SCOTT

2016
STANDARD POSTAGE
STAMP CATALOGUE

ONE HUNDRED AND SEVENTY-SECOND EDITION IN SIX VOLUMES

VOLUME 4
COUNTRIES OF THE WORLD
J-M

EDITOR	Charles Snee
MANAGING EDITOR	Donna Houseman
EDITOR EMERITUS	James E. Kloetzel
SENIOR EDITOR /NEW ISSUES & VALUING	Martin J. Frankevicz
SENIOR VALUING ANALYST	Steven R. Myers
ADMINISTRATIVE ASSISTANT/CATALOGUE LAYOUT	Eric Wiessinger
PRINTING AND IMAGE COORDINATOR	Stacey Mahan
SENIOR GRAPHIC DESIGNER	Cinda McAlexander
ADVERTISING/SALES – EAST	Stephanie Campana
	David Pistello
ADVERTISING/SALES – MIDWEST	Mike Mandozzi
ADVERTISING/SALES – WEST & FL	Eric Roth
	Victoria Hardy
VICE PRESIDENT	Dean Horowitz
PRESIDENT	Jeff Greisch

Released July 2015

Includes New Stamp Listings through the May 2015 *Linn's Stamp News Monthly* Catalogue Update

Copyright© 2015 by

AMOS MEDIA

911 Vandemark Road, Sidney, OH 45365-4129

Publishers of *Linn's Stamp News, Linn's Stamp News Monthly, Coin World* and *Coin World Monthly*

Table of Contents

See Volume 1 for United States, United Nations and Countries of the World A-B
See Volume 2, 3, 5, 6 for Countries of the World, C-I, N-Z

Volume 2: C-F
Volume 3: G-I
Volume 5: N-Sam
Volume 6: San-Z

Scott Catalogue Mission Statement

The Scott Catalogue Team exists to serve the recreational,
educational and commercial hobby needs of stamp collectors and dealers.

We strive to set the industry standard for philatelic information and products by developing and
providing goods that help collectors identify, value, organize and present their collections.

Quality customer service is, and will continue to be, our highest priority.
We aspire toward achieving total customer satisfaction.

AMOS MEDIA
SCOTT
911 VANDEMARK ROAD, SIDNEY, OHIO 45365   937-498-0802

Greetings, Fellow Scott Catalog User:

Value changes active in Macao, Laos and Kazakhstan.

Vol. 4 of the 2016 edition of the Scott *Standard Postage Stamp Catalog* contains almost 7,500 value changes. Almost all countries in this volume — Jamaica through Mozambique Company — show some value changes. Macao tops the leaderboard, with more than 1,800. Herewith we review some of the more active countries.

The majority of the almost 750 value changes recorded for Kazakhstan are decreases. Drops of 20 percent or more are typical, with scattered larger declines. There are some bright spots, particularly among souvenir sheets. The 2001 Lake Markakol sheet (Scott 334) moves up to $12 mint and used, from $7.50 both ways in 2015. The sheet celebrating the 10th anniversary of Kazakh Railways (Scott 336) rises $3 in mint and used condition — from $12 to $15.

In South Korea, the roughly 450 value changes are concentrated in the issues of the 1940s through the early 1960s. For the most part, values drop about 10 percent to 15 percent due to a slower market and a stronger dollar against both the won and the euro.

Laos received a line-by-line examination this year, which produced more than 800 value changes. Increases predominate, and you will want to pay particular attention to postage issues from 1998 to the present. Among earlier issues, the 1982 surcharges (Scott 426A-426W) show substantial gains. The 250-kip World Telecommunications Day with black surcharge, Scott 426W, soars almost fourfold in value: from $120 mint and used in 2015 to $450 both ways this year. Please note that the editors have italicized the values for these stamps because market data is rather limited. Healthy increases also are seen for postage issues for 1999 to the present. In many cases, values for unused stamps more than double. There are a number of popular topical sets in this period, and their values are up significantly. Typical is the 2000 Year of the Dragon set (Scott 1433-1434), which advances to $5.50 mint from just $1.25 last year. Values for modern souvenir sheets are up as well. The 2000 Summer Olympics sheet of four, Scott 1454a, jumps to $10 mint and used, a 267 percent increase over its $3.75 value in 2015.

Almost 800 value changes were recorded in Libya. Market activity for this country has been rather sluggish, and the downward trend in values reflects this. A large number of changes are seen for the postage issues of 1912 through 1941 (Scott 1-101). Values for stamps from the 1950s to the present held steady, but there are a few scattered increases. Among the more notable increases is the 1986 Khadafy set of 12 (Scott 1286-1297), which moves from $480 mint and used last year to $605 both ways in the 2016 catalog. Six souvenir sheets issued in 1996 (Scott 1548-1553) each rise in value about 14 percent: from $17.50 mint and used in 2015 to $20 both ways this year. Among airmail and other back-of-the-book issues, decreases of 10 percent to 20 percent are the norm.

Macao comes out on top this year, with more than 1,800 value changes. Here we see a mixture of increases and decreases. Changes were tempered somewhat to reflect the sometimes wide range of prices seen in the marketplace. Values for stamps from the Portuguese territory period are generally down, while increases are noted for stamps issued since late 1999, when Macao became a special administrative region of the People's Republic of China. Among these later issues, values rise around 10 percent. A few issues rise between 15 percent and 20 percent. The 2007 Seng Yu Proverbs booklet pane, Scott 1223, rises $3 — from $13 in 2015 to $16 this year.

A partial examination of Malaya and its associated states produced almost 450 values changes. Increases are seen across the board, with noticeable jumps for occupation issues.

The 1942 Malaya postage due stamps issued under Japanese occupation (Scott NJ1-NJ7) move up as much as 25 percent.

A careful review of Morocco yielded almost 750 value changes. In the postage section, changes are seen throughout the listings. Increases dominate over decreases, but the changes in either direction are rather modest. There are some noticeable jumps for a handful of topical issues. Representative are the 1978 1-dirham National Folklore Festival (Scott 420), which rises in mint condition from 65¢ to $2, and the 1980 40-centime Hunting With Falcons (Scott 458), which advances to $1.75 mint from 60¢ last year.

In general, increases are more robust for stamps issued in the 1980s to the present. The souvenir sheet issued in 1989 to celebrate the 60th birthday of King Hassan II, Scott 675b, soars from $1.75 mint and used in 2015 to $15 both ways this year. A small number of stamps that were previously dashed in the value columns, such as the 2005 King Mohammed VI issues of 2005 (Scott 1007A-1007B) and 2007 (Scott 1054A-1054B), are now valued for the first time. Be sure to review the Northern Zone issues that are valued in footnotes accompanying the main listings. The set of imperforate pairs of Scott 1-8 rises from $1,500 to $2,000.

New errors added to Jordan, Mexico.

Below we highlight some of the editorial additions that were made this year. A good number of these are new error listings.

Jordan: Almost a dozen new errors have been added. Most of these are color-omitted errors scattered among a handful of sets issued in the 1960s and 1970s. Of these, perhaps the most striking is Scott 429a, which is missing the black used to print the English and Arabic script across the top and the portraits of Pope Paul VI and King Hussein at left and right, respectively.

Macao: Three new errors expand the listings for the 1898-1903 King Carlos set. Scott Nos. 75b, 76b and 77a show the black "Macau" and denomination inscriptions inverted. A clarifying footnote has been added to the listings for Nos. 159-161, explaining that the stamps were bisected before being placed on sale. One double overprint and six inverted overprint errors have been added to the overprinted King Carlos stamps of 1913. The double overprint, Scott 195a, is valued at $175 unused and used, and each of the six inverted overprints (Scott 195b//204a) is valued at $95 unused.

Malaysia: Collectors of Malaysia stamps will no doubt be pleased to see that the stamps of the Malaysia state of Sarawak, formerly tucked at the end of the Postage section for Sarawak in Vol. 6 of the Standard catalog, are now included with the rest of the Malaysia states in this volume. Specifically, we have moved the listings for the State of Malaysia issues for Sarawak after Sabah in the Malaysian States listings. Previously these stamps were listed with the other Sarawak stamps that were issued before Sarawak became a part of Malaysia. The affected Scott numbers, 215-274, remain the same with this move.

Mexico: Three new errors have been added to the 1914 Coat of Arms stamps overprinted "Victoria de Torreon Abril 2 1914" (Scott 362-368). On each of the errors, the year date in the overprint mistakenly reads "1912." The new errors are Scott 362a, 366a and 367a. An explanatory footnote has been added to the Tlacotalpan provisional, based on research suggesting that the stamp was part of a postal fraud perpetrated by the Tlacotalpan postmaster and his assistant.

Now grab your stamp album, pick up your tongs, settle in with your copy of the Scott catalog and bask in the pleasures of the world's greatest hobby. Cheers!

Charles Snee/Catalogue Editor

Acknowledgments

Our appreciation and gratitude go to the following individuals who have assisted us in preparing information included in this year's Scott Catalogues. Some helpers prefer anonymity. These individuals have generously shared their stamp knowledge with others through the medium of the Scott Catalogue.

Those who follow provided information that is in addition to the hundreds of dealer price lists and advertisements and scores of auction catalogues and realizations that were used in producing the catalogue values. It is from those noted here that we have been able to obtain information on items not normally seen in published lists and advertisements. Support from these people goes beyond data leading to catalogue values, for they also are key to editorial changes.

> A special acknowledgment to Liane and Sergio Sismondo of The Classic Collector for their assistance and knowledge sharing that have aided in the preparation of this year's Standard and Classic Specialized Catalogues.

Michael Aldrich (Michael E. Aldrich, Inc.)
Roland Austin
Robert Ausubel (Great Britain Collectors Club)
Jack Hagop Barsoumian (International Stamp Co.)
John Birkinbine II
Brian M. Bleckwenn
Roger S. Brody
Keith & Margie Brown
Mahdi Bseiso
Josh Buchsbayew (Cherrystone Auctions)
Ronald A. Burns
Peter Bylen
Tina & John Carlson (JET Stamps)
Henry Chlanda
Frank D. Correl
Steven D. Crippe (Gradedstamps.com)
Tony L. Crumbley (Carolina Coin & Stamp, Inc.)
Christopher Dahle
Stephen R. Datz
Tony Davis
Charles Deaton
Ubaldo Del Toro
Bob & Rita Dumaine (Sam Houston Duck Co.)
Sister Theresa Durand
Mark Eastzer (Markest Stamp Co.)
Paul G. Eckman
George Epstein (Allkor Stamp Co.)
Mehdi Esmaili
George Eveleth (Spink Shreves Galleries)
Henry Fisher
Jeffrey M. Forster
Ernest E. Fricks (France & Colonies Philatelic Society)
Frank Geiger (Worldstamps.com)
Bob Genisol (Sultan Stamp Center)
Allan Grant (Rushstamps, Ltd.)
Daniel E. Grau
Jan E. Gronwall
Grosvenor Auctions
Chris Harmer (Harmer-Schau Auctions)
Robin Harris
Bruce Hecht (Bruce L. Hecht Co.)
Peter Hoffman
Armen Hovsepian (Armenstamp)
Philip J. Hughes
Doug Iams

John Jamieson (Saskatoon Stamp and Coin)
N. M. Janoowalla
Peter Jeannopoulos
Stephen Joe (International Stamp Service)
William A. Jones
Sheikh Shafiqul Islam
John Kardos
Allan Katz (Ventura Stamp Co.)
Stanford M. Katz
Lewis Kaufman (The Philatelic Foundation)
Patricia A. Kaufmann (Confederate Stamp Alliance)
William V. Kriebel (Brazil Philatelic Association)
George Krieger
Frederick P. Lawrence
Ken Lawrence
John R. Lewis (The William Henry Stamp Co.)
Ulf Lindahl
Ignacio Llach (Filatelia Llach S.L.)
Larry Martin (Crown Colony Stamp Co.)
Marilyn R. Mattke
William K. McDaniel
Mark S. Miller
Gary Morris (Pacific Midwest Co.)
Bruce M. Moyer (Moyer Stamps & Collectibles)
Richard H. Muller
Behruz Nassre
Nestor Nunez
Robert P. Odenweller
Nik & Lisa Oquist
Dr. Everett Parker
Donald J. Peterson (International Philippine Philatelic Society)
Stanley M. Piller (Stanley M. Piller & Associates)
Virgil Pirvulescu
Todor Drumev Popov
Philippe & Guido Poppe (Poppe Stamps, Inc.)
Siddique Mahmudur Rahman
Ghassan D. Riachi
Eric Roberts
Peter A. Robertson
Wilford H. Ross
Robert G. Rufe

Mehrdad Sadri (Persiphila)
Theodosios Sampson PhD
Michael Schreiber
Jacques C. Schiff, Jr. (Jacques C. Schiff, Jr., Inc.)
Vincent Sgro
Guy Shaw
Jeff Siddiqui
Sergio & Liane Sismondo (The Classic Collector)
Jay Smith
Frank J. Stanley, III
Kenneth Thompson
Peter Thy
Scott R. Trepel (Siegel Auction Galleries)
Dan Undersander (United Postal Stationery Society)
Steven Unkrich
Philip T. Wall
Kristian Wang
Daniel C. Warren
Giana Wayman
William R. Weiss, Jr. (Weiss Expertizing)
Don White (Dunedin Stamp Centre)
Ralph Yorio
Val Zabijaka
Michal Zika
Steven Zirinsky
Alfonso G. Zulueta
Steven Zwillinger

Addresses, Telephone Numbers, Web Sites, E-Mail Addresses of General & Specialized Philatelic Societies

Collectors can contact the following groups for information about the philately of the areas within the scope of these societies, or inquire about membership in these groups. Aside from the general societies, we limit this list to groups that specialize in particular fields of philately, particular areas covered by the Scott Standard Postage Stamp Catalogue, and topical groups. Many more specialized philatelic society exist than those listed below. These addresses are updated yearly, and they are, to the best of our knowledge, correct and current. Groups should inform the editors of address changes whenever they occur. The editors also want to hear from other such specialized groups not listed. Unless otherwise noted all website addresses begin with http://

American Philatelic Society
100 Match Factory Place
Bellefonte PA 16823-1367
Ph: (814) 933-3803
www.stamps.org
E-mail: apsinfo@stamps.org

American Stamp Dealers Association, Inc.
P.O. Box 692
Leesport PA 19553
Ph: (800) 369-8207
www.americanstampdealer.com
E-mail: asda@americanstampdealer.com

National Stamp Dealers Association
Dick Keiser, President
2916 NW Bucklin Hill Road #136
Silverdale WA 98383-8514
Ph: (800) 875-6633
www.nsdainc.org
E-mail: gail@nsdainc.org

International Society of Worldwide Stamp Collectors
Joanne Berkowitz, MD
P.O. Box 19006
Sacramento CA 95819
www.iswsc.org
E-mail: executivedirector@iswsc.org

Royal Philatelic Society
41 Devonshire Place
London, W1G 6JY
UNITED KINGDOM
www.rpsl.org.uk
E-mail: secretary@rpsl.org.uk

Royal Philatelic Society of Canada
P.O. Box 929, Station Q
Toronto, ON, M4T 2P1
CANADA
Ph: (888) 285-4143
www.rpsc.org
E-mail: info@rpsc.org

Young Stamp Collectors of America
Janet Houser
100 Match Factory Place
Bellefonte PA 16823-1367
Ph: (814) 933-3820
www.stamps.org/ysca/intro.htm
E-mail: ysca@stamps.org

Philatelic Research Resources

(The Scott editors encourage any additional research organizations to submit data for inclusion in this listing category)
American Philatelic Research Library

Tara Murray
100 Match Factory Place
Bellefonte PA 16823
Ph: (814) 933-3803
www.stamplibrary.org
E-mail: aprl@stamps.org

Institute for Analytical Philately, Inc.
P.O. Box 8035
Holland MI 49422-8035
Ph: (616) 399-9299
www.analyticalphilately.org
E-mail: info@analyticalphilately.org

The Western Philatelic Library
P.O. Box 2219
1500 Partridge Ave.
Sunnyvale CA 94087
Ph: (408) 733-0336
www.fwpf.org

Groups focusing on fields or aspects found in worldwide philately (some might cover U.S. area only)

American Air Mail Society
Stephen Reinhard
P.O. Box 110
Mineola NY 11501
www.americanairmailsociety.org
E-mail: sreinhard1@optonline.net

American First Day Cover Society
Douglas Kelsey
P.O. Box 16277
Tucson AZ 85732-6277
Ph: (520) 321-0880
www.afdcs.org
E-mail: afdcs@afdcs.org

American Revenue Association
Eric Jackson
P.O. Box 728
Leesport PA 19533-0728
Ph: (610) 926-6200
www.revenuer.org
E-mail: eric@revenuer.com

American Topical Association
Vera Felts
P.O. Box 8
Carterville IL 62918-0008
Ph: (618) 985-5100
www.americantopicalassn.org
E-mail: americantopical@msn.com

Christmas Seal & Charity Stamp Society
John Denune
234 E. Broadway
Granville OH 43023
Ph: (740) 587-0276
www.seal-society.org
E-mail: jdenune@roadrunner.com

Errors, Freaks and Oddities Collectors Club
Scott Shaulis
P.O. Box 549
Murrysville PA 15668-0549
Ph: (724) 733-4134
www.efocc.org

First Issues Collectors Club
Kurt Streepy, Secretary
3128 E. Mattatha Drive
Bloomington IN 47401
www.firstissues.org
E-mail: secretary@firstissues.org

International Society of Reply Coupon Collectors
Peter Robin
P.O. Box 353
Bala Cynwyd PA 19004
E-mail: peterrobin@verizon.net

The Joint Stamp Issues Society
Richard Zimmermann
29A Rue Des Eviats
Lalaye F-67220
FRANCE
www.jointstampissues.net
E-mail: contact@jointstampissues.net

National Duck Stamp Collectors Society
Anthony J. Monico
P.O. Box 43
Harleysville PA 19438-0043
www.ndscs.org
E-mail: ndscs@ndscs.org

No Value Identified Club
Albert Sauvanet
Le Clos Royal B, Boulevard des Pas Enchantes
St. Sebastien-sur Loire, 44230
FRANCE
E-mail: alain.vailly@irin.univ nantes.fr

The Perfins Club
Jerry Hejduk
P.O. Box 490450
Leesburg FL 34749-0450
www.perfins.org
Ph: (352) 326-2117
E-mail: flprepers@comcast.net

Postage Due Mail Study Group
John Rawlins
13, Longacre
Chelmsford, CM1 3BJ
UNITED KINGDOM
E-mail: john.rawlins2@ukonline.co.uk

Post Mark Collectors Club
Bob Milligan
7014 Woodland Oaks
Magnolia TX 77354
Ph: (281) 359-2735
www.postmarks.org
E-mail: bob.milligan@prodigy.net
Postal History Society
Joseph F. Frasch, Jr.
P.O. Box 20387
Columbus OH 43220-0387
www.stampclubs.com
E-mail: jfrasch@ix.netcom.com

Precancel Stamp Society
Rick Podwell
P.O. Box 85
Fawn Grove PA 17321
Ph: (717) 817-8807
www.precancels.com
E-mail: pssprosec@comcast.net

United Postal Stationery Society
Stuart Leven
P.O. Box 24764
San Jose CA 95154-4764
www.upss.org
E-mail: poststat@gmail.com

United States Possessions Philatelic Society
Daniel F. Ring
P.O. Box 113
Woodstock IL 60098
www.uspps.net
E-mail: danielfring@hotmail.com

Groups focusing on U.S. area philately as covered in the Standard Catalogue

Canal Zone Study Group
Tom Brougham
737 Neilson St.
Berkeley CA 94707
www.CanalZoneStudyGroup.com
E-mail: czsgsecretary@gmail.com

Carriers and Locals Society
Martin Richardson
P.O. Box 74
Grosse Ile MI 48138
www.pennypost.org
E-mail: martinr362@aol.com

Confederate Stamp Alliance
Patricia A. Kaufmann
10194 N. Old State Road
Lincoln DE 19960
Ph. (302) 422-2656
www.csalliance.org
E-mail: trishkauf@comcast.net

Hawaiian Philatelic Society
Kay H. Hoke
P.O. Box 10115
Honolulu HI 96816-0115
Ph. (000) 521-5721

Plate Number Coil Collectors Club
Gene Trinks
16415 W. Desert Wren Court
Surprise AZ 85374
Ph: (623) 322-4619
www.pnc3.org
E-mail: gctrinks@cox.net

Ryukyu Philatelic Specialist Society
Laura Edmonds, Secy.
P.O. Box 240177
Charlotte NC 28224-0177
Ph: (336) 509-3739
www.ryukyustamps.org
E-mail: secretary@ryukyustamps.org
United Nations Philatelists
Blanton Clement, Jr.
P.O. Box 146
Morrisville PA 19067-0146
www.unpi.com
E-mail: bclemjr@yahoo.com

United States Stamp Society
Executive Secretary
P.O. Box 6634
Katy TX 77491-6631
www.usstamps.org
E-mail: webmaster@usstamps.org

U.S. Cancellation Club
Arden Calleder
Houston TX 77077
Ph: (281) 589-1075
bob.trachimowicz.org/uscchome.htm
E-mail: callenderardy@secglobal.net

U.S. Philatelic Classics Society
Rob Lund
2913 Fulton St.
Everett WA 98201-3733
www.uspcs.org
E-mail: membershipchairman@uspcs.org

Groups focusing on philately of foreign countries or regions

Aden & Somaliland Study Group
Gary Brown
P.O. Box 106
Briar Hill, Victoria, 3088
AUSTRALIA
E-mail: garyjohn951@optushome.com.au

American Society of Polar Philatelists
(Antarctic areas)
Alan Warren
P.O. Box 39
Exton PA 19341-0039
www.polarphilatelists.org

Andorran Philatelic Study Circle
D. Hope
17 Hawthorn Drive
Stalybridge, Cheshire, SK15 1UE
UNITED KINGDOM
apsc.free.fr
E-mail: apsc@free.fr

Australian States Study Circle of The Royal Sydney Philatelic Club
Ben Palmer
GPO 1751
Sydney, N.S.W., 2001
AUSTRALIA
www.philas.org.au/states

Austria Philatelic Society
Ralph Schneider
P.O. Box 23049
Belleville IL 62223
Ph: (618) 277-6152
www.austriaphilatelicsociety.com
E-mail: rschneiderstamps@att.net

American Belgian Philatelic Society
Edward de Bary
11 Wakefield Drive Apt. 2105
Asheville NC 28803

Bechuanalands and Botswana Society
Neville Midwood
69 Porlock Lane
Furzton, Milton Keynes, MK4 1JY
UNITED KINGDOM
www.nevsoft.com
E-mail: bbsoc@nevsoft.com

Bermuda Collectors Society
John Pare
405 Perimeter Road
Mount Horeb WI 53572
www.bermudacollectorssociety.org
E-mail: pare16@mhtc.net

Brazil Philatelic Association
William V. Kriebel
1923 Manning St.
Philadelphia PA 19103-5728
www.brazilphilatelic.org
E-mail: info@brazilphilatelic.org

British Caribbean Philatelic Study Group
Dr. Reuben Ramkissoon
11075 Benton St. #236
Loma Linda CA 92354-3812
Ph: (909) 796-6409
www.bcpsg.com
E-mail: rramkissoon@juno.com

The King George VI Collectors Society
(British Commonwealth)
Brian Livingstone
21 York Mansions, Prince of Wales Drive
London, SW11 4DL
UNITED KINGDOM
www.kg6.info
E-mail: livingstone484@btinternet.com

British North America Philatelic Society
(Canada & Provinces)
David G. Jones
184 Larkin Drive
Nepean, ON, K2J 1H9
CANADA
www.bnaps.org
E-mail: shibumi.management@gmail.com

British West Indies Study Circle
John Seidl
4324 Granby Way
Marietta GA 30062
Ph: (770) 642-6424
www.bwisc.org
E-mail: john.seidl@gmail.com

Burma Philatelic Study Circle
Michael Whittaker
1, Ecton Leys, Hillside
Rugby, Warwickshire, CV22 5SL
UNITED KINGDOM
www.burmastamps.homecall.co.uk
E-mail: manningham8@mypostoffice.co.uk

Cape and Natal Study Circle
Dr. Guy Dillaway
P.O. Box 181
Weston MA 02493
www.nzsc.demon.co.uk

Ceylon Study Circle
R. W. P. Frost
42 Lonsdale Road, Cannington
Bridgewater, Somerset, TA5 2JS
UNITED KINGDOM
www.ceylonsc.org
E-mail: rodney.frost@tiscali.co.uk

Channel Islands Specialists Society
Moira Edwards
86, Hall Lane, Sandon
Chelmsford, Essex, CM2 7RQ
UNITED KINGDOM
www.ciss1950.org.uk
E-mail: membership@ciss1950.org.uk

China Stamp Society
Paul H. Gault
P.O. Box 20711
Columbus OH 43220
www.chinastampsociety.org
E-mail: secretary@chinastampsociety.org

Colombia/Panama Philatelic Study Group
(COPAPHIL)
Thomas P. Myers
P.O. Box 522
Gordonsville VA 22942
www.copaphil.org
E-mail: tpmphil@hotmail.com

Association Filatelic de Costa Rica
Giana Wayman
c/o Interlink 102, P.O. Box 52-6770
Miami FL 33152
E-mail: scotland@racsa.co.cr

Society for Costa Rica Collectors
Dr. Hector R. Mena
P.O. Box 14831
Baton Rouge LA 70808
www.socorico.org
E-mail: hrmena@aol.com

International Cuban Philatelic Society
Ernesto Cuesta
P.O. Box 34434
Bethesda MD 20827
www.cubafil.org
E-mail: ecuesta@philat.com

Cuban Philatelic Society of America ®
P.O. Box 141656
Coral Gables FL 33114-1656
www.cubapsa.com
E-mail: cpsa.usa@gmail.com

Cyprus Study Circle
Colin Dear
10 Marne Close, Wem
Shropshire, SY4 5YE
UNITED KINGDOM
www.cyprusstudycircle.org/index.htm
E-mail: colindear@talktalk.net

Society for Czechoslovak Philately
Tom Cassaboom
P.O. Box 4124
Prescott AZ 86302
www.csphilately.org
E-mail: klfck1@aol.com

Danish West Indies Study Unit of the Scandinavian Collectors Club
Arnold Sorensen
7666 Edgedale Drive
Newburgh IN 47630
Ph: (812) 480-6532
www.scc-online.org
E-mail: valbydwi@hotmail.com

East Africa Study Circle
Michael Vesey-Fitzgerald
Gambles Cottage, 18 Clarence Road
Lyndhurst, SO43 7AL
UNITED KINGDOM
www.easc.org.uk
E-mail: secretary@easc.org.uk

Egypt Study Circle
Mike Murphy
109 Chadwick Road
London, SE15 4PY
UNITED KINGDOM
Trent Ruebush: North American Agent
E-mail: truebrush@usaid.gov
egyptstudycircle.org.uk
E-mail: egyptstudycircle@hotmail.com

Estonian Philatelic Society
Juri Kirsimagi
29 Clifford Ave.
Pelham NY 10803
Ph: (914) 738-3713

Ethiopian Philatelic Society
Ulf Lindahl
21 Westview Place
Riverside CT 06878
Ph: (203) 722-0769
home.comcast.net/~fbheiser/ethiopia5.htm
E-mail: ulindahl@optonline.net

Falkland Islands Philatelic Study Group
Carl J. Faulkner
615 Taconic Trail
Williamstown MA 01267-2745
Ph: (413) 458-4421
www.fipsg.org.uk
E-mail: cfaulkner@taconicwilliamstown.com

Faroe Islands Study Circle
Norman Hudson
40 Queen's Road, Vicar's Cross
Chester, CH3 5HB
UNITED KINGDOM
www.faroeislandssc.org
E-mail: jntropics@hotmail.com

Former French Colonies Specialist Society
COLFRA
BP 628
75367 Paris, Cedex 08
FRANCE
www.colfra.org
E-mail: secretaire@colfra.org

France & Colonies Philatelic Society
Edward Grabowski
111 Prospect St., 4C
Westfield NJ 07090
www.franceandcols.org
E-mail: edjjg@alum.mit.edu

Germany Philatelic Society
P.O. Box 6547
Chesterfield MO 63006
www.germanyphilatelicusa.org

Gibraltar Study Circle
David R. Stirrups
152 The Rowans, Milton
Cambridge, CB24 6YX
UNITED KINGDOM
www.gibraltarstudycircle.wordpress.com
E-mail: begglps@gmail.com

Great Britain Collectors Club
Steve McGill
10309 Brookhollow Circle
Highlands Ranch CO 80129
www.gbstamps.com/gbcc
E-mail: steve.mcgill@comcast.net

International Society of Guatemala Collectors
Jaime Marckwordt
449 St. Francis Blvd.
Daly City CA 94015-2136
www.guatemalastamps.com
E-mail: membership@guatamalastamps.com

Haiti Philatelic Society
Ubaldo Del Toro
5709 Marble Archway
Alexandria VA 22315
www.haitiphilately.org
E-mail: u007ubi@aol.com

Hong Kong Stamp Society
Ming W. Tsang
P.O. Box 206
Glenside PA 19038
www.hkss.org
E-mail: hkstamps@yahoo.com

Society for Hungarian Philately
Robert Morgan
2201 Roscomare Road
Los Angeles CA 90077-2222
Ph; (617) 645-4045
www.hungarianphilately.org
E-mail: alan@hungarianstamps.com

India Study Circle
John Warren
P.O. Box 7326
Washington DC 20044
Ph: (202) 564-6876
www.indiastudycircle.org
E-mail: warren.john@epa.gov

Indian Ocean Study Circle
E. S. Hutton
29 Patermoster Close
Waltham Abby, Essex, EN9 3JU
UNITED KINGDOM
www.indianoceanstudycircle.com
E-mail: secretary@indianoceanstudycircle.com

Society of Indo-China Philatelists
Ron Bentley
2600 N. 24th St.
Arlington VA 22207
www.sicp-online.org
E-mail: ron.bentley@verizon.net

Iran Philatelic Study Circle
Mehdi Esmaili
P.O. Box 750096
Forest Hills NY 11375
www.iranphilatelic.org
E-mail: m.esmaili@earthlink.net

Eire Philatelic Association (Ireland)
David J. Brennan
P.O. Box 704
Bernardsville NJ 07924
www.eirephilatelicassoc.org
E-mail: brennan704@aol.com

Society of Israel Philatelists
Edwin Kroft
P.O. Box 507
Northfield OH 44067
www.israelstamps.com
E-mail: israelstamps@gmail.com

Italy and Colonies Study Circle
Richard Harlow
7 Duncombe House, 8 Manor Road
Teddington, TW11 8BE
UNITED KINGDOM
www.icsc.pwp.blueyonder.co.uk
E-mail: harlowr@gmail.com

International Society for Japanese Philately
William Eisenhauer
P.O. Box 230462
Tigard OR 97281
www.isjp.org
E-mail: secretary@isjp.org

Korea Stamp Society
John E. Talmage
P.O. Box 6889
Oak Ridge TN 37831
www.pennfamily.org/KSS-USA
E-mail: jtalmage@usit.net

Latin American Philatelic Society
Jules K. Beck
30½ St. #209
St. Louis Park MN 55426-3551

Liberian Philatelic Society
William Thomas Lockard
P.O. Box 106
Wellston OH 45692
Ph: (740) 384-2020
E-mail: tlockard@zoomnet.net

Liechtenstudy USA (Liechtenstein)
Paul Tremaine
410 SW Ninth St.
Dundee OR 97115
Ph: (503) 538-4500
www.liechtenstudy.org
E-mail: editor@liechtenstudy.org

Lithuania Philatelic Society
John Variakojis
8472 Carlisle Court.
Burr Ridge IL 60527
Ph: (630) 974-6525
www.lithuanianphilately.com/lps
E-mail: variakojis@sbcglobal.net

Luxembourg Collectors Club
Gary B. Little
7319 Beau Road
Sechelt, BC, VON 3A8
CANADA
lcc.luxcentral.com
E-mail: gary@luxcentral.com

Malaya Study Group
David Tett
P.O. Box 34
Wheathampstead, Herts, AL4 8JY
UNITED KINGDOM
www.m-s-g.org.uk
E-mail: davidtett@aol.com

Malta Study Circle
Alec Webster
50 Worcester Road
Sutton, Surrey, SM2 6QB
UNITED KINGDOM
www.maltastudycircle.org.uk
E-mail: alecwebster50@hotmail.com

Mexico-Elmhurst Philatelic Society International
Thurston Bland
50 Regato
Rancho Santa Margarita CA 92688-3003
www.mepsi.org

Asociacion Mexicana de Filatelia
AMEXFIL
Jose Maria Rico, 129, Col. Del Valle
Mexico City DF, 03100
MEXICO
www.amexfil.mx
E-mail: amexfil@gmail.com

Society for Moroccan and Tunisian Philately
S.P.L.M.
206, bld. Pereire
75017 Paris
FRANCE
members.aol.com/Jhaik5814
E-mail: splm206@aol.com

Nepal & Tibet Philatelic Study Group
Roger D. Skinner
1020 Covington Road
Los Altos CA 94024-5003
Ph: (650) 968-4163
www.fuchs-online.com/ntpsc/
E-mail: colinhepper@hotmail.co.uk

American Society for Netherlands Philately
Hans Kremer
50 Rockport Court
Danville CA 94526
Ph: (925) 820-5841
www.asnp1975.com
E-mail: hkremer@usa.net

New Zealand Society of Great Britain
Michael Wilkinson
121 London Road
Sevenoaks, Kent, TN13 1BH
UNITED KINGDOM
www.nzsgb.org.uk
E-mail: mwilkin799@aol.com

Nicaragua Study Group
Erick Rodriguez
11817 SW 11th St.
Miami FL 33184-2501
clubs.yahoo.com/clubs/
nicaraguastudygroup
E-mail: nsgsec@yahoo.com

Society of Australasian Specialists/ Oceania
David McNamee
P.O. Box 37
Alamo CA 94507
www.sasoceania.org
E-mail: dmcnamee@aol.com

Orange Free State Study Circle
J. R. Stroud
24 Hooper Close
Burnham-on-sea, Somerset, TA8 1JQ
UNITED KINGDOM
orangefreestatephilately.org.uk
E-mail: richardstroudph@gofast.co.uk

Pacific Islands Study Circle
John Ray
24 Woodvale Ave.
London, SE25 4AE
UNITED KINGDOM
www.pisc.org.uk
E-mail: info@pisc.org.uk

Pakistan Philatelic Study Circle
Jeff Siddiqui
P.O. Box 7002
Lynnwood WA 98046
E-mail: jeffsiddiqui@msn.com

Centro de Filatelistas Independientes de Panama
Vladimir Berrio-Lemm
Apartado 0823-02748
Plaza Concordia Panama
PANAMA
E-mail: panahistoria@gmail.com

Papuan Philatelic Society
Steven Zirinsky
P.O. Box 49, Ansonia Station
New York NY 10023
Ph: (718) 706-0616
www.communigate.co.uk/york/pps
E-mail: szirinsky@cs.com

International Philippine Philatelic Society
Donald J. Peterson
P.O. Box 122
Brunswick MD 21716
Ph: (301) 834-6419
www.theipps.info
E-mail: dpeterson4526@gmail.com

Pitcairn Islands Study Group
Dr. Everett L. Parker
249 NW Live Oak Place
Lake City FL 32055-8906
Ph: (386) 754-8524
www.pisg.net
E-mail: eparker@hughes.net

Polonus Philatelic Society (Poland)
Robert Ogrodnik
P.O. Box 240428
Ballwin MO 63024-0428
Ph: (314) 821-6130
www.polonus.org
E-mail: rvo1937@gmail.com

International Society for Portuguese Philately
Clyde Homen
1491 Bonnie View Road
Hollister CA 95023-5117
www.portugalstamps.com
E-mail: cjh1491@sbcglobal.net

Rhodesian Study Circle
William R. Wallace
P.O. Box 16381
San Francisco CA 94116
www.rhodesianstudycircle.org.uk
E-mail: bwall8rscr@earthlink.net

Rossica Society of Russian Philately
Alexander Kolchinsky
1506 Country Lake Drive
Champaign IL 6821-6428
www.rossica.org
E-mail: alexander.kolchinsky@rossica.org

St. Helena, Ascension & Tristan Da Cunha Philatelic Society
Dr. Everett L. Parker
249 NW Live Oak Place
Lake City FL 32055-8906
Ph: (386) 754-8524
www.atlanticislands.org
E-mail: eparker@hughes.net

St. Pierre & Miquelon Philatelic Society
James R. (Jim) Taylor
2335 Paliswood Road SW
Calgary, AB, T2V 3P6
CANADA
www.stamps.org/spm

Associated Collectors of El Salvador
Joseph D. Hahn
1015 Old Boalsburg Road Apt G-5
State College PA 16801-6149
www.elsalvadorphilately.org
E-mail: jdhahn2@gmail.com

Fellowship of Samoa Specialists
Donald Mcc
23 Leo St.
Christchurch, 8051
NEW ZEALAND
www.samoaexpress.org
E-mail: donanm@xtra.co.nz

Sarawak Specialists' Society
Stu Leven
P.O. Box 24764
San Jose CA 95154-4764
Ph: (408) 978-0193
www.britborneostamps.org.uk
E-mail: stulev@ix.netcom.com

Scandinavian Collectors Club
Steve Lund
P.O. Box 16213
St. Paul MN 55116
www.scc-online.org
E-mail: steve88h@aol.com

Slovakia Stamp Society
Jack Benchik
P.O. Box 555
Notre Dame IN 46556

Philatelic Society for Greater Southern Africa
Alan Hanks
34 Seaton Drive
Aurora, ON, L4G 2KI
CANADA
Ph: (905) 727-6993
www.psgsa.thestampweb.com
Email: alan.hanks@sympatico.ca

South Sudan Philatelic Society
William Barclay
134A Spring Hill Road
South Londonerry VT 05155
E-mail: bill.barclay@wfp.org

Spanish Philatelic Society
Robert H. Penn
1108 Walnut Drive
Danielsville PA 18038
Ph: (610) 844-8963
E-mail: roberthpenn43@gmail.com

Sudan Study Group
David Sher
5 Ellis Park Road
Toronto, ON, M6S 2V2
CANADA
www.sudanstamps.org
E-mail: sh3603@hotmail.com

American Helvetia Philatelic Society (Switzerland, Liechtenstein)
Richard T. Hall
P.O. Box 15053
Asheville NC 28813-0053
www.swiss-stamps.org
E-mail: secretary2@swiss-stamps.org

Tannu Tuva Collectors Society
Ken R. Simon
P.O. Box 385
Lake Worth FL 33460-0385
Ph: (561) 588-5954
www.tuva.tk
E-mail: yurttuva@yahoo.com

Society for Thai Philately
H. R. Blakeney
P.O. Box 25644
Oklahoma City OK 73125
E-mail: HRBlakeney@aol.com

Transvaal Study Circle
Jeff Woolgar
c/o 9 Meadow Road
Gravesend, DA11 7LR
UNITED KINGDOM
www.transvaal.org.uk

Ottoman and Near East Philatelic Society (Turkey and related areas)
Bob Stuchell
193 Valley Stream Lane
Wayne PA 19087
www.oneps.org
E-mail: rstuchell@msn.com

Ukrainian Philatelic & Numismatic Society
Martin B. Tatuch
5117 8th Road N.
Arlington VA 22205-1201
www.upns.org
E-mail: treasurer@upns.org

Vatican Philatelic Society
Sal Quinonez
1 Aldersgate, Apt. 1002
Riverhead NY 11901-1830
Ph: (516) 727-6426
www.vaticanphilately.org

British Virgin Islands Philatelic Society
Giorgio Migliavacca
P.O. Box 7007
St. Thomas VI 00801-0007
www.islandsun.com/category/collectables/
E-mail: issun@candwbvi.net

West Africa Study Circle
Martin Bratzel
1233 Virginia Ave.
Windsor, ON, N8S 2Z1
CANADA
www.wasc.org.uk/
E-mail: marty_bratzel@yahoo.ca

Western Australia Study Group
Brian Pope
P.O. Box 423
Claremont, Western Australia, 6910
AUSTRALIA
www.wastudygroup.com
E-mail: black5swan@yahoo.com.au

Yugoslavia Study Group of the Croatian Philatelic Society
Michael Lenard
1514 N. Third Ave.
Wausau WI 54401
Ph: (715) 675-2833
E-mail: mjlenard@aol.com

Topical Groups

Americana Unit
Dennis Dengel
17 Peckham Road
Poughkeepsie NY 12603-2018
www.americanaunit.org
E-mail: info@americanaunit.org

Astronomy Study Unit
John W. G. Budd
728 Sugar Camp Way
Brooksville FL 34604
E-mail: jwgbudd@gmail.com

Bicycle Stamp Club
Steve Andreasen
2000 Alaskan Way, Unit 157
Seattle WA 98121
members.tripod.com/~bicyclestamps
E-mail: steven.w.andreasen@gmail.com

Biology Unit
Alan Hanks
34 Seaton Drive
Aurora, ON, L4G 2K1
CANADA
Ph: (905) 727-6993

Bird Stamp Society
S. A. H. (Tony) Statham
Ashlyns Lodge, Chesham Road,
Berkhamsted, Hertfordshire HP4 2ST
UNITED KINGDOM
www.bird-stamps.org/bss
E-mail: tony.statham@sky.com

Captain Cook Society
Jerry Yucht
8427 Leale Ave.
Stockton CA 95212
www.captaincooksociety.com
E-mail: US@captaincooksociety.com

The CartoPhilatelic Society
Marybeth Sulkowski
1117 Douglas Ave. #209
North Providence RI 02904-5374
www.mapsonstamps.org
E-mail: secretary@mapsonstamps.org

Casey Jones Railroad Unit
Roy W. Menninger MD
85 SW Pepper Tree Lane
Topeka KS 66611-2072
www.uqp.de/cjr/index.htm
E-mail: roymenn@sbcglobal.net

Cats on Stamps Study Unit
Mary Ann Brown
3006 Wade Road
Durham NC 27705
www.catsonstamps.org
E-mail: mabrown@nc.rr.com

Chemistry & Physics on Stamps Study Unit
Dr. Roland Hirsch
20458 Water Point Lane
Germantown MD 20874
www.cpossu.org
E-mail: rfhirsch@cpossu.org

Chess on Stamps Study Unit
Ray C. Alexis
608 Emery St.
Longmont CO 80501
E-mail: chessstuff911459@aol.com

Christmas Philatelic Club
Jim Balog
P.O. Box 774
Geneva OH 44041
www.web.295.ca/cpc/
E-mail: jpbstamps@windstream.net

Christopher Columbus Philatelic Society
Donald R. Ager
P.O. Box 71
Hillsboro NH 03244-0071
Ph: (603) 464-5379
ccps.maphist.nl/
E-mail: meganddon@tds.net

Collectors of Religion on Stamps
James Bailey
P.O. Box 937
Brownwood TX 76804
www.coros-society.org
E-mail: corosec@directtv.net

Dogs on Stamps Study Unit
Morris Raskin
202A Newport Road
Monroe Township NJ 08831
Ph: (609) 655-7411
www.dossu.org
E-mail: mraskin@cellurian.com

Earth's Physical Features Study Group
Fred Klein
515 Magdalena Ave.
Los Altos CA 94024
epfsu.jeffhayward.com

Ebony Society of Philatelic Events and Reflections, Inc. (African-American topicals)
Manuel Gilyard
800 Riverside Drive, Suite 4H
New York NY 10032-7412
www.esperstamps.org
E-mail: gilyardmani@aol.com

Europa Study Unit
Tonny E. Van Loij
3002 S. Xanthia St.
Denver CO 80231-4237
www.europastudyunit.org/
E-mail: tvanloij@gmail.com

Fine & Performing Arts
Deborah L. Washington
6922 S. Jeffery Blvd., #7 - North
Chicago IL 60649
E-mail: brasslady@comcast.net

Fire Service in Philately
John Zaranek
81 Hillpine Road
Cheektowaga NY 14227-2259
Ph: (716) 668-3352
E-mail: jczaranek@roadrunner.com

Gay & Lesbian History on Stamps Club
Joe Petronie
P.O. Box 190842
Dallas TX 75219-0842
www.facebook.com/glhsc
E-mail: glhsc@aol.com

Gems, Minerals & Jewelry Study Unit
Mrs. Gilberte Proteau
138 Lafontaine
Beloeil QC J3G 2G7
CANADA
Ph: (978) 851-8283
E-mail: gilberte.ferland@sympatico.ca

Graphics Philately Association
Mark H. Winnegrad
P.O. Box 380
Bronx NY 10462-0380
www.graphics-stamps.org
E-mail: indybruce1@yahoo.com

Journalists, Authors & Poets on Stamps
Ms. Lee Straayer
P.O. Box 6808
Champaign IL 61826
E-mail: lstraayer@dcbnet.com

Lighthouse Stamp Society
Dalene Thomas
8612 W. Warren Lane
Lakewood CO 80227-2352
Ph: (303) 986-6620
www.lighthousestampsociety.org
E-mail: dalene@lighthousestampsociety.org

Lions International Stamp Club
John Bargus
108-2777 Barry Road RR 2
Mill Bay, BC, V0R 2P2
CANADA
Ph: (250) 743-5782

Mahatma Gandhi On Stamps Study Circle
Pramod Shivagunde
Pratik Clinic, Akluj
Solapur, Maharashtra, 413101
INDIA
E-mail: drnanda@bom6.vsnl.net.in

Masonic Study Unit
Stanley R. Longenecker
930 Wood St.
Mount Joy PA 17552-1926
Ph: (717) 669-9094
E-mail: natsco@usa.net

Mathematical Study Unit
Monty J. Strauss
4209 88th St.
Lubbock TX 79423-2041
www.mathstamps.org
E-mail: montystrauss@gmail.com

Medical Subjects Unit
Dr. Frederick C. Skvara
P.O. Box 6228
Bridgewater NJ 08807
E-mail: fcskvara@optonline.net

Military Postal History Society
Ed Dubin
1 S. Wacker Drive, Suite 3500
Chicago IL 60606
www.militaryPHS.org
E-mail: dubine@comcast.net

Mourning Stamps and Covers Club
James Bailey, Jr.
P.O. Box 937
Brownwood TX 76804
E-mail: jfbailey238@directv.net

Napoleonic Age Philatelists
Ken Berry
4117 NW 146th St.
Oklahoma City OK 73134-1746
Ph: (405) 748-8646
www.nap-stamps.org
E-mail: krb4117@att.net

Old World Archeological Study Unit
Caroline Scannell
11 Dawn Drive
Smithtown NY 11787-1761
www.owasu.org
E-mail: editor@owasu.org

Petroleum Philatelic Society International
Dr. Chris Coggins
174 Old Bedford Road
Luton, England, LU2 7HW
UNITED KINGDOM
E-mail: WAMTECH@Luton174.fsnet.co.uk

Rotary on Stamps Unit
Gerald L. Fitzsimmons
105 Calla Ricardo
Victoria TX 77904
rotaryonstamps.org
E-mail: glfitz@suddenlink.net

Scouts on Stamps Society International
Lawrence Clay
P.O. Box 6228
Kennewick WA 99336
Ph: (509) 735-3731
www.sossi.org
E-mail: rfrank@sossi.org

Ships on Stamps Unit
Les Smith
302 Conklin Ave.
Penticton, BC, V2A 2T4
CANADA
Ph: (250) 493-7486
www.shipsonstamps.org
E-mail: lessmith440@shaw.ca

Space Unit
Carmine Torrisi
P.O. Box 780241
Maspeth NY 11378
Ph: (917) 620-5687
stargate.1usa.com/stamps/
E-mail: ctorrisi1@nyc.rr.com

Sports Philatelists International
Mark Maestrone
2824 Curie Place
San Diego CA 92122-4110
www.sportstamps.org
Email: president@sportstamps.org

Stamps on Stamps Collectors Club
Alf Jordan
156 W. Elm St.
Yarmouth ME 04096
www.stampsonstamps.org
E-mail: ajordan1@maine.rr.com

Windmill Study Unit
Walter J. Hollien
607 N. Porter St.
Watkins Glenn NY 14891-1345
Ph: (862) 812-0030
E-mail: whollien@earthlink.net

Wine On Stamps Study Unit
David Wolfersberger
768 Chain Ridge Road
St. Louis MO 63122-3259
Ph: (314) 961-5032
www.wine-on-stamps.org
E-mail: dewolf2@swbell.net

Women on Stamps Study Unit
Hugh Gottfried
2232 26th St.
Santa Monica CA 90405-1902
E-mail: hgottfried@adelphia.net

Expertizing Services

The following organizations will, for a fee, provide expert opinions about stamps submitted to them. Collectors should contact these organizations to find out about their fees and requirements before submiting philatelic material to them. The listing of these groups here is not intended as an endorsement by Amos Media Co.

General Expertizing Services

American Philatelic Expertizing Service (a service of the American Philatelic Society)
100 Match Factory Place
Bellefonte PA 16823-1367
Ph: (814) 237-3803
Fax: (814) 237-6128
www.stamps.org
E-mail: ambristo@stamps.org
Areas of Expertise: Worldwide

B. P. A. Expertising, Ltd.
P.O. Box 1141
Guildford, Surrey, GU5 0WR
UNITED KINGDOM
E-mail: sec@bpaexpertising.org
Areas of Expertise: British Commonwealth, Great Britain, Classics of Europe, South America and the Far East

Philatelic Foundation
341 W. 38th St., 5th Floor
New York NY 10018
Ph: (212) 221-6555
Fax: (212) 221-6208
www.philatelicfoundation.org
E-mail: philatelicfoundation@verizon.net
Areas of Expertise: U.S. & Worldwide

Philatelic Stamp Authentication and Grading, Inc.
P.O. Box 41-0880
Melbourne FL 32941-0880
Customer Service: (305) 345-9864
www.psaginc.com
E-mail: info@psaginc.com
Areas of Expertise: U.S., Canal Zone, Hawaii, Philippines, Canada & Provinces

Professional Stamp Experts
P.O. Box 6170
Newport Beach CA 92658
Ph: (877) STAMP-88
Fax: (949) 833-7955
www.collectors.com/pse
E-mail: pseinfo@collectors.com
Areas of Expertise: Stamps and covers of U.S., U.S. Possessions, British Commonwealth

Royal Philatelic Society Expert Committee
41 Devonshire Place
London, W1N 1PE
UNITED KINGDOM
www.rpsl.org.uk/experts.html
E-mail: experts@rpsl.org.uk
Areas of Expertise: Worldwide

Expertizing Services Covering Specific Fields Or Countries

China Stamp Society Expertizing Service
1050 W. Blue Ridge Blvd.
Kansas City MO 64145
Ph: (816) 942-6300
E-mail: hjmesq@aol.com
Areas of Expertise: China

Confederate Stamp Alliance Authentication Service
Gen. Frank Crown, Jr.
P.O. Box 278
Capshaw AL 35742-0396
Ph: (302) 422-2656
Fax: (302) 424-1990
www.csalliance.org
E-mail: csaas@knology.net
Areas of Expertise: Confederate stamps and postal history

Errors, Freaks and Oddities Collectors Club Expertizing Service
138 East Lakemont Drive
Kingsland GA 31548
Ph: (912) 729-1573
Areas of Expertise: U.S. errors, freaks and oddities

Estonian Philatelic Society Expertizing Service
39 Clafford Lane
Melville NY 11747
Ph: (516) 421-2078
E-mail: esto4@aol.com
Areas of Expertise: Estonia

Hawaiian Philatelic Society Expertizing Service
P.O. Box 10115
Honolulu HI 96816-0115
Areas of Expertise: Hawaii

Hong Kong Stamp Society Expertizing Service
P.O. Box 206
Glenside PA 19038
Fax: (215) 576-6850
Areas of Expertise: Hong Kong

International Association of Philatelic Experts United States Associate members:

Paul Buchsbayew
119 W. 57th St.
New York NY 10019
Ph: (212) 977-7734
Fax: (212) 977-8653
Areas of Expertise: Russia, Soviet Union

William T. Crowe
P.O. Box 2090
Danbury CT 06813-2090
E-mail: wtcrowe@aol.com
Areas of Expertise: United States

John Lievsay
(see American Philatelic Expertizing Service and Philatelic Foundation)
Areas of Expertise: France

Robert W. Lyman
P.O. Box 348
Irvington on Hudson NY 10533
Ph and Fax: (914) 591-6937
Areas of Expertise: British North America, New Zealand

Robert Odenweller
P.O. Box 401
Bernardsville NJ 07924-0401
Ph and Fax: (908) 766-5460
Areas of Expertise: New Zealand, Samoa to 1900

Sergio Sismondo
The Regency Tower, Suite 1109
770 James Street
Syracuse NY 13203
Ph: (315) 422-2331
Fax: (315) 422-2956
Areas of Expertise: British East Africa, Camerouns, Cape of Good Hope, Canada, British North America

International Society for Japanese Philately Expertizing Committee
132 North Pine Terrace
Staten Island NY 10312-4052
Ph: (718) 227-5229
Areas of Expertise: Japan and related areas, except WWII Japanese Occupation issues

International Society for Portuguese Philately Expertizing Service
P.O. Box 43146
Philadelphia PA 19129-3146
Ph and Fax: (215) 843-2106
E-mail: s.s.washburne@worldnet.att.net
Areas of Expertise: Portugal and Colonies

Mexico-Elmhurst Philatelic Society International Expert Committee
P.O. Box 1133
West Covina CA 91793
Areas of Expertise: Mexico

Ukrainian Philatelic & Numismatic Society Expertizing Service
30552 Dell Lane
Warren MI 48092-1862
Areas of Expertise: Ukraine, Western Ukraine

V. G. Greene Philatelic Research Foundation
P.O. Box 204, Station Q
Toronto, ON, M4T 2M1
CANADA
Ph: (416) 921-2073
Fax: (416) 921-1282
www.greenefoundation.ca
E-mail: vggfoundation@on.aibn.com
Areas of Expertise: British North America

Information on Catalogue Values, Grade and Condition

Catalogue Value

The Scott Catalogue value is a retail value; that is, an amount you could expect to pay for a stamp in the grade of Very Fine with no faults. Any exceptions to the grade valued will be noted in the text. The general introduction on the following pages and the individual section introductions further explain the type of material that is valued. The value listed for any given stamp is a reference that reflects recent actual dealer selling prices for that item.

Dealer retail price lists, public auction results, published prices in advertising and individual solicitation of retail prices from dealers, collectors and specialty organizations have been used in establishing the values found in this catalogue. Amos Media Co. values stamps, but Amos Media is not a company engaged in the business of buying and selling stamps as a dealer.

Use this catalogue as a guide for buying and selling. The actual price you pay for a stamp may be higher or lower than the catalogue value because of many different factors, including the amount of personal service a dealer offers, or increased or decreased interest in the country or topic represented by a stamp or set. An item may occasionally be offered at a lower price as a "loss leader," or as part of a special sale. You also may obtain an item inexpensively at public auction because of little interest at that time or as part of a large lot.

Stamps that are of a lesser grade than Very Fine, or those with condition problems, generally trade at lower prices than those given in this catalogue. Stamps of exceptional quality in both grade and condition often command higher prices than those listed.

Values for pre-1900 unused issues are for stamps with approximately half or more of their original gum. Stamps with most or all of their original gum may be expected to sell for more, and stamps with less than half of their original gum may be expected to sell for somewhat less than the values listed. On rarer stamps, it may be expected that the original gum will be somewhat more disturbed than it will be on more common issues. Post-1900 unused issues are assumed to have full original gum. From breakpoints in most countries' listings, stamps are valued as never hinged, due to the wide availability of stamps in that condition. These notations are prominently placed in the listings and in the country information preceding the listings. Some countries also feature listings with dual values for hinged and never-hinged stamps.

Grade

A stamp's grade and condition are crucial to its value. The accompanying illustrations show examples of Very Fine stamps from different time periods, along with examples of stamps in Fine to Very Fine and Extremely Fine grades as points of reference. When a stamp seller offers a stamp in any grade from fine to superb without further qualifying statements, that stamp should not only have the centering grade as defined, but it also should be free of faults or other condition problems.

FINE stamps (illustrations not shown) have designs that are quite off center, with the perforations on one or two sides very close to the design but not quite touching it. There is white space between the perforations and the design that is minimal but evident to the unaided eye. Imperforate stamps may have small margins, and earlier issues may show the design just touching one edge of the stamp design. Very early perforated issues normally will have the perforations slightly cutting into the design. Used stamps may have heavier than usual cancellations.

FINE-VERY FINE stamps will be somewhat off center on one side, or slightly off center on two sides. Imperforate stamps will have two margins of at least normal size, and the design will not touch any edge. For perforated stamps, the perfs are well clear of the design, but are still noticeably off center. *However, early issues of a country may be printed in such a way that the design naturally is very close to the edges. In these cases, the perforations may cut into the design very slightly.* Used stamps will not have a cancellation that detracts from the design.

VERY FINE stamps will be just slightly off center on one or two sides, but the design will be well clear of the edge. The stamp will present a nice, balanced appearance. Imperforate stamps will be well centered within normal-sized margins. *However, early issues of many countries may be printed in such a way that the perforations may touch the design on one or more sides. Where this is the case, a boxed note will be found defining the centering and margins of the stamps being valued.* Used stamps will have light or otherwise neat cancellations. This is the grade used to establish Scott Catalogue values.

EXTREMELY FINE stamps are close to being perfectly centered. Imperforate stamps will have even margins that are slightly larger than normal. Even the earliest perforated issues will have perforations clear of the design on all sides.

Amos Media Co. recognizes that there is no formally enforced grading scheme for postage stamps, and that the final price you pay or obtain for a stamp will be determined by individual agreement at the time of transaction.

Condition

Grade addresses only centering and (for used stamps) cancellation. *Condition* refers to factors other than grade that affect a stamp's desirability.

Factors that can increase the value of a stamp include exceptionally wide margins, particularly fresh color, the presence of selvage, and plate or die varieties. Unusual cancels on used stamps (particularly those of the 19th century) can greatly enhance their value as well.

Factors other than faults that decrease the value of a stamp include loss of original gum, regumming, a hinge remnant or foreign object adhering to the gum, natural inclusions, straight edges, and markings or notations applied by collectors or dealers.

Faults include missing pieces, tears, pin or other holes, surface scuffs, thin spots, creases, toning, short or pulled perforations, clipped perforations, oxidation or other forms of color changelings, soiling, stains, and such man-made changes as reperforations or the chemical removal or lightening of a cancellation.

Grading Illustrations

On the following two pages are illustrations of various stamps from countries appearing in this volume. These stamps are arranged by country, and they represent early or important issues that are often found in widely different grades in the marketplace. The editors believe the illustrations will prove useful in showing the margin size and centering that will be seen on the various issues.

In addition to the matters of margin size and centering, collectors are reminded that the very fine stamps valued in the Scott catalogues also will possess fresh color and intact perforations, and they will be free from defects.

Examples shown are computer-manipulated images made from single digitized master illustrations.

Stamp Illustrations Used in the Catalogue

It is important to note that the stamp images used for identification purposes in this catlaogue may not be indicative of the grade of stamp being valued. Refer to the written discussion of grades on this page and to the grading illustrations on the following two pages for grading information.

Fine-Very Fine

SCOTT
CATALOGUES
VALUE
STAMPS IN
THIS GRADE

Very Fine

Extremely Fine

Fine-Very Fine

SCOTT
CATALOGUES
VALUE
STAMPS IN
THIS GRADE

Very Fine

Extremely Fine

Fine-Very Fine →

SCOTT CATALOGUES VALUE STAMPS IN THIS GRADE

Very Fine →

Extremely Fine →

Fine-Very Fine →

SCOTT CATALOGUES VALUE STAMPS IN THIS GRADE

Very Fine →

Extremely Fine →

For purposes of helping to determine the gum condition and value of an unused stamp, Scott presents the following chart which details different gum conditions and indicates how the conditions correlate with the Scott values for unused stamps. Used together, the Illustrated Grading Chart on the previous pages and this Illustrated Gum Chart should allow catalogue users to better understand the grade and gum condition of stamps valued in the Scott catalogues.

Gum Categories:	MINT N.H.	ORIGINAL GUM (O.G.)				NO GUM
	Mint Never Hinged *Free from any disturbance*	**Lightly Hinged** *Faint impression of a removed hinge over a small area*	**Hinge Mark or Remnant** *Prominent hinged spot with part or all of the hinge remaining*	**Large part o.g.** *Approximately half or more of the gum intact*	**Small part o.g.** *Approximately less than half of the gum intact*	**No gum** *Only if issued with gum*
Commonly Used Symbol:	★ ★	★	★	★	★	(★)
Pre-1900 Issues (Pre-1881 for U.S.)	*Very fine pre-1900 stamps in these categories trade at a premium over Scott value*			Scott Value for "Unused"		Scott "No Gum" listings for selected unused classic stamps
From 1900 to break-points for listings of never-hinged stamps	Scott "Never Hinged" listings for selected unused stamps	Scott Value for "Unused" (Actual value will be affected by the degree of hinging of the full o.g.)				
From breakpoints noted for many countries	Scott Value for "Unused"					

Never Hinged (NH; ★★): A never-hinged stamp will have full original gum that will have no hinge mark or disturbance. The presence of an expertizer's mark does not disqualify a stamp from this designation.

Original Gum (OG; ★): Pre-1900 stamps should have approximately half or more of their original gum. On rarer stamps, it may be expected that the original gum will be somewhat more disturbed than it will be on more common issues. Post-1900 stamps should have full original gum. Original gum will show some disturbance caused by a previous hinge(s) which may be present or entirely removed. The actual value of a post-1900 stamp will be affected by the degree of hinging of the full original gum.

Disturbed Original Gum: Gum showing noticeable effects of humidity, climate or hinging over more than half of the gum. The significance of gum disturbance in valuing a stamp in any of the Original Gum categories depends on the degree of disturbance, the rarity and normal gum condition of the issue and other variables affecting quality.

Regummed (RG; (★)): A regummed stamp is a stamp without gum that has had some type of gum privately applied at a time after it was issued. This normally is done to deceive collectors and/or dealers into thinking that the stamp has original gum and therefore has a higher value. A regummed stamp is considered the same as a stamp with none of its original gum for purposes of grading.

Understanding the Listings

On the opposite page is an enlarged "typical" listing from this catalogue. Below are detailed explanations of each of the highlighted parts of the listing.

❶ Scott number — Scott catalogue numbers are used to identify specific items when buying, selling or trading stamps. Each listed postage stamp from every country has a unique Scott catalogue number. Therefore, Germany Scott 99, for example, can only refer to a single stamp. Although the Scott catalogue usually lists stamps in chronological order by date of issue, there are exceptions. When a country has issued a set of stamps over a period of time, those stamps within the set are kept together without regard to date of issue. This follows the normal collecting approach of keeping stamps in their natural sets.

When a country issues a set of stamps over a period of time, a group of consecutive catalogue numbers is reserved for the stamps in that set, as issued. If that group of numbers proves to be too few, capital-letter suffixes, such as "A" or "B," may be added to existing numbers to create enough catalogue numbers to cover all items in the set. A capital-letter suffix indicates a major Scott catalogue number listing. Scott generally uses a suffix letter only once. Therefore, a catalogue number listing with a capital-letter suffix will seldom be found with the same letter (lower case) used as a minor-letter listing. If there is a Scott 16A in a set, for example, there will seldom be a Scott 16a. However, a minor-letter "a" listing may be added to a major number containing an "A" suffix (Scott 16Aa, for example).

Suffix letters are cumulative. A minor "b" variety of Scott 16A would be Scott 16Ab, not Scott 16b.

There are times when a reserved block of Scott catalogue numbers is too large for a set, leaving some numbers unused. Such gaps in the numbering sequence also occur when the catalogue editors move an item's listing elsewhere or have removed it entirely from the catalogue. Scott does not attempt to account for every possible number, but rather attempts to assure that each stamp is assigned its own number.

Scott numbers designating regular postage normally are only numerals. Scott numbers for other types of stamps, such as air post, semi-postal, postal tax, postage due, occupation and others have a prefix consisting of one or more capital letters or a combination of numerals and capital letters.

❷ Illustration number — Illustration or design-type numbers are used to identify each catalogue illustration. For most sets, the lowest face-value stamp is shown. It then serves as an example of the basic design approach for other stamps not illustrated. Where more than one stamp use the same illustration number, but have differences in design, the design paragraph or the description line clearly indicates the design on each stamp not illustrated. Where there are both vertical and horizontal designs in a set, a single illustration may be used, with the exceptions noted in the design paragraph or description line.

When an illustration is followed by a lower-case letter in parentheses, such as "A2(b)," the trailing letter indicates which overprint or surcharge illustration applies.

Illustrations normally are 70 percent of the original size of the stamp. Oversized stamps, blocks and souvenir sheets are reduced even more. Overprints and surcharges are shown at 100 percent of their original size if shown alone, but are 70 percent of original size if shown on stamps. In some cases, the illustration will be placed above the set, between listings or omitted completely. Overprint and surcharge illustrations are not placed in this catalogue for purposes of expertizing stamps.

❸ Paper color — The color of a stamp's paper is noted in italic type when the paper used is not white.

❹ Listing styles — There are two principal types of catalogue listings: major and minor.

Major listings are in a larger type style than minor listings. The catalogue number is a numeral that can be found with or without a capital-letter suffix, and with or without a prefix.

Minor listings are in a smaller type style and have a small-letter suffix or (if the listing immediately follows that of the major number)

may show only the letter. These listings identify a variety of the major item. Examples include perforation and shade differences, multiples (some souvenir sheets, booklet panes and se-tenant combinations), and singles of multiples.

Examples of major number listings include 16, 28A, B97, C13A, 10N5, and 10N6A. Examples of minor numbers are 16a and C13Ab.

❺ Basic information about a stamp or set — Introducing each stamp issue is a small section (usually a line listing) of basic information about a stamp or set. This section normally includes the date of issue, method of printing, perforation, watermark and, sometimes, some additional information of note. *Printing method, perforation and watermark apply to the following sets until a change is noted.* Stamps created by overprinting or surcharging previous issues are assumed to have the same perforation, watermark, printing method and other production characteristics as the original. Dates of issue are as precise as Scott is able to confirm and often reflect the dates on first-day covers, rather than the actual date of release.

❻ Denomination — This normally refers to the face value of the stamp; that is, the cost of the unused stamp at the post office at the time of issue. When a denomination is shown in parentheses, it does not appear on the stamp. This includes the non-denominated stamps of the United States, Brazil and Great Britain, for example.

❼ Color or other description — This area provides information to solidify identification of a stamp. In many recent cases, a description of the stamp design appears in this space, rather than a listing of colors.

❽ Year of issue — In stamp sets that have been released in a period that spans more than a year, the number shown in parentheses is the year that stamp first appeared. Stamps without a date appeared during the first year of the issue. Dates are not always given for minor varieties.

❾ Value unused and Value used — The Scott catalogue values are based on stamps that are in a grade of Very Fine unless stated otherwise. Unused values refer to items that have not seen postal, revenue or any other duty for which they were intended. Pre-1900 unused stamps that were issued with gum must have at least most of their original gum. Later issues are assumed to have full original gum. From breakpoints specified in most countries' listings, stamps are valued as never hinged. Stamps issued without gum are noted. Modern issues with PVA or other synthetic adhesives may appear ungummed. Unused self-adhesive stamps are valued as appearing undisturbed on their original backing paper. Values for used self-adhesive stamps are for examples either on piece or off piece. For a more detailed explanation of these values, please see the "Catalogue Value," "Condition" and "Understanding Valuing Notations" sections elsewhere in this introduction.

In some cases, where used stamps are more valuable than unused stamps, the value is for an example with a contemporaneous cancel, rather than a modern cancel or a smudge or other unclear marking. For those stamps that were released for postal and fiscal purposes, the used value represents a postally used stamp. Stamps with revenue cancels generally sell for less.

Stamps separated from a complete se-tenant multiple usually will be worth less than a pro-rated portion of the se-tenant multiple, and stamps lacking the attached labels that are noted in the listings will be worth less than the values shown.

❿ Changes in basic set information — Bold type is used to show any changes in the basic data given for a set of stamps. These basic data categories include perforation gauge measurement, paper type, printing method and watermark.

⓫ Total value of a set — The total value of sets of three or more stamps issued after 1900 are shown. The set line also notes the range of Scott numbers and total number of stamps included in the grouping. The actual value of a set consisting predominantly of stamps having the minimum value of 25 cents may be less than the total value shown. Similarly, the actual value or catalogue value of se-tenant pairs or of blocks consisting of stamps having the minimum value of 25 cents may be less than the catalogue values of the component parts.

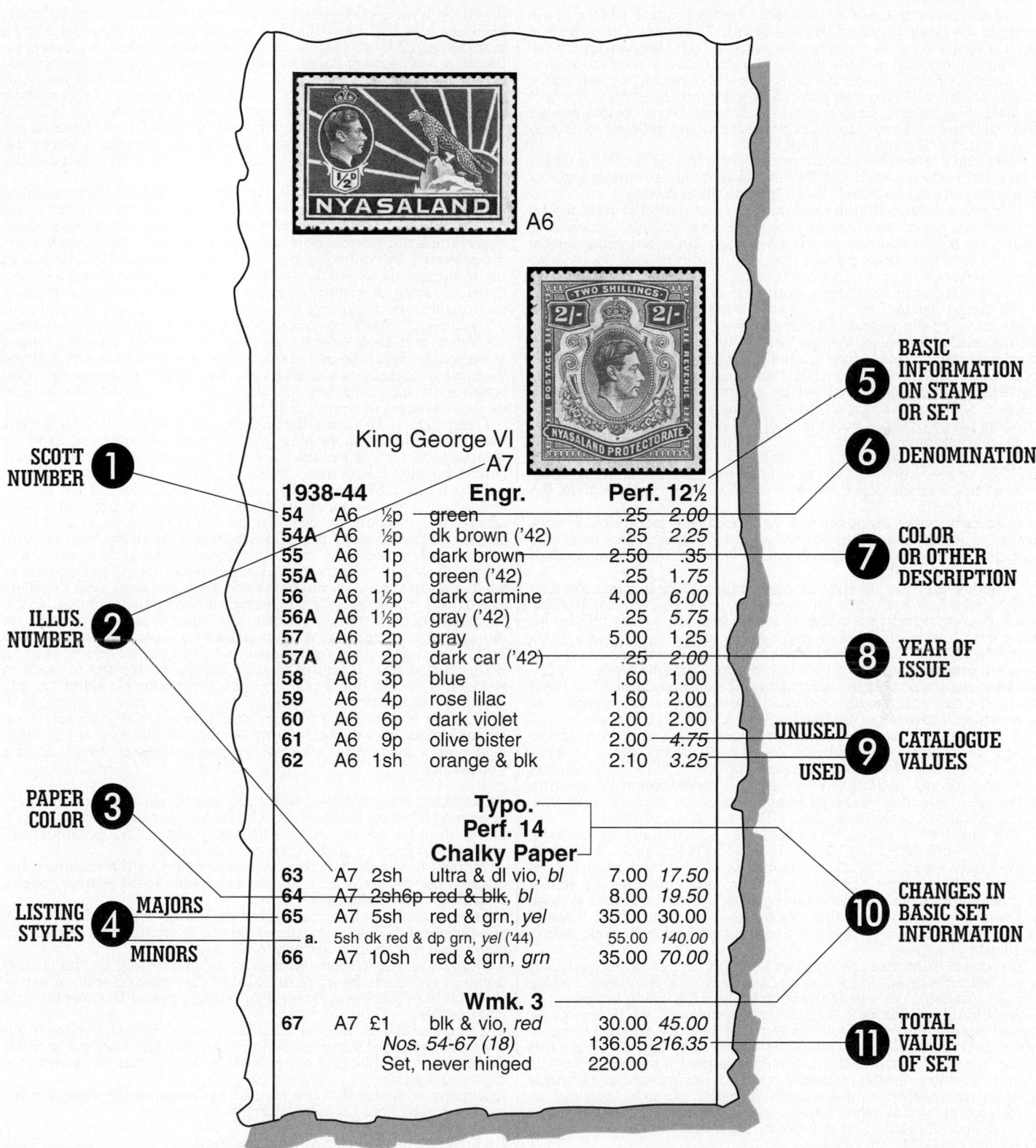

A6

King George VI
A7

SCOTT NUMBER ❶

ILLUS. NUMBER ❷

PAPER COLOR ❸

LISTING STYLES ❹ MAJORS / MINORS

❺ BASIC INFORMATION ON STAMP OR SET

❻ DENOMINATION

❼ COLOR OR OTHER DESCRIPTION

❽ YEAR OF ISSUE

❾ CATALOGUE VALUES — UNUSED / USED

❿ CHANGES IN BASIC SET INFORMATION

⓫ TOTAL VALUE OF SET

Scott	Illus.	Denom.	Description	Unused	Used
1938-44			**Engr.**	**Perf. 12½**	
54	A6	½p	green	.25	*2.00*
54A	A6	½p	dk brown ('42)	.25	*2.25*
55	A6	1p	dark brown	2.50	.35
55A	A6	1p	green ('42)	.25	1.75
56	A6	1½p	dark carmine	4.00	*6.00*
56A	A6	1½p	gray ('42)	.25	5.75
57	A6	2p	gray	5.00	1.25
57A	A6	2p	dark car ('42)	.25	*2.00*
58	A6	3p	blue	.60	1.00
59	A6	4p	rose lilac	1.60	2.00
60	A6	6p	dark violet	2.00	2.00
61	A6	9p	olive bister	2.00	*4.75*
62	A6	1sh	orange & blk	2.10	*3.25*

Typo.
Perf. 14
Chalky Paper

Scott	Illus.	Denom.	Description	Unused	Used
63	A7	2sh	ultra & dl vio, *bl*	7.00	*17.50*
64	A7	2sh6p	red & blk, *bl*	8.00	*19.50*
65	A7	5sh	red & grn, *yel*	35.00	30.00
a.		5sh	dk red & dp grn, *yel* ('44)	55.00	*140.00*
66	A7	10sh	red & grn, *grn*	35.00	*70.00*

Wmk. 3

Scott	Illus.	Denom.	Description	Unused	Used
67	A7	£1	blk & vio, *red*	30.00	*45.00*
			Nos. 54-67 (18)	136.05	*216.35*
			Set, never hinged	220.00	

Catalogue Listing Policy

It is the intent of Amos Media Co. to list all postage stamps of the world in the *Scott Standard Postage Stamp Catalogue*. The only strict criteria for listing is that stamps be decreed legal for postage by the issuing country and that the issuing country actually have an operating postal system. Whether the primary intent of issuing a given stamp or set was for sale to postal patrons or to stamp collectors is not part of our listing criteria. Scott's role is to provide basic comprehensive postage stamp information. It is up to each stamp collector to choose which items to include in a collection.

It is Scott's objective to seek reasons why a stamp should be listed, rather than why it should not. Nevertheless, there are certain types of items that will not be listed. These include the following:

1. Unissued items that are not officially distributed or released by the issuing postal authority. If such items are officially issued at a later date by the country, they will be listed. Unissued items consist of those that have been printed and then held from sale for reasons such as change in government, errors found on stamps or something deemed objectionable about a stamp subject or design.

2. Stamps "issued" by non-existent postal entities or fantasy countries, such as Nagaland, Occusi-Ambeno, Staffa, Sedang, Torres Straits and others. Also, stamps "issued" in the names of legitimate, stamp-issuing countries that are not authorized by those countries.

3. Semi-official or unofficial items not required for postage. Examples include items issued by private agencies for their own express services. When such items are required for delivery, or are valid as prepayment of postage, they are listed.

4. Local stamps issued for local use only. Postage stamps issued by governments specifically for "domestic" use, such as Haiti Scott 219-228, or the United States non-denominated stamps, are not considered to be locals, since they are valid for postage throughout the country of origin.

5. Items not valid for postal use. For example, a few countries have issued souvenir sheets that are not valid for postage. This area also includes a number of worldwide charity labels (some denominated) that do not pay postage.

6. Intentional varieties, such as imperforate stamps that look like their perforated counterparts and are usually issued in very small quantities. Also, other egregiously exploitative issues such as stamps sold for far more than face value, stamps purposefully issued in artificially small quantities or only against advance orders, stamps awarded only to a selected audience such as a philatelic bureau's standing order customers, or stamps sold only in conjunction with other products. All of these kinds of items are usually controlled issues and/or are intended for speculation. These items normally will be included in a footnote.

7. Items distributed by the issuing government only to a limited group, club, philatelic exhibition or a single stamp dealer or other private company. These items normally will be included in a footnote.

8. Stamps not available to collectors. These generally are rare items, all of which are held by public institutions such as museums. The existence of such items often will be cited in footnotes.

The fact that a stamp has been used successfully as postage, even on international mail, is not in itself sufficient proof that it was legitimately issued. Numerous examples of so-called stamps from non-existent countries are known to have been used to post letters that have successfully passed through the international mail system.

There are certain items that are subject to interpretation. When a stamp falls outside our specifications, it may be listed along with a cautionary footnote.

A number of factors are considered in our approach to analyzing how a stamp is listed. The following list of factors is presented to share with you, the catalogue user, the complexity of the listing process.

Additional printings — "Additional printings" of a previously issued stamp may range from an item that is totally different to cases where it is impossible to differentiate from the original. At least a minor number (a small-letter suffix) is assigned if there is a distinct change in stamp shade, noticeably redrawn design, or a significantly different perforation measurement. A major number (numeral or numeral and capital-letter combination) is assigned if the editors feel the "additional printing" is sufficiently different from the original that it constitutes a different issue.

Commemoratives — Where practical, commemoratives with the same theme are placed in a set. For example, the U.S. Civil War Centennial set of 1961-65 and the Constitution Bicentennial series of 1989-90 appear as sets. Countries such as Japan and Korea issue such material on a regular basis, with an announced, or at least predictable, number of stamps known in advance. Occasionally, however, stamp sets that were released over a period of years have been separated. Appropriately placed footnotes will guide you to each set's continuation.

Definitive sets — Blocks of numbers generally have been reserved for definitive sets, based on previous experience with any given country. If a few more stamps were issued in a set than originally expected,

they often have been inserted into the original set with a capital-letter suffix, such as U.S. Scott 1059A. If it appears that many more stamps than the originally allotted block will be released before the set is completed, a new block of numbers will be reserved, with the original one being closed off. In some cases, such as the U.S. Transportation and Great Americans series, several blocks of numbers exist. Appropriately placed footnotes will guide you to each set's continuation.

New country — Membership in the Universal Postal Union is not a consideration for listing status or order of placement within the catalogue. The index will tell you in what volume or page number the listings begin.

"No release date" items — The amount of information available for any given stamp issue varies greatly from country to country and even from time to time. Extremely comprehensive information about new stamps is available from some countries well before the stamps are released. By contrast some countries do not provide information about stamps or release dates. Most countries, however, fall between these extremes. A country may provide denominations or subjects of stamps from upcoming issues that are not issued as planned. Sometimes, philatelic agencies, those private firms hired to represent countries, add these later-issued items to sets well after the formal release date. This time period can range from weeks to years. If these items were officially released by the country, they will be added to the appropriate spot in the set. In many cases, the specific release date of a stamp or set of stamps may never be known.

Overprints — The color of an overprint is always noted if it is other than black. Where more than one color of ink has been used on overprints of a single set, the color used is noted. Early overprint and surcharge illustrations were altered to prevent their use by forgers.

Personalized Stamps — Since 1999, the special service of personalizing stamp vignettes, or labels attached to stamps, has been offered to customers by postal administrations of many countries. Sheets of these stamps are sold, singly or in quantity, only through special orders made by mail, in person, or through a sale on a computer website with the postal administrations or their agents for which an extra fee is charged, though some countries offer to collectors at face value personalized stamps having generic images in the vignettes or on the attached labels. It is impossible for any catalogue to know what images have been chosen by customers. Images can be 1) owned or created by the customer, 2) a generic image, or 3) an image pulled from a library of stock images on the stamp creation website. It is also impossible to know the quantity printed for any stamp having a particular image. So from a valuing standpoint, any image is equivalent to any other image for any personalized stamp having the same catalogue number. Illustrations of personalized stamps in the catalogue are not always those of stamps having generic images.

Personalized items are listed with some exceptions. These include:
1. Stamps or sheets that have attached labels that the customer cannot personalize, but which are nonetheless marketed as "personalized," and are sold for far more than the franking value.
2. Stamps or sheets that can be personalized by the customer, but where a portion of the print run must be ceded to the issuing country for sale to other customers.
3. Stamps or sheets that are created exclusively for a particular commercial client, or clients, including stamps that differ from any similar stamp that has been made available to the public.
4. Stamps or sheets that are deliberately conceived by the issuing authority that have been, or are likely to be, created with an excessive number of different face values, sizes, or other features that are changeable.
5. Stamps or sheets that are created by postal administrations using the same system of stamp personalization that has been put in place for use by the public that are printed in limited quantities and sold above face value.
6. Stamps or sheets that are created by licensees not directly affiliated or controlled by a postal administration.

Excluded items may or may not be footnoted.

Se-tenants — Connected stamps of differing features (se-tenants) will be listed in the format most commonly collected. This includes pairs, blocks or larger multiples. Se-tenant units are not always symmetrical. An example is Australia Scott 508, which is a block of seven stamps. If the stamps are primarily collected as a unit, the major number may be assigned to the multiple, with minors going to each component stamp. In cases where continuous-design or other unit se-tenants will receive significant postal use, each stamp is given a major Scott number listing. This includes issues from the United States, Canada, Germany and Great Britain, for example.

Special Notices

Classification of stamps

The *Scott Standard Postage Stamp Catalogue* lists stamps by country of issue. The next level of organization is a listing by section on the basis of the function of the stamps. The principal sections cover regular postage, semi-postal, air post, special delivery, registration, postage due and other categories. Except for regular postage, catalogue numbers for all sections include a prefix letter (or number-letter combination) denoting the class to which a given stamp belongs. When some countries issue sets containing stamps from more than one category, the catalogue will at times list all of the stamps in one category (such as air post stamps listed as part of a postage set).

The following is a listing of the most commonly used catalogue prefixes.

Prefix .... Category

C.........	Air Post
M........	Military
P.........	Newspaper
N.........	Occupation - Regular Issues
O........	Official
Q........	Parcel Post
J..........	Postage Due
RA	Postal Tax
B.........	Semi-Postal
E.........	Special Delivery
MR......	War Tax

Other prefixes used by more than one country include the following:

H.........	Acknowledgment of Receipt
I..........	Late Fee
CO......	Air Post Official
CQ......	Air Post Parcel Post
RAC....	Air Post Postal Tax
CF	Air Post Registration
CB	Air Post Semi-Postal
CBO ...	Air Post Semi-Postal Official
CE.......	Air Post Special Delivery
EY.......	Authorized Delivery
S.........	Franchise
G	Insured Letter
GY......	Marine Insurance
MC	Military Air Post
MQ	Military Parcel Post
NC......	Occupation - Air Post
NO......	Occupation - Official
NJ........	Occupation - Postage Due
NRA....	Occupation - Postal Tax
NB	Occupation - Semi-Postal
NE	Occupation - Special Delivery
QY......	Parcel Post Authorized Delivery
AR	Postal-fiscal
RAJ	Postal Tax Due
RAB	Postal Tax Semi-Postal
F.........	Registration
EB.......	Semi-Postal Special Delivery
EO	Special Delivery Official
QE	Special Handling

New issue listings

Updates to this catalogue appear each month in the *Linn's Stamp News* monthly magazine. Included in this update are additions to the listings of countries found in the *Scott Standard Postage Stamp Catalogue* and the *Specialized Catalogue of United States Stamps and Covers*, as well as corrections and updates to current editions of this catalogue.

From time to time there will be changes in the final listings of stamps from the *Linn's Stamp News* magazine to the next edition of the catalogue. This occurs as more information about certain stamps or sets becomes available.

The catalogue update section of the *Linn's Stamp News* magazine is the most timely presentation of this material available. Annual subscriptions to *Linn's Stamp News* are available from Linn's Stamp News, Box 926, Sidney, OH 45365-0926.

Number additions, deletions & changes

A listing of catalogue number additions, deletions and changes from the previous edition of the catalogue appears in each volume. See Catalogue Number Additions, Deletions & Changes in the table of contents for the location of this list.

Understanding valuing notations

The *minimum catalogue value* of an individual stamp or set is 25 cents. This represents a portion of the cost incurred by a dealer when he prepares an individual stamp for resale. As a point of philatelic-economic fact, the lower the value shown for an item in this catalogue, the greater the percentage of that value is attributed to dealer mark up and profit margin. In many cases, such as the 25-cent minimum value, that price does not cover the labor or other costs involved with stocking it as an individual stamp. The sum of minimum values in a set does not properly represent the value of a complete set primarily composed of a number of minimum-value stamps, nor does the sum represent the actual value of a packet made up of minimum-value stamps. Thus a packet of 1,000 different common stamps — each of which has a catalogue value of 25 cents — normally sells for considerably less than 250 dollars!

The *absence of a retail value* for a stamp does not necessarily suggest that a stamp is scarce or rare. A dash in the value column means that the stamp is known in a stated form or variety, but information is either lacking or insufficient for purposes of establishing a usable catalogue value.

Stamp values in *italics* generally refer to items that are difficult to value accurately. For expensive items, such as those priced at $1,000 or higher, a value in italics indicates that the affected item trades very seldom. For inexpensive items, a value in italics represents a warning. One example is a "blocked" issue where the issuing postal administration may have controlled one stamp in a set in an attempt to make the whole set more valuable. Another example is an item that sold at an extreme multiple of face value in the marketplace at the time of its issue.

One type of warning to collectors that appears in the catalogue is illustrated by a stamp that is valued considerably higher in used condition than it is as unused. In this case, collectors are cautioned to be certain the used version has a genuine and contemporaneous cancellation. The type of cancellation on a stamp can be an important factor in determining its sale price. Catalogue values do not apply to fiscal, telegraph or non-contemporaneous postal cancels, unless otherwise noted.

Some countries have released back issues of stamps in canceled-to-order form, sometimes covering as much as a 10-year period. The Scott Catalogue values for used stamps reflect canceled-to-order material when such stamps are found to predominate in the marketplace for the issue involved. Notes frequently appear in the stamp listings to specify which items are valued as canceled-to-order, or if there is a premium for postally used examples.

Many countries sell canceled-to-order stamps at a marked reduction of face value. Countries that sell or have sold canceled-to-order stamps at *full* face value include United Nations, Australia, Netherlands, France and Switzerland. It may be almost impossible to identify such stamps if the gum has been removed, because official government canceling devices are used. Postally used examples of these items on cover, however, are usually worth more than the canceled-to-order stamps with original gum.

Abbreviations

Scott uses a consistent set of abbreviations throughout this catalogue to conserve space, while still providing necessary information.

COLOR ABBREVIATIONS

amb. amber	crim. crimson	ol ..... olive
anil.. aniline	cr ..... cream	olvn . olivine
ap.... apple	dk .... dark	org... orange
aqua aquamarine	dl ..... dull	pck .. peacock
az .... azure	dp.... deep	pnksh pinkish
bis ... bister	db.... drab	Prus. Prussian
bl ..... blue	emer emerald	pur... purple
bld... blood	gldn. golden	redsh reddish
blk... black	gryshgrayish	res ... reseda
bril... brilliant	grn... green	ros ... rosine
brn... brown	grnsh greenish	ryl.... royal
brnsh brownish	hel ... heliotrope	sal ... salmon
brnz. bronze	hn.... henna	saph sapphire
brt.... bright	ind... indigo	scar . scarlet
brnt . burnt	int .... intense	sep .. sepia
car... carmine	lav ... lavender	sien . sienna
cer ... cerise	lem.. lemon	sil.... silver
chlky chalky	lil ..... lilac	sl...... slate
chamchamois	lt ...... light	stl ..... steel
chnt . chestnut	mag. magenta	turq.. turquoise
choc chocolate	man. manila	ultra ultramarine
chr... chrome	mar.. maroon	Ven.. Venetian
cit .... citron	mv ... mauve	ver ... vermilion
cl...... claret	multi multicolored	vio ... violet
cob .. cobalt	mlky milky	yel ... yellow
cop .. copper	myr.. myrtle	yelsh yellowish

When no color is given for an overprint or surcharge, black is the color used. Abbreviations for colors used for overprints and surcharges include: "(B)" or "(Blk)," black; "(Bl)," blue; "(R)," red; and "(G)," green.

Additional abbreviations in this catalogue are shown below:

Adm.	Administration
AFL	American Federation of Labor
Anniv.	Anniversary
APS	American Philatelic Society
Assoc.	Association
ASSR.	Autonomous Soviet Socialist Republic
b.	Born
BEP	Bureau of Engraving and Printing
Bicent.	Bicentennial
Bklt.	Booklet
Brit.	British
btwn.	Between
Bur.	Bureau
c. or ca.	Circa
Cat.	Catalogue
Cent.	Centennial, century, centenary
CIO	Congress of Industrial Organizations
Conf.	Conference
Cong.	Congress
Cpl.	Corporal
CTO	Canceled to order
d.	Died
Dbl.	Double
EDU	Earliest documented use
Engr.	Engraved
Exhib.	Exhibition
Expo.	Exposition
Fed.	Federation
GB	Great Britain
Gen.	General
GPO	General post office
Horiz.	Horizontal
Imperf.	Imperforate
Impt.	Imprint

Intl.	International
Invtd.	Inverted
L	Left
Lieut., lt.	Lieutenant
Litho.	Lithographed
LL	Lower left
LR	Lower right
mm	Millimeter
Ms.	Manuscript
Natl.	National
No.	Number
NY	New York
NYC	New York City
Ovpt.	Overprint
Ovptd.	Overprinted
P	Plate number
Perf.	Perforated, perforation
Phil.	Philatelic
Photo.	Photogravure
PO	Post office
Pr.	Pair
P.R.	Puerto Rico
Prec.	Precancel, precanceled
Pres.	President
PTT	Post, Telephone and Telegraph
R	Right
Rio	Rio de Janeiro
Sgt.	Sergeant
Soc.	Society
Souv.	Souvenir
SSR	Soviet Socialist Republic, see ASSR
St.	Saint, street
Surch.	Surcharge
Typo.	Typographed
UL	Upper left
Unwmkd.	Unwatermarked
UPU	Universal Postal Union
UR	Upper Right
US	United States
USPOD	United States Post Office Department
USSR	Union of Soviet Socialist Republics
Vert.	Vertical
VP	Vice president
Wmk.	Watermark
Wmkd.	Watermarked
WWI	World War I
WWII	World War II

Examination

Amos Media Co. will not comment upon the genuineness, grade or condition of stamps, because of the time and responsibility involved. Rather, there are several expertizing groups that undertake this work for both collectors and dealers. Neither will Amos Media Co. appraise or identify philatelic material. The company cannot take responsibility for unsolicited stamps or covers sent by individuals.

All letters, E-mails, etc. are read attentively, but they are not always answered due to time considerations.

How to order from your dealer

When ordering stamps from a dealer, it is not necessary to write the full description of a stamp as listed in this catalogue. All you need is the name of the country, the Scott catalogue number and whether the desired item is unused or used. For example, "Japan Scott 422 unused" is sufficient to identify the unused stamp of Japan listed as "422 A206 5y brown."

Basic Stamp Information

A stamp collector's knowledge of the combined elements that make a given stamp issue unique determines his or her ability to identify stamps. These elements include paper, watermark, method of separation, printing, design and gum. On the following pages each of these important areas is briefly described.

Paper

Paper is an organic material composed of a compacted weave of cellulose fibers and generally formed into sheets. Paper used to print stamps may be manufactured in sheets, or it may have been part of a large roll (called a web) before being cut to size. The fibers most often used to create paper on which stamps are printed include bark, wood, straw and certain grasses. In many cases, linen or cotton rags have been added for greater strength and durability. Grinding, bleaching, cooking and rinsing these raw fibers reduces them to a slushy pulp, referred to by paper makers as "stuff." Sizing and, sometimes, coloring matter is added to the pulp to make different types of finished paper.

After the stuff is prepared, it is poured onto sieve-like frames that allow the water to run off, while retaining the matted pulp. As fibers fall onto the screen and are held by gravity, they form a natural weave that will later hold the paper together. If the screen has metal bits that are formed into letters or images attached, it leaves slightly thinned areas on the paper. These are called watermarks.

When the stuff is almost dry, it is passed under pressure through smooth or engraved rollers - dandy rolls - or placed between cloth in a press to be flattened and dried.

Wove Laid Granite

Quadrille Oblong Quadrille Laid Batonne

Stamp paper falls broadly into two types: wove and laid. The nature of the surface of the frame onto which the pulp is first deposited causes the differences in appearance between the two. If the surface is smooth and even, the paper will be of fairly uniform texture throughout. This is known as *wove paper*. Early papermaking machines poured the pulp onto a continuously circulating web of felt, but modern machines feed the pulp onto a cloth-like screen made of closely interwoven fine wires. This paper, when held to a light, will show little dots or points very close together. The proper name for this is "wire wove," but the type is still considered wove. Any U.S. or British stamp printed after 1880 will serve as an example of wire wove paper.

Closely spaced parallel wires, with cross wires at wider intervals, make up the frames used for what is known as *laid paper*. A greater thickness of the pulp will settle between the wires. The paper, when held to a light, will show alternate light and dark lines. The spacing and the thickness of the lines may vary, but on any one sheet of paper they are all alike. See Russia Scott 31-38 for examples of laid paper.

Batonne, from the French word meaning "a staff," is a term used if the lines in the paper are spaced quite far apart, like the printed ruling on a writing tablet. Batonne paper may be either wove or laid. If laid, fine laid lines can be seen between the batons.

Quadrille is the term used when the lines in the paper form little squares. *Oblong quadrille* is the term used when rectangles, rather than squares, are formed. Grid patterns vary from distinct to extremely faint. See Mexico-Guadalajara Scott 35-37 for examples of oblong quadrille paper.

Paper also is classified as thick or thin, hard or soft, and by color. Such colors may include yellowish, greenish, bluish and reddish.

Brief explanations of other types of paper used for printing stamps, as well as examples, follow.

Colored — Colored paper is created by the addition of dye in the paper-making process. Such colors may include shades of yellow, green, blue and red. *Surface-colored papers*, most commonly used for British colonial issues in 1913-14, are created when coloring is added only to the surface during the finishing process. Stamps printed on surface-colored paper have white or uncolored backs, while true colored papers are colored through. See Jamaica Scott 71-73.

Pelure — Pelure paper is a very thin, hard and often brittle paper that is sometimes bluish or grayish in appearance. See Serbia Scott 169-170.

Native — This is a term applied to handmade papers used to produce some of the early stamps of the Indian states. Stamps printed on native paper may be expected to display various natural inclusions that are normal and do not negatively affect value. Japanese paper, originally made of mulberry fibers and rice flour, is part of this group. See Japan Scott 1-18.

Manila — This type of paper is often used to make stamped envelopes and wrappers. It is a coarse-textured stock, usually smooth on one side and rough on the other. A variety of colors of manila paper exist, but the most common range is yellowish-brown.

Silk — Introduced by the British in 1847 as a safeguard against counterfeiting, silk paper contains bits of colored silk thread scattered throughout. The density of these fibers varies greatly and can include as few as one fiber per stamp or hundreds. U.S. revenue Scott R152 is a good example of an easy-to-identify silk paper stamp.

Silk-thread paper has uninterrupted threads of colored silk arranged so that one or more threads run through the stamp or postal stationery. See Great Britain Scott 5-6 and Switzerland Scott 14-19.

Granite — Filled with minute cloth or colored paper fibers of various colors and lengths, granite paper should not be confused with either type of silk paper. Austria Scott 172-175 and a number of Swiss stamps are examples of granite paper.

Chalky — A chalk-like substance coats the surface of chalky paper to discourage the cleaning and reuse of canceled stamps, as well as to provide a smoother, more acceptable printing surface. Because the designs of stamps printed on chalky paper are imprinted on what is often a water-soluble coating, any attempt to remove a cancellation will destroy the stamp. *Do not soak these stamps in any fluid.* To remove a stamp printed on chalky paper from an envelope, wet the paper from underneath the stamp until the gum dissolves enough to release the stamp from the paper. See St. Kitts-Nevis Scott 89-90 for examples of stamps printed on this type of chalky paper.

India — Another name for this paper, originally introduced from China about 1750, is "China Paper." It is a thin, opaque paper often used for plate and die proofs by many countries.

Double — In philately, the term double paper has two distinct meanings. The first is a two-ply paper, usually a combination of a thick and a thin sheet, joined during manufacture. This type was used experimentally as a means to discourage the reuse of stamps.

The design is printed on the thin paper. Any attempt to remove a cancellation would destroy the design. U.S. Scott 158 and other Banknote-era stamps exist on this form of double paper.

The second type of double paper occurs on a rotary press, when the end of one paper roll, or web, is affixed to the next roll to save time feeding the paper through the press. Stamp designs are printed over the joined paper and, if overlooked by inspectors, may get into post office stocks.

Goldbeater's Skin — This type of paper was used for the 1866 issue of Prussia, and was a tough, translucent paper. The design was printed in reverse on the back of the stamp, and the gum applied over the printing. It is impossible to remove stamps printed on this type of paper from the paper to which they are affixed without destroying the design.

Ribbed — Ribbed paper has an uneven, corrugated surface made by passing the paper through ridged rollers. This type exists on some copies of U.S. Scott 156-165.

Various other substances, or substrates, have been used for stamp manufacture, including wood, aluminum, copper, silver and gold foil, plastic, and silk and cotton fabrics.

Watermarks

Watermarks are an integral part of some papers. They are formed in the process of paper manufacture. Watermarks consist of small designs, formed of wire or cut from metal and soldered to the surface of the mold or, sometimes, on the dandy roll. The designs may be in the form of crowns, stars, anchors, letters or other characters or symbols. These pieces of metal - known in the paper-making industry as "bits" - impress a design into the paper. The design sometimes may be seen by holding the stamp to the light. Some are more easily seen with a watermark detector. This important tool is a small black tray into which a stamp is placed face down and dampened with a fast-evaporating watermark detection fluid that brings up the watermark image in the form of dark lines against a lighter background. These dark lines are the thinner areas of the paper known as the watermark. Some watermarks are extremely difficult to locate, due to either a faint impression, watermark location or the color of the stamp. There also are electric watermark detectors that come with plastic filter disks of various colors. The disks neutralize the color of the stamp, permitting the watermark to be seen more easily.

Multiple watermarks of Crown Agents and Burma

Watermarks of Uruguay, Vatican City and Jamaica

WARNING: Some inks used in the photogravure process dissolve in watermark fluids (Please see the section on Soluble Printing Inks). Also, see "chalky paper."

Watermarks may be found normal, reversed, inverted, reversed and inverted, sideways or diagonal, as seen from the back of the stamp. The relationship of watermark to stamp design depends on the position of the printing plates or how paper is fed through the press. On machine-made paper, watermarks normally are read from right to left. The design is repeated closely throughout the sheet in a "multiple-watermark design." In a "sheet watermark," the design appears only once on the sheet, but extends over many stamps. Individual stamps

may carry only a small fraction or none of the watermark.

"Marginal watermarks" occur in the margins of sheets or panes of stamps. They occur on the outside border of paper (ostensibly outside the area where stamps are to be printed). A large row of letters may spell the name of the country or the manufacturer of the paper, or a border of lines may appear. Careless press feeding may cause parts of these letters and/or lines to show on stamps of the outer row of a pane.

Soluble Printing Inks

WARNING: Most stamp colors are permanent; that is, they are not seriously affected by short-term exposure to light or water. Many colors, especially of modern inks, fade from excessive exposure to light. There are stamps printed with inks that dissolve easily in water or in fluids used to detect watermarks. Use of these inks was intentional to prevent the removal of cancellations. Water affects all aniline inks, those on so-called safety paper and some photogravure printings - all such inks are known as fugitive colors. *Removal from paper of such stamps requires care and alternatives to traditional soaking.*

Separation

"Separation" is the general term used to describe methods used to separate stamps. The three standard forms currently in use are perforating, rouletting and die-cutting. These methods are done during the stamp production process, after printing. Sometimes these methods are done on-press or sometimes as a separate step. The earliest issues, such as the 1840 Penny Black of Great Britain (Scott 1), did not have any means provided for separation. It was expected the stamps would be cut apart with scissors or folded and torn. These are examples of imperforate stamps. Many stamps were first issued in imperforate formats and were later issued with perforations. Therefore, care must be observed in buying single imperforate stamps to be certain they were issued imperforate and are not perforated copies that have been altered by having the perforations trimmed away. Stamps issued imperforate usually are valued as singles. However, imperforate varieties of normally perforated stamps should be collected in pairs or larger pieces as indisputable evidence of their imperforate character.

PERFORATION

The chief style of separation of stamps, and the one that is in almost universal use today, is perforating. By this process, paper between the stamps is cut away in a line of holes, usually round, leaving little bridges of paper between the stamps to hold them together. Some types of perforation, such as hyphen-hole perfs, can be confused with roulettes, but a close visual inspection reveals that paper has been removed. The little perforation bridges, which project from the stamp when it is torn from the pane, are called the teeth of the perforation.

As the size of the perforation is sometimes the only way to differentiate between two otherwise identical stamps, it is necessary to be able to accurately measure and describe them. This is done with a perforation gauge, usually a ruler-like device that has dots or graduated lines to show how many perforations may be counted in the space of two centimeters. Two centimeters is the space universally adopted in which to measure perforations.

Perforation gauge

perce en arc   perce en lignes

perce en points   oblique roulette

perce en scie   perce serpentin

To measure a stamp, run it along the gauge until the dots on it fit exactly into the perforations of the stamp. If you are using a graduated-line perforation gauge, simply slide the stamp along the surface until the lines on the gauge perfectly project from the center of the bridges or holes. The number to the side of the line of dots or lines that fit the stamp's perforation is the measurement. For example, an "11" means that 11 perforations fit between two centimeters. The description of the stamp therefore is "perf. 11." If the gauge of the perforations on the top and bottom of a stamp differs from that on the sides, the result is what is known as *compound perforations*. In measuring compound perforations, the gauge at top and bottom is always given first, then the sides. Thus, a stamp that measures 11 at top and bottom and 10½ at the sides is "perf. 11 x 10½." See U.S. Scott 632-642 for examples of compound perforations.

Stamps also are known with perforations different on three or all four sides. Descriptions of such items are clockwise, beginning with the top of the stamp.

A perforation with small holes and teeth close together is a "fine perforation." One with large holes and teeth far apart is a "coarse perforation." Holes that are jagged, rather than clean-cut, are "rough perforations." *Blind perforations* are the slight impressions left by the perforating pins if they fail to puncture the paper. Multiples of stamps showing blind perforations may command a slight premium over normally perforated stamps.

The term *syncopated perfs* describes intentional irregularities in the perforations. The earliest form was used by the Netherlands from 1925-33, where holes were omitted to create distinctive patterns. Beginning in 1992, Great Britain has used an oval perforation to help prevent counterfeiting. Several other countries have started using the oval perfs or other syncopated perf patterns.

A new type of perforation, still primarily used for postal stationery, is known as microperfs. Microperfs are tiny perforations (in some cases hundreds of holes per two centimeters) that allows items to be intentionally separated very easily, while not accidentally breaking apart as easily as standard perforations. These are not currently measured or differentiated by size, as are standard perforations.

ROULETTING

In rouletting, the stamp paper is cut partly or wholly through, with no paper removed. In perforating, some paper is removed. Roulotting derives its name from the French roulette, a spur-like wheel. As the wheel is rolled over the paper, each point makes a small cut. The number of cuts made in a two-centimeter space determines the gauge of the roulette, just as the number of perforations in two centimeters determines the gauge of the perforation.

The shape and arrangement of the teeth on the wheels varies. Various roulette types generally carry French names:

Perce en lignes - rouletted in lines. The paper receives short, straight cuts in lines. This is the most common type of roulotting. See Mexico Scott 500.

Perce en points - pin-rouletted or pin-perfed. This differs from a small perforation because no paper is removed, although round, equidistant holes are pricked through the paper. See Mexico Scott 242-256.

Perce en arc and *perce en scie* - pierced in an arc or saw-toothed designs, forming half circles or small triangles. See Hanover (German States) Scott 25-29.

Perce en serpentin - serpentine roulettes. The cuts form a serpentine or wavy line. See Brunswick (German States) Scott 13-18.

Once again, no paper is removed by these processes, leaving the stamps easily separated, but closely attached.

DIE-CUTTING

The third major form of stamp separation is die-cutting. This is a method where a die in the pattern of separation is created that later cuts the stamp paper in a stroke motion. Although some standard stamps bear die-cut perforations, this process is primarily used for self-adhesive postage stamps. Die-cutting can appear in straight lines, such as U.S. Scott 2522, shapes, such as U.S. Scott 1551, or imitating the appearance of perforations, such as New Zealand Scott 935A and 935B.

Printing Processes

ENGRAVING (Intaglio, Line-engraving, Etching)

Master die — The initial operation in the process of line engraving is making the master die. The die is a small, flat block of softened steel upon which the stamp design is recess engraved in reverse.

Master die

Transfer roll

Photographic reduction of the original art is made to the appropriate size. It then serves as a tracing guide for the initial outline of the design. The engraver lightly traces the design on the steel with his graver, then slowly works the design until it is completed. At various points during the engraving process, the engraver hand-inks the die and makes an impression to check his progress. These are known as progressive die proofs. After completion of the engraving, the die is hardened to withstand the stress and pressures of later transfer operations.

Transfer roll — Next is production of the transfer roll that, as the name implies, is the medium used to transfer the subject from the master die to the printing plate. A blank roll of soft steel, mounted on a mandrel, is placed under the bearers of the transfer press to allow it to roll freely on its axis. The hardened die is placed on the bed of the press and the face of the transfer roll is applied to the die, under pressure. The bed or the roll is then rocked back and forth under increasing pressure, until the soft steel of the roll is forced into every engraved line of the die. The resulting impression on the roll is known as a "relief" or a "relief transfer." The engraved image is now positive in appearance and stands out from the steel. After the required number of reliefs are "rocked in," the soft steel transfer roll is hardened.

Different flaws may occur during the relief process. A defective relief may occur during the rocking in process because of a minute piece of foreign material lodging on the die, or some other cause. Imperfections in the steel of the transfer roll may result in a breaking away of parts of the design. This is known as a relief break, which will show up on finished stamps as small, unprinted areas. If a damaged relief remains in use, it will transfer a repeating defect to the plate. Deliberate alterations of reliefs sometimes occur. "Altered reliefs" designate these changed conditions.

Plate — The final step in pre-printing production is the making of the printing plate. A flat piece of soft steel replaces the die on the bed of the transfer press. One of the reliefs on the transfer roll is positioned over this soft steel. Position, or layout, dots determine the correct position on the plate. The dots have been lightly marked on the plate in advance. After the correct position of the relief is determined,

the design is rocked in by following the same method used in making the transfer roll. The difference is that this time the image is being transferred from the transfer roll, rather than to it. Once the design is entered on the plate, it appears in reverse and is recessed. There are as many transfers entered on the plate as there are subjects printed on the sheet of stamps. It is during this process that double and shifted transfers occur, as well as re-entries. These are the result of improperly entered images that have not been properly burnished out prior to rocking in a new image.

Modern siderography processes, such as those used by the U.S. Bureau of Engraving and Printing, involve an automated form of rocking designs in on preformed cylindrical printing sleeves. The same process also allows for easier removal and re-entry of worn images right on the sleeve.

Transferring the design to the plate

Following the entering of the required transfers on the plate, the position dots, layout dots and lines, scratches and other markings generally are burnished out. Added at this time by the siderographer are any required *guide lines, plate numbers* or other *marginal markings*. The plate is then hand-inked and a proof impression is taken. This is known as a plate proof. If the impression is approved, the plate is machined for fitting onto the press, is hardened and sent to the plate vault ready for use.

On press, the plate is inked and the surface is automatically wiped clean, leaving ink only in the recessed lines. Paper is then forced under pressure into the engraved recessed lines, thereby receiving the ink. Thus, the ink lines on engraved stamps are slightly raised, and slight depressions (debossing) occur on the back of the stamp. Prior to the advent of modern high-speed presses and more advanced ink formulations, paper had to be dampened before receiving the ink. This sometimes led to uneven shrinkage by the time the stamps were perforated, resulting in improperly perforated stamps, or misperfs. Newer presses use drier paper, thus both *wet* and *dry printings* exist on some stamps.

Rotary Press — Until 1914, only flat plates were used to print engraved stamps. Rotary press printing was introduced in 1914, and slowly spread. Some countries still use flat-plate printing.

After approval of the plate proof, older *rotary press plates* require additional machining. They are curved to fit the press cylinder. "Gripper slots" are cut into the back of each plate to receive the "grippers," which hold the plate securely on the press. The plate is then hardened. Stamps printed from these bent rotary press plates are longer or wider than the same stamps printed from flat-plate presses. The stretching of the plate during the curving process is what causes this distortion.

Re-entry — To execute a re-entry on a flat plate, the transfer roll is re-applied to the plate, often at some time after its first use on the press. Worn-out designs can be resharpened by carefully burnishing out the original image and re-entering it from the transfer roll. If the original impression has not been sufficiently removed and the transfer roll is not precisely in line with the remaining impression, the resulting double transfer will make the re-entry obvious. If the registration is true, a re-entry may be difficult or impossible to distinguish. Sometimes a stamp printed from a successful re-entry is identified by having a much sharper and clearer impression than its neighbors. With the advent of rotary presses, post-press re-entries were not possible. After a plate was curved for the rotary press, it was impossible to make a re-entry. This is because the plate had already been bent once (with the design distorted).

However, with the introduction of the previously mentioned modern-style siderography machines, entries are made to the preformed cylindrical printing sleeve. Such sleeves are dechromed and softened. This allows individual images to be burnished out and re-entered on the curved sleeve. The sleeve is then rechromed, resulting in longer press life.

Double Transfer — This is a description of the condition of a transfer on a plate that shows evidence of a duplication of all, or a portion of the design. It usually is the result of the changing of the registration between the transfer roll and the plate during the rocking in of the original entry. Double transfers also occur when only a portion of the design has been rocked in and improper positioning is noted. If the worker elected not to burnish out the partial or completed design, a strong double transfer will occur for part or all of the design.

It sometimes is necessary to remove the original transfer from a plate and repeat the process a second time. If the finished re-worked image shows traces of the original impression, attributable to incomplete burnishing, the result is a partial double transfer.

With the modern automatic machines mentioned previously, double transfers are all but impossible to create. Those partially doubled images on stamps printed from such sleeves are more than likely re-entries, rather than true double transfers.

Re-engraved — Alterations to a stamp design are sometimes necessary after some stamps have been printed. In some cases, either the original die or the actual printing plate may have its "temper" drawn (softened), and the design will be re-cut. The resulting impressions from such a re-engraved die or plate may differ slightly from the original issue, and are known as "re-engraved." If the alteration was made to the master die, all future printings will be consistently different from the original. If alterations were made to the printing plate, each altered stamp on the plate will be slightly different from each other, allowing specialists to reconstruct a complete printing plate.

Dropped Transfers — If an impression from the transfer roll has not been properly placed, a dropped transfer may occur. The final stamp image will appear obviously out of line with its neighbors.

Short Transfer — Sometimes a transfer roll is not rocked its entire length when entering a transfer onto a plate. As a result, the finished transfer on the plate fails to show the complete design, and the finished stamp will have an incomplete design printed. This is known as a "short transfer." U.S. Scott No. 8 is a good example of a short transfer.

TYPOGRAPHY (Letterpress, Surface Printing, Flexography, Dry Offset, High Etch)

Although the word "Typography" is obsolete as a term describing a printing method, it was the accepted term throughout the first century of postage stamps. Therefore, appropriate Scott listings in this catalogue refer to typographed stamps. The current term for this form of printing, however, is "letterpress."

As it relates to the production of postage stamps, letterpress printing is the reverse of engraving. Rather than having recessed areas trap the ink and deposit it on paper, only the raised areas of the design are inked. This is comparable to the type of printing seen by inking and using an ordinary rubber stamp. Letterpress includes all printing where the design is above the surface area, whether it is wood, metal or, in some instances, hardened rubber or polymer plastic.

For most letterpress-printed stamps, the engraved master is made in much the same manner as for engraved stamps. In this instance, however, an additional step is needed. The design is transferred to another surface before being transferred to the transfer roll. In this way, the transfer roll has a recessed stamp design, rather than one done in relief. This makes the printing areas on the final plate raised, or relief areas.

For less-detailed stamps of the 19th century, the area on the die not used as a printing surface was cut away, leaving the surface area raised. The original die was then reproduced by stereotyping or electrotyping. The resulting electrotypes were assembled in the required number and format of the desired sheet of stamps. The plate used in printing the stamps was an electroplate of these assembled electrotypes.

Once the final letterpress plates are created, ink is applied to the raised surface and the pressure of the press transfers the ink impression to the paper. In contrast to engraving, the fine lines of letterpress are impressed on the surface of the stamp, leaving a debossed surface. When viewed from the back (as on a typewritten page), the corresponding line work on the stamp will be raised slightly (embossed) above the surface.

PHOTOGRAVURE (Gravure, Rotogravure, Heliogravure)

In this process, the basic principles of photography are applied to a chemically sensitized metal plate, rather than photographic paper. The design is transferred photographically to the plate through a halftone, or dot-matrix screen, breaking the reproduction into tiny dots. The plate is treated chemically and the dots form depressions, called cells, of varying depths and diameters, depending on the degrees of shade in the design. Then, like engraving, ink is applied to the plate and the surface is wiped clean. This leaves ink in the tiny cells that is lifted out and deposited on the paper when it is pressed against the plate.

Gravure is most often used for multicolored stamps, generally using the three primary colors (red, yellow and blue) and black. By varying the dot matrix pattern and density of these colors, virtually any color can be reproduced. A typical full-color gravure stamp will be created from four printing cylinders (one for each color). The original multicolored image will have been photographically separated into its component colors.

Modern gravure printing may use computer-generated dot-matrix screens, and modern plates may be of various types including metal-coated plastic. The catalogue designation of Photogravure (or "Photo") covers any of these older and more modern gravure methods of printing.

For examples of the first photogravure stamps printed (1914), see Bavaria Scott 94-114.

LITHOGRAPHY (Offset Lithography, Stone Lithography, Dilitho, Planography, Collotype)

The principle that oil and water do not mix is the basis for lithography. The stamp design is drawn by hand or transferred from engraving to the surface of a lithographic stone or metal plate in a greasy (oily) substance. This oily substance holds the ink, which will later be transferred to the paper. The stone (or plate) is wet with an acid fluid, causing it to repel the printing ink in all areas not covered by the greasy substance.

Transfer paper is used to transfer the design from the original stone or plate. A series of duplicate transfers are grouped and, in turn, transferred to the final printing plate.

Photolithography — The application of photographic processes to lithography. This process allows greater flexibility of design, related to use of halftone screens combined with line work. Unlike photogravure or engraving, this process can allow large, solid areas to be printed.

Offset — A refinement of the lithographic process. A rubber-covered blanket cylinder takes the impression from the inked lithographic plate. From the "blanket" the impression is *offset* or transferred to the paper. Greater flexibility and speed are the principal reasons offset printing has largely displaced lithography. The term "lithography" covers both processes, and results are almost identical.

EMBOSSED (Relief) Printing

Embossing, not considered one of the four main printing types, is a method in which the design first is sunk into the metal of the die. Printing is done against a yielding platen, such as leather or linoleum. The platen is forced into the depression of the die, thus forming the design on the paper in relief. This process is often used for metallic inks.

Embossing may be done without color (see Sardinia Scott 4-6); with color printed around the embossed area (see Great Britain Scott 5 and most U.S. envelopes); and with color in exact registration with the embossed subject (see Canada Scott 656-657).

HOLOGRAMS

For objects to appear as holograms on stamps, a model exactly the same size as it is to appear on the hologram must be created. Rather than using photographic film to capture the image, holography records an image on a photoresist material. In processing, chemicals eat away at certain exposed areas, leaving a pattern of constructive and destructive interference. When the photoresist is developed, the result is a pattern of uneven ridges that acts as a mold. This mold is then coated with metal, and the resulting form is used to press copies in much the same way phonograph records are produced.

A typical reflective hologram used for stamps consists of a reproduction of the uneven patterns on a plastic film that is applied to a reflective background, usually a silver or gold foil. Light is reflected off the background through the film, making the pattern present on the film visible. Because of the uneven pattern of the film, the viewer will perceive the objects in their proper three-dimensional relationships with appropriate brightness.

The first hologram on a stamp was produced by Austria in 1988 (Scott 1441).

FOIL APPLICATION

A modern technique of applying color to stamps involves the application of metallic foil to the stamp paper. A pattern of foil is applied to the stamp paper by use of a stamping die. The foil usually is flat, but it may be textured. Canada Scott 1735 has three different foil applications in pearl, bronze and gold. The gold foil was textured using a chemical-etch copper embossing die. The printing of this stamp also involved two-color offset lithography plus embossing.

THERMOGRAPHY

In the 1990s stamps began to be enhanced with thermographic printing. In this process, a powdered polymer is applied over a sheet that has just been printed. The powder adheres to ink that lacks drying or hardening agents and does not adhere to areas where the ink has these agents. The excess powder is removed and the sheet is briefly heated to melt the powder. The melted powder solidifies after cooling, producing a raised, shiny effect on the stamps. See Scott New Caledonia C239-C240.

COMBINATION PRINTINGS

Sometimes two or even three printing methods are combined in producing stamps. In these cases, such as Austria Scott 933 or Canada 1735 (described in the preceding paragraph), the multiple-printing technique can be determined by studying the individual characteristics of each printing type. A few stamps, such as Singapore Scott 684-684A, combine as many as three of the four major printing types (lithography, engraving and typography). When this is done it often indicates the incorporation of security devices against counterfeiting.

INK COLORS

Inks or colored papers used in stamp printing often are of mineral origin, although there are numerous examples of organic-based pigments. As a general rule, organic-based pigments are far more subject to varieties and change than those of mineral-based origin.

The appearance of any given color on a stamp may be affected by many aspects, including printing variations, light, color of paper, aging and chemical alterations.

Numerous printing variations may be observed. Heavier pressure or inking will cause a more intense color, while slight interruptions in the ink feed or lighter impressions will cause a lighter appearance. Stamps printed in the same color by water-based and solvent-based inks can differ significantly in appearance. This affects several stamps in the U.S. Prominent Americans series. Hand-mixed ink formulas (primarily from the 19th century) produced under different conditions (humidity and temperature) account for notable color variations in early printings of the same stamp (see U.S. Scott 248-250, 279B, for example). Different sources of pigment can also result in significant differences in color.

Light exposure and aging are closely related in the way they affect stamp color. Both eventually break down the ink and fade colors, so that a carefully kept stamp may differ significantly in color from an identical copy that has been exposed to light. If stamps are exposed to light either intentionally or accidentally, their colors can be faded or completely changed in some cases.

Papers of different quality and consistency used for the same stamp printing may affect color appearance. Most pelure papers, for example, show a richer color when compared with wove or laid papers. See Russia Scott 181a, for an example of this effect.

The very nature of the printing processes can cause a variety of differences in shades or hues of the same stamp. Some of these shades are scarcer than others, and are of particular interest to the advanced collector.

Luminescence

All forms of tagged stamps fall under the general category of luminescence. Within this broad category is fluorescence, dealing with forms of tagging visible under longwave ultraviolet light, and phosphorescence, which deals with tagging visible only under shortwave light. Phosphorescence leaves an afterglow and fluorescence does not. These treated stamps show up in a range of different colors when exposed to UV light. The differing wavelengths of the light activates the tagging material, making it glow in various colors that usually serve different mail processing purposes.

Intentional tagging is a post-World War II phenomenon, brought about by the increased literacy rate and rapidly growing mail volume. It was one of several answers to the problem of the need for more automated mail processes. Early tagged stamps served the purpose of triggering machines to separate different types of mail. A natural outgrowth was to also use the signal to trigger machines that faced all envelopes the same way and canceled them.

Tagged stamps come in many different forms. Some tagged stamps have luminescent shapes or images imprinted on them as a form of security device. Others have blocks (United States), stripes, frames (South Africa and Canada), overall coatings (United States), bars (Great Britain and Canada) and many other types. Some types of tagging are even mixed in with the pigmented printing ink (Australia Scott 366, Netherlands Scott 478 and U.S. Scott 1359 and 2443).

The means of applying taggant to stamps differs as much as the intended purposes for the stamps. The most common form of tagging is a coating applied to the surface of the printed stamp. Since the taggant ink is frequently invisible except under UV light, it does not interfere with the appearance of the stamp. Another common application is the use of phosphored papers. In this case the paper itself either has a coating of taggant applied before the stamp is printed, has taggant applied during the papermaking process (incorporating it into the fibers), or has the taggant mixed into the coating of the paper. The latter method, among others, is currently in use in the United States.

Many countries now use tagging in various forms to either expedite mail handling or to serve as a printing security device against counterfeiting. Following the introduction of tagged stamps for public use in 1959 by Great Britain, other countries have steadily joined the parade. Among those are Germany (1961); Canada and Denmark (1962); United States, Australia, France and Switzerland (1963); Belgium and Japan (1966); Sweden and Norway (1967); Italy (1968); and Russia (1969). Since then, many other countries have begun using forms of tagging, including Brazil, China, Czechoslovakia, Hong Kong, Guatemala, Indonesia, Israel, Lithuania, Luxembourg, Netherlands, Penrhyn Islands, Portugal, St. Vincent, Singapore, South Africa, Spain and Sweden to name a few.

In some cases, including United States, Canada, Great Britain and Switzerland, stamps were released both with and without tagging. Many of these were released during each country's experimental period. Tagged and untagged versions are listed for the aforementioned countries and are noted in some other countries' listings. For at least a few stamps, the experimentally tagged version is worth far more than its untagged counterpart, such as the 1963 experimental tagged version of France Scott 1024.

In some cases, luminescent varieties of stamps were inadvertently created. Several Russian stamps, for example, sport highly fluorescent ink that was not intended as a form of tagging. Older stamps, such as early U.S. postage dues, can be positively identified by the use of UV light, since the organic ink used has become slightly fluorescent over time. Other stamps, such as Austria Scott 70a-82a (varnish bars) and Obock Scott 46-64 (printed quadrille lines), have become fluorescent over time.

Various fluorescent substances have been added to paper to make it appear brighter. These optical brightners, as they are known, greatly affect the appearance of the stamp under UV light. The brightest of these is known as Hi-Brite paper. These paper varieties are beyond the scope of the Scott Catalogue.

Shortwave UV light also is used extensively in expertizing, since each form of paper has its own fluorescent characteristics that are impossible to perfectly match. It is therefore a simple matter to detect filled thins, added perforation teeth and other alterations that involve the addition of paper. UV light also is used to examine stamps that have had cancels chemically removed and for other purposes as well.

Gum

The Illustrated Gum Chart in the first part of this introduction shows and defines various types of gum condition. Because gum condition has an important impact on the value of unused stamps, we recommend studying this chart and the accompanying text carefully.

The gum on the back of a stamp may be shiny, dull, smooth, rough, dark, white, colored or tinted. Most stamp gumming adhesives use gum arabic or dextrine as a base. Certain polymers such as polyvinyl alcohol (PVA) have been used extensively since World War II.

The Scott Standard Postage Stamp Catalogue does not list items by types of gum. The Scott Specialized Catalogue of United States Stamps and Covers does differentiate among some types of gum for certain issues.

Reprints of stamps may have gum differing from the original issues. In addition, some countries have used different gum formulas for different seasons. These adhesives have different properties that may become more apparent over time.

Many stamps have been issued without gum, and the catalogue will note this fact. See, for example, United States Scott 40-47. Sometimes, gum may have been removed to preserve the stamp. Germany Scott B68, for example, has a highly acidic gum that eventually destroys the stamps. This item is valued in the catalogue with gum removed.

Reprints and Reissues

These are impressions of stamps (usually obsolete) made from the original plates or stones. If they are valid for postage and reproduce obsolete issues (such as U.S. Scott 102-111), the stamps are reissues. If they are from current issues, they are designated as second, third, etc., printing. If designated for a particular purpose, they are called special printings.

When special printings are not valid for postage, but are made from original dies and plates by authorized persons, they are official reprints. Private reprints are made from the original plates and dies by private hands. An example of a private reprint is that of the 1871-1932 reprints made from the original die of the 1845 New Haven, Conn., postmaster's provisional. Official reproductions or imitations are made from new dies and plates by government authorization. Scott will list those reissues that are valid for postage if they differ significantly from the original printing.

The U.S. government made special printings of its first postage stamps in 1875. Produced were official imitations of the first two stamps (listed as Scott 3-4), reprints of the demonetized pre-1861 issues (Scott 40-47) and reissues of the 1861 stamps, the 1869 stamps and the then-current 1875 denominations. Even though the official imitations and the reprints were not valid for postage, Scott lists all of these U.S. special printings.

Most reprints or reissues differ slightly from the original stamp in some characteristic, such as gum, paper, perforation, color or watermark. Sometimes the details are followed so meticulously that only a student of that specific stamp is able to distinguish the reprint or reissue from the original.

Remainders and Canceled to Order

Some countries sell their stock of old stamps when a new issue replaces them. To avoid postal use, the remainders usually are canceled with a punch hole, a heavy line or bar, or a more-or-less regular-looking cancellation. The most famous merchant of remainders was Nicholas F. Seebeck. In the 1880s and 1890s, he arranged printing contracts between the Hamilton Bank Note Co., of which he was a director, and several Central and South American countries. The contracts provided that the plates and all remainders of the yearly issues became the property of Hamilton. Seebeck saw to it that ample stock remained. The "Seebecks," both remainders and reprints, were standard packet fillers for decades.

Some countries also issue stamps canceled-to-order (CTO), either in sheets with original gum or stuck onto pieces of paper or envelopes and canceled. Such CTO items generally are worth less than postally used stamps. In cases where the CTO material is far more prevalent in the marketplace than postally used examples, the catalogue value relates to the CTO examples, with postally used examples noted as premium items. Most CTOs can be detected by the presence of gum. However, as the CTO practice goes back at least to 1885, the gum inevitably has been soaked off some stamps so they could pass as postally used. The normally applied postmarks usually differ slightly from standard postmarks, and specialists are able to tell the difference. When applied individually to envelopes by philatelically minded persons, CTO material is known as favor canceled and generally sells at large discounts.

Cinderellas and Facsimiles

Cinderella is a catch-all term used by stamp collectors to describe phantoms, fantasies, bogus items, municipal issues, exhibition seals, local revenues, transportation stamps, labels, poster stamps and many other types of items. Some cinderella collectors include in their collections local postage issues, telegraph stamps, essays and proofs, forgeries and counterfeits.

A *fantasy* is an adhesive created for a nonexistent stamp-issuing authority. Fantasy items range from imaginary countries (Occusi-Ambeno, Kingdom of Sedang, Principality of Trinidad or Torres Straits), to non-existent locals (Winans City Post), or nonexistent transportation lines (McRobish & Co.'s Acapulco-San Francisco Line).

On the other hand, if the entity exists and could have issued stamps (but did not) or was known to have issued other stamps, the items are considered *bogus* stamps. These would include the Mormon postage stamps of Utah, S. Allan Taylor's Guatemala and Paraguay inventions, the propaganda issues for the South Moluccas and the adhesives of the Page & Keyes local post of Boston.

Phantoms is another term for both fantasy and bogus issues.

Facsimiles are copies or imitations made to represent original stamps, but which do not pretend to be originals. A catalogue illustration is such a facsimile. Illustrations from the Moens catalogue of the last century were occasionally colored and passed off as stamps. Since the beginning of stamp collecting, facsimiles have been made for collectors as space fillers or for reference. They often carry the word "facsimile," "falsch" (German), "sanko" or "mozo" (Japanese), or "faux" (French) overprinted on the face or stamped on the back. Unfortunately, over the years a number of these items have had fake cancels applied over the facsimile notation and have been passed off as genuine.

Forgeries and Counterfeits

Forgeries and counterfeits have been with philately virtually from the beginning of stamp production. Over time, the terminology for the two has been used interchangeably. Although both forgeries and counterfeits are reproductions of stamps, the purposes behind their creation differ considerably.

Among specialists there is an increasing movement to more specifically define such items. Although there is no universally accepted terminology, we feel the following definitions most closely mirror the items and their purposes as they are currently defined.

Forgeries (also often referred to as *Counterfeits*) are reproductions of genuine stamps that have been created to defraud collectors. Such spurious items first appeared on the market around 1860, and most old-time collections contain one or more. Many are crude and easily spotted, but some can deceive experts.

An important supplier of these early philatelic forgeries was the Hamburg printer Gebruder Spiro. Many others with reputations in this craft included S. Allan Taylor, George Hussey, James Chute, George Forune, Benjamin & Sarpy, Julius Goldner, E. Oneglia and L.H. Mercier. Among the noted 20th-century forgers were Francois Fournier, Jean Sperati and the prolific Raoul DeThuin.

Forgeries may be complete replications, or they may be genuine stamps altered to resemble a scarcer (and more valuable) type. Most forgeries, particularly those of rare stamps, are worth only a small fraction of the value of a genuine example, but a few types, created by some of the most notable forgers, such as Sperati, can be worth as much or more than the genuine. Fraudulently produced copies are known of most classic rarities and many medium-priced stamps.

In addition to rare stamps, large numbers of common 19th- and early 20th-century stamps were forged to supply stamps to the early packet trade. Many can still be easily found. Few new philatelic forgeries have appeared in recent decades. Successful imitation of well-engraved work is virtually impossible. It has proven far easier to produce a fake by altering a genuine stamp than to duplicate a stamp completely.

Counterfeit (also often referred to as *Postal Counterfeit* or *Postal Forgery*) is the term generally applied to reproductions of stamps that have been created to defraud the government of revenue. Such items usually are created at the time a stamp is current and, in some cases, are hard to detect. Because most counterfeits are seized when the perpetrator is captured, postal counterfeits, particularly used on cover, are usually worth much more than a genuine example to specialists. The first postal counterfeit was of Spain's 4-cuarto carmine of 1854 (the real one is Scott 25). Apparently, the counterfeiters were not satisfied with their first version, which is now very scarce, and they soon created an engraved counterfeit, which is common. Postal counterfeits quickly followed in Austria, Naples, Sardinia and the Roman States. They have since been created in many other countries as well, including the United States.

An infamous counterfeit to defraud the government is the 1-shilling Great Britain "Stock Exchange" forgery of 1872, used on telegraph forms at the exchange that year. The stamp escaped detection until a stamp dealer noticed it in 1898.

Fakes

Fakes are genuine stamps altered in some way to make them more desirable. One student of this part of stamp collecting has estimated that by the 1950s more than 30,000 varieties of fakes were known. That number has grown greatly since then. The widespread existence of fakes makes it important for stamp collectors to study their philatelic holdings and use relevant literature. Likewise, collectors should buy from reputable dealers who guarantee their stamps and make full and prompt refunds should a purchased item be declared faked or altered by some mutually agreed-upon authority. Because fakes always have some genuine characteristics, it is not always possible to obtain unanimous agreement among experts regarding specific items. These students may change their opinions as philatelic knowledge increases. More than 80 percent of all fakes on the philatelic market today are regummed, reperforated (or perforated for the first time), or bear forged overprints, surcharges or cancellations.

Stamps can be chemically treated to alter or eliminate colors. For example, a pale rose stamp can be re-colored to resemble a blue shade of high market value. In other cases, treated stamps can be made to resemble missing color varieties. Designs may be changed by painting, or a stroke or a dot added or bleached out to turn an ordinary variety into a seemingly scarcer stamp. Part of a stamp can be bleached and reprinted in a different version, achieving an inverted center or frame. Margins can be added or repairs done so deceptively that the stamps move from the "repaired" into the "fake" category.

Fakers have not left the backs of the stamps untouched either. They may create false watermarks, add fake grills or press out genuine grills. A thin India paper proof may be glued onto a thicker backing to create the appearance an issued stamp, or a proof printed on cardboard may be shaved down and perforated to resemble a stamp. Silk threads are impressed into paper and stamps have been split so that a rare paper variety is added to an otherwise inexpensive stamp. The most common treatment to the back of a stamp, however, is regumming.

Some in the business of faking stamps have openly advertised fool-proof application of "original gum" to stamps that lack it, although most publications now ban such ads from their pages. It is believed that very few early stamps have survived without being hinged. The large number of never-hinged examples of such earlier material offered for sale thus suggests the widespread extent of regumming activity. Regumming also may be used to hide repairs or thin spots. Dipping the stamp into watermark fluid, or examining it under longwave ultraviolet light often will reveal these flaws.

Fakers also tamper with separations. Ingenious ways to add margins are known. Perforated wide-margin stamps may be falsely represented as imperforate when trimmed. Reperforating is commonly done to create scarce coil or perforation varieties, and to eliminate the naturally occurring straight-edge stamps found in sheet margin positions of many earlier issues. Custom has made straight-edged stamps less desirable. Fakers have obliged by perforating straight-edged stamps so that many are now uncommon, if not rare.

Another fertile field for the faker is that of overprints, surcharges and cancellations. The forging of rare surcharges or overprints began in the 1880s or 1890s. These forgeries are sometimes difficult to detect, but experts have identified almost all. Occasionally, overprints or cancellations are removed to create non-overprinted stamps or seemingly unused items. This is most commonly done by removing a manuscript cancel to make a stamp resemble an unused example. "SPECIMEN" overprints may be removed by scraping and repainting to create non-overprinted varieties. Fakers use inexpensive revenues or pen-canceled stamps to generate unused stamps for further faking by adding other markings. The quartz lamp or UV lamp and a high-powered magnifying glass help to easily detect removed cancellations.

The bigger problem, however, is the addition of overprints, surcharges or cancellations - many with such precision that they are very difficult to ascertain. Plating of the stamps or the overprint can be an important method of detection.

Fake postmarks may range from many spurious fancy cancellations to a host of markings applied to transatlantic covers, to adding normally appearing postmarks to definitives of some countries with stamps that are valued far higher used than unused. With the increased popularity of cover collecting, and the widespread interest in postal history, a fertile new field for fakers has come about. Some have tried to create entire covers. Others specialize in adding stamps, tied by fake cancellations, to genuine stampless covers, or replacing less expensive or damaged stamps with more valuable ones. Detailed study of postal rates in effect at the time a cover in question was mailed, including the analysis of each handstamp used during the period, ink analysis and similar techniques, usually will unmask the fraud.

Restoration and Repairs

Scott bases its catalogue values on stamps that are free of defects and otherwise meet the standards set forth earlier in this introduction. Most stamp collectors desire to have the finest copy of an item possible. Even within given grading categories there are variances. This leads to a controversial practice that is not defined in any universal manner: stamp *restoration*.

There are broad differences of opinion about what is permissible when it comes to restoration. Carefully applying a soft eraser to a stamp or cover to remove light soiling is one form of restoration, as is washing a stamp in mild soap and water to clean it. These are fairly accepted forms of restoration. More severe forms of restoration include pressing out creases or removing stains caused by tape. To what degree each of these is acceptable is dependent upon the individual situation. Further along the spectrum is the freshening of a stamp's color by removing oxide build-up or the effects of wax paper left next to stamps shipped to the tropics.

At some point in this spectrum the concept of *repair* replaces that of restoration. Repairs include filling thin spots, mending tears by reweaving or adding a missing perforation tooth. Regumming stamps may have been acceptable as a restoration or repair technique many decades ago, but today it is considered a form of fakery.

Restored stamps may or may not sell at a discount, and it is possible that the value of individual restored items may be enhanced over that of their pre-restoration state. Specific situations dictate the resultant value of such an item. Repaired stamps sell at substantial discounts from the value of sound stamps.

Terminology

Booklets — Many countries have issued stamps in small booklets for the convenience of users. This idea continues to become increasingly popular in many countries. Booklets have been issued in many sizes and forms, often with advertising on the covers, the panes of stamps or on the interleaving.

The panes used in booklets may be printed from special plates or made from regular sheets. All panes from booklets issued by the United States and many from those of other countries contain stamps that are straight edged on the sides, but perforated between. Others are distinguished by orientation of watermark or other identifying features. Any stamp-like unit in the pane, either printed or blank, that is not a postage stamp, is considered to be a *label* in the catalogue listings.

Scott lists and values booklet panes. Modern complete booklets also are listed and valued. Individual booklet panes are listed only when they are not fashioned from existing sheet stamps and, therefore, are identifiable from their sheet stamp counterparts.

Panes usually do not have a used value assigned to them because there is little market activity for used booklet panes, even though many exist used and there is some demand for them.

Cancellations — The marks or obliterations put on stamps by postal authorities to show that they have performed service and to prevent their reuse are known as cancellations. If the marking is made with a pen, it is considered a "pen cancel." When the location of the post office appears in the marking, it is a "town cancellation." A "postmark" is technically any postal marking, but in practice the term generally is applied to a town cancellation with a date. When calling attention to a cause or celebration, the marking is known as a "slogan cancellation." Many other types and styles of cancellations exist, such as duplex, numerals, targets, fancy and others. See also "precancels," below.

Coil Stamps — These are stamps that are issued in rolls for use in dispensers, affixing and vending machines. Those coils of the United States, Canada, Sweden and some other countries are perforated horizontally or vertically only, with the outer edges imperforate. Coil stamps of some countries, such as Great Britain and Germany, are perforated on all four sides and may in some cases be distinguished from their sheet stamp counterparts by watermarks, counting numbers on the reverse or other means.

Covers — Entire envelopes, with or without adhesive postage stamps, that have passed through the mail and bear postal or other markings of philatelic interest are known as covers. Before the introduction of envelopes in about 1840, people folded letters and wrote the address on the outside. Some people covered their letters with an extra sheet of paper on the outside for the address, producing the term "cover." Used airletter sheets, stamped envelopes and other items of postal stationery also are considered covers.

Errors — Stamps that have some major, consistent, unintentional deviation from the normal are considered errors. Errors include, but are not limited to, missing or wrong colors, wrong paper, wrong watermarks, inverted centers or frames on multicolor printing, inverted or missing surcharges or overprints, double impressions, missing perforations, unintentionally omitted tagging and others. Factually wrong or misspelled information, if it appears on all examples of a stamp, are not considered errors in the true sense of the word. They are errors of design. Inconsistent or randomly appearing items, such as misperfs or color shifts, are classified as freaks.

Color-Omitted Errors — This term refers to stamps where a missing color is caused by the complete failure of the printing plate to deliver ink to the stamp paper or any other paper. Generally, this is caused by the printing plate not being engaged on the press or the ink station running dry of ink during printing.

Color-Missing Errors — This term refers to stamps where a color or colors were printed somewhere but do not appear on the finished stamp. There are four different classes of color-missing errors, and the catalog indicates with a two-letter code appended to each such listing what caused the color to be missing. These codes are used only for the United States' color-missing error listings.

FO = A *foldover* of the stamp sheet during printing may block ink from appearing on a stamp. Instead, the color will appear on the back of the foldover (where it might fall on the back of the selvage or perhaps on the back of the stamp or another stamp). FO also will be used in the case of foldunders, where the paper may fold underneath the other stamp paper and the color will print on the platen.

EP = A piece of *extraneous paper* falling across the plate or stamp paper will receive the printed ink. When the extraneous paper is removed, an unprinted portion of stamp paper remains and shows partially or totally missing colors.

CM = A misregistration of the printing plates during printing will result in a *color misregistration*, and such a misregistraion may result in a color not appearing on the finished stamp.

PS = A *perforation shift* after printing may remove a color from the finished stamp. Normally, this will occur on a row of stamps at the edge of the stamp pane.

Measurements – When measurements are given in the Scott catalogues for stamp size, grill size or any other reason, the first measurement given is always for the top and bottom dimension, while the second measurement will be for the sides (just as perforation gauges are measured). Thus, a stamp size of 15mm x 21mm will indicate a vertically oriented stamp 15mm wide at top and bottom, and 21mm tall at the sides. The same principle holds for measuring or counting items such as U.S. grills. A grill count of 22x18 points (B grill) indicates that there are 22 grill points across by 18 grill points down.

Overprints and Surcharges — Overprinting involves applying wording or design elements over an already existing stamp. Overprints can be used to alter the place of use (such as "Canal Zone" on U.S. stamps), to adapt them for a special purpose ("Porto" on Denmark's 1913-20 regular issues for use as postage due stamps, Scott J1-J7) or to commemorate a special occasion (United States Scott 647-648).

A *surcharge* is a form of overprint that changes or restates the face value of a stamp or piece of postal stationery.

Surcharges and overprints may be handstamped, typeset or, occasionally, lithographed or engraved. A few hand-written overprints and surcharges are known.

Personalized Stamps — In 1999, Australia issued stamps with se-tenant labels that could be personalized with pictures of the customer's choice. Other countries quickly followed suit, with some offering to print the selected picture on the stamp itself within a frame that was used exclusively for personalized issues. As the picture used on these stamps or labels vary, listings for such stamps are for any picture within the common frame (or any picture on a se-tenant label), be it a "generic" image or one produced especially for a customer, almost invariably at a premium price.

Precancels — Stamps that are canceled before they are placed in the mail are known as precancels. Precanceling usually is done to expedite the handling of large mailings and generally allow the affected mail pieces to skip certain phases of mail handling.

In the United States, precancellations generally identified the point of origin; that is, the city and state. This information appeared across the face of the stamp, usually centered between parallel lines. More recently, bureau precancels retained the parallel lines, but the city and state designations were dropped. Recent coils have a service inscription that is present on the original printing plate. These show the mail service paid for by the stamp. Since these stamps are not intended to receive further cancellations when used as intended, they are considered precancels. Such items often do not have parallel lines as part of the precancellation.

In France, the abbreviation *Affranchts* in a semicircle together with the word *Postes* is the general form of precancel in use. Belgian precancellations usually appear in a box in which the name of the city appears. Netherlands precancels have the name of the city enclosed between concentric circles, sometimes called a "lifesaver." Precancellations of other countries usually follow these patterns, but may be any arrangement of bars, boxes and city names.

Precancels are listed in the Scott catalogues only if the precancel changes the denomination (Belgium Scott 477-478); if the precanceled stamp is different from the non-precanceled version (such as untagged U.S. precancels); or if the stamp exists only precanceled (France Scott 1096-1099, U.S. Scott 2265).

Proofs and Essays — Proofs are impressions taken from an approved die, plate or stone in which the design and color are the same as the stamp issued to the public. Trial color proofs are impressions taken from approved dies, plates or stones in colors that vary from the final version. An essay is the impression of a design that differs in some way from the issued stamp. "Progressive die proofs" generally are considered to be essays.

Provisionals — These are stamps that are issued on short notice and intended for temporary use pending the arrival of regular issues. They usually are issued to meet such contingencies as changes in government or currency, shortage of necessary postage values or military occupation.

During the 1840s, postmasters in certain American cities issued stamps that were valid only at specific post offices. In 1861, postmasters of the Confederate States also issued stamps with limited validity. Both of these examples are known as "postmaster's provisionals."

Se-tenant — This term refers to an unsevered pair, strip or block of stamps that differ in design, denomination or overprint.

Unless the se-tenant item has a continuous design (see U.S. Scott 1451a, 1694a) the stamps do not have to be in the same order as shown in the catalogue (see U.S. Scott 2158a).

Specimens — The Universal Postal Union required member nations to send samples of all stamps they released into service to the International Bureau in Switzerland. Member nations of the UPU received these specimens as samples of what stamps were valid for postage. Many are overprinted, handstamped or initial-perforated "Specimen," "Canceled" or "Muestra." Some are marked with bars across the denominations (China-Taiwan), punched holes (Czechoslovakia) or back inscriptions (Mongolia).

Stamps distributed to government officials or for publicity purposes, and stamps submitted by private security printers for official approval, also may receive such defacements.

The previously described defacement markings prevent postal use, and all such items generally are known as "specimens."

Tete Beche — This term describes a pair of stamps in which one is upside down in relation to the other. Some of these are the result of intentional sheet arrangements, such as Morocco Scott B10-B11. Others occurred when one or more electrotypes accidentally were placed upside down on the plate, such as Colombia Scott 57a. Separation of the tete-beche stamps, of course, destroys the tete beche variety.

Pronunciation Symbols

ə .... banana, collide, abut

ˈə, ˌə .... humdrum, abut

ə .... immediately preceding \l\, \n\, \m\, \ŋ\, as in battle, mitten, eaten, and sometimes open \ˈō-pᵊm\, lock and key \-ᵊŋ-\; immediately following \l\, \m\, \r\, as often in French table, prisme, titre

ər .... further, merger, bird

ˈər-
ˈə-r } .... as in two different pronunciations of hurry \ˈhər-ē, ˈhə-rē\

a .... mat, map, mad, gag, snap, patch

ā .... day, fade, date, aorta, drape, cape

ä .... bother, cot, and, with most American speakers, father, cart

à .... father as pronounced by speakers who do not rhyme it with bother; French patte

au̇ .... now, loud, out

b .... baby, rib

ch .... chin, nature \ˈnā-chər\

d .... did, adder

e .... bet, bed, peck

ˈē, ˌē .... beat, nosebleed, evenly, easy

ē .... easy, mealy

f .... fifty, cuff

g .... go, big, gift

h .... hat, ahead

hw .... whale as pronounced by those who do not have the same pronunciation for both whale and wail

i .... tip, banish, active

ī .... site, side, buy, tripe

j .... job, gem, edge, join, judge

k .... kin, cook, ache

k̲ .... German ich, Buch; one pronunciation of loch

l .... lily, pool

m .... murmur, dim, nymph

n .... no, own

ⁿ .... indicates that a preceding vowel or diphthong is pronounced with the nasal passages open, as in French un bon vin blanc \œⁿ -bōⁿ -vaⁿ -bläⁿ\

ŋ .... sing \ˈsiŋ\, singer \ˈsiŋ-ər\, finger \ˈfiŋ-gər\, ink \ˈiŋk\

ō .... bone, know, beau

o̅ .... saw, all, gnaw, caught

œ .... French boeuf, German Hölle

œ̅ .... French feu, German Höhle

o̅i .... coin, destroy

p .... pepper, lip

r .... red, car, rarity

s .... source, less

sh .... as in shy, mission, machine, special (actually, this is a single sound, not two); with a hyphen between, two sounds as in grasshopper \ˈgras-ˌhä-pər\

t .... tie, attack, late, later, latter

th .... as in thin, ether (actually, this is a single sound, not two); with a hyphen between, two sounds as in knighthood \ˈnīt-ˌhu̇d\

th̲ .... then, either, this (actually, this is a single sound, not two)

ü .... rule, youth, union \ˈyün-yən\, few \ˈfyü\

u̇ .... pull, wood, book, curable \ˈkyu̇r-ə-bəl\, fury \ˈfyu̇r-ē\

ue .... German füllen, hübsch

u̅e .... French rue, German fühlen

v .... vivid, give

w .... we, away

y .... yard, young, cue \ˈkyü\, mute \ˈmyüt\, union \ˈyün-yən\

ʸ .... indicates that during the articulation of the sound represented by the preceding character the front of the tongue has substantially the position it has for the articulation of the first sound of yard, as in French digne \dēnʸ\

z .... zone, raise

zh .... as in vision, azure \ˈa-zhər\ (actually, this is a single sound, not two); with a hyphen between, two sounds as in hogshead \ˈhȯgz-ˌhed, ˈhägz-\

\ .... slant line used in pairs to mark the beginning and end of a transcription: \ˈpen\

ˈ .... mark preceding a syllable with primary (strongest) stress: \ˈpen-mən-ˌship\

ˌ .... mark preceding a syllable with secondary (medium) stress: \ˈpen-mən-ˌship\

- .... mark of syllable division

( ) .... indicate that what is symbolized between is present in some utterances but not in others: factory \ˈfak-t(ə-)rē\

÷ .... indicates that many regard as unacceptable the pronunciation variant immediately following: cupola \ˈkyü-pə-lə, ÷-ˌlō\

Currency Conversion

Country	Dollar	Pound	S Franc	Yen	HK $	Euro	Cdn $	Aus $
Australia	1.2779	1.9505	1.3264	0.0107	0.1648	1.4150	1.0293	—
Canada	1.2415	1.8949	1.2887	0.0104	0.1601	1.3747	—	0.9715
European Union	0.9031	1.3784	0.9374	0.0075	0.1164	—	0.7274	0.7067
Hong Kong	7.7555	11.837	8.0501	0.0648	—	8.5876	6.2469	6.0689
Japan	119.71	182.71	124.26	—	15.436	132.56	96.424	93.678
Switzerland	0.9634	1.4704	—	0.0080	0.1242	1.0668	0.7760	0.9756
United Kingdom	0.6552	—	0.6801	0.0055	0.0845	0.7255	0.5277	0.7539
United States	—	1.5263	1.0380	0.0084	0.1289	1.1073	0.8055	0.7825

Country	Currency	U.S. $ Equiv.
Jamaica	dollar	.0087
Japan	yen	.0084
Jordan	dinar	1.4110
Kazakhstan	tenge	.0054
Kenya	shilling	.0110
Kiribati	Australian dollar	.7825
Korea (South)	won	.0009
Korea (North)	won	.0072
Kosovo	euro	1.1073
Kuwait	dinar	3.3659
Kyrgyzstan	som	.0163
Laos	kip	.0001
Latvia	euro	1.1073
Lebanon	pound	.0007
Lesotho	maloti	.0849
Liberia	dollar	.0108
Libya	dinar	.7335
Liechtenstein	Swiss franc	1.0380
Lithuania	euro	1.1073
Luxembourg	euro	1.1073
Macao	pataca	.1252
Macedonia	denar	.0181
Malagasy Republic	ariary	.0039
Malawi	kwacha	.0023
Malaysia	ringgit (dollar)	.2731
Maldive Islands	rafiyaa	.0651
Mali	Community of French Africa (CFA) franc	.0017
Malta	euro	1.1073
Marshall Islands	U.S. dollar	1.000
Mauritania	ouguiya	.0034
Mauritius	rupee	.0291
Mexico	peso	.0665
Micronesia	U.S. dollar	1.000
Moldova	leu	.0548
Monaco	euro	1.1073
Mongolia	tugrik	.0005
Montenegro	euro	1.1073
Montserrat	East Caribbean dollar	.3704
Morocco	dirham	.1030
Mozambique	metical	.0297

Source: **xe.com** *Mar. 4, 2015. Figures reflect values as of Mar. 4, 2015.*

COMMON DESIGN TYPES

Pictured in this section are issues where one illustration has been used for a number of countries in the Catalogue. Not included in this section are overprinted stamps or those issues which are illustrated in each country. Because the location of Never Hinged breakpoints varies from country to country, some of the values in the listings below will be for unused stamps that were previously hinged.

EUROPA
Europa, 1956

The design symbolizing the cooperation among the six countries comprising the Coal and Steel Community is illustrated in each country.

Belgium	*496-497*
France	*805-806*
Germany	*748-749*
Italy	*715-716*
Luxembourg	*318-320*
Netherlands	*368-369*

Nos. 496-497 (2)	9.00	.70
Nos. 805-806 (2)	6.80	1.10
Nos. 748-749 (2)	7.30	1.20
Nos. 715-716 (2)	11.50	1.25
Nos. 318-320 (3)	102.50	56.35
Nos. 368-369 (2)	72.50	1.75
Set total (13) Stamps	209.60	62.35

Europa, 1958

"E" and Dove — CD1

European Postal Union at the service of European Integration.

1958, Sept. 13

Belgium	527-528
France	889-890
Germany	790-791
Italy	750-751
Luxembourg	341-343
Netherlands	375-376
Saar	317-318

Nos. 527-528 (2)	4.25	.60
Nos. 889-890 (2)	1.65	.55
Nos. 790-791 (2)	3.65	.65
Nos. 750-751 (2)	1.85	.60
Nos. 341-343 (3)	2.35	1.15
Nos. 375-376 (2)	2.50	.75
Nos. 317-318 (2)	1.05	2.30
Set total (15) Stamps	17.30	6.60

Europa, 1959

6-Link Enless Chain — CD2

1959, Sept. 19

Belgium	536-537
France	929-930
Germany	805-806
Italy	791-792
Luxembourg	354-355
Netherlands	379-380

Nos. 536-537 (2)	1.55	.60
Nos. 929-930 (2)	1.85	.90
Nos. 805-806 (2)	1.55	.65
Nos. 791-792 (2)	.80	.50
Nos. 354-355 (2)	3.50	1.40
Nos. 379-380 (2)	9.90	1.25
Set total (12) Stamps	19.15	5.30

Europa, 1960

19-Spoke Wheel CD3

First anniverary of the establishment of C.E.P.T. (Conference Europeenne des Administrations des Postes et des Telecommunications.) The spokes symbolize the 19 founding members of the Conference.

1960, Sept.

Belgium	553-554
Denmark	379
Finland	376-377
France	970-971
Germany	818-820
Great Britain	377-378
Greece	688
Iceland	327-328
Ireland	175-176
Italy	809-810
Luxembourg	374-375
Netherlands	385-386
Norway	387
Portugal	866-867
Spain	941-942
Sweden	562-563
Switzerland	400-401
Turkey	1493-1494

Nos. 553-554 (2)	1.25	.55
No. 379 (1)	.65	.65
Nos. 376-377 (2)	1.70	1.80
Nos. 970-971 (2)	.55	.50
Nos. 818-820 (3)	2.25	1.50
Nos. 377-378 (2)	9.75	5.00
No. 688 (1)	5.00	2.00
Nos. 327-328 (2)	1.30	1.30
Nos. 175-176 (2)	75.00	14.00
Nos. 809-810 (2)	.70	.50
Nos. 374-375 (2)	1.00	.80
Nos. 385-386 (2)	3.65	1.50
No. 387 (1)	1.25	1.25
Nos. 866-867 (2)	2.25	1.25
Nos. 941-942 (2)	1.50	.75
Nos. 562-563 (2)	1.05	.55
Nos. 400-401 (2)	1.25	.65
Nos. 1493-1494 (2)	2.10	1.35
Set total (31) Stamps	112.20	35.90

Europa, 1961

19 Doves Flying as One — CD4

The 19 doves represent the 19 members of the Conference of European Postal and Telecommunications Administrations C.E.P.T.

1961-62

Belgium	572-573
Cyprus	201-203
France	1005-1006
Germany	844-845
Great Britain	382-384
Greece	718-719
Iceland	340-341
Italy	845-846
Luxembourg	382-383
Netherlands	387-388
Spain	1010-1011
Switzerland	410-411
Turkey	1518-1520

Nos. 572-573 (2)	.75	.55
Nos. 201-203 (3)	2.10	1.20
Nos. 1005-1006 (2)	.50	.50
Nos. 844-845 (2)	.60	.75
Nos. 382-384 (3)	.75	.90
Nos. 718-719 (2)	.80	.50
Nos. 340-341 (2)	.90	.90
Nos. 845-846 (2)	.55	.50
Nos. 382-383 (2)	.70	.70
Nos. 387-388 (2)	.55	.50
Nos. 1010-1011 (2)	.70	.55
Nos. 410-411 (2)	1.25	.60
Nos. 1518-1520 (3)	2.45	1.30
Set total (29) Stamps	12.60	9.40

Europa, 1962

Young Tree with 19 Leaves CD5

The 19 leaves represent the 19 original members of C.E.P.T.

1962-63

Belgium	582-583
Cyprus	219-221
France	1045-1046
Germany	852-853
Greece	739-740
Iceland	348-349
Ireland	184-185
Italy	860-861
Luxembourg	386-387
Netherlands	394-395
Norway	414-415
Switzerland	416-417
Turkey	1553-1555

Nos. 582-583 (2)	.65	.65
Nos. 219-221 (3)	76.25	4.40
Nos. 1045-1046 (2)	.60	.50
Nos. 852-853 (2)	.70	.80
Nos. 739-740 (2)	2.25	1.15
Nos. 348-349 (2)	.85	.85
Nos. 184-185 (2)	2.00	1.50
Nos. 860-861 (2)	1.35	.55
Nos. 386-387 (2)	.85	.70
Nos. 394-395 (2)	1.40	.75
Nos. 414-415 (2)	2.25	2.25
Nos. 416-417 (2)	1.65	1.00
Nos. 1553-1555 (3)	3.00	1.55
Set total (28) Stamps	93.80	16.65

Europa, 1963

Stylized Links, Symbolizing Unity — CD6

1963, Sept.

Belgium	598-599
Cyprus	229-231
Finland	419
France	1074-1075
Germany	867-868
Greece	768-769
Iceland	357-358
Ireland	188-189
Italy	880-881
Luxembourg	403-404
Netherlands	416-417
Norway	441-442
Switzerland	429
Turkey	1602-1603

Nos. 598-599 (2)	1.60	.55
Nos. 229-231 (3)	54.75	5.15
No. 419 (1)	1.60	.80
Nos. 1074-1075 (2)	.60	.50
Nos. 867-868 (2)	.50	.55
Nos. 768-769 (2)	5.25	1.90
Nos. 357-358 (2)	1.50	1.50
Nos. 188-189 (2)	4.75	3.25
Nos. 880-881 (2)	.65	.50
Nos. 403-404 (2)	1.00	.80
Nos. 416-417 (2)	2.25	1.00
Nos. 441-442 (2)	4.75	3.00
No. 429 (1)	.90	.60
Nos. 1602-1603 (2)	1.40	.60
Set total (27) Stamps	81.50	20.70

Europa, 1964

Symbolic Daisy — CD7

5th anniversary of the establishment of C.E.P.T. The 22 petals of the flower symbolize the 22 members of the Conference.

1964, Sept.

Austria	738
Belgium	614-615
Cyprus	244-246
France	1109-1110
Germany	897-898
Greece	801-802
Iceland	367-368
Ireland	196-197
Italy	894-895
Luxembourg	411-412
Monaco	590-591
Netherlands	428-429
Norway	458
Portugal	931-933
Spain	1262-1263
Switzerland	438-439
Turkey	1628-1629

No. 738 (1)	1.20	.80
Nos. 614-615 (2)	1.40	.60
Nos. 244-246 (3)	35.75	3.45
Nos. 1109-1110 (2)	.50	.50
Nos. 897-898 (2)	.50	.50
Nos. 801-802 (2)	5.00	1.90
Nos. 367-368 (2)	2.00	1.65
Nos. 196-197 (2)	20.00	4.25
Nos. 894-895 (2)	.55	.50
Nos. 411-412 (2)	.90	.55
Nos. 590-591 (2)	2.50	.70
Nos. 428-429 (2)	1.80	.60
No. 458 (1)	4.50	4.50
Nos. 931-933 (3)	10.00	2.00
Nos. 1262-1263 (2)	1.30	.80
Nos. 438-439 (2)	1.60	.50
Nos. 1628-1629 (2)	2.65	1.35
Set total (34) Stamps	92.15	25.15

Europa, 1965

Leaves and "Fruit" CD8

1965

Belgium	636-637
Cyprus	262-264
Finland	437
France	1131-1132
Germany	934-935
Greece	833-834
Iceland	375-376
Ireland	204-205
Italy	915-916
Luxembourg	432-433
Monaco	616-617
Netherlands	438-439
Norway	475-476
Portugal	958-960
Switzerland	469
Turkey	1665-1666

Nos. 636-637 (2)	.50	.50
Nos. 262-264 (3)	25.35	3.80
No. 437 (1)	1.50	.65
Nos. 1131-1132 (2)	.75	.80
Nos. 934-935 (2)	.50	.50
Nos. 833-834 (2)	2.25	1.15
Nos. 375-376 (2)	2.50	1.75
Nos. 204-205 (2)	20.00	3.35
Nos. 915-916 (2)	.50	.50
Nos. 432-433 (2)	.80	.60
Nos. 616-617 (2)	3.25	1.65
Nos. 438-439 (2)	.75	.55
Nos. 475-476 (2)	4.00	3.10
Nos. 958-960 (3)	10.00	2.75
No. 469 (1)	1.15	.25
Nos. 1665-1666 (2)	3.50	2.10
Set total (32) Stamps	77.30	24.00

Europa, 1966

Symbolic Sailboat — CD9

1966, Sept.

Andorra, French	172
Belgium	675-676
Cyprus	275-277
France	1163-1164
Germany	963-964

Greece	862-863
Iceland	384-385
Ireland	216-217
Italy	942-943
Liechtenstein	415
Luxembourg	440-441
Monaco	639-640
Netherlands	441-442
Norway	496-497
Portugal	980-982
Switzerland	477-478
Turkey	1718-1719

No. 172 (1)	3.00	3.00
Nos. 675-676 (2)	.80	.50
Nos. 275-277 (3)	4.75	1.90
Nos. 1163-1164 (2)	.60	.50
Nos. 963-964 (2)	.50	.55
Nos. 862-863 (2)	2.25	1.05
Nos. 384-385 (2)	5.00	3.80
Nos. 216-217 (2)	7.00	2.00
Nos. 942-943 (2)	.50	.50
No. 415 (1)	.40	.35
Nos. 440-441 (2)	.80	.60
Nos. 639-640 (2)	2.00	.65
Nos. 441-442 (2)	1.50	.65
Nos. 496-497 (2)	5.00	3.00
Nos. 980-982 (3)	9.75	2.25
Nos. 477-478 (2)	1.60	.60
Nos. 1718-1719 (2)	3.35	1.75
Set total (34) Stamps	48.80	23.65

Europa, 1967

Cogwheels
CD10

1967

Andorra, French	174-175
Belgium	688-689
Cyprus	297-299
France	1178-1179
Germany	969-970
Greece	891-892
Iceland	389-390
Ireland	232-233
Italy	951-952
Liechtenstein	420
Luxembourg	449-450
Monaco	669-670
Netherlands	444-447
Norway	504-505
Portugal	994-996
Spain	1465-1466
Switzerland	482
Turkey	B120-B121

Nos. 174-175 (2)	10.75	6.25
Nos. 688-689 (2)	1.05	.55
Nos. 297-299 (3)	4.25	1.75
Nos. 1178-1179 (2)	.80	.70
Nos. 969-970 (2)	.55	.55
Nos. 891-892 (2)	3.75	1.00
Nos. 389-390 (2)	3.00	2.00
Nos. 232-233 (2)	6.15	2.30
Nos. 951-952 (2)	.60	.50
No. 420 (1)	.45	.40
Nos. 449-450 (2)	1.00	.70
Nos. 669-670 (2)	2.75	.70
Nos. 444-447 (4)	5.00	1.85
Nos. 504-505 (2)	3.25	2.75
Nos. 994-996 (3)	9.50	1.85
Nos. 1465-1466 (2)	.50	.50
No. 482 (1)	.70	.25
Nos. B120-B121 (2)	3.50	2.75
Set total (38) Stamps	57.55	27.35

Europa, 1968

Golden Key
with
C.E.P.T.
Emblem
CD11

1968

Andorra, French	182-183
Belgium	705-706
Cyprus	314-316
France	1209-1210
Germany	983-984
Greece	916-917
Iceland	395-396
Ireland	242-243
Italy	979-980

Liechtenstein	442
Luxembourg	466-467
Monaco	689-691
Netherlands	452-453
Portugal	1019-1021
San Marino	687
Spain	1526
Switzerland	488
Turkey	1775-1776

Nos. 182-183 (2)	16.50	10.00
Nos. 705-706 (2)	1.25	.50
Nos. 314-316 (3)	2.90	1.75
Nos. 1209-1210 (2)	.90	.55
Nos. 983-984 (2)	.50	.55
Nos. 916-917 (2)	3.75	1.65
Nos. 395-396 (2)	3.00	2.50
Nos. 242-243 (2)	3.75	3.00
Nos. 979-980 (2)	.50	.50
No. 442 (1)	.45	.40
Nos. 466-467 (2)	.80	.70
Nos. 689-691 (2)	5.40	.95
Nos. 452-453 (2)	2.10	.70
Nos. 1019-1021 (3)	9.75	2.10
No. 687 (1)	.55	.35
No. 1526 (1)	.25	.25
No. 488 (1)	.45	.25
Nos. 1775-1776 (2)	5.00	2.00
Set total (35) Stamps	57.80	28.70

Europa, 1969

"EUROPA"
and "CEPT"
CD12

Tenth anniversary of C.E.P.T.

1969

Andorra, French	188-189
Austria	837
Belgium	718-719
Cyprus	326-328
Denmark	458
Finland	483
France	1245-1246
Germany	996-997
Great Britain	585
Greece	947-948
Iceland	406-407
Ireland	270-271
Italy	1000-1001
Liechtenstein	453
Luxembourg	475-476
Monaco	722-724
Netherlands	475-476
Norway	533-534
Portugal	1038-1040
San Marino	701-702
Spain	1567
Sweden	814-816
Switzerland	500-501
Turkey	1799-1800
Vatican	470-472
Yugoslavia	1003-1004

Nos. 188-189 (2)	18.50	12.00
No. 837 (1)	.65	.30
Nos. 718-719 (2)	.75	.50
Nos. 326-328 (3)	3.00	1.35
No. 458 (1)	1.10	.75
No. 483 (1)	4.50	1.00
Nos. 1245-1246 (2)	.55	.50
Nos. 996-997 (2)	.80	.50
No. 585 (1)	.25	.25
Nos. 947-948 (2)	5.00	1.50
Nos. 406-407 (2)	4.20	2.40
Nos. 270-271 (2)	4.00	2.00
Nos. 1000-1001 (2)	.70	.50
No. 453 (1)	.45	.45
Nos. 475-476 (2)	1.00	.70
Nos. 722-724 (3)	10.50	2.00
Nos. 475-476 (2)	2.60	1.15
Nos. 533-534 (2)	3.75	2.35
Nos. 1038-1040 (3)	17.85	2.40
Nos. 701-702 (2)	.90	.90
No. 1567 (1)	.25	.25
Nos. 814-816 (3)	4.00	2.85
Nos. 500-501 (2)	1.85	.60
Nos. 1799-1800 (2)	3.85	2.25
Nos. 470-472 (3)	.75	.75
Nos. 1003-1004 (2)	4.00	4.00
Set total (51) Stamps	95.75	44.20

Europa, 1970

Interwoven
Threads
CD13

1970

Andorra, French	196-197
Belgium	741-742
Cyprus	340-342
France	1271-1272
Germany	1018-1019
Greece	985, 987
Iceland	420-421
Ireland	279-281
Italy	1013-1014
Liechtenstein	470
Luxembourg	489-490
Monaco	768-770
Netherlands	483-484
Portugal	1060-1062
San Marino	729-730
Spain	1607
Switzerland	515-516
Turkey	1848-1849
Yugoslavia	1024-1025

Nos. 196-197 (2)	20.00	8.50
Nos. 741-742 (2)	1.10	.55
Nos. 340-342 (3)	2.70	1.90
Nos. 1271-1272 (2)	.65	.50
Nos. 1018-1019 (2)	.60	.50
Nos. 985, 987 (2)	7.75	2.00
Nos. 420-421 (2)	6.00	4.00
Nos. 279-281 (3)	9.50	3.30
Nos. 1013-1014 (2)	.65	.50
No. 470 (1)	.45	.45
Nos. 489-490 (2)	.80	.80
Nos. 768-770 (3)	6.35	2.10
Nos. 483-484 (2)	2.50	1.15
Nos. 1060-1062 (3)	9.85	2.35
Nos. 729-730 (2)	.90	.55
No. 1607 (1)	.25	.25
Nos. 515-516 (2)	1.85	.60
Nos. 1848-1849 (2)	5.00	2.25
Nos. 1024-1025 (2)	.80	.80
Set total (40) Stamps	77.70	33.05

Europa, 1971

"Fraternity,
Cooperation,
Common
Effort"
CD14

1971

Andorra, French	205-206
Belgium	803-804
Cyprus	365-367
Finland	504
France	1304
Germany	1064-1065
Greece	1029-1030
Iceland	429-430
Ireland	305-306
Italy	1038-1039
Liechtenstein	485
Luxembourg	500-501
Malta	425-427
Monaco	797-799
Netherlands	488-489
Portugal	1094-1096
San Marino	749-750
Spain	1675-1676
Switzerland	531-532
Turkey	1876-1877
Yugoslavia	1052-1053

Nos. 205-206 (2)	20.00	7.75
Nos. 803-804 (2)	1.30	.55
Nos. 365-367 (3)	2.60	1.75
No. 504 (1)	5.00	.75
No. 1304 (1)	.45	.40
Nos. 1064-1065 (2)	.60	.50
Nos. 1029-1030 (2)	4.00	1.80
Nos. 429-430 (2)	5.00	3.75
Nos. 305-306 (2)	5.00	1.50
Nos. 1038-1039 (2)	.65	.50
No. 485 (1)	.45	.45
Nos. 500-501 (2)	1.00	.80
Nos. 425-427 (3)	.80	.80
Nos. 797-799 (3)	15.00	2.80
Nos. 488-489 (2)	2.50	1.15
Nos. 1094-1096 (3)	9.75	1.75
Nos. 749-750 (2)	.65	.55
Nos. 1675-1676 (2)	.75	.55
Nos. 531-532 (2)	1.85	.65
Nos. 1876-1877 (2)	5.60	2.50
Nos. 1052-1053 (2)	.50	.50
Set total (43) Stamps	83.45	31.75

Europa, 1972

Sparkles, Symbolic
of Communications
CD15

1972

Andorra, French	210-211
Andorra, Spanish	62
Belgium	825-826
Cyprus	380-382
Finland	512-513
France	1341
Germany	1089-1090
Greece	1049-1050
Iceland	439-440
Ireland	316-317
Italy	1065-1066
Liechtenstein	504
Luxembourg	512-513
Malta	450-453
Monaco	831-832
Netherlands	494-495
Portugal	1141-1143
San Marino	771-772
Spain	1718
Switzerland	544-545
Turkey	1907-1908
Yugoslavia	1100-1101

Nos. 210-211 (2)	21.00	7.00
No. 62 (1)	65.00	45.00
Nos. 825-826 (2)	.95	.55
Nos. 380-382 (3)	5.95	2.45
Nos. 512-513 (2)	8.50	1.40
No. 1341 (1)	.50	.35
Nos. 1089-1090 (2)	1.30	.50
Nos. 1049-1050 (2)	2.00	1.55
Nos. 439-440 (2)	2.90	2.65
Nos. 316-317 (2)	13.00	4.50
Nos. 1065-1066 (2)	.65	.50
No. 504 (1)	.45	.45
Nos. 512-513 (2)	1.00	.80
Nos. 450-453 (4)	1.05	1.40
Nos. 831-832 (2)	5.00	1.40
Nos. 494-495 (2)	3.25	1.15
Nos. 1141-1143 (3)	9.85	1.50
Nos. 771-772 (2)	.70	.50
No. 1718 (1)	.50	.40
Nos. 544-545 (2)	1.65	.60
Nos. 1907-1908 (2)	7.50	3.00
Nos. 1100-1101 (2)	1.20	1.20
Set total (44) Stamps	153.90	78.85

Europa, 1973

Post Horn
and Arrows
CD16

1973

Andorra, French	219-220
Andorra, Spanish	76
Belgium	839-840
Cyprus	396-398
Finland	526
France	1367
Germany	1114-1115
Greece	1090-1092
Iceland	447-448
Ireland	329-330
Italy	1108-1109
Liechtenstein	528-529
Luxembourg	523-524
Malta	469-471
Monaco	866-867
Netherlands	504-505
Norway	604-605
Portugal	1170-1172
San Marino	802-803
Spain	1753
Switzerland	580-581
Turkey	1935-1936
Yugoslavia	1138-1139

Nos. 219-220 (2)	20.00	11.00
No. 76 (1)	.65	.55
Nos. 839-840 (2)	1.00	.65
Nos. 396-398 (3)	4.25	2.10
No. 526 (1)	1.40	1.25
No. 1367 (1)	1.60	.75
Nos. 1114-1115 (2)	.90	.50
Nos. 1090-1092 (3)	2.10	1.40
Nos. 447-448 (2)	7.00	4.05

Nos. 329-330 (2)	5.25	2.00
Nos. 1108-1109 (2)	.65	.50
Nos. 528-529 (2)	.60	.60
Nos. 523-524 (2)	.90	1.00
Nos. 469-471 (3)	.90	1.20
Nos. 866-867 (2)	15.00	2.40
Nos. 504-505 (2)	2.85	1.10
Nos. 604-605 (2)	6.25	2.40
Nos. 1170-1172 (3)	13.00	2.15
Nos. 802-803 (2)	1.00	.60
No. 1753 (1)	.35	.25
Nos. 580-581 (2)	1.55	.60
Nos. 1935-1936 (2)	10.00	4.50
Nos. 1138-1139 (2)	1.15	1.10
Set total (46) Stamps	98.35	42.65

Europa, 2000

CD17

2000

Albania	2621-2622
Andorra, French	522
Andorra, Spanish	262
Armenia	610-611
Austria	1814
Azerbaijan	698-699
Belarus	350
Belgium	1818
Bosnia & Herzegovina (Moslem)	358
Bosnia & Herzegovina (Serb)	111-112
Croatia	428-429
Cyprus	959
Czech Republic	3120
Denmark	1189
Estonia	394
Faroe Islands	376
Finland	1129
Aland Islands	166
France	2771
Georgia	228-229
Germany	2086-2087
Gibraltar	837-840
Great Britain (Jersey)	935-936
Great Britain (Isle of Man)	883
Greece	1959
Greenland	363
Hungary	3699-3700
Iceland	910
Ireland	1230-1231
Italy	2349
Latvia	504
Liechtenstein	1178
Lithuania	668
Luxembourg	1035
Macedonia	187
Malta	1011-1012
Moldova	355
Monaco	2161-2162
Poland	3519
Portugal	2358
Portugal (Azores)	455
Portugal (Madeira)	208
Romania	4370
Russia	6589
San Marino	1480
Slovakia	355
Slovenia	424
Spain	3036
Sweden	2394
Switzerland	1074
Turkey	2762
Turkish Rep. of Northern Cyprus	500
Ukraine	379
Vatican City	1152

Nos. 2621-2622 (2)	13.00	13.00
No. 522 (1)	2.00	1.00
No. 262 (1)	1.60	.70
Nos. 610-611 (2)	9.00	9.00
No. 1814 (1)	1.40	1.40
Nos. 698-699 (2)	8.00	8.00
No. 350 (1)	2.00	2.00
No. 1818 (1)	1.40	1.40
No. 358 (1)	4.75	4.75
Nos. 111-112 (2)	135.00	135.00
Nos. 428-429 (2)	4.40	3.50
No. 959 (1)	2.10	1.40
No. 3120 (1)	1.00	.40
No. 1189 (1)	3.50	2.25
No. 394 (1)	1.25	1.25
No. 376 (1)	3.00	3.00
No. 1129 (1)	2.00	.90
No. 166 (1)	1.75	1.50
No. 2771 (1)	1.40	.40
No. 228-229 (1)	9.00	9.00
Nos. 2086-2087 (2)	4.15	1.90
Nos. 837-840 (4)	6.25	6.25

Nos. 935-936 (2)	2.40	2.40
No. 883 (1)	1.50	1.50
No. 1959 (1)	3.00	3.00
No. 363 (1)	1.90	1.90
Nos. 3699-3700 (2)	6.50	2.00
No. 910 (1)	2.00	2.00
Nos. 1230-1231 (2)	4.75	4.75
No. 2349 (1)	1.50	.40
No. 504 (1)	5.00	2.40
No. 1178 (1)	2.25	1.75
No. 668 (1)	1.50	1.50
No. 1035 (1)	1.40	1.00
No. 187 (1)	3.25	3.25
Nos. 1011-1012 (2)	4.35	4.35
No. 355 (1)	3.50	3.50
Nos. 2161-2162 (2)	2.80	1.40
No. 3519 (1)	1.10	.50
No. 2358 (1)	1.25	.65
No. 455 (1)	1.25	.50
No. 208 (1)	1.25	.50
No. 4370 (1)	2.50	1.25
No. 6589 (1)	2.00	.85
No. 1480 (1)	1.00	1.00
No. 355 (1)	1.10	.55
No. 424 (1)	3.25	1.60
No. 3036 (1)	.75	.40
No. 2394 (1)	3.00	2.25
No. 1074 (1)	2.10	.75
No. 2762 (1)	2.00	2.00
No. 500 (1)	2.50	2.50
No. 379 (1)	4.50	3.00
No. 1152 (1)	1.25	1.25
Set total (68) Stamps	296.35	264.35

The Gibraltar stamps are similar to the stamp illustrated, but none have the design shown above. All other sets listed above include at least one stamp with the design shown, but some include stamps with entirely different designs. Bulgaria Nos. 4131-4132, Guernsey Nos. 802-803 and Yugoslavia Nos. 2485-2486 are Europa stamps with completely different designs.

PORTUGAL & COLONIES
Vasco da Gama

Fleet Departing CD20

Fleet Arriving at Calicut — CD21

Embarking at Rastello CD22

Muse of History CD23

San Gabriel, da Gama and Camoens CD24

Archangel Gabriel, the Patron Saint CD25

Flagship San Gabriel — CD26

Vasco da Gama — CD27

Fourth centenary of Vasco da Gama's discovery of the route to India.

1898

Azores	93-100
Macao	67-74
Madeira	37-44
Portugal	147-154
Port. Africa	1-8
Port. Congo	75-98
Port. India	189-196
St. Thomas & Prince Islands	170-193
Timor	45-52

Nos. 93-100 (8)	122.00	76.25
Nos. 67-74 (8)	136.00	96.75
Nos. 37-44 (8)	44.55	34.90
Nos. 147-154 (8)	169.30	43.45
Nos. 1-8 (8)	23.95	21.70
Nos. 75-98 (24)	34.45	34.45
Nos. 189-196 (8)	20.25	12.95
Nos. 170-193 (24)	37.85	34.30
Nos. 45-52 (8)	21.50	10.45
Set total (104) Stamps	609.85	364.30

Pombal
POSTAL TAX
POSTAL TAX DUES

Marquis de Pombal — CD28

Planning Reconstruction of Lisbon, 1755 — CD29

Pombal Monument, Lisbon — CD30

Sebastiao Jose de Carvalho e Mello, Marquis de Pombal (1699-1782), statesman, rebuilt Lisbon after earthquake of 1755. Tax was for the erection of Pombal monument. Obligatory on all mail on certain days throughout the year. Postal Tax Dues are inscribed "Multa."

1925

Angola	RA1-RA3,	RAJ1-RAJ3
Azores	RA9-RA11,	RAJ2-RAJ4
Cape Verde	RA1-RA3,	RAJ1-RAJ3
Macao	RA1-RA3,	RAJ1-RAJ3
Madeira	RA1-RA3,	RAJ1-RAJ3
Mozambique	RA1-RA3,	RAJ1-RAJ3
Nyassa	RA1-RA3,	RAJ1-RAJ3
Portugal	RA11-RA13,	RAJ2-RAJ4
Port. Guinea	RA1-RA3,	RAJ1-RAJ3
Port. India	RA1-RA3,	RAJ1-RAJ3
St. Thomas & Prince Islands	RA1-RA3,	RAJ1-RAJ3
Timor	RA1-RA3,	RAJ1-RAJ3

Nos. RA1-RA3,RAJ1-RAJ3 (6)	7.50	6.00
Nos. RA9-RA11,RAJ2-RAJ4 (6)	6.60	9.30
Nos. RA1-RA3,RAJ1-RAJ3 (6)	6.00	5.40
Nos. RA1-RA3,RAJ1-RAJ3 (6)	19.50	4.20
Nos. RA1-RA3,RAJ1-RAJ3 (6)	4.35	12.45
Nos. RA1-RA3,RAJ1-RAJ3 (6)	2.55	2.70
Nos. RA1-RA3,RAJ1-RAJ3 (6)	52.50	38.25
Nos. RA11-RA13,RAJ2-RAJ4 (6)	5.80	5.20
Nos. RA1-RA3,RAJ1-RAJ3 (6)	3.30	2.70
Nos. RA1-RA3,RAJ1-RAJ3 (6)	3.45	3.45
Nos. RA1-RA3,RAJ1-RAJ3 (6)	3.60	3.60
Nos. RA1-RA3,RAJ1-RAJ3 (6)	2.10	3.90
Set total (72) Stamps	117.25	97.15

Vasco da Gama CD34

Mousinho de Albuquerque CD35

Dam CD36

Prince Henry the Navigator CD37

Affonso de Albuquerque CD38

Plane over Globe CD39

1938-39

Angola	274-291, C1-C9
Cape Verde	234-251, C1-C9
Macao	289-305, C7-C15
Mozambique	270-287, C1-C9
Port. Guinea	233-250, C1-C9
Port. India	439-453, C1-C8
St. Thomas & Prince Islands	302-319, 323-340, C1-C18
Timor	223-239, C1-C9

Nos. 274-291,C1-C9 (27)	141.35	22.25
Nos. 234-251,C1-C9 (27)	100.00	31.20
Nos. 289-305,C7-C15 (26)	701.70	135.60
Nos. 270-287,C1-C9 (27)	60.95	11.20
Nos. 233-250,C1-C9 (27)	86.05	30.70
Nos. 439-453,C1-C8 (23)	74.75	25.50
Nos. 302-319,323-340,C1-C18 (54)	319.25	190.35
Nos. 223-239,C1-C9 (26)	149.25	73.15
Set total (237) Stamps	1,633	519.95

Lady of Fatima

Our Lady of the Rosary, Fatima, Portugal — CD40

1948-49

Angola	315-318
Cape Verde	266
Macao	336
Mozambique	325-328
Port. Guinea	271
Port. India	480
St. Thomas & Prince Islands	351
Timor	254

Nos. 315-318 (4)	88.50	17.90
No. 266 (1)	8.50	4.50
No. 336 (1)	40.00	12.00
Nos. 325-328 (4)	20.00	4.50
No. 271 (1)	3.25	3.00
No. 480 (1)	2.50	2.25
No. 351 (1)	7.25	6.50
No. 254 (1)	3.00	3.00
Set total (14) Stamps	173.00	53.65

A souvenir sheet of 9 stamps was issued in 1951 to mark the extension of the 1950 Holy Year. The sheet contains: Angola No. 316, Cape Verde No. 266, Macao No. 336, Mozambique No. 325, Portuguese Guinea No. 271, Portuguese India Nos. 480, 485, St. Thomas & Prince Islands No. 351, Timor No. 254. The sheet also contains a portrait of Pope Pius XII and is inscribed "Encerramento do

Ano Santo, Fatima 1951." It was sold for 11 escudos.

Holy Year

Church Bells and Dove CD41

Angel Holding Candelabra CD42

Holy Year, 1950.

1950-51

Angola		331-332	
Cape Verde		268-269	
Macao		339-340	
Mozambique		330-331	
Port. Guinea		273-274	
Port. India		490-491, 496-503	
St. Thomas & Prince Islands		353-354	
Timor		258-259	
Nos. 331-332 (2)		7.60	1.35
Nos. 268-269 (2)		4.75	2.20
Nos. 339-340 (2)		55.00	12.50
Nos. 330-331 (2)		1.75	.85
Nos. 273-274 (2)		3.50	2.60
Nos. 490-491,496-503 (10)		12.80	5.40
Nos. 353-354 (2)		7.50	4.40
Nos. 258-259 (2)		3.75	3.25
Set total (24) Stamps		96.65	32.55

A souvenir sheet of 8 stamps was issued in 1951 to mark the extension of the Holy Year. The sheet contains: Angola No. 331, Cape Verde No. 269, Macao No. 340, Mozambique No. 331, Portuguese Guinea No. 275, Portuguese India No. 490, St. Thomas & Prince Islands No. 354, Timor No. 258, some with colors changed. The sheet contains doves and is inscribed 'Encerramento do Ano Santo, Fatima 1951.' It was sold for 17 escudos.

Holy Year Conclusion

Our Lady of Fatima — CD43

Conclusion of Holy Year. Sheets contain alternate vertical rows of stamps and labels bearing quotation from Pope Pius XII, different for each colony.

1951

Angola		357	
Cape Verde		270	
Macao		352	
Mozambique		356	
Port. Guinea		275	
Port. India		506	
St. Thomas & Prince Islands		355	
Timor		270	
No. 357 (1)		5.25	1.50
No. 270 (1)		1.50	1.25
No. 352 (1)		37.50	10.00
No. 356 (1)		2.25	1.00
No. 275 (1)		1.00	.65
No. 506 (1)		1.60	1.00
No. 355 (1)		2.50	2.00
No. 270 (1)		2.00	1.75
Set total (8) Stamps		53.60	19.15

Medical Congress

CD44

First National Congress of Tropical Medicine, Lisbon, 1952. Each stamp has a different design.

1952

Angola		358
Cape Verde		287
Macao		364

Mozambique		359
Port. Guinea		276
Port. India		516
St. Thomas & Prince Islands		356
Timor		271
No. 358 (1)	1.25	.45
No. 287 (1)	.70	.50
No. 364 (1)	9.75	4.25
No. 359 (1)	1.10	.55
No. 276 (1)	.45	.35
No. 516 (1)	4.75	2.00
No. 356 (1)	.30	.30
No. 271 (1)	1.00	1.00
Set total (8) Stamps	19.30	9.40

Postage Due Stamps

CD45

1952

Angola		J37-J42	
Cape Verde		J31-J36	
Macao		J53-J58	
Mozambique		J51-J56	
Port. Guinea		J40-J45	
Port. India		J47-J52	
St. Thomas & Prince Islands		J52-J57	
Timor		J31-J36	
Nos. J37-J42 (6)		4.05	3.15
Nos. J31-J36 (6)		2.80	2.30
Nos. J53-J58 (6)		17.45	6.85
Nos. J51-J56 (6)		1.80	1.55
Nos. J40-J45 (6)		2.55	2.55
Nos. J47-J52 (6)		6.10	6.10
Nos. J52-J57 (6)		4.15	4.15
Nos. J31-J36 (6)		3.50	3.50
Set total (48) Stamps		42.40	30.15

Sao Paulo

Father Manuel da Nobrega and View of Sao Paulo — CD46

Founding of Sao Paulo, Brazil, 400th anniv.

1954

Angola		385	
Cape Verde		297	
Macao		382	
Mozambique		395	
Port. Guinea		291	
Port. India		530	
St. Thomas & Prince Islands		369	
Timor		279	
No. 385 (1)		.80	.50
No. 297 (1)		.70	.60
No. 382 (1)		14.00	3.00
No. 395 (1)		.40	.30
No. 291 (1)		.35	.25
No. 530 (1)		.80	.40
No. 369 (1)		.80	.40
No. 279 (1)		.85	.70
Set total (8) Stamps		18.70	6.35

Tropical Medicine Congress

CD47

Sixth International Congress for Tropical Medicine and Malaria, Lisbon, Sept. 1958. Each stamp shows a different plant.

1958

Angola		409
Cape Verde		303
Macao		392
Mozambique		404
Port. Guinea		295
Port. India		569
St. Thomas & Prince Islands		371

Timor		289	
No. 409 (1)		3.50	1.10
No. 303 (1)		5.50	2.10
No. 392 (1)		8.00	3.00
No. 404 (1)		4.00	.85
No. 295 (1)		2.75	1.10
No. 569 (1)		1.75	.75
No. 371 (1)		2.75	2.25
No. 289 (1)		3.00	2.75
Set total (8) Stamps		31.25	13.90

Sports

CD48

Each stamp shows a different sport.

1962

Angola		433-438	
Cape Verde		320-325	
Macao		394-399	
Mozambique		424-429	
Port. Guinea		299-304	
St. Thomas & Prince Islands		374-379	
Timor		313-318	
Nos. 433-438 (6)		6.50	3.20
Nos. 320-325 (6)		14.25	5.20
Nos. 394-399 (6)		74.00	14.60
Nos. 424-429 (6)		5.00	2.45
Nos. 299-304 (6)		4.95	2.15
Nos. 374-379 (6)		6.75	3.20
Nos. 313-318 (6)		6.40	3.70
Set total (42) Stamps		117.85	34.50

Anti-Malaria

Anopheles Funestus and Malaria Eradication Symbol — CD49

World Health Organization drive to eradicate malaria.

1962

Angola		439	
Cape Verde		326	
Macao		400	
Mozambique		430	
Port. Guinea		305	
St. Thomas & Prince Islands		380	
Timor		319	
No. 439 (1)		2.00	.90
No. 326 (1)		1.40	.90
No. 400 (1)		6.50	2.00
No. 430 (1)		1.40	.40
No. 305 (1)		1.25	.45
No. 380 (1)		2.00	1.50
No. 319 (1)		.75	.60
Set total (7) Stamps		15.30	6.75

Airline Anniversary

Map of Africa, Super Constellation and Jet Liner — CD50

Tenth anniversary of Transportes Aereos Portugueses (TAP).

1963

Angola		490
Cape Verde		327
Mozambique		434
Port. Guinea		318
St. Thomas & Prince Islands		381
No. 490 (1)	1.25	.50
No. 327 (1)	1.10	.70
No. 434 (1)	.40	.25

No. 318 (1)		.65	.35
No. 381 (1)		.70	.60
Set total (5) Stamps		4.10	2.40

National Overseas Bank

Antonio Teixeira de Sousa — CD51

Centenary of the National Overseas Bank of Portugal.

1964, May 16

Angola		509	
Cape Verde		328	
Port. Guinea		319	
St. Thomas & Prince Islands		382	
Timor		320	
No. 509 (1)		.90	.30
No. 328 (1)		1.10	.75
No. 319 (1)		.65	.40
No. 382 (1)		.70	.50
No. 320 (1)		.75	.60
Set total (5) Stamps		4.10	2.55

ITU

ITU Emblem and the Archangel Gabriel — CD52

International Communications Union, Cent.

1965, May 17

Angola		511	
Cape Verde		329	
Macao		402	
Mozambique		464	
Port. Guinea		320	
St. Thomas & Prince Islands		383	
Timor		321	
No. 511 (1)		1.25	.65
No. 329 (1)		2.10	1.40
No. 402 (1)		5.00	2.00
No. 464 (1)		.40	.25
No. 320 (1)		1.90	.75
No. 383 (1)		1.50	1.00
No. 321 (1)		1.50	.90
Set total (7) Stamps		13.65	6.95

National Revolution

CD53

40th anniv. of the National Revolution. Different buildings on each stamp.

1966, May 28

Angola		525	
Cape Verde		338	
Macao		403	
Mozambique		465	
Port. Guinea		329	
St. Thomas & Prince Islands		392	
Timor		322	
No. 525 (1)		.45	.25
No. 338 (1)		.60	.45
No. 403 (1)		5.00	2.00
No. 465 (1)		.50	.30
No. 329 (1)		.55	.35
No. 392 (1)		.75	.50
No. 322 (1)		1.50	.90
Set total (7) Stamps		9.35	4.75

Navy Club

CD54

Centenary of Portugal's Navy Club. Each stamp has a different design.

1967, Jan. 31

Angola	527-528
Cape Verde	339-340
Macao	412-413
Mozambique	478-479
Port. Guinea	330-331
St. Thomas & Prince Islands	393-394
Timor	323-324

Nos. 527-528 (2)	2.25	1.00
Nos. 339-340 (2)	2.00	1.40
Nos. 412-413 (2)	9.50	3.75
Nos. 478-479 (2)	1.20	.65
Nos. 330-331 (2)	1.20	.90
Nos. 393-394 (2)	3.20	1.25
Nos. 323-324 (2)	4.00	2.00
Set total (14) Stamps	23.35	10.95

Admiral Coutinho

CD55

Centenary of the birth of Admiral Carlos Viegas Gago Coutinho (1869-1959), explorer and aviation pioneer. Each stamp has a different design.

1969, Feb. 17

Angola	547
Cape Verde	355
Macao	417
Mozambique	484
Port. Guinea	335
St. Thomas & Prince Islands	397
Timor	335

No. 547 (1)	1.00	.35
No. 355 (1)	.35	.25
No. 417 (1)	3.75	1.50
No. 484 (1)	.25	.25
No. 335 (1)	.35	.25
No. 397 (1)	.50	.35
No. 335 (1)	1.10	.85
Set total (7) Stamps	7.30	3.80

Administration Reform

Luiz Augusto Rebello da Silva — CD56

Centenary of the administration reforms of the overseas territories.

1969, Sept. 25

Angola	549
Cape Verde	357
Macao	419
Mozambique	491
Port. Guinea	337
St. Thomas & Prince Islands	399
Timor	338

No. 549 (1)	.25	.25
No. 357 (1)	.35	.25
No. 419 (1)	5.00	1.00
No. 491 (1)	.25	.25
No. 337 (1)	.25	.25
No. 399 (1)	.45	.45
No. 338 (1)	.40	.25
Set total (7) Stamps	6.95	2.70

Marshal Carmona

CD57

Birth centenary of Marshal Antonio Oscar Carmona de Fragoso (1869-1951), President of Portugal. Each stamp has a different design.

1970, Nov. 15

Angola	563
Cape Verde	359
Macao	422
Mozambique	493
Port. Guinea	340
St. Thomas & Prince Islands	403
Timor	341

No. 563 (1)	.45	.25
No. 359 (1)	.55	.25
No. 422 (1)	2.25	1.25
No. 493 (1)	.40	.25
No. 340 (1)	.35	.25
No. 403 (1)	.75	.45
No. 341 (1)	.25	.25
Set total (7) Stamps	5.00	3.05

Olympic Games

CD59

20th Olympic Games, Munich, Aug. 26-Sept. 11. Each stamp shows a different sport.

1972, June 20

Angola	569
Cape Verde	361
Macao	426
Mozambique	504
Port. Guinea	342
St. Thomas & Prince Islands	408
Timor	343

No. 569 (1)	.65	.25
No. 361 (1)	.65	.30
No. 426 (1)	3.25	1.00
No. 504 (1)	.30	.25
No. 342 (1)	.45	.25
No. 408 (1)	.35	.25
No. 343 (1)	.50	.50
Set total (7) Stamps	6.15	2.80

Lisbon-Rio de Janeiro Flight

CD60

50th anniversary of the Lisbon to Rio de Janeiro flight by Arturo de Sacadura and Coutinho, March 30-June 5, 1922. Each stamp shows a different stage of the flight.

1972, Sept. 20

Angola	570
Cape Verde	362
Macao	427
Mozambique	505
Port. Guinea	343
St. Thomas & Prince Islands	409
Timor	344

No. 570 (1)	.35	.25
No. 362 (1)	1.50	.30
No. 427 (1)	22.50	7.50
No. 505 (1)	.25	.25
No. 343 (1)	.25	.25
No. 409 (1)	.35	.25
No. 344 (1)	.25	.40
Set total (7) Stamps	25.45	9.20

WMO Centenary

WMO Emblem — CD61

Centenary of international meterological cooperation.

1973, Dec. 15

Angola	571
Cape Verde	363
Macao	429
Mozambique	509
Port. Guinea	344
St. Thomas & Prince Islands	410

Timor		345
No. 571 (1)	.45	.25
No. 363 (1)	.65	.30
No. 429 (1)	6.25	1.75
No. 509 (1)	.30	.25
No. 344 (1)	.45	.35
No. 410 (1)	.60	.50
No. 345 (1)	1.75	2.00
Set total (7) Stamps	10.45	5.40

FRENCH COMMUNITY
Upper Volta can be found under Burkina Faso in Vol. 1
Madagascar can be found under Malagasy in Vol. 3
Colonial Exposition

People of French Empire CD70

Women's Heads CD71

France Showing Way to Civilization CD72

"Colonial Commerce" CD73

International Colonial Exposition, Paris.

1931

Cameroun	213-216
Chad	60-63
Dahomey	97-100
Fr. Guiana	152-155
Fr. Guinea	116-119
Fr. India	100-103
Fr. Polynesia	76-79
Fr. Sudan	102-105
Gabon	120-123
Guadeloupe	138-141
Indo-China	140-142
Ivory Coast	92-95
Madagascar	169-172
Martinique	129-132
Mauritania	65-68
Middle Congo	61-64
New Caledonia	176-179
Niger	73-76
Reunion	122-125
St. Pierre & Miquelon	132-135
Senegal	138-141
Somali Coast	135-138
Togo	254-257
Ubangi-Shari	82-85
Upper Volta	66-69
Wallis & Futuna Isls.	85-88

Nos. 213-216 (4)	23.00	18.25
Nos. 60-63 (4)	22.00	22.00
Nos. 97-100 (4)	26.00	26.00
Nos. 152-155 (4)	22.00	22.00
Nos. 116-119 (4)	19.75	19.75
Nos. 100-103 (4)	18.00	18.00
Nos. 76-79 (4)	30.00	30.00
Nos. 102-105 (4)	19.00	19.00
Nos. 120-123 (4)	17.50	17.50
Nos. 138-141 (4)	19.00	19.00
Nos. 140-142 (3)	11.50	11.50
Nos. 92-95 (4)	22.50	22.50
Nos. 169-172 (4)	7.90	5.00
Nos. 129-132 (4)	21.00	21.00
Nos. 65-68 (4)	22.00	22.00
Nos. 61-64 (4)	20.50	20.50
Nos. 176-179 (4)	24.00	24.00
Nos. 73-76 (4)	22.50	22.50
Nos. 122-125 (4)	22.00	22.00
Nos. 132-135 (4)	24.00	24.00
Nos. 138-141 (4)	18.00	18.00
Nos. 135-138 (4)	26.00	26.00
Nos. 254-257 (4)	26.00	26.00

Nos. 82-85 (4)	22.00	22.00
Nos. 66-69 (4)	19.00	19.00
Nos. 85-88 (4)	35.00	35.00
Set total (103) Stamps	560.15	552.50

Paris International Exposition
Colonial Arts Exposition

"Colonial Resources"
CD74   CD77

Overseas Commerce CD75

Exposition Building and Women CD76

"France and the Empire" CD78

Cultural Treasures of the Colonies CD79

Souvenir sheets contain one imperf. stamp.

1937

Cameroun	217-222A
Dahomey	101-107
Fr. Equatorial Africa	27-32, 73
Fr. Guiana	162-168
Fr. Guinea	120-126
Fr. India	104-110
Fr. Polynesia	117-123
Fr. Sudan	106-112
Guadeloupe	148-154
Indo-China	193-199
Inini	41
Ivory Coast	152-158
Kwangchowan	132
Madagascar	191-197
Martinique	179-185
Mauritania	69-75
New Caledonia	208-214
Niger	73-83
Reunion	167-173
St. Pierre & Miquelon	165-171
Senegal	172-178
Somali Coast	139-145
Togo	258-264
Wallis & Futuna Isls.	89

Nos. 217-222A (7)	18.95	20.45
Nos. 101-107 (7)	23.60	27.60
Nos. 27-32, 73 (7)	28.10	32.10
Nos. 162-168 (7)	22.50	24.50
Nos. 120-126 (7)	24.00	28.00
Nos. 104-110 (7)	21.15	24.40
Nos. 117-123 (7)	58.50	75.00
Nos. 106-112 (7)	23.60	27.60
Nos. 148-154 (7)	19.55	21.05
Nos. 193-199 (7)	17.70	19.70
No. 41 (1)	19.00	22.50
Nos. 152-158 (7)	22.20	26.20
No. 132 (1)	9.25	11.00
Nos. 191-197 (7)	17.55	18.30
Nos. 179-185 (7)	19.95	21.70
Nos. 69-75 (7)	20.50	24.50
Nos. 208-214 (7)	39.00	50.50
Nos. 73-83 (7)	42.70	44.20
Nos. 167-173 (7)	21.70	23.20
Nos. 165-171 (7)	49.60	64.00
Nos. 172-178 (7)	19.95	21.70
Nos. 139-145 (7)	25.95	27.95
Nos. 258-264 (7)	19.40	20.90
No. 89 (1)	28.50	37.50
Set total (154) Stamps	612.90	714.55

Curie

Pierre and Marie Curie
CD80

40th anniversary of the discovery of radium. The surtax was for the benefit of the Intl. Union for the Control of Cancer.

1938

Cameroun	B1
Cuba	B1-B2
Dahomey	B2
France	B76
Fr. Equatorial Africa	B1
Fr. Guiana	B3
Fr. Guinea	B2
Fr. India	B6
Fr. Polynesia	B5
Fr. Sudan	B1
Guadeloupe	B3
Indo-China	B14
Ivory Coast	B2
Madagascar	B2
Martinique	B2
Mauritania	B3
New Caledonia	B4
Niger	B1
Reunion	B4
St. Pierre & Miquelon	B3
Senegal	B3
Somali Coast	B2
Togo	B1

No. B1 (1)	10.00	10.00
Nos. B1-B2 (2)	8.50	2.40
No. B2 (1)	9.50	9.50
No. B76 (1)	21.00	12.50
No. B1 (1)	24.00	24.00
No. B3 (1)	13.50	13.50
No. B2 (1)	8.75	8.75
No. B6 (1)	10.00	10.00
No. B5 (1)	20.00	20.00
No. B1 (1)	12.50	12.50
No. B3 (1)	11.00	10.50
No. B14 (1)	12.00	12.00
No. B2 (1)	11.00	7.50
No. B2 (1)	11.00	11.00
No. B2 (1)	13.00	13.00
No. B3 (1)	7.75	7.75
No. B4 (1)	16.50	17.50
No. B1 (1)	17.00	17.00
No. B4 (1)	14.00	14.00
No. B3 (1)	21.00	22.50
No. B3 (1)	13.00	13.00
No. B2 (1)	8.75	8.75
No. B1 (1)	20.00	20.00
Set total (24) Stamps	313.75	297.65

Caillie

Rene Caillie and Map of Northwestern Africa — CD81

Death centenary of Rene Caillie (1799-1838), French explorer. All three denominations exist with colony name omitted.

1939

Dahomey	108-110
Fr. Guinea	161-163
Fr. Sudan	113-115
Ivory Coast	160-162
Mauritania	109-111
Niger	84-86
Senegal	188-190
Togo	265-267

Nos. 108-110 (3)	1.20	3.60
Nos. 161-163 (3)	1.20	3.20
Nos. 113-115 (3)	1.20	2.80
Nos. 160-162 (3)	1.05	2.25
Nos. 109-111 (3)	1.05	3.80
Nos. 84-86 (3)	3.20	3.20
Nos. 188-190 (3)	3.20	3.20
Nos. 265-267 (3)	3.15	3.15
Set total (24) Stamps	15.25	25.20

New York World's Fair

Natives and New York Skyline
CD82

1939

Cameroun	223-224
Dahomey	111-112
Fr. Equatorial Africa	78-79
Fr. Guiana	169-170
Fr. Guinea	164-165
Fr. India	111-112
Fr. Polynesia	124-125
Fr. Sudan	116-117
Guadeloupe	155-156
Indo-China	203-204
Inini	42-43
Ivory Coast	163-164
Kwangchowan	133-134
Madagascar	209-210
Martinique	186-187
Mauritania	112-113
New Caledonia	215-216
Niger	87-88
Reunion	174-175
St. Pierre & Miquelon	205-206
Senegal	191-192
Somali Coast	179-180
Togo	268-269
Wallis & Futuna Isls.	90-91

Nos. 223-224 (2)	2.80	2.40
Nos. 111-112 (2)	1.60	3.20
Nos. 78-79 (2)	1.60	3.20
Nos. 169-170 (2)	2.60	2.60
Nos. 164-165 (2)	1.60	3.20
Nos. 111-112 (2)	3.00	3.00
Nos. 124-125 (2)	4.80	4.80
Nos. 116-117 (2)	1.60	3.20
Nos. 155-156 (2)	2.50	2.50
Nos. 203-204 (2)	2.05	2.05
Nos. 42-43 (2)	7.50	9.00
Nos. 163-164 (2)	1.50	3.00
Nos. 133-134 (2)	2.50	2.50
Nos. 209-210 (2)	3.75	3.75
Nos. 186-187 (2)	2.35	2.35
Nos. 112-113 (2)	1.40	2.80
Nos. 215-216 (2)	3.35	3.35
Nos. 87-88 (2)	2.40	2.40
Nos. 174-175 (2)	2.80	2.80
Nos. 205-206 (2)	4.80	6.00
Nos. 191-192 (2)	2.00	2.00
Nos. 179-180 (2)	2.90	2.90
Nos. 268-269 (2)	2.50	2.50
Nos. 90-91 (2)	6.00	6.00
Set total (48) Stamps	69.90	81.50

French Revolution

Storming of the Bastille
CD83

French Revolution, 150th anniv. The surtax was for the defense of the colonies.

1939

Cameroun	B2-B6
Dahomey	B3-B7
Fr. Equatorial Africa	B4-B8, CB1
Fr. Guiana	B4-B8, CB1
Fr. Guinea	B3-B7
Fr. India	B7-B11
Fr. Polynesia	B6-B10, CB1
Fr. Sudan	B2-B6
Guadeloupe	B4-B8
Indo-China	B15-B19, CB1
Inini	B1-B5
Ivory Coast	B3-B7
Kwangchowan	B1-B5
Madagascar	B3-B7, CB1
Martinique	B3-B7
Mauritania	B4-B8
New Caledonia	B5-B9, CB1
Niger	B2-B6
Reunion	B5-B9, CB1
St. Pierre & Miquelon	B4-B8
Senegal	B4-B8, CB1
Somali Coast	B3-B7
Togo	B2-B6
Wallis & Futuna Isls.	B1-B5

Nos. B2-B6 (5)	60.00	60.00
Nos. B3-B7 (5)	47.50	47.50
Nos. B4-B8,CB1 (6)	120.00	120.00
Nos. B4-B8,CB1 (6)	79.50	79.50
Nos. B3-B7 (5)	47.50	47.50
Nos. B7-B11 (5)	45.00	45.00
Nos. B6-B10,CB1 (6)	122.50	122.50
Nos. B2-B6 (5)	50.00	50.00
Nos. B4-B8 (5)	50.00	50.00
Nos. B15-B19,CB1 (6)	85.00	85.00
Nos. B1-B5 (5)	80.00	87.50
Nos. B3-B7 (5)	43.75	43.75
Nos. B1-B5 (5)	46.25	46.25
Nos. B3-B7,CB1 (6)	65.50	65.50
Nos. B3-B7 (5)	52.50	52.50
Nos. B4-B8 (5)	42.50	42.50
Nos. B5-B9,CB1 (6)	101.50	101.50
Nos. B2-B6 (5)	60.00	60.00
Nos. B5-B9,CB1 (6)	87.50	87.50
Nos. B4-B8 (5)	67.50	72.50
Nos. B4-B8,CB1 (6)	63.00	63.00
Nos. B3-B7 (5)	52.50	52.50
Nos. B2-B6 (5)	47.50	47.50
Nos. B1-B5 (5)	95.00	95.00
Set total (128) Stamps	1,612	1,625

Plane over Coastal Area
CD85

All five denominations exist with colony name omitted.

1940

Dahomey	C1-C5
Fr. Guinea	C1-C5
Fr. Sudan	C1-C5
Ivory Coast	C1-C5
Mauritania	C1-C5
Niger	C1-C5
Senegal	C12-C16
Togo	C1-C5

Nos. C1-C5 (5)	4.00	4.00
Nos. C1-C5 (5)	4.00	4.00
Nos. C1-C5 (5)	4.00	4.00
Nos. C1-C5 (5)	3.80	3.80
Nos. C1-C5 (5)	3.50	3.50
Nos. C1-C5 (5)	4.00	4.00
Nos. C12-C16 (5)	4.00	4.00
Nos. C1-C5 (5)	4.05	4.05
Set total (40) Stamps	31.35	31.35

Defense of the Empire

Colonial Infantryman — CD86

1941

Cameroun	B13B
Dahomey	B13
Fr. Equatorial Africa	B8B
Fr. Guiana	B10
Fr. Guinea	B13
Fr. India	B13
Fr. Polynesia	B12
Fr. Sudan	B12
Guadeloupe	B10
Indo-China	B19B
Inini	B7
Ivory Coast	B13
Kwangchowan	B7
Madagascar	B9
Martinique	B9
Mauritania	B14
New Caledonia	B11
Niger	B12
Reunion	B11
St. Pierre & Miquelon	B8B
Senegal	B14
Somali Coast	B9
Togo	B10B
Wallis & Futuna Isls.	B7

No. B13B (1)	1.60
No. B13 (1)	1.20
No. B8B (1)	3.50
No. B10 (1)	1.40
No. B13 (1)	1.40
No. B13 (1)	1.25
No. B12 (1)	3.50
No. B12 (1)	1.40
No. B10 (1)	1.00
No. B19B (1)	1.60
No. B7 (1)	1.75
No. B13 (1)	1.25
No. B7 (1)	.85
No. B9 (1)	1.50

No. B9 (1)	1.40
No. B14 (1)	.95
No. B11 (1)	1.60
No. B12 (1)	1.40
No. B11 (1)	1.60
No. B8B (1)	3.75
No. B14 (1)	1.25
No. B9 (1)	1.60
No. B10B (1)	1.25
No. B7 (1)	2.40
Set total (24) Stamps	40.40

Each of the CD86 stamps listed above is part of a set of three stamps. The designs of the other two stamps in the set vary from country to country. Only the values of the Common Design stamps are listed here.

Colonial Education Fund

CD86a

1942

Cameroun	CB3
Dahomey	CB4
Fr. Equatorial Africa	CB5
Fr. Guiana	CB4
Fr. Guinea	CB4
Fr. India	CB3
Fr. Polynesia	CB4
Fr. Sudan	CB4
Guadeloupe	CB3
Indo-China	CB5
Inini	CB3
Ivory Coast	CB4
Kwangchowan	CB4
Malagasy	CB5
Martinique	CB3
Mauritania	CB4
New Caledonia	CB4
Niger	CB4
Reunion	CB4
St. Pierre & Miquelon	CB3
Senegal	CB5
Somali Coast	CB4
Togo	CB3
Wallis & Futuna	CB3

No. CB3 (1)	1.10	
No. CB4 (1)	.80	5.50
No. CB5 (1)	.80	
No. CB4 (1)	1.10	
No. CB3 (1)	.40	5.50
No. CB4 (1)	.90	
No. CB4 (1)	2.00	
No. CB3 (1)	.40	5.50
No. CB5 (1)	1.10	
No. CB3 (1)	1.10	
No. CB4 (1)	1.25	
No. CB4 (1)	1.00	5.50
No. CB5 (1)	1.00	
No. CB3 (1)	.65	
No. CB4 (1)	1.00	
No. CB3 (1)	.80	
No. CB4 (1)	1.60	
No. CB4 (1)	.80	
No. CB4 (1)	.90	
No. CB3 (1)	5.25	
No. CB5 (1)	.80	6.50
No. CB3 (1)	1.75	
No. CB3 (1)	.70	
No. CB3 (1)	2.25	
Set total (24) Stamps	29.45	28.50

Cross of Lorraine & Four-motor Plane
CD87

1941-5

Cameroun	C1-C7
Fr. Equatorial Africa	C17-C23
Fr. Guiana	C9-C10
Fr. India	C1-C6
Fr. Polynesia	C3-C9
Fr. West Africa	C1-C3
Guadeloupe	C1-C2
Madagascar	C37-C43

Martinique		C1-C2
New Caledonia		C7-C13
Reunion		C18-C24
St. Pierre & Miquelon		C1-C7
Somali Coast		C1-C7

Nos. C1-C7 (7)	6.30	6.30
Nos. C17-C23 (7)	10.40	6.35
Nos. C9-C10 (2)	3.80	3.10
Nos. C1-C6 (6)	9.30	9.30
Nos. C3-C9 (7)	13.75	10.00
Nos. C1-C3 (3)	9.50	3.90
Nos. C1-C2 (2)	3.75	2.50
Nos. C37-C43 (7)	5.60	3.80
Nos. C1-C2 (2)	3.00	1.60
Nos. C7-C13 (7)	8.35	8.35
Nos. C18-C24 (7)	7.05	5.00
Nos. C1-C7 (7)	11.60	9.40
Nos. C1-C7 (7)	16.80	12.75
Set total (71) Stamps	109.20	82.35

Transport Plane CD88

Caravan and Plane CD89

1942

Dahomey		C6-C13
Fr. Guinea		C6-C13
Fr. Sudan		C6-C13
Ivory Coast		C6-C13
Mauritania		C6-C13
Niger		C6-C13
Senegal		C17-C25
Togo		C6-C13

Nos. C6-C13 (8)	7.15	
Nos. C6-C13 (8)	5.75	
Nos. C6-C13 (8)	8.00	
Nos. C6-C13 (8)	11.15	
Nos. C6-C13 (8)	9.75	
Nos. C6-C13 (8)	6.25	
Nos. C17-C25 (9)	9.45	
Nos. C0-C13 (0)	0.55	
Set total (65) Stamps	64.05	

Red Cross

Marianne CD90

The surtax was for the French Red Cross and national relief.

1944

Cameroun		B28
Fr. Equatorial Africa		B38
Fr. Guiana		B12
Fr. India		B14
Fr. Polynesia		B13
Fr. West Africa		B1
Guadeloupe		B12
Madagascar		B15
Martinique		B11
New Caledonia		B13
Reunion		B15
St. Pierre & Miquelon		B13
Somali Coast		B13
Wallis & Futuna Isls.		B9

No. B28 (1)	2.00	1.60
No. B38 (1)	1.60	1.20
No. B12 (1)	1.75	1.25
No. B14 (1)	1.50	1.25
No. B13 (1)	2.00	1.60
No. B1 (1)	6.50	4.75
No. B12 (1)	1.40	1.00
No. B15 (1)	.90	.90
No. B11 (1)	1.20	1.20
No. B13 (1)	1.50	1.50
No. B15 (1)	1.60	1.10
No. B13 (1)	2.75	2.40
No. B13 (1)	2.40	2.00
No. B9 (1)	4.50	3.25
Set total (14) Stamps	31.60	25.00

Eboue

CD91

Felix Eboue, first French colonial administrator to proclaim resistance to Germany after French surrender in World War II.

1945

Cameroun		296-297
Fr. Equatorial Africa		156-157
Fr. Guiana		171-172
Fr. India		210-211
Fr. Polynesia		150-151
Fr. West Africa		15-16
Guadeloupe		187-188
Madagascar		259-260
Martinique		196-197
New Caledonia		274-275
Reunion		238-239
St. Pierre & Miquelon		322-323
Somali Coast		238-239

Nos. 296-297 (2)	2.40	1.95
Nos. 156-157 (2)	2.55	2.00
Nos. 171-172 (2)	2.45	2.00
Nos. 210-211 (2)	2.20	1.95
Nos. 150-151 (2)	3.60	2.85
Nos. 15-16 (2)	2.40	2.40
Nos. 187-188 (2)	2.05	1.60
Nos. 259-260 (2)	1.70	1.45
Nos. 196-197 (2)	2.05	1.55
Nos. 274-275 (2)	3.40	3.00
Nos. 238-239 (2)	2.40	2.00
Nos. 322-323 (2)	4.40	3.45
Nos. 238-239 (2)	3.25	3.25
Set total (26) Stamps	34.85	29.45

Victory

Victory — CD92

European victory of the Allied Nations in World War II.

1946, May 8

Cameroun		C8
Fr. Equatorial Africa		C24
Fr. Guiana		C11
Fr. India		C7
Fr. Polynesia		C10
Fr. West Africa		C4
Guadeloupe		C3
Indo-China		C19
Madagascar		C44
Martinique		C3
New Caledonia		C14
Reunion		C25
St. Pierre & Miquelon		C8
Somali Coast		C8
Wallis & Futuna Isls.		C1

No. C8 (1)	1.60	1.20
No. C24 (1)	1.60	1.25
No. C11 (1)	1.75	1.25
No. C7 (1)	1.00	.95
No. C10 (1)	2.75	2.00
No. C4 (1)	1.60	1.20
No. C3 (1)	1.25	1.00
No. C19 (1)	1.00	.55
No. C44 (1)	.90	.35
No. C3 (1)	1.30	1.00
No. C14 (1)	2.25	1.25
No. C25 (1)	1.10	.90
No. C8 (1)	2.10	1.75
No. C8 (1)	2.00	1.60
No. C1 (1)	2.50	1.90
Set total (15) Stamps	24.70	18.15

Chad to Rhine

Leclerc's Departure from Chad — CD93

Battle at Cufra Oasis — CD94

Tanks in Action, Mareth — CD95

Normandy Invasion — CD96

Entering Paris — CD97

Liberation of Strasbourg — CD98

"Chad to the Rhine" march, 1942-44, by Gen. Jacques Leclerc's column, later French 2nd Armored Division.

1946, June 6

Cameroun		C9-C14
Fr. Equatorial Africa		C25-C30
Fr. Guiana		C12-C17
Fr. India		C8-C13
Fr. Polynesia		C11-C16
Fr. West Africa		C5-C10
Guadeloupe		C4-C9
Indo-China		C20-C25
Madagascar		C45-C50
Martinique		C4-C9
New Caledonia		C15-C20
Reunion		C26-C31
St. Pierre & Miquelon		C9-C14
Somali Coast		C9-C14
Wallis & Futuna Isls.		C2-C7

Nos. C9-C14 (6)	12.05	9.70
Nos. C25-C30 (6)	14.70	10.80
Nos. C12-C17 (6)	12.65	10.35
Nos. C8-C13 (6)	12.80	9.20
Nos. C11-C16 (6)	17.55	13.40
Nos. C5-C10 (6)	16.05	11.95
Nos. C4-C9 (6)	12.00	9.60
Nos. C20-C25 (6)	6.40	6.40
Nos. C45-C50 (6)	10.30	8.40
Nos. C4-C9 (6)	8.85	7.30
Nos. C15-C20 (6)	13.40	11.90
Nos. C26-C31 (6)	10.25	6.55
Nos. C9-C14 (6)	17.30	14.35

Nos. C9-C14 (6)	19.35	14.60
Nos. C2-C7 (6)	13.75	10.45
Set total (90) Stamps	197.40	154.95

UPU

French Colonials, Globe and Plane — CD99

Universal Postal Union, 75th anniv.

1949, July 4

Cameroun		C29
Fr. Equatorial Africa		C34
Fr. India		C17
Fr. Polynesia		C20
Fr. West Africa		C15
Indo-China		C26
Madagascar		C55
New Caledonia		C24
St. Pierre & Miquelon		C18
Somali Coast		C18
Togo		C18
Wallis & Futuna Isls.		C10

No. C29 (1)	8.00	4.75
No. C34 (1)	16.00	12.00
No. C17 (1)	11.50	8.75
No. C20 (1)	20.00	15.00
No. C15 (1)	12.00	8.75
No. C26 (1)	4.75	4.00
No. C55 (1)	4.00	2.75
No. C24 (1)	8.25	5.25
No. C18 (1)	20.00	12.00
No. C18 (1)	13.50	11.00
No. C18 (1)	8.75	7.25
No. C10 (1)	12.50	8.25
Set total (12) Stamps	139.25	99.75

Tropical Medicine

Doctor Treating Infant CD100

The surtax was for charitable work.

1950

Cameroun		B29
Fr. Equatorial Africa		B39
Fr. India		B15
Fr. Polynesia		B14
Fr. West Africa		B3
Madagascar		B17
New Caledonia		B14
St. Pierre & Miquelon		B14
Somali Coast		B14
Togo		B11

No. B29 (1)	7.25	5.50
No. B39 (1)	7.25	5.50
No. B15 (1)	6.00	4.00
No. B14 (1)	10.50	8.00
No. B3 (1)	9.50	7.25
No. B17 (1)	5.50	5.50
No. B14 (1)	6.75	5.25
No. B14 (1)	17.00	13.00
No. B14 (1)	8.75	7.25
No. B11 (1)	5.50	4.00
Set total (10) Stamps	84.00	65.25

Military Medal

Medal, Early Marine and Colonial Soldier — CD101

Centenary of the creation of the French Military Medal.

1952

Cameroun		322
Comoro Isls.		39
Fr. Equatorial Africa		186

Fr. India 233
Fr. Polynesia...............................179
Fr. West Africa 57
Madagascar.................................286
New Caledonia.............................295
St. Pierre & Miquelon....................345
Somali Coast...............................267
Togo..327
Wallis & Futuna Isls. 149

No. 322 (1)	7.25	3.25
No. 39 (1)	50.00	40.00
No. 186 (1)	8.00	5.50
No. 233 (1)	7.00	4.75
No. 179 (1)	13.50	10.00
No. 57 (1)	8.75	6.50
No. 286 (1)	3.75	2.50
No. 295 (1)	7.50	6.00
No. 345 (1)	17.00	13.00
No. 267 (1)	10.50	8.75
No. 327 (1)	6.50	4.75
No. 149 (1)	9.50	7.00
Set total (12) Stamps	149.25	112.00

Liberation

Allied Landing, Victory Sign and Cross of Lorraine — CD102

Liberation of France, 10th anniv.

1954, June 6

Cameroun.....................................C32
Comoro Isls. C4
Fr. Equatorial Africa C38
Fr. India C18
Fr. Polynesia.................................C22
Fr. West Africa C17
Madagascar...................................C57
New Caledonia...............................C25
St. Pierre & Miquelon.....................C19
Somali Coast.................................C19
Togo...C19
Wallis & Futuna Isls. C11

No. C32 (1)	7.25	4.75
No. C4 (1)	35.00	20.00
No. C38 (1)	12.00	8.00
No. C18 (1)	11.00	8.00
No. C22 (1)	10.00	8.00
No. C17 (1)	12.00	5.50
No. C57 (1)	3.25	2.00
No. C25 (1)	8.25	5.00
No. C19 (1)	18.00	12.00
No. C19 (1)	12.00	9.50
No. C19 (1)	8.00	6.50
No. C11 (1)	12.50	8.25
Set total (12) Stamps	149.25	97.50

FIDES

Plowmen CD103

Efforts of FIDES, the Economic and Social Development Fund for Overseas Possessions (Fonds d' Investissement pour le Developpement Economique et Social). Each stamp has a different design.

1956

Cameroun.............................326-329
Comoro Isls. 43
Fr. Equatorial Africa 189-192
Fr. Polynesia.................................181
Fr. West Africa 65-72
Madagascar.............................292-295
New Caledonia...............................303
St. Pierre & Miquelon....................350
Somali Coast...........................268-269
Togo..331

Nos. 326-329 (4)	6.90	3.20
No. 43 (1)	2.25	1.60
Nos. 189-192 (4)	3.20	1.65
No. 181 (1)	4.00	2.00
Nos. 65-72 (8)	16.00	6.35
Nos. 292-295 (4)	2.25	1.20
No. 303 (1)	1.90	1.10
No. 350 (1)	6.50	3.50
Nos. 268-269 (2)	5.90	3.60
No. 331 (1)	4.75	2.40
Set total (27) Stamps	53.65	26.60

Flower

CD104

Each stamp shows a different flower.

1958-9

Cameroon.....................................333
Comoro Isls. 45
Fr. Equatorial Africa 200-201
Fr. Polynesia.................................192
Fr. So. & Antarctic Terr. 11
Fr. West Africa 79-83
Madagascar.............................301-302
New Caledonia.........................304-305
St. Pierre & Miquelon....................357
Somali Coast...............................270
Togo......................................348-349
Wallis & Futuna Isls. 152

No. 333 (1)	1.60	.80
No. 45 (1)	5.50	4.50
Nos. 200-201 (2)	3.60	1.60
No. 192 (1)	6.50	4.00
No. 11 (1)	10.00	8.00
Nos. 79-83 (5)	10.45	5.60
Nos. 301-302 (2)	1.50	.55
Nos. 304-305 (2)	9.25	3.00
No. 357 (1)	4.50	2.40
No. 270 (1)	4.00	1.60
Nos. 348-349 (2)	1.00	.50
No. 152 (1)	4.50	2.50
Set total (20) Stamps	62.40	35.05

Human Rights

Sun, Dove and U.N. Emblem CD105

10th anniversary of the signing of the Universal Declaration of Human Rights.

1958

Comoro Isls. 44
Fr. Equatorial Africa 202
Fr. Polynesia.................................191
Fr. West Africa 85
Madagascar...................................300
New Caledonia...............................306
St. Pierre & Miquelon....................356
Somali Coast...............................274
Wallis & Futuna Isls. 153

No. 44 (1)	11.00	11.00
No. 202 (1)	2.40	1.25
No. 191 (1)	13.00	8.75
No. 85 (1)	2.40	2.00
No. 300 (1)	.80	.40
No. 306 (1)	3.00	1.50
No. 356 (1)	3.50	2.50
No. 274 (1)	3.25	2.40
No. 153 (1)	5.75	4.00
Set total (9) Stamps	45.10	33.80

C.C.T.A.

CD106

Commission for Technical Cooperation in Africa south of the Sahara, 10th anniv.

1960

Cameroun.....................................339
Cent. Africa 3
Chad...66
Congo, P.R......................................90
Dahomey 138
Gabon..150
Ivory Coast....................................180
Madagascar...................................317
Mali..9
Mauritania....................................117
Niger..104
Upper Volta.....................................89

No. 339 (1)	1.60	.75
No. 3 (1)	1.90	.65
No. 66 (1)	1.90	.50
No. 90 (1)	1.00	1.00
No. 138 (1)	.50	.25
No. 150 (1)	1.40	1.10
No. 180 (1)	1.10	.50
No. 317 (1)	.60	.30
No. 9 (1)	1.40	.50
No. 117 (1)	.75	.40
No. 104 (1)	.85	.45
No. 89 (1)	.45	.40
Set total (12) Stamps	13.45	6.80

Air Afrique, 1961

Modern and Ancient Africa, Map and Planes — CD107

Founding of Air Afrique (African Airlines).

1961-62

Cameroun.....................................C37
Cent. Africa C5
Chad..C7
Congo, P.R......................................C5
Dahomey C17
Gabon..C5
Ivory Coast....................................C18
Mauritania....................................C17
Niger..C22
Senegal C31
Upper Volta.....................................C4

No. C37 (1)	1.00	.50
No. C5 (1)	1.00	.55
No. C7 (1)	1.00	.25
No. C5 (1)	1.75	.90
No. C17 (1)	.80	.40
No. C7 (1)	.75	.25
No. C18 (1)	2.00	1.25
No. C17 (1)	2.50	1.25
No. C22 (1)	1.75	.90
No. C31 (1)	.80	.30
No. C4 (1)	.65	.45
Set total (11) Stamps	14.00	7.00

Anti-Malaria

CD108

World Health Organization drive to eradicate malaria.

1962, Apr. 7

Cameroun.....................................B36
Cent. Africa B1
Chad..B1
Comoro Isls. B1
Congo, P.R......................................B3
Dahomey B15
Gabon..B4
Ivory Coast....................................B15
Madagascar...................................B19
Mali..B1
Mauritania....................................B16
Niger..B14
Senegal B16
Somali Coast...............................B15
Upper Volta.....................................B1

No. B36 (1)	1.00	.45
No. B1 (1)	1.40	1.40
No. B1 (1)	1.25	.50
No. B1 (1)	4.00	4.00
No. B3 (1)	1.40	1.00
No. B15 (1)	.75	.75
No. B4 (1)	1.00	1.00
No. B15 (1)	1.25	1.25
No. B19 (1)	.90	.90
No. B1 (1)	1.25	.60
No. B16 (1)	.80	.80
No. B14 (1)	.60	.60
No. B16 (1)	1.10	.65
No. B15 (1)	7.25	7.25
No. B1 (1)	.95	.95
Set total (15) Stamps	24.90	21.70

Abidjan Games

CD109

Abidjan Games, Ivory Coast, Dec. 24-31, 1961. Each stamp shows a different sport.

1962

Cent. Africa 19-20, C6
Chad.................................83-84, C8
Congo, P.R....................103-104, C7
Gabon............................163-164, C6
Niger.................................109-111
Upper Volta.........................103-105

Nos. 19-20,C6 (3)	3.90	2.60
Nos. 83-84,C8 (3)	6.30	1.55
Nos. 103-104,C7 (3)	3.85	1.80
Nos. 163-164,C6 (3)	5.00	3.00
Nos. 109-111 (3)	2.60	1.10
Nos. 103-105 (3)	3.15	1.80
Set total (18) Stamps	24.80	11.85

African and Malagasy Union

Flag of Union CD110

First anniversary of the Union.

1962, Sept. 8

Cameroun.....................................373
Cent. Africa 21
Chad...85
Congo, P.R....................................105
Dahomey 155
Gabon..165
Ivory Coast....................................198
Madagascar...................................332
Mauritania....................................170
Niger..112
Senegal 211
Upper Volta....................................106

No. 373 (1)	2.00	.75
No. 21 (1)	1.25	.60
No. 85 (1)	1.25	.25
No. 155 (1)	1.25	.90
No. 165 (1)	1.60	1.25
No. 198 (1)	2.10	.75
No. 332 (1)	.80	.80
No. 170 (1)	.75	.50
No. 112 (1)	.80	.40
No. 211 (1)	.80	.50
No. 106 (1)	1.50	.90
Set total (12) Stamps	15.60	8.10

Telstar

Telstar and Globe Showing Andover and Pleumeur-Bodou — CD111

First television connection of the United States and Europe through the Telstar satellite, July 11-12, 1962.

1962-63

Andorra, French 154
Comoro Isls. C7
Fr. Polynesia.................................C29
Fr. So. & Antarctic Terr. C5
New Caledonia...............................C33
St. Pierre & Miquelon....................C26
Somali Coast...............................C31
Wallis & Futuna Isls. C17

No. 154 (1)	2.00	1.60
No. C7 (1)	5.00	3.00
No. C29 (1)	11.50	8.00

No. C5 (1)	29.00	21.00
No. C33 (1)	30.00	18.50
No. C26 (1)	7.25	5.50
No. C31 (1)	1.00	1.00
No. C17 (1)	3.50	3.50
Set total (8) Stamps	89.25	62.10

Freedom From Hunger

World Map and Wheat Emblem CD112

U.N. Food and Agriculture Organization's "Freedom from Hunger" campaign.

1963, Mar. 21

Cameroon	B37-B38
Cent. Africa	B2
Chad	B2
Congo, P.R.	B4
Dahomey	B16
Gabon	B5
Ivory Coast	B16
Madagascar	B21
Mauritania	B17
Niger	B15
Senegal	B17
Upper Volta	B2

Nos. B37-B38 (2)	2.25	.75
No. B2 (1)	1.25	1.25
No. B2 (1)	2.00	.50
No. B4 (1)	1.40	1.00
No. B16 (1)	.80	.80
No. B5 (1)	1.00	1.00
No. B16 (1)	1.50	1.50
No. B21 (1)	.70	.45
No. B17 (1)	.80	.80
No. B15 (1)	.60	.60
No. B17 (1)	.80	.50
No. B2 (1)	.95	.95
Set total (13) Stamps	14.05	10.10

Red Cross Centenary

CD113

Centenary of the International Red Cross.

1963, Sept. 2

Comoro Isls.	55
Fr. Polynesia	205
New Caledonia	328
St. Pierre & Miquelon	367
Somali Coast	297
Wallis & Futuna Isls.	165

No. 55 (1)	9.50	7.00
No. 205 (1)	15.00	12.00
No. 328 (1)	9.00	6.75
No. 367 (1)	12.00	6.75
No. 297 (1)	7.25	7.25
No. 165 (1)	4.00	3.50
Set total (6) Stamps	56.75	43.25

African Postal Union, 1963

UAMPT Emblem, Radio Masts, Plane and Mail CD114

Establishment of the African and Malagasy Posts and Telecommunications Union.

1963, Sept. 8

Cameroun	C47
Cent. Africa	C10
Chad	C9
Congo, P.R.	C13

Dahomey	C19
Gabon	C13
Ivory Coast	C25
Madagascar	C75
Mauritania	C22
Niger	C27
Rwanda	36
Senegal	C32
Upper Volta	C9

No. C47 (1)	2.25	1.00
No. C10 (1)	1.90	.85
No. C9 (1)	2.40	.60
No. C13 (1)	1.40	.75
No. C19 (1)	.75	.25
No. C13 (1)	1.90	.80
No. C25 (1)	2.50	1.50
No. C75 (1)	1.25	.80
No. C22 (1)	1.50	.60
No. C27 (1)	1.25	.60
No. 36 (1)	.90	.55
No. C32 (1)	1.75	.50
No. C9 (1)	1.50	.75
Set total (13) Stamps	21.25	9.55

Air Afrique, 1963

Symbols of Flight — CD115

First anniversary of Air Afrique and inauguration of DC-8 service.

1963, Nov. 19

Cameroun	C48
Chad	C10
Congo, P.R.	C14
Gabon	C18
Ivory Coast	C26
Mauritania	C26
Niger	C35
Senegal	C33

No. C48 (1)	1.25	.40
No. C10 (1)	2.40	.80
No. C14 (1)	1.60	.60
No. C18 (1)	1.40	.65
No. C26 (1)	1.00	.50
No. C20 (1)	.70	.25
No. C35 (1)	.90	.50
No. C33 (1)	2.00	.65
Set total (8) Stamps	11.25	4.15

Europafrica

Europe and Africa Linked — CD116

Signing of an economic agreement between the European Economic Community and the African and Malagasy Union, Yaounde, Cameroun, July 20, 1963.

1963-64

Cameroun	402
Cent. Africa	C12
Chad	C11
Congo, P.R.	C16
Gabon	C19
Ivory Coast	217
Niger	C43
Upper Volta	C11

No. 402 (1)	2.25	.60
No. C12 (1)	2.50	1.75
No. C11 (1)	2.00	.50
No. C16 (1)	1.60	1.00
No. C19 (1)	1.40	.75
No. 217 (1)	1.10	.35
No. C43 (1)	.85	.50
No. C11 (1)	1.50	.80
Set total (8) Stamps	13.20	6.25

Human Rights

Scales of Justice and Globe CD117

15th anniversary of the Universal Declaration of Human Rights.

1963, Dec. 10

Comoro Isls.	56
Fr. Polynesia	206
New Caledonia	329
St. Pierre & Miquelon	368
Somali Coast	300
Wallis & Futuna Isls.	166

No. 56 (1)	9.50	7.50
No. 205 (1)	15.00	12.00
No. 329 (1)	8.00	6.00
No. 368 (1)	6.50	3.50
No. 300 (1)	9.50	9.50
No. 166 (1)	8.00	7.50
Set total (6) Stamps	56.50	46.00

PHILATEC

Stamp Album, Champs Elysees Palace and Horses of Marly CD118

Intl. Philatelic and Postal Techniques Exhibition, Paris, June 5-21, 1964.

1963-64

Comoro Isls.	60
France	1078
Fr. Polynesia	207
New Caledonia	341
St. Pierre & Miquelon	369
Somali Coast	301
Wallis & Futuna Isls.	167

No. 60 (1)	4.50	4.00
No. 1078 (1)	.25	.25
No. 206 (1)	15.00	10.00
No. 341 (1)	8.50	6.75
No. 369 (1)	11.00	8.00
No. 301 (1)	8.75	8.75
No. 167 (1)	3.50	3.50
Set total (7) Stamps	51.50	41.25

Cooperation

CD119

Cooperation between France and the French-speaking countries of Africa and Madagascar.

1964

Cameroun	409-410
Cent. Africa	39
Chad	103
Congo, P.R.	121
Dahomey	193
France	1111
Gabon	175
Ivory Coast	221
Madagascar	360
Mauritania	181
Niger	143
Senegal	236
Togo	495

Nos. 409-410 (2)	2.50	.50
No. 39 (1)	1.00	.55
No. 103 (1)	1.00	.55
No. 121 (1)	.80	.35
No. 193 (1)	.80	.35
No. 1111 (1)	.25	.25
No. 175 (1)	.90	.60
No. 221 (1)	1.10	.35

No. 360 (1)	.60	.25
No. 181 (1)	.60	.35
No. 143 (1)	.80	.40
No. 236 (1)	1.60	.85
No. 495 (1)	.80	.25
Set total (14) Stamps	12.75	5.30

ITU

Telegraph, Syncom Satellite and ITU Emblem CD120

Intl. Telecommunication Union, Cent.

1965, May 17

Comoro Isls.	C14
Fr. Polynesia	C33
Fr. So. & Antarctic Terr.	C8
New Caledonia	C40
New Hebrides	124-125
St. Pierre & Miquelon	C29
Somali Coast	C36
Wallis & Futuna Isls.	C20

No. C14 (1)	20.00	10.00
No. C33 (1)	80.00	52.50
No. C8 (1)	200.00	160.00
No. C40 (1)	12.00	9.00
Nos. 124-125 (2)	40.50	34.00
No. C29 (1)	24.00	11.00
No. C36 (1)	17.50	10.50
No. C20 (1)	21.00	15.00
Set total (9) Stamps	415.00	302.00

French Satellite A-1

Diamant Rocket and Launching Installation — CD121

Launching of France's first satellite, Nov. 26, 1965.

1965-66

Comoro Isls.	C16a
France	1138a
Reunion	359a
Fr. Polynesia	C41a
Fr. So. & Antarctic Terr.	C10a
New Caledonia	C45a
St. Pierre & Miquelon	C31a
Somali Coast	C40a
Wallis & Futuna Isls.	C23a

No. C16a (1)	11.00	11.00
No. 1138a (1)	.65	.65
No. 359a (1)	3.50	3.00
No. C41a (1)	14.00	14.00
No. C10a (1)	29.00	24.00
No. C45a (1)	8.25	7.00
No. C31a (1)	15.00	15.00
No. C40a (1)	9.00	9.00
No. C23a (1)	9.25	9.25
Set total (9) Stamps	99.65	92.90

French Satellite D-1

D-1 Satellite in Orbit — CD122

Launching of the D-1 satellite at Hammaguir, Algeria, Feb. 17, 1966.

1966

Comoro Isls.	C17
France	1148

Fr. Polynesia..........................C42
Fr. So. & Antarctic Terr. C11
New Caledonia........................C46
St. Pierre & Miquelon..................C32
Somali Coast...........................C49
Wallis & Futuna Isls. C24

No. C17 (1)	4.00	4.00
No. 1148 (1)	.25	.25
No. C42 (1)	7.00	4.75
No. C11 (1)	57.50	40.00
No. C46 (1)	3.00	2.00
No. C32 (1)	10.50	6.50
No. C49 (1)	4.75	3.25
No. C24 (1)	3.50	3.50
Set total (8) Stamps	90.50	64.25

Air Afrique, 1966

Planes and Air Afrique
Emblem — CD123

Introduction of DC-8F planes by Air Afrique.

1966

Cameroun..............................C79
Cent. Africa C35
Chad....................................C26
Congo, P.R. C42
Dahomey C42
Gabon..................................C47
Ivory Coast C32
Mauritania C57
Niger...................................C63
Senegal C47
Togo C54
Upper Volta............................C31

No. C79 (1)	.80	.25
No. C35 (1)	1.00	.40
No. C26 (1)	1.00	.25
No. C42 (1)	1.00	.25
No. C42 (1)	.75	.25
No. C47 (1)	.90	.35
No. C32 (1)	1.00	.60
No. C57 (1)	.80	.30
No. C63 (1)	.60	.35
No. C47 (1)	.80	.30
No. C54 (1)	.80	.25
No. C31 (1)	.75	.50
Set total (12) Stamps	10.20	4.05

African Postal Union, 1967

Telecommunications Symbols and Map
of Africa — CD124

Fifth anniversary of the establishment of the
African and Malagasy Union of Posts and
Telecommunications, UAMPT.

1967

Cameroun..............................C90
Cent. Africa C46
Chad....................................C37
Congo, P.R. C57
Dahomey C61
Gabon..................................C58
Ivory Coast C34
Madagascar C85
Mauritania C65
Niger...................................C75
Rwanda C1-C3
Senegal C60
Togo C81
Upper Volta............................C50

No. C90 (1)	2.40	.65
No. C46 (1)	2.25	.85
No. C37 (1)	2.00	.60
No. C57 (1)	1.60	.60
No. C61 (1)	1.75	.95
No. C58 (1)	2.25	.95
No. C34 (1)	3.50	1.50
No. C85 (1)	1.25	.60
No. C65 (1)	1.25	.60
No. C75 (1)	1.40	.60

Nos. C1-C3 (3)	2.30	1.25
No. C60 (1)	1.75	.50
No. C81 (1)	1.90	.30
No. C50 (1)	1.80	.70
Set total (16) Stamps	27.40	10.65

Monetary Union

Gold Token of the
Ashantis, 17-18th
Centuries — CD125

West African Monetary Union, 5th anniv.

1967, Nov. 4

Dahomey 244
Ivory Coast 259
Mauritania 238
Niger..204
Senegal 294
Togo 623
Upper Volta.................................181

No. 244 (1)	.65	.65
No. 259 (1)	.85	.40
No. 238 (1)	.45	.25
No. 204 (1)	.45	.25
No. 294 (1)	.60	.25
No. 623 (1)	.60	.25
No. 181 (1)	.70	.35
Set total (7) Stamps	4.30	2.40

WHO Anniversary

Sun,
Flowers
and WHO
Emblem
CD126

World Health Organization, 20th anniv.

1968, May 4

Afars & Issas 317
Comoro Isls. 73
Fr. Polynesia...........................241-242
Fr. So. & Antarctic Terr. 31
New Caledonia..............................367
St. Pierre & Miquelon.......................377
Wallis & Futuna Isls. 169

No. 317 (1)	3.25	2.25
No. 73 (1)	2.75	2.00
Nos. 241-242 (2)	22.00	12.75
No. 31 (1)	65.00	45.00
No. 367 (1)	4.50	2.25
No. 377 (1)	12.00	8.00
No. 169 (1)	6.50	4.50
Set total (8) Stamps	116.00	76.75

Human Rights Year

Human Rights
Flame — CD127

1968, Aug. 10

Afars & Issas 322-323
Comoro Isls. 76
Fr. Polynesia...........................243-244
Fr. So. & Antarctic Terr. 32
New Caledonia..............................369
St. Pierre & Miquelon.......................382
Wallis & Futuna Isls. 170

Nos. 322-323 (2)	7.00	4.25
No. 76 (1)	3.50	3.50
Nos. 241-242 (2)	22.00	12.75
No. 31 (1)	65.00	45.00
No. 369 (1)	3.00	1.50
No. 382 (1)	10.00	5.50
No. 170 (1)	3.75	3.75
Set total (9) Stamps	114.25	76.25

2nd PHILEXAFRIQUE

CD128

Opening of PHILEXAFRIQUE, Abidjan, Feb.
14. Each stamp shows a local scene and
stamp.

1969, Feb. 14

Cameroun................................C118
Cent. Africa C65
Chad.....................................C48
Congo, P.R. C77
Dahomey C94
Gabon...................................C82
Ivory Coast C38-C40
Madagascar C92
Mali C65
Mauritania C80
Niger...................................C104
Senegal C68
Togo C104
Upper Volta..............................C62

No. C118 (1)	3.25	1.25
No. C65 (1)	1.90	1.90
No. C48 (1)	2.40	1.00
No. C77 (1)	2.00	1.75
No. C94 (1)	2.25	2.25
No. C82 (1)	2.25	2.25
Nos. C38-C40 (3)	14.50	14.50
No. C92 (1)	1.75	.85
No. C65 (1)	2.00	1.00
No. C80 (1)	1.90	.75
No. C104 (1)	2.75	1.90
No. C68 (1)	2.00	1.40
No. C104 (1)	2.25	.45
No. C62 (1)	4.00	3.75
Set total (16) Stamps	45.20	35.00

Concorde

Concorde in
Flight
CD129

First flight of the prototype Concorde supersonic plane at Toulouse, Mar. 1, 1969.

1969

Afars & Issas C56
Comoro Isls. C29
France......................................C42
Fr. Polynesia...............................C50
Fr. So. & Antarctic Terr. C18
New Caledonia.............................C63
St. Pierre & Miquelon......................C40
Wallis & Futuna Isls. C30

No. C56 (1)	30.00	18.00
No. C29 (1)	24.00	16.00
No. C42 (1)	1.00	.35
No. C50 (1)	55.00	35.00
No. C18 (1)	55.00	37.50
No. C63 (1)	35.00	20.00
No. C40 (1)	32.50	12.00
No. C30 (1)	15.00	10.00
Set total (8) Stamps	247.50	148.85

Development Bank

Bank
Emblem — CD130

African Development Bank, fifth anniv.

1969

Cameroun...................................499
Chad..217
Congo, P.R. 181-182

Ivory Coast 281
Mali 127-128
Mauritania 267
Niger..220
Senegal 317-318
Upper Volta.................................201

No. 499 (1)	.80	.25
No. 217 (1)	.70	.25
Nos. 181-182 (2)	.80	.50
No. 281 (1)	.70	.40
Nos. 127-128 (2)	1.25	.50
No. 267 (1)	.60	.25
No. 220 (1)	.60	.30
Nos. 317-318 (2)	1.55	.50
No. 201 (1)	.70	.30
Set total (12) Stamps	7.70	3.25

ILO

ILO Headquarters, Geneva, and
Emblem — CD131

Intl. Labor Organization, 50th anniv.

1969-70

Afars & Issas 337
Comoro Isls. 83
Fr. Polynesia...........................251-252
Fr. So. & Antarctic Terr. 35
New Caledonia..............................379
St. Pierre & Miquelon.......................396
Wallis & Futuna Isls. 172

No. 337 (1)	3.00	2.25
No. 83 (1)	1.25	.75
Nos. 251-252 (2)	24.00	12.50
No. 35 (1)	18.50	11.00
No. 379 (1)	2.25	1.10
No. 396 (1)	10.00	5.50
No. 172 (1)	3.00	2.90
Set total (8) Stamps	62.00	36.00

ASECNA

Map of
Africa,
Plane and
Airport
CD132

10th anniversary of the Agency for the
Security of Aerial Navigation in Africa and
Madagascar (ASECNA, Agence pour la
Securite de la Navigation Aerienne en Afrique
et a Madagascar).

1969-70

Cameroun...................................500
Cent. Africa 119
Chad..222
Congo, P.R. 197
Dahomey 269
Gabon......................................260
Ivory Coast 287
Mali 130
Niger..221
Senegal 321
Upper Volta.................................204

No. 500 (1)	2.00	.60
No. 119 (1)	2.25	.80
No. 222 (1)	1.00	.25
No. 197 (1)	2.00	.40
No. 269 (1)	.90	.55
No. 260 (1)	1.75	.75
No. 287 (1)	.90	.40
No. 130 (1)	1.00	.40
No. 221 (1)	1.25	.70
No. 321 (1)	1.60	.50
No. 204 (1)	1.75	1.00
Set total (11) Stamps	16.40	6.35

U.P.U. Headquarters

CD133

New Universal Postal Union headquarters,
Bern, Switzerland.

1970

Afars & Issas	342
Algeria	443
Cameroun	503-504
Cent. Africa	125
Chad	225
Comoro Isls.	84
Congo, P.R.	216
Fr. Polynesia	261-262
Fr. So. & Antarctic Terr.	36
Gabon	258
Ivory Coast	295
Madagascar	444
Mali	134-135
Mauritania	283
New Caledonia	382
Niger	231-232
St. Pierre & Miquelon	397-398
Senegal	328-329
Tunisia	535
Wallis & Futuna Isls.	173

No. 342 (1)	3.25	1.75
No. 443 (1)	1.10	.40
Nos. 503-504 (2)	2.60	.55
No. 125 (1)	1.90	.70
No. 225 (1)	1.00	.25
No. 84 (1)	5.50	2.00
No. 216 (1)	.80	.25
Nos. 261-262 (2)	20.00	10.00
No. 36 (1)	45.00	29.00
No. 258 (1)	.90	.55
No. 295 (1)	1.10	.50
No. 444 (1)	.55	.25
Nos. 134-135 (2)	1.25	.50
No. 283 (1)	.60	.30
No. 382 (1)	3.00	1.50
Nos. 231-232 (2)	1.10	.60
Nos. 397-398 (2)	34.00	17.50
Nos. 328-329 (2)	1.55	.55
No. 535 (1)	1.25	.25
No. 173 (1)	4.00	4.00
Set total (26) Stamps	130.45	71.40

De Gaulle

CD134

First anniversay of the death of Charles de Gaulle, (1890-1970), President of France.

1971-72

Afars & Issas	356-357
Comoro Isls.	104-105
France	1325a
Fr. Polynesia	270-271
Fr. So. & Antarctic Terr.	52-53
New Caledonia	393-394
Reunion	380a
St. Pierre & Miquelon	417-418
Wallis & Futuna Isls.	177-178

Nos. 356-357 (2)	16.00	9.50
Nos. 104-105 (2)	9.00	5.75
No. 1325a (1)	4.50	4.00
Nos. 270-271 (2)	51.50	29.50
Nos. 52-53 (2)	47.00	33.50
Nos. 393-394 (2)	25.00	11.75
No. 380a (1)	9.25	8.00
Nos. 417-418 (2)	57.50	30.00
Nos. 177-178 (2)	24.00	16.25
Set total (16) Stamps	243.75	148.25

African Postal Union, 1971

UAMPT Building, Brazzaville, Congo — CD135

10th anniversary of the establishment of the African and Malagasy Posts and Telecommunications Union, UAMPT. Each stamp has a different native design.

1971, Nov. 13

Cameroun	C177
Cent. Africa	C89
Chad	C94

Congo, P.R.	C136
Dahomey	C146
Gabon	C120
Ivory Coast	C47
Mauritania	C113
Niger	C164
Rwanda	C8
Senegal	C105
Togo	C166
Upper Volta	C97

No. C177 (1)	2.00	.50
No. C89 (1)	2.25	.85
No. C91 (1)	1.50	.50
No. C136 (1)	1.60	.75
No. C146 (1)	1.75	.80
No. C120 (1)	1.75	.70
No. C47 (1)	2.00	1.00
No. C113 (1)	1.20	.65
No. C164 (1)	1.25	.60
No. C8 (1)	2.75	2.25
No. C105 (1)	1.60	.50
No. C166 (1)	1.25	.40
No. C97 (1)	1.50	.70
Set total (13) Stamps	22.40	10.20

West African Monetary Union

African Couple, City, Village and Commemorative Coin — CD136

West African Monetary Union, 10th anniv.

1972, Nov. 2

Dahomey	300
Ivory Coast	331
Mauritania	299
Niger	258
Senegal	374
Togo	825
Upper Volta	280

No. 300 (1)	.65	.25
No. 331 (1)	1.00	.50
No. 299 (1)	.75	.25
No. 258 (1)	.55	.30
No. 374 (1)	.50	.30
No. 825 (1)	.60	.25
No. 280 (1)	.60	.25
Set total (7) Stamps	4.65	2.10

African Postal Union, 1973

Telecommunications Symbols and Map of Africa — CD137

11th anniversary of the African and Malagasy Posts and Telecommunications Union (UAMPT).

1973, Sept. 12

Cameroun	574
Cent. Africa	194
Chad	294
Congo, P.R.	289
Dahomey	311
Gabon	320
Ivory Coast	361
Madagascar	500
Mauritania	304
Niger	287
Rwanda	540
Senegal	393
Togo	849
Upper Volta	297

No. 574 (1)	1.75	.40
No. 194 (1)	1.25	.75
No. 294 (1)	1.75	.40
No. 289 (1)	1.60	.50
No. 311 (1)	1.25	.55
No. 320 (1)	1.40	.75
No. 361 (1)	2.50	1.00
No. 500 (1)	1.00	.35
No. 304 (1)	1.10	.40
No. 287 (1)	.90	.60
No. 540 (1)	3.75	2.00
No. 393 (1)	1.60	.50

No. 849 (1)	1.25	.35
No. 297 (1)	1.25	.70
Set total (14) Stamps	22.35	9.25

Philexafrique II — Essen

CD138

CD139

Designs: Indigenous fauna, local and German stamps. Types CD138-CD139 printed horizontally and vertically se-tenant in sheets of 10 (2x5). Label between horizontal pairs alternately commemorative Philexafrique II, Libreville, Gabon, June 1978, and 2nd International Stamp Fair, Essen, Germany, Nov. 1-5.

1978-1979

Benin	C286a
Central Africa	C201a
Chad	C239a
Congo Republic	C246a
Djibouti	C122a
Gabon	C216a
Ivory Coast	C65a
Mali	C357a
Mauritania	C186a
Niger	C292a
Rwanda	C13a
Senegal	C141a
Togo	C364a

No. C286a (1)	9.00	8.50
No. C201a (1)	7.50	7.50
No. C239a (1)	8.00	4.00
No. C246a (1)	7.00	7.00
No. C122a (1)	8.50	8.50
No. C216a (1)	6.50	4.00
No. C65a (1)	9.00	9.00
No. C357a (1)	7.50	3.00
No. C186a (1)	4.50	4.00
No. C292a (1)	6.00	5.00
No. C13a (1)	4.00	4.00
No. C147a (1)	10.00	4.00
No. C364a (1)	5.00	5.00
Set total (13) Stamps	92.50	73.50

BRITISH COMMONWEALTH OF NATIONS

The listings follow established trade practices when these issues are offered as units by dealers. The Peace issue, for example, includes only one stamp from the Indian state of Hyderabad. The U.P.U. issue includes the Egypt set. Pairs are included for those varieties issued with bilingual designs se-tenant.

Silver Jubilee

Windsor Castle and King George V CD301

Reign of King George V, 25th anniv.

1935

Antigua	77-80
Ascension	33-36
Bahamas	92-95
Barbados	186-189
Basutoland	11-14

Bechuanaland Protectorate	117-120
Bermuda	100-103
British Guiana	223-226
British Honduras	108-111
Cayman Islands	81-84
Ceylon	260-263
Cyprus	136-139
Dominica	90-93
Falkland Islands	77-80
Fiji	110-113
Gambia	125-128
Gibraltar	100-103
Gilbert & Ellice Islands	33-36
Gold Coast	108-111
Grenada	124-127
Hong Kong	147-150
Jamaica	109-112
Kenya, Uganda, Tanzania	42-45
Leeward Islands	96-99
Malta	184-187
Mauritius	204-207
Montserrat	85-88
Newfoundland	226-229
Nigeria	34-37
Northern Rhodesia	18-21
Nyasaland Protectorate	47-50
St. Helena	111-114
St. Kitts-Nevis	72-75
St. Lucia	91-94
St. Vincent	134-137
Seychelles	118-121
Sierra Leone	166-169
Solomon Islands	60-63
Somaliland Protectorate	77-80
Straits Settlements	213-216
Swaziland	20-23
Trinidad & Tobago	43-46
Turks & Caicos Islands	71-74
Virgin Islands	69-72

The following states have different designs but are included in the omnibus set:

Great Britain	226-229
Offices in Morocco (Sp. Curr.)	67-70
Offices in Morocco (Br. Curr.)	226-229
Offices in Morocco (Fr. Curr.)	422-425
Offices in Morocco (Tangier)	508-510
Australia	152-154
Canada	211-216
Cook Islands	98-100
India	142-148
Nauru	31-34
New Guinea	46-47
New Zealand	199-201
Niue	67-69
Papua	114-117
Samoa	163-165
South Africa	68-71
Southern Rhodesia	33-36
South-West Africa	121-124

Nos. 77-80 (4)	21.50	22.75
Nos. 33-36 (4)	61.00	127.50
Nos. 92-95 (4)	25.00	43.00
Nos. 186-189 (4)	30.15	49.30
Nos. 11-14 (4)	12.10	21.50
Nos. 117-120 (4)	17.00	29.25
Nos. 100-103 (4)	18.00	58.25
Nos. 223-226 (4)	18.35	35.50
Nos. 108-111 (4)	15.25	15.35
Nos. 81-84 (4)	16.95	17.75
Nos. 260-263 (4)	12.60	23.35
Nos. 136-139 (4)	39.75	34.40
Nos. 90-93 (4)	18.85	19.85
Nos. 77-80 (4)	51.00	13.75
Nos. 110-113 (4)	15.25	29.00
Nos. 125-128 (4)	12.65	29.25
Nos. 100-103 (4)	34.35	50.00
Nos. 33-36 (4)	37.00	53.50
Nos. 108-111 (4)	26.25	62.25
Nos. 124-127 (4)	18.60	45.00
Nos. 147-150 (4)	76.50	21.00
Nos. 109-112 (4)	22.80	42.00
Nos. 42-45 (4)	9.25	12.50
Nos. 96-99 (4)	35.75	49.60
Nos. 184-187 (4)	25.00	34.70
Nos. 204-207 (4)	47.60	58.25
Nos. 85-88 (4)	10.25	30.25
Nos. 226-229 (4)	17.50	12.05
Nos. 34-37 (4)	13.25	59.75
Nos. 18-21 (4)	15.75	16.25
Nos. 47-50 (4)	37.25	80.25
Nos. 111-114 (4)	31.15	33.25
Nos. 72-75 (4)	11.55	18.50
Nos. 91-94 (4)	16.00	20.80
Nos. 134-137 (4)	9.45	21.25
Nos. 118-121 (4)	17.50	31.00
Nos. 166-169 (4)	18.50	55.00
Nos. 60-63 (4)	27.50	38.00
Nos. 77-80 (4)	17.75	46.00
Nos. 213-216 (4)	15.00	25.10
Nos. 20-23 (4)	6.05	13.00
Nos. 43-46 (4)	12.30	27.75
Nos. 71-74 (4)	9.25	16.25
Nos. 69-72 (4)	22.20	47.50
Nos. 226-229 (4)	7.25	7.45

Nos. 67-70 (4)	14.35	*26.10*
Nos. 226-229 (4)	8.20	*28.90*
Nos. 422-425 (4)	3.90	*2.00*
Nos. 508-510 (3)	18.80	*23.85*
Nos. 152-154 (3)	45.75	*60.35*
Nos. 211-216 (6)	27.85	*13.35*
Nos. 98-100 (3)	6.75	*14.00*
Nos. 142-148 (7)	23.25	*11.80*
Nos. 31-34 (4)	12.60	*13.85*
Nos. 46-47 (2)	4.10	*1.70*
Nos. 199-201 (3)	21.75	*31.75*
Nos. 67-69 (3)	7.80	*22.50*
Nos. 114-117 (4)	9.20	*17.00*
Nos. 163-165 (3)	4.40	*5.50*
Nos. 68-71 (4)	62.50	*167.00*
Nos. 33-36 (4)	29.00	*45.25*
Nos. 121-124 (4)	14.50	*36.10*
Set total (245) Stamps	1,349	*2,120*

Coronation

Queen Elizabeth and King George VI CD302

1937

Aden	13-15
Antigua	81-83
Ascension	37-39
Bahamas	97-99
Barbados	190-192
Basutoland	15-17
Bechuanaland Protectorate	121-123
Bermuda	115-117
British Guiana	227-229
British Honduras	112-114
Cayman Islands	97-99
Ceylon	275-277
Cyprus	140-142
Dominica	94-96
Falkland Islands	81-83
Fiji	114-116
Gambia	129-131
Gibraltar	104-106
Gilbert & Ellice Islands	37-39
Gold Coast	112-114
Grenada	128-130
Hong Kong	151-153
Jamaica	113-115
Kenya, Uganda, Tanzania	60-62
Leeward Islands	100-102
Malta	188-190
Mauritius	208-210
Montserrat	89-91
Newfoundland	230-232
Nigeria	50-52
Northern Rhodesia	22-24
Nyasaland Protectorate	51-53
St. Helena	115-117
St. Kitts-Nevis	76-78
St. Lucia	107-109
St. Vincent	138-140
Seychelles	122-124
Sierra Leone	170-172
Solomon Islands	64-66
Somaliland Protectorate	81-83
Straits Settlements	235-237
Swaziland	24-26
Trinidad & Tobago	47-49
Turks & Caicos Islands	75-77
Virgin Islands	73-75

The following have different designs but are included in the omnibus set:

Great Britain	234
Offices in Morocco (Sp. Curr.)	82
Offices in Morocco (Fr. Curr.)	439
Offices in Morocco (Tangier)	514
Canada	237
Cook Islands	109-111
Nauru	35-38
Newfoundland	233-243
New Guinea	48-51
New Zealand	223-225
Niue	70-72
Papua	118-121
South Africa	74-78
Southern Rhodesia	38-41
South-West Africa	125-132

Nos. 13-15 (3)	3.00	*6.10*
Nos. 81-83 (3)	2.00	*4.50*
Nos. 37-39 (3)	2.75	*2.75*
Nos. 97-99 (3)	1.15	*3.05*
Nos. 190-192 (3)	1.10	*1.95*
Nos. 15-17 (3)	1.25	*3.00*
Nos. 121-123 (3)	.95	*3.35*
Nos. 115-117 (3)	1.25	*5.00*
Nos. 227-229 (3)	1.45	*3.05*
Nos. 112-114 (3)	1.20	*2.35*
Nos. 97-99 (3)	1.10	*2.30*
Nos. 275-277 (3)	8.25	*10.35*

Nos. 140-142 (3)	3.75	*6.50*
Nos. 94-96 (3)	.85	*2.40*
Nos. 81-83 (3)	2.90	*2.30*
Nos. 114-116 (3)	1.35	*5.75*
Nos. 129-131 (3)	1.00	*4.70*
Nos. 104-106 (3)	2.60	*6.45*
Nos. 37-39 (3)	.95	*2.00*
Nos. 112-114 (3)	3.10	*10.00*
Nos. 128-130 (3)	1.00	*.85*
Nos. 151-153 (3)	27.00	*12.50*
Nos. 113-115 (3)	1.95	*1.25*
Nos. 60-62 (3)	1.25	*2.35*
Nos. 100-102 (3)	1.55	*4.00*
Nos. 188-190 (3)	1.35	*1.65*
Nos. 208-210 (3)	2.05	*3.75*
Nos. 89-91 (3)	1.00	*3.35*
Nos. 230-232 (3)	7.00	*2.80*
Nos. 50-52 (3)	3.25	*8.50*
Nos. 22-24 (3)	1.35	*2.00*
Nos. 51-53 (3)	1.05	*1.30*
Nos. 115-117 (3)	1.45	*2.05*
Nos. 76-78 (3)	.95	*2.05*
Nos. 107-109 (3)	1.05	*2.05*
Nos. 138-140 (3)	.80	*4.75*
Nos. 122-124 (3)	1.20	*1.90*
Nos. 170-172 (3)	1.95	*5.65*
Nos. 64-66 (3)	.90	*2.00*
Nos. 81-83 (3)	1.10	*3.40*
Nos. 235-237 (3)	3.25	*1.60*
Nos. 24-26 (3)	1.05	*1.75*
Nos. 47-49 (3)	1.00	*1.00*
Nos. 75-77 (3)	1.30	*1.55*
Nos. 73-75 (3)	1.20	*5.00*

No. 234 (1)	.25	*.25*
No. 82 (1)	.80	*.80*
No. 439 (1)	.35	*.25*
No. 514 (1)	.55	*.55*
No. 237 (1)	.35	*.25*
Nos. 109-111 (3)	.85	*.80*
Nos. 35-38 (4)	1.15	*5.50*
Nos. 233-243 (11)	34.50	*30.40*
Nos. 48-51 (4)	1.40	*7.90*
Nos. 223-225 (3)	1.40	*2.75*
Nos. 70-72 (3)	.80	*2.05*
Nos. 118-121 (4)	1.60	*5.25*
Nos. 74-78 (5)	9.25	*11.05*
Nos. 38-41 (4)	4.00	*16.25*
Nos. 125-132 (8)	5.50	*8.45*
Set total (189) Stamps	171.70	*259.40*

Peace

King George VI and Parliament Buildings, London CD303

Return to peace at the close of World War II.

1945-46

Aden	28-29
Antigua	96-97
Ascension	50-51
Bahamas	130-131
Barbados	207-208
Bermuda	131-132
British Guiana	242-243
British Honduras	127-128
Cayman Islands	112-113
Ceylon	293-294
Cyprus	156-157
Dominica	112-113
Falkland Islands	97-98
Falkland Islands Dep.	1L9-1L10
Fiji	137-138
Gambia	144-145
Gibraltar	119-120
Gilbert & Ellice Islands	52-53
Gold Coast	128-129
Grenada	143-144
Jamaica	136-137
Kenya, Uganda, Tanzania	90-91
Leeward Islands	116-117
Malta	206-207
Mauritius	223-224
Montserrat	104-105
Nigeria	71-72
Northern Rhodesia	46-47
Nyasaland Protectorate	82-83
Pitcairn Islands	9-10
St. Helena	128-129
St. Kitts-Nevis	91-92
St. Lucia	127-128
St. Vincent	152-153
Seychelles	149-150
Sierra Leone	186-187
Solomon Islands	80-81
Somaliland Protectorate	108-109
Trinidad & Tobago	62-63
Turks & Caicos Islands	90-91
Virgin Islands	88-89

The following have different designs but are included in the omnibus set:

Great Britain	264-265

Offices in Morocco (Tangier)	523-524
Aden	
Kathiri State of Seiyun	12-13
Qu'aiti State of Shihr and Mukalla	
	12-13
Australia	200-202
Basutoland	29-31
Bechuanaland Protectorate	137-139
Burma	66-69
Cook Islands	127-130
Hong Kong	174-175
India	195-198
Hyderabad	51-53
New Zealand	247-257
Niue	90-93
Pakistan-Bahawalpur	O16
Samoa	191-194
South Africa	100-102
Southern Rhodesia	67-70
South-West Africa	153-155
Swaziland	38-40
Zanzibar	222-223

Nos. 28-29 (2)	.70	*2.30*
Nos. 96-97 (2)	.50	*.80*
Nos. 50-51 (2)	.90	*1.75*
Nos. 130-131 (2)	.50	*1.40*
Nos. 207-208 (2)	.50	*1.10*
Nos. 131-132 (2)	.55	*.55*
Nos. 242-243 (2)	1.05	*1.40*
Nos. 127-128 (2)	.50	*.50*
Nos. 112-113 (2)	.60	*.80*
Nos. 293-294 (2)	.60	*2.10*
Nos. 156-157 (2)	1.00	*.70*
Nos. 112-113 (2)	.50	*.50*
Nos. 97-98 (2)	.90	*1.35*
Nos. 1L9-1L10 (2)	1.40	*1.00*
Nos. 137-138 (2)	.50	*1.75*
Nos. 144-145 (2)	.50	*.95*
Nos. 119-120 (2)	.75	*1.00*
Nos. 52-53 (2)	.50	*.50*
Nos. 128-129 (2)	1.85	*3.75*
Nos. 143-144 (2)	.50	*.95*
Nos. 136-137 (2)	5.55	*7.50*
Nos. 90-91 (2)	.65	*.65*
Nos. 116-117 (2)	.50	*1.50*
Nos. 206-207 (2)	.65	*2.00*
Nos. 223-224 (2)	.50	*1.05*
Nos. 104-105 (2)	.50	*.50*
Nos. 71-72 (2)	.70	*2.75*
Nos. 46-47 (2)	1.25	*2.00*
Nos. 82-83 (2)	.50	*.50*
Nos. 9-10 (2)	1.40	*1.40*
Nos. 128-129 (2)	.65	*.70*
Nos. 91-92 (2)	.50	*.50*
Nos. 127-128 (2)	.50	*.60*
Nos. 152-153 (2)	.50	*.50*
Nos. 149-150 (2)	.55	*.50*
Nos. 186-187 (2)	.50	*.50*
Nos. 80-81 (2)	.50	*1.30*
Nos. 108-109 (2)	.50	*.50*
Nos. 62-63 (2)	.50	*.50*
Nos. 90-91 (2)	.50	*.50*
Nos. 88-89 (2)	.50	*.50*

Nos. 264-265 (2)	.50	*.70*
Nos. 523-524 (2)	1.50	*3.00*
Nos. 12-13 (2)	.50	*.90*
Nos. 12-13 (2)	.50	*1.05*
Nos. 200-202 (3)	1.60	*3.00*
Nos. 29-31 (3)	2.10	*2.60*
Nos. 137-139 (3)	2.05	*4.75*
Nos. 66-69 (4)	1.60	*1.30*
Nos. 127-130 (4)	2.20	*2.00*
Nos. 174-175 (4)	7.25	*3.15*
Nos. 195-198 (4)	4.75	*3.60*
Nos. 51-53 (3)	1.50	*1.70*
Nos. 247-257 (11)	3.95	*3.90*
Nos. 90-93 (4)	1.70	*2.20*
No. O16 (1)	5.50	*7.00*
Nos. 191-194 (4)	2.05	*1.00*
Nos. 100-102 (3)	1.20	*4.00*
Nos. 67-70 (4)	1.40	*1.75*
Nos. 153-155 (3)	2.55	*3.50*
Nos. 38-40 (3)	2.40	*5.50*
Nos. 222-223 (2)	.65	*1.00*
Set total (151) Stamps	80.15	*109.20*

Silver Wedding

King George VI and Queen Elizabeth

CD304   CD305

1948-49

Aden	30-31
Kathiri State of Seiyun	14-15
Qu'aiti State of Shihr and Mukalla	
	14-15

Antigua	98-99
Ascension	52-53
Bahamas	148-149
Barbados	210-211
Basutoland	39-40
Bechuanaland Protectorate	147-148
Bermuda	133-134
British Guiana	244-245
British Honduras	129-130
Cayman Islands	116-117
Cyprus	158-159
Dominica	114-115
Falkland Islands	99-100
Falkland Islands Dep.	1L11-1L12
Fiji	139-140
Gambia	146-147
Gibraltar	121-122
Gilbert & Ellice Islands	54-55
Gold Coast	142-143
Grenada	145-146
Hong Kong	178-179
Jamaica	138-139
Kenya, Uganda, Tanzania	92-93
Leeward Islands	118-119
Malaya	
Johore	128-129
Kedah	55-56
Kelantan	44-45
Malacca	1-2
Negri Sembilan	36-37
Pahang	44-45
Penang	1-2
Perak	99-100
Perlis	1-2
Selangor	74-75
Trengganu	47-48
Malta	223-224
Mauritius	229-230
Montserrat	106-107
Nigeria	73-74
North Borneo	238-239
Northern Rhodesia	48-49
Nyasaland Protectorate	85-86
Pitcairn Islands	11-12
St. Helena	130-131
St. Kitts-Nevis	93-94
St. Lucia	129-130
St. Vincent	154-155
Sarawak	174-175
Seychelles	151-152
Sierra Leone	188-189
Singapore	21-22
Solomon Islands	82-83
Somaliland Protectorate	110-111
Swaziland	48-49
Trinidad & Tobago	64-65
Turks & Caicos Islands	92-93
Virgin Islands	90-91
Zanzibar	224-225

The following have different designs but are included in the omnibus set:

Great Britain	267-268
Offices in Morocco (Sp. Curr.)	93-94
Offices in Morocco (Tangier)	525-526
Bahrain	62-63
Kuwait	82-83
Oman	25-26
South Africa	106
South-West Africa	159

Nos. 30-31 (2)	37.90	*47.50*
Nos. 14-15 (2)	21.50	*16.00*
Nos. 14-15 (2)	22.00	*18.50*
Nos. 98-99 (2)	15.00	*14.25*
Nos. 52-53 (2)	58.15	*60.60*
Nos. 148-149 (2)	45.25	*40.30*
Nos. 210-211 (2)	18.35	*13.05*
Nos. 39-40 (2)	50.30	*50.25*
Nos. 147-148 (2)	45.35	*50.25*
Nos. 133-134 (2)	47.75	*55.25*
Nos. 244-245 (2)	24.25	*28.45*
Nos. 129-130 (2)	22.75	*53.20*
Nos. 116-117 (2)	22.75	*28.50*
Nos. 158-159 (2)	58.50	*78.05*
Nos. 114-115 (2)	25.25	*32.75*
Nos. 99-100 (2)	112.10	*83.60*
Nos. 1L11-1L12 (2)	4.25	*6.00*
Nos. 139-140 (2)	18.20	*10.75*
Nos. 146-147 (2)	22.75	*25.25*
Nos. 121-122 (2)	71.00	*90.50*
Nos. 54-55 (2)	16.25	*24.25*
Nos. 142-143 (2)	35.25	*37.75*
Nos. 145-146 (2)	25.25	*25.25*
Nos. 178-179 (2)	363.90	*136.60*
Nos. 138-139 (2)	20.35	*77.75*
Nos. 92-93 (2)	52.75	*72.75*
Nos. 118-119 (2)	7.00	*8.25*
Nos. 128-129 (2)	29.25	*53.25*
Nos. 55-56 (2)	35.25	*50.25*
Nos. 44-45 (2)	35.75	*62.75*
Nos. 1-2 (2)	35.40	*49.75*
Nos. 36-37 (2)	28.10	*38.20*
Nos. 44-45 (2)	28.00	*38.05*
Nos. 1-2 (2)	40.50	*37.80*

Nos. 99-100 (2)	27.80	37.75
Nos. 1-2 (2)	33.50	58.00
Nos. 74-75 (2)	30.25	25.30
Nos. 47-48 (2)	35.25	62.75
Nos. 223-224 (2)	40.55	45.25
Nos. 229-230 (2)	17.75	45.25
Nos. 106-107 (2)	9.25	18.25
Nos. 73-74 (2)	17.85	22.80
Nos. 238-239 (2)	35.30	45.75
Nos. 48-49 (2)	92.80	80.25
Nos. 85-86 (2)	19.25	32.75
Nos. 11-12 (2)	56.75	53.50
Nos. 130-131 (2)	32.80	42.80
Nos. 93-94 (2)	11.25	7.25
Nos. 129-130 (2)	22.25	45.25
Nos. 154-155 (2)	27.75	30.25
Nos. 174-175 (2)	52.90	55.40
Nos. 151-152 (2)	16.25	45.75
Nos. 188-189 (2)	24.75	26.25
Nos. 21-22 (2)	146.25	55.40
Nos. 82-83 (2)	13.40	13.40
Nos. 110-111 (2)	7.00	8.25
Nos. 48-49 (2)	40.30	47.75
Nos. 64-65 (2)	32.75	38.25
Nos. 92-93 (2)	15.25	20.30
Nos. 90-91 (2)	18.85	21.35
Nos. 224-225 (2)	29.60	38.00
Nos. 267-268 (2)	40.40	40.25
Nos. 93-94 (2)	20.10	25.35
Nos. 525-526 (2)	23.10	29.25
Nos. 62-63 (2)	38.45	72.50
Nos. 82-83 (2)	45.50	45.50
Nos. 25-26 (2)	46.00	47.50
No. 106 (1)	.70	1.25
No. 159 (1)	1.25	.35
Set total (136) Stamps	**2,620**	**2,801**

U.P.U.

Mercury and Symbols of Communications — CD306

Plane, Ship and Hemispheres — CD307

Mercury Scattering Letters over Globe CD308

U.P.U. Monument, Bern CD309

Universal Postal Union, 75th anniversary.

1949

Aden	32-35
Kathiri State of Seiyun	16-19
Qu'aiti State of Shihr and Mukalla	16-19
Antigua	100-103
Ascension	57-60
Bahamas	150-153
Barbados	212-215
Basutoland	41-44
Bechuanaland Protectorate	149-152
Bermuda	138-141
British Guiana	246-249
British Honduras	137-140
Brunei	79-82
Cayman Islands	118-121
Cyprus	160-163
Dominica	116-119
Falkland Islands	103-106
Falkland Islands Dep.	1L14-1L17
Fiji	141-144
Gambia	148-151
Gibraltar	123-126

Gilbert & Ellice Islands	56-59
Gold Coast	144-147
Grenada	147-150
Hong Kong	180-183
Jamaica	142-145
Kenya, Uganda, Tanzania	94-97
Leeward Islands	126-129
Malaya	
Johore	151-154
Kedah	57-60
Kelantan	46-49
Malacca	18-21
Negri Sembilan	59-62
Pahang	46-49
Penang	23-26
Perak	101-104
Perlis	3-6
Selangor	76-79
Trengganu	49-52
Malta	225-228
Mauritius	231-234
Montserrat	108-111
New Hebrides, British	62-65
New Hebrides, French	79-82
Nigeria	75-78
North Borneo	240-243
Northern Rhodesia	50-53
Nyasaland Protectorate	87-90
Pitcairn Islands	13-16
St. Helena	132-135
St. Kitts-Nevis	95-98
St. Lucia	131-134
St. Vincent	170-173
Sarawak	176-179
Seychelles	153-156
Sierra Leone	190-193
Singapore	23-26
Solomon Islands	84-87
Somaliland Protectorate	112-115
Southern Rhodesia	71-72
Swaziland	50-53
Tonga	87-90
Trinidad & Tobago	66-69
Turks & Caicos Islands	101-104
Virgin Islands	92-95
Zanzibar	226-229

The following have different designs but are included in the omnibus set:

Great Britain	276-279
Offices in Morocco (Tangier)	546-549
Australia	223
Bahrain	68-71
Burma	116-121
Ceylon	304-306
Egypt	281-283
India	223-226
Kuwait	89-92
Oman	31-34
Pakistan-Bahawalpur	26-29, O25-O28
South Africa	109-111
South-West Africa	160-162

Nos. 32-35 (4)	6.60	8.95
Nos. 16-19 (4)	2.40	6.80
Nos. 16-19 (4)	2.55	3.25
Nos. 100-103 (4)	3.95	6.60
Nos. 57-60 (4)	10.90	9.00
Nos. 150-153 (4)	5.60	9.55
Nos. 212-215 (4)	4.40	14.15
Nos. 41-44 (4)	4.75	10.00
Nos. 149-152 (4)	3.35	7.25
Nos. 138-141 (4)	4.75	5.55
Nos. 246-249 (4)	2.65	4.20
Nos. 137-140 (4)	3.35	4.75
Nos. 79-82 (4)	7.75	6.75
Nos. 118-121 (4)	4.00	6.40
Nos. 160-163 (4)	4.60	8.30
Nos. 116-119 (4)	2.30	5.65
Nos. 103-106 (4)	14.90	17.10
Nos. 1L14-1L17 (4)	15.50	14.00
Nos. 141-144 (4)	3.35	14.00
Nos. 148-151 (4)	3.50	7.85
Nos. 123-126 (4)	6.75	9.50
Nos. 56-59 (4)	4.85	8.75
Nos. 144-147 (4)	3.05	6.95
Nos. 147-150 (4)	2.30	3.55
Nos. 180-183 (4)	74.25	23.60
Nos. 142-145 (4)	2.70	6.00
Nos. 94-97 (4)	2.90	3.40
Nos. 126-129 (4)	3.05	9.60
Nos. 151-154 (4)	4.70	8.90
Nos. 57 60 (4)	4.80	12.00
Nos. 46-49 (4)	4.25	12.65
Nos. 18-21 (4)	4.25	17.30
Nos. 59-62 (4)	3.50	10.75
Nos. 46-49 (4)	3.00	7.25
Nos. 23-26 (4)	5.10	11.75
Nos. 101-104 (4)	3.65	10.75
Nos. 3-6 (4)	3.95	14.25
Nos. 76-79 (4)	4.90	12.30
Nos. 49-52 (4)	4.95	9.75
Nos. 225-228 (4)	4.50	5.35
Nos. 231-234 (4)	4.35	6.70
Nos. 108-111 (4)	3.40	3.85
Nos. 62-65 (4)	1.60	4.10
Nos. 79-82 (4)	24.25	24.25

Nos. 75-78 (4)	2.80	9.25
Nos. 240-243 (4)	7.15	6.50
Nos. 50-53 (4)	5.00	6.50
Nos. 87-90 (4)	4.05	4.05
Nos. 13-16 (4)	24.00	18.75
Nos. 132-135 (4)	4.85	7.10
Nos. 95-98 (4)	3.35	4.70
Nos. 131-134 (4)	2.55	3.85
Nos. 170-173 (4)	2.20	5.05
Nos. 176-179 (4)	9.00	11.10
Nos. 153-156 (4)	3.25	4.10
Nos. 190-193 (4)	3.00	5.10
Nos. 23-26 (4)	24.25	14.20
Nos. 84-87 (4)	4.35	4.90
Nos. 112-115 (4)	2.45	7.95
Nos. 71-72 (2)	1.95	2.25
Nos. 50-53 (4)	2.80	4.65
Nos. 87-90 (4)	3.25	5.25
Nos. 66-69 (4)	3.15	3.15
Nos. 101-104 (4)	3.65	4.00
Nos. 92-95 (4)	2.60	4.60
Nos. 226-229 (4)	5.45	13.50
Nos. 276-279 (4)	1.85	2.40
Nos. 546-549 (4)	3.20	10.15
No. 223 (1)	.60	.55
Nos. 68-71 (4)	5.00	16.75
Nos. 116-121 (6)	7.15	5.30
Nos. 304-306 (3)	3.35	4.25
Nos. 281-283 (3)	5.75	2.70
Nos. 223-226 (4)	35.50	10.50
Nos. 89-92 (4)	6.10	10.25
Nos. 31-34 (4)	5.55	15.75
Nos. 26-29, O25-O28 (8)	2.00	42.00
Nos. 109-111 (3)	3.00	3.00
Nos. 160-162 (3)	3.95	6.00
Set total (313) Stamps	**504.25**	**693.45**

University

Arms of University College CD310

Alice, Princess of Athlone CD311

1948 opening of University College of the West Indies at Jamaica.

1951

Antigua	104-105
Barbados	228-229
British Guiana	250-251
British Honduras	141-142
Dominica	120-121
Grenada	164-165
Jamaica	146-147
Leeward Islands	130-131
Montserrat	112-113
St. Kitts-Nevis	105-106
St. Lucia	149-150
St. Vincent	174-175
Trinidad & Tobago	70-71
Virgin Islands	96-97

Nos. 104-105 (2)	1.35	3.25
Nos. 228-229 (2)	1.85	1.55
Nos. 250-251 (2)	1.10	1.25
Nos. 141-142 (2)	1.40	2.15
Nos. 120-121 (2)	1.40	1.75
Nos. 164-165 (2)	1.20	1.60
Nos. 146-147 (2)	.95	.85
Nos. 112-113 (2)	.85	1.50
Nos. 105-106 (2)	.90	1.50
Nos. 149-150 (2)	1.40	1.50
Nos. 174-175 (2)	1.00	2.15
Nos. 70-71 (2)	.75	.75
Nos. 96-97 (2)	1.50	3.40
Set total (26) Stamps	**15.65**	**23.20**

Coronation

Queen Elizabeth II — CD312

1953

Aden	47
Kathiri State of Seiyun	28
Qu'aiti State of Shihr and Mukalla	28

Antigua	106
Ascension	61
Bahamas	157
Barbados	234
Basutoland	45
Bechuanaland Protectorate	153
Bermuda	142
British Guiana	252
British Honduras	143
Cayman Islands	150
Cyprus	167
Dominica	141
Falkland Islands	121
Falkland Islands Dependencies	1L18
Fiji	145
Gambia	152
Gibraltar	131
Gilbert & Ellice Islands	60
Gold Coast	160
Grenada	170
Hong Kong	184
Jamaica	153
Kenya, Uganda, Tanzania	101
Leeward Islands	132
Malaya	
Johore	155
Kedah	82
Kelantan	71
Malacca	27
Negri Sembilan	63
Pahang	71
Penang	27
Perak	126
Perlis	28
Selangor	101
Trengganu	74
Malta	241
Mauritius	250
Montserrat	127
New Hebrides, British	77
Nigeria	79
North Borneo	260
Northern Rhodesia	60
Nyasaland Protectorate	96
Pitcairn Islands	19
St. Helena	139
St. Kitts-Nevis	119
St. Lucia	156
St. Vincent	185
Sarawak	196
Seychelles	172
Sierra Leone	194
Singapore	27
Solomon Islands	88
Somaliland Protectorate	127
Swaziland	54
Trinidad & Tobago	84
Tristan da Cunha	13
Turks & Caicos Islands	118
Virgin Islands	114

The following have different designs but are included in the omnibus set:

Great Britain	313-316
Offices in Morocco (Tangier)	579-582
Australia	259-261
Bahrain	92-95
Canada	330
Ceylon	317
Cook Islands	145-146
Kuwait	113-116
New Zealand	280-284
Niue	104-105
Oman	52-55
Samoa	214-215
South Africa	192
Southern Rhodesia	80
South-West Africa	244-248
Tokelau Islands	4

No. 47 (1)	1.25	1.25
No. 28 (1)	.40	1.50
No. 28 (1)	1.10	.60
No. 106 (1)	.50	.75
No. 61 (1)	1.25	2.50
No. 157 (1)	1.25	.75
No. 234 (1)	1.00	.25
No. 45 (1)	.50	.60
No. 153 (1)	.75	.35
No. 142 (1)	.85	.40
No. 252 (1)	.45	.25
No. 143 (1)	.55	.40
No. 150 (1)	.40	1.00
No. 167 (1)	1.50	1.00
No. 141 (1)	.40	.40
No. 121 (1)	.90	1.50
No. 1L18 (1)	1.50	1.50
No. 145 (1)	1.75	.00
No. 152 (1)	.50	.50
No. 131 (1)	.50	.50
No. 60 (1)	.65	2.25
No. 160 (1)	.95	.25
No. 170 (1)	.30	.25
No. 184 (1)	7.00	.35
No. 153 (1)	1.50	.25

No. 101 (1)	.40	.25
No. 132 (1)	1.00	2.25
No. 155 (1)	1.40	.30
No. 82 (1)	2.25	.60
No. 71 (1)	1.60	1.60
No. 27 (1)	1.10	1.50
No. 63 (1)	1.40	.65
No. 71 (1)	2.25	.25
No. 27 (1)	1.75	.30
No. 126 (1)	1.60	.25
No. 28 (1)	1.75	4.00
No. 101 (1)	1.75	.25
No. 74 (1)	1.50	1.00
No. 241 (1)	.55	.25
No. 250 (1)	1.00	.25
No. 127 (1)	.65	.50
No. 77 (1)	.75	.60
No. 79 (1)	.45	.25
No. 260 (1)	2.00	1.00
No. 60 (1)	.70	.25
No. 96 (1)	.75	.75
No. 19 (1)	2.50	2.50
No. 139 (1)	1.25	1.25
No. 119 (1)	.35	.25
No. 156 (1)	.70	.35
No. 185 (1)	.50	.30
No. 196 (1)	2.00	2.25
No. 172 (1)	.80	.80
No. 194 (1)	.40	.40
No. 27 (1)	2.75	.40
No. 88 (1)	1.10	1.10
No. 127 (1)	.40	.25
No. 54 (1)	.30	.25
No. 84 (1)	.25	.25
No. 13 (1)	1.10	1.75
No. 118 (1)	.40	1.10
No. 114 (1)	.40	1.00
Nos. 313-316 (4)	16.35	8.75
Nos. 579-582 (4)	7.40	5.20
Nos. 259-261 (3)	4.60	3.25
Nos. 92-95 (4)	15.25	12.75
No. 330 (1)	.25	.25
No. 317 (1)	1.50	.25
Nos. 145-146 (2)	2.90	2.90
Nos. 113-116 (4)	16.00	8.50
Nos. 280-284 (5)	5.65	6.85
Nos. 104-105 (2)	1.75	1.75
Nos. 52-55 (4)	15.25	6.50
Nos. 214-215 (2)	2.10	1.00
No. 192 (1)	.30	.25
No. 80 (1)	7.25	7.25
Nos. 244-248 (5)	4.90	3.50
No. 4 (1)	3.75	2.75
Set total (106) Stamps	174.70	122.90

Separate designs for each country for the visit of Queen Elizabeth II and the Duke of Edinburgh.

Royal Visit 1953

1953

Aden	62
Australia	267-269
Bermuda	163
Ceylon	318
Fiji	146
Gibraltar	146
Jamaica	154
Kenya, Uganda, Tanzania	102
Malta	242
New Zealand	286-287

No. 62 (1)	.65	2.00
Nos. 267-269 (3)	2.35	1.90
No. 163 (1)	.50	.25
No. 318 (1)	1.25	.25
No. 146 (1)	.65	.35
No. 146 (1)	.50	.35
No. 154 (1)	.55	.25
No. 102 (1)	.50	.25
No. 242 (1)	.35	.25
Nos. 286-287 (2)	.50	.50
Set total (13) Stamps	7.80	6.35

West Indies Federation

Map of the Caribbean
CD313

Federation of the West Indies, April 22, 1958.

1958

Antigua	122-124
Barbados	248-250
Dominica	161-163
Grenada	184-186
Jamaica	175-177
Montserrat	143-145
St. Kitts-Nevis	136-138
St. Lucia	170-172
St. Vincent	198-200

Trinidad & Tobago	86-88

Nos. 122-124 (3)	5.80	3.80
Nos. 248-250 (3)	1.60	2.90
Nos. 161-163 (3)	1.95	1.85
Nos. 184-186 (3)	1.50	1.20
Nos. 175-177 (3)	3.10	4.20
Nos. 143-145 (3)	2.35	1.35
Nos. 136-138 (3)	3.00	1.85
Nos. 170-172 (3)	2.05	2.80
Nos. 198-200 (3)	1.50	1.75
Nos. 86-88 (3)	.75	.90
Set total (30) Stamps	23.60	22.60

Freedom from Hunger

Protein Food
CD314

U.N. Food and Agricultural Organization's "Freedom from Hunger" campaign.

1963

Aden	65
Antigua	133
Ascension	89
Bahamas	180
Basutoland	83
Bechuanaland Protectorate	194
Bermuda	192
British Guiana	271
British Honduras	179
Brunei	100
Cayman Islands	168
Dominica	181
Falkland Islands	146
Fiji	198
Gambia	172
Gibraltar	161
Gilbert & Ellice Islands	76
Grenada	190
Hong Kong	218
Malta	291
Mauritius	270
Montserrat	150
New Hebrides, British	93
North Borneo	296
Pitcairn Islands	35
St. Helena	173
St. Lucia	179
St. Vincent	201
Sarawak	212
Seychelles	213
Solomon Islands	109
Swaziland	108
Tonga	127
Tristan da Cunha	68
Turks & Caicos Islands	138
Virgin Islands	140
Zanzibar	280

No. 65 (1)	1.75	1.75
No. 133 (1)	.35	.35
No. 89 (1)	1.00	1.00
No. 180 (1)	.65	.65
No. 83 (1)	.50	.25
No. 194 (1)	.50	.50
No. 192 (1)	1.00	.50
No. 271 (1)	.45	.25
No. 179 (1)	.65	.25
No. 100 (1)	3.25	2.25
No. 168 (1)	.50	.30
No. 181 (1)	.30	.30
No. 146 (1)	11.50	3.50
No. 198 (1)	5.25	2.75
No. 172 (1)	.50	.25
No. 161 (1)	4.00	2.25
No. 76 (1)	1.40	.40
No. 190 (1)	.30	.25
No. 218 (1)	57.50	8.75
No. 291 (1)	2.25	2.75
No. 270 (1)	.50	.50
No. 150 (1)	.55	.45
No. 93 (1)	.60	.25
No. 296 (1)	1.90	.75
No. 35 (1)	17.50	7.00
No. 173 (1)	2.25	1.10
No. 179 (1)	.40	.40
No. 201 (1)	.90	.50
No. 212 (1)	1.60	1.75
No. 213 (1)	.85	.35
No. 109 (1)	2.00	.85
No. 108 (1)	.50	.50
No. 127 (1)	.70	.35
No. 68 (1)	1.00	.40
No. 138 (1)	.50	.50
No. 140 (1)	.50	.50
No. 280 (1)	1.50	.80
Set total (37) Stamps	127.35	46.20

Red Cross Centenary

Red Cross and Elizabeth II
CD315

1963

Antigua	134-135
Ascension	90-91
Bahamas	183-184
Basutoland	84-85
Bechuanaland Protectorate	195-196
Bermuda	193-194
British Guiana	272-273
British Honduras	180-181
Cayman Islands	169-170
Dominica	182-183
Falkland Islands	147-148
Fiji	203-204
Gambia	173-174
Gibraltar	162-163
Gilbert & Ellice Islands	77-78
Grenada	191-192
Hong Kong	219-220
Jamaica	203-204
Malta	292-293
Mauritius	271-272
Montserrat	151-152
New Hebrides, British	94-95
Pitcairn Islands	36-37
St. Helena	174-175
St. Kitts-Nevis	143-144
St. Lucia	180-181
St. Vincent	202-203
Seychelles	214-215
Solomon Islands	110-111
South Arabia	1-2
Swaziland	109-110
Tonga	134-135
Tristan da Cunha	69-70
Turks & Caicos Islands	139-140
Virgin Islands	141-142

Nos. 134-135 (2)	1.10	1.50
Nos. 90-91 (2)	8.25	2.70
Nos. 183-184 (2)	2.30	2.55
Nos. 84-85 (2)	1.20	.90
Nos. 195-196 (2)	1.05	1.05
Nos. 193-194 (2)	2.75	2.55
Nos. 272-273 (2)	1.05	.80
Nos. 180-181 (2)	1.00	2.25
Nos. 169-170 (2)	.95	2.00
Nos. 182-183 (2)	.70	1.05
Nos. 147-148 (2)	19.75	6.00
Nos. 203-204 (2)	4.00	3.55
Nos. 173-174 (2)	.85	.85
Nos. 162-163 (2)	7.05	5.40
Nos. 77-78 (2)	2.25	3.25
Nos. 191-192 (2)	.80	.50
Nos. 219-220 (2)	39.50	8.85
Nos. 203-204 (2)	.75	1.65
Nos. 292-293 (2)	3.25	5.00
Nos. 271-272 (2)	.90	.90
Nos. 151-152 (2)	1.00	.80
Nos. 94-95 (2)	1.00	.50
Nos. 36-37 (2)	12.40	7.00
Nos. 174-175 (2)	1.70	2.30
Nos. 143-144 (2)	.90	.90
Nos. 180-181 (2)	1.25	1.25
Nos. 202-203 (2)	.90	.90
Nos. 214-215 (2)	1.10	.90
Nos. 110-111 (2)	1.25	1.15
Nos. 1-2 (2)	1.25	1.25
Nos. 109-110 (2)	1.10	1.10
Nos. 134-135 (2)	1.00	1.25
Nos. 69-70 (2)	2.00	1.00
Nos. 139-140 (2)	.95	1.10
Nos. 141-142 (2)	.80	.80
Set total (70) Stamps	128.05	75.50

Shakespeare

Shakespeare Memorial Theatre, Stratford-on-Avon — CD316

400th anniversary of the birth of William Shakespeare.

1964

Antigua	151
Bahamas	201
Bechuanaland Protectorate	197
Cayman Islands	171

Dominica	184
Falkland Islands	149
Gambia	192
Gibraltar	164
Montserrat	153
St. Lucia	196
Turks & Caicos Islands	141
Virgin Islands	143

No. 151 (1)	.40	.25
No. 201 (1)	.60	.35
No. 197 (1)	.35	.35
No. 171 (1)	.35	.30
No. 184 (1)	.35	.35
No. 149 (1)	1.75	.50
No. 192 (1)	.35	.25
No. 164 (1)	.65	.55
No. 153 (1)	.35	.25
No. 196 (1)	.45	.25
No. 141 (1)	.40	.40
No. 143 (1)	.45	.45
Set total (12) Stamps	6.45	4.25

ITU

ITU Emblem
CD317

Intl. Telecommunication Union, cent.

1965

Antigua	153-154
Ascension	92-93
Bahamas	219-220
Barbados	265-266
Basutoland	101-102
Bechuanaland Protectorate	202-203
Bermuda	196-197
British Guiana	293-294
British Honduras	187-188
Brunei	116-117
Cayman Islands	172-173
Dominica	185-186
Falkland Islands	154-155
Fiji	211-212
Gibraltar	167-168
Gilbert & Ellice Islands	87-88
Grenada	205-206
Hong Kong	221-222
Mauritius	291-292
Montserrat	157-158
New Hebrides, British	108-109
Pitcairn Islands	52-53
St. Helena	180-181
St. Kitts-Nevis	163-164
St. Lucia	197-198
St. Vincent	224-225
Seychelles	218-219
Solomon Islands	126-127
Swaziland	115-116
Tristan da Cunha	85-86
Turks & Caicos Islands	142-143
Virgin Islands	159-160

Nos. 153-154 (2)	1.65	1.35
Nos. 92-93 (2)	1.90	1.50
Nos. 219-220 (2)	1.35	1.35
Nos. 265-266 (2)	1.50	1.25
Nos. 101-102 (2)	.85	.65
Nos. 202-203 (2)	1.20	.75
Nos. 196-197 (2)	2.15	2.25
Nos. 293-294 (2)	.60	.55
Nos. 187-188 (2)	.85	.85
Nos. 116-117 (2)	1.75	1.75
Nos. 172-173 (2)	1.00	1.00
Nos. 185-186 (2)	.55	.55
Nos. 154-155 (2)	7.75	3.65
Nos. 211-212 (2)	2.70	2.70
Nos. 167-168 (2)	11.25	5.95
Nos. 87-88 (2)	.95	.75
Nos. 205-206 (2)	.50	.50
Nos. 221-222 (2)	32.00	4.55
Nos. 291-292 (2)	1.20	.65
Nos. 157-158 (2)	1.25	1.15
Nos. 108-109 (2)	.65	.50
Nos. 52-53 (2)	14.50	8.55
Nos. 180-181 (2)	.80	.80
Nos. 163-164 (2)	.60	.60
Nos. 197-198 (2)	1.25	1.25
Nos. 224-225 (2)	.80	.90
Nos. 218-219 (2)	.90	.90
Nos. 126-127 (2)	.70	.55
Nos. 115-116 (2)	.75	.75
Nos. 85-86 (2)	1.50	.65
Nos. 142-143 (2)	.90	.90
Nos. 159-160 (2)	.95	.85
Set total (64) Stamps	97.25	50.50

Intl. Cooperation Year

ICY Emblem CD318

1965

Antigua	155-156
Ascension	94-95
Bahamas	222-223
Basutoland	103-104
Bechuanaland Protectorate	204-205
Bermuda	199-200
British Guiana	295-296
British Honduras	189-190
Brunei	118-119
Cayman Islands	174-175
Dominica	187-188
Falkland Islands	156-157
Fiji	213-214
Gibraltar	169-170
Gilbert & Ellice Islands	104-105
Grenada	207-208
Hong Kong	223-224
Mauritius	293-294
Montserrat	176-177
New Hebrides, British	110-111
New Hebrides, French	126-127
Pitcairn Islands	54-55
St. Helena	182-183
St. Kitts-Nevis	165-166
St. Lucia	199-200
Seychelles	220-221
Solomon Islands	143-144
South Arabia	17-18
Swaziland	117-118
Tristan da Cunha	87-88
Turks & Caicos Islands	144-145
Virgin Islands	161-162

Nos. 155-156 (2)	.60	.50
Nos. 94-95 (2)	1.30	1.50
Nos. 222-223 (2)	.65	1.40
Nos. 103-104 (2)	.75	.85
Nos. 204-205 (2)	1.00	1.15
Nos. 199-200 (2)	2.25	1.25
Nos. 295-296 (2)	.65	.60
Nos. 189-190 (2)	.60	.55
Nos. 118-119 (2)	.85	.85
Nos. 174-175 (2)	1.00	.95
Nos. 187-188 (2)	.55	.55
Nos. 156-157 (2)	7.00	1.90
Nos. 213-214 (2)	2.60	2.35
Nos. 169-170 (2)	1.35	3.00
Nos. 104-105 (2)	.95	.60
Nos. 207-208 (2)	.50	.50
Nos. 223-224 (2)	26.00	4.10
Nos. 293-294 (2)	.70	.70
Nos. 176-177 (2)	.80	.65
Nos. 110-111 (2)	.50	.50
Nos. 126-127 (2)	12.00	12.00
Nos. 54-55 (2)	14.35	6.75
Nos. 182-183 (2)	.95	.50
Nos. 165-166 (2)	.70	.60
Nos. 199-200 (2)	.55	.55
Nos. 220-221 (2)	.90	.65
Nos. 143-144 (2)	.70	.60
Nos. 17-18 (2)	1.20	.50
Nos. 117-118 (2)	.75	.75
Nos. 87-88 (2)	1.65	.75
Nos. 144-145 (2)	.85	.85
Nos. 161-162 (2)	.80	.50
Set total (64) Stamps	86.00	49.75

Churchill Memorial

Winston Churchill and St. Paul's, London, During Air Attack CD319

1966

Antigua	157-160
Ascension	96-99
Bahamas	224-227
Barbados	281-284
Basutoland	105-108
Bechuanaland Protectorate	206-209
Bermuda	201-204
British Antarctic Territory	16-19
British Honduras	191-194
Brunei	120-123
Cayman Islands	176-179
Dominica	189-192
Falkland Islands	158-161
Fiji	215-218

Gibraltar	171-174
Gilbert & Ellice Islands	106-109
Grenada	209-212
Hong Kong	225-228
Mauritius	295-298
Montserrat	178-181
New Hebrides, British	112-115
New Hebrides, French	128-131
Pitcairn Islands	56-59
St. Helena	184-187
St. Kitts-Nevis	167-170
St. Lucia	201-204
St. Vincent	241-244
Seychelles	222-225
Solomon Islands	145-148
South Arabia	19-22
Swaziland	119-122
Tristan da Cunha	89-92
Turks & Caicos Islands	146-149
Virgin Islands	163-166

Nos. 157-160 (4)	3.05	2.55
Nos. 96-99 (4)	10.00	7.15
Nos. 224-227 (4)	2.30	3.20
Nos. 281-284 (4)	3.00	4.45
Nos. 105-108 (4)	2.80	2.75
Nos. 206-209 (4)	2.80	2.30
Nos. 201-204 (4)	4.00	4.00
Nos. 16-19 (4)	46.35	20.00
Nos. 191-194 (4)	2.55	1.80
Nos. 120-123 (4)	8.00	7.25
Nos. 176-179 (4)	3.40	3.55
Nos. 189-192 (4)	1.15	1.15
Nos. 158-161 (4)	12.75	7.80
Nos. 215-218 (4)	5.15	3.45
Nos. 171-174 (4)	3.80	5.45
Nos. 106-109 (4)	1.75	1.30
Nos. 209-212 (4)	1.10	1.10
Nos. 225-228 (4)	68.00	12.15
Nos. 295-298 (4)	4.05	4.05
Nos. 178-181 (4)	1.60	1.55
Nos. 112-115 (4)	2.30	1.00
Nos. 128-131 (4)	10.25	10.25
Nos. 56-59 (4)	19.75	12.90
Nos. 184-187 (4)	1.85	1.95
Nos. 167-170 (4)	1.70	1.70
Nos. 201-204 (4)	1.50	1.50
Nos. 241-244 (4)	1.50	1.75
Nos. 222-225 (4)	3.20	3.60
Nos. 145-148 (4)	1.75	1.75
Nos. 19-22 (4)	3.80	2.50
Nos. 119-122 (4)	1.70	2.55
Nos. 89-92 (4)	7.00	2.70
Nos. 146-149 (4)	1.60	1.75
Nos. 163-166 (4)	1.90	1.90
Set total (136) Stamps	247.40	144.80

Royal Visit, 1966

Queen Elizabeth II and Prince Philip CD320

Caribbean visit, Feb. 4 - Mar. 6, 1966.

1966

Antigua	161-162
Bahamas	228-229
Barbados	285-286
British Guiana	299-300
Cayman Islands	180-181
Dominica	193-194
Grenada	213-214
Montserrat	182-183
St. Kitts-Nevis	171-172
St. Lucia	205-206
St. Vincent	245-246
Turks & Caicos Islands	150-151
Virgin Islands	167-168

Nos. 161-162 (2)	3.80	2.60
Nos. 228-229 (2)	3.05	3.05
Nos. 285-286 (2)	3.00	2.00
Nos. 299-300 (2)	3.35	1.60
Nos. 180-181 (2)	3.45	1.80
Nos. 193-194 (2)	3.00	.60
Nos. 213-214 (2)	.90	.50
Nos. 182-183 (2)	1.70	1.00
Nos. 171-172 (2)	.80	.75
Nos. 205-206 (2)	1.50	1.35
Nos. 245-246 (2)	2.75	1.35
Nos. 150-151 (2)	1.20	.70
Nos. 167-168 (2)	2.25	2.25
Set total (26) Stamps	30.75	19.55

World Cup Soccer

Soccer Player and Jules Rimet Cup CD321

World Cup Soccer Championship, Wembley, England, July 11-30.

1966

Antigua	163-164
Ascension	100-101
Bahamas	245-246
Bermuda	205-206
Brunei	124-125
Cayman Islands	182-183
Dominica	195-196
Fiji	219-220
Gibraltar	175-176
Gilbert & Ellice Islands	125-126
Grenada	230-231
New Hebrides, British	116-117
New Hebrides, French	132-133
Pitcairn Islands	60-61
St. Helena	188-189
St. Kitts-Nevis	173-174
St. Lucia	207-208
Seychelles	226-227
Solomon Islands	167-168
South Arabia	23-24
Tristan da Cunha	93-94

Nos. 163-164 (2)	.85	.50
Nos. 100-101 (2)	2.50	1.80
Nos. 245-246 (2)	.65	.65
Nos. 205-206 (2)	1.75	1.75
Nos. 124-125 (2)	1.40	1.00
Nos. 182-183 (2)	.75	.75
Nos. 195-196 (2)	1.20	.75
Nos. 219-220 (2)	2.00	1.20
Nos. 175-176 (2)	2.00	1.80
Nos. 125-126 (2)	.80	.60
Nos. 230-231 (2)	.65	.95
Nos. 116-117 (2)	1.00	1.00
Nos. 132-133 (2)	7.00	7.00
Nos. 60-61 (2)	8.00	4.75
Nos. 188-189 (2)	1.25	.60
Nos. 173-174 (2)	.85	.80
Nos. 207-208 (2)	1.15	.90
Nos. 226-227 (2)	.85	.85
Nos. 167-168 (2)	.70	.70
Nos. 23-24 (2)	1.90	.55
Nos. 93-94 (2)	1.50	.80
Set total (42) Stamps	38.75	29.70

WHO Headquarters

World Health Organization Headquarters, Geneva — CD322

1966

Antigua	165-166
Ascension	102-103
Bahamas	247-248
Brunei	126-127
Cayman Islands	184-185
Dominica	197-198
Fiji	224-225
Gibraltar	180-181
Gilbert & Ellice Islands	127-128
Grenada	232-233
Hong Kong	229-230
Montserrat	184-185
New Hebrides, British	118-119
New Hebrides, French	134-135
Pitcairn Islands	62-63
St. Helena	190-191
St. Kitts-Nevis	177-178
St. Lucia	209-210
St. Vincent	247-248
Seychelles	228-229
Solomon Islands	169-170
South Arabia	25-26
Tristan da Cunha	99-100

Nos. 165-166 (2)	1.05	.55
Nos. 102-103 (2)	6.60	3.50
Nos. 247-248 (2)	.80	.80
Nos. 126-127 (2)	1.35	1.00
Nos. 184-185 (2)	2.25	1.40
Nos. 197-198 (2)	.75	.75
Nos. 224-225 (2)	5.10	3.90
Nos. 180-181 (2)	7.50	4.75
Nos. 127-128 (2)	.80	.70
Nos. 232-233 (2)	.80	.50
Nos. 229-230 (2)	14.25	2.30
Nos. 184-185 (2)	1.00	1.00
Nos. 118-119 (2)	.75	.50
Nos. 134-135 (2)	8.75	8.75
Nos. 62-63 (2)	13.00	7.00
Nos. 190-191 (2)	3.50	1.50
Nos. 177-178 (2)	.65	.65
Nos. 209-210 (2)	.80	.80
Nos. 247-248 (2)	1.15	1.05
Nos. 228-229 (2)	1.25	.75
Nos. 169-170 (2)	.80	.80

Nos. 25-26 (2)	2.10	.70
Nos. 99-100 (2)	2.25	1.25
Set total (46) Stamps	77.25	44.90

UNESCO Anniversary

"Education" — CD323

"Science" (Wheat ears & flask enclosing globe). "Culture" (lyre & columns). 20th anniversary of the UNESCO.

1966-67

Antigua	183-185
Ascension	108-110
Bahamas	249-251
Barbados	287-289
Bermuda	207-209
Brunei	128-130
Cayman Islands	186-188
Dominica	199-201
Gibraltar	183-185
Gilbert & Ellice Islands	129-131
Grenada	234-236
Hong Kong	231-233
Mauritius	299-301
Montserrat	186-188
New Hebrides, British	120-122
New Hebrides, French	136-138
Pitcairn Islands	64-66
St. Helena	192-194
St. Kitts-Nevis	179-181
St. Lucia	211-213
St. Vincent	249-251
Seychelles	230-232
Solomon Islands	171-173
South Arabia	27-29
Swaziland	123-125
Tristan da Cunha	101-103
Turks & Caicos Islands	155-157
Virgin Islands	176-178

Nos. 183-185 (3)	1.90	2.50
Nos. 108-110 (3)	11.00	6.15
Nos. 249-251 (3)	2.35	2.35
Nos. 287-289 (3)	2.50	2.15
Nos. 207-209 (3)	4.30	3.90
Nos. 128-130 (3)	5.00	7.40
Nos. 186-188 (3)	2.50	1.70
Nos. 199-201 (3)	1.60	.75
Nos. 183-185 (3)	7.50	3.75
Nos. 129-131 (3)	2.50	1.65
Nos. 234-236 (3)	1.10	1.20
Nos. 231-233 (3)	89.00	20.00
Nos. 299-301 (3)	2.10	1.50
Nos. 186-188 (3)	2.40	2.40
Nos. 120-122 (3)	1.90	1.90
Nos. 136-138 (3)	7.75	7.75
Nos. 64-66 (3)	12.85	7.10
Nos. 192-194 (3)	5.25	3.65
Nos. 179-181 (3)	.90	.90
Nos. 211-213 (3)	1.15	1.15
Nos. 249-251 (3)	2.30	1.35
Nos. 230-232 (3)	2.40	2.40
Nos. 171-173 (3)	2.00	1.50
Nos. 27-29 (3)	5.65	6.30
Nos. 123-125 (3)	1.45	1.45
Nos. 101-103 (3)	2.50	1.40
Nos. 155-157 (3)	1.05	1.05
Nos. 176-178 (3)	1.30	1.30
Set total (84) Stamps	184.20	96.60

Silver Wedding, 1972

Queen Elizabeth II and Prince Philip — CD324

Designs: borders differ for each country.

1972

Anguilla	161-162
Antigua	295-296
Ascension	164-165
Bahamas	344-345
Bermuda	296-297
British Antarctic Territory	43-44
British Honduras	306-307
British Indian Ocean Territory	48-49

Brunei.....186-187
Cayman Islands.....304-305
Dominica.....352-353
Falkland Islands.....223-224
Fiji.....328-329
Gibraltar.....292-293
Gilbert & Ellice Islands.....206-207
Grenada.....466-467
Hong Kong.....271-272
Montserrat.....286-287
New Hebrides, British.....169-170
Pitcairn Islands.....127-128
St. Helena.....271-272
St. Kitts-Nevis.....257-258
St. Lucia.....328-329
St.Vincent.....344-345
Seychelles.....309-310
Solomon Islands.....248-249
South Georgia.....35-36
Tristan da Cunha.....178-179
Turks & Caicos Islands.....257-258
Virgin Islands.....241-242

Nos. 161-162 (2) 1.80 1.50
Nos. 295-296 (2) .50 .50
Nos. 164-165 (2) .80 .80
Nos. 344-345 (2) .60 .60
Nos. 296-297 (2) .50 .50
Nos. 43-44 (2) 7.75 6.10
Nos. 306-307 (2) .90 .90
Nos. 48-49 (2) 2.30 1.00
Nos. 186-187 (2) .65 .85
Nos. 304-305 (2) .75 .75
Nos. 352-353 (2) .65 .65
Nos. 223-224 (2) 1.10 1.10
Nos. 328-329 (2) 1.00 1.00
Nos. 292-293 (2) .50 .50
Nos. 206-207 (2) .50 .50
Nos. 466-467 (2) .70 .70
Nos. 271-272 (2) 2.10 1.75
Nos. 286-287 (2) .55 .55
Nos. 169-170 (2) .50 .50
Nos. 127-128 (2) 1.15 .80
Nos. 271-272 (2) .70 1.20
Nos. 257-258 (2) .65 .50
Nos. 328-329 (2) .75 .75
Nos. 344-345 (2) .55 .55
Nos. 309-310 (2) .95 .95
Nos. 248-249 (2) .60 .60
Nos. 35-36 (2) 1.40 1.40
Nos. 178-179 (2) .75 .70
Nos. 257-258 (2) .50 .50
Nos. 241-242 (2) .50 .50
Set total (60) Stamps 32.65 29.20

Princess Anne's Wedding

Princess Anne and Mark Phillips — CD325

Wedding of Princess Anne and Mark Phillips, Nov. 14, 1973.

1973

Anguilla.....179-180
Ascension.....177-178
Belize.....325-326
Bermuda.....302-303
British Antarctic Territory.....60-61
Cayman Islands.....320-321
Falkland Islands.....225-226
Gibraltar.....305-306
Gilbert & Ellice Islands.....216-217
Hong Kong.....289-290
Montserrat.....300-301
Pitcairn Islands.....135-136
St. Helena.....277-278
St. Kitts-Nevis.....274-275
St. Lucia.....349-350
St. Vincent.....358-359
St. Vincent Grenadines.....1-2
Seychelles.....311-312
Solomon Islands.....259-260
South Georgia.....37-38
Tristan da Cunha.....189-190
Turks & Caicos Islands.....286-287
Virgin Islands.....260-261

Nos. 179-180 (2) .55 .55
Nos. 177-178 (2) .65 .65
Nos. 325-326 (2) .50 .50
Nos. 302-303 (2) .50 .50
Nos. 60-61 (2) 1.10 1.10
Nos. 320-321 (2) .55 .55
Nos. 225-226 (2) .75 .75
Nos. 305-306 (2) .70 .70

Nos. 216-217 (2) .50 .50
Nos. 289-290 (2) 3.25 2.25
Nos. 300-301 (2) .65 .65
Nos. 135-136 (2) .90 .60
Nos. 277-278 (2) .50 .50
Nos. 274-275 (2) .50 .50
Nos. 349-350 (2) .50 .50
Nos. 358-359 (2) .50 .50
Nos. 1-2 (2) .65 .65
Nos. 311-312 (2) .70 .70
Nos. 259-260 (2) .70 .70
Nos. 37-38 (2) .75 .75
Nos. 189-190 (2) .50 .50
Nos. 286-287 (2) .50 .50
Nos. 260-261 (2) .50 .50
Set total (46) Stamps 16.90 15.60

Elizabeth II Coronation Anniv.

CD326   CD327

CD328

Designs: Royal and local beasts in heraldic form and simulated stonework. Portrait of Elizabeth II by Peter Grugeon. 25th anniversary of coronation of Queen Elizabeth II.

1978

Ascension.....229
Barbados.....474
Belize.....397
British Antarctic Territory.....71
Cayman Islands.....404
Christmas Island.....87
Falkland Islands.....275
Fiji.....384
Gambia.....380
Gilbert Islands.....312
Mauritius.....464
New Hebrides, British.....258
St. Helena.....317
St. Kitts-Nevis.....354
Samoa.....472
Solomon Islands.....368
South Georgia.....51
Swaziland.....302
Tristan da Cunha.....238
Virgin Islands.....337

No. 229 (1) 2.25 2.25
No. 474 (1) 1.35 1.35
No. 397 (1) 1.75 1.75
No. 71 (1) 6.00 6.00
No. 404 (1) 2.00 2.50
No. 87 (1) 3.75 4.25
No. 275 (1) 4.00 4.00
No. 384 (1) 2.75 2.75
No. 380 (1) 1.50 1.50
No. 312 (1) 1.25 1.25
No. 464 (1) 2.75 2.75
No. 258 (1) 1.75 1.75
No. 317 (1) 1.75 1.75
No. 354 (1) 1.00 1.00
No. 472 (1) 2.00 2.00
No. 368 (1) 3.00 3.00
No. 51 (1) 3.00 3.00
No. 302 (1) 1.75 1.75
No. 238 (1) 1.60 1.60
No. 337 (1) 2.25 2.25
Set total (20) Stamps 47.45 48.45

Queen Mother Elizabeth's 80th Birthday

CD330

Designs: Photographs of Queen Mother Elizabeth. Falkland Islands issued in sheets of 50; others in sheets of 9.

1980

Ascension.....261
Bermuda.....401
Cayman Islands.....443
Falkland Islands.....305
Gambia.....412
Gibraltar.....393
Hong Kong.....364
Pitcairn Islands.....193
St. Helena.....341
Samoa.....532
Solomon Islands.....426
Tristan da Cunha.....277

No. 261 (1) .50 .50
No. 401 (1) .45 .45
No. 443 (1) .45 .45
No. 305 (1) .40 .40
No. 412 (1) .40 .50
No. 393 (1) .35 .35
No. 364 (1) 1.10 1.00
No. 193 (1) .70 .70
No. 341 (1) .50 .50
No. 532 (1) .55 .55
No. 426 (1) .50 .50
No. 277 (1) .45 .45
Set total (12) Stamps 6.35 6.35

Royal Wedding, 1981

Prince Charles and Lady Diana — CD331   CD331a

Wedding of Charles, Prince of Wales, and Lady Diana Spencer, St. Paul's Cathedral, London, July 29, 1981.

1981

Antigua.....623-627
Ascension.....294-296
Barbados.....547-549
Barbuda.....497-501
Bermuda.....412-414
Brunei.....268-270
Cayman Islands.....471-473
Dominica.....701-705
Falkland Islands.....324-326
Falkland Islands Dep.....1L59-1L61
Fiji.....442-444
Gambia.....426-428
Ghana.....759-764
Grenada.....1051-1055
Grenada Grenadines.....440-443
Hong Kong.....373-375
Jamaica.....500-503
Lesotho.....335-337
Maldive Islands.....906-909
Mauritius.....520-522
Norfolk Island.....280-282
Pitcairn Islands.....206-208
St. Helena.....353-355
St. Lucia.....543-549
Samoa.....558-560
Sierra Leone.....509-518
Solomon Islands.....450-452
Swaziland.....382-384
Tristan da Cunha.....294-296
Turks & Caicos Islands.....486-489
Caicos Island.....8-11
Uganda.....314-317
Vanuatu.....308-310
Virgin Islands.....406-408

Nos. 623-627 (5) 7.55 2.55
Nos. 294-296 (3) 1.10 1.10
Nos. 547-549 (3) .90 .90
Nos. 497-501 (5) 10.95 10.95
Nos. 412-414 (3) 2.00 2.00
Nos. 268-270 (3) 2.15 4.50
Nos. 471-473 (3) 1.35 1.35
Nos. 701-705 (5) 8.35 2.35
Nos. 324-326 (3) 1.65 1.70
Nos. 1L59-1L61 (3) 1.45 1.45
Nos. 442-444 (3) 1.70 1.70
Nos. 426-428 (3) .80 .80
Nos. 759-764 (9) 5.00 5.00
Nos. 1051-1055 (5) 9.85 1.85
Nos. 440-443 (4) 2.35 2.35
Nos. 373-375 (3) 3.30 3.10
Nos. 500-503 (4) 1.50 1.25

Nos. 335-337 (3) 1.10 1.10
Nos. 906-909 (4) 1.70 1.80
Nos. 520-522 (3) 2.75 2.75
Nos. 280-282 (3) 1.35 1.35
Nos. 206-208 (3) 1.35 1.35
Nos. 353-355 (3) .85 .85
Nos. 543-549 (5) 8.50 8.50
Nos. 558-560 (3) .85 .85
Nos. 509-518 (10) 15.50 15.50
Nos. 450-452 (3) 1.05 1.05
Nos. 382-384 (3) 1.30 1.25
Nos. 294-296 (3) .95 .95
Nos. 486-489 (4) 2.20 2.20
Nos. 8-11 (4) 6.25 6.25
Nos. 314-317 (3) 3.30 3.00
Nos. 308-310 (3) 1.15 1.15
Nos. 406-408 (3) 1.30 1.30
Set total (131) Stamps 113.40 96.10

Princess Diana

CD332

CD333

Designs: Photographs and portrait of Princess Diana, wedding or honeymoon photographs, royal residences, arms of issuing country. Portrait photograph by Clive Friend. Souvenir sheet margins show family tree, various people related to the princess. 21st birthday of Princess Diana of Wales, July 1.

1982

Antigua.....663-666
Ascension.....313-316
Bahamas.....510-513
Barbados.....585-588
Barbuda.....544-547
British Antarctic Territory.....92-95
Cayman Islands.....486-489
Dominica.....773-776
Falkland Islands.....348-351
Falkland Islands Dep.....1L72-1L75
Fiji.....470-473
Gambia.....447-450
Grenada.....1101A-1105
Grenada Grenadines.....485-491
Lesotho.....372-375
Maldive Islands.....952-955
Mauritius.....548-551
Pitcairn Islands.....213-216
St. Helena.....372-375
St. Lucia.....591-594
Sierra Leone.....531-534
Solomon Islands.....471-474
Swaziland.....406-409
Tristan da Cunha.....310-313
Turks and Caicos Islands.....531-534
Virgin Islands.....430-433

Nos. 663-666 (4) 9.70 9.70
Nos. 313-316 (4) 3.95 3.95
Nos. 510-513 (4) 6.00 3.85
Nos. 585-588 (4) 3.40 3.25
Nos. 544-547 (4) 9.75 7.70
Nos. 92-95 (4) 5.30 3.45
Nos. 486-489 (4) 5.40 2.70
Nos. 773-776 (4) 7.05 7.05
Nos. 348-351 (4) 3.10 3.10
Nos. 1L72-1L75 (4) 2.50 2.60
Nos. 470-473 (4) 4.50 4.50
Nos. 447-450 (4) 2.85 2.85
Nos. 1101A-1105 (7) 16.05 15.55
Nos. 485-491 (7) 17.65 17.65
Nos. 372-375 (4) 4.00 4.00
Nos. 952-955 (4) 7.25 7.25
Nos. 548-551 (4) 5.50 5.50
Nos. 213-216 (4) 3.40 3.40
Nos. 372-375 (4) 2.95 2.95
Nos. 591-594 (4) 9.90 9.90
Nos. 531-534 (4) 7.60 7.60
Nos. 471-474 (4) 2.90 2.90
Nos. 406-409 (4) 3.85 2.25
Nos. 310-313 (4) 4.75 1.45
Nos. 486-489 (4) 2.20 2.20
Nos. 430-433 (4) 3.55 3.55
Set total (110) Stamps 155.05 140.85

250th anniv. of first edition of Lloyd's List (shipping news publication) & of Lloyd's marine insurance.

CD335

Designs: First page of early edition of the list; historical ships, modern transportation or harbor scenes.

1984

Ascension	351-354
Bahamas	555-558
Barbados	627-630
Cayes of Belize	10-13
Cayman Islands	522-526
Falkland Islands	404-407
Fiji	509-512
Gambia	519-522
Mauritius	587-590
Nauru	280-283
St. Helena	412-415
Samoa	624-627
Seychelles	538-541
Solomon Islands	521-524
Vanuatu	368-371
Virgin Islands	466-469

Nos. 351-354 (4)	3.30	2.55
Nos. 555-558 (4)	4.55	2.95
Nos. 627-630 (4)	6.10	5.15
Nos. 10-13 (4)	3.05	3.05
Nos. 522-526 (5)	9.30	8.45
Nos. 404-407 (4)	3.65	4.00
Nos. 509-512 (4)	6.15	6.15
Nos. 519-522 (4)	4.20	4.30
Nos. 587-590 (4)	8.95	8.95
Nos. 280-283 (4)	2.40	2.35
Nos. 412-415 (4)	2.40	2.40
Nos. 624-627 (4)	2.75	2.55
Nos. 538-541 (4)	5.25	5.25
Nos. 521-524 (4)	4.65	3.95
Nos. 368-371 (4)	2.40	2.40
Nos. 400-409 (4)	5.00	5.00
Set total (65) Stamps	74.10	69.45

Queen Mother 85th Birthday

CD336

Designs: Photographs tracing the life of the Queen Mother, Elizabeth. The high value in each set pictures the same photograph taken of the Queen Mother holding the infant Prince Henry.

1985

Ascension	372-376
Bahamas	580-584
Barbados	660-664
Bermuda	469-473
Falkland Islands	420-424
Falkland Islands Dep.	1L92-1L96
Fiji	531-535
Hong Kong	447-450
Jamaica	599-603
Mauritius	604-608
Norfolk Island	364-368
Pitcairn Islands	253-257
St. Helena	428-432
Samoa	649-653
Seychelles	567-571
Zil Elwannyen Sesel	101-105
Solomon Islands	543-547
Swaziland	476-480
Tristan da Cunha	372-376
Vanuatu	392-396

Nos. 372-376 (5)	5.35	5.35
Nos. 580-584 (5)	7.95	6.45
Nos. 660-664 (5)	8.00	6.70
Nos. 469-473 (5)	9.90	9.90
Nos. 420-424 (5)	8.80	8.80
Nos. 1L92-1L96 (5)	8.25	8.25
Nos. 531-535 (5)	7.05	7.05

Nos. 447-450 (4)	10.25	8.50
Nos. 599-603 (5)	7.50	8.00
Nos. 604-608 (5)	11.80	11.80
Nos. 364-368 (5)	5.05	5.05
Nos. 253-257 (5)	6.00	6.15
Nos. 428-432 (5)	5.25	5.25
Nos. 649-653 (5)	8.65	7.80
Nos. 567-571 (5)	8.70	8.70
Nos. 101-105 (5)	7.15	7.15
Nos. 543-547 (5)	4.45	4.45
Nos. 476-480 (5)	8.00	7.50
Nos. 372-376 (5)	5.40	5.40
Nos. 392-396 (5)	5.25	5.25
Set total (99) Stamps	148.75	143.50

Queen Elizabeth II, 60th Birthday

CD337

1986, April 21

Ascension	389-393
Bahamas	592-596
Barbados	675-679
Bermuda	499-503
Cayman Islands	555-559
Falkland Islands	441-445
Fiji	544-548
Hong Kong	465-469
Jamaica	620-624
Kiribati	470-474
Mauritius	629-633
Papua New Guinea	640-644
Pitcairn Islands	270-274
St. Helena	451-455
Samoa	670-674
Seychelles	592-596
Zil Elwannyen Sesel	114-118
Solomon Islands	562-566
South Georgia	101-105
Swaziland	490-494
Tristan da Cunha	388-392
Vanuatu	414-418
Zambia	343-347

Nos. 389-393 (5)	2.80	2.80
Nos. 592-596 (5)	2.75	3.70
Nos. 675-679 (5)	3.35	3.20
Nos. 499-503 (5)	4.90	4.90
Nos. 555-559 (5)	4.55	4.45
Nos. 441-445 (5)	3.95	4.95
Nos. 544-548 (5)	4.05	4.05
Nos. 465-469 (5)	9.60	6.85
Nos. 620-624 (5)	2.95	3.05
Nos. 470-474 (5)	2.10	2.10
Nos. 629-633 (5)	3.70	3.70
Nos. 640-644 (5)	4.50	4.50
Nos. 270-274 (5)	3.85	3.85
Nos. 451-455 (5)	3.05	3.05
Nos. 670-674 (5)	2.90	2.90
Nos. 592-596 (5)	2.70	2.70
Nos. 114-118 (5)	2.25	2.25
Nos. 562-566 (5)	2.50	2.50
Nos. 101-105 (5)	3.55	3.55
Nos. 490-494 (5)	2.30	2.30
Nos. 388-392 (5)	3.60	3.60
Nos. 414-418 (5)	3.10	3.10
Nos. 343-347 (5)	2.25	2.25
Set total (115) Stamps	81.25	80.30

Royal Wedding

Marriage of Prince Andrew and Sarah Ferguson
CD338

1986, July 23

Ascension	399-400
Bahamas	602-603
Barbados	687-688
Cayman Islands	560-561
Jamaica	629-630
Pitcairn Islands	275-276
St. Helena	460-461
St. Kitts	181-182
Seychelles	602-603
Zil Elwannyen Sesel	119-120
Solomon Islands	567-568
Tristan da Cunha	397-398
Zambia	348-349

Nos. 399-400 (2)	1.60	1.60
Nos. 602-603 (2)	2.75	2.75

Nos. 687-688 (2)	2.25	1.25
Nos. 560-561 (2)	1.50	2.15
Nos. 629-630 (2)	1.75	1.75
Nos. 275-276 (2)	2.75	2.75
Nos. 460-461 (2)	1.05	1.05
Nos. 181-182 (2)	1.50	1.50
Nos. 602-603 (2)	2.50	2.50
Nos. 119-120 (2)	2.30	2.30
Nos. 567-568 (2)	1.00	1.00
Nos. 397-398 (2)	1.50	1.50
Nos. 348-349 (2)	1.30	1.45
Set total (26) Stamps	23.75	23.55

Queen Elizabeth II, 60th Birthday

Queen Elizabeth II & Prince Philip, 1947 Wedding Portrait — CD339

Designs: Photographs tracing the life of Queen Elizabeth II.

1986

Anguilla	674-677
Antigua	925-928
Barbuda	783-786
Dominica	950-953
Gambia	611-614
Grenada	1371-1374
Grenada Grenadines	749-752
Lesotho	531-534
Maldive Islands	1172-1175
Sierra Leone	760-763
Uganda	495-498

Nos. 674-677 (4)	8.00	8.00
Nos. 925-928 (4)	6.75	6.75
Nos. 783-786 (4)	25.60	25.60
Nos. 950-953 (4)	7.15	7.15
Nos. 611-614 (4)	8.25	7.90
Nos. 1371-1374 (4)	6.80	6.80
Nos. 749-752 (4)	6.75	6.75
Nos. 531-534 (4)	5.50	5.50
Nos. 1172-1175 (4)	7.00	7.00
Nos. 760-763 (4)	6.30	6.30
Nos. 495-498 (4)	8.50	8.50
Set total (44) Stamps	96.60	96.25

Royal Wedding, 1986

CD340

Designs: Photographs of Prince Andrew and Sarah Ferguson during courtship, engagement and marriage.

1986

Antigua	939-942
Barbuda	809-812
Dominica	970-973
Gambia	635-638
Grenada	1385-1388
Grenada Grenadines	758-761
Lesotho	545-548
Maldive Islands	1181-1184
Sierra Leone	769-772
Uganda	510-513

Nos. 939-942 (4)	8.25	8.25
Nos. 809-812 (4)	15.90	15.80
Nos. 970-973 (4)	7.25	7.25
Nos. 635-638 (4)	8.55	8.55
Nos. 1385-1388 (4)	8.30	8.30
Nos. 758-761 (4)	9.00	9.00
Nos. 545-548 (4)	7.95	7.95
Nos. 1181-1184 (4)	10.20	10.20
Nos. 769-772 (4)	5.55	5.55
Nos. 510-513 (4)	9.50	10.25
Set total (40) Stamps	90.45	91.10

Lloyds of London, 300th Anniv.

CD341

Designs: 17th century aspects of Lloyds, representations of each country's individual connections with Lloyds and publicized disasters insured by the organization.

1986

Ascension	454-457
Bahamas	655-658
Barbados	731-734
Bermuda	541-544
Falkland Islands	481-484
Liberia	1101-1104
Malawi	534-537
Nevis	571-574
St. Helena	501-504
St. Lucia	923-926
Seychelles	649-652
Zil Elwannyen Sesel	146-149
Solomon Islands	627-630
South Georgia	131-134
Trinidad & Tobago	484-487
Tristan da Cunha	439-442
Vanuatu	485-488

Nos. 454-457 (4)	5.00	5.00
Nos. 655-658 (4)	8.90	4.95
Nos. 731-734 (4)	12.50	8.35
Nos. 541-544 (4)	8.25	5.60
Nos. 481-484 (4)	6.30	4.55
Nos. 1101-1104 (4)	5.25	5.25
Nos. 534-537 (4)	11.00	7.85
Nos. 571-574 (4)	8.35	8.35
Nos. 501-504 (4)	8.70	7.15
Nos. 923-926 (4)	9.40	9.40
Nos. 649-652 (4)	13.10	13.10
Nos. 146-149 (4)	11.25	11.25
Nos. 627-630 (4)	7.90	4.45
Nos. 131-134 (4)	6.30	3.70
Nos. 484-487 (4)	11.85	8.50
Nos. 439-442 (4)	0.75	0.75
Nos. 485-488 (4)	5.90	5.90
Set total (68) Stamps	146.70	120.10

Moon Landing, 20th Anniv.

CD342

Designs: Equipment, crew photographs, spacecraft, official emblems and report profiles created for the Apollo Missions. Two stamps in each set are square in format rather than like the stamp shown; see individual country listings for more information.

1989

Ascension	468-472
Bahamas	674-678
Belize	916-920
Kiribati	517-521
Liberia	1125-1129
Nevis	586-590
St. Kitts	248-252
Samoa	760-764
Seychelles	676-680
Zil Elwannyen Sesel	154-158
Solomon Islands	643-647
Vanuatu	507-511

Nos. 468-472 (5)	9.40	8.60
Nos. 674-678 (5)	23.00	19.70
Nos. 916-920 (5)	27.40	23.50
Nos. 517-521 (5)	12.50	12.50
Nos. 1125-1129 (5)	10.65	10.65
Nos. 586-590 (5)	7.50	7.50
Nos. 248-252 (5)	8.00	8.00
Nos. 760-764 (5)	9.60	9.05
Nos. 676-680 (5)	16.65	16.65
Nos. 154-158 (5)	26.85	26.85

Nos. 643-647 (5)	12.75	11.60
Nos. 507-511 (5)	9.90	9.90
Set total (60) Stamps	174.20	164.50

Queen Mother, 90th Birthday

CD343   CD344

Designs: Portraits of Queen Elizabeth, the Queen Mother. See individual country listings for more information.

1990

Ascension	.491-492
Bahamas	.698-699
Barbados	.782-783
British Antarctic Territory	.170-171
British Indian Ocean Territory	.106-107
Cayman Islands	.622-623
Falkland Islands	.524-525
Kenya	.527-528
Kiribati	.555-556
Liberia	.1145-1146
Pitcairn Islands	.336-337
St. Helena	.532-533
St. Lucia	.969-970
Seychelles	.710-711
Zil Elwannyen Sesel	.171-172
Solomon Islands	.671-672
South Georgia	.143-144
Swaziland	.565-566
Tristan da Cunha	.480-481

Nos. 491-492 (2)	4.75	5.65
Nos. 698-699 (2)	5.65	5.65
Nos. 782-783 (2)	4.00	3.70
Nos. 170-171 (2)	6.75	6.75
Nos. 106-107 (2)	20.75	21.25
Nos. 622-623 (2)	5.10	6.75
Nos. 524-525 (2)	5.25	5.25
Nos. 527-528 (2)	7.00	7.00
Nos. 555-556 (2)	5.60	5.60
Nos. 1145-1146 (2)	4.25	4.25
Nos. 336-337 (2)	5.25	5.25
Nos. 532-533 (2)	5.25	5.25
Nos. 969-970 (2)	5.25	5.25
Nos. 710-711 (2)	6.60	6.60
Nos. 171-172 (2)	8.25	8.25
Nos. 671-672 (2)	6.50	6.40
Nos. 143-144 (2)	5.75	5.75
Nos. 565-566 (2)	4.35	4.35
Nos. 480-481 (2)	6.25	5.60
Set total (38) Stamps	122.55	124.55

Queen Elizabeth II, 65th Birthday, and Prince Philip, 70th Birthday

CD345

CD346

Designs: Portraits of Queen Elizabeth II and Prince Philip differ for each country. Printed in sheets of 10 + 5 labels (3 different) between. Stamps alternate, producing 5 different triptychs.

1991

Ascension	.506a
Bahamas	.731a
Belize	.970a
Bermuda	.618a
Kiribati	.572a

Mauritius	.734a
Pitcairn Islands	.349a
St. Helena	.555a
St. Kitts	.319a
Samoa	.791a
Seychelles	.724a
Zil Elwannyen Sesel	.178a
Solomon Islands	.689a
South Georgia	.150a
Swaziland	.587a
Vanuatu	.541a

No. 506a (1)	3.50	3.75
No. 731a (1)	4.00	4.00
No. 970a (1)	3.75	3.75
No. 618a (1)	4.00	4.00
No. 572a (1)	4.00	4.00
No. 734a (1)	3.75	3.75
No. 349a (1)	3.50	3.50
No. 555a (1)	2.75	2.75
No. 319a (1)	3.00	3.00
No. 791a (1)	4.25	4.25
No. 724a (1)	5.00	5.00
No. 178a (1)	6.50	6.50
No. 689a (1)	4.50	4.50
No. 150a (1)	7.00	7.00
No. 587a (1)	4.25	4.25
No. 541a (1)	2.50	2.50
Set total (16) Stamps	66.25	66.50

Royal Family Birthday, Anniversary

CD347

Queen Elizabeth II, 65th birthday, Charles and Diana, 10th wedding anniversary: Various photographs of Queen Elizabeth II, Prince Philip, Prince Charles, Princess Diana and their sons William and Henry.

1991

Antigua	.1446-1455
Barbuda	.1229-1238
Dominica	.1328-1337
Gambia	.1080-1089
Grenada	.2006-2015
Grenada Grenadines	.1331-1340
Guyana	.2440-2451
Lesotho	.871-875
Maldive Islands	.1533-1542
Nevis	.666-675
St. Vincent	.1485-1494
St. Vincent Grenadines	.769-778
Sierra Leone	.1387-1396
Turks & Caicos Islands	.913-922
Uganda	.918-927

Nos. 1446-1455 (10)	21.95	20.30
Nos. 1229-1238 (10)	146.25	139.90
Nos. 1328-1337 (10)	29.85	29.85
Nos. 1080-1089 (10)	24.65	24.40
Nos. 2006-2015 (10)	25.45	22.10
Nos. 1331-1340 (10)	23.85	23.35
Nos. 2440-2451 (12)	37.05	36.70
Nos. 871-875 (5)	13.55	13.55
Nos. 1533-1542 (10)	29.60	29.60
Nos. 666-675 (10)	25.65	25.65
Nos. 1485-1494 (10)	26.75	25.90
Nos. 769-778 (10)	27.10	27.10
Nos. 1387-1396 (10)	26.55	26.55
Nos. 913-922 (10)	31.65	30.00
Nos. 918-927 (10)	26.60	26.60
Set total (147) Stamps	516.50	501.55

Queen Elizabeth II's Accession to the Throne, 40th Anniv.

CD348

CD349

Various photographs of Queen Elizabeth II with local Scenes.

1992 - CD348

Antigua	.1513-1518

Barbuda	.1306-1311
Dominica	.1414-1419
Gambia	.1172-1177
Grenada	.2047-2052
Grenada Grenadines	.1368-1373
Lesotho	.881-885
Maldive Islands	.1637-1642
Nevis	.702-707
St. Vincent	.1582-1587
St. Vincent Grenadines	.829-834
Sierra Leone	.1482-1487
Turks and Caicos Islands	.978-987
Uganda	.990-995
Virgin Islands	.742-746

Nos. 1513-1518 (6)	16.00	14.10
Nos. 1306-1311 (6)	144.50	98.75
Nos. 1414-1419 (6)	12.50	12.50
Nos. 1172-1177 (6)	16.60	16.35
Nos. 2047-2052 (6)	15.95	15.95
Nos. 1368-1373 (6)	17.00	15.35
Nos. 881-885 (5)	11.90	11.90
Nos. 1637-1642 (6)	17.55	17.55
Nos. 702-707 (6)	13.80	13.80
Nos. 1582-1587 (6)	14.40	14.40
Nos. 829-834 (6)	20.55	20.55
Nos. 1482-1487 (6)	22.50	22.50
Nos. 913-922 (10)	31.65	30.00
Nos. 990-995 (6)	19.50	19.50
Nos. 742-746 (5)	15.50	15.50
Set total (92) Stamps	389.90	338.70

1992 - CD349

Ascension	.531-535
Bahamas	.744-748
Bermuda	.623-627
British Indian Ocean Territory	.119-123
Cayman Islands	.648-652
Falkland Islands	.549-553
Gibraltar	.605-609
Hong Kong	.619-623
Kenya	.563-567
Kiribati	.582-586
Pitcairn Islands	.362-366
St. Helena	.570-574
St. Kitts	.332-336
Samoa	.805-809
Seychelles	.734-738
Zil Elwannyen Sesel	.183-187
Solomon Islands	.708-712
South Georgia	.157-161
Tristan da Cunha	.508-512
Vanuatu	.555-559
Zambia	.561-565

Nos. 531-535 (5)	6.35	6.35
Nos. 744-748 (5)	6.90	4.70
Nos. 623-627 (5)	8.20	7.30
Nos. 119-123 (5)	24.75	21.00
Nos. 648-652 (5)	7.60	7.10
Nos. 549-553 (5)	6.80	8.20
Nos. 605-609 (5)	6.55	7.00
Nos. 619-623 (5)	5.65	2.65
Nos. 563-567 (5)	9.10	9.10
Nos. 582-586 (5)	3.85	3.85
Nos. 362-366 (5)	6.55	6.55
Nos. 570-574 (5)	5.70	5.70
Nos. 332-336 (5)	6.60	5.50
Nos. 805-809 (5)	8.10	6.15
Nos. 734-738 (5)	10.80	10.80
Nos. 183-187 (5)	9.40	9.40
Nos. 708-712 (5)	7.95	7.30
Nos. 157-161 (5)	5.85	5.75
Nos. 508-512 (5)	9.45	8.30
Nos. 555-559 (5)	3.65	3.65
Nos. 561-565 (5)	6.40	6.40
Set total (105) Stamps	166.20	152.75

Royal Air Force, 75th Anniversary

CD350

1993

Ascension	.557-561
Bahamas	.771-775
Barbados	.842-846
Belize	.1003-1008
Bermuda	.648-651
British Indian Ocean Territory	.136-140
Falkland Is.	.573-577
Fiji	.687-691
Montserrat	.830-834
St. Kitts	.351-355

Nos. 557-561 (5)	15.55	14.05
Nos. 771-775 (5)	26.00	22.20
Nos. 842-846 (5)	12.90	11.60
Nos. 1003-1008 (6)	19.40	18.70
Nos. 648-651 (4)	10.50	9.95
Nos. 136-140 (5)	17.50	17.50
Nos. 549-553 (5)	6.80	8.20
Nos. 687-691 (5)	18.95	18.95

Nos. 830-834 (5)	14.35	14.35
Nos. 351-355 (5)	24.45	23.95
Set total (50) Stamps	166.40	159.45

Royal Air Force, 80th Anniv.

Design CD350 Re-inscribed

1998

Ascension	.697-701
Bahamas	.907-911
British Indian Ocean Terr	.198-202
Cayman Islands	.754-758
Fiji	.814-818
Gibraltar	.755-759
Samoa	.957-961
Turks & Caicos Islands	.1258-1265
Tuvalu	.763-767
Virgin Islands	.879-883

Nos. 697-701 (5)	17.35	17.35
Nos. 907-911 (5)	14.25	13.55
Nos. 136-140 (5)	17.50	17.50
Nos. 754-758 (5)	15.75	15.75
Nos. 814-818 (5)	15.50	15.50
Nos. 755-759 (5)	12.20	12.20
Nos. 957-961 (5)	16.70	15.90
Nos. 1258-1265 (2)	32.00	32.00
Nos. 763-767 (5)	9.75	9.75
Nos. 879-883 (5)	17.00	17.00
Set total (47) Stamps	168.00	166.50

End of World War II, 50th Anniv.

CD351

CD352

1995

Ascension	.613-617
Bahamas	.824-828
Barbados	.891-895
Belize	.1047-1050
British Indian Ocean Territory	.163-167
Cayman Islands	.704-708
Falkland Islands	.634-638
Fiji	.720-724
Kiribati	.662-668
Liberia	.1175-1179
Mauritius	.803-805
St. Helena	.646-654
St. Kitts	.389-393
St. Lucia	.1018-1022
Samoa	.890-894
Solomon Islands	.799-803
South Georgia	.198-200
Tristan da Cunha	.562-566

Nos. 613-617 (5)	21.50	21.50
Nos. 824-828 (5)	22.00	18.70
Nos. 891-895 (5)	14.20	11.90
Nos. 1047-1050 (4)	7.45	6.75
Nos. 163-167 (5)	16.25	16.25
Nos. 704-708 (5)	18.15	14.45
Nos. 634-638 (5)	17.90	17.40
Nos. 720-724 (5)	21.35	21.35
Nos. 662-668 (7)	16.30	16.30
Nos. 1175-1179 (5)	19.60	19.60
Nos. 803-805 (3)	7.50	7.50

Nos. 646-654 (9)   26.10   26.10
Nos. 389-393 (5)   13.60   13.60
Nos. 1018-1022 (5)   14.25   11.15
Nos. 890-894 (5)   14.25   13.50
Nos. 799-803 (5)   17.50   17.50
Nos. 198-200 (3)   14.00   14.00
Nos. 562-566 (5)   22.85   22.85
Set total (91) Stamps   304.75   290.40

UN, 50th Anniv.

CD353

1995

Bahamas	839-842
Barbados	901-904
Belize	1055-1058
Jamaica	847-851
Liberia	1187-1190
Mauritius	813-816
Pitcairn Islands	436-439
St. Kitts	398-401
St. Lucia	1023-1026
Samoa	900-903
Tristan da Cunha	568-571
Virgin Islands	807-810

Nos. 839-842 (4)   8.00   7.05
Nos. 901-904 (4)   7.00   5.75
Nos. 1055-1058 (4)   5.70   5.60
Nos. 847-851 (5)   6.30   5.85
Nos. 1187-1190 (4)   15.00   15.00
Nos. 813-816 (4)   3.90   3.90
Nos. 436-439 (4)   11.25   11.25
Nos. 398-401 (4)   6.15   6.15
Nos. 1023-1026 (4)   7.50   7.25
Nos. 900-903 (4)   9.35   8.20
Nos. 568-571 (4)   14.90   14.90
Nos. 807-810 (4)   9.45   9.45
Set total (49) Stamps   104.50   100.35

Queen Elizabeth, 70th Birthday

CD354

1996

Ascension	632-635
British Antarctic Territory	240-243
British Indian Ocean Territory	176-180
Falkland Islands	653-657
Pitcairn Islands	446-449
St. Helena	672-676
Samoa	912-916
Tokelau	223-227
Tristan da Cunha	576-579
Virgin Islands	824-828

Nos. 632-635 (4)   5.90   5.90
Nos. 240-243 (4)   10.50   8.90
Nos. 176-180 (5)   11.50   11.50
Nos. 653-657 (5)   13.75   13.75
Nos. 446-449 (4)   10.50   10.50
Nos. 672-676 (5)   12.70   12.70
Nos. 912-916 (5)   11.50   11.50
Nos. 223-227 (5)   11.35   11.35
Nos. 576-579 (4)   9.15   9.15
Nos. 824-828 (5)   11.80   11.80
Set total (46) Stamps   108.65   107.05

Diana, Princess of Wales (1961-97)

CD355

1998

Ascension 696

Bahamas	901A-902
Barbados	950
Belize	1091
Bermuda	753
Botswana	659-663
British Antarctic Territory	258
British Indian Ocean Terr.	197
Cayman Islands	752A-753
Falkland Islands	694
Fiji	819-820
Gibraltar	754
Kiribati	719A-720
Namibia	909
Niue	706
Norfolk Island	644-645
Papua New Guinea	937
Pitcairn Islands	487
St. Helena	711
St. Kitts	437A-438
Samoa	955A-956
Seychelles	802
Solomon Islands	866-867
South Georgia	220
Tokelau	252B-253
Tonga	980
Niuafo'ou	201
Tristan da Cunha	618
Tuvalu	762
Vanuatu	718A-719
Virgin Islands	878

No. 696 (1)   5.50   5.50
Nos. 901A-902 (2)   5.30   5.30
No. 950 (1)   5.00   5.00
No. 1091 (1)   5.50   5.50
No. 753 (1)   5.50   5.50
Nos. 659-663 (5)   10.25   10.10
No. 258 (1)   6.25   6.25
No. 197 (1)   6.50   6.50
Nos. 752A-753 (3)   7.75   7.75
No. 694 (1)   4.75   4.75
Nos. 819-820 (2)   6.00   6.00
No. 754 (1)   5.50   5.50
Nos. 719A-720 (2)   4.85   4.85
No. 909 (1)   1.90   1.90
No. 706 (1)   5.50   5.50
Nos. 644-645 (2)   5.25   5.25
No. 937 (1)   6.50   6.50
No. 487 (1)   5.25   5.25
No. 711 (1)   4.25   4.25
Nos. 437A-438 (2)   5.15   5.15
Nos. 955A-956 (2)   7.00   7.00
No. 802 (1)   6.25   6.25
Nos. 866-867 (2)   6.90   6.90
No. 220 (1)   5.25   5.25
Nos. 252B-253 (2)   6.75   6.75
No. 980 (1)   5.75   5.75
No. 201 (1)   7.75   7.75
No. 618 (1)   6.00   6.00
No. 762 (1)   4.00   4.00
Nos. 718A-719 (2)   8.00   8.00
No. 878 (1)   5.50   5.50
Set total (46) Stamps   181.60   181.45

Wedding of Prince Edward and Sophie Rhys-Jones

CD356

1999

Ascension	729-730
Cayman Islands	775-776
Falkland Islands	729-730
Pitcairn Islands	505-506
St. Helena	733-734
Samoa	971-972
Tristan da Cunha	636-637
Virgin Islands	908-909

Nos. 729-730 (2)   5.90   5.90
Nos. 775-776 (2)   5.50   5.50
Nos. 729-730 (2)   15.00   15.00
Nos. 505-506 (2)   9.00   9.00
Nos. 733-734 (2)   5.00   5.00
Nos. 971-972 (2)   5.00   5.00
Nos. 636-637 (2)   8.00   8.00
Nos. 908-909 (2)   8.30   8.30
Set total (16) Stamps   61.70   61.70

1st Manned Moon Landing, 30th Anniv.

CD357

1999

Ascension	731-735
Bahamas	942-946
Barbados	967-971
Bermuda	778
Cayman Islands	777-781
Fiji	853-857
Jamaica	889-893
Kirbati	746-750
Nauru	465-469
St. Kitts	460-464
Samoa	973-977
Solomon Islands	875-879
Tuvalu	800-804
Virgin Islands	910-914

Nos. 731-735 (5)   13.90   13.90
Nos. 942-946 (5)   14.10   14.10
Nos. 967-971 (5)   8.65   7.75
No. 778 (1)   8.00   8.00
Nos. 777-781 (5)   10.30   10.30
Nos. 853-857 (5)   10.40   10.40
Nos. 889-893 (5)   10.20   10.00
Nos. 746-750 (5)   8.85   8.85
Nos. 465-469 (5)   8.90   10.15
Nos. 460-464 (5)   12.00   12.00
Nos. 973-977 (5)   13.45   13.30
Nos. 875-879 (5)   10.00   9.85
Nos. 800-804 (5)   7.45   7.45
Nos. 910-914 (5)   15.00   15.00
Set total (66) Stamps   151.20   151.05

Queen Mother's Century

CD358

1999

Ascension	736-740
Bahamas	951-955
Cayman Islands	782-786
Falkland Islands	734-738
Fiji	858-862
Norfolk Island	688-692
St. Helena	740-744
Samoa	978-982
Solomon Islands	880-884
South Georgia	231-235
Tristan da Cunha	638-642
Tuvalu	805-809

Nos. 736-740 (5)   17.00   17.00
Nos. 951-955 (5)   14.00   12.90
Nos. 782-786 (5)   9.15   9.15
Nos. 734-738 (5)   29.85   29.85
Nos. 858-862 (5)   15.00   15.00
Nos. 688-692 (5)   10.30   10.30
Nos. 740-744 (5)   16.15   16.15
Nos. 978-982 (5)   13.25   13.25
Nos. 880-884 (5)   10.00   9.00
Nos. 231-235 (5)   30.25   29.75
Nos. 638-642 (5)   20.00   20.00
Nos. 805-809 (5)   8.65   8.65
Set total (60) Stamps   193.60   191.45

Prince William, 18th Birthday

CD359

2000

Ascension	755-759
Cayman Islands	797-801
Falkland Islands	762-766
Fiji	889-893
South Georgia	257-261
Tristan da Cunha	664-668
Virgin Islands	925-929

Nos. 755-759 (5)   17.75   17.75
Nos. 797-801 (5)   13.05   12.75
Nos. 762-766 (5)   27.15   23.75
Nos. 889-893 (5)   14.00   14.00
Nos. 257-261 (5)   29.00   29.00
Nos. 664-668 (5)   21.00   21.00
Nos. 925-929 (5)   14.75   14.75
Set total (35) Stamps   136.70   133.00

Reign of Queen Elizabeth II, 50th Anniv.

CD360

2002

Ascension	790-794
Bahamas	1033-1037
Barbados	1019-1023
Belize	1152-1156
Bermuda	822-826
British Antarctic Territory	307-311
British Indian Ocean Territory	239-243
Cayman Islands	844-848
Falkland Islands	804-808
Gibraltar	896-900
Jamaica	952-956
Nauru	491-495
Norfolk Island	758-762
Papua New Guinea	1019-1023
Pitcairn Islands	552
St. Helena	788-792
St. Lucia	1146-1150
Solomon Islands	931-935
South Georgia	274-278
Swaziland	706-710
Tokelau	302-306
Tonga	1059
Niuafo'ou	239
Tristan da Cunha	706-710
Virgin Islands	967-971

Nos. 790-794 (5)   16.25   16.25
Nos. 1033-1037 (5)   15.75   15.75
Nos. 1019-1023 (5)   13.15   13.15
Nos. 1152-1156 (5)   15.50   15.15
Nos. 822-826 (5)   18.50   18.50
Nos. 307-311 (5)   25.00   25.00
Nos. 239-243 (5)   22.00   22.00
Nos. 844-848 (5)   14.25   14.25
Nos. 804-808 (5)   23.50   22.50
Nos. 896-900 (5)   8.00   8.00
Nos. 952-956 (5)   18.25   18.25
Nos. 491-495 (5)   18.75   18.75
Nos. 758-762 (5)   19.50   19.50
Nos. 1019-1023 (5)   14.50   14.50
No. 552 (1)   11.50   11.50
Nos. 788-792 (5)   19.75   19.75
Nos. 1146-1150 (5)   12.25   12.25
Nos. 931-935 (5)   16.00   16.00
Nos. 274-278 (5)   28.50   28.50
Nos. 706-710 (5)   12.75   12.75
Nos. 302-306 (5)   17.00   17.00
No. 1059 (1)   8.00   8.00
No. 239 (1)   7.00   7.00
Nos. 706-710 (5)   19.00   19.00
Nos. 967-971 (5)   19.00   19.00
Set total (113) Stamps   413.65   412.30

Queen Mother Elizabeth (1900-2002)

CD361

2002

Ascension	799-801
Bahamas	1044-1046
Bermuda	834-836
British Antarctic Territory	312-314

British Indian Ocean Territory 245-
247
Cayman Islands........................857-861
Falkland Islands 812-816
Nauru..499-501
Pitcairn Islands.......................561-565
St. Helena 808-812
St. Lucia 1155-1159
Seychelles 830
Solomon Islands......................945-947
South Georgia 281-285
Tokelau 312-314
Tristan da Cunha....................715-717
Virgin Islands...........................979-983

Nos. 799-801 (3)	9.75	9.75
Nos. 1044-1046 (3)	9.35	9.35
Nos. 834-836 (3)	12.50	12.50
Nos. 312-314 (3)	19.25	19.25
Nos. 245-247 (3)	19.50	19.50
Nos. 857-861 (5)	15.00	15.00
Nos. 812-816 (5)	32.00	32.00
Nos. 499-501 (3)	16.00	16.00
Nos. 561-565 (5)	18.50	18.50
Nos. 808-812 (5)	12.00	12.00
Nos. 1155-1159 (5)	13.00	13.00
No. 830 (1)	6.50	6.50
Nos. 945-947 (3)	11.00	11.00
Nos. 281-285 (5)	20.00	20.00
Nos. 312-314 (3)	14.25	13.75
Nos. 715-717 (3)	16.00	16.00
Nos. 979-983 (5)	26.50	26.50
Set total (63) Stamps	271.10	270.60

Head of Queen Elizabeth II

CD362

2003

Ascension.......................................822
Bermuda...865
British Antarctic Territory.................322
British Indian Ocean Territory 261
Cayman Islands...............................878
Falkland Islands 828
St. Helena 820
South Georgia 294
Tristan da Cunha.............................731
Virgin Islands.................................1003

No. 822 (1)	13.50	13.50
No. 865 (1)	55.00	55.00
No. 322 (1)	10.00	10.00
No. 261 (1)	12.50	12.50
No. 878 (1)	17.00	17.00
No. 828 (1)	10.00	10.00
No. 820 (1)	9.00	9.00
No. 294 (1)	9.00	9.00
No. 731 (1)	11.00	11.00
No. 1003 (1)	10.00	10.00
Set total (10) Stamps	157.00	157.00

Coronation of Queen Elizabeth II, 50th Anniv.

CD363

2003

Ascension 823-825
Bahamas 1073-1075
Bermuda...................................866-868
British Antarctic Territory..........323-325
British Indian Ocean Territory 262-
264
Cayman Islands........................879-881
Jamaica 970-972
Kiribati 825-827
Pitcairn Islands........................577-581
St. Helena 821-823
St. Lucia 1171-1173
Tokelau 320-322
Tristan da Cunha....................732-734
Virgin Islands........................1004-1006

Nos. 823-825 (3)	13.50	13.50
Nos. 1073-1075 (3)	13.00	13.00
Nos. 866-868 (3)	14.25	14.25
Nos. 323-325 (3)	26.00	26.00
Nos. 262-264 (3)	31.00	31.00
Nos. 879-881 (3)	20.25	20.25

Nos. 970-972 (3)	11.75	11.75
Nos. 825-827 (3)	13.50	13.50
Nos. 577-581 (5)	18.50	18.50
Nos. 821-823 (3)	7.25	7.25
Nos. 1171-1173 (3)	8.75	8.75
Nos. 320-322 (3)	20.00	20.00
Nos. 732-734 (3)	17.00	17.00
Nos. 1004-1006 (3)	25.00	25.00
Set total (44) Stamps	239.75	239.75

Prince William, 21st Birthday

CD364

2003

Ascension.......................................826
British Indian Ocean Territory 265
Cayman Islands........................882-884
Falkland Islands 829
South Georgia 295
Tokelau 323
Tristan da Cunha.............................735
Virgin Islands.........................1007-1009

No. 826 (1)	7.50	7.50
No. 265 (1)	9.00	9.00
Nos. 882-884 (3)	7.65	7.65
No. 829 (1)	14.50	14.50
No. 295 (1)	9.00	9.00
No. 323 (1)	7.25	7.25
No. 735 (1)	7.00	7.00
Nos. 1007-1009 (3)	10.00	10.00
Set total (12) Stamps	71.90	71.90

British Commonwealth of Nations

Dominions, Colonies, Territories, Offices and Independent Members

Comprising stamps of the British Commonwealth and associated nations.

A strict observance of technicalities would bar some or all of the stamps listed under Burma, Ireland, Kuwait, Nepal, New Republic, Orange Free State, Samoa, South Africa, South-West Africa, Stellaland, Sudan, Swaziland, the two Transvaal Republics and others but these are included for the convenience of collectors.

1. Great Britain

Great Britain: Including England, Scotland, Wales and Northern Ireland.

2. The Dominions, Present and Past

AUSTRALIA

The Commonwealth of Australia was proclaimed on January 1, 1901. It consists of six former colonies as follows:

New South Wales	Victoria
Queensland	Tasmania
South Australia	Western Australia

The following islands and territories are, or have been, administered by Australia: Australian Antarctic Territory, Christmas Island, Cocos (Keeling) Islands, Nauru, New Guinea, Norfolk Island, Papua.

CANADA

The Dominion of Canada was created by the British North America Act in 1867. The following provinces were former sepa- rate colonies and issued postage stamps:

British Columbia and Vancouver Island	Newfoundland
New Brunswick	Nova Scotia
	Prince Edward Island

FIJI

The colony of Fiji became an independent nation with dominion status on Oct. 10, 1970.

GHANA

This state came into existence Mar. 6, 1957, with dominion status. It consists of the former colony of the Gold Coast and the Trusteeship Territory of Togoland. Ghana became a republic July 1, 1960.

INDIA

The Republic of India was inaugurated on January 26, 1950. It succeeded the Dominion of India which was proclaimed August 15, 1947, when the former Empire of India was divided into Pakistan and the Union of India. The Republic is composed of about 40 predominantly Hindu states of three classes: governor's provinces, chief commissioner's provinces and princely states. India also has various territories, such as the Andaman and Nicobar Islands.

The old Empire of India was a federation of British India and the native states. The more important princely states were autonomous. Of the more than 700 Indian states, these 43 are familiar names to philatelists because of their postage stamps.

CONVENTION STATES

Chamba	Jhind
Faridkot	Nabha
Gwalior	Patiala

FEUDATORY STATES

Alwar	Jammu and Kashmir
Bahawalpur	Jasdan
Bamra	Jhalawar
Barwani	Jhind (1875-76)
Bhopal	Kashmir
Bhor	Kishangarh
Bijawar	Kotah
Bundi	Las Bela
Bussahir	Morvi
Charkhari	Nandgaon
Cochin	Nowanuggur
Dhar	Orchha
Dungarpur	Poonch
Duttia	Rajasthan
Faridkot (1879-85)	Rajpeepla
Hyderabad	Sirmur
Idar	Soruth
Indore	Tonk
Jaipur	Travancore
Jammu	Wadhwan

NEW ZEALAND

Became a dominion on September 26, 1907. The following islands and territories are, or have been, administered by New Zealand:

Aitutaki	Ross Dependency
Cook Islands (Rarotonga)	Samoa (Western Samoa)
Niue	Tokelau Islands
Penrhyn	

PAKISTAN

The Republic of Pakistan was proclaimed March 23, 1956. It succeeded the Dominion which was proclaimed August 15, 1947. It is made up of all or part of several Moslem provinces and various districts of the former Empire of India, including Bahawalpur and Las Bela. Pakistan withdrew from the Commonwealth in 1972.

SOUTH AFRICA

Under the terms of the South African Act (1909) the self-governing colonies of Cape of Good Hope, Natal, Orange River Colony and Transvaal united on May 31, 1910, to form the Union of South Africa. It became an independent republic May 3, 1961.

Under the terms of the Treaty of Versailles, South-West Africa, formerly German South-West Africa, was mandated to the Union of South Africa.

SRI LANKA (CEYLON)

The Dominion of Ceylon was proclaimed February 4, 1948. The island had been a Crown Colony from 1802 until then. On May 22, 1972, Ceylon became the Republic of Sri Lanka.

3. Colonies, Past and Present; Controlled Territory and Independent Members of the Commonwealth

Aden	Bechuanaland
Aitutaki	Bechuanaland Prot.
Antigua	Belize
Ascension	Bermuda
Bahamas	Botswana
Bahrain	British Antarctic Territory
Bangladesh	British Central Africa
Barbados	British Columbia and
Barbuda	Vancouver Island
Basutoland	British East Africa
Batum	British Guiana

British Honduras
British Indian Ocean Territory
British New Guinea
British Solomon Islands
British Somaliland
Brunei
Burma
Bushire
Cameroons
Cape of Good Hope
Cayman Islands
Christmas Island
Cocos (Keeling) Islands
Cook Islands
Crete,
  British Administration
Cyprus
Dominica
East Africa & Uganda
  Protectorates
Egypt
Falkland Islands
Fiji
Gambia
German East Africa
Gibraltar
Gilbert Islands
Gilbert & Ellice Islands
Gold Coast
Grenada
Griqualand West
Guernsey
Guyana
Heligoland
Hong Kong
Indian Native States
  (see India)
Ionian Islands
Jamaica
Jersey

Kenya
Kenya, Uganda & Tanzania
Kuwait
Labuan
Lagos
Leeward Islands
Lesotho
Madagascar
Malawi
Malaya
  Federated Malay States
  Johore
  Kedah
  Kelantan
  Malacca
  Negri Sembilan
  Pahang
  Penang
  Perak
  Perlis
  Selangor
  Singapore
  Sungei Ujong
  Trengganu
Malaysia
Maldive Islands
Malta
Man, Isle of
Mauritius
Mesopotamia
Montserrat
Muscat
Namibia
Natal
Nauru
Nevis
New Britain
New Brunswick
Newfoundland
New Guinea

New Hebrides
New Republic
New South Wales
Niger Coast Protectorate
Nigeria
Niue
Norfolk Island
North Borneo
Northern Nigeria
Northern Rhodesia
North West Pacific Islands
Nova Scotia
Nyasaland Protectorate
Oman
Orange River Colony
Palestine
Papua New Guinea
Penrhyn Island
Pitcairn Islands
Prince Edward Island
Queensland
Rhodesia
Rhodesia & Nyasaland
Ross Dependency
Sabah
St. Christopher
St. Helena
St. Kitts
St. Kitts-Nevis-Anguilla
St. Lucia
St. Vincent
Samoa
Sarawak
Seychelles
Sierra Leone
Solomon Islands
Somaliland Protectorate
South Arabia
South Australia
South Georgia

Southern Nigeria
Southern Rhodesia
South-West Africa
Stellaland
Straits Settlements
Sudan
Swaziland
Tanganyika
Tanzania
Tasmania
Tobago
Togo
Tokelau Islands
Tonga
Transvaal
Trinidad
Trinidad and Tobago
Tristan da Cunha
Trucial States
Turks and Caicos
Turks Islands
Tuvalu
Uganda
United Arab Emirates
Victoria
Virgin Islands
Western Australia
Zambia
Zanzibar
Zululand

POST OFFICES IN FOREIGN COUNTRIES
Africa
  East Africa Forces
  Middle East Forces
Bangkok
China
Morocco
Turkish Empire

Colonies, Former Colonies, Offices, Territories Controlled by Parent States

Belgium
Belgian Congo
Ruanda-Urundi

Denmark
Danish West Indies
Faroe Islands
Greenland
Iceland

Finland
Aland Islands

France
COLONIES PAST AND PRESENT, CONTROLLED TERRITORIES
Afars & Issas, Territory of
Alaouites
Alexandretta
Algeria
Alsace & Lorraine
Anjouan
Annam & Tonkin
Benin
Cambodia (Khmer)
Cameroun
Castellorizo
Chad
Cilicia
Cochin China
Comoro Islands
Dahomey
Diego Suarez
Djibouti (Somali Coast)
Fezzan
French Congo
French Equatorial Africa
French Guiana
French Guinea
French India
French Morocco
French Polynesia (Oceania)
French Southern & Antarctic Territories
French Sudan
French West Africa
Gabon
Germany
Ghadames
Grand Comoro
Guadeloupe
Indo-China
Inini
Ivory Coast
Laos
Latakia
Lebanon
Madagascar
Martinique
Mauritania
Mayotte
Memel
Middle Congo
Moheli
New Caledonia
New Hebrides
Niger Territory

Nossi-Be
Obock
Reunion
Rouad, Ile
Ste.-Marie de Madagascar
St. Pierre & Miquelon
Senegal
Senegambia & Niger
Somali Coast
Syria
Tahiti
Togo
Tunisia
Ubangi-Shari
Upper Senegal & Niger
Upper Volta
Viet Nam
Wallis & Futuna Islands

POST OFFICES IN FOREIGN COUNTRIES
China
Crete
Egypt
Turkish Empire
Zanzibar

Germany
EARLY STATES
Baden
Bavaria
Bergedorf
Bremen
Brunswick
Hamburg
Hanover
Lubeck
Mecklenburg-Schwerin
Mecklenburg-Strelitz
Oldenburg
Prussia
Saxony
Schleswig-Holstein
Wurttemberg

FORMER COLONIES
Cameroun (Kamerun)
Caroline Islands
German East Africa
German New Guinea
German South-West Africa
Kiauchau
Mariana Islands
Marshall Islands
Samoa
Togo

Italy
EARLY STATES
Modena
Parma
Romagna
Roman States
Sardinia
Tuscany
Two Sicilies
    Naples
    Neapolitan Provinces
    Sicily

FORMER COLONIES, CONTROLLED TERRITORIES, OCCUPATION AREAS
Aegean Islands
    Calimno (Calino)
    Caso
    Cos (Coo)
    Karki (Carchi)
    Leros (Lero)
    Lipso
    Nisiros (Nisiro)
    Patmos (Patmo)
    Piscopi
    Rodi (Rhodes)
    Scarpanto
    Simi
    Stampalia
Castellorizo
Corfu
Cyrenaica
Eritrea
Ethiopia (Abyssinia)
Fiume
Ionian Islands
    Cephalonia
    Ithaca
    Paxos
Italian East Africa
Libya
Oltre Giuba
Saseno
Somalia (Italian Somaliland)
Tripolitania

POST OFFICES IN FOREIGN COUNTRIES
"ESTERO"*
Austria
China
    Peking
    Tientsin
Crete
Tripoli
Turkish Empire
    Constantinople
    Durazzo
    Janina
Jerusalem
Salonika
Scutari
Smyrna
Valona
*Stamps overprinted "ESTERO" were used in various parts of the world.

Netherlands
Aruba
Caribbean Netherlands
Curacao
Netherlands Antilles (Curacao)
Netherlands Indies
Netherlands New Guinea
St. Martin
Surinam (Dutch Guiana)

Portugal
COLONIES PAST AND PRESENT, CONTROLLED TERRITORIES
Angola
Angra
Azores

Cape Verde
Funchal
Horta
Inhambane
Kionga
Lourenco Marques
Macao
Madeira
Mozambique
Mozambique Co.
Nyassa
Ponta Delgada
Portuguese Africa
Portuguese Congo
Portuguese Guinea
Portuguese India
Quelimane
St. Thomas & Prince Islands
Tete
Timor
Zambezia

Russia
ALLIED TERRITORIES AND REPUBLICS, OCCUPATION AREAS
Armenia
Aunus (Olonets)
Azerbaijan
Batum
Estonia
Far Eastern Republic
Georgia
Karelia
Latvia
Lithuania
North Ingermanland
Ostland
Russian Turkestan
Siberia
South Russia
Tannu Tuva
Transcaucasian Fed. Republics
Ukraine
Wenden (Livonia)
Western Ukraine

Spain
COLONIES PAST AND PRESENT, CONTROLLED TERRITORIES
Aguera, La
Cape Juby
Cuba
Elobey, Annobon & Corisco
Fernando Po
Ifni
Mariana Islands
Philippines
Puerto Rico
Rio de Oro
Rio Muni
Spanish Guinea
Spanish Morocco
Spanish Sahara
Spanish West Africa

POST OFFICES IN FOREIGN COUNTRIES
Morocco
Tangier
Tetuan

Dies of British Colonial Stamps

DIE A:

1. The lines in the groundwork vary in thickness and are not uniformly straight.
2. The seventh and eighth lines from the top, in the groundwork, converge where they meet the head.
3. There is a small dash in the upper part of the second jewel in the band of the crown.
4. The vertical color line in front of the throat stops at the sixth line of shading on the neck.

DIE B:

1. The lines in the groundwork are all thin and straight.
2. All the lines of the background are parallel.
3. There is no dash in the upper part of the second jewel in the band of the crown.
4. The vertical color line in front of the throat stops at the eighth line of shading on the neck.

DIE I:

1. The base of the crown is well below the level of the inner white line around the vignette.
2. The labels inscribed "POSTAGE" and "REVENUE" are cut square at the top.
3. There is a white "bud" on the outer side of the main stem of the curved ornaments in each lower corner.
4. The second (thick) line below the country name has the ends next to the crown cut diagonally.

DIE Ia.	DIE Ib.
1 as die II.	1 and 3 as die II.
2 and 3 as die I.	2 as die I.

DIE II:

1. The base of the crown is aligned with the underside of the white line around the vignette.
2. The labels curve inward at the top inner corners.
3. The "bud" has been removed from the outer curve of the ornaments in each corner.
4. The second line below the country name has the ends next to the crown cut vertically.

**Wmk. 1
Crown and C C**

**Wmk. 2
Crown and C A**

**Wmk. 3
Multiple Crown
and C A**

**Wmk. 4
Multiple Crown
and Script C A**

Wmk. 4a

**Wmk. 314
St. Edward's Crown
and C A Multiple**

Wmk. 373

Wmk. 384

Wmk. 406

British Colonial and Crown Agents Watermarks

Watermarks 1 to 4, 314, 373, 384 and 406, common to many British territories, are illustrated here to avoid duplication.

The letters "CC" of Wmk. 1 identify the paper as having been made for the use of the Crown Colonies, while the letters "CA" of the others stand for "Crown Agents." Both Wmks. 1 and 2 were used on stamps printed by De La Rue & Co.

Wmk. 3 was adopted in 1904; Wmk. 4 in 1921; Wmk. 314 in 1957; Wmk. 373 in 1974; Wmk. 384 in 1985; Wmk 406 in 2008.

In Wmk. 4a, a non-matching crown of the general St. Edwards type (bulging on both sides at top) was substituted for one of the Wmk. 4 crowns which fell off the dandy roll. The non-matching crown occurs in 1950-52 printings in a horizontal row of crowns on certain regular stamps of Johore and Seychelles, and on various postage due stamps of Barbados, Basutoland, British Guiana, Gold Coast, Grenada, Northern Rhodesia, St. Lucia, Swaziland and Trinidad and Tobago. A variation of Wmk. 4a, with the non-matching crown in a horizontal row of crown-CA-crown, occurs on regular stamps of Bahamas, St. Kitts-Nevis and Singapore.

Wmk. 314 was intentionally used sideways, starting in 1966. When a stamp was issued with Wmk. 314 both upright and sideways, the sideways varieties usually are listed also – with minor numbers. In many of the later issues, Wmk. 314 is slightly visible.

Wmk. 373 is usually only faintly visible.

JAMAICA

jə-'mā-kə

LOCATION — Caribbean Sea, about 90 miles south of Cuba
GOVT. — Independent state in the British Commonwealth
AREA — 4,411 sq. mi.
POP. — 2,652,443 (1999 est.)
CAPITAL — Kingston

Jamaica became an independent state in the British Commonwealth in August 1962. As a colony, it administered two dependencies: Cayman Islands and Turks and Caicos Islands.

12 Pence = 1 Shilling
20 Shillings = 1 Pound
100 Cents = 1 Dollar (1969)

> Catalogue values for unused stamps in this country are for Never Hinged items, beginning with Scott 129 in the regular postage section and Scott B4 in the semi-postal section.

Watermarks

Wmk. 45 —
Pineapple

Wmk. 352 — J and Pineapple,
Multiple

Values for unused stamps are for examples with original gum as defined in the catalogue introduction. Very fine examples of Nos. 1-12 will have perforations touching the design on at least one side due to the narrow spacing of the stamps on the plates. Stamps with perfs clear on all four sides are scarce and will command higher prices.

Queen Victoria
A1   A2

A3

A4

A5

A6

1860-63   Typo.   Wmk. 45   Perf. 14

1	A1	1p blue	72.50	16.00
a.		Diagonal half used as ½p on cover		825.00
b.		1p deep blue	145.00	37.50
c.		1p pale blue	77.50	20.00
d.		1p pale greenish blue	100.00	24.00
2	A2	2p rose	225.00	60.00
a.		2p deep rose	220.00	60.00
3	A3	3p green ('63)	170.00	32.50
4	A4	4p brown org	275.00	62.50
a.		4p orange	250.00	25.00
5	A5	6p lilac	240.00	25.00
a.		6p deep lilac	1,050.	60.00
b.		6p gray lilac	350.00	40.00
6	A6	1sh brown	230.00	35.00
a.		1sh lilac brown	650.00	30.00
b.		1sh yellow brown	575.00	32.50

All except No. 3 exist imperforate.

1870-71   Wmk. 1

7	A1	1p blue	100.00	.90
8	A2	2p rose	110.00	.85
a.		2p brownish rose	120.00	1.10
9	A3	3p green	155.00	9.25
10	A4	4p brown org ('72)	325.00	13.50
a.		4p red orange	450.00	6.50
11	A5	6p lilac ('71)	100.00	6.00
12	A6	1sh brown ('73)	27.50	9.50
		Nos. 7-12 (6)	817.50	40.00

The 1p and 4p exist imperf.
See Nos. 17-23, 40, 43, 47-53.

A7

1872, Oct. 29

13	A7	½p claret	21.00	4.00
a.		½p deep claret	26.50	6.00

Exists imperf. See No. 16.

A8

A9

1875, Aug. 27   Perf. 12½

14	A8	2sh red brown	50.00	30.00
15	A9	5sh violet	125.00	175.00

Exist imperf.
See Nos. 29-30, 44, 54.

1883-90   Wmk. 2   Perf. 14

16	A7	½p blue green ('85)	9.00	1.75
a.		½p gray green	2.75	.25
17	A1	1p blue ('84)	350.00	7.75
18	A1	1p carmine ('85)	72.50	1.00
a.		1p rose	87.50	2.25
19	A2	2p rose ('84)	240.00	5.25
20	A2	2p slate ('85)	105.00	.70
a.		2p gray	160.00	9.00
21	A3	3p ol green ('86)	2.75	2.25
22	A4	4p red brown	2.25	.40
a.		4p orange brown	450.00	25.00
23	A5	6p orange yel ('90)	6.00	5.00
a.		6p yellow	40.00	8.75
		Nos. 16-23 (8)	787.50	24.10

Nos. 18 and 20 exist imperf. Perf. 12 stamps are considered to be proofs.
For surcharge, see No. 27.

A10

1889-91

24	A10	1p lilac & red vio	10.00	.25
25	A10	2p deep green	22.50	8.00
a.		2p green	37.50	5.50
26	A10	2½p lilac & ultra ('91)	8.75	.75
		Nos. 24-26 (3)	41.25	9.00

No. 22 Surcharged in Black

1890, June

27	A4	2½p on 4p red brn	40.00	17.50
b.		Double surcharge	350.00	250.00
d.		"PFNNY"	100.00	70.00
f.		As "d," double surcharge	70.00	—

Three settings of surcharge.

1897

28	A6	1sh brown	9.50	6.50
29	A8	2sh red brown	32.50	30.00
30	A9	5sh violet	70.00	100.00
		Nos. 28-30 (3)	112.00	136.50

The 2sh exists imperf.

Llandovery
Falls — A12

1900, May 1   Engr.   Wmk. 1

31	A12	1p red	11.50	.25

1901, Sept. 25

32	A12	1p red & black	10.00	.25
a.		Pair, imperf. horiz.	25,000.	
b.		Bluish paper	120.00	110.00

Arms of Jamaica — A13

1903-04   Typo.   Wmk. 2

33	A13	½p green & black	1.75	.40
b.		"SERᵥ ET" for "SERVIET"	45.00	50.00
34	A13	1p car & black ('04)	4.50	.25
b.		"SERᵥ ET" for "SERVIET"	35.00	40.00
35	A13	2½p ultra & blk	8.25	.45
a.		"SERᵥ ET" for "SERVIET"	72.50	85.00
36	A13	5p yel & black ('04)	17.50	26.00
a.		"SERᵥ ET" for "SERVIET"	075.00	1,100.
		Nos. 33-36 (4)	32.00	27.10

1905-11   Chalky Paper   Wmk. 3

37	A13	½p green & black	4.50	.25
b.		"SERᵥ ET" for "SERVIET"	32.50	45.00
38	A13	1p car & black	20.00	2.00
39	A13	2½p ultra & blk ('07)	5.50	7.50
39A	A3	3p vio, yel ('10)	2.25	1.60
40	A4	4p black, yel ('10)	14.00	60.00
41	A13	5p yel & black ('07)	67.50	80.00
a.		"SERᵥ ET" for "SERVIET"	1,425.	1,600.
42	A13	6p red vio & vio ('11)	15.50	19.00
42A	A13	6p purple ('10)	11.50	30.00
43	A6	1sh black, green ('10)	8.25	10.00
44	A8	2sh vio, blue	10.00	6.50
45	A13	5sh vio & black	52.50	55.00
		Nos. 37-45 (11)	211.50	271.85

1905-11   Ordinary Paper

46	A13	2½p ultra ('10)	5.00	1.40
47	A3	3p sage green ('07)	7.00	3.25
a.		3p olive green ('05)	10.00	4.50
48	A3	3p pale purple, yel ('10)	7.00	3.75
49	A4	4p red brn ('08)	77.50	80.00
50	A4	4p red, yel ('11)	1.75	7.50
51	A5	6p dull vio ('09)	30.00	60.00
52	A5	6p org yel ('09)	35.00	67.50
a.		6p orange ('06)	17.00	27.50
53	A6	1sh brown ('06)	25.00	50.00
54	A8	2sh red brn ('08)	160.00	170.00
		Nos. 46-54 (9)	348.25	443.40

A14

A15

1906

58	A14	½p green	4.00	.25
a.		Booklet pane of 6	—	
59	A15	1p carmine	1.60	.25
a.		Booklet pane of 6	—	

For overprints see Nos. MR1, MR4, MR7, MR10.

Edward VII — A16

1911, Feb. 3

60	A16	2p gray	8.00	15.00

George V — A17

1912-20

61	A17	1p scarlet ('16)	8.00	.80
a.		1p carmine ('12)	1.75	.25
b.		Booklet pane of 6	—	
62	A17	1½p brown org ('16)	1.50	.70
a.		1½p yellow orange	17.00	1.25
63	A17	2p gray	2.25	2.00
64	A17	2½p dp br blue	.80	1.25
a.		2½p ultra ('13)	1.75	.25

Chalky Paper

65	A17	3p violet, yel	.60	.50
66	A17	4p scar & blk, yel ('13)	.60	4.00
67	A17	6p red vio & dl vio	1.90	2.00
68	A17	1sh black, green	2.60	2.25
a.		1sh blk, bl grn, olive back ('20)	3.50	9.00
69	A17	2sh ultra & vio, blue ('19)	24.00	35.00
70	A17	5sh scarlet & green, yel ('19)	82.50	105.00

Surface-colored Paper

71	A17	3p violet, yel ('13)	.55	.45
72	A17	4p scar & black, yel ('14)	.85	4.25
73	A17	1sh black, green ('15)	4.75	5.00
		Nos. 61-73 (13)	130.90	163.20

See Nos. 101-102. For overprints see Nos. MR2-MR3, MR5-MR6, MR8-MR9, MR11.

Exhibition Buildings of 1891 — A18

Arawak Woman Preparing Cassava — A19

World War I Contingent Embarking for Overseas Duty — A20

King's House, Spanish Town — A21

Return of Overseas Contingent, 1919 — A22

Columbus Landing in Jamaica — A23

Cathedral in Spanish Town — A24

Statue of Queen Victoria — A26

Memorial to Admiral Rodney — A27

Monument to Sir Charles Metcalfe — A28

Woodland Scene — A29

King George V — A30

1919-21   Typo.   Wmk. 3   Perf. 14
Chalky Paper

75	A18	½p ol grn & dk grn ('20)	1.10	1.10
76	A19	1p org & car ('21)	2.00	1.90

Engr.
Ordinary Paper

77	A20	1½p green	.45	1.10
78	A21	2p grn & bl ('21)	1.25	4.50
79	A22	2½p blue-black & blue	1.50	1.75
a.		2½ blue & dark blue ('21)	15.00	3.50
80	A23	3p blue & grn ('21)	5.50	2.75
81	A24	4p green & dk brown ('21)	2.75	10.00
83	A26	1sh brt org & org ('20)	4.25	5.75
a.		Frame inverted	40,000.	25,000.
		As "a," revenue cancel		2,500.
84	A27	2sh brn & bl ('20)	12.50	30.00
85	A28	3sh org & violet ('20)	24.00	120.00
86	A29	5sh ocher & blue ('21)	55.00	82.50
87	A30	10sh dk myrtle grn ('20)	85.00	160.00
		Nos. 75-87 (12)	195.30	421.35

See note after No. 100. Watermark varieties exist and sell for much higher values.
A 6p stamp depicting the abolition of slavery was sent to the Colony but was not issued. "Specimen" examples exist with wmk. 3 or 4. Value $750 each.
Without "Specimen," values: wmk. 3, $52,500; wmk. 4, $32,500.

Port Royal in 1853 A31

1921-23   Typo.   Wmk. 4   Perf. 14
Chalky Paper

88	A18	½p ol grn & dk grn ('22)	.60	.60
a.		Booklet pane of 4		
89	A19	1p orange & car ('22)	1.75	.25
a.		Booklet pane of 6		

Engr.
Ordinary Paper

90	A20	1½p green	3.00	.55
91	A21	2p grn & blue	7.50	.90
92	A22	2½p bl & dk bl	6.50	2.00
93	A23	3p bl & grn ('22)	5.00	.80
94	A24	4p grn & dk brn	1.25	.35
95	A31	6p bl & blk ('22)	15.00	2.25
96	A26	1sh brn org & dl org	2.00	.90
97	A27	2sh brn & bl ('22)	3.75	.75
98	A28	3sh org & violet	18.50	11.00
99	A29	5sh ocher & bl ('23)	35.00	29.00
a.		5sh orange & blue	80.00	80.00
100	A30	10sh dk myrtle green ('22)	60.00	80.00
		Nos. 88-100 (13)	159.85	129.35
		Set, never hinged	380.00	

No. 89 differs from No. 76 in having the words "Postage and Revenue" at the bottom.
On No. 79 the horizontal bar of the flag at the left has a broad white line below the colored line. On No. 92 this has been corrected and the broad white line placed above the colored line.
Watermark is sideways on Nos. 76-77, 87, 89-90.

Type of 1912-19 Issue
1921-27   Typo.   Wmk. 4

101	A17	½p green ('27)	3.50	.25
a.		Booklet pane of 6		
102	A17	6p red vio & dl vio	17.50	4.50

No. 102 is on chalky paper.

A32

Type I

Type II

Type II — Cross shading beneath "Jamaica."

1929-32   Engr.   Perf. 13½x14, 14

103	A32	1p red, type I	14.00	.25
a.		1p red, type II ('32)	14.00	.25
b.		Booklet pane of 6, type II		
104	A32	1½p brown	8.50	.25
105	A32	9p violet brown	8.50	1.25
		Nos. 103-105 (3)	31.00	1.75
		Set, never hinged	35.00	

The frames on Nos. 103 to 105 differ.

Coco Palms at Columbus Cove — A33

Scene near Castleton, St. Andrew — A34

Priestman's River, Portland Parish — A35

1932   Perf. 12½

106	A33	2p grn & gray blk	35.00	3.50
a.		Vertical pair, imperf. between	15,000.	
107	A34	2½p ultra & sl blue	6.50	1.75
a.		Vertical pair, imperf. between	21,000.	21,000.
108	A35	6p red vio & gray black	35.00	4.50
		Nos. 106-108 (3)	76.50	9.75
		Set, never hinged	125.00	

Common Design Types pictured following the introduction.

Silver Jubilee Issue
Common Design Type

1935, May 6   Perf. 11x12

109	CD301	1p car & blue	.55	.25
a.		Booklet pane of 6	175.00	
110	CD301	1½p black & ultra	.75	1.75
111	CD301	6p indigo & grn	13.00	20.00
112	CD301	1sh brn vio & ind	8.50	20.00
		Nos. 109-112 (4)	22.80	42.00
		Set, never hinged	32.50	

Coronation Issue
Common Design Type

1937, May 12   Perf. 13½x14

113	CD302	1p carmine	.30	.25
114	CD302	1½p gray black	.65	.30
115	CD302	2½p bright ultra	1.00	.70
		Nos. 113-115 (3)	1.95	1.25
		Set, never hinged	2.25	

King George VI — A36

Coco Palms at Columbus Cove — A37

Scene near Castleton, St. Andrew — A38

Bananas A39

Citrus Grove A40

Priestman's River, Portland Parish — A41

Kingston Harbor A42

Sugar Industry A43

Bamboo Walk — A44

Woodland Scene — A45

King George VI — A46

1938-51   Perf. 13½x14

116	A36	½p dk blue grn	1.40	.25
a.		Booklet pane of 6	9.00	
b.		Wmkd. sideways		8,500.
117	A36	1p carmine	1.00	.25
a.		Booklet pane of 6	13.00	
118	A36	1½p brown	1.00	.25

Perf. 12½, 13x13½, 13½x13, 12½x13

119	A37	2p grn & gray blk, perf. 12½	1.00	1.00
a.		Perf. 13x13½ ('39)	2.25	.60
b.		Perf. 12½x13 ('51)	1.00	.25
120	A38	2½p ultra & sl bl	5.00	2.25
121	A39	3p grn & lt ultra	.90	1.75
122	A40	4p grn & yel brn	.65	.25
123	A41	6p red vio & gray blk, perf. 13½x13 ('50)	2.00	.25
a.		Perf. 12½	5.50	.35
b.		As "a," double impression of gray blk	—	
124	A42	9p rose lake	.65	.55
125	A43	1sh dk brn & brt grn	8.00	.25
126	A44	2sh brn & brt bl	22.50	.25

Perf. 13, 14

127	A45	5sh ocher & bl, perf. 13 ('50)	6.00	4.25
a.		Bluish paper, perf. 13 ('49)	6.00	3.50
b.		Perf. 14	11.50	4.00
128	A46	10sh dk myrtle grn, perf. 14	9.00	10.50
a.		Perf. 13 ('50)	11.50	8.00
		Nos. 116-128 (13)	59.10	23.05
		Set, never hinged	110.00	

See Nos. 140, 148, 149, 152.

Catalogue values for unused stamps in this section, from this point to the end of the section, are for Never Hinged items.

Courthouse, Falmouth A47

Kings Charles II and George VI A48

House of Assembly, 1762-1869 A50

Institute of Jamaica — A49

Allegory of Labor and Learning — A51

Constitution and Flag of Jamaica A52

Perf. 12½
			Wmk. 4	
1945, Aug. 20		Engr.		
129	A47	1½p brown	.30	.35
a.		Booklet pane of 4	37.50	
b.		Perf. 12½x13½ ('46)	10.00	1.75
130	A48	2p dp grn, perf. 12½x13½	.35	.55
a.		Perf. 12½	14.00	1.10
131	A49	3p bright ultra	.25	.55
a.		Perf. 13 ('46)	3.25	3.25
132	A50	4½p slate black	.60	.35
a.		Perf. 13 ('46)	4.50	4.75
133	A51	2sh chocolate	1.25	.50
134	A52	5sh deep blue	3.50	1.10
135	A49	10sh green	3.00	2.60
		Nos. 129-135 (7)	9.25	6.00

Granting of a new Constitution in 1944.

Peace Issue
Common Design Type
			Wmk. 4	Perf. 13½
1946, Oct. 14				
136	CD303	1½p black brown	.30	4.50
a.		Perf. 13½x14	2.75	.25
		Perf. 13½x14		
137	CD303	3p deep blue	5.25	3.00
a.		Perf. 13½	.60	7.25

Silver Wedding Issue
Common Design Types
			Photo.	Perf. 14x14½
1948, Dec. 1				
138	CD304	1½p red brown	.35	.25
		Engr.; Name Typo.		
		Perf. 11½x11		
139	CD305	£1 red	20.00	77.50

Type of 1938 and

Tobacco Industry A53

				Perf. 12½
1949, Aug. 15		Engr.		
140	A39	3p ultra & slate blue	4.50	1.25
141	A53	£1 purple & brown	60.00	40.00

UPU Issue
Common Design Types
Perf. 13½, 11x11½
				Wmk. 4
1949, Oct. 10				
142	CD306	1½p red brown	.25	.25
143	CD307	2p dark green	1.40	2.75
144	CD000	3p indigo	.50	1.25
145	CD309	6p rose violet	.55	1.75
		Nos. 142-145 (4)	2.70	6.00

University Issue
Common Design Types
Perf. 14x14½
1951, Feb. 16				
146	CD310	2p brown & gray blk	.35	.35
147	CD311	6p rose lilac & gray blk	.60	.50

George VI Type of 1938
				Perf. 13½x14
1951, Oct. 25				
148	A36	½p orange	2.75	.35
a.		Booklet pane of 6	16.50	
149	A36	1p blue green	3.50	.25
a.		Booklet pane of 6	22.50	

Boy Scout Emblem with Map — A54

Map and Emblem A55

Perf. 13½x13, 13x13½
			Typo.	Wmk. 4
1952, Mar. 5				
150	A54	2p blk, yel grn & blue	.30	.25
151	A55	6p blk, yel grn & dk red	.70	.60

1st Caribbean Boy Scout Jamboree, 1952.

Banana Type of 1938
			Engr.	Perf. 12½
1952, July 1				
152	A39	3p rose red & green	4.50	.40

Coronation Issue
Common Design Type
				Perf. 13½x13
1953, June 2				
153	CD312	2p dk green & black	1.50	.25

Type of 1938 with Portrait of Queen Elizabeth II and Inscription: "ROYAL VISIT 1953"
				Perf. 13
1953, Nov. 25				
154	A37	2p green & gray black	.55	.25

Visit of Queen Elizabeth II and the Duke of Edinburgh, 1953.

Warship off Port Royal A56

Designs: 2½p, Old Montego Bay. 3p, Old Kingston. 6p, Proclaiming abolition of slavery.

			Engr.	Perf. 12x12½
1955, May 10				
		Center in Black		
155	A56	2p olive green	.85	.25
156	A56	2½p light ultra	.25	.35
157	A56	3p deep plum	.25	.30
158	A56	6p rose red	.30	.25
		Nos. 155-158 (4)	1.65	1.15

300th anniv. of Jamaica's establishment as a British territory.

Palm Trees — A57

Blue Mountain Peak — A58

Arms of Jamaica — A59

Arms of Jamaica — A60

1p, Sugar cane. 2p, Pineapple. 2½p, Bananas. 3p, Mahoe flower. 4p, Breadfruit. 5p, Ackee fruit. 6p, Streamer (hummingbird). 1sh, Royal Botanic Gardens, Hope. 1sh6p, Rafting on the Rio Grande. 2sh, Fort Charles.

1956			Wmk. 4	Perf. 12½
159	A57	½p org ver & black	.25	.25
a.		Booklet pane of 6	.30	
160	A57	1p emer & blk	.25	.25
a.		Booklet pane of 6	.50	
161	A57	2p rose red & blk	.25	.25
a.		Booklet pane of 6	.85	
162	A57	2½p lt ultra & black	.75	.55
a.		Booklet pane of 6	4.50	
163	A57	3p brown & green	.25	.25
164	A57	4p dk blue & ol grn	.30	.25
165	A57	5p ol green & car	.30	2.75
166	A57	6p car & blk	3.25	.25
		Perf. 13½		
167	A58	8p red org & brt ultra	2.00	.25
168	A58	1sh blue & yel grn	2.00	.25
169	A58	1sh6p dp cl & ultra	1.00	.25
170	A58	2sh ol grn & ultra	15.00	3.25
		Perf. 11½		
171	A59	3sh blue & black	3.00	3.50
172	A59	5sh carmine & blk	4.25	7.00
173	A60	10sh blue grn & blk	35.00	22.00
174	A60	£1 purple & blk	35.00	22.00
		Nos. 159-174 (16)	102.85	63.30

For overprints see Nos. 185-196. For types overprinted see Nos. 208-216.

West Indies Federation
Common Design Type
Perf. 11½x11
			Engr.	Wmk. 314
1958, Apr. 22				
175	CD313	2p green	.75	.25
176	CD010	5p blue	1.10	0.50
177	CD313	6p carmine rose	1.25	.45
		Nos. 175-177 (3)	3.10	4.20

Britannia Plane over 1860 Packet Boat A61

1sh Stamps of 1860 and 1956 — A62

6p, Victorian post cart and mail truck.

1960, Jan. 4				Perf. 13x13½
178	A61	2p lilac & blue	.60	.25
179	A61	6p ol grn & car rose	.60	.50
		Perf. 13		
180	A62	1sh blue, yel grn & brn	.60	.55
		Nos. 178-180 (3)	1.80	1.30

Centenary of Jamaican postal service.

Independent State

Zouave Bugler and Map of Jamaica A63

1sh6p, Gordon House (Legislature) & hands of three races holding banner. 5sh, Map & symbols of agriculture & industry.

1962, Aug. 8			Photo.	Perf. 13
181	A63	2p multicolored	1.75	.25
182	A63	4p multicolored	1.10	.25
a.		Yellow omitted		

183	A63	1sh6p red, black & brn	4.00	1.00
184	A63	5sh multicolored	6.00	6.00
		Nos. 181-184 (4)	12.85	7.50

Issue of 1956 Overprinted

a

b

Perf. 12½
1962, Aug. 8			Wmk. 4	Engr.
185	A57(a)	½p org ver & blk	.25	1.00
186	A57(a)	1p emer & blk	.25	1.00
187	A57(a)	2½p lt ultra & blk	.25	1.50
188	A57(b)	3p brn & grn	.25	.25
189	A57(b)	5p ol grn & car	.25	.80
190	A57(b)	6p car & black	2.75	.25
		Perf. 13½		
191	A58(b)	8p red org & brt ultra	.30	.25
192	A58(b)	1sh bl & yel grn	.30	.25
193	A58(b)	2sh ol green & ultra	1.00	1.75
		Perf. 11½		
194	A59(a)	3sh blue & blk	1.25	1.75
195	A60(a)	10sh bl grn & blk	4.00	5.00
196	A60(a)	£1 pur & black	4.25	6.00
		Nos. 185-196 (12)	15.10	19.05

Nos. 181-196 issued to commemorate Jamaica's independence. "Independence" measures 17½x1½mm on Nos. 185-187; 18x1mm on Nos. 194-196. See Nos. 208-216.

Weight Lifting, Soccer, Boxing and Cycling A64

Designs: 6p, Various water sports. 8p, Running and jumping. 2sh, Arms and runner.

Perf. 14½x14
1962, Aug. 11			Photo.	Wmk. 314
197	A64	1p car & dk brown	.25	.25
198	A64	6p blue & brown	.25	.25
199	A64	8p olive & dk brown	.25	.25
200	A64	2sh multicolored	.30	.85
		Nos. 197-200 (4)	1.05	1.60

IX Central American and Caribbean Games, Kingston, Aug. 11-25.

A souvenir sheet containing one each of Nos. 197-200, imperf., was sold exclusively by National Sports, Ltd., at 5sh (face 3sh3p). The Jamaican Post Office sold the entire issue of this sheet to National Sports at face value, plus the printing cost. The stamps are postally valid. The sheet has marginal inscriptions and simulated perforations in ultramarine. Value $14.

Freedom from Hunger Issue

Man Planting Mango Tree and Produce A65

Perf. 12½
1963, June 4			Unwmk.	Litho.
201	A65	1p blue & multi	.25	.25
202	A65	8p rose & multi	.80	.60

See note after CD314, Common Design section.

Red Cross Centenary Issue
Common Design Type
1963, Sept. 2			Wmk. 314	Perf. 13
203	CD315	2p black & red	.25	.25
204	CD315	1sh6p ultra & red	.50	1.40

Carole Joan Crawford — A66

Unwmk.

1964, Feb. 14   Photo.   Perf. 13

205	A66	3p multicolored	.25	.25
206	A66	1sh olive & multi	.35	.25
207	A66	1sh6p multicolored	.65	.65
a.		Souvenir sheet of 3	2.00	2.00
		Nos. 205-207 (3)	1.25	1.15

Carole Joan Crawford, Miss World, 1963.
No. 207a contains one each of Nos. 205-207 with simulated perforations. Issued May 25. Sold for 4sh.

Types of 1956 Overprinted like 1962 Independence Issue

Wmk. 314

1963-64   Engr.   Perf. 12½

208	A57(a)	½p org ver & blk	.25	.25
209	A57(a)	1p emer & blk ('64)	.25	1.75
210	A57(a)	2½p lt ultra & blk ('64)	.40	2.75
211	A57(b)	3p brn & grn	.30	.25
212	A57(b)	5p ol grn & car ('64)	.60	2.75

Perf. 13½

213	A58(a)	8p red org & brt ultra ('64)	.45	.75
214	A58(b)	1sh bl & yel grn	.55	.75
215	A58(b)	2sh ol grn & ultra ('64)	.70	7.00

Perf. 11½

216	A59(a)	3sh bl & blk ('64)	2.75	5.00
		Nos. 208-216 (9)	6.25	21.25

Overprint is at bottom on Nos. 214-215, at top on Nos. 192-193.

Lignum Vitae, National Flower, and Map — A67

1½p, Ackee, national fruit, and map. 2p, Blue Mahoe, national tree, and map, vert. 2½p, Land shells (snails). 3p, Flag over map. 4p, Murex antillarum, sea shell. 6p, Papilio homerus. 8p, Streamer (hummingbird). 9p, Gypsum industry. 1sh, Stadium and statue of runner. 1sh6p, Palisadoes International Airport. 2sh, Bauxite mining. 3sh, Blue marlin and boat. 5sh, Port Royal exploration of sunken city, map, ship and artifacts. 10sh, Coat of arms, vert. £1, Flag and Queen Elizabeth II.

Perf. 14½, 14x14½

1964, May 4   Photo.   Wmk. 352

Size: 26x22mm, 22x26mm

217	A67	1p bis, vio bl & green	.25	.25
a.		Booklet pane of 6	.35	
218	A67	1½p multicolored	.25	.25
219	A67	2p multicolored	.25	.25
a.		Booklet pane of 6	.85	
220	A67	2½p multicolored	1.00	.60
221	A67	3p emer, yel & black	.25	.25
a.		Booklet pane of 6	3.00	
222	A67	4p violet & buff	.50	.25
223	A67	6p multicolored	2.25	.25
a.		Ultramarine omitted	95.00	
b.		Denomination omitted	2,000.	
224	A67	8p multicolored	2.50	1.50
a.		Red omitted	200.00	

Perf. 14½x14, 13½x14½, 14x14½

Size: 32x26mm, 26x32mm

225	A67	9p blue & yel	1.50	.25
226	A67	1sh yel brn & blk	.25	.25
a.		Yellow brown omitted	3,000.	
b.		Black omitted	2,200.	
227	A67	1sh6p sl, buff & bl	4.00	.25
228	A67	2sh bl, brn red & black	2.75	.35
229	A67	3sh grn, saph & dk bl, perf. 14½x14	.40	.70
a.		Perf. 14x14½	1.00	1.00

230	A67	5sh bl, blk & bis	1.25	1.00
231	A67	10sh multicolored	1.25	1.25
a.		Blue ("Jamaica" etc.) omitted	450.00	
232	A67	£1 multicolored	2.75	1.00
		Nos. 217-232 (16)	21.40	8.65

See Nos. 306-318. For overprints & surcharges see Nos. 248-251, 279-291, 305.

Scout Hat, Globe, Neckerchief — A68

Scout Emblem, American Crocodile — A69

Design: 3p, Scout belt buckle.

Perf. 14½x14, 14

1964, Aug. 27   Wmk. 352

233	A68	3p pink, black & red	.25	.25
234	A68	8p ultra, black & olive	.25	.25
235	A69	1sh ultra & gold	.25	.45
		Nos. 233-235 (3)	.75	.95

6th Inter-American Scout Conference, Kingston, Aug. 25-29.

Gordon House, Kingston, and Commonwealth Parliamentary Association Emblem — A70

6p, Headquarters House, Kingston. 1sh6p, House of Assembly, Spanish Town.

1964, Nov. 16   Photo.   Perf. 14½x14

236	A70	3p yel green & blk	.25	.25
237	A70	6p red & black	.35	.25
238	A70	1sh6p ultra & black	.45	.25
		Nos. 236-238 (3)	1.05	.75

10th Commonwealth Parliamentary Conf.

Eleanor Roosevelt — A71

1964, Dec. 10   Wmk. 352

239	A71	1sh lt green, blk & red	.25	.25

Eleanor Roosevelt (1884-1962) on the 16th anniv. of the Universal Declaration of Human Rights.

Map of Jamaica and Girl Guide Emblem — A72

Girl Guide Emblems — A73

Perf. 14x14½, 14

1965, May 17   Photo.   Wmk. 352

240	A72	3p lt blue, yel & yel grn	.25	.25
241	A73	1sh lt yel grn, blk & bis	.25	.30

50th anniv. of the Girl Guides of Jamaica.

Salvation Army Cap — A74

1sh6p, Flag bearer, drummer, globe, vert.

Perf. 14x14½, 14½x14

1965, Aug. 23   Photo.   Wmk. 352

242	A74	3p dp blue, yel, mar & blk	.25	.25
243	A74	1sh6p emerald & multi	.50	.40

Centenary of the Salvation Army.

Paul Bogle, William Gordon and Morant Bay Court House A75

1965, Dec. 29   Unwmk.   Perf. 14x13

244	A75	3p vio blue, blk & brn	.25	.25
245	A75	1sh6p yel grn, blk & brn	.25	.25
246	A75	3sh pink & brown	.30	.80
		Nos. 244-246 (3)	.80	1.30

Cent. of the Morant Bay rebellion against governor John Eyre.

ITU Emblem, Telstar, Telegraph Key and Man Blowing Horn — A76

Perf. 14x14½

1965, Dec. 29   Photo.   Wmk. 352

247	A76	1sh gray, black & red	.50	.25

Cent. of the ITU.

Nos. 221, 223, 226-227 Overprinted

Perf. 14½, 14½x14

1966, Mar. 3   Photo.   Wmk. 352

Size: 26x22mm

248	A67	3p emer, yel & black	.30	.25
249	A67	6p multicolored	2.25	.40

Size: 32x26mm

250	A67	1sh yel brown & blk	.75	.25
251	A67	1sh6p slate, buff & blue	3.50	2.50
		Nos. 248-251 (4)	6.80	3.40

See note after Antigua No. 162.

Winston Churchill A77

1966, Apr. 18   Perf. 14, 14x14½

252	A77	6p olive green & gray	.60	.35
253	A77	1sh violet & sepia	.85	.95

Sir Winston Leonard Spencer Churchill (1874-1965), statesman and WWII leader.

Runner, Flags of Jamaica, Great Britain and Games' Emblem A78

Designs: 6p, Bicyclists and waterfall. 1sh, Stadium. 3sh, Games' Emblem.

Perf. 14½x14

1966, Aug. 4   Photo.   Wmk. 352

254	A78	3p multicolored	.25	.25
255	A78	6p multicolored	.40	.25
256	A78	1sh multicolored	.25	.25
257	A78	3sh gold & dk vio blue	.40	.45
a.		Souvenir sheet of 4	5.75	5.75
		Nos. 254-257 (4)	1.30	1.20

8th British Empire and Commonwealth Games, Aug. 4-13, 1966.
No. 257a contains 4 imperf. stamps with simulated perforations similar to Nos. 254-257. Issued Aug. 25, 1966.

Bolivar Statue, Kingston, Flags of Jamaica and Venezuela — A79

1966, Dec. 5   Perf. 14x14½

258	A79	8p multicolored	.35	.25

150th anniv. of the "Bolivar Letter," written by Simon Bolivar, while in exile in Jamaica.

Jamaican Pavilion — A80

1967, Apr. 28   Perf. 14½x14

259	A80	6p multicolored	.25	.25
260	A80	1sh multicolored	.25	.25

EXPO '67 Intl. Exhibition, Montreal, Apr. 28-Oct. 27.

Donald Burns Sangster — A81

Perf. 13x13½

1967, Aug. 28   Unwmk.

261	A81	3p multicolored	.25	.25
262	A81	1sh6p multicolored	.25	.25

Sir Donald Burns Sangster (1911-1967), Prime Minister.

Traffic Police and Post Office A82

Designs: 1sh, Officers representing various branches of police force in front of Police Headquarters. 1sh6p, Constable, 1867, Old House of Assembly, and 1967 constable with New House of Assembly.

JAMAICA
5

Perf. 13½x14
1967, Nov. 28   Photo.   Wmk. 352
Size: 42x25mm
263 A82   3p red brown & multi   .40 .25
Size: 56½x20½mm
Perf. 13½x14½
264 A82   1sh yellow & multi   .40 .25
Size: 42x25mm
Perf. 13½x14
265 A82   1sh6p gray & multi   .70 .75
Nos. 263-265 (3)   1.50 1.25
Centenary of the Constabulary Force.

A Human Rights set of three (3p, 1sh, 3sh) was prepared and announced for release on Jan. 2, 1968. The Crown Agents distributed sample sets, but the stamps were not issued. On Dec. 3, Nos. 271-273 were issued instead. Designs of the unissued set show bowls of food, an abacus and praying hands. Value, $160.

Wicketkeeper, Emblem of West Indies Cricket Team — A82a

Designs: No. 266, Wicketkeeper and emblem of West Indies Cricket Team. No. 267, Batsman and emblem of Marylebone Cricket Club. No. 268, Bowler and emblem of West Indies Cricket Team.

1968, Feb. 8   Photo.   Perf. 14
266 A82a 6p multicolored   .45 .45
267 A82a 6p multicolored   .45 .45
268 A82a 6p multicolored   .45 .45
a.   Horiz. strip of 3, #266-268   2.25 2.50
Nos. 266-268 (3)   1.35 1.35
Visit of the Marylebone Cricket Club to the West Indies, Jan.-Feb. 1968.

Sir Alexander and Lady Bustamante — A83

1968, May 23   Perf. 14½
269 A83   3p brt rose & black   .25 .25
270 A83   1sh olive green & black   .25 .25
Labor Day, May 23, 1968.

Human Rights Flame and Map of Jamaica A84

Designs: 1sh, Hands shielding Human Rights flame, vert. 3sh, Man kneeling on Map of Jamaica, and Human Rights flame.

1968, Dec. 3   Wmk. 352   Perf. 14½
271 A84   3p multicolored   .25 .25
a.   Gold (flame) omitted   150.00
272 A84   1sh multicolored   .25 .25
273 A84   3sh multicolored   .45 .90
a.   Gold (flame) omitted   175.00
Nos. 271-273 (3)   .95 1.40
International Human Rights Year.

ILO Emblem A85

Unwmk.
1969, May 23   Litho.   Perf. 14
274 A85   6p black & orange yel   .25 .25
275 A85   3sh black & brt green   .30 .30
50th anniv. of the ILO.

WHO Emblem, Children and Nurse — A86

Designs: 1sh, Malaria eradication, horiz. 3sh, Student nurses.

1969, May 30   Photo.   Perf. 14
276 A86   6p org, black & brown   .25 .25
277 A86   1sh blue grn, blk & brn   .25 .25
278 A86   3sh ultra, black & brn   .25 .90
Nos. 276-278 (3)   .75 1.40
WHO, 20th anniv.

Nos. 217-219, 221-223, 225-232 Surcharged

1969, Sept. 8   Wmk. 352   Perf. 14½
Size: 26x22mm, 22x26mm
279 A67   1c on 1p multi   .25 .25
280 A67   2c on 2p multi   .25 .25
281 A67   3c on 3p multi   .25 .25
282 A67   4c on 4p multi   1.10 .25
283 A67   5c on 6p multi   1.10 .25
a.   Blue (wing dots) omitted   100.00
Perf. 14½x14, 13½x14½, 14x14½
Size: 32x26mm, 26x32mm
284 A67   8c on 9p multi   .25 .25
285 A67   10c on 1sh multi   .25 .25
286 A67   15c on 1sh6p multi   .50 .75
287 A67   20c on 2sh multi   1.25 1.50
288 A67   30c on 3sh multi   2.00 3.00
289 A67   50c on 5sh multi   1.10 3.00
290 A67 $1 on 10sh multi   1.10 6.00
291 A67 $2 on £1 multi   1.75 6.00
Nos. 279-291 (13)   11.15 22.00
Introduction of decimal currency.
The old denomination is obliterated by groups of small rectangles on the 1c and 5c, and with a square on the 2c, 4c and 8c; old denominations not obliterated on others.

Madonna and Child with St. John, by Raphael — A87

Christmas (Paintings): 2c, The Adoration of the Kings, by Vincenzo Foppa. 8c, The Adoration of the Kings, by Dosso Dossi.

1969, Oct. 25   Litho.   Perf. 13
292 A87   2c vermilion & multi   .25 .40
293 A87   5c multicolored   .25 .40
294 A87   8c orange & multi   .25 .40
Nos. 292-294 (3)   .75 1.20

First Jamaica Penny — A88

Design: 3c, First Jamaica halfpenny.

1969, Oct. 27   Perf. 12x12½
295 A88   3c brt pink, blk & silver   .25 .25
296 A88   15c emerald, blk & silver   .25 .25
Centenary of the first Jamaican coinage.

George William Gordon — A89

Portraits: 3c, Sir Alexander Bustamante (1884-1977). 5c, Norman W. Manley (1893-1969). 10c, Marcus M. Garvey (1887-1940). 15c, Paul Bogle (1820-1865).

Perf. 12x12½
1970, Mar. 11   Photo.   Unwmk.
297 A89   1c lt violet & multi   .25 .25
298 A89   3c lt blue & multi   .25 .25
299 A89   5c lt gray & multi   .25 .25
300 A89   10c pale rose & multi   .25 .25
301 A89   15c pale green & multi   .25 .25
Nos. 297-301 (5)   1.25 1.25
National heroes connected with Jamaica's independence.

Crucifixion, by Antonello da Messina — A90

Easter: 3c, Christ Appearing to St. Peter, by Annibale Carracci. 20c, Easter lily.

1970, Mar. 23
302 A90   3c pink & multi   .25 .25
303 A90   10c gray green & multi   .25 .25
304 A90   20c gray & multi   .30 .60
Nos. 302-304 (3)   .80 1.10

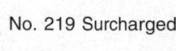

No. 219 Surcharged

1970, July 16   Wmk. 352   Perf. 14½
305 A67   2c on 2p multicolored   .30 .25

Type of Regular Issue, 1964
Values in Cents and Dollars

Designs: 1c, Lignum vitae and map. 2c, Blue mahoe and map, vert. 3c, Flag over map. 4c, Murex antillarum, coa choll. 5c, Papilio homerus. 8c, Gypsum industry. 10c, Stadium and statue of runner. 15c, Palisadoes International Airport. 20c, Bauxite mining. 30c, Blue marlin and boat. 50c, Port Royal exploration of sunken city, map, ship and artifacts. $1, Coat of arms, vert. $2, Flag and Queen Elizabeth II.

1970   Wmk. 352   Photo.   Perf. 14½
Size: 26x22mm, 22x26mm
306 A67   1c bister & multi   .65 1.00
307 A67   2c gray grn & multi   .35 .25
308 A67   3c emer, yel & black   .50 .80
309 A67   4c violet & buff   2.50 .35
310 A67   5c green & multi   2.75 .65

Perf. 14½x14, 13½x14½, 14x14½
Size: 32x26mm, 26x32mm
311 A67   8c blue & yellow   1.75 .25
312 A67   10c yel brn & black   .60 .25
313 A67   15c multicolored   2.50 3.00
314 A67   20c multicolored   1.25 3.00
315 A67   30c multicolored   4.00 6.50
316 A67   50c multicolored   1.25 3.75
317 A67 $1 multicolored   1.00 5.50
318 A67 $2 multicolored   1.50 4.00
Nos. 306-318 (13)   20.60 29.30
Issued: Nos. 306-312, 9/7; Nos. 313-318, 11/2.

Bright's Cable Gear on "Dacia" A91

Designs: 3c, Telegraph cable ship "Dacia." 50c, Double current Morse key, 1870, and map of Jamaica.

1970, Oct. 12   Litho.   Perf. 14½
319 A91   3c red orange & multi   .25 .25
320 A91   10c blue green & multi   .25 .25
321 A91   50c emerald & multi   .85 .85
Nos. 319-321 (3)   1.35 1.35
Centenary of telegraph service.

Bananas, Citrus Fruit, Sugar Cane and Tobacco — A92

1970, Nov. 2   Wmk. 352   Perf. 14
322 A92   2c brown & multi   .25 .30
323 A92   10c black & multi   .35 .25
Jamaica Agricultural Society, 75th anniv.

"The Projector," 1845 — A93

Locomotives: 15c, Engine 54, 1944. 50c, Engine 102, 1967.

1970, Nov. 21   Litho.   Perf. 13½
324 A93   3c green & multi   .25 .25
325 A93   15c org brown & multi   .80 .80
326 A93   50c multicolored   2.00 2.00
Nos. 324-326 (3)   3.05 3.05
125th anniv. of the Jamaican railroad.

Kingston Cathedral — A94

30c, Arms of Jamaica Bishopric. 10c, 20c, like 3c.

1971, Feb. 22   Perf. 14½
327 A94   3c lt green & multi   .25 .25
328 A94   10c dull orange & multi   .25 .25
329 A94   20c ultra & multi   .30 .30
330 A94   30c gray & multi   .30 .60
Nos. 327-330 (4)   1.10 1.40
Centenary of the disestablishment of the Church of England.

Henry Morgan, Ships in Port Royal Harbor A95

Designs: 15c, Mary Read, Anne Bonny and pamphlet on their trial. 30c, 18th century merchantman surrendering to pirate schooner.

1971, May 10   Litho.   Wmk. 352

331	A95	3c red brown & multi	1.00	.25
332	A95	15c gray & multi	1.40	.35
333	A95	30c lilac & multi	2.00	1.60
		Nos. 331-333 (3)	4.40	2.20

Pirates and buccaneers.

Dummer Packet Letter, 1705 — A96

Designs: 5c, Stampless cover, 1793. 8c, Post office, Kingston, 1820. 10c, Modern date cancellation on No. 312. 20c, Cover with stamps of Great Britain and Jamaica cancellations, 1859. 50c, Jamaica No. 83a, vert.

1971, Oct. 30   Perf. 13½

334	A96	3c dk carmine & black	.25	.25
335	A96	5c lt ol grn & black	.25	.25
336	A96	8c purple & black	.25	.25
337	A96	10c slate, black & brn	.25	.25
338	A96	20c multicolored	.35	.35
339	A96	50c dk gray, blk & org	.60	.60
		Nos. 334-339 (6)	1.95	1.95

Tercentenary of Jamaica Post Office.

Earth Station and Satellite — A97

1972, Feb. 17   Perf. 14x13½

340	A97	3c red & multi	.25	.25
341	A97	15c gray & multi	.35	.35
342	A97	50c multicolored	.75	.75
		Nos. 340-342 (3)	1.35	1.35

Jamaica's earth satellite station.

Bauxite Industry — A98

National Stadium A99

1c, Pimento, vert. 2c, Red ginger, vert. 4c, Kingston harbor. 5c, Oil refinery. 6c, Senate Building, Univ. of the West Indies. 9c, Devon House, Hope Road. 10c, Stewardess and Air Jamaica plane. 15c, Old Iron Bridge, vert. 20c, College of Arts, Science & Technology. 30c, Dunn's River Falls, vert. 50c, River raft. $1, Jamaica House. $2, Kings House. $5, Map and arms of Jamaica ('79).

Perf. 14½x14, 14x14½

1972-79   Litho.   Wmk. 352

343	A98	1c multicolored	.25	.25
344	A98	2c multicolored	.25	.25
345	A98	3c shown	.25	.25
346	A98	4c multicolored	.25	.25
347	A98	5c multicolored	.25	.25
348	A98	6c multicolored	.25	.25

Perf. 13½

349	A99	8c shown	.30	.25
350	A99	9c multicolored	.25	.25
351	A99	10c multicolored	.25	.25
352	A99	15c multicolored	1.75	.25
353	A99	20c multicolored	.30	.25
354	A99	30c multicolored	.65	.25
355	A99	50c multicolored	1.60	.40
356	A99	$1 multicolored	.75	1.50
357	A99	$2 multicolored	1.00	1.50

Perf. 14½x14
Size: 37x26½mm

358	A99	$5 multicolored	1.50	1.75
		Nos. 343-358 (16)	9.85	8.15

For overprints see Nos. 360-362, 451.

Nos. 345, 351, 355 Overprinted

1972, Aug. 8   Perf. 14½x14, 13½

360	A98	3c multicolored	.30	.30
361	A99	10c multicolored	.30	.25
362	A99	50c multicolored	.75	1.50
		Nos. 360-362 (3)	1.35	2.05

Arms of Kingston — A100

Design: 5c, 30c, Arms of Kingston, vert.

1972, Dec. 4   Perf. 13½x14, 14x13½

363	A100	5c pink & multi	.25	.25
364	A100	30c lemon & multi	.25	.25
365	A100	50c lt blue & multi	.55	1.75
		Nos. 363-365 (3)	1.05	2.25

Centenary of Kingston as capital.

Mongoose and Map of Jamaica A101

40c, Mongoose & rat. 60c, Mongoose & chicken.

Perf. 14x14½

1973, Apr. 9   Litho.   Wmk. 352

366	A101	8c yel green & blk	.25	.25
367	A101	40c blue & black	.45	.45
368	A101	60c salmon & black	.75	1.25
a.		Souvenir sheet of 3, #366-368	2.25	2.25
		Nos. 366-368 (3)	1.45	1.95

Centenary of the introduction of the mongoose to Jamaica.

Euphorbia Punicea — A102

Flowers: 6c, Hylocereus triangularis. 9c, Columnea argentea. 15c, Portlandia

grandiflora. 30c, Samyda pubescens. 50c, Cordia sebestena.

1973, July 9   Perf. 14

369	A102	1c dp green & multi	.25	.25
370	A102	6c vio blue & multi	.25	.25
371	A102	9c orange & multi	.30	.25
372	A102	15c brown & multi	.35	.25
373	A102	30c olive & multi	.60	.60
374	A102	50c multicolored	.90	1.25
		Nos. 369-374 (6)	2.65	2.85

Broughtonia Sanguinea — A103

Orchids: 10c, Arpophyllum jamaicense, vert. 20c, Oncidium pulchellum, vert. $1, Brassia maculata.

1973, Oct. 8   Perf. 14x13½, 13½x14

375	A103	5c multicolored	.50	.25
376	A103	10c multicolored	.70	.25
377	A103	20c slate & multi	1.40	.50
378	A103	$1 ultra & multi	3.50	4.00
a.		Souv. sheet of 4, #375-378, perf 12	5.75	5.75
		Nos. 375-378 (4)	6.10	5.00

Mailboat "Mary" (1808-1815) — A104

Mailboats: 10c, "Queensbury" (1814-27). 15c, "Sheldrake" (1829-34). 50c, "Thames" (1842).

Perf. 13½ (5c, 50c), 14½ (10c, 15c)

1974, Apr. 8   Wmk. 352

379	A104	5c shown	.85	.25
a.		Perf. 14½	2.50	1.25
380	A104	10c multicolored	.85	.35
381	A104	15c multicolored	1.25	.55
382	A104	50c multicolored	2.25	2.25
a.		Souv. sheet of 4, #379-382, perf 13½	5.50	5.50
		Nos. 379-382 (4)	5.20	3.40

Jamaican Dancers — A105

Designs: Dancers.

1974, Aug. 1   Litho.   Perf. 13½

383	A105	5c green & multi	.25	.25
384	A105	10c black & multi	.25	.25
385	A105	30c brown & multi	.30	.30
386	A105	50c lilac & multi	.50	.50
a.		Souvenir sheet of 4, #383-386	2.50	2.50
		Nos. 383-386 (4)	1.30	1.30

National Dance Theatre.

Globe, Letter, UPU Emblem A106

1974, Oct. 9   Perf. 14

387	A106	5c plum & multi	.25	.25
388	A106	9c olive & multi	.25	.25
389	A106	50c multicolored	.30	.30
		Nos. 387-389 (3)	.80	.80

Centenary of Universal Postal Union.

Senate Building and Sir Hugh Wooding A107

10c, 50c, Chapel & Princess Alice. 30c, like 5c.

1975, Jan. 13   Wmk. 352

390	A107	5c yellow & multi	.25	.25
391	A107	10c salmon & multi	.25	.25
392	A107	30c dull orange & multi	.25	.25
393	A107	50c multicolored	.35	.35
		Nos. 390-393 (4)	1.10	1.10

University College of the West Indies, 25th anniversary.

Commonwealth Symbol — A108

Commonwealth Symbol and: 10c, Arms of Jamaica. 30c, Dove of peace. 50c, Jamaican flag.

1975, Apr. 29   Litho.   Perf. 13½

394	A108	5c buff & multi	.25	.25
395	A108	10c rose & multi	.25	.25
396	A108	30c violet blue & multi	.25	.25
397	A108	50c multicolored	.30	.30
		Nos. 394-397 (4)	1.05	1.05

Commonwealth Heads of Government Conference, Jamaica, Apr.-May.

Graphium Marcellinus A109

Butterflies: 20c, Papilio thoas melonius. 25c, Papilio thersites. 30c, Papilio homerus.

1975, Aug. 25   Litho.   Perf. 14

398	A109	10c lt green & multi	1.10	.35
399	A109	20c lt green & multi	1.60	1.10
400	A109	25c lt green & multi	1.75	2.00
401	A109	30c lt green & multi	2.40	2.75
a.		Souvenir sheet of 4, #398-401	8.50	8.50
		Nos. 398-401 (4)	6.85	6.20

See Nos. 423-426, 435-438.

Koo Koo, "Actor-boy" — A110

Christmas: 10c, Red "set-girls." 20c, French "set-girls." 50c, Jawbone or "House John Canoe." Festival dancers drawn by I. M. Belisario in Kingston, 1837.

1975, Nov. 3   Litho.   Wmk. 352

402	A110	8c multicolored	.25	.25
403	A110	10c olive & multi	.25	.25
404	A110	20c ultra & multi	.45	.45
405	A110	50c multicolored	.95	.95
a.		Souv. sheet of 4, #402-405, perf. 13½	2.50	2.50
		Nos. 402-405 (4)	1.90	1.90

See Nos. 416-418.

Map of Jamaica, by Benedetto Bordone, 1528 — A111

Maps of Jamaica by: 20c, Tommaso Porcacchi, 1576. 30c, Theodor DeBry, 1594. 50c, Barent Langenes, 1598.

1976, Mar. 12   *Perf. 13½x14*

406	A111	10c brown, buff & red	.35	.25
407	A111	20c bister & multi	.60	.40
408	A111	30c lt blue & multi	.80	.80
409	A111	50c multicolored	1.10	1.50
		Nos. 406-409 (4)	2.85	2.95

See Nos. 419-422.

Olympic Rings — A112

1976, June 14   **Litho.**   *Perf. 13½x14*

410	A112	10c black & multi	.25	.25
411	A112	20c blue & multi	.30	.30
412	A112	25c red & multi	.30	.30
413	A112	50c green & multi	.55	.55
		Nos. 410-413 (4)	1.40	1.40

21st Olympic Games, Montreal, Canada, July 17-Aug. 1.

Map of West Indies, Bats, Wicket and Ball A112a

Prudential Cup — A112b

1976, Aug. 9   **Unwmk.**   *Perf. 14*

414	A112a	10c lt blue & multi	.30	.30
415	A112b	25c lilac rose & blk	.70	.70

World Cricket Cup, won by West Indies Team, 1975.

Christmas Type of 1975

Belisario Prints, 1837: 10c, Queen of the "set-girls." 20c, Band of Jawbone John Canoe. 50c, Koo Koo, "actor-boy."

1976, Nov. 8   **Wmk. 352**   *Perf. 13½*

416	A110	10c brick red & multi	.25	.25
417	A110	20c bister & multi	.25	.25
418	A110	50c tan & multi	.45	.60
a.		Souv. sheet of 3, #416-418, perf. 14	1.40	1.40
		Nos. 416-418 (3)	.95	1.10

Christmas.

Map Type of 1976

Maps of Jamaica by: 9c, Edmund Hickeringill, 1661. 10c, John Ogilby, 1671. 25c, House of Visscher, 1680. 40c, John Thornton, 1689.

1977, Feb. 28   **Litho.**   *Perf. 13*

419	A111	9c lt blue & multi	.30	.25
420	A111	10c buff & multi	.50	.45
421	A111	25c multicolored	.75	.80
422	A111	40c multicolored	1.00	.75
		Nos. 419-422 (4)	2.55	2.25

Butterfly Type of 1975

10c, Eurema elathea. 20c, Dynamine egaea. 25c, Atlantea pantoni. 40c, Hypolimnas misippus.

1977, May 9   **Wmk. 352**   *Perf. 13½*

423	A109	10c black & multi	.45	.25
424	A109	20c black & multi	.95	.95
425	A109	25c black & multi	1.40	1.40
426	A109	40c black & multi	2.50	4.00
a.		Souv. sheet of 4, #423-426, perf. 14½	7.50	7.50
		Nos. 423-426 (4)	5.30	6.60

Scout Emblem, Doctor Bird, Outline of Jamaica — A113

1977, Aug. 5   **Litho.**   *Perf. 14*

427	A113	10c multicolored	.75	.25
428	A113	20c multicolored	1.00	.30
429	A113	25c multicolored	1.25	.45
430	A113	50c multicolored	1.75	1.75
		Nos. 427-430 (4)	4.75	2.75

6th Caribbean Jamboree, Hope Gardens, Kingston, Aug. 3-17.

Trumpeter A114

10c, 2 clarinetists and oboist. 20c, kettle drummer and oboist, vert. 25c, Cellist and trumpeter, vert.

1977, Dec. 19   **Litho.**   *Perf. 14*

431	A114	9c multicolored	.25	.25
432	A114	10c multicolored	.25	.25
433	A114	20c multicolored	.45	.35
434	A114	25c multicolored	.60	.60
a.		Souvenir sheet of 4, #431-434	3.25	3.25
		Nos. 431-434 (4)	1.55	1.45

Jamaica Military Band, 50th anniversary.

Butterfly Type of 1975

Butterflies: 10c, Callophrys crethona. 20c, Siproeta stelenes. 25c, Urbanus proteus. 50c, Anaea troglodyta.

1978, Apr. 17   **Litho.**   *Perf. 14½*

435	A109	10c black & multi	.60	.25
436	A109	20c black & multi	1.10	.25
437	A109	25c black & multi	1.40	.75
438	A109	50c black & multi	2.50	3.25
a.		Souvenir sheet of 4, #435-438	6.50	6.50
		Nos. 435-438 (4)	5.60	4.50

Half Figure with Canopy — A115

Arawak Artifacts, found 1792: 20c, Standing figure. 50c, Birdman.

1978, July 10   **Litho.**   *Perf. 13½x13*

439	A115	10c multicolored	.25	.25
440	A115	20c multicolored	.25	.25
441	A115	50c multicolored	.50	.50
a.		Souv. sheet of 3, #439-441, perf. 14	1.10	1.10
		Nos. 439-441 (3)	1.00	1.00

Norman Manley Statue — A116

Designs: 20c, Alexander Bustamante statue. 25c, Kingston coat of arms. 40c, Gordon House Chamber, House of Representatives.

1978, Sept. 25   **Litho.**   **Wmk. 352**

442	A116	10c multicolored	.25	.25
443	A116	20c multicolored	.25	.25
444	A116	25c multicolored	.30	.25
445	A116	40c multicolored	.35	.35
		Nos. 442-445 (4)	1.15	1.10

24th Commonwealth Parliamentary Conf.

Salvation Army Band A117

Designs: 20c, Trumpeter. 25c, "S" and Cross entwined on pole of Army flag. 50c, William Booth and Salvation Army shield.

1978, Dec. 4   *Perf. 14*

446	A117	10c multicolored	.25	.25
447	A117	20c multicolored	.35	.25
448	A117	25c multicolored	.35	.30
449	A117	50c multicolored	.65	.75
		Nos. 446-449 (4)	1.60	1.55

Christmas; Salvation Army centenary.

"Negro Aroused," by Edna Manley — A118

1978, Dec. 11   *Perf. 13*

450	A118	10c multicolored	.40	.25

International Anti-Apartheid Year.

No. 351 Overprinted

1979, Apr. 2   **Litho.**   *Perf. 13½*

451	A99	10c multicolored	.50	.50

Arawak Grinding Stone, c. 400 B.C. — A119

Arawak Artifacts (all A.D.): 10c, Stone implements, c. 500, horiz. 20c, Cooking pot, c. 300, horiz. 25c, Serving boat, c. 300, horiz. 50c, Storage jar fragment, c. 300.

1979, Apr. 23   *Perf. 14*

452	A119	5c multicolored	.25	.25
453	A119	10c multicolored	.25	.25
454	A119	20c multicolored	.25	.25
455	A119	25c multicolored	.25	.25
456	A119	50c multicolored	.25	.25
		Nos. 452-456 (5)	1.25	1.25

Jamaica No. 183, Hill Statue A120

Hill Statue and Stamps of Jamaica: 20c, No. 83a. 25c, No. 5. 50c, No. 271.

1979, Aug. 13   **Litho.**   *Perf. 14*

457	A120	10c multicolored	.25	.25
458	A120	20c multicolored	.25	.25
a.		Souvenir sheet of 1	.70	.70
459	A120	25c multicolored	.25	.25
460	A120	50c multicolored	.25	.60
		Nos. 457-460 (4)	1.00	1.35

Sir Rowland Hill (1795-1879), originator of penny postage.

Children, IYC Emblem A121

International Year of the Child: 20c, Doll, vert. 25c, "The Family." 25c, "House on the Hill." 25c, 50c are children's drawings.

1979, Oct. 1

461	A121	10c multicolored	.25	.25
462	A121	20c multicolored	.25	.25
463	A121	25c multicolored	.25	.25
464	A121	50c multicolored	.25	.25
		Nos. 461-464 (4)	1.00	1.00

Tennis, Montego Bay — A122   Jamaican Tody — A123

Designs: 2c, Golfing, Tryall Hanover. 4c, Horseback riding, Negril Beach. 5c, Old Waterwheel, Tryall Hanover. 6c, Fern Gully, Ocho Rios. 7c, Dunn's River Falls, Ocho Rios. 10c, Doctorbird. 12c, Yellow-billed parrot. 15c, Hummingbird. 35c, White-chinned thrush. 50c, Jamaican woodpecker. 65c, Rafting Martha Brae Trelawny. 75c, Blue marlin fishing, Port Antonio. $1, Scuba diving. Ocho Rios. $2, Sail boats, Montego Bay.

Wmk. 352

1979-80   **Litho.**   *Perf. 13½*

465	A122	1c multicolored	.75	.50
466	A122	2c multicolored	2.25	1.75
467	A122	4c multicolored	.60	2.25
468	A122	5c multicolored	1.50	.30
469	A122	6c multicolored	1.75	2.50
470	A122	7c multicolored	.60	.30
472	A123	8c multicolored	1.25	1.25
473	A123	10c multicolored	1.25	.25
474	A123	12c multicolored	1.25	2.00
475	A123	15c multicolored	1.25	.30
476	A123	35c multicolored	1.75	.35
477	A123	50c multicolored	2.25	.35
478	A122	65c multicolored	2.25	2.75
479	A122	75c multicolored	2.50	2.25
480	A122	$1 multicolored	2.50	2.25
481	A122	$2 multicolored	2.75	.75
		Nos. 465-481 (16)	26.45	20.10

Issued: Nos. 465-470, 11/26/79; Nos 472-481, 5/80.

For surcharges see Nos. 581-582, 665-666.

Institute of Jamaica Centenary — A124

15c, Institute building, 1980. 35c, "The Ascension" on microfilm reader, vert. 50c, Hawksbill and green turtles. 75c, Jamaican owl, vert.

1980, Feb. 25   Litho.   Perf. 13½
484	A124	5c shown	.25	.25
485	A124	15c multicolored	.25	.25
486	A124	35c multicolored	.35	.30
487	A124	50c multicolored	.60	.60
488	A124	75c multicolored	1.90	1.90
		Nos. 484-488 (5)	3.35	3.30

Don Quarrie, 1976 Gold Medalist, 200-Meter Race, Moscow '80 Emblem A125

1952 4x400-meter Relay Team: a, Arthur Wint. b, Leslie Laing. c, Herbert McKenley. d, George Rhoden.

1980, July 21   Litho.   Perf. 13
489	A125	15c shown	.40	.25
490		Strip of 4	3.25	3.25
a.-d.	A125	35c any single	.50	.50

22nd Summer Olympic Games, Moscow, July 19-Aug. 3.

Parish Church, Kingston A126

20c, Coke Memorial. 25c, Church of the Redeemer. $5, Holy Trinity Cathedral.

1980, Nov. 24   Litho.   Perf. 14
491	A126	15c shown	.25	.25
492	A126	20c multicolored	.25	.25
493	A126	25c multicolored	.25	.25
494	A126	$5 multicolored	1.25	1.25
a.		Souvenir sheet of 4, #491-494	2.25	2.25
		Nos. 491-494 (4)	2.00	2.00

Christmas.

Tube Sponge A127

1981, Feb. 27   Wmk. 352   Perf. 14
495	A127	20c Blood cup sponge, vert.	.25	.25
496	A127	45c shown	.35	.35
497	A127	60c Black coral, vert.	.50	.50
498	A127	75c Tire reef	.60	.60
		Nos. 495-498 (4)	1.70	1.70

See Nos. 523-527.

Indian Coney A128

Designs: b, Facing left. c, Eating. d, Family.

1981, May 25   Wmk. 352   Perf. 14
499		Strip of 4	1.25	1.25
a.-d.	A128	20c any single	.25	.25

Royal Wedding Issue
Common Design Type

1981, July 29   Litho.   Perf. 15
500	CD331	20c White orchid	.25	.25
501	CD331	45c Royal coach	.25	.25
502	CD331	60c Couple	.25	.25

Perf. 13½
503	CD331	$5 St. James' Palace	.75	.50
a.		Souvenir sheet of 1	.90	.90
b.		Bkit. pane of 4, perf 14x14½	1.60	
		Nos. 500-503 (4)	1.50	1.25

Also issued in sheets of 5 + label, perf. 13½.

Intl. Year of the Disabled A129

1981, Sept. 14   Wmk. 352   Perf. 13½
504	A129	20c Blind weaver	.25	.25
505	A129	45c Artist	.40	.40
506	A129	60c Learning sign language	.50	.50
507	A129	1.50 Basketball players	2.25	2.25
		Nos. 504-507 (4)	3.40	3.40

World Food Day — A130

Perf. 13x13½, 13½x13
1981, Oct. 16   Litho.   Wmk. 352
508	A130	20c No. 218	.40	.25
509	A130	45c No. 76, vert.	.75	.45
510	A130	2.50 No. 121	2.25	1.40
511	A130	$4 No. 125	3.25	2.50
		Nos. 508-511 (4)	6.65	4.60

Bob Marley (1945-1981), Reggae Musician — A131

Portraits of Bob Marley and song titles.

1981, Oct. 20   Wmk. 373   Perf. 14½
512	A131	1c multicolored	.70	1.00
513	A131	2c multicolored	.70	1.00
514	A131	3c multicolored	.70	1.00
515	A131	15c multicolored	3.25	.30
516	A131	20c multicolored	3.50	.30
517	A131	60c multicolored	4.50	3.00
518	A131	$3 multicolored	6.75	11.00
		Nos. 512-518 (7)	20.10	17.60

Souvenir Sheet
519	A131	$5.25 multicolored	8.50	6.50

Christmas A132

1981, Dec. 11   Wmk. 352   Perf. 14
520	A132	10c Webb Memorial Baptist Church	.25	.25
521	A132	45c Church of God	.35	.35
522	A132	$5 Bryce United Church	2.00	2.00
a.		Souvenir sheet of 3, #520-522, perf. 12½x12	4.00	4.00
		Nos. 520-522 (3)	2.60	2.60

See Nos. 547-549.

Marine Life Type of 1981

1982, Feb. 22   Litho.   Perf. 14
523	A127	20c Gorgonian coral, vert.	.55	.25
524	A127	45c Hard sponge	.85	.25
525	A127	60c Sea cow	1.00	.55
526	A127	75c Plume worm	1.10	.65

527	A127	$3 Coral-banded shrimp	3.25	1.75
		Nos. 523-527 (5)	6.75	3.45

Scouting Year — A133

20c, 45c, 60c, Various scouts. $2, Baden-Powell.

1982, July 12   Litho.   Perf. 13½
528	A133	20c multicolored	.60	.25
529	A133	45c multicolored	1.00	.40
530	A133	60c multicolored	1.40	.90
531	A133	$2 multicolored	2.25	2.00
a.		Souvenir sheet of 4, #528-531	7.50	7.50
		Nos. 528-531 (4)	5.25	3.55

Princess Diana, 21st Birthday — A134

20c, Lignum vitae. 45c, Couple in coach. 60c, Wedding portrait. 75c, Saxifraga longifolia. $2, Diana. $3, Viola gracilis major. $5, Honeymoon.

1982, Sept. 1   Perf. 14½
532	A134	20c multicolored	.40	.25
533	A134	45c multicolored	.60	.35
534	A134	60c multicolored	.75	.60
a.		Booklet pane of 3, #532-534	2.00	
535	A134	75c multicolored	1.25	1.50
536	A134	$2 multicolored	1.90	1.90
537	A134	$3 multicolored	2.10	3.50
a.		Booklet pane of 3, #535-537	7.50	
		Nos. 532-537 (6)	7.00	8.10

Souvenir Sheet
538	A134	$5 multicolored	3.25	3.25

Nos. 535, 537 in sheets of 5.

Nos. 532-538 Overprinted

1982, Sept. 13
539	A134	20c multicolored	.35	.25
540	A134	45c multicolored	.40	.40
541	A134	60c multicolored	.55	.55
a.		Booklet pane of 3, #539-541	2.00	
542	A134	75c multicolored	.90	1.50
543	A134	$2 multicolored	1.25	1.25
544	A134	$3 multicolored	1.50	2.00
a.		Booklet pane of 3, #542-544	7.00	
		Nos. 539-544 (6)	4.95	5.95

Souvenir Sheet
545	A134	$5 multicolored	3.25	3.25

Birth of Prince William of Wales, June 21.

Lizard Cuckoo Capturing Prey — A135

Designs: b, Searching for prey. c, Calling. d, Landing. e, Flying.

1982, Oct. 25
546		Strip of 5	10.00	10.00
a.-e.	A135	$1 any single	1.30	1.30

Christmas Type of 1981

20c, United Pentecostal Church. 45c, Disciples of Christ Church. 75c, Open Bible Church.

Perf. 13x13½
1982, Dec. 8   Wmk. 352
547	A132	20c multicolored	.75	.25
548	A132	45c multicolored	1.00	.35
549	A132	75c multicolored	2.00	2.50
		Nos. 547-549 (3)	3.75	3.10

Visit of Queen Elizabeth II — A136

1983, Feb. 14   Litho.   Perf. 14
550	A136	$2 Queen Elizabeth II	4.25	3.50
551	A136	$3 Arms	5.25	6.50

A136a

1983, Mar. 14   Litho.   Wmk. 352
552	A136a	20c Dancers	.25	.25
553	A136a	45c Bauxite mining	.40	.45
554	A136a	75c Map	.55	.55
555	A136a	$2 Arms, citizens	1.25	1.50
		Nos. 552-555 (4)	2.45	2.75

Commonwealth Day.

25th Anniv. of Intl. Maritime Org. A137

1983, Mar. 17   Litho.   Perf. 14
556	A137	15c Cargo ship	1.00	.30
557	A137	20c Cruise liner	1.75	.40
558	A137	45c Container vessel	2.50	.85
559	A137	$1 Intl. Seabed Headquarters	3.75	5.00
		Nos. 556-559 (4)	9.00	6.55

21st Anniv. of Independence A138

Prime Ministers Alexander Bustamante and Norman Washington Manley.

1983, July 25   Litho.   Perf. 14
560	A138	15c blue & multi	.25	.25
561	A138	20c lt green & multi	.25	.25
562	A138	45c yellow & multi	.30	.30
		Nos. 560-562 (3)	.80	.80

World Communications Year — A139

1983, Oct. 18   Wmk. 352   Perf. 14
563	A139	20c Ship-to-shore radio	.80	.25
564	A139	45c Postal services	1.40	.40
565	A139	75c Telephone commu-nication	1.60	2.50
566	A139	$1 TV satellite	2.00	3.00
		Nos. 563-566 (4)	5.80	6.15

Christmas 1983
A140

Paintings: 15c, Racing at Caymanas, by Sidney McLaren. 20c, Seated Figures, by Karl Parboosingh. 75c, The Petitioner, by Henry Daley, vert. $2, Banana Plantation, by John Dunkley, vert.

1983, Dec. 12   Litho.   Perf. 13½
567	A140	15c multicolored	.25	.25
568	A140	20c multicolored	.25	.50
569	A140	75c multicolored	.50	.60
570	A140	$2 multicolored	1.50	3.50
		Nos. 567-570 (4)	2.50	4.85

Alexander Bustamante (1884-1977), First Prime Minister — A141

1984, Feb. 24   Litho.   Perf. 14
571		20c Portrait	.90	.90
572		20c Blenheim (birthplace)	.90	.90
a.	A141	Pair, #571-572	2.50	3.50

Sea Planes A142

1984, June 11   Litho.   Perf. 14
573	A142	25c Gypsy Moth	2.00	.30
574	A142	55c Consolidated Commodore	2.25	.80
575	A142	$1.50 Sikorsky S-38	4.25	4.00
576	A142	$3 Sikorsky S-40	5.00	6.00
		Nos. 573-576 (4)	13.50	11.10

1984 Summer Olympics A143

1984, July 11
577	A143	25c Bicycling	2.00	.50
578	A143	55c Relay race	.90	.30
579	A143	$1.50 Running	1.90	4.50
580	A143	$3 Women's run-ning	2.40	4.50
a.		Souvenir sheet of 4, #577-580	7.00	7.00
		Nos. 577-580 (4)	7.20	9.80

Nos. 469, 474 Surcharged

1984, Aug. 7   Litho.   Perf. 13½
581	A122	5c on 6c #469	.45	.45
582	A123	10c on 12c #474	1.50	.60

Early Steam Engines — A144

25c, Enterprise, 1845. 55c, Tank Locomotive, 1880. $1.50, Kitson-Meyer Tank, 1904. $3, Superheater, 1916.

1984, Nov. 16   Litho.   Perf. 13½
583	A144	25c multicolored	1.50	.35
584	A144	55c multicolored	2.25	.75
585	A144	$1.50 multicolored	4.00	3.50
586	A144	$3 multicolored	5.00	5.50
		Nos. 583-586 (4)	12.75	10.10

See Nos. 608-611.

Christmas — A145

Local sculptures: 20c, Accompong Madonna, by Namba Roy. 25c, Head, by Alvin Marriott. 55c, Moon, by Edna Manley. $1.50, All Women are Five Women, by Mallica Reynolds.

1984, Dec. 6   Wmk. 352   Perf. 14
587	A145	20c multicolored	.35	.25
588	A145	25c multicolored	.40	.25
589	A145	55c multicolored	1.10	.50
590	A145	$2 multicolored	2.00	2.50
		Nos. 587-590 (4)	3.85	3.50

Jamaican Boas — A146

1984, Oct. 22   Litho.   Perf. 14½
591	A146	25c Head of boa	10.00	.75
592	A146	55c Boa over water	12.50	1.40
593	A146	70c Boa with young	15.00	4.50
594	A146	$1 Boa on branch	22.50	5.00
a.		Souv. sheet of 4, #591-594	12.00	12.00
		Nos. 591-594 (4)	60.00	11.65

Stamps in No. 594a do not have WWF emblem.

Brown Pelicans — A147

1985, Apr. 15   Wmk. 352   Perf. 13
595	A147	20c multicolored	1.10	.25
596	A147	55c multicolored	2.00	.45
597	A147	$2 multicolored	3.25	3.25
598	A147	$5 multicolored	4.50	5.00
a.		Souvenir sheet of 4, #595-598	11.00	11.00
		Nos. 595-598 (4)	10.85	8.95

Birth bicentenary of artist and naturalist John J. Audubon (1785-1851).

Queen Mother 85th Birthday
Common Design Type

25c, Holding photograph album, 1963. 55c, With Prince Charles, Windsor Castle, 1983.

$1.50, At Belfast University. $3, Holding Prince Henry.
$5, With limousine.

1985, June 7   Litho.   Perf. 14½x14
599	CD336	25c multicolored	.40	.25
600	CD336	55c multicolored	.65	.25
601	CD336	$1.50 multicolored	1.00	1.00
602	CD336	$3 multicolored	1.75	3.00
		Nos. 599-602 (4)	3.80	4.50

Souvenir Sheet
603	CD336	$5 multicolored	3.50	3.50

Maps of Americas and Jamaica, IYY and Jamboree Emblems A148

1985, July 30   Litho.   Perf. 14
604	A148	25c multicolored	1.00	.25
605	A148	55c multicolored	1.25	.35
606	A148	70c multicolored	1.75	1.50
607	A148	$4 multicolored	3.50	6.50
		Nos. 604-607 (4)	7.50	8.60

Intl. Youth Year and 5th Pan-American Scouting Jamboree.

Locomotives Type of 1984

1985, Sept. 30   Size: 39x25mm
608	A144	25c Baldwin	1.50	.30
609	A144	55c Rogers	2.00	.35
610	A144	$1.50 Projector	3.25	3.00
611	A144	$4 Diesel	4.25	5.75
		Nos. 608-611 (4)	11.00	9.40

The Old Settlement, by Ralph Campbell — A149

Christmas (Paintings by local artists): 55c, The Vendor, by Albert Huie, vert. 75c, Road Menders, by Gaston Tabois. $4, Woman, Must I Not Be About My Father's Business? by Carl Abrahams, vert.

1985, Dec. 9
612	A149	20c multicolored	.25	.25
613	A149	55c multicolored	.25	.25
614	A149	75c multicolored	.25	.25
615	A149	$4 multicolored	1.10	1.10
		Nos. 612-615 (4)	1.85	1.85

Birds — A150

25c, Chestnut-bellied cuckoo. 55c, Jamaican becard. $1.50, White-eyed thrush. $5, Rufous-tailed flycatcher.

1986, Feb. 10   Litho.   Perf. 14
616	A150	25c multicolored	.80	.25
617	A150	55c multicolored	1.00	.30
618	A150	$1.50 multicolored	1.50	1.50
619	A150	$5 multicolored	3.00	3.75
		Nos. 616-619 (4)	6.30	5.80

Queen Elizabeth II 60th Birthday
Common Design Type

Designs: 20c, With Princess Margaret, 1939. 25c, Leaving Liverpool Street Station for Sandringham with Princes Charles and Andrew, 1962. 70c, Visiting the Montego Bay war memorial, Jamaica, 1983. $3, State visit to Luxembourg, 1976. $5, Visiting Crown Agents' offices, 1983.

1986, Apr. 21   Perf. 14½
620	CD337	20c scar, blk & sil	.35	.25
621	CD337	25c ultra & multi	.35	.25
622	CD337	70c green & multi	.40	.30
623	CD337	$3 violet & multi	.75	.75
624	CD337	$5 rose vio & multi	1.10	1.50
		Nos. 620-624 (5)	2.95	3.05

A151

AMERIPEX '86: 25c, Bustamante Childrens Hospital. 55c, Vacation cities. $3, Norman Manley Law School. $5, Exports.

1986, May 19
625	A151	25c multicolored	.75	.25
626	A151	55c multicolored	2.00	.45
627	A151	$3 multicolored	1.25	1.25
628	A151	$5 multicolored	7.25	7.25
a.		Souvenir sheet of 4, #625-628	11.00	11.00
		Nos. 625-628 (4)	11.25	9.20

Royal Wedding Issue, 1986
Common Design Type

Designs: 20c, At the races. $5, Andrew addressing the press.

Perf. 14½x14
1986, July 23   Wmk. 352
629	CD338	20c multicolored	.25	.25
630	CD338	$5 multicolored	1.50	1.50

Boxing Champions A152

Champions: 45c, Richard "Shrimpy" Clarke, 1986 Commonwealth flyweight. 70c, Michael McCallum, 1984 WBA junior middleweight. $2, Trevor Berbick, 1986 WBC heavyweight. $4, Clarke, McCallum and Berbick.

1986, Oct. 27   Litho.   Perf. 14
631	A152	45c multicolored	.30	.25
632	A152	70c multicolored	.40	.30
633	A152	$2 multicolored	.95	1.25
634	A152	$4 multicolored	1.75	2.50
		Nos. 631-634 (4)	3.40	4.30

Flowers A153

20c, Heliconia wagneriana, vert. 25c, Heliconia psittacorum. 55c, Heliconia rostrata, vert. $5, Strelitzia reginae.

1986, Dec. 1   Perf. 14
635	A153	20c multicolored	.25	.25
636	A153	25c multicolored	.25	.25
637	A153	55c multicolored	.25	.25
638	A153	$5 multicolored	2.25	3.25
		Nos. 635-638 (4)	3.00	4.00

Christmas. See Nos. 675-678, 706-709.

Shells — A154

1987, Feb. 23   Litho.   Perf. 15
639	A154	35c Crown cone	.65	.25
640	A154	75c Measled cowrie	.80	.65
641	A154	$1 Trumpet triton	.90	.90
642	A154	$5 Rooster-tail conch	1.60	2.75
		Nos. 639-642 (4)	3.95	4.55

Prime
Ministers
A155

Natl. Coat of
Arms
A156

Designs: 1c-9c, 55c, Norman Washington Manley. 10c-50c, 60c-90c, Sir Alexander Bustamante.

1987-94   *Perf. 12½x13*
No inscription below design unless noted

643	A155	1c dull red	.25	.75
644	A155	2c rose pink	.25	.75
645	A155	3c light olive	.25	*.75*
646	A155	4c dull green	.25	*.75*
647	A155	5c slate blue	.45	*.75*
a.		Inscribed "1988"	.60	*.75*
648	A155	6c ultramarine	.30	*.75*
649	A155	7c dull magenta	.85	.75
650	A155	8c red lilac	.35	.25
651	A155	9c brown olive	.90	.25
652	A155	10c deep rose	.40	*.45*
a.		Inscribed "1993"	1.50	.75
b.		Inscribed "1994"	3.00	.75
653	A155	20c bright org	.80	.25
a.		Inscribed "1988"	.80	.25
b.		Inscribed "1989"	.80	.25
c.		Inscribed "1992"	.80	.25
d.		Inscribed "1993"	.80	.25
e.		Inscribed "1994"	.45	.30
654	A155	30c emerald	.70	.25
a.		Inscribed "1994"	1.50	1.50
655	A155	40c lt blue green	.80	.30
a.		Inscribed "1991"	1.00	.75
b.		Inscribed "1992"	1.00	*.75*
c.		Inscribed "1994"	.60	*.75*
656	A155	50c gray olive	.90	.40
a.		Inscribed "1991"	1.50	.75
b.		Inscribed "1992"	.70	*.75*
c.		Inscribed "1993"	.70	*.75*
d.		Inscribed "1994"	.70	*.75*
656A	A155	55c olive brown, inscr. "1994"	1.50	1.25
657	A155	60c light ultra	.45	.25
658	A155	70c pale violet	.45	.35
659	A155	80c violet	.85	.85
660	A155	90c light brown	1.25	.70
a.		Inscribed "1992"	2.25	.90
b.		Inscribed "1993"	1.00	1.50
661	A156	$1 dull brn & buff	.90	.45
a.		Inscribed "1991"	1.00	.50
b.		Inscribed "1992"	1.00	.50
c.		Inscribed "1993"	1.00	.50
d.		Inscribed "1997"	.90	.50
661A	A156	$1.10 dull brn & buff, inscr. "1994"	3.00	.65
662	A156	$2 orange	1.50	.90
a.		Inscribed "1997"	2.00	1.25
663	A156	$5 gray olive & greenish buff	1.50	1.25
a.		Inscribed "1997"	2.00	1.50
664	A156	$10 royal blue & pale blue	2.50	1.75
		Perf. 13x13½		
664A	A156	$25 vio & pale vio, inscr. "1991"	3.50	2.00
664B	A156	$50 lilac & pale lilac, inscr. "1991"	6.50	3.25
		Nos. 643-664B (26)	31.35	21.05

Issued: $25, $50 (dated "1991"), 10/9/91; 55c, $1.10 (dated "1994"), 10/10/94; others (undated), 5/18/87.
Reprints issued: No. 647a, 653a, 6/6/88; 653b, 1989; 645a, 656a, 2/12/91; 661a, 6/6/91; 661b, 1992; 653c, 655b, 656b, 660a, 5/92; 653d, 656c, 660b, 661c, 1993; 652a, 11/93; 654d, 655c, 656c, 1994; 652b, 654a, 10/10/94; 661d, 662a, 663a, 4/30/97.

Nos. 477-478
Surcharged

1986, Nov. 3   *Perf. 13½*
665	A123	5c on 50c multi	3.75	3.75
666	A122	10c on 65c multi	2.25	2.25

A157

Wmk. 352
1987, July 27   Litho.   *Perf. 14*
667	A157	55c Flag, sunset	1.75	.75
668	A157	70c Flag, horiz.	1.75	1.75

Natl. Independence, 25th anniv.

A158

1987, Aug. 17
669	25c Portrait	1.60	*1.60*
670	25c Statue	1.60	*1.60*
a.	A158 Pair, #669-670	4.25	*4.50*

Marcus Mosiah Garvey (1887-1940), natl. hero. No. 670a has a continuous design.

Salvation
Army in
Jamaica,
Cent.
A159

Designs: 25c, School for the Blind. 55c, Col. Mary Booth, Bramwell-Booth Memorial Hall. $3, "War Chariot," 1929. $5, Arrival of col. Abram Davey on the S.S. Alene, 1887.

1987, Oct. 8   *Perf. 13*
671	A159	25c multicolored	1.75	.40
672	A159	55c multicolored	1.75	.40
673	A159	$3 multicolored	5.25	5.25
674	A159	$5 multicolored	6.50	8.00
a.		Souvenir sheet of 4, #671-674	18.50	18.50
		Nos. 671-674 (4)	15.25	14.05

Flower Type of 1986

20c, Hibiscus hybrid. 25c, Hibiscus elatus. $4, Hibiscus cannabinus. $5, Hibiscus rosa sinensis.

1987, Nov. 30   Litho.   *Perf. 14½*
675	A153	20c multicolored	.25	.25
676	A153	25c multicolored	.25	.25
677	A153	$4 multicolored	3.00	2.75
678	A153	$5 multicolored	3.25	3.25
		Nos. 675-678 (4)	6.75	6.50

Christmas. Nos. 675-678 vert.

Birds — A160

Designs: No. 679, Chestnut-bellied cuckoo, black-billed parrot, Jamaican euphonia. No. 680, Jamaican white-eyed vireo, rufous-throated solitaire, yellow-crowned elaenia. No. 681, Snowy plover, little blue heron, great white heron. No. 682, Common stilt, snowy egret, black-crowned night heron.

1988, Jan. 22   Litho.   *Perf. 14*
679		45c multicolored	1.75	1.75
680		45c multicolored	1.75	1.75
a.	A160	Pair, #679-680	6.00	*7.00*
681		$5 multicolored	5.00	5.00
682		$5 multicolored	5.00	5.00
a.	A160	Pair, #681-682	14.00	*15.00*
		Nos. 679-682 (4)	13.50	13.50

Nos. 680a, 682a have continuous designs.

Marine
Mammals
A161

20c, Blue whales. 25c, Gervais's whales. 55c, Killer whales. $5, Common dolphins.

1988, Apr. 14   Litho.   *Perf. 14*
683	A161	20c multicolored	2.75	.85
684	A161	25c multicolored	2.75	.85
685	A161	55c multicolored	4.50	1.00
686	A161	$5 multicolored	6.75	*7.50*
		Nos. 683-686 (4)	16.75	10.20

Cricket
A162

Bat, wicket posts, ball, 18th cent. belt buckle and batsmen: 25c, Jackie Hendriks. 55c, George Headley. $2, Michael Holding. $3, R.K. Nunes. $4, Allan Rae.

1988, June 6   Litho.   *Perf. 14*
687	A162	25c multicolored	2.00	.50
688	A162	55c multicolored	2.00	.50
689	A162	$2 multicolored	4.00	4.00
690	A162	$3 multicolored	4.50	4.50
691	A162	$4 multicolored	5.25	5.25
		Nos. 687-691 (5)	17.75	14.75

Intl. Red Cross
and Red
Crescent
Organizations,
125th
Annivs. — A163

Anniversary emblem, Jamaica Red Cross emblem and: 55c, Ambulances. $5, Jean-Henri Dunant, 1828-1910, treating the wounded after the Battle of Solferino, 1859.

1988, Aug. 8   Litho.   *Perf. 14½*
692	A163	55c multicolored	.75	.40
693	A163	$5 multicolored	3.00	3.00

1988
Summer
Olympics,
Seoul
A164

1988, Aug. 24   Wmk. 352   *Perf. 14*
694	A164	25c Boxing	.50	.25
695	A164	45c Cycling	2.25	.75
696	A164	$4 Women's running	2.25	2.25
697	A164	$5 Hurdling	2.50	2.50
a.		Souvenir sheet of 4, #694-697	8.50	8.50
		Nos. 694-697 (4)	7.50	5.75

No. 697a sold for $9.90. For surcharges see Nos. B4-B7.

Natl.
Olympic
Bobsled
Team
A165

1988, Nov. 4   Litho.   *Perf. 14*
698	A165	25c Team members	.50	.50
699	A165	25c Two-man bobsled	.50	.50
a.		Pair, #698-699	2.75	*3.00*
700	A165	$5 Team members, diff.	2.25	2.25
701	A165	$5 Four-man bobsled	2.25	2.25
a.		Pair, #700-701	7.00	*8.00*
		Nos. 698-701 (4)	5.50	5.50

Nos. 699a, 701a have continuous designs.

Labor
Year — A166

**   *Perf. 14½x14***
1988, Nov. 24   Wmk. 352
702	A166	25c Medicine, fire fighting	1.75	.50
703	A166	55c Handicrafts	.60	.50
704	A166	$3 Garment industry	1.50	1.50
705	A166	$5 Fishing	2.00	2.00
		Nos. 702-705 (4)	5.85	4.50

Flower Type of 1986

25c, Euphorbia pulcherrima, vert. 55c, Spathodea campanulata. $3, Hylocereus triangularis, vert. $4, Broughtonia sanguinea.

1988, Dec. 15
706	A153	25c multicolored	.85	.25
707	A153	55c multicolored	.95	.25
708	A153	$3 multicolored	2.00	1.75
709	A153	$4 multicolored	2.50	2.00
		Nos. 706-709 (4)	6.30	4.25

Christmas.

Methodist Church in Jamaica,
Bicent. — A167

25c, Old York Castle School. 45c, Parade Chapel, Kingston, Rev. Thomas Coke. $5, Fr. Hugh Sherlock, St. John's Church.

1989, Jan. 19   *Perf. 13½*
710	A167	25c multicolored	.35	.25
711	A167	45c multicolored	.45	.25
712	A167	$5 multicolored	3.25	3.25
		Nos. 710-712 (3)	4.05	3.75

Indigenous
Moths — A168

25c, Syntomidopsis variegata. 55c, Himantoides undata-perkinsi. $3, Hypercompe nigriplaga. $5, Sthenognatha toddi.

**   Wmk. 352**
1989, Aug. 30   Litho.   *Perf. 14*
713	A168	25c multicolored	1.00	.25
714	A168	55c multicolored	1.50	.30
715	A168	$3 multicolored	2.50	2.50
716	A168	$5 multicolored	4.25	4.25
		Nos. 713-716 (4)	9.25	7.30

See Nos. 725-728, 752-755. For surcharges & overprints see Nos. 729-732, 756-759.

A169

Discovery of America, 500th Anniv. (in 1992): 25c, Arawak spear fisherman. 70c, Smoking tobacco. $5, Ferdinand and Isabella inspecting caravels. $10, Columbus studying chart.

1989, Dec. 22   *Perf. 13½*
717	A169	25c multicolored	.30	.25
718	A169	70c multicolored	.60	.40
719	A169	$5 multicolored	3.25	3.25
720	A169	$10 multicolored	6.50	7.50
a.		Souvenir sheet of 4, #717-720, perf. 12½	20.00	20.00
		Nos. 717-720 (4)	10.65	11.40

No. 720a exists imperf. Value $25.

A171

Wmk. 352
1990, June 28   **Litho.**   *Perf. 14*
721	A171	45c multicolored	1.75	.40
722	A171	55c multi, diff.	1.75	.40
723	A171	$5 multi, diff.	6.50	8.00
		Nos. 721-723 (3)	10.00	8.80

Girl Guides of Jamaica, 75th anniv.

Indigenous Moths Type of 1989

25c, Eunomia rubripunctata. 55c, Perigonia jamaicensis. $4, Uraga haemorrhoa. $5, Empyreuma pugione.

Wmk. 352
1990, Sept. 12   **Litho.**   *Perf. 14*
725	A168	25c multicolored	1.00	.50
726	A168	55c multicolored	1.50	.50
727	A168	$4 multicolored	3.50	3.50
728	A168	$5 multicolored	3.50	3.50
		Nos. 725-728 (4)	9.50	8.00

Nos. 725-728
Ovptd. in Black

1990, Sept. 12
729	A168	25c No. 725	1.00	.50
730	A168	55c No. 726	1.50	.50
731	A168	$4 No. 727	3.50	3.50
732	A168	$5 No. 728	3.50	3.50
		Nos. 729-732 (4)	9.50	8.00

Expo '90, International Garden and Greenery Exposition, Osaka, Japan.

Intl.
Literacy
Year
A172

Wmk. 352
1990, Oct. 10   **Litho.**   *Perf. 14*
733	A172	55c shown	1.00	.35
734	A172	$5 Mathematics class	5.75	6.25

Christmas — A173

Children's art — 20c, To the market. 25c, Untitled (houses). 55c, Jack and Jill. 70c, Untitled (market). $1.50, Lonely (beach). $5, Market woman, vert.

Perf. 13½x14
1990, Dec. 7   **Litho.**   **Wmk. 352**
735	A173	20c multicolored	.70	.25
736	A173	25c multicolored	.70	.25
737	A173	55c multicolored	.85	.25
738	A173	70c multicolored	1.10	.50
739	A173	$1.50 multicolored	2.00	2.00
740	A173	$5 multicolored	4.00	4.00
		Nos. 735-740 (6)	9.35	7.25

See Nos. 760-763.

Discovery of
America,
500th Anniv.
(in 1992)
A174

Maps of Columbus' voyages.

1990, Dec. 19   *Perf. 14*
741	A174	25c First, 1492	1.75	.55
742	A174	45c Second, 1493	2.25	.55
743	A174	$5 Third, 1498	5.75	5.75
744	A174	$10 Fourth, 1502	8.50	8.50
		Nos. 741-744 (4)	18.25	15.35

Souvenir Sheet
745		Sheet of 4	16.00	16.00
a.	A174	25c Cuba, Jamaica	1.00	1.00
b.	A174	45c Hispaniola, Puerto Rico	1.25	1.25
c.	A174	$5 Central America	4.00	4.00
d.	A174	$10 Venezuela	7.00	7.00

Souvenir sheet also exists imperf. Value, $25.
See Nos. 764-767.

Natl. Meteorological Service — A175

1991, May 20   **Litho.**   **Wmk. 352**
746	A175	50c multicolored	.75	.25
747	A175	$10 multicolored	8.00	8.00

11th World Meteorological Congress.

Intl. Council of Nurses Council of Natl. Representatives, Jamaica — A176

50c, Mary Seacole. $1.10, Mary Seacole House. $8, Hospital at Scutari.

Wmk. 352
1991, June 24   **Litho.**   *Perf. 13½*
748	A176	50c multicolored	1.25	.35
749	A176	$1.10 multicolored	2.25	2.25

Souvenir Sheet
750	A176	$8 multicolored	4.50	4.50

Cyclura Collei
(Jamaican
Iguana) — A177

Designs: a. Head pointed to UR. b, Facing right. c, Climbing rock. d, Facing left. e, Head pointed to UL.

Wmk. 352
1991, July 29   **Litho.**   *Perf. 13*
751	A177	$1.10 Strip of 5, #a.-e.	5.25	5.25

Natural History Soc. of Jamaica, 50th anniv.

Moths Type of 1989

50c, Urania sloanus. $1.10, Phoenicoprocta jamaicensis. $1.40, Horama grotei. $8, Amplypterus gannascus.

1991, Aug. 12   *Perf. 14*
752	A168	50c multicolored	1.10	.25
753	A168	$1.10 multicolored	1.25	.70
754	A168	$1.40 multicolored	1.50	1.00
755	A168	$8 multicolored	4.50	4.50
		Nos. 752-755 (4)	8.35	6.45

Nos. 752-755
Overprinted

1991, Sept. 23
756	A168	50c on No. 752	1.50	.25
757	A168	$1.10 on No. 753	1.75	.75
758	A168	$1.40 on No. 754	2.00	1.25
759	A168	$8 on No. 755	5.50	7.25
		Nos. 756-759 (4)	10.75	9.50

Children's Christmas Art Type

Children's drawings.

1991, Nov. 27   *Perf. 14x15*
760	A173	50c Doctor bird	.80	.25
761	A173	$1.10 Road scene	1.25	.30
762	A173	$5 House, people	4.00	4.00
763	A173	$10 Cows grazing	7.00	7.00
		Nos. 760-763 (4)	13.05	11.55

Christmas.

Discovery of America Type of 1990

Designs: 50c, Explorers did not land at Santa Gloria because of hostile Indians. $1.10, Fierce dog used to subdue the Indians. $1.40, Indians brought gifts of fruit. $25, Columbus describes Jamaica with crumpled paper.

1991, Dec. 16   *Perf. 13½x14*
764	A174	50c multicolored	.75	.25
765	A174	$1.10 multicolored	1.00	.50
766	A174	$1.40 multicolored	1.00	.50
767	A174	$25 multicolored	8.25	8.25
a.		Souvenir sheet of 4, #764-767	11.50	11.50
		Nos. 764-767 (4)	11.00	9.50

Souvenir sheet also exists imperf. Same value as perf.

First Provincial
Grand Master of
English
Freemasonry in
Jamaica, 250th
Anniv. — A178

Masonic symbols: 50c, Square and compass. $1.10, Stained glass window. $1.40, Square and compass on Bible. $25, Seeing eye.

1992, May 1   *Perf. 13½*
768	A178	50c multicolored	1.25	.40
769	A178	$1.10 multicolored	1.50	.50
770	A178	$1.40 multicolored	1.50	.50
771	A178	$25 multicolored	11.00	11.00
a.		Souvenir sheet of 4, #768-771	20.00	20.00
		Nos. 768-771 (4)	15.25	12.40

Destruction of Port Royal by
Earthquake, 300th Anniv. — A179

Scenes of destruction: 50c, Ship in harbor. $1.10, Homes, church. $1.40, Homes toppling.

$5, Port Royal from contemporary broadsheet. $25, Fissure in street.

1992, June 7   *Perf. 14x13½*
772	A179	50c multicolored	.75	.45
773	A179	$1.10 multicolored	1.00	.55
774	A179	$1.40 multicolored	1.00	.55
775	A179	$25 multicolored	9.00	9.00
		Nos. 772-775 (4)	11.75	10.55

Souvenir Sheet
Perf. 13x12
776	A179	$5 multicolored	7.00	7.00

No. 776 inscribed on reverse.

Independence, 30th Anniv. — A180

1992, Aug. 6   *Perf. 13½*
777	A180	50c black & multi	.35	.25
778	A180	$1.10 green & multi	.45	.30
779	A180	$25 yellow & multi	4.00	4.00
		Nos. 777-779 (3)	4.80	4.55

Credit Union Movement in Jamaica,
50th Anniv. — A181

1992, Aug. 24   *Perf. 14x15*
780	A181	50c Emblem	1.25	.60
781	A181	$1.40 Emblem, O'Hare Hall	2.50	2.50

Pottery — A182

Designs: 50c, "Rainbow" vase, by Cecil Baugh O.D. $1.10, "Yabba Pot," by Louisa Jones (MaLou) O.D. $1.40, "Sculptured Vase," by Gene Pearson. $25, "Lidded Form," by Norma Rodney Harrack.

1993, Apr. 26   *Perf. 13½*
782	A182	50c multicolored	.30	.25
783	A182	$1.10 multicolored	.50	.25
784	A182	$1.40 multicolored	.50	.25
785	A182	$25 multicolored	4.75	4.75
		Nos. 782-785 (4)	6.05	5.50

Girls'
Brigade,
Cent.
A183

1993, Aug. 9   *Perf. 14x13½*
786	A183	50c Parade	1.25	.75
787	A183	$1.10 Brigade members	1.50	1.25

Jamaica Combined Cadet Force, 50th
Anniv. — A184

Designs: 50c, Tank, cadet, vert. $1.10, Airplane, female cadet. $1.40, Ships, female cadet, vert. $3, Cap badge, cadet.

1993, Nov. 8   **Perf. 14**
788	A184	50c	multicolored	.55	.45
789	A184	$1.10	multicolored	.85	.45
790	A184	$1.40	multicolored	.85	.45
791	A184	$3	multicolored	1.00	1.50
		Nos. 788-791 (4)		3.25	2.65

Golf Courses A185

50c, $1.10, Constant Spring. $1.40, $2, Half Moon. $3, $10, Jamaica Jamaica. $25, Tryall, vert.

1993-94   **Litho.**   **Wmk. 352**   **Perf. 14**
792	A185	50c	yellow & multi	.45	.25
793	A185	$1.10	blue & multi	.50	.25
794	A185	$1.40	brn org & multi	.70	.25
795	A185	$2	lilac & multi	1.00	1.00
796	A185	$3	dark blue & multi	1.10	1.10
797	A185	$10	tan & multi	2.75	2.75
		Nos. 792-797 (6)		6.50	5.60

Souvenir Sheets
798	A185	$25	green & multi	7.00	7.00
799	A185	$25	#798 inscribed with Hong Kong '94 emblem.	7.00	7.00

Issued: Nos. 792-797, 12/21/93; No. 798, 12/16/93; No. 799, 2/18/94.

A186

1994, Jan. 12   **Perf. 14x15**
800	A186	$25	Portrait	2.50	2.50
801	A186	$50	Portrait, diff.	3.00	3.00
a.		Pair, #800-801		8.50	10.00

Norman Washington Manley, birth cent.

A187

Royal Visit: $1.10, Jamaican, United Kingdom flags. $1.40, Royal yacht Britannia. $25, Queen Elizabeth II. $50, Prince Philip, Queen.

1994, Mar. 1   **Perf. 14**
802	A187	$1.10	multicolored	.75	.25
803	A187	$1.40	multicolored	1.60	.40
804	A187	$25	multicolored	3.25	3.25
805	A187	$50	multicolored	5.25	6.50
		Nos. 802-805 (4)		10.85	10.40

Air Jamaica, 25th Anniv. — A188

Wmk. 352
1994, Apr. 26   **Litho.**   **Perf. 14**
806	A188	50c	Douglas DC9	.55	.25
807	A188	$1.10	Douglas DC8	.60	.35
808	A188	$5	Boeing 727	1.10	1.10
809	A188	$50	Airbus A300	4.00	4.00
		Nos. 806-809 (4)		6.25	5.70

Giant Swallowtail A189

Various views of the butterfly.

Perf. 14x13½
1994, Aug. 18   **Litho.**   **Wmk. 352**
810	A189	50c	multicolored	.50	.30
811	A189	$1.10	multicolored	.50	.30
812	A189	$10	multicolored	2.00	2.00
813	A189	$25	multicolored	3.75	3.75
		Nos. 810-813 (4)		6.75	6.35

Souvenir Sheet
814	189	$50	multicolored	10.00	10.00

A190

Tourism A191

Designs: 50c, Royal Botanical Gardens, by Sidney McClaren. $1.10, Blue Mountains, coffee beans, leaves. $5, Woman in hammock, waterfalls.
Tourist poster: No. 818a, Flowers, birds (c). b, Diver (d). c, Vegetation, coastline (a, d). d, Guide, tourists on raft.

Wmk. 352
1994, Sept. 7   **Litho.**   **Perf. 14**
815	A190	50c	multicolored	.75	.25
816	A190	$1.10	multicolored	1.10	.40
817	A190	$5	multicolored	3.25	3.25
		Nos. 815-817 (3)		5.10	3.90

Souvenir Sheet
818	A191	$25	Sheet of 4, #a.-d.	8.50	8.50

Caribbean Tourism Conf. (No. 818).

Red Poll Cattle A192

1994, Nov. 16   **Perf. 14x13½**
819	A192	50c	Calf	.25	.25
820	A192	$1.10	Heifer	.25	.25
821	A192	$25	Cow	1.50	1.50
822	A192	$50	Bull	3.75	3.75
		Nos. 819-822 (4)		5.75	5.75

Christmas — A193

Paintings by Children: 50c, Clean-up crew. 90c, Hospital Room. $1.10, House. $50, Meadow.

1994, Dec. 1   **Perf. 14x14½**
823	A193	50c	multicolored	.25	.25
824	A193	90c	multicolored	.25	.25
825	A193	$1.10	multicolored	.25	.25
826	A193	$50	multicolored	3.75	3.75
		Nos. 823-826 (4)		4.50	4.50

Birds — A194

50c, Ring-tailed pigeon. 90c, Yellow-billed parrot. $1.10, Black-billed parrot. No. 830, Brown owl.
No. 831, Streamertail.

Wmk. 384
1995, Apr. 24   **Litho.**   **Perf. 14**
827	A194	50c	multicolored	.70	.35
828	A194	90c	multicolored	.80	.35
829	A194	$1.10	multicolored	.80	.35
830	A194	$50	multicolored	5.50	7.00
		Nos. 827-830 (4)		7.80	8.05

Souvenir Sheet
831	A194	$50	multicolored	8.00	8.00
a.		Ovptd. in sheet margin		6.75	6.75

No. 831 is a continuous design.
No. 831a ovptd. with Singapore '95 emblem. Issued: 9/1/95.

Caribbean Development Bank, 25th Anniv. — A195

Anniversary emblem and: 50c, $1, Jamaican flag, graph, vert. $1.10, Industries, agriculture. $50, Bank notes, coins.

Wmk. 352
1995, May 11   **Litho.**   **Perf. 13½**
832	A195	50c	green & multi	.25	.25
833	A195	$1	black & multi	.25	.25
834	A195	$1.10	multicolored	.25	.25
835	A195	$50	multicolored	4.00	4.00
		Nos. 832-835 (4)		4.75	4.75

Bob Marley (1945-81), Reggae Musician — A196

Marley performing songs: 50c, Songs of Freedom, by Adrian Boot. $1.10, Fire, by Neville Garrick. $1.40, Time Will Tell, by Peter Murphy. $3, Natural Mystic, by Boot. $10, Live at Lyceum, by Boot.
$100, Legend, by Boot.

Wmk. 352
1995, July 31   **Litho.**   **Perf. 14**
836	A196	50c	multicolored	.40	.25
837	A196	$1.10	multicolored	.60	.25
838	A196	$1.40	multicolored	.65	.35
839	A196	$3	multicolored	1.00	1.00
840	A196	$10	multicolored	1.90	1.90
		Nos. 836-840 (5)		4.55	3.75

Souvenir Sheet
841	A196	$100	multicolored	10.00	10.00

Souvenir Sheet

Queen Mother, 95th Birthday — A197

1995, Aug. 4   **Perf. 14x13½**
842	A197	$75	multicolored	6.00	6.00

Order of the Caribbean Community — A198

Designs: 50c, Michael Manley, former prime minister, Jamaica. $1.10, Sir Alister McIntyre, Vice Chancellor, UWI, Jamaica. $1.40, P. Telford Georges, former Chief Justice, Bahamas. $50, Dame Nita Barrow, Governor General, Barbados.

1995, Aug. 23   **Perf. 14x14½**
843	A198	50c	multicolored	.25	.25
844	A198	$1.10	multicolored	.35	.25
845	A198	$1.40	multicolored	.35	.25
846	A198	$50	multicolored	4.50	4.50
		Nos. 843-846 (4)		5.45	5.25

UN, 50th Anniv.
Common Design Type

Designs: 50c, Signals Land Rover. $1.10, Antonov AN-32. $3, Bedford Articulated Tanker. $5, Fairchild DC-119 Flying Boxcar. $50, Observation vehicles.

Wmk. 352
1995, Oct. 24   **Litho.**   **Perf. 14**
847	CD353	50c	multicolored	.40	.25
848	CD353	$1.10	multicolored	.70	.30
849	CD353	$3	multicolored	.90	.90
850	CD353	$5	multicolored	1.00	1.00
		Nos. 847-850 (4)		3.00	2.45

Souvenir Sheet
851	CD353	$50	multicolored	3.50	3.50

No. 851 has continuous design.

Arrival of East Indians in Jamaica, 150th Anniv. A199

Wmk. 352
1996, May 22   **Litho.**   **Perf. 14**
852	A199	$2.50	Coming ashore	.25	.25
853	A199	$10	Musicians, dancers	1.10	1.10

UNICEF, 50th Anniv. — A200

1996, Sept. 2   **Perf. 14½x14**
854 A200 $2.50 multicolored   .75 .75
855 A200 $8 multicolored   1.40 1.40
856 A200 $10 multicolored   1.50 1.50
    Nos. 854-856 (3)   3.65 3.65

Jamaican Hutia (Indian Coney) A201

$2.50, Two in den. $10, One on ledge. $12.50, Mother, young. $25, One up close.

1996, Sept. 23   **Perf. 13½x14**
857 A201 $2.50 multicolored   .30 .25
858 A201 $10 multicolored   .75 .75
859 A201 $12.50 multicolored   1.00 1.00
860 A201 $25 multicolored   2.00 *3.00*
    Nos. 857-860 (4)   4.05 5.00

World Wildlife Fund.

Kingston Parish Church of St. Thomas the Apostle, 300th Anniv. A202

$2, High altar. $8, Exterior view. $12.50, Carving, "The Angel," by Edna Manley, vert. $60, Exterior view at sunset.

Unwmk.
1997, Feb. 7   **Litho.**   **Perf. 14**
861 A202 $2 multicolored   .60 .25
862 A202 $8 multicolored   1.25 1.25
863 A202 $12.50 multicolored   1.75 1.75
    Nos. 861-863 (3)   3.60 3.25

Souvenir Sheet
864 A202 $60 multicolored   4.50 4.50

No. 864 contains one 42x50mm stamp.

Chernobyl's Children — A203

Perf. 13½x14
1997, Apr. 7   **Litho.**   **Unwmk.**
865 A203 $55 multicolored   4.50 4.50

Caribbean Integration, 50th Anniv. — A203a

$2.50, Map of Caribbean. $8, $10, View of coastline.

Wmk. 352
1997, June 30   **Litho.**   **Perf. 14**
865A A203a $2.50 multi   0.50 0.50
865B A203a $8 multi   9.50 4.50
865C A203a $10 multi   11.00 4.50
    Nos. 865A-865C (3)   29.00 17.50

Orchids A204

$1, Coelia triptera. $2, Oncidium pulchellum. $2.50, Oncidium triquetrum. $3, Broughtonia negrilensis. $5, Encyclia frangrans.

Wmk. 352
1997, Oct. 6   **Litho.**   **Perf. 14**
866 A204 $1 multi, vert.   .30 .25
867 A204 $2 multi   .35 .25
868 A204 $2.50 multi, vert.   .40 .25
869 A204 $3 multi, vert.   .45 .30
870 A204 $5 multi   .50 .40
    Nos. 866-870 (5)   2.00 1.45

See Nos. 873-877.

Diana, Princess of Wales (1961-97) — A205

Unwmk.
1998, Feb. 24   **Litho.**   **Perf. 14**
871 A205 $20 Portrait   1.50 1.50

Souvenir Sheet
872 A205 $80 With Mother Teresa   8.00 8.00

No. 871 was issued in sheets of 6. No. 872 contains one 42x56mm stamp.

Orchid Type of 1997

Designs: $4.50, Oncidium gauntlettii. $8, Broughtonia sanguinea. $12, Phaius tankervilleae, vert. $25, Cochleanthes flabelliformis. $50, Broughtonia sanguinea (3 varieties).

Wmk. 352
1997, Dec. 1   **Litho.**   **Perf. 14**
873 A204 $4.50 multicolored   .70 .55
874 A204 $8 multicolored   .90 .85
875 A204 $12 multicolored   1.10 1.00
876 A204 $25 multicolored   2.25 2.25
    a. Inscribed "1999"   2.50 2.50
877 A204 $50 multicolored   1.75 1.75
    Nos. 873-877 (5)   6.70 6.40

CARICOM, 25th Anniv. — A206

Perf. 13½
1998, Sept. 17   **Litho.**   **Unwmk.**
878 A206 $30 multicolored   3.75 3.75

University of the West Indies, Mona, 50th Anniv. A207

$8, Chapel. $10, Philip Sherlock Centre for the Creative Arts. $50, University arms.

1998, July 31   **Wmk. 352**
879 A207 $8 multi   .55 .50
880 A207 $10 multi   .65 .60
881 A207 $50 multi, vert.   2.75 2.75
    Nos. 879-881 (3)   3.95 3.85

1998 World Cup Soccer Championships, France, Jamaica's Debut in Tournament — A208

Wmk. 373
1998, Sept. 28   **Litho.**   **Perf. 13½**
882 A208 $10 Player, vert.   .65 .55
883 A208 $25 Team picture   1.60 1.60
884 A208 $100 Team picture, diff.   5.50 *6.00*
    Nos. 882-884 (3)   7.75 8.15

Intl. Year of the Ocean A209

Designs: $10, Underwater scene. $30, Fishermen, Negril. $50, Long spiny black urchin. $100, Design elements from Nos. 885-887, vert.

Wmk. 352
1998, Dec. 23   **Litho.**   **Perf. 14**
885 A209 $10 multicolored   1.75 .60
886 A209 $30 multicolored   4.00 4.00
887 A209 $50 multicolored   5.50 5.50

Size: 28x42mm
888 A209 $100 multicolored   11.00 *11.00*
    Nos. 885-888 (4)   22.25 21.10

Christmas.

1st Manned Moon Landing, 30th Anniv.

Common Design Type

Designs: $7, Michael Collins. $10, Service module reverses to dock with lunar module. $25, Aldrin walks on lunar surface. $30, Command module back in earth orbit.
$100, Looking at earth from moon.

Perf. 14x13¾
1999, July 20   **Wmk. 352**
889 CD357 $7 multicolored   .45 .35
890 CD357 $10 multicolored   .60 .50
891 CD357 $25 multicolored   1.40 1.40
892 CD357 $30 multicolored   1.75 1.75
    Nos. 889-892 (4)   4.20 4.00

Souvenir Sheet
Perf. 14
893 CD357 $100 multicolored   6.00 6.00

No. 893 contains one 40mm circular stamp.

Athletes A210

Designs: $5, Polo player Lesley Ann Masterton Fong-Yee. $10, Men's cricketers Collie Smith, Lawrence Rowe and Alfred Valentine. $20, Women's cricketer Vivalyn Latty-Scott, vert. $25, Soccer player Lindy Delapenha, vert. $30, Netball player Joy Grant-Charles, vert. $50, Boxers Percy Hayles, Gerald Gray and Bunny Grant.
$100, Delapenha and Grant-Charles.

Perf. 13¼x13¾, 13¾x13¼
1999, Aug. 3   **Litho.**   **Wmk. 352**
894 A210 $5 multicolored   .80 .35
895 A210 $10 multicolored   1.40 1.40
896 A210 $20 multicolored   1.60 1.60
897 A210 $25 multicolored   1.75 1.75
898 A210 $30 multicolored   2.00 2.00
899 A210 $50 multicolored   2.50 2.50
    Nos. 894-899 (6)   10.05 9.60

Souvenir Sheet
900 A210 $100 multicolored   7.50 7.50

No. 900 contains one 52x38mm stamp.

UPU, 125th Anniv. A211

Designs: $7, Mail ship "Spey." $10, Mail ship "Jamaica Planter." $25, Lockheed Constellation. $30, Airbus A-310.

Air Jamaica, 30th Anniv. — A212

Wmk. 352
1999, Oct. 8   **Litho.**   **Perf. 14**
901 A211 $7 multicolored   1.25 .40
902 A211 $10 multicolored   1.50 .60
903 A211 $25 multicolored   2.50 2.50
904 A211 $30 multicolored   2.75 2.75
    Nos. 901-904 (4)   8.00 6.25

Wmk. 352
1999, Nov. 1   **Litho.**   **Perf. 14**
905 A212 $10 A-310   1.00 .45
906 A212 $25 A-320   1.60 1.60
907 A212 $30 A-340   2.00 *2.50*
    Nos. 905-907 (3)   4.60 4.55

Dogs — A213

1999, Nov. 25   **Perf. 14¼**
908 A213 $7 Shih tzu   1.50 .60
909 A213 $10 German shepherd   2.00 .80
910 A213 $30 Doberman pinscher   3.50 3.50
    Nos. 908-910 (3)   7.00 4.90

Parks A214

Designs: $7, Nelson Mandela Park. $10, St. William Grant Park. $25, Seaview Park. $30, Holruth Park.

1999, Dec. 15   **Perf. 14**
911 A214 $7 multi   .50 .40
912 A214 $10 multi   .65 .45
913 A214 $25 multi   1.25 1.25
914 A214 $30 multi   1.50 1.50
    Nos. 911-914 (4)   3.90 3.60

Edna Manley (1900-87), Sculptor A215

Designs: $10, The Prophet, 1935. $25, Horse of the Morning, 1943. $30, The Angel, 1970. $100, Portrait of Manley.

2000, Mar. 1   **Litho.**   **Perf. 13¾**
915 A215 $10 multi   .70 .70
916 A215 $25 multi   1.60 1.60
917 A215 $30 multi   1.90 1.90
918 A215 $100 multi   5.25 5.25
    a. Souvenir sheet, #915-918   9.50 9.50
    Nos. 915-918 (4)   9.45 9.45

Lennox Lewis, Heavyweight Boxing Champion of the World — A216

a, $10, With belt & Empire State Building. b, $10, Holding up arm. c, $10, Holding up belt. d, $25, In ring with opponent. e, $25, Close-up. f, $25, In ring with referee. g, $30, Holding up belt, diff. h, $30, Holding 4 belts. i, $30, Holding belts in front of buildings.

2000, Mar. 24   Litho.   *Perf. 14*
919   A216   Sheet of 9, #a.-i.   10.00   10.00

Ferrari Automobiles — A217

Unwmk.
2000, May 26   Litho.   *Perf. 14*
920   A217 $10   1947 125S   .90   .90
921   A217 $10   1950 375F1   .90   .90
922   A217 $10   1966 312F1   .90   .90
923   A217 $25   1965 Dino 166P   1.75   1.75
924   A217 $25   1971 312P   1.75   1.75
925   A217 $25   1990 F190   1.75   1.75
     Nos. 920-925 (6)   7.95   7.95

Queen Mother, 100th Birthday — A218

Various photos.

2000, Aug. 4   Wmk. 352
926   A218 $10 multi   .75   .55
927   A218 $25 multi   1.25   1.25
928   A218 $30 multi   1.75   1.75
929   A218 $50 multi   3.75   3.75
     Nos. 926-929 (4)   7.50   7.30

2000 Summer Olympics, Sydney — A219

Jamaican flag and various views of sculpture, "The Runner," by Alvin Marriott. Denominations, $10, $25, $30, vert., $50, vert.

Wmk. 352
2000, Sept. 1   Litho.   *Perf. 14*
930-933   A219   Set of 4   7.50   7.50

Trees — A220

Designs: $10, Bull thatch palm. $25, Blue mahoe. $30, Silk cotton. $50, Yellow pout.

2000, Oct. 6
934-937   A220   Set of 4   8.75   8.75
Souvenir Sheet
938   A220 $100 Lignum vitae, horiz.   9.00   9.00

Christmas — A221

Designs: $10, Madonna and Child, by Osmond Watson, vert. $20, Boy in the Temple, by Carl Abrahams. $25, Ascension, by Abrahams, vert. $30, Jah Lives, by Watson.

Wmk. 352
2000, Dec. 6   Litho.   *Perf. 13¾*
939-942   A221   Set of 4   5.00   5.00

Commonwealth Day, 25th Anniv. — A222

Wmk. 352
2001, Mar. 12   Litho.   *Perf. 12½*
943   A222 $30 multi   2.00   2.00

Father Andrew Duffus Mowatt, Founder of Jamaica Burial Scheme Society — A223

Wmk. 352
2001, Oct. 12   Litho.   *Perf. 13¼*
944   A223 $15 multi   1.50   1.50

Lithographs of Daguerrotypes by Adolphe Duperly (1801-64) — A224

Designs: $15, The Market, Falmouth. $40, Ferry Inn, Spanish Town Road. $45, Coke Chapel. $60, King Street, Kingston.

2001, Nov. 14   *Perf. 13*
945-948   A224   Set of 4   10.50   10.50
   a.   Souvenir sheet, #945-948   10.00   10.00

Christmas — A225

Poinsettias with background colors of: $15, Light blue. $30, Pink. $40, Pale orange.

2001, Dec. 10   *Perf. 13¼*
949-951   A225   Set of 3   7.00   7.00

Reign Of Queen Elizabeth II, 50th Anniv. Issue
Common Design Type

Designs: Nos. 952, 956a, $15, Princess Elizabeth. Nos. 953, 956b, $40, Wearing striped dress. Nos. 954, 956c, $45, In 1953. Nos. 955, 956d, $60, In 1995. No. 956e, $30, 1955 portrait by Annigoni (38x50mm).

Perf. 14¼x14½, 13¾ (#956e)
2002, Feb. 6   Litho.   Wmk. 373
With Gold Frames
952   CD360 $15 multicolored   .75   .75
953   CD360 $40 multicolored   2.25   2.25
954   CD360 $45 multicolored   2.50   2.50
955   CD360 $60 multicolored   3.50   3.50
     Nos. 952-955 (4)   9.00   9.00
Souvenir Sheet
Without Gold Frames
956   CD360   Sheet of 5, #a-e   9.25   9.25

Visit of Queen Elizabeth II and Prince Philip, Feb. 18-20 — A226

Designs: $15, Queen and Prince in 1983, flag of the Royal Standard. $45, Queen in 1983, Jamaican arms.

Perf. 13¼x13¾
2002, Feb. 18   Litho.   Wmk. 352
957-958   A226   Set of 2   6.50   6.50

Sir Philip Sherlock (1902-2000), Educator — A227

2002, Mar. 11   *Perf. 13¾*
959   A227 $40 multi   2.00   2.00

Pan-American Health Organization, Cent. — A228

Wmk. 352
2002, Dec. 2   Litho.   *Perf. 13¾*
960   A228 $40 multi   2.25   2.25

Christmas — A229

Art: $15, Masquerade, by Osmond Watson, vert. $40, John Canoe in Guanaboa Vale, by Gaston Tabois. $45, Mother and Child, sculpture, by Kapo, vert. $60, Hills of Papine, sculpture by Edna Manley.

2002, Dec. 6
961-964   A229   Set of 4   7.75   7.75

Natl. Dance Theater Company, 40th Anniv. — A230

2002, Dec. 27   *Perf. 14*
965   A230 $15 multi   1.75   1.75

Independence, 40th Anniv. — A231

Flag and: $15, Natl. Dance Theater Company performers. $40, Sir Alexander Bustamante, Michael Manley. $60, Factory workers.

2002, Dec. 27
966-968   A231   Set of 3   8.50   8.50

Kingston, Bicent. — A232

Historical views of Kingston and panel colors of: a, Brown. b, Olive green. c, Indigo.

2002, Dec. 31   *Perf. 13¾*
969   A232   Horiz. strip of 3   4.00   4.00
   a.-c. $15 Any single   1.00   1.00

Coronation of Queen Elizabeth II, 50th Anniv.
Common Design Type

Designs: Nos. 970, $15, 972b, $100, Queen in chair awaiting crown. Nos. 971, $45, 972a, $50, Queen and Prince Philip in carriage.

Perf. 14¼x14½
2003, June 2   Litho.   Wmk. 352
Vignettes Framed, Red Background
970   CD363 $15 multicolored   1.00   1.00
971   CD363 $45 multicolored   3.50   3.50
Souvenir Sheet
Vignettes Without Frame, Purple Panel
972   CD363   Sheet of 2, #a-b   7.25   7.25

Caribbean Community (CARICOM), 30th Anniv. — A233

Wmk. 352

2003, July 4		**Litho.**		***Perf. 14***
973	A233	$40 multi	3.50	3.50

Bird Life International — A234

Designs: $15, Jamaican stripe-headed tanager, vert. $40, Crested quail dove. $45, Jamaican tody. $60, Blue Mountain vireo.
No. 978 — Jamaican blackbird: a, With beak open (35x30mm). b, Chicks in nest (35x30mm). c, In palm fronds, vert. (30x35mm). d, With beak open, vert. (30x35mm) e, With insect in beak (35x30mm).

2003, Sept. 19				***Perf. 14***
974-977	A234	Set of 4	10.00	10.00

Souvenir Sheet

Perf. 14¼x14½, 14½x14¼

978	A234	$30 Sheet of 5, #a-e	10.00	10.00

Maritime Heritage — A235

No. 979: a, Map, sailing ships. b, Sailing ships, ship with passengers. c, The Sugar Refiner and barges.

2003, Sept. 25				***Perf 14x14¾***
979	A235	Horiz. strip of 3	9.00	9.00
a.-c.		$40 Any single	2.50	2.50

Christmas — A236

Flowers and: $15, Adoration of the Magi. $30, Christ child. $60, Holy Family.

2003, Dec.				***Perf. 13¼***
980-982	A236	Set of 3	7.25	7.25

Haitian Revolution, Bicent. — A237

Wmk. 352

2004, Jan. 30		**Litho.**		***Perf. 13½***
983	A237	$40 multi	3.50	3.50

Caribbean Bird Festival A238

No. 984: a, Yellow-billed amazon. b, Jamaican oriole. c, Orangequit. d, Yellow-shouldered grassquit. e, Jamaican woodpecker. f, Red-

billed streamertail. g, Jamaican mango. h, White-eyed thrush. i, Jamaican lizard cuckoo. j, Arrow-headed warbler.

Wmk. 352

2004, May 17		**Litho.**		***Perf. 13¾***
984		Block of 10	11.00	11.00
a.-j.	A238	$10 Any single	.90	.85

Miniature Sheet

World Environment Day — A239

No. 985: a, $10, Water lilies. b, $10, Hawksbill turtle. c, $10, Tube sponge. d, $10, Boater on Parattee Pond. e, $40, Vase sponge, star coral. f, $40, Sea fan, black and white crinoid. g, $40, Glassy sweepers. h, $40, Giant sea anemone.

Unwmk.

2004, June 4		**Litho.**		***Perf. 14***
985	A239	Sheet of 8, #a-h	9.50	9.50

2004 Summer Olympics, Athens — A240

Jamaican athletes: $30, Women's hurdles. $60, Running. $70, Swimming. $90, Rifle shooting, women's badminton.

Wmk. 352

2004, Aug. 10		**Litho.**		***Perf. 14***
986-989	A240	Set of 4	11.00	11.00

FIFA (Fédération Internationale de Football Association), Cent. — A241

FIFA emblem and various soccer players: $10, $30, $45, $50.

Wmk. 352

2004, Oct. 13		**Litho.**		***Perf. 14***
990-993	A241	Set of 4	7.75	7.75

Jamaica Hotels Law, Cent. A242

Designs: No. 994, Ralph Lauren, Doctors Cave Beach, Montego Bay.
No. 995 — Ambassador John Pringle, Round Hill Hotel and: a, Pink panel. b, Lilac panel.
No. 996 — Tower Isle Hotel and: a, Abe Issa, yellow green panels. b, John Issa, green panels. c, Abe Issa, red panels. d, John Issa, yellow green panels. e, Abe Issa, green panels. f, John Issa, red panels.

2004	**Unwmk.**		**Perf. 13¼x13½**	
994	A242	$40 multi	2.50	2.50
995	A242	$40 Pair, #a-b	5.00	5.00
996	A242	$40 Sheet of 6, #a-f	15.00	15.00
		Nos. 994-996 (3)	22.50	22.50

Issued: No. 994, 11/19, Nos. 995-996, 11/12. No. 994 printed in sheets of six; No. 995 printed in sheets containing three pairs. Value, set of three sheets $45.

Christmas — A243

White sorrel stalks: $10, $20, $50, $60. $50 and $60 are horiz.

Wmk. 352

2004, Nov. 22		**Litho.**		***Perf. 14¼***
997-1000	A243	Set of 4	8.00	8.00

Founding of Moravian Church in Jamaica, 250th Anniv. A244

Designs: 90c, Mary Morris Knibb, Mizpah Moravian Church. $10, Rev. W. O'Meally, Mizpah Moravian Church. $50, Bishop S. U. Hastings, Redeemer Moravian Church.

2004, Dec. 14				
1001-1003	A244	Set of 3	4.00	4.00

Buildings — A245

Designs: 90c, Rose Hall Great House, St. James. $5, Holy Trinity Cathedral. $30, National Commercial Bank, New Kingston. $60, Court House, Falmouth.

2005, Jan. 13	**Wmk. 352**		**Perf. 13¼**	
1004	A245	90c multi	.25	.25
1004A	A245	$5 multi	.30	.25
1005	A245	$30 multi	1.50	1.10
a.		Dated 2006 at bottom	2.00	1.50
b.		Dated 2008 at bottom	1.00	.75
1006	A245	$60 multi	3.00	2.75
a.		Dated 2008 at bottom	2.00	1.50
		Nos. 1004-1006 (4)	5.05	4.35

Self-Adhesive

Serpentine Die Cut 12¼x12½

Unwmk.

1008	A245	$5 multi	.40	.25
1008A	A245	$30 multi	1.50	1.50
b.		Booklet pane of 10	15.00	
		Complete booklet, #1008Ab	15.00	
c.		Dated 2006 at right	2.00	2.00
1009	A245	$60 multi	3.50	3.50

See Nos. 1038-1053.

Chinese in Jamaica, 150th Anniv. A246

Flags of People's Republic of China and Jamaica and: $30, Food and fruits from China and Jamaica. $60, Chinatown. $90, Chinese Benevolent Association Building.

2005, Feb. 5	**Wmk. 352**		**Perf. 14¼**	
1010-1012	A246	Set of 3	10.00	10.00

European Philatelic Cooperation, 50th Anniv. (in 2006) — A247

Designs: $60, Green square. $70, Yellow diamond. $100 Blue square.

Perf. 13½

2005, June 1		**Litho.**		**Unwmk.**
1013-1015	A247	Set of 3	9.00	9.00
1015a		Souvenir sheet, #1013-1015	9.00	9.00

Europa stamps, 50th anniv. (in 2006).

Battle of Trafalgar, Bicent. — A248

Designs: $20, Gun captain holding powder cartridge. $30, Admiral Horatio Nelson, vert. $50, British 12-pounder cannon. $60, HMS Africa, vert. $70, HMS Leviathan being attacked by the Intrepide, vert. $90, HMS Victory.
$200, HMS Africa at Port Royal, Jamaica.

Wmk. 352, Unwmkd. ($90)

2005, June 23		**Litho.**		***Perf. 13¼***
1016-1021	A248	Set of 6	14.50	14.50

Souvenir Sheet

Perf. 13½

1022	A248	$200 multi	11.00	11.00

No. 1021 has particles of wood from the HMS Victory embedded in areas covered by a thermographic process that produces a raised, shiny effect. No. 1022 contains one 44x44mm stamp.

Rotary International, Cent. — A249

2005, June 30		**Wmk. 352**		***Perf. 13¾***
1023	A249	$30 multi	2.00	2.00

Pope John Paul II (1920-2005) A250

Unwmk.

2005, Aug. 18		**Litho.**		***Perf. 14***
1024	A250	$30 multi	1.75	1.75

Battle of Trafalgar, Bicent. — A251

Designs: $50, HMS Victory. $90, Ships in battle, horiz. $100, Admiral Horatio Nelson.

Perf. 13¼

2005, Oct. 18		**Litho.**		**Unwmk.**
1025-1027	A251	Set of 3	13.50	13.50

Mary Seacole (1805-81), Nurse — A252

Seacole and: $30, Herbal remedies and medicines. $50, Seacole Hall, University of the West Indies. $60, Crimean War soldiers. $70, Medals.

Wmk. 352

2005, Nov. 21	Litho.		Perf. 13½	
1028-1031 A252	Set of 4		8.00	8.00

World AIDS Day — A253

2005, Dec. 1		Perf. 14¾x14	
1032 A253 $30 multi		1.50	1.50

Christmas A254

Star of Bethlehem and poinsettia with various frame designs: $20, $30, $50, $80.

2005, Dec. 1		
1033-1036 A254 Set of 4	6.75	6.75

Jessie Ripoll (Sister Mary Peter Claver), Founder of Alpha Schools — A255

2005, Dec. 12		Perf. 13½	
1037 A255 $30 multi		1.25	1.25

Alpha Schools, 125th anniv.

Buildings Type of 2005

Designs: $10, Court House, Morant Bay. $15, Spanish Town Square, St. Catherine. $20, Mico College. $25, Simms Building, Jamaica College. $50, Devon House, St. Andrew. $70, Ward Theater, Kingston. $90, Vale Royal, St. Andrew. $100, Falmouth Post Office.

Perf. 14x13¼

2006, May 12	Litho.		Wmk. 352	
No date inscription below design				
1038 A245	$10 multi		.70	.40
a.	Inscribed "2008"		.35	.35
1039 A245	$15 multi		.60	.50
a.	Inscribed "2008"		.70	.65
1040 A245	$20 multi		1.25	1.00
a.	Inscribed "2008"		.90	.80
1041 A245	$25 multi		.90	.80
1042 A245	$50 multi		2.75	1.75
a.	Inscribed "2008"		1.75	1.00
1043 A245	$70 multi		3.25	3.25
a.	Inscribed "2008"		2.25	1.75

1044 A245	$90 multi		4.50	4.50
a.	Inscribed "2008"		2.75	2.25
1045 A245	$50 multi		3.25	3.25
	Nos. 1038-1045 (8)		17.20	15.45

Self-Adhesive
Unwmk.
Serpentine Die Cut 13¼x14

1046 A245	$10 multi		.40	.40
1047 A245	$15 multi		.65	.65
1048 A245	$20 multi		.75	.75
1049 A245	$25 multi		.90	.90
1050 A245	$50 multi		2.00	2.00
1051 A245	$70 multi		2.50	2.50
1052 A245	$90 multi		3.00	3.00
1053 A245	$100 multi		3.25	3.25
	Nos. 1046-1053 (8)		13.45	13.45

Worldwide Fund for Nature (WWF) A256

Black-billed Amazon parrot: $5, Chicks. $10, Head of adult bird. $30, Bird on branch. $50, Two birds.

Perf. 13¼x13½

2006, Nov. 30	Litho.		Wmk. 352	
1054-1057 A256	Set of 4		7.00	7.00
1057a	Sheet, 4 each #1054-1057		28.00	28.00

Christmas A257

Flowers: $20, Cup and saucer. $30, Lignum vitae. $50, Neocogniauxia monophylla, vert. $60, Ghost orchid, vert.

Perf. 13¼x13¾, 13¾x13¼

2006, Nov. 30			
1058-1061 A257	Set of 4	7.00	7.00

2007 ICC Cricket World Cup, West Indies — A258

Designs: No. 1062, $30, Courtney Walsh. No. 1063, $30, Collie Smith. $40, New Sabrina Park, horiz. $50, Like #1062. $70, Trelawney Multi-purpose Sports Complex, horiz. $200, ICC Cricket World Cup.

Wmk. 352

2007, Feb. 28	Litho.		Perf. 14	
1062-1066 A258	Set of 5		11.00	11.00
Souvenir Sheet				
1067 A258 $200 multi			10.00	10.00

British Abolition of the Slave Trade, Bicent. — A259

Wmk. 352

2007, June 7	Litho.		Perf. 14
1068 A259 $30 multi		1.50	1.50

Scouting, Cent. A260

Designs: $5, Boy scout, Jamaican flag, Scout salute. $10, Scouts, compass. $30, Scouts handling Jamaican flag, Scout making craft.
No. 1073, vert.: a, $50, Scouts on parade. b, $100, Lord Robert Baden-Powell blowing kudu horn.

2007, July 9		Perf. 13¾	
1069-1072 A260	Set of 4	5.00	5.00
Souvenir Sheet			
1073 A260	Sheet of 2, #a-b	8.00	8.00

Christmas — A261

Flowers: $20, Tolumnia triquetra. $30, Broughtonia negrilensis, horiz. $50, Broughtonia sanguinea, horiz. $60, Spathelia sorbifolia.

Wmk. 352

2007, Nov. 9	Litho.		Perf. 14
1074-1077 A261	Set of 4	7.00	7.00

2008 Summer Olympics, Beijing A262

Designs: $20, Fish, Asafa Powell. $60, Lanterns, Veronica Campbell-Brown.
No. 1079: a, Bamboo, Aleen Bailey, Veronica Campbell-Brown. b, Sherone Simpson, Tayna Lawrence, dragon.

Wmk. 352

2008, Apr. 30	Litho.		Perf. 13¼	
1078 A262	$20 multi		1.00	1.00
1079 A262	$30 Horiz. pair, #a-b		3.00	3.00
1080 A262	$60 multi		3.00	3.00
	Nos. 1078-1080 (3)		7.00	7.00

University of Technology, 50th Anniv. — A263

2008, May 26	Litho.		Perf. 14	
1081 A263	$30 multi		2.00	2.00
a.	Souvenir sheet of 1		2.10	2.10

Associated Board of the Royal Schools of Music in Jamaica, Cent. — A264

Map of Jamaica and: $30, Piano keyboard. $70, Violin.

Wmk. 352

2008, Oct. 30	Litho.		Perf. 14
1082-1083 A264	Set of 2	5.00	5.00

Christmas A265

Various ferns: $20, $30, $50, $60.

Wmk. 352

2008, Nov. 21	Litho.		Perf. 13¾
1084-1087 A265	Set of 4	7.00	7.00

George Headley (1909-83), Cricket Player — A266

Designs: $10, Head of Headley. $30, Headley in front of wickets. $200, Statue of Headley.
$250, Statue of Headley, Sabina Park, Kingston.

Wmk. 352

2009, Sept. 25	Litho.		Perf. 14	
1088-1090 A266	Set of 3		8.00	8.00
Souvenir Sheet				
Perf. 14¼x14				
1091 A266 $250 multi			8.50	8.50

No. 1091 contains one 43x57mm stamp.

Christmas — A267

Paintings by Juanita Isabel Ramos: $20, Guardian Angel. $30, Madonna and Child. $50, Madonna and Flowers, horiz.

Wmk. 352

2009, Nov. 20	Litho.		Perf. 13½
1092-1094 A267	Set of 3	3.50	3.50

Christmas A268

Musical groups: $40, NDTC Singers. $60, Kingston College Chapel Choir. $120, The University Singers. $160, The Jamaican Folk Singers.

Wmk. 352

2010, Dec. 13	Litho.		Perf. 13¾
1095-1098 A268	Set of 4	11.00	11.00

Souvenir Sheet

Wedding of Prince William and Catherine Middleton — A269

2011, Apr. 29   **Perf. 14¾x14¼**
1099 A269 $400 multi   11.00 11.00

Lighthouses — A270

Designs: $20, Negril Lighthouse. $50, Morant Point Lighthouse. $60, Lover's Leap Lighthouse, vert. $200, Galina Lighthouse, vert.

2011, July 4   **Perf. 14**
1100 A270 $20 multi   .50 .50
  a. Dated "2012"   .50 .50
  b. Dated "2013"   .40 .40
1101 A270 $50 multi   1.25 1.25
  a. Dated "2012"   1.25 1.25
  b. Dated "2013"   1.00 1.00
1102 A270 $60 multi   1.40 1.40
  a. Dated "2012"   1.40 1.40
  b. Dated "2013"   1.25 1.25
1103 A270 $200 multi   4.75 4.75
  a. Dated "2012"   4.75 4.75
  b. Dated "2013"   4.00 4.00
    Nos. 1100-1103 (4)   7.90 7.90

Issued: Nos. 1100a, 1101a, 1102a, 1103a, 3/23/12. Nos. 1100b, 1101b, 1102b, 1103b, 6/13/13.

Independence, 50th Anniv. — A271

Designs: $60, Fiftieth anniversary emblem. $120, Coat of arms, vert.

Perf. 14x14¾, 14¾x14
2012, Aug. 31
1104-1105 A271 Set of 2   4.25 4.25

Medalists at 2008 Summer Olympics A272

Designs: No. 1106, $60, Usain Bolt, Men's 100-meter and 200-meter gold medalist (orange panel). No. 1107, $60, Melaine Walker, Women's 400-meter hurdles gold medalist (red panel). No. 1108, $60, Veronica Campbell-Brown, women's 200-meter gold medalist (blue panel). No. 1109, $60, Men's 4x100-meter relay team (Bolt, Michael Frater, Nesta Carter, Asafa Powell) (green panel). No. 1110, $60, Shelly-Ann Fraser, gold medalist, Sherone Simpson and Kerron Stewart, silver medalists in women's 100-meter (black panel).

2013, May 3   **Perf. 13¼**
1106-1110 A272 Set of 5   6.25 6.25

Christmas A273

Bells and: $20, Night-blooming cereus. $60, Coffee berries and flowers. $120, Century palm. $160, Cactus flower.

Wmk. 352
2013, Dec. 6   **Litho.**   **Perf. 13¼**
1111-1114 A273 Set of 4   7.50 7.50

St. Andrew Parish Church, 350th Anniv. — A274

Various views of church's exterior: $20, $60, $120.
$200, Stained-glass windows, vert.

Perf. 14¼x14¾
2014, Dec. 11   **Litho.**
1115-1117 A274 Set of 3   3.50 3.50
Souvenir Sheet
Perf. 14¾x14¼
1118 A274 $200 multi   3.50 3.50

SEMI-POSTAL STAMPS

Native Girl — SP1   Native Boy — SP2

Native Boy and Girl — SP3

1923, Nov. 1   **Engr.**   **Perf. 12**
B1 SP1 ½p green & black   1.25 6.25
B2 SP2 1p car & black   3.50 12.00
B3 SP3 2½p blue & black   22.50 20.00
    Nos. B1-B3 (3)   27.25 38.25

Each stamp was sold for ½p over face value. The surtax benefited the Child Saving League of Jamaica.

> **Catalogue values for unused stamps in this section, from this point to the end of the section, are for Never Hinged items.**

Nos. 694-697 Surcharged in Black

Wmk. 352
1988, Nov. 11   **Litho.**   **Perf. 14**
B4 A164 25c +25c multi   .25 .25
B5 A164 45c +45c multi   .30 .25
B6 A164 $4 +$4 multi   2.50 3.00
B7 A164 $5 +$5 multi   2.50 3.00
    Nos. B4-B7 (4)   5.55 6.50

Red Surcharge
B4a A164 25c + 25c   .25 .25
B5a A164 45c + 45c   .30 .25
B6a A164 $4 + $4   2.50 3.00
B7a A164 $5 + $5   2.50 3.00
    Nos. B4a-B7a (4)   5.55 6.50

WAR TAX STAMPS

Regular Issues of 1906-19 Overprinted

1916   **Wmk. 3**   **Perf. 14**
MR1 A14 ½p green   .25 .40
  a. Without period   17.50 27.50
  b. Double overprint   140.00 160.00
  c. Inverted overprint   130.00 150.00
  d. As "c," without period   350.00
MR2 A17 3p violet, *yel*   2.50 22.00
  a. Without period   40.00 100.00

Surface-colored Paper
MR3 A17 3p violet, *yel*   27.50 45.00
    Nos. MR1-MR3 (3)   30.25 67.40

Regular Issues of 1906-18 Overprinted

MR4 A14 ½p green   .25 .30
  a. Without period   20.00 55.00
  b. Pair, one without ovpt.   6,500. 5,250.
  c. "R" inserted by hand   1,800. 1,500.
  d. "WAR" only   125.00
MR5 A17 1½p orange   .25 .25
  a. Without period   5.75 8.50
  b. "TAMP"   190.00 200.00
  c. "S" inserted by hand   425.00
  d. "H" omitted   3,500. 3,100.
  e. "R" inserted by hand   1,550. 1,250.
MR6 A17 3p violet, *yel*   7.00 1.10
  a. Without period   70.00 75.00
  b. "TAMP"   1,000. 1,000.
  c. "S" inserted by hand   225.00 225.00
  d. Inverted overprint   325.00 175.00
  e. As "a," inverted
    Nos. MR4-MR6 (3)   7.50 1.65

Regular Issues of 1906-19 Overprinted

1917, Mar.
MR7 A14 ½p green   2.00 .35
  a. Without period   17.50 30.00
  b. Overprinted on back instead of face   250.00
  c. Inverted overprint   25.00 57.50
MR8 A17 1½p orange   .25 .25
  a. Without period   4.00 20.00
  b. Double overprint   92.50 100.00
  c. Inverted overprint   92.50 85.00
  d. As "a," inverted   400.00
MR9 A17 3p violet, *yel*   2.25 1.60
  a. Without period   27.50 50.00
  b. Vertical overprint   425.00 425.00
  c. Inverted overprint   160.00 190.00
  d. As "a," inverted   450.00
    Nos. MR7-MR9 (3)   4.50 2.20

There are many minor varieties of Nos. MR1-MR9.

Regular Issues of 1906-19 Overprinted in Red

1919, Oct. 4
MR10 A14 ½p green   .25 .25
MR11 A17 3p violet, *yel*   15.50 3.25

OFFICIAL STAMPS

No. 16 Overprinted in Black

Type I — Word 15 to 16mm long.
Type II — Word 17 to 17½mm long.

1890   **Wmk. 2**   **Perf. 14**
O1 A7 ½p green (II)   18.00 2.25
  a. Type I   45.00 30.00
  b. Inverted overprint (II)   100.00 110.00
  c. Double overprint (II)   100.00 110.00
  d. Dbl. ovpt., one invtd. (II)   550.00 550.00
  e. Dbl. ovpt., one vert. (II)   1,100.
  f. Double overprint (I)   825.00

Missing "O," "L" or one or both "I's" known.

No. 16 and Type of 1889 Overprinted

1890-91
O2 A7 ½p green   11.00 1.75
O3 A10 1p carmine rose   8.00 1.50
O4 A10 2p slate   27.50 1.50
    Nos. O2-O4 (3)   46.50 4.75

JAPAN
ja-'pan

LOCATION — North Pacific Ocean, east of China
GOVT. — Constitutional monarchy
AREA — 142,726 sq. mi.
POP. — 126,182,077 (1999 est.)
CAPITAL — Tokyo

1000 Mon = 10 Sen
100 Sen = 1 Yen (or En)
10 Rin = 1 Sen

> **Catalogue values for unused stamps in this country are for Never Hinged items, beginning with Scott 375 in the regular postage section, Scott B8 in the semipostal section, and Scott C9 in the airpost section.**

Watermarks

Wmk. 141 —
Zigzag Lines

Wmk. 142 —
Parallel Lines

Wmk. 257 — Curved
Wavy Lines

After 1945, Wmk. 257 exists also in a narrow spacing on a small number of issues.

Counterfeits of Nos. 1-71 are plentiful. Some are excellent and deceive many collectors.

Nos. 1-54A were printed from plates of 40 with individually engraved subjects. Each stamp in the sheet is slightly different.

Pair of Dragons Facing
Characters of
Value — A1

Plate I   Plate II

48 mon:
Plate I — Solid dots in inner border.
Plate II — Tiny circles replace dots.

Plate I

Plate II

100 mon:
Plate I — Lowest dragon claw at upper right and at lower left point upward.
Plate II — Same two claws point downward.

Plate I   Plate II

200 mon:
Plate I — Dot in upper left corner.
Plate II — No dot. (Some Plate I copies show dot faintly; these can be mistaken for Plate II.)

Plate I   Plate II

500 mon:
Plate I — Lower right corner of Greek-type border incomplete
Plate II — Short horizontal line completes corner border pattern.

Unwmk.
1871, Apr. 20   Engr.   Imperf.
Native Laid Paper Without Gum
Denomination in Black

1	A1	48m brown (I)	260.	260.
a.		48m red brown (I)	375.	375.
b.		Wove paper (I)	300.	300.
c.		48m brown (II)	350.	350.
d.		Wove paper (II)	400.	400.
2	A1	100m blue (I)	260.	260.
a.		Wove paper (I)	350.	350.
b.		Plate II	550.	550.
c.		Wove paper (II)	800.	800.
3	A1	200m vermilion (I)	450.	425.
a.		Wove paper (I)	525.	450.
b.		Plate II	2,500.	2,000.
c.		Wove paper (II)		4,000.
4	A1	500m blue green (I)	650.	650.
a.		500m greenish blue (I)	700.	675.
b.		500m green (I)	2,000.	1,400.
c.		500m yellow green (I)	3,500.	1,500.
d.		Wove paper (I)	750.	650.
e.		500m blue green (II)	775.	4,000.
f.		500m greenish blue (II)	775.	4,000.
g.		Wove paper (II)	2,750.	5,000.
h.		Denomination inverted (I)		175,000.

Perforations, Nos. 5-8
Perforations on Nos. 5-8 generally are rough and irregular due to the perforating equipment used and the quality of the paper. Values are for stamps with rough perfs that touch the frameline on one or more sides.

Dragons and
Denomination — A1a

½ sen:
Plate I — Same as 48m Plate II. Measures not less than 19.8x19.8mm. Some subjects on this plate measure 20.3x20.2mm.
Plate II — Same as 48m Plate II. Measures not more than 19.7x19.3mm. Some subjects measure 19.3x18.7mm.

Plate I & II   Plate III

1 sen:

Plate I — Same as 100m Plate I. Narrow space between frameline and Greek-type border.
Plate II — Same as 100m Plate II. Same narrow space between frameline and border.
Plate III — Space between frameline and border is much wider. Frameline thinner. Shading on dragon heads heavier than on Plates I and II.

Native Laid Paper
With or Without Gum

1872   Perf. 9-12 & compound
Denomination in Black

5	A1a	½s brown (II)	130.00	130.00
a.		½s red brown (II)	130.00	130.00
b.		½s gray brown (II)	130.00	130.00
c.		Wove paper (II)	725.00	675.00
d.		½s brown (I)	200.00	200.00
e.		½s red brown (I)	200.00	200.00
f.		½s gray brown (I)	200.00	200.00
g.		Wove paper (I)	275.00	275.00
6	A1a	1s blue (II)	425.00	425.00
a.		Wove paper (II)	675.00	675.00
b.		Plate I	1,400.	3,000.
c.		Wove paper (I)	7,000.	
d.		Plate III	15,000.	2,500.
e.		Wove paper (III)		7,500.
7	A1a	2s vermilion	575.00	575.00
a.		Wove paper	625.00	625.00
8	A1a	5s blue green	850.00	850.00
a.		5s yellow green	875.00	875.00
b.		Wove paper	900.00	900.00

In 1896 the government made imperforate imitations of Nos. 6-7 to include in a presentation book.

Beginning with No. 9, Japanese stamps intended for distribution outside the Postal Ministry were overprinted with three characters, as shown above, reading "Mihon" (specimen). These specimens were included in ministry announcements detailing forthcoming issues and were in presentation booklets given to government officials, foreign governments, etc.

Expect perforations on Nos. 9-71 to be rough and irregular.

Imperial Crest and
Branches of Kiri
Tree — A2

Dragons and
Chrysanthemum
Crest — A3

Imperial
Chrysanthemum
Crest — A4

Imperial Crest and
Branches of Kiri
Tree — A5

Perf. 9 to 13 and Compound
1872-73
Native Wove or Laid Paper of Varying Thickness

9	A2	½s brown, hard wove	25.00	20.00
a.		Upper character in left label has 2 diagonal top strokes missing	2,100.	1,250.
b.		Laid paper	80.00	—
c.		As "a," laid paper	2,200.	—
d.		½s gray brown, soft porous native wove	80.00	—

Nos. 9, 9a are on stiff, brittle wove paper. Nos. 9b, 9c and 9d on a soft, fibrous paper. Nos. 9b, 9c and 9d probably were never put in use, though genuine used examples do exist.

10	A2	1s blue, wove	50.00	26.00
a.		Laid paper	52.50	29.00
11	A2	2s ver, wove	100.00	50.00
12	A2	2s dull rose, laid	75.00	35.00
a.		Wove paper	100.00	50.00
13	A2	2s yel, laid ('73)	75.00	21.00
a.		Wove paper ('73)	175.00	26.00
14	A2	4s rose, laid ('73)	67.50	26.00
a.		Wove paper ('73)	210.00	32.00
15	A3	10s blue grn, wove	260.00	160.00
16	A3	10s yel grn, laid	475.00	325.00
a.		Wove paper ('73)	1,150.	500.00
17	A4	20s lilac, wove	700.00	425.00
b.		20s violet, wove	750.00	425.00
b.		20s red violet, laid		
18	A5	30s gray, wove	625.00	375.00

See Nos. 24-25, 30-31, 37-39, 51-52.

1874   Foreign Wove Paper

24	A2	4s rose	650.	300.
25	A5	30s gray	30,000.	7,500.

A6   A7

Design A6 differs from A2 by the addition of a syllabic character in a box covering crossed kiri branches above SEN. Stamps of design A6 differ for each value in border and spandrel designs.

In design A7, the syllabic character appears just below the buckle. In design A8, it appears in an oval frame at bottom center below SE of SEN.

With Syllabic Characters

イ ロ ハ ニ ホ ヘ ト チ
i ro ha ni ho he to chi
1 2 3 4 5 6 7 8

リ ヌ ル ヲ ワ カ ヨ タ
ri nu ru wo wa ka yo ta
9 10 11 12 13 14 15 16

レ ソ ツ ネ ナ ラ ム
re so tsu ne na ra mu
17 18 19 20 21 22 23

Perf. 9½ to 12½ and Compound
1874   Native Laid or Wove Paper

28	A6	2s yellow (syll. 1)	27,000.	400.00
		Syllabic 16	425.00	
29	A7	6s vio brn (Syll. 1)	1,700.	475.00
		Syllabic 2	1,900.	500.00
		Syllabic 3	20,000.	1,100.
		Syllabic 4	20,000.	600.00
		Syllabic 5	20,000.	600.00
		Syllabic 6	20,000.	700.00
		Syllabic 7	25,000.	550.00
		Syllabic 8	25,000.	550.00
		Syllabic 9	20,000.	700.00
		Syllabic 10		3,500.
		Syllabic 11		3,000.
		Syllabic 12	20,000.	1,900.
30	A4	20s red vio (Syll. 3)	10,000.	
		Syllabic 1	150,000.	
		Syllabic 2	10,000.	

31　A5　30s gray (Syll.
　　　　1)　　　　　　　3,000.　3,000.
　a.　Very thin laid paper　3,000.　3,000.
　　　No. 30, syll. 1, comes only with small, elliptical specimen dot (*Sumiten*, "secret mark").

Perf. 11 to 12½ and Compound
1874　　　　　**Foreign Wove Paper**
32　A6　½s brown (Syll.
　　　　1)　　　　　　　25.00　　20.00
　　Syllabic 2　　　　　40.00　　40.00
33　A6　1s blue (Syll. 4)　160.00　40.00
　　Syllabic 1　　　　　150.00　35.00
　　Syllabic 2　　　　　225.00　40.00
　　Syllabic 4　　　　　200.00　40.00
　　Syllabic 5　　　　　650.00　150.00
　　Syllabic 6, 9　　　　150.00　45.00
　　Syllabic 7　　　　　350.00　50.00
　　Syllabic 8　　　　　150.00　40.00
　　Syllabic 10　　　　　225.00　70.00
　　Syllabic 11　　　　　215.00　60.00
　　Syllabic 12　　　　　250.00　65.00
34　A6　2s yel (Syll. 2-4,
　　　　15, 17, 20)　　　200.00　30.00
　　Syllabic 1　　　　　400.00　35.00
　　Syllabic 5　　　　　450.00　30.00
　　Syllabic 6　　　　2,000.　　50.00
　　Syllabic 7　　　　2,000.　　30.00
　　Syllabic 8　　　　　200.00　55.00
　　Syllabic 9　　　　　200.00　35.00
　　Syllabic 10　　　　2,750.　　50.00
　　Syllabic 11　　　　　200.00　30.00
　　Syllabic 12,22　　　2,650.　　30.00
　　Syllabic 13　　　　2,500.　　30.00
　　Syllabic 14　　　　2,650.　　45.00
　　Syllabic 16　　　　2,500.　　35.00
　　Syllabic 18,19　　　200.00　30.00
　　Syllabic 21　　　　　250.00　30.00
　　Syllabic 23　　　　　265.00　30.00
35　A6　4s rose (Syll. 1)　3,500.　475.00
36　A7　6s vio brn (Syll.
　　　　16)　　　　　　200.00　70.00
　　Syllabic 10　　　　　650.00　650.00
　　Syllabic 11　　　　　500.00
　　Syllabic 13　　　14,000.　　5,000.
　　Syllabic 14　　　　　300.00　275.00
　　Syllabic 15　　　25,000.　　3,000.
　　Syllabic 17　　　　　240.00　85.00
　　Syllabic 18　　　　　325.00　115.00
37　A3　10s yel grn (Syll.
　　　　2)　　　　　　425.00　100.00
　　Syllabic 1　　　　　525.00　85.00
　　Syllabic 3　　　　1,000.　　300.00
38　A4　20s violet (Syll. 5)　500.00　95.00
　　Syllabic 4　　　　　525.00　100.00
39　A5　30s gray (Syll. 1)　575.00　100.00

1875　　**Perf. 9 to 13 and Compound**
40　A6　½s gray (Syll.
　　　　2, 3)　　　　　25.00　　20.00
　　Syllabic 4　　　　　30.00　1,000.
41　A6　1s brn (Syll.
　　　　15)　　　　　　35.00　　22.50
　　Syllabic 5　　　　　375.00　50.00
　　Syllabic 7　　　　2,250.　　275.00
　　Syllabic 8　　　32,500.　　275.00
　　Syllabic 12　　　　1,300.　　225.00
　　Syllabic 13　　　　　50.00　22.50
　　Syllabic 14　　　　　50.00　22.50
　　Syllabic 16-17　　　45.00　　25.00
42　A6　4s green
　　　　(Syll. 1)　　　130.00　29.00
　　Syllabic 2　　　　　200.00　29.00
　　Syllabic 3　　　　　130.00　29.00
43　A7　6s orange
　　　　(Syll.
　　　　16,17)　　　　　90.00　　25.00
　　Syllabic 10　　　　　175.00　55.00
　　Syllabic 11　　　　　150.00　50.00
　　Syllabic 13　　　　　325.00　45.00
　　Syllabic 14　　　　　160.00　32.50
　　Syllabic 15　　　　　　　　162,500.
44　A8　6s orange
　　　　(Syll. 20)　　　90.00　　25.00
　　Syllabic 19　　　　　125.00　25.00
　　Syllabic 21　　　　　100.00　25.00
　　Syllabic 22　　　　4,250.　　1,750.

Dragons A9　　Wild Goose A10

Wagtail — A11　　Imperial Crest — A11a

Kiri Branches — A11b

Goshawk — A12

45　A9　10s ultra (Syll. 4)　175.00　27.50
　　Syllabic 5　　　　　4,150.　　350.00
46　A10　12s rose (Syll. 1)　450.00　150.00
　　Syllabic 2　　　　　500.00　175.00
　　Syllabic 3　　　　3,500.　　500.00
47　A11　15s lilac (Syll. 1)　350.00　160.00
　　Syllabic 2　　　　　400.00　165.00
　　Syllabic 3　　　　　350.00　175.00
48　A11a　20s rose (Syll. 8)　140.00　25.00
　　Syllabic 9
49　A11b　30s vio (Syll. 2-4)　180.00　70.00
50　A12　45s lake (Syll. 1)　600.00　275.00
　　Syllabic 2　　　　1,250.　　550.00
　　Syllabic 3　　　　1,200.　　425.00

　　Issued: No. 46, syll. 2, 1882; No. 46, syll. 3,
1883; others, 1875.
　　The 1s brown on laid paper, type A6, formerly listed as No. 50A, is one of several
stamps of the preceding issue which exist on a
laid type paper. They are difficult to identify
and mainly of interest to specialists.

1875　　**Without Syllabic Characters**
51　A2　1s brown　　　6,500.　700.00
52　A2　4s green　　　　525.00　100.00

Branches of　　　Imperial Crest
Kiri Tree Tied　　and Kiri
with Ribbon　　　Branches
A13　　　　　　A14

1875-76
53　A13　1s brown　　　80.00　　12.00
54　A13　2s yellow　　　95.00　　20.00
54A　A14　4s green ('76)　200.00　100.00
　　Nos. 53-54A (3)　　375.00　132.00

Postal Cancellations

Beta Cancel　　　Postal Cancel

Telegraph Cancellation

　　Nos. 58, 61-62, 64-65, 71-84 are
found with telegraph or telephone office
cancellations. These sell at considerably lower prices than postally used
examples.

A15　　　　　　A16

Imperial　　　　Sun, Kikumon
Crest, Star　　　and Kiri
and Kiri　　　　Branches
Branches　　　　A18
A17

Perf. 8 to 14 and Compound
1876-77　　　　　　　　**Typo.**
55　A15　5r slate　　　25.00　　10.00
56　A16　1s black　　　37.50　　4.75
　a.　Horiz. pair, imperf. btwn.
57　A16　2s brown ol　　52.50　　3.00
58　A16　4s blue grn　　42.50　　5.00
　a.　4s green　　　　　42.50　　5.00
59　A17　5s brown　　　65.00　　25.00
60　A17　6s orange ('77)　160.00　65.00
61　A17　8s vio brn ('77)　67.50　6.00
62　A17　10s blue ('77)　　55.00　2.50
63　A17　12s rose ('77)　250.00　150.00
64　A18　15s yel grn ('77)　160.00　2.50
65　A18　20s dk blue ('77)　175.00　12.00
66　A18　30s violet ('77)　250.00　110.00
　a.　30s red violet　　250.00　110.00
67　A18　45s carmine ('77)　775.00　525.00

1879
68　A16　1s maroon　　　15.00　　1.25
69　A16　2s dk violet　　40.00　　2.00
70　A16　3s orange　　　60.00　　30.00
71　A18　50s carmine　　225.00　15.00
　　Nos. 68-71 (4)　　340.00　48.25

1883
72　A16　1s green　　　11.50　　.80
73　A16　2s car rose　　15.00　　.25
74　A17　5s ultra　　　25.00　　.60
　　Nos. 72-74 (3)　　51.50　1.65

Imperial　　　　Kikumon
Crest and Kiri　　A20
Branches
A19

1888-92
75　A15　5r gray blk ('89)　5.00　.45
76　A16　3s lilac rose ('92)　15.00　.45
77　A16　4s olive bis　　13.00　　.45
78　A17　8s blue lilac　　19.00　　1.60
79　A17　10s brown org　17.00　　.45
80　A18　15s purple　　　57.50　　.50
81　A18　20s orange　　　75.00　　1.50
　a.　20s yellow　　　　75.00　　1.50
82　A19　25s blue green　150.00　1.50
83　A19　50s brown　　100.00　　3.25
84　A20　1y carmine　　160.00　　4.25
　　Nos. 75-84 (10)　　611.50　14.40

　　Stamps of types A16-A18 differ for each
value, in backgrounds and ornaments.

Cranes and
Imperial
Crest — A21

Perf. 11½ to 13 and Compound
1894, Mar. 9
85　A21　2s carmine　　24.00　　3.00
86　A21　5s ultra　　　37.50　　11.00

　　25th wedding anniv. of Emperor Meiji (Mut-
suhito) and Empress Haru.

Gen. Yoshihisa Kitashirakawa
A22　　　　　　A23

Field Marshal Akihito
Arisugawa
A24　　　　　　A25

1896, Aug. 1　　　　　　**Engr.**
87　A22　2s rose　　　26.00　　3.00
88　A23　5s deep ultra　52.50　　3.00
89　A24　2s rose　　　26.00　　3.00
90　A25　5s deep ultra　52.50　　3.00
　　Nos. 87-90 (4)　　157.00　12.00

　　Victory in Chinese-Japanese War (1894-95).

A26　　　　　　A27

A28　　　　　　A29

Perf. 11½ to 14 and Compound
1899-1907　　　　　　　**Typo.**
91　A26　5r gray　　　　5.50　　1.00
92　A26　½s gray ('01)　3.00　　.25
93　A26　1s lt red brn　3.50　　.25
94　A26　1½s ultra ('00)　12.00　.85
95　A26　1½s violet ('06)　9.00　.25
96　A26　2s lt green　　9.00　　.25
97　A26　3s violet brn　8.50　　.25
　a.　Double impression
98　A26　3s rose ('06)　5.00　　.25
99　A26　4s rose　　　6.00　　1.25
　a.　4s pink ('06)　　7.00　　1.75
100　A26　5s orange yel　18.00　.25
101　A27　6s maroon ('07)　32.50　3.50
102　A27　8s olive grn　34.00　　5.00
103　A27　10s deep blue　11.00　　.25
104　A27　15s purple　　42.50　　2.00
105　A27　20s red orange　21.00　.25
106　A28　25s blue green　67.50　1.00
107　A28　50s red brown　70.00　2.25
108　A29　1y carmine　　80.00　　3.25
　　Nos. 91-108 (18)　438.00　22.35

　　For overprints see Nos. M1, Offices in
China, 1-18, Offices in Korea, 1-14.

Boxes for Rice
Cakes and
Marriage
Certificates — A30

Perf. 11½ to 12½ and Compound
1900, May 10
109　A30　3s carmine　　28.00　2.50

　　Wedding of the Crown Prince Yoshihito and
Princess Sadako.
　　For overprints see Offices in China No. 19,
Offices in Korea No. 15.

Symbols of Korea and
Japan — A31

1905, July 1
110　A31　3s rose red　　80.00　20.00

　　Issued to commemorate the amalgamation
of the postal services of Japan and Korea.
Korean stamps were withdrawn from sale
June 30, 1905, but remained valid until Aug.
31. No. 110 was used in the Korea and China
Offices of Japan, as well as in Japan proper.

Field-piece and
Japanese Flag — A32

1906, Apr. 29
111 A32 1½s blue 26.00 4.00
112 A32 3s carmine rose 55.00 16.00
Triumphal military review following the Russo-Japanese War.

Empress Jingo — A33

1908 Engr.
113 A33 5y green 875.00 6.00
114 A33 10y dark violet 1,200. 10.00
The frame of No. 114 differs slightly from the illustration.
See Nos. 146-147.
For overprints see Offices in China Nos. 20-21, 48-49.

A34 A35

A36

Perf. 12, 12x13, 13x13½
1913 Typo. Unwmk.
115 A34 ½s brown 7.00 .85
116 A34 1s orange 14.00 .85
117 A34 1½s lt blue 18.00 1.25
  a. Booklet pane of 6 175.00
118 A34 2s green 19.00 .85
119 A34 3s rose 26.00 .45
  a. Booklet pane of 6 175.00
120 A35 4s red 27.50 14.00
121 A35 5s violet 35.00 1.25
122 A35 10s deep blue 110.00 .60
123 A35 20s claret 110.00 1.25
124 A35 25s olive green 110.00 2.75
125 A36 1y yel grn & mar 775.00 45.00
  Nos. 115-125 (11) 1,251. 69.10

1914-25 Wmk. 141 Granite Paper
Size: 19x22½mm ("Old Die")
127 A34 ½s brown 2.10 .25
128 A34 1s orange 2.10 .25
129 A34 1½s blue 2.10 .25
  a. Booklet pane of 6 72.50
  d. As "a," imperf.
130 A34 2s green 4.25 .25
  a. Booklet pane of 6 72.50
131 A34 3s rose 1.60 .25
  a. Booklet pane of 6 60.00
132 A35 4s red 14.00 1.00
  a. Booklet pane of 6 72.50
133 A35 5s violet 13.00 .45
134 A35 6s brown ('19) 18.00 9.00
136 A35 8s gray ('19) 15.00 9.00
137 A35 10s deep blue 17.50 .25
  a. Booklet pane of 6 110.00
138 A35 13s olive brn ('25) 35.00 1.90
139 A35 20s claret 80.00 .60
140 A35 25s olive grn 12.00 .85
141 A36 30s orange brn ('19) 18.00 .50
143 A36 50s dk brown ('19) 26.00 1.00
145 A36 1y yel grn & mar 140.00 1.50
  b. Imperf., pair
146 A36 5y green 475.00 6.00
147 A36 10y violet 650.00 9.50
  Nos. 127-147 (18) 1,525. 36.20

"New Die" Size: 18½x22mm (Flat Plate) or 18½x22½mm (Rotary)
1924-33
127a A34 ½s brown 1.75 .95
128a A34 1s orange 1.75 .95
129b A34 1½s blue 2.75 .30
  c. Bklt. pane of 6 ('30) 19.00
131b A34 3s rose 1.10 .25
  c. Bklt. pane of 6 ('28) 45.00
133a A35 5s violet 15.00 .25
135 A35 7s red org ('30) 7.75 .25
138a A35 13s bister brn ('25) 6.00 .25
140a A35 25s olive green 45.00 .25
142 A36 30s org & grn ('29) 17.00 .30
144 A36 50s yel brn & dk bl ('29) 12.00 .50
145a A36 1y yel grn & mar 67.50 1.00
  Nos. 127a-145a (11) 177.60 5.25

See Nos. 212-213, 239-241, 243, 245, 249-252, 255. For overprints see Nos. C1-C2, M2-M5, Offices in China, 22-47.

Ceremonial Cap — A37   Imperial Throne — A38

Enthronement Hall, Kyoto — A39

Perf. 12½
1915, Nov. 10 Typo. Unwmk.
148 A37 1½s red & blk 2.00 .55
149 A38 3s orange & vio 2.50 .80
Engr.
Perf. 12x12½
150 A39 4s carmine rose 12.00 10.00
151 A39 10s ultra 25.00 16.00
  Nos. 148-151 (4) 41.50 27.35
Enthronement of Emperor Yoshihito.

Mandarin Duck — A40   Ceremonial Cap — A41

1916, Nov. 3 Typo. Perf. 12½
152 A40 1½s green, red & yel 4.00 1.75
153 A40 3s red & yellow 7.00 2.00
154 A41 10s ultra & dk blue 825.00 275.00
Nomination of the Prince Heir Apparent, later Emperor Hirohito.

A42

Dove and Olive Branch — A43

Perf. 12, 12½, 13½x13
1919, July 1 Engr.
155 A42 1½s dark brown 2.00 .60
156 A43 3s gray green 2.50 1.00
157 A42 4s rose 5.50 3.75
158 A43 10s dark blue 23.00 12.00
  Nos. 155-158 (4) 33.00 17.35
Restoration of peace after World War I.

Census Officer, A.D. 652 — A44

Meiji Shrine, Tokyo — A45

Perf. 12½
1920, Sept. 25 Typo. Unwmk.
159 A44 1½s red violet 6.50 2.75
160 A44 3s vermilion 7.00 3.60
Taking of the 1st modern census in Japan. Not available for foreign postage except to China.

1920, Nov. 1 Engr.
161 A45 1½s dull violet 2.50 1.10
162 A45 3s rose 2.50 1.10
Dedication of the Meiji Shrine. Not available for foreign postage except to China.

National and Postal Flags — A46

Ministry of Communications Building, Tokyo — A47

Typographed (A46), Engraved (A47)
1921, Apr. 20 Perf. 12½, 13x13½
163 A46 1½s gray grn & red 1.60 .90
164 A47 3s violet brn 2.10 1.00
165 A46 4s rose & red 42.50 18.00
166 A47 10s dark blue 200.00 125.00
  Nos. 163-166 (4) 246.20 144.90
50th anniv. of the establishment of postal service and Japanese postage stamps.

Battleships "Katori" and "Kashima" — A48

1921, Sept. 3 Litho. Perf. 12½
167 A48 1½s violet 2.00 1.00
168 A48 3s olive green 2.25 1.00
169 A48 4s rose red 32.50 15.00
170 A48 10s deep blue 45.00 18.00
  Nos. 167-170 (4) 81.75 35.00
Return of Crown Prince Hirohito from his European visit.

Mount Fuji — A49

Perf. 13x13½
1930-37 Typo. Wmk. 141
Granite Paper
Size: 18½x22mm ("New Die")
171 A49 4s green ('37) 2.40 .35
172 A49 4s orange 5.50 .25
174 A49 8s olive green 8.50 .25
175a A49 20s blue ('37) 19.00 26.00
176 A49 20s brown violet 26.00 .25
  Nos. 171-176 (5) 61.40 27.10

1922-29
Size: 19x22½mm ("Old Die")
171a A49 4s green 7.50 2.60
172a A49 4s orange ('29) 75.00 7.50
173 A49 8s rose 15.00 5.25
174a A49 8s olive green ('29) 225.00 70.00
175 A49 20s deep blue 17.00 .50
176a A49 20s brown vio ('29) 75.00 1.25
  Nos. 171a-176a (6) 414.50 87.10
See Nos. 242, 246, 248.

Mt. Niitaka, Taiwan — A50

Perf. 12½
1923, Apr. 16 Unwmk. Engr.
177 A50 1½s orange 9.50 6.75
178 A50 3s dark violet 14.00 5.75
1st visit of Crown Prince Hirohito to Taiwan. The stamps were sold only in Taiwan, but were valid throughout the empire.

Cherry
Blossoms
A51

Sun and
Dragonflies
A52

Without Gum; Granite Paper

				Imperf.
1923		**Wmk. 142**	**Litho.**	
179	A51	½s gray	4.50	2.25
180	A51	1½s lt blue	5.00	1.00
181	A51	2s red brown	4.50	1.00
182	A51	3s brt rose	3.25	.80
183	A51	4s gray green	40.00	12.00
184	A51	5s dull violet	15.00	1.00
185	A51	8s red orange	65.00	21.00
186	A52	10s deep brown	27.50	1.00
187	A52	20s deep blue	30.00	1.50
		Nos. 179-187 (9)	194.75	41.55

Nos. 179-187 exist rouletted and with various perforations. These were made privately.

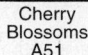

Empress Jingo — A53

Granite Paper

Perf. 12, 13x13½

				Wmk. 141
1924		**Engr.**		
188	A53	5y gray green	250.00	3.50
189	A53	10y dull violet	375.00	3.00
		See Nos. 253-254.		

Cranes — A54

Phoenix — A55

Perf. 10½ to 13½ and Compound

				Unwmk.
1925, May 10			**Litho.**	
190	A54	1½s gray violet	2.00	1.00
191	A55	3s silver & brn org	2.60	1.50
a.		Vert. pair, imperf. btwn.	425.00	
192	A54	8s light red	20.00	11.00
193	A55	20s silver & gray grn	45.00	35.00
		Nos. 190-193 (4)	69.60	48.50

25th wedding anniv. of the Emperor Yoshihito (Taisho) and Empress Sadako.

Mt. Fuji — A56

Yomei Gate,
Nikko — A57

Nagoya
Castle — A58

Perf. 13½x13

1926-37	**Typo.**	**Wmk. 141**	
	Granite Paper		
194	A56	2s green	1.60	.25
195	A57	6s carmine	6.00	.25
196	A58	10s dark blue	7.00	.25
197	A58	10s carmine ('37)	8.00	7.00
	Nos. 194-197 (4)	22.60	7.75

See Nos. 244, 247. For surcharges see People's Republic of China No. 2L5-2L6.

Baron Hisoka
Maeshima — A59

Map of World on Mollweide's
Projection — A60

Perf. 12½, 13x13½

				Unwmk.
1927, June 20				
198	A59	1½s lilac	2.50	1.00
199	A59	3s olive green	2.50	1.00
200	A60	6s carmine rose	55.00	45.00
201	A60	10s blue	67.50	45.00
		Nos. 198-201 (4)	127.50	92.00

50th anniv. of Japan's joining the UPU. Baron Maeshima (1835-1919) organized Japan's modern postal system and was postmaster general.

Phoenix — A61

Enthronement Hall,
Kyoto — A62

1928, Nov. 10	**Engr.**	*Perf. 12½*	
	Yellow Paper		
202	A61	1½s deep green	1.25	.50
203	A62	3s red violet	1.25	.50
204	A61	6s carmine rose	2.25	1.60
205	A62	10s deep blue	3.00	2.10
		Nos. 202-205 (4)	7.75	4.70

Enthronement of Emperor Hirohito.

Great Shrines of
Ise — A63

1929, Oct. 2		*Perf. 12½*	
206	A63	1½s gray violet	1.00	1.00
207	A63	3s carmine	1.50	1.10

58th rebuilding of the Ise Shrines.

Map of Japanese
Empire — A64

1930, Sept. 25		**Unwmk.**	
208	A64	1½s deep violet	2.00	1.25
209	A64	3s deep red	2.25	1.50

2nd census in the Japanese Empire.

Meiji
Shrine — A65

1930, Nov. 1		**Litho.**	
210	A65	1½s green	1.50	.85
211	A65	3s brown org	2.00	1.00

10th anniv. of dedication of Meiji Shrine.

Coil Stamps

Wmk. Zigzag Lines (141)

1933	**Typo.**	*Perf. 13 Horiz.*	
212	A34	1½s light blue	13.00	17.00
213	A34	3s rose	14.00	21.00

Japanese Red
Cross
Badge — A66

Red Cross Building,
Tokyo — A67

Perf. 12½

				Unwmk.
1934, Oct. 1		**Engr.**		
214	A66	1½s green & red	1.50	1.00
215	A67	3s dull vio & red	1.75	1.25
216	A66	6s dk car & red	8.00	5.00
217	A67	10s blue & red	12.00	8.00
		Nos. 214-217 (4)	23.25	15.25

15th International Red Cross Congress. Sheets of 20 with commemorative marginal inscription. One side of sheet is perf. 13.

White Tower of
Liaoyang and
Warship
"Hiei" — A68

Akasaka Detached
Palace,
Tokyo — A69

1935, Apr. 2			
218	A68	1½s olive green	1.00	.60
219	A69	3s red brown	1.50	1.00
220	A68	6s carmine	6.25	3.00
221	A69	10s blue	9.00	6.00
		Nos. 218-221 (4)	17.75	10.60

Visit of Emperor Kang Teh of Manchukuo (Henry Pu-yi) to Tokyo, April 6, 1935. Sheets of 20 with commemorative marginal inscription. One side of sheet is perf. 13.

Mt. Fuji — A70

1935	**Typo.**	*Perf. 13x13½*	
	Granite Paper		
222	A70	1½s rose carmine	10.00	.75
a.		Miniature sheet of 20	700.00	500.00

Issued to pay postage on New Year's cards from Dec. 1-31, 1935. After Jan. 1, 1936, used for ordinary letter postage. No. 222 was issued in sheets of 100.

Mt. Fuji
A71

Fuji from
Lake Ashi
A72

Fuji from Lake Kawaguchi — A73

Fuji from
Mishima
A74

1936, July 10	**Photo.**	**Wmk. 141**	
	Granite Paper		
223	A71	1½s red brown	3.00	2.00
224	A72	3s dark green	4.50	3.00
225	A73	6s carmine rose	10.00	8.00
226	A74	10s dark blue	12.00	10.00
		Nos. 223-226 (4)	29.50	23.00

Fuji-Hakone National Park.

Dove, Map of
Manchuria and
Kwantung — A75

Shinto Shrine, Port
Arthur — A76

Headquarters of
Kwantung
Government
A77

1936, Sept. 1	**Litho.**	*Perf. 12½*	
	Granite Paper		
227	A75	1½s gray violet	18.00	10.00
228	A76	3s red brown	14.00	12.00
229	A77	10s dull green	210.00	135.00
		Nos. 227-229 (3)	242.00	157.00

30th anniv. of Japanese administration of Kwantung Leased Territory and the South Manchuria Railway Zone.

Imperial
Diet
Building
A78

Grand
Staircase
A79

1936, Nov. 7		**Engr.**	*Perf. 13*
230	A78	1½s green	2.00	1.00
231	A79	3s brown vio	3.00	1.50
232	A79	6s carmine	6.00	4.00
233	A78	10s blue	10.00	5.75
		Nos. 230-233 (4)	21.00	12.25

Opening of the new Diet Building, Tokyo.

"Wedded Rocks,"
Futamigaura — A80

1936, Dec. 10   **Photo.**

234   A80   1½s rose carmine   3.50   .25

Issued to pay postage on New Year's greeting cards.

Types of 1913-26
Perf. 13½x13, 13x13½

			Wmk. 257	
1937		**Typo.**		
239	A34	½s brown	1.90	1.00
240	A34	1s orange yel	2.75	1.25
241	A34	3s rose	1.00	.25
242	A49	4s green	3.75	.25
243	A35	5s violet	5.00	.25
244	A57	6s crimson	8.00	.95
245	A35	7s red org	8.00	.25
246	A49	8s olive bister	8.50	.50
247	A58	10s carmine	7.00	.25
248	A49	20s blue	13.50	.50
249	A35	25s olive grn	40.00	2.00
250	A36	30s org & grn	30.00	.50
251	A36	50s brn org & dk bl	125.00	2.00
252	A36	1y yel grn & mar	60.00	1.50
		Nos. 239-252 (14)	314.40	11.45

Engr.

253	A53	5y gray green	300.00	3.25
254	A53	10y dull violet	425.00	3.00

For overprint see People's Republic of China No. 2L6.

Coil Stamps

1938		**Typo.**	*Perf. 13 Horiz.*	
255	A34	3s rose	4.00	4.00

New Year's
Decoration — A81

1937, Dec. 15   **Photo.**   *Perf. 13*

256   A81   2s scarlet   6.25   .25

Issued to pay postage on New Year's cards, later for ordinary use.

Trading Ship
A82

Harvesting
A83

Gen.
Maresuke
Nogi — A84

Power
Plant — A85

Admiral
Heihachiro
Togo
A86

Mount
Hodaka
A87

Garambi
Lighthouse,
Taiwan — A88

Diamond
Mountains,
Korea — A89

Meiji Shrine,
Tokyo — A90

Yomei Gate,
Nikko — A91

Plane and
Map of
Japan — A92

Kasuga
Shrine,
Nara — A93

Mount Fuji
and Cherry
Blossoms
A94

Horyu Temple,
Nara
A95

Miyajima Torii,
Itsukushima
Shrine — A96

Golden
Pavilion,
Kyoto — A97

Great
Buddha,
Kamakura
A98

Kamatari
Fujiwara
A99

Plum
Blossoms — A100

Typographed or Engraved

1937-45		**Wmk. 257**	*Perf. 13*	
257	A82	½s purple	.50	.30
258	A83	1s fawn	1.50	.25
259	A84	2s crimson	.35	.25
a.		Booklet pane of 20	50.00	
b.		2s pink, perf. 12 ('45)	1.25	.85
c.		2s vermilion ('44)	2.10	1.60
260	A85	3s green ('39)	.35	.25
261	A86	4s dark green ('39)	.75	.25
a.		Booklet pane of 20	13.00	
262	A87	5s dark ultra ('39)	.75	.25
263	A88	6s orange ('39)	1.50	.60
264	A89	7s deep green ('39)	.50	.25
265	A90	8s dk pur & pale vio ('39)	.45	.25
266	A91	10s lake ('38)	2.50	.25
267	A92	12s indigo ('39)	.50	.30
268	A93	14s rose lake & pale rose ('38)	.50	.25
269	A94	20s ultra ('40)	.50	.25
270	A95	25s dk brn & pale brn ('38)	.50	.25
271	A96	30s pck blue ('39)	1.25	.25
a.		Imperf., pair	400.00	
272	A97	50s ol & pale ol ('39)	.60	.25
a.		Pale olive (forest) omitted		
273	A98	1y brn & pale brn ('39)	3.50	1.00
274	A99	5y dp gray grn ('39)	25.00	2.50
275	A100	10y dk brn vio ('39)	16.50	2.00
		Nos. 257-275 (19)	58.00	9.95

Nos. 257-261, 265, 268, 270, 272-273 are typographed; the others are engraved.

Coil Stamps

1938-39		**Typo.**	*Perf. 13 Horiz.*	
276	A82	½s purple ('39)	2.75	4.50
277	A84	2s crimson	3.25	4.25
278	A86	4s dark green	3.75	4.25
279	A93	14s rose lake & pale rose	125.00	80.00
		Nos. 276-279 (4)	134.75	93.00

See Nos. 329, 331, 333, 341, 351, 360 and 361. For surcharges see Nos. B4-B5, Burma 2N4-2N27, China-Taiwan, 8-9, People's Republic of China 2L3, 2L7, 2L9-2L10, 2L39, Korea 55-56. For overprints see Ryukyu Islands (Scott US Specialized catalogue) Nos. 2X1-2X2, 2X4-2X7, 2X10, 2X13-2X14, 2X17, 2X20, 2X23, 2X27, 2X29, 2X33-2X34, 3X2-3X7, 3X10-3X11, 3X14, 3X17, 3X19, 3X21, 3X23, 3X26-3X30, 5X1-5X3, 5X5-5X8, 5X10.

Mount
Nantai — A101

Kegon
Falls — A102

Sacred
Bridge,
Nikko
A103

Mount
Hiuchi
A104

Unwmk.

1938, Dec. 25		**Photo.**	*Perf. 13*	
280	A101	2s brown orange	1.00	.50
281	A102	4s olive green	1.00	.50
282	A103	10s deep rose	5.75	3.75
283	A104	20s dark blue	5.75	3.75
a.		Souvenir sheet of 4, #280-283	45.00	75.00
		Never hinged	80.00	
		Nos. 280-283 (4)	13.50	8.50
		Set, never hinged	32.50	

Nikko National Park.
No. 283a sold for 50s.

Many souvenir sheets were sold in folders. Values are for sheets without folders.

Mount
Daisen
A106

Yashima
Plateau,
Inland
Sea
A107

Abuto
Kwannon
Temple
A108

Tomo
Bay,
Inland
Sea
A109

1939, Apr. 20

285	A106	2s lt brown	1.00	.50
286	A107	4s yellow grn	1.60	1.00
287	A108	10s dull rose	6.50	4.00
288	A109	20s blue	6.50	4.00
a.		Souvenir sheet of 4, #285-288	25.00	40.00
		Never hinged	50.00	
		Nos. 285-288 (4)	15.60	9.50
		Set, never hinged	32.50	

Daisen and Inland Sea National Parks.
No. 288a sold for 50s.

View from
Kuju
Village,
Kyushu
A111

Mount
Naka
A112

Crater of
Mount
Naka
A113

Volcanic
Cones of
Mt. Aso
A114

1939, Aug. 15

290	A111	2s olive brown	1.00	.50
291	A112	4s yellow green	3.00	2.00
292	A113	10s carmine	15.00	9.00
293	A114	20s sapphire	22.50	10.00
a.		Souvenir sheet of 4, #290-293	85.00	100.00
		Never hinged	140.00	
		Nos. 290-293 (4)	41.50	21.50
		Set, never hinged	85.00	

Aso National Park. No. 293a sold for 50s.

Globe — A116

Tsunetami
Sano — A117

1939, Nov. 15   *Perf. 12½*
Cross in Carmine

295	A116	2s brown	1.50	.90
296	A117	4s yellow green	1.60	1.00
297	A116	10s crimson	7.00	6.50
298	A117	20s sapphire	7.00	6.50
		Nos. 295-298 (4)	17.10	14.90
		Set, never hinged	32.50	

Intl. Red Cross Society founding, 75th anniv.

Sacred Golden
Kite — A118

Mount
Takachiho — A119

Five Ayu Fish
and Sake
Jar — A120

Kashiwara
Shrine — A121

1940   Engr.   Perf. 12

299	A118	2s brown orange	.80	.80
300	A119	4s dark green	.60	.60
301	A120	10s dark carmine	3.25	3.00
302	A121	20s dark ultra	.80	.80
		Nos. 299-302 (4)	5.45	5.20
		Set, never hinged	7.50	

2,600th anniv. of the legendary date of the founding of Japan.

Mt.
Hokuchin,
Hokkaido
A122

Mt.
Asahi,
Hokkaido
A123

Sounkyo
Gorge — A124

Tokachi
Mountain
Range
A125

1940, Apr. 20   Photo.   Perf. 13

303	A122	2s brown	1.00	1.00
304	A123	4s yellow green	2.75	2.00
305	A124	10s carmine	6.00	5.25
306	A125	20s sapphire	6.00	5.50
a.		Souvenir sheet of 4, #303-306	190.00	200.00
		Never hinged	350.00	
		Nos. 303-306 (4)	15.75	13.75
		Set, never hinged	32.50	

Daisetsuzan National Park. No. 306a sold for 50s.

Mt.
Karakuni,
Kyushu
A127

Mt.
Takachiho
A128

Torii of
Kirishima
Shrine
A129

Lake of
the Six
Kwannon
A130

1940, Aug. 21

308	A127	2s brown	1.00	.75
309	A128	4s green	1.75	1.50
310	A129	10s carmine	6.00	4.75
311	A130	20s deep ultra	7.00	5.75
a.		Souvenir sheet of 4, #308-311	175.00	175.00
		Never hinged	325.00	
		Nos. 308-311 (4)	15.75	12.75
		Set, never hinged	37.50	

Kirishima National Park.
No. 311a sold for 50s.

Education
Minister with
Rescript on
Education
A132

Characters
Signifying Loyalty
and Filial Piety
A133

1940, Oct. 25   Engr.   Perf. 12½

313	A132	2s purple	.75	.75
314	A133	4s green	1.00	1.00
		Set, never hinged	2.25	

50th anniv. of the imperial rescript on education, given by Emperor Meiji to clarify Japan's educational policy.

Mt.
Daiton,
Taiwan
A134

Central
Peak of
Mt.
Niitaka
A135

Buddhist
Temple
on Mt.
Kwannon
A136

View from
Mt.
Niitaka
A137

1941, Mar. 10   Photo.   Perf. 13

315	A134	2s brown	1.00	.80
316	A135	4s brt green	1.75	1.50
317	A136	10s rose red	5.50	3.50
318	A137	20s brilliant ultra	7.25	5.25
a.		Souv. sheet of 4, #315-318	80.00	125.00
		Never hinged	175.00	
		Nos. 315-318 (4)	15.50	11.05
		Set, never hinged	45.00	

Daiton and Niitaka-Arisan National Parks.
No. 318a sold with No. 323a in same folder for 90s.

Seisui Precipice,
East Taiwan
Coast — A139

Taroko
Gorge — A141

Mt.
Tsugitaka
A140

Upper
River
Takkiri
District
A142

1941, Mar. 10

320	A139	2s brown	1.00	.80
321	A140	4s brt green	1.75	1.00
322	A141	10s rose red	5.50	2.00
323	A142	20s bril ultra	7.25	4.00
a.		Souv. sheet of 4, #320-323	80.00	100.00
		Never hinged	175.00	
		Nos. 320-323 (4)	15.50	7.80
		Set, never hinged	30.00	

Tsugitaka-Taroko National Park.
See note after No. 318.

War Factory
Girl — A144

Building of
Wooden
Ship — A145

Hyuga
Monument
and Mt. Fuji
A146

War Worker
and Planes
A147

Palms and
Map of
"Greater East
Asia"
A148

"Enemy
Country
Surrender"
A149

Aviator
Saluting and
Japanese
Flag
A150

Torii of
Yasukuni
Shrine
A151

Mt. Fuji and
Cherry
Blossoms
A152

Torii of
Miyajima
A153

Garambi Lighthouse,
Taiwan — A154

Typographed; Engraved

1942-45   Wmk. 257   Perf. 13

325	A144	1s orange brn ('43)	.25	.40
328	A145	2s green	.40	.30
329	A84	3s brown ('44)	.70	.35
330	A146	4s emerald	.25	.25
331	A86	5s brown lake	.40	.30
332	A147	6s lt ultra ('44)	.60	.30
a.		Imperf., pair		
333	A86	7s org ver ('44)	.40	.35
334	A148	10s crim & dl rose	.80	.25
a.		Dull rose (map) omitted	475.00	475.00
335	A149	10s lt gray ('45)	2.75	2.75
336	A150	15s dull blue	2.00	1.50
337	A151	17s gray vio ('43)	.80	.50
338	A152	20s blue ('44)	.80	.25
339	A151	27s rose brn ('45)	.80	.75
340	A153	30s bluish grn ('44)	2.00	1.00
341	A88	40s dull violet	.60	.25
342	A154	40s dk violet ('44)	1.10	1.00
		Nos. 325,328-342 (16)	14.65	10.50

Nos. 325-335, 337-340 and 342 are engr. Nos. 336 and 341 are typo.

Nos. 329, 331, 333-334, 342 issued with and without gum. No. 335 issued only without gum. These are valued without gum.

Nos. 328, 342 exist with watermark sideways. No. 328 exists printed on gummed side. Most stamps of the above series exist in numerous shades.

For overprints and surcharges see North Borneo Nos. N34, N37, N41-N42, People's Republic of China 2L4, 2L8, Korea 57-60, Ryukyu Islands (US Specialized) Nos. 2X3, 2X9, 2X12, 2X15-2X16, 2X18-2X19, 2X21-2X22, 2X24-2X26, 2X28, 3X1, 3X8-3X9, 3X12-3X13, 3X15-3X16, 3X18, 3X20, 3X25, 3X31, 4X1-4X2, 5X4.

Kenkoku Shrine,
Hsinking — A155

Boys of Japan
and Manchukuo
A156

Orchid Crest of
Manchukuo
A157

1942   Unwmk.   Engr.   Perf. 12

343	A155	2s brown	.45	.45
344	A156	5s olive	.70	.70
345	A155	10s red	.95	.95
346	A157	20s dark blue	1.75	2.25
		Nos. 343-346 (4)	3.85	4.35
		Set, never hinged	7.50	

The 2s and 10s were issued Mar. 1 for the 10th anniv. of the creation of Manchukuo; 5s and 20s on Sept. 15 for the 10th anniv. of Japanese diplomatic recognition of Manchukuo.

C-59 Locomotive
A158

1942, Oct. 14   **Photo.**
347 A158 5s Prus green   3.50   3.50
    Never hinged   5.00

70th anniv. of Japan's 1st railway.

Yasukuni Shrine, Tokyo — A159

1944, June 29   **Perf. 13**
348 A159 7s Prus green   .55   .55
    Never hinged   .85

75th anniversary of Yasukuni Shrine.

Kwantung Shrine and Map of Kwantung Peninsula — A160

1944, Oct. 1
349 A160 3s red brown   3.75   *9.00*
350 A160 7s gray violet   4.25   *9.50*
    Set, never hinged   13.00

Dedication of Kwantung Shrine, Port Arthur.

Sun and Cherry Blossoms A161   Sunrise at Sea and Plane A162

Coal Miners A163   Yasukuni Shrine A164

Lithographed, Typographed
1945-47   **Wmk. 257**   **Imperf.**
Without Gum
351 A84   2s rose red   .30   .30
352 A161   3s rose carmine   .25   .30
353 A162   5s green   .25   .25
   a.   5s blue   9.00   6.75
354 A149   10s lt gray   10.00   7.50
354A A149   10s blue   22.50
355 A152   10s red orange   .25   .25
356 A152   20s ultra ('46)   .35   .25
357 A153   30s brt blue ('46)   1.50   .75
358 A163   50s dark brown ('46)   .30   .25
   a.   Souvenir sheet of 5 ('47)   10.50   12.50
359 A164   1y dp ol grn ('46)   1.00   .75
360 A99   5y dp gray grn   5.00   .65
361 A100   10y dk brown vio   32.50   .75
   Nos. 351-361 (12)   74.20
   Nos. 351-354,355-361 (11)   11.80

Nos. 351 and 354 are typographed. The other stamps in this set are printed by offset lithography.

No. 358a was issued with marginal inscriptions to commemorate the Sapporo (Hokkaido) Philatelic Exhibition, Nov., 1947.

Nos. 351 to 361 are on grayish paper, and Nos. 355 to 361 also exist on white paper.

Most stamps of the above series exist in numerous shades and with private perforation or roulette.

Beware of forgeries of Nos. 352, 353, 355-357 and 360 on unwatermarked paper.

See No. 404. For overprints see Ryukyu Islands (US Specialized) Nos. 2X8, 2X11, 2X30, 3X22, 4X3, 5X9.

Baron Hisoka Maeshima A165   Horyu Temple Pagoda A166

"Thunderstorm below Fuji," by Hokusai A167   "First Geese," Print by Hokusai A168

Kintai Bridge, Iwakuni A169   Kiyomizu Temple, Kyoto A170

Goldfish A171   Noh Mask A172

Plum Blossoms — A173

Characters Read Right to Left
1946-47   **Wmk. 257**   **Litho.**   **Imperf.**
Without Gum
362 A165   15s dark green   .45   .35
363 A166   30s dull lilac   .65   .30
364 A167   1y ultra   .70   .30
   a.   1y deep ultramarine   1.75   .30
   b.   1y light blue   .75   .30
365 A168   1.30y olive bister   2.50   1.00
366 A169   1.50y dark gray   2.25   .75
367 A170   2y vermilion ('47)   2.00   .30
   a.   Souvenir sheet of 5 ('47)   21.00   20.00
368 A171   5y lilac rose   7.50   .85
   Nos. 362-368 (7)   16.05   3.85

Engr.
369 A172   50y bister brn   62.50   .90
370 A173   100y brn car ('47)   62.50   .90

Perf. 13
371 A172   50y bis brn, with gum ('47)   62.50   .40
372 A173   100y brn car, with gum ('47)   62.50   .40

Litho.
Perf. 13x13½, 12, 12x12½
373 A166   30s dull lilac   3.00   2.75

Rouletted in Colored Lines
Typo.   **Unwmk.**
With Gum
374 A166   30s deep lilac   .95   *1.40*

Nos. 363, 368, 373 exist with and without gum, valued without gum, as are Nos. 371-372, 374.

No. 367a for the "Know Your Stamps" exhibition, Kyoto, Aug. 19-24, 1947. Size: 113x71mm

Nos. 362, 369 exist with watermark horizontal.

Beware of Nos. 362-364, 364a, 364b, 365 and 367 on unwatermarked paper.

See Nos. 384-387, 512A. For overprints see Ryukyu Islands (US Specialized) Nos. 2X32, 3X24, 4X4.

> **Catalogue values for unused stamps in this section, from this point to the end of the section, are for Never Hinged items.**

Medieval Postman's Bell A175   Baron Hisoka Maeshima A176

Design of First Japanese Stamp — A177

Communication Symbols — A178

Perf. 12½, 13½x13
1946, Dec. 12   **Engr.**   **Unwmk.**
375 A175   15s orange   5.00   3.00
376 A176   30s deep green   6.00   4.00
377 A177   50s carmine   3.00   2.00
378 A178   1y deep blue   3.00   2.00
   a.   Souvenir sheet of 4, #375-378, imperf.   160.00   140.00
     Hinged   75.00
   Nos. 375-378 (4)   17.00   11.00

Government postal service in Japan, 75th anniv.

No. 378a measures 180-183x125-127mm and is ungummed. There were 2 printings: I — The 4 colors were printed simultaneously. Arched top inscription and other inscriptions in high relief (no more than 2,000 sheets). II — Stamps were printed in one step, sheet inscriptions and 15s orange stamp in another. Lines of top inscription and inscriptions at lower left and lower right (flanking the 1y blue stamp) are much flatter (less raised) than the lines of the green, carmine and blue stamps, almost level with paper's surface (about 49,000 sheets). 1st printing value $800.

Mother and Child, Diet Building — A180   Bouquet of Japanese May Flowers — A181

Wmk. 257
1947, May 3   **Litho.**   **Perf. 12½**
Without Gum
380 A180   50s rose brown   .25   .30
381 A181   1y brt ultra   .50   .40
   a.   Souv. sheet of 2, #380-381, imperf, without gum   9.50   5.00
   b.   As "a," 50s stamp omitted   800.00
   c.   As "a," 1y stamp omitted   800.00

Inauguration of the constitution of May 3, 1947.

A182

1947, Aug. 15   **Photo.**   **Perf. 12½**
382 A182   1.20y brown   2.10   1.00
383 A182   4y brt ultra   4.25   1.40

Reopening of foreign trade on a private basis.

The ornaments on No. 383 differ from those shown in the illustration.

Types of 1946 Redrawn Characters Read Left to Right
1947-48   **Wmk. 257**   **Typo.**   **Perf. 13**
384 A166   30s deep lilac   1.50   1.25
385 A166   1.20y lt olive grn   1.00   .35
   a.   Souvenir sheet of 15   150.00   110.00
386 A170   2y vermilion ('48)   4.00   .25
387 A168   4y lt ultra   2.60   .25
   Nos. 384-387 (4)   9.10   2.10

No. 385a was issued with marginal inscriptions to commemorate the "Know Your Stamps" Exhibition, Tokyo, May, 1947.

On No. 386, the chrysanthemum crest has been eliminated and the top inscription centered.

Plum Blossoms — A183

1947   **Typo.**   **Imperf.**
Without Gum
388 A183   10y dk brown vio   40.00   .80

This stamp is similar to type A100 but with new inscription "Nippon Yubin" (Japan Post), reading from left to right. The characters for the denomination are likewise transposed.

A184   A185

Baron Hisoka Maejima A186   Whaling A187

National Art, Imperial Treasure House, Nara — A188

1947   **Typo.**   **Perf. 13x13½**
389 A184   35s green   .40   .30
Litho.
390 A185   45s lilac rose   .55   .50
   a.   Imperf., pair   700.00
   b.   Perf. 11x13½   3.75   3.75
391 A186   1y dull brown   2.40   .35
Typo.
392 A187   5y blue   5.50   .25
   a.   Imperf., pair   500.00
   b.   Perf. 11x13½   19.00   2.40
Engr.
Perf. 13½x13
393 A188   10y lilac   15.00   .25
   a.   Imperf., pair   —
   Nos. 389-393 (5)   23.85   1.65

No. 389 was produced on both rotary and flat press. Sheets of the rotary press printing have a border. Those of the flat press printing have none.

Lily of the
Valley — A188a

1947, Sept. 13   Unwmk.   Perf. 12½
394 A188a 2y dk Prus green   3.00 1.25
Relief of Ex-convicts Day, Sept. 13, 1947.

Souvenir Sheet

A189

1947   Wmk. 257   Litho.   Imperf.
Without Gum
395 A189 Sheet of 5, ultra   3.50 2.60
Stamp Hobby Week, Nov. 1-7, 1947. Sheet size: 113½x71½mm, on white or grayish paper.
For overprint, see No. 408.

"Benkei," 1880 Locomotive — A190

1947, Oct. 14   Unwmk.   Engr.
Without Gum
396 A190 4y deep ultra   17.50 16.50
75th anniv. of railway service in Japan.

Hurdling — A191   Diving — A192
Discus Throwing   Volleyball
A193   A194

1947, Oct. 25   Photo.   Perf. 12½
397 A191 1.20y red violet   9.00 6.00
398 A192 1.20y red violet   9.00 6.00
399 A193 1.20y red violet   9.00 6.00
400 A194 1.20y red violet   9.00 6.00
a.   Block of 4, #397-400   52.50 30.00
2nd Natl. Athletic Meet, held in Kanazawa, Oct. 30-Nov. 3.

Souvenir Sheets

A195

1948   Wmk. 257   Litho.   Imperf.
Without Gum
401 A195 Sheet of 2, As #368, rose carmine   13.50 15.00
Same, Inscribed with Three instead of Two Japanese Characters at Bottom Center
402 A195 Sheet of 2, #368   15.00 17.00
Philatelic exhibitions at Osaka (No. 401) and Nagoya (No. 402).
For Nos. 401-402 overprinted in green, see Nos. 407, 407b.

Stylized Tree — A196

Perf. 12½
1948, Apr. 1   Unwmk.   Photo.
403 A196 1.20y dp yellow grn   1.25   .90
Forestation movement. Sheets of 30, marginal inscription.

Coal Miners Type of 1946 and

National Art Treasure, Nara — A197

Perf. 13x13½
1948   Wmk. 257   Litho.
404 A163 50s dark brown   1.50   .95
Typo.
Perf. 13x13½
405 A197 10y rose violet   13.50   .25
a.   Imperf., pair
See No. 515A.

School Children — A198

Perf. 12½
1948, May 3   Unwmk.   Photo.
406 A198 1.20y dark carmine   1.25   .80
Reorganization of Japan's educational system. Sheets of 30, marginal inscription.

No. 402 Overprinted at Top, Bottom and Sides with Japanese Characters and Flowers in Green
1948, Apr. 3   Souvenir Sheets
407 A195 Sheet of 2   60.00 37.50
a.   Overprint inverted   125.00 125.00
b.   Overprint on No. 401   100.00 95.00
Mishima Philatelic Exhibition, Apr. 3-9.

No. 395 Overprinted at Top and Bottom With Japanese Characters in Plum
1948, Apr. 18
408 A189 Sheet of 5, ultra   22.50 19.00
Centenary of the death of Katsushika Hokusai, painter.

Sampans on Inland Sea, Near Suma — A199

Engr. & Litho.
1948, Apr. 22   Unwmk.   Imperf.
Without Gum
409 A199 Sheet of 2, grn & rose car   12.00 7.50
Communications Exhib., Tokyo, Apr. 27-May 3, 1948. Sheet contains two 2y deep carmine stamps.
Sheet exists with green border omitted.

1948, May 20   Without Gum
410 A199 Sheet of 2, ultra & rose car   14.50 13.50
Aomori Newspaper and Stamp Exhibition. Border design of apples and apple blossoms.

Type A199 With Altered Border and Inscriptions
1948, May 23   Without Gum
411 A199 Sheet of 2, blue & rose car   14.50 13.50
Fukushima Stamp Exhibition. Border design of cherries and crossed lines.

Horse Race — A200

1948, June 6   Photo.   Perf. 12½
412 A200 5y brown   2.50   .95
25th anniv. of the enforcement of Japan's horse racing laws. Each sheet contains 30 stamps and 2 labels, with marginal inscription.

A201   A202

Wmk. 257
1948, Sept. 10   Litho.   Perf. 13
413 A201 1.50y blue   2.25   .45
414 A202 3.80y lt brown   6.50 5.25
Souvenir Sheet
Without Gum
Imperf
415   Sheet of 4   32.50 30.00
Kumamoto Stamp Exhibition, Sept. 20. Souvenir sheet, issued Sept. 20, contains two each of 1.50y deep blue (A201) and 3.80y brown (A202).

Rectifying Tower — A203

Perf. 12½
1948, Sept. 14   Photo.   Unwmk.
416 A203 5y dark olive bister   2.75 1.50
Government alcohol monopoly.

Swimmer — A204

Runner — A205

Designs: No. 419, High jumper. No. 420, Baseball players. No. 421, Bicycle racers.

1948
417 A204 5y blue   3.75 1.75
418 A205 5y green   7.50 3.50
419 A205 5y green   7.50 3.50
420 A205 5y green   7.50 3.50
421 A205 5y green   7.50 3.50
a.   Block of 4, #418-421   40.00 35.00
Nos. 417-421 (5)   33.75 15.75
3rd Natl. Athletic Meet. Swimming matches held at Yawata, Sept. 16-19, field events, Fukuoka, Oct. 29-Nov. 3.

"Beauty Looking Back," Print by Moronobu A206

1948, Nov. 29   Perf. 13
422 A206 5y brown   47.50 30.00
a.   Sheet of 5   300.00 225.00
Sheet, hinged   200.00
Philatelic Week, Nov. 29-Dec. 5.
See Nos. 2418-2419.

Souvenir Sheets
1948, Dec. 3   Without Gum   Imperf.
423 A206 5y brown, sheet of 1   40.00 27.50
Kanazawa and Takaoka stamp exhibitions.

Child Playing Hanetsuki — A207

1948, Dec. 13   Litho.   Perf. 13
424 A207 2y scarlet   3.75 3.00
Issued to pay postage on New Year's cards, later for ordinary use.

Farm Woman   Whaling
A208   A209

Miner
A210

Tea Picking
A211

Girl Printer
A212

Factory Girl
with Cotton
Bobbin
A213

Mt.
Hodaka
A214

Planting
A215

Postman
A216

Blast Furnace
A217

Locomotive
Assembly
A218

Typographed, Engraved
1948-49   Wmk. 257   Perf. 13x13½

425	A208	2y green	1.50	.25
a.		Overprinted with 4 characters in frame	.55	.75
b.		As "a," overprint inverted	57.50	
426	A209	3y lt grnsh bl ('49)	4.25	.25
427	A210	5y olive bis	15.00	.25
a.		Booklet pane of 20	225.00	10.00
		Hinged	120.00	
428	A211	5y blue grn ('49)	30.00	4.75
429	A212	6y red org ('49)	6.75	.25
430	A210	8y brown org ('49)	6.75	.25
a.		Booklet pane of 20	300.00	8.50
		Hinged	175.00	
431	A213	15y blue	3.00	.25
432	A214	16y ultra ('49)	8.00	3.50
433	A215	20y dk green ('49)	27.50	.25
434	A216	30y violet bl ('49)	45.00	.25
435	A217	100y car lake ('49)	650.00	3.00
436	A218	500y deep blue ('49)	525.00	4.00
		Nos. 425-436 (12)	1,322.	17.25
		Set, hinged	625.00	

No. 425a has a red control overprint of four characters ("Senkyo Jimu," or "Election Business") arranged vertically in a rectangular frame. Each candidate received 1,000 copies.
Nos. 432, 435-436 are engraved.
See Nos. 442, 511-512, 514-515, 518, 520, 521A-521B.

Souvenir Sheets
Typo. and Litho.
1948, Oct. 16   Imperf.

437	A213	15y blue, sheet of 1	30.00	30.00

Nagano Stamp Exhibition, Oct. 16.

1948, Nov. 2   Imperf.

438	A210	5y ol bis, sheet of 2	40.00	35.00

Shikoku Traveling Stamp Exhib., Nov. 1948.

Sampans
on Inland
Sea
A219

1949   Wmk. 257   Engr.   Perf. 13x13½

439	A219	10y rose lake	40.00	15.00
440	A219	10y car rose	25.00	14.00
441	A219	10y orange ver	27.50	13.50
442	A214	16y brt blue	12.00	4.50
		Nos. 439-442 (4)	104.50	47.00
		Set, hinged	57.50	

Issued in sheets of 20 stamps with marginal inscription publicizing expositions at Takamatsu (No. 439), Okayama (No. 440) and Matsuyama (No. 441), Nagano Peace Exposition, Apr. 1-May 31, 1949 (No. 442).

Ice
Skater — A221

Ski
Jumper — A222

1949   Unwmk.   Photo.   Perf. 12

444	A221	5y violet	2.75	1.25
445	A222	5y ultra	3.00	1.25

Winter events of the 4th Natl. Athletic Meet: skating at Suwa Jan. 27-30, skiing at Sapporo Mar. 3-6. Issued: No. 444, 1/27; No. 445, 3/3.

Steamer in
Beppu
Bay — A223

1949, Mar. 10   Engr.   Perf. 13x13½

446	A223	2y carmine & ultra	1.25	.65
447	A223	5y green & ultra	4.00	1.00

Scene at
Fair — A224

1949, Mar. 15   Photo.   Imperf.

448	A224	5y brt rose	2.00	1.60
a.		Perf. 13	3.00	1.50
b.		Sheet of 20, imperf.	65.00	45.00

Issued to publicize the Japan Foreign Trade Fair, Yokohama, 1949.
No. 448a was printed in sheets of 50 (10x5); No. 448 in sheets of 20 (4x5) with marginal inscriptions (No. 448b).

Stylized
Trees — A225

1949, Apr. 1   Unwmk.   Perf. 12

449	A225	5y bright green	8.00	1.50

Issued to publicize the forestation movement.

Lion Rock
A226

Daiho-zan (Mt. Ohmine) — A227

Doro
Gorge
A228

Bridge
Pier
Rocks
A229

1949, Apr. 10   Photo.   Perf. 13

450	A226	2y brown	1.10	.75
451	A227	5y yellow grn	3.50	1.10
452	A228	10y scarlet	14.50	8.25
453	A229	16y blue	7.25	3.75
a.		Souv. sheet of 4, #450-453, no gum	29.00	24.00
b.		As "a," 10y stamp omitted		
		Nos. 450-453 (4)	26.35	13.85

Yoshino-Kumano National Park.
No. 453a sold for 40y.

Boy — A230

1949, May 5   Perf. 12

455	A230	5y rose brn & org	4.25	1.40
a.		Orange omitted	275.00	

Children's Day, May 5, 1949.

Souvenir Sheets
1949, May 5   Imperf.

456	A230	5y rose brn & org, sheet of 10	350.00	225.00
		Hinged	150.00	

Children's Exhib., Inuyama, Apr. 1-May 31.

Radio Tower and Star — A231

1949, May 11   Perf. 13

457	A231	20y dp blue	110.00	75.00
		Hinged	55.00	

Electrical Communication Week, May 11-18.

Symbols of
Communication
A232

1949, June 1   Wmk. 257   Engr.   Perf. 12

458	A232	8y brt ultra	3.00	1.50

Establishment of the Post Ministry and the Ministry of Electricity and Communication.

Central
Meteorological
Observatory,
Tokyo — A233

1949, June 1   Unwmk.   Perf. 12½

459	A233	8y deep green	3.50	1.50

75th anniv. of the establishment of the Central Meteorological Observatory.

Mt. Fuji in
Autumn
A234

Lake Kawaguchi — A235

Mt. Fuji from Mt. Shichimen — A236

Shinobuno Village and Mt.
Fuji — A237

1949, July 15   Photo.   Perf. 13

460	A234	2y yellow brown	3.00	.75
461	A235	8y yellow green	3.50	1.10
462	A236	14y carmine lake	1.50	.45
463	A237	24y blue	5.00	.60
a.		Souv. sheet of 4, #460-463	50.00	35.00
		Nos. 460-463 (4)	13.00	2.90

Fuji-Hakone National Park.
No. 463a sold for 55y.

Allegory
of Peace
A238

Doves over
Nagasaki — A239

Perf. 13x13½, 13½x13

1949 **Photo.** **Unwmk.**
465 A238 8y yellow brown 6.50 1.75
466 A239 8y green 4.25 1.75

Establishment of Hiroshima as the City of Eternal Peace and of Nagasaki as the International City of Culture. Issued: No. 465, 8/6; No. 466, 8/9.

Boy Scout — A240

1949, Sept. 22 **Perf. 13x13½**
467 A240 8y brown 5.75 1.90

Natl. Boy Scout Jamboree.

Pen Nib of
Newspaper
Stereotype
Matrix — A241

1949, Oct. 1 **Perf. 13½x13**
468 A241 8y deep blue 4.75 1.90

Natl. Newspaper Week.

Racing Swimmer
Poised for
Dive — A242

Javelin
Thrower — A243

1949 **Perf. 13½**
469 A242 8y dull blue 3.00 1.10

Perf. 12
470 A243 8y shown 5.50 2.10
471 A243 8y Yacht Racing 5.50 2.10
472 A243 8y Relay Race 5.50 2.10
473 A243 8y Tennis 5.50 2.10
　a. Block of 4, #470-473 27.50 32.50
　Nos. 469-473 (5) 25.00 9.50

4th Natl. Athletic Meet. The swimming matches were held at Yokohama, Sept. 15-18 and the fall events at Tokyo, Oct. 30. Issued: No. 469, 9/15; Nos. 470-473, 10/30. Nos. 470-473 exist perf 12½. Values 50 percent above those of perf 12 copies.

Map and Envelopes
Forming
"75" — A244

Symbols of
UPU — A245

1949, Oct. 10 **Engr.** **Perf. 12, 13½**
474 A244 2y dull green 2.25 1.00
475 A245 8y maroon 3.00 1.00
　a. Souv. sheet of 2, #474-475,
　　imperf. 4.75 4.75
476 A244 14y carmine 7.50 4.00
477 A245 24y aqua 11.50 4.50
　a. Imperf., pair
　Nos. 474-477 (4) 24.25 10.50

75th anniv. of the UPU.
No 745a was issued without gum.

Floating Zenith
Telescope — A246

1949, Oct. 30 **Photo.** **Perf. 12**
478 A246 8y dk blue grn 3.00 1.25

50th anniv. of the Mizusawa Latitudinal Observatory.

"Moon and
Geese," Print by
Hiroshige — A247

1949, Nov. 1 **Perf. 13x13½**
479 A247 8y purple 75.00 40.00
　a. Sheet of 5 425.00 325.00
　　Sheet, hinged 300.00

Postal Week, Nov. 1-7. See Nos. 2420-2421.

Dr. Hideyo
Noguchi
A248

Yukichi Fukuzawa
A249

Soseki Natsume
A250

Shoyo Tsubouchi
A251

Danjuro
Ichikawa — A252

Joseph Hardy
Niijima — A253

Hogai Kano
A254

Kanzo Uchimura
A255

Ichiyo
Higuchi — A256

Ogai
Mori — A257

Shiki
Masaoka — A258

Shunso
Hishida — A259

Amane
Nishi — A260

Kenjiro
Ume — A261

Hisashi
Kimura — A262

Inazo
Nitobe — A263

Torahiko
Terada — A264

Tenshin
Okakura — A265

1949-52 **Unwmk.** **Engr.** **Perf. 12½**
480 A248 8y green 8.00 .95
　a. Imperf., pair
481 A249 8y deep olive ('50) 3.25 .95
　a. Imperf., pair
482 A250 8y dk Prus grn
　　 ('50) 3.25 .95
483 A251 8y Prus grn ('50) 3.00 .95
　a. Imperf., pair
484 A252 8y dk violet ('50) 8.75 3.00
485 A253 8y vio brn ('50) 3.00 .95
486 A254 8y dk green ('51) 9.00 1.90
487 A255 8y dp purple ('51) 10.00 1.90
488 A256 8y carmine ('51) 15.00 1.90
489 A257 8y vio brn ('51) 25.00 2.10
490 A258 8y choc ('51) 15.00 2.10
491 A259 8y dk blue ('51) 12.50 2.10
492 A260 10y dk green ('52) 60.00 3.75
493 A261 10y brn vio ('52) 10.00 1.25
494 A262 10y carmine ('52) 3.00 1.10
495 A263 10y dk grn ('52) 5.25 1.10
496 A264 10y choc ('52) 4.25 1.10
497 A265 10y dk blue ('52) 4.25 1.10
　Nos. 480-497 (18) 202.50 29.15
　Set, hinged 100.00

Tiger — A266

1950, Feb. 1 **Photo.** **Perf. 12**
498 A266 2y dark red 5.25 1.50

6th prize (lottery), sheet of 5, value $190.

Microphones of 1925
and 1950 — A267

1950, Mar. 21 **Perf. 13**
499 A267 8y ultra 3.25 1.25

25th anniversary of broadcasting in Japan. Sheets of 20 with marginal inscription.

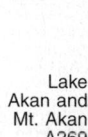

Dove and Olive Twig
on Letter
Box — A268

1950, Apr. 20 **Perf. 12**
500 A268 8y dp yellow grn 3.00 1.10

Day of Posts, Apr. 20.

Lake
Akan and
Mt. Akan
A269

Lake
Kutcharo,
Hokkaido
A270

Mt. Akan-
Fuji
A271

Lake
Mashu
A272

1950, July 15 **Unwmk.** **Perf. 13**
501 A269 2y yellow brn 1.50 .75
502 A270 8y dp yellow grn 2.25 1.10
503 A271 14y rose car 10.50 3.75
504 A272 24y brt blue 11.50 4.50
　a. Souv. sheet of 4, #501-504 50.00 32.50
　Nos. 501-504 (4) 25.75 10.10

Akan National Park.
No. 504a sold for 55y.

Gymnast on
Rings — A273

Designs: No. 506, Pole vault. No. 507, Soccer. No. 508, Equestrian.

1950, Oct. 28   *Perf. 13½x13*
505	A273	8y rose brown	35.00	8.25
506	A273	8y rose brown	35.00	8.25
507	A273	8y rose brown	35.00	8.25
508	A273	8y rose brown	35.00	8.25
a.		Strip of 4, #505-508	160.00	110.00
b.		Block of 4, #505-508	175.00	125.00
		As "b," hinged	80.00	

5th National Athletic Meet. Sheets of 20 stamps in which each horizontal row contains all four designs. Value, sheet $850.

Types of 1947-49 and

Ishiyama-dera Pagoda A274

Hisoka Maeshima A275

Long-tailed Cock of Tosa A276

Goddess Kannon A277

Himeji Castle A278

Nyoirin Kannon of Chuguji A280

Phoenix Hall, Byodoin Temple A279

Perf. 13x13½, 13½x13 (14y)
1950-52   Typo.   Unwmk.
509	A274	80s carmine ('51)	2.50	1.25
a.		Sheet of 1	8.00	9.50

Photo.
510	A275	1y dk brown ('51)	4.00	.55
a.		Souvenir sheet of 4	17.50	15.00

Typo.
511	A208	2y green ('51)	2.00	.25
512	A209	3y lt grnsh bl ('51)	50.00	.95
512A	A168	4y lt ultra ('52)	40.00	1.10
513	A276	5y dp grn & org brn ('51)	6.00	.25
a.		Orange brown omitted	425.00	
514	A212	6y red org ('51)	7.00	.45
515	A210	8y dk org brn ('51)	35.00	.55
515A	A197	10y rose vio ('51)	75.00	5.00
516	A277	10y red brn & lil ('51)	25.00	.25

Engr.
517	A278	14y brn & car ('51)	55.00	30.00
a.		Sheet of 1	70.00	60.00

Typo.
518	A215	20y dk green ('51)	65.00	.95

Engr.
519	A279	24y dp ultra ('51)	40.00	15.00
a.		Sheet of 1	60.00	40.00

Typo.
520	A216	30y vio bl ('52)	200.00	1.10

Photo.
521	A280	50y dk brown ('51)	150.00	1.25
		Hinged	85.00	
c.		Sheet of 1	250.00	250.00
		Hinged	125.00	

Engr.
521A	A217	100y car lake ('52)	475.00	1.25
521B	A218	500y dp blue ('52)	475.00	2.00
		Nos. 509-521B (17)	1,706.	62.15

No. 510a for the 80th anniv. of Japan's postal service. On No. 512A, characters read from left to right.

Compare designs: A274 with A314c; A275 with A314a, A447, A563a; A277 with A332a; A278 with A373a; A279 with A385a; A280 with A314b and A565f.

Girl and Rabbit — A281

1951, Jan. 1   Photo.   Perf. 12
522	A281	2y rose pink	5.00	1.00

9th prize (lottery), sheet of 5, value $42.50. See No. 2655a.

Scenic Spots Issue

Skiers on Mt. Zao
A282   A283

1951, Feb. 15   Perf. 13
523	A282	8y olive	13.50	2.00
524	A283	24y blue	17.50	4.50

Tea Picking — A284

Mt. Fuji Seen from Nihon Plateau A285

Nihon-daira Plateau.

1951, Apr. 2
525	A284	8y olive green	14.00	2.75
526	A285	24y bright blue	82.50	20.00

Hot Springs, Hakone — A286

Lake Ashi, Hakone A287

1951, May 25
527	A286	8y chestnut brown	9.00	2.10
528	A287	24y deep blue	7.50	2.50

Senju Waterfall — A288

Ninai Waterfall A289

Akame 48 Waterfalls.

1951, June 1
529	A288	8y deep green	10.00	2.10
530	A289	24y deep blue	9.75	2.50

Pavilion, Wakanoura Bay — A290

Wakanoura Bay — A291

Wakanoura & Tomogashima.

1951, June 25
531	A290	8y brown	7.50	2.10
532	A291	24y brt blue	7.00	2.50

Uji River — A292

View from Uji Bridge A293

Perf. 13x13½, 13½x13
1951, Aug. 1   Engr.
533	A292	8y brown	7.50	2.10
534	A293	24y deep blue	7.00	2.50

Oura Catholic Church, Nagasaki — A294

Sofuku Temple A295

1951, Sept. 15   Photo.   Perf. 13½
535	A294	8y carmine rose	10.00	2.10
536	A295	24y dull blue	8.75	2.50

Marunuma — A296

Sugenuma A297

1951, Oct. 1
537	A296	8y rose violet	11.50	2.10
a.		Imperf., pair		
538	A297	24y dull blue grn	6.25	2.50

Kakuenpo (peak) — A298

Nagatoro Bridge A299

Shosenkyo Gorge.

1951, Oct. 15
539	A298	8y brown red	10.00	2.10
540	A299	24y dp Prus grn	10.50	2.50
		Nos. 523-540 (18)	249.75	61.45

Boy's Head and Seedling — A300

1951, May 5   Perf. 13½
541	A300	8y orange brown	22.50	2.25

Issued to publicize Children's Day, May 5, 1951.

Oirase River A301

Lake Towada A302

View from Kankodai A303

Mt. Hakkoda from Mt. Yokodake A304

1951, July 20   Photo.   Perf. 13x13½
542 A301 2y brown   2.50 .95
543 A302 8y green   10.00 1.40
544 A303 14y dark red   11.50 4.75
545 A304 24y blue   12.00 5.50
  a.   Souv. sheet of 4, #542-545   47.50 30.00
    Nos. 542-545 (4)   36.00 12.60
Towada Natl. Park. No. 545a sold for 55y.

Chrysanthemum   National Flag
A305   A306

1951, Sept. 9   Perf. 13½
546 A305 2y orange brown   1.90 .95
547 A306 8y slate blue & red 5.75 2.25
548 A305 24y blue green   17.00 6.00
    Nos. 546-548 (3)   24.65 9.20
Signing of the peace treaty of 1951.

Putting the   Hockey — A308
Shot — A307

1951, Oct. 27
549 A307 2y orange brown   3.25 1.60
550 A308 2y gray blue   3.25 1.60
  a.   Pair, #549-550   8.75 8.75
6th Natl. Athletic Meet, Hiroshima, 10/27-31.

Okina Mask — A309

1952, Jan. 16   Photo.   Perf. 13½x13
551 A309 5y crimson rose   9.50 .75
Sheets reproducing four of these stamps with Japanese inscriptions and floral ornament at left were awarded as sixth prize in the national lottery. Value $120.

Southern Cross   Earth and Big
from   Dipper — A311
Ship — A310

1952, Feb. 19
552 A310 5y purple   5.00 1.00
553 A311 10y dark green   14.50 2.00
75th anniv. of Japan's admission to the UPU.

Red Cross and   Red Cross
Lilies — A312   Nurse — A313

1952, May 1
554 A312 5y rose red & dk red 4.25 .95
555 A313 10y dk green & red   10.00 2.00
  a.   Red cross omitted   500.00
  b.   Imperf., pair   75.00
75th anniv. of the formation of the Japanese Red Cross Society.

Goldfish — A314

A314a   A314b

A314c

1952   Perf. 13x13½
556 A314 35y red orange   10.00 .25
  a.   Imperf., pair
Types of 1951
Redrawn; Zeros Omitted
Unwmk.
557 A314a 1y dark brown   .55 .25
558 A314b 50y dark brown   5.00 .30
Typo.
559 A314c 4y dp cl & pale 1.75 .30
        rose
  a.   Background (pale rose) omitted
Ornamental frame and background added, denomination at upper left, Japanese characters at upper right.

Japanese
Serow — A315

Photo.
560 A315 8y brown   .30 .25
    Nos. 556-560 (5)   17.60 1.35

Mt. Yari — A316   Kurobe
                  Valley — A317

Mt.
Shirouma
A318

Mt.
Norikura
A319

1952, July 5   Perf. 13½x13, 13x13½
561 A316 5y brown   4.50 .50
562 A317 10y blue green   22.50 1.75
563 A318 14y bright red   5.75 3.00

564 A319 24y bright blue   9.50 3.00
  a.   Souv. sheet of 4, #561-564,
    imperf.   100.00 60.00
    Nos. 561-564 (4)   42.25 8.25
Japan Alps (Chubu-Sangaku) National Park. No. 564a sold for 60y.

Yasuda Hall, Tokyo
University — A320

1952, Oct. 1   Engr.   Perf. 13
565 A320 10y dull green   16.00 2.00
75th anniversary of the founding of Tokyo University.

Yomei Gate,
Nikko — A321

1952, Oct. 15   Photo.   Perf. 13x13½
566 A321 45y blue   3.50 .25

Mountain
Climber — A322

1952, Oct. 18   Dated "1952"
567 A322 5y shown   6.00 1.50
568 A322 5y Wrestlers   6.00 1.50
  a.   Pair, #567-568   17.50 9.00
7th Nat.l Athletic Meet, Fukushima, 10/18-22.

Mt.
Azuma
A323

Mt. Asahi
A324

Mt.
Bandai
A325

Mt.
Gatsun
A326

Unwmk.
1952, Oct. 18   Photo.   Perf. 13
569 A323 5y brown   3.75 .60
570 A324 10y olive grn   11.50 1.50
571 A325 14y rose red   4.50 2.25
572 A326 24y blue   10.00 4.00
  a.   Souv. sheet of 4, #569-572,
    imperf.   80.00 60.00
    Nos. 569-572 (4)   29.75 8.35
Bandai-Asahi National Park. No. 572a sold for 60y.

Kirin — A327   Flag of Crown
               Prince — A328

Engr. and Photo.
1952, Nov. 10   Perf. 13½
573 A327 5y red org & pur 1.90 .55
574 A327 10y red org & dk 2.25 .80
        grn
575 A328 24y deep blue   12.00 4.50
  a.   Souv. sheet of 3, #573-575,
    imperf.   70.00 90.00
    Nos. 573-575 (3)   16.15 5.85
Issued to commemorate the nomination of Crown Prince Akihito as Heir Apparent.
No. 575a measures 130x129mm, and has a background design of phoenix and clouds in violet brown and blue. Sold for 50y.

Sambaso
Doll — A329

Perf. 13½x13
1953, Jan. 1   Photo.   Unwmk.
576 A329 5y carmine   6.75 .75
For postage on New Year's cards, later for ordinary use.
Sheets of 4 were awarded as 6th prize in the natl. lottery. Value $80.

First Electric Lamp
in Japan — A330

1953, Mar. 25
577 A330 10y brown   6.25 1.90
75th anniv. of electric lighting in Japan.

"Kintai Bridge," Print
by Hiroshige — A331

Kintai Bridge
as Rebuilt in
1953 — A332

1953, May 3   Perf. 13
578 A331 10y chestnut   6.50 2.10
579 A332 24y blue   6.00 3.00

Kannon Type of 1951
Redrawn; Zeros Omitted

A332a

1953-54   **Typo.**
580 A332a 10y red brn & lilac   4.00   .25
a. Booklet pane 10 + 2 la-
bels (souvenir) ('54)   125.00 100.00
b. Bkt. pane 10 + 2 labels
('54)   67.50   60.00

No. 580a was issued in honor of Philatelic Week 1954. The inscriptions on the two labels are arranged in two columns of boldface characters.

On No. 580b, the left-hand label inscriptions are arranged in three columns of mixed heavy and thin characters.

See Nos. 611a-611b and 672.

Lake Shikotsu, Hokkaido A333

Mt. Yotei A334

1953, July 25   **Photo.**   **Perf. 13**
581 A333 5y ultra   2.00   .55
582 A334 10y green   5.00   1.10
a. Souv. sheet of 2, #581-582,
imperf., no gum   32.50 29.00

Shikotsu-Toya National Park.
No. 582a sold for 20 yen.

Akita Dog A335   Cormorant Fishing A336

1953   **Unwmk.**
583 A335 2y gray   .25   .25
Engr.
584 A336 100y dark red 35.00   .25
a. Imperf., pair   2,750.

See No. 1622.

Futamigaura Beach — A337

Namikiri Coast A338

1953, Oct. 2   **Photo.**
585 A337 5y red   1.90   .55
586 A338 10y blue   3.75   1.10
a. Souv. sheet of 2, #585-586,
imperf., no gum   20.00 17.50

Ise-Shima National Park.

Phoenix — A339

Design: 10y, Japanese crane in flight.

1953, Oct. 12   **Engr.**   **Perf. 12½**
587 A339 5y brown carmine 2.75 1.10
Photo.
588 A339 10y dark blue   5.50 1.90

Nos. 587-588 were issued on the occasion of the return of Crown Prince Akihito from his visit to Europe and America. Issued in sheets of 20 with marginal inscription.

Rugby Match — A340

Judo — A341

1953, Oct. 22   **Perf. 13½**
589 A340 5y black   5.75 1.25
590 A341 5y blue green 5.75 1.25
a. Pair, #589-590   13.50 7.50

8th Natl. Athletic Meet, Matsuyama, Oct. 22-26.

Sky and Top of Observatory A342

1953, Oct. 29
591 A342 10y dk gray blue 9.00 1.50

75th anniversary of the Tokyo Astronomical Observatory.

Mt. Unzen from Golf Course A343

Mt. Unzen from Chijiwa Beach A344

1953, Nov. 20   **Perf. 13**
592 A343 5y red   1.75   .55
593 A344 10y blue   4.50   1.10
a. Souv. sheet of 2, #592-593,
imperf., no gum   20.00 17.50

Unzen National Park.

Toy Horse — A345

1953, Dec. 25   **Perf. 13½x13**
594 A345 5y rose   5.25   .55

Issued to pay postage on New Year's cards, later for ordinary use. A sheet reproducing four of these stamps was awarded as sixth prize in the national lottery. Value $37.50.

Racing Skaters — A346

1954, Jan. 16
595 A346 10y blue   4.50   1.40

World Speed Skating Matches for Men, Sapporo City, Jan. 16-17, 1954.

Golden Hall, Chusonji Temple — A347

1954, Jan. 20
596 A347 20y olive green 1.00 .25

Thread, Pearls, Gears, Buttons and Globe — A348

1954, Apr. 10
597 A348 10y dark red   3.25 1.00

International Trade Fair, Osaka, Apr. 10-23.

Little Cuckoo — A349

1954, May 10   **Perf. 13x13½**
598 A349 3y blue green   .25   .25
a. Imperf., pair   500.00

For stamp inscribed "NIPPON," see No. 1067.

Wrestlers A350

1954, May 22   **Engr.**
599 A350 10y deep green 2.75 1.00

World Free Style Wrestling Championship Matches, Tokyo, 1954.

Mt. Asama A351

Mt. Tanikawa A352

1954, June 25   **Perf. 13**
600 A351 5y dk gray brn 2.00   .55
601 A352 10y dk blue grn 3.50 1.10
a. Souvenir sheet of 2, #600-601, no gum 17.50 15.00

Jo-Shin-etsu National Park.

Table Tennis — A353

Archery — A354

1954, Aug. 22   **Engr.**   **Perf. 12**
602 A353 5y dull brown   4.00 1.00
603 A354 5y gray green   4.00 1.00
a. Pair, #602-603   9.00 5.75

9th Natl. Athletic Meet, Sapporo, Aug. 22-26.

Morse Telegraph Instrument A355   ITU Monument A356

1954, Oct. 13   **Perf. 13x13½, 13½x13**
604 A355 5y dark purple brown 1.75 .55
605 A356 10y deep blue   4.75 1.10

75th anniv. of Japanese membership in the ITU.

Daruma Doll — A357

1954, Dec. 20 **Photo.** **Perf. 13½x13**
606 A357 5y black & red   5.25 .55

Sheets reproducing four of these stamps with Japanese inscriptions and ornaments were awarded as fifth prize in the national lottery. Value $37.50.

Mountain Stream, Tama Gorge — A358

Chichibu Mountains — A359

1955, Mar. 1   **Engr.**   **Perf. 13**
607 A358 5y blue   1.50   .55
608 A359 10y red brown   1.90   .75
a. Souv. sheet of 2, #607-608,
imperf., no gum   20.00 17.50

Chichibu-Tama National Park.

Bridge and Iris — A360

1955, Mar. 15   **Perf. 13x13½**
609   A360   500y deep plum   50.00   .60

Paper Carp as Flown on Boys' Day — A361

1955, May 16   **Unwmk.**   **Perf. 13**
610   A361   10y multicolored   4.25   1.10

   15th congress of the International Chamber of Commerce, Tokyo, May 16-21, 1955.

Mandarin Ducks — A362

1955-64
611   A362   5y lt bl & red brn   .25   .25
   a.   Bklt. pane, 4 #611, 8 #580   50.00
         ('59)
   b.   Bklt. pane, 4 #611, 8 #725   35.00   17.00
         ('63)
   c.   Bklt. pane of 4 ('64)   4.25   2.75
   d.   Imperf., pair   1,400.

   See Nos. 738, 881d, 914b.

Benten Cape — A363

Jodo Beach A364

1955, Sept. 30
612   A363   5y deep green   1.40   .45
613   A364   10y rose lake   1.90   .75
   a.   Souv. sheet of 2, #612-613,
         imperf., no gum   20.00   17.50

   Rikuchu-Kaigan National Park.
   No. 613a sold for 20y.

Gymnastics   Runners
A365   A366

1955, Oct. 30   **Engr.**
614   A365   5y brown lake   1.75   .75
615   A366   5y bluish black   1.75   .75
   a.   Pair, #614-615   6.50   5.00

   10th National Athletic Meet, Kanagawa Prefecture.
   See Nos. 639-640, 657.

"A Girl Blowing Glass Toy," by Utamaro A367

1955, Nov. 1   **Photo.**
616   A367   10y multicolored   10.00   5.75

   150th anniv. of the death of Utamaro, woodcut artist, and to publicize Philatelic Week, Nov. 1955. Issued in sheets of 10.

Kokeshi Dolls — A368

1955, Dec. 30   **Unwmk.**   **Perf. 13**
617   A368   5y olive grn & red   1.75   .25

   Sheets reproducing four of these stamps, were awarded as fifth prize in the New Year's lottery. Value $27.50.

Table Tennis — A369

1956, Apr. 2   **Perf. 13x13½**
618   A369   10y red brown   1.25   .75

   Intl. Table Tennis Championship, Tokyo, 4/2-11.

Judo — A370

1956, May 2   **Perf. 13**
619   A370   10y green & lilac   1.50   .75

   Issued to publicize the first World Judo Championship Meet, Tokyo, May 3, 1956.

Boy and Girl with Paper Carp A371

1956, May 5
620   A371   5y lt blue & blk   1.10   .55

   Establishment of World Children's Day, 5/5/56.

Water Plants,   Big Purple
Lake Akan   Butterfly
A372   A373

1956   **Unwmk.**   **Perf. 13**
621   A372   55y lt blue, grn & blk   12.50   .55
622   A373   75y multicolored   7.00   .55

   See Nos. 887A, 917.

Castle Type of 1951
Redrawn; Zeros Omitted

A373a

1956   **Engr.**   **Perf. 13½x13**
623   A373a   14y gray olive   5.00   1.75

Osezaki Promontory — A374

Kujuku Island A375

1956, Oct. 1   **Photo.**
624   A374   5y red brown   1.00   .45
          Engr. & Photo.
625   A375   10y lt blue & indigo   1.25   .75
   a.   Souv. sheet of 2, #624-625,
         imperf., no gum   17.00   16.00

   Saikai National Park.
   No. 625a sold for 20y.

Palace Moat and Modern Tokyo A376

1956, Oct. 1   **Engr.**
626   A376   10y dull purple   1.90   .75

   500th anniv. of the founding of Tokyo.

Sakuma Dam — A377

1956, Oct. 15   **Unwmk.**   **Perf. 13**
627   A377   10y dark blue   1.90   .75

   Completion of Sakuma Dam.

Long Jump   Basketball
A378   A379

1956, Oct. 28   **Perf. 13½x13**
628   A378   5y brown violet   1.00   .55
629   A379   5y steel blue   1.00   .55
   a.   Pair, #628-629   3.00   2.50

   11th Natl. Athletic Meet, Hyogo Prefecture.
   See No. 658.

Kabuki Actor Ebizo Ichikawa by Sharaku A380

1956, Nov. 1   **Photo.**   **Perf. 13**
630   A380   10y multicolored   8.50   5.50

   Stamp Week. Sheets of 10.

Mount Manaslu A381

1956, Nov. 3
631   A381   10y multicolored   3.00   1.60

   Japanese expedition which climbed Mount Manaslu in the Himalayas on May 9 and 11, 1956.

Electric Locomotive and Hiroshige's "Yui Stage" — A382

1956, Nov. 19   **Unwmk.**   **Perf. 13**
632   A382   10y dk ol bis, blk & grn   4.00   2.00

   Electrification of Tokaido Line.

Cogwheel, Vacuum Tube and Ship — A383

1956, Dec. 18   **Engr.**
633   A383   10y ultra   .90   .75

   Japanese Machinery Floating Fair.

Toy Whale — A384

1956, Dec. 20   **Photo.**
634   A384   5y multicolored   1.25   .25
   a.   Imperf., pair

   Sheets reproducing four of these stamps, with inscriptions and ornaments, were awarded as sixth prize in the national lottery. Value $13.50.

United Nations Emblem A385

Photogravure and Engraved
1957, Mar. 8   **Unwmk.**   **Perf. 13½x13**
635   A385   10y lt blue & dk car   .70   .55

   Japan's admission to the UN, Dec. 18, 1956.

Temple Type of 1950
Redrawn; Zeros Omitted

A385a

1957-59 Engr. Perf. 13x13½
636 A385a 24y violet | 17.50 | 3.00
636A A385a 30y rose lilac ('59) | 45.00 | .90
  b. Imperf., pair | 6,000. | 2,000.

IGY Emblem, Penguin and "Soya" — A386

1957, July 1 Photo. Perf. 13
637 A386 10y blue, yel & blk | 1.00 | .50

International Geophysical Year.

Atomic Reactor — A387

1957, Sept. 18 Engr. Perf. 13
638 A387 10y dark purple | .45 | .25

Completion of Japan's atomic reactor at Tokai-Mura, Ibaraki Prefecture.

Sports Type of 1955

No. 639, Girl on parallel bars. No. 640, Boxers.

1957, Oct. 26 Unwmk. Perf. 13
639 A366 5y ultra | .35 | .25
640 A366 5y dark red | .35 | .25
  a. Pair, #639-640 | 1.00 | .75

12th Natl. Athletic Meet, Shizuoka Prefecture.

"Girl Bouncing Ball," by Suzuki Harunobu A388

1957, Nov. 1 Photo.
641 A388 10y multicolored | 1.50 | 1.25

1957 Stamp Week. Issued in sheets of 10. See Nos. 646, 671, 728, 757.

Lake Okutama and Ogochi Dam — A389

1957, Nov. 26 Engr. Perf. 13½
642 A389 10y ultra | .30 | .25

Completion of Ogochi Dam, part of the Tokyo water supply system.

Modern and First Japanese Blast Furnaces A390

1957, Dec. 1 Photo. Unwmk.
643 A390 10y orange & dk pur | .25 | .25

Centenary of Japan's iron industry.

Toy Dog (Inu-hariko) — A391

1957, Dec. 20 Perf. 13½x13
644 A391 5y multicolored | .25 | .25

New Year 1958. Sheets reproducing 4 No. 644, with inscriptions and ornaments, were awarded as 5th prize in the New Year lottery. Value $5.

Shimonoseki-Moji Tunnel — A392

1958, Mar. 9 Perf. 13x13½
645 A392 10y multicolored | .25 | .25

Completion of the Kan-Mon Underwater Highway connecting Honshu and Kyushu Islands.

Stamp Week Type of 1957

Design: 10y, Woman with Umbrella, woodcut by Kiyonaga.

1958, Apr. 20 Unwmk. Perf. 13
646 A388 10y multicolored | .65 | .25

Stamp Week, 1958. Sheets of 10.

Statue of Ii Naosuke and Harbor A393

Unwmk.
1958, May 10 Engr. Perf. 13
647 A393 10y gray blue & car | .25 | .25

Cent. of the opening of the ports of Yokohama, Nagasaki and Hakodate to foreign powers.

National Stadium — A394

3rd Asian Games, Tokyo: 10y, Torch and emblem. 14y, Runner. 24y, Woman diver.

1958, May 24 Photo.
648 A394 5y bl grn, bis & pink | .25 | .25
649 A394 10y multicolored | .25 | .30
650 A394 14y multicolored | .30 | .25
651 A394 24y multicolored | .35 | .30
  Nos. 648-651 (4) | 1.15 | 1.10

Kasato Maru, Map and Brazilian Flag A395

1958, June 18
652 A395 10y multicolored | .25 | .25

50 years of Japanese emigration to Brazil.

Sado Island and Local Dancer A396

Mt. Yahiko and Echigo Plain — A397

1958, Aug. 20 Unwmk. Perf. 13
653 A396 10y multicolored | .70 | .25
654 A397 10y multicolored | .55 | .25

Sado-Yahiko Quasi-National Park.

Stethoscope A398

1958, Sept. 7 Photo. Perf. 13
655 A398 10y Prussian green | .25 | .25

5th Intl. Cong. on Diseases of the Chest and the 7th Intl. Cong. of Bronchoesophagology.

"Kyoto" (Sanjo Bridge), Print by Hiroshige A399

1958, Oct. 5
656 A399 24y multicolored | 2.00 | .70

Issued for International Letter Writing Week, Oct. 5-11. See No. 679.

Sports Types of 1955-56

Designs: No. 657, Weight lifter. No. 658, Girl badminton player.

1958, Oct. 19 Engr.
657 A365 5y gray blue | .25 | .25
658 A379 5y claret | .25 | .25
  a. Pair, #657-658 | 1.00 | 2.00

13th Natl. Athletic Meet, Toyama Prefecture.

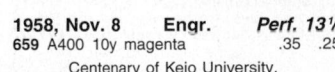

Keio University and Yukichi Fukuzawa — A400

1958, Nov. 8 Engr. Perf. 13½
659 A400 10y magenta | .35 | .25

Centenary of Keio University.

Globe and Playing Children A401

1958, Nov. 23 Photo. Perf. 13
660 A401 10y deep green | .25 | .25

9th Intl. Conf. of Social Work and the 2nd Intl. Study Conf. on Child Welfare.

Flame: Symbol of Human Rights — A402

1958, Dec. 10 Unwmk. Perf. 13
661 A402 10y multicolored | .25 | .25

10th anniv. of the signing of the Universal Declaration of Human Rights.

Toy of Takamatsu (Tai-Ebisu) — A403

1958, Dec. 20 Perf. 13½
662 A403 5y multicolored | .70 | .25

New Year 1959. Sheets reproducing 4 No. 662, with inscriptions and ornaments, were awarded as prizes in the New Year lottery. Size: 103x89mm. Value $5.

Tractor and Map of Kojima Bay — A404

1959, Feb. 1 Perf. 12½
663 A404 10y claret & bister brn | .25 | .25

Completion of the embankment closing Kojima Bay for reclamation.

Karst Plateau A405

Akiyoshi Cave — A406

1959, Mar. 16 Photo. Perf. 13½
664 A405 10y green, bl & ocher | .90 | .25
665 A406 10y multicolored | 1.50 | .25

Akiyoshidai Quasi-National Park.

Map of Southeast Asia — A407

1959, Mar. 27
666 A407 10y deep carmine .25 .25
Asian Cultural Cong., Tokyo, Mar. 27-31, marking the 2,500th anniv. of the death of Buddha.

Ceremonial Fan — A408

Prince Akihito and Princess Michiko — A409

Photogravure; Portraits Engraved
1959, Apr. 10
667 A408 5y magenta & violet .25 .25
668 A409 10y red brn & dull pur .50 .25
a. Souv. sheet of 2, #667-668, imperf. 4.75 4.75
669 A408 20y org brn & brn .85 .25
670 A409 30y yel grn & dk grn 2.50 .30
Nos. 667-670 (4) 4.10 1.05
Wedding of Crown Prince Akihito and Princess Michiko, Apr. 10, 1959.

Type of 1957
Women Reading Poetry, print by Eishi Fujiwara.

1959, May 20 Photo. Perf. 13
671 A388 10y multicolored 2.10 .90
Stamp Week. Issued in sheets of 10.

Redrawn Kannon Type of 1953
Coil Stamp
Perf. 13 Horiz.
1959, Jan. 20 Typo. Unwmk.
672 A332a 10y red brn & lilac 18.00 20.00

Measuring Glass, Tape Measure and Scales — A410

1959, June 5 Photo. Perf. 13
673 A410 10y lt blue & blk .25 .25
Adoption of the metric system.

Nurses Carrying Stretcher A411

1959, June 24
674 A411 10y olive grn & red .25 .25
Centenary of the Red Cross idea.

Mt. Fuji and Lake Motosu A412

1959, July 21 Engr. Perf. 13
675 A412 10y green, bl & sepia .50 .25
Establishment of Natural Park Day and 1st Natural Park Convention, Yumoto, Nikko, July 21, 1959.

Ao Cave Area of Yabakei A413

Hita, Mt. Hiko and Great Cormorant A414

1959, Sept. 25 Photo. Perf. 13
676 A413 10y multicolored .90 .25
677 A414 10y multicolored .90 .25
Yaba-Hita-Hiko Quasi National Park.

Golden Dolphin, Nagoya Castle — A415

1959, Oct. 1
678 A415 10y brt bl, gold & blk .60 .25
350th anniversary of Nagoya.

Hiroshige Type of 1958
Design: 30y, "Kuwana," the 7-ri Crossing Point, print by Hiroshige.

1959, Oct. 4 Unwmk.
679 A399 30y multicolored 6.00 1.25
Intl. Letter Writing Week, Oct. 4-10.

Japanese Crane, IATA Emblem — A416

1959, Oct. 12 Engr.
680 A416 10y brt grnsh blue .35 .25
15th General Meeting of the International Air Transport Association.

Shoin Yoshida and PTA Symbol — A417

1959, Oct. 27 Photo. Perf. 13
681 A417 10y brown .25 .25
Centenary of the death of Shoin Yoshida, educator, and in connection with the Parent-Teachers Association convention.

Throwing the Hammer — A418

Design: No. 683, Woman Fencer.

1959, Oct. 25 Engr.
682 A418 5y gray blue .35 .25
683 A418 5y olive bister .35 .25
a. Pair, #682-683 1.00 1.00
14th National Athletic Meet, Tokyo.

Globes A419

1959, Nov. 2 Photo.
684 A419 10y brown red .25 .25
15th session of GATT (General Agreement on Tariffs & Trade), Tokyo, Oct. 12-Nov. 21.

Toy Mouse of Kanazawa — A420

1959, Dec. 19 Unwmk. Perf. 13½
685 A420 5y gold, red, grn & blk .75 .25
New Year 1960. Sheets reproducing 4 No. 685, with marginal inscription and ornaments, were awarded as prizes in natl. lottery. Value $5.50.

Yukio Ozaki and Clock Tower, Ozaki Memorial Hall — A421

1960, Feb. 25 Photo. Perf. 13½
686 A421 10y red brn & dk brn .25 .25
Completion of Ozaki Memorial Hall, erected in memory of Yukio Ozaki (1858-1954), statesman.

Nara Period Artwork, Shosoin Treasure House — A422

1960, Mar. 10
687 A422 10y olive gray .40 .25
Transfer of the capital to Nara, 1250th anniv.

Scenic Trio Issue

Bay of Matsushima A423

Ama-no-hashidate (Heavenly Bridge) — A424

Miyajima from the Sea — A425

1960 Engr.
688 A423 10y maroon & bl grn 1.25 .45
689 A424 10y green & lt bl 1.60 .45
690 A425 10y vio blk & bl grn 1.60 .45
Nos. 688-690 (3) 4.45 1.35
Issued: No. 688, 3/15; No. 689, 7/15; No. 690, 11/15.

Takeshima, off Gamagori A426

1960, Mar. 20 Photo. Perf. 13½
691 A426 10y multicolored .75 .25
Mikawa Bay Quasi-National Park.

Poetess Isé, 13th Century Painting — A427

1960, Apr. 20 Unwmk. Perf. 13
692 A427 10y multicolored 1.75 1.75
Stamp Week, 1960.

Kanrin Maru — A428

Design: 30y, Pres. Buchanan receiving first Japanese diplomatic mission.

1960, May 17 Engr.
693 A428 10y bl grn & brn .40 .25
694 A428 30y car & indigo 1.25 .40
Cent. of the Japan-US Treaty of Amity and Commerce. Nos. 694 and 693 form pages of an open book when placed next to each other. Souvenir sheet is No. 703.

Crested Ibis (Toki) — A429

1960, May 24 Photo. Perf. 13½
695 A429 10y gray, pink & red .50 .40
12th Intl. Congress for Bird Preservation.

Radio Waves Encircling Globe — A430

1960, June 1 Engr.
696 A430 10y carmine rose .30 .25
25th anniv. of the Intl. Radio Program by the Japanese Broadcasting Corporation.

Flower Garden (Gensei Kaen) — A431

1960, June 15   **Photo.**
697 A431 10y multicolored   1.00 .40
Abashiri Quasi-National Park.

Cape Ashizuri A432

1960, Aug. 1   **Unwmk.**
698 A432 10y multicolored   .65 .40
Ashizuri Quasi-National Park.

Rainbow Spanning Pacific, Cherry Blossoms and Pineapples A433

1960, Aug. 20   **Perf. 13½**
699 A433 10y multicolored   .60 .25
75th anniversary of Japanese contract emigration to Hawaii.

Henri Farman's Biplane and Jet — A434

1960, Sept. 20   **Perf. 13**
700 A434 10y brn & chlky bl   .35 .25
50th anniversary of Japanese aviation.

Seat Plan of Diet — A435

"Red Fuji" by Hokusai and Diet Building — A436

1960, Sept. 27
701 A435 5y indigo & org   .25 .25
702 A436 10y blue & red brn   .40 .25
49th Inter-Parliamentary Conference.

Souvenir Sheet

1960, Sept. 27   **Engr.**
703 A428 Sheet of 2, #693-694   22.50 22.50
Visit of Prince Akihito and Princess Michiko to the US.

"Night Snow at Kambara," by Hiroshige A437

1960, Oct. 9   **Photo.**
704 A437 30y multicolored   11.00 3.75
Issued for International Letter Writing Week, Oct. 9-15. See Nos. 735, 769.

Japanese Fencing (Kendo) — A438

No. 706, Girl gymnast and vaulting horse.

1960, Oct. 23   **Engr.**   **Perf. 13½**
705 A438 5y dull blue   .35 .25
706 A438 5y rose violet   .35 .25
   a.   Pair, #705-706   1.00 1.00
15th National Athletic Meet, Kumamoto.

Okayama Astrophysical Observatory A439

1960, Oct. 19
707 A439 10y brt violet   .50 .25
Opening of the Okayama Astrophysical Observatory.

Lt. Naoshi Shirase and Map of Antarctica A440

1960, Nov. 29   **Photo.**
708 A440 10y fawn & black   .55 .25
50th anniv. of the 1st Japanese Antarctic expedition.

Little Red Calf of Aizu, Gold Calf of Iwate — A441

1960, Dec. 20   **Unwmk.**   **Perf. 13½**
709 A441 5y multicolored   .50 .25
New Year 1961. Sheets reproducing 4 No. 709 were awarded as prizes in the New Year lottery. Size: 102x89mm. Value $6.

Diet Building at Night — A442

Opening of First Session — A443

1960, Dec. 24   **Photo.; Engr. (10y)**
710 A442 5y gray & dk bl   .35 .25
711 A443 10y carmine   .45 .25
70th anniversary of the Japanese Diet.

Narcissus — A444

No. 713, Plum blossoms. No. 714, Camellia japonica. No. 715, Cherry blossoms. No. 716, Peony. No. 717, Iris. No. 718, Lily. No. 719,

Morning glory. No. 720, Bellflower. No. 721, Gentian. No. 722, Chrysanthemum. No. 723, Camellia sasanqua.

1961   **Photo.**   **Perf. 13½**
712 A444 10y lilac, yel & grn   3.50 .75
713 A444 10y brown, grn & yel   1.50 .75
714 A444 10y lem, grn, pink & yel   1.25 .75
715 A444 10y gray, brn, pink, yel & blk   1.25 .75
716 A444 10y blk, grn, pink & yel   .95 .70
717 A444 10y gray, pur, grn & yel   .60 .40
718 A444 10y gray grn, yel & brn   .45 .35
719 A444 10y lt bl, grn & lil   .45 .35
720 A444 10y lt yel grn, vio & grn   .45 .35
721 A444 10y org, vio bl & grn   .45 .35
722 A444 10y blue, yel & grn   .45 .35
723 A444 10y sl, pink, yel & grn   .45 .35
   Nos. 712-723 (12)   11.75 6.20

Nojima Cape Lighthouse and Fisherwomen A445

1961, Mar. 15
724 A445 10y multicolored   .55 .25
South Boso Quasi-National Park.

Cherry Blossoms — A446

Unwmk.
1961, Apr. 1   **Photo.**   **Perf. 13**
725 A446 10y lilac rose & gray   .30 .25
   a.   Lilac rose omitted   300.00
   b.   Imperf., pair   1,100.
   c.   Booklet pane of 4   5.50 2.25
   d.   Gray omitted   200.00
See No. 611b.

Coil Stamp
1961, Apr. 25   **Perf. 13 Horiz.**
726 A446 10y lil rose & gray   5.00 1.90

Hisoka Maeshima — A447

1961, Apr. 20   **Perf. 13**
727 A447 10y olive & black   1.10 .25
90th anniv. of Japan's modern postal service from Tokyo to Osaka, inaugurated by Deputy Postmaster General Hisoka Maeshima.

Type of 1957
"Dancing Girl" from a "Screen of Dancers."

1961, Apr. 20   **Perf. 13½**
728 A388 10y multicolored   1.00 .60
Stamp Week, 1961. Sheets of 10 (5x2).

Lake Biwa — A448

1961, Apr. 25
729 A448 10y blk, dk bl & yel grn   .55 .25
Lake Biwa Quasi-National Park.

Rotary Emblem and People of Various Races — A449

1961, May 29   **Engr.**   **Perf. 13**
730 A449 10y gray & orange   .25 .25
52nd convention of Rotary Intl., Tokyo, May 29-June 1, 1961.

Faucet, Wheat, Insulator & Cogwheel — A450

1961, July 7   **Photo.**   **Perf. 13½**
731 A450 10y violet & aqua   .30 .25
Aichi irrigation system, Kiso river.

Sun, Earth and Meridian — A451

1961, July 12
732 A451 10y yellow, red & blk   .30 .25
75th anniv. of Japanese standard time.

Parasol Dance on Dunes of Tottori A452

1961, Aug. 15
733 A452 10y multicolored   .55 .25
San'in Kaigan Quasi-National Park

Onuma Lake and Komagatake Volcano A453

1961, Sept. 15
734 A453 10y grn, red brn & bl   .60 .25
Onuma Quasi-National Park.

Hiroshige Type of 1960
Design: 30y, "Hakone," print by Hiroshige from the 53 Stages of the Tokaido.

1961, Oct. 8   **Perf. 13**
735 A437 30y multicolored   5.25 4.25
Intl. Letter Writing Week, Oct. 8-14.

Gymnast on Horizontal Bar — A454

Design: No. 737, Women rowing.

1961, Oct. 8   **Engr.**   **Perf. 13½**
736 A454 5y blue green   .30 .25
737 A454 5y ultra   .30 .25
   a.   Pair, #736-737   1.00 1.00
16th National Athletic Meet, Akita.
See Nos. 770-771, 816-817, 852-853.

Duck Type of 1955
Coil Stamp
1961, Oct. 2   Photo.   *Perf. 13 Horiz.*
738 A362 5y lt bl & red brn   2.50 2.00

National Diet Library and Book — A455

1961, Nov. 1   *Perf. 13½*
739 A455 10y dp ultra & gold   .25 .25
Opening of the new Natl. Diet Library, Tokyo.

Paper Mâché Tiger — A456

1961, Dec. 15   *Perf. 13½*
740 A456 5y multicolored   .65 .25
New Year 1962. Sheets reproducing 4 No. 740 were awarded as 5th prize in the New Year lottery. Size: 102x90, Value $6.

Mt. Fuji from Lake Ashi — A457

Minokake-Iwa at Irozaki A458

Mt. Fuji from Mitsu Pass — A459

Mt. Fuji from Cape of Ose — A460

1962, Jan. 16   Unwmk.   Photo.
741 A457 5y deep green   .40 .25
742 A458 5y dark blue   .40 .25
743 A459 10y red brown   1.10 .25
744 A460 10y black   1.10 .30
   Nos. 741-744 (4)   3.00 1.05
Fuji-Hakone-Izu National Park.

Omishima A461

1962, Feb. 15   *Perf. 13½*
745 A461 10y ultra, red & yel   .55 .25
Kitanagato-Kaigan Quasi-National Park.

Perotrochus Hirasei A462

Sacred Bamboo A463

Shari-den of Engakuji A464

Yomei Gate, Nikko A465

Noh Mask — A466

Copper Pheasant A466a

Wind God, Fujin, by Sotatsu A467

Japanese Crane A468

Mythical Winged Woman, Chusonji A469

1962-65   Unwmk.   *Perf. 13*
746 A462 4y dk brn & red ('63)   .25 .25
747 A463 6y gray grn & car   .25 .25
748 A464 30y violet black   4.00 .25
749 A465 40y rose red   4.50 .25
750 A466 70y yel brn & blk ('65) 2.00 .25
751 A466a 80y crim & brn ('65)   1.00 .25
752 A467 90y brt blue grn   26.00 .35
753 A468 100y pink & blk ('63) 8.00 .25
754 A469 120y purple   8.00 .65
   Nos. 746-754 (9)   54.00 2.75
See Nos. 888, 888A, 1076, 1079, 1257.

Coil Stamp
Perf. 13 Horiz.
755 A464 30y dull violet ('63) 3.75 3.00

Hinamatsuri, Doll Festival — A470

1962, Mar. 3   *Perf. 13½*
756 A470 10y brn, blk, bl & car 1.00 .50
The Doll Festival is celebrated Mar. 3 in honor of young girls.

Type of 1957
Design: Dancer from "Flower Viewing Party" by Naganobu Kano.

1962, Apr. 20 Photo.   *Perf. 13½*
757 A388 10y multicolored   1.00 .75
Stamp Week, 1962. Sheets of 10.

Sakurajima Volcano and Kagoshima Bay — A471

1962, Apr. 30
758 A471 10y multicolored   .35 .25
Kinkowan Quasi-National Park.

Mount Kongo A472

1962, May 15   *Perf. 13½*
759 A472 10y gray bl, dk grn & sal .35 .25
Kongo-Ikoma Quasi-National Park.

Suigo Park Scene and Iris — A473

1962, June 1   *Perf. 13½*
760 A473 10y multicolored   .35 .25
Suigo Quasi-National Park.

Train Emerging from Hokuriku Tunnel — A474

1962, June 10   Photo.
761 A474 10y olive gray   .85 .40
Opening of Hokuriku Tunnel between Tsuruga and Imajo, Fukui Prefecture.

Star Festival (Tanabata Matsuri) — A475

1962, July 7   Unwmk.   *Perf. 13½*
762 A475 10y multicolored   .30 .25
The Tanabata festival is celebrated on the evening of July 7.

Boy Scout Hat on Map of Southeast Asia — A476

1962, Aug. 3
763 A476 10y red org, blk & bis .30 .25
Asian Boy Scout Jamboree, Mt. Fuji, Aug. 3-7.

Ozegahara Swampland and Mt. Shibutsu A477

Fumes on Mt. Chausu, Nasu — A478

Lake Chuzenji and Mt. Nantai A479

Senryu-kyo Narrows, Shiobara A480

1962, Sept. 1
764 A477 5y greenish blue   .30 .25
765 A478 5y maroon   .30 .25
766 A479 10y purple   .40 .25
767 A480 10y olive   .40 .25
   Nos. 764-767 (4)   1.40 1.00
Nikko National Park.

Wakato Suspension Bridge — A481

Perf. 13½x13
1962, Sept. 26 Engr.   Unwmk.
768 A481 10y rose red   .65 .25
Opening of Wakato Bridge over Dokai Bay in North Kyushu.

Hiroshige Type of 1960
Design: 40y, "Nihonbashi," print by Hiroshige from the 53 Stages of the Tokaido.

1962, Oct. 7   Photo.   *Perf. 13*
769 A437 40y multicolored   4.50 3.75
Intl. Letter Writing Week, Oct. 7-13.

Sports Type of 1961
Design: No. 770, Woman softball pitcher. No. 771, Rifle shooting.

1962, Oct. 21 Engr.   *Perf. 13½*
770 A454 5y bluish black   .25 .25
771 A454 5y brown violet   .25 .25
a.   Pair, #770-771   .85 .85
17th National Athletic Meeting, Okayama.

Shichi-go-san Festival — A482

1962, Nov. 15 Photo.   *Perf. 13½*
772 A482 10y multicolored   .30 .25
This festival for 7 and 3-year-old girls and 5-year-old boys is celebrated on Nov. 15.

Rabbit Bell — A483

1962, Dec. 15
773 A483 5y multicolored .35 .25
New Year 1963. Sheets reproducing 4 No. 773 were awarded as prizes in the New Year lottery. Value $6.
See No. 2655b.

Mt. Ishizuchi
A484

1963, Jan. 11   Unwmk.   Perf. 13½
774 A484 10y multicolored .35 .25
Ishizuchi Quasi-National Park.

Setsubun, Spring Festival, Bean Scattering Ceremony — A485

1963, Feb. 3   Photo.
775 A485 10y multicolored .30 .25

Map of City, Birds, Ship and Factory — A486

1963, Feb. 10
776 A486 10y chocolate .25 .25
Consolidation of the communities of Moji, Kokura, Wakamatsu, Yawata and Tobata into Kita-Kyushu City.

"Frost Flowers" on Mt. Fugen A487

Amakusa Island and Mt. Unzen A488

1963, Feb. 15
777 A487 5y gray blue .25 .25
778 A488 10y carmine rose .35 .25
Unzen-Amakusa National Park.

Green Pond, Midorigaike
A489

Hakusan Range
A490

Perf. 13½
1963, Mar. 1   Unwmk.   Photo.
779 A489 5y violet brown .25 .25
780 A490 10y dark green .35 .25
Hakusan National Park.

Keya-no-Oto Rock — A491

1963, Mar. 15
781 A491 10y multicolored .30 .25
Genkai Quasi-National Park.

Wheat Emblem and Globe — A492

1963, Mar. 21
782 A492 10y dark green .25 .25
FAO "Freedom from Hunger" campaign.

"Girl Reading Letter," Yedo Screen A493

1963, Apr. 20   Perf. 13½
783 A493 10y multicolored .45 .45
Issued to publicize Stamp Week, 1963.

World Map and Centenary Emblem A494

1963, May 8
784 A494 10y multicolored .25 .25
Centenary of the International Red Cross.

Globe and Leaf with Symbolic River System — A495

1963, May 15   Photo.
785 A495 10y blue .25 .25
5th Congress of the Intl. Commission on Irrigation and Drainage.

Ito-dake, Asahi Range A496

Lake Hibara and Mt. Bandai A497

1963, May 25   Unwmk.   Perf. 13½
786 A496 5y green .25 .25
787 A497 10y red brown .35 .25
Bandai-Asahi National Park.

Lidth's Jay — A498

No. 789, Rock ptarmigan. No. 790, Eastern turtle dove. No. 791, Japanese white stork. No. 792, Bush warbler. No. 792A, Meadow bunting.

1963-64   Perf. 13½
Design and Inscription
788 A498 10y lt green .65 .40
789 A498 10y blue .30 .25
790 A498 10y pale yellow .30 .25
791 A498 10y grnsh blue ('64) .30 .25
792 A498 10y green ('64) .30 .25
792A A498 10y lt rose brn ('64) .30 .25
Nos. 788-792A (6) 2.15 1.65

Intersection at Ritto, Shiga — A499

1963, July 15   Unwmk.   Perf. 13½
793 A499 10y bl grn, blk & org .25 .25
Opening of the Nagoya-Kobe expressway, linking Nagoya with Kyoto, Osaka and Kobe.

Girl Scout and Flag — A500

1963, Aug. 1   Photo.
794 A500 10y multicolored .30 .25
Asian Girl Scout and Girl Guides Camp, Togakushi Heights, Nagano, Aug. 1-7.

View of Nashu A501

Whirlpool at Naruto A502

1963, Aug. 20
795 A501 5y olive bister .25 .25
796 A502 10y dark green .35 .25
Inland Sea National Park.

Lake Shikaribetsu, Hokkaido A503

Mt. Kurodake from Sounkyo Valley — A504

1963, Sept. 1   Unwmk.   Perf. 13½
797 A503 5y deep Prus blue .25 .25
798 A504 10y rose violet .35 .25
Daisetsuzan National Park.

Parabolic Antenna for Space Communications A505

1963, Sept. 9   Photo.
799 A505 10y multicolored .25 .25
14th General Assembly of the International Scientific Radio Union, Tokyo.

"Great Wave off Kanagawa," by Hokusai A506

1963, Oct. 10   Perf. 13
800 A506 40y gray, dk bl & yel 3.00 1.25
Issued for International Letter Writing Week, Oct. 6-12. Design from Hokusai's "36 Views of Fuji." Printed in sheets of 10 (5x2).

Diver, Pole Vaulter and Relay Runner — A507

1963, Oct. 11   Perf. 13½
801 A507 10y bl, ocher, blk & red .25 .25
Tokyo Intl. (Pre-Olympic) Sports Meet, Tokyo, Oct. 11-16.

Woman Gymnast — A508

No. 803, Japanese wrestling (sumo).

Perf. 13½
1963, Oct. 27   Unwmk.   Engr.
802 A508 5y slate green .25 .25
803 A508 5y brown .25 .25
a. Pair, #802-803 .60 .85
18th National Athletic Meet, Yamaguchi.

Phoenix Tree and Hachijo Island — A509

1963, Dec. 10   Photo.
804 A509 10y multicolored .30 .25
Izu Islands Quasi-National Park.

Toy Dragons of Tottori and Yamanashi — A510

1963, Dec. 16
805 A510 5y gold, pink, aqua, ind & red   .25 .25
  a. Aqua omitted

New Year 1964. Sheets containing 4 No. 805 were awarded as 5th prize in the New Year lottery. Value $4.25.

Wakasa-Fuji from Takahama A511

1964, Jan. 25   *Perf. 13½*
806 A511 10y multicolored   .30 .25

Wakasa Bay Quasi-National Park.

Agave and View from Horikiri Pass — A512

1964, Feb. 20   *Unwmk.*
807 A512 10y multicolored   .30 .25

Nichinan-Kaigan Quasi-National Park.

Uji Bridge A513

View of Toba — A514

1964, Mar. 15   *Photo.*
808 A513 5y sepia   .25 .25
809 A514 10y red lilac   .30 .25

Ise-Shima National Park.

Takayama Festival Float and Mt. Norikura — A515

No. 811, Yamaboko floats & Gion Shrine, Kyoto.

1964   *Photo.*   *Perf. 13½*
810 A515 10y lt green & multi   .25 .25
811 A515 10y grnsh blue & multi   .25 .25

No. 810 issued for the annual Takayama spring and autumn festivals, Takayama City, Gifu Prefecture. No. 811 for the annual Gion festival of Kyoto, July 10-30.
Issue dates: No. 810, 4/15. No. 811, 7/15.

Yadorigi Scene from Genji Monogatari Scroll — A516

1964, Apr. 20
814 A516 10y multicolored   .25 .25
Stamp Week, 1964. Sheets of 10 (2x5).

Himeji Castle — A517

1964, June 1   *Perf. 13½*
815 A517 10y dark brown   .25 .25
Restoration of Himeji Castle.

Sports Type of 1961
1964, June 6   *Perf. 13½*
816 A454 5y Handball   .25 .25
817 A454 5y Woman on beam   .25 .25
  a. Pair, #816-817   .65 .65

19th National Athletic Meeting, Niigata.

Cable Cross Section, Map of Pacific Ocean A518

1964, June 19
818 A518 10y gray grn, dp mag & yel   .25 .25
Opening of the transpacific cable.

Tokyo Expressway Crossing Nihonbashi — A519

1964, Aug. 1   *Photo.*
819 A519 10y green, silver & blk   .25 .25
Opening of the Tokyo Expressway.

Coin-like Emblems A520

1964, Sept. 7   *Unwmk.*   *Perf. 13½*
820 A520 10y scarlet, gold & blk   .25 .25

Annual general meeting of the Intl. Monetary Fund, Intl. Bank for Reconstruction and Development, Intl. Financial Corporation and the Intl. Development Assoc., Tokyo, Sept. 7-11.

Athletes, Olympic Flame and Rings — A521

National Stadium, Tokyo — A522

30y, Nippon Bodokan (fencing hall). 40y, Natl. Gymnasium. 50y, Komazawa Gymnasium.

1964
821 A521 5y multicolored   .25 .25
822 A522 10y multicolored   .25 .25
823 A522 30y multicolored   .35 .25
824 A522 40y multicolored   .45 .25
825 A522 50y multicolored   .50 .25
  a. Souvenir sheet of 5, #821-825   3.75 4.25
    Nos. 821-825 (5)   1.80 1.25

18th Olympic Games, Tokyo, Oct. 10-25.
Issue dates: 5y, Sept. 9. Others, Oct. 10.

Hand with Grain, Cow and Fruit — A523

1964, Sept. 15   *Perf. 13½*
826 A523 10y violet brn & gold   .25 .25
Draining of Hachirogata Lagoon, providing new farmland for the future.

Express Train — A524

1964, Oct. 1
827 A524 10y blue & black   .35 .25
Opening of the new Tokaido railroad line.

Mt. Fuji Seen from Tokaido, by Hokusai A525

1964, Oct. 4   *Perf. 13*
828 A525 40y multicolored   1.00 .50
Issued for International Letter Writing Week, Oct. 4-10. Issued in sheets of 10 (5x2). See Nos. 850, 896, 932, 971, 1016.

"Straw Snake" Mascot — A526

1964, Dec. 15   *Photo.*   *Perf. 13½*
829 A526 5y crimson, blk & yel   .25 .25
New Year 1965. Sheets containing 4 No. 829 were awarded as prizes in the New Year lottery (issued Jan. 20, 1965). Value $1.75.

Mt. Daisen A527

Paradise Cove, Oki Islands A528

1965, Jan. 20   *Unwmk.*   *Perf. 13½*
830 A527 5y dark blue   .25 .25
831 A528 10y brown orange   .30 .25
Daisen-Oki National Park.

Niseko-Annupuri — A529

1965, Feb. 15   *Photo.*
832 A529 10y multicolored   .30 .25
Niseko-Shakotan-Otarukaigan Quasi-Natl. Park.

Meteorological Radar Station on Mt. Fuji — A530

1965, Mar. 10   *Photo.*   *Perf. 13½*
833 A530 10y multicolored   .25 .25
Completion of the Meteorological Radar Station on Kengamine Heights of Mt. Fuji.

Kiyotsu Gorge — A531

Lake Nojiri and Mt. Myoko A532

1965, Mar. 15
834 A531 5y brown   .25 .25
835 A532 10y magenta   .30 .25
Jo-Shin-etsu Kogen National Park.

Communications Museum, Tokyo — A533

1965, Mar. 25   *Unwmk.*   *Perf. 13½*
836 A533 10y green   .25 .25
Philatelic Exhibition celebrating the completion of the Communications Museum.

"The Prelude" by Shoen Uemura A534

1965, Apr. 20   *Photo.*
837 A534 10y gray & multi   .30 .25
Issued for Stamp Week, 1965.

Playing Children, Cows and Swan A535

1965, May 5   *Unwmk.*   *Perf. 13½*
838 A535 10y pink & multi   .25 .25
Opening of the National Garden for Children, Tokyo-Yokohama.

Stylized Tree and Sun — A536

1965, May 9
839 A536 10y multicolored .25 .25
Issued to publicize the forestation movement and the forestation ceremony, Tottori Prefecture.

Globe, Old and New Communication Equipment — A537

1965, May 17
840 A537 10y brt blue, yel & blk .25 .25
Cent. of the ITU.

Crater of Mt. Naka, Kyushu A538

Five Central Peaks of Aso and Mountain Road — A539

1965, June 15 Photo. Perf. 13½
841 A538 5y carmine rose .25 .25
842 A539 10y deep green .30 .25
Aso National Park.

ICY Emblem and Doves A540

1965, June 26 Unwmk.
843 A540 40y multicolored .45 .25
Intl. Cooperation Year, 1965, and 20th anniv. of the UN.

Horse Chase, Soma A541

Chichibu Festival Scene A542

1965 Photo. Perf. 13x13½
844 A541 10y multicolored .25 .25
845 A542 10y multicolored .25 .25
No. 844 issued to publicize the ancient Soma Nomaoi Festival, Fukushima Prefecture; No. 845, to publicize the festival dedicated to the Chichibu Myoken Shrine (built 1584).
Issue dates: No. 844, 7/16; No. 845, 12/3.

Meiji Maru, Black-tailed Gulls — A543

1965, July 20 Perf. 13½
846 A543 10y grn, gray, blk & yel .25 .25
25th Maritime Day, July 20.

Drop of Blood, Girl's Face and Bloodmobile A544

1965, Sept. 1 Perf. 13½
847 A544 10y yel, grn, blk & red .25 .25
Issued to publicize the national campaign for blood donations, Sept. 1-30.

Tokai Atomic Power Station and Structure of Alpha Uranium — A545

1965, Sept. 21 Photo.
848 A545 10y multicolored .25 .25
9th General Conf. of the Intl. Atomic Energy Agency, IAEA, Tokyo, Sept. 21-30.

People and Flag — A546

1965, Oct. 1
849 A546 10y multicolored .25 .25
Tenth national census.

Hokusai Type of 1964
Design: No. 850, "Waters at Misaka" by Hokusai (Mt. Fuji seen across Lake Kawaguchi).

1965, Oct. 6 Unwmk. Perf. 13
850 A525 40y multicolored .75 .40
Issued for International Letter Writing Week, Oct. 6-12. Issued in sheets of 10 (5x2).

Emblems and Diagram of Seats in National Diet — A547

1965, Oct. 15 Perf. 13½
851 A547 10y multicolored .25 .25
75th anniv. of natl. suffrage, 40th anniv. of universal suffrage and 20th anniv. of women's suffrage.

Sports Type of 1961
Designs: No. 852, Gymnast on vaulting horse. No. 853, Walking race.

1965, Oct. 24 Engr. Perf. 13½
852 A454 5y red brown .25 .25
853 A454 5y yellow green .25 .25
a. Pair, #852-853 .55 .65
20th National Athletic Meeting, Gifu.

Profile and Infant A548

1965, Oct. 30 Photo. Perf. 13
854 A548 30y car lake, yel & lt bl .35 .25
8th Intl. Conf. of Otorhinolaryngology and the 11th Intl. Conf. of Pediatrics.

Mt. Iwo from Shari Coast, Hokkaido — A549

Rausu Lake and Mt. Rausu A550

1965, Nov. 15 Perf. 13½
855 A549 5y Prus green .25 .25
856 A550 10y bright blue .30 .25
Shiretoko National Park.

Aurora Australis, Map of Antarctica and "Fuji" — A551

1965, Nov. 20
857 A551 10y bl, yel & dk bl .25 .25
Issued to publicize the Antarctic expedition, which left on the observation ship "Fuji," Nov. 20, 1965.

"Secret Horse" Straw Toy, Iwate Prefecture — A552

1965, Dec. 10
858 A552 5y lt blue & multi .25 .25
Issued for New Year 1966. Sheets containing four of No. 858 were awarded as prizes in the New Year lottery (issued Jan. 20, 1966). Value $1.50.

Telephone Dial and 1890 Switchboard — A553

1965, Dec. 16
859 A553 10y multicolored .25 .25
75th anniversary of telephone service in Japan.

Japanese Spiny Lobster A554

Carp — A555

Bream A555a

Skipjack Tuna A555b

Three Ayu — A555c

Eel A555d

Jack Mackeral A555e

Chum Salmon A555f

Yellowtail A555g

Tiger Puffer A555h

Squid A555i

Turbo Cornutus A555j

1966-67   Photo.   *Perf. 13*
Multicolored; Background in Colors Indicated

860	A554	10y green & ultra	.25	.25
861	A555	10y blue green	.25	.25
862	A555a	10y dk blue	.25	.25
863	A555b	10y dk ultra	.25	.25
864	A555c	10y bis & dk grn	.25	.25
865	A555d	15y grnsh bl & yel	.30	.25
866	A555e	15y brt grn	.30	.25
867	A555f	15y brt grn & bl	.30	.25
868	A555g	15y lt bl grn ('67)	.30	.25
869	A555h	15y brt grn ('67)	.30	.25
870	A555i	15y ultra & grn ('67)	.30	.25
871	A555j	15y chlky bl ('67)	.55	.25
		Nos. 860-871 (12)	3.60	3.00

Famous Gardens Issue

A556

A557

A558

10y, Kobuntei Pavilion and plum blossoms, Kairakuen Garden, Ibaraki. No. 873, Japanese cranes and Okayama Castle, Korakuen Garden, Okayama. No. 874, Kenrokuen Garden in the snow.

1966-67   *Perf. 13½*

872	A556	10y gold, blk & grn	.25	.25
873	A557	15y blue, blk & mag	.35	.25
874	A558	15y silver, grn & dk brn	.35	.25
		Nos. 872-874 (3)	.95	.75

Issued: 10y, 2/25; No. 873, 11/3; No. 874, 1/25/67.

Crater Lake, Zao — A559

1966, Mar. 15

875   A559   10y multicolored   .30 .25

Zao Quasi-National Park.

Muroto Cape — A560

Senba Cliffs, Anan Coast — A561

1966, Mar. 22   *Perf. 13½*

876	A560	10y multicolored	.30	.25
877	A561	10y multicolored	.30	.25

Muroto-Anan Coast Quasi-National Park.

AIPPI Emblem A562

1966, Apr. 11   *Perf. 13*

878   A562   40y multicolored   .75 .25

26th General Assembly of the Intl. Association for the Protection of Industrial Properties, Tokyo, Apr. 11-16.

"Butterflies" by Takeji Fujishima — A563

Photogravure and Engraved
1966, Apr. 20   *Perf. 13½*

879   A563   10y gray & multi   .30 .25

Stamp Week, 1966. Sheets of 10 (2x5). See No. 907.

Hisoka Maeshima — A563a

Goldfish — A564

Chrysanthemums A565

Wisteria A565a

Hydrangea A565b

Golden Hall, Chusonji A565c

Yomei Gate, Nikko A565d

Nyoirin Kannon of Chuguji — A565f

Central Hall, Enryakuji Temple — A566

Ancient Clay Horse (Haniwa) — A567

A567a

A567b

A567c

Katsura Palace Garden — A568

A569

Bodhisattva Playing Flute (from Todaiji Lantern) — A570

Designs: 20y, Wisteria. 25y, Hydrangea. 35y, Luminescent squid. 45y, Lysichiton camtschatsense (white flowers). 500y, Deva King statue, South Gate, Todaiji.

1966-69   Photo.   *Perf. 13*

879A	A563a	1y olive bis ('68)	.25	.25
880	A564	7y ol & dp org	1.50	.25
881	A565	15y bl & yel (bl "15")	.95	.25
b.		Bklt. pane of 2 + label ('67)	3.25	
c.		Bklt. pane of 4 ('67)	2.25	
d.		Bklt. pane of 4 (2 #881 + 2 #611) ('67)	6.00	
e.		Imperf., pair	400.00	
881A	A565a	20y vio & multi ('67)	2.25	2.50
882	A565b	25y grn & lt ultra	.50	.25
882A	A565c	30y dp ultra & gold ('68)	.55	.25
883	A564	35y blue, gray & blk	1.25	.25
883A	A565d	40y bl grn & brn ('68)	.60	.25
884	A565	45y blue & multi ('67)	.55	.25
885	A565f	50y dk car rose	7.50	.25
		Engr.		
886	A566	60y slate green	1.75	.25
		Photo.		
887	A567	65y orange brown	9.00	.25
887A	A567a	75y rose, blk, yel & pur	1.00	.25
888	A567b	90y gold & brn	2.00	.25
888A	A567c	100y ver & blk ('68)	1.90	.25
		Engr.		
889	A568	110y brown	1.90	.25
890	A569	120y red	2.50	.25
891	A570	200y Prus grn (22x33mm)	4.00	.25
891A	A570	500y dull pur ('69)	9.50	.25
		Nos. 879A-891A (19)	49.45	7.00

Nos. 880-881 were also issued with fluorescent frame on July 18, 1966.
Compare type A563a with type A2682.
See Nos. 913-916, 918, 926, 1072, 1079, 1081, 1244, 1256.

UNESCO Emblem — A571

1966, July 2   Photo.   *Perf. 13*

892   A571   15y multicolored   .30 .25

20th anniv. of UNESCO.

Map of Pacific Ocean — A572

1966, Aug. 22   *Perf. 13*

893   A572   15y bis brn, dl bl & rose   .30 .25

11th Pacific Science Congress, Tokyo, Aug. 22-Sept. 10.

Amakusa Bridges, Kyushu — A573

1966, Sept. 24   Photo.   *Perf. 13*

894   A573   15y multicolored   .30 .25

Completion of five bridges linking Misumi Harbor, Kyushu, with Amakusa islands.

Emblem of Post Office Life Insurance and Family — A574

1966, Oct. 1

895   A574   15y yellow grn & multi   .30 .25

Post office life insurance service, 50th anniv.

Hokusai Type of 1964

50y, "Sekiya on the Sumida" (horseback riders and Mt. Fuji) from Hokusai's "36 Views of Fuji."

1966, Oct. 6

896   A525   50y multicolored   .95 .70

Intl. Letter Writing Week, Oct. 6-12. Printed in sheets of 10 (5x2).

Sharpshooter A575

Design: No. 898, Hop, skip and jump.

1966, Oct. 23   Engr.   *Perf. 13½*

897	A575	7y ultra	.25	.25
898	A575	7y carmine rose	.25	.25
a.		Pair, #897-898	.55	.55

21st Natl. Athletic Meet, Oita, Oct. 23-28.

National Theater A576

Kabuki Scene — A577

Bunraku Puppet Show — A578

1966, Nov. 1 ***Perf. 13, 13½***

899 A576 15y multicolored .25 .25
900 A577 25y multicolored .45 .30
901 A578 50y multicolored .85 .45
Nos. 899-901 (3) 1.55 1.00

Inauguration of first National Theater in Japan. Nos. 900-901 issued in sheets of 10.

Rice Year Emblem — A579

1966, Nov. 21 ***Perf. 13½***

902 A579 15y red, blk & ocher .30 .25

FAO International Rice Year.

Ittobori Carved Sheep, Nara Prefecture — A580

1966, Dec. 10 **Photo.** ***Perf. 13½***

903 A580 7y bl, gold, blk & pink .25 .25

New Year 1967. Sheets containing 4 No. 903 were awarded as prizes in the New Year lottery. Value $1.25.

International Communications Satellite, Lani Bird 2 — A581

1967, Jan. 27 ***Perf. 13½***

904 A581 15y dk Prus bl & sepia .30 .25

Inauguration in Japan of Intl. commercial communications service via satellite.

Around the World Air Route and Jet Plane — A582

1967, Mar. 6 **Photo.** ***Perf. 13½***

905 A582 15y multicolored .30 .25

Issued to publicize the inauguration of Japan Air Lines Tokyo-London service via New York, which completes the around the world air route.

Library of Modern Japanese Literature A583

1967, Apr. 11

906 A583 15y grnsh bl, lt & dk brn .30 .25

Opening of the Library of Modern Japanese Literature, Komaba Park, Meguro-ku, Tokyo.

Painting Type of 1966

Design: 15y, Lakeside (seated woman), by Seiki (Kiyoteru) Kuroda.

1967, Apr. 20

907 A563 15y multicolored .40 .25

Stamp Week, 1967. Sheets of 10 (2x5).

Kobe Harbor A584

1967, May 8 **Photo.** ***Perf. 13x13½***

908 A584 50y multicolored .95 .25

5th Cong. of the Intl. Association of Ports and Harbors, Tokyo, May 8-13.

Welfare Commissioner's Emblem — A585

1967, May 12 ***Perf. 13½***

909 A585 15y dk brown & gold .30 .25

50th anniversary of the Welfare Commissioner System.

Traffic Light, Automobile and Children — A586

1967, May 22 ***Perf. 13x13½***

910 A586 15y emer, red, blk & yel .30 .25

Issued to publicize traffic safety.

Kita and Kai-Koma Mountains A587

Akaishi and Hijiri Mountains A588

1967, July 10

911 A587 7y Prus blue .25 .25
912 A588 15y rose lilac .30 .25

South Japan Alps National Park.

Types of 1966-69 Redrawn and

A588a

Original 20y No. 881A

Redrawn 20y No. 915

1967-69 **Photo.** ***Perf. 13***

913 A564 7y brt yel grn & dp org .25 .25
914 A565 15y bl & yel (white "15") .30 .25
a. Pane of 10 (5x2) ('68) 2.75
b. Bklt. panes of 4 with gutter (6 #914 + 2 #611) ('68) 7.00
c. Imperf., pair 500.00
d. Blue shading omitted
e. Bklt. panes of 2 & 4 with gutter ('68) 45.00 45.00
915 A565a 20y vio & multi ('69) 1.10 .25
916 A565f 50y brt carmine .90 .25
917 A588a 55y lt bl, grn & blk ('69) .85 .25
918 A567 65y deep orange 1.10 .25
Nos. 913-918 (6) 4.50 1.50

Issued for use in facer-canceling machines. Issue dates: 7y, Aug. 1; 15y, 50y, July 1; 65y, July 20, 1967; 20y, Apr. 1, 1969; 55y, Sept. 1, 1969.

On No. 913 the background has been lightened and a frame line of shading added at top and right side.

No. 914a is imperf. on four sides.

The two panes of Nos. 914b and 914e are connected by a vertical creased gutter 21mm wide. The left pane of No. 914b consists of 2 No. 914 and 2 No. 611; the right pane, 4 of No. 914. The left pane of 2 of No. 914e includes a 4-line inscription.

On No. 915 the wisteria leaves do not touch frame at left and top. On No. 881A they do.

Coil Stamp

1968, Jan. 9 ***Perf. 13 Horiz.***

926 A565 15y bl & yel (white "15") .55 .30

Mitochondria and Protein Model A589

1967, Aug. 19 **Photo.** ***Perf. 13***

927 A589 15y gray & multi .30 .25

7th Intl. Biochemistry Cong., Tokyo, Aug. 19-25.

Gymnast on Horizontal Bar — A590

Universiade Emblem — A591

1967, Aug. 26

928 A590 15y red & multi .30 .25
929 A591 50y yellow & multi .95 .25

World University Games, Universiade 1967, Tokyo, Aug. 26-Sept. 4.

Paper Lantern, ITY Emblem — A592

"Sacred Mt. Fuji" by Taikan Yokoyama — A593

1967, Oct. 2 **Photo.** ***Perf. 13***

930 A592 15y ultra & multi .25 .25
931 A593 50y multicolored 1.25 1.00

International Tourist Year, 1967. No. 931 issued in sheets of 10.

Hokusai Type of 1964

50y, "Kajikazawa, Koshu" (fisherman and waves) from Hokusai's "36 Views of Fuji."

1967, Oct. 6

932 A525 50y multicolored 1.25 .55

Issued for International Letter Writing Week, Oct. 6-12. Sheets of 10 (5x2).

Athlete, Wild Primrose and Chichibu Mountains — A594

1967, Oct. 22 **Photo.** ***Perf. 13***

933 A594 15y gold & multi .30 .25

22nd Natl. Athletic Meet, Saitama, 10/22-27.

Miroku Bosatsu, Koryuji Temple, Kyoto — A595

Kudara Kannon, Horyuji Temple, Nara — A596

Golden Hall and Pagoda, Horyuji Temple, Nara — A597

1967, Nov. 1 **Photo.**

934 A595 15y multicolored .30 .25

Engr.

935 A596 15y pale grn, blk & red .30 .25

Photo. & Engr.

936 A597 50y multicolored 1.25 .75
Nos. 934-936 (3) 1.85 1.25

National treasures of Asuka Period (6th-7th centuries). No. 936 issued in sheets of 10.

Highway and Congress Emblem A598

1967, Nov. 5 **Photo.** ***Perf. 13***

937 A598 50y multicolored .95 .25

13th World Road Cong., Tokyo, Nov. 5-11.

Mt. Kumotori
A599

Lake Chichibu
A600

1967, Nov. 27
938 A599 7y olive   .25 .25
939 A600 15y red lilac   .30 .25

Chichibu-Tama National Park

Climbing Monkey
Toy (Noborizaru),
Miyazaki
Prefecture — A601

1967, Dec. 11   Photo.   Perf. 13
940 A601 7y multicolored   .25 .25

New Year 1968. Sheets containing 4 No.
940 were awarded as prizes in the New Year
lottery. Value $1.25.

Mt.
Sobo — A602

Takachiho
Gorge — A603

1967, Dec. 20
941 A602 15y multicolored   .30 .25
942 A603 15y multicolored   .30 .25

Sobo Katamuki Quasi-National Park.

Girl, Boy and
Sakura
Maru — A604

1968, Jan. 19   Photo.   Perf. 13
943 A604 15y ultra, ocher & blk   .30 .25

Cent. of the Meiji Era, and 1st Japanese
Youth Good Will Cruise in celebration of the
centenary.

Ashura,
Kofukuji
Temple,
Nara — A605

Gakko Bosatsu,
Todaiji Temple,
Nara — A606

Kichijo Ten,
Yakushiji
Temple,
Nara — A607

1968, Feb. 1   Engr.   Perf. 13
944 A605 15y sepia & car   .30 .25
Engr. & Photo.
945 A606 15y dk brn, pale grn &
            org   .30 .25
Photo.
946 A607 50y multicolored   .95 .95
      Nos. 944-946 (3)   1.55 1.45

Issued to show National Treasures of the
Nara Period (710-784).

Grazing Cows
and Mt.
Yatsugatake
A608

Mt. Tateshina
A609

1968, Mar. 21   Photo.   Perf. 13
947 A608 15y multicolored   .30 .25
948 A609 15y multicolored   .30 .25

Yatsugatake-Chushin-Kogen Quasi-Natl.
Park.

Young Dancer
(Maiko) in
Tenjuan
Garden, by
Bakusen
Tsuchida
A610

1968, Apr. 20   Photo.   Perf. 13
949 A610 15y multicolored   .30 .25
Stamp Week, 1968. Sheets of 10 (5x2).

Rishiri Isl.
Seen from
Rebun
Isl. — A611

1968, May 10   Photo.   Perf. 13
950 A611 15y multicolored   .30 .25
Rishiri-Rebun Quasi-National Park.

Gold Lacquer and
Mother-of-Pearl
Box — A612

"The Origin of Shigisan" Painting from
Chogo-sonshiji, Nara — A613

Bodhisattva Samantabhadra — A614

1968, June 1   Engr. & Photo.
951 A612 15y lt blue & multi   .30 .25
Photo.
952 A613 15y tan & multi   .30 .25
953 A614 50y sepia & multi   1.75 1.50
      Nos. 951-953 (3)   2.35 2.00

Issued to show national treasures of the
Heian Period (8-12th centuries).

Memorial Tower and
Badge of
Hokkaido — A615

1968, June 14
954 A615 15y grn, vio bl, bis & red .30 .25
Centenary of development of Hokkaido.

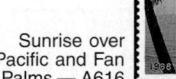

Sunrise over
Pacific and Fan
Palms — A616

1968, June 26   Photo.   Perf. 13
955 A616 15y blk, org & red org   .30 .25
Return of Bonin Islands to Japan by US.

Map of Japan Showing
Postal Codes — A617

Two types of inscription:
Type I (enlarged)

あなたの住所にも郵便番号を

"Postal code also on your address"

Type II (enlarged)

あて名に郵便番号を

"Don't omit postal code on the
address"

1968, July 1
956 A617 7y yel grn & red (I)   2.00 .30
957 A617 7y yel grn & red (II)   2.00 .30
  a.   Pair, #956-957   5.00 1.50
958 A617 15y sky bl & car (I)   .60 .30
  a.   Bkt. panes of 4 with gutter (4
         #958 + 2 #959 + 2 #611)   65.00 65.00
959 A617 15y sky bl & car (II)   .60 .30
  d.   Pair, #958-959   1.75 1.25
      Nos. 956-959 (4)   5.20 1.20

Introduction of the postal code system.
The double booklet pane, No. 958a, comes
in two forms, the positions of the Postal Code
types being transposed.

**Coil Stamps
Perf. 13 Horiz.**
959A A617 15y sky blue & car (I)   1.10 .75
959B A617 15y sky blue & car
            (II)   1.10 .75
  c.   Pair, #959A-959B   2.75 2.75

Kiso River — A618

Inuyama
Castle
A619

1968, July 20   Perf. 13½
960 A618 15y multicolored   .30 .25
961 A619 15y multicolored   .30 .25

Hida-Kisogawa Quasi-National Park.

Youth Hostel
Emblem,
Trees and
Sun — A620

1968, Aug. 6   Photo.   Perf. 13
962 A620 15y citron & multi   .30 .25

27th Intl. Youth Hostel Cong., Tokyo, 8/6-20.

Boys Forming
Tournament
Emblem
A621

Pitcher and
Tournament
Flag — A622

1968, Aug. 9
963 A621 15y yel grn, yel, blk & red .30 .25
964 A622 15y red, yellow & blk   .30 .25
  a.   Pair, #963-964   .65 .60

50th All-Japan High School Baseball Championship Tournament, Koshi-en Baseball
Grounds, Aug. 9. Nos. 963-964 printed
checkerwise.

Minamoto
Yoritomo, Jingoji,
Kyoto — A623

Heiji Monogatari Scroll Painting — A624

Red-threaded Armor, Kasuga Shrine, Nara — A625

1968, Sept. 16   Photo.   Perf. 13
965 A623 15y black & multi   .35 .25
966 A624 15y tan & multi   .35 .25
Photo. & Engr.
967 A625 50y multicolored   1.00 1.00
Nos. 965-967 (3)   1.70 1.50
National treasures of Kamakura period (1180-1192 to 1333).

Mt. Iwate, seen from Hachimantai A626

Lake Towada, seen from Mt. Ohanabe A627

1968, Sept. 16   Photo.
968 A626 7y red brown   .25 .25
969 A627 15y green   .30 .25
Towada-Hachimantai National Park.

Gymnast, Tojimbo Cliff and Narcissus — A628

1968, Oct. 1   Photo.   Perf. 13
970 A628 15y multicolored   .30 .25
23rd National Athletic Meet, Fukui Prefecture, Oct. 1-6.

Hokusai Type of 1964
Design: 50y, "Fujimihara in Owari Province" (cooper working on a barrel) from Hokusai's "36 Views of Fuji."

1968, Oct. 7
971 A525 50y multicolored   1.00 .60
Issued for International Letter Writing Week, Oct. 7-13. Sheets of 10 (5x2).

Centenary Emblem, Sun and First Western Style Warship — A629

Imperial Carriage Arriving in Tokyo (1868), by Tomote Kobori A630

1968, Oct. 23
972 A629 15y vio bl, red, gold & gray   .30 .25
973 A630 15y multicolored   .30 .25
a.   Imperf., pair
Meiji Centenary Festival.

Old and New Lighthouses A631

1968, Nov. 1   Photo.
974 A631 15y multicolored   .30 .25
Centenary of the first western style lighthouse in Japan.

Ryo'o Court Dance and State Hall, Imperial Palace — A632

1968, Nov. 14
975 A632 15y multicolored   .30 .25
Completion of the new Imperial Palace.

Mt. Takachiho A633

Mt. Motobu, Yaku Island A634

1968, Nov. 20
976 A633 7y purple   .25 .25
977 A634 15y orange   .30 .25
Kirishima-Yaku National Park.

Carved Toy Cock of Yonezawa, Yamagata Prefecture — A635

1968, Dec. 5   Photo.   Perf. 13
978 A635 7y lt blue & multi   .25 .25
New Year 1969. Sheets containing 4 No. 978 were awarded as prizes in the New Year lottery. Value $1.50.

Human Rights Flame, Dancing Children and Globe — A636

1968, Dec. 10
979 A636 50y orange & multi   .95 .25
International Human Rights Year.

Striped Squirrel — A637

1968, Dec. 14
980 A637 15y emerald & blk   .30 .25
Issued to promote saving.

Kochomon Cave and Road — A638

1969, Jan. 27   Photo.
981 A638 15y multicolored   .30 .25
Echizen-Kaga-Kaigan Quasi-National Park.

Silver Pavilion, Jishoji Temple, Kyoto — A639

Pagoda, Anrakuji Temple, Nagano — A640

Winter Landscape by Sesshu A641

1969, Feb. 10   Photo.   Perf. 13
982 A639 15y multicolored   .30 .25
Photo. & Engr.
983 A640 15y lt green & multi   .30 .25
Photo.
984 A641 50y tan, blk & ver   1.10 .75
Nos. 982-984 (3)   1.70 1.25
Issued to show national treasures of the Muromachi Period (1333-1572).

Mt. Chokai, seen from Tobishima Island — A642

1969, Feb. 25   Photo.
985 A642 15y brt blue & multi   .30 .25
Chokai Quasi-National Park.

Mt. Koya Seen from Jinnogamine A643

Mt. Gomadan and Rhododendron — A644

1969, Mar. 25   Photo.   Perf. 13
986 A643 15y multicolored   .30 .25
987 A644 15y multicolored   .30 .25
Koya-Ryujin Quasi-National Park.

Hair (Kami), by Kokei Kobayashi A645

1969, Apr. 20   Photo.   Perf. 13
988 A645 15y multicolored   .30 .25
Issued for Philatelic Week.

Mother, Son Crossing Street — A646

1969, May 10   Photo.   Perf. 13
989 A646 15y lt blue, red & grn   .30 .25
National traffic safety campaign.

Tokyo-Nagoya Expressway and Sakawagawa Bridge A647

1969, May 26
990 A647 15y multicolored   .30 .25
Completion of Tokyo-Nagoya Expressway.

Nuclear Ship Mutsu and Atom Diagram A648

1969, June 12
991 A648 15y gray, blk, pink & bl   .30 .25
Issued to publicize the launching of the first Japanese nuclear ship, Mutsu.

Museum of Modern Art and Palette A649

1969, June 11   Photo.   Perf. 13½
992 A649 15y lt bl, brn, yel & blk   .30 .25
Opening of the new National Museum of Modern Art, Tokyo.

Cable Ship KKD Maru and Map of Japan Sea — A650

1969, June 25
993 A650 15y lt bl, blk & ocher   .30 .25
Completion of the Japan sea cable between Naoetsu, Japan, and Nakhodka, Russia.

Postcards, Postal Code Symbol A651

Mailbox, Postal Code Symbol A652

1969, July 1   Photo.   Perf. 13
997 A651 7y yellow grn & car   .25 .25
998 A652 15y sky blue & car   .30 .25
1st anniv. of the postal code system and to promote its use.

Lions Emblem and Rose — A653

1969, July 2
999 A653 15y bl, blk, rose & gold   .30 .25
52nd Convention of Lions Intl., Tokyo, July 2-5.

Hotoke-ga-ura on Shimokita Peninsula, Northern Honshu A654

1969, July 15
1000 A654 15y multicolored   .30 .25
Shimokita Hanto Quasi-National Park.

Himeji Castle, Hyogo Prefecture A655

"Pine Forest" (Detail), by Tohaku Hasegawa A656

"Cypresses," Attributed to Eitoku Kano — A657

1969, July 21   Photo. & Engr.
1001 A655 15y lt blue & multi   .30 .25
Photo.
1002 A656 15y pale brown & blk   .30 .25
1003 A657 50y gold & multi   1.10 .60
Nos. 1001-1003 (3)   1.70 1.10
Issued to show national treasures of the Momoyama period (1573-1614). The 50y is in sheets of 10 (2x5); Nos. 1001-1002 in sheets of 20 (5x4).

Harano-fudo Waterfall — A658

Mt. Nagisan A659

1969, Aug. 20
1004 A658 15y multicolored   .30 .25
1005 A659 15y multicolored   .30 .25
Hyobosen-Ushiroyama-Nagisan Quasi-Natl. Park.

Mt. O-akan, Hokkaido — A660

Mt. Iwo — A661

1969, Aug. 25   Photo.   Perf. 13
1006 A660 7y bright blue   .25 .25
1007 A661 15y sepia   .30 .25
Akan National Park.

Angling, by Taiga Ikeno — A662

The Red Plum, by Korin Ogata — A663

Pheasant-shaped Incense Burner — A664

No. 1010, The White Plum, by Korin Ogata.

1969, Sept. 25   Photo.   Perf. 13x13½
1008 A662 15y multicolored   .30 .25
Perf. 13
1009 A663 15y gold & multi   .30 .25
1010 A663 15y gold & multi   .30 .25
a.   Pair, #1009-1010   .75 .75
Photo. & Engr.
1011 A664 50y multicolored   1.00 .65
Nos. 1008-1011 (4)   1.90 1.40
Natl. treasures, Edo Period (1615-1867).

Birds Circling Globe and UPU Congress Emblem A665

Woman Reading Letter, by Utamaro A666

Designs (UPU Congress Emblem and): 50y, Two Women Reading a Letter, by Harunobu. 60y, Man Reading a Letter (Miyako Dennai), by Sharaku.

1969, Oct. 1   Photo.   Perf. 13
1012 A665 15y red & multi   .30 .25
1013 A666 30y multicolored   .55 .40
1014 A666 50y multicolored   .90 .50
1015 A666 60y multicolored   1.00 .65
Nos. 1012-1015 (4)   2.75 1.80
16th UPU Congress, Tokyo, 10/1-11/16. 15y issued in sheets of 20, others in sheets of 10.

Hokusai Type of 1964
Design: 50y, "Passing through Koshu down to Mishima" from Hokusai's 36 Views of Fuji.

1969, Oct. 7   Photo.   Perf. 13
1016 A525 50y multicolored   1.00 .55
Issued for International Letter Writing Week Oct. 7-13. Sheets of 10 (5x2).

Rugby Player, Camellia and Oura Catholic Church — A667

1969, Oct. 26
1017 A667 15y lt ultra & multi   .30 .25
24th Natl. Athletic Meet, Nagasaki, 10/26-31.

Cape Kitayama — A668

Goishi Coast — A669

1969, Nov. 20   Photo.   Perf. 13
1018 A668 7y gray & dk blue   .25 .25
1019 A669 15y salmon & dk red   .30 .25
Rikuchu Coast National Park.

Worker in Hard Hat — A670

1969, Nov. 26
1020 A670 15y ultra, blk yel & brn   .30 .25
50th anniv. of the ILO.

Dog Amulet, Hokkeji, Nara — A671

1969, Dec. 10
1021 A671 7y orange & multi   .25 .25
New Year 1970. Sheets containing 4 No. 1021 were awarded as prizes in the New Year lottery. Value $1.50.

Aso Bay and Tsutsu Women with Horse — A672

1970, Feb. 25   Photo.   Perf. 13
1022 A672 15y multicolored   .30 .25
Iki-Tsushima Quasi-National Park.

Fireworks over EXPO '70 — A673

Cherry Blossoms Around Globe — A674

Pole Lanterns at EXPO — A679

View of EXPO Within Globe — A680

Girl Scout — A686

1970, July 26
1037 A686 15y multicolored   .30 .25
50th anniversary of Japanese Girl Scouts.

Equestrian, Mt. Iwate and Paulownia — A693

1970, Oct. 10   Photo.   *Perf. 13*
1044 A693 15y silver & multi   .30 .25
25th Natl. Athletic Meet, Morioka, 10/10-16.

Irises, by Korin Ogata (1658-1716) — A675

1970, Mar. 14   Photo.   *Perf. 13*
1023 A673 7y red & multi   .25 .25
1024 A674 15y gold & multi   .30 .25
1025 A675 50y gold & multi   .90 .45
  a. Souv. sheet of 3, #1023-1025 1.75 1.75
  b. Bklt. pane of 4 & 3 with gutter 3.00
  Nos. 1023-1025 (3)   1.45 .95
EXPO '70 Intl. Exposition, Senri, Osaka, Mar. 15-Sept. 13.
No. 1025b contains a pane of 4 No. 1023 and a pane with Nos. 1023-1025. A 35mm gutter separates the panes.

Grass in Autumn Wind, by Hoitsu Sakai (1761-1828) — A681

1970, June 15   Photo.   *Perf. 13*
1029 A679 7y red & multi   .25 .25
1030 A680 15y blue & multi   .30 .25
1031 A681 50y silver & multi   .90 .45
  a. Souv. sheet of 3, #1029-1031 1.75
  b. Bklt. panes of 4 & 3 with gutter 3.00
  Nos. 1029-1031 (3)   1.45 .75
EXPO '70, 2nd issue.
No. 1031b contains a pane of 4 No. 1029 and a pane with Nos. 1029-1031. A 35mm gutter separates the panes.

Kinoura Coast and Festival Drum — A687

Tate Mountains Seen from Himi Coast — A688

1970, Aug. 1
1038 A687 15y multicolored   .30 .25
1039 A688 15y multicolored   .30 .25
Noto Hanto Quasi-National Park.

Tree and UN Emblem A695

50y, UN emblem and Headquarters with flags.

1970, Oct. 24
1046 A695 15y olive, ap grn & gold .30 .25
1047 A695 50y multicolored   .90 .25
25th anniversary of United Nations.

Woman with Hand Drum, by Saburosuke Okada A676

1970, Apr. 20   Photo.   *Perf. 13*
1026 A676 15y multicolored   .45 .25
Issued for Stamp Week, Apr. 20-26.

Buildings and Postal Code Symbol — A682

1970, July 1   Photo.   *Perf. 13*
1032 A682 7y emerald & vio   .35 .25
1033 A682 15y brt blue & choc   .40 .25
Postal code system.

Sunflower and UN Emblem — A689

1970, Aug. 17
1040 A689 15y lt blue & multi   .30 .25
Issued to publicize the 4th United Nations Congress on the Prevention of Crime and the Treatment of Offenders, Kyoto, Aug. 17-26.

Hodogaya Stage, by Hiroshige III — A694

1970, Oct. 20
1045 A694 15y silver & multi   .30 .25
Centenary of telegraph service in Japan.

Vocational Training Competition Emblem — A696

1970, Nov. 10   Photo.   *Perf. 13*
1048 A696 15y multicolored   .30 .25
The 19th International Vocational Training Competition, Chiba City, Nov. 10-19.

Mt. Yoshino — A677

Nachi Waterfall A678

1970, Apr. 30   Photo.   *Perf. 13*
1027 A677 7y gray & pink   .25 .25
1028 A678 15y pale blue & grn   .30 .25
Yoshino-Kumano National Park.

"Maiden at Dojo Temple" A683

Scene from "Sukeroku" A684

"The Subscription List" (Kanjincho) — A685

1970, July 10
1034 A683 15y multicolored   .30 .25
1035 A684 15y multicolored   .30 .25
1036 A685 50y multicolored   .90 .30
  Nos. 1034-1036 (3)   1.50 .80
Issued to publicize the Kabuki Theater.

Mt. Myogi — A690

Mt. Arafune A691

1970, Sept. 11   Photo.   *Perf. 13*
1041 A690 15y multicolored   .30 .25
1042 A691 15y multicolored   .30 .25
Myogi-Arafune-Sakukogen Quasi-Natl. Park.

G.P.O., Tokyo, by Hiroshige III — A692

1970, Oct. 6
1043 A692 50y multicolored   .95 :30
Intl. Letter Writing Week, Oct. 6-12. Sheets of 10 (5x2). Design from wood block series, "Noted Places in Tokyo."

Diet Building and Doves A697

1970, Nov. 29
1049 A697 15y multicolored   .30 .25
80th anniversary of Japanese Diet.

Wild Boar, Folk Art, Arai City, Niigata Prefecture — A698

1970, Dec. 10
1050 A698 7y multicolored   .25 .25
New Year 1971. Sheets containing 4 No. 1050 were awarded as prizes in the New Year lottery. Value $1.50.

Gen-jo-raku
A699

Ko-cho
A700

Tai-hei-raku — A701

1971, Apr. 1   **Photo.**   **Perf. 13**
1051 A699 15y multicolored .30 .25
1052 A700 15y multicolored .30 .25
1053 A701 50y multicolored .90 .25
     Nos. 1051-1053 (3) 1.50 .75

Gagaku, classical Japanese court entertainment.

Woman Voter and Parliament — A702

1971, Apr. 10   **Photo.**   **Perf. 13**
1054 A702 15y orange & multi .30 .25

25th anniversary of woman suffrage.

Pines and Maple Leaves — A703

1971, Apr. 18
1055 A703 7y emerald & violet .25 .25

National forestation campaign.

Woman of Tokyo, by Kiyokata Kaburagi — A704

1971, Apr. 19
1056 A704 15y gray & multi .35 .25

Philatelic Week, Apr. 19-25.

Mailman
A705

Mailbox
A706

Railroad Post Office — A707

1971, Apr. 20
1057 A705 15y blk & org brn .30 .25
1058 A706 15y multicolored .30 .25
1059 A707 15y multicolored .30 .25
     Nos. 1057-1059 (3) .90 .75

Centenary of Japanese postage stamps.

Titmouse — A708

1971, May 10   **Photo.**   **Perf. 13**
1060 A708 15y emer, blk & bis .30 .25

25th Bird Week.

Penguins — A709

1971, June 23   **Photo.**   **Perf. 13**
1061 A709 15y dk blue, yel & grn .30 .25

Antarctic Treaty pledging peaceful uses of and scientific co-operation in Antarctica, 10th anniv.

Goto Wakamatsu Seto Region — A710

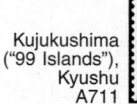

Kujukushima ("99 Islands"), Kyushu A711

1971, June 26   **Photo.**   **Perf. 13**
1062 A710 7y dark green .25 .25
1063 A711 15y deep brown .30 .25

Saikai National Park.

Arabic Numerals and Postal Code Symbol — A712

1971, July 1
1064 A712 7y emerald & red .25 .25
1065 A712 15y blue & carmine .30 .25

Promotion for postal code system.

**Inscribed "NIPPON"
Types of 1962-67 and**

Little Cuckoo
A713

Mute Swan
A714

Sika Deer
A715

Beetle
A716

Pine — A717

Noh Mask
A717a

Pheasant
A717b

Golden Eagle — A717c

Bronze Phoenix, Uji — A718

Buddha, Sculpture, 685 A718b

Burial Statue of Warrior, Ota — A718a

Tentoki Sculpture, 11th Century A718c

Bazara-Taisho, c. 710-794 A718d

Goddess Kissho A718e

Photo., Engr. (No. 1087)
1971-75   **Perf. 13**
1067 A713 3y emerald .25 .25
    a.   Bklt. pane of 20 ('72) 3.00
1068 A714 5y bright blue .25 .25
1069 A715 10y yel grn & sep ('72) .25 .25
    a.   Bklt. pane of 6 (2 #1069, 4 #1071 with gutter btwn.) ('72) 3.00
1070 A716 12y deep brown .25 .25
1071 A717 20y grn & sep ('72) .25 .25
    a.   Pane of 10 (5x2) ('72) 4.00
1072 A565b 25y emer & lt ultra ('72) .40
1074 A717a 70y dp org & blk 1.00
1075 A717b 80y crimson & brn 1.25
1076 A467 90y org & dk brn 1.50
1077 A717c 90y org & brn ('73) 1.50
1079 A569 120y dk brn & lt grn ('72) 2.00
1080 A718 150y lt & dk green 2.50 .25

1081 A570 200y dp car (18x22mm; '72) 3.50 .25
1082 A718a 200y red brn ('74) 3.50 .30
1083 A718b 300y dk blue ('74) 5.50 .25
1084 A718c 400y car rose ('74) 7.00 .25
1085 A718d 500y green ('74) 9.00 .35
1087 A718e 1000y multi ('75) 17.50 .75
    a.   Miniature sheet of 1 22.50 22.50
    Nos. 1067-1087 (18) 57.40 5.15

No. 1071a is imperf. on four sides. Compare type A718a with types A1207 and A2686. Compare types A713, A714 and A718d with types A2683, A2684 and A2687. See Nos. 1249-1250, 1254.

Coil Stamp
Perf. 13 Horiz.
1088 A717 20y green & sep ('72) .45 .30

Boy Scout Bugler — A719

1971, Aug. 2
1090 A719 15y lt blue & multi .30 .25

13th World Boy Scout Jamboree, Asagiri Plain, Aug. 2-10.

Rose and Rings — A720

1971, Oct. 1
1091 A720 15y ultra & multi .30 .25

50th anniv. of Japanese Conciliation System.

Tokyo Horsedrawn Streetcar, by Yoshimura A721

1971, Oct. 6
1092 A721 50y multicolored .95 .30

Intl. Letter Writing Week. Sheets of 10 (5x2).

Emperor's Flag, Chrysanthemums and Phoenix — A722

"Beyond the Sea," by Empress Nagako A723

1971, Oct. 14
1093 A722 15y gold, vio, red & bl .30 .25
1094 A723 15y gold, vio, red & bl .30 .25
    a.   Souv. sheet of 2, #1093-1094, imperf. .85 .85
    b.   Pair, #1093-1094 .60 .25

European trip of Emperor Hirohito and Empress Nagako, Sept. 28-Oct. 15. No. 1094a has violet map of Asia, Africa and Europe in background.

Tennis, Cape Shiono-misaki, Plum Blossoms — A724

1971, Oct. 24   Photo.   *Perf. 13*
1095 A724 15y orange & multi   .30   .25
26th National Athletic Meet, Wakayama Prefecture, Oct. 24-29.

Child's Face and "100" — A725

1971, Oct. 27
1096 A725 15y pink, car & blk   .30   .25
Centenary of Japanese Family Registration System.

Tiger, by Gaho Hashimoto A726

Design: No. 1098, Dragon, from "Dragon and Tiger," by Gaho Hashimoto.

1971, Nov. 1   Engr.   *Perf. 13*
1097 A726 15y olive & multi   .30   .25
1098 A726 15y olive & multi   .30   .25
  a.   Pair, #1097-1098   .75   .65
Centenary of Government Printing Works. Nos. 1097-1098 printed checkerwise.

Mt. Yotei from Lake Toya — A727

Mt. Showa-Shinzan — A728

1971, Dec. 6
1099 A727   7y slate grn & yel   .25   .25
1100 A728 15y pink & vio bl   .30   .25
Shikotsu-Toya National Park.

Treasure Ship — A729

1971-72
1101 A729   7y emerald, gold & org   .25   .25
1102 A729 10y lt blue, org & gold   .25   .25
New Year 1972. Sheets containing 3 No. 1102 were awarded as prizes in the New Year lottery. Value $1.75.
Issued: 7y, 12/10; 10y, 1/11/72.

Downhill Skiing — A730

No. 1104, Bobsledding. 50y, Figure skating, pairs.

1972, Feb. 3   Photo.   *Perf. 13*
Size: 24x34mm
1103 A730 20y ultra & multi   .40   .25
1104 A730 20y ultra & multi   .40   .25
Size: 49x34mm
1105 A730 50y ultra & multi   .90   .25
  a.   Souv. sheet of 3, #1103-1105 1.60 1.60
  Nos. 1103-1105 (3)   1.70   .75
11th Winter Olympic Games, Sapporo, Feb. 3-13. No. 1105a has continuous design extending into margin.

Bunraku, Ningyo Jyoruri Puppet Theater
A731   A732

A733

1972, Mar. 1   Photo.   *Perf. 13½*
1106 A731 20y gray & multi   .40   .25
Perf. 12½x13
1107 A732 20y multicolored   .40   .25
Lithographed and Engraved
Perf. 13½x13
1108 A733 50y multicolored   .90   .25
  Nos. 1106-1108 (3)   1.70   .75
Japanese classical entertainment.

Express Train on New Sanyo Line — A734

1972, Mar. 15   Photo.   *Perf. 13*
1109 A734 20y multicolored   .40   .25
Centenary of first Japanese railroad.

Taishaku-kyo Valley — A735

Hiba Mountains Seen from Mt. Dogo — A736

1972, Mar. 24
1110 A735 20y gray & multi   .40   .25
1111 A736 20y green & multi   .40   .25
Hiba-Dogo-Taishaku Quasi-National Park.

Heart and UN Emblem A737

1972, Apr. 15
1112 A737 20y gray, red & black   .40   .25
"Your heart is your health," World Health Day.

"A Balloon Rising," by Gakuryo Nakamura A738

1972, Apr. 20
1113 A738 20y violet bl & multi   .40   .25
Philatelic Week, Apr. 20-26.

Shurei Gate, Okinawa — A739

1972, May 15
1114 A739 20y ultra & multi   .40   .25
Ratification of the Reversion Agreement with US under which the Ryukyu Islands were returned to Japan.

Camellia — A740

1972, May 20
1115 A740 20y brt grn, vio bl & yel   .40   .25
National forestation campaign and 23rd Arbor Day, May 21.

Mt. Kurikoma and Kijiyama Kokeshi Doll — A741

Naruko-kyo Gorge and Naruko Kokeshi Doll — A742

1972, June 20   Photo.   *Perf. 13*
1116 A741 20y blue & multi   .40   .25
1117 A742 20y red & multi   .40   .25
Kurikoma Quasi-National Park.

Envelope, Postal Code Symbol A743   Mailbox, Postal Code Symbol A744

1972, July 1
1118 A743 10y blue, blk & gray   .25   .25
1119 A744 20y emerald & org   .40   .25
Publicity for the postal code system.

Mt. Hodaka A745

Mt. Tate — A746

1972, Aug. 10   Photo.   *Perf. 13*
1120 A745 10y rose & violet   .25   .25
1121 A746 20y blue & buff   .40   .25
Chubu Sangaku National Park.

Ghost in "Tamura" A747   Lady Rokujo in "Lady Hollyhock" A748

"Hagoromo" (Feather Robe) — A749

1972, Sept. 20   Engr.
1122 A747 20y multicolored   .40   .25
Photo.
1123 A748 20y multicolored   .40   .25
Perf. 13½x13
1124 A749 50y multicolored   .90   .25
  Nos. 1122-1124 (3)   1.70   .75
Noh, classical public entertainment.

School Children — A750

1972, Oct. 5   Photo.   *Perf. 13*
1125 A750 20y lt ultra, vio bl & car .40   .25
Centenary of modern education system.

Eitai Bridge, Tokyo, by Hiroshige III — A751

1972, Oct. 9
1126 A751 50y multicolored .90 .25
Intl. Letter Writing Week, Oct. 9-15.

Inauguration of Railway Service, by Hiroshige III — A752

Locomotive, Class C62 — A753

1972, Oct. 14
1127 A752 20y multicolored .40 .25
1128 A753 20y multicolored .40 .25
Centenary of Japanese railroad system.

Kendo (Fencing) and Sakurajima Volcano — A754

1972, Oct. 22
1129 A754 10y yellow & multi .30 .25
27th National Athletic Meet, Kagoshima Prefecture, Oct. 22-27.

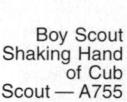

Boy Scout Shaking Hand of Cub Scout — A755

1972, Nov. 4
1130 A755 20y yellow & multi .40 .25
50th anniversary of the Boy Scouts of Japan.

US Ship, Yokohama Harbor — A756

1972, Nov. 28 **Photo.** **Perf. 13**
1131 A756 20y multicolored .40 .25
Centenary of Japanese customs. Wood block by Hiroshige III (d. 1896).

"Clay Plate with Plum Blossoms" — A757

1972, Dec. 11
1132 A757 10y blue & multi .25 .25
New Year 1973. Art work by Kenzan Ogata (1663-1743). Sheets containing 3 No. 1132

were awarded as prizes in the New Year lottery. Value $1.75.

Mt. Tsurugi A758

Oboke Valley — A759

1973, Feb. 20 **Photo.** **Perf. 13**
1133 A758 20y multicolored .30 .25
1134 A759 20y multicolored .30 .25
Mt. Tsurugi Quasi-National Park.

Mt. Takao — A760

Minoo Falls — A761

1973, Mar. 12 **Photo.** **Perf. 13**
1135 A760 20y multicolored .30 .25
1136 A761 20y multicolored .30 .25
Meiji Forests Quasi-National Park.

Phoenix Tree — A762

1973, Apr. 7 **Photo.** **Perf. 13**
1137 A762 20y brt grn, yel & dk bl .30 .25
National forestation campaign.

Sumiyoshi Shrine Visitor — A763

1973, Apr. 20
1138 A763 20y multicolored .30 .25
Philatelic Week, Apr. 20-26. Design from painting by Ryusei Kishida (1891-1929) of his daughter, "A Portrait of Reiko Visiting Sumiyoshi Shrine."

Mt. Kamagatake A764

Mt. Haguro A765

1973, May 25 **Photo.** **Perf. 13**
1139 A764 20y multicolored .30 .25
1140 A765 20y multicolored .30 .25
Suzuka Quasi-National Park.

Chichijima Beach A766

Coral Reef on Minami Island — A767

1973, June 26
1141 A766 10y grnsh bl & Prus bl .30 .25
1142 A767 20y lilac & dk pur .30 .25
Ogasawara National Park.
5th anniversary of the return of the Bonin (Ogasawara Islands) to Japan.

Tree, Postal Code Symbol A768

Mailman, Postal Code Symbol A769

1973, July 1 **Photo.** **Perf. 13**
1143 A768 10y brt green & gold .25 .25
1144 A769 20y blue, purple & car .40 .25
Postal code system, 5th anniversary.

Sandan Gorge — A770

Mt. Shinnyu A771

1973, Aug. 28 **Photo.** **Perf. 13**
1145 A770 20y multicolored .40 .25
1146 A771 20y multicolored .40 .25
Nishi-Chugoku-Sanchi Quasi-National Park.

Tenryu Valley — A772

Mt. Horaiji — A773

1973, Sept. 18 **Photo.** **Perf. 13**
1147 A772 20y lilac & multi .40 .25
1148 A773 20y vio bl, lt bl & sil .40 .25
Tenryu-Okumikawa Quasi-National Park.

Cock, by Jakuchu Ito (1716-1800) A774

1973, Oct. 6
1149 A774 50y gold & multi .90 .25
International Letter Writing Week, Oct. 7-13. Sheets of 10.

Woman Runner at Start — A775

1973, Oct. 14
1150 A775 10y silver & multi .25 .25
28th National Athletic Meet, Chiba Prefecture, Oct. 14-19.

Kan Mon Bridge A776

1973, Nov. 14 **Engr.** **Perf. 13**
1151 A776 20y black, rose & yel .40 .25
Opening of Kan Mon Bridge connecting Honshu and Kyushu.

Old Man and Dog — A777

Designs: No. 1153, Old man and wife pounding rice mortar, which yields gold. No. 1154, Old man sitting in tree and landlord admiring tree.

1973, Nov. 20 **Photo.**
1152 A777 20y multicolored .40 .25
1153 A777 20y multicolored .40 .25
1154 A777 20y multicolored .40 .25
Nos. 1152-1154 (3) 1.20 .75
Folk tale "Hanasaka-jijii" (The Old Man Who Made Trees Bloom).

Bronze Lantern, Muromachi Period — A778

1973, Dec. 10
1155 A778 10y emerald, blk & org .25 .25
New Year 1974. Sheets containing 3 No. 1155 were awarded as prizes in the New Year lottery. Value $1.50.

Nijubashi, Tokyo A779

Imperial
Palace,
Tokyo
A780

1974, Jan. 26   **Photo.**   **Perf. 13**
1156 A779 20y gold & multi   .40 .25
1157 A780 20y gold & multi   .40 .25
   a.   Souv. sheet of 2, #1156-1157   .90 .40
   50th anniversary of the wedding of Emperor
Hirohito and Empress Nagako.

Young Wife
A781

Crane
Weaving
A782

Cranes in
Flight
A783

1974, Feb. 20   **Photo.**   **Perf. 13**
1158 A781 20y multicolored   .40 .25
1159 A782 20y multicolored   .40 .25
1160 A783 20y multicolored   .40 .25
   Nos. 1158-1160 (3)   1.20 .75
   Folk tale "Tsuru-nyobo" (Crane becomes
wife of peasant).

Marudu
Falls — A784

Marine
Scene — A785

1974, Mar. 15
1161 A784 20y multicolored   .40 .25
1162 A785 20y multicolored   .40 .25
   Iriomote National Park.

"Finger," by
Ito Shinsui
A786

1974, Apr. 20   **Photo.**   **Perf. 13**
1163 A786 20y multicolored   .40 .25
   Philatelic Week, Apr. 20-27.

Nambu Red Pine
Sapling & Mt.
Iwate — A787

1974, May 18
1164 A787 20y multicolored   .30 .25
   National forestation campaign.

Supreme
Court
Building
A788

1974, May 23   **Engr.**
1165 A788 20y redsh brown   .30 .25
   Completion of Supreme Court Building,
Tokyo.

Midget
Using Bowl
as Boat
A789

   Designs: No. 1167, Midget fighting demon.
No. 1168, Princess and midget changed into
prince with magic hammer.

1974, June 10   **Photo.**   **Perf. 13**
1166 A789 20y yellow & multi   .40 .25
1167 A789 20y bister & multi   .40 .25
1168 A789 20y bister & multi   .40 .25
   Nos. 1166-1168 (3)   1.20 .75
   Folk tale "Issun Hoschi" (The Story of the
Mini-mini Boy).

"Police," by
Kunimasa
Baido — A790

1974, June 17   **Perf. 13**
1169 A790 20y multicolored   .30 .25
   Centenary of the Tokyo Metropolitan Police
Department.

Japanese
Otter
A791

   No. 1170, Mayailurus iriomotensis. No.
1172, Pentalagus furnessi. No. 1173, Pteropus pselaphon.

**Litho. and Engr.; Photo. and Engr.
(Nos. 1172-1173)**
1974
1170 A791 20y multicolored   .40 .25
1171 A791 20y multicolored   .40 .25
1172 A791 20y multicolored   .40 .25
1173 A791 20y multicolored   .40 .25
   Nos. 1170-1173 (4)   1.60 1.00
   Nature conservation.
   Issue dates: No. 1170, 3/25; No. 1171, 6/25;
No. 1172, 8/30; No. 1173, 11/15.

Transfusion Bottle,
Globe,
Doves — A794

1974, July 1   **Photo.**
1174 A794 20y brt blue & multi   .40 .25
   Intl. Red Cross Blood Donations Year.

Discovery of
Kaguya
Hime in
Shining
Bamboo
A795

Kaguya
Hime as
Grown-up
Beauty
A796

Kaguya
Hime and
Escorts
Returning to
Moon
A797

1974, July 29   **Photo.**   **Perf. 13**
1175 A795 20y multicolored   .40 .25
1176 A796 20y multicolored   .40 .25
1177 A797 20y multicolored   .40 .25
   Nos. 1175-1177 (3)   1.20 .75
   Folk tale "Kaguya Hime" or "Tale of the Bamboo Cutter."

Rich and
Poor Men
with Wens
A798

Poor Man
Dancing
With Spirits
A798a

   Design: No. 1180, Rich man with two wens,
poor man without wen, spirits.

1974, Sept. 9   **Photo.**   **Perf. 13**
1178 A798 20y multicolored   .40 .25
1179 A798a 20y multicolored   .40 .25
1180 A798 20y multicolored   .40 .25
   Nos. 1178-1180 (3)   1.20 .75
   Folk tale "Kobutori Jiisan," or "The Old Man
who had his Wen Taken by Spirits."

Goode's
Projection and
Diet — A799

"Aizen" by Ryushi Kawabata — A800

1974, Oct. 1   **Photo.**   **Perf. 13**
1181 A799 20y multicolored   .30 .25
1182 A800 50y multicolored   .90 .25
   Interparliamentary Union, 61st Meeting,
Tokyo, Nov. 2-11.

Pine and Hawk, by
Sesson — A801

1974, Oct. 7
1183 A801 50y sepia, blk & dk brn   .90 .25
   Intl. Letter Writing Week, Oct. 6-12.

UPU
Emblem — A802

Tending Cow, Fan by Sotatsu
Tawaraya — A803

1974, Oct. 9
1184 A802 20y multicolored   .30 .25
1185 A803 50y multicolored   .90 .25
   Centenary of Universal Postal Union.

Soccer Players and
Sailboat — A804

1974, Oct. 20   **Photo.**
1186 A804 10y multicolored   .25 .25
   29th National Athletic Meet, Ibaraki Prefecture, Oct. 20-25.

Various
Mushrooms — A805

1974, Nov. 2
1187 A805 20y multicolored   .40 .25
   9th International Congress on the Cultivation of Edible Fungi, Japan, Nov. 4-13.

Steam Locomotive Class D51 — A806

Class C57 — A807

Designs: Steam locomotives.

1974, Nov. 26   Photo.   Perf. 13
1188 A806 20y shown   .45 .25
1189 A807 20y shown   .45 .25
  a.   Pair, #1188-1189   .95 .60

1975, Feb. 25
1190 A806 20y Class D52   .45 .25
1191 A807 20y Class C58   .45 .25
  a.   Pair, #1190-1191   .95 .60

Class 8620 — A808   Class C11 — A809

1975, Apr. 3
1192 A808 20y shown   .45 .25
1193 A809 20y shown   .45 .25
  a.   Pair, #1192-1193   .95 .60

1975, May 15
1194 A806 20y Class 9600   .45 .25
1195 A807 20y Class C51   .45 .25
  a.   Pair, #1194-1195   .95 .60

1975, June 10   Photo. & Engr.
1196 A806 20y Class 7100   .45 .25
1197 A806 20y Class 150   .45 .25
  a.   Pair, #1196-1197   .95 .60
    Nos. 1188-1197 (10)   4.50 2.50

Japanese National Railways.

Ornamental Nail Cover, Katsura Palace — A810

1974, Dec. 10
1198 A810 10y blue & multi   .25 .25
New Year 1975. Sheets containing 3 No. 1198 were awarded as prizes in the New Year Lottery. Value $1.50.

Short-tailed Albatrosses A811

Bonin Island Honey-eater A812

Temminck's Robin A813

Ryukyu-Yamagame Tortoise — A814

Design: No. 1200, Japanese cranes.

1975-76   Photo. & Engr.   Perf. 13
1199 A811 20y multicolored   .40 .25
1200 A811 20y multicolored   .40 .25
1201 A812 20y multicolored   .40 .25
1202 A813 50y multicolored   .90 .25
1203 A814 50y multicolored   .90 .25
    Nos. 1199-1203 (5)   3.00 1.25
Nature conservation.
Issued: No. 1199, 1/16; No. 1200, 2/13; No. 1201, 8/8; No. 1202, 2/27/76; No. 1203, 3/25/76.

Taro Urashima Releasing Turtle A815

Palace of the Sea God and Fish A816

Smoke from Casket Making Taro an Old Man A817

1975, Jan. 28   Photo.   Perf. 13
1204 A815 20y multicolored   .40 .25
1205 A816 20y multicolored   .40 .25
1206 A817 20y multicolored   .40 .25
    Nos. 1204-1206 (3)   1.20 .75
Folk tale "Legend of Taro Urashima."

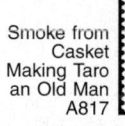

Kan-mon-sho (Seeing and Hearing), by Shiko Munakata — A818

1975, Mar. 20   Photo.   Perf. 13
1207 A818 20y brown & multi   .40 .25
Japan Broadcasting Corp., 50th anniv.

Old Man Feeding Mouse A819

Man Following Mouse Underground — A820

Mice Entertaining and Bringing Gifts A821

1975, Apr. 15   Photo.   Perf. 13
1208 A819 20y multicolored   .40 .25
1209 A820 20y multicolored   .40 .25
1210 A821 20y multicolored   .40 .25
    Nos. 1208-1210 (3)   1.20 .75
Folk tale "Paradise for the Mice."

Matsuura Screen (detail), 16th Century — A822

1975, Apr. 21
1211   20y denomination at lower left   .40 .25
1212   20y denomination at lower right   .40 .25
  a.   A822 Pair, #1211-1212   .80 .65
Philatelic Week, Apr. 21-27.

Oil Derricks, Congress Emblem — A824

1975, May 10   Photo.   Perf. 13
1213 A824 20y multicolored   .30 .25
9th World Petroleum Cong., Tokyo, May 11-16.

Trees and River — A825

1975, May 24
1214 A825 20y green & multi   .30 .25
National forestation campaign.

IWY Emblem, Sun and Woman — A826

1975, June 23
1215 A826 20y orange & multi   .30 .25
International Women's Year 1975.

Okinawan Dancer, EXPO 75 Emblem A827   Birds in Flight (Bingata) A828

Aquapolis and Globe — A829

1975, July 19   Photo.   Perf. 13
1216 A827 20y ultra & multi   .30 .25
1217 A828 30y blue grn & multi   .50 .25
1218 A829 50y ultra & multi   .90 .25
  a.   Souv. sheet of 3, #1216-1218 1.75 1.75
    Nos. 1216-1218 (3)   1.70 .75
Oceanexpo 75, 1st Intl. Ocean Exposition, Okinawa, July 20, 1975-Jan. 18, 1976.

Historic Ship Issue

Kentoshi-sen 7th-9th Centuries — A830

Ships: No. 1220, Kenmin-sen, 7th-9th cent. No. 1221, Goshuin-sen, merchant ship, 16th-17th cent. No. 1222, Tenchi-maru, state barge, built 1630. No. 1223, Sengoku-bune (cargo ship) and fishing vessel. No. 1224, Shoheimaru, 1852, European-type sailing ship. No. 1225, Taisei-maru, four-mast bark training ship, 1903. No. 1226, Tenyomaru, first Japanese passenger liner, 1907. No. 1227, Asama-maru, passenger liner. No. 1228, Kinai-maru, transpacific freighter and Statue of Liberty. No. 1229, Container ship. No. 1230, Tanker.

1975-76   Engr.   Perf. 13
1219 A830 20y rose red   .40 .25
1220 A830 20y sepia   .40 .25
  a.   Pair, #1219-1220   .80 .65
1221 A830 20y lt olive   .40 .25
1222 A830 20y dark blue   .40 .25
  a.   Pair, #1221-1222   .80 .65
1223 A830 50y violet blue   .90 .25
1224 A830 50y lilac   .90 .25
  a.   Pair, #1223-1224   1.90 1.00
1225 A830 50y gray   .90 .25
1226 A830 50y dark brown   .90 .25
  a.   Pair, #1225-1226   1.90 1.00
1227 A830 50y olive green   .90 .25
1228 A830 50y olive brown   .90 .25
  a.   Pair, #1227-1228   1.90 1.00
1229 A830 50y ultra   .90 .25
1230 A830 50y violet blue   .90 .25
  a.   Pair, #1229-1230   1.90 1.00
    Nos. 1219-1230 (12)   8.80 3.00
Printed checkerwise in sheets of 20.
Issued: Nos. 1219-1220, 8/30; Nos. 1221-1222, 9/25; Nos. 1223-1224, 3/11/76; Nos. 1225-1226, 4/12/76; Nos. 1227-1228, 6/1/76; Nos. 1229-1230, 8/18/76.

Apple and Apple Tree — A831

1975, Sept. 17   Photo.   Perf. 13
1231 A831 20y gray, black & red   .35 .25
Centenary of apple cultivation in Japan.

Peacock, by Korin
Ogata — A832

1975, Oct. 6   Photo.   Perf. 13
1232 A832 50y gold & multi   .90 .25
Intl. Letter Writing Week, Oct. 6-12.

American
Flag and
Cherry
Blossoms
A833

Japanese
Flag and
Dogwood
A834

1975, Oct. 14
1233 A833 20y ultra & multi   .35 .25
1234 A834 20y green & multi   .35 .25
    a. Souv. sheet of 2, #1233-1234 1.00 .75
Visit of Emperor Hirohito and Empress
Nagako to the United States, Oct. 1-14.

Savings Box
and
Coins — A835

1975, Oct. 24
1235 A835 20y multicolored   .30 .25
Japan's Postal Savings System, centenary.

Weight
Lifter — A836

1975, Oct. 25
1236 A836 10y multicolored   .25 .25
30th National Athletic Meet, Mie Prefecture,
Oct. 26-31.

Papier-mache Dragon,
Fukushima
Prefecture — A837

1975, Dec. 13   Photo.   Perf. 13
1237 A837 10y multicolored   .25 .25
New Year 1976. Sheets containing 3 No.
1237 were awarded as prizes in the New Year
Lottery. Value $1.50.

Inscribed "NIPPON"
Types of 1963-74 and

Japanese
Narcissus
A841

Noh Mask,
Old Man
A843

Guardian
Dog, Katori
Shrine
A845

Sho-Kannon,
Yakushiji
Temple
A846

Designs: 50y, Nyoirin Kannon, Chuguji Temple. 150y, Bronze phoenix, Uji. 200y, Clay burial figure of warrior, Ota.

1976-79   Photo.   Perf. 13
1244 A565f 50y emerald   .90 .25
    a. Bklt. panes of 2 & 4 with gut-
        ter   6.00
1245 A841 60y multicolored   1.10 .25
1248 A843 140y lil rose & lil   2.50 .25
1249 A718 150y red org & brn   2.75 .25
1250 A718a 200y red orange   3.75 .25
1251 A845 250y blue   4.50 .25
1253 A846 350y dk violet brn   6.25 .25
    Nos. 1244-1253 (7)   21.75 1.75

Coil Stamps
Perf. 13 Horiz.
1254 A715 10y yel grn & sep
            ('79)   .25 .25
1256 A565f 50y emerald   1.25 .25
1257 A567c 100y ver & blk ('79) 1.90 .30
    Nos. 1254-1257 (3)   3.40 .80

    See No. 1631.

Hikone Folding Screen (detail), 17th
Century — A850

1976, Apr. 20   Photo.   Perf. 13
1258 50y denomination at lower
       right   .90 .25
1259 50y denomination at upper
       right   .90 .25
    a. A850 Pair, #1258-1259 1.90 1.25
    Philatelic Week, Apr. 20-26.

Plum Blossoms,
Cedars, Mt.
Tsukuba — A852

1976, May 22
1260 A852 50y multicolored   .90 .25
National forestation campaign.

Green Tree
Frog — A853

Bitterlings
A854

Sticklebacks
A855

1976   Photo. & Engr.   Perf. 13
1261 A853 50y multicolored   .90 .25
1262 A854 50y multicolored   .90 .25
1263 A855 50y multicolored   .90 .25
    Nos. 1261-1263 (3)   2.70 .75
Nature conservation.
Issued: No. 1261, 7/20; No. 1262, 8/26; No.
1263, 9/16.

Crows, by Yosa
Buson — A856

1976, Oct. 6   Photo.   Perf. 13
1264 A856 100y gray, blk & buff 1.75 .25
Intl. Letter Writing Week, Oct. 6-12.

Gymnasts and
Stadium — A857

1976, Oct. 23   Photo.   Perf. 13
1265 A857 20y multicolored   .30 .25
31st National Athletic Meet, Saga Prefecture, Oct. 24-29.

Cable, Cable
Ship, Map of
East China
Sea — A858

1976, Oct. 25
1266 A858 50y blue, blk & silver .90 .25
Opening of Sino-Japanese cable between
Shanghai and Reihoku-cho, Kumamoto
Prefecture.

Classical
Court
Dance
A859

Imperial
Coach
A860

1976, Nov. 10   Photo.   Perf. 13
1267 A859 50y multicolored   .90 .25
1268 A860 50y multicolored   .90 .25
    a. Souv. sheet of 2, #1267-1268 1.90 1.90
Emperor Hirohito's accession to the throne,
50th anniversary.

Kindergarten
Class — A861

1976, Nov. 16
1269 A861 50y multicolored   .90 .25
Centenary of first kindergarten in Japan.

Healthy
Family
A862

1976, Nov. 24
1270 A862 50y multicolored   .90 .25
Natl. Health Insurance, 50th anniv.

Bamboo Toy
Snake — A863

1976, Dec. 1   Photo.   Perf. 13
1271 A863 20y multicolored   .35 .25
New Year 1977. Sheets containing 2 No.
1271 were awarded as prizes in the New Year
lottery. Value $1.65.

National Treasures

East Pagoda,
Yakushiji Temple,
c. 730 — A864

Deva King in
Armor
Holding
Spear, Nara
Period
A865

1976, Dec. 9   Photo.   Perf. 13
1272 A864 50y multicolored   .90 .25
                    Engr.
1273 A865 100y green & multi   1.75 .30

Golden Pavilion, Toshodai-ji Temple,
8th Century — A866

Praying
Women, from
Heike Nokyo
Sutra, 12th
Century
A867

Photogravure and Engraved
1977, Jan. 20   *Perf. 13*
1274 A866 50y multicolored   .90 .25
Photo.
1275 A867 100y multicolored   1.75 .30

Comic Picture Scroll, Attributed to
Toba Sojo Kakuyu (1053-
1140) — A868

Saint on
Cloud, 11th
Century
Wood
Carving,
Byodoin
Temple
A869

1977, Mar. 25   **Photo.**   *Perf. 13*
1276 A868 50y multicolored   .90 .25
Engr.
1277 A869 100y multicolored   1.75 .30

Noblemen on Way to Court, from
Picture Scroll, Heian Period — A870

Statue of
Seitaka-doji,
Messenger,
Kamakura
Period
A871

1977, June 27   **Photo.**   *Perf. 13*
1278 A870 50y multicolored   .90 .25
Engr.
1279 A871 100y multicolored   1.75 .30

The Recluse Han
Shan, 14th
Century
Painting — A872

Tower, Matsumoto Castle, 16th
Century — A873

1977, Aug. 25   **Photo.**   *Perf. 13*
1280 A872 50y multicolored   .90 .25
Photogravure and Engraved
1281 A873 100y black & multi   1.75 .30

Pine and Flowers, Chishakuin Temple,
Kyoto, 1591 — A874

Main Hall, Kiyomizu Temple,
1633 — A875

1977, Nov. 16   **Photo.**   *Perf. 13*
1282 A874 50y multicolored   .90 .25
Engr.
1283 A875 100y multicolored   1.75 .30

Scene from Tale of Genji, by Sotatsu
Tawaraya — A876

Inkstone Case, by Koetsu
Honami — A877

1978, Jan. 26   **Photo.**   *Perf. 13*
1284 A876 50y multicolored   .90 .25
Photogravure and Engraved
1285 A877 100y black & multi   1.75 .30

Family Enjoying Cool Evening, by
Morikage Kusumi — A878

Yomeimon, Toshogu Shrine,
1636 — A879

1978, Mar. 3   **Photo.**   *Perf. 13*
1286 A878 50y gray & multi   .90 .25
Photogravure and Engraved
1287 A879 100y multicolored   1.75 .30

Horseshoe
Crabs
A884

Graphium Doson
Albidum — A885

Firefly
A886

Cicada — A887   Dragonfly — A888

1977   **Photo.**   *Perf. 13*
1292 A884 50y multicolored   .95 .25
Photogravure and Engraved
1293 A885 50y multicolored   .95 .25
1294 A886 50y multicolored   .95 .25
1295 A887 50y multicolored   .95 .25
Photo.
1296 A888 50y multicolored   .95 .25
     Nos. 1292-1296 (5)   4.75 1.25
  Issued: No. 1292, 2/18; No. 1293, 5/18; No.
1294, 7/22; No. 1295, 8/15; No. 1296, 9/14.

Figure
Skating — A889

Figure
Skating
Pair — A890

1977, Mar. 1
1297 A889 50y silver & multi   .90 .25
1298 A890 50y silver & multi   .90 .25
  World Figure Skating Championships,
National Yoyogi Stadium, March 1-6.

Sun Shining on
Forest — A891

1977, Apr. 16   **Photo.**   *Perf. 13*
1299 A891 50y green & multi   .90 .25
  National forestation campaign.

Weavers and Dyers (Detail from
Folding Screen) — A892

1977, Apr. 20
1300   50y denomination at lower
             left   .90 .25
1301   50y denomination at upper
             left   .90 .25
    a. A892 Pair, #1300-1301   1.90 .90
  Philatelic Week, Apr. 20-26.

Nurses
A894

1977, May 30   **Photo.**   *Perf. 13*
1302 A894 50y multicolored   .90 .25
  16th Quadrennial Congress of the Intl.
Council of Nurses, Tokyo, May 30-June 3.

Fast Breeder
Reactor, Central
Part — A895

1977, June 6
1303 A895 50y multicolored   .90 .25
  Experimental fast breeder reactor "Joyo,"
which began operating Apr. 24, 1977.

Workers and   Work on
Safety   High-rise
Emblems   Buildings
A896   A897

Cargo
Unloading
A898

Machinery
Work
A899

1977, July 1
1304	A896 50y multicolored	.90	.25
1305	A897 50y multicolored	.90	.25
1306	A898 50y multicolored	.90	.25
1307	A899 50y multicolored	.90	.25
a.	Block or strip of 4, #1304-1307	4.00	1.00

National Safety Week, July 1-July 7.

Carrier
Pigeons,
Mail Box,
UPU
Emblem
A900

UPU
Emblem,
Postal
Service Flag
of Meiji Era,
world Map
A900a

1977, June 20   Photo.   Perf. 13
1308	A900 50y multicolored	.90	.25
1309	A900a 100y multicolored	1.75	.30
a.	Souv. sheet of 2, #1308-1309	2.75	2.00

Cent. of Japan's admission to the UPU.

Surgeon in
Operating
Room — A901

1977, Sept. 3   Photo.   Perf. 13
1310	A901 50y multicolored	.90	.25

27th Cong. of the Intl. Surgeon's Society on
the 75th anniv. of its founding, Kyoto, 9/3-8.

Child Using
Telephone,
Map of New
Cable
Route — A902

1977, Aug. 26
1311	A902 50y multicolored	.90	.25

Inauguration of underwater telephone cable
linking Okinawa, Luzon and Hong Kong.

Early Speaker,
Waves and
Telegraph
Key — A903

1977, Sept. 24   Photo.   Perf. 13
1312	A903 50y multicolored	.90	.25

50th anniversary of amateur radio in Japan.

Bicyclist, Mt. Iwaki
and Iwaki
River — A904

1977, Oct. 1
1313	A904 20y multicolored	.35	.25

32nd National Athletic Meet, Aomori Prefecture, Oct. 2-7.

Flowers and
Ducks, Attributed
to Hasegawa
Tohaku — A905

1977, Oct. 6
1314	A905 100y multicolored	1.75	.30

Intl. Letter Writing Week, Oct. 6-12.

Dinosaur,
Stars,
Museum
A906

1977, Nov. 2   Photo.   Perf. 13
1315	A906 50y multicolored	.90	.25

Centenary of National Science Museum.

Decorated Horse,
Fushimi Toy — A907

1977, Dec. 1   Photo.   Perf. 13
1316	A907 20y multicolored	.35	.25

New Year 1978. Sheets containing 2 No.
1316 were awarded as prizes in the New Year
lottery. Value $1.50.

Tokyo
Subway,
1927
A908

1977, Dec. 6
1317	50y shown	.90	.25
1318	50y Subway, 1977	.90	.25
a.	A908 Pair, #1317-1318	2.00	.90

Tokyo Subway, 50th anniversary.

Primrose — A909

Pinguicula
Ramosa — A910

Dicentra — A911

1978   Photo. & Engr.   Perf. 13
1319	A909 50y multicolored	.90	.25
1320	A910 50y multicolored	.90	.25
1321	A911 50y multicolored	.90	.25
	Nos. 1319-1321 (3)	2.70	.75

Nature protection.
Issued: No. 1319, 4/12; No. 1320, 6/8; No.
1321, 7/25.

Kanbun Bijinzu Folding Screen, Edo
Period — A912

1978, Apr. 20   Photo.   Perf. 13
1322	50y inscribed at left	.90	.25
1323	50y inscribed at right	.90	.25
a.	A912 Pair, #1322-1323	1.90	.90

Philatelic Week, Apr. 16-22.

Rotary Emblem,
Mt. Fuji — A914

1978, May 13   Photo.   Perf. 13
1324	A914 50y multicolored	.90	.25

69th Rotary International Convention,
Tokyo, May 14-18.

Congress Emblem,
by Taro
Okamoto — A915

1978, May 15
1325	A915 50y multicolored	.90	.25

23rd International Ophthalmological Congress, Kyoto, May 14-20.

Narita
International
Airport,
Tokyo — A916

1978, May 20
1326	A916 50y multicolored	.90	.25

Opening of Tokyo International Airport.

Rainbow, Japanese
Cedars, Cape
Ashizuri — A917

1978, May 20
1327	A917 50y multicolored	.90	.25

National forestation campaign.

Lion, by Sotatsu
Tawaraya, Lions
Emblem — A918

1978, June 21   Photo.   Perf. 13
1328	A918 50y multicolored	.90	.25

61st Lions Intl. Convention, Tokyo, 6/21-24.

Sumo Print Issues

Grand Champion Hidenoyama with
Sword Bearer and Herald, by
Kunisada I (Toyokuni III) — A919

Ekoin Drum Tower,
Ryogoku, by
Hiroshige — A921

Photogravure and Engraved
1978, July 1   Perf. 13
1329	50y multicolored	.90	.25
1330	50y multicolored	.90	.25
a.	A919 Pair, #1329-1330	1.90	.90

Photo.
1331	A921 50y multicolored	.95	.25
	Nos. 1329-1331 (3)	2.75	.75

Champions Tanikaze and Onogawa in
Ring-entry Ceremony, 1782, by
Shunsho — A922

Jimmaku, Raiden and Referee Shonosuke, 1791 Bout, by Shun'ei — A924

Photogravure and Engraved
1978, Sept. 9 *Perf. 13*
1332	50y multicolored	.90	.25
1333	50y multicolored	.90	.25
a.	A922 Pair, #1332-1333	1.90	.90
1334	A924 50y multicolored	.90	.25
	Nos. 1332-1334 (3)	2.70	.75

Referee Shonosuke and Champion Onomatsu, by Kunisada I — A925

Children's Sumo Play, by Utamaro — A927

1978, Nov. 11 *Perf. 13*
1335	50y multicolored	.90	.25
1336	50y multicolored	.90	.25
a.	A925 Pair, #1335-1336	1.90	.90
1337	A927 50y multicolored	.90	.25
	Nos. 1335-1337 (3)	2.70	.75

Wrestlers on Ryogoku Bridge, by Kunisada I — A928

Bow-receiving Ceremony at Tournament, by Kunisada II — A930

1979, Jan. 13 *Perf. 13*
1338	50y multicolored	.90	.25
1339	50y multicolored	.90	.25
a.	A928 Pair, #1338-1339	1.90	.90
1340	A930 50y multicolored	.90	.25
	Nos. 1338-1340 (3)	2.70	.75

Takekuma and Iwamigata (Hidenoyama) Wrestling, by Kuniyoshi — A931

Daidozan (Great Child Mountain) in Ring-entry Ceremony, by Sharaku — A933

1979, Mar. 10 *Perf. 13*
1341	50y multicolored	.90	.25
1342	50y multicolored	.90	.25
a.	A931 Pair, #1341-1342	1.90	.90
1343	A933 50y multicolored	.90	.25
	Nos. 1341-1343 (3)	2.70	.75

Radio Gymnastics Emblem — A934

1978, Aug. 1 **Photo.** *Perf. 13*
1344	A934 50y multicolored	.90	.25

Radio gymnastics program exercises, 50th anniversary.

Chamber of Commerce and Industry — A935

1978, Aug. 28 **Photo.** *Perf. 13*
1345	A935 50y multicolored	.90	.25

Tokyo Chamber of Commerce, centenary.

Symbolic Sculptures, Tokyo Stock Exchange — A936

1978, Sept. 14 **Engr.** *Perf. 13*
1346	A936 50y lilac, grn & brn	.90	.25

Centenary of the Tokyo and Osaka Stock Exchanges.

Flowering Plum with Pheasant, from Screen, Tenkyuin Temple — A937

1978, Oct. 6 **Photo.** *Perf. 13*
1347	A937 100y multicolored	1.75	.30

Intl. Letter Writing Week, Oct. 6-12.

Softball and Mt. Yarigatake — A938

1978, Oct. 14
1348	A938 20y multicolored	.35	.25

33rd National Athletic Meet, Nagano Prefecture, Oct. 15-20.

Artificial Hip, Orthopedists' Emblem — A939

1978, Oct. 16
1349	A939 50y multicolored	.90	.25

14th World Cong. of Intl. Soc. of Orthopedic Surgeons (50th anniv.), Kyoto, Oct. 15-20.

Telescope and Stars — A940

1978, Dec. 1 **Photo.**
1350	A940 50y multicolored	.90	.25

Tokyo Astronomical Observatory, cent.

Sheep Bell, Nakayama Toy — A941

1978, Dec. 4
1351	A941 20y multicolored	.35	.25

New Year 1979. Sheets containing 2 No. 1351 were awarded as prizes in the New Year Lottery. Value $1.50.

Family, Human Rights Emblem — A942

1978, Dec. 4
1352	A942 50y multicolored	.90	.25

Human Rights Week, Dec. 4-10.

Hands Shielding Children — A943

1979, Feb. 16 **Photo.** *Perf. 13*
1353	A943 50y multicolored	.90	.25

Education of the handicapped, centenary.

Telephone Dials — A944

1979, Mar. 14 **Photo.** *Perf. 13*
1354	A944 50y multicolored	.90	.25

Nation-wide telephone automatization completion.

Sketch of Man, by Leonardo da Vinci — A945

Photogravure and Engraved
1979, Apr. 7 *Perf. 13*
1355	A945 50y multicolored	.90	.25

Centenary of promulgation of State Medical Act, initiating modern medicine.

Standing Beauties, Middle Edo Period — A946

1979, Apr. 20 **Photo.**
1356	50y multicolored	.90	.25
1357	50y multicolored	.90	.25
a.	A946 Pair, #1356-1357	1.90	.90

Philatelic Week, Apr. 16-22.

Mt. Horaiji and Maple — A948

1979, May 26 **Photo.** *Perf. 13*
1358	A948 50y multicolored	.90	.25

National forestation campaign.

Modern Japanese Art Issue

Merciful Mother Goddess, by Kano Hogai — A949

Sea God's Princess, by Aoki Shigeru — A950

1979, May 30 **Photo.** *Perf. 13*
1359	A949 50y multicolored	.90	.25
1360	A950 50y multicolored	.90	.25

Fire Dance, by
Gyoshu
Hayami — A951

Leaning Figure,
by Tetsugoro
Yorozu — A952

1979, June 25   Photo.   Perf. 13
1361 A951 50y red & multi   .90 .25
Photogravure and Engraved
1362 A952 50y red & multi   .90 .25

The Black Cat, by
Shunso
Hishida — A953

Kinyo, by
Sotaro
Yasui — A954

1979, Sept. 21   Photo.   Perf. 13
1363 A953 50y multicolored   .90 .25
1364 A954 50y multicolored   .90 .25

Nude, by
Kagaku
Murakami
A955

Harvest, by Asai Chu — A956

Photogravure and Engraved
1979, Nov. 22   Perf. 13
1365 A955 50y multicolored   .90 .25
1366 A956 50y multicolored   .90 .25

Salmon, by Yuichi
Takahashi
A956a

Hall of the
Supreme
Buddha, by Kokei
Kabayashi
A956b

Photogravure and Engraved
1980, Feb. 22   Perf. 13½
1367 A956a 50y multicolored   .90 .25
Photo.
1368 A956b 50y multicolored   .90 .25

Quarantine
Officers,
Ships, Plane,
Microscope
A957

1979, July 14   Photo.
1369 A957 50y multicolored   .90 .25
Centenary of Japanese Quarantine system.

Girl Mailing
Letter — A958

Hakata Doll with
Letter-paper
Roll — A959

1979, July 23
1370 A958 20y multicolored   .30 .25
1371 A959 50y multicolored   .90 .25
Letter Writing Day.

Pitcher, Baseball
with Black Lion
Emblem — A960

1979, July 27
1372 A960 50y multicolored   .90 .25
50th National Inter-city Amateur Baseball
Tournament, Tokyo, August.

Girl Floating
in Space
A961

Design: No. 1374, Boy floating in space.

1979, Aug. 1
1373 A961 50y magenta & multi   .90 .25
1374 A961 50y blue & multi   .90 .25
  a. Souv. sheet of 2, #1373-1374   1.90 1.90
International Year of the Child.

Japanese Song Issue

Moon over Castle,
by Rentaro Taki
A962

Evening Glow, by
Shin Kusakawa
A963

1979, Aug. 24   Photo. & Engr.
1375 A962 50y multicolored   .90 .25
1376 A963 50y multicolored   .90 .25

Maple
Leaves, by
Teiichi Okano
A964

The Birthplace, by
Teiichi
Okano — A965

1979, Nov. 26
1377 A964 50y multicolored   .90 .25
1378 A965 50y multicolored   .90 .25

Winter
Landscape
A966

Mt.
Fuji — A967

1980, Jan. 28   Perf. 13
1379 A966 50y multicolored   .90 .25
1380 A967 50y multicolored   .90 .25

Spring Brook
A968

Cherry
Blossoms
A969

1980, Mar. 21
1381 A968 50y multicolored   .90 .25
1382 A969 50y multicolored   .90 .25
  Nos. 1375-1382 (8)   7.20 2.00

Great Owl, by
Okyo
Maruyama — A970

1979, Oct. 8   Photo.   Perf. 13
1383 A970 100y multicolored   1.75 .30
Intl. Letter Writing Week, Oct. 8-14.

Runner — A971

1979, Oct. 13
1384 A971 20y multicolored   .35 .25
34th National Athletic Meet, Miyazaki, Oct.
4-19.

"ITU," Globe — A972

1979, Oct. 13   Litho.   Perf. 13½
1385 A972 50y multicolored   .90 .25
Admission to ITU, cent.

Woman and
Fetus — A973

1979, Nov. 12   Photo.
1386 A973 50y multicolored   .90 .25
9th World Congress of Gynecology and
Obstetrics, Tokyo, Oct. 25-31.

Happy Monkeys,
Osaka Toy — A974

1979, Dec. 1   Photo.   Perf. 13x13½
1387 A974 20y multicolored   .35 .25
New Year 1980. Sheets of 2 No. 1387 were
New Year Lottery prizes. Value $1.50.

56 JAPAN

Government
Auditing
Centenary
A975

1980, Mar. 5   Photo.   Perf. 13½
1388 A975 50y multicolored   .90 .25

Scenes of Outdoor Play in Spring, by
Sukenobu Nishikawa — A976

1980, Apr. 21   Photo.   Perf. 13½
1389   50y multicolored   .90 .25
1390   50y multicolored   .90 .25
  a. A976 Pair, #1389-1390   1.90 .90

Philatelic Week, Apr. 21-27. Sheets of 10.

Japanese Song Issue

The
Sea — A978

The Night of the   Memories of
Hazy   Summer — A981
Moon — A979

The Sun
Flag — A980

1980   Photo. & Engr.   Perf. 13
1391 A978 50y multicolored   .90 .25
1392 A979 50y multicolored   .90 .25
1393 A980 50y multicolored   .90 .25
1394 A981 50y multicolored   .90 .25
      Nos. 1391-1394 (4)   3.60 1.00

Issued: Nos. 1391-1392, 4/28; Nos. 1393-
1394, 6/16.

The Red
Dragonfly
A982

Song by the
Sea — A983

1980, Sept. 18   Perf. 13
1395 A982 50y multicolored   .90 .25
1396 A983 50y multicolored   .90 .25

Lullaby
A984

Coconut, by Toraji
Ohnaka — A985

1981, Feb. 9   Perf. 13
1397 A984 60y multicolored   1.00 .25
1398 A985 60y multicolored   1.00 .25

Spring Has Come,
by Tatsuyuki
Takano — A986

Cherry
Blossoms, by
Hagoromo
Takeshima
A987

1981, Mar. 10   Perf. 13
1399 A986 60y multicolored   1.00 .25
1400 A987 60y multicolored   1.00 .25

Modern Japanese Art Issue

Dancers, by
Seiki
Kuroda — A988

Mother and
Child, by Shoen
Uemura
A989

1980, May 12   Photo.   Perf. 13½
1401 A988 50y multicolored   .90 .25
1402 A989 50y multicolored   .90 .25

The Black Fan, by
Takeji
Fujishima — A990

Dear Me . . .
It's a Shower,
by Seiho
Takeuchi
A991

1980, July 7   Photo.   Perf. 13½
1403 A990 50y multicolored   .90 .25
1404 A991 50y multicolored   .90 .25

Woman, by Morie
Ogiwara — A992

Kurofuneya, by
Yumeji
Takehisa — A993

1980, Oct. 27   Photo.   Perf. 13½
1405 A992 50y multicolored   .90 .25
1406 A993 50y multicolored   .90 .25

Nippon Maru,
Institute
Emblem — A994

1980, May 17
1407 A994 50y multicolored   .90 .25

Institute for Nautical Training, training ships
Nippon Maru and Kaio Maru, 50th
anniversary.

Mt. Gozaisho-dake,
Cedars,
Flowers — A995

1980, May 24   Perf. 13x13½
1408 A995 50y multicolored   .90 .25

National forestation campaign.

Yayosu Fire Brigade
Review, by Hiroshige
III — A996

1980, May 31
1409 A996 50y multicolored   .90 .25

Fire fighting centenary.

A997   A997a

Letter Writing Day: 20y, Teddy Bear holding
letter. 50y, Folded and tied letter of good
wishes, horiz.

1980, July 23   Perf. 13x13½, 13½x13
1410 A997 20y multicolored   .40 .25
1411 A997a 50y multicolored   .90 .25

Lühdorfla
Japonica
A998

1980, Aug. 2   Perf. 13½
1412 A998 50y multicolored   .90 .25

16th Intl. Cong. of Entomology, Kyoto, Aug.
3-9.

Three-dimensional World Map — A999

1980, Aug. 25   Photo.
1413 A999 50y multicolored   .90 .25

24th Intl. Geographic Cong. and 10th Intl.
Cartographic Conf., Tokyo, August.

Integrated
Circuit
A1000

1980, Sept. 29
1414 A1000 50y multicolored   .90 .25

Intl. Federation for Information Processing
Cong. '80, Tokyo, Oct. 6-9 and World Conf. on
Medical Informatics '80, Tokyo, 9/29-10/4.

Camellia — A1001

1980, Oct. 1

1415	A1001	30y shown	.50	.25
1416	A1001	40y Rape flower, cabbage butterflies	.75	.25
1417	A1001	50y Cherry blossoms	.90	.25
		Nos. 1415-1417 (3)	2.15	.75

See No. 1437.

Cranes, by Motooki Watanabe A1002

1980, Oct. 6   Perf. 13

| 1418 | A1002 | 100y multicolored | 1.75 | .30 |

24th Intl. Letter Writing Week, Oct. 6-12.

Archery, Mt. Nantai — A1003

1980, Oct. 11

| 1419 | A1003 | 20y multicolored | .35 | .25 |

35th National Athletic Meet, Tochigi, Oct.

Globe, Jaycee Emblem — A1004

1980, Nov. 8   Perf. 13

| 1420 | A1004 | 50y multicolored | .90 | .25 |

35th Jaycee (Intl. Junior Chamber of Commerce) World Congress, Osaka, Nov. 9-15.

Diet Building and Doves — A1005

1980, Nov. 29   Perf. 13½

| 1421 | A1005 | 50y multicolored | .90 | .25 |

90th anniversary of Japanese Diet.

Type of 1980 and

Amur Adonis A1006

White Trumpet Lily A1007

Hanging Bell, Byodoin Temple A1008

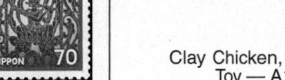

Bronze Buddhist Ornament, 7th Century A1009

Writing Box Cover A1010

Mirror with Figures A1011

Heart-shaped Figurine A1012

Silver Crane A1013

Maitreya, Horyuji Temple A1014

Ichiji Kinrin, Chusonji Temple A1015

Komokuten, Todaiji Temple A1016

Lady Maya A1017

Enamel Jar, by Ninsei Nonomura A1018

Miroku Bosatsu, Koryuji Temple A1019

1980-82   Photo.   Perf. 13x13½

1422	A1006	10y multicolored	.25	.25
1423	A1007	20y multicolored	.30	.25
1424	A1008	60y multicolored	1.00	.25
a.		Bklt. pane (#1424, 4 #1424 with gutter btwn.) ('81)	5.50	
1425	A1009	70y multicolored	1.50	.30
1426	A1010	70y multicolored	1.25	.25
1427	A1011	80y multicolored	1.60	.25
1428	A1012	90y multicolored	1.75	.25
1429	A1013	100y multicolored	1.90	.25
1430	A1014	170y multicolored	3.00	.25
1431	A1015	260y multicolored	4.50	.30
1432	A1016	310y multicolored	5.50	.25
1433	A1017	410y multicolored	8.50	.60
1434	A1018	410y multicolored	7.50	.40
1435	A1019	600y multicolored	10.00	.60
		Nos. 1422-1435 (14)	48.55	4.50

Coil Stamps
Perf. 13 Horiz.

1436	A1006	10y multi ('82)	.25	.25
1437	A1001	40y as #1416	.90	.30
1438	A1008	60y multi ('82)	1.00	.30
1439	A1013	100y multi ('82)	1.75	.35
		Nos. 1436-1439 (4)	3.90	1.20

Compare type A1013 with type A2685. See Nos. 1627-1628.

Clay Chicken, Folk Toy — A1026

1980, Dec. 1   Perf. 13 Horiz.

| 1442 | A1026 | 20y multicolored | .35 | .25 |

New Year 1981.
Sheets of two were New Year Lottery Prizes. Value $1.50.

Modern Japanese Art Issue

Snow-Covered Power Station, by Shikanosuke Oka — A1027

NuKada-no-Ohkimi and Nara in Spring, by Yukihiko Yasuda — A1028

1981, Feb. 26   Perf. 13½

| 1443 | A1027 | 60y multicolored | 1.00 | .25 |

Photo.

| 1444 | A1028 | 60y multicolored | 1.00 | .25 |

Artist's Family, by Narashige Koide — A1029

Bamboo Shoots, by Heihachiro Fukuda A1030

Photo. & Engr., Photo.

1981, June 18   Perf. 13½

| 1445 | A1029 | 60y multicolored | 1.00 | .25 |
| 1446 | A1030 | 60y multicolored | 1.00 | .25 |

Portrait of Ichiyo, by Kiyokata Kaburagi (1878-1972) A1031

Portrait of Reiko, by Ryusei Kishida (1891-1929) A1032

Photo., Photo. and Engr.

1981, Nov. 27   Engr.   Perf. 13½

| 1447 | A1031 | 60y multicolored | 1.00 | .25 |
| 1448 | A1032 | 60y multicolored | 1.00 | .25 |

Yoritomo in a Cave, by Seison Maeda — A1033

Advertisement of a Terrace, by Yuzo Saeki — A1034

1982, Feb. 25   Photo.   Perf. 13½

| 1449 | A1033 | 60y multicolored | 1.00 | .25 |
| 1450 | A1034 | 60y multicolored | 1.00 | .25 |

Emblem, Port Island A1035

1981, Mar. 20   Perf. 13

| 1451 | A1035 | 60y multicolored | 1.00 | .25 |

Portopia '81, Kobe Port Island Exhibition, Mar. 20-Sept. 15.

Agriculture, Forestry and Fishery Promotion Centenary A1036

1981, Apr. 7

| 1452 | A1036 | 60y multicolored | 1.00 | .25 |

Moonflower, by Harunobu
Suzuki — A1037

1981, Apr. 20   Photo.   Perf. 13½
1453   60y multicolored   1.00 .25
1454   60y multicolored   1.00 .25
  a. A1037 Pair, #1453-1454   2.25 .90

Philatelic Week, Apr. 21-27.

Cherry
Blossoms — A1039

1981, May 23   Photo.   Perf. 13x13½
1455 A1039 60y multicolored   1.00 .25

Cargo Ship
and Crane
A1040

1981, May 25   Perf. 13
1456 A1040 60y multicolored   1.00 .25
International Port and Harbor Association,
12th Convention, Nagoya, May 23-30.

Land Erosion
Control
Cent. — A1041

1981, June 27   Perf. 13½
1457 A1041 60y multicolored   1.00 .25

Stylized Man
and Spinal
Cord Dose
Response
Curve
A1042

1981, July 18   Photo.   Perf. 13
1458 A1042 60y multicolored   1.00 .25
  8th Intl. Pharmacology Cong., Tokyo, July
19-24.

Girl Writing
Letter — A1043

1981, July 23
1459 A1043 40y shown   .75 .25
1460 A1043 60y Boy, stamp   1.00 .25
Letter Writing Day (23rd of each month).

Japanese Crested
Ibis — A1044

1981, July 27   Litho.
1461 A1044 60y multicolored   1.00 .25

Plug, faucet   Plugs
A1044a   A1045

1981, Aug. 1   Photo.
1462 A1044a 40y multicolored   .75 .25
1463 A1045 60y multicolored   1.00 .25
Energy conservation.

Western Architecture Issue

Oura
Cathedral — A1046

Hyokei Hall,
Tokyo
A1047

Photogravure and Engraved
1981, Aug. 22
1464 A1046 60y multicolored   1.00 .25
1465 A1047 60y multicolored   1.00 .25

Old Kaichi
School,
Nagano
A1048

Doshisha
University
Chapel,
Kyoto
A1049

1981, Nov. 9   Perf. 13
1466 A1048 60y multicolored   1.00 .25
1467 A1049 60y multicolored   1.00 .25

St. John's Church,
Meiji-mura
A1050

Military
Exercise
Hall (Former
Sapporo
Agricultural
School),
Sapporo
A1051

1982, Jan. 29   Perf. 13
1468 A1050 60y multicolored   1.00 .25
1469 A1051 60y multicolored   1.00 .25

Former
Kyoto
Branch of
Bank of
Japan
A1052

Main Building,
Former Saiseikan
Hospital — A1053

1982, Mar. 10   Perf. 13
1470 A1052 60y multicolored   1.00 .25
1471 A1053 60y multicolored   1.00 .25

Oyama Shrine
Gate, Kanazawa
A1054

Former
Iwasaki
Family
Residence,
Tokyo
A1055

1982, June 12   Perf. 13
1472 A1054 60y multicolored   1.00 .25
1473 A1055 60y multicolored   1.00 .25

Hokkaido
Prefectural
Govt.
Building,
Sapporo
A1056

Former
Residence
of
Tsugumichi
Saigo
A1057

1982, Sept. 10   Perf. 13
1474 A1056 60y multicolored   1.00 .25
1475 A1057 60y multicolored   1.00 .25

Old Mutsuzawa
School — A1058

Sakuranomiya Public Hall — A1059

1983, Feb. 15
1476 A1058 60y multicolored   1.00 .25
1477 A1059 60y multicolored   1.00 .25

Globe on
Brain
A1060

1981, Sept. 12   Photo.
1478 A1060 60y multicolored   1.00 .25
  Intl. medical conferences, Kyoto: 12th Neu-
rology, Sept. 20-25; 10th Brainwaves and
Clinical Neurophysiology, Sept. 13-17; 1981
Intl. Epilepsy Conference, Sept. 17-21.

Congress
Emblem — A1061

1981, Sept. 16
1479 A1061 60y multicolored   1.00 .25
  24th World PTTI (Post, Telegraph and Telephone Intl. Labor Federation) Cong., Tokyo,
Sept. 16-22.

Plum Trees and
Fowl, by Sanraku
Kano — A1062

1981, Oct. 6   Photo.
1480 A1062 130y multicolored   2.10 .30
  25th Intl. Letter Writing Week, Oct. 6-12.

A1063

1981, Oct. 9   Photo. & Engr.
1481 A1063 60y No. 1   1.00 .25
1482 A1063 60y No. 2   1.00 .25
1483 A1063 60y No. 3   1.00 .25
1484 A1063 60y No. 4   1.00 .25
  a.   Strip or block of 4, #1481-
          1484   4.50 4.50

Philatokyo '81 Intl. Stamp Exhibition, Tokyo,
Oct. 9-18.

1981, Oct. 13 Photo.
1485 A1064 40y multicolored .75 .25
36th Natl. Athletic Meet, Oct. 13-18.

A1065

1981, Dec. 1 Photo. Perf. 13x13½
1486 A1065 40y multicolored .75 .25
New Year of 1982 (Year of the Dog). Sheets of 2 were lottery prizes. Value $1.50.

A1066

Ueno Zoo Centenary: a, Gorilla, flamingo. b, Penguins, lion. c, Panda, elephants. d, Zebras, giraffe.

1982, Mar. 20 Photo.
1487 A1066 Strip of 4 4.50 1.75
a.-d. 60y any single 1.00 .30

Views of the Snow on Matsuchiyama, by Kiyonaga Torii — A1067

1982, Apr. 20 Photo. Perf. 13½
1488 60y multicolored 1.00 .30
1489 60y multicolored 1.00 .30
a. A1067 Pair, #1488-1489 2.25 .90
Philatelic Week.

Shisa (Lion-shaped Guard Dog) — A1069

1982, May 15 Photo.
1490 A1069 60y multicolored 1.10 .30
10th anniv. of Reversion Agreement returning Ryukyu Islands.

Natl. Forestation Campaign — A1070

1982, May 22 Perf. 13x13½
1491 A1070 60y multicolored 1.00 .25

16th Intl. Dermatology Conference Tokyo, May 23-28 — A1071

1982, May 24 Perf. 13
1492 A1071 60y Noh mask 1.00 .25

Tohoku-Shinkansen Railroad Line Opening — A1072

1982, June 23
1493 60y Diesel locomotive 1.00 .30
1494 60y Steam model 1290 1.00 .30
a. A1072 Pair, #1493-1494 2.25 .90

Letter Writing Day — A1073

1982, July 23 Perf. 13x13½, 13½x13
1495 A1073 40y Sea gull, letter .75 .25
1496 A1073 60y Fairy, letter, horiz. 1.00 .30

Modern Japanese Art Issue

Kimono Patterned with Irises, by Saburosuke Okada (1869-1939) A1074

Bodhisattva Kuan-yin on Potalaka Island, by Tessai Tomioka (1837-1924) A1075

1982, Aug. 5 Photo. Perf. 13½
1497 A1074 60y multicolored 1.00 .30
1498 A1075 60y multicolored 1.00 .30

The Sarasvati, by Shiko Munakata (1903-1975) A1076

Saltim-banque, by Seiji Togo (1897-1978) A1077

1982, Nov. 24
1499 A1076 60y multicolored 1.00 .30
1500 A1077 60y multicolored 1.00 .30

Snowstorm, by Shinsui Ito — A1078

Spiraeas and Callas with Persian Pot, by Zenzaburo Kojima A1079

1983, Jan. 24 Photo.
1501 A1078 60y multicolored 1.00 .30
1502 A1079 60y multicolored 1.00 .30

Innocence, by Taikan Yokoyama (1868-1958) A1080

Roen, by Koun Takamura (1852-1934) A1081

Photo., Photo. and Engr.
1983, Mar. 10 Perf. 13½
1503 A1080 60y multicolored 1.00 .30
1504 A1081 60y multicolored 1.00 .30

A1082

A1083

A1084

1982, Aug. 23 Perf. 13x13½
1505 A1082 60y Wreath 1.00 .35
1506 A1083 60y Crane 1.00 .35
1507 A1084 70y Tortoise 1.25 .35
Nos. 1505-1507 (3) 3.25 1.05
For use on greeting (Nos. 1506-1507) and condolence (No. 1505) cards.
See Nos. 1555-1556, 1836-1839, 2227-2230 and footnotes after Nos. 1708, 1765.

400th Anniv. of Boys' Delegation to Europe, Tensho Era — A1085

1982, Sept. 20 Photo. Perf. 13
1508 A1085 60y 16th cent. ship, map 1.00 .25

10th Anniv. of Japanese-Chinese Relations Normalization — A1086

Design: Hall of Prayer for Good Harvests, Temple of Heaven, Peking, by Ryuzaburo Umehara.

1982, Sept. 29
1509 A1086 60y multicolored 1.10 .30

Table Tennis — A1087

1982, Oct. 2
1510 A1087 40y multicolored .75 .25
37th Natl. Athletic Meet, Matsue, Oct. 3-8.

"Amusement," Doll
by Goyo
Hirata — A1088

1982, Oct. 6
1511 A1088 130y multicolored   2.10 .45
Intl. Letter Writing Week, Oct. 6-12.

Central Bank
System
Centenary
A1089

Design: The Bank of Japan near Eitaibashi
in Snow, by Yasuji Inoue.

Photogravure and Engraved
1982, Oct. 12   **Perf. 13½**
1512 A1089 60y multicolored   1.00 .25

Opening of Joetsu Shinkansen
Railroad Line — A1090

1982, Nov. 15
1513   60y Locomotive, 1982   1.00 .30
1514   60y Locomotive, 1931   1.00 .30
  a. A1090 Pair, #1513-1514   2.25 .90

New Year
1983 — A1092

1982, Dec. 1   **Perf. 13x13½**
1515 A1092 40y Kintaro on Wild
             Boar   .75 .25
Sheets of 2 were lottery prizes. Value, $1.50.

Natl. Museum
of History and
Folklore
Opening
A1093

1983, Mar. 16 Photo.   Perf. 13½x13
1516 A1093 60y multicolored   1.00 .25

Women Working in the Kitchen, by
Utamaro Kitagawa (1753-
1806) — A1094

1983, Apr. 20   Photo.   Perf. 13
1517   60y multicolored   1.00 .30
1518   60y multicolored   1.00 .30
  a. A1094 Pair, #1517-1518   2.25 .90
Philatelic Week.

Natl. Forestation
Campaign — A1096

Hakusan Mountains, black lily, forest.

1983, May 21   Perf. 13
1519 A1096 60y multicolored   1.00 .25

50th Nippon
Derby — A1097

1983, May 28
1520 A1097 60y Colt, racing horse 1.00 .25

Islands Cleanup
Campaign — A1098

1983, June 13   Photo.   Perf. 13½
1521 A1098 60y multicolored   1.00 .25

Western Architecture Series

Hohei Hall
Sapporo
A1099

Old Glover
House,
Nagasaki
A1100

Photogravure and Engraved
1983, June 23   Perf. 13
1522 A1099 60y multicolored   1.00 .30
1523 A1100 60y multicolored   1.00 .30

Gojyuku
Bank,
Hirosaki
A1101

Gakushuin
Elementary
School,
Tokyo
A1102

1983, Aug. 15
1524 A1101 60y multicolored   1.00 .30
1525 A1102 60y multicolored   1.00 .30

Bank of
Japan,
Tokyo
A1103

Old Hunter
House,
Kobe
A1104

1984, Feb. 16
1526 A1103 60y multicolored   1.00 .30
1527 A1104 60y multicolored   1.00 .30
  Nos. 1522-1527 (6)   6.00 1.80

Official Gazette
Centenary
A1107

Design: First issue, Drawing of the Government Bulletin Board at Nihonbashi, by
Hiroshige Ando III.

1983, July 2   Photo.
1530 A1107 60y multicolored   1.00 .25

Letter Writing
Day — A1108

1983, July 23   Perf. 13x13½, 13½x13
1531 A1108 40y Boy writing letter   .75 .25
1532 A1108 60y Fairy bringing let-
             ter, horiz.   1.00 .30

Opening of
Natl. Noh
Theater,
Tokyo
A1109

1983, Sept. 14   Photo.   Perf. 13
1533 A1109 60y Masked actor,
             theater   1.00 .25

Endangered Birds Issue

Rallus Okinawae
A1110

Ketupa
Blakistoni
A1111

Photo. and Engr., Photo.
1983, Sept. 22   Perf. 13
1534 A1110 60y multicolored   1.00 .30
1535 A1111 60y multicolored   1.00 .30

Photo., Photo. & Engr.
1983, Nov. 25
1536 A1110 60y Sapheopipo
             noguchii   1.00 .30
1537 A1111 60y Branta canaden-
             sis leucopareia   1.00 .30

Photo., Photo. and Engr.
1984, Jan. 26
1538 A1111 60y Megalurus pry-
             eri pryeri   1.00 .30
1539 A1110 60y Spilornis cheela
             perplexus   1.00 .30

1984, Mar. 15   Photo.
1540 A1110 60y Columba
             janthina nitens   1.00 .30
1541 A1111 60y Tringa guttifer   1.00 .30

1984, June 22
1542 A1110 60y Falco per-
             egrinus frutti   1.00 .30

Photo. and Engr.
1543 A1111 60y Dendrocopus
             leucutus aus-
             toni   1.00 .30
  Nos. 1534-1543 (10)   10.00 3.00

Souvenir Sheet
1984, Dec. 10   Photo. & Engr.
1544   Sheet of 3   3.50 3.50
  a. A1111 60y Prus grn., engr.,
             #1535   1.00 .30
  b. A1110 60y vio brn., engr., #1539 1.00 .30
  c. A1110 60y ol blk., engr., #1542   1.00 .30

Intl. Letter Writing
Week — A1124

Chikyu Doll by Juzo Kagoshima (1898-
1982).

1983, Oct. 6   Photo.   Perf. 13
1548 A1124 130y multicolored   2.10 .40

38th Natl. Athletic
Meet — A1125

1983, Oct. 15   Perf. 13
1549 A1125 40y Naginata event   .75 .25

A1126

World
Communications
Year — A1127

1983, Oct. 17   Photo.   Perf. 13
1550 A1126 60y multicolored   1.00 .25
1551 A1127 60y multicolored   1.00 .25

Showa
Memorial
National Park
Opening
A1128

1983, Oct. 26   Photo.   Perf. 13
1552 A1128 60y multicolored   1.00 .30

1983, Nov. 14   Photo.
1553 A1129 60y multicolored   1.00 .25
71st World Dentistry Congress.

A1130

1983, Nov. 14   Photo.   *Perf. 13*
1554 A1130 60y multicolored   1.00 .30
Shirase, Antarctic observation ship, maiden voyage.

Type of 1982
1983, Nov. 22   Photo.   *Perf. 12½*
1555 A1082 40y Wreath   .75 .25
1556 A1083 40y Crane   .75 .25
For use on condolence and greeting cards.

A1131

1983, Dec. 1   Photo.   *Perf. 13x13½*
1557 A1131 40y Rat riding hammer .75 .25
New Year 1984. Sheets of 2 were lottery prizes. Value, $1.50.

A1132

1983, Dec. 5   Photo.   *Perf. 13½*
1558 A1132 60y Emblem   1.00 .25
Universal Declaration of Human Rights, 35th anniv.

20th Grand Confectionery Fair, Tokyo, Feb. 24-Mar. 12 — A1133

1984, Feb. 24   Photo.
1559 A1133 60y Confection, tea whisk   1.00 .25

Natl. Bunraku Theater Opening, Osaka A1134

1984, Apr. 6   Photo.   *Perf. 13*
1560 A1134 60y Bunraku puppet 1.00 .25

A1135

Philatelic Week (Sharaku Prints): No. 1561, Hanshiro Iwai IV (facing right) Playing Shige-noi. No. 1562, Oniji Otani (facing left) Playing Edobe.

Photogravure and Engraved
1984, Apr. 20   *Perf. 13½*
1561   60y multicolored   1.00 .30
1562   60y multicolored   1.00 .30
  a. A1135 Pair, #1561-1562   2.25 .90

Natl. Forestation Campaign A1137

1984, May 19   Photo.
1563 A1137 60y Cedar Forest, Sakurajima   1.00 .25

Weather Forecasting Centenary A1138

1984, June 1   *Perf. 13x13½*
1564 A1138 60y Himawari satel-lite, map   1.00 .30

UNESCO Emblem, Doves — A1139

1984, July 16   Photo.
1565 A1139 60y multicolored   1.00 .25
UNESCO Clubs and Associations World Congress, July 16-24.

Letter Writing Day — A1140

1984, July 23   *Perf. 13x13½, 13½x13*
1566 A1140 40y Birds in tree   .75 .25
1567 A1140 60y Bird holding letter, horiz.   1.00 .30

Disaster Relief A1141

Perf. 13x12½, 12½x13
1984, Aug. 23   Photo.
1568 A1141 40y Fire, wind   .75 .25
1569 A1141 60y Mother, child, vert.   1.00 .30

Alpine Plant Series

Leontopodium Fauriei — A1142

Lagotis Glauca A1143

Photogravure and Engraved
Perf. 12½x13, 13x12½
1984, Aug. 27
1570 A1142 60y multicolored   1.00 .30
1571 A1143 60y multicolored   1.00 .30

Trollius Riederianus A1144   Primula Cuneifolia A1145

1984, Sept. 21   *Perf. 13*
1572 A1144 60y multicolored   1.00 .30
1573 A1145 60y multicolored   1.00 .30

Rhododendron Aureum — A1146

Oxytropis Nigrescens Var. Japonica A1147

1985, Jan. 25   *Perf. 13*
1574 A1146 60y multicolored   1.00 .30
1575 A1147 60y multicolored   1.00 .30

Draba Japonica — A1148

Dryas Octopetala A1149

1985, Feb. 28
1576 A1148 60y multicolored   1.00 .30
1577 A1149 60y multicolored   1.00 .30

Callianthemum Insigne Var. Miyabeanum A1150   Gentiana Nipponica A1151

1985, July 31   *Perf. 13*
1578 A1150 60y multicolored   1.00 .30
1579 A1151 60y multicolored   1.00 .30

Campanula Chamissonis A1152

Viola Crassa A1153

1985, Sept. 27
1580 A1152 60y multicolored   1.00 .30
1581 A1153 60y multicolored   1.00 .30

Diapensia Lapponica A1154   Pedicularis Apodochila A1155

1986, Feb. 13   *Perf. 13*
1582 A1154 60y multicolored   1.00 .30
1583 A1155 60y multicolored   1.00 .30

Basho's Street, Sendai — A1156

1984, Sept. 1   Photo.   *Perf. 13*
1584 A1156 60y multicolored   1.00 .25
Intl. Microbiological Association's 6th Intl. Congress of Virology, Sendai, Sept. 1-7.

Electronic Mail — A1157

1984, Oct. 1   Photo.
1585 A1157 500y multicolored   9.50 4.50

28th Intl. Letter Writing Week, Oct. 6-12 — A1158

1984, Oct. 6
1586 A1158 130y Wooden doll 2.10 .50

17th Intl. Internal Medicine Congress, Kyoto, Oct. 7-12 A1159

1984, Oct. 8
1587 A1159 60y Ginkakuji Temple 1.00 .25

39th Natl. Athletic Meet, Nara City, Oct. 12-17 — A1160

1984, Oct. 12
1588 A1160 40y Field hockey .75 .25

Traditional Crafts Series

Kutaniyaki Plates — A1161

Nishijinori Weavings — A1163

1984, Nov. 2   Photo.   Perf. 12½x13
1589 60y Birds 1.00 .30
1590 60y Flowers 1.00 .30
   a. A1161 Pair, #1589-1590 2.25 .90
1591 60y Flowers 1.00 .30
1592 60y Leaves 1.00 .30
   a. A1163 Pair, #1591-1592 2.25 .90

Edokimekomi Dolls — A1165

Ryukyubingata Cloth — A1167

1985, Feb. 15   Photo.   Perf. 13
1593 60y Adult figures 1.00 .30
1594 60y Child and pet 1.00 .30
   a. A1165 Pair, #1593-1594 2.25 .90
1595 60y Bird and branch 1.00 .30
1596 60y Birds 1.00 .30
   a. A1167 Pair, #1595-1596 2.25 .90

Ichii-ittobori Carved Birds — A1169

Imariyaki & Aritayaki Ceramic Ware — A1171

1985, May 23   Photo.   Perf. 13
1597 60y Bird 1.00 .30
1598 60y Birds 1.00 .30
   a. A1169 Pair, #1597-1598 2.25 .90
1599 60y Bowl 1.00 .30
1600 60y Plate 1.00 .30
   a. A1171 Pair, #1599-1600 2.25 .90

Kamakurabori Wood Carvings — A1173

Ojiyachijimi Weavings — A1175

1985, June 24   Photo. & Engr.
1601 60y Bird and flower panel 1.00 .30
1602 60y Round flower panel 1.00 .30
   a. A1173 Pair, #1601-1602 2.25 .90

Litho.
1603 60y Hemp star pattern 1.00 .30
1604 60y Hemp linear pattern 1.00 .30
   a. A1175 Pair, #1603-1604 2.25 .90

Hakata Ningyo Clay Figures — A1177

Nanbu Tekki Iron Ware — A1179

1985, Aug. 8   Photo.
1605 60y Man 1.00 .30
1606 60y Woman and child 1.00 .30
   a. A1177 Pair, #1605-1606 2.25 .90

Photogravure and Engraved
1607 60y Silver kettle 1.00 .30
1608 60y Black kettle 1.00 .30
   a. A1179 Pair, #1607-1608 2.25 .90

Wajimanuri Lacquerware — A1181

Izumo-ishidoro Sandstone Sculptures — A1183

Photo., Photo. & Engr. (#1611-1612)
1985, Nov. 15
1609 60y Bowl on table 1.00 .30
1610 60y Bowl 1.00 .30
   a. A1181 Pair, #1609-1610 2.25 .90
1611 60y Columnar lantern 1.00 .30
1612 60y Lantern on four legs 1.00 .30
   a. A1183 Pair, #1611-1612 2.25 .90

Kyo-sensu Silk Fans — A1185

Tobeyaki Porcelain — A1187

1986, Mar. 13   Photo.   Perf. 13
1613 60y Flower bouquets 1.00 .30
1614 60y Sun and trees 1.00 .30
   a. A1185 Pair, #1613-1614 2.25 .90

1615 60y Jug 1.00 .30
1616 60y Jar 1.00 .30
   a. A1187 Pair, #1615-1616 2.25 .90
   Nos. 1613-1616 (4) 4.00 1.20

Japanese Professional Baseball, 50th Anniv. — A1189

1984, Nov. 15   Perf. 13½
1617 60y Pitcher 1.00 .30
1618 60y Batter 1.00 .30
   a. A1189 Pair, #1617-1618 2.25 .90
1619 A1189 60y Matsutaro Shoriki 1.00 .30
   Nos. 1617-1619 (3) 3.00 .90

Industrial Education Centenary A1190

1984, Nov. 20   Perf. 13x12½
1620 A1190 60y Workers, symbols 1.00 .25

New Year 1984 — A1191

1984, Dec. 1   Photo.   Perf. 13½x13
1621 A1191 40y Sakushu Cattle Folk Toy .75 .25

Sheets of 2 were lottery prizes. Value, $1.50.

A1200 — Akita   A1201 — Ivory Shell

A1202 — Hiougi-gai (Bivalve)   A1203 — Rinbo Shell

A1204   A1205

A1206   A1207

A1208   A1209

Photo., Engr. (300y)

1984-89   **Perf. 13x13½**

1622	A1200	2y turq blue ('89)	.25	.25
1623	A1201	40y multi ('88)	.90	.25
1624	A1202	41y multi ('89)	.80	.25
1624B	A1202	41y Imperf., self-adhesive	.80	.25
1625	A1203	60y multi ('88)	1.10	.25
a.		Bklt. pane, 5 each #1623, 1625	9.25	
1626	A1204	62y multi ('89)	1.10	.25
a.		Bklt. pane, 2 #1624, 4 #1626	6.00	
1626B	A1204	62y Imperf., self-adhesive	1.10	.25
c.		Bklt. pane, 2 #1624B, 4 #1626B ('89)	6.00	
1627	A1205	72y dark vio, blk & org yel ('89)	1.25	.25
1628	A1206	175y multi ('89)	2.75	.25
1629	A1207	210y multi ('89)	3.25	.30
1630	A1208	300y dk red brown	5.00	.35
1631	A1209	360y dull pink & brn ('89)	6.00	.35
	Nos. 1622-1631 (12)		24.30	3.25

Coil Stamps
Perf. 13 Horiz.

1636	A1202	41y multi ('89)	.80	.25
1637	A1204	62y multi ('89)	1.10	.25

No. 1622 inscribed "Nippon," unlike No. 583.
No. 1626Bc is adhered to the booklet cover, made of peelable paper, folded in half and rouletted down the center fold.
Issued: 40y, 60y, 4/1; 300y, 4/3; 2y, 72y, 4/1; 42y, Nos. 1626, 1626a, 41y, No. 1637, 3/24; 175y, 210y, 360y, 6/1; No.1626d, 7/3.

A1210

EXPO '85 — A1211

1985, Mar. 16   **Photo.**   **Perf. 13**

1640	A1210	40y multicolored	.75	.25
1641	A1211	60y multicolored	1.00	.30
a.		Souv. sheet of 2, #1640-1641	2.25	2.00

University of the Air — A1212

1985, Apr. 1   **Photo.**   **Perf. 13½**

1642 A1212 60y University broadcast tower   1.00 .30

Inauguration of adult education through broadcasting.

Nippon Telegraph & Telephone Co. — A1213

1985, Apr. 1

1643 A1213 60y Satellite receiver   1.00 .25

Inauguration of Japan's new telecommunications system.

World Import Fair, Nagoya A1214

1985, Apr. 5   **Photo.**   **Perf. 13**

1644 A1214 60y 16th century map of Japan   1.00 .25

Industrial Proprietary System Cent. — A1215

Design: Portrait of Korekiyo Takashashi, system promulgator, inscriptions in English.

1985, Apr. 18   **Photo.**   **Perf. 13½**

1645 A1215 60y multicolored   1.00 .25

Winter in the North — A1216   To the Morning Light — A1217

Paintings by Yumeji Takehisa (1884-1934).

1985, Apr. 20   **Perf. 13**

1646	A1216	60y multicolored	1.00	.30
1647	A1217	60y multicolored	1.00	.30
a.		Pair, #1646-1647	2.25	.90

Philatelic Week. Printed in sheets of 10.

Natl. Land Forestation Project — A1218

Intl. Year of the Forest: Autumn bellflower, camphor tree, cattle and Mt. Aso.

1985, May 10   **Perf. 13½**

1648 A1218 60y multicolored   1.00 .25

Radio Japan, 50th Anniv. — A1219

Painting: Cherry Blossoms at Night, by Taikan Yokoyama.

1985, June 1   **Photo.**   **Perf. 13**

1649		60y multi (Left)	1.00	.30
1650		60y multi (Right)	1.00	.30
a.	A1219	Pair, #1649-1650	2.25	.90

Hisoka Maejima, 1st Postmaster General — A1220

1985, June 5   **Photo.**   **Perf. 13**

1651 A1220 60y Portrait, former P.O. building   1.00 .30

Oonaruto Bridge Opening A1221

1985, June 7   **Perf. 13½**

1652 A1221 60y multicolored   1.00 .25

Intl. Youth Year A1222

1985, July 20   **Photo.**   **Perf. 13**

1653 A1222 60y Emblem, silhouette   1.00 .25

Owl Carrying Letter — A1223

Perf. 13½x13, 13x13½

1985, July 23   **Photo.**

1654	A1223	40y shown	.75	.25
1655	A1223	60y Girl, cat, bird, letter	1.00	.30

Letter Writing Day (23rd of each month).

Electronic Mail — A1224

1985, Aug. 1   **Photo.**   **Perf. 13x13½**

1656 A1224 500y multicolored   9.50 2.75

Meson Theory, 50th Anniv. A1225

1985, Aug. 15   **Photo.**   **Perf. 13**

1657 A1225 60y Portrait, nuclear particles   1.00 .25

Dr. Hideki Yukawa was presented the Nobel Prize for Physics for the Meson Theory in 1949, which is the foundation for high-energy physics.

A1226

1985, Aug. 24   **Photo.**   **Perf. 13½**

1658 A1226 60y Gymnast, horse   1.00 .25

Universiade 1985, Kobe.

A1227

1985, Sept. 13   **Photo.**

1659 A1227 40y Emblem, competitor   .75 .25

28th Intl. Vocational Training Competition, Oct. 21-27.

Normalization of Diplomatic Relations Between Japan and the Republic of Korea, 20th Anniv. — A1228

1985, Sept. 18

1660 A1228 60y Rose of Sharon   1.00 .30

Kan-Etsu Tunnel Opening A1229

60y, Mountains, diagram, cross sections.

1985, Oct. 2   **Perf. 13**

1661 A1229 60y multicolored   1.00 .25

Seisen Doll by Goyo Hirata (1903-1981) A1230

1985, Oct. 7

1662 A1230 130y multicolored   2.10 .50

Intl. Letter Writing Week, Oct. 6-12.

30th Intl. Apicultural Congress, Oct. 10-16, Nagoya A1231

1985, Oct. 9

1663 A1231 60y Honeybee, strawberry plants   1.00 .25

Japanese Overseas Cooperation Volunteers, 20th Anniv. A1232

1985, Oct. 9   Litho.
1664 A1232 60y Planting crop   1.00 .30

40th Natl. Athletic Meet, Oct. 20-25, Tottori City Sports Arena — A1233

1985, Oct. 19   Photo.
1665 A1233 40y Handball player, Mt. Daisen   .75 .25

New Year 1986 — A1234

1985, Dec. 2   Photo.   Perf. 13x13½
1666 A1234 40y Shinno papier-mache tiger   .75 .25

Sheets of 2 were lottery prizes. Value, $1.40.

Natl. Ministerial System of Government, Cent. A1235

1985, Dec. 20   Litho.   Perf. 13½
1667 A1235 60y Official seal, Cabinet emblem   1.00 .25

Building Institute, Cent. — A1236

1986, Apr. 9   Photo.   Perf. 13
1668 A1236 60y multicolored   1.00 .25

Philately Week — A1237

Southern Hateroma (details), by Keigetsu Kikuchi.

1986, Apr. 15
1669   60y Woman standing   1.00 .30
1670   60y Seated woman   1.00 .30
   a.   A1237 Pair, #1669-1670   2.25 .90

Kyoto Imperial Palace, Phoenix A1238

No. 1672, Imperial chrysanthemum crest & partridges.

1986, Apr. 28
1671 A1238 60y multicolored   1.00 .30
1672 A1238 60y multicolored   1.00 .30
   a.   Souv. sheet of 2, #1671-1672   2.40 2.40

Reign of Emperor Hirohito, 60th anniv.

6th Intl. Summit, Tokyo A1239

1986, May 2
1673 A1239 60y Mt. Fuji   1.00 .30

Shrike on Reed, Emperor Nintoku's Mausoleum A1240

1986, May 9   Perf. 13½
1674 A1240 60y multicolored   1.00 .30

Natl. Land Afforestation Campaign.

Japanese Pharmaceutical Regulatory Syst., Cent. — A1241

1986, June 25   Photo.   Perf. 13½
1675 A1241 60y multicolored   1.00 .30

Japanese Standard Time, Cent. — A1242

1986, July 11   Litho.   Perf. 13
1676 A1242 60y Meridian, clock   1.00 .30

Letter Writing Day — A1243

1986, July 23   Photo.   Perf. 13x13½
1677 A1243 40y Bird   .75 .25
1678 A1243 60y Girl, rabbit, birds   1.00 .30
   a.   Bklt. pane, 5 each #1677-1678   9.25

Sheets of 2 were lottery prizes. Value, $60.

Merchant Marine Education, 110th Anniv. A1244

Training ship Nihonmaru & navigation training institute founders Makoto Kondo, Yataro Iwasaki.

1986, July 26   Perf. 13
1679 A1244 60y multicolored   1.00 .30

CTO's exist for Nos. 1680-1681, 1684-1685, 1688-1689, 1694-1695, 1696-1697. They read "Japan" between two arcs in a corner.

Insects

Parnassius Eversmanni — A1245

Photogravure and Engraved
1986, July 30   Perf. 13
1680   60y shown   1.00 .35
1681   60y Poecilocoris lewisi   1.00 .35
  a. A1245 Pair, #1680-1681   2.25 1.00
1682   60y Rasalia batesi   1.00 .35
1683   60y Epiophlebia super-stes   1.00 .35
  a. A1245 Pair, #1682-1683   2.25 1.00
1986, Sept. 26
1684   60y Dorcus hopei   1.00 .35
1685   60y Thermo- zephyrus ataxus   1.00 .35
  a. A1245 Pair, #1684-1685   2.25 1.00
1686   60y Sympetrum pedemontanum   1.00 .35
1687   60y Damaster blaptoides   1.00 .35
  a. A1245 Pair, #1686-1687   2.25 1.00
1986, Nov. 21
1688   60y Elcysma westwoodii   1.00 .35
1689   60y Rhyothemis variegata   1.00 .35
  a. A1245 Pair, #1688-1689   2.25 1.00
1690   60y Tibicen japonicus   1.00 .35
1691   60y Chrysochroa holstii   1.00 .35
  a. A1245 Pair, #1690-1691   2.25 1.00
1987, Jan. 23
1692   60y Parantica sita   1.00 .35
1693   60y Cheirotonus jambar   1.00 .35
  a. A1245 Pair, #1692-1693   2.25 1.00
1694   60y Lucanus macu-lifemoratus   1.00 .35
1695   60y Anotogaster sieboldii   1.00 .35
  a. A1245 Pair, #1694-1695   2.25 1.00
1987, Mar. 12
1696   60y Ascaraphus ramburi   1.00 .35
1697   60y Polyphylla laticollis   1.00 .35
  a. A1245 Pair, #1696-1697   2.25 1.00
1698   60y Kallima inachus   1.00 .35
1699   60y Calopteryx cornelia   1.00 .35
  f. A1245 Pair, #1698-1699   2.25 1.00
  Nos. 1680-1699 (20)   20.00 7.00

Miniature Sheet
1699A   Sheet of 4 (#1680, 1692, 1699b-1699c)   3.75 3.75
  b. 40y Anthocaris cardamines   .75 .35
  c. 40y Sasakia charonda   .75 .35
  d. Bklt. pane, 5 #1680, 5 #1699b   9.25
  e. Bklt. pane, 5 #1692, 5 #1699c   9.25
  g. A1245 Pair, #1699b, 1680   1.90
  h. A1245 Pair, #1699c, 1692   1.90

Booklet panes are perf. 13x13½ on 2 or 3 sides.

Folkways in Twelve Months (Detail), by Shunsho Katsukawa A1265

1986, Aug. 23   Photo.   Perf. 13
1700 A1265 60y multicolored   1.00 .30

52nd conference of the Intl. Federation of Library Associations, Tokyo, Aug. 24-29.

Electron Microscope A1266

1986, Aug. 30
1701 A1266 60y multicolored   1.00 .30

11th Int. Congress of Electron Microscopy, Kyoto, Aug. 31-Sept. 7.

23rd Intl. Conference on Social Welfare, Tokyo, Aug. 31-Sept. 5 — A1267

1986, Aug. 30   Litho.
1702 A1267 60y multicolored   1.00 .25

Ohmorimiyage Doll, by Juzoh Kagoshima A1268

1986, Oct. 6   Photo.
1703 A1268 130y multicolored   2.10 .60

Intl. Letter Writing Week.

41st Natl. Athletic Meet, Oct. 12-17, Kofu — A1269

1986, Oct. 9
1704 A1269 40y multicolored   .75 .25

5th World Ikebana Convention A1270

Painting: Flower in Autumn and a Girl in Rakuhoku.

1986, Oct. 17   Photo.   Perf. 13½x13
1705 A1270 60y multicolored   1.00 .30

A1271

Intl. Peace Year A1272

Lithographed, Photogravure (#1707)
1986, Nov. 28
1706 A1271 40y multicolored   .75 .25
1707 A1272 60y multicolored   1.00 .30

New Year 1987 (Year of the Hare) — A1273

Design: A Couple of Rabbits Making Rice Cake, Nagoya clay figurine.

1986, Dec. 1   Photo.   Perf. 13x13½
1708 A1273 40y multicolored   .75   .25

Sheets of two containing Nos. 1506 and 1708 were lottery prizes. Value, $1.75.
See No. 2655c.

Real Estate Registry System, Cent.
A1274

1987, Jan. 30   Photo.   Perf. 13½
1709 A1274 60y multicolored   1.00   .25

Basho Series, Part I

A1275

A1277

A1279

A1281

A1283

A1285

A1287

A1289

A1291

A1293

No. 1710, Basho. No. 1711, Basho's haiku. No. 1712, Kegon Falls. No. 1713, Haiku. No. 1714, Cuckoo. No. 1715, Horse and haiku. No. 1716, Willow Tree. No. 1717, Rice Paddy and haiku. No. 1718, Chestnut Tree in Bloom. No. 1719, Chestnut Leaves and haiku. No. 1720, Planting Rice Paddy. No. 1721, Fern Leaves and haiku. No. 1722, Sweetflags. No. 1723, Sweetflags and haiku. No. 1724, Prosperous Man, 17th Cent. No. 1725, Summer Grass and haiku. No. 1726, Safflowers in Bloom. No. 1727, Haiku. No. 1728, Yamadera (Temple). No. 1729, Forest and haiku.

1987-89   Photo.   Perf. 13x13½
1710   60y multicolored   1.00   .35
1711   60y multicolored   1.00   .35
  a. Sheet of 2, #1710-1711, imperf. ('89)   2.50   2.50
  b. A1275 Pair, #1710-1711   2.25   1.00
1712   60y multicolored   1.00   .35
1713   60y multicolored   1.00   .35
  a. Sheet of 2, #1712-1713, imperf. ('89)   2.50   2.50
  b. A1277 Pair, #1712-1713   2.25   1.00
1714   60y multicolored   1.00   .35
1715   60y multicolored   1.00   .35
  a. Sheet of 2, #1714-1715, imperf. ('89)   2.50   2.50
  b. A1279 Pair, #1714-1715   2.25   1.00
1716   60y multicolored   1.00   .35
1717   60y multicolored   1.00   .35
  a. Sheet of 2, #1716-1717, imperf. ('89)   2.50   2.50
  b. A1281 Pair, #1716-1717   2.25   1.00
1718   60y multicolored   1.00   .35
1719   60y multicolored   1.00   .35
  a. Sheet of 2, #1718-1719, imperf. ('89)   2.50   2.50
  b. A1283 Pair, #1718-1719   2.25   1.00
1720   60y multicolored   1.00   .35
1721   60y multicolored   1.00   .35
  a. Sheet of 2, #1720-1721, imperf. ('89)   2.50   2.50
  b. A1285 Pair, #1720-1721   2.25   1.00
1722   60y multi ('88)   1.00   .35
1723   60y multi ('88)   1.00   .35
  a. Sheet of 2, #1722-1723, imperf. ('89)   2.50   2.50
  b. A1287 Pair, #1722-1723   2.25   1.00
1724   60y multi ('88)   1.00   .35
1725   60y multi ('88)   1.00   .35
  a. Sheet of 2, #1724-1725, imperf. ('89)   2.50   2.50
  b. A1289 Pair, #1724-1725   2.25   1.00
1726   60y multi ('88)   1.00   .35
1727   60y multi ('88)   1.00   .35
  a. Sheet of 2, #1726-1727, imperf. ('89)   2.50   2.50
  b. A1291 Pair, #1726-1727   2.25   1.00

1728   60y multi ('88)   1.00   .35
1729   60y multi ('88)   1.00   .35
  a. Sheet of 2, #1728-1729, imperf. ('89)   2.50   2.50
  b. A1293 Pair, #1728-1729   2.25   1.00
  Nos. 1710-1729 (20)   20.00   7.00

Issued to commemorate the 300th anniversary of a trip from Edo (now Tokyo) to northern Japan by the famous haiku poet Matsuo Munefusa "Basho" (1644-1694). His prose account of the journey, *Oku no hosomichi* (*Narrow Road to a Far Province*), contains numerous 17-syllable poems (*haiku*), which are shown on the stamps.

In each setenant pair, a complete *haiku* by Basho is inscribed vertically at right on the left stamp and in the center of the right stamp. The same poem appears on both stamps in each pair.

Issued: Nos. 1710-1713, 2/26; Nos. 1714-1717, 6/23; Nos. 1718-1721, 8/25; Nos. 1722-1725, 1/3; Nos. 1726-1729, 3/26.
See Nos. 1775-1794.

12th World Orchid Congress, Tokyo
A1295   A1296

1987, Mar. 19   Photo.   Perf. 13
1730 A1295 60y multicolored   1.00   .30
1731 A1296 60y multicolored   1.00   .30

Railway Post Office Termination, Oct. 1, 1986
A1297

1987, Mar. 26   Litho.   Perf. 13½
1732   60y Mail car   1.00   .30
1733   60y Loading mail on car 1.00   .30
  a. A1297 Pair, #1732-1733   2.25   1.00

Privatization of Japan Railways
A1298

No. 1734, Locomotive No. 137, c. 1900. No. 1735, Linear induction train, 1987.

1987, Apr. 1   Photo.   Perf. 13½
1734 A1298 60y multicolored   1.00   .35
1735 A1298 60y multicolored   1.00   .35

Natl. Marine Biology Research, Cent.
A1299

1987, Apr. 2   Perf. 13
1736 A1299 60y Sea slugs   1.00   .25

Paintings by Hashiguchi Goyo (1880-1921) — A1300

1987, Apr. 14
1737   60y denomination at upper right   1.00   .30
1738   60y denomination at lower left   1.00   .30
  a. A1300 Pair, #1737-1738   2.25   1.00

Philately Week.

Map of Asia and Oceania
A1302

1987, Apr. 27   Photo.   Perf. 13½
1739 A1302 60y multicolored   1.00   .25

20th annual meeting of the Asian Development Bank.

Nat'l. Land Afforestation Campaign
A1303

1987, May 23
1740 A1303 60y Magpie, seashore 1.00 .25

National Treasures Series

A1304

A1305

Designs: No. 1741, Yatsuhashi gold inkstone box, by Kohrin Ogata. No. 1742, Donjon of Hikone Castle, c. 1573-1592.

1987, May 26   Photo.   Perf. 13
1741 A1304 60y multicolored   1.00   .35
Photo. & Engr.   Perf. 13½
1742 A1305 110y multicolored   1.90   .50

Golden Turtle Sharito — A1306

Imuyama Castle Donjon, 1469 — A1307

1987, July 17   Photo.   Perf. 13
1743 A1306 60y multicolored   1.00   .35

Photo. & Engr.

Perf. 13½

1744 A1307 110y multicolored 1.90 .50

Kongo Sanmai in Tahotoh Temple, Kamakura Era — A1308

Wood Ekoh-Dohji Statue in the Likeness of Kongobuji Fudodo, Kamakura Era, by Unkei — A1309

1988, Feb. 12 Photo. *Perf. 13*

1745 A1308 60y multicolored 1.00 .35

Photo. & Engr.

Perf. 13½

1746 A1309 110y multicolored 1.90 .50

Itsukushima Shrine, Heian Period A1310

Kozakura-gawa, Braided Armor Worn by Minamoto-no-Yoshimitsu, Heian Period War Lord, Kai Province — A1311

1988, June 23 Photo. *Perf. 13*

1747 A1310 60y multicolored 1.00 .35

Photo. & Engr.

Perf. 13½

1748 A1311 100y multicolored 1.75 .50

Statue of *Nakatsu-hime-no-mikoto,* a Hachiman Goddess, Heian Period, Yakushiji Temple — A1312

Murou-ji Temple Pagoda, 9th Cent. — A1313

1988, Sept. 26 Photo. *Perf. 13*

1749 A1312 60y multicolored 1.00 .35

Photo. & Engr.

Perf. 13½

1750 A1313 100y multicolored 1.75 .50
Nos. 1741-1750 (10) 14.20 4.25

Letter Writing Day — A1314

1987, July 23 Photo. *Perf. 13x13½*

1751 A1314 40y Flowers, envelope .75 .30
1752 A1314 60y Elephant 1.00 .35
a. Bklt. pane, 5 ea #1751-1752 9.00

Sheets of 2, Nos. 1751-1752, were lottery prizes. Value, *$4.25.*

Kiso Three Rivers Flood Control, Cent. A1315

1987, Aug. 7 Photo. *Perf. 13½*

1753 A1315 60y Kiso, Nagara and Ibi Rivers 1.00 .25

Japan — Thailand Diplomatic Relations, Cent. A1316

Design: Temple of the Emerald Buddha and cherry blossoms.

1987, Sept. 26 *Perf. 13*

1754 A1316 60y multicolored 1.00 .30

Intl. Letter Writing Week — A1317

Dolls by Goyo Hirata: 130y, Gensho Kanto, by Royojo Hori (1898-1984). 150y, Utage-no-Hana (Fair Woman at the Party).

1987, Oct. 6 Photo. *Perf. 13*

1755 A1317 130y multicolored 2.10 .75
1756 A1317 150y multicolored 2.50 .85

13th World Congress of Certified Public Accountants, Tokyo, Oct. 11-15 — A1318

Design: Three Beauties (adaptation), by Toyokuni Utagawa (1769-1825).

1987, Oct. 9 *Perf. 13*

1757 A1318 60y multicolored 1.00 .35

Modern Waterworks, Cent. — A1319

Design: Lion's head public fountain, 1887, Waterworks Museum, Yokohama.

1987, Oct. 16 Engr.

1758 A1319 60y multicolored 1.00 .25

Shurei Gate, Okinawa, Basketball Players — A1320

1987, Oct. 24 Photo.

1759 A1320 40y multicolored .75 .25

42nd Natl. Athletic Meet, Okinawa.

6th World Cong. on Smoking & Health, Nov. 9-12, Tokyo — A1321

1987, Nov. 9

1760 A1321 60y multicolored 1.00 .25

World Telecommunications Conf., Nov. 15-18, Tokyo — A1322

Design: Microwave dish antenna at Kashima Station Radio Research Laboratory.

1987, Nov. 13 *Perf. 13½*

1761 A1322 60y multicolored 1.00 .25

World Conference on Large Historic Cities, Nov. 18-21, Kyoto A1323

Design: Nijo Castle guardhouse roof and Ninomaru Hall, 17th cent.

1987, Nov. 18 *Perf. 13*

1762 A1323 60y multicolored 1.00 .30

Intl. Year of Shelter for the Homeless A1324

Prize-winning illustrations by: 40y, Takahiro Nahahama. 60y, Yoko Sasaki.

1987, Nov. 25

1763 A1324 40y multicolored .75 .25
1764 A1324 60y multicolored 1.00 .30

New Year 1988 (Year of the Dragon) — A1325

Design: Kurashiki papier-mache dragon, 1869, by Tajuro Omizu.

1987, Dec. 1 *Perf. 13x13½*

1765 A1325 40y multicolored .75 .30

Sheets of 2, Nos. 1506, 1765, were lottery prizes. Value, $2.25.

Seikan Tunnel Opening A1326

1988, Mar. 11 Photo. *Perf. 13¼*

1766 A1326 60y ED 79 locomotive, map 1.00 .35
a. Booklet pane of 10 12.00

Opening of Seto-Oohashi Bridge

Kagawa Side

A1327 A1328

Okayama Side

A1329 A1330

1988, Apr. 8 Engr. *Perf. 13½*

1767 A1327 60y multicolored 1.00 .35
1768 A1328 60y multicolored 1.00 .35
1769 A1329 60y multicolored 1.00 .35
1770 A1330 60y multicolored 1.00 .35
a. Strip of 4, #1767-1770 4.50 4.50

Nos. 1767-1768 and 1769-1770 have continuous designs.

Philately Week — A1331

Prints by Kotondo Torii (1900-76): No. 1771, Long Undergarment. No. 1772, Kimono Sash.

1988, Apr. 19 Photo. *Perf. 13*

1771 60y denomination at lower right 1.00 .35
1772 60y denomination at upper left 1.00 .35
a. A1331 Pair, #1771-1772 2.50 1.50

Souv. sheet of 2 exists. Value $6.

Silk Road
Exposition, Apr.
24-Oct. 23,
Nara — A1333

Design: Plectrum guard playing the biwa,
detail of Raden-Shitan-no-Gogen-Biwa, a five-
panel work of gold lacquer nacre on sandalwood preserved at Shosoin.

1988, Apr. 23   Photo. & Engr.
1773 A1333 60y multicolored   1.00 .30

Natl. Afforestation
Campaign
A1334

Design: Yahsima, site of the Genji-Heike
war, and cuckoo on olive tree branch.

1988, May 20   Photo.   Perf. 13½
1774 A1334 60y multicolored   1.00 .25

Basho Series, Part II

A1335

A1337

No. 1775, Mogami River. No. 1776, Haiku
and flower. No. 1777, Mt. Gassan. No. 1778,
Haiku and mountain.

1988, May 30   Photo.   Perf. 13x13½
1775   60y multicolored   1.00 .35
1776   60y multicolored   1.00 .35
  a.   Souv. sheet of 2, #1775-1776,
        imperf. ('89)   2.50 2.50
  b.   A1335 Pair, #1775-1776   2.25 1.00
1777   60y multicolored   1.00 .35
1778   60y multicolored   1.00 .35
  a.   Souv. sheet of 2, #1777-1778,
        imperf. ('89)   2.50 2.50
  b.   A1337 Pair, #1777-1778   2.25 1.00

A1339

A1341

No. 1779, Mimosa in bloom. No. 1780,
Verse, birds, Kisagata Inlet. No. 1781, Ocean
waves. No. 1782, Verse and current.

1988, Aug. 23
1779   60y multicolored   1.00 .35
1780   60y multicolored   1.00 .35
  a.   Souv. sheet of 2, #1779-1780,
        imperf. ('89)   2.50 2.50
  b.   A1339 Pair, #1779-1780   2.25 1.00
1781   60y multicolored   1.00 .35
1782   60y multicolored   1.00 .35
  a.   Souv. sheet of 2, #1781-1782,
        imperf. ('89)   2.50 2.50
  b.   A1341 Pair, #1781-1782   2.25 1.00

A1343

A1345

No. 1783, Rice. No. 1784, Birds in flight,
haiku. No. 1785, Sun glow. No. 1786, Rice,
haiku.

1988, Nov. 11
1783   60y multicolored   1.00 .35
1784   60y multicolored   1.00 .35
  a.   Souv. sheet of 2, #1783-1784,
        imperf. ('89)   2.50 2.50
  b.   A1343 Pair, #1783-1784   2.25 1.00
1785   60y multicolored   1.00 .35
1786   60y multicolored   1.00 .35
  a.   Souv. sheet of 2, #1785-1786,
        imperf. ('89)   2.50 2.50
  b.   A1345 Pair, #1785-1786   2.25 1.00

A1347

A1349

No. 1787, Nata-dera Temple. No. 1788,
Haiku, white grass. No. 1789, Trees. No. 1790,
Haiku, moonlit forest.

1989, Feb. 13
1787   60y multicolored   1.00 .35
1788   60y multicolored   1.00 .35
  a.   Souv. sheet of 2, #1787-1788,
        imperf.   2.50 2.50
  b.   A1347 Pair, #1787-1788   2.25 1.00
1789   60y multicolored   1.00 .35
1790   60y multicolored   1.00 .35
  a.   Souv. sheet of 2, #1789-1790,
        imperf.   2.50 2.50
  b.   A1349 Pair, #1789-1790   2.25 1.00

A1351

A1353

No. 1791, Autumn on the beach. No. 1792,
Haiku. No. 1793, Clams. No. 1794, Haiku.

1989, May 12
1791   62y multicolored   1.00 .35
1792   62y multicolored   1.00 .35
  a.   Souv. sheet of 2, #1791-
        1792, imperf.   2.50 2.50
  b.   A1351 Pair, #1791-1792   2.25 1.00
1793   62y multicolored   1.00 .35
1794   62y multicolored   1.00 .35
  a.   Souv. sheet of 2, #1793-
        1794, imperf.   2.50 2.50
  b.   A1353 Pair, #1793-1794   2.25 1.00

Haiku from *Oku-no-hosomichi*, "Narrow
Road to a Far Province," 1694, a travel
description written by Matsuo Munefusa
(1644-94), a haiku poet best known by his
pen-name Basho.
In each setenant pair, a complete *haiku* by
Basho is inscribed vertically at right on the left
stamp and in the center of the right stamp. The
same poem appears on both stamps in each
pair.
Issued: Nos. 1776a-1794a, Aug. 1, 1989.

Intl.
Conference
on Volcanoes,
Kagoshima
A1355

1988, July 19   Photo.   Perf. 14
1795 A1355 60y multicolored   1.00 .30

A1356

A1357

A1358

Letter Writing
Day, 10th
Anniv. — A1359

Designs and contest-winning children's
drawings: No. 1796, Cat and letter. No. 1797,
Crab and Letter, by Katsuyuki Yamada. No.
1798, Fairy and letter. No. 1799, *Girl and Letter*, by Takashi Ukai.

Photo., Litho. (Nos. 1797, 1799)
1988, July 23   Perf. 13x13½
1796   A1356 40y multicolored   .75 .30
1796A A1356 40y Imperf., self-
              adhesive   .75 .30
1797   A1357 40y multicolored   1.00 .30
1798   A1358 60y multicolored   1.00 .30
  a.   Bklt. pane, 5 each #1796,
        1798   9.25
1798B A1358 60y Imperf., self-
              adhesive   1.00 .30
  c.   Bklt. pane, 3 each #1796A,
        1798B   7.50
1799   A1359 60y multicolored   1.00 .30
       Nos. 1796-1799 (6)   5.25 1.80

No. 1798c is adhered to the booklet cover,
made of peelable paper, folded in half and
rouletted down the center fold, with No. 1796a
at left and No. 1798b at right of the roulette.
Sheets of 2 containing Nos. 1796, 1798
were lottery prizes. Value, $5.

15th World Puppetry Festival, July 27-
Aug. 11 — A1360

Puppets: No. 1800, *Ohana*, string puppet
from the film *Spring and Fall in the Meiji Era*,
by Kinosuke Takeda (1923-1979), Japan. No.
1801, Girl, stick puppet from the Natl. Radost
Puppet Theater, Brno, Czechoslovakia. No.
1802, Woman, shadow puppet from China.
No. 1803, Knight, a marionette from Sicily.

1988, July 27   Photo.   Perf. 13
1800   60y multicolored   1.00 .35
1801   60y multicolored   1.00 .35
1802   60y multicolored   1.00 .35
1803   60y multicolored   1.00 .35
  a.   A1360 Block or strip of 4, #1800-
        1803   4.50 1.75

Japan-China Treaty, 10th
Anniv. — A1364

1988, Aug. 12   Photo.
1804 60y Peony   1.00 .35
1805 60y Panda   1.00 .35
  a.   A1364 Pair, #1804-1805 2.25 1.00

18th World Poultry
Congress, Nagoya,
Sept. 4-9 — A1366

1988, Sept. 3   Perf. 13½
1806 A1366 60y multicolored 1.00 .30

Rehabilitation
Intl. 16th
World
Congress,
Tokyo, Sept.
5-9 — A1367

Photo. & Embossed
1988, Sept. 5 *Perf. 13*
1807 A1367 60y multicolored   1.00 .25

A1368

Prints: 80y, *Kumesaburo Iwai as Chiyo,* by Kunimasa Utagawa (1773-1810), late Edo Period. 120y, *Komazo Ichikawa III as Ganryu Sasaki,* by Toyokuni Utagawa (1769-1825).

1988, Oct. 6 *Photo.*
1808 A1368 80y multicolored   1.40 .50
1809 A1368 120y multicolored   2.00 .50
Intl. Letter-Writing Week.

A1369

Design: Gymnast on parallel bars and "Kinkakuji," Temple of the Golden Pavilion.

1988, Oct. 14
1810 A1369 40y multicolored   .75 .25
43rd Natl. Athletic Meet, Kyoto.

Japan-Mexico Trade Agreement, Cent. — A1370

1988, Nov. 30 *Photo.*
1811 A1370 60y multicolored   1.00 .30

New Year 1989 (Year of the Snake) — A1371

Clay bell snake by Masanobu Ogawa.

1988, Dec. 1
1812 A1371 40y multicolored   .75 .35
Sheets of two containing Nos. 1506, 1812 were lottery prizes. Value, $2.50.

UN Declaration of Human Rights, 40th Anniv. — A1372

1988, Dec. 5 *Litho.* *Perf. 13½*
1813 A1372 60y multicolored   1.00 .25

National Treasures Series

Votive Silver Lidded Bowl Used in Todai-ji Temple Ground-Breaking Ceremony, 8th Cent. — A1373

Bronze Yakushi-nyorai Buddha, Asuka Period, 7th Cent. — A1374

Photo., Photo & Engr. (100y)
1989, Jan. 20 *Perf. 13, 13½ (100y)*
1814 A1373 60y multicolored   1.00 .35
1815 A1374 100y multicolored   1.75 .50

Kondo-Sukashibori-Kurakanagu, Bronze Saddle from Ohjin Imperial Mausoleum — A1375

Tamamushi-no-Zushi, Buddhist Altar in Lacquered Cypress from the Asuka Era — A1376

1989, June 30
1816 A1375 62y multicolored   1.10 .35
1817 A1376 100y multicolored   1.75 .50

Kin-in, a Gokan Era Gold Seal Given to the King of Na by Emperor Kobutei — A1377

Shinninshaba-gazokyo, a 5th Cent. European Bronze Mirror Back — A1378

1989, Aug. 15
1818 A1377 62y multicolored   1.10 .35
1819 A1378 100y multicolored   1.75 .50
    Nos. 1814-1819 (6)   8.45 2.55

Asian-Pacific Expo, Fukuoka, Mar. 17-Sept. 3 — A1383

1989 *Photo.* *Perf. 13*
1822 A1383 60y multicolored   1.00 .30
1823 A1383 62y multicolored   1.50 .50
Issue dates: 60y, Mar. 16; 62y, Apr. 18.

Yokohama Exposition (Space and Children), Yokohama City, Mar. 25 to Oct. 1 — A1384

Design: Detail of *Russian Lady Sight-seeing at the Port,* by Yoshitora, and entrance to the Yokohama City Art Museum.

1989, Mar. 24 *Litho.*
1824 A1384 60y multicolored   1.00 .30
1825 A1384 62y multicolored   1.50 .50

World Bonsai Convention, Omiya, Apr. 6-9 — A1385

1989, Apr. 6 *Photo.* *Perf. 13*
1826 A1385 62y multicolored   1.10 .35

Awa-odori, by Tsunetomi Kitano (b. 1880) — A1386

1989, Apr. 18 *Perf. 13*
1827   62y multicolored   1.10 .35
1828   62y multicolored   1.10 .35
  a. A1386 Pair, #1827-1828   2.25 1.00
Philately Week. Sheets of 2 containing Nos. 1827-1828 were lottery prizes. Value, $5.

Holland Festival 1989 — A1388

1989, Apr. 19 *Perf. 13½*
1829 A1388 62y Ship   1.10 .30

Fiber-optic Cable, the 3rd Transpacific Line Relay Linking Japan and the US — A1389

1989, May 10 *Perf. 13½x13*
1830 A1389 62y Station tower, map 1.10 .30

Natl. Afforestation Campaign — A1390

1989, May 19 *Perf. 13½*
1831 A1390 62y Bayberry, lime, Mt. Tsurugi   1.10 .30

World Design Exposition, Nagoya, July 15-Nov. 26
A1391   A1392

1989, July 14
1832 A1391 41y multicolored   .80 .35
1833 A1392 62y multicolored   1.10 .35

Letter Writing Day
A1393   A1394

1989, July 21 *Perf. 13x13½*
1834 A1393 41y multicolored   .80 .35
1835 A1394 62y multicolored   1.10 .30
  a.   Bklt. pane, 5 each #1834-1835   9.50
Sheets of 2 containing Nos. 1834-1835 were lottery prizes. Value, $3.

Congratulations and Condolences Types of 1982
1989, Aug. 10 *Photo.* *Perf. 13x13½*
1836 A1082 41y Wreath   .80 .25
1837 A1083 41y Crane   .80 .25
1838 A1083 62y Crane   1.10 .30
1839 A1084 72y Tortoise   1.30 .35
    Nos. 1836-1839 (4)   4.00 1.20

6th Interflora World Congress, Tokyo, Aug. 27-30 — A1395

1989, Aug. 25 *Photo.* *Perf. 13½*
1840 A1395 62y multicolored   1.10 .35

Prefecture Issues
Nos. 1841-1990 have been changed to Nos. Z1-Z150. The listings can be found in the section immediately following the postage section and preceding the semi-postal listings.

Far East and South Pacific Games for the Disabled (FESPIC), Kobe, Sept. 15-20
A1546

1989, Sept. 14 *Photo.* *Perf. 13½*
1991 A1546 62y multicolored   1.10 .30

Okuni Kabuki Screen
A1547   A1548

1989, Sept. 18   **Perf. 13**
1992 A1547 62y multicolored   1.10 .35
1993 A1548 70y multicolored   1.25 .40
EUROPALIA '89, Japan.

A1549

A1550

Scenes from the Yadorigi and Takekawa Chapters of the Tales of the Genji picture scroll, attributed to Fujiwara-no-Takeyoshi, late Heian Period (897-1185).

1989, Oct. 6   Photo.   Perf. 13½
1994 A1549 80y multicolored   1.40 .45
1995 A1550 120y multicolored   2.00 .55
Intl. Letter Writing Day.

Intl. Conference on Irrigation and Drainage — A1551

1989, Oct. 13
1996 A1551 62y Rice   1.10 .30

100th Tenno Sho Horse Race — A1552

1989, Oct. 27   Perf. 13
1997 A1552 62y Jockey riding Shinzan   1.10 .30

9th Hot Air Balloon World Championships, Saga — A1553

1989, Nov. 17   Photo.   Perf. 13x13½
1998 A1553 62y multicolored   1.10 .35

Copyright Control System, 50th Anniv. A1554

1989, Nov. 17   Perf. 13
1999 A1554 62y Conductor   1.10 .30

New Year 1990 (Year of the Horse)
A1555   A1556

41y, *Yawata-Uma* festival horse. 62y, *Kazari-Uma*, Meiji Period.

1989, Dec. 1   Perf. 13x13½, 13½
2000 A1555 41y multicolored   .80 .30
2001 A1556 62y multicolored   1.10 .35

No. 2001 was sold through Jan. 10, 1990, serving as a lottery ticket.
Sheets of two containing Nos. 1838, 2000 were lottery prizes. Value, $2.

Electric Locomotives

10,000
A1557

Photo. & Engr., Photo.
1990   Perf. 13
2002 A1557 62y shown   1.10 .35
2003 A1557 62y EF58   1.10 .35
2004 A1557 62y ED40   1.10 .35
2005 A1557 62y EH10   1.10 .35
2006 A1557 62y EF53   1.10 .35
2007 A1557 62y ED70   1.10 .35
2008 A1557 62y EF55   1.10 .35
2009 A1557 62y ED61   1.10 .35
2010 A1557 62y EF57   1.10 .35
2011 A1557 62y EF30   1.10 .35
   Nos. 2002-2011 (10)   11.00 3.50

Issued two stamps at a time, the first photo. & engr., the second photo.
Issued: Nos. 2002-2003, 1/31; Nos. 2004-2005, 2/28; Nos. 2006-2007, 4/23; Nos. 2008-2009, 5/23; Nos. 2010-2011, 7/18.

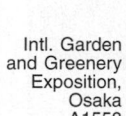
Intl. Garden and Greenery Exposition, Osaka A1558

1990, Mar. 30   Photo.   Perf. 13
2021 A1558 62y multicolored   1.10 .30
See No. B45.

A1559
Painting: *Women Gazing at the Stars*, by Chou Ohta.

1990, Apr. 20   Photo.   Perf. 13
2022 A1559 62y multicolored   1.10 .30
a.   Souvenir sheet of 1   1.25 1.25
Philately Week.

A1560

1990, May 18   Photo.   Perf. 13½
2023 A1560 62y Azalea, Mt. Unzen   1.10 .30
Natl. Land Afforestation Campaign.

Flower, Butterfly A1561

Abstract Art — A1561a

1990, June 1   Photo.   Perf. 13
2024 A1561 62y multicolored   1.10 .35
2025 A1561a 70y multicolored   1.25 .35

Japan-Turkey Relations, Cent. — A1562

1990, June 13
2026 A1562 62y multicolored   1.10 .30

Horses Series

Horses at Stable from Umaya-zu Byobu — A1563

Foals A1564

Lacquered Saddle, 16th Cent. A1565

Lacquered Stirrups, 16th Cent. A1566

Horse by S. Nishiyama A1567

Kettei A1568

"Kamo-Kurabeuma-Monyo-Kosode" A1569

Perf. 13x13½, 13
1990   Litho. & Engr.
Color of Horse
2027 62y red brown   1.10 .35
2028 62y gray   1.10 .35
2029 62y beige   1.10 .35
2030 62y tan   1.10 .35
2031 62y mottled   1.10 .35
a.   A1563 Strip of 5, #2027-2031   6.75 2.75

Photo.
2032 A1564 62y shown   1.10 .35

Photo. & Engr.
2033 A1565 62y shown   1.10 .35
2034 A1566 62y shown   1.10 .35
a.   Pair, #2033-2034   2.75 1.00

Photo.
2035 A1567 62y multicolored   1.10 .35
2036 A1568 62y multicolored   1.10 .35
2037 A1569 62y multicolored   1.10 .35

Postal Carriages — A1569a

Inkstone Case "Sano-no-Watashi" — A1570

"Bushu-Senju-zu" by Hokusai — A1571

"Shudan" by Kogetsu Saigo A1571a

Photo. & Engr., Photo. (#2040, 2042)
1991 *Perf. 12½x13*
2038 62y one horse 1.10 .35
2039 62y two horses 1.10 .35
a. A1569a Pair, #2038-2039 2.75 1.00
Perf. 13½x13
2040 A1570 62y multicolored 1.10 .35
2041 A1571 62y multicolored 1.10 .35
2042 A1571a 62y multicolored 1.10 .35
Nos. 2027-2042 (16) 17.60 5.60
Issued: Nos. 2027-2032, 6/20; Nos. 2033-2035, 7/31; Nos. 2036-2037, 9/27; Nos. 2038-2040, 1/31. Nos. 2041-2042, 2/28.

38th Intl. Youth Hostel Fed. Conference A1573

1990, June 25 **Litho.** *Perf. 13*
2057 A1573 62y multicolored 1.10 .30

Letter Writing Day A1574 A1575
1990, July 23 **Photo.** *Perf. 13½*
2058 A1574 41y multicolored .80 .35
2059 A1575 62y multicolored 1.10 .40
a. Souv. sheet of 1 1.25 1.25
b. Bklt. pane, 5 ea #2058-2059 9.50
See No. 2117.

21st Intl. Congress of Mathematicians — A1576
1990, Aug. 17 **Photo.** *Perf. 13*
2060 A1576 62y multicolored 1.10 .30

World Cycling Championships A1577
1990, Aug. 20 **Litho.** *Perf. 13½*
2061 A1577 62y multicolored 1.10 .30

Ogai Mori, Educator A1578
1990, Aug. 27 **Photo.**
2062 A1578 62y multicolored 1.10 .30
Intl. Assoc. for Germanic Studies (IVG), 8th Congress.

Character "Ji" in Shape of Rosetta Stone — A1579
1990, Sept. 7 *Perf. 13*
2063 A1579 62y multicolored 1.10 .30
Intl. Literacy Year.

Decade for Natural Disaster Reduction A1580
1990, Sept. 27 **Photo.**
2064 A1580 62y multicolored 1.10 .30

Intl. Confederation of Midwives, 22nd Congress A1581
1990, Oct. 5 **Photo.**
2065 A1581 62y multicolored 1.10 .30

A1582

"Choju-Jinbutsu-Giga" — A1583
Photo. & Engr.
1990, Oct. 5 *Perf. 13½*
2066 A1582 80y multicolored 1.40 .45
2067 A1583 120y multicolored 2.00 .55
Intl. Letter Writing Week.

"Fumizukai-zu" by Harunobu Suiendo A1584
1990, Oct. 16 **Photo.**
2068 A1584 100y multicolored 1.75 .55
a. Souv. sheet of 1 1.75 1.75
No. 2068a exists with surcharge which paid admission to PHILANIPPON '91. These were not sold by the post office.

Court System, Cent. — A1585
1990, Nov. 1 **Photo.** *Perf. 13x13½*
2069 A1585 62y "Justice" 1.10 .35

Japanese Braille, Cent. A1586
Photo & Embossed
1990, Nov. 1 *Perf. 13½*
2070 A1586 62y multicolored 1.10 .30

Enthronement of Akihito — A1587
No. 2071, Chinese phoenix depicted on Emperor's chair. No. 2072, Diamond pattern for costume worn at banquet ceremony.
1990, Nov. 9 **Photo.** *Perf. 13*
2071 A1587 62y multicolored 1.10 .35
2072 A1587 62y multicolored 1.10 .35
a. Souv. sheet of 2, #2071-2072 2.50 2.50

Japanese Diet, Cent. — A1588
1990, Nov. 29 **Litho.**
2073 A1588 62y multicolored 1.10 .35

New Year 1991 (Year of the Sheep)
A1589 A1590
1990, Dec. 3 **Photo.** *Perf. 13x13½*
2074 A1589 41y multicolored .80 .30
Photo. & Engr.
Perf. 13½
2075 A1590 41y multicolored .80 .35
2076 A1590 62y multi, diff. 1.10 .45
Nos. 2074-2076 (3) 2.70 1.10
Sheets of 2 No. 2074 were lottery prizes. Value, $1.50.

Dr. Yoshio Nishina, Physicist — A1591
1990, Dec. 6 **Photo.** *Perf. 13*
2077 A1591 62y multicolored 1.10 .30
Use of radio isotopes in Japan, 50th anniv.

Telephone Service, Cent. — A1592
1990, Dec. 14
2078 A1592 62y multicolored 1.10 .30

A1593
1991, Mar. 1 **Photo.** *Perf. 13½*
2079 A1593 41y Figure skating .80 .30
Perf. 13½x13
2080 A1593 62y Speed skating, horiz. 1.10 .30
1991 Winter Universiade.

A1594
1991, Apr. 1 **Photo.** *Perf. 13*
2081 A1594 62y multicolored 1.10 .30
Postal Life Insurance System.

Philately Week
A1595 A1596
No. 2082, Beauty Looking Back by Moronobu. No. 2083, Opening Dance by Shuho Yamakawa.
1991, Apr. 19
2082 A1595 62y multicolored 1.10 .35
2083 A1596 62y multicolored 1.10 .35
a. Souv. sheet of 2, #2082-2083 2.40 2.40
b. Pair, #2082-2083 2.40 2.40
Postal Service, 120th anniv. Pairs of Nos. 2082-2083 with label between are available from sheets of 20.

Kabuki Series

A1597

1991, Apr. 19   *Perf. 13½*
2084 A1597 62y multicolored   1.10   .30
Ceramic World Shigaraki '91.

A1598

1991, May 24   Photo.   *Perf. 13½*
2085 A1598 41y multicolored   .80   .30
Natl. Land Afforestation Campaign.

Standard Datum of
Leveling,
Cent. — A1599

1991, May 30   Photo.   *Perf. 13*
2086 A1599m 62y mutlicolored   1.10   .35

Int'l Stamp Design Contest Winning Entries

A1600

A1601

A1601a

A1601b

1991, May 31   Photo.   *Perf. 13*
2087 A1600 41y Flowers   .80   .30
2088 A1601 62y Couple in
         Ethnic Dress   1.10   .30
2089 A1601a 70y World peace   1.25   .40
2090 A1601b 100y Butterfly   1.75   .50
    Nos. 2087-2090 (4)   4.90   1.50
Int'l. Stamp Design Contest winning entries.

Kagamijishi
A1602

Yaegakihime
A1603

Koshiro
Matsumoto VII
A1604

Danjuro
Ichikawa XI
A1605

Baigyoku
Nakamura III
A1606

Ganjiro
Nakamura II
A1607

Kichiemon
Nakamura
I — A1608

Nizaemon
Kataoka
XIII — A1609

Enjaku
Jitsukawa II
A1610

Hakuo
Matsumoto I
A1611

Fuji-Musume
A1612

Kotobuki-Soganotaimen — A1613

Perf. 13 (62y), 13½ (100y)

1991-92			**Photo.**	
2091	A1602	62y dp bl grn & gold	1.10	.35
2092	A1603	100y multicolored	1.75	.55
2093	A1604	62y multicolored	1.10	.35
2094	A1605	100y multicolored	1.75	.55
2095	A1606	62y multicolored	1.10	.35
2096	A1607	100y multicolored	1.75	.55
2097	A1608	62y multicolored	1.10	.35
2098	A1609	100y multicolored	1.75	.55
2099	A1610	62y multicolored	1.10	.35
2100	A1611	100y multicolored	1.75	.55
2101	A1612	62y multicolored	1.10	.35
2102	A1613	100y multicolored	1.75	.55
		Nos. 2091-2102 (12)	17.10	5.40

Issued: Nos. 2091-2092, 6/28; Nos. 2093-2094, 9/27; Nos. 2095-2096, 11/20; Nos. 2097-2098, 2/20/92; Nos. 2099-2100, 4/10/92; Nos. 2101-2102, 6/30/92.

Waterbird Series

Gallinago
Hardwickii
(Latham's
Snipe)
A1614

No. 2104, Sula leucogaster. No. 2105, Larus crassirostris. No. 2106, Podiceps ruficollis. No. 2107, Lunda cirrhata. No. 2108, Grus monacha. No. 2109, Cygnus cygnus. No. 2110, Rostratula benghalensis. No. 2111, Calonectris leucomelas. No. 2112, Halcyon coromanda. No. 2113, Alcedo atthis. No. 2114, Bubulcus ibis.

1991-93		**Photo.**	*Perf. 13½*	
2103	A1614	62y multicolored	1.10	.35
2104	A1614	62y multicolored	1.10	.35
2105	A1614	62y multicolored	1.10	.35
2106	A1614	62y multicolored	1.10	.35
2107	A1614	62y multicolored	1.10	.35
2108	A1614	62y multicolored	1.10	.35
2109	A1614	62y multicolored	1.10	.35
2110	A1614	62y multicolored	1.10	.35
2111	A1614	62y multicolored	1.10	.35
2112	A1614	62y multicolored	1.10	.35
2113	A1614	62y multicolored	1.10	.35
2114	A1614	62y multicolored	1.10	.35
		Nos. 2103-2114 (12)	13.20	4.20

Nos. 2103-2104 printed in blocks of 12 with gutter between in sheet of 24.
Issued: Nos. 2103-2104, 6/28; Nos. 2105-2106, 9/27; Nos. 2107-2108, 1/30/92; Nos. 2109-2110, 3/25/92; Nos. 2111-2112, 8/31/92; Nos. 2113-2114, 1/29/93.
See Nos. 2192-2195.

Intl. Conf. on
Superconductivity — A1620

1991, July 19   Litho.   *Perf. 13½*
2115 A1620 62y multicolored   1.10   .30

Type of Letter Writing Day of 1990 and

A1621

1991, July 23   Photo.   *Perf. 13x13½*
2116 A1621 41y multicolored   .80   .35
2117 A1575 62y multicolored   1.10   .35
   a.   Souvenir sheet of 1   1.25   1.25
   b.   Bklt. pane, 5 each #2116-2117 9.50

Nos. 2117, 2117a have light blue frameline and inscription and violet denomination.

3rd IAAF World
Track & Field
Championships,
Tokyo — A1622

1991, Aug. 23   *Perf. 13*
2118 A1622 41y High jump   .80   .30
2119 A1622 62y Shot put   1.10   .30

Intl. Symposium on Environmental
Change and Geographical Information
Systems — A1623

1991, Aug. 23
2120 A1623 62y multicolored   1.10   .30

Intl. Letter Writing Week
A1624

Bandainagon-emaki picture scroll probably by Mitsunaga Tokiwa: 80y, Crowd of people. 120y, People, house.

Photo. & Engr.
1991, Oct. 7   **Perf. 13½**
2121 A1624 80y multicolored   1.40   .45
2122 A1624 120y multicolored   2.00   .55

A1625

62y, Breezy Fine Weather by Hokusai.

1991, Oct. 8   Photo.   Perf. 13
2123 A1625 62y multicolored   1.10   .35
Summit Conf. on Earthquake and Natural Disasters Countermeasures.

A1626

1991, Oct. 31   Litho.   Perf. 13
2124 A1626 62y multicolored   1.10   .35
Japanese Green Tea, 800th anniv.

A1627

Koshaku-Musume by Kunisada Utagawa.

Photo. & Engr.
1991, Nov. 15   **Perf. 13**
2125 A1627 62y multicolored   1.10   .35
  a.   Sheet of 2   3.00 3.00
World Stamp Exhibition, Nippon '91.

A1628

1991, Nov. 20   Photo.
2126 A1628 62y multicolored   1.10   .30
Administrative Counselors System, 30th anniv.

A1629

A1630

New Year 1992 (Year of the Monkey)
A1631   A1632

1991, Dec. 2   Photo.   Perf. 13½
2127 A1629 41y multicolored   .80   .40
2128 A1630 62y multicolored   1.10   .40
2129 A1631 41y +3y, multi   .85   .50
2130 A1632 62y +3y, multi   1.25   .50
      Nos. 2127-2130 (4)   4.00 1.80
Sheets of 2 No. 2127 were lottery prizes. Value, $2.

8th Conference on Intl. Trade in Endangered Species (CITES)
A1633

1992, Mar. 2   Photo.   Perf. 13
2131 A1633 62y multicolored   1.10   .30

A1634

Flowers on the Chair, by Hoshun Yamaguchi.

1992, Apr. 20
2132 A1634 62y multicolored   1.10   .30
Philately Week.

A1635

1992, May 15
2133 A1635 62y multicolored   1.10   .35
Return of Ryukyu Islands to Japan, 20th anniv.

Intl. Space Year — A1636

1992, July 7   Photo.   Perf. 13
2134 62y satellite at left   1.10   .35
2135 62y space station upper
      right   1.10   .35
  a. A1636 Pair, #2134-2135   2.25 1.25

Letter Writing Day
A1638   A1639

1992, July 23   Perf. 13x13½
2136 A1638 41y multicolored   .80   .35
          Perf. 13½
2137 A1639 62y multicolored   1.10   .35
  a.   Souvenir sheet of 1   1.25 1.25
  b.   Bklt. pane, 5 each #2136-2137 9.50

29th Intl. Geological Congress, Kyoto
A1640

1992, Aug. 24 Photo. Perf. 13½x13
2138 A1640 62y multicolored   1.10   .30

47th Natl. Athletic Meet, Yamagata Prefecture — A1641

1992, Sept. 4   Perf. 13½
2139 A1641 41y multicolored   .80   .30

Normalization of Japanese-Chinese Relations, 20th Anniv. — A1642

Photo. & Engr.
1992, Sept. 29   **Perf. 13**
2140 62y jug   1.10   .35
2141 62y long-neck jar   1.10   .35
  a. A1642 Pair, #2140-2141   2.25 1.00

Intl. Letter Writing Week — A1644

Heiji picture scroll: 80y, Nobles, servants in carriages by Taikenmon gate. 120y, Fujiwara-no Nobuyori seated before samurai.

Photo. & Engr.
1992, Oct. 6   **Perf. 13½**
2142 A1644 80y multicolored   1.40   .45
2143 A1644 120y multicolored   2.00   .55

Cat and Birds
A1644a

Design: 70y, Santa Claus, snow scene, vert.

Perf. 13½x13, 13x13½
1992, Oct. 9   Photo.
2144 A1644a 62y multicolored   1.10   .30
2145 A1644a 70y multicolored   1.25   .30
Winners of Third Postage Stamp Design contest.

30th Congress of Intl. Cooperative Alliance, Tokyo — A1644b

1992, Oct. 27   Perf. 13x13½
2146 A1644b 62y multicolored   1.10   .30

A1645

Cultural Pioneers: No. 2147, Takakazu Seki (1642?-1708), mathematician. No. 2148, Akiko Yosano (1878-1942), poet.

Photo. & Engr.
1992, Nov. 4   **Perf. 13**
2147 A1645 62y multicolored   1.10   .30
2148 A1645 62y multicolored   1.10   .30
   See Nos. 2217-2219, 2434-2435, 2642, 2717-2718.

A1646

1992, Nov. 9 Photo. Perf. 13x13½
2149 A1646 62y multicolored   1.10   .30
Certified Public Tax Accountant System, 50th anniv.

A1647

A1648

New Year 1993 (Year of the Rooster)

A1649   A1650

1992, Nov. 16   *Perf. 13x13½*
2150	A1647	41y multicolored	.80	.35
2151	A1648	62y multicolored	1.10	.35
a.		Souvenir sheet of 2, #2150-2151	2.00	1.10

Perf. 13½
2152	A1649	41y +3y multi	.85	.45
2153	A1650	62y +3y multi	1.25	.45
	Nos. 2150-2153 (4)		4.00	1.60

Surtax on Nos. 2152-2153 for lottery.

Flora and Fauna — A1651

9y, Dragonfly. 15y, Swallowtail. 18y, Ladybug. 41y, Mandarin duck. No. 2158, 50y, Japanese white-eye. No. 2159, 62y, Rufous turtle dove. 72y, Varied tit. 80y, Pied kingfisher. 90y, Spotbill duck. 130y, Bullfinch. 190y, Fringed orchid. 270y, Wild pink. 350y, Adder's tongue lily. 420y, Japanese iris. 430y, Violet.

1992-94   **Photo.**   *Perf. 13x13½*
2154	A1651	9y multi	.25	.25
2155	A1651	15y multi	.30	.25
2156	A1651	18y multi	.35	.25
2157	A1651	41y multi	.80	.35
2158	A1651	50y multi	.90	.30
2159	A1651	62y multi	1.10	.25
a.		Bklt. pane, 5 ea #2157, 2159	9.50	
b.		Booklet pane of 10	11.00	
2160	A1651	72y multi	1.30	.40
2161	A1651	80y multi	1.40	.25
a.		Miniature sheet, 5 #2158, 10 #2161 + 3 labels	45.00	
2162	A1651	90y multi	1.60	.50
2163	A1651	130y multi	2.10	.65
2164	A1651	190y multi	3.50	.75
2165	A1651	270y multi	4.75	1.00
2166	A1651	350y multi	6.25	1.10
2167	A1651	420y multi	6.75	1.25
2167A	A1651	430y multi	7.00	1.50
	Nos. 2154-2167A (15)		38.35	9.05

Coil Stamps
Perf. 13 Horiz.
2168	A1651	50y like #2158	.90	.40
2169	A1651	80y like #2161	1.40	.55

Booklet Stamps
Self-Adhesive
Die Cut
2170	A1651	41y like #2157	.80	.35
2171	A1651	50y like #2158	.95	.45
2172	A1651	62y like #2159	1.10	.50
a.		Bklt. pane, 2 #2170, 4 #2172	6.00	
2173	A1651	80y like #2161	1.50	.70
a.		Bklt. pane, 4 #2171, 4 #2173	10.00	

Issued: 41y, 62y, 72y, 11/30/92; 9y, 18y, Nos. 2158, 2161, 90y, 1/13/94; 270y, 350y, 420y, 1/24/94; 15y, 130y, 190y, 430y, 4/25/94. Nos. 2172a, 2173a are adhered to the booklet cover, made of peelable paper, folded in half and rouletted down the center fold.
See Nos. 2475-2483, 2486-2488. Compare No. 2166 with No. 3446.

World Alpine Skiing Championships, Morioka-Shizukuishi — A1657

1993, Feb. 3   **Photo.**   *Perf. 13*
2174	A1657	41y shown	.80	.40
2175	A1657	62y Skier, diff.	1.10	.55

Seasonal Flowers Series

Poppy   Cherry Blossoms
A1658   A1659

Lily — A1660   Thistle — A1661

Chinese Bellflowers A1662   Chrysanthemums A1663

Plum Blossom A1664   Winter Camellia A1665

Perf. 13½ (41y, 50y), 13 (62y, 80y)
1993-94   **Photo.**
2176	A1658	41y multicolored	.80	.35

Perf. 13
2177	A1659	62y multicolored	1.10	.35
2178	A1660	41y multicolored	.80	.35

Perf. 13
2179	A1661	62y multicolored	1.10	.35
2180	A1662	41y multicolored	.80	.35
2181	A1663	62y multicolored	1.10	.35
2182	A1664	50y multicolored	.90	.35
2183	A1665	80y multicolored	1.40	.55
	Nos. 2176-2183 (8)		8.00	3.00

Issued: Nos. 2176-2177, 3/12; Nos. 2178-2179, 6/18; Nos. 2180-2181, 9/16; Nos. 2182-2183, 1/28/94.

Waterbird Type
1993   **Photo.**   *Perf. 13½*
2192	A1614	62y Grus vipio	1.10	.35
2193	A1614	62y Ansner albifrons	1.10	.35
2194	A1614	62y Anas formosa	1.10	.35
2195	A1614	62y Haliaeetus albicilla	1.10	.35
	Nos. 2192-2195 (4)		4.40	1.40

Issued: Nos. 2192-2193, 3/31; Nos. 2194-2195, 5/25.

Philately Week — A1674

Painting: In the Studio, by Nampu Katayama.

1993, Apr. 20   **Photo.**   *Perf. 13*
2196	A1674	62y multicolored	1.10	.30

Natl. Land Afforestation Campaign — A1675

1993, Apr. 23   *Perf. 13½*
2197	A1675	41y multicolored	.80	.30

Mandarin Duck in the Nest — A1676   Gardenia in the Nest — A1677

Design: 70y, Mandarin Duck and Gardenia emblems, horiz.

1993, June 8   **Photo.**   *Perf. 13*
2198	A1676	62y multicolored	1.10	.35
2199	A1677	62y multicolored	1.10	.35
a.		Pair, #2198-2199	2.25	1.25
2200	A1676	70y multicolored	1.25	.40
	Nos. 2198-2200 (3)		3.45	1.10

Royal Wedding of Crown Prince Naruhito and Masako Owada.

5th Meeting of Signatories to Ramsar, Iran Convention on Wetlands and Waterfowl Habitats A1678

1993, June 10   **Photo.**   *Perf. 13½*
2201	A1678	62y Crane with young	1.10	.35
2202	A1678	62y Crane's head	1.10	.35
a.		Pair, #2201-2202	2.50	2.00

Commercial Registration System, Cent. — A1679

1993, July 1   **Photo.**   *Perf. 13x13½*
2203	A1679	62y multicolored	1.10	.30

Letter Writing Day
A1680   A1681

1993, July 23   *Perf. 13x13½*
2204	A1680	41y multicolored	.80	.35

Perf. 13½x13
2205	A1681	62y multicolored	1.10	.35
a.		Souvenir sheet of 1	1.25	1.25
b.		Booklet pane, 5 each #2204-2205	10.00	

15th Intl. Botanical Congress, Tokyo A1682

Designs: No. 2206, Glaucidium palmatum. No. 2207, Sciadopitys verticillata.

1993, Aug. 23   **Photo.**   *Perf. 13½x13*
2206		62y multicolored	1.10	.35
2207		62y multicolored	1.10	.35
a.	A1682	Pair, #2206-2207	2.50	1.25

World Federation for Mental Health Congress, Chiba City — A1683

1993, Aug. 23   *Perf. 13½x13*
2208	A1683	62y multicolored	1.10	.30

A1684

1993, Sept. 3   **Photo.**   *Perf. 13½*
2209		41y Swimming	.80	.30
2210		41y Karate	.80	.30
a.	A1684	Pair, #2209-2210	1.75	1.00

48th natl. athletic meet, Kagawa Prefecture.

A1685

Japanese-Portuguese Relations, 450th Anniv.: No. 2211, Arrival of Portuguese, folding screen, c. 1560-1630. No. 2212, Mother-of-Pearl Host Box, Jesuit symbols and grape motif.

1993, Sept. 22   **Photo.**   *Perf. 13*
2211		62y multicolored	1.10	.35
2212		62y multicolored	1.10	.35
a.	A1685	Pair, #2211-2212	2.50	1.25

Intl. Letter Writing Wook A1686

Portraits from Picture Scrolls of the Thirty-Six Immortal Poets: 80y, Ki no Tsurayuki. 120y, Kodai no Kimi.

1993, Oct. 6 — Perf. 13½

2213	A1686	80y multicolored	1.40	.40
2214	A1686	120y multicolored	2.00	.50

10th World Veterans' Track and Field Championships, Miyazaki Prefecture
A1687

1993, Oct. 7 — Perf. 14

2215	A1687	62y multicolored	1.10	.30

Souvenir Sheet

Wedding of Crown Prince Naruhito and Princess Masako — A1688

1993, Oct. 13 — Photo. — Perf. 13½

2216	A1688	62y multicolored	1.25	1.25

Cultural Pioneers Type of 1992

No. 2217, Kazan Watanabe (1793-1841), artist. No. 2218, Umetaro Suzuki (1874-1943), chemist. No. 2219, Toson Shimazaki (1872-1943), poet.

1993, Nov. 4 — Photo. — Perf. 13

2217	A1645	62y multicolored	1.10	.30

Photo. & Engr.

2218	A1645	62y multicolored	1.10	.30
2219	A1645	62y multicolored	1.10	.30
		Nos. 2217-2219 (3)	3.30	.90

Agricultural Research Center, Cent. — A1689

1993, Nov. 17 — Perf. 13½

2220	A1689	62y multicolored	1.10	.30

A1690   A1691

New Year 1994 (Year of the Dog)
A1692   A1693

1993, Nov. 17 — Perf. 13x13½

2221	A1690	41y multicolored	.80	.35
2222	A1691	62y multicolored	1.10	.35

Perf. 13½

2223	A1692	41y +3y multi	.85	.40
2224	A1693	62y +3y multi	1.25	.40
		Nos. 2221-2224 (4)	4.00	1.50

Sheets of 2, Nos. 2221-2222, were lottery prizes. Value, $2.25.

Declaration of Human Rights, 45th Anniv. — A1694

Designs: 62y, Man with bird perched on head. 70y, Globe, dove, person breaking chains, peace symbol.

1993, Dec. 10 — Photo. — Perf. 13

2225	A1694	62y multicolored	1.10	.30
2226	A1694	70y multicolored	1.25	.40

Congratulations and Condolences Types of 1982

1994, Mar. 10 — Photo. — Perf. 13x13½

2227	A1082	50y Wreath	.90	.35
2228	A1083	50y Crane	.90	.35
2229	A1083	80y Crane	1.40	.40
2230	A1084	90y Tortoise	1.60	.40
		Nos. 2227-2230 (4)	4.80	1.50

For use on condolence and greeting cards.

1994 World Figure Skating Championships, Tokyo — A1695

1994, Mar. 17 — Photo. — Perf. 13

2231	A1695	50y Ice dancing	.90	.35
2232	A1695	50y Women's singles	.90	.35
a.		Pair, #2231-2232	2.25	1.25
2233	A1695	80y Men's singles, vert.	1.40	.40
2234	A1695	80y Pairs, vert.	1.40	.40
a.		Pair, #2233-2234	3.00	1.50
		Nos. 2231-2234 (4)	4.60	1.50

Philately Week — A1696

1994, Apr. 20 — Photo. — Perf. 13

2235	A1696	80y Irises	1.40	.40

Intl. Year of the Family — A1697

Designs: No. 2236, "Love" spelled by people. No. 2237, Faces in flowers. No. 2238, Sun shining on people, homes. No. 2239, Family flying inside bird.

1994, May 13 — Photo. — Perf. 13

2236	A1697	50y multicolored	.90	.30
2237	A1697	50y multicolored	.90	.30
2238	A1697	80y multicolored	1.40	.40
a.		Pair, #2236, 2238	2.50	1.25
2239	A1697	80y multicolored	1.40	.40
a.		Pair, #2237, 2239	2.50	1.25
		Nos. 2236-2239 (4)	4.60	1.30

Natl. Land Afforestation Campaign
A1698

1994, May 20

2240	A1698	50y multicolored	.90	.35

Intl. Conference on Natural Disaster Reduction
A1699

1994, May 23

2241	A1699	80y multicolored	1.40	.35

No. 2241 printed in sheets of 16 with 4 labels.

A1700

1994, May 24

2242	A1700	80y multicolored	1.40	.35

Prototype Fast Breeder Reactor, Monju.

A1701

1994, June 3 — Photo. — Perf. 13

2243	A1701	80y multicolored	1.40	.40

Environment day.

Letter Writing Day
A1702   A1703

1994, July 22

2244	A1702	50y multicolored	.90	.35
2245	A1703	80y multicolored	1.40	.40
a.		Souvenir sheet of 1	1.60	1.60
b.		Bklt. pane, 5 each #2244-2245	12.50	

Prefecture Issues

Nos. 2246-2400B have been changed to #Z151-Z307. The listings can be found in a new section immediately following the postage section and preceding the semi-postal listings.

10th Intl. Conference on AIDS, Yokohama — A1859

1994, Aug. 5 — Photo. — Perf. 13

2401	A1859	80y multicolored	1.40	.35

Postal History Series

A1860

First Japanese stamps (Baron Hisoka Maeshima and): No. 2402, #1. No. 2403, #2. No. 2404, #3. No. 2405, #4.
CTO's exist for Nos. 2402-2405. They read "Japan" between two arcs in a corner.

Photo. & Engr.

1994, Aug. 10 — Perf. 13

2402	A1860	80y brown & black	1.40	.40
2403	A1860	80y blue & black	1.40	.40
2404	A1860	80y ver & black	1.40	.40
2405	A1860	80y olive grn & blk	1.40	.40
a.		Strip of 4, #2402-2405	6.00	6.00

A1861

Early Japanese stamps (Edoardo Chiossone and): No. 2406, #55. No. 2407, Type A16. No. 2408, #63. No. 2409, #65.

1994, Nov. 18 — Perf. 13½

2406	A1861	80y buff, slate & blk	1.40	.40
2407	A1861	80y gray & dk brown	1.40	.40
2408	A1861	80y gray lilac & rose	1.40	.40
2409	A1861	80y lt blue & dk blue	1.40	.40
a.		Strip of 4, #2406-2409	6.00	6.00

A1862

Designs: No. 2410, #85, transporting mail by ricksha. No. 2411, #86, transporting mail by horse-drawn carriage.

1995, Jan. 25

2410	A1862	80y multicolored	1.40	.40
2411	A1862	80y multicolored	1.40	.40
		Nos. 2402-2411 (10)	14.00	4.00

A1863

Designs: No. 2412, #C3, First Osaka-Tokyo airmail flight. No. 2413, #C6, Workers loading freight onto airplane.

Photo. & Engr.

1995, May 25   *Perf. 13½*
2412 A1863 110y multicolored   2.00   .50
2413 A1863 110y multicolored   2.00   .50

Nos. 2412-2413 printed in blocks of 10 with gutter between in sheets of 20.

A1864

No. 2414, Light mail van, #436. No. 2415, Cherub commemorative mail box, #428. No. 2416, Mail box, #435. No. 2417, Van, #433.

Photo. & Engr.

1995, Sept. 19   *Perf. 13½*
2414 A1864 80y multicolored   1.40   .40
2415 A1864 80y multicolored   1.40   .40
2416 A1864 80y multicolored   1.40   .40
2417 A1864 80y multicolored   1.40   .40
   a.   Block of 4, #2414-2417   6.00   6.00

Postal History Series
Types of 1948-49 With "NIPPON" Inscribed at Bottom
Size: 22x47mm
Photo. & Engr.

1996, June 3   *Perf. 13½*
2418 A206 80y like #422, brown   1.40   .40
2419 A206 80y like #422, multi   1.40   .40
2420 A247 80y like #479, purple   1.40   .40
2421 A247 80y like #479, multi   1.40   .40
   a.   Strip of 4, #2418-2421   6.00   6.00

Opening of Kansai Intl. Airport — A1877

Designs: No. 2422, Airport, part of plane's vertical stabilizer. No. 2423, Aft section of airplane. No. 2424, Airport, jet.

1994, Sept. 2   Photo.   *Perf. 13*
2422 A1877 80y multicolored   1.40   .35
2423 A1877 80y multicolored   1.40   .35
   a.   Vert. pair, #2422-2423   3.00   3.00
   b.   Vert. strip of 3, #2422-2424   4.50   4.50
2424 A1877 80y multicolored   1.40   .35
   Nos. 2422-2424 (3)   4.20   1.05

A1878

1994, Sept. 19
2425 A1878 80y multicolored   1.40   .35
ITU Plenipotentiary Conference, Kyoto.

A1879

1994, Sept. 30
2426 A1879 50y Kick volleyball   .90   .30
2427 A1879 80y Steeplechase   1.40   .35
2428 A1879 80y Synchronized swimming   1.40   .35
   a.   Pair, #2427-2428   3.00   1.75
   Nos. 2426-2428 (3)   3.70   1.00
12th Asian Games, Hiroshima.

Intl. Letter Writing Week A1880

Screen paintings of popular indoor games, Momoyama, Edo periods: 90y, Sugoroku. 110y, Japanese chess. 130y, Go.

1994, Oct. 6   Photo.   *Perf. 13x13½*
2429 A1880 90y multicolored   1.60   .45
2430 A1880 110y multicolored   1.90   .55
2431 A1880 130y multicolored   2.10   .55
   Nos. 2429-2431 (3)   5.60   1.55

49th Natl. Athletic Meet, Aichi Prefecture — A1881

1994, Oct. 28   *Perf. 13½*
2432 A1881 50y multicolored   .90   .30

A1882

1994, Nov. 4   Photo.   *Perf. 13*
2433 A1882 80y multicolored   1.40   .35
Intl. Diabetes Federation, 15th Congress, Kobe.

Cultural Pioneers Type of 1992
Cultural pioneers: No. 2434, Michio Miyagi (1894-1956), Musician. No. 2435, Gyoshu Hayami (1894-1935), artist.

1994, Nov. 4   Photo. & Engr.
2434 A1645 80y multicolored   1.40   .35
2435 A1645 80y multicolored   1.40   .35

A1884

Heiankyo (Kyoto), 1200th Anniv. — A1885

Kanpuzu, by Hideyori Kano, Momoyama period depicts autumn scene on Kiyotakigawa River: No. 2436, People seated, white birds. No. 2437, Bridge, people. No. 2438, Bridge, birds flying. No. 2439, People, Jingoji Temple, Atago-Jinja Shrine. No. 2440, People seated, tree.
No. 2441, Painting of Dry Garden (Sekitei), Ryoanji Temple, by Eizo Kato. No. 2442, Painting of artificial pond, Shugakuin Rikyu, by Kanji Kawai, horiz.

1994, Nov. 8   Photo.   *Perf. 13x13½*
2436   80y multicolored   1.40   .40
2437   80y multicolored   1.40   .40
2438   80y multicolored   1.40   .40
2439   80y multicolored   1.40   .40
2440   80y multicolored   1.40   .40
   a.   A1884 Strip of 5, #2436-2440   8.50   8.50
2441 A1885 80y multicolored   1.40   .40

Perf. 13½x13
2442 A1885 80y multicolored   1.40   .40
   Nos. 2436-2442 (7)   9.80   2.80

A1886   A1887

New Year 1995 (Year of the Boar)
A1888   A1889

1994, Nov. 15   *Perf. 13x13½*
2443 A1886 50y multicolored   .90   .35
2444 A1887 80y multicolored   1.40   .40

Perf. 13½
2445 A1888 50y +3y multi   .95   .40
2446 A1889 80y +3y multi   1.50   .40
   Nos. 2443-2446 (4)   4.75   1.55
Sheets of two containing Nos. 2443-2444 were lottery prizes. Value $2.50.

World Heritage Series

Himeji Castle
A1890   A1891

1994, Dec. 14   Photo.   *Perf. 13*
2447 A1890 80y multicolored   1.40   .40
2448 A1891 80y multicolored   1.40   .40

A1892

Horyuji Temple A1893

Designs: 80y, Goddess Kannon from inner temple wall. 110y, Temple exterior.

1995, Feb. 22
2449 A1892 80y multicolored   1.40   .40
2450 A1893 110y multicolored   1.90   .55

Cryptomeria Japonica A1894   Cervus Nippon Yakushimae A1895

1995, July 28
2451 A1894 80y multicolored   1.40   .40
2452 A1895 80y multicolored   1.40   .40

Virgin Beech Forest A1896   Black Woodpecker A1897

1995, Nov. 21
2453 A1896 80y multicolored   1.40   .40
2454 A1897 80y multicolored   1.40   .40
   Nos. 2447-2454 (8)   11.70   3.35

Japan-Brazil Friendship, Cent. A1898

Designs: No. 2455, Natl. emblems, flowers. No. 2456, Soccer players.

1995, Mar. 3   Photo.   *Perf. 13½*
2455 A1898 80y multicolored   1.40   .35
2456 A1898 80y multicolored   1.40   .35

A1899 | Fujiwara-Kyo Palace, 1300th Anniv. — A1900

Designs: 50y, Unebiyama, Nijozan Mountains, roofing tile from palace. 80y, Portrait of a Woman, in Asuka and Hakuho era style, by Okada, 1925.

1995, Mar. 28
2457 A1899 50y multicolored .90 .35
2458 A1900 80y multicolored 1.40 .40

Modern Anatomical Education A1901

1995, Mar. 31   Perf. 13
2459 A1901 80y multicolored 1.40 .35

A1902

1995, Apr. 12   Photo.   Perf. 13
2460 A1902 80y multicolored 1.40 .40

1995 Census.

A1903

1995, Apr. 20
2461 A1903 80y multicolored 1.40 .40

Japanese Overseas Cooperation Volunteers, 30th anniv.

A1904

A1905

A1906

A1907

A1908

1995, Apr. 25   Perf. 13x13½
2462 A1904 50y multicolored .90 .30
2463 A1905 50y multicolored .90 .30
2464 A1906 80y multicolored 1.40 .35
2465 A1907 80y multicolored 1.40 .35
2466 A1908 90y multicolored 1.75 .55
Nos. 2462-2466 (5) 6.35 1.85

For use on condolence and greeting cards.

A1909

1995, May 19   Photo.   Perf. 13½x13
2467 A1909 50y multicolored .90 .30

Natl. land afforestation campaign.

A1910

Greetings: No. 2468, Rainbow, hearts. No. 2469, Girl holding heart-shaped balloon. No. 2470, Flower holding pencil, sign. No. 2471, Star, sun, moon as flowers, fauna. No. 2472, Person, dog with flowers, butterfly in hair.

Self-Adhesive

1995, June 1   Die Cut Perf. 13½
2468 A1910 80y multicolored 1.40 .40
2469 A1910 80y multicolored 1.40 .40
2470 A1910 80y multicolored 1.40 .40
2471 A1910 80y multicolored 1.40 .40
2472 A1910 80y multicolored 1.40 .40
a. Miniature sheet, #2468-2472 + 5 labels 8.00 8.00

Letter Writing Day
A1911   A1912

1995, July 21   Photo.   Perf. 13½
2473 A1911 50y multicolored .90 .30
2474 A1912 80y multicolored 1.40 .35
a. Souvenir sheet of 1 1.60 1.60
b. Bklt. pane, 5 ea #2473-2474 12.50
Complete booklet, #2474b 12.50

Flora & Fauna Type of 1992 and

Shikikacho-zu
A1926

Matsutaka-Zu
A1926a

10y, Scarab, dandelions. 20y, Honey bee, flower. 30y, Hairstreak, flowers. 70y, Great tit. 110y, Plover. 120y, Shrike. 140y, Japanese grosbeak. 160y, Jay. 390y, Dayflower.

1995-98   Photo.   Perf. 13½
2475 A1651 10y multi .25 .25
2476 A1651 20y multi .30 .25
2477 A1651 30y multi .50 .35
2478 A1651 70y multi 1.25 .40
2479 A1651 110y multi 1.90 .50
2480 A1651 120y multi 2.00 .50
2481 A1651 140y multi 2.25 .50
2482 A1651 160y multi 2.75 .60

**   Perf. 13x13½**
2483 A1651 390y multi 7.50 1.25

**   Perf. 13½**
2484 A1926 700y multi 13.00 3.50

Photo. & Engr.

Self-Adhesive
Die Cut Perf. 13x13½
2486 A1651 50y Like #2158 .75 .40
2487 A1651 80y Like #2161 1.10 .35

Coil Stamp
Perf. 13 Horiz.
2488 A1651 10y like #2475 .25 .25

Issued: 700y, 7/4/95; 390y, 1000y, 3/28/96; 70y, 110y, 7/22/97; No. 2475, 20y, 30y, 11/28/97; 120y, 140y, 2/16/98 160y, 2/23/98; No. 2488, 9/11/98. Nos. 2486-2487, 3/25/02. Nos. 2486 and 2487 were issued in panes of 10.

2485 A1926a 1000y multi 17.50 3.75

End of World War II, 50th Anniv.
A1937   A1938

Design: No. 2491, Children holding hands behind stained glass window, peace dove, earth from space.

1995, Aug. 1   Photo.   Perf. 13
2489 A1937 50y multicolored .90 .30
2490 A1938 80y multicolored 1.40 .35
2491 A1938 80y multicolored 1.40 .35
Nos. 2489-2491 (3) 3.70 1.00

A1939

1995, Aug. 23
2492 A1939 80y multicolored 1.40 .35

18th Universiade, Fukuoka.

A1940

50y, Radio controlled plane, transmitter. 80y, Radio controlled helicopter, competitor, assistant.

1995, Aug. 25
2493 A1940 50y multicolored .90 .30
2494 A1940 80y multicolored 1.40 .35

1995 Aeromodel World Championships, Okayama Prefecture.

World Veterinary Congress, Yokohama A1941

1995, Sept. 1   Photo.   Perf. 13
2495 A1941 80y Dog, cow & horse 1.40 .35

World Sports Championships A1942

No. 2496, 1995 World Judo Championships, Chiba Prefecture. No. 2497, 1995 World Gymnastics Championships, Sabae, Fukui Prefecture.

1995, Sept. 28
2496 A1942 80y multicolored 1.40 .35
2497 A1942 80y multicolored 1.40 .35

Letter Writing Week A1943

Screen paintings: 90y, Shell-matching game. 110y, Battledore and shuttlecock. 130y, Playing cards.

1995, Oct. 6   Perf. 13½
2498 A1943 90y multicolored 1.60 .45
2499 A1943 110y multicolored 1.90 .55
2500 A1943 130y multicolored 2.40 .55
Nos. 2498-2500 (3) 5.90 1.55

A1944

1995, Oct. 13   Perf. 13x13½
2501 A1944 50y multicolored .90 .30

50th Natl. athletic meet, Fukushima prefecture.

A1945

1995, Oct. 24   Perf. 13
2502 A1945 80y UN, hearts 1.40 .35
2503 A1945 80y UNESCO, children 1.40 .35

UN, UNESCO, 50th anniv.

Cultural Pioneers Type of 1992

No. 2504, Tadataka Ino (1745-1818), cartographer. No. 2505, Kitaro Nishida (1870-1945), philosopher.

Photo. & Engr.
1995, Nov. 6   Perf. 13
2504 A1645 80y multicolored 1.40 .40
2505 A1645 80y multicolored 1.40 .40

A1947

A1948

109450   739450

New Year 1996 (Year of the Rat)
A1949   A1950

1995, Oct. 15   **Photo.**   *Perf. 13x13½*
2506 A1947 50y multicolored .90 .35
2507 A1948 80y multicolored 1.40 .40
      Perf. 13½
2508 A1949 50y +3y multi .95 .40
2509 A1950 80y +3y multi 1.50 .45
   Nos. 2506-2509 (4) 4.75 1.60
Sheets of two containing Nos. 2506-2507
were lottery prizes. Value $2.50.

Japanese-Korean
Diplomatic
Relations, 30th
Anniv. — A1951

1995, Dec. 18   *Perf. 13*
2510 A1951 80y multicolored 1.40 .35

Nos. 2511-2512 are unassigned.

A1952

1996, Feb. 16   **Photo.**   *Perf. 13*
2513 A1952 80y multicolored 1.40 .35
Philipp Franz von Siebold (1796-1866),
naturalist.

A1953

1996, Mar. 1
2514 A1953 80y multicolored 1.40 .35
Labor Relations Commissions, 50th anniv.

Senior
Citizens — A1954

1996, Mar. 21   *Perf. 13½*
2515 A1954 80y multicolored 1.40 .35
No. 2515 issued in sheets of 5.

50th Postwar Memorial Year
A1955   A1956

No. 2516, Crowd, Emperor's limosine
approaching Diet. No. 2517, Prime Minister
Yoshida signing Peace Treaty, San Francisco,
9/8/51. No. 2518, Women performing traditional Okinawan dance.

1996, Apr. 1   **Photo.**   *Perf. 13*
2516 A1955 80y multicolored 1.40 .40
2517 A1955 80y multicolored 1.40 .40
  a.   Pair, Nos. 2516-2517 3.00 2.25
2518 A1956 80y multicolored 1.40 .40
   Nos. 2516-2518 (3) 4.20 1.20
Promulgation of the the Constitution,
11/7/46 (No. 2517a). Return of Okinawa,
5/15/72 (No. 2518).

Woman Suffrage,
50th Anniv. — A1957

1996, Apr. 10   *Perf. 13½*
2519 A1957 80y multicolored 1.40 .35

Philately
Week — A1958

1996, Apr. 19   *Perf. 13*
2520 A1958 80y multicolored 1.40 .40

UNICEF, 50th
Anniv. — A1959

1996, May 1   **Photo.**   *Perf. 13*
2521 A1959 80y multicolored 1.40 .35

Child Welfare
Week, 50th
Anniv. — A1960

1996, May 1
2522 A1960 80y multicolored 1.40 .35

Bird Week, 50th Anniv. — A1961

1996, May 10
2523   80y Birds 1.40 .40
2524   80y Field Glasses 1.40 .40
  a.   A1961 Pair, #2523-2524 3.00 1.75

Natl. Afforestation
Campaign — A1963

1996, May 17
2525 A1963 50y multicolored .90 .30

50th Postwar Memorial Year
A1964   A1965

1996, June 24   **Photo.**   *Perf. 13*
2526 A1964 80y multicolored 1.40 .40
2527 A1965 80y multicolored 1.40 .40

River Administration System,
Cent. — A1966

1996, July 5   **Photo.**   *Perf. 13½*
2528   80y denomination lower
    right 1.40 .40
2529   80y denomination lower left 1.40 .40
  a.   A1966 Pair, #2528-2529 3.00 1.75

A1968

Marine Day's
Establishment
A1969

1996, July 19
2530 A1968 50y multicolored .90 .35
2531 A1969 80y multicolored 1.40 .40

Letter Writing Day
A1970   A1971

1996, July 23
2532 A1970 50y multicolored .90 .35
2533 A1971 80y multicolored 1.40 .40
  a.   Souvenir sheet of 1 1.50 1.50
  b.   Bklt. pane, 5 ea #2532-2533 12.00
    Complete booklet 12.50

Cultural Pioneers Type of 1992

No. 2534, Kenji Miyazaw (1896-1933). No.
2535, Hokiichi Hanawa (1746-1821).

     Photo. & Engr.
1996, Aug. 27   *Perf. 13*
2534 A1645 80y multicolored 1.40 .35
2535 A1645 80y multicolored 1.40 .35

A1974   A1975

Designs: No. 2536, Advances of women in
society, diffusion of home electrical products.
No. 2537, Modern highway, railway systems.

1996, Aug. 27   **Photo.**   *Perf. 13*
2536 A1974 80y multicolored 1.40 .40
2537 A1975 80y multicolored 1.40 .40

51st Natl. Athletic
Meet — A1976

1996, Sept. 6   **Photo.**   *Perf. 13½*
2538 A1976 50y Archery .90 .30

Community Chest,
50th Anniv. — A1977

1996, Sept. 30
2539 A1977 80y multicolored 1.40 .35

Intl. Music
Day — A1978

1996, Oct. 1   **Perf. 13**
2540 A1978 80y multicolored   1.40   .35

A1979

A1980

A1980a

Intl.
Letter
Writing
Week —
A1980b

Paintings: No. 2541, Water wheel, Mt. Fuji.
No. 2543, Mt. Fuji in Clear Weather (Red Fuji),
by Hokusai. No. 2545, Mt. Fuji, lake.

1996, Oct. 7   **Perf. 13½**
2541	A1979	90y multicolored	1.60	.50
2542	A1980	90y multicolored	1.60	.50
a.		Pair, #2541-2542	3.50	1.75
2543	A1979	110y multicolored	1.90	.55
2544	A1980a	110y multicolored	1.90	.55
a.		Pair, #2543-2544	4.25	2.00
2545	A1979	130y multicolored	2.25	.60
2546	A1980b	130y multicolored	2.25	.60
a.		Pair, #2545-2546	5.00	2.25
		Nos. 2541-2546 (6)	11.50	3.30

18th World
Congress of
Savings
Banks — A1981

1996, Oct. 23   **Perf. 13**
2547 A1981 80y multicolored   1.40   .35

50th Postwar Memorial Year
A1982   A1983

No. 2548, Earth from space. No. 2549, Cellular telephone, fiber optic cable, satellite in
orbit.

1996, Nov. 8   **Photo.**   **Perf. 13**
2548 A1982 80y multicolored   1.40   .40
2549 A1983 80y multicolored   1.40   .40

A1984   A1985

New Year 1997 (Year of the Ox)
A1986   A1987

1996, Nov. 15   **Photo.**   **Perf. 13x13½**
2550 A1984 50y multicolored   .90   .35
2551 A1985 80y multicolored   1.40   .40

Perf. 13½
2552 A1986 50y +3y multi   .95   .40
2553 A1987 80y +3y multi   1.50   .50
      Nos. 2550-2553 (4)   4.75   1.65

Sheets of 2 containing Nos. 2550-2551
were lottery prizes. Value $3.

Yujiro Ishihara, Actor — A1988

Hibari Misora, Entertainer — A1990

Osamu Tezuka, Cartoonist — A1992

1997, Jan. 28   **Photo.**   **Perf. 13**
2554		80y multicolored	1.40	.40
2555		80y multicolored	1.40	.40
a.	A1988	Pair, #2554-2555	3.00	1.75
2556		80y multicolored	1.40	.40
2557		80y multicolored	1.40	.40
a.	A1990	Pair, #2556-2557	3.00	1.75
2558		80y multicolored	1.75	.45
2559		80y multicolored	1.75	.45
a.	A1992	Pair, #2558-2559	4.00	2.25
		Nos. 2554-2559 (6)	9.10	2.50

Sparrow, Rice   Sparrow,
Plant,   Maple,
Camellia   Camellia
A1994   A1995

Perf. 14 Horiz. Syncopated Type A
1997, Apr. 10   **Photo.**
2560	A1994	50y multi	1.25	.50
2560A	A1994	80y multi	1.75	.50
2560B	A1994	90y multi	2.00	.60
2560C	A1994	120y multi	2.75	.65
2560D	A1994	130y multi	25.00	11.50
2561	A1995	270y multi	5.50	2.00
		Nos. 2560-2561 (6)	38.25	15.75

Denominations of Nos. 2560-2561 were
printed by machine at point of sale, and were
limited to the denominations listed.

Daigo, by
Okumura
Dogyu (1889-
1990)
A1996

1997, Apr. 18   **Litho.**   **Perf. 13½**
2562 A1996 80y multicolored   1.40   .35

Philately Week.

Supreme Court,
50th
Anniv. — A1997

1997, May 2   **Photo.**   **Perf. 13**
2563 A1997 80y Main court room   1.40   .35

Doraemon — A1998

Designs: No. 2564, Shown. No. 2565, With
envelope. No. 2566, Standing on hand. No.
2567, With propeller. No. 2568, In love.

Booklet Stamps
Serpentine Die Cut 13½
1997, May 2   **Self-Adhesive**
2564	A1998	80y multicolored	1.40	.40
2565	A1998	80y multicolored	1.40	.40
2566	A1998	80y multicolored	1.40	.40
2567	A1998	80y multicolored	1.40	.40
2568	A1998	80y multicolored	1.40	.40
a.		Pane of 5, #2564-2568	7.50	7.50

Japanese Migration
to Mexico,
Cent. — A1999

1997, May 12   **Perf. 13**
2569 A1999 80y multicolored   1.40   .35
     See Mexico No. 2035.

A2000

1997, May 16   **Perf. 13½**
2570 A2000 50y Miyagi bush clo-
            ver   .90   .30

Natl. afforestation campaign.

A2001

1997, May 20   **Perf. 13**
2571 A2001 80y Natl. Diet   1.40   .35

Natl. House of Councilors, 50th anniv.

Letter Writing Day

A2002   A2003

A2004   A2005

1997, July 23   **Photo.**   **Perf. 13**
2572	A2002	50y multicolored	.90	.30
2573	A2003	70y multicolored	1.25	.35
2574	A2004	80y multicolored	1.40	.35
a.		Souvenir sheet of 1	1.60	1.60
b.		Bklt. pane, 5 ea #2572, 2574	13.00	
		Complete booklet, #2574b	13.00	
2575	A2005	90y multicolored	1.60	.45
		Nos. 2572-2575 (4)	5.15	1.45

A2006

1997, Aug. 11   **Photo.**   **Perf. 13**
2576 A2006 50y multicolored   .90   .30

Part-time and correspondence education at
upper secondary schools, 50th anniv.

A2007

1997, Sept. 1
2577 A2007 80y multicolored   1.40   .35

Labor Standards Law, 50th anniv.

Friendship Between Japan and Chile, Cent. — A2008

1997, Sept. 1   *Perf. 13½*
2578   A2008   80y multicolored   1.40   .35
    See Chile No. 1217.

52nd Natl. Sports Festival — A2009

1997, Sept. 12
2579   A2009   50y multicolored   .90   .30

A2010

A2010a

A2010b

Intl. Letter Writing Week — A2010c

Paintings of Tokaido's 53 Stations by Hiroshige: No. 2580, Hodogaya (bridge over waterway). No. 2582, Kameyama snow-covered mountain slope).
No. 2584, Sumida Riverbank Snowscape (woman in traditional attire beside river), by Hiroshige
From Scrolls of Flowers and Birds of the Four Seasons by Hoitsu Sakai: No. 2581, Bird on tree. No. 2583, Leaves and berries. No. 2585, Bird on tree branch of blossoms.

1997, Oct. 6   **Photo.**   *Perf. 13½*
2580   A2010   90y multicolored   1.40   .45
2581   A2010a   90y multicolored   1.40   .45
   a.   Pair, #2580-2581   3.50   2.00
2582   A2010   110y multicolored   1.80   .50
2583   A2010b   110y multicolored   1.80   .50
   a.   Pair, #2582-2583   4.25   2.00
2584   A2010   130y multicolored   2.25   .55
2585   A2010c   130y multicolored   2.25   .55
   a.   Pair, #2584-2585   5.00   2.25
    Nos. 2580-2585 (6)   10.90   3.00

Grand Opening of the Natl. Theater of Tokyo — A2011

1997, Oct. 9   *Perf. 13*
2586   A2011   80y multicolored   1.40   .35

Favorite Songs
A2012   A2013

50y Departure on a Fine Day, by Tanimura Shinji. 80y, Desert Under the Moon, by Kato Masao & Sakasi Suguru.

1997, Oct. 24
2587   A2012   50y multicolored   .90   .30
2588   A2013   80y multicolored   1.40   .40

Cultural Pioneers Type of 1992
No. 2589, Rohan Kouda (1867-1947), writer. No. 2590, Ando Hiroshige (1797-1858), artist.

1997, Nov. 4
2589   A1645   80y multicolored   1.40   .35
2590   A1645   80y multicolored   1.40   .35

A2016   A2017

New Year 1997 (Year of the Tiger)
A2018   A2019

1997, Nov. 14   *Perf. 13x13½*
2591   A2016   50y multicolored   .90   .40
2592   A2017   80y multicolored   1.40   .45
         Perf. 13½
2593   A2018   50y +3y multi   .95   .45
2594   A2019   80y +3y multi   1.50   .50
   Sheets of two containing Nos. 2591-2592 were lottery prizes. Value $2.50.

Return of Okinawa to Japan, 25th Anniv. — A2020

1997, Nov. 21   *Perf. 13*
2595   A2020   80y multicolored   1.40   .35

Shibuya Family's House A2021

Tomizawa Family's House A2022

Photo. & Engr.
1997, Nov. 28   *Perf. 13½*
2596   A2021   80y multicolored   1.40   .45
2597   A2022   80y multicolored   1.40   .45

A2023

Woodprints: No. 2598, Mother Sea. No. 2599, Mother Earth.

1997, Dec. 1   **Photo.**   *Perf. 13*
2598   A2023   80y multicolored   1.40   .35
2599   A2023   80y multicolored   1.40   .35
   a.   Pair, #2598-2599   3.00   2.00
   3rd Conference of the Parties to the UN Framework Convention on Climate Change, Kyoto.

A2024

1997, Dec. 2
2600   A2024   80y multicolored   1.40   .35
   Agricultural Insurance System, 50th anniv.

Favorite Songs

A2025   A2026

A2027   A2028

1997, Dec. 8
2601   A2025   50y Sunayama   .90   .30
2602   A2026   80y Jingle Bells   1.40   .35

1998, Jan. 26   **Photo.**   *Perf. 13*
2603   A2027   50y Shabondama   .90   .30
2604   A2028   80y Kitaguni no Haru   1.40   .35

1998 Winter Olympic & Paralympic Games, Nagano
A2029   A2030

Paralympic logo and: No. 2605, Glaucidium palmatum. No. 2606, Ice hockey.
Olympic rings and: No. 2607: a, Gentiana nipponica. b, Caltha palustris. c, Fritillaria camtschatcensis. d, Paeonia japonica. e, Erythronium japonicum. f, Snowboarding. g, Curling. h, Speed skating. i, Cross-country skiing. j, Downhill skiing.

1998, Feb. 5
2605   A2029   50y multicolored   .90   .30
2606   A2030   80y multicolored   1.40   .35
   a.   Pair, #2605-2606   2.50   1.00
2607   Sheet of 10   12.50   12.50
   a.-e.   A2029 50y Any single   .90   .30
   f.-j.   A2030 80y Any single   1.40   .35

Historic Houses

A2031

A2032

Photo. & Engr.
1998, Feb. 23   *Perf. 13½*
2608   A2031   80y multicolored   1.40   .45
2609   A2032   80y multicolored   1.40   .45

Japanese Fire Service, 50th Anniv. — A2033

1998, Mar. 6   **Photo.**   *Perf. 13*
2610   80y multicolored   1.40   .40
2611   80y multicolored   1.40   .40
   a.   A2033 Pair, #2610-2611   3.00   1.25

Favorite Songs
A2035   A2036

1998   **Photo.**   *Perf. 13*
2612   A2035   50y Medaka-no-Gak-ko   .90   .30
2613   A2036   80y Aoi Sanmyaku   1.40   .35
   Issued: 50y, 3/23; 80y, 3/16.

Greetings Stamps — A2037

Designs: a, Puppy. b, Kitten. c, Parakeets. d, Pansies. e, Bunny.

1998, Mar. 13　Photo.　Die Cut
Self-Adhesive
2614		Sheet of 5	7.50	
	a.-e.	A2037 80y any single	1.40	.75

Philately
Week — A2038

"Poppies," by Kokei Kobayashi (1883-1957).

1998, Apr. 17　　　　　Perf. 13½
2615	A2038 80y multicolored	1.40	.35

1998
Year of
France
in Japan
A2039

"Liberty Leading the People," by Delacroix.

1998, Apr. 28　　　　　Perf. 13½
2616	A2039 110y multicolored	1.90	.55

Natl. Afforestation
Campaign — A2040

1998, May 8
2617	A2040 50y Trout, Renge azalea	.90	.30

Favorite Songs

A2041　　　　　A2042

Designs: 50y, "Wild Roses," by Franz Schubert. 80y, "Hill Abloom with Tangerine Flowers," by Minoru Uminuma and Shogo Kato.

1998, May 25　　　　　Perf. 13
2618	A2041 50y multicolored	.90	.30
2619	A2042 80y multicolored	1.40	.35

Historic Houses

Kowata
Residence
A2043

Kamihaga
Residence
A2044

Photo. & Engr.
1998, June 22　　　　　Perf. 13½
2620	A2043 80y multicolored	1.40	.45
2621	A2044 80y multicolored	1.40	.45

Favorite Songs

A2045　　　　　A2046

50y, Kono Michi, "This Road." 80y, Ware Wa Umino Ko, "I'm a Boy of the Sea."

1998, July 6　　Photo.　Perf. 13
2622	A2045 50y multicolored	.90	.30
2623	A2046 80y multicolored	1.40	.35

Letter Writing
Day — A2047

Stylized drawings of children: No. 2624, Child writing letter. No. 2625, Child wearing glasses, letter on table. No. 2626, Child with ink pen, flowers overhead. No. 2627, Child with ink pen, dove overhead. No. 2628, Children holding letters, envelopes.

1998, July 23　　　　　Perf. 13
2624	A2047 50y multi	.90	.30
2625	A2047 50y multi	.90	.30
a.	Pair, #2624-2625	1.90	1.10
2626	A2047 80y multi	1.40	.35
2627	A2047 80y multi	1.40	.35
2628	A2047 80y multi, horiz.	1.40	.35
a.	Souvenir sheet of 1	1.60	1.60
b.	Sheet, 4 each #2626-2627, 2 #2628	17.50	17.50
c.	Bklt. pane, 2 ea #2624-2628	14.00	14.00
	Complete booklet, #2628c	15.00	

See Nos. 2682-2686, 2738-2742, 2779-2783, 2824-2828. See Nos. 2733h-2733j for self-adhesive stamps.

Historic Houses

Kamio
Residence
A2048

Nakamura
Residence
A2049

Photo. & Engr.
1998, Aug. 24　　　　　Perf. 13½
2629	A2048 80y multicolored	1.40	.45
2630	A2049 80y multicolored	1.40	.45

53rd Natl. Sports
Festival,
Kanagawa — A2050

1998, Sept. 11　Photo.　Perf. 13½
2631	A2050 50y multicolored	.90	.30

A2051

A2051a

A2051b

A2051c

Intl. Letter Writing Week, Greetings — A2051c

Details or complete paintings by Jakuchu Ito: No. 2632, "Birds & Autumn Maple." No. 2633, "Parakeet in Oak Tree." No. 2634, "Mandarin Ducks in the Snow." No. 2635, "Golden Pheasant & Bamboo in Snow." No. 2636, "Leafy Peonies & Butterflies." No. 2637, "Parakeet in Rose Bush."

1998, Oct. 6　　Photo.　Perf. 13½
2632	A2051　90y multicolored	1.60	.45
2633	A2051a 90y multicolored	1.60	.45
a.	Pair, #2632-2633	3.50	1.75
2634	A2051　110y multicolored	1.90	.55
2635	A2051b 110y multicolored	1.90	.55
a.	Pair, #2634-2635	4.25	1.75
2636	A2051　130y multicolored	2.10	.65
2637	A2051c 130y multicolored	2.10	.65
a.	Pair, #2636-2637	5.00	1.75
	Nos. 2632-2637 (6)	11.20	3.30

Nos. 2632, 2634, 2636 are from "Plants and Animals" and are inscribed for Intl. Letter Writing Week. Nos. 2633, 2635, 2637 are from "Painted Woodcuts of Flowers and Birds."

1998 World
Volleyball
Championships for
Men and Women,
Japan — A2052

1998, Nov. 2　　　　　Perf. 13
2638	A2052 80y Serve	1.40	.35
2639	A2052 80y Receive	1.40	.35
2640	A2052 80y Set & spike	1.40	.35
2641	A2052 80y Block	1.40	.35
a.	Strip of 4, #2638-2641	6.00	6.00

Cultural Pioneer Type of 1992 and

Yoshie Fujiwara(1898-1976) — A2053

No. 2642, Bakin Takizawa (1767-1848).

Photo. & Engr.
1998, Nov. 4　　　　　Perf. 13
2642	A1645 80y multicolored	1.40	.35
2643	A2053 80y multicolored	1.40	.35

See Nos. 2719, 2747-2748, 2839-2840.

A2054　　　　　A2055

New Year 1999 (Year of the
Rabbit)
A2056　　　　　A2057

1998, Nov. 13　Photo.　Perf. 13x13½
2644	A2054 50y multicolored	.90	.35
2645	A2055 80y multicolored	1.40	.40

Perf. 13½x13
2646	A2056 50y +3y multi	1.00	.40
2647	A2057 80y +3y multi	1.50	.50
	Nos. 2644-2647 (4)	4.80	1.65

Sheets of two containing Nos. 2644-2645 were lottery prizes. Value $2.50.
See No. 2655.

Favorite Songs

A2058　　　　　A2059

50y, The Apple Song. 80y, Toys Cha-Cha-Cha at Night.

1998, Nov. 24　　　　　Perf. 13x13½
2648	A2058 50y multicolored	.90	.30
2649	A2059 80y multicolored	1.40	.35

Japan-Argentina Friendship Treaty, Cent. — A2060

1998, Dec. 2   Photo.   Perf. 13
2650 A2060 80y multicolored   1.40 .35

A2061   A2062

Universal Declaration of Human Rights, 50th Anniv.
A2063   A2064

1998, Dec. 10
2651 A2061 50y multicolored   .90 .35
2652 A2062 70y multicolored   1.25 .40
2653 A2063 80y multicolored   1.40 .35
2654 A2064 90y multicolored   1.60 .45
      Nos. 2651-2654 (4)   5.15 1.55

Greetings Types of 1951, 1962, 1986 and 1998

1998, Dec. 15   Photo.   Perf. 13x13½
2655 50y Sheet of 8, 2 each
      #a, c., 2644   7.75 7.75
  a. A281 rose pink, like #522   .90 .40
  b. A483 multi, like #773   .90 .40
  c. A1273 multi, like #1708   .90 .40

Favorite Songs

A2065   A2066

50y, Flowing Like a River. 80y, Song of the Four Seasons.

1999, Jan. 26   Photo.   Perf. 13
2656 A2065 50y multicolored   .90 .30
2657 A2066 80y multicolored   1.40 .35

Traditional Houses

Iwase Family House, Gokayama District A2067

Gassho-Zukuri Houses, Shirakawa-mura District — A2068

Gassho-Zukuri House — A2069

Photo. & Engr.
1999, Feb. 16   Perf. 13½
2658 A2067 80y multicolored   1.40 .45
2659 A2068 80y multicolored   1.40 .45
2660 A2069 80y multicolored   1.40 .45
  a. Pair, #2659-2660   3.50 3.50
      Nos. 2658-2660 (3)   4.20 1.35

Rakugo (Comic Storytellers) Stamps

Kokontei Shinshou V — A2070   Katsura Bunraku VIII — A2071

Sanyutei Enshou VI — A2072   Yanagiya Kosan V — A2073

Katsura Beichou III — A2074

1999, Mar. 12   Photo.   Perf. 13
2661 A2070 80y multicolored   1.40 .55
2662 A2071 80y multicolored   1.40 .55
2663 A2072 80y multicolored   1.40 .55
2664 A2073 80y multicolored   1.40 .55
2665 A2074 80y multicolored   1.40 .55
  a. Sheet, 2 each #2661-2665   15.00 15.00

Favorite Songs

Sukiyaki Song   Soushunfu
A2075   A2076

1999, Mar. 16
2666 A2075 50y multicolored   .90 .30
2667 A2076 80y multicolored   1.40 .35

Greetings Stamps — A2077

a, Kitten, daisies. b, Checks, flowers, roses. c, Tartan, puppy. d, Flowers, brown rabbit. e, Gray and white rabbit, moon and stars.

1999, Mar. 23   Die Cut
Self-Adhesive
2668 Sheet of 5   7.50
  a.-e. A2077 80y Any single   1.40 .75

25th General Assembly of Japan Medical Congress A2078

1999, Apr. 2   Perf. 13
2669 A2078 80y multicolored   1.40 .35

Philately Week — A2079

Rabbits Playing in the Field in Spring, by Doumoto Inshou (1891-1975): No. 2670, Three rabbits. No. 2671, Two rabbits.

1999, Apr. 20   Perf. 13½
2670 80y three rabbits   1.40 .40
2671 80y Two rabbits   1.40 .40
  a. A2079 Pair, #2670-2671   3.00 1.50

No. 2671a is a continuous design. No. 2671a also exists as a strip of two with central label. Value, $6.50.

A2080

1999, May 18   Photo.   Perf. 13
2672 A2080 80y multicolored   1.40 .35

Japanese migration to Peru, cent.

A2081

1999, May 28   Perf. 13¼
2673 A2081 50y multicolored   .90 .30

Natl. afforestation campaign.

A2082

Painting: Ruins of Tholos, by Masayuki Murai.

1999, June 1   Photo.   Perf. 13
2674 A2082 80y multicolored   1.40 .35

Japanese-Greek Treaty of Commerce & Navigation, cent.

A2083

1999, June 3
2675 A2083 80y multicolored   1.40 .35

Japanese emigration to Bolivia, cent.

Land Improvement System, 50th Anniv. — A2084

1999, June 4
2676 A2084 80y multicolored   1.40 .35

Family Court, 50th Anniv. — A2085

1999, June 16
2677 A2085 80y multicolored   1.40 .35

Patent Attorney System in Japan, Cent. — A2086

1999, July 1   Photo.   Perf. 13
2678 A2086 80y multicolored   1.40 .35

A2087

1999, July 1
2679 A2087 80y multicolored   1.40 .35

Japanese Community-Based Treatment of Offenders System, 50th anniv.

A2088

Enforcement of Civil and Commercial Codes, Cent.: Masaakira Tomii (1858-1935), Kenjiro Ume (1860-1910) and Nobushige Hozumi (1856-1926), drafters of Civil and Commerical Codes.

1999, July 19
2680 A2088 80y multicolored   1.40   .35

Copyright System in Japan, Cent. — A2089

1999, July 22
2681 A2089 80y multicolored   1.40   .35

Letter Writing Day Type of 1998

Stylized drawings of children and toys: No. 2682, Boy and clown, letter. No. 2683, Teddy bear seated on pencil. No. 2684, Girl, ink pen. No. 2685, Clown with yellow hat, jumping up out of envelope.

No. 2686: a, Giraffes. b, Kite, bird, horiz. c, Boy holding kite string. d, Girl with pencil and paper. e, Bunny and bear. f, Boy blowing trumpet. g, Girl playing cello. h, Girl in red. i, Girl in yellow holding envelope. j, Three ducks.

1999, July 23		**Photo.**	**Perf. 13**
2682	A2047	50y multicolored	.90	.30
2683	A2047	50y multicolored	.90	.30
2684	A2047	50y multicolored	.90	.30
2685	A2047	50y multicolored	.90	.30
a.		Strip of 4, #2682-2685	4.00	3.50
2686		Sheet of 10	16.00	16.00
a.-j.	A2047 80y any single		1.40	.35
k.	Booklet pane, #2682-2685, 2 each #2686c, 2686g, 2686i		14.00	
	Complete booklet, #2686k		14.50	
l.	Sheet of 2, #2682, 2686g		2.75	2.75

Nos. 2686a is 53x27mm. Nos. 2686d, 2686h, 2686j are 30mm in diameter. No. 2686f is 38x39mm. Sheet numbers are in center of rectangles at top of sheets.

The 20th Century — A2090

1900-10 (Sheet 1) — No. 2687: a, 50y, 1905-06 Serialized novel "Wagahai wa Neko de aru," by Soseki Natsume (stamp 7). b, 50y, 1906 Novel "Bochan," by Natsume (stamp 8). c, 80y, 1901 Collection of poems "Midaregami," by Akiko Yosano (stamp 1). d, 80y, Opening of Denkikan movie theater in Asakusa, 1903 (stamp 2). e, 80y, Electrification of streetcars, 1903 (stamp 3). f, 80y, Otojirou Kawakami & Sadayakko, actors (stamp 4). g, 80y, Westernization of fashion (stamp 9). h, 80y, Completion of Ryogoku Kokugikan sumo arena, 1909 (stamp 10). i,

---

80y, Russo-Japanese War soldiers on horseback (stamp 5). j, 80y, Russo-Japanese War soldiers in tent (stamp 6).

A2090a

1910-13 (Sheet 2) — No. 2688: a, 50y, 1st Japanese-produced airship, tail of 1st Japanese airplane (stamp 3). b, 50y, Front of 1st Japanese airplane (stamp 4). c, 80y, Elementary school song book published by Education ministry, 1910 (stamp 1). d, 80y, Antarctic expedition led by Nobu Shirase, 1910 (stamp 2). e, 80y, Dr. Hideyo Noguchi (stamp 5). f, 80y, Extinction of Japanese wolves (stamp 6). g, 80y, Runner Shizo Kanaguri at 1st participation in Olympic Games, 1912 (stamp 7). h, Takarazuka Musical Review founded, 1913 (stamp 8). i, 80y, "Song of Kachusha," by Sumako Matsui & Hogetsu Shimamura (stamp 9). j, 80y, 1st sale of caramels, 1913 (stamp 10).

A2090b

1914-20 (Sheet 3) — No. 2689: a, 50y, Painting of couple in boat by Yumeji Takehisa (stamp 9). b, 50y, Takehisa, painting of flowers (stamp 10). c, 80y, 1914 Opening of Tokyo train station (blimp in sky) (stamp 1). d, 80y, Tokyo train station main entrance (stamp 2). e, 80y, Japanese WWI seamen (stamp 3). f, 80y, Western-style women's hair styles (stamp 4). g, 80y, 1915 Poetry book "Rashomon," by Ryunosuke Akutagawa (stamp 5). h, 80y, 1916 Start of postal life insurance (goddess in clouds) (stamp 6). i, 80y, Sakuzo Yoshino, political scientist & democracy advocate, & tree (stamp 7). j, 80y, 1918 Rice riots (painting, photo of crowds) (stamp 8).

A2090c

1920-25 (Sheet 4) — No. 2690: a, 50y, Silent film star Matsunosuke Onoe (denomination at UR) (stamp 8). b, 50y, Silent film star Tsumasaburo Bandoh (denomination at UL) (stamp 9). c, 80y, 1st Hakone Relay Marathon, 1920 (stamp 1). d, 80y, Popularity of "Gondola Song" recording, spread of phonographs (stamp 2). e, 80y, Ruins from 1923 Kanto earthquake (stamp 3). f, "Nonki na Tosan" comic strip (man with dog) (stamp 4). g, 80y, "Adventures of Sho-chan" comic strip (man with vulture) (stamp 5). h, 80y, Japanese crane nears extinction (stamp 6). i, 80y, 1924 Opening of Koshien Stadium (stamp 7). j, 80y, Man, woman in Western-style clothing (stamp 10).

A2090d

1927-28 (Sheet 5) — No. 2691: a, 50y, 1927 Opening of Tokyo subway (close-up of car) (stamp 2). b, 50y, Subway car approaching station (stamp 3). c, 80y, Movie "Kurama Tengu" (Samurai) (stamp 1). d, 80y, Radio broadcast of "National Health Gymnastics" exercise program (stamp 4). e, 80y, Yoshiyuki Tsuruta, 1928 Olympic swimming champion (stamp 5). f, 80y, Mikio Oda, 1928 Olympic triple jump champion (stamp 6). g, 80y, Olympic Games program (stamp 7). h, 80y, Runner Kinue Hitomi, 1st female Japanese Olympic medalist (stamp 8). i, 80y, Man in Western clothing, cafe (stamp 9). j, 1928 Publishing of "Horoki," by Fumiko Hayashi (stamp 10).

A2090e

1929-32 (Sheet 6) — No. 2692: a, 50y, Mass production of Japanese automobiles (green 1932 Datsun Model 10) (stamp 4). b, 50y, Black 1936 Toyota Model AA (stamp 5). c, 80y, Volcano, Mt. Asama (stamp 1). d, 80y, Takiji Kobayashi, writer of "Kani-kosen," crane, smokestacks (stamp 2). e, 80y, Man with shirt with open collar, woman with handbag (stamp 3). f, 80y, "Norakuro" comic strip (cat, brick wall) (stamp 6). g, 80y, 1932 Nippon Derby winner Wakataka & jockey (stamp 7). h, 80y, Nippon Derby winner Kabutoyama (stamp 8). i, 80y, Song "Longing for Your Shadow" (woman with closed eyes) (stamp 9). j, 80y, 1932, 1936 Political assassinations (soldiers, truck, building) (stamp 10).

A2090f

1932-36 (Sheet 7) — No. 2693: a, 50y, Front of D51 steam locomotive (stamp 8). b, 50y, Rear of D51 (stamp 9). c, 80y, Fumihiko Otsuki, lexicographer (Otsuki, geometric design) (stamp 1). d, 80y, Song "Tokyo Ondo" (woman, buildings) (stamp 2). e, 80y, Keinichi Enomoto, comic actor, with feather (stamp 3). f, 80y, Formation of Japanese Baseball League (catcher, umpire) (stamp 4). g, 80y, Batter (stamp 5). h, 80y, Hachiko, dog that waited for dead owner, statue of Hachiko (stamp 6). i, 80y, Eiji Yoshikawa, author of "Miyamoto Musashi." (stamp 7). j, 80y, Extinct species Okinawan pigeon (stamp 10).

A2090g

A2090i

A2090k

A2090m

1937-40 (Sheet 8) — No. 2694: a, 50y, Nose of Kamikaze plane, tail of Nippon cargo plane (stamp 2). b, 50y, Nose of Nippon cargo plain, tail of Kamikaze plane (stamp 3). c, 80y, Helen Keller's 1st trip to Japan (stamp 1). d, 80y, Women with senninbari cloths, monpe work pants, man with kokumln-fuku unlform (stamp 4). e, 80y, Yuzo Yamamoto, author of "Robo No Ishi" (stamp 5). f, 80y, Woman & man embracing in movie, "Aizenkatsura" (stamp 6). g, 80y, Sumo wrestler Yokozuna Futabayama, winner of 69 consecutive matches (stamp 7). h, 80y, Baseball pitcher Eiji Sawamura (stamp 8). i, 80y, Song, "Dareka Kokyo" (ducks in flight) (stamp 9). j, 80y, Woodblock art of Shiko Munakata (stamp 10).

1945-52 (Sheet 10) — No. 2696: a, 50y, "Captain Atom" cartoon by Osamu Tezuka (stamp 7). b, 50y, "Astro Boy," cartoon by Tezuka (stamp 8). c, 80y, Song, "Ringo No Uta" (Apple Song) (stamp 1). d, 80y, "Sazae San," cartoon by Machiko Hasegawa (stamp 2). e, 80y, Promulgation of Japanese Constitution (woman, child, buildings) (stamp 3). f, 80y, Swimming records by Hironoshin Furuhashi (stamp 4). g, 80y, Dr. Hideki Yukawa, Nobel laureate for Physics (stamp 5). h, 80y, New Year's Eve radio program "Kohaku Uta Gassen" on NHK (stamp 6). i, 80y, Radio soap opera "Kimino Na Wa" (woman and man) (stamp 9). j, 80y, Novel "Nijyu-Yon No Hitomi," by Sakae Tsuboi (stamp 10).

1959-64 (Sheet 12) — No. 2698: a, 50y, Dog Taro, survivor of abandonment in Antarctica, ship's stern (stamp 1). b, 50y, Dog Giro, survivor of abandonment in Antarctic, ship's bow (stamp 2). c, 80y, Commemorative cake box from Wedding of Crown Prince Akihito (stamp 3). d, 80y, Weather map of Isewan Typhoon (stamp 4). e, 80y, "Sukiyaki Song," by Rokusuke Ei (stamp 5). f, 80y, Novelist Ryotaro Shiba and cover from "Ryomaga Yuku," depicting Ryoma Sakamoto (stamp 6). g, 80y, Baby doll, and song "Konnichiwa Akachan," by Ei (stamp 7). h, 80y, Inauguration of Bullet Train (stamp 8). i, 80y, Poster depicting swimmer from Tokyo Olympics (stamp 9). j, 80y, Poster depicting torchbearer from Tokyo Olympics (stamp 10).

1972-74 (Sheet 14) — No. 2700: a, 50y, Baseball player Sadaharu Oh (leg in air) (stamp 7). b, 50y, Baseball player Shigeo Nagashima (Tokyo uniform) (stamp 8). c, 80y, Two men from Takamatsu Zuka wall paintings, Asuka (stamp 1). d, 80y, Four women from Takamatsu Zuka wall paintings (stamp 2). e, 80y, Pandas Kankan and Ranran, gift from China (stamp 3). f, Shureimon, Return of Okinawa to Japanese control (stamp 4). g, 80y, Oscar, from cartoon "Roses of Versailles," by Riyoko Ikeda (stamp 5). h, 80y, Conductor Seiji Ozawa (stamp 6). i, 80y, Erimo Cape, and song "Erimo Misaki" (stamp 9). j, 80y, Space battleship Yamato from cartoon "Uchu Senkan Yamato," by Reiji Matsumoto (stamp 10).

A2090h

A2090j

A2090l

A2090n

1940-45 (Sheet 9) — No. 2695: a, 50y, "Ohgon Bat," cartoon by Ichiro Suzuki (character without hat) (stamp 9). b, 50y, "Ohgon Bat" character wearing hat (stamp 10). c, 80y, Chiune Sugihara, vice-consul in Lithuania who saved Jews from Holocaust (stamp 1). d, 80y, Start of Kokumin Gakko school system (children exercising) (stamp 2). e, 80y, Airplane in attack on Pearl Harbor (stamp 3). f, 80y, Kotaro Takamura, poet, winner of 1st Imperial Art Academy prize, & Japanese characters (stamp 4). g, 80y, Eruption of Mt. Showashin-zan (stamp 5). h, 80y, Atomic Bomb Memorial Dome (stamp 6). i, 80y, Statue at Nagasaki Atomic Bomb Museum (stamp 7). j, Signing of World War II surrender documents on USS Missouri (stamp 8).

1953-58 (Sheet 11) — No. 2697: a, 50y, Tokyo Tower (olive green panel) (stamp 9). b, 50y, Tokyo Tower from ground (stamp 10). c, 80y, Popularity of radio and television (stamp 1). d, 80y, Director Akira Kurosawa, camera, two Samurai from "Shinchinin No Samurai," (stamp 2). e, 80y, Five Samurai from "Shinchinin No Samurai." (stamp 3). f, 80y, Sumo wrestler Rikidozan and championship belt (stamp 4). g, 80y, Rikidozan in action (stamp 5). h, 80y, Movie "Godzilla" (stamp 6). i, 80y, Taiyozoku fashions (man, woman at seaside) (stamp 7), j, 80y, Portrait of Shotokutaishi from 10,000-yen bank note (stamp 8, 31x42mm oval stamp).

1964-71 (Sheet 13) — No. 2699: a, 50y, TV show puppets Don Gabacho and Torahige (stamp 1, 31x30mm semi-oval stamp with straight side at right). b, 50y, TV show puppets Hakase and Lion (stamp 2, 31x30mm semi-oval stamp with straight side at left). c, 80y, Color television, automobile and air conditioner (stamp 3). d, 80y, TV character, Ultraman (stamp 4). e, 80y, Baltan Seijin, character from Ultraman TV series (stamp 5). f, 80y, Electric guitars (stamp 6). g, 80y, Yasunari Kawabata and Kenzaburo Oe, Nobel laureates for Literature (stamp 7). h, 80y, Scene from movie "Otokowa Tsuraiyo" (man holding basket) (stamp 8). i, 80y, Tower from Expo '70, Osaka (stamp 9). j, 80y, Youth fashions and song "Senso O Shiranai Kodomotachi" (stamp 10).

1975-83 (Sheet 15) — No. 2701: a, 50y, Gundam and Zaku, from TV cartoon series "Kidosenshi Gundam" (blue background) (stamp 7). b, 50y, Amuro and Gundam, from "Kidonsenshi Gundam" (orange background) (stamp 8). c, 80y, Guitar, and song "Jidai" (stamp 1). d, 80y, Fish character Taiyaki Kun, from children's song "Oyoge! Taiyaki Kun" (stamp 2). e, 80y, Musical notes and microphones (popularity of karaoke) (stamp 3). f, 80y, Flower, and song "Cosmos" (stamp 4). g, 80y, UFO, and song "UFO" (stamp 5). h, 80y, Students from TV series, "San Nen B Gumi Kinpachi Sensei" (stamp 6). i, 80y, Musical notes and electronic synthesizer (stamp 9). j, 80y, Oshin, from TV series "Oshin" (stamp 10).

A2090o

1986-93 (Sheet 16) — No. 2702: a, 50y, Character from cartoon show "Soreike! Anpanman" (stamp 3). b, 50y, Four characters from "Soreike! Anpanman" (stamp 4). c, 80y, Return of Halley's Comet (stamp 1, pentagonal). d, 80y, Opening of Seikan Railroad Tunnel (stamp 2). e, 80y, Watchtower excavated at Yoshinogari Iseki ruins (stamp 5). f, 80y, Singer Hibari Misora, National Medal of Honor recipient (stamp 6). g, 80y, Mascot of J-League Soccer Games (stamp 7, 34x28mm semi-oval stamp with straight side at bottom). h, 80y, Soccer ball (stamp 8, 34x28mm stamp with straight side at top). i, 80y, Selection of Dunjuang as World Heritage Site (Cliffside, stamp 9). j, 80y, Selection of Horyuji Temple as World Heritage Site (Temple and sun, stamp 10).

A2090p

1993-98 (Sheet 17) — No. 2703: a, 50y, Nagano Winter Olympics emblem (stamp 7). b, 50y, Four owl mascots of Nagano Winter Olympics (stamp 8). c, 80y, Wedding of Crown Prince Naruhito and Masako Owada (stamp 1). d, 80y, Phoenix and damage from Hanshin-Awaji earthquake (stamp 2). e, 80y, Cellular phone and computer (stamp 3). f, 80y, Launch of Japanese astronaut aboard Space Shuttle Endeavor (stamp 4). g, 80y, Astronaut Mamoru Mohri in space (stamp 5). h, 80y, Details from Kyoto Climate Change Conf. stamps, #2598-2599 (stamp 6). i, 80y, Poster for Nagano Winter Olympics (stamp 9). j, Soccer player at 1998 World Cup Championships (stamp 10, 42x31mm elliptical stamp).
Illustrations reduced.

1999-2000	Photo.	Perf. 13x13¼		
	Sheets of 10			
2687	A2090	#a.-j.	17.50	17.50
a.-b.		50y any single	.90	.50
c.-j.		80y any single	1.40	.50
2688	A2090a	#a.-j.	17.50	17.50
a.-b.		50y any single	.90	.50
c.-j.		80y any single	1.40	.50
2689	A2090b	#a.-j.	17.50	17.50
a.-b.		50y any single	.90	.50
c.-j.		80y any single	1.40	.50
2690	A2090c	#a.-j.	17.50	17.50
a.-b.		50y any single	.90	.50
c.-j.		80y any single	1.40	.50

2691	A2090d	#a.-j.	17.50	17.50
a.-b.		50y any single	.90	.50
c.-j.		80y any single	1.40	.50
2692	A2090e	#a.-j.	17.50	17.50
a.-b.		50y any single	.90	.50
c.-j.		80y any single	1.40	.50
2693	A2090f	#a.-j.	17.50	17.50
a.-b.		50y any single	.90	.50
c.-j.		80y any single	1.40	.50
2694	A2090g	#a.-j	17.50	17.50
a.-b.		50y any single	.90	.50
c.-j.		80y any single	1.40	.50
2695	A2090h	#a.-j	17.50	17.50
a.-b.		50y Any single	.90	.50
c.-j.		80y any single	1.40	.50
2696	A2090i	#a.-j	17.50	17.50
a.-b.		50y any single	.90	.50
c.-j.		80y any single	1.40	.50
2697	A2090j	#a.-j	17.50	17.50
a.-b.		50y any single	.90	.50
c.-j.		80y any single	1.40	.50
2698	A2090k	#a.-j	17.50	17.50
a.-b.		50y any single	.90	.50
c.-j.		80y any single	1.40	.50
2699	A2090l	#a.-j	17.50	17.50
a.-b.		50y any single	.90	.50
c.-j.		80y any single	1.40	.50
2700	A2090m	#a.-j	17.50	17.50
a.-b.		50y any single	.90	.50
c.-j.		80y any single	1.40	.50
2701	A2090n	#a.-j	17.50	17.50
a.-b.		50y any single	.90	.50
c.-j.		80y any single	1.40	.50
2702	A2090o	#a.-j	17.50	17.50
a.-b.		50y any single	.90	.50
c.-j.		80y any single	1.40	.50
2703	A2090p	#a.-j	17.50	17.50
a.-b.		50y Any single	.90	.50
c.-j.		80y any single	1.40	.50

Sheet numbers are in UR corner of sheets or in center of rectangles at top of sheet. Stamp numbers are in sheet margin.
Issued: No. 2687, 8/23; No. 2688, 9/22; No. 2689, 10/22; No. 2690, 12/22; No. 2691, 1/21/00; No. 2692, 2/9/00; No. 2693, 2/23/00; No. 2694, 3/23/00; No. 2695, 4/21/00; No. 2696, 5/23/00; No. 2697, 6/23/00; No. 2698, 7/21/00; No. 2699, 8/23/00; No. 2700, 9/22/00; No. 2701, 10/23/00; No. 2702, 11/22; No. 2703, 12/22.

Hearts and Doves A2092

Celebration A2093

Red-crowned Crane — A2094

1999, Aug. 16	Photo.	Perf. 13¼	
2704	A2092	50y multi	.90	.30
2705	A2093	80y multi	1.40	.35
2706	A2094	90y multi	1.60	.40
	Nos. 2704-2706 (3)		3.90	1.05

A2095

1999, Sept. 10
2707	A2095	50y multi		.90	.30

54th Natl. Sports Festival.

A2096

1999, Oct. 1   Perf. 12¾x13
2708	A2096	80y multi		1.40	.35

Intl. Year of Older Persons.

A2097

A2098

A2099

Intl. Letter Writing Week A2100

Hokusai Paintings: No. 2709, Sea Route in Kazusa Area. No. 2710, Roses & a Sparrow. No. 2711, Rain Beneath the Mountaintop. No. 2712, Chrysanthemums & a Horsefly. No. 2713, Under the Fukagawa Bridge. No. 2714, Peonies & a Butterfly.

1999, Oct. 6			Perf. 13¼	
2709	A2097	90y multi	1.50	.45
2710	A2098	90y multi	1.50	.45
a.		Pair, #2709-2710	3.50	1.75
2711	A2097	110y multi	2.00	.55
2712	A2099	110y multi	2.00	.55
a.		Pair, #2711-2712	4.25	1.75
2713	A2097	130y multi	2.10	.60
2714	A2100	130y multi	2.10	.60
a.		Pair, #2713-2714	5.00	1.75
	Nos. 2709-2714 (6)		11.20	3.20

Central and Pacific Baseball Leagues, 50th Anniv. — A2101

Mascots wearing uniforms of: a, Yokohama Bay Stars. b, Chunichi Dragons. c, Seibu Lions. d, Nippon Ham Fighters. e, Yomiuri Giants. f, Yakult Swallows g, Orix Blue Wave. h, Fukuoka Daiei Hawks. i, Hiroshima Toyo Carp. j, Hanshin Tigers. k, Kintetsu Buffaloes. l, Chiba Lotte Marines.

1999, Oct. 22   Die Cut
Self-Adhesive
2715	A2101	Sheet of 12		18.00	
a.-l.		80y any single		1.40	.35

Natl. Science Council, 50th Anniv. — A2102

1999, Oct. 28   Perf. 13x13¼
2716	A2102	80y multi		1.40	.35

Cultural Pioneers Types of 1992-98
No. 2717, Hokusai (1760-1849), painter. No. 2718: Yasunari Kawabata (1899-1972), writer. No. 2719, Shoen Uemura (1875-1949), painter.

1999, Nov. 4   Photo.   Perf. 12¾x13
2717	A1645	80y multi	1.40	.35
	Photo. & Engr.			
	Perf. 13			
2718	A1645	80y multi	1.40	.35
2719	A2053	80y multi	1.40	.35
	Nos. 2717-2719 (3)		4.20	1.05

Reign of Emperor Akihito, 10th Anniv. A2103

Designs: No. 2720, Paulownia and bamboo crest. No. 2721, Phoenix crest.

1999, Nov. 12   Photo.   Perf. 12¼
2720	A2103	80y red & multi	1.40	.35
2721	A2103	80y yel & multi	1.40	.35
a.		Souvenir sheet, #2720-2721	3.00	3.00

A2104

A2105

A2106

A2107

New Year 2000 (Year of the Dragon)

1999, Nov. 15   Perf. 13x13¼
2722	A2104	50y multi	.90	.35
2723	A2105	80y multi	1.40	.40
	Perf. 13¼			
2724	A2106	50y +3y multi	.90	.40
2725	A2107	80y +3y multi	1.40	.50

Sheets of 2 containing Nos. 2722-2723 were lottery prizes. Value $2.50.

子どもの本の日／国際子ども図書館開館記念

Children's Book Day — A2108

a, Flower with child reading, bird in flight. b, Flower with child reading, bird perched. c, Child, left half of new Intl. Library of Children's Literature. d, Child, right half of library. e, Butterfly with child's head. f, Two children, library.

Perf. 12¾x13¼

2000, Mar. 31   **Photo.**

2726	A2108	Sheet of 10, #e-f, 2 each #a-d	17.50 17.50
a.-f.		80y any single	1.40 .35

Seishu Hanaoka (1760-1835), Physician, and Flower — A2109

2000, Apr. 11   **Perf. 12¾x13**

2727	A2109	80y multi	1.40 .35

Japan Surgical Society, 100th congress.

Japan-Netherlands Relations, 400th Anniv. — A2110

2000, Apr. 19   **Perf. 13**

2728	80y multi	1.40 .35
2729	80y multi	1.40 .35
a.	A2110 Pair, #2728-2729	3.00 1.50

Dragon and Tiger by Gaho Hashimoto — A2112

2000, Apr. 20   **Perf. 13¼**

2730	80y multi	1.40 .40
2731	80y multi	1.40 .40
a.	A2112 Pair, #2730-2731	3.25 2.50

Philately week.

Natl. Land Afforestation Campaign — A2114

2000, Apr. 21   **Perf. 13¼**

2732	A2114	50y multi	.90 .40

Phila Nippon 2001, Tokyo — A2115

Designs: a, Wild goose (dull green frame background). b, Wagtail (dull violet frame background). c, Goshawk (dull rose frame background). d, A Girl Blowing Glass Toy, by Utamaro. e, Kabuki Actor Ebizo Ichikawa, by Sharaku. f, Flowers. g, Dog and cat. h, Children with pen and envelope (blue background). i, Child with clown. j, Children with pen and envelope (red background).

2000, May 19   **Photo.**   **Die Cut**

Self-Adhesive

2733	A2115	Sheet of 10, #a-j	17.50
a.-j.		80y any single	1.40 .55

Kyushu-Okinawa Summit — A2116

2000, June 21   **Photo.**   **Perf. 12¾x13**

2734	80y multi	1.40 .35
2735	80y multi	1.40 .35
a.	A2116 Pair, #2734-2735	3.00 1.50

A2117

2000, June 30

2736	80y Three flowers	1.40 .35
2737	80y Two flowers	1.40 .35
a.	A2117 Pair, #2736-2737	3.00 1.50

Crime Prevention Campaign, 50th anniv.

Letter Writing Day Type of 1998

Designs: No. 2738, Girl with bows in hair, pen. No. 2739, Birds, house, letter. No. 2740, Clown with red hat, open envelope. No. 2741, Boy reading letter, puppy.

No. 2742: a, Child, dog, in basket. b, Apple tree, flower (circular stamp). c, Parrots holding envelope (elliptical stamp). d, Bicycle, rabbit, flower (oval stamp). e, Boy, girl, dove. f, Girl, letter, snail, porcupine (oval stamp). g, Child playing harp. h, Child playing recorder. i, Child playing bass (semicircular stamp). j, Girl with blue hat, pen, birds holding envelope.

2000, July 21   **Perf. 12¾x13¼**

2738	A2047	50y multi	.90 .35
2739	A2047	50y multi	.90 .35
2740	A2047	50y multi	.90 .35
2741	A2047	50y multi	.90 .35
a.		Strip of 4, #2738-2741	4.00 4.00
2742		Sheet of 10	17.50 17.50
a.-j.	A2047	80y Any single	1.40 .40
k.		Booklet pane, #2738-2741, 2742g, 2742h, 2 #2742e, 2742j	14.50
		Booklet, #2742k	14.50
l.		Souvenir sheet, #2739, 2742e	2.50 2.50

No. 2742b is 30mm in diameter, No. 2742c is 23x34mm, Nos. 2742d, 2742f are 28x40mm, and No. 2742i is 24x40mm.

Women's Private Higher Education, Cent. — A2118

2000, Sept. 22   **Photo.**   **Perf. 13**

2743	A2118	80y multi	1.40 .35

Intl. Letter Writing Week — A2119

Artwork by Hiroshige: 90y, Okabe. 110y, Maisaka. 130y, Okazaki.

2000, Oct. 6   **Perf. 13¼**

2744	A2119	90y multi	1.60 .50
2745	A2119	110y multi	2.00 .60
2746	A2119	130y multi	2.25 .65
	Nos. 2744-2746 (3)		5.85 1.75

See Nos. 2791-2793, 2835-2837, 2865-2867, 2904-2906, 2938-2940, 2999-3001, 3064-3066.

Cultural Pioneers Type of 1998 and

Ukichiro Nakaya (1900-62), Snow Crystal Researcher A2120

Designs: No. 2747, Hantaro Nagaoka (1865-1950), physicist. No. 2748, Teijo Nakamura (1900-88), poet.

Photo. & Engr.

2000, Nov. 6   **Perf. 13**

2747	A2053	80y multi	1.40 .35
2748	A2053	80y multi	1.40 .35
2749	A2120	80y multi	1.40 .35
	Nos. 2747-2749 (3)		4.20 1.05

See No. 2841.

A2121   A2122

New Year 2001 (Year of the Snake)

A2123   A2124

2000, Nov. 15   **Photo.**   **Perf. 13x13¼**

2750	A2121	50y multi	.90 .35
2751	A2122	80y multi	1.40 .40

Perf. 13¼x13½

2752	A2123	50y +3y multi	.95 .40
2753	A2124	80y +3y multi	1.50 .50
	Nos. 2750-2753 (4)		4.75 1.65

Sheets of 2, Nos. 2750-2751, were lottery prizes.

Diet, 110th Anniv. — A2125

2000, Nov. 29   **Perf. 13**

2754	A2125	80y multi	1.40 .35

Internet Expo 2001 — A2126

2001, Jan. 5   **Perf. 13x13¼**

2755		80y Denom. at L	1.40 .35
2756		80y Denom. at R	1.40 .35
a.	A2126	Pair, #2755-2756	3.00 1.50

Intl. Volunteers Year — A2127

2001, Jan. 17   **Perf. 13½x13¼**

2757	A2127	80y multi	1.40 .35

Administrative Scriveners System, 50th Anniv. — A2128

2001, Feb. 22   **Photo.**   **Perf. 13¼**

2758	A2128	80y multi	1.40 .35

World Heritage Sites

Sheet 1 — A2129

Sheet 2 — A2130

Sheet 3 — A2131

Sheet 4 — A2132

Sheet 5 — A2133

Sheet 6 — A2134

No. 2759 — Nikko: a, Bridge (stamp 1). b, Shrine with pillars in foreground (stamp 2). c, Temple gate (stamp 3). d, Dragon (stamp 4). e, Peacock (stamp 5). f, Cat (stamp 6). g, Statue of blue green figure (stamp 7). h, Statue of red figure (stamp 8). i, Shrine (stamp 9). j, Shrine and walkways (stamp 10).

No. 2760 — Itsukushima: a, Marodo Jinjya and pillar in water (stamp 1). b, Marodo Jinjya (stamp 2). c, Honsha (shrine entrance with steps, stamp 3). d, Koma-inu (lion statue, stamp 4). e, Marodo Jinjya and Gojyuno-tou (stamp 5). f, Bugakumen (sculpture with blue water background, stamp 6). g, Kazari-uma (horse statue, stamp 7). h, Noubutai (building with brown eaves, stamp 8). i, Tahoutou (building with cherry blossoms, stamp 9). j, Oomoto Jinjya (building with red fence, stamp 10).

No. 2761 — Kyoto: a, Hosodono Hall, Maidono Hall and Tsuchinoya Hall, Kamowakeikazuchi Shrine (buildings with cones in foreground, stamp 1). b, Romon Gate, Kamowakeikazuchi Shrine (building with stream, stamp 2). c, East Main Hall, Kamomioya Shrine (building with guardian dog statue on landing, stamp 3). d, Guardian dog statue, Kamomioya Shrine (stamp 4). e, South Great Gate and 5-Story Pagoda (deep blue sky, stamp 5). f, Fukuu Joju Nyorai Statue, Toji Temple (gold statue, stamp 6). g, Nyoirin Kannon, Toji Temple (painting, stamp 7). h, Daiitoku Myoo Statue, Toji Temple (stone statue, stamp 8). i, West Gate, 3-Story Pagoda, Kiyomizudera Temple (red gate and temple, stamp 9). j, Main Hall, Kiyomizudera Temple (building with cherry blooosms, stamp 10).

No. 2762 — Kyoto: a, Konpon Chudo Hall, Enryakuji Temple (roof, stamp 1). b, Eternal Flame, Enryakuji Temple (stamp 2). c, Ninai-do Hall, Enryakuji Temple (building with large trees in foreground, stamp 3). d, Sanbo-in Temple Garden, Daigoji Temple (building, one end of small bridge, stamp 4). e, Sanbo-in Temple Garden (end of bridge, trees, stamp 5). f, 5-Story Pagoda, Daigoji Temple (white sky, stamp 6). g, Goten, Ninnaji Temple (buildings with walkways, stamp 7). h, 5-Story Pagoda (cherry trees in foreground, stamp 8). i, Phoenix Hall, Byodoin Temple (black sky, stamp 9). j, Wooden carving of Bodhisattvas Floating on Clouds, Byodoin Temple (stamp 10).

No. 2763 — Kyoto: a, Ujikami Shrine (low fence around shrine with denomination at UL, stamp 1). b, Kaeru Mata, Ujikami Shrine (thin, crossing diagonal strips, stamp 2). c, Front approach to Kozanji Temple (walkway of square panels, stamp 3). d, Sekisuiin, Kozanji Temple (yellow tree blossoms in front of temple, stamp 4). e, Kasumijima Garden, Saihoji Temple (moss-covered bridge, stamp 5) f, Kojokan Garden, Saihoji Temple (Stone stairs and rocks, stamp 6). g, View of garden and pond from under roof, Tenryuji Temple (denomination at left, stamp 7). h, View of garden and pond from under roof, Tenryuji Temple (denomination at right, stamp 8). i, Rokuonji Temple in autumn (Building on lake, green leaves on trees, stamp 9). j, Rokuonji Temple in winter (snow covered roofs and trees, stamp 10).

No. 2764 — Kyoto: a, Snow-covered Silver Pavilion, Jishoji Temple (stamp 1). b, Silver Pavilion without snow (stamp 2). c, Moss-covered rock, Hojo Garden, Ryoanji Temple (stamp 3). d, Rock and snow, Hojo Garden (stamp 4). e, Karamon, Honganji Temple (gate with curved roof, stamp 5). f, Hiunkaku, Honganji Temple (building near pond, stamp 6). g, Shoin, Honganji Temple (wall with landscape, stamp 7). h, Ninomaur Palace, Nijo Castle (roof with chrysanthemum crest at peak, stamp 8). i, Detail from "Hawks on Pine," Nijo Castle (hawk looking left, stamp 9). j, Detail from "Hawks on Pine," Nijo Castle (hawk looking down, stamp 10).

2001		Photo.	Perf. 13x13¼	
2759	A2129	Sheet of 10	18.00	18.00
a.-j.		80y Any single	1.40	.55
2760	A2130	Sheet of 10	18.00	18.00
a.-j.		80y Any single	1.40	.55
2761	A2131	Sheet of 10	18.00	18.00
a.-j.		80y Any single	1.40	.55
2762	A2132	Sheet of 10	18.00	18.00
a.-j.		80y Any single	1.40	.55
2763	A2133	Sheet of 10	18.00	18.00
a.-j.		80y Any single	1.40	.55
2764	A2134	Sheet of 10	18.00	18.00
a.-j.		80y Any single	1.40	.55

Issued: No. 2759, 2/23; No. 2760, 3/23; No. 2761, 6/22; No. 2762, 8/23. No. 2763, 12/21. No. 2764, 2/22/02.

Sheet numbers are in center of colored rectangles at top of sheet. Stamp numbers are in sheet margins.

Exhibit of Italian Art at Museum of Western Art, Tokyo — A2135

Designs: 80y, Show emblem. No. 2766, Angel, from The Annunciation, by Botticelli. No. 2767, Virgin Mary, from The Annunciation.

2001, Mar. 19		Photo.	Perf. 13	
2765	A2135	80y multi	1.40	.35

Size: 33x44mm
Perf. 13¼

2766	A2135	110y multi	1.90	.55
2767	A2135	110y multi	1.90	.55
a.		Pair, #2766-2767	5.00	3.00
		Nos. 2765-2767 (3)	5.20	1.45

Japanese Dermatological Association, 100th Annual Meeting — A2136

2001, Apr. 6			Perf. 13¼	

Color of Triangle Behind "0" in Denomination

2768	A2136	80y pink	1.40	.35
2769	A2136	80y orange	1.40	.35
2770	A2136	80y yellow	1.40	.35
2771	A2136	80y green	1.40	.35
2772	A2136	80y blue	1.40	.35
a.		Vert. strip of 5, #2768-2772	7.50	5.00

Depositing Mail, by Senseki Nakamura A2137

2001, Apr. 20			Perf. 13x13¼	
2773	A2137	80y multi	1.40	.35

Philately Week, Cent. of red cylindrical mailboxes.

Membership in UNESCO, 50th Anniv. — A2138

2001, July 2			Perf. 13¼	
2774	A2138	80y multi	1.40	.35

9th FINA World Swimming Championships, Fukuoka A2139

Designs: No. 2775, Swimming race. No. 2776, Synchronized swimming. No. 2777, Diving. No. 2778, Water polo.

2001, July 16			Perf. 13x13¼	
2775	A2139	80y multi	1.40	.35
2776	A2139	80y multi	1.40	.35
2777	A2139	80y multi	1.40	.35
2778	A2139	80y multi	1.40	.35
a.		Horiz. strip of 4, #2775-2778	6.00	6.00

Letter Writing Day Type of 1998

Designs: No. 2779, Three rabbits, tulip background. No. 2780, Girl with pencil, pencil background. No. 2781, Boy with envelope, bird background. No. 2782, Girl, flower background.

No. 2783: a, Girl with rabbit, bird, flower (oval stamp). b, Bird in tree (circular stamp). c, Boy with pen behind back. d, Girl with envelope and dog. e, Girl on bicycle, flowers (semi-circular stamp). f, Flowers, bird with envelope, insect (circular stamp). g, Bird flying, bird on roof. h, Chicken, chicks, pig (oval stamp). i, Rabbit, flowers (elliptical stamp). j, Boy with hat, rabbit (oval stamp).

2001, July 23			Perf. 13x13¼	
2779	A2047	50y multi	.90	.30
2780	A2047	50y multi	.90	.30
2781	A2047	50y multi	.90	.30
2782	A2047	50y multi	.90	.30
a.		Horiz. strip of 4, #2779-2782	4.00	4.00
2783		Sheet of 10	15.00	15.00
a.-j.		A2047 50y Any single	1.40	.35
k.		Booklet pane, #2779-2782, 2 each #2783c, 2783d, 2783g	13.50	
		Booklet, #2783k	14.00	
l.		Souvenir sheet, #2780, 2783g	2.50	2.50

Phila Nippon '01 (Nos. 2783, 2783l). Nos. 2783a and 2783e are 35x29mm; Nos. 2783b and 2783f are 29mm in diameter; No. 2783h is 40x28mm; No. 2783i is 35x23mm; No. 2783j is 34x28mm.

On No. 2783e, the bicycle appears in the selvage below the stamp.

Phila Nippon '01 — A2140

Art: a, Oniji Otani as Edobei (striped kimono), by Sharaku. b, Hanshiro Iwai as Shigenoi (flowered kimono, facing left), by Sharaku. c, Hangoro Sakata as Mizuemon Fujikawa (brown kimono), by Sharaku. d, Kikunojo Segawa as Oshizu, Bunzo Tanabe's Wife (kimono with stars), by Sharaku. e, Omezo Ichikawa as Ippei Yakko (with sword), by Sharaku. f, Beauty Looking Back (flowered kimono), by Moronobu Hishikawa. g, A Girl Whistling a Vidro (checkered kimono), by Utamaro. h, Nishiki Fuzoku Higashino Returning From a Bathhouse in the Rain (with umbrella), by Kiyonaga Torii. i, Kumesaburo Iwai as Chiyo (blue background), by Kunimasa Utagawa. j, Komazo Ichikawa as Ganryu Sasaki (with sword), by Toyokuni Utagawa.

2001, Aug. 1   **Perf. 13**
2784	A2140	Sheet of 10+10 labels	12.50 12.50
a.-e.		50y Any single	.90 .50
f.-j.		80y Any single	1.40 .50

Labels could be personalized by customers at Phila Nippon stamp exhibition.

2001 World Games, Akita — A2141

Designs: No. 2785, Fishing, Frisbee throwing. No. 2786, Aerobics, billiards. No. 2787, Life saving, water skiing. No. 2788, Body building, tug-of-war.

2001, Aug. 16   **Perf. 13**
2785	A2141	50y multi	.90 .30
2786	A2141	50y multi	.90 .30
a.		Pair, #2785-2786	1.90 1.00
2787	A2141	80y multi	1.40 .35
2788	A2141	80y multi	1.40 .35
a.		Pair, #2787-2788	3.00 1.50
		Nos. 2785-2788 (4)	4.60 1.30

Phila Nippon '01 — A2142

Designs: a, Hanshiro Iwai as Shigenoi (figure with stick in hair), by Sharaku. b, Oniji Otani as Edobei (figure with fingers splayed), by Sharaku. c, Mandarin duck in water. d, White-eye on branch. e, Children with letters. f, Kumesaburo Iwai as Chiyo (lilac background), by Kunimasa Utagawa. g, Komazo Ichikawa as Ganryu Sasaki (brown background), by Toyokuni Utagawa. h, Turtledove (blue background). i, Greater pied kingfisher (green background). j, Japan #1.

2001, Aug. 1   **Photo.**   **Die Cut**
Self-Adhesive
2789	A2142	Sheet of 10	14.00
a.-e.		50y Any single	.90 .30
f.-j.		80y Any single	1.40 .35

San Francisco Peace Treaty, 50th Anniv. — A2143

2001, Sept. 7   **Perf. 13**
2790	A2143	80y multi	1.40 .35

Intl. Letter Writing Week Type of 2000

Hiroshige paintings from 53 Stations of the Tokaido: 90y, Hara. 110y, Oiso. 130y, Sakanoshita.

2001, Oct. 5   **Perf. 13¼**
2791	A2119	90y multi	1.40 .50
2792	A2119	110y multi	1.90 .55
2793	A2119	130y multi	2.10 .60
		Nos. 2791-2793 (3)	5.40 1.65

Town Safety Campaign — A2144

Designs: No. 2794, Boy, duck chicks, owl, frogs, insects. No. 2795, Girl, dogs, cats, birds, insects.

2001, Oct. 11   **Perf. 13x13¼**
2794		80y multi	1.40 .35
2795		80y multi	1.40 .35
a.		A2144 Horiz. pair, #2794-2795	3.00 1.50

1st National Games for the Disabled — A2145

Designs: No. 2796, Disc throwing. No. 2797, Wheelchair race.

2001, Oct. 26   **Perf. 12¾x13**
2796		80y multi	1.40 .35
2797		80y multi	1.40 .35
a.		A2145 Horiz. pair, #2796-2797	3.00 1.50

Norinaga Motoori (1730-1801), Physician, Scholar — A2146   Gidayu Takemoto (1651-1714), Joruri Chanter — A2147

Photo. & Engr.

2001, Nov. 5   **Perf. 12¾x13**
2798	A2146	80y multi	1.40 .35
2799	A2147	80y multi	1.40 .35

Commercial Broadcasting, 50th Anniv. — A2148

2001, Nov. 15   **Photo.**
2800	A2148	80y multi	1.40 .35

A2149   A2150

New Year 2002 (Year of the Horse)

A2151   A2152

2001, Nov. 15   **Perf. 13x13¼**
2801	A2149	50y multi	.90 .30
2802	A2150	80y multi	1.40 .35

Perf. 13¼x13½
2803	A2151	50y +3y multi	.95 .40
2804	A2152	80y +3y multi	1.50 .50
		Nos. 2801-2804 (4)	4.75 1.55

Sheets of two containing Nos. 2801-2802 were lottery prizes.

Legal Aid System, 50th Anniv. — A2153

2002, Jan. 24   **Perf. 12¾x13**
2805	A2153	80y multi	1.40 .35

Japan — Mongolia Diplomatic Relations, 30th Anniv. — A2154

2002, Feb. 15
2806	A2154	80y multi	1.40 .35

Lions Clubs in Japan, 50th Anniv. — A2155

2002, Mar. 1   **Photo.**   **Perf. 13x13¼**
2807	A2155	80y multi	1.40 .35

2002 World Figure Skating Championships, Nagano — A2156

2002, Mar. 8
2808		80y Men's Singles	1.40 .90
2809		80y Pairs	1.40 .90
a.		A2156 Horiz. pair, #2808-2809	3.00 1.90

Diplomatic Relations Anniversaries A2157

Designs: No. 2810, Taj Mahal, India. No. 2811, Sculpture of "Priest King," Mohenjo Daro excavations, Pakistan. No. 2812, Sigiriya goddess, Lion's Rock, Sri Lanka. No. 2813, Carving from Buddhist Vihara, Paharpur, Bangladesh.

2002, Apr. 12
2810	A2157	80y multi	1.40 .40
2811	A2157	80y multi	1.40 .40
2812	A2157	80y multi	1.40 .40
2813	A2157	80y multi	1.40 .40
		Nos. 2810-2813 (4)	5.60 1.60

Japanese diplomatic relations with India, 50th anniv. (No. 2810); Pakistan, 50th anniv. (No. 2811). Sri Lanka, 50th anniv. (No. 2812), and Bangladesh, 30th anniv. (No. 2813).

Philately Week — A2158

Folding screen panels depicting horse racing scenes: No. 2814, Denomination at bottom. No. 2815, Denomination at top.

2002, Apr. 19   **Perf. 13¼**
2814		80y multi	1.40 .40
2815		80y multi	1.40 .40
a.		A2158 Horiz. pair, #2814-2815	3.00 1.75

Fulbright Exchange Program, 50th Anniv. — A2159

2002, May 8   **Perf. 12¾x13**
2816	A2159	80y multi	1.40 .35

Return of Okinawa, 30th Anniv. — A2160

2002, May 15   **Perf. 13x13¼**
2817	A2160	80y multi	1.40 .35

2002 World Cup Soccer Championships, Japan and Korea — A2161

2002, May 24

2818	80y	Soccer field	1.40	.35
2819	80y	World Cup	1.40	.35
a.	A2161	Horiz. pair, #2818-2819	3.00	1.75

Nos. 2818-2819 were issued in sheets of 10 stamps, containing five of each. Thirteen different sheet margins exist.

World Heritage Sites

Sheet 7 — A2162

No. 2820 — Todaiji and Koufukuji Temples, Nara: a, Great Buddha Hall, Todaiji Temple (stamp 1). b, Underside of roof of Nandaimon Gate, Todaiji Temple (stamp 2). c, Engraving on lotus petal, Todaiji Temple (stamp 3). d, Head of Koumokuten, Todaiji Temple (stamp 4). e, Hokkedo Hall and steps, Todaiji Temple (stamp 5). f, Five-story pagoda, Koufukuji Temple (stamp 6). g, Hokuendo Hall (with roof ornament), Koufukuji Temple (stamp 7). h, Ashura (statue with four arms), Koufukuji Temple (stamp 8). i, Head of Buddha, Koufukuji Temple (stamp 9). j, Ogre under dragon lantern, Koufukuji Temple (stamp 10).

2002 Photo. Perf. 13x13¼

2820	A2162	Sheet of 10	16.00	16.00
a.-j.		80y Any single	1.40	.55

Issued: No. 2820, 6/21.
Numbers have been reserved for additional sheets. Sheet numbers are in center of colored rectangle at top of sheet. Stamp numbers are in sheet margins.

World Heritage Series

Sheet 8 — A2163

Sheet 9 — A2164

Sheet 10 — A2165

No. 2821 — Nara: a, Covered passageway, Kasuga Taisha Shrine (stamp 1). b, Chumon, Kasuga Taisha Shrine (stamp 2). c, Deer in Kasuga-yama Primeval Forest (stamp 3). d, Gokurakubo Zenshitsu and Gokurakubo Hondo, Gango-ji Temple (stamp 4). e, Gokurakubo Five-story Pagoda, Gango-ji Temple (stamp 5). f, East and West Pagodas, Yakushi-ji Temple (stamp 6). g, Yakushi Nyorai (seated Buddha), Yakushi-ji Temple (stamp 7). h, Golden Hall, Toshodai-ji Temple (stamp 8). i, Senju Kannon Ryu-zo (standing image with hands together of Thousand-handed Goddess of Mercy), Toshodai-ji Temple (stamp 9). j, Suzakumon Gate, Heijo Imperial Palace (stamp 10).

No. 2822 — Villages of Shirakawa-go and Gokayama: a, House with large tree at left,

Ogimachi (stamp 1). b, Two houses, trees in fall colors Ogimachi (stamp 2). c, House with flowers, Ogimachi (stamp 3). d, Myozen-ji Temple and house, Ogimachi (stamp 4). e, Two houses covered in snow at night, Ogimachi (stamp 5). f, Neighborhood of houses, Ainokura (stamp 6). g, Sonen-ji Temple with stone wall, Ainokura (stamp 7). h, Two houses, Ainokura (stamp 8). i, House with shrub in front, Suganuma (stamp 9). j, House covered in snow, Suganuma (stamp 10).

No. 2823 — Gusuku Sites of the Ryukyu Kingdom: a, Stone lion at royal mausoleum (stamp 1). b, Three steps and stone gate to Sonohyan'utaki Sanctuary (stamp 2). c, Cherry blossoms and ruins of Nakijinjou Castle (stamp 3). d, Steps and stone gate at ruins of Zakimijou Castle (stamp 4). e, Ruins of Katsurenjou Castle walls (stamp 5). f, Ruins of Nakagusukujou Castle citadel (walls with gate, stamp 6). g Kankaimon, main gate of Shurijou Castle (stamp 7). h, Main hall of Shurijou Castle (red building, stamp 8). i, Shikina'en, royal garden (stamp 9). j, Seifautaki Sanctuary (niche in rocks, stamp 10).

2002 Photo. Perf. 13x13¼

2821	A2163	Sheet of 10	16.00	16.00
a.-j.		80y Any single	1.40	.55
2822	A2164	Sheet of 10	16.00	16.00
a.-j.		80y Any single	1.40	.55
2823	A2165	Sheet of 10	16.00	16.00
a.-j.		80y Any single	1.40	.55

Issued: No. 2821, 7/23; No. 2822, 9/20; No. 2823, 12/20. Sheet numbers are in center of colored rectangle at top of sheet. Stamp numbers are in sheet margins.

Letter Writing Day Type of 1998

Designs: No. 2824, Girl with bows in hair holding envelope. No. 2825, Monkey in tree holding envelope. No. 2826, House and flowers. No. 2827, Boy with arms raised, fence.

No. 2828: a, Cow and bird (triangular stamp). b, Boy and sheep (elliptical stamp). c, Caterpillar and ladybug under magnifying glass (round stamp). d, Girl with bows in hair, flowers (oval stamp). e, Boy with soccer ball. f, Girl with tennis racquet and ball. g, Man on bicycle. h, Girl with flower in vase (round stamp). i, Truck and automobile. j, Woman holding gift and coat, boy holding envelope

Perf. 13x13¼, 13 (#2828a)

2002, July 23 Photo.

2824	A2047	50y multi	.90	.40
2825	A2047	50y multi	.90	.40
2826	A2047	50y multi	.90	.40
2827	A2047	50y multi	.90	.40
a.		Strip of 4, #2824-2827	4.00	2.75
2828		Sheet of 10	16.00	16.00
a.-j.	A2047	80y Any single	1.40	.45
k.		Booklet pane, #2824-2827, 3 each #2828g, 2828j	16.00	
		Booklet, #2828k	16.00	
l.		Souvenir sheet, #2825, 2828j	2.50	2.50

No. 2828a is 34x28mm; No. 2828b is 29x26mm; No. 2828c is 29mm in diameter; No. 2828d is 28x40mm; Nos. 2828e and 2828f are 22x36mm; No. 2828h is 28mm in diameter; No. 2828i is 25x25mm.

12th World Congress of Psychiatry, Yokohama — A2166

2002, Aug. 1 Photo. Perf. 12¾x13

2829	A2166	80y multi	1.40	.35

World Wheelchair Basketball Championships, Kitakyushu — A2167

2002, Aug. 9

2830	A2167	80y multi	1.40	.35

Civil Aviation, 50th Anniv. — A2168

2002, Sept. 6

2831	A2168	80y multi	1.40	.35

Normalization of Diplomatic Relations Between Japan and People's Republic of China, 30th Anniv. — A2169

Designs: No. 2832, Purple wisteria flowers. No. 2833, Goldfish and cherry blossoms.

2002, Sept. 13 Perf. 13x13¼

2832		80y multi	1.40	.55
2833		80y multi	1.40	.55
a.	A2169	Horiz. pair, #2832-2833	3.00	2.50

Intl. Fleet Review, Tokyo Bay — A2170

2002, Oct. 1

2834	A2170	80y multi	1.40	.40

Letter Writing Week Type of 2000

Hiroshige paintings from 53 Stations of the Tokaido Highway: 90y, Yui. 110y, Shono. 130y, Tozuka.

2002, Oct. 7 Perf. 13¼

2835	A2119	90y multi	1.40	.50
2836	A2119	110y multi	1.90	.55
2837	A2119	130y multi	2.10	.60
	Nos. 2835-2837 (3)		5.40	1.65

Asian and Pacific Decade of Disabled Persons — A2171

2002, Oct. 10 Perf. 12¾x13

2838	A2171	80y multi	1.40	.40

Cultural Pioneers Types of 1998-2000

Designs: No. 2839, Shiki Masaoka (1867-1902), poet. No. 2840, Ookawabata Yusuzumi-zu, by Kiyonaga Torii (1752-1815), artist. No. 2841, Aikitu Tanakadate (1856-1952), physicist.

Photo. & Engr., Photo. (#2840)

2002, Nov. 5 Perf. 13

2839	A2053	80y multi	1.40	.40
2840	A2053	80y multi	1.40	.40
2841	A2120	80y multi	1.40	.40
	Nos. 2839-2841 (3)		4.20	1.20

A2172   A2173

New Year 2003 (Year of the Ram)

A2174   A2175

2002, Nov. 15   Photo.   Perf. 13x13¼
2842 A2172 50y multi   .90   .40
2843 A2173 80y multi   1.40   .45
               Perf. 13½x13¼
2844 A2174 50y +3y multi   1.00   .55
2845 A2175 80y +3y multi   1.60   .65
       Nos. 2842-2845 (4)   4.90   2.05

Sheets of two containing Nos. 2842-2843 were lottery prizes.

Kabuki, 400th Anniv. — A2176

Designs: No. 2846, Shibaraku and Tsuchigumo. No. 2847, Okuni Kabuki-zu, detail from painted screen.

2003, Jan. 15   Photo.   Perf. 13x13¼
2846   80y multi   1.40   .50
2847   80y multi   1.40   .50
  a. A2176 Horiz. pair, #2846-2847 3.50 2.00

Japanese Television, 50th Anniv.
A2177   A2178

2003, Jan. 31
2848 A2177 80y multi   1.40   .40
2849 A2178 80y multi   1.40   .40

A2179

Greetings — A2180

No. 2850: a, Roses. b, Reindeer. c, Cat and butterfly. d, Rabbits in automobile. e, White flowers.
No. 2851: a, Heart and flower. b, Dog with noisemaker. c, Bird and snowman. d, Bird and strawberries. e, Cranes and turtle.

2003, Feb. 10   Die Cut Perf. 13½
Self-Adhesive
2850 A2179 Pane of 5 + 5 labels   10.00 10.00
  a.-e. 80y Any single   1.40   .75
2851 A2180 Pane of 5 + 5 labels   10.00 10.00
  a.-e. 80y Any single   1.40   .75

World Heritage Series

Sheet 11 — A2181

No. 2852 — Hiroshima buildings and stamps on theme of "Peace": a, Atomic Bomb Dome (stamp 1). b, Hiroshima Prefectural Commercial Exhibit Hall (stamp 2). c, Dove over Atomic Bomb Dome, yellow denomination (stamp 3). d, Child's drawing of person with flower (stamp 4). e, Dove over Atomic Bomb Dome, blue denomination (stamp 5). f, Dove over Atomic Bomb Dome, red denomination (stamp 6). g, Doves, stylized person holding child (stamp 7). h, People on hill (stamp 8). i, Bird (stamp 9). j, Rabbit, butterflies and flowers (stamp 10).

2003, Mar. 20   Photo.   Perf. 13x13¼
2852 A2181 Sheet of 10   16.00 16.00
  a.-j.   80y Any single   1.40   .55

Sheet numbers are in center of colored rectangle at top of sheet. Stamp numbers are in sheet margin.

Inauguration of Japan Post — A2182

No. 2853 — Flowers: a, Adonis (yellow flowers). b, Primrose (pink flowers). c, Violets and Japanese quince (violet and red flowers). d, Field horsetail (flowerless). e, Japanese wisteria (white hanging flowers). f, Weeping cherry tree (pink buds and flowers) and swallow. g, Hydrangea (lilac flowers). h, Japanese magnolia (white and pink flowers). i, Candock (yellow flower) and moorhen. j, Peony (pink flower and bud) and butterfly.

2003, Apr. 1   Die Cut Perf. 13¼
Self-Adhesive
2853 A2182 Sheet of 10   16.00 16.00
  a.-j.   80y Any single   1.40   .55

Japan Post Mascots — A2183

Designs: a, Aichan (squirrel with pink bow). b, Male Kanchan (with heart on shorts). c, Posuton (with hands extended). d, Yuchan (squirrel with cap). e, Female Kanchan (with flower). f, Posuton (with letter). g, Posuton (with letter). h, Aichan (with pink bow), diff. i, Female Kanchan (with flower), diff. j, Posuton (with hands extended), diff. k, Yuchan (with cap), diff. l, Male Kanchan (waving).

2003, Apr. 1   Die Cut Perf. 13¼
Self-Adhesive
2854 A2183 Sheet of 12   16.00 16.00
  a.-f. 50y Any single   .85   .40
  g.-l. 80y Any single   1.25   .55

Ram and Tree
Batik Soroon
Design — A2184

2003, Apr. 18   Perf. 13¼
2855 A2184 80y multi   1.40   .40
       Philately Week.

Edo Shogunate, 400th Anniv.

Screen Depicting   Wall Decoration,
Edo — A2185   Edo
                        Castle — A2186

Armor of Ieyasu   Detail from
Tokugawa   Writing Box
A2187   A2188

Noh Mask and
Costume — A2189

Sheet 2 — A2190

A2191

No. 2857 — Sheet 2: a, Nihonbashi, from 53 Stations of the Tokaido Road, by Hiroshige (stamp 1). b, Fireman's coat (stamp 2). c, Screen depicting Kabuki theater (stamp 3). d, Hina-matsuri fesitval doll of empress (no number). e, Hina-matsuri festival doll of emperor (stamp 4). f, Danjurou Ichikawa playing role of Goro Takenuki (stamp 5).

No. 2858 — Sheet 3: a, Stern of USS Powhatan (stamp 1). b, Bow of USS Powhatan (no number). c, Screen art depicting return of Commodore Perry's fleet to Japan (stamp 2). d, Ceramic platter for export to Europe (stamp 3). e, Portrait of a European Woman, probably by Gennai Hiraga (stamp 4). f, Perpetual clock (stamp 5).

2003   Perf. 13x13¼
2856   Vert. strip of 5   7.00   7.00
  a. A2185 80y multi   1.40   .55
  b. A2186 80y multi   1.40   .55
  c. A2187 80y multi   1.40   .55
  d. A2188 80y multi   1.40   .55
  e. A2189 80y multi   1.40   .55
          Sheet, 2 #2856 (Sheet 1) 16.50 16.50
2857 A2190 Sheet of 10,
             #2857d-
             2857e, 2 each
             #2857a-2857c,
             2857f   16.50 16.50
  a.-f. 80y Any single   1.40   .55
2858 A2191 Sheet of 10,
             #2858a-
             2858b, 2 each
             #2858c-2858f   16.50 16.50
  a.-f. 80y Any single   1.40   .55

Issued: No. 2856, 5/23; No. 2857, 6/12; No. 2858, 7/1. Sheet numbers are in center of arrows at top of sheet. Stamp numbers are in sheet margins.

ASEAN — Japan Exchange
Year — A2192

No. 2859: a, Omar Ali Saifuddien Mosque, Brunei (stamp 1). b, Angkor Wat, Cambodia (stamp 2). c, Borobudur Temple, Indonesia (stamp 3). d, That Luang, Laos (stamp 4). e, Sultan Abdul Samad Building, Malaysia (stamp 5). f, Shwedagon Pagoda, Myanmar (stamp 6). g, Rice terraces, Philippines (stamp 7). h, Merlion Statue, Singapore (stamp 8). i, Wat Phra Kaeo, Thailand (stamp 9). j, Van Mieu, Viet Nam (stamp 10).

2003, June 16   Photo.   Perf. 13x13¼
2859 A2192 Sheet of 10   16.50 16.50
  a.-j.   80y Any single   1.40   .55

Letter Writing
Day — A2193

Designs: No. 2860, Bear with guitar, bird. No. 2861, Monkey with letter. No. 2862, Crocodile with accordion, bird. No. 2863, Cat with camera, letter.
No. 2864: a, Hippopotamus with umbrella, flowers, birds (oval stamp). b, Parakeet with letter. c, Owl (round stamp). d, Bear with letter, bird (oval stamp). e, Elephant with flowers. f, Giraffe with letter (semi-circular stamp). g, Rabbit with letter, flowers (semi-circular stamp). h, Lion with letter, lantern. i, Goat with letter. j, Gorilla with koala, bird and owl.

2003, July 23   Photo.   Perf. 13x13¼
2860 A2193 50y multi   .85   .35
2861 A2193 50y multi   .85   .35
2862 A2193 50y multi   .85   .35
2863 A2193 50y multi   .85   .35
  a.   Horiz. strip of 4, #2860-
        2863   3.50 2.25
2864   Sheet of 10   16.50 16.50
  a.-j. A2193 80y Any single   1.40   .55
  k.   Booklet pane of 10, #2860-
        2863, 2 each #2864b, 2864h,
        2864i   14.00   —
        Complete booklet, #2864k   14.00
  l.   Souvenir sheet, #2860, #2864b 2.50 2.50

Nos. 2864a, 2864d and 2864f are 28x40mm; No. 2864c is 30mm in diameter; No. 2864g is 40x24mm.

Intl. Letter Writing Week Type of 2000

Hiroshige paintings from 53 Stations of the Tokaido Highway: 90y, Kawasaki. 110y, Miya. 130y, Otsu.

2003, Oct. 6   Perf. 13¼
2865 A2119 90y multi   1.60   .45
2866 A2119 110y multi   1.90   .55
2867 A2119 130y multi   2.10   .65
      Nos. 2865-2867 (3)   5.60 1.65

Cultural
Pioneers — A2194

Designs: No. 2868, Mokichi Saito (1882-1953), poet. No. 2869, Shibasaburo Kitasato (1853-1931), bacteriologist.

Photo. & Engr.
2003, Nov. 4   Perf. 13
2868 A2194 80y multi   1.40   .40
2869 A2194 80y multi   1.40   .40
      See Nos. 2907-2909.

Reversion of the
Amami Islands to
Japanese Control,
50th
Anniv. — A2195

2003, Nov. 7   Photo.
2870 A2195 80y multi   1.40   .40

A2196   A2197

New Year 2004 (Year of the
Monkey)
A2198   A2199

2003, Nov. 14   Perf. 13x13¼
2871 A2196 50y multi   .90   .35
2872 A2197 80y multi   1.40   .40

Photo. & Litho.
Perf. 13½x13¼
2873 A2198 50y +3y multi   1.00   .45
2874 A2199 80y +3y multi   1.60   .55
      Nos. 2871-2874 (4)   4.90 1.75

Sheets of two containing Nos. 2871-2872 were lottery prizes.

Happy Face —
A2199a

Sky — A2199b

Serpentine Die Cut 9¼x9
2003, Dec. 1   Photo.
Self-Adhesive
2874A A2199a 80y multi + label   1.90 1.25
Serpentine Die Cut 6½x5½
Stamp + Label
Color of Japanese Inscription
2874B A2199b 80y blue   1.90 1.25
2874C A2199b 80y red orange   1.90 1.25
2874D A2199a 80y white   —
      Nos. 2874A-2874C (3)   5.70 3.75

Stamps and labels are separated by a line of rouletting on Nos. 2874B-2874D. Labels could be personalized. No. 2874A was printed in sheets of 4 stamps and 4 labels that sold for 500y, and sheets of 10 stamps and 10 labels that sold for 1000y. Nos. 2874B-2874C were printed in sheets containing five of each stamp and 10 labels that sold for 1000y. No. 287D was printed in sheets of 10 and 10 labels and sold for 1000y.

Bubbles —
A2199c

Bubbles —
A2199d

Rose —
A2199e

Serpentine Die Cut 6
2004, Jan. 23   Photo.
Self-Adhesive
2874E A2199c 50y multi + label   1.25 1.25
2874F A2199d 50y multi + label   1.25 1.25
2874G A2199e 90y multi + label   2.00 1.50
      Nos. 2874E-2874G (3)   4.50 4.00

Stamps and labels are separated by a line of rouletting. Labels could be personalized. Nos. 2874E-2874F were printed in sheets containing ten of each stamp and 20 labels that sold for 1200y. No. 2874G was printed in a sheet of 20 stamps and 20 labels that sold for 2000y.

Science, Technology and Animation

Astro   Bowman
Boy — A2200   Doll — A2201

Hantaro Nagaoka   H-II Rocket
A2202   A2203

Morph   Astro
3 — A2204   Boy — A2205

Astro   Astro
Boy — A2206   Boy — A2207

Super   Japanese
Jetter — A2208   Clock — A2209

Otomo — A2210   KAZ — A2211

Stratospheric Platform Airship — A2212

Super Jetter — A2213

Super Jetter — A2214

Super Jetter — A2215

2003-2004   Photo.   Perf. 13x13¼

2875	Vert. strip of 5	8.00	8.00
a.	A2200 80y multi	1.40	.55
b.	A2201 80y multi	1.40	.55
c.	A2202 80y multi	1.40	.55
d.	A2203 80y multi	1.40	.55
e.	A2204 80y multi	1.40	.55
	Sheet, 2 #2075	17.50	17.50
2876	Sheet, #2875b-2875e, 2 each #2876a-2876c	17.50	17.50
a.	A2205 80y multi	1.40	.55
b.	A2206 80y multi	1.40	.55
c.	A2207 80y multi	1.40	.55
2877	Vert. strip of 5	8.00	8.00
a.	A2208 80y multi	1.40	.55
b.	A2209 80y multi	1.40	.55
c.	A2210 80y multi	1.40	.55
d.	A2211 80y multi	1.40	.55
e.	A2212 80y multi	1.40	.55
	Sheet, 2 #2875	17.50	17.50
2878	Sheet, #2877b-2877e, 2 each #2878a-2878c	17.50	17.50
a.	A2213 80y multi	1.40	.55
b.	A2214 80y multi	1.40	.55
c.	A2215 80y multi	1.40	.55

Issued: Nos. 2875-2876, 12/16/03; Nos. 2877-2878, 1/23/04.

Science, Technology and Animation

Marvelous Melmo and Baby — A2216

Seishu Hanaoka (1760-1835), Surgeon — A2217

Wooden Microscope A2218

Jokichi Takamine (1854-1922), Chemist A2219

Drug Delivery System — A2220

Marvelous Melmo with Mother — A2221

Marvelous Melmo with Man — A2222

Marvelous Melmo and Others in Bottle — A2223

Science Ninja Team Gatchaman A2224

Proposed Perpetual Motion Machine of Michitaka Kume A2225

OHSUMI Satellite — A2226

Conducting Polymer — A2227

Tissue and Organ Reproduction A2228

Science Ninja Team Gatchaman A2229

Science Ninja Team Gatchaman A2230

Science Ninja Team Gatchaman A2231

2004   Photo.   Perf. 13x13¼

2879	Vert. strip of 5	8.00	8.00
a.	A2216 80y multi	1.40	.55
b.	A2217 80y multi	1.40	.55
c.	A2218 80y multi	1.40	.55
d.	A2219 80y multi	1.40	.55
e.	A2220 80y multi	1.40	.55
	Sheet, 2 #2879	17.50	17.50
2880	Sheet, #2879b-2879e, 2 each #2880a-2880c	17.50	17.50
a.	A2221 80y multi	1.40	.55
b.	A2222 80y multi	1.40	.55
c.	A2223 80y multi	1.40	.55
2881	Vert. strip of 5	8.00	8.00
a.	A2224 80y multi	1.40	.55
b.	A2225 80y multi	1.40	.55
c.	A2226 80y multi	1.40	.55
d.	A2227 80y multi	1.40	.55
e.	A2228 80y multi	1.40	.55
	Sheet, 2 #2881	17.50	17.50
2882	Sheet, #2881b-2881e, 2 each #2882a-2882c	17.50	17.50
a.	A2229 80y multi	1.40	.55
b.	A2230 80y multi	1.40	.55
c.	A2231 80y multi	1.40	.55

Issued: Nos. 2879-2880, 2/23/04. Nos. 2881-2882, 3/23/04.

Hello Kitty

A2232

Hello Kitty — A2233

No. 2883: a, Red, white and blue flowers under chin. b, Red flower under chin, beige background. c, No flower under chin. d, Blue and red flowers under chin. e, Red flower under chin. f, Two blue flowers under chin. g, White flowers with green leaves under chin. h, Two pink flowers under chin. i, One blue flower under chin. j, Pink, yellow and green flower under chin.

No. 2884 — Head of Kitty with: a, Cherries. b, Bow. c, Strawberries. d, Blue flower. e, Spray of flowers.

Die Cut Perf. 13¼

2004, Feb. 6   Litho.
Self-Adhesive

2883	A2232	Sheet of 10	9.50	
a.-j.		50y Any single	.90	.55
2884	A2233	Sheet of 5	8.00	
a.-e.		80y Any single	1.40	.55

Uchu-no Sakura Gohiki-no Saru-zu, by Sosen Mori — A2234

Perf. 12½x12¾ Syncopated

2004, Apr. 20   Photo.

2885	A2234	80y multi	1.40	.45

Philatelic Week.

Japanese Racing Association, 50th Anniv. — A2235

Designs: No. 2886, Ten Point and Tosho Boy, 22nd Armia Memorial Stakes. No. 2007, Narita Brian, 61st Tolyo Yushun.

2004, May 28   Perf. 13x13¼

2886	80y green & multi	1.40	.45
2887	80y blue & multi	1.40	.45
a.	A2235 Horiz. pair, #2886-2887	3.00	2.25

Police Law, 50th Anniv. — A2236

2004, June 21   Perf. 13

2888	80y Police car	1.40	.45
2889	80y Police motorcycle	1.40	.45
a.	A2236 Horiz. pair, #2888-2889	3.00	2.25

Letter Writing Day — A2237

Designs: No. 2890, Donkichi with pencil. No. 2891, Hime (woman with letter). No. 2892, Shouchan (man with ski cap). No. 2893, Owl with letter.

No. 2894: a, Dove with letter, rainbow. b, Squirrel with wings, rainbow. c, Stork (round stamp). d, Hime with wings (oval stamp). e, Donkichi with wings, letter. f, Kuriko (elf in pink) with wings. g, Megami (woman in white) (oval stamp). h, Shouchan with wings. i, Squirrel with flowers, letter. j, Rabbit (round stamp).

2004, July 23 Photo. Perf. 13x13¼
2890	A2237 50y multi	.90	.35
2891	A2237 50y multi	.90	.35
2892	A2237 50y multi	.90	.35
2893	A2237 50y multi	.90	.35
a.	Horiz. strip of 4, #2890-2893	4.00	2.75
2894	Sheet of 10	16.50	16.50
a.-j.	A2237 80y Any single	1.40	.55
k.	Booklet pane of 10, #2890-2893, 2 each #2894b, 2894e, 2894f	14.00	—
	Complete booklet, #2894k	14.00	
l.	Souvenir sheet, #2890, #2894f	2.50	2.50

Nos. 2894c, 2894j are 30mm in diameter; No. 2894d is 28x37mm; No. 2894g is 28x40mm; No. 2894i is 28x29mm.

2004 Summer Olympics, Athens — A2238

Olympic rings and: No. 2895, Olympic Flame, Olympia. No. 2896, 2004 Athens Olympics emblem.

2004, Aug. 6 Perf. 13
2895	80y multi	1.40	.45
2896	80y multi	1.40	.45
a.	A2238 Horiz. pair, #2895-2896	3.00	2.25

Science, Technology and Animation

Mazinger-Z A2239   Steam Locomotive A2240

New KS Steel A2241   Shinkai 6500 Research Submarine A2242

Fuel Cell A2243   Mazinger-Z A2244

Mazinger-Z A2245   Mazinger-Z A2246

2004, Aug. 23 Photo. Perf. 13x13¼
2897	Vert. strip of 5	8.00	8.00
a.	A2239 80y multi	1.40	.55
b.	A2240 80y multi	1.40	.55
c.	A2241 80y multi	1.40	.55
d.	A2242 80y multi	1.40	.55

e.	A2243 80y multi	1.40	.55
	Sheet, 2 #2897	17.50	17.50
2898	Sheet, #2897b-2897e, 2 each #2898a-2898c	17.50	17.50
a.	A2244 80y multi	1.40	.55
b.	A2245 80y multi	1.40	.55
c.	A2246 80y multi	1.40	.55

Science, Technology and Animation

Doraemon A2247   Gennai Hiraga A2248

Mechanical Netsuke A2249   Television A2250

Optical Fiber A2251   Doraemon A2252

Doraemon A2253   Doraemon A2254

2004, Nov. 22 Photo. Perf. 13x13¼
2899	Vert. strip of 5	8.00	8.00
a.	A2247 80y multi	1.40	.55
b.	A2248 80y multi	1.40	.55
c.	A2249 80y multi	1.40	.55
d.	A2250 80y multi	1.40	.55
e.	A2251 80y multi	1.40	.55
	Sheet, 2, #2899	17.50	17.50
2900	Sheet, #2899b-2899e, 2 each #2900a-2900c	17.50	17.50
a.	A2252 80y multi	1.40	.55
b.	A2253 80y multi	1.40	.55
c.	A2254 80y multi	1.40	.55

Japan — United States Relationships, 150th Anniv. — A2255

Designs: No. 2901, Mt. Fuji, by Frederick Harris. No. 2902, Cafe, by Yasuo Kuniyoshi.

2004, Sept. 22 Perf. 13
2901	80y multi	1.40	.50
2902	80y multi	1.40	.50
a.	A2255 Horiz. pair, #2901-2902	3.00	2.25

World Medical Association General Assembly, Tokyo — A2256

2004, Oct. 6 Perf. 12¾x13
2903	A2256 80y multi	1.40	.40

International Letter Writing Week Type of 2000

Hiroshige paintings from 53 Stations of the Tokaido Highway: 90y, Hiratsuka. 110y, Yokkaichi. 130y, Tsuchiyama.

2004, Oct. 8 Perf. 13¼
2904	A2119 90y multi	1.60	.45
2905	A2119 110y multi	1.90	.55
2906	A2119 130y multi	2.10	.65
	Nos. 2904-2906 (3)	5.60	1.65

Cultural Pioneers Type of 2003

Designs: No. 2907, Lafcadio Hearn (1850-1904), writer. No. 2908, Isamu Noguchi (1904-88), sculptor. No. 2909, Masao Koga (1904-78), composer.

Litho. & Engr.

2004, Nov. 4 Perf. 12¾x13
2907	A2194 80y multi	1.40	.40
2908	A2194 80y multi	1.40	.40
2909	A2194 80y multi	1.40	.40
	Nos. 2907-2909 (3)	4.20	1.20

A2257   A2258

New Year 2005 (Year of the Cock) A2259   A2260

2004, Nov. 15 Photo. Perf. 13x13¼
2910	A2257 50y multi	.90	.45
2911	A2258 80y multi	1.40	.55

Photo. & Typo.
Perf. 13½x13¼
2912	A2259 50y +3y multi	1.00	.65
2913	A2260 80y +3y multi	1.60	.75
	Nos. 2910-2913 (4)	4.90	2.40

Miniature Sheet

Eto Calligraphy — A2261

Word "tori" in: a, Tensho style. b, Kinbun style (red). c, Kinbun style (black). d, Pictographic tensho style. e, Kana style. f, Sousho style. g, Kobun style (denomination at UR). h, Reisho style. i, Koukotsumoji style. j, Kobun style (denomination at LR).

Photo. & Embossed
2004, Dec. 1 Perf. 13
2914	A2261 Sheet of 10	17.50	17.50
a.-j.	80y Any single	1.40	.55

"Japan Post" — A2261a

A2261b

A2261c

Rose — A2261d

A2261e

A2261f

Die Cut Perf. 12½

2004, Dec. 15 Photo.

Stamp + Label
Denomination Color

2914K	A2261a	80y rose	2.00	1.25
2914L	A2261a	80y blue	2.00	1.25
2914M	A2261b	80y lilac	2.00	2.00
2914N	A2261c	80y green	2.00	2.00
2914O	A2261d	80y rose	2.00	2.00
2914P	A2261e	80y gray	2.00	2.00
2914Q	A2261f	80y rose	2.00	2.00
	Nos. 2914K-2914Q (7)		14.00	12.50

Stamps and labels are separated by a line of rouletting. Labels could be personalized. Nos. 2914K-2914L were printed in sheets containing five of each stamp and 10 labels that sold for 1000y. Nos. 2914M-2914Q were printed in sheets of two of each stamp and 10 labels that sold for 1000y.

World Conference on Disaster Reduction A2262

2005, Jan. 11 Photo. **Perf. 13**
2915 A2262 80y multi   1.40   .40

Opening of Chubu Natl. Airport — A2263

2005, Feb. 1
2916 A2263 80y multi   1.40   .40

Science, Technology and Animation

Time Bokan — A2264

Circular Loom — A2265

Bullet Train — A2266

Micromachines A2267

International Space Station — A2268

Time Bokan — A2269

Time Bokan — A2270

Time Bokan — A2271

2005, Mar. 23 Photo. **Perf. 13x13¼**

2917		Vert. strip of 5	8.00	8.00
a.	A2264	80y multi	1.40	.55
b.	A2265	80y multi	1.40	.55
c.	A2266	80y multi	1.40	.55
d.	A2267	80y multi	1.40	.55
e.	A2268	80y multi	1.40	.55
		Sheet, 2 #2917	17.50	17.50
2918		Sheet, #2917b-2917e, 2 each #2918a-2918c	17.50	17.50
a.	A2269	80y multi	1.40	.55
b.	A2270	80y multi	1.40	.55
c.	A2271	80y multi	1.40	.55

Pokémon

Gonbe — A2272

Rayquaza A2273

Mew — A2274

Rizadon — A2275

Pikachu — A2276

2005, June 23 Litho. **Perf. 13x13¼**

2919		Vert. strip of 5	6.50	6.50
a.	A2272	50y multi	.90	.55
b.	A2273	50y multi	.90	.55
c.	A2274	80y multi	1.40	.55
d.	A2275	80y multi	1.40	.55
e.	A2276	80y multi	1.40	.55
		Sheet, 2 #2919	14.00	14.00

Self-Adhesive
Booklet Stamps

2919F	A2272	50y multi	1.25	1.00
i.		Booklet pane of 2	3.00	3.00
2919G	A2276	80y multi	1.75	1.25
2919H	A2274	80y multi	1.75	1.25
j.		Booklet pane, #2919G-2919H	4.75	4.75
		Complete booklet, #2919Fi, 2919Hj + 8 postal cards	19.00	

Complete booklet sold for 1000y.

Mobile Suit Gundam

Freedom Gundam and Kira Yamato — A2277

Justice Gundam and Athrun Zala — A2278

Gundam W — A2279

Hiiro — A2280

Kamille Bidan — A2281

Z Gundam
A2282

Zaku — A2283

Char
Aznable — A2284

Amuro
Ray — A2285

Gundam
A2286

2005, Aug. 1

2920		Sheet of 10	17.50	17.50
a.	A2277	50y multi	.90	.55
b.	A2278	50y multi	.90	.55
c.	A2279	50y multi	.90	.55
d.	A2280	50y multi	.90	.55
e.	A2281	80y multi	1.40	.55
f.	A2282	80y multi	1.40	.55
g.	A2283	80y multi	1.40	.55
h.	A2284	80y multi	1.40	.55
i.	A2285	80y multi	1.40	.55
j.	A2286	80y multi	1.40	.55

Expo 2005, Aichi — A2287

Designs: No. 2921, Earth and mammoth skull and tusks. No. 2922, Earth and mammoth.

2005, Mar. 25   Photo.   Perf. 13x13¼

2921		80y multi	1.40	.45
2922		80y multi	1.40	.45
a.	A2287	Horiz. pair, #2921-2922	3.00	2.25

Daikei-shiyu-zu, by Jakuchu
Itou — A2288

Perf. 12½x12¾ Syncopated

2005, Apr. 20

2923	A2288	80y multi	1.40	.45

Philately Week.

Rotary
International,
Cent. — A2289

2005, Apr. 28   Litho.   Perf. 12¾x13

2924	A2289	80y multi	1.40	.40

Hodakadake
A2290

Hakusan-ichige
A2291

Yarigatake
A2292

Miyama-odamaki
A2293

2005, May 2   Perf. 13¼

2925	A2290	50y multi	.90	.40
2926	A2291	50y multi	.90	.40
2927	A2292	50y multi	.90	.40
2928	A2293	50y multi	.90	.40
a.		Horiz. strip of 4, #2925-2928	5.00	5.00

Japanese Alpine Club, cent.

Letter Writing
Day — A2294

Designs: No. 2929, Owl on branch with envelope. No. 2930, Kuriko with letter. No. 2931, Squirrel with acorn. No. 2932, Rabbit and flowers.

No. 2933: a, Pigeon with pink letter. b, Donkichi in tree (round stamp). c, Castle and rainbow (oval stamp). d, Shochan with blue ski cap. e, Rabbit with pink letter (round stamp). f, Kuriko with flute on horse. g, Hime with bows in hair. h, Squirrel. i, Fox with letter (round stamp). j, Violets (oval stamp).

2005, July 22   Photo.   Perf. 13x13¼

2929	A2294	50y multi	.90	.35
2930	A2294	50y multi	.90	.35
2931	A2294	50y multi	.90	.35
2932	A2294	50y multi	.90	.35
a.		Horiz. strip of 4, #2929-2932	5.00	2.75

2933		Sheet of 10	16.50	16.50
a.-j.	A2294	80y Any single	1.40	.55
k.		Booklet pane of 10, #2929-2932, 2 each #2933d, 2933f, 2933g	14.00	—
		Complete booklet, #2933k	14.00	
l.		Souvenir sheet, #2932, #2933d	2.50	2.50

Nos. 2933a, 2933h are 28x29mm, Nos. 2933b, 2933e, 2933i are 30mm in diameter; No. 2933c, 2933j are 28x40mm.

Poetry Collections — A2295

Poets: No. 2934, Ono no Komachi. No. 2935, Fujiwara no Teika.

2005, Sept. 1   Litho.   Perf. 12¾x13

2934		80y multi	1.40	.45
2935		80y multi	1.40	.45
a.	A2295	Horiz. pair, #2934-2935	3.00	2.25

Kokin Wakashu, 1100th anniv. (No. 2934), Shinkokin Wakashu, 800th anniv. (No. 2935).

Intl Astronautics Congress,
Fukuoka — A2296

Designs: No. 2936, Himawari-6 satellite. No. 2937, H-IIA rocket launch.

2005, Oct. 3

2936		80y multi	1.40	.55
2937		80y multi	1.40	.55
a.	A2296	Horiz. pair, #2934-2935	3.00	2.25

Intl. Letter Writing Week Type of 2000

Hiroshige paintings from 53 Stations of the Tokaido Highway: 90y, Mariko. 110y, Minakuchi. 130y, Shinagawa.

2005, Oct. 7   Photo.   Perf. 13¼

2938	A2119	90y multi	1.40	.45
2939	A2119	110y multi	1.60	.55
2940	A2119	130y multi	2.10	.65
		Nos. 2938-2940 (3)	5.10	1.65

Souvenir Sheets

A2297

Greetings Stamps — A2298

No. 2941: a, Cyclamen. b, Elf and flower. c, Bear and bird. d, Owl, gorilla playing banjo. e, Snowman.

No. 2942: a, Santa Claus. b, Poinsettias and candle. c, Angel with gift. d, Hamster and strawberries. e, Owl, cat playing drums.

Litho. With Foil Application
Serpentine Die Cut 13¼

2005, Oct. 21   Self-Adhesive

2941	A2297	Sheet of 5	5.50	
a.-e.		50y Any single	.90	.90

Serpentine Die Cut 13¼x13½

2942	A2298	Sheet of 5	8.50	
a.-e.		80y Any single	1.40	.90

A2299   A2300

New Year 2006 (Year of the Dog)
A2301   A2302

2005, Nov. 15   Photo.   Perf. 13x13¼

2943	A2299	50y multi	.90	.35
2944	A2300	80y multi	1.40	.40

Photo. & Typo.
Perf. 13¼

2945	A2301	50y +3y multi	1.00	.45
2946	A2302	80y +3y multi	1.60	.55
		Nos. 2943-2946 (4)	4.90	1.75

Miniature Sheet

Germany — Japan Exchange
Year — A2303

No. 2947: a, Ludwig van Beethoven. b, Benz automobile. c, Meissen porcelain figurine of Japanese man playing drum. d, Meissen porcelain figurine of female musician. e, Meissen porcelain figurine of woman on circus horse. f, Meissen porcelain figurine of a harlequin.

2005, Dec. 1   Photo.   Perf. 13

2947	A2303	Sheet of 10, #a-b, 2 each #c-f	17.50	17.50
a.-f.		80y Any single	1.40	.55

Miniature Sheet

Eto Calligraphy — A2304

Word "inu" in: a, Tensho style (connected lines). b, Kinbun style (on brown red panel). c, Pictograph (denomination at UL). d, Phonetic letters (2 lines unconnected, denomination at LR). e, Tensho style (2 red chops). f, Tensho style (blue half-circle). g, Symbolic characters (red). h, Semi-cursive style (red chop at L, denomination at LL). i, Semi-cursive style (oval chop in red at L). j, Koukotsumoji style (denomination at L, red chop at R).

Photo. & Embossed

2005, Dec. 1			Perf. 13x13¼	
2948	A2304	Sheet of 10	17.50	17.50
a.-j.		80y Any single	1.40	.55

Animation

Galaxy Express 999 — A2305

No. 2949: a, Tetsuro and Galaxy Express 999 in flight. b, Matael and passenger cars. c, Claire holding book. d, The Conductor. e, Freija and Matael. f, Tetsuro and Moriki Yutaka. g, Emeraldas and Count Mecha. h, Herlock. i, Matael and galaxy. j, Galaxy Express 999.

2006, Feb. 1		Litho.	Perf. 13x13¼	
2949	A2305	Sheet of 10	17.50	17.50
a.-j.		80y Any single	1.40	.55

Detective Conan — A2306

No. 2950: a, Conan in green jacket. b, Conan wearing glasses, with woman in light blue jacket. c, With Shinichi, scratching chins. d, Ran holding letter. e, Dr. Agasa, Ayumi, front of car. f, Mitsuhiko, Genta, rear of car. g, Haibara Ai. h, Conan with backpack. i, Mysterious Thief Kid. j, Shinichi and Conan, city in background.

2006, Apr. 3		Litho.	Perf. 13x13¼	
2950	A2306	Sheet of 10	17.50	17.50
a.-j.		80y Any single	1.40	.55

International Exchanges and Friendships A2307

Designs: No. 2951, Rabbit and flowers. No. 2952, Children kissing. No. 2953, Bears and caught fish. No. 2954, Children's drawing of two animals. No. 2955, Chick, cat, dog, rabbit, squirrel and rocket.

2006, Mar. 1		Photo.	Perf. 13	
2951	A2307	80y multi	1.40	.55
2952	A2307	80y multi	1.40	.55
2953	A2307	80y multi	1.40	.55
2954	A2307	80y multi	1.40	.55
2955	A2307	80y multi	1.40	.55
a.		Vert. strip of 5, #2951-2955	8.50	5.00
		Sheet, 2 each #2951-2955	17.50	17.50

Morning Glories and Puppies, Door Painting by Okyu Maruyama — A2308

Designs: No. 2956, Morning glories. No. 2957, Puppies.

Perf. 13½x13 Syncopated

2006, Apr. 20			Photo.	
2956		80y multi	1.40	.55
2957		80y multi	1.40	.55
a.	A2308	Horiz. pair, #2956-2957	5.00	3.00

Philately Week.

Miniature Sheet

Australia-Japan Year of Exchange — A2309

No. 2958: a, Australian flag, Ayers Rock. b, Kangaroo and Ayers Rock. c, Sydney Opera House. d, Australian flag and Sydney Opera House. e, Fish of Great Barrier Reef. f, Heart Reef. g, Golden wattle flowers. h, Bottlebrush flowers. i, Koalas. j, Kookaburra.

2006, May 23		Photo.	Perf. 13	
2958	A2309	Sheet of 10	17.50	17.50
a.-j.		80y Any single	1.40	.55

Miniature Sheet

Sacred Sites and Pilgrimage Routes of the Kii Mountains World Heritage Site — A2310

No. 2959: a, Kumano Hongu-Taisha Shrine Building 3 (brown roof, part of stairs seen at bottom). b, Kumano Hongu-Taisha Shrine Building 4 (brown roof, full set of stairs at LR). c, Great Waterfall of Nachi. d, Overhead view of Kumano Nachi-Taisha Shrine (denomination at LL). e, Nachi Fire Festival. f, Seigantoji Temple (dark blue roof). g, Kongobuji Temple (blue green roof). h, Wooden Kongara-Doji-Ryuzo (statue, denomination at UL). i, Kinpusenji Temple (gray roof). j, Wooden Zao-Gongen-Ryuzo (statue, denomination at LL).

2006, June 23			Perf. 13x13¼	
2959	A2310	Sheet of 10	17.50	17.50
a.-j.		80y Any single	1.40	.55

Miniature Sheets

A2311

Greetings Stamps — A2312

No. 2960: a, Fairy and flower. b, Church bell. c, Flower bouquet and ribbons. d, Dolphin. e, Hibiscus and hummingbird.

No. 2961: a, Pink cattleya orchid. b, Fairy, flowers and trees. c, Flower and oranges. d, Parrot and flowers. e, Fairy with pail and orange flowers.

Litho. With Foil Application
Serpentine Die Cut 13¼

2006, June 30			Self-Adhesive	
2960	A2311	Sheet of 5	6.00	
a.-e.		50y Any single	.90	.80

Serpentine Die Cut 13½

2961	A2312	Sheet of 5	9.00	
a.-e.		80y Any single	1.40	1.00

No. 2960 sold for 300y; No. 2961 for 500y.

Taifu Iseno, Poet — A2313

Sadaijin Gotokudaijino, Poet — A2314

Mitsune Ooshikochino, Poet — A2315

Akahito Yamabeno, Poet — A2316

Naishi Suono, Poet — A2317

ふみの日「百人一首」

Poets and Poetry — A2318

No. 2963: a, Double Cherry Blossoms, by Yasuko Koyama. b, Iseno and poetry. c, Pale Morning Moon, by Keiso Mitsuoka. d, Gotokudaijino and poetry. e, White Chrysanthemum, by Shiko Miyazaki. f, Ooshikochino and poetry. g, Mt. Fuji, by Eiko Matsumoto. h, Yamabeno and poetry. i, Spring Night, by Soshu Miyake. j, Suono and poetry.

2006, July 21   Photo.   Perf. 13¼

2962		Vert. strip of 5	6.00	4.00
a.	A2313	50y multi	.90	.45
b.	A2314	50y multi	.90	.45
c.	A2315	50y multi	.90	.45
d.	A2316	50y multi	.90	.45
e.	A2317	50y multi	.90	.45
		Sheet, 2 #2962	13.00	13.00

Perf. 13

2963	A2318	Sheet of 10	16.00	16.00
a.-j.		80y Any single	1.60	1.00

Letter Writing Day.

Horizontal
Lines and
Colored Circles
— A2318a

Die Cut Perf. 13¼

2006, Sept. 1   Litho.
Self-Adhesive

2963K	A2318a	80y multi	2.50	2.50

Printed in sheets of 10 that sold for 1000y. The image portion could be personalized. The image shown is a generic image.

Blue Flowers
— A2318b

Pink Flowers
— A2318c

Die Cut Perf. 13¼
2006, Sept. 1   Litho.
Self-Adhesive

2963L	A2318b	80y multi	2.50	2.50
2963M	A2318c	80y multi	2.50	2.50

Nos. 2963L-2963M were printed in sheets of 10, containing five of each stamp, that sold for 1000y. The image portions could be personalized. The images shown are generic images.

Accession to the United Nations, 50th
Anniv. — A2319

Paintings by Toshiro Sawanuki: 90y, Glorious World To Come. 110y, Eternity.

2006, Sept. 29   Litho.   Perf. 13¾x14

2964	A2319	90y multi	1.50	.60
2965	A2319	110y multi	1.90	.90

Miniature Sheet

Greetings — A2320

No. 2966: a, Mokara Lion's Gold orchid. b, Renanthera Singaporean orchid. c, Vanda Miss Joaquim orchid. d, Vanda Mimi Palmer orchid. e, Hollyhocks and Egret, by Hoitsu Sakai, horiz. f, Irises and Moorhens, by Sakai, horiz.

Litho. With Foil Application
2006, Oct. 3   Die Cut Perf. 13½x13¾
Self-Adhesive

2966	A2320	Sheet of 6	10.00	10.00
a.-b.		50y Either single	.90	.90
c.-d.		80y Either single	1.40	.90
e.		90y multi	1.50	.90
f.		110y multi	1.90	.90

Roulettes separate adjacent 50y and 80y stamps. No. 2966 sold for 500y. See Singapore Nos. 1225-1231.

Miniature Sheets

日本映画Ⅰ

A2321

日本映画Ⅱ

Scenes From Japanese
Movies — A2322

No. 2967: a, Tange Sazen (scarred samurai, green). b, Carmen Kokyo-Ni-Kaeru (women waving, lilac). c, Ugetsu Monogatari (man and woman, maroon). d, Tokyo Monogatari (man and woman, brown). e, Shichinin-No-Samurai (helmeted samurai, deep green). f, Hawaii-No-Yoru (man and woman, olive green). g, Nemuri Kyoshiro (samurai, blue green). h, Guitar-Wo-Motta-Wataridori (man with guitar, blue). i, Miyamoto Musashi (swordsman, blue gray). j, Cupola-No-Aru-Machi (girl, brown).

No. 2968: a, Sailor-Fuku-To-Kikanju (woman with gun). b, Otoko-Ha-Tsuraiyo (man in light blue kimono). c, Kamata Koshin Kyoku (Three people). d, Yomigaeru Kinro (man in chair). e, Setouchi-Shonen-Yakyu-Dan (woman with baseball glove). f, HANA-BI (man standing). g, Shitsurakuen (Woman hugging man). h, Gamera (monster, denomination at UL). i, Tasogare Seibei (woman grooming man). j, Godzilla (monster, denomination at UR).

2006, Oct. 10   Photo.   Perf. 13

2967	A2321	Sheet of 10	17.50	17.50
a.-j.		80y Any single	1.40	.55
2968	A2322	Sheet of 10	17.50	17.50
a.-j.		80y Any single	1.40	.55

Ikebana International Ninth World
Convention — A2323

2006, Oct. 23   Litho.   Perf. 13x13¼
Background Colors

2969		80y grn & lt grn	1.40	.55
2970		80y red & yel	1.40	.55
a.	A2323	Horiz. pair, #2969-2970	3.00	2.00

A2324

A2325

A2326

A2327

New Year 2007 (Year of the Pig)

2006, Nov. 1   Photo.   Perf. 13x13¼

2971	A2324	50y multi	.90	.45
2972	A2325	80y multi	1.40	.55

Photo. & Typo.
Perf. 13¼

2973	A2326	50y +3y multi	1.10	.60
2974	A2327	80y +3y multi	1.75	.65
		Nos. 2971-2974 (4)	5.15	2.25

New Year Greetings
— A2327a

Inscribed "'07 New Year"
Stamp + Label
Panel Color

2006, Nov. 1   Photo.   Perf. 13¼

2974A	A2327a	50y blue	.90	.40
2974B	A2327a	50y red violet	.90	.40
c.		Pair, #2974A-2974B + 2 labels	2.50	2.50

Labels could be personalized.
See Nos. 3010P-3010Q, 3074-3075.

Miniature Sheets

A2328

Greetings Stamps — A2329

No. 2975: a, Squirrel in mug. b, Bell with flowers. c, Clown with flower. d, Skating polar bear. e, Bear in Santa Claus suit, guitar, birds. No. 2976: a, Cat in Santa Claus suit ringing bell. b, Fairy and cyclamen. c, Snowman with gift. d, Reindeer and star. e, Floral wreath.

Litho. with Foil Application
Die Cut Perf. 13½x13¼

2006, Nov. 24		**Self-Adhesive**	
2975	A2328	Sheet of 5	6.00	
a.-e.		50y Any single	.90	.90

Die Cut Perf. 13

2976	A2329	Sheet of 5	9.00	
a.-e.		80y Any single	1.40	.90

No. 2975 sold for 300y; No. 2976 for 500y.

Miniature Sheet

Eto Calligraphy — A2330

No. 2977: a, Semicursive style (white background, red chop at lower left). b, Kinbun style (blue background). c, Reisho style (red background). d, Japanese cursive syllabary (white background, red chop at lower right, character with small arc at top). e, Kinbun style (white background, red chop at lower right, character with funnel-shaped line at top). f, Kinbun style (red character). g, Kinbun style (white background, red chop at lower left, character with flat line at top. h, Kinbun style (white background. red chop at lower right, character with large blotch at top). i, Tensho style (white background, red chop at lower left, character with long curved arc and circle at top) j, Reisho style (white background, red chop at lower right, character with dot and straight line at top).

Litho. & Embossed

2006, Dec. 1			**Perf. 13x13¼**	
2977	A2330	Sheet of 10	17.50	17.50
a.-j.		80y Any single	1.40	.55

Miniature Sheet

A2331

Japanese Antarctic Research
Expeditions, 50th Anniv. — A2332

No. 2978: a, Observation ship Fuji. b, Spotter plane. c, Adult emperor penguin and chick. d, Adult emperor penguins and five chicks. e, Observation ship Soya and Adelie penguins. f, Adult Adelie penguins and chick. g, Dog, Jiro, in snow, dog team. h, Dog, Taro, standing, dog sled. i, Scientist, observation ship Shirase. j, Snowmobile with cabin.

No. 2979: a, Snowmobile with cabin (26x28mm). b, Spotter plane (28mm diameter). c, Soya and dog sled (34x26mm). d, Weddell seal (28x23mm ellipse). e, Head of emperor penguin (26x37mm oval). f, Two Adelie penguins (26x28mm). g, Dog, Taro, standing with mouth open (28mm diameter). h, Emperor penguin chicks (28mm diameter). i, Adult emperor penguin and chick (26x28mm). j, Dog, Jiro, in snow (26x37mm oval).

2007, Jan. 23		**Litho.**	**Perf. 13**	
2978	A2331	Sheet of 10	16.50	16.50
a.-j.		80y Any single	1.40	.40

Self-Adhesive
Die Cut Perf. 13¾x13½

2979	A2332	Sheet of 10	20.00	
a.-j.		80y Any single	1.40	.55

Animation
Miniature Sheet

Neon Genesis Evangelion — A2333

No. 2980: a, Evangelion Unit 01. b, Shinji Ikari. c, Rei Ayanami. d, Evangelion Unit 00. e, Soryu Asuka Langley. f, Evangelion Unit 02. g, Rei Ayanami and Soryu Asuka Langley. h, Misato Katsuragi. i, Kawora Nagisa. j, Sachiel, the third angel.

2007, Feb. 23			**Perf. 13x13¼**	
2980	A2333	Sheet of 10	16.50	16.50
a.-j.		80y Any single	1.40	.55

Animation
Miniature Sheet

Future Boy Conan — A2334

No. 2981: a, Conan (with name). b, Lana (with name). c, Lana (without name). d, Conan (without name). e, Monsley and airplane. f, Lepka. g, Jimsy and Umaso. h, Dyce on running robot. i, Dr. Lao and hovering craft. j, Grandpa.

2007, June 22		**Litho.**	**Perf. 13x13¼**	
2981	A2334	Sheet of 10	16.50	16.50
a.-j.		80y Any single	1.40	.55

World Heritage Sites
Miniature Sheet

Sacred Sites and Pilgrimage Routes of
the Kii Mountains World Heritage
Site — A2335

No. 2982: a, Yoshino Mikumari Shrine, cherry blossoms at left. b, Pictoral and rope decoration at Yoshino Mikumari shrine. c, Omine-Okugake-Michi trail. d, Kumano Hayatama-Taisha Shrine (black-roofed building with red trim). e, Kumano Hayatama-Taisha Shrine, diff. f, Wooden icon of Kumano-Fusumino-Okami-Zazo. g, Cherry trees in bloom at Kumano Sankei-Michi Nakahechi. h, Stone sculpture of Emperor Kazan riding ox and horse. i, Kongo-Sanmaiin Temple. j, Steps to Kong-Sanmaiin Temple.

2007, Mar. 23		**Photo.**	**Perf. 13x13¼**	
2982	A2335	Sheet of 10	16.50	16.50
a.-j.		80y Any single	1.40	.55

World Heritage Sites
Miniature Sheet

Shiretoko World Heritage
Site — A2336

No. 2983: a, Lake and mountain, cloudless sky. b, Lake and mountain, cloud in sky. c, Blakiston's fish owl. d, Sea ice, Mt. Rausu. e, Cherry blossoms. f, Brown bear. g, Harbor seal. h, Ezo deer. i, Sea eagle. j, Shiretoko violets (white and yellow flowers).

2007, July 6		**Photo.**	**Perf. 13x13¼**	
2983	A2336	Sheet of 10	16.50	16.50
a.-j.		80y Any single	1.40	.55

Sleeping Boar, by
Ippo
Mori — A2337

Boar Loping
Across Fields, by
Mori — A2338

Sparrow, by
Mori — A2339

Cherry Blossoms,
by Mori — A2340

Bird Flock, by
Mori — A2341

Great Tits Sitting
In a Japanese
Bush Clover, by
Mori — A2342

Perf. 13¼x13 Syncopated

2007, Apr. 20			Photo.
2984	A2337	80y multi	1.40	.55
2985	A2338	80y multi	1.40	.55
a.		Horiz. pair, #2984-2985	3.00	2.00
		Sheet, 5 #2985a	16.00	16.00
2986	A2339	80y multi	1.40	.55
2987	A2340	80y multi	1.40	.55
2988	A2341	80y multi	1.40	.55
2989	A2342	80y multi	1.40	.55
a.		Vert. strip of 4, #2986-2989	7.50	4.00
		Sheet, 2 each #2985-2989	16.00	16.00
		Nos. 2984-2989 (6)	8.40	3.30

Miniature Sheet

Japan - India Friendship
Year — A2343

No. 2990: a, Taj Mahal. b, Taj Mahal and
camels. c, Bengal tiger. d, Peacock. e, Buddhist monastery, Sanchi, India. f, Statue of
goddess, Sanchi. g, Painting of Indian woman
facing left. h, Calico print of Indian facing right.
i, Indian folk dancer. j, Character from
Kathakali, Indian dance drama.

2007, May 23			Perf. 13
2990	A2343	Sheet of 10	17.50	17.50
a.-j.		80y Any single	1.40	.55

Tsurayuki Kino,
Poet — A2344

Empress Jito,
Poet — A2345

Dayu Sarumaru,
Poet — A2346

Kanemasa
Minamotono,
Poet — A2347

Sanuki Nijoinno,
Poet — A2348

Poetry — A2349

No. 2996 — Poetry in Japanese calligraphy
and: a, Plum blossoms. b, Tsurayuki Kino. c,
Mount Kagu. d, Empress Jito. e, Deer. f, Dayu
Sarumaru. g, Plovers. h, Kanemasa
Minamotono. i, Stone in sea. j, Sanuki
Nijoinno.

2007, July 23			Photo.	Perf. 13½
2991	A2344	50y multi	.90	.45
2992	A2345	50y multi	.90	.45
2993	A2346	50y multi	.90	.45
2994	A2347	50y multi	.90	.45
2995	A2348	50y multi	.90	.45
a.		Vert. strip of 5, #2991-2995	5.75	4.00

			Perf. 13
2996	A2349	Sheet of 10	17.50	17.50
a.-j.		80y Any single	1.40	.55

Letter Writing Day.

Miniature Sheet

11th World Track and Field
Championships, Osaka — A2350

No. 2997: a, Dai Tamesue (athlete 545),
hurdler. b, Kumiko Ikeda (athlete 426),
sprinter. c, Yuzo Kanemaru (athlete 300), runner. d, Shingo Suetsugu (athlete 526), runner.
e, Kayoko Fukushi (athlete 422), runner. f,
Masato Naito running over hurdle. g, Naoyuki
Daigo high jumping. h, Kenji Narisako (athlete
531), hurdler. i, Daichi Sawano pole vaulting. j,
Koji Murofushi (athlete 774), hammer throw.

2007, Aug. 23		Litho.	Perf. 13x13¼
2997	A2350	Sheet of 10	17.50	17.50
a.-j.		80y Any single	1.40	.55

Miniature Sheet

Diplomatic Relations Between Japan
and Thailand, 120th Anniv. — A2351

No. 2998: a, Maple leaves, bamboo. b,
Cherry blossoms. c, Ratchaphruek (yellow
flower) blossom. d, Rhynchostylis
gigantea (purple and white orchids). e, Mother-of-pearl
elephant. f, Mother-of-pearl flower. g, Thai
dancer. h, Statue, Wat Phra Keo. i, Elephant
with head at left, from Toshogu Shrine, Japan,
horiz. j, Elephant with head at right, from
Toshogu Shrine, horiz.

**Die Cut Perf. and Serpentine Die
Cut**

2007, Sept. 26			Litho.
		Self-Adhesive	
2998	A2351	Sheet of 10	16.50	16.50
a.-j.		80y any single	1.40	.55

Vertical stamps are die cut perf. 13 at top
and bottom, serpentine die cut 10¼ on side
adjacent to another stamp, and die cut perf.
12½ on remaining side. Horizontal stamps are
die cut perf. 13 at top and bottom, serpentine
die cut 10¼ on side adjacent to another
stamp, and die cut perf. 12¾ on remaining
side.

See Thailand No. 2316.

**International Letter Writing Week
Type of 2000**

Hiroshige paintings from 53 Stations of the
Tokaido Highway: 90y, Hodogaya. 110y, Arai.
130y, Kusatsu.

2007, Sept. 28		Litho.	Perf. 14
2999	A2119	90y multi	1.50	.45
3000	A2119	110y multi	1.90	.45
3001	A2119	130y multi	2.10	.65
		Nos. 2999-3001 (3)	5.50	1.65

Mandarin
Duck
A2352

Eastern Turtle
Dove
A2353

2007, Oct. 1		Photo.	Perf. 13x13½
3002	A2352	50y multi	.85	.50
3003	A2353	80y multi	1.40	.55

See No. 3281.

Miniature Sheets

A2354

Establishment of Japan Post
Corporation — A2355

No. 3004: a, Baron Hisoka Maejima (red
panels). b, Japan #2 (red panels). c, Post
office counter (orange panels). d, Postal workers loading mail coach (dark red panels). e,
Postal saving counter (green panels). f, People
at post office counters (blue panels).

No. 3005 — Paintings of flowers: a, Sunflower, by Hoitsu Sakai. b, Confederate Roses,
by Sakai. c, Chrysanthemums, by Sakai. d,
Maple Leaves, by Kiitsu Suzuki (showing
branch). e, Maple Leaves, by Suzuki (no
branch). f, Camellia, by Sakai. g, Cherry Tree,
by Sakai (bird in tree). h, Tree Peony, by
Sakai. i, Iris, by Sakai. j, Hydrangeas, by
Sakai.

2007, Oct. 1	Photo.	Perf. 13¼	
3004	A2354	Sheet of 10,	16.50 16.50
		#a-b, 2 each	
		#c-f	
a.-f.		80y Any single	1.40 .55
3005	A2355	Sheet of 10	16.50 16.50
a.-j.		80y Any single	1.40 .55

Miniature Sheet

Intl. Skills Festival For All — A2356

No. 3006: a, Computer operator and robot.
b, Computer operator. c, Plasterer and Geisha. d, Plasterer and pillar. e, Pastry chef and
cake. f, Pastry chef and bowls. g, Flower
arranger and flowers. h, Flower arranger holding scissors. i, Sheet metal worker and automobile. j, Sheet metal worker hammering
metal.

2007, Oct. 23	Litho.	Perf. 13	
3006	A2356	Sheet of 10	17.50 17.50
a.-j.		80y Any single	1.40 .55

A2357   A2358

New Year 2008 (Year of the Rat)
A2359   A2360

2007, Nov. 1	Photo.	Perf. 13x13½	
3007	A2357	50y multi	.90 .45
3008	A2358	80y multi	1.40 .50

Photo. & Typo.
Perf. 13¼

3009	A2359	50y +3y multi	1.10 .55
3010	A2360	80y +3y multi	1.60 .60
		Nos. 3007-3010 (4)	5.00 2.10

Diamonds —
A2360a

Die Cut Perf. 13¼
2007, Nov. 1			Litho.

Self-Adhesive
Green Diamonds
Color of Country Name

3010A	A2360a	50y blue	4.00 4.00
3010B	A2360a	50y green	4.00 4.00
3010C	A2360a	50y red	4.00 4.00
3010D	A2360a	50y purple	4.00 4.00
3010E	A2360a	50y black	4.00 4.00

Blue Diamonds

3010F	A2360a	80y blue	3.50 3.50
3010G	A2360a	80y green	3.50 3.50
3010H	A2360a	80y red	3.50 3.50
3010I	A2360a	80y purple	3.50 3.50
3010J	A2360a	80y black	3.50 3.50

Nos. 3010A-3010E were printed in sheets of
10, containing two of each stamp, that sold for
900y. Nos. 3010F-3010J were printed in
sheets of 10, containing two of each stamp,
that sold for 1200y. The image portion could
be personalized. The image shown is a
generic image.

New Year Greetings Type of 2006
Inscribed "'08 New Year"
Stamp + Label
Panel Color

2007, Nov. 1	Photo.	Perf. 13¼	
3010P	A2327a	50y red violet	1.75 1.75
3010Q	A2327a	50y orange	1.75 1.75
r.		Pair, #3010P-3010Q + 2 la-	
		bels	4.00 4.00

Labels could be personalized.

Miniature Sheets

A2361

Greetings Stamps — A2362

No. 3011: a, White buildings. b, Fairies on
flying swans. c, Santa Claus. d, Flowers and
snow-covered trees. e, Cat and candy cane.
No. 3012: a, Santa Claus and reindeer. b,
Fairy and flowers. c, Snowman with green cap.
d, Strawberries. e, Snowman and flying
reindeer.

2007, Nov. 26	Litho.	Die Cut Perf.	

Self-Adhesive

3011	A2361	Sheet of 5	5.00	
a.-e.		50y Any single	.90	.80

Die Cut Perf. 13

3012	A2362	Sheet of 5	7.50	
a.-e.		80y Any single	1.40	.80

Miniature Sheet

Edo Calligraphy — A2363

No. 3013 — Charters for "rat": a, In Kinbun
style (red character). b, Black character with
three long vertical lines at top, with red chop at
LR. c, In Tensho style (gold character on red
and brown background). d, In Reisho style
(black character resembling a "3" with line
through it, with red chop at LR). e, In Shoden
style (gold character on blue and pink background). f, In Kana style (black characters
resembling "12" with a check mark, with red
chop at LR). g, In Reisho style (black characters, with red chop at LL). h, In Sosho style
(black character with pink lines, with red chop
at LL). i, Black character resembling stick figure with raised arms, with red chop at LR. j, In
Kinbun style (black character with five short
vertical lines at top, red chop at LL).

Litho. & Embossed
2007, Dec. 3			Perf. 13
3013	A2363	Sheet of 10	17.50 17.50
a.-j.		80y Any single	1.40 .55

Mt. Fuji
A2364

Mt. Fuji
A2365

Mt. Fuji
A2366

Mt. Fuji
A2367

Mt. Fuji
A2368

Bamboo — A2369

Someiyoshino Blossoms — A2370

Hydrangea Blossoms — A2371

Maple
Leaves
A2372

Narcissuses — A2373

2008, Jan. 23	Litho.	Perf. 13¾x14	
3014		Sheet of 10	17.50 17.50
a.	A2364	80y multi	1.40 .55
b.	A2365	80y multi	1.40 .55
c.	A2366	80y multi	1.40 .55
d.	A2367	80y multi	1.40 .55
e.	A2368	80y multi	1.40 .55
f.	A2369	80y multi	1.40 .55
g.	A2370	80y multi	1.40 .55
h.	A2371	80y multi	1.40 .55
i.	A2372	80y multi	1.40 .55
j.	A2373	80y multi	1.40 .55

Yokoso! Japan Weeks.

Souvenir Sheet

New Year 2008 (Year of the
Rat) — A2374

No. 3015: a, Two rats. b, One rat.

2008, Jan. 28	Photo.	Perf. 13	
3015 A2374	Sheet of 2	2.50	2.50
a.	50y multi	.90	.45
b.	80y multi	1.40	.55

Miniature Sheet

Animated Folktales — A2375

No. 3016: a, Man on horse, cherry trees, pagoda. b, Man in cherry tree. c, Moon Princess in bamboo stump, woodsman with ax. d, Moon Princess, flying horse and wagon, archers. e, Four statues in snow. f, Two statues in snow, man with basket. g, Boy in ship. h, Demons. i, Woman carrying roll of cloth. j, Man, woman, crane.

2008, Feb. 22	Litho.	Perf. 13	
3016 A2375	Sheet of 10	17.50	17.50
a.-j.	80y Any single	1.40	.55

Folktales "The Old Man Who Made Cherry Trees Blossom" (No. 3016a-3016b), "The Moon Princess" (Nos. 3016c-3016d), "Six Little Statues" (Nos. 3016e-3016f), "The Peach Boy" (NOs. 3016g-3016h), "The Grateful Crane" (Nos. 3016i-3016j).

Miniature Sheet

Astronomical Society of Japan,
Cent. — A2376

No. 3017: a, Jupiter. b, Saturn. c, Spiral galaxy. d, Suzaku X-ray satellite. e, Hayabusa probe. f, Asteroids and Earth. g, Subaru Telescope. h, Stars. i, Mars. j, Nobeyama Radio Telescope.

2008, Mar. 21			
3017 A2376	Sheet of 10	17.50	17.50
a.-j.	80y Any single	1.40	.55

Miniature Sheet

Diplomatic Relations Between Japan
and Indonesia, 50th Anniv. — A2377

No. 3018: a, Kelimutu Volcano, Indonesia. b, Mt. Fuji, Japan, and cherry blossoms. c, Borobudur, Indonesia. d, Toji Temple, Kyoto. e, Rafflesia arnoldii. f, Cherry blossoms. g, Angklung (Indonesian musical instrument). h, Gaku biwa (Japanese musical instrument). i, Red arowana fish, horiz. j, Three koi, horiz.

2008, June 23	Photo.	Perf. 13	
3018 A2377	Sheet of 10	15.00	15.00
a.-j.	80y Any single	1.40	.55

See Indonesia Nos. 2135-2139.

Small Bird in
Cherry Blossom,
by Seitei
Watanabe
A2378

Butterfly in Peony
Branch, by
Watanabe
A2379

Egrets in the Rain
Beneath Willow
Trees, by
Watanabe
A2380

Grapes, by
Watanabe
A2381

Sea Birds on a
Rocky Crag, by
Watanabe
A2382

Perf. 13½x13 Syncopated

2008, Apr. 18		Photo.	
3019 A2378	80y multi	1.40	.55
3020 A2379	80y multi	1.40	.55
3021 A2380	80y multi	1.40	.55
3022 A2381	80y multi	1.40	.55
3023 A2382	80y multi	1.40	.55
a.	Vert. strip of 5, #3019-3023	8.75	8.75
	Sheet, 2 #3023a	17.50	17.50

Philately Week.

See note after No. Z827 in the Prefecture Stamp listings.

Miniature Sheet

Home Towns — A2383

No. 3024 — Paintings by Taiji Harada of views of towns: a, Water Shield (Yamamoto District, Akita prefecture). b, Bell of Time (Kawago, Saitama prefecture). c, Enjoying the Evening Cool (Gujo, Gifu prefecture). d, The Little Electric Train (Choshi, Chiba prefecture).

e, Sea of the Heart (Shozu District, Kagawa prefecture). f, Lake in the Evening Sun (Gamo District, Shiga prefecture). g, Tanabata Dolls (Matsumoto, Nagano prefecture). h, Town of Outdoor Warehouses (Ise, Mie prefecture). i, The Farm Clock (Aki, Kochi prefecture). j, Late Summer Heat in the Street (Hakusan, Ishikawa prefecture).

2008, May 2	Photo.	Perf. 13	
3024 A2383	Sheet of 10	16.00	16.00
a.-j.	80y Any single	1.40	.55

Hideyo Noguchi Africa Prize — A2384

2008, May 23	Litho.	Perf. 13	
3025	80y Noguchi	1.40	.55
3026	80y Map of Africa	1.40	.55
a. A2384	Horiz. pair, #3025-3026	3.25	2.50

Miniature Sheet

National Afforestation
Campaign — A2385

No. 3027 — Scenes from Akita prefecture: a, Aleutian avens and Mt. Moriyoshi, denomination at UL. b, Aleutian avens and Mt. Moriyoshi, denomination at UR. c, Fringed galax flowers, denomination at LL. d, Fringed galax flowers, denomination at LR. e, Autumn leaves, denomination at LL. f, Autumn leaves, denomination at UR. g, Beech forest in autumn, denomination at UL. h, Beech forest in autumn, denomination in UR. i, Weigela. j, Waterfall.

2008, June 13	Photo.	Perf. 13	
3027 A2385	Sheet of 10	9.50	9.50
a.-j.	50y Any single	.90	.55

Miniature Sheet

Year of Exchange Between Japan and Brazil — A2386

No. 3028: a, Roasted coffee beans, seal of Brazilian vice-consulate in Kobe. b, Coffee cherries, ship. c, Christ the Redeemer Statue, Rio de Janeiro. d, Sugarloaf Mountain, Rio de Janeiro. e, Iguaçu Falls, denomination at UL. f, Iguaçu Falls, denomination at UR. g, Houses, denomination at LL. h, Houses, denomination at LR. i, Butterflies. j, Toucan.

2008, June 18   Litho.   Perf. 13
3028	A2386	Sheet of 10	16.00	16.00
a.-j.		80y Any single	1.40	.55

See Brazil No. 3051.

Miniature Sheet

Publication of *Anne of Green Gables*, by Lucy Maud Montgomery, Cent. — A2387

No. 3029: a, Anne holding buttercups. b, Green Gables House. c, Matthew Cuthbert, wearing hat, vert. d, Marilla Cuthbert, wearing hat, vert. e, Anne, Diana Barry holding hands, vert. f, Diana, vert. g, Anne in black dress, vert. h, Anne and Gilbert Blythe, vert. i, Matthew Cuthbert, without hat, vert. j, Anne, Marilla Cuthbert, vert.

Perf. 13¼x13 (#3029a-3029b), 13x13¼

2008, June 20
3029	A2387	Sheet of 10	16.00	16.00
a.-j.		80y Any single	1.40	.55

See Canada Nos. 2276-2278.

Lily — A2388

Rugosa Rose — A2389

Rhododendron A2390

Safflower A2391

Gentian — A2392

Lily — A2393

Rugosa Rose A2394

Rhododendron A2395

Safflower A2396

Gentian A2397

2008, July 1   Photo.   Perf. 13¼
3030	A2388	50y multi	.90	.50
3031	A2389	50y multi	.90	.50
3032	A2390	50y multi	.90	.50
3033	A2391	50y multi	.90	.50
3034	A2392	50y multi	.90	.50
a.		Vert. strip of 5, #3030-3034	5.50	5.00
3035	A2393	80y multi	1.40	.60
3036	A2394	80y multi	1.40	.60
3037	A2395	80y multi	1.40	.60
3038	A2396	80y multi	1.40	.60
3039	A2397	80y multi	1.40	.60
a.		Vert. strip of 5, #3035-3039	8.75	8.00
		Nos. 3030-3039 (10)	11.50	5.50

Flowers of Kanagawa, Hokkaido, Fukushima, Yamagata and Nagano prefectures.

Miniature Sheet

Hokkaido Local Autonomy Law, 60th Anniv. — A2398

No. 3040: a, Lake Toya, cranes (32x39mm). b, Goryokaku Fortress (28x33mm). c, Hills around Biei (28x33mm). d, Sea angel (28x33mm). e, Otaru Canal (28x33mm).

2008, July 1   Perf. 13¼ (#3040a), 13
3040	A2398	Sheet of 5	7.50	7.50
a.-e.		80y Any single	1.40	.55

Miniature Sheet

G8 Summit, Toyako — A2399

No. 3041: a, Mt. Yotei (stamp 1). b, Showa Shinzan (stamp 2). c, Mt. Yotei and Lake Toya (stamp 3). d, Mt. Yotei and Fukidashi Park (stamp 4). e, Mt. Eniwa and Lake Shikotsu (stamp 5). f, Pink Japanese wood poppies (stamp 6). g, Squirrel (stamp 7). h, Beardtongue flowers (stamp 8). i, Mountain ash leaves and berries (stamp 9). j, Northern fox (stamp 10).

2008, July 7   Litho.   Perf. 13¾x14
3041	A2399	Sheet of 10	15.00	15.00
a.-j.		80y Any single	1.50	1.10

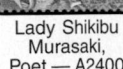
Lady Shikibu Murasaki, Poet — A2400

Sanekata Fujiwara, Poet — A2401

Lady Shonagon Sei, Poet — A2402

Kinto Dainagon, Poet — A2403

Lady Shikibu Izumi, Poet — A2404

Poetry — A2405

No. 3047 — Poetry in Japanese calligraphy and: a, Moon behind cloud. b, Lady Shikibu Murasaki. c, Mugwort. d, Sanekata Fujiwara. e, Waterfall. f, Lady Shonagon Sei. g, Barrier. h, Kinto Dainagon. i, Bare branches. j, Lady Shikibu Izumi.

2008, July 23   Photo.   Perf. 13¼
3042	A2400	50y multi	.90	.45
3043	A2401	50y multi	.90	.45
3044	A2402	50y multi	.90	.45
3045	A2403	50y multi	.90	.45
3046	A2404	50y multi	.90	.45
a.		Vert. strip of 5, #3042-3046	5.50	3.75

Perf. 12¾x13
3047	A2405	Sheet of 10	17.50	17.50
a.-j.		80y Any single	1.40	.55

Letter Writing Day.

Miniature Sheets

A2406

Hello Kitty — A2407

No. 3048 — Hello Kitty characters with: a, Gold denomination at UR. b, Green denomination at UR. c, Yellow denomination at UL, Kitty with pink flowers on head. d, Yellow denomination at UR, Kitty wearing green patterned kimono. e, Green denomination at UL, Kitty wearing black kimono. f, Green denomination at UL, Kitty with pink and blue flowers on head. g, Green denomination at UL, Kitty with bow and flowers on head. h, Yellow denomination at UL, Kitty wearing dark green kimono. i, Green denomination at UL, Kitty wearing brown kimono. j, Green denomination at UL, Kitty with purple and green flowers on head.

No. 3049 — Hello Kitty characters with: a, Green denomination at LL (41x27mm). b, Gold denomination at LR, one Kitty with two pink flowers on head (41x27mm). c, Gold denomination at LR, Kitty at right with purple and green flowers on head (41x27mm). d, Green denomination at UR (41x27mm). e, Gold denomination at LR, Kitty at left with bow and flower on head (41x27mm). f, Blue denomination (34mm diameter). g, Gold denomination, Kitty wearing gray kimono (34mm diameter). h, Gold denomination, Kitty holding fan (34mm diameter). i, Gold denomination, Kitty with snowflakes in background

---

(34mm diameter). j, Blue denomination (40x28mm oval stamp).

Die Cut Perf. and Serpentine Die Cut (see note)

2008, July 23   Litho.

Self-Adhesive

3048   A2406   Sheet of 10   9.50
a.-j.   50y Any single   .90   .45

Die Cut Perf. 13x13¼ (#3049a-3049e), Die Cut Perf.

3049   A2407   Sheet of 10   15.00 15.00
a.-j.   80y Any single   1.50   1.10

Stamps on No. 3048 are arranged in five rows of se-tenant pairs. Each pair is die cut perf. 13¾ at top and bottom, die cut perf. 13½ on the outer sides, and serpentine die cut 11¼ between the stamps in the pair.

Love That Meets the Night, by Utamaro
A2408

Yatsumi Bridge, by Hiroshige
A2409

Mannen Bridge, Fukagawa, by Hiroshige
A2410

Koshiro Matsumoto IV as Gorobe Sakanaya of San'ya, by Sharaku
A2411

Hanazuma From Hyogoya, by Utamaro
A2412

Ayase River at Kanegafuchi, by Hiroshige
A2413

Tsukiji Hongan-ji Temple, Teppozu, by Hiroshige
A2414

Hikosaburo Bando III as Sanai Sagisaka, by Sharaku
A2415

Roko of Tatsumi, by Utamaro
A2416

Kameido Plum Gardens, by Hiroshige
A2417

2008, Aug. 1   Litho.   ***Perf. 13¼***
3050   Sheet of 10   17.50 17.50
a.   A2408 80y multi   1.40   .55
b.   A2409 80y multi   1.40   .55
c.   A2410 80y multi   1.40   .55
d.   A2411 80y multi   1.40   .55
e.   A2412 80y multi   1.40   .55
f.   A2413 80y multi   1.40   .55
g.   A2414 80y multi   1.40   .55
h.   A2415 80y multi   1.40   .55
i.   A2416 80y multi   1.40   .55
j.   A2417 80y multi   1.40   .55

Life in Edo (Tokyo).

Miniature Sheet

Hometown Festivals — A2418

No. 3051: a, Streamers for Sendai Tanabata Festival, Miyagi prefecture (light green background, denomination at UR). b, Streamers for Sendai Tanabata Festival (light green background, denomination at UL). c, Portable shrine for Kanda Festival, Tokyo prefecture (yellow background, denomination in red at LL). d, Portable shrine for Kanda Festival (yellow background, denomination in blue at UR). e, Dancers from Awa Dance Festival, Tokushima prefecture (pink background, denomination at LR). f, Dancers from Awa Dance Festival (pink background, denomination at UR). g, Participants and lanterns for Hakata Gion Yamakasa Festival, Fukuoka prefecture (light blue background, denomination at UL). h, Participants and float for Hakata Gion Yamakasa Festival (light blue background, denomination at UR). i, Drummers for Eisa Festival, Okinawa prefecture (yellow background, denomination in red at LR). j, Drummers for Eisa Festival (yellow background, denomination in blue at UR).

2008, Aug. 1   Photo.   ***Perf. 13½x13¼***
3051   A2418   Sheet of 10   9.50   9.50
a.-j.   50y Any single   .90   .45

Miniature Sheet

Treaty of Peace and Friendship Between Japan and People's Republic of China, 30th Anniv. — A2419

No. 3052: a, Temple of Heaven, Beijing. b, Huangshan Mountains, China. c, Mogao Cave Shrines, China. d, Temple of the Flourishing Law, Ikaruga, Japan. e, Female mandarin duck. f, Male mandarin duck. g, Panel from painting by Wang Chuanfeng depicting three stylized fish and red Japanese apricot flower. h, Panel from painting by Wang Chuanfeng depicting two stylized fish and water lily. i, Panel from painting by Wang Chuanfeng depicting one stylized fish and autumn leaves. j, Panel from painting by Wang Chuanfeng depicting two staylized fish and white and red narcissus. Nos. 3052a-3052d, 3052g-3052j are 28x49mm; Nos. 3052e-3052f, 32x49mm.

2008, Aug. 12   Photo.   ***Perf. 13***
3052   A2419   Sheet of 10   15.00 15.00
a.-j.   80y Any single   1.40   .55

Animation
Miniature Sheet

Patlabor — A2420

No. 3053: a, Ingfram Model 1 robot. b, Noa Izumimn, with "2" on sleeve patch. c, Isao Ota, with crossed arms. d, Ingram Model 2 robot. e, Shinobu Nagumo, with long hair. f, Ingram Model 3 robot. g, Robot, diff. h, Asumo Shinohara, with hand on head. i, Ingram Model 1 robot and eight characters. j, Ingram Model 2 robot and three characters.

2008, Aug. 22   Litho.   ***Perf. 13x13¼***
3053   A2420   Sheet of 10   15.00 15.00
a.-j.   80y Any single   1.40   .55

Miniature Sheet

Home Towns — A2421

No. 3054 — Paintings by Taiji Harada of views of towns: a, Idyllic Village (Farmhouses, Tonami, Toyama prefecture). b, Blessing (Wedding at Yamate Catholic Church, Yokohama, Kanagawa prefecture). c, Approaching Winter (Lake Nojiri, Kamiminochi District, Nagano prefecture). d, Konjac Field (Farmers planting, Numata, Gunma prefecture). e, Vespers (Family in garden near houses, Nara, Nara prefecture). f, Cosmos (Flowers, boats and boathouses, Mikatakaminaka District, Fukui prefecture). g, Voices of Excited Children (Farmhouse and hill, Haga District, Tochigi prefecture). h, Autumn Colors Everywhere (Farmhouse and train car, Namegata, Ibaraki prefecture). i, Small Market (Family at roadside market, Asakura District, Fukuoka prefecture). j, Lullaby Village (Village and bridge, Kuma District, Kumamoto prefecture).

2008, Sept. 1   Photo.   Perf. 13
3054	A2421	Sheet of 10	15.00	15.00
a.-j.		80y Any single	1.40	.55

Miniature Sheet

Kyoto Travel Scenes — A2422

No. 3055: a, Otagi Nebutsu Temple and stone sculptures (stamp 1). b, Toriimoto (stamp 2). c, Adashino Nenbutsu Temple (stamp 3). d, Gio Temple (stamp 4). e, Buddha sculptures, Nison Temple (stamp 5). f, Hut of Fallen Persimmons, persimmons on tree (stamp 6). g, Jojakko Temple (stamp 7). h, Sagano Scenic Railway bridge and trains (stamp 8). i, Rowboats on Hozu River (stamp 9). J, Togetsu Bridge (stamp 10).

2008, Sept. 1   Litho.   Perf. 13x13¼
3055	A2422	Sheet of 10	15.00	15.00
a.-j.		80y Any single	1.40	.55

Personalized Stamp — A2423

Die Cut Perf. 12¾ Syncopated
2008, Aug. 7   Litho.
Self-Adhesive
Color of Denomination
3056	A2423	80y blue	2.00	2.00
3057	A2423	80y red	2.00	2.00
3058	A2423	80y orange	2.00	2.00
3059	A2423	80y green	2.00	2.00
3060	A2423	80y black	2.00	2.00
		Nos. 3056-3060 (5)	10.00	10.00

Nos. 3056-3060 were printed in sheets of 10 containing 2 of each stamp that sold for 1200y. The image portion could be personalized. The image shown is a generic image.

A2424

A2425

A2426

A2427

A2428

A2429

A2430

A2431

A2432

The Tale of Genji, by Shikibu Murasaki — A2433

2008, Sept. 22   Photo.   Perf. 13¼
3061		Sheet of 10	16.00	16.00
a.	A2424	80y multi	1.40	.55
b.	A2425	80y multi	1.40	.55
c.	A2426	80y multi	1.40	.55
d.	A2427	80y multi	1.40	.55
e.	A2428	80y multi	1.40	.55
f.	A2429	80y multi	1.40	.55
g.	A2430	80y multi	1.40	.55
h.	A2431	80y multi	1.40	.55
i.	A2432	80y multi	1.40	.55
j.	A2433	80y multi	1.40	.55

Kyushu Oil Dome, Oita Sports Park — A2435

Fencing — A2436

Hurdler — A2437

Kayaker — A2438

2008, Sept. 26   Perf. 13x13¼
3062		Sheet of 10, 2 each #3062a, 3062b, 3062d, 4 #3062c	9.50	9.50
a.	A2435	50y multi	.90	.50
b.	A2436	50y multi	.90	.50
c.	A2437	50y multi	.90	.50
d.	A2438	50y multi	.90	.50

Miniature Sheet

Travel Scenes — A2439

No. 3063: a, Sanjunoto Pagoda (stamp 1). b, Kiyomizudera Temple (stamp 2). c, Detail from painted sliding partition showing flowers from Chishaku Temple, denomination at LL (stamp 3). d, Like "c," denomination at LR (stamp 4). e, Kodai Temple (stamp 5). f, Temple garden (stamp 6). g, Sannei Hill (stamp 7). h, Yasaka Pagoda (stamp 8). i, Apprentice geisha (stamp 9). j, Kamo River and waterfront (stamp 10).

2008, Oct. 1   Litho.   Perf. 13x13¼
3063	A2439	Sheet of 10	16.00	16.00
a.-j.		80y Any single	1.40	.55

International Letter Writing Week Type of 2000

Hiroshige paintings from 53 Stations of the Tokaido Highway: 90y, Kanagawa. 110y, Mishima. 130y, Ishibe.

2008, Oct. 9   Photo.   Perf. 13¼x13½
3064	A2119	90y multi	1.60	.45
3065	A2119	110y multi	1.90	.55
3066	A2119	130y multi	2.10	.65
		Nos. 3064-3066 (3)	5.60	1.65

World Heritage Sites
Miniature Sheet

Iwami Silver Mine World Heritage
Site — A2440

No. 3067: a, Map of Tartary by Abraham Ortelius (stamp 1). b, Ryugenji mine shaft (stamp 2). c, Smelting plant and ruins of Shimizudani smelting works (stamp 3). d, Painting of dragon, ceiling of Kigami Shinto shrine (stamp 4). e, Rakanji Temple (stamp 5). f, Omori silver mine district (stamp 6). g, Silver guardian dog (stamp 7). h, Interior of Kumagai family residence (stamp 8). i, Silver coin for official use and picture scroll (stamp 9). j, Naito Mansion, Yunotsu (stamp 10).

2008, Oct. 23			**Perf. 13x13¼**	
3067	A2440	Sheet of 10	16.00	16.00
a.-j.		80y Any single	1.40	.55

Miniature Sheet

Kyoto Prefecture Local Autonomy Law,
60th Anniv. — A2441

No. 3068: a, Scene from The Tale of Genji, by Shikibu Murasaki (33x39mm). b, Cherry blossoms, Kyoto Prefectural Botanical Garden (28x33mm). c, Thatched-roof house, Nantan (28x33mm). d, Kaijusen Pagoda, Wazuka tea plantation (28x33mm). e, Amanohashidate Sandbar (28x33mm).

Perf. 13¼ (#3068a), 13x13¼				
2008, Oct. 27			**Photo.**	
3068	A2441	Sheet of 5	8.00	8.00
a.-e.		80y Any single	1.40	.55

Miniature Sheet

Home Towns — A2442

No. 3069 — Paintings by Taiji Harada of views of towns: a, Stove Train (train, Kitatsugaru District, Aomori prefecture). b, New Year (buildings with snow-covered roofs, man shoveling snow, Nishimurayama District, Yamagata prefecture). c, Seaside Station (train station and telephone pole, Abashiri, Hokkaido prefecture). d, Incense Waterwheel (mill with waterwheel, Tsuyama, Okayama prefecture). e, Harness Straps (horse dragging log, Kurayoshi, Tottori prefecture). f, Life in the Snow Country (postman delivering mail to people at snow-covered house, Waga District, Iwate prefecture). g, Good Friends (people on town street in snowfall, Aizu Wakamatsu, Fukushima prefecture). h, Community of Stone Walls (people walking by stone wall, Minamiuwa District, Ehime prefecture). i, Village on Steep Slope (houses on mountainside, Miyoshi, Toskushima prefecture). j, Sedge-woven Hat (woman standing outside of building in snowstorm, Nakaonuma District, Niigata prefecture).

2008, Nov. 4			**Perf. 13**	
3069	A2442	Sheet of 10	16.00	16.00
a.-j.		80y Any single	1.40	.55

A2443   A2444

New Year 2009 (Year of the Ox)
A2445   A2446

2008, Nov. 4		**Photo.**	**Perf. 13x13¼**	
3070	A2443	50y multi	.90	.45
3071	A2444	80y multi	1.40	.55
			Perf. 13¼	
3072	A2445	50y +3y multi	1.00	.65
3073	A2446	80y +3y multi	1.60	.75
		Nos. 3070-3073 (4)	4.90	2.40

New Year Greetings Type of 2006
Inscribed "'09 New Year"
Stamp + Label
Panel Color

2008, Nov. 4		**Photo.**	**Perf. 13¼**	
3074	A2327a	50y blue green	1.40	1.40
3075	A2327a	50y red	1.40	1.40
a.		Pair, #3074-3075 + 2 labels	3.50	3.50

Labels could be personalized.

Miniature Sheet

Keio University, 150th Anniv. — A2447

No. 3076: a, Yukichi Fukuzawa (1835-1901), founder (stamp 1). b, University emblem (stamp 2). c, Old Library, denomination at LL (stamp 3). d, Old Library, denomination at LR (stamp 4). e, Keio and Waseda University rugby players (stamp 5). f, Keio and Waseda University baseball players (stamp 6). g, Stained-glass window depicting horse's head (stamp 7). h, Stained-glass window depicting goddess with upraised arm (stamp 8). i, Stained-glass window depicting feudal warrior (stamp 9). j, Stained-glass window with Latin inscription "Calamus Gladio Fortior" (stamp 10).

2008, Nov. 7			**Perf. 13**	
3076	A2447	Sheet of 10	16.00	16.00
a.-j.		80y Any single	1.40	.55

Miniature Sheet

Edo Calligraphy — A2448

No. 3077 — Characters for "ox": a, Depiction of ox head (Kinbun style) with red chop at LL. b, Blue character on lilac background, in Kokotsubun style. c, Character with three horizontal lines and two vertical lines, in standard script, with red chop at LR. d, Red character in Kinbun style. e, Character with two horizontal lines and one vertical line, in standard script, with red chop at left center. f, Character in Tensho style with red chop at right center. g, Character with arc and crossed lines in Tensho style, with red chop at LR. h, Character with two crossing curves in Kokotsubun style, with red chop in center. i, Character with two components in Reisho style, with red chop at left. j, Character with dot above sinuous line in Hiragana style, with red chop at LR.

Litho. & Embossed

2008, Nov. 21			**Perf. 13x13¼**	
3077	A2448	Sheet of 10	17.50	17.50
a.-j.		80y Any single	1.40	.55

A2449

A2450

A2451

A2452

A2453

Iron and Steel
Industry, 150th
Anniv. — A2454

2008, Dec. 1		**Photo.**	**Perf. 12¾x13**	
3078		Sheet of 10, #3078a,		
		3078b, 2 each		
		#3078c-3078f	17.50	17.50
a.	A2449	80y multi	1.40	.55
b.	A2450	80y multi	1.40	.55
c.	A2451	80y multi	1.40	.55
d.	A2452	80y multi	1.40	.55
e.	A2453	80y multi	1.40	.55
f.	A2454	80y multi	1.40	.55

Daffodils
A2455

Plum Blossoms
A2456

Fuki
A2457

Plum Blossoms
A2458

Weeping Cherry
Blossoms
A2459

Daffodils
A2460

Plum Blossoms
A2461

Fuki
A2462

Plum Blossoms
A2463

Weeping Cherry
Blossoms
A2464

2008, Dec. 1   Photo.   Perf. 13¼

3079	A2455	50y multi	.90	.45
3080	A2456	50y multi	.90	.45
3081	A2457	50y multi	.90	.45
3082	A2458	50y multi	.90	.45
3083	A2459	50y multi	.90	.45
a.		Vert. strip of 5, #3079-3083	5.50	4.25
3084	A2460	80y multi	1.40	.55
3085	A2461	80y multi	1.40	.55
3086	A2462	80y multi	1.40	.55
3087	A2463	80y multi	1.40	.55
3088	A2464	80y multi	1.40	.55
a.		Vert. strip of 5, #3084-3088	8.75	7.00
		Nos. 3079-3088 (10)	11.50	5.00

Flowers of Fukui, Wakayama, Akita, Fukuoka and Kyoto prefectures.

Miniature Sheets

A2465

Greetings Stamps — A2466

No. 3089: a, Santa Claus holding star (26x30mm). b, Stylized man, woman as bell (26x30mm). c, Kittens (26x30mm). d, Teddy bears and gift box (26x30mm). e, Chick, flowers (29mm diameter).
No. 3090: a, Kittens (34x28mm oval). b, Elf with bag of toys (25x34mm). c, Bluebirds in bouquet of roses (25x34mm). d, Santa Claus with horn (25x34mm). e, Fruit and flowers (25x34mm).

Die Cut Perf. 13¼

2008, Dec. 8   Litho.

3089	A2465	Sheet of 5	5.50	5.50
a.-e.		50y Any single	.90	.45

Die Cut Perf. 13

3090	A2466	Sheet of 5	8.75	8.75
a.-e.		80y Any single	1.40	.55

Miniature Sheet

Shimane Prefecture Local Autonomy Law, 60th Anniv. — A2467

No. 3091: a, Tree peony, silver coin for official use (33x39mm). b, Kuniga Coast (28x33mm). c, Matsue Castle (28x33mm). d, Tsuwano (28x33mm). e, Bronze bell (28x33mm).

Perf. 13¼ (#3091a), 13x13¼

2008, Dec. 8   Photo.

3091	A2467	Sheet of 5	8.75	8.75
a.-e.		80y Any single	1.40	.55

Miniature Sheet

Travel Scenes — A2468

No. 3092: a, Dragon from Shuri Castle Main Hall (stamp 1). b, Shuri Castle Main Hall (stamp 2). c, Ryukyuan dancer with arm raised at left (stamp 3). d, Ryukyuan dancer with arm raised at right (stamp 4). e, Shurei Gate (stamp 5). f, Zuisen Gate and Rokoku Gate, Shuri Castle (stamp 6). g, Shikina Garden (stamp 7). h, Stone pavement, Kinjo (stamp 8).

i, Guardian lion, International Street, Naha (stamp 9). j, Yui Monorail, Naha (stamp 10).

2009, Jan. 23   Litho.   Perf. 13x13¼

3092	A2468	Sheet of 10	18.00	18.00
a.-j.		80y Any single	1.40	.60

Miniature Sheet

Travel Scenes — A2469

No. 3093: a, Guardian Lion (stamp 1). b, Indian coral tree, Iejima (stamp 2). c, Fish in Okinawa Churaumi Aquarium, denomination at UR (stamp 3). d, As "c," denomination at LL (stamp 4). e, People watching fish in Okinawa Churaumi Aquarium, denomination at LL (stamp 5). f, As "e," denomination at LR (stamp 6). g, Nakijin Castle ruins (stamp 7). h, Okinawa rail (stamp 8). i, Cape Hedo, Okinawa (stamp 9). j, Mangroves, Gesashi Inlet (stamp 10).

2009, Feb. 2

3093	A2469	Sheet of 10	16.00	16.00
a.-j.		80y Any single	1.40	.60

Yoshino Cherry
Blossoms
A2470

Azaleas
A2471

Tulips
A2472

Rhododendron
A2473

Nara Cherry
Blossoms
A2474

Yoshino Cherry
Blossoms
A2475

Azaleas
A2476

Tulips
A2477

Rhododendrons
A2478

Nara Cherry
Blossoms
A2479

2009, Feb. 2   Photo.   Perf. 13¼

3094	A2470	50y multi	.90	.50
3095	A2471	50y multi	.90	.50
3096	A2472	50y multi	.90	.50
3097	A2473	50y multi	.90	.50
3098	A2474	50y multi	.90	.50
a.		Vert. strip of 5, #3094-3098	5.00	3.75
3099	A2475	80y multi	1.40	.60
3100	A2476	80y multi	1.40	.60
3101	A2477	80y multi	1.40	.60
3102	A2478	80y multi	1.40	.60
3103	A2479	80y multi	1.40	.60
a.		Vert. strip of 5, #3099-3103	8.00	6.25
		Nos. 3094-3103 (10)	11.50	5.50

Flowers of Tokyo, Tochigi, Niigata, Shiga and Nara prefectures.

Animation
Miniature Sheet

GeGeGe no Kitaro — A2480

No. 3104: a, Kitaro and Otoko Nezumi. b, Daddy Eyeball in bowl. c, Kitaro kicking. d, Kitaro in fire. e, Villain with elongated head, villain with blades for arms. f, Villains with red face, villain with snake. g, Kitaro and mermaid. h, Musume Neko. i, Otoko Nezumi, Musume Neko, Babaa Sunakake and Nurikabe. j, Kitaro, Daddy Eyeball, Jijii Konaki, Momen Ittan.

2009, Feb. 23   Litho.   Perf. 13x13¼

3104	A2480	Sheet of 10	16.00	16.00
a.-j.		80y Any single	1.40	.60

Miniature Sheet

Travel Scenes — A2481

No. 3105: a, Todai Temple (stamp 1). b, Buddha, Todai Temple (stamp 2). c, Asura, Kofuku Temple (stamp 3). d, Nara National Museum (stamp 4). e, Kasuga Taisha Shrine (stamp 5). f, Roof of Kasuga Taisha Shrine and overhanging roof (stamp 6). g, Japanese deer, Wakakusa Hill (stamp 7). h, Inanuishi family residence (stamp 8). i, Gazebo, Nara Park (stamp 9). j, Bridge to gazebo, Nara Park (stamp 10).

2009, Mar. 2
3105 A2481 Sheet of 10 16.00 16.00
a.-j. 80y Any single 1.40 .60

Miniature Sheet

Home Towns — A2482

No. 3106 — Paintings by Taiji Harada of views of towns: a, Cultivating (farmer in field, Nishitama District, Tokyo prefecture). b, Children Planting Rice (children in rice paddy, Katta District, Miyagi prefecture). c, I'm Home (child running up hill to farmhouse, Yamagata District, Hiroshima prefecture). d, Northern Springtime (farmer and wheelbarrow in field of yellow flowers, Iwanai District, Hokkaido prefecture). e, Chinese Milk Vetch Field (people near farmhouse, Kyoto, Kyoto prefecture). f, Water Mortar (farmer near water mortar, Hita, Oita prefecture). g, Short Rest (woman resting on bench in front of building, Numazu, Shizuoka prefecture). h, Red Train (street scene with train in background, Izumo, Shimane prefecture). i, Oven-shaped Thatch Roofs (woman, children with toy car in front of farm house, Kishima District, Saga prefecture). j, Little Post Office (people outside of post office, Hosu District, Ishikawa prefecture).

2009, Mar. 2 Photo. Perf. 13
3106 A2482 Sheet of 10 16.00 16.00
a.-j. 80y Any single 1.40 .60

Miniature Sheets

A2483

Weekly Comic Books For Boys, 50th Anniv — A2484

No. 3107: a, Osomatsu-kun (boy's face, green panel at top). b, Makoto Chan (boy with broom). c, Kamui Gaiden (swordsman with black hair). d, Gambare Genki (boxer, dark blue background). e, Paman (three characters with masks and capes). f, Urusei Yatsura (boy in cap, girl in bikini). g, Dame Oyaji (man holding radish and knife). h, Saibogu 009 (characters with galaxy in background). i, Purogorufa Saru (golfer). j, Tacchi (boy and girl looking over their shoulders).

No. 3108: a, Eitoman (android with "8" on chest). b, Taiga Masuku (caped man with tiger mask). c, Kyojin no Hoshi (Yomiuri Giants pitcher). d, Karate Baka Ichidai (karate master with green hair). e, GeGeGe no Kitaro (Kitaro, Daddy Eyeball and Otoko Nezumi). f, Ai to Makoto (girl with orange hair, boy with green hair). g, Tensai Bakabon (woman with yellow hair bow, screaming man). h, Tsurikichi Sanpei (boy holding fish). i, Ashita no Jo (boxer, pale blue background). j, Tonda Kappuru (boy, girl with green dress and orange bow).

2009, Mar. 17 Litho. Perf. 13
3107 A2483 Sheet of 10 16.00 16.00
a.-j. 80y Any single 1.40 .60
3108 A2484 Sheet of 10 16.00 16.00
a.-j. 80y Any single 1.40 .60

Wedding of Emperor Akihito and Empress Michiko, 50th Anniv. — A2485

Designs: No. 3109, Confectionery box. No. 3110, Fan.

2009, Apr. 10 Photo. Perf. 13¼
3109 80y multi 1.40 .60
3110 80y multi 1.40 .60
a. A2485 Pair, #3109-3110 3.20 2.50
b. Souvenir sheet, #3109-3110 3.25 3.25

Animation
Miniature Sheet

Detective Conan — A2486

No. 3111: a, Ai Haibara and Conan and brick wall. b, Mitsuhiko Tsuburaya, Ayumi Yoshida, and Genta Kojima and brick wall. c, Heiji Hattori and cherry blossoms. d, Kazuha Toyama and cherry blossoms. e, Conan and night sky. f, Gin and night sky. g, Conan and fence. h, Ran Mori and fence. i, Kiddo Kaito holding Christmas gift. j, Conan, Moon and hang-glider.

2009, Apr. 17 Litho. Perf. 13x13¼
3111 A2486 Sheet of 10 17.50 17.50
a.-j. 80y Any single 1.40 .60

Peonies, by Yu Fei'an A2487

Peonies, by Ren Bonian A2488

Peonies, by Keika Kanashima A2489

Peonies, by Keika Kanashima A2490

Peonies, by Keika Kanashima A2491

Peonies, by Keika Kanashima A2492

2009, Apr. 20 Photo. Perf. 13¼
3112 Sheet of 10, #3112c-3112f, 3 each, #3112a-3112b 17.50 17.50
a. A2487 80y multi 1.40 .60
b. A2488 80y multi 1.40 .60
c. A2489 80y multi 1.40 .60
d. A2490 80y multi 1.40 .60
e. A2491 80y multi 1.40 .60
f. A2492 80y multi 1.40 .60

Philately Week.

Red Cross, 150th Anniv. — A2493

Designs: No. 3113, Henri Dunant (1828-1910), founder of Red Cross. No. 3114, Japanese Red Cross Day poster, 1933.

2009, May 8   Litho.   Perf. 13

3113	80y multi	1.40	.60
3114	80y multi	1.40	.60
a.	A2493 Pair, #3113-3114	3.50	2.50

Miniature Sheet

Nagano Prefecture Local Autonomy
Law, 60th Anniv. — A2494

No. 3115: a, Kappa Bridge, Azusa River, Mt.
Hodaka (33x39mm). b, Nanohana Park and
Chikuma River, Iiyama City (28x33mm). c,
Anraku Temple (28x33mm). d, Matsumoto
Castle (28x33mm). e, Manji Buddha statue
(28x33mm).

Perf. 13¼ (#3115a), 13x13¼

2009, May 14   Photo.

| 3115 | A2494 | Sheet of 5 | 8.75 | 8.75 |
| a.-e. | 80y Any single | | 1.40 | .60 |

Inauguration of Lay Judge
System — A2495

Designs: No. 3116, Lay Judge System
emblem. No. 3117, Birds on scale.

2009, May 21   Litho.   Perf. 13x13¼

3116	80y multi	1.40	.60
3117	80y multi	1.40	.60
a.	A2495 Pair, #3116-3117	3.50	2.50

Miniature Sheets

A2496

Weekly Comic Books For Boys, 50th
Anniv — A2497

No. 3118: a, Gu-Gu Ganmo (child and
chicken-like alien). b, Major (baseball player
with bat, ball and glove). c, Patlabor Mobile
Police (man standing on robot). d, Rekka no
Hono (boy with gloved hand raised). e, Ushio
to Tora (monster and boy holding torch). f,
ARMS (boy with extended hand and slash
marks in background). g, GS Mikami
Gakuraku Daisakusen (woman with long red
hair). h, Kekkaishi (magician pointing finger
forward). i, Detective Conan (boy pointing forward wearing glasses and bow tie). j, Hayate
no Gotoku (girl, boy and tower).
No. 3119: a, 1, 2 no Sanshiro (judo fighter
with flame in background). b, Hajime no Ippo
(boxer). c, Kabocha Wain (boy and tall girl). d,
Kindaichi Shonen no Jikenbo (two boys and
girl). e, Kotaro Makari Tooru (boy and girl in
white clothes). f, GTO (boy with GTO tattoo).
g, Bari Bari Densetsu (motorcyclist). h, RAVE
(swordsman and other characters). i, Misuta
Ajikko (chef). j, Daiya no A (baseball pitcher).

2009, May 22   Perf. 13

3118	A2496	Sheet of 10	17.50	17.50
a.-j.	80y Any single		1.40	.60
3119	A2497	Sheet of 10	17.50	17.50
a.-j.	80y Any single		1.40	.60

**Opening of Japanese Ports, 150th
Anniv.**
Miniature Sheets

Nagasaki — A2498

Yokohama — A2499

Hakodate — A2500

No. 3120: a, 19th century woodblock print of
Nagasaki Port (denomination at left in black).
b, 19th century woodblock print of Nagasaki
Port (denomination at right in black). c, Nagasaki Port at night (denomination at UL in
white). d, Nagasaki Port at night (denomination at UR in black). e, Drawing of boats and
ships (denomination at UL in black). f, Drawing
of boats and ships (denomination at LR in
white). g, Nagasaki Port at night (denomination at LL in white). h, Oura Catholic Church. i,
Goddess Great Bridge, Nippon Maru cruise
ship. j, Glover Garden, Nagasaki Port (lamppost in foreground).
No. 3121: a, Woodblock print of Yokohama
Port, 1871 (denomination at LL in black). b,
Woodblock print of Yokohama Port, 1871
(denomination at LR in black). c, Yokohama
Port at night (denomination at UL in white, tall
building at right). d, Yokohama Port at night
(denomination at LR in white). e, Yokohama
Bay Bridge. f, Yokohama City Port Opening
Memorial Hall. g, Sailing ship Nippon Maru. h,
Yokohama International Passenger Boat Ter-
minal and cruise ship.
No. 3122: a, Woodblock print of Hakodate
Port, 1882 (denomination at LL in black). b,
Woodblock print of Hakodate Port, 1882
(denomination at UL in black). c, Hakodate
Port at night (denomination at UR in white). d,
Hakodate Port at night (denomination at UL in
white). e, Street on Hachiman Slope, Hako-
date Port at night. f, Hakodate Orthodox Christian Church. g, Ship, lamppost at Old Pier at
night. h, Hakodate Park, Hakodate Port
(denomination at UL in black).

2009, June 2   Litho.   Perf. 13

3120	A2498	Sheet of 10	17.50	17.50
a.-j.	80y Any single		1.40	.60
3121	A2499	Sheet of 10, #3120e-3120f, 3121a-3121h	17.50	17.50
a.-h.	80y Any single		1.40	.60
3122	A2500	Sheet of 10, #3120e-3120f, 3122a-3122h	17.50	17.50
a.-h.	80y Any single		1.40	.60
	Nos. 3120-3122 (3)		52.50	52.50

Miniature Sheet

国土緑化
ふるさと・24 福井県

National Afforestation
Campaign — A2501

No. 3123 — Flora from Fukui Prefecture: a, Weeping cherry blossoms. b, Japanese zelkova tree. c, Japanese red pine tree. d, Japanese bird cherry tree. e, Magnolia blossoms. f, Camellia. g, Japanese horse chestnut tree. h, Kousa dogwood blossoms. i, Narcissi (denomination at UL). j, Narcissi (denomination at UR).

2009, June 5   Litho.   Perf. 13
3123 A2501   Sheet of 10   11.00 11.00
a.-j.   50y Any single   .90   .50

Miniature Sheet

Home Towns — A2502

No. 3124 — Paintings by Taiji Harada of views of towns: a, Flowers Blooming in the Rain (mother and daughter under umbrellas on path by flower field, Tone District, Gumma prefecture). b, Potato Blossoms (train car near potato field, Nakagawa District, Hokkaido prefecture). c, High Country Flowers (people in flower field, Suwa, Nagano prefecture). d, Memories on the Wind (farmer with wheelbarrow on path near farmhouse, Hagi, Yamaguchi

prefecture). e, Tranquility (people near stone wall in front of house, Sumoto, Hyogo prefecture). f, Sunset Skies (adult and child on hillside path near house, Nishiusuki District, Miyazaki prefecture). g, Island Post Office (people standing in front of post office, Yaeyama District, Okinawa prefecture). h, Lotus Blossoms (field of lotus with house and large tree in background, Hakusan, Ishikawa prefecture). i, Flower Garden (two women picking flowers with house and telephone pole in background, Minamiboso, Chiba prefecture). j, Peach Blossoms (adult and child picnicking under trees, Fuefuki, Yamanashi prefecture).

2009, June 23   Photo.   Perf. 13
3124 A2502   Sheet of 10   17.50 17.50
a.-j.   80y Any single   1.40   .60

Miniature Sheet

Intl. Polar Year — A2503

No. 3125: a, Polar bears. b, Weddell seal. c, Arctic fox. d, Adélie penguin.

Litho. With Hologram Affixed
2009, June 30   Die Cut Perf. 13
Self-Adhesive
3125 A2503   Sheet of 4   7.00 7.00
a.-d.   80y Any single   1.40   .60

Gentian
A2504

Chrysanthemums
A2505

Miyagi Bush
Clover — A2506

Black
Lilies — A2507

Japanese
Maple — A2508

Gentian — A2509

Chrysanthemums
A2510

Miyagi Bush
Clover
A2511

Black
Lilies — A2512

Japanese
Maple — A2513

2009, July 1   Photo.   Perf. 13¼
3126 A2504   50y multi   .90   .50
3127 A2505   50y multi   .90   .50
3128 A2506   50y multi   .90   .50
3129 A2507   50y multi   .90   .50
3130 A2508   50y multi   .90   .50
a.   Vert. strip of 5, #3126-3130   5.50   4.00
3131 A2509   80y multi   1.40   .60
3132 A2510   80y multi   1.40   .60
3133 A2511   80y multi   1.40   .60
3134 A2512   80y multi   1.40   .60
3135 A2513   80y multi   1.40   .60
a.   Vert. strip of 5, #3131-3135   8.75   6.25
Nos. 3126-3135 (10)   11.50   5.50

Flora of Kumamoto, Hyogo, Miyagi, Ishikawa and Hiroshima prefectures.

Miniature Sheet

新潟県

Niigata Prefecture Local Autonomy
Law, 60th Anniv. — A2514

No. 3136: a, Japanese crested ibis over Sado Island (33x39mm). b, Cherry blossoms, Takada Castle (28x33mm). c, Fireworks over Nagaoka (28x33mm). d, Imori Pond, Mt. Myoko (28x33mm). e, Fireworks at Tokamichi Snow Festival (28x33mm).

Perf. 13¼ (#3136a), 13x13¼
2009, July 8   Photo.
3136 A2514   Sheet of 5   8.75 8.75
a.-e.   80y Any single   1.40   .60

Statue of Eki
Doji — A2515

2009, July 23   Photo.   Perf. 13x13½
3137 A2515 300y multi   6.25   4.75

Ono no Komachi,
Poet — A2516

Ietaka Junii,
Poet — A2517

Hoshi Jakuren,
Poet — A2518

Sakanoue no
Korenori,
Poet — A2519

Daini no Sanmi,
Poet — A2520

平成21年 ふみの日「百人一首」

Poetry — A2521

No. 3143 — Poetry in Japanese calligraphy and: a, Tree with white blossoms. b, Ono no Komachi. c, Tree near pond. d, Ietaka Junii. e, Tree with green leaves. f, Hoshi Jakuren. g, House. h, Sakanoue no Korenori. i, Leaves. j, Daini no Sanmi.

2009, July 23   Photo.   Perf. 13¼
3138 A2516   50y multi   .90   .50
3139 A2517   50y multi   .90   .50
3140 A2518   50y multi   .90   .50
3141 A2519   50y multi   .90   .50
3142 A2520   50y multi   .90   .50
a.   Vert. strip of 5, #3138-3142   5.50   5.50

Perf. 12¾x13
3143 A2521   Sheet of 10   17.50 17.50
a.-j.   80y Any single   1.40   .90

Letter Writing Day.

Miniature Sheets

A2522

Hello Kitty and Dear Daniel — A2523

No. 3144: a, Hello Kitty with envelope. b, Hello Kitty, Dear Daniel, birds in pond. c, Hello Kitty, Dear Daniel, two trees. d, Hello Kitty and Dear Daniel with envelopes. e, Hello Kitty, Dear Daniel, three trees.

No. 3145: a, Hello Kitty with envelope (35mm diameter). b, Hello Kitty, two birds (35x28mm, heart-shaped). c, Hello Kitty, tree, three birds. d, Bird carrying envelope flying over Hello Kitty. e, Hello Kitty, bird, two trees. f, Hello Kitty, Dear Daniel, bird, squirrel and rabbit.

Die Cut Perf. 13½

2009, July 23   Litho.

3144	A2522	Sheet of 10, 2 each #a-e	11.00
a.-e.		50y Any single	.90	.50

Die Cut Perf. (#3145a-3145b), Die Cut Perf. 13½

3145	A2523	Sheet of 10, #a-b, 2 each #c-f	17.50
a.-f.		80y Any single	1.40	.90

Suwa Bluff, Nippori, by Hiroshige A2524

Pensive Love, by Utamaro A2525

Tokuji Otani as Yakko Sodesuke, by Sharaku A2526

Kumano Junisha Shrine, by Hiroshige A2527

Moon Promontory, by Hiroshige A2528

Woman Reading a Letter, by Utamaro A2529

Wadaemon Nakajima as Bodara Chozaemon and Konozo Nakamura as Funayado Kanagaway no Gon, by Sharaku A2530

Pagoda at Zojo Temple, by Hiroshige A2531

Clear Weather After Snowfall at Japan Bridge, by Hiroshige A2532

Kameikichi of Sodegaura, by Utamaro A2533

2009, Aug. 3   Litho.   **Perf. 13¼**

3146		Sheet of 10	17.50	17.50
a.	A2524	80y multi	1.40	.90
b.	A2525	80y multi	1.40	.90
c.	A2526	80y multi	1.40	.90
d.	A2527	80y multi	1.40	.90
e.	A2528	80y multi	1.40	.90
f.	A2529	80y multi	1.40	.90
g.	A2530	80y multi	1.40	.90
h.	A2531	80y multi	1.40	.90
i.	A2532	80y multi	1.40	.90
j.	A2533	80y multi	1.40	.90

Life in Edo (Tokyo).

Gujo Dance (Gifu) — A2534

Fukagawa Hachiman Festival (Tokyo) — A2535

Denomination at: No. 3147, Right. No. 3148, Left. No. 3149, Right. No. 3150, Left.

2009, Aug. 10

3147		50y multi	.90	.50
3148		50y multi	.90	.50
a.	A2534	Horiz. pair, #3147-3148	2.20	2.20
3149		50y multi	.90	.50
3150		50y multi	.90	.50
a.	A2535	Horiz. pair, #3149-3150	2.20	2.20
		Nos. 3147-3150 (4)	3.60	2.00

Miniature Sheet

Travel Scenes — A2536

No. 3151: a, Asuka, denomination at LL (stamp 1). b, Asuka, denomination at LR (stamp 2). c, Tachibana Temple, denomination at LL (stamp 3). d, Tachibana Temple, denomination at LR (stamp 4). e, Sculpture, Asuka Historical Museum (stamp 5). f, Stone burial mound (stamp 6). g, Tanzan Shrine, denomination at UR (stamp 7). h, Tanzan Shrine, denomination at UL (stamp 8). i, Picture scroll, denomination at UL (stamp 9). j, Picture scroll, denomination at LL (stamp 10).

2009, Aug. 21   **Perf. 13x13¼**

3151	A2536	Sheet of 10	17.50	17.50
a.-j.		80y Any single	1.40	.90

Persimmons and Haiku by Shiki Masaoka — A2537

Roofs of Dogo Onsen and Haiku by Shiki Masaoka — A2538

Mountain, Field and Haiku by Kyoshi Takahama A2539

House and Haiku by Soseki Natsume — A2540

Cherry Blossoms and Haiku by Hekigoto Kawahigashi A2541

2009, Sept. 1   Litho.

3152	A2537	80y multi	1.40	.90
3153	A2538	80y multi	1.40	.90
3154	A2539	80y multi	1.40	.90
3155	A2540	80y multi	1.40	.90
3156	A2541	80y multi	1.40	.90
a.		Vert. strip of 5, #3152-3156	8.75	8.75

Miniature Sheet

National Athletic Meet (Niigata) — A2542

No. 3157: a, Tohoku Electric Power Big Swan Stadium. b, Soccer player. c, Boxer. d, Basketball player.

2009, Sept. 25   **Perf. 13x13¼**
3157 A2542 Sheet of 10, 2
                        each #3157a-
                        3157c, 4
                        #3157d   11.00 11.00
a.-d.   50y Any single   .90   .50

Takayama Festival (Gifu) — A2543

Hakone Feudal Lord's Procession (Kanagawa) — A2544

Designs: No. 3158, Crowd at Night Festival. No. 3159, Shakkyo float puppet. No. 3160, Three men and box. No. 3161, Three men.

2009, Oct. 1   **Perf. 13¼**
3158   50y multi   .90   .50
3159   50y multi   .90   .50
a. A2543 Pair, #3158-3159   2.20   2.20
3160   50y multi   .90   .50
3161   50y multi   .90   .50
a. A2544 Horiz. pair, #3160-3161   2.20   2.20
        Nos. 3158-3161 (4)   3.60   2.00

Miniature Sheet

Home Towns — A2545

No. 3162 — Paintings by Taiji Harada of views of towns: a, Nagasaki Kunchi (palanquin in parade, Nagasaki, Nagasaki prefecture). b, Rice Paddy Spirit Festival (people in rice paddy, Satsumasendai, Kagoshima prefecture). c, Carp Streamers (people making carp streamers, Iwakura, Aichi prefecture). d, Doll Send-off (winter parade, Waga District, Iwate prefecture). e, Deer Dance (musicians, people in blue, white, red and yellow costumes holding poles with banners, Kitauwa District, Ehime prefecture). f, Business Success Festival (crowd in front of Ebisu Shrine, Naniwa Ward, Osaka prefecture). g, Amahage Festival (masked man visiting children and parents, Akumi District, Yamagata prefecture). h, Lion Dance (large crowd surrounding float with dancers on tower, Wakayama, Wakayama prefecture). i, Floating Doll Festival (women dropping dolls into Sendai River, Tottori, Tottori prefecture). j, Gruel Doll Festival (children at table near Kama River, Tano District, Gumma prefecture).

2009, Oct. 8   **Photo.**   **Perf. 13**
3162 A2545 Sheet of 10   17.50 17.50
a.-j.   80y Any single   1.40   .90

International Letter Writing Week Type of 2000

Hiroshige paintings from 53 Stations of the Tokaido Highway: 90y, Fujisawa. 110y, Okitsu. 130y, Chiryu.

2009, Oct. 9   **Photo.**   **Perf. 13¼**
3163 A2119 90y multi   1.60   .80
3164 A2119 110y multi   1.90   .90
3165 A2119 130y multi   2.10   1.00
        Nos. 3163-3165 (3)   5.60   2.70

Miniature Sheet

Diplomatic Relations Between Japan and Austria, 140th Anniv. — A2546

No. 3166: a, Portrait of Emilie Flöge, by Gustav Klimt (45x30mm). b, Autumn Clothing, by Shoen Uemura (45x30mm). c, Vienna Art History Museum and fountain (39x30mm). d, Empress Elizabeth of Austria, by Franz Winterhalter (39x30mm). e, Melk Abbey (steeple at right), Austria (39x30mm). f, Melk Abbey (steeple at left, 39x30mm). g, Wolfgang Amadeus Mozart and Salzburg (39x30mm). h, Salzburg (39x30mm). i, Hallstatt waterfront (39x30mm). j, Mountainside buildings, Hallstatt (39x30mm).

2009, Oct. 16   **Litho.**   **Perf. 13¼x13**
3166 A2546 Sheet of 10   17.50 17.50
a.-j.   80y Any single   1.40   .90
        See Austria No. 2227.

Miniature Sheet

Diplomatic Relations Between Japan and Hungary, 140th Anniv. — A2547

No. 3167: a, Hungarian flask. b, Mount Fuji, horiz. c, Jar from Japanese tea service. d, Hungarian Parliament (flag above building). e, Hungarian Parliament (building with dome). f, Matyo folk embroidery, Hungary. g, Elizabeth Bridge, Hungary, horiz. h, Crane and leaves fabric pattern from Japanese kimono. i, Herend porcelain figurine (Hussar examining sword blade). j, Herend porcelain vase.

Perf. 13x13¼, 13¼x13
2009, Oct. 16   **Litho.**
3167 A2547 Sheet of 10   17.50 17.50
a.-j.   80y Any single   1.40   .90
        See Hungary No. 4141.

Animation
Miniature Sheet

Naruto: Hurricane Chronicles — A2548

No. 3168: a, Naruto Uzumaki (yellow hair, black and orange shirt). b, Sasuke Uchiha (with open shirt). c, Sakura Haruno (girl with pink hair). d, Kakashi Hatake (with red spiral on sleeve). e, Sai (with sword). f, Shikamaru Nara (clasping hands). g, Deidara (girl with yellow hair and raised hand). h, Itachi Uchiha (with black hair and black and red robe). i, Jiraiya (with white hair). j, Fourth Hokage (yellow hair, white, gray and red robe).

2009, Oct. 23   **Litho.**   **Perf. 13x13¼**
3168 A2548 Sheet of 10   17.50 17.50
a.-j.   80y Any single   1.40   .90

Miniature Sheet

Ibaraki Prefecture Local Autonomy Law, 60th Anniv. — A2549

No. 3169: a, H-2 rocket, Mt. Tsukuba (33x39mm). b, Fukuroda Falls (28x33mm). c, Mitsukuni Tokugawa (1628-1700), Mito daimyo (28x33mm). d, Boat on Kasumigaura (28x33mm). e, Fireworks over Tsuchiura (28x33mm).

Perf. 13¼ (#3169a), 13x13¼
2009, Nov. 4   **Photo.**
3169 A2549 Sheet of 5   9.00   9.00
a.-e.   80y Any single   1.40   .90

A2550   A2551

New Year 2010 (Year of the Tiger)
A2552   A2553

2009, Nov. 11 **Photo.** **Perf. 13x13½**
3170 A2550 50y multi   .90   .60
3171 A2551 80y multi   1.40   .90

                              Perf. 13¼
3172 A2552 50y +3y multi   1.10   .80
3173 A2553 80y +3y multi   1.60   1.25
        Nos. 3170-3173 (4)   5.00   3.55

Phoenix — A2554

Kirin Facing Right A2555

Kirin Facing Left A2556

2009, Nov. 12   **Photo.**   **Perf. 13¼**
3174 A2554 80y multi   1.40   .90
3175 A2555 80y multi   1.40   .90
3176 A2556 80y multi   1.40   .90
a.   Souvenir sheet, #3175-3176   3.50   2.80
        Nos. 3174-3176 (3)   4.20   2.70

Enthronement of Emperor Akihito, 20th anniv. Nos. 3174-3176 were printed in sheets containing two each of Nos. 3175 and 3176 and six of No. 3174.

Miniature Sheet

Calligraphy — A2557

No. 3177 — Characters for "tiger" by calligraphers: a, Chikusei Hayashi (character in running script with red background). b, Chosho Kneko (character in clerical style, with denomination at LR, and large red chop at LL). c, Gakufu Toriyama (character in kinbun style in gold with blue green background). d, Hosen Takeuchi (character in kinbun style with denomination at LL, red chop at LR). e, Shiko Miyazaki (character in hiragana script with denomination above Japanese characters and "Nippon" at LL). f, Setsuzan Kitano (character in kokotsubun style with denomination and red chop at LL). g, Masato Seki (character in kinbun style in red). h, Junichi Yanagida (characters in running script with denomination at LL above Japanese characters and "Nippon" at LR). i, Kukoku Tamura (character in clerical script in blue with light blue and white background). j, Bokushun Kito (character in kinbun style with denomination at LR and small red chop at LL).

Litho. & Embossed
2009, Nov. 20   Perf. 13x13¼
3177 A2557 Sheet of 10   17.50 17.50
  a.-j.   80y Any single   1.40   .90

Miniature Sheets

A2558

Greetings Stamps — A2559

No. 3178: a, Girl and apples. b, Snowman and stars. c, Angel holding toy rabbit. d, Apple, ribbon, ring of roses. e, Figures with blue and pink faces, horiz.

No. 3179: a, Christmas wreath. b, Santa Claus playing violin on chimney. c, Oil lamp and flowers. d, Angel with gift. e, Figure made of fir branches, candle.

Die Cut Perf. 12¾x13, 13x12¾
2009, Nov. 24   Litho.
Self-Adhesive
3178 A2558 Sheet of 5   5.50 5.50
  a.-e.   50y Any single   .90   .50
Die Cut Perf. 12¾x13
3179 A2559 Sheet of 5   9.00 9.00
  a.-e.   80y Any single   1.40   .90

Peach Blossoms
A2560

Rape Blossoms
A2561

Plum Blossoms
and Primrose
A2562

Bayberry
A2563

Bungo Plum
Blossoms
A2564

Peach Blossoms
A2565

Rape Blossoms
A2566

Plum Blossoms
and Primrose
A2567

Bayberry
A2568

Bungo Plum
Blossoms
A2569

2009, Dec. 1   Photo.   Perf. 13¼
3180 A2560 50y multi   .90   .50
3181 A2561 50y multi   .90   .50
3182 A2562 50y multi   .90   .50
3183 A2563 50y multi   .90   .50
3184 A2564 50y multi   .90   .50
  a.   Vert. strip of 5, #3180-3184   5.50 5.50
3185 A2565 80y multi   1.40   .90
3186 A2566 80y multi   1.40   .90
3187 A2567 80y multi   1.40   .90
3188 A2568 80y multi   1.40   .90
3189 A2569 80y multi   1.40   .90
  a.   Vert. strip of 5, #3185-3189   8.75 8.75
    Nos. 3180-3189 (10)   11.50 7.00

Flowers of Okayama, Chiba, Osaka, Kochi and Oita prefectures.

Prefecture Types of 1991-2007

Designs as before.

Die Cut Perf. 13¼ at T, L and R, Serpentine Die Cut 11¾ at B
2009   Litho.   Self-Adhesive
3189B ZA684 50y multi   .90   .50
Serpentine Die Cut 11¾ at T and B, Die Cut Perf. 13¼ at L and R
3189C ZA685 50y multi   .90   .50
3189D ZA686 50y multi   .90   .50
3189E ZA687 50y multi   .90   .50
Serpentine Die Cut 11¾ at T, Die Cut Perf. 13¼ at L, R and B
3189F ZA688 50y multi   .90   .50
  j.   Vert. strip of 5, #3189B-3189F   5.50

Serpentine Die Cut 11½ at T, Die Cut Perf. 13½ at L, R and B
3189G ZA115 80y multi   1.40   .90
Serpentine Die Cut 11¾
3189H 80y Katsura Beach   1.40   .90
3189I 80y Sakamoto Ryoma   1.40   .90
  k.   ZA352 Horiz. pair, #3189H-3189I   3.50
    Nos. 3189B-3189I (8)   8.70 5.20
    Issued: Nos. 3189B-3189F, Oct.; No. 3189G, 3/19; Nos. 3189H-3189I, Nov.

Animation
Miniature Sheet

Sergeant Keroro — A2570

No. 3190: a, Sergeant Keroro, wearing helmet, holding post card. b, Fuyuki Hinata holding post card. c, Natsumi Hinata holding gift. d, Corporal Giroro, wearing helmet, with arms crossed. e, Private Tamama holding gift above head. f, Momoka Nishizawa holding letter. g, Saburo holding stamps. h, Sergeant Major Kururu with stamp on forehead. i, Lance Corporal Dororo, with white helmet, holding scroll. j, Koyuki Azumaya, holding scroll.

2010, Jan. 22   Litho.   Perf. 13
3190 A2570 Sheet of 10   17.50 17.50
  a.-j.   80y Any single   1.40   .90

Miniature Sheets

A2571

Greetings Stamps — A2572

No. 3191: a, Fairy with watering can. b, Fairy giving letter to bird. c, Fairies holding flower basket. d, Fairy with horn on back of flying bird. e, Fairy with violin on flower leaf.

No. 3192: a, Flower bouquet in red wrapping paper, butterflies. b, Woman with flute. c, Flower bouquet in white wrapping paper, butterflies. d, Flowers, G clef. e, Flowers, rabbit.

Die Cut Perf. 12¾x13
2010, Jan. 25   Litho.
Self-Adhesive
3191 A2571 Sheet of 5   5.50 5.50
  a.-e.   50y Any single   .90   .50
3192 A2572 Sheet of 5   9.00 9.00
  a.-e.   80y Any single   1.40   .90

Miniature Sheet

Travel Scenes — A2573

No. 3193: a, Matsushima, denomination at LL (stamp 1). b, Matsushima, denomination at LR (stamp 2). c, Sendai Castle ruins (stamp 3). d, Suit of armor and crested helmet (stamp 4). e, Sendai tourist bus (stamp 5). f, A Bathing Woman, sculpture by Venanzo Crocetti, Sendai (stamp 6). g, Tanabata Festival, Sendai (stamp 7). h, Zuihoden Mausoleum (stamp 8). i, Rinno Temple, denomination at LL (stamp 9). j, Garden and pond at Rinno Temple (stamp 10).

2010, Jan. 29   Litho.   Perf. 13
3193 A2573 Sheet of 10   17.50 17.50
  a.-j.   80y Any single   1.40   .90

Tulips — A2574

Chinese Milk
Vetch — A2575

Nijisseiki Pear
Blossoms
A2576

Coral Tree
Blossoms
A2577

Fuji Cherry
Blossoms
A2578

Tulips
A2579

Chinese Milk
Vetch
A2580

Nijisseiki Pear
Blossoms
A2581

Coral Tree
Blossoms
A2582

Fuji Cherry
Blossoms
A2583

2010, Feb. 1   Photo.   Perf. 13¼

3194	A2574	50y multi	.90	.50
3195	A2575	50y multi	.90	.50
3196	A2576	50y multi	.90	.50
3197	A2577	50y multi	.90	.50
3198	A2578	50y multi	.90	.50
a.		Vert. strip of 5, #3194-3198	5.50	5.50
3199	A2579	80y multi	1.40	.90
3200	A2580	80y multi	1.40	.90
3201	A2581	80y multi	1.40	.90
3202	A2582	80y multi	1.40	.90
3203	A2583	80y multi	1.40	.90
a.		Vert. strip of 5, #3199-3203	8.75	8.75
		Nos. 3194-3203 (10)	11.50	7.00

Flowers of Toyama, Gifu, Tottori, Okinawa and Yamanashi prefectures.

Miniature Sheet

Nara Prefecture Local Autonomy Law,
60th Anniv. — A2584

No. 3204: a, Great Hall of State, cherry blossoms, kemari players (33x39mm). b, Hase Temple, peonies (28x33mm). c, Ukimodo during Nara Candlelight Festival (28x33mm). d, Muro Temple pagoda (28x33mm). e, Mt. Yoshino and cherry blossoms (28x33mm).

Perf. 13¼ (#3204a), 13x13¼

2010, Feb. 8   Photo.

3204	A2584	Sheet of 5	9.00	9.00
a.-e.		80y Any single	1.40	.90

Miniature Sheet

Travel Scenes — A2585

No. 3205: a, Kurashiki District buildings, denomination at LL (stamp 1). b, Kurashiki District buildings, swans, denomination at UR (stamp 2). c, Ohara Museum of Art (stamp 3). d, Belgian Girl in Kimono, painting by Torajiro Kojima (stamp 4). e, Seto Great Bridge, from distance (stamp 5). f, Arches and roadway of Seto Great Bridge (stamp 6). g, Kotohira Shrine (stamp 7). h, Mt. Iino (stamp 8). i, Bridge, Ritsurin Park, Takamatsu, denomination at LL (stamp 9). j, Bridge, Ritsurin Park, and cherry blossoms, denomination at UR (stamp 10).

2010, Mar. 1   Litho.   Perf. 13

3205	A2585	Sheet of 10	17.50	17.50
a.-j.		80y Any single	1.40	.90

Miniature Sheet

Characters From Peanuts Comic
Strip — A2586

No. 3206: a, Snoopy reading letter (33x32mm). b, Woodstock reading letter under lamp (33x32mm). c, Peppermint Patty reading letter (33x32mm). d, Snoopy hugging Woodstock (35mm diameter). e, Sally reading letter (33x32mm). f, Snoopy and Woodstock on doghouse (35x29mm heart-shaped). g, Snoopy giving letter to Woodstock (33x32mm). h, Charlie Brown writing letter (33x32mm).

Die Cut Perf. 13½

2010, Mar. 3   Litho.

Self-Adhesive

3206	A2586	Sheet of 10, #3206c-3206h, 2 each #3206a-3206b	17.50	17.50
a.-h.		80y Any single	1.40	.90

Peony
A2587

Sudachi Flowers
A2588

Unzen Azalea
Flowers
A2589

Kakitsubata
Irises
A2590

Camphor
Blossoms
A2591

Peonies
A2592

Sudachi Flowers
A2593

Unzen Azalea
Flowers
A2594

Kakitsubata
Irises
A2595

Camphor
Blossoms
A2596

2010, Mar. 8   Photo.   Perf. 13¼

3207	A2587	50y multi	.90	.50
3208	A2588	50y multi	.90	.50
3209	A2589	50y multi	.90	.50
3210	A2590	50y multi	.90	.50
3211	A2591	50y multi	.90	.50
a.		Vert. strip of 5, #3207-3211	5.50	5.50
3212	A2592	80y multi	1.40	.90
3213	A2593	80y multi	1.40	.90
3214	A2594	80y multi	1.40	.90
3215	A2595	80y multi	1.40	.90
3216	A2596	80y multi	1.40	.90
a.		Vert. strip of 5, #3212-3216	8.75	8.75
		Nos. 3207-3216 (10)	11.50	7.00

Flowers of Shimane, Tokushima, Nagasaki, Aichi and Saga prefectures.

Miniature Sheet

Friendship With San Marino — A2597

No. 3217: a, La Repubblica, statue by Vittorio Pocchini, San Marino (stamp 1). b, First Tower, San Marino (stamp 2). c, Saint Marinus, angel and crowd from Appearance of Saint Marinus to His People, mural by Emilio Retrosi (stamp 3). d, Angel and crowd from Appearance of Saint Marinus to His People (stamp 4). e, Statue of Liberty, San Marino Government Building (stamp 5). f, Basilica of Saint Marinus (stamp 6). g, Second Tower, San Marino (stamp 7). h, Bell tower, First Tower (stamp 8). i, St. Mary Magdalene, painting by Francesco Menzocchi (stamp 9). j, St. Marinus, painting by unknown artist (stamp 10).

2010, Mar. 23   Litho.   Perf. 13

3217	A2597	Sheet of 10	17.50	17.50
a.-j.		80y Any single	1.40	.90

See San Marino No. 1818.

Miniature Sheet

Hometown Festival — A2598

No. 3218 — Suwa Grand Shrine Sacred Pillar Festival, Nagano Prefecture: a, Honmiya Shrine, denomination in yellow. b, Maemiya Shrine, denomination in pink. c, Akimiya Shrine, denomination in greenish black. d, Harumiya Shrine, denomination in light blue. e, Men dragging logs to Miya River, denomination in pink. f, Nagamochi, denomination in black. g, Men dragging log down hill, denomination in blue.

2010, Apr. 1   Litho.   Perf. 13¼
Self-Adhesive

3218	A2598	Sheet of 10, #3218a-3218d, 2 each #3218e-3218g	11.00	11.00
a.-g.		50y Any single	.90	.50

Philately Week — A2599

No. 3219: a, Tiger from screen painting by Gaho Hashimoto, denomination at UL. b, Peonies from screen painting by Hashimoto, denomination at LL. c, Peonies and birds from screen painting by Hashimoto, denomination at UL. d, Tiger, by Zhang Shanzi, denomination at LR.

Perf. 12¾x12½ Syncopated
2010, Apr. 20   Photo.

3219	A2599	Block of 4	7.00	7.00
a.-d.		80y Any single	1.40	.90

Miniature Sheet

Treasures of Nara — A2600

No. 3220: a, Restored Heijo Palace (stamp 1). b, Inner gate, Kasuga Grand Shrine (stamp 2). c, Tanjo Shaka statue, denomination in white at UR (stamp 3). d, Aizen Myo-o statue, denomination in white at UL (stamp 4). e, Tentoki holding lantern, denomination in gold at UL (stamp 5). f, Buddha Yakushi, denomination in gold at UL (stamp 6). g, Thousand-armed Kannon statue, denomination in white at UR (stamp 7). h, Standing Bodhisattva statue, denomination in white at LR (stamp 8). i, Tamonten statue, denomination in gold at LL (stamp 9). j, Basara Taisho statue, denomination in gold at LR (stamp 10).

2010, Apr. 23   Litho.   Perf. 14x13¾

3220	A2600	Sheet of 10	17.50	17.50
a.-j.		80y Any single	1.40	.90

Move of Imperial capital to Nara, 1300th anniv.

Hanashobu Iris
A2601

Olive Blossoms
A2602

Azalea Flowers
A2603

Paulownia Blossoms
A2604

Crinum Flowers
A2605

Hanashobu Irises
A2606

Olive Blossoms
A2607

Azalea Flowers
A2608

Paulownia Blossoms
A2609

Crinum Flowers
A2610

2010, Mar. 8   Photo.   Perf. 13¼

3221	A2601	50y multi	.90	.50
3222	A2602	50y multi	.90	.50
3223	A2603	50y multi	.90	.50
3224	A2604	50y multi	.90	.50
3225	A2605	50y multi	.90	.50
a.		Vert. strip of 5, #3221-3225	5.50	5.50
3226	A2606	80y multi	1.40	.90
3227	A2607	80y multi	1.40	.90
3228	A2608	80y multi	1.40	.90
3229	A2609	80y multi	1.40	.90
3230	A2610	80y multi	1.40	.90
a.		Vert. strip of 5, #3226-3230	8.75	8.75
		Nos. 3221-3230 (10)	11.50	7.00

Flowers of Mie, Kagawa, Gumma, Iwate and Miyazaki prefectures.

Miniature Sheet

A2611

Hello Kitty — A2612

No. 3231 — Hello Kitty: a, With butterflies and flowers (28x31mm heart-shaped). b, In kimono, flowers (28x31mm heart-shaped). c, With dragon (28x28mm). d, With mountain (28x28mm). e, With peonies (28x28mm). f, With origami cranes (28x28mm).

No. 3232 — Hello Kitty: a, And Shanghai skyline (30x32mm). b, And pagoda in Shanghai (30x32mm). c, And Tiger (30x32mm). d, With peonies (31x28mm heart-shaped). e, Holding fan (31mm diameter).

Die Cut Perf. 13½
2010, May 6   Litho.
Self-Adhesive

3231	A2611	Sheet of 10, #3231a-3231b, 2 each #3231c-3231f	11.00	11.00
a.-f.		50y Any single	.90	.50

Die Cut Perf. 12½

3232	A2612	Sheet of 10, 2 each #3232a-3232e	17.50	17.50
a.-e.		80y Any single	1.40	.90

Miniature Sheet

Kochi Prefecture Local Autonomy Law, 60th Anniv. — A2613

No. 3233: a, Ryoma Sakamoto (1836-67), samurai, and Katsura Beach (33x39mm). b, Farmhouse clock, Aki (28x33mm). c, Harimaya Bridge, streetcar (28x33mm). d, Paper carp streamers (28x33mm). e, Cape Ashizuri Lighthouse (28x33mm).

Perf. 13¼ (#3233a), 13x13¼
2010, May 14   Photo.

3233	A2613	Sheet of 5	8.75	8.75
a.-e.		80y Any single	1.40	.90

Miniature Sheet

Kanagawa Prefecture Afforestation — A2614

No. 3234. a, Pinks. b, Japanese cedar. c, Sawtooth oak. d, Japanese maple. e, Golden-rayed lilies. f, Evergreen oak. g, Japanese chinquapin. h, Ginkgo. i, Beech. j, Gentians.

2010, May 21   Litho.   Perf. 13

3234	A2614	Sheet of 10	11.00	11.00
a.-j.		50y Any single	.90	.50

114 JAPAN

Miniature Sheets

SAMURAI BLUE

A2615

2010 World Cup Soccer
Championships, South Africa — A2616

No. 3235: a, Soccer ball, African animals (33x39mm). b, World Cup trophy (29x38mm). c, Poster for 2010 World Cup tournament (29x38mm). d, Emblem of 2010 World Cup (29x38mm). e, Emblem of Japan Soccer Association (29x38mm).

No. 3236 — Posters for World Cup tournaments of: a, 1930. b, 1934. c, 1938. d, 1950. e, 1954. f, 1958. g, 1962. h, 1970. i, 1978. j, 1986. k, 1990. l, 1994. m, 1998. n, 2002. o, 2006. p, Jules Rimet Cup. q, Jules Rimet Cup and hand.

Litho., Litho. & Embossed (#3235a)
Perf. 13, 14x13½ (#3235a)
2010, May 31
3235	A2615	Sheet of 5	8.75	8.75
a.-e.		80y Any single	1.40	.90

Litho.
Perf. 13
3236	A2616	Sheet of 20,		
		#3236a-3236o,		
		3 #3236p, 2		
		#3236q	35.00	35.00
a.-q.		80y Any single	1.40	.90

Miniature Sheet

Asia-Pacific Economic Cooperation
Economic Leader's Meeting,
Yokohama — A2617

No. 3237: a, Flowers at top and left, denomination at LR. b, Flowers at top and right, denomination at LL. c, Purple flower at center right, denomination at UR. d, Purple flower at center left, denomination at UL. e, Pink rose at center right, denomination at LL. f, Pink rose at center left, denomination at LR. g, White flowers at center right, denomination at UR. h, White flowers at center left, denomination at UL. i, Flowers at bottom and left, red flowers at LR, denomination at UR. j, Flowers at bottom and right, red flowers at LL, denomination at UL.

2010, June 4   Litho.   *Perf. 13*
3237	A2617	Sheet of 10	17.50	17.50
a.-j.		80y Any single	1.40	.90

Emblem of Japan
Academy
A2618

Certificate and
Photograph of
First Awards
Ceremony
A2619

Venue of First
Awards
Ceremony
A2620

Former Japan
Academy Hall
A2621

Rooster — A2622

2010, June 7   Litho.   *Perf. 13*
3238	A2618	80y multi	1.40	.90
3239	A2619	80y multi	1.40	.90
3240	A2620	80y multi	1.40	.90
3241	A2621	80y multi	1.40	.90
3242	A2622	80y multi	1.40	.90
a.		Vert. strip of 5, #3238-3242	8.75	8.75
		Nos. 3238-3242 (5)	7.00	4.50

Japan Academy Prizes, cent.

Animation
Miniature Sheet

Full Metal Alchemist — A2623

No. 3243: a, Edward Elric (with yellow hair and hand on his shoulder). b, Alphonse Elric (in black armor). c, Riza Hawkeye (holding gun). d, Roy Mustang with symbol on back of hand. e, Xiao Mei (panda). f, May Chang (with braided hair). g, Ling Yao holding sword. h, Lan Fan holding dagger. i, Winry Rockbell (girl in tank top). j, Edward Elric with dog, Den.

2010, June 14   Litho.   *Perf. 13x13¼*
3243	A2623	Sheet of 10	19.00	19.00
a.-j.		80y Any single	1.40	.90

Miniature Sheet

Gifu Local Autonomy Law, 60th
Anniv. — A2624

No. 3244: a, Cormorant fishing on Nagara River (32x39mm). b, Gifu Castle (28x33mm). c, Yokokura Temple (28x33mm). d, Art exhibition, Mino (28x33mm). e, Restored buildings, Magome (28x33mm).

Perf. 13¼ (#3244a), 13x13¼
2010, June 18   Photo.
3244	A2624	Sheet of 5	9.50	9.50
a.-e.		80y Any single	1.40	.90

Revision of Japan-United States
Security Treaty, 50th Anniv. — A2625

Designs: No. 3245, Flags of U.S. and Japan, Japanese Prime Minister Nobusuke Kishi and U.S. President Dwight D. Eisenhower. No. 3246, Japanese Diet and U.S. Capitol.

2010, June 23   Litho.   *Perf. 13*
3245	80y multi	1.40	.90
3246	80y multi	1.40	.90
a.	A2625 Pair, #3245-3246	3.80	3.80

Miniature Sheet

National Fireworks Competition,
Omagari, Akita Prefecture — A2626

No. 3247 — Various fireworks with denomination in: a, Yellow green at UL, country name in Japanese characters at LL. b, Yellow green at UR. c, Pale orange at LL. d, Blue at LL. e, Rose at UL. f, Rose at LR, country name in Japanese characters at LR. g, Rose at LR, country name in Japanese characters at LL. h, Blue green at LR. i, Yellow green at UL, country name in Japanese characters at LR. j, Yellow green at LR.

2010, July 1   Litho.   *Perf. 13¼*
3247	A2626	Sheet of 10	11.50	11.50
a.-j.		50y Any single	.90	.50

Miniature Sheet

Travel Scenes — A2627

No. 3248: a, Kurushima-Kaikyo Great Bridge, denomination at LL (stamp 1). b, Kurushima-Kaikyo Great Bridge, denomination at LR (stamp 2). c, Jodo Temple, denomination at UR (stamp 3). d, Jodo Temple, denomination at UL (stamp 4). e, Bridge, sculptures on Mt. Shirataki (stamp 5). f, Kojoji three-story pagoda (stamp 6). g, Oyamazumi Shrine (stamp 7). h, Omishima Bridge, boat (stamp 8). i, Building with red window shutters at Imabari Castle (stamp 9). j, Six-story donjon at Imabari Castle (stamp 10).

2010, July 8   Litho.   Perf. 13x13¼
3248   A2627   Sheet of 10   19.00   19.00
a.-j.   80y Any single   1.40   .90

Emperor Koko, Poet — A2628 / Lady Ise, Poet — A2629

Saki no Daisojo Gyoson, Poet — A2630 / Yushi Naishinno-ke no Kii, Poet — A2631

Sutoku In, Poet — A2632

Poetry — A2633

No. 3254 — Poetry in Japanese calligraphy and: a, Purple flowers. b, Emperor Koko. c, Pond. d, Lady Ise. e, Hill and flowering trees. f, Saki no Daisojo Gyoson. g, Ocean waves. h, Yushi Naishinno-ke no Kii. i, Waterfall. j, Sutoku In.

2010, July 23   Photo.   Perf. 13¼
3249   A2628   50y multi   .90   .50
3250   A2629   50y multi   .90   .50
3251   A2630   50y multi   .90   .50
3252   A2631   50y multi   .90   .50
3253   A2632   50y multi   .90   .50
a.   Vert. strip of 5, #3249-3253   6.25   6.25

Perf. 12¾x13
3254   A2633   Sheet of 10   19.00   19.00
a.-j.   80y Any single   1.40   .90

Letter Writing Day.

Suruga Street, by Hiroshige A2634 / Woman Reading a Letter, by Utamaro A2635

Dyer's Quarters, Kanda, by Hiroshige A2636 / Sojuro Sawamura II as Kurando Ogishi, by Sharaku A2637

Asakusa Ricefields and Torinomachi Festival, by Hiroshige A2638 / White Uchikake, by Utamaro A2639

Takinogawa, Oji, by Hiroshige A2640 / Torazo Tanimura as Yaheiji Washizuka, by Sharaku A2641

Yamashita Park, Ueno, by Hiroshige A2642 / Glass Goblet, by Utamaro A2643

2010, Aug. 2   Litho.   Perf. 13¼
3255   Sheet of 10   19.00   19.00
a.   A2634   80y multi   1.40   .90
b.   A2635   80y multi   1.40   .90
c.   A2636   80y multi   1.40   .90
d.   A2637   80y multi   1.40   .90
e.   A2638   80y multi   1.40   .90
f.   A2639   80y multi   1.40   .90
g.   A2640   80y multi   1.40   .90
h.   A2641   80y multi   1.40   .90
i.   A2642   80y multi   1.40   .90
j.   A2643   80y multi   1.40   .90

Life in Edo (Tokyo).

Miniature Sheet

Fukui Local Autonomy Law, 60th Anniv. — A2644

No. 3256: a, Dinosaur at Tojimbo (32x39mm). b, Narcissus (28x33mm). c, Lake and flowers (28x33mm). d, Ichijodani ruins, cherry tree (28x33mm). e, Crab, Echizen-Kaga Kaigan Quasi-National Park (28x33mm).

Perf. 13¼ (#3256a), 13x13¼
2010, Aug. 9   Photo.
3256   A2644   Sheet of 5   9.50   9.50
a.-e.   80y Any single   1.40   .90

Miniature Sheet

Home Towns — A2645

No. 3257 — Paintings by Taiji Harada of views of Hokkaido prefecture towns: a, Shiranuka Line (Farmhouses, haystack, two cows, Shiranuka). b, Shiranuka Line (Train, three cows, Shiranuka). c, Red-crowned Cranes (Building near forest in snow, Tsurui). d, Red-crowned Cranes (Woman feeding cranes, Tsurui). e, Flowers of the Land (Houses, trees hills, Biei). f, Flowers of the Land (Tractor, hills, trees, Biei). g, Farm (Farm buildings, mail box cows, Ishikari). h, Farm (Farm buildings, silo, farmer tending cow, Ishikari). i, Hibernation (Building in snow, fishing boats, Wakkanai). j, Canal in Spring (Boats in canal, Otaru).

2010, Sept. 10   Photo.   Perf. 13
3257   A2645   Sheet of 10   19.00   19.00
a.-j.   80y Any single   1.40   .90

Biplane of Henri Farman A2646

Aeronautical Research Plane A2647

Asuka A2648

Boeing 747-400 A2649

Mitsubishi Regional Jet — A2650

Monoplane of Hans Grade A2651

YS-11 A2652

Kawasaki T-4 A2653

US-2 A2654

Supersonic Plane A2655

2010, Sept. 21　Litho.　Perf. 13

3258		Sheet of 10	20.00	20.00
a.	A2646	80y multi	1.40	.90
b.	A2647	80y multi	1.40	.90
c.	A2648	80y multi	1.40	.90
d.	A2649	80y multi	1.40	.90
e.	A2650	80y multi	1.40	.90
f.	A2651	80y multi	1.40	.90
g.	A2652	80y multi	1.40	.90
h.	A2653	80y multi	1.40	.90
i.	A2654	80y multi	1.40	.90
j.	A2655	80y multi	1.40	.90

Aviation in Japan, cent.

Animation
Miniature Sheet

Chibi Maruko-chan — A2656

No. 3259: a, Sakura family members, Maruko, Sakiko, and mother Sumire (denomination in red at UL). b, Sakura family members father Hiroshi, grandfather Tomozo, and grandmother Kotake (denomination in white at LL). c, Maruko blowing bubbles (holding gun). d, Tomozo and bubbles. e, Hiroshi and Maruko with glow worm. f, Sakiko with glow worm. g, Sumire preparing food. h, Maruko and Kotake preparing food. i, Hamaji and Butaro (boys and snowflakes). j, Maruko and Tama-chan (and snowflakes).

2010, Sept. 22　Litho.　Perf. 13x13¼

3259	A2656	Sheet of 10	20.00	20.00
a.-j.		80y Any single	1.40	.90

Chiba Central Sports Center and Chiba Marine Stadium — A2657

Hammer Throw — A2658

Equestrian A2659

Rock Climbing A2660

Pole Vault — A2661

2010, Sept. 24　Litho.　Perf. 13x13¼

3260	Sheet of 10, 2 each		
	#a-e	12.50	12.50
a.	A2657 50y multi	.90	.50
b.	A2658 50y multi	.90	.50
c.	A2659 50y multi	.90	.50
d.	A2660 50y multi	.90	.50
e.	A2661 50y multi	.90	.50

65th National Athletics Meet, Chiba.

Miniature Sheet

Travel Scenes — A2662

No. 3261: a, Akashi Strait Great Bridge, denomination in blue at UL (stamp 1). b, Akashi Strait Great Bridge, Sun Yat-sen Memorial Hall, Kobe, denomination at UR (stamp 2). c, Flowers, Awaji Island, denomination at UR to right of "Nippon" (stamp 3). d, Flowers, Awaji Island, denomination at UR below "Nippon" (stamp 4). e, Awaji puppet theater, denomination at UR (stamp 5). f, Awaji puppet theater, denomination at UL (stamp 6). g, Onaruto Bridge, denomination in white at LL (stamp 7). h, Onaruto Bridge, denomination in white at UR(stamp 8). i, Bridge, Naruto Whirlpools (stamp 9). j, Esaki Lighthouse (stamp 10).

2010, Oct. 1　Litho.　Perf. 13x13¼

3261	A2662	Sheet of 10	20.00	20.00
a.-j.		80y Any single	1.40	.90

Miniature Sheet

Aichi Local Autonomy Law, 60th Anniv. — A2663

No. 3262: a, Golden dolphin sculpture at Nagoya Castle, irises, Atsumi Peninsula (32x39mm). b, Eurasian scops owl (28x33mm). c, Ginkgo leaves (28x33mm). d, Seto ceramic jar (28x33mm). e, Cherry blossoms (28x33mm).

Perf. 13¼ (#3262a), 13x13¼

2010, Oct. 4　　　　　Photo.

3262	A2663	Sheet of 5	10.00	10.00
a.-e.		80y Any single	1.40	.90

Intl. Letter Writing Week — A2664

Painting details: 90y, Michitose, by Shinsui Ito. 110y, Nozaki Village, by Kiyokata Kaburagi. 130y, Botanyuki, by Shoen Uemura, horiz.

2010, Oct. 8　　Photo.　　Perf. 13¼

3263	A2664	90y multi	1.60	1.00
3264	A2664	110y multi	2.00	1.40
3265	A2664	130y multi	2.50	1.60
		Nos. 3263-3265 (3)	8.25	6.25

Miniature Sheet

Tenth Conference of Parties to the Convention on Biological Diversity, Nagoya — A2665

No. 3266: a, Lake Mashu, frost-covered trees. b, Spotted seal. c, Mt. Tsurugi. d, Japanese antelope. e, Buildings in mountains. f, Common tree frog and flowers. g, Banks of Shimanto River. h, Common kingfisher. i, Flowers at Cape Tamatori. j, False clownfish and sea anemone.

2010, Oct. 18　Litho.　Perf. 13x13¼

3266	A2665	Sheet of 10	20.00	20.00
a.-j.		80y Any single	2.00	1.50

Miniature Sheet

Friendship Between Japan and Portugal, 150th Anniv. — A2666

No. 3267: a, Japanese screen painting depicting bow of Portuguese ship, denomination at LL (30x45mm, stamp 1). b, Japanese screen painting depicting stern of Portuguese ship, denomination at LR (30x45mm, stamp 2). c, Belém Tower, Lisbon (30x43mm, stamp 3). d, Statue of St. Vincent (30x43mm, stamp 4). e, Monastery of the Hieronymites, Lisbon (30x43mm, stamp 5). f, Ruins of Roman Temple of Evora, Portugal (30x43mm, stamp 6). g, Oporto, Portugal, and boat (30x43mm, stamp 7). h, Batalha Monastery, Batalha, Portugal (30x43mm, stamp 8). i, Portuguese decorative tiles (30x43mm, stamp 9). j, Puppet of St. Isabel of Portugal (30x43mm, stamp 10).

2010, Oct. 22　Litho.　Perf. 13¼x13

3267	A2666	Sheet of 10	20.00	20.00
a.-j.		80y Any single	1.40	.90

See Portugal No. 3271.

Seven People — A2667 Eight People — A2668

Congress Emblem A2669 Peace Statue, Nagasaki A2670

2010, Nov. 5 **Photo.** *Perf. 13*
3268   Sheet of 10, 2 each
        #3268a-3268c, 4
        #3268d   20.00 20.00
  a. A2667 80y multi   1.40   .90
  b. A2668 80y multi   1.40   .90
  c. A2669 80y multi   1.40   .90
  d. A2670 80y multi   1.40   .90
Third UNI Global Union World Congress, Nagasaki.

Miniature Sheets

A2671

A2672

Greetings — A2673

No. 3269: a, Star and Santa Claus with sack. b, Poinsettias, ribbon and bell. c, Sleigh of Santa Claus over church, horiz. d, Heart-shaped wreath. e, Reindeer and Aurora Borealis.
No. 3270: a, Santa Claus. b, Christmas tree. c, Sleigh of Santa Claus over mountain, horiz. d, Wreath with pine cones. e, Reindeer and Aurora Borealis, diff.
No. 3271: a, Fairy with horn flying above town. b, Snowman juggling snowballs. c, Children singing, horiz. d, Rose in box. e, Cakes.

Die Cut Perf. 13
2010, Nov. 8   **Litho.**
Self-Adhesive
3269 A2671 Sheet of 5   6.25 6.25
  a.-e. 50y Any single   1.25   .50
3270 A2672 Sheet of 5   10.00 10.00
  a.-e. 80y Any single   1.40   .90
3271 A2673 Sheet of 5   11.50 11.50
  a.-e. 90y Any single   1.60 1.00

A2674   A2675

New Year 2011 (Year of the Rabbit)
A2676   A2677
2010, Nov. 10 **Photo.** *Perf. 13x13½*
3272 A2674 50y multi   .90   .50
3273 A2675 80y multi   1.40   .90
Photo. & Typo.
Perf. 13¼
3274 A2676 50y +3y multi 1.25 1.10
3275 A2677 80y +3y multi 1.75 1.60
    Nos. 3272-3275 (4)   6.75 5.15
Sheets of two containing Nos. 3272-3273 were lottery prizes.

Miniature Sheet

Aomori Local Autonomy Law, 60th Anniv. — A2678

No. 3276: a, Apples, Nebuta Festival floats (32x39mm). b, Hirosaki Castle and cherry blossoms (28x33mm). c, Three Shrines Festival, Hachinohe (28x33mm). d, Lake Towada (28x33mm). e, Horse and Shiriyazaki Lighthouse (28x33mm).

Perf. 13¼ (#3276a), 13x13¼
2010, Nov. 15   **Photo.**
3276 A2678 Sheet of 5   10.00 10.00
  a.-e. 80y Any single   1.40   .90

Miniature Sheet

Edo Calligraphy — A2679

No. 3277 — Charcters for "rabbit": a, In Kinbun style (red character). b, In Six Dynasties style standard script (heavy black characters with red chop at LL, denomination at UR. c, In oracle bone script (single black character resembling animal with legs and tail, denomination at LR). d, In oracle bone script (three characters having horizontal line at UL, with red chop at LR, denomination at LR). e, In clerical script (silver character on green background). f, In small seal script (denomination at UL, "Nippon" at LR). g, In seal script (two black characters, with red chop, denomination and "Nippon" at LR). h, In Hirigana style (black character with denomination and "Nippon" at UL, red chop near center). i, In running script (black character with small dot at top, with denomination at LR and "Nippon" at LL). j, In standard script (two black characters with red chop and denomination at LR, "Nippon" at LL).

Litho. & Embossed
2010, Dec. 3   *Perf. 13x13¼*
3277 A2679 Sheet of 10   20.00 20.00
  a.-j. 80y Any single   1.40   .90

Japanese Diet, 120th Anniv. — A2680

Stained-glass window from Central Hall, old and new Diet buildings with entranceway of: No. 3278, New Diet. No. 3279, Old Diet.

2010, Nov. 29   **Litho.** *Perf. 13*
3278 80y multi   1.40   .90
3279 80y multi   1.40   .90
  a. A2680 Horiz. pair, #3278-3279 4.00 3.00

Miniature Sheet

Home Towns — A2681

No. 3280 — Paintings by Taiji Harada of views of Tohoku region towns: a, Paulownia Village (Cyclist near house, Mishima, Fukushima prefecture). b, Paulownia Village (Farmers and tree near water, Mishima). c, Bonnet Bus (White bus, Hiraizumi, Iwate prefecture). d, Bonnet Bus (Houses, people under umbrella, Hiraizumi). e, Bent House by the Sea (Mother with children near sea, Yurihonjo, Akita prefecture). f, After the Snowfall (Person and houses in snow, Akita, Akita prefecture). g, Railbus (Railbus and station, Kamikita District, Aomori prefecture). h, Railbus (People at station, Kamikita District). i, Dear Home (People on path near house, Tsuruoka, Yamagata prefecture). j, Kokeshi Doll (Children and adults near doll vendor's stall, Shiroishi, Miyagi prefecture).

2010, Dec. 1   **Photo.** *Perf. 13*
3280 A2681 Sheet of 10   20.00 20.00
  a.-j. 80y Any single   2.00 1.50

Mandarin Duck Type of 2007
Perf. 13¾x13½ Syncopated
2010, Jan.   **Litho.**
3281 A2352 50y multi   1.10   .85

Prefecture Type of 1990 Redrawn and Prefecture Types of 1991-96
Designs as before.

Serpentine Die Cut 10¾x11½
2010   **Litho.** **Self-Adhesive**
3282 ZA85   80y multi   1.40   .90
3283 ZA86   80y multi   1.40   .90
3284 ZA87   80y multi   1.40   .90
3285 ZA88   80y multi   1.40   .90
  a. Horiz. strip of 4, #3282-3285   7.00 7.00
3286 ZA97   80y multi   1.40   .90
3287 ZA98   80y multi   1.40   .90
3288 ZA99   80y multi   1.40   .90
3289 ZA100 80y multi   1.40   .90
  a. Horiz. strip of 4, #3286-3289   7.00 7.00

Serpentine Die Cut 11½x11¾
3290 ZA186 80y multi   1.40   .90
    Nos. 3282-3290 (9)   12.60 8.10
  Issued: Nos. 3282-3289, Mar.; No. 3290, Apr.

Hisoka Maeshima (1835-1919), Founder of Japanese Postal Service A2682   Little Cuckoo A2683

Mute Swan
A2684

Silver Crane
A2685

Burial Statue
of Warrior, Ota
A2686

Bazara-Taisho,
c. 710-794
A2687

2010-11   Photo.   Perf. 13x13½

3293	A2682	1y brown	.25	.25
3294	A2683	3y green	.25	.25
3295	A2684	5y blue & lt bl	.25	.25
3296	A2685	100y multi	1.75	1.20
3297	A2686	200y vermilion	3.75	2.50
3298	A2687	500y dark green	9.50	6.00
		Nos. 3293-3298 (6)	19.90	15.00

Issued: 1y, 1/7/11; 3y, 12/8; 5y, 12/6; 100y, 12/27; 200y, 2/10/11; 500y, 12/15. Compare type A2682 with type A563a, types A2683-A2687 with types A713, A714, A718a, A718d, A1013 and A1207.

Miniature Sheet

Saga Local Autonomy Law, 60th
Anniv. — A2688

No. 3299: a, Shigenobu Okuma (1838-1922), politician, and Arita porcelain (32x39mm). b, Yoshinogari ruins (28x33mm). c, Yutoku Inari shrine and bridge (28x33mm). d, Hot-air balloons, Saga International Balloon Festival (28x33mm). e, Sea bream float, Karatsu Festival (28x33mm).

Perf. 13¼ (#3299a), 13x13¼

2011, Jan. 14   Photo.

3299	A2688	Sheet of 5	10.00	10.00
a.-e.		80y Any single	1.40	.90

Miniature Sheet

Phila Nippon'11, Yokohama — A2689

No. 3300: a, Mighty Atom (blue background, 28x48mm). b, Doraemon (green background, 28x48mm). c, Pikachu (purple background, 28x48mm). d, Hello Kitty (red background, 28x48mm). e, Rabbit riding donkey from 11th cent. scroll (28x48mm). f, Mighty Atom, diff. (28x32mm). g, Doraemon, diff. (28x32mm). h, Pikachu, diff. (28x32mm). i, Hello Kitty, diff. (28x32mm). j, Rabbit riding donkey, diff. (28x32mm).

Die Cut Perf. 12¾x13

2011, Jan. 21   Litho.

Self-Adhesive

3300	A2689	Sheet of 10	20.00	20.00
a.-j.		80y Any single	1.40	.90

Miniature Sheet

Friendship Between Japan and
Germany, 150th Anniv. — A2690

No. 3301 — UNESCO World Heritage Sites and other landmarks: a, Old Town, Regensburg, horiz. (45x26mm, stamp 1). b, Yakushi-ji, Historic Monuments of Ancient Nara, Japan, horiz. (45x26mm, stamp 2). c, Quadriga of Brandenburg Gate, Berlin (27x38mm, stamp 3). d, Frauenkirche, Dresden (27x38mm, stamp 4). e, Schwerin Castle (two tall spires, 27x38mm, stamp 5). f, Schwerin Castle (three tall spires, 27x38mm, stamp 6). g, Old Town, Bamberg (bridge at right, 27x38mm, stamp 7). h, Old Town, Bamberg (bridge at left, 27x38mm, stamp 8). i, Neuschwanstein Castle (27x38mm, stamp 9). j, Tower at Zollverein Coal Mine Industrial Complex, Essen (27x38mm, stamp 10).

2011, Jan. 24   Litho.   Perf. 13

3301	A2690	Sheet of 10	20.00	20.00
a.-j.		80y Any single	1.40	.90

Miniature Sheet

Travel Scenes — A2691

No. 3302: a, Snow sculpture of Frauenkirche of Dresden, Germany at Sapporo Snow Festival, German and Japanese flags (stamp 1). b, Penguins walking at Asahiyama Zoo (stamp 2). c, Lamp post along canal at Otaru Snow Light Path (stamp 3). d, Building along canal in Otaru (stamp 4). e, Lake Toya in winter (stamp 5). f, Hakodate Orthodox Christian Church (stamp 6). g, Lake and snow-capped mountains at Shiretoko UNESCO World Heritage Site, denomination at LL (stamp 7). h, Lake and snow-capped mountains at Shiretoko UNESCO World Heritage Site, denomination at LR (stamp 8). i, Red-crowned cranes (stamp 9). j, Ice on Sea of Okhotsk near Abashiri (stamp 10).

2011, Feb. 1   Litho.   Perf. 13x13¼

3302	A2691	Sheet of 10	20.00	20.00
a.-j.		80y Any single	1.40	.90

Miniature Sheets

A2692

Greetings Stamps — A2693

No. 3303: a, Fawn, yellow crocuses. b, Bluebird, blue lilies. c, Rose, butterfly made of pink violets. d, Swans, blue roses. e, Hares, strawberries and flowers.

No. 3304: a, Flowers trailing from fairy's hat. b, Fairy blowing horn in daffodils. c, Fairy on back of bird delivering mail, horiz. d, Fairy with letter on rainbow. e, Fairy writing in purple flowers.

2011, Feb. 4   Litho.   Die Cut Perf.

Self-Adhesive

3303	A2692	Sheet of 5	6.25	6.25
a.-e.		50y Any single	.90	.50

Die Cut Perf. 13

3304	A2693	Sheet of 5	10.00	10.00
a.-e.		80y Any single	1.40	.90

Rose
A2694

Apple Blossoms
A2695

Primroses
A2696

Japanese
Grapefruit
Blossoms
A2697

Kyushu Azalea
Flowers
A2698

Roses
A2699

Apple Blossoms
A2700

Primroses
A2701

Japanese
Grapefruit
Blossoms
A2702

Kyushu Azalea
Flowers
A2703

2011, Feb. 8   Photo.   Perf. 13¼

3305	A2694	50y multi	.90	.50
3306	A2695	50y multi	.90	.50
3307	A2696	50y multi	.90	.50
3308	A2697	50y multi	.90	.50
3309	A2698	50y multi	.90	.50
a.		Vert. strip of 5, #3305-3309	6.25	6.25
3310	A2699	80y multi	1.40	.90
3311	A2700	80y multi	1.40	.90
3312	A2701	80y multi	1.40	.90
3313	A2702	80y multi	1.40	.90
3314	A2703	80y multi	1.40	.90
a.		Vert. strip of 5, #3310-3314	10.00	10.00
		Nos. 3305-3314 (10)	16.25	12.25

Flowers of Ibaraki, Aomori, Saitama, Yamaguchi and Kagoshima prefectures.

Miniature Sheet

Home Towns — A2704

No. 3315 — Paintings by Taiji Harada of views of towns of Kanto region: a, Rice Nursery (farmers in rice field, Hitachi, Ibaraka prefecture, denomination at UL). b, Rice Nursery (farmers in rice field, Hitachi, denomination at LL). c, Spring Breeze (woman and child near farmhouse, Kumagaya, Saitama prefecture, denomination at LL). d, Spring Breeze (farm buildings, trees in bloom in orchard, Kumagaya, denomination at UL). e, Spring Garden (tall tree, farmer with pole near shed, Tone District, Gumma prefecture). f, Spring Garden (boy with dog near mailbox near farmhouse, Tone District). g, Wheat Field (farmer and dog in field, Haga District, Tochigi prefecture). h, Home Inside a Tree Grove (house amidst trees, Kisarazu, Chiba prefecture). i, Roadside Zelkova Trees (city street with trees, Shibuya Ward, Tokyo prefecture). j, Westernized Building (building with lamp post, Yokohama, Kanagawa prefecture).

2011, Mar. 1   Photo.   Perf. 13

3315	A2704	Sheet of 10	20.00	20.00
a.-j.		80y Any single	1.40	.90

Miniature Sheets

Characters From Children's Stories by
Beatrix Potter — A2705

Scenes From *The Tale of Peter
Rabbit,* by Beatrix Potter — A2706

No. 3316: a, Peter Rabbit running. b, Mouse
of Gloucester. c, Peter Rabbit standing. d,
Benjamin Bunny. e, Pigling Bland. f, Old Mr.
Brown and Nutkin. g, Mrs. Tiggy-winkle. h,
Jemima Puddle-duck. i, Squirrel Nutkin. j, Tom
Kitten.
No. 3317: a, Rabbit family's home under fir
tree. b, Mother and younger sisters (27x37mm
oval). c, Peter Rabbit and back of sisters. d,
Mother dressing Peter (29mm diameter) e,
Mother holding basket. f, Peter near pots in
garden, robin. g, Peter going under garden
fence (27x37mm oval). h, Peter eating vegeta-
bles. i, Peter encountering Mr. McGregor
(29mm diameter). j, Peter running from Mr.
McGregor (29mm diameter).

2011, Mar. 3   Litho.   Die Cut Perf.
Self-Adhesive
3316 A2705 Sheet of 10   12.50 12.50
a.-j.   50y Any single   .90   .50
**Die Cut Perf. 13¼x13¾, Die Cut
Perf.**
3317 A2706 Sheet of 10   20.00 20.00
a.-j.   80y Any single   1.40   .90

Animation
Miniature Sheet

One Piece — A2707

No. 3318: a, Monkey D. Luffy wearing hat
and red shirt. b, Chopper wearing large top
hat. c, Sanji wearing blue shirt. d, Zoro wearing white shirt. e, Robin wearing red striped
blouse. f, Nami wearing beige shirt. g, Usopp
and Brook. h, Franky with chain on chest. i, D
Successor 1 with fire coming from hand. j, D
Successor 2 with clouds.

2011, Mar. 23   Litho.   Perf. 13x13¼
3318 A2707 Sheet of 10   19.00 19.00
a.-j.   80y Any single   1.90   1.40

Samisen Player   Samisen Player
A2708   and Children
                  A2709

Matsubashi   Matsubashi
Parade   Parade
Participants,   A2711
Decorated
Bamboo
A2710

2011, Apr. 4   Litho.   Perf. 13¼
3319   Block of 6, #3319c-
        3319d, 2 each
        #3319a-3319b   7.50   7.50
a. A2708 50y green & multi   .90   .50
b. A2709 50y red violet & multi .90   .50
c. A2710 50y blue & multi   .90   .50
d. A2711 50y blue & multi   .90   .50
Hakata Dontaku Port Festival, Fukuoka,
Fukuoka prefecture. Printed in sheets of 10
containing Nos. 3319c-3319d and 4 each Nos.
#3319a-3319b.

Administrative Counselors System,
50th Anniv. — A2712

2011, Apr. 15   Perf. 13
3320 80y Denomination at LL   1.40   .90
3321 80y Denomination at LR   1.40   .90
a. A2712 Horiz. pair, #3320-3321 4.00 4.00

Digital Television
Broadcasting
Towers — A2713

Designs: No. 3322, Tokyo Sky Tree, emblem
at LR. No. 3323, Tokyo Tower, emblem at LL.

2011, Apr. 15   Perf. 14x14¼
3322 80y multi   1.40   .90
3323 80y multi   1.40   .90
a. A2713 Pair, #3322-3323   4.00 4.00

Kabuki Actor
Kikugoro Onoe
V as Postman,
by Kunichika
Toyohara
A2714

Yokkaichi Postal Communications
Bureau, by Hiroshige III — A2715

A Quick Primer
on
Modernization,
by Kunimasa
Baido — A2716

Perf. 12½x12¾ Syncopated
2011, Apr. 20   Photo.
3324 A2714 80y multi   1.40   .90
3325 A2715 80y multi   1.40   .90
3326 A2716 80y multi   1.40   .90
a. Vert. strip of 3, #3324-3326 6.00 6.00
Philately Week. Printed in sheets of 10 containing 4 No. 3325 and 3 each Nos. 3324,
3326.

Azalea Flowers   Satsuma Orange
A2717   Blossoms
                  A2718

Azalea Flowers   Satsuma Orange
A2719   Blossoms
                  A2720

2011, May 2   Photo.   Perf. 13¼
3327 A2717 50y multi   .90   .50
3328 A2718 50y multi   .90   .50
a. Horiz. pair, #3327-3328 2.50 2.50
b. Sheet of 47 + label (see
    contents below)   62.50 62.50
3329 A2719 80y multi   1.40   .90
3330 A2720 80y multi   1.40   .90
a. Horiz. pair, #3329-3330 4.00 4.00
b. Sheet of 47 + label (see
    contents below)   100.00 100.00
Nos. 3327-3330 (4)   4.60 2.80
Flowers of Shizuoka and Ehime prefectures.
Issued: Nos. 3328b, 3330b, 7/15.
No. 3328b contains Nos. 3030-3034, 3079-
3083, 3094-3098, 3126-3130, 3180-3184,
3194-3198, 3207-3211, 3221-3225, 3305-
3309, 3327-3328 + label.
No. 3330b, contains Nos. 3035-3039, 3084-
3088, 3099-3103, 3131-3135, 3185-3189,
3199-3203, 3212-3216, 3226-3230, 3310-
3314, 3329-3330 + label.

Miniature Sheet

Kumamoto Local Autonomy Law, 60th
Anniv. — A2721

No. 3331: a, Mt. Azo (32x39mm). b, Kumamoto Castle (28x33mm). c, Kikuchi Castle
(octagonal tower, 28x33mm). d, Utasebune
(sailboat, 28x33mm). e, Matsushima and
Maejima Bridges (28x33mm).

Perf. 13¼ (#3331a), 13x13¼
2011, May 13   Photo.
3331 A2721 Sheet of 5   10.00 10.00
a.-e.   80y Any single   1.40   .90

Miniature Sheet

Intl. Year of Forests — A2722

No. 3332: a, Japanese cypress (denomination in white at LL, Japanese text in green, date at UR). b, Cherry blossoms (denomination in white at UR, Japanese text in blue, date at LL). c, Persea thunbergii (denomination in white at LL, Japanese text in blue, date at LR). d, Japanese umbrella pine (denomination in blue at UR, Japanese text in green, date at UL). e, Plum blossoms (denomination in white at UR, Japanese text in green, date at LL). f, Boat oak (denomination in white at UR, Japanese text in blue, date at LL). g, Nageia nagi (denomination in white at LL, Japanese text in blue, date at UL). h, Michelia compressa blossom (denomination in white at UR, Japanese text in green, date at UL). i, Japanese Douglas fir (denomination in white at UL, Japanese text in green, date at LL). j, Intl. Year of Forests emblem.

2011, May 20   Litho.   Perf. 13
3332 A2722   Sheet of 10   12.50 12.50
a.-j.   50y Any single   .90   .50

Miniature Sheet

Travel Scenes — A2723

No. 3333: a, Spotted seal (stamp 1). b, Wheat field, Biei (stamp 2). c, Lavender field, Furano, denomination at LR (stamp 3). d, Lavender field, Furano, denomination at LL (stamp 4). e, Statue of Dr. William Smith Clark, Hitsujigaoka (stamp 5). f, Cattle in pasture, Kamishihoro (stamp 6). g, Rugosa roses, Mt. Rishiri, denomination at UL (stamp 7). h,

Rugosa roses, Mt. Rishiri, denomination at UR (stamp 8). i, Trees on hill at Higashimokoto Moss Pink Park, denomination at UL (stamp 9). j, Trees on hill at Higashimokoto Moss Pink Park, denomination at UR (stamp 10).

2011, May 30   Litho.   Perf. 13x13¼
3333 A2723   Sheet of 10   20.00 20.00
a.-j.   80y Any single   1.40   .90

Animation
Miniature Sheet

Rose of Versailles — A2724

No. 3334: a, Marie Antoinette holding rose (blue denomination at LL). b, Oscar François de Jarjayes holding sword (blue denomination at LR). c, André Grandier (pink denomination at LL). d, Jarjayes wearing green shirt (pink denomination at UR). e, Hans Axel von Fersen in brown cape (trees in background, blue denomination at LL). f, Marie Antoinette (pink denomination at LR). g, Von Fersen (bubbles in background, blue denomination at LL). h, Jarjayes in blue dress (bubbles in background, blue denomination at IR) i, Rosalie Lamorlière in pink dress (blue denomination at UL). j, Jeanne de Valois-Saint Rémy (pink denomination at UR).

2011, June 10   Perf. 13x13¼
3334 A2724   Sheet of 10   20.00 20.00
a.-j.   80y Any single   1.40   .90

Miniature Sheet

Toyama Local Autonomy Law, 60th Anniv. — A2725

No. 3335: a, Tateyama Mountains (32x39mm). b, Kurobe Dam (28x33mm). c, Japanese rock ptarmigan (28x33mm). d, Zuiryu Temple (28x33mm). e, Gokayama farmhouse (28x33mm).

Perf. 13¼ (#3335a), 13x13¼
2011, June 15   Photo.
3335 A2725   Sheet of 5   10.00 10.00
a.-e.   80y Any single   1.40   .90

A2726

A2727

A2728

A2729

A2730

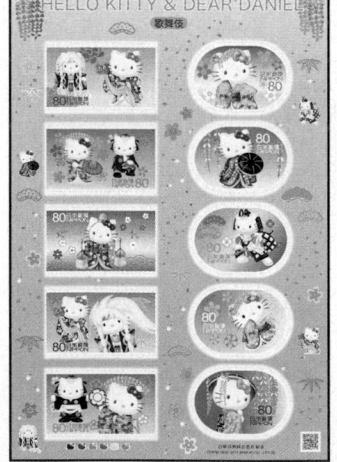

Hello Kitty — A2731

No. 3341: a, Dear Daniel at left, and Hello Kitty, rectangular stamp with green background, denomination in green at LL. b, Hello Kitty and Dear Daniel, rectangular stamp with pink background. c, Hello Kitty, rectangular stamp with blue gray background, denomination in white at UL. d, Hello Kitty and Dear Daniel, rectangular stamp with green background, denomination in purple at LL. e, Dear Daniel and Hello Kitty, rectangular stamp with purple background, denomination in gold at LL. f, Hello Kitty, oval stamp with pink background and gold denomination at right. g, Hello Kitty, oval stamp with blue gray background, denomination in white at UR. h, Dear Daniel, oval stamp with green background. i, Hello Kitty, oval stamp with pink background and white denomination at left. j, Hello Kitty, oval stamp with purple background, denomination in purple at LR.

Die Cut Perf. 13½
2011, June 22   Litho.
Self-Adhesive
3336 A2726   50y multi   .90   .50
3337 A2727   50y multi   .90   .50
3338 A2728   50y multi   .90   .50
3339 A2729   50y multi   .90   .50
3340 A2730   50y multi   .90   .50
a.   Vert. strip of 5, #3336-3340   6.25 6.25
Die Cut Perf. 11½x13¼ (#3341a-3341e), 12 (#3341f-3341j)
3341 A2731   Sheet of 10   20.00
a.-j.   80y Any single   1.40   .90

Nos. 3336-3340 were printed in sheets containing 2 of each stamp.

Adélie
Penguin — A2732

Chinstrap
Penguin — A2733

Gentoo
Penguin — A2734

Emperor
Penguin — A2735

Macaroni
Penguin — A2736

Map of Antarctica
and Snowflakes
A2737

2011, June 23   Perf. 13
3342   Sheet of 10, #3342a-3342f, 5 #3342f   20.00 20.00
a.   A2732 80y multi   1.40   .90
b.   A2733 80y multi   1.40   .90
c.   A2734 80y multi   1.40   .90
d.   A2735 80y multi   1.40   .90
e.   A2736 80y multi   1.40   .90
f.   A2737 80y multi   1.40   .90

Antarctic Treaty, 50th Anniv.

Miniature Sheet

Constellations — A2738

No. 3343: a, Libra (scales). b, Scorpius (scorpion). c, Sagittarius (archer). d, Lyra (lyre). e, Aquila (eagle). f, Cygnus (swan). g, Hercules. h, Ophiuchus and Serpens (man and snake). i, Delphinus (dolphin). j, Fishhook asterism.

Litho. With Foil Application
2011, July 7   **Die Cut Perf. 13**
Self-Adhesive

3343	A2738	Sheet of 10	20.00	
a.-j.		80y Any single	1.40	.90

Miniature Sheet

Japan Sports Association,
Cent. — A2739

No. 3344: a, Jigoro Kano (1860-1938), and Seiichi Kishi (1867-1933), presidents of Japan Amateur Sports Association (stamp 1). b, Athletes in parade at 1912 Stockholm Olympics (stamp 2). c, Women's volleyball, horse jumping, and emblem of National Athletic Meet (stamp 3). d, Hironoshin Furuhashi (1928-2009), swimmer (stamp 4). e, Baseball players and boy with martial arts stick (stamp 5). f, Weight lifter, gymnast and women's volleyball team members from 1964 Tokyo Summer Olympics (stamp 6). g, Skiers from 1972 Sapporo Winter Olympics (stamp 7). h, Skier and skater from 1998 Nagano Winter Olympics (stamp 8). i, Emblem of Sports Masters Japan Tournament (stamp 9). j, Woman wrestler, swimmer and women's softball team members from 2008 Beijing Summer Olympics (stamp 10).

2011, July 8   **Litho.**   **Perf. 13**

3344	A2739	Sheet of 10	20.00	20.00
a.-j.		80y Any single	1.40	.90

A2740

A2741

PhilaNippon 2011 Intl. Philatelic
Exhibition, Yokohama — A2742

No. 3345 — Woodblock prints by Hokusai depicting Mt. Fuji: a, Shower Below the Summit (Mt. Fuji and clouds, denomination in gold at LL). b, Fujimigahara in Owari Province (cooper making cask). c, Hodogaya on the Tokaido (people on road near Mt. Fuji). d, Mishima Pass in Kai Province (large tree and Mt. Fuji). e, The Surface of the Water at Misaka (boat and reflection of Mt. Fuji in lake). f, Clear Day with a Southern Breeze (Mt. Fuji and clouds, denomination in white at LR). g, The Village of Sekiya on the Sumida River (horsemen on road). h, Sea Route to Kazusa (sailing ship). i, Hongan Temple at Asakusa (kite and temple roof). j, Senju in Musashi Province (fishermen, man with horse).

No. 3346: a, Writing box depicting rabbit, bamboo and chrysanthemum. b, Japan #1.

No. 3347: a, Astro Boy (32x47mm). b, Doraemon (cat, 28x47mm). c, Pikachu (28x47mm). d, Hello Kitty (28x47mm). e, Emblem of PhilaNippon 2011, Mt. Fuji (28x47mm). f, Astro Boy, diff. (28x32mm). g, Doraemon, diff. (28x32mm). h, Pikachu, diff. (28x32mm). i, Hello Kitty, diff. (28x 32mm). j, Emblem, diff. (28x32mm).

2011, July 28   **Litho.**   **Perf. 13**

3345	A2740	Sheet of 10 +		
		10 labels	21.00	21.00
a.-j.		80y Any single + label	1.40	.90

Souvenir Sheet
Litho. & Embossed With Foil Application
Perf. 14x13¾

3346	A2741	Sheet of 2	32.50	32.50
a.-b.		500y Either single	9.50	9.50

Self-Adhesive
Litho. With Foil Application
Die Cut Perf. 13

3347	A2742	Sheet of 10	21.00	21.00
a.-j.		00y Any single	1.40	.90

No. 3346 sold for 1200y inside a folder that was sealed in plastic.

Sazae Hall, by
Hiroshige
A2743

Kisegawa of
Matsubaya, by
Utamaro
A2744

Tanabata Festival
in a Prospering
City, by Hiroshige
A2745

Komazo Ishikawa
III as Daishichi
Shiga, by
Sharaku
A2746

Plum Garden at
Kamata, by
Hiroshige
A2747

Three Beauties
of the Present
Day, by Utamaro
A2748

Yatsukoji, Inside
Sujikai Gate, by
Hiroshige
A2749

Tomisaburo
Segawa II as
Yadorigi, by
Sharaku
A2750

Old Man's Tea
House, Meguro,
by Hiroshige
A2751

Hanaogi of
Ogiya, by
Utamaro
A2752

2011, Aug. 1   **Litho.**   **Perf. 13¼**

3348		Sheet of 10	21.00	21.00
a.	A2743	80y multi	1.40	.90
b.	A2744	80y multi	1.40	.90
c.	A2745	80y multi	1.40	.90
d.	A2746	80y multi	1.40	.90
e.	A2747	80y multi	1.40	.90
f.	A2748	80y multi	1.40	.90
g.	A2749	80y multi	1.40	.90
h.	A2750	80y multi	1.40	.90
i.	A2751	80y multi	1.40	.90
j.	A2752	80y multi	1.40	.90

Life in Edo (Tokyo).

A2753

A2754

A2755

A2756

A2757

Lantern Float
Festival,
Aomori — A2758

2011, Aug. 2

3349		Sheet of 10, #3349a-		
		3349b, 3349e-3349f,		
		3 each #3349c-		
		3349d	13.00	13.00
a.	A2753	50y multi	.90	.50
b.	A2754	50y multi	.90	.50
c.	A2755	50y multi	.90	.50
d.	A2756	50y multi	.90	.50
e.	A2757	50y multi	.90	.50
f.	A2758	50y multi	.90	.50

Miniature Sheet

Tottori Local Autonomy Law, 60th
Anniv. — A2759

No. 3350: a, Tottori Sand Dunes and San'in Coast (32x39mm). b, Japanese pear (28x33mm). c, Kirin lion mask (28x33mm). d, Nageire Hall, Sanbutsu Temple (28x33mm). e, Mt. Daisen (28x33mm).

Perf. 13¼ (#3350a), 13x13¼
2011, Aug. 15   **Photo.**

3350	A2759	Sheet of 5	10.50	10.50
a.-e.		80y Any single	1.40	.90

Tsushima
Leopard
Cat — A2760

Saunders's
Gull — A2761

Rebun Large-flowered
Cypripedium — A2762

Green Sea
Turtle
A2763

Shijimiaeoides Divinus — A2764

2011, Aug. 23   Perf. 13¼

3351	A2760	80y multi	1.40	.90
3352	A2761	80y multi	1.40	.90
3353	A2762	80y multi	1.40	.90
3354	A2763	80y multi	1.40	.90
3355	A2764	80y multi	1.40	.90
a.		Vert. strip of 5, #3351-3355	10.50	10.50

Endangered species. Nos. 3351-3355
printed in sheets containing two vertical strips.

Airplane and Old
Control
Tower — A2765

Airplane and New
Control
Tower — A2766

Airplane and Map
of
Airport — A2767

Airplane and New
Control
Tower — A2768

2011, Aug. 25   Litho.   Perf. 13

3356	A2765	80y multi	1.40	.90
3357	A2766	80y multi	1.40	.90
3358	A2767	80y multi	1.40	.90
3359	A2768	80y multi	1.40	.90
a.		Block of 4, #3356-3359	8.50	8.50
		Nos. 3356-3359 (4)	5.60	3.60

Nos. 3356-3359 were printed in a sheet of
10 containing Nos. 3356-3357, and 4 each
Nos. 3358-3359.

Bellflower
A2769

Pink
A2770

Sweet Olive
Flowers
A2771

Cosmos
A2772

Bush Clover
A2773

Bellflowers
A2774

Pinks
A2775

Sweet Olive
Flowers
A2776

Cosmos
A2777

Bush Clover
A2778

2011, Sept. 1   Photo.   Perf. 13¼

3360	A2769	50y multi	.90	.50
3361	A2770	50y multi	.90	.50
3362	A2771	50y multi	.90	.50
3363	A2772	50y multi	.90	.50
3364	A2773	50y multi	.90	.50
a.		Vert. strip of 5, #3360-3364	6.50	6.50
3365	A2774	80y multi	1.40	.90
3366	A2775	80y multi	1.40	.90
3367	A2776	80y multi	1.40	.90
3368	A2777	80y multi	1.40	.90
3369	A2778	80y multi	1.40	.90
a.		Vert. strip of 5, #3365-3369	10.50	10.50
		Nos. 3360-3369 (10)	11.50	7.00

Miniature Sheet

Travel Scenes — A2779

No. 3370: a, Midori Swamp, denomination
at LL (stamp 1). b, Lake Mashu in autumn,
denomination at LR (stamp 2). c, Old Hokkaido Central Government Building, denomination at UR (stamp 3). d, Sapporo Clock
Tower, denomination at LR (stamp 4). e, Lake
Toya, Nakajima and tree top in autumn,
denomination at LL (stamp 5). f, Lake Toya,
Nakajima and tree in autumn, denomination at
LR (stamp 6). g, Hagoromo Falls (stamp 7). h,
Glasswort in Lake Notoro (red plants in lake)
(stamp 8). i, Ezo sable, denomination at UR
(stamp 9). j, Ezo flying squirrel, denomination
at UL (stamp 10).

2011, Sept. 9   Litho.   Perf. 13x13¼

3370	A2779	Sheet of 10	21.00	21.00
a.-j.		80y Any single	1.40	.90

Mt. Fuji
A2780

Mt. Bandai
A2781

Hakusan
A2782

Mt. Hiei
A2783

Mt. Ishizuchi
A2784

Mt. Iwate
A2785

Mt. Tanigawa
A2786

Mt. Akaishi
A2787

Hiruzen
A2788

Mt. Aso
A2789

2011, Sept. 22   Perf. 13

3371		Sheet of 10	21.00	21.00
a.	A2780	80y multi	1.40	.90
b.	A2781	80y multi	1.40	.90
c.	A2782	80y multi	1.40	.90
d.	A2783	80y multi	1.40	.90
e.	A2784	80y multi	1.40	.90
f.	A2785	80y multi	1.40	.90
g.	A2786	80y multi	1.40	.90
h.	A2787	80y multi	1.40	.90
i.	A2788	80y multi	1.40	.90
j.	A2789	80y multi	1.40	.90

66th National
Athletic
Meet — A2790

2011, Sept. 30

3372	A2790	50y	Sailing	.90	.50
3373	A2790	50y	Wrestling	.90	.50
3374	A2790	50y	Rock climbing	.90	.50
3375	A2790	50y	Handball	.90	.50
3376	A2790	50y	Softball	.90	.50
a.			Vert. strip of 5, #3372-3376	6.50	6.50

2011 Artistic
Gymnastics World
Championships,
Tokyo — A2791

Designs: No. 3377, Female gymnast. No. 3378, Male gymnast.

2011, Oct. 6   Litho.   Perf. 13
3377 A2791 80y red vio & multi   1.40   .90
3378 A2791 80y blue & multi   1.40   .90
a.   Horiz. pair, #3377-3378   4.25   4.25

Intl. Letter Writing Week A2792

Designs: 90y, Sound of the Tsuzumi, by Shoen Uemura. 110y, Backstage, by Shinsui Ito. 130y, Midori, Heroine of Takekurabe, by Kiyokata Kaburagi.

2011, Oct. 7   Photo.   Perf. 13¼
3379 A2792 90y multi   1.60   1.00
3380 A2792 110y multi   1.90   1.40
3381 A2792 130y multi   2.10   1.60
      Nos. 3379-3381 (3)   5.60   4.00

Miniature Sheet

Shiga Local Autonomy Law, 60th Anniv. — A2793

No. 3382: a, Ukimido Temple, grebes on Lake Biwa (32x39mm). b, Boats in canal, Omihachiman (28x33mm). c, Boat tied to tree limb (28x33mm). d, Ishiyama Temple, Japanese red maples (28x33mm). e, Hikone Castle in winter (28x33mm).

Perf. 13¼ (#3382a), 13x13¼
2011, Oct. 14   Photo.
3382 A2793 Sheet of 5   10.50 10.50
a.-e.   80y Any single   1.40   .90

Miniature Sheet

Travel Scenes — A2794

No. 3383: a, Yoyogi National Gymnasium, denomination at UR (stamp 1). b, Bench in Yoyogi Park, denomination at LR (stamp 2). c, Illumination of Omotesando trees at left, denomination at LL (stamp 3). d, Illumination of Otmotesando, trees at right, denomination at LR (stamp 4). e, Sidewalk and buildings along Omotesando, denomination at UL (stamp 5). f, Meiji Memorial Picture Gallery, denomination at UL (stamp 6). g, Ginkgo trees in Meiji Shrine Outer Garden, trees at left, denomination in blue at UL (stamp 7). h, Ginkgo trees in Meiji Shrine Outer Garden, trees at right, denomination in blue at UR (stamp 8). i, Nezu Museum, denomination at UL (stamp 9). j, Irises, painted screen, by Korin Ogata, denomination at LR (stamp 10).

2011, Oct. 21   Litho.   Perf. 13x13¼
3383 A2794 Sheet of 10   21.00 21.00
a.-j.   80y Any single   1.40   .90

Tokyo Metropolitan Festival Hall, 50th Anniv. — A2795

No. 3384: a, Stage and seating of Main Hall. b, Piano on stage of Small Hall. c, Ballet slippers, reflection of swan. d, Opera glasses, camellia. e, Piano keyboard. f, Violin.

2011, Oct. 31   Litho.   Perf. 13
3384 A2795 Block of 6   13.00 13.00
a.-f.   80y Any single   1.40   .90

No. 3384 was pritned in a sheet of 10 containing Nos. 3384a, 3384b and 2 each Nos. 3384c-3384f.

Miniature Sheets

A2796

A2797

Greetings — A2798

No. 3385: a, Wreath and dog (29mm diameter). b, Children and three Christmas trees (28x36mm). c, Christmas tree (28x38mm, Christmas tree-shaped). d, Santa Claus (28x36mm). e, Wreath and cat (29mm diameter).

No. 3386: a, Children starting to decorate Christmas tree. b, Children and decorated Christmas tree. c, Santa Claus, Christmas tree, children in bed. d, Santa Claus at Christmas tree. e, Children with Christmas presents.

No. 3387: a, Dog in snow (28x34mm oval). b, Flower bouquet (28x34mm oval). c, Snowman and animals on child's hat (38x28mm). d, Fairy and flowers (28x34mm oval). e, Children and cat looking at rabbit in snow (28x34mm oval).

2011, Nov. 10   Die Cut Perf. 13
Self-Adhesive
3385 A2796 Sheet of 5   6.50   6.50
a.-e.   50y Any single   .90   .50
3386 A2797 Sheet of 5   10.50 10.50
a.-e.   80y Any single   1.40   .90
3387 A2798 Sheet of 5   12.00 12.00
a.-e.   90y Any single   1.60   1.00

A2799   A2800

New Year 2012 (Year of the Dragon)
A2801   A2802

2011, Nov. 11   Photo.   Perf. 13x13½
3388 A2799 50y multi   .90   .50
3389 A2800 80y multi   1.40   .90

Photo. & Typo.
Perf. 13¼
3390 A2801 50y +3y multi   1.25   1.10
3391 A2802 80y +3y multi   2.00   1.60
      Nos. 3388-3391 (4)   5.55   4.10

Sheets of two containing Nos. 3388-3389 were lottery prizes.

Miniature Sheet

Iwate Local Autonomy Law, 60th Anniv. — A2803

No. 3392: a, Golden Hall, Chuson-ji, lotus flower (32x39mm). b, Cherry trees in bloom (28x33mm). c, Hayachine Kagura folk performers (28x33mm). d, Rocks at Jodogahama (28x33mm). e, Joboji lacquer trees (28x33mm).

Perf. 13¼ (#3392a), 13x13¼
2011, Nov. 15   Photo.
3392 A2803 Sheet of 5   10.50 10.50
a.-e.   80y Any single   1.40   .90

Miniature Sheet

Edo Calligraphy — A2804

No. 3393 — Characters for "dragon": a, In running script (black chracter with small red chop at LR). b, In Kinbun style (blue background). c, In Kinbun style (red background). d, In Sosho cursive stylo (black character with large dot, red chop at LL). e, In Kana (black character with five lines not touching each other, red chop at left). f, In Reisho script (complex black character, red chop of right angle and circle at lower left). g, In Reisho script (black character with thick diagonal line over denomination, red chop at left). h, In seal script form (black character with two thick parallel horizontal lines at top, red chop at LL). i, In Tensho seal style (in red). j, In Kana black character with thin curved line well above rest of character, red chop at left).

Litho. & Embossed
2011, Nov. 21   **Perf. 13x13¼**
3393	A2804	Sheet of 10	21.00 21.00
a.-j.		80y Any single	1.40 .90

Ministry of Agriculture, Forestry and Fisheries Festival, 50th Anniv. — A2805

Designs: No. 3394, Rice, chickens, tomatoes, fruit trees. No. 3395, Rice and fish.

2011, Nov. 22   **Litho.**   **Perf. 13**
3394		80y multi	1.40 .90
3395		80y multi	1.40 .90
a.	A2805	Horiz. pair, #3394-3395	4.20 4.20

Miniature Sheet

Home Towns — A2806

No. 3396 — Paintings by Taiji Harada of views of towns of Shinetsu region: a, Excursion (children, farmhouse, field of flowers, Iiyama, Nagano prefecture, denomination at LL). b, Excursion (children, hosue, river, field of flowers, Iiyama, denomination at UL). c, Kite Flying (three children near houses, Oshino Hakkai, Yamanashi prefecture, denomination at UL). d, Kite Flying (women and children, kites in air, Oshino Hakkai, denomination at UL). e, Riverbank Homes (person with dog in front of house, Kashiwazaki, Niigata prefecture). f, Riverbank Homes (man on scooter in front of house, Kashiwazaki). g, Yamakoshi in Springtime (koi breeding pool and building, Nagaoka, Niigata prefecture, denomination at LL). h, Yamakoshi in Springtime (building, man along path beside breeding pool, Nagaoka, denomination at UR). i, Town with a View of Fuji (adult and child, building, Mount Fuji, Yamanashi, Yamanashi prefecture). j, Snow Removal (adults cleaning snow, children playing, Naganao, Nagano prefecture).

2011, Dec. 1   **Photo.**   **Perf. 13**
3396	A2806	Sheet of 10	21.00 21.00
a.-j.		80y Any single	1.40 .90

Miniature Sheet

Akita Local Autonomy Law, 60th Anniv. — A2807

No. 3397: a, Nobu Shirase (1861-1946), Antarctic explorer, and two namahage (32x39mm). b, Korakukan Theater, Kosaka (28x33mm). c, Weeping cherry trees, Kakunodate (28x33mm). d, Statue of Tatsuko, Lake Tazawa (28x33mm). e, Kamakura Snow Festival, Yokote (28x33mm).

Perf. 13¼ (#3397a), 13x13¼
2012, Jan. 13
3397	A2807	Sheet of 5	10.50 10.50
a.-e.		80y Any single	1.40 .90

Animation
Miniature Sheet

Dragon Ball Kai — A2808

No. 3398: a, Vegeta on rock (white denomination at UL). b, Son Goku (purple denomination at LL). c, Son Gohan (red denomination at LL). d, Piccolo (purple denomination at LR). e, Trunks facing left(white denomination at LL). f, Vegeta facing right (white denomination at UR). g, Son Goku with fist extended(red denomination at LR). h, Piccolo flying (white denomination at LR) i, Son Gohan with white cape (white denomination at LL). j, Son Goku with brown tunic (white denomination at LR).

2012, Jan. 23   **Litho.**   **Perf. 13x13¼**
3398	A2808	Sheet of 10	21.00 21.00
a.-j.		80y Any single	1.40 .90

Miniature Sheets

Greetings Stamps — A2810

No. 3399: a, Child on bird. b, Child with boxes and pail, cat, flowers. c, Tree, bear, rabbit, bird, flowers. d, Swan, flower bouquet. e, Children on cherry blossom petals.
No. 3400: a, Cat and flowers in box. b, Dog, falling cherry blossom petals. c, Bouquet of cherry blossoms. d, Birds in basket of flowers. e, Girl with letter, mailbox.

Die Cut Perf. 13¼x13½
2012, Feb. 1   **Litho.**
Self-Adhesive
3399	A2809	Sheet of 5	7.00
a.-e.		50y Any single	.90 .50

Die Cut Perf. 13
3400	A2810	Sheet of 5	10.50
a.-e.		80y Any single	1.40 .90

Violets — A2811

Rose — A2812

Flowering Dogwood A2813

Muscari A2814

Poppy — A2815

Violets — A2816

Roses A2817

Flowering Dogwood A2818

Muscari A2819

Poppies A2820

2012, Mar. 1   **Photo.**   **Perf. 13¼**
3401	A2811	50y multi	.90 .50
3402	A2812	50y multi	.90 .50
3403	A2813	50y multi	.90 .50
3404	A2814	50y multi	.90 .50
3405	A2815	50y multi	.90 .50
a.		Vert. strip of 5, #3401-3405	6.25 6.25
3406	A2816	80y multi	1.40 .90
3407	A2817	80y multi	1.40 .90
3408	A2818	80y multi	1.40 .90
3409	A2819	80y multi	1.40 .90
3410	A2820	80y multi	1.40 .90
a.		Vert. strip of 5, #3406-3410	10.00 10.00
		Nos. 3401-3410 (10)	11.50 7.00

Miniature Sheets

A2821

Disney Characters — A2822

No. 3411: a, Mickey and Minnie Mouse holding each other with arms extended (36x29mm heart-shaped stamp). b, Mickey with arm raised (27x28mm). c, Minnie with arms at side (27x28mm). d, Mickey with arms behind back (27x28mm). e, Minnie winking (27x28mm). f, Mickey with hands on hips (27x28mm). g, Minnie and Mickey, Minnie at left (36x29mm heart-shaped stamp). h, Mickey and Minnie not touching, Mickey's arm extended (36x29mm heart-shaped stamp). i, Mickey and Minnie, tails crossing (36x29mm heart-shaped stamp). j, Mickey and Minnie, Minnie's arms extended (36x29mm heart-shaped stamp).
No. 3412: a, Mickey (yellow background, 28mm diameter). b, Minnie (yellow background, 28mm diameter). c, Mickey, Minnie, Goofy, Pluto, Daisy Duck, Donald Duck (yellow background, 37mm diameter). d, Minnie and Daisy (pink background, 28mm diameter). e, Daisy (pink background, 28mm diameter). f, Donald (blue background, 28mm diameter). g, Mickey and Pluto (blue background, 28mm diameter). h, Mickey with arms raised (white, beige and blue background, oval). i, Goofy, Mickey and Donald (pink background, 37mm diameter). j, Minnie, Pluto and Mickey (blue background, 37mm diameter).

Die Cut Perf., Die Cut Perf. 13¼x13½ (#3411b-3411f)
2012, Mar. 2   **Litho.**
Self-Adhesive
3411	A2821	Sheet of 10	12.50 12.50
a.-j.		50y Any single	.90 .50
3412	A2822	Sheet of 10	20.00 20.00
a.-j.		80y Any single	1.40 .90

Miniature Sheet

U.S. Cherry Blossom
Centennial — A2823

No. 3413: a, Cherry trees in bloom, Washington Monument. b, Cherry trees in bloom, Jefferson Memorial. c, Cherry blossoms, bright blue background. d, Cherry blossoms, dark green background. e, Cherry blossoms, gray blue background. f, Cherry blossoms, olive brown background. g, Cherry blossoms, pink background.

2012, Mar. 27   Perf. 13
3413 A2823 Sheet of 10,
      #3413a-3413f,
      4 #3413g   20.00 20.00
  a.-g. 80y Any single   1.40   .90
    See U.S. Nos. 4651-4652.

Miniature Sheet

Okinawa Local Autonomy Law, 60th
Anniv. — A2824

No. 3414: a, Shuri Castle and Kumiodori dancer (32x39mm). b, Shurei Gate, Shuri Castle (28x33mm). c, Ryukyuan bingata (28x33mm). d, Ryukyuan dancers (28x33mm). e, Coral tree blossoms (28x33mm).

Perf. 13¼ (#3414a), 13x13¼
2012, Apr. 13   Photo.
3414 A2824 Sheet of 5   10.00 10.00
  a.-e. 80y Any single   1.40   .90

Fence with Grasses and Flowers,
From Paper Partition by Unknown
Artist — A2825

Dragon, From Screen by Sanraku
Kano — A2826

Peonies, From Screen by Eino
Kano — A2827

Perf. 12¾ Syncopated
2012, Apr. 20   Photo.
3415 A2825 80y multi   1.40   .90
3416 A2826 80y multi   1.40   .90
3417 A2827 80y multi   1.40   .90
    Nos. 3415-3417 (3)   4.20 2.70
  Philately Week. Nos. 3415-3417 were printed in a sheet of 10 containing 3 each Nos. 3415 and 3417 and 4 No. 3416.

Miniature Sheet

Travel Scenes — A2828

No. 3418: a, Giant panda with open mouth (stamp 1). b, Giant panda with closed mouth (stamp 2). c, Shinobazo Pond, Ueno Park, Tokyo, denomination at UL (stamp 3). d, Shinobazo Pond, Ueno Park and Tokyo Buildings in distance, denomination at UR (stamp 4). e, Thunder Gate, Senso-ji Temple, denomination at LL (stamp 5). f, Senso-ji pagodas, denomination at UL (stamp 6). g, Boat on Sumida River, buildings, denomination at UR (stamp 7). h, Asahi Beer Buildings along Sumida River, denomination at UR (stamp 8). i, Cherry blossoms, Sumida Park, denomination at UL (stamp 9). j, Fireworks display along Sumida River, denomination at LR (stamp 10).

2012, Apr. 23 Litho. Perf. 13x13¼
3418 A2828 Sheet of 10 20.00 20.00
  a.-j. 80y Any single   1.40   .90

Japanese Bush
Cranberry
A2829

Yellow-flowered
Toad Lily — A2830

Phedimus
Sikokianus
A2831

Japanese Wild
Orchid — A2832

Stigmatodactylus
Sikokianus
A2833

2012, Apr. 24   Perf. 12¾x13
3419 A2829 80y multi   1.40   .90
3420 A2830 80y multi   1.40   .90
3421 A2831 80y multi   1.40   .90
3422 A2832 80y multi   1.40   .90
3423 A2833 80y multi   1.40   .90
  a.   Vert. strip of 5, #3419-3423 10.00 10.00
    Nos. 3419-3423 (5)   7.00 4.50
  Plant illustrations by Tomitaro Makino (1862-1957), botanist.

Miniature Sheet

Return of Okinawa to Japanese
Control, 40th Anniv. — A2834

No. 3424: a, Shuri Castle, denomination at LL. b, Shuri Castle, denomination at UR. c, Bitter melon, denomination at LL. d, Mangos, denomination at UR. e, Pink and white orchids, denomination at LL. f, White orchids, denomination at UR. g, Whale shark and fish, denomination at LL. h, Whale shark and fish, denomination at UR. i, Okinawa Urban Monorail, denomination at LL. j, Bridge between islands, denomination at UR.

2012, May 15 Photo. Perf. 13
3424 A2834 Sheet of 10 20.00 20.00
  a.-j. 80y Any single   1.40   .90

Miniature Sheet

Yamaguchi Prefecture
Afforestation — A2835

No. 3425: a, Camphor tree, denomination at UR. b, Japanese maple, denomination at LR in yellow. c, Ginkgo (yellow leaves on branch), denomination at LL in yellow. d, Wild camellia, denomination at UR. e, Citrus natsudaiidai (single white flower), denomination at UR. f, Japanese red pine, denomination at UR in green. g, Rape blossoms (yellow flowers), denomination at LR in yellow. h, Japanese cypress, denomination at LL. i, Boat oak, denomination at LL in green . j, Cherry blossoms, denomination at LL.

2012, May 25		Litho.		
3425	A2835	Sheet of 10	13.00	13.00
a.-j.		50y Any single	.90	.50

A2836

A2837

A2838

A2839

A2840

A2841

A2842

A2843

A2844

Ikebana, 550th
Anniv. — A2845

2012, May 31			
3426		Sheet of 10	20.00	20.00
a.	A2836	80y multi	1.40	.90
b.	A2837	80y multi	1.40	.90
c.	A2838	80y multi	1.40	.90
d.	A2839	80y multi	1.40	.90
e.	A2840	80y multi	1.40	.90
f.	A2841	80y multi	1.40	.90
g.	A2842	80y multi	1.40	.90
h.	A2843	80y multi	1.40	.90
i.	A2844	80y multi	1.40	.90
j.	A2845	80y multi	1.40	.90

Miniature Sheet

Modern Art — A2846

No. 3427: a, Bathhouse Girls, by Bakusen Tsuchida (detail of bird in tree). b, Bathouse Girls, by Tsuchida (detail of girl). c, Young Girl, by Kunzo Minami (girl at table writing). d, Portrait of Encho San'yutei, by Kiyokata Kaburagi (man kneeling on mat). e, Road, Cut Bank and Fence, by Ryusei Kishida. f, Mother and Child, by Shoen Uemura. g, Reading by the Window, by Kijiro Ota (woman reading book). h, Back Garden After the Rain, by Shinsen Tokuoka (bird under flowering bush). i, Portrait of a Lady, by Sotaro Yasui (woman seated in chair). j, Study of Flowers, by Heihachiro Fukuda (pond with iris shoots and fallen cherry blossoms).

2012, June 1		Photo.		Perf. 13	
3427	A2846	Sheet of 10	20.00	20.00
a.-j.		80y Any single	1.40	.90

Wisteria
A2847

Lily of the Valley
A2848

Hydrangea
A2849

Sunflower
A2850

Morning Glories
A2851

Wisteria
A2852

Lily of the Valley
A2853

Hydrangea
A2854

Sunflowers
A2855

Morning Glories
A2856

2012, June 7		Photo.		Perf. 13¼	
3428	A2847	50y multi	.90	.50
3429	A2848	50y multi	.90	.50
3430	A2849	50y multi	.90	.50
3431	A2850	50y multi	.90	.50
3432	A2851	50y multi	.90	.50
a.		Vert. strip of 5, #3428-3432	6.25	6.25
3433	A2852	80y multi	1.40	.90
3434	A2853	80y multi	1.40	.90
3435	A2854	80y multi	1.40	.90
3436	A2855	80y multi	1.40	.90
3437	A2856	80y multi	1.40	.90
a.		Vert. strip of 5, #3433-3437	10.00	10.00
		Nos. 3428-3437 (10)	11.50	7.00

Tenjin Festival (Osaka) — A2857

2012, June 15		Litho.		Perf. 13¼	
3438		50y	Denomination at UR	.90	.50
3439		50y	Denomination at UL	.90	.50
a.	A2857	Horiz. pair, #3438-3439	2.50	2.50

Japanese Forces in United Nations
Peacekeeping Operations, 20th
Anniv. — A2858

2012, June 19			Perf. 13	
3440		80y pink & multi	1.40	.90
3441		80y blue & multi	1.40	.90
a.	A2858	Pair, #3440-3441	4.00	4.00

Miniature Sheet

Ogaswara Islands UNESCO World
Heritage Site — A2859

No. 3442: a, Bonin white-eye, denomination at UL (stamp 1). b, Bonin peonies, denomination at LR (stamp 2). c, Heart Rock, denomination at UL (stamp 3). d, Snail on leaf, denomination at LL (stamp 4). e, Ogi Pond and rock arch, denomination at LL (stamp 5). f, Semifossilized shells, denomination at UL (stamp 6). g, Bonin camellia, denomination at LL (stamp 7). h, Chichijima Forests, denomination at LR (stamp 8). i, Southern bottlenose dolphins, denomination at UR (stamp 9). j, Pandanus boninensis, denomination at UR (stamp 10).

2012, June 20 Photo. Perf. 13x13¼
3442 A2859 Sheet of 10   20.00 20.00
a.-j.   80y Any single   1.40   .90

Miniature Sheets

A2860

Hello Kitty — A2861

No. 3443: a, Hello Kitty and Dear Daniel (25x38mm fan-shaped stamp). b, Hello Kitty (25x38mm fan-shaped stamp). c, Hello Kitty, pink panel (25x25mm). d, Hello Kitty, lilac panel (25x25mm). e, Hello Kitty, yellow panel (25x25mm).
No. 3444: a, Hello Kitty and Dear Daniel (42x27mm rectangular stamp). b, Hello Kitty, rabbit, building with blue roof (40x29mm building-shaped stamp). c, Hello Kitty, denomination in red at R (29mm diameter). d, Hello Kitty, bear, building with red roof (40x29mm building shaped stamp). e, Hello Kitty, white denomination at L (29mm diameter). f, Hello Kitty and Dear Daniel, building with orange

roof (40x29mm building-shaped stamp). g, Hello Kitty and Dear Daniel, fireworks overhead (28x38mm oval stamp). h, Hello Kitty and Dear Daniel holding fans (28x38mm oval stamp).

Die Cut Perf. 13¼ (#3443a-3443b),
Die Cut Perf. 13¼x13½ (#3443c-3443e)
2012, June 22   Litho.
        Self-Adhesive
3443 A2860 Sheet of 10, 2
      each #3443a-
      3443e   12.50
a.-e.   50y Any single   .90   .50

Die Cut Perf. 13½
3444 A2861 Sheet of 10,
      #3444a-3444f,
      2 each #3444g-
      3444h   20.00
a.-h.   80y Any single   1.40   .90

Miniature Sheet

Hiraizumi UNESCO World Heritage Site — A2862

No. 3445: a, Golden Hall, Chuson-ji, denomination at LR in gold (stamp 1). b, Hanging ornament, denomination at LL (stamp 2). c, Kyozo buildings, Chuson-ji, denomination at UL (stamp 3). d, People under umbrellas at Motsuji, denomination at LL (stamp 4). e, Motsuji Jodo Garden and pond, denomination at UL (stamp 5). f, Motsuji Jodo Garden and pond, denomination at UR (stamp 6). g, Kanjizaio-in temple garden and pond, denomination at LR (stamp 7). h, Kanjizaio-in temple garden and pond, denomination at LL (stamp 8). i, Muryoko-in ruins, trees and mountain, denomination at LR (stamp 9). j, Lotus blossoms, denomination at LL (stamp 10).

2012, June 29 Photo. Perf. 13x13¼
3445 A2862 Sheet of 10   20.00 20.00
a.-j.   80y Any single   1.40   .90

Adder's Tongue Lily A2863

Bazara-Taisho (c. 710-794) A2864

2012, July 2 Photo. Perf. 13x13¼
3446 A2863 350y multi   7.00 6.00
3447 A2864 500y multi   9.50 8.00
No. 3446 has a vignette different from No. 2166.

Miniature Sheet

Season's Memories in My Heart — A2865

No. 3448: a, Woman on bench near water, denomination at UL (stamp 1). b, Street vendor booths at festival, denomination at LR in gold (stamp 2). c, Child running stick against fence posts, denomination at UR (stamp 3). d, Children and animals in fog, denomination at UR (stamp 4). e, Girl with flower, boy with fishing pole and bucket, denomination at UL (stamp 5). f, Children on steps near sea, denomination at LR (stamp 6). g, Children, boats on shore, flying gull, denomination at UL (stamp 7). h, Children on hill looking at boat, denomination at UL in gold (stamp 8). i, Boat on shore, children looking at jellyfish, denomination at UL (stamp 9). j, Cricket with leaf cello, child, bottle, denomination at UL in gold (stamp 10).

2012, July 3 Photo. Perf. 13
3448 A2865 Sheet of 10   20.00 20.00
a.-j.   80y Any single   1.40   .90

Miniature Sheet

Constellations — A2866

No. 3449: a, Capricornus (goat). b, Aquarius (water bearer). c, Pisces (fish). d, Cassiopeia (woman in chair). e, Pegasus. f, Andromeda (woman in chains). g, Perseus (swordsman). h, Cepheus (king with scepter). i, Cetus (creature with two front legs and tail). j, Cassiopeia (anchor).

Litho. With Foil Application
2012, July 6   Die Cut Perf. 13
        Self-Adhesive
3449 A2866 Sheet of 10   20.00
a.-j.   80y Any single   1.40   .90

Miniature Sheet

Kanagawa Local Autonomy Law, 60th Anniv. — A2867

No. 3450: a, Tsurugaoka Hachimangu, Kamakura, and mounted archer (32x39mm). b, Minato Mirai 21 buildings, Yokohama (28x33mm). c, Jogashima Lighthouse (28x33mm). d, Tanzawa Mountains and Lake Miyagase (28x33mm). e, Lake Ashi (28x33mm).

Perf. 13¼ (#3450a), 13x13¼
2012, July 13   Photo.
3450 A2867 Sheet of 5   10.50 10.50
a.-e.   80y Any single   1.40   .90

Susanoo, Shinto God of the Sea — A2868

Legendary Princess Inada — A2869

Legendary Princess Konohanasakuya A2870

Legendary Prince Yamatotakeru A2871

2012, July 20   Litho.   *Perf. 13*

3451	A2868	80y multi	1.40	.90
3452	A2869	80y multi	1.40	.90
3453	A2870	80y multi	1.40	.90
3454	A2871	80y multi	1.40	.90
a.	Block of 4, #3451-3454		8.40	8.40
	Nos. 3451-3454 (4)		5.60	3.60

Nos. 3451-3454 were printed in sheets of 10 containing 3 each Nos. 3451-3452 and 2 each Nos. 3453-3454.

Inpumon In no Taifu, Poet — A2872

Fujiwara no Toshiyuki Ason, Poet — A2873

Shune-hoshi, Poet — A2874

Kokamon In no Betto, Poet — A2875

Sone no Yoshitada, Poet — A2876

Poetry — A2877

No. 3460 — Poetry in Japanese calligraphy and: a, Boat in lake, denomination at LL. b, Inpumon In no Taifu. c, Hill near water, denomination at UL. d, Fujiwara no Toshiyuki Ason. e, Building and tree. f, Shune-hoshi. g, Eddies in river, denomination at UR. h, Kokamon In no Betto. i, Man rowing boat. j, Sone no Yoshitada.

2012, July 23   Photo.   *Perf. 13¼*

3455	A2872	50y multi	.90	.50
3456	A2873	50y multi	.90	.50
3457	A2874	50y multi	.90	.50
3458	A2875	50y multi	.90	.50
3459	A2876	50y multi	.90	.50
a.	Vert. strip of 5, #3455-3459		6.50	6.50
	Nos. 3455-3459 (5)		4.50	2.50

Perf. 12¾x13

3460	A2877	Sheet of 10	21.00	21.00
a.-j.	80y Any single		2.10	1.60

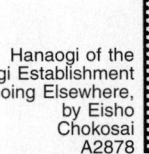
Hanaogi of the Ogi Establishment Going Elsewhere, by Eisho Chokosai A2878

The Moon Crossing Bridge at Arashiyama in Yamashiro Province, by Hiroshige A2879

Tosei Onna Fuzuoku Tsuu Hokkoku no Keisei, by Utamaro A2880

The Brocade Bridge at Iwakuni in Suo Province, by Hiroshige A2881

Furyu Setsugekka Tsuki, by Eizan Kikukawa A2882

Mt. Kyodai and the Moon Reflected in the Rice Fields at Sarashina in Shinano Province, by Hiroshige A2883

Ogiya Uchi Hanaogi Yoshino Tatsuta, by Utamaro A2884

Rough Sea at Naruto in Awa Province, by Hiroshige A2885

Furyu Mutamagawa Chofu no Tamagawa, by Eizan Kikukawa A2886

The Monkey Bridge in Kai Province, by Hiroshige A2887

2012, Aug. 1   Litho.   *Perf. 13*

3461		Sheet of 10	21.00	21.00
a.	A2878	80y multi	1.40	.90
b.	A2879	80y multi	1.40	.90
c.	A2880	80y multi	1.40	.90
d.	A2881	80y multi	1.40	.90
e.	A2882	80y multi	1.40	.90
f.	A2883	80y multi	1.40	.90
g.	A2884	80y multi	1.40	.90
h.	A2885	80y multi	1.40	.90
i.	A2886	80y multi	1.40	.90
j.	A2887	80y multi	1.40	.90

Miniature Sheet

Miyazaki Local Autonomy Law, 60th Anniv. — A2888

No. 3462: a, Miyazaki Prefectural Office and dancer (32x39mm). b, Koibitono-oka (hill with gazebo) (28x33mm). c, Yellow flowers, Saitobaru Burial Grounds (28x33mm). d, Pink flowers, Ebino-kogen Highlands (28x33mm). e, Terraced rice fields (28x33mm).

Perf. 13¼ (#3462a), 13x13¼

2012, Aug. 15   Photo.

3462	A2888	Sheet of 5	10.50	10.50
a.-e.	80y Any single		1.40	.90

Sorex Minutissimus A2889

Aquila Chrysaetos A2890

Paeonia Obovata A2891

Oryzias Latipes A2892

Tachypleus Tridentatus A2893

2012, Aug. 23   *Perf. 13¼*

3463	A2889	80y multi	1.40	.90
3464	A2890	80y multi	1.40	.90
3465	A2891	80y multi	1.40	.90
3466	A2892	80y multi	1.40	.90
3467	A2893	80y multi	1.40	.90
a.	Vert. strip of 5, #3463-3467		10.50	10.50
	Nos. 3463-3467 (5)		7.00	4.50

Normalization of Diplomatic Relations Between Japan and People's Republic of China, 40th Anniv. — A2894

2012, Sept. 4   *Perf. 13*

3468	A2894	80y multi	1.40	.90

Miniature Sheet

Travel Scenes — A2895

No. 3469 — Sites in Nagasaki: a, Urakami Cathedral, denomination at UR (stamp 1). b, Peace Statue, Nagasaki (stamp 2). c, Megane Bridge, denomination at LL (stamp 3). d, Megane Bridge, denomination at LR (stamp 4). e, Lantern Festival, denomination at UL below country name (stamp 5). f, Sofuku Temple, denomination at UL, to left of country name (stamp 6). g, Glover House, Glover Gardens, denomination at UR (stamp 7). h, Glover House , Glover Gardens, denomination at LR (stamp 8). i, People carrying dragon at Kunchi Festival, denomination at LL (stamp 9). j, Tall Ships Festival, denomination at UR (stamp 10).

2012, Sept. 11   Litho.   Perf. 13x13¼
3469 A2895   Sheet of 10   21.00 21.00
a.-j.   80y Any single   1.40   .90

Miniature Sheets

A2896

Teddy Bears — A2897

No. 3470 — Teddy bear with: a, Blue cap, pink background, red bow at top (28x28mm). b, Blue cap, light blue background, blue bow at top (28x28mm). c, Blue and white box with red ribbon, pink background, pink bow at top (28x28mm). d, Gold box with yellow ribbon, yellow background, yellow bow at top (28x28mm). e, Card with red ribbon, lilac

background, red bow at top(28x28mm). f, Card with blue ribbon, light green background, gray green bow at top (28x28mm). g, Red box with white ribbon, plaid bow around neck (26x30mm). h, Blue box with red ribbon, dark blue bow around neck (26x30mm). i, Card with red ribbon, green bow around neck (26x30mm). j, Blue and white box with red ribbon, blue bow around neck (26x30mm).

No. 3471: a, Bear with blue and white box with yellow ribbon (26x38mm). b, Bear with green box with red ribbon (26x38mm). c, Bear with card with red ribbon (26x38mm). d, Two bears, lilac denomination (42x27mm). e, Two bears, blue denomination (27x38mm oval). f, Two bears, red denomination (27x38mm oval). g, Bear with black and brown bow around neck, red denomination (27x38mm oval). h, Bear with card with red ribbon, red denomination (27x38mm oval). i, Bear with flower (27x38mm oval). j, Bear with cap, two boxes (42x27mm).

Die Cut Perf. 14, Die Cut Perf. ½ (#3470g-3470j)

2012, Sept. 21   Litho.
Self-Adhesive
3470 A2896   Sheet of 10   13.00
a.-j.   50y Any single   .90   .50

Die Cut Perf. 14½x14 (#3471a-3471c), 11¼x13½ (#3471d, 3471j), 13¾
3471 A2897   Sheet of 10   21.00
a.-j.   80y Any single   1.40   .90

 Badminton A2898
 Rhythmic Gymnastics A2899
 Rowing — A2900
 Cycling — A2901

Field Hockey — A2902

2012, Sept. 28   Litho.   Perf. 13
3472 A2898 50y multi   .90   .50
3473 A2899 50y multi   .90   .50
3474 A2900 50y multi   .90   .50
3475 A2901 50y multi   .90   .50
3476 A2902 50y multi   .90   .50
a.   Vert. strip of 5, #3472-3476   6.50 6.50

67th National Athletic Meet, Gifu. Compare with type A2790.

Miniature Sheet

Horse Racing in Japan, 150th Anniv. — A2903

No. 3477: a, Orfevre (horse #9, jockey with green helmet). b, Apapane (horse #9, jockey with yellow helmet, blue and yellow silks). c, Deep Impact (horse #5, jockey with red helmet, yellow and gray silks). d, Still in Love (horse #9, jockey with yellow helmet, red and blue silks). e, Narita Brian (horse #4, jockey with red helmet). f, Mejiro l'Amone (horse #13). g, Symboli Rudolf (horse #5, jockey with red helmet, blue and red silks). h, Mr. C.B. (horse #12, jockey with green and white silks).

i, Shinzan (horse #4, jockey with brown helmet). j, Saint Lite (horse #12, black-and-white photograph).

2012, Oct. 2   Photo.   Perf. 13
3477   A2903 80y Any single   21.00 21.00
a.- j.   1.40   .90

Intl. Letter Writing Week A2904

Designs: 90y, Hatsugochi, by Kiyokata Kaburaki. 110y, Shunpo, by Shoen Uemura. 130y, Hubuki, by Shinsui Ito.

2012, Oct. 9   Photo.   Perf. 13¼
3478 A2904 90y multi   1.60 1.00
3479 A2904 110y multi   1.90 1.40
3480 A2904 130y multi   2.10 1.60
    Nos. 3478-3480 (3)   5.60 4.00

Miniature Sheet

Annual Meeting of Intl. Monetary Fund and World Bank Group, Tokyo — A2905

No. 3481: a, Silver and copper Wado Kaichin coins, 708 (gold frame). b, Oval copper Tempo Tsuho coin, 1835, round Kanei Tsuho coin, 1636 (gold frame). c, Six round Chinese copper coins, 12th-15th cent. (silver frame). d, Moneychanger's balance, 19th cent. (silver frame). e, Hirumokin gold slug, Sekishugin silver slug, Yuzurihakin gold plate, 16th cent. (gold frame). f, Yamada Hagaki paper money, 17th-19th cent. (gold frame). g, Gold Keicho Oban, 1601 (silver frame). h, Molded coins attached to sprues, c. 1863 (silver frame). i, Silver Keicho Chogin coin and five Silver Keicho Mameitagin coins, 1601 (silver frame). j, 1871 gold 20-yen, silver 50-yen and copper 2-sen coins (gold frame).

2012, Oct. 12   Photo.   Perf. 13
3481 A2905   Sheet of 10   20.00 20.00
a.- j.   80y Any single   1.40   .90

Miniature Sheet

Tochigi Local Autonomy Law, 60th Anniv. — A2906

No. 3482: a, Yomei Gate, Toshogu Shrine (32x39mm). b, Gate at Ashikaga School (28x33mm). c, Carp amulets on sticks (28x33mm). d, Moka Railway steam locomotive and flowers (28x33mm). e, Cherry blossoms and mountain, Nasu Kogen (28x33mm).

Perf. 13¼ (#3482a), 13x13¼
2012, Oct. 15   Photo.
3482 A2906   Sheet of 5   10.00 10.00
a.-e.   80y Any single   1.40   .90

Animation
Miniature Sheet

Rascal — A2907

No. 3483: a, Rascal the Raccoon on tree (white denomination at UR). b, Sterling and Alice (white denomination at UL). c, Rascal with book and lamp (white denomination at UL). d, Sterling and book (white denomination at UR). e, Three raccoon babies, butterflies (black denomination at UL). f, Rascal facing left (black denomination at UR). g, Rascal drinking from bottle (white denomination at UL). h, Sterling drinking from bottle (white denomination at UL). i, Rascal, Rascal in canoe (black denomination at UR). j, Sterling, Sterling in canoe (white denomination at UR).

2012, Oct. 23   Litho.   Perf. 13x13¼
3483 A2907   Sheet of 10   20.00 20.00
a.-j.   80y Any single   1.40   .90

Miniature Sheet

Traditional Crafts — A2908

No. 3484: a, Hakata doll depicting man holding fan (Fukuoka Prefecture). b, Black rectangular inkstone and lid (Miyagi Prefecture). c, Banana-fiber handbag (Okinawa Prefecture). d, Container and two cups (Fukushima Prefecture). e, Two lacquerware bowls (Aomori Prefecture). f, Folding fan (Kyoto Prefecture). g, Kaga dyed screen (Ishikawa Prefecture). h, Decorated Kutani plate (Ishikawa Prefecture). i, Cast-iron kettle (Iwate Prefecture). j, Tsuboya ceramic urn with handles (Okinawa Prefecture).

2012, Oct. 25   Photo.   Perf. 13½
3484 A2908   Sheet of 10   20.00 20.00
  a.-j.   80y Any single   1.40   .90

Miniature Sheets

A2909

A2910

Greetings — A2911

No. 3485: a, Star, Santa Clauses, gift (29x39mm). b, Kitten in stocking (26x34mm). c, Wreath, children, squirrel (29mm diameter).

d, Puppy in stocking (26x34mm). e, Christmas tree and cardinal (29x39mm).

No. 3486: a, Santa Claus and reindeer on building roof. b, Fireplace, Christmas tree, two children, cat and bird. c, Fireplace, three children, bird. d, Fireplace, Christmas tree, two children, two cats, bird. e, Fireplace, two children, Christmas tree being decorated, bird.

No. 3487: a, Cat on roof, envelope in night sky (37x28mm). b, Angel with violin, bird carrying letter (35x28mm ellipse). c, Snowman, squirrel, mailbox, child (28x37mm). d, Roses and open letter (35x28mm ellipse). e, three children in pajamas, candles (37x28mm).

Self-Adhesive
Die Cut Perf. 13

2012, Nov. 9   Litho.
3485 A2909   Sheet of 5   6.25   6.25
  a.-e.   50y Any single   .90   .50
3486 A2910   Sheet of 5   10.00 10.00
  a.-e.   80y Any single   1.40   .90
3487 A2911   Sheet of 5   11.50 11.50
  a.-e.   90y Any single   1.60   1.00

A2912   A2913

New Year 2013 (Year of the Snake)

A2914   A2915

2012, Nov. 12   Photo.   Perf. 13x13½
3488 A2912   50y multi   .90   .50
3489 A2913   80y multi   1.40   .90

Photo. & Typo.
Perf. 13¼
3490 A2914   50y +3y multi   1.25   1.00
3491 A2915   80y +3y multi   1.75   1.60
    Nos. 3488-3491 (4)   6.65   5.05

Miniature Sheet

Oita Local Autonomy Law, 60th Anniv. — A2916

No. 3492: a, Usa Jingu Shrine, Oita, Futabayama (1912-68), sumo wrestler (32x39mm). b, Plum blossoms, Japanese white-eye (28x33mm). c, Fukiji Temple (28x33mm). d, Hita Gion Festival (28x33mm). e, Sunrise at Bungofutamigaura (28x33mm).

Perf. 13¼ (#3492a), 13x13¼
2012, Nov. 15   Photo.
3492 A2916   Sheet of 5   10.00 10.00
  a.-e.   80y Any single   1.40   .90

Miniature Sheets

A2917

Disney Characters — A2918

No. 3493: a, Winnie the Pooh (27x27mm). b, Piglet (27x27mm). c, Alice in Wonderland (27x38mm oval). d, Donald Duck (26x34mm). e, Daisy Duck (26x34mm). f, Cinderella (27x38mm oval). g, Dumbo (29mm diameter). h, Marie the Cat (26x34mm). i, Goofy (26x34mm). j, Three Dalmatians (29mm diameter).

No. 3494: a, Tinker Bell (27x27mm). b, Mickey Mouse (27x38mm oval). c, Minnie Mouse (27x38mm oval). d, Bambi (27x27mm). e, Pinocchio (27x35mm). f, Snow White (27x38mm oval). g, Pluto (27x35mm). h, Ariel (35x27mm). i, Stitch (29mm diameter). j, Three Little Pigs (35x27mm).

Die Cut Perf. 13½, Die Cut Perf. 13 (#3493d, 3493e, 3493h, 3493i), Die Cut Perf. 13¼x13¾ (#3494e, 3494g), Die Cut Perf. 13¾x13¼ (#3494h, 3494j) Die Cut Perf. (#3493g, 3493i, 3494i)

2012, Nov. 20   Litho.
Self-Adhesive
3493 A2917   Sheet of 10   12.50
  a.-j.   50y Any single   .90   .50
3494 A2918   Sheet of 10   20.00
  a.-j.   80y Any single   1.40   .90

Miniature Sheet

Edo Calligraphy — A2919

No. 3495 — Characters for "snake": a, In Gyosho style (red background). b, In Reisho style (black character with red chop at bottom center). c, From Qing Dynaasty seal (black curved character with circle with small red chop at left). d, In Reisho style (pink background, red chop at bottom center). e, In Kana (black character similar to "3", red chop at LR). f, In Kaisho script (black character, red chop at LL). g, In Sosho stylet (black character with thick line similar to "2" and thin curved line, red chop at LR). h, In Gyosho style (green background). i, In small seal cutting (character in red). j, In Kinbun style (character in gold, brown background).

Litho. & Embossed

2012, Nov. 21		Perf. 13x13¼		
3495	A2919	Sheet of 10	20.00	20.00
a.-j.		80y Any single	1.40	.90

Camellia
A2920

Plum Blossom
A2921

Adonis Flower
A2922

Cyclamen
A2923

Hellebore
A2924

Camellia
A2925

Plum Blossoms
A2926

Adonis Flowers
A2927

Cyclamen
A2928

Hellebores
A2929

2012, Dec. 3		Photo.	Perf. 13¼	
3496	A2920	50y multi	.90	.50
3497	A2921	50y multi	.90	.50
3498	A2922	50y multi	.90	.50
3499	A2923	50y multi	.90	.50
3500	A2924	50y multi	.90	.50
a.		Vert. strip of 5, #3496-3500	6.25	6.25
3501	A2925	80y multi	1.40	.90
3502	A2926	80y multi	1.40	.90
3503	A2927	80y multi	1.40	.90
3504	A2928	80y multi	1.40	.90
3505	A2929	80y multi	1.40	.90
a.		Vert. strip of 5, #3501-3505	10.00	10.00
		Nos. 3496-3505 (10)	11.50	7.00

Miniature Sheet

Hyogo Local Autonomy Law, 60th
Anniv. — A2930

No. 3506: a, Flying crane, Himeji Castle (32x39mm). b, Meriken Park, Kobe, and waterfront buildings (28x33mm). c, Shinkoro Tower, Izushi (28x33mm). d, Shinmaiko Beach (28x33mm). e, Narcissuses, Awaji-shima (28x33mm).

Perf. 13¼ (#3506a), 13x13¼

2013, Jan. 15				
3506	A2930	Sheet of 5	8.75	8.75
a.-e.		80y Any single	1.40	.90

Animation
Miniature Sheet

Heidi, Girl of the Alps — A2931

No. 3507: a, Lamb and flowers. b, Heidi picking flowers). c, Dog and chalet. d, Heidi and chalet. e, Hoidi's grandfather. f, Heidi pointing. g, Heidi and Peter on sled. h, Rabbits. i, Heidi running, mountain in background. j, Clara in blue dress.

2013, Jan. 23		Litho.	Perf. 13x13¼	
3507	A2931	Sheet of 10	17.50	17.50
a.-j.		80y Any single	1.40	.90

Miniature Sheets

A2932

Greetings:Spring

Greetings — A2933

No. 3508: a, Cherry blossom, boy, birds with letter (30x29mm flower-shaped stamp). b, Wreath with strawberries (29mm diameter). c, Boy, girl, cat, wreath of cherry blossoms (29mm diameter). d, Tulips, cats and rabbit (28x28mm). e, Girl carrying potted plant up stairs, cat with broom (28x28mm).

No. 3509: a, Gril with letter, cherry blossoms (30x29mm flower shaped stamp). b, Bouquet of red and pink flowerst (24x34mm oval). c, Bouquet of blue and white flowers (24x34mm oval). d, Bouquet of yellow and orange flowers (24x34mm oval). e, Teddy bear with letter and mail bag, mail box (23x30mm).

Die Cut Perf., Die Cut Perf 13¼ (#3508d, 3508e, 3509b-3509d), Die Cut Perf. 13¼x12¾ (#3509e)

2013, Feb. 1				
		Self-Adhesive		
3508	A2932	Sheet of 5	5.50	5.50
a.-e.		50y Any single	.90	.50
3509	A2933	Sheet of 5	8.75	8.75
a.-e.		80y Any single	1.40	.90

Dianthus
Caryophyllus
A2934

Tulip
A2935

Cherry
Blossoms
A2936

Gerbera Daisy
A2937

Myosotis
Scorpioides
A2938

Dianthus
Caryophyllus
A2939

Tulip
A2940

Cherry
Blossoms
A2941

Gerbera Daisy
A2942

Myosotis
Scorpioides
A2943

2013, Feb. 8　Photo.　Perf. 13¼

3510	A2934	50y multi	.90 .50
3511	A2935	50y multi	.90 .50
3512	A2936	50y multi	.90 .50
3513	A2937	50y multi	.90 .50
3514	A2938	50y multi	.90 .50
a.	Vert. strip of 5, #3510-3514		5.50 5.50
3515	A2939	80y multi	1.40 .90
3516	A2940	80y multi	1.40 .90
3517	A2941	80y multi	1.40 .90
3518	A2942	80y multi	1.40 .90
3519	A2943	80y multi	1.40 .90
a.	Vert. strip of 5, #3515-3519		8.75 8.75
Nos. 3510-3519 (10)			14.25 11.25

Mt.
Fuji — A2944

Mt. Tsukuba
A2945

Mt. Kasa
A2946

Mt. Ibuki
A2947

Mt.
Iino — A2948

Mt.
Zao — A2949

Mt. Gassan
A2950

Mt. Ryokami
A2951

Mt.
Nijo — A2952

Mt. Kuju — A2953

2013, Feb. 22　Litho.　Perf. 13¼x13

3520	Sheet of 10		17.50 17.50
a.	A2944	80y multi	1.40 .90
b.	A2945	80y multi	1.40 .90
c.	A2946	80y multi	1.40 .90
d.	A2947	80y multi	1.40 .90
e.	A2948	80y multi	1.40 .90
f.	A2949	80y multi	1.40 .90
g.	A2950	80y multi	1.40 .90
h.	A2951	80y multi	1.40 .90
i.	A2952	80y multi	1.40 .90
j.	A2953	80y multi	1.40 .90

A2954

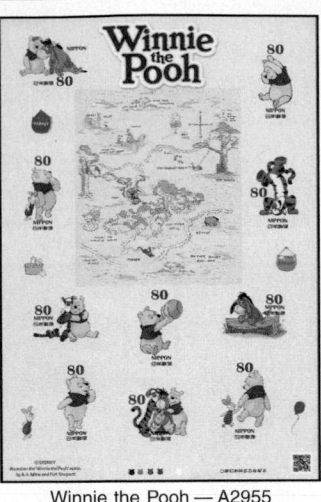

Winnie the Pooh — A2955

No. 3521: a, Winnie, Piglet, two beamed sixteenth notes in blue, eighth note in black. b, Winnie, sixteenth notes in black and green. c, Winnie, staff in pink, two beamed eighth notes in black. d, Tigger, staff in pink, eighth note in black. e, Winnie, staff in yellow, black and red sixteenth notes. f, Tigger, staff in yellow, two beamed eighth notes in black, eighth note in blue. g, Piglet, staff in yellow, three beamed sixteenth notes, eighth notes in black and pink, half note. h, Eeyore, staff in yellow, sixteenth note and two beamed sixteenth notes in black, eighth note in lilac. i, Winnie, staff in pink, sixteenth note and two beamed sixteenth notes in black. j, Winnie, staff in pink, eighth note, sixteenth note and two beamed sixteenth notes in black.

No. 3522, oval stamps: a, Winnie and Eeyore. b, Winnie seated, touching his nose and with arm wrapped over his head, vert. c, Winnie and Piglet standing, vert. d, Tigger, vert. e, Winnie and Tigger. f, Winnie and honey jar, vert. g, Eeyore and log. h, Winnie standing with arm near mouth. i, Tigger, Eeyore and Winnie. j, Winnie and Piglet walking, vert.

2013, Mar. 1　Die Cut Perf. 13x12¾
Self-Adhesive

3521	A2954	Sheet of 10	11.00
a.-j.		50y Any single	.90 .50

Die Cut Perf. 13

3522	A2955	Sheet of 10	17.50
a.-j.		80y Any single	1.40 .90

Grand Canyon, United States A2956

Pyramids, Egypt A2957

Mont-Saint-Michel, France — A2958

Macchu Picchu, Peru A2959

Angkor Wat, Cambodia A2960

2013, Mar. 14　Perf. 13¼x13

3523	A2956	80y multi	1.40 .90
3524	A2957	80y multi	1.40 .90
3525	A2958	80y multi	1.40 .90
3526	A2959	80y multi	1.40 .90
3527	A2960	80y multi	1.40 .90
a.	Horiz. strip of 5, #3523-3527		8.75 8.75
Nos. 3523-3527 (5)			7.00 4.50

Foreign UNESCO World Heritage Sites.

Hirosaki Cherry Blossom Festival (Aomori) — A2961

Designs: No. 3528, Weeping cherry branch, Mt. Iwaki (denomination in green). No. 3529, Yoshino cherry blossoms, Hirosaki Castle (denomination in lilac).

2013, Mar. 22　Perf. 13¼

3528	50y multi		.90 .50
3529	50y multi		.90 .50
a.	A2961 Horiz. pair, #3528-3529		2.20 2.20

Miniature Sheet

Season's Memories in My Heart — A2962

No. 3530: a, Girl in yellow dress staring at cherry blossom petals (stamp 1). b, Two children and flower cart (stamp 2). c, Three children, falling cherry blossom petals (stamp 3). d, Girl holding fiddlehead fern in field (stamp 4). e, Girl and flowers (stamp 5). f, Boy and girl looking at flowers (stamp 6). g, Boy in tulips, cat (stamp 7). h, Boy playing flute, girl reading book, flowers (stamp 8). i, Girl with doll, girl with dog, flowers (stamp 9). j, Girls playing house with doll, lawn chair (stamp 10).

2013, Apr. 3　Photo.　Perf. 13

3530	A2962	Sheet of 10	17.50 17.50
a.-j.		80y Any single	1.40 .90

JAPAN

133

Miniature Sheet

Travel Scenes — A2963

No. 3531 — Sites in Tateyama and Kurobe areas of Toyama: a, Ptarmigan (stamp 1). b, Bus and tourists in Great Snow Valley (stamp 2). c, Shomyo Falls (stamp 3). d, Tateyama gentians, denomination at LL (stamp 4). e, Midagahara Wetlands, denomination at UL (stamp 5). f, Midagahara Wetlands, denomination at UR (stamp 6). g, Murodo Highland, yellow day lilies (stamp 7). h, Stoat (stamp 8). i, Aleutian avens flowers, denomination at LR (stamp 9). j, Cable car at Daikanbo (stamp 10).

2013, Apr. 16 Litho. Perf. 13x13¼
3531	A2963	Sheet of 10	16.00 16.00
a.-j.		80y Any single	1.40 .90

A2964   A2965

A2966   A2967

A2968   A2969

A2970   A2971

Sections of Painted Screen by Motonobu Kano (1476-1559)
A2972   A2973

2013, Apr. 19 Photo. Perf. 13¼
3532		Sheet of 10	16.00 16.00
a.	A2964	80y multi	1.40 .90
b.	A2965	80y multi	1.40 .90
c.	A2966	80y multi	1.40 .90
d.	A2967	80y multi	1.40 .90
e.	A2968	80y multi	1.40 .90
f.	A2969	80y multi	1.40 .90
g.	A2970	80y multi	1.40 .90
h.	A2971	80y multi	1.40 .90
i.	A2972	80y multi	1.40 .90
j.	A2973	80y multi	1.40 .90

Philately Week.

Lily — A2974   Day Lily — A2975

Lilac A2976   Clematis A2977

Skunk Cabbage A2978   Lilies A2979

Day Lilies — A2980   Lilac — A2981

Clematis A2982   Skunk Cabbages A2983

2013, Apr. 24 Perf. 13¼
3533	A2974	50y multi	.90 .50
3534	A2975	50y multi	.90 .50
3535	A2976	50y multi	.90 .50
3536	A2977	50y multi	.90 .50
3537	A2978	50y multi	.90 .50
a.		Vert. strip of 5, #3533-3537	5.00 5.00
3538	A2979	80y multi	1.40 .90
3539	A2980	80y multi	1.40 .90
3540	A2981	80y multi	1.40 .90
3541	A2982	80y multi	1.40 .90
3542	A2983	80y multi	1.40 .90
a.		Vert. strip of 5, #3538-3542	8.00 8.00

Miniature Sheet

Miyagi Local Autonomy Law, 60th Anniv. — A2984

No. 3543: a, Statue of Masamune Date, replica of Date Maru ship (32x39mm). b, Mt. Kurikoma and cherry tree (28x33mm). c, Sendai Tanabata Festival (28x33mm). d, Bridge, Narukokyo Gorge (28x33mm). e, Sendai Pageant of Starlight (28x33mm).

Perf. 13¼ (#3543a), 13x13¼
2013, May 15 Photo.
3543	A2984	Sheet of 5	8.75 8.75
a.-e.		80y Any single	1.75 1.40

Martes Zibellina Brachyura A2985

Luscinia Komadori Namiyei A2986

Primula Kisoana Miquel A2987

Neolucanus Insulicola Donan A2988

Meretrix Lusoria A2989

2013, May 23 Perf. 13¼
3544	A2985	80y multi	1.40 .90
3545	A2986	80y multi	1.40 .90
3546	A2987	80y multi	1.40 .90
3547	A2988	80y multi	1.40 .90
3548	A2989	80y multi	1.40 .90
a.		Vert. strip of 5, #3544-3548	8.75 8.75
		Nos. 3544-3548 (5)	7.00 4.50

Miniature Sheet

Tottori Prefecture Afforestation — A2990

No. 3549: a, Quercus serrata (tree), denomination at LL. b, Lilium japonicum (pink flower), denomination at LL. c, Prunus jamasakura (cherry blossoms), denomination at LR. d, Taxus cuspidata (Japanese yew with red arils), denomination at LR. e, Castanopsis sieboldii (tree), denomination at UR. f, Iris sanguinea (purple flowers), denomination at UL. g, Nijisseiki pear tree blossoms, denomination at LR. h, Japanese persimmons on branch, denomination at LR. i, Castanea crenata (Japanese chestnut), denomination at UR. j, Magnolia obovata flower, denomination at LL.

2013, May 24   Litho.   **Perf. 13**
3549   A2990   Sheet of 10   11.00   11.00
a.-j.   50y Any single   .90   .50

Second Hideyo Noguchi Africa
Prize — A2991

Noguchi (1876-1928), bacteriologist, and:
No. 3550, Microscope and flowers. No. 3551,
Globe.

2013, May 31   Photo.
3550   80y multi   1.40   .90
3551   80y multi   1.40   .90
a.   A2991 Horiz. pair, #3550-3551   3.50   3.50

Animation

Doraemon — A2992

No. 3552: a, Doraemon with wings, two children with wings. b, Three children with wings.
c, Doraemon paddling raft. d, Children on fish.
e, Doraemon, machine, woman near doorway
carrying tray with bottles and glasses. f, Man
and boy in indoor fountain. g, Three children
with helicopter rotor on head flying. h,
Doraemon and child with helicopter rotor on
head flying. i, Boy and girl on orse, boy with
smokestack on head, boy with umbrella in
flight. j, Doraemon and cat on flying
seahorses.

2013, June 4   Litho.   **Perf. 13x13¼**
3552   A2992   Sheet of 10   17.50   17.50
a.-j.   80y Any single   1.40   .90

Miniature Sheet

Hiroshima Local Autonomy Law, 60th
Anniv. — A2993

No. 3553: a, Itsukushima Shrine, Bugaku
dancer, maple leaves (32x39mm). b, Mibo no
Hana Taue rice-planting ritual (28x33mm). c,
Taishakukyo Valley (28x33mm). d, Lemons
(28x33mm). e, Lighthouse and street,
Tomonoura (28x33mm).

Perf. 13¼ (#3553a), 13x13¼
2013, June 14   Photo.
3553   A2993   Sheet of 5   8.75   8.75
a.-e.   80y Any single   1.40   .90

Japan Women's Association for
Rehabilitation Aid, 50th
Anniv. — A2994

Designs: No. 3554, Two women. No. 3555,
Three women.

2013, June 18   Litho.   **Perf. 13**
3554   80y multi   1.40   .90
3555   80y multi   1.40   .90
a.   A2994 Horiz. pair, #3554-3555   3.50   3.50

Miniature Sheets

A2995

Greetings — A2996

No. 3556: a, Hello Kitty reading book
(30x27mm heart-shaped stamp). b, Hello Kitty

and house (27x30mm house-shaped stamp).
c, Mimmy riding tricycle (23x23mm). d, Dear
Daniel with letter at mailbox (22x30mm oval
stamp). f, Hello Kitty watering flowers from
mouse on tree stump (28mm diameter). f,
Hello Kitty watering flowers (27x21mm). g, My
Melody, bird in mailbox holding letter
(21x27mm). h, My Melody and mouse jumping
(30x27mm heart-shaped stamp). i, Little Twin
Stars on crescent moon (28mm diameter). j,
Little Twin Stars with music book and harp
(23x23mm).
No. 3557: a, Little Twin Stars on cloud
(27x21mm). b, Little Twin Stars, stars
(24x28mm). c, Hello Kitty in airplane (28mm
diameter). d, Hello Kitty holding teddy bear
and letter (23x23mm). e, Hello Kitty on back of
envelope (27x21mm). f, Hello Kitty and Mimmy
on tricycles (27x21mm). g, Dear Daniel reaching to insert letter in mailbox (26x29mm). h,
Hello Kitty holding apple (29x27mm heart-
shaped stamp). i, My Melody receiving letter
from bird in mailbox (29x26mm). j, My Melody
receiving kiss from mouse (30x27mm oval
stamp).

Die Cut Perf. 13¼, Die Cut Perf. 14
(#3556c, 3556j, 3557d), Die Cut Perf.
13¼x14 (#3556f, 3557a, 3557e,
3557f), Die Cut Perf. 14x13¾
(#3556g), Die Cut Perf. (#3556e,
3556i, 3557b, 3557c)

2013, June 21   Litho.
Self-Adhesive
3556   A2995   Sheet of 10   10.00
a.-j.   50y Any single   .90   .50
3557   A2996   Sheet of 10   16.00
a.-j.   80y Any single   1.40   .90

Miniature Sheet

Travel Scenes — A2997

No. 3558 — Sites in Chiba: a, Narita-san
Temple (stamp 1). b, Tourists in boat, flowers
at Suigo Sarawa Aquatic Botanical Gardens
(stamp 2). c, Chiba Port Tower (stamp 3). d,
Nokogiriyama Cable Car (stamp 4). e, Yellow
and red Kominato Railway train car (stamp 5).
f, Waterfall, Yoro-keikoku Valley (stamp 6). g,
Tsuki-no-Sabaku Statues, Onjuku Beach
(stamp 7). h, Yellow and green Isumi Railway
train car (stamp 8). i, Light green Choshi Electric Railway train car (stamp 9). j, Inubosaki
Lighthouse (stamp 10).

2013, June 25   Litho.   **Perf. 13x13¼**
3558   A2997   Sheet of 10   16.00   16.00
a.-j.   80y Any single   1.40   .90

Gion Festival, Kyoto — A2998

Various festival scenes with denomination in purple at: No. 3559, UL. No. 3560, UR. No. 3561, LL. No. 3562, LR.

2013, July 1		**Perf. 13¼**	
3559	50y multi	.90	.50
3560	50y multi	.90	.50
3561	50y multi	.90	.50
3562	50y multi	.90	.50
a.	A2998 Block of 4, #3559-3562	4.00	4.00
	Nos. 3559-3562 (4)	3.60	2.00

Miniature Sheet

Constellations — A2999

No. 3563: a, Cancer (crab). b, Leo (lion). c, Virgo (virgin). d, Ursa Major (large bear, tail at left). e, Ursa Minor (small bear, tail at top). f, Boötes (herdsman). g, Corvus (crow). h, Corona Borealis (crown). i, Canes Venatici (hunting dogs). j, Big Dipper asterism.

Litho. With Foil Application
2013, July 5   **Die Cut Perf. 13**
Self-Adhesive

3563	A2999 Sheet of 10	16.00	
a.-j.	80y Any single	1.40	.90

Miniature Sheet

Gunma Local Autonomy Law, 60th Anniv. — A3000

No. 3564: a, Tomioka Silk Mill, woman (32x39mm). b, Red rhododendrons (28x33mm). c, Usui Railway Bridge (28x33mm). d, Fukiware Falls (28x33mm). e, Yellow day lilies (28x33mm).

Perf. 13¼ (#3564a), 13x13¼

2013, July 12		**Photo.**	
3564	A3000 Sheet of 5	8.00	8.00
a.-e.	80y Any single	1.40	.90

Boy Writing
Postcard
A3001

Goldfish in Bowl
A3002

Mailbox,
Dragonfly,
Net — A3003

Japanese
Morning Glories
and
Trellis — A3004

Cucumbers,
Eggplants, and
Tomatoes — A3005

A3006

No. 3570: a, Girl writing a letter. b, Mailbox, dragonfly, net, diff. c, Beans and bowl of rice. d, Tea kettle and glasses. e, Corn. f, Japanese morning glories and trellis, diff. g, Postal truck on bridge. h, Spiral mosquito repellent coils. i, Bowls of noodles and sauce. j, Tomatoes.

2013, July 23		**Perf. 13¼**	
3565	A3001 50y multi	.90	.50
3566	A3002 50y multi	.90	.50
3567	A3003 50y multi	.90	.50
3568	A3004 50y multi	.90	.50
3569	A3005 50y multi	.90	.50
a.	Vert strip of 5, #3565-3569	5.50	5.50
	Nos. 3565-3569 (5)	4.50	2.50

		Perf. 13	
3570	A3006 Sheet of 10	17.50	17.50
a.-j.	80y Any single	1.40	.90

Letter Writing Day.

Kisegawa of
Matsubaya, by
Eishi Chobunsai
A3007

Pine Grove at
Miho, by
Hiroshige
A3008

Midorigi of the
Wakamatsu
House, by Eisho
Chokosai
A3009

Oyashirazu, by
Hiroshige
A3010

Woman Holding
an Umbrella, by
Eizan Kikukawa
A3011

Waka Bay, by
Hiroshige
A3012

Koito of Itoya, by
Utamaro
A3013

Festival at the
Itsukushima
Shrine, by
Hiroshige
A3014

Geisha of
Tachibana Street,
by Kiyonaga Torii
A3015

Amanohashidate,
by Hiroshige
A3016

2013, Aug. 1	**Litho.**	**Perf. 13**	
3571	Sheet of 10	17.50	17.50
a.	A3007 80y multi	1.75	1.40
b.	A3008 80y multi	1.75	1.40
c.	A3009 80y multi	1.75	1.40
d.	A3010 80y multi	1.75	1.40
e.	A3011 80y multi	1.75	1.40
f.	A3012 80y multi	1.75	1.40
g.	A3013 80y multi	1.75	1.40
h.	A3014 80y multi	1.75	1.40
i.	A3015 80y multi	1.75	1.40
j.	A3016 80y multi	1.75	1.40

Miniature Sheets

A3017

Disney Characters — A3018

No. 3572: a, Mickey Mouse on blue box. b, Minnie Mouse on pink box. c, Donald Duck on blue box. d, Daisy Duck on pink box. e, Tinker Bell on pink box. f, Marie the Cat on blue box. g, Buzz Lightyear and Woody on pink box. h, Lightning McQueen on blue box. i, Winnie the Pooh on blue box. j, Alice on pink box.

No. 3573: a, Tinker Bell (29mm diameter). b, Winnie the Pooh and Piglet in balloon gondola (21x30mm oval). c, Alice in balloon gondola (29mm diameter). d, Marie the Cat in balloon gondola (21x30mm oval). e, Oswald the Rabbit in balloon gondola (23x23mm). f, Mike Wazowski and James P. Sullivan in balloon gondola (21x30mm oval). g, Goofy, Chip, Donald Duck, Pluto, Mickey Mouse, Minnie Mouse, Daisy Duck in balloon gondola (44x35mm). h, Woody and Buzz Lightyear in balloon gondola (21x30mm oval). i, Snow White, Rapunzel and Cinderella in balloon gondola (29mm diameter). j, Dumbo (30x21mm oval).

Die Cut Perf. 13¼
2013, Aug. 8   Litho.
Self-Adhesive
3572	A3017	Sheet of 10	10.00	
a.-j.		50y Any single	1.00	.75

Die Cut Perf., Die Cut Perf. 13¼ (oval stamps), Die Cut Perf. 14 (#3573e), Die Cut Perf. 13½ (#3573g)
3573	A3018	Sheet of 10	16.00	
a.-j.		80y Any single	1.60	1.25

Kayak on Tama River — A3019

Sailboats Near Tokyo Gate Bridge — A3020

Bonin Islands — A3021

Tokyo Skyline — A3022

Tokyo Stadium — A3023

2013, Aug. 25   Litho.   Perf. 13
3574	A3019	80y multi	1.60	1.25
3575	A3020	80y multi	1.60	1.25
3576	A3021	80y multi	1.60	1.25
3577	A3022	80y multi	1.60	1.25
3578	A3023	80y multi	1.60	1.25
a.		Vert. strip of 5, #3574-3578	8.00	6.25
		Nos. 3574-3578 (5)	8.00	6.25

68th National Athletic Meet, Tokyo.

Persimmon A3024

Bok Choy A3025

Chestnut A3026

Sweet Potato A3027

Pear A3028

Apple A3029

Taro Roots A3030

Japanese Pears A3031

Turnip Greens A3032

Grapes A3033

Die Cut Perf. 13x13¼, 13¼x13
2013, Aug. 30   Photo.
Self-Adhesive
3579		Sheet of 10, 2 each #3579a-3579e	10.00	
a.	A3024	50y multi	1.00	.75
b.	A3025	50y multi	1.00	.75
c.	A3026	50y multi	1.00	.75
d.	A3027	50y multi	1.00	.75
e.	A3028	50y multi	1.00	.75
3580		Sheet of 10, 2 each #3580a-3580e	16.00	
a.	A3029	80y multi	1.60	1.25
b.	A3030	80y multi	1.60	1.25
c.	A3031	80y multi	1.60	1.25
d.	A3032	80y multi	1.60	1.25
e.	A3033	80y multi	1.60	1.25

Dahlia A3034

Chrysanthemum A3035

Cockscomb A3036

Asiatic Dayflower A3037

Rose A3038

Dahlias A3039

Chrysanthemums A3040

Cockscombs A3041

Asiatic Dayflowers A3042

Roses A3043

2013, Sept. 13   Photo.   Perf. 13¼
3581	A3034	50y multi	1.00	.75
3582	A3035	50y multi	1.00	.75
3583	A3036	50y multi	1.00	.75
3584	A3037	50y multi	1.00	.75
3585	A3038	50y multi	1.00	.75
a.		Vert. strip of 5, #3581-3585	5.00	3.75
3586	A3039	80y multi	1.60	1.25
3587	A3040	80y multi	1.60	1.25
3588	A3041	80y multi	1.60	1.25
3589	A3042	80y multi	1.60	1.25
3590	A3043	80y multi	1.60	1.25
a.		Vert. strip of 5, #3586-3590	8.00	6.25
		Nos. 3581-3590 (10)	13.00	10.00

Ambulance Service Legislation, 50th Anniv. — A3044

2013, Sept. 9   Litho.   Perf. 13
3591		80y Helicopter ambulance	1.60	1.25
3592		80y Ambulance	1.60	1.25
a.	A3044	Horiz. pair, #3591-3592	3.20	2.50

Miniature Sheets

Greetings:Autumn
ぽすくまの1日

A3045

Greetings:Autumn
Greetings — A3046

No. 3593 — Teddy bear wearing postman's cap: a, In bed (21x30mm oval). b, Alone at table (21x30mm oval). c, At right of pillar box (23x23mm). d, At left of pillar box (23x23mm). e, Delivering letter to large teddy bear (23x23mm). f, Delivering gift to large teddy bear (23x23mm). g, Holding flower bouquet with light blue ribbon (27x30mm). h, Holding flower bouquet with yellow ribbon (27x30mm). i, With two other teddy bears at table (21x30mm oval). j, Reading book in bed (21x30mm oval).

No. 3594: a, Teddy bear delivering letter to large teddy bear (27x21mm). b, Teddy bear walking on path, holding letter (21x30mm oval). c, Teddy bear delivering gift to large teddy bear (27x21mm). d, Teddy bear delivering letter to bird (21x30mm oval). e, Teddy bear on bicycle (27x21mm). f, Teddy bear delivering letter to bear with pail and fishing pole (27x21mm). g, Small teddy bear without cap holding letter near pillar box (21x30mm oval). h, Teddy bear with cap, small teddy bear with flower bouquet (27x21mm). i, Teddy bear with cap lifting small teddy bear to slot of pillar box (21x27mm). j, Small teddy bear behind teddy bear with cap (29mm diameter).

Die Cut Perf. 13¼ (oval stamps), Die Cut Perf. 14 (square stamps), Die Cut Perf. (#3593g, 3593h)
2013, Sept. 19   Litho.
Self-Adhesive
3593	A3045	Sheet of 10	10.00	
a.-j.		50y Any single	1.00	.75

Die Cut Perf. 13¼x13¾, Die Cut Perf. 13¼ (oval stamps), Die Cut Perf. 13¾x13¼ (#3594i), Die Cut Perf. (#3594j)
3594	A3046	Sheet of 10	16.00	
a.-j.		80y Any single	1.60	1.25

Baby Elephant A3047

Baby and Adult Killer Whales A3048

Black-tailed Prairie Dog A3049

Adult and Juvenile Gentoo Penguins A3050

Kangaroo
A3051

Amur Tiger Cub
A3052

Timber Wolf
Pups — A3053

Ring-tailed
Lemurs
A3054

Polar
Bear — A3055

White
Oryx — A3056

Die Cut Perf. 13¼

2013, Sept. 20   **Litho.**

Self-Adhesive

3595		Sheet of 10, 2 each	
		#3595a-3595e	10.00
a.	A3047 50y multi	1.00	.75
b.	A3048 50y multi	1.00	.75
c.	A3049 50y multi	1.00	.75
d.	A3050 50y multi	1.00	.75
e.	A3051 50y multi	1.00	.75
3596		Sheet of 10, 2 each	
		#3596a-3596e	16.00
a.	A3052 80y multi	1.60	1.25
b.	A3053 80y multi	1.60	1.25
c.	A3054 80y multi	1.60	1.25
d.	A3055 80y multi	1.60	1.25
e.	A3056 80y multi	1.60	1.25

Miniature Sheet

Diplomatic Relations Between Japan
and Spain, 400th Anniv. — A3057

No. 3597: a, Potted geraniums on decorative shelf. b, Japanese bush clover. c, Guggenheim Museum, Bilbao, Spain (white denomination at UR, numeral to right of "Nippon."). d, Santiago de Compostela Cathedral (gold denomination at UR). e, Museum of Contemporary Art, León, Spain (white denomination at UR, numeral below "Nippon."). f, Alcazar of Segovia (castle with spires). g, Royal Palace, Madrid (building with dome). h, Archos and columns, Córdoba Cathedral, Spain. i, Courtyard and archway, Palace of Generalife, Granada, Spain. j, Field of sunflowers.

2013, Oct. 1   **Litho.**   **Perf. 13**

3597	A3057	Sheet of 10	16.00 16.00
a.-j.		80y Any single	1.60 1.25

See Spain No. 3944.

Miniature Sheet

Okayama Local Autonomy Law, 60th
Anniv. — A3058

No. 3598: a, Korakuen Gardens, Momotaro with animals (32x39mm). b, Bridge and buildings, Kurashiki Bikan (28x33mm). c, Shizutani School (28x33mm). d, Cattle grazing, Hiruzenkogen Highlands (28x33mm). e, Tsuyama Castle and cherry blossoms (28x33mm).

Perf. 13¼ (#3598a), 13x13¼

2013, Oct. 4   **Photo.**

3598	A3058	Sheet of 5	8.00 8.00
a.-e.		80y Any single	1.60 1.25

Intl. Letter
Writing
Week
A3059

Posting stations from The Fifty-three Stations of the Tokaido, by Hiroshige: 70y, Shirasuka. 90y, Odawara. 110y, Hamamatsu. 130y, Ishiyakushi.

2013, Oct. 9   **Photo.**   **Perf. 13**

3599	A3059 70y multi	1.50	1.10
3600	A3059 90y multi	1.90	1.50
3601	A3059 110y multi	2.25	1.75
3602	A3059 130y multi	2.60	2.00
	Nos. 3599-3602 (4)	8.25	6.35

Tokyo
Railroad
Station
A3060

Odakyu 3000
Series
Locomotive
A3061

JNR 151
Series
Locomotive
A3062

Kintetsu
10100 Series
Locomotive
A3063

JNR Kiha 81
Series
Locomotive
A3064

Meitetsu 7000
Series
Locomotive
A3065

Kintetsu
20100 Series
Locomotive
A3066

Odakyu 3100
Series
Locomotive
A3067

JNR
Shinkansen 0
Series
Locomotive
A3068

Shinkansen
E5 Series
Locomotive
A3069

2013, Oct. 11   **Photo.**   **Perf. 13¼x13**

3603		Sheet of 10	16.00 16.00
a.	A3060 80y multi	1.60	1.25
b.	A3061 80y multi	1.60	1.25
c.	A3062 80y multi	1.60	1.25
d.	A3063 80y multi	1.60	1.25
e.	A3064 80y multi	1.60	1.25
f.	A3065 80y multi	1.60	1.25
g.	A3066 80y multi	1.60	1.25
h.	A3067 80y multi	1.60	1.25
i.	A3068 80y multi	1.60	1.25
j.	A3069 80y multi	1.60	1.25

Miniature Sheet

Shizuoka Local Autonomy Law, 60th
Anniv. — A3070

No. 3604: a, Mount Fuji and clouds (32x39mm). b, Mount Fuji and yellow flowers (28x33mm). c, Mount Fuji reflected in Lake Tanuki (28x33mm). d, Mount Fuji and trees (28x33mm). e, Mount Fuji, ships and coastal rocks (28x33mm).

Perf. 13¼ (#3604a), 13x13¼

2013, Oct. 15   **Photo.**

3604	A3070	Sheet of 5	8.00 8.00
a.-e.		80y Any single	1.60 1.25

Tortoise on
Galapagos
Islands,
Ecuador
A3071

Taj Mahal,
India
A3072

Venice,
Italy — A3073

Victoria Falls, Zambia and Zimbabwe
A3074

Cologne Cathedral, Germany
A3075

2013, Oct. 23 Litho. *Perf. 13¼x13*

3605	A3071	80y	multi	1.60	1.25
3606	A3072	80y	multi	1.60	1.25
3607	A3073	80y	multi	1.60	1.25
3608	A3074	80y	multi	1.60	1.25
3609	A3075	80y	multi	1.60	1.25
a.	Horiz. strip of 5, #3605-3609			8.00	6.25
	Nos. 3605-3609 (5)			8.00	6.25

Foreign UNESCO World Heritage Sites.

Miniature Sheet

Traditional Crafts — A3076

No. 3610: a, Kishu lacquerware vase (Wakayama Prefecture). b, Two Edo Kiriko glasses (Tokyo Prefecture). c, Owari Shippo porcelain bowl with lid (Aichi Prefecture). d, Two Kyo Kumihimo braids (Kyoto Prefecture). e, Chibana Okinawa weavings (Okinawa Prefecture). f, Ainu ceremonial costume (Hokkaido Prefecture). g, Kishu lacquered utensil handles (Wakayama Prefecture). h, Mashiko-yaki pottery bowl (Tochigi Prefecture). i, Kokeshi dolls (Miyagi Prefecture). j, Takaoka copper vessel (Toyama Prefecture).

2013, Oct. 25 Litho. *Perf. 13½*

3610	A3076	Sheet of 10	16.00	16.00
a.-j.	80y Any single		1.60	1.25

A3077 A3078

New Year 2014 (Year of the Horse)
A3079 A3080

2013, Nov. 1 Photo. *Perf. 13x13½*

3611	A3077	50y	multi	1.00	.75
3612	A3078	80y	multi	1.60	1.25

Photo. & Typo.

Perf. 13¼

3613	A3079	50y +3y	multi	1.10	.85
3614	A3080	80y +3y	multi	1.75	1.40
	Nos. 3611-3614 (4)			5.45	4.25

Miniature Sheet

Edo Calligraphy — A3081

No. 3615 — Characters for "horse": a, In Manyo-kana style (black character with dot at top, red chop at center left). b, In oracle bone script (red character). c, In Qin Dynasty bamboo roll calligraphy (black character with curved arc crossing center line, red chop at center left). d, In Western Zhou Dynasty Kinbun style (black character with teardrop shaped top with dot in center, red chop at LL). e, In Sosho style (black character of one continuous curved line, red chop at LL). f, In Kaisho style (black character, red chop at bottom center). g, In Gyosho style (black character with red chop at LR. h, In Kana (black character with lilac background). i, In Seal style calligraphy (black character with two horizontal lines at bottom, red chop at center right). j, In Katakana (gold character on blue violet background).

Litho. & Embossed

2013, Nov. 1 *Perf. 13x13¼*

3615	A3081	Sheet of 10	16.00	16.00
a.-j.	80y Any single		1.60	1.25

Two Snowmen
A3082

Snowman With Broom
A3083

Three Snowmen
A3084

Snowman With Gift
A3085

Snowman on Skis
A3086

Snowflake Jewelry With Sapphires
A3087

Snowflake Jewelry With Emeralds
A3088

Snowflake Jewelry With Aquamarines
A3089

Snowflake Jewelry With Peridots
A3090

Snowflake Jewelry With Rubies
A3091

Two Wine Glasses
A3092

Two Candles
A3093

Two Champagne Flutes
A3094

Candle
A3095

Two Martini Glasses — A3096

Die Cut Perf. 13¼

2013, Nov. 7 Litho.

Self-Adhesive

3616	Sheet of 10, 2 each #3616a-3616e	10.00	
a.	A3082 50y multi	1.00	.75
b.	A3083 50y multi	1.00	.75
c.	A3084 50y multi	1.00	.75
d.	A3085 50y multi	1.00	.75
e.	A3086 50y multi	1.00	.75
3617	Sheet of 10	16.00	
a.	A3087 80y multi	1.60	1.25
b.	A3088 80y multi	1.60	1.25
c.	A3089 80y multi	1.60	1.25
d.	A3090 80y multi	1.60	1.25
e.	A3091 80y multi	1.60	1.25
f.	A3092 80y multi	1.60	1.25
g.	A3093 80y multi	1.60	1.25
h.	A3094 80y multi	1.60	1.25
i.	A3095 80y multi	1.60	1.25
j.	A3096 80y multi	1.60	1.25

Miniature Sheet

Yamanashi Local Autonomy Law, 60th Anniv. — A3097

No. 3618: a, Mount Fuji, grapes, and maglev test train (32x39mm). b, Shosenkyo Gorges (28x33mm). c, Nishizawa Valley waterfalls (28x33mm). d, Pagoda and cherry blossoms (28x33mm). e, Saruhashi Bridge (28x33mm).

Perf. 13¼ (#3618a), 13x13¼

2013, Nov. 15 Photo.

3618	A3097	Sheet of 5	8.00	8.00
a.-e.	80y Any single		1.60	1.25

Mt. Iwakisan
A3098

Mt. Tsurugidake
A3099

Mt. Hirugatake
A3100

Mt. Gozaishodake — A3101

Mt. Daisen
A3102

Mt. Myokosan
A3103

80 NIPPON 日本郵便
Mt. Aobasan
A3104

80 NIPPON 日本郵便
Mt. Kaikomagatake — A3105

Mt. Oodaigahara
A3106
80 NIPPON 日本郵便

80 NIPPON 日本郵便
Mt. Tenzan
A3107

2013, Nov. 19   Litho.   Perf. 13¼x13

3619		Sheet of 10	16.00	16.00
a.	A3098	80y multi	1.60	1.25
b.	A3099	80y multi	1.60	1.25
c.	A3100	80y multi	1.60	1.25
d.	A3101	80y multi	1.60	1.25
e.	A3102	80y multi	1.60	1.25
f.	A3103	80y multi	1.60	1.25
g.	A3104	80y multi	1.60	1.25
h.	A3105	80y multi	1.60	1.25
i.	A3106	80y multi	1.60	1.25
j.	A3107	80y multi	1.60	1.25

Volunteer Fire Service, 120th
Anniv. — A3108

Paintings by Kunichida Toyohara of Kabuki actors wearing costumes of fire fighters: No. 3620, Jyuzaburo Nakamura (denomination at right). No. 3621, Hikosaburo Bando (denomination at left).

2013, Nov. 25   Litho.   Perf. 13

3620		80y multi	1.60	1.25
3621		80y multi	1.60	1.25
a.	A3108	Horiz. pair, #3620-3621	3.20	2.50

Japanese Allspice
A3109

Snowdrop
A3110

Christmas Camellia
A3111

Narcissus
A3112

Leopard Plant Flowers
A3113

Japanese Allspice
A3114

Snowdrops
A3115

Christmas Camellias
A3116

Narcissi
A3117

Leopard Plant Flowers
A3118

2013, Dec. 3   Photo.   Perf. 13¼

3622	A3109	50y multi	1.00	.75
3623	A3110	50y multi	1.00	.75
3624	A3111	50y multi	1.00	.75
3625	A3112	50y multi	1.00	.75
3626	A3113	50y multi	1.00	.75
a.		Vert. strip of 5, #3622-3626	5.00	3.75
3627	A3114	80y multi	1.60	1.25
3628	A3115	80y multi	1.60	1.25
3629	A3116	80y multi	1.60	1.25
3630	A0117	00y multi	1.00	1.25
3631	A3118	80y multi	1.60	1.25
a.		Vert. strip of 5, #3627-3631	8.00	6.25
		Nos. 3622-3631 (10)	13.00	10.00

Miniature Sheet

Constellations — A3119

No. 3632: a, Aries (ram). b, Taurus (bull). c, Gemini (twins). d, Orion (hunter with shield). e, Auriga (man holding goat). f, Canis Major (dog on hind legs). g, Canis Minor (dog on four legs). h, Lepus (rabbit). i, Monoceros (unicorn). j, Tsuzumiboshi (Japanese drum, Japanese version of Orion).

Litho. With Foil Application
2013, Dec. 4   Die Cut Perf. 13
Self-Adhesive

3632	A3119	Sheet of 10	16.00	
a.-j.		80y Any single	1.60	1.25

Wakamatsu Castle — A3120

Odawara Castle — A3121

Hikone Castle — A3122

Nijo Castle — A3123

Okayama Castle — A3124

2013, Dec. 10   Litho.   Perf. 13

3633	A3120	80y multi	1.60	1.25
3634	A3121	80y multi	1.60	1.25
3635	A3122	80y multi	1.60	1.25
3636	A3123	80y multi	1.60	1.25
3637	A3124	80y multi	1.60	1.25
a.		Vert. strip of 5, #3633-3637	8.00	6.25
		Nos. 3633-3637 (5)	8.00	6.25

Diplomatic Relations Between Japan and Kenya, 50th Anniv. A3125

African wildlife: No. 3638, Giraffes. No. 3639, Cheetahs. No. 3640, Elephants. No. 3641, Zebras. No. 3642, Lion.

2013, Dec. 12   Litho.   Perf. 13¼x13

3638	A3125	80y multi	1.60	1.25
3639	A3125	80y multi	1.60	1.25
3640	A3125	80y multi	1.60	1.25
3641	A3125	80y multi	1.60	1.25
3642	A3125	80y multi	1.60	1.25
a.		Horiz. strip of 5, #3638-3642	8.00	6.25
		Nos. 3638-3642 (5)	8.00	6.25

Miniature Sheet

Kagoshima Local Autonomy Law, 60th Anniv. — A3126

No. 3643: a, Jomon Sugi tree, rhododendrons (32x39mm). b, Sakurajima Volcano (28x33mm). c, Kaimondake Volcano and coastal rocks (28x33mm). d, Flowers on Kirishima Mountains (28x33mm). e, Cranes (28x33mm).

Perf. 13¼ (#3643a), 13x13¼

2013, Dec. 13   Photo.

3643	A3126	Sheet of 5	8.00	8.00
a.-e.		80y Any single	1.60	1.25

Teddy Bear, Gift and Dog — A3127

Boy, Gift, Birds With Ribbon — A3128

Girl With Broom, Squirrel and Turtle
A3129

Animals, Gift, Flowers and Strawberries
A3130

Roses — A3131

Cherry Blossoms — A3132

Mt. Fuji and Cherry
Blossoms
A3133

Rose Bouquet
A3134

Tulips and
Girl With
Letter and
Flower
Bouquet
A3135

Teddy Bears,
Flowers and
Mailbox
A3136

Die Cut Perf., Die Cut Perf. 13
(#3644d, 3644e, 3645e)

2014, Jan. 16   Litho.

Self-Adhesive

3644	Sheet of 10, 2 each		
	#3644a-3644e	10.00	
a.	A3127 50y multi	1.00	.75
b.	A3128 50y multi	1.00	.75
c.	A3129 50y multi	1.00	.75
d.	A3130 50y multi	1.00	.75
e.	A3131 50y multi	1.00	.75
3645	Sheet of 10, 2 each		
	#3645a-3645e	16.00	
a.	A3132 80y multi	1.60	1.25
b.	A3133 80y multi	1.60	1.25
c.	A3134 80y multi	1.60	1.25
d.	A3135 80y multi	1.60	1.25
e.	A3136 80y multi	1.60	1.25

Miniature Sheet

Diplomatic Relations Between Japan
and Switzerland, 150th
Anniv. — A3137

No. 3646: a, Swiss mountains in spring. b,
Mount Fuji and cherry blossoms. c, Aletsch
Glacier, Switzerland. d, Bern, Switzerland. e,
Lavaux Vineyard Terraces. f, Rhaetian Railway
train on bridge. g, Jungfrau Railway train, flow-
ers and mountains. h, Narcissus Path, Les
Avants, Switzerland. i, Fluhalp Mountain
Lodge. j, Meadow in Bernina Alps.

2014, Feb. 6   Litho.   Perf. 13

3646	A3137 Sheet of 10	16.00	16.00
a.-j.	80y Any single	1.60	1.25

See Switzerland Nos. 1507-1508.

Hokkaido
Mountain
Hare
A3138

Cherry
Blossoms
A3139

Plum
Blossoms
A3140

Violets
A3141

Cedar
Tree — A3142

Nachi
Falls — A3143

Rishiri Island — A3144

2014, Mar. 3   Photo.   Perf. 13x13¼

3647	A3138	2y multi	.25	.25
3648	A3139	52y multi	1.00	.75
3649	A3140	82y multi	1.60	1.25
3650	A3141	92y multi	1.90	1.40
3651	A3142	205y multi	4.00	3.00
3652	A3143	280y multi	5.50	4.25
3653	A3144	310y multi	6.00	4.50
	Nos. 3647-3653 (7)		20.25	15.40

Flowers For
Mourning — A3145

2014, Mar. 3   Photo.   Perf. 13x13¼

3654	A3145 52y multi		1.00	.75

Fan With
Plum
Blossoms
A3146

Fan With
Bamboo
A3147

Fan With Tree
Branches — A3148

2014, Mar. 3   Photo.   Perf. 13x13¼

3655	A3146 52y multi		1.00	.75
3656	A3147 82y multi		1.60	1.25
3657	A3148 92y multi		1.90	1.40
	Nos. 3655-3657 (3)		4.50	3.40

A3149

A3150

A3151

A3152

A3153

A3154

A3155

A3156

A3157

Takarazuka
Revue,
100th Anniv.
A3158

2014, Apr. 1   Litho.   Perf. 13

3658	Sheet of 10		16.00	16.00
a.	A3149 82c multi		1.60	1.25
b.	A3150 82c multi		1.60	1.25
c.	A3151 82c multi		1.60	1.25
d.	A3152 82c multi		1.60	1.25
e.	A3153 82c multi		1.60	1.25
f.	A3154 82c multi		1.60	1.25
g.	A3155 82c multi		1.60	1.25
h.	A3156 82c multi		1.60	1.25
i.	A3157 82c multi		1.60	1.25
j.	A3158 82c multi		1.60	1.25

Organization for Economic
Cooperation, 50th Anniv. — A3159

Designs: No. 3659, Emblem, Organization
Headquarters, Paris. No. 3660, Symbols for
cooperation and development.

2014, Apr. 2   Litho.   Perf. 13

3659	82y multi		1.60	1.25
3660	82y multi		1.60	1.25
a.	A3159 Pair, #3659-3660		3.20	2.50

Daisy and
Sweet Peas
A3160

Lily
A3161

Cherry
Blossoms
A3162

Water Lily
A3163

Poppies and
Ranunculus
A3164

Peony
A3165

Roses
A3166

Magnolias
A3167

2014, Apr. 3   Litho.   Perf. 14x14¼

3661	A3160 52y multi		1.00	.75
3662	A3161 52y multi		1.00	.75
3663	A3162 52y multi		1.00	.75
3664	A3163 52y multi		1.00	.75
a.	Horiz. strip of 4, #3661-3664		4.00	3.00
3665	A3164 82y multi		1.60	1.25
3666	A3165 82y multi		1.60	1.25
3667	A3166 82y multi		1.60	1.25
3668	A3167 82y multi		1.60	1.25
a.	Horiz. strip of 4, #3665-3668		6.40	5.00
	Nos. 3661-3668 (8)		10.40	8.00

Miniature Sheet

Ehime Local Autonomy Law, 60th
Anniv. — A3168

No. 3669: a, Oranges, Dogo Hot Springs
Building (32x39mm). b, Matsuyama Castle
(28x33mm). c, Mount Ichizuchi (28x33mm). d,
Terraced fields, Yusumizugaura (28x33mm).
e, Sadamisaki Lighthouse (28x33mm).

Perf. 13¼ (#3669a), 13x13¼

2014, Apr. 17			Photo.	
3669	A3168	Sheet of 5	8.00	8.00
a.-e.		82y Any single	1.60	1.25

Philatelic Week — A3169

Details from folding screens by Eishuku
Kano: No. 3670, Seven small birds near tree.
No. 3671, Two birds below tree branch. No.
3672, Three adult and three juvenile cranes,
white and yellow flowers. No. 3673, Adult
cranes and flowers.

2014, Apr. 18		Photo.	Perf. 13¼	
3670		82y multi	1.60	1.25
3671		82y multi	1.60	1.25
3672		82y multi	1.60	1.25
3673		82y multi	1.60	1.25
a.		A3169 Block of 4, #3670-3673	6.40	5.00
		Nos. 3670-3673 (4)	6.40	5.00

Nos. 3670-3673 were printed in sheets of 10
containing 3 each of Nos. 3670-3671 and 2
each of Nos. 3672-3673.

Mount Akita-Komagatake — A3170

Mount Iyo — A3171

Mount Oku-Hotakadake — A3172

Mount Fuji — A3173

Mount Rokko A3174

Mount Mikura A3175

Mount Tsurugi A3176

Mount Unzen A3177

Mount Okue A3178

Mount Tama A3179

2014, May 1		Litho.	Perf. 13¼x13	
3674		Sheet of 10	16.00	16.00
a.	A3170	82y multi	1.60	1.25
b.	A3171	82y multi	1.60	1.25
c.	A3172	82y multi	1.60	1.25
d.	A3173	82y multi	1.60	1.25
e.	A3174	82y multi	1.60	1.25
f.	A3175	82y multi	1.60	1.25
g.	A3176	82y multi	1.60	1.25
h.	A3177	82y multi	1.60	1.25
i.	A3178	82y multi	1.60	1.25
j.	A3179	82y multi	1.60	1.25

Souvenir Sheets

A3180

A3181

2014 World Cup Soccer
Championships, Brazil — A3182

No. 3675 — Trophy with: a, Denomination at
UL, "Nippon" at UR. b, Denomination at LR. c,
Denomination and "Nippon" at UL.
No. 3676: a, Emblem. b, Emblem, design
with stylized soccer player dribbling ball at left.
c, Emblem, design with stylized goalie making
save at right.
No. 3677 — Mascot: a, Carrying flag. b,
Holding soccer ball. c, Dribbling soccer ball.

2014, May 12		Litho.	Perf. 13	
3675	A3180	Sheet of 3	5.00	5.00
a.-c.		82c Any single	1.60	1.25
3676	A3181	Sheet of 3	5.00	5.00
a.-c.		82c Any single	1.00	1.25
3677	A3182	Sheet of 3	5.00	5.00
a.-c.		82c Any single	1.60	1.25
		Nos. 3675-3677 (3)	15.00	15.00

Miniature Sheet

Yamagata Local Autonomy Law, 60th
Anniv. — A3183

No. 3678: a, Mogami River and cherries
(32x39mm). b, Mt. Haguro five-story pagoda
(28x33mm). c, Kubo cherry tree blossoming
(28x33mm). d, Hayashi Family court dancer
(28x33mm). e, Shinjo Festival (28x33mm).

Perf. 13¼ (#3678a), 13x13¼

2014, May 14			Photo.	
3678	A3183	Sheet of 5	8.00	8.00
a.-e.		82y Any single	1.60	1.25

Pentalagus Furnessi A3184

Lagopus Muta Japonica A3185

Polemonium Kiushianum A3186

Tanakia Tanago A3187

Cuora Flavomarginata
Evelynae — A3188

2014, May 15		Litho.	Perf. 13¼	
3679	A3184	82y multi	1.60	1.25
3680	A3185	82y multi	1.60	1.25
3681	A3186	82y multi	1.60	1.25
3682	A3187	82y multi	1.60	1.25
3683	A3188	82y multi	1.60	1.25
a.		Vert. strip of 5, #3679-3683	8.00	6.25
		Nos. 3679-3683 (5)	8.00	6.25

Miniature Sheets

A3189

Characters From Disney Animated Films — A3190

No. 3684: a, Snow White and bird. b, Sleeping Beauty. c, Cinderella. d, Peter Pan with Wendy, John and Michael Darling. e, March Hare, Alice and Mad Hatter. f, Dumbo and Timothy. g, Thumper, Bambi and Flower. h, Lady and the Tramp. i, 101 Dalmatians. j, Geppetto and Pinocchio.

No. 3685: a, Winnie the Pooh seated, looking in honey jar. b, Winnie standing, looking in honey jar. c, Winnie and Eeyore. d, Winnie and Tigger. e, Winnie, Kanga and Roo. f, Winnie and Piglet. g, Winnie holding note. h, Winnie reaching for honey jar. i, Winnie turning over honey jar. j, Winnie standing in large honey pot.

Die Cut Perf. 14

		2014, May 23	Self-Adhesive	Litho.
3684	A3189	Sheet of 10	10.00	
a.-j.		52y Any single	1.00	.75
3685	A3190	Sheet of 10	16.00	
a.-j.		82y Any single	1.60	1.25

Miniature Sheet

National Afforestation — A3191

No. 3686: a, Tulipa gesneria. b, Magnolia salicifolia flowers. c, Magnolia obovata flowers. d, Erythronium japonicum. e, Fagus crenata leaves. f, Camellia rusticana. g, Maple leaves on branches. h, Hepatica nobilis. i, Narcissus tazetta. j, Azalea flowers.

		2014, May 30		Perf. 13	Litho.
3686	A3191	Sheet of 10	10.00	10.00	
a.-j.		52y Any single	1.00	.75	

Palace of Versailles, France A3192

Thebes, Egypt A3193

Roman Colosseum, Italy — A3194

Great Barrier Reef, Australia A3195

La Pedrera, Barcelona, Spain A3196

		2014, June 3	Litho.	Perf. 13¼x13
3687	A3192	82y multi	1.60	1.25
3688	A3193	82y multi	1.60	1.25
3689	A3194	82y multi	1.60	1.25
3690	A3195	82y multi	1.60	1.25
3691	A3196	82y multi	1.60	1.25
a.		Horiz. strip of 5, #3687-3691	8.00	6.25
		Nos. 3687-3691 (5)	8.00	6.25

UNESCO World Heritage sites.

Cherries A3197

Bell Peppers A3198

Japanese Plums A3199

Corn A3200

Watermelons A3201

Tomato A3202

Japanese Apricots A3203

Eggplants A3204

Cucumbers A3205

Peach A3206

Die Cut Perf. 13x13¼, 13¼x13

2014, June 4   **Self-Adhesive**   Litho.

3692		Sheet of 10, 2 each #3692a-3692e	10.00	
a.	A3197	52y multi	1.00	.75
b.	A3198	52y multi	1.00	.75
c.	A3199	52y multi	1.00	.75
d.	A3200	52y multi	1.00	.75
e.	A3201	52y multi	1.00	.75
3693		Sheet of 10, 2 each #3693a-3693e	16.00	
a.	A3202	82y multi	1.60	1.25
b.	A3203	82y multi	1.60	1.25
c.	A3204	82y multi	1.60	1.25
d.	A3205	82y multi	1.60	1.25
e.	A3206	82y multi	1.60	1.25

Miniature Sheet

Mie Local Autonomy Law, 60th Anniv. — A3207

No. 3694: a, Uji Bridge and Isuzu River (32x39mm). b, Iris ensata (28x33mm). c, Wedded Rocks, Ise-Shima National Park (28x33mm). d, Lion Rock and fireworks (28x33mm). e, Ago Bay (28x33mm).

Perf. 13¼ (#3694a), 13x13¼

		2014, June 19		Photo.
3694	A3207	Sheet of 5	8.00	8.00
a.-e.		82y Any single	1.60	1.25

Miniature Sheets

A3208

Sanrio Cartoon Characters — A3209

No. 3695: a, Hello Kitty on bicycle (29x26mm heart-shaped stamp). b, Hello Kitty on elephant (29mm diameter). c, Hello Kitty and Mimmy on telephone (23x23mm). d, Hello Kitty and Mimmy on see-saw (22x30mm oval stamp). e, Hello Kitty in airplane (23x23mm). f, Hello Kitty on scale (27x22mm). g, My Melody on swing with squirrel, Blanco (22x27mm). h, My Melody on ground with mouse, Flat (29x26mm heart-shaped stamp). i, Pompompurin and Macaroon (29mm diameter). j, Pompompurin and stuffed toys (23x23mm).

No. 3696: a, Hello Kitty, umbrella, cherries, pencils and candy bag (22x27mm). b, Hello Kitty with balloon (29x26mm heart-shaped stamp). c, Hello Kitty and Mimmy on telephone with apples (29mm diameter). d, Hello Kitty with watering can (27x22mm). e, Hello Kitty and Mimmy in go-karts (23x23mm). f, Hello Kitty with hair brush (22x30mm oval stamp). g, My Melody at mailbox (27x22mm). h, My Melody reading letter (30x22mm oval stamp). i, Pompompurin and Muffin (29x26mm heart-shaped stamp). j, Pompompurin and "PURIN" (27x22mm).

Die Cut Perf. 14 (square stamps), 13¼x13¾, 13¾x13¼ (rectangular stamps), 13¼ (oval stamps), Die Cut Perf.

2014, June 23   Litho.
              Self-Adhesive
3695 A3208   Sheet of 10   10.00
   a.-j.   52y Any single   1.00   .75
3696 A3209   Sheet of 10   16.00
   a.-j.   82y Any single   1.60   1.25

Miniature Sheet

Mount Fuji UNESCO World Heritage Site — A3210

No. 3697 — Various views of Mount Fuji: a, Clouds above mountain, denomination at LL. b, Clouds obscuring base, denomination at LH. c, Framed by cherry trees in bloom, denomination at UL. d, With farm fields below, denomination at LL. e, With cherry blossoms at top, denomination at UL. f, In winter, with hills below, denomination at LL. g, With lake below, denomination at UL. h, With clouds and forest below, denomination at LL. i, With forest and waterfall below, denomination at LL. j, With swan on lake below, denomination at UR.

2014, June 26 Photo.   Perf. 13x13¼
3697 A3210   Sheet of 10   16.00 16.00
   a.-j.   82y Any single   1.60   1.25

Miniature Sheet

Constellations — A3211

No. 3698: a, Cancer. b, Leo. c, Virgo. d, Vega (without white frame).

Litho. With Foil Application
2014, July 7   Die Cut Perf. 13x13¼
              Self-Adhesive
3698 A3211   Sheet of 10, 3
              each #3698a-
              3698c, 1
              #3698d   16.00
   a.-d.   82y Any single   1.60   1.25

Matsumae Castle — A3212

Inuyama Castle — A3213

Matsue Castle — A3214

Takamatsu Castle — A3215

Kumamoto Castle — A3216

2014, July 15   Litho.   Perf. 13
3699 A3212 82y multi   1.60 1.25
3700 A3213 82y multi   1.60 1.25
3701 A3214 82y multi   1.60 1.25
3702 A3215 82y multi   1.60 1.25
3703 A3216 82y multi   1.60 1.25
   a.   Vert. strip of 5, #3699-3703
                            8.00 6.25
         Nos. 3699-3703 (5) 8.00 6.25

Irises A3217

Goldfish A3218

Flowers A3219

Rabbits A3220

Birds in Plum Tree A3221

Raspberries A3222

Morning Glories A3223

Gourds A3224

Cranes A3225

Cherry Blossoms and Water Wheels A3226

Geometric Pattern A3227

Poppies A3228

Grapevines A3229

Flowers A3230

Rape Blossoms A3231

Loquats A3232

Morning Glory and Fan A3233

Leaves and Nuts A3234

Pine Trees A3235

Cherry Blossoms A3236

Die Cut Perf. 13x13½
2014, July 23   Litho.
           Booklet Stamps
           Self-Adhesive
3704 A3217 52y multi   1.00   .75
3705 A3218 52y multi   1.00   .75
3706 A3219 52y multi   1.00   .75
3707 A3220 52y multi   1.00   .75
3708 A3221 52y multi   1.00   .75
3709 A3222 52y multi   1.00   .75
3710 A3223 52y multi   1.00   .75
3711 A3224 52y multi   1.00   .75
3712 A3225 52y multi   1.00   .75
3713 A3226 52y multi   1.00   .75
   a.   Booklet pane of 10, #3704-
         3713   10.00
3714 A3227 82y multi   1.60 1.25
3715 A3228 82y multi   1.60 1.25
3716 A3229 82y multi   1.60 1.25
3717 A3230 82y multi   1.60 1.25
3718 A3231 82y multi   1.60 1.25
3719 A3232 82y multi   1.60 1.25
3720 A3233 82y multi   1.60 1.25
3721 A3234 82y multi   1.60 1.25
3722 A3235 82y multi   1.60 1.25
3723 A3236 82y multi   1.60 1.25
   a.   Booklet pane of 10, #3714-
         3723   16.00
         Nos. 3704-3723 (20) 26.00 20.00

The Ide Tama River: Karuta of the Choji-ya, by Eizan Kikukawa
A3237

Karokoyama, by Hiroshige Utagawa
A3238

Hitomoto of the Mojiro, by Utamaro Kitagawa
A3239

Fishing Boats Netting Flounder, by Hiroshige Utagawa
A3240

Washing and Starching Fabric, by Eizan Kikukawa
A3241

Tsushima Tenno Festival, by Hiroshige Utagawa
A3242

Girl with a Fan, by Utamaro Kitagawa
A3243

Cherry Island, by Hiroshige Utagawa
A3244

The Doll Festival, by Eisho Chokosai
A3245

Basket Ferry, by Hiroshige Utagawa
A3246

2014, Aug. 1   Litho.   Perf. 13½
3724   Sheet of 10   16.00   16.00
a. A3237 82y multi   1.60   1.25
b. A3238 82y multi   1.60   1.25
c. A3239 82y multi   1.60   1.25
d. A3240 82y multi   1.60   1.25
e. A3241 82y multi   1.60   1.25
f. A3242 82y multi   1.60   1.25
g. A3243 82y multi   1.60   1.25
h. A3244 82y multi   1.60   1.25
i. A3245 82y multi   1.60   1.25
j. A3246 82y multi   1.60   1.25

Mount Asahi
A3247

Mount Sanbe
A3248

Mount Nantai
A3249

Mount Tokusa
A3250

Mount Takao
A3251

Mount Hiko
A3252

Mount Mitsuse-Myojin — A3253

Mount Miune
A3254

Kumano Kodo
A3255

Mount Shinmoe
A3256

2014, Aug. 11   Litho.   Perf. 13¼x13
3725   Sheet of 10   16.00   16.00
a. A3247 82y multi   1.60   1.25
b. A3248 82y multi   1.60   1.25
c. A3249 82y multi   1.60   1.25
d. A3250 82y multi   1.60   1.25
e. A3251 82y multi   1.60   1.25
f. A3252 82y multi   1.60   1.25
g. A3253 82y multi   1.60   1.25

h. A3254 82y multi   1.60   1.25
i. A3255 82y multi   1.60   1.25
j. A3256 82y multi   1.60   1.25

Miniature Sheets

A3257

Characters From Peanuts Comic Strip — A3258

No. 3726: a, Sally, Woodstock and Snoopy drawing (26x22mm). b, Snoopy and heart (26x25mm). c, Snoopy holding slice of bread, Woodstock near mug (26x22mm). d, Snoopy, Linus, Woodstock and cookies (26x22mm). e, Snoopy on Charlie Brown's head, woodstock on books (26x22mm). f, Sally and Snoopy eating (26x22mm). g, Snoopy, Lucy and Woodstock with flowers (26x22mm). h, Woodstock flying, Snoopy attempting to fly (26x22mm). i, Snoopy and Woodstock on dog house roof (29x36mm). j, Snoopy, Woodstock, umbrella and musical notes (26x22mm).

No. 3727: a, Snoopy and Woodstock with letters, bird flying (22x27mm). b, Charlie Brown with letter near mailbox (22x27mm). c, Snoopy wearing mailman's uniform (22x27mm). d, Snoopy with nose in mailbox (22x27mm). e, Snoopy reading letter near mailbox (27x22mm). f, Snoopy and Woodstock at typewriter (27x22mm). g, Snoopy watching Sally write letter (27x22mm). h, Snoopy sitting and reading letter with Woodstock (27x22mm). i, Charlie Brown and stream of letters in mailbox (27x22mm). j, Charlie Brown and Sally looking at letter (27x22mm).

Die Cut Perf. 14, 12¼ (#3726b, 3726i)
2014, Aug. 19   Litho.
         Self-Adhesive
3726 A3257   Sheet of 10   10.00
a.-j.   52y Any single   1.00   .75
Die Cut Perf. 14x13½, 13½x14
3727 A3258   Sheet of 10   16.00
a.-j.   52y Any single   1.60   1.25

Miniature Sheet

Japan Society of Civil Engineers,
Cent. — A3259

No. 3728: a, Tunnel, sun over mountains. b, Dam. c, Ships and jetties, airport runway. d, Harbor and airport. e, Floodgate ar mouth of river. f, Highway bridges over river and interchange. g, Farm feilds near coast, rocks in water. h, Small harbor and highway tunnel. i, Terraces and irrigation canal. j, Train and irrigation canal.

2014, Sept. 1   Litho.   Perf. 13
3728 A3259 Sheet of 10   16.00 16.00
a.-j.   82y Any single   1.60 1.25

Miniature Sheet

Season's Memories in My
Heart — A3260

No. 3729: a, Houses near water, denomination in black at LL. b, Farm houses, denomination in white at LR. c, Farm house near river, denomination in white at UL. d, Sunset, denomination in white at UL. e, Village in mist, denomination in white at LL. f, Cars near church and building, denomination in black at UR. g, Church at end of path, denomination in white at left. h, Large cloud over church, flowers in air, denomination in white at UL. i, House near water, denomination in black at UR. j, Houses and path, denomination in black at UR.

2014, Sept. 2   Photo.   Perf. 13
3729 A3260   Sheet of 10   16.00 16.00
a.-j.   82y Any single   1.60 1.25

Λ3261

Teddy Bears — A3262

No. 3730: a, Bear with gray fur and pearl necklace, pink rose (22x30mm). b, Bear with brown fur and red ribbon, yellow flowers (22x30mm). c, Bear with light brown fur and blue bow tie, red rose (22x30mm). d, Bear with beige fur and yellow bow tie, pink flower (22x30mm). e, Bear with light brown fur, wearing cap and red ribbon, with flower bouquet (22x30mm). f, Bear with light brown fur and green ribbon, with pink lily (22x30mm). g, Three bears wearing caps, pink flowers (28x28mm). h, Five bears and yellow flowers (28x28mm). i, Two bears, pink flowers, red ribbon at top (28x28mm). j, Two bears, pink flowers, blue ribbon at top (28x28mm).

No. 3731: a, Bear with letter, yellow door (23x30mm). b, Bear with gift, green door (23x30mm). c, Bear with cap, mail bag and letter, blue door (23x30mm). d, Bear with letter, white door (23x30mm). e, Bear with cap in yellow envelope (25x25mm). f, Bear in light blue envelope (25x25mm). g, Four bears and mail box (23x30mm). h, Bear with letter at mail box (23x30mm). i, Pink bear with pink gift (27x30mm). j, Bear with blue gift (27x30mm).

Die Cut Perf. 13¼x13¾, 13¾x13½
2014, Sept. 5   Litho.
Self-Adhesive
3730 A3261   Sheet of 10   10.00
a.-j.   52y Any single   1.00   .75

***Die Cut Perf. 13x12¾, 13 (#3731e,
3731f)***
3731 A3262   Sheet of 10   15.00
a.-j.   82y Any single   1.50 1.10

Miniature Sheet

Kagawa Local Autonomy Law, 60th
Anniv. — A3263

No. 3732: a, Ritsurin Koen Park (32x39mm). b, Gennai Hiraga and his electrostatic generator (28x33mm). c, Marugame Castle (28x33mm). d, Kotohiki Park (28x33mm). e, Olives (28x33mm).

Perf. 13¼ (#3732a), 13x13¼
2014, Sept. 10   Photo.
3732 A3263   Sheet of 5   7.50 7.50
a.-e.   82y Any single   1.50 1.10

Intl. Congress on
Child Abuse and
Neglect,
Nagoya — A3264

2014, Sept. 12   Litho.   Perf. 13
3733 A3264 82y multi   1.50 1.10

Miniature Sheet

69th National Sports Festival — A3265

No. 3734: a, Gymnast on rings. b, Blue hydrangeas. c, Runner in starting blocks. d, Pink rhododendrons. e, Archer. f, Pink day lily. g, Soccer players. h, Lilac pink rhododendrons. i, Kendoka. j, Red camellias.

2014, Sept. 12   Litho.   Perf. 13
3734 A3265 82y Sheet of 10   15.00 15.00
a.-j.   82y Any single   1.50 1.10

Tortoise
A3266

Spotted Seals
A3267

Tapir
A3268

Giraffes
A3269

Orangutans
A3270

Koalas
A3271

Giant Pandas
A3272

Capybara
A3273

Lion — A3274

Fennec
Fox — A3275

Die Cut Perf. 13x13¼

2014, Sept. 19   **Litho.**

Self-Adhesive

3735	Sheet of 10, 2 each		
	#3735a-3735e	10.00	
a.	A3266 52y multi	1.00	.75
b.	A3267 52y multi	1.00	.75
c.	A3268 52y multi	1.00	.75
d.	A3269 52y multi	1.00	.75
e.	A3270 52y multi	1.00	.75

Die Cut Perf. 13¼

3736	Sheet of 10, 2 each		
	#3736a-3736e	15.00	
a.	A3271 82y multi	1.50	1.10
b.	A3272 82y multi	1.50	1.10
c.	A3273 82y multi	1.50	1.10
d.	A3274 82y multi	1.50	1.10
e.	A3275 82y multi	1.50	1.10

Miniature Sheet

Shinkansen High-Speed Rail Lines,
50th Anniv. — A3276

No. 3737: a, Train with thick blue stripe (Tokaido and Sanyo 0 series). b, Three trains (Tokaido and Sanyo 100, 0 and 300 series), top train with thick blue stripe above thin blue stripe, bottom train with thin blue strip over thick blue stripe. c, Train with two thin blue stripes (Tokaido and Sanyo N700A). d, Three trains (Tokaido and Sanyo 700 series, N700A, and T4 model), top train with two thin blue stripes, bottom train yellow with two blue stripes. e, Light blue train with one blue stripe (Sanyo and Kyushu N700). f, Three trains (Sanyo 700 series Rail Star, Sanyo and Kyushu N700, Sanyo 500 series), top train with gray and yellow stripes along windows. g, Train with thin red stripe (Kyushu New 800 series). h, Three trains (Tohuku E2 series, Kyushu New 800 series, Yamagata 400 series), top train with red stripe under window above blue along bottom of train. i, Train with blue green top and red stripe (Tohuku E5 series). j, Three trains (Joetsu E1 series, Tohuku E5 series, Akita E6 series, light blue top train with blue green stripe.

2014, Oct. 1   **Litho.**   **Perf. 13½x13¼**

3737	A3276	Sheet of 10	15.00 15.00
a.-j.		82y Any single	1.50 1.10

Miniature Sheet

Saitama Local Autonomy Law, 60th
Anniv. — A3277

No. 3738: a, Eiichi Shibusawa, industrialist, Bell of Time (32x39mm). b, Saitama Stadium (28x33mm). c, Chichibu Night Festival (28x33mm). d, Shoden Hall, Kangi Temple (28x33mm). e, Stairway at Sakitama ancient tomb complex (28x33mm).

Perf. 13¼ (#3738a), 13x13¼

2014, Oct. 8   **Photo.**

3738	A3277	Sheet of 5	7.50 7.50
a.-e.		82y Any single	1.50 1.10

A3278

International
Letter
Writing
Week
A3279

Paintings by Hiroshige: 70y, Sparrows and Camellia in the Snow. 90y, The Fifty-three Stations of the Tokaido: Ejiri. 110y, The Fifty-three Stations of the Tokaido: Kanaya. 130y, The Fifty-three Stations of the Tokaido: Fukuroi.

2014, Oct. 9   **Photo.**   **Perf. 13¼**

3739	A3278	70y multi	1.25 .95

Perf. 13

3740	A3279	90y multi	1.60 1.25
3741	A3279	110y multi	2.00 1.50
3742	A3279	130y multi	2.25 1.75
		Nos. 3739-3742 (4)	7.10 5.45

Fronts of Five
Passenger
Train Cars
A3280

Nagoya
Railroad KiHa
8000 Series
Locomotive
A3281

Kintetsu
18200 Series
Locomotive
A3282

Japan
National
Railways 581
Series
Locomotive
A3283

Japan
National
Railways
Class EF66
Locomotive
A3284

Seibu
Railways
5000 Series
Locomotive
A3285

Japan
National
Railways 14
Series
Sleeping
Car — A3286

East Japan
Railway E259
Series
Locomotive
A3287

Keisei Electric
Railway AE
Series
Locomotive
A3288

Tokyo
Underground
Railway 1000
Series Train
A3289

2014, Oct. 10   **Photo.**   **Perf. 13¼x13**

3743	Sheet of 10	15.00 15.00
a.	A3280 82y multi	1.50 1.10
b.	A3281 82y multi	1.50 1.10
c.	A3282 82y multi	1.50 1.10
d.	A3283 82y multi	1.50 1.10
e.	A3284 82y multi	1.50 1.10
f.	A3285 82y multi	1.50 1.10
g.	A3286 82y multi	1.50 1.10
h.	A3287 82y multi	1.50 1.10
i.	A3288 82y multi	1.50 1.10
j.	A3289 82y multi	1.50 1.10

Sandalwood Go
Game Board and
Pieces — A3290

Gold and Silver
Inlaid Lacquered
Kin — A3291

Glass
Goblet — A3292

Decorated
Catapult
Sticks — A3293

Sandalwood
Lute — A3294

2014, Oct. 17   **Photo.**   **Perf. 13**

3744	A3290	82y multi	1.50 1.10
3745	A3291	82y multi	1.50 1.10
3746	A3292	82y multi	1.50 1.10
3747	A3293	82y multi	1.50 1.10
3748	A3294	82y multi	1.50 1.10
a.	Vert. strip of 5, #3744-3748	7.50 5.50
	Nos. 3744-3748 (5)	7.50 5.50

Treasures of the Shosoin.

Fish
A3295

"Happy" and
Stars
A3296

2014, Oct. 23   **Litho.**   **Perf. 13x13¼**

3749	A3295	52y multi	.90 .70

Background Color

3750	A3296	52y rose lilac	.90 .70
3751	A3296	52y orange	.90 .70
a.	Vert. pair, #3750-3751	1.80 1.40
	Nos. 3749-3751 (3)	2.70 2.10

Miniature Sheet

Traditional Crafts — A3297

No. 3752: a, Imari-Arita ceramic ware (Saga Prefecture). b, Inshu hand-made paper (Tottori Prefecture). c, Echizen chest of drawers (Fukui Prefecture). d, Chichibu-meisen silk textiles (Saitama Prefecture). e, Kagawa lacquered container (Kagawa Prefecture). f, Ise katagami paper stencils (Mie Prefecture). g, Yamaga lantern (Kumamoto Prefecture). h, Koshu carved crystal (Yamanashi Prefecture). i, Hakone parquet containers (Kanagawa Prefecture). j, Arimatsu-Narumi tie-dyed fabrics (Aichi Prefecture).

2014, Oct. 24   **Litho.**   **Perf. 13½**

3752	A3297	Sheet of 10	15.00 15.00
a.-j.		82y Any single	1.50 1.10

Miniature Sheet

Edo Calligraphy — A3298

No. 3753 — Characters for "sheep": a, In Kobun style (blue character). b, In Han Dynasty document style (character in black with two red chops at left). c, In small seal script (character in black with thick lines, small red chop at LR. d, In cursive script (character in black with small red chop at LL). e, In running script (Black character on brown red background). f, In Kana characters (surved black character with dots with large red chop at LR). g, In oracle bone script (black character with curved and straight lines, large red chop at LR). h, In Chou Dyansty bronze vessel style (character in thick black lines with small red chop at LL). i, In seal script (character in red). j, In clerical script (character in thick black lines with large red chop at LL).

Litho. & Embossed

2014, Oct. 30		Perf. 13x13¼	
3753	A3298	Sheet of 10	15.00 15.00
a.-j.		82y Any single	1.50 1.10

Japanese Foods — A3299

Designs: No. 3754, Sushi (denomination at LL). No. 3755, Tempura (denomination at LR).

2014, Oct. 30		Litho.	Perf. 13¼x13	
3754		18y multi	.35	.25
3755		18y multi	.35	.25
a.	A3299	Horiz. pair, #3754-3755	.70	.50

A3300   A3301

New Year 2015 (Year of the Ram)
A3302   A3303

2014, Oct. 30		Photo.	Perf. 13x13¼	
3756	A3300	52y multi	.90	.70
3757	A3301	82y multi	1.50	1.10

Photo. & Typo.
Perf. 13¼

3758	A3302	52y +3y multi	1.00	.75
3759	A3303	82y +3y multi	1.50	1.10
		Nos. 3756-3759 (4)	4.90	3.65

Lady Shikibu
Murasaki Scroll
and
Books — A3304

Flower
Arrangement and
Go
Players — A3305

Noh and Bunraku
Theater
A3306

Lute Player and
Entertainers
A3307

Tale of the Genji
Scroll — A3308

2014, Oct. 31		Litho.	Perf. 13	
3760	A3304	82y multi	1.50	1.10
3761	A3305	82y multi	1.50	1.10
3762	A3306	82y multl	1.50	1.10
3763	A3307	82y multi	1.50	1.10
3764	A3308	82y multi	1.50	1.10
a.		Vert. strip of 5, #3760-3764	7.50	5.50
		Nos. 3760-3764 (5)	7.50	5.50

Classics Day.

Narcissus
A3309

Plum
Blossoms
A3310

Adonis
Ramosa
A3311

Cyclamen
A3312

Matthiola
Incana
A3313

Camellia
Japonica
A3314

Brassica
Oleracea
A3315

Poinsettia
A3316

2014, Nov. 6		Litho.	Perf. 14x14¼	
3765	A3309	52y multi	.90	.70
3766	A3310	52y multi	.90	.70
3767	A3311	52y multi	.90	.70
3768	A3312	52y multi	.90	.70
a.		Horiz. strip of 4, #3765-3768	3.60	2.80
3769	A3313	82y multi	1.50	1.10
3770	A3314	82y multi	1.50	1.10
3771	A3315	82y multi	1.50	1.10
3772	A3316	82y multi	1.50	1.10
a.		Horiz. strip of 4, #3769-3772	6.00	4.40
		Nos. 3765-3772 (8)	9.60	7.20

Miniature Sheets

A3317

Winter Greetings — A3318

No. 3773: a, Cookie with snowman design. b, Cookies in shape of man and woman. c, Cookie with mailbox design. d, Cookie with polar bear design. e, Cookie in shape of rabbit. f, Cookie with Christmas tree design. g, Cookie in shape of horse. h, Cookie in shape of woman. i, Cookie with poinsettia design. j, Cookie in shape of man.

No. 3774 — Needlepoint designs: a, House with brown door standing in front of trees. b, Post office with red mailbox at left. c, House with red door. d, House with brown door and shrubbery. e, Automobile. f, Onowman. g, One sheep. h, Two sheep. i, Boy and dog. j, Mailbox and fence.

Die Cut Perf. 13x13¼

2014, Nov. 7			Litho.	
Self-Adhesive				
3773	A3317	Sheet of 10	9.00	
a.-j.		52y Any single	.90	.70
3774	A3318	Sheet of 10	15.00	
a.-j.		82y Any single	1.50	1.10

Miniature Sheet

Season's Memories in My
Heart — A3319

No. 3775 — Illustrations from children's book Guri and Gura, by Yuriko Yamawaki: a, Guri, Gura and rabbits on sled. b, Child looking out of window. c, Guri and Gura making snowman. d, Guri and Gura reading near fireplace. e, Guri picking strawberries. f, Guri cooking. g, Gura looking at head-shaped cake. h, Guri and Gura holding basket. i, Stove and

---

various animals. j, Guri, Gura, various animals and table.

2014, Nov. 20		Litho.	Perf. 13½	
3775	A3319	Sheet of 10	14.00	14.00
a.-j.		82y Any single	1.40	1.10

Miniature Sheet

Ishikawa Local Autonomy Law, 60th
Anniv. — A3320

No. 3776: a, Stone lantern, trees in Kenrokuen Garden (32x39mm). b, Terraced rice fields at sunset (28x33mm). c, Mitsukejima (28x33mm). d, Mount Hakusan (28x33mm). e, Fritillaria cantschatcensis (28x33mm).

Perf. 13¼ (#3776a), 13x13¼

2014, Nov. 26			Photo.	
3776	A3320	Sheet of 5	7.00	7.00
a.-e.		82y Any single	1.40	1.10

Matsumoto
Castle — A3321

Takeda
Castle — A3322

Nagoya
Castle — A3323

Bitchu-Matsuyama
Castle — A3324

Shuri
Castle — A3325

2014, Dec. 10		Litho.	Perf. 12¾x13	
3777	A3321	82y multi	1.40	1.10
3778	A3322	82y multi	1.40	1.10
3779	A3323	82y multi	1.40	1.10
3780	A3324	82y multi	1.40	1.10
3781	A3325	82y multi	1.40	1.10
a.		Vert. strip of 5, #3777-3781	7.00	5.50
		Nos. 3777-3781 (5)	7.00	5.50

Miniature Sheets

A3326

Illustrations From *Peter Rabbit*, by Beatrix Potter — A3327

No. 3782: a, Jemima Puddleduck. b, Peter Rabbit holding placard. c, Squirrel Nutkin. d, Owl reading "Squirrel Nutkin" book. e, Tom Kitten. f, Benjamin Bunny. g, Peter holding shovel. h, Peter and Benjamin Bunny. i, Mother Rabbit and young. j, Rabbits holding towel.

No. 3783: a, Peter with shovel and flower box. b, Peter posting letter. c, Rabbit with mail bag, facing forward. d, Rabbit with mail bag, facing backward. e, Rabbit holding letter and cauliflower. f, Rabbits with basket. g, Peter and female rabbit on windy day. h, Cat, Peter with daffodil. i, Peter and Benjamin carrying sticks. j, Peter and Benjamin harvesting apples.

2015, Jan. 9 Litho. *Die Cut Perf. 14*
Self-Adhesive

3782	A3326	Sheet of 10	9.00	
a.-j.		52y Any single	.90	.70

Die Cut Perf. 14x13¼

3783	A3327	Sheet of 10	14.00	
a.-j.		82y Any single	1.40	1.10

Flowers, Musical Notes, Clef and Staff — A3328

Flowers in Music Box — A3329

Four Teddy Bears — A3330

Musicians and Bird — A3331

Animals With Musical Instruments A3332

Cherry Blossoms and Bird A3333

Roses A3334

Violas A3335

Girl and Carnations A3336

Teddy Bear and Flowers A3337

Die Cut Perf. 14
2015, Jan. 16 **Litho.**
Self-Adhesive

3784		Sheet of 10, 2 each		
		#3784a-3784e	9.00	
a.	A3328	52y multi	.90	.70
b.	A3329	52y multi	.90	.70
c.	A3330	52y multi	.90	.70
d.	A3331	52y multi	.90	.70
e.	A3332	52y multi	.90	.70

Die Cut Perf. 14x13¼, 13¼x14

3785		Sheet of 10, 2 each		
		#3785a-3785e	14.00	
a.	A3333	82y multi	1.40	1.10
b.	A3334	82y multi	1.40	1.10
c.	A3335	82y multi	1.40	1.10
d.	A3336	82y multi	1.40	1.10
e.	A3337	82y multi	1.40	1.10

Wombats A3338

Baby Rhinoceros A3340

Porcupines A3342

Puppy A3344

Snow Leopard A3346

Lamb A3339

Chick A3341

Red Pandas A3343

Japanese Macaque A3345

California Sea Lions A3347

Die Cut Perf. 13¼
2015, Jan. 23 **Litho.**
Self-Adhesive

3786		Sheet of 10, 2 each		
		#3786a-3786e	9.00	
a.	A3338	52y multi	.90	.70
b.	A3339	52y multi	.90	.70
c.	A3340	52y multi	.90	.70
d.	A3341	52y multi	.90	.70
e.	A3342	52y multi	.90	.70
3787		Sheet of 10, 2 each		
		#3787a-3787e	14.00	
a.	A3343	82y multi	1.40	1.10
b.	A3344	82y multi	1.40	1.10
c.	A3345	82y multi	1.40	1.10
d.	A3346	82y multi	1.40	1.10
e.	A3347	82y multi	1.40	1.10

Hisoka Maeshima (1835-1919), Founder of Japanese Postal Service A3348

Japanese Macaque A3350

Siberian Chipmunk A3349

Crested Ibis A3351

Sika Deer A3352

Japanese Serow A3354

Japanese Wisteria A3356

Red Fox A3353

Japanese Primrose A3355

Kerria Japonica A3357

Stream, Towada-Hachimantai National Park — A3358

Mt. Fuji, by Chikuden Tanomura — A3359

2015, Feb. 2 **Photo.** ***Perf. 13x13¼***

3788	A3348	1y brown	.25	.25
3789	A3349	3y multi	.25	.25
3790	A3350	5y multi	.25	.25
3791	A3351	10y multi	.25	.25
3792	A3352	20y multi	.35	.25
3793	A3353	30y multi	.50	.40
3794	A3354	50y multi	.85	.65
3795	A3355	100y multi	1.75	1.40
3796	A3356	120y multi	2.10	1.60
3797	A3357	140y multi	2.40	1.90
3798	A3358	500y multi	8.50	6.50

Photo. & Engr.
Perf. 13¼

3799	A3359	1000y multi	17.00	13.00
	Nos. 3788-3799 (12)		34.45	26.70

Cabbage A3360

Peas A3362

Onion A3364

Satsuma Orange A3361

Mango A3363

Oranges A3365

Asparagus
A3366

Strawberries
A3367

Lettuce
A3368

Pineapple
A3369

Die Cut Perf. 13¼x13, 13x13¼

2015, Feb. 23   **Litho.**
Self-Adhesive

3800	Sheet of 10, 2 each #3800a-3800e	9.00	
a.	A3360 52y multi	.90	.70
b.	A3361 52y multi	.90	.70
c.	A3362 52y multi	.90	.70
d.	A3363 52y multi	.90	.70
e.	A3364 52y multi	.90	.70
3801	Sheet of 10, 2 each #3801a-3801e	14.00	
a.	A3365 82y multi	1.40	1.10
b.	A3360 82y multi	1.40	1.10
c.	A3367 82y multi	1.40	1.10
d.	A3368 82y multi	1.40	1.10
e.	A3369 82y multi	1.40	1.10

PREFECTURE ISSUES

Japan has 47 prefectures (political subdivisions) and 13 postal regions (12 until 2004). Since 1989, the national postal ministry has issued stamps to publicize each prefecture. These prefectural stamps are valid throughout Japan and were issued not only in the prefecture named on the stamp but in all other prefectures in the postal region, and in one or more post offices in the other 11 or 12 postal regions. Prefectural stamps are distinguishable from other Japanese stamps by the style of the ideographic characters of "Nippon yubin" on each stamp:

日本郵便

Inscr. on National Stamps since 1948

日本郵便

Inscr. on Prefectural Stamps

Monkeys
(Nagano) — ZA1

Cherries on Tree
(Yamagata) — ZA2

Shurei-mon, Gate
of Courtesy
(Okinawa) — ZA3

Dogo Hot Spa
(Ehime) — ZA4

Blue-eyed Doll
(Kanagawa)
ZA5

Seto Inland Sea (Hiroshima) — ZA6

Memorial Hall and
Mandai Bridge
(Niigata) — ZA8

Nagoya
Castle and
Shachihoko
(Aichi) — ZA9

Mt. Takasaki
Monkey Holding
Perilla Leaf, Fruit
(Oita) — ZA10

City Hall, 1888
(Hokkaido)
ZA11

Runner, Flower
(Hokkaido)
ZA12

Kumamoto Castle
(Kumamoto)
ZA13

Stone Lantern,
Kenroku-en Park
(Ishikawa) — ZA14

Bunraku Puppets
and Theater
(Osaka) — ZA15

Shigaraki
Ware
Raccoon Dog
and Lake
Biwa (Shiga)
ZA16

Apples and
Blossoms
(Aomori) — ZA17

Raccoon Dogs
Dancing
(Chiba) — ZA18

Blowfish Lanterns
(Yamaguchi)
ZA19

Tokyo Station
(Tokyo) — ZA20

2nd Asian Winter
Olympics
(Hokkaido)
ZA21

Waterfalls
(Toyama)
ZA22

Perf. 13, 13½ (#Z4, Z11, Z20),
13x13½ (#Z12-Z19)

1989-90   Photo., Litho. (#Z16-Z17)

Z1	ZA1	62y multicolored	1.10	.70
Z2	ZA2	62y multicolored	1.10	.70
Z3	ZA3	62y multicolored	1.10	.70
Z4	ZA4	62y multicolored	1.10	.70
Z5	ZA5	62y multicolored	1.10	.70
Z6		62y sampan, bridge	1.10	.70
Z7		62y islands, stairs, starbursts	1.10	.70
a.	ZA6	Pair, #Z6-Z7	2.25	2.25
Z8	ZA8	62y multicolored	1.10	.70
Z9	ZA9	62y multicolored	1.10	.70
Z10	ZA10	62y multicolored	1.10	.70
Z11	ZA11	62y multicolored	1.10	.70
Z12	ZA12	62y multicolored	1.10	.70
Z13	ZA13	62y multicolored	1.10	.70
Z14	ZA14	62y multicolored	1.10	.70
Z15	ZA15	62y multicolored	1.10	.70
Z16	ZA16	62y multicolored	1.10	.70
Z17	ZA17	62y multicolored	1.10	.70
Z18	ZA18	62y multicolored	1.10	.70
Z19	ZA19	62y multicolored	1.10	.70
Z20	ZA20	62y multicolored	1.10	.70
Z21	ZA21	62y multicolored	1.10	.70
Z22	ZA22	62y multicolored	1.10	.70
		Nos. Z1-Z22 (22)	24.20	15.40

Sheets containing 4 Nos. Z1, Z2, Z4, Z11 or 3 No. Z14 + label, 3 No. Z19 + label were lottery prizes.
Issued: Nos. Z1-Z2, 4/1; No. Z3, 5/15; No. Z4, 6/1; No. Z5, 6/2; NO6, Z6-Z7, 7/7; No. Z8, 7/14; No. Z9, 8/1; Nos. Z10-Z11, 8/15; No. Z12, 9/1; No. Z13, 9/29; Nos. Z14-Z17, 10/2; No. Z18, 10/27; Nos. Z19-Z20, 11/1; No. Z21, 3/1/90; No. Z22, 4/18/90.
See Nos. Z263, Z285, Z363.

Nos. Z23-Z69 were issued as one set. It is broken into sections for ease of reference. See No. Z69a for sheet containing all 47 stamps.

Hokkaido
ZA23

Aomori
ZA24

Iwate — ZA25

Miyagi — ZA26

Akita
ZA27

Yamagata
ZA28

Fukushima
ZA29

Ibaraki
ZA30

Flowers of the Prefectures.

1990, Apr. 27   Litho.   Perf. 13½

Z23	ZA23	62y Sweet briar	3.50	.70
Z24	ZA24	62y Apple blossom	1.25	.70
Z25	ZA25	62y Paulownia	1.25	.70
Z26	ZA20	02y Japanese bush clover	1.25	.70
Z27	ZA27	62y Butterbur flower	1.25	.70
Z28	ZA28	62y Safflower	1.25	.70
Z29	ZA29	62y Alpine rose	1.25	.70
Z30	ZA30	62y Rose	1.25	.70
		Nos. Z23-Z30 (8)	12.25	5.60

See Nos. Z190, Z614-Z619.

Tochigi — ZA31

Gunma — ZA32

Saitama — ZA33

Chiba — ZA34

Tokyo
ZA35

Kanagawa
ZA36

Yamanashi
ZA37

Nagano
ZA38

Niigata — ZA39   Toyama — ZA40

No. Z31, Yashio azalea. No. Z32, Japanese azalea. No. Z33, Primrose. No. Z34, Rape blossom. No. Z35, Cherry blossom. No. Z36, Gold-banded lily. No. Z37, Cherry blossom. No. Z38, Autumn bellflower. No. Z39, Tulip. No. Z40, Tulip.

Z31	ZA31 62y multicolored	1.25	.70
Z32	ZA32 62y multicolored	1.25	.70
Z33	ZA33 62y multicolored	1.25	.70
Z34	ZA34 62y multicolored	1.25	.70
Z35	ZA35 62y multicolored	1.25	.70
Z36	ZA36 62y multicolored	1.25	.70
Z37	ZA37 62y multicolored	1.25	.70
Z38	ZA38 62y multicolored	3.50	.70
Z39	ZA39 62y multicolored	1.25	.70
Z40	ZA40 62y multicolored	1.25	.70
	Nos. Z31-Z40 (10)	14.75	7.00

See No. Z197.

Ishikawa
ZA41

Fukui
ZA42

Gifu
ZA43   Shizuoka
ZA44

Aichi — ZA45   Mie — ZA46

Shiga — ZA47   Kyoto — ZA48

Osaka — ZA49   Hyogo — ZA50

No. Z41, Black lily. No. Z42, Daffodil. No. Z43, Chinese milk vetch. No. Z44, Azalea. No. Z45, Rabbit-ear iris. No. Z46, Iris. No. Z47,

Alpine rose. No. Z48, Drooping cherry blossom. No. Z49, Japanese apricot and primrose. No. Z50, Chrysanthemum.

Z41	ZA41 62y multicolored	1.25	.70
Z42	ZA42 62y multicolored	1.25	.70
Z43	ZA43 62y multicolored	1.50	.70
Z44	ZA44 62y multicolored	2.00	.70
Z45	ZA45 62y multicolored	1.25	.70
Z46	ZA46 62y multicolored	1.25	.70
Z47	ZA47 62y multicolored	3.00	.70
Z48	ZA48 62y multicolored	3.00	.70
Z49	ZA49 62y multicolored	1.25	.70
Z50	ZA50 62y multicolored	1.25	.70
	Nos. Z41-Z50 (10)	17.00	7.00

Nara
ZA51

Wakayama
ZA52

Tottori
ZA53

Shimane
ZA54

Okayama
ZA55

Hiroshima
ZA56

Yamaguchi
ZA57

Tokushima
ZA58

Kagawa — ZA59

Ehime — ZA60

No. Z51, Double cherry blossom. No. Z52, Japanese apricot. No. Z53, Pear blossom. No. Z54, Peony. No. Z55, Peach blossom. No. Z56, Japanese Maple. No. Z57, Summer orange blossom. No. Z58, Sudachi orange blossom. No. Z59, Olive blossom. No. Z60, Mandarin orange blossom.

Z51	ZA51 62y multicolored	2.00	.70
Z52	ZA52 62y multicolored	1.50	.70
Z53	ZA53 62y multicolored	1.25	.70
Z54	ZA54 62y multicolored	1.25	.70
Z55	ZA55 62y multicolored	1.25	.70
Z56	ZA56 62y multicolored	1.25	.70
Z57	ZA57 62y multicolored	1.25	.70
Z58	ZA58 62y multicolored	1.50	.70
Z59	ZA59 62y multicolored	5.00	.70
Z60	ZA60 62y multicolored	2.50	.70
	Nos. Z51-Z60 (10)	18.75	7.00

Kochi
ZA61

Fukuoka
ZA62

Saga
ZA63

Nagasaki
ZA64

Kumamoto
ZA65

Oita
ZA66

Miyazaki
ZA67

Kagoshima
ZA68

Okinawa — ZA69

No. Z61, Myrica. No. Z62, Japanese apricot. No. Z63, Laurel. No. Z64, Unzen azalea. No. Z65, Autumn bellflower. No. Z66, Japanese apricot of bungo. No. Z67, Crinum. No. Z68, Rosebay. No. Z69, Coral tree.

Z61	ZA61 62y multicolored	2.00	.70
Z62	ZA62 62y multicolored	1.25	.70
Z63	ZA63 62y multicolored	1.25	.70
Z64	ZA64 62y multicolored	1.25	.70
Z65	ZA65 62y multicolored	1.25	.70
Z66	ZA66 62y multicolored	1.25	.70
Z67	ZA67 62y multicolored	1.25	.70
Z68	ZA68 62y multicolored	1.25	.70
Z69	ZA69 62y multicolored	1.25	.70
a.	Sheet of 47 + 3 labels, #Z23-Z69	110.00	
	Nos. Z61-Z69 (9)	12.00	6.30

Nos. Z23-Z69 were issued in sheets of 20. No. Z69a was released in all prefectures.

Seven Baby Crows
(Ibaraki) — ZA70

Inns of Tsumago & Magome
(Nagano)
ZA71   ZA72

Mt. Fuji and Tea Picking (Shizuoka)
ZA73

Two Peaches
(Fukushima)
ZA74

Mt. Sakurajima
(Kagoshima)
ZA75

Fireworks Festival of Omagari (Akita)
ZA76

Travel Expo '90, Nagasaki
(Nagasaki) — ZA77

Tokyo Shin Post Office (Tokyo)
ZA78

Yasukibushi Folk Song (Shimane)
ZA79

Ryukyu Dancer
(Okinawa)
ZA80

Litho., Litho. & Engr. (#Z70-Z71)

1990   *Perf. 13*

Z70	ZA70 62y multicolored	1.10	.70
Z71	ZA71 62y blk & buff	1.10	.70
Z72	ZA72 62y blk & pale grn	1.10	.70
a.	Pair, #Z71-Z72	2.25	2.25
Z73	ZA73 62y multicolored	1.10	.70
Z74	ZA74 62y multicolored	1.10	.70
Z75	ZA75 62y multicolored	1.10	.70
Z76	ZA76 62y multicolored	1.10	.70
Z77	ZA77 62y multicolored	1.10	.70
Z78	ZA78 62y multicolored	1.10	.70
Z79	ZA79 62y multicolored	1.10	.70
Z80	ZA80 62y multicolored	1.10	.70
	Nos. Z70-Z80 (11)	12.10	7.70

Issued: Nos. Z70-Z72, 5/1; No. Z73, 5/2; No. Z74, 6/1; Nos. Z75-Z76, 7/2; No. Z77, 8/1; No. Z78, 8/6; Nos. Z79-Z80, 8/15.
Sheets of 3 + label of Nos. Z70, Z73, Z80 were lottery prizes. Value, each $3.25.
See Nos. Z332-Z333.

Dancing Girl
(Kyoto)
ZA81

Old Path of
Kumano
(Wakayama)
ZA82

45th Natl. Athletic
Meet (Fukuoka)
ZA83

Izu Swamp,
Swans (Miyagi)
ZA84

Spring
(Gifu) — ZA85

Summer
(Gifu) — ZA86

Autumn
(Gifu) — ZA87

Winter
(Gifu) — ZA88

Nursery Rhyme,
Toryanse
(Saitama) — ZA89

Japanese
Cranes
(Hokkaido)
ZA90

1990

Z81	ZA81	62y multicolored	1.10	.70
Z82	ZA82	62y multicolored	1.10	.70
Z83	ZA83	62y multicolored	1.10	.70
Z84	ZA84	62y multicolored	1.10	.70
Z85	ZA85	62y multicolored	1.10	.70
Z86	ZA86	62y multicolored	1.10	.70
Z87	ZA87	62y multicolored	1.10	.70
Z88	ZA88	62y multicolored	1.10	.70
a.		Strip of 4, #Z85-Z88	4.50	4.50
Z89	ZA89	62y multicolored	1.10	.70
Z90	ZA90	62y multicolored	1.10	.70
		Nos. Z81-Z90 (10)	11.00	7.00

Issued: Nos. Z81-Z83, 9/3; No. Z84, 10/1;
Nos. Z85-Z88, 10/9; No. Z89, 10/12; No. Z90,
10/30.
Sheets of 3 No. Z82 + label were lottery
prizes. Value, $3.25.
See Nos. 3282-3285, Z171-Z174.

Bizen Ware (Okayama) — ZA92

Battle of Yashima
(Kagawa) — ZA91

Yoshinogari Ruins
(Saga) — ZA94

Bride Under
Cherry Blossoms
(Yamanashi)
ZA95

Carp (Niigata)
ZA96

Lily Bell
(Hokkaido)
ZA97

Lilac (Hokkaido)
ZA98

Day Lily
(Hokkaido)
ZA99

Rowanberry
(Hokkaido)
ZA100

Litho., Photo. (#Z94-Z95)

1991			**Perf. 13**	
Z91	ZA91	62y multicolored	1.10	.70
Z92		62y pedestal	1.10	.70
Z93		62y bowl	1.10	.70
a.		ZA92 Pair, #Z92-Z93	2.25	2.25
Z94	ZA94	62y multicolored	1.10	.70
Z95	ZA95	62y multicolored	1.10	.70
Z96	ZA96	62y multicolored	1.10	.70
Z97	ZA97	62y multicolored	1.10	.70
Z98	ZA98	62y multicolored	1.10	.70
Z99	ZA99	62y multicolored	1.10	.70
Z100	ZA100	62y multicolored	1.10	.70
a.		Strip of 4, #Z97-Z100	4.50	4.50
		Nos. Z91-Z100 (10)	11.00	7.00

Issued: No. Z91, 2/19; Nos. Z92-Z93, 4/5;
No. Z94, 4/12; No. Z95, 4/18; No. Z96, 5/1;
Nos. Z97-Z100, 5/31.
See Nos. 3286-3289, Z304-Z307.

Nikkou Mountains
(Tochigi) — ZA101

Mt. Iwate by Yaoji
Hashimoto
(Iwate) — ZA102

Wooden Puppet
(Tokushima)
ZA103

Whales (Kochi)
ZA104

Fringed Orchids
(Tokyo)
ZA105

Cape Toi, Horses
(Miyazaki)
ZA106

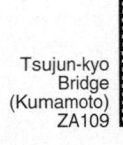

Black Pearls of
Kabira Bay
(Okinawa)
ZA107

Japanese Pears
(Tottori)
ZA108

Tsujun-kyo
Bridge
(Kumamoto)
ZA109

1991 | **Photo.**

Z101	ZA101	62y multicolored	1.10	.70
Z102	ZA102	62y multicolored	1.10	.70
a.		Booklet pane of 10	11.00	
		Complete booklet, #Z102a	11.00	
Z103	ZA103	62y multicolored	1.10	.70
a.		Pane of 10	11.00	
Z104	ZA104	62y multicolored	1.10	.70
a.		Pane of 10	11.00	
Z105	ZA105	41y multicolored	2.50	1.00
a.		Booklet pane of 10	15.00	
		Complete booklet, #Z105a	15.00	
Z106	ZA106	62y multicolored	1.10	.70
a.		Booklet pane of 10	15.00	
		Complete booklet, #Z106a	15.00	
Z107	ZA107	41y multicolored	.80	.50
Z108	ZA108	62y multicolored	1.10	.70
Z109	ZA109	62y multicolored	1.10	.70
a.		Booklet pane of 10	15.00	
		Complete booklet, #Z108a	15.00	
		Nos. Z101-Z109 (9)	11.00	6.40

Issued: No. Z101, 5/29; No. Z102, 6/10;
Nos. Z103-Z104, 6/26; Nos. Z105-Z106, 7/1;
Nos. Z107-Z108, 8/1; No. Z109, 8/26.
Sheets of 3 No. Z106 + label were lottery
prizes. Value, $3.

Ninja, Iga
Ueno Castle
(Mie)
ZA111

46th Natl.
Athletic Meet
(Ishikawa)
ZA110

Eyeglass Industry
(Fukui)
ZA112

Nursery Rhyme,
Tortoise and the
Hare — ZA113

Kobe City
Weathervane
(Hyogo) — ZA114

Spring
(Nara) — ZA115

Autumn (Nara,
Gunma) — ZA116

Litho., Photo. (#Z110, Z112)

1991			**Perf. 13, 13½ (#Z110)**	
Z110	ZA110	41y multicolored	.80	.50
a.		Pane of 10	8.00	
Z111	ZA111	62y multicolored	1.10	.70
a.		Booklet pane of 10	14.00	
		Complete booklet, #Z111a	14.00	
Z112	ZA112	62y multicolored	1.10	.70
a.		Booklet pane of 10	14.00	
		Complete booklet, #Z112a	14.00	
Z113	ZA113	62y multicolored	1.10	.70
a.		Booklet pane of 10	14.00	
		Complete booklet, #Z113a	14.00	
Z114	ZA114	62y multicolored	1.10	.70
a.		Booklet pane of 10	14.00	
		Complete booklet, #Z114a	14.00	
Z115	ZA115	62y multicolored	1.10	.70
Z116	ZA116	62y multicolored	1.10	.70
a.		Pair, #Z115-Z116	2.25	2.25
b.		Booklet pane, 5 #Z116a	14.00	
		Complete booklet, #Z116b	14.00	
		Nos. Z110-Z116 (7)	7.40	4.70

Issued: No. Z110, 9/2; No. Z111, 9/10; No.
Z112, 10/1; No. Z113, 10/23; Nos. Z114-Z116,
10/25.
See Nos. 3189G, Z177-Z178.

Gogo-An
Temple, Sea of
Japan (Niigata)
ZA117

Natl. Land
Afforestation
Campaign
(Fukuoka)
ZA118

Arctic Fox
(Hokkaido)
ZA119

Tateyama
Mountain Range
(Toyama)
ZA120

Rikuchu Coast
(Iwate) — ZA121

Kurushima
Strait (Ehime)
ZA122

Tsurusaki
Dance (Oita)
ZA123

Tanabata
Lantern Festival
(Yamaguchi)
ZA124

Shasui-no-taki
Waterfall
(Kanagawa)
ZA125

Kurodabushi
Dance
(Fukuoka)
ZA126

Boat Race
(Okinawa)
ZA127

Osaka Castle,
Business Park
(Osaka)
ZA128

Owl, Mt. Horaiji
(Aichi) — ZA129

1992   **Litho.**   **Perf. 13½**
Z117 ZA117 41y multicolored   .80   .50
  a.   Pane of 10   8.00
      Photo.
Z118 ZA118 41y multicolored   .80   .50
Z119 ZA119 62y multicolored   1.10   .70
  a.   Souvenir sheet of 3   3.50   3.50
      Litho.
Z120 ZA120 62y multicolored   1.10   .70
  a.   Pane of 10   11.00
      Photo.
Z121 ZA121 62y multicolored   1.10   .70
  a.   Pane of 10   11.00
Z122 ZA122 62y multicolored   1.10   .70
  a.   Pane of 10   11.00
Z123 ZA123 62y multicolored   1.10   .70
Z124 ZA124 62y multicolored   1.10   .70
Z125 ZA125 62y multicolored   1.10   .70
  a.   Pane of 10   11.00
  b.   Souvenir sheet of 3   3.50   3.50
      Litho.
Z126 ZA126 62y multicolored   1.10   .70
Z127 ZA127 62y multicolored   1.10   .70
Z128 ZA128 41y multicolored   .80   .60

      Photo.
Z129 ZA129 62y multicolored   1.10   .70
  a.   Souvenir sheet of 3   3.50   3.50
  b.   Pane of 10   11.00
      Nos. Z117-Z129 (13)   13.40   8.60

Issued: No. Z117, 5/1; No. Z118, 5/8; No.
Z119, 5/29; No. Z120, 6/10; Nos. Z121-Z122,
6/23; No. Z124, 7/7; No. Z123, 7/23; No. Z125,
7/24; No. Z126, 8/3; No. Z127, 8/17; No. Z129,
10/15.
    See also No. Z320.

Oga Peninsula
(Akita)
ZA130

Fukuroda
Waterfall
(Ibaraki)
ZA131

Notojima
Bridge, Nanao
Bay
(Ishikawa)
ZA132

Tama District
Mountains
(Metropolitan
Tokyo)
ZA133

Harbor Seal
(Hokkaido) — ZA134

Peace Statue
(Kagawa)
ZA135

Hana Ta'ue Rice
Planting Festival
(Hiroshima)
ZA136

Paradise
Flycatcher and
Mt. Fuji
(Shizuoka)
ZA137

Sailboats on
Lake Biwa
(Shiga)
ZA138

Matumoto Castle
& Japan Alps
(Nagano)
ZA139

Ohara Festival
(Kagoshima)
ZA140

Oirase Mountain
Stream (Aomori)
ZA141

Yourou Valley
(Chiba) — ZA142

1993   **Litho.**   **Perf. 13½**
Z130 ZA130 41y multicolored   .80   .50
  a.   Pane of 10   8.00
Z131 ZA131 62y multicolored   1.10   .70
  a.   Pane of 10   11.00
      Photo.
Z132 ZA132 62y multicolored   1.10   .70
  a.   Pane of 10   11.50
Z133 ZA133 62y multicolored   1.10   .70
  a.   Booklet pane of 10   11.50
     Complete booklet, #Z133a   11.50
Z134 ZA134 62y multicolored   1.10   .70
Z135 ZA135 62y multicolored   1.10   .70
  a.   Pane of 10   11.50
Z136 ZA136 62y multicolored   1.25   .70
  a.   Pane of 10   12.00
Z137 ZA137 41y multicolored   .80   .50
  a.   Pane of 10   8.00
Z138 ZA138 62y multicolored   1.25   .70
  a.   Pane of 10   12.00
Z139 ZA139 62y multicolored   1.25   .70
  a.   Pane of 10   12.00
Z140 ZA140 41y multicolored   .80   .50
  a.   Pane of 10   8.00
      Perf. 13x13½
Z141 ZA141 62y multicolored   1.10   .70
  a.   Pane of 10   11.00
      Perf. 13½
Z142 ZA142 41y multicolored   .80   .50
  a.   Pane of 10   8.00
      Nos. Z130-Z142 (13)   13.55   8.30

Issued: No. Z130, 2/12; No. Z131, 3/26; No.
Z132, 4/2; No. Z133, 4/23; No. Z134, 5/17; No.
Z135, 5/21; No. Z136, 6/4; No. Z137, 6/23; No.
Z138, 7/1; No. Z139, 7/16; No. Z140, 9/1; No.
Z141, 9/22; No. Z142, 10/1.
    See also No. Z321.

Dream Bridge
(Metropolitan
Tokyo)
ZA143

Kurobe Canyon
& Dam
(Toyama)
ZA144

Haiku,
Storehouse of
Poet Issa (1763-
1827) (Nagano)
ZA145

Okuni, Izumo
Great Shrine,
Taisha
(Shimane)
ZA146

Fukiwari Falls
(Gunma)
ZA147

Ezoshika
(Hokkaido)
ZA148

Watch Tower,
Festival in
Tajima (Hyogo)
ZA149

Wakura Coast
(Wakayama)
ZA150

1994   **Photo.**   **Perf. 13**
Z143 ZA143 50y multicolored   .90   .50
  a.   Pane of 10   9.50
Z144 ZA144 80y multicolored   1.40   .90
  a.   Pane of 10   15.00
Z145 ZA145 80y multicolored   1.40   .90
  a.   Pane of 10   15.00
Z146 ZA146 80y multicolored   1.40   .90
  a.   Pane of 10   15.00
      Litho.
Z147 ZA147 80y multicolored   1.40   .90
  a.   Pane of 10   15.00
Z148 ZA148 50y multicolored   .90   .50
  a.   Pane of 10   10.00
Z149 ZA149 50y multicolored   .90   .50
  a.   Pane of 10   10.00
Z150 ZA150 80y multicolored   1.40   .90
  a.   Pane of 10   15.00
      Nos. Z143-Z150 (8)   9.70   6.00

Issued: No. Z143, 3/23; No. Z144, 4/25;
Nos. Z145-Z146, 5/2; No. Z147, 6/6; No.
Z148, 6/7; No. Z149, 6/23; No. Z150, 7/15.

Kentish Plovers
(Mie)
ZA151

Awaodori Dance
(Tokushima)
ZA152

Tug-of-War
(Okinawa)
ZA153

Kehi Pine Wood
(Fukui)
ZA154

Matsushima
(Miyagi)
ZA155

Kunchi
Festival
(Nagasaki)
ZA156

1994   **Photo.**   **Perf. 13**
Z151 ZA151 80y multicolored   1.40   .90
  a.   Pane of 10   15.00
Z152 ZA152 50y multicolored   .90   .90
  a.   Pane of 10   10.00

Z153	ZA153 50y multicolored		.90	.50
Z154	ZA154 50y multicolored		.90	.50
a.	Pane of 10		10.00	
Z155	ZA155 80y multicolored		1.40	.90
a.	Pane of 10		16.50	
Z156	ZA156 80y multicolored		1.40	.90
a.	Pane of 10		16.50	
	Nos. Z151-Z156 (6)		6.90	4.20

Issued: No. Z151, 7/22; Nos. Z152-Z153, 8/1; No. Z154, 9/1; No. Z155, 9/20; No. Z156, 10/3.

Hokkaido Chipmunks (Hokkaido) — ZA157

Ushiwakamaru and Benkei (Kyoto) — ZA158

Utopia Flower (Gifu) ZA159

Jade Bead, Gyofu Soma (1883-1950), Lyricist (Niigata) ZA160

Cape Ashizuri-Misaki Lighthouse (Kochi) ZA161

Ishikawamon Gate, Kanazawa Castle (Ishikawa) ZA162

Akamon Gate, University of Tokyo (Tokyo) ZA163

Three Waterfalls, Kuroyama (Saitama) ZA164

Lady's Slipper, Rebun Island (Hokkaido) ZA165

Street with Zelkova Trees (Miyagi) ZA166

Eisa Festival (Okinawa) — ZA167

1995	**Photo.**		**Perf. 13**	
Z157	ZA157 80y multicolored		1.40	.90
a.	Pane of 10		19.00	
		Perf. 13½		
Z158	ZA158 80y multicolored		1.40	.90
a.	Pane of 10		19.00	
Z159	ZA159 80y multicolored		1.40	.90
a.	Pane of 10		19.00	
Z160	ZA160 80y multicolored		1.40	.90
a.	Pane of 10		19.00	
Z161	ZA161 80y multicolored		1.40	.90
a.	Pane of 10		19.00	
Z162	ZA162 80y multicolored		1.40	.90
a.	Pane of 10		19.00	
Z163	ZA163 50y multicolored		.90	.50
a.	Pane of 10		11.00	
Z164	ZA164 80y multicolored		1.40	.90
a.	Pane of 10		17.50	
Z165	ZA165 80y multicolored		1.40	.90
a.	Pane of 10		17.50	
Z166	ZA166 50y multicolored		.90	.50
a.	Pane of 10		10.00	
Z167	ZA167 80y multicolored		1.40	.90
	Nos. Z157-Z167 (11)		14.40	9.10

Issued: No. Z157, 3/3; No. Z158, 4/3; No. Z159, 4/26; No. Z160, 5/1; Nos. Z161-Z162, 6/1; Nos. Z163-Z165, 7/7; Nos. Z166-Z167, 8/1.

Seasons Types of 1990-91 Redrawn and

Kishiwada Danjiri Festival (Osaka) ZA168

Yamadera Temple (Yamagata) ZA169

Karatsu Kunchi Festival (Saga) ZA170

Niimi-No-Shou Festival (Okayama) ZA171

Kirifuri Waterfall (Tochigi) ZA172

10th All-Japan Holstein Show (Chiba) ZA173

Nos. Z171-Z174: (Gifu).
No. Z177, (Nara). No. Z178, (Nara, Gunma).

1995	**Photo.**		**Perf. 13½**	
Z168	ZA168 80y multicolored		1.40	.90
a.	Pane of 10		16.00	
Z169	ZA169 80y multicolored		1.40	.90
a.	Pane of 10		16.00	
Z170	ZA170 80y multicolored		1.40	.90
a.	Pane of 10		16.00	
		Perf. 13		
Z171	ZA85 80y Spring		1.40	.90
Z172	ZA86 80y Summer		1.40	.90
Z173	ZA87 80y Autumn		1.40	.90

Z174	ZA88 80y Winter		1.40	.90
a.	Strip of 4, #Z171-Z174		6.50	6.50
		Perf. 13½		
Z175	ZA171 80y multicolored		1.40	.90
Z176	ZA172 50y multicolored		.90	.50
a.	Pane of 10		10.00	
Z177	ZA115 80y Spring		1.40	.90
Z178	ZA116 80y Autumn		1.40	.90
a.	Pair, #Z177-Z178		3.00	3.00
Z179	ZA173 80y multicolored		1.40	.90
a.	Pane of 10		15.00	
	Nos. Z168-Z179 (12)		16.30	10.40

Issued: No. Z168, 9/1; No. Z169, 9/15; Nos. Z170-Z174, 10/2; No. Z175, 10/13; No. Z176, 10/27; Nos. Z177-Z178, 11/6; No. Z179, 11/21.

For self-adhesives, see Nos. 3282-3285.

Clione Limancia (Hokkaido) ZA174

Ushibuka Haiya Festival (Kumamoto) ZA175

Peony of Sukagawa (Fukushima) ZA176

Hamayu (Mie) ZA177

Ama Divers (Mie) — ZA178

World Ceramics Expo '96 (Saga) — ZA179

Shosenkyo Gorge (Yamanashi) ZA180

Murasaki Shikibu of Takefu (Fukui) ZA181

1996	**Litho.**		**Perf. 13½x13**	
Z180	ZA174 80y multicolored		1.40	.90
a.	Pane of 10		11.50	
		Photo.		
Z181	ZA175 80y multicolored		1.40	.90
a.	Pane of 10		15.00	
Z182	ZA176 80y multicolored		1.40	.90
a.	Pane of 10		15.00	
Z183	ZA177 80y multicolored		1.40	.90
Z184	ZA178 80y multicolored		1.40	.90
a.	Pair, #Z183-Z184		3.00	3.00
b.	Pane, 5 #Z184a		15.00	
Z185	ZA179 80y multicolored		1.40	.90
		Perf. 13½		
Z186	ZA180 50y multicolored		.90	.50
a.	Pane of 10		9.50	
Z187	ZA181 80y multicolored		1.40	.90
	Nos. Z180-Z187 (8)		10.70	6.80

Issued: No. Z180, 2/6; No. Z181, 4/1; No. Z182, 4/26; Nos. Z183-Z184, 5/1; No. Z185, 5/17; No. Z186, 6/3; No. Z187, 6/24.

Flower Types of 1990 and

Ancient Trees, Kompon-chudo of Mt. Hiei (Shiga) ZA182

Nishiumi Marine Park (Ehime) ZA183

Nebuta Festival (Aomori) ZA184

Main Palace, Shuri Castle (Okinawa) ZA186

Shimozuru Usudaiko Odori Folk Dance (Miyazaki) ZA185

Asakusa Kaminarimon Gate (Metropolitan Tokyo) ZA187

Tottori Shanshan Festival (Tottori) ZA188

Saito Kinen Festival Matsumoto (Nagano) ZA189

No. Z190, (Hokkaido). No. Z197, (Nagano).

1996	**Photo.**		**Perf. 13½**	
Z188	ZA182 80y multicolored		1.40	.90
a.	Pane of 10		15.00	
Z189	ZA183 80y multicolored		1.40	.90
a.	Pane of 10		15.00	
Z190	ZA23 80y Sweetbriar		1.40	.90
Z191	ZA184 80y multicolored		1.40	.90
a.	Pane of 10		15.00	
Z192	ZA185 80y multicolored		1.40	.90
a.	Pane of 10		15.00	
Z193	ZA186 80y multicolored		1.40	.90
a.	Pane of 10		15.00	
Z194	ZA187 80y multicolored		1.40	.90
a.	Pane of 10		15.00	
Z195	ZA188 80y multicolored		1.40	.90
Z196	ZA189 80y multicolored		1.40	.90
a.	Pane of 10		15.00	
Z197	ZA38 80y Autumn bell-flower		1.40	.90
	Nos. Z188-Z197 (10)		14.00	9.00

Issued: Nos. Z188-Z189, 7/1; No. Z190, 7/5; No. Z191, 7/23; Nos. Z192-Z193, 8/1; No. Z194, 8/8; No. Z195, 8/16; Nos. Z196-Z197, 8/22.

For self-adhesive, see No. 3290.

Sengokubara Marsh
(Kanagawa)
ZA190

Nagoya Festival (Aichi) — ZA191

Grass-burning
Rite on Mt.
Wakakusa
(Nara)
ZA193

1997 Men's
Handball World
Championships
(Kumamoto)
ZA194

Tea Picking
(Shizuoka)
ZA195

Dahurian
Rhododendron
(Hokkaido)
ZA196

Mt. Fuji (Shizuoka) — ZA197

1996-97	Photo.	Perf. 13½	
Z198	ZA190 80y multicolored	1.40	.90
a.	Pane of 10	15.00	
Z199	80y horse, rider	1.40	.90
Z200	80y two floats	1.40	.90
a.	ZA191 Pair, #Z199-Z200	3.00	3.00
b.	Pane, 5 #Z200a	15.00	
Z201	ZA193 50y multicolored	.90	.50
a.	Pane of 10	9.50	
Z202	ZA194 80y multicolored	1.40	.90
a.	Pane of 10	15.00	
Z203	ZA195 50y multicolored	.90	.50
a.	Pane of 10	9.50	
Z204	ZA196 80y multicolored	1.40	.90
a.	Pane of 10	15.00	
Z205	80y cattle	1.40	.90
Z206	80y orange grasses	1.40	.90
a.	ZA197 Pair, #Z205-Z206	2.50	2.50
b.	Pane, 5 #Z206a	12.50	
	Nos. Z198-Z206 (9)	11.60	7.30

Issued: No. Z198, 9/6; Nos. Z199-Z200, 10/1; No. Z201, 11/15; No. Z202, 4/17/97; Nos. Z203-Z206, 4/25/97.

Marugame
Castle (Kagawa)
ZA199

Hokkaido
Ermine
(Hokkaido)
ZA200

Okayama Castle
(Okayama)
ZA201

Okinawan Fruits
(Okinawa)
ZA202

ZA204   ZA205

ZA206   ZA207
Nagasaki Kaido Highway
(Nagasaki, Saga, Fukuoka)

Fukiya Koji's
Hanayome
Ningyo, Doll of
Bride (Niigata)
ZA208

The Clock Tower
of Kyoto
University
(Kyoto)
ZA209

1997	Photo.	Perf. 13½	
Z207	ZA199 80y multicolored	1.40	.90
a.	Pane of 10	15.00	
Z208	ZA200 50y multicolored	.90	.50
a.	Pane of 10	9.50	
Z209	ZA201 80y multicolored	1.40	.90
a.	Pane of 10	15.00	
Z210	50y pineapple	.90	.50
Z211	50y mango	.90	.50
a.	ZA202 Pair, #Z210-Z211	1.90	1.90
Z212	ZA204 80y multicolored	1.40	.90
Z213	ZA205 80y multicolored	1.40	.90
Z214	ZA206 80y multicolored	1.40	.90
Z215	ZA207 80y multicolored	1.40	.90
a.	Strip of 4, #Z212-Z215	6.00	6.00
Z216	ZA208 50y multicolored	.90	.50
a.	Pane of 10	9.50	
Z217	ZA209 80y multicolored	1.40	.90
a.	Pane of 10	15.00	
	Nos. Z207-Z217 (11)	13.40	8.30

Issued: No. Z207, 5/15; Nos. Z208-Z209, 5/30; Nos. Z210-Z211, 6/2; Nos. Z212-Z215, 6/3; Nos. Z216-Z217, 6/18.

Kanto Festival
(Akita)
ZA210

San-in Yume
Minato
Exposition
(Tottori)
ZA211

Waterwheel
Plant, Hozoji-
numa Pond
(Saitama)
ZA212

Lake
Kasumigaura
(Ibaraki)
ZA215

Bon Wind Festival, Owara
(Toyama) — ZA213

Tokyo Big Site
(Tokyo)
ZA216

Telecom Center
(Tokyo)
ZA217

Rainbow Bridge
(Tokyo)
ZA218

Intl. Forum
(Tokyo)
ZA219

Tokyo Museum
(Tokyo)
ZA220

First World
Walking Festival
(Saitama)
ZA221

1997	Photo.	Perf. 13½	
Z218	ZA210 80y multicolored	1.40	.90
a.	Pane of 10	15.00	
Z219	ZA211 80y multicolored	1.40	.90
a.	Pane of 10	15.00	
Z220	ZA212 50y multicolored	.90	.50
a.	Pane of 10	9.50	
Z221	80y woman	1.40	.90
Z222	80y man	1.40	.90
a.	ZA213 Pair, #Z221-Z222	3.00	3.00
b.	Pane, 5 #Z222a	15.00	
Z223	ZA215 80y multicolored	1.40	.90
a.	Pane of 10	15.00	

Z224	ZA216 80y multicolored	1.40	.90
Z225	ZA217 80y multicolored	1.40	.90
Z226	ZA218 80y multicolored	1.40	.90
Z227	ZA219 80y multicolored	1.40	.90
Z228	ZA220 80y multicolored	1.40	.70
a.	Strip of 5, #Z224-Z228	7.50	7.50
b.	Pane, 2 #Z228a	15.00	
Z229	ZA221 80y multicolored	1.40	.70
a.	Pane of 10	15.00	
	Nos. Z218-Z229 (12)	16.30	10.00

Issued: No. Z218, 7/7; No. Z219, 7/11; No. Z220, 8/1; Nos. Z221-Z222, 8/20; No. Z223, 9/1; Nos. Z224-Z228, 10/1; No. Z229, 10/28.

Kanagawa-Chiba Bridge Tunnel
(Chiba, Kanagawa) — ZA222

Snow-Covered
Tree (Hokkaido)
ZA224

Flower in a
Dream
(Hokkaido)
ZA225

Hiyoshi Dam
(Kyoto)
ZA226

Sanshin
(Okinawa)
ZA227

Okoshi Daiko
(Gifu)
ZA228

Kobe-Awaji Expressway (Tokushima,
Hyogo) — ZA229

1997-98	Litho.	Perf. 13½	
Z230	80y denomination upper right	1.40	.90
Z231	80y denomination lower left	1.40	.90
a.	ZA222 Pair, #Z230-Z231	3.00	3.00
b.	Pane, 5 #Z231a	15.00	
Z232	ZA224 80y multicolored	1.40	.90
Z233	ZA225 80y multicolored	1.40	.90
a.	Pair, #Z232-Z233	3.00	3.00
b.	Pane, 5 #Z233a	15.00	
	Photo.		
	Perf. 13		
Z234	ZA226 80y multicolored	1.40	.90
a.	Pane of 10	15.00	
	Perf. 13½		
Z235	ZA227 80y multicolored	1.40	.90
a.	Pane of 10	15.00	
Z236	ZA228 80y multicolored	1.40	.90
a.	Pane of 10	15.00	
Z237	80y bridge, whirl-pool	1.40	.90

Z238	80y bridge, flowers	1.40	.90
a.	ZA229 Pair, #Z237-Z238	3.00	3.00
b.	Pane, 5 #Z238a	15.00	

Issued: Nos. Z230-Z231, 12/18; Nos. Z232-Z233, 2/5/98; No. Z234, 3/2/98; No. Z235, 3/4/98; No. Z236, 3/19/98; Nos. Z237-Z238, 3/20/98.

Jomon Figurine (Nagano) ZA231

Chaguchagu Umakko, Mt. Iwate (Iwate) ZA232

Tokyo '98 Business Show (Tokyo) ZA233

Mt. Heisei Shinzan (Nagasaki) ZA234

Oze (Gunma) — ZA235

Hanagasa Matsuri (Yamagata) ZA237

9th Women's World Softball Championships (Shizuoka) ZA238

1998	**Photo.**	**Perf. 13½**	
Z239	ZA231 80y multicolored	1.40	.90
a.	Pane of 10	15.00	
Z240	ZA232 80y multicolored	1.40	.90
a.	Pane of 10	15.00	
Z241	ZA233 80y multicolored	1.40	.90
a.	Pane of 10	15.00	
Z242	ZA234 80y multicolored	1.40	.90
a.	Pane of 10	15.00	
Z243	80y blue & multi	1.40	.90
Z244	80y brown & multi	1.40	.90
a.	ZA235 Pair, #Z243-Z244	3.00	3.00
b.	Pane, 5 #Z244a	15.00	
Z245	ZA237 50y multicolored	.90	.50
a.	Pane of 10	9.50	
Z246	ZA238 80y multicolored	1.40	.90
a.	Pane of 10	15.00	
	Nos. Z239-Z246 (8)	10.70	6.80

Issued: No. Z239, 4/1; No. Z240, 4/24; No. Z241, 5/19; No. Z242, 5/20/98; Nos. Z243-Z244, 5/21; No. Z245, 6/5; No. Z246, 6/22.

Mt. Hakusan (Ishikawa) ZA239

Hita Gion (Ohita) ZA240

World Puppetry Festival (Nagano) — ZA241

Views of Seto (Hiroshima) — ZA243

First Postage Stamps of Ryukyu Islands, 50th Anniv. (Ryukyu Islands) — ZA245

1998	**Photo.**	**Perf. 13½**	
Z247	ZA239 50y multicolored	.90	.50
a.	Pane of 10	9.50	
Z248	ZA240 50y multicolored	.90	.50
a.	Pane of 10	9.50	
Z249	50y stage left	.90	.50
Z250	50y stage right	.90	.50
a.	ZA241 Pair, #Z249-Z250	1.90	1.90
b.	Pane, 5 #Z250a	9.50	
Z251	80y harbor	1.40	.90
Z252	80y highway	1.40	.90
a.	ZA243 Pair, #Z251-Z252	3.00	3.00
b.	Pane, 5 #Z252a	15.00	
Z253	80y Ryukyu Islands #1	1.40	.90
Z254	80y Ryukyu Islands #228	1.40	.90
a.	ZA245 Pair, #Z253-Z254	3.00	3.00
	Nos. Z247-Z254 (8)	9.20	5.60

Issued: Nos. Z247-Z248, 7/1; Nos. Z249-Z252, 7/17; Nos. Z253-Z254, 7/23.

Satsuma Pottery, 400th Anniv. (Kogoshima) — ZA247

Seto Ohashi Bridge (Kagawa) ZA249

Kobe Luminaries (Hyogo) ZA250

Apples (Aomori) ZA251

Kumano Path (Wakayama) ZA252

Tama Monorail (Tokyo) — ZA253

1998	**Photo.**	**Perf. 13½**	
Z255	80y bowl	1.40	.90
Z256	80y vase	1.40	.90
a.	ZA247 Pair, #Z255-Z256	3.00	3.00
b.	Pane, 5 #Z256a	15.00	
Z257	ZA249 80y multicolored	1.40	.90
a.	Pane of 10	15.00	
Z258	ZA250 80y multicolored	1.40	.90
a.	Pane of 10	15.00	
	Perf. 13		
Z259	ZA251 80y multicolored	1.40	.90
a.	Pane of 10	15.00	
Z260	ZA252 80y multicolored	1.40	.90
	Perf. 13½		
Z261	ZA253 80y multicolored	1.40	.90
a.	Pane of 10	15.00	
	Nos. Z255-Z261 (7)	9.80	6.30

Issued: Nos. Z255-Z256, 10/1; Nos. Z257-Z258, 11/9; Nos. Z259-Z260, 11/13; No. Z261, 11/26.

Dogo Hot Spa (Ehime) Type of 1989 and

Ibara Line (Okayama, Hiroshima) — ZA254

ZA255

Ao-no-Domon (Oita) — ZA256

ZA257   ZA258

Snow World (Hokkaido) ZA259   ZA260

Tokamachi Snow Festival (Niigata) — ZA261

Orchids (Tokyo) — ZA262

Dinosaurs (Fukui) — ZA264

1999	**Photo.**	**Perf. 13½**	
Z262	ZA254 80y multicolored	1.40	.70
a.	Pane of 10	15.00	
Z263	ZA4 80y multicolored	1.40	.70
Z264	ZA255 80y multicolored	1.40	.70
Z265	ZA256 80y multicolored	1.40	.70
a.	Vert. pair, #Z264-Z265	3.00	3.00
b.	Pane, 5 #Z265a	15.00	
Z266	ZA257 50y multicolored	.90	.50
Z267	ZA258 50y multicolored	.90	.50
Z268	ZA259 80y multicolored	1.40	.70
Z269	ZA260 80y multicolored	1.40	.70
a.	Strip of 4, #Z266-Z269	5.00	3.50
Z270	ZA261 80y multicolored	1.40	.70
a.	Pane of 10	15.00	
Z271	80y white flowers	1.40	.70
Z272	80y purple flowers	1.40	.70
a.	ZA262 Pair, #Z271-Z272	3.00	3.00
b.	Pane, 5 #Z272a	15.00	
Z273	80y denomination upper left	1.40	.70
Z274	80y denomination lower left	1.40	.70
a.	ZA264 Pair, #Z273-Z274	3.00	3.00
b.	Pane, 5 #Z274a	15.00	
	Nos. Z262-Z274 (13)	17.20	8.70

Issued: No. Z262, 1/1; Nos. Z263-Z265, 2/1; Nos. Z266-Z269, 2/5; Nos. Z270-Z272, 2/12; Nos. Z273-Z274, 2/22.

Lake Chuzenji (Tochigi) — ZA266

Renowned Cherry Tree (Gifu) ZA268

Kiso Observatory, Mt. Ontake (Nagano) ZA271

Postal Service in Okinawa, 125th Anniv. (Okinawa) — ZA269

ZA272

ZA273

ZA274

The Old Path for
Kumano
(Mie) — ZA275

No. Z275, Spring. No. Z276, Fall. No. Z278, Traditional costume. No. Z279, Laughing lions. No. Z281, Tsuzurato Pass. No. Z282, Matsumoto Pass. No. Z283, Umagoshi Pass. No. Z284, Touri Pass.

	1999	Photo.	Perf. 13½	
Z275		80y multicolored	1.40	.90
Z276		80y multicolored	1.40	.90
a.	ZA266 Pair, #Z275-Z276		3.00	3.00
b.	Pane, 5 #Z276a		15.00	
Z277	ZA268	80y multicolored	1.40	.90
a.	Pane of 10		15.00	
Z278		80y multicolored	1.40	.90
Z279		80y multicolored	1.40	.90
a.	ZA269 Pair, #Z278-Z279		3.00	3.00
b.	Pane, 5 #Z279a		15.00	
Z280	ZA271	80y multicolored	1.40	.90
a.	Pane of 10		15.00	
Z281	ZA272	80y multicolored	1.40	.70
Z282	ZA273	80y multicolored	1.40	.70
Z283	ZA274	80y multicolored	1.40	.70
Z284	ZA275	80y multicolored	1.40	.70
a.	Strip of 4, #Z281-Z284		6.00	6.00
	Nos. Z275-Z284 (10)		14.00	8.20

Issued: Nos. Z275-Z276, 3/1. No. Z277, 3/16. Nos. Z278-Z279, 3/23. No. Z280, 4/9. Nos. Z281-Z284, 4/16.

**Cherries (Yamagata) Type of 1989
and**

Taiko-Mon Gate,
Matsumoto
Castle (Nagano)
ZA276

Firefly Squid
(Toyama)
ZA277

ZA278

ZA279

**Four Seasons, Kenrokuen Garden
(Ishikawa)**

ZA280   ZA281

No. Z288, Kaisekitou Pagoda, Spring. No. Z289, Fountain, Summer. No. Z290, Kinjoureitaku spring, Autumn. No. Z291, Kotoji stone lantern and yukitsuri, Winter.

	1999, Apr. 26	Photo.	Perf. 13	
Z285	ZA2	80y like #Z2	1.40	.90
		Perf. 13½		
Z286	ZA276	80y multicolored	1.40	.90
a.	Pane of 10		15.00	
Z287	ZA277	80y multicolored	1.40	.90
a.	Pane of 10		15.00	
Z288	ZA278	80y multicolored	1.40	.90
Z289	ZA279	80y multicolored	1.40	.90
Z290	ZA280	80y multicolored	1.40	.90
Z291	ZA281	80y multicolored	1.40	.90
a.	Strip of 4, #Z288-Z291		6.00	6.00
b.	Souvenir sheet, #Z288-Z291			
	Nos. Z285-Z291 (7)		9.80	6.30

ZA282   ZA283

ZA284   ZA285

ZA286   ZA287

ZA288   ZA289

**Opening of Shimanami Seaside
Highway (Hiroshima & Ehime)**

ZA290   ZA291

Designs: No. Z292, Onomichi-suido Channel. No. Z293, Kurushima-kaikyo Straits. No. Z294, Old, new Onomichi-oohashi Bridges. No. Z295, Kurushima-kaikyo-oohashi Bridge. No. Z296, Innoshima-oohashi Bridge. No. Z297, Kurushima-kaikyo-oohashi Bridge, diff. No. Z298, Ikuchibashi Bridge. No. Z299,

---

Hakatabashi, Ooshima-oohashi Bridges. No. Z300, Tatara-oohashi Bridge. No. Z301, Oomishimabashi Bridge.

	1999, Apr. 26	Photo.	Perf. 13½	
Z292	ZA282	80y multicolored	1.40	.90
Z293	ZA283	80y multicolored	1.40	.90
Z294	ZA284	80y multicolored	1.40	.90
Z295	ZA285	80y multicolored	1.40	.90
Z296	ZA286	80y multicolored	1.40	.90
Z297	ZA287	80y multicolored	1.40	.90
Z298	ZA288	80y multicolored	1.40	.90
Z299	ZA289	80y multicolored	1.40	.90
Z300	ZA290	80y multicolored	1.40	.90
Z301	ZA291	80y multicolored	1.40	.90
a.	Block of 10, #Z292-Z301		15.00	15.00
b.	Sheet of 8, # Z294-Z301		12.00	12.00

Flora (Hokkaido) Type of 1991 and

**Southern Kii Peninsula
(Wakayama) — ZA292**

Designs: No. Z302, Nachi-no-taki Falls. No. Z303, Engetsutou Island.

	1999, Apr. 28	Photo.	Perf. 13½	
Z302		80y multicolored	1.40	.90
Z303		80y multicolored	1.40	.90
a.	ZA292 Pair, #Z302-Z303		3.00	3.00
b.	Pane, 5 #Z303a		15.00	
		Perf. 13		
Z304	ZA97	80y Lily bell	1.40	.90
Z305	ZA98	80y Lilac	1.40	.90
Z306	ZA99	80y Daylily	1.40	.90
Z307	ZA100	80y Rowanberry	1.40	.90
a.	Strip of 4, #Z304-Z307		6.00	6.00

Sendai Tanabata
Festival (Miyagi)
ZA294

Souma Nomaoi
Festival
(Fukushima)
ZA295

	1999, May 14	Photo.	Perf. 13½	
Z310	ZA294	80y multicolored	1.40	.90
Z311	ZA295	80y multicolored	1.40	.90
a.	Pair, #Z310-Z311		3.00	3.00
b.	Pane, 5 #Z311a		15.00	

Ryukyu Dance
(Okinawa) — ZA296

	1999, May 14			
Z312	ZA296	80y multicolored	1.40	.90
a.	Pane of 10		15.00	

ZA297

**Northern Paradise
(Hokkaido)
ZA298**

	1999, May 25			
Z313	ZA297	50y Lavender field	.90	.50
Z314	ZA298	80y Wheat field	1.40	.90

**Kurashiki
Sightseeing District
(Okayama) — ZA299**

	1999, May 25	Photo.	Perf. 13½	
Z316	ZA299	80y multicolored	1.40	.90
a.	Pane of 10		15.00	

Shirone Big Kite Battle (Niigata)

ZA300   ZA301

	1999, June 1	Litho.	Perf. 13½	
Z317	ZA300	80y multicolored	1.40	.90
Z318	ZA301	80y multicolored	1.40	.90
a.	#Z317-Z318		3.00	3.00
b.	Pane, 5 #Z318a		15.00	

Noto Kiriko Festival
(Ishikawa) — ZA302

	1999, June 11			
Z319	ZA302	80y multicolored	1.40	.90
a.	Pane of 10		15.00	

Hokkaido Types of 1992-93

	1999, June 25	Photo.	Perf. 13½	
Z320	ZA119	80y Arctic fox	1.40	.90
		Litho.		
Z321	ZA134	80y Largha seals	1.40	.90

ZA303

Tokyo: No. Z323, morning glories. No. Z324, starburst fireworks over Sumida River. No. Z325, flower burst fireworks.

	1999, July 1	Photo.	Perf. 13½	
Z323		80y multicolored	1.40	.90
Z324		80y multicolored	1.40	.90
Z325		80y multicolored	1.40	.90
a.	ZA303 Block of 3, #Z323-Z325		4.50	4.50
b.	Souv. sheet of 2, #Z324-Z325		3.00	3.00

**Hakata Gion
Yamagasa Festival
(Fukuoka) — ZA306**

1999, July 1   Litho.
Z326 ZA306 80y multicolored   1.40   .90
a.   Pane of 10   15.00

ZA307   ZA308

ZA309   ZA310

Five Fuji Lakes (Yamanashi) ZA311

1999, July 1
Z327 ZA307 80y Yamanakako   1.40   .90
Z328 ZA308 80y Kawaguchiko   1.40   .90
Z329 ZA309 80y Saiko   1.40   .90
Z330 ZA310 80y Shoujiko   1.40   .90
Z331 ZA311 80y Motosuko   1.40   .90
a.   Strip of 5, #Z327-Z331   7.70   7.50
b.   Pane, 2 #Z331a   15.00

Inns of Tsumago, Magome Types of 1990
Photo. & Engr.
1999, July 16   Perf. 13
Z332 ZA71 80y like #Z71   1.40   .90
Z333 ZA72 80y like #Z72   1.40   .90
a.   Pair, #Z332-Z333   3.00   3.00

ZA312

Toki (Japanese Crested Ibis) (Niigata) ZA313

1999, July 16   Litho.   Perf. 13½
Z334 ZA312 80y Youyou, Yangyang   1.40   .90
Z335 ZA313 80y Kin   1.40   .90
a.   Pair, #Z334-Z335   3.00   3.00
b.   Pane, 5 #Z335a   15.00

ZA314

Design: Amanohashidate sandbar, Miyatsu Bay (Kyoto).

1999, July 16
Z336 ZA314 80y multicolored   1.40   .90

ZA315

Design: Ooga lotus (Chiba).

1999, July 16
Z337 ZA315 80y multicolored   1.40   .90
a.   Pane of 10   15.00

ZA316   ZA317

ZA318   ZA319

Birds (Hokkaido): No. Z338, Steller's sea-eagle. No. Z339, Tufted puffin. No. Z340, Blakiston's fish owl. No. Z341, Red-crowned crane.

1999, July 23   Photo.   Perf. 13½
Z338 ZA316 50y multicolored   .90   .50
Z339 ZA317 50y multicolored   .90   .50
Z340 ZA318 50y multicolored   .90   .50
Z341 ZA319 50y multicolored   .90   .50
a.   Strip of 4, #Z337-Z340   4.00   4.00

Hill on Ie Island, Sabani Boat (Okinawa) — ZA320

1999, July 23   Litho.   Perf. 13¼
Z343 ZA320 80y multicolored   1.40   .90
a.   Pane of 10   15.00

National Treasures (Wakayama) — ZA321

No. Z344, Kouyasan, Buddhist monastic complex. No. Z345, Natl. treasure, Kongaradouji.

1999, July 26   Perf. 13½
Z344   80y multicolored   1.40   .90
Z345   80y multicolored   1.40   .90
a.   ZA321 Pair, #Z344-Z345   3.00   3.00
b.   Pane, 5 #Z345a   15.00

Autumn Bellflowers (Iwate) — ZA323

1999, July 30
Z346 ZA323 50y multicolored   .90   .50
a.   Pane of 10   9.50

Shimizu Port, Cent. (Shizuoka) ZA324   Fishing Boat (Kumamoto) ZA325

1999, Aug. 2   Litho.   Perf. 13¼
Z347 ZA324 80y multi   1.40   .90
a.   Pane of 10   15.00
Z348 ZA325 80y multi   1.40   .90
a.   Pane of 10   15.00

Ritsurin Park (Kagawa) — ZA326

1999, Aug. 2   Perf. 13¼
Z349 ZA326 80y multi   1.40   .90
a.   Pane of 10   15.00

Artificial Island, Dejima (Nagasaki) ZA327

1999, Sept. 1   Photo.
Z350 ZA327 80y multi   1.40   .90
a.   Pane of 10   15.00

Yoritomo Minamotono (1174-99), Shogun (Kanagawa) ZA328

1999, Sept. 2   Litho.
Z351 ZA328 80y multi   1.40   .90
a.   Pane of 10   15.00

Shirakami Mountains (Aomori) ZA329

1999, Sept. 6
Z352 ZA329 80y multi   1.40   .90
a.   Pane of 10   15.00

Gassho-zukuri Farmhouses and Kokiriko Dance (Toyama) — ZA330

1999, Sept. 14   Photo.
Z353 ZA330 80y multi   1.40   .90

Corn (Hokkaido) ZA331   Potatoes (Hokkaido) ZA332

Asparagus (Hokkaido) ZA333   Muskmelon (Hokkaido) ZA334

1999, Sept. 17   Litho.
Z354 ZA331 50y multi   .90   .50
Z355 ZA332 50y multi   .90   .50
Z356 ZA333 50y multi   .90   .50
Z357 ZA334 50y multi   .90   .50
a.   Strip, #Z354-Z357   4.00   4.00

(Gumma) — ZA335

1999, Sept. 17   Perf. 13¼
Z358 ZA335 80y multi   1.40   .90
a.   Pane of 10   15.00

Iwajuku Paleolithic Site Excavations, 50th anniv.

(Osaka) — ZA336

1999, Sept. 27
Z359 ZA336 80y multi   1.40   .90

23rd Rhythmic Gymnastics World Championships.

Nihonmatsu Chrysanthemum Exhibition (Fukushima) ZA337

1999, Oct. 1
Z360 ZA337 80y multi   1.40   .90

Town of Obi (Miyazaki) — ZA338

Designs: No. Z361, Taihei dance, front gate of Obi Castle. No. Z362, Shintokudou School, Komura Jutarou (1855-1911).

1999, Oct. 1   *Perf. 13¼*

Z361	80y multi	1.40	.90
Z362	80y multi	1.40	.90
a.	ZA338 Pair, #Z361-Z362	3.00	3.00
b.	Pane, 5 #Z362a	15.00	

Nagano Monkey Type of 1989

1999, Oct. 13   Photo.   *Perf. 12¾x13*

Z363	ZA1 80y multi	1.50	.75

(Aichi) — ZA340

No. Z364, Ichiei Sato. No. Z365, "Beautiful Yamato."

1999, Oct. 13   Photo.   *Perf. 13¼*

Z364	80y multi	1.40	.90
Z365	80y multi	1.40	.90
a.	ZA340 Pair, #Z364-Z365	3.00	3.00
b.	Pane, 5 #Z365a	15.00	

ZA342

No. Z366, Hagi (Yamaguchi). No. Z367, Tsuwano (Shimane).

1999, Oct. 13

Z366	80y multi	1.40	.90
Z367	80y multi	1.40	.90
a.	ZA342 Vert. pair, #Z366-Z367	3.00	3.00
b.	Pane, 5 #Z367a	15.00	

(Nara) — ZA344

No. Z368, Yamato Three Mountains. No. Z369, Ishibutai Tomb.

1999, Oct. 28   Litho.   *Perf. 13¼*

Z368	80y multi	1.40	.90
Z369	80y multi	1.40	.90
a.	ZA344 Pair, #Z368-Z369	3.00	3.00
b.	Pane, 5 #Z369a	15.00	

Shikina-en Garden (Okinawa) — ZA346

1999, Oct. 28

Z370	50y multi	.90	.50
Z371	50y multi	.90	.50
a.	ZA346 Pair, #Z370-Z371	1.90	1.90
b.	Pane, 5 #Z371a	9.50	

(Fukui) — ZA348

No. Z372, Echizen Crab. No. Z373, Tojinbou Cliff.

1999, Nov. 4

Z372	80y multi	1.40	.90
Z373	80y multi	1.40	.90
a.	ZA348 Pair, #Z372-Z373	3.00	3.00
b.	Pane, 5 #Z373a	15.00	

Children in Santa's Sleigh (Hokkaido) ZA350

Yoshinogari Dig Site (Saga) ZA351

1999, Nov. 11   *Perf. 13¼*

Z374	ZA350 80y multi	1.40	.90
a.	Pane of 10	15.00	
Z375	ZA351 80y multi	1.40	.90
a.	Pane of 10	15.00	

(Kochi) — ZA352

No. Z376, Katsura Beach. No. Z377, Sakamoto Ryoma.

1999, Nov. 15   Photo.

Z376	80y multi	1.40	.90
Z377	80y multi	1.40	.90
a.	ZA352 Pair, #Z376-Z377	3.00	3.00
b.	Pane, 5 #Z377a	15.00	

For self-adhesives, see Nos. 3189H-3189I.

Samurai House, Kakunodate (Akita) — ZA354

1999, Dec. 17   Litho.   *Perf. 13¼*

Z378	ZA354 80y multi	1.40	.90
a.	Pane of 10	15.00	

ZA355

ZA356

ZA357

ZA358

Tokyo Scenes (Tokyo) — ZA359

2000, Jan. 12   Litho.   *Perf. 13¼*

Z379	ZA355 50y multi	.90	.50
Z380	ZA356 50y multi	.90	.50
Z381	ZA357 50y multi	.90	.50
Z382	ZA358 50y multi	.90	.50
Z383	ZA359 50y multi	.90	.50
a.	Horiz. strip, #Z379-Z383	4.75	4.75
b.	Pane, 2 each #Z379-Z383	9.50	

ZA360   ZA361

ZA362   ZA363
Snow World (Hokkaido)

2000, Feb. 7   Photo.

Z384	ZA360 80y multi	1.40	.90
Z385	ZA361 80y multi	1.40	.90
Z386	ZA362 80y multi	1.40	.90
Z387	ZA363 80y multi	1.40	.90
a.	Strip, #Z384-Z387	6.00	6.00

ZA364

Japan Flora 2000 (Hyogo) — ZA365

2000, Mar. 1   Litho.   *Perf. 13¼*

Z388	ZA364 50y multi	.90	.50
Z389	ZA365 80y multi	1.40	.90
a.	Pane, 5 each #Z388-Z389	12.50	

ZA366   ZA367

ZA368   ZA369
Korakuen Gardens, 300th Anniv.
(Okayama)

2000, Mar. 2   Photo.

Z390	ZA366 80y multi	1.40	.70
Z391	ZA367 80y multi	1.40	.70
Z392	ZA368 80y multi	1.40	.70
Z393	ZA369 80y multi	1.40	.70
a.	Strip, #Z390-Z393	6.00	6.00
b.	Souvenir sheet, #Z390-Z393	6.00	6.00

Cherry Blossoms in Takato (Nagano) — ZA370

2000, Mar. 3

Z394	ZA370 80y multi	1.40	.90
a.	Pane of 10	15.00	

Dyed Fabrics (Okinawa) ZA371

2000, Mar. 17   Litho.

Z395	ZA371 50y multi	.90	.50
a.	Pane of 10	9.50	

Azumino (Nagano) — ZA372

2000, Mar. 23   Photo.

Z396	ZA372 80y multi	1.40	.90
a.	Pane of 10	15.00	

Cherry Blossoms (Aomori) ZA373

Cherry Blossoms (Fukushima) ZA374

Cherry Blossoms
(Iwate) — ZA375

Cherry Blossoms
(Miyagi) — ZA376

Cherry Blossoms
(Akita) — ZA377

Cherry Blossoms
(Yamagata)
ZA378

2000, Apr. 3   **Litho.**

Z397	ZA373 80y multi	1.40	.90
a.	Pair, #Z397, Z399	3.00	3.00
b.	Pair, #Z397, Z400	3.00	3.00
c.	Pair, #Z397, Z401	3.00	3.00
d.	Pair, #Z397, Z402	3.00	3.00
Z398	ZA374 80y multi	1.40	.90
a.	Pair, #Z398, Z399	3.00	3.00
b.	Pair, #Z398, Z400	3.00	3.00
c.	Pair, #Z398, Z401	3.00	3.00
d.	Pair, #Z398, Z402	3.00	3.00
Z399	ZA375 80y multi	1.40	.90
Z400	ZA376 80y multi	1.40	.90
Z401	ZA377 80y multi	1.40	.90
Z402	ZA378 80y multi	1.40	.90
a.	Vert. strip, #Z399-Z402	6.00	6.00
	Nos. Z397-Z402 (6)	8.40	5.40

Printed in sheets containing one column of
four stamps of Nos. Z397 and Z398 at left and
right respectively with 3 No. Z402a between.

Tulips (Toyama) — ZA379

2000, Apr. 28   **Photo.**   **Perf. 13¼**

Z403	50y multi	.90	.50
Z404	80y multi	1.40	.90
a.	ZA379 Pair, #Z403-Z404	2.50	2.50
b.	Pane, 5 #Z404a	12.50	

Uwajima Castle
(Ehime) — ZA381

2000, Apr. 28   **Perf. 13½x13¼**

Z405	ZA381 80y multi	1.40	.90

New Urban Center (Saitama) — ZA382

2000, May 1   **Perf. 13¼**

Z406	50y multi	.90	.50
Z407	50y multi	.90	.50
a.	ZA382 Pair, #Z406-Z407	1.90	1.90
b.	Pane, 5 #Z407a	9.50	

Flowers of the Chugoku Region

(Tottori)
ZA384

(Shimane)
ZA385

(Okayama)
ZA386

(Hiroshima)
ZA387

(Yamaguchi)
ZA388

2000, May 1   **Litho.**   **Perf. 13¼**

Z408	ZA384 50y multi	.90	.50
Z409	ZA385 50y multi	.90	.50
Z410	ZA386 50y multi	.90	.50
Z411	ZA387 50y multi	.90	.50
Z412	ZA388 50y multi	.90	.50
a.	Vert. strip, #Z408-Z412	4.75	4.75
b.	Pane, 2# Z412a	9.50	

Cosmos (Tokyo)
ZA389

Roses (Tokyo)
ZA390

Bird of Paradise
Flowers (Tokyo)
ZA391

Sasanquas
(Tokyo)
ZA392

Freesias
(Tokyo) — ZA393

2000, June 1   **Photo.**   **Perf. 13¼**

Z413	ZA389 50y multi	.90	.50
Z414	ZA390 50y multi	.90	.50
Z415	ZA391 50y multi	.90	.50
Z416	ZA392 50y multi	.90	.50
Z417	ZA393 50y multi	.90	.50
a.	Vert. strip of 5, #Z413-Z417	4.75	4.75
b.	Pane, 2 #Z417a	9.50	

Shonan Hiratsuka Tanabata Festival
(Kanagawa) — ZA394

2000, June 2   **Litho.**

Z418	50y multi	.90	.50
Z419	50y multi	.90	.50
a.	ZA394 Pair, #Z418-Z419	1.90	1.90
b.	Pane, 5 #Z419a	9.50	

Bankoku Shinryokan
(Okinawa) — ZA396

2000, June 21   **Photo.**   **Perf. 13¼**

Z420	ZA396 80y multi	1.40	.90
a.	Pane of 10	15.00	

World Performing
Arts Festival
(Osaka) — ZA397

2000, June 28   **Litho.**

Z421	ZA397 80y multi	1.40	.90
a.	Pane of 10	15.00	

Kujuku Islands
(Akita) — ZA398

2000, July 7   **Photo.**

Z422	ZA398 80y multi	1.40	.90
a.	Pane of 10	15.00	

Potato Field (Hokkaido) — ZA399

Hillside and Hay Rolls
(Hokkaido) — ZA400

2000, July 19

Z423	50y Flowers, barn	.90	.50
Z424	50y Barn, silo	.90	.50
a.	ZA399 Pair, #Z423-Z424	1.90	1.90

Z425	80y + 20y Hayrolls, houses	1.90	1.00
Z426	80y + 20y Hayrolls, barns	1.90	1.00
a.	ZA400 Pair, #Z425-Z426	4.00	4.00
	Nos. Z423-Z426 (4)	5.60	3.00

Surtax on Nos. Z425-Z426 for refugees of
eruption of Mt. Usu.

Awa-odori
(Tokushima)
ZA401

2000, July 31   **Litho.**

Z427	ZA401 80y multi	1.40	.90
a.	Pane of 10	15.00	

Golden Hall of
Chusonji Temple
(Iwate) — ZA402

2000, Aug. 1

Z428	ZA402 80y multi	1.40	.90
a.	Pane of 10	15.00	

Hakata Doll
(Fukuoka) — ZA403

2000, Aug. 2

Z429	ZA403 80y multi	1.40	.90
a.	Pane of 10	15.00	

55th Natl. Athletic
Meet
(Toyama) — ZA404

2000, Sept. 1   **Photo.**

Z430	ZA404 50y multi	.90	.50
a.	Pane of 10	9.50	

25th World Parachuting
Championships (Mie) — ZA405

2000, Sept. 13

Z431	80y 2 skydivers	1.40	.90
Z432	80y 3 skydivers	1.40	.90
a.	ZA405 Pair, #Z431-Z432	3.00	3.00
b.	Pane, 5 #Z432a	15.00	

Friendly Tokyo
(Tokyo) — ZA406

2000, Sept. 29 Litho.
Z433 ZA406 80y multi 1.40 .90
a. Pane of 10 15.00

Iwakuni Kintaikyo Bridge (Yamaguchi) ZA407

2000, Oct. 10
Z434 ZA407 80y multi 1.40 .90
a. Pane of 10 15.00

Intl. Wheelchair Marathon (Oita) — ZA408

2000, Oct. 11
Z435 ZA408 80y multi 1.40 .90
a. Pane of 10 15.00

Willow and Frog (Aichi) — ZA409

2000, Oct. 20 Photo.
Z436 ZA409 80y multi 1.40 .90
a. Pane of 10 15.00

ZA410   ZA411

ZA412   ZA413
Four Seasons (Kyoto)

2000, Oct. 20 Litho.
Z437 ZA410 80y multi 1.40 .90
Z438 ZA411 80y multi 1.40 .90
a. Pane, 5 each #Z437-Z438 15.00
Z439 ZA412 80y multi 1.40 .90
Z440 ZA413 80y multi 1.40 .90
a. Horiz. strip, #Z437-Z440 6.00 3.50
b. Pane, 5 each #Z439-Z440 15.00

Odawarajo Castle (Kanagawa) — ZA414

2000, Oct. 27
Z441 50y multi .90 .50
Z442 50y multi .90 .50
a. ZA414 Pair, #Z441-Z442 1.90 1.90
b. Pane, 5 #Z442a 9.50

Intl. Balloon Festival (Saga) — ZA415

2000, Nov. 1 Litho. Perf. 13¼
Z443 ZA415 80y multi 1.40 .90
a. Pane of 10 15.00

Chichibu Night Festival (Saitama) — ZA416

2000, Nov. 1 Photo.
Z444 80y Yatai, fireworks 1.40 .90
Z445 80y Kasahoko 1.40 .90
a. ZA416 Pair, #Z444-Z445 3.00 3.00
b. Pane, 5 #Z445a 15.00

Scenic Izu (Shizuoka) — ZA417

2000, Nov. 29 Litho.
Z446 50y Garden .90 .50
Z447 50y Waterfall .90 .50
a. ZA417 Pair, #Z446-Z447 1.90 1.90
b. Pane, 5 #Z447a 9.50

Hata Festival, Kohata (Fukushima) ZA418

2000, Dec. 1 Photo.
Z448 ZA418 80y multi 1.40 .90
a. Pane of 10 15.00

Sekino'o-taki Falls and Kirishima (Miyazaki) — ZA419

2000, Dec. 12 Photo.
Z449 80y Waterfall 1.40 .90
Z450 80y Mountain 1.40 .90
a. ZA419 Pair, #Z449-Z450 3.00 3.00
b. Pane, 5 #Z450a 15.00

Megane-bashi Bridge (Gunma) — ZA420

2000, Dec. 15 Litho.
Z451 50y Bridge .90 .50
Z452 50y Transformer substation .90 .50
a. ZA420 Pair, #Z451-Z452 1.90 1.90

Song "Shinano-no Kuni" (Nagano) — ZA421

2000, Dec. 15 Photo.
Z453 50y Denom. at L .90 .50
Z454 50y Denom. at R .90 .50
a. ZA421 Pair, #Z453-Z454 1.90 1.90

Kobe Earthquake Restoration (Hyogo) — ZA422

2001, Jan. 17 Photo. Perf. 13¼
Z455 50y Pandas .90 .50
Z456 80y Kobe Port 1.40 .90
a. ZA422 Pair, #Z455-Z456 2.50 2.50
b. Pane, 5 #Z456a 12.50

Ooe Kouwaka-mai (Fukuoka) — ZA423

2001, Jan. 19 Litho.
Z457 ZA423 80y multi 1.40 .90
a. Pane of 10 15.00

Kairakuen Garden (Ibaraki) — ZA424

Designs: No. Z458, Koubuntei Pavilion, tree blossoms. No. Z459, Path, Chumon Gate. No. Z460, Togyokusen Spring, path. No. Z461, Koubuntei Pavilion in winter.

2001, Feb. 1 Photo.
Z458 50y multi .90 .50
Z459 50y multi .90 .50
Z460 50y multi .90 .50
Z461 50y multi .90 .50
a. ZA424 Horiz. strip, #Z458-Z461 4.00 4.00
b. Souvenir sheet, #Z461a 4.00 4.00

Ezo Sable (Hokkaido) — ZA425

2001, Feb. 6 Litho.
Z462 ZA425 80y multi 1.40 .90
a. Pane of 10 15.00
b. Horiz. pair, #Z321, Z462 3.00 3.00
Issued: No. Z462b, Sept. 2007.

Kochi Castle and Sunday Market (Kochi) — ZA426

2001, Mar. 1 Photo. Perf. 13¼
Z463 80y multi 1.40 .90
Z464 80y multi 1.40 .90
a. ZA426 Pair, #Z463-Z464 3.00 3.00
b. Pane, 5 #Z464a 15.00

Takarazuka Revue Dancers (Hyogo) — ZA427   Violets (Hyogo) — ZA428

2001, Mar. 21 Litho.
Z465 ZA427 80y multi 1.40 .90
Z466 ZA428 80y multi 1.40 .90
a. Pane, 5 each #Z465-Z466 15.00

Matsue Castle and Meimei-an Teahouse (Shimane) — ZA429

2001, Mar. 21
Z467 80y multi 1.40 .90
Z468 80y multi 1.40 .90
a. ZA429 Pair, #Z467-Z468 3.00 3.00
b. Pane, 5 #Z468a 15.00

Grapes, Jewelry and Mt. Fuji (Yamanashi) ZA430

2001, Mar. 30 Photo.
Z469 ZA430 80y multi 1.40 .90
a. Pane of 10 15.00

Sports Paradise (Osaka) — ZA431

Designs: No. Z470, Thunder god (red) playing table tennis. No. Z471, Wing god (green) playing table tennis. No. Z472, Bowling. No. Z473, Taekwondo.

2001, Apr. 3

Z470	50y multi	.90	.50
Z471	50y multi	.90	.50
Z472	50y multi	.90	.50
Z473	50y multi	.90	.50
a.	ZA431 Horiz. strip, #Z470-Z473	4.00	4.00

Beautiful Fukushima Future Expo (Fukushima) ZA432

2001, Apr. 10

Z474	ZA432 80y multi	1.40	.90
a.	Pane of 10	15.00	

Cherry Blossoms at Takada Castle (Niigata) — ZA433

2001, Apr. 10   Litho.

Z475	ZA433 80y multi	1.40	.90
a.	Pane of 10	15.00	

Hamamatsu Festival (Shizuoka) — ZA434

Designs: No. Z476, Palace Festival. No. Z477, Kite fighting.

2001, May 1

Z476	80y multi	1.40	.90
Z477	80y multi	1.40	.90
a.	ZA434 Pair, #Z476-Z477	3.00	3.00
b.	Pane, 5 #Z477a	15.00	

Ashikaga School Gate (Tochigi) ZA435   Ashikaga School (Tochigi) ZA436

2001, May 11   Photo.

Z478	ZA435 80y multi	1.40	.90
Z479	ZA436 50y multi	1.40	.90
a.	Pane, 5 each #Z478-Z479	15.00	

Natl. Afforestation Campaign (Yamanashi) ZA437

2001, May 18

Z480	ZA437 50y multi	.90	.50
a.	Pane of 10	9.50	

Sendai, 400th Anniv. (Miyagi) — ZA438

2001, May 18   Litho.

Z481	ZA438 80y multi	1.40	.90
a.	Pane of 10	15.00	

Zenkoji Temple and Mt. Iizunayama (Nagano) — ZA439

2001, May 23

Z482	80y multi	1.40	.90
Z483	80y multi	1.40	.90
a.	ZA439 Pair, #Z482-Z483	3.00	3.00
b.	Pane, 5 #Z483a	15.00	

Ducks (Yamaguchi) ZA440   Kirara Band, Japan Expo Site (Yamaguchi) ZA441

2001, May 25

Z484	ZA440 50y multi	.90	.50
Z485	ZA441 80y multi	1.40	.90
a.	Pane, 5 each #Z484-Z485	12.25	

Cherry Blossoms (Tokyo) — ZA442   Hydrangea (Tokyo) — ZA443

Salvia (Tokyo) — ZA444   Chrysanthemums (Tokyo) — ZA445

Camellias (Tokyo) — ZA446

2001, June 1   Photo.

Z486	ZA442 50y multi	.90	.50
Z487	ZA443 50y multi	.90	.50
Z488	ZA444 50y multi	.90	.50
Z489	ZA445 50y multi	.90	.50

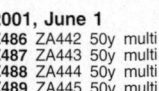

Z490	ZA446 50y multi	.90	.50
a.	Vert. strip, #Z486-Z490	4.75	4.75
b.	Pane, 2 #Z490a	9.50	

ZA447

Sites (Tottori) — ZA448

Designs: No. Z491, Snow crab, Uradome Coast. No. Z492, Tottori Dunes. No. Z493, Paper Hina dolls in river. No. Z494, Mt. Daisen. No. Z495, Nageiredo Hall. No. Z496, Mukibanda Yayoi Period.
Illustration ZA447 reduced.

2001, June 1

Z491	50y multi	.90	.50
Z492	50y multi	.90	.50
Z493	50y multi	.90	.50
Z494	50y multi	.90	.50
a.	ZA447 Horiz. strip, #Z491-Z494	4.00	4.00
Z495	80y multi	1.40	.90
Z496	80y multi	1.40	.90
a.	ZA448 Horiz. pair, #Z495-Z496	3.00	3.00
	Nos. Z491-Z496 (6)	6.40	3.80

Prosperity in Kaga (Ishikawa) — ZA449

2001, June 4   Litho.

Z497	ZA449 80y multi	1.40	.90
a.	Pane of 10	15.00	

Poppies (Hokkaido) ZA450   Calanthe (Hokkaido) ZA451

2001, June 22   Litho.

Z498	ZA450 50y multi	.90	.50
a.	Pane of 10	9.50	
Z499	ZA451 50y multi	.90	.50
a.	Pane of 10	9.50	

Cornerstone of Peace (Okinawa) — ZA452

2001, June 22   Photo.

Z500	ZA452 80y multi	1.40	.90

Peach Blossoms, Shirane-sanzan Mountains (Yamanashi) ZA453   Irises, Mt. Kitadake (Yamanashi) ZA454

Horses, Mt. Yatsugatake (Yamanashi) ZA455   Oshino-hakkai Pond (Yamanashi) ZA456

Cherry Blossoms, Minobu (Yamanashi) ZA457

2001, July 2

Z501	ZA453 50y multi	.90	.50
Z502	ZA454 50y multi	.90	.50
Z503	ZA455 50y multi	.90	.50
Z504	ZA456 50y multi	.90	.50
Z505	ZA457 50y multi	.90	.50
a.	Vert. strip, #Z501-Z505	4.75	4.75
b.	Pane, 2 #Z505a	9.50	

Automobile City, Toyota (Aichi) — ZA458

Designs: No. Z506, Toyota-oohashi Bridge. No. Z507, Toyota Stadium.

2001, July 2

Z506	50y multi	.90	.50
Z507	50y multi	.90	.50
a.	ZA458 Pair, #Z506-Z507	1.90	1.90
b.	Pane, 5 #Z507a	9.50	

Kitakyushu Expo Festival (Fukuoka) — ZA459

2001, July 4

Z508	ZA459 80y multi	1.40	.90
a.	Pane of 10	15.00	

World Trade Organization, 14th General Assembly (Osaka) — ZA460

Designs: No. Z509, Namdaemun, Seoul, and Doton-bori, Osaka. No. Z510, Bunraku, Nong-ak.

2001, July 6		**Litho.**	
Z509	80y multi	1.40	.90
Z510	80y multi	1.40	.90
a.	ZA460 Pair, #Z509-Z510	3.00	3.00

Grand Fireworks of Nagaoka
(Niigata) — ZA461

2001, July 23			
Z511	50y yel & multi	.90	.50
Z512	50y pink & multi	.90	.50
a.	ZA461 Pair, #Z511-Z512	1.90	1.90
b.	Pane, 5 #Z512a	9.50	

Poplars
(Hokkaido)
ZA462

Statue, Sheep
(Hokkaido)
ZA463

2001, Sept. 3	**Litho.**	**Perf. 13¼**	
Z513	ZA462 80y multi	1.40	.90
Z514	ZA463 80y multi	1.40	.90
a.	Pane, 5 each #Z513-Z514	15.00	

56th Natl. Athletic
Meets
(Miyagi) — ZA464

2001, Sept. 7		**Photo.**	
Z515	ZA464 50y multi	.90	.50
a.	Pane of 10	9.50	

Matsuyama Castle, Masaoki Shiki
(1867-1902), Poet (Ehime) — ZA465

2001, Sept. 12			
Z516	50y Castle	.90	.50
Z517	50y Poet	.90	.50
a.	ZA465 Horiz. pair, #Z516-Z517	1.90	1.90

Ibi Traditions (Gifu) — ZA466

Designs: No. Z518, Tanigumi-Odori dance.
No. Z519, Train, persimmons.

2001, Sept. 28	**Photo.**	**Perf. 13¼**	
Z518	50y multi	.90	.50
Z519	50y multi	.90	.50
a.	ZA466 Horiz. pair, #Z518-Z519	1.90	1.90
b.	Pane, 5 #Z519a	9.50	

Kamakura Igloo
(Akita) — ZA467

2001, Oct. 1		**Litho.**	
Z520	ZA467 80y multi	1.40	.90
a.	Pane of 10	15.00	

9th Intl. Conference
on Lake
Conservation &
Management
(Shiga) — ZA468

2001, Oct. 1			
Z521	ZA468 50y multi	.90	.50
a.	Pane of 10	9.50	

World Indoor Cycling
Championships
(Kagoshima)
ZA469

2001, Oct. 1			
Z522	ZA469 80y multi	1.40	.90

Okuma Auditorium,
Waseda University
(Tokyo) — ZA470

2001, Oct. 19			
Z523	ZA470 80y multi	1.40	.90
a.	Pane of 10	15.00	

Wild Narcissi
(Fukui)
ZA471

Echizen Coast
and Wild
Narcissi (Fukui)
ZA472

2001, Nov. 6			
Z524	ZA471 50y multi	.90	.50
a.	Pane of 10	9.50	
Z525	ZA472 80y multi	1.40	.90
a.	Pane of 10	15.00	

Tokyo Millenalio
(Tokyo) — ZA473

2001, Dec. 3		**Photo.**	
Z526	ZA473 80y multi	1.40	.90
a.	Pane of 10	15.00	

Ezo Flying Squirrels
(Hokkaido) — ZA474

2002, Feb. 5			
Z527	ZA474 80y multi	1.40	.90

Scenes North of Hiroshima
(Hiroshima) — ZA475

Designs: No. Z528, Nukui Dam. No. Z529,
On-bashi Bridge.

2002, Feb. 22		**Litho.**	
Z528	80y multi	1.40	.90
Z529	80y multi	1.40	.90
a.	ZA475 Horiz. pair, #Z528-Z529	3.00	3.00

Azaleas (Wakayama)
ZA476

2002, Mar. 1	**Photo.**	**Perf. 13¼**	
Z530	ZA476 80y multi	1.40	.90

Glover Garden (Nagasaki) — ZA477

Designs: No. Z531, Houses, fountain, roses.
No. Z532, House, tulips.

2002, Mar. 1		**Litho.**	
Z531	50y multi	.90	.50
Z532	50y multi	.90	.50
a.	ZA477 Horiz. pair, #Z531-Z532	1.90	1.90

Cherry
Blossoms,
Hiikawa River
(Shimane)
ZA478

Cherry
Blossoms,
Bicchu-
Kokubunji
Temple
(Okayama)
ZA479

2002, Mar. 18			
Z533	ZA478 50y multi	.90	.50
Z534	ZA479 50y multi	.90	.50
a.	Horiz. pair, #Z533-Z534	1.90	1.90
b.	Pane, 5 #Z534a	9.50	—

Tangerine, Sata
Cape (Ehime)
ZA480

Citrus Fruit, Mt.
Tsurugisan
(Tokushima)
ZA481

Bayberry, Tengu
Highlands
(Kochi)
ZA482

Olives, Shodo
Island (Kagawa)
ZA483

2002, Mar. 20		**Photo.**	
Z535	ZA480 50y multi	.90	.50
Z536	ZA481 50y multi	.90	.50
Z537	ZA482 50y multi	.90	.50
Z538	ZA483 50y multi	.90	.50
a.	Horiz. strip of 4, #Z535-Z538	4.00	4.00

Flowers (Hokkaido) — ZA484

2002, Apr. 25		**Litho.**	
Z539	80y Tulips, windmills	1.40	.90
Z540	80y Sunflowers, field	1.40	.90
a.	ZA484 Horiz. pair, #Z539-Z540	3.00	3.00

54th Intl. Whaling
Commission
(Yamaguchi)
ZA485

2002, Apr. 25			
Z541	ZA485 80y multi	1.40	.90

Bonsai Village
(Saitama) — ZA486

2002, Apr. 26		**Photo.**	
Z542	ZA486 80y multi	1.40	.90

Yokohama (Kanagawa) — ZA487

Designs: No. Z543, Sailing ships. No. Z544,
Modern ship, skyline, woman.

2002, May 1			
Z543	50y multi	.90	.50
Z544	50y multi	.90	.50
a.	ZA487 Horiz. pair, #Z543-Z544	1.90	1.90
b.	Pane, 5 #Z544a	9.50	

Flowers (Niigata) — ZA488

Designs: No. Z545, Red camellias. No. Z546, Yellow daylilies. No. Z547, Purple and pink irises. No. Z548, Pink iwakagami flowers.

2002, May 1   **Litho.**
Z545	50y multi	.90	.50
Z546	50y multi	.90	.50
Z547	50y multi	.90	.50
Z548	50y multi	.90	.50
a.	ZA488 Horiz. strip of 4, #Z545-Z548	4.00	4.00

Natl. Afforestation Campaign (Yamagata) — ZA489

2002, May 31   **Photo.**
Z549	ZA489 50y multi	.90	.50
a.	Pane of 10	9.50	

Oze (Fukushima) — ZA490

Designs: No. Z550, Flowers, bare trees, walkway. No. Z551, Flowers, evergreens.

2002, June 28   **Litho.**
Z550	50y multi	.90	.50
Z551	50y multi	.90	.50
a.	ZA490 Horiz. pair, #Z550-Z551	1.90	1.90

Mt. Tanigawadake (Gunma) — ZA491

Mountains and: No. Z552, Rhododendrons. No. Z553, Trees in autumn.

2002, June 28
Z552	80y multi	1.40	.90
Z553	80y multi	1.40	.90
a.	ZA491 Horiz. pair, #Z552-Z553	3.00	3.00

Tokyo Fair and Market (Tokyo) — ZA492

Designs: No. Z554, Morning Glory Fair. No. Z555, Hozuki Fair.

2002, June 28   **Photo.**
Z554	80y multi	1.40	.90
Z555	80y multi	1.40	.90
a.	ZA492 Horiz. pair, #Z554-Z555	3.00	3.00

Alpine Flora (Ishikawa) — ZA493

2002, July 1   **Flower Color**
Z556	50y Purple	.90	.50
Z557	50y Brown	.90	.50
Z558	50y Bright pink	.90	.50
Z559	50y White	.90	.50
a.	ZA493 Horiz. strip of 4, #Z556-Z559	4.00	4.00

Gujou-odori Dance (Gifu) — ZA494

2002, July 1
Z560	ZA494 50y multi	.90	.50

85th Lions Club Intl. Convention (Osaka) — ZA495

2002, July 1
Z561	ZA495 80y multi	1.40	.90

23rd Asia-Pacific Scout Jamboree (Osaka) — ZA496

2002, July 15
Z562	ZA496 50y multi	.90	.50

Yachiyoza Theater (Kumamoto) — ZA497

2002, July 15   **Litho.**
Z563	ZA497 80y multi	1.40	.90

Hikan-zakura, Iejima (Okinawa) ZA498

Hibiscus, Kaichudouro Highway (Okinawa) ZA499

Bougainvillea, House in Tsuboya (Okinawa) ZA500

Lily, Higashihennazaki (Okinawa) ZA501

Seishika Flower, Seishika Bridge (Okinawa) — ZA502

2002, Aug. 23   **Photo.**   *Perf. 13¼*
Z564	ZA498 50y multi	.90	.50
Z565	ZA499 50y multi	.90	.50
Z566	ZA500 50y multi	.90	.50
Z567	ZA501 50y multi	.90	.50
Z568	ZA502 50y multi	.90	.50
a.	Vert. strip of 5, #Z564-Z568	4.75	4.75

Printed in sheets containing two No. Z568a.

Flora (Tokyo) — ZA503

Designs: No. Z569, Azalea (pink flower, blue denomination). No. Z570, Lily. No. Z571, Crape myrtle (pink flower and denomination). No. Z572, Ginkgo leaves.

2002, Sept. 2
Z569	50y multi	.90	.50
Z570	50y multi	.90	.50
Z571	50y multi	.90	.50
Z572	50y multi	.90	.50
a.	ZA503 Horiz. strip of 4, #Z569-Z572	4.00	4.00

57th Natl. Athletic Meet (Kochi) — ZA504

2002, Sept. 5
Z573	ZA504 50y multi	.90	.50

Iga-Ueno (Mie) — ZA505

Designs: No. Z574, Basho Matsuo, Iga-Ueno Castle. No. Z575, Iga-Ueno Castle, Haisei-den Hall.

2002, Sept. 10   **Litho.**
Z574	80y multi	1.40	.90
Z575	80y multi	1.40	.90
a.	ZA505 Horiz. pair, #Z574-Z575	3.00	3.00

Tohoku's Four Season Story (Aomori) — ZA506

2002, Oct. 23   **Photo.**   *Perf. 13¼*
Z576	ZA506 80y multi	1.40	.90

Fifth Winter Asian Games (Aomori) — ZA507

2003, Jan. 24   **Photo.**   *Perf. 13¼*
Z577	ZA507 50y multi	1.40	.90

Nobeoka, City of Noh Theater (Miyazaki) — ZA508

Designs: No. Z570, Actor on stage, audience. No. Z579, Actor with red kimono.

2003, Feb. 3
Z578	80y multi	1.40	.90
Z579	80y multi	1.40	.90
a.	ZA508 Horiz. pair, #Z578 Z570	3.00	3.00

Hokkaido Heritage (Hokkaido) — ZA509

2003, Feb. 5   **Photo.**   *Perf. 13¼*
Z580	80y Ainu design	1.40	.90
Z581	80y Lake Mashuko	1.40	.90
a.	ZA509 Horiz. pair, #Z580-Z581	3.00	3.00

Flora (Nagano) — ZA510

Designs: No. Z582, Dogtooth Violet (pink flowers) and mountain. No. Z583, Skunk Cabbage (white flower). No. Z584, Nikkoday Lily (yellow flower. No. Z585, Cosmos (white, pink and red flowers).

2003, Mar. 5   **Photo.**   *Perf. 13¼*
Z582	50y multi	.85	.50
Z583	50y multi	.85	.50
Z584	50y multi	.85	.50
Z585	50y multi	.85	.50
a.	ZA510 Horiz. strip of 4, #Z582-Z585	3.50	3.50

Kibitsu Shrine (Okayama) — ZA511

2003, Mar. 5
Z586	ZA511 80y multi	1.40	.90

Kompira-Ohshibai Theater (Kagawa) — ZA512

2003, Mar. 24   Litho.
Z587   ZA512 80y multi   1.40   .90

Imari-Arita Ceramics (Saga) — ZA513

2003, Apr. 10
Z588   ZA513 80y multi   1.40   .90

Kaneko Misuzu and Poem "Tairyo" (Yamaguchi) — ZA514

2003, Apr. 11   Photo.
Z589   80y Misuzu   1.40   .90
Z590   80y Poem   1.40   .90
   a.   ZA514 Horiz. pair, #Z589-Z590   2.80   2.80

Cormorant Fishing and Gifu Castle (Gifu) — ZA515

2003, May 1   Perf. 13¼
Z591   50y Fishermen   .85   .50
Z592   50y Castle   .85   .50
   a.   ZA515 Horiz. pair, #Z591-Z592   1.75   1.75

Traditional Events (Kyoto) — ZA516

Designs: No. Z593, Aoi-matsuri (wagon decorated with flowers). No. Z594, Gion-matsuri festival float (tower on wheels). No. Z595, Okuribi (fire on mountain). No. Z596, Jidai-matsuri (parade procession).

2003, May 1   Litho.
Z593   50y multi   .85   .50
Z594   50y multi   .85   .50
Z595   50y multi   .85   .50
Z596   50y multi   .85   .50
   a.   ZA516 Horiz. strip of 4, #Z593-Z596   3.50   3.50

Natl. Afforestation Campaign (Chiba) — ZA517

2003, May 16   Photo.
Z597   ZA517 50y multi   .85   .50

Mt. Tsukuba and Iris (Ibaraki) — ZA518

2003, May 20   Litho.
Z598   ZA518 80y multi   1.40   .90

Tsurugajou Castle, Persimmons (Fukushima) ZA519

2003, July 1   Photo.   Perf. 13¼
Z599   ZA519 80y multi   1.40   .90

Kyuya Fukada, Mountineer, Birth Cent. (Ishikawa) — ZA520

2003, July 1   Litho.
Z600   ZA520 80y multi   1.40   .90

Okinawa Urban Monorail (Okinawa) — ZA521

2003, Aug. 8
Z601   50y Shurijo Castle   .85   .50
Z602   50y Naha Airport   .85   .50
   a.   ZA521 Horiz. pair, #Z601-Z602   1.75   1.75

58th Natl. Athletics Meets (Shizuoka) — ZA522

2003, Aug. 29   Photo.
Z603   ZA522 50y multi   .85   .65

Sweet Briar (Tokyo) ZA523

Wisterias (Tokyo) ZA524

Irises (Tokyo) ZA525

Tea Blossoms (Tokyo) ZA526

2003, Sept. 1
Z604   ZA523 50y multi   .85   .50
Z605   ZA524 50y multi   .85   .50
Z606   ZA525 50y multi   .85   .50
Z607   ZA526 50y multi   .85   .50
   a.   Horiz. strip, #Z604-Z607   3.50   3.50

Chiyojo, Haiku Poet (Ishikawa) — ZA527

2003, Oct. 3   Litho.
Z608   80y Haiku text   1.40   .90
Z609   80y Chiyojo   1.40   .90
   a.   ZA527 Horiz. pair, #Z608-Z609   3.00   3.00

Yasujiro Ozu (1903-63), Film Director (Mie) — ZA528

2003, Oct. 23   Photo.
Z610   ZA528 80y multi   1.40   .90

Kiritappu Wetland and Wakka Primeval Garden (Hokkaido) — ZA529

2004, Feb. 5   Litho.   Perf. 13¼
Z611   80y Yellow flowers   1.40   .90
Z612   80y Orange flowers   1.40   .90
   a.   ZA529 Horiz. pair, #Z611-Z612   3.00   3.00

Kyushu Bullet Train (Kagoshima) ZA530

2004, Mar. 12   Photo.   Perf. 13¼
Z613   ZA530 50y multi   .90   .65

Flower Types of 1990

Designs as before.

2004, Mar. 19
Z614   ZA24 50y multi   .90   .50
Z615   ZA25 50y multi   .90   .50
Z616   ZA26 50y multi   .90   .50
Z617   ZA27 50y multi   .90   .50
Z618   ZA28 50y multi   .90   .50
Z619   ZA29 50y multi   .90   .50
   Nos. Z614-Z619 (6)   5.40   3.00

Zuiryuji Temple (Toyama) — ZA531

2004, Mar. 19   Litho.
Z620   ZA531 80y multi   1.40   .90

Hana-Kairou Flower Park (Tottori) — ZA532

2004, Mar. 23
Z621   ZA532 80y multi   1.40   .90

Gerbera (Shizuoka) ZA533

Carnation (Shizuoka) ZA534

Rose (Shizuoka) ZA535

Lisianthus (Shizuoka) ZA536

2004, Apr. 8
Z622   ZA533 80y multi   1.40   .90
Z623   ZA534 80y multi   1.40   .90
Z624   ZA535 80y multi   1.40   .90
Z625   ZA536 80y multi   1.40   .90
   a.   Horiz. strip of 4, #Z622-Z625   6.00   6.00

Pacific Flora 2004.

National Afforestation Campaign (Miyazaki) — ZA537

2004, Mar. 23   Photo.
Z626   ZA537 50y multi   .90   .50

Murouji's Five Story Pagoda (Nara) — ZA538

2004, Apr. 26
Z627   ZA538 80y multi   1.40   .90

Rotary International Convention (Osaka) — ZA539

2004, May 21
Z628   ZA539 80y multi   1.40   .90

Ice Breaker Garinko-go, Steller's Sea Eagle (Hokkaido) — ZA540

2004, May 28
Z629 ZA540 80y multi   1.40 .90

Kanto Festival Performer, Namahage (Akita) — ZA541

2004, June 1   Litho.
Z630   50y blue & multi   .90 .50
Z631   50y red & multi   .90 .50
  a.   ZA541 Horiz. pair, #Z630-Z631   1.80 1.80

Akita City, 400th anniv.

Magnolia (Tokyo) — ZA542   Azalea (Tokyo) — ZA543

Wildflower (Tokyo) — ZA544   Bush Clover (Tokyo) — ZA545

2004, June 1   Photo.
Z632 ZA542 50y multi   .90 .50
Z633 ZA543 50y multi   .90 .50
Z634 ZA544 50y multi   .90 .50
Z635 ZA545 50y multi   .90 .50
  a.   Horiz. strip of 4, #Z632-Z635   3.75 3.75

Roses and Buildings (Kanagawa) ZA546   Gold-banded Lily and Buildings (Kanagawa) ZA547

Wisteria and Enoshima Island (Kanagawa) ZA548   Hydrangea and Lake Ashinoko (Kanagawa) ZA549

2004, June 1
Z636 ZA546 50y multi   .90 .50
Z637 ZA547 50y multi   .90 .50
Z638 ZA548 50y multi   .90 .50
Z639 ZA549 50y multi   .90 .50
  a.   Horiz. strip of 4, #Z636-Z639   3.75 3.75

Daimyo Processions of Lord Takachika Mouri (Yamaguchi) — ZA550

2004, June 21   Litho.
Z640   80y red & multi   1.40 .90
Z641   80y green & multi   1.40 .90
  a.   ZA550 Horiz. pair, #Z640-Z641   3.00 3.00

Rose, Mt. Tsukubasan (Ibaraki) ZA551   Yashio-tsutsuji and Lake Chuzenjiko (Tochigi) ZA552

Renge-tsutsuji and Mt. Akagisan (Gunma) ZA553   Primrose and Tajimagahara Native Primrose Field (Saitama) ZA554

Rape Blossoms and Nojimazaki Lighthouse (Chiba) — ZA555

2004, June 23   Photo.
Z642 ZA551 50y multi   .90 .50
Z643 ZA552 50y multi   .90 .50
Z644 ZA553 50y multi   .90 .50
Z645 ZA554 50y multi   .90 .50
Z646 ZA555 50y multi   .90 .50
  a.   Vert. strip of 5, #Z642-Z646   4.75 4.75

Owara Dance (Toyama) — ZA556

Designs: No. Z647, Children. No. Z648, Dancers in pink kimonos. No. Z648, Dancers in black clothes. No. Z649, Dancers in blue kimonos.

2004, Aug. 20   Litho.
Z647   50y multi   .90 .50
Z648   50y multi   .90 .50
Z649   50y multi   .90 .50
Z650   50y multi   .90 .50
  a.   ZA556 Horiz. strip of 4, #Z647-Z650   3.75 3.75

59th National Athletic Meets (Saitama) — ZA557

2004, Sept. 10   Photo.   Perf. 13¼
Z651 ZA557 50y multi   .90 .50

Miniature Sheet

88 Temples (Shikoku) — ZA558

No. Z652: a, Ryozenji (Temple 1). b, Gokurakuji (Temple 2). c, Konsenji (Temple 3). d, Dainchiji (Temple 4). e, Tatsueji (Temple 19). f, Kakurinji (Temple 20). g, Tairyuji (Temple 21). h, Byoudouji (Temple 22). i, Iwamotoji (Temple 37). j, Kongoufukuji (Temple 38). k, Enkouji (Temple 39). l, Kanjizaiji (Temple 40). m, Nankoubou (Temple 55). n, Taizanji (Temple 56). o, Eifukuji (Temple 57). p, Senyuji (Temple 58) q, Shusshakaji (Temple 73). r, Kouyamaji (Temple 74). s, Zentsuji (Temple 75). t, Kouzouji (Temple 76).

2004, Nov. 5
Z652 ZA558 Sheet of 20   30.00 30.00
  a.-t.   80y Any single   1.40 .90

Temple numbers are found in the first group of small Japanese characters on each stamp. The numbers used are the same as those found under "China" in the Illustrated Identifier at the back of the book. The left and right Japanese characters in this first group of small characters, which ranges from 3 to 5 characters in length, are the same on each stamp. The characters between these two constant characters represent the temple number. As there is no character for zero, the number "20" will show the character for "2" (=) to the left of the character for "10" (+). Numbers 11-19 will have the unit's character to the right of the character for "10." Thus, the numbers "12" and "20" will have the same characters, just in a different order. Two-digit numbers beginning with 21 that are not divisible by 10 will be three characters long. Number 21, as an example, will show the characters for "2," "10," and "1" reading from left to right (= + -).

National Theater (Okinawa) — ZA559

2005, Jan. 21   Litho.   Perf. 13¼
Z653 ZA559 50y multi   .90 .50

Apple Blossoms (Nagano) ZA560   Renge Azalea (Nagano) ZA561

Lily of the Valley (Nagano) ZA562   Gentian (Nagano) ZA563

2005, Apr. 1   Litho.   Perf. 13¼
Z654 ZA560 50y multi   .90 .50
Z855 ZA561 50y multi   .90 .50
Z656 ZA562 50y multi   .90 .50
Z657 ZA563 50y multi   .90 .50
  a.   Horiz. strip of 4, #Z654-Z657   3.75 3.75

Tulip (Toyama, Ishikawa, Fukui) — ZA564   Hydrangea (Toyama, Ishikawa, Fukui) — ZA565

Rhododendron (Toyama, Ishikawa, Fukui) — ZA566   Lily (Toyama, Ishikawa, Fukui) — ZA567

2005, Apr. 1
Z658 ZA564 50y multi   .90 .50
Z659 ZA565 50y multi   .90 .50
Z660 ZA566 50y multi   .90 .50
Z661 ZA567 50y multi   .90 .50
  a.   Horiz. strip of 4, #Z658-Z661   3.75 3.75

Peace Memorial Park (Hiroshima) — ZA568

Designs: No. Z662, Birds, Cenotaph for Atomic Bomb Victims. No. Z663, Fountains, Hiroshima Peace Memorial Museum.

2005, Apr. 22
Z662   50y multi   .90 .50
Z663   50y multi   .90 .50
  a.   ZA568 Horiz. pair, #Z662-Z663   1.90 1.90

Sweetbrier (Hokkaido) ZA569   Lavender (Hokkaido) ZA570

Cowslip (Hokkaido) ZA571   Lily of the Valley (Hokkaido) ZA572

2005, Apr. 26

Z664	ZA569	50y multi	.90	.50
Z665	ZA570	50y multi	.90	.50
Z666	ZA571	50y multi	.90	.50
Z667	ZA572	50y multi	.90	.50
a.	Horiz. strip of 4, #Z664-Z667		3.75	3.75

Momordica Charantia (Okinawa) — ZA573

2005, May 6

Z668	ZA573	50y multi	.90	.50

Sunflower, Mt. Yatsugatake (Yamanashi) ZA574   Gentian, Mt. Kitadake (Yamanashi) ZA575

Evening Primrose, Mt. Fuji (Yamanashi) ZA576   Lady's Slipper, Mt. Fuji (Yamanashi) ZA577

2005, May 16   Litho.   Perf. 13¼

Z669	ZA574	80y multi	1.40	.90
Z670	ZA575	80y multi	1.40	.90
Z671	ZA576	80y multi	1.40	.90
Z672	ZA577	80y multi	1.40	.90
a.	Horiz. strip of 4, #Z669-Z672		6.00	6.00

National Afforestation Campaign (Ibaraki) ZA578

2005, May 27   Photo.

Z673	ZA578	50y multi	.90	.50

Orchid (Tokyo) — ZA579   Crinum (Tokyo) — ZA580

Kerria (Tokyo) — ZA581   Azalea (Tokyo) — ZA582

2005, June 1

Z674	ZA579	50y multi	.90	.50
Z675	ZA580	50y multi	.90	.50
Z676	ZA581	50y multi	.90	.50
Z677	ZA582	50y multi	.90	.50
a.	Horiz. strip of 4, #Z674-Z677		3.75	3.75

Une, Dazaifu-Tenmangu (Fukuoka) ZA583   Cherry Blossoms, Kanmon Bridge (Fukuoka) ZA584

Camphor Blossoms, Ariake Sea (Saga) ZA585   Azaleas, Mt. Fugendake (Nagasaki) ZA586

Tulips, Huis Ten Bosch (Nagasaki) ZA587   Gentians, Mt. Aso (Kumamoto) ZA588

Bungo-ume, Mt. Takasaki (Oita) ZA589   Crinums, Nichinan Beach (Miyazaki) ZA590

Azaleas, Kirishima Mountains (Kagoshima) ZA591   Hibiscus, Screw Pine (Kagoshima) ZA592

2005, June 1

Z678	ZA583	50y multi	.90	.50
Z679	ZA584	50y multi	.90	.50
Z680	ZA585	50y multi	.90	.50
Z681	ZA586	50y multi	.90	.50
Z682	ZA587	50y multi	.90	.50
Z683	ZA588	50y multi	.90	.50
Z684	ZA589	50y multi	.90	.50
Z685	ZA590	50y multi	.90	.50
Z686	ZA591	50y multi	.90	.50
Z687	ZA592	50y multi	.90	.50
a.	Block of 10, #Z678-Z687		9.50	9.50

Reintroduction of Oriental White Stork (Hyogo) — ZA593

2005, June 6   Litho.

Z688	ZA593	80y multi	1.40	.90

Azaleas, Tsutsujigaoka Park (Gunma) ZA594   Nikko Day Lily, Kirifuri Heights (Tochigi) ZA595

Sunflowers, Hana-hotaru (Chiba) ZA596   Bush Clover, Kairakuen Garden (Ibaraki) ZA597

Allspice, Mt. Bukosan (Saitama) — ZA598

2005, June 23

Z689	ZA594	50y multi	.90	.50
Z690	ZA595	50y multi	.90	.50
Z691	ZA596	50y multi	.90	.50
Z692	ZA597	50y multi	.90	.50
Z693	ZA598	50y multi	.90	.50
a.	Vert. strip of 5, #Z689-Z693		4.50	4.50

Apples (Aomori) ZA599   Apples (Iwate) ZA600

Cherries (Yamagata) ZA601   Peaches (Fukushima) ZA602

2005, June 28   Litho.

Z694	ZA599	50y multi	.90	.50
Z695	ZA600	50y multi	.90	.50
Z696	ZA601	50y multi	.90	.50
Z697	ZA602	50y multi	.90	.50
a.	Horiz. strip of 4, #Z694-Z697		3.75	3.75

Miniature Sheet

88 Temples (Shikoku) — ZA603

No. Z698: a, Zizouji (Temple 5). b, Anrakuji (Temple 6). c, Juurakuji (Temple 7). d, Kumadaniji (Temple 8). e, Yakuooji (Temple 23). f, Hotsumisakiji (Temple 24). g, Shinjouji (Temple 25). h, Kongouchouji (Temple 26). i, Ryukouji (Temple 41). j, Butsumokuji (Temple 42). k, Meisekiji (Temple 43). l, Daihouji (Temple 44). m, Kokubunji (Temple 59). n, Yokomineji (Temple 60). o, Kouonji (Temple 61). p, Houjuji (Temple 62). q, Douryuji (Temple 77). r, Goushouji (Temple 78). s, Tennouji (Temple 79). t, Kokubunji (Temple 80).

2005, July 8   Photo.

Z698	ZA603	Sheet of 20	30.00	30.00
a.-t.	80y Any single		1.40	.90

See note under No. Z652 for information on identifying temple numbers.

Swwtbriar, Old Shana Post Office (Hokkaido) ZA604   Sea Otter (Hokkaido) ZA605

Cherry Blossoms (Hokkaido) ZA606   Tufted Puffins (Hokkaido) ZA607

2005, Aug. 22

Z699	ZA604	80y multi	1.40	.90
Z700	ZA605	80y multi	1.40	.90
Z701	ZA606	80y multi	1.40	.90
Z702	ZA607	80y multi	1.40	.90
a.	Horiz. strip of 4, #Z699-Z702		6.00	6.00

60th Natl. Athletic Meets (Okayama) — ZA608

2005, Sept. 1
Z703 ZA608 50y multi .90 .50

Kobe Luminarie (Hyogo) — ZA609

2005, Dec. 9 — Litho.
Z704 50y Yellow denomination .85 .50
Z705 50y Blue denomination .85 .50
a. ZA609 Horiz. pair, #Z704-Z705 1.75 1.75

Kawazu Cherry Blossoms (Shizuoka) — ZA610

2006, Feb. 1 — Photo. — Perf. 13¼
Z706 50y With bird .85 .50
Z707 50y Without bird .85 .50
a. ZA610 Horiz. pair, #Z706-Z707 1.75 1.75

Japanese Characters (Fukui) — ZA611

Maruoka Castle, Hills (Fukui) — ZA612

Maruoka Castle, Clouds (Fukui) — ZA613

Maruoka Castle, Sun (Fukui) — ZA614

Maruoka Castle, Moon (Fukui) — ZA615

2006, Apr. 3 — Litho.
Z708 ZA611 80y multi 1.40 .90
Z709 ZA612 80y multi 1.40 .90
Z710 ZA613 80y multi 1.40 .90
Z711 ZA614 80y multi 1.40 .90
Z712 ZA615 80y multi 1.40 .90
a. Horiz. strip of 4, #Z709-Z712 5.75 5.75
Nos. Z708-Z712 (5) 7.00 4.50

Printed in sheets of 20 consisting of 12 No. ZA708, and 2 each Nos. Z709-Z712.

Primroses (Osaka) ZA616

Cherry Blossoms (Nara) ZA617

Wild Chrysanthemums (Hyogo) ZA618

Rhododendrons (Shiga) ZA619

Ume Blossoms (Wakayama) ZA620

Weeping Cherry Blossoms (Kyoto) ZA621

2006, Apr. 3
Z713 ZA616 50y multi .85 .50
Z714 ZA617 50y multi .85 .50
Z715 ZA618 50y multi .85 .50
Z716 ZA619 50y multi .85 .50
Z717 ZA620 50y multi .85 .50
a. Horiz. strip of 4, #Z714-Z717 3.50 3.50
Z718 ZA621 50y multi .85 .50
Nos. Z713-Z718 (6) 5.10 3.00

Printed in sheets containing 4 each nos. Z713, Z718, 3 each Nos. Z714-Z717.

Pear Blossoms, Yumigahama Beach (Tottori) ZA622

Peonies, Hinomisaki Lighthouse (Shimane) ZA623

Peach Blossoms, Seto-oohashi Bridge (Okayama) ZA624

Scarlet Maple Leaves, Miyajima Shrine (Hiroshima) ZA625

Citron Blossoms, Oomi Island (Yamaguchi) ZA626

2006, May 1 — Photo.
Z719 ZA622 50y multi .90 .50
Z720 ZA623 50y multi .90 .50
Z721 ZA624 50y multi .90 .50
Z722 ZA625 50y multi .90 .50
Z723 ZA626 50y multi .90 .50
a. Vert. strip of 5, #Z719-Z723! 4.50 4.50
Nos. Z719-Z723 (5) 4.50 2.50

National Afforestation Campaign (Gifu) — ZA627

2006, May 19
Z724 ZA627 50y multi .90 .50

Mt. Echigo (Niigata, Nagano) ZA628

Sankayou Flowers (Niigata, Nagano) ZA629

Mt. Asama (Niigata, Nagano) ZA630

Sakurasou Flowers (Niigata, Nagano) ZA631

2006, June 1 — Litho.
Z725 ZA628 80y multi 1.40 .90
Z726 ZA629 80y multi 1.40 .90
Z727 ZA630 80y multi 1.40 .90
Z728 ZA631 80y multi 1.40 .90
a. Horiz. strip of 4, #Z725-Z728 6.00 6.00
Nos. Z725-Z728 (4) 5.60 3.60

Daffodils, Nokonoshima Island (Fukuoka) ZA632

Bellflowers, Hirodai (Fukuoka) ZA633

Hydrangeas, Mikaerinotaki Falls (Saga) ZA634

Cosmos, Kujukushima Islands (Nagasaki) ZA635

Camellias, Amakusa Bridges (Kumamoto) ZA636

Flowers, Mt. Aso (Kumamoto) ZA637

Primroses, Mt. Yufudake (Oita) — ZA638

Lavender, Kujurenzan (Oita) — ZA639

Poppies, Mt. Hinamoridake (Miyazaki) ZA640

Nanohana, Mt. Kaimondake (Kagoshima) ZA641

2006, June 1 — Photo.
Z729 ZA632 80y multi 1.40 .90
Z730 ZA633 80y multi 1.40 .90
Z731 ZA634 80y multi 1.40 .90
Z732 ZA635 80y multi 1.40 .90
Z733 ZA636 80y multi 1.40 .90
Z734 ZA637 80y multi 1.40 .90
Z735 ZA638 80y multi 1.40 .90
Z736 ZA639 80y multi 1.40 .90
Z737 ZA640 80y multi 1.40 .90
Z738 ZA641 80y multi 1.40 .90
a. Block of 10, #Z729-Z738 15.00 15.00
Nos. Z729-Z738 (10) 14.00 9.00

Fox (Hokkaido) ZA642

Bears (Hokkaido) ZA643

Squirrel (Hokkaido) ZA644

Owl (Hokkaido) ZA645

2006, June 3
Z739 ZA642 50y multi .90 .50
Z740 ZA643 50y multi .90 .50
Z741 ZA644 50y multi .90 .50
Z742 ZA645 50y multi .90 .50
a. Horiz. strip of 4, #Z739-Z742 3.75 3.75
Nos. Z739-Z742 (4) 3.60 2.00

Aomori Nebuta
Festival (Aomori)
ZA646

Akita Kanto
Festival (Akita)
ZA647

Yamagata
Hanagasa
Festival
(Yamagata)
ZA648

Sendai Tanabata
Festival (Miyagi)
ZA649

2006, June 3　　　　　　**Litho.**
Z743	ZA646	80y multi	1.40	.90
Z744	ZA647	80y multi	1.40	.90
Z745	ZA648	80y multi	1.40	.90
Z746	ZA649	80y multi	1.40	.90
a.		Horiz. strip of 4, #Z743-Z746	5.75	5.75
		Nos. Z743-Z746 (4)	5.60	3.60

Azaleas, Eboshi-
iwa, Mt. Fuji
(Kanagawa)
ZA650

Daffodils,
Sakawagawa
River (Kanagawa)
ZA651

Pinks, Tanzawa
Mountains
(Kanagawa)
ZA652

Balloon Flowers,
Mt. Fuji
(Kanagawa)
ZA653

2006, Aug. 1　　　　　　**Photo.**
Z747	ZA650	80y multi	1.40	.90
Z748	ZA651	80y multi	1.40	.90
Z749	ZA652	80y multi	1.40	.90
Z750	ZA653	80y multi	1.40	.90
a.		Horiz. strip of 4, #Z747-Z750	5.75	5.75
		Nos. Z747-Z750 (4)	5.60	3.60

Miniature Sheet

88 Temples (Shikoku) — ZA654

No. Z751: a, Hourinji (Temple 9). b, Kirihata
(Temple 10). c, Fujiidera (Temple 11). d,
Shouzanji (Temple 12). e, Kounomineji (Tem-
ple 27). f, Dainichiji (Temple 28). g, Kokubunji
(Temple 29). h, Zenrakuji (Temple 30). i,
Iwayaji (Temple 45). j, Joururiji (Temple 46). k,
Yasakaji (Temple 47). l, Sairinji (Temple 48).
m, Kichijouji (Temple 63). n, Maegamiji (Tem-
ple 64). o, Sankakuji (Temple 65). p, Unbenji
(Temple 66). q, Shiromineji (Temple 81). r,
Negoroji (Temple 82). s, Ichinomiyaji (Temple
83). t, Yashimaji (Temple 84).

2006, Aug. 1
| Z751 | ZA654 | Sheet of 20 | 28.00 | 28.00 |
| a.-t. | | 80y Any single | 1.40 | .90 |

See note under No. Z652 for information on
identifying temple numbers.

61st National
Athletic Meets
(Hyogo) — ZA655

2006, Sept. 1
| Z752 | ZA655 | 50y multi | | .85 | .50 |

Loquats,
Byobugaura
(Chiba)
ZA656

Umes, Fukuroda
Waterfall
(Ibaraki)
ZA657

Apples, Oze
(Gunma)
ZA658

Japanese Pears,
Nagatoro
(Saitama)
ZA659

Strawberries, Kegon
Waterfall
(Tochigi) — ZA660

2006, Sept. 1
Z753	ZA656	80y multi	1.40	.90
Z754	ZA657	80y multi	1.40	.90
Z755	ZA658	80y multi	1.40	.90
Z756	ZA659	80y multi	1.40	.90
Z757	ZA660	80y multi	1.40	.90
a.		Vert. strip of 5, #Z753-Z757	7.00	7.00
		Nos. Z753-Z757 (5)	7.00	4.50

Roses
(Aichi) — ZA661

Chrysanthemums
(Aichi) — ZA662

Orchids
(Aichi) — ZA663

Cyclamen
(Aichi) — ZA664

2006, Oct. 2　　　　　　**Litho.**
Z758	ZA661	50y multi	.85	.50
Z759	ZA662	50y multi	.85	.50
Z760	ZA663	50y multi	.85	.50
Z761	ZA664	50y multi	.85	.50
a.		Horiz. strip of 4, #Z758-Z761	3.50	3.50
		Nos. Z758-Z761 (4)	3.40	2.00

Cherry Blossoms,
Chidorigafuchi
(Tokyo) — ZA665

Roses, Akasaka
Palace
(Tokyo) — ZA666

Cosmos, Shouwa
Kinen Park
(Tokyo) — ZA667

Japanese Apricot
Blossoms,
Yushima Tenjin
Shrine
(Tokyo) — ZA668

2006, Oct. 2　　　　　　**Photo.**
Z762	ZA665	80y multi	1.40	.90
Z763	ZA666	80y multi	1.40	.90
Z764	ZA667	80y multi	1.40	.90
Z765	ZA668	80y multi	1.40	.90
a.		Horiz. strip of 4, #Z762-Z765	5.75	5.75
		Nos. Z762-Z765 (4)	5.60	3.60

Iris, Takeshima
(Aichi, Mie, Gifu,
Shizuoka)
ZA669

Chinese Milk
Vetch,
Shirakawa
Village (Aichi,
Mie, Gifu,
Shizuoka)
ZA670

Lily, Nagoya
Castle (Aichi,
Mie, Gifu,
Shizuoka)
ZA671

Japanese Iris,
Couple Rock
(Aichi, Mie, Gifu,
Shizuoka)
ZA672

Azalea, Jogasaki
Coast (Aichi, Mie,
Gifu,
Shizuoka) — ZA673

2007, Apr. 2　　**Photo.**　　**Perf. 13¼**
Z766	ZA669	80y multi	1.40	.90
Z767	ZA670	80y multi	1.40	.90
Z768	ZA671	80y multi	1.40	.90
Z769	ZA672	80y multi	1.40	.90
Z770	ZA673	80y multi	1.40	.90
a.		Vert. strip of 5, #Z766-Z770	7.00	7.00

Cherry Blossom,
Yatsugatake
(Yamanashi)
ZA674

Grapes,
Katsunuma
Vineyard
(Yamanashi)
ZA675

Azalea,
Syosenkyo
(Yamanashi)
ZA676

Lavender, Mt.
Fuji (Yamanashi)
ZA677

Peaches, Southern
Japanese Alps
(Yamanashi)
ZA678

2007, Apr. 2

Z771	ZA674	80y multi	1.40	.90
Z772	ZA675	80y multi	1.40	.90
Z773	ZA676	80y multi	1.40	.90
Z774	ZA677	80y multi	1.40	.90
Z775	ZA678	80y multi	1.40	.90
a.	Vert. strip of 5, #Z771-Z775	7.00	7.00

Tulips (Niigata)
ZA679

Rice (Niigata)
ZA680

Pears (Niigata)
ZA681

Mealy Primrose
(Niigata)
ZA682

Iris
(Niigata) — ZA683

2007, Apr. 2   Litho.

Z776	ZA679	80y multi	1.40	.90
Z777	ZA680	80y multi	1.40	.90
Z778	ZA681	80y multi	1.40	.90
Z779	ZA682	80y multi	1.40	.90
Z780	ZA683	80y multi	1.40	.90
a.	Vert. strip of 5, #Z776-Z780	7.00	7.00

Cherry Blossom
(Saitama)
ZA684

Japanese Rose
(Ibaraki)
ZA685

Skunk Cabbage
(Gunma)
ZA686

Adder's Tongue
Lily (Tochigi)
ZA687

Poppies
(Chiba) — ZA688

2007, May 1   Photo.   Perf. 13¼

Z781	ZA684	50y multi	.85	.50
Z782	ZA685	50y multi	.85	.50
Z783	ZA686	50y multi	.85	.50
Z784	ZA687	50y multi	.85	.50
Z785	ZA688	50y multi	.85	.50
a.	Vert. strip of 5, #Z781-Z785	4.25	4.25

For self-adhesives, see Nos. 3189B-3189F.

Mandarin Ducks
(Tottori)
ZA689

Swans (Shimane)
ZA690

Pheasants
(Okayama)
ZA691

Red-throated
Loons
(Hiroshima)
ZA692

Hooded Cranes
(Yamaguchi)
ZA693

2007, May 1   Litho.

Z786	ZA689	80y multi	1.40	.90
Z787	ZA690	80y multi	1.40	.90
Z788	ZA691	80y multi	1.40	.90
Z789	ZA692	80y multi	1.40	.90
Z790	ZA693	80y multi	1.40	.90
a.	Vert. strip of 5, #Z786-Z790	7.00	7.00

Japanese Cranes
(Hokkaido)
ZA694

Hokkaido
Mountain Hares
(Hokkaido)
ZA695

Flying Squirrels
(Hokkaido)
ZA696

Hokkaido Deer
(Hokkaido)
ZA697

Spotted Seals
(Hokkaido)
ZA698

2007, May 1   Litho.

Z791	ZA694	80y multi	1.40	.90
Z792	ZA695	80y multi	1.40	.90
Z793	ZA696	80y multi	1.40	.90
Z794	ZA697	80y multi	1.40	.90
Z795	ZA698	80y multi	1.40	.90
a.	Horiz. strip of 5, #Z791-Z795	7.00	7.00

Koriyama Castle
(Nara) — ZA699

Hikone Castle
(Shiga) — ZA700

Himeji Castle
(Hyogo) — ZA701

Osaka Castle
(Osaka) — ZA702

Wakayama Castle
(Wakayama)
ZA703

2007, June 1   Photo.

Z796	ZA699	50y multi	.85	.50
Z797	ZA700	50y multi	.85	.50
Z798	ZA701	50y multi	.85	.50
Z799	ZA702	50y multi	.85	.50
Z800	ZA703	50y multi	.85	.50
a.	Vert. strip of 5, #Z796-Z800	4.25	4.25

Whale Shark
(Okinawa)
ZA704

Longfin
Bannerfish
(Okinawa)
ZA705

False Clownfish
(Okinawa)
ZA706

Blue Damselfish
(Okinawa)
ZA707

Manta Ray
(Okinawa)
ZA708

2007, June 1   Photo.

Z801	ZA704	80y multi	1.40	.90
Z802	ZA705	80y multi	1.40	.90
Z803	ZA706	80y multi	1.40	.90
Z804	ZA707	80y multi	1.40	.90
Z805	ZA708	80y multi	1.40	.90
a.	Horiz. strip of 5, #Z801-Z805	7.00	7.00

National
Afforestation
Campaign
(Hokkaido)
ZA709

2007, June 22   Perf. 12½x12¾

Z806	ZA709	50y multi	.85	.60

Dancers, Owara
Wind Festival
(Toyama)
ZA710

Dancers, Owara
Wind Festival
(Toyama)
ZA711

Dancers, Owara
Wind Festival
(Toyama)
ZA712

Dancers, Owara
Wind Festival
(Toyama)
ZA713

Dancers, Owara
Wind Festival
(Toyama) — ZA714

2007, July 2   Litho.   Perf. 13¼

Z807	ZA710	80y multi	1.40	.90
Z808	ZA711	80y multi	1.40	.90
Z809	ZA712	80y multi	1.40	.90
Z810	ZA713	80y multi	1.40	.90
Z811	ZA714	80y multi	1.40	.90
a.	Vert. strip of 5, #Z807-Z811	7.00	7.00

Tokyo Tower,
Japanese
Allspice
(Tokyo) — ZA715

Double Bridge,
Chinese Violet
Cress
(Tokyo) — ZA716

Meiji shrine Outer
Garden, Sweet
Olive
(Tokyo) — ZA717

Lake Okutama,
Gentian
(Tokyo) — ZA718

Japan Bridge,
Camellia
(Tokyo) — ZA719

2007, July 2   **Photo.**

Z812	ZA715	80y multi	1.40	.90
Z813	ZA716	80y multi	1.40	.90
Z814	ZA717	80y multi	1.40	.90
Z815	ZA718	80y multi	1.40	.90
Z816	ZA719	80y multi	1.40	.90
a.	Vert. strip of 5, #Z812-Z8161	7.00	7.00

Oirase Mountain Stream (Aomori) ZA720

Hirosaki Castle (Aomori) ZA721

Chuson Temple (Iwate) — ZA722

Jodogahama (Iwate) — ZA723

Matsushima (Miyagi) ZA724

Mt. Zao Crater Lake (Miyagi, Yamagata) ZA725

Oga Peninsula (Akita) ZA726

Mt. Chokai (Akita, Yamagata) ZA727

Oze (Fukushima) ZA728

Gassan Volcano (Yamagata) ZA729

2007, July 2

Z817		Sheet of 10	14.00	14.00
a.	ZA720 80y multi	1.40	.90
b.	ZA721 80y multi	1.40	.90
c.	ZA722 80y multi	1.40	.90
d.	ZA723 80y multi	1.40	.90
e.	ZA724 80y multi	1.40	.90
f.	ZA725 80y multi	1.40	.90
g.	ZA726 80y multi	1.40	.90
h.	ZA727 80y multi	1.40	.90
i.	ZA728 80y multi	1.40	.90
j.	ZA729 80y multi	1.40	.90

Main Tower, Kumamoto Castle, Cherry Blossoms (Kumamoto) ZA730

Uto Turret, Kumamoto Castle, in Summer (Kumamoto) ZA731

Main Tower, Kumamoto Castle, Gingko Trees (Kumamoto) ZA732

Uto Turret, Kumamoto Castle, in Winter (Kumamoto) ZA733

Three Towers, Kumamoto Castle (Kumamoto) ZA734

2007, Aug. 1   **Litho.**

Z818	ZA730	80y multi	1.40	.90
Z819	ZA731	80y multi	1.40	.90
Z820	ZA732	80y multi	1.40	.90
Z821	ZA733	80y multi	1.40	.90
Z822	ZA734	80y multi	1.40	.90
a.	Vert. strip of 5, #Z818-Z822	7.00	7.00

Edo Bridge from Japan Bridge, by Hiroshige (Tokyo) — ZA735

Ohisa Takashima, by Utamaro (Tokyo) — ZA736

Yaozo Ichikawa II as Bunzo Tanabe, by Sharaku (Tokyo) — ZA737

Horikiri Irises, by Hiroshige (Tokyo) — ZA738

Kinryuzan Temple, by Hiroshige (Tokyo) — ZA739

Seven Women Applying Makeup Using a Full Length Mirror, by Utamaro (Tokyo) — ZA740

Ryuzo Arashi II as Kinkichi Ishibe, Moneylender, by Sharaku (Tokyo) — ZA741

Suido Bridge and Surugadai, by Hiroshige (Tokyo) — ZA742

Moon Pine, Ueno Temple, by Hiroshige (Tokyo) — ZA743

Hanaogi from Ogiya, No. 1 District, Edo Town, by Utamaro (Tokyo) — ZA744

2007, Aug. 1

Z823		Sheet of 10	14.00	14.00
a.	ZA735 80y multi	1.40	.90
b.	ZA736 80y multi	1.40	.90
c.	ZA737 80y multi	1.40	.90
d.	ZA738 80y multi	1.40	.90
e.	ZA739 80y multi	1.40	.90
f.	ZA740 80y multi	1.40	.90
g.	ZA741 80y multi	1.40	.90
h.	ZA742 80y multi	1.40	.90
i.	ZA743 80y multi	1.40	.90
j.	ZA744 80y multi	1.40	.90

88 Temples (Shikoku) — ZA746

No. Z824: a, Dainchiji (Temple 13). b, Jorakuji (Temple 14). c, Kokubunji (Temple 15). d, Kanonji (Temple 16). e, Chikurinji (Temple 31). f, Zenjibuji (Temple 32). g, Sekkeiji (Temple 33). h, Tanemaji (Temple 34). i, Jodoji (Temple 49). j, Hantaji (Temple 50). k, Ishiteji (Temple 51). l, Taisanji (Temple 52). m, Daikoji (Temple 67). n, Jinnein (Temple 68). o, Kanonji (Temple 69). p, Motoyamaji (Temple 70). q, Yakuriji (Temple 85). r, Shidoji (Temple 86). s, Nagaoji (Temple 87). t, Okuboji (Temple 88).

No. Z825: a, Idoji (Temple 17). b, Onzanji (Temple 18). c, Kiyotakiji (Temple 35). d, Shoryuji (Temple 36). e, Emmyoji (Temple 53). f, Emmeiji (Temple 54). g, Iyadaniji (Temple 71). h, Mandaraji (Temple 72). i, Deities Cave (no temple number). j, Painting of Daishi Kobo (no temple number).

2007, Aug. 1   **Photo.**   **Perf. 13¼**

Z824	ZA745	Sheet of 20	28.00	28.00
a.-t.	80y Any single	1.40	.90
Z825	ZA746	Sheet of 10	14.00	14.00
a.-j.	80y Any single	1.40	.90

See note under No. Z652 for information on identifying temple numbers.

62nd National Athletic Meet (Akita) — ZA747

2007, Sept. 3   **Litho.**

Z826	ZA747	50y multi	.90	.50

ZA745

Miniature Sheet

Nagoya Port (Aichi) — ZA748

No. Z827: a, Hibiscus and Antarctic survey. b, Hibiscus and Port Tower. c, Azaleas, killer whale at Nagoya Aquarium. d, Azaleas, dolphins at Nagoya Aquarium. e, Yellow chrysanthemums, Meiko Triton Bridge. f, Orange and yellow chrysanthemums, two bridges. g, Snapdragons and fireworks. h, Sailing ship and snapdragons. i, Azaleas, bridge, Nagoya Aquarium and half of Ferris wheel. j, Azaleas, Port Tower, Nagoya Castle, and half of Ferris wheel.

2007, Nov. 5   Litho.   Perf. 13¼

Z827	ZA748	Sheet of 10	15.00	15.00
a.-j.		80y Any single	1.40	.90

Beginning in 2008 the planning and design of prefecture stamps, previously done by regional postal authorities, was taken over by national postal authorities. The national authorities planned issues for 2008 that would be available in more of postal regions, thus making prefectural issues more nationwide and less local in scope. Additionally, the style of the "Nippon yubin" ideographic characters that had been used solely for prefecture stamps reverted to the style used on the national issues for most issues. Because of these changes, prefecture stamps will be listed in the regular postage listings starting with the 2008 issues.

PREFECTURE SEMI-POSTAL STAMPS

Earthquake and Volcano Eruption Refugee Relief (Tokyo) — ZSP1

2000, Nov. 15   Photo.

ZB1	80y +20y Pink ribbon	1.75	1.25
ZB2	80y +20y Blue ribbon	1.75	1.25
a.	ZSP1 Pair, #ZB1-ZB2	4.00	4.00

SEMI-POSTAL STAMPS

Douglas Plane over Japan Alps — SP1

Wmk. Zigzag Lines (141)

1937, June 1   Photo.   Perf. 13

B1	SP1 2s + 2s rose carmine	1.75	.75
B2	SP1 3s + 2s purple	1.75	1.25
B3	SP1 4s + 2s green	2.50	1.00
	Nos. B1-B3 (3)	6.00	3.00
	Set, never hinged	8.00	

The surtax was for the Patriotic Aviation Fund to build civil airports.

Nos. 259 and 261 Surcharged in Blue or Red

1942, Feb. 16   Wmk. 257   Perf. 13

B4	A84 2s +1s crimson (Bl)	1.00	.90
B5	A86 4s +2s dk grn (R)	1.25	1.10
	Set, never hinged	3.75	

Fall of Singapore to Japanese forces.

Tank Corps Attack, Bataan — SP2

Pearl Harbor Under Japanese Attack — SP3

Unwmk.

1942, Dec. 8   Photo.   Perf. 12

B6	SP2 2s +1s rose brown	2.00	1.00
B7	SP3 5s +2s sapphire	2.25	1.50
	Set, never hinged	6.00	

1st anniv. of the "Greater East Asia War." The surtax was for national defense.

> **Catalogue values for unused stamps in this section, from this point to the end of the section, are for Never Hinged items.**

SP4

1947, Nov. 25   Wmk. 257   Perf. 12½

B8	SP4 1.20y + 80s dk rose red	1.00	.85

Japan's 1st Community Chest drive. The surtax was for charitable purposes.

Nurse — SP5

Bird Feeding Young — SP6

1948, Oct. 1   Unwmk.   Perf. 12½

B9	SP5 5y + 2.50y bright red	12.50	9.00
B10	SP6 5y + 2.50y emerald	12.50	9.00

Souvenir Sheet

Wmk. 257

Imperf

Without Gum

B11	Sheet of 2	55.00	55.00

The surtax on Nos. B9-B11 was divided between the Red Cross and Community Chest organizations.

No. B11 contains Nos. B9-B10, imperf.

Javelin Thrower SP8

No. B13, Wrestlers. No. B14, Diver. No. B15, Water polo. No. B16, Woman gymnast. No. B17, Judo. No. B18, Fencing. No. B19, Basketball. No. B20, Rowing. No. B21, Sailing. No. B22, Boxing. No. B23, Volleyball. No. B24, Bicyclist. No. B25, Equestrian. No. B26, Field hockey. No. B27, Pistol shooting. No. B28, Modern pentathlon. No. B29, Weight lifter. No. B30, Women's kayak doubles. No. B31, Soccer.

Perf. 13½

1961, Oct. 11   Unwmk.   Engr.

B12	SP8 5y + 5y bister	.75	1.00
B13	SP8 5y + 5y dk green	.75	1.00
B14	SP8 5y + 5y carmine	.75	1.00
a.	Souvenir sheet of 3 ('64)	4.25	4.75

1962, June 23

B15	SP8 5y + 5y green	.45	.75
B16	SP8 5y + 5y dk purple	.45	.75
B17	SP8 5y + 5y dk carmine	.45	.75
a.	Souvenir sheet of 3 ('64)	2.75	3.25

1962, Oct. 10

B18	SP8 5y + 5y brick red	.25	.40
B19	SP8 5y + 5y slate grn	.25	.40
B20	SP8 5y + 5y violet	.25	.40
a.	Souvenir sheet of 3 ('64)	2.25	2.50

1963, June 23

B21	SP8 5y + 5y blue	.25	.40
B22	SP8 5y + 5y dk brown	.25	.40
B23	SP8 5y + 5y brown	.25	.40
a.	Souvenir sheet of 3 ('64)	4.75	5.25

1963, Nov. 11

B24	SP8 5y + 5y dk blue	.25	.25
B25	SP8 5y + 5y olive	.25	.25
B26	SP8 5y + 5y black	.25	.25
B27	SP8 5y + 5y claret	.25	.25
a.	Souvenir sheet of 4 ('64)	4.75	5.25

1964, June 23

B28	SP8 5y + 5y bluish vio	.25	.25
B29	SP8 5y + 5y dp olive	.25	.25
B30	SP8 5y + 5y grnsh blue	.25	.25
B31	SP8 5y + 5y rose claret	.25	.25
a.	Souvenir sheet of 4 ('64)	4.75	5.25
	Nos. B12-B31 (20)	7.10	9.65

Issued to raise funds for the 1964 Olympic Games in Tokyo.

The souvenir sheets were issued Aug. 20, 1964. Each contains one each of the stamps in the set it follows. Nos. B14a, B20a, B23a and B27a, exist imperf.

Cobalt Treatment Unit — SP9

Early Cancer Detection with X-rays — SP10

1966, Oct. 21   Photo.   Perf. 13

B32	SP9 7y + 3y yel org & blk	.25	.25
B33	SP10 15y + 5y multicolored	.40	.25

9th Intl. Anticancer Congress, Tokyo, Oct. 23-29. The surtax was for the fight against cancer and for research.

EXPO '70 Emblem and Globe — SP11

Cherry Blossoms, Screen, Chishakuin Temple — SP12

1969, Mar. 15   Photo.   Perf. 13

B34	SP11 15y + 5y bl, ocher & ver	.60	.60
B35	SP12 50y + 10y gold, brn & grn	1.25	1.25

Issued to publicize EXPO '70, International Exhibition, Osaka, 1970.

Ice Hockey, Sapporo Olympic Emblem SP13

Design: No. B37, Ski jump and Sapporo Olympic Games emblem, vert.

1971, Feb. 6   Photo.   Perf. 13

B36	SP13 15y + 5y multi	.40	.25
B37	SP13 15y + 5y multi	.40	.25

To promote the 11th Winter Olympic Games, Sapporo, Japan, 1972.

Blue Dragon, East Wall — SP14

Murals from ancient tomb mound: No. B39, Two men, east wall, vert. 50y+10y, Four women, west wall, vert.

1973, Mar. 26   Photo.   Perf. 13
Size: 48x27mm, 27x48mm

B38	SP14 20y + 5y multi	.50	.50
B39	SP14 20y + 5y multi	.50	.40

Photogravure and Engraved
Size: 33x48mm

B40	SP14 50y + 10y multi	1.10	.75
	Nos. B38-B40 (3)	2.10	1.65

Surtax was for restoration work on the murals of the Takamatsu-zuka tomb mound, discovered in March, 1972, and excavated in Nara Prefecture.

Reefs, by Hyakusui Hirafuku — SP15

1974, Mar. 2   Photo.   *Perf. 13*
B41 SP15 20y + 5y multi   .50   .30

The surtax was for the International Ocean Exposition, Okinawa, 1975.

Intl. Year of the Disabled — SP16

Photogravure and Embossed
1981, Sept. 1   *Perf. 13½*
B42 SP16 60y + 10y multi   1.25   .25

Surtax was for education of the disabled.

TSUKUB'85 Intl. Exposition, Mar. 17-Sept. 16, 1985 — SP17

1984, Feb. 19   Photo.   *Perf. 13½*
B43 SP17 60y + 10y multi   1.25   .45

Intl. Garden and Greenery Exposition, Osaka — SP18

1989, June 1   Photo.   *Perf. 13*
B44 SP18 62y + 10y multi   1.40   .75

Surtax for the preparation and management of the exposition.

Intl. Garden and Greenery Exposition, Osaka SP19

1990, Mar. 30
B45 SP19 41y + 4y multi   .85   .45

SP20

1991, July 5   Photo.   *Perf. 13*
B46 SP20 62y + 10y multi   1.40   .85

11th World Congress of the World Federation of the Deaf.

SP21

1995, Apr. 20   Photo.   *Perf. 13*
B47 SP21 80y + 20y multi   2.40   1.75

Philately week. Surtax for benefit of victims of Kobe earthquake.

1998 Winter Olympic Games, Nagano — SP22

1997, Feb. 7   Photo.   *Perf. 13*
B48 80y + 10y emblem   1.75   1.10
B49 80y + 10y stylized owls   1.75   1.10
a.   SP22 Pair, #B48-B49   3.50   2.25

2002 Soccer World Cup, Japan and Korea — SP23

Colors of mascots: No. B50, Purple, yellow and blue. No. B51, Purple. No. B52, Blue.

2001, May 31   Photo.   *Perf. 13x13¼*
B50 SP23 80y + 10y multi   1.75   1.10
B51 SP23 80y + 10y multi   1.75   1.10
B52 SP23 80y + 10y multi   1.75   1.10
a.   Horiz. pair, #B51-B52   3.50   2.20

Wall Paintings, Kitora Tumulus, Asuka — SP24

Designs: No. B53, White Tiger of the West. No. B54, Red Bird fo the South.

2003, Oct. 15   Photo.   *Perf. 13*
B53 80y + 10y multi   1.75   1.25
B54 80y + 10y multi   1.75   1.25
a.   SP24 Horiz. pair, #B53-B54   3.50   2.50

2005 World Exposition, Aichi — SP25

Exposition mascots and: No. B55, Earth. No. B56, Cherry blossoms.

2004, Mar. 25   Photo.   *Perf. 13x13¼*
B55 80y + 10y multi   1.75   1.75
B56 80y + 10y multi   1.75   1.75
a.   SP25 Horiz. pair, #B55-B56   3.50   3.50

Miniature Sheet

Be Kind to Animals Week — SP26

No. B57: a, Dog, flower background. b, White cat, red background. c, White Yorkshire terrier, green curtain. d, Cat, bubbles in background. e, Black Labrador retriever puppy sitting. f, Cat, brown striped background. g, Shiba puppy standing. h, Scottish Fold cat, dots and stripes in background. i, Dog in doorway. j, Cat, crescent moon.

2009, Sept. 18   Litho.   *Perf. 13¼*
B57   SP26   Sheet of 10   12.50   12.50
a.-j.   50y+5y Any single   1.25   1.25

Surtax for animal welfare organizations.

SP27

SP28

SP29

SP30

Mar. 11, 2011 Earthquake and Tsunami Relief — SP31

2011, June 21   Photo.   *Perf. 13*
B58 SP27 80y+20y multi   2.50   2.50
B59 SP28 80y+20y multi   2.50   2.50
B60 SP29 80y+20y multi   2.50   2.50
B61 SP30 80y+20y multi   2.50   2.50
B62 SP31 80y+20y multi   2.50   2.50
a.   Vert. strip of 5, #B58-B62 12.50   12.50

Nos. B58-B62 were printed in sheets containing two strips.

AIR POST STAMPS

Regular Issue of 1914 Overprinted in Red or Blue

Wmk. Zigzag Lines (141)
1919, Oct. 3   *Perf. 13x13½*
Granite Paper
C1 A34 1½s blue (R)   260.00   72.50
C2 A34 3s rose (Bl)   450.00 210.00

Excellent counterfeits exist.

Passenger Plane over Lake Ashi — AP1

1929-34   Engr.   *Perf. 13½x13*
Granite Paper
C3 AP1 8½s orange brn   27.50   14.00
C4 AP1 9½s rose   9.00   3.75
C5 AP1 16½s yellow grn   9.00   4.00
C6 AP1 18s ultra   10.00   3.75
C7 AP1 33s gray   20.00   3.25
    Nos. C3-C7 (5)   75.50   28.75
    Set, never hinged   190.00

Souvenir Sheet
C8 AP1 Sheet of 4,
         #C4-C7   1,250. 1,250.
         Never hinged

Issued: 9½s, 3/1/34; No. C8, 4/20/34; others, 10/6/29. No. C8 for Communications Commemoration Day (1st observance of establishment of the postal service and issuance of #1-4). Sold only at Phil. Exhib. p.o., Tokyo, 4/20-27. Size: 110x100mm.

Catalogue values for unused stamps in this section, from this point to the end of the section, are for Never Hinged items.

Southern Green Pheasant AP3

Perf. 13x13½

1950, Jan. 10 — Engr. — Unwmk.
			Unwmk.	
C9	AP3	16y gray	37.50	10.00
C10	AP3	34y brown violet	52.50	12.00
C11	AP3	59y carmine	72.50	7.00
C12	AP3	103y orange yellow	47.50	20.00
C13	AP3	144y olive	57.50	22.50
		Nos. C9-C13 (5)	267.50	71.50
		Set, hinged	150.00	

Pagoda and Plane — AP4

Plane and Mt. Tsurugi-dake — AP5

1951-52 — Photo.
C14	AP4	15y purple	3.50	2.75
C15	AP4	20y blue	30.00	1.25
C16	AP4	25y yellow grn	27.50	.45
C17	AP4	30y brown red	20.00	.45
C18	AP4	40y gray blk	8.00	.55
C19	AP5	55y brt blue	250.00	60.00
C20	AP5	75y brnsh red	160.00	35.00
C21	AP5	80y magenta	22.50	3.00
C22	AP5	85y black	27.50	7.25
C23	AP5	125y olive bis	14.00	3.25
C24	AP5	160y Prus green	30.00	3.75
		Nos. C14-C24 (11)	593.00	117.70
		Set, hinged	350.00	

Issue dates: 25y, 30y, Dec. 20; 15y, 20y, 40y, Sept. 1; 55y-160y, Feb. 11, 1952.

Redrawn; Underlined Zeros Omitted
1952-62
C25	AP4	15y purple ('62)	1.75	.60
C26	AP4	20y blue	60.00	1.00
C27	AP4	25y yel grn ('53)	1.25	.35
C28	AP4	30y brown red	8.00	.45
C29	AP4	40y gray blk ('53)	5.50	.45
C30	AP5	55y brt blue	75.00	4.00
C32	AP5	75y brnsh red	160.00	9.00
C33	AP5	80y magenta	110.00	3.00
C34	AP5	85y black	6.50	1.50
C36	AP5	125y olive bis	10.00	1.75
C38	AP5	160y Prus green	40.00	2.00
		Nos. C25-C38 (11)	478.00	24.10
		Set, hinged	225.00	

See No. C43.

Great Buddha of Kamakura — AP6

1953, Aug. 15 — Perf. 13½
C39	AP6	70y red brown	5.25	.25
C40	AP6	80y blue	7.50	.25
C41	AP6	115y olive green	3.75	.50
C42	AP6	145y Prus green	25.00	3.00
		Nos. C39-C42 (4)	41.50	4.00

Redrawn Type of 1952-62 Coil Stamp
1961, Oct. 2 — Perf. 13 Horiz.
C43	AP4	30y brown red	37.50	27.50

MILITARY STAMPS

Nos. 98, 119, 131 Overprinted

1910-14 — Unwmk. — Perf. 11½ to 13½
M1	A26	3s rose	225.00	35.00
M2	A34	3s rose ('13)	350.00	140.00

Wmk. 141
M3	A34	3s rose ('14)	35.00	16.00
		Nos. M1-M3 (3)	610.00	191.00

Nos. M1-M3 overprint type I has 3.85mm between characters; type II, 4-4.5mm (movable type).

1921 — On Offices in China No. 37
M4	A34	3s rose	5,750.	4,750.

No. M4 is a provisional military stamp issued at the Japanese Post Office, Tsingtao, China. The overprint differs from the illustration, being 12mm high with thicker characters. Counterfeits are plentiful.

Overprint 16mm High
1924 — On No. 131
M5	A34	3s rose	100.00	72.50
a.		3s rose (#131b)	100.00	75.00

Excellent forgeries exist of Nos. M1-M5.

JAPANESE OFFICES ABROAD

Offices in China

1899-1907 Regular Issues of Japan Overprinted in Red or Black

Perf. 11½, 12, 12½, 13½, 13x13½
1900-06 — Unwmk.
1	A26	5r gray (R)	3.50	2.75
2	A26	½s gray (R) ('01)	2.10	.70
3	A26	1s lt red brn (R)	2.10	.70
4	A26	1½s ultra	9.50	2.10
5	A26	1½s vio ('06)	5.25	.95
6	A26	2s lt grn (R)	5.25	.70
7	A26	3s violet brn	5.75	.70
8	A26	3s rose ('06)	4.25	.50
9	A26	4s rose	4.75	1.25
10	A26	5s org yel (R)	9.50	1.25
11	A27	6s maroon ('06)	18.00	12.00
12	A27	8s ol grn (R)	9.50	6.00
13	A27	10s deep blue	9.50	1.00
14	A27	15s purple	20.00	1.75
15	A27	20s red org	18.00	1.00
16	A28	25s blue grn (R)	37.50	4.00
17	A28	50s red brown	40.00	3.00
18	A29	1y carmine	60.00	3.00
		Nos. 1-18 (18)	264.45	43.35

No. 6 with black overprint is bogus.
Nos. 5, 6, 8, 9 and 13 exist as booklet panes of 6, made from sheet stamps. They are rare.

1900
19	A30	3s carmine	27.50	15.00

Wedding of Crown Prince Yoshihito and Princess Sadako.

Japan Nos. 113 & 114 Overprinted

1908
20	A33	5y green	400.00	47.50
21	A33	10y dark violet	700.00	110.00

On #20-21 the space between characters of the overprint is 6½mm instead of 1½mm.

Stamps of 1913-33 Issues Overprinted

1913 — Perf. 12, 12x13, 13x13½
22	A34	½s brown	15.00	15.00
23	A34	1s orange	16.00	16.00
24	A34	1½s lt blue	42.50	19.00
25	A34	2s green	50.00	21.00
26	A34	3s rose	24.00	8.00
27	A35	4s red	70.00	70.00
28	A35	5s violet	70.00	55.00
29	A35	10s deep blue	70.00	22.50
30	A35	20s claret	275.00	150.00
31	A35	25s olive green	100.00	22.50
32	A36	1y yel grn & mar	825.00	550.00
		Nos. 22-32 (11)	1,557.	949.00

Nos. 24, 25, 26, 27 and 29 exist in booklet panes of 6, made from sheet stamps. The No. 26 pane is very rare.

Japan Nos. 127-137, 139-147 Overprinted
1914-21 — Wmk. 141
Granite Paper
33	A34	½s brown	3.25	.80
34	A34	1s orange	3.75	.80
35	A34	1½s blue	4.25	.80
36	A34	2s green	2.75	.95
37	A34	3s rose	2.40	.80
38	A35	4s red	10.50	4.75
39	A35	5s violet	19.00	1.75
40	A35	6s brown ('20)	32.50	19.00
41	A35	8s gray ('20)	40.00	21.00
42	A35	10s dp blue	13.50	1.25
43	A35	20s claret	45.00	3.25
44	A35	25s olive grn	55.00	3.50
45	A36	30s org brn ('20)	80.00	29.00
46	A36	50s dk brn ('20)	95.00	32.50
47	A36	1y yel grn & mar ('18)	140.00	6.75
48	A33	5y green	1,900.	550.00
49	A33	10y violet ('21)	2,700.	1,700.
		Nos. 33-49 (17)	5,146.	2,376.

On Nos. 48-49 the space between characters of overprint is 4½mm, instead of 6½mm on Nos. 20-21 and 1½mm on all lower values. See No. M4.
No. 42 exists as a booklet pane of 6, made from sheet stamps. It is very rare.
Counterfeit overprints exist of Nos. 1-49.

Offices in Korea

Regular Issue of Japan Overprinted in Red or Black

1900 — Unwmk. — Perf. 11½, 12, 12½
1	A26	5r gray (R)	19.00	8.75
2	A26	1s lt red brn (R)	20.00	5.00
3	A26	1½s ultra	250.00	130.00
4	A26	2s lt green (R)	19.00	10.00
5	A26	3s violet brn	17.00	4.75
6	A26	4s rose	65.00	27.50
7	A26	5s org yel (R)	67.50	27.50
8	A27	8s ol grn (R)	250.00	120.00
9	A27	10s deep blue	35.00	9.00
10	A27	15s purple	62.50	6.00
11	A27	20s red orange	62.50	5.00
12	A28	25s blue grn (R)	220.00	55.00
13	A28	50s red brown	175.00	18.00
14	A29	1y carmine	475.00	14.00
		Nos. 1-14 (14)	1,737.	440.50

1900
15	A30	3s carmine	125.00	55.00

Wedding of Crown Prince Yoshihito and Princess Sadako.
Counterfeit overprints exist of Nos. 1-15.

Taiwan (Formosa)

Numeral of Value and Imperial Crest — A1

1945 — Unwmk. — Litho. — Imperf.
Without Gum
1	A1	3s carmine	30.00	30.00
2	A1	5s blue green	22.50	22.50
3	A1	10s pale blue	35.00	35.00
		Nos. 1-3 (3)	87.50	87.50

Additional values, prepared, but not issued, were: 30s, 40s, 50s, 1y, 5y and 10y. The entire set of nine was overprinted by Chinese authorities after World War II and issued for use in Taiwan.
For overprints see China-Taiwan Nos. 1-7.

JORDAN

ˈjor-dən

Trans-Jordan

LOCATION — In the Near East, separated from the Mediterranean Sea by Israel
GOVT. — Kingdom
AREA — 38,400 sq. mi.
POP. — 4,561,147 (1999 est.)
CAPITAL — Amman

The former Turkish territory was mandated to Great Britain following World War I. It became an independent state in 1946.

10 Milliemes = 1 Piaster
1000 Mils = 1 Palestine Pound (1930)
1000 Fils = 100 piasters = 1 Jordan Dinar (1951)

Catalogue values for unused stamps in this country are for Never Hinged items, beginning with Scott 221 in the regular postage section, Scott B13 in the semi-postal section, Scott C1 in the air post section, Scott J47 in the postage due section, Scott RA1 in the postal tax section, Scott N1 in the occupation section, Scott NJ1 in the occupation postage due section, and Scott NRA1 in the occupation postal tax section.

Watermarks

Wmk. 305 — Roman and Arabic Initials

Wmk. 328 — UAR

Wmk. 388 — Multiple "SPM"

British Mandate

Stamps and Type of Palestine 1918 Overprinted in Black or Silver

Perf. 14, 15x14

1920, Nov. **Wmk. 33**
1	A1	1m dark brown		2.00	3.00
a.		Inverted overprint		140.00	275.00
b.		Perf. 14		2.50	2.50
c.		As "b," inverted overprint		170.00	
2	A1	2m blue green		2.00	2.00
a.		Perf. 15x14		20.00	21.00
b.		2m blue green (S)			
3	A1	3m light brown		2.50	3.00
a.		Perf. 14		20.00	25.00
4	A1	4m scarlet		2.75	2.75
a.		Perf. 14		19.00	40.00
5	A1	5m orange		5.00	1.00
a.		Perf. 15x14		5.75	2.00

6	A1	1pi dark blue (S)		3.75	2.50
a.		Perf. 15x14		2,250.	
7	A1	2pi olive green		6.00	5.00
a.		Perf. 15x14		7.00	11.00
8	A1	5pi plum		5.50	7.50
a.		Perf. 15x14		40.00	50.00
9	A1	9pi bister		7.25	30.00
a.				1,000.	1,500.
10	A1	10pi ultramarine		9.25	30.00
11	A1	20pi gray		17.50	50.00
		Nos. 1-11 (11)		63.50	136.25

The overprint reads "Sharqi al-ardan" (East of Jordan).
For overprints see Nos. 12-63, 83A.

Stamps of 1920 Issue Handstamp Surcharged "Ashir el qirsh" (tenth of piaster) and numeral in Black, Red or Violet

1922
12	A1	⅒pi on 1m dk brn		35.00	32.50
13	A1	⅒pi on 1m dk brn (R)		90.00	67.50
13A	A1	⅒pi on 1m dk brn (V)		77.50	70.00
14	A1	²⁄₁₀pi on 2m bl grn		40.00	29.00
a.		³⁄₁₀pi on 2m bl grn (error)		125.00	110.00
15	A1	²⁄₁₀pi on 2m bl grn (R)		100.00	80.00
16	A1	²⁄₁₀pi on 2m bl grn (V)		135.00	100.00
17	A1	³⁄₁₀pi on 3m lt brn		17.50	15.00
17A	A1	³⁄₁₀pi on 3m lt brn (V)		175.00	150.00
18	A1	⁴⁄₁₀pi on 4m scar		70.00	50.00
19	A1	⁵⁄₁₀pi on 5m org		225.00	100.00
c.		Perf. 15x14		200.00	100.00
19A	A1	⁵⁄₁₀pi on 5m dp org (R)		250.00	
19B	A1	⁵⁄₁₀pi on 5m org (V)		325.00	

For overprint see No. 83B.

Handstamp Surcharged "El qirsh" (piaster) and numeral in Black, Red or Violet

20	A1	1pi dk bl (R)		210.00	60.00
20A	A1	1pi dk bl (V)		425.00	
21	A1	2pi ol grn (Bk)		300.00	75.00
22	A1	2pi ol grn (R)		350.00	80.00
22A	A1	2pi ol grn (V)		325.00	90.00
23	A1	5pi plum (Bk)		65.00	70.00
23A	A1	5pi plum (V)		325.00	
24	A1	9pi bister (Bk)		350.00	350.00
25	A1	9pi bister (R)		175.00	140.00
a.		Perf. 14		600.00	600.00
26	A1	10pi ultra (Bk)		975.00	1,000.
27	A1	20pi gray (Bk)		800.00	850.00
27A	A1	20pi gray (V)		1,000.	950.00

Same Surcharge in Black on Palestine Nos. 13-14
28	A1	10pi on 10pi ultra		2,000.	2,500.
29	A1	20pi on 20pi gray		2,600.	3,000.

For overprints see Nos. 86, 88, 94, 97, 98.

Stamps of 1920 Handstamped in Violet, Black or Red

1922, Dec. **Perf. 15x14, 14**
30	A1	1m dk brn (V)		32.50	20.00
31	A1	1m dk brn (Bk)		27.50	18.00
32	A1	1m dk brn (R)		17.50	15.00
33	A1	2m bl grn (V)		12.50	10.00
34	A1	2m bl grn (Bk)		15.00	15.00
35	A1	2m bl grn (R)		32.50	25.00
36	A1	3m lt brn (V)		12.50	9.00
37	A1	3m lt brn (Bk)		14.00	10.00
38	A1	3m lt brn (R)		55.00	40.00
39	A1	4m scar (V)		65.00	65.00
39A	A1	4m scar (Bk)		60.00	60.00
40	A1	4m scar (R)		60.00	60.00
41	A1	5m orange (V)		22.50	12.00
42	A1	5m orange (R)		45.00	12.00
a.		Perf. 14		325.00	75.00
43	A1	1pi dk blue (V)		22.50	9.00
44	A1	1pi dk blue (R)		37.50	15.00
45	A1	2pi ol grn (V)		30.00	15.00
a.		Perf. 14		82.50	80.00
46	A1	2pi ol grn (Bk)		17.50	50.00
47	A1	2pi ol grn (R)		75.00	40.00
48	A1	5pi plum (V)		80.00	85.00
a.		Perf. 14		110.00	120.00
49	A1	5pi plum (R)		100.00	120.00
50	A1	9pi bister (V)		250.00	250.00
50A	A1	9pi bister (Bk)		72.50	85.00
50B	A1	9pi bister (R)		450.00	450.00

51	A1	10pi ultra (V)		1,250.	1,600.
51A	A1	10pi ultra (R)		2,000.	1,900.
52	A1	20pi gray (V)		1,250.	1,800.
52A	A1	20pi gray (R)		1,750.	2,000.

The overprint reads "Hukumat al Sharqi al Arabia" (Arab Government of the East) and date, 1923. The surcharges or overprints on Nos. 12 to 52A inclusive are handstamped and, as usual, are found inverted and doubled. Ink pads of several colors were in use at the same time and the surcharges and overprints frequently show a mixture of two colors.
For overprints see Nos. 84, 87, 89, 92-93, 95-96.

Stamps of 1920 Overprinted in Gold or Black

1923, Mar. 1 **Perf. 14, 15x14**
53	A1	1m dark brn (G)		22.50	32.50
a.		Inverted overprint		750.00	
b.		Perf. 15x14		1,600.	1,800.
54	A1	2m blue grn (G)		20.00	20.00
a.		Double overprint		300.00	
b.		Inverted overprint		375.00	350.00
c.		Black overprint		300.00	
d.		As "c," inverted overprint		300.00	
55	A1	3m lt brn (G)		17.50	15.00
a.		Double overprint		550.00	
b.		Inverted overprint		550.00	
c.		Black overprint		82.50	85.00
56	A1	4m scarlet (Bk)		20.00	17.50
57	A1	5m orange (Bk)		17.50	12.00
a.		Perf. 15x14		60.00	50.00
58	A1	1pi dk blue (G)		17.50	17.50
a.		Double overprint		500.00	475.00
b.		Black overprint		875.00	850.00
59	A1	2pi ol grn (G)		23.00	21.00
a.		Black overprint		275.00	250.00
b.		Overprint on back		275.00	
60	A1	5pi plum (G)		75.00	100.00
a.		Inverted overprint		250.00	
b.		"922" for "921"			
c.		Black overprint (inverted)		1,500.	
61	A1	9pi bister (Bk)		95.00	130.00
a.		Perf. 15x14			
62	A1	10pi ultra (G)		85.00	130.00
63	A1	20pi gray (G)		85.00	130.00
a.		Inverted overprint		400.00	
b.		Double overprint		475.00	
c.		Double ovpt., one inverted		475.00	
d.		Black overprint		850.00	
e.		As "d," inverted		1,100.	
f.		As "d," double, one inverted		1,300.	

The overprint reads "Hukumat al Sharqi al Arabia, Nissan Sanat 921" (Arab Government of the East, April, 1921).
For overprints see Nos. 85, 99, 100, 102.

Stamps of Hejaz, 1922, Overprinted in Black

Coat of Arms (Hejaz A7)

1923, Apr. **Unwmk.** **Perf. 11½**
64	A7	⅛pi orange brn		4.50	3.75
a.		Double overprint		225.00	
b.		Inverted overprint		100.00	
65	A7	½pi red		4.50	3.75
a.		Inverted overprint		125.00	
66	A7	1pi dark blue		3.75	1.50
a.		Inverted overprint		140.00	140.00
67	A7	1½pi violet		3.75	2.50
a.		Double overprint		160.00	
b.		Pair, one without overprint		250.00	
c.		Pair, imperf. between		175.00	
68	A7	2pi orange		4.50	8.00
69	A7	3pi olive brn		5.00	13.00
a.		Inverted overprint		250.00	
b.		Double overprint		250.00	250.00
c.		Pair, one without overprint		400.00	
70	A7	5pi olive green		22.50	32.50
		Nos. 64-70 (7)		48.50	65.00

The overprint is similar to that on the preceding group but is differently arranged. There are numerous varieties in the Arabic letters.
For overprints see Nos. 71-72, 91, J1-J5.

a   b

With Additional Surcharge of New Value in Arabic

71	A7(a)	¼pi on ⅛pi		11.00	11.00
a.		Inverted surcharge		175.00	
b.		Surcharge doubled		—	200.00
72	A7(b)	10pi on 5pi		32.50	37.50

Independence Issue

Palestine Stamps and Type of 1918 Overprinted Vertically in Black or Gold

1923, May **Wmk. 33** **Perf. 15x14**
73	A1	1m dark brn (Bk)		22.50	17.00
a.		Double ovpt., one reversed		725.00	650.00
73B	A1	1m dark brn (G)		175.00	175.00
a.		Double ovpt., one reversed		1,000.	
74	A1	2m blue grn		42.50	50.00
75	A1	3m lt brown		14.00	17.50
76	A1	4m scarlet		14.00	17.50
77	A1	5m orange		70.00	80.00
78	A1	1pi dk blue (G)		95.00	110.00
a.		Double overprint		750.00	850.00
79	A1	2pi olive grn		70.00	90.00
80	A1	5pi plum (G)		80.00	90.00
a.		Double overprint (G)		725.00	
b.		Double overprint (Bk)		1,500.	
81	A1	9pi bis, perf. 14		70.00	85.00
82	A1	10pi ultra, perf. 14		80.00	100.00
83	A1	20pi gray		85.00	110.00
		Nos. 73-83 (12)		818.00	942.00

The overprint reads, "Arab Government of the East (abbreviated), Souvenir of Independence, 25th, May, 1923 ('923')."
There were printed 480 complete sets and a larger number of the 1, 2, 3 and 4m. A large number of these sets were distributed to high officials. The overprint was in a setting of twenty-four and the error "933" instead of "923" occurs once in the setting. Value about five times the "923" stamps.
The overprint exists reading downward on all values, as illustrated, and reading upward on all except the 5m and 2pi.
Forged overprints exist.
For overprint see No. 101.

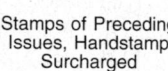

Stamps of Preceding Issues, Handstamp Surcharged

83A	A1	2½ / 10ths pi on 5m dp org		175.00	175.00
83B	A1	⁵⁄₁₀pi on 3m (#17)		—	
84	A1	⁵⁄₁₀pi on 3m (#36)		50.00	60.00
85	A1	⁵⁄₁₀pi on 3m (#55)		27.50	40.00
86	A1	⁵⁄₁₀pi on 5pi (#23)		75.00	85.00
87	A1	⁵⁄₁₀pi on 5pi (#48)		10.00	17.50
88	A1	⁵⁄₁₀pi on 5pi (#23)		75.00	85.00
89	A1	1pi on 5pi (#48)		2,500.	

Same Surcharge on Palestine Stamp of 1918
90	A1	⁵⁄₁₀pi on 3m lt brn		17,000.	

No. 90 is valued in the grade of fine-very fine. Very fine examples are not known.
As is usual with handstamped surcharges these are found double, inverted, etc.

No. 67 Surcharged by Handstamp

Unwmk. **Perf. 11½**
91	A7	½pi on 1 ½pi vio		12.00	14.00
a.		Surcharge typographed		55.00	55.00
b.		As "a," inverted surcharge		150.00	

c. As "a," double surcharge 180.00
d. As "a," pair, one with surcharge 500.00

The surcharge reads: "Nusf el qirsh" (half piastre). See note after No. 90.
Handstamped surcharge exists double; inverted; double, one inverted, etc.

Stamps of Preceding Issues Surcharged by Handstamp

No. 92

Perf. 14, 15x14

1923, Nov. **Wmk. 33**

92	A1	½pi on 2pi (#45)	60.00	80.00
93	A1	½pi on 2pi (#47)	100.00	120.00
94	A1	½pi on 5pi (#23)	75.00	85.00
95	A1	½pi on 5pi (#48)	3,000.	2,000.
96	A1	½pi on 5pi (#49)	2,000.	2,750.
97	A1	½pi on 9pi (#24)	6,500.	
98	A1	½pi on 9pi (#25)	95.00	160.00
99	A1	½pi on 9pi (#61)	200.00	160.00

Surcharged by Handstamp

No. 102

100	A1	1pi on 10pi (#62)	2,250.	2,500.
101	A1	1pi on 10pi (#82)	3,000.	3,000.
102	A1	2pi on 20pi (#63)	65.00	80.00

Of the 25 examples of No. 100, a few were handstamped in violet. Value, unused $2,750.

Stamp of Hejaz, 1922, Overprinted by Handstamp

1923, Dec. **Unwmk.** **Perf. 11½**
103 A7 ½pi red 7.50 4.25

Two settings of No. 103 exist. They differ in the spacing of the characters and the position of the bottom line of the overprint, either to the left or centered.
Nos. 92-103 handstamps exist inverted, doubled, etc.

Stamp of Hejaz, 1922, Overprinted

1924 **Typo.**
104 A7 ½pi red 13.50 14.00

King Hussein Issue

Stamps of Hejaz, 1922, Overprinted

1924 **Gold Overprint**
105 A7 ½pi red 3.25 3.25
a.

106	A7	1pi dark blue	3.50	3.25
107	A7	1½pi violet	4.25	4.50
108	A7	2pi orange	10.00	10.00

Black Overprint

109	A7	1pi red	2.50	2.50
110	A7	1pi dark blue	3.00	3.00
111	A7	1½pi violet	3.25	3.25
112	A7	2pi orange	10.00	10.00
		Nos. 105-112 (8)	39.75	39.75

The overprint reads: "Arab Government of the East. In commemoration of the visit of H. M. the King of the Arabs, 11 Jemad el Than i 1342 (17th Jan. 1924)." The overprint was in a setting of thirty-six and the error "432" instead of "342" occurs once in the setting and is found on all values. Value, $75 each.

Stamps of Hejaz, 1922-24, Overprinted in Black or Red

Coat of Arms (Hejaz A8)

1924

113	A7	⅛pi red brown	1.00	.50
a.		Inverted overprint	130.00	
114	A7	¼pi yellow green	1.00	.65
a.		Tête bêche pair	9.00	12.00
b.		As "a," one overprint inverted	300.00	
c.		Inverted overprint	85.00	
115	A7	½pi red	1.00	.65
116	A7	1pi dark blue	7.50	2.50
a.		Inverted overprint		
117	A7	1½pi violet	5.75	5.75
118	A7	2pi orange	4.25	3.50
a.		Double overprint		
119	A7	3pi dark brown	3.75	3.75
a.		Double overprint	100.00	—
b.		Inverted overprint	100.00	—
120	A7	5pi olive green	5.00	5.75
121	A8	10pi vio & dk brn (R)	11.50	13.00
a.		Pair, one without overprint		—
b.		Black overprint	250.00	—
		Nos. 113-121 (9)	40.75	36.05

The overprint reads: "Hukumat al Sharqi al Arabia, 1342." (Arab Government of the East, 1924.)

Stamps of Hejaz, 1925, Overprinted in Black or Red

(Hejaz A9)

(Hejaz A10)

(Hejaz A11)

1925, Aug.

122	A9	⅛pi chocolate	.80	1.25
a.		Inverted overprint	70.00	
123	A9	¼pi ultramarine	1.00	1.50
a.		Inverted overprint	70.00	
124	A9	½pi carmine rose	1.10	.65
a.		Inverted overprint	70.00	
125	A10	1pi yellow green	1.00	.65
126	A10	1½pi orange	2.50	.85
a.		Inverted overprint	70.00	
127	A10	2pi deep blue	4.00	4.50
128	A11	3pi dark green (R)	4.25	7.00
a.		Inverted overprint	00.00	—
129	A11	5pi orange brn	7.75	12.00
a.		Inverted overprint	85.00	
		Nos. 122-129 (8)	22.40	28.40

The overprint reads: "Hukumat al Sharqi al Arabi. 1343 Sanat." (Arab Government of the East, 1925). Nos. 122-129 exist imperforate, and with overprint double.

Type of Palestine, 1918

1925, Nov. 1 **Wmk. 4** **Perf. 14**

130	A1	1m dark brown	.40	2.75
131	A1	2m yellow	.65	.50
132	A1	3m Prussian bl	1.50	1.25
133	A1	4m rose	1.50	2.75
134	A1	5m orange	2.00	.55
135	A1	6m blue green	1.50	2.00
136	A1	7m yel brown	1.50	2.00
137	A1	8m red	1.50	1.10
138	A1	1pi gray	1.50	.70
139	A1	13m ultramarine	1.75	1.75
140	A1	2pi olive green	3.25	3.50
141	A1	5pi plum	6.00	8.00
142	A1	9pi bister	8.75	19.00
143	A1	10pi light blue	22.50	320.00
144	A1	20pi violet	35.00	50.00
		Nos. 130-144 (15)	89.30	415.85

This overprint reads: "Sharqi al-ardan" (East of Jordan).
For overprints see Nos. J12-J23.

Perf. 15x14

142a	A1	9pi	900.	1,425.
143a	A1	10pi	100.	110.
144a	A1	20pi	1,100.	1,100.
		Nos. 142a-144a (3)	2,100.	2,635.

Amir Abdullah ibn Hussein
A1   A2

1927-29 **Engr.** **Perf. 14**

145	A1	2(m) Prus blue	1.00	1.00
146	A1	3(m) rose	1.75	1.75
147	A1	4(m) green	2.25	3.00
148	A1	5(m) orange	1.50	.35
149	A1	10(m) red	1.75	2.00
150	A1	15(m) ultra	1.75	.35
151	A1	20(m) olive grn	2.00	2.00
152	A2	50(m) claret	3.75	7.50
153	A2	90(m) bister	9.75	17.50
154	A2	100(m) lt blue	11.00	16.00
155	A2	200(m) violet	22.50	37.50
156	A2	500(m) dp brn ('29)	87.50	110.00
157	A2	1000(m) gray ('29)	175.00	210.00
		Nos. 145-157 (13)	321.50	408.95

For overprints see Nos. 158-168, B1-B12, J24-J29.

Stamps of 1927 Overprinted in Black

1928, Sept. 1

158	A1	2(m) Prus blue	1.75	2.00
159	A1	3(m) rose	2.00	3.00
160	A1	4(m) green	2.25	4.00
161	A1	5(m) orange	2.25	2.25
162	A1	10(m) red	2.50	5.00
163	A1	15(m) ultra	2.50	2.00
164	A1	20(m) olive grn	7.50	12.50
165	A2	50(m) claret	14.00	15.00
166	A2	90(m) bister	22.50	45.00
167	A2	100(m) lt blue	32.50	65.00
168	A2	200(m) violet	90.00	160.00
		Nos. 158-168 (11)	179.75	315.75

The overprint is the Arabic word "Dastour," meaning "Constitution." The stamps were in commemoration of the enactment of the law setting forth the Constitution.

A3

"MILS" or "L. P." at lower right and Arabic equivalents at upper left.

1930-36 **Engr.** **Perf. 14**
Size: 17¼x21mm

169	A3	1m red brn ('34)	1.00	1.10
170	A3	2m Prus blue	.50	.60
171	A3	3m rose	1.50	.85
172	A3	3m green ('34)	2.00	1.25
173	A3	4m green	1.75	3.75
174	A3	4m rose ('34)	3.75	1.50
175	A3	5m orange	1.25	.35
a.		Perf. 13½x14 (coil) ('36)	32.50	18.00
176	A3	10m red	2.00	.25
177	A3	15m ultra	2.00	.25
a.		Perf. 13½x14 (coil) ('36)	30.00	17.50
178	A3	20m olive grn	3.00	.55

Size: 19¼x23½mm

179	A3	50m red violet	3.50	2.00
180	A3	90m bister	4.25	6.00
181	A3	100m light blue	5.00	6.00
182	A3	200m violet	16.00	18.00
183	A3	500m deep brown	30.00	57.50
184	A3	£1 gray	82.50	125.00
		Nos. 169-184 (16)	160.00	224.95

See Nos. 199-220, 230-235. For overprint see No. N15a.

1939 **Perf. 13½x13**
Size: 17¼x21mm

169a	A3	1m red brown	6.00	4.00
170a	A3	2m Prussian blue	15.00	3.75
172a	A3	3m green	25.00	6.50
174a	A3	4m rose	90.00	27.50
175b	A3	5m orange	75.00	4.50
176a	A3	10m red	150.00	5.75
177b	A3	15m ultramarine	47.50	5.50
178a	A3	20m olive grn	72.50	17.50
		Nos. 169a-178a (8)	481.00	75.00

For overprint see No. N3a.

Mushetta — A4

Nymphaeum, Jerash — A5

Kasr Kharana — A6

Kerak Castle — A7

Temple of Artemis, Jerash — A8

Aijalon Castle — A9

Khazneh, Rock-hewn Temple, Petra — A10

Allenby Bridge,
River
Jordan — A11

Ancient
Threshing
Floor — A12

Amir Abdullah ibn
Hussein — A13

1933, Feb. 1   **Perf. 12**

185	A4	1m dk brn & blk	1.50	1.25
186	A5	2m claret & blk	2.00	1.00
187	A6	3m blue green	2.50	1.50
188	A7	4m bister & blk	3.00	3.00
189	A8	5m orange & blk	3.50	1.25
190	A9	10m brown red	4.00	3.50
191	A10	15m dull blue	4.50	1.75
192	A11	20m ol grn & blk	6.50	5.50
193	A12	50m brn vio & blk	20.00	15.00
194	A6	90m yel & black	22.50	27.50
195	A8	100m blue & blk	25.00	30.00
196	A9	200m dk vio & blk	60.00	80.00
197	A10	500m brn & ver	180.00	250.00
198	A13	£1 green & blk	600.00	900.00
		Nos. 185-198 (14)	935.00	1,321.

Nos. 194-197 are larger than the lower values in the same designs.

Amir Abdullah ibn
Hussein — A14

      Perf. 13x13½

1942, May 18   **Litho.**   **Unwmk.**

199	A14	1m dull red brn	1.25	*5.00*
200	A14	2m dull green	2.75	2.25
201	A14	3m dp yel green	3.50	*5.25*
202	A14	4m rose pink	3.50	*5.25*
203	A14	5m orange yel	5.00	1.50
204	A14	10m dull ver	6.50	3.75
205	A14	15m deep blue	14.50	4.00
206	A14	20m dull ol grn	25.00	25.00
		Nos. 199-206 (8)	62.00	52.00

Type A14 differs from A3 in the redrawn inscription above the head and in the form of the "millieme" character at upper left.
For overprint see No. N1.

Abdullah Type of 1930-39
White Paper

1943-44   **Engr.**   **Wmk. 4**   **Perf. 12**
Size: 17¾x21½mm

207	A3	1m red brown	.30	.70
208	A3	2m Prussian grn	1.50	1.25
209	A3	3m blue green	1.75	1.25
210	A3	4m deep rose	1.60	1.25
211	A3	5m orange	1.60	.30
212	A3	10m scarlet	3.25	1.25
213	A3	15m blue green	3.25	1.50
214	A3	20m olive ('44)	3.25	1.00

Size: 20x24mm

215	A3	50m red lil ('44)	3.25	1.10
216	A3	90m ocher	5.50	7.00
217	A3	100m dp bl ('44)	9.25	1.75
218	A3	200m dk vio ('44)	11.50	9.00
219	A3	500m dk brn ('44)	22.50	14.00
220	A3	£1 black ('44)	37.50	27.50
		Nos. 207-220 (14)	106.00	68.85

See Nos. 230-235. For overprints see Nos. 255-256, 259, 264-269, RA23, N2-N4, N7, N12-N17.

Catalogue values for unused stamps in this section, from this point to the end of the section, are for Never Hinged items.

Independent Kingdom

Symbols of Peace
and Liberty — A15

      Perf. 11½

1946, May 25   **Unwmk.**   **Litho.**

221	A15	1m sepia	.30	.25
222	A15	2m yel orange	.30	.25
223	A15	3m dl ol grn	.30	.25
224	A15	4m lt violet	.30	.25
225	A15	10m orange brn	.30	.25
226	A15	12m rose red	.30	.25
227	A15	20m dark blue	.35	.25
228	A15	50m ultra	.90	.60
229	A15	200m green	3.00	3.00
		Nos. 221-229 (9)	6.05	5.35

Independence of the Kingdom of Trans-Jordan.
Nos. 221-229 exist imperforate.

Abdullah Type of 1930-39

1947   **Wmk. 4**   **Engr.**   **Perf. 12**

230	A3	3m rose carmine	.40	.30
231	A3	4m deep yel green	.40	.30
232	A3	10m violet	.60	.30
233	A3	12m deep rose	1.10	.80
234	A3	15m dull olive grn	1.25	.90
235	A3	20m deep blue	1.40	1.00
		Nos. 230-235 (6)	5.15	3.60

For overprints see Nos. 257-258, 260-263, RA24-RA25, N5-N6, N8-N11.

Parliament
Building,
Amman
A16

1947, Nov. 1   **Engr.**   **Unwmk.**

236	A16	1m purple	.45	.25
237	A16	3m red orange	.45	.25
238	A16	4m yel green	.45	.25
239	A16	10m dk vio brn	.45	.25
240	A16	12m carmine	.45	.25
241	A16	20m deep blue	.60	.25
242	A16	50m red vio	.95	.35
243	A16	100m rose	1.25	.65
244	A16	200m dark green	1.90	1.50
		Nos. 236-244 (9)	6.95	4.00

Founding of the new Trans-Jordan parliament, 1947.
Nos. 236-244 exist imperforate.

Symbols
of the
UPU
A17

King
Abdullah
ibn
Hussein
A18

1949, Aug. 1   **Wmk. 4**   **Perf. 13**

245	A17	1m brown	.50	.50
246	A17	4m green	.90	.90
247	A17	10m red	1.10	1.10
248	A17	20m ultramarine	2.00	2.00
249	A18	50m dull green	2.75	2.75
		Nos. 245-249 (5)	7.25	7.25

UPU, 75th anniv. For overprints see Nos. N18-N22.

Nos. 207-208, 211,
215-220, 230-235
Surcharged in Carmine,
Black or Green

1952   **Wmk. 4**   **Perf. 12**
Size: 17¾x21½mm

255	A3	1f on 1m red brn (Bk)	.55	.55
256	A3	2f on 2m Prus grn	.55	.55
257	A3	3f on 3m rose car (Bk)	.55	.55
258	A3	4f on 4m dp yel grn	.55	.55
259	A3	5f on 5m org (G)	1.25	.75
260	A3	10f on 10m vio	1.25	1.00
261	A3	12f on 12m dp rose (Bk)	1.25	1.00
262	A3	15f on 15m dl ol grn	1.50	.75
263	A3	20f on 20m dp bl	2.50	1.10

Size: 20x24mm

264	A3	50f on 50m red lil (G)	2.50	1.75
265	A3	90f on 90m ocher (G)	17.50	11.50
266	A3	100f on 100m dp bl	10.00	3.75
267	A3	200f on 200m dk vio	15.00	4.75
268	A3	500f on 500m dk brn	32.50	17.50
269	A3	1d on £1 black	80.00	20.00
		Nos. 255-269 (15)	167.45	66.05

This surcharge also exists on Nos. 199-203, 205, 209-210, 212-214. Numerous inverted, double and wrong color surcharges exist.

Relief Map — A19

      Perf. 13½x13

1952, Apr. 1   **Engr.**   **Wmk. 4**

270	A19	1f red brn & yel grn	.40	.40
271	A19	2f dk bl grn & red	.40	.40
272	A19	3f car & gray blk	.40	.40
273	A19	4f green & orange	.50	.50
274	A19	5f choc & rose vio	.50	.50
275	A19	10f violet & brown	.50	.50
276	A19	20f dark bl & blk	1.25	.75
277	A19	100f dp blue & brn	4.75	3.25
278	A19	200f purple & orange	11.50	6.00
		Nos. 270-278 (9)	20.20	12.70

Unity of Jordan, Apr. 24, 1950.
For overprints see Nos. 297-305.

Amir Abdullah ibn
Hussein — A20

1952   **Wmk. 4**   **Perf. 11½**

279	A20	5f orange	.40	.30
280	A20	10f violet	.40	.30
281	A20	12f carmine	1.25	.95
282	A20	15f olive	.75	.30
283	A20	20f deep blue	.75	.40

Size: 20x24½mm
Perf. 12x12½

284	A20	50f plum	1.60	.75
285	A20	90f brn orange	4.50	2.50
286	A20	100f deep blue	5.00	1.60
		Nos. 279-286 (8)	14.65	7.10

Nos. RA5-RA7 Overprinted in Black or Carmine
Perf. 11½x12½

1953   **Unwmk.**   **Engr.**

286A	PT1	10m carmine	32.50	25.00
286B	PT1	15m gray (C)	3.00	1.25
286C	PT1	20m dark brown	70.00	47.50

Same Overprint on Nos. NRA4-NRA7

286D	PT1	5m plum	45.00	25.00
286E	PT1	10m carmine	45.00	25.00
286F	PT1	15m gray (C)	45.00	25.00
286G	PT1	20m dk brn (C)	45.00	25.00
		Nos. 286A-286G (7)	285.50	173.75

In addition a few sheets of Nos. RA9, NRA1, NRA3, NRA8-NRA9 and RA37-RA41 have been reported with this overprint. It is doubtful whether they were regularly issued. See Nos. 344-347.

Nos. RA28-RA31
Overprinted in Black
or Carmine

1953   **Wmk. 4**   **Perf. 11½x12½**

287	PT1	5f plum	.35	.25
288	PT1	10f carmine	.40	.25
289	PT1	15f gray (C)	.75	.75
290	PT1	20f dark brown (C)	1.40	1.10
		Nos. 287-290 (4)	2.90	2.35

King
Hussein
A21

Unwmk.

1953, Oct. 1   **Engr.**   **Perf. 12**
Portrait in Black

291	A21	1f dark green	.35	.25
292	A21	4f deep plum	.35	.25
293	A21	15f deep ultra	1.10	.30
294	A21	20f dark purple	2.10	.30
295	A21	50f dark blue grn	4.75	2.25
296	A21	100f dark blue	9.25	6.50
		Nos. 291-296 (6)	17.90	9.85

Accession of King Hussein, May 2, 1953.

Nos. 270-278
Overprinted in Black

1953   **Wmk. 4**   **Perf. 13½x13**

297	A19	1f red brn & yel grn	.40	.25
298	A19	2f dk bl grn & red	.40	.25
299	A19	3f car & gray blk	.40	.25
300	A19	4f green & orange	.40	.25
301	A19	5f choc & rose vio	.40	.25
302	A19	10f violet & brown	1.00	.45
303	A19	20f dark bl & blk	1.00	.60
304	A19	100f dp blue & brn	5.25	1.50
305	A19	200f purple & org	7.00	4.50
		Nos. 297-305 (9)	16.25	8.30

Two main settings of the bars exist on Nos. 297-300 and 304 — the "normal" 1½mm spacing, and the "narrow" ½mm spacing. Values above are for normal spacing. Value of set with narrow spacing, $150.

El Deir Temple,
Petra — A22

Dome of the Rock
— A23

Designs: 2f, 4f, 500f, 1d, King Hussein. 3f, 5f, Treasury Bldg., Petra. 12f, 50f, 100f, 200f, Al Aqsa Mosque. 20f, as 10f.

1954   **Unwmk.**   **Engr.**   **Perf. 12½**

306	A22	1f dk bl grn & red brn	.35	.25
307	A22	2f red & black	.35	.25
308	A22	3f dp plum & vio bl	.35	.25
309	A22	4f org brn & dk grn	.40	.30
310	A22	5f vio & dk grn	.40	.30
311	A23	10f pur & dk grn	.50	.35
312	A23	12f car rose & sep	1.25	.70
313	A23	20f dp bl & dk grn	1.25	.35
314	A23	50f dk bl & dp rose	3.75	3.50
315	A23	100f dk grn & dp bl	2.75	.75
316	A23	200f dp cl & pck bl	12.00	2.25
317	A22	500f choc & purple	32.50	12.50
318	A22	1d dk ol grn & rose brn	50.00	20.00
		Nos. 306-318 (13)	105.85	41.75

See Nos. 324-337. For overprint see No. 425.

Globe — A23a

Perf. 13½x13

1955, Jan. 1   Photo.   Wmk. 195
319	A23a	15f green	.45 .30
320	A23a	20f violet	.45 .30
321	A23a	25f yellow brown	.60 .40
		Nos. 319-321 (3)	1.50 1.00

Founding of the APU, July 1, 1954.

Princess Dina Abdul Hamid and King Hussein — A24

1955, Apr. 19   Perf. 11x11½
322	A24	15f ultramarine	1.50 .65
323	A24	100f rose brown	5.75 2.50

Marriage of King Hussein and Princess Dina Abdul Hamid.

Types of 1954

Design: 15f, Dome of the Rock.

Wmk. 305
1955-64   Engr.   Perf. 12½
324	A22	1f dk bl grn & red brn ('57)	.40 .25
325	A22	2f red & blk ('57)	.40 .25
326	A22	3f dp plum & vio bl ('56)	.40 .25
327	A22	4f org brn & dk grn ('56)	.40 .25
328	A22	5f vio & dk grn ('56)	.40 .25
329	A23	10f pur & grn ('57)	.50 .25
330	A23	12f car rose & sep	1.25 .25
331	A23	15f dp brn & rose red	.75 .25
332	A23	20f dp bl & dk grn ('57)	.60 .25
333	A23	50f dk bl & dp rose	1.50 .35
334	A23	100f dk grn & dp bl ('62)	2.75 .90
335	A23	200f dp cl & pck bl ('65)	7.50 1.75
336	A22	500f choc & pur ('65)	24.00 9.00
337	A22	1d dk ol grn & rose brn ('65)	40.00 15.00
		Nos. 324-337 (14)	80.85 29.25

Envelope A25

Wmk. 305
1956, Jan. 15   Engr.   Perf. 14
"Postmarks" in Black
338	A25	1f light brown	.30 .25
339	A25	4f dark car rose	.30 .25
340	A25	15f blue	.30 .25
341	A25	20f yellow olive	.35 .25
342	A25	50f slate blue	.55 .25
343	A25	100f vermilion	.85 .50
		Nos. 338-343 (6)	2.65 1.75

1st Arab Postal Congress in Amman.

Nos. HA1, HA3, HA8 and RA33 Overprinted in Carmine or Black

Perf. 11½x12½

1956, Jan. 5   Unwmk.
344	PT1	1m ultramarine	.30 .25
345	PT1	3m emerald	.35 .25
346	PT1	50m purple	.60 .50

Wmk. 4
347	PT1	100f orange (Bk)	3.25 1.90
		Nos. 344-347 (4)	4.50 2.90

Numerous inverted, double and wrong color surcharges exist.

Torch of Liberty — A26

1958   Wmk. 305   Engr.   Perf. 12½
348	A26	5f blue & red brown	.45 .40
349	A26	15f bister brn & blk	.45 .40
350	A26	35f blue grn & plum	1.10 1.00
351	A26	45f car & olive grn	10.00 8.50
		Nos. 348-351 (4)	12.00 10.30

10th anniv. of the Universal Declaration of Human Rights.

King Hussein — A27

Perf. 12x11½
1959   Wmk. 305   Engr.
Centers in Black
352	A27	1f deep green	.35 .25
353	A27	2f violet	.35 .25
354	A27	3f deep carmine	.35 .25
355	A27	4f brown black	.40 .25
356	A27	7f dark green	.40 .25
357	A27	12f deep carmine	.50 .25
358	A27	15f dark red	.50 .25
359	A27	21f green	.50 .25
360	A27	25f ocher	.70 .25
361	A27	35f dark blue	1.00 .30
362	A27	40f olive green	1.50 .30
363	A27	50f red	2.25 .30
364	A27	100f blue green	3.00 .50
365	A27	200f rose lake	7.00 3.00
366	A27	500f gray blue	17.50 7.50
367	A27	1d dark purple	35.00 19.00
		Nos. 352-367 (16)	71.30 33.15

For overprints see Nos. 423-424, 425a, 426-427.

Arab League Center, Cairo, and King Hussein A28

Perf. 13x13½
1960, Mar. 22   Photo.   Wmk. 328
368	A28	15f dull green & blk	.35 .25

Opening of the Arab League Center and the Arab Postal Museum in Cairo.

World Refugee Year Emblem A29

Wmk. 305
1960, Apr. 7   Litho.   Perf. 13½
369	A29	15f pale blue & red	.35 .25
370	A29	35f bister & black	.50 .45

World Refugee Year, 7/1/59-6/30/60.
For overprints see Nos. 377-378.

Shah of Iran, King Hussein and Flags A30

Perf. 13x13½
1960, May 15   Wmk. 305
Flags in Green, Red & Black
371	A30	15f yellow & black	.55 .55
372	A30	35f blue & black	.80 .80
373	A30	50f salmon & black	1.10 1.10
		Nos. 371-373 (3)	2.45 2.45

Visit of Mohammed Riza Pahlavi, Shah of Iran, to Jordan, Nov. 2, 1959.

Oil Refinery, Zarka A31

1961, May 1   Engr.   Perf. 14x13
374	A31	15f dull vio & blue	.35 .25
375	A31	35f dl vio & brick red	.55 .40

Opening of oil refinery at Zarka.

Urban and Nomad Families and Chart A32

Perf. 13x13½
1961, Oct. 15   Photo.   Unwmk.
376	A32	15f orange brown	.30 .25

First Jordanian census, 1901.

Nos. 369-370 Overprinted in English and Arabic, "In Memorial of Dag Hammarskjoeld 1904-1961," and Laurel Leaf Border

1961   Wmk. 305   Litho.   Perf. 13½
377	A29	15f pale blue & red	3.75 3.50
378	A29	35f bister & black	4.25 3.75

Dag Hammarskjold, Secretary General of the UN, 1953-1961.

Malaria Eradication Emblem — A33

Perf. 11x11½
1962, Apr. 15   Unwmk.
379	A33	15f bright pink	.35 .25
380	A33	35f bister red	.45 .30

WHO drive to eradicate malaria. A souvenir sheet exists with one each of Nos. 379-380. Value $5.50.

Dial and Exchange Building, Amman A34

1962, Dec. 11   Engr.   Wmk. 305
381	A34	15f blue & lilac	.30 .25
382	A34	35f lilac & emer	.35 .25

Telephone automation in Amman (in 1960).

Opening of the Port of 'Aqaba A35

1962, Dec. 11
383	A35	15f lilac & blk	.40 .25
384	A35	35f violet bl & blk	.60 .30
a.	Souvenir sheet of 2, #383-384		5.00 5.00

No. 384a imperf., same value.

Dag Hammarskjold and UN Headquarters, NY — A36

Perf. 14x14½
1963, Jan. 24   Photo.   Unwmk.
385	A36	15f ultra, ol grn & brn red	.45 .25
386	A36	35f ol, brn red & ultra	.80 .45
387	A36	50f brn red, ol & ultra	1.25 .80
		Nos. 385-387 (3)	2.50 1.50

17th anniv. of the UN and in memory of Dag Hammarskjold, Secretary General of the UN, 1953-61. An imperf. souvenir sheet contains one each of Nos. 385-387 with simulated perforations. Value $9.

Imperforates
Starting with No. 385, imperforates exist of many Jordanian stamps.

Church of St. Virgin's Tomb, Jerusalem — A37

Designs: No. 389, Basilica of the Agony, Gethsemane. No. 390, Church of the Holy Sepulcher, Jerusalem. No. 391, Church of the Nativity, Bethlehem. No. 392, Haram el-Khalil (tomb of Abraham), Hebron. No. 393, Dome of the Rock, Jerusalem. No. 394, Mosque of Omar el-Khatab, Jerusalem. No. 395, Al Aqsa Mosque, Jerusalem.

1963, Feb. 5   Perf. 14½x14
Center Multicolored
388	A37	50f blue	1.50 1.00
389	A37	50f dull red	1.50 1.00
390	A37	50f bright blue	1.50 1.00
391	A37	50f olive green	1.50 1.00
a.	Vert. strip of 4, #388-391		15.00
392	A37	50f gray	1.50 1.00
a.	Yellow (in center) omitted		—
393	A37	50f purple	1.50 1.00
a.	Yellow (in center) omitted		—
394	A37	50f dull red	1.50 1.00
a.	Yellow (in center) omitted		—
395	A37	50f light purple	1.50 1.00
a.	Vert. strip of 4, #392-395		15.00
b.	Yellow (in center) omitted		—
		Nos. 388-395 (8)	12.00 8.00

Arab League Building, Cairo — A38

1963, July 16 Photo. *Perf. 13½x13*
396 A38 15f slate blue   .45 .25
397 A38 35f orange red   .65 .25

Arab League.

Wheat and UN Emblem — A39

Perf. 11½x12½
1963, Sept. 15 Litho. Wmk. 305
398 A39 15f lt bl, grn & black .30 .25
399 A39 35f lt grn, grn & blk   .30 .25
a. Souvenir sheet of 2, #398-399 1.50 1.50

FAO "Freedom from Hunger" campaign. No. 399a imperf., same value.

East Ghor Canal, Pylon, Gear Wheel and Wheat A40

1963, Sept. 20 *Perf. 14½x14*
400 A40 1f dull yel & black   .35 .25
401 A40 4f blue & black   .35 .25
402 A40 5f lilac & black   .35 .25
403 A40 10f brt yel grn & blk   .40 .25
404 A40 35f orange & black   1.25 .50
Nos. 400-404 (5)   2.70 1.50

East Ghor Canal Project.

UNESCO Emblem, Scales and Globe A41

Perf. 13½x13
1963, Dec. 10 Unwmk.
405 A41 50f pale vio bl & red   .70 .60
406 A41 50f rose red & blue   .70 .60

15th anniv. of the Universal Declaration of Human Rights.

Red Crescent and King Hussein — A42

1963, Dec. 24 Photo. *Perf. 14x14½*
407 A42 1f red & red lilac   .30 .25
408 A42 2f red & bl green   .30 .25
409 A42 3f red & dk blue   .30 .25
410 A42 4f red & dk green   .30 .25
411 A42 5f red & dk brown   .30 .25
412 A42 85f red & dp green   1.10 .95

Design: Red Cross at right, no portrait
413 A42 1f red lilac & red   .30 .25
414 A42 2f blue grn & red   .30 .25
415 A42 3f dk blue & red   .30 .25
416 A42 4f dk green & red   .30 .25
417 A42 5f dk brown & red   .30 .25
418 A42 85f dp green & red   4.00 1.50
Nos. 407-418 (12)   8.10 4.95

Centenary of the Intl. Red Cross. Two 100f imperf. souvenir sheets, red and red lilac, exist in the Red Crescent and Red Cross designs. Value, pair of sheets $50.

Hussein ibn Ali and King Hussein A43

Perf. 11x11½
1963, Dec. 25 Litho. Unwmk.
419 A43 15f yellow & multi   .50 .25
420 A43 25f multicolored   .75 .35
421 A43 35f brt pink & multi   1.75 .85
422 A43 50f lt blue & multi   2.75 2.00
Nos. 419-422 (4)   5.75 3.45

Arab Renaissance Day, June 10, 1916. Perf. and imperf. souvenir sheets exist containing one each of Nos. 419-422. Value: perf, $6.50; imperf, $9.

Nos. 359, 312, 357 and 361 Surcharged

Wmk. 305, Unwmk.
Perf. 12x11½, 12½
1963, Dec. 16 Engr.
423 A27 1f on 21f grn & blk   .40 .30
424 A27 2f on 21f grn & blk   .40 .30
425 A23 4f on 12f car rose & sepia .45 .40
a. 4f on 12f dp car & blk (#357) 19.00 22.50
426 A27 5f on 21f grn & blk   .85 .50
427 A27 25f on 35f dk bl & blk 3.25 1.50
Nos. 423-427 (5)   5.35 3.00

Pope Paul VI, King Hussein and Al Aqsa Mosque, Jerusalem — A44

Portraits and: 35f, Dome of the Rock. 50f, Church of the Holy Sepulcher. 80f, Church of the Nativity, Bethlehem.

1964, Jan. 4 Litho. *Perf. 13x13½*
428 A44 15f emerald & blk   .80 .30
429 A44 35f car rose & blk   1.00 .40
a. Black omitted   —   —
430 A44 50f brown & black   1.75 .90
431 A44 80f vio bl & blk   3.25 2.00
Nos. 428-431 (4)   6.80 3.60

Visit of Pope Paul VI to the Holy Land, Jan. 4-6. An imperf. souvenir sheet contains 4 stamps similar to Nos. 428-431. Value $27.50.

Crown Prince Abdullah ben Al-Hussein — A46

Design: 5f, Crown Prince standing, vert.

1964, Mar. 30 Photo. *Perf. 14*
432 A46 5f multicolored   .55 .25
433 A46 10f multicolored   .65 .50
434 A46 35f multicolored   1.50 1.00
Nos. 432-434 (3)   2.70 1.75

2nd birthday of Crown Prince Abdullah ben Al-Hussein (b. Jan. 30, 1962).

A47

Mercury Astronauts, Spacecraft — A48

Designs: b, M. Scott Carpenter. c, Entering space. d, Alan Shepard. e, At launch pad. f, Virgil Grissom. g, After separation. h, Walter Schirra. i, Lift-off. j, John Glenn. Stamp has point down on b, d, f, h, j.

1964, Mar. 25 Photo. *Perf. 14*
435 A47 20f Block of 10, #a.-j. 12.00 6.50

Imperf
Size: 111x80mm
436 A48 100f multicolored   20.00 20.00

Table Tennis A49

Designs: 1f, 2f, 3f, 5f vertical.

Perf. 14½x14, 14x14½
1964, June 1 Litho. Unwmk.
446 A49 1f Basketball   .50 .25
447 A49 2f Volleyball   .50 .25
448 A49 3f Soccer   .50 .25
449 A49 4f shown   .50 .25
450 A49 5f Running   .50 .25
451 A49 35f Bicycling   1.75 1.10
452 A49 50f Fencing   2.50 1.50
453 A49 100f Pole vault   4.50 2.75
Nos. 446-453 (8)   11.25 6.60

1964 Olympic Games, Tokyo, Oct. 10-25. An imperf. 200f greenish blue souvenir sheet in design of 100f exists. Value $35.

Mother and Child — A50

1964, June 1 Wmk. 305 *Perf. 14*
454 A50 5f multicolored   .30 .25
455 A50 10f multicolored   .30 .25
456 A50 25f multicolored   .30 .25
Nos. 454-456 (3)   .90 .75

Social Studies Seminar, fourth session.

Pres. John F. Kennedy — A51

1964, July 15 Unwmk.
457 A51 1f brt violet   .50 .40
458 A51 2f carmine rose   .50 .40
459 A51 3f ultramarine   .50 .40
460 A51 4f orange brown   .50 .40
461 A51 5f bright green   .50 .40
462 A51 85f rose red   18.50 11.00
Nos. 457-462 (6)   21.00 13.00

President John F. Kennedy (1917-1963). An imperf. 100f brown souvenir sheet exists. Size of stamp: 58x83mm. Value $18.50.

Ramses II A52

Perf. 14½x14
1964, July Litho. Wmk. 305
463 A52 4f lt blue & dark brn   .30 .25
464 A52 15f yellow & violet   .30 .25
465 A52 25f lt yel grn & dk red .30 .25
Nos. 463-465 (3)   .90 .75

UNESCO world campaign to save historic monuments in Nubia.

King Hussein and Map of Jordan and Israel — A53

1964, Sept. 5 Unwmk. *Perf. 12*
466 A53 10f multicolored   .40 .25
467 A53 15f multicolored   .40 .25
468 A53 25f multicolored   .40 .25
469 A53 50f multicolored   .70 .25
470 A53 80f multicolored   1.00 .45
Nos. 466-470 (5)   2.90 1.45

Council of the Heads of State of the Arab League (Arab Summit Conference), Cairo, Jan. 13, 1964. An imperf. souvenir sheet contains Nos. 466-470 with simulated perforations. Value $4.

Pope Paul VI, King Hussein and Patriarch Athenagoras; Church of St. Savior, Church of the Holy Sepulcher and Dome of the Rock — A54

1964, Aug. 17 Litho.
471 A54 10f dk grn, sep & org   .50 .25
472 A54 15f claret, sep & org   .50 .25
473 A54 25f choc, sepia & org   .50 .25
474 A54 50f blue, sepia & org 1.00 .70
475 A54 80f brt grn, sep & org 2.25 .60
Nos. 471-475 (5)   4.75 2.05

Meeting between Pope Paul VI and Patriarch Athenagoras of the Greek Orthodox Church in Jerusalem, Jan. 5, 1964. An imperf. souvenir sheet contains Nos. 471-475 with simulated perforations. Value $12.

A two-line bilingual overprint, "Papa Paulus VI World Peace Visit to United Nations 1965", was applied to Nos. 471-475 and the souvenir sheet. These overprints were issued Apr. 27, 1966. Value, unused: set, $6; souvenir sheet, $12.

Pagoda, Olympic Torch and Emblem — A55

1964, Nov. 21   Litho.   Perf. 14
476 A55   1f dark red   .45   .25
477 A55   2f bright violet   .55   .25
478 A55   3f blue green   .65   .25
479 A55   4f brown   .75   .30
480 A55   5f henna brown   .85   .35
481 A55 35f indigo   1.25 1.00
482 A55 50f olive   2.00 1.50
483 A55 100f violet blue   4.25 3.00
       Nos. 476-483 (8)   10.75 6.90

18th Olympic Games, Tokyo, Oct. 10-25. An imperf. 100f carmine rose souvenir sheet exists. Size of stamp: 82mm at the base. Value $20.

Scouts Crossing Stream on Log Bridge — A56

Designs: 2f, First aid. 3f, Calisthenics. 4f, Instruction in knot tying. 5f, Outdoor cooking. 35f, Sailing. 50f, Campfire.

1964, Dec. 7   Unwmk.
484 A56   1f brown   .70   .25
485 A56   2f bright violet   .70   .25
486 A56   3f ocher   .70   .25
487 A56   4f maroon   .70   .25
488 A56   5f yellow green   .70   .25
489 A56 35f bright blue   2.00 1.25
490 A56 50f dk slate green   3.50 1.75
       Nos. 484-490 (7)   9.00 4.25

Jordanian Boy Scouts. An imperf. 100f dark blue souvenir sheet in campfire design exists. Size of stamp: 104mm at the base. Value $22.50.

Yuri A. Gagarin — A57

Russian Cosmonauts: No. 492, Gherman Titov. No. 493, Andrian G. Nikolayev. No. 494, Pavel R. Popovich. No. 495, Valeri Bykovski. No. 496, Valentina Tereshkova.

1965, Jan. 20   Litho.   Perf. 14
491 A57 40f sepia & vio bl   1.25   .75
492 A57 40f pink & dk grn   1.25   .75
493 A57 40f lt bl & vio blk   1.25   .75
494 A57 40f olive & dk vio   1.25   .75
495 A57 40f lt grn & red brn   1.25   .75
496 A57 40f chlky bl & blk   1.25   .75
       Nos. 491-496 (6)   7.50 4.50

Russian cosmonauts. A blue 100f souvenir sheet exists showing portraits of the 6 astronauts and space-ship circling globe. This sheet received later an additional overprint honoring the space flight of Komarov, Feoktistov and Yegorov. Value $20, each.
For overprints see Nos. 527-527E.

UN Headquarters and Emblem — A58

1965, Feb. 15   Perf. 14x15
497 A58 30f yel brn, pur & lt bl .60   .25
498 A58 70f vio, lt bl & yel brn 1.00   .70

19th anniv. of the UN (in 1964). A souvenir sheet contains Nos. 497-498, imperf. Value $14.

Dagger in Map of Palestine — A59

1965, Apr. 9   Photo.   Perf. 11x11½
499 A59 25f red & olive   4.50 1.25
  a.   Red omitted   —

Deir Yassin massacre, Apr. 9, 1948.
See Iraq Nos. 372-373 and Kuwait Nos. 281-282.

Volleyball Player and Cup — A60

1965, June   Litho.   Perf. 14½x14
500 A60 15f lemon   1.25   .25
501 A60 35f rose brown   1.50   .25
502 A60 50f greenish blue   2.25   .75
       Nos. 500-502 (3)   5.00 1.25

Arab Volleyball Championships. An imperf. 100f orange brown souvenir sheet exists. Size of stamp: 33x57mm. Value $22.50.

Cavalry Horsemanship A61

Army Day: 10f, Tank. 35f, King Hussein and aides standing in army car.

1965, May 24
503 A61   5f green   .50   .25
504 A61 10f violet blue   .55   .25
505 A61 35f brown red   1.50   .55
       Nos. 503-505 (3)   2.55 1.05

John F. Kennedy — A62

1965, June 1   Wmk. 305   Perf. 14
506 A62 10f black & brt green   .30   .25
507 A62 15f violet & orange   .50   .25
508 A62 25f brown & lt blue   .50   .30
509 A62 50f deep claret & emer   1.50   .60
       Nos. 506-509 (4)   2.80 1.40

John F. Kennedy (1917-63). An imperf. 50f salmon and dark blue souv. sheet exists. Value $17.50.

Pope Paul VI, King Hussein and Dome of the Rock — A63

Perf. 13½x14
1965, June 15   Litho.   Wmk. 305
510 A63   5f brown & rose lil   .50   .25
511 A63 10f vio brn & lt yel grn .90   .40
512 A63 15f ultra & salmon   1.10   .50
513 A63 50f black & rose   3.25 1.60
       Nos. 510-513 (4)   5.75 2.75

1st anniversary of the visit of Pope Paul VI to the Holy Land. An imperf. 50f violet and light blue souvenir sheet exists with simulated perforations. Value $25.

Jordan's Pavilion and Unisphere — A64

Perf. 14x13½
1965, Aug.   Unwmk.   Photo.
514 A64 15f silver & multi   .45   .25
515 A64 25f bronze & multi   .45   .25
516 A64 50f gold & multi   .85   .40
  a.   Souvenir sheet of 1, 100f 3.25 3.00
       Nos. 514-516 (3)   1.75   .90

New York World's Fair, 1964-65.
No. 516a contains a 100f gold and multicolored stamp, type A64, imperf.

Library Aflame and Lamp A64a

1965, Aug.   Wmk. 305   Perf. 11½x11
517 A64a 25f black, grn & red   .50   .25
Burning of the Library of Algiers, 6/7/62.

ITU Emblem, Old and New Telecommunication Equipment — A65

1965, Aug.   Litho.   Perf. 14x13½
518 A65 25f lt blue & dk bl   .40   .25
519 A65 45f grnsh gray & blk   .60   .35

ITU, centenary. An imperf. 100f salmon and carmine rose souvenir sheet exists with carmine rose border. Size of stamp: 39x32mm. Value $3.

Syncom Satellite over Pagoda — A66

Designs: 10f, 20f, Rocket in space. 15f, Astronauts in cabin.

1965, Sept.   Perf. 14
521 A66   5f multicolored   .30   .25
521A A66 10f multicolored   .30   .25
521B A66 15f multicolored   .50   .25
521C A66 20f multicolored   .60   .30
521D A66 50f multicolored   1.50   .75
       Nos. 521-521D (5)   3.20 1.80

Achievements in space research. A 50f multicolored imperf. souvenir sheet shows earth and Syncom satellite. Value $17.50.

Dead Sea A66a

Designs: b, Qumran Caves. c, Dead Sea. d, Dead Sea Scrolls.

1965, Sept. 23   Photo.   Perf. 14
522 A66a 35f Strip of 4, #a.-d.   6.00 6.00

Visit of King Hussein to France and U.S. — A66b

10f, With Charles DeGaulle. 20f, With Lyndon Johnson.

Wmk. 305
1965, Oct. 5   Litho.   Perf. 14
523 A66b 5f shown   .30   .25
523A A66b 10f multicolored   .30   .25
523B A66b 20f multicolored   .65   .50
523C A66b 50f like #523   1.50 1.10
       Nos. 523-523C (4)   2.75 2.10

No. 523C exists in a 50f imperf. souvenir sheet. Value $12.

Intl. Cooperation Year — A66c

1965, Oct. 24   *Perf. 14x13½*
524	A66c	5f brt org & dk org	.40	.25
524A	A66c	10f brt bl & dk bl	.75	.35
524B	A66c	45f brt grn & dk violet	2.10	1.40
		Nos. 524-524B (3)	3.25	2.00

Arab Postal Union, 10th Anniv. — A66d

1965, Nov. 5   *Perf. 15x14*
525	A66d	15f violet bl & blk	.30	.25
525A	A66d	25f brt yel grn & blk	.50	.35

Dome of the Rock A66e

1965, Nov. 20   *Perf. 14x15*
526	A66e	15f multicolored	1.10	1.10
526A	A66e	25f multicolored	1.60	1.60

Nos. 491-496 with Spaceship & Bilingual Ovpt. in Blue

1966, Jan. 15   Litho.   *Perf. 14*
527	A57	40f on No. 491	3.75	3.50
527A	A57	40f on No. 492	3.75	3.50
527B	A57	40f on No. 493	3.75	3.50
527C	A57	40f on No. 494	3.75	3.50
527D	A57	40f on No. 495	3.75	3.50
527E	A57	40f on No. 496	3.75	3.50
		Nos. 527-527E (6)	22.50	21.00

Both souvenir sheets mentioned after No. 496 exist overprinted in red violet. Value, $50 each.

King Hussein A67

Perf. 14½x14
1966, Jan. 15   Photo.   Unwmk.
Portrait in Slate Blue
528	A67	1f orange	.40	.25
528A	A67	2f ultramarine	.40	.25
528B	A67	3f dk purple	.40	.25
528C	A67	4f plum	.40	.25
528D	A67	7f brn orange	.40	.25
528E	A67	12f cerise	.40	.25
528F	A67	15f olive brn	.40	.25

Portrait in Violet Brown
528G	A67	21f green	.55	.35
528H	A67	25f greenish bl	.55	.35
528I	A67	35f yel bister	.80	.35
528J	A67	40f orange yel	1.00	.35
528K	A67	50f olive grn	1.10	.25
528L	A67	100f lt yel grn	2.10	.40
528M	A67	150f violet	3.00	1.00
		Nos. 528-528M,C43-C45 (17)	52.90	19.85

Anti-tuberculosis Campaign — A67a

1966, May 17   Photo.   *Perf. 14x15*
Blue Overprint
529	A67a	15f multicolored	.65	.50
529A	A67a	35f multicolored	1.10	.95
529B	A67a	50f multicolored	1.50	1.25
		Nos. 529-529B (3)	3.25	2.70

Unissued Freedom from Hunger stamps overprinted. Two imperf. souvenir sheets exist, one with simulated perforations. Value, each $10.

Nos. 529-529B with Added Surcharge Obliterated with Black Bars

1966, May 17   Photo.   *Perf. 14x15*
530	A67a	15f on 15f + 15f	.75	.30
530A	A67a	35f on 35f + 35f	1.50	.75
530B	A67a	50f on 50f + 50f	2.75	1.25
		Nos. 530-530B (3)	5.00	2.30

A67b

Stations on Jesus' walk to Calvary along Via Dolorosa (Stations of the Cross): 1f, Condemned to death. 2f, Takes up cross. 3f, Falls the 1st time. 4f, Meets His mother. 5f, Simon helps carry cross. 6f, Woman wipes Jesus' brow. 7f, Falls 2nd time. 8f, Tells women not to weep. 9f, Falls 3rd time. 10f, Stripped of His garment. 11f, Nailed to cross. 12f, Death on cross. 13f, Removal from cross. 14f, Burial. Denominations expressed in Roman numerals.

1966, Sept. 14   Photo.   *Perf. 15x14*
531	A67b	1f multi	.40	.25
531A	A67b	2f multi	.40	.25
531B	A67b	3f multi	.40	.25
531C	A67b	4f multi	.50	.25
531D	A67b	5f multi	.60	.30
531E	A67b	6f multi	.60	.30
531F	A67b	7f multi	.80	.40
531G	A67b	8f multi	.90	.45
531H	A67b	9f multi	1.00	.50
531I	A67b	10f multi	1.10	.55
531J	A67b	11f multi	1.25	.60
531K	A67b	12f multi	1.40	.65
531L	A67b	13f multi	1.50	.70
531M	A67b	14f multi	1.60	.75
		Nos. 531-531M (14)	12.45	6.20

Souvenir Sheet
Imperf
531N	A67b	100f like #531	30.00	27.50

A67c

Astronauts and spacecraft from Gemini Missions 6-8: 1f, Walter M. Schirra. 2f, Thomas P. Stafford. 3f, Frank Borman. 4f, James A. Lovell. 30f, Neil Armstrong. 60f, David R. Scott.
100f, Gemini 6-8 astronauts.

1966, Nov. 15   Photo.   *Perf. 15x14*
532	A67c	1f multi	.35	.25
532A	A67c	2f multi	.35	.25
532B	A67c	3f multi	.35	.25
532C	A67c	4f multi	.35	.25
532D	A67c	30f multi	1.50	.90
532E	A67c	60f multi	2.10	1.50
		Nos. 532-532E (6)	5.00	3.20

Imperf
Size: 119x89mm
532F	A67c	100f multi	22.50	20.00

Christmas — A67d

5f, Magi following star. 10f, Adoration of the Magi. 35f, Flight to Egypt, vert.

Perf. 14x15, 15x14
1966, Dec. 21   Photo.
533	A67d	5f multi	.35	.25
533A	A67d	10f multi	.35	.25
533B	A67d	35f multi	3.25	1.10
		Nos. 533-533B (3)	3.95	1.60

Souvenir Sheet
Imperf
533C	A67d	50f like #533A	22.50	20.00

King Hussein — A67e

Builders of World Peace: No. 534, Dag Hammarskjold. No. 534A, U Thant. No. 534B, Jawaharlal Nehru. No. 534C, Charles DeGaulle. No. 534D, John F. Kennedy. No. 534E, Lyndon B. Johnson. No. 534F, Pope John XXIII. No. 534G, Pope Paul VI. No. 534H, King Abdullah of Jordan.

1967, Jan. 5   Photo.   *Perf. 15x14*
Background Color
534	A67e	5f gray	.35	.25
534A	A67e	5f brt yel grn	.35	.25
534B	A67e	10f rose lilac	.35	.25
a.		"FILS" omitted	—	
534C	A67e	10f red brown	.35	.25
534D	A67e	35f olive green	.95	.70
534E	A67e	35f orange	.95	.70
a.		Gold (frame) omitted	—	
534F	A67e	50f rose claret	1.10	1.00
534G	A67e	50f yel bister	1.10	1.00
534H	A67e	100f brt blue	2.50	2.10
534I	A67e	100f dull blue	2.50	2.10
		Nos. 534-534I (10)	10.50	8.60

Imperf
Size: 99x64mm
534J	A67e	100f Kennedy, etc.	22.50	22.50
534K	A67e	100f DeGaulle, etc.	22.50	22.50

King Hussein A67f

Photo. & Embossed
1967, Feb. 7   *Imperf.*
Gold Portrait and Border
Diameter: 50f, 100f, 48mm; 200f, 54mm
Portrait of King Hussein
535	A67f	5f dk bl & sal	.75	.75
535A	A67f	10f pur & sal	.75	.75
535B	A67f	50f blk brn & vio	4.25	4.25
535C	A67f	100f dk ol grn & pink	5.00	5.00
535D	A67f	200f dp bl & bl	7.75	7.75

Portrait of Crown Prince Hassan
536	A67f	5f brt yel grn & blk	.75	.75
536A	A67f	10f vio & blk	.75	.75
536B	A67f	50f bl & blk	4.25	4.25
536C	A67f	100f bister & blk	5.00	5.00
536D	A67f	200f brt pink & blk	7.75	7.75

Portrait of John F. Kennedy
537	A67f	5f brt bl & lt grn	.75	.75
537A	A67f	10f dp grn & pink	.75	.75
537B	A67f	50f brt rose & org yel	3.25	3.25
537C	A67f	100f brn & apple grn	4.25	4.25
537D	A67f	200f dk purple & pale grn	5.00	5.00
		Nos. 535-537D (15)	51.00	51.00

1968 Summer Olympic Games, Mexico — A67g

Olympic torch and: 1f, Natl. University Library with O'Gormans mosaics, statue, Mexico City. 2f, Fishermen on Lake Patzcuaro. 3f, Natl. University buildings. 4f, Paseo de la Reforma, Mexico City. 30f, Guadalajara Cathedral. 60f, 100f, Palace of Fine Arts, Mexico City.

Perf. 14x15
1967, Mar.   Photo.   Unwmk.
538	A67g	1f lake, dk bl vio & blk	.30	.25
538A	A67g	2f blk, lake & dk bl vio	.30	.25
538B	A67g	3f dark bl vio, blk & lake	.30	.25
538C	A67g	4f bl, grn & brn	.30	.25
538D	A67g	30f grn, brn & bl	.60	.60
538E	A67g	60f brn, bl & grn	1.10	1.10
		Nos. 538-538E (6)	2.90	2.70

Souvenir Sheet
Imperf
538F	A67g	100f brn, dark bl & grn	22.50	22.50

Symbolic Water Cycle A68

Perf. 14½x14
1967, Mar. 1   Litho.   Wmk. 305
539 A68 10f dp org, blk & gray .50 .25
540 A68 15f grnsh bl, blk & gray .50 .35
541 A68 25f brt rose lil, blk & gray .75 .50
Nos. 539-541 (3) 1.75 1.10
Hydrological Decade (UNESCO), 1965-74.

UNESCO Emblem — A69

1967, Mar. 16
542 A69 100f multicolored 1.10 1.10
20th anniv. of UNESCO.

Dromedary — A70

Animals: 2f, Karakul. 3f, Angora goat.

Perf. 14x15
1967, Feb. 11   Photo.   Unwmk.
543 A70 1f dark brn & multi 1.10 .25
544 A70 2f yellow & multi 1.10 .25
545 A70 3f lt blue & multi 1.10 .25
Nos. 543-545,C46-C48 (6) 12.30 2.45
A souvenir sheet exists with a 100f in design and colors of No. C47, simulated perforation and marginal animal design. Value $35.

Inauguration of WHO Headquarters, Geneva — A71

1967, Apr. 7   Wmk. 305
546 A71 5f emerald & blk .40 .25
547 A71 45f dl orange & blk .50 .30

Arab League Emblem and Hands Reaching for Knowledge — A72

1968, May 5   Unwmk.   Perf. 11
548 A72 20f org & slate grn .45 .25
549 A72 20f brt pink & dk bl .45 .25
Issued to publicize the literacy campaign.

"20" and WHO Emblem A73

Perf. 14½x14
1968, Aug. 10   Wmk. 305
550 A73 30f multicolored .60 .25
551 A73 100f multicolored 1.75 1.10
20th anniv. of the WHO.

European Goldfinch — A74

Protected Game: 10f, Rock partridge, vert. 1f, Ostriches, vert. 20f, Sand partridge. 30f, Dorcas gazelle. 40f, Oryxes. 50f, Houbara bustard.

1968, Oct. 5   Unwmk.   Perf. 13½
552 A74 5f multicolored 3.25 1.25
553 A74 10f multicolored 6.50 1.25
554 A74 15f multicolored 8.50 1.50
555 A74 20f multicolored 8.50 1.75
556 A74 30f multicolored 5.25 1.25
557 A74 40f multicolored 8.00 1.50
558 A74 50f multicolored 12.50 3.00
Nos. 552-558,C49-C50 (9) 81.00 23.00

Human Rights Flame — A75

1968, Dec. 10   Litho.   Perf. 13
559 A75 20f dp org, lt org & blk .40 .25
560 A75 60f grn, lt blue & blk .75 .45
International Human Rights Year.

Dome of the Rock, Jerusalem A76

5f, 45f, Holy Kaaba, Mecca, & Dome of the Rock.

1969, Oct. 8   Photo.   Perf. 12
Size: 56x25mm
561 A76 5f dull vio & multi .80 .25
Size: 36x25mm
562 A76 10f vio blue & multi .80 .50
563 A76 20f Prus bl & multi 1.25 .60
Size: 56x25mm
564 A76 45f Prus bl & multi 2.10 .70
Nos. 561-564 (4) 4.95 2.05

ILO Emblem A77

1969, June 10   Perf. 13½x14
565 A77 10f blue & black .35 .25
566 A77 20f bister brn & blk .35 .25
567 A77 25f lt olive & black .35 .25
568 A77 45f lil rose & black .50 .30
569 A77 60f orange & black .75 .35
Nos. 565-569 (5) 2.30 1.40
ILO, 50th anniversary.

Horses A78

20f, White stallion. 45f, Mare and foal.

1969, July 6   Unwmk.   Perf. 13½
570 A78 10f dark bl & multi 1.50 .25
571 A78 20f dl green & multi 3.50 .60
572 A78 45f red & multi 6.50 1.75
Nos. 570-572 (3) 11.50 2.60

Prince Hassan and Princess Tharwat A79

Designs: 60f, 100f, Prince Hassan and bride in western bridal gown.

1969, Dec. 2   Photo.   Perf. 12½
573 A79 20f gold & multi .50 .25
573A A79 60f gold & multi 1.00 .65
573B A79 100f gold & multi 1.50 1.25
 c. Strip of 3, #573-573B 3.25 3.25
Wedding of Crown Prince Hassan, 11/14/68.

The Tragedy and the Flight of the Refugees — A79a

Different design on each stamp. Each strip of 5 has five consecutive denominations.

Perf. 14½x13½
1969, Dec. 10   Photo.
574 A79a 1f-5f Strip of 5 11.00 11.00
 f.-j. A79a 1f-5f Any single
574A A79a 6f-10f Strip of 5 11.00 11.00
 a.-e. A79a 6f-10f Any single
574B A79a 11f-15f Strip of 5 11.00 11.00
 a.-e. A79a 11f-15f Any single
574C A79a 16f-20f Strip of 5 11.00 11.00
 a.-e. A79a 16f-20f Any single
574D A79a 21f-25f Strip of 5 11.00 11.00
 a.-e. A79a 21f-25f Any single
574E A79a 26f-30f Strip of 5 11.00 11.00
 a.-e. A79a 26f-30f Any single
For surcharges see Nos. 870-875.

Inscribed: Tragedy in the Holy Lands
Different design on each stamp. Each strip of 5 has five consecutive denominations.

Perf. 14½x13½
1969, Dec. 10   Photo.
575 A79a 1f-5f Strip of 5 5.00 5.00
 f.-j. A79a 1f-5f Any single
575A A79a 6f-10f Strip of 5 5.00 5.00
 a.-e. A79a 6f-10f Any single
575B A79a 11f-15f Strip of 5 5.00 5.00
 a.-e. A79a 11f-15f Any single
575C A79a 16f-20f Strip of 5 5.00 5.00
 a.-e. A79a 16f-20f Any single
575D A79a 21f-25f Strip of 5 5.00 5.00
 a.-e. A79a 21f-25f Any single
575E A79a 26f-30f Strip of 5 5.00 5.00
 a.-e. A79a 26f-30f Any single
For surcharges see Nos. 876-881.

Pomegranate Flower (inscribed "Desert Scabius") — A80

Oranges — A81

Black Bush Robin — A82

Designs: 15f, Wattle flower ("Caper"). 20f, Melon. 25f, Caper flower ("Pomegranate"). 30f, Lemons. 35f, Morning glory. 40f, Grapes. 45f, Desert scabius ("Wattle"). 50f, Olive-laden branch. 75f, Black iris. 100f, Apples. 180f, Masked shrike. 200f, Palestine sunbird. (Inscriptions incorrect on 5f, 15f, 25f and 45f.)

Perf. 14x13½ (flowers), 12 (fruit), 13½x14 (birds)
1969-70   Photo.
576 A80 5f yel & multi ('70) .40 .25
577 A81 10f blue & multi .40 .25
578 A80 15f tan & multi ('70) .70 .25
579 A81 20f sepia & multi .60 .25
580 A80 25f multi ('70) 1.00 .25
581 A81 30f vio bl & multi 1.00 .25
582 A80 35f multi ('70) 1.50 .25
583 A81 40f dull yel & multi 1.50 .25
584 A80 45f gray & multi ('70) 2.00 .25
585 A81 50f car rose & multi 2.00 .40
586 A80 75f multi ('70) 3.00 1.00
587 A01 100f dk gray & multi 3.25 1.25
588 A82 120f org & multi ('70) 10.00 2.00
589 A82 180f multi ('70) 17.50 4.75
590 A82 200f multi ('70) 20.00 7.00
Nos. 576-590 (15) 64.85 18.65
Issued: Fruits, 11/22; flowers, 3/21; birds, 9/1.

Soccer A83

Designs: 10f, Diver. 15f, Boxers. 50f, Runner. 100f, Bicyclist, vert. 150f, Basketball, vert.

1970, Aug.   Perf. 13½x14, 14x13½
651 A83 5f green & multi 1.00 .25
652 A83 10f lt bl & multi 1.00 .25
653 A83 15f gray & multi 1.00 .25
654 A83 50f gray & multi 1.50 .65
655 A83 100f yellow & multi 2.25 1.25
656 A83 150f multicolored 3.25 2.25
Nos. 651-656 (6) 10.00 4.90

Refugee Children A84

Emblems and: 10F, Boy Fetching Water, UNICEF and Refugee Emblems. 15f, Girl and tents. 20f, Boy in front of tent.

1970, Aug.
657 A84 5f multicolored .30 .25
658 A84 10f multicolored .40 .25
659 A84 15f multicolored .50 .25
660 A84 20f multicolored .70 .25
Nos. 657-660 (4) 1.90 1.00
Issued for Childhood Day.

Nativity Grotto, Bethlehem A85

Church of the Nativity, Bethlehem: 10f, Manger. 20f, Altar. 25f, Interior.

1970, Dec. 25   Photo.   Perf. 13½
661 A85 5f blue & multi   .45   .25
662 A85 10f scarlet & multi   .45   .25
663 A85 20f rose lilac & multi   .80   .30
664 A85 25f green & multi   1.00   .35
        Nos. 661-664 (4)   2.70   1.15
                    Christmas.

Flag and
Map of
Arab
League
Countries
A85a

1971, May 10 Photo.   Perf. 11½x11
665 A85a 10f orange & multi   .40   .25
666 A85a 20f lt blue & multi   .40   .25
667 A85a 30f olive & multi   .40   .25
        Nos. 665-667 (3)   1.20   .75

    25th anniversary of the Arab League.

Emblem and Doves — A86

Designs: 5f, Emblem and 4 races, vert. 10f,
Emblem as flower, vert.

1971, July
668 A86 5f green & multi   .35   .30
669 A86 10f brick red & multi   .40   .30
670 A86 15f dk blue & multi   .50   .30
        Nos. 668-670 (3)   1.25   .90

    Intl. Year Against Racial Discrimination.

Dead Sea
A87

Views of the Holy Land: 30f, Excavated
building, Petra. 45f, Via Dolorosa, Jerusalem,
vert. 60f, Jordan River. 100f, Christmas bell,
Bethlehem, vert.

1971, Aug.   Perf. 14x13½, 13½x14
671 A87 5f blue & multi   .90   .30
672 A87 30f pink & multi   1.75   .60
673 A87 45f blue & multi   2.25   .90
674 A87 60f gray & multi   3.75   1.50
675 A87 100f gray & multi   5.50   3.00
        Nos. 671-675 (5)   14.15   6.30
                  Tourist publicity.

Opening of UPU Headquarters, Bern
in 1970 — A88

1971, Oct.   Perf. 11
676 A88 10f brn, brn & yel grn   .40   .25
677 A88 20f dk vio, grn & yel grn   .70   .25

Averroes (1126-
1198)
A89

Arab Scholars: 5f, Avicenna (980-1037).
20f, ibn-Khaldun (1332-1406). 25f, ibn-Tufail
(?-1185). 30f, Alhazen (965?-1039?).

1971, Sept.   Perf. 12
678 A89 5f gold & multi   .35   .25
679 A89 10f gold & multi   .35   .25
680 A89 20f gold & multi   .65   .25
681 A89 25f gold & multi   1.00   .25
682 A89 30f gold & multi   1.50   .75
        Nos. 678-682 (5)   3.85   1.85

Child Learning to
Write — A90

1972, Feb. 9   Photo.   Perf. 11
683 A90 5f ultra, brn & grn   .35   .25
684 A90 15f mag, brn & blue   .35   .25
685 A90 20f grn, brn & blue   .35   .25
686 A90 30f org, brn & blue   .75   .30
        Nos. 683-686 (4)   1.80   1.05

    International Education Year.

Arab Mother and
Child — A91

Mother's Day: 10f, Mothers and children,
horiz. 20f, Mother and child.

1972, Mar.   Perf. 14x13½
687 A91 10f lt grn & multi   .50   .25
688 A91 20f red brown & blk   .50   .25
689 A91 30f blue, brn & blk   .75   .25
        Nos. 687-689 (3)   1.75   .75

Pope Paul VI and
Holy
Sepulcher — A92

1972, Apr.   Photo.   Perf. 14x13½
690 A92 30f black & multi   1.00   .25
            Easter. See Nos. C51-C52.

UNICEF
Emblem,
Children
A93

UNICEF Emblem and: 20f, Child playing
with blocks spelling "UNICEF," vert. 30f,
Mother and child.

1972, May   Perf. 11½x11, 11x11½
691 A93 10f bl, vio bl & blk   .40   .25
692 A93 20f multicolored   .40   .25
693 A93 30f blue & multi   .50   .25
        Nos. 691-693 (3)   1.30   .75

    25th anniv. (in 1971) of UNICEF.

UN Emblem, Dove
and Grain — A94

1972, July   Perf. 11x11½
694 A94 5f vio & multi   .50   .25
695 A94 10f multicolored   .50   .25
696 A94 15f black & multi   .50   .25

---

697 A94 20f green & multi   .50   .25
698 A94 30f multicolored   .85   .50
        Nos. 694-698 (5)   2.85   1.50
      25th anniv. (in 1970) of the UN.

Al Aqsa Mosque, Jerusalem — A95

Designs: 60f, Al Aqsa Mosque on fire. 100f,
Al Aqsa Mosque, interior.

1972, Aug. 21   Litho.   Perf. 14½
699 A95 30f green & multi   1.60   .25
700 A95 60f blue & multi   3.50   .85
701 A95 100f ocher & multi   5.50   1.50
        Nos. 699-701 (3)   10.60   2.60

3rd anniversary of the burning of Al Aqsa
Mosque, Jerusalem.

House in
Desert
A96

1972, Nov.   Perf. 14x13½, 13½x14
702 A96 5f Falconer, vert   .55   .25
703 A96 10f shown   .55   .25
704 A96 15f Man on camel   .55   .25
705 A96 20f Pipe line construc-
            tion   .95   .25
706 A96 25f Shepherd   .95   .25
707 A96 30f Camels at water
            trough   1.25   .45
708 A96 35f Chicken farm   1.50   .65
709 A96 45f Irrigation canal   2.00   1.10
        Nos. 702-709 (8)   8.30   3.45
            Life in the Arab desert.

Wasfi el
Tell and
Dome of
the Rock
A97

Wasfi el Tell,
Map of
Palestine and
Jordan — A98

Perf. 13x13½, 13½x13
1972, Dec.   Photo.
710 A97 5f citron & multi   .45   .25
711 A97 10f red & multi   .50   .25
712 A97 20f dl blue & multi   1.00   .25
713 A98 30f green & multi   1.10   .85
        Nos. 710-713 (4)   3.05   1.60

In memory of Prime Minister Wasfi el Tell,
who was assassinated in Cairo by Black September terrorists.

Trapshooting
A99

Designs: 75f, Trapshooter facing right,
horiz. 120f, Trapshooter facing left, horiz.

1972, Dec.   Perf. 14x13½, 13½x14
714 A99 25f multicolored   .80   .25
715 A99 75f multicolored   1.10   .80
716 A99 120f multicolored   2.10   1.00
        Nos. 714-716 (3)   4.00   2.05
    World Trapshooting Championships.

Aero Club
Emblem
A100

1973, Jan.   Photo.   Perf. 13½x14
717 A100 5f blue, blk & yel   .50   .25
718 A100 10f blue, blk & yel   .50   .25
        Nos. 717-718,C53-C55 (5)   4.45   1.45
        Royal Jordanian Aero Club.

Peace
Dove and
Jordanian
Flag
A101

10f, Emblem. 15f, King Hussein. 30f, Map of
Jordan.

1973, Mar.   Perf. 11½
719 A101 5f blue & multi   .45   .25
720 A101 10f pale grn & multi   .45   .25
721 A101 15f olive & multi   .45   .25
722 A101 30f yel grn & multi   .90   .45
        Nos. 719-722 (4)   2.25   1.20

Hashemite Kingdom of Jordan, 50th anniv.

Battle, Flag and Map of
Palestine — A102

10f, 2 soldiers in combat, map of Palestine.
15f, Map of Palestine, olive branch, soldier on
tank.

1973, Apr. 10   Photo.   Perf. 11
723 A102 5f crimson & multi   1.00   .40
724 A102 10f crimson & multi   1.50   .60
725 A102 15f grn, blue & brn   2.25   1.25
        Nos. 723-725 (3)   4.75   2.25

    5th anniversary of Karama Battle.

Father and
Child — A103

Father's Day: 20f, Father & infant. 30f,
Family.

1973, Apr. 20   Perf. 13½
726 A103 10f citron & multi   .50   .25
727 A103 20f lt blue & multi   .75   .25
728 A103 30f multicolored   1.25   .55
        Nos. 726-728 (3)   2.50   1.05

Phosphate Mine A104

1973, June 25 Litho. Perf. 13½x14
729 A104 5f shown .40 .25
730 A104 10f Cement factory .40 .25
731 A104 15f Sharmasil Dam .50 .25
732 A104 20f Kafrein Dam .70 .25
  Nos. 729-732 (4) 2.00 1.00
Development projects.

Camel Racer A105

Designs: Camel racing.

1973, July 21
733 A105 5f multicolored .80 .25
734 A105 10f multicolored .80 .25
735 A105 15f multicolored .80 .25
736 A105 20f multicolored .80 .25
  Nos. 733-736 (4) 3.20 1.00

Book Year Emblem — A106

1973, Aug. 25 Photo. Perf. 13x13½
737 A106 30f dk grn & multi .75 .25
738 A106 60f purple & multi 1.00 .35
Intl. Book Year. For overprints see Nos. 781-782.

Family A107

Family Day: 30f, Family around fire. 60f, Large family outdoors.

1973, Sept. 18 Litho. Perf. 13½
739 A107 20f multicolored .50 .25
740 A107 30f multicolored .50 .25
741 A107 60f multicolored 1.00 .35
  Nos. 739-741 (3) 2.00 .85

Kings of Iran and Jordan, Tomb of Cyrus the Great and Mosque of Omar — A108

1973, Oct. Litho. Perf. 13
742 A108 5f ver & multi .50 .25
743 A108 10f brown & multi .50 .25
744 A108 15f gray & multi .75 .25
745 A108 30f blue & multi 1.00 .40
  Nos. 742-745 (4) 2.75 1.15
2500th anniversary of the founding of the Persian Empire by Cyrus the Great.

Palestine Week Emblem A109

Palestine Week: 10f, Torch and laurel. 15f, Refugee family behind barbed wire, vert. 30f, Children, Map of Palestine, globe. Sizes: 5f, 10f, 30f; 38½x22mm. 15f, 25x46mm.

1973, Nov. 17 Photo. Perf. 11
746 A109 5f multicolored .50 .25
747 A109 10f dl bl & multi .65 .25
748 A109 15f yel grn & multi .85 .25
749 A109 30f brt grn & multi 1.50 .40
  Nos. 746-749 (4) 3.50 1.15

Traditional Harvest A110

Traditional and modern agricultural methods.

1973, Dec. 25 Perf. 13½
750 A110 5f shown .65 .25
751 A110 10f Harvesting machine .65 .25
752 A110 15f Traditional seeding .65 .25
753 A110 20f Seeding machine .65 .25
754 A110 30f Ox plow 1.00 .25
755 A110 35f Plowing machine 1.10 .25
756 A110 45f Pest control 1.25 .25
757 A110 60f Horticulture 1.75 1.10
  Nos. 750-757,C56 (9) 10.20 3.85

Red Sea Fish A111

Designs: Various Red Sea fishes.

1974, Feb. 15 Photo. Perf. 14
758 A111 5f multicolored .50 .25
759 A111 10f multicolored .60 .25
760 A111 15f multicolored .75 .25
761 A111 20f multicolored .90 .35
762 A111 25f multicolored 1.25 .40
763 A111 30f multicolored 2.00 .50
764 A111 35f multicolored 2.25 .80
765 A111 40f multicolored 2.75 1.00
766 A111 45f multicolored 3.00 1.10
767 A111 50f multicolored 5.00 1.25
768 A111 60f multicolored 6.25 1.75
  Nos. 758-768 (11) 25.25 7.90

Battle of Muta, 1250 A112

20f, Yarmouk Battle, 636. 30f, Hitteen Battle, 1187.

1974, Mar. 15 Photo. Perf. 13½
769 A112 10f shown .65 .25
770 A112 20f multicolored 1.25 .40
771 A112 30f multicolored 1.60 .65
  Nos. 769-771 (3) 3.50 1.30

Clubfooted Boy, by Murillo — A113

Paintings: 10f, Praying Hands, by Dürer. 15f, St. George and the Dragon, by Paolo Uccello. 20f, Mona Lisa, by Da Vinci. 30f, Hope, by Frederic Watts. 40f, Angelus, by Jean F. Millet, horiz. 50f, The Artist and her Daughter, by Angelica Kauffmann. 60f, Portrait of my Mother, by James Whistler, horiz. 100f, Master Hare, by Reynolds.

Perf. 14x13½, 13½x14
1974, Apr. 15 Litho.
772 A113 5f black & multi 1.50 .25
773 A113 10f black & gray 1.50 .25
774 A113 15f black & multi 1.50 .25
775 A113 20f black & multi 1.50 .25
776 A113 30f black & multi 1.50 .25
777 A113 40f black & multi 1.75 .25
778 A113 50f black & multi 2.00 .95
779 A113 60f black & multi 2.50 1.00
780 A113 100f black & multi 3.50 1.75
  Nos. 772-780 (9) 17.25 5.20

Nos. 737-738 Overprinted

1974, Apr. 20 Photo. Perf. 13x13½
781 A106 30f dk grn & multi .70 .25
782 A106 60f purple & multi 1.00 .50
Intl. Conf. for Damascus History, Apr. 20-25.

Camel Caravan at Sunset A115

3f, 30f, Palm at shore of Dead Sea. 4f, 40f, Hotel at shore. 5f, 50f, Jars from Qumran Caves. 6f, 60f, Copper scrolls, vert. 10f, 100f, Cracked cistern steps, vert. 20f, like 2f.

1974, June 25 Photo. Perf. 14
786 A115 2f multicolored .50 .25
787 A115 3f multicolored .50 .25
788 A115 4f multicolored .50 .25
789 A115 5f multicolored .75 .25
790 A115 6f multicolored .75 .25
791 A115 10f multicolored .75 .25
792 A115 20f multicolored .50 .25
793 A115 30f multicolored .65 .25
794 A115 40f multicolored .75 .50
795 A115 50f multicolored 1.75 .40
796 A115 60f multicolored 2.25 .50
797 A115 100f multicolored 3.50 .85
  Nos. 786-797 (12) 13.15 4.25

UPU Emblem — A114

1974 Perf. 10x12½
783 A114 10f yel grn & multi .40 .25
784 A114 30f blue & multi .50 .25
785 A114 60f multicolored .85 .30
  Nos. 783-785 (3) 1.75 .80
Centenary of Universal Postal Union.

WPY Emblem — A116

1974, Aug. 20 Photo. Perf. 11
798 A116 5f lt green, blk & pur .30 .25
799 A116 10f lt green, blk & car .30 .25
800 A116 20f lt green, blk & org .40 .25
  Nos. 798-800 (3) 1.00 .75
World Population Year.

Water Skiing — A117

Water Skiing: 10f, 100f, Side view, horiz. 20f, 200f, Turning, horiz. 50f, like 5f.

Perf. 14x13½, 13½x14
1974, Sept. 20
801 A117 5f multicolored .50 .25
802 A117 10f multicolored .50 .25
803 A117 20f multicolored .50 .25
804 A117 50f multicolored .65 .25
805 A117 100f multicolored 1.25 .50
806 A117 200f multicolored 2.10 .95
  Nos. 801-806 (6) 5.50 2.45

Holy Kaaba, Mecca, and Pilgrims — A118

1974, Nov. Photo. Perf. 11
807 A118 10f blue & multi .75 .25
808 A118 20f yellow & multi .80 .25
Pilgrimage season.

Amrah Palace A119

Ruins: 20f, Hisham Palace. 30f, Kharraneh Castle.

1974, Nov. 25 Photo. Perf. 14x13½
809 A119 10f black & multi .50 .25
810 A119 20f black & multi .75 .30
811 A119 30f black & multi 1.25 .50
  Nos. 809-811 (3) 2.50 1.05

Jordanian Woman — A120

Designs: Various women's costumes.

1975, Feb. 1 Photo. Perf. 12
812 A120 5f lt green & multi .45 .25
813 A120 10f yellow & multi .50 .25
814 A120 15f lt blue & multi .75 .30
815 A120 20f ultra & multi 1.10 .40
816 A120 25t green & multi 1.50 .85
  Nos. 812-816 (5) 4.30 2.05

Treasury,
Petra — A121

Ommayyad
Palace,
Amman
A122

Designs: 30f, Dome of the Rock, Jerusalem. 40f, Columns, Forum of Jerash.

Perf. 14x13½, 13½x14

1975, Mar. 1   **Photo.**
824	A121	15f lt blue & multi	1.00	.25
825	A122	20f pink & multi	1.00	.25
826	A122	30f yellow & multi	1.25	.25
827	A122	40f lt blue & multi	1.60	.25
	Nos. 824-827,C59-C61 (7)		10.25	3.25

King Hussein — A123

1975, Apr. 8   **Photo.**   *Perf. 14*
Size: 19x23mm
831	A123	5f green & ind	.50	.25
832	A123	10f vio & indigo	.50	.25
833	A123	15f car & indigo	.50	.25
834	A123	20f brn ol & ind	.50	.25
835	A123	25f vio bl & ind	.50	.25
836	A123	30f brown & ind	.50	.25
837	A123	35f vio & indigo	.50	.25
838	A123	40f orange & ind	.50	.25
839	A123	45f red lil & ind	.50	.25
840	A123	50f bl green & ind	.65	.25
	Nos. 831-840,C62-C68 (17)		21.65	11.40

Globe, "alia" and
Plane — A125

Designs: 30f, Boeing 727 connecting Jordan with world, horiz. 60f, Globe and "alia."

1975, June 15   **Photo.**   *Perf. 11*
853	A125	10f multicolored	.70	.25
854	A125	30f multicolored	.75	.25
855	A125	60f multicolored	1.40	.85
	Nos. 853-855 (3)		2.85	1.35

Royal Jordanian Airline, 30th anniversary.

Satellite Transmission System, Map of
Mediterranean — A126

1975, Aug. 1   **Photo.**   *Perf. 11*
856	A126	20f vio bl & multi	.90	.25
857	A126	30f green & multi	1.10	.75

Opening of satellite earth station.

Chamber of
Commerce
Emblem — A127

1975, Oct. 15   **Photo.**   *Perf. 11*
858	A127	10f yellow & blue	.35	.25
859	A127	15f yel, red & blue	.35	.25
860	A127	20f yel, grn & blue	.35	.25
	Nos. 858-860 (3)		1.05	.75

Amman Chamber of Commerce, 50th anniv.

Hand Holding Wrench, Wall and
Emblem — A128

1975, Nov.   **Photo.**   *Perf. 11½*
861	A128	5f green, car & blk	.35	.25
862	A128	10f car, green & blk	.35	.25
863	A128	20f blk, green & car	.35	.25
	Nos. 861-863 (3)		1.05	.75

Three-year development plan.

Family and
IWY Emblem
A129

IWY Emblem and: 25f, Woman scientist
with microscope. 60f, Woman graduate.

1976, Apr. 27   **Litho.**   *Perf. 14x13½*
864	A129	5f multicolored	.50	.25
865	A129	25f multicolored	.50	.25
866	A129	60f multicolored	1.00	.40
	Nos. 864-866 (3)		2.00	.90

International Women's Year.

Salt
Industry — A130

Arab Labor Organization Emblem and: 30f,
Welders. 60f, Ship at 'Aqaba.

1976, June 1   **Litho.**   *Perf. 13½x14*
867	A130	10f gray & multi	.50	.25
868	A130	30f bister & multi	.50	.25
869	A130	60f brown & multi	.75	.40
	Nos. 867-869 (3)		1.75	.90

Arab Labor Organization.

Nos. 574-
574E
Srchd.

Perf. 14½x13½

1976, July 18   **Photo.**
Strips of 5
870	A79a	25f on 1f-5f	32.50	32.50
a.-e.	Any single, 1f-5f			
871	A79a	25f on 6f-10f	32.50	32.50
a.-e.	Any single, 6f-10f			
872	A79a	40f on 11f-15f	32.50	32.50
a.-e.	Any single, 11f-15f			
873	A79a	50f on 16f-20f	32.50	32.50
a.-e.	Any single, 16f-20f			
874	A79a	75f on 21f-25f	32.50	32.50
a.-e.	Any single, 21f-25f			
875	A79a	125f on 26f-30f	32.50	32.50
a.-e.	Any single, 26f-30f			

**Nos. 575-575E Surcharged Same as
Nos. 870-875**
876	A79a	25f on 1f-5f	32.50	32.50
a.-e.	Any single, 1f-5f			
877	A79a	25f on 6f-10f	32.50	32.50
a.-e.	Any single, 6f-10f			
878	A79a	40f on 11f-15f	32.50	32.50
a.-e.	Any single, 11f-15f			
879	A79a	50f on 16f-20f	32.50	32.50
a.-e.	Any single, 16f-20f			
880	A79a	75f on 21f-25f	32.50	32.50
a.-e.	Any single, 21f-25f			
881	A79a	125f on 26f-30f	32.50	32.50
a.-e.	Any single, 26f-30f			

Tennis — A132

Designs: 10f, Athlete and wreath. 15f, Soccer. 20f, Equestrian and Jordanian flag. 30f,
Weight lifting. 100f, Stadium, Amman.

1976, Nov. 1   **Litho.**   *Perf. 14x13½*
990	A132	5f buff & multi	.75	.25
991	A132	10f lt bl & multi	.75	.25
992	A132	15f green & multi	.75	.25
993	A132	20f green & multi	.75	.25
994	A132	30f green & multi	1.00	.25
995	A132	100f multicolored	2.00	1.25
	Nos. 990-995 (6)		6.00	2.50

Sports and youth.

Dam — A133

Designs: Various dams.

1976, Dec. 7   **Litho.**   *Perf. 14x13½*
996	A133	30f multicolored	1.00	.25
997	A133	60f multicolored	1.25	.70
998	A133	100f multicolored	2.25	1.10
	Nos. 996-998 (3)		4.50	2.05

Telephones, 1876
and 1976 — A134

125f, 1876 telephone and 1976 receiver.

1977, Feb. 17   **Litho.**   *Perf. 11½x12*
999	A134	75f rose & multi	1.50	.95
1000	A134	125f blue & multi	2.00	1.25

Centenary of first telephone call by Alexander Graham Bell, Mar. 10, 1876.

Street
Crossing,
Traffic
Light — A135

Designs: 75f, Traffic circle and light. 125f,
Traffic light and signs, motorcycle policeman.

1977, May 4   **Litho.**   *Perf. 11x12*
1001	A135	5f rose & multi	.55	.25
1002	A135	75f black & multi	1.50	.85
1003	A135	125f yellow & multi	2.25	1.40
	Nos. 1001-1003 (3)		4.30	2.50

International Traffic Day.

Plane over
Ship — A136

Coat of Arms and: 25f, Factories and power
lines. 40f, Fertilizer plant and trucks. 50f,
Ground to air missile. 75f, Mosque and wor-
shippers. 125f, Radar station and TV emblem.

1977, Aug. 11   **Photo.**   *Perf. 11½x12*
1004	A136	10f sil & multi	.40	.25
1005	A136	25f sil & multi	.40	.25
1006	A136	40f sil & multi	.70	.35
1007	A136	50f sil & multi	.80	.40
1008	A136	75f sil & multi	.95	.60
1009	A136	125f sil & multi	1.75	1.00
	Nos. 1004-1009 (6)		5.00	2.85

Imperf
Size: 100x70mm
1009A	A136	100f multicolored	8.50	8.50

25th anniv. of the reign of King Hussein.

Child with Toy
Bank — A137

Postal Savings Bank: 25f, Boy with piggy
bank. 50f, Postal Savings Bank emblem. 75f,
Boy talking to teller.

1977, Sept. 1   **Litho.**   *Perf. 11½x12*
1010	A137	10f multicolored	.40	.25
1011	A137	25f multicolored	.60	.25
1012	A137	50f multicolored	.75	.40
1013	A137	75f multicolored	1.10	.65
	Nos. 1010-1013 (4)		2.85	1.55

King Hussein and
Queen Alia — A138

1977, Nov. 1   **Litho.**   *Perf. 11½x12*
1014	A138	10f lt grn & multi	.40	.25
1015	A138	25f rose & multi	.40	.25
1016	A138	40f yellow & multi	.50	.25
1017	A138	50f blue & multi	.70	.25
	Nos. 1014-1017 (4)		2.00	1.00

Queen Alia — A139

1977, Dec. 1   **Litho.**   *Perf. 11½x12*
1018	A139	10f green & multi	.50	.25
1019	A139	25f brown & multi	.50	.25
1020	A139	40f blue & multi	.70	.25
1021	A139	50f yellow & multi	.95	.25
	Nos. 1018-1021 (4)		2.65	1.00

Queen Alia, died in 1977 air crash.

Jinnah, Flags of Pakistan and Jordan — A140

1977, Dec. 20 — *Perf. 11½*
1022 A140 25f multicolored .30 .25
1023 A140 75f multicolored .70 .40

Mohammed Ali Jinnah (1876-1948), 1st Governor General of Pakistan.

APU Emblem, Members' Flags — A141

1978, Apr. 12 *Litho.* — *Perf. 12x11½*
1024 A141 25f yellow & multi .75 .50
1025 A141 40f buff & multi 1.25 .75

25th anniv. (in 1977), of Arab Postal Union.

Copper Coffee Set — A142

Handicraft: 40f, Porcelain plate and ashtray. 75f, Vase and jewelry. 125f, Pipe holder.

1978, May 30 *Photo.* — *Perf. 11½x12*
1026 A142 25f olive & multi .50 .25
1027 A142 40f lilac & multi .65 .25
1028 A142 75f ultra & multi 1.10 .65
1029 A142 125f orange & multi 1.75 1.00
   Nos. 1026-1029 (4) 4.00 2.15

Roman Amphitheater, Jerash A143

Tourist Views: 20f, Roman Columns, Jerash. 40f, Goat, grapes and man, Roman mosaic, Madaba. 75f, Rock formations, Rum, and camel rider.

1978, July 30 *Litho.* — *Perf. 12*
1030 A143 5f multicolored .55 .25
1031 A143 20f multicolored .55 .25
1032 A143 40f multicolored 1.00 .25
1033 A143 75f multicolored 1.40 .75
   Nos. 1030-1033 (4) 3.50 1.50

King Hussein and Pres. Sadat — A144

Designs: No. 1035, King Hussein and Pres. Assad, Jordanian and Syrian flags, horiz. No. 1036, King Hussein, King Khalid, Jordanian and Saudi Arabian flags, horiz.

1978, Aug. 20 — *Perf. 11½x12*
1034 A144 40f multicolored .90 .50
1035 A144 40f multicolored .90 .50
1036 A144 40f multicolored .90 .50
   Nos. 1034-1036 (3) 2.70 1.50

Visits of Arab leaders to Jordan.

Cement Factory A145

Designs: 10f, Science laboratory. 25f, Printing press. 75f, Artificial fertilizer plant.

1978, Sept. 25 *Litho.* — *Perf. 12*
1037 A145 5f multicolored .60 .25
1038 A145 10f multicolored .60 .25
1039 A145 25f multicolored .80 .25
1040 A145 75f multicolored 1.60 .90
   Nos. 1037-1040 (4) 3.60 1.65

Industrial development.

"UNESCO" Scales and Globe — A146

1978, Dec. 5 *Litho.* — *Perf. 12x11½*
1041 A146 40f multicolored .75 .35
1042 A146 75f multicolored 1.25 .70

30th anniversary of UNESCO.

1976-1980 Development Plan — A147

1979, Oct. 25 *Litho.* — *Perf. 12½x12*
1043 A147 25f multicolored .30 .25
1044 A147 40f multicolored .70 .25
1045 A147 50f multicolored .95 .25
   Nos. 1043-1045 (3) 1.95 .75

IYC Emblem, Flag of Jordan — A148

1979, Nov. 15 *Litho.* — *Perf. 12x12½*
1046 A148 25f multicolored .50 .25
1047 A148 40f multicolored .75 .25
1048 A148 50f multicolored 1.25 .35
   Nos. 1046-1048 (3) 2.50 .85

International Year of the Child.

1979 Population and Housing Census A149

1979, Dec. 25 *Litho.* — *Perf. 12½x12*
1049 A149 25f multicolored .50 .25
1050 A149 40f multicolored .70 .25
1051 A149 50f multicolored .80 .30
   Nos. 1049-1051 (3) 2.00 .80

King Hussein — A150

1980 *Litho.* — *Perf. 13½x13*
1052 A150 5f multicolored .30 .25
   b. Inscribed 1981 .30 .25
1053 A150 10f multicolored .30 .25
   b. Inscribed 1981 .30 .25
1055 A150 20f multicolored .30 .25
   b. Inscribed 1981 .30 .25
1056 A150 25f multicolored .30 .25
   a. Inscribed 1979 .30 .25
   b. Inscribed 1981 .30 .25
1058 A150 40f multicolored .60 .25
   a. Inscribed 1979 .50 .25
   b. Inscribed 1981 .60 .25
1059 A150 50f multicolored .80 .25
1060 A150 75f multicolored 1.00 .30
1061 A150 125f multicolored 1.50 .35
   a. Complete booklet, 4 each
      #1056, 1058-1061 17.50
   Nos. 1052-1061 (8) 5.10 2.15

International Nursing Day — A151

1980, May 12 *Litho.* — *Perf. 12x12½*
1062 A151 25f multicolored .50 .25
1063 A151 40f multicolored .70 .25
1064 A151 50f multicolored .85 .25
   Nos. 1062-1064 (3) 2.05 .75

El Deir Temple, Petra — A152

1980 *Litho.* — *Perf. 14½*
1065 A152 25f multicolored .60 .25
1066 A152 40f multicolored .90 .50
1067 A152 50f multicolored 1.25 .60
   Nos. 1065-1067 (3) 2.75 1.35

World Tourism Conf., Manila, Sept. 27.

Hegira (Pilgrimage Year) — A153

1980, Nov. 11 *Litho.* — *Perf. 14½*
1068 A153 25f multicolored .30 .25
1069 A153 40f multicolored .45 .25
1070 A153 50f multicolored .75 .30
1071 A153 75f multicolored 1.50 .40
1072 A153 100f multicolored 1.50 .70
   Nos. 1068-1072 (5) 4.50 1.90

Souvenir Sheet
Imperf
1073 A153 290f multicolored 6.50 6.50

No. 1073 contains designs of Nos. 1068-1071.

11th Arab Summit Conference, Amman — A153a

1980, Nov. 25 *Litho.* — *Perf. 14½*
1073A A153a 25f multi .40 .25
1073B A153a 40f multi .60 .25
1073C A153a 50f multi .80 .30
1073D A153a 75f multi 1.00 .45
1073E A153a 100f multi 1.10 .65
   f. Souv. sheet of 5, #1073A-
      1073E, imperf. 6.50 6.50
   Nos. 1073A-1073E (5) 3.90 1.90

A154

1981, May 8 *Litho.* — *Perf. 14½*
1074 A154 25f multicolored .50 .25
1075 A154 40f multicolored .80 .60
1076 A154 50f multicolored .95 .70
   Nos. 1074-1076 (3) 2.25 1.55

Red Crescent Society.

A155

1981, June 17 *Litho.* — *Perf. 14x14½*
1077 A155 25f multicolored .75 .25
1078 A155 40f multicolored .90 .90
1079 A155 50f multicolored 1.25 .90
   Nos. 1077-1079 (3) 2.90 2.05

13th World Telecommunications Day.

Nos. 174 and 832 — A156

Perf. 13½x14½, 14½x13½
1981, July 1 *Litho.*
1080 A156 25f shown .55 .25
1081 A156 40f Nos. 313, 189, vert. 1.00 .65
1082 A156 50f Nos. 272, 222 1.10 .90
   Nos. 1080-1082 (3) 2.65 1.80

Postal Museum opening.

A157

Arab Women: 25f, Khawla Bint El-Azwar, Ancient Warrior. 40f, El-Khansa (d.645), writer. 50f, Rabia El-Adawiyeh, religious leader.

1981, Aug. 25 *Litho.* — *Perf. 14½x14*
1083 A157 25f multicolored .25 .25
1084 A157 40f multicolored 2.00 1.25
1085 A157 50f multicolored 3.00 1.50
   Nos. 1083-1085 (3) 5.25 3.00

A158

1981, Oct. 16 *Litho.* — *Perf. 14x14½*
1086 A158 25f multicolored .25 .25
1087 A158 40f multicolored .80 .55
1088 A158 50f multicolored 1.00 .65
   Nos. 1086-1088 (3) 2.05 1.45

World Food Day.

Intl. Year of
the Disabled
A159

1981, Nov. 14   Litho.   Perf. 14½x14
1089 A159 25f multicolored   .25   .25
1090 A159 40f multicolored   1.00   .70
1091 A159 50f multicolored   1.40   .90
      Nos. 1089-1091 (3)   2.65 1.85

Hands Reading
Braille — A160

1981, Nov. 14   Perf. 14x14½
1092 A160 25f multicolored   .25   .25
1093 A160 40f multicolored   1.00   .70
1094 A160 50f multicolored   1.40   .90
      Nos. 1092-1094 (3)   2.65 1.85

A161

Design: Hand holding jug and stone tablet.

1982, Mar. 10   Litho.   Perf. 14x14½
1095 A161 25f multicolored   .50   .25
1096 A161 40f multicolored   1.10   .60
1097 A161 50f multicolored   1.25   .80
      Nos. 1095-1097 (3)   2.85 1.65

Nos. 1095-1097 inscribed 1981.

A162

1982, Apr. 12   Litho.   Perf. 14x14½
1098 A162 10f multicolored   .25   .25
1099 A162 25f multicolored   .65   .25
1100 A162 40f multicolored   .90   .65
1101 A162 50f multicolored   1.10   .80
1102 A162 100f multicolored   2.40 1.60
      Nos. 1098-1102 (5)   5.30 3.55

30th anniv. of Arab Postal Union.

King Hussein
and Rockets
A163

1982, May 25   Litho.   Perf. 14½x14
1103 A163 10f shown   .25   .25
1104 A163 25f Tanks crossing
                  bridge   .65   .25
1105 A163 40f Jet   .90   .65
1106 A163 50f Tanks, diff.   1.25   .75
1107 A163 100f Raising flag   2.25 1.50
      Nos. 1103-1107 (5)   5.30 3.40

Independence and Army Day; 30th anniv. of
King Hussein's accession to the throne.

Salt
Secondary
School
A164

1982, Sept. 12   Litho.   Perf. 14½x14
1108 A164 10f multicolored   .25   .25
1109 A164 25f multicolored   .60   .25
1110 A164 40f multicolored   .85   .60
1111 A164 50f multicolored   1.10   .65
1112 A164 100f multicolored   2.25 1.25
      Nos. 1108-1112 (5)   5.05 3.00

International
Heritage of
Jerusalem — A165

1982, Nov. 14   Litho.   Perf. 14x14½
1113 A165 10f Gate to Old City   .25   .25
1114 A165 25f Minaret   1.00   .45
1115 A165 40f Al Aqsa   1.25   .80
1116 A165 50f Dome of the
                  Rock   1.60   .90
1117 A165 100f Dome of the
                  Rock, diff.   3.25 1.75
      Nos. 1113-1117 (5)   7.35 4.15

Yarmouk
Forces
A166

1982, Nov. 14   Perf. 14½x14
1118 A166 10f multicolored   .25   .25
1119 A166 25f multicolored   .45   .25
1120 A166 40f multicolored   .80   .45
1121 A166 50f multicolored   .95   .60
1122 A166 100f multicolored   2.10 1.40
      Nos. 1118-1122 (5)   4.55 2.95

Size: 71x51mm
Imperf
1123 A166 100f Armed Forces
                  emblem   15.00 15.00

2nd UN Conf.
on Peaceful
Uses of Outer
Space,
Vienna, Aug.
9-21 — A167

1982, Dec. 1   Perf. 14½x14
1124 A167 10f multicolored   .25   .25
1125 A167 25f multicolored   .50   .25
1126 A167 40f multicolored   .75   .50
1127 A167 50f multicolored   .95   .60
1128 A167 100f multicolored   2.00 1.25
      Nos. 1124-1128 (5)   4.45 2.85

Birth Centenary of
Amir Abdullah ibn
Hussein — A168

1982, Dec. 13   Litho.   Perf. 14½
1129 A168 10f multicolored   .25   .25
1130 A168 25f multicolored   .40   .25
1131 A168 40f multicolored   .60   .45
1132 A168 50f multicolored   .95   .80
1133 A168 100f multicolored   2.25 1.40
      Nos. 1129-1133 (5)   4.45 3.15

Roman
Ruins of
Jerash
A169

1982, Dec. 29   Litho.   Perf. 15
1134 A169 10f Temple colon-
                  nade   .25   .25
1135 A169 25f Arch   .90   .25
1136 A169 40f Columns   1.40   .90
1137 A169 50f Ampitheater   1.75 1.00
1138 A169 100f Hippodrome   3.25 2.10
      Nos. 1134-1138 (5)   7.55 4.50

King
Hussein — A170

1983   Litho.   Perf. 14½x14
1139 A170 10f multicolored   .25   .25
1140 A170 25f multicolored   .25   .25
1141 A170 40f multicolored   .40   .30
1142 A170 60f multicolored   .60   .40
1143 A170 100f multicolored   1.00   .65
1144 A170 125f multicolored   1.25   .70
      Nos. 1139-1144 (6)   3.75 2.55

Issue dates: 10f, 60f, Feb. 1; 40f, Feb. 8;
25f, 100f, 125f, Mar. 3. Inscribed 1982.

Massacre at
Shatilla and
Sabra
Palestinian
Refugee
Camps
A171

10f, 25f, 50f, No. 1149, Various victims. 40f,
Children. No. 1150, Wounded child.

1983, Apr. 9   Litho.   Perf. 14½
1145 A171 10f multicolored   .50   .25
1146 A171 25f multicolored   1.00   .70
1147 A171 40f multicolored   1.50   .90
1148 A171 50f multicolored   2.00 1.25
1149 A171 100f multicolored   3.00 2.00
      Nos. 1145-1149 (5)   8.00 5.10

Souvenir Sheet
Imperf
1150 A171 100f multicolored   18.00

Opening of
Queen Alia
Intl. Airport
A172

10f, Aerial view. 25f, Terminal buildings. 40f,
Hangar. 50f, Terminal buildings, diff. 100f,
Embarkation Bridge.

1983, May 25   Litho.   Perf. 12½
1151 A172 10f multicolored   .25   .25
1152 A172 25f multicolored   .80   .25
1153 A172 40f multicolored   1.10   .80
1154 A172 50f multicolored   1.40   .90
1155 A172 100f multicolored   2.75 1.75
      Nos. 1151-1155 (5)   6.30 3.95

Royal
Jordanian
Radio
Amateurs'
Society
A173

1983, Aug. 11   Litho.   Perf. 12
1156 A173 10f multicolored   .25   .25
1157 A173 25f multicolored   .65   .25
1158 A173 40f multicolored   .90   .65
1159 A173 50f multicolored   1.25   .75
1160 A173 100f multicolored   2.40 1.50
      Nos. 1156-1160 (5)   5.45 3.40

Royal
Academy
for Islamic
Cultural
Research
A174

1983, Sept. 16   Litho.   Perf. 12
1161 A174 10f Academy Bldg.   .25   .25
1162 A174 25f Silk carpet   .70   .50
1163 A174 40f Mosque, Amman   1.10   .70
1164 A174 50f Dome of the
                  Rock   1.50   .90

1165 A174 100f Islamic city
                  views   2.75 1.75
      Nos. 1161-1165 (5)   6.30 4.10

A 100f souvenir sheet shows letter from
Mohammed. Value $15.

World
Food Day
A175

1983, Oct. 16   Litho.   Perf. 12
1166 A175 10f Irrigation canal   .25   .25
1167 A175 25f Greenhouses   .60   .25
1168 A175 40f Light-grown
                  crops   1.00   .60
1169 A175 50f Harvest   1.25   .70
1170 A175 100f Sheep farm   2.50 1.40
      Nos. 1166-1170 (5)   5.60 3.20

World Communications Year — A176

10f, Radio switchboard operators. 25f, Earth
satellite station. 40f, Symbols of communication. 50f, Emblems. 100f, Airmail letter.

1983, Nov. 14
1171 A176 10f multicolored   .25   .25
1172 A176 25f multicolored   1.00   .25
1173 A176 40f multicolored   1.25 1.00
1174 A176 50f multicolored   1.50 1.00
1175 A176 100f multicolored   3.25 1.75
      Nos. 1171-1175 (5)   7.25 4.25

Intl.
Palestinian
Solidarity
Day
A177

Dome of the Rock, Jerusalem.

1983, Nov. 29   Perf. 12
1176 A177 5f   multicolored   .90   .45
1177 A177 10f multicolored   1.50   .70

35th Anniv.
of UN
Declaration
of Human
Rights
A178

1983, Dec. 10
1178 A178 10f multicolored   .25   .25
1179 A178 25f multicolored   .65   .25
1180 A178 40f multicolored   .75   .65
1181 A178 50f multicolored   1.25   .75
1182 A178 100f multicolored   2.50 1.50
      Nos. 1178-1182 (5)   5.40 3.40

Anti-Paralysis — A179

1984, Apr. 7   Perf. 13½x11½
1183 A179 40f multicolored   1.10   .70
1184 A179 60f multicolored   1.60   .95
1185 A179 100f multicolored   2.75 1.60
      Nos. 1183-1185 (3)   5.45 3.25

Anti-Polio Campaign.

Israeli Bombing of Iraq Nuclear
Reactor — A180

Various designs.

1984, June 7 Litho. Perf. 13½x11½
1186	A180	40f multicolored	1.60	.55
1187	A180	60f multicolored	2.00	.70
1188	A180	100f multicolored	3.25	1.25
	Nos. 1186-1188 (3)		6.85	2.50

Independence and Army Day — A181

King Hussein and various armed forces.

1984, June 10
1189	A181	10f multicolored	.25	.25
1190	A181	25f multicolored	.65	.35
1191	A181	40f multicolored	1.00	.65
1192	A181	60f multicolored	1.60	.90
1193	A181	100f multicolored	2.75	1.60
	Nos. 1189-1193 (5)		6.25	3.65

1984 Summer Olympics, Los
Angeles — A182

1984, July 28
1194	A182	25f shown	.30	.25
1195	A182	40f Swimming	.50	.30
1196	A182	60f Shooting, archery	1.10	.45
1197	A182	100f Gymnastics	1.60	.75
	Nos. 1194-1197 (4)		3.50	1.75

An imperf. 100f souvenir sheet exists picturing pole vaulting. Value $14.

Water and Electricity Year — A183

25f, Power lines, factory. 40f, Amman Power Station. 60f, Irrigation. 100f, Hydro-electric dam.

1984, Aug. 11
1198	A183	25f multicolored	.45	.25
1199	A183	40f multicolored	.70	.45
1200	A183	60f multicolored	1.10	.60
1201	A183	100f multicolored	1.75	1.10
	Nos. 1198-1201 (4)		4.00	2.40

Coins
A184

40f, Omayyad gold dinar. 60f, Abbasid gold dinar. 125f, Hashemite silver dinar.

1984, Sept. 26 Photo. Perf. 13
1202	A184	40f multicolored	1.10	.60
1203	A184	60f multicolored	1.40	.80
1204	A184	125f multicolored	3.00	1.75
	Nos. 1202-1204 (3)		5.50	3.15

Royal Society for the Conservation of
Nature — A185

25f, Four antelopes. 40f, Grazing. 60f, Three antelopes. 100f, King Hussein, Queen Alia, Duke of Edinburgh.

1984, Oct. 18
1205	A185	25f multicolored	.70	.25
1206	A185	40f multicolored	1.10	.70
1207	A185	60f multicolored	1.60	.95
1208	A185	100f multicolored	2.75	1.60
	Nos. 1205-1208 (4)		6.15	3.50

Natl. Universities — A186

Designs: 40f, Mu'ta Military University, Karak. 60f, Yarmouk University, Irbid. 125f, Jordan University, Amman.

1984, Nov. 14 Perf. 13x13½
1209	A186	40f multicolored	.55	.40
1210	A186	60f multicolored	.95	.55
1211	A186	125f multicolored	2.00	1.10
	Nos. 1209-1211 (3)		3.50	2.05

Al
Sahaba
Tombs
A187

Designs: 10f, El Harath bin Omier el-Azdi and Derer bin El-Azwar. 25f, Sharhabil bin Hasna and Abu Obaidah Amer bin el-Jarrah. 40f, Muath bin Jabal. 50f, Zaid bin Haretha and Abdullah bin Rawaha. 60f, Amer bin Abi Waqqas. 100f, Jafar bin Abi Taleb.

1984, Dec. 5 Litho. Perf. 13½x11½
1212	A187	10f multicolored	.25	.25
1213	A187	25f multicolored	.50	.25
1214	A187	40f multicolored	.75	.50
1215	A187	50f multicolored	.95	.55
1216	A187	60f multicolored	1.25	.65
1217	A187	100f multicolored	2.00	1.25
	Nos. 1212-1217 (6)		5.70	3.45

Independence and Army Day — A188

Designs: 25f, King Hussein, soldier descending mountain. 40f, King Hussein, Arab revolt flag, globe, Sharif Hussein. 60f, Flag, natl. arms, equestrian. 100f, Natl. flag, arms, Sharif Hussein.

1985, June 10 Perf. 13x13½
1218	A188	25f multicolored	.45	.25
1219	A188	40f multicolored	.90	.45
1220	A188	60f multicolored	1.40	.75
1221	A188	100f multicolored	2.25	1.40
	Nos. 1218-1221 (4)		5.00	2.85

Men in
Postal
History
A189

40f, Sir Rowland Hill. 60f, Heinrich von Stephan. 125f, Yacoub al-Sukkar.

1985, July 1
1222	A189	40f multicolored	.75	.45
1223	A189	60f multicolored	1.10	.65
1224	A189	125f multicolored	2.40	1.40
	Nos. 1222-1224 (3)		4.25	2.50

1st
Convention
of
Jordanian
Expatriates
A190

Various designs.

1985, July 20 Photo.
1225	A190	40f multicolored	.75	.45
1226	A190	60f multicolored	1.10	.65
1227	A190	125f multicolored	2.40	1.40
	Nos. 1225-1227 (3)		4.25	2.50

Intl. Youth
Year — A191

Various designs.

1985, Aug. 11 Litho. Perf. 13½x13
1228	A191	10f multicolored	.25	.25
1229	A191	25f multicolored	.50	.25
1230	A191	40f multicolored	.80	.50
1231	A191	60f multicolored	1.25	.70
1232	A191	125f multicolored	2.50	1.50
	Nos. 1228-1232 (5)		5.30	3.20

World Tourism Organization, 10th
Anniv. — A192

10f, Ruins of the Treasury, Petra. 25f, Jerash Temple. 40f, Roman baths. 50f, Jordanian valley town. 60f, Aqaba Bay. 125f, Roman amphitheater.

1985, Sept. 13 Perf. 13½x13
1233	A192	10f multicolored	.25	.25
1234	A192	25f multicolored	.50	.25
1235	A192	40f multicolored	.80	.50
1236	A192	50f multicolored	1.00	.60
1237	A192	60f multicolored	1.25	.70
1238	A192	125f multicolored	2.50	1.40
	Nos. 1233-1238 (6)		6.30	3.70

An imperf. 100f souvenir sheet exists picturing flower, 10 and natl. flag. Value $6.50.

UN Child
Survival
Campaign
A193

Various designs.

1985, Oct. 7
1239	A193	25f multicolored	.50	.25
1240	A193	40f multicolored	.75	.50
1241	A193	60f multicolored	1.25	.70
1242	A193	125f multicolored	2.50	1.50
	Nos. 1239-1242 (4)		5.00	2.95

An imperf. 100f souvenir sheet exists picturing campaign emblem and the faces of healthy children. Value $12.

5th
Jerash
Festival
A194

1985, Oct. 21
1243	A194	10f Opening ceremony, 1980	.25	.25
1244	A194	25f Folk dancers	.45	.25
1245	A194	40f Dancers	.90	.45
1246	A194	60f Choir, Roman theater	1.50	.75
1247	A194	100f King and Queen	2.40	1.50
	Nos. 1243-1247 (5)		5.50	3.20

UN, 40th
Anniv. — A195

1985, Oct. 25 Photo. Perf. 13x13½
1248	A195	60f multicolored	1.25	1.00
1249	A195	125f multicolored	2.50	2.00

King
Hussein,
50th
Birthday
A196

Various photos of King.

1985, Nov. 14 Litho. Perf. 14½
1250	A196	10f multicolored	.25	.25
1251	A196	25f multicolored	.50	.25
1252	A196	40f multicolored	.90	.50
1253	A196	60f multicolored	1.50	.75
1254	A196	100f multicolored	2.40	1.50
	Nos. 1250-1254 (5)		5.55	3.25

An imperf. 200f souvenir sheet exists picturing flags, King Hussein and Dome of the Rock. Value $15.

Restoration
of Al Aqsa
Mosque,
Jerusalem
A196a

1985, Nov. 25 Litho. Perf. 13x13½
1254A	A196a	5f multicolored	1.10	1.10
1254B	A196a	10f multicolored	2.40	2.25

Police
A197

1985, Dec. 18
1255 A197 40f Patrol car   1.10 .25
1256 A197 60f Crossing guard   1.40 1.10
1257 A197 125f Police academy   3.00 2.00
     Nos. 1255-1257 (3)   5.50 3.35

Launch of ARABSAT-1, 1st
Anniv. — A198

1986, Feb. 8   Litho.   Perf. 13½x13
1258 A198 60f Satellite in orbit   .85 .25
1259 A198 100f Over map of Arab
               countries   1.40 .85

Arabization of
the Army,
30th Anniv.
A199

40f, King Hussein presenting flag. 60f,
Greeting army sergeant. 100f, Hussein
addressing army.

1986, Mar. 1   Perf. 11½x12½
1260 A199 40f multicolored   .75 .25
1261 A199 60f multicolored   .90 .25
1262 A199 100f multicolored   1.60 .90
     Nos. 1260-1262 (3)   3.25 1.40

An imperf. souvenir sheet exists with design
of 100f. Value $10.

Natl. Independence, 40th
Anniv. — A200

Design: King Abdullah decorating soldier.

1986, May 25   Perf. 12½x11½
1263 A200 160f multicolored   2.75 2.10

Arab Revolt against Turkey, 70th
Anniv. — A201

Unattributed paintings (details): 40f, The
four sons of King Hussein, Prince of Mecca,
vert. 60f, Sharif Hussein, retainers and bodyguard. 160f, Abdullah and followers on
horseback.

Perf. 12½x11½, 11½x12½
1986, June 10
1264 A201 40f multicolored   .65 .25
1265 A201 60f multicolored   .85 .25
1266 A201 160f multicolored   2.50 1.25
     Nos. 1264-1266 (3)   4.00 1.75

An imperf. 200f souvenir sheet exists picturing the Arab Revolt flag, Sharif Hussein and
text from independence declaration. Value $9.

Intl.
Peace
Year
A202

1986, July 1   Litho.   Perf. 13½x13
1267 A202 160f multicolored   2.25 1.25
1268 A202 240f multicolored   3.25 1.90

King
Hussein
Medical
City
Cardiac
Center
A203

1986, Aug. 11
1269 A203 40f Cardiac Center   .90 .25
1270 A203 60f Surgery   1.10 .90
1271 A203 100f Surgery, diff. 1.75 .95
     Nos. 1269-1271 (3)   3.75 2.10

UN, 40th Anniv. — A204

Excerpts from King Hussein's speech: 40f,
In Arabic. 80f, Arabic, diff. 100f, English.

1986, Sept. 27   Perf. 12½x11½
1272 A204 40f multicolored   .75 .25
1273 A204 80f multicolored   1.25 .85
1274 A204 100f multicolored   1.60 .85
     Nos. 1272-1274 (3)   3.60 1.95

An imperf. 200f stamp 90x70mm exists picturing speech in Arabic and English, King Hussein at podium. Value $8.50.

Arab
Postal
Union,
35th
Anniv.
A205

1987, Apr. 12   Litho.   Perf. 13½x13
1275 A205 80f Old post office   .85 .60
1276 A205 160f New post office 1.90 1.10

Chemical Soc. Emblem and
Chemists — A206

Designs: 60f, Jaber ibn Hayyan al-Azdi
(720-813). 80f, Abu-al-Qasem al-Majreeti
(950-1007). 240f, Abu-Bakr al-Razi (864-932).

1987, Apr. 24
1277 A206 60f multicolored   .75 .50
1278 A206 80f multicolored   1.00 .60
1279 A206 240f multicolored   2.75 1.60
     Nos. 1277-1279 (3)   4.50 2.70

SOS Children's Village — A207

1987, May 7
1280 A207 80f Village in Am-
               man   1.25 .70
1281 A207 240f Child, bird mural 3.25 1.90

4th
Brigade,
40th
Anniv.
A208

80f, Soldiers in armored vehicle. 160f, Four
veterans.

1987, June 10
1282 A208 60f shown   1.40 .95
1283 A208 80f multicolored   1.60 1.10

Size: 70x91mm
Imperf
1284 A208 160f multicolored   8.00 7.50
     Nos. 1282-1284 (3)   11.00 9.55

Indigenous Birds — A209

10f, Hoopoe. 40f, Palestine sunbird. 50f,
Black-headed bunting. 60f, Spur-winged
plover. 80f, Greenfinch. 100f, Black-winged
stilt.

1987, June 24
1285 A209 10f multicolored   1.60 .55
1286 A209 40f multicolored   1.60 .55
1287 A209 50f multicolored   2.00 .60
1288 A209 60f multicolored   2.50 .90
1289 A209 80f multicolored   3.00 1.25
1290 A209 100f multicolored   4.00 1.75
     Nos. 1285-1290 (6)   14.70 5.60

King
Hussein — A210

1987, June 24   Litho.   Perf. 13x13½
1291 A210 60f multicolored   .40 .30
1292 A210 80f multicolored   .85 .40
1293 A210 160f multicolored   1.75 1.10
1294 A210 240f multicolored   2.50 1.75
     Nos. 1291-1294 (4)   5.50 3.55

Battle of
Hittin,
800th
Anniv.
A211

H.K. OF JORDAN

BATTLE OF HITTIN
800th
ANNIVERSARY
1187-1987

Dome of the Rock and Saladin (1137-
1193), Conqueror of
Jerusalem — A212

60f, Battle, Jerusalem. 80f, Horseman,
Jerusalem, Dome of the Rock. No. 1297, 100f,
Saladin.

1987, July 4
1295 A211 60f multicolored   .75 .70
1296 A211 80f multicolored   1.50 .85
1297 A211 100f multicolored   2.25 1.50
     Nos. 1295-1297 (3)   4.50 3.05

Souvenir Sheet
Perf. 12x12½
1298 A212 100f shown   8.00 7.75

No. 1298 exists imperf.

Natl. Coat of
Arms — A213

1987, Aug. 11   Perf. 11½x12½   Litho.
1299 A213 80f multicolored   1.00 .65
1300 A213 160f multicolored   2.00 1.25

Amman Industrial Park at
Sahab — A214

1987, Aug. 11   Perf. 13½x13
1301 A214 80f multicolored   1.00 .80

University
Crest
A215

University Entrance — A216

1987, Sept. 2

Perf. 11½x11, 12½x11½

1302	A215	60f multicolored	.80	.50
1303	A216	80f multicolored	.95	.65

University of Jordan, 25th anniv.

UN Child Survival Campaign A217

1987, Oct. 5   Litho.   *Perf. 13x13½*

1304	A217	60f Oral vaccine	.75	.60
1305	A217	80f Natl. flag, child	1.25	.80
1306	A217	160f Growth monitoring	2.50	1.60
		Nos. 1304-1306 (3)	4.50	3.00

Parliament, 40th Anniv. — A218

1987, Oct. 20   *Perf. 13½x13*

1307	A218	60f Opening ceremony, 1947	1.00	.60
1308	A218	80f In session, 1987	1.25	.80

A219

Special Arab Summit Conference, Amman — A220

1987, Nov. 8

1309	A219	60f multicolored	.55	.50
1310	A219	80f multicolored	.90	.55
1311	A219	160f multicolored	2.00	1.25
1312	A219	240f multicolored	2.75	2.00
		Nos. 1309-1312 (4)	6.20	4.30

Size: 90x66mm

Imperf

1313	A220	100f multicolored	7.50	7.50

King Hussein, Dag Hammarskjold Peace Prize Winner for 1987 — A221

1988, Feb. 6   Litho.   *Perf. 12½*

1314	A221	80f Hussein, woman, vert.	.95	.75
1315	A221	160f shown	1.90	1.25

Natl. Victory at the 1987 Arab Military Basketball Championships — A222

60f, Golden Sword Award. 80f, Hussein congratulating team. 160f, Jump ball.

1988, Mar. 1   *Perf. 13½x13*

1316	A222	60f multicolored	.80	.50
1317	A222	80f multicolored	1.10	.65
1318	A222	160f multicolored	2.10	1.25
		Nos. 1316-1318 (3)	4.00	2.40

WHO, 40th Anniv. — A223

1988, Apr. 7   Photo.   *Perf. 13x13½*

1319	A223	60f multicolored	1.00	.70
1320	A223	80f multicolored	1.25	.90

Arab Scouts, 75th Anniv. — A224

1988, July 2   Litho.   *Perf. 13x13½*

1321	A224	60f multicolored	1.00	.90
1322	A224	80f multicolored	1.25	1.10

Birds A225

1988, July 21   Litho.   *Perf. 11½x12*

1323	A225	10f Crested lark	2.25	.70
1324	A225	20f Stone curlew	2.25	.80
1325	A225	30f Redstart	2.25	.90
1326	A225	50f Blackbird	3.25	1.00
1327	A225	50f Rock dove	4.00	1.10
1328	A225	160f Smyrna kingfisher	11.00	1.75
		Nos. 1323-1328 (6)	25.00	6.25

Size: 71x90mm

Imperf

1328A	A225	310f Six species	17.50	15.00

Restoration of San'a, Yemen Arab Republic A226

1988, Aug. 11   Litho.   *Perf. 12x11½*

1329	A226	80f multicolored	.95	.70
1330	A226	160f multicolored	1.90	1.50

Historic Natl. Sites A227

1988, Aug. 11   *Perf. 13½x13*

1331	A227	60f Umm Al-rasas	.70	.50
1332	A227	80f Umm Qais	.90	.70
1333	A227	160f Iraq Al-amir	1.90	1.50
		Nos. 1331-1333 (3)	3.50	2.70

An imperf. souvenir sheet of 3 exists containing one each Nos. 1331-1333. Value $5.

1988 Summer Olympics, Seoul — A228

1988, Sept. 17   Litho.   *Perf. 13x13½*

1334	A228	10f Tennis	.25	.25
1335	A228	60f Character trademark	.90	.70
1336	A228	80f Running, swimming	1.40	.90
1337	A228	120f Basketball	1.75	1.50
1338	A228	160f Soccer	2.50	1.75
		Nos. 1334-1338 (5)	6.80	5.10

Size: 70x91mm

Imperf

1339	A228	100f Emblems	17.50	17.50

Royal Jordanian Airlines, 25th Anniv. — A229

1988, Dec. 15   Litho.   *Perf. 11½x12*

1340	A229	60f Ruins of Petra	1.00	.75
1341	A229	80f Aircraft, world map	1.25	1.00

UN Declaration of Human Rights, 40th Anniv. — A230

1988, Dec. 10

1342	A230	80f multicolored	.75	.60
1343	A230	160f multicolored	1.75	1.10

Arab Cooperation Council, Feb. 16 — A231

1989   Litho.   *Perf. 13½x13*

1344	A231	10f shown	.25	.25
1345	A231	30f multi, diff.	.25	.25
1346	A231	40f multi, diff.	.25	.25
1347	A231	60f multi, diff.	1.00	.95
		Nos. 1344-1347 (4)	1.75	1.70

Martyrs of Palestine and Their Families — A232

1989   *Perf. 14½*

1348	A232	5f multicolored	.90	.30
1349	A232	10f multicolored	.90	.30

Interparliamentary Union, Cent. — A233

1989   Litho.   *Perf. 12*

1350	A233	40f multicolored	.35	.25
1351	A233	60f multicolored	.55	.35

Arab Housing Day and World Refugee Day A234

Designs: 5f, Housing complex, emblems, vert. 60f, Housing complex, emblem.

1989

1352	A234	5f multicolored	.25	.25
1353	A234	40f shown	.55	.25
1354	A234	60f multicolored	.75	.55
		Nos. 1352-1354 (3)	1.55	1.05

Ministry of Agriculture, 50th Anniv. — A235

40f, Tree, anniv. emblem. 60f, Fruit tree, emblem, apiary.

1989   Litho.   *Perf. 12*

1355	A235	5f shown	.25	.25
1356	A235	40f multicolored	.25	.25
1357	A235	60f multicolored	2.25	.25
		Nos. 1355-1357 (3)	2.75	.75

Arabian Horse Festival A236

40f, Horse, building facade. 60f, Horse's head, vert. 100f, Mare and foal.

1989			Perf. 12	
1358	A236	5f shown	.40	.25
1359	A236	40f multicolored	.85	.25
1360	A236	60f multicolored	2.40	.25
		Nos. 1358-1360 (3)	3.65	.75

Size: 90x70mm
Imperf

1361	A236	100f multicolored	25.00	22.50

Natl. Library Assoc. A237

1989			Perf. 12	
1362	A237	40f multicolored	.25	.25
1363	A237	60f multicolored	1.00	.25

Mosque of the Martyr King Abdullah — A238

1989			Perf. 12	
1364	A238	40f multicolored	.25	.25
1365	A238	60f multicolored	1.00	.25

Size: 90x70mm
Imperf

1366	A238	100f multicolored	6.75	6.75

Mosaics A239

1989, Dec. 23		Litho.	Perf. 12	
1367	A239	5f Man with Basket	.60	.30
1368	A239	10f Building	.60	.30
1369	A239	40f Deer	1.50	.50
1370	A239	60f Man with stick	2.00	.65
1371	A239	80f Town, horiz.	2.50	.90
		Nos. 1367-1371 (5)	7.20	2.65

Size: 90x70mm
Imperf

1372	A239	100f like #1371, horiz.	17.50	17.50

Arab Cooperation Council, 1st Anniv. — A240

1990, Feb. 16			Perf. 13	
1373	A240	5f multicolored	.25	.25
1374	A240	20f multicolored	.25	.25
1375	A240	60f multicolored	.75	.45
1376	A240	80f multicolored	1.00	.65
		Nos. 1373-1376 (4)	2.25	1.60

Nature Conservation — A241

1990, Apr. 22				
1377	A241	40f Horses	.25	.25
1378	A241	60f Mountain	.50	.25
1379	A241	80f Oasis	.65	.35
		Nos. 1377-1379 (3)	1.40	.85

Prince Abdullah's Arrival in Ma'an, 70th Anniv. — A243

1990		Litho.	Perf. 13½x13	
1382	A243	40f org & multi	.25	.25
1383	A243	60f grn & multi	.40	.25

Size: 90x70mm
Imperf

1384	A243	200f multicolored	7.00	7.00

UN Development Program, 40th Anniv. — A244

1990			Perf. 13	
1385	A244	60f multicolored	.25	.25
1386	A244	80f multicolored	.55	.25

King Hussein — A245

1990-92		Litho.	Perf. 12x13½	
1387	A245	5f yel org & multi	.25	.25
a.		Slightly larger vignette, inscr. 1991	.25	.25
1390	A245	20f blue green & multi	.25	.25
1391	A245	40f orange & multi	.25	.25
1393	A245	60f blue & multi	.45	.45
1395	A245	80f pink & multi	.70	.70
a.		Slightly larger vignette, inscr. 1991	.70	.70
1397	A245	240f brown & multi	.70	.70
1398	A245	320f red lilac & multi	1.75	1.25
1399	A245	1d yel green & multi	2.75	2.40
		Nos. 1387-1399 (8)	7.65	6.45

No. 1390 dated 1991.
Issued: 20f, 1992; 5f, 60f, 80f 1990; others 1991.

Endangered Animals A246

1991, Sept. 1		Litho.	Perf. 13x13½	
1401	A246	5f Nubian ibex	.25	.25
1402	A246	40f Onager	.50	.25
1403	A246	80f Arabian gazelle	2.25	.40
1404	A246	160f Arabian oryx	1.60	1.10
		Nos. 1401-1404 (4)	4.60	2.00

Energy Rationalization Program — A247

Designs: 5f, Light bulbs. 40f, Solar panels, sun, vert. 80f, Electric table lamp, vert.

		Perf. 13½x13, 13x13½		
1991, Oct. 3				Litho.
1405	A247	5f multicolored	.25	.25
1406	A247	40f multicolored	.25	.25
1407	A247	80f multicolored	.70	.25
		Nos. 1405-1407 (3)	1.20	.75

Grain Production for Food Security — A248

1991, Oct. 16			Perf. 13½x13	
1408	A248	5f Different grains	.25	.25
1409	A248	40f shown	.25	.25
1410	A248	80f Wheat stalk, kernels	.70	.25
		Nos. 1408-1410 (3)	1.20	.75

Palestinian Uprising — A249

1991, Nov. 29		Litho.	Perf. 11	
1411	A249	20f multicolored	2.00	.75

Blood Donation Campaign — A250

1991, Nov. 14		Litho.	Perf. 13½x13	
1412	A250	80f multicolored	.75	.25
1413	A250	160f multicolored	1.50	.75

Expo '92, Seville A251

1992, Feb. 20				
1414	A251	80f multicolored	.65	.25
1415	A251	320f multicolored	1.60	.95

Healthy Hearts A252

80f, Man & woman, heart at center of scale, vert.

		Perf. 13x13½, 13½x13		
1992, Apr. 7				Litho.
1416	A252	80f multicolored	.70	.25
1417	A252	125f multicolored	.80	.50

SOS Children's Village, 'Aqaba — A253

1992, Apr. 30		Litho.	Perf. 13½x13	
1418	A253	80f shown	.70	.25
1419	A253	125f Village	.80	.50

1992 Summer Olympics, Barcelona — A254

Stylized designs with Barcelona Olympic emblem: 5fr, Judo. 40f, Runner, vert. 80f, Diver. 125f, Flag, Cobi, map, vert. 160f, Table tennis.
100f, Incorporates all designs of set.

		Perf. 13½x13, 13x13½		
1992, July 25				Litho.
1420	A254	5f multicolored	.25	.25
1421	A254	40f multicolored	.25	.25
1422	A254	80f multicolored	.50	.25
1423	A254	125f multicolored	.75	.35
1424	A254	160f multicolored	1.10	.50
		Nos. 1420-1424 (5)	2.85	1.60

Size: 70x90mm
Imperf

1425	A254	100f multicolored	15.00	12.00

King Hussein, 40th Anniv. of Accession — A255

Designs: 40f, Flags, King in full dress uniform, vert. 125f, King wearing headdress, flags. 160f, King in business suit, crown. 200f, Portrait.

1992, Aug. 11   *Perf. 13x13½*
| 1426 | A255 | 40f multicolored | .25 | .25 |

Perf. 13½x13
1427	A255	80f shown	.45	.25
1428	A255	125f multicolored	.75	.35
1429	A255	160f multicolored	1.10	.50
		Nos. 1426-1429 (4)	2.55	1.35

Size: 90x70mm

Imperf
| 1430 | A255 | 200f multicolored | 7.25 | 7.25 |

Butterflies — A256

5f, Danaus chrysippus. 40f, Aporia cartaegi. 80f, Papilio machaon. 160f, Pseudochazara telephassa. 200f, Same as Nos. 1431-1434.

1992, Dec. 20   Litho.   *Perf. 13½x13*
1431	A256	5f multicolored	.50	.25
1432	A256	40f multicolored	1.00	.25
1433	A256	80f multicolored	2.00	.50
1434	A256	160f multicolored	4.50	1.25
		Nos. 1431-1434 (4)	8.00	2.25

Imperf
Size: 90x70mm
| 1435 | A256 | 200f multicolored | 17.50 | 17.50 |

See Nos. 1448-1452.

Intl. Customs Day — A257

1993, Jan. 26   Litho.   *Perf. 13½x13*
| 1436 | A257 | 80f green & multi | .60 | .25 |
| 1437 | A257 | 125f pale orange & multi | .90 | .45 |

Royal Scientific Society — A258

1993, June 10   Litho.   *Perf. 12½x13*
| 1438 | A258 | 80f multicolored | .50 | .25 |

Es Salt Municipality, Cent. — A259

1993, Sept. 1   Litho.   *Perf. 12*
1439	A259	80f pink & multi	.60	.25
1440	A259	125f green & multi	.90	.45
a.		Souvenir sheet of 2, #1439-1440, imperf.	6.25	6.25

No. 1440a sold for 200f.

Great Arab Revolt and Army Day A260

Designs: 5f, Rockets, planes, tank, King Hussein, 40f, King Hussein, military activities. 80f, Amir Abdullah ibn Hussein, Dome of the Rock, map, flags. 125f, Amir Abdullah ibn Hussein, Dome of the Rock, riders. 100f, King Hussein, flags.

1993, June 10
1441	A260	5f multicolored	.25	.25
1442	A260	40f multicolored	.25	.25
1443	A260	80f multicolored	.50	.25
1444	A260	125f multicolored	.85	.35
		Nos. 1441-1444 (4)	1.85	1.10

Size: 90x70mm

Imperf
| 1445 | A260 | 100f multicolored | 6.00 | 6.00 |

White Cane Day A261

Design: 125f, Lighted world, cane, eye, vert.

1993, Oct. 23   Litho.   *Perf. 12*
| 1446 | A261 | 80f shown | .60 | .25 |
| 1447 | A261 | 125f multicolored | .90 | .45 |

Butterfly Type of 1992

Designs: 5f, Lampides boeticus. 40f, Melanargria titea. 80f, Allancastria deyrollei. 160f, Gonepteryx cleopatra. 100f, Same designs as Nos. 1448-1451.

1993, Oct. 10   Litho.   *Perf. 12*
1448	A256	5f multicolored	.40	.25
1449	A256	40f multicolored	.75	.30
1450	A256	80f multicolored	1.00	.40
1451	A256	160f multicolored	2.50	1.00
		Nos. 1448-1451 (4)	4.65	1.95

Size: 83x65mm

Imperf
| 1452 | A256 | 100f multicolored | 25.00 | 25.00 |

UN Declaration of Human Rights, 45th Anniv. — A262

1993, Dec. 10   *Perf. 12*
| 1453 | A262 | 40f yellow & multi | .25 | .25 |
| 1454 | A262 | 160f red & multi | 1.10 | .75 |

Recovery & Homecoming, 1st Anniv. — A263

King Hussein: 80f, Crowd. 125f, Waving to people. 160f, Embracing woman. 100f, Standing on airplane ramp.

1993, Nov. 25
1455	A263	80f multicolored	.50	.25
1456	A263	125f multicolored	.85	.40
1457	A263	160f multicolored	1.00	.50
		Nos. 1455-1457 (3)	2.35	1.15

Size: 85x65

Imperf
| 1458 | A263 | 100f multicolored | 5.50 | 3.75 |

World AIDS Day — A264

1993, Dec. 1   *Perf. 12*
| 1459 | A264 | 80f red & multi | .50 | .25 |
| 1460 | A264 | 125f green & multi | .85 | .45 |

Size: 83x70mm

Imperf
| 1461 | A264 | 200f like #1459-1460 | 6.25 | 4.50 |

King Hussein A265

King Hussein wearing: 40f, Military uniform. 80f, Traditional costume. 125f, Business suit. 160f, 100f, Dress uniform in portrait with Queen Noor, horiz.

1993, Nov. 14   *Perf. 12*
1462	A265	40f multi, horiz.	.25	.25
1463	A265	80f multi, horiz.	.50	.25
1464	A265	125f multi, horiz.	.80	.35
1465	A265	160f multicolored	1.25	.50
		Nos. 1462-1465 (4)	2.80	1.35

Size: 82x68mm

Imperf
| 1466 | A265 | 100f multicolored | 8.00 | 5.75 |

Assumption of Constitutional Powers by King Hussein, 40th anniv.

Saladin (1138-1193), Dome of the Rock — A266

1993, Nov. 25   *Perf. 12*
1467	A266	40f blue & multi	.25	.25
1468	A266	80f gray & multi	.55	.25
1469	A266	125f yellow & multi	.75	.40
		Nos. 1467-1469 (3)	1.55	.90

Triumphal Arch, Jerash — A267

Perf. 12x13½ (5f, No. 80f, 1473A, 1475, 160f, 320f, 1d), 12 (25f, 40f, 50f, #1474C, 240f, No. 1478C, No. 1479), 14x13½ (75f, No. 1474, 150f, 200f, 300f, 400f), 13½x14 (#1201), 12¾x13¼ (#1479B)

1993-2003   Litho.
1470	A267	5f blue & multi	.25	.25
1471	A267	25f pale violet & multi	.25	.25
b.		Perf 12½x13¼, inscr. "2003"	.25	.25

1471A	A267	40f grn & multi	.25	.25
1472	A267	50f yel & multi	.25	.25
a.		Perf 12, inscr. "1996"	.25	.25
b.		Perf 12¾x13¼	.25	.25
c.		Perf 13½x14	.25	.25
d.		As "b," inscr. "2003"	.25	.25
1472E	A267	75f buff & multi	.40	.40
1473	A267	80f grn & multi	.35	.25
1473A	A267	100f red & multi	.40	.40
b.		Perf. 12	.25	
c.		As "b," inscribed "1996"	.40	.25
1474	A267	100f apple grn & multi	.50	.50
a.		Perf. 12	.50	.50
d.		As "a," inscr. "1996"	.50	.50
1474B	A267	120f bl grn & multi	.65	.65
1474C	A267	125f lt bl & multi	.60	.60
1475	A267	125f buff & multi	.50	.25
a.		Perf. 12	.50	.25
1475B	A267	150f sal pink & multi	.90	.90
1476	A267	160f yel & multi	.65	.25
b.		Perf. 12	.75	.25
c.		As "b," inscribed "1994"	.75	.25
1476A	A267	200f gray & multi	1.10	1.10
d.		Perf. 12	1.10	
1477	A267	240f pink & multi	1.00	.25
b.		Perf. 12	.90	.25
c.		perf 12, inscribed "1994"	1.25	1.25
1477A	A267	300f pink & multi	1.75	1.75
d.		Perf. 12	1.75	1.75
1478	A267	320f brn & multi	1.25	.35
1478A	A267	320f sal & multi	1.25	.35
1478C	A267	400f brt blue & multi	2.50	2.50
b.		Perf. 13x13¼	2.50	2.50
1479	A267	500f bister & multi	2.00	.85
a.		Perf 12x13½	2.00	.85
1479B	A267	500f yel & multi	2.50	2.50
1480	A267	1d olive & multi	4.00	1.25
a.		Perf. 12¾x13¼	5.00	1.25
		Nos. 1470-1480 (22)	23.30	15.95

Nos. 1472E, 1473, 1473A, 1477b, 1479a are dated 1992; Nos. 1471A, 1473Ab, 1476b, 1993; No. 1474, 1994; No. 1477Ac, 1995; Nos. 1478Ab, 1479B, 1480a, 1997.

Issued: 5f, 320f, 1/13/93 (dated 1992); 25f, 1/18/96 (dated 1995); 40f, 1994; 100f, 200f, 300f, 5/15/96; 1d, 1/13/93; 125f, 160f, 1/13/93; 240f, 3/23/94; 50f, 1995; 150f, 400f, 5/15/96; 500f, 10/25/96; 75f, 5/15/96; No. 1478Ab, 5/10/98. 80f, Nos. 1473A, 1477b, 1479a, 1/13/93; Nos. 1473Ab, 1476b, 3/23/94; 120f, 5/15/96; No. 1474C, 2/13/95; Nos. 1476Ad, 1477Ad, 1/18/96; No. 1478C, 1993; Nos. 1479B, 1480a, 5/10/98.

Hashemite Charity Organization — A268

Designs: 80f, Loading supplies into plane. 125f, People gathering at plane.

1994, Mar. 20   Litho.   *Perf. 12*
| 1481 | A268 | 80f multicolored | .55 | .25 |
| 1482 | A268 | 125f multicolored | .80 | .50 |

Third Hashemite Restoration of Al Aqsa Mosque, Dome of the Rock — A269

King Hussein with various scenes of restoration.

1994, Apr. 18   Litho.   *Perf. 12x12½*
1483	A269	80f yellow & multi	.40	.25
1484	A269	125f lt orange & multi	.70	.35
1485	A269	240f lilac & multi	1.25	.60
		Nos. 1483-1485 (3)	2.35	1.20

Imperf
Size: 90x70mm
| 1486 | A269 | 100f green & multi | 8.00 | 5.50 |

ILO,
75th
Anniv.
A270

1994, June 13   Litho.   Perf. 12
1487 A270 80f yellow & multi   .45   .25
1488 A270 125f brt pink & multi   .70   .35

Intl. Red Cross and Red Crescent
Societies, 75th Anniv. — A271

1994, May 8   Perf. 12
1489 A271 80f shown   .45   .25
1490 A271 160f Doves, em-
            blems, vert   .80   .45

Size: 61x78mm
Imperf
1491 A271 200f #1489-1490   11.00 8.25

Intl.
Year of
the
Family
A272

1994, Aug. 11   Litho.   Perf. 12
1492 A272 80f green & multi   .45   .25
1493 A272 125f pink & multi   .80   .40
1494 A272 160f yellow & multi 1.00   .45
        Nos. 1492-1494 (3)   2.25 1.10

Intl. Olympic Committee,
Cent. — A273

Olympic rings and: 80f, Globe, venue symbols, vert. 100f, Jordanian colors. 125f, Venue
symbols, diff., vert. 160f, shown. 240f, Torch.

1994, June 23
1495 A273 80f blue & multi   .40   .25
1496 A273 125f multicolored   .65   .30
1497 A273 160f multicolored   1.10   .40
1498 A273 240f multicolored   1.60   .65
        Nos. 1495-1498 (4)   3.75 1.60

Size: 90x70mm
Imperf
1499 A273 100f multicolored   8.50 8.50

Jordanian Participation in UN
Peacekeeping Forces — A274

Designs: 80f, King Hussein greeting troops.
125f, King inspecting troops. 160f,
Checkpoint.

1994, Aug. 11   Litho.   Perf. 12
1500 A274 80f multicolored   .45   .25
1501 A274 125f multicolored   .70   .35
1502 A274 160f multicolored   .85   .45
        Nos. 1500-1502 (3)   2.00 1.05

Water Conservation Day — A275

80f, Hands, water droplet. 125f, Water faucet, foods, factory. 160f, Child, rain drops.

1994, Nov. 14   Litho.   Perf. 14
1503 A275 80f multicolored   .60   .25
1504 A275 125f multicolored   1.00   .55
1505 A275 160f multicolored   1.25   .60
        Nos. 1503-1505 (3)   2.85 1.40

ICAO,
50th
Anniv.
A276

1994, Oct. 25   Perf. 12
1506 A276 80f green & multi   .45   .25
1507 A276 125f red & multi   .70   .35
1508 A276 160f blue & multi   .85   .45
        Nos. 1506-1508 (3)   2.00 1.05

Crown
Prince's
Award,
10th
Anniv.
A277

1994, Dec. 11   Litho.   Perf. 12
1509 A277 80f yel grn & multi   .70   .25
1510 A277 125f org brn & multi .90   .55
1511 A277 160f vio bl & multi 1.25   .70
        Nos. 1509-1511 (3)   2.85 1.50

UN,
50th
Anniv.
A278

1995, Apr. 1   Litho.   Perf. 14
1512 A278 80f green & multi   .65   .25
1513 A278 125f pink & multi   .95   .55

May
Day
A279

80f, Emblem, workers, flag. 125f, Emblem,
world map, worker. 160f, Hands holding
wrench, torch, Jordanian map, emblem.

1995, May 1
1514 A279 80f multicolored   .45   .25
1515 A279 125f multicolored   .65   .40
1516 A279 160f multicolored   .90   .45
        Nos. 1514-1516 (3)   2.00 1.10

Jordan
Week in
Japan
A280

Globe in two hemispheres with olive
branches and: 125f, Japanese, Jordanian
flags. 160f, Flags above wall.

1995, May 22   Litho.   Perf. 14
1517 A280 80f green & multi   .45   .25
1518 A280 125f pink & multi   .70   .30
1519 A280 160f gray & multi   .85   .45
        Nos. 1517-1519 (3)   2.00 1.00

Opening of Al
al-Bayt
University
A281

1995, Feb. 8   Litho.   Perf. 12
1520 A281 80f grn blue & multi .50   .25
1521 A281 125f ol grn & multi   .75   .40
  a.   Souvenir sheet, #1520-1521,
       imperf.   3.75 3.25

No. 1521a sold for 200f. Nos. 1520-1521
are dated 1994.

Petra,
the
Rose
City
A282

Archaeological discoveries: 50f, Amphitheater. 75f, Facial carvings, bowl, pitcher. 80f,
Columns of building, vert. 160f, Front of building with columns, vert. 200f, Building in side of
mountain.

1995, Aug. 11   Litho.   Perf. 14
1524 A282 50f multicolored   .25   .25
1525 A282 75f multicolored   .85   .25
1526 A282 80f multicolored   .95   .25
1527 A282 160f multicolored   1.75   .95
        Nos. 1524-1527 (4)   3.80 1.70

Size: 90x70mm
Imperf
1528 A282 200f multicolored   20.00 20.00

Arab
League,
50th
Anniv.
A283

1995, Sept. 20   Litho.   Perf. 14
1529 A283 80f green & multi   .45   .25
1530 A283 125f pink & multi   .70   .25
1531 A283 160f gray & multi   .85   .45
        Nos. 1529-1531 (3)   2.00   .95

FAO,
50th
Anniv.
A284

Designs: 125f, "50," FAO emblem, shafts of
grain. 160f, UN, FAO emblems, "50."

1995, Oct. 16   Litho.   Perf. 14
1532 A284 80f shown   .50   .25
1533 A284 125f multicolored   .85   .40
1534 A284 160f multicolored   1.00   .50
        Nos. 1532-1534 (3)   2.35 1.15

Middle East and North Africa
Economic Summit, Amman — A285

1995, Oct. 29   Perf. 12
1535 A285 80f brt pink & multi .50   .25
1536 A285 125f org yel & multi .75   .40

The
Deaf
A286

1995, Nov. 30   Perf. 14
1537 A286 80f shown   .50   .25
1538 A286 125f Emblems, hand
            sign   .75   .35

King
Hussein,
60th
Birthday
A287

Designs: 40f, Crown over King's picture in
business suit. 80f, Crown, flag, dove, ruins of
Petra, King in traditional head wear, military
uniform. 100f, King dress uniform, crown, "60."
125f, King in traditional head wear, business
suit, crown, flag, olive branch. 160f, Flag, King
in business suit. 200f, "60," Dome of the Rock,
King in dress uniform, olive branch.

1995, Nov. 14
1539 A287 25f multicolored   .25   .25
1540 A287 40f multicolored   .25   .25
1541 A287 80f multicolored   .45   .25
1542 A287 100f multicolored   .50   .25
1543 A287 125f multicolored   1.00   .35
1544 A287 160f multicolored   1.25   .45
        Nos. 1539-1544 (6)   3.70 1.80

Size: 83x63mm
Imperf
1545 A287 200f multicolored   6.25 6.25

Independence, 50th Anniv. — A288

King Hussein and: No. 1547, Outline map of
Jordan, crown, dove of peace, Amir Abdullah
ibn Hussein. 300f, Jordanian monuments, flag.
No. 1549, Map of Jordan surrounded by
wreath, dove, national flags.

1996, May 25   Perf. 12
1546 A288 100f multicolored   .55   .25
1547 A288 200f multicolored   1.10   .40
1548 A288 300f multicolored   1.75   .65
        Nos. 1546-1548 (3)   3.40 1.30

Size: 86x66mm
1549 A288 200f multicolored   7.50 7.50

1996
Summer
Olympic
Games,
Atlanta
A289

1996 Olympic Games Emblem and: 50f, Natl. flag, Olympic rings, sports pictograms. 100f, Sports pictograms. 200f, Hands. 300f, Torch, Olympic rings, natl. flag.

1996, July 19   Litho.   Perf. 12
1550	A289	50f multicolored	.25	.25
1551	A289	100f multicolored	.70	.25
1552	A289	200f multicolored	1.60	.70
1553	A289	300f multicolored	2.50	1.10
	Nos. 1550-1553 (4)	5.05	2.30

Protection of the Ozone Layer — A290

1996, Sept. 16
1554	A290	100f multicolored	1.25	.25

UNICEF, 50th Anniv. — A291

1996, Dec. 11   Litho.   Perf. 12
1555	A291	100f green & multi	.60	.25
1556	A291	200f gray lilac & multi	1.00	.60

Crown Prince El-Hassan, 50th Birthday — A292

Designs: 50f, On horseback. 100f, Wearing suit & tie, vert. No. 1559, Natl. flag, wearing traditional attire.
No. 1560, Wearing graduation cap.

1997, Mar. 20   Litho.   Perf. 12
1557	A292	50f multicolored	.25	.25
1558	A292	100f multicolored	.70	.25
1559	A292	200f multicolored	1.10	.70
	Nos. 1557-1559 (3)	2.05	1.20

Size: 84x64mm
Imperf
1560	A292	200f multicolored	8.25	8.25

Heinrich von Stephan (1831-97) A293

1997, Apr. 8   Litho.   Perf. 12
1561	A293	100f multicolored	.90	.25
1562	A293	200f multicolored	1.60	.80

Discovery of the Madeba Mosaic Map, Cent. — A294

1997, Apr. 7
1563	A294	100f Karak, vert.	.75	.35
1564	A294	200f River Jordan	1.50	.50
1565	A294	300f Jerusalem, vert.	2.50	.90
	Nos. 1563-1565 (3)	4.75	1.75

Size: 86x67mm
Imperf
1566	A294	100f Entire map	15.00	15.00

Jordanian Rosefinch — A295

1997, May 25   Litho.   Perf. 12
1567	A295	50f multicolored	.25	.25
1568	A295	100f multi, diff.	.65	.25
1569	A295	150f multi, diff.	1.00	.45
1570	A295	200f multi, diff.	1.50	.65
	Nos. 1567-1570 (4)	3.40	1.60

Jerash Festival, 15th Anniv. A296

Designs: 50f, Couples in traditional costumes, ruins. 100f, Symphony orchestra, silhouettes of buildings. 150f, Pillars, parade of dignitaries. 200f, Women in traditional costumes, crowd, ruins.
15d, Queen Noor lighting torch.

1997, July 23   Litho.   Perf. 12
1571	A296	50f multicolored	.25	.25
1572	A296	100f multicolored	.60	.25
1573	A296	150f multicolored	.95	.45
1574	A296	200f multicolored	1.50	.65
	Nos. 1571-1574 (4)	3.30	1.60

Size: 90x70mm
Imperf
1575	A296	15d multicolored	8.50	8.50

Natl. Forum for Women A297

Emblem and: 50f, Women in tradtional and modern dress, vert. 100f, Natl. flag, flame, book. 150fr, Natl. flag, women seated at conference table.

1997, Dec. 20   Litho.   Perf. 12
1576	A297	50f multicolored	.25	.25
1577	A297	100f multicolored	.50	.25
1578	A297	150f multicolored	.80	.35
	Nos. 1576-1578 (3)	1.55	.85

Jordanian Team, 1997 Arab Soccer Champions — A298

Designs: 50f, Team parading in stadium. 75f, Team in red uniforms. 100f, Team in white uniforms, ceremony.
200f, Formal presentation to King Hussein, motorcade.

1997, Dec. 15
1579	A298	50f multicolored	.25	.25
1580	A298	75f multicolored	.40	.25
1581	A298	100f multicolored	.55	.25
	Nos. 1579-1581 (3)	1.20	.75

Size: 91x70mm
Imperf
1582	A298	200f multicolored	9.00	7.50

House of Parliament, 50th Anniv. — A299

100f, Outside view of building, drawing. 200f, Speaker, members assembled in chamber.

1997, Nov. 1   Perf. 12½
1583	A299	100f multicolored	.60	.25
1584	A299	200f multicolored	.90	.60

53rd General Meeting of Intl. Air Transport Association A300

1997, Nov. 3   Litho.   Perf. 13x13½
1585	A300	100f lt blue & multi	1.00	1.00
1586	A300	200f red & multi	1.00	1.00
1587	A300	300f gray & multi	1.00	1.00

Two additional stamps were issued in this set. The editors would like to examine them.

King Hussein II, 62nd Birthday A301

1997, Nov. 14   Litho.   Perf. 13x13½
Frame Color
1588	A301	100f red	1.00	1.00
1589	A301	200f gold	1.00	1.00
1590	A301	300f blue	1.00	1.00

Souvenir Sheet
Perf. 12
1590A	A301	200f gold	8.50	8.50

No. 1590A contains one 44x60mm stamp.

Earth Day A302

Children's drawings: 50f, Various ways of polluting air and water. 100f, Pollution from factory smoke, automobiles. 150f, Earth chained to various methods of pollution, vert.

1998, Apr. 29   Litho.   Perf. 14
1591	A302	50f multicolored	.25	.25
1592	A302	100f multicolored	.50	.25
1593	A302	150f multicolored	.80	.50
	Nos. 1591-1593 (3)	1.55	1.00

Trans-Jordan Emirate, 75th Anniv. — A303

Designs: 100f, Camel rider holding flag, Amir Abdullah ibn Hussein. 200f, Camel rider holding flag, King Hussein. 300f, King Hussein, arms, #81, Amir Abdullah ibn Hussein.

1998, May 25   Perf. 12
1594	A303	100f multicolored	.50	.50
1595	A303	200f multicolored	1.00	1.00
1596	A303	300f multicolored	1.75	1.75
	Nos. 1594-1596 (3)	3.25	3.25

Size: 80x70mm
Imperf
1597	A303	300f like #1596	8.50	8.50

Mosaics, Um Ar-Rasas A304

1998, July 22   Litho.   Perf. 14
1598	A304	100f multicolored	.50	.50
1599	A304	200f multi, diff.	1.00	1.00
1600	A304	300f multi, diff.	1.75	1.75
	Nos. 1598-1600 (3)	3.25	3.25

Flowers A305

1998, July 7
1601	A305	50f purple & white, thorns	.30	.25
1602	A305	100f Poppies	.60	.55
1603	A305	150f shown	1.00	.75
	Nos. 1601-1603 (3)	1.90	1.55

Size: 60x80mm
Imperf
1604	A305	200f Flower, map of Jordan	8.50	8.50

2nd Arab Beekeepers
Conference — A306

Various pictures of bees, flowers,
honeycomb.

1998, Aug. 3   Litho.   Perf. 14
1605 A306 50f multicolored   .50 .40
1606 A306 100f multi, vert.   .85 .50
1607 A306 150f multicolored   1.25 .60
   Nos. 1605-1607 (3)   2.60 1.50
Size: 80x60mm
Imperf
1608 A306 200f Bees, flowers,
emblem   9.00 9.00

World
Stamp
Day
A307

1998, Oct. 9   Litho.   Perf. 14
1609 A307 50f shown   .25 .25
1610 A307 100f World map, em-
blems   .90 .90
1611 A307 150f Globe, stamps   1.75 1.75
   Nos. 1609-1611 (3)   2.90 2.90

Universal Declaration of Human
Rights, 50th Anniv. — A308

1998, Dec. 10
1612 A308 100f shown   .60 .60
1613 A308 200f Emblems, people 1.00 1.00

King
Hussein,
63rd
Birthday
A309

1998, Nov. 14   Litho.   Perf. 14x14½
1614 A309 100f green & multi   .65 .45
1615 A309 200f violet & multi   1.25 1.00
1616 A309 300f violet blue &
multi   2.25 1.50
   Nos. 1614-1616 (3)   4.15 2.95
Size: 90x70mm
Imperf
1617 A309 300f gold & multi   8.50 8.50

Arab Police and Security Chiefs
Meeting, 25th Anniv. (in 1997)
A310

Map of Arab world and: 100f, King Hussein,
emblem. 200f, Flags of Arab countries,
emblem, flame, vert. 300f, Beret.

1998, Nov. 18   **Perf. 14**
1618 A310 100f multicolored   .65 .65
1619 A310 200f multicolored   1.10 1.10
1620 A310 300f multicolored   2.00 1.75
   Nos. 1618-1620 (3)   3.75 3.50

Mustafa Wahbi
(1899-1949),
Poet — A311

1999, May 25   Litho.   Perf. 14¼
1621 A311 100f multicolored   .90 .90

Environmental Protection — A312

Designs: 100f, Children, bandaged Earth.
200f, Earth as fruit in hands.

1999, Oct. 14   Litho.   Perf. 13¼x13¾
1622 A312 100f multi   .50 .50
1623 A312 200f multi   1.00 1.00

Hijazi
Railway
Museum
A313

Train and: 100f, 200f, Map of Jordan,
museum building. 300f, Museum building.

1999, Sept. 7   Litho.   Perf. 13½x13¾
1624-1626 A313   Set of 3   6.00 6.00

9th Arab Sports Tournament — A314

Bird mascot, emblem and: 50f, Weight lifting, tennis, wrestling, soccer. 100f, Torch. No.
1629, Shooting, fencing, swimming, track &
field, vert. 300f, Flag, map, discus thrower,
tennis player.
No. 1631, Basketball, volleyball, boxing,
swimming.

Perf. 13¼x13¾, 13¾x13¼
1999, Aug. 15   Litho.   **Litho.**
1627 A314 50f multi   .25 .25
1628 A314 100f multi   .65 .65
1629 A314 200f multi   1.40 1.40
1630 A314 300f multi   2.25 2.25
   Nos. 1627-1630 (4)   4.55 4.55
Imperf
Size: 90x70mm
1631 A314 200f multi   3.25 3.25

UPU,
125th
Anniv.
A315

Designs: 100f, "125," UPU emblems, stripes
of airmail envelope. No. 1633, Airmail envelope with UPU emblem.
No. 1634, Like No. 1633, yellow
background.

1999, Oct. 9   Perf. 13¼x13¾
1632 A315 100f multi   .65 .65
1633 A315 200f multi   1.10 1.10
Imperf
Size: 90x70mm
1634 A315 200f multi   2.50 2.50

Gulf of
Aqaba
Corals
A316

Designs: 50f, Pachyseris speciosa. 100f,
Acropora digitifera. No. 1637, 200f, Oxypora
lacera. 300f, Fungia echinata.
No. 1639, 200f, Gorgonia.

1999, Oct. 2   Litho.   Perf. 13½x13¾
1635-1638 A316   Set of 4   4.00 4.00
Imperf
Size: 90x70mm
1639 A316 200f multi   12.00 12.00

Cradle of Civilizations — A317

Archaeological sites — Petra: No. 1640,
100f, Al-Deir. No. 1641, 200f, Khazneh. No.
1642, 300f, Obelisk tomb.
Jerash: No. 1643, 100f, Cardo Maximus.
No. 1644, 200f, Temple of Artemis. No. 1645,
300f, Nymphaeum.
Amman: No. 1646, 100f, Roman Theater.
No. 1647, 200f, Citadel. No. 1648, 300f, Ain
Ghazal statues.
Wadi Rum and Aqaba: No. 1649, 100f,
Camel riders, Wadi Rum. No. 1650, 200f,
House, Aqaba. No. 1651, Ruins, Aqaba.
Madaba: No. 1652, 100f, Mosaic. No. 1653,
200f, Church. No. 1654, 300f, Mosaic map of
Jerusalem.
Baptism Site (Bethany): No. 1655, Plant life
near water. No. 1656, 200f, Aerial view. No.
1657, 300f, Excavation site.
Ajloun: No. 1658, 100f, Ruins. No. 1659,
200f, Ruins diff. No. 1660, 300f, Ruins, diff.
Pella: No. 1661, 100f, Ruins of Byzantine
cathedral. No. 1662, 200f, Three large pillars.
No. 1663, 300f, Ruins.

1999-2000   Litho.   Perf. 13½x14
1640-1663 A317 Set of 12   23.00 23.00
Issued: Nos. 1640-1645, 10/24; Nos. 1646-
1651, 10/31; Nos. 1652-1654, 12/22; Nos.
1655-1657, 12/23; Nos. 1658-1663, 3/7/00.
See Nos. 1688-1693.

Museum of Political History — A318

100f, Building interior. 200f, Museum
entrance and plaza. 300f, Museum entrance.

1999, Nov. 14   Litho.   Perf. 13½x14
1664-1666 A318   Set of 3   3.75 3.75

Jordan Philatelic Club, 20th
Anniv. — A318a

Designs: 100f, #534H and other stamps.
200f, #284 and other stamps.

1999, Nov. 14   Perf. 14¼
1666A-1666B A318a Set of 2   1.50 1.50

SOS
Children's
Village,
Irbid — A318b

100f, SOS Children's Village 50th anniv.
emblem, Jordanian flag. 200f, Woman,
children.

1999, Nov. 23
1666C-1666D A318b Set of 2   1.50 1.50

Coronation of King Abdullah II — A319

1999, Dec. 27   Litho.   Perf. 11¾
Frame Color
1667 A319 100f red   .90 .90
1668 A319 200f green   .90 .90
1669 A319 300f blue   .90 .90
Souvenir Sheet
1670 A319 200f gold   1.00 1.00

King Abdullah II and Queen Rania
A319a

1999, Dec. 27   Litho.   Perf. 11¾
1670A A319a 100f red   .95 .95
1670B A319a 200f green   .95 .95
1670C A319a 300f blue   .95 .95
Souvenir Sheet
1670D A319a 200f gold   5.25 5.25
   Issued: 1670D, 12/27/99.

Numbers have been reserved for three additional stamps in this set. The editors would like to examine any examples of them.

King Abdullah II, 38th Birthday A320

King, crown and: 100f, Olive branches. 200f, Nos. #1672-#1674, Flag, "38," horiz. 300f, Flag, "38," eagle, olive branch, horiz.

Perf 12, Imperf (#1674)

2000, Jan. 30			Litho.	
1671-1673	A320	Set of 3	3.00	3.00

Size: 90x74mm

| 1674 | A320 | 200f multi | 3.50 | 3.50 |

Geneva Convention, 50th Anniv. — A321

Perf. 13½x13¾

2000, Feb. 15		Litho.	
1675	Horiz. strip of 3	3.50	3.50
a.	A321 100f lt bl & multi	.50	.50
b.	A321 200f ocher & multi	1.00	1.00
c.	A321 300f gray & multi	1.50	1.50

Dated 1999.

Millennium A322

No. 1678: a, Jordanian flag, "Jordan, The River & The Land of the Baptism" in English. b, Fish in river. c, As "a," with Arabic inscription.

Perf. 13¼x13¾

2000, Feb. 22		Litho.	
1678	Strip of 3	3.25	3.25
a.	A322 100f multi	.45	.45
b.	A322 200f multi	.90	.90
c.	A322 300f multi	1.25	1.25

King Abdullah II, Houses of Worship and Pope John Paul II — A323

Color of lower panel: 100f, Dull blue green. 200f, Lilac. 300f, Bright yellow green.

2000, Mar. 20		Litho.	Perf. 12	
1679-1681	A323	Set of 3	3.25	3.25

Visit of Pope Paul VI to Jordan, 36th anniv.

Visit of Pope John Paul II to Jordan A324

Pope John Paul II, King Abdullah II and: 100f, "2000." 200f, River. 300f, Vatican and Jordanian flags, map of Jordan. No. 1685, Pope, baptism of Christ, vert.

Perf 12, Imperf (#1685)

2000, Mar. 20			
1682-1684	A324	Set of 3	3.25	3.25

Size: 70x90mm

| 1685 | A324 | 200f multi | 17.50 | 17.50 |

World Meteorological Organization, 50th Anniv. — A325

Designs: 100f, Globe, emblem, anniversary emblem. 200f, Globe with arrows, emblem, anniversary emblem.

2000, Mar. 23		Litho.	Perf. 12	
1686	A325	100f multi	.75	.75
1687	A325	200f multi	1.25	1.25

Cradle of Civilizations Type of 1999

Archaeological sites — Palaces: No. 1688, 100f, Mushatta. No. 1689, 200f, Kharaneh. No. 1690, 300f, Amra.
Um Qais: No. 1691, 100f, Decumanus. No. 1692, 200f, Amphitheater. No. 1693, 300f, Ruins.

2000, Apr. 7		Litho.	Perf. 13½x14	
Palaces				
1688-1690	A317	Set of 3	4.00	4.00
Um Qais				
1691-1693	A317	Set of 3	4.00	4.00
a.	Sheet, #1640-1663, 1688-1693		40.00	—

Scouting in Jordan, 90th Anniv. A326

"90" and: 100f, Emblem, Jordanian flag. 200f, Tents. 300f, Tents, Jordanian flag. No. 1697, Like No. 1694.

Perf 12, Imperf (#1697)

2000, May 11		Litho.	
1694-1696	A326	Set of 3	5.00	5.00

Size: 90x70mm

| 1697 | A326 | 200f multi | 7.50 | 7.50 |

Expo 2000, Hanover — A327

Designs: No. 1698, 200f, Inscribed clay tablet. 300f, Artifact with two heads.
No. 1700, 200f, King, Queen, Jordan pavilion interior.

2000, June 1	Litho.	Perf. 11¾
Granite Paper		
1698-1699	A327	Set of 2	3.50	3.50

Imperf
Size: 90x70mm

| 1700 | A327 | 200f multi | 3.00 | 3.00 |

Palace of Justice A328

Palace and: 100f, Scales of justice. 200f, Scales, Jordanian flag.

2000, June 25	Unwmk.	Perf. 12	
1701	A328	100f multi	.75	.75

Wmk. 388

| 1702 | A328 | 200f multi | 1.25 | 1.25 |

A number has been reserved for an additional stamp in this set. The editors would like to examine it.

Al-Amal Cancer Center — A329

Emblem and: 200f, Building. 300f, Family.

Perf. 11¾

2000, July 17	Litho.	Unwmk.
Granite Paper		
1704-1705	A329	Set of 2	3.75	3.75

Flora and Fauna — A330

Designs: 50f, Dove. 100f, Arabian oryx. 150f, Caracal. 200f, Red fox. 300f, Jal'ad iris. 400f, White broom.

2000, Sept. 28			Perf. 14¼	
Booklet Stamps				
1706	A330	50f multi	.35	.30
1707	A330	100f multi	.75	.50
a.	Booklet pane, 2 each #1706-1707		4.00	—
1708	A330	150f multi	1.25	.60
1709	A330	200f multi	1.50	.80
a.	Booklet pane, 2 each #1708-1709		7.00	—
1710	A330	300f multi	2.50	1.75
1711	A330	400f multi	3.00	1.90
a.	Booklet pane, 2 each #1710-1711		13.00	—
	Booklet, #1707a, 1709a, 1711a		30.00	

World Conservation Union — A331

Background color: 200f, Green. 300f, Blue.

2000, Oct. 4			Perf. 11¾	
Granite Paper				
1712-1713	A331	Set of 2	3.50	3.50

Tourist Sites A332

Designs: 50f, Petra. 100f, Jerash. 150f, Mount Nebo. 200f, Dead Sea. 300f, Aqaba. 400f, Wadi Rum.

2000, Oct. 9			Perf. 14¼	
Booklet Stamps				
1714	A332	50f multi	.35	.35
1715	A332	100f multi	.75	.60
a.	Booklet pane, 2 each #1714-1715		2.25	—
1716	A332	150f multi	1.25	.90
1717	A332	200f multi	1.75	1.10
a.	Booklet pane, 2 each #1716-1717		6.00	—
1718	A332	300f multi	2.25	1.50
1719	A332	400f multi	2.75	2.25
a.	Booklet pane, 2 each #1718-1719		10.00	—
	Booklet, #1715a, 1717a, 1719a		22.50	

King Hussein (1935-99) A333

Designs: 50f, King, vert. No. 1721, 150f, No. 1723, 200f, King and wreath. No. 1722, 200f, King, symbols of industry and agriculture.

2000, Nov. 14	Litho.	Perf. 11¾	
Granite Paper			
1720-1722	A333	Set of 3	2.75	2.75

Size: 90x70mm
Imperf

| 1723 | A333 | 200f multi | 4.50 | 4.50 |

UN High Commissioner for Refugees, 50th Anniv. — A334

Designs: 200f, Man, women, child. 300f, Emblem.

2000, Dec. 3	Litho.	Perf. 11¾	
Granite Paper			
1724-1725	A334	Set of 2	3.50	3.50

13th Arab Summit Conference A335

Emblem, map of Middle East and: 50f, Jordanian flag. 200f, Jordanian flags. 250f, King Abdullah II.

2001, Aug. 1			Perf. 14	
1726-1728	A335	Set of 3	3.00	3.00

Palestinian Intifada A336

Dome of the Rock and: 200f, Rock throwers, man carrying flag. 300f, Rock throwers, Israeli troops.

2001, Aug. 5
1729-1730 A336 Set of 2   3.00 3.00

Mohammed Al-Dorra, Boy Killed in Intifada Crossfire A337

Designs: 200f, Al-Dorra and father, Dome of the Rock. 300f, Close-up of Al-Dorra, Al-Dorra dead on father's lap.

2001, Aug. 5
1731-1732 A337 Set of 2   3.00 3.00

Healthy Non-smoking Students — A338

Designs: 200f, Students. 300f, Cartoon character, vert.

2001, Sept. 1
1733-1734 A338 Set of 2   3.00 3.00

Sports For People With Special Needs — A339

Stylized figures and: 200f, Man in wheelchair. 300f, Woman.

2001, Sept. 15
1735-1736 A339 Set of 2   3.00 3.00

Olive Trees A340

Designs: 200f, Olives on branch, tree, map of Jordan. 300f, Woman picking olives, vert.

2001, Oct. 1
1737-1738 A340 Set of 2   3.00 3.00

Year of Dialogue Among Civilizations A341

Emblem and: 200f, Family, handshake, world map. 300f, Other stylized drawings.

2001, Oct. 21
1739-1740 A341 Set of 2   3.00 3.00

Cooperation Between Jordan and Japan — A342

Designs: 200f, Sheikh Hussein Bridge, flags. 300f, King Hussein Bridge, handshake.

2001, Nov. 12 Litho. **Perf. 14¼**
1741-1742 A342 Set of 2   3.00 3.00

Jordan - People's Republic of China Diplomatic Relations, 25th Anniv. A343

Designs: 200f, Dove with envelope. 300f, King Abdullah II and Chinese Pres. Jiang Zemin.

2002   **Perf. 12**
1743-1744 A343 Set of 2   2.25 2.25

Amman, 2002 Arab Cultural Capital A344

Designs: 100f, Arabic script, star. 200f, Pen, torch. 300f, Amphitheater.

2002   **Perf. 14¼**
1745-1747 A344 Set of 3   3.00 3.00

Paintings A345

Paintings by, 100f, Rafiq Laham. 150f, Mahmoud Taha, horiz. 200f, Mohanna Durra. 300f, Wijdan, horiz.

2002, July 2   **Perf. 13¼**
1748-1751 A345 Set of 4   4.50 4.50

Vision 2020 — A346

Designs: 200f, Symbols of business and technology. 300f, Fingers, electronic device.

2002   Litho.   **Perf. 13¼**
1752-1753 A346 Set of 2   2.25 2.25

Migratory Birds A347

Designs: 100f, Goldfinch. No. 1755, 200f, Rufous bush robin. 300f, White stork.
No. 1757, 200f, Golden oriole, goshawk, ortolan bunting, hoopoe.

2002   **Perf. 13¼**
1754-1756 A347 Set of 3   4.00 4.00
Imperf
Size: 70x90mm
1757 A347 200f multi   8.50 8.50

Hashemite Rulers A348

No. 1758: a, Sherif Hussein bin Ali. b, King Abdullah. c, King Talal bin Abdullah. d, King Hussein bin Talal. e, King Abdullah II.

2003, July 2 Litho.   **Perf. 14**
1758   Miniature sheet of 5   4.50 4.50
a.-e. A348 200f Any single   .75   .75

Salt Museum A349

Views of building exterior: 150f, 250f.

2003, July 2
1759-1760 A349 Set of 2   1.75 1.75

Trees A350

Designs: 50f, Cupressus sempervirens. 100f, Pistacia atlantica. 200f, Quercus aegilops.

2003, Aug. 7
1761-1763 A350 Set of 3   2.25 2.25

Flowers A351

Designs: 50f, Cistanche tubulosa. 100f, Ophioglossum polyphyllum, vert. 150f, Narcissus tazetta. 200f, Gynandriris sisyrinchium, vert.

2003, Aug. 7
1764-1767 A351 Set of 4   3.00 3.00

Birds of Prey — A352

Designs: 100f, Ciraetus gallicus. No. 1769, 200f, Falco peregrinus. 300f, Accipiter nisus. No. 1771, 200f, Ciraetus gallicus, diff.

2003, Dec. 9 Litho.   **Perf. 14**
1768-1770 A352 Set of 3   3.50 3.50
Imperf
Size: 70x90mm
1771 A352 200f multi   6.00 6.00

Royal Cars Museum A353

Designs: 100f, Red sports car. 150f, Black limousine. 300f, White limousine. 200f, Three automobiles.

2003, Dec. 23 Litho.   **Perf. 14**
1772-1774 A353 Set of 3   3.50 3.50
Size: 90x70mm
Imperf
1775 A353 200f multi   4.50 4.50

Jordan Post Company A354

Emblem and: 50f, Arch. 100f, Pillars, vert.

2003, Dec. 23 Litho.   **Perf. 14**
1776-1777 A354 Set of 2   1.00 1.00

Triumphal Arch Type of 1993-98
2003   Litho.   **Perf. 12¾x13¼**
              Granite Paper
1777A A267 25f gray & multi   —   —

Arabian Horses A355

Various horses: 5pi, 7.50pi, 12.50pi, 15pi, 25pi. 10pi, Two horses, horiz.

2004, Dec. 27 Litho.   **Perf. 14¼**
                Granite Paper
1778-1782 A355 Set of 5   3.25 3.25
Imperf
Size: 90x70mm
1783 A355 10pi multi   8.50 8.50

Ain Ghazal
Statues
A356

Various statues: 5pi, 7.50pi, 12.50pi, 15pi, 25pi.
10pi, Two statues.

2004, Dec. 29 **Granite Paper**
1784-1788 A356 Set of 5 3.00 3.00
Imperf
Size: 70x90mm

1789 A356 10pi multi 5.00 5.00

Children's Paintings — A357

Various paintings: 5pi, 7.50pi, 12.50pi, 15pi, 25pi.
10pi, Parts of various paintings.

2004, Dec. 27 **Granite Paper**
1790-1794 A357 Set of 5 2.75 2.75
Imperf
Size: 90x70mm

1795 A357 10pi multi 5.50 5.50

Miniature Sheet

Nazareth Iris — A358

No. 1796 — Various photographs of Nazareth Iris: a, 5pi. b, 7.50pi. c, 10pi (70x90mm). d, 12.50pi. e, 15pi. f, 25pi.

2004, Dec. 29 **Perf. 14¼**
Granite Paper
1796 A358 Sheet of 6, #a-f 6.00 6.00

Miniature Sheet

Details From Mosaic Floor of Church
of the Holy Martyrs Lot and Procopius,
Mount Nebo — A359

No. 1797: a, 10pi, Man with scythe (68x90mm). b, 10pi, Man with flute, grapes. c, 15pi, Building. d, 25pi, Man with Basket.

2004, Dec. 27 **Litho.**
Granite Paper
1797 A359 Sheet of 4, #a-d 6.00 6.00

Expo 2005,
Aichi, Japan
A360

No. 1798: a, Dead Sea salt crystal. b, Dead Sea salt crystal, diff. c, Dead Sea salt crystal, diff. d, Dead Sea (70x70mm).

2005, Aug. 7 **Litho.** **Perf. 13¾**
1798 Sheet of 4 3.25 3.25
a. A360 5pi multi .30 .30
b. A360 7.50pi multi .45 .45
c. A360 12.50pi multi .75 .75
d. A360 20pi multi .90 .90

Fish — A361

Various Red Sea fish: 5f, 5pi, 7.50pi, 12.50pi.

Perf. 13½x13¾
2005, Dec. 27 **Litho.**
1799-1802 A361 Set of 4 2.50 2.50
Souvenir Sheet
1803 A361 20pi Lionfish 5.00 5.00

Intl. Sports
Year — A362

Children's drawings of: 1pi, Tennis player. 10pi, Medal winner. 15pi, Soccer game, horiz. No. 1807, 20pi, Swimmer, horiz. No. 1808, Basketball player.

Perf. 13½x13¾, 13¾x13½
2005, Dec. 27
1804-1807 A362 Set of 4 3.50 3.50
Size: 71x90mm
Imperf
1808 A362 20pi multi 6.00 6.00

Worldwide Fund for Nature — A363

Arabian oryx: 1.50pi, Grazing. 5pi, Three oryx. 7.50pi, Adults and juvenile. 12.50pi, Two adults.
20pi, Adult, three oryx in background.

2005, Dec. 27 **Perf. 13¾x13½**
1809-1812 A363 Set of 4 7.25 7.25
Souvenir Sheet
1813 A363 20pi multi 22.50 22.50

Child Protection — A364

Designs: 7.50pi, Hands of adult and child. 10pi, Mother holding infant. 12.50pi, Adult hugging child.
20pi, Child.

2005, Dec. 27 **Perf. 13¾**
1814-1816 A364 Set of 3 3.00 3.00
Size: 70x90mm
Imperf
1817 A364 20pi multi 6.50 6.50

Friendship of Jordan and
Japan — A365

Design: 7.50pi, Gallery of Japanese calligraphy. 12.50pi, Building. 15pi, Building at night. 20pi, Pottery in museum gallery.

2005, Dec. 27 **Perf. 13¾x13½**
1818-1820 A365 Set of 3 2.75 2.75
Size: 70x90mm
Imperf
1821 A365 20pi multi 5.75 5.75

Islamic
Art
Revival
A366

Designs: 5pi, Woodworker. 7.50pi, Engraver. 10pi, Calligrapher. 15pi, Woodworker, diff.
20pi, Calligrapher, diff.

2005, Dec. 27 **Perf. 13¾x13½**
1822-1825 A366 Set of 4 3.00 3.00
Size: 90x71mm
Imperf
1826 A366 20pi multi 6.00 6.00

Modern
Architecture
A367

Various buildings with panel color of: 7.50pi, Green. 10pi, Lemon, horiz. 12.50pi, Red brown.
20pi, Brown, horiz.

2006, Jan. 1 **Litho.** **Perf. 14**
1827-1829 A367 Set of 3 3.50 3.50
Imperf
Size: 90x70mm
1830 A367 20pi multi 4.50 4.50

Government Vehicles — A368

Designs: 10pi, Police car. 12.50pi, Fire truck. 17.50pi, Garbage truck. No. 1834, 20pi, Mail vans.
No. 1835, 20pi, Ambulance.

2006, Jan. 1 **Perf. 14**
1831-1834 A368 Set of 4 3.75 3.75
Imperf
Size: 90x70mm
1835 A368 20pi multi 4.50 4.50

Ancient
Coins — A369

Various coins with background color of: 5pi, Purple. 7.50pi, Yellow brown. 10pi, Gray. 12.50pi, Blue. 15pi, Dark red.
30pi, Dark blue, horiz.

2006, Jan. 1 **Perf. 13¾**
1836-1840 A369 Set of 5 4.50 4.50
Imperf
Size: 90x70mm
1841 A369 30pi multi 6.50 6.50

2006 World Cup
Soccer
Championships,
Germany
A370

Background color: 5pi, Light blue. 7.50pi, Yellow. 10pi, Tan. 12.50pi, Green. 15pi, Blue. 30pi, Yellow green, horiz.

2006, Jan. 1 **Perf. 14**
1842-1846 A370 Set of 5 4.50 4.50
Imperf
Size: 90x70mm
1847 A370 30pi multi 5.50 5.50

Art — A371

Various works of art by unnamed artists: 5pi, 10pi, 15pi. 20pi.
No. 1852, Four works of art, horiz.

2006, Oct. 21 **Litho.** **Perf. 14¼**
Granite Paper
1848-1851 A371 Set of 4 3.50 3.50
Imperf
Size: 90x70mm
1852 A371 20pi multi 6.00 6.00

Desert Reptiles A372

Designs: 5pi, Lizard. 7.50pi, Snake. 10pi, Lizards. 12.50pi, Lizard, diff. 15pi, Lizard, horiz. 20pi, Snake, diff.
No. 1859, Lizard, diff., horiz.

2006, Oct. 21   **Perf. 14¼**
Granite Paper
1853-1858 A372   Set of 6   3.25 3.25
Imperf
Size: 90x70mm
1859 A372 20pi multi   5.25 5.25

Information and Communications Technology in Education — A373

Design: 7.50pi, Man at computer. 12.50pi, Woman punching keys on keypad. 15pi, Man and computer screen. 20pi, Man using cellular phone.
No. 1864, Circuit board, design of unissued 50f stamp showing finger punching keypad.

2006, Nov. 11   **Perf. 14¼**
Granite Paper
1860-1863 A373   Set of 4   2.75 2.75
Imperf
Size: 70x90mm
1864 A373 20pi multi   5.50 5.50

National Symbols A374

Designs: 5pi, King Abdullah II in dress uniform. 7.50pi, King Abdullah II in suit and tie. 10pi, Jordanian soldiers, horiz. 12.50pi, King Abdullah II in camouflage uniform. 15pi, Flag, horiz. 20pi, Men in army uniforms and native garb, horiz. 25pi, Parade of tanks, horiz. 30pi, Flag and rose, horiz.

2006, Nov. 11   **Perf. 14¼**
Granite Paper
1865-1872 A374   Set of 8   6.25 6.25

Pitchers and Spouted Pots — A375

Designs: 10pi, Spouted pot. 20pi, Spouted pot with legs. 30pi, Pitcher. 25pi, Spouted pot, horiz.

Perf. 13½x13¾
2007, Dec. 31   **Litho.**
1873-1875 A375   Set of 3   1.75 1.75
Imperf
Size: 90x70mm
1876 A375 25pi multi   2.25 2.25

Culture and Identity A376

Designs: 10pi, Books. No. 1878, 20pi, Lute. 25pi, Bottle. 30pi, Arabic text.
No. 1881, 20pi, Arabic text, paint brushes, bottle, lute, books.

2007, Dec. 31   **Perf. 13½x13¾**
1877-1880 A376   Set of 4   2.40 2.40
Imperf
Size: 70x90mm
1881 A376 20pi multi   1.50 1.50

Butterflies A377

Various butterflies with denomination color of: 10pi, Orange. 15pi, Yellow green. 20pi, Gray. 25pi, Olive gray, horiz. 30pi, Orange, horiz.
40pi, Olive green, horiz.

Perf. 13½x13¾, 13¼x13½
2007, Dec. 31
1882-1886 A377   Set of 5   3.00 3.00
Imperf
Size: 90x70mm
1887 A377 40pi multi   4.50 4.50

Aqaba A378

Designs: 10pi, Arch and beach. 15pi, Scuba diver. 20pi, Motor boats. 30pi, Double-masted ship.

2008, July 16   **Litho.**   **Perf. 14¼**
Granite Paper
1888-1891 A378   Set of 4   2.10 2.10

Traditional Women's Clothing A379

Designs: 10pi, Mafraq. 15pi, Ma'an. 20pi, Amman. 25pi, Jerash. 30pi, Salt.

2008, July 16   **Granite Paper**
1892-1896 A379   Set of 5   3.00 3.00

Fruit — A380

Designs: 10pi, Oranges. 15pi, Cherries. 20pi, Figs. 25pi, Pomegranates. 30pi, Grapes.

2008, July 16
1897-1901 A380   Set of 5   3.00 3.00

Petra — A381

Designs: 10pi, Sculpture of face. 15pi, Ceramic plate. 20pi, Sculpture of grapevine. 25pi, Siq al Barid fresco. 30pi, Rock formations. 40pi, Treasury.

2008, July 16   **Litho.**   **Perf. 14¼**
Granite Paper
1902-1906 A381   Set of 5   3.00 3.00
Size: 66x86mm
1907 A381 40pi multi   1.25 1.25
Imperf
1908 A381 40pi multi   1.25 1.25

Bridge A382

50th Anniversary Emblem of Engineer's Association A383

2008, Sept. 22   **Litho.**   **Perf. 14¼**
Granite Paper
1909 A382 15pi shown   .45 .45
1910 A382 20pi shown   .60 .60
1911 A382 25pi Power station   .70 .70
    Nos. 1909-1911 (3)   1.75 1.75

2008 Summer Olympics, Beijing A384

Desings: 20pi, Taekwondo. 30pi, Equestrian. 40pi, Table tennis. 50pi, Running.

2008, Sept. 22   **Litho.**
Granite Paper
1912-1915 A384   Set of 4   4.00 4.00

Musical Instruments A385

Designs: 20pi, Oud. 40pi, Rebab. 60pi, Zither. 80pi, Flutes. 100pi, Tambourine and drum.
50pi, Oud, rebab, zither, flutes, tambourine and drum, horiz.

2008, Sept. 22   **Perf. 14¼**
Granite Paper
1916-1920 A385   Set of 5   8.50 8.50
Imperf
Size: 90x70mm
1921 A385 50pi multi   1.40 1.40

Flowers A386

Designs: 5pi, Egyptian catchfly. 10pi, Lupine. 15pi, Judean viper's bugloss. 20pi, Pimpernel. 30pi, Asiatic crowfoot. 40pi, Grape hyacinth. No. 1928, 50pi, Large flowered sage. 60pi, Star of Bethlehem. 80pi, Pyramidalis. 100pi, Calotropis.
No. 1932, 50pi, Cyclamen, horiz.

2008, Nov. 25   **Litho.**   **Perf. 14¼**
Granite Paper
1922-1931 A386   Set of 10   12.00 12.00
Imperf
Size: 90x70mm
1932 A386 50pi multi   1.40 1.40

Art From Quseir Amra UNESCO World Heritage Site — A387

Designs: 40pi, Woman with arm raised. 60pi, Grapes. 80pi, Hunters on horseback, bath. 100pi, Face of woman.
50pi, Quseir Amra Palace.

2008, Nov. 25   **Perf. 14¼x14**
Granite Paper
1933-1936 A387   Set of 4   8.00 8.00
Imperf
Size: 90x69mm
1937 A387 50pi multi   1.40 1.40

Hejaz Railway, Cent. A388

Designs: 20pi, Train on bridge. 30pi, Locomotive and tender. 50pi, Station and road.

2009, Feb. 1   **Litho.**   **Perf. 14¼**
Granite Paper
1938-1940 A388   Set of 3   3.00 3.00
    Dated 2008.

Birds
A389

Designs: 10pi, Mallard duck. 15pi, Saker. 20pi, Crouser cream. 30pi, Palestine sunbird. 40pi, Hoopoe. No. 1946, 50pi, Black francolin. 60pi, Little green bee-eater. 80pi, Sinai rosefinch.
No. 1949, 50pi, Kingfisher.

2009, Feb. 1   *Perf. 14¼*
Granite Paper
1941-1948 A389   Set of 8   8.75   8.75
Imperf
Size: 90x70mm
1949   A389   50pi multi   4.75   4.75
Dated 2008.

Arabian Coffee
Tools — A390

Designs: 40pi, Mortar and pestle. 60pi, Coffee pots and roasting pan. 80pi, Coffee pot and cups. 100pi, Bowl, roasting pan and shovel.
50pi, Mortar, pestle, coffee pot, bowl, roasting pan and shovel.

2009, Mar. 1   *Perf. 14¼*
Granite Paper
1950-1953 A390   Set of 4   8.00   8.00
Imperf
Size: 70x90mm
1954   A390   50pi multi   1.25   1.25
Dated 2008.

Traditional
Costumes
A391

Close-ups of costumes and: 40pi, Woman. 60pi, Woman, diff. 80pi, Woman, diff. 100pi, Man and woman.
50pi, Woman only.

2009, Mar. 1   *Perf. 14¼*
Granite Paper
1955-1958 A391   Set of 4   8.00   8.00
Imperf
Size: 70x90mm
1959   A391   50pi multi   4.25   4.25

Visit of
Pope
Benedict
XVI to
Jordan
A392

Designs: 20pi, Pope Benedict XVI, King Abdullah II, walkway to river. 30pi, Pope Benedict XVI. 40pi, Pope and King shaking hands. 50pi, Pope and King shaking hands, walkway to river, crucifix.

2009, May 8   *Perf. 14¼*
Granite Paper
1960-1962 A392   Set of 3   2.60   2.60
Imperf
Size: 90x70mm
1963   A392   50pi multi   4.75   4.75

King Abdullah II,
10th Anniv. of
Accession to
Throne — A393

2009, June 9   *Perf. 13¾*
Granite Paper
Background Color
1964   A393   10pi maroon   .30   .30
1965   A393   15pi dark blue   .45   .45
1966   A393   20pi bright blue   .60   .60
1967   A393   25pi tan   .70   .70
1968   A393   30pi dark green   .85   .85
1969   A393   35pi blue   1.00   1.00
1970   A393   40pi purple   1.10   1.10
1971   A393   45pi black   1.25   1.25
1972   A393   50pi brown   1.40   1.40
1973   A393   1d blue gray   3.00   3.00
Nos. 1964-1973 (10)   10.65   10.65

E-Government
A394

Designs: 20pi, Computer cables. 30pi, Spiral emblem. 40pi, Internet address of Jordanian government. 50pi, Letter, compass, Earth.

2009, Aug. 25   Litho.   *Perf. 13¼*
Granite Paper
1974-1977 A394   Set of 4   4.00   4.00

A395   A396

A397   A398

A399

University emblems: No. 1983, Al-Hussein Bin Jalal University. No. 1984, Tafila Technical University. No. 1985, German-Jordanian University. No. 1986, Al-Balqa Applied University. No. 1987, Yarmouk University.

2009, Aug. 25   *Perf. 13¼*
Granite Paper
1978   A395   20pi multi   .60   .60
1979   A396   20pi multi   .60   .60
1980   A397   20pi multi   .60   .60
1981   A398   20pi multi   .60   .60
1982   A399   20pi multi   .60   .60
1983   A399   20pi multi   .60   .60

1984   A399   20pi multi   .60   .60
1985   A399   20pi multi   .60   .60
1986   A399   20pi multi   .60   .60
1987   A399   20pi multi   .60   .60
Nos. 1978-1987 (10)   6.00   6.00

Waterfalls,
Ma'een — A400

Designs: 10pi, Waterfall, orange brown panel. 20pi, Building and mountain, fawn panel. 30pi, Waterfall, black panel. 40pi, Waterfall, gray green panel. 50pi, Waterfall, olive brown panel.
60pi, Waterfall, blue panel.

2009, Aug. 25   Litho.
Granite Paper
1988-1992 A400   Set of 5   4.25   4.25
Size: 70x91mm
Imperf
1993   A400   60pi multi   1.75   1.75

Animals
A401

Designs: 10pi, Horse. 20pi, Rabbits. 30pi, Fox. 40pi, Maha gazelle. 50pi, Gazelle. 60pi, Camel.

2009, Aug. 25   Litho.
Granite Paper
1994-1998 A401   Set of 5   4.25   4.25
Size: 70x91mm
Imperf
1999   A401   60pi multi   1.75   1.75

Vegetables
A402

No. 2000: a, Corn. b, Onions, garlic. c, Beans, peas, okra. d, Cabbages. e, Eggplants. f, Pumpkins. g, Bell peppers. h, Hot peppers. i, Radishes, turnips, beets. j, Tomatoes, zucchini.

2009, Aug. 25   *Perf. 13¼*
Granite Paper
2000   Sheet of 10   6.00   6.00
   a.-j.   A402 20pi Any single   .60   .60

Environmental
Protection — A403

Designs: 20pi, Tree, shrub, flower. 30pi, Man and fire. 40pi, Animals grazing. 50pi, Litter in stream.

2009   **Granite Paper**   Litho.
2001-2004 A403   Set of 4   4.00   4.00

Insects — A404

Designs: 10pi, Beetle. 15pi, Butterfly. 20pi, Ladybug. 25pi, Bee. 30pi, Mantis. 40pi, Moth. 50pi, Dragonfly. 60pi, Fly. 80pi, Grasshopper. 100pi, Dragonflies.

2009, Dec. 13   Litho.   *Perf. 13¼*
Granite Paper
2005-2014 A404   Set of 10   12.50   12.50

Nos. 588-590
Surcharged

Methods and Perfs As Before
2009, Dec. 20
2015   A82   80pi on 120f #588   2.25   2.25
2016   A82   80pi on 180f #589   2.25   2.25
2017   A82   80pi on 200f #590   2.25   2.25
Nos. 2015-2017 (3)   6.75   6.75

No. 1471b
Surcharged

Perf. 12¾x13¼
2009, Dec. 20   Litho.
2018   A267   80pi on 25f multi   2.25   2.25

Tourism
A405

Sites in: 10pi, Ajlun. 20pi, Amman. 30pi, Karak. 40pi, Showbak.
50pi, Jerash.

2010, Oct. 3   *Perf. 14*
2019-2022 A405   Set of 4   3.00   3.00
Size: 90x70mm
Imperf
2023   A405   50pi multi   1.50   1.50

Miniature Sheet

Mushrooms — A406

No. 2024: a, Cortinarius balteatus. b, Russula bicolor. c, Red fly agaric. d, Amanita muscaria. e, Boletus edulis. f, Amanita albocreata. g, Agaricus anderwij. h, Agaricus bisporus.

2010, Oct. 3   *Perf. 14*
2024   A406   20pi Sheet of 8, #a-h   4.50   4.50

Mosques in
Jordan
A407

Designs: 10pi, Jordan University Mosque. 20pi, Abu-Darwiesh Mosque. 30pi, Al Hussainy Mosque. 40pi, King Abdullah Mosque. 50pi, King Hussein bin Talal Mosque.

2010, Nov. 30
2025-2029 A407   Set of 5   4.25   4.25

Sports — A408

Designs: 10pi, Skydiving. 20pi, Swimming. 30pi, Hot-air ballooning. 40pi, Racing boats. 50pi, Jordan Rally.

2010, Nov. 30   **Perf. 14**
2030-2033 A408   3.00 3.00
Size: 70x90mm
Imperf
2034 A408 50pi multi   1.50 1.50

Old Farming Tools A409

Designs: 20pi, Millstone. 30pi, Flail. 40pi, Pitchfork. 50pi, Olive crushing wheel.

2011, Feb. 27   **Perf. 14**
2035-2038 A409 Set of 4   4.00 4.00
Dated 2010.

Development Zones — A410

Emblem of: No. 2039, 20pi, Dead Sea Development Zone. No. 2040, 20pi, Irbid Development Area. No. 2041, 20pi, Jabal Ajloun Development Area. No. 2042, 20pi, King Hussein Bin Talal Development Area. No. 2043, 20pi, Ma'an Development Area.

2011, Feb. 27
2039-2043 A410 Set of 5   3.00 3.00
Dated 2010.

Wild Herbs — A411

Designs: No. 2044, 20pi, Artemisia herba alba. No. 2045, 20pi, Capparis spinosa. No. 2046, 20pi, Lavandula vera. No. 2047, 20pi, Matricaria chamomilla. No. 2048, 20pi, Ocimum basilicum. No. 2049, 20pi, Salvia officinalis. No. 2050, 20pi, Thymus serpyllum. No. 2051, 20pi, Trigonella foenum-graecum.

2011, Feb. 27
2044-2051 A411 Set of 8   4.50 4.50
Dated 2010. Latin names of plants are misspelled on Nos. 2044, 2045, 2046, 2050 and 2051.

Junior and Cadet World Fencing Championships, Jordan — A412

Fencers and stylized fencer in panel in: 10pi, Red brown. 20pi, Blue violet. 30pi, Greenish blue. 40pi, Olive green. No. 2056, 50pi, Gray.
No. 2057, 50pi, Fencers, vert.

2011, Apr. 6   **Perf. 13x12¾**
2052-2056 A412 Set of 5   4.25 4.25
Size: 75x94mm
Imperf
2057 A412 50pi multi   *6.00 6.00*

Jordan Rally — A413

Various race cars: 10pu, 20pi, 30pi, 40pi, 50pi.
No. 2063, 50pi, Race car, ruins, helicopter.

2011, Apr. 14   **Perf. 13x12¾**
2058-2062 A413 Set of 5   4.25 4.25
Size: 95x74mm
Imperf
2063 A413 50pi multi   *5.75 5.75*

Jewelry — A414

Designs: 20pi, Pendant on necklace. No. 2065, 30pi, Pendants, necklace and bracelet. 40pi, Ring. 50i, Necklace with pendants. No. 2068, 30pi, Ring, diff.

2011, May 10   **Perf. 13¼x13**
Granite Paper
2064-2067 A414 Set of 4   4.00 4.00
Size: 77x77mm
Imperf
2068 A414 30pi multi   *5.00 5.00*
Dated 2010.

A415

A416

A417

A418

A419

A420

A421

A422

A423

Dams A424

2011, May 10   **Perf. 13x13¼**
Granite Paper
2069 A415 20pi multi   .60 .60
2070 A416 20pi multi   .60 .60
2071 A417 20pi multi   .60 .60
2072 A418 20pi multi   .60 .60
2073 A419 20pi multi   .60 .60
2074 A420 20pi multi   .60 .60
2075 A421 20pi multi   .60 .60
2076 A422 20pi multi   .60 .60
2077 A423 20pi multi   .60 .60
2078 A424 20pi multi   .60 .60
     Nos. 2069-2078 (10)   6.00 6.00
Size: 90x70mm
Imperf
2079 A424 30pi multi   *6.75 6.75*
Dated 2010.

Red Sea Coral Reefs A425

Designs: 20pi, Brain coral. 30pi, Coral, fish. No. 2082, 40pi, Coral. 50pi, Coral, diff. 60pi, Coral, diff. No. 2085, 40p, Coral, fish, diff.

2011, Sept. 28 **Litho.** **Perf. 14**
2080-2084 A425 Set of 5   5.75 5.75
Size: 90x70mm
Imperf
2085 A425 40pi multi   1.25 1.25

Ceramics A426

Designs: 10pi, Jug with handle, head. 20pi, Item on pedestal. No. 2088, 30pi, Jug with handle. 40pi, Item with Arabic script. 50pi, Item with Arabic script and people. 60pi, Sphere on pedestal. No. 2092, 30p, Abstract tile designs.

2011, Sept. 28   **Perf. 14**
2086-2091 A426 Set of 5   6.00 6.00
Size: 70x90mm
Imperf
2092 A426 30pi multi   .85 .85

A427

A428

A429

A430

A431

A432

A433

A434

A435

Historical
Path — A436

2011, Sept. 28   *Perf. 14*
2093 A427 20pi multi   .60   .60
2094 A428 20pi multi   .60   .60
2095 A429 20pi multi   .60   .60
2096 A430 20pi multi   .60   .60
2097 A431 20pi multi   .60   .60
2098 A432 20pi multi   .60   .60
2099 A433 20pi multi   .60   .60
2100 A434 20pi multi   .60   .60
2101 A435 20pi multi   .60   .60
2102 A436 20pi multi   .60   .60
   Nos. 2093-2102 (10)   6.00 6.00

Crown Prince
Hussein
A437

Denominations: 20pi, 30pi, 50pi.

2011   *Perf. 13½x13¼*
   Granite Paper
2103-2105 A437 Set of 3   3.00 3.00

Old
Astronomical
Instruments
A438

Designs: 10pi, Astrolabe. 20pi, Telescope.
30pi, Sextant. 40pi, Sundial.

2011   *Perf. 13½x13¼*
   Granite Paper
2106-2109 A438 Set of 4   3.00 3.00

Royal Jordanian Falcons Aerobatic
Squad — A439

Designs: 10pi, Line of four airplanes. 20pi,
Pilot in cockpit, three other airplanes. 30pi,
Three airplanes. 40pi, Four airplanes in
formation.
50pi, Four airplanes, Jordanian flag.

2011   *Perf. 13¼x13½*
   Granite Paper
2110-2113 A439 Set of 4   3.00 3.00
    Size: 90x70mm
     Imperf
2114 A439 50pi multi   1.40 1.40

   Souvenir Sheet

Preervation of Polar Regions and
Glaciers — A440

No. 2115: a, 80pi, Penguins. b, 1d, Polar
bear.

2011 **Granite Paper**   *Perf. 13½*
2115 A440 Sheet of 2, #a-b   5.25 5.25

A441

A442

A444

A445

King Abdullah
II — A446

Design: 50pi, King Abdullah II and mosque,
horiz.

2012, Jan. 30   *Perf. 13½x13¼*
   Granite Paper
2116 A441 20pi multi   .60   .60
2117 A442 20pi multi   .60   .60
2118 A443 20pi multi   .60   .60
2119 A444 20pi multi   .60   .60
2120 A445 20pi multi   .60   .60
2121 A446 20pi multi   .60   .60
   Nos. 2116-2121 (6)   3.60 3.60
    Size: 90x70mm
     Imperf
2122 A446 50pi multi   1.40 1.40

Labor
Day — A447

Designs: 20pi, Raised fists. 30pi, Man with
shovel. 40pi, Man with pick, woman and child.
50pi, Man with hard hat.

2012   *Perf. 13½x13¼*
   Granite Paper
2123-2126 A447 Set of 4   4.00 4.00

World Telecommunications
Day — A448

Designs: 30pi, Hands holding Earth. 40pi,
Dish antennas. 50pi, Computer.

2012 **Granite Paper**   **Litho.**
2127-2129 A448 Set of 3   3.50 3.50

2012 Summer
Olympics,
London
A449

Designs: 20pi, Equestrian. 30pi, Soccer.
40pi, Tennis. 50pi, Kayaking.

2012   **Granite Paper**
2130-2133 A449 Set of 4   4.00 4.00

Chess
A450

Various chess pieces: 30pi, 40pi, 50pi.

2012 **Litho.**   *Perf. 11¾*
2134-2136 A450 Set of 3   3.50 3.50

Citrus
Fruits — A451

Designs: 10pi, Kumquats. 20pi, Oranges.
30pi, Lemons. 40pi, Oranges, diff. 50pi,
Pomelos.

2012 **Litho.**   *Perf. 11¾*
2137-2141 A451 Set of 5   4.25 4.25

   Miniature Sheets

A452

Prehistoric Animals — A453

No. 2142: a, Pteranodon in flight, back of
Apatosaurus. b, Tyrannosaurus Rex and volcano. c, Triceratops and Stegosaurus. d,
Horned dinosaur, legs of Tyrannosaurus Rex.
No. 2143: a, Head of Tyrannosaurus rex,
waterfall. b, Apatosauruses. c, Raptors on
shore. d, Three dinosaurs in water.

2012 **Litho.**   *Perf. 11¾*
2142 A452 20pi Sheet of 4, #a-d 2.25 2.25
2143 A453 20pi Sheet of 4, #a-d 2.25 2.25

A454

A454a

A454b

A454c

A454d

A454e

Artists —
A454g

A454f

2012		**Litho.**		**Perf. 11¾**
2144	A454	20pi multi	.60	.60
2145	A454a	20pi multi	.60	.60
2146	A454b	20pi multi	.60	.60
2147	A454c	20pi multi	.60	.60
2148	A454d	20pi multi	.60	.60
2149	A454e	20pi multi	.60	.60
2150	A454f	20pi multi	.60	.60
2151	A454g	20pi multi	.60	.60
	Nos. 2144-2151 (8)		4.80	4.80

Jordan Library and
Information
Association, 50th
Anniv. — A455

Designs: 40pi, Association emblem. 50pi,
50th anniversary emblem.

2013		**Litho.**	**Perf. 14**
2152-2153	A455	Set of 2	2.60 2.60

Horses — A456

Designs: 10pi, Two horses. 20pi, One horse,
horiz. 30pi, Two horses, horiz. 40pi, Head of
horse, horiz. No. 2158, 50pi, Horse in water,
horiz.
No. 2159, 50pi, Six horses, horiz.

2013, Dec. 2		**Litho.**	**Perf. 11¾**
2154-2158	A456	Set of 5	4.25 4.25
		Size: 90x70mm	
		Imperf	
2159	A456	50pi multi	1.40 1.40
		Dated 2012.	

Ships
A457

Various ships, 20pi, 30pi, 40pi, 50pi.
No. 2164, 50pi, Fleet of ships.

2013, Dec. 2		**Litho.**	**Perf. 11¾**
2160-2163	A457	Set of 4	4.00 4.00
		Size: 90x70mm	
		Imperf	
2164	A457	50pi multi	1.40 1.40
		Dated 2012.	

Nature
Reserves — A458

Designs: 10pi, Rocks. 20pi, Flowers, horiz.
30pi, Lake, horiz. 40pi, Plateaus, horiz. No.
2169, 50pi, Antelopes, horiz.
No. 2170, 50pi, Hillside village, horiz.

2014, Feb. 9		**Litho.**	**Perf. 14**
2165-2169	A458	Set of 5	4.25 4.25
		Size: 90x70mm	
		Imperf	
2170	A458	50pi multi	1.40 1.40
		Dated 2013.	

Doors and
Windows
A459

Designs: No. 2171, 20pi, Door, King Hussein's Mosque. No. 2172, 20pi, Door and window, Umayyad Palace. No. 2173, 20pi, Door,
Royal Hashemite Court, vert. No. 2174, 20pi,
Door and windows, Justice Palace, vert. No.
2175, 20pi, Window, Raghadan Palace, vert.
No. 2176, 20pi, Door, Al-Salt School, vert. No.
2177, 20pi, Window, Al-Salt, vert.

2014, Feb. 9		**Litho.**	**Perf. 14**
2171-2177	A459	Set of 7	4.00 4.00
		Dated 2013.	

A460

A461

A462

A463

A464

A465

A466

Birds — A467

2014, Feb. 9		**Litho.**		**Perf. 14**
2178	A460	20pi multi	.60	.60
2179	A461	20pi multi	.60	.60
2180	A462	20pi multi	.60	.60
2181	A463	20pi multi	.60	.60
2182	A464	20pi multi	.60	.60
2183	A465	20pi multi	.60	.60
2184	A466	20pi multi	.60	.60
2185	A467	20pi multi	.60	.60
	Nos. 2178-2185 (8)		4.80	4.80
		Dated 2013.		

1933 Stamps and Map of
Jordan — A468

Map of Jordan and stamp: No. 2186, 80pi,
Jordan #191. No. 2187, 80pi, Jordan #197.

2014, Feb. 9		**Litho.**	**Imperf.**
2186-2187	A468	Set of 2	4.50 4.50

Visit of
Pope
Francis
to
Jordan
A469

Designs: 20pi, Pope Francis. 30pi, Pope
Francis and King Abdullah II. 40pi, Pope Francis and dove, vert.
50pi, Flags of Vatican City and Jordan, Jordan #474, 1683, 1961, 2188.

2014, May 24		**Litho.**	**Perf. 14¼**
2188-2190	A469	Set of 3	2.60 2.60
		Imperf	
		Size: 90x70mm	
2191	A469	50pi multi	1.40 1.40

First Papal visit to Jordan, 50th anniv. (No.
2191).

A470

A471

A472

A473

A474

Cartoons — A475

2014, July 1   Litho.   Perf. 14
2192	A470	20pi multi	.60	.60
2193	A471	20pi multi	.60	.60
2194	A472	20pi multi	.60	.60
2195	A473	20pi multi	.60	.60
2196	A474	20pi multi	.60	.60
2197	A475	20pi multi	.60	.60
	Nos. 2192-2197 (6)		3.60	3.60

Dated 2013.

SEMI-POSTAL STAMPS

Locust Campaign Issue

Nos. 145-156
Overprinted

1930, Apr. 1   Wmk. 4   Perf. 14
| B1 | A1 | 2(m) Prus blue | 1.75 | 3.50 |
| a. | Inverted overprint | | 200.00 | |

B2	A1	3(m) rose	1.75	3.50
B3	A1	4(m) green	2.00	4.75
B4	A1	5(m) orange	20.00	16.75
a.	Double overprint		300.00	
B5	A1	10(m) red	2.25	3.50
B6	A1	15(m) ultra	2.25	3.50
a.	Inverted overprint		200.00	
B7	A1	20(m) olive grn	2.25	5.00
B8	A2	50(m) claret	7.50	11.50
B9	A2	90(m) bister	16.00	45.00
B10	A2	100(m) lt blue	20.00	47.50
B11	A2	200(m) violet	47.50	110.00
B12	A2	500(m) brown	150.00	160.00
a.	"C" of "Locust" omitted		750.00	
	Nos. B1-B12 (12)		273.25	414.50

These stamps were issued to raise funds to help combat a plague of locusts.

> **Catalogue values for unused stamps in this section, from this point to the end of the section, are for Never Hinged items.**

Jerusalem — SP1

1997, Nov. 29   Litho.   Perf. 13½x13
B13	SP1	100f +10f bl & multi	.90	.75
B14	SP1	200f +20f yel & multi	1.75	1.50
B15	SP1	300f +30f bl grn & multi	2.50	2.25
	Nos. B13-B15 (3)		5.15	4.50

Breast Cancer Prevention — SP2

2009, Aug. 25   Litho.   Perf. 13¼
Granite Paper
| B16 | SP2 | 30pi +50pi multi | 2.75 | 2.25 |

Jerusalem, Capital of Arab Culture — SP3

Panel color: 20pi+25pi, Orange. 30pi+25pi, Purple. 40pi+25pi, Red. 50pi+25pi, Gray green.

2009, Dec. 13   Perf. 13¼
Granite Paper
| B17-B20 | SP3 | Set of 4 | 7.25 | 6.75 |

AIR POST STAMPS

> **Catalogue values for unused stamps in this section are for Never Hinged items.**

Plane and Globe — AP1

Perf. 13½x13
1950, Sept. 16   Engr.   Wmk. 4
C1	AP1	5f org & red vio	1.50	.25
C2	AP1	10f pur & brown	1.50	.25
C3	AP1	15f ol grn & rose car	1.50	.25
C4	AP1	20f deep blue & blk	1.75	.60
C5	AP1	50f rose pink & dl grn	2.00	.75
C6	AP1	100f blue & brown	3.50	1.50
C7	AP1	150f blk & red org	5.00	2.25
	Nos. C1-C7 (7)		16.75	5.85

Temple of Artemis, Jerash — AP2

1954   Unwmk.   Perf. 12
C8	AP2	5f blue blk & org	.80	.25
C9	AP2	10f vio brn & ver	.80	.25
C10	AP2	25f bl grn & ultra	.90	.25
C11	AP2	35f dp plum & grnsh bl	1.25	.25
C12	AP2	40f car rose & blk	1.50	.25
C13	AP2	50f dp ultra & org yel	1.75	.40
C14	AP2	100f dk bl & vio brn	2.00	.75
C15	AP2	150f stl bl & red brn	3.00	1.00
	Nos. C8-C15 (8)		12.00	3.40

1958-59   Wmk. 305   Perf. 12
C16	AP2	5f blue blk & org	.90	.25
C17	AP2	10f vio brn & ver	.90	.25
C18	AP2	25f bl grn & ultra	.90	.25
C19	AP2	35f dp plum grnsh bl	.90	.25
C20	AP2	40f car rose & blk	1.10	.50
C21	AP2	50f dp ultra & org yel ('59)	1.75	1.00
	Nos. C16-C21 (6)		6.45	2.50

Stadium and Torch AP3

Perf. 11x11½
1964, July 12   Litho.   Wmk. 305
C22	AP3	1f yellow & multi	.50	.25
C23	AP3	4t red & multi	.50	.25
C24	AP3	10f blue & multi	.50	.25
C25	AP3	35f yel grn & multi	1.00	.40
a.	Souvenir sheet of 4, #C22-C25		3.00	1.25
	Nos. C22-C25 (4)		2.50	1.15

Opening of Hussein Sports City. No. C25a also exists imperf.

Gorgeous Bush-Shrike — AP4

Birds: 500f, Ornate hawk-eagle, vert. 1d, Gray-headed kingfisher, vert.

Perf. 14x14½
1964, Dec. 18   Photo.   Unwmk.
Birds in Natural Colors
C26	AP4	150f lt grn, blk & car	30.00	11.00
C27	AP4	500f brt bl, blk & grn	75.00	30.00
C28	AP4	1d lt ol grn & blk	135.00	50.00
	Nos. C26-C28 (3)		240.00	91.00

Pagoda, Olympic Torch and Emblem — AP5

1965, Mar. 5   Litho.   Perf. 14
C29	AP5	10f deep rose	.50	.60
C30	AP5	15f violet	.60	.70
C31	AP5	20f blue	.75	.85
C32	AP5	30f green	.90	1.00
C33	AP5	40f brown	1.40	1.50
C34	AP5	60f carmine rose	2.00	2.25
	Nos. C29-C34 (6)		6.15	6.90

18th Olympic Games, Tokyo, Oct. 10-25, 1964. An imperf. 100f violet blue souvenir sheet exists. Size of stamp: 60x60mm. Value $12.50.
For overprints see Nos. C42A-C42F.

Forum, Jerash — AP6

Antiquities of Jerash: No. C36, South Theater. No. C37, Triumphal arch. No. C38, Temple of Artemis. No. C39, Cathedral steps. No. C40, Artemis Temple, gate. No. C41, Columns. No. C42, Columns and niche, South Theater. Nos. C39-C42 are vertical.

1965, June 22   Photo.   Perf. 14x15
Center Multicolored
C35	AP6	55f bright pink	1.75	1.00
C36	AP6	55f light blue	1.75	1.00
C37	AP6	55f green	1.75	1.00
C38	AP6	55f black	1.75	1.00
C39	AP6	55f light green	1.75	1.00
C40	AP6	55f carmine rose	1.75	1.00
C41	AP6	55f gray	1.75	1.00
C42	AP6	55f blue	1.75	1.00
	Nos. C35-C42 (8)		14.00	8.00

Nos. C35-C38 are printed in horizontal rows of 4; Nos. C39-C42 in vertical rows of 4; sheets of 16.

Nos. C29-C34 with Bilingual Ovpt. and Rocket in Black

1965, Sept. 25   Litho.   Perf. 14
C42A	AP5	10f deep rose	1.75	.95
C42B	AP5	15f violet	2.50	1.40
C42C	AP5	20f blue	3.00	2.00
C42D	AP5	30f green	4.75	3.00
C42E	AP5	40f brown	6.00	4.00
C42F	AP5	60f carmine rose	7.50	5.75
	Nos. C42A-C42F (6)		25.50	17.10

The imperf. 100f blue souvenir sheet exists overprinted. Value $21.50.

King Hussein Type of Regular Issue

1966, Jan. 15   Photo.   Perf. 14½x14
Portrait in Brown

C43	A67	200f brt blue grn	6.50	1.25
C44	A67	500f light green	12.00	5.00
C45	A67	1d light ultra	22.50	9.00
		Nos. C43-C45 (3)	32.75	15.25

Animal Type of Regular Issue, 1967

Animals: 4f, Striped hyena. 30f, Arabian stallion. 60f, Persian gazelle.

1967, Feb. 11   Photo.   Perf. 14x15

C46	A70	4f dk brn & multi	2.00	.25
C47	A70	30f lt bl & multi	2.50	.45
C48	A70	60f yellow & multi	4.50	1.00
		Nos. C46-C48 (3)	8.00	1.65

Game Type of Regular Issue, 1968

Protected Game: 60f, Nubian ibex, vert. 100f, Wild ducks.

1968, Oct. 5   Litho.   Perf. 13½

C49	A74	60f multicolored	11.00	4.50
C50	A74	100f multicolored	17.50	7.00

Easter Type of Regular Issue

Designs: 60f, Altar, Holy Sepulcher. 100f, Feet Washing, Holy Gate, Jerusalem.

1972, Apr.   Photo.   Perf. 14x13½

C51	A92	60f dk bl & multi	1.50	.70
C52	A92	100f multicolored	2.00	1.10

Aero Club Type of Regular Issue

15f, Two Piper 140s. 20f, R.J.A.C. Beechcraft. 40f, Aero Club emblem with winged horse.

1973, Jan.   Photo.   Perf. 13½x14

C53	A100	15f blue, blk & red	.85	.25
C54	A100	20f blue, blk & red	.85	.25
C55	A100	40f mag, blk & yel	1.75	.45
		Nos. C53-C55 (3)	3.00	.85

Agriculture Type of Regular Issue

Design: 100f, Soil conservation.

1973, Dec. 25   Perf. 13½

C56	A110	100f multicolored	2.50	1.00

King Hussein
Driving Car — AP7

1974, Dec. 20   Perf. 12

C57	AP7	30f multicolored	.80	.25
C58	AP7	60f multicolored	1.50	.75

Royal Jordanian Automobile Club.

Building Type of Regular Issue

Designs: 50f, Palms, Aqaba. 60f, Obelisk tomb. 80f, Fort of Wadi Rum.

1975, Mar. 1   Photo.   Perf. 13½x14

C59	A121	50f pink & multi	1.40	.65
C60	A121	60f lt bl & multi	1.75	.80
C61	A121	80f yellow & multi	2.25	.80
		Nos. C59-C61 (3)	4.85	2.25

Hussein Type of Regular Issue

1975, Apr. 8   Photo.   Perf. 14x13½
Size: 22x27mm

C62	A123	60f dk grn & brn	1.25	.35
C63	A123	100f org brn & brn	2.00	.40
C64	A123	120f dp bl & brn	1.50	.65
C65	A123	180f brt mag & brn	2.00	1.00
C66	A123	200f grnsh bl & brn	2.25	1.25
C67	A123	400f pur & brown	3.25	2.00
C68	A123	500f orange & brn	4.25	3.25
		Nos. C62-C68 (7)	14.00	8.90

POSTAGE DUE STAMPS

Stamps of Regular Issue (Nos. 69, 66-68 Surcharged with New Value like No. 91) Overprinted

This overprint reads: "Mustahaq" (Tax or Due)

1923   Unwmk.   Perf. 11½
Typo. Ovpt. "Mustahaq" 10mm long

J1	A7	½pi on 3pi ol brn	47.50	55.00
a.		Inverted overprint	175.00	175.00
b.		Double overprint	175.00	175.00

Handstamped Overprint 12mm long

J2	A7	½pi on 3pi ol brn	13.50	15.00
a.		Inverted overprint	50.00	—
b.		Double overprint	50.00	—
J3	A7	1pi dark blue	9.00	9.50
a.		Inverted overprint	45.00	—
b.		Double overprint	50.00	—
J4	A7	1 ½pi violet	9.00	9.50
a.		Inverted overprint	45.00	—
b.		Double overprint	50.00	—
J5	A7	2pi orange	10.00	11.00
a.		Inverted overprint	60.00	—
b.		Double overprint	65.00	—
		Nos. J1-J5 (5)	89.00	100.00

Stamps of Hejaz Handstamped

J6	A7	½pi red	1.50	1.75
J7	A7	1pi dark blue	1.60	2.00
J8	A7	1 ½pi violet	2.00	2.25
J9	A7	2pi orange	2.50	3.00
J10	A7	3pi olive brown	3.50	5.50
J11	A7	5pi olive green	6.00	8.00
		Nos. J6-J11 (6)	17.10	22.50

Type of Palestine, 1918, Overprinted

The overprint reads: "Mustahaq. Sharqi al'Ardan." (Tax. Eastern Jordan).

1925   Wmk. 4   Perf. 14

J12	A1	1m dark brown	2.25	5.00
J13	A1	2m yellow	3.00	3.25
J14	A1	4m rose	4.75	5.00
J15	A1	8m red	5.50	8.50
J16	A1	13m ultramarine	7.50	8.50
J17	A1	5pi plum	8.25	11.50
a.		Perf. 15x14	67.50	77.50
		Nos. J12-J17 (6)	31.25	41.75

Stamps of Palestine, 1918, Surcharged

1926

J18	A1	1m on 1m dk brn	4.00	5.00
J19	A1	2m on 1m dk brn	4.00	5.00
J20	A1	4m on 3m Prus bl	4.00	6.75
J21	A1	8m on 3m Prus bl	4.25	7.50
J22	A1	13m on 13m ultra	4.25	8.50
J23	A1	5pi on 13m ultra	5.75	10.50
		Nos. J18-J23 (6)	26.25	43.25

The surcharge reads "Tax—Eastern Jordan" and New Value.

Stamps of Regular Issue, 1927, Overprinted

1929

J24	A1	2m Prussian bl	2.50	6.00
J25	A1	10m red	2.50	6.00
J26	A2	50m claret	6.50	19.00
		Nos. J24-J26 (3)	11.50	31.00

With Additional Surcharge

J27	A1	1(m) on 3(m) rose	1.75	7.00
J28	A1	4(m) on 15(m) ultra	3.00	7.50
a.		Inverted surch. and ovpt.	95.00	
J29	A2	20(m) on 100(m) lt bl	6.50	19.00
		Nos. J27-J29 (3)	11.25	33.50

D1

1929   Engr.   Perf. 14
Size: 17¼x21mm

J30	D1	1m brown	1.00	3.25
a.		Perf. 13½x13	90.00	45.00
J31	D1	2m orange	1.00	3.75
J32	D1	4m green	1.00	4.25
J33	D1	10m carmine	2.25	4.75
J34	D1	20m olive green	8.50	15.00
J35	D1	50m blue	10.50	19.00
		Nos. J30-J35 (6)	24.25	50.00

See Nos. J39-J43 design with larger type. For surcharge see No. J52. For overprints see Nos. NJ1a, NJ3, NJ5a, NJ6-NJ7.

D2

1942   Unwmk.   Litho.   Perf. 13x13½

J36	D2	1m dull red brn	.35	.35
J37	D2	2m dl orange yel	3.75	3.75
J38	D2	10m dark carmine	4.75	4.75
		Nos. J36-J38 (3)	8.85	8.85

For overprints see Nos. NJ8-NJ10.

Type of 1929
1943-44   Engr.   Wmk. 4   Perf. 12
Size: 17¾x21 ¼mm

J39	D1	1m orange brn	.35	.35
J40	D1	2m yel orange	.35	.35
J41	D1	4m yel green	.35	.35
J42	D1	10m rose carmine	.35	.35
J43	D1	20m olive green	11.00	11.00
		Nos. J39-J43 (5)	12.40	12.40

For overprints see Nos. J47-J51, NJ1-NJ2, NJ3a, NJ5, NJ6a.

> **Catalogue values for unused stamps in this section, from this point to the end of the section, are for Never Hinged items.**

Nos. J39-J43, J35 Srchd. "FILS" & its Arabic Equivalent in Black, Green or Carmine

1952   Wmk. 4   Perf. 12

J47	D1	1f on 1m org brn (Bk)	2.25	.25
J48	D1	2f on 2m yel org (G)	2.25	.25
J49	D1	4f on 4m yel grn	2.25	.25
J50	D1	10f on 10m rose car (Bk)	2.75	1.75
J51	D1	20f on 20m ol grn	5.00	2.50

Perf. 14

J52	D1	50f on 50m blue	5.50	3.25
		Nos. J47-J52 (6)	20.00	8.25

This overprint exists on Nos. J34, J36-J38. Exists inverted, double and in wrong color.

D3

Inscribed: "The Hashemite Kingdom of the Jordan"

1952   Engr.   Perf. 11½

J53	D3	1f orange brown	.65	.45
J54	D3	2f yel orange	.65	.45
J55	D3	4f yel green	.65	.45
J56	D3	10f rose carmine	1.25	.80
J57	D3	20f yel brown	1.25	.95
J58	D3	50f blue	3.00	2.25
		Nos. J53-J58 (6)	7.45	5.35

Type of 1952 Redrawn

Inscribed: "The Hashemite Kingdom of Jordan"

1957   Wmk. 305   Perf. 11½

J59	D3	1f orange brown	1.00	.40
J60	D3	2f yel orange	1.00	.40
J61	D3	4f yel green	1.00	.60
J62	D3	10f rose carmine	1.25	.55
J63	D3	20f yel brown	1.75	1.25
		Nos. J59-J63 (5)	6.00	3.20

OFFICIAL STAMP

Saudi Arabia No. L34 Overprinted

1924, Jan.   Typo.   Perf. 11½

O1	A7	½pi red	100.00	—

Overprint reads: "(Government) the Arabian East 1342."

POSTAL TAX STAMPS

> **Catalogue values for unused stamps in this section are for Never Hinged items.**

Mosque at Hebron — PT1

Designs: 10m, 15m, 20m, 50m, Dome of the Rock. 100m, 200m, 500m, £1, Acre.

Perf. 11½x12½

			Unwmk.	Engr.
RA1	PT1	1m ultra	.40	.25
RA2	PT1	2m carmine	.40	.25
RA3	PT1	3m emerald	.55	.25
RA4	PT1	5m plum	.65	.25
RA5	PT1	10m carmine	.80	.30
RA6	PT1	15m gray	1.10	.30
RA7	PT1	20m dk brown	3.75	1.40
RA8	PT1	50m purple	8.50	3.50
RA9	PT1	100m orange red	16.00	8.00
RA10	PT1	200m dp blue	37.50	24.00
RA11	PT1	500m green	57.50	40.00
RA12	PT1	£1 dk brown	100.00	90.00
		Nos. RA1-RA12 (12)	227.15	168.50

Issued to help the Welfare Fund for Arabs in Palestine. Required on foreign-bound letters to the amount of half the regular postage.

For overprints and surcharges see Nos. 286A-286C, 344-346, RA37-RA46, NRA1-NRA12.

Nos. 211, 232 and 234 Overprinted in Black

1950   Wmk. 4   Perf. 12

RA23	A3	5m orange	13.50	
RA24	A3	10m violet	22.50	
RA25	A3	15m dull olive grn	25.00	
		Nos. RA23-RA25 (3)	61.00	

Arch and
Colonnade,
Palmyra,
Syria — PT2

Two types of 5m:
Type I — "A" with serifs. Arabic ovpt. 8mm
wide.
Type II — "A" without serifs. Arabic ovpt.
5mm wide.

Black or Carmine Overprint

1950-51		Engr.		Perf. 13½x13
RA26	PT2	5m orange (I)		22.50
a.		Type II ('51)		27.50
RA27	PT2	10m violet (C)		22.50

The overprint on No. RA27 is similar to that
on RA23-RA25 but slightly bolder.

Type of 1947

Designs: 5f, Hebron Mosque. 10f, 15f, 20f,
Dome of the Rock. 100f, Acre.

1951		Wmk. 4	Perf. 11½x12½	
RA28	PT1	5f plum	.30	.30
RA29	PT1	10f carmine	.30	.30
RA30	PT1	15f gray	.30	.30
RA31	PT1	20f dk brown	.95	.95
RA33	PT1	100f orange	6.00	6.00
		Nos. RA28-RA33 (5)	7.85	7.85

The tax on Nos. RA1-RA33 was for Arab aid
in Palestine.
For overprints see Nos. 287-290, 347.

Postal Tax Stamps of
1947 Srchd. "FILS" or
"J.D." & Their Arabic
Equivalents & Bars in
Carmine or Black

1952			Unwmk.	
RA37	PT1	1f on 1m ultra	.80	.25
RA38	PT1	3f on 3m emer	.80	.25
RA39	PT1	10f on 10m car	1.30	.75
RA40	PT1	15f on 15m gray	1.75	1.25
RA41	PT1	20f on 20m dk brown	2.50	1.60
RA42	PT1	50f on 50m pur	6.00	3.75
RA43	PT1	100f on 100m org red	16.00	9.50
RA44	PT1	200f on 200m dp blue	42.50	12.00
RA45	PT1	500f on 500m grn	70.00	24.00
RA46	PT1	1d on £1 dk brn	105.00	60.00
		Nos. RA37-RA46 (10)	246.65	113.35

"J.D." stands for Jordanian Dinar.

OCCUPATION STAMPS

Catalogue values for unused
stamps in this section are for
Never Hinged items.

For Use in Palestine

Stamps of Jordan
Overprinted in Red,
Black, Dark Green,
Green or Orange Red

On No. 200

1948		Unwmk.	Perf. 13x13½	
N1	A14	2m dull green (R)	2.50	2.00

On #207-209, 211, 230-235, 215-220

1948	Wmk. 4	Perf. 12, 13½x13, 14		
N2	A3	1m red brown	.75	.60
N3	A3	2m Prus grn (R)	.75	.60
a.		2m Prussian blue, perf. 13½x13 (R) (#170a)	1.00	1.25
N4	A3	3m blue grn (R)	.90	.75
N5	A3	3m rose carmine	.50	.35
N6	A3	4m dp yel grn (R)	.50	.35
N7	A3	5m orange (R)	.50	.35
N8	A3	10m violet (OR)	1.25	1.00
N9	A3	12m deep rose	1.25	.80
N10	A3	15m dl ol grn (R)	1.75	1.00
N11	A3	20m dp blue (R)	2.25	1.40
N12	A3	50m red lil (Dk G)	2.75	1.75

N13	A3	90m ocher (Dk G)	10.75	4.75
N14	A3	100m dp blue (R)	12.50	5.50
N15	A3	200m dk vio (R)	8.00	7.00
a.		200m vio, perf. 14 (R) (#182)	35.00	25.00
N16	A3	500m dk brn (R)	45.00	14.00
N17	A3	£1 black (R)	80.00	42.50
		Nos. N2-N17 (16)	169.40	82.70

The first overprinting of these stamps
include Nos. N1-N6, N9-N17. The second
overprinting includes Nos. N1, N3, N5-N17, in
inks differing in shade from the originals.
Many values exist with inverted or double
overprint.

Jordan Nos. 245-249 Overprinted in Black or Red

1949, Aug.		Wmk. 4	Perf. 13	
N18	A17	1m brown (Bk)	1.25	1.25
N19	A17	4m green	1.25	1.25
a.		"PLAESTINE"	25.00	
N20	A17	10m red	1.60	1.60
N21	A17	20m ultra	1.60	1.60
N22	A18	50m dull green	3.00	3.00
a.		"PLAESTINE"	25.00	
		Nos. N18-N22 (5)	8.70	8.70

The overprint is in one line on No. N22.
UPU, 75th anniversary.

OCCUPATION POSTAGE DUE STAMPS

Catalogue values for unused
stamps in this section are for
Never Hinged items.

Jordan Nos. J39, J30a, J40, J32, J41-J43, J34 and J35 Overprinted in Black, Red or Carmine

1948-49	Wmk. 4	Perf. 12, 14		
NJ1	D1	1m org brn, perf. 12	1.50	1.25
a.		Perf. 13½x13 (#J30a)	50.00	45.00
NJ2	D1	2m yel orange	1.50	1.25
NJ3	D1	4m grn (R) (#J32)	2.75	2.50
a.		4m yel grn (C) (#J41) ('49)	5.00	
NJ5	D1	10m rose car (#J42) ('49)	4.50	3.75
a.		Perf. 14 (#J33)	80.00	
NJ6	D1	20m ol grn (R), perf. 14	2.75	2.50
a.		Perf. 12 (R) (#J43)	62.50	
NJ7	D1	50m blue (R)	4.25	2.50
		Nos. NJ1-NJ3,NJ5-NJ7 (6)	17.25	13.75

The second overprinting of these stamps
includes Nos. NJ1-NJ3, NJ3a and NJ5-NJ7, in
inks differing in shade from the originals.
Double and inverted overprints exist.

Same Overprint in Black on Jordan Nos. J36-J38

1948-49		Unwmk.	Perf. 13x13½	
NJ8	D2	1m dl red brn	115.00	115.00
NJ9	D2	2m dl org yel ('49)	12.00	11.00
NJ10	D2	10m dark car	10.00	9.00

OCCUPATION POSTAL TAX STAMPS

Catalogue values for unused
stamps in this section are for
Never Hinged items.

Postal Tax Stamps of
1947 Overprinted in
Red or Black

1950				
NRA1	PT1	1m ultra (R)	.40	.35
NRA2	PT1	2m carmine	.45	.35
NRA3	PT1	3m emer (R)	.60	.35
NRA4	PT1	5m plum	1.00	.35
NRA5	PT1	10m carmine	1.75	.50
NRA6	PT1	15m gray (R)	2.75	.90
NRA7	PT1	20m dk brn (R)	4.00	1.10
NRA8	PT1	50m purple (R)	4.75	1.75
NRA9	PT1	100m org red	7.00	2.40
NRA10	PT1	200m dp blue (R)	19.00	6.00
NRA11	PT1	500m green (R)	50.00	18.00
NRA12	PT1	£1 dk brn (R)	105.00	35.00
		Nos. NRA1-NRA12 (12)	196.70	67.05

For overprints see Nos. 286D-286G.

KARELIA

kə-'rē-lə-ə

LOCATION — In northwestern Soviet
Russia
GOVT. — An autonomous republic of
the Soviet Union
AREA — 55,198 sq. mi. (approx.)
ПОР. — 270,000 (approx.)
CAPITAL — Petrozavodsk (Kalininsk)

In 1921 the Karelians rebelled and for
a short period a form of sovereignty
independent of Russia was maintained.

100 Pennia = 1 Markka

Bear — A1

1922	Unwmk.	Litho.	Perf. 11½, 12	
1	A1	5p dark gray	15.00	50.00
2	A1	10p light blue	15.00	50.00
3	A1	20p rose red	15.00	50.00
4	A1	25p yellow brown	16.00	50.00
5	A1	40p magenta	16.00	50.00
6	A1	50p gray green	16.00	50.00
7	A1	75p orange yellow	25.00	50.00
8	A1	1m pink & gray	25.00	50.00
9	A1	2m yel grn & gray	27.50	110.00
10	A1	3m lt blue & gray	27.50	140.00
11	A1	5m red lil & gray	27.50	175.00
12	A1	10m lt brn & gray	30.00	275.00
13	A1	15m green & car	30.00	275.00
14	A1	20m rose & green	30.00	275.00
15	A1	25m yellow & blue	40.00	275.00
		Nos. 1-15 (15)	355.50	1,925.
		Set, never hinged	475.00	

Nos. 1-15 were valid Jan. 31-Feb. 16, 1922.
Use probably ended Feb. 3, although cancel-
lations of the 4th and 5th exist.
Counterfeits abound.

OCCUPATION STAMPS

Issued under Finnish Occupation

Issued in the Russian territory of
Eastern Karelia under Finnish military
administration.

Types of Finland Stamps, 1930 Overprinted in Black

On A26   On A27-A28

1941		Unwmk.	Perf. 14	
N1	A26	50p brt yel grn	.45	1.00
N2	A26	1.75m dk gray	1.25	1.75
N3	A26	2m dp org	1.75	4.50
N4	A26	2.75m yel org	.75	1.25
N5	A26	3½m lt ultra	2.50	4.50
N6	A27	5m rose vio	6.00	10.00
N7	A28	10m pale brn	6.75	12.00
		Nos. N1-N7 (7)	19.45	35.00
		Set, never hinged	32.00	

Types of Finland Stamps, 1930 Overprinted in Green

On A26   On A27-A29

N8	A26	50p brt yel grn	.45	.70
N9	A26	1.75m dk gray	.60	1.00
N10	A26	2m dp org	1.00	2.00
N11	A26	2.75m yel org	.55	1.25
N12	A26	3½m lt ultra	1.25	1.25
N13	A27	5m rose vio	1.75	5.00
N14	A29	10m pale brown	4.25	8.50
N15	A29	25m green	4.50	9.00
		Nos. N8-N15 (8)	14.35	28.70
		Set, never hinged	32.50	

Mannerheim Type of
Finland Overprinted

1942				
N16	A48	50p dk yel grn	.95	2.25
N17	A48	1.75m slate bl	.95	2.25
N18	A48	2m red org	.95	2.25
N19	A48	2.75m brn org	.80	2.25
N20	A48	3.50m brt ultra	.80	2.25
N21	A48	5m brn vio	.80	2.25
		Nos. N16-N21 (6)	5.25	13.50
		Set, never hinged	9.50	

Same Overprint on Ryti Type of Finland

N22	A49	50p dk yel grn	.80	2.25
N23	A49	1.75m slate bl	.80	2.25
N24	A49	2m red org	.80	2.25
N25	A49	2.75m brn org	.95	2.25
N26	A49	3.50m brt ultra	.95	2.25
N27	A49	5m brn vio	.95	2.25
		Nos. N22-N27 (6)	5.25	13.50
		Set, never hinged	9.50	

The overprint translates, "East Karelia Military Administration."

OCCUPATION SEMI-POSTAL STAMP

Arms of East
Karelia — SP1

1943	Unwmk.	Engr.	Perf. 14	
NB1	SP1	3.50m + 1.50m dk ol	.75	2.50
		Never hinged	2.00	

This surtax aided war victims in East Karelia.

KATANGA

kə-'täŋ-gə

LOCATION — Central Africa
GOVT. — Republic
CAPITAL — Elisabethville

Katanga province seceded from the Congo (ex-Belgian) Republic in July, 1960, but established nations did not recognize it as an independent state. The UN declared the secession ended in Sept, 1961. The last troops surrendered Sept. 1963.

During the secession Katanga stamps were tolerated in the international mails, but the government authorizing them was not recognized.

100 Centimes = 1 Franc

Catalogue values for all unused stamps in this country are for Never Hinged items.

Belgian Congo Nos. 318-322 Overprinted "KATANGA"
Perf. 11½

		1960, Sept. 12	Photo.	Unwmk.
1	A94	50c golden brn, ocher & red brn		
2	A94	1fr dk bl, pur & red brn		
3	A94	2fr gray, brt bl & red brn		
		Nos. 1-3 (3)	1.00	1.00

Inscription in French

| 4 | A95 | 3fr gray & red | 8.00 | 8.00 |

Inscription in Flemish

| 5 | A95 | 3fr gray & red | 8.00 | 8.00 |

Inverted overprints exist on No. 1-5. Values: 1-3 $4 each; 4-5 $10 each.
For surcharges see Nos. 50-51.

Animal Type of Belgian Congo, Nos. 306-317, Overprinted "KATANGA"

		1960, Sept. 19	Granite Paper	
6	A92	10c bl & brn		
7	A93	20c red org & slate		
8	A92	40c brn & bl		
9	A93	50c brt ultra, red & sep		
10	A92	1fr brn, grn & blk		
11	A93	1.50fr blk & org yel		
12	A92	2fr crim, blk & brn		
13	A93	3fr blk, gray & lil rose		
14	A92	5fr brn, dk brn & brt grn		
15	A93	6.50fr bl, brn & org yel		
16	A92	8fr org brn, ol bis & lil		
17	A93	10fr multi		
		Nos. 6-17 (12)	65.00	27.50

Inverted overprints exist. Value $10 each.

Flower Type of Belgian Congo, Nos. 263-271, 274-281, Overprinted "KATANGA"
Flowers in Natural Colors

		1960, Sept. 22	Granite Paper	
18	A86	10c dp plum & ocher		
19	A86	15c red & yel grn		
20	A86	20c grn & gray		
21	A86	25c dk grn & dl org		
22	A86	40c grn & sal		
23	A86	50c dk car & aqua		
24	A86	60c bl grn & pink		
25	A86	75c dp plum & gray		
26	A86	1fr car & yel		
27	A86	2fr ol grn & buff		
28	A86	3fr ol grn & pink		
29	A86	4fr choc & lil		
30	A86	5fr dp plum & lt bl grn		
31	A86	6.50fr dk car & lil		
32	A86	7fr dk grn & fawn		
33	A86	8fr grn & lt yel		
34	A86	10fr dp plum & pale ol		
		Nos. 18-34 (17)	85.00	27.50

Inverted overprints exist. Value $12 each.

Carving and Mask Type of Belgian Congo, Nos. 241, 246, 254-256, Surcharged or Overprinted

		1960, Sept. 22	Perf. 12½	
35	A82	1.50fr on 1.25fr	2.00	.60
36	A82	3.50fr on 2.50fr	2.50	.75
37	A82	20fr red org & vio brn	8.00	4.00
38	A82	50fr dp org & blk	19.00	10.00
39	A82	100fr crim & blk brn	90.00	30.00
		Nos. 35-39 (5)	121.50	45.35

Inverted surcharges and overprints exist. Values, No. 37 $42.50, No. 38 $50, No. 39 $80.

Map Type of Congo Democratic Republic, Nos. 356-365, Overprinted "11 / JUILLET / DE / L'ETAT DU KATANGA"

		1960, Oct. 26	Perf. 11½	
		Granite Paper		
40	A93a	20c brown	.25	.25
41	A93a	50c rose red	.25	.25
42	A93a	1fr green	.25	.25
43	A93a	1.50fr red brn	.25	.25
44	A93a	2fr rose car	.25	.25
45	A93a	3.50fr lilac	.25	.25
46	A93a	5fr brt bl	.25	.25
47	A93a	6.50fr gray	.25	.25
48	A93a	10fr orange	.30	.25
49	A93a	20fr ultra	.40	.25
		Nos. 40-49 (10)	2.70	2.50

Inverted and double surcharges exist.

Belgian Congo Nos. 321-322 Surcharged

		1961, Jan. 16		
50	A95	3.50fr on 3fr #321	4.50	4.50
51	A95	3.50fr on 3fr #322	4.50	4.50

Inverted surcharges exist. Value $5.50 each.

A1

Katangan Wood Carvings: 3.50fr-8fr, Preparing meal. 10fr-100fr, Family group.

		1961, Mar. 1	Perf. 11½	
		Granite Paper		
52	A1	10c grn & lt grn	.25	.25
53	A1	20c purple & lil	.25	.25
54	A1	50c blue & lt bl	.25	.25
55	A1	1.50fr ol grn & lt ol grn	.25	.25
56	A1	2fr red brn & lt brn	.25	.25
57	A1	3.50fr dk blue & lt bl	.25	.25
58	A1	5fr bl grn & lt bl grn	.25	.25
59	A1	6fr org brn & tan	.25	.25
60	A1	6.50fr bl vio & gray vio	.25	.25
61	A1	8fr claret & pink	.25	.25
62	A1	10fr dk brn & lt brn	.25	.25
63	A1	20fr dk ol & lt grn	.35	.25
64	A1	50fr brn & lt brn	.65	.45
65	A1	100fr Prus bl & lt bl	1.10	.75
		Nos. 52-65 (14)	4.85	4.20

A2

1fr, 5fr, Abstract vehicle. 2.50fr, 6.50fr, Gear.

Granite Paper

		1961, July 8	Perf. 11½	
66	A2	50c blk, grn & red	.25	.25
67	A2	1fr blk & blue	.25	.25
68	A2	2.50fr blk & yellow	.25	.25
69	A2	3.50fr blk, brn & scar	.25	.25
70	A2	5fr blk & purple	.40	.40
71	A2	6.50fr blk & orange	.75	.65
		Nos. 66-71 (6)	2.15	2.05

Katanga International Fair.
Imperfs exist. Value, set $45.

Air Katanga
A3

Design: 6.50fr, 10fr, Plane on ground.

		1961, Aug. 1	Perf. 11½	
		Granite Paper		
72	A3	3.50fr multicolored		
73	A3	6.50fr multicolored		
74	A3	8fr multicolored		
75	A3	10fr multicolored		
		Nos. 72-75 (4)	9.50	8.50

Imperfs exist. Value, set $60.

Katanga Gendarmerie — A4

		1962, Oct. 1	Perf. 11½	
		Granite Paper		
76	A4	6fr multicolored		
77	A4	8fr multicolored		
78	A4	10fr multicolored		
		Nos. 76-78 (3)	7.00	6.00

Imperfs exist. Value, set $40.

SEMI-POSTAL STAMPS

Pres. Moise Tshombe — SP1

		1961, July 11	Perf. 11½	
		Granite Paper		
B1	SP1	6.50fr + 5fr multi		
B2	SP1	8fr + 5fr multi		
B3	SP1	10fr + 5fr multi		
		Nos. B1-B3 (3)	10.00	6.50

Imperf exist. Value, set $65.

POSTAGE DUE STAMPS

Belgian Congo Nos. J8a-J10a, J16-J19 Handstamped "KATANGA" in Blue

		1960, Dec. 30	Unwmk.	Perf. 12½
J1	D2	10c olive green		
J2	D2	20c dark ultra		
J3	D2	50c green		

			Perf. 11½	
J4	D3	1fr light blue		
J5	D3	2fr vermilion		
J6	D3	4fr purple		
J7	D3	6fr violet blue		
		Nos. J1-J7 (7)	45.00	45.00

This overprint also exists on Belgian Congo Nos. J11a-J12a, J13-J15. Value, set $180.

KAZAKHSTAN

ˌka-ˌzak-'stan

(Kazakstan)

LOCATION — Bounded by southern Russia, Uzbekistan, Kyrgyzstan, and China.
GOVT. — Independent republic, member of the Commonwealth of Independent States.
AREA — 1,049,155 sq. mi.
POP. — 16,824,825 (1999 est.)
CAPITAL — Astana

With the breakup of the Soviet Union on Dec. 26, 1991, Kazakhstan and ten former Soviet republics established the Commonwealth of Independent States.

100 Kopecks = 1 Ruble
100 Tijn = 1 Tenge (1993)

Catalogue values for all unused stamps in this country are for Never Hinged items.

Overprinted Stamps
The Philatelic Club of Alma Ata, Kazakhstan, has announced that various overprinted stamps of the USSR were not generally available nor were they in values reflecting actual postal rates.

A1

Perf. 12x12½

		1992, Mar. 23	Litho.	Unwmk.
1	A1	50k multicolored	.30	.25

For surcharge, see No. 667.

Saiga Tatarica
A2

		1992, Sept. 11	Litho.	Perf. 12
2	A2	75k multicolored	.30	.25

Camels and Train, by K. Kasteev — A3

		1992, Sept. 11	Litho.	Perf. 12½x12
3	A3	1r multicolored	.30	.30

Day of the Republic
A3a

		1992, Dec. 16	Litho.	Perf. 12
4	A3a	5r multicolored	.40	.40

Space Ship
and Yurt — A4

Natl. Flag — A5

1993, Jan. 24   Litho.   Perf. 13x12½

22	A4	1r green	.25	.25
23	A4	3r red	.25	.25
24	A4	10r golden brown	.25	.25
25	A4	25r purple	.75	.75

Perf. 14

| 26 | A5 | 50r multicolored | 1.40 | 1.40 |
| | | Nos. 22-26 (5) | 2.90 | 2.90 |

See Nos. 64, 69, 108-115.

Space
Mail
A6

1993, Mar. 5   Litho.   Perf. 13½

| 35 | A6 | 100r multicolored | 1.50 | 1.25 |

New Year 1993
(Year of the
Rooster) — A7

1993, Mar. 22   Litho.   Perf. 13x13½

| 36 | A7 | 60r yellow, black & red | 1.25 | 1.25 |

See Nos. 54, 98, 141, 187A, 220, 268.

Cosmonauts' Day — A8

1993, Apr. 12   Perf. 13½x13

| 37 | A8 | 90r multicolored | 1.75 | 1.25 |

Pres. Nursultan Nazarbayev — A9

1993, Aug. 2   Litho.   Perf. 14

| 38 | A9 | 50r multicolored | .90 | .70 |

Bukar Zhirav Kalkaman (1668-1781),
Poet — A10

1993, Aug. 18   Perf. 13½x13

| 39 | A10 | 15r multicolored | .40 | .25 |

Map, Pres. Nursultan
Nazarbayev — A11

1993, Sept. 24   Litho.   Perf. 13

| 40 | A11 | 100r multicolored | 1.50 | 1.10 |

Wildlife
A12

Designs: 5r, Selevinia betpakdalensis. 10r,
Hystrix leucura. 15r, Vormela peregusna. 20r,
Equis hemionus onager. 25r, Ovis orientalis.
30r, Acinonyx jubatus venaticus.

1993, Nov. 11   Perf. 12x12½

41	A12	5r multicolored	.30	.25
42	A12	10r multicolored	.40	.30
43	A12	15r multicolored	.45	.35
44	A12	20r multicolored	.50	.40
45	A12	25r multicolored	.55	.45
46	A12	30r multicolored	.60	.50
		Nos. 41-46 (6)	2.80	2.25

Nos. 1-46 were sold after the currency changeover as stamps denominated in one or both of the new currency units. Nos. 47-50, 54, 64 and 69
were sold as stamps denominated in
tijn, and later as tenge.

1994 Winter
Olympics,
Lillehammer
A13

1994, Jan. 24   Litho.   Perf. 13½x13

47	A13	15te Ice hockey	.30	.30
48	A13	25te Slalom skiing	.45	.45
49	A13	90te Ski jumping	1.50	1.50
50	A13	150te Speed skating	2.25	2.25
		Nos. 47-50 (4)	4.50	4.50

1994 Winter Olympics,
Lillehammer — A14

No. 53 With 2 Line Cyrillic Inscription

Designs: 2te, Skiers Vladimir Smirnov,
Kazakhstan; Bjorn Daehlie, Norway. 6.80te,
12te, Smirnov.

1994, Feb. 19   Litho.   Perf. 13x13½

51		2te multicolored	.35	.25
52		6.80te multicolored	.80	.80
a.		A14 Pair, #51-52	1.60	1.60
53	A14	12te like No. 52	1.10	1.10
		Nos. 51-53 (3)	2.25	2.15

No. 53 has an additional two line Cyrillic
inscription.

New Year Type of 1993
Size: 26x38mm

1994, Mar. 22   Perf. 12

| 54 | A7 | 30te green, black & blue | .65 | .25 |

New Year 1994 (Year of the Dog).

Space
Program
A15

1994, Apr. 12   Perf. 13½x13

| 55 | A15 | 2te multicolored | .50 | .50 |

Souvenir Sheet

Russian Space Shuttle,
Cosmonaut — A16,

1994, July 12   Perf. 13

| 56 | A16 | 6.80te Sheet of 4 | 3.25 | 3.25 |

Space Ship and Yurt Type of 1993

1994, July 12   Litho.   Perf. 11½

| 64 | A4 | 15ti blue | .95 | .80 |
| 69 | A4 | 80ti lake | 2.10 | 1.60 |

For surcharges see Nos. 70-76, 122.

Nos. 64, 69
Surcharged in Lake or
Purple

1995-2004   Litho.   Perf. 11½

70	A4	1te on 15ti #64	.30	.30
71	A4	2te on 15ti #64	.30	.30
72	A4	3te on 80ti #69 (P)	.35	.35
73	A4	4te on 80ti #69 (P)	.45	.45
74	A4	6te on 80ti #69 (P)	.50	.50
75	A4	8te on 80ti #69 (P)	.75	.75
76	A4	12te on 80ti #69 (P)	.75	.75
77	A4	20te on 80ti #69 (P)	.95	.95
78	A4	200te on 80ti #69 (P)	4.50	4.50
		Nos. 70-78 (9)	8.85	8.85

Issued: 1te, 2te, 12te, 2/2/95. 3te, 4te, 6te,
20te, 2/10/95. 8te, 9/25/95. 200te, 1/29/04.
Inverted surcharges exist.

Music
Competition
Festival
A18

Designs: 10te, Snow-covered mountain top.
15te, Aerial view of stadium at night.

1994, Aug. 1   Perf. 13½

| 81 | A18 | 10te multicolored | .50 | .50 |
| 82 | A18 | 15te multicolored | .70 | .70 |

For surcharges see Nos. 119A-119B.

Reptiles
A19

Designs: 1te, Agrionemys horsfieldi. 1.20te,
Phrynocephalus mystaceus. 2te, Agkistrodon

halys. 3te, Teratoscincus scincus. 5te, Trape-
lus sanguinolenta. 7te, Ophisaurus apodus.
10te, Varanus griseus.

1994, Oct. 10   Perf. 12½x12

83	A19	1te multicolored	.25	.25
84	A19	1.20te multicolored	.25	.25
85	A19	2te multicolored	.25	.25
86	A19	3te multicolored	.25	.25
87	A19	5te multicolored	.35	.35
88	A19	7te multicolored	.40	.40
		Nos. 83-88 (6)	1.75	1.75

Souvenir Sheet

| 89 | A19 | 10te multicolored | 1.10 | 1.10 |

Prehistoric
Animals
A20

1994, Nov. 24   Litho.   Perf. 12½x12

90	A20	1te Entelodon	.25	.25
91	A20	1.20te Saurolophus	.25	.25
92	A20	2te Plesiosaurus	.25	.25
93	A20	3te Sordes pilosus	.30	.30
94	A20	5te Mosasaurus	.35	.35
95	A20	7te Megaloceros gi-
ganteum	.40	.40
		Nos. 90-95 (6)	1.80	1.80

Souvenir Sheet

| 96 | A20 | 10te Koelodonta anti-
quitatis | 1.25 | 1.25 |

Day of the
Republic
A21

1994, Oct. 25   Perf. 11½

| 97 | A21 | 2te multicolored | .50 | .50 |

For surcharge see No. 160B.

New Year Type of 1993

1995, Mar. 22   Litho.   Perf. 14
Size: 27x32mm

| 98 | A7 | 10te blue, black & ultra | .85 | .85 |

New Year 1995 (Year of the Boar).

Abai (Ibraghim)
Kynanbaev (1845-
1904), Poet — A22

1995, Mar. 31

| 99 | A22 | 4te Portrait | .30 | .30 |
| 100 | A22 | 9te Portrait, diff. | .60 | .60 |

Nos. 99-100 exist with "Kazakstan" spelled
"Kazakstah." Value, set $9.

Space Day — A23

Designs: 10te, Cosmonauts Malenchenko,
Musabaev and Merbold.

1995, Apr. 12   Litho.   Perf. 14

| 101 | A23 | 2te multicolored | 2.50 | 2.50 |
| 102 | A23 | 10te multicolored | 11.00 | 11.00 |

Mahatma Gandhi (1869-1948) — A24

1995, Oct. 2
103	A24	9te multicolored	2.00	2.00
104	A24	22te multicolored	5.00	5.00

End of World War II, 50th Anniv. A25

Designs: 1te, Hero, battle scene. 3te, Heroine, tank. 5te, Dove, monument.

1995, May 9   Litho.   Perf. 14
105	A25	1te multicolored	.85	.85
106	A25	3te multicolored	2.50	2.50
107	A25	5te multicolored	4.25	4.25
		Nos. 105-107 (3)	7.60	7.60

Spaceship and Yurt Type of 1993

1995, Mar. 24   Litho.   Perf. 14x14½
108	A4	20ti orange	.25	.25
109	A4	25ti yellow brown	.30	.25
110	A4	50ti gray	.35	.25
111	A4	1te green	.45	.25
112	A4	2te blue	.60	.25
113	A4	4te bright pink	.75	.50
114	A4	6te gray green	.90	.75
115	A4	12te lilac	1.90	1.50
		Nos. 108-115 (8)	5.50	4.00

Nos. 108-115 are inscribed "1995."

Paintings — A26

Designs: 4te, "Springtime," by S. Mambeev. 9te, "Mountains," by Z. Shchardenov. 15te, "Kulash Baiseitova in role of Kyz Zhibek," by G. Ismailova, vert. 28te, "Kokpar," by K. Telzhanov.

1995, June 23   Litho.   Perf. 14
116	A26	4te multicolored	.75	.75
117	A26	9te multicolored	1.25	1.25
118	A26	15te multicolored	2.50	2.50
119	A26	28te multicolored	4.50	4.50
		Nos. 116-119 (4)	9.00	9.00

Nos. 81-82 Ovptd.

1995, July 25   Litho.   Perf. 13½
119A	A18	10te multicolored	1.10	1.10
119B	A18	15te multicolored	1.50	1.50

Dauletkerey (1820-87), Composer — A27

1995, Sept. 1   Litho.   Perf. 14
120	A27	2te yellow & multi	.75	.75
121	A27	28te lake & multi	6.50	6.50

UN, 50th Anniv. — A28

1995, Nov. 24   Litho.   Perf. 14
123	A28	10te multicolored	1.50	1.50
124	A28	36te gold & lt blue	5.00	5.00

Resurrection Cathedral A29

Circus A29a

Buildings in Alma-Ata: 2te, Culture Palace. 3te, Opera and Ballet House. 6te, Kazakh Science Academy. 48te, Dramatics Theatre.

Perf. 14, 13x12 (#126, 129)

1995-96   Litho.
125	A29	1te green	.25	.25
126	A29a	1te green	.25	.25
127	A29	2te blue	.55	.50
128	A29	3te red	.75	.65
129	A29a	6te olive	.60	.60
130	A29	48te brown	7.50	7.00
		Nos. 125-130 (6)	9.90	9.25

Issued: Nos. 125, 127-128, 130, 10/25/95; Nos. 126, 129, 7/5/96.

Raptors A30

1te, Haliaeetus albicilla. 3te, Pandion haliaetus. 5te, Gypaetus barbatus. 6te, Gyps himalayensis. 30te, Falco cherrug. 50te, Aquila chrysaetus.

1995, Dec. 20   Litho.   Perf. 14
131	A30	1te multicolored	.25	.25
132	A30	3te multicolored	.25	.25
133	A30	5te multicolored	.45	.45
134	A30	6te multicolored	.55	.55
135	A30	30te multicolored	1.75	1.75
136	A30	50te multicolored	3.25	3.25
		Nos. 131-136 (6)	6.50	6.50

New Year Type of 1993
Size: 27x32mm

1996, Mar. 21   Litho.   Perf. 14
141	A7	25te lil, blk & red	1.50	1.50

New Year 1996 (Year of the Rat).

Space Day — A32

1996, Apr. 12
142	A32	6te Earth	1.75	1.75
143	A32	15te Cosmonaut	2.75	2.75
144	A32	20te Space station Mir	4.50	4.50
		Nos. 142-144 (3)	9.00	9.00

Souvenir Sheet

Save the Aral Sea — A33

Designs: a, Felis caracal. b, Salmo trutta aralensis. c, Hyaena hyaena. d, Pseudoscaphirhynchus kaufmanni. e, Aspiolucius esocinus.

1996, Apr. 20   Litho.   Perf. 14
145	A33	20te Sheet of 5, #a.-e.	4.00	4.00

See Kyrgyzstan No. 107, Tadjikistan No. 91, Turkmenistan No. 52, Uzbekistan No. 113.

1996 Summer Olympic Games, Atlanta — A34

1996, June 19   Litho.   Perf. 14
146	A34	4te Cycling	.50	.50
147	A34	6te Wrestling	1.25	1.25
148	A34	30te Boxing	4.75	4.75
		Nos. 146-148 (3)	6.50	6.50

Souvenir Sheet
149	A34	50te Hurdles	3.50	3.50

Issued: Nos. 146-148, 6/19/96; No. 149, 7/19/96.

Architectural Sites — A35

1te, Tomb, 8-9th cent. 3te, Mausoleum, 11-12th cent. 6te, Mausoleum, 13th cent. 30te, Hadji Ahmet Yassauy's Mausoleum, 14th cent.

1996, Sept. 27   Litho.   Perf. 14
150	A35	1te multicolored	.40	.40
151	A35	3te multicolored	1.25	1.25
152	A35	6te multicolored	2.50	2.50
		Nos. 150-152 (3)	4.15	4.15

Souvenir Sheet
153	A35	30te multicolored	2.50	2.50

World Post Day — A37

1996, Oct. 9   Litho.   Perf. 14
156	A37	9te shown	.90	.90
157	A37	40te UPU emblem	3.00	3.00

A38

1996, Aug. 21
158	A38	12te multicolored	1.00	1.00

Schambyl Schabaev (1846-1945).

Space Station Mir — A39

1996, Oct. 2
159	A39	46te multicolored	2.25	2.00
160	A39	46te T. Aubakirov	2.25	2.00
a.		Pair, #159-160	5.00	5.00

T. Aubakirov, 1st Kazak cosmonaut.

No. 97 Surcharged

1997, Oct. 25   Litho.   Perf. 11½
160B	A21	21te on 2te multi	1.00	1.00

Surcharge adds numeral 1 to existing value to appear as 21, obliterates original date and adds new date.

Butterflies A40

4te, Saturnia schenki. 6te, Parnassius patricius. 12te, Parnassius ariadne. 46te, Colias draconis.

1996, Nov. 21   Litho.   Perf. 14
161	A40	4te multicolored	.30	.25
162	A40	6te multicolored	.40	.30
163	A40	12te multicolored	.60	.50
164	A40	46te multicolored	2.00	1.75
a.		Sheet of 10, 2 ea. #161-162, 3 ea. #163-164	12.00	12.00
		Nos. 161-164 (4)	3.30	2.80

Hunting Dogs A41

1996, Nov. 29
165	A41	5te multicolored	.55	.55

Souvenir Sheet
166	A41	100te like #165	4.50	4.50

No. 166 is a continuous design.

A42

Traditional Costumes, Furnishings: a, 10te, Woman outside tent. b, 16te, Man outside tent. c, 45te, Interior view of furnishings.

1996, Dec. 5
167	A42	Strip of 3, #a.-c.	6.00	6.00

Nos. 167a-167b have continuous design.

A43

Archives, Bicent.: 4te, Quill pen, candle, documents. 68te, Scroll, papers, book.

1996, Dec. 24
168	A43	4te brown	.30	.30
169	A43	68te purple	2.25	2.25

Motion Pictures, Cent. — A44

Film scenes: a, Man in hat holding up fingers. b, Horse, woman, man. c, Two men, from "His Time Arrives." d, Woman holding paper, boy holding hat.

1996, Dec. 25   Litho.   Perf. 14
170	A44	24te Sheet of 4, #a.- d.	9.00	9.00

Vormela Peregusna — A45

1997, Feb. 12   Litho.   Perf. 14
171	A45	6te shown	.60	.60
172	A45	10te Adult	.70	.70
173	A45	32te Two young	1.75	1.75
174	A45	46te Adult, tail up	2.25	2.25
a.		Vert. strip of 4, #171-174, with horiz. gutters	6.00	6.00
b.		Souv. sheet of 8, 2 ea. #171-174	12.00	12.00
		Nos. 171-174 (4)	5.30	5.30

World Wildlife Fund.
Nos. 171-174 each printed in sheets of 10. No. 174b has no gutters between stamps.

Zodiac Constellations A47

1997, Mar. 26   Litho.   Perf. 14
176	A47	1te Aries	.25	.25
177	A47	2te Taurus	.25	.25
178	A47	3te Gemini	.25	.25
179	A47	4te Cancer	.25	.25
180	A47	5te Leo	.25	.25
181	A47	6te Virgo	.25	.25
182	A47	7te Libra	.25	.25
183	A47	8te Scorpio	.25	.25
184	A47	9te Sagittarius	.30	.30
185	A47	10te Capricorn	.35	.35
186	A47	12te Aquarius	.45	.45
187	A47	20te Pisces	.70	.70
b.		Sheet of 12, #176-187	5.50	5.50

New Year Type of 1993 With Kazakhstan Inscribed in Both Cyrillic & Roman Letters

1997, Mar. 22   Litho.   Perf. 14
187A	A7	40te multicolored	1.50	1.50

New Year 1997 (Year of the Ox).

A48

Cosmonauts' Day: a, Earth, Sputnik. b, Space vehicle, Saturn. c, Space shuttle, space station.

1997, Apr. 12
188	A48	10te Strip of 3, #a.-c.	3.25	3.25

No. 188 has continuous design.

A49

1997, Apr. 23
189	A49	15te org yel & grn	.50	.50
190	A49	60te org yel & grn	2.10	2.10

UNESCO World Book Day.

Mukhtar Auezov (1897-1961), Writer — A50

1997, May
191	A50	25te House	1.00	1.00
192	A50	40te Auezov at his desk	1.60	1.60

Orders and Medals — A51

Various medals.

1997, June 30   Litho.   Perf. 14
193	A51	15te grn & yel ribbon	.50	.50
194	A51	15te grn, red & pink ribbon	.50	.50
195	A51	20te grn bl & multi	.75	.75
196	A51	30te grn yel & multi	1.00	1.00
		Nos. 193-196 (4)	2.75	2.75

Tulips — A52

15te, Tulipa regelii. No. 198, Tulipa greigii. No. 199, Tulipa alberti.

1997, Aug. 7   Litho.   Perf. 13½
197	A52	15te multicolored	.40	.40
198	A52	35te multicolored	1.25	1.25
199	A52	35te multicolored	1.25	1.25
		Nos. 197-199 (3)	2.90	2.90

Paintings — A53

Designs: No. 200, Roping of a Wild Horse, by Moldakhmet S. Kenbaev. No. 201, Shepherd, by Sh. T. Sariev, vert. No. 202, Fantastic Still Life, by Sergei I. Kalmykov, vert.

1997, Sept. 10   Litho.   Perf. 14
200	A53	25te multicolored	1.00	1.00
201	A53	25te multicolored	1.00	1.00
202	A53	25te multicolored	1.00	1.00
		Nos. 200-202 (3)	3.00	3.00

Agate — A54   Azurite — A55

1997, Oct. 15   Litho.   Perf. 14
203	A54	15te shown	.60	.60
204	A54	15te Chalcedony	.60	.60
205	A55	20te shown	.90	.90
206	A55	20te Malachite	.90	.90
a.		Souvenir sheet, #203-206	3.25	3.25
		Nos. 203-206 (4)	3.00	3.00

Desert Fauna — A56

Designs: No. 207, Gylippus rickmersi. No. 208, Anemelobathus rickmersi. No. 209, Latrodectus pallidus. No. 210, Oculicosa supermirabilis.

1997, Nov. 26   Litho.   Perf. 14
207	A56	30te multicolored	1.10	1.10
208	A56	30te multicolored	1.10	1.10
209	A56	30te multicolored	1.10	1.10
210	A56	30te multicolored	1.10	1.10
		Nos. 207-210 (4)	4.40	4.40

Souvenir Sheet

Nature Park — A57

Designs: a, Mountain goat. b, Trees on side of mountain. c, Rock formations, wildflowers.

1997, Dec. 22
211	A57	30te Sheet of 3, #a.-c.	3.00	3.00

See No. 257A.

A58

Sports A59

Designs: No. 212, Woman, man riding horses. No. 213, Wrestling match. No. 214, Group of men on galloping horses.

1997, Dec. 30   Litho.   Perf. 14
212	A58	20te multicolored	1.40	1.40
213	A58	20te multicolored	1.40	1.40
214	A58	20te multicolored	1.40	1.40
215	A59	20te multicolored	1.40	1.40
		Nos. 212-215 (4)	5.60	5.60

1998 Winter Olympic Games, Nagano — A60

1998, Mar. 13   Litho.   Perf. 14
216	A60	15te Figure skating	.70	.50
217	A60	30te Biathlon	1.25	1.00

Children's Paintings — A61

1998, Mar. 20
218	A61	15te shown	.50	.50
219	A61	15te Outdoor scene, horiz.	.50	.50

New Year Type of 1993 with "Kazakhstan" inscribed in both Cyrillic and Roman letters

1998, Mar. 22   Litho.   Perf. 14
220	A7	30te yellow, black & brown	1.75	1.75

New Year 1998 (Year of the Tiger).

Kurmangazy (1823-96), Composer — A62

No. 222, Ahmet Baitursynov (1873-1937), poet.

1998   Litho.   Perf. 14
221	A62	30te multicolored	.75	.75
222	A62	30te multicolored	.75	.75

Issued: No. 221, 4/10/98. No. 222, 4/28/98.

Ancient Gold Folk Art A63

15te, Ram's heads. 30te, Jeweled pendants, vert. 40te, Animal filigree diadem fragment.

1998, Apr. 30
223	A63	15te multicolored	.55	.55
224	A63	30te multicolored	.95	.95
225	A63	40te multicolored	2.00	2.00
		Nos. 223-225 (3)	3.50	3.50

Cosmonaut's Day — A64

No. 226, Apollo 8, moon, sun. No.227, Apollo 8, moon, Earth. 50te, Vostok 6, Earth.

1998, May 4
226	A64	30te multi, vert.	.75	.75
227	A64	30te multi, vert.	.75	.75
a.		Pair, #226-227, with tabs	3.00	3.00
228	A64	50te multi	1.25	1.25
		Nos. 226-228 (3)	2.75	2.75

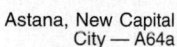

Astana, New Capital City — A64a

A65

Buildings: 10te, Mosque. 15te, Govt., vert. 20te, Parliament, vert. 25te, Office. 100te, Presidential office.

1998   Litho.   Perf. 13½
229	A64a	10te brown	.35	.35
230	A64a	15te dark blue	.55	.55
231	A64a	15te blue	.55	.55
232	A64a	20te green blue	.65	.65
232A	A64a	25te purple	.90	.90
		Nos. 229-232A (5)	3.00	3.00

Souvenir Sheet
233	A65	100te multicolored	3.00	3.00

Issued: Nos. 229-232, 233, 6/10; 25te, 12/98. No. 230 is inscribed "AKMOLA" in Cyrillic. No. 231 is inscribed "ACTANA."

Souvenir Sheet

Climbing Mt. Everest — A67

1998, July 29   Litho.   Perf. 14
239	A67	100te multicolored	3.75	3.75

Fauna — A68

Birds: No. 240, Ciconia nigra. No. 241, Phoenicopterus roseus. No. 242, Grus leucogeranus.

Wild cats: No. 243, Lynx lynx isabellinus. No. 244, Felis margarita. No. 245, Uncia uncia.

1998, July 31
240	A68	15te multicolored	.60	.60
241	A68	30te multicolored	1.00	1.00
242	A68	50te multicolored	1.75	1.75
		Nos. 240-242 (3)	3.35	3.35

1998, Aug. 8
243	A68	15te multicolored	.60	.60
244	A68	30te multicolored	1.00	1.00
245	A68	50te multicolored	1.75	1.75
		Nos. 243-245 (3)	3.35	3.35

Souvenir Sheet

Admission of Kazakhstan to UPU — A69

1998, Oct. 9   Litho.   Perf. 14
246	A69	50te multicolored	3.00	3.00

Natl. Arms
A70

World Stamp Day
A71

Republic, 5th Anniv. — A72

1998   Litho.   Perf. 13½
Inscribed "1998"
247	A70	1te green	.25	.25
a.		Inscribed "1999"	.25	.25
248	A70	2te blue	.25	.25
a.		Inscribed "1999"	.25	.25
249	A70	3te red	.25	.25
250	A70	4te bright pink	.25	.25
251	A70	5te orange yellow	.25	.25
a.		Inscribed "1999"	.25	.25
252	A70	8te orange	.45	.45
253	A71	30te olive	1.25	1.25
254	A72	40te orange	1.50	1.50
		Nos. 247-254 (8)	4.45	4.45

Issued: 1te-5te, 6/29; 8te-40te, 11/12. "1999" varieties issued: 1te, 1/28/00; 2te, 9/7/99; 5te, 11/12/99.
See Nos. 296, 299. Compare with Nos. 444-455.

Natl. Epic
A73

Horseman: 20te, Holding sword. 30te, Shooting bow and arrow. 40te, Charging with spear.

1998, Dec.   Perf. 14
255	A73	20te multicolored	1.50	1.50
256	A73	30te multicolored	2.25	2.25
257	A73	40te multicolored	2.75	2.75
		Nos. 255-257 (3)	6.50	6.50

Souvenir Sheet
Nature Park Type of 1997

Designs: a, Island in middle of lake, mountains. b, Lake, mountain peaks.

1998, Dec.   Litho.   Perf. 14
257A	A57	30te Sheet of 2, #a.-b.	2.75	2.75

1999
Census
A74

Space
Communications
A77

K. Satpayev (1899-1964)
A75   A76

1999   Litho.   Perf. 13½
258	A74	1te green	.25	.25
259	A75	15te rose lake	.50	.50
260	A76	20te brown	.65	.65
261	A77	30te olive	1.25	1.25
		Nos. 258-261 (4)	2.65	2.65

Issued: 1te, 2/5/99; 30te, 3/19/99.
See Nos. 270, 272.

Trains — A78

Map showing Orenburg-Tashkent Rail Line, 1890-1906, and: 40te, Steam train. 50te, Diesel locomotive. 60te, Bullet train. 80te, Interurban train.

1999   Perf. 14
262	A78	40te yel & multi	1.25	1.25
263	A78	50te pink & multi	1.75	1.75
264	A78	60te grn & multi	2.00	2.00
265	A78	80te blue & multi	2.50	2.50
		Nos. 262-265 (4)	7.50	7.50

Space Achievements — A79

50te, Soviet spacecraft, vert. 90te, Apollo 11 mission.

1999
266	A79	50te multicolored	6.75	6.75
267	A79	90te multicolored	13.00	13.00

Cosmonaut Day (No. 266), first manned lunar landing, 30th anniv. (No. 267).

New Year Type of 1993
with "Kazakhstan" inscribed in both
Cyrillis and Roman letters

1999, Mar. 19   Litho.   Perf. 14
268	A7	40te multicolored	2.75	2.75

New Year 1999 (Year of the Rabbit).

Space Communications Type of 1999 and

A79a   A79b

1999   Litho.   Perf. 13½
270	A77	3te red	.25	.25
271	A79a	4te bright pink	.30	.30
272	A77	9te bright green	.50	.50
273	A79b	10te purple	.75	.75
274	A79a	30te olive green	.90	.90
		Nos. 270-274 (5)	2.70	2.70

No. 273 is for the UPU, 125th Anniv.

Flowers — A80

Designs: 20te, Pseudoeremostachys severzowii. 30te, Rhaphidophyton regelii. 90te, Niedzwedkia semiretscenskia.

1999, June 28   Litho.   Perf. 14¼x14
276	A80	20te multicolored	1.00	1.00
277	A80	30te multicolored	1.25	1.25
278	A80	90te multicolored	3.25	3.25
		Nos. 276-278 (3)	5.50	5.50

Movies — A81

No. 279: a, 15te, Film scene from 1929. b, 20te, Scenes from 1988, 1997, M. Berkovich. c, 30te, Scenes from 1935, 1938, 1957. d, 35te, Scenes from 1989, 1994, 1997. e, 50te, Alfred Hitchcock. f, 60te, Sergei Eisenstein.

1999   Litho.   Perf. 14
279	A81	Sheet of 10, #e.-f., 2 each #a.-d.	7.50	7.50

Foxes
A82

Designs: 20te, Vulpes vulpes. 30te, Cuon alpinus. 90te, Vulpes corsac.

1999   Litho.   Perf. 14x 14¼
280	A82	20te multicolored	1.00	.75
281	A82	30te multicolored	1.50	1.25
282	A82	90te multicolored	4.00	3.50
		Nos. 280-282 (3)	6.50	5.50

Souvenir Sheet

Environmental Protection — A83

Designs: a, 15te, Cessation of nuclear tests at Semipalatinsk, 10th anniv. b, 45te, Save the ozone layer. c, 60te, Save nature.

1999   Litho.   Perf. 14x13¾
283	A83	Sheet of 3, #a.-c.	3.00	3.00

Kazakhstan Hockey Team — A84

1999   **Litho.**   *Perf. 14*
284   A84   20te   Face-off   1.25   1.25
285   A84   30te   Team photo   1.50   1.50

10th Gusman Kosanov Memorial Track
& Field Meet — A85

1999
286   A85   40te   multi   1.75   1.75

Cosmonauts — A86

1999   *Perf. 14*
287   A86   40te   Talgat Musabayev   1.50   1.50
288   A86   50te   Toktar Aubakirov,
          vert.   1.75   1.75

Souvenir Sheet

UPU, 125th Anniv. — A87

1999, Dec. 20   **Litho.**   *Perf. 14x13¾*
289   A87   20te   multi   1.00   1.00

Arms Type of 1998 and

Spireanthus   Echo
Schrenhianus   Satellite
A88   A89

Oil Rig
A90

Mukhammed Khaidar Dulati (1499-
1551), Historian
A91

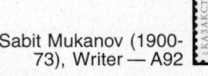

Sabit Mukanov (1900-
73), Writer — A92

2000   **Litho.**   *Perf. 13½*
290   A88   1te   green   .25   .25
291   A88   2te   bright blue   .25   .25
291A   A89   5te   orange yellow   .25   .25
292   A90   7te   red   .40   .40
293   A91   8te   dark blue   .30   .30
294   A92   10te   olive green   .40   .40
295   A93   15te   violet blue   .50   .50
296   A70   20te   orange   .75   .65
297   A89   20te   indigo   .60   .35

299   A70   50te   blue   1.75   1.60
300   A88   50te   blue   1.75   1.60
    Nos. 290-300 (11)   7.20   6.75
    Issued: 7te, 20te, 50te, 1/18/00; 1te, 2te, No. 300, 11/24; 5te, 15te, No. 297, 9/28; 8te, 8/25; 10te, 6/30. 20te and 50te are dated 1999.

Navruz
Bayram — A93

2000, Mar. 21   **Litho.**   *Imperf.*
301   A93   20te   multi   1.50   1.50

Millennium — A94

2000, Mar. 24   **Litho.**   *Perf. 13½*
302   A94   30te   org & blue green   2.25   2.25

Victory in World War
II, 55th Anniv. — A95

2000, May 8   **Litho.**   *Perf. 13½*
303   A95   3te   brown & red   .25   .25

Souvenir Sheet

Millennium — A96

2000, June 1   *Perf. 14x13¾*
304   A96   70te   multi   2.50   2.50

Containers — A97

    No. 305: a, 15te, Leather vessel for koumiss, Kazakhstan. b, 50te, Teapot, China.

2000, June 28   *Perf. 12½x12*
305   A97   Horiz. pair, #a-b   2.50   2.50
    See China (PRC) Nos. 3042-3043.

2000 Summer Olympics,
Sydney — A98

    Designs: 35te, Rowing. No. 307, 40te, Taekwondo. No. 308, 40te, Men's gymnastics. 50te, Triathlon.

2000, Sept. 15   *Perf. 12*
306-309   A98   Set of 4   7.00   7.00

Souvenir Sheet

Turkistan, 1500th Anniv. — A99

    Mausoleums of: a, 50te, Arystan Bab, 12th-20th cents. b, 50te, Karashash Ana, 12th-18th cents. c, 70te, Hadji Ahmet Yassauy, 14th cent.

2000, Oct. 19   *Perf. 13½*
310   A99   Sheet of 3, #a-c   5.50   5.50
    Complete booklet, #310   *14.00*

Bourzhan Momush-Uly
(1910-82), Hero of the
Soviet Union — A100

2000, Dec. 22   *Perf. 13½*
311   A100   4te   black & brown   .50   .50

No. B1 Surcharged in Dark Blue

Method and Perf. as Before
2001, Jan. 26
    Block of 3, #a-c, + Label
312   SP1   10te on 1te+30ti multi   1.00   1.00
    No. 312 exists with double surcharge and inverted surcharge.

**New Year Type of 1993 with
"Kazakhstan" Inscribed in Both
Cyrillic and Roman Letters**
2001, Mar. 2   **Litho.**   *Perf. 13¾x14*
313   A7   40te   org, blk & blue   1.75   1.75
    Dated 2000. New Year 2000 (Year of the Snail).

Cosmonaut's Day — A101

    Designs: 40te, Dogs Belka and Strelka. 70te, Rocket launch, vert.

2001, Mar. 6   *Perf. 14*
314-315   A101   Set of 2   *3.50 3.50*
    Dated 2000. Spaceflight of Belka and Strelka, 40th anniv., Baikonur Cosmodrome, 45th anniv.

**New Year Type of 1993 with
"Kazakhstan" Inscribed in Both
Cyrillic and Roman Letters**
2001, Mar. 21   **Litho.**   *Perf. 13¾x14*
316   A7   40te   grn, blk & brn   1.25   1.25
    New Year 2001 (Year of the Snake).

Souvenir Sheet

Ministry of Communications, 10th
Anniv. — A102

2001, Apr. 4   *Perf. 11½*
317   A102   100te   multi   *12.00 12.00*

Cosmonaut's Day — A103

    Designs: 45te, Soyuz 11 and Salyut. 60te, Yuri Gagarin, Earth.

2001, Apr. 12   *Perf. 14*
318-319   A103   Set of 2   3.50   3.50

Aquilegia   School,
Karatavica   Almaty
A104   A105

Phodopus
Roborovskii — A106

Perf. 13½, 14 (#321, 326)
2001   **Litho.**
320   A104   3te   olive green   .25   .25
321   A105   7te   red violet   .25   .25
322   A106   8te   orange   .30   .30
323   A104   10te   yellow green   .35   .35
324   A106   15te   dark blue   .50   .50
325   A106   20te   deep blue   .60   .60
326   A105   30te   greenish gray   .75   .75
327   A106   50te   brown   1.25   1.25
    Nos. 320-327 (8)   4.25   4.25
    See Nos. 399, 403-405.
    Issued: 7te, 30te, 10/19/01.

Kazakh State
Khans — A107

    Designs: 50te, Abulkhair Khan (1693-1748). 60te, Abylai Khan (1711-81).

2001, May 24   **Litho.**   *Perf. 13¾x14*
328-329   A107   Set of 2   3.75   3.75
    Dated 2000.

Owls
A108

    Designs: 30te, Bubo bubo. 40te, Asio otus. 50te, Surnia ulula.

2001, June 7   *Perf. 14*
330-332   A108   Set of 3   7.00   7.00
    Dated 2000.

Communications
Program
2030 — A109

2001, June 21   *Perf. 14x13¾*
333 A109 40te multi   1.40 1.40
    Dated 2000.

Souvenir Sheet

Lake Markakol — A110

No. 334: a, Cervus elaphus. b, Ursus
arctos. c, Brachymystax lenok.

2001, July 5   *Perf. 13¾x14*
334 A110 30te Sheet of 3, #a-
    c   12.00 12.00

Souvenir Sheet

Flora & Fauna — A111

No. 335: a, 9te, Marmota bobac. b, 12te,
Otis tarda. c, 25te, Larus relictus. d, 60te, Felis
libyca. e, 90te, Nymphaea alba. f, 100te, Pelecanus crispus.

2001, July 19   *Perf. 14x14¼*
335 A111 Sheet of 6, #a-f   6.50 6.50

Souvenir Sheet

Kazakh Railways, 10th Anniv. — A112

No. 336: a, 15te, Building. b, 20te, Turkestan-Siberia locomotive. c, 50te, Railroad
workers.

2001, Aug. 4   *Perf. 14x13¾*
336 A112 Sheet of 3, #a-c   15.00 15.00

Medicine — A113

Designs: 1te, WHO emblem, lungs (tuberculosis prevention). 5te, Ribbon, book (AIDS
prevention).

2001, Aug. 9   *Perf. 13½*
337-338 A113 Set of 2   .50 .50

Intl. Year of Mountains (in
2002) — A114

Various mountains: 35te, 60te.

2001, Sept. 26   *Perf. 14*
339-340 A114 Set of 2   3.25 3.25

Space Achievements
A115

Designs: 50te, Alexei Leonov's walk in
space, 1965, vert. 70te, Apollo-Soyuz mission,
1975.

2001, Oct. 2
341-342 A115 Set of 2   6.00 6.00
    Dated 2000.

Year of Dialogue
Among Civilizations
A116

2001, Oct. 9   *Perf. 13¾x14*
343 A116 45te multi   1.50 1.50

Worldwide Fund for Nature
(WWF) — A117

Various views of Equus hemionus kulan:
9te, 12te, 25te, 50te.

2001, Nov. 1   *Perf. 14*
344-347 A117 Set of 4   3.25 3.25

Commonwealth of
Independent States,
10th Anniv. — A118

2001, Dec. 12   Litho.   *Perf. 14*
348 A118 40te multi   1.75 1.75

Visit of Pope John Paul II — A119

No. 349: a, 20te, Pres. Nazarbayev, Pope.
b, 50te, Pope, Pres. Nazarbayev.

2001, Dec. 14   *Perf. 11½*
349 A119 Horiz. pair, #a-b   5.00 5.00

A120

Independence, 10th Anniv. — A121

No. 351: a, 9te, Monument of Independence, Almaty. b, 25te, Parliament, Astana. c,
35te, Pres. Nazarbayev.

2001   *Perf. 13½*
350 A120 40te multi   1.75 1.75

Souvenir Sheet
Perf. 13¾x14
351 A121   Sheet of 3, #a-c   6.50 6.50
    Issued: 40te, 12/18; No. 351, 12/16.

Native Attire — A122

No. 352: a, 25te, Male attire. b, 35te,
Female attire.

2001, Dec. 25   *Perf. 14x13¾*
352 A122   Horiz. pair, #a-b   2.40 2.40

2002
Winter
Olympics,
Salt Lake
City
A123

Designs: 50te, Women's ice hockey. 150te,
Freestyle skiing.

2002, Feb. 14   *Perf. 14*
353-354 A123 Set of 2   8.00 8.00

**New Year Type of 1993 With
"Kazakhstan" Inscribed in Both
Cyrillic and Roman Letters**
2002, Mar. 21   *Perf. 11½*
355 A7 50te multi   1.75 1.75
    New Year 2002 (Year of the Horse).

Pterygo-
stemon
Spathulatus
A125

Gani
Muratbaev
(1902-25),
Political Leader
A126

Salpingotus
Pallidus
A127

Trade House,
Petropavlovsk
A128

Monument,
Petro-
pavlovsk
A129

Gabiden
Mustafin
(1902-85),
Writer
A130

2002   Litho.   *Perf. 13½*
359 A125 1te blue green   .25 .25
360 A125 2te blue   .25 .25
361 A125 3te green   .25 .25
362 A125 3te brown   .25 .25
363 A127 5te rose lilac   .25 .25
364 A128 6te red   .25 .25
365 A128 7te lilac   .25 .25
366 A129 8te orange   .25 .25
367 A125 10te violet   .25 .25
368 A130 10te blue   .25 .25
369 A125 12te pink   .40 .40
370 A127 15te dark blue   .40 .40
371 A125 23te gray blue   .70 .70
372 A125 25te purple   .70 .70
373 A125 35te olive green   .95 .95
374 A127 40te bister brown   1.10 1.10
375 A127 50te brown   1.60 1.60
    Nos. 359-375 (17)   8.35 8.35

Petropavlovsk, 250th anniv. (Nos. 364-366,
371). Issued: 1te, 2te, 5/7; nos. 360, 367,
35te, 4/30; 5te, 15te, 40te, 50te, 4/4; 6te, 7te,
8te, 23te, 7/9; 12te, 25te, 5/14; No. 362,
12/19; No. 368, 12/18.

Cosmonauts Day — A131

Designs: 30te, Cosmonauts Yuri Baturin,
Talgat Musabaev and first space tourist Den-
nis Tito. 70te, Globe, rocket, flags of US,
Kazakhstan and Russia.

2002, Apr. 10   Litho.   *Perf. 11¾*
376-377 A131 Set of 2   3.00 3.00

2002 World Cup Soccer
Championships, Japan and
Korea — A132

Two players, one with: No. 378, 10te, Jersey
No. 8. No. 379, 10te, Jersey No. 7.

2002, May 31
378-379 A132 Set of 2   1.25 1.25

Horses
A124

Horses: 9te, English. 25te, Kustenai. 60te,
Akhalteka.

2002, Mar. 28
356-358 A124 Set of 3   5.00 5.00

Transeurasia 2002
Conference — A133

2002, June 6   **Perf. 13½**
380 A133 30te multi   1.00 1.00

Souvenir Sheet

Flora and Fauna — A134

No. 381: a, Leontopodium fedt-schenkoanum. b, Mustela erminea. c, Aport Alexander apples.

2002, June 6   **Perf. 11¾x11½**
381 A134 30te Sheet of 3, #a-c   3.00 3.00

Art — A135

Designs. 8te, Kazakh Folk Epos, by E. Sidorkin, 1961. 9te, Makhambet, by M. Kisamedinov, 1973. 60te, Batyr, by Sidorkin, 1979.

2002, July 19   **Perf. 11¾**
382-384 A135 Set of 3   2.75 2.75

Birds — A136

No. 385: a, 10te, Larus ichthyaetus pallas. b, 15te, Anthropoides virgo.

2002, Aug. 29   **Perf. 12**
385 A136 Horiz. pair, #a-b   1.50 1.50
See Russia No. 6709.

Marine Life — A137

No. 386: a, 20te, Huso huso ponticus. b, 35te, Phoca caspica.

2002, Sept. 6
386 A137 Horiz. pair, #a-b   2.25 2.25
See Ukraine No. 483.

Souvenir Sheet

Taraz, 2000th Anniv. — A138

2002, Sept. 25
387 A138 70te multi   2.25 2.25

Souvenir Sheet

International Year of
Mountains — A139

2002, Oct. 4   **Perf. 11½x11¾**
388 A139 50te multi   1.90 1.90

Gabit Musrepov
(1902-85)
A140

2002, Dec. 30   **Litho.**   **Perf. 11½**
389 A140 20te multi   .65 .65

Airplanes
A141

Designs: 20te, Ilyushin-86. 40te, Tupolev-144 and map.

    Perf. 11½x11¾
2002, Dec. 23   Set of 2   **Litho.**
390-391 A141   2.40 2.40
First Moscow to Alma Ata flight of Tupolev-144, 25th anniv. (No. 391).

**Type of 1999, Types of 2000-01
Redrawn and**

Monument to Victims of Political Reprisals A142			Selevinia Betpak-dalensis A143	

2003   **Litho.**   **Perf. 13½**
392	A88	1te green	.25	.25
393	A142	1te red violet	.25	.25
394	A88	2te bright blue	.25	.25
394A	A77	3te red	.25	.25
395	A143	4te brown	.25	.25
396	A143	5te bister	.25	.25
397	A143	6te gray green	.25	.25
398	A143	7te dull green	.25	.25
399	A106	8te orange	.25	.25
400	A142	8te red brown	.25	.25
401	A77	9te dark blue	.25	.25
402	A143	10te blue	.25	.25
403	A106	15te deep blue	.45	.45
404	A106	20te gray blue	.55	.55
405	A106	35te dark green	1.00	1.00
406	A143	63te fawn	1.90	1.90

407	A77	84te purple	2.40	2.40
408	A77	100te orange	2.75	2.75
409	A143	150te claret	4.00	4.00
		Nos. 392-409 (19)	16.05	16.05

Issued: No. 392, 2te, 2/24; Nos. 393, 400, 4/17; 4te, 5te, 6te, 7te, 10te, 63te, 150te, 1/31; No. 399, 15te, 20te, 35te, 3/28; 84te, 100te, 5/30; 3te, 9te, 9/12.

Nos. 392 and 394 are dated "2003" and have smaller Cyrillic inscription of country name, and longer Roman inscription of country name than Nos. 290-291.

Nos. 394A is dated "2003" and has a smaller denomination with thinner zeroes than No. 270.

Nos. 399, 403 and 404 are dated "2003" and have taller Cyrillic inscription of country name than Nos. 322, 324-325.

Domestic and
Wild
Sheep — A144

Various rams, ewes and lambs: 20te, 40te, 50te.

2003, Feb. 26   **Perf. 11½x11¾**
410-412 A144 Set of 3   3.25 3.25

**New Year Type of 1993 With
"Kazakhstan" Inscribed in Both
Cyrillic and Roman Letters**

2003, Mar. 21   **Perf. 11½**
413 A7 40te lt bl, blk & dk bl   1.25 1.25
New Year 2003 (Year of the Ram).

Cosmonaut's Day — A145

Designs: 40te, Pioneer 10 and Jupiter. 70te, Mir Space Station, vert.

2003, Apr. 12   **Perf. 11¾**
414-415 A145 Set of 2   3.25 3.25

Intl. Association of
Academies of
Science, 10th
Anniv. — A146

2003, Apr. 23   **Litho.**   **Perf. 11½**
416 A146 50te multi   1.60 1.60

Souvenir Sheet

Ethnic Groups in Kazakhstan — A147

No. 417: a, Kazakhs (woman with red vest). b, Russians (woman with yellow blouse). c, Ukrainians (woman with blue vest).

2003, Apr. 29   **Litho.**   **Perf. 11¾x11½**
417 A147 35te Sheet of 3, #a-c   3.25 3.25

Musical Instruments
A148

Designs: 25te, Dombra. 50te, Kobyz.

2003, May 26
418-419 A148 Set of 2   2.25 2.25

Fairy
Tales
A149

Designs: 30te, Aldar Kose and Alasha Khan. 40te, Aldar Kose and Karynbaj.

2003, June 27   **Perf. 11½**
420-421 A149 Set of 2   1.75 1.75

Art — A150

Designs: 20te, Chess Match, by Arturo Ricci (1854-1919). 35te, Portrait of the Shepherd, sculpture by H. Nauryzbaev. 45te, Bowls of Koumiss, by Aisha Galimbaeva (1917-).

2003, July 7   **Perf. 11¾**
422-424 A150 Set of 3   3.00 3.00

Famous
Men — A151

Designs: No. 425, 60te, Tole Bey (1663-1756). No. 426, 60te, Kazybek Bey (1667-1763). No. 427, 60te, Aiteke Bey (1689-1766).

2003, Aug. 11   **Perf. 11¾x11½**
425-427 A151 Set of 3   4.00 4.00

Halyk
Bank,
80th
Anniv.
A152

2003, Aug. 15   **Perf. 11½x11¾**
428 A152 23te multi   .60 .60

International Transit Conference,
Almaty — A153

2003, Aug. 28
429 A153 40te multi   1.25 1.25

World Post
Day — A154

2003, Oct. 9   **Perf. 13½**
430 A154 23te pur & blue   .65 .65

Houses of
Worship,
Almaty — A155

Designs: No. 431, 50te, Cathedral. No. 432, 50te, Mosque.

2003, Oct. 10   **Perf. 11¾x11½**
431-432 A155 Set of 2   2.25 2.25

Tenge Currency, 10th
Anniv. — A156

2003, Nov. 15   **Perf. 13½**
433 A156 25te blue & yel org   .65 .65

Paintings — A157

No. 434: a, Baxt, by S. Ayitbaev, 1966. b, Tong. Onalik, by R. Ahmedov, 1962.

2003, Nov. 25   **Perf. 12**
434 A157 100te Horiz. pair, #a-b   4.50 4.50
See Uzbekistan No. 385.

Populus
Diversifolia
A158

2003, Dec. 10   **Perf. 11½**
435 A158 100te multi   2.00 2.00

Petroglyphs, Tamgaly — A159

Designs: 25te, Cows. 30te, Man as sun on bull, vert.

Perf. 11½x11¾, 11¾x11½
2003, Dec. 19
436-437 A159 Set of 2   1.75 1.75

Abylkhan Kasteev
(1904-73),
Artist — A160

2004, Feb. 28   **Litho.**   **Perf. 11¾**
439 A160 115te multi   2.50 2.50

**New Year Type of 1993 With
"Kazakhstan" Inscribed in Both
Cyrillic and Roman Letters**
2004, Mar. 23   **Perf. 11½**
440 A7 35te lt bl, dk bl & org   .85 .85
New Year 2004 (Year of the Monkey).

Cosmonaut's Day — A161

Designs: 40te, Mariner 10, vert. 50te, Luna 3.

Perf. 11¾x11½, 11½x11¾
2004, Apr. 12
441-442 A161 Set of 2   2.00 2.00

Kazakhstan
Flag — A162

2004, Apr. 19   **Perf. 13½**
443 A162 25te yel & brt blue   .70 .70

Arms Type of 1998 Redrawn
2004   **Litho.**   **Perf. 13½**
444 A70 1te green   .25 .25
445 A70 2te bright blue   .25 .25
446 A70 4te bright pink   .25 .25
447 A70 5te orange yellow   .25 .25
448 A70 10te olive green   .25 .25
449 A70 16te brt purple   .40 .40
450 A70 20te purple   .50 .50
451 A70 35te bright yellow   .85 .85
452 A70 50te brt green   1.25 1.25
453 A70 72te orange   1.75 1.75
454 A70 100te greenish blue   2.50 2.50
455 A70 200te vermilion   4.75 4.75
   Nos. 444-455 (12)   13.25 13.25

Issued: 1te, 2te, 4te, 4/19; 20te, 35te, 72te, 100te, 200te, 5/11; 5te, 10te, 16te, 50te, 6/10.
Nos. 444-455 are dated "2004," arms and "Kazakhstan" in Roman letters are larger and denominations are smaller than those features on Nos. 247-254.
No. 447 is dated "2004," arms and "Kazakhstan" in Roman letters are larger and denomination is smaller than those features on No. 251.

Souvenir Sheet

Kazakhstan Railways, Cent. — A163

2004, Apr. 22   **Litho.**   **Perf. 11¾x11½**
456 A163 150te multi   3.00 3.00

Souvenir Sheet

Ethnic Groups in Kazakhstan — A164

No. 457: a, Uzbeks (denomination at left). b, Germans (denomination at right).

2004, May 12
457 A164 65te Sheet of 2, #a-b   3.00 3.00

FIFA (Fédération Internationale de
Football Association), Cent. — A165

FIFA emblem, soccer player and soccer ball at: No. 458, 100te, Left. No. 459, 100te, Center.

2004, May 21   **Litho. & Embossed**
458-459 A165 Set of 2   4.00 4.00

Children's
Art — A166

Designs: No. 460, 45te, Yurts and sheep, by A. Sadykov. No. 461, 45te, Woman, by D. Iskhanova, vert.

2004, June 20   **Litho.**   **Perf. 11½**
460-461 A166 Set of 2   1.75 1.75

Souvenir Sheet

2004 Summer Olympics,
Athens — A167

No. 462: a, 70te, Boxing. b, 115te, Shooting.

Litho., Margin Embossed
2004, June 28
462 A167   Sheet of 2, #a-b   3.25 3.25

Souvenir Sheet

Fauna in Altyn Emel Reserve — A168

No. 463: a, Acgypius monacus. b, Capra sibirica. c, Gazella subgutturosa.

2004, Aug. 11   **Perf. 11½x11¾**
463 A168 50te Sheet of 3, #a-c   3.50 3.50

Souvenir Sheet

Kazaktelecom, 10th Anniv. — A169

Perf. 11½x11¾
2004, Aug. 18   **Litho.**
464 A169 70te multi   1.50 1.50

Alkei Khakan
Margulan
(1904-85),
Archaeologist
A170

2004, Sept. 23
465 A170 115te multi   2.25 2.25

Flowers — A171

2004, Oct. 4   **Perf. 12¼x11½**
466 A171 25te multi + label   .60 .60
Printed in sheets of 12 + 12 labels.

World Post Day Type of 2003
2004, Oct. 9   **Perf. 13½**
467 A154 3te red vio & blue   .30 .30
468 A154 30te yel org & blue   .80 .80

New Year
2005 — A172

2004, Nov. 23   **Perf. 13¼**
469 A172 65te multi   1.50 1.50

Musical Instruments — A173

No. 470: a, Adyma. b, Gizhak and bow.

2004, Nov. 29   *Perf. 11½x11¾*
470 A173 100te Horiz. pair, #a-b   4.50 4.50
See Tajikistan No. 248.

Saken Seifullin
(1894-1939),
Writer — A174

2004, Dec. 28
471 A174 35te multi   .75 .75

Women's Headdresses — A175

No. 472: a, Kazakh headdress, denomination at left. b, Mongol headdress, denomination at right.

2004, Dec. 30
472 A175 72te Horiz. pair, #a-b   3.75 3.75
See Mongolia No. 2590.

Veterinary Research
Institute, Cent. — A176

2005, Jan. 14   *Perf. 13½*
473 A176 7te multi   .30 .30

Constitution, 10th
Anniv. — A177

2005, Apr. 8   Litho.   *Perf. 13½*
474 A177 1te blue & brn   .25 .25
475 A177 2te vio & brn   .25 .25
476 A177 3te brt grn & brn   .25 .25
477 A177 8te brt bl & brn   .25 .25
478 A177 10te red & brn   .25 .25
479 A177 A red vio & brn   .70 .70
480 A177 50te olive & brn   1.25 1.25
481 A177 65te bl grn & brn   1.50 1.50
   Nos. 474-481 (8)   4.70 4.70

No. 479 sold for 25te on day of issue.

Europa — A178

2005, Apr. 14   Litho.   *Perf. 11½x12¼*
482 A178 90te multi   4.25 4.25

End of World
War II, 60th
Anniv. — A179

2005, Apr. 28   Litho.   *Perf. 13¼x13*
483 A179 72te multi   1.25 1.25

Souvenir Sheet

Baikonur Space Complex, 50th
Anniv. — A180

No. 484: a, Rocket. b, Buran space shuttle. c, Capsule and parachute.

2005, June 2   *Perf. 11½x11¾*
484 A180 72te Sheet of 3, #a-c   4.25 4.25

Peace and Harmony Palace — A181

Litho. & Embossed
2005, July 6   *Perf. 13¼*
485 A181 65te multi   1.50 1.50

Minerals — A182

Designs: 50te, Azurite. 70te, Agate.

2005, July 12   Litho.   *Perf. 11¾x11½*
486-487 A182   Set of 2   2.75 2.75

Fairy Tales Type of 2003

Designs: 35te, Aldar Kose and the Musician. 45te, Aldar Kose and the Raiser of Asses.

2005, Aug. 11
488-489 A149   Set of 2   1.75 1.75

Constitution, 10th
Anniv. — A183

2005, Aug. 26
490 A183 72te multi   1.60 1.60

Souvenir Sheet

Olympic Gold Medalists — A184

No. 491: a, Zaksylik Ushkempirov, 1980, 48kg Greco-Roman wrestling. b, Vitaly Savin, 1988, 4x100m relay. c, Vasily Zhirov, 1996, light heavyweight boxing. d, Bekzat Sattarkhanov, 2000, featherweight boxing.

2005, Sept. 22   Litho.   *Perf. 11¾*
491 A184 100te Sheet of 4, #a-d   7.50 7.50

Akhmet
Baitursynov (1873-
1937),
Writer — A185

Litho. with Foil Application
2005, Oct. 6   *Perf. 13¾x14*
492 A185 30te multi   .70 .70

No. 492 not issued without gold overprint.

World Post
Day — A186

2005, Oct. 8   Litho.   *Perf. 13½*
493 A186 35te blue & pur   .80 .80
494 A186 40te pur & red   .95 .95

Dogs — A187

No. 495: a, Kazakh hound (dog with curled tail). b, Estonian hound (white, black and brown dog).

2005, Oct. 19   *Perf. 11½x11¾*
495 A187 138te Horiz. pair, #a-b   4.50 4.50
See Estonia No. 523.

United Nations, 60th
Anniv. — A188

2005, Oct. 31   *Perf. 13½*
496 A188 150te multi   3.25 3.25

New Year
2006 — A189

2005, Nov. 10   Litho.   *Perf. 13¼*
497 A189 65te multi   1.25 1.25

Evgeny Brusilovsky (1905-81),
Composer — A190

2005, Nov. 18   *Perf. 11½x11¾*
498 A190 150te multi   2.75 2.75

Assembly of Peoples of
Kazakhstan, 10th
Anniv. — A191

2005, Nov. 24   *Perf. 13½*
499 A191 80te multi   1.75 1.75

Souvenir Sheet

National Symbols — A192

No. 500: a, 70te, Flag and eagle. b, 70te, National anthem. c, 300te, Arms.

Litho. & Embossed
2005, Dec. 22   *Perf. 13¼*
500 A192   Sheet of 3, #a-c   6.50 6.50

Turgen
Waterfall
A193

Mountain Lake
A194

2005, Dec. 23   Litho.   *Perf. 13½*
501 A193 12te multi   .30 .30
502 A194 100te multi   2.40 2.40

Hans Christian Andersen (1805-75),
Author — A195

2005, Dec. 30   *Perf. 11¾x11½*
503 A195 200te multi   3.75 3.75

Parliament,
10th
Anniv. — A196

2006, Jan. 17   Litho.   *Perf. 11½x11¾*
504 A196 50te multi   1.25 1.25

Abylai Khan, by Aubakir Ismailov A197

Litho. With Foil Application
2006, Jan. 27   *Perf. 13x13¼*
505 A197 94te multi   1.90 1.90

2006 Winter Olympics, Turin — A198

Perf. 11½x11¾
2006, Feb. 20   Litho.
506 A198 138te multi   2.25 2.25

Cosmonaut's Day — A199

Paintings of cosmonauts by: 100te, P. M. Popov. 120te, A. M. Stepanov.

2006, Apr. 12   *Perf. 11¾x11½*
507-508 A199   Set of 2   3.75 3.75

Traditional Jewelry — A200

No. 509: a, Bracelet, Kazakhstan. b, Brooch, Latvia.

2006, Apr. 19   *Perf. 11½x11¾*
509 A200 110te Horiz. pair, #a-b 4.00 4.00
See Latvia No. 650.

Saksaul Tree — A201

2006, Apr. 27   *Perf. 11¾x11½*
510 A201 25te multi   .60 .60

Europa — A202

2006, May 3
511 A202 210te multi   3.50 3.50
  a.   Tete-beche pair   10.00 10.00

Turkestan-Siberia Railway, 75th Anniv. — A203

2006, May 31   *Perf. 13x13¼*
512 A203 200te multi   4.00 4.00

2006 World Cup Soccer Championships, Germany — A204

2006, June 2   *Perf. 11½x11¾*
513 A204 150te multi   2.75 2.75

Intl. Year of Deserts and Desertification — A205

2006, July 7   *Perf. 13¼*
514 A205 110te multi   2.00 2.00

Mosque, Astana — A206

2006   Litho.   *Perf. 13½x13¾*
515 A206   5te emerald   .25 .25
516 A206   8te Prus blue   .25 .25
517 A206   10te olive grn   .30 .25
518 A206   A purple   .55 .45
518A A206   100te dark blue   2.00 2.00
519 A206   110te brown   2.00 1.75
520 A206   120te green   2.25 2.00
521 A206   200te red violet   4.25 3.25
     Nos. 515-521 (8)   11.85 10.20

No. 518 sold for 25te on day of issue. Issued: 100te, 10/10/06; rest, 7/20/06.

Akzhan Mashani, Geologist, Cent. of Birth — A207

2006, July 21 Litho. *Perf. 11½x11¾*
522 A207 85te multi   2.00 2.00

Houses of Worship in Almaty — A208

Designs: No. 523, 25te, Catholic Church (denomination in orange). No. 524, 25te, Synagogue (denomination in white).

2006, Aug. 17   *Perf. 11¾x11½*
523-524 A208   Set of 2   1.10 1.10

Souvenir Sheet

Famous Men — A209

No. 525: a, Chokan Valikhanov (1835-65), diplomat. b, Saken Sejfullin (1894-1938), poet. c, Nazir Tjurjakulov (1893-1937). d, Kanysh Satpaev (1899-1964), geologist.

2006, Aug. 20   *Perf. 11½*
525 A209 90te Sheet of 4, #a-d 5.75 5.75

Third Meeting of Economic Cooperation Organization Postal Authorities, Turkey — A210

2006, Sept. 15   *Perf. 12*
526 A210 210te multi   4.00 4.00
See Iran No. 2917, Pakistan No. 1101 and Turkey No. 3041.

No. 526 Overprinted in Gold

2006, Sept. 22
527 A210 210te multi   4.00 4.00
Overprint corrects site of meeting from Istanbul to Ankara.

Ahmet Zhubanov (1906-68), Composer A211

2006, Oct. 13   *Perf. 11½*
528 A211 85te multi   1.50 1.50

Coats of Arms — A212

Arms of: 17te, Almaty. 80te, Astana.

2006, Oct. 20 Litho. *Perf. 13½x13¾*
529-530 A212   Set of 2   2.25 2.25

New Year 2007 — A213

2006, Nov. 1   Litho.   *Perf. 13¼*
531 A213 25te multi   .55 .55

Latif Khamidi (1906-83), Composer A214

2006, Nov. 9   *Perf. 11½x11¾*
532 A214 110te multi   2.00 2.00

Mukagali Makataev (1931-76), Writer — A215

2006, Nov. 29   *Perf. 13½x13¾*
533 A215   1te dark red   .25 .25
534 A215   4te olive grn   .25 .25
535 A215   7te rose claret   .25 .25
536 A215   15te red brown   .30 .30
     Nos. 533-536 (4)   1.05 1.05

Manash Kozybaev (1931-2002), Historian — A216

2006, Nov. 29
537 A216 20te brown   .45 .45
538 A216 30te brn lake   .65 .65

Character From Opera *Silk Girl* — A217

2006, Dec. 15   *Perf. 13¼*
539 A217 80te multi   1.25 1.25
Values are for stamps with surrounding selvage.

18th Century Helmet — A218

2006, Dec. 15   *Perf. 13x12¾*
540 A218 85te multi   1.75 1.75

Nikolai Repinsky (1906-69), Architect — A219

2006, Dec. 20   *Perf. 13½x13¾*
541 A219 2te brown   .25   .25
542 A219 3te yel brn   .25   .25
543 A219 105te gray grn   2.00   2.00
544 A219 150te blue   3.00   3.00
545 A219 500te rose claret   9.00   9.00
   Nos. 541-545 (5)   14.50   14.50

Miniature Sheet

Kurgalzhinsky Nature Reserve — A220

No. 546: a, 25te, Phoenicopterus roseus. b, 100te, Cygnus cygnus. c, 120te, Meles meles.

2006, Dec. 29   *Perf. 11½x11¾*
546 A220   Sheet of 3, #a-c   5.50   5.50

KazTransOil, 10th Anniv. — A221

2007, Apr. 12   Litho.   *Perf. 12¾*
547 A221 25te multi   .55   .55

Cosmonaut's Day — A222

Designs: 80te, Konstantin E. Tsiolkovsky (1857-1935), rocket pioneer. 110te, Sergei P. Korolev (1906-66), aeronautical engineer.

2007, Apr. 12   *Perf. 12¼x11¾*
548-549 A222   Set of 2   2.50   2.50

Europa — A223

No. 550 — Children's art: a, 25te, Scout bugler and tents. b, 65te, Scouts with backpacks, dog.

2007, May 8   *Perf. 11½x11¾*
550 A223   Pair, #a-b   1.75   1.75
   Scouting, cent.

63rd Session of UN Economic and Social Commission for Asia and the Pacific, Almaty — A224

2007, May 17   *Perf. 12¾*
551 A224 25te multi   .55   .55

Gali Ormanov (1907-78), Poet — A225

2007, Sept. 28   Litho.   *Perf. 11½*
552 A225 25te multi   .55   .55

Conference on Interaction and Confidence-Building Measures in Asia, 15th Anniv. — A226

2007, Oct. 17   *Perf. 13½*
553 A226 80te multi   1.75   1.75

Maulen Balakaev (1907-95), Philologist — A227

2007, Oct. 29   Litho.   *Perf. 13½*
554 A227 1to rod brown   .25   .25
555 A227 4te green   .25   .25
556 A227 5te dk brown   .25   .25
   Nos. 554-556 (3)   .75   .75

Almaty Zoo Animals — A228

No. 557: a, 25te, Zebras. b, 110te, Elephant.

2007, Oct. 31   Litho.   *Perf. 11½*
557 A228   Pair, #a-b   2.50   2.50
   Printed in sheets containing 4 each of Nos. 557a and 557b, with a central label.

Hirundo Rustica — A229

2007, Nov. 15   *Perf. 13½*
558 A229 20te multi   .45   .35
559 A229 25te multi   .55   .45
560 A229 50te multi   1.00   .75
561 A229 100te multi   2.25   1.75
   Nos. 558-561 (4)   4.25   3.30

Saddle A230

2007, Nov. 27   *Perf. 12*
562 A230 80te multi   1.50   1.50

Launch of Sputnik 1, 50th Anniv. — A231

2007, Nov. 27   *Perf. 12½x12¾*
563 A231 500te multi   8.50   8.50

Karagand Arms — A232   Pavlodar Arms — A233

2007, Dec. 10   *Perf. 13½x13¼*
564 A232 10te multi   .40   .40
565 A233 10te multi   .40   .40

Miniature Sheet

Olympic Gold Medalists — A234

No. 566: a, Vladimir Smirnov, 1994, 50-kilometer skiing. b, Yuri Melinichenko, 1996, Greco-Roman wrestling. c, Olga Shishigina, 2000, 100-meter hurdles. d, Ermahan Ibraimov, 2000, boxing.

2007, Dec. 28   *Perf. 12x11½*
566 A234 150te Sheet of 4, #a-d   11.00   11.00

Souvenir Sheet

Peoples of Kazakhstan — A235

No. 567: a, Uighur man and woman (denomination at left). b, Tatar man and woman (denomination at right).

2007, Dec. 28   *Perf. 11½*
567 A235 105te Sheet of 2, #a-b   3.75   3.75

New Year — A236

2008, Jan. 23   Litho.   *Perf. 13¼*
568 A230 25te multi   .65   .65
   Printed in sheets of 8 + central label.

Miniature Sheet

Women's Day — A237

No. 569 — Various flowers with: a, Denomination at LL. b, Denomination at LR. c, Denomination and country name at UL. d, Denomination and country name at UR, Kazakh text in lower panel justified at right. e, Denomination at L, country name at LL. f, Denomination and country name at UR, Kazakh text in lower panel justified at left.

2008, Mar. 14   *Perf. 13¼*
569 A237 25te Sheet of 6, #a-f, + 3 labels   4.50   4.50

Navruz Bayram — A238

2008, Mar. 21   *Perf. 12¾*
570 A238 25te multi   .55   .55

2008 Summer Olympics, Beijing — A239

2008, Apr. 2   *Perf. 14x14¼*
571 A239 25te multi   .55   .55

Kazakhstan Postal Service, 15th Anniv. — A240

2008, Apr. 4   *Perf. 12¾*
572 A240 25te multi   .55   .55

Cosmonaut's Day — A241

Designs: 100te, Space Station Mir. 150te, International Space Station.

2008, Apr. 10   *Perf. 14x14¼*
573-574 A241   Set of 2   5.00   5.00

Europa — A242

No. 575 — Color of dove: a, Blue. b, Red.

2008, May 6   **Perf. 14x14¼**
575 A242 150te Horiz. pair, #a-b   5.00 5.00

2008 Summer Olympics,
Beijing — A243

No. 576: a, Judo. b, Handball.

2008, Aug. 10   Litho.   Perf. 14x14¼
576 A243 100te Horiz. pair, #a-b   3.75 3.75

Deer — A244

No. 577: a, Cervus elaphus sibiricus. b,
Cervus nippon.

2008, Sept. 18
577 A244 110te Horiz. pair, #a-b   3.75 3.75

    See Moldova No. 596.

Ancient Jewelry From Iran and
Kazakhstan — A245

No. 578: a, Buckle depicting snow leopard
and mountains, 4th-5th cent. B.C., Kazakhstan. b, Gold medal depicting lions, 7th cent.
B.C., Iran.

2008, Oct. 3   **Perf. 14x14¼**
578   Horiz. pair + flanking la-
     bel   4.50 4.50
  a.   A245 25te multi   .55 .55
  b.   A245 150te multi   3.50 3.50

    See Iran No. 2965.

Universal Declaration of Human
Rights, 60th Anniv. — A246

Perf. 11¾x11½
2008, Dec. 10   **Litho.**
579 A246 25te multi   .55 .55

Taiyr Zharakov
(1908-65),
Poet — A247

2008, Dec. 12   **Perf. 11½**
580 A247 25te multi   .55 .55

Shakarim
Kudaiberdyuly
(1859-1931),
Poet — A248

2008, Dec. 12
581 A248 25te multi   .55 .55

Alash Movement,
90th
Anniv. — A249

2008, Dec. 18
582 A249 25te multi   .55 .55

Musical Instruments — A250

No. 583: a, 25te, Zhelbuaz. b, 100te,
Dauylpaz.

2008, Dec. 19
583 A250   Pair, #a-b   2.25 2.25

Paintings — A251

No. 584: a, 25te, Portrait of Kenesary, by A.
Kasteev. b, 100te, Guest, by S. Aitbayev.

2008, Dec. 19
584 A251   Pair, #a-b   2.25 2.25

Insects — A252

No. 585: a, 25te, Callisthenes semenovi. b,
100te, Dorcadion acharlense.

2008, Dec. 22
585 A252   Pair, #a-b   2.25 2.25

Peter Aravin (1908-
79), Musicologist
A253

Perf. 13¾x13½
2008, Dec. 25   **Litho.**
586 A253 10te multi   .35 .35

Eagle — A254

2008, Dec. 25
587 A254 20te multi   .50 .50

Arms of   Arms of
Atyrau — A255   Taraz — A256

2008, Dec. 25   Litho.   Perf. 14x13½
588 A255 A multi   .70 .70
589 A256 A multi   .70 .70
    On day of issue, Nos. 588-589 each sold for
25te.

Preservation of Polar Regions and
Glaciers — A257

2009, Mar. 12   Litho.   Perf. 12¾
590 A257 230te multi   3.75 3.75

Navruz Bayram — A258

2009, Mar. 20
591 A258 25te multi   .50 .50

Louis Braille (1809-
52), Educator of
the Blind — A259

2009, Mar. 26   **Perf. 11½**
592 A259 230te multi   3.75 3.75

Europa — A260

    Telescopes and: No. 593, 230te, Galileo
Galilei, Moon. No. 594, 230te, Taurus constellation, Kazakhs looking at sky.

2009, Apr. 3
593-594 A260   Set of 2   7.50 7.50
    Intl. Year of Astronomy.

Earrings — A261

No. 595 — Earring from: a, Korea, 5th-6th
cent. b, Mongolia, 18th-19th cent. c, Kazakhstan, 2nd-1st cent. B.C.

2009, June 12   Litho.   Perf. 13x12¾
595 A261   Horiz. strip of 3   9.00 9.00
  a.-c.   180te Any single   2.75 2.75
    See South Korea No. 2313, Mongolia No.
2674.

Astronomy
A262

    Designs: 180te, Telescope. 230te,
Observatories.

2009, June 25   **Perf. 13**
596-597 A262   Set of 2   6.25 6.25

Horsemen and Shield — A263

2009, July 9   **Perf. 12¾x12½**
598 A263 190te multi   3.00 3.00
  a.   Tête bêche pair   7.00 7.00

Maria Lizogub
(1909-98),
Painter — A264

2009, Aug. 25   **Perf. 11½**
599 A264 180te multi   3.00 3.00

Kenen Azerbaev (1884-1976), Composer A265

2009, Sept. 2
600 A265 180te multi   3.00 3.00

Garifolla Kurmangaliev (1909-93), Singer — A266

2009, Sept. 8
601 A266 180te multi   3.00 3.00

18th Session of World Tourism Organization, Astana — A267

2009, Oct. 5
602 A267 140te multi   2.10 2.10

Miniature Sheet

Ballet — A268

No. 603: a, 180te, Dancers from Giselle (woman in white, man in black). b, 180te, Dancers from Don Quixote (woman in red, man in black and white). c, 180te, Dancers from Swan Lake (man and woman in white). d, 180te, Dancer from Tilep and Sarykyz. e, 230te, Dancer in red from Legend About Love. f, 230te, Dancer in blue from Bahchisarayski Fountain.

2009, Oct. 8   *Perf. 13¼*
603 A268   Sheet of 6, #a-f   17.00 17.00

National Games — A269

No. 604: a, 140te, Blindfolded man on horseback. b, 180te, Horsemen in competition.

2009, Nov. 16   *Perf. 12*
604 A269   Pair, #a-b   5.00 5.00

Abdilda Tazhibaev (1909-98), Writer — A270

2009, Nov. 16   *Perf. 11½*
605 A270 180te multi   2.75 2.75

Flora and Fauna A271

Designs: No. 606, 180te, Crataegus ambigua. No. 607, 180te, Mellivora capensis.

2009, Dec. 3   *Litho.*   *Perf. 13*
606-607 A271   Set of 2   5.50 5.50

Iskander Tynyshpaev (1909-95), Cinematographer — A272

2009, Dec. 9   *Perf. 11½x11¾*
608 A272 25te multi   .50 .50

Tuleu Basenov (1909-76), Architect A273

2009, Dec. 30
609 A273 25te multi   .50 .50

Birzhan Sal Kozhagululy (1834-97), Composer A274

2009, Dec. 30
610 A274 25te multi   .50 .50

Construction of Central Asian Gas Pipeline — A275

Perf. 12½x12¾
2009, Dec. 30   *Litho.*
611 A275 25te multi   .50 .50

Kazakhstan Chairmanship of Organization for Security and Cooperation in Europe — A276

2010, Jan. 6   *Litho.*   *Perf. 12*
612 A276 230te multi   4.00 4.00

Navruz Bayram — A277

2010, Apr. 15   *Perf. 12¾*
613 A277 32te multi   .55 .55

Victory in World War II, 65th Anniv. A278

2010, Apr. 15   *Perf. 12*
614 A278 32te multi   .55 .55

2010 Winter Olympics, Vancouver A279

Designs: 32te, Ski jumper. 190te, Alpine skier.

2010, Apr. 29   *Litho.*   *Perf. 12*
615-616 A279   Set of 2   3.50 3.50

Europa — A280

2010, May 5   *Perf. 12¾*
617 A280 240te multi   3.50 3.50

Temirtau, 50th Anniv. A281

2010, June 1   *Litho.*   *Perf. 14x14¼*
618 A281 32te multi   .65 .65

Khan Shatyr Entertainment Center, Astana — A282

2010, July 1
619 A282 32te multi   .65 .65

2010 World Cup Soccer Championships, South Africa — A283

2010, July 12
620 A283 240te multi   4.00 4.00

Arms of Chimkent   Arms of Aktyubinsk
A284   A285

2010   *Perf. 14¼ Syncopated*
621 A284 5te multi   .25 .25
622 A285 10te multi   .25 .25
   Issued: 5te, 8/17; 10te, 7/27.

Constitution, 15th Anniv. — A286

2010, Aug. 20   *Perf. 14x14¼*
623 A286 32te multi   .65 .65

Musa Baijanuly (1835-1929), Composer A287

Perf. 13¾x13½ Syncopated
2010, Aug. 24
624 A287 (32te) multi   .65 .65

Baikonur Cosmodrome, 55th Anniv. — A288

2010, Aug. 27   *Perf. 13x13¼*
625 A288 190te multi   3.00 3.00

Mukhamedzhan Karataev (1910-95), Encyclopedia Editor — A289

Perf. 13¾x13½ Syncopated
2010, Sept. 22
626 A289 20te multi   .45 .45

Souvenir Sheet

Baurjan Momasuhly (1910-82), World War II Hero — A290

2010, Sept. 24   *Perf. 14x14¼*
627 A290 140te multi   2.50 2.50

Shokan Valikhanov (1835-65), Diplomat, Engineer — A291

2010, Oct. 21   **Perf. 14¼x14**
628 A291 140te multi   2.75 2.75
See Russia No. 7246.

Frédéric Chopin (1810-49), Composer — A292

2010, Oct. 28   **Perf. 14¼x14**
629 A292 240te multi   3.75 3.75

Water Agreement Between Kazakhstan and Kyrgyzstan, 10th Anniv. — A293

2010, Nov. 17   **Perf. 14x14¼**
630 A293 32te multi   .65 .65

Souvenir Sheet

Organization for Security and Cooperation in Europe Summit, Astana — A294

No. 631: a, 32te, Independence Monument and Kazakhstan flag. b, 140te, Pyramid of Peace. c, 190te, Ak Orda (Presidential Palace), Pyramid of Peace.

2010, Nov. 23   **Perf. 14¼x14**
631 A294   Sheet of 3, #a-c   6.25 6.25

Birds of the Caspian Sea — A295

No. 632: a, Phoenicopterus roseus. b, Ardeola ralloides.

2010, Nov. 24   **Litho.**
632 A295 140te Pair, #a-b   4.75 4.75
See Azerbaijan No. 938.

Seventh Asian Winter Games, Astana and Almaty — A296

No. 633: a, 190te, Games emblem. b, 190te, Mascot freestyle skiing. c, 240te, Mascot ski jumping. d, 240te, Mascot ice skating.

2010, Dec. 21
633 A296   Block or horiz.
             strip of 4, #a-d   13.00 13.00

Mirzhakyp Dulatov (1885-1935), Poet — A297

Perf. 13½x13¾ Syncopated
2010, Dec. 28
634 A297 50te multi   .80 .80

Fish in Astana Oceanarium — A298

No. 635: a, 32te, Rhinecanthus aculeatus. b, 190te, Zebrasoma veliferum.

2010, Dec. 30   **Perf. 13½x13¾**
635 A298   Pair, #a-b   3.50 3.50

Souvenir Sheet

Fauna of Bayanaul Nature Reserve — A299

No. 636: a, 32te, Tadorna ferruginea. b, 140te, Mustela nivalis. c, 190te, Capreolus pygargus.

2010, Dec. 30   **Perf. 14x14¼**
636 A299   Sheet of 3, #a-c   10.00 10.00
On Nos. 636a-636c, country name is misspelled "Kazakhstah."

Souvenir Sheet

Peoples of Kazakhstan — A300

No. 637: a, 32te, Korean man and woman. b, 190te, Belarussian man and woman.

2010, Dec. 30   **Perf. 14¼x14**
637 A300   Sheet of 2, #a-b   3.50 3.50

First Man in Space, 50th Anniv. A301

2011, Feb. 28   **Perf. 14x14¼**
638 A301 190te multi   3.00 3.00

Europa A302

2011, Apr. 21   **Litho.**
639 A302 250te multi   3.75 3.75
Intl. Year of Forests.

Shanghai Cooperation Organization, 10th Anniv. — A303

2011, May 5   **Perf. 14¼x14**
640 A303 210te multi   3.25 3.25

Campaign Against AIDS, 30th Anniv. — A304

2011, June 3 Litho.   Perf. 14x13½
641 A304 32te multi   .60 .60

Eurasian Economic Community, 10th Anniv. — A305

2011, June 14   **Perf. 14¼x14**
642 A305 32te multi   .60 .60

Kasym Amanzholov (1911-55), Poet — A306

2011, July 14   **Perf. 13½x14**
643 A306 32te multi   .65 .65

Coins — A307

No. 644 — Coin from: a, 7th cent. b, 13th cent. c, 14th cent. d, 16th cent.

2011, Sept. 7   **Perf. 14x14¼**
644 A307 32te Block of 4, #a-d   2.00 2.00

Orymbek Zhautykov (1911-89), Mathematician A308

2011, Sept. 15
645 A308 32te multi   .60 .60

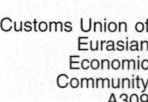

Customs Union of Eurasian Economic Community A309

2011, Sept. 22   **Perf. 14¼x14**
646 A309 32te multi   .65 .65

Regional Communications Commonwealth, 20th Anniv. — A310

2011, Sept. 22   **Perf. 14x13½**
647 A310 150te multi   2.25 2.25

Gabdol Slanov (1911-69), Writer — A311

2011, Sept. 30   **Perf. 14x14¼**
648 A311 32te multi   .65 .65

National Coat of Arms — A312

Perf. 14x14¼ Syncopated

2011, Oct. 5
649	A312	A multi	.50	.50
650	A312	50te multi	.85	.85
651	A312	80te multi	1.25	1.25
652	A312	100te multi	1.50	1.50
653	A312	200te multi	3.00	3.00
654	A312	500te multi	8.00	8.00
	Nos. 649-654 (6)		15.10	15.10

No. 649 sold for 32te on day of issue.

Umirzak Sultangazin (1936-2005), Director of Kazakhstan Space Reseach Institute — A313

2011, Oct. 20 *Perf. 14x14¼*
655 A313 32te multi .65 .65

Dina Nurpeisova (1861-1955), Musician — A314

2011, Oct. 25 *Perf. 14x14¼*
656 A314 32te multi .65 .65

Commonwealth of Independent States, 20th Anniv. — A315

2011, Nov. 10 *Perf. 14¼x14*
657 A315 150te multi 2.50 2.50

Independence, 20th Anniv. — A316

2011, Dec. 5
658 A316 32te multi .55 .55

Isatai Isabayev (1936-2007), Painter — A317

2011, Dec. 14 *Perf. 14x14¼*
659 A317 32te multi .60 .60

Miniature Sheet

Birds — A318

No. 660: a, Turdus merula. b, Acridotheres tristis. c, Parus major. d, Corvus frugilegus. e, Pica pica. f, Columba livia. g, Corvus cornix. h, Passer domesticus.

2011, Dec. 14
660 A318 250te Sheet of 8, #a-h 25.00 25.00

Independence, 20th Anniv. — A319

2011, Dec. 15
661 A319 20te multi .30 .30

First Kazakh Antarctic Expedition A320

2011, Dec. 16
662 A320 190te multi 3.50 3.50

Petro Kazakhstan Kumkol Resources, 25th Anniv. — A321

2011, Dec. 22
663 A321 150te multi 2.25 2.25

Kazakhstan E-Government — A322

2011, Dec. 31
664 A322 32te multi .55 .55

Dinmukhamed Konayev (1912-93), Politician — A323

2012, Jan. 27 *Perf. 14¼x14*
665 A323 100te multi 1.75 1.75

Katynkaragay National Park — A324

2012, Mar. 20 *Perf. 13½x13¾*
666 A324 110te multi 2.00 2.00

No. 1 Surcharged in Gold

Method and Perf. As Before
2012, Apr. 4
667 A1 50te on 50k #1 1.00 1.00

Europa A325

2012, Apr. 11 Litho. *Perf. 14x14¼*
668 A325 250te multi 3.50 3.50

Hedgehogs — A326

No. 669: a, Erinaceus europaeus. b, Hemiechinus auritus.

2012, June 20
669 A326 190te Pair, #a-b 6.25 6.25
See Belarus Nos. 827-828.

Navruz Bayram A327

2012, July 25
670 A327 190te multi 3.00 3.00

Space Vehicle A328

2012, July 25
671 A328 250te multi 3.75 3.75

Ufa Ahmedsafin (1912-84), Hydrogeologist A329

2012, Aug. 9 *Perf. 14¼x14*
672 A329 150te multi 2.50 2.50

Conference on a Nuclear Weapons-Free World, Astana — A330

2012, Aug. 27
673 A330 50te multi .80 .80

Mezhit Begalin (1922-78), Film Director — A331

2012, Oct. 4 *Perf. 14x14¼*
674 A331 90te multi 1.40 1.40

Lev Gumilev (1912-92), Anthropologist A332

2012, Oct. 11
675 A332 100te multi 1.50 1.50

Dmitri Snegin (1912-2001), Writer — A333

2012, Oct. 17 *Perf. 13¾ Syncopated*
676 A333 80te multi 1.50 1.50

Shara Zhienkulova (1912-91), Dancer — A334

2012, Oct. 17
677 A334 100te multi 1.90 1.90

Paintings — A335

No. 678: a, Warriors, by P. Zaltsman, 1973. b, Milking a Red Camel, by A. Sadykhanov, 1986-87.

2012, Oct. 17   *Perf. 14¼x14*
678 A335 250te Vert. pair, #a-b   6.50 6.50

Mir Broadcasting Company, 20th Anniv. — A336

2012, Oct. 25
679 A336 10te multi   .25 .25

Collective Security Treaty Organization, 10th Anniv. — A337

2012, Oct. 25
680 A337 80te multi   1.25 1.25

Zein Shashkin (1912-66), Writer — A338

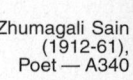

Zhamal Omarova (1912-76), Singer — A339

Zhumagali Sain (1912-61), Poet — A340

Perf. 13¾ Syncopated
2012, Nov. 12
681 A338 5te multi   .25 .25
682 A339 10te multi   .25 .25
683 A340 20te multi   .40 .40
    Nos. 681-683 (3)   .90 .90

Kulyash Baiseitova (1912-57), Opera Singer — A341

Denominations: 2te, 50te, A.

Perf. 13¾ Syncopated
2012, Nov. 12
684-686 A341   Set of 3   2.25 2.25
No. 686 sold for 60te on day of issue.

Coat of Arms and Flag of Kazakhstan, 20th Anniv. — A342

2012, Nov. 20   *Perf. 14¼x14*
687 A342 190te multi   3.00 3.00

Union of Designers, 25th Anniv. — A343

2012, Nov. 22
688 A343 80te multi   1.60 1.60

Diplomatic Relations Between Kazakhstan and Bulgaria, 20th Anniv. — A344

No. 689: a, Gold buckle depicting bird and deer, 8th-7th cent. B.C. b, Gold rhyton with design of deer's head, 4th cent. B.C.

2012, Dec. 14   *Perf. 14¼x14*
689 A344 250te Horiz. pair, #a-b   7.50 7.50
Printed in sheets containing 4 pairs. See Bulgaria No. 4622.

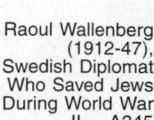

Raoul Wallenberg (1912-47), Swedish Diplomat Who Saved Jews During World War II — A345

2012, Dec. 19   *Perf. 14x14¼*
690 A345 250te multi   4.00 4.00

School, Astana — A346

Lev N. Gumilev University, Astana — A347

Mangylik El Triumphal Arch, Astana — A348

2012, Dec. 20
691 A346 100te multi   1.50 1.50
692 A347 100te multi   1.50 1.50
693 A348 100te multi   1.50 1.50
    Nos. 691-693 (3)   4.50 4.50

Traditional Costumes — A349

Designs: 150te, Man and woman, emblem of Regional Communications Commonwealth. 250te, Man and woman, no emblem.

2013, Jan. 23   *Perf. 14¼x14*
694-695 A349   Set of 2   5.75 5.75

Miniature Sheet

2012 Summer Olympics Gold Medalists — A350

No. 696: a, Ilya Ilin, weight lifting (wearing blue and white uniform). b, Serik Sapiyev, boxing. c, Olga Rypakova, triple jump. d, Alexander Vinokourov, cycling. e, Svetlana Podobedova, weight lifting (wearing yellow uniform, with hand over heart). f, Zulfiya Chinshanlo, weight lifting (holding medal around neck, denomination at left). g, Maiya Maneza, weight lifting (holding medal around neck, denomination at right).

2013, Jan. 23
696 A350 150te Sheet of 7,
    #a-g, + label   17.50 17.50

Postman, by Nikolai Khludov — A351

2013, Apr. 25
697 A351 200te multi   2.75 2.75
   a.   Tête bêche pair   6.25 6.25

Miniature Sheet

Lunar Calendar Animals — A352

No. 698: a, Mouse. b, Calf. c, Snow leopard. d, Rabbit. e, Snail. f, Snake. g, Horse. h, Sheep. i, Monkey. j, Chicks. k, Dog. l, Pig.

2013, Apr. 25   *Perf. 14x14¼*
698 A352 100te Sheet of 12,
    #a-l   17.50 17.50

Rocket, Dove, Space Capsule and Parachute A353

Cosmonaut Valentina Tereshkova A354

Perf. 13½x13¾ Syncopated
2013, July 2   Litho.
699 A353 150te multi   2.00 2.00
700 A354 200te multi   3.00 3.00
   a.   Pair, #699-700   6.00 6.00

Space flight of Tereshkova (first woman in space), 50th anniv. Nos. 699-700 each were printed in sheets of 6. No. 700a is from sheet containing three each of Nos. 699-700.

Souvenir Sheets

Pres. Nursultan Nazarbayev, Map of Kazakhstan — A355

Perf. 13½x13¾ Syncopated
2013, July 2   Litho.
701 A355 250te multi   4.00 4.00
Litho. With Foil Application
Perf. 14
Granite Paper
702 A355 900te multi   13.00 13.00

Establishment of diplomatic relations with various countries, 20th anniv. No. 701 contains one 55x33mm stamp. No. 702 contains one 50x30mm stamp.

Miniature Sheets

A356

Renaming of Akmola to Astana, 15th
Anniv. — A357

No. 703: a, Presidential Palace. b, Palace of
Independence and fountain. c, Bayterek
Tower. d, Kazakh Eli Monument. No. 704: a,
Pres. Nursultan Nazarbayev. b, Emblem of
Astana with "1998." c, New cost of arms. d,
Emblem of Expo 2017.

Perf. 13¾x13½ Syncopated
2013, July 4   **Litho.**
703 A356 100te Sheet of 4, #a-d   6.50 6.50
704 A357 100te Sheet of 4, #a-d   6.50 6.50

Miniature Sheet

Navruz Bayram — A358

No. 705: a, Coat of arms of Kazakhstan. b,
Pres. Nursultan Nazarbayev waving at Navruz
celebrations. c, Pres. Nazarbayev playing
stringed instrument at Navruz celebrations. d,
Emblem of Congress of Leaders of World and
Traditional Religions, Astana.

Perf. 13¾x13½ Syncopated
2013, July 5   **Litho.**
705 A358 150te Sheet of 4,
         #a-d   8.00 8.00

Miniature Sheet

Victory Day — A359

No. 706: a, Pres. Nursultan Nazarbayev with
hand over heart, floral bouquet. b, Flowers,
Pres. Nazarbayev folding Kazakhstan flag. c,
Eternal flame, flowers, parade. d, Pres.
Nazarbayev shaking hands with veteran.

Perf. 13½ Syncopated
2013, July 5   **Litho.**
706 A359 90te Sheet of 4, #a-d,
         + 2 labels   5.75 5.75

Souvenir Sheet

Olympic Champions — A360

No. 707 — Kazakhstan flag and: a, Bakh-
tiyar Artayev, boxing, 2004 (denomination at
UR). b, Alexander Parygin, pentathlon, 1996
(denomination at UL, Parygin not touching
medal). c, Bakhyt Sarsekbayev, boxing, 2008
(denomination at UL, Sarsekbayev touching
medal).

Perf. 13½x13¾ Syncopated
2013, July 16   **Litho.**
707 A360 150te Sheet of 3, #a-c,
         + label   7.00 7.00

Souvenir Sheet

Kazakhstan's Participation in 2010 and
2012 Nuclear Security
Summits — A361

No. 708: a, Pres. Nursultan Nazarbayev at
lectern at 2010 summit. b, U.S. Pres. Barack
Obama, Pres. Nazarbayev, and Russian Pres.
Dmitry Medvedev at 2012 summit.

Perf. 13¾x13½ Syncopated
2013, Aug. 28   **Litho.**
708 A361 150te Sheet of 2, #a-b   6.00 6.00

Miniature Sheet

Flowers — A362

No. 709: a, 60te, Tulipa behmiana. b, 60te,
Tulipa ostrowskiana. c, 100te, Papaver tian-
schanicum. d, 100te, Papaver pavoninum.

Perf. 13¼x13¾ Syncopated
2013, Oct. 4   **Litho.**
709 A362 Sheet of 4, #a-d   6.50 6.50

Souvenir Sheet

Kazakhstan Postal Service, 20th
Anniv. — A363

Perf. 13½x13¾ Syncopated
2013, Oct. 9   **Litho.**
710 A363 200te multi   4.00 4.00

Miniature Sheet

Kazakhstan Coins — A364

No. 711: a, Obverse of 100,000-tenge gold
coin. b, Reverse of 100,000-tenge gold coin of
2013. c, Obverse of 500-tenge silver coin. d,
Reverse of 500-tenge silver coin of 2013.

Perf. 13¾x13¼ Syncopated
2013, Nov. 29   **Litho.**
711 A364 60te Sheet of 4, #a-d   4.75 4.75
   Introduction of tenge currency, 20th anniv.

Miniature Sheet

Birds — A365

No. 712: a, Chettusia gregaria. b, Tetrax
tetrax. c, Aquila nipalensis. d, Numenius
arquata. e, Oxyura leucocephala. f, Mela-
nocorypha yeltoniensis.

Perf. 13½x14 Syncopated
2013, Dec. 25   **Litho.**
712 A365 150te Sheet of 6,
         #a-f   18.00 18.00

Souvenir Sheet

Wildlife of the Ustyurt Game
Reserve — A366

No. 713: a, 60te, Acinonyx jubatus. b, 150e,
Saga pedo. c, 190te, Circaetus gallicus.

Perf. 13½x14 Syncopated
2013, Dec. 25   **Litho.**
713 A366   Sheet of 3, #a-c   8.00 8.00

Mukan
Tolebayev
(1913-60),
Composer
A367

Amre
Kashaubayev
(1888-
1938),
Singer
A368

Valentina
Tereshkova,
First
Woman in
Space
A369

Saiga
A370

Perf. 13½x14½ Syncopated
2013, Dec. 27   **Litho.**
714 A367   1te pale yel & blk   .25   .25
715 A368   3te lt grn & blk   .25   .25
716 A369   5te lt bl & blk   .25   .25
Perf. 14½x13½ Syncopated
717 A370 10te yel & blk   .25   .25
   Nos. 714-717 (4)   1.00 1.00
Tereshkova's space flight, 50th anniv. (No.
716).

Souvenir Sheet

Yurt Furnishings — A371

No. 718: a, Pillows and blankets on chest,
edge of table. b, Trunks and chests, table with
bowls and tureen. c, Curtains above bed with
pillows.

Perf. 13½ Syncopated
2014, Jan. 15   **Litho.**
718 A371 200te Sheet of 3,
         #a-c   12.00 12.00

Souvenir Sheet

Communications History — A372

Perf. 13½x13¾ Syncopated

2014, Jan. 15   Litho.
719 A372 200te multi   4.00 4.00

SEMI-POSTAL STAMP

Cartoons
SP1

a, Mother and child. b, Cow, rabbit. c, Horses.

1994, Nov. 3   Litho.   **Perf. 12½x12**
B1 SP1 1te +30ti Block of 3 +
       label   .75   .75

KENYA

'ke-nyə

LOCATION — East Africa, bordering on the Indian Ocean
GOVT. — Republic
AREA — 224,960 sq. mi.
POP. — 28,808,658 (1999 est.)
CAPITAL — Nairobi

Formerly a part of the British colony of Kenya, Uganda, Tanganyika, Kenya gained independence Dec. 12, 1963.

100 Cents = 1 Shilling

Catalogue values for all unused stamps in this country are for Never Hinged items.

Treetop Hotel and Elephants — A1

Designs: 5c, Cattle ranching. 10c, Wood carving. 15c, Riveter. 20c, Timber industry. 30c, Jomo Kenyatta facing Mt. Kenya. 40c, Fishing industry. 50c, Flag and emblem. 65c, Pyrethrum industry (daisies). 1sh, National Assembly bldg. 2sh, Harvesting coffee. 5sh, Harvesting tea. 10sh, Mombasa port. 20sh, Royal College, Nairobi.

Perf. 14x14½

1963, Dec. 12   Photo.   Unwmk.
Size: 21x17½mm
1   A1 5c bl, buff & dk brn   .25   .60
2   A1 10c brown   .25   .25
a.   Booklet pane of 4   .30
3   A1 15c deep magenta   1.00   .25
a.   Booklet pane of 4   4.00
4   A1 20c yel grn & dk brn   .25   .25
a.   Booklet pane of 4   .40
5   A1 30c yel & black   .25   .25
a.   Booklet pane of 4   .55

6   A1 40c blue & brown   .25   .45
7   A1 50c grn, blk & dp car .60   .25
a.   Booklet pane of 4   2.50
8   A1 65c steel blue & yel   .55   .70
Perf. 14½
Size: 41½x25½mm
9   A1 1sh multicolored   .25   .25
10 A1 1.30sh grn, brn & blk 5.00   .30
11 A1 2sh multicolored   1.25   .40
12 A1 5sh ultra, yel grn &
         brn   1.25 1.00
13 A1 10sh brn & dark brn   8.75 3.00
14 A1 20sh pink & grnsh blk 4.50 8.50
      Nos. 1-14 (14)   24.40 16.45

President Jomo Kenyatta and Flag of Kenya — A2

Flag and: 15c, Cockerel. 50c, African lion. 1.30sh, Hartlaub's touraco. 2.50sh, Nandi flame flower.

1964, Dec. 12   Photo.   **Perf. 13x12½**
15 A2 15c lt violet & multi .25   .25
16 A2 30c dk blue & multi   .25   .25
17 A2 50c dk brown & multi   .25   .25
18 A2 1.30sh multicolored   2.75   .50
19 A2 2.50sh multicolored   .85 3.75
      Nos. 15-19 (5)   4.35 5.00

Establishment of the Republic of Kenya, Dec. 12, 1964.

Greater Kudu A3

Animals: 5c, Thomson's gazelle. 10c, Sable antelope. 15c, Aardvark. 20c, Senegal bush baby. 30c, Warthog. 40c, Zebra. 50c, Buffalo. 65c, Black rhinoceros. 70c, Ostrich. 1.30sh, Elephant. 1.50sh, Bat-eared fox. 2.50sh, Cheetah. 5sh, Vervet monkey. 10sh, Giant pangolin. 20sh, Lion.

1966-69   Unwmk.   **Perf. 14x14½**
Size: 21x17mm
20 A3 5c gray, black &
         org   .30   .25
21 A3 10c blk & yel grn   .25   .25
22 A3 15c dp org & blk   .25   .25
23 A3 20c ultra, lt brn &
         blk   .25   .25
24 A3 30c lt ultra & blk   .25   .25
25 A3 40c ocher & blk   .60   .25
26 A3 50c dp orange & blk   .60   .25
27 A3 65c dp yel grn & blk 1.25 2.00
28 A3 70c rose lake &
         black   4.75 1.75
Perf. 14½
Size: 41x25mm
29 A3 1sh gray bl, ol &
         blk   1.00   .25
30 A3 1.30sh yel grn & blk 4.00   .35
31 A3 1.50sh brn org, brn &
         black   3.25 3.00
32 A3 2.50sh ol bis, yel &
         blk   4.00 1.25
33 A3 5sh brt grn, ultra &
         black   1.00   .75
34 A3 10sh red brn, bis &
         black   2.75 3.00
35 A3 20sh ocher, bis,
         gold & black   8.00 12.00
      Nos. 20-35 (16)   32.50 26.10
Issued: No. 28, 31, 9/15/69; others, 12/12/66.

Branched Murex — A4

Sea shells: 5c, Morning pink. 10c, Episcopal miter. 15c, Strawberry-top shell. 20c, Hump-back cowrie. 30c, variable abalone. 40c, Flame-top shell. 50c, Violet sailor. 60c, Bull's-mouth helmet. 70c, Pearly nautilus. 1.50sh, Neptune's trumpet. 2.50sh, Mediterranean tulip shell. 5sh, Fluctuating turban. 10sh, Textile cone. 20sh, Scorpion shell.

1971 Dec. 13   Photo.   **Perf. 14½x14**
Size: 17x21mm
36 A4 5c bister & multi   .25   .45
37 A4 10c dull grn & multi   .25   .25
a.   Booklet pane of 4   .60
38 A4 15c tan & multi   .25   .25
a.   Booklet pane of 4   .60
39 A4 20c tan & multi   .25   .25
a.   Booklet pane of 4   .75
40 A4 30c yellow & multi   .25   .25
a.   Booklet pane of 4   2.25
41 A4 40c gray & multi   .25   .25
a.   Booklet pane of 4   2.25
42 A4 50c buff & multi   .40   .30
         (Janthina globosa)
a.   Booklet pane of 4   3.50
43 A4 60c lilac & multi   .35 1.75
         (Nautilus
         pompileus)
44 A4 70c gray grn & multi
         (Nautilus
         pompileus)   .50 1.50
a.   Booklet pane of 4   5.00
Perf. 14½
Size: 25x41mm
45 A4 1sh ocher & multi   .40   .35
46 A4 1.50sh pale grn & multi 1.00 .30
47 A4 2.50sh vio gray & multi 1.50 .30
48 A4 5sh lemon & multi   1.75   .25
49 A4 10sh multicolored   2.00   .25
50 A4 20sh gray & multi   3.00   .25
      Nos. 36-50 (15)   12.40 6.95

Used values of Nos. 48-50 are for stamps with printed cancellations.
For surcharges see Nos. 53-55.

Nos. 42, 44 with Revised Inscription
1974, Jan. 20   **Perf. 14½x14**
51 A4 50c (Janthina janthina) 16.00 3.50
52 A4 70c (Nautilus pompili-
         us)   12.00 6.50

Nos. 46-47, 50 Surcharged with New Value and 2 Bars
1975, Nov. 17   Photo.   **Perf. 14½**
53 A4 2sh on 1.50sh multi   7.00 7.00
54 A4 3sh on 2.50sh multi   12.00 23.00
55 A4 40sh on 20sh multi   7.00 16.00
      Nos. 53-55 (3)   26.00 45.00

Microwave Tower — A5

Designs: 1sh, Cordless switchboard and operators, horiz. 2sh, Telephones of 1880, 1930 and 1976. 3sh, Message switching center, horiz.

1976, Apr. 15   Litho.   **Perf. 14½**
56 A5 50c blue & multi   .25   .25
57 A5 1sh red & multi   .25   .25
58 A5 2sh yellow & multi   .25   .35
59 A5 3sh multicolored   .45   .45
a.   Souvenir sheet of 4   2.50 2.50
      Nos. 56-59 (4)   1.20 1.30

Telecommunication development in East Africa. No. 59a contains 4 stamps similar to Nos. 56-59 with simulated perforations.

Akii Bua, Ugandan Hurdler — A6

Designs: 1sh, Filbert Bayi, Tanzanian runner. 2sh, Steve Muchoki, Kenyan boxer. 3sh, Olympic torch, flags of Kenya, Tanzania and Uganda.

1976, July 5   Litho.   **Perf. 14½**
60 A6 50c blue & multi   .25   .25
61 A6 1sh red & multi   .25   .25
62 A6 2sh yellow & multi   .50   .40

63 A6 3sh blue & multi   1.00   .75
a.   Souv. sheet of 4, #60-63, perf. 13 8.00 8.00
      Nos. 60-63 (4)   2.00 1.65
21st Olympic Games, Montreal, Canada, July 17-Aug. 1.

Tanzania-Zambia Railway — A7

Designs: 1sh, Nile Bridge, Uganda. 2sh, Nakuru Station, Kenya. 3sh, Class A locomotive, 1896.

1976, Oct. 4   Litho.   **Perf. 14½**
64 A7 50c lilac & multi   .50   .25
65 A7 1sh emerald & multi   .60   .25
66 A7 2sh brt rose & multi 1.75 1.00
67 A7 3sh yellow & multi   1.90 1.75
a.   Souv. sheet of 4, #64-67, perf.
       13   10.00 10.00
      Nos. 64-67 (4)   4.75 3.25
Rail transport in East Africa.

Nile Perch — A8

Game Fish: 1sh, Tilapia. 3sh, Sailfish. 5sh, Black marlin.

1977, Jan. 10   Litho.   **Perf. 14½**
68 A8 50c multicolored   .25   .25
69 A8 1sh multicolored   .55   .25
70 A8 3sh multicolored   1.50   .75
71 A8 5sh multicolored   1.50 1.00
a.   Souvenir sheet of 4, #68-71 12.00 12.00
      Nos. 68-71 (4)   3.80 2.25

Festival Emblem and Masai Tribesmen Bleeding Cow — A9

Festival Emblem and: 1sh, Dancers from Uganda. 2sh, Makonde sculpture, Tanzania. 3sh, Tribesmen skinning hippopotamus.

1977, Jan. 15   **Perf. 13½x14**
72 A9 50c multicolored   .25   .25
73 A9 1sh multicolored   .40   .25
74 A9 2sh multicolored   1.25 1.25
75 A9 3sh multicolored   1.50 1.50
a.   Souvenir sheet of 4, #72-75 6.50 6.50
      Nos. 72-75 (4)   3.40 3.25

2nd World Black and African Festival, Lagos, Nigeria, Jan. 15-Feb. 12.

Automobile Passing through Village — A10

Safari Rally Emblem and: 1sh, Winner at finish line. 2sh, Car going through washout. 5sh, Car, elephants and Mt. Kenya.

1977, Apr. 5   Litho.   **Perf. 14**
76 A10 50c multicolored   .25   .25
77 A10 1sh multicolored   .40   .25
78 A10 2sh multicolored   .75   .75

79	A10 5sh multicolored	2.25	2.25
a.	Souvenir sheet of 4, #76-79	5.50	5.50
	Nos. 76-79 (4)	3.65	3.50

25th Safari Rally, Apr. 7-11.

Rev. Canon Apolo Kivebulaya — A11

1sh, Uganda Cathedral. 2sh, Early grass-topped Cathedral. 5sh, Early tent congregation, Kigezi.

1977, June 20   Litho.   Perf. 14

80	A11 50c multicolored	.25	.25
81	A11 1sh multicolored	.25	.25
82	A11 2sh multicolored	.40	.40
83	A11 5sh multicolored	1.75	1.75
a.	Souvenir sheet of 4, #80-83	3.25	3.25
	Nos. 80-83 (4)	2.65	2.65

Church of Uganda, centenary.

Elizabeth II and Prince Philip at Sagana Lodge — A12

Designs: 5sh, "Treetops" observation hut, Aberdare Forest, and elephants, vert. 10sh, Pres. Jomo Kenyatta, Elizabeth II, crossed spears and shield. 15sh, Elizabeth II and Pres. Kenyatta in open automobile. 50sh, Elizabeth II and Prince Philip at window in Treetops.

1977, July 20   Litho.   Perf. 14

84	A12 2sh multicolored	.25	.25
85	A12 5sh multicolored	.25	.25
86	A12 10sh multicolored	.60	.60
87	A12 15sh multicolored	.75	.75
a.	Souvenir sheet of 1	1.50	1.50
	Nos. 84-87 (4)	1.85	1.85

Souvenir Sheet

88	A12 50sh multicolored	4.50	4.50

Reign of Queen Elizabeth II, 25th anniv.

Pancake Tortoise — A13

Wildlife Fund Emblem and; 1sh, Nile crocodile. 2sh, Hunter's hartebeest. 3sh, Red colobus monkey. 5sh, Dugong.

1977, Sept. 26   Litho.   Perf. 14x13½

89	A13 50c multicolored	.55	.25
90	A13 1sh multicolored	.75	.30
91	A13 2sh multicolored	2.50	1.50
92	A13 3sh multicolored	3.00	2.50
93	A13 5sh multicolored	3.50	3.50
a.	Souvenir sheet of 4, #90-93	10.00	10.00
	Nos. 89-93 (5)	10.30	8.05

Endangered species.

Kenya-Ethiopia Border Point — A14

Designs: 1sh, Station wagon at Archer's Post. 2sh, Thika overpass. 5sh, Marsabit Game Lodge and elephant.

1977, Nov. 10   Litho.   Perf. 14

94	A14 50c multicolored	.25	.25
95	A14 1sh multicolored	.25	.25
96	A14 2sh multicolored	.40	.40

97	A14 5sh multicolored	.80	.80
a.	Souvenir sheet of 4, #94-97	3.75	3.75
	Nos. 94-97 (4)	1.70	1.70

Opening of Nairobi-Addis Ababa highway.

Minerals Found in Kenya — A15

A16

Perf. 14½x14, 14½ (A16)

1977, Dec. 13   Photo.

98	A15 10c Gypsum	1.60	.25
99	A15 20c Trona	2.40	.25
100	A15 30c Kyanite	2.40	.25
101	A15 40c Amazonite	1.90	.25
102	A15 50c Galena	1.90	.25
103	A15 70c Silicified wood	8.00	1.00
104	A15 80c Fluorite	8.00	1.00
105	A16 1sh Amethyst	1.90	.25
106	A16 1.50sh Agate	1.90	.40
107	A16 2sh Tourmaline	1.90	.45
108	A16 3sh Aquamarine	2.40	.95
109	A16 5sh Rhodolite garnet	2.40	1.50
110	A16 10sh Sapphire	2.40	2.50
111	A16 20sh Ruby	5.00	5.25
112	A16 40sh Green grossular garnet	20.00	24.00
	Nos. 98-112 (15)	64.10	38.55

The 10c, 20c, 40c, 50c and 80c were also issued in booklet panes of 4. The 50c was also issued in a booklet pane of 2.
For surcharge see No. 242.

Soccer, Joe Kadenge and World Cup — A17

World Cup and: 1sh, Mohammed Chuma receiving trophy, and his portrait. 2sh, Shot on goal and Omari S. Kidevu. 3sh, Backfield defense and Polly Ouma.

1978, Apr. 10   Litho.   Perf. 14x13½

113	A17 50c green & multi	.25	.25
114	A17 1sh lt brown & multi	.25	.25
115	A17 2sh lilac & multi	.40	.40
116	A17 3sh dk blue & multi	.75	.75
a.	Souvenir sheet of 4, #113-116	5.00	5.00
	Nos. 113-116 (4)	1.65	1.65

World Soccer Cup Championships, Argentina 78, June 1-25.

Boxing and Games' Emblem A18

Games Emblem and: 1sh, Pres. Kenyatta welcoming 1968 Olympic team. 3sh, Javelin. 5sh, Pres. Kenyatta, boxing team and trophy.

1978, July 15   Photo.   Perf. 13x14

117	A18 50c multicolored	.25	.25
118	A18 1sh multicolored	.25	.25
119	A18 3sh multicolored	.70	.70
120	A18 5sh multicolored	.85	.85
	Nos. 117-120 (4)	2.05	2.05

Commonwealth Games, Edmonton, Canada, Aug. 3-12.

Overloaded Truck — A19

Road Safety: 1sh, Observe speed limit. 1.50sh, Observe traffic lights. 2sh, School crossing. 3sh, Passing. 5sh, Railroad crossing.

1978, Sept. 18   Litho.   Perf. 13½x14

121	A19 50c multicolored	.65	.25
122	A19 1sh multicolored	.90	.45
123	A19 1.50sh multicolored	1.10	.90
124	A19 2sh multicolored	1.60	1.00
125	A19 3sh multicolored	1.90	1.90
126	A19 5sh multicolored	2.75	3.00
	Nos. 121-126 (6)	8.90	7.50

Pres. Kenyatta at Harambee Water Project Opening — A20

Kenyatta Day: 1sh, Prince Philip handing over symbol of independence, 1963. 2sh, Pres. Jomo Kenyatta addressing independence rally. 3sh, Stage at 15th independence anniversary celebration. 5sh, Handcuffed Kenyatta led by soldiers, 1952.

1978, Oct. 16   Litho.   Perf. 14

127	A20 50c multicolored	.35	.35
128	A20 1sh multicolored	.35	.35
129	A20 2sh multicolored	.45	.45
130	A20 3sh multicolored	1.00	1.00
131	A20 5sh multicolored	1.30	1.30
	Nos. 127-131 (5)	3.45	3.45

Soldiers and Emblem A21

Anti-Apartheid Emblem and: 1sh, Anti-Apartheid Conference. 2sh, Stephen Biko, South African Anti-Apartheid leader. 3sh, Nelson Mandela, jailed since 1961. 5sh, Bishop Lamont, expelled from Rhodesia in 1977.

1978, Dec. 11   Litho.   Perf. 14x14½

132	A21 50c multicolored	.30	.30
133	A21 1sh multicolored	.30	.30
134	A21 2sh multicolored	.45	.45
135	A21 3sh multicolored	.70	.70
136	A21 5sh multicolored	.90	.90
	Nos. 132-136 (5)	2.65	2.65

Anti-Apartheid Year and Namibia's struggle for independence.

Children on School Playground — A22

Children's Year Emblem and: 2sh, Boy catching fish. 3sh, Children dancing and singing. 5sh, Children and camel caravan.

1979, Feb. 5   Litho.   Perf. 14

137	A22 50c multicolored	.35	.35
138	A22 2sh multicolored	.75	.75
139	A22 3sh multicolored	.80	.80
140	A22 5sh multicolored	1.50	1.50
	Nos. 137-140 (4)	3.40	3.40

International Year of the Child.

"The Lion and the Jewel" A23

National Theater: 1sh, Dancers and drummers. 2sh, Programs of various productions. 3sh, View of National Theater. 5sh, "Genesis," performed by Nairobi City Players.

1979, Apr. 6   Litho.   Perf. 13½x14

141	A23 50c multicolored	.25	.25
142	A23 1sh multicolored	.40	.40
143	A23 2sh multicolored	.60	.60
144	A23 3sh multicolored	.90	.90
145	A23 5sh multicolored	1.50	1.50
	Nos. 141-145 (5)	3.65	3.65

Village Workshop — A24

Salvation Army Emblem and: 50c, Blind telephone operator, vert. 1sh, Care for the aged, vert. 5sh, Vocational training (nurse).

1979, June 4   Perf. 13½x13, 13x13½

146	A24 50c multicolored	.30	.30
147	A24 1sh multicolored	.50	.50
148	A24 3sh multicolored	1.25	1.25
149	A24 5sh multicolored	2.50	2.50
	Nos. 146-149 (4)	4.55	4.55

Salvation Army Social Services, 50th anniv.

Funeral Procession — A25

Kenyatta: 1sh, Taking oath of office. 3sh, Addressing crowd. 5sh, As young man with wooden trying plane.

1979, Aug. 22   Litho.   Perf. 13½x14

150	A25 50c multicolored	.25	.25
151	A25 1sh multicolored	.35	.35
152	A25 3sh multicolored	.60	.60
153	A25 5sh multicolored	1.00	1.00
	Nos. 150-153 (4)	2.20	2.20

Jomo Kenyatta (1893-1978), first president of Kenya.

British East Africa No. 2, Hill, Signature — A26

Hill, Signature and: 1sh, Kenya, Uganda and Tanzania #54. 2sh, Penny Black. 5sh, Kenya #10.

1979, Nov. 27   Litho.   Perf. 14

154	A26 50c multicolored	.25	.25
155	A26 1sh multicolored	.25	.25
156	A26 3sh multicolored	.35	.35
157	A26 5sh multicolored	.75	.75
	Nos. 154-157 (4)	1.60	1.60

Sir Rowland Hill (1795-1879), originator of penny postage.

Highways, Globe, Conference
Emblem — A27

Conference Emblem and: 1sh, Truck at Athi
River, New Weighbridge. 3sh, New Nyali
Bridge, Mombasa. 5sh, Jomo Kenyatta Airport
Highway.

1980, Jan. 10   Litho.   Perf. 14
158 A27 50c multicolored   .25   .25
159 A27 1sh multicolored   .25   .25
160 A27 3sh multicolored   .60   .60
161 A27 5sh multicolored   1.00 1.00
    Nos. 158-161 (4)   2.10 2.10

4th IRF African Highway Conference, Nairobi, Jan. 20-25.

Patient
Airlift
A28

1980, Mar. 20   Litho.   Perf. 14½
162 A28 50c Outdoor clinic   .25   .25
163 A28 1sh Mule transport of
         patient, vert.   .40   .35
164 A28 3sh Surgery, vert.   .85   .85
165 A28 5sh shown   1.25 1.25
  a.   Souvenir sheet of 4, #162-165   3.25 3.25
    Nos. 162-165 (4)   2.75 2.70

Flying doctor service.

Hill Statue,
Kidderminster and
Mt. Kenya — A29

1980, May 6   Litho.   Perf. 14
166 A29 25sh multicolored   1.40 1.40
  a.   Souvenir sheet   2.10 2.10

London 1980 International Stamp Exhibition, May 6-14.

Pope
John
Paul II
and
Crowd
A30

Visit of Pope John Paul II to Kenya: 1sh,
Pope, Nairobi Cathedral, papal flag and arms,
vert. 5sh, Pope, papal and Kenya flags, dove,
vert. 10sh, Pres. arap Moi of Kenya, Pope, flag
of Kenya on map of Africa.

1980, May 8   Perf. 13½
167 A30 50c multicolored   .35   .25
168 A30 1sh multicolored   .55   .35
169 A30 5sh multicolored   1.40 1.40
170 A30 10sh multicolored   3.00 3.00
    Nos. 167-170 (4)   5.30 5.00

Sting Ray — A31

1980, June 27   Litho.   Perf. 14½
171 A31 50c shown   .65   .65
172 A31 2sh Alkit snapper   1.40   .90
173 A31 3sh Sea slug   2.00 2.00
174 A31 5sh Hawksbill turtle   2.40 2.40
    Nos. 171-174 (4)   6.45 5.95

National
Archives,
1904
A32

1sh, Commissioner's Office, Nairobi, 1913.
1.50sh, Nairobi House, 1913. 2sh, Norfolk
Hotel, 1904. 3sh, McMillan Library, 1929. 5sh,
Kipande House, 1913.

1980, Oct. 9   Litho.   Perf. 14
175 A32 50c shown   .25   .25
176 A32 1sh multicolored   .25   .25
177 A32 1.50sh multicolored   .30   .30
178 A32 2sh multicolored   .45   .45
179 A32 3sh multicolored   .60   .60
180 A32 5sh multicolored   .90   .90
    Nos. 175-180 (6)   2.75 2.75

Woman in Wheelchair and
Child — A33

1sh, Pres. arap Moi, team captain. 3sh,
Blind mountain climbers, Mt. Kenya, 1965.
5sh, Disabled artist.

1981, Feb. 10   Litho.   Perf. 14x13½
181 A33 50c shown   .25   .25
182 A33 1sh multicolored   .25   .25
183 A33 3sh multicolored   .85   .85
184 A33 5sh multicolored   1.40 1.40
    Nos. 181-184 (4)   2.75 2.75

International Year of the Disabled.

Longonot Earth Station
Complex — A34

1981, Apr. 4   Litho.   Perf. 14x14½
185 A34 50c shown   .30   .30
186 A34 2sh Intelsat V   .50   .50
187 A34 3sh Longonot I   .70   .70
188 A34 5sh Longonot II   .90   .90
    Nos. 185-188 (4)   2.40 2.40

Conference Center, OAU Flag — A35

18th Organization for African Unity Conference, Nairobi: 1sh, Map of Africa showing
Panaftel earth stations. 3sh, Parliament Building, Nairobi. 5sh, Jomo Kenyatta Intl. Airport.
10sh, OAU flag.

1981, June 24   Wmk. 373   Perf. 13½
189 A35 50c multicolored   .25   .25
190 A35 1sh multicolored   .25   .25
191 A35 3sh multicolored   .60   .60
192 A35 5sh multicolored   .75   .75
193 A35 10sh multicolored   1.75 1.75
  a.   Souvenir sheet of 1, perf. 14½   2.25 2.25
    Nos. 189-193 (5)   3.60 3.60

St. Paul's
Cathedral — A36

1981, July 29   Litho.   Perf. 14, 12
194 A36 50c Charles, Pres.
         arap Moi   .25   .25
195 A36 3sh shown   .25   .25
196 A36 5sh Britannia   .25   .30
197 A36 10sh Charles   .25   .60
    Nos. 194-197 (4)   1.00 1.40

Souvenir Sheet
198 A36 25sh Couple   1.50 1.50

Royal Wedding.

Reticulated
Giraffe — A37

1981, Aug. 31   Litho.   Perf. 14½
199 A37 50c shown   .40   .40
200 A37 2sh Bongo   .70   .70
201 A37 5sh Roan antelope   1.60 1.60
202 A37 10sh Mangabey   3.25 3.25
    Nos. 199-202 (4)   5.95 5.95

World Food
Day — A38

1981, Oct. 16   Litho.   Perf. 14
203 A38 50c Plowing   .25   .25
204 A38 1sh Rice field   .25   .25
205 A38 2sh Irrigation   .45   .45
206 A38 5sh Cattle   1.10 1.10
    Nos. 203-206 (4)   2.05 2.05

Ceremonial
Tribal Costumes
A39

Perf. 14½x13½
1981, Dec. 18   Litho.
207 A39 50c Kamba   .55   .25
208 A39 1sh Turkana   .65   .55
209 A39 2sh Giriama   1.50 1.10
210 A39 3sh Masai   2.00 2.00
211 A39 5sh Luo   3.00 4.00
    Nos. 207-211 (5)   7.70 7.90

Australopithecus Boisei — A40

1982, Jan. 16   Litho.   Perf. 14
212 A40 50c shown   2.00 1.00
213 A40 2sh Homo erectus   4.00 2.10
214 A40 3sh Homo habilis   4.00 3.75
215 A40 5sh Proconsul afri-
         canus   4.75 4.75
    Nos. 212-215 (4)   14.75 11.60

Scouting
Year
A41

No. 216, Tree planting. No. 217, Paying
homage. No. 218, Be Prepared. No. 219, Intl.
friendship. No. 220, Helping disabled. No.
221, Community service. No. 222, Paxtu Cottage. No. 223, Lady Baden-Powell.

1982, June 2   Litho.   Perf. 14½
216 A41 70c multicolored   .50   .50
217 A41 70c multicolored   .50   .50
  a.   Pair, #216-217   1.25 1.25
218 A41 3.50sh multicolored   1.25 1.25
219 A41 3.50sh multicolored   1.25 1.25
  a.   Pair, #218-219   3.00 3.00
220 A41 5sh multicolored   1.60 1.60
221 A41 5sh multicolored   1.60 1.60
  a.   Pair, #220-221   4.50 4.50
222 A41 6.50sh multicolored   2.25 2.25
223 A41 6.50sh multicolored   2.25 2.25
  a.   Pair, #222-223   6.25 6.25
    Nos. 216-223 (8)   11.20 11.20

Souvenir Sheet
224   Sheet of 4   6.50 6.50
  a.   A41 70c like #216   .25   .25
  b.   A41 3.50sh like #218   1.25   .45
  c.   A41 5sh like #220   1.90   .70
  d.   A41 6.50sh like #222   2.25   .85

1982 World Cup — A42

Various soccer players on world map.

1982, July 5   Litho.   Perf. 12½
225 A42 70c multicolored   1.50   .50
226 A42 3.50sh multicolored   3.25 2.50
227 A42 5sh multicolored   4.50 4.25
228 A42 10sh multicolored   6.50 6.50
    Nos. 225-228 (4)   15.75 13.75

Souvenir Sheet
Perf. 13½x14
229 A42 20sh multicolored   8.25 8.25

A43

1982, Sept. 28   Litho.   Perf. 14½
230 A43 70c Cattle judging   1.00 1.00
231 A43 2.50sh Farm machinery   1.75 1.40
232 A43 3.50sh Musical ride   2.25 2.25
233 A43 6.50sh Emblem   3.25 3.25
    Nos. 230-233 (4)   8.25 7.40

Agricultural Society, 80th anniv.

A44

70c, Microwave radio system. 3.50sh, Ship-to-shore communication. 5sh, Rural telecommunication. 6.50sh, Emblem.

1982, Oct. 27   Photo.   Perf. 11½
Granite Paper

234	A44	70c multicolored	.25	.25
235	A44	3.50sh multicolored	2.00	1.75
236	A44	5sh multicolored	2.75	2.50
237	A44	6.50sh multicolored	4.00	3.75
		Nos. 234-237 (4)	9.00	8.25

ITU Plenipoteniaries Conf., Nairobi, Sept.

5th Anniv. of Kenya Ports Authority
A45

70c, Container cranes. 2sh, Cranes, diff. 3.50sh, Cranes, diff. 5sh, Mombasa Harbor map.

1983, Jan. 20   Litho.   Perf. 14

238	A45	70c multicolored	.90	.90
239	A45	2sh multicolored	1.60	1.60
240	A45	3.50sh multicolored	2.75	2.75
241	A45	5sh multicolored	4.25	4.25
a.		Souvenir sheet of 4, #238-241	10.00	10.00
		Nos. 238-241 (4)	9.50	9.50

No. 104 Surcharged

1983, Jan.   Photo.   Perf. 14½x14

242	A15	70c on 80c multicolored	2.00 2.00

A45a

70c, Coffee picking, vert. 2sh, Pres. arap Moi, vert. 5sh, Globe. 10sh, Masai dance.

1983, Mar. 14   Litho.   Perf. 14½

243	A45a	70c multicolored	.25	.25
244	A45a	2sh multicolored	.30	.25
245	A45a	5sh multicolored	.50	.50
246	A45a	10sh multicolored	1.00	1.00
		Nos. 243-246 (4)	2.05	2.00

Commonwealth Day.

Dichrostachys Cinerea
A46

Dombeya Burgessiae
A47

20c, Rhamphicarpa montana. 30c, Barleria eranthemoides. 40c, Commelina. 50c, Canarina abyssinica. 70c, Aspilia mossambicensis. 1sh, Dombeya burgessiae. 1.50sh, Lantana trifolia. 2sh, Adenium obesum. 2.50sh, Terminalia orbicularis. 3.50sh, Ceropegia ballyana. 5sh, Ruttya fruticosa. 10sh, Pentanisia ouranogyne. 20sh, Brillantaisia nyanzarum. 40sh, Crotalaria axillaris.

Perf. 14½x14, 14x14½
1983, Feb. 15   Photo.

247	A46	10c shown	.45	.25
248	A46	20c multicolored	.65	.25
249	A46	30c multicolored	.65	.25
250	A46	40c multicolored	.65	.25
251	A46	50c multicolored	.65	.25
252	A46	70c multicolored	.70	.25
253	A47	1sh multicolored	.75	.25
254	A47	1.50sh multicolored	2.25	.60
255	A47	2sh multicolored	2.50	.85
256	A47	2.50sh multicolored	3.00	1.00
257	A47	3.50sh multicolored	2.75	1.50
258	A47	5sh multicolored	2.75	1.90
259	A47	10sh multicolored	3.00	5.25
260	A47	20sh multicolored	3.50	6.25
261	A47	40sh multicolored	5.75	10.00
		Nos. 247-261 (15)	30.00	29.10

See Nos. 350-354.

30th Anniv. of Customs Cooperation Council — A48

70c, Parcel check. 2.50sh, Headquarters, Mombasa. 3.50sh, Headquarters, Brussels. 10sh, Patrol boat.

1983, May 11   Litho.   Perf. 14½

262	A48	70c multicolored	.35	.25
263	A48	2.50sh multicolored	.80	.35
264	A48	3.50sh multicolored	.90	.60
265	A48	10sh multicolored	2.75	2.75
		Nos. 262-265 (4)	4.80	3.95

World Communications Year — A49

70c, Satellite, dish antenna, vert. 2.50sh, Mailbox, birthday card, telephone, vert. 3.50sh, Jet, ship. 5sh, Railroad bridge, highway.

1983, July 4   Litho.   Perf. 14½

266	A49	70c multicolored	.70	.25
267	A49	2.50sh multicolored	1.90	1.40
268	A49	3.50sh multicolored	2.50	2.50
269	A49	5sh multicolored	3.75	3.75
		Nos. 266-269 (4)	8.85	7.90

Intl. Maritime Organization, 25th Anniv. — A50

70c, Kilindini Harbor. 2.50sh, Life preserver. 3.50sh, Mombasa Container Terminal. 10sh, Marine Park.

1983, Sept. 22   Litho.   Perf. 14½

270	A50	70c multicolored	1.25	.25
271	A50	2.50sh multicolored	2.25	1.75
272	A50	3.50sh multicolored	3.00	3.00
273	A50	10sh multicolored	4.00	4.00
		Nos. 270-273 (4)	10.50	9.00

29th Commonwealth Parliamentary Conference — A51

2.50sh, Parliament Bldg., vert. 5sh, State Opening, vert.

1983, Oct. 31   Litho.   Perf. 14

274	A51	70c shown	.40	.25
275	A51	2.50sh multicolored	1.40	1.40
276	A51	5sh multicolored	2.50	2.50
a.		Souv. sheet of 3, #274-276 + label	5.00	5.00
		Nos. 274-276 (3)	4.30	4.15

Royal Visit
A52

70c, Flags. 3.50sh, Sagana State Lodge. 5sh, Tree Tops Hotel. 10sh, Elizabeth II and Daniel arap Moi.

1983, Nov. 10   Litho.   Perf. 14

277	A52	70c multicolored	.95	.30
278	A52	3.50sh multicolored	2.60	1.90
279	A52	5sh multicolored	3.00	3.00
280	A52	10sh multicolored	4.50	4.50
		Nos. 277-280 (4)	11.05	9.70

Souvenir Sheet

281	A52	25sh multicolored	6.25	6.25

No. 281 contains Nos. 277-280 without denominations showing simulated perforations.

President Daniel arap Moi, Monument — A53

2sh, Tree planting. 3.50sh, Map, flag, emblem. 5sh, School, milk program. 10sh, People, flag, banner.

1983, Dec. 9   Litho.   Perf. 14½

282	A53	70c shown	.30	.30
283	A53	2sh multicolored	.30	.30
284	A53	3.50sh multicolored	.40	.40
285	A53	5sh multicolored	.70	.70
286	A53	10sh multicolored	1.25	1.25
		Nos. 282-286 (5)	2.95	2.95

Souvenir Sheet
Imperf

287	A53	25sh multicolored	2.75	2.75

Independence, 20th Anniv. No. 287 contains Nos. 282, 284-286 without denominations.

Rare Local Birds — A54

70c, White-backed night heron. 2.50sh, Quail plover. 3.50sh, Heller's ground thrush. 5sh, Papyrus gonolek. 10sh, White-winged Apalis.

1984, Feb. 6   Litho.   Perf. 14½x13½

288	A54	70c multicolored	2.75	2.75
289	A54	2.50sh multicolored	4.00	3.50
290	A54	3.50sh multicolored	5.00	5.00
291	A54	5sh multicolored	5.75	5.75
292	A54	10sh multicolored	7.25	7.25
		Nos. 288-292 (5)	24.75	24.25

Intl. Civil Aviation Org., 40th Anniv.
A55

70c, Radar, vert. 2.50sh, Kenya School of Aviation. 3.50sh, Jet, Moi Intl. Airport. 5sh, Air traffic control center, vert.

1984, Apr. 2   Litho.   Perf. 14

293	A55	70c multicolored	.25	.25
294	A55	2.50sh multicolored	.65	.65
295	A55	3.50sh multicolored	1.00	1.00
296	A55	5sh multicolored	1.50	1.50
		Nos. 293-296 (4)	3.40	3.40

1984 Summer Olympics — A56

1984, May 21   Perf. 14½

297	A56	70c Running	.25	.25
298	A56	2.50sh Hurdles	1.00	1.00
299	A56	5sh Boxing	2.50	2.40
300	A56	10sh Field Hockey	4.75	4.75
		Nos. 297-300 (4)	8.50	8.40

Souvenir Sheet
Imperf

301	A56	25sh Torch bearers	6.00	6.00

No. 301 contains designs of Nos. 297-300.

Bookmobile — A57

1984, Aug. 10   Litho.   Perf. 14½

302	A57	70c Emblem	.25	.25
303	A57	3.50sh shown	.70	.70
304	A57	5sh Adult library	1.10	1.10
305	A57	10sh Children's library	2.00	2.00
		Nos. 302-305 (4)	4.05	4.05

Intl. Fed. of Library Associations, 50th Conf.

Kenya Export Year (KEY)
A58

1984, Oct. 1   Litho.   Perf. 14

306	A58	70c Emblem, vert.	.25	.25
307	A58	3.50sh Airport	1.90	1.90
308	A58	5sh Harbor, vert.	3.50	3.50
309	A58	10sh Exports	5.50	5.50
		Nos. 306-309 (4)	11.15	11.15

A59

70c, Doves, cross. 2.50sh, Doves, Hinduism symbol. 3.50sh, Doves, Sikhism symbol. 6.50sh, Doves, Islam symbol.

1984, Aug. 23   Litho.   Perf. 14x14½

310	A59	70c multicolored	.25	.25
311	A59	2.50sh multicolored	1.50	1.50
312	A59	3.50sh multicolored	2.25	2.25
313	A59	6.50sh multicolored	4.00	4.00
		Nos. 310-313 (4)	8.00	8.00

World Conference on Religion and Peace, Nairobi, Aug. 23-31, 1984.

Tribal Costumes A60

1984, Nov. 5   Litho.   Perf. 14½x13½
314 A60   70c Luhya   .90   .90
315 A60   2sh Kikuyu   2.25 2.25
316 A60   3.50sh Pokomo   3.25 3.25
317 A60   5sh Nandi   3.50 3.50
318 A60   10sh Rendile   5.75 5.75
    Nos. 314-318 (5)   15.65 15.65

60th Anniv., World Chess Federation — A61

70c, Nyayo Stadium, knight. 2.50sh, Fort Jesus, rook. 3.50sh, National Monument, bishop. 5sh, Parliament, queen. 10sh, Nyayo Fountain, king.

1984, Dec. 21   Litho.   Perf. 14½
319 A61   70c multicolored   2.25   .40
320 A61   2.50sh multicolored   3.25 2.10
321 A61   3.50sh multicolored   4.00 4.50
322 A61   5sh multicolored   4.50 4.50
323 A61   10sh multicolored   7.25 7.25
    Nos. 319-323 (5)   21.25 18.75

Energy Conservation — A62

1985, Jan. 22   Litho.   Perf. 13½
324 A62   70c Stove, fire pit   .35   .35
325 A62   2sh Solar panel   .40   .40
326 A62   3.50sh Biogas tank   .65   .65
327 A62   10sh Plowing field   2.25 2.25
328 A62   20sh Energy conservation 4.00 4.00
    Nos. 324-328 (5)   7.65 7.65

No. 328 contains Nos. 324-327 without denominations.

Girl Guides, 75th Anniv. A63

1sh, Girl Guide, handicrafts. 3sh, Community service. 5sh, Lady Baden-Powell, Kenyan leader. 7sh, Food project.

1985, Mar. 27   Litho.   Perf. 13½
329 A63   1sh multicolored   1.00 1.00
330 A63   3sh multicolored   2.25 1.60
331 A63   5sh multicolored   2.75 2.75
332 A63   7sh multicolored   4.25 4.25
    Nos. 329-332 (4)   10.25 9.60

Intl. Red Cross Day A64

1985, May 8   Perf. 14½
333 A64   1sh Emblem   1.10 1.00
334 A64   4sh First Aid   3.50 3.50
335 A64   5sh Blood donation   4.00 4.00

---

336 A64   7sh Famine relief, cornucopia 5.25 5.25
    Nos. 333-336 (4)   13.85 13.75

A65

Diseases caused by microorganisms carried by insects.

1985, June 25
337 A65   1sh Malaria   2.25   .30
338 A65   3sh Leishmaniasis   4.00 2.75
339 A65   5sh Trypanosomiasis   4.75 4.25
340 A65   7sh Babesiosis   7.50 7.50
    Nos. 337-340 (4)   18.50 14.80

7th Intl. Congress on Protozoology, Nairobi, June 22-29.

A66

1sh, Repairing water pipes. 3sh, Traditional food processing. 5sh, Basket weaving. 7sh, Dress making.

1985, July 15
341 A66   1sh multicolored   .30   .30
342 A66   3sh multicolored   .80   .80
343 A66   5sh multicolored   1.60 1.60
344 A66   7sh multicolored   2.25 2.25
    Nos. 341-344 (4)   4.95 4.95

UN Decade for Women.

43rd Intl. Eucharistic Congress, Nairobi, Aug. 11-18 — A67

1sh, The Last Supper. 3sh, Afro-Christian family. 5sh, Congress altar, Uhuru Park. 7sh, St. Peter Claver's Church. 25sh, Pope John Paul II.

1985, Aug. 15   Perf. 13½
345 A67   1sh multicolored   1.10 1.10
346 A67   3sh multicolored   2.25 2.25
347 A67   5sh multicolored   3.25 3.25
348 A67   7sh multicolored   4.00 3.50
    Nos. 345-348 (4)   10.60 10.10

Souvenir Sheet
349 A67   25sh multicolored   8.50 8.50

Flower Types of 1983
1sh, Dombeya burgessiae. 3sh, Calotropis procera. 4sh, Momordica foetida. 7sh, Oncoba spinosa.

1985   Photo.   Perf. 14½x14, 14½
350 A46   80c like #250   4.50 2.50
351 A46   1sh multicolored   4.50 1.60
352 A47   3sh multicolored   8.50 5.00
353 A47   4sh multicolored   5.25 6.75
354 A47   7sh multicolored   7.00 7.00
    Nos. 350-354 (5)   29.75 22.85

Endangered Wildlife — A68

1sh, Diceros bicornis. 3sh, Acinonyx jubatus. 5sh, Cercopithecus neglectus. 10sh, Equus greyvi. 25sh, Hunter pursuing game.

1985, Dec. 10   Litho.   Perf. 14½
355 A68   1sh multicolored   2.75 1.50
356 A68   3sh multicolored   3.75 3.25
357 A68   5sh multicolored   4.00 4.00
358 A68   10sh multicolored   7.00 7.00
    Nos. 355-358 (4)   17.50 15.75

Size: 130x122mm
Imperf
359 A68   25sh multicolored   12.00 12.00

Trees A69

1sh, Borassus aethiopum. 3sh, Acacia xanthophloea. 5sh, Ficus natalensis. 7sh, Spathodea nilotica. 25sh, Glade.

1986, Jan. 24   Perf. 14½
360 A69   1sh multicolored   1.40   .25
361 A69   3sh multicolored   3.50 2.75
362 A69   5sh multicolored   4.75 4.75
363 A69   7sh multicolored   6.75 6.75
    Nos. 360-363 (4)   16.40 14.50

Size: 117x97mm
Imperf
364 A69   25sh multicolored   6.50 6.50

Intl. Peace Year — A70

1986, Apr. 17   Perf. 14½
365 A70   1sh Dove, UN emblem   .55   .55
366 A70   3sh UN General Assembly, horiz. 1.25 1.25
367 A70   7sh Mushroom cloud   2.40 2.40
368 A70   10sh Isaiah 2:4, horiz. 3.75 3.75
    Nos. 365-368 (4)   7.95 7.95

1986 World Cup Soccer Championships, Mexico — A71

1986, May 9
369 A71   1sh Dribbling   1.10   .55
370 A71   3sh Penalty shot   2.25 1.10
371 A71   5sh Tackling   3.50 2.25
372 A71   7sh Champions   4.50 4.50
373 A71   10sh Heading the ball 5.75 5.75
    Nos. 369-373 (5)   17.10 14.15

Size: 110x86mm
Imperf
374 A71   30sh Harambee Stars   6.50 6.50

EXPO '86, Vancouver — A72

1986, June 11   Perf. 13½x13
375 A72   1sh Rural post office 1.25   .60
376 A72   3sh Container depot, Embakasi 2.40 1.25
377 A72   5sh Plane landing   3.75 2.40
378 A72   7sh Shipping exports 4.75 4.75
379 A72   10sh Goods transport 6.25 6.25
    Nos. 375-379 (5)   18.40 15.25

TELECOM '86, Nairobi, Sept. 16-23 — A73

1sh, Telephone-computer links. 3sh, Telephones, 1876-1986. 5sh, Satellite communications. 7sh, Switchboards.

1986, Sept. 16   Litho.   Perf. 14½
380 A73   1sh multicolored   .30   .30
381 A73   3sh multicolored   1.25 1.25
382 A73   5sh multicolored   2.10 2.10
383 A73   7sh multicolored   3.50 3.50
    Nos. 380-383 (4)   7.15 7.15

A74

Dhows (Ships) — A75

1986, Oct. 30   Litho.   Perf. 14½
384 A74   1sh Mashua   .90   .25
385 A74   3sh Mtepe   2.25 1.50
386 A74   5sh Dau la Mwao   3.25 3.00
387 A74   10sh Jahazi   6.75 6.75
    Nos. 384-387 (4)   13.15 11.50

Souvenir Sheet
388 A75   25sh Lamu, map   8.00 8.00

Christmas A76

1986, Dec. 5   Perf. 12
389 A76   1sh Nativity, vert.   .35   .25
390 A76   3sh Shepherd boy, vert. 1.75 1.75
391 A76   5sh Angel, map   2.50 2.50
392 A76   7sh Magi   3.75 3.75
    Nos. 389-392 (4)   8.35 8.25

UNICEF, 40th Anniv. — A77

Child Survival Campaign: 1sh, Universal immunization by 1990. 3sh, Food and nutrition. 4sh, Oral rehydration. 5sh, Family planning. 10sh, Literacy of women.

1987, Jan. 6   Litho.   Perf. 14½

393	A77	1sh multicolored	.60	.60
394	A77	1.25sh multicolored	1.25	1.25
395	A77	4sh multicolored	1.75	1.75
396	A77	5sh multicolored	2.25	2.25
397	A77	10sh multicolored	3.50	3.50
		Nos. 393-397 (5)	9.35	9.35

Tourism — A79

1987, Mar. 25   Litho.   Perf. 14½

398	A78	1sh Akamba carvers	.60	.25
399	A78	3sh Beach	3.25	2.00
400	A78	5sh Escarpment	4.00	4.00
401	A78	7sh Pride of lions	6.00	6.00
		Nos. 398-401 (4)	13.85	12.25

Souvenir Sheet

402	A79	30sh Kenya geysers	14.00	14.00

Ceremonial Costumes A80

1987, May 20   Perf. 14½x13½

403	A80	1sh Embu	1.25	.60
404	A80	3sh Kisii	2.75	1.40
405	A80	5sh Samburu	4.25	2.40
406	A80	7sh Taita	4.75	4.75
407	A80	10sh Boran	5.00	5.00
		Nos. 403-407 (5)	18.00	14.15

See Nos. 505-509.

Posts & Telecommunications Corp., 10th Anniv. — A81

1sh, Telecommunications satellite. 3sh, Rural post office, Kajiado. 4sh, Athletics. 5sh, Rural communication. 7sh, Speedpost. 25sh, Natl. Flag.

1987, July 1   Litho.   Perf. 13½

408	A81	1sh multicolored	.75	.30
409	A81	3sh multicolored	1.75	1.75
410	A81	4sh multicolored	2.25	2.25
411	A81	5sh multicolored	2.40	2.40
412	A81	7sh multicolored	3.25	3.25
		Nos. 408-412 (5)	10.40	9.95

Souvenir Sheet

413	A81	25sh multicolored	4.50	4.50

A82

1987, Aug. 5   Perf. 14½x14

414	A82	1sh Volleyball	.25	.25
415	A82	3sh Cycling	.55	.55
416	A82	4sh Boxing	.75	.75
417	A82	5sh Swimming	.90	.90
418	A82	7sh Steeple chase	1.25	1.25
		Nos. 414-418 (5)	3.70	3.70

Souvenir Sheet
Perf. 14x14½

419	A82	30sh Kasarani Sports Complex	5.00	5.00

4th All Africa Games, Nairobi, Aug. 1-12. Nos. 414-418, vert.

A83

Medicinal herbs: 1sh, Aloe volkensii. 3sh, Cassia didymobotrya. 5sh, Erythrina abyssinica. 7sh, Adenium obesum. 10sh, Herbalist's clinic.

1987, Oct. 27   Litho.   Perf. 13½x14

420	A83	1sh multicolored	1.10	.65
421	A83	3sh multicolored	2.25	1.50
422	A83	5sh multicolored	3.00	2.40
423	A83	7sh multicolored	3.75	3.75
424	A83	10sh multicolored	5.00	5.00
		Nos. 420-424 (5)	15.10	13.30

Butterflies — A84

10c, Cyrestis camillus. 20c, Iolaus sidus. 40c, Vanessa cardui. 50c, Colotis euippe omphale. 70c, Precis westermanni. 80c, Colias electo. 1sh, Eronia leda. 1.50sh, Papilio dardanus planemoides. 2sh, Papilio rex. 2.50sh, Colotis phisadia. 3sh, Papilio desmondi teita. 3.50sh, Papilio demodocus. 4sh, Papilio phorcas. 5sh, Charaxes druceanus teita. 7sh, Cymothoe teita. 10sh, Charaxes zoolina. 20sh, Papilio dardanus. 40sh, Charaxes cithaeron kennethi.

1988-90   Photo.   Perf. 15x14

424A	A84	10c multicolored	1.25	1.25
425	A84	20c multicolored	.35	.40
426	A84	40c multicolored	.50	.40
427	A84	50c multicolored	.50	.40
428	A84	70c multicolored	.50	.40
429	A84	80c multicolored	.50	.40
430	A84	1sh multicolored	.50	.30
430A	A84	1.50sh multicolored	5.00	1.25

Size: 25x41mm
Perf. 14½

431	A84	2sh multicolored	.75	.95
432	A84	2.50sh multicolored	.80	.95
433	A84	3sh multicolored	.80	.95
434	A84	3.50sh multicolored	.85	.95
435	A84	4sh multicolored	.90	1.75
436	A84	5sh multicolored	1.25	.70
437	A84	7sh multicolored	1.50	2.50
438	A84	10sh multicolored	2.50	1.75
439	A84	20sh multicolored	4.00	3.50
440	A84	40sh multicolored	7.25	8.00
		Nos. 424A-440 (18)	29.70	26.80

Issued: 10c, 9/1/89; 1.50sh, 5/18/90; others, 2/14/88.

Game Lodges A85

1sh, Samburu. 3sh, Naro Moru River. 4sh, Mara Serena. 5sh, Voi Safari. 7sh, Kilimanjaro Buffalo Lodge. 10sh, Meru Mulika.

1988, May 31   Litho.   Perf. 14½

441	A85	1sh multicolored	.75	.35
442	A85	3sh multicolored	1.10	1.10
443	A85	4sh multicolored	1.75	1.75
444	A85	5sh multicolored	1.90	1.90
445	A85	7sh multicolored	2.25	2.25
446	A85	10sh multicolored	2.75	2.75
		Nos. 441-446 (6)	10.50	10.10

World Expo '88, Brisbane A86

EXPO '88 and Australia bicentennial emblems plus: 1sh, Stadium, site of the 1982 Commonwealth Games, and runners. 3sh, Flying Doctor Service aircraft. 4sh, HMS Sirius, a 19th cent. immigrant ship. 5sh, Ostrich and emu. 7sh, Pres. Daniel arap Moi, Queen Elizabeth II and Robert Hawke, prime minister of Australia. 30sh, Kenya Pavilion at EXPO '88.

1988, June 10

447	A86	1sh multicolored	.60	.60
448	A86	3sh multicolored	1.75	1.75
449	A86	4sh multicolored	3.00	3.00
450	A86	5sh multicolored	4.00	4.00
451	A86	7sh multicolored	5.00	5.00
		Nos. 447-451 (5)	14.35	14.35

Souvenir Sheet

452	A86	30sh multicolored	4.50	4.50

World Health Organization, 40th Anniv. — A87

1988, July 1   Litho.   Perf. 14½

453	A87	1sh shown	.35	.35
454	A87	3sh Nutrition	1.40	1.40
455	A87	5sh Immunization	2.50	2.50
456	A87	7sh Water supply	3.75	3.75
		Nos. 453-456 (4)	8.00	8.00

1988 Summer Olympics, Seoul — A88

1988, Aug. 1   Litho.   Perf. 14½x14

457	A88	1sh Handball	.50	.25
458	A88	3sh Judo	1.00	.80
459	A88	5sh Weight lifting	1.50	1.50
460	A88	7sh Javelin	2.00	2.00
461	A88	10sh 400-meter relay	2.50	2.50
		Nos. 457-461 (5)	7.50	7.05

Souvenir Sheet

462	A88	30sh Tennis	5.00	5.00

Utensils A89

Perf. 14½x14, 14x14½
1988, Sept. 20   Litho.

463	A89	1sh Calabashes, vert.	.55	.25
464	A89	3sh Milk gourds, vert.	1.10	.65
465	A89	5sh Cooking pots	1.50	1.10
466	A89	7sh Winnowing trays	1.90	1.90
467	A89	10sh Reed baskets	2.50	2.50
		Nos. 463-467 (5)	7.55	6.40

Souvenir Sheet

468	A89	25sh Gourds, calabash, horn	4.50	4.50

10-Year Presidency of Daniel arap Moi — A90

Designs: 1sh, Swearing-in ceremony, 1978. 3sh, Promoting soil conservation. 3.50sh, Public transportation (bus), Nairobi. 4sh, Jua Kali artisans at market. 5sh, Moi University, Eldoret, established in 1985. 7sh, Hospital ward expansion. 10sh, British Prime Minister Margaret Thatcher and Pres. Moi inaugurating the Kapsabet Telephone Exchange, Jan. 6, 1988.

1988, Oct. 13   Litho.   Perf. 13½x14½

469	A90	1sh multicolored	.70	.70
470	A90	3sh multicolored	1.75	1.75
471	A90	3.50sh multicolored	2.00	2.00
472	A90	4sh multicolored	2.25	2.25
473	A90	5sh multicolored	2.75	2.75
474	A90	7sh multicolored	3.50	3.50
475	A90	10sh multicolored	5.50	5.50
		Nos. 469-475 (7)	18.45	18.45

Independence, 25th Anniv. — A91

1sh, Natl. flag. 3sh, Coffee picking. 5sh, Model of postal headquarters. 7sh, Harambee Star Airbus A310-300. 10sh, Locomotive 9401.

1988, Dec. 9   Litho.   Perf. 11½

476	A91	1sh multicolored	.35	.35
477	A91	3sh multicolored	1.90	1.90
478	A91	5sh multicolored	3.25	3.25
479	A91	7sh multicolored	4.75	4.75
480	A91	10sh multicolored	6.50	6.50
		Nos. 476-480 (5)	16.75	16.75

Natl. Monuments — A92

1.20sh, Gedi Ruins, Malindi. 3.40sh, Vasco Da Gama Pillar, Malindi, vert. 4.40sh, Ishiakani Monument, Kiunga. 5.50sh, Ft. Jesus, Mombasa. 7.70sh, She Burnan Omwe, Lamu, vert.

1989, Mar. 15   Litho.   Perf. 14½

481	A92	1.20sh multicolored	.40	.40
482	A92	3.40sh multicolored	1.00	1.00
483	A92	4.40sh multicolored	2.00	2.00
484	A92	5.50sh multicolored	2.50	2.50
485	A92	7.70sh multicolored	3.00	3.00
		Nos. 481-485 (5)	8.90	8.90

Red Cross, 125th Anniv. A93

1.20sh, Anniv. and natl. soc. emblems. 3.40sh, First aid. 4.40sh, Disaster relief. 5.50sh, Jean-Henri Dunant. 7.70sh, Blood donation.

1989, May 8   Litho.   Perf. 14x13½

486	A93	1.20sh multicolored	.35	.35
487	A93	3.40sh multicolored	1.25	1.25
488	A93	4.40sh multicolored	1.75	1.75
489	A93	5.50sh multicolored	2.40	2.40
490	A93	7.70sh multicolored	3.75	3.75
		Nos. 486-490 (5)	9.50	9.50

World Wildlife
Fund — A94

Giraffes, Giraffa Camelopardalis Reticulata.

1989, July 12   Litho.   Perf. 14½

491	A94	1.20sh multicolored	2.50	2.25
492	A94	3.40sh multicolored	5.25	5.00
493	A94	4.40sh multicolored	6.00	6.00
494	A94	5.50sh multicolored	7.25	8.00
		Nos. 491-494 (4)	21.00	21.25

Size: 80x110mm
Imperf

495	A94	30sh multicolored	15.00	15.00

No. 495 contains four labels like Nos. 491-494, perf. 14½, without denominations or WWF emblem.

Mushrooms — A95

1989, Sept. 6   Litho.   Perf. 14½

496	A95	1.20sh Oyster	2.40	.65
497	A95	3.40sh Chestnut	3.50	2.40
498	A95	4.40sh White button	4.00	3.25
499	A95	5.50sh Termite	4.75	3.75
500	A95	7.70sh Shiitake	6.50	6.50
		Nos. 496-500 (5)	21.15	16.55

Jawaharlal Nehru,
1st Prime Minister
of Independent
India — A96

1989, Nov. 9   Litho.   Perf. 13½x14

501	A96	1.20sh Independence struggle	2.00	1.50
502	A96	3.40sh Education	2.50	2.00
503	A96	5.50sh Portrait	4.50	4.50
504	A96	7.70sh Industry	7.50	7.50
		Nos. 501-504 (4)	16.50	15.50

Costume Type of 1980

1989, Dec. 8   Litho.   Perf. 14½x13½

505	A80	1.20sh Kipsigis	1.25	.45
506	A80	3.40sh Rabai	2.50	2.50
507	A80	5.50sh Duruma	3.25	2.40
508	A80	7.70sh Kuria	4.50	3.75
509	A80	10sh Bajuni	5.50	5.50
		Nos. 505-509 (5)	17.00	14.60

Pan-African Postal Union, 10th
Anniv. — A97

Perf. 14x13½, 13½x14
1990, Jan. 31   Litho.

510	A97	1.20sh EMS Speedpost	.30	.30
511	A97	3.40sh Mail runner	.90	.90
512	A97	5.50sh Mandera P.O.	1.10	1.10
513	A97	7.70sh EMS, diff., vert.	1.40	1.40
514	A97	10sh PAPU emblem, vert.	1.75	1.75
		Nos. 510-514 (5)	5.45	5.45

Soccer
Trophies — A98

Designs:1.50sh, Moi Golden Cup. 4.50sh, East & Central Africa Challenge Cup. 6.50sh, East & Central Africa Club Championship Cup. 9sh, World Cup.

1990, May 21   Litho.   Perf. 14½

515	A98	1.50sh multicolored	.50	.50
516	A98	4.50sh multicolored	3.00	3.00
517	A98	6.50sh multicolored	4.00	4.00
518	A98	9sh multicolored	5.00	5.00
		Nos. 515-518 (4)	12.50	12.50

Penny Black
150th Anniv.,
Stamp World
London
'90 — A99

4.50sh, Great Britain No. 1. 6.50sh, Early British cancellations. 9sh, Main P.O.

1990, Apr. 27   Litho.   Perf. 11½

519	A99	1.50sh shown	.45	.35
520	A99	4.50sh multicolored	1.60	1.60
521	A99	6.50sh multicolored	2.40	2.40
522	A99	9sh multicolored	3.50	3.50
a.		Souvenir sheet of 4, #519-522	8.50	8.50
		Nos. 519-522 (4)	7.95	7.85

No. 522a sold for 30 shillings.

ITU,
125th
Anniv.
A100

Designs: 4.50sh, Telephone assembly. 6.50sh, ITU Anniv. emblem. 9sh, Telecommunications development.

1990, July 12

523	A100	1.50sh multicolored	.45	.25
524	A100	4.50sh multicolored	.90	.65
525	A100	6.50sh multicolored	1.25	1.10
526	A100	9sh multicolored	1.60	1.60
		Nos. 523-526 (4)	4.20	3.60

Common Design Types pictured following the introduction.

Queen Mother, 90th Birthday
Common Design Types

10sh, Queen Mother. 40sh, At garden party, 1947.

Perf. 14x15
1990, Aug. 4   Litho.   Wmk. 384

527	CD343	10sh multicolored	1.50	1.50

Perf. 14½

528	CD344	40sh multicolored	5.50	5.50

Kenya
African
National
Union
(KANU),
50th
Anniv.
A101

1.50sh, KANU flag. 2.50sh, Nyayo Monument. 4.50sh, KICC Party Headquarters. 5sh, Jomo Kenyatta. 6.50sh, Daniel T. arap Moi. 9sh, KANU mass meeting. 10sh, Voters.

1990, June 11

529	A101	1.50sh multicolored	.35	.25
530	A101	2.50sh multicolored	.40	.35
531	A101	4.50sh multicolored	.85	.85
532	A101	5sh multicolored	1.00	1.00
533	A101	6.50sh multicolored	1.10	1.10
534	A101	9sh multicolored	1.75	1.75
535	A101	10sh multicolored	1.75	1.75
		Nos. 529-535 (7)	7.20	7.05

Kenya Postage
Stamps,
Cent. — A102

Designs: 1.50sh, Kenya #431. 4.50sh, East Africa and Uganda Protectorates #2. 6.50sh, British East Africa #1. 9sh, Kenya and Uganda #25. 20sh, Kenya, Uganda, Tanzania #232.

1990, Sept. 5   Litho.   Perf. 14x14½

536	A102	1.50sh multicolored	1.50	.45
537	A102	4.50sh multicolored	3.00	2.50
538	A102	6.50sh multicolored	4.00	3.75
539	A102	9sh multicolored	5.25	4.75
540	A102	20sh multicolored	8.50	8.50
		Nos. 536-540 (5)	22.25	19.95

Intl. Literacy
Year — A103

1.50sh, Adult literacy class. 4.50sh, Radio teaching program. 6.50sh, Technical training. 9sh, Literacy year emblem.

1990, Nov. 30   Litho.   Perf. 13½x14

541	A103	1.50sh multicolored	.65	.65
542	A103	4.50sh multicolored	1.60	1.60
543	A103	6.50sh multicolored	2.25	2.25
544	A103	9sh multicolored	3.50	3.50
		Nos. 541-544 (4)	8.00	8.00

1992 Summer Olympics,
Barcelona — A106

1991, Nov. 29   Litho.   Perf. 14x13½

554	A106	2sh National flag	.45	.45
555	A106	6sh Basketball	1.90	1.90
556	A106	7sh Field hockey	2.50	2.50
557	A106	8.50sh Table tennis	3.00	3.00
558	A106	11sh Boxing	4.50	4.50
		Nos. 554-558 (5)	12.35	12.35

Fight
AIDS — A107

2sh, You too can be infected. 6sh, Has no cure. 8.50sh, Casual sex is unsafe. 11sh, Sterilize syringe before use.

1991, Oct. 31   Litho.   Perf. 13½x14

559	A107	2sh multicolored	1.25	.25
560	A107	6sh multicolored	2.50	2.25
561	A107	8.50sh multicolored	3.50	3.00
562	A107	11sh multicolored	4.75	4.75
		Nos. 559-562 (4)	12.00	10.25

Queen Elizabeth II's Accession to the Throne, 40th Anniv.
Common Design Type

1992, Feb. 6   Litho.   Perf. 14x13½

563	CD349	3sh multicolored	.25	.25
564	CD349	8sh multicolored	1.10	1.10
565	CD349	11sh multicolored	1.40	1.40
566	CD349	14sh multicolored	1.60	1.60
567	CD349	40sh multicolored	4.75	4.75
		Nos. 563-567 (5)	9.10	9.10

Wildlife — A108

1992, May 8   Perf. 14½

568	A108	3sh Leopard	2.00	.35
569	A108	8sh Lion	2.75	2.00
570	A108	10sh Elephant	5.75	3.00
571	A108	11sh Buffalo	3.50	3.00
572	A108	14sh Rhinoceros	9.50	5.00
		Nos. 568-572 (5)	23.50	13.35

Vintage
Cars
A109

Designs: 3sh, Intl. Harvester S.S. motor truck, 1926. 8sh, Fiat 509, 1924. 10sh, "R" Hupmobile, 1923. 11sh, Chevrolet Box Body, 1928. 14sh, Bentley Parkward, 1934.

1992, June 24   Perf. 14½

573	A109	3sh multicolored	2.25	.70
574	A109	8sh multicolored	3.00	1.90
575	A109	10sh multicolored	3.50	2.50
576	A109	11sh multicolored	4.00	3.50
577	A109	14sh multicolored	5.50	5.50
		Nos. 573-577 (5)	18.25	14.10

1992 Summer
Olympics,
Barcelona — A110

3sh, Runners. 8sh, Judo. 10sh, Women's volleyball. 11sh, 4x100-meter relay. 14sh, 10,000-meter run.

1992, July 24   Litho.   Perf. 14½

578	A110	3sh multicolored	.60	.60
579	A110	8sh multicolored	2.10	2.10
580	A110	10sh multicolored	3.50	3.50
581	A110	11sh multicolored	3.50	3.50
582	A110	14sh multicolored	4.75	4.75
		Nos. 578-582 (5)	14.45	14.45

Christmas — A111

Designs: 3sh, Joseph, Jesus & animals in stable. 8sh, Mary holding Jesus in stable.

11sh, Map of Kenya, Christmas tree. 14sh, Adoration of the Magi.

1992, Dec. 14   Litho.   Perf. 13½x14

583	A111	3sh multicolored	.50	.50
584	A111	8sh multicolored	1.25	1.25
585	A111	11sh multicolored	1.75	1.75
586	A111	14sh multicolored	2.00	2.00
		Nos. 583-586 (4)	5.50	5.50

Lighthouses
A112

Designs: 3sh, Asembo Bay, Lake Victoria. 8sh, Ras Serani, Mombasa. 11sh, Ras Serani, Mombasa, diff. 14sh, Gingira, Lake Victoria.

1993, Jan. 25   Perf. 14½

587	A112	3sh multicolored	2.75	1.10
588	A112	8sh multicolored	4.75	3.25
589	A112	11sh multicolored	6.00	5.25
590	A112	14sh multicolored	8.00	8.00
		Nos. 587-590 (4)	21.50	17.60

Birds — A113

Designs: 50c, Superb starling. 1sh, Red and yellow barbet. 1.50sh, Ross's turaco. 3sh, Greater honeyguide. 5sh, African fish eagle. 6sh, Vulturine guineafowl. 7sh, Malachite kingfisher. 8sh, Speckled pigeon. 10sh, Cinnamon-chested bee-eater. 11sh, Scarlet-chested sunbird. 14sh, Reichenow's weaver. 50sh, Yellow-billed hornbill. 80sh, Lesser flamingo. 100sh, Hadada ibis.

1993-99   Photo.   Perf. 15x14
Granite Paper

594	A113	50c multi	.25	.25
597	A113	1sh multi	.25	.25
598	A113	1.50sh multi	.25	.25
600	A113	3sh multi	.25	.25
601	A113	5sh multi	.25	.25
601A	A113	6sh multi	5.00	1.00
602	A113	7sh multi	.45	.45
603	A113	8sh multi	.55	.55
604	A113	10sh multi	.65	.65
605	A113	11sh multi	.70	.70
606	A113	14sh multi	.90	.90

Size: 25x42mm
Perf. 14½

608	A113	50sh multi	3.25	3.25
609	A113	80sh multi	5.00	5.00
610	A113	100sh multi	6.50	6.50
		Nos. 594-610 (14)	24.25	20.25

Issued: 1.50sh, 5sh, 2/14/94; 6sh, 1999; others, 2/22/93.
This is an expanding set. Numbers may change.

17th World Congress of Rehabilatation Intl. — A114

3sh, Health care, vert. 8sh, Recreation. 10sh, Vocational training. 11sh, Recreation & sports. 14sh, Emblem, vert.

1993, July 1   Litho.   Perf. 14½

611	A114	3sh multicolored	.90	.25
612	A114	8sh multicolored	1.40	.75
613	A114	10sh multicolored	1.75	1.75
614	A114	11sh multicolored	1.75	1.75
615	A114	14sh multicolored	2.10	2.10
		Nos. 611-615 (5)	7.90	6.60

Maendeleo ya Wanawake
Organization, 42th Anniv. — A115

Designs: 3.50sh, Maendeleo House. 9sh, Planting trees. 11sh, Rural family planning services, vert. 12.50sh, Water nearer the people. 15.50sh, Maendeleo improved wood cookstove, vert.

Perf. 14x13½, 13½x14

1994, Mar. 17   Litho.

616	A115	3.50sh multicolored	1.10	.25
617	A115	9sh multicolored	1.60	.60
618	A115	11sh multicolored	1.25	1.25
619	A115	12.50sh multicolored	2.25	2.25
620	A115	15.50sh multicolored	2.50	2.50
		Nos. 616-620 (5)	8.70	6.85

Orchids — A116

Designs: 3.50sh, Ansellia africana. 9sh, Aerangis lutecalba. 12.50sh, Polystachya bella. 15.50sh, Brachycorythis kalbreyeri. 20sh, Eulophia guineensis.

1994, June 27   Litho.   Perf. 13½x14

621	A116	3.50sh multicolored	2.40	.25
622	A116	9sh multicolored	3.25	1.00
623	A116	12.50sh multicolored	3.50	2.50
624	A116	15.50sh multicolored	4.25	4.25
625	A116	20sh multicolored	5.50	5.50
		Nos. 621-625 (5)	18.90	13.50

African Development Bank, 30th
Anniv. — A117

1994, Nov. 21   Litho.   Perf. 14½

626	A117	6sh KICC, Nairobi	1.25	.25
627	A117	25sh Isinya, Kajiado	4.50	4.50

Intl. Year of the
Family — A118

6sh, Family planning. 14.50sh, Health. 20sh, Education, horiz. 25sh, Emblem, horiz.

1994, Dec. 22

628	A118	6sh multi	1.00	.25
629	A118	14.50sh multi	3.50	1.50
630	A118	20sh multi	4.00	4.00
631	A118	25sh multi	4.00	4.00
		Nos. 628-631 (4)	12.50	9.75

Rotary, 50th
Anniv. — A119

Designs: 6sh, Paul P. Harris, founder. 14.50sh, Rotary Club of Mombasa. 17.50sh, Polio plus vaccine. 20sh, Water projects. 25sh, Emblem, motto.

1994, Dec. 29   Perf. 13½x14

632	A119	6sh multicolored	.60	.25
633	A119	14.50sh multicolored	1.60	.75
634	A119	17.50sh multicolored	2.00	2.00
635	A119	20sh multicolored	2.25	2.25
636	A119	25sh multicolored	2.75	2.75
		Nos. 632-636 (5)	9.20	8.00

SPCA — A120

1995, Jan. 13   Litho.   Perf. 14½

637	A120	6sh Donkey	.55	.25
638	A120	14.50sh Cattle	1.50	.55
639	A120	17.50sh Sheep	1.90	1.10
640	A120	20sh Dog	2.10	2.10
641	A120	25sh Cat	2.60	2.60
		Nos. 637-641 (5)	8.65	6.60

Kenya Society for Prevention of Cruelty to Animals.

Golf — A121

1995, Feb. 28   Litho.   Perf. 14½

642	A121	6sh Man in vest	1.10	.25
643	A121	17.50sh Woman	3.50	1.10
644	A121	20sh Man in red shirt	3.75	1.80
645	A121	25sh Golf club	5.00	1.60
		Nos. 642-645 (4)	13.35	4.75

Traditional Crafts — A122

6sh, Perfume containers. 14.50sh, Basketry. 17.50sh, Preservation pots. 20sh, Gourds. 25sh, Wooden containers.

1995, Mar. 24   Litho.   Perf. 14x13½

646	A122	6sh multicolored	.50	.25
647	A122	14.50sh multicolored	1.00	.95
648	A122	17.50sh multicolored	1.40	1.40
649	A122	20sh multicolored	1.75	1.75
650	A122	25sh multicolored	2.40	2.40
		Nos. 646-650 (5)	7.05	6.75

UN, 50th
Anniv.
A123

Designs: 23sh, UN Headquarters, Nairobi. 26sh, People holding UN emblem. 32sh, UN Peacekeeper's helmet. 40sh, UN emblem.

1995, Oct. 24   Litho.   Perf. 13½

651	A123	23sh multicolored	1.40	.70
652	A123	26sh multicolored	1.50	.90
653	A123	32sh multicolored	2.10	2.10
654	A123	40sh multicolored	2.25	2.25
		Nos. 651-654 (4)	7.25	5.95

A124

1995, Sept. 29   Litho.   Perf. 13½

655	A124	14sh Tse-tse fly	.75	.35
656	A124	26sh Tick	1.40	.90
657	A124	32sh Wild silk moth	1.75	1.25
658	A124	33sh Maize borer	1.90	1.90
659	A124	40sh Locust	2.25	2.25
		Nos. 655-659 (5)	8.05	6.65

ICIPE, 25th anniv.

A125

1995, Oct. 16

660	A125	14sh Maize production	.90	.35
661	A125	28sh Cattle rearing	2.00	1.00
662	A125	32sh Poultry keeping	2.25	2.00
663	A125	33sh Fishing	2.25	2.25
664	A125	40sh Fruits	2.75	2.75
		Nos. 660-664 (5)	10.15	8.35

FAO, 50th anniv.

Miniature Sheets

1996 Summer Olympics,
Atlanta — A126

No. 665: a, 14sh, Swimming. b, 20sh, Archery. c, 32sh, Javelin. d, 40sh, Fencing. e, 50sh, Discus. f, 20sh, Weight lifting.
No. 666: a, Pole vault. b, Equestrian. c, Diving. d, Track e, Torch bearer. f, Hurdles. g, Kayak. h, Boxing. i, Gymnastics.
No. 667 — Medal winners: a, Greg Louganis, diving. b, Muhammed Ali, boxing. c, Nadia Comaneci, gymnastics. d, Daley Thompson, decathlon. e, Kipchoge "Kip" Keino, track and field. f, Kornelia Enders, swimming. g, Jackie Joyner-Kersee, track and field. h, Michael Jordan, basketball. i, Shun Fujimoto, gymnastics.

No. 668, 100sh, Torch bearer. No. 669, 100sh, Gold medalist.

1996, Jan. 5   **Litho.**   **Perf. 14**
665 A126   Sheet of 6,   11.50 11.50
       #a.-f.
666 A126 20sh Sheet of 9,   12.50 12.50
       #a.-i.
667 A126 25sh Sheet of 9,   13.50 13.50
       #a.-i.
    Souvenir Sheets
668-669 A126   Set of 2   11.00 11.00

World Tourism Organization, 20th Anniv. — A127

1996, Jan. 31   **Litho.**   **Perf. 13½**
670 A127 6sh Lions   .50 .25
671 A127 14sh Mount Kenya   1.00 .35
672 A127 20sh Water sports   1.50 .80
673 A127 25sh Hippopotomus   2.00 2.00
674 A127 40sh Culture   3.00 3.00
    Nos. 670-674 (5)   8.00 6.40
    Perf. 13x13½
675 A127 50sh Giraffes, vert.   5.00 5.00

Wild Animals A128

1996   **Perf. 13x13½**
    Booklet Stamps
676 A128 20sh Water buck   1.40 1.10
677 A128 20sh Rhinoceros   1.40 1.10
678 A128 20sh Cheetah   1.40 1.10
679 A128 20sh Oryx   1.40 1.10
680 A128 20sh Reticulated giraffe   1.40 1.10
681 A128 20sh Bongo   1.40 1.10
  a.   Booklet pane of 6, #676-681   11.00
     Complete booklet, 4 #681a   45.00

Nos. 676-681 appear in No. 681a in two different orders. Complete booklet contains 2 of each type of pane.

1996 Summer Olympic Games, Atlanta — A129

1996, July 18   **Litho.**   **Perf. 13½x14**
682 A129 6sh Woman running   .30 .30
683 A129 14sh Steeple chase   .60 .60
684 A129 20sh Victory lap   .90 .90
685 A129 25sh Boxing   1.10 1.10
686 A129 40sh Man running   1.90 1.90
    Nos. 682-686 (5)   4.80 4.80

Red Cross — A130

1996, Aug. 30   **Litho.**   **Perf. 14**
687 A130 6sh Emblem   .40 .40
688 A130 14sh Blood donation   .80 .80
689 A130 20sh Immunization   1.25 1.25
690 A130 25sh Refugees   1.50 1.50
691 A130 40sh Clean environment   2.50 2.50
    Nos. 687-691 (5)   6.45 6.45

A131

1996, Sept. 10   **Litho.**   **Perf. 14½**
693 A131 6sh Impala   .45 .45
694 A131 20sh Colobus monkey   1.60 1.60
695 A131 25sh Elephant   2.00 2.00
696 A131 40sh Black rhino   3.75 3.75
    Nos. 693-696 (4)   7.80 7.80
East African Wildlife Society.

A132

1996, Oct. 31   **Litho.**   **Perf. 13½**
697 A132 6sh Logo   .30 .30
698 A132 14sh Eye camps   .95 .95
699 A132 20sh Wheel chair   1.50 1.50
700 A132 25sh Ambulance   1.75 1.75
    Nos. 697-700 (4)   4.50 4.50
Lions Club Intl.

COMESA (Common Market for Eastern and Southern Africa — A133

1997, Jan. 15   **Litho.**   **Perf. 13½x14**
701 A133 6sh COMESA logo   .25 .25
702 A133 20sh Natl. flag   1.40 1.40

Fish of Lake Victoria A134

Haplochromis: No. 703, Orange rock hunter. No. 704, Chilotes. No. 705, Cinctus. No. 706, Nigricans.

1997, Jan. 31   **Perf. 14x13½**
703 A134 25sh multicolored   3.00 1.75
704 A134 25sh multicolored   3.00 1.75
705 A134 25sh multicolored   3.00 1.75
706 A134 25sh multicolored   3.00 1.75
    Nos. 703-706 (4)   12.00 7.00
World Wildlife Fund.

Locomotives — A135

1997, Feb. 20   **Litho.**   **Perf. 14x13½**
707 A135 6sh Class 94, 1981   .80 .25
708 A135 14sh Class 87, 1964   1.25 .45
709 A135 20sh Class 59, 1955   1.60 .70
710 A135 25sh Class 57, 1939   1.60 1.25

711 A135 30sh Class 23, 1923   2.00 2.00
712 A135 40sh Class 10, 1914   2.25 2.25
    Nos. 707-712 (6)   9.50 6.90
    Dated 1996.

Fruits — A136

1997, Feb. 28   **Perf. 14½**
713 A136 6sh Orange   .25 .25
714 A136 14sh Pineapple   2.10 .90
715 A136 20sh Mango   3.00 2.00
716 A136 25sh Papaya   3.75 2.50
    Nos. 713-716 (4)   9.10 5.25

A137

Scouting Organizations: No. 717, Girl Guides, 75th anniv. No. 718, Lord Baden Powell. No. 719, Girl scouts hiking. No. 720, Rangers camping. No. 721, Girl Guides planting trees. No. 722, Boy Scouts first aid. No. 723, Boy Scouts camping. No. 724, Brownies.

1997, Sept. 1   **Litho.**   **Perf. 14½**
717 A137 10sh multicolored   .35 .35
718 A137 10sh multicolored   .35 .35
  a.   Pair, #717-718   .75 .75
719 A137 27sh multicolored   .90 .90
720 A137 27sh multicolored   .90 .90
  a.   Pair, #719-720   2.25 2.25
721 A137 33sh multicolored   1.25 1.25
722 A137 33sh multicolored   1.25 1.25
  a.   Pair, #721-722   3.00 3.00
723 A137 42sh multicolored   1.50 1.50
724 A137 42sh multicolored   1.50 1.50
  a.   Pair, #723-724   3.50 3.50
    Nos. 717-724 (8)   8.00 8.00

Tourist Attractions — A138

Designs: 10sh, Crocodile. 27sh, Hot Springs, Lake Bogoria. 30sh, Warthogs. 33sh, Wind surfing. 42sh, Traditional huts.

1997, Oct. 9   **Perf. 13½**
725 A138 10sh multicolored   1.25 .25
726 A138 27sh multicolored   2.00 1.60
727 A138 30sh multicolored   2.00 1.90
728 A138 33sh multicolored   2.25 2.25
729 A138 42sh multicolored   2.50 2.50
    Nos. 725-729 (5)   10.00 8.50

Vasco da Gama's Stop in Malindi, 500th Anniv. A139

Designs: 10sh, Residents greeting ships as they arrive. 24sh, Three ships. 33sh, Map of voyage. 42sh, Ships in bay, monument.

1998, Apr. 4   **Litho.**   **Perf. 13**
730 A139 10sh multicolored   .60 .30
731 A139 24sh multicolored   1.40 .75
732 A139 33sh multicolored   2.00 2.00
733 A139 42sh multicolored   2.50 2.50
    Nos. 730-733 (4)   6.50 5.55

Pan African Postal Union (PAPU) A140

1998, June 10   **Litho.**   **Perf. 14½**
734 A140 10sh Lion   2.10 .30
735 A140 24sh Buffalo   2.75 .85
736 A140 33sh Grant's gazelle   3.75 3.75
737 A140 42sh Cheetah   5.00 5.00
    Nos. 734-737 (4)   13.60 9.90
    Souvenir Sheet
738 A140 50sh Hirola gazelle   4.50 4.50

Pres. Daniel arap Moi Taking Oath of Office, 1998 A141

1998, Dec. 8   **Litho.**   **Perf. 13½**
739 A141 14sh multicolored   1.50 .80

Turtles A142

Designs: 17sh, Leatherback. 20sh, Green sea. 30sh, Hawksbill. 47sh, Olive Ridley. 59sh, Loggerhead.

2000, Apr. 13   **Litho.**   **Perf. 13½x13¾**
740 A142 17sh multi   1.00 .35
741 A142 20sh multi   1.25 .40
742 A142 30sh multi   1.75 1.00
743 A142 47sh multi   2.50 2.50
744 A142 59sh multi   3.00 3.00
    Nos. 740-744 (5)   9.50 7.25

Emblems of East African Postal Administrations — A143

Designs: 17sh, Postal Corporation of Kenya. 35sh, Uganda Posta Limited. 50sh, Tanzania Posts Corporation. 70sh, Postal Corporation of Kenya.

2000, May 31   **Perf. 13¾x13½**
745 A143 17sh multi   .85 .35
746 A143 35sh multi   1.60 1.25
747 A143 50sh multi   2.25 2.25
    Nos. 745-747 (3)   4.70 3.85
    Souvenir Sheet
    Perf. 13¼x13
748 A143 70sh multi   4.50 4.50

Crops — A144

2001, Feb. 28   **Photo.**   **Perf. 14½x14**
749 A144 2sh Cotton   .25 .25
750 A144 4sh Bananas   .25 .25
751 A144 5sh Avocados   .25 .25
752 A144 6sh Cassava   .25 .25
753 A144 8sh Arrowroot   .25 .25
754 A144 10sh Papayas   .25 .25
755 A144 19sh Oranges   .50 .35
756 A144 20sh Pyrethrum   .50 .35
757 A144 30sh Peanuts   .75 .60
758 A144 35sh Coconuts   .90 .60
759 A144 40sh Sisal   1.00 .75
760 A144 50sh Cashews   1.25 .90

Size: 25x42mm
Perf. 14¼

761	A144	60sh Tea	1.50	1.00
762	A144	80sh Corn	2.00	1.50
763	A144	100sh Coffee	2.50	1.75
764	A144	200sh Finger millet	5.00	3.50
765	A144	400sh Sorghum	10.00	7.00
766	A144	500sh Sugar cane	12.50	8.50
		Nos. 749-766 (18)	39.90	28.30

2001   Photo.   Perf. 14¾ Horiz.
Coil Stamps

766A	A144	5sh Avocados	—	—
766B	A144	10sh Papayas	—	—

Historic Sites of East Africa A145

Designs: 19sh, Source of Nile River, Jinja, Uganda. 35sh, Lamu Fort, Kenya (28x28mm). 40sh, Olduvai Gorge, Tanzania. 50sh, Thimlich Ohinga, Kenya (28x28mm).

Perf. 14¼, 13½ (35sh, 50sh)

2002   Litho.

767-770	A145	Set of 4	9.50 9.50

Kenya - People's Republic of China Diplomatic Relations, 40th Anniv. — A146

Flags of Kenya and People's Republic of China and: 21sh, Section of Mombasa Road. 66sh, Kasarani Stadium.

2003, Dec. 14   Litho.   Perf. 12

771-772	A146	Set of 2	6.00 6.00

Mammals — A147

Designs: 21sh, Lioness and baby oryx. 60sh, Leopard and cub. 66sh, Zebra and calf. 88sh, Bongo and calf.

2004, Nov. 19   Litho.   Perf. 14½

773-776	A147	Set of 4	11.00 11.00

Easter — A148

Designs: 25sh, Jesus with hand raised. 65sh, Jesus condemned to death. 75sh, Crucifixion. 95sh, Jesus praying.

2005, Apr. 1   Litho.   Perf. 13½

777-780	A148	Set of 4	10.50 10.50

Rotary International, Cent. — A149

Rotary emblem and: 25sh, Polio vaccination. 65sh, Donation of Jaipur feet. 75sh, Don Bosco Center, Nairobi. 95sh, Donation of sewing machine.

2005, May 26

781-784	A149	Set of 4	12.00 12.00

Native Costumes A150

Designs: 21sh, Gabbra. 60sh, Pokot. 66sh, Meru. 88sh, Digo.

2005, Dec. 6   Litho.   Perf. 14½

785-788	A150	Set of 4	8.00 8.00

Fish A151

Designs: 25sh, Elephant snout fish. 55sh, Sudan catfish. 75sh, Nile perch. 95sh, Redbreast tilapia.

2006, May 4   Litho.   Perf. 13½x13

789	A151	25sh multi	— —
790	A151	55sh multi	— —
791	A151	75sh multi	— —
792	A151	95sh multi	— —

24th Universal Postal Union Congress, Nairobi — A152

2006, Oct. 11   Litho.   Perf. 13½

793	A152	25sh multi	1.25 1.25

Values are for stamps with surrounding selvage. Due to political unrest in Kenya, the UPU Congress was moved to Geneva, Switzerland.

Hippopotamus and Tortoise — A153

2006, Dec. 15   Litho.   Perf. 12½x13

794	A153	25sh multi	2.00 2.00

Tourism A155

2006, Dec. 15   Perf. 13
Booklet Stamps

795	A155	25sh Roan antelope	2.60	2.60
796	A155	25sh Weaver bird	2.60	2.60
797	A155	25sh Monkey	2.60	2.60
a.		Booklet pane of 3, #795-797	8.00	—
798	A155	25sh Turkana hut	2.60	2.60
799	A155	25sh Sports	2.60	2.60
800	A155	25sh Golf course	2.60	2.60
a.		Booklet pane of 3, #798-800	8.00	—
801	A155	25sh Abadares Waterfall	2.60	2.60
802	A155	25sh Balloon safari	2.60	2.60
803	A155	25sh Bull fighting	2.60	2.60
a.		Booklet pane of 3, #801-803	8.00	—
804	A155	25sh Chimpanzee	2.60	2.60
805	A155	25sh Maasai	2.60	2.60
806	A155	25sh Kit Mikaye	2.60	2.60
a.		Booklet pane of 3, #804-806	8.00	—
		Complete booklet, #797a, 800a, 803a, 806a	32.00	
		Nos. 795-806 (12)	31.20	31.20

Mountains — A156

Designs: 25sh, Mt. Kenya, Kenya. 75sh, Mt. Ruwenzori, Uganda. 95sh, Mt. Kilimanjaro, Tanzania.

2007, Feb. 28   Litho.   Perf. 13½

807-809	A156	Set of 3	6.25 6.25

Breast Cancer Awareness A157

2007, Oct. 28   Perf. 13¼

810	A157	25sh multi	1.25 1.25

Ceremonial Costumes — A158

Men's and women's costumes: 25sh, Ogiek. 65sh, Sabaot. 75sh, Ribe. 95sh, Elmolo.

2007, Nov. 21   Perf. 14½

811-814	A158	Set of 4	8.25 8.25

National Arboretum, Cent. — A159

Designs: 25sh, Cape chestnut tree and blossom. 65sh, Bhutan cypress tree, Tree Center. 75sh, Nandi flame tree and blossom. 95sh, Calabash nutmeg tree and blossom.

2007, Dec. 13   Litho.   Perf. 13¾

815-818	A159	Set of 4	8.25 8.25

24th UPU Congress — A160

Design: 25sh, Sitalunga gazelle in Saiwa Swamp. 65sh, Jackson's hartebeest at Ruma Park. 75sh, Steeplechase runner. 95sh, Kenyatta Intl. Conference Center, Nairobi.

2008, Feb. 7   Litho.   Perf. 14½

819	A160	25sh multi	1.00	.50
820	A160	65sh multi	2.50	1.50
821	A160	75sh multi	3.00	2.25
822	A160	95sh multi	3.75	3.75
		Nos. 819-822 (4)	10.25	8.00

Because of political turmoil in Kenya, the 24th UPU Congress was moved from Nairobi to Geneva, Switzerland.

2008 Summer Olympics, Beijing — A161

Designs: 25sh, Kenyan athletes holding Kenyan flag. 65sh, Women's volleyball, vert. 75sh, Women runners. 95sh, Boxing.

2008, Aug. 21   Litho.   Perf. 14½

823-826	A161	Set of 4	7.50 7.50

Heroes of Kenya — A162

Designs: 25sh, Vice-president Oginga Odinga (c. 1911-94), Pio Gama Pinto (1927-65), politician, Tom Mboya (1930-69), politician, Ronald Ngala (1923-72), politician. 65sh, The Kapenguria Six. 75sh, Dedan Kimathi (1920-57), rebel leader, Elijah Masinde (c. 1910-87), Bukusu tribal leader, Mekatilili Wa Menza, female leader of 1914 rebellion, Koitalel Samoei (1860-1905), Nandi chief. 95sh, Kenya Army Peacekeeping Force.

2008, Oct. 17   Perf. 12¾x13¼

827-830	A162	Set of 4	8.50 8.50

Theosophical Order of Service, Cent. — A163

2008, Nov. 17   Litho.   Perf. 14x13¾

831	A163	25sh multi	1.25 1.25

Aga Khan, 50th Anniv. of Reign
A164

Designs: 25sh, Madrasa program (40x40mm). 65sh, Coastal rural support program (40x40mm). 75sh, Aga Khan Academy, Mombasa (44x30mm). 95sh, Aga Khan University Hospital, Nairobi (44x30mm).

Perf. 13, 14½ (75sh, 95sh)
2008, Dec. 13
832-835 A164 Set of 4 7.50 7.50

Blind Man — A165

2009, July 20   **Perf. 14½**
836 A165 25sh multi .65 .65
Louis Braille (1809-52), educator of the blind.

Postal Services — A166

Designs: No. 837, 25sh, Man greeting woman, PostaPay emblem. No. 838, 25sh, Parcels, Posta Parcel emblem. No. 839, 25sh, Mailman and trucks, Posta Dispatch emblem. No. 840, 25sh, Stamp collector and stamps, Posta Philately emblem. No. 841, 25sh, Open post office box, Posta Direct Mail emblem. No. 842, 25sh, Agency services, Posta Kenya emblem. No. 843, 25sh, Woman reading letter, Posta Mail emblem. No. 844, 25sh, Man at open post office box, Posta Kenya emblem. No. 845, 25sh, Financial Services clerk and client, computer, Posta Money Order emblem. No. 846, 65sh, Postal worker with package at airport, EMS Kenya emblem. No. 847, 75sh, Narok Post Office, Posta Kenya emblem. No. 848, 95sh, People at water spigot, Posta Kenya emblem.

2009, Dec. 9   **Perf. 14x13¾**
837-848 A166 Set of 12 12.50 12.50
845a Sheet of 9, #837-845 6.00 6.00

East Africa Natural History Society, Cent. A167

Bird on branch and: 25sh, Taita African violet, Amegilla bee. 65sh, Reed frog. 75sh, Great blue turaco. 95sh, Golden-rumped sengi.

2010, Mar. 25   **Perf. 13**
Granite Paper
849-852 A167 Set of 4 6.75 6.75

Insects A168

No. 853: a, Danaus chrysippus (African monarch). b, Pontia helice. c, Junonia hierta (Yellow pansy). d, Chiasmia subcurvaria. e, Catopsilia florella (African migrant). f, Belenois thysa (False dotted border). g, Leucinodes orbonalis sp. h, Gelechioidea sp. i, Eupitheca sp. cf. festiva. j, Nymphalidae. k, Paraccra mimesa. l, Hodebertia testalis. m, Alucitidae sp. n, Anthozela sp. n. o, Eucosmini gen. n. sp. n. p, Eucosmini sp. q, Zalaca snelleni. r, Yponomeuta strigillata. s, Tortrix dinota. t, Parotis sp. nr. prasinalis. u, Precis hierta. v, Colotis antevippe. w, Cryptophlebia semilunana. x, Hypolimnas misippus. y, Yponomeuta fumigatus.
No. 854: a, Oplostomus haroldi (Large hive beetle). b, Cartoblatta sp. (Cockroaches). c, Mormotomyia hirsuta. d, Cicindellidae. e, Nosognatha ruficollis. f, Hetrodinae sp. g, Helopeltis schoutedeni. h, Ceroctis sp. (Blister beetle). i, Bagrada cruciferarum. j, Popillia aeneipennis (Chafer). k, Lampetis sp. (Jewel beetle). l, Oryctes sp. (Rhinoceros beetle). m, Homoderus mellyi. n, Zonocerus variegatus. o, Leucospidae. p, Agnoscelis versicolor. q, Hispinae (Tortoise beetle). r, Curculionidae. s, Cypholoba perspicillaris. t, Lycidae. u, Milkweed bugs. v, Mylabris tristigma. w, Paederus sp. x, Pyrops turritus. y, Tenebrionidae.
No. 855: a, Fig wasp in flight. b, Ptyelus flavescens (Rain tree bug). c, Phlebotomus feeding. d, Fig wasp, head at bottom. e, Trithemis annulata (Dragonfly). f, Braconid wasp. g, Polistes sp. (Paper wasps). h, Helopeltis schoutedeni. i, Trithemis sp. (Dragonfly). j, Cicada. k, Silverfish. l, Stingless bee. m, Lipotriches sp. n, Bombyliidae. o, Bromophila caffra. p, Schistocerca gregaria. q, Plagiotryptus hippiscus. r, Reduviidae. s, Diopsidae (Stalk-eyed fly). t, Lamyra gulo and wasp prey. u, Dictyopharidae. v, Rhiniidae cf. Fainia sp. w, Locust. x, Megastigmus sp. m. y, Glossina morsitans feeding.
No. 856: a, Bactrocera invadens, head at top. b, Trihrithrum culcasiae. c, Trirhithrum coffeae. d, Bactrocera invadens, head at bottom. e, Bactrocera munroi. f, Caprophthoromyia dimidiata. g, Celidodacus obnubilus. h, Ceratitis caetrata. i, Ceratitis captiata. j, Ceratitis copelandi. k, Ceratitis cosyra. l, Ceratitis cuthbertsoni. m, Ceratitis rosa. n, Ceratitis stictica. o, Ceratitis whartoni. p, Conradtina acroleuca. q, Dacus apostata. r, Dacus frontalis. s, Dacus sphaeristicus. t, Dacus telfairae. u, Munromyia whartoni. v, Craspedoxantha sp. w, Taomyia marshalli. x, Themarictera laticeps. y, Trirhithrum albomaculatum.

2011, Nov. 16   **Perf. 13x13¼**
853 Sheet of 25 14.00 14.00
a.-y. A168 25sh Any single .55 .55
854 Sheet of 25 37.50 37.50
a.-y. A168 65sh Any single 1.50 1.50
855 Sheet of 25 44.00 44.00
a.-y. A168 75sh Any single 1.75 1.75
856 Sheet of 25 52.50 52.50
a.-y. A168 95sh Any single 2.10 2.10
Nos. 853-856 (4) 148.00 148.00

Intl. Center of Insect Physiology and Endocrinology, 40th anniv.

Promulgation of New Constitution A169

2011   **Perf. 14½**
857 A169 25sh multi .60 .60

United Nations Environment Program, 40th Anniv. — A170

Designs: 30sh, Flags at UNEP regional office, Nairobi. 90sh, Buildings in Stockholm, Sweden. 110sh, Christ the Redeemer Statue, Rio de Janeiro.

2012   **Perf. 14**
858-860 A170 Set of 3 5.50 5.50

United Nations Environment Program, 40th Anniv. — A171

United Nations Environment Program emblem and emblem for: 30sh, Convention on International Trade in Endangered Species of Wild Fauna and Flora. 90sh, Montreal Protocol on Substances that Deplete the Ozone Layer. 110sh, Green Economy,

2012, June 22 **Litho.** **Perf. 14**
861-863 A171 Set of 3 5.50 5.50

Wangari Muta Maathai (1940-2011), 2004 Nobel Peace Laureate — A173

2012, Sept. 25 **Litho.** **Perf. 14**
867 A173 30sh multi .70 .70

Independence, 50th Anniv. — A174

No. 868: a, First airplane to land in Kenya, 1920. b, 1904 locomotive. c, East Africa Railway & Harbor train car. d, Jamhuri High School. e, Prince of Wales School. f, Machakos Girls School. g, Royal Technical College, University of Nairobi. h, Kenyatta University. i, Jomo Kenyatta University of Agriculture & Technology. j, Nairobi skyline. k, King George VI Hospital. l, Kenyatta National Hospital. m, Jomo Kenyatta International Airport. n, Mobile library. o, Kenya National Library, Nairobi. p, Horticulture. q, Poultry farming. r, Corn farming (maize). s, Beef farming. t, Dairy farming. u, Compulsory free primary education. v, Kenya National Adult Literacy Survey. w, Murang's Road Junction. x, Globe Cinema Complex. y, Oil prospecting.
No. 869: a, Pres. Uhuru Kenyatta and Deputy Pres. William Ruto. b, Queen Elizabeth II and Prince Philip, 1953. c, Lancaster House Conference, 1963. d, Dedan Kimathi. e, Mau Mau movement. f, Kapenguria Six. g, Kapenguria cells. h, Lowering of the Union Jack, 1963. i, Munyao Kisol hoisting Kenyan flag on Mt. Kenya, 1963. j, Promulgation of new constitution. k, First transition. l, Second transition. m, Third transition. n, Fourth transition. o, Parliament Building. p, First Cabinet, 1963. q, Colonial and current coats of arms. r, Colonial and current flags. s, Maps showing the eight provinces and 47 counties. t, Judiciary Building. u, Kenyatta Mausoleum. v, Old Provincial Commissioner's Office, 1913. w, Nyayo House. x, Baron Delamere, first governor of Nairobi. y, Kenya Defense Forces in Somalia.
No. 870: a, Fort Jesus, 1565. b, Kenya-Uganda railway line, 1896. c, Nyali Bridge, 1900. d, Gedi Ruins, 13th cent. e, First Post Office in Mombasa, 1902. f, First General Post Office in Mombasa, 1920. g, First General Post Office in Nairobi, 1944. h, Kenya National Archives, 1944. i, Macmillan Library, 1925. j, Nairobi National Museum, 1890. k, 1885 Mombasa coins. l, Maasai Morans. m, Luo traditional homestead. n, Karen Blixen Museum. o, Kipande House, 1913. p, Laikipia camel caravan. q, East Africa and Uganda Protectorates #53, Kenya #8. r, Chaka drummers. s, Obokano musical instrument. t, Vasco da Gama Pillar, Malindi. u, Naftali Temu, first Kenyan Olympic gold medalist. v, Pamela Jelimo, Janeth Jepkosgei, runners. w, Ezekiel

Kemboi, 2004 Olympic steeplechase gold medalist. x, David Rudisha, 2012 Olympic 800-meter gold medalist. y, Kenya Rugby Union national team.
No. 871: a, Lion. b, Elephant. c, Leopard. d, Rhinoceros. e, Buffalo. f, Hippopotamus. g, Cheetah. h, Giraffe. i, Zebra. j, Warthog. k, Wildebeest migration. l, Bongo. m, Impala. n, Hyena. o, Jackal. p, Crocodiles on Tana River. q, Flamingos at Lake Nakuru. r, Ostriches. s, Colobus monkey. t, Falcon. u, Longonot Crater. v, Thompson Falls, Nyahururu. w, Mt. Kenya. x, Lake Turkana. y, Solar eclipse.

Perf. 13½x13¼ Syncopated
2013, Dec. 13   **Litho.**
868 Sheet of 25 17.50 17.50
a.-y. A174 30sh Any single .70 .70
869 Sheet of 25 44.00 44.00
a.-y. A174 75sh Any single 1.75 1.75
870 Sheet of 25 52.50 52.50
a.-y. A174 90sh Any single 2.10 2.10
871 Sheet of 25 65.00 65.00
a.-y. A174 110sh Any single 2.60 2.60
Nos. 868-871 (4) 179.00 179.00

Diplomatic Relations Between Kenya and People's Republic of China, 50th Anniv. — A175

Flags of Kenya and People's Republic of China and: 30sh, Ship, Kenyan and Chinese containers. 110sh, Cranes, Kenyan Pres. Uhuru Kenyatta, Chinese Pres. Xi Jinping.

2013, Dec. 20 **Litho.** **Perf. 12**
875-876 A175 Set of 2 3.25 3.25

POSTAGE DUE STAMPS

D1

Perf. 14x13½
1967-85 **Litho.** **Unwmk.**
"POSTAGE DUE" 12½mm long
J1 D1 5c dark red .25 2.75
J2 D1 10c green .35 2.75
J3 D1 20c dark blue .70 3.25
J4 D1 30c reddish brown 1.00 4.00
J5 D1 40c brt red lilac 1.25 6.75
Perf. 14
J6 D1 80c brick red 1.00 6.25
Perf. 14x13½
J7 D1 1sh orange 3.00 9.00
"POSTAGE DUE" 11½mm long
Perf. 14¾x14
J8 D1 2sh pale violet .90 .90
Nos. J1-J8 (8) 8.45 35.65
Issued: 80c, 1978. 2sh, 1985; others, 1/3/67. See Nos. J9-J14.

1969-70   **Perf. 14**
J1a D1 5c .25 5.25
J2a D1 10c .25 5.25
J3a D1 20c .45 5.75
J4a D1 30c .70 6.75
J5a D1 40c .90 10.50
J7a D1 1sh 2.00 13.50
Nos. J1a-J7a (6) 4.55 47.00
Issued: 1sh, 2/18/70; others, 12/16/69.

1971-73   **Perf. 14x15**
J1b D1 5c 1.75 5.25
J2b D1 10c 1.75 5.25
J3b D1 20c 1.50 5.75
J4b D1 30c 10.50 13.50
J5b D1 40c 1.25 9.00
J7b D1 1sh 2.50 13.50
Nos. J1b-J7b (6) 19.25 52.25
Issued: 30c, 7/13/71; others, 2/20/73. The 10c, 20c, 1sh on chalky paper were issued 7/13/71.

1973, Dec. 12 **Perf. 15**

J1c	D1	5c	.45	4.00
J2c	D1	10c	.45	4.00
J3c	D1	20c	.45	5.00
J4c	D1	30c	.45	5.75
J5c	D1	40c	5.25	10.00
J7c	D1	1sh	1.75	12.50
	Nos. J1c-J7c (6)		8.80	41.25

1983 **Wmk. 373** **Perf. 14x14¼**

J2d	D1	10c	.45	2.00
J3d	D1	20c	.45	2.00
J5d	D1	40c	8.50	10.00

Nos. J5, J7-J8 Redrawn
Perf. 14¾x14

1987-98 **Litho.** **Unwmk.**

J8A	D1	30c brown	.25	.25
J9	D1	40c bright red lilac	.25	.25
J10	D1	50c dark green	.25	.25
J10A	D1	80c red brown	.25	.25
J11	D1	1sh light orange	.80	.80
a.		light orange	.25	.25
J12	D1	2sh pale violet	.25	.25
J13	D1	3sh dark blue	.45	.45
J14	D1	5sh red brown	.45	.45
J15	D1	10sh brown	.45	.45
J16	D1	20sh red lilac	.80	.80
	Nos. J8A-J16 (10)		4.20	4.20

"KENYA" is 9mm wide on Nos. J9, J11. "CENTS" is 4½mm wide and "SHILLING" has cross bar on "G"; both are in a new font.
"KENYA" is 8½mm wide on No. J12. "POST-AGE DUE" is 11mm wide on Nos. J10, J11a, J15, J16.
Issued: 40c, 1sh, 1987; 10sh, 20sh, 1998; others, Dec. 6, 1993.

OFFICIAL STAMPS

Nos. 1-5 and 7
Overprinted

Perf. 14x14½

1964, Oct. 1 **Photo.** **Unwmk.**
Size: 21x17½mm

O1	A1	5c blue, buff & dk brn	.25	.25
O2	A1	10c brown	.25	.25
O3	A1	15c dp magenta	1.50	.30
O4	A1	20c yel green & dk brn	.30	.45
O5	A1	30c yellow & black	.40	.65
O6	A1	50c green, blk & dp car	2.75	1.10
	Nos. O1-O6 (6)		5.45	3.00

KENYA, UGANDA, & TANZANIA

ˈke-nyə, ü-ˈgan-də, ˌtan-zə-ˈnē-ə

LOCATION — East Africa, bordering on the Indian Ocean
GOVT. — States in British Commonwealth
AREA — 679,802 sq. mi.
POP. — 42,760,000 (est. 1977)
CAPITAL — Nairobi (Kenya), Kampala (Uganda), Dar es Salaam (Tanzania)

Kenya became a crown colony in 1906, including the former East Africa Protectorate leased from the Sultan of Zanzibar and known as the Kenya Protectorate. In 1963 the colony became independent. Its stamps are listed under "Kenya."
The inland Uganda Protectorate, lying west of Kenya Colony, was declared a British Protectorate in 1894. Uganda became independent in 1962.
Tanganyika, a trust territory larger than Kenya or Uganda, was grouped with them postally from 1935 under the East African Posts & Telecommunications Administration. Tanganyika became independent in 1961. When it merged with Zanzibar in 1964, "Zanzibar" was added to the inscriptions on stamps issued under the E.A.P. & T. Administration. In 1965 the multiple inscription was changed to "Kenya, Uganda, Tanzania," variously arranged.

Zanzibar withdrew its own stamps in 1968, and K., U. & T. stamps became valid Jan. 1, 1968.

100 Cents = 1 Rupee
100 Cents = 1 Shilling (1922)
20 Shillings = 1 Pound

Catalogue values for unused stamps in this country are for Never Hinged items, beginning with Scott 90.

East Africa and Uganda Protectorates

King George V
A1   A2

1921 **Typo.** **Wmk. 4** **Perf. 14**
Ordinary Paper

1	A1	1c black	.90	1.90
2	A1	3c green	6.75	12.00
3	A1	6c rose red	9.00	17.50
4	A1	10c orange	9.75	1.40
5	A1	12c gray	9.00	140.00
6	A1	15c ultramarine	12.50	19.00

Chalky Paper

7	A1	50c gray lilac & blk	16.50	120.00
8	A2	2r blk & red, blue	82.50	190.00
9	A2	3r green & violet	150.00	350.00
10	A2	5r gray lil & ultra	190.00	275.00
11	A2	50r gray grn & red	5,250.	8,250.
	Nos. 1-10 (10)		486.90	1,126.

The name of the colony was changed to Kenya in August, 1920, but stamps of the East Africa and Uganda types were continued in use. Stamps of types A1 and A2 watermarked Multiple Crown and C A (3) are listed under East Africa and Uganda Protectorates.
For stamps of Kenya and Uganda overprinted "G. E. A." used in parts of former German East Africa occupied by British forces, see Tanganyika Nos. 1-9.

Kenya and Uganda

King George V
A3   A4

1922-27 **Wmk. 4**

18	A3	1c brown	1.10	4.25
19	A3	5c violet	5.00	1.00
20	A3	5c grn ('27)	2.40	.55
21	A3	10c green	1.75	.35
22	A3	10c blk ('27)	4.50	.25
23	A3	12c black	12.00	29.00
24	A3	15c car rose	1.40	.25
25	A3	20c orange	3.75	.25
26	A3	30c ultra	4.25	.60
27	A3	50c gray	2.75	.25
28	A3	75c ol bister	9.00	15.00
29	A4	1sh green	5.50	3.00
30	A4	2sh gray lil	10.00	18.00
31	A4	2sh50c brn ('25)	24.00	110.00
32	A4	3sh gray blk	20.00	7.50
33	A4	4sh gray	35.00	125.00
		('25)		
34	A4	5sh carmine	27.50	27.50
35	A4	7sh50c org ('25)	120.00	275.00
36	A4	10sh ultra	70.00	70.00
37	A4	£1 org & blk	225.00	300.00
		Revenue cancel		20.00
38	A4	£2 brn vio & grn	1,100.	1,850.
		('25)		
		Revenue cancel		120.00
39	A4	£3 yel & dl vio	1,650.	—
		('25)		
		Revenue cancel		180.00
40	A4	£4 rose lil & blk	5,000.	—
		('25)		
		Revenue cancel		225.00
41	A4	£5 blue & blk	5,500.	—
		Revenue cancel		375.00

41A	A4	£10 grn & blk	14,000.	
		Revenue cancel		475.00
41B	A4	£20 grn & red	34,500.	
		('25)		
		Revenue cancel		850.00
41C	A4	£25 red & blk	37,500.	
		Revenue cancel		800.00
41D	A4	£50 brn & blk	45,000.	
		Revenue cancel		900.00
41E	A4	£75 gray & purple	140,000.	
		Revenue cancel		1,750.
41F	A4	£100 blk & red	150,000.	
		Revenue cancel		1,800.
	Nos. 18-37 (20)		584.90	987.75

High face value stamps are known with revenue cancellations removed and forged postal cancellations added.

Common Design Types pictured following the introduction.

Kenya, Uganda, Tanganyika
Silver Jubilee Issue
Common Design Type

1935, May **Engr.** **Perf. 13½x14**

42	CD301	20c ol grn & lt bl	2.00	.25
43	CD301	30c blue & brown	3.00	3.50
44	CD301	65c indigo & green	2.00	3.25
45	CD301	1sh brt vio & indigo	2.25	5.50
	Nos. 42-45 (4)		9.25	12.50
	Set, never hinged		16.00	

Kavirondo Cranes — A5

Dhow on Lake Victoria — A6

Lion — A7

Mount Kilimanjaro — A8

Jinja Bridge by Ripon Falls — A9

Mount Kenya — A10

Lake Naivasha A11

FIVE CENTS
Type I — Left rope does not touch sail.
Type II — Left rope touches sail.

Perf. 13, 14, 11½x13, 13x11½
Engr.; Typo. (10c, £1)

1935, May 1

46	A5	1c red brn & blk	1.00	1.50
47	A6	5c grn & blk (I)	3.25	.50
a.		Type II	35.00	7.50
b.		Perf. 13x11½ (I)	9,250.	1,000.
c.		Perf. 13x11½ (II)	825.00	225.00
48	A7	10c black & yel	6.50	.65
49	A8	15c red & black	3.50	.25
50	A5	20c red org & blk	3.50	.25
51	A9	30c dk ultra & blk	4.75	1.00
52	A6	50c blk & red vio	5.00	.25
53	A10	65c yel brn & blk	7.00	2.00
54	A11	1sh grn & black	5.00	1.00
a.		Perf. 13x11½ ('36)	1,425.	135.00
55	A8	2sh red vio & rose brn	12.00	4.50
56	A11	3sh blk & ultra	17.50	17.50
a.		Perf. 13x11½	2,500.	
57	A9	5sh car & black	35.00	35.00
58	A5	10sh ultra & red vio	95.00	125.00
59	A7	£1 blk & scar	275.00	400.00
	Nos. 46-59 (14)		464.00	589.40
	Set, never hinged		900.00	

Coronation Issue
Common Design Type

1937, May 12 **Engr.** **Perf. 13½x14**

60	CD302	5c deep green	.25	.25
61	CD302	20c deep orange	.40	.35
62	CD302	30c brt ultra	.60	1.75
	Nos. 60-62 (3)		1.25	2.35
	Set, never hinged		2.00	

Kavirondo Cranes — A12

Dhow on Lake Victoria — A13

Lake Naivasha — A14   Jinja Bridge, Ripon Falls — A16

Mt. Kilimanjaro A15

Lion — A17

Type II

FIFTY CENTS:
Type I — Left rope does not touch sail.
Type II — Left rope touches sail.

1938-54   Engr.   Perf. 13x13½

66	A12	1c vio brn & blk ('42)	.25	.50
a.		1c red brown & gray black, perf. 13	2.75	.85

Perf. 13x11½

67	A13	5c grn & blk	3.00	.50
68	A13	5c red org & brn ('49)	1.00	6.00
a.		Perf. 13x12½ ('50)	1.75	4.00
69	A14	10c org & brn	1.90	.25
a.		Perf. 14 ('41)	95.00	10.00
70	A14	10c grn & blk ('49)	.25	2.00
a.		Perf. 13x12½ ('50)	2.40	.25

Perf. 13x12½

71	A14	10c gray & red brn ('52)	1.00	.55

Perf. 13½x13, 13x13½

72	A15	15c car & gray blk ('43)	3.50	3.75
a.		Booklet pane of 4	15.00	
b.		Perf. 13	25.00	.55
73	A15	15c grn & blk ('52)	1.75	6.00
74	A12	20c org & gray blk ('42)	5.75	.25
a.		Booklet pane of 4	24.00	
b.		Imperf., pair		
c.		Perf. 13	35.00	.30
d.		Perf. 14 ('41)	45.00	3.00

Perf. 13x12½

75	A13	25c car & blk ('52)	1.25	2.25

Perf. 13x13½

76	A16	30c dp bl & gray blk ('42)	2.00	.35
a.		Perf. 14 ('41)	130.00	12.50
b.		Perf. 13	40.00	.40
77	A16	30c brn & pur ('52)	1.25	.40
78	A12	40c brt bl & gray blk ('52)	1.50	5.00

Perf. 13x12½

79	A13	50c gray blk & red vio (II) ('49)	5.75	.60
a.		Perf. 13x11½ (II)	14.00	1.10
b.		Perf. 13x11½ (I)	175.00	250.00

Perf. 13x11½

80	A14	1sh yel brn & gray blk	18.00	.30
a.		Perf. 13x12½ ('49)	10.00	.60

Perf. 13½x13

81	A15	2sh red vio & org brn ('44)	27.50	.30
a.		Perf. 13	110.00	17.50
b.		Perf. 14 ('41)	62.50	17.50

Perf. 13x12½

82	A14	3sh gray blk & ultra ('50)	30.00	8.00
a.		Perf. 13x11½	35.00	8.00

Perf. 13x13½

83	A16	5sh car rose & gray blk ('44)	30.00	1.75
a.		Perf. 13	125.00	20.00
b.		Perf. 14 ('41)	35.00	2.75
84	A12	10sh ultra & red vio ('44)	40.00	7.50
a.		Perf. 13	110.00	30.00
b.		Perf. 14 ('41)	32.50	22.50

Typo.
Perf. 14

85	A17	£1 blk & scar ('41)	22.50	27.50
a.		Perf. 11½x13	300.00	170.00
b.		Perf. 12½ ('54)	12.00	40.00
		Nos. 66-85 (20)	198.15	73.75
		Set, never hinged	300.00	

Nos. 85-85b were printed on chalky paper. No. 85 also exists on ordinary paper, from a 1944 printing. Values are the same.
See Nos. 98-99.

South Africa Nos. 48, 57, 60 and 62 Surcharged

Basic stamps of Nos. 86-89 are inscribed alternately in English and Afrikaans.

1941-42   Wmk. 201   Perf. 15x14, 14

86	A6	5c on 1p car & gray, pair	1.00	2.00
a.		Single, English	.25	.25
b.		Single, Afrikaans	.25	.25
87	A17	10c on 3p ultra, pair	3.00	10.00
a.		Single, English	.30	.35
b.		Single, Afrikaans	.30	.35
88	A7	20c on 6p org & grn, pair	2.50	3.75
a.		Single, English	.25	.25
b.		Single, Afrikaans	.25	.25
89	A11	70c on 1sh lt bl & ol brn, pair	15.00	7.00
a.		Single, English	.50	.45
b.		Single, Afrikaans	.50	.45
		Nos. 86-89 (4)	21.50	22.75
		Set, never hinged	30.00	

Issued: Nos. 86-88, 7/1/41; No. 89, 4/20/42.

Values are for horizontal pairs. Vertical pairs are worth substantially less.

> **Catalogue values for unused stamps in this section, from this point to the end of the section, are for Never Hinged items.**

Peace Issue
Common Design Type
Perf. 13½x14

1946, Nov. 11		**Engr.**		**Wmk. 4**
90	CD303	20c red orange	.25	.25
91	CD303	30c deep blue	.40	.40

Silver Wedding Issue
Common Design Types

1948, Dec. 1		**Photo.**		**Perf. 14x14½**
92	CD304	20c orange	.25	.25

Engr.; Name Typo.
Perf. 11½x11

93	CD305	£1 red	52.50	72.50

UPU Issue
Common Design Types
Engr.; Typo. on Nos. 95 and 96

1949, Oct. 10			**Perf. 13, 11x11½**	
94	CD306	20c red orange	.25	.25
95	CD307	30c indigo	1.75	2.25
96	CD308	50c gray	.40	.40
97	CD309	1sh red brown	.50	.50
		Nos. 94-97 (4)	2.90	3.40

Type of 1949 with Added Inscription: "Royal Visit 1952"

1952, Feb. 1		**Engr.**		**Perf. 13x12½**
98	A14	10c green & black	.30	1.60
99	A14	1sh yel brn & gray blk	1.25	2.25

Visit of Princess Elizabeth, Duchess of Edinburgh, and the Duke of Edinburgh, 1952.

Coronation Issue
Common Design Type

1953, June 2			**Perf. 13½x13**	
101	CD312	20c red orange & blk	.40	.25

Owen Falls Dam — A18

1954, Apr. 28   Perf. 12½x13
Inscribed "ROYAL VISIT 1954"

102	A18	30c dp ultra & black	.50	.25

Visit of Queen Elizabeth II and the Duke of Edinburgh, 1954.

Owen Falls Dam — A18a

Giraffe — A19

Mt. Kilimanjaro A20

Elizabeth II — A21

5c, 30c, Owen Falls Dam (without "Royal Visit 1954"). 20c, 40c, 1sh, Lion. 15c, 1.30sh, 5sh, Elephants. 10sh, Royal Lodge, Sagana.

1954-59   Perf. 12½x13, 13x12½

103	A18a	5c choc & blk	1.75	.65
a.		Booklet pane of 4	7.00	
		Vignette (dam) inverted		67,500.
104	A19	10c carmine	1.75	.25
a.		Booklet pane of 4	7.00	
105	A20	15c lt blue & blk (no period below "c") ('58)	1.00	1.60
a.		Booklet pane of 4	4.00	
106	A20	15c lt blue & blk (period below "c") ('59)	1.00	1.60
a.		Booklet pane of 4	4.00	
107	A19	20c org & black	2.00	.25
a.		Booklet pane of 4	8.00	
b.		Imperf., pair	1,300.	1,500.
108	A18a	30c ultra & black	1.50	.25
a.		Booklet pane of 4	6.00	
b.		Vignette (dam) inverted		32,500.
109	A19	40c brown ('58)	1.50	1.00
110	A19	50c dp red lilac	3.50	.25
a.		Booklet pane of 4	14.00	
111	A20	65c brn car & grn ('55)	3.50	2.00
112	A19	1sh dp mag & blk	3.75	.25
113	A20	1.30sh pur & red org ('55)	17.50	.25
114	A20	2sh dp grn & gray	16.00	1.50
115	A20	5sh black & org	32.50	3.50
116	A20	10sh ultra & black	40.00	8.75
117	A21	£1 black & ver	21.00	20.00
		Nos. 103-117 (15)	148.25	42.10

No. 103b is unique.
For "Official" overprints see Tanganyika Nos. O1-O12.

Map Showing Lakes Victoria and Tanganyika A22

Perf. 12½x13

1958, July 30		**Engr.**		**Wmk. 314**
118	A22	40c green & blue	.90	.40
119	A22	1.30sh violet & green	.90	1.00

Cent. of the discovery of Lakes Victoria and Tanganyika by Sir Richard F. Burton and Capt. J. H. Speke.

Sisal — A23

A25

Mount Kenya and Giant Plants A24

10c, Cotton. 15c, Coffee. 20c, Gnu. 25c, Ostriches. 30c, Thompson's gazelles. 40c, Manta ray. 50c, Zebras. 65c, Cheetah. 1.30sh, Murchison Falls & hippopotamuses. 2sh, Mt. Kilimanjaro & giraffes. 2.50sh, Candelabra tree & black rhinoceroses. 5sh, Crater Lake & Mountains of the Moon. 10sh, Ngorongoro Crater & buffaloes.

Perf. 14½x14

1960, Oct. 1		**Photo.**		**Wmk. 314**
120	A23	5c dull blue	.25	.25
121	A23	10c lt olive green	.25	.25
a.		Booklet pane of 4	.60	
122	A23	15c dull purple	.40	.25
a.		Booklet pane of 4	1.75	
123	A23	20c brt lilac rose	.25	.25
a.		Booklet pane of 4	1.20	
124	A23	25c olive gray	4.00	1.25
125	A23	30c brt vermilion	.25	.25
a.		Booklet pane of 4	.90	
126	A23	40c bright blue	.30	.25
127	A23	50c dull violet	.45	.25
a.		Booklet pane of 4	1.90	
128	A23	65c lemon	.65	1.75

Engr.
Perf. 14

129	A24	1sh vio & red lilac	1.00	.25
130	A24	1.30sh choc & dk car	6.50	.25
131	A24	2sh dk bl & dull bl	8.50	.55
132	A24	2.50sh ol grn & dull bl	11.00	2.75
133	A24	5sh rose red & lil	4.75	.60
134	A24	10sh sl bl & ol grn	15.00	7.00

Perf. 13½x13

135	A25	20sh lake & bluish violet	26.00	30.00
		Nos. 120-135 (16)	79.55	46.15

Booklets issued in 1961.
On Nos. 120-134, positions of "Kenya," "Uganda" and "Tanganyika" are rotated.
For "Official" overprints see Tanganyika Nos. O13-O20.

Agricultural Development — A26

Design: 30c, 1.30sh, Farmer picking corn.

Unwmk.

1963, Mar. 21		**Photo.**		**Perf. 14**
136	A26	15c lt ol grn & ultra	.25	.25
137	A26	30c yel & red brown	.35	.25
138	A26	50c dp org & ultra	.50	.25
139	A26	1.30sh lt blue & red brn	1.10	1.00
		Nos. 136-139 (4)	2.20	1.75

FAO "Freedom from Hunger" campaign.

Scholars and Open Book A27

1963, June 28		**Unwmk.**		**Perf. 14**
140	A27	30c multicolored	.25	.25
141	A27	1.30sh multicolored	.30	.30

Inauguration of University of East Africa.

Red Cross A28

1963, Sept. 2				
142	A28	30c blue & red	1.25	.30
143	A28	50c bister brown & red	1.50	1.25

Centenary of International Red Cross.

Kenya, Uganda, Tanganyika and Zanzibar
Issued by the East African Common Services Organization. Not used in Zanzibar.

Japanese Crest and Olympic Rings — A29

Olympic Rings and Banners A30

Unwmk.
1964, Oct. 25   Photo.   Perf. 14
144	A29	30c org & dk purple	.25	.25
145	A29	50c dk purple & org	.25	.25
146	A30	1.30sh blue, grn & org	.35	.25
147	A30	2.50sh blue, vlo & lil rose	.40	.75
		Nos. 144-147 (4)	1.25	1.50

18th Olympic Games, Tokyo, Oct. 10-25.

Kenya, Uganda, Tanzania
Issued by the East African Common Services Organization.

Safari Rally Emblem and Leopard — A31

1.30sh, 2.50sh, Car on road through national park & emblem of the East African Safari Rally.

1965, Apr. 15   Unwmk.   Perf. 14
148	A31	30c blue grn, yel & blk	.25	.25
149	A31	50c brown, yel & blk	.25	.25
150	A31	1.30sh lt ultra, ocher & green	.25	.25
151	A31	2.50sh blue, dk grn & dull red	.60	1.25
		Nos. 148-151 (4)	1.35	2.00

13th East African Safari Rally, 4/15-19/65.

ITU Emblem, Old and Modern Communication Equipment — A32

1965, May 17   Photo.
152	A32	30c lilac rose, gold & brn	.25	.25
153	A32	50c gray, gold & brown	.25	.25
154	A32	1.30sh lt vio bl, gold & brn	.40	.25
155	A32	2.50sh brt bl grn, gold & brn	1.25	1.25
		Nos. 152-155 (4)	2.15	2.00

Cent. of the ITU.

ICY Emblem — A33

1965, Aug. 4   Unwmk.   Perf. 14
156	A33	30c green & gold	.25	.25
157	A33	50c slate blk & gold	.25	.25
158	A33	1.30sh ultra & gold	.40	.25
159	A33	2.50sh car & gold	1.00	1.00
		Nos. 156-159 (4)	1.90	1.75

International Cooperation Year.

Game Park Lodge A34

Tourist Publicity: 50c, Murchison Falls, Uganda. 1.30sh, Lake Nakuru, Kenya. 2.50sh, Deep-sea fishing, Tanzania.

1966, Apr. 4   Photo.   Perf. 14
160	A34	30c ocher & multi	.50	.25
161	A34	50c green & multi	.60	.25
	a.	Blue omitted	400.00	
162	A34	1.30sh multicolored	3.00	.35
163	A34	2.50sh gray & multi	2.00	2.50
		Nos. 160-163 (4)	6.10	3.35

Javelin Thrower and Games' Emblem A35

1966, Aug. 2   Unwmk.   Perf. 14
164	A35	30c multicolored	.25	.25
165	A35	50c multicolored	.25	.25
166	A35	1.30sh multicolored	.25	.25
167	A35	2.50sh multicolored	.30	1.25
		Nos. 164-167 (4)	1.05	2.00

8th British Commonwealth and Empire Games, Jamaica, Aug. 4-13, 1966.

UNESCO Emblem — A36

1966, Oct. 3   Photo.   Perf. 14
168	A36	30c rose red, brt grn & blk	.45	.25
169	A36	50c lt brn, brt grn & blk	.55	.25
170	A36	1.30sh gray, brt grn & blk	1.50	.25
171	A36	2.50sh yel, brt grn & blk	2.00	4.75
		Nos. 168-171 (4)	4.50	5.50

20th anniv. of UNESCO.

Dragon Rapide A37

Planes: 50c, Super VC10. 1.30sh, Comet 4. 2.50sh, F.27 Friendship.

1967, Jan. 23   Unwmk.
172	A37	30c multicolored	.30	.25
173	A37	50c multicolored	.40	.25
174	A37	1.30sh multicolored	.85	.30
175	A37	2.50sh multicolored	1.40	3.00
		Nos. 172-175 (4)	2.95	3.80

21st anniversary of East African Airways.

Pillar Tomb, East African Coast — A38

Designs: 50c, Man hunting elephant, petroglyph, Tanzania. 1.30sh, Clay head, Luzira, Uganda. 2.50sh, Proconsul skull, Rusinga Island, Kenya.

1967, May 2   Photo.   Perf. 14
176	A38	30c rose lake, blk & yel	.25	.25
177	A38	50c gray, black & ver	.60	.25
178	A38	1.30sh green, yel & blk	.85	.25
179	A38	2.50sh cop red, yel & blk	1.35	2.50
		Nos. 176-179 (4)	3.05	3.25

Archaeological relics of East Africa.

Emblems of Kenya, Tanzania and Tanganyika — A39

Photo.; Gold Impressed
1967, Dec. 1   Perf. 14½x14
180	A39	5sh gray, black & gold	.55	1.00

Establishment of East African Community.

Mountain climber A40

30c Mountain climber. 50c, Mount Kenya. 1.30sh, Mount Kilimanjaro. 2.50sh, Ruwenzori Mountains.

1968, Mar. 4   Photo.   Perf. 14½
181	A40	30c multicolored	.25	.25
182	A40	50c multicolored	.35	.25
183	A40	1.30sh multicolored	.60	.25
184	A40	2.50sh multicolored	1.10	2.00
		Nos. 181-184 (4)	2.30	2.75

Family and Rural Hospital A41

Family and: 50c, Student nurse. 1.30sh, Microscope. 2.50sh, Mosquito and hand holding hypodermic.

1968, May 13   Photo.   Perf. 13½
185	A41	30c multicolored	.25	.25
186	A41	50c rose vio, blk & brt pink	.25	.25
187	A41	1.30sh brn org, blk & brt pink	.25	.25
188	A41	2.50sh gray, blk & brt pink	.30	1.25
		Nos. 185-188 (4)	1.05	2.00

20th anniv. of the WHO.

Stadium A42

Designs: 50c, Diving tower. 1.30sh, Pylons and tracks. 2.50sh, Boxing ring, vert.

Perf. 14½x14, 14x14½
1968, Oct. 14   Photo.
189	A42	30c dull pur & gray grn	.25	.25
190	A42	50c brt blu, blk & gray	.25	.25
191	A42	1.30sh gray grn, blk & dk car	.30	.25
192	A42	2.50sh buff, brn org & brn blk	.35	1.25
		Nos. 189-192 (4)	1.15	2.00

19th Olympic Games, Mexico City, 10/12-27.

Railroad Ferry MV Umoja A43

Water Transport: 50c, Transatlantic liner S.S. Harambee. 1.30sh, Lake motor vessel Victoria. 2.50sh, Ferry St. Michael.

1969, Jan. 20   Photo.   Perf. 14
193	A43	30c blue, gray & dk bl	.40	.25
194	A43	50c blue, gray & scar	.45	.25
195	A43	1.30sh bl, dk bl & dk green	.80	.25
196	A43	2.50sh bl, dk bl & org	1.50	3.00
		Nos. 193-196 (4)	3.15	3.75

Farm Workers and ILO Emblem A44

ILO Emblem and: 50c, Construction. 1.30sh, Industry. 2.50sh, Shipping.

1969, Apr. 14   Photo.   Perf. 14
197	A44	30c green, blk & yel	.25	.25
198	A44	50c car rose, blk & car	.25	.25
199	A44	1.30sh dp org, blk & org	.25	.25
200	A44	2.50sh grnsh bl, blk & ultra	.30	.75
		Nos. 197-200 (4)	1.05	1.50

50th anniv. of the ILO.

Pope Paul VI, Mountains of the Moon, Papal Arms, Crested Crane — A45

1969, July 31   Photo.   Perf. 14
201	A45	30c dk blue, blk & gold	.25	.25
202	A45	70c plum, blk & gold	.25	.25
203	A45	1.50sh gray bl, blk & gold	.25	.25
204	A45	2.50sh dp vio, blk & gold	.30	1.25
		Nos. 201-204 (4)	1.05	2.00

Visit of Pope Paul VI to Uganda, 7/31-8/2.

Euphorbia Tree in Shape of Africa, Development Bank Emblem — A46

Perf. 14x13½
1969, Dec. 8   Litho.   Unwmk.
205	A46	30c brt grn, dk grn & gold	.25	.25
206	A46	70c plum, dk grn & gold	.25	.25

207 A46 1.50sh grnsh bl, dk grn
         & gold   .25   .25
208 A46 2.50sh brn org, dk grn &
         gold   .35   .60
   Nos. 205-208 (4)   1.10 1.35
African Development Bank, 5th anniv.

Amadinda, Uganda — A47

Musical Instruments: 30c, Marimba,
Tanzania. 1.50sh, Nzomari (trumpet), Kenya.
2.50sh, Adeudeu, Kenya.

1970, Feb. 16   Litho.   Perf. 11x12
209 A47 30c multicolored   .25   .25
210 A47 70c multicolored   .30   .25
211 A47 1.50sh dk rose brn &
         org   .50   .25
212 A47 2.50sh multicolored   .90   1.50
   Nos. 209-212 (4)   1.95 2.25

Satellite
Earth
Station
A48

Designs: 70c, Radar station by day. 1.50sh,
Radar station by night. 2.50sh, Satellite trans-
mitting communications to and from earth.

1970, May 18   Litho.   Perf. 14½
213 A48 30c multicolored   .25   .25
214 A48 70c multicolored   .25   .25
215 A48 1.50sh org, blk & vio .30   .25
216 A48 2.50sh dull bl & multi .50 2.00
   Nos. 213-216 (4)   1.30 2.75

Opening of the East African Satellite Earth
Station, Mt. Margaret, Kenya.

Runner — A49

1970, July 16   Litho.   Perf. 14½
217 A49 30c org brn, dk brn &
         blk   .25   .25
218 A49 70c grn, dk brn & blk .25   .25
219 A49 1.50sh dull pur, dk brn
         & blk   .25   .25
220 A49 2.50sh grnsh bl, dk brn
         & blk   .30   1.00
   Nos. 217-220 (4)   1.05 1.75

9th British Commonwealth Games, Edinburgh, July 16-25.

UN
Emblem
and
People
A50

1970, Oct. 19   Photo.   Perf. 14½
221 A50 30c org brn, gold &
         black   .25   .25
222 A50 70c bl grn, gold &
         black   .25   .25
223 A50 1.50sh dull red brn, gold
         & blk   .25   .25
224 A50 2.50sh olive, gold & blk .45 1.75
   Nos. 221-224 (4)   1.20 2.50

25th anniversary of the United Nations.

Conversion from Pounds to
Kilograms — A51

Designs: 70c, Conversion from Fahrenheit
to centigrade. 1.50sh, Conversion from gallons
to liters. 2.50sh, Conversion from miles to
kilometers.

1971, Jan. 4   Photo.   Perf. 14½
225 A51 30c silver & multi   .25   .25
226 A51 70c silver & multi   .25   .25
227 A51 1.50sh silver & multi .25   .25
228 A51 2.50sh silver & multi .30   .80
   Nos. 225-228 (4)   1.05 1.55

Conversion to metric system of weights and
measures.

Locomotive — A52

Designs: Various locomotives.

1971, Apr. 19   Photo.   Perf. 14½
229 A52 30c gold & multi   .30   .25
230 A52 70c gold & multi   .35   .25
231 A52 1.50sh gold & multi   .90   .25
232 A52 2.50sh gold & multi   1.25 2.25
 a.   Souvenir sheet of 4, #229-232 9.00 9.00
   Nos. 229-232 (4)   2.80 3.00

70th anniversary of the completion of the
Mombasa to Kisumu line.

Campaign Emblem and Cow — A53

Designs: 1.50sh, Like 30c. 70c, 2.50sh, Bull
and Campaign Emblem.

1971, July 5   Photo.   Perf. 14½
233 A53 30c yel grn, blk & bis .25   .25
234 A53 70c gray bl, blk & bis .25   .25
235 A53 1.50sh mag, blk & bis   .25   .25
236 A53 2.50sh red org, blk & blk .25 .65
   Nos. 233-236 (4)   1.00 1.40

Rinderpest campaign by the Organization
for African Unity.

Meeting of Stanley and
Livingstone — A54

1971, Oct. 28   Litho.   Perf. 14
237 A54 5sh multicolored   .40   .40

Centenary of the meeting at Ujiji of Dr.
David Livingstone, missionary, and Henry M.
Stanley, journalist, who had been sent to find
Livingstone.

Modern Farming Village — A55

Designs: 30c, Pres. Julius K. Nyerere carried in triumph, 1961, vert. 1.50sh, University

of Dar es Salaam. 2.50sh, Kilimanjaro International Airport.

1971, Dec. 9   Perf. 14
238 A55 30c bister & multi   .25   .25
239 A55 70c lt blue & multi   .25   .25
240 A55 1.50sh lt green & multi .25 .25
241 A55 2.50sh yel & multi   .65   2.00
   Nos. 238-241 (4)   1.40 2.75

10th anniv. of independence of Tanzania.

Flags of African Nations and Fair
Emblem — A56

1972, Feb. 23   Perf. 13½x14
242 A56 30c lt bl & multi   .25   .25
243 A56 70c gray & multi   .25   .25
244 A56 1.50sh yel & multi   .25   .25
245 A56 2.50sh multicolored   .25   .75
   Nos. 242-245 (4)   1.00 1.50

First All-Africa Trade Fair, Nairobi, Kenya,
Feb. 23-Mar. 5.

Child
Drinking
Milk,
UNICEF
Emblem
A57

25th Anniv. (in 1971) of UNICEF: 70c, Children playing ball. 1.50sh, Child writing on
blackboard. 2.50sh, Boy playing with tractor.

1972, Apr. 24   Litho.   Perf. 14½x14
246 A57 30c brn org & multi   .25   .25
247 A57 70c lt ultra & multi .25   .25
248 A57 1.50sh yel & multi   .25   .25
249 A57 2.50sh green & multi .25   .75
   Nos. 246-249 (4)   1.00 1.50

Hurdles, Olympic and Motion
Emblems — A58

1972, Aug. 28
250 A58 40c shown   .25   .25
251 A58 70c Running   .25   .25
252 A58 1.50sh Boxing   .25   .25
253 A58 2.50sh Hockey   .30   1.50
 a.   Souvenir sheet of 4, #250-253 7.00 7.00
   Nos. 250-253 (4)   1.05 2.25

20th Olympic Games, Munich, 8/26-9/11.

Uganda Kob, Semliki Game
Reserve — A59

70c, Intl. Conf. Center. 1.50sh, Makerere
Univ., Kampala. 2.50sh, Uganda arms.

1972, Oct. 9   Litho.   Perf. 14
254 A59 40c shown   .30   .25
255 A59 70c multicolored   .30   .25
256 A59 1.50sh multicolored   .65   .30
257 A59 2.50sh multicolored   1.10 2.25
 a.   Souvenir sheet of 4, #254-257,
      perf. 13x14   4.75 4.75
   Nos. 254-257 (4)   2.35 3.05

Uganda's independence, 10th anniv. No.
256 also for 50th anniv. of Makerere University, Kampala.

Flag of East Africa — A60

1972, Dec. 1   Litho.   Perf. 14½x14
258 A60 5sh multicolored   .90   .90
5th anniv. of the East African Community.

Anemometer, Lake Victoria
Station — A61

WMO Emblem and: 70c, Release of
weather balloon, vert. 1.50sh, Hail suppres-
sion by meteorological rocket. 2.50sh, Meteorological satellite receiving antenna.

1973, Mar. 5   Litho.   Perf. 14
259 A61 40c multicolored   .25   .25
260 A61 70c ultra & multi   .25   .25
261 A61 1.50sh emer & multi   .30   .25
262 A61 2.50sh multicolored   .50   1.00
   Nos. 259-262 (4)   1.30 1.75

Cent. of intl. meteorological cooperation.

Scouts Laying
Bricks — A62

Designs: 70c, Baden-Powell's gravestone,
Nyeri, Kenya. 1.50sh, World Scout emblem.
2.50sh, Lord Baden-Powell.

1973, July 16   Litho.   Perf. 14
263 A62 40c ocher & multi   .25   .25
264 A62 70c multicolored   .30   .25
265 A62 1.50sh multicolored   .50   .30
266 A62 2.50sh grn & ultra   1.25 1.60
   Nos. 263-266 (4)   2.30 2.40

24th Boy Scout World Conference (1st in
Africa), Nairobi, Kenya, July 16-21.

International Bank for Reconstruction
and Development and Affiliates'
Emblems — A63

Designs: 40c, Arrows dividing 4 bank affiliate emblems. 70c, Vert. lines dividing 4
emblems. 1.50sh, Kenyatta Conference
Center, Nairobi, vert.

1973, Sept. 24   Litho.   Perf. 14x13½
267 A63 40c gray, blk & grn   .25   .25
268 A63 70c brn, gray & blk   .25   .25
269 A63 1.50sh lem, gray & blk .25 .30
270 A63 2.50sh blk, org & gray .40 1.75
 a.   Souvenir sheet of 4   2.75 2.75
   Nos. 267-270 (4)   1.15 2.55

Intl. Bank for Reconstruction and Development and Affiliate Intl. Monetary Fund Meet-
ings, Nairobi.

No. 270a contains stamps similar to Nos.
267-270 with simulated perforations.

INTERPOL
Emblem,
Policeman and
Dog — A64

Designs: 70c, East African policemen and emblem. 1.50sh, INTERPOL emblem. 2.50sh, INTERPOL Headquarters, St. Cloud, France.

1973-74		Litho.	Perf. 14x14½	
271	A64	40c yellow & multi	.55	.25
272	A64	70c multicolored	.80	.25
273	A64	1.50sh violet & multi	1.40	.90
274	A64	2.50sh lemon & multi (St. Clans)	3.75	6.00
275	A64	2.50sh lemon & multi (St. Cloud) ('74)	6.00	6.00
		Nos. 271-275 (5)	12.50	13.40

50th anniv. of Intl. Criminal Police Org. Issued: Nos. 271-274, Oct. 24, 1973.

Tea Factory, Nandi Hills — A65

1973, Dec. 12		Photo.	Perf. 13x14	
276	A65	40c shown	.25	.25
277	A65	70c Kenyatta Hospital	.25	.25
278	A65	1.50sh Nairobi Airport	.55	.25
279	A65	2.50sh Kindaruma hydroelectric plant	.85	1.75
		Nos. 276-279 (4)	1.90	2.50

10th anniversary of independence.

Afro-Shirazi Party
Headquarters — A66

Designs: 70c, Michenzani housing development. 1.50sh, Map of East Africa and television screen with flower. 2.50sh, Amaan Stadium.

1974, Jan. 12		Litho.	Perf. 13½x14	
280	A66	40c multicolored	.25	.25
281	A66	70c multicolored	.25	.25
282	A66	1.50sh black & multi	.35	.25
283	A66	2.50sh black & multi	.70	2.50
		Nos. 280-283 (4)	1.55	3.25

10th anniversary of Zanzibar revolution.

Symbol
of Union
A67

Designs: 70c, Map of Tanganyika and Zanzibar, and handshake. 1.50sh, Map of Tanganyika and Zanzibar, and communications symbols. 2.50sh, Flags of Tanu, Tanzania and Afro-Shirazi Party.

1974, Apr. 24		Litho.	Perf. 14½	
284	A67	40c sepia & multi	.25	.25
285	A67	70c blue grn & multi	.25	.25
286	A67	1.50sh ultra & multi	.35	.25
287	A67	2.50sh multicolored	.70	2.50
		Nos. 284-287 (4)	1.55	3.25

Union of Tanganyika and Zanzibar, 10th anniv.

Family
and
Home
A68

Designs: 70c, Drummer at dawn. 1.50sh, Family hoeing, and livestock. 2.50sh, Telephonist, train, plane, telegraph lines.

1974, July 15		Litho.	Perf. 14½	
288	A68	40c multicolored	.25	.25
289	A68	70c multicolored	.25	.25
290	A68	1.50sh multicolored	.25	.25
291	A68	2.50sh multicolored	.80	1.25
		Nos. 288-291 (4)	1.55	2.00

17th Intl. Conf. on Social Welfare, 7/14-20.

Post and Telegraph Headquarters,
Kampala — A69

Cent. of the UPU: 70c, Mail train and truck. 1.50sh, UPU Headquarters, Bern. 2.50sh, Loading mail on East African Airways VC-10.

1974, Oct. 9		Litho.	Perf. 14	
292	A69	40c lt green & multi	.25	.25
293	A69	70c gray & multi	.25	.25
294	A69	1.50sh yel & multi	.25	.25
295	A69	2.50sh lt blue & multi	.50	1.25
		Nos. 292-295 (4)	1.25	2.00

Family
Planning
Clinic
A70

World Population Year: 70c, "Tug of War." 1.50sh, Scales and world population figures. 2.50sh, World Population Year emblem.

1974, Dec. 16		Litho.	Perf. 14½	
296	A70	40c multicolored	.25	.25
297	A70	70c purple & multi	.25	.25
298	A70	1.50sh multicolored	.25	.25
299	A70	2.50sh blue blk & multi	.30	1.50
		Nos. 296-299 (4)	1.05	2.25

Seronera Wild Life Lodge,
Tanzania — A71

Game lodges of East Africa: 70c, Mweya Safari Lodge, Uganda. 1.50sh, Ark-Aberdare Forest Lodge, Kenya. 2.50sh, Paraa Safari Lodge, Uganda.

1975, Feb. 24		Litho.	Perf. 14½	
300	A71	40c multicolored	.25	.25
301	A71	70c multicolored	.25	.25
302	A71	1.50sh multicolored	.25	.30
303	A71	2.50sh multicolored	.85	2.00
		Nos. 300-303 (4)	1.60	2.80

Wooden Comb,
Bajun,
Kenya — A72

African Artifacts: 1sh, Earring, Chaga, Tanzania. 2sh, Armlet, Acholi, Uganda. 3sh, Kamba gourd, Kenya.

1975, May 5		Litho.	Perf. 13½	
304	A72	50c gray & multi	.25	.25
305	A72	1sh gray & multi	.25	.25
306	A72	2sh multicolored	.35	.35
307	A72	3sh multicolored	.75	1.50
		Nos. 304-307 (4)	1.60	2.35

Map Showing OAU
Members, Ugandan
Flag — A73

OAU Emblem and: 50c, Entebbe Airport, horiz. 2sh, Nile Hotel, Kampala, horiz. 3sh, Ugandan Martyrs' Shrine, Namugongo.

		Perf. 11½x11, 11x11½		
1975, July 28			Litho.	
308	A73	50c multicolored	.35	.25
309	A73	1sh multicolored	.35	.25
310	A73	2sh multicolored	.35	.50
311	A73	3sh multicolored	.65	1.50
		Nos. 308-311 (4)	1.70	2.50

Organization for African Unity (OAU), Summit Conf., Kampala, July 28 - Aug. 1.

Elephant,
Kenya — A74

Protected animals: 1sh, Albino buffalo, Uganda. 2sh, Elephant, exhibit in National Museum, Kenya. 3sh, Abbott's duiker, Tanzania.

1975, Sept. 11		Litho.	Perf. 11x11½	
312	A74	50c multicolored	.65	.25
313	A74	1sh brown & multi	.65	.25
314	A74	2sh yel green & multi	1.75	1.50
315	A74	3sh blue grn & multi	2.50	2.50
		Nos. 312-315 (4)	5.55	4.50

Masai Villagers Bleeding Cow, Masai,
Kenya — A75

Festival Emblem and: 1sh, Ugandan dancers. 2sh, Family, Makonde sculpture, Tanzania. 3sh, Skinning hippopotamus, East Africa.

1975, Nov. 3		Litho.	Perf. 13½x14	
316	A75	50c org brown & multi	.25	.25
317	A75	1sh brt green & multi	.25	.25
318	A75	2sh dk blue & multi	.55	.80
319	A75	3sh lilac & multi	.95	1.40
		Nos. 316-319 (4)	2.00	2.70

2nd World Black and African Festival of Arts and Culture, Lagos, Nigeria, Jan. 5 - Feb. 12.

Fokker Friendship, Nairobi
Airport — A76

East African Airways, 30th anniv.: 1sh, DC-9 Kilimanjaro Airport. 2sh, Super VC10,

Entebbe Airport. 3sh, East African Airways emblem.

1976, Jan. 2		Litho.	Perf. 11½	
320	A76	50c ultra & multi	1.25	.75
321	A76	1sh rose & multi	1.50	.75
322	A76	2sh orange & multi	4.00	3.50
323	A76	3sh black & multi	5.50	4.25
		Nos. 320-323 (4)	12.25	9.25

POSTAGE DUE STAMPS

Kenya and Uganda

D1

		Perf. 14½x14		
1928-33		Typo.		Wmk. 4
J1	D1	5c deep violet	2.75	1.00
J2	D1	10c orange red	2.75	.60
J3	D1	20c yel green	3.25	4.00
J4	D1	30c ol brn ('31)	22.50	16.00
J5	D1	40c dull blue	7.50	15.00
J6	D1	1sh grnsh gray ('33)	72.50	140.00
		Nos. J1-J6 (6)	111.25	176.60
		Set, never hinged	200.00	

Kenya, Uganda, Tanganyika

D2

1935, May 1			Perf. 13½x14	
J7	D2	5c violet	3.25	2.00
J8	D2	10c red	.35	.65
J9	D2	20c green	.55	.65
J10	D2	30c brown	1.25	.80
J11	D2	40c ultramarine	1.75	3.50
J12	D2	1sh gray	22.50	25.00
		Nos. J7-J12 (6)	29.65	32.60
		Set, never hinged	50.00	

OFFICIAL STAMPS

The 1959-60 "OFFICIAL" overprints on Nos. 103-104, 106-108, 110, 112-117, 120-123, 125, 127, 129, 133 are listed under Tanganyika, as they were used by the Tanganyika government.

KIAUCHAU
(Kiautschou)

LOCATION — A district of China on the south side of the Shantung peninsula.
GOVT. — German colony
AREA — 200 sq. mi.
POP. — 192,000 (approx. 1914).

The area was seized by Germany in 1897 and through negotiations that followed was leased to Germany by China.

100 Pfennig = 1 Mark
100 Cents = 1 Dollar (1905)

TSINGTAU ISSUES

Stamps of Germany, Offices in China 1898, with Additional Surcharge

a   b

c

On Nos. 1-9, a blue or violet line is drawn through "PF. 10 PF." All exist without this line. All examples of Nos. 1b, 2b and 3b lack the colored line.
The three surcharge types can most easily be distinguished by the differences in the lower loop of the "5."

1900
"China" Overprint at 56 degree Angle

1	A10(a)	5pfg on 10pf car	45.00	52.50
c.		Dbl. surch., one inverted	750.00	
2	A10(b)	5pfg on 10pf car	45.00	52.50
c.		Dbl. surch., one inverted	750.00	
3	A10(c)	5pfg on 10pf car	45.00	52.50
c.		Dbl. surch., one inverted	750.00	
		Nos. 1-3 (3)	135.00	157.50

"China" Overprint at 45 degree Angle

1a	A10(a)	5pfg on 10pf car	145.00	130.00
b.		Double surcharge	450.00	575.00
2a	A10(b)	5pfg on 10pf car	145.00	130.00
b.		Double surcharge	450.00	575.00
3a	A10(c)	5pfg on 10pf car	145.00	130.00
b.		Double surcharge	450.00	575.00
		Nos. 1a-3a (3)	435.00	390.00

Surcharged

d   e

5 Pf.

f

"China" Overprint at 48 degree Angle on Nos. 4-9

4	A10(d)	5pf on 10pf car	3,250.	4,000.
a.		Double surcharge	8,250.	18,000.
5	A10(e)	5pf on 10pf car	3,250.	4,000.
a.		Double surcharge	8,250.	18,000.
6	A10(f)	5pf on 10pf car	3,250.	4,000.
a.		Double surcharge	8,250.	18,000.
b.		5fP		18,000.
c.		As "b," double surcharge		

5

With Additional Handstamp

7	A10(d)	5pf on 10pf car	40,000.	50,000.
8	A10(f)	5pf on 10pf car	40,000.	50,000.
a.		On No. 6b	—	

With Additional Handstamp

9	A10(f)	5pf on 10pf car	8,250.	12,500.
a.		Double surcharge	37,500.	
b.		On No. 6a		
c.		On No. 6b		
d.		On No. 6c		

Kaiser's Yacht "Hohenzollern"
A1   A2

1901, Jan.   Unwmk.   Typo.   Perf. 14

10	A1	3pf brown	2.00	2.00
11	A1	5pf green	2.00	1.75
12	A1	10pf carmine	2.50	2.10
13	A1	20pf ultra	7.50	8.50
14	A1	25pf org & blk, *yel*	13.50	17.00
15	A1	30pf org & blk, *sal*	13.50	16.50
16	A1	40pf lake & blk	16.00	21.00
17	A1	50pf pur & blk, *sal*	16.00	22.50
18	A1	80pf lake & blk, *rose*	30.00	52.50

Engr.   Perf. 14½x14

19	A2	1m carmine	50.00	92.50
20	A2	2m blue	75.00	110.00
21	A2	3m blk vio	75.00	200.00
22	A2	5m slate & car	210.00	650.00
		Nos. 10-22 (13)	513.00	1,196.
		Set, never hinged	1,350.	

A3   A4

1905   Typo.

23	A3	1c brown	1.25	1.75
24	A3	2c green	2.00	1.75
25	A3	4c carmine	4.50	1.75
26	A3	10c ultra	8.50	5.50
27	A3	20c lake & blk	34.00	20.00
28	A3	40c lake & blk, *rose*	100.00	100.00

Engr.

29	A4	$½ carmine	72.50	85.00
30a	A4	$1 blue	150.00	130.00
31	A4	$1½ blk vio	1,200.	1,700.
32	A4	$2½ slate & car, 26x17 holes	1,500.	5,000.
a.		$2½ slate & car, 25x16 holes	2,100.	3,500.
		Nos. 23-32 (10)	3,072.	7,040.
		Set, never hinged	8,000.	

1905-16   Wmk. 125   Typo.

33	A3	1c brown ('06)	1.25	1.50
a.		1c yellow brown ('16)	.50	
34	A3	2c green ('09)	1.10	1.10
a.		2c dark green ('14)	.50	1.75
35	A3	4c carmine ('09)	1.00	1.10
36	A3	10c ultra ('09)	1.10	3.25
a.		10c blue	12.00	5.00
37	A3	20c lake & blk ('08)	3.00	16.00
38	A3	40c lake & blk, *rose*	3.25	52.50

Engr.

39	A4	$½ carmine, 26x17 holes ('07)	10.00	65.00
40	A4	$1 blue, 26x17 holes ('06)	12.50	67.50
41	A4	$1½ blk violet	11.00	225.00
42	A4	$2½ slate & car	60.00	475.00
		Nos. 33-42 (10)	104.20	907.95
		Set, never hinged	550.00	

Four values of the design A3 and A4 stamps in recognizably different shades were printed and released in 1918, but by then Germany had lost control of Kiauchau, and these stamps are not known used. The four stamps and their unused values are: 20c red & black, $1.75; $½ pale rose, $5.50; $1 bright blue, $6.75; $1½ gray violet, $20.

KIONGA
ˈkyoŋ-gə

LOCATION — Southeast Africa and northeast Mozambique, on Indian Ocean south of Rovuma River
GOVT. — Part of German East Africa
AREA — 400 sq. mi.

This territory, occupied by Portuguese troops during World War I, was allotted to Portugal by the Treaty of Versailles. Later it became part of Mozambique.

100 Centavos = 1 Escudo

Lourenco Marques No. 149 Surcharged in Red

1916, May 29   Unwmk.   Perf. 11½

1	A2	½c on 100r bl, *bl*	30.00	20.00
2	A2	1c on 100r bl, *bl*	24.00	17.00
3	A2	2½c on 100r bl, *bl*	24.00	17.00
4	A2	5c on 100r bl, *bl*	24.00	17.00
		Nos. 1-4 (4)	102.00	71.00

Most of the stock of Lourenço Marques No. 149 used for these surcharges lacked gum. Unused examples with original gum are worth approximately 50% more than the values shown.

KIRIBATI
ˈkir-ə-ˌbas

LOCATION — A group of islands in the Pacific Ocean northeast of Australia
GOVT. — Republic
AREA — 277 sq. mi.
POP. — 85,501 (1999 est.)
CAPITAL — Tarawa

100 Cents = 1 Australian Dollar

Kiribati, former Gilbert Islands, consists of the Gilbert, Phoenix, Ocean and Line Islands.

> **Catalogue values for all unused stamps in this country are for Never Hinged items.**

Watermark

Wmk. 380 — "POST OFFICE"

Kiribati Flag
A50

Parliament, London, Assembly, Tarawa — A51

Wmk. 373
1979, July 12   Litho.   Perf. 14

325	A50	10c multicolored	.25	.30
326	A51	45c multicolored	.25	.50

Independence.

Training Ship Teraaka A52

Designs: 3c, Passenger launch Tautunu. 5c, Hibiscus. 7c, Cathedral, Tarawa. 10c, House of Assembly, Bikenibeu Island. 12c, Betio harbor. 15c, Reef egret. 20c, Flamboyant tree. 25c, Moorish idol (fish). 30c, Frangipani blossoms. 35c, Chapel, Tangintebu Island. 50c, Hypolimnas bolina elliciana (butterfly). $1, Tarawa Lagoon ferry, Tabakea. $2, Sunset over lagoon. $5, Natl. flag.

1979-80   Wmk. 373

327	A52	1c multicolored	.25	.65
328	A52	3c multicolored	.25	.35
329	A52	5c multicolored	.25	.25
330	A52	7c multicolored	.25	.25
331	A52	10c multicolored	.25	.25
332	A52	12c multicolored	.25	.25
333	A52	15c multicolored	.30	.30
334	A52	20c multicolored	.25	.30
335	A52	25c multicolored	.25	.30
336	A52	30c multicolored	.25	.30
337	A52	35c multicolored	.25	.30
338	A52	50c multicolored	.70	.55
339	A52	$1 multicolored	.55	.60
340	A52	$2 multicolored	.55	.70
340A	A52	$5 multicolored	1.25	3.00
		Nos. 327-340A (15)	5.85	8.35

Issued: $5, 8/27/80; others, 7/12/79.

1980-81   Unwmk.

327a	A52	1c multi ('81)	.25	.35
328a	A52	3c multi ('81)	.25	.35
329a	A52	5c multi	.25	.35
330a	A52	7c multi	.25	.35
331a	A52	10c multi	.25	.35
332a	A52	12c multi	.25	.35
333a	A52	15c multi	.65	.35
334a	A52	20c multi ('81)	.25	.35
335a	A52	25c multi	.35	.35
336a	A52	30c multi ('81)	.25	.75
337a	A52	35c multi ('81)	.25	.75
338a	A52	50c multi ('81)	.90	1.10
339a	A52	$1 multi	.75	.75
340b	A52	$2 multi	1.40	1.05
340c	A52	$5 multi ('80)	2.25	3.75
		Nos. 327a-340c (15)	8.55	11.30

For overprints see Nos. O1-O15.

Gilbert and Ellice Islands No. 1 — A53

Simulated Cancel and: 20c, Gilbert and Ellice No. 70. 25c, Great Britain No. 139. 45c, Gilbert and Ellice No. 31.

Wmk. 373
1979, Oct. 4   Litho.   Perf. 14

341	A53	10c multicolored	.25	.25
342	A53	20c multicolored	.25	.25
343	A53	25c multicolored	.25	.25
344	A53	45c multicolored	.25	.25
a.		Souvenir sheet of 4, #341-344	1.25	1.25
		Nos. 341-344 (4)	1.00	1.00

Sir Rowland Hill (1795-1879), originator of penny postage.

Boy Climbing Coconut Palm, IYC
Emblem — A54

IYC Emblem, Coat of Arms and: 10c, Boy
and giant clam shell. 45c, Girl reading book.
$1, Boy wearing garlands. All vert.

Perf. 14x13½, 13½x14

1979, Nov. 28			Litho.	
345	A54	10c multicolored	.25	.25
346	A54	20c multicolored	.25	.25
347	A54	45c multicolored	.25	.25
348	A54	$1 multicolored	.25	.25
		Nos. 345-348 (4)	1.00	1.00

International Year of the Child.

Downrange Station — A55

National Space Development Agency of
Japan (NASDA) Satellite Tracking: 45c, Experimental satellite trajectory (map). $1, Rocket
launch, Tanegashima, Japan, vert.

1980, Feb. 20			Litho.	Perf. 14½
349	A55	25c multicolored	.25	.25
350	A55	45c multicolored	.25	.25
351	A55	$1 multicolored	.25	.25
		Nos. 349-351 (3)	.75	.75

T.S.
Teraaka,
London
1980
Emblem
A56

1980, Apr. 30			Litho.	Unwmk.
352	A56	12c shown	.25	.25
353	A56	25c Air Tungaru plane, Bonriki Airport	.25	.25
354	A56	30c Radio operator	.25	.25
355	A56	$1 Bairiki post office	.25	.35
a.		Souvenir sheet of 4, #352-355	.75	.85
		Nos. 352-355 (4)	1.00	1.10

London 1980 Intl. Stamp Exhib., May 6-14.

Achaea
Janata
A57

1980, Aug. 27			Litho.	Perf. 14
356	A57	12c shown	.25	.25
357	A57	25c Ethmia nigroapicella	.25	.25
358	A57	30c Utetheisa pulchel- loides	.30	.30
359	A57	50c Anua coronata	.45	.45
		Nos. 356-359 (4)	1.25	1.25

Capt.
Cook
Hotel
A58

1980, Nov. 19		Wmk. 373	Perf. 13½
360	A58	10c shown	.25	.25
361	A58	20c Stadium	.25	.25
362	A58	25c Intl. Airport, Bonriki	.25	.25
363	A58	35c National Library	.25	.25
364	A58	$1 Otintai Hotel	.25	.25
		Nos. 360-364 (5)	1.25	1.25

Acalypha
Godseffiana
A59

30c, Hibiscus schizopetalus. 35c, Calotropis
gigantea. 50c, Euphorbia pulcherrima.

Perf. 14x13½

1981, Feb. 18		Litho.	Wmk. 373
365	A59	12c shown	.25	.25
366	A59	30c multicolored	.25	.25
367	A59	35c multicolored	.25	.25
368	A59	50c multicolored	.25	.25
		Nos. 365-368 (4)	1.00	1.00

Abaiang and Marakei Islands, String
Figures — A60

30c, Butaritari, Little Makin, house. 35c,
Maiana, Coral Road. $1, Christmas Island,
Resolution.

1981, May 6		Wmk. 380	Litho.	Perf. 14
369	A60	12c shown	.25	.25
370	A60	30c multicolored	.25	.25
371	A60	35c multicolored	.25	.25
372	A60	$1 multicolored	.45	.45
		Nos. 369-372 (4)	1.20	1.20

Prince
Charles,
Lady
Diana,
Royal
Yacht
Charlotte
A60a

Prince Charles and Lady
Diana — A60b

Wmk. 380

1981, July 29		Litho.	Perf. 14
373	A60a	12c Couple, The Katherine	.25	.25
a.		Bklt. pane of 4, perf. 12, unwmkd.	.75	
374	A60b	12c Couple	.30	.25
375	A60b	50c The Osborne	.85	.50
376	A60b	50c like #374	.90	.50
a.		Bklt. pane of 2, perf. 12, unwmkd.	2.25	
377	A60b	$2 Britannia	2.25	1.60
378	A60b	$2 like #374	2.25	1.60
		Nos. 373-378 (6)	6.80	4.70

Souvenir Sheet

Perf. 12

379	A60b	$1.20 like #374	3.00	3.00

Royal wedding.
Stamps of the same denomination issued in
sheets of 7 (6 type A60a and 1 type A60b).

Bonriki
Tuna Fish
Bait
Breeding
Center
A61

1981, Nov. 19			
380	A61	12c shown	.25	.25
381	A61	30c Fishing boat	.25	.25
382	A61	35c Cold storage, Betio	.25	.25
383	A61	50c Nei Manganibuka	.25	.25
a.		Souvenir sheet of 4, #380-383	1.25	1.25
		Nos. 380-383 (4)	1.00	1.00

Pomarine
Jaegers
A62

2c, Mallards. 4c, Collared petrels. 5c, Blue-
faced boobies. 7c, Friendly quail dove. 8c,
Shovelers. 12c, Christmas Island warblers.
15c, Pacific plovers. 20c, Reef herons. 25c,
Brown noddies. 30c, Brown boobies. 35c,
Audubon's shearwaters. 40c, White-throated
storm petrels, vert. 50c, Bristle-thighed
curlews, vert. 55c, Fairy tern. $1, Scarlet-
breasted lorikeets, vert. $2, Long-tailed
cuckoo, vert. $5, Great frigate birds, vert.

1982-85		Litho.	Perf. 14
384	A62	1c shown	.25	.25
385	A62	2c multicolored	.25	.25
386	A62	4c multicolored	.25	.25
387	A62	5c multicolored	.25	.25
388	A62	7c multicolored	.25	.25
389	A62	8c multicolored	.25	.25
390	A62	12c multicolored	.30	.25
391	A62	15c multicolored	.35	.35
392	A62	20c multicolored	.40	.50
392A	A62	25c multi ('83)	2.75	1.75
393	A62	30c multicolored	.55	.60
394	A62	35c multicolored	.75	.70
395	A62	40c multicolored	.70	.80
396	A62	50c multicolored	.75	.65
396A	A62	55c multi ('85)	12.50	17.00
397	A62	$1 multicolored	1.60	.85
398	A62	$2 multicolored	2.25	1.10
399	A62	$5 multicolored	4.50	4.00
		Nos. 384-399 (18)	28.90	30.05

Issued: 25c, 1/31/83; 55c, 11/19/85; others,
2/18/82.
For overprints see Nos. O16-O20.

Air
Tungaru
A63

12c, De Havilland DH114 Heron. 30c, Brit-
ten-Norman Trislander. 35c, Casa 212 Avio-
car. 50c, Boeing 727.

1982, Feb. 18			Wmk. 380
400	A63	12c multicolored	.25	.25
401	A63	30c multicolored	.25	.25
402	A63	35c multicolored	.25	.25
403	A63	50c multicolored	.40	.40
		Nos. 400-403 (4)	1.15	1.15

21st Birthday of
Princess Diana,
July 1 — A64

1982, May 19			
404	A64	12c Mary of Teck, 1893	.25	.25
405	A64	50c Teck arms	.40	.40
406	A64	$1 Diana	.60	.60
		Nos. 404-406 (3)	1.25	1.25

**Nos. 404-406 Overprinted: "ROYAL
BABY"**

1982, July 14			
407	A64	12c multicolored	.25	.25
408	A64	50c multicolored	.40	.40
409	A64	$1 multicolored	.60	.60
		Nos. 407-409 (3)	1.25	1.25

Birth of Prince William of Wales, June 21.

Scouting Year — A65

1982, Aug. 12			
410	A65	12c First aid	.25	.25
411	A65	25c Repairing boat	.25	.25
412	A65	30c Saluting	.30	.30
413	A65	50c Gilbert Islds. #304	.40	.40
		Nos. 410-413 (4)	1.20	1.20

Visit of
Queen
Elizabeth
II and
Prince
Philip
A66

Wmk. 380

1982, Oct. 23		Litho.	Perf. 14
414	A66	12c Couple, dancer	.25	.25
415	A66	25c Couple, boat	.25	.25
416	A66	35c Philatelic Bureau	.45	.45
		Nos. 414-416 (3)	.95	.95

Souvenir Sheet

417	A66	50c Queen Elizabeth II, vert.	1.30	1.30

Nos. 414-416 also issued in sheets of 6.

A67

12c, Obala the Feathered legend. 30c, Robert Louis Stevenson Hotel, Abemama. 50c,
Betio Harbor. $1, Map.

1983, Mar. 14		Wmk. 380	Perf. 14
418	A67	12c multicolored	.25	.25
419	A67	30c multicolored	.25	.25
420	A67	50c multicolored	.25	.25
421	A67	$1 multicolored	.30	.30
		Nos. 418-421 (4)	1.05	1.05

Commonwealth day.

Map of Beru and Nikunau Islds.,
Canoe — A68

1983, May 19		Litho.	Perf. 14
422	A68	12c shown	.25	.25
423	A68	25c Abemama, Kuria, Aranuka	.25	.25
424	A68	35c Nonouti, vert.	.25	.25
425	A68	50c Tarawa, vert.	.25	.25
		Nos. 422-425 (4)	1.00	1.00

See Nos. 436-439, 456-459, 475-479, 487-
490.

Copra
Industry
A69

Designs: 12c, Collecting fallen Coconuts.
25c, Selecting Coconuts for Copra. 30c,
Removing Husk from Coconuts. 35c, Drying
Copra in the Sun. 50c, Loading Copra, Betio
Harbor.

1983, Aug. 8   Litho.   Perf. 14
426 A69 12c multicolored   .25   .25
427 A69 25c multicolored   .40   .35
428 A69 30c multicolored   .50   .45
429 A69 35c multicolored   .55   .55
430 A69 50c multicolored   .70   .70
        Nos. 426-430 (5)   2.40   2.30

Battle of
Tarawa,
40th
Anniv.
A70

1983, Nov. 17   Litho.   Wmk. 380
431 A70 12c War memorials   .25   .25
432 A70 30c Battle map   .25   .25
433 A70 35c Defense gun   .25   .25
434 A70 50c Scenes, 1943, 1983   .30   .30
435 A70 $1 Amphibious Assault
           Ship USS Tarawa   .45   .45
        Nos. 431-435 (5)   1.50   1.50

Map Type of 1983

1984, Feb. 14   Wmk. 380   Perf. 14
436 A68 12c Teraina   .25   .25
437 A68 30c Nikumaroro   .35   .35
438 A68 35c Kanton   .40   .40
439 A68 50c Banaba   .60   .60
        Nos. 436-439 (4)   1.60   1.60

Local
Ships
A71

1984, May 9   Litho.   Wmk. 380
440 A71 12c Tug boat   .50   .25
441 A71 35c Ferry landing craft   .85   .50
442 A71 50c Ferry   1.10   .75
443 A71 $1 Cargo and pas-
           sanger boat   1.75   1.75
  a.   Souvenir sheet of 4, #440-443,
        perf. 13½   5.00   5.00
        Nos. 440-443 (4)   4.20   3.25

Ausipex '84 — A72

12c, South Tarawa sewer & water system.
30c, Fishing boat Nouamake. 35c, Overseas
communications training. 50c, Intl. telecommunications link.

1984, Aug. 21   Litho.   Perf. 14
444 A72 12c multicolored   .25   .25
445 A72 30c multicolored   .25   .25
446 A72 35c multicolored   .25   .25
447 A72 50c multicolored   .35   .35
        Nos. 444-447 (4)   1.10   1.10

Legends
A73

Designs: 12c, Tabakea supporting Banaba
on his back. 30c, Nakaa, Judge of the Dead.
35c, Naareau and Tiku-Tiku-Tamoamoa. 50c,
Whistling Ghosts.

1984, Nov. 21   Wmk. 380   Perf. 14
448 A73 12c multicolored   .25   .25
449 A73 30c multicolored   .25   .25
450 A73 35c multicolored   .25   .25
451 A73 50c multicolored   .25   .25
        Nos. 448-451 (4)   1.00   1.00

        See Nos. 464-467.

Reef Fish
A74

1985, Feb. 19   Litho.   Perf. 14
452 A74 12c Tang   .75   .35
453 A74 25c White-barred trig-
           gerfish   1.30   .80
454 A74 35c Surgeon fish   1.50   1.25
455 A74 80c Squirrel fish   3.25   3.25
  a.   Souvenir sheet of 4, #452-455 7.50 7.50
        Nos. 452-455 (4)   6.80   5.65

        See Nos. 540-554, 567.

Map Type of 1983

1985, May 9   Litho.   Perf. 13½
456 A68 12c Tabuaeran, frigate
           bird   1.40   .45
457 A68 35c Rawaki, coconuts   1.75   .70
458 A68 50c Arorae, xanthid crab 2.00   1.10
459 A68 $1 Tamana, fish hook   2.50   2.50
        Nos. 456-459 (4)   7.65   4.75

Intl. Youth
Year
A76

1985, Aug. 5
460 A76 15c Boys playing soccer   .75   .50
461 A76 35c Emblems   1.10   1.10
462 A76 40c Girl processing fruit,
           vert.   1.25   1.25
463 A76 55c Intl. youth exchange 1.75   1.75
        Nos. 460-463 (4)   4.85   4.60

Legends Type of 1984

15c, Nang Kineia & the Tickling Ghosts.
35c, Myth of Auriaria & Tituabine. 40c, First
Coming of Babai at Arorae. 55c, Riiki & the
Milky Way.

1985, Nov. 19   Wmk. 380   Perf. 14
464 A73 15c multicolored   .60   .60
465 A73 35c multicolored   .85   .85
466 A73 40c multicolored   1.00   1.00
467 A73 55c multicolored   1.40   1.40
        Nos. 464-467 (4)   3.85   3.85

Transport and Telecommunications
Decade 1985-95 — A77

1985, Dec. 9   Litho.   Perf. 14
468 A77 15c Satellite network   3.00   2.75
469 A77 40c Tarawa-Suva feeder
           service   4.00   3.50

Common Design Types
pictured following the introduction.

Queen Elizabeth II 60th Birthday
Common Design Type

15c, Review of Girl Guides, Windsor Castle,
1938. 35c, Birthday parade, Buckingham Palace, 1980. 40c, With Prince Philip during royal
tour, 1982. 55c, Banquet, Austrian embassy in
London, 1966. $1, Visiting Crown Agents'
offices, 1983.

1986, Apr. 21   Perf. 14½x14
470 CD337 15c scar, black & sil   .25   .25
471 CD337 35c ultra & multi   .25   .25
472 CD337 40c green & multi   .25   .25
473 CD337 55c violet & multi   .40   .40
474 CD337 $1 rose vio & multi   .95   .95
        Nos. 470-474 (5)   2.10   2.10

        For overprints see Nos. 495-499.

Map Type of 1983

1986, June 17   Wmk. 380   Perf. 14
475 A68 15c Manra   3.25   1.50
476 A68 30c Birnie, McKean   4.25   2.00
477 A68 35c Orona   5.00   2.50
478 A68 40c Malden   5.25   3.00

479 A68 55c Vostok, Caroline,
           Flint   5.50   3.50
        Nos. 475-479 (5)   23.25 12.50

Lizards
A79

15c, Lepidodactylus lugubris. 35c, Gehyra
mutilata. 40c, Hemidactylus frenatus. 55c,
Gehyra oceanica.

1986, Aug. 26   Unwmk.   Perf. 14
480 A79 15c multicolored   2.25   1.00
481 A79 35c multicolored   3.00   1.75
482 A79 40c multicolored   3.50   2.25
483 A79 55c multicolored   5.00   4.50
        Nos. 480-483 (4)   13.75   9.50

        See Nos. 491-494.

America's Cup — A80

Perf. 14x14½
1986, Dec. 29   Unwmk.
484 A80   Strip of 3   2.25   2.25
  a.   15c Map of Australia   .25   .25
  b.   55c Course, trophy   .55   .55
  c. $1.50 Australia II   1.30   1.30

        No. 484 has a continuous design.

Transport and Telecommunications
Decade (1985-1995) — A81

Designs: 30c, Nei Moamoa, flagship of
Kiribati overseas shipping line. 55c, Manual
and electronic telephone switching systems.

1987, Mar. 31   Litho.   Perf. 14
485 A81 30c multicolored   3.75   3.75
486 A81 55c multicolored   5.00   5.00

Map Type of 1983

15c, Starbuck, red-tailed tropicbird. 30c,
Enderbury, white tern. 55c, Tabiteuea, pandanus. $1, Onotoa, Okai house.

1987, Sept. 22   Litho.   Unwmk.
487 A68 15c multicolored   .70   .55
488 A68 30c multicolored   .75   .55
489 A68 55c multicolored   1.00   .65
490 A68 $1 multicolored   1.50   2.00
        Nos. 487-490 (4)   3.95   3.75

        Nos. 487-490 vert.

Lizard Type of 1986

1987, Oct. 27   Perf. 15
491 A79 15c Emoia nigra   .40   .40
492 A79 35c Cryptoblepharus   .55   .60
493 A79 40c Emoia cyanura   .55   .75
494 A79 $1 Lipinia noctua   1.20   1.75
  a.   Souvenir sheet of 4, #491-494 3.00 3.00
        Nos. 491-494 (4)   2.70   3.50

Nos. 470-474
Overprinted in
Silver

Perf. 14½x14
1987, Nov. 30   Litho.   Unwmk.
495 CD337 15c scar, black & sil   .25   .25
496 CD337 35c ultra & multi   .25   .30
497 CD337 40c green & multi   .35   .35
498 CD337 55c violet & multi   .50   .45
499 CD337 $1 rose vio & multi   1.00   1.50
        Nos. 495-499 (5)   2.35   2.85

Intl. Red Cross
and Red
Crescent
Organizations,
125th
Annivs. — A83

15c, Jean Henri Dunant (1828-1910),
founder. 35c, Red Cross volunteers on
parade. 40c, Stretcher bearers. 55c, Gilbert
and Ellice Islands #159.

Perf. 14½x14
1988, May 8   Litho.   Unwmk.
500 A83 15c multicolored   .90   .60
501 A83 35c multicolored   1.10   1.50
502 A83 40c multicolored   1.30   1.50
503 A83 55c multicolored   2.75   3.50
        Nos. 500-503 (4)   6.05   7.10

A84

SYDPEX '88, Australia
Bicentennial — A85

Emblem and: 15c, Australia-assisted causeway construction. 35c, Capt. Cook, map of
Australia and Kiribati. No. 506, Australia bicentennial banknote obverse. No. 507, Bank note
reverse. $2, "Logistic Ace."

1988, July 30   Litho.   Perf. 14½
504 A84 15c multicolored   .30   .30
505 A84 35c multicolored   .60   .60
506 A84 $1 multicolored   1.75   1.75
507 A84 $1 multicolored   1.75   1.75
  a.   Pair, #506-507   3.75   3.75
        Nos. 504-507 (4)   4.40   4.40

Souvenir Sheet
Perf. 13½x14
508 A85 $2 multicolored   6.50   6.50

Robert F. Stockton, 1st propeller-driven
steamship, 150th anniv.

Transport and Telecommunications
Decade (1985-1995) — A86

35c, Telephone operator, map. 45c, Betio-
Bairiki Causeway.

Wmk. 373
1988, Dec. 28   Litho.   Perf. 14
509 A86 35c multicolored   1.25   1.25
510 A86 45c multicolored   1.75   1.75

Ships
A87

15c, Brigantine Hound, 1835. 30c, Brig
Phantom, 1854. 40c, HMS Alacrity, 1873. $1,
Whaler Charles W. Morgan, 1851.

Wmk. 384

1989, May 26		**Litho.**	**Perf. 14½**	
511	A87	15c multicolored	1.25	.90
512	A87	30c multicolored	2.00	1.50
513	A87	40c multicolored	2.40	2.40
514	A87	$1 multicolored	3.75	3.75
		Nos. 511-514 (4)	9.40	8.55

See Nos. 557-561, 687-690.

A88

Perf. 13½x14

1989, July 12		**Litho.**	**Wmk. 384**	
515	A88	15c House of Assembly	.40	.40
516	A88	$1 Constitution	2.60	2.60

Natl. Independence, 10th anniv.

Moon Landing, 20th Anniv.
Common Design Type

Apollo 10: 20c, Service and command mod-
ules, launch escape system. 50c, Eugene A.
Cernan, Thomas P. Stafford and John W.
Young. 60c, Mission emblem. 75c,
Splashdown, Honolulu. $2.50, Apollo 11 com-
mand module in space.

1989, July 20			**Perf. 14**	
Size of Nos. 518-519: 29x29mm				
517	CD342	20c multicolored	.50	.50
518	CD342	50c multicolored	.90	.90
519	CD342	60c multicolored	1.10	1.10
520	CD342	75c multicolored	1.25	1.25
		Nos. 517-520 (4)	3.75	3.75

Souvenir Sheet

521	CD342	$2.50 multicolored	8.75	8.75

Birds — A89

No. 522, Eastern reef heron. No. 523, Brood
in nest. No. 524, White-tailed tropicbird in
flight. No. 525, Seated tropicbird.

Perf. 14½x14

1989, June 28		**Litho.**	**Wmk. 384**	
522	A89	15c multicolored	1.60	1.60
523	A89	15c multicolored	1.60	1.60
a.		Pair, #522-523	3.75	3.75
524	A89	$1 multicolored	3.00	3.00
525	A89	$1 multicolored	3.00	3.00
a.		Pair, #524-525	6.50	6.50
		Nos. 522-525 (4)	9.20	9.20

Nos. 523a, 525a have continuous designs.
For overprints see Nos. 534-535.

Souvenir Sheets

A90

Perf. 14x13½

1989, Aug. 7		**Litho.**	**Wmk. 384**	
526	A90	$2 Gilbert & Ellice Isls.		
		#58	6.00	6.00

A91

Workmen renovating the Statue of Liberty:
a, Torch. b, Drilling copper sheeting. c, Glanc-
ing at a sketch of the statue.

Perf. 14x13½

1989, Sept. 25		**Litho.**	**Unwmk.**	
527	A91	Sheet of 3	5.50	5.50
a.-c.		35c any single	1.60	1.60

World Stamp Expo '89, Washington, DC,
PHILEXFRANCE '89, Paris. No. 526 margin
pictures #435, France #634 and US #2224.

Transport and Telecommunications
Decade, 1985-95 — A92

1989, Oct. 16		**Wmk. 384**	**Perf. 14**	
528	A92	30c shown	2.75	2.75
529	A92	75c MV *Mataburo*	4.25	4.25

Christmas — A93

Paintings: 10c, *Adoration of the Holy Child*
(detail), by Denys Calvert. 15c, *Adoration of
the Holy Child* (entire painting). 55c, *The Holy
Family and St. Elizabeth*, by Rubens. $1,
Madonna with Child and Mary Magdalene,
School of Corregio.

1989, Dec. 1				
530	A93	10c multicolored	1.10	.70
531	A93	15c multicolored	1.40	.85
532	A93	55c multicolored	3.75	2.25
533	A93	$1 multicolored	5.25	7.50
		Nos. 530-533 (4)	11.50	11.30

Nos. 524-525
Ovptd.

1989, Oct. 21		**Litho.**	**Perf. 14½x14**	
534	A89	$1 on No. 524	5.00	5.00
535	A89	$1 on No. 525	5.00	5.00
a.		Pair, #534-535	10.50	10.50

STAMPSHOW '89, Melbourne.

Penny
Black
150th
Anniv.,
Stamp
World
London
'90 — A94

Stamps on stamps: 15c, Gilbert & Ellice
#15, Great Britain #2. 50c, Gilbert & Ellice #8,
Great Britain #1 canceled. 60c, Kiribati #384,
Great Britain #58. $1, Gilbert Islands #269,
Great Britain #3.

1990, May 1		**Litho.**	**Perf. 14**	
536	A94	15c multicolored	1.50	1.50
537	A94	50c multicolored	2.75	2.75
538	A94	60c multicolored	3.00	3.00
539	A94	$1 multicolored	4.50	4.50
		Nos. 536-539 (4)	11.75	11.75

Fish Type of 1985

Fish: 1c, Blue-barred orange parrotfish. 5c,
Honeycomb rock cod. 10c, Bluefin jack. 15c,
Paddle tail snapper. 20c, Variegated emperor.
25c, Rainbow runner. 30c, Black saddled coral
trout. 35c, Great barracuda. 40c, Convict
surgeonfish. 50c, Violet squirrelfish. 60c,
Freckled hawkfish. 75c, Pennant coral fish. $1,
Yellow and blue sea perch. $2, Pacific sailfish.
$5, Whitetip reef shark.

Wmk. 373

1990, July 12		**Litho.**	**Perf. 14**	
540	A74	1c multicolored	.40	.40
541	A74	5c multicolored	.50	.50
542	A74	10c multicolored	.65	.65
543	A74	15c multicolored	.75	.75
544	A74	20c multicolored	.90	.90
545	A74	25c multicolored	1.00	.95
546	A74	30c multicolored	1.10	1.00
547	A74	35c multicolored	1.25	1.10
548	A74	40c multicolored	1.50	1.25
549	A74	50c multicolored	1.75	1.75
550	A74	60c multicolored	2.00	2.00
551	A74	75c multicolored	2.25	2.25
552	A74	$1 multicolored	3.00	2.50
553	A74	$2 multicolored	4.50	4.50
554	A74	$5 multicolored	7.75	9.00
		Nos. 540-554 (15)	29.30	29.50

Dated 1990. See No. 567. For overprints
see Nos. 587-590.

Queen Mother 90th Birthday
Common Design Types

1990, Aug. 4		**Wmk. 384**	**Perf. 14x15**	
555	CD343	75c Queen Mother	1.60	1.60
			Perf. 14½	
556	CD344	$2 King, Queen &		
		WWII bombing		
		victim, 1940	4.00	4.00

Ships Type of 1989

15c, Whaling ship Herald, 1851. 50c, Bark
Belle, 1849. 60c, Schooner Supply, 1851. 75c,
Whaling ship Triton, 1848.
$2, Convict transport Charlotte, 1789.

1990, Nov. 5		**Litho.**	**Perf. 14½**	
557	A87	15c multicolored	1.10	.70
558	A87	50c multicolored	2.25	1.75
559	A87	60c multicolored	2.75	2.75
560	A87	75c multicolored	3.25	3.25
		Nos. 557-560 (4)	9.35	8.45

Souvenir Sheet

561	A87	$2 multicolored	12.00	12.00

Manta
Ray
A95

1991, Jan. 17		**Wmk. 373**	**Perf. 14**	
562	A95	15c shown	1.75	1.25
563	A95	20c Manta ray, diff.	2.00	1.75
564	A95	30c Whale shark	2.50	2.50
565	A95	35c Whale shark, diff.	3.00	3.00
		Nos. 562-565 (4)	9.25	8.50

World Wildlife Fund.

Fish Type of 1985

Design: 23c, Bennett's pufferfish.

1991, Apr. 30		**Wmk. 384**		
567	A74	23c multicolored	2.00	2.00

For overprint see No. 587.

Elizabeth & Philip, Birthdays
Common Design Types

1991, June 17			**Perf. 14½**	
571	CD345	65c multicolored	1.75	1.75
572	CD346	70c multicolored	1.75	1.75
a.		Pair, #571-572 + label	4.00	4.00

Phila Nippon '91 — A96

Opening of new Tungaru Central Hospital:
23c, Aerial view. 50c, Traditional dancers. 60c,
Main entrance. 75c, Foundation stone, plaque.
$5, Ambulance, nursing staff.

1991, Nov. 16			**Perf. 13½x14**	
573	A96	23c multicolored	.50	.50
574	A96	50c multicolored	1.00	1.00
575	A96	60c multicolored	1.40	1.40
576	A96	75c multicolored	1.60	1.60
		Nos. 573-576 (4)	4.50	4.50

Souvenir Sheet

577	A96	$5 multicolored	9.00	9.00

Christmas
A97

Designs: 23c, Island mother and child. 50c,
Family in island hut. 60c, Nativity Scene. 75c,
Adoration of the Shepherds.

1991, Dec. 2		**Wmk. 373**		
578	A97	23c multicolored	.75	.60
579	A97	50c multicolored	1.25	1.25
580	A97	60c multicolored	1.75	1.75
581	A97	75c multicolored	2.25	2.25
		Nos. 578-581 (4)	6.00	5.85

**Queen Elizabeth II's Accession to
the Throne, 40th Anniv.**
Common Design Type

		Wmk. 373		
1992, Feb. 6		**Litho.**	**Perf. 14**	
582	CD349	23c multicolored	.35	.35
583	CD349	30c multicolored	.50	.50
584	CD349	50c multicolored	.80	.80
585	CD349	60c multicolored	1.00	1.00
586	CD349	75c multicolored	1.20	1.20
		Nos. 582-586 (5)	3.85	3.85

Nos. 550-
551, 553,
& 567
Ovptd.

Wmk. 384, 373

1992, June 1 Litho. *Perf. 14*
587	A74	23c on No. 567	1.00	.85
588	A74	60c on No. 550	2.25	2.25
589	A74	75c on No. 551	2.75	2.75
590	A74	$2 on No. 553	3.00	3.50
		Nos. 587-590 (4)	9.00	9.35

Marine Training Center, 25th Anniv. A98

1992, Aug. 28 *Perf. 14*
591	A98	23c Entrance	.65	.65
592	A98	50c Cadets at morning parade	1.00	1.00
593	A98	60c Fire school	1.20	1.20
594	A98	75c Lifeboat training	1.50	1.50
		Nos. 591-594 (4)	4.35	4.35

FAO, WHO A99

Wmk. 373

1992, Dec. 1 Litho. *Perf. 14*
595	A99	23c Children running	1.10	1.10
596	A99	50c Night fishing	1.30	1.30
597	A99	60c Fruit	1.75	1.75
598	A99	75c Ship	3.00	3.00
		Nos. 595-598 (4)	7.15	7.15

Water Birds — A100

Wmk. 373

1993, May 28 Litho. *Perf. 14½*
599	A100	23c Phoenix petrel	.70	.70
600	A100	23c Cooks petrel	.70	.70
a.		Pair, #599-600	1.50	1.50
601	A100	60c Northern pintail	1.30	1.30
602	A100	60c Eurasian widgeon	1.30	1.30
a.		Pair, #601-602	2.75	2.75
603	A100	75c Spectacled tern	1.60	1.60
604	A100	75c Black naped tern	1.60	1.60
a.		Pair, #603-604	3.50	3.50
605	A100	$1 Stilt wader	1.75	1.75
606	A100	$1 Wandering tattler	1.75	1.75
a.		Pair, #605-606	4.00	4.00
		Nos. 599-606 (8)	10.70	10.70

Insects — A101

23c, Chilocorus nigritus. 60c, Rodolia pumila. 75c, Rodolia cardinalis. $1, Cryptolaemus montrouzieri.

Perf. 14½x14
1993, Aug. 23 Litho. Wmk. 373
607	A101	23c multicolored	1.25	1.25
608	A101	60c multicolored	2.00	2.00
609	A101	75c multicolored	2.50	2.50
610	A101	$1 multicolored	3.00	3.50
		Nos. 607-610 (4)	8.75	9.25

Liberation of Kiribati, 50th Anniv. — A102

No. 611: a, Air reconnaissance of Tarawa Atoll. b, USS Nautilus surveys Tarawa. c, USS Indianapolis. d, USS Pursuit leads seaborne assault. e, Kingfisher spotter plane. f, Destroyers USS Ringgold and USS Dashiell. g, Sherman tank on seabed. h, Fighter plane in lagoon. i, Naval gun on seabed. j, First US aircraft to land on Betio Island.
No. 612: a, Transports disembark landing craft. b, Marines assault Betio Island. c, Sea and air assault of Betio. d, Marines pinned down in surf. e, USS Maryland firing broadside. f, Betio from the air. g, Memorial to US Navy dead. h, Memorial to expatriates. i, Memorial to Japanese dead. j, Battle map of Betio.

Wmk. 373
1993, Nov. 1 Litho. *Perf. 14*
Sheets of 10
611	A102	23c #a.-j. + label	8.50	8.50
612	A102	75c #a.-j. + label	22.50	22.50

Christmas — A103

Perf. 13½x14
1993, Dec. 1 Litho. Wmk. 373
613	A103	23c Shepherds	.65	.40
614	A103	40c Three kings	1.00	1.00
615	A103	60c Holy Family	1.40	1.75
616	A103	75c Mother, children	1.75	2.10
		Nos. 613-616 (4)	4.80	5.25

Souvenir Sheet
617	A103	$3 Madonna and Child	6.50	6.50

Stampcards — A104

Rouletted 6 on 2 or 3 Sides
1993, Nov. 1 Litho.
Self-Adhesive
Cards of 6 + 6 labels
618	A104	40c #a.-f.	5.00
619	A104	$1 #a.-f.	12.00
620	A104	$1.20 #a.-f.	15.00
621	A104	$1.60 #a.-f.	22.50
		Nos. 618-621 (4)	54.50

Nos. 619-621 are airmail. Individual stamps measure 70x9mm and have a card backing. Se-tenant labels on No. 618 inscribed "economique." Se-tenant labels on Nos. 619-621 inscribed "prioritaire AIR MAIL."
It has been stated that these stamps were available only from the Philatelic Bureau and were not accepted by local post offices as valid for postage, though this is contradicted by the Controller of Postal Services.

Souvenir Sheet

New Year 1994 (Year of the Dog) — A105

Wmk. 373
1994, Feb. 18 Litho. *Perf. 14*
622	A105	$3 multicolored	7.00	7.00

Hong Kong '94.

Whales A106

Designs: 23c, Bryde's whale. 40c, Blue whale. 60c, Humpback whale. 75c, Killer whale.

1994, May 2
623	A106	23c multicolored	1.40	1.40
624	A106	23c multicolored	1.40	1.40
a.		Pair, #623-624	3.00	3.00
625	A106	40c multicolored	1.60	1.60
626	A106	40c multicolored	1.60	1.60
a.		Pair, #625-626	3.50	3.50
627	A106	60c multicolored	2.50	2.50
628	A106	60c multicolored	2.50	2.50
a.		Pair, #627-628	5.50	5.50
629	A106	75c multicolored	2.75	2.75
630	A106	75c multicolored	2.75	2.75
a.		Pair #629-630	6.00	6.00
		Nos. 623-630 (8)	16.50	16.50

Value at UL on Nos. 623, 625, 627, 629; at UR on others.
Nos. 624a-630a have continuous designs.

Environmental Protection — A107

Designs: 40c, Family on beach at sunset. 60c, Fish. 75c, Frigate birds.

1994, July 12
631	A107	40c multicolored	1.00	.90
632	A107	60c multicolored	1.10	1.10
633	A107	75c multicolored	1.60	1.60
		Nos. 631-633 (3)	3.70	3.60

Independence, 15th anniv.

Butterflies A108

Designs: 1c, Diaphania indica. 5c, Herpetogramma licarsisalis. 10c, Parotis suralis. 12c, Sufetula sunidesalis. 20c, Aedia sericea. 23c, Anomis vitiensis. 30c, Anticarsia irrorata. 35c, Spodoptera litura. 40c, Mocis frugalis. 45c, Agrius convolvuli. 50c, Cephonodes picus. 55c, Gnathothlibus erotus. 60c, Macroglossum hirundo. 75c, Badamia exclamationis. $1, Precis villida. $2, Danaus plexippus. $3, Hypolimnas bolina (male). $5, Hypolimnas bolina (female).

1994, Aug. 19 *Perf. 14½x14*
634	A108	1c multicolored	.25	.25
635	A108	5c multicolored	.25	.25
636	A108	10c multicolored	.25	.25

637	A108	12c multicolored	.25	.25
638	A108	20c multicolored	.35	.35
639	A108	23c multicolored	.45	.45
640	A108	30c multicolored	.60	.55
641	A108	35c multicolored	.70	.65
642	A108	40c multicolored	.80	.70
643	A108	45c multicolored	.85	.80
644	A108	50c multicolored	.90	.85
645	A108	55c multicolored	1.10	.95
646	A108	60c multicolored	1.10	1.00
647	A108	75c multicolored	1.25	1.25
648	A108	$1 multicolored	1.75	1.75
a.		Souvenir sheet of 1	2.75	2.75
649	A108	$2 multicolored	3.25	4.00
650	A108	$3 multicolored	5.25	6.00
651	A108	$5 multicolored	9.00	10.00
		Nos. 634-651 (18)	28.35	30.30

No. 648a issued 2/12/97 for Hong Kong '97. For overprints see Nos. 763-767.

Flowers — A109

23c, Nerium oleander. 60c, Catharanthus roseus. 75c, Ipomea pes-caprae. $1, Calophyllum mophyllum.

1994, Oct. 31
652	A109	23c multicolored	.65	.65
653	A109	60c multicolored	1.10	1.10
654	A109	75c multicolored	1.50	1.50
655	A109	$1 multicolored	2.00	2.00
		Nos. 652-655 (4)	5.25	5.25

A110

Constellations.

1995, Jan. 31
656	A110	50c Gemini	1.20	1.20
657	A110	60c Cancer	1.30	1.30
658	A110	75c Cassiopeia	1.50	1.50
659	A110	$1 Southern cross	2.00	2.00
		Nos. 656-659 (4)	6.00	6.00

A111

Scenes of Kiribati: No. 660: a, Architecture. b, Men, canoe, sailboat. c, Gun emplacement, Tarawa. d, Children, shells. e, Outdoor sports.
No. 661: a, Women traditionally attired. b, Windsurfing. c, Filleting fish. d, Snorkeling, scuba diving. e, Weaving.

Wmk. 384
1995, Apr. 3 Litho. *Perf. 14½*
660	A111	30c Strip of 5, #a.-e.	4.50	4.50
661	A111	40c Strip of 5, #a.-e.	6.50	6.50
f.		Booklet pane, #660, #661 + 5 labels	12.00	12.00
		Complete booklet, #661f	13.00	

Visit South Pacific Year.

End of World War II, 50th Anniv.
Common Design Type

Designs: 23c, Grumman TBM-3E Avenger. 40c, Curtiss SOC. 3-1 seagull. 50c, Consolidated B-24J Liberator. 60c, Grumman Goose. 75c, Martin B-26 Marauder. $1, Northrop P-61B Black Widow. $2, Reverse of War Medal 1939-45.

Perf. 14x13½
1995, May 8 Wmk. 373
662	CD351	23c multicolored	1.10	1.10
663	CD351	40c multicolored	1.30	1.30
664	CD351	50c multicolored	1.50	1.50
665	CD351	60c multicolored	1.75	1.75

666	CD351	75c multicolored	2.40	2.40
667	CD351	$1 multicolored	3.25	3.25
		Nos. 662-667 (6)	11.30	11.30

Souvenir Sheet
Perf. 14

668	CD352	$2 multicolored	5.00	5.00

For overprints see Nos. 691-697.

Souvenir Sheet

Environmental Protection — A112

Marine life: a, Electus parrot, great frigate bird, coconut crab. b, Red-tailed tropic bird, common dolphin, pantropical spotted dolphin. c, Yellow & blue sea perch, green turtle, blue-barred orange parrot fish. d, Pennant coral fish, red-banded wrasse, violet squirrel fish.

Wmk. 373

1995, July 12	Litho.		**Perf. 14**
669 A112	60c #a.-d. + 4 labels	5.00	5.00

For overprint see No. 672.

Souvenir Sheet

New Year 1995 (Year of the Boar) — A113

$2, Sow, piglets.

1995, Sept. 1	Litho.		**Perf. 13**
670 A113	$2 multicolored	4.75	4.75

Singapore '95.

Souvenir Sheet

Beijing '95 — A114

Design: $2, like #670.

1995, Sept. 14			
671 A114	$2 multicolored	4.75	4.75

No. 669 Overprinted for Jakarta '95

Wmk. 373

1995, Aug. 19	Litho.		**Perf. 14**
672 A112	60c #a.-d. + 4 labels	10.00	10.00

Police Maritime Unit — A115

Patrol boat RKS Teanoai: No. 673, In harbor. No. 674, Under way.

Wmk. 373

1995, Nov. 30	Litho.			**Perf. 13**
673	75c multicolored		2.25	2.25
674	75c multicolored		2.25	2.25
	a.	A115 Pair, #673-674	4.75	4.75

Dolphins A116

Designs: 23c, Pantropical spotted. 60c, Spinner. 75c, Fraser's. $1, Rough-toothed.

Wmk. 384

1996, Jan. 15	Litho.			**Perf. 14**
675	A116	23c multicolored	1.60	.90
676	A116	60c multicolored	2.25	1.30
677	A116	75c multicolored	3.00	2.25
678	A116	$1 multicolored	3.50	3.75
		Nos. 675-678 (4)	10.35	8.20

UNICEF, 50th Anniv. — A117

Portion of UNICEF emblem and: a, Water faucet, clean water. b, Documents, chilren's rights. c, Hypodermic, health care. d, Open book, education.

Wmk. 373

1996, Apr. 22	Litho.			**Perf. 13**
679 A117	30c Block of 4, #a.-d.	2.75	2.75

No. 679 is a continuous design.

Souvenir Sheet

CHINA '96, 9th Intl. Philatelic Exhibition — A118

1996, Apr. 30	**Wmk. 384**			**Perf. 13½**
680 A118	50c multicolored		2.00	2.00

New Year 1996, Year of the Rat.

Souvenir Sheet

No. 5609 Gilbert and Ellice Islands LMS Jubilee Class 4-6-0 Locomotive — A119

Wmk. 373

1996, June 8	Litho.			**Perf. 12**
681 A119	$2 multicolored		4.25	4.25

CAPEX '96.

Sea Crabs A120

Wmk. 373

1996, Aug. 6	Litho.			**Perf. 14**
682	A120	23c Rathbun red	.65	.50
683	A120	60c Red & white painted	1.50	1.10
684	A120	75c Red spotted	1.75	1.75
685	A120	$1 Red spotted white	2.25	2.75
		Nos. 682-685 (4)	6.15	6.10

Souvenir Sheet

Taipei '96 — A121

Wmk. 384

1996, Oct. 21	Litho.			**Perf. 14½**
686 A121	$1.50 Outrigger canoe		4.25	4.25

Ships Type of 1989

23c, Whaling ship, "Potomac," 1843. 50c, Barkentine "Southern Cross IV," 1891. 60c, Bark "John Williams III," 1890. $1, HMS Dolphin, 1765.

Wmk. 384

1996, Dec. 2	Litho.			**Perf. 14½**
687	A87	23c multicolored	.70	.55
688	A87	50c multicolored	1.10	1.10
689	A87	60c multicolored	1.30	1.30
690	A87	$1 multicolored	2.25	2.25
		Nos. 687-690 (4)	5.35	5.20

Nos. 662-668 Ovptd.

Perf. 14x13½

1997, May 29	Litho.		**Wmk. 373**	
691	CD351	23c multicolored	.70	.50
692	CD351	40c multicolored	.95	.80
693	CD351	50c multicolored	1.25	1.10
694	CD351	60c multicolored	1.50	1.50
695	CD351	75c multicolored	1.75	1.75
696	CD351	$1 multicolored	2.25	2.25
		Nos. 691-696 (6)	8.40	7.90

Souvenir Sheet

697	CD351	$2 multicolored	5.00	5.00

Queen Elizabeth II and Prince Philip, 50th Wedding Anniv. — A122

No. 698, Queen Elizabeth II. No. 699, Horse team going down river bank. No. 700, Queen in open carriage. No. 701, Prince Philip. No. 702, Prince, Queen. No. 703, Riding horse. $2, Queen, Prince in open carriage, horiz.

Perf. 14½x14

1997, July 10	Litho.		**Wmk. 373**	
698		50c multicolored	1.40	1.40
699		50c multicolored	1.40	1.40
	a.	A122 Pair, #698-699	3.00	3.00
700		60c multicolored	1.60	1.60
701		60c multicolored	1.60	1.60
	a.	A122 Pair, #700-701	3.50	3.50
702		75c multicolored	2.40	2.40
703		75c multicolored	2.40	2.40
	a.	A122 Pair, #702-703	5.25	5.25
		Nos. 698-703 (6)	10.80	10.80

Souvenir Sheet

704	A122	$2 multicolored	6.50	6.50

Birds — A123

Nos. 705-706, Rock dove. Nos. 707-708, Pacific pigeon. Nos. 709-710, Micronesian pigeon.

Wmk. 373

1997, Dec. 1	Litho.			**Perf. 14**
705		50c Immature	1.10	1.10
706		50c Adult	1.10	1.10
	a.	A123 Pair, #705-706	2.40	2.40
707		60c Adult	1.50	1.50
708		60c Immature	1.50	1.50
	a.	A123 Pair, #707-708	3.25	3.25
709		75c Adult	1.75	1.75
710		75c Immature	1.75	1.75
	a.	A123 Pair, #709-710	3.75	3.75
		Nos. 705-710 (6)	8.70	8.70

Nos. 705-706, 709-710 With Added Inscription

Wmk. 373

1997, Dec. 5   Litho.   Perf. 14

711	50c on #705	1.25	1.25
712	50c on #706	1.25	1.25
a.	A123 Pair, #711-712	2.75	2.75
713	75c on #709	2.00	2.00
714	75c on #710	2.00	2.00
a.	A123 Pair, #713-714	4.25	4.25
	Nos. 711-714 (4)	6.50	6.50

Asia '97.

Spiny Lobster A124

Wmk. 373

1998, Feb. 2   Litho.   Perf. 14

715	A124	25c shown	.70	.70
716	A124	25c Crawling right	.70	.70
717	A124	25c Crawling left	.70	.70
718	A124	25c Looking upward	.70	.70
a.	Strip of 4, #715-718		3.00	3.00

Souvenir Sheet

719	A124	$1.50 Looking straight forward	3.50	3.50

World Wildlife Fund.

Diana, Princess of Wales (1961-97)
Common Design Type

Various portraits — No. 720: a, 50c. b, 60c. c, 75c.

Perf. 14½x14

1998, Mar. 31   Litho.   Wmk. 373

719A	CD355	25c multicolored	.60	.60

Sheet of 4

720	CD355	#a.-c., 719A	4.25	4.25

No. 720 sold for $2.10 + 50c, with surtax from international sales being donated to the Princess Diana Memorial Fund, and surtax from national sales being donated to designated local charity.

Intl. Year of the Ocean — A125

Whales and dolphins: No. 721, Indo-Pacific humpbacked dolphin. No. 722, Bottlenose dolphin. No. 723, Short-snouted spinner dolphin. No. 724, Risso's dolphin. No. 725, Striped dolphin. No. 726, Sei whale. No. 727, Fin whale. No. 728, Minke whale.

Wmk. 373

1998, Oct. 1   Litho.   Perf. 14

721	25c multicolored	.60	.60
722	25c multicolored	.60	.60
a.	A125 Pair, #721-722	1.50	1.50
723	60c multicolored	1.25	1.25
724	60c multicolored	1.25	1.25
a.	A125 Pair, #723-724	2.75	2.75
725	75c multicolored	1.75	1.75
726	75c multicolored	1.75	1.75
a.	A125 Pair, #725-726	3.75	3.75
727	$1 multicolored	2.00	2.00
728	$1 multicolored	2.00	2.00
a.	A125 Pair, #727-728	4.50	4.50
	Nos. 721-728 (8)	11.20	11.20

Souvenir Sheet

Children of Kiribati — A125a

1998, Sept. 15

729	A125a	$1 multicolored	2.25	2.25

Souvenir Sheet

Reuben K. Uatioa Stadium — A126

Wmk. 373

1998, Oct. 23   Litho.   Perf. 14

730	A126	$2 multicolored	3.75	3.75

Italia '98 World Philatelic Exhibition.

Greenhouse Effect — A127

Designs: 25c, Contributors to Greenhouse gases. 50c, Explanation of the Greenhouse Effect. 60c, Greenhouse Effect on Tarawa Atoll. 75c, Greenhouse Effect on Kiritimati Island.
$1.50, People in sailboat, "Kiribati way of life."

Wmk. 373

1998, Dec. 1   Litho.   Perf. 13½

731	A127	25c multicolored	.60	.60
732	A127	50c multicolored	.90	.90
733	A127	60c multicolored	1.25	1.25
734	A127	75c multicolored	1.75	1.75
	Nos. 731-734 (4)		4.50	4.50

Souvenir Sheet

735	A127	$1.50 multicolored	4.75	4.75

Souvenir Sheet

HMS Resolution at Christmas Island — A128

Wmk. 373

1999, Mar. 19   Litho.   Perf. 14

736	A128	$2 multicolored	4.25	4.25

Australia '99 World Stamp Expo.

IBRA '99, Philatelic Exhibition, Nuremberg — A129

Ducks: 25c, Northern shoveller, male. 50c, Northern shoveller, female. 60c, Green-winged teal, male. 75c, Green-winged teal, female and ducklings.
$3, Green winged teal, male, duckling.

Wmk. 373

1999, Apr. 27   Litho.   Perf. 14

737	A129	25c multicolored	.65	.50
738	A129	50c multicolored	1.25	.80
739	A129	60c multicolored	1.40	1.40
740	A129	75c multicolored	1.75	2.00
	Nos. 737-740 (4)		5.05	4.70

Souvenir Sheet

741	A129	$3 multicolored	6.00	6.00

Independence, 20th Anniv. — A130

Designs: 25c, Millennium Island. 60c, Map of Kiribati. 75c, Map of Nikumaroro. $1, Amelia Earhart, Lockheed 10E Electra airplane.

Wmk. 373

1999, July 12   Litho.   Perf. 13½

742	A130	25c multicolored	.60	.60
743	A130	60c multicolored	1.10	1.10
744	A130	75c multicolored	1.40	1.40
745	A130	$1 multicolored	3.00	3.00
a.	Souvenir sheet, #744-745		4.00	4.00
	Nos. 742-745 (4)		6.10	6.10

1st Manned Moon Landing, 30th Anniv.
Common Design Type

Designs: 25c, Edwin Aldrin. 60c, Service module docks with lander. 75c, Apollo 11 on lunar surface. $1, Command module separates from service module.
$2, Earth as seen from moon.

Perf. 14x13¾

			Wmk. 384	
746	CD357	25c multicolored	.60	.60
747	CD357	60c multicolored	1.10	1.10
748	CD357	75c multicolored	1.40	1.40
749	CD357	$1 multicolored	1.75	1.75
	Nos. 746-749 (4)		4.85	4.85

Souvenir Sheet
Perf. 14

750	CD357	$2 multicolored	4.00	4.00

No. 750 contains one 40mm circular stamp 40mm.

UPU, 125th Anniv., Christmas A131

Wmk. 373

1999, Oct. 9   Litho.   Perf. 13½

751	A131	25c Santa in canoe	.55	.45
752	A131	60c Santa on dock	1.00	.85
753	A131	75c Santa in sleigh	1.25	1.25
754	A131	$1 Santa at computer	1.50	1.50
	Nos. 751-754 (4)		4.30	4.05

Millennium A132

Perf. 13¼x13

2000, Jan. 1   Litho.   Wmk. 373

755	A132	25c Faith	.55	.45
756	A132	40c Harmony	.80	.70
757	A132	60c Hope	1.10	1.10
758	A132	75c Enlightenment	1.75	1.75
759	A132	$1 Peace	2.00	2.00
	Nos. 755-759 (5)		6.20	6.00

Sesame Street Characters — A133

No. 760: a, Bert. b, Baby Bear. c, Grover. d, Elmo, Cookie Monster. e, Telly Monster. f. Zoe. g, Ernie. h, Big Bird, Rosita. i, Oscar the Grouch.
No. 761, Grover as mailman.

Perf. 14½x14¾

2000, Mar. 22   Litho.   Wmk. 373

760	A133	20c Sheet of 9, #a-i	3.75	3.75

Souvenir Sheet

761	A133	$1.50 multi	2.75	2.75

Souvenir Sheet

The Stamp Show 2000, London — A134

2000, May 8   Wmk. 373   Perf. 13¾

762	A134	$5 Queen Elizabeth II	7.50	7.50

Nos. 635, 636, 638, 648 and 650 Ovptd.

Perf. 14½x14

2000, June 1   Wmk. 373

763	A108	5c multi	.40	.40
764	A108	10c multi	.40	.40
765	A108	20c multi	.50	.50
766	A108	$1 multi	1.50	1.50
767	A108	$3 multi	4.00	4.00
	Nos. 763-767 (5)		6.80	6.80

Prince William, 18th Birthday A135

Various views of Prince William with Prince Charles.

Wmk. 373

2000, July 24	**Litho.**		**Perf. 12¾**
768	A135 25c multi	.40	.40
769	A135 60c multi	.90	.90
770	A135 75c multi	1.25	1.25
771	A135 $1 multi	1.50	1.50
	Nos. 768-771 (4)	4.05	4.05

Ducks
A136

Designs: No. 772, 25c, Blue duck. No. 773, 25c, Green-winged teal. No. 774, 25c, Mallard. No. 775, 25c, Northern shoveler. No. 776, 25c, Pacific black duck. No. 777, 25c, Wandering whistling duck.

Wmk. 373

2001, Jan. 22	**Litho.**		**Perf. 14**
772-777	A136 Set of 6	9.00	9.00
Souvenir Sheet			
778	A136 $1 Gray teal	8.50	8.50

Water Conservation
A137

Children's art by: 25c, Tiare Hongkai. 50c, Gilbert Z. Tluanga. 60c, Mantokataake Tebaiuea, vert. 75c, Tokaman Karanebo, vert. $2, Taom Simon.

2001, July 12	**Litho.**		**Perf. 13¼**
779-783	A137 Set of 5	6.25	6.25

Phila Nippon '01
A138

Development projects: 75c, Betio Port. $2, New Parliament House.

2001, Aug. 1			
784-785	A138 Set of 2	5.00	5.00

Tourism — A139

Designs: 75c, Norwegian Cruise Line ship, map of cruise to Fanning Island. $3, The Betsey, map of Fanning Island.

			Perf. 13¼
2001, Nov. 14	**Litho.**		**Unwmk.**
786-787	A139 Set of 2	5.75	5.75

Fish — A140

Designs: 5c, Paracanthurus hepatus. 10c, Centropyge flavissimus. 15c, Anthias squamipinnis. 20c, Centropyge loriculus. 25c, Acanthurus lineatus. 30c, Oxycirrhites typus. 40c, Dascyllus trimaculatus. 50c, Acanthurus achilles. 60c, Pomacentrus coeruleus. 75c, Acanthurus glaucopareus. 80c, Thalassoma lunare. 90c, Arothron meleagris. $1, Odonus

niger. $2, Cephalopholis miniatus. $5, Pomacanthus imperator. $10, Balistoides conspicillum.

2002, Feb. 28	**Unwmk.**		**Perf. 13**
788	A140 5c multi	.25	.25
789	A140 10c multi	.30	.30
790	A140 15c multi	.35	.35
791	A140 20c multi	.40	.40
792	A140 25c multi	.45	.45
793	A140 30c multi	.50	.50
794	A140 40c multi	.70	.70
795	A140 50c multi	.80	.80
796	A140 60c multi	.90	.90
797	A140 75c multi	1.00	1.00
798	A140 80c multi	1.25	1.25
799	A140 90c multi	1.60	1.60
800	A140 $1 multi	1.75	1.75
801	A140 $2 multi	3.50	3.50
802	A140 $5 multi	8.00	8.00
803	A140 $10 multi	14.50	14.50
	Nos. 788-803 (16)	36.25	36.25

For overprints, see Nos. 988-990.

Pacific Explorers
A141

Designs: 25c, Adm. Fabian von Bellingshausen and the Vostok, 1820. 40c, Capt. Charles Wilkes and the Vincennes, 1838-42. 60c, Capt. Edmund Fanning and the Betsey, 1798. 75c, Capt. Coffin and the Transit, 1823. $1, Commodore John Byron and the Dolphin, 1765. $2, Capt. Broughton and HMS Providence, 1795.
$5, Capt. James Cook, 1777, vert.

2002, Mar. 25	**Wmk. 373**		**Perf. 14**
804-809	A141 Set of 6	9.00	9.00
Souvenir Sheet			
810	A141 $5 multi	9.00	9.00

In Remembrance of Sept. 11, 2001 Terrorist Attacks — A142

No. 811: a, 25c. b, $2.

2002, May 3	**Wmk. 373**		**Perf. 13¾**
811	A142 Vert. pair, #a-b	5.00	5.00
Issued in sheets of 2 pairs.			

Reign of Queen Elizabeth II, 50th Anniv. — A143

Various photographs by Dorothy Wilding. Panel colors: 25c, Purple.
No. 812: a, Maroon. b, Purple.

2002, June 3	**Wmk. 373**		**Perf. 14**
812	A143 25c multi	1.25	1.25
Souvenir Sheet			
813	A143 $2 Sheet of 2, #a-b	10.00	10.00

Christmas
A144

Ribbons and bow with various basketry weaves: 25c, 60c, 75c, $1, $2.50.

2002, Dec. 2	**Litho.**		**Perf. 13x13¼**
814-818	A144 Set of 5	7.00	7.00

Cowrie Shells — A145

Designs: 25c, Cypraea mappa. 50c, Cypraea eglantina. 60c, Cypraea mauritiana. 75c, Cypraea cribaria. $1, Cypraea talpa. $2.50, Cypraea depressa.

Perf. 14½x14¼

2003, May 12	**Litho.**		**Unwmk.**
819-824	A145 Set of 6	8.50	8.50
824a	A145 Souvenir sheet, #819-824	8.50	8.50

Coronation of Queen Elizabeth II, 50th Anniv.
Common Design Type

Designs: Nos. 825, 25c, 827a, $2, Queen and Prince Philip waving. Nos. 826, $3, 827b, $5, Prince Philip paying homage to Queen at coronation.

Perf. 14¼x14½

2003, June 2	**Litho.**		**Wmk. 373**
Vignettes Framed, Red Background			
825	CD363 $2 multicolored	1.75	1.75
826	CD363 $3 multicolored	2.50	2.50
Souvenir Sheet			
Vignettes Without Frame, Purple Panel			
827	CD363 Sheet of 2, #a-b	9.25	9.25

Powered Flight, Cent. — A146

Designs: 25c, Sopwith Camel. 50c, Northrop Alpha. No. 830, 60c, DeHavilland Comet. 75c, Boeing 727. $1, English Electric Canberra. $2.50, Lockheed Martin F-22.
No. 834: a, 40c, Mitsubishi A6M-5 Zero. b, 60c, Grumman F6F Hellcat.

Wmk. 373

2003, Aug. 29	**Litho.**		**Perf. 14**
Stamp + Label			
828-833	A146 Set of 6	10.00	10.00
Souvenir Sheet			
834	A146 Sheet of 2, #a-b	3.50	3.50

Christmas — A147

Christmas Island scenes: 25c, Teareba Taomeka, Tabwakea. 40c, Seventh Day Adventist Church, London. 50c, St. Teresa Catholic Church, Tabakea Village. 60c, Betaera Fou, London. 75c, Children, church bells, London. $1.50, Emanuira Church, London. $2.50, Church of Christ (60x24mm).

2003, Dec. 20	**Unwmk.**		**Perf. 13¼**
835-841	A147 Set of 7	10.00	10.00
841a	Souvenir sheet, #835-841	10.00	10.00

Road Safety — A148

No. 842: a, Accident. b, Automobile. c, Beverage can, drink, cigarette. d, Children.

2004, Apr. 7	**Litho.**		**Perf. 13x13¼**
842	A148 Horiz. strip of 4	6.50	6.50
a.	30c multi	.75	.75
b.	40c multi	1.10	1.10
c.	50c multi	1.30	1.10
d.	60c multi	1.60	1.40
e.	Souvenir sheet, #842	6.50	6.50

World Health Day.

Bird Life International
A149

Designs: 25c, Pacific golden plover. 40c, Whimbrel. 50c, Wandering tattler. 60c, Sanderling. 75c, Bar-tailed godwit. $2.50, Ruddy turnstone.
No. 849 — Bristle-thighed curlew: a, One in tree, one at water's edge. b, Head of bird. c, Front of bird, head facing right, vert. d, Back of bird, head facing left, vert. e, Two birds at water's edge.

Perf. 14¼x13¾

2004, Apr. 29	**Litho.**		**Unwmk.**
843-848	A149 Set of 6	13.00	13.00
Souvenir Sheet			
Perf. 14¼x14½			
849	A149 $1 Sheet of 5, #a-e	15.00	15.00

2004 Summer Olympics, Athens — A150

Designs: 25c, Runners. 50c, Taekwondo. 60c, Weight lifting. 75c, Women's running.

2004, July 12	**Wmk. 373**		**Perf. 14**
850-853	A150 Set of 4	4.50	4.50

Souvenir Sheet

Celebration Games — A151

No. 854: a, Runners on track. b, Athletes, dancer, building.

2004, July 12			
854	A151 $2.50 Sheet of 2, #a-b	10.00	10.00

Orchids — A152

No. 855: a, Dendrobium anosmum. b, Dendrobium chrysotoxum. c, Dendrobium laevifolium. d, Dendrobium mohlianum. e,

Dendrobium pseudoglomeratum. f, Dendrobium purpureum. g, Grammatophyllum speciosum. h, Dendrobium williamsianum. i, Spathoglottis plicata. j, Vanda hindsii.

2004, Aug. 28　Unwmk.　Perf. 13½
855　A152　Block of 10　18.00　18.00
a.-j.　$1 Any single　1.60　1.50

Merchant Ships
A153

Designs: 50c, MV Montelucia. 75c, MS Pacific Princess. $2.50 MS Prinsendam. $5, MS Norwegian Wind.

2004, Oct. 25　Litho.　Perf. 13¼
856-859　A153　Set of 4　17.50　17.50

Battle of Trafalgar, Bicent. — A154

Designs: 25c, French 16-pounder cannon. 50c, San Ildefonso in action against HMS Defence. 75c, HMS Victory lashed to the Redoubtable. $1, Emperor Napoleon Bonaparte, vert. $1.50, HMS Victory. No. 865, $2.50, Vice-admiral Sir Horatio Nelson, vert. No. 866: a, Admiral Federico Gravina. b, Santissima Trinidad.

2005, Mar. 29　Litho.　Perf. 13¼
860-865　A154　Set of 6　15.00　15.00
Souvenir Sheet
866　A154　$2.50 Sheet of 2,
　　　　#a-b　10.00　10.00

No. 864 has particles of wood from the HMS Victory embedded in the areas covered by a thermographic process that produces a raised, shiny effect.

End of World War II, 60th Anniv. — A155

No. 867: a, Japanese Type 95 Ha-Go tank invading Gilbert Islands. b, Japanese A6M Zero fighter on Gilbert Islands. c, USS Argonaut and Nautilus land Marines at Butaritari in Carlson Raid. d, Pacific Fleet Admiral Chester W. Nimitz. e, USS Liscome Bay sunk by Japanese submarine. f, US Higgins landing craft approaching Tarawa Red Beach. g, F6F-3 Hellcats provide air cover over Tarawa Red Beach. h, LVTs hit the shore at Tarawa Red Beach. i, Sherman tank at Tarawa Red Beach. j, US Marines take cover on Tarawa Red Beach.
$5, Australian Prime Minister John Curtin, British Prime Minister Winston Churchill.

2005, Apr. 21　Perf. 13¾
867　A155　75c Sheet of 10, #a-j 20.00　20.00
Souvenir Sheet
868　A155　$5 multi　15.00　15.00
Pacific Explorer 2005 World Stamp Expo, Sydney (No. 868).

BirdLife International — A156

No. 869, 25c — Birds of Christmas Island: a, Lesser frigatebird. b, Red-tailed tropicbird. c, Blue noddy. d, Christmas shearwater. e, Sooty tern. f, Masked booby.
No. 870, $2 — Birds of Kiribati: a, Whitetailed tropicbird. b, Black noddy. c, Red-footed booby. d, Wedge-tailed shearwater. e, White tern. f, Great frigatebird.

2005, Aug. 15　Perf. 13¼x13
Sheets of 6, #a-f
869-870　A156　Set of 2　32.50　32.50

Pope John Paul II (1920-2005)
A157

2005, Aug. 18　Litho.　Perf. 14
871　A157　$1 multi　3.50　3.50

Battle of Trafalgar, Bicent. — A158

Designs: 25c, HMS Victory. 50c, Ships, horiz. $5, Admiral Horatio Nelson

2005, Oct. 18　Litho.　Perf. 13½
872-874　A158　Set of 3　16.00　16.00

Worldwide Fund for Nature (WWF) — A159

Various depictions of harlequin shrimp: 50c, 60c, 75c, $5.

2005, Dec. 1　Perf. 14
875-878　A159　Set of 4　16.50　16.50
878a　Miniature sheet, 2 each
　　　　#875-878　34.00　34.00

Queen Elizabeth II, 80th Birthday
A160

Queen: 50c, As young woman. 75c, Wearing tiara, sepia photograph. $1, Wearing tiara, color photograph. $2, Wearing pink hat.
No. 883: a, $1.50, Like $1. b, $2.50, Like 75c.

2006, Apr. 21　Litho.　Perf. 14
Stamps With White Frames
879-882　A160　Set of 4　10.00　10.00

Souvenir Sheet
Stamps Without White Frames
883　A160　Sheet of 2, #a-b　14.00　14.00
For footnotes, see Nos. 991-994.

Europa Stamps, 50th Anniv. — A161

Flags of European Union and Kiribati with gradiating background colors of: $2, Gray green. $2.50, Purple. $3, Yellowish brown. $5, Blue.

2006, May 4　Perf. 13¼
884-887　A161　Set of 4　22.00　22.00
887a　Souvenir sheet, #884-887　22.00　22.00

Anniversaries — A162

No. 888, 25c: a, Charles Darwin and marine life. b, Fish and marine life.
No. 889, 50c: a, Isambard Kingdom Brunel. b, Glowing rivet.
No. 890, 75c: a, Christopher Columbus. b, Ship.
No. 891, $1: a, Thomas Alva Edison. b, Tin foil phonograph.
No. 892, $1.25: a, Wolfgang Amadeus Mozart. b, Violin and quill pen.
No. 893, $1.50: a, Concorde. b, Wing of Concorde, Concorde in flight.

2006, May 27　Perf. 13x12½
Horiz. Pairs, #a-b
888-893　A162　Set of 6　22.50　22.50
Darwin's voyage on the Beagle, 250th anniv., Birth of Brunel, bicent., Death of Columbus, 500th anniv., Death of Edison, 75th anniv., Birth of Mozart, 250th anniv., Inaugural Concorde flights, 30th anniv.

Dinosaurs
A163

Designs: 25c, Ultrasaurus. 50c, Rhamphorhynchus. 60c, Dilophosaurus. 75c, Brachiosaurus. No. 898, $1, Minmi paravertebra. No. 899, $1, Eoraptor. $1.25, Stegosaurus. $1.50, Gigantosaurus.

2006, Sept. 15　Perf. 13¼x13½
894-901　A163　Set of 8　12.50　12.50

Victoria Cross, 150th Anniv. — A164

No. 902: a, Troop Sergeant Major John Berryman with Captain Webb at Balaclava. b, Private W. Norman bringing in two Russian prisoners. c, Sergeant Major John Greive saving officer's life at Balaclava. d, Private Thomas Beach rescuing Colonel Carpenter at Inkerman. e, Brevet Major C. H. Lumley engaged with Russian gunners in the Redan. f, Major F. C. Elton working in trenches.

2006, Oct. 20　Litho.　Perf. 13¼x12½
902　A164　$1.50 Sheet of 6,
　　　　#a-f, + 6 la-
　　　　bels　19.00　19.00

60th Wedding Anniversary of Queen Elizabeth II and Prince Philip — A165

Designs: 50c, Portrait of Elizabeth and Philip. 75c, Wedding procession. $1, Bride and groom waving. $1.50, Queen reading. $5, Wedding portrait.

2007, Jan. 31　Litho.　Perf. 13¾
903-906　A165　Set of 4　6.00　6.00
Souvenir Sheet
Perf. 14
907　A165　$5 multi　7.75　7.75
No. 907 contains one 42x56mm stamp

Scouting, Cent. A166

Designs: 25c, Scouts with Kiribati flag, hands tying neckerchief. 50c, Scouts learning about AIDS, Scout saluting. 75c, Scout leaders, hand with compass. $2, 1962 Scout shelter, hands lashing rope.
No. 912, vert.: a, $1, Emblem of Kiribati Scouts. b, $1.50, Lord Robert Baden-Powell.

Perf. 13x13¼
2007, Sept. 21　Litho.　Wmk. 373
908-911　A166　Set of 4　7.50　7.50
Souvenir Sheet
Perf. 13¼x13
912　A166　Sheet of 2, #a-b　5.25　5.25

Princess Diana
(1961-97)
A167

Designs: No. 913, 25c, Wearing white dress, facing right. No. 914, 25c, Wearing pink dress, facing left. 50c, Wearing pink dress, diff. No. 916, 75c, Wearing emerald necklace. No. 917, 75c, Wearing black and white dress. $1, Wearing red dress.

Perf. 13¼x12½

2007, Nov. 1   Litho.   Unwmk.
913-918 A167 Set of 6   7.00 7.00

Military
Uniforms — A168

Uniforms of: 25c, Royal Engineers. 40c, 95th Rifles. 50c, 24th Regiment of Foot. 60c, New Zealand soldiers. 75c, 93rd Sutherland Highlanders. 90c, Irish Guard. $1, Japanese soldiers. $1.50, United States Marine Corps.

2007, Nov. 20   Wmk. 373   Perf. 14
919-926 A168 Set of 8   12.00 12.00

Birds — A169

Designs: 5c, Great crested tern. 10c Eurasian teal. 15c, Laughing gull. 20c, Black-tailed godwit. 25c, Pectoral sandpiper. 50c, Band-rumped storm petrel. 60c, Sharp-tailed sandpiper. 75c, Gray-tailed tattler. 90c, Red phalarope. $1, Pink-footed shearwater. $2, Ring-billed gull. $5, Bonin petrel.

Wmk. 373
2008, Feb. 9   Litho.   Perf. 13¾
927 A169 5c multi   .25   .25
928 A169 10c multi   .25   .25
929 A169 15c multi   .30   .30
930 A169 20c multi   .40   .40
931 A169 25c multi   .45   .45
932 A169 50c multi   .95   .95
933 A169 60c multi   1.10 1.10
934 A169 75c multi   1.40 1.40
935 A169 90c multi   1.75 1.75
936 A169 $1 multi   2.00 2.00
937 A169 $2 multi   4.25 4.25
  a. Souvenir sheet, #929, 933-
      937   10.00 10.00
938 A169 $5 multi   10.50 10.50
  a. Souvenir sheet, #927-928,
      930-932, 938   12.50 12.50
  Nos. 927-938 (12)   23.60 23.60

For surcharges, see Nos. 984-987.

A170

Royal Air Force, 90th Anniv. — A171

Designs: 25c, Avro Shackleton. 50c, Harrier GR3. 75c, Eurofighter Typhoon. $1, Vickers Valiant. $2.50, Dambusters Raid.

Wmk. 373
2008, Apr. 1   Litho.   Perf. 14
939-942 A170 Set of 4   5.50 5.50
Souvenir Sheet
943 A171 $2.50 multi   5.50 5.50

Phoenix
Island
Protected
Area
A172

Designs: 40c, Huts. 75c, Map of Kanton Island. 80c, Map of various islands. 85c, Phoenix petrel. $1.25, Acropora nobilis and reef fish. $1.75, Blacktip reef shark.

2008, July 12   Perf. 13¾
944-949 A172 Set of 6   11.50 11.50
949a   Souvenir sheet of 6, #944-
        949   11.50 11.50

2008
Summer
Olympics,
Beijing
A173

Designs: 25c, Bamboo, weight lifting. 50c, Dragon, running. 60c, Lanterns, cycling. 75c, Fish, javelin.

Wmk. 373
2008, Aug. 8   Perf. 13½
950-953 A173 Set of 4   3.75 3.75

Christmas — A174

No. 954, 25c: a, Lady Sacred Heart Church, Bairiki. b, Kiribati Protestant Church, Bikenibeu.
No. 955, 40c: a, Kaotitaeka Roman Catholic Church, Betio. b, Mormon Church, Iesu Kristo.
No. 956, 50c: a, Moaningaina Church, Eita. b, Sacred Heart Cathedral, Tarawa.
No. 957, 75c: a, St. Paul's Millennium Church, Betio. b, Kainkatikun Kristo Church, Naninimo.

Wmk. 406
2008, Dec. 8   Litho.   Perf. 13
Pairs, #a-b
954-957 A174 Set of 4   5.00 5.00
957c   Souvenir sheet, #954a-954b,
        955a-955b, 956a-956b, 957a-
        957b   5.00 5.00

Explorers — A175

Designs: 25c, Sir Ernest Shackleton (1874-1922). 40c, Robert Falcon Scott (1868-1912). 50c, Captain James Cook (1728-79). 75c, Marco Polo (1254-1324). $1.50, Matthew Flinders (1774-1814). $1.75, John Cabot (c. 1450-99).

Wmk. 406
2009, Mar. 9   Litho.   Perf. 14
958-963 A175 Set of 6   9.00 9.00

Naval
Aviation,
Cent.
A176

Aircraft: 40c, Grumman Avenger. 50c, Chance Vought Corsair. 75c, Westland Whirlwind helicopter. $1.25, McDonnell Douglas Phantom. $3, Helicopter on deck of HMS Ark Royal.

Wmk. 406
2009, May 12   Litho.   Perf. 14
964-967 A176 Set of 4   4.75 4.75
Souvenir Sheet
968 A176 $3 multi   4.75 4.75
  Nos. 964-968 each were printed in sheets of 8 + central label.

Space
Exploration
A177

Designs: 40c, Mars Science Laboratory. 50c, International Space Station. 75c, Space Shuttle Endeavour and Boeing transporter plane. $1.25, Launch of Apollo 12. No. 973, $3, Luna 16.
No. 974, $3, Astronaut on Moon, painting by Capt. Alan Bean, vert.

Wmk. 406
2009, July 20   Litho.   Perf. 13¼
969-973 A177 Set of 5   9.25 9.25
Souvenir Sheet
Perf. 13x13½
974 A177 $3 multi   4.75 4.75
  First man on the Moon, 40th anniv. No. 974 contains one 40x60mm stamp.

Battle of Britain,
70th
Anniv. — A178

Stained-glass windows of Biggin Hill Memorial Chapel depicting: 25c, Aircraft servicing. 40c, Knight, English flag, airplanes. 50c, Parachute packing. 75c, Ground control. $1, Rescue services. $1.50, Royal Air Force emblem. $3, Photograph of Sir Douglas Bader.

Wmk. 406
2010, Apr. 14   Litho.   Perf. 13
975-980 A178 Set of 6   8.25 8.25
Souvenir Sheet
981 A178 $3 multi   5.75 5.75

Souvenir Sheet

Wedding of Prince William and
Catherine Middleton — A179

Perf. 14¾x14¼
2011, Apr. 29   Litho.   Wmk. 406
982 A179 $5 multi   11.00 11.00

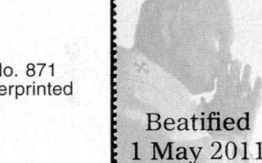

No. 871
Overprinted

Unwmk.
2011, June 13   Litho.   Perf. 14
983 A157 $1 multi   2.10 2.10

Nos. 927-930
Surcharged

Methods, Perfs and Watermarks As
Before
2011, July
984 A169 25c on 5c #927   .50   .50
985 A169 30c on 10c #928   .60   .60
986 A169 50c on 20c #930   .95   .95
987 A169 75c on 15c #929   1.40 1.40
  Nos. 984-987 (4)   3.45 3.45

Nos. 794,
801 & 803
Ovptd.

Methods and Perfs As Before
2011, July
988 A140 40c on #794   .75   .75
989 A140 $2 on #801   3.75 3.75
990 A140 $10 on #803   19.00 19.00
  Nos. 088-000 (3)   23.50 23.50

Nos. 879-882 Overprinted in Silver

Methods and Perfs. As Before

2012, June 4
991	A160	50c on #879	1.00 1.00
992	A160	75c on #880	1.50 1.50
993	A160	$1 on #881	2.00 2.00
994	A160	$2 on #882	4.00 4.00
		Nos. 991-994 (4)	8.50 8.50

Worldwide Fund for Nature (WWF) A180

Various views of Giant trevally.

2012, July 11   Litho.   Perf. 14¼x14
995		Horiz. strip of 4	11.50 11.50
a.	A180	80c multi	1.75 1.75
b.	A180	$1 multi	2.10 2.10
c.	A180	$1.50 multi	3.25 3.25
d.	A180	$2 multi	4.25 4.25

Printed in sheets containing two each Nos. 995a-995d.

Miniature Sheet

Marine Life of Phoenix Islands Protected Area — A181

No. 996: a, 40c, Manta ray. b, 50c, Napoleon wrasse. c, 60c, Yellow and blueback fusiliers. d, 75c, Rainbow runners. e, $1, Green turtle. f, $1.50, Ornate butterflyfish. g, $2, Chrysiptera albata. h, $2.50, Small giant clam.

2012, Sept. 12   Perf. 14¼x14
996	A181	Sheet of 8, #a-h	19.00 19.00

Watercraft A182

Designs: 5c, Christmas Island outrigger. 10c, Ferry to shore. 15c, Inter-island ferries. 20c, Fishing boats. 25c, Inter-island ferry. 30c, Te Tia Awaka and cargo boat. 35c, Bwaan Tetangira II. 40c, Passengers diving off outrigger Te Okarsi. 45c, Akenraoi in Abaiang Lagoon. 50c, Native house with outrigger. 55c, Moamoa. 60c, Container ship Kiribati Chief. 75c, Cruise liner Pride of Aloha. $1, Kiribati 36 yacht. $2, Pilot boat Teeitei. $5, Traditional outrigger.

Perf. 13¾

2013, Oct. 5   Litho.   Unwmk.
997	A182	5c multi	.25 .25
998	A182	10c multi	.25 .25
999	A182	15c multi	.30 .30
1000	A182	20c multi	.40 .40
1001	A182	25c multi	.50 .50
1002	A182	30c multi	.60 .60
1003	A182	35c multi	.65 .65
1004	A182	40c multi	.75 .75
1005	A182	45c multi	.85 .85
1006	A182	50c multi	.95 .95
1007	A182	55c multi	1.00 1.00
1008	A182	60c multi	1.10 1.10
1009	A182	75c multi	1.40 1.40
1010	A182	$1 multi	1.90 1.90
1011	A182	$2 multi	3.75 3.75
1012	A182	$5 multi	9.50 9.50
		Nos. 997-1012 (16)	24.15 24.15

Mangroves — A183

Designs: 45c, Building and mangroves. 75c, Man and boys on beach near mangroves. $1, People near mangroves. $3, People planting mangroves.

2014, June 16   Litho.   Perf. 14x14½
1013-1016	A183	Set of 4	10.00 10.00

POSTAGE DUE STAMPS

Natl. Arms — D1

1981, Aug. 27   Litho.   Perf. 14
J1	D1	1c brt pink & black	.25 .25
J2	D1	2c greenish blue & blk	.25 .25
J3	D1	5c brt yel grn & black	.25 .25
J4	D1	10c lt red brown & blk	.25 .25
J5	D1	20c ultra & black	.25 .25
J6	D1	30c yel bister & black	.25 .35
J7	D1	40c brt pur & black	.25 .45
J8	D1	50c green & black	.25 .50
J9	D1	$1 red orange & blk	.25 .90
		Nos. J1-J9 (9)	2.25 3.45

Imperfs exist from the liquidation of Format International. They are not errors.

OFFICIAL STAMPS

Nos. 327a-340c Overprinted "O.K.G.S."

1981, May   Litho.   Unwmk.   Perf. 14
O1	A52	1c multicolored	.25 .25
O2	A52	3c multicolored	.25 .25
O3	A52	5c multicolored	.25 .25
O4	A52	7c multicolored	.25 .25
O5	A52	10c multicolored	.25 .25
O6	A52	12c multicolored	.25 .25
O7	A52	15c multicolored	.25 .25
O8	A52	20c multicolored	.25 .25
O9	A52	25c multicolored	.25 .25
O10	A52	30c multicolored	.25 .25
O11	A52	35c multicolored	.30 .30
O12	A52	50c multicolored	.40 .40
O13	A52	$1 multicolored	.70 .70
O14	A52	$2 multicolored	1.20 1.20
O15	A52	$5 multicolored	3.00 3.00
		Nos. O1-O15 (15)	8.10 8.10

Nos. O1-O15 have thick overprint.

1981   Wmk. 373
O1a	A52	1c multi	4.00 4.25
O5a	A52	10c multi	20.00 21.00
O6a	A52	12c multi	6.00 6.00
O7a	A52	15c multi	20.00 20.00
O8a	A52	20c multi	13.00 13.00
O10a	A52	30c multi	8.00 9.00
O12a	A52	50c multi	7.50 7.50
O13a	A52	$1 multi	14.00 14.00
O14a	A52	$2 multi	16.00 17.00
O15a	A52	$5 multi	4.50 4.50
		Nos. O1a-O15a (10)	113.00 116.25

Nos. 390, 393-394, 396, 398 Overprinted "O.K.G.S."

1983, June 28   Litho.   Perf. 14
O16	A62	12c multicolored	.45 .45
O17	A62	30c multicolored	.80 .80
O18	A62	35c multicolored	.90 .90
O19	A62	50c multicolored	1.25 1.25
O20	A62	$2 multicolored	3.75 3.75
		Nos. O16-O20 (5)	7.15 7.15

This overprint has shorter, thinner letters than the one used for Nos. O1-O15. It also exists on Nos. 327, 331-334, 336-340. These have been questioned.

KOREA

kə-'rē-ə

(Corea)

(Chosen, Tyosen, Tae Han)

LOCATION — Peninsula extending from Manchuria between the Yellow Sea and the Sea of Japan (East Sea)
GOVT. — Republic
AREA — 38,221 sq. mi.
POP. — 48,860,500 (2011 est.)
CAPITAL — Seoul

Korea (or Corea) an independent monarchy for centuries under Chinese influence, came under Japanese influence in 1876. Chinese and Japanese stamps were used there as early as 1877. Administrative control was assumed by Japan in 1905 and annexation followed in 1910. Postage stamps of Japan were used in Korea from 1905 to early 1946.

At the end of World War II, American forces occupied South Korea and Russian forces occupied North Korea, with the 38th parallel of latitude as the dividing line. A republic was established in 1948 following an election in South Korea. North Korea issues its own stamps.

```
100 Mon = 1 Poon
5 Poon = 1 Cheun
1000 Re = 100 Cheun = Weun
100 Weun = 1 Hwan (1953)
100 Chun = 1 Won (1962)
```

> **Catalogue values for unused stamps in this country are for Never Hinged items, beginning with Scott 283 in the regular postage section, Scott B5 in the semipostal section, and Scott C23 in the airpost section.**

Watermarks

Wmk. 257 — Curved Wavy Lines

Wmk. 312 — Zigzag Lines

Wmk. 317 — Communications Department Emblem

Stylized Yin Yang
A1   A2

Perf. 8½ to 11½

1884   Typo.   Unwmk.
1	A1	5m rose	65.00 6,750.
2	A2	10m blue	55.00 6,750.

Reprints and counterfeits of Nos. 1-2 exist.

These stamps were never placed in use. Values: 25 and 50 mon, each $19; 100 mon $20.
Counterfeits exist.

Yin Yang — A6

Two types of 50p:
I — No period after "50."
II — Period after "50."

Perf. 11½, 12, 12½, 13 and Compound

1895   Litho.
6	A6	5p green	27.50 16.00
a.		5p pale yellow green	75.00 27.50
b.		Vert. pair, imperf horiz.	425.00 —
c.		Horiz. pair, imperf. vert.	425.00 —
d.		Vertical pair, imperf. between	425.00 —
e.		Horiz. pair, imperf. btwn.	425.00 —
7	A6	10p deep blue	150.00 40.00
a.		Horiz. pair, imperf. between	425.00
b.		Vert. pair, imperf. horiz.	425.00
8	A6	25p maroon	67.50 30.00
a.		Horiz. pair, imperf. between	375.00 375.00
b.		Vert. pair, imperf. horiz.	375.00 375.00
9	A6	50p purple (II)	24.00 14.00
a.		Horiz. pair, imperf. between	400.00 400.00
b.		Vert. pair, imperf. horiz.	400.00 400.00
c.		Horiz. pair, imperf. vert.	400.00 400.00
d.		Type I	75.00 40.00
		Nos. 6-9 (4)	269.00 100.00

For overprints and surcharges see Nos. 10-17C, 35-38.
Counterfeits exist of Nos. 6-9 and all surcharges and overprints.

Overprinted "Tae Han" in Korean and Chinese Characters

1897   Red Overprint
10	A6	5p green	100.00 10.00
a.		5p pale yellow green	200.00 10.00
b.		Inverted overprint	150.00 150.00
c.		Without ovpt. at bottom	150.00 130.00
d.		Without overprint at top	150.00 130.00
f.		Double overprint at top	140.00 140.00
g.		Overprint at bottom in blk	160.00 160.00
h.		Pair, one without overprint	450.00 450.00
i.		Double overprint at top, inverted at bottom	550.00
11	A6	10p deep blue	110.00 15.00
a.		Without ovpt. at bottom	150.00 150.00
b.		Without overprint at top	150.00 150.00
c.		Double overprint at top	150.00 150.00
d.		Bottom overprint inverted	140.00 140.00
e.		Top ovpt. dbl., one in blk	210.00 210.00
f.		Top overprint omitted, bottom overprint inverted	450.00
12	A6	25p maroon	120.00 17.00
a.		Overprint at bottom invtd.	150.00 150.00
b.		Overprint at bottom in blk	210.00 210.00
c.		Bottom overprint omitted	150.00 150.00
e.		Top ovpt. dbl., one in blk	225.00 225.00
f.		Top and bottom overprints double, one of each in blk	250.00 250.00
g.		Pair, one without overprint	425.00 425.00

13	A6	50p purple	100.00	12.00
a.		Without ovpt. at bottom	120.00	110.00
b.		Without overprint at top	120.00	110.00
c.		Bottom overprint double	120.00	110.00
e.		Pair, one without overprint	275.00	275.00
		Nos. 10-13 (4)	430.00	54.00

1897   **Black Overprint**

13F	A6	5p green	400.00	85.00
13G	A6	10p deep blue	400.00	100.00
h.		Without ovpt. at bottom	450.00	
14	A6	25p maroon	400.00	100.00
a.		Without ovpt. at bottom	450.00	
b.		Without overprint at top	450.00	
c.		Double overprint at bottom	450.00	
15	A6	50p purple	400.00	80.00
a.		Without ovpt. at bottom	450.00	
		Nos. 13F-15 (4)	1,600.	

These stamps with black overprint, also No. 16A, are said not to have been officially authorized.

Nos. 6, 6a and 8
Surcharged in Red or
Black

1900

15B	A6	1p on 5p grn (R)	3,500.	750.00
c.		Yellow green		
16	A6	1p on 25p mar	100.00	60.00

Same Surcharge in Red or Black on Nos. 10, 10a, 12, 12c and 14

16A	A6	1p on 5p grn (R)	1,000.	
b.		1p on 5p pale yellow green	1,000.	
17	A6	1p on 25p (#12)	60.00	22.50
a.		Figure "1" omitted	100.00	
b.		On #12c	90.00	70.00
17C	A6	1p on 25p (#14)	775.00	175.00

Counterfeit overprints and surcharges of Nos. 10-17C exist. See note after No. 15.

A8   A9

A10   A11

A12   A13

A14   A15

A16   A17

A18   A19

A20   A21

1900-01   **Typo.**   **Perf. 11**

18	A8	2re gray	8.00	3.50
19	A9	1ch yellow grn	12.00	4.50
20B	A11	2ch pale blue	27.50	12.00
21	A12	3ch org red	12.00	10.00
a.		Vert. pair, imperf. horiz.	200.00	200.00
b.		Horiz. pair, imperf. btwn.		500.00
c.		3c brnsh org	12.00	10.00
d.		As "c," vert. pair, imperf. btwn.		500.00
22	A13	4ch carmine	40.00	16.00
23	A14	5ch pink	32.50	8.00
24	A15	6ch dp blue	40.00	7.25
25	A16	10ch pur ('01)	47.50	27.50
26	A17	15ch gray vio	72.50	45.00
27	A18	20ch red brown	140.00	47.50
31	A19	50ch ol grn & pink	600.00	240.00
32	A20	1wn rose, blk & bl	1,200.	300.00
33	A21	2wn pur & yel grn	1,500.	650.00
		Nos. 18-33 (13)	3,732.	1,371.

Nos. 22, 23, 25, 26, 33 exist imperf.
Some examples of Nos. 18-27 exist with forged Tae Han overprints in red. It is believed that Nos. 18 and 21 exist with genuine Tae Han overprints.
Reprints of No. 24 were made in light blue, perf. 12x13, in 1905 for a souvenir booklet. See Nos. 52-54.
See note after No. 54.

Perf. 10

18a	A8	2re	17.50	5.25
19a	A9	1ch	17.50	5.50
20	A10	2ch blue	75.00	45.00
a.		Horiz. pair, imperf. btwn.	725.00	
20Ba	A11	2ch pale blue	50.00	45.00
21e	A12	3ch	16.00	9.00
22a	A13	4ch	45.00	20.00
23a	A14	5ch	40.00	10.00
24a	A15	6ch	47.50	12.00
26a	A17	15ch	160.00	140.00
27a	A18	20ch	225.00	225.00
		Nos. 18a-27a (10)	693.50	516.75

Emperor's
Crown — A22

1902, Oct. 18   **Perf. 11½**

34	A22	3ch orange	67.50	35.00

40th year of the reign of Emperor Kojong. An imperf. single was part of the 1905 souvenir booklet. See note following No. 54. Counterfeits exist.

Nos. 8 and 9 Handstamp Surcharged in Black

1ch

2ch

3ch

Perf. 11½, 12, 12½, 13 and Compound

1902

35	A6	1ch on 25p maroon	25.00	6.00
b.		Horiz. pair, imperf. btwn.	275.00	
c.		Imperf.	90.00	
d.		Vert. pair, imperf. horiz.	275.00	
e.		On No. 12	—	—

36	A6	2ch on 25p maroon	29.00	7.00
b.		Imperf.	75.00	
d.		On No. 12	90.00	90.00
36E	A6	2ch on 50p purple	175.00	175.00
f.		Character "cheun" unabbreviated (in two rows instead of one)	250.00	175.00
37	A6	3ch on 50p purple	27.50	8.00
b.		With character "cheun" unabbreviated (in two rows instead of one)	2,400.	950.00
d.		Horiz. pair, imperf. btwn.		200.00
e.		Vert. pair, imperf. btwn.		200.00
g.		On No. 13		240.00
38	A6	3ch on 25p maroon	65.00	65.00
		Nos. 35-38 (5)	321.50	261.00

There are several sizes of these surcharges. Being handstamped, inverted and double surcharges exist.
Counterfeit surcharges exist.

Falcon — A23

1903   **Perf. 13½x14**

39	A23	2re slate	10.00	6.25
40	A23	1ch violet brn	11.00	7.50
41	A23	2ch green	15.00	7.50
42	A23	3ch orange	13.00	7.50
43	A23	4ch rose	22.50	9.50
44	A23	5ch yellow brn	22.50	11.00
45	A23	6ch lilac	26.00	12.50
46	A23	10ch blue	32.50	16.00
47	A23	15ch red, *straw*	45.00	22.50
48	A23	20ch vio brn, *straw*	67.50	32.50
49	A23	50ch red, *grn*	210.00	120.00
50	A23	1wn vio, *lav*	550.00	300.00
51	A23	2wn vio, *org*	550.00	300.00
		Nos. 39-51 (13)	1,575.	852.75

Values are for stamps with perfs touching the design.

Types of 1901
1903   **Perf. 12½**
Thin, Semi-Transparent Paper

52	A19	50ch pale ol grn & pale pink	400.00	160.00
53	A20	1wn rose, blk & bl	600.00	200.00
54	A21	2wn lt vio & lt grn	875.00	250.00
		Nos. 52-54 (3)	1,875.	610.00

No. 24, perf. 12x13, No. 34 imperf. and most examples of Nos. 52-54 unused are from souvenir booklets made up in 1905 when the Japanese withdrew all Korean stamps from circulation.

WARNING

In 1957 the Ministry of Communications issued 4000 presentation booklets containing Nos. 1-54 reproduced on watermark 312 paper.

Other presentation booklets included full-color reproductions of Nos. 1-54 and Japan No. 110 printed on the pages. Beware of wide-margined imperfs cut from these booklets.

Issued under US Military Rule

Stamps of Japan Nos. 331, 268, 342, 332, 339 and 337 Surcharged in Black

1946, Feb. 1   **Wmk. 257**   **Perf. 13**

55	A86	5ch on 5s brn lake	8.00	17.50
56	A93	5ch on 14s rose lake & pale rose	1.25	3.00
a.		5ch on 40s dark violet (error)	125.00	
57	A154	10ch on 40s dk vio	1.25	3.00
58	A147	20ch on 6s lt ultra	1.25	3.00
a.		20ch on 27s rose brown (error)	125.00	
b.		Double surcharge	30.00	

59	A151	30ch on 27s rose brn	1.25	3.00
a.		30ch on 6s light ultra (error)	125.00	
b.		Double surcharge	25.00	
60	A151	5wn on 17s gray vio	8.00	17.50
		Nos. 55-60 (6)	21.00	47.00
		Set, never hinged	40.00	

Five essays for this provisional issue exist both with and without additional overprint of two Chinese characters ("specimen") in vermilion. The essays are: 20ch on Japan No. 269; 50ch on No. 272; 1wn on No. 336; 1wn on No. 273; 10wn on No. 265. Values, each: $1,200 never hinged, $750 hinged. Other denominations have been reported.

Korean Family
and Flag — A24
Arms of
Korea — A25

Wmk. 257
1946, May 1   **Litho.**   **Perf. 10½**

61	A24	3ch orange yellow	.75	1.60
62	A24	5ch green	.75	1.60
63	A24	10ch carmine	.75	1.60
64	A24	20ch dark blue	.75	1.60
65	A25	50ch brown violet	3.25	2.50
66	A25	1wn lt brown	5.50	3.25
		Nos. 61-66 (6)	11.75	12.15
		Set, never hinged	21.00	

Liberation from Japan.

Imperfs., Part Perfs.

Imperforate and part-perforate examples of a great many Korean stamps from No. 61 onward exist.

The imperfs. include Nos. 61-90, 93-97, 116-117, 119-126, 132-173, 182-186, 195, 197-199, 202A, 203, 204-205, 217, etc.

The part-perfs. include Nos. 62-65, 69, 72-73, 109, 111-113, 132, etc.

Printers waste includes printed on both sides, etc.

As the field is so extensive, the editors believe that they belong more properly in a specialized catalogue.

Dove — A26

1946, Aug. 15   **Unwmk.**

67	A26	50ch deep violet	8.00	5.50
		Never hinged	15.00	

First anniversary of liberation.

Perforations often are rough on stamps issued between Aug. 1946 and the end of 1954. This is not considered a defect.

Flags of
US and
Korea
A27

1946, Sept. 9   **Perf. 11**

68	A27	10wn carmine	6.00	4.75
		Never hinged	11.00	

Resumption of postal communication with the US.

Astronomical Observatory, Kyongju — A28

Hibiscus with Rice — A29

Map of Korea — A30

Gold Crown of Silla Dynasty — A31

Admiral Li Sun-sin — A32

1946					**Rouletted 12**
69	A28	50ch dark blue	1.10	2.25
70	A29	1wn buff	1.00	2.50
71	A30	2wn indigo	2.00	3.25
72	A31	5wn magenta	12.00	22.50
73	A32	10wn emerald	12.50	20.00
		Nos. 69-73 (5)	28.60	50.50
		Set, never hinged	45.00	

Perf. 11
70a	A29	1wn	2.00	3.25
71a	A30	2wn	75.00	120.00
72a	A31	5wn	75.00	120.00
		Nos. 70a-72a (3)	152.00	243.25
		Set, never hinged	300.00	

Korean Phonetic Alphabet — A33

1946, Oct. 9					**Perf. 11**
74	A33	50ch deep blue	4.50	4.50
		Never hinged	9.00	

500th anniv. of the introduction of the Korean phonetic alphabet (Hangul).

Li Jun — A34

Admiral Li Sun-sin — A35

Perf. 11½x11, 11½
1947, Aug. 1	**Litho.**	**Wmk. 257**
75	A34	5wn lt blue green	7.50	9.00
76	A35	10wn light blue	7.50	9.00
		Set, never hinged	28.00	

Presentation Sheets
Starting in 1947 with No. 75, nearly 100 Korean stamps were printed in miniature or souvenir sheets and given to government officials and others. These sheets were released in quantities of 300 to 4,000. In 1957 the Ministry of Communications began to sell the souvenir sheets at post offices at face value to be used for postage. They are listed from No. 264a onward.

Letter-encircled Globe — A36

1947, Aug. 1					**Perf. 11½x11**
77	A36	10wn light blue	11.00	9.50
		Never hinged	19.00	

Resumption of international mail service between Korea and all countries of the world.

Granite Paper
Starting with No. 77, most Korean stamps through No. 751, except those on Laid Paper, are on Granite Paper. Granite Paper is noted above listing if the issue was printed on both ordinary and Granite Paper, such as Nos. 360a-374A.

Arch of Independence, Seoul — A37

Tortoise Ship, First Ironclad War Vessel — A38

1948, Apr.
78	A37	20wn rose	5.00	4.00
79	A38	50wn dull red brown	80.00	40.00
		Set, never hinged	160.00	

Republic

Flag and Ballot — A39

Woman and Man Casting Ballots — A40

Perf. 11x11½
1948, May 10	**Litho.**	**Wmk. 257**
80	A39	2wn orange	13.00	10.00
81	A39	5wn lilac rose	20.00	12.00
82	A39	10wn lt violet	30.00	20.00
83	A40	20wn carmine	42.50	27.50
84	A40	50wn blue	30.00	22.50
		Nos. 80-84 (5)	135.50	92.00
		Set, never hinged	250.00	

South Korea election of May 10, 1948.

Korean Flag and Olive Branches — A41

Olympic Torchbearer and Map of Korea — A42

National Assembly — A43

1948, June 1	**Perf. 11x11½, 11½x11**
85	A41	5wn green	100.00	65.00
86	A42	10wn purple	45.00	24.00
		Set, never hinged	240.00	

Korea's participation in the 1948 Olympic Games.

1948, July 1	**Wmk. 257**	**Perf. 11½**
87	A43	4wn orange brown	16.00	12.00
		Never hinged	27.50	

Opening of the Assembly July 1, 1948. Exists without period between "5" and "31."

Korean Family and Capitol — A44

Flag of Korea A45

1948, Aug. 1					**Litho.**
88	A44	4wn emerald	85.00	40.00
89	A45	10wn orange brown	37.50	25.00
		Set, never hinged	210.00	

Signing of the new constitution, 7/17/48.

Pres. Syngman Rhee — A46

1948, Aug. 5
90	A46	5wn deep blue	250.00	200.00
		Never hinged	375.00	

Inauguration of Korea's first president, Syngman Rhee.

Dove — A47

Hibiscus — A48

Two types of 5wn:
I — "1948" 3mm wide; top inscription 9mm wide; periods in "8.15." barely visible.
II — "1948" 4mm wide; top inscription 9½mm wide; periods in "8.15." bold and strong.

Li Jun — A49

Observatory, Kyongju — A50

1948					**Perf. 11, 11x11½**
91	A47	4wn blue	30.00	32.50
92	A48	5wn rose lilac (II)	45.00	40.00
a.		Type I	120.00	100.00
		Set, never hinged	160.00	

Issued to commemorate the establishment of Korea's republican government.

1948, Oct. 1					**Perf. 11½x11**
93	A49	4wn rose carmine	.75	1.25
94	A50	14wn deep blue	.75	1.25
a.		14wn light blue	200.00	75.00
		Never hinged	375.00	
		Set, never hinged	3.50	

For surcharges see Nos. 127, 174, 176.

Doves over UN Emblem — A51

1949, Feb. 12	**Wmk. 257**	**Perf. 11**
95	A51	10wn blue	30.00	21.00
		Never hinged	55.00	

Arrival of the UN Commission on Korea, Feb. 12, 1949.

Korean Citizen and Census Date — A52

1949, Apr. 25
96	A52	15wn purple	40.00	22.50
		Never hinged	75.00	

Census of May 1, 1949.

Korean Boy and Girl A53

1949, May 5

97	A53	15wn purple	20.00	12.00
		Never hinged	40.00	

20th anniv. of Children's Day, May 5, 1949.

Postman — A54 Worker and Factory — A55

Rice Harvesting A56 Japanese Cranes A57

Diamond Mountains A58 Ginseng Plant A59

South Gate, Seoul — A60 Tabo Pagoda, Kyongju — A61

1949 Litho. Perf. 11

98	A54	1wn rose	3.25	3.25
99	A55	2wn dk blue gray	3.00	3.00
100	A56	5wn yellow green	14.00	9.50
101	A57	10wn blue green	1.20	1.20
102	A58	20wn orange brown	.80	1.20
103	A59	30wn blue green	.80	1.20
104	A60	50wn violet blue	.80	1.20
105	A61	100wn dull yellow grn	.80	1.20
		Nos. 98-105 (8)	24.65	21.75
		Set, never hinged	50.00	

For surcharges see Nos. 129-131, 175, 177B-179, 181.

Phoenix and Yin Yang — A62

1949, Aug. 25

106	A62	15wn deep blue	27.50	14.00
		Never hinged	55.00	

1st anniv. of Korea's independence.

Express Train "Sam Chun Li" A63

1949, Sept. 18 Perf. 11½x12

107	A63	15wn violet blue	110.00	40.00
		Never hinged	195.00	

50th anniversary of Korean railroads.

Korean Flag — A64

Perf. 11½x11

1949, Oct. 15 Wmk. 257

108	A64	15wn red org, yel & dk bl	15.00	15.00
		Never hinged	35.00	

75th anniv. of the UPU.
No. 108 exists unwatermarked. These are counterfeit.

Hibiscus — A65 Magpies and Map of Korea — A66

Stylized Bird and Globe — A67

Diamond Mountains A68

Admiral Li Sun-sin A69

1949 Wmk. 257 Litho. Perf. 11

109	A65	15wn vermilion	.60	1.10
110	A66	65wn deep blue	2.25	2.25
111	A67	200wn green	.60	1.10
112	A68	400wn brown	.60	1.10
113	A69	500wn deep blue	.60	1.10
		Nos. 109-113 (5)	4.65	6.65
		Set, never hinged	7.50	

For surcharges see Nos. 128, 177, 180.

Canceled to Order

More than 100 Korean stamps and souvenir sheets were canceled to order, the cancellation incorporating the date "67.9.20." These include 81 stamps between Nos. 111 and 327, 18 airmail stamps between Nos. C6 and C26, and 5 souvenir sheets between Nos. 313 and 332, etc.

Also exists with later dates and on other stamps.

These c-t-o stamps and souvenir sheets are sold for much less than the values shown below, which are for postally used examples.

A70

Ancient postal medal (Ma-Pae).

1950, Jan. 1

114	A70	15wn yellow green	22.50	16.00
115	A70	65wn red brown	12.00	8.00
		Set, never hinged	70.00	

50th anniv. of Korea's entrance into the UPU.

Revolutionists — A71

1950, Mar. 10 Perf. 11½

116	A71	15wn olive	25.00	16.00
117	A71	65wn light violet	12.00	8.00
		Set, never hinged	72.50	

41st anniversary of Korea's declaration of Independence.

Korean Emblem and National Assembly — A72

1950, May 30

118	A72	30wn bl, red, brn & grn	16.00	8.00
		Never hinged	27.50	

2nd natl. election of the Korean Republic.

Syngman Rhee — A73

Korean Flag and White Mountains — A74

Flags of UN and Korea, Map of Korea A75

1950, Nov. 20 Wmk. 257 Perf. 11

119	A73	100wn blue	5.00	3.25
120	A74	100wn green	4.25	3.25
121	A75	200wn dark green	3.75	2.50
		Nos. 119-121 (3)	13.00	9.00
		Set, never hinged	24.00	

Crane — A76

Tiger Mural — A77 Dove and Flag — A78

Postal Medal — A79 Mural from Ancient Tomb — A80

1951 Unwmk. Perf. 11
Ordinary Paper

122	A76	5wn orange brown	1.75	2.00
123	A77	20wn purple	2.25	2.75
124	A78	50wn green	16.00	15.00
125	A79	100wn deep blue	32.50	15.00
126	A80	1000wn green	32.50	15.00
		Nos. 122-126 (5)	85.00	49.75
		Set, never hinged	135.00	

Rouletted 12

122a	A76	5wn orange brown	1.00	1.75
123a	A77	20wn purple	1.00	1.75
124a	A78	50wn green	3.00	4.50
125a	A79	100wn blue	4.50	4.50
		Nos. 122a-125a (4)	9.50	12.50
		Set, never hinged	18.00	

No. 126 also exists perforated 12½. See Nos. 187-189.

No. 93 Surcharged with New Value and Wavy Lines in Blue

1951 Wmk. 257 Perf. 11½x11

127	A49	100wn on 4wn rose car	3.25	4.50
a.		Inverted surcharge	32.50	65.00
		Never hinged	65.00	

Nos. 109, 101, 102 and 104 Surcharged in Blue or Brown

Perf. 11

128	A65	200wn on 15wn	4.00	7.50
a.		Inverted surcharge	32.50	65.00
		Never hinged	65.00	
129	A57	300wn on 10wn (Br)	5.75	4.50
a.		Inverted surcharge	32.50	
		Never hinged	65.00	
130	A58	300wn on 20wn	4.50	4.50
a.		Inverted surcharge	35.00	
		Never hinged	75.00	
131	A60	300wn on 50wn (Br)	7.00	4.00
		Nos. 127-131 (5)	24.50	25.00
		Set, never hinged	80.00	

Size and details of surcharge varies. Numeral upright on Nos. 129 and 131; numeral slanted on Nos. 175 and 179. See Nos. 174-181.

On No. 130, the zeros in "300" are octagonal; on No. 177B they are oval.

Flags of US and Korea and Statue of Liberty — A81

Design (blue stamps). Flag of same country as preceding green stamp, UN emblem and doves.

1951-52 Wmk. 257 Perf. 11
Flags in Natural Colors, Participating Country at Left

132	A81	500wn green	5.50	9.50
133	A81	500wn blue	5.50	9.50
134	A81	500wn grn (Australia)	6.00	11.00
135	A81	500wn blue	6.00	11.00
136	A81	500wn grn (Belgium)	6.00	11.00

137	A81	500wn blue	6.00	11.00
138	A81	500wn grn (Britain)	6.00	11.00
139	A81	500wn blue	6.00	11.00
140	A81	500wn grn (Canada)	6.00	11.00
141	A81	500wn blue	6.00	11.00
142	A81	500wn grn (Colombia)	6.00	11.00
143	A81	500wn blue	6.00	11.00
144	A81	500wn grn (Denmark)	30.00	40.00
145	A81	500wn blue	30.00	40.00
146	A81	500wn grn (Ethiopia)	6.00	11.00
147	A81	500wn blue	6.00	11.00
148	A81	500wn grn (France)	6.00	11.00
149	A81	500wn blue	6.00	11.00
150	A81	500wn grn (Greece)	6.00	11.00
151	A81	500wn blue	6.00	11.00
152	A81	500wn grn (India)	26.00	40.00
153	A81	500wn blue	26.00	40.00
154	A81	500wn grn (Italy)	6.50	24.00
a.		Flag without crown ('52)	32.50	47.50
155	A81	500wn blue	6.50	24.00
a.		Flag without crown ('52)	32.50	47.50
156	A81	500wn grn (Luxembourg)	26.00	40.00
157	A81	500wn blue	26.00	40.00
158	A81	500wn grn (Netherlands)	6.00	11.00
159	A81	500wn blue	6.00	11.00
160	A81	500wn grn (New Zealand)	6.00	11.00
161	A81	500wn blue	6.00	11.00
162	A81	500wn grn (Norway)	26.00	40.00
163	A81	500wn blue	26.00	40.00
164	A81	500wn grn (Philippines)	6.00	11.00
165	A81	500wn blue	6.00	11.00
166	A81	500wn grn (Sweden)	6.00	11.00
167	A81	500wn blue	6.00	11.00
168	A81	500wn grn (Thailand)	6.00	11.00
169	A81	500wn blue	6.00	11.00
170	A81	500wn grn(Turkey)	6.00	11.00
171	A81	500wn blue	6.00	11.00
172	A81	500wn grn (Union of So. Africa)	6.00	11.00
173	A81	500wn blue	6.00	11.00
		Nos. 132-173 (42)	420.00	717.00
		Set, never hinged	975.00	

Twenty-two imperf. souvenir sheets of two, containing the green and the blue stamps for each participating country (including both types of Italy) were issued. Size: 140x90mm. Value, set hinged $800; never hinged $1,300.

Nos. 93-94, 101-105, 109-110 Surcharged Like Nos. 128-131 in Blue or Brown

1951   Wmk. 257   Perf. 11½x11, 11

174	A49	300wn on 4wn	3.00	4.75
a.		Inverted surcharge	32.50	65.00
		Never hinged	65.00	
175	A57	300wn on 10wn (Br)	8.00	6.00
a.		Inverted surcharge	32.50	65.00
		Never hinged	65.00	
176	A50	300wn on 14wn (Br)	5.50	4.75
a.		300wn on 14wn lt bl	2,000.	900.00
		Never hinged	4,000.	
b.		Inverted surcharge	32.50	65.00
		Never hinged	65.00	
177	A65	300wn on 15wn	3.00	4.75
a.		Inverted surcharge	32.50	65.00
		Never hinged	65.00	
177B	A58	300wn on 20wn	6.50	6.00
178	A59	300wn on 30wn (Br)	3.25	4.75
a.		Inverted surcharge	32.50	65.00
		Never hinged	65.00	
179	A60	300wn on 50wn (Br)	2.75	3.25
180	A66	300wn on 65wn (Br)	3.25	4.75
a.		Inverted monad	47.50	95.00
		Never hinged	95.00	
181	A61	300wn on 100wn	3.00	4.75
a.		Inverted surcharge	45.00	90.00
		Never hinged	90.00	
		Nos. 174-181 (9)	38.25	43.75
		Set, never hinged	75.00	

"300" slanted on Nos. 175, 177B and 179; "300" upright on Nos. 129 and 131. The surcharge exists double on several of these stamps.
No. 177B differs from No. 130 in detail noted after No. 131.

Syngman Rhee and "Happiness" — A82

1952, Sept. 10   Litho.   Perf. 12½

182	A82	1000wn dark green	7.50	7.50
		Never hinged	14.00	

Second inauguration of President Syngman Rhee, Aug. 15, 1952.

Sok Kul Am, Near Kyongju — A83

Bool Gook Temple, Kyongju — A84

Tombstone of Mu Yal Wang — A85

Choong Yul Sa Shrine, Tongyung — A86

1952   Wmk. 257   Typo.   Perf. 12½

183	A83	200wn henna brown	2.00	1.60
184	A84	300wm green	1.50	.80
185	A85	500wn carmine	2.50	1.60
186	A86	2000wn deep blue	2.00	.75

Rough Perf. 10-11, 11½x11 and Compound Litho.

186A	A83	200wn henna brown	1.50	1.50
186B	A84	300wn green	1.40	.85
		Nos. 183-186B (6)	10.90	7.10
		Set, never hinged	22.50	

Types of 1951 Designs slightly smaller

1952-53   Rough Perf. 10-11

187	A77	20wn purple	12.00	3.00
187A	A78	50wn green	24.00	25.00
187B	A79	100wn deep blue	2.25	1.60
187C	A80	1000wn green	140.00	30.00
		Nos. 187-187C (4)	178.25	59.60
		Set, never hinged	375.00	

Designs slightly larger Perf. 12½

187D	A78	50wn green	2.50	2.40
188	A79	100wn deep blue	1.75	2.00
189	A80	1000wn green ('53)	5.50	.85
		Nos. 187D-189 (3)	9.75	5.25
		Set, never hinged	22.50	

Type of 1952

1953

189A	A85	500wn deep blue	24.00	160.00
		Never hinged	45.00	

All examples of No. 189A were affixed to postal cards before sale. Values are for stamps removed from the cards.
See Nos. 191-192, 203B, 248.

Types of 1952 and

Planting Trees — A87

Wmk. 257

1953, Apr. 5   Litho.   Perf. 12½

190	A87	1h aqua	.80	.65
191	A85	2h aqua	.80	.45
192	A85	5h bright green	1.00	.45
193	A87	10h bright green	2.75	1.50
194	A86	20h brown	3.75	1.60
		Nos. 190-194 (5)	9.10	4.65
		Set, never hinged	18.00	

See Nos. 203A, 247.

Map and YMCA Emblem — A88

1953, Oct. 25   Perf. 13½

195	A88	10h dk slate bl & red	5.00	4.00
		Never hinged	10.00	

50th anniv. of the Korean YMCA.

Tombstone of Mu Yal Wang — A88a

A89   Sika Deer — A90

1954, Apr.   Perf. 12½

196	A88a	5h dark green	1.10	1.25
197	A89	100h brn car	8.00	3.00
198	A90	500h brn org	45.00	6.00
199	A90	1000h bister brown	100.00	7.00
		Nos. 196-199 (4)	154.10	17.25
		Set, never hinged	350.00	

See Nos. 203C, 203D, 238-239, 248A, 250-251, 259, 261-262, 269-270, 279, 281-282.

Dok Do (Dok Island) — A91

Design: 10h, Dok Do, lateral view.

1954, Sept. 15

200	A91	2h claret	2.25	2.50
201	A91	5h blue	5.00	2.50
202	A91	10h blue green	8.00	2.50
		Nos. 200-202 (3)	15.25	7.50
		Set, never hinged	30.00	

Moth and Flag — A92   Pagoda Park, Seoul — A92a

1954, Apr. 16   Wmk. 257   Perf. 12½

202A	A92	10h brown	8.00	2.00
203	A92a	30h dark blue	1.00	1.50
		Set, never hinged	20.00	

See Nos. 203E, 260, 280.

Types of 1952-54

1955-56   Unwmk.   Perf. 12½
Laid Paper

203A	A87	1h aqua ('56)	.30	.50
203B	A85	2h aqua ('56)	.30	.50
203C	A88a	5h brt grn ('56)	.40	.45
203D	A89	100h brn car	45.00	6.50
203E	A92a	200h brn car	7.00	2.50
		Nos. 203A-203E (5)	53.00	10.45
		Set, never hinged	140.00	

On No. 203C the right hand character is redrawn as in illustration above No. 212D. Nos. 203A and 203C are found on horizontally and vertically laid paper.

Erosion Control on Mountainside A93

1954, Dec. 12   Wmk. 257

204	A93	10h dk grn & yel grn	3.00	1.25
205	A93	19h dk grn & yel grn	3.00	2.00
		Set, never hinged	11.00	

Issued to publicize the 1954 forestation campaign.

Presidents Rhee and Eisenhower Shaking Hands — A94

1954, Dec. 25   Perf. 13½

206	A94	10h violet blue	2.25	1.60
207	A94	19h brown	2.25	1.60
208	A94	71h dull green	4.00	2.50
		Nos. 206-208 (3)	8.50	5.70
		Set, never hinged	16.50	

Adoption of the US-Korea mutual defense treaty.

"Reconstruction" A95

1955, Feb. 10   Wmk. 257   Perf. 12½   Litho.

209	A95	10h brown	3.50	3.00
210	A95	15h violet	3.50	3.00
211	A95	20h blue	700.00	20.00
		Never hinged	1,500.	
212	A95	50h plum	8.00	3.25
		Nos. 209-210,212 (3)	15.00	
		Nos. 209-212 (4)		29.25
		Set, #209-210, 212, never hinged	30.00	

Korea's industrial reconstruction.

1955, Oct. 19   Unwmk.   Perf. 12½
Laid Paper

212A	A95	15h violet	2.75	2.40
212B	A95	20h blue	2.75	1.60
212C	A95	50h plum	5.00	.80
		Nos. 212A-212C (3)	10.50	4.80
		Set, never hinged	20.00	

No. 212B is found on horizontally and vertically laid paper.

Same with Right Character at Top Redrawn

Original   Redrawn

1956, June 5   Unwmk.   Perf. 12½
Laid Paper

212D	A95	10h brown	3.00 2.50
212E	A95	15h violet	3.00 2.50
212F	A95	20h blue	3.00 .85
a.		Booklet pane of 6	175.00
		Nos. 212D-212F (3)	9.00 5.85
		Set, never hinged	18.00

Nos. 212D-212F are found on horizontally and vertically laid paper. See Nos. 248B, 256, 272, 276.

Rotary Emblem — A96

1955, Feb. 23   Wmk. 257   Perf. 13½

213	A96	20h violet	4.00 3.00
214	A96	25h dull green	2.00 1.50
215	A96	71h magenta	2.00 1.50
		Nos. 213-215 (3)	8.00 6.00
		Set, never hinged	16.00

Rotary International, 50th anniversary.

Syngman Rhee, 80th Birthday, Apr. 26 — A98

1955, Mar. 26

217	A98	20h deep blue	13.50 8.00
		Never hinged	28.50

Flag and Arch of Independence A99

1955, Aug. 15   Litho.   Perf. 13½

218	A99	40h Prus green	4.50 2.00
219	A99	100h lake	4.50 2.75
		Set, never hinged	20.00

Tenth anniversary of independence.

UN Emblem in Circle of Clasped Hands — A100

1955, Oct. 24

221	A100	20h bluish green	2.00 1.60
222	A100	55h aqua	2.00 1.60
		Set, never hinged	10.00

United Nations, 10th anniversary.

Olympic Torch and Runners — A101

1955, Oct. 23

223	A101	20h claret	3.50 2.00
224	A101	55h dark green	3.50 2.00
		Set, never hinged	13.50

36th National Athletic Meet.

Adm. Li Sun-sin, Navy Flag and Tortoise Ship A102

Perf. 13x13½
1955, Nov. 11   Unwmk.
Laid Paper

225	A102	20h violet blue	4.00 3.00
		Never hinged	10.00

Korean Navy, 10th anniversary.

Rhee Monument near Seoul — A103

1956, Mar. 26   Perf. 13½x13

226	A103	20h dull green	3.00 3.00
		Never hinged	7.50

81st birthday of Pres. Syngman Rhee. No. 226 is found on horizontally and vertically laid paper.

Third Inauguration of Pres. Syngman Rhee — A104

1956, Aug. 15   Perf. 13x13½

227	A104	20h brown	45.00 25.00
228	A104	55h violet blue	20.00 12.00
		Set, never hinged	140.00

Olympic Rings and Torch — A105

1956, Nov. 1   Litho.   Perf. 12½
Laid Paper

229	A105	20h red orange	2.50 2.50
230	A105	55h brt green	2.50 2.50
		Set, never hinged	11.00

16th Olympic Games in Melbourne, 11/22-12/8.

Central Post Office, Seoul A107

Stamp of 1884 — A108

Mail Delivered by Donkey A109

1956, Dec. 4   Laid Paper   Unwmk.

232	A107	20h lt blue green	6.50 2.75
233	A108	50h lt carmine	10.00 4.50
234	A109	55h green	4.50 2.00
		Nos. 232-234 (3)	21.00 9.25
		Set, never hinged	45.00

Issued to commemorate Postal Day.

Types of 1954 Redrawn and

Hibiscus — A110

King Sejong — A111

Kyongju Observatory A112

No Hwan Symbol; Redrawn Character

1956, Dec. 4   Unwmk.   Perf. 12½
Laid Paper

235	A110	10h lilac rose	1.00 .75
236	A111	20h lilac	2.00 .75
237	A112	50h violet	2.00 .75
238	A89	100h brn car	12.50 4.50
239	A90	500h brn org	32.50 5.00
		Nos. 235-239 (5)	50.00 11.75
		Set, never hinged	105.00

On Nos. 238-239, the character after numeral has been omitted and the last character of the inscription has been redrawn as illustrated above No. 212D.

Nos. 235-236 are found on horizontally and vertically laid paper.

See Nos. 240-242, 253, 255, 258, 273, 275, 278, 291Bd, 291Bf, B3-B4.

Types of 1956

1957, Jan. 21   Wmk. 312   Perf. 12½

240	A110	10h lilac rose	1.00 .65
241	A111	20h red lilac	2.40 1.25
242	A112	50h violet	3.75 .65
		Nos. 240-242 (3)	7.15 2.55
		Set, never hinged	16.00

Telecommunication Symbols — A117

1957, Jan. 31   Perf. 13½

243	A117	40h lt ultra	1.50 1.40
244	A117	55h brt green	1.50 1.40
		Set, never hinged	5.00

5th anniv. of Korea's joining the ITU.

Boy Scout and Emblem A118

1957, Feb. 27   Wmk. 312

245	A118	40h pale purple	1.25 1.40
246	A118	55h lt magenta	1.25 1.40
		Set, never hinged	5.50

50th anniversary of Boy Scout movement.

Types of 1953-56
Top Right Character Redrawn;
Hwan Symbol Retained

1957   Wmk. 312   Perf. 12½

247	A87	1h aqua	.35 .55
248	A85	2h aqua	.45 .55
248A	A88a	5h brt green	.45 .55
248B	A95	15h violet	3.50 2.00
		Nos. 247-248B (4)	4.75 3.65
		Set, never hinged	13.00

Redrawn Types of 1954, 1956 and

Planting Trees — A119

South Gate, Seoul — A120

Tiger A121

Diamond Mountains A122

No Hwan Symbol; Redrawn Character

1957   Wmk. 312   Litho.   Perf. 12½

249	A119	2h aqua	.30 .40
250	A88a	4h aqua	.45 .40
251	A88a	5h emerald	.45 .40
252	A120	10h green	.50 .75
253	A110	20h lilac rose	.65 .40
254	A121	30h pale lilac	.65 .40
255	A111	40h red lilac	.75 .35
a.		Booklet pane of 6	80.00
256	A95	50h lake	3.25 .65
257	A122	55h violet brn	1.50 1.50
258	A112	100h violet	1.75 .50
259	A89	200h brown car	2.00 .50
260	A92a	400h brt violet	32.50 4.75
261	A90	500h ocher	32.50 6.00
262	A90	1000h dk ol bis	70.00 11.50
		Nos. 249-262 (14)	147.25 28.50
		Set, never hinged	300.00

The "redrawn character" is illustrated above No. 212D.

See Nos. 268, 271, 274, 277, 291c, 291e.

Mercury and Flags of Korea and US A123

1957, Nov. 7   Wmk. 312   Perf. 13½

263	A123	40h dp orange	1.00 .90
264	A123	205h emerald	2.00 1.90
a.		Souv. sheet of 2, #263-264, imperf.	850.00
		Never hinged	1,500.
		Set, never hinged	7.00

Treaty of friendship, commerce and navigation between Korea and the US.

Star of Bethlehem
and Pine
Cone — A124

Designs: 25h, Christmas tree and tassel.
30h, Christmas tree, window and dog.

1957, Dec. 11   Litho.   Perf. 12½
265 A124 15h org, brn & grn   4.00   2.00
  a.   Souv. sheet of 1, imperf.   625.00
    Never hinged   1,000.
266 A124 25h lt grn, yel &
    red   3.25   2.00
  a.   Souv. sheet of 1, imperf.   625.00
    Never hinged   1,000.
267 A124 30h bl, lt grn & yel   9.00   3.00
  a.   Souv. sheet of 1, imperf.   625.00
    Never hinged   1,000.
    Nos. 265-267 (3)   16.25   7.00
    Set, never hinged   40.00

Issued for Christmas and the New Year.

Redrawn Types of 1954-57
Wmk. 317
1957-59   Litho.   Perf. 12½
268 A119 2h aqua   .35   .45
269 A88a 4h aqua   .45   .45
270 A88a 5h emerald
    ('58)   .45   .45
271 A120 10h green   .75   .45
272 A95 15h violet ('58)   2.50   2.25
273 A110 20h lilac rose   .90   .35
274 A121 30h pale lil ('58)   .90   .35
275 A111 40h red lilac   .85   .35
276 A95 50h lake ('58)   5.00   .80
277 A122 55h vio brn
    ('59)   1.95   .85
278 A112 100h violet   1.75   .45
279 A89 200h brn car
    ('59)   2.40   .45
280 A92a 400h brt vio ('59)   45.00   3.00
281 A90 500h ocher ('58)   35.00   3.00
282 A90 1000h dk ol bis
    ('58)   75.00   7.75
    Nos. 268-282 (15)   173.25   21.40
    Set, never hinged   450.00

Nos. 268-282 have no hwan symbol, and
final character of inscription is the redrawn one
illustrated above No. 212D.
See No. 291B.

> Catalogue values for unused
> stamps in this section, from this
> point to the end of the section, are
> for Never Hinged items.

Winged
Envelope — A125

1958, May 20   Wmk. 317
283 A125 40h dk blue & red   2.10   .80
  a.   Souv. sheet of 1, imperf.   2,000.

Issued for the Second Postal Week.

Children
Looking at
Industrial
Growth
A126

Design: 40h, Hibiscus forming "10".

1958, Aug. 15   Perf. 13½
284 A126 20h gray   2.00   .65
285 A126 40h dk carmine   2.50   .90
  a.   Souv. sheet of 2, # 284-285,
    imperf.   500.00

10th anniversary of Republic of Korea.

UNESCO
Building,
Paris
A127

1958, Nov. 3   Wmk. 317
286 A127 40h orange & green   1.50   .60
  a.   Souv. sheet of 1, imperf.   175.00

Opening of UNESCO. headquarters in
Paris, Nov. 3.

Children Flying
Kites — A128

Christmas Tree
and Fortune
Screen — A129

Children in
Costume — A130

1958, Dec. 11   Litho.   Perf. 12½
287 A128 15h yellow green   2.25   .75
  a.   Souv. sheet of 1, imperf.   70.00
288 A129 25h blue, red & yel   2.25   .75
  a.   Souv. sheet of 1, imperf.   70.00
289 A130 30h yell, ultra & red   3.75   1.25
  a.   Souv. sheet of 1, imperf.   70.00
    Nos. 287-289 (3)   8.25   2.75
    Nos. 287a-289a (3)   210.00

Issued for Christmas and the New Year.

Flag and
Pagoda
Park
A131

1959, Mar. 1   Perf. 13½
290 A131 40h rose lilac &
    brn   1.50   .65
  a.   Souv. sheet of 1, imperf.   120.00   120.00

40th anniv. of Independence Movement Day.

Korean
Marines
Landing
A132

1959, Apr. 15
291 A132 40h olive grn   1.50   .65
  a.   Souv. sheet of 1, imperf.   15.00   15.00

Korean Marine Corps, 10th anniversary.

Types of 1956-57
Souvenir Sheet
Wmk. 317
1959, May 20   Litho.   Imperf.
291B   Sheet of 4   10.00   10.00
  c. A120 10h green   1.40   .60
  d. A110 20h lilac rose   1.40   .60
  e. A121 30h pale lilac   1.40   .60
  f. A111 40h red lilac   1.40   .60

3rd Postal Week, May 20-26.

WHO
Emblem
and
Family
A133

1959, Aug. 17   Wmk. 317   Perf. 13½
292 A133 40h pink & rose vio   1.50   .65
  a.   Souv. sheet of 1, imperf.   12.00   12.00

10th anniv. of Korea's joining the WHO.

Diesel
Train
A134

1959, Sept. 18   Litho.
293 A134 40h brown & bister   2.50   1.00
  a.   Souv. sheet of 1, imperf.   30.00   30.00

60th anniversary of Korean railroads.

Relay
Race and
Emblem
A135

1959, Oct. 3
294 A135 40h lt bl & red brn   1.50   .70
  a.   Souv. sheet of 1, imperf.   17.00   17.00

40th National Athletic Meet.

Red
Cross and
Korea
Map
A136

55h, Red Cross superimposed on globe.

1959, Oct. 27   Perf. 13½
295 A136 40h red & bl grn   1.50   .50
296 A136 55h pale lilac & red   1.50   .50
  a.   Souv. sheet of 2, #295-296,
    imperf.   40.00   40.00

Centenary of the Red Cross idea.

Old Postal Flag and New
Communications Flag — A137

1959, Dec. 4
297 A137 40h blue & red   1.50   .60
  a.   Souv. sheet of 1, imperf.   21.00   21.00

75th anniv. of the Korean postal system.

Mice and Chinese
Happy New Year
Character — A138

Designs: 25h, Children singing Christmas
hymns. 30h, Red-crested crane.

1959, Dec. 15   Perf. 12½
298 A138 15h gray, vio bl &
    pink   1.50   .40
  a.   Souv. sheet of 1, imperf.   30.00   30.00

299 A138 25h blue, red & em-
    er   1.50   .40
  a.   Souv. sheet of 1, imperf.   30.00   30.00
300 A138 30h lt lilac, blk & red   3.00   .60
  a.   Souv. sheet of 1, imperf.   30.00   30.00
    Nos. 298-300 (3)   6.00   1.40
    Nos. 298a-300a (3)   90.00

Issued for Christmas and the New Year.

UPU Monument and Means of
Transportation — A139

Wmk. 317
1960, Jan. 1   Litho.   Perf. 13½
301 A139 40h grnsh bl & brn   1.75   .80
  a.   Souv. sheet of 1, imperf.   35.00   35.00

60th anniv. of Korean membership in the
UPU.

Bee, Honeycomb
and
Clover — A140

Snail and Money
Bag — A141

1960, Apr. 1   Wmk. 317   Perf. 12½
302 A140 10h emer, brn & org   6.00   .80
303 A141 20h pink, bl & brn   1.75   .80

Issued to encourage systematic saving by
children. See No. 313, souvenir sheet.
See Nos. 377-380.

Uprooted Oak
Emblem and Yin
Yang — A142

1960, Apr. 7   Wmk. 312   Perf. 13½
304 A142 40h emer, car & ul-
    tra   1.50   .60
  a.   Souv. sheet of 1, imperf.   35.00   35.00

Issued to publicize World Refugee Year,
July 1, 1959-June 30, 1960.

Dwight D.
Eisenhower
A143

1960, June 19   Litho.   Wmk. 317
305 A143 40h bl, red & bluish
    grn   4.25   2.00
  a.   Souv. sheet of 1, imperf.   30.00   30.00

Pres. Eisenhower's visit to Korea, June 19.

Children
in School
and
Ancient
Home
Teaching
A144

1960, Aug. 3 Wmk. 317 Perf. 13½
306 A144 40h multicolored 1.50 .50
a. Souv. sheet of 1, imperf. 9.00 9.00

75th anniv. of the modern educational system.

Hibiscus and House of Councilors A145

1960, Aug. 8
307 A145 40h blue 1.50 .50
a. Souv. sheet of 1, imperf. 9.00 9.00

Inaugural session, House of Councilors.

Woman Holding Torch and Man with Flag — A146

1960, Aug. 15
308 A146 40h bis, lt bl & brn 1.75 .60
a. Souv. sheet of 1, imperf. 9.00 9.00

15th anniversary of liberation.

Weight Lifter A147

40h, South Gate, Seoul, & Olympic emblem.

1960, Aug. 25 Litho.
309 A147 20h brn, lt bl & sal 1.50 .75
310 A147 40h brn, lt bl & dk bl 1.50 .75
a. Souv. sheet of 2, #309-310, imperf. 27.50 27.50

17th Olympic Games, Rome, 8/25-9/11.

Swallow and Telegraph Pole — A148

1960, Sept. 28 Perf. 13½
311 A148 40h lt bl, lil & gray 1.75 .75
a. Souv. sheet of 1, imperf. 8.25 8.25

Establishment of telegraph service, 75th anniv.

Students and Sprout A149

1960, Oct. 1 Wmk. 317
312 A149 40h bl, sal pink & emer 1.50 .50
a. Souv. sheet of 1, imperf. 7.50 7.50

Rebirth of the Republic.

Savings Types of 1960
Souvenir Sheet

1960, Oct. 7 Imperf.
313 Sheet of two 5.50 5.50
a. A140 10h emer, brn & org 2.25 2.25
b. A141 20h pink, blue & brown 2.25 2.25

4th Postal Week, Oct. 7-13, and Intl. Letter Writing Week, Oct. 3-9.

Torch — A150

1960, Oct. 15 Perf. 13½
314 A150 40h dk bl, lt bl & yel 1.50 .50
a. Souv. sheet of 1, imperf. 7.50 7.50

Cultural Month (October).

UN Flag, Globe and Laurel — A151

1960, Oct. 24 Litho.
315 A151 40h rose lil, bl & grn 1.50 .50
a. Souv. sheet of 1, imperf. 7.25 7.25

15th anniversary of United Nations.

UN Emblem and Grave Markers — A152

1960, Nov. 1 Wmk. 317
316 A152 40h salmon & brn 1.50 .50
a. Souv. sheet of 1, imperf. 7.25 7.25

Establishment of the UN Memorial Cemetery, Tanggok, Pusan, Korea.

"Housing, Agriculture, Population" — A153

1960, Nov. 15 Perf. 13½
317 A153 40h multicolored 1.50 .50
a. Souv. sheet of 1, imperf. 7.50 7.50

Issued to publicize the 1960 census.

Boy and Head of Ox — A154

Star of Bethlehem and Korean Sock — A155

Girl Giving New Year's Greeting — A156

1960, Dec. 15 Litho. Perf. 12½
318 A154 15h gray, brn & org yel 2.25 .40
a. Souv. sheet of 1, imperf. 10.00 10.00
319 A155 25h vio bl, red & grn 3.00 .40
a. Souv. sheet of 1, imperf. 10.00 10.00
320 A156 30h red, vio bl & yel 3.75 .75
a. Souv. sheet of 1, imperf. 10.00 10.00
Nos. 318-320 (3) 9.00 1.55
Nos. 318a-320a (3) 30.00

Issued for Christmas and the New Year.

UN Emblem, Windsock and Ancient Rain Gauge A157

1961, Mar. 23 Perf. 13½
321 A157 40h lt blue & ultra 1.60 .50
a. Souv. sheet of 1, imperf. 4.50 4.50

1st World Meteorological Day.

Children, Globe and UN Emblem A158

1961, Apr. 7 Wmk. 317
322 A158 40h salmon & brown 1.60 .50
a. Souv. sheet of 1, imperf. 4.50 4.50

10th World Health Day.

Students Demonstrating — A159

1961, Apr. 19 Litho.
323 A159 40h red, grn & ultra 2.00 .80
a. Souv. sheet of 1, imperf. 11.00 11.00

1st anniv. of the Korean April revolution.

Workers — A160

1961, May 6
324 A160 40h brt green 1.50 .60
a. Souv. sheet of 1, imperf. 6.50 6.50

International Conference on Community Development, Seoul.

Girl Scout A161

1961, May 10
325 A161 40h brt green 2.00 .60
a. Souv. sheet of 1, imperf. 15.00 15.00

15th anniversary of Korea's Girl Scouts.

Soldier's Grave — A162

Wmk. 317
1961, June 6 Litho. Perf. 13½
326 A162 40h blk & ol gray 3.00 1.25
a. Souv. sheet of 1, imperf. 11.00 11.00

6th National Mourning Day.

Soldier with Torch — A163

1961, June 16
327 A163 40h brown & yellow 3.00 1.25
a. Souv. sheet of 1, imperf. 10.00 10.00

Military Revolution of May 16, 1961.

Map of Korea, Torch and Broken Chain — A164

1961, Aug. 15 Wmk. 317 Perf. 13½
328 A164 40h dk bl, ver & aqua 3.00 1.25
a. Souv. sheet of 1, imperf. 6.00 6.00

16th anniv. of liberation.

Flag and Servicemen — A165

1961, Oct. 1 Litho.
329 A165 40h vio bl, red & brn 3.00 1.25
a. Souv. sheet of 1, imperf. 5.50 5.50

Issued for Armed Forces Day.

Kyongbok Palace Art Museum — A166

1961, Nov. 1 Wmk. 317 Perf. 13½
330 A166 40h beige & dk brn 2.00 .60
a. Souv. sheet of 1, imperf. 4.50 4.50

10th Natl. Exhibition of Fine Arts.

"UNESCO," Candle and Laurel — A167

1961, Nov. 4
331 A167 40h lt grn & dk bl   2.00   .60
   a.   Souv. sheet of 1, imperf.   4.50   4.50
         15th anniv. of UNESCO.

Mobile X-Ray Unit A168

1961, Nov. 16
332 A168 40h rose beige & red brn   1.60   .60
   a.   Souv. sheet of 1, imperf.   4.50   4.50
         Tuberculosis Prevention Week.

Ginseng — A169   King Sejong and Hangul Alphabet — A170

Tristram's Woodpecker A171   Rice Farmer A172

Ancient Drums — A173

1961-62   Unwmk.   Litho.   Perf. 12½
338 A169 20h rose brn ('62)   2.10   .65
339 A170 30h pale purple   6.50   .65
340 A171 40h dk blue & red   5.50   .65
341 A172 40h dk green ('62)   9.50   .80
342 A173 100h red brown   12.50   1.60
     Nos. 338-342 (5)   36.10   4.35

   See Nos. 363-366, 368, 388-392, 517-519, B5-B7.

Globe with Map of Korea and ITU Emblem A175

1962, Jan. 31   Unwmk.   Perf. 13½
348 A175 40h ver & dk blue   2.00   1.00
   a.   Souv. sheet of 1, imperf.   12.00   12.00
         10th anniv. of Korea's joining the ITU.

Atomic Reactor and Atom Symbol A176

1962, Mar. 30   Litho.   Perf. 13½
349 A176 40h lt bl, sl grn & ol gray 2.10 .50
     Inauguration of the Triga Mark II atomic reactor.

Malaria Eradication Emblem and Mosquito — A177

1962, Apr. 7   Unwmk.
350 A177 40h green & red org   1.60   .75
   a.   Souv. sheet of 1, imperf.   4.00   4.00
         WHO drive to eradicate malaria.

YWCA Emblem and Girl A178

1962, Apr. 20   Perf. 13½
351 A178 40h pink & dk blue   3.25   .60
     40th anniv. of the Korean Young Women's Christian Association.

South Gate and FPA Emblem A179

1962, May 12   Wmk. 317
352 A179 40h lt bl, dk vio & red   3.25   .75
     Meeting of the Federation of Motion Picture Producers in Asia, May 12-16.

Men Pushing Cogwheel A180

 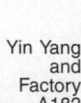

Soldiers on Hang Kang Bridge — A181

Yin Yang and Factory A182

Wmk. 317
1962, May 16   Litho.   Perf. 13½
353 A180 30h brn & pale olive   3.25   1.00
   a.   Souv. sheet of 1, Korean text   15.00   15.00
   b.   Souv. sheet of 1, English text   25.00   20.00
354 A181 40h brn, lt bl & citron   3.25   1.00
   a.   Souv. sheet of 1, Korean text   15.00   15.00
   b.   Souv. sheet of 1, English text   25.00   20.00
355 A182 200h ultra, yel & red   35.00   9.00
   a.   Souv. sheet of 1, Korean text   50.00   50.00
   b.   Souv. sheet of 1, English text   110.00   100.00
     Nos. 353-355 (3)   41.50   11.00

   1st anniv. of the May 16th Revolution. The souvenir sheets are imperf.
   The sheets with English text also exist with "E" in "POSTAGE" omitted. The English-text sheets are not watermarked except those with "E" omitted. Value, each $120.

Tortoise Warship, 16th Century A183

   Design: 4w, Tortoise ship, heading right.

1962, Aug. 14   Unwmk.   Perf. 13½
356 A183 2w dk bl & pale bl   16.00   1.50
357 A183 4w blk, bluish grn & lil   19.00   2.50
   370th anniv. of Korea's victory in the naval battle with the Japanese off Hansan Island.

Flag, Scout Emblem and Tents — A184

1962, Oct. 5   Wmk. 312
                  Litho.   Perf. 13½
358 A184 4w brown, bl & red   2.00   .75
   a.   Souv. sheet of 1, imperf., unwmkd.   8.00   8.00

Wmk. 317
359 A184 4w green, bl & red   2.00   .75
   a.   Souv. sheet of 1, imperf., unwmkd.   8.00   8.00

     40th anniv. of Korean Boy Scouts.

Types of 1961-62 and

Hanabusaya Asiatica — A185   Miruk Bosal — A186

Folk Dancers — A185a   Long-horned Beetle — A186a

Symbols of Thrift and Development A186b   Meesun Blossoms and Fruit A186c

Library of Early Buddhist Scriptures A186d   Sika Deer A186e

King Songdok Bell, 8th Cent. — A186f   Bodhisattva in Cavern Temple, Silla Dynasty — A187

Tile of Silla Dynasty — A187a

   Designs: 20ch, Jin-Do dog. 1.50w, Miruk Bosal. 2w, Ginseng. 3w, King Sejong. 4w, Rice farmer. 5w, Dragon waterpot. 10w, Ancient drums. 500w, Blue dragon fresco, Koguryo dynasty.

1962-63   Unwmk.   Litho.   Perf. 12½
Ordinary Paper
Size: 22x25mm, 25x22mm
360 A186 20ch gldn brown   1.60   .40
361 A185 40ch blue   1.60   .40
362 A186 50ch claret brn   1.60   .40
363 A185a 1w brt blue ('63)   3.25   .40
364 A169 2w red brown   4.75   .40
365 A170 3w violet brown   5.25   .40
366 A172 4w green   5.50   .40
367 A186 5w grnsh blue   6.50   .90
368 A173 10w red brown   95.00   4.00
369 A186c 20w lil rose ('63)   16.00   2.00
370 A186d 40w dl pur ('63)   140.00   5.00
     Nos. 360-370 (11)   281.05   14.70

1964-66   Granite Paper
360a A186 20ch org brn   .90   .25
361a A185 40ch blue   .95   .25
362a A186 50ch claret brn   .95   .25
362B A186a 60ch black ('66)   .95   .30
363a A185a 1w bright blue   3.50   .25
363B A186 1.50w dk sl grn ('66)   .70   .30
364a A169 2w red brown   5.50   .40
365a A170 3w vio brown   15.00   .30
366a A172 4w green   6.75   .30
367a A186 5w grnsh blue   32.50   1.50
367B A186b 7w lilac rose ('66)   3.25   .75
368a A173 10w red brown   5.00   .40
369a A186c 20w lilac rose   5.00   .40
370a A186d 40w vio brown   50.00   2.25
371 A186e 50w red brn   62.50   1.50
372 A186f 100w slate grn   100.00   3.00
373 A187 200w dk & lt grn ('65)   27.50   3.00
374 A187a 300w sl grn & buff ('65)   55.00   4.00
374A A187a 500w dk & lt bl ('65)   27.50   4.00
     Nos. 360a-374A (19)   403.45   23.40

   The paper of Nos. 360a to 374A contains a few colored fibers; the paper of Nos. 385-396 contains many fibers.
   Postal counterfeits exist of Nos. 369a, 370a, 371 and 372.
   See Nos. 385-396, 516, 521-522, 582-584, 1076-1079, B8.

Map, Mackerel and Trawler
A188

1962, Oct. 10   *Perf. 13½*
375 A188 4w dk bl & grnsh bl   4.00 .75
10th anniv. of the Pacific Fishery Council.

ICAO Emblem and Plane
A189

1962, Dec. 11   *Perf. 13½*
376 A189 4w blue & brown   2.40 .75
   a.   Souv. sheet of 1, imperf.   10.00 10.00
10th anniv. of Korea's joining the ICAO.

Savings Types of 1960
1962-64   **Unwmk.**   *Perf. 12½*
377 A140 1w emer, brn & org
          ('63)   7.25 1.25
   a.   Granite paper   16.00 12.50
378 A141 2w pink, bl & brn   12.00 1.50
   a.   Granite paper   14.00 2.50
          Wmk. 317
379 A140 1w emer, brn & org
          ('64)   95.00 10.00
380 A141 2w pink, bl & brn
          ('64)   14.00 1.75
   Nos. 377-380 (4)   128.25 14.50

Wheat Emblem
A190

          Wmk. 317
1963, Mar. 21   **Litho.**   *Perf. 13½*
381 A190 4w emer, dk bl & ocher 1.60 .75
   a.   Souv. sheet of 1, imperf.   4.75 4.75
FAO "Freedom from Hunger" campaign.

Globe and Letters
A191

1963, Apr. 1
382 A191 4w rose lil, ol & dk bl   2.40 .60
   a.   Souv. sheet of 1, imperf.   4.75 4.75
1st anniv. of the formation of the Asian-Oceanic Postal Union, AOPU.

Centenary Emblem and World Map
A192

1963, May 8   **Litho.**
383 A192 4w org, red & gray   1.50 .60
384 A192 4w lt bl, red & gray   1.50 .60
   a.   Souv. sheet of 2, #383-384, imperf.   14.00 14.00
Cent. of the Intl. Red Cross.

Types of 1961-63
Designs as before.

1963-64   **Wmk. 317**   *Perf. 12½*
       Granite Paper
    Size: 22x25mm, 25x22mm
385 A186 20ch gldn brn
          ('64)   .85 .25
386 A185 40ch blue   .85 .25
387 A186 50ch cl brn ('64)   .85 .25
388 A185a 1w brt blue   3.50 .35
389 A169 2w red brown   5.25 .40
390 A170 3w vio brown   15.00 .35
391 A172 4w green   6.75 .60
392 A173 10w red brown   5.50 .60
393 A186c 20w lil rose ('64)   12.00 1.75
394 A186d 40w dull purple   55.00 2.50
395 A186e 50w brown   72.50 2.00
396 A186f 100w slate grn   110.00 4.00
   Nos. 385-396 (12)   288.05 13.30

Hibiscus and "15"
A193

1963, Aug. 15   **Wmk. 317**   *Perf. 13½*
398 A193 4w vio bl, pale bl & red 3.25 1.25
15th anniversary of the Republic.

Army Nurse and Corps Emblem
A194

1963, Aug. 26   **Litho.**
399 A194 4w citron, grn & blk   2.40 .85
Army Nurses Corps, 15th anniversary.

First Five-Year Plan Issue

Transformer and Power Transmission Tower
A195

Irrigated Rice Fields
A196

No. 402, Cement factory. No. 403, Coal Miner. No. 404, Oil refinery. No. 405, Fishing industry (ships). No. 406, Cargo ship and cargo. No. 407, Fertilizer plant and grain. No. 408, Radar and telephone. No. 409, Transportation (plane, train, ship and map).

1962-66   **Unwmk.**   *Perf. 12½*
400 A195 4w org & dk vio   24.00 1.50
401 A196 4w lt bl & vio bl   24.00 1.50
          Wmk. 317
402 A195 4w dk bl & gray   5.50 1.25
403 A196 4w buff & brn   5.50 1.25
404 A195 4w yel & ultra   2.40 1.20
405 A196 4w lt bl & blk   2.40 1.20
          Unwmk.
406 A195 4w pale pink & vio bl   2.40 1.00
407 A196 4w bis brn & blk   2.40 1.00
408 A195 7w yel bis & blk   4.00 1.00
409 A196 7w vio bl & lt bl   4.00 1.00
   Nos. 400-409 (10)   76.60 11.90
Economic Development Five-Year Plan.
Issued: Nos. 400-401, 12/28/62; Nos. 402-403, 9/1/63; Nos. 404-405, 6/15/64; Nos. 406-407, 6/1/65; Nos. 408-409, 6/1/66.

Ramses Temple, Abu Simbel — A197

         Wmk. 317
1963, Oct. 1   *Perf. 13½*
410 3w gray & ol gray   5.50 2.25
411 4w gray & ol gray   5.50 2.25
   a.   Souv. sheet of 2, #410-411, imperf.   10.00 10.00
   b.   A197 Pair, #410-411   12.00 5.50
UNESCO world campaign to save historic monuments in Nubia.

Rugby and Torch Bearer
A199

1963, Oct. 4   **Wmk. 317**   *Perf. 13½*
412 A199 4w pale bl, red brn & dk grn   4.00 1.40
44th National Athletic Games.

Nurse & Mobile X-Ray Unit — A200

1963, Nov. 6   *Perf. 13½*
413 A200 4w org & bluish blk   2.00 .75
10h anniv. of the Korean Natl. Tuberculosis Association.

Eleanor Roosevelt
A201

Design: 4w, Hands holding torch and globe.

1963, Dec. 10   **Litho.**   **Wmk. 317**
414 A201 3w lt red brn & dk bl   1.60 .55
415 A201 4w dl org, ol & dk bl   1.60 .55
   a.   Souv. sheet of 2, 414-415, imperf.   6.00 6.00
Eleanor Roosevelt; 15th anniv. of the Universary Declaration of Human Rights.

Korean Flag and UN Headquarters
A202

1963, Dec. 12   **Wmk. 317**   *Perf. 13½*
416 A202 4w grnsh bl, ol & blk   1.60 .50
   a.   Souv. sheet of 1, imperf.   5.25 5.25
15th anniv. of Korea's recognition by the UN.

Tang-piri (Recorder)
A203

Musical Instruments: No. 418, Pyen-kyeng (chimes). No. 419, Chang-ko (drums). No. 420, Tai-keum (large flute). No. 421, Taipyeng-so (Chinese oboe). No. 422, Na-bal (brass trumpet). No. 423, Hyang-pipa (Chinese short lute). No. 424, Wul-keum (banjo). No. 425, Kaya-ko (zither), horiz. No. 426, Wa-kong-hu (harp), horiz.

1963, Dec. 17   **Unwmk.**
417 A203 4w pink, blk & car   6.50 1.40
418 A203 4w bl, bl grn & blk   6.50 1.40
419 A203 4w rose, vio bl & brn   6.50 1.40
420 A203 4w tan, dk grn & brn   6.50 1.40
421 A203 4w yel, vio bl & brn   6.50 1.40
422 A203 4w gray, brn & vio   6.50 1.40
423 A203 4w pink, vio bl & red brn   6.50 1.40
424 A203 4w grnsh bl, blk & bl   6.50 1.40
425 A203 4w rose, red brn & blk   6.50 1.40
426 A203 4w lil, blk & bl   6.50 1.40
   Nos. 417-426 (10)   65.00 14.00

Pres. Park and Capitol
A204

1963, Dec. 17   **Wmk. 317**
427 A204 4w black & brt grn   65.00 16.00
Inauguration of Pres. Park Chung Hee.

Symbols of Metric System
A205

1964, Jan. 1   **Litho.**
428 A205 4w multicolored   1.60 .50
   a.   Imperf., pair   75.00
Introduction of the metric system.

UNESCO Emblem and Yin Yang — A206

1964, Jan. 30   **Wmk. 317**   *Perf. 13½*
429 A206 4w red, lt bl & ultra   2.00 .75
Korean Natl. Commission for UNESCO, 10th anniv.

Industrial Census
A207

1964, Mar. 23   **Wmk. 317**   *Perf. 13½*
430 A207 4w gray, blk & red brn   2.00 .75
National Mining and Industrial Census.

YMCA Emblem and Head A208

1964, Apr. 12   **Litho.**
431   A208   4w ap grn, dk bl & red   1.60   .50
    50th anniv. of the Korean YMCA.

Unisphere, Ginseng and Cargo Ship — A209

Design: 100w, Korean pavilion and globe.

1964, Apr. 22   **Wmk. 317**   **Perf. 13½**
432   A209   40w buff, red brn & grn   4.00   1.40
433   A209   100w bl red brn & ultra   40.00   8.00
   a.   Souv. sheet of 2, imperf.   110.00   80.00
    New York World's Fair, 1964-65.

Secret Garden, Changdok Palace, Seoul A210

Views: 2w, Whahong Gate, Suwon. 3w, Uisang Pavilion, Yangyang-gun. 4w, Maitreya Buddha, Bopju Temple at Mt. Songni. 5w, Paekma River and Rock of Falling Flowers. 6w, Anab Pond, Kyongju. 7w, Choksok Pavilion, Chinju. 8w, Kwanghan Pavilion. 9w, Whaom Temple, Mt. Chiri. 10w, Chonjeyon Falls, Soguipo.

1964, May 25   **Wmk. 317**   **Perf. 13½**
Light Blue Background
434   A210   1w green   1.60   .50
435   A210   2w gray   1.60   .50
436   A210   3w dk green   1.60   .50
437   A210   4w emerald   3.25   1.00
438   A210   5w violet   5.50   1.50
439   A210   6w vio blue   8.00   2.00
   a.   Souv. sheet of 2 (5w, 6w)   19.00   19.00
440   A210   7w dk brown   12.50   2.75
   a.   Souv. sheet of 2 (4w, 7w)   19.00   19.00
441   A210   8w brown   15.00   2.75
   a.   Souv. sheet of 2 (3w, 8w)   19.00   19.00
442   A210   9w lt violet   16.00   2.75
   a.   Souv. sheet of 2 (2w, 9w)   19.00   19.00
443   A210   10w slate grn   20.00   3.25
   a.   Souv. sheet of 2 (1w, 10w)   19.00   19.00
    Nos. 434-443 (10)   85.05   17.50
    Nos. 439a-443a (5)   95.00   95.00

The five souvenir sheets are imperf.

Globe and Wheel A211

1964, July 1   **Litho.**   **Perf. 13½**
444   A211   4w lt ol grn, dl brn & ocher   1.60   .60
   a.   Souv. sheet of 1, imperf.   5.50   5.50
    Colombo Plan for co-operative economic development of south and southeast Asia.

Hands and World Health Organization Emblem — A212

1964, Aug. 17   **Wmk. 317**   **Perf. 13½**
445   A212   4w brt yel grn, yel grn & blk   1.60   .60
   a.   Souv. sheet of 1, imperf.   5.50   5.50
    15th anniv. of Korea's joining the UN.

Runner A213

1964, Sept. 3
446   A213   4w red lil, grn & pink   4.00   1.40
    45th Natl. Athletic Meet, Inchon, Sept. 3-8.

UPU Monument, Bern — A214

1964, Sept. 15
447   A214   4w pink, red brn & bl   1.60   .60
   a.   Souv. sheet of 1, imperf.   6.00   6.00
    1st Intl. Cong. for establishing the UPU, 90th anniv.

Crane Hook and Emblem — A215

1964, Sept. 29   **Wmk. 317**   **Perf. 13½**
448   A215   4w red brn & dull grn   1.60   .60
    5th Convention of the Intl. Federation of Asian and Western Pacific Contractors' Assoc. (IFAWPCA), Seoul, Sept. 29-Oct. 7.

Marathon Runners A216

No. 453, "V," Olympic rings, laurel & track, vert.

1964, Oct. 10   **Litho.**
449   A216   4w shown   3.25   1.00
450   A216   4w Equestrian   3.25   1.00
451   A216   4w Gymnast   3.25   1.00
452   A216   4w Rowing   3.25   1.00
453   A216   4w multicolored   3.25   1.00
    Nos. 449-453 (5)   16.25   5.00
    18th Olympic Games, Tokyo, Oct. 10-25.

Souvenir Sheets of 1, Imperf., Unwmk.
449a   A216   4w   4.75   4.75
450a   A216   4w   4.75   4.75
451a   A216   4w   4.75   4.75
452a   A216   4w   4.75   4.75
453a   A216   4w   4.75   4.75
    Nos. 449a-453a (5)   23.75   23.75

Stamp of 1885 — A217

Yong Sik Hong — A218

1964, Dec. 4   **Unwmk.**   **Perf. 13½**
454   A217   3w lilac, vio & dl bl grn   4.00   1.00
455   A218   4w gray, vio bl & blk   5.50   1.25
    80th anniv. of the Korean postal system. Hong Yong-Sik (1855-84) was Korea's 1st general postmaster.

Pine Branch and Cones — A219

No. 457, Plum Blossoms. No. 458, Forsythia. No. 459, Azalea. No. 460, Lilac. No. 461, Sweetbrier. No. 462, Garden balsam. No. 463, Hibiscus. No. 464, Crape myrtle. No. 465, Chrysanthemum lucidum. No. 466, Paulownia coreana. No. 467, Bamboo.

1965   **Litho.**   **Perf. 13½**
456   A219   4w pale grn, dp grn & brn   2.40   .75
457   A219   4w gray, blk, rose & yel   2.40   .75
458   A219   4w lt bl, yel & brn   2.40   .75
459   A219   4w brt grn, lil rose & sal   2.40   .75
460   A219   4w red lil & brt grn   2.40   .75
461   A219   4w yel grn, grn, car & brn   2.40   .75
462   A219   4w bl, grn & red   2.40   .75
463   A219   4w bluish gray, rose red & grn   2.40   .75
464   A219   4w multicolored   2.40   .75
465   A219   4w pale grn, dk brn, grn & car rose   2.40   .75
466   A219   4w buff, ol grn & brn   2.40   .75
467   A219   4w ultra & emer   2.40   .75
    Nos. 456-467 (12)   28.80   9.00

Souvenir Sheets of 1, Imperf.
456a   A219   4w   3.25   3.25
457a   A219   4w   3.25   3.25
458a   A219   4w   3.25   3.25
459a   A219   4w   3.25   3.25
460a   A219   4w   3.25   3.25
461a   A219   4w   3.25   3.25
462a   A219   4w   3.25   3.25
463a   A219   4w   3.25   3.25
464a   A219   4w   3.25   3.25
465a   A219   4w   3.25   3.25
466a   A219   4w   3.25   3.25
467a   A219   4w   3.25   3.25
    Nos. 456a-467a (12)   39.00   39.00

Dancing Women, PATA Emblem and Tabo Tower A220

1965, Mar. 26
468   A220   4w lt bl grn, dk brn & dk vio bl   1.40   .50
   a.   Souv. sheet of 1, imperf.   4.00   4.00
    14th conf. of the Pacific Travel Association, Seoul, Mar. 26-Apr. 2.

Map of Viet Nam and Flag of Korean Assistance Group — A221

1965, Apr. 20   **Perf. 13½**
469   A221   4w blk, lt yel grn & grnsh bl   1.25   .50
   a.   Souv. sheet of 1, imperf.   4.00   4.00
    Issued to honor the Korean military assistance group in Viet Nam.

Symbols of 7-Year Plan — A222

1965, May 1   **Litho.**
470   A222   4w emer, dk grn & dk brn   1.25   .50
    Issued to publicize the 7-year plan for increased food production.

Scales with Families and Homes A223

1965, May 8
471   A223   4w lt & dk grn & gray   1.25   .50
   a.   Souv. sheet of 1, imperf.   3.50   3.50
    May as Month of Family Planning.

ITU Emblem, Old and New Communication Equipment — A224

1965, May 17
472   A224   4w lt bl, car & blk   1.25   .50
   a.   Souv. sheet of 1, imperf.   3.50   3.50
    Cent. of the ITU.

UN Emblem and Flags of Australia, Belgium, Great Britain, Canada and Colombia A225

Gen. Douglas MacArthur and Flags of Korea, UN and US A226

UN Emblem and Flags: No. 474, Denmark, Ethiopia, France, Greece and India. No. 475, Italy, Luxembourg, Netherlands, New Zealand and Norway. No. 476, Philippines, Sweden, Thailand, Turkey and South Africa.

1965, June 25
Flags in Original Colors

473	A225	4w gray & vio bl	1.60	.75
474	A225	4w grnsh bl & vio bl	1.60	.75
475	A225	4w grnsh bl & vio bl	1.60	.75
476	A225	4w grnsh bl & vio bl	1.60	.75
477	A226	10w lt bl, blk, vio bl & red	5.50	1.50
	Nos. 473-477 (5)		11.90	4.50

15th anniv. of the participation of UN Forces in the Korean war.

Souvenir Sheets of 1, Imperf.

473a	A225	4w	2.00	2.00
474a	A225	4w	2.00	2.00
475a	A225	4w	2.00	2.00
476a	A225	4w	2.00	2.00
477a	A226	10w	4.00	4.00
	Nos. 473a-477a (5)		12.00	12.00

Flag, Factories and "20" — A227

South Gate, Seoul, Fireworks and Yin Yang — A228

1965, Aug. 15 — Litho.

478	A227	4w lt bl, vio bl & red	3.25	.60
479	A228	10w vio bl, lt bl & red	4.00	.80

20th anniv. of liberation from the Japanese.

Factory, Leaf and Ants — A229

1965, Sept. 20 — Perf. 13½

480	A229	4w brt yel grn, brn & bister	1.25	.50

Issued to publicize the importance of saving.

Parabolic Antenna, Telephone Dial and Punched Tape A230

Telegraph Operator, 1885 A231

1965, Sept. 28

481	A230	3w lt bl, blk & ol	2.00	.50
482	A231	10w citron, Prus bl & blk	4.75	.75

80th anniv. of telegraph service between Seoul and Inchon.

Korean Flag and Capitol, Seoul — A232

1965, Sept. 28

483	A232	3w org, slate grn & bl grn	3.25	1.25

15th anniversary of recapture of Seoul.

Pole Vault A233

1965, Oct. 5

484	A233	3w black, lil & sal	2.40	1.00

46th Natl. Athletic Meet, Kwangju, Oct. 5-10.

ICY Emblem A234

UN Flag and Headquarters, NY — A235

1965, Oct. 24 — Litho.

485	A234	3w lt & dk grn & org brn	1.20	.50
a.	Souv. sheet of 1, imperf.		4.00	4.00
486	A235	10w lt bl, vio bl & grn	2.40	.75
a.	Souv. sheet of 1, imperf.		4.00	4.00

ICY, 1965, and 20th anniv. of the UN.

Child Posting Letter A236

Design: 10w, Airmail envelope, telephone.

1965, Dec. 4 — Perf. 13½

487	A236	3w bl grn, blk, grn & red	3.25	1.00
488	A236	10w ol, dk bl & red	6.50	1.75

Tenth Communications Day.

Children with Sled — A237

Children and South Gate — A238

1965, Dec. 11 — Litho. — Perf. 12½

489	A237	3w pale grn, vio bl & red	2.40	.60
490	A238	4w lt bl, grn, vio bl & red	4.00	.60
a.	Souv. sheet of 2, #489-490, imperf.		4.75	4.75

Issued for Christmas and the New Year.

Freedom House A239

1966, Feb. 15 — Unwmk. — Perf. 12½

491	A239	7w brt grn, blk & cit	2.40	.75
492	A239	39w lil, blk & pale grn	14.00	3.25
a.	Souv. sheet of 2, #491-492, imperf.		24.00	17.50

Opening of "Freedom House" at Panmunjom.

Wildlife Issue

Mandarin Ducks A240

Birds: 5w, Japanese cranes. 7w, Ring-necked pheasants.

1966, Mar. 15 — Litho. — Perf. 12½

493	A240	3w multicolored	2.75	1.40
494	A240	5w multicolored	2.75	1.40
495	A240	7w multicolored	4.00	1.40

Alaska Pollack A241

Fish: 5w, Manchurian trout. 7w, Yellow corvina.

1966, June 15

496	A241	3w bl, dk brn & yel	3.25	.90
497	A241	5w grnsh bl, blk & mag	4.00	.90
498	A241	7w brt grnsh bl, blk & yel	4.75	1.00

Firefly A242

Insects: 5w, Grasshopper. 7w, Silk butterfly (sericinus telamon).

1966, Sept. 15

499	A242	3w multicolored	2.40	.90
500	A242	5w dp yellow & multi	3.25	.90
501	A242	7w lt blue & multi	3.25	1.00

Badger A243

Animals: 5w, Asiatic black bear. 7w, Tiger.

1966, Dec. 15

502	A243	3w multicolored	3.25	1.10
503	A243	5w multicolored	3.25	1.10
504	A243	7w multicolored	4.00	1.10
	Nos. 493-504 (12)		40.90	13.10

Souvenir Sheets of 1, Imperf.

493a	A240	3w	4.00	4.00
494a	A240	5w	4.00	4.00
495a	A240	7w	6.50	6.50
496a	A241	3w	3.25	3.25
497a	A241	5w	4.00	4.00
498a	A241	7w	4.75	4.75
499a	A242	3w	3.25	3.25
500a	A242	5w	3.25	3.25
501a	A242	7w	4.00	4.00
502a	A243	3w	4.75	4.75
503a	A243	5w	4.75	4.75
504a	A243	7w	5.50	5.50
	Nos. 493a-504a (12)		52.00	52.00

Hwansung-gun and Kwangnung Forests — A244

1966, Apr. 5 — Unwmk. — Perf. 12½

505	A244	7w green & brown	1.60	.60

Forestation Movement.

Symbolic Newspaper Printing and Pen — A245

1966, Apr. 7 — Litho.

506	A245	7w lt bl, vio brn & yel	1.40	.60

Tenth Newspaper Day.

Proper Guidance of Young People — A246

1966, May 1 — Unwmk. — Perf. 12½

507	A246	7w Children & bell	1.40	.60

Opening of WHO Headquarters, Geneva — A247

1966, May 3 — Litho.

508	A247	7w lt bl, blk & yel	1.60	.60
a.	Souv. sheet of 1, imperf.		4.75	4.75
509	A247	39w bluish gray, yel & red	12.00	3.50

Girl Scout and Flag — A248

1966, May 10

510	A248	7w yel, emer & dk bl	2.40	.80

Girl Scouts of Korea, 20th anniversary.

Pres. Park and Flags of Korea, Malaysia, Thailand and Republic of China A249

1966, May 10

511	A249	7w multicolored	8.00	2.50

State visits of President Chung Hee Park.

Women's Ewha University, Seoul, and Student A250

1966, May 31
512 A250 7w lt bl, vio bl & dp org 1.40 .50
80th anniv. of modern education for women.

Types of 1961-66 Inscribed "Republic of Korea," and

Porcelain Incense Burner, 11th-12th Centuries — A253

Celadon Vessel, 12th Century — A254

Unjin Miruk Buddha, Kwanchok Temple — A255

60ch, Long-horned beetle. 1w, Folk dancers. 2w, Ginseng. 3w, King Sejong. 5w, Dragon waterpot. 7w, Symbols of thrift & development.

Perf. 12½
1966, Aug. 20   Unwmk.   Litho.
Size: 22x19mm, 19x22mm
Granite Paper
516 A186a 60ch gray green .80 .25
517 A185a 1w green 4.50 .40
518 A169 2w blue green .50 .25
519 A170 3w dull red brn .50 .25
521 A186 5w gray green 5.50 .80
522 A186b 7w grnsh blue 5.50 .30
Size: 22x25mm
523 A253 13w vio blue 5.50 .75
524 A254 60w green 32.50 1.50
525 A255 80w slate grn 8.50 1.50
Nos. 516-525 (9) 63.80 6.00

Souvenir Sheet

Carrier Pigeons — A258

1966, July 13   Wmk. 317   Imperf.
Red Brown Surcharge
534 A258 7w on 40h emer & dk
grn 4.00 4.00
6th Intl. Letter Writing Week, June 13-19. No. 534 was not issued without surcharge.

Children and World Map Projection A259

1966, July 28   Unwmk.   Perf. 12½
535 A259 7w lt & dk vio bl & gray 2.40 .50
a. Souv. sheet of 1, imperf. 4.00 4.00
15th annual assembly of WCOTP (World Conf. of Teaching Profession), Seoul, July 28-Aug. 9.

Factory, Money Bag and Honeycomb A260

1966, Sept. 1   Unwmk.   Perf. 12½
536 A260 7w multicolored 1.40 .50
Issued to publicize systematic saving.

Map of Korea, and People A261

1966, Sept. 1   Litho.
537 A261 7w multicolored 1.40 .50
Ninth national census.

CISM Emblem and Round-Table Conference A262

1966, Sept. 29   Unwmk.   Perf. 12½
538 A262 7w multicolored 1.40 .50
a. Souv. sheet of 1, imperf. 4.00 4.00
21st General Assembly of the Intl. Military Sports Council (CISM), Seoul, 9/29-10/9.

Flags of Korea and Viet Nam and Korean Soldiers A263

1966, Oct. 1
539 A263 7w multicolored 9.50 2.40
1st anniv. of Korean combat troops in Viet Nam.

Wrestlers A264

1966, Oct. 10
540 A264 7w red brn, buff & blk 2.50 1.00
47th Natl. Athletic Meet, Seoul, Oct. 10-15.

Lions Emblem and Map of Southeast Asia — A265

1966, Oct. 15
541 A265 7w multicolored 1.60 .50
a. Souv. sheet of 1, imperf. 4.00 4.00
5th East and Southeast Asia Lions Convention, Seoul, Oct. 15-17.

Seoul University Emblem A266

1966, Oct. 15   Litho.
542 A266 7w multicolored 1.60 .50
20th anniversary of Seoul University.

Anticommunist League Emblem — A267

1966, Oct. 31   Unwmk.   Perf. 12½
543 A267 7w multicolored 1.60 .50
a. Souv. sheet of 1, imperf. 3.50 3.50
12th Conf. of the Asian Anticommunist League, Seoul, Oct. 31-Nov. 7.

Presidents Park and Johnson, Flags of US and Korea A268

1966, Oct. 31   Litho.   Perf. 12½
544 A268 7w multicolored 2.40 .75
545 A268 83w multicolored 14.00 4.00
a. Souv. sheet of 2, #544-545,
imperf. 16.00 16.00
Visit of Pres. Lyndon B. Johnson to Korea.

UNESCO Emblem and Symbols of Learning — A269

1966, Nov. 4
546 A269 7w multicolored 1.60 .40
a. Souvenir sheets 4.00 4.00
20th anniv. of UNESCO.

Good Luck Bag and "Joy" A270

Ram and "Completion" A271

1966, Dec. 10   Perf. 12½x13, 13x12½
547 A270 5w multicolored 2.40 .35
a. Souv. sheet of 1, imperf. 4.00 4.00
548 A271 7w multicolored 4.00 .35
a. Souv. sheet of 1, imperf. 4.00 4.00
Issued for Christmas and the New Year.

Syncom Satellite over Globe — A272

1967, Jan. 31   Litho.   Perf. 12½
549 A272 7w dk blue & multi 1.60 .60
a. Souv. sheet of 1, imperf. 4.50 4.50
15th anniv. of Korea's membership in the ITU.

Presidents Park and Lübke A273

Perf. 12½
1967, Mar. 2   Unwmk.
550 A273 7w multicolored 2.50 1.40
a. Souv. sheet of 1, imperf. 4.75 4.75
Visit of Pres. Heinrich Lübke of Germany, Mar. 2-6.

Hand Holding Coin, Industrial and Private Buildings A274

1967, Mar. 3
551 A274 7w lt green & blk brn 1.60 .50
1st anniv. of the Natl. Taxation Office.

Folklore Series

Okwangdae Clown — A275

5w, Sandi mask & dance, horiz. 7w, Hafoe mask.

1967, Mar. 15   Litho.   Perf. 12½
552 A275 4w gray, blk & yel 2.40 .70
553 A275 5w multicolored 2.40 .80
554 A275 7w multicolored 3.25 1.00

Perfect Peace Dance — A276

Designs: 4w, Sword dance, horiz. 7w, Buddhist Monk dance.

1967, June 15
555 A276 4w multicolored 4.00 .80
556 A276 5w multicolored 4.75 .85
557 A276 7w multicolored 5.50 1.20

Girls on Seesaw — A277

Designs: 4w, Girls on swing, horiz. 7w, Girls dancing in the moonlight.

1967, Sept. 15
558 A277 4w multicolored 4.00 .75
559 A277 5w multicolored 4.00 1.00
560 A277 7w multicolored 6.50 1.20

Korean
Shuttlecock — A278

Designs: 5w, Girls celebrating full moon, horiz. 7w, Archery.

1967, Dec. 15

561	A278	4w multicolored	3.25	.85
562	A278	5w multicolored	3.50	1.10
563	A278	7w multicolored	3.50	1.00
		Nos. 552-563 (12)	47.05	11.25

Souvenir Sheets of 1, Imperf.

552a	A275	4w	3.25	3.25
553a	A275	5w	3.25	3.25
554a	A275	7w	4.75	4.75
555a	A276	4w	6.50	3.25
556a	A276	5w	6.50	3.25
557a	A276	7w	8.00	4.75
558a	A277	4w	6.50	6.50
559a	A277	5w	6.50	6.50
560a	A277	7w	8.00	8.00
561a	A278	4w	4.00	4.00
562a	A278	5w	4.00	4.00
563a	A278	7w	4.75	4.75
		Nos. 552a-563a (12)	66.00	56.25

JCI Emblem and Kyunghoe Pavilion A279

1967, Apr. 13   Litho.   Perf. 12½

564	A279	7w dk brn, brt grn, bl & red	1.40	.40
a.		Souv. sheet of 1, imperf.	4.00	4.00

Intl. Junior Chamber of Commerce Conf., Seoul, Apr. 13-16.

Emblem, Map of Far East — A280

1967, Apr. 24   Unwmk.   Perf. 12½

565	A280	7w vio bl & multi	1.40	.40
a.		Souv. sheet of 1, imperf.	4.00	4.00

Issued to publicize the 5th Asian Pacific Dental Congress, Seoul, Apr. 24-28.

EXPO '67 Korean Pavilion A281

1967, Apr. 28

566	A281	7w yel, blk & red	4.00	.75
567	A281	83w lt bl, blk & red	24.00	5.50
a.		Souv. sheet of 2, #566-567, imperf.	20.00	20.00

EXPO '67, Intl. Exhibition, Montreal, Apr. 28-Oct. 27, 1967.

Worker, Soldier, Emblem and Buildings — A282

1967, May 1

568	A282	7w multicolored	1.60	.45

Veterans' Day, May 1.

Second Five-Year Plan Issue

Nut and Arrows A283

No. 570, Iron wheel and rail. No. 571, Express highway. No. 572, Cloverleaf intersection. No. 573, Rising income for fishermen and farmers (oysters, silk worm, mushrooms and bull's head). No. 574, Machine industry (cogwheels, automobile, wrench and motor). No. 575, Harbor. No. 576, Housing projects plans. No. 577, Atomic power plant. No. 578, Four Great River Valley development.

1967-71   Litho.   Perf. 12½

569	A283	7w blk, red brn & dl org	7.25	1.20
570	A283	7w dl org, yel & blk	7.25	1.20
571	A283	7w grn, bl & ol	14.00	1.00
572	A283	7w dk brn, yel & grn	8.00	1.00

Perf. 13x12½

573	A283	7w brn, grn, yel & org	1.60	.40
574	A283	7w dk bl, lil rose & buff	1.60	.40
575	A283	10w dk bl, bl, yel & grn	1.60	.40
576	A283	10w lt bl, bl, grn & red	1.60	.40

Photo.   Perf. 13

577	A283	10w blk, car & bl	1.60	.40
578	A283	10w blk, grn & brn	1.60	.40
		Nos. 569-578 (10)	46.10	6.80

Second Economic Development Five-Year Plan.
Issued: Nos. 569-570, 6/1/67; Nos. 571-572, 12/5/68; Nos. 573-574, 12/5/69; Nos. 575-576, 12/5/70; Nos. 577-578, 12/5/71.

President Park and Phoenix A284

1967, July 1   Unwmk.   Perf. 12½

579	A284	7w multicolored	24.00	4.00
a.		Souv. sheet of 1, imperf.	67.50	67.50

Inauguration of President Park Chung Hee for a 2nd term, July 1, 1967.

Korean Boy Scout, Emblem and Tents — A285

20w, Korean Boy Scout emblem, bridge & tents.

1967, Aug. 10   Litho.   Perf. 12½

580	A285	7w multicolored	1.60	.60
a.		Souv. sheet of 1, imperf.	5.50	5.50
581	A285	20w multicolored	5.50	2.25
a.		Souv. sheet of 1, imperf.	5.50	5.50

3rd Korean Boy Scout Jamboree, Hwarangdae, Seoul, Aug. 10-15.

Types of 1962-66 Redrawn
(Inscribed "Republic of Korea")

Designs: 20w, Meesun blossoms and fruit. 40w, Library of early Buddhist scriptures. 50w, Deer.

1967, Aug. 25   Granite Paper

582	A186c	20w green & lt bl grn	80.00	1.50
583	A186d	40w dk grn & lt ol	47.50	1.50
584	A186e	50w dk brn & bister	9.00	1.50
		Nos. 582-584 (3)	136.50	4.50

The printing of redrawn designs of the regular issue of 1962-66 became necessary upon discovery of large quantities of counterfeits, made to defraud the post. The position of the denominations was changed and elaborate fine background tracings were added.

Freedom Center and Emblem A286

Hand Breaking Chain — A287

1967, Sept. 25   Litho.   Perf. 12½

586	A286	5w multicolored	1.60	.40
a.		Souv. sheet of 1, imperf.	5.50	5.50
587	A287	7w multicolored	1.60	.40
a.		Souv. sheet of 1, imperf.	5.50	5.50

1st Conf. of the World Anti-Communist League, WACL, Taipei, China, Sept. 25-29.

Boxing — A288

Design: 7w, Women's basketball.

1967, Oct. 5

588	A288	5w tan & multi	2.40	.75
589	A288	7w pale rose & multi	3.25	.75

48th Natl. Athletic Meet, Seoul, Oct. 5-10.

Students' Memorial, Kwangjoo — A289

1967, Nov. 3   Litho.   Perf. 12½

590	A289	7w lt green & multi	1.60	.40

Issued for Student Day commemorating 1929 students' uprising against Japan.

Symbolic Water Cycle — A290

1967, Nov. 20

591	A290	7w multicolored	1.60	.40

Hydrological Decade (UNESCO), 1965-74.

Children Spinning Top — A291   Monkey and Oriental Zodiac — A292

1967, Dec. 10

592	A291	5w sal, org & vio bl	3.25	.35
a.		Souv. sheet of 1, imperf.	4.00	4.00
593	A292	7w yel bis, brn & vio bl	4.00	.35
a.		Souv. sheet of 1, imperf.	4.00	4.00

Issued for Christmas and New Year.

Parabolic Antenna and Electric Waves — A293

1967, Dec. 21

594	A293	7w lt bl, blk & yel	1.60	.70
a.		Souv. sheet of 1, imperf.	4.00	4.00

Opening of the natl. microwave communications network, Dec. 21.

Carving from King Songdok Bell — A294

Earrings, 6th Cent. — A295   Flag — A296

Perf. 13x12½

1968, Feb. 1   Litho.   Unwmk.
Granite Paper

595	A294	1w yellow & brown	.40	.25
596	A295	5w dk green & yellow	3.50	.55
597	A296	7w dark blue & red	1.60	.25
		Nos. 595-597 (3)	5.50	1.05

WHO, 20th Anniv. — A297

1968, Apr. 7   Unwmk.   Perf. 12½

598	A297	7w multicolored	1.60	.45
a.		Souv. sheet of 1, imperf.	4.00	4.00

EATA Emblem and Korean Buildings — A298

1968, Apr. 9   Litho.

599	A298	7w multicolored	1.60	.45
			4.75	4.75

2nd General Meeting of the East Asia Travel Association (EATA), Seoul, Apr. 9-13.

Door Knocker, Factories and Emblem A299

1968, May 6   Unwmk.   Perf. 12½
600 A299 7w multicolored   1.60   .45
  a.   Souv. sheet of 1, imperf.   4.50 4.50
2nd Conf. of the Confederation of Asian Chambers of Commerce and Industry, Seoul.

Pres. Park and Emperor Haile Selassie A300

1968, May 18   Litho.
601 A300 7w multicolored   4.00 1.50
  a.   Souv. sheet of 1, imperf.   8.00 8.00
Visit of Haile Selassie I, May 18-20.

Mailman's Pouch A301

Mailman A302

1968, May 31   Unwmk.   Perf. 12½
602 A301 5w multicolored   1.60   .70
603 A302 7w multicolored   1.60   .70
First Postman's Day, May 31, 1968.

Atom Diagram and Symbols of Development A303

1968, June 1   Litho.
604 A303 7w dk bl, citron & ver   1.60   .45
Issued to promote science and technology.

Kyung Hee University and Conference Emblem A304

1968, June 18   Unwmk.
605 A304 7w bl, pink & blk   1.60   .45
  a.   Souv. sheet of 1, imperf.   5.50 5.50
2nd Conf. of the Intl. Association of University Presidents.

Liberated People A305

1968, July 1   Litho.   Perf. 12½
606 A305 7w multicolored   1.60   .45
Issued to publicize the movement to liberate people under communist rule.

Peacock and Industrial Plant — A306

1968, Aug. 15   Unwmk.   Perf. 12½
607 A306 7w multicolored   1.60   .45
Republic of Korea, 20th anniversary.

Fair Entrance A307

1968, Sept. 9   Unwmk.   Perf. 12½
608 A307 7w lilac & multi   1.60   .45
Issued to publicize the first Korean Trade Fair, Seoul, Sept. 9-Oct. 18.

Assembly Emblem and Pills — A308

1968, Sept. 16   Litho.
609 A308 7w multicolored   1.60   .45
3rd General Assembly of the Federation of Asian Pharmaceutical Associations, Seoul, Sept. 16-21.

Soldier, Insigne and Battle Scene — A309

No. 611, Sailor, insigne & ship's guns. No. 612, Servicemen & flags. No. 613, Aviator, insigne & planes. No. 614, Marine, insigne & landing group.

1968, Oct. 1
610 A309 7w green & org   8.00 2.40
611 A309 7w lt & dk blue   8.00 2.40
612 A309 7w dk blue & org   8.00 2.40
613 A309 7w dk & lt blue   8.00 2.40
614 A309 7w orange & grn   8.00 2.40
  a. Vert. strip of 5, #610-614 47.50 16.00
20th anniv. of the Korean armed forces.

Colombo Plan Emblem and Globe — A310

1968, Oct. 8   Litho.   Perf. 12½
615 A310 7w dk brn, pale sal & grn   1.60   .35
19th meeting of the Consultative Committee of the Colombo Plan, Seoul, Oct. 8-28.

Bicycling (Type I) — A311   Type II — (2nd line flush left)

No. 617, Bicycling, Type II. No. 618-619, Wrestling. No. 620-621, Boxing. No. 622-623, Olympic flame, "68" & symbols of various sports events.

1968, Oct. 12   Unwmk.   Perf. 12½
616 A311 7w pink & multi (I)   16.00 4.75
617 A311 7w pink & multi (II)   16.00 4.75
  a. Souv. sheet of 2, #616-617, imperf. 12.00 12.00
  b. Pair, #616-617   40.00 40.00
618 A311 7w olive & multi (I)   16.00 16.00
619 A311 7w olive & multi (II) 16.00 16.00
  a. Souv. sheet of 2, #618-619, imperf. 12.00 12.00
  b. Pair, #618-619   40.00 40.00
620 A311 7w orange & multi (I) 16.00 16.00
621 A311 7w orange & multi (II) 16.00 16.00
  a. Souv. sheet of 2, #620-621, imperf. 12.00 12.00
  b. Pair, #620-621   40.00 40.00
622 A311 7w bluish grn & multi (I) 16.00 16.00
623 A311 7w bluish grn & multi (II) 16.00 16.00
  a. Souv. sheet of 2, #622-623, imperf. 12.00 12.00
  b. Pair, #622-623   40.00 40.00
  Nos. 616-623 (8)   128.00 105.50
19th Olympic Games, Mexico City, 10/12-27. The position of the "7" is reversed on Nos. 619, 621, 623 as are the designs of Nos. 619, 621.

"Search for Knowledge" and School Girls — A312

1968, Oct. 15
624 A312 7w multicolored   1.60   .40
60th anniv. of public secondary education for women.

Coin and Statistics A313

1968, Nov. 1
625 A313 7w multicolored   1.60   .40
National Wealth Survey.

Memorial to Students' Uprising — A314

1968, Nov. 23
626 A314 7w gray & multi   2.00   .55
Issued to commemorate the anti-communist students' uprising, Nov. 23, 1945.

Men With Banners Declaring Human Rights A315

1968, Dec. 10
627 A315 7w multicolored   1.60   .40
Declaration of Human Rights, 20th anniv.

Christmas Decorations A316   Cock and Good Luck Characters A317

1968, Dec. 11
628 A316 5w salmon & multi   9.50   .55
  a.   Souv. sheet of 1, imperf.   8.00 8.00
629 A317 7w multicolored   9.50   .55
  a.   Souv. sheet of 1, imperf.   8.00 8.00
Issued for Christmas and the New Year.

UN Emblems and Korean House A318

1968, Dec. 12
630 A318 7w lt blue & multi   1.60   .40
20th anniv. of the recognition of the Republic of Korea by the UN.

Regional Boy Scout Conf. — A319

Design: Boy Scout Emblem.

1968, Sept. 30   Litho.   Perf. 12½
631 A319 7w black & multi   2.40   .75

Sam-il Movement, 50th Anniv. — A320

Design: Torch, map and students Demonstrating against Japan, 1919.

1969, Mar. 1   Unwmk.   Perf. 12½
632 A320 7w multicolored   1.60   .45

Hyun Choong Sa Shrine and Tortoise Ships A321

1969, Apr. 28   Unwmk.   Perf. 12½
633 A321 7w deep bl, grn & brn   1.60   .45
Completion of the Hyun Choong Sa Shrine at Onyang, dedicated to the memory of Adm. Li Sun-sin.

Pres. Park and Tuanku Nasiruddin of Malaysia
A322

1969, Apr. 29 Litho.
634 A322 7w yellow & multi 4.00 1.25
  a. Souv. sheet of 1, imperf. 67.50 67.50
Visit of Tuanku Ismail Nasiruddin, ruler of Malaysia, Apr. 29, 1969.

Hanabusaya Asiatica
A323

Flag of Korea
A324

Ancient Drums
A325

Red-crested Cranes
A326

Highway and Farm
A327

Pitcher (12-13th Centuries)
A328

Ceramic Duck (Water Jar)
A329

Library of Early Buddhist Scriptures
A330

Vase, Yi dynasty (17th-18th Centuries)
A331

Miruk Bosal
A333

1w, Old man's mask. No. 637, Stone lamp, 8th cent. No. 638, Chipmunk. No. 644, Tiger lily. No. 649, Bee. No. 653, Gold crown, Silla Dynasty.
Zeros Omitted except 7w, No. 639
Granite Paper (Lithographed); Ordinary Paper (Photogravure)
  Perf. 13x12, 12x13 (Litho.);
  13½x12½, 12½x13½ (Photo.)
Litho. (40ch, Nos. 641, 650); Photo.
1969-74 Unwmk.
635 A323 40ch green 1.60 .40
636 A326 1w dk rose brn
    ('74) .45 .25
637 A328 5w brt plum 1.10 .25
638 A326 5w maroon ('74) .40 .25
639 A324 7w blue ("7.00") 4.00 .40
640 A324 7w blue ("7") 1.60 .30
641 A325 10w ultra 32.50 .70
642 A324 10w ultra ("10")
    ('70) 1.60 .25
643 A326 10w bl & dk bl
    ('73) 1.60 .40
644 A323 10w grn & multi
    ('73) .95 .25

645 A327 10w grn, red &
    gray ('73) .80 .25
647 A328 20w green 2.00 .40
648 A329 30w dull grn ('70) 4.00 .75
649 A326 30w yel & dk brn
    ('74) .75 .25
650 A330 40w vio bl & pink 47.50 2.25
651 A331 40w ultra & lilac 2.00 .75
652 A333 100w dp claret &
    yel 100.00 2.25
653 A333 100w brn & yel
    ('74) 40.00 2.40
  Nos. 635-653 (18) 242.85 12.75
See No. 1090. For surcharge see No. B18.
Counterfeits exist of No. 653.

Red Cross, Faces and Doves
A336

1969, May 5 Litho. *Perf. 12½*
654 A336 7w multicolored 2.00 .45
  a. Souv. sheet of 1, imperf. 5.50 5.50
50th anniv. of the League of Red Cross Societies.

Savings Bank, Factories and Highway — A337

1969, May 20 Unwmk. *Perf. 12½*
655 A337 7w yellow grn & multi 1.60 .45
Second Economy Drive.

Pres. Park, Pres. Thieu and Flags of Korea and Viet Nam — A338

1969, May 27 Litho.
656 A338 7w pink & multi 3.25 1.25
  a. Souv. sheet of 1, imperf. 8.75 8.75
Visit of Pres. Nguyen Van Thieu of Viet Nam, May 27.

"Reforestation and Parched Fields" — A339

Growing and Withering Plants — A340

1969, June 10
657 A339 7w multicolored 1.60 .40
658 A340 7w multicolored 1.60 .40
Issued to publicize the need for prevention of damages from floods and droughts.

Apollo 11, Separation of Second Stage
A341

No. 660, Apollo 11, separation of 3rd Stage. No. 661, Orbits of command & landing modules around moon. No. 662, Astronauts gathering rock samples on moon. 40w, Spacecraft splashdown.

1969, Aug. 15 Unwmk. *Perf. 12½*
659 A341 10w indigo, bl & red 4.00 1.00
660 A341 10w indigo, bl & red 4.00 1.00
661 A341 20w indigo, bl, red &
    lem 4.00 1.00
662 A341 20w indigo, bl, red &
    lem 4.00 1.00
663 A341 40w indigo, bl & red 4.00 1.00
  a. Souv. sheet of 5, #659-663,
    imperf. 35.00 35.00
  b. Strip of 5, #659-663 24.00 12.00
Man's 1st landing on the moon, July 20, 1969. US astronauts Neil A. Armstrong and Col. Edwin E. Aldrin, Jr., with Lieut. Col. Michael Collins piloting Apollo 11.

Fable Issue

Girl and Stepmother
A342

Kongji and Patji (Cinderella): 7w, Sparrows help Kongji separate rice. 10w, Ox helps Kongji to weed a field. 20w, Kongji in a sedan chair on the way to the palace.

1969, Sept. 1 Litho. *Perf. 12½*
664 A342 5w apple grn & multi 4.00 .90
665 A342 7w yellow & multi 4.00 .90
666 A342 10w lt violet & multi 6.50 1.25
667 A342 20w lt green & multi 6.50 1.25

The Sick Princess
A343

"The Hare's Liver": 7w, Hare riding to the palace on back of turtle. 10w, Hare telling a lie to the King to save his life. 20w, Hare mocking the turtle.

1969, Nov. 1 *Perf. 13x12½*
668 A343 5w yellow & multi 2.25 .65
669 A343 7w lt vio & multi 2.25 .65
670 A343 10w lt grnsh bl & multi 2.25 1.00
671 A343 20w lt yel grn & multi 4.00 1.00

Mother Meeting Tiger — A344

"The Sun and the Moon": 7w, Tiger disguised as mother at children's house. 10w, Tiger, and children on tree. 20w, Children safe on cloud, and tiger falling to his death.

1970, Jan. 5
672 A344 5w orange & multi 2.25 .65
673 A344 7w gray grn & multi 2.25 .65
674 A344 10w lt green & multi 2.25 .90
675 A344 20w gray & multi 4.00 .90

Woodcutter Stealing Fairy's Clothes
A345

Designs: No. 677, Woodcutter with wife and children. No. 678, Wife taking children to heaven. No. 679, Husband joining family in heaven.

1970, Mar. 5
676 A345 10w dull bl grn & multi 2.75 1.00
677 A345 10w buff & multi 2.75 1.00
678 A345 10w lt grnsh bl & multi 2.75 1.00
679 A345 10w pink & multi 2.75 1.00

Heungbu and Wife Release Healed Swallow
A346

Designs: No. 681, Heungbu and wife finding gold treasure in gourd. No. 682, Nolbu and wife with large gourd. No. 683, Demon emerging from gourd punishing evil Nolbu and wife.

1970, May 5 *Perf. 12½*
680 A346 10w lt grnsh bl &
    multi 6.50 1.20
681 A346 10w orange &
    multi 6.50 1.20
682 A346 10w apple grn &
    multi 6.50 1.20
683 A346 10w tan & multi 6.50 1.20
  Nos. 664-683 (20) 79.50 19.50

Souvenir Sheets of 1, Imperf.
664a A342 5w 6.50 6.50
665a A342 7w 6.50 6.50
666a A342 10w 6.50 6.50
667a A342 20w 6.50 6.50
668a A343 5w 5.50 5.50
669a A343 7w 5.50 5.50
670a A343 10w 5.50 5.50
671a A343 20w 5.50 5.50
672a A344 5w 5.50 5.50
673a A344 7w 5.50 5.50
674a A344 10w 5.50 5.50
675a A344 20w 5.50 5.50
676a A345 10w 5.50 5.50
677a A345 10w 5.50 5.50
678a A345 10w 5.50 5.50
679a A345 10w 5.50 5.50
680a A346 10w 16.00 16.00
681a A346 10w 16.00 16.00
682a A346 10w 16.00 16.00
683a A346 10w 16.00 16.00
  Nos. 664a-683a (20) 156.00 156.00

1869 Locomotive and Diesel Train — A347

Design: No. 685, Early locomotive.

Perf. 12½
1969, Sept. 18 Litho. Unwmk.
684 A347 7w yellow & multi 2.00 .70
685 A347 7w green & multi 2.00 .70
70th anniversary of Korean Railroads.

Formation of F-5A Planes
A348

Design: No. 687, F-4D Phantom.

1969, Oct. 1 Photo. *Perf. 13½x13*
686 A348 10w blue, blk & car 5.00 .75

Litho. *Perf. 13x12½*
687 A348 10w multicolored 7.00 .75
20th anniversary of Korean Air Force.

Cha-jun Game
A349

1969, Oct. 3
688 A349 7w ap grn, dk bl & blk 1.20 .35
10th National Festival of Traditional Skills.

Institute of Science and Technology A350

1969, Oct. 23
689 A350 7w bister, grn & choc 1.20 .35
Completion of the Korean Institute of Science and Technology, Hongnung, Seoul.

Pres. Park and Diori Hamani A351

1969, Oct. 27
690 A351 7w yel grn & multi 2.25 1.00
a. Souv. sheet of 1, imperf. 14.00 14.00
Visit of Diori Hamani, Pres. of Niger, Oct. 27.

Korean Wrestling A352

No. 692, Fencing. No. 693, Korean karate (taekwondo). No. 694, Volleyball, vert. No. 695, Soccer, vert.

1969, Oct. 28 Perf. 13x12½, 12½x13
691 A352 10w yel grn & multi 3.25 .75
692 A352 10w blue & multi 3.25 .75
693 A352 10w green & multi 3.25 .75
694 A352 10w olive & multi 3.25 .75
695 A352 10w ultra & multi 3.25 .75
Nos. 691-695 (5) 16.25 3.75
50th Natl. Athletic Meet, Seoul, Oct. 28-Nov. 2.

Allegory of National Education Charter — A353

1969, Dec. 5 Litho. Perf. 12½x13
696 A353 7w dull yel & multi 1.20 .35
1st anniv. of the proclamation of the Natl. Education Charter.

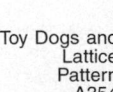

Toy Dogs and Lattice Pattern A354

Candle, Lattice Door and Fence A355

1969, Dec. 11 Photo. Perf. 13½
697 A354 5w green & multi 1.50 .45
698 A355 7w blue & multi 1.50 .45
Issued for New Year 1970.

UPU Monument, Bern, and Korean Woman — A356

1970, Jan. 1 Photo. Perf. 13x13½
699 A356 10w multicolored 12.00 4.00
70th anniv. of Korea's admission to the UPU.

Education Year Emblem and Book — A357

1970, Mar. 10 Litho. Perf. 12½x13
700 A357 10w pink & multi 6.50 2.25
International Education Year 1970.

EXPO '70 Emblem, Seated Buddha, Korean Pavilion A358

1970, Mar. 15 Perf. 13x12½
701 A358 10w multicolored 6.50 1.50
Issued to publicize EXPO '70 International Exhibition, Osaka, Japan, March 15-Sept. 13.

Korean Youths and 4-H Club Emblem — A359

1970, Mar. 28 Perf. 12½x13
702 A359 10w yellow & multi 3.50 .75
Issued to publicize the 15th Korean 4-H Club Central Contest, Suwon, March 28.

Money and Bank Emblem A360

1970, Apr. 9 Litho. Perf. 13x12½
703 A360 10w yellow & multi 2.00 .75
3rd annual Board of Governors' meeting of the Asian Development Bank, Seoul, 4/9-11.

Royal Palanquin — A361

1899 Streetcar A362

Historic Means of Transportation: No. 706, Emperor Sunjong's Cadillac, 1903. No. 707, Nieuport biplane, 1922.

Perf. 13x13½, 13½x13
1970, May 20 Photo.
704 A361 10w citron & multi 2.75 .90
705 A362 10w yellow & multi 2.75 .90
706 A362 10w ocher & multi 2.75 .90
707 A362 10w aqua & multi 2.75 .90
Nos. 704-707 (4) 11.00 3.60

UPU Headquarters A363

1970, May 30 Perf. 13½x13
708 A363 10w multicolored 1.25 .35
New UPU Headquarters in Bern, Switzerland.

Map, Radar and Satellite — A364

1970, June 2 Perf. 13x13½
709 A364 10w sky bl, vio bl & blk 2.00 .75
Issued to commemorate the completion of the Kum San Earth Station of the International Satellite Consortium (INTELSAT).

"PEN" and Manuscript Paper — A365

1970, June 28 Photo. Perf. 13x13½
710 A365 10w bl grn, bl & car 1.25 .35
37th Intl. P.E.N. Cong. (Poets, Playwrights, Editors, Essayists and Novelists), Seoul, June 28-July 4.

Seoul-Pusan Expressway — A366

1970, June 30
711 A366 10w multicolored 2.00 .75
Opening of Seoul-Pusan Expressway.

Postal Code Symbol and Number — A367

1970, July 1
712 A367 10w multicolored 1.25 .40
Issued to publicize the introduction of postal zone numbers, July 1, 1970.

Mail Sorting Machine — A368

1970, July 2
713 A368 10w lt violet & multi 1.25 .40
a. Souv. sheet, 2 each #712-713 110.00 110.00
Mechanization of Korean postal system.

Boy and Children's Hall — A369

1970, July 25
714 A369 10w pink & multi 1.25 .40

Paintings Issue

Jongyangsa Temple and Mt. Kumgang, by Chong Son (1676-1759) — A370

The Fierce Tiger, by Shim Sa-yung (1707-1769) A371

Paintings: No. 716, Mountains and Rivers, by Yi In-moon (1745-1821). No. 717, Mountains and Rivers in Moonlight, by Kim Doo-ryang (1696-1763).

Perf. 13x13½, 13½x13
1970, Aug. 31 Photo.
715 A370 10w blue & multi 2.75 .75
716 A370 10w buff & multi 2.75 .75
717 A371 10w multicolored 2.75 .75

1970, Oct. 30
Paintings: No. 719, Cats and Sparrows, by Pyun Sang-byuk (18th century). No. 720, Dog with puppies, by Yi Am (1499-?).
718 A371 30w multicolored 10.00 2.00
719 A371 30w multicolored 10.00 2.00
720 A371 30w multicolored 10.00 2.00
Nos. 718-720 exist imperf. Value, set $50.

1970, Dec. 30
Paintings: No. 721, Cliff and Boat, by Kim Hong-do (1745-?). No. 722, Cock, Hens and Chick, by Pyun Sang-byuk (early 18th century). No. 723, Woman Playing Flute, by Shin Yun-bok (late 18th century).
721 A371 10w yel brn, blk & red 2.75 .75
722 A371 10w pale rose, blk & grn 2.75 .75
723 A371 10w multicolored 2.75 .75
Nos. 715-723 (9) 46.50 10.50

Souvenir Sheets of 2
715a A370 10w 5.50 5.50
716a A370 10w 5.50 5.50
717a A371 10w 5.50 5.50
718a A371 30w Imperf 35.00 35.00
719a A371 30w Imperf 35.00 35.00
720a A371 30w Imperf 35.00 35.00
721a A371 10w 9.00 9.00

722a	A371	10w	9.00	9.00
723a	A371	10w	9.00	9.00

Nos. 715a-723a (9) 148.50 148.50

Nos. 715a-717a have simulated perforations. Background color of stamps on No. 717a is yellow instead of greenish gray as on No. 717.

Nos. 718a-720a exist perf, twice the imperf values.

Nos. 721a-723a exist imperf. Value, each $3.50.

P.T.T.I. Emblem and Map of Far East — A372

1970, Sept. 6 Litho. Perf. 13x12½
724 A372 10w lt yel grn, bl & dk bl 1.75 .40

Opening of the Councillors' Meeting of the Asian Chapter of the Postal, Telegraph and Telephone Intl. Org., Sept. 6-12.

Korean WAC and Emblem — A373

1970, Sept. 6 Photo. Perf. 13x13½
725 A373 10w blue & multi 1.75 .40

20th anniv. of the founding of the Korean Women's Army Corps.

Pres. Park, Korean Flag and Means of Transportation — A374

Pres. Park, Highways, Factories A375

1970 Perf. 13x13½, 13½x13
726 A374 10w vio bl, blk & car 9.50 4.00
727 A375 10w dk bl, grnsh bl & blk 15.00 4.00

Presidents Park and Hernandez, Flags of Korea, Salvador A376

1970, Sept. 28 Litho. Perf. 13x12½
728 A376 10w dk bl, red & blk 3.25 1.50
a. Souv. sheet of 1, imperf. 100.00 100.00

Visit of Gen. Fidel Sanchez Hernandez, President of El Salvador.

The first printing of 30,000 of No. 728a spelled "Salvadol." Second printing, also 30,000, corrected the error. Value is for first printing. Value, 2nd printing $40, unused or used.

People and Houses A377

1970, Oct. 1 Litho. Perf. 13x12½
729 A377 10w lilac & multi 1.40 1.40

Natl. census of population & housing, Oct. 1.

Diver A378

1970, Oct. 6 Photo. Perf. 12½x13½
730 A378 10w shown 4.50 1.00
a. Souv. sheet of 2, imperf. 10.00 10.00
731 A378 10w Field hockey 4.50 1.00
a. Souv. sheet of 2, imperf. 10.00 10.00
732 A378 10w Baseball 4.50 1.00
a. Souv. sheet of 2, imperf. 10.00 10.00
Nos. 730-732 (3) 13.50 3.00
Nos. 730a-732a (3) 30.00

51st Natl. Athletic Games, Seoul, Oct. 6-11.

Police Emblem and Activities A379

1970, Oct. 21 Litho. Perf. 12½
733 A379 10w ultra & multi 1.60 .55

The 25th Policemen's Day.

Freedom Bell, UN Emblem over Globe — A380

1970, Oct. 24 Photo. Perf. 13x13½
734 A380 10w blue & multi 1.60 .45

25th anniversary of United Nations.

Kite and Holly — A380a

Boar — A381

1970, Dec. 1 Litho. Perf. 13
735 A380a 10w lt blue & multi 1.50 .35
a. Souvenir sheet of 3 7.50 7.50
736 A381 10w green & multi 1.50 .35
a. Souvenir sheet of 3 7.50 7.50

New Year 1971.

Pres. Park Quotation, Globe and Telecommunications Emblems — A382

1970, Dec. 4 Photo.
737 A382 10w multicolored 1.75 .55

For the 15th Communications Day.

Power Dam — A383

Coal Mining A384

Highway Intersection — A385

No. 739, Crate wrapped in world map, & ships. No. 740, Irrigation project & farm, vert. No. 742, Cement factory, vert. No. 743, Fertilizer factory. No. 744, Increased national income (scales). No. 745, Increased savings (factories, bee & coins).

1971 Perf. 13x13½, 13½x13
738 A383 10w blue & multi 2.50 .55
739 A383 10w pale lil & multi 2.50 .55
740 A383 10w green & multi 2.50 .55
741 A384 10w bl grn, lt bl & blk 1.25 .35
742 A384 10w lt bl, vio & brt mag 1.25 .35
743 A384 10w vio, grn & bis 1.25 .35
744 A384 10w pink & multi 1.50 .40
745 A384 10w lt bl grn & multi 1.50 .40
746 A385 10w violet & multi 1.50 .40
Nos. 738-746 (9) 15.75 3.90

Economic Development.

Souvenir Sheets of 1, Imperf.
738a A383 10w 6.50 6.50
739a A383 10w 6.50 6.50
740a A383 10w 6.50 6.50

Souvenir Sheets of 2, Imperf.
741a A384 10w 6.50 6.50
742a A384 10w 6.50 6.50
743a A384 10w 6.50 6.50
744a A384 10w 5.00 5.00
745a A384 10w 5.00 5.00
746a A385 10w 5.00 5.00
Nos. 738a-746a (9) 54.00 54.00

No. 739a exists without date. Value $40.

Torch, Globe and Spider — A386

1971, Mar. 1 Litho. Perf. 12½x13
747 A386 10w gray & multi 1.75 .45

March, the month for anti-espionage and victory over communism.

Reservist, Reserve Forces Emblem A387

1971, Apr. 3 Photo. Perf. 13½x13
748 A387 10w lt ultra & multi 1.75 .45

Home Reserve Forces Day, Apr. 3.

WHO Emblem, Stethoscope, Microscope A388

1971, Apr. 7
749 A388 10w lt bl, pur & yel 1.75 .50

20th World Health Day, Apr. 7.

Subway Tunnel and Train — A389

1971, Apr. 12 Litho. Perf. 12½x13
750 A389 10w multicolored 1.75 .35

Seoul subway construction start.

First Asian Soccer Games, Seoul, May 2-13 — A390

1971, May 2
751 A390 10w grn, dk brn & blk 2.00 .60

Veterans Flag and Veterans — A391

1971, May 8 Photo. Perf. 13x13½
752 A391 10w ultra & multi 1.50 .45

20th Korean Veterans Day.

Girl Scouts and Emblem — A392

1971, May 10
753 A392 10w lilac & multi 1.60 .30

25th anniversary of the Korean Federation of Girl Scouts.

Torch and Development A393

1971, May 16
754 A393 10w lt blue & multi 1.50 .35

10th anniversary of May 16th revolution.

"Telecommunication" — A394

1971, May 17
755 A394 10w blue & multi   1.50   .45
3rd World Telecommunications Day.

UN Organizations A395

Korean Flag — A396

No. 756, ILO. No. 757, FAO. No. 758, General Assembly (UN Headquarters). No. 759, UNESCO. No. 760, WHO. No. 761, World Bank. No. 762, Intl. Development Association (IDA). No. 763, Security Council. No. 764, Intl. Finance Corp. (IFC). No. 765, Intl. Monetary Fund. No. 766, ICAO. No. 767, Economic and Social Council. No. 768, Korean Flag. No. 769, Trusteeship Council. No. 770, UPU. No. 771, ITU. No. 772, World Meteorological Org. (WMO). No. 773, Intl. Court of Justice. No. 774, Intl. Maritime Consultative Org. No. 775, UNICEF. No. 776, Intl. Atomic Energy Agency. No. 777, UN Industrial Development Org. No. 778, UN Commission for the Unification and Rehabilitation of Korea. No. 779, UN Development Program. No. 780, UN Conf. on Trade and Development.

1971, May 30   **Perf. 13½x13**
756 A395 10w green, blk & pink   4.00   1.25
757 A395 10w pink, blk & bl   4.00   1.25
758 A395 10w bl, blk, grn & pink   4.00   1.25
759 A395 10w pink, blk & bl   4.00   1.25
760 A395 10w green, blk & pink   4.00   1.25
761 A395 10w pink, blk & bl   4.00   1.25
762 A395 10w blue, blk & pink   4.00   1.25
763 A395 10w green, blk & pink   4.00   1.25
764 A395 10w blue, blk & pink   4.00   1.25
765 A395 10w pink, blk & bl   4.00   1.25
766 A395 10w blue, blk & pink   4.00   1.25
767 A395 10w green, blk & pink   4.00   1.25
768 A396 10w blue, blk & pink   4.00   1.25
769 A395 10w green, blk & pink   4.00   1.25
770 A395 10w blue, blk & pink   4.00   1.25
771 A395 10w pink, blk & bl   4.00   1.25
772 A395 10w blue, blk & pink   4.00   1.25
773 A395 10w green, blk & pink   4.00   1.25
774 A395 10w blue, blk & pink   4.00   1.25
775 A395 10w pink, blk & bl   4.00   1.25
776 A395 10w green, blk & pink   4.00   1.25
777 A395 10w pink, blk & bl   4.00   1.25
778 A395 10w blue, blk & pink   4.00   1.25
779 A395 10w pink, blk & bl   4.00   1.25
780 A395 10w green, blk & pink   4.00   1.25
    Nos. 756-780 (25)   100.00   31.25
Sheet of 50 incorporates 2 each of Nos. 756-780.

Boat Ride, by Shin Yun-bok — A397

Man and Boy under Pine Tree — A398

Paintings by Shin Yun-bok: No. 782, Greeting travelers. No. 783, Sword dance. No. 784, Lady traveling with servants. No. 785, Man and woman on the road.

     Perf. 13x13½, 13½x13
1971, June 20   **Photo.**
781 A397 10w multicolored   6.50   2.00
782 A397 10w multicolored   6.50   2.00
783 A397 10w multicolored   6.50   2.00
784 A397 10w multicolored   6.50   2.00
785 A397 10w multicolored   6.50   2.00
   b.   Vert. strip of 5, #781-785   39.00   39.00
786 A398 10w multicolored   6.50   2.00
    Nos. 781-786 (6)   39.00   12.00
     Souvenir Sheets of 2
781a A397 10w   12.00   12.00
782a A397 10w   12.00   12.00
783a A397 10w   12.00   12.00
784a A397 10w   12.00   12.00
785a A397 10w   12.00   12.00
786a A398 10w   12.00   12.00
    Nos. 781a-786a (6)   72.00   72.00

Types A397-A398 with Inscription at Left

Paintings: No. 787, Farmyard scene, by Kim Deuk-shin. No. 788, Family living in valley, by Lee Chae-kwan. No. 789, Man reading book under pine tree, by Lee Chae-kwan.

1971, July 20
787 A397 10w pale grn & multi   3.50   1.25
788 A398 10w pale grn & multi   3.50   1.25
789 A398 10w lt yel grn & multi   3.50   1.25
    Nos. 787-789 (3)   10.50   3.75
     Souvenir Sheets of 2
787a A397 10w   9.00   9.00
788a A398 10w   9.00   9.00
789a A398 10w   9.00   9.00
    Nos. 787a-789a (3)   27.00   27.00

Teacher and Students, by Kim Hong-do A399

Paintings by Kim Hong-do (Yi Dynasty): No. 791, Wrestlers. No. 792, Dancer and musicians. No. 793, Weavers. No. 794, At the Well.

1971, Aug. 20   **Perf. 13½x13**
790 A399 10w blk, lt grn & rose   6.50   3.25
791 A399 10w blk, lt grn & rose   6.50   3.25
792 A399 10w blk, lt grn & rose   6.50   3.25
793 A399 10w blk, lt grn & rose   6.50   3.25
794 A399 10w blk, lt grn & rose   6.50   3.25
   b.   Horiz. strip of 5, #790-794   35.00   35.00
     Souvenir Sheets of 2
790a A399 10w   12.00   12.00
791a A399 10w   12.00   12.00
792a A399 10w   12.00   12.00

793a A399 10w   12.00   12.00
794a A399 10w   12.00   12.00
    Nos. 790a-794a (5)   60.00   60.00

Pres. Park, Highway and Phoenix A400

1971, July 1   **Perf. 13½x13**
795 A400 10w grn, blk & org   20.00   2.00
   a.   Souvenir sheet of 2   70.00   70.00
Inauguration of President Park Chung Hee for a third term, July 1.

Campfire and Tents — A401

1971, Aug. 2   **Photo.**   **Perf. 13x13½**
796 A401 10w blue grn & multi   1.60   .35
13th Boy Scout World Jamboree, Asagiri Plain, Japan, Aug. 2-10.

Symbol of Conference A402

1971, Sept. 27   **Perf. 13**
797 A402 10w multicolored   1.25   .45
   a.   Souvenir sheet of 2   50.00   50.00
Asian Labor Ministers' Conference, Seoul, Sept. 27-30.

Archers — A403

1971, Oct. 8   **Photo.**   **Perf. 13x13½**
798 A403 10w shown   2.00   .75
   a.   Souvenir sheet of 3   35.00   35.00
799 A403 10w Judo   2.00   .75
   a.   Souvenir sheet of 3   35.00   35.00
52nd National Athletic Meet.

Taeguk on Palette A404

1971, Oct. 11   **Perf. 13½x13**
800 A404 10w yellow & multi   1.25   .25
20th National Fine Arts Exhibition.

Physician, Globe and Emblem A405

1971, Oct. 13
801 A405 10w multicolored   1.25   .25
7th Congress of the Confederation of Medical Associations in Asia and Oceania.

Symbols of Contest Events — A406

1971, Oct. 20   **Photo.**   **Perf. 13x13½**
802 A406 10w multicolored   1.25   .25
   a.   Souvenir sheet of 2   40.00   40.00
2nd National Skill Contest for High School Students.

Slide Caliper and KS Emblem A407

1971, Nov. 11   **Perf. 13x13½**
803 A407 10w multicolored   1.25   .25
10th anniversary of industrial standardization in Korea.

Rats — A408

Japanese Crane — A409

1971, Dec. 1
804 A408 10w multicolored   1.75   .35
   a.   Souvenir sheet of 3   25.00   25.00
805 A409 10w multicolored   1.75   .35
   a.   Souvenir sheet of 3   25.00   25.00
New Year 1972.

Emblem of Hangul Hakhoe and Hangul Letters — A410

1971, Dec. 3   **Photo.**
806 A410 10w dk blue & multi   1.00   .25
50th anniversary of Korean Language Research Society (Hangul Hakhoe).

Red Cross Headquarters and Map of Korea A411

1971, Dec. 31   **Perf. 13½x13**
807 A411 10w multicolored   1.90   .60
   a.   Souvenir sheet of 2   12.50   12.50
First South and North Korean Red Cross Conference, Panmunjom, Aug. 20, 1971.

Globe and
Book — A412

1972, Jan. 5   **Perf. 13x13½**
808 A412 10w multicolored   1.10   .30
     a.   Souvenir sheet of 2   12.50   12.50
International Book Year 1972.

Intelsat 4
Sending
Signals to
Korea
A413

1972, Jan. 31   **Perf. 13½x13**
809 A413 10w dk blue & multi   1.10   .30
Korea's entry into ITU, 20th anniv.

Figure Skating,
Sapporo '72
Emblem — A414

Design: No. 811, Speed skating.

1972, Feb. 3   **Perf. 13x13½**
810 A414 10w lt & dk bl & car   1.90   .60
811 A414 10w lt & dk bl & car   1.90   .60
     a.   Souvenir sheet of 2, #810-
        811   12.50   12.50
11th Winter Olympic Games, Sapporo,
Japan, Feb. 3-13.

Map of Korea with
Forest Sites — A415

1972, Mar. 10   **Photo.**   **Perf. 13x13**
812 A415 10w buff, bl grn & red   1.25   .30
Publicity for forests planted to mark hope for
re-unification of Korea.

Junior
Chamber of
Commerce
Emblem and
Beetles
A416

1972, Mar. 19   **Perf. 13½x13**
813 A416 10w pink & multi   1.25   .30
Junior Chamber of Commerce, 20th
anniversary.

UN Emblem,
Agriculture and
Industry — A417

1972, Mar. 28   **Perf. 13x13½**
814 A417 10w violet, grn & car   1.25   .30
Economic Commission for Asia and the Far
East (ECAFE), 25th anniversary.

Flags — A418

1972, Apr. 1   **Perf. 13½x13**
815 A418 10w blue & multi   1.25   .30
Asian-Oceanic Postal Union, 10th anniv.

Homeland Reserve
Forces Flag — A419

1972, Apr. 1   **Photo.**   **Perf. 13x13½**
816 A419 10w yellow & multi   1.50   .40
Homeland Reserve Forces Day, Apr. 1.

YWCA Emblem,
Butterflies — A420

1972, Apr. 20
817 A420 10w violet & multi   1.75   .40
50th anniv. of the YWCA of Korea.

Community
Projects — A421

1972, May 1   **Perf. 13x13½**
818 A421 10w pink & multi   1.25   .40
Rural rehabilitation and construction
movement.

Korean Flag &
Inscription — A422

1972, May 1
819 A422 10w green & multi   1.25   .40
Anti-espionage and victory over communism month.

Children with
Balloons
A423

1972, May 5   **Perf. 13½x13**
820 A423 10w yellow & multi   1.25   .40
Children's Day, May 5.

King
Munyong's
Gold Earrings
A424

Design: No. 822, Gold ornament from King's
crown, vert.

1972, May 10   **Perf. 13½x13, 13x13½**
821 A424 10w green & multi   1.40   .40
822 A424 10w green & multi   1.40   .40
National treasures from tomb of King Munyong of Paekche, who reigned 501-523.

Kojo
Island — A425

National parks: No. 823, Crater Lake.

1972, May 30   **Perf. 13½x13**
823 A425 10w blue grn & multi   3.25   .40
824 A425 10w green & multi   3.25   .40

UN Conference on
Human
Environment,
Stockholm, June 5-
16 — A426

10w, Daisy, environment emblem.

1972, May 30   **Litho.**   **Perf. 13x13½**
825 A426 10w multicolored   1.25   .35
     a.   Souvenir sheet of 2   8.50   8.50

7th Meeting of
Asian-Pacific
Council
(ASPAC) — A427

10w, Gwanghwa Gate, flags of participants.

1972, June 14
826 A427 10w multicolored   1.25   .35

Farm and
Fish Hatchery
A428

Third Five-Year Plan Issue
1972, July 1   **Photo.**   **Perf. 13½x13**
827 A428 10w shown   2.00   .50
828 A428 10w Steel industry and
        products   2.00   .50
829 A428 10w Globe and cargo   2.00   .50
     Nos. 827-829 (3)   6.00   1.50
3rd Economic Development Five-Year Plan.

Weight
Lifting — A429

1972, Aug. 26   **Photo.**   **Perf. 13x13½**
830 A429 20w shown   1.25   .50
831 A429 20w Judo   1.25   .50
     a.   Souvenir sheet of 2, #830-831   6.00   6.00
     b.   Pair, #830-831   5.00   2.50
832 A429 20w Boxing   1.25   .50
833 A429 20w Wrestling   1.25   .50
     a.   Souvenir sheet of 2, #832-833   6.00   6.00
     b.   Pair, #832-833   5.00   2.50
     Nos. 830-833 (4)   5.00   2.00
20th Olympic Games, Munich, Aug. 26-
Sept. 11. Nos. 831b, 833b each printed
checkerwise.

Families
Reunited by
Red Cross
A430

1972, Aug. 30   **Photo.**   **Perf. 13x13½**
834 A430 10w lt blue & multi   1.00   .70
     a.   Souvenir sheet of 2   27.50   27.50
Plenary meeting of the South-North Red
Cross Conference, Pyongyang, Aug. 30, 1972.

Bulkuk-sa
Temple,
Kyongju
Park — A431

Bopju-sa
Temple, Mt.
Sokri
Park — A432

1972, Sept. 20   **Photo.**   **Perf. 13½x13**
835 A431 10w brown & multi   1.50   .45
836 A432 10w blue & multi   1.50   .45
National parks.

"5" and Conference
Emblem — A433

1972, Sept. 25   **Perf. 13x13½**
837 A433 10w vio blue & multi   1.20   .35
Fifth Asian Judicial Conf., Seoul, 9/25-29.

Lions
Emblem,
Taeguk
Fan — A434

1972, Sept. 28   **Perf. 13½x13**
838 A434 10w multicolored   1.40   .35
11th Orient and Southeast Asian Lions Convention, Seoul, Sept. 28-30.

Scout Taking Oath, Korean Flag and Scout Emblem A435

1972, Oct. 5
839 A435 10w yellow & multi 2.00 .45
Boy Scouts of Korea, 50th anniversary.

Children and Ox — A436

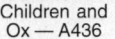

Children in Balloon — A437

1972, Dec. 1 Photo. Perf. 13x13½
840 A436 10w green & multi 1.40 .40
  a. Souvenir sheet of 2 5.00 5.00
841 A437 10w blue & multi 1.40 .40
  a. Souvenir sheet of 2 5.00 5.00
New Year 1973.

Mt. Naejang Park and Temple — A438

Mt. Sorang and Madeungryong Pass — A439

1972, Dec. 10 Perf. 13x13½, 13½x13
842 A438 10w multicolored 1.50 .40
843 A439 10w multicolored 1.50 .40
National parks.

Pres. Park, Korean Flag and Modern Landscape — A440

1972, Dec. 27 Perf. 13x13½
844 A440 10w multicolored 7.50 1.50
  a. Souvenir sheet of 2 67.50 67.50
Inauguration of Park Chung Hee for a 4th term as president of Korea.

Tourism Issue

Kyongbok Palace (National Museum) A441

Mt. Sorak and Kejo-am Temple A442

1973, Feb. 20 Photo. Perf. 13½x13
845 A441 10w multicolored 1.25 .40
846 A442 10w multicolored 1.25 .40

Palmi Island and Beach — A443

Sain-am Rock, Mt. Dokjol — A444

1973, Apr. 20 Perf. 13x13½
847 A443 10w multicolored 1.50 .40
848 A444 10w multicolored 1.50 .40

Shrine for Adm. Li Sun-sin — A445

Limestone Cavern, Kusan-ni — A446

1973, June 20
849 A445 10w multicolored 1.50 .40
850 A446 10w multicolored 1.50 .40

Namhae Bridge A447

Hongdo Island — A448

1973, Aug. 20 Perf. 13½x13
851 A447 10w multicolored 1.50 .30
852 A448 10w multicolored 1.50 .30

Mt. Mai — A449

Tangerine Orchard, Cheju Island A450

1973, Oct. 20
853 A449 10w multicolored 1.00 .25
854 A450 10w multicolored 1.00 .25
  Nos. 845-854 (10) 13.50 3.50

Praying Family — A451

1973, Mar. 1 Perf. 13x13½
855 A451 10w yellow & multi 1.25 .30
Prayer for national unification.

Flags of Korea and South Viet Nam, Victory Sign — A452

1973, Mar. 1
856 A452 10w violet & multi 1.25 .30
Return of Korean Expeditionary Force from South Viet Nam.

Workers, Factory, Cogwheel — A453

1973, Mar. 10 Unwmk.
857 A453 10w blue & multi 1.10 .30
10th Labor Day.

Satellite, WMO Emblem — A454

1973, Mar. 23
858 A454 10w blue & multi 1.10 .30
  a. Souvenir sheet of 2 5.50 5.50
Cent. of Intl. Meteorological Cooperation.

King's Ceremonial Robe — A455

Traditional Korean Costumes (Yi dynasty): No. 860, Queen's ceremonial dress. No. 861, King's robe. No. 862, Queen's robe. No. 863, Crown Prince. No. 864, Princess. No. 865, Courtier. No. 866, Royal bridal gown. No. 867, Official's wife. No. 868, Military official.

1973 Photo. Perf. 13½x13
859 A455 10w ocher & multi 3.50 .70
860 A455 10w salmon & multi 3.50 .70
861 A455 10w rose lil & multi 3.25 .60
862 A455 10w apple grn & multi 3.25 .60
863 A455 10w lt blue & multi 3.00 .60
864 A455 10w lil rose & multi 3.00 .60
865 A455 10w yellow & multi 1.50 .50
866 A455 10w lt blue & multi 1.50 .50
867 A455 10w ocher & multi 1.25 .35
868 A455 10w lil rose & multi 1.25 .35
  Nos. 859-868 (10) 25.00 5.50

Issued: Nos. 859-860, 3/30; Nos. 861-862, 5/30; Nos. 863-864, 7/30; Nos. 865-866, 9/30; Nos. 867-868, 11/30.

Souvenir Sheets of 2
859a A455 10w (#1) 7.50 7.50
860a A455 10w (#2) 7.50 7.50
861a A455 10w (#3) 7.50 7.50
862a A455 10w (#4) 7.50 7.50
863a A455 10w (#5) 7.50 7.50
864a A455 10w (#6) 7.50 7.50
865a A455 10w (#7) 5.00 5.00
866a A455 10w (#8) 5.00 5.00
867a A455 10w (#9) 5.00 5.00
868a A455 10w (#10) 5.00 5.00
  Nos. 859a-868a (10) 65.00 65.00

Parenthetical numbers after souvenir sheet listings appear in top marginal inscriptions.

Nurse Holding Lamp — A456

1973, Apr. 1 Perf. 13½x13
869 A456 10w rose & multi 1.25 .25
50th anniv. of Korean Nurses Association.

Homeland Reservists and Flag — A457

1973, Apr. 7 Perf. 13x13½
870 A457 10w yellow & multi 1.50 .30
Homeland Reserve Forces Day on 5th anniversary of their establishment.

Table Tennis Player, and Globe — A458

1973, May 23 Perf. 13x13½
871 A458 10w pink & multi 2.50 .70
Victory of Korean women's table tennis team, 32nd Intl. Table Tennis Championships, Sarajevo, Yugoslavia, Apr. 5-15.

World Vision Children's Choir — A459

1973, June 25 Perf. 13x13½
872 A459 10w multicolored 1.50 .30
20th anniversary of World Vision International, a Christian service organization.

Converter, Pohang Steel Works — A460

1973, July 3 Perf. 13x13½
873 A460 10w blue & multi 1.00 .45
Inauguration of Pohang iron and steel plant.

INTERPOL Emblem A461

1973, Sept. 3 Perf. 13½x13
874 A461 10w lt violet & multi 1.25 .25
50th anniversary of the International Criminal Police Organization (INTERPOL).

Children with
Stamp
Albums
A462

1973, Oct. 12   *Perf. 13½x13*
875   A462 10w dp grn & multi   .90   .30
a.   Souvenir sheet of 2   16.00 16.00
Philatelic Week, Oct. 12-18.

Woman Hurdler — A463

1973, Oct. 12   *Perf. 12½x13½*
876   A463 10w shown   1.20   .30
877   A463 10w Tennis player   1.20   .30
54th Natl. Athletic Meet, Pusan, Oct. 12-17.

Soyang River
Dam, Map
Showing
Location
A464

1973, Oct. 15   *Perf. 13½x13*
878   A464 10w blue & multi   .50   .25
Inauguration of Soyang River Dam and
hydroelectric plant.

Fire from Match and
Cigarette — A465

1973, Nov. 1   *Perf. 13x13½*
879   A465 10w multicolored   .70   .25
10th Fire Prevention Day.

Tiger and   Toys — A467
Candles — A466

1973, Dec. 1 Photo.   *Perf. 13x13½*
880   A466 10w emerald & multi   1.00   .30
a.   Souvenir sheet of 2   5.00 5.00
881   A467 10w blue & multi   1.00   .30
a.   Souvenir sheet of 2   5.00 5.00
New Year 1974.

Human Rights
Flame, and
Head — A468

1973, Dec. 10   *Perf. 13½x13*
882   A468 10w orange & multi   .80   .25
25th anniversary of Universal Declaration of
Human Rights.

Musical Instruments Issue

Komunko, Six-stringed Zither — A469

Design: 30w, Nagak, shell trumpet.

1974, Feb. 20 Photo.   *Perf. 13x13½*
883   A469 10w lt bl, blk & brn   1.10   .30
884   A469 30w orange & multi   3.00   .60

1974, Apr. 20
Designs: 10w, Tchouk; wooden hammer in
slanted box, used to start orchestra. 30w, Eu;
crouching tiger, used to stop orchestra.
885   A469 10w brt blue & multi   1.25   .25
886   A469 30w lt green & multi   2.50   .35

1974, June 20
Designs: 10w, A-chaing, 7-stringed instrument. 30w, Kyobang-ko, drum.
887   A469 10w dull yel & multi   1.50   .25
888   A469 30w salmon pink &
              multi   2.50   .35

1974, Aug. 20
Designs: 10w, So, 16-pipe ritual instrument.
30w, Kaikeum, 2-stringed fiddle.
889   A469 10w lt blue & multi   1.00   .30
890   A469 30w brt pink & multi   2.00   .45

1974, Oct. 20
10w, Pak (clappers). 30w, Pyenchong (bell
chimes).
891   A469 10w lt lilac & multi   1.00   .30
892   A469 30w lemon & multi   2.00   .45
        Nos. 883-892 (10)   17.85 3.60

Souvenir Sheets of 2
883a   A469 10w (#1)   5.00   5.00
884a   A469 30w (#2)   7.50   7.50
885a   A469 10w (#3)   4.00   4.00
886a   A469 30w (#4)   6.00   6.00
887a   A469 10w (#5)   4.00   4.00
888a   A469 30w (#6)   6.00   6.00
889a   A469 10w (#7)   3.00   3.00
890a   A469 30w (#8)   5.00   5.00
891a   A469 10w (#9)   3.00   3.00
892a   A469 30w (#10)   5.00   5.00
        Nos. 883a-892a (10)   48.50 48.50

Fruit Issue

Apricots — A470

1974, Mar. 30 Photo.   *Perf. 13x13½*
893   A470 10w shown   1.00   .30
894   A470 30w Strawberries   2.50   .45

1974, May 30
895   A470 10w Peaches   1.00   .30
896   A470 30w Grapes   2.50   .45

1974, July 30
897   A470 10w Pears   .60   .30
898   A470 30w Apples   2.25   .45

1974, Sept. 30
899   A470 10w Cherries   .80   .30
900   A470 30w Persimmons   2.00   .45

1974, Nov. 30
901   A470 10w Tangerines   .65   .30
902   A470 30w Chestnuts   1.60   .35
        Nos. 893-902 (10)   14.90 3.65

Souvenir Sheets of 2
893a   A470 10w (#1)   3.50   3.50
894a   A470 30w (#2)   7.50   7.50
895a   A470 10w (#3)   3.50   3.50
896a   A470 30w (#4)   7.00   7.00
897a   A470 10w (#5)   3.00   3.00
898a   A470 30w (#6)   7.50   7.50
899a   A470 10w (#7)   2.50   2.50
900a   A470 30w (#8)   3.50   3.50
901a   A470 10w (#9)   3.00   3.00
902a   A470 30w (#10)   3.50   3.50
        Nos. 893a-902a (10)   44.50 44.50

Reservist and
Factory
A471

1974, Apr. 6 Photo.   *Perf. 13½x13*
903   A471 10w yellow & multi   .80   .25
Homeland Reserve Forces Day.

WPY Emblem and
Scales — A472

1974, Apr. 10   *Perf. 13x13½*
904   A472 10w salmon & multi   .65   .25
a.   Souvenir sheet of 2   5.00 5.00
World Population Year 1974.

Train and Communications
Emblem — A473

1974, Apr. 22   *Perf. 13½x13*
905   A473 10w multicolored   .75   .25
19th Communications Day.

Emblem and
Stylized
Globe — A474

1974, May 6 Photo.   *Perf. 13*
906   A474 10w red lilac & multi   .65   .25
22nd Session of Intl. Chamber of Commerce (Eastern Division), Seoul, May 6-8.

New Dock at
Inchon
A475

1974, May 10
907   A475 10w yellow & multi   .80   .25
Dedication of dock, Inchon.

UNESCO Emblem,
"20" and Yin
Yang — A476

1974, June 14 Photo. *Perf. 13*
908   A476 10w org yel & multi   .65   .25
20th anniversary of the Korean National
Commission for UNESCO.

EXPLO '74
Emblems — A477

Design: No. 910, EXPLO emblem rising
from map of Korea.

1974, Aug. 13 Photo.   *Perf. 13*
909   A477 10w orange & multi   .55   .25
910   A477 10w blue & multi   .55   .25
EXPLO '74, International Christian Congress, Yoido Islet, Seoul, Aug. 13-18.

Subway, Bus and
Plane — A478

1974, Aug. 15
911   A478 10w green & multi   1.00   .25
Inauguration of Seoul subway (first in
Korea), Aug. 15, 1974.

Target Shooting — A479

1974, Oct. 8 Photo.   *Perf. 13x13½*
912   A479 10w shown   .65   .25
913   A479 30w Rowing   1.90   .40
55th National Athletic Meet.

UPU Emblem
A480

1974, Oct. 9   *Perf. 13*
914   A480 10w yellow & multi   .50   .25
a.   Souvenir sheet of 2   5.50 5.50
Cent. of UPU. See No. C43.

International
Landmarks — A481

1974, Oct. 11
915   A481 10w multicolored   .65   .25
Intl. People to People Conf., Seoul, 10/11-14.

Korea Nos. 1-
2 — A482

1974, Oct. 17
916   A482 10w lilac & multi   .80   .25
a.   Souvenir sheet of 2   8.00 8.00
Philatelic Week, Oct. 17-23 and 90th anniversary of first Korean postage stamps.

Taekwondo and Kukkiwon Center A483

1974, Oct. 18
917 A483 10w yellow grn & multi .65 .25
First Asian Taekwondo (self-defense) Games, Seoul, Oct. 18-20.

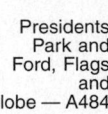

Presidents Park and Ford, Flags and Globe — A484

1974, Nov. 22 Photo. Perf. 13
918 A484 10y multicolored 1.10 .30
a. Souvenir sheet of 2 8.50 8.50
Visit of Pres. Gerald R. Ford to South Korea.

Yook Young Soo — A485

1974, Nov. 29
919 A485 10w green 1.00 .30
920 A485 10w orange 1.00 .30
921 A485 10w lilac 1.00 .30
922 A485 10w blue 1.00 .30
a. Souvenir sheet of 4, #919-922 35.00 35.00
b. Block of 4, #919-922 4.00 3.00
Yook Young Soo (1925-1974), wife of Pres. Park.

Rabbits — A486   Good-luck Purse — A487

1974, Dec. 1 Litho. Perf. 12½x13
923 A486 10w multicolored .75 .25
a. Souvenir sheet of 2 4.50 4.50
924 A487 10w multicolored .75 .25
a. Souvenir sheet of 2 4.50 4.50
New Year 1975.

Good-luck Key and Pigeon A488

1975, Jan. 1 Photo. Perf. 13
925 A488 10w lt blue & multi .65 .25
Introduction of Natl. Welfare Insurance System.

UPU Emblem and "75" — A489   UPU Emblem and Paper Plane — A490

1975, Jan. 1
926 A489 10w yellow & multi .60 .25
927 A490 10w lt blue & multi .60 .25
75th anniv. of Korea's membership in UPU.

Dr. Albert Schweitzer, Map of Africa, Hypodermic Needle A491

1975, Jan. 14
928 A491 10w olive 1.00 .35
929 A491 10w brt rose 1.00 .35
930 A491 10w orange 1.00 .35
931 A491 10w brt green 1.00 .35
a. Block of 4, #928-931 5.00 3.00

Folk Dance Issue

Dancer — A492   Bupo Nori — A492a

No. 933, Dancer with fan. No. 934, Woman with butterfly sleeves. No. 935, Group of Women. No. 936, Pongsan mask dance. No. 937, Pusan mask dance. No. 938, Buddhist drum dance. No. 939, Bara (cymbals) dance. No. 940, Sogo dance.

1975, Feb. 20 Photo. Perf. 13
932 A492 10w emerald & multi .85 .25
933 A492 10w brt blue & multi .85 .25
1975, Apr. 20
934 A492 10w yel grn & multi .90 .25
935 A492 10w yellow & multi .90 .25
1975, June 20
936 A492 10w pink & multi .90 .25
937 A492 10w blue & multi .90 .25
1975, Aug. 20
938 A492 20w yellow & multi 1.40 .45
939 A492 20w salmon & multi 1.40 .45
1975, Oct. 20
940 A492 20w blue & multi 1.40 .45
941 A492a 20w yellow & multi 1.40 .45
Nos. 932-941 (10) 10.90 3.30

Souvenir Sheets of 2
932a A492 10w (#1) 2.25 2.25
933a A492 10w (#2) 2.25 2.25
934a A492 10w (#3) 2.00 2.00
935a A492 10w (#4) 2.00 2.00
936a A492 10w (#5) 2.00 2.00
937a A492 10w (#6) 2.00 2.00
938a A492 20w (#7) 3.00 3.00
939a A492 20w (#8) 3.00 3.00
940a A492 20w (#9) 2.75 2.75
941a A492a 20w (#10) 2.75 2.75
Nos. 932a-941a (10) 24.00 24.00

Globe and Rotary Emblem A493

1975, Feb. 23
942 A493 10w multicolored .65 .25
Rotary International, 70th anniversary.

Women and IWY Emblem A494

1975, Mar. 8
943 A494 10w multicolored .65 .25
International Women's Year 1975.

Flower Issue

Violets A495   Anemones A496

Clematis Patens — A496a   Broad-bell Flowers — A496b

Designs: No. 946, Rhododendron. No. 948, Thistle. No. 949, Iris. No. 951, Bush clover. No. 952, Camellia. No. 953, Gentian.

1975, Mar. 15
944 A495 10w orange & multi .80 .25
945 A496 10w yellow & multi .80 .25
1975, May 15
946 A495 10w dk green & multi .90 .25
947 A496a 10w yellow grn & multi .90 .25
1975, July 15
948 A495 10w emerald & multi .90 .25
949 A495 10w blue & multi .90 .25
1975, Sept. 15
950 A496b 20w yellow & multi 1.40 .30
951 A495 20w blue grn & multi 1.40 .30
1975, Nov. 15
952 A495 20w yellow & multi 2.00 2.00
953 A496 20w salmon & multi 2.00 .50
Nos. 944-953 (10) 12.00 4.60

Forest and Water Resources — A497

1975, Mar. 20
954 A497 Strip of 4 5.00 3.00
a. 10w Saemaeul forest .75 .30
b. 10w Dam and reservoir .75 .30
c. 10w Green forest .75 .30
d. 10w Timber industry .75 .30
Natl. Tree Planting Month, Mar. 21-Apr. 20.

Map of Korea, HRF Emblem — A498

1975, Apr. 12 Photo. Perf. 13
955 A498 10w blue & multi .80 .25
Homeland Reserve Forces Day.

Lily — A499   Ceramic Jar — A500

Ceramic Vase A501   Adm. Li Sun-sin A502

1975 Photo. Perf. 13½x13
963 A499 6w green & bl grn .65 .25
964 A500 50w gray grn & brn .85 .25
965 A501 60w brown & yellow 1.10 .25
966 A502 100w carmine 2.25 .25
Nos. 963-966 (4) 4.85 1.00
Issued: Nos. 964-965, 3/15/75; Nos. 963, 966, 10/10/75.

Metric System Symbols A507

1975, May 20 Perf. 13
975 A507 10w salmon & multi .65 .25
Centenary of International Meter Convention, Paris, 1875.

Praying Soldier, Incense Burner A508

1975, June 6 Photo. Perf. 13
976 A508 10w multicolored .65 .25
20th Memorial Day.

Flags of Korea, UN and US — A509

Designs (Flags of): No. 978, Ethiopia, France, Greece, Canada, South Africa. No. 979, Luxembourg, Australia, Great Britain, Colombia, Turkey. No. 980, Netherlands, Belgium, Philippines, New Zealand, Thailand.

1975, June 25 Photo. Perf. 13
977 A509 10w dk blue & multi .75 .30
978 A509 10w dk blue & multi .75 .30
979 A509 10w dk blue & multi .75 .30
980 A509 10w dk blue & multi .75 .30
a. Strip of 4, #977-980 5.00 3.00
25th anniv. of beginning of Korean War.

Presidents Park and Bongo, Flags of Korea and Gabon A510

1975, July 5
981 A510 10w blue & multi   .65 .25
  a.   Souvenir sheet of 2   3.00 3.00
Visit of Pres. Albert Bongo of Gabon, 7/5-8.

Scout Emblem, Tents and Neckerchief — A511

1975, July 29   **Photo.**   *Perf. 13*
982 A511 10w shown   .90 .30
983 A511 10w Pick and oath   .90 .30
984 A511 10w Tents   .90 .30
985 A511 10w Ax, rope and tree   .90 .30
986 A511 10w Campfire   .90 .30
  a.   Strip of 5, #982-986   5.50 3.50
Nordjamb 75, 14th Boy Scout Jamboree, Lillehammer, Norway, July 29-Aug. 7.

Flame and Broken Chain A512

Balloons with Symbols of Development over Map — A513

1975, Aug. 15   *Perf. 13½x13*
987 A512 20w gold & multi   .85 .25
988 A513 20w silver & multi   .85 .25
30th anniversary of liberation.

Taekwondo — A514

1975, Aug. 26   *Perf. 13*
989 A514 20w multicolored   .65 .25
2nd World Taekwondo Championships, Seoul, Aug. 25-Sept. 1.

National Assembly and Emblem A515

1975, Sept. 1   **Photo.**   *Perf. 13½x13*
990 A515 20w multicolored   .65 .25
Completion of National Assembly Building.

Convention Emblem and Dump Truck — A516

1975, Sept. 7   **Photo.**   *Perf. 13½x13*
991 A516 20w ultra & multi   .65 .25
14th Convention of the Intl. Fed. of Asian and Western Pacific Contractors.

Cassegrainian Telescope and Morse Key — A517

1975, Sept. 28
992 A517 20w red lil, org & blk   .65 .25
90th anniversary of Korean telecommunications system.

Stalactite Cave, Yeongweol A518

View of Mt. Sorak A519

1975, Sept. 28
993 A518 20w multicolored   .65 .25
994 A519 20w multicolored   .65 .25
International Tourism Day.

Armed Forces Flag and Missiles — A519a

1975, Oct. 1   **Photo.**   *Perf. 13*
994A A519a 20w multicolored   .65 .25
Armed Forces Day.

Gymnastics A520

Handball A521

1975, Oct. 7   **Photo.**   *Perf. 13*
995 A520 20w yellow & multi   .50 .25
996 A521 20w multicolored   .50 .25
56th Natl. Athletic Meet, Taegu, Oct. 7-12.

Stamp Collecting Kangaroo — A522

1975, Oct. 8
997 A522 20w multicolored   .65 .25
Philatelic Week, Oct. 8-14.

Hands and UN Emblem — A523

1975, Oct. 24
998 A523 20w multicolored   .65 .25
United Nations, 30th anniversary.

Red Cross and Activities — A524

1975, Oct. 30
999 A524 20w orange, red & brn   .65 .25
Korean Red Cross, 70th anniversary.

Emblem and Dove — A525

1975, Nov. 30   **Photo.**   *Perf. 13*
1000 A525 20w multicolored   .65 .25
Asian Parliamentary Union, 10th anniv.

Children Playing — A526

Dragon — A527

1975, Dec. 1
1001 A526 20w multicolored   .70 .25
  a.   Souvenir sheet of 2   2.00 2.00
1002 A527 20w multicolored   .70 .25
  a.   Souvenir sheet of 2   2.00 2.00
New Year 1976.

Inchong-Bukpyong Railroad — A528

1975, Dec. 5   **Photo.**   *Perf. 13*
1003 A528 20w multicolored   .65 .25
Opening of electric cross-country railroad.

Butterfly Issue

Dilipa Fenestra A529

Byasa Alcinous Klug — A529a

Graphium Sarpedon A529b

Fabriciana Nerippe A529c

Nymphalis Xanthomelas A529d

Butterflies: No. 1005, Luehdorfia puziloi. No. 1006, Papilio xuthus linne. No. 1007, Parnassius bremeri. No. 1008, Colias erate esper. No. 1010, Hestina assimilis.

1976, Jan. 20   **Photo.**   *Perf. 13*
1004 A529 20w dp rose & multi   2.00 .30
1005 A529 20w dp blue & multi   2.00 .30
1976, Mar. 20
1006 A529 20w yellow & multi   2.00 .30
1007 A529 20w yel grn & multi   2.00 .30
1976, June 20
1008 A529 20w lt violet & multi   2.00 .30
1009 A529a 20w citron & multi   2.00 .30
1976, Aug. 20
1010 A529 20w tan & multi   2.25 .75
1011 A529b 20w lt gray & multi   2.25 .75
1976, Oct. 20
1012 A529c 20w lt grn & multi   2.25 .90
1013 A529d 20w lilac & multi   2.25 .90
  Nos. 1004-1013 (10)   21.00 5.10

Emblems of Science, Industry and KIST — A530

1976, Feb. 10   **Photo.**   *Perf. 13*
1014 A530 20w multicolored   .65 .25
Korean Institute of Science and Technology (KIST), 10th anniversary.

Birds Issue

A531

A532

A532a

A532b

A532c

A532d

A532e

A532f

A532g

A532h

No. 1015, Siberian Bustard. No. 1016, White-naped Crane. No. 1017, Blue-winged pitta. No. 1018, Tristam's woodpecker. No. 1019, Wood pigeon. No. 1020, Oyster catcher. No. 1021, Black-faced spoonbill. No. 1022, Black stork. No. 1023, Whooper swan. No. 1024, Black vulture.

1976, Feb. 20   Photo.   Perf. 13x13½
1015 A531 20w multicolored   1.50 .35
1016 A532 20w multicolored   1.50 .35
1976, May 20
1017 A532a 20w multicolored   1.50 .35
1018 A532b 20w multicolored   1.50 .35
1976, July 20
1019 A532c 20w multicolored   1.50 .35
1020 A532d 20w multicolored   1.50 .35
1976, Sept. 20
1021 A532e 20w multicolored   1.50 .35
1022 A532f 20w multicolored   1.50 .35
1976, Nov. 20
1023 A532g 20w multicolored   3.50 1.40
1024 A532h 20w multicolored   3.50 1.40
Nos. 1015-1024 (10)   19.00 5.60

1876 and 1976 Telephones, Globe — A533

1976, Mar. 10
1025 A533 20w multicolored   .65 .25
Centenary of first telephone call by Alexander Graham Bell, Mar. 10, 1876.

Homeland Reserves A534

1976, Apr. 3   Photo.   Perf. 13½x13
1026 A534 20w multicolored   .65 .25
8th Homeland Reserve Forces Day.

"People and Eye" — A535

1976, Apr. 7   Perf. 13x13½
1027 A535 20w multicolored   .65 .25
World Health Day; "Foresight prevents blindness."

Pres. Park, New Village Movement Flag — A536

Intellectual Pursuits — A537

No. 1030, Village improvement. No. 1031, Agriculture. No. 1032, Income from production.

1976, Apr. 22
1028 A536 20w shown   1.50 .45
1029 A537 20w shown   1.50 .45
1030 A537 20w multicolored   1.50 .45
1031 A537 20w multicolored   1.50 .45
1032 A537 20w multicolored   1.50 .45
  a. Strip of 5, #1028-1032   10.00 6.00
6th anniv. of Pres. Park's New Village Movement for National Prosperity.

Mohenjo-Daro A538

1976, May 1   Perf. 13½x13
1033 A538 20w multicolored   .65 .25
UNESCO campaign to save the Mohenjo-Daro excavations in Pakistan.

13-Star and 50-Star Flags — A539

American Bicentennial (Bicentennial Emblem and): No. 1035, Statue of Liberty. No. 1036, Map of US and Mt. Rushmore monument. No. 1037, Liberty Bell. No. 1038, First astronaut on moon.

1976, May 8   Perf. 13x13½
1034 A539 100w blk, dp bl & red   3.00 1.00
  a. Souvenir sheet of 1   6.00 6.00
1035 A539 100w blk, dp bl & red   3.00 1.00
1036 A539 100w blk, dp bl & red   3.00 1.00
1037 A539 100w blk, dp bl & red   3.00 1.00
1038 A539 100w blk, dp bl & red   3.00 1.00
Nos. 1034-1038 (5)   15.00 5.00

Girl Scouts, Campfire and Emblem — A540

1976, May 10
1039 A540 20w orange & multi   1.25 .25
Korean Federation of Girl Scouts, 30th anniv.

Stupas, Buddha of Borobudur — A541

1976, June 10
1040 A541 20w multicolored   .65 .25
UNESCO campaign to save the Borobudur Temple, Java.

"Life Insurance" — A542

1976, July 1   Photo.   Perf. 13x13½
1041 A542 20w multicolored   .65 .25
National Life Insurance policies: "Over 100 billion-won," Apr. 30, 1976.

Volleyball — A543

1976, July 17
1042 A543 20w shown   .50 .25
1043 A543 20w Boxing   .50 .25
21st Olympic Games, Montreal, Canada, July 17-Aug. 1.

Children and Books A544

1976, Aug. 10   Perf. 13½x13
1044 A544 20w brown & multi   .65 .25
Books for children.

Civil Defense Corps, Flag and Members — A545

1976, Sept. 15   Perf. 13x13½
1045 A545 20w multicolored   .65 .25
Civil Defense Corps, first anniversary.

Chamsungdan, Mani Mountain — A546

Front Gate, Tongdosa Temple A547

1976, Sept. 28   Perf. 13½x13
1046 A546 20w multicolored   .75 .25
1047 A547 20w multicolored   .75 .25
International Tourism Day.

Cadets and Academy A548

1976, Oct. 1
1048 A548 20w multicolored   .65 .25
Korean Military Academy, 30th anniversary.

Leaves and Stones, by Cheong Ju — A549

1976, Oct. 5   Perf. 13x13½
1049 A549 20w blk, gray & red   .65 .25
  a. Souvenir sheet of 2   5.00 5.00
Philatelic Week, Oct. 5-11.

Snake-headed Figure, Bas-relief A550

Door-pull and Cranes A551

1976, Dec. 1   Photo.   Perf. 13x13½
1050 A550 20w multicolored   .70 .25
  a. Souvenir sheet of 2   2.50 2.50
1051 A551 20w multicolored   .70 .25
  a. Souvenir sheet of 2   2.50 2.50
New Year 1977.

Arrows, Cogwheels, Worker at Lathe — A552

No. 1053, Arrows, Cogwheels, ship in dock.

1977, Jan. 20   Photo.   Perf. 13½x13
1052 A552 20w multicolored   .65 .25
1053 A552 20w multicolored   .65 .25
4th Economic Development Five-Year Plan.

Satellite Antenna and Microwaves — A553

1977, Jan. 31 *Perf. 13x13½*
1054 A553 20w multicolored .65 .25
Membership in ITU, 25th anniv.

Korean Broadcasting Center A554

1977, Feb. 16 *Perf. 13½x13*
1055 A554 20w multicolored .65 .25
50th anniversary of broadcasting in Korea.

Parents and Two Children — A555

1977, Apr. 1 Photo. Perf. 13½x13
1056 A555 20w brt grn & orange 2.25 .25
Family planning.

Reservist on Duty — A556

1977, Apr. 2 *Perf. 13x13½*
1057 A556 20w multicolored .65 .25
9th Homeland Reserve Forces Day.

Head with Symbols — A557

1977, Apr. 21 Photo. Perf. 13x13½
1058 A557 20w dp lilac & multi .65 .25
10th anniversary of Science Day.

Book, Map, Syringe A558

1977, Apr. 25
1059 A558 20w blue & multi .65 .25
35th Intl. Meeting on Military Medicine.

Boy with Flowers and Dog — A559

1977, May 5
1060 A559 20w multicolored .65 .25
Proclamation of Children's Charter, 20th anniversary.

Veteran's Emblem and Flag — A560

1977, May 8
1061 A560 20w multicolored .65 .25
25th anniversary of Korean Veterans' Day.

Buddha, 8th Century, Sokkulam Grotto — A561

1977, May 25 Photo. Perf. 13x13½
1062 A561 20w sepia & olive .65 .25
a.   Souvenir sheet of 2 5.00 5.00
"2600th" anniversary of birth of Buddha.

Ceramic Issues

Jar with Grape Design, 17th Century — A562   Celadon Vase, Bamboo Design, 12th Century — A563

1977, Mar. 15 Photo. Perf. 13x13½
1063 A562 20w vio brn & multi 2.00 .30
1064 A563 20w gray, grn & bis 2.00 .30

Celadon Jar with Peonies A564

Vase with Willow Reed Peony Pattern — A565

Perf. 13x13½, 13½x13
1977, June 15 Photo.
1065 A564 20w multicolored 1.10 .30
1066 A565 20w multicolored 1.10 .30

Celadon Manshaped Wine Jug — A566   Celadon Melon-shaped Vase — A567

1977, July 15
1067 A566 20w multicolored 1.10 .25
1068 A567 20w multicolored 1.10 .25

1977, Aug. 15

Designs: No. 1069, White porcelain bowl with inlaid lotus vine design. No. 1070, Black Koryo ware vase with plum blossom vine.

1069 A564 20w multicolored 1.10 .25
1070 A565 20w multicolored 1.10 .25

Punch'ong Jar — A568   Celadon Cylindrical Vase — A569

1977, Nov. 15
1071 A568 20w multicolored 1.10 .25
1072 A569 20w multicolored 1.10 .25
Nos. 1063-1072 (10) 12.80 2.70

Types of 1962-66
Designs as Before

1976-77 Litho. *Perf. 12½*
Granite Paper
1076 A187 200w brn & lt grn 25.00 7.00
1077 A187a 300w sl grn & sal ('76) 50.00 8.00
1078 A187a 300w brn & sal 50.00 8.00
1079 A107a 500w pur & lt grn 100.00 10.00

Magpie A570   Nature Protection A571

"Family Planning" A572   Children on Swing A573

Ceramic Horseman A574   Muryangsu Hall, Busok Temple A575

Pagoda, Pobjusa Temple A576   Gold Crown, from Chonmachong Mound A577

Monster Mask Tile, 6th or 7th Century — A578

Flying Angels from Bronze Bell from Sangwon-sa, 725 A.D. — A579

Perf. 12½x13½, 13½x12½
1977-79 Photo.
1088 A570 3w lt blue & blk .75 .25
1090 A326 10w emer & blk .70 .25
1091 A571 20w multicolored .75 .25
1092 A572 20w emer & blk ('78) .50 .25
1093 A573 20w grn & org ('79) .50 .25
1097 A574 80w lt brn & sep 1.75 .40
1099 A575 200w salmon & brn 2.00 .50
1100 A576 300w brn purple 2.75 .60
1101 A577 500w multicolored 27.50 1.50

Perf. 13½x13
1102 A578 500w brown & pur 17.50 1.00

Perf. 13
1103 A579 1000w slate grn ('78) 10.00 1.50
Nos. 1088-1103 (11) 64.70 6.75

Ulleung Island — A580

Design: No. 1105, Haeundae Beach.

1977, Sept. 28 Photo. Perf. 13
1104 A580 20w multicolored .65 .25
1105 A580 20w multicolored .65 .25
World Tourism Day.

Armed Forces Day — A581

1977, Oct. 1 Photo. Perf. 13
1106 A581 20w green & multi .65 .25

Mt. Inwang after the Rain, by Chung Seon (1676-1759) — A582

1977, Oct. 4
1107   20w mountain, clouds   .90   .25
1108   20w mountain, house   .90   .25
   a.   Souvenir sheet of 2   8.50   8.50
   b.   A582 Pair, #1107-1108   2.25   1.50
    Philatelic Week, Oct. 4-10.

Rotary Emblem on Bronze Bell, Koryo Dynasty — A584

1977, Nov. 10   Photo.   *Perf. 13*
1109   A584   20w multicolored   .65   .25
   Korean Rotary Club, 50th anniversary.

Korean Flag on Mt. Everest A585

1977, Nov. 11
1110   A585   20w multicolored   1.10   .25
   Korean Mt. Everest Expedition, reached peak, Sept. 15, 1977.

Children and Kites A586   Horse-headed Figure, Bas-relief A587

1977, Dec. 1   Photo.   *Perf. 13*
1111   A586   20w multicolored   .45   .25
   a.   Souvenir sheet of 2   2.25   2.25
1112   A587   20w multicolored   .45   .25
   a.   Souvenir sheet of 2   2.25   2.25
    New Year 1978.

Clay Pigeon Shooting A588

Designs: No. 1114, Air pistol shooting. No. 1115, Air rifle shooting and target.

1977, Dec. 3
1113   A588   20w multicolored   .60   .25
   a.   Souvenir sheet of 2 ('78)   4.50   4.50
1114   A588   20w multicolored   .60   .25
   a.   Souvenir sheet of 2 ('78)   4.50   4.50
1115   A588   20w multicolored   .60   .25
   a.   Souvenir sheet of 2 ('78)   4.50   4.50
   Nos. 1113-1115 (3)   1.80   .75
   Nos. 1113a-1115a (3)   13.50
   42nd World Shooting Championships, Seoul, 1978.

Boeing 727 over Globe, ICAO Emblem A589

1977, Dec. 11
1116   A589   20w multicolored   .65   .25
   25th anniv. of Korea's membership in the ICAO.

Plane, Cargo, Freighter and Globe A590

1977, Dec. 22   Photo.   *Perf. 13*
1117   A590   20w multicolored   .65   .25
   Korean exports.

Ships and World Map — A591

1978, Mar. 13   Photo.   *Perf. 13*
1118   A591   20w multicolored   .65   .25
   Maritime Day.

Stone Pagoda Issue

Four Lions Pagoda, Hwaom-sa — A592

Seven-storied Pagoda, T'appyongri — A592a

1978, Mar. 20   Photo.   *Perf. 13*
1119   A592   20w lt green & multi   1.40   .30
1120   A592a   20w ocher & multi   1.40   .30

Punhwang-sa Temple A593

Miruk-sa Temple — A593a

1978, May 20
1121   A593   20w lt green & blk   1.40   .30
1122   A593a   20w grn, brn & yel   1.40   .30

Tabo Pagoda, Pulguk-sa — A592b   Three-storied pagoda, Pulguk-sa — A592c

1978, June 20
1123   A592b   20w gray, lt grn & blk   1.20   .25
1124   A592c   20w lilac & black   1.20   .25

Kyongch'on sa Temple — A594

Octagonal Pagoda, Wolchong-sa Temple — A594a

1978, July 20   *Perf. 13½x12½*
1125   A594   20w gray & brn   1.25   .30
1126   A594a   20w lt green & blk   1.25   .30

13-storied Pagoda, Jeonghye-sa — A592d   Three-storied Pagoda, Jinjeon-sa — A592e

1978, Nov. 20   *Perf. 13x13½*
1127   A592d   20w pale grn & multi   .70   .25
1128   A592e   20w lilac & multi   .70   .25
   Nos. 1119-1128 (10)   11.90   2.80

Ants and Coins — A595

1978, Apr. 1
1129   A595   20w multicolored   .65   .25
   Importance of saving.

Reservist with Flag — A596

1978, Apr. 1
1130   A596   20w multicolored   .65   .25
   10th Homeland Reserve Forces Day.

Seoul Cultural Center A597

1978, Apr. 1
1131   A597   20w multicolored   .95   .25
   Opening of Seoul Cultural Center.

National Assembly in Plenary Session A598

1978, May 31
1132   A598   20w multicolored   .65   .25
   30th anniversary of National Assembly.

Hands Holding Tools, Competition Emblem — A599

1978, Aug. 5   Photo.   *Perf. 13*
1133   A599   20w multicolored   .65   .25
   a.   Souvenir sheet of 2   3.50   3.50
   24th World Youth Skill Olympics, Busan, Aug. 30-Sept. 15.

Bell of Joy and Crater Lake, Mt. Baegdu — A600

1978, Aug. 15
1134   A600   20w multicolored   .65   .25
   Founding of republic, 30th anniversary.

Nurse, Badge and Flowers — A601

1978, Aug. 26
1135   A601   20w multicolored   .65   .25
   Army Nurse Corps, 30th anniversary.

Sobaeksan Observatory A602

1978, Sept. 13   Photo.   *Perf. 13*
1136   A602   20w multicolored   .65   .25
   Opening of Sobaeksan Natl. Observatory.

Kyunghoeru
Pavilion,
Kyongbok
Palace, Seoul
A603

Design: No. 1138, Baeg Do (island).

1978, Sept. 28
1137 A603 20w multicolored   .50   .25
1138 A603 20w multicolored   .50   .25

Tourist publicity.

Customs Flag
and Officers
A604

1978, Sept. 28
1139 A604 20w multicolored   .50   .25

Cent. of 1st Korean Custom House, Busan.

Armed Forces
A605

1978, Oct. 1   Photo.   Perf. 13
1140 A605 20w multicolored   .50   .25

Armed Forces, 30th anniversary.

Clay Figurines, Silla
Dynasty — A606

1978, Oct. 1
1141 A606 20w lt green & blk   .50   .25

Culture Month, October 1978.

Portrait of a Lady,
by Shin Yoon-
bok — A607

1978, Oct. 24
1142 A607 20w multicolored   .50   .25
  a.   Souvenir sheet of 2   4.00   4.00

Philatelic Week, Oct. 24-29.

Young Men,
YMCA
Emblem
A608

1978, Oct. 28
1143 A608 20w multicolored   .50   .25

75th anniv. of founding of Korean YMCA.

Hand Protecting
Against Fire — A609

1978, Nov. 1   Photo.   Perf. 13
1144 A609 20w multicolored   .50   .25

Fire Prevention Day, Nov. 1.

Winter
Landscape
A610

Ram-headed
Figure, Bas-relief
A611

1978, Dec. 1   Photo.   Perf. 13x13½
1145 A610 20w multicolored   .65   .25
  a.   Souvenir sheet of 2   2.00   2.00
1146 A611 20w multicolored   .65   .25
  a.   Souvenir sheet of 2   2.00   2.00

New Year 1979.

Hibiscus, Students,
Globe — A612

1978, Dec. 5
1147 A612 20w multicolored   .50   .25

Proclamation of National Education Charter,
10th anniversary.

President
Park — A613

1978, Dec. 27
1148 A613 20w multicolored   .60   .25
  a.   Souvenir sheet of 2   12.50 12.50

Inauguration of Park Chung Hee for fifth
term as president.

Nature Conservation Issue

Golden
Mandarinfish
A614

Lace-bark Pines
A615

Mandarin
Ducks — A616

Neofinettia
Orchid — A617

Goral — A618

Lilies of the
Valley — A619

Rain Frog
A620

Asian Polypody
A621

Firefly — A622

Meesun
Tree — A623

1979, Feb. 20   Photo.   Perf. 13x13½
1149 A614 20w multicolored   2.00   .25
1150 A615 20w multicolored   2.00   .25
1979, May 20
1151 A616 20w multicolored   2.00   .25
1152 A617 20w multicolored   2.00   .25
1979, June 20
1153 A618 20w multicolored   2.00   .25
1154 A619 20w multicolored   2.00   .25
1979, Nov. 25
1155 A620 20w multicolored   2.00   .25
1156 A621 20w multicolored   2.00   .25
1980, Jan. 20
1157 A622 30w multicolored   2.00   .25
1158 A623 30w multicolored   2.00   .25
  Nos. 1149-1158 (10)   20.00   2.50

Samil
Monument — A624

1979, Mar. 1   Photo.   Perf. 13x13½
1159 A624 20w multicolored   .50   .25

Samil independence movement, 60th anniv.

Worker and
Bulldozer
A625

1979, Mar. 10   Perf. 13½x13
1160 A625 20w multicolored   .50   .25

Labor Day.

Hand Holding Tools,
Gun and
Grain — A626

1979, Apr. 1   Perf. 13x13½
1161 A626 20w multicolored   .50   .25

Strengthening national security.

Tabo Pagoda,
Pulguk-sa
Temple — A627

Women, Silk Screen — A628

Art Treasures: No. 1163, Statue. No. 1164,
Crown. No. 1165, Celadon Vase.

1979, Apr. 1
1162 A627 20w gray bl & multi   .60   .25
1163 A627 20w bister & multi   .60   .25
1164 A627 20w violet & multi   .60   .25
1165 A627 20w brt grn & multi   .60   .25
1166 A628 60w multicolored   1.00   .30
  a.   Souvenir sheet of 2   4.00   4.00
  Nos. 1162-1166 (5)   3.40   1.30

5000 years of Korean art.
See Nos. 1175-1179, 1190.

Pulguk-sa
Temple and
PATA Emblem
A629

1979, Apr. 16   Perf. 13½x13
1167 A629 20w multicolored   .50   .25

28th Pacific Area Travel Association (PATA)
Conf., Seoul, Apr. 16-18, and Gyeongju, Apr.
20-21.

Presidents
Park and
Senghor
A630

1979, Apr. 22   Perf. 13½x13
1168 A630 20w multicolored   .50   .25
  a.   Souvenir sheet of 2   2.00   2.00

Visit of Pres. Leopold Sedar Senghor of
Senegal.

Basketball — A631

1979, Apr. 29   Perf. 13x13½
1169 A631 20w multicolored   .50   .25

8th World Women's Basketball Championship, Seoul, Apr. 29-May 13.

Children and IYC Emblem A632

1979, May 5　Photo.　Perf. 13½x13
1170　A632　20w multicolored　　.50　.25
　a.　Souvenir sheet of 2　　2.00　2.00

International Year of the Child.

Traffic Pollution — A633

1979, June 5　Photo.　Perf. 13x13½
1171　A633　20w green & dk brn　.90　.25

Pollution control.

Flags, Presidents Park and Carter A634

1979, June 29　　　Perf. 13½x13
1172　A634　20w multicolored　　.50　.25
　a.　Souvenir sheet of 2　　2.00　2.00

Visit of Pres. Jimmy Carter.

Korean Exhibition Center A635

1979, July 3
1173　A635　20w multicolored　　.50　.25

Opening of Korean Exhibition Center.

Jet, Globe, South Gate — A636

1979, Aug. 1　Photo.　Perf. 13½x13
1174　A636　20w multicolored　　.50　.25

10th anniversary of Korean airlines.

Art Treasure Types

Designs: No. 1175, Porcelain jar, 17th century. No. 1176, Man on horseback, ceremonial pitcher, horiz. No. 1177, Sword Dance, by Shin Yun-bok. No. 1178, Golden Amitabha with halo, 8th century. No. 1179, Hahoe ritual mask.

1979　Photo.　Perf. 13x13½, 13½x13
1175　A627　20w lilac & multi　　.65　.25
1176　A627　20w multicolored　　.65　.25
1177　A628　60w multicolored　1.10　.30
　a.　Souvenir sheet of 2　　5.00　5.00
　　Nos. 1175-1177 (3)　　2.40　.80

Issued: No. 1177, 9/1; Nos. 1175-1176, 10/15.

1979, Nov. 15
1178　A627　20w dp green & multi　.50　.25
1179　A627　20w multicolored　　.50　.25

Yongdu Rock — A637

1979, Sept. 28
1180　A637　20w shown　　　.50　.25
1181　A637　20w Mt. Mai, vert.　.50　.25

World Tourism Day.

People, Blood and Heart — A637a

1979, Oct. 1　　　Perf. 13½x13
1182　A637a　20w multicolored　.75　.25

Blood Banks, 4th anniversary.

"My Life in the Year 2000" — A638

1979, Oct. 30　　　Perf. 13½x13
1183　A638　20w multicolored　　.50　.25
　a.　Souvenir sheet of 2　　1.75　1.75

Philatelic Week, Oct. 30-Nov. 4.

Monkey-headed Figure, Bas-relief A639　　Children Playing Yut A640

1979, Dec. 1
1184　A639　20w multicolored　　.50　.25
　a.　Souvenir sheet of 2　　1.50　1.50
1185　A640　20w multicolored　　.50　.25
　a.　Souvenir sheet of 2　　1.50　1.50

New Year 1980.

Inauguration of Pres. Choi Kyu-hah A641

1979, Dec. 21
1186　A641　20w multicolored　　.50　.25
　a.　Souvenir sheet of 2　　5.00　5.00

President Park — A642

1980, Feb. 2　Photo.　Perf. 13x13½
1187　A642　30w orange brn　　.95　.25
1188　A642　30w dull purple　　.95　.25
　a.　Souvenir sheet of 2　　4.00　4.00
　b.　Pair, #1187-1188　　2.50　2.50

President Park Chung Hee (1917-1979) memorial.

Art Treasure Type of 1979 and

Dragon-shaped Kettle — A643

Design: 60w, Landscape, by Kim Hong-do.

Perf. 13½x13, 13x13½
1980, Feb. 20　　　　　Photo.
1189　A643　30w multicolored　　.60　.25
1190　A628　60w multicolored　1.00　.30
　a.　Souvenir sheet of 2　　4.00　4.00

Art Treasure Issue

Heavenly Horse, Saddle A644

Dragon Head, Banner Staff A645　　Tiger, Granite Sculpture A647

Mounted Nobleman Mural — A646

Human Face, Roof Tile — A648　　Deva King Sculpture — A650

White Tiger Mural — A649

Earthenware Ducks — A651

Tiger, Folk Painting — A653

Perf. 13½x13, 13x13½
1980-83　　　　　　Photo.
1191　A644　30w multicolored　　.75　.25
1192　A645　30w multicolored　　.75　.25
1193　A646　30w multicolored　　.75　.25
1194　A647　30w multicolored　　.75　.25
1195　A648　30w multicolored　　.75　.25
1196　A649　30w multicolored　　.75　.25
**　　　　　Engr.　　Perf. 12½x13**
1197　A650　30w black　　　1.00　.25
1198　A650　30w red　　　1.00　.25
1983　　　Litho.　　Perf. 13
1199　　　1000w bis brn & red
　　　　　　　　　brn　　6.00　.80
1200　　　1000w bis brn & red
　　　　　　　　　brn　　6.00　.80
　a.　A651　Pair, #1199-1200　12.00　5.00

1201　A653　5000w multicolored　25.00　5.00
　a.　Souvenir sheet, perf. 13½x13　30.00
　　Nos. 1191-1201 (11)　　43.50　8.60

Issued: Nos. 1191-1192, 4/20; Nos. 1193-1194, 5/20; Nos. 1195-1196, 8/20; Nos. 1197-1198, 11/20. Nos. 1199-1200, 11/25/83. No. 1201, 12/1/83.
No. 1201a for PHILAKOREA '84. No. 1201a exists imperf. Value $150.

Lotus Blossoms and Ducks — A656

Tiger and Magpie A657

1980, Mar. 10　Perf. 13x13½, 13½x13
1203　A656　30w multicolored　　.60　.25
1204　A657　60w multicolored　1.50　.50

Red Phoenix (in Form of Rooster) — A658

Moon Over Mt. Konryun — A659

No. 1207, Sun over Mt. Konryun. No. 1207a has continuous design.

1980, May 10　　　Perf. 13x13½
1205　A658　30w multicolored　　.55　.25
1206　A659　60w multicolored　1.75　.45
1207　A659　60w multicolored　1.75　.45
　a.　Souvenir sheet of 2, #1206-
　　　1207　　　　5.50　5.50
　b.　Pair, #1206-1207　　4.50　3.50
　　Nos. 1205-1207 (3)　　4.05　1.15

Rabbits Pounding Grain in a Mortar — A660　　Dragon in the Clouds — A661

1980, July 10　Photo.　Perf. 13x13½
1208　A660　30w multicolored　　.70　.25
1209　A661　30w multicolored　　.70　.25

Pine Tree,
Pavilion,
Mountain
A662

Flowers and Birds,
Bridal Room
Screen
A663

1980, Aug. 9   Photo.   Perf. 13x13½
1210 A662 30w multicolored   .55   .25
1211 A663 30w multicolored   1.10   .30

Tortoises and Cranes — A664

Symbols of longevity: a, cranes, tortoises. b,
buck. c, doe. d, waterfall.

1980, Nov. 10   Photo.   Perf. 13½x13
1212 A664   Strip of 4   8.00   4.50
a.-d.   30w any single   1.50   .25

New Community
Movement, 10th
Anniv. — A668

1980, Apr. 22   Perf. 13x13½
1216 A668 30w multicolored   .50   .25

Freighters at
Sea — A669

1980, Mar. 13
1217 A669 30w multicolored   .50   .25
 Increase of Korea's shipping tonnage to 5
million tons.

Soccer — A670

1980, Aug. 23   Perf. 13x13½
1218 A670 30w multicolored   .50   .25
 10th President's Cup Soccer Tournament,
Aug. 23-Sept. 5.

Mt.
Sorak — A671

Paikryung
Island — A672

Perf. 12½x13½
1980, Apr. 10   Photo.
1219 A671 15w multicolored   .40   .25
1220 A672 90w multicolored   1.10   .25

Flag — A673

1980, Sept. 10   Perf. 13½x13
1221 A673 30w multicolored   .45   .25
Coil Stamp
Perf. Vert.
1221A A673 30w multicolored   1.40   .25
 No. 1221A issued 2/1/87.

UN Intervention,
30th Anniv. — A674

1980, June 25   Perf. 13x13½
1222 A674 30w multicolored   .60   .25

Election of Miss
World in
Seoul — A675

1980, July 8
1223 A675 30w multicolored   .60   .25

Women's
Army Corps,
30th
Anniversary
A676

1980, Sept. 6   Perf. 13½x13
1224 A676 30w multicolored   .60   .25

Baegma
River — A677

Three Peaks
of Dodam
A678

1980, Sept. 28
1225 A677 30w multicolored   .40   .25
1226 A678 30w multicolored   .40   .25

Inauguration
of Pres. Chun
Doo-hwan
A679

1980, Sept. 1
1227 A679 30w multicolored   .60   .25
a.   Souvenir sheet of 2   3.50   3.50

Ear of Corn — A680

1980, Oct. 20   Perf. 13x13½
1228 A680 30w multicolored   .60   .25
 12th population and housing census.

Symbolic
Tree — A681

1980, Oct. 27
1229 A681 30w multicolored   .60   .25
 National Red Cross, 75th anniversary.

"Mail-Delivering Angels" — A682

1980, Nov. 6   Perf. 13½x13
1230 A682 30w multicolored   .60   .25
a.   Souvenir sheet of 2   1.75   1.75
 Philatelic Week, Nov. 6-11.

Korea-Japan
Submarine Cable
System Inauguration
A683

1980, Nov. 28   Perf. 13x13½
1231 A683 30w multicolored   .60   .25

Rooster — A684   Cranes — A685

1980, Dec. 1
1232 A684 30w multicolored   .60   .25
a.   Souvenir sheet of 2   1.75   1.75
1233 A685 30w multicolored   .60   .25
a.   Souvenir sheet of 2   1.75   1.75
 New Year 1981.

Second
Inauguration
of Pres. Chun
Doo-hwan
A686

1981, Mar. 3   Photo.   Perf. 13½x13
1234 A686 30w multicolored   .60   .25
a.   Souvenir sheet of 2   1.75   1.75

Ship Issue

Oil Tanker
A687

Cargo Ship — A688

Oil Tanker
A689

Cargo
Ship — A690

Tug
Boat — A691

Stern Trawler
A692

Log Carrier
A693

Auto Carrier
A694

Chemical
Carrier
A695

Passenger
Boat
A696

1981, Mar. 13   Perf. 13½x13, 13x13½
1235 A687 30w multicolored   .55   .25
1236 A688 90w multicolored   .85   .25
 5th Maritime Day.

1981, May 10   Photo.   Perf. 13½x13
1237 A689 30w multicolored   .55   .25
1238 A690 90w multicolored   .95   .30

1981, July 10   *Perf. 13½x13*
1239 A691 40w multicolored   .70   .25
1240 A692 100w multicolored   1.20   .30
1981, Aug. 10
1241 A693 40w multicolored   .70   .25
1242 A694 100w multicolored   1.20   .30
1981, Nov. 10 Engr.   *Perf. 13x12½*
1243 A695 40w black   .65   .25
1244 A696 100w dk blue   1.10   .30
    Nos. 1235-1244 (10)   8.45 2.70

11th Natl.
Assembly
Opening
Session
A697

1981, Apr. 17 Photo.   *Perf. 13½x13*
1245 A697 30w gold & dk brn   .50   .25

Hand Reading
Braille, Helping
Hands — A698

1981, Apr. 20 Photo.   *Perf. 13x13½*
1246 A698 30w shown   .40   .25
1247 A698 90w Man in wheel-
          chair   .75   .25

International Year of the Disabled.

Ribbon and Council
Emblem — A699

1981, June 5 Photo.   *Perf. 13x13½*
1248 A699 40w multicolored   .50   .25

Advisory Council on Peaceful Unification
Policy (North and South Korea) anniv.

Clena River and
Mountains — A700

1981, June 5
1249 A700 30w shown   .40   .25
1250 A700 90w Seagulls   .85   .25

10th World Environment Day.

Pres. Chun
and Pres.
Suharto of
Indonesia
A701

Pres. Chun Visit to Asia: b, King of Malay-
sia. c, Korean, Singapore flags. d, King
Bhumibol Adulyadej of Thailand. e, Pres.
Marcos of Philippines.

1981, June 25   *Perf. 13½x13*
1251   Strip of 5   4.75 4.00
a.-e. A701 40w, any single   .65   .25
f.   Souvenir sheet of 5, imperf. 2.75 2.75

      Size: 49x33mm
      Perf. 13x13½
1252 A701 40w multicolored   .65   .25
a.   Souvenir sheet of 2, imperf. 2.75 2.75

36th Anniv. of
Liberation — A702

1981, Aug. 15 Photo.   *Perf. 13x13½*
1253 A702 40w multicolored   .50   .25

Tolharubang,   Rose of
"Stone   Sharon
Grandfather"   A705
A704

Porcelain Jar,   Chomsongdae
17th   Observatory,
Cent. — A706   7th
                      Cent. — A707

Mounted   Family Planning
Warrior,   A709
Earthenware
Jug, 5th Cent.
A708

Walking Stick   Ryu Kwan-
A710   soon (1904-
                      20), Martyr
                      A711

"Tasan" Chung   Ahn Joong-
Yak-yong, Lee   geun (1879-
Dynasty   1910), Martyr
Scholar   A713
A712

Ahn Chang-ho   Koryo Celadon
(1878-1938),   Incense
Independence   Burner
Fighter   A715
A714

Kim Ku (1876-   Mountain
1949),   Landscape
Statesman   Brick Bas-
A716   relief
                      A717

Mandarin Duck,
Celadon Incense
Burner — A718

Perf. 13½x12½ (Nos. 1256, 1257, 1266), 13, 13½x13, 13x13½

1981-89   **Photo., Engr.**
1255 A704 20w multi   .50   .25
1256 A705 40w multi ('86)   .70   .25
1257 A706 60w multi   .70   .25
1258 A707 70w multi   .75   .25
1259 A708 80w multi ('83)   .85   .25
1260 A709 80w multi ('86)   1.00   .25
1261 A710 80w multi ('89)   2.50   .25
1262 A711 100w lilac   1.00   .25
1263 A712 100w gray blk
            ('86)   3.50   .25
1264 A713 200w lt ol grn &
            ol   1.50   .25
1265 A714 300w dl lil ('83)   2.25   .25
1266 A715 400w multi   6.00   .50
1267 A715 400w pale grn &
            multi ('83)   4.00   .40
1268 A716 450w dk vio brn
            ('86)   2.75   .40
1269 A717 500w multi   4.00   .75
1270 A718 700w multi ('83)   5.00   .80
    Nos. 1255-1270 (16)   37.00 5.60

Inscription and denomination of No. 1266,
colorless, No. 1267, dark brown.
See Nos. 1449, 1449C, 1594F.

Coil Stamp
Photo.   Perf. 13 Horiz.
1271 A707 70w multicolored   2.00   .50

Girl Flying Model
Plane — A721

Air Force Chief of Staff Cup, 3rd Aeronautic
Competition: Various model planes.

1981, Sept. 20   *Perf. 13½x13*
1272   Strip of 5   4.50 3.75
a. A721 10w multi   .50   .25
b. A721 20w multi   .50   .25
c. A721 40w multi   .50   .25
d. A721 50w multi   .65   .30
e. A721 80w multi   .90   .40

WHO Emblem,
Citizens — A722

1981, Sept. 22   *Perf. 13x13½*
1273 A722 40w multicolored   .50   .25
WHO, 32nd Western Pacific Regional Committee Meeting, Seoul, Sept. 22-28.

World Tourism
Day — A723

1981, Sept. 28
1274 A723 40w Seoul Tower   .40   .25
1275 A723 40w Ulreung Isld.   .40   .25

Bicycle
Racing
A724

1981, Oct. 10   *Perf. 13½x13*
1276 A724 40w shown   .45   .25
1277 A724 40w Swimming   .45   .25
62nd Natl. Sports Festival, Seoul, 10/10-15.

Flags,
Presidents
Chun and
Carazo
A725

1981, Oct. 12   *Perf. 13½x13*
1278 A725 40w multicolored   .50   .25
Visit of Pres. Rodrigo Carazo Odio of Costa
Rica, Oct. 12-14.

World Food
Day — A726

1981, Oct. 16   *Perf. 13x13½*
1279 A726 40w multicolored   .50   .25

First Natl.
Aviation
Day — A727

1981, Oct. 30   *Perf. 13½x13*
1280 A727 40w multicolored   .50   .25

1988 Olympic
Games,
Seoul — A728

1981, Oct. 30   *Perf. 13x13½*
1281 A728 40w multicolored   .65   .25

9th Philatelic
Week, Nov.
18-24 — A729

1981, Nov. 18   *Perf. 13½x13*
1282 A729 40w multicolored   .50   .25
a.   Souvenir sheet of 2   2.00 2.00

Camellia and Dog — A730

Children Flying Kite — A731

1981, Dec. 1   **Perf. 13x13½**
1283 A730 40w multicolored   .55   .25
  a. Souvenir sheet of 2   2.00 2.00
1284 A731 40w multicolored   .55   .25
  a. Souvenir sheet of 2   2.00 2.00

New Year 1982 (Year of the Dog).

Hangul Hakhoe Language Society, 60th Anniv. A732

1981, Dec. 3   **Perf. 13½x13**
1285 A732 40w multicolored   .50   .25

Centenary of US-Korea Treaty of Amity — A739

Telecommunications Authority Inauguration A733

1982, Jan. 4   **Photo.**   **Perf. 13x13½**
1286 A733 60w multicolored   .50   .25

Scouting Year — A734

1982, Feb. 22
1287 A734 60w multicolored   .50   .25

60th Anniv. of YWCA in Korea — A735

1982, Apr. 20   **Photo.**   **Perf. 13x13½**
1288 A735 60w multicolored   .50   .25

Intl. Polar Year Centenary A736

1982, Apr. 21   **Perf. 13½x13**
1289 A736 60w multicolored   .65   .25

60th Children's Day — A737

1982, May 5   **Perf. 13½x13**
1290 A737 60w multicolored   .50   .25

Visit of Liberian Pres. Samuel K. Doe, May 9-13 A738

1982, May 9   **Litho.**   **Perf. 13x12½**
1291 A738 60w multicolored   .60   .25
  a. Souvenir sheet of 2, imperf.   2.00 2.00

Centenary of US-Korea Treaty of Amity — A739

1982, May 18   **Photo.**   **Perf. 13½x13**
1292 A739 60w Statue of Liberty,
      pagoda   .80   .25
1293 A739 60w Emblem   .80   .25
  a. Souvenir sheet of 2   3.50 3.50
  b. Pair, #1292-1293   1.75 1.75

Visit of Zaire Pres. Mobutu Sese Seko, June 7-10 A740

1982, June 7   **Litho.**   **Perf. 13x12½**
1294 A740 60w multicolored   .50   .25
  a. Souvenir sheet of 2, imperf.   2.00 2.00

Historical Painting Issue

Gen. Kwon Yul's Victory at Haengju, by Oh Seung-woo — A747

Designs: No. 1295, Territorial Expansion by Kwanggaeto the Great, by Lee Chong-sang, 1975. No. 1296, Gen. Euljimunduck's Victory at Salsoo, by Park Kak-soon, 1975. No. 1297, Shilla's Repulse of Tang's Army, by Oh Seung-woo. No. 1298, Gen. Kang Kam-chan's Victory at Kyiju, by Lee Yong-hwan. No. 1299, Admiral Yi Sun-sin's Victory at Hansan, 1592, by Kim Hyung-ku. No. 1300, Gen. Kim Chwa-jin's Battle at Chungsanri, by Sohn Soo-kwang. No. 1302, Kim Chong-suh's Exploitation of Yukjin, 1434, by Kim Tae.

1982   **Photo.**   **Perf. 13x13½**
1295 A747 60w multicolored   .75   .40
1296 A747 60w multicolored   1.50   .60
1297 A747 60w multicolored   1.00   .30
1298 A747 60w multicolored   1.00   .30
1299 A747 60w multicolored   1.00   .40
1300 A747 60w multicolored   1.00   .40
1301 A747 60w shown   1.25   .40
1302 A747 60w multicolored   1.25   .40
    Nos. 1295-1302 (8)   8.75 3.20

Issued: Nos. 1295-1296, 6/15; Nos. 1297-1298, 7/15; Nos. 1299-1300, 10/15; Nos. 1301-1302, 12/15.

55th Intl. YMCA Convention, Seoul, July 20-23 — A749

1982, July 20
1303 A749 60w multicolored   .50   .25

Flags, Presidents Chun and Arap Moi — A750

Pres. Chun's Visit to Africa & Canada: No. 1304, Kenya (Pres. Daniel T. Arap Moi), Aug. 17-19. No. 1305, Nigeria (Pres. Alhaji Shehe Shagari), Aug. 19-22. No. 1306, Gabon (Pres. El Hadj Omar Bongo), Aug. 22-24. No. 1307, Senegal (Pres. Abdou Diouf), Aug. 24-26. No. 1308, Canada, Aug. 28-31.

1982, Aug. 17   **Perf. 13½x13**
1304 A750 60w multicolored   .50   .25
1305 A750 60w multicolored   .50   .25
1306 A750 60w multicolored   .50   .25
1307 A750 60w multicolored   .50   .25
1308 A750 60w multicolored   .50   .25
    Nos. 1304-1308 (5)   2.50 1.25

Souvenir Sheets of 2

1304a A750   60w   2.50 2.50
1305a A750   60w   2.50 2.50
1306a A750   60w   2.50 2.50
1307a A750   60w   2.50 2.50
1308a A750   60w   2.50 2.50
   Nos. 1304a-1308a (5)   12.50 12.50

Natl. Flag Centenary A751

1982, Aug. 22
1309 A751 60w multicolored   .50   .25
  a. Souvenir sheet of 2   2.75 2.75

2nd Seoul Open Intl. Table Tennis Championship, Aug. 25-31 — A752

1982, Aug. 25
1310 A752 60w multicolored   .60   .25

27th World Amateur Baseball Championship Series, Seoul, Sept. 4-18 — A753

1982, Sept. 4   **Engr.**   **Perf. 13**
1311 A753 60w red brn   .90   .25

Seoul Intl. Trade Fair (SITRA '82), Sept. 24-Oct. 18 — A754

1982, Sept. 17   **Photo.**   **Perf. 13½x13**
1312 A754 60w multicolored   .50   .25

Philatelic Week, Oct. 15-21 — A755

Design: Miners reading consolatory letters.

1982, Oct. 15
1313 A755 60w multicolored   .50   .25
  a. Souvenir sheet of 2   2.00 2.00

Visit of Indonesian Pres. Suharto, Oct. 16-19 — A756

1982, Oct. 16   **Litho.**   **Perf. 13x12½**
1314 A756 60w multicolored   .50   .25
  a. Souvenir sheet of 2, imperf.   1.75 1.75

37th Jaycee (Intl. Junior Chamber of Commerce) World Congress, Seoul, Nov. 3-18 — A757

1982, Nov. 3   **Perf. 13½x13**
1315 A757 60w multicolored   .50   .25

2nd UN Conference on Peaceful Uses of Outer Space, Vienna, Aug. 9-21 — A758

1982, Nov. 20   **Perf. 13x13½**
1316 A758 60w multicolored   .50   .25

New Year 1983 (Year of the Boar) — A759

1982, Dec. 1
1317 A759 60w Magpies, money
      bag   .50   .25
  a. Souvenir sheet of 2   2.40 2.40
1318 A759 60w Boar, bas-relief   .50   .25
  a. Souvenir sheet of 2   2.40 2.40

Flags of Korea and Turkey — A760

1982, Dec. 20   **Perf. 13**
1319 A760 60w multicolored   .50   .25
  a. Souvenir sheet of 2, imperf.   2.00 2.00

Visit of Pres. Kenan Evren of Turkey, Dec. 20-23.

Letter Writing
Campaign — A761

1982, Dec. 31 Photo. Perf. 13x13½
1320 A761 60w multicolored   .50 .25

First Intl.
Customs
Day — A762

1983, Jan. 26   Perf. 13½x13
1321 A762 60w multicolored   .60 .25

Korean-made Vehicle Issue

Hyundai
Pony-2
A764

Daewoo
Maepsy
A765

Super Titan
Truck — A768

Flat-bed
Truck — A770

1983   Photo.   Perf. 13½x13
1322 A764 60w Keohwa Jeep   .90 .25
1323 A764 60w shown   .90 .25
  a.   Pair, #1322-1323   2.50 2.50
1324 A765 60w shown   .90 .25
1325 A764 60w Kia minibus   .90 .25
  a.   Pair, #1324-1325   2.50 2.50
1326 A764 60w Highway bus   .90 .25
1327 A768 60w shown   .90 .25
1328 A764 70w Dump truck   1.25 .25
1329 A770 70w shown   1.25 .25
1330 A764 70w Cement mixer   1.25 .25
1331 A764 70w Oil truck   1.25 .25
     Nos. 1322-1331 (10)   10.40 2.50

Issued: Nos. 1322-1323, 2/25; Nos. 1324-
1325, 3/25; Nos. 1326-1327, 5/25; Nos. 1328-
1329, 7/25; Nos. 1330-1331, 8/25.

Visit of
Malaysian
Seri Paduka
Baginda, Mar.
22-26 — A773

1983, Mar. 22
1332 A773 60w multicolored   .50 .25
  a.   Souvenir sheet of 2   1.40 1.40

Postal Service Issue

General
Bureau of
Postal
Administration
Building
A774

Mailman,
1884 — A776

Ancient Mail
Carrier
A778

Nos. 1-
2 — A780

Pre-modern
Period Postal
Symbol,
Mailbox
A782

Designs: No. 1334, Seoul Central PO. No.
1336, Mailman on motorcycle, 1983. No.
1338, Modern mail transport. No. 1340, No.
1201. No. 1342, Current postal symbol,
mailbox.

1983-84   Photo.   Perf. 13½x13
1333 A774 60w multicolored   .70 .25
1334 A774 60w multicolored   .70 .25
1335 A776 60w multicolored   .90 .25
1336 A776 70w multicolored   .90 .25
1337 A778 70w multicolored   .90 .25
1338 A778 70w multicolored   .90 .25
1339 A780 70w multicolored   .70 .25
1340 A780 70w multicolored   .70 .25
1341 A782 70w multicolored   .70 .25
1342 A782 70w multicolored   .70 .25
     Nos. 1333-1342 (10)   7.80 2.50

PHILAKOREA '84, Seoul, Oct. 22-31, 1984.
Issued: Nos. 1333-1334, 4/22; Nos. 1335-
1336, 6/10; Nos. 1337-1338, 8/10; Nos. 1339-
1340, 2/10/84; Nos. 1341-1342, 3/10/84.

Teachers'
Day — A784

1983, May 15   Photo.   Perf. 13x13½
1343 A784 60w Village school-
               house, score   .60 .25
  a.   Souvenir sheet of 2   2.00 2.00

World Communications Year — A785

1983, June 20
1344 A785 70w multicolored   .60 .25
  a.   Souvenir sheet of 2   1.75 1.75

Communications Life Insurance
Inauguration — A786

1983, July 1   Photo.   Perf. 13½x13
1345 A786 70w multicolored   .70 .25

Science and
Technology
Symposium,
Seoul, July 4-
8 — A787

1983, July 4
1346 A787 70w multicolored   .60 .25

 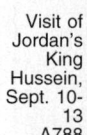

Visit of
Jordan's
King
Hussein,
Sept. 10-
13
A788

1983, Sept. 10   Litho.   Perf. 13x12½
1347 A788 70w Pres. Hwan, King
               Hussein, flags   .60 .25
  a.   Souvenir sheet of 2, imperf. 1.75 1.75

ASTA, 53rd World
Travel Congress,
Seoul — A789

1983, Sept. 25   Photo.   Perf. 13
1348 A789 70w multicolored   .60 .25

A790

1983, Oct. 4   Photo.   Perf. 13
1349 A790 70w multicolored   .60 .25
  a.   Souvenir sheet of 2   1.75 1.75

70th Inter-Parliamentary Union Conference.

A791

1983, Oct. 6   Photo.   Perf. 13
1350 A791 70w Gymnastics   .65 .25
1351 A791 70w Soccer   .65 .25

64th National Sports Festival.

Pres. Chun
and Pres. U
San Yu of
Burma
A791a

Pres. Chun's Curtailed Visit to Southwest
Asia: No. 1351B, India. No. 1351C, Pres.
Junius R. Jayawardene, Sri Lanka. No.
1351D, Australia, flag. No. 1351E, New Zealand, flag. Withdrawn after one day due to
political assassination.

1983, Oct. 8   Photo.   Perf. 13½x13
1351A A791a 70w multicolored   1.50 .75
1351B A791a 70w multicolored   1.50 .75
1351C A791a 70w multicolored   1.50 .75
1351D A791a 70w multicolored   1.50 .75
1351E A791a 70w multicolored   1.50 .75
      Nos. 1351A-1351E (5)   7.50 3.75

Souvenir Sheets of 2

1351f A791a 70w   5.00 5.00
1351g A791a 70w   5.00 5.00
1351h A791a 70w   5.00 5.00
1351i A791a 70w   5.00 5.00
1351j A791a 70w   5.00 5.00
      Nos. 1351f-1351j (5)   25.00 25.00

Water Resource
Development
A792

1983, Oct. 15   Litho.   Perf. 13
1352 A792 70w multicolored   .60 .25

Newspaper
Publication
Cent. — A793

1983, Oct. 31   Litho.   Perf. 13
1353 A793 70w multicolored   .60 .25

Natl. Tuberculosis
Assoc., 30th
Anniv. — A794

1983, Nov. 6   Photo.   Perf. 13
1354 A794 70w multicolored   .60 .25

Presidents Chun and Reagan, Natl. Flags — A795

1983, Nov. 12   Photo.   *Perf. 13*
1355 A795 70w multicolored .... .75 .25
  a.   Souvenir sheet of 2 ..... 3.00 3.00
Visit of Pres. Ronald Reagan, Nov. 12-14.

11th Philatelic Week — A796

1983, Nov. 18   Photo.   *Perf. 13*
1356 A796 70w multicolored .... .60 .25
  a.   Souvenir sheet of 2 ..... 2.75 2.75

New Year 1984
A797   A798

1983, Dec. 1   Photo.   *Perf. 13*
1357 A797 70w Mouse, stone
    wall relief .... .75 .25
  a.   Souvenir sheet of 2 ..... 2.75 2.75
1358 A798 70w Cranes, pine tree ... .75 .25
  a.   Souvenir sheet of 2 ..... 2.75 2.75

Bicentenary of Catholic Church in Korea — A799

1984, Jan. 4   Photo.   *Perf. 13x13½*
1359 A799 70w Cross .... .60 .25
  a.   Souvenir sheet of 2 ..... 3.25 3.25

Visit of Brunei's Sultan Bolkiah-Apr. 7-9 — A800

1984, Apr. 7   Litho.   *Perf. 13x12½*
1360 A800 70w multicolored .... .60 .25
  a.   Souvenir sheet of 2, imperf. 1.75 1.75

Visit of Qatar's Sheik Khalifa, Apr. 20-22 A801

1984, Apr. 20
1361 A801 70w multicolored .... .60 .25
  a.   Souvenir sheet of 2, imperf. 1.75 1.75

Girl Mailing Letter — A802

Mailman in City — A803

1984, Apr. 22   Photo.   *Perf. 13½x13*
1362 A802 70w multicolored .... .60 .25
  a.   Souvenir sheet of 2 ..... 1.75 1.75
1363 A803 70w multicolored .... .60 .25
  a.   Souvenir sheet of 2 ..... 1.75 1.75
Korean postal service.

Visit of Pope John Paul II, May 3-7 — A808

1984, May 3   Engr.   *Perf. 12½*
1368 A808 70w dk brn .... .70 .25

Photogravure & Engraved
1369 A808 70w multicolored .... .70 .25
  a.   Souvenir sheet of 2, #1368-
    1369, perf. 13½ 2.75 2.75

Tools, Brushes, Flower — A809

1984, May 11   Photo.   *Perf. 13x13½*
1370 A809 70w multicolored .... .60 .25
Workers' Cultural Festival.

Jet, Ship, Asia Map — A810

1984, May 21   Photo.   *Perf. 13x13½*
1371 A810 70w multicolored .... .60 .25
Customs Cooperation Council 63rd-64th Sessions, Seoul, May 21-25.

Visit of Sri Lanka's Pres. Jayewardene, May 27-30 — A811

1904, May 27   *Perf. 13½x13*
1372 A811 70w Asia map, flags,
    flowers .... .60 .25
  a.   Souvenir sheet of 2 ..... 1.75 1.75

Advertising Congress Emblem — A812

1984, June 18   Photo.   *Perf. 13x13½*
1373 A812 70w multicolored .... .60 .25
14th Asian Advertising Cong., Seoul, June 18-21.

'88 Olympic Expressway Opening — A813

1984, June 22
1374 A813 70w multicolored .... .70 .25

Intl. Olympic Committee, 90th Anniv. — A814

1984, June 23
1375 A814 70w multicolored .... .60 .25

Asia-Pacific Broadcasting Union, 20th Anniv. A815

1984, June 30   *Perf. 13½x13*
1376 A815 70w Emblem,
    microphone .... .60 .25

Visit of Senegal's Pres. Diouf, July 9-12 A816

1984, July 9   Litho.   *Perf. 13x12½*
1377 A816 70w Flags of Korea &
    Senegal .... .60 .25
  a.   Souvenir sheet of 2, imperf. 2.00 2.00

1984 Summer Olympics A817

Lithographed and Engraved
1984, July 28   *Perf. 12½*
1378 A817 70w Archery .... 75 .25
1379 A817 440w Fencing .... 3.00 .75

Korean Protestant Church Cent. — A818

Stained glass windows.

1984, Aug. 16   *Perf. 13*
1380 A818 70w Crucifixion .... .75 .25
1381 A818 70w Cross, dove .... .75 .25
  a.   Souvenir sheet of 2 ..... 6.00 6.00
  b.   Pair, #1380-1381 ..... 2.00 2.00

Groom on Horseback — A819

Wedding Procession: a, Lantern carrier. b, Groom. c, Musician. d, Bride in sedan chair (52x33mm).

1984, Sept. 1   Photo.   *Perf. 13x13½*
1382   Strip of 4 .... 4.50 1.50
  a.-d.   A819 70w any single ..... .75 .75
  e.   Souvenir sheet 2.50 2.50
No. 1382e contains No. 1382d.

Pres. Chun's Visit to Japan, Sept. 6-8 A820

1984, Sept. 6   Litho.   *Perf. 13x12½*
1383 A820 70w Chun, flag, Mt.
    Fuji .... .60 .25
  a.   Souvenir sheet of 2, imperf. 2.00 2.00

Visit of Gambia's Pres. Jawara, Sept. 12-17 A821

1984, Sept. 12
1384 A821 70w Flags of Korea &
    Gambia .... .60 .25
  a.   Souvenir sheet of 2, imperf. 2.00 2.00

Visit of Gabon's Pres. Bongo, Sept. 21-23 — A822

1984, Sept. 21   *Perf. 13*
1385 A822 70w Flags of Korea &
    Gabon .... .60 .25
  a.   Souvenir sheet of 2, imperf. 2.00 2.00

Seoul Intl. Trade Fair — A823

1984, Sept. 18   Photo.   *Perf. 13x13½*
1386 A823 70w Products   .60   .25

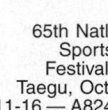

65th Natl. Sports Festival, Taegu, Oct. 11-16 — A824

1984, Oct. 11   Photo.   *Perf. 13½x13*
1387 A824 70w Badminton   .65   .25
1388 A824 70w Wrestling   .65   .25

Philakorea '84 Stamp Show, Seoul, Oct. 22-31 A825

No. 1389, South Gate, stamps. No. 1390, Emblem under magnifier, vert.

1984, Oct. 22   *Perf. 13½x13, 13x13½*
1389 A825 70w multicolored   .60   .25
   a.   Souvenir sheet of 4   4.00   4.00
1390 A825 70w multicolored   .60   .25
   a.   Souvenir sheet of 4   4.00   4.00

Visit of Maldives Pres. Maumoon Abdul Gayoom, Oct. 29-Nov. 1 A826

1984, Oct. 29   Litho.   *Perf. 13x12½*
1392 A826 70w multicolored   .60   .25
   a.   Souvenir sheet of 2, imperf. 2.00   2.00

Chamber of Commerce and Industry Cent. — A827

1984, Oct. 31   Photo.   *Perf. 13x13½*
1393 A827 70w "100"   .60   .25

Children Playing Jaegi-chagi — A828

New Year 1985 (Year of the ox).

1984, Dec. 1   Photo.   *Perf. 13x13½*
1394 A828 70w Ox, bas-relief   .60   .25
   a.   Souvenir sheet of 2   2.00   2.00
1395 A828 70w shown   .60   .25
   a.   Souvenir sheet of 2   2.00   2.00

Intl. Youth Year — A829

1985, Jan. 25   Photo.   *Perf. 13½x13*
1396 A829 70w IYY emblem   .60   .25

Korean Folkways Series

A830

1985   Photo.   *Perf. 13x13½*
1397 A830 70w Pounding rice   .80   .25
1398 A830 70w Welcoming full moon   .80   .25
1399 A830 70w Wrestling   1.00   .25
1400 A830 70w Janggi, Korean chess   1.00   .25

Issued: Nos. 1397-1398, 2/19; Nos. 1399-1400, 8/20.

Modern Art Series

Rocky Mountain in the Early Spring, 1915, by Shimjoen, (Ahn Jung-shik) A831

Still-life with a Doll, 1927, by Suhlcho, (Lee Chong-woo) A832

Spring Day on a Farm, 1961, by Eijai, (Huh Paik-ryun, 1903-1977) A833

The Exorcist, 1941, by Chulma, (Kim Chung-hyun, 1901-1953) — A834

Chunhyang-do, by Kim Un-ho — A835

Flowers, by Lee Sang-bum A836

Image of A Friend, by Ku Bon-wung A837

Woman in a Ski Suit, by Son Ung-seng A838

Valley of the Peach Blossoms, 1964, by Pyen Kwan-Sik (1899-1976) A839

Rural Landscape, 1940, by Lee Yong-Wu (1904-1952) A840

Male, 1932, by Lee Ma-Dong A841

Woman with a Water Jar on Her Head, 1944, by Yun Hyo-Chung (1917-1967) A842

Photo.; Litho. & Engr. (#1411-1412)
1985-87   *Perf. 13½x13, 13x13½*
1401 A831 70w multicolored   .90   .25
1402 A832 70w multicolored   .90   .25
1403 A833 70w multicolored   .90   .25
1404 A834 70w multicolored   .90   .25
1405 A835 80w multi ('86)   1.25   .40
1406 A836 80w multi ('86)   1.25   .40
1407 A837 80w multi ('86)   1.25   .40
1408 A838 80w multi ('86)   1.25   .40
1409 A839 80w multi ('87)   3.50   .90
1410 A840 80w multi ('87)   3.50   .90
1411 A841 80w multi ('87)   3.50   .90
1412 A842 80w multi ('87)   3.50   .90
   Nos. 1401-1412 (12)   22.60   6.20

Issued: Nos. 1401-1402, 4/10; Nos. 1403-1404, 7/5; Nos. 1405-1408, 12/1; Nos. 1409-1412, 6/12.

State Visit of Pres. Chun to the US — A843

Photo. & Engr.
1985, Apr. 24   *Perf. 13*
1413 A843 70w multicolored   .60   .25
   a.   Souvenir sheet of 2   2.00   2.00

Coastal and Inland Fish Series

Gak-si- Bung-eo (silver carp) — A844

Dot-sac-chi (sword fish) — A845

Eoreumchi A846

Sweetfish
A847

Sardine
A848

Hammerhead
Shark
A849

Cham-jung-
go-ji — A850

Swi-ri — A851

Oar
Fish — A852

Devil-ray
A853

1985-87   Photo.   Perf. 13½x13
1414 A844 70w multicolored   .75   .25
1415 A845 70w multicolored   .75   .25
1416 A846 70w multi ('86)   2.00   .55
1417 A847 70w multi ('86)   2.00   .55
1418 A848 70w multi ('86)   2.00   .55
1419 A849 70w multi ('86)   2.00   .55
1420 A850 80w multi ('87)   2.75   1.00
1421 A851 80w multi ('87)   2.75   1.00
1422 A852 80w multi ('87)   2.75   1.00
1423 A853 80w multi ('87)   2.75   1.00
        Nos. 1414-1423 (10)   20.50   6.70

Issued: Nos. 1414-1415, 5/30; Nos. 1416-1423, 7/25.

Yonsei
University
and
Medical
School,
Cent.
A854

Photogravure and Engraved
1985, May 6   Perf. 13
1424 A854 70w Underwood Hall   .60   .25

State Visit of Pres.
Mohammad Zia-Ul-
Haq of Pakistan,
May 6-10 — A855

1985, May 6   Photo.   Perf. 13x13½
1425 A855 70w multicolored   .60   .25
 a.   Souvenir sheet of 2   2.00   2.00

State Visit of
Pres. Luis
Alberto
Monge of
Costa Rica,
May 19-
23 — A856

1985, May 18   Perf. 13½x13
1426 A856 70w multicolored   .60   .25
 a.   Souvenir sheet of 2   2.00   2.00

State Visit of
Pres. Hussain
Muhammad
Ershad of
Bangladesh,
June 15-19
A857

1985, June 15
1427 A857 70w multicolored   .60   .25
 a.   Souvenir sheet of 2, imperf. 2.00 2.00

State Visit of Pres. Joao Bernardo
Vieira of Guinea-Bissau, June 25-
28 — A858

1985, June 25
1428 A858 70w multicolored   .60   .25
 a.   Souvenir sheet of 2, imperf. 2.00 2.00

Liberation from Japanese Occupation
Forces, 40th Anniv. — A859

Heavenly Lake, Mt. Paektu, natl. flower.

1985, Aug. 14   Litho.   Perf. 13x12½
1429 A859 70w multicolored   .60   .25

Music Series

The Spring of My
Home, Music by
Hong Nan-pa
and Lyrics by
Lee Won-su
A860

A Leaf Boat,
Music by Yun
Yong-ha and
Lyrics by Park
Hong-Keun
A861

Half Moon,
1924, by Yun
Keuk-Young
A862

Let's Go and
Pick the Moon,
by Yun Seok-
Jung and Park
Tae Hyun
A863

Barley Field, by
Park Wha-mok
and Yun Yong-
ha — A865

Magnolia, by
Cho Young-Shik
and Kim Dong-
jin — A866

1985-86   Photo.   Perf. 13x13½
1430 A860 70w multicolored   .90   .25
1431 A861 70w multicolored   .90   .25
1432 A862 70w multicolored   1.00   .30
1433 A863 70w multicolored   1.75   .60

Issued: Nos. 1430-1431, 9/10; Nos. 1432-1433, 6/25/86.

Korean Folkways Series

Korean Farm
Music
A864

No. 1434 — Musicians with: a, Flag, hand gong. b, Drum flute. c, Drum, hand gong. d, Taborets, ribbons. e, Taboret, sun, woman, child. Has continuous design.

1986, Aug. 26 Photo.   Perf. 13½x13
1434   Strip of 5   7.50   7.50
 a.-e. A864 70w, any single   1.25   .25

Music Series

Barley Field, by
Park Wha-mok
and Yun Yong-
ha — A865

Magnolia, by
Cho Young-Shik
and Kim Dong-
jin — A866

1987, Mar. 25 Photo.   Perf. 13x13½
1435 A865 80w multicolored   3.00   1.00
1436 A866 80w multicolored   3.00   1.00

Korean Folkways Series

Chusok, Harvest Moon
Festival — A867

No. 1437—Harvest moon dance: a, Eight dancers, harvest moon. b, Four dancers, festival wheels, balloons. c, Three dancers, children on see-saw. d, Four dancers, women preparing meal.

1987, Sept. 10 Photo.   Perf. 13x13½
1437 A867 Strip of 4   17.50 17.50
 a.-d. 80w any single   3.25   1.00

Folkways and Music Series

Tano, Spring Harvest Festival — A868

No. 1438: a, Woman on shore, riding a swing. b, Sweet flag coiffures. c, Boy picking flowers, girl on swing. d, Boys wrestling.

1988, Aug. 25 Photo.   Perf. 13x13½
1438 A868 Strip of 4   6.50   6.50
 a.-d. 80w multicolored   1.25   .40

Sick for Home,
by Lee Eun-sang
and Kim Kong-jin
A869

Pioneer, by Yoon
Hae-young and
Cho Doo-nam
A870

1988, Nov. 15
1439 A869 80w multicolored   .75   .25
1440 A870 80w multicolored   .75   .25

Mask Dance (Talchum) — A871

No. 1441: a, Two mask dancers with scarves. b, Dancers with fans. c, Dancers with scarf and laurel or fan. d, Three dancers, first as an animal and two more carrying fan and bells or torch.

1989, Feb. 25
1441 A871 Strip of 4   6.00   6.00
 a.-d. 80w any single   1.25   .40

Korean Telecommunications,
Cent. — A872

70w, Satellite, emblem, dish receiver.

1985, Sept. 28   Perf. 13½x13
1442 A872 70w multicolored   .60   .25

World Bank
Conference, Seoul,
Oct. 8-11 — A873

1985, Oct. 8   Perf. 13x13½
1443 A873 70w Emblem   .60   .25

Intl. Bank for Reconstruction & Development, 40th Anniv.

UN, 40th
Anniv.
A874

1985, Oct. 24   Perf. 13½x13
1444 A874 70w Emblem, doves   .60   .25

Natl. Red
Cross, 80th
Anniv.
A875

1985, Oct. 26
1445 A875 70w red, blk & bl   .60   .25

Segment of
Canceled
Cover — A876

1985, Nov. 18 Photo.   Perf. 13½x13
1446 A876 70w multicolored   .60   .25
12th Philatelic Week, Nov. 18-23.

New Year
1986 — A877

Lithographed and Engraved
1985, Dec. 2   Perf. 13x13½
1447 A877 70w multicolored   .60   .25

Mt. Fuji, Korean Airlines Jet — A878

1985, Dec. 18   Photo.
1448 A878 70w brt bl, blk & red   .75   .30
Normalization of diplomatic relations
between Korea and Japan, 20th anniv.
See No. C44.

**Statesman Type of 1986 and Types
of 1981-86**
Engr., Photo. (40w)
1986-87   Perf. 13
1449 A716 550w indigo   3.00   .40
Coil Stamps
Perf. 13 Vert.
1449A A704 20w multicolored   .75   .40
1449B A705 40w multicolored   .90   .30
1449C A708 80w multicolored   1.50   .60
  Nos. 1449A-1449C (3)   3.15 1.30
Issue dates: 550w, Dec. 10; others, 1987.

Intl. Peace
Year — A879

1986, Jan. 15   Photo.   Perf. 13x13½
1450 A879 70w multicolored   .60   .25
See No. C45.

State Visits of
Pres.
Chun — A880

Portrait, natl. flags and: No. 1452, Parlia-
ment, Brussels. No. 1453, Eiffel Tower, Paris.
No. 1454, Cathedral, Cologne. No. 1455, Big
Ben, London.

1986, Apr. 4   Litho.   Perf. 12½x13
1452 A880 70w multicolored   .75   .30
1453 A880 70w multicolored   .75   .30
1454 A880 70w multicolored   .75   .30
1455 A880 70w multicolored   .75   .30
  Nos. 1452-1455 (4)   3.00 1.20
Souvenir Sheets of 2
Perf. 13½
1452a A880 70w   3.50 3.50
1453a A880 70w   3.50 3.50
1454a A880 70w   3.50 3.50
1455a A880 70w   3.50 3.50
  Nos. 1452a-1455a (4)   14.00 14.00

Science Series

Observatories — A881

Designs: No. 1456, Chomsongdae Observatory, Satellites. No. 1457, Kwanchondae
Observatory, Halley's Comet.

1986, Apr. 21   Perf. 13½x13
1456   70w multicolored   3.00   .85
1457   70w multicolored   3.00   .85
  a. A881 Pair, #1456-1457   7.50 2.75

Weather — A883

Designs: No. 1458, Wind observatory stone
foundation, Chosun Dynasty. No. 1459, Rain
gauge, Sejong Period to Chosun Dynasty.

1987, Apr. 21   Photo.   Perf. 13½
1458   80w multicolored   3.00 1.00
1459   80w multicolored   3.00 1.00
  a. A883 Pair, #1458-1459   7.50 4.00

Clocks — A885

Designs: No. 1460, Chagyokru, water clock
invented by Chang Yongshil and Kim Bin in
1434. No. 1461, Angbuilgu, sundial completed
during King Sejong's reign (1418-1450).

1988, Apr. 21   Photo.   Perf. 13½x13
1460   80w multicolored   .85   .30
1461   80w multicolored   .85   .30
  a. A885 Pair, #1460-1461   2.25 2.25

Early Printing Methods — A887

Designs: No. 1462, Sutra manuscript
(detail) printed from wood type, Shila Dynasty,
c.704-751. No. 1463, Two characters from a
manuscript printed from metal type, Koryo,
c.1237.

1989, Apr. 21
1462   80w buff & sepia   1.60   .40
1463   80w buff & sepia   1.60   .40
  a. A887 Pair, #1462-1463   3.25 3.25

A889

Designs: No. 1464, 7th century gilt bronze
Buddha. No. 1465, Bronze Age dagger, spear
molds.

1990, Apr. 21
1464   100w multicolored   .60   .25
1465   100w multicolored   .60   .25
  a. A889 Pair, #1464-1465   1.50 1.50
  Complete bklt., 2 each #1464-
  1465   2.50
  Nos. 1456-1465 (10)   18.10 5.60
Pairs have continuous designs.

Souvenir Booklets
Booklets containing the stamps listed
below have a stamp, pair or strip of
stamps, tied to the booklet cover with a
first day cancel.
  1464-1465, 1523-1524, 1529-1532,
1535-1536, 1539-1540, 1553, 1559-
1566, 1572-1576, 1583-1584, 1595-
1608, 1613-1621, 1622-1623B, 1624,
1635-1650, 1655-1656, 1657-1668,
1669-1676, 1678-1690, 1693-1699,
1700-1702, 1713-1714, 1745-1748,
1751-1758, 1763-1764, 1767-1768,
1770-1773, 1776-1787, 1797, 1799-
1802, 1803-1806, 1810-1811.

Assoc. of Natl.
Olympic
Committees, 5th
General Assembly,
Seoul, Apr. 21-
25 — A891

1986, Apr. 21   Perf. 13x13½
1466 A891 70w multicolored   .60   .25

Souvenir Sheet

Butterflies — A892

1986, May 22   Litho.   Perf. 13½
1467   Sheet of 6   29.00 29.00
  a. A892 70w multicolored   3.00 1.50
  b. A892 370w multicolored   3.00 1.50
  c. A892 400w multicolored   3.00 1.50
  d. A892 440w multicolored   3.00 1.50
  e. A892 450w multicolored   3.00 1.50
  f. A892 470w multicolored   3.00 1.50

AMERIPEX '86, Chicago, May 22-June 1.
No. 1467 contains stamps of different sizes
(370w, 42x41mm; 400w, 42x33mm; 440w,
39x45mm; 450w, 32x42mm; 470w,
33x44mm); margin continues the designs.

Women's
Education,
Cent.
A893

1986, May 31   Perf. 13x12½
1468 A893 70w multicolored   .60   .25

State Visit
of Pres.
Andre
Kolingba,
Central
Africa
A894

1986, June 10   Perf. 13
1469 A894 70w multicolored   .60   .25
  a. Souvenir sheet of 2, imperf. 1.75 1.75

Completion of Han River Development
Project — A895

1986, Sept. 10   Litho.   Perf. 13
1470   Strip of 3   4.50 4.50
  a. A895 30w Bridge   1.20   .30
  b. A895 60w Buildings   1.20   .30
  c. A895 80w Seoul Tower, buildings 1.20   .30
Printed in a continuous design.

Fireworks, Seoul Tower — A896   Games Emblem — A897

1986, Sept. 20 Photo. Perf. 13x13½
1471 A896 80w multicolored .70 .30
  a. Souvenir sheet of 2 7.50 7.50
1472 A897 80w multicolored .70 .30
  a. Souvenir sheet of 2 7.50 7.50

Souvenir Sheet

10th Asian Games, Seoul, Sept. 20-Oct. 5 — A898

1986, Oct. 31
1473 A898 550w multicolored 21.00 21.00

Juan Antonio Samaranch, Korean IOC Delegation, 1981 — A899

1986, Sept. 30
1474 A899 80w multicolored 1.10 .40
Intl. Olympic Committee decision to hold 24th Olympic Games in Seoul, 5th anniv.

Philatelic Week — A900

1986, Nov. 18 Photo. Perf. 13½x13
1475 A900 80w Boy fishing for stamp .70 .25

New Year 1987 (Year of the Hare) — A901

1986, Dec. 1 Photo. Perf. 13x13½
1476 A901 80w multicolored 1.00 .30

Birds — A902

1986, Dec. 20 Perf. 13x14
1477 A902 80w Waxwing 1.50 .40
1478 A902 80w Oriole 1.50 .40
1479 A902 80w Kingfisher 1.50 .40
1480 A902 80w Hoopoe 1.50 .40
1481 A902 80w Roller 1.50 .40
  a. Strip of 5, #1477-1481 8.50 8.50

Coil Stamps
Perf. 14 Horiz.
1481B A902 80w like No. 1479 3.00 .75
1481C A902 80w like No. 1480 3.00 .75
1481D A902 80w like No. 1481 3.00 .75
1481E A902 80w like No. 1477 3.00 .75
1481F A902 80w like No. 1478 3.00 .75
  g. Strip of 5, #1481B-1481F 25.00 25.00

Wildlife Conservation A903

Endangered species: No. 1482, Panthera tigris altaica. No. 1483, Felis bengalensis. No. 1484, Vulpes vulpes. No. 1485, Sus scrofa.

1987, Feb. 25 Photo. Perf. 13½x13
1482 A903 80w multicolored 2.50 .70
1483 A903 80w multicolored 2.50 .70
1484 A903 80w multicolored 2.50 .70
1485 A903 80w multicolored 2.50 .70
  a. Strip of 4, #1482-1485 12.00 12.00

Flowers — A904

No. 1486, Dicentra spectabilis. No. 1487, Hanabusaya asiatica. No. 1488, Erythronium japonicum. No. 1489, Dianthus chinensis. No. 1490, Chrysanthemum zawadskii coreanum.

1987, Mar. 20 Photo. Perf. 14x13
1486 A904 550w multicolored 2.50 .60
1487 A904 550w multicolored 2.50 .60
1488 A904 550w multicolored 2.50 .60
1489 A904 550w multicolored 2.50 .60
1490 A904 550w multicolored 2.50 .60
  a. Strip of 5, #1486-1490 14.00 14.00

Coil Stamps
Perf. 13 Vert.
1490B A904 550w like No. 1486 3.00 1.00
1490C A904 550w like No. 1487 3.00 1.00
1490D A904 550w like No. 1488 3.00 1.00
1490E A904 550w like No. 1489 3.00 1.00
1490F A904 550w like No. 1490 3.00 1.00
  g. Strip of 5, #1490B-1490F 17.50 17.50

State Visit of Pres. Ahmed Abdallah Abderemane of the Comoro Isls., Apr. 6-9 — A905

1987, Apr. 6 Litho. Perf. 13½x13
1491 A905 80w multicolored .60 .25
  a. Souvenir sheet of 2 2.25 2.25

Electrification of Korea, Cent. — A906

1987, Apr. 10 Photo.
1492 A906 80w multicolored .60 .25

Int'l. Assoc. of Ports and Harbors, 15th General Session, Seoul — A907

1987, Apr. 25 Photo. Perf. 13½x13
1493 A907 80w multicolored .60 .25

State Visit of Pres. U San Yu of Burma A908

1987, June 8 Litho. Perf. 13½x13
1494 A908 80w multicolored .60 .25
  a. Souvenir sheet of 2 2.00 2.00

Year of The Communications for Information Society — A909

1987, June 30 Perf. 13x13½
1495 A909 80w Map, digital telephone .70 .25
1496 A909 80w Emblem .70 .25
Introduction of automatic switching telephone system.

Independence Hall, Monument to the Nation — A910

Statue of Indomitable Koreans, Nat'l. Flag — A911

1987, Aug. 14 Photo. Perf. 13½x13
1497 A910 80w multicolored 1.00 .30
  a. Souvenir sheet of 2 12.50 12.50
1498 A911 80w multicolored 1.00 .30
  a. Souvenir sheet of 2 12.50 12.50
Opening of Independence Hall, Aug. 15.

16th Pacific Science Congress, Seoul, Aug. 20-30 — A912

1987, Aug. 20 Perf. 13x13½
1499 A912 80w multicolored .75 .25
  a. Souvenir sheet of 2 3.50 3.50

State Visit of Pres. Virgilio Barco of Colombia A913

1987, Sept. 8 Litho. Perf. 13½x13
1500 A913 80w multicolored .60 .25
  a. Souvenir sheet of 2 2.25 2.25

Installation of 10-millionth Telephone A914

1987, Sept. 28 Perf. 13½x13
1501 A914 80w multicolored .60 .25

Armed Forces, 39th Anniv. — A915

Armed Forces Day: Servicemen, flags of three military services.

1987, Sept. 30 Litho. Perf. 13
1502 A915 80w multicolored .90 .25

14th Philatelic Week, Nov. 18-24 — A916

1987, Nov. 18 Photo. Perf. 13½
1503 A916 80w Boy playing the nalrali .75 .25

A917

1987, Nov. 28 Litho.
1504 A917 80w multicolored 1.10 .40
Signing of the Antarctic Treaty by Korea, 1st anniv.

A918

1987, Dec. 1 Photo.
1505 A918 80w multicolored 1.20 .30
New Year 1988 (Year of the Dragon).

Natl. Social
Security
Program
A919

1988, Jan. 4   Litho.   *Perf. 13½x13*
1506 A919 80w multicolored   .75   .25

Completion of the
Korean Antarctic
Base — A919a

1988, Feb. 16   Photo.   *Perf. 13x13½*
1506A A919a 80w multicolored   1.25   .30

Inauguration
of Roh Tae-
Woo, 13th
President
A920

1988, Feb. 24   Photo.   *Perf. 13½x13*
1507 A920 80w multicolored   1.25   .40
   a.   Souvenir sheet of 2   22.50 22.50

World Wildlife
Fund — A921

White-naped crane (*Grus vipio*) displaying
various behaviors: a, Calling (1). b, Running
(2). c, Spreading wings (3). d, Flying (4).

1988, Apr. 1   *Perf. 13x13½*
1508   Strip of 4   9.00   9.00
  a.-d. A921 80w any single   1.40   .80

Intl. Red Cross &
Red Crescent
Organizations,
125th
Annivs. — A922

1988, May 7   Photo.   *Perf. 13x13½*
1509 A922 80w multicolored   .75   .25

Telepress Medium,
1st Anniv. — A923

1988, June 1   Litho.
1510 A923 80w multicolored   .60   .25

Pierre de
Coubertin,
Olympic
Flag — A924

Olympic
Temple
A925

View of   Folk
Seoul — A926   Dancers — A927

Litho. & Engr.
1988, Sept. 16   *Perf. 13½x13*
1511 A924 80w multicolored   1.00   .30
1512 A925 80w multicolored   1.00   .30
Photo.
**   *Perf. 13x13½***
1513 A926 80w multicolored   1.00   .30
1514 A927 80w multicolored   1.00   .30
     Nos. 1511-1514 (4)   4.00   1.20
1988 Summer Olympics, Seoul.
Souvenir Sheets of 2
1511a A924   80w   2.25   2.25
1512a A925   80w   2.25   2.25
1513a A926   80w   2.25   2.25
1514a A927   80w   2.25   2.25
    Nos. 1511a-1514a (4)   9.00   9.00

Margin inscriptions on Nos. 1511a-1512a
are photo.

OLYMPHILEX '88,
Sept. 19-28,
Seoul — A928

1988, Sept. 19   Photo.   *Perf. 13x13½*
1515 A928 80w multicolored   .60   .25
   a.   Souvenir sheet of 2   2.00   2.00

22nd
Congress
of the Intl. Iron
and Steel
Institute,
Seoul
A929

1988, Oct. 8   *Perf. 13½x13*
1516 A929 80w multicolored   .60   .25

A930

1988, Oct. 15   *Perf. 13x13½*
1517 A930 80w shown   1.00   .60
1518 A930 80w Archer seated in
          wheelchair   .75   .30
**1988 Natl. Special Olympics (Paralympics),
Seoul.**

A931

1988, Dec. 1   Photo.   *Perf. 13x13½*
1519 A931 80w multicolored   1.00   .25
   New Year 1989 (Year of the Snake).

Souvenir Sheet

Successful Completion of the 1988
Summer Olympics, Seoul — A932

1988, Dec. 20   Litho.   *Perf. 13x12½*
1520 A932 550w Opening cer-
       emony   16.00 16.00

Music Series

Arirang — A933   Doraji — A934

Pakyon Falls   Chonan-Samkori
A935   A936

Natl. ballads.

1989-90   Photo.   *Perf. 13x13½*
1521 A933 80w multicolored   .75   .25
1522 A934 80w multicolored   .75   .25
Litho.
1523 A935 80w multicolored   .75   .25
    Complete booklet, 4 #1523   6.50
1524 A936 80w multicolored   .75   .25
    Complete booklet, 4 #1524   6.50
  Issued: Nos. 1521-1522, 3/27; Nos. 1523-
1524, 2/26/90.

Korean Folkways Series

Willowing
Bow — A937

Spinning
Wheel
A938

Treating
Threads
A939

Weaving
Fabric
A940

Litho. & Engr.
1990, Sept. 25   *Perf. 13½x13*
1525 A937 100w multicolored   1.00   .30
1526 A938 100w multicolored   1.00   .30
1527 A939 100w multicolored   1.00   .30
1528 A940 100w multicolored   1.00   .30
   a.   Strip of 4, #1525-1528   4.50   4.50

Music Series

Orchard   In Flower
Avenue — A941   Garden — A942

A Swing   Longing for Mt.
A943   Keumkang
                A944

1991-92   Litho.   *Perf. 13x13½*
1529 A941 100w multicolored   .85   .30
    Complete booklet, 4 #1529   8.00
1530 A942 100w multicolored   .85   .30
    Complete booklet, 4 #1530   8.00
1531 A943 100w multicolored   .75   .25
    Complete booklet, 4 #1531   8.00
1532 A944 100w multicolored   .75   .25
    Complete booklet, 4 #1532   8.00
  Issued: Nos. 1529-1530, 3/27; Nos. 1531-
1532, 7/13/92.

14th Asian-Pacific
Dental
Congress — A945

1989, Apr. 26   Photo.   *Perf. 13x13½*
1533 A945 80w multicolored   .60   .25

Rotary Intl.
Convention, Seoul,
May 21-25 — A946

1989, May 20   Photo.   *Perf. 13x13½*
1534 A946 80w multicolored   .75   .25

19th Cong. of the Intl. Council of Nurses, Seoul, May 28-June 2 — A947

1989, May 27
1535 A947 80w multicolored .75 .25
   Complete booklet, 4 #1535 5.00

Information Industry Month — A948

1989, June 1
1536 A948 80w multicolored .75 .25
   Complete booklet, 4 #1536 5.00

World Environment Day — A949

1989, June 5
1537 A949 80w multicolored .75 .25

Asia-Pacific Telecommunity, 10th Anniv. — A950

1989, July 1 Photo. *Perf. 13x13½*
1538 A950 80w multicolored .75 .25

French Revolution, Bicent. A951

1989, July 14 Litho. *Perf. 13½x13*
1539 A951 80w multicolored .60 .25
   Complete booklet, 4 #1539 5.00

Federation of Asian and Oceanian Biochemists 5th Congress A952

1989, Aug. 12 Photo.
1540 A952 80w multicolored .60 .25
   Complete booklet, 4 #1540 5.00

Modern Art Series

A White Ox, by Lee Joong-Sub — A953

A Street Stall, by Park Lae-hyun A954

A Little Girl, by Lee Bong-Sang A955

An Autumn Scene, by Oh Ji-ho — A956

Litho. & Engr.; Photo. (#1542, 1544)
1989, Sept. 4 *Perf. 13x13½, 13½x13*
1541 A953 80w multicolored .80 .30
1542 A954 80w multicolored .80 .30
1543 A955 80w multicolored .80 .30
1544 A956 80w multicolored .80 .30
   Nos. 1541-1544 (4) 3.20 1.20

Allegory: The Valiant Spirit of Koreans A965

1989, Sept. 12 Litho. *Perf. 13½x13*
1553 A965 80w multicolored .60 .25
   Complete booklet, 4 #1553 5.00
1988 Seoul Olympics and the World Korean Sports Festival.

Personification of Justice and Ancient Codex — A966

1989, Sept. 18
1554 A966 80w multicolored .75 .25
Constitutional Court, 1st anniv.

Fish

A967

A968

A969

A970

No. 1555, Oplegnathus fasciatus. No. 1556, Cobitis multifasciata. No. 1557, Liobagrus mediadiposalis. No. 1558, Monocentris japonicus.

1989, Sept. 30 Photo. *Perf. 13½x13*
1555 A967 80w multicolored .85 .30
1556 A968 80w multicolored .85 .30
1557 A969 80w multicolored .85 .30
1558 A970 80w multicolored .85 .30

A971

A972

A973

A974

No. 1559, Hapalogenys mucronatus. No. 1560, Fugu niphobles. No. 1561, Oncorhynchus masou. No. 1562, Rhodeus ocellatus.

1990, July 2
1559 A971 100w multicolored .80 .30
   Complete booklet, 4 #1559 10.00
1560 A972 100w multicolored .80 .30
   Complete booklet, 4 #1560 10.00
1561 A973 100w multicolored .80 .30
   Complete booklet, 4 #1561 10.00
1562 A974 100w multicolored .80 .30
   Complete booklet, 4 #1562 10.00

A975

A976

A977

A978

No. 1563, Microphyso- gobio longidorsalis. No. 1564, Gnathopogon majimae. No. 1565, Therapon oxyrhnchus. No. 1566, Psettina ijimae.

1991, June 8
1563 A975 100w multicolored .85 .25
   Complete booklet, 4 #1563 10.00
1564 A976 100w multicolored .85 .25
   Complete booklet, 4 #1564 10.00
1565 A977 100w multicolored .85 .25
   Complete booklet, 4 #1565 10.00
1566 A978 100w multicolored .85 .25
   Complete booklet, 4 #1566 10.00
   Nos. 1555-1566 (12) 10.00 3.40

Light of Peace Illuminating the World — A979

1989, Oct. 4
1567 A979 80w multicolored .60 .25
44th Intl. Eucharistic Cong., Seoul, Oct. 4-8.

29th World Congress of the Intl. Civil Airports Assoc., Seoul, Oct. 17-19 — A980

1989, Oct. 17
1568 A980 80w multicolored .60 .25

Philatelic Week — A981

1989, Nov. 18 Photo. *Perf. 13x13½*
1569 A981 80w Lantern .60 .25
   a.   Souvenir sheet of 2 2.00 2.00

Two Cranes — A982

Folk Festival Customs A983

1989, Dec. 1 *Perf. 13x13½, 13½x13*
1570 A982 80w multicolored .70 .25
   a.   Souvenir sheet of 2 1.75 1.75
1571 A983 80w multicolored .70 .25
   a.   Souvenir sheet of 2 1.75 1.75
New Year 1990.

World Meteorological Day — A984

1990, Mar. 23 *Perf. 13½x13*
1572 A984 80w multicolored .60 .25
Complete booklet, 4 #1572 7.50

UNICEF in Korea, 40th Anniv. — A985

1990, Mar. 24 *Perf. 13x13½*
1573 A985 80w multicolored .60 .25
Complete booklet, 4 #1573 7.50

Cheju-Kohung Fiber Optic Submarine Cable A986

1990, Apr. 21 *Perf. 13½x13*
1574 A986 80w multicolored .60 .25
Complete booklet, 4 #1574 7.50

Saemaul Movement, 20th Anniv. A987

1990, Apr. 21
1575 A987 100w multicolored .60 .25
Complete booklet, 4 #1575 7.50

Youth Month A988

1990, May 1
1576 A988 100w multicolored .75 .25
Complete booklet, 4 #1576 7.50

Type of 1981 and

Korean Flag — A989

Korean Stork — A990

White Magnolia A991

Korean White Pine A991a

Cart-shaped Earthenware A992

Fire Safety A993

Environmental Protection A994

Traffic Safety A995

Waiting One's Turn A996

Saving Energy A997

Child Protection A997a

Purification of Language Movement A997b

Rose of Sharon A997c

Give Life to Water A997d

Ginger Jar — A998

Chong-IP'um-Song, Pine Tree Natl. Monument — A999

Drum, Drum Dance A1001

Mask, Wrestlers A1002

Hong Yong-Sik A1003

King Sejong, Korean Alphabet A1004

Dragon Head, Banner Staff — A1005

Gilt-bronze Buddha Triad with Inscription of Keymi — A1006

Photo., Litho. (#1582), Litho. & Engr. (#1594)

1990-96 *Perf. 13½x13, 13x13½*

No.	Type	Denom.		
1577	A989	10w multi	.45	.25
1578	A990	20w multi	.45	.25
1579	A991	30w multi	.50	.25
1580	A991a	40w multi	.45	.25
1581	A992	50w multi	.60	.25
1582	A993	80w multi	3.00	.30
1583	A994	100w multi	6.00	.40
		Complete booklet, 10 #1583	50.00	
1584	A995	100w multi	2.00	.40
		Complete booklet, 10 #1584	15.00	
1585	A996	100w multi	2.00	.25
1586	A997	100w multi	1.25	.25
1587	A997a	100w multi	1.25	.25
1588	A997b	100w multi	1.25	.25
1589	A997c	110w multi	1.00	.25
1590	A997d	110w multi	1.00	.25
1591	A998	150w multi	1.50	.25
a.		Booklet pane, 20 #1591	20.00	
		Complete booklet, #1591a	22.50	
1592	A999	160w multi	1.50	.25
1593	A1001	370w multi	3.00	.50
1594	A1002	440w multi	4.00	.60
1594A	A1003	600w multi	4.00	.80
1594B	A1004	710w multi	5.00	1.00
1594C	A1005	800w multi	5.00	1.00
1594D	A1006	900w multi	6.50	.85
		Nos. 1577-1594D (22)	51.70	9.10

Issued: No. 1583, 6/5; 600w, 6/25; 150w, 7/2; 800w, 7/10; No. 1584, 7/25; 50w, 9/28; 80w, 11/1; No. 1585, 6/26/91; No. 1586, 11/1/91; No. 1587, 4/5/92; No. 1588, 11/2/92; 370w, 440w, 3/22/93; 10w, 1589, 3/30/93; 160w, 710w, 4/30/93; 20w, 30w, 40w, 5/24/93; No. 1590, 7/1/93; 900w, 9/20/93; #1591a, 3/20/96.

See Nos. 1715-1738, 1846, 1851-1852, 1860, 1862.

Coil Stamps

1990 Litho. *Perf. 13 Horiz.*
1594E A992 50w multicolored 1.00 .30

Perf. 13 Vert.
1594F A706 60w multicolored .75 .25
1594G A994 100w multicolored 1.75 .75
1594H A997c 110w multicolored 1.25 .25
Nos. 1594E-1594H (4) 4.75 1.55

Seoul Mail Center A1007

1990, July 4 Litho. *Perf. 13½x13*
1595 A1007 100w multicolored .75 .25
a. Souvenir sheet of 2 2.25 2.25
Complete booklet, 4 #1595 5.00

8th Korean Boy Scout Jamboree — A1008

1990, Aug. 8 *Perf. 13x13½*
1596 A1008 100w multicolored .75 .25
Complete booklet, 4 #1596 6.00

Wild Flowers

A1009 A1010

A1011 A1012

1990, Aug. 25 Photo.
1597 A1009 370w Lilium 1.75 .85
Complete booklet, 4 #1597 17.50
1598 A1010 400w Aster 2.25 1.00
Complete booklet, 4 #1598 22.50
1599 A1011 440w Adonis 2.00 .90
Complete booklet, 4 #1599 20.00
1600 A1012 470w Scabiosa 2.40 1.00
Complete booklet, 4 #1600 24.00

A1013

No. 1601, Aerides japonicum. No. 1602, Helioniopsis orientalis. No. 1603, Aquilegia buergeriana. No. 1604, Gentiana zollingeri.

1991, July 26
1601 A1013 100w multicolored .65 .25
Complete booklet, 4 #1601 5.00
1602 A1013 100w multicolored .65 .25
Complete booklet, 4 #1602 5.00
1603 A1013 370w multicolored 1.90 .65
Complete booklet, 4 #1603 14.00
1604 A1013 440w multicolored 2.00 .75
Complete booklet, 4 #1604 16.00

1992, June 22 Photo. *Perf. 13x13½*

No. 1605, Lychnis wilfordii. No. 1606, Lycoris radiata. No. 1607, Commelina communis. No. 1608, Calanthe striata.

1605 A1013 100w multicolored .60 .30
Complete booklet, 4 #1605 5.00
1606 A1013 100w multicolored .60 .30
Complete booklet, 4 #1606 5.00
1607 A1013 370w multicolored 1.60 .65
Complete booklet, 4 #1607 13.00
1608 A1013 440w multicolored 1.90 .70
Complete booklet, 4 #1608 15.00
Nos. 1597-1608 (12) 18.30 7.60

See Nos. 1751-1762, 1869-1872, 1907-1910.

A1021

1990, Sept. 29 Litho. *Perf. 13x13½*
1609 A1021 100w .75 .25

Anglican Church of Korea, cent.

A1022

1990, Oct. 15
1610 A1022 100w blk, red & bl .75 .25

Opening of Seoul Tower, 10th anniv.

National
Census — A1023

1990, Oct. 20 *Perf. 13x13½*
1611 A1023 100w multicolored 60 25

UN
Development
Program, 40th
Anniv.
A1024

1990, Oct. 24
1612 A1024 100w multicolored .60 .25

Philatelic
Week — A1025

Litho. & Engr.
1990, Nov. 16 *Perf. 13x13½*
1613 A1025 100w multicolored .75 .25
a. Souvenir sheet of 2 4.50 4.50
Complete booklet, 4 #1613 6.00

New Year 1991
(Year of the
Sheep) — A1026

Two
Cranes — A1027

1990, Dec. 1 **Litho.** *Perf. 13x13½*
1614 A1026 100w multicolored .70 .25
Complete booklet, 4 #1614 5.00
1615 A1027 100w multicolored .70 .25
Complete booklet, 4 #1615 5.00
a. Souv. sheet of 2, #1614-1615 6.00 6.00

Taejon Expo '93

A1028

A1029

A1030

A1031

A1032

A1033

Government
Pavilion
A1034

Intl. Pavilion
A1035

Recycling Art
Pavilion
A1035a

Telcom
Pavilion
A1035b

1990, Dec. 12
1616 A1028 100w multicolored .85 .30
a. Souvenir sheet of 2 1.75 1.75
Complete booklet, 4 #1616 7.50
1617 A1029 440w multicolored 2.00 .90
a. Souvenir sheet of 2 5.25 5.25
Complete booklet, 4 #1617 17.50

1991, Mar. 23
1618 A1030 100w multicolored .85 .30
a. Souvenir sheet of 2 1.75 1.75
Complete booklet, 4 #1618 7.00
1619 A1031 100w multicolored .85 .30
a. Souvenir sheet of 2 1.75 1.75
Complete booklet, 4 #1619 7.00

1992, Aug. 7 **Photo.** *Perf. 13½x13*
1620 A1032 100w multicolored .70 .25
a. Souvenir sheet of 2 1.50 1.50
Complete booklet, 4 #1620 4.00
1621 A1033 100w multicolored .70 .25
a. Souvenir sheet of 2 1.50 1.50
Complete booklet, 4 #1621 4.00

1993, Aug. 7
1622 A1034 110w multi .75 .25
Souvenir sheet of 2 1.25 1.25
Complete booklet, 4 #1622 5.00
1623 A1035 110w multi .75 .25
c. Souvenir sheet of 2 1.25 1.25
Complete booklet, 4 #1623 5.00
1623A A1035a 110w multi .75 .25
d. Souvenir sheet of 2 1.25 1.25
Complete booklet, 4
#1623A 5.00
1623B A1035b 110w multi .75 .25
e. Souvenir sheet of 2 1.25 1.25
Complete booklet, 4
#1623B 5.00
Nos. 1616-1623B (10) 8.95 3.30

Saemaul
Minilibrary,
30th Anniv.
A1036

1991, Feb. 1 **Litho.** *Perf. 13½x13*
1624 A1036 100w multicolored 65 25
Complete booklet, 4 #1624 4.75

Moth
A1037

Beetle
A1038

Butterfly
A1039

Beetle
A1040

Cicada — A1041

1991, Apr. 8 **Photo.** *Perf. 13½x13*
1625 A1037 100w shown 1.00 .25
1626 A1038 100w shown 1.00 .25
1627 A1039 100w shown 1.00 .25
1628 A1040 100w shown 1.00 .25
1629 A1041 100w shown 1.00 .25
1630 A1040 100w Water beetle 1.00 .25
1631 A1040 100w Bee 1.00 .25
1632 A1040 100w Lady bug 1.00 .25
1633 A1037 100w Dragonfly 1.00 .25
1634 A1037 100w Grasshop-
per 1.00 .25
a. Strip of 10, #1625-1634 12.00 12.00
Printed in sheets of 100 with each row
shifted one design.

Traditional
Performing Arts
Center, 40th
Anniv. — A1042

1991, Apr. 10 *Perf. 13x13½*
1635 A1042 100w multicolored .75 .25
Complete booklet, 4 #1635 5.00

Provisional
Government,
72nd Anniv.
A1043

1991, Apr. 13 *Perf. 13½x13*
1636 A1043 100w multicolored .75 .25
Complete booklet, 4 #1636 5.00

Hire the
Handicapped
A1044

1991, Apr. 20
1637 A1044 100w multicolored .75 .25
Complete booklet, 4 #1637 6.00

Teachers'
Day, 10th
Anniv.
A1045

1991, May 15 **Litho.** *Perf. 13½x13*
1638 A1045 100w multicolored .75 25
Complete booklet, 4 #1638 5.00

A1046

1991, Aug. 8 **Litho.** *Perf. 13x13½*
1639 A1046 100w multicolored .75 .25
a. Souvenir sheet of 2 2.00 2.00
Complete booklet, 4 #1639 9.00
17th World Scouting Jamboree.

A1047

1991, Aug. 22 **Litho.** *Perf. 13x13½*
1640 A1047 100w multicolored .75 .25
Complete booklet, 4 #1640 9.00
YMCA World Assembly.

Natl. Desire for
Reunification
A1048

1991, Sept. 11 **Litho.** *Perf. 13x13½*
1641 A1048 100w multicolored .75 .25
Complete booklet, 4 #1641 8.00

Admission to
UN — A1049

1991, Sept. 18 *Perf. 13½x13*
1642 A1049 100w multicolored .75 .25
Complete booklet, 4 #1642 6.00

Musical Instruments

Deerskin Drum
(Galgo)
A1050

Mouth Organ
(Saenghwang)
A1051

Seated
Drum — A1052

Small
Gong — A1053

Designs: No. 1645, Brass chimes (Unra).
No. 1646, Large gong (Jing). No. 1649,
Dragon drum. No. 1650, Single bell chime.

1991-92 **Photo.** *Perf. 13x13½*
Background color
1643 A1050 100w gray .75 .30
Complete booklet, 4 #1643 5.00
1644 A1051 100w tan .75 .30
Complete booklet, 4 #1644 5.00
1645 A1050 100w lt violet .75 .30
Complete booklet, 4 #1645 5.00
1646 A1050 100w pale green .75 .30
Complete booklet, 4 #1646 5.00
1647 A1052 100w gray .80 .30
Complete booklet, 4 #1647 5.00
1648 A1053 100w tan .80 .30
Complete booklet, 4 #1648 5.00
1649 A1052 100w pale violet .80 .30
Complete booklet, 4 #1649 5.00

1650 A1053 100w pale green   .80   .30
   Complete booklet, 4 #1650   5.00
   Nos. 1643-1650 (8)   6.20 2.40
   Issued: Nos. 1643-1646, 9/26; others,
2/24/92.

Month of
Culture — A1056

1991, Oct. 1   Litho.   Perf. 13x13½
1655 A1056 100w multicolored   .75   .25
   Complete booklet, 4 #1655   5.00

Telecom
'91 — A1057

1991, Oct. 7   Photo.
1656 A1057 100w multicolored   .75   .25
   Complete booklet, 4 #1656   6.00

Sixth World Telecommunication Exhibition &
Forum, Geneva, Switzerland.

Beauty Series

A1058   A1059

Kottam Architectural Patterns
A1060   A1061

1991, Oct. 26
1657 A1058 100w multicolored   .85   .30
1658 A1059 100w multicolored   .85   .30
1659 A1060 100w multicolored   .85   .30
1660 A1061 100w multicolored   .85   .30
  a. Block or strip of 4, #1657-
      1660   4.50 4.50
   Complete booklet, 2 #1660a

A1062   A1063

Norigae
A1064   A1065

1992, Sept. 21   Photo. & Engr.
1661 A1062 100w multicolored   .75   .30
1662 A1063 100w multicolored   .75   .30
1663 A1064 100w multicolored   .75   .30
1664 A1065 100w multicolored   .75   .30
  a. Block or strip of 4, #1661-
      1664   4.00 4.00
   Complete booklet, 2 #1664a

A1066   A1067

Tapestries
A1068   A1069

1993, Oct. 11   Photo.   Perf. 13x13½
1665 A1066 110w multicolored   .60   .30
1666 A1067 110w multicolored   .60   .30
1667 A1068 110w multicolored   .60   .30
1668 A1069 110w multicolored   .60   .30
  a. Block or strip of 4, #1665-
      1668   3.25 3.25
   Complete booklet, 2 #1668a   —

Philatelic
Week — A1070

1991, Dec. 5   Photo.   Perf. 13x13½
1669 A1070 100w multicolored   .75   .25
  a. Souvenir sheet of 2   1.75 1.75
   Complete booklet, 4 #1669   5.00

New Year 1992, Year of the Monkey
A1071   A1072

1991, Dec. 2   Photo. & Engr.
1670 A1071 100w multicolored   .70   .25
  a. Souvenir sheet of 2   2.00 2.00
   Complete booklet, 4 #1670   5.00
1671 A1072 100w multicolored   .70   .25
  a. Souvenir sheet of 2   2.00 2.00
   Complete booklet, 4 #1671   5.00

Hibiscus Syriacus,
Natl.
Flower — A1073

1992, Mar. 9   Photo.   Perf. 13x13½
Background color
1672 A1073 100w lt green   1.10   .40
1673 A1073 100w lt blue   1.10   .40

Im-Jin War,
400th Anniv.
A1074

1992, May 23   Photo.   Perf. 13½x13
1674 A1074 100w multicolored   .60   .25
   Complete booklet, 4 #1674   5.00

Science Day,
25th Anniv.
A1075

1992, Apr. 21   Photo.   Perf. 13½x13
1675 A1075 100w multicolored   .60   .25
   Complete booklet, 4 #1675   6.00

Pong-Gil Yoon,
Assassin of
Japanese
Occupation
Leaders, 60th
Anniv. of
Execution — A1076

Photo. & Engr.
1992, Apr. 29   Perf. 13x13½
1676 A1076 100w multicolored   .60   .25
   Complete booklet, 4 #1676   5.00

A1077

Photo & Engr.
1992, May 25   Perf. 13x13½
1678 A1077 100w multicolored   .60   .25
   Complete booklet, 4 #1678   5.00

60th Intl. Fertilizer Assoc. conf.

A1078

1992, July 25   Photo.   Perf. 13x13½
1679 A1078 100w Pole vault   .75   .25
   Complete booklet, 4 #1679   5.00
1680 A1078 100w Rhythmic gym-
    nastics   .75   .25
   Complete booklet, 4 #1680   5.00

1992 Summer Olympics, Barcelona.

21st Universal
Postal
Congress,
Seoul, 1994
A1079

Designs: No. 1681, Korean Exhibition
Center, Namdae-mun Gate. No. 1682, Stone
statue of Tolharubang, Songsan Ilchulbong
Peak.

1992, Aug. 22   Photo.   Perf. 13½x13
1681 A1079 100w red vio & multi   .65   .25
  a. Souvenir sheet of 2   1.75 1.75
   Complete booklet, 4 #1681   5.00
1682 A1079 100w brown & multi   .65   .25
  a. Souvenir sheet of 2   1.75 1.75
   Complete booklet, 4 #1682   5.00

A1086

Litho. & Engr.
1992, Oct. 10   Perf. 13x13½
1683 A1086 100w salmon & red
    brn   .60   .25
   Complete booklet, 4 #1683   5.00

Pong-Chang Yi (1900-1932), would-be
assassin of Japanese Emperor Hirohito.

A1087

Design: No. 1684, Hwang Young-Jo, 1992
Olympic marathon winner. No. 1685, Shon
Kee-Chung, 1936 Olympic Marathon Winner.

1992, Oct. 10   Litho.
1684 A1087 100w multicolored   .75   .25
1685 A1087 100w grn & multi   .75   .25
  a. Pair, #1684-1685   2.00 2.00
  b. Souv. sheet of 2, #1684-
     1685   4.50 4.50
   Complete booklet, 2 #1685a   10.00

Discovery of
America, 500th
Anniv. — A1088

1992, Oct. 12   Photo.
1686 A1088 100w multicolored   .85   .25
   Complete booklet, 4 #1686   10.00

Philatelic
Week
A1089

1992, Nov. 14   Photo.   Perf. 13½x13
1687 A1089 100w multicolored   .60   .25
  a. Souvenir sheet of 2   2.00 2.00
   Complete booklet, 4 #1687   5.00

New Year 1993 (Year of the
Rooster)
A1090   A1091

1992, Dec. 1   Photo.   Perf. 13x13½
1688 A1090 100w multicolored   .70   .25
  a. Souvenir sheet of 2   2.00 2.00
   Complete booklet, 4 #1688   5.00
1689 A1091 100w multicolored   .70   .25
  a. Souvenir sheet of 2   2.00 2.00
   Complete booklet, 4 #1689   5.00

Intl.
Conference
on Nutrition,
Rome
A1092

1992, Dec. 5   *Perf. 13½x13*
1690 A1092 100w multicolored   .60   .25
Complete booklet, 4 #1690   5.00

Seoul Art Center, Grand Opening A1093

1993, Feb. 15 Photo.   *Perf. 13½x13*
1691 A1093 110w multicolored   .60   .25
Complete booklet, 4 #1691   5.00

Inauguration of Kim Young Sam, 14th President A1094

1993, Feb. 24
1692 A1094 110w multicolored   1.00   .30
a.   Souvenir sheet of 2   6.50   6.50

A1095

1993, May 27 Photo.   *Perf. 13x13½*
1693 A1095 110w lilac & silver   .60   .25
Complete booklet, 4 #1693   6.00

Student Inventions Exhibition.

A1096

1993, June 14 Photo.   *Perf. 13x13½*
1694 A1096 110w multicolored   .60   .25
Complete booklet, 4 #1694   6.00

UN Conference on Human Rights, Vienna.

Mushrooms A1098

No. 1696, Ganoderma lucidum. No. 1697, Pleurotus ostreatus. No. 1698, Lentinula edodes. No. 1699, Tricholoma matsutake.

1993, July 26 Photo.   *Perf. 13x13½*
1696 A1098 110w multicolored   .50   .25
Complete booklet, 4 #1696   5.00
1697 A1098 110w multicolored   .50   .25
Complete booklet, 4 #1697   5.00
1698 A1098 110w multicolored   .50   .25
Complete booklet, 4 #1698   5.00
1699 A1098 110w multicolored   .50   .25
Complete booklet, 4 #1699   5.00
Nos. 1696-1699 (1)   2.00   1.00

See Nos. 1770-1773, 1803-1806, 1883-1886, 1912-1915, 1935.

A1099

1993, Aug. 28 Photo.   *Perf. 13x13½*
1700 A1099 110w multicolored   .75   .25
Complete booklet, 4 #1700   4.00

19th World Congress of Intl. Society of Orthopedic Surgery and Trauma Study.

O-Dol-Odo-Gi A1100   Ong-He-Ya A1101

1993, Sept. 13
1701 A1100 110w multicolored   .70   .25
Complete booklet, 4 #1701   4.00
1702 A1101 110w multicolored   .70   .25
Complete booklet, 4 #1702   4.00

Visit Korea Year '94
A1112   A1113

1993, Sept 27 Photo.   *Perf. 13x13½*
1713 A1112 110w multicolored   .60   .25
Complete booklet, 4 #1713   4.00
1714 A1113 110w multicolored   .60   .25
Complete booklet, 4 #1714   4.00

Type of 1993 and

Squirrel A1114   Physalis Alkekengi A1115

Scops Owl A1116   Reduce Garbage A1117

Narcissus A1118   Little Tern A1119

Sea Turtle — A1120

Airplane A1122

Passenger Airplane A1123

Porcelain Chicken Water Dropper A1124   Celadon Water Dropper A1125

Gilt Bronze Bongnae-san Incense Burner — A1127   Celadon Pitcher — A1128

Designs: 300w, Van. 540w, Train. 1190w, Passenger ship.

Perf. 13½x13, 13x13½ (210w, 1050w, #1728, 1732, 1734), 13½x12½ (60w, 90w), 12½x13½ (180w, 200w)
Photo., Litho. (#1726), Photo. & Engr. (#1734)
1993-95
1715 A1114   60w multi   .60   .25
1716 A1115   70w multi   .50   .25
1717 A1116   90w multi   .75   .25
1718 A1117   110w multi   1.00   .25
1719 A997c   120w multi   1.00   .25
1720 A1118   130w multi   1.00   .25
a.   Booklet pane of 20   20.00
Complete booklet, #1720a   20.00
1721 A1119   180w multi   1.50   .25
1722 A1120   200w multi   2.00   .30
1723 A1119   210w multi   1.60   .25
1724 A1123   300w multi   2.00   .40
1725 A1122   330w multi   3.25   .25
1726 A1123   390w multi   3.00   .50
a.   Booklet pane of 10   35.00
Complete booklet, #1726a   35.00
1727 A1122   400w multi   2.25   .40
a.   Booklet pane, 10 #1727   25.00
Complete booklet, #1727a   25.00
1728 A1124   400w multi   2.25   .40
1729 A1125   500w multi   2.25   .65
1730 A1123   540w multi   3.50   .75
1731 A1122   560w multi   3.50   .60
1732 A1127   700w multi   4.00   .95
1733 A1004   910w like #1594B   6.00   1.25
1734 A1128   930w blue & multi   6.00   1.10
1735 A1128   930w tan & multi   6.00   1.25
a.   Booklet pane of 10   80.00
Complete booklet, #1735a   80.00
1736 A1128   1050w multi   6.00   1.00
1737 A1123   1190w multi   8.00   1.50
1738 A1122   1300w multi   8.00   1.25
Nos. 1715-1738 (24)   75.95   14.55

Issued: No. 1718, 11/1/93; 910w, 2/15/94; 90w, 4/22/94; 130w, 8/20/94; 80w, 9/12/94; 390w, No. 1734, 1190w, 10/1/94; 540w, 11/1/94; 300w, 11/18/94; 60w, 200w, 12/19/94; No. 1720a, 2/28/95; 70w, 3/15/95; No. 1737, 3/11/95; No. 1735a, 3/20/95; 700w, 6/15/95; No. 1728, 8/28/95; No. 1727, 10/16/95; 1050w, 1300w, 10/25/95; 210w, 560w, 11/1/95; 500w, 11/6/95; 120w, 330w, 11/11/95; No. 1727a, 3/27/96.
Five versions of booklets with No. 1720a exist with blocks of different colors at the top of the booklet cover. The blocks of color match color bars printed in the selvage of the attached booklet pane.
See Nos. 1847-1848, 1857.

Coil Stamp
1990   Litho.   *Perf. 13 Vert.*
1739 A1118 130w multicolored   1.25   .25

Philatelic Week — A1144

1993, Nov. 13 Photo.   *Perf. 13x13½*
1745 A1144 110w multicolored   .75   .25
a.   Souvenir sheet of 2   1.50   1.50
Complete booklet, 4 #1745   10.00

21st UPU Congress, Seoul — A1145

No. 1746, Dancer, muscians. No. 1747, Weavers, horiz.

Perf. 13x13½, 13½x13
1993, Nov. 18
1746 A1145 110w multicolored   .60   .25
a.   Souvenir sheet of 2   1.50   1.50
Complete booklet, 4 #1746   5.00
1747 A1145 110w multicolored   .60   .25
a.   Souvenir sheet of 2   1.50   1.50
Complete booklet, 4 #1747   5.00

Trade Day, 30th Anniv. A1146

1993, Nov. 30   *Perf. 13½x13*
1748 A1146 110w multicolored   .60   .25
Complete booklet, 4 #1748   5.00

New Year 1994 (Year of the Dog) A1147

1993, Dec. 1   *Perf. 13½x13, 13x13½*
1749 A1147 110w shown   1.00   .25
a.   Souvenir sheet of 2   2.00   2.00
1750 A1147 110w Stuffed toy dog, vert.   1.00   .25
a.   Souvenir sheet of 2   2.00   2.00

Flower Type of 1991

No. 1751, Weigela bortensis. No. 1752, Caltha palustris. No. 1753, Iris ruthenica. No. 1754, Aceriphyllum rosii. No. 1755, Leontopodium japonicum. No. 1756, Geranium eriostemon. No. 1757, Lycoris aurea. No. 1758, Gentiana jamesii. No. 1759, Halenia corniculata. No. 1760, Erthyronium japonicum. No. 1761, Iris odaesanensis. No. 1762, Leontice microrrhyncha.

1993-95   Photo.   *Perf. 13x13½*
1751 A1013 110w multicolored   .70   .25
Complete booklet, 4 #1751   3.50
1752 A1013 110w multicolored   .70   .25
Complete booklet, 4 #1752   3.50
1753 A1013 110w multicolored   .70   .25
Complete booklet, 4 #1753   3.50
1754 A1013 110w multicolored   .70   .25
Complete booklet, 4 #1754   3.50
1755 A1013 130w multicolored   1.00   .25
Complete booklet, 4 #1755   5.00
1756 A1013 130w multicolored   1.00   .25
Complete booklet, 4 #1756   5.00
1757 A1013 130w multicolored   1.00   .25
Complete booklet, 4 #1757   5.00
1758 A1013 130w multicolored   1.00   .25
Complete booklet, 4 #1758   5.00
1759 A1013 130w multicolored   1.00   .25
Complete booklet, 6 #1759   5.00
1760 A1013 130w multicolored   1.00   .25
Complete booklet, 6 #1760   5.00
1761 A1013 130w multicolored   1.00   .25
Complete booklet, 6 #1761   5.00

1762 A1013 130w multicolored 1.00 .25
Complete booklet, 6 #1762 5.00
Nos. 1751-1762 (12) 10.80 3.00
Issued: Nos. 1751-1754, 12/20/93; Nos. 1755-1758, 10/4/94; Nos. 1759-1762, 7/24/95.

Visit Korea Year
A1148   A1149
1994, Jan. 11 Photo. Perf. 13x13½
1763 A1148 110w Masked dancer .65 .25
Complete booklet, 4 #1763 2.75
1764 A1149 110w Piper, clouds .65 .25
Complete booklet, 4 #1764 2.75

21st UPU
Congress,
Seoul
A1150

1994, Jan. 24 Perf. 13½x13
1765 A1150 300w multicolored 1.40 .50
a. Souvenir sheet of 2 3.25 3.25
b. Booklet pane of 10 30.00
Complete booklet, #1765b 30.00

Samil Independence
Movement, 75th
Anniv. — A1151
1994, Feb. 28 Photo. Perf. 13x13½
1766 A1151 110w multicolored .60 .25

Wildlife
Protection
A1152

No. 1767, Sasakia charonda. No. 1768, Allomyrina dichotoma.

1994, Mar. 7 Photo. Perf. 13½x13
1767 A1152 110w multicolored .75 .25
a. Souvenir sheet of 2 2.00 2.00
Complete booklet, 4 #1767 3.75
1768 A1152 110w multicolored .75 .25
a. Souvenir sheet of 2 2.00 2.00
Complete booklet, 4 #1768 3.75

Intl. Year of
the Family
A1153
1994, May 14 Photo. Perf. 13
1769 A1153 110w multicolored .60 .25

Mushroom Type of 1993
No. 1770, Oudemansiella platyphylla. No. 1771, Morchella esculenta. No. 1772, Cortinarius purpurascens. No. 1773, Gomphus floccosus.

1994, May 30 Photo. Perf. 13x13½
1770 A1098 110w multicolored .50 .25
a. Souvenir sheet of 2 1.50 1.50
Complete booklet, 4 #1770 2.50
1771 A1098 110w multicolored .50 .25
a. Souvenir sheet of 2 1.50 1.50
Complete booklet, 4 #1771 2.50
1772 A1098 110w multicolored .50 .25
a. Souvenir sheet of 2 1.50 1.50
Complete booklet, 4 #1772 2.50

1773 A1098 110w multicolored .50 .25
a. Souvenir sheet of 2 1.50 1.50
Complete booklet, 4 #1773 2.50
Nos. 1770-1773 (4) 2.00 1.00
Nos. 1770a-1773a (4) 6.00 6.00

Opening of
War Memorial
Center
A1154
1994, June 10 Photo. Perf. 13
1774 A1154 110w multicolored .60 .25

PHILAKOREA
'94, Seoul
A1155
1994, June 13 Perf. 13
1775 A1155 910w multicolored 4.00 1.50
a. Souvenir sheet of 1 4.50 4.50
b. Booklet pane of 10 40.00
Complete booklet, #1775b 40.00
Stamps from No. 1775b have a straight edge at either top or bottom.

Beauty Series

Fans — A1156
1994, July 18 Photo. Perf. 13x13½
1776 110w Taeguk .60 .25
1777 110w Crane .60 .25
1778 110w Pearl .60 .25
1779 110w Wheel .60 .25
a. A1156 Strip of 4, #1776-1779 3.00 3.00
Complete booklet, 2 #1779a 15.00

Gates — A1160

No. 1780, Lofty Gate, traditional Yungban residence. No. 1781, Pomosa Temple. No. 1782, Osumun (Fish Water) Gate, Changdukkung Palace. No. 1783, Pullomun Gate, Changdukkung Palace.

1995, May 22 Photo. Perf. 13x13½
1780 130w multicolored .60 .25
1781 130w multicolored .60 .25
1782 130w multicolored .60 .25
1783 130w multicolored .60 .25
a. A1160 Strip of 4, #1780-1783 3.25 3.25
Complete booklet, 2 #1783a 15.00

Pouches — A1164
1996, Nov. 1 Photo. Perf. 13x13½
1784 150w multicolored .60 .25
1785 150w multicolored .60 .25
1786 150w multicolored .60 .25
1787 150w multicolored .60 .25
a. A1164 Strip of 4, #1784-1787 3.00 3.00
Complete booklet, 2 #1787a 15.00
Nos. 1776-1787 (12) 7.20 3.00

A1168

PHILAKOREA
'94 — A1169
1994, Aug. 16 Photo. Perf. 13
1788 A1168 130w Winter scene 1.25 .25
a. Souvenir sheet of 2 1.50 1.50
b. Booklet pane of 10 12.50
Complete booklet, #1788b 12.50
1789 A1168 130w Grape vines 1.25 .25
a. Souvenir sheet of 2 1.50 1.50
b. Booklet pane of 10 12.50
Complete booklet, #1789b 12.50
1790 A1168 130w Cranes 1.25 .25
a. Souvenir sheet of 2 1.50 1.50
b. Booklet pane of 10 12.50
Complete booklet, #1790b 12.50
Nos. 1788-1790 (3) 3.75 .75

Souvenir Sheet
Litho. & Engr.
1791 Sheet of 7 10.00 10.00
a. A1169 130w Crane, mountaine .40 .25
b. A1169 300w Two cranes, sun .95 .40
c. A1169 370w Two cranes in trees 1.20 .50
d. A1169 400w Two deer 1.30 .55
e. A1169 440w Turtle, rapids 1.50 .60
f. A1169 470w River 1.50 .60
g. A1169 930w Trees 3.00 1.25

A1170

21st UPU Congress, Seoul: No. 1792, Pens, glasses, stamps. No. 1793, Sword dance. No. 1794, Dove holding envelope. No. 1795, Hong Yong-sik, Heinrich Von Stephan, horiz.

1994, Aug. 22 Photo. Perf. 13
1792 A1170 130w multicolored .55 .25
a. Souvenir sheet of 2 1.50 1.50
b. Booklet pane of 10 6.50
Complete booklet, #1792b 6.50
1793 A1170 130w multicolored .55 .25
a. Souvenir sheet of 2 1.50 1.50
b. Booklet pane of 10 6.50
Complete booklet, #1793b 6.50
1794 A1170 130w multicolored .55 .25
a. Souvenir sheet of 2 1.50 1.50
b. Booklet pane of 10 6.50
Complete booklet, #1794b 6.50
1795 A1170 370w multicolored 1.50 .60
a. Souvenir sheet of 2 3.25 3.25
b. Souvenir sheet of 4, #1792-1795 7.00 7.00
c. Booklet pane of 10 45.00
Complete booklet, #1795b 45.00
Nos. 1792-1795 (4) 3.15 1.35

A1171

1994, Sept. 27
1796 A1171 130w multicolored .60 .25
Seoul, Capital of Korea, 600th anniv.

A1172

1994, Nov. 19 Photo. Perf. 13x13½
1797 A1172 130w multicolored .60 .25
a. Souvenir sheet of 2 1.75 1.75
Complete booklet, 4 #1797 6.00
Philatelic Week. Complete booklet has one No. 1797 tied to cover with first day cancel.

A1173
1994, Nov. 29
1798 A1173 130w multicolored .60 .25
Seoul becomes Korea's capital, 600th anniv.

New Year
1995 (Year of
the Boar)
A1174
1994, Dec. 1 Perf. 13½x13
1799 A1174 130w shown .60 .25
a. Souvenir sheet of 2 1.50 1.50
Complete booklet, 4 #1799 6.00
1800 A1174 130w Family outing .60 .25
a. Souvenir sheet of 2 1.50 1.50
Complete booklet, 4 #1800 6.00

Wildlife
Protection
A1175
1995, Jan. 23 Photo. Perf. 13½x13
1801 A1175 130w Rana plancyi .70 .30
a. Souv. sheet of 2, imperf. 2.00 2.00
Complete booklet, 4 #1801 5.50
1802 A1175 130w Bufo bufo .70 .30
a. Souv. sheet of 2, imperf. 2.00 2.00
Complete booklet, 4 #1802 5.50

Mushroom Type of 1993
Designs: No. 1803, Russula virescens. No. 1804, Lentinus lepideus. No. 1805, Coprinus comalus. No. 1806, Laetiporus sulphureus.

1995, Mar. 31 Photo. Perf. 13x13½
1803 A1098 130w multicolored .70 .30
a. Souvenir sheet of 2 1.50 1.50
Complete booklet, 4 #1803 5.50
1804 A1098 130w multicolored .70 .30
a. Souvenir sheet of 2 1.50 1.50
Complete booklet, 4 #1804 5.50
1805 A1098 130w multicolored .70 .30
a. Souvenir sheet of 2 1.50 1.50
Complete booklet, 4 #1805 5.50
1806 A1098 130w multicolored .70 .30
a. Souvenir sheet of 2 1.50 1.50
Complete booklet, 4 #1806 5.50
Nos. 1803-1806 (4) 2.80 1.20

Completion of
HANARO
Research
Reactor
A1176
1995, Apr. 7 Perf. 13½x13
1807 A1176 130w multicolored .75 .35
Complete booklet, 4 #1807 5.50

Modern Judicial
System,
Cent. — A1177

1995, Apr. 25 Litho. Perf. 13x13½
1808 A1177 130w multicolored .60 .25

Modern Legal
Education,
Cent.
A1178

1995, Apr. 25   *Perf. 13½x13*
1809 A1178 130w multicolored   .60   .25

Cartoons
A1179

130w, "Dooly, the Little Dinosaur," baby,
porpoise. 440w, "Kochuboo," riding in
airplane.

1995, May 4
1810 A1179 130w multicolored   .70   .35
a.   Souvenir sheet of 1   1.50   1.50
          Complete booklet, 4 #1810   5.50
1811 A1179 440w multicolored   1.75   .65
a.   Souvenir sheet of 1   3.25   3.25
          Complete booklet, 4 #1811   12.50

78th Lions
Clubs Intl.
Convention
A1180

1995, July 4   Photo.   Perf. 13½x13
1812 A1180 130w multicolored   .75   .25

Liberation
Day, 50th
Anniv.
A1181

Design: 440w, Mountain, yin/yang symbol.

1995, Aug. 14   Photo.   Perf. 13½x13
1813 A1181 130w multicolored   .60   .25
a.   Booklet pane of 10   12.00
          Complete booklet, #1813a   12.00
b.   Souvenir sheet of 2   1.50   1.50

Size: 97x19mm
Perf. 13x13½
1814 A1181 440w multicolored   1.75   .65
a.   Souvenir sheet of 1   2.50   2.50

Opening of
Bohyunsan Optical
Astronomical
Observatory
A1183

1995, Sept. 13   Litho.   Perf. 13x13½
1816 A1183 130w multicolored   .75   .25
          Complete booklet, 6 #1816   7.50

Literature Series

Kuji-ga Song (The
Turtle's Back
Song) — A1184

Chongeop-sa
Song
A1185

A1186

A1187

Record of Travel to
Five Indian
Kingdoms — A1188

A Poem to the
Sui General
Yu Zhong
Wen — A1189

A1190

A1191

A1192

A1193

A1194   A1195

Perf. 13x13½, 13½x13
1995-99   **Photo.**
1817 A1184 130w multi   .65   .25
a.   Souvenir sheet of 2   1.40   1.40
          Complete booklet, 6 #1817   6.00
1818 A1185 130w multi   .65   .25
a.   Souvenir sheet of 2   1.40   1.40
          Complete booklet, 6 #1818   6.00
1819 A1186 150w multi   .65   .25
a.   Souvenir sheet of 2   1.50   1.50
          Complete booklet, 10 #1819   12.00
1820 A1187 150w multi   .65   .25
a.   Souvenir sheet of 2   1.50   1.50
          Complete booklet, 10 #1820   12.00

1821 A1188 170w multi   .70   .25
a.   Souvenir sheet of 2   1.40   1.40
          Complete booklet, 10 #1821   9.00
1822 A1189 170w multi   .70   .25
a.   Sheet of 2   1.40   1.40
          Complete booklet, 10 #1822   9.00
Photo. & Engr.
1823 A1190 170w multi   .60   .25
          Complete booklet, 10 #1823   9.00
a.   Souvenir sheet of 1   1.20   1.20
1824 A1191 170w multi   .60   .25
          Complete booklet, 10 #1824   9.00
a.   Souvenir sheet of 1   1.20   1.20
1825 A1192 170w multi   .60   .30
          Complete booklet, 10 #1825   9.00
1826 A1193 170w multi   .60   .30
          Complete booklet, 10 #1826   9.00
1827 A1194 170w multi   .60   .30
          Complete booklet, 10 #1827   9.00
1828 A1195 170w multi   .60   .30
          Complete booklet, 10 #1828   9.00
Nos. 1817-1828 (12)   7.60   3.20
Souvenir Sheets
1828A A1192 340w multi   1.75   1.75
1828B A1193 340w multi   1.75   1.75
1828C A1194 340w multi   1.75   1.75
1828D A1195 340w multi   1.75   1.75

Issued: Nos. 1817-1818, 9/25/95; Nos.
1819-1820, 9/16/96; Nos. 1821-1822,
12/12/97; Nos. 1823-1824, 9/14/98; Nos.
1825-1828D, 10/20/99.

FAO, 50th
Anniv.
A1196

Litho. & Engr.
1995, Oct. 16   *Perf. 13*
1829 A1196 150w dp vio & blk   .75   .25
          Complete booklet, 10 #1829   10.00

Korean Bible
Society, Cent.
A1197

1995, Oct. 18   **Litho.**
1830 A1197 150w multicolored   .65   .25
          Complete booklet, 10 #1830   10.00

Population and
Housing
Census — A1198

1995, Oct. 20
1831 A1198 150w multicolored   .65   .25
          Complete booklet, 10 #1831   10.00

UN, 50th
Anniv.
A1199

1995, Oct. 24   **Photo.**
1832 A1199 150w multicolored   .75   .25
          Complete booklet, 10 #1832   10.00

Wilhelm
Röntgen
(1845-1923),
Discovery of
the X-Ray,
Cent.
A1200

1995, Nov. 8   *Perf. 13½x13*
1833 A1200 150w multicolored   1.50   .25
          Complete booklet, 10 #1833   20.00

Philatelic
Week — A1201

1995, Nov. 18   Photo.   Perf. 13x13½
1834 A1201 150w multicolored   .75   .25
a.   Souvenir sheet of 2   1.50   1.50
          Complete booklet, 10 #1834   10.00

A1202

New Year
1996 (Year of
the
Rat) — A1203

1995, Dec. 1   Perf. 13x13½, 13½x13
1835 A1202 150w multicolored   .75   .25
a.   Souvenir sheet of 2   2.00   2.00
          Complete booklet, 10 #1835   10.00
1836 A1203 150w multicolored   .75   .25
a.   Souvenir sheet of 2   2.00   2.00
          Complete booklet, 10 #1836   10.00

Normalization of
Korea-Japan
Relations, 30th
Anniv. — A1204

1995, Dec. 18   Litho.   Perf. 13x13½
1837 A1204 420w multicolored   2.00   .70
          Complete booklet, 4 #1837   10.00

Types of 1993-97 and

Gallicrex   Zosterops
Cinerea   Japonica
A1206   A1208

Luffa   Numenius
Cylindrica   Madagascariensis
A1209   A1210

Cambaroides
Similis — A1211

747 Airplane
A1215

Mare and Colt — A1221

Soksu Stone Carving A1223

Bronze Incense Burner in Shape of Lotus Flowers — A1224

Photo., Photo. & Embossed (#1844)

1996-98   *Perf. 13x13½, 13½x13*

1839	A1206	50w multi	.65	.25
1840	A1208	80w multi	.65	.25
1841	A1209	100w multi	.60	.25
1842	A1118	140w multi	1.00	.25

Perf. 13

1843	A1210	170w multi	2.50	.25
1844	A1210	170w like #1843, braille inscription	2.00	.45

Perf. 13x13½, 13½x13

1845	A1211	170w multi	1.25	.30
1846	A997c	190w multi	1.50	.30
1847	A1119	260w multi	2.00	.40

Perf. 13x14

1848	A1119	300w Alauda arvensis	1.75	.40

Perf. 13½x13, 13x13½, 13 (#1855)

1849	A1215	340w green blue & multi	2.25	.45
1850	A1215	380w lt lilac & multi	2.75	.50
1851	A1001	420w like #1593	3.25	.45
1852	A1002	480w like #1594	3.50	.50
1854	A1221	800w multi	3.25	.60
1855	A1223	1000w multi	4.00	1.25
1856	A1224	1170w multi	6.00	1.00
1857	A1128	1190w multi	7.00	2.00
1858	A1215	1340w brt green & multi	8.00	1.60
1859	A1215	1380w pink & multi	8.00	1.90
	Nos. 1839-1859 (20)		61.90	14.35

Coil Stamps
Perf. 13 Horiz., 13 Vert. (#1860, 1862)

1996-97   **Photo.**

1860	A998	150w like #1591	1.40	.75
1861	A1211	170w like No. 1845	1.40	.30
1862	A997c	190w like No. 1846	1.50	.30
	Nos. 1860-1862 (3)		4.30	1.35

Issued: 300w, 1/22/96; No. 1860, 2/1/96; 420w, 480w, 3/20/96; 1000w, 12/16/96; 100w, 3/5/97; 80w, 7/1/97; Nos. 1845-1846, 9/1/97; 340w, 380w, 1340w, 1380w, 9/12/97; Nos. 1842, 1847, 1856, 1857, 11/1/97; Nos. 1861, 1862, 11/18/97; No. 1843, 12/15/97; 50w, 2/19/98; 800w, 4/4/98; No. 1844, 10/15/98.

Opening of China-Korea Submarine Fiber Optic Cable System A1229

1996, Feb. 8   Litho.   *Perf. 13½x13*

1863	A1229	420w multicolored	2.00	.50
	Complete booklet, 4 #1863		10.00	

See People's Republic of China No. 2647.

Korea Institute of Science and Technology, 30th Anniv. A1230

1996, Feb. 10   Photo.   *Perf. 13½x13*

1864	A1230	150w multicolored	.75	.25
	Complete booklet, 10 #1864		10.00	

Protection of Nature A1231

No. 1865, Geoclemys reevesii. No. 1866, Scincella laterale.

1996, Mar. 5   Photo.   *Perf. 13½x13*

1865	A1231	150w multicolored	.75	.25
a.		Souvenir sheet of 2	1.75	1.75
	Complete booklet, 10 #1865		12.00	
1866	A1231	150w multicolored	.75	.25
a.		Souvenir sheet of 2	1.75	1.75
	Complete booklet, 10 #1866		12.00	

Successful Launches of Mugunghwa Satellites A1232

1996, Mar. 18   Photo.   *Perf. 13*

1867	A1232	150w multicolored	.75	.25
	Complete booklet, 10 #1867		10.00	

Tongnip Shinmun, First Privately Published Newspaper, Cent. A1233

So Chae-p'il, lead article of first issue.

Litho. & Engr.

1996, Apr. 6   *Perf. 13*

1868	A1233	150w multicolored	.75	.25
	Complete booklet, 10 #1868		12.00	

Wildflower Type of 1992

No. 1869, Cypripedium macranthum. No. 1870, Trillium tschonoskii. No. 1871, Viola variegata. No. 1872, Hypericum ascyron.

1996, Apr. 22   Photo.   *Perf. 13*

1869	A1013	150w multicolored	1.00	.25
	Complete booklet, 10 #1869		12.50	
1870	A1013	150w multicolored	1.00	.25
	Complete booklet, 10 #1870		12.50	
1871	A1013	150w multicolored	1.00	.25
	Complete booklet, 10 #1871		12.50	
1872	A1013	150w multicolored	1.00	.25
	Complete booklet, 10 #1872		12.50	
	Nos. 1869-1872 (4)		4.00	1.00

Korea Military Academy, 50th Anniv. A1234

1996, May 1   Litho.   *Perf. 13½x13*

1873	A1234	150w multicolored	.75	.25
	Complete booklet, 10 #1873		10.00	

Cartoons A1235

No. 1874, Gobau running. No. 1875, Kkach'i in swordfight.

1996, May 4   Photo.

1874	A1235	150w multicolored	.75	.25
a.		Souvenir sheet of 1	1.75	1.75
	Complete booklet, 10 #1874		10.00	
1875	A1235	150w multicolored	.75	.25
a.		Souvenir sheet of 1	1.75	1.75
	Complete booklet, 10 #1875		10.00	

Girl Scouts of Korea, 50th Anniv. A1236

1996, May 10   Litho.

1876	A1236	150w multicolored	.75	.25
	Complete booklet, 10 #1876		12.00	

35th IAA World Advertising Congress — A1237

1996, June 8   Litho.   *Perf. 13*

1877	A1237	150w multicolored	.75	.25
	Complete booklet, 10 #1877		9.50	

Campaign Against Illegal Drugs A1238

1996, June 26   Photo.   *Perf. 13½x13*

1878	A1238	150w multicolored	.75	.25
	Complete booklet, 10 #1878		12.00	

Winter Universiade '97, Muju-Chonju A1239

1996, July 1   *Perf. 13½x13, 13x13½*

1879	A1239	150w shown	.75	.25
	Complete booklet, 10 #1879		10.00	
1880	A1239	150w Emblem, vert.	.75	.25
	Complete booklet, 10 #1880		10.00	

1996 Summer Olympic Games, Atlanta

A1240   A1241

1996, July 20   *Perf. 13x13½*

1881	A1240	150w multicolored	.75	.25
	Complete booklet, 10 #1881		15.00	
1882	A1241	150w multicolored	.75	.25
	Complete booklet, 10 #1882		15.00	

Mushroom Type of 1993

Designs: No. 1883, Paxillus atrotomentosus. No. 1884, Sarcodon imbricatum. No. 1885, Rhodophyllus crassipes. No. 1886, Amanita inaurata.

1996, Aug. 19   Photo.   *Perf. 13x13½*

1883	A1098	150w multicolored	.75	.25
a.		Souvenir sheet of 2	1.50	1.50
	Complete booklet, 10 #1883		15.00	
1884	A1098	150w multicolored	.75	.25
a.		Souvenir sheet of 2	1.50	1.50
	Complete booklet, 10 #1884		15.00	
1885	A1098	150w multicolored	.75	.25
a.		Souvenir sheet o 2	1.50	1.50
	Complete booklet, 10 #1885		15.00	
1886	A1098	150w multicolored	.75	.25
a.		Souvenir sheet of 2	1.50	1.50
	Complete booklet, 10 #1886		15.00	
	Nos. 1883-1886 (4)		3.00	1.00

Souvenir Sheets

2002 World Cup Soccer Championships, Korea — A1242

No. 1887, Players, Korean flag. No. 1888, 2 players.

1996, Aug. 1   Photo.   *Perf. 13½*

1887	A1242	400w Sheet of 4	7.50	7.50
1888	A1242	400w Sheet of 4	7.50	7.50

Korean Alphabet, 550th Anniv. — A1243

Litho. & Engr.

1996, Oct. 9   *Perf. 13x13½*

1889	A1243	150w multicolored	.75	.25
a.		Souvenir sheet of 2	1.50	1.50
	Complete booklet, 10 #1889		12.50	

Suwon Castle, Bicent. A1244

Photo. & Engr.

1996, Oct. 10   *Perf. 13½x13*

1890	A1244	400w multicolored	2.00	.60

Seoul Natl. University, 50th Anniv. A1245

1996, Oct. 15   Photo.   *Perf. 13½x13*

1891	A1245	150w multicolored	.75	.25
	Complete booklet, 10 #1891		11.00	

Philatelic Week — A1246

Painting: Poppy and a Lizard, by Shin Saimdang.

1996, Nov. 18   Photo.   *Perf. 13½x13*

1892	A1246	150w multicolored	.75	.25
a.		Souvenir sheet of 2	1.60	1.60
	Complete booklet, 10 #1892		13.00	

A1247

New Year 1997 (Year of the Ox) — A1248

1996, Dec. 2   *Perf. 13*
1893 A1247 150w multicolored   .85   .25
    a.   Souvenir sheet of 2   1.50   1.50
       Complete booklet, 10 #1893   14.50
1894 A1248 150w multicolored   .85   .25
    a.   Souvenir sheet of 2   1.50   1.50
       Complete booklet, 10 #1894   14.50

Winter Universiade
'97, Muju-Chonju
A1249

1997, Jan. 24   **Photo.**   *Perf. 13*
1895 A1249 150w Skier   .70   .25
       Complete booklet, 10 #1895   14.00
1896 A1249 150w Ice skater   .70   .25
       Complete booklet, 10 #1896   14.00

Modern
Banking
System in
Korea, Cent.
A1250

1997, Feb. 19   **Litho.**   *Perf. 13½x13*
1897 A1250 150w multicolored   .75   .25
       Complete booklet, 10 #1897   12.00

A1251

1997, Apr. 10   *Perf. 13½x13*
1898 A1251 150w multicolored   .60   .25
       Complete booklet, 10 #1898   12.00

97th Inter-Parliamentary Conference, 160th
Inter-Parliamentary Council.

A1252

1997, Apr. 23   **Litho.**
1899 A1252 150w multicolored   .75   .25
       Complete booklet, 10 #1899   12.00

World Book & Copyright Day.

Cartoons
A1253

No. 1900, Mother holding child from "A
Long, Long Journey in Search of Mommy."
No. 1901, Girl in air holding medal from "Run,
Run, Hannie."

1997, May 3   **Photo.**   *Perf. 13½x13*
1900 A1253 150w multicolored   .70   .25
    a.   Souvenir sheet of 1   1.10   1.10
       Complete booklet, 10 #1900   16.00
1901 A1253 150w multicolored   .70   .25
    a.   Souvenir sheet of 1   1.10   1.10
       Complete booklet, 10 #1901   16.00

Nos. 1900a, 1901a are continuous designs.

2nd Pusan East
Asian
Games — A1254

1997, May 10   **Litho.**   *Perf. 13x13½*
1902 A1254 150w multicolored   .75   .25
       Complete booklet, 10 #1900   12.00

2002 World Cup Soccer,
Korea/Japan
A1255   A1256

No. 1903, Jules Rimet, founder of World
Cup. No. 1904, Painting of Ch'ukkuk match.

1997, May 31   **Photo.**   *Perf. 13x13½*
1903 A1255 150w multicolored   .85   .25
    a.   Souvenir sheet of 2   2.00   2.00
       Complete booklet, 10 #1903   14.00
1904 A1256 150w multicolored   .85   .25
    a.   Souvenir sheet of 3   2.25   2.25
       Complete booklet, 10 #1904   14.00

Wildlife
Protection
A1257

Fish: No. 1905, Pungitius sinensis. No.
1906, Coreoperca kawamebari.

1997, June 5   *Perf. 13*
1905 A1257 150w multicolored   .75   .25
    a.   Souvenir sheet of 2   1.25   1.25
       Complete booklet, 10 #1905   14.00
1906 A1257 150w multicolored   .75   .25
    a.   Souvenir sheet of 2   1.25   1.25
       Complete booklet, 10 #1906   14.00

Wildflower Type of 1992

No. 1907, Belamcanda chinensis. No. 1908,
Hylomecon ernale. No. 1909, Campanula
takesimana. No. 1910, Magnolia sieboldii.

1997, June 19   **Photo.**   *Perf. 13*
1907 A1013 150w multicolored   .75   .25
       Complete booklet, 10 #1907   15.00
1908 A1013 150w multicolored   .75   .25
       Complete booklet, 10 #1908   15.00
1909 A1013 150w multicolored   .75   .25
       Complete booklet, 10 #1909   15.00
1910 A1013 150w multicolored   .75   .25
       Complete booklet, 10 #1910   15.00
       Nos. 1907-1910 (4)   3.00   1.00

1997 Kwangju
Biennale — A1258

1997, July 1
1911 A1258 150w multicolored   .60   .25
       Complete booklet, 10 #1911   11.00

Mushroom Type of 1993

Designs: No. 1912, Inocybe fastigiata. No.
1913, Panaeolus papilionaceus. No. 1914,
Ramaria flava. No. 1915, Amanita muscaria.

1997, July 21   **Photo.**   *Perf. 13x13½*
1912 A1098 150w multicolored   .75   .25
    a.   Souvenir sheet of 2   1.40   1.40
1913 A1098 150w multicolored   .75   .25
    a.   Souvenir sheet of 2   1.40   1.40
1914 A1098 150w multicolored   .75   .25
    a.   Souvenir sheet of 2   1.40   1.40
1915 A1098 150w multicolored   .75   .25
    a.   Souvenir sheet of 2   1.40   1.40
       Nos. 1912-1915 (4)   3.00   1.00

85th World
Dental
Congress,
Seoul
A1259

1997, Sept. 5   **Photo.**   *Perf. 13½x13*
1916 A1259 170w multicolored   .70   .25

Opening of
Port of
Mokpo, Cent.
A1260

Litho. & Engr.
1997, Oct. 1   *Perf. 13½x13*
1917 A1260 170w multicolored   .70   .25

Soongsil
Academy,
Cent.
A1261

1997, Oct. 10   **Photo. & Engr.**
1918 A1261 170w multicolored   .70   .25

Beauty Series

Wrapping Cloths — A1262

1997, Nov. 3   **Photo.**   *Perf. 13½x13½*
1919   170w multicolored   .85   .25
1920   170w multicolored   .85   .25
1921   170w multicolored   .85   .25
1922   170w multicolored   .85   .25
    a.   A1262 Strip of 4, #1919-1922   4.00   4.00

Philatelic
Week — A1266

1997, Nov. 18
1923 A1266 170w multicolored   .85   .25
    a.   Souvenir sheet of 2   1.25   1.25

New Year 1998 (Year of the Tiger)
A1267   A1268

1997, Dec. 1   **Photo.**   *Perf. 13x13½*
1924 A1267 170w multicolored   1.00   .25
    a.   Souvenir sheet of 2   1.75   1.75
1925 A1268 170w multicolored   1.00   .25
    a.   Souvenir sheet of 2   1.75   1.75

Pulguksa Temple — A1269

Litho. & Engr.
1997, Dec. 9   *Perf. 13½x13½*
1926 A1269 Sheet of 14   35.00   35.00
    a.   170w Buddha, Sokkuram
         Grotto   1.00   1.00
    b.   380w Temple   4.00   4.00

Top part of No. 1926 contains one each
Nos. 1926a-1926b and is separated from the
bottom portion of the sheet by a row of perforations. The lower part of No. 1926 contains 9
No. 1926a and 3 No, 1926b.

Electric Power
in Korea,
Cent.
A1271

1998, Jan. 26   **Photo.**   *Perf. 13½x13*
1927 A1271 170w multicolored   .75   .25

Inauguration
of the 15th
President,
Kim Dae-jung
A1272

1998, Feb. 25   **Litho.**   *Perf. 13½x13*
1928 A1272 170w multicolored   1.00   .40
    a.   Souvenir sheet of 1   6.00   6.00

Protection of Wild
Animals and
Plants — A1273

Designs: a, Panthera pardus orientalis. b,
Selenarctos thibetanus ussuricus. c, Lutra
lutra. d, Moschus moschiferus.

1998, Mar. 21   *Perf. 13x13½*
1929   Sheet of 12   25.00   25.00
    a.-d.   A1273 340w Any single   1.50   .30

Top part of No. 1929 contains one each No.
1929a-1929d and is separated from the bottom portion of the sheet by a row of perforations. The lower part of No. 1929 contains 2
each Nos. 1929a-1929d.

Cartoons A1274

Designs: 170w, Boy daydreaming while holding flower, from "Aktong-i," by Lee Hi-jae. 340w, Mother on motorcycle, son making fists from "Challenger," by Park Ki-jong.

1998, May 4 Photo. *Perf. 13½x13*

1930 A1274 170w multicolored .75 .25
a. Souvenir sheet of 1 .75 .75
b. Booklet pane of 10 20.00
Complete booklet, #1930b 20.00

Photo. & Engr.

1931 A1274 340w multicolored 1.50 1.50
a. Souvenir sheet of 1 1.50 1.50
b. Booklet pane of 10 26.00
Complete booklet, #1931b 26.00

Natl. Assembly, 50th Anniv. A1275

1998, May 30 Litho. *Perf. 13½x13*

1932 A1275 170w multicolored .75 .25

2002 World Cup Soccer Championships, Korea/Japan — A1276

Designs: a, Player. b, Two players. c, Player heading ball. d, Player performing bicycle kick.

1998, May 30 *Perf. 13x13½*

1933 A1276 Strip of 4, #a.-d. 4.00 4.00
a.-d. 170w any single .70 .25
e. Souvenir sheet, #1933 3.25 3.25

Information Culture Special A1277

Communication through the ages: a, Rock drawings. b, Horseback messenger, beacon fire. c, Telephone, mailbox. d, Computers.

1998, June 1 Litho. *Perf. 13½x13*

1934 Strip of 4 4.00 4.00
a.-c. A1277 170w any single .60 .25
d. A1277 340w multicolored 1.25 .45

No. 1934d is 68x70mm.

Mushroom Type of 1993

Designs: a, Pseudocolus schellenbergiae. b, Cyptotrama asprata. c, Laccaria vinaceoavellanea. d, Phallus rugulosus.

1998, July 4

1935 Sheet of 16 17.50 17.50
a.-d. A1098 170w Any single .75 .30

Left part of No. 1935 contains 3 each Nos. 1935a-1935d, with each strip in a different order. This is separated from the right portion of the sheet by a row of perforations. The right part of No. 1935 contains 1 each Nos. 1935a-1935d.

Republic of Korea, 50th Anniv. A1278

1998, Aug. 14 Photo. *Perf. 13½x13*

1937 A1278 170w multicolored .75 .25

A1279

1998, Aug. 19 *Perf. 13x13½*

1938 A1279 170w multicolored .75 .25
a. Souvenir sheet of 2 1.25 1.25

Philatelic Week.

A1280

1998, Sept. 24 Photo. *Perf. 13x13½*

1939 A1280 170w multicolored .75 .25
Complete booklet, 10 #1939 12.00

1998 Pusan Intl. Film Festival.

Founding of Songkyunkwan, 600th Anniv. — A1281

Photo. & Engr.

1998, Sept. 25 *Perf. 13*

1940 A1281 170w multicolored .75 .25
Complete booklet, 5 #1940 5.00

A1282

1998, Oct. 1

1941 A1282 170w multicolored .75 .25
Complete booklet, 10 #1941 7.50

Korean Armed Forces, 50th anniv.

A1283

1998, Oct. 9

1942 A1283 170w multicolored .85 .25
Complete booklet, 10 #1942 6.50

World Stamp Day.

Beauty Series

Ceramics — A1284

No. 1944, Box with cranes on lid. No. 1945, Fish. No. 1946, Red, white blossom with blue leaf. No. 1947, Frog. No. 1948, Dragon. No. 1949, Monkeys. No. 1950, Pagoda.

1998, Nov. 20 Photo. *Perf. 13*

1943 A1284 170w multicolored .85 .40
1944 A1284 170w multicolored .85 .40
1945 A1284 170w multicolored .85 .40
1946 A1284 170w multicolored .85 .40
1947 A1284 170w multicolored .85 .40
1948 A1284 170w multicolored .85 .40
1949 A1284 170w multicolored .85 .40
1950 A1284 170w multicolored .85 .40
a. Block of 8, #1243-1250 8.50 7.50

New Year 1999 (Year of the Rabbit) — A1286

1998, Dec. 1 *Perf. 13x13½*

1952 A1286 170w multicolored .75 .25
Complete booklet, 10 #1952 9.00

Woodblock of Buddhist Tripitaka Koreana, Haeinsa Temple A1287

Haeinsa Temple Changgyong P'anjon Complex — A1288

Litho. & Engr.

1998, Dec. 9 *Perf. 13½*

1953 Sheet of 12 30.00 30.00
a. A1287 170w multicolored .95 .50
b. A1288 380w multicolored 2.75 2.00

Top part of No. 1953 contains one each Nos. 1953a-1953b and is separated from the bottom portion of the sheet by a row of perforations. The lower part of No. 1953 contains 6 No. 1953a and 4 No. 1953b.

Opening of Kunsan Port, Cent. A1289

1999, May 1 Litho. *Perf. 13¼*

1954 A1289 170w multicolored .75 .25

Opening of Masan Port, Cent. — A1290

1999, May 1

1955 A1290 170w multicolored 1.00 .25

Cartoons A1291

No. 1956, Boy and dog, "Tokgo T'ak," by Lee Sang-mu. No. 1957, Choson Dynasty robber, "Im Kkuk-jung," by Lee Du-ho. No. 1958, Fighter against alien invaders, "Rai-Fi," by Kim San-ho, vert.

1999, May 3 Photo. *Perf. 13½*

1956 A1291 170w multicolored .75 .30
1957 A1291 170w multicolored .75 .30
1958 A1291 170w multicolored .75 .30
Nos. 1956-1958 (3) 2.25 .90

Souvenir Sheets

1959 A1291 340w like #1956 1.50 1.25
1960 A1291 340w like #1957 1.50 1.25
1961 A1291 340w like #1958 1.50 1.25
Nos. 1959-1961 (3) 4.50 3.75

Nos. 1959-1961 are continuous designs.

A1292

Raptors: a, Falco peregrinus. b, Accipiter soloensis. c, Bubo bubo. d, Haliaeetus pelagicus.

1999, June 5 Litho. *Perf. 13x13¼*

1962 Sheet of 12 30.00 30.00
a.-b. A1292 170w each 1.00 .30
c.-d. A1292 340w each 2.00 .60

Top part of No. 1962 contains one each Nos. 1962a-1962d and is separated from the bottom portion of the sheet by a row of perforations. The lower part of No. 1962 contains 2 blocks of Nos. 1962a-1962d.

A1293

1999, June 12 Photo. *Perf. 13x13¼*

1963 A1293 170w multicolored .75 .25
Complete booklet, 10 #1963 15.00

1999 Intl. Olympic Committee Congress, Seoul.

Johann Wolfgang von Goethe, German Poet (1749-1832) A1294

Litho. & Engr.

1999, Aug. 12 *Perf. 13x13½*

1964 A1294 170w multicolored 1.00 .30

Souvenir Sheet

1965 A1294 480w multicolored 2.50 2.50

See Germany No. 2052.

Kumgang Mountain by Kyomjae (1676-1759) — A1295

1999, Aug. 13 Litho.

1966 A1295 170w multicolored .75 .30

Souvenir Sheet

1967 A1295 340w multicolored 1.25 1.25

Korean National Railroad,
Cent. — A1296

Litho. & Engr.
1999, Sept. 18   *Perf. 13x13¼*
1968 A1296 170w multicolored   .85   .30
      Complete booklet, 10 #1968   12.00

Millennium — A1297

A1297a

A1297b

A1297c

A1297d

A1297e

A1297f

A1297g

A1297h

A1297i

A1297j

Prehistoric sites and artifacts — No. 1969: a, Paleolithic ruins, Chungok-ri (black denomination at LL). b, Neolithic sites, Amsa-dong (white denomination at UR). c, Neolithic shell mound ruins, Tongsam-dong (black denomination at LR). d, Dolmen, Pukon-ri (black denomination at UR). e, Bronze Age artifacts and ruins, Songguk-ri. f, Rock carvings, Ulsan.

Three Countries Era artifacts — No. 1970: a, Tiger-shpaed belt buckle from tomb of Sarari, duck-shaped earthenware container, Kyongsang. b, Gold crown, silver cup from Hwangnamdae tomb. c, Wall painting of hunting scene from Tomb of the Dancers, Chibanri. d, Gold diadem ornaments, curved jade pieces from tomb of King Muryong. e, Gold crown from Koryong, armor from Kimhae. f, Decorative tiles, Anapji Pond.

Ancient Choson to Unified Shilla periods — No. 1971: a, Writing, site of Asadal, ancient capital of Choson. b, Korean wrestlers. c, King Kwanggaet'o, stone stele, and circular artifact with writing. d, Archers on horseback. e, Admiral Chang Po-go, ship.

Koryo dynasty — No. 1972: a, Writing and buildings (civil service examinations). b, Monk and Tripitaka Koreana wood blocks. c, Jade and movable metal type. d, Scholar An-hyang, writing and buildings. e, Mun Ik-jom, cotton plants and spinning wheel.

Early Choson dynasty — No. 1973: a, King Sejong and Korean alphabet. b, Korean script and Lady Shin Saimdang, calligrapher and painter. c, Yi Hwang and Yi I and Confucian academy building. d, Admiral Yi Sun-shin and turtle boat. e, Sandae-nori mask dance dramas.

Late Choson Dynasty — No. 1974: a, Tongui Pogam, medical treatises by Huh Joon (anatomic diagram, mortar and pestle) b, Dancer and Musicians, by Kim Hong-do. c, Plum Blossoms and Bird, by Chong Yak-yong and building. d, Map of Korea, by Kim Chongho and compass. e, Carved stone monument at Tongchak Peasant Uprsing Memorial Hall.

Historic relics of Koryo and Choson Dynasties — No. 1975: a, Container, pitcher, Kangjin kiln site. b, Fenced-off monument and Nirvana Hall, Pongjungsa Temple (yellow building). c, Hahoe and Pyongsan wooden masks. d, Kunjong Hall, Kyongbok Palace. e, Dream Journey to the Peach Blossom land, by An Kyon. f, Water clock of King Sejong.

Joseon Dynasty — No. 1976: a, Spring Outing, by Sin Yun-bok. b, Chusa-style calligraphy, birthplace of Kim Jeong-hui. c, Beacon Lighthouse, book of technical drawings. d, Myeongdong Cathedral. e, Wongaksa Theater, performers. f, KITSAT-1 satellite.

Vision of the Future — No. 1977: a, Bicycle with wheels represening the two Koreas. b, Rainbow (environmental protection). c, Human genome project. d, IMT 2000 and satellites. e, Children's drawing of space travel. f, Solarpowered vehicle, windmills.

Pre-independence historic events and personalities — No. 1978: a, Kim Ku. b, March 1 Independence Movement, Declaration of Independence. c, Establishment of Korean interim government. d, Ahn Ik-tae, composer of national anthem. e, Yun Dong-ju, poet.

Historic events since independence — No. 1979: a, Liberation after World War II (People with flag). b, Korean War (soldiers, barbed wire). c, Construction of Seoul-Busan Expressway. d, Saemaul Undong movement (workers and flag). e, 1988 Summer Olympics, Seoul.

1999-2001	Litho.	Perf. 13x13½		
1969	A1297	Sheet of 6	6.00	6.00
a.-f.		170w any single	.70	.30
1970	A1297a	Sheet of 6	6.00	6.00
a.-f.		170w any single	.70	.30
		Perf. 13½		
1971	A1297b	Sheet of 5 + label	6.50	6.50
a.-e.		170w any single	.75	.30
		Photo.		
1972	A1297c	Sheet of 5 + label	6.50	6.50
a.-e.		170w any single	.75	.30
1973	A1297d	Sheet of 5 + label	6.50	6.50
a.-e.		170w any single	.75	.30
1974	A1297e	Sheet of 5 + label	8.50	8.50
a.-e.		170w any single	.75	.30
		Perf. 13		
1975	A1297f	Sheet of 6	9.00	9.00
a.-f.		170w Any single	1.00	.30
1976	A1297g	Sheet of 6	7.00	7.00
a.-f.		170w any single	.75	.30
1977	A1297h	Sheet of 6	6.50	6.50
a.-f.		170w Any single	.75	.30
		Perf. 13½		
1978	A1297i	Sheet of 5 + label	9.00	9.00
a.-e.		170w any single	1.00	.30
1979	A1297j	Sheet of 5 + label	6.00	6.00
a.-e.		170w Any single	.75	.30
		Nos. 1969-1979 (11)	77.50	77.50

Issued: No. 1969, 10/2; No. 1970, 11/16; No. 1971, 1/3/00; No. 1972, 3/2/00; No. 1973, 5/1/00; No. 1974, 7/1/00; No. 1975, 9/1/00; No. 1976, 11/1/00; No. 1977, 1/2/01; No. 1978, 4/2/01; No. 1979, 7/2/01.

UPU, 125th Anniv. — A1298

1999, Oct. 9   Litho.   *Perf. 13x13½*
1980 A1298 170w multi   .85 .25

Beauty Series

A1299

a, Purple panel, 4 orange flowers in purple and blue vase, rabbit, duck. b, Blue green panel, red jar, rooster. c, Orange panel, 4 orange flowers in yellow vase. d, Purple panel, fish, purple vase with flower decoration. e, Blue green panel, fish in net. f, Red panel, crab. g, Purple panel, birds, red flowers. h, Orange panel, deer, 3 orange flowers.

1999, Nov. 3   Litho.   *Perf. 13x13¼*
1981 A1299 Sheet of 8, #a.-h. 15.00 15.00
a.-h.   340w any single   1.75 .60

New Year 2000 (Year of the Dragon) — A1300

1999, Dec. 1   Photo.
1982 A1300 170w multi   .85 .30
a.   Souvenir sheet of 2   1.60 1.60

A1301

Registration of Korean Sites on World Heritage List — A1302

Litho. & Engr.
1999, Dec. 9   *Perf. 13x13¼*
1983   Sheet of 10   20.00 20.00
a. A1301 170w multicolored   .80 .30
b. A1302 340w multicolored   3.00 .70

Top part of No. 1983 contains one each Nos. 1983a-1983b. The lower part of No. 1983 contains 4 each Nos. 1983a-1983b.

Flag
A1303

Vitis Amurensis
A1305

Nycticorax Nycticorax
A1304

Purpuricenus Lituratus
A1306

Eophona Migratoria
A1307

Limenitis Populi
A1310

Plow
A1311

Sseore
A1311a

Sowing Basket, Namtae
A1311b

Hoes
A1311c

Namu-janngun, Jaetbak
A1311d

Yongdurei
A1311e

Winnower, Thresher
A1311f

Meongseok, Wicker Tray
A1311g

Mortar, Pestle, Grindstone
A1311h

Carrier, Rice Chest
A1311i

Hibiscus Syriacus
A1312

Chionectes Opilio
A1313

Falco Tinnunculus — A1314

Hibiscus Syriacus
A1314a

Hibiscus Syriacus
A1314b

Ficedula Zanthopygia — A1315

Hibiscus Syriacus
A1315a

Celadon Pitcher
A1316

Porcelain Container
A1316a

Hong Yong-Sik, 1st General Postmaster
A1317

Koryo Jade Ornament — A1319

Kylin Roof-End Tile — A1320

Ridge-End Tile — A1321

Porcelain Vase With Bamboo Design — A1322

Malus Asiatica
A1326

Crown From Tombs of Shinch'on-ni
A1323

Aquilegia Flabeliata — A1327

Perf. 13¼x13 (#2000, 2002, 2004, 2005), 13x13¼ (#2001, 2003, 2006, 2007), 12¾x13¾ (#1984-1990, 1996), 13¾x12¾ (#1986, 1991, 1993, 1994, 1995, 1997, 1998)

		Photo.	
1999-2003			
1984	A1303	10w multi	.35 .25
1985	A1304	20w multi	.50 .30
1986	A1305	30w multi	.50 .35
1987	A1306	40w multi	.50 .30
1988	A1307	60w multi	.55 .35
1989	A1310	160w multi	.80 .35
1990		Horiz. strip of 10	20.00 12.50
a.	A1311	170w multi	1.25 .30
b.	A1311a	170w multi	1.25 .30
c.	A1311b	170w multi	1.25 .30
d.	A1311c	170w multi	1.25 .30
e.	A1311d	170w multi	1.25 .30
f.	A1311e	170w multi	1.25 .30
g.	A1311f	170w multi	1.25 .30
h.	A1311g	170w multi	1.25 .30
i.	A1311h	170w multi	1.25 .30
j.	A1311i	170w multi	1.25 .30
1991	A1312	190w multi	.95 .30
1992	A1313	200w multi	1.25 .35
1993	A1314	210w multi	.95 .30
1994	A1314a	220w multi	.95 .30
1995	A1314b	240w multi	.95 .45
1996	A1315	280w multi	1.20 .45
1997	A1315a	310w multi	1.25 .60
1998	A1316	400w multi	1.50 .90
1999	A1316a	500w multi	2.00 1.00
2000	A1317	600w multi	3.00 1.00
2001	A1319	700w multi	3.50 1.00
2002	A1320	1290w multi	7.00 2.50
2003	A1321	1310w multi	6.00 2.50
2004	A1320	1490w buff & multi	7.00 3.50
2005	A1321	1510w brn & multi	7.00 3.50
2006	A1322	1520w multi	6.00 3.50
2007	A1323	2000w multi	8.00 1.50

Booklet Stamps
Self-Adhesive
Serpentine Die Cut 11¼x11½, 11½x11¼

2008	A1326	190w multi	1.75 .35
a.		Booklet pane of 20	27.50
2008A	A1327	190w multi	1.75 .35
a.		Booklet pane of 20	27.50

Nos. 1984-2008A (26)   85.20 38.70

Issued: 600w, 11/15; 2000w, 11/1; 20w, 700w, 1/17/00; 40w, 6/10/00; No. 1990, 1/20/01; 200w, 3/5/01. 160w, 210w, 280w, 1290w, 1310w, 1/15/02; 10w, 3/6/03; 30w, 9/10/01; 60w, 3/15/02; 400w, 4/11/03; 1490w, 1510w, 1/1/03; Nos. 2008-2008A, 7/1/03; 500w, 7/11/03; No. 1991, 220w, 240w, 310w, 1520w, 11/1/04.

2002 World Cup Soccer Championships, Korea & Japan — A1328

Various players in action.

1999, Dec. 31   Photo.   *Perf. 13x13½*
Denomination   Color

2009	170w	orange	.70 .35
2010	170w	green	.70 .35
2011	170w	red	.70 .35
2012	170w	blue	.70 .35
a.	A1328	Strip of 4, #2009-2012	3.25 3.25
b.		Souvenir sheet, #2009-2012	3.50 3.50

Korea's Entry into UPU, Cent.
A1329

2000, Jan. 3   Photo.   *Perf. 13¼x13*
2013 A1329 170w multi   .85 .30
    Booklet, 10 #2013   15.00

Steam Locomotives — A1330

Designs: No. 2014, Pashi. No. 2015, Teho. No. 2016, Mika. No. 2017, Hyouki.

2000, Feb. 1 Photo. Perf. 13¾x12¾
2014	A1330	170w tan, blk & vio	.75	.30
2015	A1330	170w pink, blk & vio	.75	.30
2016	A1330	170w gray, blk & vio	.75	.30
2017	A1330	170w cit, blk & vio	.75	.30
a.		Block of 4, #2014-2017	4.00	4.00
		Booklet, 2 #2017a	—	

Endangered Flowers — A1331

a, Lilium cernuum. b, Hibiscus hamabo. c, Sedirea japonica. d, Cypripedium japonicum.

2000, Feb. 25 Perf. 13x13¼
2018		Sheet of 12	20.00	20.00
a.-d.	A1331	170w any single	1.25	.30

Top part of No. 2018 contains one each of Nos. 2018a-2018d and the lower part contains two each. No. 2018 is impregnated with floral scent.

World Water Day — A1332

2000, Mar. 22 Photo. Perf. 13¼x13
2019	A1332	170w multi	.75	.30
		Booklet, 10 #2019	12.00	

World Meteorological Organization, 50th Anniv. — A1333

2000, Mar. 23 Perf. 13x13¼
2020	A1333	170w multi	.85	.30
		Booklet, 10 #2020	12.00	

Love A1334

2000, Apr. 20 Photo. Perf. 13¼
2021	A1334	170w multi	1.25	.30

No. 2021 has floral scent. Value is for copy with surrounding selvage.

Cyber Korea 21 Technology Plan — A1335

2000, Apr. 22 Litho. Perf. 13¼x13
2022	A1335	170w multi	.85	.30
		Booklet, 10 #2022	12.00	

Cartoons — A1336

Designs: No. 2023: Goindol, by Park Soo-dong (cavemen). No. 2024, Youngsim-i, by Bae Gum-taek (girl with lipstick).

2000, May 4 Photo. Perf. 13x13¼
2023	A1336	170w multi	.75	.40
a.		Souvenir sheet of 1	1.00	1.00
		Booklet, 10 #2023	12.00	
2024	A1336	170w multi	.75	.40
a.		Souvenir sheet of 1	1.00	1.00
		Booklet, 10 #2024	12.00	

Summit Meeting Between North and South Korea A1337

2000, June 12 Photo. Perf. 13¼x13
2025	A1337	170w multi	.75	.50

41st Intl. Mathematical Olympiad — A1338

2000, July 13 Photo. Perf. 13x13¼
2026	A1338	170w multi	1.00	.35
		Booklet, 10 #2026	12.00	

Literature Series

The Nine Cloud Dream, by Kim Man-jung A1339

From the Sea to a Child, by Chun Nam-seon A1340

Tears of Blood, by Yi In-jik A1341

Yolha Diary, by Park Ji-won A1342

The Fisherman's Calendar, by Yun Seon-do A1343

2000, Aug. 1 Perf. 13¼x13, 13x13¼
2027	A1339	170w multi	.85	.35
a.		Souvenir sheet of 1	1.00	1.00
2028	A1340	170w multi	.85	.35
a.		Souvenir sheet of 1	1.00	1.00
2029	A1341	170w multi	.85	.35
a.		Souvenir sheet of 1	1.00	1.00
2030	A1342	170w multi	.85	.35
a.		Souvenir sheet of 1	1.00	1.00
2031	A1343	170w multi	.85	.35
a.		Souvenir sheet of 1	1.00	1.00
		Nos. 2027-2031 (5)	4.25	1.75

The Puljongdae Cliff of Mt. Kumgang, by Chong Son — A1344

2000, Aug. 2 Litho. Perf. 13¼x13
2032	A1344	340w multi	1.50	.70
a.		Souvenir sheet of 1	1.75	1.75

Philately Week.

2000 Summer Olympics, Sydney — A1345

2000, Sept. 15 Photo. Perf. 13x13¼
2033	A1345	170w multi	.75	.45

Public Secondary Schools, Cent. — A1346

2000, Oct. 2 Litho. & Engr. Perf. 13
2034	A1346	170w multi	.75	.45

Third Asia-Europe Summit Meeting, Seoul A1347

2000, Oct. 20 Photo. Perf. 13¼x13
2035	A1347	170w multi	.75	.35

Intl. Council of Graphic Design Associations Millennium Congress — A1348

2000, Oct. 25 Perf. 13x13¼
2036	A1348	170w org & blk	.75	.35

Cartoon Character Gobau, 50th Anniv. — A1349

2000, Nov. 1 Litho. Perf. 13¼
2037	A1349	170w multi	.75	.35

Beauty Series

Tortoise-shell Comb A1350

Woman's Ceremonial Headdress A1351

Butterfly-shaped Hair Pin — A1352

Dragon and Phoenix Hair Pins — A1353

2000, Nov. 16 Photo. Perf. 13¼x13
2038		Horiz. strip of 4	4.50	4.50
a.	A1350	170w multi	.75	.40
b.	A1351	170w multi	.75	.40
c.	A1352	170w multi	.75	.40
d.	A1353	170w multi	.75	.40

Seoul World Cup Stadium A1354

Busan Sports Complex Main Stadium A1355

Daegu Sports Complex Stadium A1356

Incheon Munhak Stadium A1357

Gwangju World Cup Stadium A1358

Daejeon World Cup Stadium A1359

Ulsan Munsu
Soccer
Stadium
A1360

Suwon World
Cup Stadium
A1361

Jeonju World
Cup Stadium
A1362

Jeju World
Cup Stadium
A1363

2000, Nov. 24   Photo.   Perf. 13¼x13

2039		Block of 10	15.00	10.00
a.	A1354 170w multi		1.40	.40
b.	A1355 170w multi		1.40	.40
c.	A1356 170w multi		1.40	.40
d.	A1357 170w multi		1.40	.40
e.	A1358 170w multi		1.40	.40
f.	A1359 170w multi		1.40	.40
g.	A1360 170w multi		1.40	.40
h.	A1361 170w multi		1.40	.40
i.	A1362 170w multi		1.40	.40
j.	A1363 170w multi		1.40	.40
k.	Souvenir sheet, #2039a-2039b		3.50	3.50
l.	Souvenir sheet, #2039c-2039d		3.50	3.50
m.	Souvenir sheet, #2039e-2039f		3.50	3.50
n.	Souvenir sheet, #2039g-2039h		3.50	3.50
o.	Souvenir sheet, #2039i-2039j		3.50	3.50

New Year
2001 (Year of
the Snake)
A1364

2000   Photo.   Perf. 13¼

2040	A1364 170w multi	1.00	.35
a.	Souvenir sheet of 2	2.00	2.00

Self-Adhesive
Serpentine Die Cut 10¼

2041	A1364 170w multi	1.50	.35

Issued: No. 2040, 12/1; No. 241, 12/22. No. 2041 issued in sheets of 10.

King Sejong and Hunmin Chongun
Manuscript — A1365

Annals of the Choson Dynasty and
Repository — A1365a

Litho. & Engr.

2000, Dec. 9   Perf. 13x13¼

2042	Sheet of 8	17.00	17.00
a.	A1365 340w multi	1.50	1.10
b.	A1365a 340w multi	1.50	1.10

Addition of Hunmin Chongun manuscript and Annals of the Choson Dynasty to UNESCO Memory of the World Register. Top part of No. 2042 contains one each Nos. 2042a-2042b the lower part contains three each Nos. 2042a-2042b.

Awarding of
Nobel
Peace
Prize to
Pres. Kim
Dae-jung
A1366

2000, Dec. 9   Photo.

2043	A1366 170w multi	.85	.35
a.	Souvenir sheet of 1	2.50	2.50

Oksun Peaks,
by Kim Hong-
do
A1367

2001, Jan. 10   Photo.   Perf. 13¼

2044	A1367 170w multi	.85	.35

Visit Korea Year.

A1368

A1369

A1370

Diesel
and
Electric
Trains
A1371

2001, Feb. 1   Photo.   Perf. 13¾x12¾

2045	Block of 4	4.00	4.00
a.	A1368 170w multi	.85	.45
b.	A1369 170w multi	.85	.45
c.	A1370 170w multi	.85	.45
d.	A1371 170w multi	.85	.45

Endangered
Flowers — A1372

Designs: a, Diapensia lapponica. b, Rhodo-dendron aureum. c, Jeffersonia dubia. d, Sedum orbiculatum.

2001, Feb. 26   Perf. 13x13¼

2046	Sheet of 12	16.00	16.00
a.-d.	A1372 170w Any single	.90	.50

Top part of No. 2046 contains one each Nos. 2046a-2046d, the lower part contains two each Nos. 2046a-2046d.

Opening of
Inchon Intl.
Airport
A1373

2001, Mar. 29

2047	A1373 170w multi	.75	.40

Intl. Olympic
Fair, Seoul
A1374

2001, Apr. 27   Perf. 13¼x13

2048	A1374 170w multi	.75	.40
a.	Souvenir sheet of 2	2.00	2.00

Personalized Greetings — A1375

Designs: No. 2049, 170w, Hugging bears. No. 2050, 170w, Carnation. No. 2051, 170w, Congratulations. No. 2052, 170w, Birthday cake.

2001   Photo.   Perf. 13¼
Stamps + Labels

2049-2052	A1375 Set of 4	8.00	4.00

Issued: Nos. 2049-2050, 4/30; No. 2051, 6/1; No. 2052, 7/2. Each stamp was issued in sheets of 20+20 labels that could be personalized. Each sheet sold for 700w.

Cartoons — A1376

Designs: No. 2053, Iljimae, by Ko Woo-young (shown). No. 2054, Kkeobeongi, by Kil Chang-duk (student at desk).

2001, May 4   Photo.   Perf. 13x13¼

2053	A1376 170w multi	.75	.40
a.	Souvenir sheet of 1	1.00	1.00
2054	A1376 170w multi	.75	.40
a.	Souvenir sheet of 1	1.00	1.00

2002 World Cup Soccer
Championships, Japan and
Korea — A1377

Years of previous championships, soccer players, flags and scenes from host countries: a, 1954, Switzerland, mountains. b, 1986, Mexico, Chichen Itza. c, 1990, Italy, Colosseum. d, 1994, US, World Trade Center and Statue of Liberty. e, 1998, France, Eiffel Tower.

2001, May 31   Perf. 13¼x13

2055	A1377 Horiz. strip of 5	6.00	5.00
a.-e.	170w Any single	.90	.40
f.	Souvenir sheet, 2 #2055a	2.00	2.00
g.	Souvenir sheet, 2 #2055b	2.00	2.00
h.	Souvenir sheet, 2 #2055c	2.00	2.00
i.	Souvenir sheet, 2 #2055d	2.00	2.00
j.	Souvenir sheet, 2 #2055e	2.00	2.00

Kkakdugi
A1378

Bossam
Kimchi
A1379

Dongchimi
A1380

Baechu
Kimchi
A1381

2001, June 15   Perf. 13x13¼

2056	Vert. strip of 4	4.00	4.00
a.	A1378 170w multi	.75	.40
b.	A1379 170w multi	.75	.40
c.	A1380 170w multi	.75	.40
d.	A1381 170w multi	.75	.40

Roses
A1382

2001, July 18   Photo.   Perf. 13¼

2057	A1382 170w Red Queen	.75	.40
a.	Souvenir sheet of 2	2.00	2.00
2058	A1382 170w Pink Lady	.75	.40
a.	Souvenir sheet of 2	2.00	2.00

Phila Korea 2002, (Nos. 2057a, 2058a).

Love — A1383

2001, Aug. 2

2059	A1383 170w multi	.75	.40
a.	Souvenir sheet of 2	2.00	2.00

World Ceramics
Exhibition — A1384

2001, Aug. 10   Perf. 13x13¼

2060	A1384 170w multi	.75	.40

53rd Session
of the Intl.
Statistical
Institute
A1385

2001, Aug. 22   Litho.   Perf. 13¼x13

2061	A1385 170w multi	.75	.40

Korea Minting and Security Printing Corp., 50th Anniv. — A1386

Litho. & Engr.

2001, Sept. 28   *Perf. 13¼*
2062   A1386   170w multi   .75   .40

Intl. Council of Industrial Design Societies Congress, Seoul — A1387

2001, Oct. 8   Photo.   *Perf. 13x13¼*
2063   A1387   170w multi   .75   .40

Year of Dialogue Among Civilizations — A1388

2001, Oct. 9   Litho.
2064   A1388   170w multi   .75   .40

Intl. Organization of Supreme Audit Institutions, 17th Congress — A1389

2001, Oct. 19   *Perf. 13¼x13*
2065   A1389   170w blue & red   .75   .40

Orchids — A1390

No. 2066: a, Habenaria radiata. b, Orchis cyclochila. c, Dendrobium moniliforme. d, Gymnadenia camschatica.

2001, Nov. 12   Photo.   *Perf. 13¼x13*
2066   A1390   Horiz. strip of 4   5.00   5.00
   a.-d.   170w Any single   .80   .40

No. 2066 is impregnated with orchid scent.

New Year 2002 (Year of the Horse) — A1391

2001, Dec. 3   *Perf. 13x13¼*
2067   A1391   170w multi   75   40
   a.   Souvenir sheet of 2   2.00   2.00

Seonjeongjeon Hall, Changdeok Palace — A1392

Injeongjeon Hall, Changdeok Palace — A1393

Litho. & Engr.

2001, Dec. 10   *Perf. 13x13¼*
2068   Sheet of 10   20.00   15.00
   a.   A1392   170w multi   1.00   .40
   b.   A1393   340w multi   2.00   .75

Top part of No. 2068 contains one each Nos. 2068a-2068b. The lower part of No. 2068 contains 4 each Nos. 2068a-2068b.

Priority Mail — A1394

2002, Jan. 15   Photo.   *Perf. 13¼x13*
Background Color

2069	A1394	280w orange	1.75	.45
2070	A1394	310w blue	1.90	.50
2071	A1394	1380w green	5.00	2.75
2072	A1394	1410w red	5.00	2.75
		Nos. 2069-2072 (4)	13.65	6.45

See Nos. 2113-2114.

Lily — A1395

Roses — A1395a

Fish — A1396

Chick — A1396a

2002, Jan. 15   Photo.   *Perf. 13¼*
Stamp + Label

2073	A1395	190w multi	2.00	1.00
2073A	A1395a	190w multi	2.00	1.00
2074	A1396	190w multi	2.00	1.00
2074A	A1396a	190w multi	2.00	1.00
		Nos. 2073-2074A (4)		

Nos. 2073, 2073A and 2074 are impregnated with scents of items depicted. Labels could be personalized.

Korea's Entrance in Intl. Telecommunications Union, 50th Anniv. — A1397

2002, Jan. 31   Photo.   *Perf. 13x13¼*
2075   A1397   190w multi   .75   .40

Trains — A1398

No. 2076: a, Blue and white locomotive. b, Green, yellow and white locomotive. c, Green, yellow and white locomotive pulling cars. d, Red, yellow and white locomotive pulling cars.

2002, Feb. 4   Photo.   *Perf. 13¾x12¾*
2076   A1398   190w Block of 4,
         #a-d   4.50   4.50

Dye Plants — A1399

No. 2077: a, Carthamus tinctorius. b, Lithospermum erythrorhizon. c, Fraxinus rhynchophylla. d, Persicaria tinctoria.

2002, Feb. 25   Photo.   *Perf. 13¼x13*
2077   A1399   190w Block of 4,
         #a-d   4.50   3.50

See No. 2117, 2140, 2170.

Intl. Flower Exhibition, Anmyeon Island — A1400

2002, Apr. 26   *Perf. 13¼*
2078   A1400   190w multi   1.00   .40

Cartoons — A1401

Designs: No. 2079, Girl from "Wogdoggle Dugdoggle," by Mi-Na Hwang. No. 2080, Schoolmaster and children from "Mengkkong-i Seodang Village School," by Seung-woon Yoon.

2002, May 4   *Perf. 13¼x13*
2079   A1401   190w multi   1.00   .40
   a.   Souvenir sheet of 1   1.25   1.25
2080   A1401   190w multi   1.00   .40
   a.   Souvenir sheet of 1   1.25   1.25

64th Rally of Intl. Federation of Camping and Caravanning, Donghae — A1402

2002, May 16
2081   A1402   190w multi   2.00   .40

2002 World Cup Soccer Championships, Japan and Korea — A1403

No. 2082: a, Player with pink feet, part of map of Europe. b, Player with blue green feet, part of map of North and Central America. c, Player with blue violet feet, part of map of southeast Asia. d, Player with purple feet, part of map of southern Africa. e, Player with brown orange feet, part of map of South America.

2002, May 31   *Perf.*
2082   A1403   190w Shoot, 2
         each #a-e,
         + label   10.00   10.00
   f.   Souvenir sheet, 2 #2082a   1.00   .40
   g.   Souvenir sheet, 2 #2082b   1.00   .40
   h.   Souvenir sheet, 2 #2082c   1.00   .40
   i.   Souvenir sheet, 2 #2082d   1.00   .40
   j.   Souvenir sheet, 2 #2082e   1.00   .40

Korean Cuisine — A1404

No. 2083: a, Jeolpyeon (blue background). b, Shirutteok (red background). c, Injeolmi (tan background). d, Songpyeon (green background).

2002, June 15   *Perf. 13x13¼*
2083   A1404   190w Block of 4,
         #a-d   4.00   4.00

Women's Week — A1405

2002, July 1   Litho.   *Perf. 13x13¼*
2084   A1405   190w multi   .75   .40

Philakorea 2002 World Stamp Exhibition, Seoul A1406

Designs: No. 2085, Children, globe. No. 2086, Child, stamps showing flags of the world.

2002, July 1 Photo. Perf. 13¼
2085	A1406 190w multi	.85	.40
a.	Souvenir sheet of 2	2.00	2.00
2086	A1406 190w multi	.85	.40
a.	Souvenir sheet of 2	2.00	2.00

Regions of Korea

Busan — A1407

Chungbuk — A1408

Chungnam — A1409

Daegu — A1410

Daejeon — A1411

Gangwon — A1412

Gwangju — A1413

Gyeongbuk — A1414

Gyeonggi — A1415

Gyeongnam — A1416

Incheon — A1417

Jeju — A1418

Jeonbuk — A1419

Jeonnam — A1420

Seoul — A1421

Ulsan — A1422

No. 2087: a, Dongnaeyaryu Festival. b, Cliffs.
No. 2088: a, Martial arts. b, Beopju Temple.
No. 2089: a, Weaver. b, Men in sailboat.
No. 2090: a, Forest and river. b, Gwanbong Seokjoyeorae statue.
No. 2091: a, Daeok Science Town, scientist at work. b, Expo Science Park.
No. 2092: a, Gangneung mask drama. b, Ulsanbawi Rock.
No. 2093: a, Men playing tug-of-war game. b, Statues and tower at May 18th Cemetery.
No. 2094: a, Men playing game with tied logs. b, Dokdo Island.
No. 2095: a, Yangjubyeol Sandaenori mask dance. b, Panmunjom Freedom House.
No. 2096: a, Goseong Ogwangdae clowns performing. b, Rock formations in Hallyeo Haesang Natl. Maritime Park.
No. 2097: a, Chamseongdam dancers. b, Cliffs.
No. 2098: a, Traditional house and gate. b, Mt. Halla.
No. 2099: a, Iri folk band. b, Mt. Mai.
No. 2100: a, Ganggang Sullae circle dance. b, Odong Island.
No. 2101: a, Songpa Sandaenori mask dance. b, Heung-injimun Fortress.
No. 2102: a, Cheoyongmu mask dance. b, Cheonjeonnigakseok prehistoric inscriptions.

2002, Aug. 1 Perf. 13x13¼
2087	A1407 190w Horiz. pair,		
	#a-b	1.75	.75
2088	A1408 190w Horiz. pair,		
	#a-b	1.75	.75
2089	A1409 190w Horiz. pair,		
	#a-b	1.75	.75
2090	A1410 190w Horiz. pair,		
	#a-b	1.75	.75
2091	A1411 190w Horiz. pair,		
	#a-b	1.75	.75
2092	A1412 190w Horiz. pair,		
	#a-b	1.75	.75
2093	A1413 190w Horiz. pair,		
	#a-b	1.75	.75
2094	A1414 190w Horiz. pair,		
	#a-b	1.75	.75
2095	A1415 190w Horiz. pair,		
	#a-b	1.75	.75
2096	A1416 190w Horiz. pair,		
	#a-b	1.75	.75
2097	A1417 190w Horiz. pair,		
	#a-b	1.75	.75
2098	A1418 190w Horiz. pair,		
	#a-b	1.75	.75
2099	A1419 190w Horiz. pair,		
	#a-b	1.75	.75
2100	A1420 190w Horiz. pair,		
	#a-b	1.75	.75
2101	A1421 190w Horiz. pair,		
	#a-b	1.75	.75
2102	A1422 190w Horiz. pair,		
	#a-b	1.75	.75
	Nos. 2087-2102 (16)	28.00	12.00

Philakorea 2002 World Stamp Exhibition, Seoul A1423

2002, Aug. 2 Perf. 13¼x13
| 2103 | A1423 190w multi | .75 | .40 |
| a. | Sheet of 2, imperf. | 2.25 | 2.25 |

Philately Week A1424

2002, Aug. 2 Perf. 13¼
| 2104 | A1424 190w multi | .75 | .40 |
| a. | Souvenir sheet of 2 | 2.25 | 2.25 |

South Korean Soccer Team's Fourth Place Finish at World Cup Championships — A1425

No. 2105: a, Coach Guus Hiddink. b, Goalie (jersey #1). c, Player with red shirt with white accents. d, Player with red shirt with white accents, with white sock. e, Player with white shirt with red accents, ball near shoulder. f, Player (jersey #5). g, Player (jersey #6). h, Player (jersey #7). i, Player (jersey #8.) j, Player (jersey #9). k, Player (jersey #10). l, Player with ball hiding part of head. m, Goalie with red hair, white gloves with dark trim. n, Player (jersey #13). o, Player (jersey #14). p, Player (jersey #15). q, Player with white shirt with red accents, with white sock. r, Player (jersey #17). s, Player (jersey #18). t, Player (jersey #19). u, Player (jersey #20). v, Player (jersey #21). w, Player (jersey #22). x, Goalie with brown hair, black gloves with red trim.

2002, Aug. 7 Perf. 13¼x13
| 2105 | A1425 190w Sheet of 24, | | |
| | #a-x | 20.00 | 20.00 |

14th Asian Games, Busan — A1426

8th Far East and South Pacific Games for the Disabled, Busan — A1427

2002, Sept. 28 Litho. Perf. 13
| 2106 | A1426 190w multi | .85 | .40 |
| a. | Souvenir sheet of 2 | 2.25 | 2.25 |

2002, Oct. 26 Photo. Perf. 13x13¼
| 2107 | A1427 190w multi | .85 | .40 |

Orchids — A1428

No. 2108: a, Cymbidium kanran. b, Gastrodia elata. c, Pogonia japonica. d, Cephalanthera falcata.

2002, Nov. 12 Perf. 13¼x13
| 2108 | A1428 190w Block of 4, | | |
| | #a-d | 4.50 | 4.50 |

No. 2108 is impregnated with orchid scent.

Martial Arts — A1429

No. 2109: a, Taekwondo (white clothes). b, Kung Fu (red clothes).

2002, Nov. 20 Perf. 13x13¼
| 2109 | A1429 190w Horiz. pair, #a- | | |
| | b | 2.00 | 2.00 |

See People's Republic of China No. 3248.

New Year 2003 (Year of the Ram) — A1430

2002, Dec. 2
| 2110 | A1430 190w multi | .85 | .40 |
| a. | Souvenir sheet of 2 | 2.00 | 2.00 |

Gongsimdon Observation Tower, Hwaseong Fortress — A1431

Banghwasuryu Pavilion, Hwaseong
Fortress — A1432

2002, Dec. 9   **Litho. & Engr.**
2111   Sheet of 10   15.00 15.00
   a.   A1431 190w multi   .80   .40
   b.   A1432 280w multi   1.25   .65
   Top part of No. 2111 contains one each of
Nos. 2111a-2111b. The lower part contains 4
each Nos. 2111a-2111b.

South Korea — Viet Nam Diplomatic
Relations, 10th Anniv. — A1433

   No. 2112: a, Dabo Pagoda, Gyeongju
(denomination at right). b, Mot Cot Pagoda,
Hanoi, Viet Nam (denomination at left).

2002, Dec. 21   **Photo.**   **Perf. 13¼x13**
2112 A1433 190w Horiz. pair, #a-
         b   2.00 1.50
   See Viet Nam Nos. 3167-3168.

Priority Mail Type of 2002
2003, Jan. 1   **Photo.**   **Perf. 13¼x13**
             Background Color
2113 A1394 1580w lilac   6.00 6.00
2114 A1394 1610w brown   6.00 6.00

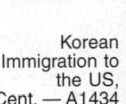

Korean
Immigration to
the US,
Cent. — A1434

2003, Jan. 13 Photo.   **Perf. 13¼x13**
2115 A1434 190w multi   .85   .40

Gondola
Car
A1435

Box Car
A1436

Tanker
Car
A1437

Hopper
Car
A1438

2003, Feb. 4   **Perf. 13¾x13**
2116   Block of 4   5.00 4.00
   a.   A1435 190w multi   .85   .40
   b.   A1436 190w multi   .85   .40
   c.   A1437 190w multi   .85   .40
   d.   A1438 190w multi   .85   .40

Dye Plants Type of 2002
   No. 2117: a, Rubia akane. b, Rhus javanica.
c, Sophora japonica. d, Isatis tinctoria.

2003, Feb. 22   **Photo.**   **Perf. 13¼x13**
2117 A1399   190w Horiz. strip of
          4, #a-d   4.50 3.00

Inauguration
of Pres.
Roh Moo-
hyun
A1439

2003, Feb. 25   **Perf. 13x13¼**
2118 A1439 190w multi   .80   .40
   a.   Souvenir sheet of 1   2.00 2.00

Traditional Culture

Footwear — A1440

Sedan Chairs — A1441

Lighting Implements — A1442

Tables — A1443

   No. 2119: a, Unhye (denomination at LL,
date at LR). b, Mokhwa (denomination at UR,
date at L). c, Jipsin (denomination at UL, date
at LH). d, Namaksin (denomination at LH, date
at LL).
   No. 2120: a, Eoyeon (no handles). b,
Choheon (wheeled). c, Sainqyo (with handles
and roof). d, Nanyeo (with handles only).
   No. 2121: a, Jojokdeung (round lantern). b,
Deungjan (lamp oil container). c, Juchilmokje
Yukgakjedeung (hexagonal lantern). d, Brass
candlestick holder with butterfly design.
   No. 2122: a, Gujok-ban (round table with
legs connected at base. b, Punghyeol-ban
(12-sided table, denomination at top). c, Iilju-
ban (12-sided table, denomination at top). d,
Haeju-ban (octagonal table).

2003   **Engr.**   **Perf. 12½**
2119 A1440 190w Horiz. strip
          of 4, #a-d   4.50 3.00
2120 A1441 190w Horiz. strip
          of 4, #a-d   4.50 3.00
2121 A1442 190w Horiz. strip
          of 4, #a-d   4.50 3.00
2122 A1443 190w Horiz. strip
          of 4, #a-d   4.50 3.00
   Nos. 2119-2122 (4)   18.00 12.00

   Issued: No. 2119, 3/19; No. 2120, 5/19; No.
2121, 7/25; No. 2122, 9/25.

Cartoons — A1444

   Designs: No. 2123, The Goblin's Cap, by
Shin Moon-soo (shown). No. 2124, The Sword
of Fire, by Kim Hye-rin (woman with sword).

2003, May 2   **Photo.**   **Perf. 13x13¼**
2123 A1444 190w multi   .85   .40
   a.   Souvenir sheet of 1   1.25 1.25
2124 A1444 190w multi   .85   .40
   a.   Souvenir sheet of 1   1.25 1.25

Lighthouse
Construction in
Korea,
Cent. — A1445

2003, May 30   **Perf. 13¼x13**
2125 A1445 190w multi   .85   .40

Dasik
A1446

Yeot
Gangjeong
A1447

Yakgwa
A1448

Yuqwa
A1449

2003, June 13   **Perf. 13x13¼**
2126   Block of 4   2.75 2.25
   a.   A1446 190w multi   .55   .40
   b.   A1447 190w multi   .55   .40
   c.   A1448 190w multi   .55   .40
   d.   A1449 190w multi   .55   .40
   Nos. 2126a-2126d were printed in sheets of
20 that yield four No. 2126 and one vertical
strip of four of Nos. 2126a-2126d.

Priority Mail Type of 2002
2003, July 1   **Photo.**   **Perf. 13¼x13**
             Background Color
2127 A1394 420w blue green   2.00 1.00

Philately Week
A1450

2003, Aug. 1   **Perf. 13¼**
2128 A1450 190w multi   .85   .40
   a.   Souvenir sheet of 2, imperf.   2.25 2.25

2003 Summer
Universiade,
Daegu — A1451

2003, Aug. 21   **Perf. 13x13¼**
2129 A1451 190w multi   .85   .40
   a.   Souvenir sheet of 2   2.25 2.25

YMCA in Korea,
Cent. — A1452

2003, Oct. 28 Photo.   **Perf. 13¼x13**
2130 A1452 190w multi   .85   .40

Soong Eui School,
Cent. — A1453

2003, Oct. 31   **Perf. 13x13¼**
2131 A1453 190w multi   .85   .40

Natl. Tuberculosis
Association, 50th
Anniv. — A1454

2003, Nov. 6   **Litho.**
2132 A1454 190w black & red   .85   .40

Orchids — A1455

   No. 2133: a, Cremastra appendiculata. b,
Cymbidium lancifolium. c, Orchis graminifolia.
d, Bulbophyllum drymoglossum.

2003, Nov. 12 Photo.   Perf. 13¼x13
2133 A1455 190w Block of 4,
         #a-d   4.50 3.50
   No. 2133 is impregnated with a floral scent.

New Year 2004 (Year
of the
Monkey) — A1456

2003, Dec. 1   **Perf. 13x13¼**
2134 A1456 190w multi   .85   .40
   a.   Souvenir sheet of 2   2.25 2.25

A1457

Dolmens — A1458

Litho. & Engr.
2003, Dec. 9   *Perf. 13x13¼*
2135   Sheet of 10   15.00 15.00
a. A1457 190w multi   .90 .40
b. A1458 280w multi   1.25 .50

Top part of No. 2135 contains one each of Nos. 2135a-2135b. The lower part contains 4 each Nos. 2135a-2135b.

South Korea — India Diplomatic Relations, 30th Anniv. — A1459

No. 2136: a, Cheomsongdae Astronomical Observatory, Gyeongju, South Korea. b, Jantar Mantar, Jaipur, India.

2003, Dec. 10   Photo.   *Perf. 13¼x13*
2136 A1459 190w Horiz. pair,
       #a-b   2.25 2.00

Dokdo Island Flora and Fauna — A1460

No. 2137: a, Calystegia soldanella. b, Aster spathulifolius, butterfly. c, Calonectris laucomelas. d, Larus crassirostris.

2004, Jan. 16   *Perf. 13x13¼*
2137 A1460   Horiz. strip of 4   18.00 —
a.-d.   190w Any single   4.50 4.50

Korean National Commission for UNESCO, 50th Anniv. — A1461

2004, Jan. 30
2138 A1461 190w multi   .80 .25

Multiple Tie Tamper A1462

Ballast Regulator A1463

Track Inspection Car — A1464

Ballast Cleaner A1465

2004, Feb. 4   *Perf. 13¾x12¾*
2139   Block of 4   4.00 4.00
a. A1462 190w brown & multi   .75 .40
b. A1463 190w lilac & multi   .75 .40
c. A1464 190w blue green & multi   .75 .40
d. A1465 190w blue & multi   .75 .40

Dye Plants Type of 2002

No. 2140: a, Juglans regia. b, Acer ginnala. c, Pinus densiflora. d, Punica granatum.

2004, Feb. 25   *Perf. 13¼x13*
2140 A1399 190w Block of 4,
       #a-d   3.50 3.50

A1466

2004, Mar. 22   Litho.   *Perf. 13x13¼*
2141 A1466 190w multi   .80 .40

12th World Water Day.

A1467

2004, Mar. 25   Photo.
2142 A1467 190w multi   .85 .40

Korean Meteorological Service, cent.

Inauguration of High Speed Railroads A1468

2004, Apr. 1   *Perf. 13¼x13*
2143 A1468 190w multi   .85 .40

A1469

Winners of Future of Science Stamp Design Contest — A1470

Perf. 13¼x13, 13x13¼
2004, Apr. 21   Photo.
2144 A1469 190w multi   .85 .40
2145 A1470 190w multi   .85 .40

A1471

Cartoons: No. 2146, Wicked Boy Sim-sultong, by Lee Jeong-moon (shown). No. 2147, Nation of Winds, by Kim Jin.

2004, May 4   Photo.   *Perf. 13¼*
2146 A1471 190w multi   .85 .40
a.   Souvenir sheet of 1   1.10 1.10
2147 A1471 190w multi   .85 .40
a.   Souvenir sheet of 1   1.10 1.10

A1472

2004, May 21
2148 A1472 190w multi   .50 .40

FIFA (Fédération Internationale de Football Association), cent.

Korean Cuisine — A1473

No. 2149: a, Sinseollo (blue background). b, Hwayangjeok (green background). c, Bibimbap (pink background). d, Gujeolpan (orange background).

2004, June 15
2149 A1473 190w Block of 4,
       #a-d   3.50 3.50

Traditional Culture

Needlework Equipment — A1474

Head Coverings — A1475

No. 2150: a, Octagonal storage basket. b, Thimbles with flower decorations. c, Cylindrical bobbin, bobbin and thread. d, Needle cases.
No. 2151: a, Gold crown with tassels. b, Bamboo hat with untied neck band. c, Gauze hat. d, Horsehair hat with tied neck band.

2004   Engr.   *Perf. 12½*
2150 A1474 190w Horiz. strip of
       4, #a-d   4.00 4.00
2151 A1475 190w Horiz. strip of
       4, #a-d   4.00 4.00

Issued: No. 2150, 6/24; No. 2151, 8/20.

National Academies, 50th Anniv. — A1476

No. 2152: a, National Academy of Science. b, National Academy of Arts.

2004, July 16   Litho.   *Perf. 13x13¼*
2152 A1476 190w Horiz. pair, #a-
       b   1.75 1.75

Congratulations — A1477

2004, July 22   Photo.   *Perf. 13¼*
2153 A1477 190w multi   .85 .40
a.   Souvenir sheet of 2   2.00 2.00

2004 Summer Olympics, Athens — A1478

2004, Aug. 13   *Perf. 13x13¼*
2154 A1478 190w multi   .85 .40

Bridges — A1479

No. 2155: a, Geumcheongyo Bridge (two arches). b, Jeongotgyo Bridge (pillars and flat slabs). c, Jinchcon Nongdari Bridge (loose rocks). d, Seungseongyo Bridge (single arch).

Perf. 13¼ Syncopated
2004, Sept. 24
2155 A1479 190w Block fo 4,
       #a-d   4.00 4.00

Intl. Council of Museums, 20th General Conference, Seoul — A1480

2004, Oct. 1   *Perf. 13x13¼*
2156 A1480 190w multi   .85 .40

Obaegnahan — A1481

Seonjakjiwat — A1482

Baengnokdam — A1483

Oreum
A1484

2004, Oct. 18

2157	Block of 4	4.00	4.00
a.	A1481 190w multi	.75	.40
b.	A1482 190w multi	.75	.40
c.	A1483 190w multi	.75	.40
d.	A1484 190w multi	.75	.40

Flag — A1485

Flowers — A1486

Flower and Bee — A1487

Lamb, Church and Bible — A1488

Children and Lotus Flower — A1489

Stylized Animals — A1490

Teddy Bear — A1491

Dinosaur — A1492

Flower and Envelope — A1493

2004, Nov. 1   Photo.   *Perf. 13¼*

2158	A1485 220w multi + label	2.50	1.50
2159	A1486 220w multi + label	2.50	1.50
2160	A1487 220w multi + label	2.50	1.50
2161	A1488 220w multi + label	2.50	1.50
2162	A1489 220w multi + label	2.50	1.50
2163	Strip of 4 + 4 alter-	10.00	10.00
	nating labels		
a.	A1490 220w multi + label	2.50	2.50
b.	A1491 220w multi + label	2.50	2.50
c.	A1492 220w multi + label	2.50	2.50
d.	A1493 220w multi + label	2.50	2.50
	Nos. 2158-2163 (6)	22.50	17.50

Labels attached to Nos. 2158-2163 could be personalized.

Orchids — A1494

No. 2164: a, Goodyera maximowicziana. b, Sarcanthus scolopendrifolius. c, Calanthe sieboldii. d, Bletilla striata.

2004, Nov. 12   *Perf. 13¼x13*

2164	A1494 220w Block of 4,		
	#a-d	4.00	4.00

No. 2164 is impregnated with orchid scent.

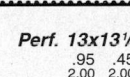

New Year 2005
(Year of the
Chicken) — A1495

2004, Dec. 1   *Perf. 13x13¼*

2165	A1495 220w multi	.95	.45
a.	Souvenir sheet of 2	2.00	2.00

Daenungwon Tumuli Park,
Seosuhyeong Ceramics, Royal Crown
of Geumgwanchong — A1496

Anapji Pond, Scissors, Buddha, Lion
Incense Burner — A1497

2004, Dec. 9   Litho. & Engr.

2166	Sheet of 10	15.00	15.00
a.	A1496 310w multi	1.00	.55
b.	A1497 310w multi	1.00	.55

Top part of No. 2166 contains one each of Nos. 2166a-2166b. The lower part contains 4 each of Nos. 2166a-2166b.

Fish of
Marado
Island
A1498

No. 2167: a, Girella punctata. b, Epinephe-lus septemfasciatus. c, Chromis notata. d, Sebastiscus marmoratus.

2005, Jan. 18   Photo.

2167	Horiz. strip of 4	7.00	7.00
a.-d.	A1498 220w Any single	1.40	.50

Cloning of Human Embryonic Stem
Cells, 1st Anniv. — A1499

2005, Feb. 12   *Perf. 12¾x13½*

2168	A1499 220w multi	3.00	.50

Rotary
International,
Cent.
A1500

2005, Feb. 23   *Perf. 13¼x13*

2169	A1500 220w multi	.80	.40

Dye Plants Type of 2002

No. 2170: a, Taxus cuspidata. b, Smilax china. c, Clerodendron trichotomum. d, Gardenia jasminoides.

2005, Feb. 25

2170	A1399 220w Block of 4,		
	#a-d	4.00	4.00

Gyeonggi Province
Tourism — A1501

2005, Mar. 10   Litho.   *Perf. 13x13¼*

2171	A1501 220w multi	.75	.40

A1502

Information and
Communication of
the Future — A1503

2005, Apr. 22   Photo.   *Perf. 13¼x13*

2172	A1502 220w multi	.75	.40

              Perf. 13¼x13¼

2173	A1503 220w multi	.75	.40

Korea
University,
Cent.
A1504

2005, May 4   Litho.   *Perf. 13x13¼*

2174	A1504 220w multi	.85	.40

57th Intl.
Whaling
Commission
Meeting,
Ulsan
A1505

2005, May 27   Photo.   *Perf. 13¼x13*

2175	A1505 220w multi	1.00	.40

Neobani
(Broiled
Beef)
A1506

Bindaetteok
(Fried
Ground
Mung
Beans)
A1507

Jeongol
(Stew)
A1508

Hwajeon (Fried Rice Cakes and Flower Petals) A1509

2005, June 15   **Perf. 13x13¼**
2176		Block of 4	4.00	4.00
a.	A1506	220w multi	.85	.40
b.	A1507	220w multi	.85	.40
c.	A1508	220w multi	.85	.40
d.	A1509	220w multi	.85	.40

Goguryeo Kingdom — A1510

No. 2177: a, Sword, armored soldier on horse. b, Armored soldiers on horses, Onyeo Fortress, Baek-am Castle.

Perf. 13x13¼ Syncopated
2005, July 1
2177	A1510	310w Vert. pair, #a-b	3.25	3.25

Strix Aluco A1513   Arctous Ruber A1514

Parus Major A1516   Crinum Asiaticum A1517

Planned City — A1521   Brown Hawk Owl — A1522

Rose of Sharon — A1523

Sungnyemun Gate — A1524   Suwon Hwaseong Fortress — A1524a

Haeundae Dongbaek Island — A1524b

Dodamsambong Peaks — A1524c

Hongdo Island — A1524d

Cheomseongdae Observatory — A1524e

Gwanghallu Pavilion — A1524f   Gyeongpodae Pavilion — A1524g

Baengnokdam Lake — A1524h

Whistling Swans A1525   Charonia Sauliae A1526

Celadon Incense Burner — A1527   Buncheong Jar — A1529

Buncheong Jar — A1530   Jar With Clay Figurines — A1530a

Gilt Bronze Pagoda — A1531   Euryale Ferox — A1532

Flag — A1533

2005-13   **Photo.**   **Perf. 13¾x12¾**
2180	A1513	50w multi	.95	.25
2181	A1514	70w multi	.50	.25

Perf. 12¾x13¾
2183	A1516	90w multi	.50	.25

Perf. 13¾x12¾
2184	A1517	100w multi	.50	.25

Perf. 13x13¼
2188	A1521	220w multi	1.00	.25
2189	A1522	250w multi	1.25	.40

Perf. 13½
2190	A1523	250w multi + label	2.00	.40

Perf. 13x13¾
2191		Horiz. strip of 9	5.00	2.50
a.	A1524	300w multi	.55	.25
b.	A1524a	300w multi	.55	.25
c.	A1524b	300w multi	.55	.25
d.	A1524c	300w multi	.55	.25
e.	A1524d	300w multi	.55	.25
f.	A1524e	300w multi	.55	.25
g.	A1524f	300w multi	.55	.25
h.	A1524g	300w multi	.55	.25
i.	A1524h	300w multi	.55	.25

Perf. 13¾x13
2192	A1525	340w multi	1.00	.40

Perf. 12¾x13¾
2193	A1526	360w multi	.65	.30

Perf. 13x13¾
2193A	A1526	390w multi	.75	.25

Perf. 13x13¼
2194	A1527	1000w multi	2.00	.85
2196	A1529	1720w multi	5.00	1.75

Perf. 13x13½
2197	A1530	1750w multi	6.00	1.90

Perf. 13x13¼
2197A	A1530a	1770w multi	3.00	1.50

Perf. 13x13½
2197B	A1530a	1930w multi	3.75	.90
2198	A1531	2000w multi	4.00	1.60

Self-Adhesive
Serpentine Die Cut 11¾x11½
2199	A1532	250w multi	1.50	.25

Serpentine Die Cut 11½x11¼
2200	A1533	270w multi	.50	.25
		Nos. 2180-2200 (19)	39.85	14.50

Issued: 50w, 9/1; 1720w, 8/1; 90w, 6/5/06; 100w, 3/2/06; 220w, 12/27/05. Nos. 2189, 2190, 2192, 2197, 11/1/06. 70w, 7/10/07. No. 2199, 6/30/08. No. 2194, 11/17/09; No. 2198, 5/25/09. Nos. 2193, 2197A, 2200, 10/1/11. Nos. 2191, 2193A, 2197B, 11/11/13.

No. 2190 was printed in sheets of 20 stamps and 20 labels that could be personalized.

Happy Birthday A1536

2005, Aug. 3   **Photo.**   **Perf. 13¼**
2203	A1536	220w multi	.85	.35
a.		Souvenir sheet of 2	2.00	2.00

Philately Week. Portions of the design were printed with a thermochromic ink that changes color when warmed.

Liberation of Korea, 60th Anniv. A1537

No. 2204: a, Charter and headquarters of provisional government. b, Proclamation of Korean Independence. c, Soldiers taking oath. d, Emblem of 60th anniv. of Korean liberation.

2005, Aug. 12   **Perf. 13¼x13**
2204		Horiz. strip of 4	8.00	8.00
a.	A1537	480w multi	1.25	.75
b.	A1537	520w multi	1.25	1.00
c.	A1537	580w multi	1.50	1.10
d.	A1537	600w multi	1.50	1.25

Fusion of Eastern and Western Cultures — A1538

2005, Aug. 18   **Litho.**   **Perf. 13x13¼**
2205	A1538	220w multi	.85	.45

Hangang Bridge — A1539

Expogyo — A1540

Banghwa Bridge — A1541

Tongyeong Bridge — A1542

Perf. 13¼ Syncopated
2005, Sept. 23   **Photo.**
2206		Block of 4	4.00	4.00
a.	A1539	220w multi	.75	.40
b.	A1540	220w multi	.75	.40
c.	A1541	220w multi	.75	.40
d.	A1542	220w multi	.75	.40

Ikki Falls A1543

Piagol Valley A1544

Cheonwangbong Peak — A1545

Baraebong Peak A1546

2005, Oct. 18 *Perf. 13x13¼*
2207   Horiz. strip of 4   6.00   6.00
a.   A1543 220w multi   1.00   .40
b.   A1544 220w multi   1.00   .40
c.   A1545 220w multi   1.00   .40
d.   A1546 220w multi   1.00   .40

Korean Red Cross, Cent. — A1547

2005, Oct. 27
2208   A1547 220w multi   .85   .50

Relocation and Reopening of National Museum A1548

2005, Oct. 28 *Perf. 13¼x13*
2209   A1548 220w multi   .85   .50

Orchids — A1549

No. 2210: a, Epipactis thunbergii. b, Cymbidium goeringii. c, Cephalanthera erecta. d, Spiranthes sinensis.

2005, Nov. 11
2210   A1549 220w Block of 4, #a-d   4.00   4.00

2005 Asian-Pacific Economic Cooperation Economic Leaders' Meeting, Busan — A1550

No. 2211: a, The Sun, the Moon and Five Peaks. b, Murimaru APEC House, Dongbaek Island.

2005, Nov. 18 Photo. *Perf. 13x13¼*
2211   A1550 220w Horiz. pair, #a-b   1.75   1.75

New Year 2006 (Year of the Dog) — A1551

2005, Dec. 1
2212   A1551 220w multi   .85   .50
a.   Souvenir sheet of 2   2.00   2.00

Jikjisimcheyojeol, Book Produced in 1377 by Movable Type — A1552

Seungjeongwon Ilgi, Diaries of the Joseon Dynasty — A1553

2005, Dec. 9 **Litho. & Engr.**
2213   Sheet of 10   15.00   15.00
a.   A1552 310w multi   1.25   .60
b.   A1553 310w multi   1.25   .60

Top part of No. 2213 contains one each of Nos. 2213a-2213b. The lower part contains 4 each of Nos. 2213a-2213b.

Wildlife of Baengnyeongdo — A1554

Designs: No. 2214, Phoca vitulina largha. No. 2215, Phalacrocorax pelagicus. No. 2216, Orithyia sinica. No. 2217, Ammodytes personatus.

2006, Jan. 18 **Photo.**
2214   A1554 220w multi   1.00   .50
2215   A1554 220w multi   1.00   .50
2216   A1554 220w multi   1.00   .50
2217   A1554 220w multi   1.00   .50
a.   Horiz. strip of 4, #2214-2217   4.50   4.50
b.   Sheet, 1 each #2214-2217, 3 #2217a + 2 labels   20.00
    Nos. 2214-2217 (4)   4.00   2.00

Designation of Cheju Island as Island of World Peace — A1555

2006, Jan. 27 *Perf. 13¾x12¾*
2218   A1555 220w multi   .85   .50

Exports

Automobiles — A1556

Semiconductors — A1557

Petrochemicals — A1558

Electronics — A1559

Machinery A1560

Ships A1561

Steel A1562

Textiles A1563

2006, Mar. 15 *Perf. 13x13¼*
2219   Block of 8   6.50   6.50
a.   A1556 220w multi   .75   .50
b.   A1557 220w multi   .75   .50
c.   A1558 220w multi   .75   .50
d.   A1559 220w multi   .75   .50
e.   A1560 220w multi   .75   .50
f.   A1561 220w multi   .75   .50
g.   A1562 220w black   .75   .50
h.   A1563 220w multi   .75   .50

Gyeongnam Goseong Dinosaur World Expo — A1564

Serpentine Die Cut 11¼x11
2006, Apr. 14
2220   A1564   Horiz. pair   2.00   1.50
a.   220w Iguanodon   .85   .50
b.   220w Megaraptor   .85   .50

A1565

Children's Drawings on Automated World A1566

2006, Apr. 21 *Perf. 13x13¼, 13¼x13*
2221   A1565 220w multi   .85   .50
2222   A1566 220w multi   .85   .50

Dongguk University, Cent. — A1567

2006, May 8 Litho. *Perf. 13x13¼*
2223   A1567 220w multi   .85   .40

Sookmyung Women's University, Cent. — A1568

Perf. 12¾x13¾
2006, May 22 **Photo.**
2224   A1568 220w multi   .85   .40

2006 World Cup Soccer Championships, Germany — A1569

2006, June 2 **Photo.** *Perf. 13¼*
2225   A1569 220w multi + label   4.00   —

No. 2225 was printed in sheets of 14 stamps + 14 labels picturing members of South Korean World Cup soccer team + one large label picturing entire team. Sheets sold for 6000w.

A1570

2006 World Cup Soccer
Championships, Germany — A1571

Perf. 12¾x13¾

2006, June 9   Photo.
2226   Pair   2.00 1.50
  a. A1570 220w multi   .85   .50
  b. A1571 220w multi   .85   .50

Goguryeo
Kingdom
A1572

No. 2227: a, Janggun Tomb and Sanse-
ongha Tombs. b, Sun and Moon Gods from
Ohoebun Tomb No. 4.

Perf. 13x13¼ Syncopated

2006, July 3   Photo.
2227 A1572 480w Vert. pair, #a-b 4.00 4.00

No. 2227 was printed in sheets containing
seven of each stamp.

Philately
Week
A1573

No. 2228: a, Denomination below heart. b,
Denomination above heart.

2006, Aug. 3   Photo.   **Perf. 13¼**
2228 A1573 220w Pair, #a-b   1.50 1.50
  c. Souvenir sheet, #2228a-2228b 2.00 2.00

Skateboarding — A1574

No. 2229: a, Tail stole. b, Drop in. c, Backside spin. d, Backside grab.

Serpentine Die Cut 11¾x11¼

2006, Sept. 5   Self-Adhesive
2229 A1574 220w Block of 4, #a-
       d   4.00 4.00

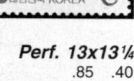

World Ginseng
Expo,
Geumsan — A1575

2006, Sept. 22   **Perf. 13x13¼**
2230 A1575 220w multi   .85   .40

Jindo Bridge — A1576

Changseon-Samcheonpo
Bridge — A1577

Olympic Bridge — A1578

Seohae Bridge — A1579

Perf. 13¼ Syncopated

2006, Sept. 26
2231   Block of 4   4.00 4.00
  a. A1576 220w multi   .75   .40
  b. A1577 220w multi   .75   .40
  c. A1578 220w multi   .75   .40
  d. A1579 220w multi   .75   .40

Hangeul
Day — A1580

2006, Oct. 9   **Perf. 13x13¼**
2232 A1580 (220w) multi   .85   .40

Use of Hangeul as official Korean writing
system, 560th anniv.

Sahmyook
University,
Cent. — A1581

2006, Oct. 10
2233 A1581 220w multi   .85   .40

Lineage — A1582

Maple
Story — A1583

Ragnarok
A1584

Gersang
A1585

Legend of Mir
III — A1586

Kartrider
A1587

Mu — A1588

Pangya — A1589

Fortress 2
Forever
Blue — A1590

Mabinogi
A1591

Serpentine Die Cut 11¾

2006, Nov. 9
2234   Block of 10   10.00 10.00
  a. A1582 250w multi   .90   .60
  b. A1583 250w multi   .90   .60
  c. A1584 250w multi   .90   .60
  d. A1585 250w multi   .90   .60
  e. A1586 250w multi   .90   .60
  f. A1587 250w multi   .90   .60
  g. A1588 250w multi   .90   .60
  h. A1589 250w multi   .90   .60
  i. A1590 250w multi   .90   .60
  j. A1591 250w multi   .90   .60

Internet games.

Janggunbong Peak — A1592

Ulsanbawi
Rock
A1593

Daecheongbong Peak — A1594

Sibiseonnyeotang Valley — A1595

2006, Nov. 16   **Perf. 13x13¼**
2235   Block of 4   4.00 3.50
  a. A1592 250w multi   .85   .60
  b. A1593 250w multi   .85   .60
  c. A1594 250w multi   .85   .60
  d. A1595 250w multi   .85   .60

New Year 2007
(Year of the
Pig) — A1596

2006, Dec. 1   Photo.   Perf. 13x13¼
2236 A1596 250w multi   .85   .40
  a.   Souvenir sheet of 2   2.00   2.00

Text of Heungboga and Pansori
Singer — A1597

Mo Heung-gap, Pansori
Singer — A1598

Litho. & Engr.
2006, Dec. 8   Perf. 13¼x13¼
2237   Sheet of 10   25.00 25.00
  a.   A1597 480w multi   2.25   1.75
  b.   A1598 480w multi   2.25   1.75
  Top part of No. 2237 contains one each of
Nos. 2237a-2237b. The lower part contains 4
each of Nos. 2237a-2237b.

A1599

Sharing and
Caring
A1600

2006, Dec. 14   Photo.   Perf. 13¼x13¼
2238 A1599 250w multi   .85   .25

Perf. 13¼x13
2239 A1600 250w multi   .85   .25
  No. 2238 is impregnated with a pine scent;
No. 2239 with a chocolate scent.

Nakdong River in Autumn — A1601

Nakdong River in Winter — A1602

Nakdong River in Spring — A1603

Nakdong River in Summer — A1604

Perf. 13¼ Syncopated
2007, Jan. 18   Photo.
2240   Block of 4   3.50   3.00
  a.   A1601 250w multi   .75   .25
  b.   A1602 250w multi   .75   .25
  c.   A1603 250w multi   .75   .25
  d.   A1604 250w multi   .75   .25

Megatron/Matrix — A1605

TV
Buddha
A1606

The More
the Better
A1607

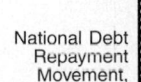

Oh-Mah
(Mother)
A1608

2007, Jan. 29   Perf. 13¼
2241   Sheet of 12, 3 each   12.00 12.00
        #a-d
  a.   A1605 250w multi   .75   .25
  b.   A1606 250w multi   .75   .25
  c.   A1607 250w multi   .75   .25
  d.   A1608 250w multi   .75   .25
  Art by Nam June Paik (1932-2006).

National Debt
Repayment
Movement,
Cent. — A1609

2007, Feb. 21   Photo.   Perf. 13¼x13¼
2242 A1609 250w multi   .85   .25

Maps of
Korea
A1610

  No. 2243: a, Map from Atlas of Korea, 1780.
b, Complete Territorial Map of the Great East,
19th cent. c, Map of the Eight Provinces, 1531.
d, Comprehensive Map of the World and
Nation's Successive Capitals, 1402.

2007, Feb. 28   Photo.   Perf. 13½x13
2243   Sheet of 8, 2 each 17.50 17.50
        #a-d
  a.   A1610 480w multi   1.20   1.20
  b.   A1610 520w multi   1.50   1.50
  c.   A1610 580w multi   1.75   1.75
  d.   A1610 600w multi   1.75   1.75

Daehan Hospital,
Seoul,
Cent. — A1611

2007, Mar. 15   Litho.   Perf. 13x13¼
2244 A1611 250w multi   .85   .25

Ninth Asia Pacific
Orchid Conference,
Goyang — A1612

2007, Mar. 16   Photo.
2245 A1612 250w multi   .85   .25

Biology
Year — A1613

2007, Mar. 19   Perf. 13¼x13
2246 A1613 250w multi   .85   .25
  a.   Souvenir sheet of 2   2.25   2.25

Sunflower — A1614

2007, Mar. 21   Litho.   Perf. 13¼
2247 A1614 250w multi + label   2.50   2.50
  Printed in sheets of 20 stamps + 20 labels
and 14 stamps + 14 labels that sold for 7500w.
Labels could be personalized.

Clover — A1615

Pig — A1616

2007, Mar. 21   Photo.   Perf. 13¼
2248 A1615 250w multi + label   2.75   2.75
2249 A1616 250w multi + label   2.75   2.75
  Nos. 2248-2249 were each printed in sheets
of 9 stamps + 9 labels. Each sheet sold for
4300w. Labels could be personalized.

Chinese Bride
and
Groom — A1617

Indian Bride and
Groom — A1618

Malaysian Bride
and
Groom — A1619

Eurasian Bride
and
Groom — A1620

  No. 2250 — Korean brides and grooms
with: e, Mountains in background. f, Flowers
on orange background. g, Flowers and foliage
in background. h, Ducks in background.

2007, Mar. 30   Perf. 13¼x13
2250   Block of 8   9.00   9.00
  a.   A1617 250w multi   .60   .40
  b.   A1618 250w multi   .60   .40
  c.   A1619 250w multi   .60   .40
  d.   A1620 250w multi   .60   .40
  e.   A1620 480w multi   1.25   1.00
  f.   A1620 520w multi   1.40   1.25
  g.   A1620 580w multi   1.75   1.50
  h.   A1620 600w multi   1.90   1.50
  See Singapore No. 1241.

Opening of Fortress Wall in Mt.
Bugaksan — A1621

2007, Apr. 5   Photo.   Perf. 13¾x12¾
2251 A1621 250w multi   .85   .30

312   KOREA

A1622

Internet
Culture
A1623

2007, Apr. 20   Litho.   Perf. 13¼x13
2252 A1622 250w multi   .85   .30
Photo.
2253 A1623 250w multi   .85   .30

Children's
Charter, 50th
Anniv. — A1624

Serpentine Die Cut
2007, May 4   Photo.
Self-Adhesive
2254 A1624 250w multi   .85   .30
No. 2254 is impregnated with a strawberry
scent.

Dispatch of Special
Envoys to Second
Hague Peace
Conference,
Cent. — A1625

Litho. & Engr.
2007, June 27   Perf. 13x13¼
2255 A1625 250w multi   .85   .30

A1626

Goguryeo
Kingdom
A1627

No. 2256: a, Cooks preparing food. b, Host
welcoming guest.

Perf. 13 Syncopated
2007, July 2   Photo.
2256 Sheet of 14, 7 each   20.00 20.00
a. A1626 480w multi   1.25   .60
b. A1627 480w multi   1.25   .60

Philately Week — A1628

No. 2257: a, Korea #1. b, Korea #2.

2007, Aug. 1   Photo.   Perf. 13x13¼
2257 Horiz. pair   2.00   2.00
a.-b. A1628 250w Either single   .75   .30
c. Souvenir sheet, #2257   2.25   2.25

Rollerblading — A1629

No. 2258: a, Drop-in. b, Flip. c, Spin. d,
Grind.

Serpentine Die Cut 11¾x11¼
2007, Sept. 5   Photo.
Self-Adhesive
2258 A1629 250w Block of 4, #a-
       d   4.00   4.00

Korean Bar
Association,
Cent. — A1630

2007, Sept. 21   Litho.   Perf. 13x13¼
2259 A1630 250w multi   .85   .30

Gwangan Bridge — A1631

Seongsu Bridge — A1632

Seongsan Bridge — A1633

Yeongjong Bridge — A1634

Perf. 13¼x13½ Syncopated
2007, Sept. 28   Photo.
2260 Block of 4   3.50   3.50
a. A1631 250w multi   .75   .30
b. A1632 250w multi   .75   .30
c. A1633 250w multi   .75   .30
d. A1634 250w multi   .75   .30

Inter-Korean
Summit,
Pyongyang,
North
Korea — A1635

2007, Oct. 2   Perf. 13x13¼
2261 A1635 250w multi   .85   .30

Hyeongje
Falls
A1636

Rimyeongsu Falls — A1637

Lake
Samjiyeon
A1638

Lake
Chonji
A1639

2007, Oct. 18 Photo.   Perf. 13x13½
2262 Block of 4   3.50   3.50
a. A1636 250w multi   .75   .30
b. A1637 250w multi   .75   .30
c. A1638 250w multi   .75   .30
d. A1639 250w multi   .75   .30

A1640

A1641

A1642

Korean
Films
A1643

No. 2263: a, Arirang, 1926. b, The Own-
erless Ferryboat, 1932. c, Looking for Love,
1928. d, Chunhyangjeon, 1935.

2007, Oct. 26   Perf. 13x13¼
2263 Sheet of 16, 4 each   16.00 16.00
a. A1640 250w multi   .75   .30
b. A1641 250w multi   .75   .30
c. A1642 250w multi   .75   .30
d. A1643 250w multi   .75   .30

A1644

Protection of
Children's
Rights
A1645

2007, Nov. 20 Photo.   Perf. 13x13¼
2264 A1644 250w multi   .85   .30
Litho.
Perf. 13¼x13
2265 A1645 250w multi   .85   .30

Opening of New Central Post Office,
Seoul — A1646

No. 2266: a, Hanseong Post Office, 1915,
and new building. b, New building.

2007, Nov. 22 Photo.   Perf. 13x13¼
2266 A1646 250w Horiz. pair, #a-
       b   2.00   2.00
No. 2266 printed in sheet containing 7 pairs.

New Year 2008
(Year of the
Rat) — A1647

2007, Nov. 30
2267 A1647 250w multi   .85   .30
a. Souvenir sheet of 2   1.50   1.50

Tapdeunggut Exorcism, Dano Festival,
Gangneung — A1648

Gwanno Mask Drama, Dano
Festival — A1649

2007, Dec. 7   **Litho. & Engr.**
2268   Sheet of 10, 5 each
      #a-b   18.00   18.00
   a.   A1648 480w multi   1.50   .75
   b.   A1649 480w multi   1.50   .75

   Top part of No. 2268 contains one each of
Nos. 2268a-2268b. The lower part contains 4
each of Nos. 2268a-2268b.

Seomjin River in Autumn — A1650

Seomjin River in Winter — A1651

Seomjin River in Spring — A1652

Seomjin River in Summer — A1653

Perf. 13½x13¼ Syncopated
2008, Jan. 18   **Photo.**
2269   Block of 4   3.25   3.25
   a.   A1650 250w multi   .75   .30
   b.   A1651 250w multi   .75   .30
   c.   A1652 250w multi   .75   .30
   d.   A1653 250w multi   .75   .30

Miniature Sheet

King Sejong Antarctic Station — A1654

   No. 2270 — Penguins and: a, Scientists on
snowmobiles. b, Station.

2008, Feb. 15   **Photo.**   *Perf. 13¼*
2270   A1654 250w Sheet of 10,
       5 each #a-
       b   12.50   12.50

Inauguration of Pres. Lee Myung-
Bak — A1655

2008, Feb. 25   **Photo.**   *Perf. 13x13¼*
2271   A1655 250w multi   .85   .30
   a.   Souvenir sheet of 1   2.00   2.00

African Savanna — A1656

   No. 2272: a, African child and mask. b,
Leopard. c, Elephant. d, Zebra.

Die Cut Perf. (outer edge) x
Serpentine Die Cut 11 (radial sides)
x Die Cut (inner edge)
2008, Mar. 26   **Self-Adhesive**
2272   A1656 250w Block of 4, #a-
       d, + central
       label   4.00   4.00

Philakorea 2009
Intl. Stamp
Exhibition,
Seoul — A1657

   No. 2273 — Dancers: a, Buchaechum
(orange background). b, Salpurichum (pink
background). c, Seungmu (blue background).
d, Taepyeongmu (green background).

2008, Apr. 10   *Perf. 13¼x13*
2273   Horiz. strip or block of
       4   3.25   3.25
  a.-d.   A1657 250w Any single   .75   .30
   e.   Souvenir sheet, #2273a-2273d, +
       label   3.00   3.00

A1658

Winning Designs in
"Mailboxes of the
Future" Children's
Stamp Design
Contest — A1659

2008, Apr. 22   **Photo.**   *Perf. 13¼x13*
2274   A1658 250w multi   .85   .30
            Litho.
        Perf. 13x13¼
2275   A1659 250w multi   .85   .30

Nurturing of Children
   A1660   A1661
2008, May 8   **Litho., Engr. & Embossed**
            Perf. 13x13¼
2276   A1660 250w multi   .85   .30
           Litho.
2277   A1661 250w multi   .85   .30

Sun and Moon — A1662

Hands Making Heart — A1663

Tree-lined Path — A1664

Roses — A1665

2008, May 19   **Photo.**   *Perf. 13¼*
2278   A1662 250w multi + label   1.50   1.50
2279   A1663 250w multi + label   1.50   1.50
2280   A1664 250w multi + label   1.50   1.50
2281   A1665 250w multi + label   1.50   1.50
      Nos. 2278-2281 (4)   6.00   6.00

   Nos. 2278-2279 each were printed in sheets
of 3 stamps + 3 labels, No. 2280 was printed
in sheets of 14 stamps + 15 labels, and No.
2281 was printed in sheets of 20 stamps + 20
labels. Labels could be personalized.

Organization for Economic
Cooperation and Development
Ministerial Meeting, Seoul — A1666

2008, June 17   *Perf. 13¼*
2282   A1666 250w multi   .85   .30

Yun Bong-Gil
(1908-32),
Assassin of
Japanese
Colonial
Generals
A1667

2008, June 20
2283   A1667 250w multi   .85   .30

Miniature Sheet

Dangun Wanggeom — A1668

   No. 2284: a, Hwanung descending from
heavens at Taebaek Mountain. b, Bear and
tiger who prayed to become human. c, Birth of
Dangun Wanggeom. d, Dangun Wanggeom
as adult.

2008, July 10   **Photo.**   *Perf. 13¼x13*
2284   A1668 250w Sheet of 12, 3
       each #a-d   6.00   6.00

Energy Conservation — A1669

   No. 2285: a, Open electrical circuit, car,
refrigerator, light bulb, fan, meter. b, Hand-
straps for public transportation. c, Electrical
plugs on flower stems. d, Thermometers.

2008, Aug. 1   **Photo.**   *Perf. 13¼x13*
2285   A1669 250w Block or horiz.
       strip of 4, #a-
       d   3.00   3.00

Philately Week — A1670

   No. 2286: a, South Korea #34. b, South
Korea #176.

2008, Aug. 7　Photo.　Perf. 13¼x13
2286　A1670　250w Pair, #a-b　　　　1.50　1.50
　　c.　Souvenir sheet, #2286a-2286b　2.00　2.00

2008
Summer
Olympics,
Beijing
A1671

2008, Aug. 8　Photo.　Perf. 13¼x13
2287　A1671　250w multi　　　　　　.85　.30

Republic of
Korea, 60th
Anniv. — A1672

2008, Aug. 14
2288　A1672　250w multi　　　　　　.85　.30

Korean Language Society,
Cent. — A1673

2008, Aug. 29　　　Perf. 12¾x13½
2289　A1673　250w multi　　　　　　.85　.30

Seoul Water Works,
Cent. — A1674

2008, Sept. 1　Litho.　Perf. 13x13¼
2290　A1674　250w multi　　　　　　.85　.30

Amateur Radio
Direction Finding
Championships,
Hwaseong
A1675

2008, Sept. 2
2291　A1675　250w multi　　　　　　.85　.30

Snowboarding — A1676

No. 2292: a, Carving turn. b, Indy grab. c,
Nose grab. d, Air.

Serpentine Die Cut 11¾x11¼
2008, Sept. 5　　　　　　　Photo.
Self-Adhesive
2292　A1676　250w Block of 4, #a-
　　　　　　d　　　　　　　　　3.50　3.50

Salvation Army in
Korea,
Cent. — A1677

2008, Oct. 1　Photo.　Perf. 13x13¼
2293　A1677　250w multi　　　　　　.85　.30

Republic of
Korea
Armed
Forces,
60th Anniv.
A1678

2008, Oct. 1
2294　A1678　250w multi　　　　　　.85　.30

Diplomatic Relations Between South
Korea and Thailand, 50th
Anniv. — A1679

No. 2295: a, Chakri Mahaprasat Hall, Thailand (denomination at left). b, Juhamnu Pavilion, South Korea (denomination at right).

2008, Oct. 1　Litho.　　Perf. 13¼
2295　A1679　250w Pair, #a-b　2.50　2.50
　　　See Thailand No. 2383.

Manmulsang — A1680

Gwimyeonam Rock — A1681

Outer Geumgangsan — A1682

Sangpaldam Pools — A1683

2008, Oct. 17　Photo.　Perf. 13x13½
2296　　Block of 4　　　　　3.25　3.25
　　a.　A1680 250w multi　　　　.75　.30
　　b.　A1681 250w multi　　　　.75　.30
　　c.　A1682 250w multi　　　　.75　.30
　　d.　A1683 250w multi　　　　.75　.30

Korean Films — A1684

No. 2297: a, A Coachman, 1961 (blue background). b, Wedding Day, 1956 (dull lilac background). c, The Seashore Village, 1965 (dull
green background). d, Mother and a Guest,
1961 (gray olive background).

2008, Oct. 27　Litho.　Perf. 13x13½
2297　A1684　250w Block of 4, #a-
　　　　　　d　　　　　　　　　3.25　3.25

Upo Wetlands — A1685

2008, Oct. 28　Photo.　Perf. 13¼
2298　A1685　250w multi　　　　　　.85　.30
Tenth Ramsar Convention Meeting,
Changwon.

Masks — A1686

No. 2299: a, Chwibari Mask, Korea (denomination at LL). b, Big head Buddha mask,
Hong Kong (denomination at LR).

2008, Nov. 6　　　　　Perf. 13¼x13
2299　A1686　250w Horiz. pair,
　　　　　　#a-b　　　　　　　2.00　2.00
　　　See Hong Kong Nos. 1337-1338.

New Year 2009
(Year of the
Ox) — A1687

2008, Dec. 1　　　　　Perf. 13x13¼
2300　A1687　250w multi　　　　1.00　1.00
　　a.　Souvenir sheet of 2　　　2.00　2.00

Louis Braille (1809-52), Educator of
the Blind — A1688

2009, Jan. 2　　　　Perf. 12¾x13½
2301　A1688　250w multi　　　　　　.85　.30

Intl. Year of Astronomy — A1689

No. 2302: a, Whirlpool Galaxy M51. b, Planetary Nebula NGC 3132.

2009, Jan. 15　Photo.　Perf. 13x13¼
2302　A1689　250w Horiz. pair,
　　　　　　#a-b　　　　　　　1.50　1.50

Geum River in Autumn — A1690

Geum River in Winter — A1691

Geum River in Spring — A1692

Geum River in Summer — A1693

Perf. 13¼ Syncopated
2009, Feb. 10
2303　　Block or horiz. strip of 4　3.25　3.25
　　a.　A1690 250w multi　　　　.70　.30
　　b.　A1691 250w multi　　　　.70　.30
　　c.　A1692 250w multi　　　　.70　.30
　　d.　A1693 250w multi　　　　.70　.30

Diplomatic Relations Between South
Korea and the Philippines, 60th Anniv.
A1694

Designs: No. 2304, 250w, Panagbenga
Flower Festival, Baguio, Philippines. No. 2305,
250w, Cow Play, Hangawi, South Korea.

2009, Mar. 3　Photo.　Perf. 13x13¼
2304-2305　A1694　Set of 2　　　1.50　1.50

Historic Trees — A1695

No. 2306: a, Fir tree (Natural Monument No.
495) (22x50mm). b, Zelkova tree (Natural

Monument No. 478), horiz. (44x25mm). c, Ginkgo tree (Natural Monument No. 30) (22x50mm). d, Seosongnyeong tree (Natural Monument No. 294), horiz. (44x25mm).

2009, Apr. 3   Litho.   Perf. 12¾
2306 A1695 250w Block of 4, #a-
               d   3.25 3.25

Republic of Korea Marine Corps, 60th Anniv. — A1696

2009, Apr. 15   Perf. 12½
2307 A1696 250w multi   .85 .30

A1697

Asia Becoming One — A1698

2009, Apr. 22   Photo.   Perf. 13¼x13
2308 A1697 250w multi   .85 .30
Litho.   Perf. 13x13¼
2309 A1698 250w multi   .85 .30

A1699

Love For the Earth — A1700

2009, Apr. 22   Litho.   Perf. 13¼x13
2310 A1699 250w multi   .85 .30
Photo.   Perf. 13x13¼
2311 A1700 250w multi   .85 .30

Cartooning in Korea, Cent. A1701

2009, June 2   Litho.   Perf. 13x13¼
2312 A1701 250w multi   .85 .30

Earrings From Korea, 5th-6th Cent. A1702

Earrings From Mongolia, 18th-19th Cent. A1703

Earrings From Kazakhstan, 2nd-1st Cent. B.C. — A1704

2009, June 12   Photo.   Perf. 13x13¼
2313   Strip of 3   2.50 2.50
  a. A1702 250w multi   .65   .30
  b. A1703 250w multi   .65   .30
  c. A1704 250w multi   .65   .30

See Kazakhstan No. 595, Mongolia No. 2674.

Cave Lake and Lava Tubes — A1705

Lava Tubes, Stalactites and Stalagmite — A1706

Litho. & Engr.
2009, June 26   Perf. 13x13¼
2314   Sheet of 10, 5 each
         #a-b   7.00 7.00
  a. A1705 250w multi   .75   .30
  b. A1706 250w multi   .75   .30

Jeju Volcanic Island and Lava Tubes UNESCO World Heritage Site.

Philately Week — A1707

No. 2315: a, Korea #19. b, South Korea #639.

2009, July 30   Photo.   Perf. 13¼x13
2315   Pair   1.50 1.50
  a.-b. A1707 250w Either single   .70 .30
  c.   Souvenir sheet, #2315   .70   .30

A1708

A1709

A1710

A1711

A1712

A1713

A1714

Bird Drawings A1715

2009, July 30   Litho.   Perf. 13¼x13
2316   Block of 8   4.50 4.50
  a. A1708 250w multi   .50   .30
  b. A1709 250w multi   .50   .30
  c. A1710 250w multi   .50   .30
  d. A1711 250w multi   .50   .30
  e. A1712 250w multi   .50   .30
  f. A1713 250w multi   .50   .30
  g. A1714 250w multi   .50   .30
  h. A1715 250w multi   .50   .30
  i.   Souvenir sheet of 2, #2316a,
       2316e   2.00 2.00
  j.   Souvenir sheet of 2, #2316b,
       2316f   2.00 2.00

  k.   Souvenir sheet of 2, #2316c,
       2316g   2.00 2.00
  l.   Souvenir sheet of 2, #2316d,
       2316h   2.00 2.00

Philakorea 2009, Seoul.

Command From God To Move Country's Capital A1716

Establishment of East Buyeo — A1717

Birth of King Geumwawang — A1718

King Geumwawang on Throne — A1719

2009, Aug. 18   Photo.   Perf. 13x13¼
2317   Sheet of 12, 3 each #a-
         d   7.00 7.00
  a. A1716 250w multi   .50   .30
  b. A1717 250w multi   .50   .30
  c. A1718 250w multi   .50   .30
  d. A1719 250w multi   .50   .30

Legend of King Geumwawang of the Buyeo Kingdom.

Green Energy — A1720

No. 2318: a, House with solar panels, bicycle. b, Automobile with solar panels. c, Wind turbines. d, Dam.

2009, Aug. 21   Photo.   Perf. 13¼
2318 A1720 250w Block of 4, #a-
               d   2.00 2.00

Groundbreaking for Taekwondo Park, Muju-gun — A1721

2009, Sept. 4   Perf. 13¾x12¾
2319 A1721 250w multi   .85 .30

BMX Bicycling — A1722

No. 2320: a, X-up. b, No hand jump. c, One foot can can. d, Superman seat grab.

Serpentine Die Cut 11¾x11¼
2009, Sept. 8 **Photo.**
2320 A1722 250w Block of 4, #a-
d 2.00 2.00

Rice — A1723

No. 2321: a, Rice flowers and plants. b, Red, black and white rice grains.

2009, Sept. 25 Litho. Perf. 13¼
2321 Pair 1.00 1.00
a.-b. A1723 250w Either single .50 .30

Third Organization for Economic Cooperation and Development World Forum, Busan — A1724

2009, Oct. 27 Litho. Perf. 13¼
2322 A1724 250w multi .75 .30

A1725

A1726

Korean Films A1728

No. 2323: a, Chilsu and Mansu, 1988. b, Never, Never Forget Me, 1976. c, A Road to Sampo, 1975. d, Yalkae, A Joker in High School, 1976.

2009, Oct. 27 Perf. 13x13¼
2323 Block or strip of 4 2.50 2.50
a. A1725 250w multi .50 .30
b. A1726 250w multi .50 .30
c. A1727 250w multi .50 .30
d. A1728 250w multi .50 .30

Diplomatic Relations Between South Korea and Brazil, 50th Anniv. — A1729

No. 2324: a, Octavio Frias de Oliveira Bridge, Brazil (denomination at UL). b, Incheon Bridge, South Korea (denomination at UR).

2009, Oct. 30 Perf. 13¼
2324 A1729 250w Pair, #a-b 1.25 1.25
See Brazil No. 3113.

New Year 2010 (Year of the Tiger) — A1730

2009, Dec. 1 Photo. Perf. 13x13¼
2325 A1730 250w multi .75 .30
a. Souvenir sheet of 2 1.25 1.25

Visit Korea Year — A1731

No. 2326: a, Stylized face, denomination in blue. b, People as Korean flag, denomination in white.

2010, Jan. 4 Photo. Perf. 13¼x13
2326 A1731 250w Pair, #a-b 1.00 1.00

2010 Winter Olympics, Vancouver — A1732

No. 2327: a, Figure skater. b, Speed skater.

2010, Feb. 12 Perf. 12¾x13½
2327 A1732 250w Pair, #a-b 1.00 1.00

Diplomatic Relations Between South Korea and Malaysia, 50th Anniv. — A1733

No. 2328: a, Panthera tigris altaica. b, Panthera tigris jacksoni.

2010, Feb. 23 Litho. Perf. 13¼
2328 A1733 250w Pair, #a-b 1.00 1.00

Ahn Jung-geun (1879-1910), Assassin of Ito Hirobumi, Japanese Resident-General of Korea — A1734

No. 2329 — Ahn Jung-geun and: a, Handprint. b, Characters written on Korean flag with blood from his severed finger.

Litho. & Engr.
2010, Mar. 26 Perf. 13¼
2329 A1734 250w Pair, #a-b 1.00 1.00

Seoul National University of Technology, Cent. — A1735

Jinju National University, Cent. — A1736

2010, Apr. 1 Photo. Perf. 12¾x13½
2330 A1735 250w multi .50 .30
2331 A1736 250w multi .50 .30

Historic Trees — A1737

No. 2332: a, Old Buddha's plum tree (Natural Monument No. 486) (22x50mm). b, Pine tree (Natural Monument No. 290), horiz (44x25mm). c, Entwined Chinese junipers (Natural Monument No. 88) (22x50mm). d, Three Thunbergii camphor trees (Natural Monument No. 481), horiz. (44x25mm).

2010, Apr. 5 Litho. Perf. 12¾
2332 A1737 250w Block of 4, #a-
d 2.00 2.00

Mo Tae Bum A1738

Le Sang Hwa A1739

Lee Seung Hoon A1740

Kim Yu Na A1741

Kwak Yoon Gy A1742

Kim Seoung Il A1743

Park Seung Hi A1744

Sung Si Bak A1745

Lee Eun Byul A1746

Lee
Jung Su
A1747

Lee Ho
Suk
A1748

2010, May 6 Photo. Perf. 13½x12¾

2333		Sheet of 11 + label	7.00	7.00
a.	A1738	250w multi	.60	.30
b.	A1739	250w multi	.60	.30
c.	A1740	250w multi	.60	.30
d.	A1741	250w multi	.60	.30
e.	A1742	250w multi	.60	.30
f.	A1743	250w multi	.60	.30
g.	A1744	250w multi	.60	.30
h.	A1745	250w multi	.60	.30
i.	A1746	250w multi	.60	.30
j.	A1747	250w multi	.60	.30
k.	A1748	250w multi	.60	.30

Medalists at 2010 Winter Olympics,
Vancouver.

Han River in Spring — A1749

Han River in Summer — A1750

Han River in Autumn — A1751

Han River in Winter — A1752

2010, May 11 Perf. 13½ Syncopated

2334		Block or strip of 4	2.00	2.00
a.	A1749	250w multi	.50	.30
b.	A1750	250w multi	.50	.30
c.	A1751	250w multi	.50	.30
d.	A1752	250w multi	.50	.30

2010 World Cup Soccer
Championships, South Africa — A1753

Perf. 13¼x13½

2010, June 11   Photo.

2335	A1753	250w multi	.75	.30

World Refugee Day, 10th
Anniv. — A1754

2010, June 18   Perf. 13¼

2336	A1754	250w multi	.60	.30

Diplomatic Relations Between South
Korea and United Arab Emirates, 30th
Anniv. — A1755

No. 2337: a, Flag of United Arab Emirates
and air-conditioning tower. b, Flag of South
Korea and Mt. Amisan Chimney,
Gyeongbokgung Palace.

2010, June 18 Photo. Perf. 13x13¼

2337	A1755	250w Pair, #a-b	1.00	1.00

See United Arab Emirates No. 990.

Start of
Korean War,
60th Anniv.
A1756

2010, June 25   Perf. 13½x13

2338	A1756	250w multi	.60	.30

Philately Week — A1757

No. 2339: a, South Korea #1197. b, South
Korea #1198.

2010, July 29   Perf. 13¼x13¼x13

2339		Pair, #a-b	1.00	1.00
a.-b.	A1757	250w Either single	.50	.30
c.		Souvenir sheet, #2339a-2339b	1.25	1.25

Dinosaurs — A1758

No. 2340: a, Herrerasaurus. b, Coelophysis.
c, Plateosaurus. d, Riojasaurus.

Perf. 13¼ Syncopated

2010, Aug. 5   Litho. & Engr.

2340		Sheet of 12, 3 each		
		#2340a-2340d	7.50	7.50
a.-b.	A1758	250w Either single	.50	.30
c.-d.	A1758	340w Either single	.50	.30

23rd Intl.
Union of
Forest
Research
Organizations
World
Congress,
Seoul
A1759

Litho. & Embossed

2010, Aug. 23   Perf. 12½

2341	A1759	340w multi	.75	.30

Legend of Goguryeo Jumong — A1760

No. 2342: a, King Geumwa and soldiers
meet woman. b, Baby Jumong, birds and animals. c, Jumong and others fleeing King
Geumwa on horseback. d, Jumong on horse
and followers at Jolboncheon.

2010, Sept. 14 Photo. Perf. 13x13½

2342	A1760	250w Block of 4, #a-d	2.00	2.00

A1761

A1762

A1763

Korean
Films
A1764

No. 2343: a, Seopyeonje, 1993. b, Shiri,
1999. c, Tae Guk Gi: The Brotherhood of War,
2004. d, Take Off, 2009.

2010, Oct. 27 Litho. Perf. 13x13¼

2343		Block of 4	2.00	2.00
a.	A1761	250w multi	.50	.30
b.	A1762	250w multi	.50	.30
c.	A1763	250w multi	.50	.30
d.	A1764	250w multi	.50	.30

Recycling
A1765

No. 2344: a, Flowers in pot. b, Recycling
robot.

2010, Nov. 11 Photo. Perf. 13¼x13

2344	A1765	250w Pair, #a-b	1.00	1.00

Miniature Sheet

G20 Summit, Seoul — A1766

No. 2345 — Summit emblem and: a, World
map. b, Gato.

2010, Nov. 11   Perf. 13x13¼

2345	A1766	Sheet of 14, 7		
		each #a-b	10.00	10.00
a.-b.		250w Either single	.60	.35

New Year 2011
(Year of the
Rabbit) — A1767

2010, Dec. 1   Perf. 13x13¼

2346	A1767	250w multi	.50	.30
a.		Souvenir sheet of 2	1.00	1.00

A1768

Personalized
Stamps
A1769

2010, Dec. 1 Photo. Perf. 13x13¼
Denomination Color

2347	A1768	250w green	2.00	2.00
2348	A1768	250w blue	2.00	2.00
2349	A1768	250w red brown	2.00	2.00

Perf. 13¼x13½

2350	A1769	250w green	2.25	2.25
2351	A1769	250w blue	2.25	2.25
2352	A1769	250w red brown	2.25	2.25
		Nos. 2347-2352 (6)	12.75	12.75

Nos. 2347-2349 each were available in
sheets of 6 that sold for 5500w and sheets of
20 that sold for 9500w. Nos. 2350-2352 each
were sold in sheets of 14 that sold for 8000y.
images could be personalized.

Miniature Sheet

Characters in Pororo, the Little
Penguin — A1770

No. 2353: a, Eddy, the Fox. b, Crong, the
Baby Dinosaur on balloon. c, Pororo wearing
helmet. d, Petty, the girl Penguin. e, Pipi and

Popo, the Aliens. f, Poby, the Polar Bear. g, Harry, the Hummingbird on ball. h, Loopy, the Beaver with basket. i, Tong Tong, the Dragon. j, Rody, the Robot.

2011, Feb. 22   Photo.   *Die Cut*
Self-Adhesive
2353 A1770   Sheet of 10   5.50 5.50
a.-j.   250w Any single   .50   .30

Historic Trees — A1771

No. 2354: a, Japanese black pine trees at Sancheondan (Natural Monument No. 160) (22x50mm). b, Ginkgo tree at Yogwang-ri (Natural Monument No. 84), horiz. (44x25mm). c, Pine tree at Chukji-ri (Natural Monument No. 491) (22x50mm). d, Zelkova tree at Haksaru (Natural Monument No. 407), horiz. (44x25mm).

2011, Apr. 5   Litho.   *Perf. 12¾*
2354 A1771 250w Block of 4,
                  #a-d   2.25 2.25

Diplomatic Relations Between South Korea and Portugal, 50th Anniv. A1772

No. 2355: a, Korean turtle ship, denomination at UL. b, Portuguese nau, denomination at UR.

2011, Apr. 15   Photo.   *Perf. 13x13¼*
2355   Sheet of 14, 7 each
            #2355a-2355b   12.00 12.00
a.-b. A1772 250w Either single   .75   .30

See Portugal Nos. 3305-3306.

Family — A1773

No. 2356: a, Stick-figure family and house. b, Heads in bunch of grapes.

2011, May 13   Photo.   *Perf. 13x13¼*
2356 A1773 250w Pair, #a-b   1.25 1.25

Bamboo Grove, Damyang — A1774

Tea Field, Boesong — A1775

Upo Swamp, Changnyeong — A1776

Jusanji Pond, Cheongsong — A1777

2011, May 27   *Perf. 13¼*
2357   Block of 4   2.50 2.50
a. A1774 250w multi   .55   .30
b. A1775 250w multi   .55   .30
c. A1776 250w multi   .55   .30
d. A1777 250w multi   .55   .30

Preservation of Polar Regions and Glaciers — A1778

No. 2358: a, Polar bears. b, Penguins.

2011, June 3   Litho.   *Perf. 13x13¼*
2358 A1778 250w Pair, #a-b   1.25 1.25

Shinheung Military Academy, Chugaga, Cent. A1779

2011, June 10   Photo.
2359 A1779 250w multi   .75   .30

Tomb of King Taejo — A1780

Tomb of King Sejong — A1781

Litho. & Engr.
2011, June 30   *Perf. 13x13¼*
2360   Sheet of 10, 5 each
            #2360a-2360b   6.50 6.50
a. A1780 250w multi   .60   .30
b. A1781 250w multi   .60   .30
Royal Tombs of the Joeson Dynasty UNESCO World Heritage Site.

Korea Disaster Relief Association, 50th Anniv. — A1782

2011, July 13   Photo.   *Perf. 13x13¼*
2361 A1782 250w multi   .75   .30

Philately Week — A1783

No. 2362 — Paintings: a, Sansu (mountain and houses), by Jo Seok-jin (denomination in green). b, Jangsongnakil (rider on horse), by Ji Woon-young (denomination in bister brown). c, Unnangjasang (portrait), by Chae Yong-sin (denomination in red brown). d, Gunmado (horses), by Kim Ki-chang (denomination in gold).

2011, July 28   *Perf. 13*
2362 A1783 250w Block of 4, #a-
                  d   2.50 2.50
e.   Souvenir sheet of 4, #2362a-
            2362d   3.00 3.00

Selection of Pyeongchang as Host of 2018 Winter Olympics — A1784

2011, Aug. 3   *Perf. 13x13¼*
2363 A1784 250w multi   .75   .30

Dinosaurs — A1785

No. 2364: a, Scelidosaurus. b, Stegosaurus. c, Allosaurus. d, Dilophosaurus.

**   *Perf. 13¼ Syncopated***
2011, Aug. 11   Litho. & Engr.
2364   Sheet of 12, 3 each
            #2364a-2364d   12.00 12.00
a.-d. A1785 340w Any single   .65   .30

Intl. Association of Athletics Federations World Championships, Daegu — A1786

No. 2365: a, Runners. b, Pole vault.

2011, Aug. 26   Litho.   *Perf. 13¼*
2365 A1786 250w Pair, #a-b   1.50 1.50

Tripitaka Koreana, 1000th Anniv. A1787

2011, Sept. 23   Photo.   *Perf. 13x13¼*
2366 A1787 250w multi   .75   .30

Tenth Session of the Conference of the Parties to the United Nations Convention to Combat Desertification, Changwon — A1792

2011, Oct. 10   Photo.   *Perf. 13¼x13*
2371 A1792 270w multi   .75   .30

Ipo Weir, Han River — A1793

Gongju Weir, Geum River — A1794

Seungchon Weir, Yeongsan River — A1795

Gangjeong-Goryeong Weir, Nakdong River — A1796

2011, Oct. 21   *Perf. 13¼*
2372   Block of 4   2.25 2.25
a. A1793 270w multi   .55   .30
b. A1794 270w multi   .55   .30
c. A1795 270w multi   .55   .30
d. A1796 270w multi   .55   .30

Diplomatic Relations Between South Korea and Australia, 50th Anniv. — A1797

No. 2373: a, Korean woman playing haegeum. b, Australian aborigine playing didgeridoo.

2011, Oct. 28   Photo.   Perf. 13¼x13
2373 A1797 270w Horiz. pair, #a-
b   1.25 1.25
See Australia Nos. 3587-3588.

A1798

A1799

A1800

Daejoyong
of the
Balhae
Kingdom
A1801

2011, Nov. 17   Perf. 13x13¼
2374 Sheet of 12, 3 each #a-
d, + label   6.00 6.00
a. A1798 270w multi   .50 .25
b. A1799 270w multi   .50 .25
c. A1800 270w multi   .50 .25
d. A1801 270w multi   .50 .25

New Year 2012
(Year of the
Dragon) — A1802

2011, Dec. 1
2375 A1802 270w multi   .75 .30
a. Souvenir sheet of 2   1.25 1.25

South Korean Achievement of One
Trillion Dollars in Trade — A1803

No. 2376: a, Automobile, computer chip,
smart phone, container ship. b, Flag of South
Korea, skyscraper.

2011, Dec. 7
2376 A1803 270w Horiz. pair, #a-
b   1.25 1.25

Diplomatic Relations Between South
Korea and Mexico, 50th
Anniv. — A1804

No. 2377: a, Juvenile gray whale, denomination at right. b, Adult gray whale, denomination at left.

2012, Jan. 26   Litho.   Perf. 13¼
2377 A1804 270w Vert. pair, #a-b 1.25 1.25
See Mexico Nos. 2771-2772.

Miniature Sheet

Characters in Pucca Animated
Television Series — A1805

No. 2378: a, Ssoso, with stick and birds
(blue green, light blue and gray background).
b, Abyo, with frog (green andd light green
background). c, Pucca, with heart (yellow and
orange background). d, Garu, with cat (orange
and light orange background. e, Ching, with
mirror (pink and light pink background). f,
Bruce, with guns (purple and gray background). g, Ho-Oh, with flame (purple and pink
background). h, Santa (bright blue and light
blue background). i, Nini, with earrings (gray
blue background). j, Woo-Wuh, with rolling
pins and dishes (dark blue and purple
background).

Serpentine Die Cut 10¼ Vert.
2012, Feb. 22   Photo.
Self-Adhesive
2378 A1805 Sheet of 10   6.00 6.00
a.-j.   270w Any single   .55 .30

Diplomatic
Relations
Between
South
Korea and
Colombia,
50th Anniv.
A1806

No. 2379: a, Coffee beans and bush. b, Ginseng flowers and root.

2012, Mar. 9   Perf. 13x13¼
2379 A1806 270w Pair, #a-b   1.25 1.25
See Colombia No. 1374.

2012 Nuclear Security Summit,
Seoul — A1807

No. 2380 — Ribbon and: a, World map. b,
Dove, flag of South Korea.

2012, Mar. 26   Perf. 13¼x13
2380 A1807 270w Horiz. pair, #a-
b   1.25 1.25

Historic Trees — A1808

No. 2381: a, Zelkova tree at Segan-ri (Natural Monument No. 493) (22x50mm). b, Trifoli-
ate orange tree at Gapgot-ri (Natural Monument No. 78), horiz. (44x25mm). c, Spring
cherry tree at Hwaeomsa Temple (Natural
Monument No. 38) (22x50mm). d, Asian fringe
trees at Gwangyang-eup (Natural Monument
No. 235), horiz. (44x25mm).

2012, Apr. 5   Litho.   Perf. 12¾
2381 A1808 270w Block of 4, #a-
d   1.90 .95

Winning Art in Stamp Design
Contest — A1809

No. 2382: a, Hearts in ski cap, by Yeonju
Chung. b, Children carrying rainbow, by Glen
M. Isaac.

2012, Apr. 25   Photo.   Perf. 13¼x13
2382 A1809 270w Horiz. pair, #a-
b   .95 .50

Expo 2012,
Yeosu — A1810

Nos. 2383 and 2384 — Expo 2012 emblem
and mascot, fish and: a, Korea Pavilion. b,
Theme Pavilion. c, Big-O. d, Sky Tower.

2012, May 11
2383   Horiz. strip of 4   1.90 .95
a.-d. A1810 270w Any single   .45 .25
Perf. 13x13¼
2384   Horiz. strip of 4   1.90 .95
a.-d. A1810 270w Any single,
26x36mm   .45 .25
No. 2383 was printed in sheets containing
five strips. No. 2384 was printed in sheets of
10 containing two strips and two additional
examples of No. 2384d.

Korea Trade Investment Promotion
Agency (KOTRA), 50th
Anniv. — A1811

No. 2385: a, 50th anniversary emblem,
world map. b, Agency headquarters.

2012, June 14   Perf. 13¼x13
2385 A1811 270w Horiz. pair, #a-
b   .95 .50

Gungnamji Pond, Buyeo — A1812

Daegwallyeong Sheep
Ranch — A1813

Cheonjiyeon Waterfalls, Jeju
Island — A1814

Dinosaur Ridge, Mt.
Seoraksan — A1815

2012, June 20   Perf. 13¼
2386   Block of 4   1.90 .95
a. A1812 270w multi   .45 .25
b. A1813 270w multi   .45 .25
c. A1814 270w multi   .45 .25
d. A1815 270w multi   .45 .25

2012 Summer
Olympics,
London — A1816

No. 2387: a, Swimming, Tower Bridge. b,
Archery, Big Ben.

2012, July 27   Perf. 13x13¼
2387 A1816 270w Vert. pair, #a-b .95 .50

Dinosaurs — A1819

No. 2384: a, Pachycephalosaurus. b, Tyrannosaurus. c, Oviraptor. d, Protoceratops.

Perf. 13¼ Syncopated

2012, Aug. 8   Litho.
2389   Sheet of 12, 3 each   12.00 12.00
    # 2389a-2389d
   a.-d.   A1819 360w Any single   1.00 1.00

Philately Week — A1820

No. 2390 — Paintings: a, The Back Alley, by Dong Jin Seo (yellow green panel). b, Namhyangjip (A House Facing South), by Ji Ho Oh (blue panel). c, Tugye (Cockfighting), by Joong Seop Lee (pink panel). d, Chodong (Early Winter), by Sang Beom Lee (dull orange panel).

2012, Aug. 9   Photo.   Perf. 13
2390   A1820 270w Block of 4, #a-
        d   1.90 .95
   e.   Souvenir sheet of 4, #2390a-
     2390d   1.90 .95

World Conservation Congress, Jeju Island — A1821

2012, Sept. 6   Perf. 13¼
2391   A1821 270w multi   .50 .25

A1822

A1823

A1824

A1825

Park Hyeokgeose (69 B.C.-4 A.D.), Silla Kingdom Monarch — A1826

2012, Nov. 21   Perf. 13x13¼
2392   Horiz. strip of 5   2.50 1.25
   a.   A1822 270w multi   .50 .25
   b.   A1823 270w multi   .50 .25
   c.   A1824 270w multi   .50 .25
   d.   A1825 270w multi   .50 .25
   e.   A1826 270w multi   .50 .25

New Year 2013 (Year of the Snake)
A1827   A1828

2012, Dec. 3   Perf. 13x13¼
2393   A1827 270w multi   .50 .25
2394   A1828 270w multi   .50 .25
   a.   Souvenir sheet of 2, #2393-
     2394   1.00 .50

Inauguration of 18th President, Park Geun-hye A1830

2013, Feb. 25   Photo.   Perf. 13¼
2396   A1830 270w multi   .50 .25

Miniature Sheet

Characters in Robocar Poli — A1831

No. 2397: a, Roy the Fire Truck. b, Amber the Ambulance. c, Poli the Police Car. d, Helly the Helicopter. e, Dumpoo the Dump Truck. f, Cap the Taxi. g, Posty the Postal Van. h, Spooky the Tow Truck. i, School B the School Bus. j, Cleany the Street Sweeper.

Serpentine Die Cut 11½x9

2013, Mar. 12   Self-Adhesive
2397   A1831   Sheet of 10   5.00
   a.-j.   270w Any single   .50 .25

Korean Baseball Players — A1832

No. 2398: a, Jang Hyo-Jo (1956-2011) at bat. b, Choi Dong-Won (1958-2011) pitching.

2013, Mar. 29   Photo.   Perf. 13¼x13
2398   A1832 (270w) Pair, #a-b   —   —

Diplomatic Relations Between Peru and South Korea, 50th Anniv. — A1833

No. 2399: a, Seongsan Ilchulbong, South Korea, South Korean and Peruvian flags at

---

LR. b, Machu Picchu, Peru, South Korean and Peruvian flags at LL.

2013, Apr. 1   Photo.   Perf. 13x13¼
2399   A1833 270w Horiz. pair, #a-
        b   .95 .50
     See Peru No. 1810.

Suncheon Bay Garden Expo 2013 — A1834

2013, Apr. 19   Photo.   Perf. 13¾x13
2400   A1834 270w multi   .50 .25

Information and Communication Day — A1835

No. 2401: a, Boy and girl holding envelope with heart, satellite, smartphone (blue background). b, Mailbox with letter in slot, robot, girl with parcels (orange yellow background). c, Boy on satellite dish, girl on television with legs (yellow background). d, Girl and robot in rocket circling Earth (purple background).

2013, Apr. 22   Photo.   Perf. 13¼x13
2401   Horiz. strip of 4   2.00 1.00
   a.-d.   A1835 270w Any single   .50 .25

Law Day A1836

2013, Apr. 25   Photo.   Perf. 13x13¼
2402   A1836 270w multi   .50 .25

Restoration of Sungnyemun Gate A1837

2013, May 10   Litho.   Perf. 13¼x13
2403   A1837 270w multi   .50 .25

Ahn Chang-ho (1878-1938), Founder of Young Korean Academy — A1838

2013, May 13   Photo.   Perf. 13x13¼
2404   A1838 270w multi   .50 .25

Diplomatic Relations Between Slovakia and South Korea, 20th Anniv. — A1839

No. 2405: a, Pansori performers, South Korea (woman and drummer). b, Lúcnica Art Ensemble dancers, Slovakia.

2013, May 31   Photo.   Perf. 13x13¼
2405   A1839 270w Pair, #a-b   1.00 .50
     See Slovakia Nos. 663-664.

Diplomatic Relations Between Germany and Korea, 130th Anniv. — A1840

No. 2406: a, Gyeongbokgung Palace, Seoul. b, Temple of the Sun, Bayreuth, Germany.

2013, June 5   Litho.   Perf. 12¾x13
2406   A1840 270w Horiz. pair, #a-
        b   1.00 .50
     See Germany Nos. 2739-2740.

Energy Conservation — A1841

No. 2407: a, Leaves and smokestacks. b, Coin entering slot in piggy bank with electric cord as tail. c, Air conditioner and fans on balance with melting iceberg. d, Boy on stylized bicycle.

2013, June 26   Photo.   Perf. 13¼
2407   A1841 270w Block or horiz.
     strip of 4, #a-
        d   2.00 1.00

Philately Week A1846

No. 2412: a, Girl writing letter. b, Girl placing letter in mailbox. c, Boy with magnifying glass examining stamp. d, Boy looking at stamp album.
   600w, Combined design elements of Nos. 2412a-2412d (108x26mm).

2013, Aug. 8   Photo.   Perf. 13¼x13
2412   Block or horiz. strip of
     4   2.25 1.25
   a.-d.   A1846 300w Any single   .55 .30
       Souvenir Sheet
2413   Sheet of 2 #2413a   2.25 1.25
   a.   A1846 600w Single stamp   1.10 .60
     Philakorea 2014 World Stamp Exhibition, Seoul.

Korean Coast Guard, 60th Anniv. A1847

2013, Sept. 10   Photo.   Perf. 13x13¼
2414   A1847 300w multi   .55 .30

Diplomatic Relations Between Indonesia and South Korea, 40th Anniv. — A1848

No. 2415: a, Small lion figure from Korean folk play, large bull figure from Indonesian folk play (denomination at left). b, Large lion figure, small bull figure (denomination at UR).

2013, Sept. 17 Photo. Perf. 13x13¼
2415 A1848 300w Pair, #a-b   1.10 .55
See Indonesia No. 2363.

Conference on Cyberspace, Seoul — A1849

2013, Oct. 17 Litho. Perf. 13x13¼
2416 A1849 300w multi   .55 .30

A1850

A1851

A1852

A1853

Onjo of the Baekje Kingdom A1854

2413, Nov. 20 Photo. Perf. 13x13¼
2417   Horiz. strip of 5   3.00 1.50
  a. A1850 300w multi   .60 .30
  b. A1851 300w multi   .60 .30
  c. A1852 300w multi   .60 .30
  d. A1853 300w multi   .60 .30
  e. A1854 300w multi   .60 .30

New Year 2014 (Year of the Horse) — A1855

No. 2418 — Snowflakes and: a, Close-up of horse's head. b, Horses and heart (yellow background). c, Line drawing of horse with multicolored squares and rectangles in background. d, Boy inside of horse raising horse's head.
No. 2419 — Combined designs of No. 2418 with cropped design of: a, No. 2418a at left. b, No. 2418b at left. c, No. 2418c at left. d, No. 2418d at left.

2013, Dec. 2 Photo. Perf. 13¼
2418 A1855 300w Block of 4, #a-d   2.40 1.25
Souvenir Sheet
2419 A1855 630w Sheet of 4, #a-d   5.00 2.50
No. 2419 contains four 108x36mm stamps.

Miniature Sheet

Characters from *Larva* Animated Television Series — A1856

No. 2420: a, Red at microphone. b, Pink and flowers. c, Brown and dung ball. d, Black with boxing gloves. e, Prussian (bird). f, Yellow eating roll and sweating, Red. g, Red, Yellow with open mouth. h, Yellow and Red with basketball. i, Red, Yellow holding lollipop. j, Yellow with open mouth.

Serpentine Die Cut 10
2014, Feb. 28   Photo.
2420 A1856   Sheet of 10   9.50
  a.-e. 300w Any single   .55 .25
  f.-h. 390w Any single   .75 .35
  i. 400w multi   .75 .40
  j. 1930w multi   3.75 1.90

Cadastral Resurveying A1857

No. 2421: a, 300w, Map of South Korea, surveying equipment. b, 390w, Smart phone.

2014, Mar. 20 Photo. Perf. 13¼x13
2421 A1857   Pair, #a-b   1.40 .70

Poets — A1858

No. 2422: a, Han Yongun (1879-1944), pink background. b, Lee Yuksa (1904-44), green background. c, Yun DongJu (1917-45), blue background.

2014, Apr. 9 Photo. Perf. 13x13¼
2422 A1858 (300w) Horiz. strip of 3, #a-c   1.75 .85

Philakorea 2014 World Stamp Exhibition, Seoul — A1859

No. 2423: a, 300w, Minhwa painting of birds and flowers. b, 300w, Hahoe wooden mask. c, 300w, Four Onggi pots. d, 300w, Neck of gayageum (stringed instrument). e, 300w, Baekja porcelain moon jar. f, 300w, Building roofs. g, 540w, Hanbok (traditional clothing). h, 540w, Hangeul (Korean text).

2014, May 16 Litho. Perf. 13¼x13
2423 A1859   Block of 8, #a-h   5.75 3.00

2014 World Cup Soccer Championships, Brazil — A1860

No. 2424 — Emblem and: a, 300w, Player and ball running toward goal. b, 540w, Players and ball.

2014, June 3 Photo. Perf. 13x13¼
2424 A1860   Pair, #a-b   1.75 .85

SEMI-POSTAL STAMPS

Catalogue values for unused stamps in this section are for Never Hinged items.

Field Hospital SP1

Nurses Supporting Patient — SP2

Perf. 13½x14, 14x13½
1953, Aug. 1 Litho. Wmk. 257
Crosses in Red
B1 SP1 10h + 5h bl grn   20.00 5.00
B2 SP2 10h + 5h bl grn   20.00 5.00
The surtax was for the Red Cross. Nos. B1-B2 exist imperf.

Type of Regular Issue, 1956, with Added inscription at Upper Left
1957, Sept. 1 Wmk. 312 Perf. 12½
Granite Paper
B3 A111 40h + 10h lt bl grn   12.50 2.40
Wmk. 317
B4 A111 40h + 10h lt bl grn   12.00 2.40
The surtax was for flood relief.

Rice Farmer Type of Regular Issue, 1961-62
1963, July 10 Wmk. 317 Perf. 12½
B5 A172 4w + 1w dk bl   9.00 1.25
The surtax was for flood victims in southern Korea.

1965, Oct. 1 Unwmk. Perf. 12½
B6 A172 4w + 2w indigo   4.75 1.25
The surtax was for flood relief.

1965, Oct. 11
B7 A172 4w + 2w magenta   4.75 1.25
The surtax was for a scholarship fund.

Type of Regular Issue 1964-66
1966, Nov. 10 Litho. Perf. 12½
Granite Paper
B8 A186b 7w + 2w car rose   6.50 1.75
The surtax was to help the needy.

Soldier with Wife and Child — SP3

1967, June 20 Perf. 12½x13
B9 SP3 7w + 3w rose lil & blk   8.00 1.25
The surtax was for veterans of the war in Viet Nam and their families.

Reservist — SP4

1968, Aug. 1 Litho. Perf. 13x12½
B10 SP4 7w + 3w grn & blk   13.00 1.75
Issued for the fund-raising drive to arm reservists.

Flag — SP5

1968, Nov. 1 Litho. Unwmk.
B11 SP5 7w + 3w dk bl & red   40.00 8.00
The surtax was for disaster relief.

1969, Feb. 15
B12 SP5 7w + 3w lt grn, dk bl & red   12.00 1.25
Surtax for military helicopter fund.

Flag Type of 1968 Redrawn Zeros Omitted
1969, Nov. 1 Litho. Perf. 13x12½
B13 SP5 7w + 3w dk bl & red   37.50 1.75
The surtax was for the searchlight fund.

"Pin of Love" — SP6

1972, Aug. 1   Photo.   Perf. 13½x12½
B14 SP6 10w + 5w blue & car   2.00   .75
Disaster relief.

"Pin of Love" — SP7

1973, July 1   Photo.   Perf. 12½x13½
B15 SP7 10w + 5w multicolored   1.20   .45
Disaster relief.

Paddle and Ball — SP8

1973, Aug. 1   Photo.   Perf. 13½x12½
B16 SP8 10w + 5w multicolored   1.25   .30

Surtax was for gymnasium to be built to commemorate the victory of the Korean women's table tennis team at the 32nd World Table Tennis Championships.

Lungs — SP9

1974, Nov. 1   Perf. 13½x12½
B17 SP9 10w + 5w green & red   .95   .25

Surtax was for tuberculosis control.

No. 647 Surcharged

Perf. 13½x12½
1977, July 25   Photo.
B18 A328 20w + 10w green   12.50   12.50

Surtax was for flood relief.

Seoul 1988 Olympic Games Series

'88 Seoul Games Emblem — SP10   Korean Tiger, Mascot — SP11

1985, Mar. 20   Photo.   Perf. 13x13½
B19 SP10 70w + 30w blk & multi   .70   .30
B20 SP11 70w + 30w blk & multi   .70   .30
a.   Souvenir sheet of 2, #B19-20   1.75   1.75

Track and Field — SP12

1985, June 10
B21 SP12 70w + 30w shown   .70   .30
B22 SP12 70w + 30w Rowing   .70   .30
a.   Souvenir sheet of 2, #B21-B22   1.75   1.75

1985, Sept. 16
B23 SP12 70w + 30w Boxing   .70   .30
B24 SP12 70w + 30w Women's basketball   .70   .30
a.   Souvenir sheet of 2, #B23-B24   1.75   1.75

1985, Nov. 1
B25 SP12 70w + 30w Canoeing   .70   .30
B26 SP12 70w + 30w Cycling   .70   .30
a.   Souvenir sheet of 2, #B25-B26   1.75   1.75

Surtax for the 24th Summer Olympic Games, Sept. 17-Oct. 2, 1988.

Equestrian — SP18

Designs: No. B28, Fencing. No. B29, Soccer. No. B30, Gymnastic rings.

1986, Mar. 25   Photo.   Perf. 13x13½
B27 SP18 70w + 30w multi   .60   .35
B28 SP18 70w + 30w multi   .60   .35
B29 SP18 70w + 30w multi   .60   .35
B30 SP18 70w + 30w multi   .60   .35

Souvenir Sheets
B31   Sheet of 4   12.00   12.00
a.   SP18 370w + 100w like #B27   2.75   2.75
B32   Sheet of 4   12.00   12.00
a.   SP18 400w + 100w like #B28   2.75   2.75
B33   Sheet of 4   12.00   12.00
a.   SP18 440w + 100w like #B29   2.75   2.75
B34   Sheet of 4   12.00   12.00
a.   SP18 470w + 100w like #B30   2.75   2.75

1986   Photo.   Perf. 13x13½
No. B35, Weight lifting. No. B36, Team handball. No. B37, Judo. No. B38, Field hockey.
B35 SP18 80w +50w multi   1.50   .75
B36 SP18 80w +50w multi   1.50   .75
B37 SP18 80w +50w multi   1.50   .75
B38 SP18 80w +50w multi   1.50   .75

Souvenir Sheets
B39   Sheet of 4   10.00   10.00
a.   SP18 370w + 100w like #B35   2.50   2.50
B40   Sheet of 4   10.00   10.00
a.   SP18 400w + 100w like #B36   2.50   2.50
B41   Sheet of 4   12.00   12.00
a.   SP18 440w + 100w like #B37   3.00   3.00
B42   Sheet of 4   13.50   13.50
a.   SP18 470w + 100w like #B38   3.50   3.50

Issue dates: Nos. B35-B36, B39-B40, Oct. 10; others, Nov. 1.

1987, May 25   Photo.   Perf. 13x13½
No. B43, Women's tennis. No. B44, Wrestling. No. B45, Show jumping. No. B46, Diving.
B43 SP18 80w +50w multi   1.00   .50
B44 SP18 80w +50w multi   1.00   .50
B45 SP18 80w +50w multi   1.00   .50
B46 SP18 80w +50w multi   1.00   .50

1987, Oct. 10
No. B47, Table Tennis. No. B48, Men's shooting. No. B49, Women's archery. No. B50, Women's volleyball.
B47 SP18 80w +50w multi   1.00   .40
B48 SP18 80w +50w multi   1.00   .40
B49 SP18 80w +50w multi   1.00   .40
B50 SP18 80w +50w multi   1.00   .40

1988, Mar. 5   Photo.   Perf. 13x13½
B51 SP18 80w +20w Sailing   .75   .35
B52 SP18 80w +20w Taekwondo   .75   .35

1988, May 6   Photo.   Perf. 13½x13
No. B53, Torch relay, horiz. No. B54, Olympic Stadium, horiz.
B53 SP18 80w +20w multi   .75   .35
Litho. & Engr.
B54 SP18 80w +20w multi   .75   .35
See Greece No. 1627.

Souvenir Sheets of 2
B43a SP18 80w +50w   3.00   3.00
B44a SP18 80w +50w   3.00   3.00
B45a SP18 80w +50w   3.00   3.00
B46a SP18 80w +50w   3.00   3.00
B47a SP18 80w +50w   3.00   3.00
B48a SP18 80w +50w   3.00   3.00
B49a SP18 80w +50w   3.00   3.00
B50a SP18 80w +50w   3.00   3.00
B51a SP18 80w +20w   3.00   3.00
B52a SP18 80w +20w   3.00   3.00
B53a SP18 80w +20w   3.00   3.00
B54a SP18 80w +20w   3.00   3.00

AIR POST STAMPS

Four-motor Plane and Globe — AP1

Perf. 11½x11
1947-50   Litho.   Wmk. 257
C1 AP1 50wn carmine rose   5.00   4.00
a.   Horiz. pair, imperf. btwn.   150.00
Perf. 11
C2 AP1 150wn blue ('49)   2.00   1.50
a.   "KORFA"   20.00   35.00
C3 AP1 150wn green ('50)   6.00   —
    Nos. C1-C3 (3)   13.00
    Set, never hinged   45.00

Nos. C2-C3 are redrawn and designs differ slightly from type AP1.
Issued: 50wn, 10/1.
For surcharge see No. C5.

Plane and Korea Map — AP2

1950, Jan. 1
C4 AP2 60wn light blue   20.00   8.00
    Never hinged   35.00

No. C2 Surcharged with New Value and Wavy Lines in Black

1951, Oct. 10
C5 AP1 500wn on 150wn bl   4.00   4.00
    Never hinged   8.50
a.   "KORFA"   40.00   70.00
    Never hinged   65.00
b.   Surcharge inverted   125.00

Douglas C-47 and Ship — AP3

Perf. 13x12½
1952, Oct. 15   Litho.   Wmk. 257
C6 AP3 1200wn red brown   1.50   .75
C7 AP3 1800wn lt blue   1.50   .75
C8 AP3 4200wn purple   5.00   1.50
    Nos. C6-C8 (3)   8.00   3.00
    Set, never hinged   12.50

Nos. C6-C8 exist imperf.

1953, Apr. 5
C9 AP3 12h dp blue   1.75   .75
C10 AP3 18h purple   2.25   .75
C11 AP3 42h Prus green   3.00   1.50
    Nos. C9-C11 (3)   7.00   3.00
    Set, never hinged   12.50

Douglas DC-7 over East Gate, Seoul — AP4

1954, June 15   Perf. 12½
C12 AP4 25h brown   3.00   1.40
C13 AP4 35h deep pink   3.00   1.60
C14 AP4 38h dark green   3.00   1.60
C15 AP4 58h ultra   3.00   2.00
C16 AP4 71h deep blue   8.00   2.50
    Nos. C12-C16 (5)   20.00   9.10
    Set, never hinged   40.00

Nos. C12-C16 exist imperf.
Counterfeits exist of Nos. C12-C16.

Type of 1954 Redrawn

1956, July 20   Unwmk.
Laid Paper
C17 AP4 70h brt bluish grn   6.50   4.00
C18 AP4 110h brown   6.50   4.00
C19 AP4 205h magenta   9.00   4.50
    Nos. C17-C19 (3)   22.00   12.50
    Set, never hinged   40.00

Nos. C18-C19 are found on horizontally and vertically laid paper.

1957, July   Wmk. 312   Perf. 12½
Granite Paper
C20 AP4 70h brt bluish grn   7.00   3.75
C21 AP4 110h brown   7.00   3.75
C22 AP4 205h magenta   9.00   3.75
    Nos. C20-C22 (3)   23.00   11.25
    Set, never hinged   45.00

On the redrawn stamps, Nos. C17-C22, the lines of the entire design are lighter, and the colorless character at right end of bottom row has been redrawn as in illustration above No. 212D.

Catalogue values for unused stamps in this section, from this point to the end of the section, are for Never Hinged items.

Girl on Palace Balcony AP5

Designs: 100h, Suwon Castle. 200h, Songnyu Gate, Tuksu Palace. 400h, Kyunghoeru Pavilion.

Perf. 12½
1961, Dec. 1   Unwmk.   Litho.
C23 AP5 50h lt blue & violet   20.00   5.50
C24 AP5 100h pale grn & sepia   27.50   9.00
C25 AP5 200h pale grn & brn   42.50   11.50
C26 AP5 400h grn & pale bl   47.50   12.00
    Nos. C23-C26 (4)   137.50   38.00

Values in Won; Same Designs; Underlined Zeros Added

1962-63
C27 AP5 5w lt bl & vio ('63)   95.00   16.00
C28 AP5 10w pale grn & sepia   90.00   16.00
C29 AP5 20w pale grn & brn ('63)   240.00   27.50
C30 AP5 40w grn & pale bl ('63)   90.00   27.50
    Nos. C27-C30 (4)   515.00   87.00

1964, May 10   Wmk. 317   Perf. 12½
Granite Paper
C32 AP5 10w pale grn & sepia   14.00   4.50
C33 AP5 20w pale grn & brn   50.00   7.50
C34 AP5 40w pale bl & grn   27.50   6.00
    Nos. C32-C34 (3)   91.50   18.00

1964, Oct.   Unwmk.   Perf. 12½
Designs: 39w, Girl on palace balcony. 64w, Suwon Castle. 78w, Songnyu Gate, Tuksu Palace. 112w, Kyunghoeru Pavilion.

Granite Paper

C35	AP5	39w vio bl & gray olive	11.00	2.25
C36	AP5	64w bl & grnsh gray	9.00	2.50
C37	AP5	78w grnsh bl & ultra	25.00	4.50
C38	AP5	112w blue & green	12.00	2.50
		Nos. C35-C38 (4)	57.00	11.75

World Map and Plane — AP6

Designs: 135w, Plane over eastern hemisphere. 145w, Plane over world map. 180w, Plane over world map.

1973, Dec. 30   Photo.   Perf. 13x12½

C39	AP6	110w pink & multi	9.25	3.75
C40	AP6	135w yel grn & red	10.00	3.75
C41	AP6	145w lt bl & rose	12.50	4.50
C42	AP6	180w lilac & yellow	30.00	6.50
		Nos. C39-C42 (4)	61.75	18.50

UPU Type of 1974

1974, Oct. 9   Photo.   Perf. 13

C43	A480	110w blue & multi	2.25	1.00
a.		Souvenir sheet of 2	14.00	14.00

Mt. Fuji, Korean Airlines Jet Type

1985, Dec. 18   Photo.   Perf. 13x13½

C44	A878	370w brt bl, blk & red	2.75	1.00

Int'l Year of Peace Type

1986, Jan. 15   Photo.   Perf. 13x13½

C45	A879	400w multicolored	3.50	1.50

Issued in sheets with two blocks of four.

KOREA, DEMOCRATIC PEOPLE'S REPUBLIC

kə-ˈrē-ə

LOCATION — Peninsula extending from Manchuria between the Yellow Sea and the Sea of Japan (East Sea)
GOVT. — Republic
AREA — 47,398 sq. mi.
POP. — 24,589,122 (2011 est.)
CAPITAL — Pyongyang

At the end of World War II, American forces occupied South Korea and Russian forces occupied North Korea, with the 38th parallel of latitude as the dividing line. North Korea was administered by a Provisional People's Committee after Feb. 9, 1946. Unoverprinted Japanese stamps continued to be used until the first North Korean issue of March 12, 1946. On Sept. 9, 1948, the Democratic People's Republic of Korea was established, and the last Soviet troops left Korea by the end of the year.

100 Chon = 1 Won (1962)

Catalogue values for unused stamps in this country are for Never Hinged items.

North Korean stamps were issued without gum, unless otherwise noted.
Early issues typically exist in a variety of color shades.
Used values are for cancelled-to-order stamps from 1957-on. Postally used stamps are worth more. Examples on non-philatelic covers are scarce, especially for 1946-1960 issues.

REPRINTS

During 1955-57 the North Korean Postal Administration created "reprints," actually imitations, of most 1946-56 issues for sale to collectors. These reprints were postally valid, and in some cases may have served real postal needs, but most were created for and sold to overseas collectors.
The reprints are more finely printed than the original stamps and are normally printed on a higher quality white wove paper. They often differ from the original printings in both size and design details. Specific distinguishing characteristics are provided below, with the descriptions of each issue.
Value of reprints, $2-$5 each, unused or cto, unless otherwise noted.

SOVIET OCCUPATION

Rose of Sharon — A1

Diamond Mountains (small "50") — A2

Diamond Mountains (large "50") — A3

Perf 11, rouletted 12(#3), 11x Imperf or Imperf x11 (#4,5)

1946, Mar. 12-1955   Litho.

1	A1 20ch red	85.00	300.00
2	A2 50ch apple grn ('46)	55.00	82.50
a.	50ch yel green, buff	55.00	82.50
3	A2 50ch car rose	2,800.	2,300.
4	A3 50ch rose red	165.00	125.00
a.	Perf 12 ('48)	165.00	125.00
c.	Perf 10 ('55)	—	—
5	A3 50ch violet	18.00	—
a.	Perf 11 ('50)	300.00	—
b.	Imperf ('55)	55.00	—
c.	Perf 10 ('55)	—	—
d.	ImperfxPerf 11, soft paper, vert. lines	20.00	
e.	Vert. pair, tete-beche	1,250.	
	Nos. 1-5 (5)	3,123.	2,807.

No. 4 has lines of colored dots along the horizontal rouletting.
Design sizes: No. 1, 18x21.5-22mm; No. 4, 17.5-18x22-23mm.
Reprints of No. 1 are in yellow green, perf 8½, 8½x9½, 10 or imperf, and measure 18-18.5x23mm. Denomination panel is 4mm high, rather than 3mm. Value $10.
Reprints of No. 4 are perf 10, 10x10½, 11 or imperf, on gummed paper, and measure 17.5-18x22-22.5mm. The double frame lines are clearly separated, and the figures of value are thin and well-formed. Value $10.

Gen. Kim Il Sung (1912-1994) — A4

1946, Aug. 15   Litho.   Pin-Perf

6	A4 50ch brown	700.00	700.00

First anniversary of liberation from Japan.
No. 6 has lines of colored dots along the horizontal pin perforations.
No. 6 is inscribed in Korean, Chinese and Russian.
No. 6 in deep violet brown and a 50ch red, similar in design, were printed for presentation to officials and privileged people. Value, $1,900 and $2,250, respectively.

Peasants — A5

Pin-Perf 12, Imperf (#10)

1947, Apr. 22-1955   Litho.

7	A5 1w turquoise	450.00	55.00
8	A5 1w violet ('49)	800.00	175.00
9	A5 1w dark blue, buff ('50)	110.00	55.00
10	A5 1w dark blue ('50)	60.00	60.00
a.	Perf 11ximperf ('50)	6.00	60.00
b.	Perf 10 ('55)	—	—

1st anniversary of agrarian reform.
Nos. 7-9 have lines of colored dots along the horizontal pin perforations.
Reprints of type A5 measure 21x24mm, versus the originals' 21-21.5x24-25mm, are finely printed in light blue and are perf 9, 10½, 11 or imperf. Value $10.

Worker and Factory — A6

1948, June 5   Litho.   Perf. 11

11	A6 50ch dark blue	3,200.	1,000.

Second anniversary of the Labor Law.
Design size: 20-20.5x31mm.
Reprints measure 20x30-30.5mm and are perf 9, 10½, 11 or imperf. Value, $10 perf, $10 imperf.

Workers and Flag — A7

1948, Aug. 15

12	A7 50ch red brown	4,000.	1,500.

Third anniversary of liberation from Japan.

Flag and Map — A8

1948, Aug. 20

13	A8 50ch indigo & red	2,500.	450.00

Adoption of the Constitution of the Democratic People's Republic of Korea, July 10, 1948.

DEMOCRATIC PEOPLE'S REPUBLIC

North Korean Flag — A9

1948, Sept. 19   Rouletted 12

14	A9 25ch reddish violet	15.00	100.00
15	A9 50ch gray blue	20.00	50.00
a.	Perf 10½	40.00	75.00

Establishment of the People's Republic, 9/9/48.
Design size: 23x30mm.
Reprints of No. 14 are in blue, on gummed paper, perf 9, 10½ or imperf. Size 20.5x28mm. Value, $10.
No. 15a is perforated over rouletting.

North Korean Flag — A10

1949, Feb. 9

16	A10 6w red & blue	4.00	12.00
a.	Perf 10¼	35.00	35.00

No. 16 exists on both brownish wove and white wove papers.
Design size: 24x32.5-33mm.
Reprints are perf 10¼, 11 or imperf. Size 19x26.5mm. On the originals, the top and bottom panels are blue, with the center field red. On the reprints, these colors are reversed. Value, $10.
For surcharge see No. 42. For overprint see No. 76.

A11

Kim Il Sung University, Pyongyang A12

1949

17	A11 1w violet	400.00	200.00
18	A12 1w blue	1,200.	125.00

Issue dates: No. 17, 8/9; No. 18, Sept.
Design size: 34x21mm.
Reprints of No. 17 are in slate lilac to reddish lilac, perf 8½, 9, 9x9½, 10 or imperf, on gummed paper. Size 31.5-32x20-20.5mm. Value, $10 perf, $10 imperf.

North Korean Flags
A13   A14

Perf 11 or Rouletted 12 (#19)

1949, Aug. 15
With or Without Gum

19	A13 1w red, grn & blue	1,000.	250.00
a.	Imperfx11	1,000.	250.00
20	A14 1w red, grn & turq	1,200.	200.00

4th anniversary of Liberation from Japan.
Design sizes: No. 19, 20.5x31mm; No. 20, 20x29.5mm

Order of the National Flag — A15

#21c Control overprint

Rouletted 12, Imperf (#23)

1950, Apr. 4-1956   Litho.

21	A15 1w pale sage green	7.00	12.00
a.	1w olive green	7.00	12.00
b.	1w yellow green	7.00	12.00
c.	With control overprint ('51)	—	—
22	A15 1w red orange	20.00	125.00

Typographed

23	A15 1w brown orange	7,000.	1,500.
24	A15 1w dark green ('51)	60.00	25.00
a.	Perf 10¼ ('56)	90.00	—
25	A15 1w light green	150.00	60.00

Design sizes: No. 21, 23-23.5x35mm; No. 22, 20x32mm; No. 23, 22.5-23x36-37mm; No. 24, 22x35.5mm; No. 25, 22.5x36mm.
No. 21c bears the seal of the DPRK Ministry of Posts and Telecommunications, which was applied to validate various stamps during the chaotic months following the landing of United Nations' forces at Inchon in mid-September, 1950, the retreat of North Korean forces to the far north by October, and their renewed advance, after the entry of the Chinese Volunteer Army into the war.
Reprints of type A15 are in dull blue green on white paper, perf 10¼ or imperf, size 22x35mm, or in red orange on white paper, perf 8½, 9, 10½, 10ximperf or imperf, size 20-20.5x32.5mm. Value (orange), $10 perf.

Flags, Liberation Monument A16

Flags, Soldier A17

Peasant and Worker — A18   Tractor — A19

1950, June 20-1956
Lithographed, Thin Paper
Roul. 12xImperf, Roul. 12 (#28, 29)

26	A16	1w indigo, lt blue & red	3.50	17.50
a.		Perf 10¼ ('55)	12.00	24.50
27	A16	1w brown orange	9.00	60.00
28	A17	2w red, steel blue & black	5.00	17.50
a.		Perf 10¼ ('55)	12.00	24.00
29	A18	6w green	6.50	—
30	A19	10w brown	9.50	—

Typographed, Thin Paper, Roul. 12

31	A18	6w red	3.50	17.50
a.		Perf 10¼ ('55)	29.00	24.00
b.		Thick brownish paper, imperf x roul. 12	29.00	24.00
32	A19	10w brown	3.50	—
a.		Thick brownish paper, imperf x roul. 12	36.00	32.50
		Nos. 26-32 (7)	40.50	112.50

Fifth anniversary of liberation from Japan.
Design sizes: No. 30, 20x27.5mm; No. 31, 22x33mm; No. 32, 22x30mm.
Reprints of No. 26 are on medium white paper, distinguishable by numerous design differences, among which are: characters in top inscription are 1½mm high, rather than 1mm, with 3 short lines at either side, rather than 2; top corner ornaments have a dark center, rather than white; 4 ray beams at left of monument, rather than 3; no dots on right face of spire, while originals have 3 small dots; value numerals within well-formed circles.
Reprints of Nos. 28 and 29 are on medium white paper, perf 10¼, 11 or imperf. No. 28 reprints are in light green, No. 29 in rose red, dull blue and black. Value, $10 each.
Reprints of type A19 are 22x31mm in size, on medium white paper and are perf 10¼ or imperf.

Capitol, Seoul — A20

1950, July 10   Litho.   Roul. 12
33	A20	1w bl grn, red & blue	45.00	500.00

Capture of Seoul.

Order of Ri Sun Sin — A21

1951, Apr. 5   Typo.   Imperf
34	A21	6w orange	15.00	15.00
a.		Perf 10¼	30.00	

No. 34 also exists perf 9x10½.
No. 34 is on brownish laid paper. Design size: 21.5-22x29.5-30mm.
Reprints are on white paper, perf 10¼ or imperf. Size 21.5x30mm. On the reprints, the center of the lower left point of the star is open; on the originals, it is hatched. Value, $10 each.
For surcharge see No. 43.

Hero Kim Ki Ok — A22

1951, Apr. 17
35	A22	1w blue	19.50	19.50
a.		Perf 10¼	180.00	

No. 35 was printed on unbleached and off-white wood-pulp laid papers, with wood chips visible. The laid lines are often difficult or impossible to detect.
Design size: 23-23.5x35.5-36mm.
Reprints are on white wove paper, perf 10¼, 10½ or imperf. Size 22.5x33.5mm. Value, $10 each.

Soviet and North Korean Flags A23

Hero Kim Ki U A24

N. Korean, Chinese & Russian Soldiers — A25

1951, Aug. 15-1955   Litho.   Roul. 12
36	A23	1w dark blue	105.00	105.00
37	A23	1w red	275.00	275.00
38	A24	1w dark blue	170.00	170.00
39	A24	1w red	170.00	170.00
40	A25	2w dark blue	65.00	65.00
41	A25	2w red	65.00	65.00
		Nos. 36-41 (11)	1,720.	1,720.

Perf 10¼ Over Roulette (1955)
36a	A23	1w dark blue)	75.00	75.00
37a	A23	1w red	275.00	275.00
38a	A24	1w dark blue	275.00	275.00
39a	A24	1w red	170.00	170.00
40a	A25	2w dark blue °	75.00	75.00
41a	A25	2w red	40.00	40.00
		Nos. 36a-41a (11)	1,655.	1,655.

Nos. 36-41 and 36a-41a exist on both coarse buff and white wove papers. Values are the same. Various perfs and roulettes and roulettes exists; not all combinations are known.
Design sizes: Nos. 36 and 37, 17x23.5mm; Nos. 38 and 39, 16x23mm; Nos. 40 and 41, 23x16.5mm.
Reprints of No. 36 are perf 9, 10½x10 or imperf. Size 15.5-16x22.5mm.
Reprints of No. 38 are perf 9, 10 or imperf. They have no lines of shading between the characters in the top inscription.
Reprints of No. 40 are perf 9, 10 or imperf. Size 22-22.5x16.5mm. The Korean "Won" character at lower right is in 4 parts, rather than 3.
Reprints are all light ultramarine. Value, $10 each.

Nos. 16, 34 Surcharged

On No. 16   On No. 34

1951, Nov. 1   Imperf
42	A10	5w on 6w red & blue (#16)	150.00	60.00
43	A21	5w on 6w org (#34)	1,000.	725.00

Order of Soldier's Honor — A26

1951, Nov. 15-1956
44	A26	40w scarlet (16.5x25mm)	22.50	4.50
a.		Perf 10¼ ('56)	22.50	7.75
45	A26	40w scarlet (17x24mm)	12.00	4.50
a.		Perf 10¼ ('56)	12.00	7.75

Victory Propaganda — A27

1951, Nov. 15-1956
46	A27	10w dark blue	15.00	7.75
47	A27	10w dark blue	15.00	7.75
a.		Perf 10¼ ('56)	22.50	22.50

No. 47 also exists perf 8½.
Design sizes: No. 46, 17x25.5mm; No. 47, 16.5-17x25mm.
Reprints are in light blue, perf 10¼, 11 or imperf. Size 16.5-17x25mm. Value and inscription at bottom are outlined and clear against cross-hatched background. Value, $10 each.

Ri Su Dok, Guerilla Hero — A28

1952, Jan. 10-1955
48	A28	70w brown	15.00	3.50
a.		Perf 10¼ ('55)	25.00	12.00
b.		70w black brown	120.00	
c.		As "b," perf 10¼	60.00	

Dove, Flag & Globe — A29

1952, Jan. 20-1957
49	A29	20w scarlet, deep blue & lt blue	24.00	6.00
a.		Perf 10¼ ('55)	24.00	12.00

Peace Propaganda.
No. 49 also exists perf 8½, 11 and rouletted 11½.
No. 49 was printed on off-white or buff paper, with broken lines between stamps. Design size: 22x31-31.5mm.
Reprints are perf 10¼ or imperf, in red, slate blue and pale turquoise blue on white paper. Size 22x31mm. They lack the broken lines between stamps. Value, each $50.

Gen. Pang Ho-san — A30

1952, Apr.
50	A30	10w dull purple	60.00	24.00

Honoring North Korean General Bang Ho San.
No. 50 is also known with locally-applied rough perforation.

Labor Day — A31

1952, Apr. 20-1955   Imperf
51	A31	10w rose red	300.00	300.00
a.		Perf 10¼ ('55)	300.00	300.00

Enforcement of the Labor Law, 6th Anniv. — A32

1952, June 1-1955
52	A32	10w light blue	500.00	500.00
a.		Perf 10¼ ('55)	—	500.00

Design size: 18x26mm. Broken lines between stamps.
Reprints are in dull or slate blue, on thick, gummed paper, with no broken lines between stamps. Size 17.5x25.5-26mm. Value, $10 each.

Day of Anti-U.S. Imperialist Struggle — A33

1952, June 4-1956
53	A33	10w rose red	180.00	150.00
a.		Perf 10¼ ('56)	180.00	

Design size: 17.5x25.5-26mm. Broken lines between stamps.
Reprints are in bright rose red, perf 10, 10¼, 11 or imperf. on thick, gummed paper, with no broken lines between stamps. Size 17.5x26mm. Value, $10 each.

North Korean-Chinese Friendship — A34

1952, July 25-1956
54	A34	20w deep blue	50.00	24.00
a.		Perf 10¼ ('56)		50.00

Design size: 18x21.5mm. Printed on thin white wove paper, with clearly discernible mesh pattern.
Reprints are perf 10¼, 11 or imperf, on thick white wove paper, with no pattern visible. Size 18.5-19x21.5-22mm. Value, $10 each.

Flags & Monument A35   Soldier & Monument A36

1952-55
55	A35	10w carmine	150.00	150.00
a.		Perf 10¼ ('55)	200.00	—
56	A36	10w scarlet	275.00	275.00
a.		Perf 10¼ ('55)	350.00	350.00

Seventh Anniversary of Liberation from Japan.
Issue dates: No. 55, 7/25/52; No. 56, 8/1/52.
Design sizes: No. 55, 20.5-21x27.5-28mm; No. 56, 29.5-30x18.5mm.
Reprints of No. 55 are in vermilion, on thick paper, perf 10½, 11 or imperf. Size 20.5x27-27.5mm. Value, $10 each.
Reprints of No. 56 are in rose red, perf 10, 10¼, 11 or imperf. Size 30.5-31x18.5-19mm. Value, $10 each.

Note: Original are typographed; reprints are lithographed on thin white paper.

International Youth Day — A37

1952, Oct. 20-1955

57   A37   10w deep green   72.50   80.00
   a.   Perf 10¼ ('55)   72.50   —

No. 57 is on thick paper, with very thin gum. Design size: 20.5-21x28mm.
Reprints are on thin to medium paper, without gum, perf 10¼, 11 or imperf. Size 20x27mm. Value, $10 each.

Soldiers in Battle — A38   Soldier and Flag — A39

1953, Jan. 20-1955

58   A38   10w rose carmine   130.00   130.00
   a.   Perf 10¼ ('55)   130.00   —
59   A39   40w red brown   60.00   60.00
   a.   Perf 10¼ ('55)   75.00   —

Fifth Anniversary of the Founding of the Korean People's Army.
Design sizes: No. 58, 21.5-22x26-26.5mm; No. 59, 21.5x27mm.
Reprints of No. 58 are on thick, gummed paper, perf 10¼, 11 or imperf. Size: 21.5-22x26.5mm. Value, $10 each.
Reprints of No. 59 are on thick, gummed paper, perf 10, 10½, 11 or imperf. Size: 21.5x26.5mm. Value, $10 each.

Woman with Flag — A40   Women and Globe — A41

1953, Mar. 1-1955

60   A40   10w carmine   60.00   60.00
   a.   Perf 10¼ ('55)   60.00   —
61   A41   40w yellow green   72.50   72.50
   a.   Perf 10¼ ('55)   72.50   —

International Women's Day.
Design sizes: No. 60, 20x29.5mm; No. 61, 21x29mm.
Reprints of No. 60 are in rose carmine, on thin paper, perf 10¼, 11 or imperf. Size 20.5x30mm.
Reprints of No. 61 may be distinguished from the originals by design differences: the dove's wing consists of many small feathers (3 large feathers on original), the women's mouths are all open (closed on original), and 3 thin connected lines on center woman's shirt (3 thick separate lines on original). Value, $10 each.

Worker — A42   Workers Marching — A43

1953, Apr. 15-1955

62   A42   10w yellow green   60.00   60.00
   a.   Perf 10¼ ('55)   72.50   —
63   A43   40w orange brown   60.00   60.00
   a.   Perf 10¼ ('55)   72.50   —

May Day
Reprints of No. 62 are in green or emerald green, perf 9½x8½, 10¼, 11 or imperf. Among

many design differences, they have 4 horizontal lines between flag and frame line at upper left, many short hatching lines between frame line and top inscription, many horizontal lines between flag and flag pole at upper right, and won letter clear. On originals, there are one or no lines at upper left, no lines between frame line and top inscription, no lines between flag and flag pole, and the won character is not clearly defined. Value, $10 each.
Reprints of No. 63 are perf 10, 10¼ or imperf. On the reprints, the right flag pole touches the frame line, and the left center element of the won character resembles a "T." On the originals, the right flag pole does not touch the frame line, and the center element of the won character resembles an inverted "L." Value, $10 each.

Soldier — A44   Battle — A45

1953, June 1-1955

64   A44   10w greenish blue   110.00   110.00
   a.   Perf 10¼ ('55)   110.00   —
65   A45   40w scarlet   110.00   130.00
   a.   Perf 10¼ ('55)   110.00   —

Day of Anti-U.S. Imperialist Struggle.
Nos. 64 and 65 were issued with gum. Design sizes: 10w, 24x33mm; 40w, 24-24.5x33mm.
Reprints of No. 64 and 65 are on thick paper, perf 10¼, 11 or imperf. Design sizes: 10w, 23.5-24x32mm; 40w, 24x32-32.5mm. No. 64 is in turquoise blue; No. 65 in vermilion or orange vermilion. Value, $10 each.

4th World Festival of Youth & Students

A46   A47

1953, June 10-1955   **With Gum**

66   A46   10w dp dull blue &   pale turq. blue   72.50   72.50
   a.   Perf 10¼ ('55)   85.00   —
67   A47   20w gray grn &pink   60.00   36.00
   a.   Perf 10¼ ('55)   72.50   —

Two types of reprints of No. 66 exist. On the reprints, the forelocks of the center and right heads have detailed hairlines, and the right head shows eye and eyebrow. On the originals, both features are solid. Value, $10 each.

Victory Issue — A48

1953, June 1-1955   **With Gum**

68   A48   10w brn & yel   360.00   400.00
   a.   Perf 10¼ ('55)   325.00   500.00

8th Anniversary of Liberation from Japan — A49

1953, Aug. 5-1955

69   A49   10w red orange   *4,000.*   *4,000.*

Design size: 25x35.5mm.

Reprints are perf 10¼ or imperf. Size: 24.5-25x34.5-35mm. Left side of monument is shaded, and windows are fully drawn and shaded. On the originals, the monument is unshaded, and the windows are only partially drawn and half shaded. Value, $10 each.

5th Anniv. Founding of D.P.R.K. — A50

1953, Aug. 25-1955

70   A50   10w dp blue & red   72.50   72.50
   a.   Perf 10¼ ('55)   95.00   —

Design size: 21.5-22x29.5-30mm. Inscribed "1948-1953."
Reprints are in blue and vermilion, perf 9x9½ or imperf and are inscribed "1948-1955." Size: 22.5x30mm. Value, each $100.

Liberation Monument — A51

1953, Dec. 25-1955   **With Gum**

71   A51   10w deep slate   72.50   47.50
   a.   Perf 10¼ ('55)   72.50   —

Design size: 20x31mm.
Reprints are in deep gray. Size: 19-19.5x30.5-31mm. Value, $10 each.

Worker & Crane — A52

1954, Jan. 25-1955   **With Gum**

72   A52   10w light blue   85.00   55.00
   a.   Perf 10¼ ('55)   110.00   —

Reconstruction and Economic Development.
Design size: 22x31.5mm.
Reprints are in greenish blue or dull blue, without gum. Size: 21.5x31mm. The horizontal lines defining the sky and clouds are clear and even, and the details of the crane are distinct. Value, $10 each.

Korean People's Army, 6th Anniv. — A53

1954, Jan. 25-1955   **With Gum**

73   A53   10w dp car red   500.00   —
   a.   Perf 10¼ ('55)   500.00   —
   b.   Rouletted   500.00   —

Design size: 23.5-24x38mm.
Reprints are in vermilion or orange vermilion. Size: 23-23.5x37.5-38mm. The design is much clearer than in the originals, with thin distinct characters in top inscription and complete unbroken frame line at right. Value, $10 each.

International Women's Day — A54

1954, Feb. 25-1955   **With Gum**

74   A54   10w carmine   250.00   250.00
   a.   Perf 10¼ ('55)   300.00   —

Design size: 19.5-20x29-29.5mm.
Reprints are in vermilion. Size: 20-20.5x29.5-30mm. The USSR and PRC flags at top right are legible, and the shading under the center and right women's chins is represented by several fine lines (solid on originals). Value, $10 each.

Labor Day — A55

1954, Apr. 15-1955   **With Gum**

75   A55   10w vermilion   72.50   72.50
   a.   Perf 10¼ ('55)   72.50   —

Design size: 20x27-27.5mm.
Reprints are in orange vermilion, perf 8½x9, 9, 10¼ or imperf. Size: 19-19.5x26-26.5. Value, $10 each.

No. 16 overprinted "Fee Collected" in Korean

1954, May (?)

76   A10   6w red & blue   1,500.   1,500.

Day of Anti-U.S. Imperialist Struggle — A56

1954, June 10-1955   **With Gum**

77   A56   10w red brown   210.00   *210.00*
   a.   Perf 10¼ ('55)   210.00   *210.00*

National Congress of Young Activists — A57

1954, July 20-1955   **With Gum**

78   A57   10w blue, red &   slate   600.00   300.00
   a.   Perf 10¼ ('55)   —   —

Design size: 20x30mm.
Reprints are in blue, scarlet vermilion & deep slate. Size: 19.5-20x29-29.5mm. On the originals, the worker's hand is beneath the tassel of the flag and is less than 1mm from the frame line. On the reprints, hand is to the right of the tassel and 2mm from frame line. Value, $10 each.

Liberation from Japan, 9th Anniv. — A58

1954, Aug. 1-1955   **With Gum**

79   A58   10w chestnut   50.00   50.00

Design size: 20-20.5x30mm.
Reprints of No. 79 are perf 10¼, 11 or imperf. Size: 20x29-29.5mm. Soldier's nose

line straight and strong, 3 lines of cooling holes in gun barrel (2 on originals). Value, $10 each.

North Korean Flag — A59

1954, Aug. 25-1955 **With Gum**
80 A59 10w blue & dp red 100.00 100.00
a. Perf 10¼ ('55) 120.00 —

Design size: 24x31.5-32mm.
Reprints are in dull blue and bright rose red. Size: 25-25.5x30.5-31mm. Value, $10 each.

Taedong Gate, Pyongyang A60

1954, Sept. 1-1956 **With Gum**
81 A60 5w reddish brown 15.00 3.75
a. Perf 10¼ ('56) 22.50
82 A60 5w lilac brown 15.00 3.75
a. Perf 10¼ ('56) 22.50

Hwanghae Iron Works — A61
Hwanghae Iron Works & Workers — A61a

No. 84, Hwanghae Iron Works & workers, horiz.

1954, Nov. 1-1956
83 A61 10w light blue 22.50 3.00
a. Perf 10¼ ('55) 45.00 —
84 A61a 10w chocolate 22.50 3.00
a. Perf 10¼ ('55) 45.00 —
b. Roul. 9x8½ ('56) 50.00 50.00

Korean People's Army, 7th Anniversary — A62

1955, Jan. 25 **With Gum**
85 A62 10w rose red 36.00 36.00
a. Perf 10¼ 36.00 —

International Women's Day — A63

1955, Feb. 25 **With Gum**
86 A03 10w deep blue 36.00 36.00
a. Perf 10¼ 45.00

Reprints are in blue, perf 10¼, imperf and imperf x 10¼. Corners of design are clearly and uniformly indented. Value, $10 each.

A63a A63b

Labor Day

1955, Apr. 16 **With Gum**
86A A63a 10w green 60.00 30.00
a. Perf 10¼ — —
86B A63b 10w violet brown 60.00 30.00
a. Perf 10¼ 60.00 —

Design sizes: No. 86A, 19.5-20x30mm. No. 86B, 19x30mm.
Reprints of No. 86A measure 19.5x29mm. Reprints of 86B measure 19x29.5mm and are without gum. Value, $10 each.

Admiral Ri Sun-Sin — A64

1955, May 14-1956
87 A64 1w blue, *pale green* 15.00 15.00
a. Perf 10¼ ('56) 18.00
88 A64 2w rose, *buff* 15.00 1.50
a. Perf 10¼ ('56) 22.00
89 A64 2w rose red ('56) 30.00 2.75
a. Perf 10¼ 30.00 —
Nos. 87-89 (3) 60.00 19.25

No. 89 is redrawn, with a larger "2."
Design sizes: Nos. 87, 88, 20x29-30mm.
Reprints of No. 87 are in dull blue, on pale apple green, perf 10¼, 11½x10½, imperf, or roul. 8½. Size 19x28-28.5mm. Reprints of No. 88 are 19-19.5x28.-28.5mm in size. Value, $10 each.

Labor Law, 9th Anniv. — A65

1955, May 30
90 A65 10w rose 90.00 90.00
a. Perf 10¼ — —

No. 90 was issued with a very thin yellow gum. Design size: 18.5-19x27.5-28mm.
Reprints exist perf 10¼, 11 or imperf. Size 18-18.5x27-27.5mm. Value unused, $10 each.

Korea-U.S.S.R. Friendship Month
A66 A67

1955, July **Perf. 10**
91 A66 10w rose red 30.00 —
a. Imperf 30.00 21.00
92 A66 10w org red & vio blue 30.00 —
a. Imperf 30.00 21.00
93 A67 20w red & lt blue 30.00 —
a. Imperf 30.00 24.00
b. Inscription below flag in two colors — —
c. As "b," imperf — —
94 A67 20w ver & lt blue 24.00 —
a. Imperf 24.00 21.00
Nos. 91-94 (4) 114.00

Issue dates: Nos. 91, 93, 7/16; Nos. 92, 94, 7/20.
Design sizes: No. 91, 22x32.5mm; No. 92, 29.5x43mm; No. 93, 18.5x32mm; No. 94, 24.5-25x42.5x43mm.
Reprints of No. 94 are in light vermilion and light blue, perf 10¼, 11 or imperf, with a very thin gum. Size: 24-24.5x42-43mm. The two

blue bands of the flag are solidly colored, with many white spots. On the originals, this area consists of fine lines with few or no white areas. Value, $10 each.

Liberation from Japan, 10th Anniv. — A68

1955, July 20 **Perf. 10¼**
95 A68 10w dull green 24.00 —
a. Imperf 24.00 18.00
96 A68 10w ver, dull blue & chestnut 24.00 —
a. Imperf 24.00 18.00

Design sizes: No. 95, 21.5-22x31.5-32mm; No. 96, 29-29.5-42-43mm.
Reprints of No. 95 are in dull blue green, perf 10¼, 11 or imperf, on gummed paper. Size: 21-21.5x31mm. Reprints of No. 96 are in rose red, dull to greenish blue and yellow brown, perf 10¼ or imperf. Size: 28-28.5x42.5-43mm. Value, $10 each.

Standing Rock in Sea-Kumgang Maritime Park — A69

1956, Jan. 20
97 A69 10w blue, *bluish* 20.00 —
a. Imperf 25.00 25.00

People's Army, 8th Anniv. — A70

1956, Jan. 20
98 A70 10w lt brn, *pale yel grn* 100.00 100.00
a. Imperf 90.00 90.00

Design size: 20x27-27.5mm.
Reprints are in chestnut on pale sage green paper, perf 10¼, 11 or imperf. Size: 19.5-20x27mm. Creases in the soldier's shirt are distinct, and nose and eyes are strongly shaded. Value, $10 each.

May Day — A71

1956, Apr. 29
99 A71 10w blue 100.00 100.00
a. Imperf 100.00 100.00

Design size: 23.5-24x35-35.5mm.
Reprints are perf 10¼, 11 or imperf, on gummed paper. Size: 23.5x35mm. Clear hatching lines at right of top inscription; many feathers in dove's wing. Value, $10 each.

Ryongwang Pavilion and Taedong Gate, Pyongyang — A72

1956, May 8
100 A72 2w light blue 55.00 55.00
a. Imperf 55.00 55.00
b. Rouletted 85.00 —

Reprints of No. 100 are on thicker, gummed paper. The tail of the central left element in the "won" inscription at lower right extends beyond the left edge of the L-shaped character beneath it. Value, $10.

Moranbong Theater, Pyongyang A73

1956, May 8
101 A73 40w light green 30.00 12.00
a. Imperf 85.00 72.50

Labor Law, 10th Anniv. — A74

1956, June 7
102 A74 10w dark brown 8.00 2.50
a. Perf 9 80.00 60.00
b. Imperf 180.00 120.00

Korean Children's Union, 10th Anniv. A75

1956, June 7
103 A75 10w dk brown 15.00 6.50
a. Imperf 160.00 35.00

Law on Equality of the Sexes, 10th Anniv. A76

1956, July 10
104 A76 10w dark brown 10.00 3.75
a. Perf 9 25.00 15.00
b. Imperf 35.00 17.50

Nationalization of Major Industries, 10th Anniv. — A77

1956, July 10
105 A77 10w dark brown 90.00 —
a. Imperf 210.00

Liberation from Japan, 11th Anniv. — A78

1956, July 24

106	A78	10w rose red	14.00	3.25
a.		Imperf	160.00	30.00

Machinist
A79

1956, July 28

107	A79	1w dark brown	3.75	2.00
a.		Perf 9	12.50	8.00
b.		Imperf	32.50	14.00

Kim Il Sung
University, 10th
Anniv. — A80

1956, Sept. 30

108	A80	10w dark brown	10.00	9.00
a.		Imperf	32.50	14.00

4th Congress, Korean Democratic
Youth League — A81

1956, Nov. 3

109	A81	10w dark brown	14.00	3.25
a.		Imperf	32.50	18.00

Model
Peasant — A82

1956, Nov. 14

110	A82	10w rose	7.50	2.25
a.		Imperf	21.00	11.00
b.		Rouletted	—	—

220th Anniv. Birth
of Pak Ji Won
(1737-1805)
A83

1957, Mar. 4

111	A83	10w blue	5.00	1.25
a.		Imperf	19.00	10.00

Tabo Pagoda
in Pulguk
Temple
A84

Ulmil Pavilion,
Pyongyang
A85

1957, Mar. 20

112	A84	5w light blue	6.00	2.50
a.		Rouletted	—	—
b.		Perf 11 (with gum)	—	—
c.		Imperf	87.50	21.00
113	A85	40w gray green	7.50	3.25
a.		Perf 11	—	—
b.		Imperf	22.50	11.00

No. 113b was issued both with and without gum.

Productivity
Campaign — A86

1957, July 4   With or Without Gum

114	A86	10w ultramarine	6.75	4.50
a.		Perf 11	—	—
b.		Imperf	32.50	15.00

Steelworker — A87

Voters Marching — A88

1957, Aug.

115	A87	1w orange	3.50	.75
a.		Imperf	9.50	4.25
116	A87	2w brown	3.50	.75
a.		Imperf	9.50	4.25
117	A88	10w vermilion	17.50	3.25
a.		Imperf	65.00	35.00
		Nos. 115-117 (3)	24.50	4.75

Second General Election.
There are two types of the 1w. On type 1,
the won character is approx. 2½mm in diameter and is distinct. On type 2, the character is
approx. 1½mm in diameter and is virtually
illegible.
Issued: 10w, 8/10; 1w, 2w, 8/13.

Founding of
Pyongyang,
1530th
Anniv. — A89

1957, Sept. 28   Perf. 10

118	A89	10w blue green	3.00	.65
a.		Imperf	30.00	9.00

Lenin — A90

Lenin &
Flags — A91

Kim Il Sung at
Pochonbo
A92

Pouring Steel
A93

1957

119	A90	10w gray blue	2.00	.95
a.		Imperf	30.00	9.00
120	A91	10w blue green	2.00	.95
a.		Imperf	30.00	9.00
b.		Rouletted 13	—	—
121	A92	10w red	2.00	.95
a.		Imperf	30.00	9.00
b.		Rouletted 13	—	—
122	A93	10w red orange	4.50	.95
a.		Imperf	120.00	13.00
b.		Rouletted 13	—	—
		Nos. 119-122 (4)	10.50	3.80

40th Anniversary of the Russian October
Revolution.
Issued: Nos. 119, 120, 9/30; No. 121, 10/3;
122, 10/16.
No. 120 exists with gum.

4th Congress
World
Federation of
Trade
Unions — A94

1957, Oct. 3

123	A94	10w ultra & lt grn	2.50	1.10
a.		Imperf	30.00	11.00

No. 123a exists with or without gum.

Russian Friendship
Month — A95

1957, Oct. 16

124	A95	10w green	4.50	1.10
a.		Imperf	210.00	140.00

Doctor Weighing
Baby — A96

Bandaging
Hand — A97

1957, Nov. 1

125	A96	1w red	9.00	1.25
a.		Imperf	65.00	12.00
126	A96	2w red	9.00	1.25
a.		Imperf	65.00	12.00
b.		Rouletted	—	—
127	A97	10w red	35.00	3.75
a.		Imperf	130.00	35.00
		Nos. 125-127 (3)	53.00	6.25

Red Cross.
No. 126 exists without or without gum. No.
126a was issued with gum.

Flying Dragon
Kettle — A98

Flying Dragon
Incense
Burner — A99

1958, Jan. 14

128	A98	10w blue	12.00	1.60
a.		Imperf	87.50	20.00
129	A99	10w gray green	12.00	1.60
a.		Imperf	87.50	20.00

Nos. 128a and 129a exist with or without
gum.

Woljong Temple
Pagoda — A100

1958, Feb. 21   10 (#130), 10½ (#131)

130	A100	5w lt green	1.90	.75
a.		Imperf	26.00	13.00
b.		Rouletted	—	—
131	A100	10w lt blue	5.50	2.50
a.		Imperf	32.50	18.00
b.		Rouletted	—	—

No. 130 was issued with gum.

Soldier — A101

Soldier, Flag & Hwanghae Iron
Works — A102

Photo (#132), Litho (#133)

1958, Feb.   Perf. 10

132	A101	10w blue	8.00	1.10
a.		Imperf	52.50	21.00
b.		Rouletted	—	—
c.		Perf 11	—	—
133	A102	10w rose	11.00	1.25
a.		Imperf	52.50	21.00

10th Anniversary of the Korean People's
Army.
No. 133 was issued with or without gum.

Rocket Launch,
Sputnik — A103

Sputnik in
Orbit — A104

Designs: 40w, Sputnik over observatory.

1958, Mar. 26   **Photo.**
134	A103 10w dull blue green	8.50	5.00
a.	Imperf	65.00	21.00
135	A104 20w dull blue green	8.50	5.00
a.	Imperf	65.00	21.00
b.	Rouletted		
136	A104 40w dull blue green	8.50	5.00
a.	Imperf	65.00	21.00
137	A103 70w dull blue green	10.00	9.00
a.	Imperf	100.00	35.00
	Nos. 134-137 (4)	35.50	24.00

International Geophysical Year.
Nos. 134-137 exist with or without gum.

Young Socialist
Constructors
Congress — A105

1958, May 12   **Litho.**
138	A105 10w blue	4.50	1.25
a.	Imperf	30.00	11.00

Opening of
Hwanghae Iron
Works — A106

1958, May 22
139	A106 10w lt blue	8.50	1.25
a.	Imperf	42.50	14.00

Commemorative
Badge — A107

1958, May 27
140	A107 10w multicolored	7.00	1.50
a.	Imperf	27.50	6.50
b.	Perf 11		
c.	Rouletted		

Departure of Chinese People's Volunteers.
See No. 150.

4th International
Democratic Women's
Congress — A108

1958, June 5
141	A108 10w blue	1.90	.75
a.	Imperf	42.50	11.00

Congress
Emblem
A109

1958, July 4
142	A109 10w grn & red brn	3.75	2.50
a.	Imperf	30.00	6.50
b.	Perf 11	12.50	

First Congress of the Young Workers of the
World Federation of Trade Unions.

Apartment
House, East
Pyongyang
A110

1958, July 24
143	A110 10w lt blue	5.00	1.25
a.	Imperf	26.00	9.00
b.	Perf 11		

Workers'
Apartment
House,
Pyongyang
A111

1958, Aug. 21
144	A111 10w blue green	5.00	1.25
a.	Imperf	26.00	9.00

Hungnam
Fertilizer
Plant — A112

Pyongyang
Railway
Station
A113

DPRK
Arms — A114

Weaver — A115

Dam,
Pyongyang
A116

1958   **Litho, Photo (#148, 149)**
145	A112 10w blue green	6.00	.95
a.	Imperf	130.00	18.00
b.	Perf 11		
146	A113 10w dp blue green	22.50	3.25
a.	Imperf	150.00	42.50
b.	Perf 11		
147	A114 10w red brn & yel grn	4.50	.95
a.	Imperf	325.00	110.00
148	A115 10w sepia	18.00	3.75
a.	Imperf	210.00	57.50
149	A116 10w sepia	30.00	12.50
a.	Imperf	150.00	35.00
	Nos. 145-149 (5)	81.00	21.40

10th Anniversary Korean People's Republic.
Issued: Nos. 145, 146, 8/21; No. 147, 9/7;
Nos. 148, 149, 9/10.

Soldier and
Troop
Train — A117

1958, Sept. 10   **Photo.**   **Perf. 10**
150	A117 10w sepia	45.00	12.50
a.	Imperf	360.00	77.50

Departure of Chinese People's Volunteers.

Transplanting
Rice Seedlings
A118

1958, Sept. 10   **Litho.**
With or Without Gum
151	A118 10w sepia	2.00	.65
a.	Imperf	15.00	6.50

Winged Horse of
Chollima — A119

1958, Sept. 16
152	A119 10w brick red	3.50	.60
a.	Imperf	32.50	4.25

National Congress of the Innovators in
Production.

North Korea-China
Friendship
Month — A120

1958, Oct. 8   **With or Without Gum**
153	A120 10w multicolored	2.25	.55
a.	Imperf	18.00	4.25
b.	Rouletted		

National
Congress of
Agricultural
Cooperatives
A121

1959, Jan. 5   **With or Without Gum**
154	A121 10w dk grnish blue	2.50	.60
a.	Imperf	18.00	4.00

Gen. Ulji
Mundok — A122

1959, Feb. 11   **With Gum**
155	A122 10w lilac brn & yel	5.50	1.10
a.	Imperf	32.50	14.00

See Nos. 157-159 and 209-212.

National Women's
Workers
Congress — A123

1959, Mar. 29
With or Without Gum
156	A123 10ch brown & red	3.75	1.25
a.	Imperf	52.50	

Jon Pong
Jun — A124

Kang Kam
Chan — A125

Ulji Mundok — A126

1959, Apr. 1
157	A124 2ch blue, *lt green*	2.50	.45
a.	Imperf	110.00	
158	A125 5ch lilac brn, *buff*	2.90	.50
a.	Imperf	150.00	
159	A126 10ch red brn, *cream*	5.75	.65
a.	Imperf	150.00	
	Nos. 157-159 (3)	11.15	1.60

Nos. 157-159 were issued with gum. Nos.
157a-159a were issued with or without gum.

Soviet Luna 1
Moon Rocket
Launch
A127

1959, May 4   **Perf. 10, 10½**
160	A127 2ch dk violet, *pale buff*	12.50	6.50
a.	Imperf	260.00	57.50
161	A127 10ch blue, *pale green*	25.00	9.50
a.	Imperf	260.00	57.50

Issued with gum (perf 10) or without gum
(perf 10½). Nos. 160a and 161a were issued
with gum.

Land Irrigation
Program — A128

1959, May 27   **Perf. 10**
162	A128 10ch multicolored	10.00	2.75
a.	Imperf	42.50	11.00

Slogan-inscribed
Tree, Chongbong
Bivouac — A129

Statue of Kim Il
Sung — A130

Mt. Paektu
A131

1959, June 4   **10, 10¾ (#164)**
163	A129 5ch multicolored	3.25	1.25
a.	Imperf	87.50	18.00
b.	Perf 10¾		
c.	Rouletted		
164	A130 10ch blue & grnsh bl	3.75	1.25
a.	Imperf	65.00	18.00
165	A131 10ch violet blue	5.00	
a.	Imperf	65.00	
	Nos. 163-165 (3)	12.00	2.50

22nd Anniversary of the Battle of Pochondo.
No. 163 also exists perf 10¾.
No. 164 was issued with gum.

Chollima Tractor A132

Jongihwa-58 Electric Locomotive — A133

Red Star-58 Bulldozer A134

Chollima Excavator A135

SU-50 Universal Lathe A136

Sungri-58 Truck A137

With or without gum

1959, June 12   *Perf. 10¾*

166	A132	1ch multicolored	1.50	.50
a.		Imperf	65.00	35.00
b.		Rouletted		
167	A133	2ch multicolored	11.00	3.25
a.		Imperf	130.00	55.00
b.		Rouletted		
168	A134	2ch multicolored	2.50	.65
a.		Imperf	87.50	18.00
b.		Rouletted		
169	A135	5ch multicolored	2.50	1.25
a.		Imperf	210.00	
b.		Rouletted		
170	A136	10ch multicolored	2.50	.95
a.		Imperf	210.00	
b.		Rouletted		
171	A137	10ch multicolored	4.50	.65
a.		Imperf	210.00	
		Nos. 166-171 (6)	24.50	7.25

Machine-building Industry.

Armistice Building, Panmunjom — A138

Anti-U.S. Protester A139

Anti-South Korean Emigration Campaign A140

Peaceful Reunification of Korea — A141

1959, June 25   **With Gum**

172	A138	10ch dk blue & blue	5.00	.30
a.		Imperf	175.00	—
b.		Perf 10¼	—	—
173	A139	20ch dk blue & lt blue	1.50	.50
174	A140	20ch sepia & brn	7.00	1.90
175	A141	70ch dk brn & lt brn	45.00	12.50
a.		Imperf	175.00	—
b.		Perf 10¼xRoul	—	—
		Nos. 172-175 (4)	58.50	15.20

Day of Struggle for the withdrawal of U.S. troops from South Korea.

Metal Type A142

Samil Wolgan Monthly Breaking Chains — A143

Flag with Symbols of Peace and Literature A144

Korean Alphabet of 1443 — A145

1959, Aug. 1

176	A142	5ch sepia	25.00	9.50
177	A143	5ch green & red	7.50	2.90
178	A144	10ch bright blue	7.50	2.90
179	A145	10ch dp bl & pale bl	11.50	4.75
a.		Souvenir sheet of 4, #176-179 imperf	110.00	55.00
		Nos. 176-179 (4)	51.50	20.05

International Book and Fine Arts Exhibition, Leipzig.
Nos. 176 and 178 were issued with gum. Nos. 177, 179 and 179a were issued without gum.

Milk Cow Farm A146

Pig Farm — A147

1959, Sept. 20

180	A146	2ch multicolored	4.00	.95
181	A147	5ch multicolored	5.50	1.25

No. 180 was issued without gum, No. 181 with gum.

Economic Development

Cement Making A148

Hydroelectrical Dam — A149

Salt Making — A150

Construction A151

Grain A152

Sugar A153

Steel-Making A154

Fishing A155

Iron-Making A156

Coal Mining A157

Textile Production A158

Fruit — A159

Perf. 10½ (#182), 11
1959, Sept. 20-1960

182	A148	1ch multicolored	.75	.55
a.		Imperf	175.00	
183	A149	2ch multicolored	1.90	.55
a.		Imperf	175.00	
184	A150	5ch multicolored	3.00	.70
a.		Imperf	175.00	
185	A151	10ch multicolored	3.50	1.00
a.		Imperf	175.00	
186	A152	10ch multicolored	1.50	.55
a.		Imperf	175.00	
187	A153	10ch multicolored	2.75	.55
a.		Imperf	175.00	
188	A154	10ch multicolored	2.50	.55
a.		Imperf	175.00	
189	A155	10ch multicolored	2.25	.55
a.		Imperf	175.00	
190	A156	10ch multicolored	1.50	.55
191	A157	10ch multicolored	2.75	.55
192	A158	10ch multicolored	1.50	.55
a.		Imperf	175.00	
193	A159	10ch multicolored ('60)	4.00	.55
		Nos. 182-193 (12)	27.90	7.20

No. 193 issued August 1960.
Nos. 183 and 185 were issued with gum, the other values without gum.

Musk Deer
A160

Sable
A161

Marten
A162

Otter
A163

Sika Deer — A164

Pheasant
A165

1959-62   **Perf. 11**
194 A160 5ch multicolored 6.50 .75
195 A161 5ch multicolored 6.50 .75
196 A162 5ch multicolored 6.50 .75
197 A163 5ch multicolored 6.50 .75
198 A164 10ch multicolored 6.50 .75
199 A165 10ch multicolored 30.00 2.50
    Nos. 194-199 (6)   62.50 6.25
       Game Preservation.
Issued: No. 198, 10/24/59; No. 199, 3/25/60; No. 194, 11/11/60; Nos. 195-197, 1/24/62.
Nos. 198 and 199 were issued with gum, Nos. 194-197 without gum.

3rd Korean Trade
Unions Congress
A166

1959, Nov. 4   **With Gum**
200 A166 5ch multicolored 1.40 .35

Electric Locomotive — A167

Freighter
A168

1959, Nov. 5   **With Gum**
201 A167 5ch brnish purple 20.00 2.90
202 A168 10ch slate green 8.25 2.25

Korean
People's
Army, 12th
Anniv.
A169

1960, Feb. 8   **With Gum**
203 A169 5ch blue 225.00 125.00

Sword
Dance — A170

Janggo
Dance — A171

Peasant
Dance — A172

1960, Feb. 25
204 A170 5ch multicolored 5.00 .45
205 A171 5ch multicolored 5.00 .45
206 A172 10ch multicolored 5.00 .45
    Nos. 204-206 (3)   15.00 1.35

Women of 3
Races,
Dove — A173

Woman
Worker — A174

1960, Mar. 8   **With Gum**
207 A173 5ch grnish blue & red
            vio 2.75 .25
208 A174 10ch grn & org 2.75 .50
   50th Anniv. of International Women's Day.

Kim Jong
Ho,
Geographer
A175

Kim Hong Do,
Painter
A176

Pak Yon,
Musician
A177

Jong Ta San,
Scholar
A178

1960   **With Gum**
209 A175 1ch gray & pale grn 2.75 .25
210 A176 2ch dp blue & yel
            buff 3.50 .25
211 A177 5ch grnish blue &
            grnish yel 12.75 .25
212 A178 10ch brn & yel 3.50 .25
    Nos. 209-212 (4)   22.50 1.00
   Issued: 1ch-5ch, 3/16/60; 10ch 6/60.

Grapes — A179

Wild fruits: No. 214, Fruit of Actinidia arguta planch. No. 215, Pine-cone. No. 216, Hawthorn berries. No. 217, Chestnuts.

1960, Apr. 8   **With Gum**
213 A179 5ch multicolored 3.25 1.00
214 A179 5ch multicolored 3.25 1.00
215 A179 5ch multicolored 3.25 1.00
216 A179 10ch multicolored 3.75 1.25
217 A179 10ch multicolored 3.75 1.25
    Nos. 213-217 (5)   17.25 5.50
   Nos. 214-215 also exist imperf.

Lenin, 90th
Birthday — A180

1960, Apr. 22   **With Gum**
218 A180 10ch violet brown 1.75 .30

Koreans and
Caricature of U.S.
Soldier — A181

1960, June 20   **With Gum**
219 A181 10ch dark blue 7.75 .75
Day of Struggle for Withdrawal of U.S. Troops from South Korea.

Mao Tse-Tung
Plaza — A182

Taedong River
Promenade
A183

Youth
Street — A184

People's Army
Street — A185

Stalin
Street — A186

1960, June 29   **With Gum**
220 A182 10ch gray green 1.25 .25
221 A183 20ch dk bl green 2.50 .30
222 A184 40ch blackish green 4.00 .75
223 A185 70ch emerald 7.25 1.75
224 A186 1w blue 10.00 2.75
    Nos. 220-224 (5)   25.00 5.80
    Views of rebuilt Pyongyang.

Luna 3 — A187

Luna 2 — A188

1960, July 15
225 A187 5ch multicolored 7.75 6.00
226 A188 10ch multicolored 11.00 3.00
    Soviet space flights.
The 5ch was issued with gum, the 10ch without gum.

Mirror
Rock — A189

Devil-faced
Rock — A190

Dancing
Dragon
Bridge
A191

Nine Dragon
Falls — A192

Mt.
Diamond
on the
Sea
A193

1960, July 15-1961
227 A189 5ch multicolored   1.75   .25
228 A190 5ch multicolored   1.75   .25
229 A191 10ch multicolored
         ('61)   6.25   .35
230 A192 10ch multicolored   5.50   .35
231 A193 10ch multicolored   2.10   .25
    Nos. 227-231 (5)   17.35 1.45
    Diamond Mountains scenery.
    No. 229 issued 2/8/61.
    See Nos. 761-764.

Lily
A194

Rhododendron
A195

Hibiscus
A196

Blue Campanula
A197

Mauve Campanula
A198

1960, July 15-1961   **With Gum**
232 A194 5ch multicolored   1.90   .30
233 A195 5ch multicolored   1.90   .30
234 A196 10ch multicolored   2.75   .50
235 A197 10ch multicolored   2.75   .50
236 A198 10ch multicolored
         ('61)   2.75   .50
    Nos. 232-236 (5)   12.05 2.10
    No. 236 issued 6/1/61.
    Nos. 232-234 and 236 also exist without
gum.

"The
Arduous
March"
A199

Crossing
the
Amnok
River
A200

Young Communist League
Meeting — A201

Showing
the Way
at
Pochonbo
A202

Return to Pyongyang — A203

1960, July 26
237 A199 5ch carmine red   .85   .25
238 A200 10ch deep blue   1.50   .25
239 A201 10ch deep blue   1.50   .25
240 A202 10ch carmine red   1.50   .25
241 A203 10ch carmine red   1.50   .25
    Nos. 237-242 (5)   6.85 1.25
    Revolutionary activities of Kim Il Sung.

15th Anniv.
Liberation
from Japan
A204

1960, Aug. 6
242 A204 10ch multicolored   5.50   .25

North Korean-Soviet
Friendship
Month — A205

1960, Aug. 6
243 A205 10ch lake, *cream*   1.40   .25

Okryu
Bridge
A206

Grand
Theater
A207

Okryu
Restaurant
A208

1960, Aug. 11
244 A206 10ch gray blue   4.00   .35
245 A207 10ch dull violet   3.50   .25
246 A208 10ch turquoise   1.40   .25
    Nos. 244-246 (3)   8.90   .85
    Pyongyang buildings.

Tokro River
Dam — A209

1960, Sept. 9   **With Gum**
247 A209 5ch slate blue   2.50   .25
    Inauguration of Tokro River Hydroelectric
Power Station.

World Federation of
Trade Unions, 15th
Anniv. — A210

1960, Sept. 16
248 A210 10ch blue & lt blue   1.60   .25

Repatriation of
Korean Nationals
from Japan — A211

1960, Sept. 26
249 A211 10ch brnish violet   5.50   .30

Korean-Soviet
Friendship — A212

1960, Oct. 5   **With Gum**
250 A212 10ch brn & org   1.75   .25

Liberation Day
Sports Festival,
Pyongyang
A213

    Designs: 5ch (No. 251), Runner. 5ch (No.
252), Weight-lifter. 5ch (No. 253), Cyclist. 5ch
(No. 254), Gymnast. 5ch (No. 255), Soccer
players, horiz. 10ch (No. 256), Swimmer,
horiz. 10ch (No. 257), Moranbong Stadium,
horiz.

1960, Oct. 5
251-257 A213 Set of 7   13.50 2.25

Chinese &
North Korean
Soldiers
A214

Friendship
Monument — A215

1960, Oct. 20   **With Gum**
258 A214 5ch rose   1.40   .25
259 A215 10ch dp blue   1.40   .25
    10th Anniversary of Chinese People's Vol-
unteers' Entry Into Korean War.

World Federation
of Democratic
Youth, 15th
Anniv. — A216

1960, Nov. 11
260 A216 10ch multicolored   1.40   .25

Woodpecker
A217

Mandarin
Ducks
A218

Scops Owl — A219

Oriole — A220

1960-61
261 A217 2ch yel grn & multi   7.25   .40
262 A218 5ch blue & multi   7.75   .50
263 A219 5ch lt blue & multi   12.50 1.00
264 A220 10ch lt bl grn & multi   7.75 1.00
    Nos. 261-264 (4)   35.25 2.90
    Issued: No. 262, 12/15/60; No. 264,
3/15/61; No. 261, 4/22/61; No. 263, 6/1/61.

Wrestling
A221

Swinging — A222

Archery
A223

Seesaw — A224

1960, Dec. 15-1961
265 A221 5ch dull grn & multi   1.00   .25
266 A222 5ch yel & multi ('61)   1.00   .25
267 A223 5ch yel gold & multi   4.50   .45
268 A224 10ch lt bl grn & multi   1.00   .25
    Nos. 265-268 (4)   7.50   1.20
    No. 266 issued 1/6/61.

Agriculture
A225

Light
Industry
A226

Korean Workers'
Party
Flag — A227

Power
Station
A228

Steel-Making — A229

1960, Dec. 15-1961
269 A225 5ch multicolored   1.90   .25
270 A226 5ch multicolored   3.50   .25
271 A227 10ch multicolored   .95   .25
272 A228 10ch multicolored   1.90   .25
273 A229 10ch multicolored   1.40   .25
    Nos. 269-273 (5)   9.65   1.25

Wild Ginseng — A230

Design: 10ch, cultivated ginseng

1961
274 A230 5ch multicolored   5.00   .25
275 A230 10ch multicolored   5.00   .25
    Issued: 10ch, 1/5; 5ch, 3/15.

A231

A232

A233

A234

Factories
A234

1961, Feb. 8   **With Gum**
276 A231 5ch red & pale yel   1.40   .25
277 A232 10ch bl grn & pale
           yel   3.00   .25
278 A233 10ch dp vio blue &
           pale yel   3.00   .25
279 A234 20ch vio & pale yel   3.75   .55
    Nos. 276-279 (4)   11.15   1.30
Construction of Vinalon Factory.
See Nos. 350-353.

Pyongyang
Students' and
Children's
Palace
A235

1961, Feb. 8   **With Gum**
280 A235 2ch red, yellow   1.00   .25

Korean
Revolution
Museum
A236

1961, Feb. 8   **With Gum**
281 A236 10ch red   .85   .25

Soviet Venus
Rocket
A237

1961, Feb. 8
282 A237 10ch turq bl & multi   6.25   .30

Tractor-Plow
A238

Disk-Harrow
A239

Wheat
Harvester
A240

Corn
Harvester
A241

Tractors
A242

1961, Feb. 21   **With Gum**
283 A238 5ch violet   .95   .25
284 A239 5ch blue green   .95   .25
285 A240 5ch dp gray green   .95   .25
286 A241 10ch violet blue   1.40   .25
287 A242 10ch purple   1.40   .25
    Nos. 283-287 (5)   5.65   1.25

Opening of
Industrial
College — A243

1961, Mar. 1   **With Gum**
288 A243 10ch red brn, buff   3.00   .25

Agrarian
Reform
Law, 15th
Anniv.
A244

1961, Mar. 1   **With Gum**
289 A244 10ch dull green, yel   2.10   .25

20-Point
Political
Program,
20th Anniv.
A245

1961, Mar. 15   **With Gum**
290 A245 10ch dull vio, pale yel   1.00   .25

Mackerel
A246

Dolphin
A247

Whale
A248

Tunny — A249

Walleye
Pollack
A250

1961, Apr. 3
291 A246 5ch yel grn & multi   5.00   .50
292 A247 5ch lt blue & multi   12.00   1.50
293 A248 10ch lt grnish blue &
           multi   13.50   .50
294 A249 10ch gray & multi   5.00   .50
295 A250 10ch dk grn & multi   5.00   .50
    Nos. 291-295 (5)   40.50   3.50

Crane-Mounted
Tractor — A251

"Sungri-1010"
Truck
A252

Vertical Milling
Machine
A253

Victory April-15
Automobile
A254

8-Meter Turning
Lathe
A255

Radial Boring Lathe — A256

750-Kg Air Hammer A258

3,000-Ton Press A260

Ssangma-15 Excavator A262

400-HP Diesel Engine — A264

Trolley — A266

Boring Lathe — A268

Tunnel Drill — A270

Hydraulic Press — A257

200mm Boring Lathe A259

3-Ton Air Hammer A261

Jangbaek Excavator A263

Honing Lathe — A265

8-Meter Planer — A267

Hobbing Lathe — A269

1961-65

296	A251	1ch red brown	2.75	.25
297	A252	2ch dk brown	2.75	.25
298	A253	2ch dk green	1.00	.25
299	A253	2ch grayish brn	50.00	12.50
300	A254	4ch dk blue	7.00	.25
301	A255	5ch dk green	4.00	.25
302	A256	5ch dk bl gray	2.10	.25
a.		5ch dark gray green	50.00	12.50
303	A257	5ch bl green	2.10	.25
304	A258	5ch red brown	1.75	.25
305	A259	5ch sl violet	2.50	.25
306	A260	10ch gray violet	3.75	.25
a.		10ch dark blue	50.00	.25
307	A261	10ch blue	3.50	.25
308	A261	10ch brown	200.00	50.00
309	A262	10ch dk vio gray	1.75	.25
310	A263	10ch dk green	3.75	.25
311	A264	10ch dk sl blue	3.75	.25
312	A265	10ch dk blue	3.25	.25

313	A266	40ch dk blue	13.50	.25
314	A267	90ch dk bl green	6.00	.30
315	A268	1w dk vio brown	17.50	.50
316	A269	5w dk brown	37.50	3.75
317	A270	10w vio brown	50.00	7.50
		Nos. 296-317 (22)	420.20	78.55

Issued: 1ch, 4/22/61; 2ch, 4/27/61; Nos. 301, 306, 5/20/61; Nos. 307, 308, 3/13/62; Nos. 302, 317, 7/30/62; 5w, 9/5/62; No. 302a, 9/15/62; No. 308, 12/26/62; Nos. 297, 298, 2/11/63; No. 303, 4/9/63; 90ch, 5/15/63; 4ch, 6/15/63; 40ch, 9/13/63; 1w, 10/16/63; No. 310, 3/20/64; No. 305, 4/28/64; No. 311, 6/25/64; No. 312, 1/1/65.

Nos. 296, 297, 301, 303, 306 and 316 are perf 10¾. Other values are perf 12½.

Nos. 296-302, 304-307 and 309-315 were issued with gum. Nos. 303, 308, 316 and 317 were issued without gum.

Nos. 296-297, 301, 303, 306-308 and 316 are lithographed. Other values are engraved.

Reforestation Campaign — A271

1961, Apr. 27   With Gum
318   A271   10ch green   2.50   .35

Peaceful Reunification of Korea — A272

1961, May 9
319   A272   10ch multicolored   30.00   2.50

Young Pioneers (Children's Union) of Korea, 15th Anniv. — A273

Designs: 5ch, Pioneers swimming. 10ch (No. 321), Pioneer bugler. 10ch (No. 322) Pioneer visiting battlefield.

1961, June 1
320-322   A273   Set of 3   6.50   1.00

Labor Law, 15th Anniv. A274

1961, June 21   With Gum
323   A274   10ch dp blue, *pale yel*   1.75   .30

Plums — A275

Peaches A276

Apples A277

Persimmons A278

Pears — A279

1961, July 11
324	A275	5ch multicolored	1.60	.25
325	A276	5ch multicolored	1.60	.25
326	A277	5ch multicolored	1.60	.25
327	A278	10ch multicolored	1.60	.25
328	A279	10ch multicolored	1.60	.25
		Nos. 324-328 (5)	8.00	1.25

Yuri Gagarin & Vostok I — A280

1961, July 11
329   A280   10ch dp bl & pale bl   2.50   .50
330   A280   10ch red vio & pale bl   2.50   .50

First manned space flight, April 12.

Nationalization of Industry, 15th Anniv. — A281

1961, July 11   With Gum
331   A281   10ch lt red brown   20.00   .90

Sex Equality Law, 15th Anniv. A282

1961, July 27   With Gum
332   A282   10ch brn red & rose   1.25   .25

Children Planting Tree — A283

Children: 5ch (No. 334), Reading book. 10ch (No. 335), Playing with ball. 10ch (No.

336), Building a toy house. 10ch (No. 337), Waving banner.

1961, Aug. 29
333-337   A283   Set of 5   6.50   .90

Livestock Breeding — A284

Fishing Industry A285

Farming A286

Textile Industry — A287

1961, Aug. 29
338	A284	5ch multicolored	2.25	.25
339	A285	10ch multicolored	1.90	.25
340	A286	10ch multicolored	3.50	.25
341	A287	10ch multicolored	3.25	.30
		Nos. 338-341 (4)	10.90	1.05

Improvement of living standards.

Kim Il Sung Writing Under Tree A288

Kim Il Sung at Desk A289

Soldiers Studying A290

1961, Sept. 8   With Gum
342	A288	10ch violet	.85	.35
343	A289	10ch dull violet	.85	.35
344	A290	10ch dp blue & yel	1.60	.35
		Nos. 342-344 (3)	3.30	1.05

15th Anniv. of Kim Il Sung's "Ten-Point Program of the Association for the Restoration of the Fatherland."

Kim Il Sung & Party Banner A291

Party Emblem, Workers — A292

Chollima Statue — A293

1961, Sept. 8   With Gum
345 A291 10ch brown red   .70   .35
346 A292 10ch green   .70   .35
347 A293 10ch violet   .70   .35
      Nos. 345-347 (3)   2.10   1.05

4th Korean Workers' Party Congress.

Miners' Day — A294

1961, Sept. 12   With Gum
348 A294 10ch brown   13.00   .75

Pak In Ro (1561-1642), Poet — A295

1961, Sept. 12
349 A295 10ch dk blue & gray
                   blue   3.75   .25

Aldehyde Shop A296

Polymerization & Saponification Shops — A297

Glacial Acetic Acid Shops A298

Spinning Shop A299

1961, Oct. 17   With Gum
350 A296 5ch red & pale yel   1.40   .25
351 A297 10ch dp blue & pale
                   yel   2.10   .25
352 A298 10ch dk brn & pale yel 2.10   .25
353 A299 20ch purple & pale yel 3.25   .40
      Nos. 350-353 (4)   8.85   1.15

Completion of Vinalon Factory.

Korean & Soviet Flags — A300

Korean & Chinese Flags A301

1961, Oct. 26
354 A300 10ch multicolored   1.40   .35
355 A301 10ch multicolored   1.40   .35

North Korean Friendship Treaties with the Soviet Union and China.

Day of Sports and Physical Culture — A302

Sports: 2ch, Table tennis. 5ch, Flying model glider. 10ch (No. 358), Basketball. 10ch (No. 359), Rowing. 10ch (No. 360), High jump. 20ch, Emblem.

1961, Nov. 4   With Gum
356-361 A302 Set of 6   10.00   1.75

No. 209 Surcharged in Violet

1961, Nov. 5
362   5ch on 1ch gray &
                   pale grn   200.00 150.00

Centenary of publication of "Taedongyojido," map.

Janggun Rock — A303

Chonbul Peak A304

Mansa Peak — A305

Kiwajip Rock A306

Mujigao Rock A307

1961, Nov. 29   With Gum
363 A303 5ch slate   1.50   .25
364 A304 5ch brown   1.50   .25
365 A305 10ch br lilac   2.75   .25
366 A306 10ch sl blue   2.75   .25
367 A307 10ch dk blue   2.75   .25
      Nos. 363-367 (5)   11.25   1.25

Mt. Chilbo scenes.

Protection of State Property — A308

1961, Nov. 29   With Gum
368 A308 10ch gray green   1.40   .25

WFTU Emblem — A309

1961, Nov. 29   With Gum
369 A309 10ch multicolored   .85   .25

5th Congress of World Federation of Trade Unions.

"Red Banner" Electric Locomotive A310

1961, Nov. 29   With Gum
370 A310 10ch vio & buff   19.00   1.75

Railway Electrification.

Winter Sports A311

Designs (all 10ch): No. 371, Figure skater. No. 372, Speed skater. No. 373, Ice hockey. No. 374, Skiier.

Figures in Sepia

1961, Dec. 12   With Gum
371-374 A311 Set of 4   11.00   1.00

Six Objectives of Production

Steel — A312

Coal — A313

Grain — A314

Textiles — A315

Sea-Foods — A316

Apartments — A317

1962, Jan. 1   **With Gum**
375	A312	5ch multicolored	1.25	.25
376	A313	5ch multicolored	8.75	.50
377	A314	10ch multicolored	1.25	.25
378	A315	10ch multicolored	4.00	.25
379	A316	10ch multicolored	3.75	.25
380	A317	10ch multicolored	1.25	.25
		Nos. 375-380 (6)	20.25	1.75

See Nos. 442-447.

Animals

Korean Tiger — A318

Racoon Dog — A319

Badger A320

Bear — A321

1962, Jan. 24
381	A318	2ch multicolored	5.25	.25
382	A319	2ch lt grn & brn	3.75	.25
383	A320	5ch lt bl grn & lt red brn	2.50	.25
384	A321	10ch grn & brn	3.75	.25
		Nos. 381-384 (4)	15.25	1.00

Traditional Musical Instruments

Kayagum — A322

Jotae (Flute) — A323

Wolgum — A324

Haegum — A325

Wagonghu A326

1962, Feb. 2
385	A322	10ch multicolored	3.75	.25
386	A323	10ch multicolored	3.75	.25
387	A324	10ch multicolored	3.75	.25
388	A325	10ch multicolored	3.75	.25
389	A326	10ch multicolored	3.75	.25
		Nos. 385-389 (5)	18.75	1.25

See Nos. 472-476.

Butterflies

Luehdorfia puziloi — A327

Sericinus telamon — A328

Parnassius nomion — A329

Inachusio A330

1962, Mar. 13
390	A327	5ch multicolored	4.50	.25
391	A328	10ch multicolored	4.50	.25
392	A329	10ch multicolored	4.50	.25
393	A330	10ch multicolored	4.50	.25
		Nos. 390-393 (4)	18.00	1.00

G. Titov & Vostok 2 A331

1962, Mar. 13
394	A331	10ch multicolored	3.75	.30

Second Soviet Manned Space Flight.

Kim Il Sung Commanding Troops — A332

Kim Il Sung Adressing Workers — A333

Perf. 10¾ (#397), 12½
1962, Apr. 14   **Engr.**   **With Gum**
395	A332	10ch blue	1.10	.30
396	A333	10ch green	1.10	.30
397	A333	10ch rose red	1.10	.30
		Nos. 395-397 (3)	3.30	.90

Marshall Kim Il Sung's 50th Birthday.

Kim Chaek — A334

Kang Kon — A335

An Kil — A336

Ryu Kyong Su — A337

Kim Jong Suk — A338

Choe Chun Guk — A339

1962, Apr. 23   **Perf. 12½**
With Gum
398	A334	10ch dark brown	7.00	.25
399	A335	10ch dark blue	7.00	.25
400	A336	10ch rose	7.00	.25
401	A337	10ch dark brown	7.00	.25
402	A338	10ch dark blue gray	7.00	.25
403	A338	10ch dark blue green	7.00	.25
404	A339	10ch violet brown	7.00	.25
		Nos. 398-404 (7)	49.00	1.75

Anti-Japanese Revolutionary Fighters.
See Nos. 480-484.

National Mothers' Meeting, Pyongyang — A340

1962, May 23   **Litho.**   **Perf. 10¾**
405	A340	10ch multicolored	.85	.25

Black-faced Spoonbill — A341

Brown Hawk Owl — A342

Eastern Broad-billed Roller — A343

Black Paradise Flycatcher A344

Whistling Swan — A345

1962, May 23   **Perf. 10¾**
406	A341	5ch multicolored	3.25	.40
407	A342	5ch multicolored	12.00	.50
408	A343	10ch multicolored	7.00	.50
409	A344	10ch multicolored	7.00	.50
410	A345	20ch multicolored	8.75	.55
		Nos. 406-410 (5)	38.00	2.45

Beneficial birds.

Battle of Pochonbo, 25th Anniv. — A346

1962, May 23
411	A346	10ch multicolored	1.90	.25

Croaker A347

Hairtail
A348

Japanese
Croaker
A349

Japanese
Sea Bass
A350

Brush
Case — A352

Gizzard
Shad
A351

1962, June 28

412	A347	5ch dp grn & multi	1.90	.25
413	A348	5ch dp blue & multi	1.90	.25
414	A349	10ch apple grn & multi	3.25	.25
415	A350	10ch vio blue & multi	3.25	.25
416	A351	10ch grn & multi	3.25	.25
	Nos. 412-416 (5)		13.55	1.25

Sea Fish.

Ink
Container — A353

Ink Slab
Case
A354

Writing
Brush
Stand
A355

Paperweight — A356

Ink Slab
A357

Filing
Cabinet
A358

Kettle — A359

1962, July 30   Centers in Black

417	A352	4ch pale blue	1.40	.25
418	A353	5ch ochre	1.40	.25
419	A354	10ch pale green	1.90	.25
420	A355	10ch salmon	1.90	.25
421	A356	10ch violet	1.90	.25
422	A357	10ch orange brown	1.90	.25
423	A358	10ch pale yellow	1.90	.25
424	A359	40ch gray	4.50	.50
	Nos. 417-424 (8)		16.80	2.25

Antiques of the Koryo and Yi Dynasties.
Nos. 418 and 420 were issued with gum, the
other values without gum.

Jong Ta
San — A360

1962, July 30   Engr.   Perf. 12½
425 A360 10ch dp brnish violet   1.60   .25
200th Anniv. birth of Jong Ta San,
philosopher.

National Assembly Elections
A361   A362
1962, Oct. 3   Litho.   Perf. 10¾
426 A361 10ch multicolored   1.60   .30
427 A362 10ch multicolored   1.60   .30

Pyongyang, 1535th Anniv. — A363

1962, Oct. 15   With Gum
428 A363 10ch pale blue & blk   1.10   .25

Launch of Soviet
Manned Rockets
Vostok 3 &
4 — A364

1962, Nov. 12
429 A364 10ch multicolored   3.75   .75

Spiraea — A365

Echinosophoora
koreensis — A366

Codonopsis
sylvestris — A367

Ginseng — A368

1962, Nov. 30

430	A365	5ch multicolored	1.90	.25
431	A366	10ch multicolored	1.90	.25
432	A367	10ch multicolored	1.90	.25
433	A368	10ch multicolored	1.90	.25
	Nos. 430-433 (4)		7.60	1.00

Korean plants.

Uibangryuchui
A369

1962, Dec. 26
434 A369 10ch multicolored   5.50   .40
485th anniversary of publication of the medical encyclopedia *Uibangryuchui*, printed with
moveable type.

Korean
Academy of
Sciences,
10th Anniv.
A370

1962, Dec. 26
435 A370 10ch dull ultra & pale
turq grn   2.25   .25

Fishing — A371

1962, Dec. 30
436 A371 10ch ultra   5.50   .25

European
Mink
A372

Korean
Hare
A373

Eurasian Red
Squirrel — A374

Goral — A375

Siberian
Chipmunk
A376

1962, Dec. 30-1963

437	A372	4ch apple green & red brown	1.60	.40
438	A373	5ch lt green & gray ('63)	1.60	.40
439	A374	10ch yellow & gray	2.75	.40
440	A375	10ch pale grn & dk brn	2.75	.40
441	A376	20ch lt gray blue & red brown	5.00	.40
		Nos. 437-441 (5)	13.70	2.00

Fur-bearing animals.
No. 438 issued 12/30/63.

Coal
A377

Grain
A378

Textiles
A379

Apartment Construction — A380

Steel
A381

Seafood — A382

1963, Jan. 1

442	A377	5ch multicolored	1.40	.25
443	A378	10ch multicolored	1.10	.25
444	A379	10ch multicolored	1.40	.25
445	A380	10ch multicolored	1.10	.25
446	A381	10ch multicolored	1.10	.25
447	A382	40ch multicolored	3.25	.45
		Nos. 442-447 (6)	9.35	1.70

Consolidation of the Achievement of the 6 Objectives. For surcharge, see No. 4539.

Korean People's
Army, 15th
Anniv. — A383

Designs: 5ch, Airman. 10ch (No. 449), Soldier. 10ch (No. 450), Sailor.

1963, Feb. 1   Engr.   Perf. 12½
With Gum

448-450	A383	Set of 3	6.50	.60

Peony — A384

Rugosa
Rose — A385

Rhododendron
A386

Campion
A387

Orchid — A388

1963, Mar. 21   Litho.   Perf. 10¾

451	A384	5ch gray & multi	1.10	.25
452	A385	10ch grnsh yel & multi	1.60	.25
453	A386	10ch lemon & multi	1.60	.25
454	A387	10ch br yel & multi	1.60	.25
455	A388	40ch green & multi	5.00	.45
		Nos. 451-455 (5)	10.90	1.45

Korean flowers.

Sword
Dance — A389

Fan
Dance — A390

1963, Apr. 15

456	A389	10ch multicolored	7.75	.30
457	A390	10ch multicolored	7.75	.30

International Music and Dance Competition, Pyongyang, April 16-May 17.

South
Korea
Uprising
of April
19, 3rd
Anniv.
A391

1963, Apr. 19

458	A391	10ch multicolored	1.60	.25

Karl Marx — A392

1963, Apr. 23   Engr.   Perf. 12½
With Gum

459	A392	10ch ultra	2.75	.25

Youth
Day — A393

Designs: 2ch, Children in chemistry class. 5ch, Children running. 10ch (No. 462), Girl chasing butterfly. 10ch (No. 463), Boy leading chorus.

1963, June 15   Litho.   Perf. 10¾

460-463	A393	Set of 4	13.00	1.00

Armed Koreans & Caricature of
American Soldier — A394

1963, June 25

464	A394	10ch multicolored	1.90	.25

Month of Struggle for the Withdrawal of U.S. Troops from South Korea.

Cyrtoclytus
caproides
A395

Cicindela
chinensis
A396

Purpuricenus
lituratus
A397

Agapanthia
pilicornus
A398

1963, July 24

465	A395	5ch multicolored	2.50	.25
466	A396	10ch multicolored	3.50	.25
467	A397	10ch multicolored	3.50	.25
468	A398	10ch multicolored	3.50	.25
		Nos. 465-468 (4)	13.00	1.00

Korean beetles.

Victory in Korean
War, 10th
Anniv. — A399

1963, July 27

469	A399	10ch multicolored	1.90	.25

National
Emblem — A400

North Korean
Flag — A401

1963, Aug. 15

470	A400	10ch multicolored	.65	.30
471	A401	10ch multicolored	.65	.30

No. 471 exists with background in blue. Not issued. Value $750.

Ajaeng
(Zither) — A402

Phyongyong (Jade
Chimes) — A403

Saenap
(Flute) — A404

Rogo
(Drums) — A405

Phiri
(Pipe) — A406

1963, Sept. 13

472	A402	5ch multicolored	1.60	.25
473	A403	5ch multicolored	1.60	.25
474	A404	10ch multicolored	2.25	.25
475	A405	10ch multicolored	2.25	.25
476	A406	10ch multicolored	2.25	.25
		Nos. 472-476 (5)	9.95	1.25

Korean traditional musical instruments.
Nos. 472 and 475 were issued with gum, the
other values without gum.

South Gate,
Kaesong
A407

Taedong Gate,
Pyongyang
A408

Pothong Gate,
Pyongyang
A409

1963, Sept. 13   Engr.   Perf. 12½
With Gum

477	A407	5ch black	.50	.25
478	A408	10ch brown	1.25	.25
479	A409	10ch black green	1.25	.25
		Nos. 477-479 (3)	3.00	.75

Korean historic buildings.
See Nos. 537-538.

Kwon Yong
Byok — A410

Ma Tong
Hui — A411

Pak Tal — A412

Ri Je
Sun — A413

Kim Yong
Bom — A414

1963, Oct. 10   With Gum

480	A410	5ch brown	9.00	—
481	A411	5ch brown purple	9.00	—
482	A412	10ch grnsh slate	9.00	—
483	A413	10ch carmine rose	9.00	—
484	A414	10ch black brown	70.00	50.00

Anti-Japanese revolutionary fighters.

Nurse & Children
at Playground
A415

Teacher &
Children at
Fairground
A416

1963, Nov. 30   Litho.   Perf. 10¾

485	A415	10ch multicolored	.85	.25
486	A416	10ch multicolored	.85	.25

Child welfare.

Hwajang
Temple — A417

Hyangsan
Stream
A418

Kwanum
Pavilion
& Pagoda
A419

Sangwon
Temple — A420

1963, Nov. 30

487	A417	5ch multicolored	1.10	.25
488	A418	10ch multicolored	5.75	.25
489	A419	10ch multicolored	2.75	.25
490	A420	10ch multicolored	2.75	.25
		Nos. 487-490 (4)	12.35	1.00

Mount Myohyang.

Arming the
People — A421

Technical
Innovation
A422

Mining Industry
A423

Building
Homes — A424

1963, Dec. 5   Engr.   Perf. 12½
With Gum

491	A421	5ch dp rose red	.55	.25
492	A422	10ch red brown	3.50	.25
493	A423	10ch gray violet	1.90	.30
494	A424	10ch gray black	3.75	.30
		Nos. 491-494 (4)	9.70	1.10

Seven-Year Plan.

Sowing
Gourd
Seeds
A425

Saving a
Swallow
A426

Swallow
Carrying
Gourd
Seed
A427

Sawing
Gourd
A428

Treasure
Pouring
from
Gourd
A429

1963, Dec. 5   Litho.   Perf. 10¾

495	A425	5ch multicolored	1.25	.30
496	A426	10ch multicolored	2.50	.30
497	A427	10ch multicolored	2.50	.30
498	A428	10ch multicolored	1.90	.30
499	A429	10ch multicolored	1.90	.30
		Nos. 495-499 (5)	10.05	1.50

Tale of Hung Bu.

Pistol
Shooting
A430

Small-Caliber Rifle Shooting — A431

Rifle
Shooting
A432

1963, Dec. 15
500 A430 5ch multicolored   .65   .25
501 A431 10ch multicolored   1.25   .25
502 A432 10ch multicolored   1.25   .25
    Nos. 500-502 (3)   3.15   .75
Marksmanship Competition.

Chongjin Mill — A433

Sinuiju Mill — A434

1964, Jan. 10   Engr.   Perf. 12½
With Gum
503 A433 10ch brn violet   1.25   .25
504 A434 10ch gray   1.25   .25
Chemical fiber industry.

Wonsan General Strike, 35th Anniv. A435

1964, Jan. 14   With Gum
505 A435 10ch brown   1.40   .25

Korean Alphabet, 520th Anniv. — A436

1964, Jan. 15   Litho.   Perf. 10¾
506 A436 10ch multicolored   1.40   .25

Lenin's Death, 40th Anniv. — A437

1964, Jan. 22   Engr.   Perf. 12½
With Gum
507 A437 10ch rose red   1.10   .25

Whaler A438

Trawler A439

Purse-Seine Boat — A440

Dragnet Boat A441

1964, Feb. 10   Litho.   Perf. 10¾
508 A438 5ch multicolored   1.60   .25
509 A439 5ch multicolored   1.60   .25
510 A440 10ch multicolored   3.25   .30
511 A441 10ch multicolored   3.25   .30
    Nos. 508-511 (4)   9.70 1.10
Korean fishing industry.

March 1 Popular Uprising, 45th Anniv. A442

1964, Feb. 10   Engr.   Perf. 12½
With Gum
512 A442 10ch dark violet   1.10   .25

Kabo Peasant War, 70th Anniv. — A443

1964, Feb. 15   With Gum
513 A443 10ch violet black   1.10   .25

Students' and Children's Palace, Pyongyang A444

1964, Mar. 3   With Gum
514 A444 10ch grnsh black   .85   .25

5th Congress, Democratic Youth League of Korea — A445

1964, May 12   Litho.   Perf. 10¾
515 A445 10ch multicolored   1.10   .25

Electric Train A446

1964, May 21
516 A446 10ch multicolored   10.00   .35
Electrification of Railway between Pyongyang and Sinuiju.

Popular Movement in Chongsan-ri — A447

1964, June 4   Engr.   Perf. 12½
With Gum
517 A447 5ch chestnut   275.00 125.00

Drum Dance — A448

Dance of Ecstasy — A449

Small Drum Dance — A450

1964, June 15   Litho.   Perf. 10¾
518 A448 2ch multicolored   1.60   .50
519 A449 5ch multicolored   2.50   .50
520 A450 10ch multicolored   3.25   .50
    Nos. 518-520 (3)   7.35 1.50
Korean folk dances.

For the Sake of the Fatherland A451

1964, June 15   Engr.   Perf. 12½
With Gum
521 A451 5ch carmine red   1.90   .25
Li Su Bok, soldier.

Nampho Smelter A452

Hwanghae Iron Works A453

1964   With Gum
522 A452 5ch bronze green   6.50   .25
523 A453 10ch gray   4.50   .25
    Issued: 5ch, 6/15. 10ch, 10/15.

Asian Economic Seminar, Pyongyang A454

Design: 10ch, Flags, industrial skyline and cogwheel.

1964, June 15   Litho.   Perf. 10¾
524 A454 5ch multicolored   .90   .25
525 A454 10ch multicolored   1.40   .25

Koreans and Statue of Kang Ho Yong, War Hero A455

1964, June 25
526 A455 10ch multicolored   1.60   .25
Korean Reunification

Domestic Poultry — A456

Designs: 2ch, Chickens. 4ch, White chickens. 5ch (No. 529), Black chickens. 5ch (No. 530), Varicolored chickens. 40ch, Helmet guineafowl.

1964, Aug. 5
527-531 A456 Set of 5   7.75 2.00

9th Winter Olympic Games, Innsbruck A457

Designs: 5ch, Skier. 10ch (No. 533), Slalom skier. 10ch (No. 534), Speed skater.

1964, Aug. 5
532-534 A457 Set of 3   4.50   .50

Flags & "Tobolsk," Repatriation Ship — A458

Welcoming Repatriates A459

1964, Aug. 13
535 A458 10ch multicolored   2.50   .25
536 A459 30ch multicolored   2.50   .25
5th anniversary of agreement for the repatriation of Korean nationals in Japan.

Thonggun Pavilion, Uiju — A460

Inphung Pavilion, Kanggye City — A461

1964, Aug. 22   Engr.   *Perf. 12½*
With Gum

537	A460	5ch black violet	.75	.25
538	A461	10ch emerald	.90	.25

Korean historic sites.

18th Olympic Games, Tokyo A462

Designs: 2ch, Rifleman. 5ch, Cyclists, vert. 10ch (No. 541), Runner. 10ch (No. 542), Wrestlers, vert.. 40ch, Volleyball, vert.

Photo, Centers Litho
1964, Sept. 5   *Perf. 10¾*

539-543	A462	Set of 5	5.50 1.00

Nos. 539-543 exist imperf. Value, $18 unused, $5 canceled.

Sinking of the *General Sherman*, 1866 A463

1964, Sept. 28   Engr.   *Perf. 12½*
With Gum

544	A463	30ch red brown	6.00 .50

Kim Il Sung & Guerrilla Fighters A464

Kim Il Sung Speaking to Peasants A465

Battle of Xiaowangqing — A466

1964, Sept. 28   Engr.   *Perf. 12½*
With Gum

545	A464	2ch brt violet	.65	.25
546	A465	5ch blue	1.00	.25
547	A466	10ch grnsh black	1.10	.25
		Nos. 545-547 (3)	2.75	.75

Revolutionary paintings.

Kwangju Students' Uprising, 35th Anniv. A467

1964, Oct. 15   With Gum

548	A467	10ch blue violet	2.25 .25

Weight Lifter — A468   Runner — A469

Boxers A470

Soccer Goalie A471

GANEFO Emblem A472

1964, Oct. 15   Litho.   *Perf. 10¾*

549	A468	2ch multicolored	.65	.25
550	A469	5ch multicolored	.65	.25
551	A470	5ch multicolored	.65	.25
552	A471	10ch multicolored	1.40	.25
553	A472	10ch multicolored	1.10	.25
		Nos. 549-553 (5)	4.45	1.25

1st Games of New Emerging Forces (GANEFO), Djakarta, Indonesia, 1963.
Nos. 549-553 exist imperf. Value, $12 unused, $5 canceled.

Wild Animals A473

Animals: 2ch, Lynx. 5ch, Leopard cat. 10ch (No. 556), Yellow-throated marten. 10ch (No. 559), Leopard.

1964, Nov. 20   Engr.   *Perf. 12½*
With Gum

554-557	A473	Set of 4	14.50 1.00

Fighting South Vietnam A474

1964, Dec. 20   Litho.   *Perf. 10¾*

558	A474	10ch multicolored	1.40	.25

Support for North Vietnam.

Prof. Kim Bong Han A475

"Bonghan" Duct — A476

"Bonghan" Corpuscle A477

1964, Dec. 20   Photo.   *Perf. 10¾*

559	A475	2ch olv grn & brown	1.00	.25
560	A476	5ch multicolored	1.40	.25
561	A477	10ch multicolored	2.00	.25
		Nos. 559-561 (3)	4.40	.75

Kyongrak Biological System.

Technical Revolution — A478

Ideological Revolution — A479

Cultural Revolution — A480

1964, Dec. 30   Litho.

562	A478	5ch multicolored	.30	.25
563	A479	10ch multicolored	.55	.25
564	A480	10ch multicolored	.55	.25
		Nos. 562-564 (3)	1.40	.75

Ideological, Technical and Cultural Revolutions in the Countryside.

"For Arms" A481

1964, Dec. 30   Engr.   *Perf. 12½*
With Gum

565	A481	4ch brown	1.10	.25

Revolutionary painting.

Consumer Goods — A482

Livestock Breeding A483

"All for the Grand Chollima March" — A484

1964, Dec. 30   Litho.   *Perf. 10¾*

566	A482	5ch multicolored	1.60	.25
567	A483	10ch multicolored	1.60	.25
568	A484	10ch multicolored	1.10	.25
		Nos. 566-568 (3)	4.30	.75

Seven-Year Plan.
No. 566 was issued with gum, Nos. 567 and 568 without gum.
Nos. 566-568 also exist imperf. Value, unused $100.

Battle of Luozigou A485

Battle of Fusong County Seat A486

Battle of Hongqihe A487

1965, Jan. 20   Engr.   *Perf. 12½*
With Gum

569	A485	10ch dp slate green	1.10	.25
570	A486	10ch deep violet	1.10	.25
571	A487	10ch slate violet	1.10	.25
		Nos. 569-571 (3)	3.30	.75

Guerrilla warfare against Japan 1934-1940.

Tuman River A488

Taedong River — A489

Amnok River A490

1965, Feb. 27   Litho.   *Perf. 10¾*

572	A488	2ch multicolored	.85 .25
573	A489	5ch multicolored	3.25 .25
574	A490	10ch multicolored	1.40 .25
		Nos. 572-574 (3)	5.50 .75

Korean rivers.

1st Congress of the Union of Agricultural Working People of Korea — A491

1965, Mar. 25   With Gum

575	A491	10ch multicolored	1.60 .25

Furnacemen, Workers — A492

1965, Mar. 25   With Gum

576	A492	10ch multicolored	1.10 .25

Ten Major Tasks of Seven-Year Plan.

Sinhung Colliery A493

Tanchou A494

1965, Mar. 31   Engr.   *Perf. 12½*
With Gum

577	A493	10ch olive black	1.90 .25
578	A494	40ch violet	1.90 .25

35th anniversary of workers' uprisings.

Sunhwa River Works A495

1965, Mar. 31   Litho.   *Perf. 10¾*
With Gum

579	A495	10ch multicolored	.85 .25

A496

South Korean Uprising of April 19, 5th Anniv. — A497

1965, Apr. 10   With Gum

580	A496	10ch multicolored	.85 .25
581	A497	40ch multicolored	1.40 .25

Nos. 580-581 exist imperf. Value, $5 unused.

Construction of Pyongyang Thermal Power Station A498

1965, Apr. 10   With Gum

582	A498	5ch dp brn & lt blue	2.10 .25

No. 582 exists imperf. Value, $5 unused.

1st Afro-Asian Conf., Bandung, 10th Anniv. — A499

1965, Apr. 18   With Gum

583	A499	10ch multicolored	.95 .25

Crowd Rejoicing — A500

Japanese Koreans Demonstrating for Reunification — A501

1965, Apr. 27   Photo.   With Gum

584	A500	10ch blue & red	1.10 .25
585	A501	40ch multicolored	1.40 .25

10th Anniv. of the General Association of Koreans in Japan.
    Nos. 584-585 exist imperf. Value, $25 unused.

Workers Demonstrating — A502

1965, May 10   Engr.   *Perf. 12½*
With Gum

586	A502	10ch brown	2.75 .25

35th Anniv. of General Strike at Pyongyang Rubber Goods Factory.

Workers in Battle — A503

Korean & African Soldiers A504

1965, June 20   Photo.   *Perf. 10¾*
With Gum

587	A503	10ch multicolored	1.75 .25
588	A504	40ch multicolored	3.25 .30

2nd Asian-African Conference, Algiers (subsequently canceled).
    Nos. 587-588 exist imperf. Value, $18 unused.

Victory-64 10-Ton Truck — A505

1965, June 20   Engr.   *Perf. 12½*
With Gum

589	A505	10ch grnsh blue	2.50 .25

Kim Chang Gol A506

Jo Kun Sil A507

An Hak Ryong A508

1965, June 20   With Gum

590	A506	10ch slate	.85 .25
591	A507	10ch red brown	.85 .25
592	A508	40ch violet	2.75 .30
		Nos. 590-592 (3)	4.45 .80

War heroes.
See Nos. 775-777 and 827-830.

Postal Ministers' Conference, Peking A509

1965, June 20   Photo.   *Perf. 10¾*
With Gum

593	A509	10ch red, yel & blk	2.25 .30

Lake Samil A510

Jipson Peak A511

Kwanum Waterfalls A512

1965, June 20   Litho.   With Gum

594	A510	2ch multicolored	.95 .25
595	A511	5ch multicolored	1.60 .25
596	A512	10ch multicolored	4.50 .25
		Nos. 594-596 (3)	7.05 .75

Diamond Mountain Scenery.
    Nos. 594-596 exist imperf. Value, unused $100.

Kusimuldong — A513

Lake Samji A514

1965, June 20   Photo.   With Gum

597	A513	5ch slate blue	.85 .25
598	A514	10ch grnsh blue	1.10 .25

Revolutionary battle sites.

Soccer Player — A515

Emblem & Stadium — A516

1965, Aug. 1   Litho.   With Gum
599 A515 10ch multicolored   1.60   .25
600 A516 10ch multicolored   1.60   .25
GANEFO Games, Pyongyang. Nos. 599-600 exist imperf, with gum. Value, $20 unused.

Liberation from Japan, 20th Anniv. — A517

1965, Aug. 15   With Gum
601 A517 10ch multicolored   1.10   .25

Friedrich Engels, 145th Anniv. Birth — A518

1965, Sept. 10   Engr.   Perf. 12½
With Gum
602 A518 10ch brown   .55   .25

Sports — A519

Designs: 2ch, Pole vault. 4ch, Javelin. 10ch (No. 605), Discus. 10ch (No. 606), High jump. 10ch (No. 607), Shot put.

1965, Sept. 24   Litho.   Perf. 11
With Gum
603-607 A519 Set of 5   4.50   1.00
Nos. 603-607 exist imperf, without gum. Value $18 unused.

Korean Workers' Party, 20th Anniv. — A520

Designs: No. 608, 10ch, Korean fighters. No. 609, 10ch, Party emblem. No. 610, 10ch, Lenin & Marx. No. 611, 10ch, Workers marching. No. 612, 10ch, Soldiers & armed workers. No. 613, 40ch, Workers.

1965, Oct. 10   Photo.   Perf. 13X13½
With Gum
608-613 A520   Set of 6   11.00   5.00
613a A520   Block of 6, #608-613   55.00   25.00
613b   Souvenir sheet of 6, #608-613   600.00   400.00

Chongjin Steel Mill A521

Kim Chaek Iron Works A522

1965, Nov. 25   Engr.   Perf. 12½
With Gum
614 A521 10ch deep violet   5.50   .25
615 A522 10ch sepia   5.50   .25

Rainbow Trout — A523

Dolly Trout — A524

Grass Carp — A525

Carp — A526

Manchurian Trout — A527

Crucian Carp — A528

1965, Dec. 10   Photo.   Perf. 13½
With Gum
616 A523 2ch multicolored   .85   .25
617 A524 4ch multicolored   1.00   .25
618 A525 10ch multicolored   2.25   .25
619 A526 10ch multicolored   2.25   .25

620 A527 10ch multicolored   2.25   .25
621 A528 40ch multicolored   3.75   .50
Nos. 616-621 (6)   12.35   1.75
Freshwater fishes. Nos. 616-621 exist imperf, without gum. Value $20 unused.

House Building — A529

Hemp Weaving — A530

Blacksmith A531

Wrestling A532

School — A533

Dance — A534

1965, Dec. 15   Engr.   Perf. 12½
With Gum
622 A529 2ch green   .70   .25
623 A530 4ch maroon   1.40   .25
624 A531 10ch violet   1.75   .25
625 A532 10ch carmine red   2.00   .25
626 A533 10ch blue   1.25   .25
627 A534 10ch brown   1.10   .25
Nos. 622-627 (6)   8.20   1.50
Paintings by Kim Hong Do, 18th century Korean artist.

Students' Extracurricular Activities A535

Designs: 2ch, Children in workshop. 4ch, Boxing. 10ch (No. 630), Playing violin. 10ch (No. 631), Chemistry lab.

1965, Dec. 15   Litho.   Perf. 13¼
With Gum
628-631 A535   Set of 4   3.00   .50
Nos. 628-631 exist imperf. Value, unused $75.

Whaler A536

Service Vessel A537

1965, Dec. 15   Engr.   Perf. 12½
With Gum
632 A536 10ch deep blue   1.90   .25
633 A537 10ch slate green   1.90   .25
Korean fishing boats.

Black-capped Kingfisher — A538

Korean Great Tit — A539

Blue Magpie A540

White-faced Wagtail A541

Migratory Korean Grosbeak A542

Perf. 11, 13½ (#640)
1965, Dec. 30   Litho.   With Gum
634 A538 4ch pale yel & multi   2.50   .25
635 A539 10ch pale salmon & multi   3.25   .25
636 A540 10ch pale grnsh blue & multi   3.25   .25
637 A541 10ch yel & multi   3.25   .25
638 A542 40ch pale yel grn & multi   9.50   .85
Nos. 634-638 (5)   21.75   1.85
Korean birds. Nos. 634-638 exist imperf, without gum. Value $27.50 unused.

Korean sericulture — A543

Designs: 2ch, Silkworm moth & cocoon. No. 640, 10ch, Ailanthus silk moth. No. 641, 10ch, Chinese Oak silk moth.

1965, Dec. 30   Engr.   Perf. 12½
With Gum
639-641 A543 Set of 3   100.00   3.00

Hooded Crane — A544

Japanese White-necked Crane — A545

Manchurian Crane — A546

Gray Heron — A547

1965, Dec. 30   **With Gum**
642 A544 2ch olive brown   3.25 .25
643 A545 10ch dp vio blue   3.75 .40
644 A546 10ch slate purple   3.75 .40
645 A547 40ch slate green   6.50 .70
    Nos. 642-645 (4)   17.25 1.75

Wading birds. For surcharge, see No. 4540.

Mollusks A548

Designs: 5ch, Japanese common squid. 10ch, Giant Pacific octopus.

1965, Dec. 31   **Litho.**   *Perf. 11*
    With Gum
646-647 A548   Set of 2   5.50 .40

Nos. 646-647 exist imperf, without gum. Value $8 unused.

Korean Ducks — A549

Designs: 2ch, Spotbill. 4ch, Ruddy shelduck. 10ch, Mallard. 40ch, Baikal teal.

1965, Dec. 31   **Litho.**   *Perf. 11*
    With Gum
648-651 A549   Set of 4   16.50 2.00

Nos. 648-651 exist imperf. Value $30 unused.

Circus, Pyongyang — A550

Trapeze Performers A551

Balancing Act — A552

Seesawing A553

Tightrope Walker — A554

1965, Dec. 31   **Photo.**
652 A550 2ch multicolored   .85 .25
653 A551 10ch multicolored   2.25 .25
654 A552 10ch multicolored   2.25 .25
655 A553 10ch multicolored   2.25 .25
656 A554 10ch multicolored   2.25 .25
    Nos. 652-656 (5)   9.85 1.25

Korean acrobatics.
Nos. 652-655 were issued with gum, No. 656 without gum.

Korean Flowers — A555

Designs: No. 657, 4ch, Marvel-of-Peru. No. 658, 10ch, Peony (violet background). No. 659, 10ch, Moss rose (yellow background). No. 660, 10ch, Magnolia (light blue background).

1965, Dec. 31   **Litho.**
657-660 A555   Set of 4   13.00 1.00

No. 657 was issued without gum, Nos. 658-60 with gum.
Nos. 657-660 exist imperf, without gum. Value $20 unused.

Yachts — A556

Designs: No. 661, 2ch, Finn Class. No. 662, 10ch, Dragon Class (blue background). No. 663, 10ch, 5.5 Class (violet background). No. 664, 40ch, Star Class.

1965, Dec. 31   **With Gum**   *Perf. 13½*
661-664 A556   Set of 4   6.50 2.00

Nos. 661-664 exist imperf, without gum. Value $10 unused.
10ch depicting Netherlands class yacht, with blue background, not issued. Value $750.

1st Congress of the Org. of Solidarity of Peoples of Asia, Africa and Latin America — A557

1966, Jan. 3   **With Gum**   *Perf. 11*
665 A557 10ch multicolored   .55 .25

Hosta — A558

Dandelion — A559

Lily of the Valley — A560

Pink Convolvulus A561

Catalpa Blossom — A562

1966, Jan. 15   **With Gum**
666 A558 2ch multicolored   1.40 .25
667 A559 4ch multicolored   1.40 .25
668 A560 10ch multicolored   1.90 .25
669 A561 10ch multicolored   1.90 .25
670 A562 40ch multicolored   6.00 .75
    Nos. 666-670 (5)   12.60 1.75

Korean wildflowers.
Imperfs exist, without gum. Value, $25 unused.

Primrose — A563

Brillian Campion — A564

Amur Pheasant's Eye — A565

Orange Lily — A566

Rhododendron A567

1966, Feb. 10   **With Gum**
671 A563 2ch multicolored   1.10 .25
672 A564 4ch multicolored   1.10 .25
673 A565 10ch multicolored   1.60 .25
674 A566 10ch multicolored   1.60 .25
675 A567 90ch multicolored   7.75 1.00
    Nos. 671-675 (5)   13.15 2.00

Korean wildflowers.

Land Reform Law, 20th Anniv. — A568

1966, Mar. 5   **With Gum**
676 A568 10ch multicolored   1.00 .25

Battle of Jiansanfen A569

Battle of Taehongdan — A570

Battle of Dashahe A571

1966, Mar. 25   **Engr.**   *Perf. 12½*
677 A569 10ch violet brown   .65 .25
678 A570 10ch dp blue green   .65 .25
679 A571 10ch brown carmine   .65 .25
    Nos. 677-679 (3)   1.95 .75

Battles of the anti-Japanese revolution.
No. 678 was issued without gum, the other values with gum.

Art Treasures of the Silla Dynasty — A572

Designs: 2ch, Covered bowl. 5ch, Jar. 10ch, Censer.

1966, Apr. 30   **With Gum**
680-682   A572   Set of 3   5.00   .60

Labor Day, 80th Anniv. — A573

1966, May 1   **Litho.**   **Perf. 11**
        With Gum
683   A573   10ch multicolored   .85   .25

Assoc. for the Restoration of the Fatherland, 30th Anniv. — A574

1966, May 5   **Photo.**   **With Gum**
684   A574   10ch brn red & yel   .85   .25

Farmer A575

Worker A576

1966, May 30   **Litho.**   **With Gum**
685   A575   5ch multicolored   .55   .25
686   A576   10ch multicolored   .85   .25

Young Pioneers, 20th Anniv. A577

1966, June 6   **With Gum**
687   A577   10ch multicolored   .85   .25

Kangson Steel Works A578

Pongung Chemical Works A579

1966, June 10   **Engr.**   **Perf. 12½**
        With Gum
688   A578   10ch gray   5.50   .25
689   A579   10ch deep red   5.50   .25
     Korean Factories.

Fish — A580

Designs: 2ch, Saury. 5ch, Pacific cod. No. 692, Chum salmon. No. 693, Mackerel. 40ch, Pink salmon.

1966, June 10   **Photo.**   **Perf. 11**
690-694   A583   Set of 5   16.50   5.00
    Nos. 690-692 were issued with gum, Nos. 693-694 without gum.
    Nos. 690-694 exist imperf, without gum. Value, $22, either unused or cancelled.

Prof. Kim Bong Han & Kyongrak Biological System — A581

1966, June 30   **Photo.**   **With Gum**
695-702   Set of 8   6.50   1.60
702a   A581   Block of 8, #695-702   12.00   9.00
702b   A581   Souvenir sheet of 8, #695-702   125.00   100.00

Voshkod 2 A582

Luna 9 A583

Luna 10 A584

1966, June 30
703   A582   5ch multicolored   .35   .25
704   A583   10ch multicolored   1.10   .30
705   A584   40ch multicolored   1.90   .40
     Nos. 703-705 (3)   3.35   .95
     Space Flight Day.
    Nos. 703-705 exist imperf. Value, $8 unused.

Jules Rimet Cup A585

Dribbling A586

Goal-keeper A587

1966, July 11   **Litho.**
706   A585   10ch multicolored   1.90   .25
707   A586   10ch multicolored   1.90   .25
708   A587   10ch multicolored   1.90   .25
     Nos. 706-708 (3)   5.70   .75
     World Cup Championship.
    Nos. 706-708 exist imperf. Value, $20 unused.

Battle of Naphalsan A588

Battle of Seoul A589

Battle of Height 1211 A590

1966, July 27   **Engr.**   **Perf. 12½**
        With Gum
709   A588   10ch red violet   .85   .25
710   A589   10ch deep green   .85   .25
711   A590   10ch violet   .85   .25
     Nos. 709-711 (3)   2.55   .75
     Korean War of 1950-53.

Sex Equality Law, 20th Anniv. A591

1966, July 30   **Litho.**   **Perf. 11**
        With Gum
712   A591   10ch multicolored   .85   .25

Nationalization of Industry, 20th Anniv. — A592

1966, Aug. 10   **With Gum**
713   A592   10ch multicolored   1.10   .25

Water Jar Dance — A593

Bell Dance — A594

Dancer in Mural Painting — A595

Sword Dance — A596

Golden Cymbal Dance — A597

1966, Aug. 10
714   A593   5ch multicolored   1.60   .25
715   A594   10ch multicolored   2.75   .25
716   A595   10ch multicolored   2.75   .25
717   A596   15ch multicolored   2.75   .25
718   A597   40ch multicolored   5.00   .30
     Nos. 714-718 (5)   14.85   1.30
     Korean Folk Dances.
    5ch and 10ch issued with or without gum. Other values issued without gum.
    Nos. 714-718 exist imperf, without gum. Value, $20 unused.

Attacking U.S. Soldier — A598

Worker with Child — A599

Industrialization A600

1966, Aug. 15   **Engr.**   **Perf. 12½**
        With Gum
719   A598   10ch deep green   1.40   .25
720   A599   10ch red violet   1.40   .25
721   A600   10ch violet   6.50   .45
     Nos. 719-721 (3)   9.30   .95
     Korean Reunification Campaign.

Crop-spraying — A601

Observing Forest Fire — A602

Geological Survey — A603

Fish
Shoal
Detection
A604

1966, Sept. 30   Photo.   Perf. 11

722	A601	2ch multicolored	.55	.25
723	A602	5ch multicolored	7.75	.25
724	A603	10ch multicolored	1.90	.25
725	A604	40ch multicolored	1.90	.25
		Nos. 722-725 (4)	12.10	1.00

Industrial uses of aircraft.
2ch, 5ch issued without gum. 10ch, 40ch issued with gum.
Nos. 722-725 exist imperf, without gum. Value, $20 unused.

A three-value set honoring revolutionary fighters, with designs similar to types A334-A339, was prepared but not issued. Value $3,500.

Kim Il Sung University, 20th
Anniv. — A605

1966, Oct. 1   Engr.   Perf. 12½
With Gum

| 726 | A605 | 10ch slate violet | .90 | .25 |

Imperforate Stamps
Imperforate varieties are without gum, unless otherwise noted.

1st Asian
GANEFO
Games
A606

Designs: a, 5ch, Judo. b, 10ch, Basketball. c, 10ch, Table tennis.

1966, Oct. 30   Litho.   Perf. 11

| 727 | A606 | Strip of 3, #a-c | 2.25 | .60 |
| | | Strip of 3, #a-c imperf | 50.00 | — |

Scarlet
Finch — A607

Hoopoe — A608

Korean
Crested
Lark — A609

Brown Thrush
A610

White-bellied
Black Woodpecker
A611

1966, Oct. 30

730	A607	2ch multicolored	2.50	.25
731	A608	5ch multicolored	2.75	.25
732	A609	10ch multicolored	3.25	.30
733	A610	10ch multicolored	3.25	.30
734	A611	40ch multicolored	6.50	.80
		Nos. 730-734 (5)	18.25	1.90
		Set of 5, imperf	35.00	

Korean birds. For surcharge, see No. 4513.

Construction — A612

Machine-Tool Production — A613

Worker
&
Graph
A614

Miners
A615

1966, Nov. 20

735	A612	5ch multicolored	.35	.25
736	A613	10ch multicolored	.60	.25
737	A614	10ch multicolored	.60	.25
738	A615	40ch multicolored	1.90	.40
		Nos. 735-738 (4)	3.45	1.15

Propaganda for increased production.
Nos. 735-737 issued with gum. No. 738 issued without gum.

Parachuting — A616

Show
Jumping
A617

Motorcycling — A618

Telegraphists' Competition — A619

1966, Nov. 30   Engr.   Perf. 12½
With Gum

739	A616	2ch dark brown	.95	.25
740	A617	5ch org vermilion	.70	.25
741	A618	10ch dp violet blue	3.25	.30
742	A619	40ch deep green	2.25	.25
		Nos. 739-742 (4)	7.15	1.05

National Defense sports.

Samil Wolgan Magazine, 30th
Anniv. — A620

1966, Dec. 1   Photo.   Perf. 11
743 A620 10ch multicolored   — —

Korean
Deer — A621

Designs: 2ch, Red deer. 5ch, Sika deer. No. 746, 10ch, Reindeer (grazing). No. 747, 10ch, Japanese sambar (erect). 70ch, Fallow deer.

1966, Dec. 20   Litho.
744-748 A627 Set of 5   20.00 5.00
            Imperf, #744-748

No. 747 was issued with gum. Other values issued without gum. For surcharge, see No. 4560.

Wild
Fruit — A622

Designs: 2ch, Blueberries. 5ch, Pears. 10ch (No. 751), Plums. 10ch (No. 752), Schizandra. 10ch (No. 753), Raspberries. 40ch, Jujube.

1966, Dec. 30

| 749-754 | A622 | Set of 6 | 6.50 | 1.00 |
| | | Imperf, #749-754 | 14.00 | |

Samson
Rocks — A623

Ryonju
Pond — A624

Jinju
Pond — A625

The Ten Thousand Rocks, Manmulsang A626

1966, Dec. 30   **Litho.**   *Perf. 11*

755	A623	2ch multicolored	1.10	.25
756	A624	4ch multicolored	4.50	.25
757	A625	10ch multicolored	1.10	.25
758	A626	10ch multicolored	4.50	.25
		Nos. 755-758 (4)	11.20	1.00

Diamond Mountains scenery.
Nos. 755-758 are inscribed "1964" but were actually issued in 1966.
2ch and 4ch issued without gum. 10ch values issued with gum.

Onpo A627

Myohyang — A628

Songdowon — A629

Hongwon A630

1966, Dec. 30   **Engr.**   *Perf. 12½*
With Gum

759	A627	2ch blue violet	.50	.25
760	A628	4ch turquoise green	.55	.25
761	A629	10ch dp blue green	.90	.25
762	A630	40ch black	1.60	.35
		Nos. 759-762 (4)	3.55	1.10

Korean rest homes.

Korean People's Army, 19th Anniv. A631

1967, Feb. 8   **Photo.**   *Perf. 11*

763	A631	10ch multicolored	.85	.25

Livestock Farming A632

Designs: 5ch, Sow. 10ch, Goat. 40ch, Bull.

1967, Feb. 28   **Litho.**

764-766	A632	Set of 3	7.50	1.75
		Imperf, #764-766	55.00	—

5ch, 10ch issued without gum. 40ch issued both with and without gum.

Battle of Pochonbo, 30th Anniv. — A633

1967, Feb. 28   **Photo.**   **With Gum**

767	A633	10ch multicolored	.85	.25

Universal Compulsory Technical Education A634

1967, Apr. 1

768	A634	10ch multicolored	.85	.25

29th World Table Tennis Championships, Pyongyang — A635

10ch, 40ch designs similar to 5ch.

1967, Apr. 11   **Litho.**

769-771	A635	Set of 3	3.50	.60
		Imperf, #769-771	100.00	—

5ch issued with or without gum. 10ch, 40ch issued without gum. For surcharge, see No. 4514.

People Helping Guerrillas, Wangyugou — A636

Blowing Up Railway Bridge A637

Shooting Down Japanese Plane A638

1967, Apr. 25   **Engr.**   **With Gum**

772	A636	10ch deep violet	.55	.25
773	A637	10ch dk vio brown	4.50	.25
774	A638	10ch slate	.55	.25
		Nos. 772-774 (3)	5.60	.75

Paintings of the guerrilla war against Japan.

Ri Tae Hun A639

Choe Jong Un A640

Kim Hwa Ryong A641

1967, Apr. 25   **With Gum**

775	A639	10ch slate	1.10	.25
776	A640	10ch reddish violet	3.25	.25
777	A641	10ch ultramarine	1.10	.25
		Nos. 775-777 (3)	5.45	.75

Heroes of the Republic.

Labor Day A642

1967, May 1   **Litho.**

778	A642	10ch multicolored	.80	.25

Pre-School Education — A643

Designs of children: 5ch, Learning to count. 10ch, Making model tractor. 40ch, Playing with ball.

1967, June 1

779-781	A643	Set of 3	4.00	.60

Victory Monument, Battle of Pochonbo — A644

1967, June 4

782	A644	10ch multicolored	1.10	.25

Military Sculpture A645

Designs: 2ch, Soldier attacking tank. 5ch, Soldiers with musical instruments. 10ch, Soldier in heroic pose. 40ch, Soldier and child.

1967, June 25   **Photo.**

783-786	A645	Set of 4	3.25	.80

2ch issued with or without gum. Other values issued without gum.

Medicinal Plants — A646

Designs: 2ch, Polygonatum japonicum. 5ch, Abelmoschus manihat. 10ch (No. 789), Rehmannia glutinosa (olive yellow). 10ch (No. 790), Scutellaria baicalensis (turquoise blue background). 10ch (No. 791), Pulsatilla koreana (violet blue). 40ch, Tanacetum boreale.

1967, July 20   **Photo.**

787-792	A646	Set of 6	12.50	1.20

Nos. 787-789, 791 issued with or without gum. Nos. 790, 792 issued without gum.

Korean People's Army — A647

Designs: 5ch, Aviator, sailor, soldier. 10ch (No. 794), Officer decorating soldier. 10ch (No. 795), Soldier and farmer.

1967, July 25

793-795	A647	Set of 3	1.60	.50

5ch issued with or without gum. 10ch values issued without gum.

Freighter "Chollima" A648

1967, July 30   **Engr.**   **With Gum**

796	A648	10ch deep green	1.90	.25

Drilling Rock — A649

Felling
Trees — A650

Reclaiming Tideland — A651

1967, Aug. 5
797 A649 5ch black brown   .65   .25
798 A650 10ch blue green   .90   .25
799 A651 10ch slate   1.25   .25
  Nos. 797-799 (3)   2.80   .75
  Revolutionary paintings.
5ch issued without gum. 10ch values issued with gum.

Crabs
A652

Designs: 2ch, Erimaculus isenbeckii. 5ch, Neptunus trituberculatus. 10ch, Paralithodes camtschatica. 40ch, Chionoecetes opilio.

1967, Aug. 10   Photo.
800-803 A652 Set of 4   8.75 1.00

Reunification of Korea
Propaganda — A653

1967, Aug. 15   Litho.
804 A653 10ch multicolored   4.00   .40

A five-value set, featuring details from famous Korean paintings of the 15th-16th centuries, was prepared for release in August, 1967, but was not issued. Value $2,500.
A 10ch stamp celebrating the 10th anniversary of the launch of the first USSR space satellite was prepared for release on Sept. 10 but was not issued. Value $1,500.

Waterfalls
A654

Designs: 2ch, Tongrim waterfalls 10ch, Sanju waterfall, Mt. Myohyang. 40ch, Sambang waterfall, Mt. Chonak.

1967, Oct. 10
805-807 A654 Set of 3   13.00   .80
  2ch issued with or without gum. 10ch, 40ch issued without gum.

"For Fresh Great Revolutionary
Upsurge" — A655

Designs: 5ch, Ship, train and truck. 10ch (No. 809), Machine industry. 10ch (No. 810), Truck, bulldozer, tractor and farmers. 10ch (No. 811), Construction machinery, buildings. 10ch (No. 812), Chollima flying horse and banners.

1967, Nov. 1   Engr.
808-812 A655 Set of 5   11.00 1.00

Russian Revolution, 50th
Anniv. — A656

1967, Nov. 7   Photo.
813 A656 10ch Multicolored   1.10   .25

Korean Elections — A657

Designs: 10ch (No. 814), Voters and flags. 10ch (No. 815), Woman casting ballot (vert.)

1967, Nov. 23   Litho.
814-815 A657 Set of 2   1.40   .40

Raptors
A658

Designs: 2ch, Black vulture. 10ch, Rough-legged buzzard. 40ch, White-tailed eagle.

1967, Dec. 1   Photo.
816-818 A658 Set of 3   16.00 2.00
  2ch issued with or without gum. 10ch, 40ch issued without gum. For surcharge, see No. 4512.

Chongjin — A659

Hamhung — A660

Sinuiju
A661

1967, Dec. 20   Engr.   With Gum
819 A659 5ch bronze green   1.10   .25
820 A660 10ch violet   1.10   .25
821 A661 10ch red violet   1.10   .25
  Nos. 819-821 (3)   3.30   .75
  Korean cities.

Whaler
Firing
Harpoon
A662

With or Without Gum
1967, Dec. 30
822 A662 10ch ultramarine   2.50   .30

Soldier
with
Red
Book
A663

Soldier Mounting Bayonet — A664

Worker and Bayoneted Rifle — A665

Litho or Photo (#829)
1967, Dec. 30
823 A663 10ch multicolored   .55   .25
824 A664 10ch multicolored   .55   .25
825 A665 10ch multicolored   .55   .25
  Nos. 823-825 (3)   1.65   .75

Korean People's Army, 20th
Anniv. — A666

Designs: a, Airman, soldier and sailor. b, Soldier, battle in background. c, Soldier & KDPR arms. d, Soldier & flag. e, Soldier with Red Book. f, Three soldiers, North Korean flag. g, Soldier & worker. h, Soldier saluting. i, Soldier attacking. j, Soldier, sailor & airman beneath flag.

1968, Feb. 3   Litho.
826 A666 Sheet of 10   80.00 30.00
  a.-j.   10ch, any single   .45   .25

Ri Su Bok (1934-51) — A667

Han Kye Ryol (1926-51) — A668

1968, Feb. 10   Engr.   With Gum
827 A667 10ch dark rose   550.00
828 A667 10ch light violet   .55   .25
829 A668 10ch dark green   550.00
830 A668 10ch lt blue violet   .55   .25
  Nos. 827-830 (4)   1,101.   .50
  War heroes.
Nos. 827 and 829 were prepared but not issued.

Apartment Building,
Pyongyang — A669

1968, Mar. 5   Litho.   With Gum
831 A669 10ch bright blue   .85   .25

Kim Il
Sung, 56th
Birthday
A670

1968, Apr. 15   With Gum
832 A670 40ch multicolored   1.10   .40
  Printed in sheets of four stamps.
Exists in a miniature sheet of one, which is rare (2 examples reported).

Kim Il Sung's Family Home in
Mangyongdae — A671

Leaving Home at Age 13 — A672

Mangyong Hill — A673

Kim Il Sung with Father — A674

Kim Il Sung with Mother — A675

1968, Apr. 15

833	A671	10ch multicolored	.65	.25
834	A672	10ch multicolored	.65	.25
835	A673	10ch multicolored	.65	.25
836	A674	10ch multicolored	.65	.25
837	A675	10ch multicolored	.65	.25
		Nos. 833-837 (5)	3.25	1.25

Childhood of Kim Il Sung.
See Nos. 883-887, 927-930.

Dredger 2
September
A676

1968, June 5

838	A676	5ch green	1.60	.25
839	A676	5ch blue	850.00	600.00

Matsutake
Mushroom
A677

Shiitake
Mushroom — A678

Meadow
Mushroom
A679

1968, Aug. 10   Photo.   With Gum

840	A677	5ch multicolored	22.50	.60
841	A678	10ch multicolored	45.00	1.00
842	A679	10ch multicolored	45.00	1.00
		Nos. 840-842 (3)	112.50	2.60

Founding of the Korean Democratic
People's Republic, 20th Anniv. — A680

Designs: a, Statue of national arms. b,
North Korean flag. c, Worker, peasant & flag.
d, Soldier & flag. e, Flying Horse of Chollima. f,
Soldiers & tanks. g, Battle scene. h, Workers,
banner & monument.

1968, Sept. 2   Litho.   With Gum

843	A680	Block of 8, #a.-h.	45.00	40.00
	a.-h.	10ch, any single	1.40	.25

Kaesong
Students'
and
Children's
Palace
A681

1968, Oct. 5   With Gum

844	A681	10ch greenish blue	.55	.25

Domestic
Goods — A682

Designs: 2ch, Shopper with domestic items.
5ch, Textile manufacturing. 10ch, Cannery.

1968, Nov. 5   Photo.   With Gum

845-847	A688	Set of 3	2.75	.60

Kim Il
Sung's 10-
Point
Program
A683

Design: 10ch, Two soldiers, Red Book,
horiz.

1968, Dec. 5   Litho.

848-849	A683	Set of 2	1.10	.25

Increasing Agricultural
Production — A684

Designs: 5ch, Woman carrying eggs. 10ch
(No. 851), Woman harvesting wheat. 10ch
(No. 852), Woman holding basket of fruit.

1968, Dec. 10   Photo.   With Gum

850-852	A684	Set of 3	1.40	.50

Shellfish
A685

Designs: 5ch (No. 853), Scallop. 5ch (No.
854), Clam. 10ch, Mussel.

1968, Dec. 20   With Gum

853-855	A685	Set of 3	6.50	.50

Details of Battle of Pochonbo Victory
Monument — A686

Designs (all 10ch): No. 856, Kim Il Sung at
head of columns, vert. No. 857, shown. No.
858, Figures marching to right, green sky at
right (42.75x28mm). No. 859, Figures marching to left (55.5x28mm). No. 860, Figures
marching to right (55.5x28mm). No. 861,
Figures marching to left, sky at right
(42.75x28mm). No. 862, Figures marching
to left, sky at left (42.75x28mm).

1968, Dec. 30

856-862	A686	Set of 7	3.75	1.40

Grand Theater, Pyongyang — A687

1968, Dec. 30

863	A687	10ch dark brown	1.10	.25

Revolutionary Museum,
Pochonbo — A688

1968, Dec. 30

864	A688	2ch dark green	.55	.25

Rural Technical Development — A689

Designs: 2ch, Irrigation. 5ch, Mechanization
of agriculture. 10ch, Electrification. 40ch,
Mechanical fertilization and spraying.

1969, Feb. 25

865-868	A689	Set of 4	2.50	.80

Rabbits
A690

Designs: 2ch, Gray rabbits. 10ch (No. 870),
White rabbits. 10ch (No. 871), Black rabbits.
10ch (No. 872), Brown rabbits. 40ch, White
rabbits.

1969, Mar. 10

869-873	A690	Set of 5	11.00	1.25

Nos. 869-873 were issued both with and
without gum.

Public
Health
A691

Designs: 2ch, Old man & girl. 10ch, Nurse
with syringe. 40ch, Doctor with woman & child.

1969, Apr. 1

874-876	A691	Set of 3	4.50	.60

Farm Machines — A692

Designs: 10ch (No. 877), Rice sower. 10ch
(No. 878), Rice harvester. 10ch (No. 879),
Herbicide sprayer. 10ch (No. 880), Wheat &
barley thresher.

1969, Apr. 10   Engr.

877-880	A692	Set of 4	3.50	.80

Mangyongdae — A693

Ponghwa — A694

1969, Apr. 15   Litho.

881	A693	10ch multicolored	1.90	.25
882	A694	10ch multicolored	1.90	.25

Revolutionary historical sites.

Early Revolutionary Years of Kim Il
Sung — A695

Designs (all 10ch): No. 883, Kim crossing
into Manchuria 1926, aged 13. No. 884, Kim
talking to four students around table (blue
green frame). No. 885, Kim speaking outdoors

to Young Communist League meeting (apple green frame). No. 886, Kim speaking to Young Communist League meeting indoors (lilac frame). No. 887, Kim leading demonstration against teachers (peach frame).

1969, Apr. 15
883-887 A695 Set of 5   3.25 1.00
No. 884 was issued with gum. The other values were issued without gum.

Kang Pan Sok (1892-1932), Mother of Kim Il Sung — A696

Designs (all 10ch): No. 888, Birthplace at Chilgol. No. 889, Resisting Japanese police in home. No. 890, Meeting with women's revolutionary association.

1969, Apr. 21   Photo.
888-890 A696 Set of 3   4.50 .60

Bivouac Sites in War against Japan — A697

Designs: 5ch, Pegaebong. 10ch (No. 892), Mupho, horiz. 10ch (No. 893), Chongbong. 40ch, Konchang, horiz.

1969, Apr. 21
891-894 A697 Set of 4   3.00 .80

Chollima Statue — A698

1969, May 1
895 A698 10ch blue   .85 .25

Poultry A699

Designs: 10ch (No. 896), Mangyong chickens. 10ch (No. 897), Kwangpho ducks.

1969, June 1   Engr.
896-897 A699 Set of 2   5.75 .50

Socialist Education System — A700

Designs: 2ch, Kim Il Sung & children. 10ch, Student & worker with books. 40ch, Male & female students, figure "9."

1969, June 1   Photo.
898-900 A700 Set of 3   2.25 .60

Pochonbo Battlefield Memorials — A701

Designs: 5ch, Machine gun platform on mountainside. 10ch (No. 902), Statue of Kim Il Sung, vert. 10ch (No. 903), Aspen Tree monument (stele & enclosed tree trunk). 10ch (No. 904), Konjang Hill monument (within forest).

1969, June 4
901-904 A701 Set of 4   2.25 .80

Kim Hyong Jik (1894-1926), Father of Kim Il Sung — A702

Designs: 10ch (No. 905), Teaching at Myongsin School. 10ch (No. 906), Outdoor meeting with five other members of Korean National Association.

1969, July 10
905-906 A702 Set of 2   1.90 .40

A 10ch stamp honoring the Juvenile Chess Game of Socialist Countries was prepared for release Aug. 5, 1969, but was not issued. Value $1,000.

Sports Day, 20th Anniv. — A703

1969, Sept. 10
907 A703 10ch multicolored   1.10 .25

Korean Revolution Museum, Pyongyang A704

1969, Sept. 10   Litho.
908 A704 10ch dk blue green   .85 .25

Pres. Nixon Attacked by Pens — A705

1969, Sept. 18   Litho.
909 A705 10ch multi   3.25 .25
Anti-U.S. Imperialism Journalists' Conference, Pyongyang.

Implementation of the 10-Point Program — A706

Designs: 5ch, Soldiers, battle. 10ch (No. 911), Globe, bayonets attacking dismembered U.S. soldier. 10ch (No. 912), Workers holding Red Books & slogan, vert.

1969, Oct. 1   Photo.
910-912 A706 Set of 3   3.25 .60

Reunification of Korea — A707

Designs: 10ch (No. 913), Kim Il Sung, marching workers. 10ch (No. 914), Worker & soldier bayoneting U.S. soldier. 50ch, Armed workers in battle, horiz.

1969, Oct. 1   Litho.
913-915 A707 Set of 3   1.60 .60

Refrigerator-Transport Ship "Taesongsan" — A708

1969, Dec. 20   Engr.
916 A708 10ch slate purple   1.40 .25

Korean Fishes A709

Designs: 5ch, Yellowtail. 10ch, Dace. 40ch, Mullet.

1969, Dec. 20   Photo.
917-919 A709 Set of 3   6.00 .60

Guerrilla Conference Sites A710

Designs: 2ch, Dahuangwai, 1935. 5ch, Yaoyinggou, 1935 (log cabin). 10ch, Xiaohaerbaling, 1940 (tent).

1970, Feb. 10
920-922 A710 Set of 3   1.40 .45

Mt. Paektu, Birthplace of the Revolution — A711

Views of Mt. Paektu (all 10ch): No. 923, Lake Chon (dull green, tan, black). No. 924, Janggun Peak (pale peach, dull blue, black). No. 925, Piryu Peak (dull yellow, blue green, black). No. 926, Pyongsa Peak (brown orange, blue, red violet).

1970, Mar. 10
923-926 A711 Set of 4   2.75 .60
See Nos. 959-961.

Support for North Vietnam — A712

1970, Mar. 10
927 A712 10ch multicolored   .65 .25

Revolutionary Activities of Kim Il Sung — A713

Designs (all 10ch): No. 928, Receiving his father's pistols from his mother. No. 929, Receiving smuggled pistols from his mother (other young revolutionaries present). No. 930, Kim speaking with four farmers in field. No. 931, Kim speaking at Kalun meeting.

1970, Apr. 15   Litho.
928-931 A713 Set of 4   5.50 .90

Lenin Birth Centenary A714

Design: 10ch (No. 933), Lenin with cap, in three-quarter profile.

1970, Apr. 22   Photo.
932-933 A714 Set of 2   1.60 .40

Assoc. of Koreans in Japan, 15th Anniv. — A715

Designs (both 10ch): No. 934, Red. No. 935, Maroon.

1970, Apr. 27   Engr.
934-935 A715 Set of 2   1.40 .40

Worker-Peasant Red Guard — A716

Design: 10ch (No. 936), Factory worker in uniform, vert.

1970, May 5   **Photo.**
936-937 A716 Set of 2   1.10   .40

Peasant Education — A717

Designs: 2ch, Students & newspapers. 5ch, Peasant reading book. 10ch, Students in class.

1970, June 25
938-940 A717 Set of 3   1.60   .45

Army Electrical Engineer A718

1970, June 25
941 A718 10ch purple brown   .85   .25

Month of the Campaign for Withdrawal of U.S. Troops from South Korea — A719

Design: 10ch, Soldier & partisan.

1970, June 25
942-943 A719 Set of 2   1.50   .25

Anti-U.S., South Korea Propaganda — A720

1970, June 25   **Engr.**
944 A720 10ch deep violet   .65   .25

Campaign for Increased Productivity A721

Designs (all 10ch): No. 945, Quarryman. No. 946, Steelworker. No. 947, Machinist. No. 948, Worker with bag. No. 949, Construction worker. No. 950, Railway flagman.

1970, Sept. 10   **Photo.**
945-950 A721 Set of 6   4.50   1.20

Workers' Party Program A722

Designs: 5ch, Peasant, farm scene. 10ch, Steelworker. 40ch, Soldiers.

1970, Oct. 5   **Engr.**
951-953 A722 Set of 3   4.00   .50

Korean Workers' Party, 25th Anniv. — A723

1970, Oct. 10   **Photo.**
954 A723 10ch multicolored   .85   .25

5th Korean Workers' Party Congress — A724

Issued in miniature sheet of 10, with one 40ch value (No. 955a) and nine 10ch values. Designs: a, Kim Il Sung, marchers. b, Family & apartment buildings. c, Soldier with Red Book. d, Soldier with binoculars, various weapons. e, Steelworker. f, Workers killing U.S. soldier. g, Farmers. h, Students. i, Schoolgirl with Red Book, atomic energy symbol. j, Cooperation with South Korean guerillas.

1970, Nov. 2   **Litho.**
955   Sheet of 10, #a.-j.   900.00
   a.-i.   A724 Any single   1.40   .50
   j.   A724 10ch   600.00

Soon after release, a design error was discovered on No. 955j, and this stamp was removed from souvenir sheets remaining in stock, usually with the bottom selvage. This is the form in which this set is commonly offered. Value, $25. The full sheet of 10 is scarce.

League of Socialist Working Youth of Korea, 25th Anniv. — A725

1971, Jan. 17   **Photo.**
956 A725 10ch multicolored   .55   .25

Nanhutou Conference, 35th Anniv. — A726

1971, Feb. 28
957 A726 10ch multicolored   .55   .25

Land Reform Law, 25th Anniv. A727

1971, Mar. 5
958 A727 2ch multicolored   .55   .25

Mt. Paektu, Second Issue — A728

Designs: 2ch, Mountainscape. 5ch, Paektu Waterfalls, vert. 10ch, Western Peak.

1971, Mar. 10
959-961 A728 Set of 3   5.00   .60

Revolutionary Museums — A729

Designs (all 10ch): No. 962, Mangyongdae (red orange & ultramarine). No. 963, Phophyong (yellow & brown). No. 964, Junggang (salmon & green).

1971, Apr. 1
962-964 A729 Set of 3   1.60   .60

Coal Production 6-Year Plan — A730

1971, Apr. 1
965 A730 10ch multicolored   .85   .25

Revolutionary Activities of Kim Il Sung — A731

Designs (all 10ch): No. 966, Portrait, vert. No. 967, Kim addressing crowd at guerrilla base camp. No. 968, Kim speaking with children on hillside. No. 969, Kim reviewing Anti-Japanese Guerrilla Army 1932.

1971, Apr. 15   **Litho.**
966-969 A731 Set of 4   3.25   .80

May Day — A732

1971, May 1   **Photo.**
970 A732 1w multicolored   3.75   .40

Association for the Restoration of the Fatherland, 35th Anniv. — A733

1971, May 5
971 A733 10ch multicolored   .85   .25

Battles in the Musan Area Command (1939) — A734

Designs: 5ch, Sinsadong Monument. 10ch, Taehongdan Monument, with encased machine guns, horiz. 40ch, Musan headquarters (log cabins in forest), horiz.

1971, May 23
972-974 A734 Set of 3   2.25   .60

Koreans in Japan A735

1971, May 25
975 A735 10ch chocolate   .65   .25

A 10ch stamp commemorating the Asia-Africa Invitational Table Tennis Game for Friendship was prepared for release on May 27, 1971, but was not issued. Value $750.

Korean Children's Union, 25th Anniv. — A736

1971, June 6
976 A736 10ch multicolored   .55   .25

6th Congress, League of Socialist Working Youth of Korea — A737

Designs: 5ch, Marchers & banners. 10ch, Marchers, banners & globe with map of Korea.

1971, June 21
977-978 A737 Set of 2   1.10   .25

Labor Law,
25th Anniv.
A738

1971, June 24
979 A738 5ch multicolored   .60   .25

Sex Equality
Law, 25th
Anniv.
A739

1971, July 30
980 A739 5ch multicolored   .60   .25

Universal Compulsory Primary
Education, 15th Anniv. — A740

1971, Aug. 1
981 A740 10ch multicolored   .70   .25

South Korean Revolutionaries — A741

Designs: 5ch, Choe Yong Do (1923-69).
10ch (No. 983), Kim Jong Thae (1926-69),
portrait with rioters killing U.S. soldier. 10ch
(No. 984), Guerrilla fighter with machine gun &
Red Book, battle scene.

1971, Aug. 1
982-984 A741 Set of 3   1.40   .45

Nationalization of Industry, 25th
Anniv. — A742

1971, Aug. 10
985 A742 5ch multicolored   2.75   .25

Anti-Imperialist, Anti-U.S.
Struggle — A743

Designs: 10ch (No. 986), N. Korean soldier,
U.S. prisoners. 10ch (No. 987), S. Korean
guerrilla fighter. 10ch (No. 988), N.
Vietnamese soldiers, map. 10ch (No. 989),
Cuban soldier, map. 10ch (No. 990), African
guerrilla fighters, map. 40ch, six soldiers of
various nationalities bayoneting dismembered
U.S. soldier.

1971, Aug. 12
986-991 A743 Set of 6   5.00 1.00

Kim Il Sung
University,
25th Anniv.
A744

1971, Oct. 1
992 A744 10ch multicolored   .55   .25

Large
Machines — A745

Designs: 2ch, 6,000-ton press. 5ch, Refrig-
erated cargo ship "Ponghwasan." 10ch (No.
995), Sungrisan heavy truck. 10ch (No. 996),
Bulldozer.

1971, Nov. 2   Litho.
993-996 A745 Set of 4   6.50   .50

Tasks of the 6-Year Plan — A746

Designs (all 10ch): No. 997, Workers & text
on red field. No. 998, Mining. No. 999, Consumer goods. No. 1000, Lathe. No. 1001,
Construction equipment. No. 1002, Consumer
electronic products. No. 1003, Grains, farming. No. 1004, Railway track, transportation.
No. 1005, Freighter. No. 1006, Hand with
wrench, manufacturing scenes. No. 1007,
Crate & export goods on dock.

1971, Nov. 2   Photo.
997-1007 A746 Set of 11   14.50 1.75

Cultural Revolution — A747

Designs: 2ch, Technical students, university.
5ch, Mechanic. 10ch (No. 1010), Chemist.
10ch (No. 1011), Composer at piano. 10ch
(No. 1012), Schoolchildren.

1971, Nov. 2
1008-1012 A747 Set of 5   4.50   .40

Ideological Revolution — A748

Designs (all 10ch): No. 1013, Workers with
Red Books, banners. No. 1014, Worker with
hydraulic drill. No. 1015, Two workers reading
Red Book. No. 1016, Workers' lecture.

1971, Nov. 2
1013-1016 A748 Set of 4   2.50   .40

Improvement in Living
Standards — A749

1971, Nov. 2
1017 A749 10ch multicolored   .60   .25

Solidarity with
International
Revolutionary
Forces — A750

Designs (all 10ch): No. 1018, Revolutionary
placards being driven into U.S. soldier. No.
1019, Japanese militarists being hammered
by mallet. No. 1020, Bayoneted rifles held
aloft. No. 1021, Armed international revolutionaries advancing, horiz.

1971, Nov. 2
1018-1021 A750 Set of 4   3.25   .50

6-Year Plan — A751

1971, Nov. 2
1022 A751 10ch multicolored   1.75   .25

Three sets were prepared for release
on Nov. 2, 1971, but were not issued:
Butterflies (3 stamps), value $2,500;
Korean Reunification (2 10ch stamps),
value $750; Cultural Revolu-
tion/Improvement of the People's Living
Standards (7 10ch stamps), value
$5,000.

Samil Wolgan
Monthly, 35th
Anniv. — A752

1971, Dec. 1
1023 A752 10ch multicolored   1.10   .25

Domestic Printings
Sometime in the early 1970s, the
DPRK post office begin to produce
separate printings of some issues for
domestic use. These stamps were
generally printed on poorer quality
white or brownish unsurfaced papers
and demonstrated poorer overall production values. Serious students of
the period are now working to identify
just which stamps exist in this form
and how to easily distinguish them
from the higher-quality printings
intended for sale to foreign collectors.
At this time, these domestic-use
printings are generally sold for $5-
$20 per stamp.

Poultry Breeding — A753

Designs: 5ch, Chicks. 10ch, Chickens &
automated henhouse. 40ch, Eggs, canned
chicken, dead chickens hanging on hooks.

1972, Feb. 1
1024-1026 A753 Set of 3   2.25   .60

War
Films
A754

Designs (all 10ch): No. 1027, Man &
woman, from *Vintage Shrine*. No. 1028, Guerrilla bayoneting soldier in back, from *The Fate
of a Self-Defense Corps Member*. No. 1029,
Young woman with a pistol, from *Sea of Blood*.

1972, Apr. 1
1027-1029 A754 Set of 3   3.75   .30
A 10ch value picturing *The Flower Girl* was
prepared but not issued. Value $2,000.

Kim Il
Sung
A755

Kim at Military Conference — A756

Kim by Lake Chon — A757

Various portraits of Kim Il Sung: No. 1030,
shown. No. 1031, In heroic pose. No. 1032,
shown. No. 1033, In wheatfield. No. 1034, In
factory. No. 1035, With foundry workers. No.
1036, Aboard whaling ship. No. 1037, Visiting
hospital. No. 1038, Visiting fruit farm. No.
1039, With railroad surveyors. No. 1040, With
women workers. No. 1041, Sitting with villagers. No. 1042, Touring chicken plant. No.
1043, On park bench with children. No. 1044,
Portrait with marchers.

1972, Apr. 15   Litho.
1030 A755 5ch multicolored   .25   .25
  a.   Strip of 3, #1030-1031,
       1044   2.25

1031	A755	5ch multicolored	.25 .25
1032	A756	5ch multicolored	.25 .25
a.		Pair, #1032, 1043	1.10
1033	A756	10ch multicolored	.50 .25
a.		Block of 10, #1033-1042	10.00
1034	A756	10ch multicolored	2.25 .40
1035	A756	10ch multicolored	.25 .25
1036	A756	10ch multicolored	.65 .25
1037	A756	10ch multicolored	1.00 .25
1038	A756	10ch multicolored	.25 .25
1039	A756	10ch multicolored	2.25 .25
1040	A756	10ch multicolored	1.40 .25
1041	A756	10ch multicolored	.25 .25
1042	A756	10ch multicolored	.45 .25
1043	A756	10ch multicolored	.60 .25
1044	A756	1wn multicolored	.90 .40
		Nos. 1030-1044 (15)	11.50 4.05

Souvenir Sheet

1045	A757	3wn multicolored	10.00 6.00

60th birthday of Kim Il Sung. Nos. 1030-1031 and 1044, 1032 and 1043, and 1033-1042, respectively, were printed setenant within their sheets.

A 4-stamp set (2ch, 5ch, 10ch and 15ch values) honoring the 20th Olympic Games were prepared but not issued. Value $3,000.

Guerrilla Army, 40th Anniv. — A758

1972, Apr. 25   Photo.
1046 A758 10ch multicolored   .95 .25

Revolutionary Sites — A759

Designs: 2ch, Ryongpho. 5ch, Onjong. 10ch, Kosanjin. 40ch, Jonsung.

1972, July 27   Litho.
1047-1050 A759 Set of 4   2.25 .50

Olympic Games, Munich A760

Designs: 2ch, Volleyball. 5ch, Boxing, horiz. 10ch (No. 1053), Judo. 10ch (No. 1054), Wrestling, horiz. 40ch, Rifle-shooting.

1972, Oct. 1
1051-1055 A760 Set of 5   3.75 1.00

Chollima Street, Pyongyang — A761

Designs (street scenes): 5ch, salmon & black. 10ch (No. 1057), dull yellow & black. 10ch (No. 1058), green & black.

1972, Nov. 1
1056-1058 A766 Set of 3   5.50 .85

Resource Management — A762

Designs: 5ch, Dredging river. 10ch, Forest conservation. 40ch, Tideland reclamation.

1972, Nov. 1   Photo.
1059-1061 A762 Set of 3   2.75 .35

6-Year Plan - Metallurgical — A763

Designs (all 10ch): No. 1062, Sheet metal, ingots, smelters. No. 1063, Pipes, foundry.

1972, Nov. 1
1062-1063 A763 Set of 2   3.75 .35

6-Year Plan — Mining Industry — A764

Designs (all 10ch): No. 1064, Iron ore. No. 1065, Coal.

1972, Nov. 1   Litho.
1064-1065 A764 Set of 2   4.50 .45

Three Major Goals of the Technical Revolution — A765

Designs (all 10ch): No. 1066, Agricultural mechanization. No. 1067, Industrial automation. No. 1068, Lightening of women's household chores.

1972, Nov. 2   Photo.
1066-1068 A765 Set of 3   3.25 .45

6-Year Plan - Machine-Building — A766

Designs (all 10ch): No. 1069, Machine tools. No. 1070, Electronics & automation tools. No. 1071, Single-purpose machines.

1972, Nov. 2   Photo.
1069-1071 A766 Set of 3   2.75 .45

6-Year Plan — Chemical Industry — A767

Designs (all 10ch): No. 1072, Chemical fertilizers, herbicides, insecticides. No. 1073, Tire, tubing, various chemical products.

1972, Nov. 2
1072-1073 A767 Set of 2   2.25 .35

6-Year Plan — Light Industry — A768

Designs (all 10ch): No. 1074, Clothing, textiles. No. 1075, Clothing, kitchenware. No. 1076, Household Goods.

1972, Nov. 2
1074-1076 A768 Set of 3   2.75 .45

6-Year Plan - Rural Economy — A769

Designs (all 10ch): No. 1077, Irrigating field. No. 1078, Bulldozers levelling field. No. 1079, Applying chemical fertilizer.

1972, Nov. 2   Litho.
1077-1079 A769 Set of 3   2.50 .45

6-Year Plan - Transportation — A770

Designs (all 10ch): No. 1080, Electric train. No. 1081, New railway construction. No. 1082, Coastal & river transport.

1972, Nov. 2
1080-1082 A770 Set of 3   6.50 .45

6-Year Plan - Military — A771

Designs (all 10ch): No. 1083, Soldier with artillery shell. No. 1084, Navy gunner. No. 1085, Air Force pilot in cockpit.

1972, Nov. 2
1083-1085 A771 Set of 3   4.50 .45

6-Year Plan - Food Storage — A772

Designs (all 10ch): No. 1086, Food Processing. No. 1087, Packing foodstuffs. No. 1088, Food storage (radishes, fruit, fish).

1972, Nov. 2   Photo.
1086-1088 A772 Set of 3   8.25 .45

Struggle for Reunification of Korea — A773

Designs (all 10ch): No. 1089, South Koreans with banners praising Kim Il Sung. No. 1090, S. Korean guerrillas killing U.S. & S. Korean soldiers. No. 1091, March of armed S. Korean workers. No. 1092, S. Koreans rioting, rioters on top of U.S. tank. No. 1093, N. Koreans demonstrating in support of S. Korean revolutionaries. No. 1094, International revolutionaries condemning U.S. soldier. No. 1095, S. Korean marchers carrying banner & Red Book.

1972, Nov. 2
1089-1095 A773 Set of 7   11.00 1.00

A 10ch anti-United States propaganda stamp was prepared for release Nov. 2, 1972, but not issued. Value $750.

Machine Tools A774

Designs: 5ch, Single-axis automatic lathe. 10ch, Kusong-3 lathe. 40ch, 2,000-ton crank press.

1972, Dec. 1   Litho.
1096-1098 A774 Set of 3   2.75 .45

National Elections A775

Designs (both 10ch): No. 1099, Voter with registration card. No. 1100, Voter casting ballot.

1972, Dec. 12   Photo.
1099-1100 A775 Set of 2   1.90 .30

Korean People's Army, 25th
Anniv. — A776

Designs: 5ch, Soldier. 10ch, Sailor. 40ch,
Pilot.

1973, Feb. 8
1101-1103 A781 Set of 3   3.75   .75

Mangyongdae Historic Sites — A777

Scenes from Kim Il Sung's childhood: 2ch,
Wrestling site. 5ch, "Warship" rock. 10ch (No.
1106), Swinging tree, vert. 10ch (No. 1107),
Sliding rock. 40ch, Fishing spot on riverside.

1973, Apr. 15
1104-1108 A777 Set of 5   4.50 1.00

Mansu Hill
Monument
A778

Designs: 10ch (No. 1109), Anti-Japanese
revolutionary monument. 10ch (No. 1110),
Socialist Revolution & Construction monument. 40ch, Statue of Kim Il Sung. 3w, Korean
Revolution Museum, hrz.

1973, Apr. 15   Litho.
1109-1112 A778 Set of 4   13.00 2.25

Secret Revolutionary Camps in the
1932 Guerrilla War — A780

Designs: 10ch (No. 1113), Karajibong
Camp. 10ch (No. 1114), Soksaegoi Camp.

1973, Apr. 26
1113-1114 A780 Set of 2   1.40   .25

Anti-Japanese Propaganda — A781

1973, June 1
1115 A781 10ch multicolored   .55   .25

Reunification of
Korea — A782

Designs: 2ch, Finger pointing down at
destroyed U.S. tanks. 5ch, Electric train, crane
lifting tractor. 10ch (No. 1118), Hand holding
declaration, map of Korea. 10ch (No. 1119),
Leaflets falling on happy crowd. 40ch, Flag &
globe.

1973, June 23
1116-1120 A782 Set of 5   6.50   .75

Trucks &
Tractors
A783

Designs: 10ch (No. 1121), Trucks. 10ch (No.
1122), Bulldozer, tractors.

1973, July 1   Photo.
1121-1122 A783 Set of 2   1.60   .30

Socialist
Countries'
Junior Women's
Volleyball
Games — A784

1973, July 27   Litho.
1123 A784 10ch multicolored   1.10   .25

North
Korean
Victory
in the
Korean
War
A785

Designs: 10ch (No. 1124), Triumphant N.
Koreans & battlefield scene. 10ch (No. 1125),
N. Koreans & symbols of military & industrial
power.

1973, July 27   Photo.
1124-1125 A785 Set of 2   3.25   .30

Mansudae Art Troupe — A786

Dances: 10ch, *Snow Falls*, dancers with red
streamers. 25ch, *Bumper Harvest of Apples*.
40ch, *Azalea of the Fatherland*.

1973, Aug. 1   Litho.
1126-1128 A786 Set of 3   4.50   .75

Compulsory
Secondary
Education,
10th Anniv.
A787

1973, Sept. 1
1129 A787 10ch multicolored   .85   .25

Writings of Kim Il Sung — A788

Designs (all 10ch): No. 1130, *On Juche in
Our Revolution* (claret scene). No. 1131, *Kim Il
Sung Selected Works*, crowd holding glowing
book aloft. No. 1132, *Let Us Further
Strengthen Our Socialist System*, four figures
holding open book aloft.

1973, Sept. 1
1130-1132 A788 Set of 3   1.90   .30
          See Nos. 1180-1181.

DPRK, 25th
Anniv.
A789

Designs: 5ch, Foundation of the republic
("1948-1973"). 10ch, Korean War ("1950-
1953"). 40ch, Farmer, worker & soldier with
scenes of economic development in background ("1948-1973").

1973, Sept. 9
1133-1135 A789 Set of 3   2.75   .60

Mt. Myohyang Scenes — A790

Designs: 2ch, Popwang Peak. 5ch, Inhodae
Rock. 10ch, Taeha Falls, vert. 40ch, Ryongyon
Falls, vert.

1973, Oct. 1   Photo.
1136-1139 A790 Set of 4   8.25   .75

Party Founding Museum — A791

1973, Oct. 10
1140 A791 1w multicolored   2.25   .45

People's
Athletic
Meeting
A792

Designs: 2ch, Soccer player, basketball
players. 5ch, High jumper, women sprinters.
10ch (No. 1143), Wrestlers, skier. 10ch (No.
1144), Speed skaters, skier. 40ch, Parachutist, motorcyclists.

1973, Nov. 1   Litho.
1141-1145 A792 Set of 5   6.50   .75

Socialist
Countries'
Junior
Weightlifting
Competition
A793

1973, Nov. 21
1146 A793 10ch multicolored   1.40   .25

Moran Hill
Scenery — A794

Designs: 2ch, Chongryu Cliff. 5ch, Moran
Waterfalls. 10ch, Pubyok Pavilion. 40ch, Ulmil
Pavilion.

1973, Nov. 1
1147-1150 A794 Set of 4   9.25 1.00

Mt. Kumgang
Scenery
A795

Designs: 2ch, Mujigae (Rainbow) Bridge.
5ch, Suspension bridge, Okryu Valley, horiz.
10ch (No. 1153), Chonnyo Peak. 10ch (No.
1154), Chilchung Rock & Sonji Peak, horiz.
40ch, Sujong & Pari Peaks, horiz.

1973, Nov. 1
1151-1155 A795 Set of 5   8.25 1.00

Magnolia
A796

1973, Nov. 1
1156 A796 10ch multicolored   2.25   .40

South Korean
Revolutionary
Struggle — A797

Designs (both 10ch): No. 1157, Mob beating
U.S. soldier. No. 1158, Armed demonstrators
killing U.S. soldier.

1973, Nov. 2   **Photo.**
1157-1158 A797   Set of 2   5.25   .30

Scenes from *Butterflies and Cock*
Fairy Tale — A798

Designs: 2ch, Cock appearing in the village
of butterflies. 5ch, Butterflies discussing how to
repel cock. No. 1161, 10ch, Cock chasing
butterflies with basket. No. 1162, 10ch, Butterflies luring cock up cliff. 40ch, Cock chasing
butterflies off cliff edge. 90ch, Cock drowning.

1973, Dec. 1   **Litho.**
1159-1164 A798   Set of 6   17.50   1.20
For surcharge, see No. 4556.

Revolutionary Sites — A799

Designs: 2ch, Buildings, Yonphung. 5ch,
Buildings, iron-rail fence, Hyangha. 10ch,
Three buildings surrounding courtyard,
Changgol. 40ch, Monuments in park-like set-
ting, Paeksong.

1973, Dec. 1
1165-1168 A799   Set of 4   3.25   .60

Modern Buildings in
Pyongyang — A800

Designs: 2ch, Science Library, Kim Il Sung
University. 5ch, Building No. 2, Kim Il Sung
University, vert. 10ch, War Museum. 40ch,
People's Palace of Culture. 90ch, Pyongyang
Indoor Stadium.

1973, Dec. 1   **Photo.**
1169-1173 A800   Set of 5   4.00   1.00
Nos. 1171-1172 are 60x24mm.

Socialist Constitution of North
Korea — A801

Designs (all 10ch): No. 1174, Socialist Constitution, national scenes. No. 1175, Marchers
with Red Book & national arms. No. 1176,
Marchers with Red Books, national flag,
banners.

1973, Dec. 27   **Litho.**
1174-1176 A801   Set of 3   1.60   .60

Korean
Songbirds
A802

Designs: 5ch, Great reed warbler. 10ch (No.
1178), Gray starling (green background). 10ch
(No. 1179), Daurian starling (pink
background).

1973, Dec. 28   **Photo.**
1177-1179 A802   Set of 3   14.50   2.00

Writings
of Kim Il
Sung
A803

Designs: No. 1180, 10ch, *Let Us Intensify
the Anti-Imperialist, Anti-U.S. Struggle*, bayonets threatening U.S. soldier. No. 1181, 10ch,
*On the Chollima Movement and the Great
Upsurge of Socialist Construction*, Chollima
statue.

1974, Jan. 10   **Litho.**
1180-1181 A803   Set of 2   1.60   .30

Opening of Pyongyang Metro — A804

Designs (all 10ch): No. 1182, Train at platform. No. 1183, Escalators. No. 1184, Underground station hall.

1974, Jan. 20
1182-1184 A804   Set of 3   2.75   .45

Socialist Construction — A805

Designs (all 10ch): No. 1185, Capital con-
struction. No. 1186, Industry (foundry), vert.
No. 1187, Agriculture. No. 1188, Transport.
No. 1189, Fishing industry.

1974, Feb. 20
1185-1189 A805   Set of 5   6.50   1.00

*Theses on the Socialist Rural
Question in Our Country,* 10th Anniv.
of Publication — A806

1974, Feb. 25
1190 A806 10ch Strip of 3, #a-c   2.75   .50

Farm
Machines
A807

Designs: 2ch, Compost sprayer. 5ch, *Jonjin*
tractor. 10ch, *Taedoksan* tractor (with flat bed).

1974, Feb. 25   **Photo.**
1193-1195 A807   Set of 3   3.25   .45

N. Korean
Victories at
1973 Sports
Contests
A808

Designs: 2ch, Archery (Grenoble). 5ch,
Gymnastics (Varna). 10ch, Boxing
(Bucharest). 20ch, Volleyball (Pyongyang).
30ch, Rifle-shooting (Sofia). 40ch, Judo (Tbi-
lisi). 60ch, Model aircraft flying (Vienna), horiz.
1.50w, Table tennis (Beijing), horiz.

Perf. 11, 12 (#1196, 1202-1203)
1974, Mar. 10   **Litho.**
1196-1203 A808   Set of 8   11.00   2.00
For surcharges, see Nos. 4562, 4564, 4600.

D.P.R.K.: World's First Tax-Free
Country — A809

1974, Apr. 1   *Perf. 11*
1204 A809 10ch multicolored   1.10   .25

Revolutionary Activities of Kim Il
Sung — A810

Designs (all 10ch): No. 1205, Kim at
Nanhutou Meeting (in log room). No. 1206,
Kim writing the 10-Point Program in forest. No.
1207, Kim instructing revolutionary (sitting on
bench, outdoor winter scene). No. 1208, Kim
at Battle of Laoheishan.

1974, Apr. 15   *Perf. 12*
1205-1208 A810   Set of 4   3.00   .60

Scenes from the Revolutionary Opera
The Flower Girl — A811

Designs: 2ch, Kkot Pun's blind younger sister. 5ch, Death of Kkot Pun's mother. 10ch,
Kkot Pun resists landlord. 40ch, Kkot Pun setting out on the road of revolution.

1974, Apr. 30
1209-1212 A811   Set of 4   12.00   .60
Souvenir Sheet
1213 A811 50ch multicolored   16.50   1.50
No. 1213 contains one larger 50ch value,
depicting Kroi Pun (The Flower Girl) and the
flowers of Revolution, imperf.

Pyongyang Zoo, 15th Anniv. — A812

A813

Designs: 2ch, Wildcat. 5ch, Lynx. No. 1216,
10ch, Fox. No. 1217, 10ch, Wild boar. 20ch,
Wolf. 40ch, Bear. 60ch, Leopard. 70ch,
Korean tiger. 90ch, Lion.
No. 1223: a, 10ch, Wildcat. b, 30ch, Lynx. c,
50ch, Leopard. d, 60ch, Tiger.

1974, May 10   *Perf. 11*
1214-1222 A812   Set of 9   14.50   2.50
Souvenir Sheet
1223 A813   Sheet of 4, imperf   60.00   —
For surcharges, see Nos. 4541, 4579.

Wild
Roses — A814

Designs: 2ch, Prickly wild rose. 5ch, Yellow
sweet briar. 10ch (No. 1226), Pink aromatic
rose. 10ch (No. 1227), Aronia sweet briar (yellow centers). 40ch, Rosa rugosa.

1974, May 20
1224-1228 A814   Set of 5   8.25   1.00

Souvenir Sheet

Kim Il Sung with Children — A815

1974, June 1   *Imperf*
1229 A815 1.20w multicolored   8.25   7.50

Wild Flowering
Plants — A816

Designs: 2ch, Chinese trumpet vine. 5ch,
Day lily. 10ch, Shooting star lily. 20ch, Tiger
lily. 40ch, Azalea. 60ch, Yellow day lily.

1974, May 20   *Perf. 11*
1230-1235 A816 Set of 6   8.25 1.00

Universal Postal Union, Cent. — A817

U.P.U. emblem and: 10ch, Letter carrier and
construction site. 25ch, Chollima statue. 40ch,
World map & airplanes.

1974, June 30   *Perf. 12*
1236-1238 A817 Set of 3   6.00 .50

A 60ch souvenir sheet was prepared but not
issued. Value $750. For surcharge, see No.
4567.

Amphibians — A818

Designs: 2ch, Black spotted frog. 5ch, Oriental fire belly toad. 10ch, North American bull
frog. 40ch, Common toad.

1974, July 10   *Perf. 11*
1239-1242 A818 Set of 4   15.50 1.50

For surcharge, see No. 4542.

Soviet Space Flights — A819

Designs: 10ch, Electron 1 & 2. 20ch, Proton
1. 30ch, Venera 3. 40ch, Venera 5 & 6. 50ch,
Launch of Chinese satellite Chicomsat 1. 1w,
Space flight of dogs "Bjelka" and "Strjelka."

1974, July 10
1243-1246 A819 Set of 4   3.75 .60
Souvenir Sheets
Imperf
1247 A819 50ch multicolored   8.25 1.00
1248 A819 1w multicolored   18.50 3.00

Nos. 1247-1248 each contain one
47x72mm stamp.

Korean Paintings — A820

Designs: 2ch, Woman in Namgang Village.
5ch, Old Man on the Raktong River
(60x49mm). 10ch, Inner Kumgang in the
Morning. 20ch, Mt. Kumgang (60x49mm).
1.50w, Evening Glow Over Kangson.

1974, July 10
1249-1252 A820 Set of 4   5.75 .75
Souvenir Sheet
Imperf
1253 A820 1.50w multicolored 11.00 10.00

For surcharge, see No. 4592.

Korean
Civil
Aviation
A821

Designs: 2ch, Antonov AN-2. 5ch, Lisunov
LI-2. 10ch, Ilyushin IL-14P. 40ch, Antonov AN-
24. 60ch, Ilyushin IL-18. 90ch, Antonov AN-24.

1974, Aug. 1
1254-1258 A821 Set of 5   9.25 1.75
Souvenir Sheet
Imperf
1259 A821 90ch multicolored 13.00 6.50

No. 1264 contains one 49x30mm stamp.

Alpine
Plants — A822

Designs: 2ch, Rhododendron. 5ch, White
mountain-avens. 10ch, Shrubby cinquefoil.
20ch, Poppies. 40ch, Purple mountain
heather. 60ch, Oxytropis anertii.

1974, Aug. 10   *Perf. 12*
1260-1265 A822 Set of 6   7.00 1.75

Korean Paintings — A823

Designs: 10ch, Sobaek Stream in the Morning. 20ch, Combatants of Mt. Laohei
(60x40mm).. 30ch, Spring on the Terraced
Field. 40ch, Night of Tideland. 60ch,
Daughter.

1974, Aug. 15   *Perf. 11*
1266-1270 A823 Set of 5   12.00 2.00

For surcharge, see No. 4563.

Italian Communist Newspaper L'Unita,
50th Anniv. — A824

1974, Sept. 1   *Imperf*
1271 A824 1.50w multicolored 24.50 5.00

Revolutionary Sites — A825

Designs: 5ch, Munmyong. 10ch, Unha (log
cabin).

1974, Sept. 9   *Perf. 11*
1272-1273 A825 Set of 2   1.40 .25

Oil-producing Crops — A826

Designs: 2ch, Sesame. 5ch, Perilla-oil plant.
10ch, Sunflower. 40ch, Castor bean.

1974, Sept. 30
1274-1277 A826 Set of 4   5.50 1.00

For surcharge, see No. 4543.

Revolutionary Activities of Kim Il
Sung — A827

Designs (all 10ch): No. 1278, Portrait in
guerrilla uniform, vert. No. 1279, On horseback. No. 1280, Helping a farm family. No.
1281, Negotiating anti-Japanese united front
with Chinese commander.

1974, Oct. 10   *Perf. 12*
1278-1281 A827 Set of 4   3.25 .60

No. 1278 is 42x65mm. Nos. 1279-1281 are
52x34.5mm.

Grand Monument on Mansu
Hill — A828

Designs (all 10ch): No. 1282, Soldiers
marching right, lead figure holding rifle aloft.
No. 1283, Soldiers marching left, lead figure
holding rifle aloft. No. 1284, Workers marching
right, lead figure holding torch aloft. No. 1285,

Workers marching left, lead figure holding
torch aloft.

1974, Oct. 10   *Perf. 11*
1282-1285 A828 Set of 4   2.75 .60

Deep-Sea Fishing — A829

Designs: a, 2ch, Factory ship *Chilbosan*. b,
5ch, Factory ship *Paektusan*. c, 10ch, Cargo
ship *Moranbong*. d, 20ch, All-purpose ship. e,
30ch, Trawler. f, 40ch, Stern trawler.

1974, Nov. 20
1286 A829 Block of 6   7.75 2.00
a.-f.   Any single   1.25   .30

A830

Kim Il Sung's Crossing of the Amnok
River, 50th Anniv.

1975, Feb. 3   *Perf. 12*
1287 A830 10ch multicolored   .65   .25

Pak Yong Sun — A831

33rd World Table Tennis
Championships — A832

1975, Feb. 16   *Perf. 11x12*
1288 A831 10ch multicolored   1.90   .25
Souvenir Sheet
Imperf
1289 A832 80ch multicolored   3.25 1.50

Honoring Pak Yong Sun, winner of the 33rd
World Table Tennis Championship, Calcutta.

Pyongyang Zoo — A833

Designs: 10ch (No. 1290), Zebra. 10ch (No. 1291), African buffalo. 20ch, Giant panda, horiz. 25ch, Bactrian camel. 30ch, Indian elephant, horiz.

Perf. 12¼, 10¾ (#1291, 1294)
1975, Feb. 20
1290-1294 A833 Set of 5   6.25 1.00

Koguryo Period Tomb Paintings, 7th Century — A834

Designs: 10ch, Blue dragon. 15ch, White tiger. 25ch, Red phoenix, vert. 40ch, Turtle and snake.

1975, Mar. 20   **Perf. 12**
1295-1298 A834 Set of 4   6.50 1.00

The Guerrilla Base in Spring (1968) — A835

Guerrilla Army Landing at Unggi (1969) — A836

The Sewing Team Members (1961) — A837

North Manchuria of China in Spring (1969) — A838

Comrade Kim Jong Suk Giving Guidance to the Children's Corps Members (1970) — A839

1975, Mar. 30
1299 A835 10ch multicolored   .55   .25
1300 A836 10ch multicolored   .55   .25
1301 A837 15ch multicolored   .85   .25
1302 A838 20ch multicolored   1.75   .25
1303 A839 30ch multicolored   1.40   .25
  Nos. 1299-1303 (5)   5.10 1.25

Korean Paintings, Anti-Japanese Struggle.
Compare with Nos. 1325-1329, 1330-1335.

Cosmonauts' Day — A840

Designs: 10ch, Cosmonaut. 30ch, Lunokhod-2 on Moon, horiz. 40ch, Soyuz and Saiyut coupling, horiz.

1975, Apr. 12   **Perf. 11¾**
1304-1306 A840 Set of 3   3.25   .50

Revolutionary Activities of Kim Il Sung — A841

Multicolor portraits of Kim Il Sung: 10ch (No. 1307), Speaking with troops in tent (aqua frame). 10ch (No. 1308), Greeting peasants bringing supplies (tan frame). 10ch (No. 1309), Speaking to crowd, arm upraised (light blue frame). 10ch (No. 1310), With soldiers around winter campfire (pale tan frame). 10ch (No. 1311), Lecturing to troops (pink frame). 15ch, At head of troop column in forest. 25ch, Standing by lake. 30ch, Speaking with peasants, child in lap. 40ch, Presiding over staff meeting, in tent.

1975, Apr. 15   **Perf. 12**
1307-1315 A841 Set of 9   8.25 2.00

Souvenir Sheet

Victory Monument — A842

1975, Apr. 15   **Imperf**
1316 A842 1w multicolored   16.50 4.00

Battle of Pochonbo, 38th Anniversary.

Flower Basket & Kim Il Sung's Birthplace A843

Kim Il Sung's Birthplace, Mangyongdae — A844

1975, Apr. 15   **Perf. 12**
1317 A843 10ch multicolored   .35   .25
1318 A844 40ch multicolored   1.60   .25

63rd Birthday of Kim Il Sung.

April 19 South Korean Popular Uprising, 15th Anniv. — A845

1975, Apr. 19   **Perf. 11**
1319 A845 10ch multicolored   .65   .25

Ri Dynasty Paintings A846

Designs: 5ch, Kingfisher at Lotus Pond. 10ch, Crabs. 15ch, Rose of Sharon. 25ch, Lotus and Water Bird. 30ch, Tree Peony and Cock and Hen.

1975, May 10
1320-1324 A846 Set of 5   13.00 1.25

On the Road of Advance Southward (1966) A847

The Assigned Post (1968) A848

For the Sake of the Fatherland (1965) — A849

Retaliation (1970) — A850

The Awaited Ranks (1970) — A851

1975, May 10
1325 A847 5ch multicolored   2.25   .25
1326 A848 10ch multicolored   1.25   .25
1327 A849 15ch multicolored   1.90   .25
1328 A850 25ch multicolored   2.75   .25
1329 A851 30ch multicolored   4.50   .25
  Nos. 1325-1329 (5)   12.65 1.25

Korean Paintings, Anti-Japanese Struggle.
For surcharge, see No. 4606.

Blue
Signal
Lamp
(1960)
A852

Pine Tree
(1966)
A853

Night with Snowfall (1963) — A854

Smelters (1968) — A855

Reclamation of Tideland
(1961) — A856

Mt. Paekgum (1966) — A857

1975, May 20

1330	A852	10ch multicolored	1.10	.25
1331	A853	10ch multicolored	3.75	.25
1332	A854	15ch multicolored	1.10	.25
1333	A855	20ch multicolored	1.25	.25

1334	A856	25ch multicolored	1.25	.25
1335	A857	30ch multicolored	1.25	.25
	Nos. 1330-1335 (6)		9.70	1.50

Korean Paintings. For surcharge, see No.
4596.

Chongryon
Assoc. of
Koreans in
Japan, 20th
Anniv. — A858

1975, May 25   **Perf. 11¾**

1336	A858	10ch multicolored	1.10	
1337	A858	3w multicolored	40.00	—

Marathon Race of Socialist
Countries — A859

1975, June 8   **Imperf**

1338	A859	1w multicolored	22.50	4.00

Diving — A860

Divers: 10ch, Man entering water feet-first.
25ch, Man performing somersalt pike. 40ch,
Woman entering water head-first.

1975, June 20   **Perf. 10¾**

1339-1341	A860	Set of 3	3.25	.75

Month of Anti-U.S.
Joint
Struggle — A861

1975, June 25   **Perf. 12¼**

1342	A861	10ch multicolored	1.40	.25

Fresh-Water Fish — A862

Fish: 10ch (No. 1343), Memorial fish, swimming to left. 10ch (No. 1344), White fish, swimming to right. 15ch, Notch-jowl. 25ch, Amur

catfish. 30ch (No. 1347), Catfish, swimming to
right. 30ch (No. 1348), Snakehead, swimming
to left.

1975, June 25   **Perf. 10¾**

1343-1348	A862	Set of 6	9.25	1.25

A863

10th International Socialist Countries'
Junior Friendship Soccer
Tournament — A864

Soccer players, with diff. stadiums in background: 5ch, Green border. 10ch, Tan border.
15ch, Lilac border. 20ch, Pale violet border.
50ch, Dull gold border.

Perf. 10¾, Imperf (#1354)

1975, July 10

1349-1353	A863	Set of 5	4.50	1.00

Souvenir Sheet

1354	A864	1w multicolored	9.25	3.50

Parrots — A865

Parrots: 10ch, Blue & yellow macaw. 15ch,
Sulphur-crested cockatoo. 20ch, Blyth's parakeet. 25ch, Rainbow lory. 30ch, Budgerigar.

1975, July 10   **Perf. 12**

1355-1359	A865	Set of 5	19.50	1.50

For surcharge, see No. 4581.

Saesallim
Street
A866

Apartment
House — A867

Pothonggang Hotel — A868

1975, July 20   **Perf. 11, 12 (#1360)**

1360	A866	90ch multicolored	20.00	20.00
1361	A867	1w multicolored	25.00	25.00
1362	A868	2w multicolored	35.00	35.00
	Nos. 1360-1362 (3)		80.00	80.00

New street, buildings in Pyongyang.

Blossoms
A869

Blossoms of Flowering Trees: 10ch, White
peach. 15ch, Red peach. 20ch, Red plum.
25ch, Apricot. 30ch, Cherry.

1975, Aug. 20   **Perf. 10¾**

1363-1367	A869	Set of 5	7.75	1.50

Diamond Mts.
Landscapes
A870

Designs: 5ch, Sejon Peak. 10ch, Chonson
Rock. 15ch, Pisa Gate. 25ch, Manmulsang.
30ch, Chaeha Peak.

1975, Aug. 20   **Perf. 11¾**

1368-1372	A870	Set of 5	7.75	1.00

Flowers
A871

Designs: 5ch, Azalea. 10ch, White azalea.
15ch, Mountain rhododendron. 20ch, White
rhododendron. 25ch, Rhododendron. 30ch,
Yellow rhododendron.

1975, Aug. 30   **Perf. 10¾**

1373-1378	A871	Set of 6	6.50	1.50

A872

Aerial Sports for National
Defence — A873

Designs: 5ch (No. 1379), Gliders. 5ch (No.
1380), Remote-controlled model airplane.
10ch (No. 1381), Parachutist in free fall, vert.

10ch (No. 1382), Parachutists landing, vert. 20ch, Parachutist with bouquet of flowers. 50ch, Formation skydiving.

Perf. 12x11¾, Imperf (#1384)
1975, Sept. 9
1379-1383 A872 Set of 5   5.00   .75

Souvenir Sheet
1384 A873 50ch multicolored   6.00   .50

Flowers — A874

Fruit tree blossoms: 10ch, Wild apple. 15ch, Wild pear. 20ch, Hawthorn. 25ch, Chinese quince. 30ch, Flowering quince.

1975, Sept. 30   ***Perf. 12¼x12***
1385-1389 A874 Set of 5   5.00 1.25

Korean Workers' Party, 30th Anniv. A875

Designs: 2ch (No. 1390), Symbolic creation of the Juche Idea. 2ch (No. 1391), Korean soldiers above American graves. 5ch (No. 1392), Hand holding torch with Juche inscription. 5ch (No. 1393), Monument of Chollima, idealized city. 10ch (No. 1394), Chollima winged horse and rider with banner. 10ch (No. 1395), Worker with Red Book. 25ch, South Koreans rioting. 70ch, Map of Korea, Red Book, flowers.

90ch (No. 1398), Kim Il Sung addressing workers, horiz. stamp, vert. souvenir sheet. 90ch (No. 1399), Kim with crowd of workers, city skyline in background, horiz. stamp, horiz. souvenir sheet.

Perf. 12, Imperf (#1398-1399)
1975, Oct. 10
1390-1397 A875 Set of 8   4.50 1.00
1398-1399 A875 Set of 2 sheets 8.25 4.00

Return of Kim Il Sung to Pyongyang, 30th Anniv. — A876

1975, Oct. 14   ***Perf. 12***
1400 A876 20ch multicolored   1.00 .25

Redong Sinmun, 30th Anniv. — A877

1975, Nov. 1   ***Perf. 11***
1401 A877 10ch multicolored   .85 .25
   a.   1w, souvenir sheet, imperf   5.50 5.00

Hyonmu Gate A878

Taedong Gate A879

Pothong Gate A880

Jongum Gate A881

Chilsong Gate — A882

Perf. 12x12¼, 12¼x12 (#1406)
1975, Nov. 20
1402 A878 10ch multicolored   1.40 .25
1403 A879 10ch multicolored   1.40 .25
1404 A880 15ch multicolored   1.90 .25
1405 A881 20ch multicolored   3.50 .25
1406 A882 30ch multicolored   5.00 .40
   Nos. 1402-1406 (5)   13.20 1.40

Ancient gates of Pyongyang.

Mt. Chilbo Views — A883

Designs: No. 1407, 10ch, Mae Rock (pale green border). No. 1408, 10ch, Jangsu Peak (pale yellow border). 15ch, Suri Peak. 20ch, Jangsu Peak, diff. 30ch, Rojok Peak.

1975, Nov. 30   ***Perf. 12x11¾***
1407-1411 A883 Set of 5   10.00 1.25

Wangjaesan Monument — A884

Designs: 10ch, Workers marching. 15ch, Soldiers marching. 25ch, Monument beacon tower, vert. 30ch, Base of tower, statues of Kim Il Sung, workers and soldiers.

Perf. 11¾, 10¾ (#1413)
1975, Dec. 20
1412-1415 A884 Set of 4   2.75 .75

Banners, Slogan — A885

Banners, Workers — A886

1976, Jan. 17   ***Perf. 12***
1416 A885 2ch multicolored   .30 .25
1417 A886 70ch multicolored   1.60 .75

League of Socialist Working Youth, 30th Anniv.

Ducks & Geese A887

Designs: 10ch, Geese. 20ch, Domesticated ducks. 40ch, Kwangpo ducks.

Perf. 12, 12x12¼ (#1418)
1976, Feb. 5
1418-1420 A887 Set of 3   8.25 .50
   For surcharge, see No. 4519.

Korean People's Army, Sculpture A888

Designs: 5ch, *Oath*. 10ch (No. 1422), *Unity Between Men and Officers*, horiz. 10ch (No. 1423), *This Flag to the Height*.

Perf. 12, 12¼x12 (#1421)
1976, Feb. 8
1421-1423 A888 Set of 3   2.75 .50

Rural Road at Evening (1965) A889

Passing-on Technique (1970) — A890

Mother (1965) A891

Medical Examination in Kindergarten (1970) — A892

Doctress of the Village (1970) — A893

1976, Feb. 10   ***Perf. 12***
1424 A889 10ch multicolored   .65 .25
1425 A890 15ch multicolored   .70 .25
1426 A891 25ch multicolored   1.10 .25
1427 A892 30ch multicolored   1.90 .25
1428 A893 40ch multicolored   2.25 .35
   Nos. 1424-1428 (5)   6.60 1.35

Modern Korean paintings.

Agrarian Reform Law, 30th Anniv. — A894

1976, Mar. 5   ***Perf. 12***
1429 A894 10ch multicolored   .65 .25

Telephone Communication Centenary — A895

Designs: 2ch, Telephones and communication satellite. 5ch, Satellite and antenna. 10ch, Satellite and telecommunications systems. 15ch, Telephone and lineman. 25ch, Satellite and map of receiving stations. 40ch, Satellite and cable-laying barge.
50ch, Satellite and antique telephone.

Surface Coated Paper

1976, Mar. 12		*Perf. 13¼*	
1430-1435	A895	Set of 6	8.75	1.00
1435a		Sheet of 8, as #1430-1436 + label, ordinary paper	10.00	—

Souvenir Sheet

Imperf, Without Gum

1436	A895	50ch multicolored	3.25	.50

Flowers A896

Designs: 5ch, Cosmos. 10ch, Dahlia. 20ch, Zinnia. 40ch, China aster.

1976, Mar. 20		*Perf. 12*		
1437-1440	A896	Set of 4	3.00	1.00

Pukchong Conference, 15th Anniv. — A897

Designs: 5ch, Fruit processing industry. 10ch, Fruit and orchards.

1976, Apr. 7		*Perf. 11½x12*		
1441-1442	A897	Set of 2	2.25	.25

Locomotives — A898

Designs: 5ch, Pulgungi electric train. 10ch, Jaju underground electric train. 15ch, Saeppyol diesel locomotive.

1976, Apr. 10		*Perf. 11¾*		
1443-1445	A898	Set of 3	3.25	.50

For surcharges, see Nos. 4594, 4603.

Many North Korean issues from 1976 on were also issued imperforate. These imperfs were issued for sale for hard currency, mostly to overseas collectors, and were not valid for postage.

Limited quantities of many sets from Scott No. 1446 on were issued without gum.

Day of Space Flight — A899

Designs: 2ch, Satellite. 5ch, Space station. 10ch, Communications satellite. 15ch, Future space station. 25ch, Satellite. 40ch, Communications satellite.
50ch, Lunar surface vehicle.

1976, Apr. 12		*Perf. 13¼*		
1446-1451	A899	Set of 6	3.25	1.00

Souvenir Sheet

Imperf

1452	A899	50ch multicolored	1.60	.50

A900

Kim Il Sung, 64th Birthday — A901

1976, Apr. 15		*Perf. 12*		
1453	A900	10ch multicolored	.85	.25

Souvenir Sheet

Imperf

1454	A901	40ch multicolored	5.00	.75

A902

3rd Asian Table Tennis Championships — A903

Designs: 5ch, Paddle and ribbon. 10ch, Three female players with bouquet. 20ch, Female player. 25ch, Male player.

Without Gum

1976, Apr. 25		*Perf. 12*		
1455-1458	A902	Set of 4	2.50	1.00

Souvenir Sheet

Imperf

1459	A903	50ch multicolored	2.50	.75

For surcharges, see Nos. 4582, 4593, 4607.

Association for the Restoration of the Fatherland, 40th Anniv. — A904

1976, May 5		*Perf. 12*		
1460	A904	10ch multicolored	.50	.25

Pheasants — A905

Designs: 2ch, Golden pheasant. 5ch, Lady Amherst's pheasant. 10ch, Silver pheasant. 15ch, Reeves' pheasant. 25ch, Copper pheasant. 40ch, Albino ring-necked pheasant.
50ch, Ring-necked pheasant.

Surface Coated Paper

1976, May 5		*Perf. 11¾*		
1461-1466	A905	Set of 6	5.00	1.50
1466a		Sheet of 8, as #1461-1467 + label, perf 12, ordinary paper	7.50	7.50

Souvenir Sheet

Imperf

1467	A905	50ch multicolored	3.50	1.50

Potong River Monument A906

1976, May 21		*Perf. 11½*		
1468	A906	10ch multicolored	75.00	—

21st Olympic Games, Montreal — A907

Stadium, Olympic rings, and: 2ch, Runners. 5ch, Diver. 10ch, Judo. 15ch, Gymnast. 25ch, Gymnast. 40ch, Fencers.
50ch, Runner with Olympic Torch.

Surface Coated Paper

1976, July 17		*Perf. 13¾*		
1469-1474	A907	Set of 6	5.00	1.00
1474a		Sheet of 8, as #1469-1475 + label, perf 12, ordinary paper	9.00	—

Souvenir Sheet

Imperf

1475	A907	50ch multicolored	3.50	1.50

For overprints and surcharges, see Nos. 1632-1638, 4568.

Winners, 21st Olympic Games, Montreal A908

Designs: 2ch, Bronze Medal, Hockey — Pakistan. 5ch, Bronze Medal, Free Pistol — Rudolf Dollinger (Austria). 10ch, Silver Medal, Boxing — Li Byong Uk (DPRK). 15ch, Silver Medal, Cycling — Daniel Morelon (France). 25ch, Gold Medal, Marathon — Waldemar Cierpinski (DDR). 40ch, Gold Medal, Boxing — Ku Yong Jo (DPRK).
50ch, Gold, Silver, Bronze Medals.

Multicolored, with Winners' Inscriptions in Silver
Surface Coated Paper

1976, Aug. 2		*Perf. 13¼*		
1476-1481	A908	Set of 6	6.00	1.00
1481a		Sheet of 8, as #1476-1482 + label	9.00	—

Souvenir Sheet

Imperf

1482	A908	50ch multicolored	4.00	2.00

Same, with Different Winners' Names

Designs: 2ch, Swimming — David Wilkie (UK). 5ch, Running — Lass Viren (Finland). 10ch, Weight Lifting — Vasili Alexeev (USSR). 15ch Swimming — Kornelia Ender (DDR). 25ch, Platform Diving — Klaus Dibiasi (Italy). 40ch, Boxing — Ku Yong Jo (DPRK). No. 1489, 50ch, Gymnastics — Nadia Comaneci (Romania).
No. 1490, 50ch, Kornelia Ender.

Ordinary Paper

1976, Aug. 2		*Perf. 13¼*		
1483-1489	A908	Sheet of 7 + label	10.00	4.00

Souvenir Sheet

Imperf

1490	A908	50ch multi	4.00	2.00

For overprints, see Nos. 1639-1645.

Winners, 21st Olympic Games, Montreal A909

Designs: 2ch, Boxing — Ku Yong Jo (DPRK). 5ch, Gymnastics — Nadie Comaneci (Romania). 10ch, Pole Vault — Tadeusz Slusarski (Poland). 15ch, Hurdling — Guy Drut (France). 25ch, Cycling — Bernt Johansson (Sweden). 40ch, Soccer (DDR). 50ch, Boxing — Ko Yong Do (DPRK).

Surface Coated Paper

1976, Aug. 2		**Perf. 13¼**
1491-1496 A909 Set of 6	4.50	1.00
1496a Sheet of 12, as #1491-1497 + 5 labels, ordinary paper	8.00	—

Souvenir Sheet
Imperf

1497 A909 50ch multicolored	3.00	.50

International Activities — A910

Designs: 2ch, UPU Headquarters, Bern. 5ch, World Cup. 10ch, Montreal Olympics Stadium. 15ch, Runner with Olympic Torch. 25ch, Satellite, junk. 40ch, Satellites. 50ch, World map.

Surface Coated Paper

1976, Aug. 5		**Perf. 13¼**
1506-1511 A910 Set of 6	5.00	1.50
1511a Sheet of 8, as #1505-1512 + label, ordinary paper	7.00	—

Souvenir Sheet
Imperf

1512 A910 50ch multicolored	2.50	2.50

For overprints, see Nos. 1646-1652.

Embroidery — A911

Designs: 2ch, Marsh Magpies. 5ch, Golden Bird. 10ch, Deer. 15ch, Golden Bird. 25ch, Fairy. 40ch, Tiger. 50ch, Tiger.

Surface Coated Paper

1976, Aug. 8		**Perf. 12**
1513-1518 A911 Set of 6	7.50	1.50
1518a Sheet of 8, as #1513-1519 + label, perf 13¾, ordinary paper	18.00	—

Souvenir Sheet
Imperf

1519 A911 50ch multicolored	4.00	.50

For surcharges, see Nos. 4598, 4599, 4604.

Model Airplane Championships (1975) — A912

Designs: 5ch, Trophy, certificate and medal. 10ch, Trophy and medals. 20ch, Model airplane and emblem. 40ch, Model glider and medals.

Without Gum

1976, Aug. 15		**Perf. 12**
1520-1523 A912 Set of 4	4.75	1.00

5th Summit Conference of Non-Aligned States — A913

1976, Aug. 16		**Without Gum**
1524 A913 10ch multicolored	.50	.25

Locomotives — A914

Designs: 2ch, "Pulgungi" diesel locomotive. 5ch, "Saeppyol" diesel locomotive. 10ch, "Saeppyol" diesel locomotive (diff.). 15ch, Electric train. 25ch, "Kumsong" diesel locomotive. 40ch, "Pulgungi" electric locomotive. 50ch, "Kumsong" diesel locomotive.

Surface Coated Paper

1976, Sept. 14		**Perf. 12x11¾**
1525-1530 A914 Set of 6	5.50	1.00
1530a Sheet of 8, as #1525-1531 + label, perf 10½	15.00	—

Souvenir Sheet
Imperf

1531 A914 50ch multicolored	6.00	3.50

House of Culture A915

Without Gum

1976, Oct. 7		**Perf. 12**
1532 A915 10ch black & brown	75.00	—

Revolutionary Activities of Kim Il Sung — A916

Kim Il Sung: 2ch, Visiting the Tosongrang. 5ch, With peasants on hillside. 10ch, With boy and man at seashore. 15ch, Giving house to farm-hand. 25ch, On muddy road at front, with driver and girl. 40ch, Walking in rain with umbrella. 50ch, Watching boy draw picture by roadside.

1976, Oct. 10		**Perf. 13¼**
1533-1538 A916 Set of 6	3.00	.75

Souvenir Sheet
Imperf

1539 A916 50ch multicolored	2.00	1.50

Down-With-Imperialism Union, 50th Anniv. — A917

Without Gum

1976, Oct. 17		**Perf. 12**
1540 A917 20ch multicolored	1.00	.25

21st Olympic Games, Montreal A918

Olympic Rings, stadium and: 5ch, Fencer. 10ch, Weightlifter. 15ch, Horse racer. 20ch, Runner. 25ch, Shot putter. 40ch, Basketball player. 60ch, Yacht race.

Simulated 3-D Printing Using Plastic Overlays

1976, Dec. 21		**Imperf.**
1541-1546 A918 Set of 6	25.00	25.00

Souvenir Sheet

1547 A918 60ch multicolored	45.00	45.00

No. 1547 Overprinted with Gold Medal Winners' Names, Events

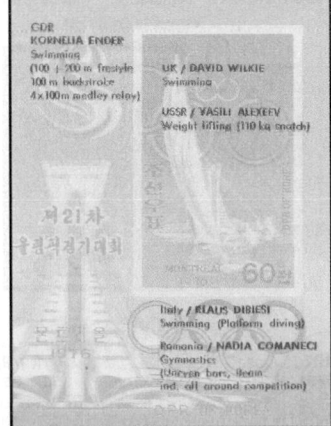

1548 A918 60ch multicolored	—	—

New Year — A919

Without Gum

1977, Jan. 1		**Perf. 12¼x12**
1549 A919 20ch multicolored	.50	.25

21st Olympic Games, Montreal (1976) — A920

Designs: 5ch, Reverse of Bronze Medal, Montreal skyline. 10ch, Obverse of Bronze Medal, diff. Montreal skyline. 15ch, Obverse of Silver Medal, stadium. 20ch, Reverse of Silver Medal, stadium. 25ch, Reverse of Gold Medal, Olympic Flame. 40ch, Obverse of Gold Medal, Olympic Flame. 60ch, Gold, Silver and Bronze Medals.

Simulated 3-D Printing Using Plastic Overlays

1977, Jan. 23		**Imperf.**
1550-1555 A920 Set of 6	25.00	25.00

Souvenir Sheet

1556 A920 60ch multicolored	55.00	55.00

No. 1556 Overprinted with Gold Medal Winners' Names, Events

1557 A920 60ch multicolored	—	—

National Costumes of Li Dynasty A921

Seasonal costumes: 10ch, Spring. 15ch, Summer. 20ch, Autumn. 40ch, Winter.

1977, Feb. 10		**Perf. 11¾x12**
1558-1561 A921 Set of 4	3.50	.75
1561a Sheet of 4, #1558-1561	5.00	—

No. 1561 is airmail.

Ships — A952

Korean ships: 2ch, Cargo ship *Mangy-ongbong.* 5ch, Freighter *Hyoksin.* 10ch, Freighter *Chongchongang.* 30ch, Tanker *Sonbang.* 50ch, Freighter *Taedonggang.*

1978, May 5   **Perf. 13¼**
1693-1697 A952 Set of 5   6.00 1.25
1697a   Sheet of 6, as #1693-1697+
             label   8.00   —

No. 1697 is airmail.

History of the World Cup — A953

World Cup Winners (all 20ch, except Nos. 1709, 1710): No. 1698, Uruguay 1930. No. 1699, Italy 1934. No. 1700, France 1938. No. 1701, Brazil 1950. No. 1702, Switzerland 1954. No. 1703, Sweden 1958. No. 1704, Chile 1962. No. 1705, England 1966. No. 1706, Mexico 1970. No. 1707, West Germany 1974. No. 1708, Argentina 1978. 50ch (No. 1709), Soccer players and emblem, horiz. 50ch (No. 1710), World Cup and championship emblem.

1978, June 1
1698-1709 A953 Set of 12   10.00 3.00
1709a   Sheet of 12, as #1698-
             1708, 1710   12.00   —
Souvenir Sheet
1710 A953 50ch multicolored   6.00   .60
No. 1709 is airmail.
For overprints, see Nos. 2051-2063.

World Cup Winners — A954

Designs: 5ch, Uruguay, 1930, 1950. 10ch, Italy, 1934, 1938. 15ch, West Germany, 1954, 1974. 25ch, Brazil, 1958, 1962, 1970. 40ch, England, 1966. 50ch, World Cup, vert. 50ch, World Cup.

1978, June 1
1711-1716 A954 Set of 6   5.00 1.25
1716a   Sheet of 6, as #1711-15,
             1717   6.00   —
Souvenir Sheet
1717 A954 50ch multicolored   4.00   .75
No. 1716 is airmail.

Art of the Revolution — A955

Designs: 10ch, Opera, *Sea of Love.* 15ch, Embroidered kerchief with floral design in the form of map of Korea. 20ch, *Tansimjul* dance. 40ch, *Song of Korea.*

1978, June 2
1718-1720 A955 Set of 3   2.50   .50
Souvenir Sheet
1721 A955 40ch multicolored   2.50   .50

Domestic Printings

Beginning in the 1970s, a number of North Korean stamps have been reprinted for sale and use within the country. Typically, these printings were on unsurfaced paper, with poorer production qualities, and without gum.

Second Seven-Year Plan — A956

Designs: 5ch, Electricity and Coal. 10ch, Steel and nonferrous metals. 15ch, Machine products and chemical fertilizers. 30ch, Cement and fishing. 50ch, Grain and tideland reclamation.

1978, June 15   **Perf. 11½x12**
1722-1726 A956 Set of 5   3.25   .90
1722a   5ch Unsurfaced white paper,
             without gum   8.00   —
1723a   10ch Unsurfaced white paper,
             without gum   8.00   —
1724a   15ch Unsurfaced white paper,
             without gum   8.00   —
1725a   30ch Unsurfaced white paper,
             without gum   5.00   —

History of Olympic Games & Winners — A957

Games emblems / medal winners (all 20ch): No. 1727, Athens 1896 / Alfred Flatow. No. 1728, Paris 1900 / Michel Theato. No. 1729, London 1908 / Wyndham Halswelle. No. 1730, Stockholm 1912 / William Kinnear. No. 1731, Antwerp 1920 / Paul Anspach. No. 1732, Paris 1924 / Ugo Frigerio. No. 1733, Amsterdam 1928 / Ahmed El Quafi. No. 1734, Berlin 1936 / Robert Charpentier. No. 1735, London 1948 / Josef Stalder. No. 1736, Helsinki 1952 / Laszlo Papp. No. 1737, Melbourne 1956 / Ronald Delany. No. 1738, Rome 1960 / Jolanda Balas. No. 1739, Tokyo 1964 / Valery Brumel. No. 1740, Mexico 1968 / Vera Caslavska. No. 1741, Munich 1972 / Li Ho Jun. 50ch, Montreal 1976 / Ku Yong Jo.

1978, June 16   **Perf. 13¼**
1727-1741 A957 Set of 15   12.00 4.50
1741a   Sheet of 16, as #1727-1741 14.00   —
Souvenir Sheet
1742 A957 50ch multicolored   2.00   .75

Passenger Aircraft — A958

Designs: 2ch, Douglas CD-8-63 jetliner and Comte AC-4 Gentleman. 10ch, Ilyushin Il-62M jetliner and Avia BH-25. 15ch, Douglas DC-8-63 jetliner and Savola Marchetti S-71. 20ch, Tupolev Tu-144 jetliner and Kalinin K-5. 25ch, Tupolev Tu-154 jetliner and Antonov An-2 biplane. 30ch, Ilyushin Il-18 airliner and '30s-era airplane. 40ch, Concorde supersonic jetliner and Wibault 283 trimotor. 50ch, Airbus.

1978, July 25
1743-1749 A958 Set of 7   7.00 1.20
1749a   Sheet of 8, as #1743-1750 10.00   —
Souvenir Sheet
1750 A958 50ch multicolored   2.50   .50
For surcharge, see No. 4586.

White-Bellied Black Woodpecker Preservation A959

Designs: 5ch, Dryocopus richardsi, map of habitat, inset map of Korea. 10ch, Woodpecker and eggs. 15ch, Woodpecker feeding young. 25ch, Woodpecker feeding young, diff. 50ch, Woodpecker on tree trunk.

1978, Aug. 5   **Perf. 11¾x12**
1751-1755 A959 Set of 5   7.50 2.00
1755a   Sheet of 6, #1751-1755 + la-
             bel   9.00   —
For surcharge, see No. 4583.

Democratic People's Republic of Korea, 30th Anniv. A960

Designs (all 10ch): No. 1756, Building and flag. No. 1757, Flag with silhouetttes of workers and peasants. No. 1758, Flag with aviator and two soldiers. No. 1759, Chollima statue and city. No. 1760, Workers demonstrating, map of Korea in background. No. 1761, Asian, European and African clasping hands, with torch and "Solidarity" in background.

Without Gum
1978, Sep. 9   **Perf. 13½x13¼**
1756-1761 A960 Set of 6   2.75   .50
1758a   10ch Unsurfaced toned pa-
             per   10.00   —
1759a   10ch Unsurfaced toned pa-
             per   15.00   —
1760a   10ch Unsurfaced toned pa-
             per   15.00   —

Paintings by Ri Am (16th Century) A961

Designs: 10ch, *Cat and Pup.* 15ch, *Cat on a Tree.* 40ch, *A Pair of Wild Geese.*

1978, Oct. 16   **Perf. 13¼**
1762-1764 A961 Set of 3   7.50 1.10
1764a   Sheet of 4, #1762-1764 +
             label   11.00   —

World Cup Winners, Argentina '78 — A962

Soccer players: 10ch, Argentina, Champion. 15ch, Holland, Sub-Champion. 25ch, Brazil, Third Place. 50ch, Argentina, Champion.

1978, Dec. 15
1765-1767 A962 Set of 3   3.00   .50
1767a   Sheet of 4, as #1765-1768 12.00   —
Souvenir Sheet
1768 A962 50ch multicolored   2.50 1.50

New Year — A963

Without Gum
1979, Jan. 1   **Perf. 12**
1769 A963 10ch multicolored   .50   .25

A964

International Year of the Child — A965

Kim Il Sung and children: 5ch, With Children's Corps members in Maanshan. 10ch, Children's Corps members in classroom. 15ch, "The New Year Gathering." 20ch, by roadside, with snowman, kite. 30ch, Looking at children's school work.

Children: 10ch, Tug of war. 15ch, Ballerinas. 20ch, Children of different races holding hands in circle around globe. 25ch, Singing at piano. 30ch, Playing on toy airplane ride.
50ch (No. 1780), Kim visiting a kindergarten. 50ch (No. 1781): As No. 1777.

1979, Jan. 1   *Perf. 13¼x13½*
1770-1774 A964 Set of 5   4.00   1.00
1775-1779 A965 Set of 5   3.00   1.00
Souvenir Sheets
Imperf
1780 A964 50ch multicolored   2.50   1.75
1781 A965 50ch multicolored   2.50   1.75

Nos. 1770-1779 were issued with setenant labels. Nos. 1780-1781 exist perf. 13¼x13½.

A set of four stamps depicting roses, similar to Type A970, was prepared for release on Jan. 5, 1979, but was not issued.

Story of Two Generals A966

Designs: 5ch, Two warriors on horseback. 10ch (No. 1783), Man blowing feather. 10ch (No. 1784), Two generals fighting Japanese invaders. 10ch (No. 1785), Two generals on horseback.

Without Gum

1979, Jan. 10   *Perf. 11¾x12*
1782-1785 A966 Set of 4   3.00   .50

Worker-Peasant Red Guards, 20th Anniv. — A967

Without Gum

1979, Jan. 14   *Perf. 12x11¾*
1786 A967 10ch multicolored   .50   .25

Airships — A968

Designs: 10ch, Clement-Bayard Airship *Fleurus.* 20ch, NI *Norge.* 50ch, *Graf Zeppelin.*

1979, Feb. 27   *Perf. 13¼*
1787-1788 A968 Set of 2   2.00   .40
1788a   Sheet of 3, as #1787-1789   5.00   —
Souvenir Sheet
1789 A968 50ch multicolored   3.00   1.75

March 1 Popular Uprising, 60th Anniv. A969

Without Gum

1979, Mar. 1   *Perf. 11¾x12*
1790 A969 10ch multicolored   .60   .25

Roses A970

Designs: 5ch, Rose. 10ch, Red star rose. 15ch, Flamerose. 20ch, Yellow rose. 30ch, White rose. 50ch, Deep pink rose.

1979, Apr. 18   *Perf. 13¼*
1791-1796 A970 Set of 6   3.50   1.00
1796a   Sheet of 6, #1791-1796   4.00   —

No. 1796 is airmail.

35th World Table Tennis Championships, Pyongyang — A971

Designs: 5ch, Championship Cup. 10ch, Female doubles. 15ch, Female singles. 20ch, Male doubles. 30ch, Male singles.
50ch, Chollima statue. "Welcome."

1979, Apr. 25
1797-1801 A971 Set of 5   3.00   .75
1801a   Sheet of 6, as #1797-1802   4.00   —
Souvenir Sheet
1802 A971 50ch multicolored   3.00   .45

For surcharges, see Nos. 4516, 4531.

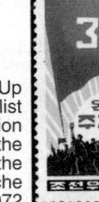

"Let Us Step Up Socialist Construction Under the Banner of the Juche Idea" — A972

Designs: 5ch, Marchers, banner. 10ch (No. 1804), Map of Korea. 10ch (No. 1805), Hand holding torch.

Without Gum

1979, Apr. 28   *Perf. 12*
1803-1805 A972 Set of 3   3.00   .25
1803a   5ch Unsurfaced dull white paper   15.00   —
1804a   10ch Unsurfaced dull white paper   15.00   —
1805a   10ch Unsurfaced dull white paper   15.00   —

Order of Honor of the Three Revolutions — A973

1979, May 2   **Without Gum**
1806 A973 10ch dp blue & lt blue   1.50   .25
a.   Unsurfaced dull white paper   15.00

World Telecommunications Day — A974

1979, May 17   **Without Gum**
1807 A974 10ch multicolored   1.00   .25

Battle in Musan Area, 40th Anniv. A975

1979, May 23   **Without Gum**
1808 A975 10ch multicolored   .60   .25

Int'l Friendship Exhibition A976

1979, May 29   **Without Gum**
1809 A976 10ch multicolored   .60   .25

Albrooht Dürer, 450th Anniv. Death A977

Details from Dürer paintings: 15ch, Peonies. 20ch, Akeley. 25ch, A Big Tuft of Grass. 30ch, Wing of a Bird.
50ch, Like 30ch.

1979, June 8   *Perf. 13¼*
1810-1813 A977 Set of 4   5.50   .75
1813a   Souvenir sheet of 4, #1810-1813   9.00   —
Souvenir Sheet
1814 A977 50ch multicolored   3.50   .60

For surcharge, see No. 4584.

Olympic Games, Moscow 1980 — A978

Olympic Torch, Moscow 1980 emblem and: 5ch, Fencers. 10ch, Gymnast. 20ch, Yacht race. 30ch, Runner. 40ch, Weightlifter. 50ch, Horse jump.

1979, July 1
1815-1819 A978 Set of 5   3.50   1.25
1819a   Sheet of 6, as #1815-1820   5.00   —
Souvenir Sheet
1820 A978 50ch multicolored   3.00   1.50

Nos. 1661-1669 Overprinted

1979, July 17
1821-1827 A946 Set of 7   10.00   3.50
1827a   Sheet of 10, as #1821-1829 + label   18.00   —
Souvenir Sheets
1828 A946 50ch multicolored   4.25   1.50
1829 A946 60ch multicolored   8.50   —

No. 1827 is airmail.

Koguryo Dynasty Horsemen — A979

Designs: 5ch, Hunting. 10ch, Archery contest. 15ch, Drummer. 20ch, Rider blowing horn. 30ch, Horse and rider in chain mail. 50ch, Hawk hunting.

1979, Aug. 1
1830-1835 A979 Set of 6   6.00   .75
1835a   Sheet of 6, as #1830-1835   9.00   —

Olympic Games, Moscow 1980 — A980

Designs: 5ch, Judo. 10ch, Volleyball. 15ch, Cycling. 20ch, Basketball. 25ch, One-oared boat. 30ch, Boxing. 40ch, Shooting. 50ch, Gymnastics.

1979, Aug. 5   *Perf. 11¾x12*
1836-1842 A980 Set of 7   5.00   1.25
1842a   Sheet of 8, as #1836-1843 + label   9.00   —
Souvenir Sheet
1843 A980 50ch multicolored   3.00   1.00

Ri Dynasty Knights' Costumes A981

Designs: 5ch, Knight in armor. 10ch, Knight in ceremonial dress. 15ch, Knight in armor (diff.) 20ch, Soldier in uniform. 30ch, Knight in armor (diff.) 50ch, Knight in armor (diff.)

1979, Aug. 6   *Perf. 11¾*
1844-1849 A981 Set of 6   3.75   .75
1849a   Sheet of 6, #1844-1849   6.00   —

No. 1849 is airmail.

1980 Summer
Olympics,
Moscow
A982

Designs: 10ch, Judo. 15ch, Handball. 20ch,
Archery. 25ch, Field hockey. 30ch, Boat race.
40ch, Soccer.
50ch, Horse race.

1979, Sept. 5   *Perf. 11¾x11½*
1850-1855 A982 Set of 6   5.25 1.25
1855a   Sheet of 8, #1850-1856 + la-   8.00 —
     bel

Souvenir Sheet

1856 A982 50ch multi   3.00 1.25

For surcharges, see Nos. 4585, 4595.

Chongbong
Monument
A983

Without Gum

1979, Sep. 10   *Perf. 12*
1857 A983 10ch multicolored   .60 .25

Sika
Deer
A984

Designs: 5ch, Breeder feeding fawn from
bottle. 10ch, Doe and suckling fawn. 15ch,
Deer drinking from stream. 20ch, Buck walking. 30ch, Deer running.
50ch, Antlers.

1979, Oct. 5   *Perf. 13½*
1858-1863 A984 Set of 6   4.00 1.25
1863a   Sheet of 6, #1858-1863   6.00

Central Zoo,
Pyongyang
A985

Designs: 5ch, Moscovy ducks. 10ch,
Ostrich. 15ch, Turkey. 20ch, Pelican. 30ch,
Guinea fowl. 50ch, Mandarin ducks.

1979, Oct. 9   *Perf. 12*
1864-1869 A985 Set of 6   5.00 1.50
1869a   Sheet of 6, #1864-1869   6.00 —

No. 1869 is airmail. For surcharge, see No.
4569.

Int'l Year of the
Child — A986

Designs: 20ch (No. 1870), Girl with toy sail
boat. 20ch (No. 1871), Boy with toy train. 20ch
(No. 1872), Boy with model biplane. 20ch (No.
1873), Boy with model spaceman. 30ch (No.
1874), Boy with toy motor boat. 30ch (No.
1875), Boy sitting on toy train. 30ch (No.
1876), Boy with model airplane. 30ch (No.
1877), Boy with model spaceman.
   Souvenir Sheets (all 80ch): No. 1878, Boy
and model ocean liner. No. 1879, Boy and girl
with model train. No. 1880, Boy and Concorde.
No. 1881, Girl and satellite.
   Miniature sheets of 4: No. 1882, Nos. 1870,
1874, 1878 + label. No. 1883, Nos. 1871,
1875, 1879 + label. No. 1884, Nos. 1872,
1876, 1880 + label. No. 1885, Nos. 1873,
1877, 1881 + label.

1979, Oct. 13   *Perf. 12x11¾*
1870-1877 A986 Set of 8   12.00 2.50

Souvenir Sheets

1878-1881 A986 Set of 4   25.00 2.50

Miniature Sheets

1882-1885 A986 Set of 4   25.00 2.50

For surcharges, see Nos. 4520, 4532.

Int'l Year of the Child — A987

Children playing soccer: 20ch, Kicking.
30ch, Dribbling.
80ch, Tackling.

1979, Nov. 15   *Perf. 12x11¾*
1886-1887 A987 Set of 2   5.00 .75
1887a   Sheet of 3, as #1886-1888   10.00 —

Souvenir Sheet

1888 A987 80ch multicolored   5.00 .75

Marine Life — A988

Designs: 20ch, Devil stinger fish (*Inimicas
japonicus*). 30ch, Black rockfish (*Sebastes
schlegeli*). 50ch, Northern sea lion
(*Eumetopias jubatus*).

1889-1891 A988 Set of 3   3.50 .75
1891a   Sheet of 3, #1889-1891   5.00

Winter Olympics Games, Lake
Placid — A989

Designs: 10ch, Figure skating (Irina
Rodnina and Aleksandr Zaitsev). 20ch, Ice
hockey (Soviet team). 30ch, Ladies' ski relay
team. 40ch, Cross-country skiing (Sergei
Saveliev, USSR), vert. 50ch, Ladies' speed
skating (Tatiana Averina), vert.

60ch, Ice dancing (Ludmila Pakhomova and
Aleksandr Gorshkov), stamp vert.

1979, Dec. 9
1892-1896 A989   Set of 5   6.00 1.50
1892a   Sheet of 3, #1892-1894   5.00 —
1895a   Sheet of 3, as #1895-1897   10.00 —

Souvenir Sheet

1897 A989 60ch multicolored   5.50 4.50

Honey
Bees — A990

Designs: 20ch, Bee gathering nectar. 30ch,
Bee and blossoms. 50ch, Bee over flower.

1979, Dec. 22
1898-1900 A990   Set of 3   6.00 .60
1900a   Sheet of 3, #1898-1900   7.50

Kim Il
Sung's
Birthplace,
Hoeryang
A991

Sinpha Revolutionary Museum — A992

1979, Dec. 24
1901 A991 10ch multicolored   .75 .25
1902 A992 10ch multicolored   .75 .25

Revolutionary historical sites.

New Year
A993

1980, Jan. 1
1903 A993 10ch multicolored   1.00 .25

Studying — A994

1980, Jan. 10   *Perf. 12x11¾*
1904 A994 10ch multicolored   .50 .25

Unryul Mine Conveyor Belt — A995

1980, Jan. 20   *Perf. 11¾x12*
1905 A995 10ch multicolored   1.00 .25

Kim Il Sung, Soldiers and
Children — A996

Children Playing — A997

Kim Visiting Kindergarten — A998

International Day of the Child

Type A997 (all 10ch): No. 1907, Black,
Asian and White children with "6" and "1." No.
1908, Children playing accordion. No. 1909,
Children on airplane ride. No. 1910, Children
on rocket ride. No. 1911, Children riding tricycles. No. 1912, Children playing with model
train.

1980, Jan. 28   *Perf. 12x11¾*
1906 A996 10ch multicolored   .35 .25
1907 A997 10ch multicolored   1.50 .35
1908 A997 10ch multicolored   .35 .25
1909 A997 10ch multicolored   .60 .25
1910 A997 10ch multicolored   2.25 .50
1911 A997 10ch multicolored   .50 .25
1912 A997 10ch multicolored   .35 .25
   Nos. 1906-1912 (7)   5.90 2.10

Souvenir Sheet
Perf. 13¼

1913 A998 50ch multicolored   3.00 1.25

Chongsan-ri Monument — A999

Chongsan-ri Party
Headquarters — A1000

1980, Feb. 5   *Perf. 11¾x12*
1914 A999 10ch multicolored   .50 .25
1915 A1000 10ch multicolored   .50 .25

Monument in Honor of Kim Jong Suk's Return A1001

1980, Feb. 16
1916 A1001 10ch multicolored   .50   .25

Explorers A1002

Designs: 10ch, Vasco Nunez be Balboa (Spain). 20ch, Francisco de Orellana (Spain). 30ch, Haroun Tazieff (France). 40ch, Sir Edmund Hillary (New Zealand) and Shri Tenzing (Nepal).
70ch, Ibn Battuta (Morocco).

1980, Feb. 18   **Perf. 13¼**
1917-1920 A1002 Set of 4   4.50 1.00
1920a   Sheet of 6, as #1917-1921
         + label   10.00   —
         Souvenir Sheet
1921 A1002 70ch multicolored   4.50 1.50

Ryongpo Revolutionary Museum — A1003

1980, Feb. 23   **Perf. 11¾**
1922 A1003 10ch lt blue & black   .50   .25

Rowland Hill (1795-1879), Centenary of Death — A1004

Rowland Hill and stamps of: 30ch, Germany, Great Britain (#1), Russia, Switzerland, DPRK and Wurttemberg. 50ch, Great Britain (#1, pair), France, Roman States, Canada, Two Sicilies and India.

1980, Mar. 1
1923-1924 A1004 Set of 2   7.00 1.00
1924a   Sheet of 2, #1923-1924 10.00   —

World Red Cross Day — A1005

Designs: No. 1925, 10ch, Emblem of DPRK Red Cross. No. 1926, 10ch, Jean-Henri Dunant. No. 1927, 10ch, Nurse and infant. No. 1928, 10ch, Red Cross ship. No. 1929, 10ch, Red Cross helicopter. No. 1930, 10ch, Nurse

with child and doll. No. 1931, 10ch, Map, Red Cross, transports.
    50ch, Nurse with syringe.

1980, Apr. 17   **Perf. 11¾x11½**
1925-1931 A1005 Set of 7   8.00 1.50
1931a   Sheet of 8, as #1925-1932 15.00   —
         Souvenir Sheet
1932 A1005 50ch multicolored   5.50 1.75

For overprints and surcharges, see Nos. 2043-2050, 4517, 4570.

Conquerors of the Sea A1006

Designs: 10ch, Fernando Magellan (Portugal). 20ch, Fridtjof Nansen (Norway). 30ch, Auguste and Jacques Piccard (Sweden). 40ch, Jacques Cousteau (France).
    70ch, Capt. James Cook (UK).

1980, Apr. 30   **Perf. 13¼**
1933-1936 A1006 Set of 4   8.00 1.50
1936a   Sheet of 6, as #1933-1937
         + label   15.00   —
         Souvenir Sheet
1937 A1006 70ch multicolored   6.50 1.50

London 1980 Int'l Philatelic Exhibition — A1007

Designs: 10ch, Great Britain #1 and Korean stamps. No. 1939, 20ch, British Guiana One-Cent Magenta and Korean cover. No. 1940, 30ch, Korea #1 (in blue) and modern Korean First Day Cover. 40ch, DPRK Nos. 1 (in green) and 1494. No. 1942, 50ch, DPRK Nos. 470-471.
    No. 1943: a, 20ch, Like 10ch. b, 30ch, Like No. 1939. c, 50ch, Like 40ch.

1980, May 6
1938-1942 A1007 Set of 5   10.00 1.50
         Souvenir Sheet
1943 A1007 Sheet of 3, #a-c   15.00 1.50

Nos. 1941, 1943c are airmail.

Conquerors of Sky and Space A1008

Designs: 10ch, Wright Brothers (USA). 20ch, Louis Bleriot (France). 30ch, Anthony Fokker (USA). 40ch, Secondo Campini (Italy) and Sir Frank Whittle (UK).
    70ch, Count Ferdinand von Zeppelin (Germany).

1980, May 10
1944-1947 A1008 Set of 4   6.00 1.25
1947a   Sheet of 6, as #1944-1948
         + label   13.00   —
         Souvenir Sheet
1948 A1008 70ch multicolored   5.00 1.25

Conquerors of the Universe A1009

Designs: 10ch, Spaceships. 20ch, Spaceship landing on another planet. 30ch, Spaceships landing on another planet, greeted by dinosaurs. 40ch, Spaceship, dinosaurs.
    70ch, Spaceman and dragons.

1980, May 20   **Perf. 11¾x12**
1949-1952 A1009 Set of 4   3.50 1.25
1952a   Sheet of 6, as #1949-1953
         + label   12.00   —
         Souvenir Sheet
1953 A1009 70ch multicolored   3.50 1.25

Chongryon, 25th Anniv. — A1010

1980, May 25   **Perf. 12¼x12**
1954 A1010 10ch multicolored   .50   .25

Chongryon is the General Association of Korean Residents in Japan.

Pyongyang Maternity Hospital — A1011

1980, May 30   **Perf. 12**
1955 A1011 10ch multicolored   1.10   .25

Changgwang Health Complex — A1012

1980, June 2   **Perf. 11¾x12**
1956 A1012 2ch black & lt blue   .60   .25

Korean Revolutionary Army, 50th Anniv. — A1013

1980, July 6   **Perf. 12**
1957 A1013 10ch multicolored   .60   .25

Regular Issue — A1014

Designs (all 10ch): No. 1958, Workers' hostel, Samjiyon. No. 1959, *Chongsanri* rice harvester. No. 1960, *Taedonggang* rice transplanter. No. 1961, corn harvester. No. 1962, Samhwa Democratic Propaganda Hall. No.

1963, Songmun-ri revolutionary historic building (with trees). No. 1964, Sundial. No. 1965, Turtle ship. No. 1966, Phungsan dog. No. 1967, Quail.

    Perf. 11¾, 11½ (#1960, 1965), 12x11¾ (#1964)
1980
1958-1967 A1014 Set of 10   25.00 3.00

Issued: Nos. 1958-1961, 7/25. Nos. 1962-1967, 8/1.

6th Congress, Workers' Party of Korea A1015

"Leading the van in the Arduous March" — A1016

"The great leader inspires and encourages colliers on the spot." — A1017

Designs (all 10ch): No. 1968, Party emblem, fireworks. No. 1969, Students, Red Book. No. 1970, Workers, banner, Red Book. No. 1971, Young workers, one with accordion. No. 1972, Worker holding wrench aloft. No. 1973, Four young workers, one with streamer, building in background. No. 1974, Map, propaganda slogans. No. 1975, Workers marching with three banners, smoke stacks in background.

1980, July 30   **Perf. 12¼x12**
1968-1975 A1015 Set of 8   6.00 1.25
         Souvenir Sheets
1976 A1016 50ch multicolored   3.00   .75
1977 A1017 50ch multicolored   2.00   .75

World Cup Soccer Championship 1978-1982 A1018

Designs: 20ch, Two soccer players dribbling ball. 30ch, Tackling. 40ch, Tackling (diff.). 60ch, Moving in to tackle.

1980, Aug. 5   **Perf. 12**
1978-1979 A1018 Set of 2   7.50 2.00
1979a   Sheet of 4, as #1978-1980
         Souvenir Sheet
1980 A1018 Sheet of 2 + label 16.00 2.00
    a.   40ch multicolored   3.00 1.00
    b.   60ch multicolored   4.00 1.00

Winter Olympic Games 1980, Gold
Medal Winners — A1019

Designs: 20ch, Irina Rodnina and Aleksandr
Zaitsev.
1w, Natalia Linitschnuk and Gennadi
Karponosov.

1980, Aug. 10   **Perf. 13¼**
1981 A1019 20ch multicolored   6.00 1.50
  a. Sheet of 2, as #1981-1982   15.00   —
Souvenir Sheet
1982 A1019 1w multicolored   6.50 2.00

Albrecht Dürer,
450th Anniv.
Death — A1020

Designs: 20ch, *Soldier with Horse.*
1w, *Horse and Rider.*

1980, Aug. 18   **Perf. 11¾x12**
1983 A1020 20ch multicolored   6.00 1.50
  a. Sheet of 2 as #1983-1984   20.00   —
Souvenir Sheet
1984 A1020 1w multicolored   9.00 2.50

Johannes
Kepler, 350th
Anniv.
Death — A1021

Designs: 20ch, Kepler, astrolabe and
satellites.
1w, Kepler, astrolabe and satellites (diff.).

1980, Aug. 25
1985 A1021 20ch multicolored   2.75 1.25
  a. Sheet of 2, as #1985-1986   12.00   —
Souvenir Sheet
1986 A1021 1w multicolored   6.00 2.00

3rd Int'l Stamp Fair Essen
1980 — A1022

Designs, Stamps from German and Russian
Zeppelin sets, respectively: 10ch, 1m and 30k.
20ch, 2m and 35k. 30ch, 4m and 1r.
50ch, Russian 2r Polar Flight stamp and
DPRK No. 1780 stamp.

1980, Sep. 25   **Perf. 13¼**
1987-1989 A1022 Set of 3   6.50 1.25
  1989a Sheet of 4, as #1987-1990 30.00   —
Souvenir Sheet
1990 A1022 50ch multicolored   9.00 2.50

A1023

Moscow Olympic Games
Winners — A1024

Designs: 10ch, Free pistol shooting — Alek-
sandr Melentiev (USSR). 20ch, 4000m Individ-
ual pursuit bicycle race — Robert Dill-Bundi
(Switzerland). 25ch, Gymnastics — Stoyan
Deltchev (Bulgaria). 30ch, Free style wrestling
— K). 35ch, Weight-lifting — Ho Bong Choi
(DPRK). 40ch, Running — Marita Koch
(DDR). 50ch, Modern pentathlon — Anatoly
Starostin (USSR).
  No. 1998, Boxing — Teofilo Stevenson
(Cuba). No. 1999, Ancient Greek rider on
horse.

1980, Oct. 20   **Perf. 12x11¾**
1991-1997 A1023 Set of 7   7.00 2.25
  1997a Sheet of 8, as #1991-1998 12.00   —
Souvenir Sheet
1998 A1023 70ch multicolored   2.75 2.00
1999 A1024 70ch multicolored   4.50 2.00

Josip Broz Tito
(1892-1980)
A1025

1980, Dec. 4   **Perf. 12¼x12**
2000 A1025 20ch multicolored   1.00   .25

First Post-
WWII
Lufthansa
Flight, 25th
Anniv.
A1026

Designs: 20ch, Convair CV 340 airliner.
1w, Airbus A 300.

1980, Dec. 10   **Perf. 13¼**
2001 A1026 20ch multicolored   5.50 2.00
  a. Sheet of 2, as #2001-2002   15.00   —
Souvenir Sheet
2002 A1026 1w multicolored   7.00 3.00

Liverpool-Manchester Railway, 150th
Anniv. — A1027

Designs: 20ch, *The Rocket.*
1w, Locomotive pulling passenger car and
horse car.

1980, Dec. 16   **Perf. 11¾**
2003 A1027 20ch multicolored   6.00 3.00
  a. Sheet of 2, as #2003-2004   15.00   —
Souvenir Sheet
2004 A1027 1w multicolored   6.00 2.50

Electric Train Centenary — A1028

Designs: 20ch, First E-type electric and
steam locomotives.
1w, Electric locomotive exhibited in Berlin,
1879.

1980, Dec. 24   **Perf. 13¼**
2005 A1028 20ch multicolored   6.00 2.00
  a. Sheet of 2, as #2005-2006   20.00   —
Souvenir Sheet
2006 A1028 1w multicolored   12.00 2.50

Dag
Hammarskjold
(1905-61), 75th
Anniv. of
Birth — A1029

Designs: 20ch, Hammarskjold and UN
Building.
1w, Hammarskjold (diff.).

1980, Dec. 26   **Perf. 11¾**
2007 A1029 20ch multicolored   3.25 2.25
  a. Sheet of 2, as #2007-2008   10.00   —
Souvenir Sheet
2008 A1029 1w multicolored   4.50 2.75

World Chess Championship,
Merano — A1030

Designs: 20ch, Bobby Fischer-Boris
Spassky chess match.
1w, Viktor Korchnoi-Anatoly Karpov chess
match.

1980, Dec. 28   **Perf. 13¼**
2009 A1030 20ch multicolored   7.00 2.00
  a. Sheet of 2, as #2009-2010   17.00   —
Souvenir Sheet
2010 A1030 1w multicolored   9.00 2.00

Robert Stolz (1880-1975), Composer,
Birth Cent. — A1031

Designs: 20ch, Stoltz with music from *At the
Flower Bed.*
1w, Stoltz working with stamp collection.

1980, Dec. 30
2011 A1031 20ch multicolored   3.00 1.00
  a. Sheet of 2, as #2011-2012   12.00   —
Souvenir Sheet
2012 A1031 1w multicolored   5.00 1.00

New
Year — A1032

1981, Jan. 1   **Perf. 12**
2013 A1032 10ch multicolored   .90   .25

Fairy Tales
A1033

Designs (all 10ch): No. 2014 Russian fairy
tale. No. 2015 Icelandic. No. 2016, Swedish.
No. 2017, Irish. No. 2018, Italian. No. 2019,
Japanese. No. 2020, German.
  70ch (No. 2021): Korean fairy tale, *A Gold
Nugget and Maize Cake.*

1981, Jan. 30   **Perf. 13¼**
2014-2020 A1033 Set of 7   10.00 3.50
  2020a Sheet of 8, as #2014-2021 15.00   —
Souvenir Sheet
2021 A1033 70ch multicolored   5.75 3.00

International Year of the Child, 1979.

Changgwang Street,
Pyongyang — A1034

1981, Feb. 16   **Perf. 11¾x12**
2022 A1034 10ch multicolored   .70   .25

World Soccer Cup Championship
ESPAÑA '82 — A1035

Designs: 10ch, Tackling. 20ch, Kicking.
30ch, Feinting.
70ch, Three players.

1981, Feb. 20   **Perf. 13¼**
2023-2025 A1035 Set of 3   9.00 2.75
2025a   Sheet of 4, as #2023-2026   17.00 —
Souvenir Sheet
2026 A1035 70ch multicolored   8.00 3.25
For overprints, see Nos. 2216.

World Soccer Cup Championship
ESPAÑA '82 (2nd issue) — A1036

Designs: 10ch, Emblem, map and cup.
20ch, Dribbling. 25ch, Tackling. 30ch, Pass.
70ch, Sliding tackle.

1981, Feb. 28
2027-2031 A1036 Set of 5   9.00 3.75
2031a   Sheet of 6, as #2027-2032   18.00 —
Souvenir Sheet
2032 A1036 70ch multicolored   9.00 3.00

Implementations
of Decisions of
6th Korean
Workers' Party
Congress
A1037

Designs: 2ch, Marchers with book, banners.
10ch (No. 2034), Worker with book. 10ch (No.
2035), Workers and factory. 10ch (No. 2036),
Electricity generation (horiz.). 10ch (No.
2037), Factory, construction scene (horiz.).
10ch (No. 2038), Cement factory, fertilizer
(horiz.). 30ch, Fishing, fabrics (horiz.). 40ch,
Grain, port facilities (horiz.). 70ch, Clasped
hands, map of Korea. 1w, Hand holding torch,
"peace" and "solidarity" slogans.

1981, Mar. 15   **Perf. 12¼**
2033-2042 A1037 Set of 10   6.00 2.50
2033a   2ch Unsurfaced white pa-
      per, without gum   10.00 —
2034a   10ch Unsurfaced white pa-
      per, without gum   10.00 —
2035a   10ch Unsurfaced white pa-
      per, without gum   10.00 —
2039a   30ch Unsurfaced white pa-
      per, without gum   10.00 —
2040a   40ch Unsurfaced white pa-
      per, without gum   10.00 —
2041a   70ch Unsurfaced white pa-
      per, without gum   10.00 —
2042a   1w Unsurfaced white pa-
      per, without gum   10.00 —

**Nos. 1925-1932 Overprinted
For Nobel Prize Winners in
Medicine**

1981, Mar. 20   **Perf. 11¾x11½**
2043-2049 A1005 Set of 7   9.00 3.00
2049a   Sheet of 8, as #2043-2050   12.00 —
Souvenir Sheet
2050 A1005 50ch multicolored   9.00

**Nos. 1698-1710 Overprinted
History of the World Cup**

1981, Mar. 20   **Perf. 13¼**
2051-2062 A953 Set of 12   24.00 —
2062a   Sheet of 12, #2051-2062   25.00 —
Souvenir Sheet
2063 A953 50ch multicolored   12.00

Copa de Oro Mini-World Cup
Championships — A1038

Designs: 20ch, Uruguayan and Brazilian
soccer players.
1w, Goalkeeper blocking ball.

1981, Mar. 27
2064 A1038 20ch multicolored   4.00 1.25
Souvenir Sheet
2065 A1038 1w multicolored   8.00 1.00

España '82 — A1039

Nos. 2066-2068 depict different designs
incorporating bleachers and crowds, with
images of soccer players and trophy that
appear or disappear, depending upon the
angle from which the stamps are viewed. This
effect is created by printing on multiple layers
of thin plastic, with gummed paper backing.

1981, Apr. 10   **Imperf.**
2066-2067 A1039 Set of 2,
     20ch, 30ch 25.00   9.00
Souvenir Sheet
2068 A1039 1w multicolored   25.00 25.00
Nos. 2066-2068 are airmail.

Naposta '81 Int'l Stamp Exhibition,
Stuttgart — A1040

Designs: 10ch, Dornier Do-X flying boat.
20ch, Count von Zeppelin and airship LZ-120.
30ch, Goetz von Berlichingen (1480-1562),
German knight and subject of poem by
Johann von Goethe (1749-1832), also
pictured.
70ch, Mercedes-Benz W 196, 1954
automobile.

1981, Apr. 28   **Perf. 12x11¾**
2069-2071 A1040 Set of 3   8.00 1.60
Souvenir Sheet
Perf. 11½x11¾
2072 A1040 70ch multicolored   5.50 2.75

World Telecommunications
Day — A1041

1981, May 17   **Perf. 11¾x11½**
2073 A1041 10ch multicolored   2.75 .25

Flowers — A1042

Designs: 10ch, Iris pseudodacorus. 20ch,
Iris pallasii. 30ch, Gladiolus gandavensis.

1981, May 20   **Perf. 12x11¾**
2074-2076 A1042 Set of 3   3.50 1.60
2076a   Sheet of 3, #2074-2076   3.75

WIPA 1981 Stamp Exhibition,
Vienna — A1043

Designs: 20ch, Austrian WIPA 1981 and
Rudolf Kirchschlager stamps. 30ch, Austrian
Maria Theresa and Franz Josef stamps.
50ch, Kim Il Sung and Korean Children's
Union choir, vert.

1981, May 22   **Perf. 13¼**
2077-2078 A1043 Set of 2   6.00 1.60
Souvenir Sheet
Perf. 11½
2079 A1043 50ch multicolored   6.00 2.75

International
Gymnastc
Federation,
Centen.
A1044

Gymnastic events: 10ch, Rings. 15ch, Pommel horse. 20ch, Long horse. 25ch, Floor.
30ch, Hoop.
70ch, Ribbon, horiz.

1981, May 25   **Perf. 11¾x12**
2080-2084 A1044 Set of 5   3.75 1.40
2084a   Sheet of 6, as #2080-2085   15.00 —
Souvenir Sheet
Perf. 11½x11¾
2085 A1044 70ch multicolored   3.00 1.00
For overprints, see Nos. 2270-2275.

Mingyuehgou
Meeting, 50th
Anniv. — A1045

1981, June 15   **Perf. 12¼x12**
2086 A1045 10ch multicolored   .50 .25

Taen
Work
System,
20th
Anniv.
A1046

1981, June 25   **Perf. 12x12¼**
2087 A1046 10ch multicolored   .50 .25

New System of Agricultural Guidance,
20th Anniv. — A1047

1981, June 25
2088 A1047 10ch multicolored   .50 .25

Anti-Japanese
Women's Assoc.,
55th
Anniv. — A1048

1981, July 5   **Perf. 12¼**
2089 A1048 5w multicolored   12.00 1.00

Opera *Sea
of Blood*,
10th
Anniv.
A1049

1981, July 17   **Perf. 12**
2090 A1049 10w multicolored   30.00 10.00

Joan of
Arc, 550th
Anniv.
Death
A1050

Designs: 10ch (No. 2091), Joan of Arc. 10ch
(No. 2092a), Archangel Michael. 70ch, Joan of
Arc in armor.
No. 2094, as No. 2092b.

1981, July 20
2091	A1050	multicolored	3.50 .75
2092		Sheet of 2, #2092a-2092b	9.00
a.		10ch multicolored	— —
b.		70ch multicolored	— —

Souvenir Sheet
Perf. 11½
2094	A1050	70ch multicolored	7.00 1.90

Down-with-Imperialism Union, 55th
Anniv. — A1051

1981, July 25　　　　　　　**Perf. 12¼**
2095	A1051	1w multicolored	6.00 2.00

Rembrandt,
375th Birth
Anniv.
A1052

Designs: 10ch, *Young Girl by the Window.*
20ch, *Rembrandt's Mother.* 30ch, *Saskia van
Uylenburgh.* 40ch, *Pallas Athenae.*
70ch, *Self-portrait.*

1981, July 25　　　　　　　**Perf. 13¼**
2096-2099	A1052	Set of 4	7.00 2.75

Souvenir Sheet
2100	A1052	70ch multicolored	5.50 3.00

Symposium of the Non-Aligned
Countries on Increasing Agricultural
Production — A1053

Designs: 10ch, Emblem, banners over
Pyongyang. 50ch, Harvesting grain. 90ch,
Marchers with banners, tractors, fields,
factories.

1981, Aug. 26　　　　　　　**Perf. 12**
2101-2103	A1053	Set of 3	2.00 1.00

Royal
Wedding
A1054

Designs: 10ch, St. Paul's Cathedral. 20ch,
Prince Charles on Great Britain #599. 30ch,
Princess Diana. 40ch, Prince Charles in military uniform.
70ch, Prince Charles and Princess Diana.

1981, Sept. 18　　　　　　　**Perf. 13¼**
2104-2107	A1054	Set of 4	10.00 3.00

Souvenir Sheet
2108	A1054	70ch multicolored	15.00 5.00

For overprints, see Nos. 2205-2209.

Reubens Paintings — A1055

Designs: 10ch, *The Four Philosophers.*
15ch, *Portrait of Helena Fourment.* 20ch, *Portrait of Isabella Brandt.* 25ch, *The Education of
Maria de Medici.* 30ch, *Helena Fourment and
Her Child.* 40ch, *Helena Fourment in Her
Wedding Dress.*
70ch, *Portrait of Nikolaas Rubens.*

1981, Sept. 20　　　　　　　**Perf. 11¾x12**
2109-2114	A1055	Set of 6	9.00 2.75

Souvenir Sheet
Perf 11½
2115	A1055	70ch multicolored	5.50 2.75

Royal Wedding — A1056

Designs: 10ch, Prince Charles and Princess
Diana wedding portrait. 20ch, Charles and
Diana with Flower Girl. 30ch, Charles and
Diana leaving St. Paul's Cathedral. 40ch,
Wedding portrait. (diff.)
70ch, Charles and Diana with Queen Eliza-
beth on balcony.

1981, Sept. 29　　　　　　　**Perf. 13¼**
2116-2119	A1056	Sheet of 4	20.00 4.50

Souvenir Sheet
2120	A1056	70ch multicolored	25.00 6.00

Philatokyo '81
International
Stamp
Exhibition,
Tokyo — A1057

Design: 10ch, Rowland Hill and first stamps
of Great Britain, Japan and DPRK. 20ch,
DPRK World Fairy Tale stamps. 30ch, Three
Japanese stamps.
70ch, Exhibition Hall.

1981, Oct. 9　　　　　　　**Perf. 11¾x11x½**
2121-2123	A1057	Set of 3	9.00 2.50
2123a		Sheet of 4, as #2121-2124,	27.50 —
		perf 12x11½	

Souvenir Sheet
2124	A1057	70ch multicolored	7.00 2.00

Philatokyo '81 — A1058

Designs (both 10ch): No. 2125, Two DPRK
stamps. No. 2126, DPRK stamp featuring
Juche torch.

1981, Oct. 9　　　　　　　**Perf. 12x12¼**
2125-2126	A1058	Set of 2	4.00 1.40

League of Socialist Working Youth of
Korea, 7th Congress — A1059

1981, Oct. 20　　　　　　　**Perf. 12x11¾**
2127	A1059	10ch multicolored	.25 .25
2128	A1059	80ch multicolored	1.00 .35

Bulgarian
State,
1300th
Anniv.
A1060

1981, Oct. 20　　　　　　　**Perf. 12x12¼**
2129	A1060	10ch multicolored	.50 .25

Georgi Dimitrov
(1882-1949), Birth
Centenary
A1061

1981, Nov. 5　　　　　　　**Perf. 12**
2130	A1061	10ch multicolored	.50 .25

Philatelia '81 Int'l Stamp Fair,
Frankfurt-am-Main — A1062

1981, Nov. 14　　　　　　　**Perf. 13¼**
2131	A1062	20ch multicolored	3.00 .45

A1063

Philexfrance
'82
International
Stamp
Exhibition,
Paris
A1064

Designs: 10ch, Count Ferdinand von
Zeppelin, *Graf Zeppelin,* Concorde. 20ch, Aircraft — Santos-Dumont 1905, Brequet 1930,
Brequet Provence 1950, Concorde 1970.
30ch, Mona Lisa, six French stamps.
No. 2135: 10ch, Hotel des Invalides, Paris.
20ch, Pres. Mitterand of France. 30ch, International Friendship Building. 70ch, Kim Il
Sung.
No. 2136: 60ch, Two French stamps picturing Rembrandt portrait and Picasso painting.

1981, Dec. 1　　　　　　　**Perf. 13¼**
2132-2134	A1063	Set of 3	10.00 2.00
2135		Sheet of 4, #a.-d.	7.50 2.50
a.	A1064	10ch multicolored	1.25 .50
b.	A1064	20ch multicolored	1.25 .50
c.	A1064	30ch multicolored	1.25 .50
d.	A1064	70ch multicolored	1.25 .50

Souvenir Sheet
2136	A1063	60ch multicolored	7.50 2.25

New
Year — A1065

1982, Jan. 1　　　　　　　**Perf. 12**
2137	A1065	10ch multicolored	.90 .25

"Korea Prospering
Under the Wise
Leadership of the
Party" — A1066

Party emblem and: 2ch, banners. 10ch (No.
2139), Iron industry. 10ch (No. 2140), Produce, city, countryside. 10ch (No. 2141), Film
industry. 10ch (No. 2142), Mining. 10ch (No.
2143), Lighthouse, helicopter. 40ch, Idealized
cityscape.

1982, Feb. 1
2138-2144	A1066	Set of 7	7.00 1.50

A1067

Pablo Picasso (1881-1973), Painter,
Birth Centenary — A1068

Designs (Nos. 2145-2148): 10ch, *La Coif-fure.* 20ch, *Woman Leaning on Arm.* 25ch, *Child with Pigeon.* 35ch, *Portrait of Gertrude Stein.*
No. 2149: 10ch, *Paulo on a Donkey.* 20ch, *Harlequin.* 25ch, *Reading a Letter.* 35ch, *Harlequin* (diff.) 80ch, *Minotaur.* 90ch, *Mother and Child.*
Nos. 2150-2151: 80ch, *Minotaur.* 90ch, *Mother and Child.*

1982, Mar. 30   *Perf. 11¾*
2145-2148	A1067	Set of 4	6.00	1.50
2149		Sheet of 6, #a.-f.	14.00	2.75
a.		A1067 10ch multicolored	2.25	.45
b.		A1067 20ch multicolored	2.25	.45
c.		A1067 25ch multicolored	2.25	.45
d.		A1067 35ch multicolored	2.25	.45
e.		A1067 80ch multicolored	2.25	.45
f.		A1067 90ch multicolored	2.25	.45

Souvenir Sheets
2150-2151	A1068	Set of 2	8.00	4.00

A1069

A1070

Kim Il Sung, 70th Birthday — A1071

Type A1069 (both 10ch): No. 2152, Kim Il Sung's Birthplace. No. 2153, Fireworks over Pyongyang.
Type A1070 (10ch), paintings of Kim Il Sung: No. 2154, "The Day Will Dawn." No. 2155, Signaling the start of the Pochonbo battle. No. 2156, Groundbreaking of Potong River Project. No. 2157, Embracing bereaved children. No. 2158, Directing operations at front. No. 2159, "On the Road of Advance." No. 2160, Speaking with workers at Kangson Steel Plant. No. 2161, Talking with peasants. No. 2162, Choosing site for reservoir.
Type A1070 (20ch): No. 2163, Visiting Komdok Valley. No. 2164, With Red Flag Company. No. 2165, With farmers. No. 2166, Opening metallurgical plant. No. 2167, Talking with smelters. No. 2168, At chemical plant. No. 2169, With fishermen.
No. 2170, Kim surrounded by adoring Koreans. No. 2171, Kim as a boy.

Perf. 11¾x12 (#2151-2152), 12x11¾
1982, Apr. 15
2152-2169		Set of 18	8.00 2.25

Souvenir Sheets
Perf. 13¼
2170-2171	A1071	60ch Set of 2	5.00 1.75

All type A1070 stamps were issued with setenant labels bearing inscriptions relating to theme of stamp. Values are for stamps with labels attached.

Korean People's Army, 50th Anniv. A1072

1982, Apr. 25   *Perf. 12*
2172	A1072	10ch multicolored	.50 .25

ESSEN '82 Int'l Stamp Fair — A1073

1982, Apr. 28   *Perf. 11¾x12*
2173	A1073	30ch multicolored	4.50 .50

Four Nature-
Remaking
Tasks — A1074

1982, Apr. 30   *Perf. 12*
2174	A1074	10ch multicolored	.60 .25

Issued to publicize the program for nature transformation contained in the Second Seven-Year Plan, which included irrigation, land reclamation, terracing, afforestation and water conservation, and reclamation of tidal lands.

Princess
Diana, 21st
Birthday
A1075

Princess Diana (Nos. 2175-2177): 10ch, As a baby. 20ch, As little girl on swing. 30ch, As little girl wearing red parka.
No. 2178: 50ch, As girl, wearing blue turtleneck sweater. 60ch, With long hair, wearing gray hat. 70ch, Wearing white hat. 80ch, Wearing white blouse and sweater.
Nos. 2179-2180: 40ch, Diana pushing her brother on swing. 80ch, As No. 2178d.

1982, May 1   *Perf. 13¼*
2175-2177	A1075	Set of 3	4.00	1.00
2178		Sheet of 4, #a.-d.	18.00	5.50
a.		A1075 50ch multicolored	3.50	1.25
b.		A1075 60ch multicolored	3.50	1.25
c.		A1075 70ch multicolored	3.50	1.25
d.		A1075 80ch multicolored	3.50	1.25

Souvenir Sheets
2179-2180	A1075	Set of 2	10.00 5.00

For overprints, see Nos. 2210-2215.

Tower of the Juche
Idea — A1076

1982, May 21   *Perf. 12*
2182	A1076	2w multicolored	7.50 2.00

Arch of
Triumph — A1077

1982, May 22
2183	A1074	3w multicolored	8.50 2.00

Tigers
A1078

Nos. 2184-2185: 20ch, Tiger cubs. 30ch, Tiger cubs. (diff.)
No. 2186 (designs horizontal): 30ch, Tiger cub with mother. 40ch, Two cubs playing. 80ch, Two cubs playing, diff.
Nos. 2187: 80ch, Two cubs, horiz.

Perf. 11¾x12 (#2185-2186), 12x11¾
1982, May 30
2184-2185	A1078	Set of 2	7.00	1.00
2186		Sheet of 3, #a.-c.	16.00	3.00
a.		A1078 30ch multicolored	3.00	.50
b.		A1078 40ch multicolored	3.00	.50
c.		A1078 80ch multicolored	3.00	.50

Souvenir Sheet
2187	A1078	80ch Multicolored	6.00 1.50

ESPANA '82 World Cup
Championship — A1079

Flags and players of: 10ch, Group 1 countries — Italy, Peru, Poland, Cameroun. 20ch, Group 2 countries — Germany, Chile, Algeria, Austria. 30ch, Group 3 countries — Argentina, Hungary, Belgium, El Salvador. 40ch, Group 4 countries — Great Britain, Czechoslovakia, France, Kuwait. 50ch, Group 5 countries — Spain, Yugoslavia, Honduras, Northern Ireland. 60ch, Group 6 countries — Brazil, Scotland, USSR, New Zealand.
1w, Soccer players, flags, trophy and ESPANA '82 emblem.

1982, June 12   *Perf. 13¼*
2188-2193	A1079	Set of 6	13.00 4.00

Souvenir Sheet
2194	A1079	1w multicolored	11.00 4.00

For overprints, see Nos. 2217-2223.

Space
Exploration
A1080

Designs: 10ch, Rocket launch. 20ch, Spaceship over planet.
No. 2197a, Spaceship between planets.
No. 2198, Spaceship exploring desert area of other planet.

1982, June 20   *Perf. 11¾x11½*
2195-2196	A1080	Set of 2	3.50	1.50
2197		Sheet of 3, #2195-2196, 2197a + label	6.00	2.50
a.		A1080 80ch multicolored	2.00	.75

Souvenir Sheet
2198	A1079	80ch multicolored	3.75 1.50

Johann von Goethe (1749-1832), Writer, 150th Death Anniv. A1081

Silhouettes: 10ch, Charlotte von Stein. 20ch, Goethe's sister. 25ch, Charlotte Buff. 35ch, Lili Schönemann.
No. 2203: 10ch, Goethe's mother. 20ch, Angelika Kauffman. 25ch, Anna Amalia. 35ch, Charlotte von Lengefeld. 80ch, Goethe.
No. 2204: 80ch, Goethe.

1982, July 25   **Perf. 11¾x12**

2199-2202	A1081 Set of 4	3.75	1.50
2203	Sheet of 5, #a.-e. + label	9.00	2.00
a.	A1081 10ch multicolored	1.75	.50
b.	A1081 20ch multicolored	1.75	.50
c.	A1081 25ch multicolored	1.75	.50
d.	A1081 35ch multicolored	1.75	.50
e.	A1081 80ch multicolored	1.75	.50

Souvenir Sheet

2204	A1081 80ch multicolored	4.00	1.75

Nos. 2104-2108 Overprinted in Blue

1982, Aug. 20

2205-2208	A1054 Set of 4	15.00	—

Souvenir Sheet

2209	A1054 70ch multicolored	15.00	—

Nos. 2175-2179 Overprinted in Blue

1982, Aug. 20

2210-2212	A1075 Set of 3	15.00	—
2213	Sheet of 4	30.00	—

Souvenir Sheet

2214-2215	A1075 Set of 2	25.00	—

Nos. 2025a, 2188-2194 Overprinted in Blue

1982, Aug. 25

2216	A1035 Sheet of 4, #a.-d.	14.00	—
a.	10ch multicolored	1.00	—
b.	20ch multicolored	2.00	—
c.	30ch multicolored	3.00	—
d.	70ch multicolored	6.00	—
2217-2222	A1079 Set of 6	15.00	—

Souvenir Sheet

2223	A1079 1w multicolored	12.50	

ESPANA '82 World Soccer Cup Winners — A1082

Designs: 20ch, Player holding World Cup aloft. 30ch, Three players with World Cup.
No. 2226: 30ch, as No. 2222. 40ch, As No. 2223. 80ch, King Juan Carlos of Spain and two players with World Cup.
No. 2227: 80ch, as No. 2226c.

1982, Aug. 30   **Perf. 13¼**

2224-2225	A1082 Set of 2	4.00	1.00
2226	Sheet of 3, #a.-c. + label	8.00	
a.	A1082 30ch multicolored	—	—
b.	A1082 40ch multicolored	—	—
c.	A1082 80ch multicolored	—	—

Souvenir Sheet

2227	A1082 80ch multicolored	9.00	2.00

A1083

1st Wedding Anniv. of Prince and Princess of Wales — A1084

1982, Sept. 21

2228	A1083 30ch multicolored	10.00	4.00

Souvenir Sheet

2229	A1084 80ch multicolored	15.00	5.00

No. 2228 was issued in sheets of four stamps and two labels.

Birth of Prince William of Wales A1085

Designs: 10ch, Charles and Diana with Prince William (Charles in suit, Diana in pink hat and dress). 20ch, Couple with William. 30ch, Couple with William (diff.). 40ch, Diana with William. 50ch, Diana with William (diff.).
No. 2235: 10ch, Diana holding bouquet. 20ch, Charles carrying William, with Diana. 30ch, Charles carrying William, with Diana (diff.). 80ch, Couple with William (diff.).
No. 2236 (horiz.): 40ch, Charles and Diana. 50ch, Charles and Diana in evening dress. 80ch, Charles holding William, with Diana.
Nos. 2237-2238 (both 80ch): Diana holding William, with Royal Family; Diana holding William, with godparents.

1982, Sept. 29

2230-2234	A1085 Set of 5	16.00	5.00
2235	Sheet of 4, #a.-d.	15.00	6.00
a.	A1085 10ch multicolored	3.25	1.25
b.	A1085 20ch multicolored	3.25	1.25
c.	A1085 30ch multicolored	3.25	1.25
d.	A1085 80ch multicolored	3.25	1.25
2236	Sheet of 3, #a.-c.	15.00	6.00
a.	A1085 40ch multicolored	4.00	1.75
b.	A1085 50ch multicolored	4.00	1.75
c.	A1085 80ch multicolored	4.00	1.75

Souvenir Sheets

2237-2238	A1085 Set of 2	20.00	8.00

A1086

Birth of Prince William of Wales — A1087

Nos. 2239-2244 are composed of layered plastic, on gummed paper, which creates two different images on each stamp, depending on the angle at which it is viewed.
30ch: No. 2239, Charles, Diana and William/Diana holding William. No. 2240, Charles, Diana and William (diff.)/Couple with William (Charles in suit, Diana in pink hat and dress). No. 2241, Diana and William/Charles and Diana with William (Charles in suit, Diana in blue dress).
80ch: No. 2242, Diana and William, Portrait of Diana/Charles. No. 2243, Diana and William, St. Paul's Church/Wedding portrait of Royal Couple. No. 2244, Charles and Diana with William/Diana holding bouquet.

1982, Oct. 1   **Imperf.**

2239-2241	A1086 Set of 3	35.00	—

Souvenir Sheets

2242-2244	A1087 Set of 3	60.00	—

Nos. 2242-2244 have simulated rouletting.

Bicentenary of Manned Flight — A1088

Designs: 10ch, Baldwin's airship *Nulli Secundus II*, 1908. 20ch, Tissandier Brothers' airship, 1883. 30ch, Parseval *PL VIII*, 1912. 40ch, Count Lennox's balloon *Eagle*, 1834.

No. 2249: 10ch, Pauley and Durs Egg's airship, *The Dolphin*, 1818. 20ch, Guyton de Morveau's balloon, 1784. 30ch, Sir George Cayley's airship, 1837. 40ch, Camille Vert's balloon *Poisson Volant*, 1859. 80ch, Dupuy de Lôme's airship, 1872.
No. 2250: Masse's oar-powered balloon, 1784, vert.

1982, Nov. 21   **Perf. 13¼**

2245-2248	A1088 Set of 4	7.00	2.00
2249	Sheet of 5, #a.-e. + label	13.00	6.00
a.	A1088 10ch multicolored	2.25	1.00
b.	A1088 20ch multicolored	2.25	1.00
c.	A1088 30ch multicolored	2.25	1.00
d.	A1088 40ch multicolored	2.25	1.00
e.	A1088 80ch multicolored	2.25	1.00

Souvenir Sheet

2250	A1085 80ch multicolored	4.50	2.00

Bicentenary of Manned Flight A1089

Designs: 10ch, Balthasar Antoine Dunker's *Utopic Balloon Post*, 1784-90. 20ch, "and they fly into heaven and have no wings." 30ch, Pierre Testu-Brissy's balloon flight with horse, 1796. 40ch, Test flight of Gaston Tissandier's balloon *Zenith*, 1875.
No. 2255: 10ch, Montgolfier balloon at Versailles, 1783. 20ch, Montgolfier Brothers' balloon, 1783. 30ch, Charles' hydrogen balloon landing at Nesle. 40ch, Blanchard and Jeffries' flight over the English Channel, 1785. 80ch, Henri Giffard's balloon *Le Grand Ballon Captif* at World's Fair, 1878.
No. 2256: "Ballons Monte" balloon mail service from besieged Paris, 1870-1871.

1982, Dec. 10

2251-2254	A1089 Set of 4	11.00	4.00
2255	Sheet of 5, #a.-e. + label	25.00	6.50
a.	A1089 10ch multicolored	4.50	1.25
b.	A1089 20ch multicolored	4.50	1.25
c.	A1089 30ch multicolored	4.50	1.25
d.	A1089 40ch multicolored	4.50	1.25
e.	A1089 80ch multicolored	4.50	1.25

Souvenir Sheet

2256	A1089 80ch multicolored	5.00	2.00

Tale of the Hare — A1090

Designs: 10ch, Turtle searching for hare. 20ch, Turtle and hare going to Dragon King Palace. 30ch, Hare swindling Dragon King, demanding her liver. 40ch, Hare cheating turtle.

1982, Dec. 25   **Perf. 12**

2257-2260	A1090 Set of 4	8.00	1.25

Socialist Constitution, 10th Anniv. — A1091

1982, Dec. 27

2261	A1091 10ch multicolored	.50	.25

New Year — A1092

1983, Jan. 1   *Perf. 12¼x12*
2262 A1092 10ch multicolored   .50 .25

Saenal Newspaper, 55th
Anniv. — A1093

1983, Jan. 15   *Perf. 11½x11¾*
2263 A1093 10ch multicolored   .90 .25

Rembrandt
Paintings
A1094

Designs: 10ch, *Man in Oriental Costume.*
20ch, *The Noble Slav.* 30ch, *Dr. Tulp's Anatomy Lesson* (detail). 40ch, *Two Scholars
Disputing.*
No. 2268: 10ch, *Child with Dead Peacocks.*
20ch, *Old Man in Fur Hat.* 30ch, *Portrait of a
Fashionable Couple.* 40ch, *Woman with Child.*
80ch, *Woman Holding an Ostrich Feather Fan.*
No. 2269: 80ch, *Self-Portrait.*

1983, Jan. 25   *Perf. 11¾x11½*
2264-2267 A1094 Set of 4   7.50 1.50
2268   Sheet of 5, #a.-e. + label 15.00 7.50
a.   A1094 10ch multicolored   2.00 1.00
b.   A1094 20ch multicolored   2.00 1.00
c.   A1094 30ch multicolored   2.00 1.00
d.   A1094 40ch multicolored   2.00 1.00
e.   A1094 80ch multicolored   2.00 1.00

Souvenir Sheet
Perf. 11¾x12
2269 A1094 80ch multicolored   4.00 1.25

**Nos. 2080-2085 Overprinted "XXIII
Summer Olympic Games 1984" and
Olympic Rings**

1983, Feb. 10
2270-2274 A1044 Set of 5   20.00   —
2274a   Sheet of 6, as #2270-2275 75.00   —

Souvenir Sheet
2275 A1044 70ch multicolored   25.00

Luposta Int'l Air Mail Exhib.,
Köln — A1095

1983, Jan. 25   *Perf. 11¾x11½*
2276 30ch multicolored   3.00 1.00
2277 40ch multicolored   3.00 1.00
a.   Pair, #2276-2277   7.00 3.00

Virgin and Child, by Stephan
Lochner — A1096

Souvenir Sheet
Perf. 13¼
2278 A1096 80ch multicolored   3.50 1.75

Wangjaesen
Meeting, 50th
Anniv.
A1097

1983, Mar. 11   *Perf. 11½x11¾*
2279 A1097 10ch multicolored   .50 .25

Karl Marx,
Centenary of
Death — A1098

1983, Mar. 14   *Perf. 11¾x12*
2280 A1098 10ch multicolored   2.25 .25

Thousand-ri Journey for Learning,
60th Anniv. — A1099

1983, Mar. 16   *Perf. 12*
2281 A1099 10ch multicolored   1.00 .25

A1100

Raphael (1483-1520), 500th Birth
Anniv. — A1101

Designs: 10ch, *Madonna of the Goldfinch.*
30ch, *Madonna of the Grand Duke.* 50ch (No.
2284), *Madonna of the Chair.*
No. 2285: 20ch, *The School of Athens*
(detail). 50ch (No. 2285b), *Madonna of the
Lamb.* 80ch, *The Beautiful Gardener.*
No. 2286: 80ch, *Madonna of St. Sixte.*

1983, Mar. 20   *Perf. 13½*
2282-2284 A1100 Set of 3   6.00 1.00
2285   Sheet of 3, #a.-c. + label 15.00 3.50
a.   A1100 20ch multicolored   4.00 .75
b.   A1100 50ch multicolored   4.00 .75
c.   A1100 80ch multicolored   4.00 .75

Souvenir Sheet
2286 A1101 80ch multicolored   4.50 1.25

Pyongyang Buildings — A1102

Designs: 2ch, Chongryu Restaurant. 10ch
(No. 2288), Munsu Street. 10ch (No. 2289),
Ice Rink. 40ch, Department Store No. 1. 70ch,
Grand People's Study House.

1983, Apr. 7   *Perf. 12¼*
2287-2291 A1102 Set of 5   6.00 .75
2287a   2ch Unsurfaced white pa-
         per, without gum   10.00 —
2288a   10ch Unsurfaced white pa-
         per, without gum   10.00 —
2289a   10ch Unsurfaced white pa-
         per, without gum   10.00 —
2290a   40ch Unsurfaced white pa-
         per, without gum   10.00 —
2291a   40ch Unsurfaced white pa-
         per, without gum   10.00 —

Int'l Institute of
the Juche Idea,
5th
Anniv. — A1103

1983, Apr. 9   *Perf. 12¼12*
2292 A1103 10ch multicolored   .50 .25

Pre-Olympic Games, Los Angeles
'84 — A1104

Designs (values in gold): 20ch (No. 2293),
Judo. 30ch (No. 2294), Judo (diff.). 40ch (No.
2295), Boxing. 50ch (No. 2296), Weightlifting.
No. 2297 (values in black): 20ch, Wrestling.
30ch, Judo (diff.). 40ch, Shooting. 50ch, Wrestling. (diff.) 80ch, Boxing (diff.).
No. 2298: 80ch, Judo (diff.)

1983, Apr. 20   *Perf. 11¼*
2293-2296 A1104 Set of 4   13.00 1.50
2297   Sheet of 5, #a.-e. + label 25.00 1.00
a.   A1104 20ch multicolored   4.00 .25
b.   A1104 30ch multicolored   4.00 .25
c.   A1104 40ch multicolored   4.00 .25
d.   A1104 50ch multicolored   4.00 .25
e.   A1104 80ch multicolored   4.00 .25

Souvenir Sheet
Perf. 13½
2298 A1104 80ch multicolored   10.00 1.00

World Communications Year — A1105

1983, Apr. 30   *Perf. 11¾x12*
2299 A1105 10ch multicolored   2.00 .25

TEMBAL '83 Int'l Topical Stamp
Exhib., Basel — A1106

Designs: 20ch, Emblem, giant panda and
stamp. 30ch, Emblem, DPRK flag and "Basel
Dove" stamp (Switzerland No. 3L1).

1983, May 21   *Perf. 12*
2300-2301 A1106 Set of 2   7.50 .75

Old Ships — A1107

Designs: 20ch, Colourful Cow (Hamburg,
1402). 35ch, Great Harry (England, 1555).
50ch, Eagle of Lübeck (Lübeck, 1567).
No. 2305: 20ch, Turtle Boat (Korea, 1592).
35ch, Admiral Li Sun Sin (1545-98), inventor
of the Turtle Boat. 50ch, Merkur (Prussia,
1847). 80ch, Duchess Elisabeth (West
Germany).
No. 2306: 80ch, Christoforo Colombo (Italy).

1983, May 30   *Perf. 11x11¼*
2302-2304 A1107 Set of 3   5.00 1.50
2305   Sheet of 4, #a.-d. + 2 la-
        bels   12.00 2.50
a.   A1107 20ch multicolored   3.00 .50
b.   A1107 35ch multicolored   3.00 .50
c.   A1107 50ch multicolored   3.00 .50
d.   A1107 80ch multicolored   3.00 .50

Souvenir Sheet
Perf. 13½x13¼
2306 A1107 80ch multicolored   6.00 3.00

Steam Locomotives — A1108

Designs: 20ch, *Locomotion* (Great Britain, 1825). 35ch, *De Adler* (Germany, 1835). 50ch, *Austria* (1837).
No. 2310: 20ch, *Drache* (Germany, 1848). 35ch, Korean Train. 50ch, Bristal and Exeter Railway locomotive (Great Britain, 1853). 80ch, Caledonian Railway locomotive (Great Britain, 1859).
No. 2311: 80ch, *Ilmarinen* (Finland, 1860).

1983, June 20		**Perf. 12x11¾**	
2307-2309	A1108 Set of 3	13.00	2.50
2310	Sheet of 4, #a.-d. + 2 labels	40.00	3.50
a.	A1108 20ch multicolored	3.00	.75
b.	A1108 35ch multicolored	3.00	.75
c.	A1108 50ch multicolored	3.00	.75
d.	A1108 80ch multicolored	3.00	.75

Souvenir Sheet
Perf. 12

2311	A1108 80ch multicolored	30.00	1.50

Publication of the Five-Point Policy for Korean Reunification, 10th Anniv. — A1109

1983, June 23		**Perf. 12¼**	
2312	A1109 10ch multicolored	1.40	.25

World Conference of Journalists Against Imperialism and for Friendship and Peace — A1110

Designs: 10ch, Emblem, Tower of Juche Idea, fireworks, "Welcome." 40ch, Emblem, clasped hands, rainbow, "Friendship." Emblem, map, hand with raised forefinger, "Korea Is One."

1983, July 2		**Perf. 12x11¾**	
2313-2315	A1110 Set of 3	1.75	.30

"Let's Create the Speed of the 80s" A1111

1983, July 10		**Perf. 12x12¼**	
2316	A1111 10ch multicolored	.50	.25

Korean War, 30th Anniv. A1112

1983, July 27
2317	A1112 10ch multicolored	.50	.25

Bangkok 1983 Int'l Stamp Exhib. — A1113

Designs: 40ch, *Gorch Foch* and DPRK #1693. 80ch, Bangkok temple, Great Britain #1 and DPRK IYC stamp.

1983, Aug. 4		**Perf. 12x11¾**	
2318	A1113 40ch multicolored	3.50	1.00

Souvenir Sheet
Perf. 11½x11¾

2319	A1113 80ch multicolored	7.00	3.50

A1114

Winter Olympic Games, Sarajevo 1984 — A1115

Designs: 10ch, Skiier. 30ch, Figure skaters. 50ch, Ski jumper.
No. 2323 (all vert.): 20ch, Woman figure skater. 50ch, Hockey player. 80ch, Speed skater.
No. 2324, 80ch, Skier shooting rifle (biathlon).

1983, Aug. 20			
2320-2322	A1114 Set of 3	8.00	1.50
2323	Sheet of 3, #a.-c., perf 11¾x12	17.00	2.75
a.	A1114 20ch multicolored	4.00	.75
b.	A1114 50ch multicolored	4.00	.75
c.	A1114 80ch multicolored	4.00	.75

Souvenir Sheet

2324	A1115 80ch multicolored	7.50	1.25

Democratic People's Republic of Korea, 35th Anniv. — A1116

1983, Sept. 9		**Perf. 13¼x13½**	
2325	A1116 10ch multicolored	.65	.25

Folk Games — A1117

Designs: 10ch (No. 2326), Archery. 40ch (No. 2327), Seesaw. No. 2328: 10ch, Flying kites. 40ch, Swinging.

1983, Sept. 20		**Perf. 11¾x12**	
2326-2327	A1117 Set of 2	5.00	.50
2328	Sheet of 2, #a.-b.	2.50	.40
a.	A1117 10ch multicolored	.75	.25
b.	A1117 40ch multicolored	.75	.25

Korean-Chinese Friendship A1118

1983, Oct. 25		**Perf. 12**	
2329	A1118 10ch multicolored	.75	.25

A1119

World Communications Year — A1120

Designs: 30ch (No. 2330), *Redong Sinmun* and magazine. 40ch (No. 2331), Letters and forms of postal transport.
No. 2332: 30ch, Communications satellite, satellite dish. 40ch, TV camera and relay tower. 80ch, Telephone and satellite dishes.
No. 2333, 80ch, Emblem, communications satellite.

1983, Oct. 30		**Perf. 13½**	
2330-2331	A1119 Set of 2	9.00	1.75
2332	Sheet of 3, #a.-c.	5.50	1.00
a.	A1119 30ch multicolored	1.00	.25
b.	A1119 40ch multicolored	1.00	.25
c.	A1119 80ch multicolored	1.00	.25

Souvenir Sheet

2333	A1120 80ch multicolored	6.00	1.25

A1121

Paintings by Peter Paul Rubens — A1122

No. 2334, *Portrait of Helene Fourmet*.
No. 2335 (both horiz.): a., Detail from *Portrait of a Young Lady*. b., *Diana Returning from Hunt*.
No. 2336: *The Bear Hunt*.

1983, Nov. 10			
2334	A1121 40ch multicolored	1.75	.45
2335	Sheet of 2, #a.-b.	4.50	1.25
a.	A1121 40ch multicolored	1.75	.45
b.	A1121 80ch multicolored	1.75	.45

Souvenir Sheet

2336	A1122 80ch multicolored	3.25	.75

Olympic Games, Los Angeles 1984 A1123

Designs: 10ch, Sprinter. 30ch, Cyclists. 50ch, Volleyball.
No. 2340: 20ch, Show jumping. 50ch, Fencing. 80ch, Gymnastics.
No. 2341: 80ch, Judo.

1983, Nov. 30		**Perf. 11½**	
2337-2339	A1123 Set of 3	10.50	1.25
2340	Sheet of 3, #a.-c.	30.00	2.00
a.	A1123 20ch multicolored	7.00	.50
b.	A1123 50ch multicolored	7.00	.50
c.	A1123 80ch multicolored	7.00	.50

Souvenir Sheet

2341	A1123 80ch multicolored	3.50	1.00

Six deluxe souvenir sheets of one, each denominated 1w, exist. Value, set of 6 sheets, $100.

A1124

Antonio Correggio (1489-1534), 450th
Death Anniv. — A1125

Designs: 20ch, *St. Catherine*. 35ch,
Madonna. 50ch, *Madonna with St. John*.
   No. 2345: a., *Morning* (detail). b., *Morning*
(diff. detail). c., *St. Catherine* (diff.). d.,
Madonna and Child.
   No. 2346: *Madonna and Child with Music-
Making Angels*.

1983, Dec. 12   **Perf. 13¼**
2342-2344 A1124 Set of 3   5.00 1.25
2345   Sheet of 4, #a.-d.   12.00 3.50
   a.   A1124 20ch multicolored 2.50 .75
   b.   A1124 35ch multicolored 2.50 .75
   c.   A1124 50ch multicolored 2.50 .75
   d.   A1124 80ch multicolored 2.50 .75
            Souvenir Sheet
2346 A1125 80ch multicolored   4.50 1.25

Cats
A1126

Domestic cats, each different, denominated
10ch. Frame color: No. 2347, green. No. 2348,
gray. No. 2349, gold. No. 2350, red. No. 2351,
blue.

1983, Dec. 20
2347-2351 A1126 Set of 5   12.00 .50

Six souvenir sheets inscribed
Sarajevo '84, each containing one 1w
stamp, were issued on Dec. 31,
1983. Value $80.

New
Year — A1127

1984, Jan. 1   **Perf. 12**
2352 A1127 10ch multicolored   1.00 .25

Korean
Workers
Party
A1128

Designs (both 10ch): No. 2353, Komdok
General Mining Enterprise, Ore-dressing Plant
No. 3, and Party flag. No. 2354, Worker hold-
ing books, and Party flag.

1984, Feb. 16
2353-2354 A1128 Set of 2   1.00 .25
2353a   10ch Unsurfaced white pa-
              per, without gum   20.00 —
2354a   10ch Unsurfaced white pa-
              per, without gum   20.00 —

Farm
Worker,
Grain
A1129

1984, Feb. 25
2355 A1129 10ch multicolored   .60 .25
Publication of the *Theses on the Socialist
Rural Question in Our Country*, 20th anniv.

Changdok
School,
Chilgol
A1130

Kim's
Birthplace,
Rejoicing
Crowd
A1131

1984, Apr. 15
2356 A1130 5ch multicolored   .50 .25
   a. Unsurfaced white paper,
              without gum   15.00 —
2357 A1131 10ch multicolored   .50 .25
   a. Unsurfaced white paper,
              without gum   20.00 —
Kim Il Sung, 72nd birthday.

A1132

España '84 Int'l Stamp
Exhib. — A1133

Designs: 10ch, *Spanish Riding School of
Vienna*, by Julius von Blaas. 20ch, *Ferdinand
of Austria*, by Rubens.
   No. 2360: 80ch, *Spanish Riding School*, by
von Blaas.

1984, Apr. 27   **Perf. 13½**
2358-2359 A1132 Set of 2   3.50 .75
            Souvenir Sheet
2360 A1133 80ch multicolored   6.50 1.25

Kiyang Irrigation System, 25th
Anniv. — A1134

1984, Apr. 30
2361 A1134 10ch multicolored   .65 .25

Raphael, 500th
Anniv. of Birth
(in
1983) — A1135

Designs: 10ch, *Portrait of Angolo Doni*.
20ch, *Portrait of La Donna Velata*. 30ch, *Portrait of Jeanne d'Aragon*. 80ch, *St. Sebastian*.

1984, Apr. 30   **Perf. 11¾x12**
2362-2364 A1135 Set of 3   4.00 1.00
            Souvenir Sheet
            Perf. 11¾x11½
2365 A1135 80ch multicolored   3.50 1.25

Socialist
Construction
A1136

1984, May 20   **Perf. 12**
2366 A1136 10ch multicolored   .65 .25

1984 Winter Olympics Games Medal
Winners — A1137

Designs: 20ch (No. 2367), Speed skating
(Karin Enke, DDR). 30ch (No. 2368), Bobsled-
ding (DDR).
   No. 2369: 10ch, Ski jumping (Matti
Nykaenen, Finland). 20ch (No. 2369b), Slalom
(Max Julen, Switzerland). 30ch (No. 2369c),
Downhill skiing (Maria Walliser, Switzerland).
   No. 2370 (both vert.): 40ch, Cross-country
skiing (Thomas Wassberg, Sweden). 80ch,
Cross-country skiing (Maria Liisa
Hamalainen).
   No. 2371 (vert.): 80ch, Biathlon (Peter
Angerer, West Germany).

1984, May 20   **Perf. 13½**
2367-2368 A1137 Set of 2   3.00 .75
2369   Sheet of 3, #a.-c.   25.00 1.25
   a.   A1137 10ch multicolored 6.00 .35
   b.   A1137 20ch multicolored 6.00 .35
   c.   A1137 30ch multicolored 6.00 .35
2370   Sheet of 2, #a.-b.   5.00 1.00
   a.   A1137 40ch multicolored 2.00 .40
   b.   A1137 80ch multicolored 2.00 .40
            Souvenir Sheet
2371 A1137 80ch multicolored   3.50 1.00

Essen '84 Int'l Stamp Exhib. — A1138

Designs: 20ch, Type "202" express locomotive (1939). 30ch, Type "E" freight locomotive
(1919).
   No. 2374: 80ch, Type "D" locomotive in
Germany.

1984, May 26   **Perf. 12x11¾**
2372-2373 A1138 Set of 2   10.00 1.00
            Souvenir Sheet
2374 A1138 80ch multicolored   9.00 1.25

Edgar Degas, 150th Birth
Anniv. — A1139

Designs: 10ch, *Mlle. Fiocre in the Ballet 'La
Source.'* 20ch, *The Dance Foyer at the Rue le
Peletier Opera*. 30ch, *Race Meeting*.
   No. 2378: 80ch, *Dancers at the Bars*.

1984, June 10   **Perf. 12**
2375-2377 A1138 Set of 3   8.00 1.25
            Souvenir Sheet
            Perf. 11½
2378 A1139 80ch multicolored   4.50 1.25

Irrigation Experts Meeting — A1140

1984, June 16   **Perf. 11¾x12**
2379 A1140 2ch multicolored   .80 .25

UPU Congress/Hamburg 1984 Stamp
Exhib. — A1141

No. 2381: 80ch, *Gorch Fock*, DPRK stamp
depicting Turtle Boat.

1984, June 19
2380 A1141 20ch multicolored   3.50 .35
            Souvenir Sheet
            Perf. 11¾x11½
2381 A1141 80ch multicolored   6.00 2.00

Tripartite Talks
Proposal — A1142

1984, June 25   **Perf. 12¼**
2382 A1142 10ch multicolored   .65   .25

Alfred
Bernhard
Nobel,
150th Birth
Anniv. (in
1983)
A1143

Designs: 20ch, Nobel in laboratory. 30ch,
Nobel portrait.
No. 2385: 80ch, Nobel portrait, diff.

1984, June 30   **Perf. 13½**
2383-2384 A1143 Set of 2   8.00   .75
Souvenir Sheet
2385 A1143 80ch multicolored   7.00 2.00

Nos. 2383 and 2384 were issued se-tenant
with labels depicting Nobel's laboratory and
home, respectively.

Improvement of Korean Living
Standards — A1144

1984, July 10   **Perf. 11¾x12**
2386 A1144 10ch multicolored   .70   .25

Kuandian
Conf.,
65th
Anniv.
A1145

1984, Aug. 17   **Perf. 12x12¼**
2387 A1145 10ch multicolored   1.25   .25

Sunhwa School,
Mangyongdae — A1146

1984, Aug. 17   **Perf. 12**
2388 A1146 10ch multicolored   1.10   .25

School of Kim Il Sung's father, Kim Hyong
Jik.

A1147

A1148

Flowers: 10ch, *Cattleya loddigesii.* 20ch,
Thunia bracteata. 30ch, *Phalaenopsis
amabilis.*
No. 2392: 80ch, *Kimilsungia.*

1984, Aug. 20
2389-2391 A1147 Set of 3   4.00   .60
Souvenir Sheet
2392 A1148 80ch multicolored   5.00 1.00

Fishing
Industry
A1149

Designs: 5ch, Swordfish and trawler. 10ch,
Marlin and trawler. 40ch, *Histiophorus
orientalis.*

1984, Aug. 25
2393-2395 A1149 Set of 3   4.50 1.00

Revolutionary Museum,
Chilgol — A1150

1984, Aug. 29
2396 A1150 10ch multicolored   .90   .25

"Let's All Become
the Kim Hyoks and
Cha Gwang Sus of
the '80s!" — A1151

1984, Aug. 31
2397 A1151 10ch multicolored   .90   .25

Orient Express, Centenary — A1152

Designs: 10ch, Inauguration of a French railway line in 1860. 20ch, Opening of a British

---

railway line in 1821. 30ch, Inauguration of
Paris-Rouen line, 1843.
No. 2401: 80ch, Interior views of passenger
cars, 1905.

1984, Sept. 7   **Perf. 13½x13¼**
2398-2400 A1152 Set of 3   8.00 1.25
Souvenir Sheet
2401 A1152 80ch multicolored   7.00 1.75

Greenwich
Meridian Time,
Centenary
A1153

Designs: 10ch, Clockface, astronomical
observatory.
No. 2403: 80ch, Clock face, buildings, Chollima statue.

1984, Sept. 15   **Perf. 12**
2402 A1153 10ch multicolored   4.00 —
Souvenir Sheet
    Perf. 11¾x11½
2403 A1153 80ch multicolored   6.00 1.25

Hamhung
Grand
Theater
A1154

1984, Sept. 21
2404 A1154 10ch multicolored   .90   .25

Automation of
Industry — A1155

1984, Sept. 25   **Perf. 12¼**
2405 A1155 10ch multicolored   .90   .25
   a.   Unsurfaced white paper, with-
      out gum   8.00 —

A1156

18th Century Korean
Paintings — A1157

Designs: 10ch, *Dragon Angler.* 20ch, *Ox
Driver,* horiz. 30ch, *Bamboo,* horiz.
80ch, *Autumn Night.*

1984, Sept. 30   **Perf. 12 (#2406), 13¼**
2406-2408 A1156 Set of 3   4.00   .60

Souvenir Sheet
    Perf. 13¼
2409 A1157 80ch multicolored   3.50 1.25

K.E.
Tsiolkovski
(1857-1935),
Russian Space
Scientist
A1158

Designs: 20ch, Portrait. 30ch, Earth,
sputnik.
No. 2412: 80ch, Rocket launch.

1984, Oct. 5   **Perf. 11¾**
2410-2411 A1158 Set of 2   2.00   .45
Souvenir Sheet
    Perf. 11¾x11½
2412 A1158 80ch multicolored   4.00   .75

Container Ships — A1159

Designs: 10ch, *Pongdaesan.* 20ch,
Ryongnamsan. 30ch, *Rungrado.*
No. 2416: 80ch, *Kumgangsan*

1984, Oct. 6   **Perf. 12x11¾**
2413-2415 A1158 Set of 3   3.50   .75
Souvenir Sheet
    Perf. 12
2416 A1159 80ch multicolored   5.00 1.25

A1160

A1161

Wild Animals: 10ch, Spotted hyenas. 20ch,
Caracal. 30ch, Black-backed jackals. 40ch,
Foxes.
80ch, Falcon.

1984, Oct. 13   **Perf. 13¼**
2417-2420 A1160 Set of 4   4.50 1.00
Souvenir Sheet
2421 A1161 80ch multicolored   6.50 1.25

Marie Curie (1867-1934), Physicist, 50th Death Anniv. A1162

No. 2423: 80ch, Portrait of Mme. Curie.

1984, Oct. 21   **Perf. 12**
2422 A1162 10ch multicolored   4.00   .25
    Souvenir Sheet
    Perf. 11¾x11½
2423 A1162 80ch multicolored   6.00   1.25

A1163

Birds: 10ch, Hoopoe. 20ch, South African crowned cranes. 30ch, Saddle-bill stork. 40ch, Chestnut-eared Aracari.
No. 2428: 80ch, Black kite.

1984, Nov. 5   **Perf. 11½**
2424-2427 Set of 4   8.50   1.25
    Souvenir Sheet
2428 A1163 80ch multicolored   8.50   1.25

Space Exploration — A1164

Designs: 10ch, Cosmonaut. 20ch, Cosmonaut on space-walk. 30ch, Cosmonaut (diff.)
No. 2432: 80ch, Moon vehicle.

1984, Nov. 15   **Perf. 12**
2429-2431 Set of 3   2.50   .50
    Souvenir Sheet
2432 A1164 80ch multicolored   4.00   1.00

Russian Icebreakers — A1165

Designs: 20ch, *Arktika.* 30ch, *Ermak.*
No. 2435: 80ch, *Lenin.*

1984, Nov. 26   **Perf. 13¼**
2433-2434 Set of 2   3.25   .60
    Souvenir Sheet
2435 A1165 80ch multicolored   5.00   1.25

A1166

Dmitri Mendeleev (1834-1907), Chemist, 150th Birth Anniv. — A1167

1984, Dec. 1   **Perf. 13¼**
2436 A1166 10ch multicolored   1.75   .25
    Souvenir Sheet
2437 A1167 80ch multicolored   4.00   1.25

Historic European Royalty, Scenes — A1168

British Monarchs — A1169

Queen Elizabeth II — A1170

No. 2438 (all 10ch): a, Konrad III, 1149 (Germany). b, Henry VIII (England). c, Henry VI (England). d, King John (England). e, Fleet of Elizabeth I (England). f, Philip II Augustus (France). g, Thames and London Bridge, 1616. h, Elizabeth I (England). i, Charles VII, parade (England).
No. 2439 (all 10ch): a, Prince Eugene, 1706 (Savoy). b, Kaiser Wilhelm II (Germany). c, Philip V (Spain). d, Ludwig II (Bavaria). e, Alfonso XIII (Spain). f, Mary Stuart (Scotland). g, Charles Edward Stuart, 1745 (Scotland). h, Marie-Louise (Austria). i, Charles V, 1547 (Spain).
No. 2440 (Horiz., all 10ch): a, Maria Theresa (Austria). b, Francis I, 1814 (Austria). c, Leopold II, 1844 (Austria). d, Louis XVIII (France). e, Versailles, 1688. f, Louis XIV (France). g, Prince Wilhelm (Germany). h, Franz Joseph I (Austria). i, Ludwig II (Bavaria).
No. 2441 (Horiz., all 10ch): a, Napoleon III (France. b, Rudolph of Habsburg, Basel 1273. c, Henry IV (France). d, Louis XII (France). e, Maximilian I (Holy Roman Empire). f, Peter the Great, Amsterdam Harbor (Russia). g, Louis VIII (France). h, Don Juan/Battle of Lepanto, 1571. i, Neuschwanstein Castle.
No. 2442 (all 10ch): a, William I. b, Richard II. c, Henry V. d, Henry VI. e, Richard III. f, Edward IV. g, Henry VII. h, Henry VIII, full length portrait. i, Henry VIII, ¾-face portrait, as young man.
No. 2443 (all 10ch): a, Henry VIII, ¾-face portrait, as middle-aged man. b, Mary I. c, Elizabeth I, facing left. d, Edward VI. e, Elizabeth I, facing right. f, Lady Jane Grey. g, Mary, Queen of Scots. h, James I. i, Charles I.
No. 2444 (all 10ch): a, Charles I. b, Henrietta Marie. c, Charles II. d, James II. e, George I, seated. f, William IV. g, Queen Anne, full-length portrait. h, George I, In profile. i, Queen Mary II.
No. 2445 (all 10ch): a, Queen Anne, with her son, William, Duke of Gloucester. b, George II, facing forward. c, George II, in profile. d, George IV. e, George III. f, William III. g, William IV. h, Queen Victoria. i, Prince Albert.
No. 2446 (all 10ch): a, Edward VII. b, Queen Alexandra. c, George V and Royal Family. d, George VI. e, George VI and Royal Family. f, Queen Elizabeth II. g, Prince Charles. h, Prince William of Wales, with Prince Charles and Princess Diana. i, Princess Diana.

1984, Dec. 20   **Perf. 12¼x12**
    Sheets of 9, #a.-i.
2438-2446   Set of 9   125.00   —
    Souvenir Sheet
    Perf. 11½
2447 A1170 80ch multicolored   20.00   12.00

Kim Il Sung's Visits to Eastern Europe — A1171

No. 2448 (all 10ch): a, USSR. b, Poland. c, DDR. d, Czechoslovakia.
No. 2249 (all 10ch): a, Hungary. b, Bulgaria. c, Romania.
No. 2450: 10ch, China.

1984, Dec. 30   **Perf. 12**
2448 A1171 Sheet of 4, #a.-d.   4.50   1.25
2449 A1171 Sheet of 3, #a.-c.   3.50   1.00
    Souvenir Sheet
    Perf. 11½
2450 A1171 10ch multicolored   2.75   1.00

New Year — A1172

1985, Jan. 1   **Perf. 12**
2451 A1172 10ch multicolored   1.90   .25

Kim Il Sung's 1,000-ri Journey, 60th Anniv. — A1173

1985, Jan. 22   **Perf. 12¼**
2452 A1173 Pair, #a.-b.   2.25   .25
   a.   5ch multicolored   .75   .25
   b.   10ch multicolored   .75   .25

A1174

History of the Motorcar — A1175

Designs: 10ch, Gugnot's Steam Car, 1769. 15ch, Goldsworthy Steam Omnibus, 1825. 20ch, Gottlieb Daimler diesel car, 1885. 25ch, Benx three-wheeled diesel car, 1886. 30ch, Peugot diesel car, 1891.
80ch, Wind-power car.

1985, Jan. 25   **Perf. 11½**
2453-2457 A1165 Set of 5   7.00   .85
    Souvenir Sheet
2458 A1175 80ch multicolored   4.50   1.25

Secret Camp, Mt. Paektu — A1176

1985, Feb. 16   **Perf. 12**
2459 A1176 10ch multicolored   .65   .25
Korean Revolution Headquarters

Lighthouses — A1177

10ch, Taechodo. 20ch, Sodo. 30ch, Pido. 40ch, Suundo.

1985, Feb. 23   *Perf. 12¼x11¾*
2460-2463 A1177   Set of 4   9.00   1.25
    For surcharges, see Nos. 4533-4534.

The Hedgehog Defeats the Tiger, Fairy Tale — A1178

Designs: 10ch, Tiger bragging about his strength. 20ch, Tiger going to stamp on rolled-up hedgehog. 30ch, Hedgehog clinging to tiger's nose. 35ch, Fleeing tiger. 40ch, Tiger crawling before hedgehog.

1985, Mar. 6   *Perf. 11½*
2464-2468 A1178   Set of 5   6.50   1.25

A1179

Mushrooms: 10ch, Pleurotus cornucopiae. 20ch, Pluerotus ostreatus. 30ch, Catathelasma ventricosum.

1985, Mar. 16
2469-2471 A1179   Set of 3   6.00   .65
    For surcharge, see No. 4521.

A1180

World Cup Soccer 1954-1966 — A1181

Designs: 10ch, W. Germany vs. Hungary, 1954. 20ch, Brazil vs. Sweden, 1958. 30ch, Brazil vs. Czechoslovakia, 1962. 40ch, England vs. W. Germany, 1966.
    80ch, DPRK team in quarter final, 1966.

1985, Mar. 20   *Perf. 13¼*
2472-2475 A1180   Set of 4   4.50   1.00
Souvenir Sheet
2476 A1181 80ch multicolored   4.00   1.25

A1182

World Cup Soccer 1970-1986 — A1183

Designs: 10ch, Brazil vs. Italy, 1970. 20ch, W. Germany vs. Netherlands, 1974. 30ch, Argentina vs. Netherlands, 1978. 40ch, Italy vs. W. Germany, 1982.
    80ch, Aztec Stadium, Mexico City.

1985, Mar. 20   *Perf. 13¼*
2477-2480 A1182   Set of 4   4.00   1.00
Souvenir Sheet
2481 A1183 80ch multicolored   4.00   1.25

Kim Il Sung, 73rd Birthday A1184

1985, April 15   *Perf. 12*
2482 A1184 10ch multicolored   .65   .25

4th Century Musical Instruments A1185

Designs: 10ch, Horn player. 20ch So (pan-pipes) player.

1985, May 7   *Perf. 11½*
2483-2484 A1185   Set of 2   3.50   .25

Chongryon Hall, Tokyo — A1186

1985, May 25
2485 A1186 10ch deep brown   .65   .25
    30th anniv. of Chongryon, the General Association of Korean Residents in Japan.

A1187

Mammals: 5ch, Common marmoset (callithrix jacchus). 10ch, Ring-tailed lemur (Lemur catta).

1985, June 7
2486-2487 A1187   Set of 2   2.50   .25

National Emblem — A1188

1985, June 20
2488 A1188 80ch multicolored   3.00   .70

A1189

Argentina '85 Int'l Stamp Exhib. — A1190

Designs: 10ch, Buenos Aires and Argentina stamp. 20ch, Iguaçu Falls and Argentine, DPRK stamps, horiz.
    80ch, Gaucho.

1985, July 5   *Perf. 11¾*
2489-2490 A1189   Set of 2   3.50   .25
Souvenir Sheet
2491 A1190 80ch multicolored   4.00   4.00

12th World Youth and Students' Festival, Moscow — A1191

Designs: 10ch, Korean dancer with streamer, gymnast. 20ch, Spassky Tower, Festival emblem. 30ch, Youths of different races.

1985, July 27   *Perf. 12¼*
2492-2494 A1191   Set of 3   3.50   .75

Pyongyang Buildings — A1192

Designs: 2ch, Phyonghwa Pavilion. 40ch, Skyscraper apartments, Chollima Street.

1985, Aug. 1   *Perf. 12*
2495-2496 A1192   Set of 2   .90   .25
2495a   2ch Thick toned unsurfaced
        paper, without gum   10.00
2496a   40ch Thick toned unsurfaced
        paper, without gum   5.00

A1193

Liberation, 40th Anniv. — A1194

Designs: 5ch, Soldiers, battle scene. 10ch (No. 2498), Korean and Russian soldier with raised arms. 10ch (No. 2499), Japanese soldiers surrendering. 10ch (No. 2500), Crowd with banners, Flame of Juche. 10ch (No. 2501), Student marchers with banners. 10ch (No. 2502), Liberation monument, vert. 40ch, Students bearing banners.
    80ch, Monument.

1985, Aug. 15   *Perf. 11½*
2497-2503 A1193   Set of 7   2.50   1.00
2497a   5ch Toned unsurfaced pa-
        per, without gum   8.00
2498a   10ch Toned unsurfaced pa-
        per, without gum   8.00
2499a   10ch Toned unsurfaced pa-
        per, without gum   8.00
2500a   10ch Toned unsurfaced pa-
        per, without gum   8.00
2501a   10ch Toned unsurfaced pa-
        per, without gum   8.00
2502a   10ch Toned unsurfaced pa-
        per, without gum   8.00
2503a   40ch Toned unsurfaced pa-
        per, without gum   8.00
Souvenir Sheet
2504 A1194 80ch multicolored   2.00   2.00

A1195

Halley's Comet — A1196

Designs: 10ch, Halley and Comet. 20ch, Comet, diagram of course, space probe. 80ch, Comet's trajectory.

1985, Aug. 25   *Perf. 13½*
2505-2506 A1195 Set of 2   2.00 .25
Souvenir Sheet
2507 A1196 80ch multicolored   4.00 1.25

Flowers — A1197

Designs: 10ch, Hippeastrum hybridum. 20ch, Camellia japonica. 30ch, Cyclamen persicum.

1985, Sept. 10   *Perf. 12*
2508-2510 A1197 Set of 3   7.00 .65

A1198

Koguryo Culture, 4th-6th Centuries A.D. — A1199

Designs: 10ch, Hero. 15ch, Heroine. 20ch, Flying fairy. 25ch, Hunting. 50ch, Pine tree.

1985, Sep. 30   *Perf. 13¼*
2511-2514 A1198 Set of 4   3.50 .65
2514a   Sheet of 4, #2511-2514   4.00 1.00
Souvenir Sheet
Perf. 12
2515 A1199 50ch multicolored   3.00 .75

Nos. 2511-2514 were issued both in separate sheets and in setenant sheets of four stamps (No. 2514a).

Korean Worker's Party, 40th Anniv. — A1200

Designs: 5ch, Party Founding Museum. 10ch (No. 2517), Soldier, workers. 10ch (No. 2518), Miner, workers. 40ch, Worker, peasant, professional worker holding up Party emblem. No. 2520: 90ch, People holding bouquets of flowers.

1985, Oct. 10   *Perf. 11½*
2516-2519 A1200 Set of 4   1.40 .75
2516a   5ch Thick toned unsurfaced paper, without gum   5.00 —

2517a   10ch Thick toned unsurfaced paper, without gum   10.00 —
2518a   10ch Thick toned unsurfaced paper, without gum   5.00 —
2519a   40ch Thick toned unsurfaced paper, without gum   10.00 —
Souvenir Sheet
2520 A1200 90ch multicolored   1.60 .50

Kim Il Sung's Return, 40th Anniv. — A1201

1985, Oct. 14   *Perf. 12*
2521 A1201 10ch red brn & lt grn 1.00 .25
a.   Dull white unsurfaced paper, without gum   8.00 —

Italia '85, Int'l Stamp Exhib., Rome A1202

Designs: 10ch, Colosseum, Rome, and DPRK stamp. 20ch, *The Holy Family*, by Raphael. 30ch. Head of Michelangelo's *David*, vert. No. 2525: 80ch, Pantheon, Rome.

1985, Oct. 25   *Perf. 11½*
2522-2524 A1200 Set of 3   2.75 .65
Souvenir Sheet
2525 A1202 80ch multicolored   4.00 1.25

South-West German Stamp Bourse, Sindelfingen — A1203

Designs, Mercedes Benz: 10ch, Type 300, 1960. 15ch, Type 770. 20ch, Type W150, 1937. 30ch, Type 600, 1966. No. 2530: 80ch, Mercedes Benz, Type W31, 1938.

1985, Oct. 25   *Perf. 11¾*
2526-2529 A1203 Set of 4   6.50 .65
Souvenir Sheet
Perf. 11¾
2530 A1203 80ch multicolored   5.25 .75

A1204

13th World Cup Championship, Mexico City — A1205

Designs: 20ch, Dribbling and sliding tackle. 30ch, Jumping kick.

80ch, Goalkeeper and Mexican monuments.
1985, Nov. 1   *Perf. 13¼*
2531-2532 A1204 Set of 2   3.25 .50
Souvenir Sheet
2533 A1205 80ch multicolored   4.50 1.10

Int'l Youth Year A1206

Designs: 10ch, Traditional dance. 20ch, Sculpture depicting gymnasts. 30ch, Scientific research. No. 2537: 80ch, Young people of different races.

1985, Nov. 9   *Perf. 11½*
2534-2536 A1206 Set of 3   3.50 .50
Souvenir Sheet
2537 A1206 80ch multicolored   4.50 1.10

A1207

13th World Cup Championship, Mexico City — A1208

Designs: 20ch, Dribbling. 30ch, Tackling. 80ch, Goalkeeper, bullfighter.

1985, Nov. 20   *Perf. 12*
2538-2539 A1207 Set of 2   3.50 .50
Souvenir Sheet
2540 A1208 80ch multicolored   5.00 1.10

Juche Torch — A1209

New Year
1986, Jan. 1   *Perf. 12x12¼*
2541 A1209 10ch multicolored   1.25 .25

History of the Motor Car A1210

Designs: 10ch, Amédée Bollée and Limousine, 1901. 20ch, Stewart Rolls, Henry Royce and Silver Ghost, 1906. 25ch, Giovanni Agnelli and Fiat car, 1912. 30ch, Ettore Bugatti and Royal coupe, 1928. 40ch, Louis Renault and fiacre, 1906. No. 2547: 80ch, Gottlieb Daimler, Karl Benz and Mercedes S, 1927.

1986, Jan. 20   *Perf. 11½*
2542-2546 A1210 Set of 5   9.50 1.25
Souvenir Sheet
2547 A1210 80ch multicolored   7.50 .75

World Chess Championship, Moscow A1211

Designs: 20ch, Gary Kasparov. No. 2549: 80ch, Kasparov-Karpov chess match.

1986, Feb. 5   *Perf. 11¾x12*
2548 A1211 20ch multicolored   2.25 .25
Souvenir Sheet
Perf. 12
2549 A1211 80ch multicolored   5.00 1.25
For surcharges, see Nos. 4522-4523.

Revolutionary Martyrs' Cemetery, Pyongyang — A1212

Designs: 5ch, Cemetery Gate. 10ch, Bronze sculpture of draped flag, soldier, workers (detail).

1986, Feb. 10   *Perf. 12*
2550-2551 A1212 Set of 2   1.50 .25

Songgan Revolutionary Site, 37th Anniv. of Kim Il Sung's Visit — A1213

1986, Feb. 16
2552 A1213 10ch multicolored   .90 .25

Mt. Myohyang Historic Buildings — A1214

Designs: 10ch, Buddhist Scriptures Museum. 20ch, Taeung Hall of the Pohyon Temple.

1986, Feb. 20   *Perf. 12¼*
2553-2554 A1214 Set of 2   2.00 .25

Tropical Fish A1215

Designs: 10ch, Heniochus acuminatus. 20ch, Amphiprion frenatus.

1986, Mar. 12   *Perf. 11½*
2555-2556 A1215 Set of 2   2.50 .30

World Cup Championship, Mexico
City — A1216

Designs, soccer players and flags of: 5ch,
Italy, Bulgaria, Argentina. 20ch, Mexico,
Belgium, Paraguay, Iraq. 25ch, France,
Canada, USSR, Hungary. 30ch, Brazil, Spain,
Algeria, Northern Ireland. 35ch, W. Germany,
Uruguay, Scotland, Denmark. 40ch, Poland,
Portugal, Morocco, England.
No. 2563: 80ch, Soccer players, World Cup,
gold soccer ball, boots.

1986, Mar. 21   ***Perf. 12***
2557-2562 A1216 Set of 6   10.00 1.60
Souvenir Sheet
2563 A1216 80ch multicolored   6.50   .65
  For overprints see Nos. 2599-2605.

4th Spring Friendship Art Festival,
Pyongyang — A1217

1986, Apr. 5
2564 A1217 1w multicolored   3.00   .65

Mercedes-Benz, 60th Anniv. — A1218

Designs: 10ch (No. 2565), Dailmer No. 1
("Motorwagen"), 1886. 10ch (No. 2566), Benz-
Velo, 1894. 20ch (No. 2567), Mercedes, 1901.
20ch (No. 2568), Benz limousine, 1909. 30ch
(No. 2569), Mercedes Tourenwagen, 1914.
30ch (No. 2570), Mercedes Benz 170/6 cylinder, 1931. 40ch (No. 2571), Mercedes Benz
380, 1933. 40ch (No. 2572), Mercedes Benz
540K, 1936.
No. 2573: 80ch, Mercedes-Simplex Phaeton, 1904.

1986, Apr. 8   ***Perf. 11½***
2565-2572 A1218 Set of 8   9.00 2.00
Souvenir Sheet
2573 A1218 80ch multicolored   5.00 1.25

Kim Il Sung, 74th
Birthday — A1219

1986, Apr. 15   ***Perf. 12***
2574 A1219 10ch multicolored   .65   .25

Association for the Restoration of the
Fatherland, 50th Anniv. — A1220

1986, May 5   ***Perf. 11¾x12***
2575 A1220 10ch multicolored   .65   .25

Intl. Year of
Peace
A1221

Designs: 10ch, Dove carrying letter. 20ch,
Dove, UN Headquarters. 30ch, Dove, globe,
broken missiles.
No. 2579: 80ch, Sculpture of children and
dove.

1986, June 18   ***Perf. 11¾x12***
2576-2578 A1221 Set of 3   4.00 1.25
Souvenir Sheet
Perf. 11¾x11½
2579 A1221 80ch multicolored   5.00   .75

Mona Lisa, by
da
Vinci — A1222

1986, July 9   ***Perf. 13½x13¼***
2580 A1222 20ch multicolored   3.00   .25

Irises — A1223

Designs: 20ch, Pink iris. 30ch, Violet iris.
No. 2583: 80ch, Magenta iris.

1986, July 20   ***Perf. 11½***
2581-2582 A1223 Set of 2   5.00   .50
Souvenir Sheet
2583 A1223 80ch multicolored   6.50 1.10

Tennis Players — A1224

Designs: 10ch, Kim Un Suk. 20ch, Ivan
Lendl. 30ch, Steffi Craf. 50ch, Boris Becker.

1986, July 30   ***Perf. 13½***
2584 A1224 Block of 4, #a.-d.   7.00 1.00
  a.   10ch multicolored   1.50   .25
  b.   20ch multicolored   1.50   .25
  c.   30ch multicolored   1.50   .25
  d.   50ch multicolored   1.50   .25
  e.   10ch Toned unsurfaced pa-
             per, without gum   10.00   —
  No. 2584 was printed in sheets containing
two setenant blocks.

No. 2584d is airmail.

Stampex '86
Stamp
Exhib.,
Adelaide
A1225

Designs: 10ch, Cockatoo; 80ch, Kangaroo,
map of Australia, emblems.

1986, Aug. 4   ***Perf. 11½***
2585 A1225 10ch multicolored   5.50   .25
Souvenir Sheet
2586 A1226 80ch multicolored   5.50 1.10

L'Unita
Festival,
Milan
A1227

Designs: 10ch, First issue of *L'Unita*. 20ch,
Milan Cathedral. 30ch, Michelangelo's *Pieta*,
vert.
No. 2590: 80ch, Enrico Berlinguer, Italian
Communist Party leader.

1986, Aug. 26
2587-2589 A1227 Set of 3   5.50 2.50
Souvenir Sheet
2590 A1227 80ch multicolored   4.50   .75
  National Festival of *L'Unita*, the Italian Communist Party newspaper.

A1228

Stockholmia '86 Int'l Stamp Exhib.,
Stockholm — A1229

Design: 10ch, Icebreaker *Express II* and
Swedish stamp.
80ch, UPU emblem, mail coach and Swedish stamps.

1986, Aug. 28
2591 A1228 10ch multicolored   2.00   .25
Souvenir Sheet
2592 A1229 80ch multicolored   7.00 1.50

DPRK Postage Stamps, 40th
Anniv. — A1230

Designs: 10ch, Perf green reprint of Scott
No. 1. 15ch, Imperf green reprint of Scott No.
1. 50ch, Scott No. 5.

1986, Sep. 12   ***Perf. 12¼x12***
2593-2595 A1230 Set of 3   6.00 1.50
  No. 2595 is airmail.

DPRK Postage Stamps, 40th
Anniv. — A1231

Designs: 10ch, Postal emblems, DPRK
#387, 2505. 15ch, Postal emblems, General
Post Office, Pyongyang, DPRK #1529, 1749.
50ch, Postal emblems, Kim Il Jung. DPRK #1,
#1 reprint in green, vert.

1986, Oct. 5   ***Perf. 12***
2596-2598 A1231 Set of 3   8.00 1.00
  No. 2598 is airmail. For surcharge, see No.
4580.

**Nos. 2557-2563 Overprinted with
World Cup Soccer Championship
Results**

1986, Oct. 14
2599-2604 A1216 Set of 6   16.00 2.50
Souvenir Sheet
2605 A1216 80ch multicolored   10.00 1.40

Down-with-Imperialism Union, 60th
Anniv. — A1232

1986, Oct. 17   ***Perf. 11½***
2606 A1232 10ch multicolored   .70   .25

Gift Animals House, 1st
Anniv. — A1233

1986, Oct. 18   ***Perf. 12x11¾***
2607 A1233 2w multicolored   8.50   .90
  a.   On toned unsurfaced paper,
          without gum   10.00   —

United Nations
Educational,
Scientific and
Cultural
Organization
(UNESCO), 40th
anniv. — A1234

Designs: 10ch, Schoolchildren. 50ch,
UNESCO emblem, Grand People's Study

House, television, communications satellite and dish, horiz.

1986, Nov. 4   **Perf. 12**
2608-2609   A1234   Set of 2   4.50 1.25

Inter-Sputnik, 15th Anniv. — A1235

1986, Nov. 15
2610   A1235   5w multicolored   10.00 2.25
  a.   On toned unsurfaced paper,
       without gum   10.00

West Sea Barrage — A1236

Designs: 10ch, Oil tanker, lock. 40ch, Aerial view of dam. 1.20w, Aerial view of dam (diff.)

1986, Nov. 20   **Perf. 12x11¾**
2611-2613   A1236   Set of 3   8.50 1.00
2611a   10ch Toned unsurfaced pa-
        per, without gum   5.00   —
2612a   40ch Toned unsurfaced pa-
        per, without gum   8.00   —
2613a   1.20w Toned unsurfaced pa-
        per, without gum   8.00   —

Mushrooms and Minerals — A1237

Designs: a, 10ch Lengenbachite. b, 10ch Clitocybe infundibuliformis. c, 15ch Rhodocrosite. d, 15ch Morchella esculenta. e, 50ch Annabergite. f, 50ch Russula.

1986, Nov. 23   **Perf. 13¼**
2614   A1237   Block of 6, #a.-f.   16.50 1.25
  a.   10ch multicolored   2.50   .25
  b.   10ch multicolored   2.50   .25
  c.   15ch multicolored   2.50   .25
  d.   15ch multicolored   2.50   .25
  e.   50ch multicolored   2.50   .25
  f.   50ch multicolored   2.50   .25

Printed in setenant blocks within the sheet. Nos. 2614e and 2614f are airmail.

A1238

Exhib. of North Korean 3-D Photos and Stamps, Lima — A1239

Design: 10ch, Machu Picchu and DPRK #1402. 80ch, Korean and Peruvian children.

1986, Nov. 25   **Perf. 13¼x13½**
2615   A1238   10ch multicolored   2.00   .25
Souvenir Sheet
2616   A1239   80ch multicolored   9.00 2.00

New
Year — A1240

Designs: 10ch, Sun, pine tree. 40ch, Hare.

1987, Jan. 1   **Perf. 12**
2617-2618   A1240   Set of 2   3.50   .50

A1241

Fungi — A1242

Designs: 10ch, *Pholiota adiposa.* 20ch, *Cantharellus cibarius.* 30ch, *Boletus impolitus.* 80ch, *Gomphidius rutilus.*

1987, Jan. 5   **Perf. 11½**
2619-2621   A1241   Set of 3   5.75   .75
Souvenir Sheet
2622   A1242   80ch multicolored   7.00 1.50

For surcharge, see No. 4535.

Famous Composers, Death
Anniv. — A1243

Designs: 10ch (No. 2623a), Maurice Ravel (1875-1937). 10ch (No. 2623b), Kim Ok Song (1916-65). 20ch, Giovanni Lully (1632-67). 30ch, Franz Liszt (1811-86). 40ch (No.2623e), Stradivarius violins (Antonio Stradivari, 1644-1737). 40ch (No. 2623f), Christoph Gluck (1714-87).

1987, Jan. 29   **Perf. 13¼**
2623   A1243   Block of 6, #a.-f.   12.00 1.10
  a.   10ch multicolored   1.50   .25
  b.   10ch multicolored   1.50   .25
  c.   20ch multicolored   1.50   .25
  d.   30ch multicolored   1.50   .25
  e.   40ch multicolored   1.50   .25
  f.   40ch multicolored   1.50   .25

No. 2623 was printed in se-tenant blocks of six within the sheet.

Kim Jong Il, 45th Birthday — A1244

1987, Feb. 16
2624   A1244   80ch multicolored   2.50   .40

Buildings — A1245

Designs: 5ch, East Pyongyang Grand Theater. 10ch, Pyongyang Koryo Hotel (vert.). 3w, Rungnado Stadium.

1987, Feb. 23   **Perf. 12**
2625-2627   A1245   Set of 3   7.50 1.20
2625a   5ch Stiff paper, without
        gum   10.00   —
2626a   10ch Stiff paper, without
        gum   5.00   —
2627a   3w Stiff paper, without
        gum   5.00   —

Sailing Ships — A1246

Designs: 20ch, *Gorch Fock.* 30ch, *Tovarisch,* vert.. 50ch (No. 2630), *Belle Poule,* vert. 50ch (No. 2631), *Sagres II,* vert. 1w (No.

2632), Merchantman, Koryo Period (918-1392). 1w (No. 2633), *Dar Mlodziezy,* vert..

1987, Feb. 25   **Perf. 13¼**
2628-2633   A1246   Set of 6   11.50 2.75
         Nos. 2630-2633 are airmail.

Fire Engines — A1247

Designs: 10ch, German fire engine. 20ch, Benz fire engine. 30ch, Chemical fire engine. 50ch, Soviet fire engine.

1987, Feb. 27   **Perf. 12**
2634-2637   A1247   Set of 4   10.00 1.20
         No. 2637 is airmail.

Road Safety — A1248

Designs (multiple traffic signs): 10ch (No. 2638), Blue sign lower center. 10ch (No. 2639), Red sign lower center. 20ch, Various signs. 50ch, Various signs (diff.)

1987, Feb. 27
2638-2641   A1248   Set of 4   7.50   .90
         Nos. 2641 is airmail.

Butterflies and Flowers — A1249

Designs: No. 2642, Apatura ilia and spiraea. No. 2643, Ypthinia argus and fuchsia. No. 2644, Neptis philyra and aguilegia. No. 2645, Papilio protenor and chrysanthemum. No. 2646, Parantica sita and celosia. No. 2847, Vanessa indica and hibiscus.

1987, Mar. 12
2642-2647   A1249   Set of 6   11.00 1.50
         For surcharge, see No. 4524.

Korean National Assoc., 70th
Anniv. — A1250

Design: 10ch, Association Monument, Pyongyang.

1987, Mar. 23   **Perf. 11½**
2648   A1250   10ch multicolored   .60   .25

5th Spring
Friendship Art
Festival — A1251

1987, Apr. 6
2649　A1251　10ch multicolored　.70　.25

A1252

Kim Il Sung, 75th Birthday — A1253

Designs: No. 2650, Mangyong Hill. No. 2651, Kim Il Sung's birthplace, Mangyongdae, horiz. No 2652, Painting, *Profound Affection for the Working Class.* No. 2653, Painting, *A Bumper Crop of Pumpkins.*

1987, Apr. 15　　　　　**Perf. 12**
2650　A1252　10ch multicolored　.50　.25
2651　A1252　10ch multicolored　.50　.25
2652　A1253　10ch multicolored　.50　.25
2653　A1253　10ch multicolored　.50　.25
　　　Nos. 2650-2653 (4)　　2.00　1.00

Horses — A1254

Designs: No. 2654a, Bay. No. 2654b, Bay, diff. No. 2654c, Gray, rearing. No. 2654d, White horse on beach.

1987, Apr. 20　　　　　**Perf. 13¼**
2654　A1254　Block of 4, #a.-d.　7.00　2.10
　a.　　10ch multicolored　　.50　.25
　b.　　10ch multicolored　　.50　.25
　c.　　40ch multicolored　　2.50　.70
　d.　　40ch multicolored　　2.50　.70

No. 2654 was printed in se-tenant blocks of four within the sheet.

Transport — A1255

Designs: No. 2655, Electric train *Juche.* No. 2656, Electric train *Mangyongdae.* No. 2657, *Sputnik I,* vert. No. 2658, Laika, first animal in space, vert. No. 2659, Tupolev Tu-144 jetliner. No. 2660, Concorde jetliner. No. 2661, Count Ferdinand von Zeppelin and LZ-4. No. 2662, Zeppelin and diagrams of airships.

1987, Apr. 30
2655　A1255　10ch multicolored　.60　.25
2656　A1255　10ch multicolored　.60　.25
　a.　　Pair, #2655-2656　　.75　.40
2657　A1255　10ch multicolored　.60　.25
2658　A1255　20ch multicolored　1.10　.25
　a.　　Pair, #2657-2658　　2.00　.40
2659　A1255　20ch multicolored　1.10　.25
2660　A1255　20ch multicolored　1.10　.25
　a.　　Pair, #2659-2660　　2.50　.40
2661　A1255　30ch multicolored　1.50　.25
2662　A1255　80ch multicolored　4.50　1.00
　a.　　Pair, #2661-2662　　7.00　1.25
　　　Nos. 2655-2662 (8)　　11.10　2.75

Nos. 2655/2656, 2657/2658, 2659/2660, 2661/2662 were printed se-tenant within their sheets.

No. 2662 is airmail.

CAPEX '87 Int'l Stamp Exhibition, Toronto — A1256

Designs: 10ch, Musk ox. 40ch, Jacques Cartier, *Grand Hermine* and modern icebreaker, horiz. 60ch, Ice hockey, Calgary '88, horiz.

1987, May 30　　　　　**Perf. 11**
2663-2665　A1256　Set of 3　6.00　1.25

Int'l Circus Festival, Monaco — A1257

Designs: No. 2666, Trapeze artists. No. 2667, "Brave Sailors" (N. Korean acrobatic troupe), vert. No. 2668, Korean performers receiving prize. No. 2669, Clown and elephant, vert. 40ch, Performing cat, horses. 50ch, Prince Rainier and family applauding.

1987, May 31　　　　　**Perf. 12**
2666-2671　A1257　Set of 6　9.50　1.50

No. 2871 is airmail.

Battle of Pochonbo, 50th
Anniv. — A1258

1987, June 4
2672　A1258　10ch multicolored　.75　.25

Chongchun Street Sports
Complex — A1259

Designs: 5ch, Various sports. 10ch, Indoor swimming pool. 40ch, Weightlifting gymnasium. 70ch, Table-tennis gymnasium. 1w, Angol football stadium. 1.20w, Handball gymnasium.

1987, June 18　　　　　**Perf. 12**
2673-2678　A1259　Set of 6　10.00　2.25
2675a　40ch　Toned unsurfaced paper, without gum　8.00　—
2676a　70ch　Toned unsurfaced paper, without gum　8.00　—
2677a　1w　Toned unsurfaced paper, without gum　8.00　—
2678a　1.20w　Toned unsurfaced paper, without gum　8.00　—

Worldwide Fund for Nature
(WWF) — A1260

Aix galericulata: No. 2679, On branch. No. 2680, On shore. No. 2681, In water and on shore. No. 2682, In water.

1987, Aug. 4　　　　　**Perf. 13¼**
2679-2682　A1260　Set of 4　11.50　2.00

For surcharge, see No. 4605.

A1261

OLYMPHILEX '87 Stamp Exhibition,
Rome — A1262

1987, Aug. 29　　　　　**Perf. 13¼**
2683　A1261　10ch multicolored　1.50　.25
Souvenir Sheet
2684　A1262　80ch multicolored　7.00　1.25

Railway Uniforms — A1263

No. 2685, Electric train and Metro dispatcher. No. 2686, Underground station and conductress. No. 2687, Train and conductress. No. 2688, Train and railway dispatcher. No. 2689, Orient Express and conductor. No. 2690, Express train and ticket inspector.

1987, Sep. 23
2685-2690　A1263　Set of 6　7.50　1.25

HAFNIA '87 Int'l Stamp Exhibition,
Copenhagen — A1264

Designs: 40ch, White stork. 60ch, The Little Mermaid and sailing ship *Danmark.*

1987, Sep. 26
2691-2692　A1264　Set of 2　5.25　.70

A1265

Winter Olympic Games,
Calgary — A1266

40ch: No. 2693, Figure skating. No. 2694, Ski jump. No. 2695, Downhill skiing. No. 2696, Cross-country skiing.

1987, Oct. 16
2693-2696　A1265　Set of 4　8.00　1.00
Souvenir Sheet
2697　A1266　80ch multicolored　5.25　1.00

PHILATELIA '87 (Koln) and 750th
Anniv. Berlin — A1267

Designs: 10ch, Victory Column. 20ch,
Reichstag, horiz. 30ch, Pfaueninsel Castle.
40ch, Charlottenburg Castle, horiz.
80ch, Olympic Stadium.

1987, Nov. 5   **Perf. 12**
2698-2701 A1267 Set of 4   150.00
Souvenir Sheet
Perf. 11½x12
2702 A1267 80ch multicolored   100.00

Roland Garros Birth Centenary and
Tennis as an Olympic Sport — A1268

Designs: 20ch (No. 2703), Roland Garros
(1888-1918), aviator; 20ch (No. 2704), Ivan
Lendl and trophy; 40ch, Steffi Graf.
No. 2706: 80ch, Steffi Graf and trophy.

1987, Nov. 10   **Perf. 13¼**
2703-2705 A1268 Set of 3   7.50   .75
Souvenir Sheet
Perf. 11½x12
2706 A1268 80ch multicolored   10.00   3.00

Kim Jong Suk (1917-49),
Revolutionary Hero — A1269

1987, Dec. 24
2707 A1269 80ch multicolored   2.50   .50

Pyongyang Buildings — A1270

Dragon — A1271

1988, Jan. 1   **Perf. 12**
2708 A1270 10ch multicolored   .60   .25
2709 A1271 40ch multicolored   1.50   .25
New Year.

Saenal Newspaper, 60th
Anniv. — A1272

1988, Jan. 15   **Perf. 11½**
2710 A1272 10ch multicolored   .90   .25

A1273

Kim Jong Il, 46th Birthday — A1274

Designs: 10ch, Kim Jong Il's birthplace, Mt.
Paektu. 80ch, Kim Jong Il.

1988, Feb. 16   **Perf. 12x11¾**
2711 A1273 10ch multicolored   .50   .25
Souvenir Sheet
2712 A1274 80ch multicolored   2.50   .50

Int'l Red Cross, 125th Anniv. — A1275

Designs: a, Henry Dunant. b, N. Korean
Red Cross emblem, map. c, International
Committee Headquarters, Geneva; d, Doctor
examining child, Pyongyang Maternity
Hospital.
80ch, Red Cross and Red Crescent, flags,
globe.

1988, Feb. 17   **Perf. 12**
2713 A1275   Sheet of 4   7.00   .90
   a.   10ch multicolored   1.75   .20
   b.   20ch multicolored   1.75   .20
   c.   20ch multicolored   1.75   .20
   d.   40ch multicolored   1.75   .20
Souvenir Sheet
2714 A1275 80ch multicolored   4.50   .75

A1276

Columbus' Discovery of America,
500th Anniv. — A1277

10ch, *Santa Maria*. 20ch, *Pinta*. 30ch, *Nina*.
80ch, Columbus.

1988, Mar. 10   **Perf. 13¼**
2718 A1276   Strip of 3   5.25   .75
   a.   10ch multicolored   1.25   .25
   b.   20ch multicolored   1.25   .25
   c.   30ch multicolored   1.25   .25
Souvenir Sheet
2719 A1277 80ch multicolored   5.25   .75
Nos. 2718a-2718c were printed together in
the sheet in se-tenant strips of three.

JUVALUX
'88 — A1278

Designs: 40ch, Hot air balloons. 60ch,
Steam engine, railroad map of Luxembourg
1900.

1988, Mar. 29
2720-2721 A1278   Set of 2   5.25   .75
JUVALUX '88 International Youth Stamp
Exhibition, Luxembourg.

6th Spring
Friendship Art
Festival — A1279

Designs: 10ch, Singer. 1.20w, Dancers.

1988, Apr. 7   **Perf. 12**
2722-2723 A1279   Set of 2   4.25   1.25
2722a   10ch, on toned unsurfaced
     paper, without gum   8.00   —

Int'l Institute of the
Juche Idea, 10th
Anniv. — A1280

1988, Apr. 9
2724 A1280 10ch multicolored   .50   .25

A1281

Kim Il Sung, 76th Birthday — A1282

Designs: 10ch, Kim Il Sung's Birthplace,
Mangyongdae.
80ch, Kim Il Sung and schoolchildren.

1988, Apr. 15
2725 A1281 10ch multicolored   .50   .25
Souvenir Sheet
2726 A1282 80ch multicolored   2.50   .40

FINLANDIA '88 Int'l Stamp Exhibition,
Helsinki — A1283

Designs: 40ch, *Urho* ice-breaker. 60ch,
Matti Nykänen, Finnish Olympic ski-jumping
gold and silver medallist.

1988, May 2   **Perf. 13¼**
2727-2728 A1283   Set of 2   5.00   .60

ITALIA '90, 14th World Soccer
Championships — A1284

Designs: 10ch, Soccer match. 20ch, Postcard for 1934 Championship. 30ch, Player
tackling, horiz.
80ch, Italian team, 1982 winners, horiz.

384 KOREA, DEMOCRATIC PEOPLE'S REPUBLIC

1988, May 19
2729-2731 A1284 Set of 3 5.25 .50
Souvenir Sheet
2732 A1284 80ch multicolored 4.50 .60

13th World Festival of Youth and Students — A1285

Designs: No. 2734, Festival emblem. No. 2735, Woman dancer. No. 2736, Woman, gymnast, Angol Sports Village. No. 2737, Map of Korea, globe and doves. No. 2738, Finger pointing at broken rockets ("Let's build a new world without nuclear weapons"). No. 2739, Three hands of different races releasing dove.

1988, May 27 **Perf. 12**
2734-2739 A1285 Set of 6 7.50 1.25
2734a 10ch Thick toned unsurfaced paper, without gum 8.00 —
2735a 10ch Thick toned unsurfaced paper, without gum 8.00 —
2736a 10ch Thick toned unsurfaced paper, without gum 8.00 —
2739a 1.20w Thick toned unsurfaced paper, without gum 8.00 —

Eight Fairies of Mt. Kumgang, Folk-Tale — A1286

Designs: 10ch, Fairy playing the *haegum*. 15ch, Fairies with rainbow. 20ch, Fairy and herdsman husband. 25ch, Couple with infant. 30ch, Couple with son and daughter. 35ch, Family on rainbow, returning to Mt. Kumgang.

1988, June 20
2740-2745 A1286 Set of 6 5.00 1.10

PRAGA '88 Int'l Stamp Exhibition, Prague — A1287

Designs: 20ch, Mallard ducks. 40ch, Vladimir Remek, Czechoslovak cosmonaut.

1988, June 26 **Perf. 13¼**
2746-2747 A1287 Set of 2 4.00 .45

Birds — A1288

Designs: 10ch, Red crossbill (*Loxia curvirostra japonica*). 15ch, Stonechat (*Saxicola torquata stejnegeri*). 20ch, European nuthatch (*Sitta eoropaea hondoensis*). 25ch, Great spotted woodpecker (*Dendrocopos*

major *japonicus*). 30ch, Common kingfisher (*Alcedo atthis bengalensis*). 35ch, Bohemian waxwing (*Bombycilla garrula centralasiae*).

1988, July 9 **Perf. 12**
2748-2753 A1288 Set of 6 10.00 1.75
For surcharge, see No. 4530.

A1289

RICCIONE '88 Int'l Stamp Fair — A1290

1988, July 25
2754 A1289 20ch multicolored .90 .25
Souvenir Sheet
2755 A1290 80ch multicolored 3.75 .50

A1291

Australia Bicentenary — A1292

Designs: 10ch, Emu. 15ch, Statin bower birds. 25ch, Kookaberra, vert. 80ch, H.M.S. *Resolution*.

1988, July 30 **Perf. 13¼**
2756-2758 A1291 Set of 3 4.00 .60
Souvenir Sheet
2759 A1292 80ch multicolored 5.00 .65

Ships — A1293

Designs: 10ch, Floating crane *5-28*. 20ch, Cargo ship *Hwanggumsan*. 30ch, Cargo ship *Jangjasan Chongnyon-ho*. 40ch, Passenger ship *Samjiyon*.

1988, Aug. 12 **Perf. 12**
2760-2763 A1293 Set of 4 5.50 .85

A1294

Count Ferdinand von Zeppelin, 150th Birth Anniv. — A1295

Designs: 10ch, LZ 13 *Hansa*. 20ch, LZ 10 *Schwaben*. 30ch, LZ 11 *Viktoria Luise*. 40ch, LZ 3. 1w, Count von Zeppelin.

1988, Aug. 21 **Perf. 11¼**
2764-2767 A1294 Set of 4 5.50 .85
Souvenir Sheet
Perf. 13¼
2768 A1295 1w multicolored 5.00 1.00

Kim Il Sung and Jambyn Batmunkh — A1296

1988, Aug. 30 **Perf. 12**
2769 A1296 10ch multicolored .75 .25
Kim Il Sung's visit to Mongolia.

National Heroes Congress — A1297

1988, Sep. 1 **Perf. 11¾**
2770 A1297 10ch multicolored 4.50 .25

A1298

Independence, 40th Anniversary — A1299

Designs: 5ch, Tower of Juche Idea. 10ch (No. 2772), Worker, factory. 10ch (No. 2773), Soldier and Mt. Paektu. 10ch (No. 2774), Map, broken U.S. missile. 10ch (No. 2775), Hand holding sign, peace march, globe, doves. 1.20w, Kim Il Sung presiding over design of DPRK flag and emblem.

1988, Sept. 9 **Perf. 12**
2771-2775 A1298 Set of 5 1.75 .75
2771a 5ch Toned unsurfaced paper, without gum 20.00 —
Souvenir Sheet
Perf. 11½
2776 A1299 1.20w multicolored 2.50 .75

FILACEPT '88 Philatelic Exhib., The Hague A1300

Designs: 40ch, *Sunflowers*, by Vincent Van Gogh. 60ch, *The Chess Game*, by Lucas van Leyden.

1988, Sept. 18 **Perf. 13½**
2777-2778 A1300 Set of 2 7.50 1.40

Emblem — A1301

1988, Sep. 23 **Perf. 11½**
2779 A1301 10ch multicolored .60 .25
16th Conference of the Ministers of Communications of Socialist Countries.

Dump Trucks A1302

Designs: 10ch, *Jaju 82* 10-ton truck. 40ch, *Kumsusan* 40-ton truck.

1988, Sept. 18 **Perf. 13½**
2780-2781 A1302 Set of 2 2.00 .75

Paintings by O Un
Byol — A1303

Designs: 10ch, *Owl.* 15ch, *Dawn.* 20ch, *The Beautiful Rose Received by the Respected Marshall.* 25ch, *The Sun and Bamboo.* 30ch, *Autumn.*

1988, Oct. 5   **Perf. 11½**
2782-2786 A1303 Set of 5   6.00   .90

Historic Locomotives — A1304

Designs: 10ch, *Junggi No. 35.* 20ch, *Junggi No. 22.* 30ch, *Jongihwa No. 3.* 40ch, *Junggi No. 307.*

1988, Oct. 28   **Perf. 12**
2787-2790 A1304 Set of 4   5.00   .75

A1305

Calgary '88 Winter Olympic Games
Winners — A1306

Designs: 10ch, Pirmin Zurbriggen (Switzerland). 20ch, Yvonne Van Gennip (Netherlands). 30ch, Marjo Matikainen (Finland). 40ch, USSR hockey team.
80ch, Katarina Witt (DDR).

1988, Nov. 1   **Perf. 13¼**
2791-2794 A1305 Set of 4   3.50 1.25
        Souvenir Sheet
2795 A1306 80ch multicolored   2.50   .50
   a.   Overprinted with names of
         winners in selvage   2.50   .50

First Man and Woman in
Space — A1307

Designs: 20ch, Yuri Gagarin. 40ch, Valentina Tereshkova.

1988, Nov. 12   **Perf. 13¼**
2796 A1307 Pair, #a.-b.   1.75   .60
   a.   20ch multicolored   .40   .25
   b.   40ch multicolored   1.10   .45

A1308

INDIA '89 Int'l Philatelic Exhib., New
Delhi — A1309

Design: 20ch, Jawaharlal Nehru (1889-1964), 100th anniversary of birth.
60ch, *Fan Dance,* Korean Folk Dance.

1988, Dec. 15   **Perf. 11¾x12**
2797 A1308 20ch multicolored   1.20   .25
        Souvenir Sheet
        Perf. 11¾x11½
2798 A1309 60ch multicolored   3.50   .40

New
Year — A1310

Designs: 10ch, Chollima Statue. 20ch, Painting, *Dragon Angler.* 40ch, *Tortoise Serpent,* Kangso tomb mural painting, horiz.

1989, Jan. 1   **Perf. 13¼**
2799-2801 A1310 Set of 3   3.50   .50

Archery — A1311

Designs: 10ch, Archery. 15ch, Rifle shooting. 20ch, Pistol shooting. 25ch, Parachuting. 30ch, Launching model glider.

1989, Jan. 10   **Perf. 12**
2802-2806 A1311 Set of 5   4.50   .75
        National defense training.

A1312

Pets Presented to Kim Il
Sung — A1313

Designs: 10ch, Dobermann pinscher. 20ch, Labrador. 25ch, German shepherd. 30ch, Border collies, horiz. 35ch, Serval, horiz. 80ch, *Felix libica.*

1989, Jan. 23   **Perf. 13½**
2807-2811 A1312 Set of 5   5.00   .90
        Souvenir Sheet
2812 A1313 80ch multicolored   4.00   .60

Kim Jong Il, 47th Birthday — A1314

1989, Feb. 16   **Perf. 11¾x12**
2813 A1314 80ch multicolored   2.00   .45

Agriculture
A1315

1989, Feb. 25   **Perf. 12**
2814 A1315 10ch multicolored   .70   .25
   a.   Toned unsurfaced paper, with-
         out gun   5.00   —

25th anniversary of publication of Kim Il Sung's *Theses on the Socialist Rural Question in Our Country.*

Mushrooms and Wild Fruits — A1316

Designs: 10ch, Rozites caperata and Vitisamurensis. 20ch, Amanita caesarea and Schizandra chinensis. 25ch, Lactarius hygrophoides and Eleagnus crispa. 30ch, Agaricus placomyces and Actinidia arguta. 35ch, Agaricus arvensis and Lycium chinense. 40ch, Suillus grevillei and Juglans cordiformis.
1w, Gomphidius roseus and Diospyros lotus.

1989, Feb. 27   **Perf. 12**
2815-2820 A1316 Set of 6   8.00 1.25
        Souvenir Sheet
        Perf. 11½x11¾
2821 A1316 1w multicolored   4.50   .90

13th World Youth
and Students'
Festival — A1317

Designs: 10ch, Girl. 20ch, Children of different races. 30ch, Fairy, rainbow. 40ch, Young people and Tower of Juche Idea.

1989, Mar. 18   **Perf. 12¼**
2822-2825 A1317 Set of 4   2.75 1.00
2822a   10ch Soft toned unsurfaced
               paper, without gum   15.00 —
2823a   20ch Soft toned unsurfaced
               paper, without gum   8.00 —
2824a   30ch Soft toned unsurfaced
               paper, without gum   8.00 —
2825a   40ch Soft toned unsurfaced
               paper, without gum   8.00 —
2825b   40ch Stiff dull white un-
               surfaced paper, with-
               out gum   8.00 —

A1318

Butterflies and Insects — A1319

Designs: 10ch, Parnassius eversmanni. 15ch, Colias heos. 20ch, Dilipa fenestra. 25ch, Buthus martensis. 30ch, Trichogramma ostriniae. 40ch, Damaster constricticollis. 80ch, Parnassius nomion.

1989, Mar. 23   **Perf. 12**
2826 A1318 Sheet of 6, #a.-f.   6.00 1.00
Souvenir Sheet
2827 A1319 80ch multicolored   3.75 .75

Spring Friendship Art Festival — A1320

1989, Apr. 6
2828 A1320 10ch multicolored   .80 .25

Kim Il Sung, 77th Birthday — A1321

1989, Apr. 15   **Perf. 11½**
2829 A1321 10ch multicolored   .50 .25
a.   Toned unsurfaced paper, without gum   10.00 —

Battle of the Musan Area, 50th Anniv. A1322

1989, May 19   **Perf. 12**
2830 A1322 10ch multicolored   1.10 .25

Jamo System of Dance Notation — A1323

Designs: 10ch, Mexican dance. 20ch, Ballet duet in *Don Quixote*. 25ch, Dance of Guinea. 30ch, Cambodian folk dance. 80ch, Korean folk dance.

1989, May 30
2831-2834 A1323 Set of 4   3.75 .65
Souvenir Sheet
2835 A1323 80ch multicolored   3.25 .50

13th World Festival of Youth and Students
A1324   A1325

1989, June 8   **Perf. 11½**
2836 A1324 5ch deep blue   .25 .25
a.   Soft toned unsurfaced paper, without gum   15.00 —
2837 A1325 10ch red brown   .30 .25

Cartoon, *Badger Measures the Height* — A1326

Designs: 10ch, Badger racing cat and bear to flag pole. 40ch, Cat and bear climbing pole, while badger measures shadow. 50ch, Badger winning the prize.

1989, June 21
2838-2840 A1326 Set of 3   4.00 .65

Astronomy A1327

20ch, Chomosongdae Observatory. 80ch, Saturn (horiz.)

1989, June 29   **Perf. 12**
2841 A1327 20ch multicolored   1.40 .25
Souvenir Sheet
2842 A1327 80ch multicolored   3.00 .50

Eugène Delacroix's *Liberty Guiding the People* — A1328

1989, July 7   **Perf. 12x11½**
2843 A1328 70ch multicolored   3.00 2.00
PHILEXFRANCE '89, Int'l Philatelic Exhib., Paris.

BRASILIANA '89, Int'l Philatelic Exhib., Rio de Janeiro — A1329

1989, July 28   **Perf. 12**
2844 A1329 40ch Pele, #1714   1.40 .30

Fire Brigade and Emergency Medical Services — A1330

Designs: 10ch, Nurse and ambulance. 20ch, Surgeon and ambulance. 30ch, Fireman and fire engine. 40ch, Fireman and fire engine (diff.)

1989, Aug. 12
2845-2848 A1330 Set of 4   6.00 .65

Plants Presented as Gifts to Kim Il Sung — A1331

Designs: 10ch, Kafir lily (Clivia miniata). 15ch, Tulips (Tulipa gesneriana). 20ch, Flamingo lily (Anthurium andreanum). 25ch, Rhododendron obtusum. 30ch, Daffodils (Narcissus pseudonarcissus). 80ch, (Gerbera hybrida).

1989, Aug. 19
2849-2853 A1331 Set of 5   5.50 1.00
Souvenir Sheet
2854 A1331 80ch multicolored   4.50 .50

150th Anniv. of Postage Stamps / STAMP WORLD LONDON '90 Int'l Philatelic Exhib. — A1332

Designs: 5ch, Letter, ship, plane, map. 10ch, Letters and mail box. 20ch, Stamps, magnifying glass, tongs. 30ch, Fiirst stamps pf DPRK. 40ch, UPU emblem, headquarters, Berne. 50ch, Sir Rowland Hill and Penny Black.

1989, Aug. 27
2855-2860 A1332 Set of 6   7.50 1.25

A1333

Alpine Flowers — A1334

Designs: 10ch, Iris setosa. 15ch, Aquilegia japonica. 20ch, Bistorta incana. 25ch, Rhodiola elongata. 30ch, Sanguisorba sitchensis. 80ch, Trollius japonicus.

1989, Sept. 8   **Perf. 11½**
2861-2865 A1333 Set of 5   5.25 1.00
Souvenir Sheet
2866 A1334 80ch multicolored   3.50 .55

Trees bearing Anti-Japanese Patriotic Slogans — A1335

Designs: 10ch, "20 million compatriots, an anti-Japanese heroine of Korea rose on Mt. Paektu," inscribed on tree, Mt. Paektu. 3w, "The future of Korea is bright with the Luminous Star of Mt. Paektu," inscribed on tree, Qun-dong, Pyongyang. 5w, "The General Star of Mt. Paektu shines three thousand-ri expanse of land," inscribed on tree, Mt. Kanbaek.

1989, Sept. 21   **Perf. 12¼**
2867-2869 A1335 Set of 3   18.00 11.00
Compare with No. 2885.

Children's Games — A1336

Designs: 10ch, Girl skipping rope. 20ch, Boy with whirligig. 30ch, Boy flying kite. 40ch, Girl spinning top.

1989, Sept. 30   **Perf. 12**
2870 A1336 Block of 4, #a.-d.   4.00 .80
a.   10ch multicolored   .25 .25
b.   20ch multicolored   1.75 .25
c.   30ch multicolored   .50 .25
d.   40ch multicolored   .60 .25

Int'l March for Peace and Reunification of Korea — A1337

1989, Oct. 1   **Perf. 11½x12**
2871 A1337 80ch multicolored   3.00 1.75

Locomotives — A1338

Designs: 10ch, Electric train entering station yard. 20ch, Electric train crossing bridge. 25ch, Diesel locomotive. 30ch, Diesel locomotive (diff.). 40ch, Steam locomotive. 50ch, Steam locomotive (diff.).

1989, Oct. 19   **Perf. 11¾x12¼**
2872-2877 A1338 Set of 6   6.00 1.25

14th World Soccer Championship, *Italia '90* — A1339

Designs: 10ch, Players and map of Italy. 20ch, Free kick. 30ch, Goal scrimmage. 40ch, Goalkeeper blocking ball.

1989, Oct. 28   **Perf. 12x11¾**
2878-2881 A1339 Set of 4   4.00 .60

Magellan
A1340

1989, Nov. 25   **Perf. 12**
2882 A1340 30ch multicolored   1.25 .25

Descobrex '89 International Philatelic Exhibition, Portugal.

A1341

A1342

10ch, Mangyong Hill and snow-covered pine branches. 20ch, Koguryo warriors.

Perf. 11½ (#2883), 12 (#2884)
1990, Jan. 1
2883 A1341 10ch multicolored   .25 .25
 a. Toned unsurfaced paper,
     without gum   15.00 —
2884 A1342 20ch multicolored   1.20 .25
 a. Toned unsurfaced paper,
     without gum   5.00 —

New Year.

Tree, Mt. Paektu, Bearing Anti-Japanese Patriotic Slogan — A1343

1990, Jan. 12   **Perf. 11½**
2885 A1343 5ch multicolored   .50 .25
 a. Toned unsurfaced paper, with-
     out gum   5.00 —

Dogs — A1344

Designs: 20ch, Ryukwoli. 30ch, Phalryuki. 40ch, Komdungi. 50ch, Olruki.

1990, Jan. 17
2886 A1344 Sheet of 4   5.50 1.50
 a. 20ch multicolored   .90 .25
 b. 30ch multicolored   .90 .25
 c. 40ch multicolored   .90 .25
 d. 50ch multicolored   .90 .25

Birthplace, Mt. Paektu — A1345

1990, Feb. 16
2887 A1345 10ch dp red brn   .50 .25
 a. Toned unsurfaced paper, with-
     out gum   5.00 —

Kim Jong Il's 48th birthday.

Stone Age Man A1346

Designs: 10ch, Primitive man, stone tools. 20ch, Paleolithic and Neolithic men, camp scene.

1990, Feb. 21
2888-2889 A1346 Set of 2   3.00 .30

Bridges — A1347

Designs: 10ch, Rungra Bridge, Pyongyang. 20ch, Pothong Bridge, Pyongyang. 30ch, Suspension bridge between Sinuiju-Ryucho Island. 40ch, Chungsongui Bridge, Pyongyang.

1990, Feb. 27   **Perf. 11½**
2890-2893 A1347 Set of 4   4.50 .60
 2890a 10ch Thin, coarse brownish
        paper, without gum   5.00 —

Traditional Warriors' Costumes A1348

Designs: 20ch, Infantryman (3rd century BC-7th century AD). 30ch, Archer. 50ch, Commander in armor (3rd century BC-7th century AD). 70ch, Koguryo Period officer (10th-14th centuries).

1990, Mar. 18
2894-2897 A1348 Set of 4   6.25 2.00
 2897a 70ch Dull white unsurfaced
        paper, without gum   5.00

Crabs A1349

Designs: 20ch, Atergatis subdentatus. 30ch, Platylambrus validus. 50ch, Uca arcuata.

1990, Mar. 25
2898-2900 A1349 Set of 3   3.00 .60

Dancers — A1350

1990, Apr. 7
2901 A1350 10ch multicolored   .50 .25

Spring Friendship Art Festival, Pyongyang.

A1351

Kim Il Sung's 78th Birthday A1352

Designs: 10ch, 'Fork in the Road' Monument, Mangyongdae Revolutionary Site. 80ch, Kim Il Sung.

1990, Apr. 15   **Perf. 11½x11¾**
2902 A1351 10ch multicolored   .50 .25
          Souvenir Sheet
2903 A1352 80ch multicolored   2.50 .50

Cacti — A1353

Designs: 10ch, Gynmocalycium sp. 30ch, Phyllocactus hybridus. 50ch, Epiphyllum truncatum.

1990, Apr. 21   **Perf. 12¼**
2904-2906 A1353 Set of 3   4.00 .60

A1354

Stamp World London '90 — A1355

Designs: 20ch, Exhibition emblem. 70ch, Sir Rowland Hill.

1990, May 3   **Perf. 11½**
2907 A1354 20ch multicolored   .90 .25
          Souvenir Sheet
2908 A1355 70ch multicolored   2.75 1.20

A1356

Peafowl — A1357

Designs: 10ch, Congo peafowl (Afropavo congensis). 20ch, Common peafowl (Pavo cristatus). 70ch, Common peafowl with tail displayed.

1990, May 10   **Perf. 11¾x12**
2909-2910 A1356 Set of 2   3.00 .60
          Souvenir Sheet
2911 A1357 70ch multicolored   3.00 .60

Bio-engineering — A1358

Designs: 10ch, Dolphin and submarine. 20ch, Bat and sonar dish, satellite. 30ch, Eagle and airplanes. 40ch, Squid and jets.

1990, May 24

2912	A1358	Sheet of 4, #a.-d.	7.00	1.25
a.		10ch multicolored	1.25	.25
b.		20ch multicolored	1.25	.25
c.		30ch multicolored	1.25	.25
d.		40ch multicolored	1.25	.25

BELGICA '90 Int'l Philatelic Exhib., Brussels A1359

Designs: 10ch, Rembrandt, *Self Portrait.* 20ch, Raphael, *Self Portrait.* 30ch, Rubens, *Self Portrait.*

1990, June 2   *Perf. 12¼x12*

2913-2915	A1359	Set of 3	2.25	.40

Düsseldorf '90, 10th Int'l Youth Philatelic Exhib. — A1360

Designs: 20ch, Steffi Graf, tennis player, with bouquet. 30ch, Exhibition emblem. 70ch, K.H. Rummenigge, German soccer player.

1990, June 20

2916-2918	A1360	Set of 3	7.00	.75

A1361

Designs: 10ch, Games mascot, Workers' Stadium, Beijing. 30ch, Chollina Statue and Korean athletes. 40ch, Games emblem, athletes.

1990, July 14

2919-2921	A1361	Set of 3	2.00	.60

11th Asian Games, Beijing (Nos. 2919-2920). Third Asian Winter Games, Samjiyon (No. 2921).

14th World Cup Soccer Championship — A1362

Designs: 15ch, Emblem of F.I.F.A. (Federation of Football Associations). 20ch, Jules Rimet. 25ch, Soccer ball. 30ch, Olympic Stadium, Rome. 35ch, Goalkeeper. 40ch, Emblem of the German Football Association. 80ch, Emblem of German Football Association and trophy.

1990, Aug. 8   *Perf. 13½*

2922-2927	A1362	Set of 6	6.00	1.00

Souvenir Sheet

2928	A1362	80ch multicolored	3.00	1.50

New Zealand '90 Int'l Philatelic Exhib., Auckland A1363

1990, Aug. 24   *Perf. 12*

2929	A1363	30ch multicolored	1.75	.40

Summer at Chipson Peak — A1364

1990, Aug. 24   *Perf. 11½*

2930	A1364	80ch multicolored	3.00	.50

Europa '90 International Stamp Fair, Riccione.

Koguryo Wedding Procession — A1365

Designs: 10ch, Man on horse blowing bugle. 30ch, Bridegroom on horse. 50ch, Bride in carriage. 1w, Man on horse beating drum.

1990, Sept. 3   *Perf. 12*

2931		Strip of 4, #a.-d.	6.00	.80
a.	A1365	10ch multicolored	1.25	.25
b.	A1365	30ch multicolored	1.25	.25
c.	A1365	50ch multicolored	1.25	.25
d.	A1365	1w multicolored	1.25	.25

Printed in setenant strips of four within the sheet.

A1366

Pan-National Rally for Peace and Reunification of Korea — A1367

Designs: 10ch, Rally emblem, crowd descending Mt. Paektu.
1w, Crowd watching dancers.

1990, Sept. 15

2932	A1366	10ch multicolored	.50	.25

Souvenir Sheet

2933	A1367	1w multicolored	2.75	.55

Insects A1368

Designs: 20ch, Praying mantis (Mantis religiosa). 30ch, Lady bug (Coccinella septempunctata). 40ch, Pheropsophus jussoensis. 70ch, Phyllium siccifolium.

1990, Sept. 20

2934-2936A	A1368	Set of 4	6.00	1.10

Soccer Players — A1369

No. 2938, North and South Korean players entering May Day Stadium.

1990, Oct. 11

2937	A1369	Pair, #a.-b.	2.75	.40
a.		10ch multicolored	1.25	.25
b.		20ch multicolored	1.25	.25

Souvenir Sheet

2938	A1369	1w multicolored	4.50	.75

North-South Reunification Soccer Games, Pyongyang.

National Reunification Concert — A1370

1990, Oct. 17

2939	A1370	10ch multicolored	.50	.25

Farm Animals — A1371

Designs: 10ch, Ox. 20ch, Pig. 30ch, Goat. 40ch, Sheep. 50ch, Horse.

1990, Oct. 18

2940-2944	A1371	Set of 5	5.75	.85
2944a		Sheet of 10, 2 ea #2940-2944	13.00	1.75

A1372

A1373

Chinese Entry Into Korean War, 40th Anniv. — A1374

Designs: 10ch, N. Korean and Communist Chinese soldiers. 20ch, Korean civilians welcoming Chinese soldiers. 30ch, Battle scene, victorious soldiers. 40ch, Postwar reconstruction.
80ch, Friendship Monument.

1990, Oct. 23

2945	A1372	10ch multicolored	.25	.25
2946	A1373	20ch multicolored	.75	.25
2947	A1373	30ch multicolored	1.00	.25
2948	A1373	40ch multicolored	1.50	.25
		Nos. 2945-2948 (4)	3.50	1.00

Souvenir Sheet
Perf. 11¾x11½

2949	A1374	80ch multicolored	3.00	.50

For overprint see No. 3282.

UN Development Program, 40th Anniv. A1375

1990, Oct. 24   *Perf. 13¼*

2950	A1375	1w multicolored	4.00	1.20

Fish — A1376

Designs: 10ch, Sturgeon (Acipenser mikadoi). 20ch, Sea bream (Sparus macrocephalus). 30ch, Flying fish (Cypsilurus agoö). 40ch, Fat greening (Heragrammos otakii). 50ch, Ray (Myliobatus tobeijei).

1990, Nov. 20   *Perf. 12*

2951-2955	A1376	Set of 5	5.75	2.00
2955a		Sheet of 10, 2 ea #2951-2955	12.00	4.00

New Year — A1377

1990, Dec. 1
2956 A1377 40ch multicolored 1.75 .25

Birds — A1378

Designs: 10ch, Moorhen (Gallinula chloropus). 20ch, Jay (Garrulus glandarius). 30ch, Three-toed woodpecker (Picodes tridactylus). 40ch, Whimbrel (Numenius phaeopus). 50ch, Water rail (Rallus aquaticus)

1990, Dec. 18 *Perf. 12*
2957-2961 A1378 Set of 5 6.50 2.00
2961a Sheet of 10, 2 ea #2957-2961 13.00 5.00

A1379

Pandas — A1380

Designs: 10ch, Giant panda. 20ch, Two giant pandas feeding. 30ch, Giant panda on limb. 40ch, Giant panda on rock. 50ch, Pair of giant pandas. 60ch, Giant panda in tree.

1991, Jan. 10 *Perf. 11¾x12*
2962-2967 A1379 Set of 6 7.00 1.75
2967a Sheet of 6, #2962-2967 7.00 1.75

Souvenir Sheet
Perf. 11½
2968 A1380 1w multicolored 3.25 .60
For surcharges, see No. 4536-4537.

A1381

Revolutionary Sites — A1382

1991, Jan. 10 *Perf. 12*
2969 A1381 5ch Changsan .25 .25
2970 A1382 10ch Oun .30 .25

Endangered Birds — A1383

Designs: 10ch, Black-faced spoonbills (Platalea minor). 20ch, Gray herons (Ardea cinerea). 30ch, Great egrets (Egretta alba). 40ch, Manchurian cranes (Grus japonensis). 50ch, Japanese white-necked cranes (Grus vipio). 70ch, White storks (Ciconia boyciana).

1991, Feb. 5
2971-2976 A1383 Set of 6 6.00 1.40
2976a Sheet of 6, #2971-2976 7.50 1.75

Alpine Butterflies — A1384

Designs: 10ch, Clossiana angarensis. 20ch, Erebia embla. 30ch, Nymphalis antiopa. 40ch, Polygonia c-album). 50ch, Colias erate. 60ch, Thecla betulae.

1991, Feb. 20 *Perf. 13¼*
2977-2982 A1384 Set of 6 7.50 2.50
2982a Sheet of 6, #2977-2982 7.50 2.50

Fungi — A1385

Designs: 10ch, Hydnum repandum. 20ch, Phylloporus rhodoxanthus. 30ch, Calvatia craniformis. 40ch, Ramaria botrytis. 50ch, Russula integra.

1991, Feb. 26 *Perf. 12x12¼*
2983-2987 A1385 Set of 5 5.00 1.25
2987a Sheet of 10, 2 ea #2983-2987 10.00 2.50
For surcharge, see No. 4546.

A1386

Revolutionary Sites — A1387

1991, Mar. 15 *Perf. 12*
2988 A1386 10ch Kumchon .30 .25
2989 A1387 40ch Samdung 1.20 .30

A1388

Silkworm Research A1389

Designs: 10ch, Dr. Kye Ung (1893-1967), silkworm researcher. 20ch, Chinese oak silk moth, Antheraea pernyi. 30ch, Attacus ricini. 40ch, Antheraea yamamai. 50ch, Bombyx mori. 60ch, Aetias artemis.

1991, Mar. 27
2990 A1388 10ch multicolored .25 .25
2991 A1389 20ch multicolored .60 .30
2992 A1389 30ch multicolored .80 .40
2993 A1389 40ch multicolored 1.20 .50
2994 A1389 50ch multicolored 1.60 .75
2995 A1389 60ch multicolored 2.00 .80
a. Sheet of 6, #2990-2995 6.50 3.50
Nos. 2990-2995 (6) 6.45 3.00

9th Spring Friendship Art Festival, Pyongyang A1390

1991, Apr. 3
2996 A1390 10ch multicolored .50 .25

Antarctic Exploration A1391

Designs: 10ch, Penguins. 20ch, Research station. 30ch, Elephant seals. 40ch, Research ship. 50ch, Black-backed gulls. 80ch, DPRK flag and map of Antarctica.

1991, Apr. 20 *Perf. 11¾x12*
2997-3001 A1391 Set of 5 6.00 1.25
3001a Sheet of 6, #2997-3002 9.00 1.80

Souvenir Sheet
Perf. 11¾
3002 A1391 80ch multicolored 3.00 .55
A single stamp like that in No. 3002 is included in No. 3001a.

85th Interparliamentary Union Conference, Pyongyang — A1392

Designs: 10ch, Peoples Palace of Culture. 1.50w, Conference emblem and azalea.

1991, Apr. 29 *Perf. 12*
3003-3004 A1392 Set of 2 5.00 1.40

Map and Kim Jong Ho — A1393

1991, May 8 *Perf. 11¾x12*
3005 A1393 90ch multicolored 2.50 .80

Dinosaurs — A1394

Designs: 10ch, Cynognathus. 20ch, Brontosaurus. 30ch, Stegosaurus and allosaurus. 40ch, Pterosauria. 50ch, Ichthyosaurus.

1991, May 21 *Perf. 12x11¾*
3006-3010 A1394 Strip of 5 + label 7.50 1.75
3010a Sheet of 5 + label 17.00 2.00

Barcelona '92 Olympic Games — A1395

Designs: No. 3011, 10ch, 100-Meter dash. No. 3012, 10ch, Hurdle race. No. 3013 20ch, Broad jump. No. 3014, 20ch, Throwing discus. No. 3015, 30ch, Shot-put. No. 3016, 30ch, Pole vault. No. 3017, 40ch, High jump. No. 3018, 40ch, Javelin throw.
No. 3019, 80ch, 400-meter race. No. 3020, 80ch, 1500-meter race.

1991, June 18
3011-3018 A1395 Set of 8 4.00 1.40
3018a Sheet of 10, #3011-3020 12.50 2.75

Souvenir Sheets
Perf. 11½x11¾
3019-3020 A1395 Set of 2 3.50 1.25
No. 3018a contains single stamps from Nos. 3019-3020 in addition to Nos. 3011-3018.

Cats — A1396

Designs: 10ch, Cats and birds. 20ch, Cat and rat. 30ch, Cat and butterfly. 40ch, Cats and ball. 50ch, Cat and frog.

1991, July 21 *Perf. 13¼*
3021-3025 A1396 Set of 5 5.25 2.25
For surcharges, see Nos. 4538, 4547.

Riccione '91 Int'l Stamp Fair — A1397

1991, Aug. 27   **Perf. 11¾x12**
3026 A1397 80ch multicolored   2.75   .60

Horses
A1398

Designs: 10ch, Equus caballus. 20ch, Equus asinus and Equus caballus. 30ch, Equus przewalskii. 40ch, Equus asinus. 50ch, Equus caballus, diff.

1991, Sept. 2   **Perf. 13½**
3027-3031 A1398 Set of 5   5.00   1.25
3031a   Sheet of 5, #3027-3031   5.00   1.40

A1399

Phila Nippon '91 International Stamp Exhibition — A1400

Fish: 10ch, Pennant coral fish (Heniochus acuminatus). 20ch, Big-spotted trigger fish (Balistoides conspicillum). 30ch, Anemone fish (Amphiprion frenatus). 40ch, Blue surgeon fish (Paracanthurus hepatus). 50ch, Angel fish (Pterophyllum eimekei).
80ch, Tetras (Hyphessobrycon innesi).

1991, Sept. 20   **Perf. 12x12¼**
3032-3036 A1399 Set of 5   5.00   1.25
3036a   Sheet of 5, #3032-3036   5.00   1.25
Souvenir Sheet
Perf. 11¾
3037 A1400 80ch multicolored   5.00   .60
No. 3036 is airmail.

Flowers
A1401

Designs: 10ch, Begonia. 20ch, Gerbera. 30ch, Rhododendrons. 40ch, Phalaenopsis. 50ch, Impatiens sultani. 60ch, Streptocarpus.

1991, Oct. 16   **Perf. 12¼x12**
3038-3043 A1401 Set of 6   6.50   1.75
3043a   Sheet of 6, #3038-3043   6.50   2.00
Nos. 3041-3043 commemorate Canada '92 International Youth Stamp Exhibition, Montreal, and include the exhibition emblem.

Panmunjon — A1402

1991, Oct. 12   **Perf. 12**
3044 A1402 10ch multicolored   .60   .25

Magnolia — A1403

1991, Nov. 1   **Perf. 11½**
3045 A1403 10ch multicolored   .60   .25
DPRK National Flower.

Women's World Soccer Championship, China — A1404

Designs: 10ch, Dribbling. 20ch, Dribbling, diff. 30ch, Heading the ball. 40ch, Overhead kick. 50ch, Tackling. 60ch, Goalkeeper.

1991, Nov. 3   **Perf. 12**
3046-3051 A1404 Set of 6   6.50   1.75
3051a   Sheet of 6, #3046-3051   6.50   2.00

A1405

Monkeys — A1406

Designs: 10ch, Squirrel monkeys (Samiri sciureus). 20ch, Pygmy marmosets (Cebuella pygmaea). 30ch, Red-handed tamarins (Saquinas midas).

80ch, Monkey leaping.

1992, Jan. 1
3052-3054 A1405 Set of 3   2.25   .70
3054a   Sheet of 3, #3052-3054   2.50   .80
Souvenir Sheet
Perf. 11¾x11½
3055 A1406 80ch multicolored   2.50   1.00

A1407

Birds of Prey — A1408

Designs: 10ch, Bubo bubo. 20ch, Buteo buteo. 30ch, Haliaeetus vocifer. 40ch, Haliaeetus pelagicus. 50ch, Aquila chrysaetos.
80ch, Falco tinnunculus.

1992, Jan. 5   **Perf. 13¼**
3056-3060 A1407 Set of 5   4.75   1.75
3060a   Sheet of 12, 2 #3056-3060
            + 2 labels   10.00   3.50
Souvenir Sheet
Perf. 11½
3061 A1408 80ch multicolored   2.50   .60
No. 3060a, Granada '92 International Stamp Exhibition. For surcharge, see No. 4609.

A1409

50th Birthday of Kim Jong II — A1410

Designs: 10ch, Birthplace, Mt. Paektu. 20ch, Mt. Paektu. 30ch, Lake Chon on top of Mt. Paektu. 40ch, Lake Samji.
80ch, *Snowstorm in Mt. Paektu.*

1992, Feb. 16   **Perf. 12x11¾**
3062-3065 A1409 Set of 4   3.25   .75
Souvenir Sheet
Perf. 11¾x11½
3066 A1410 80ch multicolored   3.00   .60

Transport
A1411

Designs: 10ch, Bus, "Jipsam 88." 20ch, Bus, "Pyongyang 86." 30ch, Trolley bus, "Chollima 84." 40ch, Bus, "Kwangbok Sonyon." 50ch, Tram. 60ch, July 17 Tram.

1992, Feb. 20   **Perf. 12¼**
3067-3072 A1411 Set of 6   6.50   1.75
3072a   Sheet of 6, #3067-3072   6.50   1.90
No. 3072a, Essen '92 International Stamp Fair.

Spring Fellowship Art Festival, Pyongyang
A1412

1992, Apr. 7
3073 A1412 10ch multicolored   .50   .25

A1413

80th Birthday of Kim II Sung — A1414

Revolutionary Sites: 10ch (No. 3074), Birthplace, Mangyongdao. 10ch (No. 3075), Party emblem, Turubong. 10ch (No. 3076), Map, Ssuksom. 10ch (No. 3077), Statue of soldier, Tongchang. 40ch (No. 3078), Chollima Statue, Kangson. 40ch (No. 3079), Cogwheels, Taean. 1.20w, Monument, West Sea Barrage.
80ch, Kim II Sung among participants in the April Spring Friendship Art Festival.

1992, Apr. 15
3074-3080 A1413 Set of 7   7.50   2.25
Souvenir Sheet
Perf. 11½
3081 A1414 80ch multicolored   3.00   .60
No. 2080 is airmail.

Kang Ban Sok, Mother of Kim II Sung, Birth Centenary — A1415

1992, Apr. 21   **Perf. 13¼**
3082 A1415 80ch multicolored   2.25   .60

Korean People's Army, 60th Anniv. A1416

Designs (all 10ch): No. 3083, Soldier, troops on parade. No. 3084, Pilot, soldiers. No. 3085, Soldier with two civilian women.

1992, Apr. 25   **Perf. 12¼**
3083-3085 A1416 Set of 3   1.10 .25
3085a   Sheet of 9, 4 #3085, 2 ea.
     #3083-3084 + label   3.00 1.00

25th Olympic Games, Barcelona '92 — A1417

Women's events: 10ch, Hurdle race. 20ch, High jump. 30ch, Shot-put. 40ch, 200-meter race. 50ch, Broad jump. 60ch, Javelin throw. 80ch, 800-meter race.

1992, May 10   **Perf. 12x11¾**
3086-3091 A1417 Set of 6   6.50 1.75
3091a   Sheet of 8, #3086-3092 + label   9.50 2.50
Souvenir Sheet
3092 A1416 80ch multicolored   2.75 .60

Prehistoric Man — A1418

Designs: 10ch, Planting crops. 20ch, Family in shelter, with cooking pot. 30ch, Plowing. 40ch, Indoor life. 50ch, Laying a dolmen.

1992, June 1   **Perf. 12x11¾**
3093-3097 A1418 Set of 5   5.00 1.25
3097a   Sheet of 5, #3093-3097 + label   6.00 1.40

Birds — A1419

Designs: 10ch, Dryocopus javensis. 20ch, Phasianis colchicus. 30ch, Ciconia boyciana. 40ch, Pitta brachyura. 50ch, Syrrhaptes paradoxus. 60ch, Lyrurus tetrix. 80ch, Sturnus sturnus.

1992, June 28   **Perf. 11½**
3098-3103 A1419 Set of 6   7.00 1.75
3103a   Sheet of 7, #3098-3104 + label   15.00 —
Souvenir Sheet
3104 A1418 80ch multicolored   3.50 1.40

No. 3103a contains a single stamp from No. 3104 in addtion to Nos. 3098-3103.

North-South Joint Statement, 20th Anniv. — A1420

1992, July 4
3105 A1420 1.50w multicolored   4.50 1.40
Souvenir Sheet
3106 A1420 3w multicolored   9.00 2.75

No. 3106 contains two copies of No. 3105 and label.

Flowers — A1421

Designs: 10ch, Bougainvillea spectabilis. 20ch, Ixora chinensis. 30ch, Dendrobium taysuwie. 40ch, Columnea gloriosa. 50ch, Crinum. 60ch, Ranunculus asiaticus.

1992, July 15   **Perf. 12¼**
3107-3112 A1421 Set of 6   6.50 1.75
3112a   Sheet of 8, #3107-3112 + 2 labels   7.00 2.00

No. 3112a, Genova '92 International Stamp Exhibition.

The Solar System — A1422

No. 3113: a, Satellite, Venus, Earth, Mars. b, Jupiter. c, Saturn. d, Uranus. e, Neptune, Pluto. 80ch, Earth, Moon.

1992, Aug. 10   **Perf. 11½**
3113 A1422 50ch Strip of 5, #a-e   8.00 2.50
3113f   Sheet of 5, #3113 + 5 labels   9.00 2.75
Souvenir Sheet
3114 A1422 80ch multicolored   2.50 1.50

Riccione '92 Int'l Stamp Fair — A1423

Designs: 10ch, C-class yacht. 20ch, Sailboard. 30ch, Rager-class yacht. 40ch, Pin-class yacht. 50ch, 470-class yacht. 60ch, Fair emblem.

1992, Aug. 27   **Perf. 12¼**
3119-3124 A1423 Set of 6   6.50 2.25
3119a   Sheet of 6 stamps, 2 ea.
     #3119, 3121, 3123   6.50 2.50
3120a   Sheet of 6 stamps, 2 ea.
     #3120, 3122, 3124   6.50 2.50

SAMPDORIA ITALIAN CHAMPION 1991

A1424

ERG THE GREATEST ITALIAN PRIVATE OIL COMPANY

U.C. Sampdoria, Italian Soccer Champion 1991 — A1425

Designs: 20ch, Moreno Mannini, defender. 30ch, Gianluca Vialli, forward. 40ch, Pietro Vierchowod, back. 50ch, Fausto Pari, center-half. 60ch, Roberto Mancini, forward. 1w, club president.
1w, Vialli and Riccardo Garrone, president of club sponsor, ERG.

1992, Aug. 31   **Perf. 12**
3125-3130 A1424 Sheet of 6   9.00 3.00
Souvenir Sheet
Perf. 11½x12
3131 A1425 1w multicolored   3.00 1.50

A1426

8th World Taekwondo Championship, Pyongyang — A1427

Designs: 10ch, Team pattern. 30ch, Side kick. 50ch, Flying high kick. 70ch, Flying twisting kick. 90ch, Black-belt breaking tiles with fist.
1.20w, Flying twin foot side kick; Choe Hong Hin, president of International Taekwon-Do Federation, in margin.

1992, Sept. 1   **Perf. 12**
3132-3136 A1426 Set of 5   8.00 2.50
3136a   Sheet of 5, #3132-3136 + label   8.00 2.50
Souvenir Sheet
3137 A1427 1.20w multicolored   4.00 1.75

No. 3137 is airmail.

Frogs and Toads A1428

Designs: No. 3138, 40ch, Rana chosenica. No. 3139, 40ch, Rana arvalis. No. 3140, 40ch, Bufo bufo. No. 3141, 70ch, Rana nigromaculata. No. 3142, 70ch, Hyla japonica. No. 3143, 70ch Rana coreana.

1992, Sept. 10   **Perf. 12¼**
3138-3143 A1428 Set of 6   10.00 3.00
3139a   Sheet of 8, 4 #3139, 2 ea.
     #3138, #3140 + label   15.00 5.00
3142a   Sheet of 8, 4 #3142, 2 ea.
     #3141, #3143 + label   15.00 5.00

No. 3143 is airmail.

World Environment Day — A1429

Designs: 10ch, Rhododendron mucronulatum. 30ch, Hirundo rustica. 40ch, Stewartia koreana. 50ch, Dictoptera aurora. 70ch, Metasequoia glyptostroboides. 90ch, Hynobius leechi. 1.20w, Gingko biloba. 1.40w, Cottus poecilopus.

1992, Oct. 20   **Perf. 12**
3144-3151 A1429 Set of 8   19.00 4.75
3151a   Sheet of 8 stamps, #3144-3151   20.00 5.25

Nos. 3150 and 3151 are airmail.

Whales and Dolphins A1430

Designs: No. 3152, 50ch, Balaenoptera physalus. No. 3153, 50ch, Delphinus delphis. No. 3154, 50ch, Orcinus orca. No. 3155, 50ch, Megaptera nodosa. No. 3156, 50ch, Berardius bairdii. No. 3157, 50ch, Physeter catadon.

1992, Oct. 20   **Set of 6**
3152-3157 A1430 Set of 6   12.00 2.75
3152a   Sheet of 3, #3152-3154   5.50 1.25
3155a   Sheet of 3, #3155-3157   5.50 1.25

No. 3157 is airmail. For surcharges, see No. 4548, 4588.

New Year (Year of the Rooster) A1431

Chickens in various cartoon forms: 10ch, Hen and chicks. 20ch, Young hen. 30ch, Strong cock. 40ch, Prince cock. 50ch, Princess hen. 60ch, King cock. 1.20w, Cock.

1992, Dec. 7   **Perf. 11½**
3158-3163 A1431 Set of 6   6.50 1.75
3163a   Sheet of 4, #3158-3160, 3163c   4.00 1.50
3163b   Sheet of 4, #3161-3163, 3163c   5.00 2.00
Souvenir Sheet
3163C A1431 1.20w multicolored   5.00 1.00

A single stamp like that in No. 3163C is included in Nos. 3163a and 3163b. For surcharges, see Nos. 4525-4526.

N. Korean Gold Medal Winners at Barcelona Olympics A1432

Designs: 10ch, Choe Chol Su (boxing). 20ch, Pae Kil Su (gymnastics). 50ch, Ri Hak Son (Wrestling). 60ch, Kim Il (wrestling).
No. 3168: a, 30ch, Archer, flame, gold medal, flags of DPRK and Spain. b, 40ch, Emblem, game mascot and Church of the Holy Family, Barcelona.

1992, Dec. 20   **Perf. 12**
3164-3167 A1432 Set of 4   4.50 1.20
Sheet of 6
3168   #3164-3167, 3168a-3168b   7.00 .60
   a.   A1432 30ch multicolored   .35 .25
   b.   A1432 40ch multicolored   .50 .30

Fungi — A1433

Designs: 10ch, Golden mushroom (Flammulina velutipes). 20ch, Shaggy caps (Coprinus comatus). 30ch, Ganoderma lucidum. 40ch, Brown mushroom (Lentinus edodes). 50ch, (Volvaria bombycina). 60ch, (Sarcodon aspratus). 1w, Scarlet caterpillar (Cordyceps militaris).

1993, Jan. 10   **Perf. 11½**
3169-3174 A1433 Set of 6   7.50 2.50
3169a   Sheet of 4, #3169, 3172, 3174, 3175   7.00 2.25
3170a   Sheet of 4, #3170, 3171, 3173, 3175   7.00 2.25
Souvenir Sheet
3175 A1433 1w multicolored   4.50 .80
A single stamp like that in No. 3175 is included in Nos. 3169a and 3170a.

A1434

Korean Plants — A1435

Designs: 10ch, Keumkangsania asiatica. 20ch, Echinosophora koreensis. 30ch, Abies koreana. 40ch, Benzoin angustifolium. 50ch, Abeliophyllum distichum. 60ch, (Abelia mosanensis). 1w, Pentactina rupicola.

1993, Jan. 20   **Perf. 12¼**
3176-3181 A1434 Set of 6   7.00 2.00
3181a   Sheet of 6, #3176-3181   7.00 2.25
Souvenir Sheet
Perf. 11½
3182 A1435 1w multicolored   3.50 2.00

8th Congress of the League of Socialist Working Youth of Korea — A1436

Designs: 10ch, Youths, banner. 20ch, Flame, emblem, motto.

1993, Jan. 25   **Perf. 12¼**
3183-3184 A1436 Set of 2   1.50 .40

Phophyong Revolutionary Site Tower & March Corps Emblem — A1437

1993, Jan. 29   **Perf. 12x12¼**
3185 A1437 10ch multicolored   .50 .25
70th anniv. of the 250-mile Journey for Learning.

Tower of the Juche Idea, Grand Monument, Mt. Wangjae A1438

1993, Feb. 11
3186 A1438 60ch multicolored   .50 .25
60th anniv. of the Wangjaesan Meeting.

A1439

Kim Jong Il, 51st Birthday — A1440

Designs: 10ch, Kimjongilia (Begonia). 1w, Kim Il Sung writing poem praising Kim Jong Il. Illustration of stamp only. Sheet measures 170mmx95mm, with marginal inscriptions that include reproductions of Kim Il Sung's poem.

1993, Feb. 16   **Perf. 12**
3187 A1439 10ch multicolored   1.00 .25
Souvenir Sheet
Perf. 13¼
3188 A1440 1w multicolored   3.50 .75

Sea Fish A1441

Designs: 10ch, Pilot fish (Naucrates ductor). 20ch, Japanese stingray (Dasyatis akajei). 30ch, Moonfish (Lampris guttatus). 40ch, Coelacanth (Latimeria chalumnae). 50ch, Grouper (Epinephelus moara). 1.20w, Mako shark (Isurus oxyrhynchus).

1993, Feb. 25   **Perf. 11½**
3189-3193 A1441 Set of 5   5.00 1.25
3189a   Sheet of 2, #3189, #3194   3.25 .45
3190a   Sheet of 2, #3190, #3193   3.25 .45
3191a   Sheet of 2, #3191, #3192   3.25 .45
Souvenir Sheet
3194 A1441 1.20w multicolored   4.50 .80
A single stamp like that in No. 3194 is included in No. 3189a.
No. 3194, Naposta '93.

Spring on the Hill, 18th century Korean Painting — A1442

1993, Mar. 20   **Perf. 12x11½**
3195 A1442 Sheet of 5   6.50 1.75
a.-e.   40ch, any single   1.00 .30

Spring Friendship Art Festival — A1443

1993, Apr. 5   **Perf. 12x12¼**
3196 A1443 10ch multicolored   .75 .25
For surcharge, see No. 4602.

A1444

Kim Il Sung, 80th Birthday, and Publication of With the Century — A1445

Designs: 10ch, With the Century, Kim Il Sung's Memoir. 1w, Kim Il Sung writing With the Century.

1993, Apr. 15
3197 A1444 10ch multicolored   .50 .25
Souvenir Sheet
Perf. 11½
3198 A1445 1w multicolored   3.50 .75

A1446

Pyongyang Scenes — A1447

Designs: 10ch, Kwangbok Street. 20ch, Chollima Street. 30ch, Munsu Street. 40ch, Moranbong Street. 50ch, Thongil Street. 1w, Changgwang Street.

1993, Apr. 20   **Perf. 12x11¾**
3199-3203 A1446 Set of 5   4.50 1.25
Souvenir Sheet
Perf. 11½
3204 A1447 1w multicolored   3.50 .75

Insects A1448

Designs: 10ch, Fly (Trichogramma dendrolimi). 20ch, Fly (Brachymeria obscurata). 30ch, Cricket (Metrioptera brachyptera). 50ch, Cricket (Gryllus campestris). 70ch, Beetle (Geocoris pallidipennis). 90ch, Wasp (Cyphononyx dorsalis).

1993, May 10   **Perf. 12x12¼**
3205-3210 A1448 Set of 6   10.00 2.25
3205a   Sheet of 3, #3205, 3207, 3210   5.00 1.25
3206a   Sheet of 3, #3206, 3208, 3209   5.00 1.25
Nos. 3205-3210 were issued both in separate sheets and in sheets of 3.

A1449

A1450

1993, May 19   **Perf. 11½**
3211 A1449 10ch multicolored   .50 .25
Souvenir Sheet
Perf. 13¼
3212 A1450 1.20w multicolored   4.00 .80
Release of Ri In Mo, North Korean war correspondent, from South Korean prison.

World Cup Soccer Championship, U.S.A. — A1451

World Cup and soccer players: 10ch, Tackling. 20ch, Kicking. 30ch, Kicking (diff.). 50ch, Tackling (diff.). 70ch, Blocking. 90ch, Feinting.

1993, May 25   **Perf. 11½**
3213-3218 A1451 Set of 6   8.50 2.25
3213a   Sheet of 3, #3213, 3215, 3218   4.25 1.25
3214a   Sheet of 3, #3214, 3216, 3217   4.25 1.25

Birds — A1452

Designs: 10ch, Gray-headed green wood-pecker (Picus canus). 20ch, King of paradise (Cicinnurus regius. 30ch, Lesser bird of paradise (Paradisea minor). 40ch, Paradise whydah (Steganura paradisaea). 50ch, Magnificent bird of paradise (Diphyllodes magnificus). 60ch, Greater bird of paradise (Paradisea apoda).

1993, May 29   **Perf. 12**
3219-3224	A1452	Set of 6	7.00	1.75
3219a	Sheet of 4, 2 ea. #3219, 3224		4.00	1.10
3220a	Sheet of 4, 2 ea. #3220, 3223		4.00	1.10
3221a	Sheet of 2, #3221, #3222		4.00	1.10

Nos. 3221, 3221a, 3222, Indopex '93 International Stamp Exhibition, Surabaya, Indonesia.

Stampcard — A1453

Map of Korean peninsula.

1993, May 29   **Rouletted**
Self-adhesive
| 3225 | A1453 | Card of 6 stamps | 20.00 | 20.00 |
| a.-f. | 1.50w, any single | | 3.00 | 3.00 |

For surcharges, see No. 3441.

Korean World Champions — A1454

Designs: 10ch, Kim Myong Nam (weight-lifting, 1990). 20ch, Kim Kwang Suk (gymnastics, 1991). 30ch, Pak Yong Sun (table tennis, 1975, 1977). 50ch, Kim Yong Ok (radio direction-finding, 1990). 70ch, Han Yun Ok (taekwondo, 1987, 1988, 1990). 90ch, Kim Yong Sik (free-style wrestling, 1986, 1989).

1993, June 15   **Perf. 12x11¾**
3226-3231	A1454	Set of 6	9.00	2.25
3226a	Sheet of 6, 2 ea. #3226, 3228, 3231		9.00	2.50
3227a	Sheet of 6, 2 ea. #3227, 3229, 3230		9.00	2.50

For surcharge, see No. 4573.

Fruits and Vegetables A1455

Designs: 10ch, Cabbage and chili peppers. 20ch, Squirrel and horse chestnuts. 30ch, Peach and grapes. 40ch, Birds and persimmons. 50ch, Tomatoes, eggplant and cherries. 60ch, Onion, radishes, garlic bulbs.

1993, June 25   **Perf. 11¾x12**
3232-3237	A1455	Set of 6	6.50	1.75
3232a	Sheet of 3, #3232, 3235, 3237		2.50	.90
3232b	As "a.," ovptd. "Polska '93"		5.00	1.25
3233c	Sheet of 3, #3233, 3234, 3236		2.50	.90

National Emblem — A1456

1993, July 5   **Perf. 12**
| 3238 | A1456 | 10ch vermilion | .60 | .25 |

Korean War, 40th Anniv. A1457

A1458

A1459

A1460

Kim Leading Soldiers on the Front — A1461

Kim Surveying Battlefield — A1462

Kim Making 1953 Victory Speech — A1463

Designs: No. 3239, 10ch, Soldiers and civilian women. No. 3240, 10ch, Officer and enlisted man. No. 3241, 10ch, Anti-aircraft missiles on military trucks. No. 3242, 10ch, Guided missiles on carriers. No. 3243, 10ch, Self-propelled missile launchers.
No. 3244, 1w, Kim Il Jong taking salute of paraders.
No. 3245, 10ch, Victory statue (soldier with flag). No. 3246, 10ch, Machine-gunners and refugees. 40ch, Soldiers and flag.
No. 3248a, 10ch, Kim Il Sung conducting planning meeting. b, 20ch, Kim inspecting artillery unit. No. 3249a, 10ch, Kim directing battle for Height 1211. b, 20ch, Kim encouraging machine gun crew. No. 3250a, 10ch, Kim at munitions factory. b, 20ch, Kim directing units of the Second Front. No. 3251a, 10ch, Kim with tank commanders. b, 20ch, Kim directing airmen. No. 3252a, 10ch, Kim with victorious soldiers. b, 20ch, Musicians.

1993, July 27
| 3239-3243 | A1457 | Set of 5 | 2.50 | .75 |

Souvenir Sheet
Perf. 13¼
| 3244 | A1458 | 1w multicolored | 4.00 | .55 |

Perf. 11¾x12
| 3245-3247 | A1459 | Set of 3 | 2.25 | .50 |
| 3247a | Sheet of 3, #3245-3247 | | 2.50 | .60 |

Souvenir Sheets of 2, #a-b
Perf. 11½
| 3248-3252 | A1460 | Set of 5 | 5.00 | 1.40 |

Souvenir Sheets
Perf. 13¼
3253	A1461	80ch multicolored	4.50	.60
3254	A1462	80ch multicolored	4.50	.60
3255	A1463	1w multicolored	6.00	.60

National Reunification Prize Winners — A1464

Designs: 10ch, Choe Yong Do (1923-69). 20ch, Kim Gu (1875-1949). 30ch, Hong Myong Hui (1888-1968). 40ch, Ryo Un Hyong (1886-1947). 50ch, Kim Jong Thae (1926-69). 60ch, Kim Chaek (1903-51).

1993, Aug. 1   **Perf. 12**
| 3256-3261 | A1464 | Set of 6 | 6.50 | 1.75 |

A1465

Taipei '93 Int'l Philatelic Exhib. — A1466

Designs: 20ch, Robina sp. 30ch, Hippeastrum cv. 1w, Deer.

1993, Aug. 14
| 3262-3263 | A1465 | Set of 2 | 1.50 | .45 |

Souvenir Sheet
| 3264 | A1466 | 1w multicolored | 3.50 | 1.50 |

350th Anniv. Birth of Sir Isaac Newton, Mathematician and Scientist A1467

Designs: 10ch, Portrait of Newton. 20ch, Apple tree and formula for Law of Gravitation. 30ch, Reflecting telescope invented by Newton. 50ch, Formula of Binomial Theorem. 70ch, Newton's works, statue.

1993, Sept. 1   **Perf. 12¼x12**
3265-3269	A1467	Set of 5	7.50	1.50
3265a	Sheet of 3, #3265, 3266, 3269		3.75	3.75
3265b	Sheet of 3, #3265, 3267, 3268		3.75	3.75

For surcharge, see No. 4597.

A1468

Restoration of the Tomb of King Tongmyong, Founder of Koguryo — A1469

Designs: 10ch, King Tongmyong shooting arrow. 20ch, King Tongmyong. 30ch, Restoration monument. 40ch, Jongrung Temple of the Tomb of King Tongmyong. 50ch, Tomb. 80ch, Kim II Sung visiting restored tomb.

1993, Sept. 10
3270-3274 A1468 Set of 5   4.50 1.25

Souvenir Sheet
Perf. 11½
3275 A1469 80ch multicolored   2.50 1.50

Bangkok '93 Int'l Philatelic
Exhib. — A1470

First stamps of North Korea and Thailand.

1993, Oct. 1
3276 A1470 1.20w multicolored   5.00 2.00

Orchids — A1471

Designs: 10ch, Cyrtopodium andresoni. 20ch, Cattleya. 30ch, Cattleya intermedia "Oculata." 40ch, Potinaria "Maysedo godonsia." 50ch, "Kimilsungia."

1993, Oct. 15   *Perf. 12*
3277-3281 A1471 Set of 5   6.00 1.25
3281a   Strip of 5, #3277-3281 6.00 6.00
3277b-3281b   Set of 5 complete
             booklets, each
             containing 5
             stamps   30.00

Nos. 3277b-3281b each contain horizontal strips of 5 of one value, taken from sheets. For surcharge, see No. 4549.

No. 2949 Overprinted

1993, Nov. 16
3282 A1373 80ch vermilion   2.50 1.50
Mao Zedong, Birth Centennial.

A1472

A1473

Mao Zedong, Birth
Centennial — A1474

Designs: 10ch, Mao in Yannan (1940). 20ch, Mao in Beijing (1960). 30ch, Mao voting (1953). 40ch, Mao with middle-school students (1959).
No. 3287: Nos. 3283-3286 and: a, Mao proclaiming People's Republic of China (1949). b, Mao and his son, Mao Anying, in Xiangshan, Beijing (1949). c, Mao and Kim II Sung (1975).
No. 3288: As No. 3287c.

1993, Dec. 26   *Perf. 11½*
3283-3286 A1472 Set of 4   3.25   .90
Souvenir Sheets
3287 A1473 Sheet of 7   6.00 6.00
  a.   25ch multicolored   .50   .30
  b.   25ch multicolored   .50   .30
  c.   1w multicolored   .90
3288 A1474 1w multicolored   2.00 2.00

A1475

A1476

New Year, Year of the Dog — A1477

Designs: 10ch, Phungsan. 20ch, Yorkshire terriers. 30ch, Gordon setter. 40ch, Pomeranian. 50ch, Spaniel with pups.
No. 3294, Pointer.
No. 3295, 2 #3289, 1 #3294a; No. 3296, 2 #3290, 1 #3294a; No. 3297, 2 #3291, 1 #3294a; No. 3298, 2 #3292, 1 #3294a; No. 3299, 2 #3293, 1 #3294a.

1994, Jan. 1   *Perf. 12*
3289-3293 A1475 Set of 5   5.00 1.00

3289a-3293a   Set of 5 complete
                 booklets, each
                 containing 5
                 stamps   25.00
Souvenir Sheet
3294 A1476 1w multicolored   4.50 1.25
Sheets of 3, #a.-c.
Perf. 12
3295-3299 A1477 Set of 5   30.00 30.00
Nos. 3289a-3293a each contain horizontal strips of 5 of one value, taken from sheets.

A1478

Kim Jong II, 52nd Birthday — A1479

Designs: 10ch, Purple hyosong flower (Prinula polyantha). 40ch, Yellow hyosong flower (Prinula polyantha).
No. 3302, Kim II Sung and Kim Jong II, from embroidery *The Sun of Juche.*

1994, Feb. 16   *Perf. 13¼*
3300-3301 A1478 Set of 2   1.50   .45
  a.   Pair, #3300-3301   1.75 1.75
Souvenir Sheet
3302 A1479 1w multicolored   3.50 1.25
Nos. 3300-3301 exist in a miniature sheet containing 4 of each value, with central label depicting Jong II Peak and *Kimjongilia.*

Goldfish — A1480

Designs: 10ch, Red and black dragon-eye. 30ch, Red and white bubble-eye. 50ch, Red and white long-finned wenyu. 70ch, Red and white fringetail.

1994, Feb. 18   *Perf. 12*
3303 A1480 Sheet of 4   6.50 1.25
  a.   10ch multicolored   1.60   .25
  b.   30ch multicolored   1.60   .25
  c.   50ch multicolored   1.60   .25
  d.   70ch multicolored   1.60   .25

A1481

Publication of the *Program of Modeling the Whole Society on the Juche Idea,* 20th Anniv. — A1482

Kim II Sung proclaiming the *Program,* 1974.

1994, Feb. 19
3307 A1481 20ch multicolored   .50   .25
Souvenir Sheet
Perf. 11½
3308 A1482 1.20w multicolored 4.25 1.25

A1483

A1484

Publication of Kim II Sung's *Theses on the Socialist Rural Question in Our Country,* 30th Anniv. — A1485

Designs: 10ch (No. 3309), Woman propagandist, sound truck. 10ch (No. 3310), Electrical generator, pylon. 10ch (No. 3311), Farm, farm equipment, piles of grain. 40ch (No. 3312), Lab technician with microscope. 40ch (No. 3313), Dancers celebrating bounty harvest.
No. 3314, Kim II Sung in field. No. 3315, Kim Jong II walking through field with peasants.

1994, Feb. 25   *Perf. 12*
3309-3313 A1483 Set of 5   3.50   .90
Souvenir Sheets
Perf. 11½
3314 A1484 1w multicolored   2.50 1.25
3315 A1485 1w multicolored   2.50 1.25

Ships
A1486

Designs: 20ch, Passenger ship, *Mangyongbong-92.* 30ch, Cargo ship, *Osandok.*

40ch, Processing stern trawler, *Ryongaksan.*
50ch, Stern trawler.
80ch, Passenger ship, *Maekjon No. 1.*

1994, Mar. 25   **Perf. 12**
3316-3319 A1486   Set of 4   4.50   1.25
3320   Sheet of 6, #3316-3319
       + 2 #3320a   10.00   2.50
   a.   A1486 80ch multicolored   2.50   .75

DPRK
Flag — A1487

1994, Mar. 30   **Perf. 13¼**
3321 A1487 10ch car & dp blue   .50   .25
   For surcharge, see No. 4571.

A1488

1994, Apr. 15   **Perf. 12**
3322-3323 A1488   Set of 2   1.50   .50
3323a   10ch Sheet of 8   7.00   2.25
3323b   40ch Sheet of 8   7.00   2.25

Souvenir Sheet
3324 A1489 2w Sheet of 5   7.00   7.00
   a.-e.   40ch any single   1.25   1.25

Kim Il Sung, 82nd Birthday — A1489

Designs: 10ch, Magnolia and Kim's home.
40ch, Kimilsungia and Kim's home.
No. 3324, Five 40ch stamps, together forming design of Lake Chon (crater lake of Mt. Paektu), with *Song of General Kim Il Sung* music within design, lyrics in sheet margin.

Alpine Plants of
the Mt. Paektu
Area — A1490

Designs: 10ch, Chrysoplenium sphaerospermum. 20ch, Campanula cephalotes. 40ch, Trollius macropetafus. 50ch, Sedum kamtschaticum.
1w, Dianthus repens.

1994, Apr. 25   **Perf. 13¼**
3325-3329 A1490   Set of 5   4.50   1.25
3325a   Sheet of 3, #3325, 3327,
      #3330   4.25   1.75
3326a   Sheet of 3, #3326, 3328,
      3329   4.25   1.75

Souvenir Sheet
3330 A1490   1w multicolored   3.50   1.50
   A single stamp like that in No. 3330 is included in No. 3325a.

A1491

Int'l Olympic Committee
Centenary — A1492

Designs: 10ch, Olympic rings, DPRK flag. 20ch, Pierre de Coubertin, founder. 30ch, Olympic flag, flame. 50ch, IOC Centenary Congress emblem.
No. 3335, Runner with Olympic Torch. No. 3336, Juan Antonio Samaranch, IOC President and new IOC headquarters.

1994, May 2   **Perf. 12**
3331-3334 A1491   Set of 4   4.00   1.00

Souvenir Sheets
Perf. 13¼
3335-3336 A1492   Set of 2   0.50   2.00

International
Federation of Red
Cross and Red
Crescent
Societies, 75th
Anniv. — A1493

Designs: 10ch, Train, pedestrians crossing on overpass ("Prevention of traffic accident"). 20ch, Medical personnel in Red Cross boat ("Relief on the Sea"). 30ch, Man and girl planting tree ("Protection of the environment"). 40ch, Dam, sailboat on lake ("Protection of drought damage").

1994, May 5
3337-3340 A1493   Strip of 4   3.50   2.50

No. 3225 Surcharged

1994, May 29   **Self-adhesive**   *Imperf*
3341 A1452 1.60w on 1.50w
       Card of 6   28.00   28.00
   a.-f.   1.60w on 1.50w, any single   7.00   7.00

Seals — A1495

Designs: 10ch, Northern fur seal (Callorhinus ursinus). 40ch, Southern elephant seal (Mirounga leonina). 60ch, Southern sea lion (Otaria byronia).
No. 3345: 20ch, California sea lion (Zalophus californianus). 30ch, Ringed seal (Phoca hispida). 50ch, Walrus (Odobenus rosmarus).
No. 3346, Harp seal (Pagophilus groenlandicus).

1994, June 10   **Perf. 11½**
3342-3344 A1494   Set of 3   4.00   .90
3345 A1494   Sheet of 3   4.50   1.00
   a.   20ch multicolored   .75   .25
   b.   30ch multicolored   1.25   .25
   c.   50ch multicolored   2.25   .50

Souvenir Sheet
3346 A1495   1w multicolored   3.50   1.00

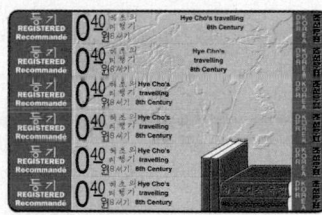

Stampcard — A1496

Map of Asia, books.

1994, June 17   *Rouletted*
Self-adhesive
3347 A1496   Card of 6 stamps   10.00   10.00
   a.-f.   40ch, any single   1.65   1.65
   Hye Cho's 8th century travels in Central Asia and India.

Stampcard — A1497

Korean Tigers.

1994, June 18   *Rouletted*
Self-adhesive
3348 A1497   Card of 6 stamps   30.00   30.00
   a.-f.   1.40w, any single   5.00   5.00

A1498

30th ANNIV. OF LEADERSHIP
OF THE DEAR LEADER
COMRADE KIM JONG IL ON
PARTY WORK

Kim Il Sung's Leadership of the
Korean Workers' Party, 30th
Anniv. — A1499

Designs (all 40ch): No. 3349, Kim and supporters on cliff ledge, overlooking lake. No. 3350, Kim on mountain top, pointing across lake to Mt. Paektu. No. 3351, Kim on film set. No. 3352, Kim visiting restaurant. No. 3353, Kim reviewing tank corps. No. 3354, Kim at conference, shaking hands onstage as audience applauds.

1994, June 19   **Perf. 12**
3349-3354 A1498   Sheetlet of 6   8.00   2.50
3350a   Booklet pane of 6, 3 ea.
      #3349-3350   8.00   —
      Complete booklet. #3350a   8.50
3353a   Booklet pane of 6, 3 ea.
      #3351, 3353   8.00   —
      Complete booklet. #3353a   8.50
3354a   Booklet pane of 6, 3 ea.
      #3352, 3354   8.00   —
      Complete booklet. #3354a   8.50

Souvenir Sheet
Perf. 11½
3355 A1499   1w multicolored   3.00   1.00

Stampcard — A1500

Turtle ship.

1994, June 20   *Rouletted*
Self-adhesive
3356 A1500   Card of 6 stamps   33.00   33.00
   a.-f.   1.80w, any single   5.50   5.50

A1501

A1502

Mollusks — A1503

Designs: 30ch, Phalium strigatum. 40ch, Gomphina veneriformis.

No. 3359: a, 10ch, Cardium muticum, No. 3358 and the stamp found in No. 3361.

No. 3360: a, 20ch, Buccinum bayani, No. 3357 and the stamp found in No. 3361.

No. 3361: Neverita didyma

1994, June 25   *Perf. 12*
3357-3358　A1501　Set of 2   2.50   .60

Sheets of 3, #a.-c.
     Perf. 13¼
3359-3360　A1502　Set of 2   14.00 10.00

Souvenir Sheet
3361　A1503　1.20w multicolored   5.00 1.40
    For surcharge, see No. 4608.

Circus Acrobats — A1504

Designs: a, 10ch, Flying trapeze. b, 20ch, Rope dance. c, 30ch, Seesaw. d, 40ch, Unicycle show.

1994, July 7   *Perf. 11½*
3362　A1504　Sheet of 4, #a.-d.   4.00 1.25

A1505

Centenary of Birth of Kim Hyong Jik (1894-1926), Father of Kim Il Sung — A1506

1994, July 10   *Perf. 13¼*
3363　A1505　10ch multicolored   .50   .25

Souvenir Sheet
     Perf. 11¾x11½
3364　A1506　1w multicolored   3.50 1.25

Jon Pong Pun & Battle Scene — A1507

1994, July 15   *Perf. 12*
3365　A1507　10ch multicolored   .60   .25
   Centenary of Kabo Peasant War.

Inoue Shuhachi — A1508

1994, July 30   *Perf. 13¼*
3366　A1508　1.20w multicolored   4.00 1.25
   Award of the First International Kim Il Sung Prize to Inoue Shuhachi, Director General of the International Institute of the Juche Idea (Japan).

Workers Marching A1509

1994, Aug. 1   *Perf. 11½*
3367　A1509　10ch multicolored   .50   .25
   Workers' Party Economic Strategy.

Fossils A1510

Designs: 40ch (No. 3368), Onsong fish. 40ch (No. 3369), Metasequoia. 40ch (No. 3370), Mammoth teeth. 80ch, Archaeopteryx.

No. 3372 contains 2 each Nos. 3368, 3371.
No. 3373 contains 2 each Nos.3369, 3371.
No. 3374 contains 2 each Nos. 3370-3371.

1994, Aug. 10   *Perf. 12*
3368-3371　A1510　Set of 4   13.00 1.75
   Complete booklet, 7 #3368   16.00
   Complete booklet, 7 #3369   16.00
   Complete booklet, 7 #3370   16.00
   Complete booklet, 7 #3371   32.00

Souvenir Sheets
3372-3374　A1510　Set of 3
     sheets   26.00 20.00

Medicinal Plants — A1511

Designs: 20ch, Acorus calamus. 30ch, Arctium lappa.

No. 3377 (133x86mm): a, 80ch, Lilium lancifolium. b, 80ch, Codonopsis lanceolata.

No. 3378 (56x83mm): 1w, Ginseng (Panax schinseng), vert.

1994, Aug. 25
3375-3376　A1511　Set of 2   1.75   .50
   Complete booklet, 10 #3375   7.00
   Complete booklet, 10 #3376   10.50

Souvenir Sheets
     Perf. 13¼
3377-3378　A1511　Set of 2
     sheets   8.00 2.00

Calisthenics — A1512

Gymnastic routines: a, 10ch, Ribbon twirling. b, 20ch, Ball. c, 30ch, Hoop. d, 40ch, Ribbon twirling (diff.). e, 50ch, Clubs.

1994, Sept. 7   *Perf. 12*
3379　A1512　Strip of 5 + label   5.50 1.50
   No. 3379 was printed in sheets of 18, containing three No. 3379 in horizontal rows, with a different label in each row.

A1513

A1514

Zhou Enlai (1898-1976), Birth Centenary — A1515

Portraits of Zhou Enlai: 10ch, As student revolutionary (1919). 20ch, Arrival in Northern Shansi after Long March (1936). 30ch, At Conference of Asian and African Countries, Bandung, Indonesia (1955). 40ch, Speaking with children.

No. 3384: 80ch, Zhou Enlai and Kim Il Sung (1970).

No. 3385: 10ch, as #3380. a, 20ch, Zhou leading Nanchang Uprising (1927). 40ch, as #3383. b, 80ch, as #3384.

No. 3386: 20ch, as #3381. a, 20ch, Zhou and Mao Tzedong at airport, horiz. 30ch, as #3383. 80ch, as #3385b.

1994, Oct. 1   *Perf. 11½*
3380-3383　A1513　Set of 4, with
     labels   3.25 1.00

Souvenir Sheets
     Perf. 13¼
3384　A1514　80ch multicolored   2.75 1.00

Perf 11½ (Vert. stamps), 11¾x12¼ (Horiz. stamps)
3385-3386　A1515　Set of 2
     sheets   9.50 4.00

   Nos. 3380-3383 were issued in sheets of 30 (6x5), with a label beneath each stamp.

World Environment Day — A1516

Each sheetlet contains two 50ch stamps with designs reflecting environmental issues. Themes: No. 3387, Prevention of air pollution. No. 3388, Preventation of water pollution. No. 3389, Protection of animal resources. No. 3390, Protection of forest resources.

1994, Oct. 5   *Perf. 12*
3387-3390　A1516　Set of 4
     sheets   12.50 12.50

A1517

A1518

위대한 수령 김일성동지는 영원히 우리와 함께 계신다

THE GREAT LEADER COMRADE
KIM IL SUNG WILL ALWAYS BE WITH US

Kim Il Sung (1912-94) — A1519

Photos of Kim Il Sung (all 40ch).
No. 3391: a, As young man (1927). b, With Kim Jong Suk, his first wife and mother of Kim Jong Il. c, As captain in Soviet army (1944).
No. 3392: Speaking at lectern upon return to Pyongyang (1945). b, Sitting at desk in office of People's Committee of North Korea. c, Speaking at microphone.

1994, Oct. 8
3391 A1517 Sheet of 3, #a.-c.   4.00   2.00
3392 A1518 Sheet of 3, #a.-c.   4.00   2.00

Souvenir Sheet
Perf. 12¼x11¾
3393 A1519 1w multicolored   3.75   1.25
Compare with Nos. 3401-3403.

A1520

World Cup '94, 15th World Soccer Championship — A1521

Soccer Players Dribbling: 10ch, Player No. 4. 20ch, Player No. 5. 30ch, Player No. 6. 40ch, Player No. 7. 1w, Player No. 8. 1.50w, Player No. 9.

1994, Oct. 13   **Perf. 13½**
3394-3399 A1520   Set of 6   12.00   6.00
3399a   Sheet of 6, #3394-3399   18.00   10.00

Souvenir Sheet
3400 A1521 2.50w multicolored   7.50   4.00
Nos. 3394-3400 were also issued imperf. Value: set, $24; souvenir sheet, $15.
Nos. 3394-3399 exist in sheetlets on one, perf and imperf. Value: perf, $24; imperf, $47.50.

A1522

위대한 수령 김일성동지는 영원히 우리와 함께 계신다

THE GREAT LEADER COMRADE
KIM IL SUNG WILL ALWAYS BE WITH US

Kim Il Sung (1912-94) — A1523

Photos of Kim Il Sung (all 40ch).
No. 3401: a, Making radio broadcast (1950). b, With soldiers (1951). c, Clapping hands, crowd of soldiers in background (1953).
No. 3402: a, Talking with workers at Chongjin Steel Plant (1959). b, Standing in field, Onchon Plain. c, Talking on telephone.
No. 3403, Kim Il Sung and Kim Jong Il.

1994, Oct. 15   **Perf. 12**
3401-3402 A1522   Set of 2
     sheets   8.00   4.00
Perf. 12¼x11¾
3403 A1523 1w multicolored   3.50   1.50
Compare with Nos. 3391-3393.

A1524

조중친선
KOREA-CHINA FRIENDSHIP

North Korean-Chinese Friendship — A1525

1w, Kim Il Sung with Mao Zedong.

1994, Oct. 25   **Perf. 11½**
3404 A1524 40ch multicolored   1.50   .50

Souvenir Sheet
Perf. 13¼
3405 A1525 1.20w multicolored   4.25   2.00

Composers
A1526

Designs: No. 3406, Ri Myon Sang (1908-89), score from *It Snows*. No. 3407, Pak Han Gyu (1919-92), score from *Nobody Knows*. No. 3408, Ludwig van Beethoven (1770-1827), score of *Piano Sonata No. 14*. No. 0400, Wolfgang Mozart (1750-91), score of *Symphony No. 39*.

1994, Nov. 25   **Perf. 11½**
3406-3409 A1526 50ch Set of 4   6.50   2.25
For surcharge, see No. 4550.

National Emblem — A1527

1994, Dec. 10   **Perf. 12**
3410 A1527 1w dp bl green   4.00   1.00
3411 A1527 3w deep brown   8.00   2.50
For surcharge, see No. 4575.

A1528

A1529

Gold Medal Winners, Winter Olympic Games, Lillehammer — A1530

Designs: 10ch, Pernilla Wiberg (Sweden), Alpine combined skiing. 20ch, Deborah Compagnoni (Italy), Slalom. 30ch, Oksana Baiul (Ukraine), Figure skating. 40ch, Dan Jansen (USA), Speed skating. 1w (No. 3416), Yubow Jegorowa (Russia), Cross-country skiing. 1w (No. 3417), Bonnie Blair (USA), Speed skating.
No. 3418, Bjorn Däehlie and Norwegian skiing team, Alpine combined skiing. No. 3419, Jekaterina Gordejewa and Serge Grinkow (Russia), Pairs figure skating. No. 3420, Vreni Schneider (Switzerland), Alpine combined skiing. No. 3421, Georg Hackl (Germany), Luge. No. 3422, Jens Weissflog (Germany), Ski jumping. No. 3423, Masashi Abe, Takanori Kono, Kenji Ogiwara (Japan), Cross-country skiing.
No. 3424, Tommy Moe (USA), Downhill skiing.

1994, Dec. 20   **Perf. 13¼**
3412-3417 A1528   Set of 6   11.00   3.00
3417a   Sheet of 6, #3412-3417   12.00   5.00

Souvenir Sheets
3418-3423 A1529 1w Set of 6   18.00   6.00
3424 A1530 2.50w multicolored   8.00   1.50

New Year — Year of the Pig A1531

Designs: 20ch, Pigs relaxing. 40ch, Pigs going to work.
Each 1w: No. 3427, Pigs carrying pumpkin. No. 3428, Piglets bowing to adult pig.

1995, Jan. 1   **Perf. 11½**
3425-3426 A1531   Set of 2   1.10   .65
3426a   Sheet of 4, 2 ea #3425-3426   3.50   3.50

Souvenir Sheets
3427-3428 A1531   Set of 2   6.00   5.00
No. 3426a inscribed in margins for Singapore '95 Intl. Stamp Exhibition. Issued, 9/1.

World Tourism Org., 20th Anniv. — A1532

Designs, each 30ch: a, Tower of the Juche Idea, Pyongyang. b, Pison Falls on Mt. Myohyang. c, Myogilsang (relief carving of Buddha), Mt. Kumgang.

1995, Jan. 2   **Perf. 12¼**
3429 A1532 Sheet of 3, #a.-c. +
     label   3.50   .90

Mangyondae, Badasgou, Emblem — A1533

1995, Jan. 22   *Perf. 11½*
3430 A1533 40ch multicolored   1.50   .90

70th anniversary of 250-Mile Journey for the Restoration of the Fatherland.

A1534

A1535

A1536

Kim Jong Il, 53rd Birthday — A1537

Designs: 10ch, Jong Il Peak (Mt. Paekdu) and 50th Birthday Ode Monument.
No. 3432 (horiz.): a, 20ch Kim Il Sung and Kim Jong Il; b, 80ch Kim Jong Il inspecting the West Sea Barrage. No. 3433 (vert.): a, 40ch Kim Jong Il in business suit; b, Kim Jong Il in uniform in Taesongsan Martyrs' Cemetary. No. 3434: 1w, Kim Jong Il inspecting the Ryongsong Machine Complex.

1995, Feb. 16   *Perf. 12¼*
3431 A1534 10ch multicolored   .25   .25

Souvenir Sheets
3432 A1535 Sheet of 2, #a.-b.   2.00   1.50
3433 A1536 Sheet of 2, #a.-b.   1.75   1.25
3434 A1537 1w multicolored   2.00   2.00

Mausoleum of King Tangun — A1537a

King Tangun and Mausoleum — A1537b

Designs: 10ch, Monument. 30ch, Straight bronze dagger tower. 50ch, Monument inscribed with King Tangun's exploits. 70ch, Gate of mausoleum.
50ch, King Tangun and Mausoleum.

1995, Feb. 25   *Perf. 12¼*
3434A-3434D A1537a Set of 4   3.00   3.00

Souvenir Sheet
Perf. 11½
3434E A1537b 1.40w multi   3.00   3.00

Lighthouses A1538

Designs: 20ch, Tamaedo Lighthouse. 1.20w, Phido Lighthouse, West Sea Barrage.

1995, Mar. 10   *Perf. 13½*
3435-3436 A1538 Set of 2   5.00   1.75

Mushrooms A1539

Designs: 20ch, Russula virescens. 30ch, Russula atropurpurea.
1w, Caesar's Mushroom (Amanita caesarea).

1995, Mar. 25
3437-3438 A1539 Set of 2   2.00   .60
3437a   Booklet pane of 10 #3437   3.50   —
   Complete booklet, #3437a   4.00
3438a   Booklet pane of 10 #3438   17.00   —
   Complete booklet, #3438a   17.50

Souvenir Sheet
3439 A1539 1w multicolored   4.50   2.50
For surcharges, see Nos. 4527-4528.

Tree Planting Day — A1540

1995, Apr. 6   *Perf. 11½*
3440 A1540 10ch multicolored   .60   .25
a.   Sheet of 6   3.50   3.50

No. 3225 Surcharged with New Values
1995, Apr. 8   *Rouletted*
3441   Card of 6 stamps   8.00   8.00
a.-f.   30ch on 1.50w, any single   1.30   1.30
Finlandia '95.

Mangyongdae, Birthplace of Kim Il Sung — A1541

Tower of Juche Idea and Kimilsungia A1542

Kim Il Sung and Children — A1543

1995, Apr. 15   *Perf. 11½*
3442 A1541 10ch multicolored   .25   .25
a.   Sheet of 6   1.50   1.50
3443 A1542 40ch multicolored   1.25   1.00
a.   Sheet of 6   7.50   7.50

Souvenir Sheet
Perf. 13½
3444 A1543 1w multicolored   3.50   3.50
Kim Il Sung, 82nd birthday. For surcharge, see No. 4610.

A1544

Kim Il Sung's Visit to China, 20th Anniv. — A1545

Designs: 10ch, Deng Xiaoping waving. 20ch, Deng sitting in armchair, vert. 50ch, Kim and Deng sitting in armchairs.

1995, Apr. 17   *Perf. 13½*
3445-3446 A1544 Set of 2   1.25   1.25

Souvenir Sheet
Perf. 11½
3447 A1545 50ch multicolored   2.00   2.00

A1546

A1547

Asian-African Conf., Bandung, 40th Anniv. — A1548

Designs: 10ch, Site of Bendung Conference. 50ch, Kim Il Sung receiving honorary doctorate from Indonesia University. 1w, Kim Il Sung and Kim Jong Il at Conference 40th Anniversary ceremony.

1995, Apr. 18   *Perf. 11½*
3448 A1546 10ch multicolored   .25   .25
3449 A1547 50ch multicolored   1.75   .70

Souvenir Sheet
3450 A1548 1w multicolored   3.50   3.50

A1549

Int'l Sports and Cultural Festival for Peace, Pyongyang — A1550

Designs: 20ch, Emblem. 40ch (No. 3452). Dancer. 40ch (No. 3453), Inoki Kanji, leader of Sports Peace Party of Japan.
1w, Nikidozan, wrestling champion.

1995, Apr. 28
3451-3453 A1549 Set of 3   3.00   2.00
3451a   Sheet of 3, 1 #3451 + 2 #3452   3.00   2.00

3453a   Sheet of 3, 2 #3453 + 1 as
      #3454   7.00   4.00

Souvenir Sheet

3454   A1550   1w multicolored   3.50   3.50

Amethyst — A1551

1995, May 2

3455   A1551   20ch multicolored   1.00   .40
  a.   Sheet of 6   7.50   7.50
  b.   Booklet pane of 10   10.00
         Complete booklet, #3455b   11.00

Finlandia '95. No. 3455a marginal selvage contains a mountain valley scene and is inscribed "Finlandia 95." No. 3455b has selvage around the block of 10 stamps.

White Animals — A1552

Each 40ch: No. 3456, Tree sparrow (*Passer montanus*). No. 3457, Sea slug (*Stichopus japonicus*).

1995, May 12   **Perf. 13½**

3456-3457   A1552   Set of 2   2.50   1.50
3457a   Sheet of 6, 3 #3456 + 3
       #3457   9.00

Fossils — A1553

Designs: a, 50ch, Ostrea. b, 1w, Cladophiebis (fern).

1995, May 15   **Perf. 12**

3458   A1553   Pair, #a.-b.   4.00   1.75

Traditional Games A1554

Designs: 30ch, Chess. 60ch, Taekwondo. 70ch, Yut.

1995, May 20   **Perf. 11½**

3459-3461   A1554   Set of 3   5.25   2.00
3459a   Sheet of 2 #3459 + label   1.75   1.75
3460a   Sheet of 2 #3460 + label   4.00   4.00
3461a   Sheet of 2 #3461 + label   6.00   6.00
3461b   Booklet pane of 6, 2 ea.
       #3459-3461   10.50
       Complete booklet. #3461b   11.00

General Assoc. of Koreans in Japan, 40th Anniv. — A1555

1995, May 25

3462   A1555   1w multicolored   3.50   .90

Atlanta '96 — A1556

Designs, each 50ch: No. 3463, Weight lifter. No. 3464, Boxing. 1w, Marksman shooting clay pigeon.

1995, June 2

3463-3464   A1556   Set of 2   3.25   1.25
3464a   Sheet of 2 #3463 + 2 #3464   7.50   7.50

Souvenir Sheet

3465   A1556   1w multicolored   5.00   5.00

Fungi — A1557

Designs: 40ch, Russula citrina. 60ch, Craterellus cornucopioides. 80ch, Coprinus comatus.

1995, July 1   **Perf. 13¼**

3466-3468   A1557   Set of 3   6.50   2.00
3466a   Booklet pane of 10 #3466   14.00   —
       Complete booklet, #3466a   14.50
3467a   Booklet pane of 10 #3467   21.00   —
       Complete booklet, #3467a   22.00
3468a   Booklet pane of 10 #3468   29.00   —
       Complete booklet, #3468a   30.00

For surcharge, see No. 4553.

A1558

A1559

A1560

Kim Il Sung, 1st Death Anniv. — A1561

No. 3469, 1w, Kim addressing conference for development of agriculture in African countries, 1981.

No. 3470: a, 10ch, Kim greeting Robert Mugabe, President of Zimbabwe. b, 70ch, Kim with King Norodom Sihanouk of Cambodia.

No. 3471: a, 20ch, Kim receiving honorary doctorate, Algeria University, 1975. b, 50ch, Kim with Fidel Castro, 1986.

No. 3472: a, 30ch, Kim talking with Ho Chi Minh, 1958. b, 40ch, Kim greeting Che Guevara, 1960.

1995, July 8

3469   A1558   1w multicolored   2.75   2.75
3470   A1559   Sheet of 2, #a.-b.   2.25   2.25
3471   A1560   Sheet of 2, #a.-b.   2.50   2.50
3472   A1561   Sheet of 2, #a.-b.   2.00   2.00

Liberation, 50th Anniv. — A1562

Designs: 10ch, Korean army officer. 30ch, Map of Korea, family. 60ch, Hero of the DPRK medal.

No. 3476, a, 20ch revolutionary soldier, #3414, 2 each.

No. 3477, a, 40ch demonstrators, #3474, 2 each.

1995, Aug. 15   **Perf. 11½**

3473-3475   A1562   Set of 3   2.75   1.25
3475a   Booklet pane of 5, #3473-
       3475, 3476a, 3477a   4.50   —
       Complete booklet, #3475a   5.00

Souvenir Sheets

3476   Sheet of 4   2.50   2.50
  a.   A1562 20ch multicolored   .50   .25
3477   Sheet of 4   4.50   4.50
  a.   A1562 40ch multicolored   1.00   .45

1st Military World Games — A1564

1995, Sept. 4

3479   A1564   40ch multicolored   1.00   .45

A1565

A1566

Korea-China Friendship — A1567

Designs: No. 3480, 80ch, Kim Il Sung and Mao Zedong. No. 3481, 80ch, Kim and Zhou Enlai.

No. 3482: a, 50ch, Kim and Zhou Enlai. b, 50ch, Kim receiving gift from Deng Ying-Chao, Premier of the State Council of the People's Republic of China.

1995, Oct. 1   **Perf. 12¼**

3480   A1565   80ch multicolored   1.50   1.50
3481   A1566   80ch multicolored   1.50   1.50
3482   A1567   Sheet of 2, #a.-b.   2.25   2.25

A1568

Korean Workers' Party, 50th Anniv. — A1569

Designs: 10ch, Korean Workers' Party Emblem and Banner. 20ch, Statue of three workers holding party symbols. 40ch, Monument to founding of Party.

No. 3486, Kim Il Sung.

1995, Oct. 10   **Perf. 11½**

3483-3485   A1568   Set of 3   1.60   .75

Souvenir Sheet
                    Perf. 13½

3486   A1569   1w multicolored   2.75   2.75

Kim Il Sung's Return to Korea, 50th Anniv. A1570

Design: 50ch, Arch of Triumph, Pyongyang.

1995, Oct. 14   **Perf. 11½**
3487   A1570   10ch multicolored   .60   .25

Great Tunny — A1571

Nos. 3488-3512 are printed in chocolate and black.

1995	**Fish**		**Perf. 13¼**	
3488	40ch	Great tunny	1.25	.35
3489	50ch	Pennant coralfish	1.50	.40
3490	50ch	Needlefish	1.50	.40
3491	60ch	Bullrout	1.75	.45
3492	5w	Imperial butterfly fish	15.00	3.50
a.		Horiz. strip of 5, #3488-3492	22.50	5.00

Machines

3493	10ch	40-ton truck *Kumsusan*	.35	.25
3494	20ch	Large bulldozer	.75	.25
3495	30ch	Hydraulic excavator	1.00	.25
3496	40ch	Wheel loader, vert.	1.60	.30
3497	10w	Tractor *Chollima-80*, vert.	27.50	7.50
a.		Horiz. strip of 5, #3493-3497	32.50	10.00

Animals

3498	30ch	Giraffe, vert.	.85	.25
3499	40ch	Ostrich, vert.	1.10	.35
3500	60ch	Bluebuck, vert.	1.60	.50
3501	70ch	Bactrian camel	2.00	.55
3502	3w	Indian rhinoceros	8.00	2.25
a.		Horiz. strip of 5, #3498-3502	16.00	4.00

Sculptures of Children

3503	30ch	Boy and pigeon, vert.	.85	.25
3504	40ch	Boy and goose, vert.	1.10	.35
3505	60ch	Girl and geese vert.	1.60	.50
3506	70ch	Boy and girl comparing heights, vert.	2.00	.50
3507	2w	Boy and girl with soccer ball, vert.	5.75	1.60
a.		Vert. strip of 5, #3503-3507	13.00	4.00

Buildings

3508	60ch	Pyongyang Circus	1.75	.50
3509	70ch	Country apartment bldg.	2.00	.55
3510	80ch	Pyongyang Hotel	2.25	.65
3511	90ch	Urban apt. towers	2.50	.75
3512	1w	Sosan Hotel	2.75	.85
a.		Horiz. strip of 5, #3508-3512	13.00	4.00

Issued: Nos. 3488-3492, 10/20; Nos. 3493-3497, 11/2; Nos. 3498-3502, 11/20; Nos. 3503-3507, 12/5; Nos. 3508-3512, 12/15.
Nos. 3488-3492, 3493-3497, 3498-3502, 3503-3507, and 3508-3512 were printed in vertical (Nos. 3503-3507) or horizontal se-tenant strips within their sheets.

No. 3512B

No. 3512D

1995, Oct. 20   *Rouletted x Imperf*
Stampcards
Self-Adhesive
3512B   black, *gold*, card of 8   6.00   6.00
   a.   20ch single stamp   .75   .75
3512D   card of 2   50.00   50.00
   e.   20ch red, *gold*   —   —
   f.   17.80w On 20ch, red, *gold*   —   —
50th anniversary of the first North Korean stamps.

Kim Hyong Gwon, Kim Il Sung's Uncle, 90th Birth Anniv. — A1572

1995, Nov. 4   **Perf. 12½x12**
3513   A1572   1w multicolored   2.75   1.50

New Year — A1573

Rodents: a, 20ch, Guinea pig. b, 20ch, Squirrel. 30ch, White mouse.

1996, Jan. 1   **Perf. 11½**
3514   A1573   Strip of 3, #a.-c.   3.00   .75
No. 3514 was issued in sheetlets of eight stamps, two each Nos. 3514a-3514b and four No. 3514c, plus one center label picturing an idyllic landscape, inscribed "1996."

League of Socialist Working Youth, 50th Anniv. — A1574

1996, Jan. 17
3517   A1574   10ch multicolored   .50   .25

Reconstruction of Tomb of King Wanggon of Koryo — A1575

Designs: 30ch, Restoration monument, horiz. 40ch, Entrance gate to royal cemetery. 50ch, King Wanggon's tomb, horiz.

1996, Jan. 30
3518-3520   A1575   Set of 3   3.50   1.00

Teng Li-Chuang (Chinese Singer) — A1576

1996, Feb. 1   **Perf. 13¼**
3521   A1576   40ch multicolored   1.50   .50

3rd Asian Winter Games, Harbin, China — A1577

Designs, each 30ch: a, Kim Song Sun, Korean speed skater. b, Ye Qiaobo, Chinese sprint skater.

1996, Feb 4   **Perf. 11½**
3522   A1577   Sheet of 2, #a.-b.   3.50   .50
See No. 3556.

A1578

Kim Jong Il, 54th Birthday — A1579

10ch, Jong Il Peak and *Kimjongilia*. 80ch, Kim Jong Il and soldiers.

1996, Feb. 16
3523   A1578   10ch multicolored   .50   .25
Souvenir Sheet
Perf. 13¼
3524   A1579   80ch multicolored   2.75   .75

5th Paektusan Prize International Figure Skating Championship. A1580

Various pairs figure skaters: 10ch, 20ch, 30ch.
50ch, Women's individual skating.

1996, Feb. 17   **Perf. 11½**
3525-3527   A1580   Set of 3   2.00   .60
3527a   Booklet pane of 4, #3525-3527, 3528a   5.50   —
   Complete booklet, #3527a   6.00
Souvenir Sheet
3528   Sheet of 4   3.50   1.00
   a.   A1580 50ch multi   3.25

Folk Tales — A1581

Screen painting by Ryu Suk: 8 stamps in continuous design, within 206mmx84mm skeetlet.

1996, Mar. 2
3529   Sheet of 8   5.00   2.25
   a.-h.   A1581 any single   .60   .25

Agrarian Reform Law, 50th Anniv. A1582

1996, Mar. 5
3530   A1582   10ch multicolored   .50   .25
No. 3530 was issued in sheetlets of six, containing 5 No. 3530 and a label depicting a music score, *Song of Plowing.*

First North Korean Stamps, 50th Anniv. — A1583

1996, Mar. 12
3531   A1583   1w multicolored   3.25   .85

Yangzhou, China — A1584

Taihou Lake, China — A1585

1996, Mar. 20
3532   A1584   50ch multicolored   1.75   .50
3533   A1585   50ch multicolored   1.75   .50
Chinese Imperial Post, Centennial.

A1586

Kim Il Sung, 83rd Birthday — A1587

Designs: 10ch, Birthplace, Mangyondae.
1w, Portrait of Kim Il Sung.

1996, Apr. 15
3534 A1586 10ch multicolored .50 .25
Souvenir Sheet
3535 A1587 1w multicolored 3.25 .85

China '96 Int'l
Stamp Exhib.,
Beijing — A1588

Designs: No. 3536, Seacoast gateway. No.
3537, Haiyin Pool.
60ch. Pantuo Stone.

1996, Apr. 22 *Perf. 13½*
3536-3537 A1588 10ch Set of 2 .50 .25
Souvenir Sheet
Perf. 11½
3538 A1588 60ch multicolored 1.60 .60

Folk Games
A1589

Designs: 20ch, Kicking stone handmill.
40ch, Shuttlecock. 50ch, Sledding.

1996, May 2
3539-3541 A1589 Set of 3 3.50 1.00
3539a-3541a Set of 3 sheets of 2 +
label 7.00 7.00

Assoc. for the
Restoration of the
Fatherland, 60th
Anniv. — A1590

1996, May 5
3542 A1590 10ch multicolored .50 .25
a. Sheet of 5 #3542 + label 2.50 1.50

Ri Po Ik — A1591

1996, May 31 *Perf. 13½*
3543 A1591 1w multicolored 3.00 .80
Ri Po Ik, Kim Il Sung's grandmother, 125th
birth anniv.

Polar Animals — A1592

Designs, 50ch: No. 3544a, Arctic fox. No.
3544b, Polar bear. No. 3545a, Emperor penguins. No. 3546b, Leopard seals.

1996, June 2 *Perf. 11½*
3544-3545 A1592 Set of 2
sheets 6.50 4.00

A1593

Korea Children's Union, 50th
Anniv. — A1594

Designs: 10ch, Boy saluting.
1w, Painting of Kim Il Sung with Children's
Union members, *There's Nothing to Envy in
the World.*

1996, June 6
3546 A1593 10ch multicolored .50 .25
Souvenir Sheet
Perf. 11½x12
3547 A1594 1w multicolored 3.00 .85

Locomotives
A1595

Designs, all 50ch: No. 3548, Steam locomotive, facing left. No. 3549, Electric locomotive,
facing right. No. 3550, Steam locomotive, facing right. No. 3551, Electric locomotive, facing
left.

1996, June 6 *Perf. 11½*
3548-3551 A1595 Set of 4 3.50 1.25
Capex '96 World Philatelic Exhibition. For
surcharge, see No. 4551.

Kim Chol Ju, Kim Il Sung's Brother,
80th Birth Anniv. — A1596

1996, June 12 *Perf. 13¼*
3552 A1596 1.50w multicolored 4.25 2.00

Open Book — A1597

1996, June 15 *Perf. 13½*
3553 A1597 40ch multicolored 1.10 .50
760th anniversary of publication of the *Complete Collection of Buddhist Scriptures Printed
from 80,000 Wooden Blocks.*

Labor Law,
50th Anniv.
A1598

1996, June 24 *Perf. 11½*
3554 A1598 50ch multicolored .50 .40

Seasonal Birds — A1599

Designs: 10ch, Broad-billed roller. 40ch, Tricolor flycatcher. 50ch, Cuckoo.

1996, July 5
3555 A1599 Sheet of 3, #a.-c. 4.00 2.00
See No. 3569.

3rd Asian Winter Games, Harbin,
China (2nd issue) — A1600

Design same as No. 3522, but with a new
30ch value picturing Ye Qiaobo replacing No,
3522b.

1996, July 5
3556 A1600 Sheet of 2 1.75 1.00
a. 30ch multi .85 .40

Kumsusan Memorial Palace — A1601

Outdoor Crowd, Statue of Kim Il
Sung — A1602

Hymn, *The Leader will be with us
forever* — A1603

Statue of Kim Il Sung in hall of the
Kumsusan Memorial Palace — A1604

1996, July 8 *Perf. 12*
3557 A1601 10ch multicolored .25 .25

Souvenir Sheets
Perf. 13¼, 12 (#3558)
3558	A1602	1w multicolored	3.00	1.00
3559	A1603	1w multicolored	3.00	1.00
3560	A1604	1w multicolored	3.00	1.00

Kim Il Sung, 2nd Death Anniv.

A1605

Designs, both 10ch: No. 3561, Kim Il Sung meeting Mao Zedong of China, 1954. No. 3562, Kim Il Sung meeting Jiang Zemin of China, 1991.

80ch, Kim shaking hands with Deng Xiaoping of China, horiz.

1996, July 11   Perf. 11½
3561-3562 A1605 Set of 2   .50 .25

Souvenir Sheet
3563 A1605 80ch multicolored   2.25 1.00

26th Olympic Games, Atlanta — A1606

Designs, each 50ch: No. 3564, Soccer. No. 3565, Tennis. No. 3566, Hammer throw. No. 3567, Baseball.

1996, July 19   Perf. 12¼
3564-3567 A1606 Set of 4   5.50 2.00

Sexual Equality Law, 50th Anniv. — A1607

1996, July 30   Perf. 11½
3568 A1607 10ch multicolored   .25 .25

Seasonal Bird Type
Designs: 10ch, Crested shelduck. 40ch, Demoiselle crane. 50ch, White swan.

1996, Aug. 5
3569 A1600 Sheet of 3, #a.-c.   2.75 1.25

Industrial Nationalization, 50th Anniv. — A1608

1996, Aug. 10   Perf. 11½
3570 A1608 50ch multicolored   .90 .40

UNICEF, 50th Anniv. — A1609

Designs: 10ch, Boy with ball, net. 20ch, Boy playing with building blocks. 50ch, Boy eating meal, holding watermelon slice. 60ch, Girl playing accordion.

1996, Aug. 20
3571-3574 A1609 Set of 4   2.75 1.10

Nos. 3571-3574 were issued in sheets of four, one containing 2 No. 3571, 1 No. 3574 and a label, the other containing 2 No. 3572, 1 No. 3573 and a different label.

1st Asian Gymnastics Championship, Changsha, China — A1610

No. 3575: a, Pae Kil Su (N. Korea), men's pommel. b, Chen Cui Ting (China), rings. c, Li Jing (China). d, Kim Kwang Suk (N. Korea), asymmetrical bars.

1996, Sept. 24
3575 A1610 15ch Sheet of 4, #a-d, + 2 labels   1.50 .60

Kim Il Sung University, 50th Anniv. A1611

1996, Oct. 1
3579 A1611 10ch multicolored   .50 .25

Tiger — A1612

Designs: 50ch: No. 3580, Tiger. No. 3581, Royal spoonbill.

80ch: Stylized dove/hand nurturing sapling, growing out of planet Earth.

1996, Oct. 13
3580-3581 A1612 Set of 2   3.00 .70

Souvenir Sheet
3582 A1612 80ch multicolored   6.50 1.50

Nos. 3580-3581 were each printed in sheets of four, containing three stamps and a label.

Down-with-Imperialism Union, 70th Anniv. — A1613

1996, Oct. 17
3583 A1613 10ch multicolored   .25 .25

A1614

Designs: a, 30ch Huang Ji Gwang. b, 10ch, Score of theme song of film Red Mountain Ridge. c, 30ch Huang Ji Gwang heroically dying in battle.

1996, Oct. 25
3584 A1614 Sheet of 3, #a.-c.   2.00 1.00

Hwang Ji Gwang, Chinese Volunteer, hero of Korean War, 44th death anniiv.

History of the Earth — A1615

Each 50ch: a, Earth 7.5 billion years ago. b, 4.5-5 billion years ago. c, 450 million-4.5 billion years ago. d, 100-450 million years ago. e, 100 million years ago to the present.

1996, Nov. 1   Perf. 13½
3585 A1615 Sheet of 5, #a.-e.   8.00 4.00

Freshwater Fish A1616

Designs, 20ch: No. 3586, Japanese eel. No. 3587, Menada gray mullet. 80ch, Silver carp.

1996, Nov. 20   Perf. 11½
3586-3587 A1616 Set of 2   1.50 .35

Souvenir Sheet
3588 A1616 80ch multicolored   3.00 .75

Kim Jong Il' Appointment as Supreme Commander of the People's Army, 5th Anniv. — A1617

1996, Dec. 24   Perf. 12
3589 A1617 20ch multicolored   .60 .25

New Year — Year of the Ox A1618

Designs: 70ch: No. 3590, Ox Driver, by Kim Tu Ryang. No. 3591, Bronze ritual plate decorated with a tiger and two bulls. No. 3592, Cowboy and bull. No. 3593, Cowboy playing flute, sitting on bull.

80ch, Kosong People's Support to the Front.

1997, Jan. 1   Perf. 11¾
| 3590-3593 | A1618 | Set of 4 | 8.00 | 2.00 |
| 3591a, 3593a | | Set of 2 sheets | 8.00 | 2.00 |

Souvenir Sheet
3594 A1618 80ch multicolored   3.00 .75

No. 3591a contains Nos. 3590 and 3591, with a central label depicting a bull's head surrounded by zodiacal signs. No. 3593a contains Nos. 3592 and 3593, with the same label.

Flowers and Butterflies, by Nam Kye-u (1811-88) — A1619

Designs, each 50ch: a, Three butterflies, flower. b, One small butterfly, flower. c, Large butterfly, leaves.

1997, Jan. 5   Perf. 12¼x11¾
3595	A1618	Sheetlet of 3, #a.-c.	4.50	1.00
d.		Booklet pane of 6, 2 each #3595a-3595b	9.00	—
		Complete booklet, #3595d	9.00	

Paintings of Cats and Dogs — A1620

Designs, 50ch: No. 3598, Puppy in basket, touching noses with kitten. No. 3599, Two dogs in basket, kitten.

No. 3600: a, Cat in basket, with dog and skein of yarn alongside. b, Kitten in basket with fruit and flowers, puppy alongside.

1997, Jan. 25   Perf. 11¾x12¼
3598-3599 A1620 Set of 2   3.25 1.00

Sheets of 4
3600		Sheet of 4, #3598, 3600b, 2 #3600a	3.50	1.50
a.		A1620 50ch multicolored	1.50	
b.		A1620 50ch multicolored	1.50	
3601		Sheet of 4, #3599, #3600a, 2 #3600b	3.50	1.50

Return of Hong Kong to China — A1621

Hong Kong nightscape, each 20ch: a, Sky-scraper with double antennae. b, Skyscraper with single spire. c, Round skyscraper, high-rise apartment buildings.

1997, Feb. 1 **Perf. 13½**
3602 A1621 Sheet of 3, #a.-c. 2.50 .65

A1622

Kim Jong Il, 55th Birthday — A1623

Designs: 10ch, Birthplace, Mt. Paekdu. No. 3604, Kim Il Sung and Kim Jong Il with farm machine. No. 3605, Kim Jong Il inspecting a Korean People's Army unit.

1997, Feb. 16 **Perf. 12**
3603 A1622 10ch multicolored .50 .25
Souvenir Sheets
3604-3605 A1623 1w Set of 2 5.50 1.75

6th Paektusan Prize Int'l Figure Skating Championships, Pyongyang — A1624

Pairs skating, different routines, 50ch: No. 3606, pale reddish brown. No. 3607, blue. No. 3608, green.

1997, Feb. 17 **Perf. 11½**
3606-3608 A1624 Set of 3 4.00 1.00
3607a Sheet of 4, 2 ea #3606, 3607 5.50 1.50
3608a Booklet pane of 6, 2 ea. #3606-3608 8.00 —
  Complete booklet, #3608a 8.50
3608b Sheet of 4, 2 ea #3607, 3608 5.50 1.50

Kye Sun Hui, Women's Judo Gold Medalist, 1996 Summer Olympic Games, Atlanta — A1625

1997, Feb. 20
3611 A1625 80ch multicolored 2.50 .60

Choe Un A — A1626

1997, Feb. 25
3612 A1626 80ch multicolored 3.00 .60
a. Booklet pane of 5
  Complete booklet, #3612a

Issued to honor Choe Un A, a seven-year-old entrant in the World Go Championships.

Apricots — A1627

Various types of apricots, 50ch: No. 3613, Prunus ansu. No. 3614, Prunus mandshurica. No. 3615, Prunus armeniaca. No. 3616, Prunus sibirica.

1997, Mar. 4 **Perf. 11¼**
3613-3616 A1627 Set of 4 6.00 1.50
3613a Sheet of 8, 2 ea#3613-3614 12.00 3.00

Foundation of Korean National Assoc., 80th Anniv. — A1628

1997, Mar. 23 **Perf. 12¼**
3617 A1628 10ch lt brn & dk grn .50 .25
a. Sheet of 8 4.00 1.00

A1629

Reforestation Day, 50th Anniv. — A1630

Designs: 10ch, Pine sapling. No. 3619, Kim Il Sung planting sapling on Munsu Hill.

1997, Apr. 6 **Perf. 11½**
3618 A1629 10ch multicolored .50 .25
a. Complete booklet, 8 #3618
Souvenir Sheet
Perf. 13¼
3619 A1630 1w multicolored 3.00 .90

A1631

A1632

Kim Il Sung, 85th Birth Anniv. — A1633

Designs: 10ch, Kim's birthplace, Mangyongdae. 20ch, Sliding rock, horiz. 40ch, Warship Rock, horiz.
Each 1w: No. 3623, Painting of Kim among crowd symbolic of the Korean people. No. 3624, Kim in business suit, surrounded by flowers.

1997, Apr. 15 **Perf. 12¼**
3620-3622 A1631 Set of 3 2.00 .55
Souvenir Sheets
Perf. 13¼ (#3623), 11¾x12¼ (#3624)
3623 A1632 1w multicolored 2.75 .90
3624 A1633 1w multicolored 2.75 .90

A1634

Korean People's Army, 65th Anniv. — A1635

Designs: 10ch, KPA cap badge, rockets and jet fighters.
1w, Kim Il Sung and Kim Jong Il at military review.

1997, Apr. 25 **Perf. 11½**
3625 A1634 10ch multicolored .50 .25
Souvenir Sheet
Perf. 12¼x11¾
3626 A1635 1w multicolored 3.00 .90

A1636

North-South Agreement, 25th Anniv. — A1637

Designs: 10ch, Map of Korea. 1w, Monument to Kim Il Sung's Autograph, Phanmunjom.

1997, May 4 **Perf. 11½**
3627 A1636 10ch multicolored 1.00 .25
Souvenir Sheet
Perf. 12x11½
3628 A1637 1w multicolored 4.00 .90

A1638

Each 10ch: No. 3629, Tower of Juche Idea, flag. No. 3630, Man with flag. No. 3631, Soldier, miner, farmer, scientist.

1997, May 25   **Perf. 12¼x12**
3629-3631 A1638 Set of 3   .90   .40

Int'l Friendship Exhib., Myohyang Mountains — A1639

Each 70ch: No. 3632, Exhibition Center. No. 3633, Statue of Kim Il Sung in exhibition entrance hall. No. 3634, Ivory sculpture *Native House in Mangyongdae*. No. 3635, Stuffed crocodile holding wooden cups, with ashtray.

1997, May 30   **Perf. 11¾**
3632-3635 A1639 Set of 4
                  sheets   7.50 5.00

Battle of Poconbo, 60th Anniv. — A1640

1997, June 4   **Perf. 11½**
3636   A1640 40ch multicolored   1.25   .35
  a.   Sheet of 6   7.50 7.50
  b.   Booklet pane of 6 #3636   7.50   —
            Complete booklet, #3636b   8.00

No. 3636b contains six stamps in a horizontal strip, within decorative selvage.

Rice Transplantation, Mirin Plain, 50th Anniv. — A1641

Each 1w: No. 3637, Kim Il Sung transplanting rice. No. 3638, Kim Il Sung inspecting a rice-transplanting machine.

1997, June 7   **Perf. 13¼**
3637-3638 A1641 Set of 2
                  sheets   5.75 1.75

A1642

Return of Hong Kong to China — A1643

No. 3639, each 20ch: a, Signing the Nanjing Treaty, 1842. b, Signing the China-Britain Joint Statement, 1984. c, Deng Xiaoping and Margaret Thatcher. d, Jiang Zenin and Tong Jianhua.
97ch, Deng Xiaoping.

1997, July 1   **Perf. 11¾**
3639   A1642 Sheet of 4, #a.-d.   3.00   .75
        Souvenir Sheet
                Perf. 13¼
3640   A1643 97ch multicolored   3.00 1.00

Fossils — A1644

Designs: 50ch, *Redlichia chinensis*. 1w, *Ptychoparia coreanica*.

1997, July 5   **Perf. 11½**
3641   A1644 Pair, #a.-b.   5.00 1.25
  c.   Booklet pane, 5 #3641a   8.75   —
            Complete booklet #3641c   9.00
  d.   Booklet pane, 5 #3641d   17.50   —
            Complete booklet #3641d   18.00

Nos. 3641c-3641d each contain horizontal strips of five stamps.

Kim Il Sung, 3rd Death Anniv. A1645

Each 50ch, Portrait of Kim Il Sung and: No. 3643, Kim speaking at party conference, 1985. No. 3644, Kim inspecting Kim Chaek Ironworks, 1985. No. 3645, Kim at Songsin Cooperative Farm, Sadong District, 1993. No. 3646, Kim being cheered by performing artists, 1986. No. 3647, Kim visiting Jonchon

Factory, Jagang Province, 1991. No. 3648, Kim receiving bouquet from soldiers.

1997, July 8   **Perf. 11¾x12**
3643-3648 A1645 Set of 6   9.00 2.25
  3645a   Sheet of 3, #3643-3645   4.50 2.00
  3648a   Sheet of 3, #3646-3648   4.50 2.00

Folk Games A1646

Designs: 30ch, Blindman's Bluff. 60ch, Jackstones. 70ch, Arm wrestling.

1997, July 26   **Perf. 11½**
3649-3651 A1646 Set of 3   4.50 1.25
  3649a-3651a   Set of 3 sheets   9.00 4.00
  3651b   Booklet pane of 6, 2 ea.
                #3649-3651   9.00   —
                Complete booklet, #3651b 9.50

Nos. 3649a-3651a each contain 2 stamps + a central label.
No. 3281b contains two each of Nos. 3649-3651, printed in a se-tenant block (3x2), with decorative selvage.

Traditional Korean Women's Clothing — A1647

Designs: 10ch, Spring costume. 40ch, Summer. 50ch, Autumn. 60ch, Winter.

1997, Aug. 10
3652-3655 A1647 Set of 4   4.50 2.00
  3652a-3654a   Set of 3 sheets   18.00 12.00

No. 3652a contains 2 each Nos. 3652-3653;
No. 3653a contains 2 each Nos. 3653-3654;
No. 3654a contains 2 each Nos. 3654-3655.

Chongryu Bridge A1648

Both 50ch: No. 3656, Night view of Chongryu Bridge. No. 3657, Panoramic view.

1997, Aug. 25
3656-3657 A1648 Set of 2   3.00 1.00
  3657a   Sheet of 2, #3656-3657   3.50 1.50
  3657b   Booklet pane of 6, 3 ea.
              #3656-3657   9.00   —
              Complete booklet, #3657b   9.50

A1649

Juche Era and Sun Day, 85th Anniv. — A1650

10ch, Sun, magnolias, banner, balloons.
Each 1w: No. 3659, Kim Il Sung, slogan, doves. No. 3660, Kim, birthplace Mongyangdae. No. 3661, Kim, Lake Chon, Mt. Paekdu. No. 3662, Kim, Kumsusan Memorial Palace.

1997, Sept. 3   **Perf. 13¼**
3658   A1649 10ch multicolored   .50   .25
        Souvenir Sheets
3659-3662 A1650 Set of 4
                  sheets   11.00 6.00

Theses on Socialist Education, 20th Anniv. of Publication A1651

1997, Sept. 5   **Perf. 11½**
3663   A1651 10ch multicolored   .50   .25

No. 3663 was issued in sheetlets of 6.

Air Koryo — A1652

Sheets of 2 stamps and central label: 20ch, TU-134. 30ch, TU-154. 50ch, IL-62.

1997, Sept. 14   **Perf. 13¼**
3664-3666 A1652 Set of 3
                  sheets   5.00 1.50
  3665a   Complete booklet, pane of 8,
            4 ea. #3664, 3666   7.00
  3666a   Complete booklet, pane of 8,
            4 ea. #3665, 3666   8.00

Korean Membership in World Tourism Org., 10th Anniv. — A1653

Views of Mt. Chilbo, each 50ch: No. 3667, Kim Chol Ung. No. 3668, Rojok Beach. No. 3669, Chonbul Peak.

1997, Sept. 22   **Perf. 12**
3667-3669 A1653 Set of 3   4.50 1.25
  3669a   Sheet, #3667-3669 + label   5.00 1.40

Kumgang
Mountains
A1654

Each 50ch: No. 3670, Kumgang Gate. No.
3671, Podok Hermitage.
1997, Oct. 2
3670-3671 A1654 Set of 2   3.00   .75
3670a   Booklet pane of 5 #3670   7.50
    Complete booklet, #3670a   8.00
3671a   Sheet of 6, 3 each #3670-
        3671   10.00   4.00
3671b   Booklet pane of 5 #3671   7.50
    Complete booklet, #3671b   8.00

Mangyongdae Revolutionary School,
50th Anniv. — A1655

1997, Oct. 12   **Perf. 11½**
3672 A1655 40ch multicolored   1.25   .30
a.   Booklet pane of 6   7.50
    Complete booklet, #3672a   8.00

Gift Animals
A1656

Animals presented to Kim Il Sung as gifts
from foreign governments: 20ch, Lion (from
Ethiopia, 1987). 30ch, Jaguar (Japan, 1992).
50ch, Barbary sheep (Czechoslovakia, 1992).
80ch, Scarlet macaw (Austria, 1979).
1997, Oct. 15
3673-3676 A1656 Set of 4   5.50   1.25
3673a   Sheet of 8, 2 each #3673-
        3676   11.00   5.00
3673b   Booklet pane of 8, 2ea.
        #3673-3676   11.00
    Complete booklet, #3673b   12.00
For surcharges, see 4554-4555.

Qu Shao Yun, Chinese Volunteer
Hero — A1657

Designs: a, 30ch, Bust of Qu Shao Yun. b,
10ch, Monument to Qu Shao Yun. c, 30ch, Qu
Shao Yun burning to death in battle.
1997, Oct. 18
3677 A1657 Sheet of 3, #a.-c.   2.25   .75

Sports — A1658

Designs: No. 3678, 50ch, Bowling. No.
3679, 50ch, Fencing. No. 3680, 50chGolf.
1997, Nov. 10   **Perf. 13¼**
3678-3680 A1658 Set of 3   5.25   1.25
3680a   Sheet, 2 each #3678-3680
        + 2 labels   11.00   5.00
For surcharge, see No. 4574.

Snails — A1659

Each 50ch: a, Two snails copulating. b,
Snail laying eggs. c, Snail.
1997, Nov. 15   **Perf. 12¼**
3681 A1659 Strip of 3, #a.-c.   4.75   2.00
d.   Sheet of 6, 2 each #3681a-
        3681c   9.50   4.00
e.   Booklet pane of 6, 2 ea.
        #3681a-3681c   9.50   —
    Complete booklet, #3681e   10.00

Shanghai Int'l Stamp & Coin
Exhib. — A1660

1997, Nov. 19   **Perf. 11½**
3684 A1660 Sheet of 2, #a.-b.   2.50   1.00
a.   30ch multicolored   1.00   .30
b.   50ch multicolored   1.50   .60

New Year — Year of the Tiger
A1661   A1662

Designs: 10ch, "Juche 87," pine boughs,
temple. 50ch (No. 3686), Tiger in rocket. 50ch
(No. 3687), Tiger in ship.
80ch, Tiger in train.

Perf. 13¼, 11½ (#3686-3687)
1997, Dec. 15
3685 A1661 10ch multicolored   .25   .25
3686 A1662 50ch multicolored   .90   .25
3687 A1662 50ch multicolored   .90   .25
a.   Sheet of 4, 1 ea #3686-#3687,
        2 #3688   4.50   2.00
    Nos. 3685-3687 (3)   2.05   .75
Souvenir Sheet
3688 A1662 80ch multicolored   2.00   .75
A single stamp like that in No. 3688 is
included in No. 3687a.

Birthplace,
Hoeryong
A1663

Kim Jong Suk, 80th Birth
Anniv. — A1664

1997, Dec. 24   **Perf. 13¼**
3689 A1663 10ch multicolored   .50   .25
Souvenir Sheet
3690 A1664 1w multicolored   3.00   .75

Winter Olympic
Games, Nagano,
Japan — A1665

Designs: 20ch, Skiing. 40ch, Speed skating.
1998, Feb. 7   **Perf. 11½**
3691-3692 A1665 Set of 2   1.25   .65
3692a   Sheet of 4, 2 ea #3691-
        #3692   2.50   1.25
3692b   Booklet pane of 8, 4 ea.
        #3691-3692   5.00   —
    Complete booklet, #3692b   5.50

A1666

Kim Jong Il, 56th Birthday — A1667

Designs: 10ch, Birth date ("2.16").
3w, Birthplace, log cabin on Mt. Paekdu.
1998, Feb. 16
3693 A1666 10ch multicolored   .50   .25
Souvenir Sheet
3694 A1667 3w multicolored   4.50   2.00

A1668

Paintings of Mt. Paekdu
Wildlife — A1669

Designs, 50ch: No. 3695, Korean tigers. No.
3696, White crane.
No. 3697, 50ch: a, Bears. b, Racoons.
1998, Mar. 6   **Perf. 11¾x12**
3695-3696 A1668 Set of 2   2.00   1.00
3696a   Booklet pane of 8, 2 ea.
        #3695-3696, 3697a-3697b   8.50
    Complete booklet, #3696a   8.50
Souvenir Sheet
3697 A1669 Sheet of 4, #3695-
        3696, 3697a-
        3697b   4.00   2.00
a.   A1668 50ch multicolored   1.00   .50
b.   A1668 50ch multicolored   1.00   .50

Kim Il
Sung's
1000-ri
Journey,
75th Anniv.
A1670

1998, Mar. 16   **Perf. 11½**
3698 A1670 10ch multicolored   .50   .25
a.   Sheet of 10   5.00   1.50

Appt. of Kim
Jong Il as
Chairman of
the Nat'l
Defense
Commission,
5th Anniv.
A1671

1998, Apr. 9
3699 A1671 10ch multicolored   .50   .25

A1672

Kim Il Sung, 86th Birth
Anniv. — A1673

Designs: 10ch, Birthplace, flags, flowers.
Circular stamps, each 80ch, within
84x155mm sheetlets, depicting portraits of
Kim Il Sung at different stages in his life:
#3701, As child. #3702, As middle school stu-
dent. 3703, As young revolutionary. #3704,
In suit and tie, ca. 1946. #3705, In military
uniform during Korean War. #3706, As middle-
aged man, in uniform. #3707, As middle-aged
man, in suit and tie. #3708, As old man in suit
and tie.

1998, Apr. 15
3700   A1672 10ch multicolored   .50   .25
       Souvenir Sheets
3701-3708 A1673 Set of 8   9.00 4.00

North-South Joint
Conference, 50th
Anniv. — A1674

1998, Apr. 21   **Perf. 13¼**
3709   A1674 10ch multicolored   .50   .25

16th World Cup Soccer Championship,
France — A1675

Designs: 30ch, Dribbling. 50ch, Kicking.

1998, May 5   **Perf. 11½**
3710-3711 A1675 Set of 2   1.60   .80
3711a   Sheet of 6, 2 ea #3710-
           #3711, #3712   6.00 3.00
3711b   Booklet pane of 10, 5 ea.
           #3710-3711   8.00   —
           Complete booklet, #3711b 8.50
           Souvenir Sheet
3712   A1675 80ch multicolored   1.60   .80
   A single stamp like that in No. 3712 is
included in No. 3711a.

A1676

Int'l Friendship Art Exhib., Mt.
Myohyang — A1677

Designs, 1w: No. 3713, *Diagram of Auto-
matic Space Station* (USSR). No. 3714,
Ceramic flower vase (Egypt). No. 3715, *Crane*
(USA).
   1w, Kim Il Sung receiving a gift from Deng
Xiaoping.

1998, May 20   **Perf. 11¾**
3713-3715 A1676 Set of 3   4.50 2.25
3714a   Sheet of 2, #3713 & #3714 2.75 1.40
3715a   Sheet of 2, #3713 & #3715 2.75 1.40
           Souvenir Sheet
           Perf. 13¼
3716   A1677 1w multicolored   2.00 1.00

A1678

Korean Art Gallery — A1679

Designs: 60ch, *A Countryside in May.*
1.40w, *Dance.*
3w, *Heart-to-heart Talk with a Peasant.*

1998, May 20
3717-3718 A1678 Set of 2   3.00 1.50
           Souvenir Sheet
3719   A1679 3w multicolored   4.50 2.25

Vegetables — A1680

Designs: 10ch, Cabbage. 40ch, Radish.
50ch, Green onion. 60ch, Cucumber. 70ch,

Pumpkin. 80ch, Carrot. 90ch, Garlic. 1w, Red
pepper.

1998, May 20   **Perf. 13¼**
3720   A1680 Sheet of 8, #a.-h.   9.00 4.50

A1681

Int'l Year of the Ocean — A1682

Designs: 10ch, Hydro-Meteorological Headquarters building, ship, oceanographic floating
balloons, dolphins, emblem. 80ch, Woman
holding child, yachts, emblem.
   5w, Vasco da Gama (1460-1524), Portuguese explorer.

1998, May 22
3730-3731 A1681 Set of 2   2.00   .90
3731a   Sheet of 4, 2 ea. #3730-3731 2.00   .90
           Souvenir Sheet
3732   A1682 5w multicolored   7.50 3.75

A1683

Korean Central History Museum,
Pyongyang — A1684

Designs: 10ch, Stone Age tool. 2.50w, Fossil monkey skull.
   4w, Kim Il Sung visiting the museum.

1998, June 15
3733-3734 A1683 Set of 2   4.00 2.00
           Souvenir Sheet
3735   A1684 4w multicolored   6.00 3.00

A1685

Dr. Ri Sung Gi (1905-96), Inventor of
Vinalon — A1686

Designs: 40ch, Dr. Ri Sung Gi and diagram
of vinalon nuclear structure.
   80ch, Gi working in laboratory.

1998, June 15   **Perf. 11½**
3736   A1685 40ch multicolored   .60   .25
   a.   Booklet pane of 10
           Complete booklet, #3736a
           Souvenir Sheet
3737   A1686 80ch multicolored   1.60 1.00

*Squirrels and
Hedgehogs*
Cartoon — A1687

Designs: 20ch, Squirrel and Commander of
Hedgehog Unit. 30ch, Commander of
Hedgehog Unit receiving invitation to banquet
celebrating bumper crop. 60ch, Weasel Commander and mouse. 1.20w, Bear falling dead-
drunk. 2w, Weasel Commander and mice
invading the flower village. 2.50w, Hedgehog
scout saving the squirrel.

1998, June 15
3738-3743 A1687 Set of 6   12.00 6.00
3743a   Sheet of 6, #3737-3743   12.00 6.00

A1688

Return of Hong Kong to China, 1st
Anniv. — A1689

Designs, 10w: No. 3744, Deng Xiaoping
(1904-97), Chinese Prime Minister. No. 3745,
Mao Zedong. No. 3746, Kim Il Sung.
   No. 3747, Deng Xiaoping, Mao Zedong and
Kim Il Sung, horiz.

1998, July 1
Embossed with gold foil application
3744-3746 A1688 Set of 3   30.00 10.00
           Souvenir Sheet
3747   A1689 10w Gold & multi   10.00 10.00

Young Wild
Mammals
A1690

Designs: 10ch, Tiger cub. 50ch, Donkey
foal. 1.60w, Elephant. 2w, Lion cubs.

1998, July 10   **Perf. 11½**
3748-3751 A1690 Set of 4   3.00   1.50

A1691

A1692

Korean War "Victory," 45th
Anniv. — A1693

Designs: 45ch, War monument, flag.
No. 3753, Kim II Sung inspecting the front.
No. 3754, Gaz-67 jeep and map of Korea,
showing Kim's inspection route.

1998, July 27   **Perf. 13¼**
3752 A1691 45ch multicolored   .25   .25
       Souvenir Sheets
3753 A1692 2w multicolored   2.00   1.00
3754 A1693 2w multicolored   2.00   1.00

Embroidery
A1694

Designs: 10ch, *White Herons in Forest.*
40ch, *Carp.* 1.20w, *Hollyhock.* 1.50w,
Cockscomb.
4w, *Pine and Cranes.*

1998, Aug. 10   **Perf. 11¾x12**
3755-3758 A1694 Set of 4   2.50   1.25
       Perf. 12x12¼
3759   Sheet of 5, #a.-e. + label   5.75   3.00
   a.   A1694 10ch multicolored   .25   .25
   b.   A1694 40ch multicolored   .40   .25
   c.   A1694 1.20w multicolored   1.00   .50
   d.   A1694 1.50w multicolored   1.00   .50
   e.   A1694 4w multicolored   2.50   1.25
       Souvenir Sheet
       Perf. 11¾x12
3760 A1694 4w multicolored   3.00   1.50

Traditional
Costumes
A1695

Designs: 10ch, Pouch. 50ch, Playthings
(dress ornaments). 1.50w, Hairpin. 1.90w,
Ornamental silver sword.

1998, Aug. 20   **Perf. 11½**
3761-3764 A1695   Set of 4   3.00   1.50
3763a   Sheet of 20, 10 se-tenant
      pairs #3761 and #3763   15.00   7.50
3764a   Sheet of 20, 10 se-tenant
      pairs #3762 and #3764   15.00   7.50

Launch of
*Kwangmyongsong
I*, DPRK's First
Earth
Satellite — A1696

Designs: 40ch, Rocket, satellite, world map
and flag.
1.50w, Rocket, earth and satellite orbit.

1998, Aug. 31   **Perf. 13¼**
3765 A1696 40ch multicolored   .35   .25
       Souvenir Sheet
3766 A1696 1.50w multicolored   1.25   .65

A1697

Acclamation of Kim Jong II as
Chairman of the DPRK National
Defense Commission — A1698

Designs: 10ch, Proclamation, *Kimjongilia.*
1w, Kim Jong II.

1998, Sept. 5   **Perf. 11½**
3767 A1697 10ch multicolored   .25   .25
       Souvenir Sheet
       Perf. 13¼
3768 A1698 1w multicolored   .75   .40

A1699

Korean DPR, 50th
Anniversary — A1700

Designs: 10ch, State Arms, Flag, Tower of
Juche Idea.
No. 3770: a, Kim II Sung saluting crowd
from balcony. b, Kim raising cap to crowd in
street. c, Kim in suit and white hat, with fruit,
stylized and idealized Korean peninsula in
background.

1998, Sept. 9   **Perf. 13¼**
3769 A1699 10ch multicolored   .25   .25
3770 A1700 1w Sheet of 6, 2
       each a-c   4.50   2.25

Poster: "Let
Us Push
Ahead with
the Forced
March for
Final
Victory"
A1701

1998, Sept. 15   **Perf. 11½**
3773 A1701 10ch multicolored   .25   .25

A1702

Korean DPR, 50th Anniversary (2nd
Issue) — A1703

1998, Sept. 20   **Perf. 13¼**
3774 A1702 40ch multicolored   .35   .25
       Perf. 11½
3775 A1703 1w multicolored   1.00   .50

Summer Olympic
Games,
Sydney — A1704

Designs: 20ch, Cyclist. 50ch, Soccer. 80ch,
Show jumping. 1.50w, Javelin throwing.
2.50w, Basketball.

1998, Sept. 25
3776-3779 A1704   Set of 4   2.50   1.25
3778a   Sheet of 3, #3777, 3778,
      as #3780   3.00   1.50
3779a   Sheet of 3, #3776, 3779,
      as #3780   3.00   1.50
       Souvenir Sheet
3780 A1704 2.50w multi   2.00   1.00
   For surcharge, see No. 4529.

Plants Presented
as Gifts to Kim
Jong II — A1705

Designs: 20ch, *Cyclamen persicum.* 2w,
Dianthus chinensis.

1998, Sept. 28   **Perf. 11½**
3781-3782 A1705 Set of 2   1.60   .80

Nat'l Vaccination
Day — A1706

1998, Oct. 20   **Perf. 13¼**
3783 A1706 40ch multicolored   .35   .25
   a.   Sheet of 6   2.10   1.00

Worldwide
Fund for
Nature
(WWF)
A1707

Panthera pardus orientalis: No. 3784, 1w,
Climbing branch. No. 3785, 1w, Walking in
snow. No. 3786, 1w, Looking to left. No. 3787,
1w, Head, full-face.

1998, Oct. 21
3784-3787 A1707 Set of 4   4.00   2.00
3787a   Sheet of 16, 4 se-tenant
   blocks of #3784-3787   16.00   8.00

For surcharges, see Nos. 4589-4590.

A1708

Land and Environment Conservation
Day — A1709

Designs: 10ch, Canal, countryside. 40ch,
Modern highway exchange, apartment towers.
1w, Kim Il Sung breaking ground for construction of Pothong River project.

1998, Oct. 23   **Perf. 11½**
3788-3789 A1708 Set of 2   .45   .25
Souvenir Sheet
Perf. 12x12¼
3790 A1709 1w multicolored   .75   .40

Italia '98 Int'l stamp Exhib.,
Milan — A1710

1998, Oct. 23   **Perf. 12¼x12**
3791 A1710 2w multicolored   1.50   .75

A1711

Designs: a, 20ch, Peng Dehuai and Kim Il
Sung. b, 20ch, Peng Dehuai, Zhou Enlai, Mao
Zedong. c, 30ch, Marshal Peng Dehuai. d,
30ch, Painting, *On the Front.*

1998, Oct. 24   **Perf. 11½**
3792 A1711 Sheet of 4, #a-d   .75   .40
Birth centenary of Peng Dehuai, Commander of the Chinese People's Volunterrs in
the Korean War.

Liu Shaoqi
A1712

Designs: 10ch, Liu Shaoqi. 20ch, Liu sitting
with Mao Zedong (1965). 30ch, Liu and his
daughter, Xiao Xiao (1964). 40ch, Liu sitting
with his wife, Wang Guangmei (1961).

1998, Nov 24   **Perf. 13¼**
3796-3799 A1712 Set of 4   .75   .40
Souvenir Sheet
Perf. 11¾x12¼
3800 A1712 1w multicolored   .75   .40

A1713

Victory in Korean-Japanese War,
400th Anniv. — A1714

Designs: 10ch, Victory monument, Yonsang
area, Yonan fortress, banners. 30ch, Naval
victory monument, Myongryang area, Gen. Ri
Sun Sin, turtleship. 1.60w, Monument to Buddhist priest Hyujong, Sosan-Chonghodang,
Hyujong, sword, helmet.
No. 3804, *Sea Battle Off Hansan Islet in
1592.*

1998, Nov. 24   **Perf. 11½**
3801-3803 A1713 Set of 3   1.50   .75
3803a   Sheet of 15, 5 se-tenant
   strips of #3801-3803   7.50   3.75
Souvenir Sheet
3804 A1714 10w multicolored   7.50   3.00

DPRK Entry into
INTERSPUTNIK, 15th
Anniv. — A1715

1998, Nov. 25   **Perf. 13¼**
3805 A1715 1w dp grn & lt grn   .75   .40

Korean
Goats — A1716

Goat with background color of: 10c, Green.
1w, Purple.

1998, Nov. 26
3806-3807 A1716 Set of 2   .80   .40
For surcharge, see No. 4576.

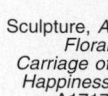

Sculpture, *A
Floral
Carriage of
Happiness*
A1717

Quotation from Kim Il Sung — A1718

Designs: 10ch, Sculpture, panoramic view
of Mangyongdae Schoolchildren's Palace.
1w, Kim Il Sung quotation, "Children are the
treasure of our country. Korea of the future is
theirs."

1998, Nov. 26   **Perf. 11½**
3808 A1717 40ch multicolored   .35   .25
   a.   Sheet of 4   2.00   1.00
Souvenir Sheet
3809 A1718 1w multicolored   .75   .40

Univeral
Declaration of
Human Rights,
50th
Anniv. — A1719

1998, Dec. 10
3810 A1719 20ch multicolored   .25   .25

Reptiles — A1720

Designs: a, 10ch, Reeves turtle. b, 40ch,
Skink. c, 60ch, Loggerhead turtle. d, 1.20w,
Leatherback turtle.

1998, Dec. 15   **Perf. 13¼**
3811 A1720 Block of 4, #a-d   1.75   .90
   e.   Sheet of 16, 4 #3811   17.00   3.50
   f.   Complete booklet, 3 ea.
     #3811   13.00

Mt.
Chilbo — A1721

Designs: 30ch, Thajong Rock. 50ch, Peasant Rock. 1.70w, Couple Rock.

1998, Dec. 15   **Perf. 11½**
3815-3817 A1721 Set of 3   1.75   .90

Tale of Chung
Hyang — A1722

Designs: 40ch, Marriage of Ri Mong Ryong
and Song Chun Hyang. 1.60w, Pyon Hak Do
watching Chun Hyang. 2.50w, Ri Mong Ryong
and Chun Hyang.
50ch, Chun Hyang in wedding veil.

1998, Dec. 20
3818-3820 A1722 Set of 3   3.50   1.75
3821   Sheet of 4, #3818-3820,
   3821a   5.00   2.50
   a.   A1722 multicolored   1.00   .50

Cholima   Arch of
Statue   Triumph
A1723   A1724

Tower of Juche
Idea — A1725

1998, Dec. 22   **Perf. 13¼**
3822 A1723 10ch red   .25   .25
3823 A1724 10ch red   .25   .25
3824 A1725 10ch red   .25   .25
3825 A1723 20ch red org   .25   .25
3826 A1725 30ch red org   .35   .25
3827 A1724 40ch yel brown   .40   .25
3828 A1725 40ch yel brown   .40   .25
3829 A1723 70ch yel grn   .65   .35
3830 A1724 70ch yel grn   .65   .35
3831 A1724 1.20w green   1.10   .55
3832 A1723 1.50w blue green   1.50   .75
3833 A1725 2w blue   2.00   1.00
3834 A1724 3w blue   2.75   1.40
3835 A1723 5w dk blue   5.00   2.50
3836 A1725 10w violet   9.75   5.00
   Nos. 3822-3836 (15)   25.55   13.65
For surcharges, see Nos. 4577, 4591, 4611.

New Year — Year
of the
Rabbit — A1726

Designs: 10ch, Rabbit meeting Lion on the
road. 1w, Rabbit using mirror to lure lion into
pit. 1.50w, Rabbit laughing at Lion in trap.
2.50w, Rabbit.

1999, Jan. 1   **Perf. 11½**
3837-3839 A1726 Set of 3   2.00   1.00
3840   Sheet of 4, #3837-3839,
   3840a   4.00   2.00
   a.   A1726 2.50w multicolored   2.00   1.00

Worker-Peasant Red
Guards, 40th
Anniv. — A1727

1999, Jan. 14   **Perf. 13¼**
3841 A1727 10ch multicolored   .25   .25

Kim Jong Il, 57th Birthday — A1728

40ch, Log cabin (birthplace) on Mt. Paekdu.

1999, Feb. 16   **Perf. 11½**
3842 A1728 40ch multicolored   .35   .25

Publication of Kim Il Sung's *Theses on the Socialist Rural Question in Our Country* — A1729

1999, Feb. 25   **Perf. 13¼**
3843 A1729 10ch multicolored   .25   .25

March 1 Popular Uprising, 80th Anniv. — A1730

1999, Feb. 25
3844 A1730 10ch olive brn & black   .25   .25

Turtle Ship — A1731

1999, Mar. 19
3845 A1731 2w multicolored   1.60   .80
Australia '99 World Stamp Expo, Melbourne.

A1732

Kim Il Sung, 87th Birth Anniv. — A1733

Designs: 10ch, Childhood Home, Mangyongdae. No. 3847, Kim Il Sung.

1999, Apr. 15   **Perf. 11½**
3846 A1732 10ch multicolored   .25   .25
Souvenir Sheet
Perf. 11½x12
3847 A1733 2w multicolored   1.60   .80

45th World Table Tennis Championships, Belgrade — A1734

1999, Apr. 26   **Perf. 11½**
3848 A1734 1.50w multicolored 1.20   .60
For surcharge, see No. 4559.

Ibra '99 Int'l Stamp Exhib., Nuremberg — A1735

1999, Apr. 27
3849 A1735 1w multicolored   .85   .40
For surcharge, see No. 4557.

Central Zoo, Pyongyang, 40th Anniv. — A1736

Designs: 50ch, Chimpanzee, rhinoceros. 60ch, Manchurian crane, deer. 70ch, Zebra, kangaroo. 2w, Tiger.

1999, Apr. 30   **Perf. 13¼**
3850-3852 A1736 Set of 3   1.60   .80
Souvenir Sheet
3853 A1736 2w multicolored   1.75   .90
For surcharge, see No. 4552.

Central Botanical Garden, Pyongyang, 40th Anniv. — A1737

Designs: 10ch, *Benzoin obtusilobum*. 30ch, *Styrax obassia*. 70ch, *Petunia hybrida*. 90ch, *Impatiens hybrida*. 2w, *Kimsungilia* and *Kimjongilia*.

1999, Apr. 30   **Perf. 11½**
3854-3857 A1737 Set of 4   1.60   .80
3857a   Sheet of 4, #3854-3857   1.75   .90
Souvenir Sheet
3858 A1737 2w multicolored   1.75   .90

Three Revolution Exhibit — A1738

Designs: 60ch, Light Industry Hall. 80ch, Heavy Industry Hall.

1999, May 2
3859-3860 A1738 Set of 2   1.20   .60
Three Revolution (ideological, technical, cultural) Exhibition, Ryonmotdong, Sosong District, Pyongyang.

Asia-Pacific Telecommunications Union, 20th Anniv. — A1739

1999, May 8   **Perf. 13¼**
3861 A1739 1w multicolored   .80   .40

Battle of Musan Area, 60th Anniv. — A1740

1999, May 19   **Perf. 11½**
3862 A1740 10ch multicolored   .25   .25

A1741

Charles Darwin, 190th Birth Anniv. — A1742

No. 3863: a, 30ch, Seagulls. b, 50ch, Bats. c, 1w, Dolphins. d, 1.20w, Rider on horseback. e, 1.50w, Korean dancer in traditional dress.

1999, May 20   **Sheet of 5 + labels**
3863 A1741 #a-e   3.00   1.50
Souvenir Sheet
Perf. 13¼x12
3864 A1742 2w multicolored   4.00   2.00

Diego Velazquez (1599-1660), Artist, 400th Birth Anniv. — A1743

Designs: 50ch: No. 3869, *Princess Margarita in a White Dress*. No. 3866, *Men Drawing Water from a Well*. 3.50w, *Self-portrait*.

1999, May 30   **Perf. 11¾**
3869-3870 A1743 Set of 2   1.00   .50
3870a   Sheet of 3, as #3869-3871   4.00   2.00
Souvenir Sheet
3871 A1743 3.50w multicolored   3.00   1.50

Medium and Small Hydroelectric Power Stations — A1744

Designs: 50ch, Rimyongsu Power Station. 1w, Janggasan Power Station.

1999, May 30   **Perf. 11½**
3872-3873 A1744 Set of 2   1.20   .60

3rd Women's World Soccer Championship, USA — A1745

Designs: a, 1w, Dribbling. b, 1.50w, Tackling. c, 1.50w, Goal shot. d, 2w, Knee kick.

1999, June 8   **Perf. 13¼**
3874 A1745 Sheet of 4, #a-d   5.00   2.50

Mars Exploration — A1746

Designs, each 2w: a, Vostock Rocket. b, Satellite over Martian crater. c, Mars probe landing, Martian moons.

1999, June 10   **Perf. 11½**
3878 A1746 Sheet of 3, #a.-c.   4.75   2.50

Movie, *The Nation and Destiny* — A1747

Scenes from film: a, Man holding candlestick. b, Man in white coat, woman with pistol. c, Old man in prison cell. d, Man in protective suit, with goggles on hat.

1999, June 10
3879 A1747 1w Sheet of 4, #a-d 3.20 1.60

Tourism — Mt. Kumgang — A1748

Designs: 20ch, Samil Lagoon. 40ch, Samson Rocks, vert. 60ch, Standing Rock. 80ch, Kuryong Waterfall. 1w, Kwimyon Rock.

1999, June 15   **Perf. 12**
3883-3887 A1748 Set of 5   2.50 1.25

UPU, 125th Anniv. — A1749

1999, June 20   **Perf. 11½**
3888 A1749 2w multicolored   1.40 .70

PHILEXFANCE '99 — A1750

2.50w, First stamps of France (1870) and DPRK (1946).

1999, July 2   **Perf. 12**
3889 A1750 2.50w multicolored   2.00 1.00

Kim Il Sung, 5th Death Anniv. — A1751

Designs: a, Kim Il Sung's Mercedes. b, Kim's railway car.

1999, July 8   **Perf. 11½**
3890 A1751 1w Sheet of 2, #a-b 1.60 .80

Kim Hyong Jik (1894-1926), Revolutionary, 105th Anniv. Birth — A1752

10ch, Chinese characters for "Jiwon" ("Aim High"), Kim Hyong Jik's motto, and Mangyong Hill.

1999, July 10
3892 A1752 10ch multicolored   .25 .25

History of Ceramics A1753

Designs: 70ch, Engraved-patterned vessel (5000 B.C.). 80ch, Wit and beauty jar (3rd-4th Centuries). 1w, Flowered jar. 1.50w, Lotus decoration celadon kettle (10th-14th Centuries). 2.50w, White china pot with blue flower (15th Century).

1999, July 15   **Perf. 13¼**
3893-3897 A1753 Set of 5   5.00 2.50

Fish Breeding A1754

Designs: 50ch, Silver carp. 1w, Common carp. 1.50w, Spotted silver carp.

1999, July 20
3898-3900 A1754 Set of 3   2.40 1.20

Year of Nat'l Independence and Great Solidarity — A1755

1999, Aug. 5
3901 A1755 40ch multicolored   .35 .25

Repatriation of Korean Nationals in Japan, 40th Anniv. A1756

1999, Aug. 16   **Perf. 11½**
3902 A1756 1.50w multicolored 1.25 .60

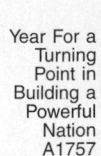

Year For a Turning Point in Building a Powerful Nation A1757

1999, Aug. 17
3903 A1757 40ch multicolored   .35 .25

7th World Athletic Championships, Seville — A1758

Designs: 30ch, 100-Meter Race. 40ch, Hurdles. 80ch, Discus.

1999, Aug. 18
3904-3906 A1758 Set of 3   1.20 .60

Gift Plants — A1759

No. 3907: a, Acalypha hispida Burm f. b, Allamanda neriifolia Hook. c, Begonia x hiemalis Fotsch. d, Fatsia japonica Decne. e, Streptocarpus hydrida hort. f, Streptocarpus rexii Lindl.

1999, Aug. 20
3907 A1759 40ch Sheet of 6, #a-f   2.00 1.00

22nd UPU Congress & China '99 World Philatelic Exhib. — A1760

Paintings by Qiu Ying: a, *Play a Flute to Call Phoenix*. b, *Six Friends in a Pine Forest*. c, *Relics Kept in the Bamboo Field*. d, *Ladies Morning Dressing*.

1999, Aug. 21
3913 A1760 40ch Sheet of 4, #a-d   1.50 .75

Mushrooms A1761

Designs: 40ch, Grifola frondosa. 60ch Lactarius volemus. 1w, Cariolus versicolor.

1999, Aug. 25
3917-3919 A1761 Set of 3   2.00 1.00
For surcharge, see No. 4558.

Cacti — A1762

Designs: 40ch, *Aporocactus flagelliformis*. 50ch *Astrophytum ornatum*. 60ch, *Gymnocalycium michanorichii*.

1999, Sept. 1
3920-3922 A1762 Set of 3   1.25 .60

Animals of the Zodiac — A1763

No. 3923: a, Rat. b, Ox. c, Tiger. d, Rabbit. e, Dragon. f, Snake.
No. 3924: a, Horse. b, Sheep. c, Monkey. d, Rooster. e, Dog. f, Pig.

1999, Sept. 10   **Perf. 12½**
     Sheets of 6, #a-f
3923-3924 A1763 10ch Set of 2 2.00 1.00

Crustacea A1764

Designs: 50ch, Pendalus hypsinotus 70ch, Penaeus orientalis. 80ch, Homarus vulgarus.

1999, Sept. 10   **Perf. 11½**
3935-3937 A1764 Set of 3   2.00 1.00

A1765

Jong Song Ok, Marathon Runner — A1766

1999, Sept. 20
3938 A1765 40ch multicolored   .35 .25
     Souvenir Sheet
3939 A1766 2w multicolored   1.60 .80

Victory of Jong Song Ok, Women's Marathon winner at 7th IAAF World Championships, Seville.

DPRK-China Diplomatic Relations, 50th Anniv. — A1767

Designs: 40ch, Mt. Kumgang, Korea. 60ch, Mt. Lushan, China.

1999, Oct. 5   *Perf. 12¼x11¼*
3940-3941 A1767 Set of 2   1.00 .50
3941a   Sheet of 4, #3940-3941 + 2
labels   3.00 1.50

Nos. 3940-3941 were printed both in sheetlets of 6, containing three vertical se-tenant pairs of the two stamps, and in sheetlets of 4, containing a horizontal se-tenant pair and two labels.

A1768

Return of Macao to China — A1769

Type A1768, 1w, Portrait of Pres. Jiang Zemin of China: No. 3942, Gold frame. No. 3943, Green frame.
Type A1769: 20ch (a), Deng Xiaoping sharing toast with Portuguese Prime Minister. 20ch (b), Jiang Zemin shaking hands with He Houhua, newly-appointed mayor of Macao special administrative region. 80ch (c), Mao Zedong at National Day Celebration, Tiananmen Square, 1951. Nos. 3944a-3944c, gold background. Nos. 3945a-3945c, green background.

1999, Nov. 10   *Perf. 13¼*
3942-3943 A1768 Set of 2
sheets   2.00 1.00
3944-3945 A1769 Set of 2
sheets, #a-c 2.50 1.25

New Year — April 19 Uprising, 40th Anniv. — A1770

2000, Jan. 1   *Perf. 11½*
3946 A1770 10ch multicolored   .25 .25

A1771

Koguryo Era (2nd Century B.C.-7th Century A.D.) — A1772

Designs, 70ch, Yellow dragon. 1.60w, Blue dragon.

2000, Jan. 1
3947 A1771 70ch multicolored   .60 .30
Souvenir Sheet
Perf. 11½x11¾
3948 A1772 1.60w multicolored   1.40 .70

Painting, *Rural Life* **(18th Century) — A1773**

No. 3949: a, Peasants weeding. b, Weaving hemp cloth. c, Peasants threshing grain. d, Riverside market.

2000, Jan. 25   *Perf. 13¼*
3949 A1773 40ch Sheet of 4, #a-
d 1.40 .70

Mt. Paekdu Rock Formations — A1774

Designs, 20ch: No. 3953, Dinosaur-shaped rock. No. 3954, Eagle-shaped rock. No. 3955, Owl-shaped rock.

2000, Jan. 30
3953-3955 A1774 Set of 3   .60 .30

Pongsan Mask Dance — A1775

Folk dances: a, 50ch, Chuibari mask dance. b, 80ch, Ryangban mask dance. c, 1w, Malttugi mask dance.

2000, Feb. 3   *Perf. 11½*
3956 A1775 Sheet of 3, #a-c 2.00 1.00

Cats — A1776

Designs, 50ch: No. 3959, Cat on windowsill. No. 3960, Kittens playing. No. 3961, Mother cat and kittens in basket.

2000, Feb. 3   *Perf. 13¼*
3959-3961 A1776 Set of 3   1.50 .75

Fauna — A1777

No. 3962: Cats: a, Singapura. b, Blue Abyssinian. c, Oriental. d, Scottish fold tabby.
No. 3963: Dogs: a, Shiba inu. b, Yorkshire terrier. c, Japanese chin. d, Afghan hound.
No. 3964: Horses: a, Przewalski's horse. b, Gray cob. c, White horse. d, Donkeys.
No. 3965: Pandas: a, In tree. b, Eating. c, Leaning against tree. d, Mother and cub.
No. 3966: Bears: a, Two polar bears. b, Mother and cub. c, Bear standing. d, Bear reclining.
No. 3967: Snakes: a, Mexican lance-headed rattlesnake (Crotalus polystictus). b, Scarlet king snake (Lampropeltis triangulum elapsoides). c, Green tree python (Chondropython viridis). d, Blood python (Python curtus).
No. 3968: Dinosaurs: a, Corythosaurus. b, Psittacosaurus. c, Megalosaurus. d, Muttaburrasaurus.
No. 3969: Marine Mammals: a, Burmeister's porpoise (Phocoena spinipinnis). b, Finless porpoise (Neophocaena phocaenoides). c, Bottle-nosed dolphin (Tursiops truncatus).d, Curvier's beaked whale (Ziphius cavirostris).
No. 3970: Sharks: a, Port Jackson shark (Heterodontus portusjacksoni). b, Great hammerhead shark (Sphyrna mokarran). c, Zebra shark (Stegostoma fasciatum). d, Ornate Wobbegong carpet shark (Orectolobus cavirostris).
No. 3971: Ducks: a, Ruddy shelduck (Tadorna ferruginea). b, European widgeon (Anas penelope). c, Mandarin drake (Aix galericulata). d, Hottentot teal (Anas hottentota).
No. 3972: Owls: a, Little owl (Athene noctua). b, Ural owl (Strix uralensis). c, Great horned owl (Bubo virginianus). d, Snowy owl (Nyctea scandiaca).
No. 3973: Parrots: a, Slaty-headed parakeet (Psittacula himalayana). b, Male eclectus parrot (Eclectus roratus). c, Major Mitchell's cockatoo (Cacatua leadbeateri). d, Female eclectus parrot (Eclectus roratus).
No. 3974: Butterflies: a, Indian leaf butterfly (Kallima paralekta). b, Spanish festoon (Zerynthia rumina). c, Male and female emerald swallowtails (Papillo palinurus). d, Bhutanitis lidderdalii.
No. 3975: Bees: a, Bumble bee. b, Bumble bee on flower. c, Honey bee (Apis mellifera). d, Honey bee fighting spider.
No. 3976: Spiders: a, Micrommata virescens. b, Araneus quadratus. c, Dolomedes fimbriatus. d, Aculepeira ceropegia.

2000, Feb. 10   **Sheets of 4, #a-d**
3962-3976 A1777 2w Set of
15 150.00 150.00

Kim Jong Il, 59th Birthday A1778

Design: Birthplace, Mt. Paekdu.

2000, Feb. 16   *Perf. 11½*
4022 A1778 40ch multicolored   .35 .25

Dinosaurs — A1779

Designs: a, Triceratops. b, Saltasaurus. c, Tyrannosaurus.

2000, Mar. 5   *Perf. 13¼*
4023 A1779 1w Sheet of 3, #a-c 3.00 1.50
d.   Sheet of 3, ovptd. with show
emblem in margin   3.00 1.50

No. 4023d, Espana 2000 International Stamp Exhibition, Madrid. Issued, 10/6/06.

A1780

Monkeys — A1781

Design, 50ch: No. 4026, Western tarsier (Tarsius spectrum). No. 4027, Patas monkey (Erythrocebus patas).
2w, Mona monkey (Cercopithecus mona).

2000, Mar. 25   *Perf. 11½*
4026-4027 A1780 Set of 2   .90 .45
4027a   Sheet of 4, 2 each #4026-
4027   2.00 1.00
Souvenir Sheet
4028 A1781 2w multicolored   1.60 .80

Nos. 4026-4027 were issued both separately in panes of 10 and together in sheets of 4.

Butterflies — A1782

No. 4029: a, 40ch Peacock (Inachus io). b, 60ch, Swallowtail (Papilio machaon). c, 80ch,

Mimic (Hypolimnas misippus Linnaeus). d, 1.20w, (Papilio bianor cramer).

2000, Mar. 25
4029 A1782 Sheet of 4, #a-d 3.00 1.50

Grand Chollima March — A1783

2000, Mar. 28
4033 A1783 10ch multicolored .25 .25
55th anniversary of the Korean Workers' Party.

April 19 Popular Uprising, 40th Anniv. A1784

2000, April 1
4034 A1784 10ch multicolored .25 .25

Sun's Day A1785

2000, April 15
4035 A1785 40ch multicolored .35 .25
88th anniversary of birth of Kim Il Sung. For surcharge, see No. 4587.

Mun Ik Hwan — A1786

2000, April 25 **Perf. 13¼**
4036 A1786 50ch multicolored .50 .25
Issued in honor of Mun Ik Hwan (1918-94), South Korean political activist, winner of 1990 National Reunification Prize.

Millennium; Korean Workers' Party, 55th Anniv. — A1787

Designs: 40ch, Chollima statue, flag, symbols of national power. 1.20w, Dove with letter, map, "2000."

2000, May 5
4037-4038 A1787 Set of 2 1.50 .75

비단란품종 주제89 (2000)

A1788

Orchids — A1789

Designs: 20ch, Cattleya intermedia. 50ch, Dendrobium moschatum. 70ch, Brassolaeliocattleya. 2w, Laeliocattleya.

2000, May 15
4039-4041 A1788 Set of 3 1.40 .70
4041a Booklet pane of 8, 2 each #4039-4040, 4 #4041 —
Complete booklet, #4041a —
Complete booklet sold for 440ch.

Souvenir Sheet
4042 A1789 2w multicolored 1.75 .90

Bridges A1790

Designs: 20ch, Okryn Bridge. 30ch, Ansan Bridge. 1w, Rungna Bridge.

2000, May 21
4043-4045 A1790 Set of 3 2.00 1.00

WIPA 2000 Int'l Stamp Exhib., Vienna — A1791

Traditional Korean musical instruments and folk dances: a, 1w, Okryugum and Jaenggang dance. b, 1.50w, Bungum and Full Moon Viewing dance. c, 1.50w, Janggo drum and "Trio" dance.

2000, May 30
4046 A1791 Sheet of 3, #a-c 3.50 1.75
Nos. 4046b-4046c are airmail stamps.

Children's Songs A1792

Designs: 40ch, Song "Halfmoon," two children in boat. 60ch, Song "Kangram Nostalgia," boy and girl. 1.50w, Song "Spring in Home Village," boy and girl with flowers.

2000, June 1 **Perf. 11¾x12¼**
4049-4050 A1792 Set of 2 .90 .45
Souvenir Sheet
4051 A1792 1.50w multicolored 1.50 .75

Cephalopods A1793

Designs: 40ch, Nautilus pompilius. 60ch, Octopus vularis. 1.50w, Ommastrephes sloanei pacificus.

2000, June 15 **Perf. 11½**
4052-4053 A1793 Set of 2 1.00 .50
Souvenir Sheet
4054 A1793 1.50w multicolored 1.50 .75
a. Booklet pane of 8, 2 each #4053-4054 —
Complete booklet, #4054a —
No. 4054a exists imperforate. Complete booklet sold for 6w.
For surcharges, see Nos. 4544-4545.

Mandarin Ducks — A1794

Designs, 50ch: No. 4055, Pair of ducks, couple on bridge. No. 4056, Pair of ducks, couple in row boat. 1w, Pair of ducks, ducklings.

2000, June 16 **Perf. 11¾x12¼**
4055-4056 A1794 Set of 2 .90 .45
4056a Sheet of 7, 3 #4055 & 4 #4056 3.25 1.60
Souvenir Sheet
4057 A1794 1w multicolored .90 .45
Nos. 4055-4056 were issued both in separate sheets of 9 (3x3) and in sheets of 7, containing 3 No. 4055 and 4 No. 4056, in an alternating arrangement.
For overprints, see Nos. 4071-4073.

Sports A1795

Designs: 80ch, Table tennis. 1w, Basketball. 1.20w, Baseball.

2000, July 7 **Perf. 13¼**
4058-4060 A1795 Set of 3 3.00 1.50

Trucks — A1796

Designs: 40ch, Sungri-61 NA. 70ch, Flat-bed truck. 1.50w, Konsol 25-50n dump truck.

2000, July 24 **Perf. 12**
4061-4063 A1796 Set of 3 2.50 1.25

Korean People's Army A1797

Portraits of KPA commanders and weapons: 60ch, Ri Tae Hun and 76mm field gun. 80ch, Ko hyon Bink and T-34 tank. 1w, Paek Ki Rah and Yak-9P pursuit plane.

2000, July 27
4064-4066 A1797 Set of 3 2.00 1.00

Minerals A1798

Designs: 30ch, Fluorite. 60ch, Graphite. 1.60w, Magnesite.

2000, Aug. 15 **Perf. 13¼**
4067-4069 A1798 Set of 3 1.00 .50
Souvenir Sheet
4070 A1798 1.60w multicolored 1.40 .70
Nos. 4067-4069 were printed together in a pane of 8, comprised of 3 No. 4067, 3 No. 4068, and 2 No. 4070. The 1.60w was also printed separately within a sheet of one (No. 4070).

Nos. 4055-4057 Overprinted

2000, Aug. 15 **Perf. 13¼**
4071-4072 Set of 2 .90 .45
Souvenir Sheet
4073 1w multicolored .90 .45
International Stamp Exhibition, Jakarta.

Sydney 2000, Summer Olympic Games — A1799

Designs: a, 80ch, Swimmer. b, 1.20, Cyclist. c, 2w, Runner.

2000, Sept. 15 **Perf. 13½**
4074 A1799 Sheet of 3, #a-c 3.75 2.00

Myohyang Mountain A1800

Designs: 40ch (No. 4077), Sanju Falls, wild pig and piglet. 40ch (No. 4078), Inho Rock, Fallow deer, pair. 1.20w, stag and fawn.

2000, Sept. 27   *Perf. 13¼*
4077-4079   A1800   Set of 3   1.75   .90

A1801

Korean Workers' Party, 55th Anniv. — A1802

Designs: 40ch, Party emblem, Party Museum.
No. 4082: a, Kim Il Sung. b, Kim Jong Il. c, Kim Jong Suk.

2000, Oct. 10   *Perf. 13¼*
4081   A1801   40ch multicolored   .25   .25
Souvenir Sheet
4082   A1802   50ch, Sheet of 3, #a-
          c   1.25   .60

Land Rezoning Project A1803

10ch, Flags, bulldozer and trucks, urban scene and rice fields.

2000, Oct. 15
4083   A1803   10ch multicolored   .25   .25

A1804

Taehongdan Potato Farms — A1805

Designs: 40ch, Potatoes, pigs, scientist, collective farm.
2w, painting, *The Great Leader President Kim Il Sung Brought a Bumper Crop of Potato in the Paektu Pleateau.*

2000, Oct. 20   *Perf. 11½*
4084   A1804   40ch multicolored   .35   .25
Souvenir Sheet
4085   A1805   2w multicolored   1.60   .80

Kim Jong Il & Pres. Jiang Zemin — A1806

2000, Oct. 21   *Perf. 11¾x12¼*
4086   A1806   1.20w multicolored   1.50   .75
Visit of Kim Jong Il to China.

Kim Jong Il & Pres. Kim Dae Jung — A1807

2000, Oct. 23   *Perf. 11½x12*
4087   A1807   2w multicolored   2.50   1.25
North-South Korean Summit Talks, Pyongyang.

Kim Jong Il & Pres. Putin — A1808

2000, Oct. 24   *Perf. 11¾x11½*
4088   A1808   1.50w multicolored   2.00   1.00
Visit of Kim Jong Il to Russia.

Chinese & Korean Soldiers — A1809

Chinese People's Volunteers' Entry Into Korean War, 50th Anniv. — A1810

No. 4090: a, 10ch, Soldiers crossing the Amnok River. b, 10ch, Battle scene. c, 50ch, Kim Il Sung and Chinese officers. d, 50ch, Mao Zedong presiding over meeting to decide upon entry into Korean War. e, 80ch, Chinese soldiers observing battle.

2000, Oct. 25   *Perf. 13¼*
4089   A1809   30ch multicolored   .55   .30
4090   A1810   Sheet of 5, #a-
          e   2.00   1.00

Alpine Flowers — A1811

Designs: 30ch, Aquilegia oxysepala. 50ch, Brilliant campion (Lychnis fulgens). 70ch, Self-heal (Prunela vulgaris).

2000, Nov. 5   *Perf. 13½*
4095-4097   A1811   Set of 3   1.25   .60
Nos. 4095-4097 were printed in sheets containing a decorative label.

A1812

Repatriation of Long-Term Prisoners of War — A1813

Designs: 80ch, Returning prisoners receiving bouquets of flowers from women in

---

Pyongyang. 1.20w, Prisoners welcomed by crowd, in front of statue of Kim Il Sung.

2000, Dec. 20
4098-4099   Set of 2 sheets   2.00   1.00

New Year — A1814

10ch, Flag, trees, factory, missiles, ship, jet planes.

2001, Jan. 1   *Perf. 11½*
4100   A1814   10ch multicolored   .25   .25

New Year (2nd Issue) — A1815

Tale of the White Snake: 10ch, White Snake meeting Xu Xian. 40ch, Stealing the Immortal Greass. 50ch, White and Green Snakes and Xu Xian. 80ch, Flooding of Jinshan Hill. 1.20w, White Snake and Green Snake.

2001, Jan. 1   *Perf. 12½x12*
4101-4104   A1815   Set of 4   3.25   1.60
4104a   Sheet of 4, #4101-4104   3.25   1.60
Souvenir Sheet
4105   A1815   1.20w multicolored   2.25   1.00
Nos. 4101-4104 were each issued singly in larger sheets and in combination in sheets of 4 (No. 4104a).

A1816

World Chess Champions — A1817

Designs: 10ch, E. Lasker (1868-1941) and J.R. Capablanca (1888-1942). 20ch, A. Alekhine (1892-1946) and E. Euwe (1901-80). 30ch, M. Botvinnik (1911-95) and V. Smylov (b. 1921). 40ch, T. Petrosian (1929-84) and M. Tal (1936-93). 50ch, B. Spassky (b. 1937) and R. Fisher (b. 1943). 1w, A. Karpov (b. 1954) and G. Kasparov (b. 1963). 2.50w, Wilhelm Steinmetz (1836-1900).

2001, Jan. 5   *Perf. 13½*
4106-4111   A1816   Set of 6   4.50   2.25
4111a   Sheet of 6, #4106-4111   4.50   2.25
4111b   Booklet pane of 6, #4106-
          4111   4.50   —
     Complete booklet, #4111b   5.00   —
Souvenir Sheet
4112   A1817   2.50w multicolored   4.50   2.25
No. 4111b contains Nos. 4106-4111 in a se-tenant vertical strip of six, with narrow decorative selvage.
For overprints, see Nos. 4129-4135.

Ri-Dynasty Men's Costumes A1818

Designs: 10ch, Trousers and jacket. 40ch, Vest. 50ch, Magoja. 70ch, Turumagi. 1.50w, Wedding attire.

2001, Jan. 19   **Perf. 12x12½**
4113-4116 A1818 Set of 4   3.00 1.50
4116a   Sheet of 5, #4113-4116,
       4117a   6.00 3.00
4116b   Booklet pane of 6, #4113-
       4114, 4116, 4117a, 2 #4115   6.75 —
       Complete booklet, #4116b   7.00

Souvenir Sheet
4117 A1818 1.50w multicolored   3.00 1.50

Nos. 4113-4116 were each issued both in large sheets and within sheets of 5, in combination with the 1.50w (No. 4117a) value contained in the souvenir sheet, No. 4117.

No. 4116b contains the six stamps in a se-tenant horizontal strip with narrow distinctive selvage.

Fire Engines — A1819

Fire-fighting vehicles and logos warning against specific fire hazards: 20ch, Small 2-door vehicle (small appliances). 30ch, Large ladder truck (oil can). 40ch, 2-door truck with closed back (match). 60ch, Small truck with ladder and external hose port (gas can). 2w, Old-fashioned fire truck with ladder (cigarette).

2001, Jan. 20   **Perf. 12½x12**
4118-4121 A1819 Set of 4   3.00 1.50
4121a   Booklet pane of 12, 3 ea.
       #4118-4121   9.00
       Complete booklet, #4121a   9.00
4121b   Sheet of 5, #4118-4121, type
       of #4122 + label   9.00

Souvenir Sheet
4122 A1819 2w multicolored   4.00 2.00

No. 4121a contains three attached se-tenant blocks of Nos. 4118-4121, arranged horizontally, with inscribed selvage on left and right sides.

Hong Kong 2001 Stamp Exhibition — A1820

1.40w, Black-naped oriole (Oriolus chinensis).

2001, Feb. 1   **Perf. 11½**
4123 A1820 1.40w multicolored   2.50 1.25

Kim Jong II, 59th Birthday — A1821

10ch, Jong II Peak in Paekdu Range, *Kimjongilia.*

2001, Feb. 10   **Perf. 13½**
4124 A1821 10ch multicolored   .30 .25

New Millenium, Joint Editorial *Rodong Sinmun, Josoninmingun* and *Chongnyonjonwi* Newspapers — A1822

10ch, Flag, symbols of Industry, Agriculture, Transportation

2001, Mar. 5
4125 A1822 10ch multicolored   .30 .25

Log Cabin at Revolutionary Headquarters on Mt. Paekdu — A1823

2001, Mar. 7   **Perf. 11½**
4126 A1823 40ch multicolored   .60 .30

Kim II Sung's Birthplace at Mangyongdae — A1824

Portraits of Kim II Sung — A1825

No. 1428 (each 80ch): a, As child. b, As Jilin-Yuwen Middle School student. c, As anti-Japanese revolutionary. d, As leader in early DPRK period. e, As supreme commander of the Korean People's Army. f, As leader during post-Korean War period. g, Portrait in middle age. h, Portrait in old age.

2001, Apr. 10   **Perf. 13½**
4127 A1824 10ch multicolored   .40 .25

Sheet of 8
4128 A1825 Sheet of 8, #a.-#g   10.00 5.00

Day of the Sun.

Nos. 4106-4112 Overprinted in Gold with Biographical Information

2001, Apr. 20
4129-4134 A1816 Set of 6   5.00 2.50

Souvenir Sheet
4135 A1817 2.50w multicolored   5.00 2.50

Kim Jong II — A1826

2001, Apr. 25   **Perf. 12**
4136 A1826 1w multicolored   1.50 .75

Propaganda issue, with the theme "Long Live the Great Victory of Songun Politics!"

Highways — A1827

Designs: 40ch, Pyongyang-Kaesong motor-way. 70ch, Pyongyang-Hyangsan tourist expressway. 1.20w, Youth Hero motorway. 1.50w, Pyongyang-Wonsan tourist expressway.

2001, May 7   **Perf. 12½x12**
4137-4140 A1827 Set of 4   5.50 2.75

Historical Pavilions A1828

Designs: 40ch, Ryongwang Pavilion in Pyongyang. 80ch, Inphung Pavilion in Kang-gye. 1.50w, Paeksang Pavilion in Anju. 2w, Thonggun Pavilion in Uiju.

2001, May 15   **Perf. 13¼**
4141-4144 A1828 Set of 4   7.00 3.50
4144a   Booklet pane of 4, #4141-
       4144   7.00 —
       Complete booklet, #4144a   7.50

No. 4144a contains Nos. 4141-4144 in a se-tenant block of four, within decorative selvage.

Education in Class Consciousness — A1829

2001, June 5
4145 A1829 10ch multicolored   .30 .25

Korean Birds — A1830

Designs: 10ch, Luscinia svecica. 40ch, Anser anser. 80ch, Diomedea albatrus. 1w, Charadrius dubius. 1.20w, Uria aalge. 1.50w, Delichon urbica.

2001, June 9   **Perf. 11½**
4146 A1830 Sheet of 6, #a.-f.   9.00 4.50
 g.   Booklet pane of 8, #4146c-
       4146f, 2 ea. #4146a-4146b 10.00 —
       Complete booklet, #4146g   10.50

BELGICA 2001 Philatelic Exhibition.
No. 4146g contains the eight stamps in a se-tenant horizontal (4x2) block with inscribed selvage on left and right sides.

Chinese Communist Party, 80th Anniv. — A1831

Designs, each 80ch: No. 4147, Mao Zedong. No. 4148, Deng Xiaoping. No. 4149, Jiang Zemin.

2001, June 15
4147-4149 A1831 Set of 3   3.75 1.75

Compare with Nos. 4226-4228.

Mt. Kumol — A1832

Designs: 10ch, Woljong Temple. 40ch, Revolutionary site. 70ch, Potnamu Pavilion. 1.30w, Rock of Tak Peak. 1.50w, Ryongyon Falls.

2001, July 9   **Perf. 12x12¼**
4150 A1832 Sheet of 5, #a.-e. +
       label   6.00 3.00
 f.   Booklet pane of 5, #4150a-
       4150e + label   6.00 —
       Complete booklet, #4150f   6.50

No. 4150f contains the stamps and labels of No. 4150 in the same format, but top and bottom marginal selvage is blank, with side selvage containing maple leaf on left and inscriptions on left and right.

Protected Plants A1833

Designs: 10ch, Rheum Coreanum. 40ch, Forsythia densiflora. 1w, Rhododendron yedoense. 2w, Iris setosa.

2001, July 20   **Perf. 13½**
4151-4154 A1833 Set of 4   5.50 2.75
4154a   Booklet pane of 6, #4152,
       4154, 2 ea. #4151, 4153   7.00 —
       Complete booklet, #4154a   7.50

No. 4154a contains the six stamps in a se-tenant vertical strip of 6, with inscribed selvage on top and bottom margins.

Orchids — A1834

Designs: 10ch, Eria pannea. 40ch, Cymbidium. 90ch, Sophrolaeliocattleya. 1.60w, Cattleya trianae.
No. 4159: 2w, Cypripedium macranthum.

2001, Aug. 1
4155-58	A1834	Set of 4	6.00	3.00
4158a		Booklet pane of 6, #4155-4156, 4158, #4159a, 2 #4157	11.00	—
		Complete booklet, #4158a	11.50	

Souvenir Sheet
4159	A1834	2w multicolored	4.00	2.00

No. 4158a contains the six stamps in a setenant horizontal strip of 6, with decorative selvage on left and right sides.

Lighthouses — A1835

Designs: 40ch, Pibaldo Lighthouse. 70ch, Soho Lighthouse. 90ch, Komalsan Lighthouse.
No. 4163: 1.50w, Alsom Lighthouse.

2001, Aug. 18
4160-4162	A1835	Set of 3	4.00	2.00
4162a		Booklet pane of 6, #4160-4161, 2 #4162, 2 #4163a	12.50	—
		Complete booklet, #4162a	13.00	
4162b		Sheet of 4, #4160-4162, 4163a	7.00	3.50

Souvenir Sheet
4163	A1835	1.50w multicolored	3.00	1.50

Nos. 4160-4162 were issued separately in large sheets and together, with the 1.50w value from No. 4163, in a sheet of 5 (No.4162b). No. 4162a contains the six stamps in a horizontal strip of 6, with thin plain selvage.

Kim Po Hyon (1871-1955), Grandfather of Kim Il Sung — A1836

2001, Aug. 19
4164	A1836	1w multicolored	1.50	.75

Protected Animals — A1837

Designs: 10ch, Ciconia nigra. 40ch, Aegypius monachus. 70ch, Hydropotes inermis. 90ch, Nemorhaedus goral. 1.30w, Bubo bubo.

2001, Sept. 2
4165-4168	A1837	Set of 4	4.00	2.00
4168a		Sheet of 5, #4165-4168, 4169a	6.50	—
4168b		Booklet pane of 6, #4165-1467, 1469a, 2 x 1468	7.50	—
		Complete booklet, #4168b	8.00	

Souvenir Sheet
4169	A1837	1.30w multicolored	2.50	1.25

Nos. 4165-4168 were issued both separately in large sheets and together, with the 1.30w value from No. No. 4169, in a sheet of 5 (No. 4168a).
No. 4168b contains the six stamps in a setenant vertical strip, within narrow decorated selvage.
For surcharge, see No. 4572.

Olympic Games 2008, Beijing — A1838

Designs, each 56ch: a, Deng Ya Ping, Gold medalist ('96), Women's Singles, Table Tennis. b, Jiang Zemin, PRC president. c, Wang Jun Xia, Chinese athlete. d, Li Ning, Chinese gymnast. e, Fu Ming Xia, Chinese diver.

2001, Sept. 10   *Perf. 12½*
4170	A1838	Sheet of 5, #a.-e.	5.00	2.50

Cycle Sports — A1839

Designs: 10ch, Cycle soccer. 40ch, Road racing. 1.50w, Mountainbike racing. 2w, Indoor race.

2001, Sept. 20   *Perf. 12*
4171	A1839	Sheet of 4, #a.-d.	7.00	3.50

Space Exploration — A1840

Designs: 10ch, Yuri Gagarin (1934-68), Soviet Cosmonaut. 40ch, Apollo 11 Moon Landing. 1.50w, Kwangmyongsong, North Korean satellite (1998). 2w, Edmund Hailey (1656-1742), Halley's Comet and Giotto satellite.

2001, Sept. 25
4172	A1840	Sheet of 4, #a.-d.	6.50	3.25
e.		Booklet pane of 5, #4172a-4172c, 2 #1472d	10.00	—
		Complete booklet, #4172e	11.00	

No. 4172e contains five stamps in a setenant horizontal strip.

Vladimir Putin and Kim Jong II — A1841

2001, Oct. 12   *Perf. 12½x12*
4173	A1841	1.50w multicolored	2.25	1.10

Visit of Kim Jong II to Russia.

Kim Jong II and Jiang Zemin — A1842

2001, Oct. 25   *Perf. 11½x12*
4174	A1842	1.50w multicolored	2.25	1.10

Meeting between Kim Jong II and Jiang Zemin, president of the People's Republic of China.

Kim Jong Suk in Battle — A1843

2001, Nov. 24   *Perf. 12½x12*
4175	A1843	1.60w multicolored	3.00	1.50

Kim Jong Suk, anti-Japanese revolutionary hero, 84th birth anniv.

Kim Jong II Inspecting
Troops — A1844

2001, Dec. 1   **Perf. 13½**
4176 A1844 1w multicolored   1.50   .75
10th anniv. of appointment of Kim Jong II as
Supreme Commander of the Korean People's
Army.

Chollima
Statue — A1845

2002, Jan. 1
4177 A1845 10ch multicolored   .30   .25
New Year.

A1846

A1847

Horses from painting *Ten Horses*, by Wang
Zhi Cheng (1702-68): 10ch, White horse.
40ch, Bay. 60ch, Pinto. 1.30w, Piebald.
1.60w, Black stallion, from painting *Horse
Master Jiu Fang Gao*, by Xu Bei Hong (1895-
1953).

2002, Jan. 1
4178-4181 A1846 Set of 4   3.75 1.75
4181a   Sheet of 5, #4178-4181,
         4182a   6.25 3.00
Souvenir Sheet
4182 A1847 1.60w multicolored   2.50 1.25
Traditional New Year — Year of the Horse.
Nos. 4178-4181 were issued both separately in large sheets and together, with the
1.60w value from No. 4182, in a sheet of 5
(No. 4181a).

Flower
Basket — A1848

Kim Jong II with Soldiers — A1849

Kim Jong II — A1850

Kim II Sung, Kim Jong II, Kim Jong
Suk — A1851

2002, Feb. 1   **Perf. 13½**
4183 A1848 10ch multicolored   .30   .25
Souvenir Sheets
4184 A1849 1.50w multicolored   2.50 1.25
Perf. 11½x12
4185 A1850 2w multicolored   3.00 1.50
Perf. 12x12½
4186 A1851 Sheet of 3, #a.-c.   6.00 3.00
Kim Jong II, 60th Birthday.
No. 4185 bears a metallic gold application.

Centenary of First Zeppelin
Flight — A1852

Designs: 40ch, LZ-1. 80ch, LZ-120. 1.20w,
Zeppelin NT.
2.40w, Zeppelin NT (different view).

2002, Feb. 5   **Perf. 12**
4187-4189 A1852 Set of 3   3.75 1.75
4189a   Sheet of 4, #4187-4189,
         4190a   7.50 3.75
Souvenir Sheet
4190 A1852 2.40w multicolored   3.75 1.75
a.   Booklet pane of 4, #4187-
     4190   13.00   —
     Complete booklet, #4190a   13.00
Nos. 4187-4187 were issued both separately in large sheets and together, with the
2.40w value from No. 4190, in a sheet of 4
(No. 4189a). Complete booklet sold for 4.90w.

Banner, Torch,
Soldiers — A1853

2002, Feb. 25   **Perf. 13½**
4191 A1853 10ch multicolored   .30   .25
Annual joint editorial of the three state
newspapers, *Rodong Sinmun, Josoninmingum* and *Chongnyonjonwi.*

Mushrooms — A1854

Designs: a, 10ch, Collybia confluons. b,
40ch, Sparassis laminosa. c, 80ch, Amanita
vaginata. d, 1.20w, Russia integra. e, 1.50w,
Pholiota squarrosa.

2002, Feb. 25   **Perf. 13½**
4192 A1854 Block of 5, #a-e
            + label   6.50 3.25
f.   Booklet pane of 5, #4192a-
     4192e, + label   16.00   —
     Complete booklet, #4192f   16.00

Complete booklet sold for 4.20w.

A1855

A1856

Kim II Sung (1912-1994) — A1857

Designs: 10ch, Kim II Sung's birthplace,
Kimsungilia.
Nos. 4198-4200 (each 1.50w): No, 4198,
Kim II Sung with Kim Jong Suk (1941). No.
4199, Kim II Sung as student, with black cap
(1927). No. 4200, Kim II Sung and Kim Chaek,
political commissar.
No. 4201: 2w, Portrait of Kim II Sung.

2002, Mar. 15   **Perf. 13½**
4197 A1855 10ch multicolored   .30   .25
Souvenir Sheets
4198-4200 A1856 1.50w Set of 3   6.00 3.00
With Gold Metallic Application
Perf. 11½x12
4201 A1857 2w multicolored   3.00 1.50

Kang Pan Suk — A1858

2002, Mar. 21   **Perf. 11½x11¾**
4202 A1858 1w multicolored   1.50   .75
Kang Pan Sok, mother of Kim II Sung, 110th
birth anniv.

20th April Spring
Friendship Art
Festival — A1859

2002, Mar. 25   **Perf. 13¼**
4203 A1859 10ch multicolored   .50   .25

Locomotives
A1860

Designs: 10ch, Kanghaenggun 1.5-01 electric train. 40ch, Samjiyon 1001 electric train. 1.50w, Steam locomotive. 2w, Steam locomotive, diff.
No. 4208, 2w, Pulgungi 5112 diesel locomotive.

2002, Apr. 10   *Perf. 11½*
4204-4207 A1860 Set of 4   6.00 3.00

Souvenir Sheet

4208 A1860 2w multicolored   3.00 1.50
   a.   Booklet pane of 5, #4204-4208   24.00 —
     Complete booklet, #4208a   24.00

For surcharge, see No. 4566. Complete booklet sold for 6.20w.

He Baozhen, 100th Anniv. Birth — A1861

Designs: a, 1w, He Baozhen and Liu Shaoqi in 1923. b, 40ch, He Baozhen's family. c, 30ch, Family home in Dao xian County, Henan Province. d, 10ch, Letter in Chinese, from Liu Ying, a wife of Zhang Wentian, Chinese Communist Party official. e, 20ch, Monument at He Baozhen's birthplace.

2002, Apr. 20   *Perf. 13¼*
4209 A1861 Sheet of 5, #a.-e.   3.00 1.50

He Baozhen, first wife of Liu Shaoqi, Chairman of the People's Republic of China 1959-68.

Shells
A1862

Designs: 10ch, Cristaria plicata. 40ch, Lanceolaria cospidata kuroda. 1w, Schistodesmus lampreyanus. 1.50w, Lamprotula coreana.

2002, Apr. 21
4210-4213 A1862 Set of 4   5.00 2.50
   4213a   Booklet pane of 6, #4212-4213, 2 each #4210-4211   13.00 —
     Complete booklet, #4213a   13.00

For surcharge, see No. 4601. Complete booklet sold for 3.70w.

A1863

Korean People's Army, 70th Anniv. — A1864

Designs: 10ch, Soldier, sailor, pilot, symbolizing the three branches of the armed forces. 1.60w, Kim Il Sung and Kim Jong Il walking with army officers and political functionaries.

2002, Apr. 25   *Perf. 12¼x11¾*
4214 A1863 10ch multicolored   .30 .25

Souvenir Sheet

4215 A1864 1.60w multicolored   2.50 1.25

Legend 'Arirang' — A1865

Designs: a, 10ch, Ri Rang and Song Bu as children. b, 40ch, As young adults. c, 50ch, Ri Rang killing the landlord. d, 1.50w, Song Bu.

2002, Apr. 28   *Perf. 13¼*
4216 A1865 Sheet of 4, #a.-d.   3.75 1.75

A1866

Mass Gymnastics and Artistic Performance of 'Arirang' — A1867

Designs: 10ch, Actors. 20ch, Cartoon characters. 30ch, Dancer holding fan. 40ch, Dancer, gymnasts with hoops. 1w, Dancer with tambourine.

2002, Apr. 28   *Perf. 12¼*
4217-4220 A1866 Set of 4   1.50 .75

Souvenir Sheet

4221 A1867 1w multicolored   1.75 .90

Nos. 4217-4220 were each issued in sheets of 6, with pictorial margins and Arirang logo.

Symbols of Modern Science & Industry
A1868

2002, May 2   *Perf. 13¼*
4222 A1868 10ch multicolored   .30 .25

Science and Technology promotion: "Science and Technology are the Driving Force of Building a Great Prosperous Powerful Nation."

Ryongmun Cavern — A1869

Designs: a, 10ch, Pink stalactite. b, 20ch, Green stalactite. c, 30ch, Golden stalagmite. d, 40ch, Rough-surfaced orange stalagmite.

2002, May 25   *Perf. 11½*
4223 A1869 Sheet of 4, #a.-d.   2.50 1.25

Monument — A1870

2002, May 2   *Perf. 13¼*
4224 A1870 10ch multicolored   .30 .25

30th Anniv. of the Elucidation of the Three Principles for National Reunification.

Butterflies — A1871

Designs: a, 10ch, Stauropus fagi. b, 40ch, Agrias claudina. c, 1.50w, Catocala nupta. d, 2w, Morpho rhetenor.

2002, June 30   *Perf. 11¾*
4225 A1871 Block of 4, #a.-d.   7.50 3.75
   e.   Booklet pane of 5, #4225a, 4225c-4225d, 2 #4225b   15.00 —
     Complete booklet, #4225e   15.00

Complete booklet sold for 4.60w.

Nos. 4147-4149 with Added Flags in Margins

A1872

2002, June 30   *Perf. 11½*
4226-4228 A1872 Set of 3 sheets   4.00 2.00

16th National Congress of the Communist Party of China, Beijing, Nov. 8-14. Compare with Nos. 4147-4149.

Elderly Man, Child, Hospital
A1873

2002, July 5   *Perf. 12¼*
4229 A1873 10ch multicolored   .30 .25

50th Anniv. of Universal Free Medical System.

Kim Jong Suk (1917-49) — A1874

Designs: a, 10ch, As child. b, 40ch, As young woman in Children's Corps. c, 1w, In army uniform. d, 1.50w, With long hair, in civilian clothing.

2002, July 20   *Perf. 13¼*
4230 A1874 Sheet of 4, #a.-d.   2.25 1.10

Kim Jong Suk, first wife of Kim Il Sung and mother of Kim Jong Il.

Soldier, Worker, Farmer — A1875

2002, July 29   *Perf. 11½*
4231 A1875 10ch multicolored   .30 .25

30th anniv. of the DPRK Constitution.

A1876

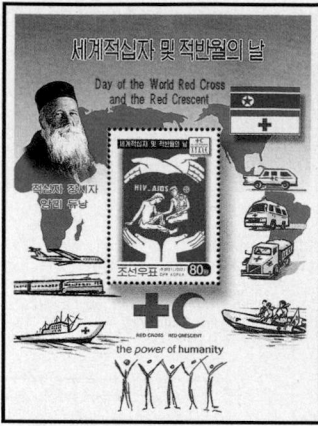

World Red Cross & Red Crescent Day — A1877

No. 4232: a, 3w, Korean returnees. b, 12w, Red Cross medics administering first aid. c, 150w, North Korean truck delivering aid to South Korean flood victims.
No. 4233: 80w, AIDS victim, family.

2002, Sept. 20   *Perf. 13¼*
Sheet of 6
4232 A1876 Sheet, 2 each #a.-c. 5.00 2.50
Souvenir Sheet
4233 A1877 80w multicolored 1.50 .75
a.   Booklet pane of 5, #4232c,
     4233, 2 each #4232a,
     4232b   9.00 —
     Complete booklet, #4233a   9.00
Complete booklet sold for 2.75w.

Hong Chang Su, 2000 World Super-Flyweight Boxing Champion — A1878

2002, Sept. 25   *Perf. 11½*
4234 A1878 75w multicolored 1.50 .75

Kim Jong Il with Pres. Putin — A1879

Kim Jong Il Shaking Hands with Pres. Putin — A1880

No. 4235 measures 85x70mm, No. 4236 120x100mm.

2002, Oct. 15   *Perf. 13¼*
Souvenir Sheets
4235 A1879 70w multicolored 1.50 .75
4236 A1880 120w multicolored 2.00 1.00
Kim Jong Il's Visit to Russia

Siamese Cat — A1881

Cavalier King Charles Spaniel — A1882

Designs:12w, Phungsan dog. 100w, White shorthair cat. 150w, Black and white shorthair cat.

2002, Oct. 20   *Perf. 12*
4237-4240 A1881 Set of 4 5.00 2.50
4240a   Booklet pane of 6, #4239-
     4240, 2 each #4237-
     4238   14.00
     Complete booklet, #4240a   14.00
Souvenir Sheet
4241 A1882 150w multicolored 3.00 1.50
a.   Inscr. "World Philatelic Exhi-
     bition Bangkok 2003" and
     emblem in margin   3.00 1.50
No. 4241a issued 10/4/2003. Complete booklet sold for 295w. No. 4240a exists imperforate.

Minerals — A1883

Designs: a, 3w, Pyrite. b, 12w, Magnetite. c, 130w, Calcite. d, 150w, Galena.

2002, Oct. 25   *Perf. 13¼*
4242 A1883 Block of 4, #a-d 5.50 2.75
e.   Booklet pane of 5, #4242am
     4242cm 4242d, 2 each
     #4242b   13.00 —
     Complete booklet, #4242e   13.00
Complete booklet sold for 322w.

Kim Jong Il and PM Junichiro Signing Declaration — A1884

Kim Jong Il with Japanese Prime Minister Koizumi Junichiro — A1885

Japan-Korea Bilateral Declaration
No. 4246 measures 90x80mm, No. 4247 75x65mm.

2002, Oct. 25   **Souvenir Sheets**
4246 A1884 120w multicolored 2.00 1.00
4247 A1885 150w multicolored 3.00 1.50

Kim Il Sung's Birthplace, Mangyongdae — A1886

Kim Jong Il's Birthplace, Mt. Paektu — A1887

Kim Jong Suk's Birthplace, Hoeryong A1888

Kimilsungia A1889

Torch, Tower of Juche Idea A1890

DPRK Flag A1891

Kimjongilia A1892

Magnolia Blossom A1893

DPRK Coat of Arms A1894

Chollima Statue A1895

Victory Monument A1896

Party Founding Monument — A1897

Perf. 11½, 13¼x13½ (#4252-4253, 4256-4259)
2002, Nov. 20
4248 A1886 1w violet brn .25 .25
4249 A1887 3w blue green .25 .25
4250 A1888 5w olive brn .25 .25
4251 A1889 10w dk lilac rose .25 .25
4252 A1890 12w dk reddish
     brn .25 .25
4253 A1891 20w dp blue & red .35 .25
4254 A1892 30w brnsh red .50 .25
4255 A1893 40w dp grnsh blue .65 .35
4256 A1894 50w dk brown .75 .40
4257 A1895 70w dk olive grn 1.00 .50
4258 A1896 100w brown 1.50 .75
4259 A1897 200w dk lilac rose 3.00 1.50
     Nos. 4248-4259 (12) 9.00 5.25
See No. 4877. For surcharges, see Nos. 4877A, 4877F.

New Year — A1898

2003, Jan. 1   *Perf. 13¼*
4260 A1898 3w multicolored .30 .25

A1899

Animated Film, *Antelopes Defeat Bald Eagles* — A1900

Designs: 3w, Mother antelope pleading with bald eagle stealing her baby. 50w, Antelopes uniting to defeat bald eagle. 70w, Bald eagle eating fish poisoned by antelopes. 100w, Mother antelope reunited with her child. 150w, Antelopes carrying litter full of fruit.

2003, Jan. 1
4261-4264 A1899 Set of 4 2.50 1.25
4264a Booklet pane of 8, 2 each #4261-4264 20.00 —
  Complete booklet, #4264a 20.00
Souvenir Sheet
4265 A1900 150w multicolored 1.50 .75

Complete booklet sold for 461w.

Folk Festivals A1901

Designs: 3w, Mother and children greeting Full Moon (Lunar New Year, Jan. 15). 12w, Dancers with Full Moon (Lunar New Year). 40w, Two girls on swing (Spring Festival). 70w, Mother and daughter laying flowers on anti-Japanese martyrs' monument (Hangawi - Harvest Moon Festival). 140w, Peasant dance (Hangawi - Harvest Moon Festival). 112w, Wrestling (Spring Festival).

2003, Jan. 20 *Perf. 11¾*
4266-4270 A1901 Set of 5 2.75 1.50
Souvenir Sheet
4271 A1901 112w multicolored 1.50 .75

Soldier A1902

2003, Feb. 14 *Perf. 13¼*
4272 A1902 12w multicolored .40 .25
Annual joint editorial of the three state newspapers, *Rodong Sinmun, Josoninmingum* and *Chongnyonjonwi.*

Weapons, Proclamation A1903

2003, Feb. 15
4273 A1903 30w multicolored .50 .25
North Korean withdrawal from the Nuclear Non-Proliferation Treaty.

Ode Monument — A1904

Sunrise at Mt. Paektu — A1905

2003, Feb. 16 *Perf. 12¼x11¼*
4274 A1904 3w multicolored .30 .25
Souvenir Sheet
4275 A1905 75w multicolored 1.00 .50
Kim Jong Il, 61st Birthday.

A1906

Ships — A1907

Designs: 15w, Cargo ship *Paekmagang.* 50w, Dredger *Konsol.* 70w, Passenger ship *Undok No. 2.* 112w, Cargo ship *Piryugang.* 150w, Excursion ship *Pyongyang No. 1.*

2003, Feb. 18 *Perf. 13½*
4276-4279 A1906 Set of 4 3.00 1.50
4279a Booklet pane of 6, #4276-4277, 2 each #4278-4279 18.00 —
  Complete booklet, #4279a 18.00
Souvenir Sheet
4280 A1907 150w multicolored 1.75 .90

Complete booklet sold for 444w.

A1908

Cars Used by Kim Il Sung — A1909

Designs: 3w, *Zis.* 14w, *Gaz.* 70w, *Pobeda.* 90w, *Mercedes Benz.* 150w, Painting by Kim San Gon *Delaying His Urgent Journey.*

2003, Feb. 20 *Perf. 11¾*
4281-4284 A1908 Set of 4 2.25 1.10
4284a Booklet pane of 6, #4281-4282, 2 each #4283-4284 16.00 —
  Complete booklet, #4284a 16.00
Souvenir Sheet
4285 A1909 150w multicolored 2.00 1.00

Complete booklet sold for 352w.

Book — A1910

2003, Mar. 15 **Souvenir Sheet**
4286 A1910 120w multicolored 1.75 .90
On the Art of Cinema, by Kim Jong Il, 30th anniv. of publication.

Army Trumpeter, Map, Soldiers Marching — A1911

2003, Mar. 16
4287 A1911 15w multicolored .30 .25
80th anniv. of Kim Il Sung's "250-mile Journey for Learning."

Soldier & Workers — A1912

2003, Mar. 29
4288 A1912 3w multicolored .25 .25
Propaganda issue: "Let us meet the requirements of Songun in ideological viewpoint, fighting spirit and way of life!"

A1913

Election of Kim Jong Il as Chairman of the DPRK National Defense Commission, 10th Anniv. — A1914

Designs: 3w, Flags, "10."
No. 4290: a, 12w, Kim Jong Il with computer. b, 70w, Kim with military officers, pointing. c, 112w, Kim, with military officers, hand raised.

2003, Apr. 9
4289 A1913 3w multicolored .25 .25
Souvenir Sheet
4290 A1914 Sheet of 3, #a.-c. 3.50 1.75

Kim Il Sung's Birthplace, Mangyongdae, *Kimsungilia* — A1915

2003, Apr. 15
4291 A1915 3w multicolored .25 .25
Day of the Sun—Kim Il Sung, 91st birth anniv.

A1916

Medals and Orders Presented to Kim Il Sung — A1917

Designs: 12w, Order of Suhbaatar (Mongolia, 1953). 35w, National Order of Grand Cross (Madagascar, 1985). 70w, Order of Lenin (USSR, 1987). 140w, Order of Playa Giron (Cuba, 1987). 120w, Kim Il Sung being presented with medal by Fidel Castro (1986).

2003, Apr. 15 *Perf. 13¼*
4292-4295 A1916 Set of 4 3.50 1.75
Souvenir Sheet
Perf. 13¼
4296 A1917 120w multicolored 1.50 .75

Insects — A1918

Designs: a, 15w, *Pantala flavescens.* b, 70w, *Tibicen japonicus.* c, 220w, Xylotrupes dichotomus. d, 300w, *Lycaena dispar.*

2003, Apr. 20　　　　**Perf. 13¼**
4297 A1918　Sheet of 4, #a.-d.　　9.00
　e.　　Booklet pane of 6, #4297c,
　　　　4297d, 2 each #4297a-
　　　　4297b　　　　　　　　　17.00　—
　　　　Complete booklet, #4297e　17.00
Complete booklet sold for 705w.

Korean National Dishes — A1919

Designs: 3w, Glutinous rice cake. 30w, Thongkimchi. 70w, Sinsollo.
120w, Pyongyang cold noodles.

2003, May 1　　　　　**Perf. 11¾**
4298-4300 A1919　Set of 3　　1.50　.75
Souvenir Sheet
4301 A1919　120w multicolored　1.50　.75

Victory Monument, Battle in Musan Area — A1920

2003, May 19　　　　**Perf. 12¾**
4302 A1920　90w multicolored　1.25　.60

Ryangchon Temple — A1921

Designs: 3w, Manse Pavilion. 12w, Buddhist statues. 40w, Painting of Buddha with two saints. 50w, Painting of Buddha with four saints.
120w, Taeung Hall, main shrine of temple.

2003, May 30　　　　**Perf. 13¼**
4303-4306 A1921　Set of 4　　1.75　.90
Souvenir Sheet
4307 A1921　120w multicolored　1.75　.90

Map, Song "We Are One" — A1922

2003, June 1
4308 A1922　60w multicolored　1.00　.50

Wild Animals — A1923

Designs: a, 3w, Tigers. b, 70w, Bears. c, 150w, Wild boars. d, 230w, Roe deer.

2003, June 10
4309 A1923　Sheet of 4, #a.-d.　　2.25
　e.　　Booklet pane of 4, #4309a-
　　　　4309d　　　　　　　　　25.00　—
　　　　Complete booklet, #4309e　25.00
Complete booklet sold for 460w.

Public Bonds of 1950, 2003
A1924

2003, July 25　　　　**Perf. 13½**
4310 A1924　140w multicolored　2.25 1.10
Campaign to promote purchase of public bonds.

A1925

A1926

DPRK "Victory" in Korean War, 50th Anniv. — A1927

Designs: 3w, Distinguished Service Medal.
No. 4312: Kim Il Sung in commander's uniform.
No. 4313: a, 12w, Kim delivering radio address. 35w, Kim talking to soldiers. c, 70w, Kim ratifying armistace agreement. d, 140w, Kim in uniform.
No. 4314: a, 12w, Kim smiling, surrounded by soldiers. 35w, Kim inspecting soldier. c, 70w, Kim Il Sung, Kim Jong Il inspecting army training. d, 140w, Middle-aged Kim Il Sung in suit and tie.
No. 4315: a, 12w, Kim Jong Il receiving bouquet from female soldier. 35w, Kim Jong Il being applauded by soldiers. c, 70w, Kim Jong Il on military inspection. d, 140w, Smiling Kim Jong Il.

2003, July 27　　　　**Perf. 13¼**
4311 A1925　3w multicolored　.25　.25
Souvenir Sheet
4312 A1926　120w multicolored　1.75　.90
Sheets of 4
Perf. 11½
4313-4315 A1927　Set of 3　12.00 6.00

Orchids — A1928

Designs: a, 3w, Minicattleya coerulea. b, 100w, Phalanopsis aphrodite. c, 150w, Calanthe discolor. d, 200w, Dendrobium snowflake.

2003, July 29　　　　**Perf. 13¼**
4316 A1928　Sheet of 4, #a.-d.　7.00 3.50
　e.　　Booklet pane of 4, #4316a-
　　　　4316d　　　　　　　　　　7.00　—
　　　　Complete booklet, #4316e　7.50
No. 4316e contains Nos. 4316a-4316d in a horizontal strip of four, with selvage similar to that of No. 4316.

A1929

Birds — A1930

Designs: 12w, Grus vipio. 70w, Nycticorax nycticorax. 100w, Columba livia var doestricus. 120w, Nymphicus hollandicus. 150w, Strix aluco.
225w, Pseudogyps africanus.

2003, Aug. 4　　　　**Perf. 13¼**
4317-4321 A1929　Set of 5　6.00 3.00
　4321a　　Booklet pane of 6, #4317-
　　　　4318, 4320-4321, 2
　　　　#4319　　　　　　　　　17.00　—
　　　　Complete booklet, #4321a　17.00
Souvenir Sheet
Perf. 11¾
4322 A1930　225w multicolored　3.00 1.50
Complete booklet sold for 567w.

Arctic & Antarctic Animals — A1931

Designs: a, 15w, Adelie penguins (Pygoscelis adeliae). b, 70w, Walrus (Odobenus rosmarus). c, 140w, Polar bear and cubs (Thalarctos maritimus). d, 150w, Bowhead whale (Balaena mysticetus). e, 220w, Spotted seals (Phoca largha).

2003, Aug. 20　　　　**Perf. 11½**
4323 A1931　Sheet of 5, #a.-e. +
　　　　label　　　　　　　　9.00 4.50
　a.　　Booklet pane of 5 + label
　　　　Complete booklet　　　13.00
No. 4323a contains one pane, with stamps and label in same arrangement as in No. 4323, surrounded by selvage containing a distinctive arrangement of Polar animals on a primarily yellowish background.

Mushrooms — A1932

Designs: a, 3w, Pholiota flammans. b, 12w, Geastrum fimbriatum. c, 70w, Coprinus atramentarius. d, 130w, Pleuotus cornucopiae. 250w, Elfvingia applanata.

2003, Sept. 5   **Perf. 13¼**
4324 A1932 Block of 4, #a-d   3.50 1.75

Souvenir Sheet
4328 A1932 250w multicolored   4.00 2.00
   a.   Booklet pane of 5, #4324a-4324d, 4328   20.00 —
     Complete booklet, #4328a   20.00

Complete booklet sold for 480w. No. 4328a exists imperforate.

Korean Stamp Exhibition Hall — A1933

Korean Stamps, Interior of Hall — A1934

2003, Sept. 5
4329 A1933 3w multicolored   .25 .25
4330 A1934 60w multicolored   1.00 .50

Korean Stamp Exhibition celebrating the 55th anniversary of the DPRK and the inauguration of the Korean Stamp Exhibition Hall.

A1935

A1936

55th Anniv. Founding of DPRK — A1937

Designs: 3w, DPRK Arms, Flag.
No. 4332: Kim Il Sung.
Sheets of 2 with central label: No. 4333: a, 60w, "The Birth of a New Korea" (Kim saluting marchers carrying DPRK flag). b, 60w, "In the Period of Building a New Korea" (Kim Jong Suk and factory workers). No. 4334: a, 60w, "Braving Through a Rain of Bullets Personally" (Kim in jeep in war zone). b, 60w, "Comrade Kim Il Sung, Ever-Victorious Iron-Willed Commander, Personally Commanding the Battle at Height 1211" (Kim on bluff, pointing to battlefield.) No. 4335: a, 60w, "We Trust and Follow Only You, the Leader" (Kim being greeted by villagers). b, 60w, "The Great Leader Kim Il Sung Giving On-the-Spot Guidance to the Pukchang Thermal Power Station" (Kim and factory workers). No. 4336: a, 60w, "The Victory of Korean Revolution Will Be Ensured by the Arms in Our Hand" (Kim speaking to soldiers, Kim Jong Il standing behind). b, 60w, "Keeping Up Songun Politics as All-Powerful Means" (Smiling Kim walking with soldiers symbolizing modern arms).

2003, Sept. 9   **Perf. 11½**
4331 A1935 3w multicolored   .25 .25

Souvenir Sheet
Perf. 13¼
4332 A1936 120w multicolored   2.00 1.00

Sheets of 2, #a.-b. + label
Perf. 12¼x12
4333-4336 A1937 Set of 4   6.00 3.00

Mao Zedong, 110th Birth Anniv. — A1938

No. 4337: a, 20w, Young Mao speaking at political meeting; b, 30w, Mao walking on shore with woman carrying manuscript. No. 4338: a, 30w, Mao addressing Red partisans; b, 30w, Mao (wearing trenchcoat) leading partisans in field. No. 4339: a, 20w, Mao talking with workers, soldiers; b, 30w, Mao in casual setting, leading discussion with soldiers. No. 4340: a, 30w, Mao addressing crowd in Beijing; b, 30w, Mao with people of various races and nationalities.
No. 4341: Sheet containing Nos. 4337-4338, with attached large label depicting 110 stamps picturing Mao and denominated 140w, the price for which the sheet was sold. No. 4342: Same, but containing Nos. 4339-4340.

2003, Dec. 26   **Perf. 13¼**
Se-Tenant Pairs with Label Between
4337-4340 A1938 Set of 4   3.50 1.75

Souvenir Sheets
4341-4342 A1938 Set of 2   4.00 2.00

New Year — A1939

Design: 2w, Soldier, workers, tower.

2004, Jan. 1   **Perf. 11½**
4343 A1939 3w multicolored   .25 .25
For surcharge, see No. 4877B.

A1940

Monkeys — A1941

Designs: 3w, Cebus apella. 60w, Papio doguera. 70w, Cercopithecus aethiops. 100w, Saguinus oedipus. 155w, Macaca mulatta.

2004, Jan. 1
4344-4347 A1940 Set of 4   4.00 2.00

Souvenir Sheet
4348 A1941 155w multicolored   2.50 2.00
   a.   Booklet pane of 5, #4344-4348   —
     Complete booklet, #4348a   20.00

Complete booklet sold for 403w. See Nos. 4351-4355.

Lunar New Year's Day — A1942

2004, Jan. 1
4349 A1942 3w multicolored   .25 .25

Souvenir Sheet

First Chinese Manned Space Flight — A1943

Designs: a, 91w, Yang Liwei, first Chinese cosmonaut (46mm diameter). b, 98w, Landing capsule, parachute, helicopter (54x45mm).

Perf. 13¼, Perf. (#4350a)
2004, Jan. 30
4350 A1943 Sheet of 2, #a.-b.   3.00 1.50
   c.   Booklet pane, 2 each #4350a-4350b   —
     Complete booklet, #4350c   —
   d.   #4350 with Hong Kong 2004 emblem opvt. in sheet margin   3.00 1.50

Booklets containing No. 4350c were issued with and without the Hong Kong 2004 emblem on the cover.

Nos. 4344-4348 with Hong Kong 2004 Emblem
2004, Jan. 30
4351-4354 A1940 Set of 4   4.00 2.00

Souvenir Sheet
4355 A1941 155w multicolored   2.50 1.25

Joint Editorial Rodong Sinmun, Josoninmingun and Chongnyonjonwi Newspapers — A1944

2004, Feb. 15   **Perf. 13¼**
4357 A1944 3w multicolored   .25 .25

A1945

Kim Jong Il, 62nd Birthday — A1946

No. 4358: 3w, Kim Jong Il's birthplace, Mt. Paektu.
No. 4359 (each 30w): a, "The Thaw of Sobaek Stream" (Spring). b, "The Thunderclap of Jong Il Peak" (Summer). c, "The Secret Camp in Autumn" (Autumn). d, "Hoarfrost in February" (Winter).

2004, Feb. 16   **Perf. 11½**
4358 A1945 3w multicolored   .25 .25

Souvenir Sheet
Perf. 13¼
4359 A1946 Sheet of 4, #a.-d.   2.00 1.00

Kim Jong Il — A1947

2004, Feb. 19   **Perf. 13¼**
4360 A1947 120w multicolored   2.00 1.00
    30th anniv. of publication of the *Program of Modelling the Whole Society on the Juche Idea.*

Rural Village
A1948

Kim Il Sung and Farmers — A1949

2004, Feb. 25   **Perf. 11½**
4361 A1948 3w multicolored   .25   .25
Souvenir Sheet
Perf. 12½ x11¾
4362 A1949 120w multicolored   1.75 1.75
    40th anniv. of publication of the "Theses on the Socialist Rural Question in Our Country."

Lighthouses — A1950

    Designs: a, 3w, Sokgundo Lighthouse. b, 12w, Yubundo Lighthouse. c, 100w, Jangdokdo Lighthouse. d, 195w, Amryongdan Lighthouse.

2004, Mar. 20   **Perf. 11¾x12½**
4363 A1950 Sheet of 4, #a.-d.   5.00 2.50
  e.   Booklet pane of 4, #4363a-
         4363d   5.00   —
       Complete booklet, #4363e   5.50
    No. 4363e contains Nos. 4363a-4363d in a horizontal strip of 4, surrounded by a seashore selvage.

A1951

Board Games — A1952

    Designs: a, 3w, Korean Chess. b, 12w, Goe. c, 90w, Yut. d, 120w, Kknoni (Chinese Checkers).
    98w, Playing Korean Chess.

2004, Mar. 20   **Perf. 13¼**
4364 A1951 Sheet of 4, #a.-d.   4.00 2.00
  e.   Booklet pane of 5, #4364a-
         4364b. 4364d, 2 x 4364c   5.00   —
       Complete booklet, #4363e   5.50
Souvenir Sheet
4365 A1952 98w multicolored   2.00 1.00
    No. 4364e contains Nos. 4364a-4364d in a horizontal strip of 5, which includes a second copy of the 90w value, with a distinctive printed selvage.

Kim Il Sung's Birthplace, Mangyongdae — A1953

Kim Il Sung — A1954

2004, Apr. 15   **Perf. 13¼**
4366 A1953 3w multicolored   .25   .25
Souvenir Sheet
Perf. 11¾
4367 A1954 120w multicolored   1.75   .90
    Kim Il Sung, 92nd birth anniv.

A1955

Tok Islands — A1956

    No. 4368: a, 3w, 19th century map of Korea. b, 12w, Western island. c, 106w, Eastern island.
    No. 4369: 116w, Both islands, sea gulls.

2004, Apr. 20   **Perf. 11½**
4368 A1955 Sheet, #a.-c. + label 2.50 1.25
Souvenir Sheet
Perf.
4369 A1956 116w multicolored   2.00 1.00
  a.   Booklet pane of 4, #4368a-
         4368c, 4369   —
       Complete booklet, #4369a   —

Fossils — A1957

    No. 4370: a, 3w, Calcinoplax antiqua. b, 12w, Podozamites lanceolatus. c, 70w, Comptonia naumannii. d, 140w, Clinocardium asagaiense.
    No. 4371: 120w, Tingia carbonica.

2004, May 20   **Perf. 13¼**
4370 A1957 Sheet of 4, #a.-d.   4.00 2.00
  e.   Booklet pane of 5, #4370a-
         4370d, #4371a   5.00   —
       Complete booklet, #4370e   5.50
Souvenir Sheet
Perf. 12½
4371 A1957 120w multicolored   2.00 1.00
  a.   single stamp   2.00 1.00

Cacti — A1958

    No. 4372: a, 70w, Notocactus leninghausii. b, 90w, Echinocactus grusonii. c, 100w, Gymnocalycium baldianum. d, 140w, Mammillaria insularis.

2004, June 2   **Perf. 11¾x12¼**
4372 A1958 Sheet of 4, #a.-d.   5.00 2.50
  e.   Ovptd. "World Stamp Champi-
         onship 2004" and Singapore
         2004 emblem in margin   5.00 2.50
  f.   Booklet pane of 4, #4372a-
         4372d   14.00 —
       Complete booklet, #4372f   14.00
    Complete booklet sold for 416w. No. 4372e was issued 8/28.

A1959

Unofficial Visit of Kim Jong Il to China — A1960

    No. 4373: a, 74w, Kim Jong Il with Hu Jintao, President of the People's Republic of China.
    No. 4374: a, 3w, Kim shaking hands with Hu Jintao. b, 12w, Kim with Jiang Zemin, President of China 1997-2003. c, 40w, Kim with Wu Bangguo, Chinese Communist Party leader. d, 60w, Kim clapping hands at outdoor reception.
    No. 4375: a, 3w, Kim with Wen Jiabao, Premier of the State Council of the PRC. b, 12w, Kim with Jia Qinglin, Chinese Communist Party leader. c, 40w, Kim with Zeng Qinghong, Vice-President of the PRC. d, 60w, Kim visiting Tianjin.

2004, June 18   **Perf. 13¼**
Souvenir Sheet
4373 A1959 74w multicolored   1.25   .60
  a.   As No. 4373, diff. (horiz.)
         selvage   1.25   .60
Sheets of 4, #a-d
4374-4375 A1960 Set of 2   3.50 1.75
  4375e   Booklet pane of 9, #4373a,
         4374a-d, 4375a-d   5.00   —
       Complete booklet, #4375e   5.50
    No. 4373a is from the booklet No. 4375e.

WPK Flag
A1961

A1962

Kim Jong Il's Appointment to the Central Committee of the Workers' Party of Korea, 40th Anniv. — A1963

No. 4377: a, 12w, Kim reading at desk. b, 100w, Kim standing in front of renderings of proposed Samjiyon Battle Site memorial.
No. 4378: a, 12w, Kim inspecting power station in Jagang Province. b, 100w, Kim with army officers.
No. 4379: a, 12w, Kim visiting the Komdok mine. b, 100w, Kim, outdoor photo portrait.
No. 4380: 130w, Kim Jong Il and Kim Il Sung.

2004, June 19
4376 A1961 3w multicolored   .25   .25
Sheets of 4
4377-4379 A1962 3 Sheets, 2 ea. #a.-b.   5.00   2.50
Souvenir Sheet
4380 A1963 130w multicolored   1.25 .60

A1964

A1965

Kim Il Sung, 10th Death Anniv. — A1966

No. 4381: 3w, *Kimilsungia*, monument to Kim Il Sung.
No. 4382: a, 12w, Kim Il Sung and Kim Jong Il visiting State Academy of Sciences. b, 116w, Kim Il Sung and Kim Jong Il on Mt. Paektu.
No. 4383: a, 12w, Kim Il Sung with workers b, 116w, Kim directing farmers at Chongan co-operative farm.
No. 4384: a, 12w, Kim with soldiers. b, 116w, Kim with children.
No. 4385: a, 12w, Kim embracing Rev. Mun Ik Hwan. 116w, Kim talking on telephone.
No. 4386: 112w, Kim waving.

2004, July 8   **Perf. 11¾**
4381 A1964 3w multicolored   .25   .25
Sheets of 4, #a-d
4382-4385 A1965 Set of 4   7.00 3.50
Souvenir Sheet
4386 A1966 112w multicolored   1.50 .75

Monument — A1967

2004, July 10   **Perf. 11¾**
4387 A1967 112w multicolored   1.50 .75
Kim Hyong Jik, father of Kim Il Sung, 110th birth anniv.

A1968

A1969

Deng Xiaoping, Birth Centennial — A1970

No. 4388: a, 3w, Deng Xiaoping as a student in France. b, 12w, Deng hiking on the Huangshan. c, 35w, Deng saluting at military review. d. 50w, Deng addressing rally celebrating the 35th anniversary of the People's Republic of China.
No. 4389a: Kim Il Sung being greeted by Deng, Chinese crowd during visit to China.
No. 4390: 80w, Deng at seashore.

2004, July 15   **Perf. 13¼**
4388 A1968 Strip of 4, #4a-d + label   1.50 .75
Sheet of 5
4389 A1969 Sheet, #4388, 4389a, label   2.50 1.25
a.   70w multicolored   .75 .40
Souvenir Sheet
4390 A1970 80w multicolored   1.25 .60

Fresh Water Fish — A1971

Designs: a, 3w, Carassius auratus. b, 12w, Tilapia nilotica. c, 140w, Ophiocephalus argus. d, 165w, Clarias gariepinus.

2004, Aug. 10
4391 A1971 Sheet of 4, #a.-d.   4.75 2.40

20th Olympic Games, Athens — A1972

Designs: a, 3w, Boxing. b, 12w, Soccer. c, 85w, Track and field events. d, 140w, Gymnastics.

2004, Aug. 10
4392 A1972 Block or strip of 4, #a.-d.   3.50 1.75
e.   Booklet pane of 4, #a.-d.   3.50
     Complete booklet, #4392e   4.00

No. 4392 was printed in panes of 8 stamps, 2 sets of Nos. 4392a-4392d, with decorative margin depicting athletes, Olympic emblems and Korean inscription. No. 4392e contains Nos. 4392a-4392d in a horizontal strip, with plain marginal selvage.
For overprints, see No. 4409.

Fire Engines — A1973

Designs: a, 3w, Mercedes Benz ladder truck. b, 12w, Fire truck. c, 40w, Jelcz pumper truck. d, 105w, Mercedes Benz fire truck. 97w, ladder truck, diff.

2004, Aug. 15
4393 A1973 Sheet of 4, #a.-d.   2.50 1.25
e.   Booklet pane of 4, #a.-d.   2.50
     Complete booklet, #4393e   3.00
f.   A1973 97w Souvenir sheet   1.50 .75

No. 4393e contains Nos. 4393a-4393d in a vertical strip, with marginal selvage similar to that of the sheet.

Airplanes — A1974

Designs: a, 3w, Airbus A340-600. b, 97w, Concorde. c, 104w, Graf Zeppelin DO-X. d, 116w, Junkers JU 52/3m.

2004, Aug. 20   **Perf. 12**
4394 A1974 Sheet of 4, #a.-d.   5.50 2.75
e.   Booklet pane of 4, #a.-d.   5.50
     Complete booklet, #4394e   6.00

No. 4394e contains Nos. 4394a-4394d in a horizontal strip, with pale yellow marginal selvage, with simple ruled lines and inscription.

Visit of Japanese Prime Minister Koizumi Zunichiro — A1975

2004, Aug. 25   **Perf. 11¾**
4395 A1975 220w multicolored   3.00 1.50

A1976

2004, Sept. 21
4396 A1976 112w multicolored   1.50 .75

An Jung Gun (1879-1910), assassin of Japanese Prime Minister Ito Hirdoumi in 1909, 125th birth anniv.

  A1977

Kim Jong Suk (1917-49), Mother of
Kim Jong II. — A1978

Designs: 3w, Kim Jong Suk's pistol.
97w, Kim Jong Suk.

2004, Sept. 22   *Perf. 13¼*
4397 A1977   3w multicolored   .25   .25
Souvenir Sheet
Perf. 12
4398 A1978   97w multicolored   1.50   .75

World
Wildlife
Fund
A1979

Swans: 3w, Swan in profile, looking left.
97w, Swan, ¾ profile, head turned to left.
104w, Two swans, one with outstretched
wings. 120w, Two swans in water.

2004, Sept. 30   *Perf. 11½*
4399-4402 A1979   Set of 4   5.00   2.50
4402a   Booklet pane of 4, #4399-
4102   5.00   —
Complete booklet, #4402a   5.50

Nos. 4399-4402 were each printed in sheets
of 4, with decorative selvage. No. 4402a contains the four stamps in a horizontal se-tenant
strip, surrounded by plain selvage.

A1980

Simwon Temple — A1981

Designs: 3w, View of Powkang Hall.
97w, Interior of Powkang Hall, with three
golden Buddha statues.

2004, Oct. 5   *Perf. 11¾*
4403 A1980   3w multicolored   .25   .25
Souvenir Sheet
Perf. 13¼
4404 A1981   97w multicolored   1.75   .90

Sidelfingen International Stamp
Fair — A1982

Electric trains: a, 3w, Red and blue train. b,
40w, Yellow train. c, 75w, Green and white
train. d, 150w, Red and green train.
120w, Vintage electric train.

2004, Nov. 5   *Perf. 11½*
4405 A1982   Sheet of 4, #a.-d.   4.50   2.25
Souvenir Sheet
4406 A1982   120w multicolored   2.00   1.00
a.   120w stamp from souvenir
sheet   2.00   1.00
b.   Booklet pane of 5, #4405a-
4405d, #4606a   6.50   —
Complete booklet, #4406b   7.00

A1983

Repatriation of Korean Nationals in
Japan, 45th Anniv. — A1984

Designs: 3w,   Repatriation ship
Mangyongbong.
80w, Kim II Sung with repatriated Korean
children.

2004, Dec. 16   *Perf. 11½*
4407 A1983   3w multicolored   .25   .25
Souvenir Sheet
Perf. 11¾
4408 A1984   80w multicolored   1.25   .60

No. 4392 Overprinted in Silver

Overprints: a, 3w, Mario Cesar Kindelan
Mesa (Boxing, Cuba). b, 12w, Argentine Soc-
cer Team. c, 85w, Yelena Slesarenko
(Women's High Jump, Russia). d, 140w, Teng
Haibin (Women's Gymnastics, China).

2004, Dec. 20   *Perf. 13¼*
4409 A1972   Block or strip of
4, #a.-d.   3.50   1.75

New Year
2005
A1985

2005, Jan. 1
4410 A1985   3w multicolored   .25   .25

A1986

New Year 2005 — Year of the
Rooster — A1987

Domestic fowl, millet stalk figures: 3w,
Rooster. 12w, Hen.
No. 4413: a, 3w, Chick. b, 70w, Rooster,
chick. c, 100w, Rooster. d, 140w, Basket of
eggs.

2005, Jan. 1
4411 A1986   3w multicolored   .25   .25
4412 A1986   12w multicolored   .60   .30
Sheet of 4
4413 A1987   Sheet, #a.-d.   4.00   .25
e.   Booklet pane of 6, #4411-
4412, #4413a-d   4.75   —
Complete booklet, #4413e   5.00

No. 4413e contains all six values of the set,
printed in a se-tenant strip of six, within a plain
yellow and green border.

Hen, Classic Chinese
Painting — A1988

Souvenir Sheet
2005, Jan. 10   *Perf. 11½*
4414 A1988   97w multicolored   1.50   .75

Kim II Sung's 250-Mile Journey, 80th
Anniv. — A1989

Souvenir Sheet
2005, Jan. 22   *Perf. 11¾*
4415 A1989   120w multicolored   1.50   .75

Statue of Kim II Sung, Chongsan-
ri — A1990

Souvenir Sheet
2005, Feb. 8   *Perf. 13¼*
4416 A1990   120w multicolored   1.50   .75
Creation of the Chongsan-ri Spirit and
Chongsan-ri Method.

Songun Scenes — A1991

Designs: a, 3w, Sunrise at Mt. Paektu. b,
12w, Snowscape. c, 40w, Royal azaleas on
Chol Pass. d, 50w, Jangja River. e, 60w, Ullim
Falls. f, 70w, Handure Plain. g, 70w, Potato
blossoms at Taehongdan. h, 100w, Poman-ri.

2005, Feb. 10   *Perf. 12¼*
4417 A1991   Sheet of 8, #a.-h.   5.00   2.50

A1992

A1993

Kim Jong II, 63rd Birthday — A1994

Design: 3w, *Kimjongilia*, mountains.
No. 4419, *216 Peaks Around Lake Chon on
Mt. Paektu,* summer scenes, each 50w: a,
Mountains, lake on lower right. b, Mountains,
lake across foreground. c, Mountains, lake in
foreground, shore at lower right.
No. 4420, *216 Peaks Around Lake Chon on
Mt. Paektu,* winter scenes, each 50w: a,
Mountains, frozen lake in foreground. b, Moun-
tains. lake in foreground, sun showing over
peaks. c, Mountains, lake in left foreground.

2005, Feb. 16   *Perf. 13¼*
4418 A1992   3w multicolored   .25   .25
Sheets of 3, #a.-c.
Perf. 12
4419 A1993   multicolored   2.00   1.00
4420 A1994   multicolored   2.00   1.00

Joint Editorial *Rodong Sinmun, Josoninmingun* and *Chongnyonjonwi* Newspapers A1995

2005, Feb. 16   *Perf. 13¼*
4421 A1995 3w multicolored   .25 .25

A1996

Naming of the *Kimilsungia*, 40th Anniv. — A1997

Designs: 3w, *Kimilsungia* and Kimilsungia-Kimjongilia Exhibition Hall.
120w: Kim Il Sung receiving a *Kimilsungia* plant from Pres. Sukarno of Indonesia.

2005, Apr. 13
4422 A1996 3w multicolored   .25 .25
Souvenir Sheet
4423 A1997 120w multicolored   1.50 .75

A1998

Kim Il Sung, 93rd Birth Anniv. — A1999

Designs: 3w, *Kimilsungia* and Mangyong Hill.
112w: Kim Il Sung standing in front of straw-thatched house at Mangyongdae.

2005, Apr. 15
4424 A1998 3w multicolored   .25 .25
Souvenir Sheet
Perf. 11¾
4425 A1999 112w multicolored   1.50 .75

48th World Table Tennis Championships, Shanghai — A2000

Designs: 3w, Pak Young Sun, Korea. b, 5w, Mao Zedong playing table tennis at the Communist base in Yanan. c, 12w, Wang Liqin, China. d, 20w, J.O. Waldner, Sweden. e, Zhang Yining, China. f, 102w, Werner Schlager, Austria.

2005, Apr. 23   *Perf. 11½*
4426 A2000 Sheet of 6, #a.-f.   3.00 1.50
  g. Booklet pane of 6, #4426a-
        4426f   3.00   —
      Complete booklet, #4426g   3.50

No. 4426g contains Nos. 4426a-4426f in a se-tenant horizontal strip of six, surrounded by blue selvage depicting the Shanghai 2005 emblem, stylized athletes and Korean inscription.

Pandas A2001

Designs: 15w, Panda on tree limb. 45w, Panda walking. 70w, Two pandas. 140w, Panda standing 120w, Panda with cub.

2005, May 3   *Perf. 13¼*
4427-4430 A2001 Set of 4   4.00   .25
4430a Booklet pane of 5, #4427-
        4430, 4432a   4.00   —
      Complete booklet, #4430a   4.50
Sheet of 5
4431 A2001 Sheet, #4427-
        4430, 4432a   6.00 3.00
Souvenir Sheet
4432 A2001 120w multicolored   3.00
  a. single stamp

Nos. 4427-4430 were each issued in separate large panes. No. 4430a contains Nos. 4427-30, 4432a in a se-tenant horizontal strip of 5, with plain white marginal selvage.
For overprints, see Nos. 4451-4455.

Ecosystem of Tok Island — A2002

Designs: a, 3w, *Dianthus superbus*. b, 3w, *Eumetopia jubata*. c, 12w, Seagull. d, 50w, *Lysimachia mauritania Lam*.
e, 97w: Eastern and Western islands, Tok Island.

Perf. 11¼, Perf. (#4433e)
2005, May 5
4433 A2002 Sheet of 9,
        #4433e, 2 each +
        #4433a-4433d +
        2 labels   12.00 6.00
  f. Booklet pane, #4433e
  g. Booklet pane of 8, 2 each
        #4433a-4433d, perf. 11¼
        on 3 sides   —   —
      Complete booklet, # 4433f,
        4433g   —

A2003

General Association of Korean Residents in Japan, 50th Anniv. — A2004

Designs: 3w, Korean family waving flag.
130w: Kim Il Sung shaking hands with man in suit.

2005, May 25   *Perf. 13¼*
4434 A2003 3w multicolored   .25 .25
Souvenir Sheet
4435 A2004 130w multicolored   1.50 .75

Fauna — A2005

Designs, each 40w: No. 4436, Korean Tiger. No. 4437, Sable.

2005, June 1
4436   40w multicolored   .75 .40
4437   40w multicolored   .75 .40
  a. 2005 Pair, #4436-4437 with
        label between   2.00 1.00
  b. Booklet pane, 2 #4437a   2.00
      Complete booklet, #4437b   2.50

See Russia No. 6911.

A2006

Koguryo Historic Site — A2007

Designs: a, Tomb of a general of Koguryo. b, 70w, Tomb mural depicting hunting scene. c, 100w, Mt. Songsan fortress. d, 130w, Gilded arrowheads.
97w: Monument at Mausoleum of King Kwanggaetho.

2005, June 14
4438 A2006 Sheet of 4, #a.-d.   4.00 2.00
  e. Booklet pane, #4436a-
        4438d, 4439a   6.00   —
      Complete booklet, #4438e   6.50
Souvenir Sheet
4439 A2007 97w multicolored   2.00 1.00
  a. 97w, single from souvenir
        sheet   2.00 1.00

No. 4438a contains Nos. 4438a-4438d in a horizontal strip of 4, with No. 4439a placed separately, within a 69mmx279mm sheetlet with selvage depicting hunting scene, artifacts and inscription.

Kim Chol Ju (1919-35), Brother of Kim Il Sung. — A2008

Souvenir Sheet
2005, June 14   *Perf. 11½*
4440 A2008 170w multicolored   1.50 .75

A2009

North-South Joint Declaration, 5th
Anniv. — A2010

Designs, all 112w: a, Kim Jong Il and S.
Korean President Kim Dae Jung shaking
hands. b, Kim Jong Il and Kim Dae Jung
standing side-by-side. c, Kim Jong Il and Kim
Dae Jung sitting together at table with large
flower arrangement. d, Kim Dae Jong and Kim
Il Jong at conference table.
167w, Kim Dae Jung and Kim Jong Il smiling, shaking hands, with representatives in
background.

2005, June 15
4441 A2009 Sheet of 4, #a.-d.   6.00   3.00
Souvenir Sheet
4442 A2010 167w multicolored   2.50   1.25

A2011

Amur Tiger — A2012

Designs: a, 3w, Tiger looking left. b, 12w,
Tiger growling. c, 130w, Tiger looking forward.
d, 200w, Tiger growling, turned to right.
150w: Tiger with cubs.

2005, July 10   **Perf. 11¾**
4443 A2011 Sheet of 4, #a.-d.   4.00   2.00
  e.   Booklet pane, #4443a-
       4443d   4.00   —
       Complete booklet, #4443e   4.50
Souvenir Sheet
Perf. 11½
4444 A2012 150w multicolored   2.00   1.00

No. 4443e contains Nos. 4443a-4443d in a
horizontal strip of 4, within selvage depicting
forest skyline and inscription "Panthera tigris
altaika."

Map of Korea — A2013

Souvenir Sheet
2005, July 25   **Perf. 11½**
4445 A2013 130w multicolored   1.50   .75

"June 25-July
27 - Period of
Joint Anti-US
Struggle"
A2014

Design: 3w, Korean soldier, U.S. POWs,
military cemetary, military vehicles.

2005, July 27   **Perf. 12**
4446 A2014 3w multicolored   .25   .25

A2015

A2016

A2017

National Liberation, 60th
Anniv. — A2018

Design: 3w, Arch of Triumph, magnolia.
No. 4448: a, 60w, Kim Il Sung receiving his
father's pistol from his mother. b, 60w, Kim Il
Sung founding the Juche-oriented revolution-
ary armed force. c, 60w, Kim Il Sung com-
manding the battle at Taehongdan. 60w, Kim Il
Sung addressing staff on eve of final offensive
against the Japanese. 102w, Kim Il Sung,
WWII-era photo.
No. 4449: a, Kim Il Sung on ship en route to
Wonsan Port landing. b, 60w, Kim Il Sung vis-
iting Kangson Steel Works. c, 60w, Kim Il
Sung delivering speech. d, 60w, Kim Il Sung
meeting his grandparents, upon his return to
Korea. e, 102w, Kim Il Sung with microphone.
No. 4450: 128w, Kim Il Sung.

2005, Aug. 15   **Perf. 13¼**
4447 A2015 3w multicolored   .25   .25
Sheets of 5
4448 A2016 Sheet, #a.-e.   4.00   2.00
4449 A2017 Sheet, #a.-e.   4.00   2.00
Souvenir Sheet
4450 A2018 128w multicolored   1.50   .75

**Nos. 4427-4430, 4432 Overprinted
"Taipei 2000" and Emblem in Red
and Blue**
2005, Aug. 19   **Perf. 13¼**
4451-4454 A2001 Set of 4   4.00   2.00
Souvenir Sheet
4455 A2001 120w multicolored   2.25   1.10

18th Asian International Stamp Exhibition,
Taipei.

A2019

National Costumes — A2020

Designs: a, 3w, Woman in red dress. b,
80w, Woman in blue dress. c, 100w, Woman
in green dress. d, 120w, Woman in white
dress with fur collar.

140w, Children.

2005, Aug. 30   **Perf. 11½**
4456 A2019 Sheet of 4, #a.-d.   3.50   1.75
  4456e   Booklet pane of 4, #4456a-d 3.50
          Complete booklet, #4456e   4.00
Souvenir Sheet
Perf. 11¾
4457 A2020 140w multicolored   1.75   .90

No. 4456e contains Nos. 4456a-d in a horizontal strip of 4, without the small decorative
labels that are printed below the stamps in No.
4456. The stamps are surrounded by a narrow
selvage similar to that of the sheet of 4.

Korean Workers' Party, 60th
Anniv. — A2021

Design: 3w, Korean soldier and workers,
banners, proclamation of Joint Slogan.

2005, Sept. 8   **Perf. 13¼**
4458 A2021 3w multicolored   .25   .25

A2022

A2023

A2024

A2025

Korean Workers' Party, 60th
Anniv. — A2026

Design: 3w, Monument to founding of Party.
No. 4460: a, 12w, Kim Il Sung organizing
Down-with-Imperialism Union. b, 30w, Kim Il
Sung forming the first Juche-oriented Party
organization. c, 60w, Kim Il Sung discussing a
draft resolution to Communist Party leaders. d,
90w, Kim Il Sung addressing Central Committee of the Communist Party.
No. 4461: a, 12w, Kim Il Sung at bank of
microphones, addressing 6th Congress of the
WPK. b, 30w, Kim Il Sung and Kim Jong Il with
military officers. c, 60w, Kim Jong Il inspecting
Tabaksol Company, a camouflaged army unit.
d, 90w, Kim Jong Il addressing crowd in
stadium.
No. 4462: 120w, Kim Il Sung. No. 4463:
120w, Kim Jong Il.

2005, Oct. 10		Perf. 13¼	
4459	A2022 3w multicolored	.25	.25

Sheets of 4
Perf. 11¾

| 4460 | A2023 Sheet, #a.-d. | 2.00 | 1.00 |
| 4461 | A2024 Sheet, #a.-d. | 2.00 | 1.00 |

Souvenir Sheets
Perf. 13¼

| 4462 | A2025 120w multicolored | 1.25 | .60 |
| 4463 | A2026 120w multicolored | 1.25 | .60 |

Bees — A2027

Designs: a, 3w, Four bees surrounding
queen. 12w, Two bees attending to larva.
128w, Bee filling comb cell with honey. 200w,
Bee flying.

2005, Oct. 20		Perf. 11½	
4464	A2027 Sheet of 4, #a.-d.	4.00	2.00
e.	Booklet pane, as #4464a- 4464d	4.00	—
	Complete booklet, #4443e	4.50	

No. 4464e contains four stamps like Nos.
4464a-4464d, but with slightly less yellow in
the comb background and a slightly paler blue
on the blue design elements. It bears a marginal selvage, with Korean inscription at left and
three bees at right.

United
States,
60th
Anniv.
A2028

2005, Oct. 24		Perf. 13¼	
4465	A2028 15w multicolored	.30	.25

A2029

Kaesong Historic Site — A2030

No 4466: a, 35w, Pogwang Hall. b, 35w,
Monument to Taegakguksa. c, 35w, Pojo Hall.
d, 75w, Ryongthong Temple.
No. 4467: a, 35w, Taesong Shrine. b, 35w,
Myongryun Hall. c, 35w, Metal type (round). d,
75w, Sam Gate.

2005, Oct. 31		Perf. 12	

Sheets of 4, #a.-d.

| 4466 | A2029 multicolored | 2.00 | 1.00 |
| 4467 | A2030 multicolored | 2.00 | 1.00 |

Nos. 4466-4467 each contain three non-
denominated labels.

Kim Hyong Gwon Monument — A2031

Souvenir Sheet

2005, Nov. 4		Perf. 11½	
4468	A2031 120w multicolored	1.50	.75

Kim Hyong Gwon (1905-36), uncle of Kim Il
Sung.

Ulsa Treaty,
Centennial
A2032

2005, Nov. 17		Perf. 11¾	
4469	A2032 12w multicolored	.30	.25

Ulsa Treaty, under which Korea became a
Japanese protectorate.

A2033

A2034

Kaesong Historic Site — A2035

No 4470: a, 35w, Kaesong Namdaemun. b,
35w, Mausoleum of King Kongmin. c, 35w,
Sonjuk Bridge. d, 35w, Sungyang Private
School. e, 35w, Anhwa Temple (Five Hundred
Rahan). f, 35w, Tomb of Pak Ji Won (Yonam).
No. 4471: a, 35w, King Wanggon, founder of
Kingdom of Koryo, 935 A.D., round. b, 35w,
Front Gate at Mausoleum of King Wanggon. c,
75w, Mausoleum of King Wanggon.
No. 4472: a, 35w, Fortress on Mt. Taehung
(North Gate). b, 35w, Marble statue of
Kwanumbosal, Kwanum Temple. c, 75w, Pakyon
Falls.

Sheet of 6, #a.-f. + 6 labels

2005, Nov. 18		Perf. 11½	
4470	A2033 multicolored	1.50	.75

Sheet of 3, #a.-c. + 2 labels
Perf. 13¼

| 4471 | A2034 multicolored | 1.50 | .75 |

Sheet of 3, #a.-c. + 4 labels
Perf. 12¼ (a, b); 11½ (c)

| 4472 | A2035 multicolored | 1.50 | .75 |

Visit to DPRK by Hu Jintao, President
of the People's Republic of
China — A2036

Design: a, 35w, Kim Jong Il meeting with Hu
Jintao. b, 35w, Kim Jong Il and Hu Jintao visiting the Taean Friendship Glass Factory. c,
35w, Kim Jong Il and Hu Jintao at state banquet. d, 102w, Kim Jong Il shaking hands with
Hu Jintao.

Perf. 11½, 13¼ (#4473d)

2005, Dec. 15	Sheet of 4, #a.-d.		
4473	A2036 multicolored	2.50	1.25

New Year
2006 — A2037

2006, Jan. 1	Litho.	Perf. 11½	
4474	A2037 3w multi	.25	.25

New Year 2006
(Year of the
Dog) — A2038

Various dogs: 3w, 70w.
No. 4477 — Various dogs: a, 15w. b, 100w.
c, 130w.

2006, Jan. 1		Perf. 13¼	
4475-4476	A2038 Set of 2	1.50	.55
4477	A2038 Sheet of 5, #4475- 4476, 4477a- 4477c	4.50	2.25
d.	Souvenir sheet of 1 #4477c	2.60	1.25

A2039

League of Socialist Working Youth,
60th Anniv. — A2040

No. 4478: a, 3w, Kim Il Sung and microphone. b, 111w, Kim Il Sung and crowd. c, 150w, Kim Jong Il receiving torch.

2006, Jan. 17   **Perf. 13¼**
4478 A2039   Sheet of 3, #a-c   5.25   2.00
Souvenir Sheet
Perf. 11½x12
4479 A2040   128w multi   2.60   1.25

A2041

New Year 2006 (Year of the Dog) — A2042

Photo. & Engr.
2006, Jan. 29   **Perf. 11x11¼**
4480 A2041   12w multi   .25   .25
Souvenir Sheet
Perf. 11½x11¼
4481 A2042   70w multi   1.00   .50

Down With Imperialism Union, 80th Anniv. — A2043

2006, Feb. 9   **Litho.**   **Perf. 13½**
4482 A2043   3w multi   .25   .25

Miniature Sheet

2006 Winter Olymics, Turin — A2044

No. 4483: a, 15w, Ice dancing. b, 85w, Ice hockey. c, 110w, Ski jumping. d, 135w, Speed skating.

2006, Feb. 10   **Perf. 13¼**
4483 A2044   Sheet of 4, #a-d   5.00   2.50
   Booklet pane of 4,
   #4483a-4483d   5.25   —
4483e   Complete booklet, #4483e   5.25
Complete booklet sold for 362w.

A2045

Kim Jong Il, 64th Birthday — A2046

No. 4485: a, 12w, Polemonium racemosum. b, 45w, Day lily. c, 100w, Dandelion. d, 140w, Parnassia palustris.

2006, Feb. 16   **Perf. 13½**
4484 A2045   3w multi   .25   .25
Souvenir Sheet
4485 A2046   Sheet of 4, #a-d   4.25   2.10

A2047

Visit of Kim Jong Il to People's Republic of China — A2048

No. 4486 — Kim Jong Il: a, 3w, At Crop Research Institute. b, 12w, At optical fiber factory. c, 35w, At Three Gorges Dam. d, 70w, At Guangzhou Intl. Conference and Exhibition Center. e, 100w, At air conditioner factory. f, 120w, At port of Yandian. 102w, Kim Jong Il and Hu Jintao.

2006, Mar. 4   **Perf. 12x12¼**
4486 A2047   Sheet of 6, #a-f   4.75   2.40
Souvenir Sheet
Perf. 11¾
4487 A2048   102w multi   1.50   .75

A2049

Agrarian Reform Law, 60th Anniv. — A2050

2006, Mar. 5   **Perf. 11½**
4488 A2049   12w multi + label   .25   .25
Souvenir Sheet
4489 A2050   150w multi   2.10   1.10

Souvenir Sheet

First North Korean Postage Stamps, 60th Anniv. — A2051

2006, Mar. 12   **Perf. 11¾**
4490 A2051   158w multi   2.25   1.10

Mt. Kumgang Scenery A2052

Designs: 3w, Pibong Falls. 12w, Podok Hermitage. 35w, Sokka Peak. 50w, Jipson Peak. 70w, Chongsok Rocks, horiz. 100w, Sejon Peak, horiz. 120w, Chonhwa Rock, horiz. 140w, Piro Peak, horiz.

2006, Mar. 15   **Perf. 11¾x12¼**
4491-4498 A2052   Set of 8   7.50   3.75

Belgica 2006 World Youth Philatelic Exhibition, Brussels A2053

Designs: No. 4499, 140w, Jules Verne (1828-1905), writer. No. 4500, 140w, Tyto alba, Volvariella speciosa, Scouting emblem. No. 4501, 140w, Disa grandiflora, Nymphalidae. No. 4502, 140w, Australopithecus afarensis, rocks. No. 4503, 140w, Alaskan malamute, Birman cat, Scouting emblem. No. 4504, 140w, Sunflowers, by Vincent Van Gogh. No. 4505, 140w, Soccer ball, chess knight, table tennis paddle and ball. No. 4506, 140w, Tursiops truncatus, Scouting emblem. No. 4507, 140w, Maglev train, horiz. No. 4508, 140w, 1962 Ernst Grube Type S 4000-1 fire truck, horiz.

2006, Apr. 13   **Perf. 11¾**
4499-4508 A2053   Set of 10   20.00   10.00

Kim Il Sung, 94th Anniv. of Birth — A2054

2006, Apr. 15   **Perf. 11½**
4509 A2054   3w multi + label   .25   .25

Association for the Restoration of the Fatherland, 70th Anniv. A2055

2006, May 5   **Perf. 13½**
4510 A2055   3w multi   .25   .25

Pothong River Improvement Project, 60th Anniv. — A2056

2006, May 21   **Perf. 12**
4511 A2056   12w multi   .25   .25

Various Stamps of 1963-2002 Surcharged in Black and Red

Methods and Perfs. As Before
2006
4512 A658   3w on 2ch #816   —   —
   (R)
4513 A608   3w on 5ch #731   —   —
4514 A635   3w on 10ch #770   —   —
4515 A932   3w on 10ch #1598   —   —
4516 A971   3w on 10ch #1798   —   —
4517 A1005   3w on 10ch #1929   —   —
4518 A926   3w on 15ch #1579   —   —
4519 A887   3w on 20ch #1419   —   —
4520 A986   3w on 20ch #1873   —   —
   (R)
4521 A1179   3w on 20ch #2470   —   —
4522 A1211   3w on 20ch #2548   —   —
4523 A1211   3w on 20ch #2548   —   —
   (R)
4524 A1249   3w on 20ch #2645   —   —
4525 A1431   3w on 20ch #3159   —   —
4526 A1431   3w on 20ch #3159   —   —
   (R)
4527 A1539   3w on 20ch #3159   —   —
4528 A1539   3w on 20ch #3159   —   —
   (R)
4529 A1704   3w on 20ch #3776   —   —
4530 A1288   3w on 25ch #2751   —   —
4531 A971   3w on 30ch #1801   —   —
4532 A986   3w on 30ch #1875   —   —
4533 A1177   3w on 30ch #2462   —   —
4534 A1177   3w on 30ch #2462   —   —
   (R)
4535 A1241   3w on 30ch #2621   —   —
4536 A1379   3w on 30ch #2964   —   —
4537 A1379   3w on 30ch #2964   —   —
   (R)

4538	A1396	3w on 30ch #3023	—	—
4539	A382	3w on 40ch #447	—	—
4540	A547	3w on 40ch #645	—	—
		(R)		
4541	A812	3w on 40ch #1219	—	—
4542	A818	3w on 40ch #1242	—	—
4543	A826	3w on 40ch #1277	—	—
4544	A1793	3w on 40ch #4052	—	—
4545	A1793	3w on 40ch #4052	—	—
		(R)		
4546	A1385	3w on 50ch #2987	—	—
4547	A1396	3w on 50ch #3025	—	—
4548	A1430	3w on 50ch #3154	—	—
a.		Double surcharge		
4549	A1471	3w on 50ch #3281	—	—
4550	A1526	3w on 50ch #3408	—	—
		(R)		
4551	A1595	3w on 50ch #3548	—	—
		(R)		
4552	A1736	3w on 60ch #3851	—	—
4553	A1557	3w on 80ch #3468	—	—
4554	A1656	3w on 80ch #3676	—	—
4555	A1651	3w on 80ch #3676	—	—
		(R)		
4556	A798	3w on 90ch #1164	—	—
4557	A1735	3w on 1w #3849	—	—
4558	A1761	3w on 1w #3919	—	—
4559	A1734	3w on 1.50w #3848	—	—
4560	A621	12w on 2ch #744	—	—
4561	A932	12w on 2ch #1597	—	—
4562	A808	12w on 2ch #1199	—	—
4563	A823	12w on 30ch #1268	—	—
4564	A808	12w on 40ch #1201	—	—
4565	A938	12w on 50ch #1622	—	—
4566	A1860	12w on 2w #4207	—	—
4567	A817	101w on 10ch #1236	—	—
4568	A907	101w on 10ch #1471	—	—
4569	A985	101w on 10ch #1865	—	—
4570	A1005	101w on 10ch #1926	—	—
4571	A1487	101w on 10ch #3321	—	—
4572	A1837	101w on 10ch #4165	—	—
4573	A1454	101w on 30ch #3228	—	—
4574	A1658	101w on 50ch #3680	—	—
4575	A1527	101w on 1w #3410	—	—
4576	A1716	101w on 1w #3807	—	—
4577	A1724	101w on 1.20w #3831	—	—
4578	A938	128w on 5ch #1619	—	—
4579	A812	128w on 10ch #1216	—	—
4580	A1231	128w on 15ch #2597	—	—
4581	A865	128w on 20ch #1357	—	—
4582	A903	128w on 20ch #1457	—	—
4583	A959	128w on 25ch #1754	—	—
4584	A977	128w on 25ch #1812	—	—
4585	A982	128w on 25ch #1853	—	—
4586	A958	128w on 40ch #1749	—	—
4587	A1785	128w on 40ch #4035	—	—
4588	A1430	128w on 50ch #3157	—	—
4589	A1707	128w on 1w #3785	—	—
4590	A1707	120w on 1w #3705	—	—
4591	A1725	128w on 2w #3833	—	—
4592	A820	134w on 5ch #1250	—	—
4593	A903	134w on 5ch #1455	—	—
4594	A898	134w on 10ch #1444	—	—
4595	A982	134w on 10ch #1850	—	—
4596	A855	134w on 20ch #1333	—	—
4597	A1467	134w on 30ch #3267	—	—
4598	A911	134w on 40ch #1518	—	—
4599	A911	134w on 40ch #1518	—	—
		(R)		
4600	A806	134w on 1.50w #1203	—	—
4601	A1862	134w on 1.50w #4213	—	—
4602	A1443	158w on 10ch #3196	—	—
4603	A898	158w on 15ch #1445	—	—
4604	A911	158w on 15ch #1516	—	—
4605	A1260	158w on 20ch #2680	—	—
4606	A850	158w on 25ch #1328	—	—
4607	A902	158w on 25ch #1458	—	—
4608	A1501	158w on 30ch #3357	—	—
4609	A1407	158w on 40ch #3059	—	—
4610	A1542	158w on 40ch #3443	—	—
4611	A1723	158w on 5w #3835	—	—

Nos. 4562-4564, 4581, 4588, 4598-4599, 4604-4605 are airmail.

Korean Children's Union, 60th Anniv. — A2057

2006, June 6   Litho.   *Perf. 13½*
4612   A2057   3w multi   .25 .25

2006 World Cup Soccer Championships, Germany
A2058

Various soccer players in action: 3w, 130w, 160w, 210w.

2006, June 9   *Perf. 13½*
4613-4616	A2058	Set of 4	7.00	3.50
4616a		Souvenir sheet, #4616 + label	3.00	1.50
4616b		Booklet pane of 4, #4613-4616	7.25	
		Complete booklet, #4616b	7.25	

Issued: No. 4616a, 10/21/09. Italia 2009 Intl. Philatelic Exhibition (No. 4616a). Complete booklet sold for 520w.

Souvenir Sheet

Kim Chol Ju (1919-35) — A2059

2006, June 12   *Perf. 11½x12*
4617   A2059   170w multi   2.40 1.25

Souvenir Sheet

Ri Su Bok (1933-51), War Hero and Poet — A2060

2006, July 27   *Perf. 11¾*
4618   A2060   120w multi   1.75 .85

Miniature Sheet

Circus Performers — A2061

Designs: a, 3w, Trapeze artists (42x35mm). b, 12w, Aerial acrobatic troupe (42x35mm). c, 130w, Seesaw jumper (42x35mm). d, 200w, Juggler (42x64mm).

Perf. 11½, 11½x12 (200w)
2006, Aug. 10   Litho.
4619   A2061   Sheet of 4, #a-d   5.00 2.50

Korean Cuisine
A2062

Designs: 3w, Kimchi. 12w, Umegi. 130w, Rice cake dumplings with bean paste. 200w, Sweet rice.

2006, Aug. 12   *Perf. 13½*
4620-4623	A2062	Set of 4	5.00	2.50
4623a		Booklet pane of 4, #4620-4623	5.00	—
		Complete booklet, #4623a	5.00	

Sea Mammals — A2063

Designs: 3w, Megaptera nodosa. 70w, Balaenoptera musculus. 160w, Physeter catodon. 240w, Inia geoffrensis.

2006, Aug. 20   *Perf. 11¾*
4624-4627	A2063	Set of 4	6.75	3.25
4627a		Booklet pane of 4, #4624-4627	6.75	—
		Complete booklet, #4627a	6.75	

Motorcycles
A2064

Various motorcycles.

2006, Sept. 1   *Perf. 11½*
4628		Horiz. strip of 4	7.00	3.50
a.	A2064	3w multi	.25	.25
b.	A2064	102w multi	1.40	.70
c.	A2064	150w multi	2.10	1.00
d.	A2064	240w multi	3.25	1.60
e.		Booklet pane of 4, #4628a-4628d	7.00	
		Complete booklet, #4628e	7.00	

Sinking of the General Sherman, 140th Anniv.
A2065

2006, Sept. 2   Litho.   *Perf. 13¼*
4629   A2065   130w multi   1.90 .95

Owls
A2066

Designs: 12w, Tyto alba. 111w, Strix uralensis. 130w, Strix aluco. 160w, Nyctea scandiaca.

Perf. 11½, 11½x12 (200w)
2006, Aug. 10   Litho.

2006, Sept. 10   *Perf. 11¾*
4630-4633	A2066	Set of 4	5.75	3.00
4633a		Booklet pane of 4, #4630-4633	5.75	—
		Complete booklet, #4633a	5.75	

For overprints see Nos. 4648-4651.

Souvenir Sheet

Kim Il Sung University, 60th Anniv. — A2067

2006, Oct. 1   *Perf. 11½x12*
4634   A2067   70w multi   1.00 .50

Famous Koreans
A2068

Designs: 3w, Ulgi Mundok, general. 12w, So Hui (942-998), diplomat and general. 35w, Kim Ung So (1564-1624), general. 70w, Kang Kam Chan (948-1031), general. 102w, Yongae Somun, general. 130w, Ri Kyu Bo (1168-1241), poet. 160w, Mun Ik Jom (1329-98), civil official.

2006, Oct. 2   *Perf. 13½*
4635-4641   A2068   Set of 7   7.25 3.75

A2069

Down With Imperialism Union, 80th Anniv. — A2070

No. 4643: a, 70w, Kim Il Sung and followers (50x38mm). b, 102w, Kim Il Sung (46mm diameter). c, 120w, Kim Il Sung and followers on railroad track (50x38mm).

2006, Oct. 17   Litho.   *Perf. 13¼*
4642   A2069   3w multi

Souvenir Sheet
Perf. 11¾ (#4643a, 4643c), Perf.
4643   A2070   Sheet of 3, #a-c   4.25 2.10

Red Cross Society of North Korea, 60th Anniv. — A2071

2006, Oct. 18   Litho.   Perf. 13½
4644 A2071 30w multi   .45   .25

Souvenir Sheet

Secondary Education for Koreans in Japan, 60th Anniv. — A2072

2006, Oct. 21   Perf. 13¼
4645 A2072 110w multi   1.60   .80

Miniature Sheet

Koguryo Tombs UNESCO World Heritage Site — A2073

No. 4646 — Murals: a, 3w, King (30x42mm). b, 70w, Queen (30x42mm). c, 130w, Subak (52x34mm). d, 135w, Procession (52x34mm). e, 160w, Kitchen (52x34mm).

Perf. 13¼ (3w, 70w), 12¼x11¾
2006, Nov. 4   Litho.
4646 A2073 Sheet of 5, #a-e   —

Souvenir Sheet

Joson University, 50th Anniv. — A2074

2006, Nov. 4   Perf. 11½
4647 A2074 110w multi + label   1.60   .80

Nos. 4630-4633 Overprinted in Gold

Methods and Perfs As Before
2006, Nov. 16
4648 A2066 12w on #4630   .25   .25
4649 A2066 111w on #4631   1.50   .75
4650 A2066 130w on #4632   1.90   .95
4651 A2066 160w on #4633   2.25 1.10
      Nos. 4648-4651 (4)   5.90 3.05

Belgica 2006 World Youth Stamp Exhibition. Location of the overprint varies.

Souvenir Sheet

Wooden Sculpture Presented by People's Army Soldiers to Kim Jong Il — A2075

2006, Dec. 24   Litho.   Perf. 11½x12
4652 A2075 130w multi   1.90   .95

New Year 2007 A2076

2007, Jan. 1   Litho.   Perf. 13½
4653 A2076 3w multi   .25   .25

New Year 2007 (Year of the Pig) A2077

Various pigs: 3w, 45w.
No. 4656 — Various pigs: a, 70w. b, 130w.

2007, Jan. 1   Perf. 11½
4654-4655 A2077 Set of 2   .70   .35
4656 A2077 Sheet, #4654-
             4655, 4656a,
             4656b   3.50 1.75
  c.   Booklet pane, #4654-4655,
       4656a, 4656b   3.50   —
       Complete booklet, #4656c   3.50
  d.   Souvenir sheet of 1 #4656a   1.00   .50

A2078

Kim Jong Il, 65th Birthday — A2079

Designs: 3w, Kimiljonghwa begonia and butterfly.
No. 4658 — Mountain, lake and musical score: a, 12w. b, 70w. c, 100w. d, 140w.

2007, Feb. 16   Perf. 13¼
4657 A2078 3w multi   .25   .25
4658 A2079 Sheet of 4, #a-d   4.50 2.25

Symbols of Progress A2080

2007, Feb. 28   Perf. 13¼
4659 A2080 3w multi   .25   .25
Annual joint editorial of state newspapers.

Butterflies — A2081

Designs: 15w, Callicore selima. 85w, Morpho rhetenor. 110w, Atrophaneura alcinous. 160w, Parnassius bremeri.

2007, Mar. 5
4660-4663 A2081 Set of 4   5.25 2.60
4663a   Booklet pane of 4, #4660-
           4663   5.25   —
           Complete booklet, #4663a 5.25

Miniature Sheet

Koguryo Tombs UNESCO World Heritage Site — A2082

No. 4664 — Anak Tomb No. 3 paintings: a, 3w, Stable (60x42mm). b, 70w, Well (60x42mm). c, 130w, Milling area (30x42mm). d, 160w, Man blowing horn (30x42mm).

2007, Mar. 10
4664 A2082 Sheet of 4, #a-d   5.25 2.60
  e.   Booklet pane of 4, #4664a-
       4664d   5.25
       Complete booklet, #4664e   5.25

Korean National Association, 90th Anniv. — A2083

2007, Mar. 23
4665 A2083 12w multi   .25   .25

Ludwig van Beethoven (1770-1827), Composer — A2084

2007, Mar. 26
4666 A2084 80w multi   1.10   .55

Mangyongdae, Birthplace of Kim Il Sung — A2085

Paintings of Kim Il Sung — A2086

Kim Il Sung and Family — A2087

No. 4668: a, 45w, The Great Leader Kim Il Sung on the 250-Mile Journey for Learning. b, 70w, The Great Leader Kim Il Sung Who Braved Through the Arduous Road of the Anti-Japanese War. c, 100w, Ever Victorious Road. d, 160w, At the Field Predicting the Rich Harvest.

2007, Apr. 15   Perf. 13¼
4667 A2085 3w multi   .25   .25

Perf. 11¾
4668 A2086 Sheet of 4, #a-d   5.25 2.60

Souvenir Sheet
Perf. 11¾x11½
4669 A2087 130w multi   1.90   .95
Kim Il Sung (1912-94).

Miniature Sheet

Rodents — A2088

No. 2088: a, 3w, Sciurus vulgaris. b, 12w, Muscardinus avellanarius. c, 20w, Hypogeomys antimena. d, 30w, Lemniscomys striatus. e, 40w, Pedetes capensis. f, 50w, Rattus norvegicus. g, 80w, Eliomys quercinus. h, 102w, Micromys minutus.

2007, Apr. 20   Perf. 13x13x12¼
4670 A2088 Sheet of 8, #a-h, +
                2 labels   4.75 2.40

Korean People's Army Soldiers and Mt. Paektu A2089

Leaders Reviewing Troops — A2090

Kim Il Sung and Kim Jong Il Reviewing Troops — A2091

No. 4672: a, 80w, Kim Il Sung and Kim Jong Il reviewing troops. b, 100w, Kim Jong Il and soldiers.

2007, Apr. 25   Perf. 13¼
4671 A2089 12w multi   .25   .25
                     Perf. 11¾
4672 A2090 Sheet of 2, #a-b   2.50 1.25
Souvenir Sheet
Perf. 12x11½
4673 A2091 120w multi   1.75   .85
Korean People's Army, 75th anniv.

Prevention of Bird Flu — A2092

2007, May 10   Perf. 13¼
4674 A2092 85w multi   1.25   .60

Miniature Sheet

First North Korean Currency, 60th Anniv. — A2093

No. 4675 — Banknotes: a, 3w, 10-won note of 1947. b, 12w, 50-chon note of 1947. c, 35w, 100-won note of 1959. d, 50w, 10-won note of 1959. e, 70w, 10-won note of 1978. f, 110w, 1-won note of 1978. g, 130w, 50-won note of 1992. h, 160w, 100-won note of 1992.

2007, May 20   Litho.
4675 A2093 Sheet of 8, #a-h   8.00 4.00

Souvenir Sheet

Battle of Pochonbo, 70th Anniv. — A2094

2007, June 4   Perf. 11½x12
4676 A2094 120w multi   1.75   .85

Fish A2095

Designs: 15w, Naso lituratus. 50w, Carassius auratus. 110w, A. citrinellus. 200w, Symphysodon discus.

2007, July 1   Perf. 13¼
4677-4680 A2095 Set of 4   5.25 2.60
4680a   Booklet pane of 4, #4677-
                 4680   5.25
           Complete booklet, #4680a 5.25

Self-disembowelment of Ri Jun at Hague Intl. Peace Conference, Cent. — A2096

2007, July 14
4681 A2096 110w brn & grn   1.60   .80

Fossils A2097

Designs: 15w, Tetracorallia. 70w, Neuropteridium. 130w, Yoldia. 200w, Rhinoceros mandible.

2007, July 20
4682-4685 A2097 Set of 4   6.00 3.00
4685a   Booklet pane of 4, #4682-
                 4685   6.00   —
           Complete booklet, #4685a 6.00

Miniature Sheet

Orchids — A2098

No. 4686: a, 3w, Oncidium wyattianum. b, 70w, Cymbidium Red Beauty "Carmen." c, 127w, Dendrobium thyrsifolium. d, 140w, Dendrobium Candy Stripe "Kodama."

2007, Aug. 3   Perf. 12¾
4686 A2098 Sheet of 4, #a-d   4.75 2.40
e.   Booklet pane of 4, #4686a-
                 4686d   4.75
           Complete booklet, #4686e 4.75

Women's Soccer — A2099

No. 4687 — Various women soccer players making plays: a, 12w. b, 40w. c, 70w. d, 110w. e, 140w.

2007, Sept. 10   Perf.
4687 A2099 Sheet of 5, #a-e   5.25 2.60
Souvenir Sheet
4688 A2099 130w shown   1.90   .95

Miniature Sheet

Flowers — A2100

No. 4689: a, Gladiolus gandavensis. b, Iris ensata. c, Rosa hybrida. d, Nelumbo nucifera.

2007, Sept. 26   Perf. 13¼
4689 A2100 30w Sheet of 4, #a-d 1.75   .85
e.   Booklet pane of 4, #4689a-
                 4689d   1.75
           Complete booklet, #4689e 1.75
           See Russia No. 7045.

Miniature Sheets

2008 Summer Olympics, Beijing — A2101

Nos. 4690 and 4691 — Mascots: a, 3w, Beibei. b, 12w, Jingjing. c, 30w, Huanhuan. d, 70w, Yingying. e, 140w, Nini.

2007, Oct. 15   Litho.   Perf.
4690 A2101 Sheet of 5, #a-e   —   —
Litho. With Three-Dimensional Plastic Affixed
4691 A2101 Sheet of 5, #a-e   —   —
No. 4691 sold for 500w, and stamps have other three-dimensional images.

Furniture and Household Furnishings — A2103

Designs: 3w, Seal box. 12w, Ornamental chest. 40w, Collapsible dressing table. 70w, Wardrobe. 110w, Chest of drawers. 130w, Chest of drawers, diff.

2007, Nov. 1   Litho.   Perf. 13¼
4694-4699 A2103 Set of 6   7.00 5.00
4699a   Booklet pane of 6, #4694-
                 4699   7.00   —
           Complete booklet, #4699a 7.00

Food A2104

Designs: 12w, Potato and rice cakes. 50w, Yongchae kimchi. 70w, Fermented flatfish. 110w, Potato cakes.

2007, Nov. 5
4700-4703 A2104 Set of 4   4.50 3.25
4703a   Booklet pane of 4, #4700-
                 4703   4.50   —
           Complete booklet, #4703a 4.50

Souvenir Sheet

Summit Meeting of Pres. Kim Jong Il and South Korean Pres. Roh Moo Hyun — A2105

2007, Nov. 10   Perf. 11½x12
4704 A2105 170w multi   3.00 2.50

Miniature Sheets

Scenes From Arirang Gymnastics Performance — A2106

No. 4705 — Various scenes: a, 12w. b, 50w.
No. 4706 — Various scenes: a, 120w. b, 155w.

2007, Nov. 15   **Perf. 11½**
Sheets of 2, #a-b, + Label
4705-4706 A2106 Set of 2   5.00 3.50

Paintings of Kim Dong Ho — A2107

Designs: 3w, Plowing. 12w, Weaving a Straw Mat. 70w, Thrashing. 130w, Archery.

2007, Nov. 18   **Perf. 13¼**
4707-4710 A2107 Set of 4   4.00 2.50
4710a   Booklet pane of 4, #4707-
             4710   4.00 —
             Complete booklet, #4710a 4.00

Souvenir Sheet

Visit of Viet Nam Communist Party Secretary General Nong Duc Manh — A2108

2007, Dec. 16   **Perf. 12x11½**
4711 A2108 120w multi   2.25 1.50

Home of Kim Jong Suk — A2109

Paintings Depicting Kim Jong Suk — A2110

No. 4713: a, 30w, Kim Jong Suk and Kim Il Sung (54x45mm). b, 70w, Kim Jong Suk (45mm diameter). c, 110w, Kim Jong Suk in battle (54x45mm).

2007, Dec. 24   **Perf. 12x11½**
4712 A2109 3w multi   .30 .25
Souvenir Sheet
Perf. 13¼, Perf. (#4713b)
4713 A2110 Sheet of 3, #a-c   4.00 3.00

New Year
2008 — A2111

2008, Jan. 1   **Litho.**   **Perf. 13¼**
4714 A2111 3w multi   .25 .25

Publication of Saenal Sinmun, 80th Anniv. — A2112

2008, Jan. 15
4715 A2112 85w multi   1.25 .60

Joint Editorials of State Newspapers — A2113

Red flag in upper left corner and: No. 4716, 3w, Arms and flag of North Korea, tower. No. 4717, 3w, Soldiers. No. 4718, 12w, Soldier and flag. No. 4719, 12w, Soldiers, factories and electrical tower, horiz. 30w, Woman and food, horiz. 120w, Musicians, children playing soccer, building. 130w, Men and woman, doves, map of Korea.

2008, Jan. 30   **Perf. 11¾**
4716-4722 A2113 Set of 7   5.75 4.00

Parrots A2114

Designs: 15w, Melopsittacus undulatus. 85w, Agapornis roseicollis. 155w, Agapornis personata, horiz. 170w, Two Melopsittacus undulatus, horiz.

2008, Feb. 5   **Perf. 13¼**
4723-4726 A2114 Set of 4   8.00 6.00
4726a   Booklet pane of 4, #4723-
             4726   8.00 —
             Complete booklet, #4726a 8.00

Souvenir Sheet

Naming of Kimjongilhwa Begonia, 20th Anniv. — A2115

2008, Feb. 13   **Perf. 11½x12**
4727 A2115 85w multi   1.75 1.25

A2116

Flowers — A2117

Designs: 3w, Pyrethrum hybridum.
No. 4729: a, 12w, Tulipa gesneriana (30x42mm). b, 70w, Adonis amurensis (30x42mm). c, 120w, Mathiola incana (30x42mm). d, 155w, Kimjongilhwa begonia (44mm diameter).

2008, Feb. 16   **Perf. 13¼**
4728 A2116 3w multi   .40 .25
4729 A2117 Sheet of 4, #a-d   6.50 4.50
   Kim Jong Il, 66th birthday.

Kim Il Sung Birthplace Type of 2002
2008, Mar. 15 **Litho.** **Perf. 11½**
4730 A1886 3w red   .40 .25
   For surcharge, see No. 4877C.

Miniature Sheet

Publication of "On the Art of Cinema," by Kim Jong Il, 35th Anniv. — A2118

No. 4731 — Various actors and actresses: a, 3w, Musician. b, 85w, Man holding gun. c, 135w, Martial artist. d, 170w, Man, woman and children.

2008, Mar. 15   **Perf. 13¼**
4731 A2118 Sheet of 4, #a-d   5.50 2.75

250-Mile Journey for Learning, 85th Anniv. — A2119

2008, Mar. 16   **Perf. 12**
4732 A2119 15w multi   .40 .25

2008 Summer Olympics, Beijing — A2120

No. 4733: a, 3w, Soccer. b, 12w, Basketball. c, 30w, Tennis. d, 70w, Table tennis.

2008, Mar. 28   **Perf. 13¼**
4733 A2120 Block or horiz.
           strip of 4, #a-d   2.25 1.10

Famous Men — A2121

Designs: 85w, Choe Yong (1316-88), military leader. 160w, Ho Jun (1546-1615), doctor.

2008, Mar. 29   **Perf. 12**
4734-4735 A2121 Set of 2   3.50 1.75

Election of Kim Jong Il as Chairman of National Defense Commission, 15th Anniv. — A2122

2008, Apr. 9   **Perf. 13¼**
4736 A2122 12w multi   .40 .25

Souvenir Sheet

Election of Kim Jong Il as Chairman of National Defense Commission, 15th Anniv. — A2123

2008, Apr. 9　　　　**Perf. 11½x12**
4737　A2123　120w multi

International Friendship Exhibition
A2124

Gifts to Kim Il Sung: 3w, Pitcher and oil lamp. 85w, Painting of rooster. 155w, Throne. 135w, Vase with two handles.

2008, Apr. 15　　　　**Perf. 11½**
4738-4740　A2124　Set of 3　3.50　1.75
Souvenir Sheet
4741　A2124　135w multi　　2.25　1.25

North-South Joint Conference, 60th Anniv. — A2125

2008, Apr. 21　　　　**Perf. 12**
4742　A2125　12w gray green　.40　.25

Mushrooms
A2126

Designs: 12w, Amanita muscaria. 50w, Armillariella mellea. 135w, Macrolepota procera. 155w, Tricholoma terreum.

2008, May 8　　　　**Perf. 11½**
4743-4746　A2126　Set of 4　5.50　3.25
4746a　　Booklet pane of 4, #4743-4746　5.50　—
　　Complete booklet, #4746a　5.50

Buildings on Mt. Ryongak
A2127

Designs: 35w, Two buildings. 155w, Building and wall.

2008, May 25　　　　**Perf. 13¼**
4747-4748　A2127　Set of 2　3.00　1.75

Musical Instruments — A2128

Designs: 15w, Hyangbipha (stringed instrument). 50w, Phiri (contrabassoon). 120w, Jangsaenap (oboe). 160w, Kayagum (zither), horiz.

2008, June 1　　　　**Perf. 13¼**
4749-4752　A2128　Set of 4　5.50　3.25
4752a　　Booklet pane of 4, #4749-4752　5.50　—
　　Complete booklet, #4752a　5.50

Opera Scenes and Scores — A2129

Designs: 3w, Sea of Blood. 12w, The Flower Girl. 85w, The True Daughter of the Party. 120w, Tell Oh Forest. 155w, The Song of Mt. Kumgang.

2008, June 5　　　　**Perf. 12x11½**
4753-4757　A2129　Set of 5　5.75　4.00

North Korea No. 1 and Romania No. 1 — A2130

2008, June 20　　　　**Perf. 12¼x11¾**
4758　A2130　85w multi　　1.50　.80
　　EFIRO 2008 Intl. Stamp Exhibition, Bucharest, Romania.

Capture of the USS Pueblo, 40th Anniv. — A2131

2008, June 25　　　　**Perf. 12¼x11¾**
4759　A2131　12w multi　　.40　.25

Souvenir Sheet

Olympic Torch Relay in Pyongyang — A2132

2008, June 26　　　　**Perf. 11¾x12¼**
4760　A2132　120w multi　　2.25　1.10

Minerals — A2133

Designs: 12w, Serpentine. 75w, Copper pyrite. 135w, Sphalerite. 155w, Molybdenite.

2008, July 5　　　　**Perf. 12¼x11¾**
4761-4764　A2133　Set of 4　6.00　3.50
4764a　　Booklet pane of 4, #4761-4764　6.00　—
　　Complete booklet, #4764a　6.00

Souvenir Sheets

A2134

A2135

Korean War Ceasefire, 55th Anniv. — A2136

No. 4765: a, 3w, Kim Il Sung leading troop crossing of Han River. b, 120w, Kim Il Sung with troops.
No. 4766: a, 35w, Kim Il Sung and seated troops. b, 155w, Celebration.
85w, Kim Il Sung at battleground.

2008, July 27　　　　**Perf. 12x11½**
4765　A2134　Sheet of 2, #a-b　2.00　1.25
4766　A2135　Sheet of 2, #a-b　3.00　1.75
　　　　　　Perf. 11½
4767　A2136　85w multi　　1.50　.85

Souvenir Sheet

Jong Il Peak, 20th Anniv. of Renaming — A2137

2008, Aug. 9　　　　**Perf. 13¼**
4768　A2137　120w multi　　2.25　1.25

Food
A2138

Designs: 3w, Rice and wormwood cakes. 70w, Rice cakes. 135w, Pancakes. 155w, Garlic in soy sauce.

2008, Aug. 20　**Litho.**　**Perf. 13¼**
4769-4772　A2138　Set of 4　5.50　3.25
4772a　　Booklet pane of 4, #4769-4772　5.50　—
　　Complete booklet, #4772a　5.50

A2139

Songun Revolutionary
Leadership — A2140

2008, Aug. 25
4773 A2139 12w multi   .25   .25
Souvenir Sheet
4774 A2140 135w multi   2.25 1.25

Miniature Sheet

Koguryo Tombs UNESCO World
Heritage Site — A2141

No. 4775 — Anak Tomb No. 3 paintings: a,
3w, Mask dance (60x42mm). b, 90w,
Janghaedok, aide to King Kogukwon
(30x42mm). c, 120w, Garage (60x42mm). d,
155w, Stable (60x42mm).

2008, Sept. 2   Litho.   Perf. 13¼
4775 A2141 Sheet of 4, #a-d, +
             label   5.50 3.25
  e.   Booklet pane of 4, #4775a-
       4775d   5.50   —
       Complete booklet, #4775e 5.50

A2142

Flag
A2143

2008, Sept. 9   Perf. 11½
4776 A2142 3w multi   .40   .25
4777 A2143 155w multi   2.50 1.50
            See No. 4876.

A2144

Creation of North Korea, 60th
Anniv. — A2145

Designs: 3w, Chollima Statue, flag of North
Korea, city and flowers. 12w, Torch, flag of the
Supreme Commander, people. 70w, Soldiers.
120w, People on horses. 160w, Handshake.
155w, Creation of National Flag and Arms.

2008, Sept. 9   Perf. 13¼
4778-4782 A2144 Set of 5   5.50 3.50
Souvenir Sheet
4783 A2145 155w multi   2.50 1.25

Transportation — A2146

Designs: No. 4784, 680w, Niña, ship of
Christopher Columbus. No. 4785, 680w, 1910
Russian steam engine. No. 4786, 680w, Hindenburg over Lake Constance. No. 4787,
680w, Siberian husky dog sled team. No.
4788, 680w, Ivan Basso, cyclist. No. 4789,
680w, Mercedes-Benz-Mets LF 16 fire truck.
No. 4790, 680w, Two Ferrari Enzos. No. 4791,
680w, Eurostar train. No. 4792, 680w, Concorde. No. 4793, 680w, Laika the dog and
Sputnik 2.

2008, Sept. 15   Perf.
4784-4793 A2146 Set of
             10   160.00 125.00
   Nos. 4784-4793 each were printed in sheets
of 2.

Souvenir Sheet

Salvelinus Malma — A2147

2008, Oct. 2   Litho.   Perf. 13¼
4794 A2147 135w multi   1.90   .95

Miniature Sheet

Moran Hill, Pyongyang — A2148

No. 4795: a, 3w, Small shelter and bridge.
b, 45w, Large shelter and walkway. c, 100w,
Flora with small shelter, bridges and Pyongyang in distance. d, 135w, Building with steps.

2008, Oct. 20
4795 A2148 Sheet of 4, #a-d   4.25 2.50

Introduction of Compulsory Secondary
Education, 50th Anniv. — A2149

2008, Nov. 1
4796 A2149 12w multi   .40   .25

Soldier
and
Flag
A2150

Woman
in Bean
Field
A2151

2008, Nov. 17
4797 A2150 12w multi   .30   .25
4798 A2151 85w multi   1.25   .60

Furniture
A2152

Designs: 50w, Haeju table. 70w, Inkstone
table. 120w, Dressing table with drawer. 170w,
Jewel box.

2008, Dec. 3
4799-4802 A2152 Set of 4   5.75 3.00
  4802a   Booklet pane of 4, #4799-
           4802   5.75   —
           Complete booklet, #4802a 5.75

Souvenir Sheet

Ulmil Pavilion, Moran Hill,
Pyongyang — A2153

**Litho. With Three-Dimensional
Plastic Affixed**
2008, Dec. 15   Perf. 13¼
Without Gum
4803 A2153 85w multi   2.00 1.00

New Year
2009
A2154

2009, Jan. 1   Litho.   Perf. 11½
4804 A2154 3w multi   .40   .25
   For surcharge, see No. 4877D.

A2155

Red Guards, 50th Anniv. — A2156

2009, Jan. 14   Perf. 11¾
4805 A2155 12w multi   .40   .25
Souvenir Sheet
4806 A2156 160w multi   2.50 1.60

Traditional Games — A2157

Designs: 3w, Tug-of-war. 120w, Knee
fighting.

2009, Jan. 25   Perf. 13¼
4807-4808 A2157 Set of 2   2.00 1.25

Kim Jong Il,
67th
Birthday
A2158

Unnamed butterfly and flowers: 3w, Crinum bracteatum. 12w, Begonia. 120w, Callistemon phoeniceus. 160w, Plumeria rubra.

2009, Feb. 16   **Perf. 11¾**
4809-4812 A2158   Set of 4   4.50 2.50

Souvenir Sheet

Proclamation of Juche Model for Society, 50th Anniv. — A2159

2009, Feb. 19   **Perf. 11½x12**
4813 A2159 170w multi   2.75 1.50

Souvenir Sheets

A2160

A2161

A2162

Joint Editorials of State Newspapers — A2163

No. 4814: a, 3w, Torch, Chollima statue. b, 170w, Symbols of industry and transportation.
No. 4815: a, 12w, Food crops, canned foods, city. b, 150w, Musical instruments, sheet music, orchestra, soccer players.
No. 4816: a, 30w, Soldiers, flag, ships, airplanes and missiles. b, 120w, Soldiers, flags, city.
No. 4817: a, 80w, Map of Korea, text. b, 100w, Hands crushing bomb.

2009, Feb. 22   **Perf. 11½**
4814 A2160   Sheet of 2, #a-b,
    + 2 labels   2.75 1.75
4815 A2161   Sheet of 2, #a-b,
    + 2 labels   2.50 1.50
4816 A2162   Sheet of 2, #a-b,
    + 2 labels   2.25 1.50
4817 A2163   Sheet of 2, #a-b,
    + 2 labels   2.75 1.75
    Nos. 4814-4817 (4)   10.25 6.50

For surcharge, see No. 4877E.

Souvenir Sheets

China 2009 World Stamp Exhibition, Luoyang — A2164

No. 4818: a, 3w, Flowers. b, 100w, Flowers, diff.
No. 4819: a, 12w, Statue of horse. b, 90w, Building, steps, sculpture.

2009, Feb. 25   **Perf. 11¾**
    Sheets of 2, #a-b
4818-4819 A2164   Set of 2   4.50 2.00
4819c   Booklet pane of 4, #4818a-
    4818b, 4819a-4819b   4.50 —
    Complete booklet, #4819c   4.50

March 1 Uprising Against Japan, 90th Anniv. — A2165

2009, Mar. 1   **Perf. 12¼x11¾**
4820 A2165 90w multi   1.50 1.00

Intl. Women's Day, Cent. — A2166

2009, Mar. 8   **Perf. 13¼**
4821 A2166 35w multi   .50 .30

Gifts to Kim Il Sung — A2167

Designs: 3w, Painting of horses. 12w, Fossil fish. 140w, Rifle. 150w, Bear skin.

2009, Apr. 15   **Perf. 13¼**
4822-4825 A2167   Set of 4   4.75 3.00
4825a   Booklet pane of 4, #4822-
    4825   4.75 —
    Complete booklet, #4825a   4.75

Complete booklet sold for 322w.

Central Zoo, Pyongyang, 50th Anniv. A2168

Birds: 12w, Anthropoides paradisea. 70w, Accipiter gentilis. 120w, Larus argentatus. 140w, Balearica pavonina.

2009, Apr. 30   **Perf. 11¾x12¼**
4826-4829 A2168   Set of 4   5.25 3.25
4829a   Booklet pane of 4, #4826-
    4829   5.25 —
    Complete booklet, #4829a   5.25

Central Botanical Garden, Pyongyang, 50th Anniv. A2169

Trees: 3w, Catalpa ovata. 50w, Betula platyphylla. 120w, Juglans cordiformis. 160w, Metasequoia glyptostroboides.

2009, Apr. 30   **Perf. 13¼**
4830-4833 A2169   Set of 4   5.25 3.25
4833a   Booklet pane of 4, #4830-
    4833   5.25 —
    Complete booklet, #4833a   5.25
Complete booklet sold for 350w.

Sports A2170

Designs: 12w, Baseball. 90w, Bowling. 160w, Fencing. 200w, Golf.

2009, May 2
4834-4837 A2170   Set of 4   6.75 3.25
4837a   Booklet pane of 4, #4834-
    4837   6.75 —
    Complete booklet, #4837a   6.75

No. 4189a Surcharged in Gold

No. 4838: a, 20w on 40ch, LZ1. b, 40w on 80ch, LZ120. c, 1w+109w on 1.20w, Zeppelin NT. d, 2w+168w on 2.40w, Zeppelin NT, diff.

Method and Perf As Before
2009, May 5
4838 A1852   Sheet of 4, #a-d   5.25 3.25

Naposta '09 and IBRA '09, Essen, Germany. On Nos. 4838c and 4838d, the obliterator covers the part of the original denomination expressed in chon.

Children's Union Camp A2171

Children: 3w, Mountaineering. 80w, Collecting butterflies. 120w, At campfire. 170w, At beach.

2009   **Litho.**   **Perf. 11½**
4839-4842 A2171   Set of 4   5.75 3.25
4842a   Booklet pane of 4, #4839-
    4842   5.75 —
    Complete booklet #4842a   5.75
4842b   Souvenir sheet of 4,
    #4839-4842   5.75 3.25

Issued: Nos. 4839-4842, 4842a, 5/6; No. 4842b, 5/14. Hong Kong 2009 Intl. Stamp Exhibition (No. 4842b).

Souvenir Sheet

Battle of Musan, 70th Anniv. — A2172

2009, May 22   **Perf. 13¼**
4843 A2172 120w multi   2.50 1.25

Miniature Sheet

Kim Jong Il as Member of Central Committee of Workers' Party, 45th Anniv. — A2173

No. 4844 — Kim Jong Il: a, 3w, At desk. b, 12w, At machine shop. c, 120w, Wearing white lab jacket. d, 170w, Looking inside cooking pot.

2009, June 19   **Perf. 11¾**
4844 A2173   Sheet of 4, #a-d   5.00 3.00

Universal Postal Union, 135th Anniv. — A2174

2009, June 20   **Perf. 13¼**
4845 A2174 50w multi   .90 .50

Insects A2175

Designs: 50w, Vespa mandarinia, rose. 90w, Cicindela japonica, dandelion. 120w, Locusta migratoria, plant. 140w, Aphaenogaster famelica, mushroom.

2009, July 1   **Perf. 11½**
4846-4849 A2175   Set of 4   6.00   4.00
4849a   Booklet pane of 4, #4846-
      4849   6.00   —
      Complete booklet, #4849a   6.00

Okryu Restaurant,
Pyongyang — A2176

Renovated Pyongyang
Buildings — A2177

No. 4851: a, 3w, Kim Chaek University
Library (35x28mm). b, 70w, Taedongmun Theater (35x28mm). c, 90w, Chongryu Restaurant
(70x28mm). d, 150w, Pyongyang Grand Theater (70x28mm).

2009, July 2   **Perf. 13¼**
4850 A2176   12w multi   .30   .25
         Perf. 11½
4851 A2177   Sheet of 4, #a-d   4.75   2.75

Miniature Sheet

Eternal Sun of Juche — A2178

No. 4852 — Paintings: a, 12w, The Great
Leader Kim Il Sung Drawing the Brush Into
Our Party's Emblem. b, 50w, First Military
Flag. c, 70w, Birth. d, 140w, Every Field With
Bumper Harvest.

2009, July 8   **Perf. 13¼**
4852 A2178   Sheet of 4, #a-d   4.50   2.75

Nurse and
Child
A2179

Ambulance and Hospital — A2180

2009, July 25
4853 A2179   12w multi   .30   .25
4854 A2180   150w multi   2.25   1.50

Souvenir Sheet

Launch of Kwangmyongsong 2
Rocket — A2181

2009, July 27   **Perf. 11½x12**
4855 A2181   120w multi   2.25   1.25

Souvenir Sheet

Northern Area Victory Monument,
Hamgyong Province — A2182

2009, Aug. 3   **Perf. 13¼**
4856 A2182   120w multi   2.25   1.25

Musical
Instruments
A2183

Designs: 12w, Saenap. 80w, Drum. 140w,
Sogoghu. 170w, Flute.

2009, Aug. 5   **Litho.**
4857-4860 A2183   Set of 4   5.75   3.00

150-Day Innovation
Campaign — A2184

2009, Aug. 10
4861 A2184   12w multi   .30   .25

Fish
A2185

Ships and: 15w, Theragra chalcogramma.
60w, Cyprinus carpio. 140w, Euthynnus
pelamis. 160w, Mugil cephalus.

2009, Sept. 1
4862-4865 A2185   Set of 4   5.50   3.25
4865a   Booklet pane of 4, #4862-
      4865   5.50
      Complete booklet, #4865a   5.50

Miniature Sheets

Intl. Year of Astronomy — A2186

No. 4866, 95w: a, Chollima Statue, solar
eclipse. b, Galileo Galilei, telescope, planets,
satellite.
No. 4867, 95w: a, Rabbits, solar eclipse. b,
Planets, galaxy.
No. 4868, 95w: a, Dogs, total solar eclipse.
b, Chomsongdae Observatory.

2009, Aug. 29   **Litho.**   **Perf. 13½**
   Sheets of 2, #a-b, + 2 Labels
4866-4868 A2186   Set of 3   8.00   6.00
4868c   Souvenir sheet of 1, #4868a   1.25   .80
4868d   Booklet pane of 6, #4866a-
      4866b, 4867a-4867b, 4868a-
      4868b   8.00
      Complete booklet, #4868d   8.00

Souvenir Sheets

A2187

Year of Friendship With People's
Republic of China — A2188

No. 4869: a, #3287c, 3384, 3716. b, #3563,
4374b, 4473c.
No. 4870: a, Five stamps. b, Six stamps.

2009, Sept. 2   **Perf. 13½**
4869 A2187   60w Sheet of 2, #a-b 2.00   1.00
4870 A2188   60w Sheet of 2, #a-b 2.00   1.00

Miniature Sheet

Birdpex 2010, Antwerp,
Belgium — A2189

No. 4871: a, 12w, Coturnicops exquisitus. b,
90w, Porzana pusilla. c, 170w, Porzana fusca.

2009, Sept. 12   **Perf. 11½**
4871 A2189   Sheet of 5,
      #4871c, 2 each
      #4871a-4871b, +
      label   5.25   2.60
d.   Booklet pane of 3, #4871a-
      4871c   4.00
      Complete booklet, #4871d   4.00

Souvenir Sheet

Intl. Red Cross and Red Crescent
Year — A2190

No. 4872 — Flags of Red Cross, North
Korea and: a, 75w, Jean-Henri Dunant,
founder of Red Cross. b, 95w, Disaster risk
reduction. c, 95w, First aid.

2009, Sept. 21   **Perf. 13½**
4872 A2190   Sheet of 3, #a-c   3.75   1.90

Souvenir Sheet

Kim Jong Suk (1917-49), Mother of
Kim Jong II — A2191

No. 4873: a, 90w, Portrait (33x45mm). b,
100w, Kim Jong Suk with troops, horiz.
(57x36mm).

2009, Sept. 22
4873 A2191   Sheet of 2, #a-b   2.75   1.40

Miniature Sheet

People's Republic of China, 60th
Anniv. — A2192

No. 4874: a, 10w, Chinese President Hu
Jintao. b, 67w, Chinese astronauts. c, 67w,
National Stadium, Beijing. d, 84w, National
Grand Theater, Beijing.

2009, Oct. 1
4874 A2192   Sheet of 4, #a-d   3.50   2.00

Worldwide Fund for Nature
(WWF) — A2193

No. 4875 — Platalea minor and: a, Snail. b,
Fish. c, Crab. d, Shrimp.

2009, Oct. 5   **Perf. 13½**
4875   Horiz. strip of 4   5.50   2.75
a.   A2193 3w multi   .25   .25
b.   A2193 12w multi   .25   .25
c.   A2193 99w multi   1.40   .70

d.	A2193 266w multi	3.75	1.90
e.	Sheet of 8, 2 each #4875a-4875d, + label	11.00	5.50

Flag and Torch Types of 2002-08

2009, Oct. 15   Litho.   Perf. 11½
4876   A2142   10w multi   .25   .25

Perf. 13¼
4877   A1890   30w multi   .45   .25

Nos. 4249, 4252, 4343, 4730, 4804 and 4814a Surcharged

Methods and Perfs As Before

2009, Oct.
4877A	A1887	10w on 3w #4249	.95	.95
4877B	A1939	10w on 3w #4343	.95	.95
4877C	A1886	10w on 3w #4730	.95	.95
4877D	A2154	10w on 3w #4804	.95	.95
4877E	A2160	10w on 3w #4814a	.95	.95
4877F	A1890	30w on 12w #4252	3.00	3.00
	Nos. 4877A-4877F (6)		7.75	7.75

Reptiles — A2194

Designs: 15w, Chamaeleo jacksonii. 50w, Naja naja. 110w, Caretta caretta, horiz. 160w, Crocodylus niloticus, horiz.

2009, Oct. 20
4878-4881	A2194	Set of 4	4.75	2.40
4881a		Booklet pane of 4, #4878-4881	4.75	—
		Complete booklet, #4881a	4.75	

Miniature Sheets

Lighthouses — A2195

No. 4882: a, Cape Palliser Lighthouse, New Zealand, and Sousa chinensis. b, Tater Du Lighthouse, United Kingdom, and Mary Rose. c, Hornby Lighthouse, Australia, and Passat, Germany. d, Rubjerg Knude Lighthouse, Denmark, and Wappen von Hamburg.

No. 4883: a, Bengtskär Lighthouse, Finland, and Phoebastria albatrus. b, Fanad Lighthouse, Ireland, and Bolma rugosa. c, Cordouan Lighthouse, France, and Sterna fuscata. d, Brandaris Lighthouse, Netherlands, and Pleurotomaria africana.

No. 4884: a, Cape St. Vincent Lighthouse, Portugal, and Sula bassana. b, Europa Point Lighthouse, Gibraltar, and Lambis scorpio. c, Vorontsov Lighthouse, Ukraine, and Grampus griseus. d, Gelendzhik Lighthouse, Russia, and Gibbula magus.

No. 4885: a, Hoy High Lighthouse, Scotland, and Delphinus delphis. b, Lindesnes Lighthouse, Norway, and Stenella coeruleoalba. c, Reykjanesviti Lighthouse, Iceland, and Chlamys varia. d, Seal Point Lighthouse, South Africa, and Chroicocephalus ridibundus.

2009, Oct. 24   Litho.   Perf. 13x13½
4882	A2195	760w Sheet of 4, #a-d	42.50	42.50
e.		Souvenir sheet of 2 #4882a	21.00	21.00
f.		Souvenir sheet of 2 #4882b	21.00	21.00
g.		Souvenir sheet of 2 #4882c	21.00	21.00
h.		Souvenir sheet of 2 #4882d	21.00	21.00

4883	A2195	760w Sheet of 4, #a-d	42.50	42.50
e.		Souvenir sheet of 2 #4883a	21.00	21.00
f.		Souvenir sheet of 2 #4883b	21.00	21.00
g.		Souvenir sheet of 2 #4883c	21.00	21.00
h.		Souvenir sheet of 2 #4883d	21.00	21.00
4884	A2195	760w Sheet of 4, #a-d	42.50	42.50
e.		Souvenir sheet of 2 #4884a	21.00	21.00
f.		Souvenir sheet of 2 #4884b	21.00	21.00
g.		Souvenir sheet of 2 #4884c	21.00	21.00
h.		Souvenir sheet of 2 #4884d	21.00	21.00
4885	A2195	760w Sheet of 4, #a-d	42.50	42.50
e.		Souvenir sheet of 2 #4885a	21.00	21.00
f.		Souvenir sheet of 2 #4885b	21.00	21.00
g.		Souvenir sheet of 2 #4885c	21.00	21.00
h.		Souvenir sheet of 2 #4885d	21.00	21.00

Souvenir Sheet

Repatriation of Korean Nationals in Japan, 50th Anniv. — A2196

2009, Dec. 16   Litho.   Perf. 11½x12
4887   A2196   160w multi   2.25   1.10

Miniature Sheet

End of Juche 98 — A2197

No. 4888: a, 10w, Launch of Kwangmyongsong No. 2 satellite. b, 20w, CNC machine tool industry. c, 20w, Oxygen separator, finished steel products, train and vehicles. d, 30w, Construction vehicles. e, 50w, Namhung Gasification Project, crane with pipe. f, 50w, Apartment buildings on Mansudae Street, Pyongyang. g, 57w, Sturgeons, ostriches, chicken, pig. h, 70w, Apples, farm, Migok-ri model village. i, 80w, Audience, soccer players, singer.

2009, Dec. 31   Litho.   Perf. 13½
4888   A2197   Sheet of 9, #a-i   5.50   2.75

Souvenir Sheet

Kim Jong Il and Workers — A2198

2009, Dec. 31   Litho.   Perf. 13¼
4889   A2198   100w multi   1.40   .70

End of Juche 98.

New Year 2010
A2199

2010, Jan. 1   Perf. 13¼
4890   A2199   10w multi   .25   .25

Tigers A2200

Tiger and: 30w, Sun. 67w, Tree. 171w, Tiger and cubs, horiz.

2010, Jan. 5   Litho.   Perf. 11¾x12¼
4891-4892	A2200	Set of 2	1.40	.70
4892a		Booklet pane of 4, 2 each #4891-4892	3.00	—
		Complete booklet, #4892a	3.00	

Souvenir Sheet
Litho. with Three-Dimensional Plastic Affixed
Perf. 13¼
Without Gum

4893   A2200   171w multi   2.40   1.25

Complete booklet sold for 213w. No. 4893 contains one 60x42mm stamp.

Wildlife A2201

Designs: 35w, Ailuropoda melanoleuca. 60w, Aix galericulata. 80w, Lagenorhynchus obliquidens. 110w, Panthera pardus.

2010, Jan. 30   Litho.   Perf. 13¼
4894-4897	A2201	Set of 4	4.00	2.00
4897a		Booklet pane of 4, #4894-4897	9.00	—
		Complete booklet, #4897a	9.00	

Complete booklet sold for 304w.

Miniature Sheet

2010 Winter Olympics, Vancouver — A2202

No. 4898: a, 10w, Ice hockey. b, 40w, Figure skating. c, 50w, Speed skating. d, 70w, Skiing.

2010, Feb. 1   Perf. 13
4898   A2202   Sheet of 8, 2 each #a-d   4.75   4.75
See No. 4919.

Kim Jong Il, 68th Birthday — A2203

No. 4899: a, 10w, Impatiens sultanii Royal Rose. b, 50w, Gazania hybrida. c, 70w, Paeonia suffructicosa. d, 110w, Bougainvillea glabra Sanderiana.

2010, Feb. 16   Perf. 11½
4899	A2203	Vert. strip or block of 4, #a-d, + 8 labels	3.50	1.75
e.		Booklet pane of 4, #4899a-4899d, + 8 labels	3.75	—
		Complete booklet, #4899e	3.75	

Complete booklet sold for 259w.

Miniature Sheet

Joint Editorials of State Newspapers — A2204

No. 4900: a, 10w, People, soldier, Party Founding Monument, flowers. b, 20w, Woman, city, manufactured items. c, 30w, Woman carrying crops, vegetables. d, 57w, Worker, factory, train, dam. e, 67w, Soldiers. f, 95w, People holding flag showing mpa of unified Korea. g, 125w, Doves, map showing unified Korea.

2010, Feb. 20   Perf. 13¼
4900   A2204   Sheet of 7, #a-g, + 2 labels   5.75   3.00

A2205

Anti-Imperialism Posters A2206

2010, Mar. 5
4901	A2205	76w multi	1.10	.55
4902	A2206	95w multi	1.40	.70

Cats
A2207

Designs: 10w, Cat, chicks. 70w, Cats, flower, butterfly. 133w, Cat, mouse. 170w, Cat, kittens, ball of yarn.

2010, Mar. 25		Perf. 11½	
4903-4906	A2207	Set of 4	5.50	2.75
4906a		Booklet pane of 4, #4903-4906	5.75	
		Complete booklet, #4906a	5.75	

Complete booklet sold for 402w.

Souvenir Sheet

Birds — A2208

No. 4907: a, 30w, Brachyramphus perdix. b, 125w, Gallinago solitaria. c, 133w, Porzana paykullii.

2010, Apr. 9			
4907	A2208	Sheet of 3, #a-c, + 3 labels	4.00	2.00
d.		Booklet pane of 3, #4907a-4907c	4.25	—
		Complete booklet, #4907d	4.25	

Antverpia 2010 International Philatelic Exhibition, Antwerp. Complete booklet sold for 307w.

Gifts to Kim Il Sung
A2209

Designs: 10w, Eagle figurine. 30w, Crane figurine. 95w, Tiger painting. 152w, Sea turtle figurine, horiz.

2010, Apr. 15			Perf. 13¼
4908-4911	A2209	Set of 4	4.00	2.00

Orchids and Insects
A2210

Designs: 30w, Sophronitella brevipendunculata, bee. 80w, Epidendrum radiatum, dragonfly. 120w, Cymbidium Lillian Stewart "Red Carpet," bee. 152w Dendrobium hybrid, butterfly.

2010, Apr. 20			Perf. 11½
4912-4915	A2210	Set of 4	5.50	2.75
4915a		Booklet pane of 4, #4912-4915	5.75	
		Complete booklet, #4915a	5.75	

Nos. 4912-4915 each were printed in sheets of 5 + label. Complete booklet sold for 401w.

Souvenir Sheet

Expo 2010, Shanghai — A2211

No. 4916: a, 10w, Chollima statue, city, flowers. b, 80w, Children watering plant, wind turbines, wildlife.

2010, May 1			Litho.
4916	A2211	Sheet of 2, #a-b, + 2 labels	1.25	.65

Miniature Sheet

Table Tennis — A2212

No. 4917: a, 10w, Man with green shirt. b, 30w, Woman with red shirt. c, 95w, Woman with blue shirt. d, 152w, Man with pink shirt.

2010, May 10			Perf.
4917	A2212	Sheet of 4, #a-d	4.00	2.00
e.		Booklet pane of 4, #4917a-4917d	4.25	—
		Complete booklet, #4917e	4.25	

Complete booklet sold for 306w.

Joint Slogans — A2213

2010, May 12			Perf. 11½
4918	A2213	10w multi	.25	.25

No. 4898 With Flags of Countries Winning Depicted Events Added at Left of Athlete
Miniature Sheet

No. 4919: a, 10w, Ice hockey, flag of Canada. b, 40w, Figure skating, flag of People's Republic of China. c, 50w, Speed skating, flag of Netherlands. d, 50w, Speed skating, flag of Czech Republic. e, 70w, Skiing, flag of Italy. f, 70w, Skiing, flag of Germany.

2010, May 25			Perf. 13
4919	A2202	Sheet of 8, #4919c-4919f, 2 each #4919a-4919b	4.75	4.75

Souvenir Sheet

Dinosaurs — A2214

No. 4920: a, 10w, Brontosaurus. b, 125w, Allosaurus. c, 152w, Pterodactylus.

2010, June 16			Perf. 12¾
4920	A2214	Sheet of 3, #a-c, + label	4.00	2.00
d.		Booklet pane of 3, #4920a-4920c	4.25	—
		Complete booklet, #4920d	4.25	
e.		As #4920, with Euro-phila 2010 emblem in sheet margin	4.50	2.25

Complete booklet sold for 306w.
Issued: No. 4920e, 10/2.

2010 World Cup Soccer Championships, South Africa — A2215

No. 4921 — Shirt colors of soccer players: a, 20w, Green, yellow. b, 57w, Yellow, blue. c, 190w, Red, white. 114w, Yellow, white.

2010, May 31			Perf. 13¼
4921	A2215	Sheet of 3, #a-c, + 3 labels	3.75	1.90
		Souvenir Sheet		
4922	A2215	114w multi	1.60	.80
a.		Booklet pane of 4, #4921a-4921c, 4922	5.75	—
		Complete booklet, #4922a	5.75	

Complete booklet sold for 400w.

Souvenir Sheet

Intl. Children's Day, 60th Anniv. — A2216

2010, June 1			Perf. 11¾
4923	A2216	95w multi	1.40	.70
a.		As #4923, with Bangkok 2010 emblem in sheet margin	1.40	.70

Issued: No. 4923a, 8/4.

Joint Declaration of June 15, 2000 on Reunification of Korea — A2217

2010, June 15			Perf. 13¼
4924	A2217	190w multi	2.75	1.40

A2218

A2219

A2220

Visit of Kim Jong Il to People's Republic of China — A2221

No. 4925 — Kim Jong Il: a, 20w, And Chinese man pointing. b, 40w, Pointing. c, 67w, Walking.
No. 4926 — Kim Jong Il: a, 20w, Standing next to woman. b, 35w, With leg raised. c, 80w, Looking through window.
No. 4927 — Kim Jong Il: a, 30w, Standing next to Chinese Pres. Hu Jintao. b, 40w, Seated at table with Pres. Hu. c, 70w, Shaking hands with Pres. Hu.
60w, Kim Jong Il and Pres. Hu.

2010, June 20			Perf. 13¼
4925	A2218	Sheet of 3, #a-c, + 6 labels	1.75	.90
4926	A2219	Sheet of 3, #a-c, + 6 labels	1.90	.95
4927	A2220	Sheet of 3, #a-c, + 3 labels	2.00	1.00
Nos. 4925-4927 (3)			5.65	2.85
		Souvenir Sheet		
		Perf. 11½x12		
4928	A2221	60w multi	.85	.40

Miniature Sheet

Children's Animated Films — A2222

No. 4929 — Scenes from children's animated films: a, 10w, Butterfly and Cock. b, 30w, A Clever Raccoon Dog. c, 95w, A Hedgehog Defeats a Tiger. d, 133w, Regret of Rabbit.

2010, June 30   **Perf. 13¼**
4929 A2222   Sheet of 4, #a-d   3.75   1.90

Souvenir Sheet

Azaleas — A2223

2010, July 1   **Litho.**
4930 A2223   85w multi   1.25   .60

Souvenir Sheet

National Anthem — A2224

2010, July 5   **Perf. 13½**
4931 A2224   50w black   .70   .35

A2225

Liberation of Korea, 65th Anniv. — A2226

No. 4932 — Paintings: a, 10w, The Great Leader Forming the Korean Revolutionary Army. b, 15w, Bloody and Long Anti-Japanese War. c, 20w, The Azalea in the Fatherland. d, 40w, Pyongyang in New Spring. e, 100w, Historical That Night.
60w, February Festival on the Eve of Korea's Liberation.

2010, Aug. 15   **Perf. 13¼**
4932 A2225   Sheet of 5, #a-e, + label   2.60   1.40

Souvenir Sheet

4933 A2226   60w multi   .85   .40

A2227

A2228

Start of Songun Revolutionary Leadership, 50th Anniv. — A2229

No. 4935 — Paintings: a, 15w, General Kim Jong Il Instilling the Traditions of Mt. Paektu in the Soldiers (63x41mm). b, 30w, Military Song of Victory (50x38mm). c, 55w, General to the Frontline, Children to the Camp (50x38mm). d, 80w, Saying He Feels Happiest Among the Soldiers (50x38mm).
70w, Blizzard on Mt. Paektu.

2010, Aug. 25   **Perf. 11½**
4934 A2227   10w multi   .25   .25
    Perf. 12x11½ (#4935a), 11¾
4935 A2228   Sheet of 4, #a-d   2.50   1.25
    Souvenir Sheet
    Perf. 11¾
4936 A2229   70w multi   1.00   .50

Souvenir Sheet

Diplomatic Relations Between North Korea and Cuba, 50th Anniv. — A2230

2010, Aug. 29   **Litho.**   **Perf. 11¾**
4937 A2230   85w multi   1.40   .70

Paintings A2231

Designs: 15w, Pine Tree and Hawk, by Sin Yun Bok. 35w, Waves of Ongchon, by Jong Son. 70w, Reeds and Wild Geese, by Jo Sok Jin. 100w, After Picking Medicinal Herbs, by Kim Hong Do.

2010, Sept. 1   **Litho.**   **Perf. 13¼**
4938-4941 A2231   Set of 4   3.25   1.60
4941a   Booklet pane of 4, #4938-4941   3.25   —
    Complete booklet, #4941a   3.25

A2232

A2233

A2234

A2235

A2236

A2237

Pres. Kim Il Sung (1912-94) — A2238

No. 4942: a, 20w, Kim Il Sung being educated by father. b, 55w, Kim Il Sung being educated by mother.
No. 4943: a, 25w, Kim Jong Suk defending Kim Il Sung (64x42mm). b, 30w, Kim Il Sung at secret camp on Mt. Paektu (45x35mm). c, 45w, Kim Il Sung on horseback leading other riders (454x35mm).
No. 4944: a, 10w, Kim Il Sung crossing Amnok River in winter. b, 30w, Kim Il Sung leading protest against Jilin-Hoeryong railway. c, 40w, Kim Il Sung reporting at Youth League meeting. d, 55w, Kang Pan Sok handing over pistols to Kim Il Sung.
No. 4945: a, 20w, Gunshot of Pochonbo. b, 30w, Kim Il Sung burning Minsaengdan documents. c, 40w, Kim Il Sung with members of children's corps. d, 45w, Kim Il Sung leading soldiers.
No. 4946: a, 10w, Kim Il Sung speaking to Anti-Japanese People's Guerilla Army. b, 20w, Kim Il Sung with people after establishing People's Revolutionary Government. c, 35w, Kim Il Sung leading soldiers, diff. d, 90w, Kim Il Sung founding Association for the Restoration of the Fatherland.
50w, Kim Il Sung at podium giving speech. 60w, Kim Il Sung leading solders, diff.

    Perf. 13¼, 12x11½ (#4943a)
2010, Sept. 5   **Litho.**
4942 A2232   Sheet of 2, #a-b, + label   1.25   .60
4943 A2233   Sheet of 3, #a-c, + label   1.60   .80
4944 A2234   Sheet of 4, #a-d   2.10   1.10
4945 A2235   Sheet of 4, #a-d   2.10   1.10
4946 A2236   Sheet of 4, #a-d   2.40   1.25
    Nos. 4942-4946 (5)   9.45   4.85
    Souvenir Sheets
    Perf. 11¾
4947 A2237   50w multi   .80   .40
4948 A2238   60w multi   .95   .45

Expo 2010, Shanghai A2239

2010, Sept. 6   **Litho.**   **Perf. 11½**
4949 A2239   25w multi   .35   .25

No. 4949 was printed in sheets of 6 + 9 labels.

A2240

Entry of Chinese People's Volunteer Army Into Korean War, 60th Anniv. — A2241

Designs: 25w, Chinese soldier and Korean woman.
No. 4951: a, 10w, Meeting to decide on the entry of Chinese Volunteer Army into the Korean War, by Gao Quan. (60x42mm). b, 15w, North Korean and Chinese soldiers fighting together (30x42mm). c, For the Peace sculpture (60x42mm). d, Korean children with doves (30x42mm).

2010, Sept. 10   **Litho.**   **Perf. 13¼**
4950 A2240   25w multi   .40   .25
4951 A2241   Sheet of 4, #a-d, + 2 labels   1.10   .55

A2242

A2243

Worker's Party of Korea, 65th
Anniv. — A2244

Designs: 10w, Flag of Worker's Party.
No. 4953 — Kim Il Sung: a, 20w, On naval
vessel. b, 25w, At rail yard. c, 50w, With farmers. d, 50w, At technology display. e, 60w,
With fabric vendor.
70w, Kim Il Sung with party flag.

2010, Oct. 10　Litho.　Perf. 11¾
4952　A2242　10w multi　　.25　.25
4953　A2243　Sheet of 6, #4952,
　　　　　4953a-4953e　3.25　1.60
Souvenir Sheet
Perf. 13½
4954　A2244　70w multi　　1.00　.50

A2245

Visit of Kim Jong Il to People's
Republic of China — A2246

Designs: No. 4955, Kim Jong Il shaking
hands with Chinese Pres. Hu Jintao.
No. 4956 — Kim Jong Il: a, 30w, Signing
guestbook at Julin Middle School. b, 42w,
Inspecting railway coach. c, 70w, Holding bottle at food processing plant.

2010, Oct. 28　Litho.　Perf. 11½x12
4955　A2245　70w multi　　1.10　.55
Perf. 11½
4956　A2246　Sheet of 3, #a-c, +
　　　　　5 labels　2.25　1.10

Conference of
Worker's Party
of Korea,
Pyongyang
A2247

2010, Oct. 30　　　Perf. 13¼
4957　A2247　30w multi　　.50　.25

New
Year
2011
(Juche
100)
A2248

2011, Jan. 1　　　Litho.
4958　A2248　10w multi　　.25　.25

Souvenir Sheet

Year of the Rabbit — A2249

Rabbits — No. 4959: a, 70w, Two rabbits. b,
140w, Two rabbits, diff.

2011, Jan. 5　　　Perf. 11½
4959　A2249　Sheet of 2, #a-b　4.00　1.60
　c.　Booklet pane of 2, #4959a-
　　　4959b, + 2 labels　4.25　—
　　　Complete booklet, #4959c　4.25
　d.　Like #4959, with inscriptions
　　　and emblems added in
　　　sheet margin　4.50　1.60
Complete booklet sold for 224w.
Issued: No. 4959d, 3/3/12. Added inscriptions on No. 4959d are for Frimung 2012 and
Huddex 2012 Stamp Shows, Huddinge,
Sweden.

Souvenir Sheet

Indipex 2011 World Philatelic
Exhibition, New Delhi — A2250

2011, Feb. 12　　　Perf. 13¼
4960　A2250　70w multi　　1.50　.55

Zoo Animals
Given to Kim
Jong Il as
Gifts — A2251

Designs: 30w, Capra hircus. 42w,
Cercopithecus aethiops. 112w, Cebuella
pygmaea. 125w, Hystrix indica, horiz.

2011, Feb. 16　　　Perf. 11½
4961-4964　A2251　Set of 4　6.00　2.40
　4964a　Horiz. strip of 4, #4961-
　　　　4964　6.25　2.40
　4964b　Booklet pane of 4, #4961-
　　　　4964　6.25
　　　　Complete booklet, #4964b　6.50
Kim Jong Il, 69th birthday. Nos. 4961-4964
were printed in sheets of 8, containing 2 of
each stamp, + 3 labels. Complete booklet sold
for 323w.

Fourth International Martial Arts
Games, Tallinn, Estonia — A2252

No. 4965: a, 42w, Emblem. b, 56w, Karate.
c, 70w, Pankration. d, 112w, Muaythai.
No. 4966, 70w, Taekwondo.

2011, Feb. 23　　　Litho.
4965　A2252　Sheet of 4, #a-d, +
　　　　　4 labels　4.50　2.25
Souvenir Sheet
4966　A2252　70w multi + label　1.10　.55

Joint Editorials — of State
Newspapers — A2253

Red flag at upper left and: No. 4967, 10w,
Two women, three men and pink ribbon. No.
4968, 10w, Man with arm extended, symbols
of progress. 30w, Farmer holding sheaf of
wheat, train, truck, tractor and food. 70w,
Soldiers and flags. 112w, Two men and
woman punching missile, map of Korea, vert.

2011, Feb. 25　　　Perf. 13¼
4967-4971　A2253　Set of 5　5.00　1.75

Birds
A2254

Designs: 30w, Paradisaea raggiana. 42w,
Cygnus olor. 75w, Pulsatrix perspicillata.
133w, Goura victoria.

2011, Mar. 2　　　Perf. 11½
4972-4975　A2254　Set of 4　6.00　2.25
　4975a　Booklet pane of 4, #4972-
　　　　4975　6.25
　　　　Complete booklet, #4975a　6.25
Nos. 4972-4975 were printed in sheets of 8
containing 2 of each stamp + 4 labels. Complete booklet sold for 294w.

Flag of North Korea, Magnolia
Flowers, North Korea No. 4 — A2255

2011, Mar. 12　　　Perf. 13¼
4976　A2255　30w multi　　.60　.25
First North Korean postage stamps, 65th
anniv.

Miniature Sheets

A2256

Treaty on Friendship Between North
Korea and People's Republic of China,
50th Anniv. — A2257

No. 4977: a, Mao Zedong at microphones
proclaiming foundation of People's Republic of
China, fireworks (30x42mm). b, Mao Zedong
and Pres. Kim Il Sung shaking hands, 1975
(54x45mm). c, Mao Zedong at microphone
holding Chinese coat of arms (30x42mm). d,
Mao Zedong at microphone in front of crowd
(56x38mm). e, Mao Zedong in front of Chinese flag (28x38mm). f, Mao Zedong and
Deng Xiaoping shaking hands (56x38mm).
No. 4978: a, Mao Zedong and Pend Dehuai,
wearing cap (45x33mm). b, Mao Zedong and
Pres. Kim Il Sung shaking hands (36x45mm).
c, Mao Zedong and Chen Yi at table with cup
and saucer (45x33mm). d, Mao Zedong and
Liu Shaoqi, pointing (56x38mm). e, Mao
Zedong and Zhou Enlai, teapot and glasses
on table (28x38mm). f, Mao Zedong and Zhu
De clapping (56x38mm).

**Perf. 13¼ (#4977a-4977c, 4978a-
4978c), 11½**
2011, Mar. 15
4977　A2256　10w Sheet of 6, #a-f　1.25　.45
4978　A2257　10w Sheet of 6, #a-f　1.25　.45

Souvenir Sheet

Intl. Year of Volunteers — A2258

No. 4979 — Red Cross and: a, 30w, Disaster risk reduction. b, 42w, Promotion activities. c, Emergency relief activities.

2011, Mar. 31 Litho. **Perf. 13¼**
4979 A2258 Sheet of 3, #a-c, +
2 labels 3.00 1.10

Apples on Branch A2259

Kim Il Sung at Fruit Orchard — A2260

2011, Apr. 7 **Perf. 12**
4980 A2259 30w multi .50 .25
Souvenir Sheet
Perf. 11¾
4981 A2260 70w multi 1.50 .55

Pukchong Enlarged Meeting of the Presidium of the Central Committee of the Workers' Party of Korea, 50th anniv.

Flowers — A2261

No. 4982: a, 30w, Kimilsungia. b, 42w, Callistephus chinensis. c, 70w, Iris ensata var. hortensis. d, 98w, Rosa hybrida. e, 112w, Lilium hybridum cv. Enchantment.

2011, Apr. 15 **Perf. 13**
4982 A2261 Sheet of 5, #a-e 6.00 2.75
f. Booklet pane of 5, #4982a-
4982e 6.25 —
Complete booklet, #4982f 6.25

Birthday of Pres. Kim Il Sung. No. 4982f sold for 366w.

Sites in Pyongyang — A2262

Designs: 30w, Yonggwang Metro Station. 42w, Mangyongdae School Children's Palace. 56w, May Day Stadium. 70w, People's Palace of Culture. 84w, Arch of Triumph. 98w, State Theater. 112w, Party Founding Museum. 140w, Birthpace of Pres. Kim Il Sung.

2011, Apr. 20 **Perf. 12¼x11¾**
4983-4990 A2262 Set of 8 11.00 4.75
4990a Booklet pane of 8, #4983-
4990 11.50 —
Complete booklet, #4990a 11.50

No. 4990a sold for 646w.

Magnolia Seiboldii A2263

Flowers — A2264

No. 4992: a, 10w, Kimilsungia. b, 30w, Kimjongilia. c, 42w, Paeonia suffructicosa.

2011, Apr. 28 **Perf. 13¼**
4991 A2263 30w multi .50 .25
Souvenir Sheet
Perf.
4992 A2264 Sheet of 3, #a-c, +
3 labels 1.25 .65
d. Booklet pane of 4, #4991,
4992a-4992c 2.00 —
Complete booklet, #4992d 2.00

2011 Intl. Horticultural Exposition, Xi'an, People's Republic of China. Complete booklet sold for 126w.

Miniature Sheet

Circus Performers — A2265

No. 4993: a, 42w, Woman suspended by neck. b, 70w, Woman juggling while hanging from trapeze. c, 98w, Unicyclist, members of rope skipping act. d, 140w, Rope skipping act.

2011, May 5 **Perf.**
4993 A2265 Sheet of 4, #a-d 7.50 2.75

Souvenir Sheet

Chollima Statue, Pyongyang — A2266

2011, May 20 **Perf. 11¾x12¼**
4994 A2266 98w multi 2.00 .75

Souvenir Sheet

Apples, Taedonggang Combined Fruit Farm — A2267

2011, June 5 **Perf. 12¼x11¾**
4995 A2267 70w multi 1.50 .55

Orchids — A2268

No. 4996: a, 10w, Vanda hybrida. b, 30w, Laeliocattleya. c, 70w, Laelia gouldiana. d, 142w, Phalaenopsis.

2011, June 20 **Perf. 13¼**
4996 A2268 Block or horiz.
strip of 4, #a-d 4.00 2.00
e. Booklet pane of 4, #4996a-
4996d 4.25
Complete booklet, #4996e 4.75

No. 4996e sold for 266w.

A2269

A2270

A2271

A2272

A2273

A2274

A2275

A2276

A2277

A2278

A2279

A2280

A2281

A2282

A2283

A2284

A2285

A2286

A2287

A2288

A2289

A2290

A2291

A2292

A2293

A2294

Pres. Kim Il Sung (1912-94) — A2295

Various paintings depicting scenes in the life of Kim Il Sung.
No. 5020: a, 25w, October Morning (64x42mm). b, 30w, Kim Il Sung Drawing the Brush Into the Party's Emblem (45x36mm). c, 45w, Kim Il Sung Making Report at Inaugural Conference of the Central Organizational Committee of the Communist Party of North Korea (45x36mm).

2011, July 5   Litho.   Perf. 13½

4997	A2269	10w multi + label	.25	.25
4998	A2270	10w multi + label	.25	.25
4999	A2271	10w multi + label	.25	.25
5000	A2272	30w multi + label	.60	.25
5001	A2273	30w multi + label	.60	.25
5002	A2274	30w multi + label	.60	.25
5003	A2275	30w multi + label	.60	.25
5004	A2276	30w multi + label	.60	.25
5005	A2277	30w multi + label	.60	.25
5006	A2278	30w multi + label	.60	.25
5007	A2279	30w multi + label	.60	.25
5008	A2280	30w multi + label	.60	.25
5009	A2281	30w multi + label	.60	.25
5010	A2282	42w multi + label	.85	.30
5011	A2283	42w multi + label	.85	.30
5012	A2284	42w multi + label	.85	.30
5013	A2285	42w multi + label	.85	.30
5014	A2286	42w multi + label	.85	.30
5015	A2287	42w multi + label	.85	.30
5016	A2288	42w multi + label	.85	.30
5017	A2289	42w multi + label	.85	.30
5018	A2290	42w multi + label	.85	.30
5019	A2291	42w multi + label	.85	.30
	Nos. 4997-5019 (23)		15.25	6.25

Miniature Sheet
Perf. 12x11½ (#5020a), 13½

5020	A2292	Sheet of 3, #a-c, + label	1.50	.75

Souvenir Sheets
Perf. 13½

5021	A2293	40w multi	.75	.30

Perf. 11¾

5022	A2294	50w multi	.90	.40
5023	A2295	60w multi	1.10	.45
	Nos. 5021-5023 (3)		2.75	1.15

Souvenir Sheets

A2296

A2297

Visit of Kim Jong Il to People's Republic of China — A2298

2011, July 15   Litho.   Perf. 12¼x11¾

5024	A2296	90w multi	2.00	.70
5025	A2297	90w multi	2.00	.70

Perf. 11¾

5026	A2298	90w multi + label	1.75	.70
	Nos. 5024-5026 (3)		5.75	2.10

Intl. Year of Chemistry A2299

2011, July 29   Perf. 13½x13¼

5027	A2299	50w multi	1.00	.40

Camellias and Birds — A2300

No. 5028: a, Denomination at LL. b, Denomination at UR.

2011, July 30   Perf. 11½

5028	A2300	20w Horiz. pair, #a-b	1.50	.30

Souvenir Sheet

Intl. Year of Forests — A2301

2011, July 30   Perf. 13¼

5029	A2301	100w multi	2.00	.80

Souvenir Sheet

Diplomatic Relations Between North Korea and the European Union, 10th Anniv. — A2302

2011, Aug. 1   Perf. 12x11½

5030	A2302	140w multi	3.00	1.50

Miniature Sheet

Cacti and Insects — A2303

No. 5031: a, 30w, Gymnocalycium schuetzianum and bee. b, 70w, Rebutia euanthema and butterfly. c, 98w, Rebutia xanthocarpa and grasshopper. d, 112w, Notocactus herteri and beetle.

2011, Aug. 5		**Perf. 11½**	
5031	A2303	Sheet of 4, #a-d	6.50 2.40
e.		Booklet pane of 4, #5031a-5031d	6.75
		Complete booklet, #5031e	7.00

Complete booklet sold for 324w.

2018 World Cup Soccer Championships, Russia — A2304

Various soccer players with city names inscribed at side: No. 5032, 200w, Nizhniy Novgorod. No. 5033, 200w, Krasnodar. No. 5034, 200w, Kaliningrad. No. 5035, 200w, Moscow. No. 5036, 200w, Sochi. No. 5037, 200w, Rostov-na-Donu. No. 5038, 200w, St. Petersburg.

2011, Aug. 31		**Stamps + Labels**	
5032-5038	A2304	Set of 7	30.00 10.50
5038a		Sheet of 7, #5032-5038, + 2 labels	30.00 10.50
5038b		Booklet pane of 7, #5032-5038, without labels	30.00 —
		Complete booklet, #5038b	30.00

Complete booklet sold for 1414w.

Dinosaurs — A2305

No. 5039: a, Megalosaurus bucklandi. b, Staurikosaurus pricei. c, Chasmosaurus belli.

2011, Sept. 5		**Perf. 12¼x11¾**	
5039		Horiz. strip of 3	4.50 2.25
a.		A2305 42w multi	.65 .30
b.		A2305 98w multi	1.50 .75
c.		A2305 140w multi	2.10 1.10
d.		Booklet pane of 3, #5039a-5039c	4.75
		Complete booklet, #5039d	4.75

Complete booklet sold for 294w.

World Leisure Expo 2011, Hangzhou, People's Republic of China — A2306

Emblems and: 10w, Samil Lagoon. 30w, Xihu.

2011, Sept. 17		**Perf. 13¼**	
5040-5041	A2306	Set of 2	.75 .30

Fire Engines — A2307

No. 5042: a, 70w, Mercedes-Benz fire engine. b, 98w, ZIL ladder truck.
No. 5043: a, 30w, ZIL fire engine. b, 140w, Mercedes-Benz ladder truck.

2011, Oct. 5		**Perf. 13¼**	
5042	A2307	Sheet of 2, #a-b, + 2 labels	3.50 1.25
5043	A2307	Sheet of 2, #a-b, + 2 labels	3.50 1.25
c.		Booklet pane of 4, #5042a-5042b, 5043a-5043b, + 2 labels	7.50 —
		Complete booklet, #5043c	7.50

Complete booklet sold for 352w.

Famous People A2308

Designs: 10w, Pak Yon (1378-1458). musician. 30w, Sinsa Im Dang (1504-51), painter. 50w, Jong Yak Yong (1762-1836), philosopher. 70w, Ryu Rin Sok (1842-1915), military leader.

2011, Oct. 15			
5044-5047	A2308	Set of 4	3.00 1.25

Souvenir Sheet

Kim Jong Il and Chinese State Councilor Dai Bingguo — A2309

2011, Oct. 18			
5048	A2309	70w multi	1.50 1.10

Miniature Sheets

A2313

A2314

A2315

A2316

Friendship Between North Korea and People's Republic of China — A2317

Design: No. 5052, 10w, Mao Zedong Going to Anyuan. No. 5053: a, 10w, Mao Zedong. b, 10w, Mao Zedong in army vehicle reviewing troops. c, 10w, Mao Zedong writing. d, 30w, Kim Il Sung in suit and tie. e, 30w, Kim Il Sung and Mao Zedong shaking hands. f, 30w, Kim Il Sung and Mao Zedong standing at military parade.
No. 5054: a, 10w, Deng Xiaoping. b, 10w, Deng Xiaoping in automobile reviewing troops. c, 10w, Deng Xiaoping saluting. d, 30w, Kim Il Sung in black shirt. e, 30w, Deng Xiaoping and Kim Il Sung embracing. f, 30w, Deng Xiaoping and Kim Il Sung standing.
No. 5055: a, 10w, Jiang Zemin. b, 10w, Jiang Zemin in automobile reviewing troops. c, 10w, Jiang Zemin at ceremony returning Hong Kong to China. d, 30w, Kim Jong Il wearing

glasses. e, 30w, Kim Jong Il and Jiang Zemin shaking hands. f, 30w, Jiang Zemin and Kim Jong Il shaking hands, cameramen.
No. 5056: a, 10w, Hu Jintao. b, 10w, Hu Jintao in automobile reviewing troops. c, 10w, Hu Jintaou holding Olympic torch. d, 30w, Kim Jong Il without glasses. e, 30w, Hu Jintao walking with Kim Jong Il. f, 30w, Kim Jong Il and Hu Jintao shaking hands.

Perf. 13¼ (#5052), 11¾x12¼			
2011, Oct. 28			**Litho.**
5052	A2313	10w multi	.25 .25
5053	A2314	Sheet of 6, #a-f	2.50 1.90
5054	A2315	Sheet of 6, #a-f	2.50 1.90
5055	A2316	Sheet of 6, #a-f	2.50 1.90
5056	A2317	Sheet of 6, #a-f	2.50 1.90
		Nos. 5052-5056 (5)	10.25 7.85

Publication of Taedongyojido Map of Korea by Kim Jong Ho, 150th Anniv. A2318

2011, Nov. 5		**Perf. 13¼**	
5057	A2318	98w multi	2.00 .75

Minerals — A2319

Designs: 30w, Limonite, crucible with molten metal. 42w, Kotoite, rocket. 58w, Wollastonite, ceramic vases. 98w, Stibnite, tractor and parts.

2011, Dec. 5			
5058-5061	A2319	Set of 4	5.00 1.75
5061a		Booklet pane of 4, #5057-5060	5.25
		Complete booklet, #5060a	5.25

Complete booklet sold for 242w.

A2320

Appointment of Kim Jong Il as Supreme Commander of Army, 20th Anniv. — A2321

No. 5062 — Kim Jong Il and: a, 10w, Pilots. b, 30w, Tank soldiers. c, 70w, Sailors. d, 98w, Soldiers carrying packs.
No. 5063, Kim Jong Il and military officer reviewing troops in military vehicle.

2011, Dec. 24			
5062	A2320	Sheet of 4, #a-d, + central label	3.25 1.60
Souvenir Sheet			
Perf. 11¾			
5063	A2321	98w multi	2.00 1.00

Souvenir Sheets

Kim Jong II (1942-2011) — A2322

Kim Jong II and Son, Kim Jong Un — A2323

2011, Dec. 29   *Perf. 12¼x11¾*
5064　A2322　70w multi　　　1.25　.55
5065　A2323　70w multi　　　1.25　.55

New Year 2012 — A2324

2012, Jan. 1   *Perf. 13¼*
5066　A2324　10w multi　　　　.25　.25

Dragons — A2325

No. 5067 — Various dragons: a, 10w. b, 30w. c, 60w.

2012, Jan. 5   *Perf. 11½*
5067　A2325　Horiz. strip of 3,
　　　#a-c　　　　　　　　2.00　.80
No. 5067 was printed in sheets containing two strips of 3.

Mt. Paektu — A2326

Designs: 20w, Lake Samji and Mt. Paektu. 30w, Lake Chon on Mt. Paektu.

2012, Jan. 17   *Perf. 12¼x11¾*
5068-5069　A2326　Set of 2　　1.00　.40

Butterflies — A2327

No. 5070: a, 30w, Pachliopta coon. b, 70w, Agrias pericles. c, 90w, Buthanitis lidderdalei. d, 120w, Cethosia biblis.

2012, Jan. 25   *Perf. 11½*
5070　A2327　Block of 4, #a-d　6.00　2.40
  e.　Booklet pane of 4, #5070a-
　　　5070d, + 2 labels　　　6.25　—
　　　Complete booklet, #5070e　6.25
Complete booklet sold for 324w.

Joint Editorials of State Newspapers A2328

Red flag at upper left and: No. 5071, 10w, Birthplace of Kim Il Sung, torch, soldier, workers. No. 5072, 10w, City buildings, packaged foods, crops and farm animals, horiz. No. 5073, 30w, Torch, symbols of industry, train and truck. No. 5074, 30w, Soldier holding rifle with bayonet, flags, missiles. 40w, Fist squashing people, U.S. Capitol. 50w, Dove, North Korea highlighted on map, rainbow.

2012, Jan. 27   *Perf. 13¼*
5071-5076　A2328　Set of 6　　3.00　1.25

Calls for Victory by Central Committee and Central Military Commission A2329

2012, Jan. 30   *Litho.*
5077　A2329　10w multi　　　　.25　.25

Architecture — A2330

Designs: 60w, Kopernik House, Moscow. Mansudae Street Apartment Buildings, Pyongyang. 100w, Patriarch House, Moscow, East Pyongyang Grand Theater. No. 5080, 140w, Grand People's Study House, Pyongyang, Gnezdikovskiy Palace, Moscow. 190w, Apartement house, Pyongyang, Egg House, Moscow. 210w, Hyangsan Hotel, Pyongyang, Weber Villa, Moscow.
No. 5083, 140w, Patriarch House, Moscow and National Theater, Pyongyang at night.

2012, Jan. 30   *Perf. 12*
5078-5082　A2330　Set of 5　14.00　5.50
Souvenir Sheet
Perf. 12x11½
5083　A2330　140w multi　　　2.75　1.10
  a.　Souvenir sheet of 6, #5078-
　　　5083, perf. 12x11½, + 3
　　　labels　　　　　　　15.00　6.75
  b.　Booklet pane of 6, #5078-
　　　5083, perf. 12x11½　　15.00　—
　　　Complete booklet, #5083b　15.00
Nos. 5078-5082 were each printed in sheets of 5 + label. Complete booklet sold for 854w.

A2331

A2332

Birthday of Kim Jong II (1942-2011) — A2333

Designs: 10w, Kimjongilia flower.
No. 5085: a, 40w, Kim Jong II, soldiers and artillery. 70w, Kim Jong II, people with flags and sled.
No. 5085, 70w, Kimg Jong II.

2012, Feb. 16   *Perf. 13¼*
5084　A2331　10w multi　　　　.25　.25
5085　A2332　Sheet of 2, #a-
　　　b, + 3 labels　　　2.25　.85
Souvenir Sheet
Perf. 11½x12
5086　A2333　70w multi　　　1.50　.55

Ceramics A2334

Designs: 30w, Container with lotus flower pattern. 40w, Container with dragon and cloud design.
70w, Pitcher and bowl.

2012, Mar. 10   *Perf. 11½*
Stamps + Labels
5087-5088　A2334　Set of 2　　1.50　.55
Souvenir Sheet
5089　A2334　70w multi + label　1.50　.55
  a.　Booklet pane of 3, #5087-
　　　5089, + 7 labels　　　4.50　—
　　　Complete booklet, #5089a　4.50
Complete booklet sold for 154w.

Posthumous Granting of Title of Generalissimo to Kim Jong II — A2335

2012, Mar. 20   *Perf. 13¼*
5090　A2335　10w multi　　　　.25　.25

Birthplace of Kim Jong II — A2336

2012, Mar. 20
5091　A2336　10w multi　　　　.25　.25
Designation of Feb. 16 (birthday of Kim Jong II) as Day of the Shining Star.

Floriade 2012 World Horticultural Expo, Venlo, Netherlands A2337

2012, Mar. 22   *Litho.*
5092　A2337　30w multi　　　　.45　.25

Korean National Association, 95th Anniv. — A2338

2012, Mar. 23   *Perf. 13¼*
5093　A2338　30w citron　　　　.75　.25

Opening of
Korean Stamp
Museum,
Pyongyang
A2339

2012, Apr. 15   **Perf. 11½**
5094 A2339 10w multi   .25   .25

A2340

A2341

A2342

A2343

A2344

A2345

A2346

A2347

A2348

A2349

Pres. Kim Il Sung (1912-94) — A2350

No. 5102 — Kim Il Sung: a, With adults and
children. b, Wearing hat, addressing men. c,
Seated behind microphone. d, With workers at
plant.
No. 5103 — Kim Il Sung: a, At trainyard. b,
With workers at textile factory. c, Holding ear
of corn, with farmers in field. d, Holding ear
of corn, with agricultural scientists.
No. 5104 — Kim Il Sung: a, With pilots. b,
Seated, talking to soldiers. c, With soldiers
inspecting artillery. d, Wearing white jacket,
walking with military.

2012, Apr. 15   **Perf. 11½**
5095 A2340 30w multi + label   .75   .25
5096 A2341 30w multi + label   .75   .25
5097 A2342 30w multi + label   .75   .25
5098 A2343 30w multi + label   .75   .25
5099 A2344 30w multi + label   .75   .25
5100 A2345 30w multi + label   .75   .25
5101 A2346 30w multi + label   .75   .25
    Nos. 5095-5101 (7)   5.25   1.75
Miniature Sheets
Perf. 13¼
5102 A2347 20w Sheet of 4, #a-d 1.75   60
5103 A2348 30w Sheet of 4, #a-d 2.50   .95
5104 A2349 40w Sheet of 4, #a-d 3.25   1.25
    Nos. 5102-5104 (3)   7.50   2.80
Souvenir Sheet
Perf. 11¾
5105 A2350 70w multi   1.75   1.00

A2351

A2352

Pres. Kim Il Sung (1912-94) — A2353

Designs: 10w, Birthplace of Kim Il Sung,
flowers.
No. 5107: a, 70w, Kim Il Sung in field with
children. b, 100w, Kim Il Sung seated, holding
hand of girl.
No. 5108, 100w, Kim Il Sung at birthplace.

2012, Apr. 15   **Perf. 13¼**
5106 A2351 10w multi   .30   .25
Miniature Sheet
Perf. 11¾
5107 A2352 Sheet of 2, #a-b   3.25   1.25
Souvenir Sheet
Perf. 11½x12
5108 A2353 100w multi   2.00   .80

Souvenir Sheet

Kang Pan Sok (1892-1932), Mother of
Kim Il Sung — A2354

2012, Apr. 21   **Perf. 11¾**
5109 A2354 70w multi   1.50   .55

Flags of
Guerilla Army,
North Korea
and Supreme
Commander
A2355

Kim Il Sung in Military
Uniform — A2356

2012, Apr. 25   **Perf. 13¼**
5110 A2355 30w multi   .75   .25
Souvenir Sheet
Perf. 11½x12
5111 A2356 70w multi   1.50   .55
Korean People's Army, 80th anniv.

Roses
A2357

Color of roses: 30w, Pink and white. 50w,
Yellow. 70w, Red.

2012, Apr. 30   **Perf. 12½**
5112-5114 A2357 Set of 3   3.00   1.25
 5114a   Booklet pane of 3, #5112-
         5114, + label   3.25   —
         Complete booklet, #5114a   3.50
Values are for stamps with surrounding
selvage. Complete booklet sold for 164w.

Principles for
National
Reunification, 40th
Anniv. — A2358

2012, May 3   **Perf. 11½**
5115 A2358 50w red & blue   1.00   .40

2012 Summer
Olympics,
London
A2359

Designs: 10w, Track and field. 30w, Judo.
70w, Rhythmic gymnastics. 110w, Swimming
and diving.

2012, May 3   **Perf. 13¼**
5116-5119 A2359 Set of 4   4.25   1.75
 5119a   Booklet pane of 4, #5116-
         5119   4.30   —
         Complete booklet, #5119a   4.75
Complete booklet sold for 234w.

Souvenir Sheet

Erection of Statues to Kim Il Sung and Kim Jong Il in Pyongyang — A2360

2012, May 30
5120 A2360 50w multi   1.00   .40

Locomotives — A2361

Designs: 50w, Songun Pulgungi 1. 70w, Velaro D407. 90w, Renfe 112.

2012, May 31
5121-5123 A2361   Set of 3   4.25 1.60
5123a   Booklet pane of 3, #5121-
    5123   4.50   —
   Complete booklet, #5123a   4.50
Complete booklet sold for 224w.

Battle of Pochonbo, 75th Anniv. — A2362

2012, June 4
5124 A2362 30w multi   .70   .25

Souvenir Sheet

2012 Planete Timbres Stamp Exhibition, Paris — A2363

2012, June 9   *Perf. 12¼x11¾*
5125 A2363 70w multi   1.50   .55

2012 World Stamp Championships, Jakarta, Indonesia A2364

2012, June 18   *Perf. 11½*
5126 A2364 30w multi   .60   .25

Birds A2365

Designs: 50w, Fringilla montifringilla. 70w, Zosterops erythropleura. 90w, Uragus sibiricus.

2012, June 30   Litho.
5127-5129 A2365   Set of 3   4.00 1.60
5129a   Booklet pane of 3, #5127-
    5129, + label   4.25   —
   Complete booklet, #5129a   4.25
Complete booklet sold for 224w.

Free Universal Medical System, 60th Anniv. A2366

2012, July 5   *Perf. 13¼*
5130 A2366 30w multi   .75   .25

Souvenir Sheets

Mao Zedong (1893-1976) and Poetry — A2367

Kim Il Sung (1912-94) and Quotes — A2368

No. 5131: a, The Yellow Crane Pavilion, poem by Mao Zedong (character at UL a diagonal line) (34x52mm). b, Mao Zedong writing (54x42mm). c, Huichang, poem by Mao Zedong (complex character with vertical line at UL).

No. 5132: a, 7 ½ lines of text from reminiscences of Kim Il Sung, and signature (34x52mm). b, Kim Il Sung writing (54x42mm). c, 8 lines of text from reminiscences of Kim Il Sung, and signature (34x52mm).

Perf. 11¾x12¼, 13¼ (#5131b, 5132b)
2012, July 15
5131 A2367 10w Sheet of 3, #a-c   .50   .25
5132 A2368 30w Sheet of 3, #a-c   1.40   .70

Souvenir Sheet

Fourth Conference of the Korean Workers' Party — A2369

No. 5133: a, Kim Jong Il wearing glasses (1941-2011). b, Kim Jong Un.

2012, July 20   *Perf. 11¾x12¼*
5133 A2369 30w Sheet of 2, #a-b   1.25   .50

A2370

Korean Children's Union, 66th Anniv. — A2371

2012, Aug. 10   *Perf. 13¼*
5134 A2370 10w multi   .25   .25

Souvenir Sheet
5135 A2371 70w multi   1.40   .55

Mother's Day — A2372

2012, Sept. 20   *Perf. 11½*
5136 A2372 10w multi   .25   .25

Miniature Sheets

A2373

Poetry of Mao Zedong (1893-1976) — A2374

No. 5137: a, The People's Liberation Army Captures Nanjing (5 ½ lines) (34x52mm). b, Swimming (large white areas at UL and LR) (54x42mm). c, Beidaihe (6 full long lines of characters, 2 shorter lines at sides) (34x52mm). d, The Long March (3mm from line at right to frame) (84x21mm). e, Mt. Liupan (6mm from line at right to frame) (84x21mm).

No. 5138: a, Changsha (line at left with 2 characters) (54x42mm). b, Reply to Comrade Guo Moruo (white area in middle of poem) (54x42mm). c, Snow (line at right three characters) (63x27mm). d, Loushan Pass (12 lines) (63x27mm). e, In Praise of the Photo Taken by Comrade Lijin of the Fairy Cave at Mt. Lushan (second line from left is single character) (63x27mm). f, The Double Ninth (13 lines with large whtie areas at top and bottom) (63x27mm).

Perf. 11¾x12¼ (#5137a, 5137c), 13¼
2012, Sept. 25
5137 A2373 10w Sheet of 5, #a-e   1.00   .40
5138 A2374 10w Sheet of 6, #a-f   1.00   .50
Beijing 2012 Intl. Stamp and Coin Exposition.

Giant Pandas — A2375

Designs: 70w, Panda on branch. 90w, Adult and juvenile panda. 120w, Two adult pandas, horiz.

2012, Dec. 14   Litho.   *Perf. 11½*
5139-5140 A2375   Set of 2   2.50 1.25
Souvenir Sheet
    Perf. 13½
5141 A2375 120w multi   1.90   .95
No. 5141 contains one 90x42mm stamp.

Souvenir Sheets

A2377

Kim Jong Il (1942-2011) — A2378

2012, Dec. 17   Litho.   *Perf. 11½x12*
5143 A2377 50w multi   1.00   .40
    Perf. 13¼
5144 A2378 50w multi   1.00   .40

Souvenir Sheet

Kim Jong Suk (1917-49) — A2379

2012, Dec. 24   **Perf.**
5145 A2379 70w multi   1.50 .55

Constitution, 40th Anniv. — A2380

2012, Dec. 27   **Perf. 13¼**
5146 A2380 30w multi   .60 .25

Souvenir Sheet

Launch of Kwangmyongsong 3-2 Satellite — A2381

2012, Dec. 30   **Litho.**   **Perf. 13¼**
5147 A2381 50w multi   .80 .40

New Year 2013 — A2382

2013, Jan. 1   **Litho.**   **Perf. 11¾**
5148 A2382 10w multi   .25 .25

Stylized Snake A2383

2013, Jan. 5   **Litho.**   **Perf. 11½**
5149 A2383 10w multi   .25 .25

No. 5149 was printed in sheets of 16 + 4 labels.

Sports — A2384

Designs: 30w, Tennis. 50w, Cricket. 70w, Cycling. 90w, Rugby.

2013, Jan. 20   **Litho.**   **Perf. 13¼**
5150-5153 A2384   Set of 4   3.75 1.90
5153a   Booklet pane of 4, #5150-5153   4.00 —
   Complete booklet, #5153a   4.00
Complete booklet sold of 254w.

A2386

A2387

Kim Jong II (1942-2011) — A2388

2013, Feb. 16   **Litho.**   **Perf. 11¾**
5155 A2386 10w multi   .25 .25
Souvenir Sheets
5156 A2387 50w multl   .80 .40
5157 A2388 50w multi   .80 .40

An additional stamp was issued in this set. The editors would like to examine any example of it.

Souvenir Sheet

Kim Jong Un Making New Year's Speech — A2390

2013, Feb. 19   **Litho.**   **Perf. 11¾**
5162 A2390 50w multi   .80 .40

A2391

A2392

A2393

Military Posters in Korean Art Gallery, Pyongyang — A2394

2013, Feb. 25   **Litho.**   **Perf. 11½**
5163 A2391 10w multi   .25 .25
5164 A2392 10w multi   .25 .25
5165 A2393 30w multi   .45 .25
5166 A2394 30w multi   .45 .25
   Nos. 5163-5166 (4)   1.40 1.00

International Red Cross, 150th Anniv. — A2395

2013, Mar. 6   **Litho.**   **Perf. 13¼**
5167 A2395 30w multi   .45 .25

Miniature Sheet

Marine Life — A2396

No. 5168: a, 30w, Carcharodon carcharias (44mm diameter). b, 50w, Caretta caretta (38x28mm). c, 90w, Peprilus simillina (28x38mm). d, 110w, Hippocampus histrix (28x38mm).

2013, Mar. 21   **Litho.**   **Perf. 11½**
5168 A2396   Sheet of 4, #a-d   4.25 2.10

Election of Kim Jong II as Chairman of National Defense Commission, 20th Anniv. — A2397

2013, Apr. 9   **Litho.**   **Perf. 13¼**
5169 A2397 30w multi   .45 .25

Souvenir Sheet

Monkeys — A2398

No. 5170: a, 10w, Monkey. b, 20w, Adult and juvenile monkey.

Litho. & Engr.
2013, Apr. 10   **Perf. 12**
5170 A2398   Sheet of 2, #a-b   .45 .25

Passage of Kumsusan Palace of the Sun Preservation Law — A2401

2013, Apr. 25   **Litho.**   **Perf. 13¼**
5176 A2401 30w multi   .45 .25

Values are for stamps with surrounding selvage.

Australia 2013
World Stamp
Exhibition,
Melbourne
A2402

2013, May 10   Litho.   Perf. 11½
5177 A2402 30w multi   .45   .25

Bees
A2407

Various bees and orchids: 30w, 70w, 110w.

2013, June 12   Litho.   Perf. 13¼
5182-5184 A2407 Set of 3   3.25 1.60

A2408

Soldiers
A2409

2013, June 25   Litho.   Perf. 13¼
5185 A2408 10w multi   .25   .25
5186 A2409 150w multi   2.25 1.10

Souvenir Sheet

Pyongyang Folk Park — A2411

No. 5189: a, Tower of the Juche Idea, Arch
of Triumph. b, Pagoda at Kumgang Temple,
vert.

2013, July 20   Litho.   Perf. 11½
5189 A2411 30w Sheet of 2, #a-b   .95   .45

Victory
Sculpture
A2413

Kim Il Sung Delivering Radio
Address — A2415

Kim Il Sung at Rally — A2416

2013, July 27   Litho.   Perf. 13¼
5194 A2413 10w multi   .25   .25

Souvenir Sheets

5196 A2415 70w multi   1.10   .55
5197 A2416 70w multi   1.10   .55

Thailand 2013
World Stamp
Exhibition,
Bangkok
A2417

2013, Aug. 2   Litho.   Perf. 13¼
5198 A2417 10w multi   .25   .25

Horses
A2420

Designs: 30w, Shire horses. 50w, Orlov
trotter.
70w, Thoroughbred horses, horiz.

2013, Aug. 28   Litho.   Perf. 13¼
5201-5202 A2420 Set of 2   1.25   .60

Souvenir Sheet

5203 A2420 70w multi   1.10   .55

A2421

Founding of the Democratic People's
Republic of Korea, 65th
Anniv. — A2422

No. 5205: a, Kim Il Sung and flags. b, Kim
Jong Il and mountain.

2013, Sept. 9   Litho.   Perf. 11½
5204 A2421 30w multi   .50   .25

Souvenir Sheet
Perf. 13¼
5205 A2422 50w Sheet of 2, #a-b 1.60   .80

Mangyongdae in Spring — A2423

Rungna
Island in
Summer
A2424

Moran Hill
in Autumn
A2425

Ryongwang Pavilion in
Winter — A2426

2013, Sept. 25   Litho.   Perf. 13¼
5206 A2423 30w multi   .50   .25
5207 A2424 50w multi   .80   .40
5208 A2425 70w multi   1.10   .55
5209 A2426 110w multi   1.75   .85
      Nos. 5206-5209 (4)   4.15 2.05

Ships
A2427

Designs: 30w, Restaurant ship Taedonggang. 50w, Cargo ship Kumrung No. 5. 90w,
Refrigerator cargo ship Rimyongsu No. 7.
110w, Refrigerator cargo ship Turubong No. 3.

2013, Oct. 15   Litho.   Perf. 11½
5210-5213 A2427 Set of 4   4.25 2.10

AIR POST STAMPS

Lisunov Li-2
Airliner over
Pyongyang
AP1

1958, Feb. 4   Photo.   Perf. 10
C1   AP1 20w blue   11.00   2.00
  a.   Imperf   22.50 10.00
  b.   Perf 11   12.00   2.50
  c.   Rouletted   15.00 10.00

Korean Civil Aviation.

REPUBLIC OF KOSOVO

'ko-sə-ˌvō

LOCATION — North of Albania and Macedonia
GOVT. — REPUBLIC
AREA — 4,212 sq. mi.
POP. — 2,100,000 (2007 est.)
CAPITAL — Pristina

From 1974 to 1990, Kosovo was an autonomous province of Serbia, a republic within Yugoslavia. In 1990, the autonomy of Kosovo was revoked. A Separatist faction declared Kosovo independence that year, but only Albania recognized it. In 1999, the United Nations Security Council placed Kosovo under a transitional United Nations Administration, and the institutions created by the independent Kosovo were replaced with the United Nations Interim Administration. Starting in 2000, postage stamps were issued by the United Nations Interim Administration, and these can be found as part of the listings for United Nations. The Kosovo Assembly declared independence on Feb. 17, 2008. Kosovo was recognized as independent by numerous countries soon thereafter, and the United Nations Interim Administration ceased issuing stamps. Serbia maintains its claim to the territory.

100 pfennigs = 1 mark
100 cents = (€)1 (2002)

Catalogue values for all unused stamps in this country are for Never Hinged items.

Peace in Kosovo — A1

Designs: 20pf, Mosaic depicting Orpheus, c. 5th-6th cent., Podujeve. 30pf, Dardinian idol, Museum of Kosovo. 50pf, Silver coin of Damastion from 4th cent. B.C. 1m, Statue of Mother Teresa, Prizren. 2m, Map of Kosovo.

Perf. 13½x13, 13½x13¼ (30pf)

		2000, Mar. 14	Litho.	Unwmk.	
1	A1	20pf multicolored		1.00	.75
2	A1	30pf multicolored		1.25	1.00
3	A1	50pf multicolored		1.60	1.40
4	A1	1m multicolored		2.75	2.00
5	A1	2m multicolored		5.50	4.00
		Nos. 1-5 (5)		12.10	9.15

Beginning with No. 6, Kosovan stamps were not available to collectors through the United Nations Postal Administration.

Peace in Kosovo — A2

Designs: 20pf, Bird. 30pf, Street musician. 50pf, Butterfly and pear. 1m, Children and stars. 2m, Globe and handprints.

		2001, Nov. 12	Litho.	Perf. 14	
6	A2	20pf multicolored		1.50	1.00
7	A2	30pf multicolored		1.75	1.25
8	A2	50pf multicolored		3.25	2.25
9	A2	1m multicolored		7.00	5.00
10	A2	2m multicolored		13.50	10.00
		Nos. 6-10 (5)		27.00	19.50

Peace in Kosovo Type of 2001 With Denominations in Euros Only

		2002, May 2	Litho.	Perf. 14	
11	A2	10c Like #6		1.50	1.00
12	A2	15c Like #7		1.75	1.25
13	A2	26c Like #8		3.25	2.25
14	A2	51c Like #9		7.50	6.00
15	A2	€1.02 Like #10		15.00	12.50
		Nos. 11-15 (5)		29.00	23.00

Christmas — A3

Designs: 50c, Candles and garland. €1, Stylized men.

		2003, Dec. 20	Litho.	Perf. 14	
16	A3	50c multicolored		14.00	12.50
17	A3	€1 multicolored		27.50	20.00

Return of Refugees — A4

Five Years of Peace — A5

		2004, June 29	Litho.	Perf. 13¼x13	
18	A4	€1 multicolored		15.00	15.00
19	A5	€2 multicolored		30.00	30.00

Musical Instruments — A6

		2004, Aug. 31	Litho.	Perf. 13¼x13	
20	A6	20c Flute		12.50	12.50
21	A6	30c Ocarina		22.50	22.50

Aprons A7

Vests — A8

Designs: 20c, Apron from Prizren. 30c, Apron from Rugova. 50c, Three vests. €1, Two vests.

		2004, Oct. 28	Litho.	Perf. 13x13¼	
22	A7	20c multicolored		8.00	8.00
23	A7	30c multicolored		11.00	11.00
24	A8	50c multicolored		18.50	18.50
25	A8	€1 multicolored		37.50	37.50
		Nos. 22-25 (4)		75.00	75.00

Mirusha Waterfall A9

		2004, Nov. 26	Litho.	Perf. 13x13¼	
26	A9	€2 multicolored		15.00	15.00

House A10

		2004, Dec. 14	Litho.	Perf. 13x13¼	
27	A10	50c multicolored		9.00	9.00

Flowers — A11

		2005, June 29	Litho.	Perf. 13½	
28	A11	15c Peony		3.00	3.00
29	A11	20c Poppies		4.00	4.00
30	A11	30c Gentian		7.00	7.00
		Nos. 28-30 (3)		14.00	14.00

A12

Handicrafts A13

		2005, July 20		Perf. 13¼x13	
31	A12	20c shown		2.50	2.50
32	A12	30c Cradle		4.00	4.00
33	A13	50c shown		6.00	6.00
34	A12	€1 Necklace		7.50	7.50
		Nos. 31-34 (4)		20.00	20.00

Village A14

Town A15

City — A16

		2005, Sept. 15		Perf. 13x13½	
35	A14	20c multicolored		4.00	4.00
36	A15	50c multicolored		7.50	7.50
37	A16	€1 multicolored		12.50	12.50
		Nos. 35-37 (3)		24.00	24.00

Archaeological Artifacts — A17

		2005, Nov. 2		Perf. 13½x13	
38	A17	20c shown		2.00	2.00
39	A17	30c Statue		3.50	3.50
40	A17	50c Sculpture		5.00	5.00
41	A17	€1 Helmet		12.50	12.50
		Nos. 38-41 (4)		23.00	23.00

Minerals A18

		2005, Dec. 10		Perf. 13x13½	
42	A18	€2 multicolored		17.50	17.50

A19

Europa — A20

		2006, July 20		Perf. 13¼x13	
43	A19	50c multicolored		3.00	3.00
44	A20	€1 multicolored		5.00	5.00

Fauna A21

		2006, May 23	Litho.	Perf. 13	
45	A21	15c Wolf		1.00	1.00
46	A21	20c Cow		1.25	1.25
47	A21	30c Pigeon		1.50	1.50
48	A21	50c Swan		1.75	1.75
49	A21	€1 Dog		3.25	3.25
a.		Souvenir sheet, #45-49, + label		10.00	10.00
		Nos. 45-49 (5)		8.75	8.75

Children
A22

Designs: 20c, Children in cradle. 30c, Children reading. 50c, Girls dancing. €1, Child in water.

2006, June 30   Litho.   Perf. 13
50	A22	20c multicolored	1.00	1.00
51	A22	30c multicolored	1.25	1.25
52	A22	50c multicolored	1.75	1.75
53	A22	€1 multicolored	4.00	4.00
a.		Souvenir sheet, #50-53	9.00	9.00
		Nos. 50-53 (4)	8.00	8.00

A23

A24

A25

Tourist Attractions — A26

2006, Sept. 1   Litho.   Perf. 13
54	A23	20c multicolored	1.00	1.00
55	A24	30c multicolored	1.25	1.25
56	A25	50c multicolored	1.75	1.75
57	A26	€1 multicolored	3.75	3.75
a.		Souvenir sheet, #54-57	11.00	11.00
		Nos. 54-57 (4)	7.75	7.75

Intl. Peace
Day — A27

2006, Sept. 21   Litho.   Perf. 13
58	A27	€2 multicolored	12.50	12.50

Ancient
Coins — A28

Various coins.

2006, Nov. 1   Litho.   Perf. 13
59	A28	20c multicolored	1.00	1.00
60	A28	30c multicolored	1.50	1.50
61	A28	50c multicolored	2.25	2.25

62	A28	€1 multicolored	4.00	4.00
a.		Souvenir sheet, #59-62	11.00	11.00
		Nos. 59-62 (4)	8.75	8.75

Sculpture — A29

2006, Dec. 1   Litho.   Perf. 13
63	A29	€2 multicolored	11.00	11.00
a.		Miniature sheet, #45-57, 59-63, + 2 labels	80.00	80.00

Convention on the
Rights of Persons
With
Disabilities — A30

Emblems of handicaps and: 20c, Children and butterfly. 50c, Handicapped women. 70c, Map of Kosovo. €1, Stylized flower.

2007, Apr. 23   Litho.   Perf. 14x14¼
64	A30	20c multicolored	1.25	1.25
65	A30	50c multicolored	2.50	2.50
66	A30	70c multicolored	3.50	3.50
67	A30	€1 multicolored	4.50	4.50
a.		Souvenir sheet, #64-67	12.50	12.50
		Nos. 64-67 (4)	11.75	11.75

Scouting,
Cent. — A31

Europa — A32

2007, May 12   Litho.   Perf. 13¼
68	A31	70c multicolored	4.50	4.50
69	A32	€1 multicolored	7.00	7.00
a.		Souvenir sheet, #68-69	110.00	110.00

A33

A34

International
Children's
Day — A36

2007, June 1   Litho.   Perf. 13¼
70	A33	20c multicolored	1.25	1.25
71	A34	30c multicolored	1.50	1.50
72	A35	70c multicolored	3.00	3.00
73	A36	€1 multicolored	5.00	5.00
		Nos. 70-73 (4)	10.75	10.75

Native
Costumes — A37

Designs: 20c, Serbian woman. 30c, Prizren Region woman. 50c, Sword dancer. 70c, Drenica Region woman. €1, Shepherd, Rugova.

2007, July 6   Litho.   Perf. 13½x13¼
74	A37	20c multicolored	1.25	1.25
75	A37	30c multicolored	1.75	1.75
76	A37	50c multicolored	2.00	2.00
77	A37	70c multicolored	3.25	3.25
78	A37	€1 multicolored	4.25	4.25
a.		Souvenir sheet, #74-78, + label	17.50	17.50
		Nos. 74-78 (5)	12.50	12.50

Masks — A38

Various masks.

Perf. 13½x13¼
2007, Sept. 11   Litho.
79	A38	15c multicolored	.75	.75
80	A38	30c multicolored	1.00	1.00
81	A38	50c multicolored	1.75	1.75
82	A38	€1 multicolored	3.50	3.50
		Nos. 79-82 (4)	7.00	7.00

Sports — A39

Designs: 20c, Soccer ball, basketball, two people standing, person in wheelchair. 50c, Wrestlers. €1, Symbols of 24 sports.

2007, Oct. 2   Litho.   Perf. 13¼x13½
83	A39	20c multicolored	1.00	1.00
84	A39	50c multicolored	2.25	2.25
85	A39	€1 multicolored	4.50	4.50
		Nos. 83-85 (3)	7.75	7.75

Architecture
A40

Designs: 30c, Stone bridge, Vushtrri. 50c, Hamam, Prizren. 70c, Tower. €1, Tower, diff.

2007, Nov. 6   Litho.   Perf. 13¼
86	A40	30c multicolored	2.00	2.00
87	A40	50c multicolored	3.50	3.50
88	A40	70c multicolored	4.00	4.00
89	A40	€1 multicolored	5.00	5.00
		Nos. 86-89 (4)	14.50	14.50

Locomotives
A41

Designs: €1, Diesel locomotive. €2, Steam locomotive

2007, Dec. 7   Litho.   Perf. 13¼
90	A41	€1 multicolored	7.50	7.50
91	A41	€2 multicolored	15.00	15.00

Skanderbeg (1405-
68), Albanian
National
Hero — A42

2008, Jan. 17   Litho.   Perf. 13¼
92	A42	€2 multicolored	8.75	8.75

Kosovo declared its independence from Serbia on Feb. 17, 2008, ending the United Nations Interim Administration. Stamps issued after Feb. 17, 2008, by the Republic of Kosovo will be listed under Kosovo in the *Scott Standard Postage Stamp Catalogue.*

Republic of Kosovo

A42

Teacher's
Day — A43

2008, Mar. 7   Litho.   Perf. 13x13¼
93	A42	70c multi	2.50	2.50
94	A43	€1 multi	3.50	3.50

Independence
A44

2008, Mar. 19   Perf. 13¼x13
Stamps With White Frames
95		Vert. pair	6.50	6.50
a.		A44 20c vio blue & multi	.75	.50
b.		A44 70c red & multi	3.00	2.00

Souvenir Sheet
Stamp With Colored Border
96	A44	70c red & multi	8.75	8.75

Earth
Day — A45

Designs: 30c, Globe, olive branch. 50c, Trees. 70c, Tree, parched land. €1, Man holding tree.

2008, Apr. 22   Perf. 13x13¼
97-100	A45	Set of 4	10.00	10.00

Europa — A46

Designs: Nos. 101, 103a, 70c, Handwritten letter, pen. Nos. 102, 103b, €1, Letter folded into paper airplane.

2008, May 9   **Litho.**
Stamps With White Frames
101-102 A46   Set of 2   8.00   8.00
Souvenir Sheet
Stamps With Colored Frames
103 A46   Sheet of 2, #a-b   20.00 20.00

Filigree — A47

Designs: 10c, Chest. 15c, Earring. 20c, Figurine of woman. 50c, Necklace. €1, Necklace, diff.

2008, June 12   **Perf. 13¼x13**
104-108 A47   Set of 5   6.75 6.75

A48   A49

Medicinal Herbs
A50   A51

2008, Sept. 9   **Litho.**   **Perf. 13¼x13**
109   Horiz. strip of 4   8.00 8.00
   a. A48 30c multi   .75 .75
   b. A49 50c multi   1.00 1.00
   c. A50 70c multi   2.00 2.00
   d. A51 €1 multi   2.75 2.75

Breast Cancer
Prevention — A52

2008, Oct. 15   **Litho.**   **Perf. 13¼x13**
110 A52   €1 multi   7.00 7.00

Albanian Alphabet, Cent. — A53

No. 111: a, 70c, Alphabet. b, €1, Notebook page for handwriting practice.

2008, Nov. 14   **Perf. 13x13¼**
111 A53   Vert. pair, #a-b   4.50 4.50

Adem Jashari (1955-98), Independence Leader — A54

2008, Nov. 28   **Perf. 13¼x13**
112 A54   €2 multi   6.50 6.50

A55

A56

A57

Visual Arts — A58

2008, Dec. 2   **Litho.**   **Perf. 13¼**
113   Horiz. strip of 4   8.50 8.50
   a. A55 20c multi   .60 .60
   b. A56 50c multi   1.25 1.25
   c. A57 70c multi   2.00 2.00
   d. A58 €1 multi   2.75 2.75

William G. Walker, Head of Kosovo Verification Mission — A59

Torn Page — A60

2009, Jan. 15
114 A59 50c multi   1.75 1.75
115 A60 70c multi   2.50 2.50
Reçak Massacre, 10th anniv.

Independence, 1st Anniv. — A61

No. 116: a, €1, Hand with pen, independence declaration. b, €2, Flag of Kosovo, date of independence.
Illustration reduced.

2009, Feb. 16   **Litho.**   **Perf. 13¼**
116 A61   Horiz. pair, #a-b   8.50 8.50

Edith Durham (1863-1944), Writer — A62

2009, Mar. 21
117 A62   €1 multi   3.25 3.25

Decan Monastery — A64

Designs: No. 118, €1, Monastery. No. 119, €2, Monastery, diff.
No. 120: a, €1, Window. b, €2, Painting of Jesus.

2009, Apr. 22
118-119 A63   Set of 2   8.00 8.00
Souvenir Sheet
120 A64   Sheet of 2, #a-b   8.00 8.00

A63

Europa — A65

Designs: €1, Map of Europe, ring of stars, man and girl at telescope. No. 122, €2, Boy and rocket on map of Europe (with white frame around stamp).
No. 123, Like #122, without white frame around stamp.

2009, May 9
121-122 A65   Set of 2   9.50 9.50
Souvenir Sheet
123 A65   €2 multi   10.00 10.00
Intl. Year of Astronomy.

A66   A67

A68   A69

Declaration of the Rights of the Child, 20th Anniv.

2009, June 1
124 A66 20c multi   .75 .75
125 A67 50c multi   2.00 2.00
126 A68 70c multi   2.75 2.75
127 A69 €1 multi   4.00 4.00
Nos. 124-127 (4)   9.50 9.50

Kosovo's Friendship With United States — A70

2009, Sept. 4
128 A70   €2 multi   7.25 7.25

Lorenc Antoni (1909-91), Composer — A71

2009, Sept. 23
129 A71   €1 multi   4.75 4.75

Germany Weeks in Kosovo — A72

2009, Oct. 3   **Litho.**   **Perf. 13¼**
130 A72   €1 multi   3.75 3.75

Pjetër Bogdani (c. 1630-89), Writer — A73

2009, Nov. 22
131 A73   €1 multi   3.50 3.50

Art — A74

Works by: 30c, M. Mulliqi. 50c, I. Kodra. 70c, G. Gjokaj. €1, M. Mulliqi, diff.

2009, Dec. 4
132-135 A74   Set of 4   7.50 7.50

A75

Film Personalities — A76

Designs: No. 136, 30c, Faruk Begolli (1944-2007), actor and director. No. 137, 70c, Melihate Qena (1939-2005), actress. €1, Abdurrahman Shala (1922-94), actor and producer. No. 139: a, 30c, Unnamed person in yellow. b, 70c, Unnamed person in brown, diff.

2010, Jan. 26
136-138 A75   Set of 3   6.00 6.00
Souvenir Sheet
139 A76   Sheet of 2, #a-b   3.25 3.25

Emblems of Kosovo Police, Defense Forces and Security Forces — A77

Police and Emblem — A78

Security Forces — A79

2010, Feb. 16   **Litho.**
140 A77 30c multi   .85 .85
141 A78 50c multi   1.40 1.40
142 A79 70c multi   1.90 1.90
      Nos. 140-142 (3)   4.15 4.15

A80

Europa — A81

Designs: €1, Child reading book under tree. No. 144, €2, Child leaving open book. No. 145, €2, Boy sitting on book.

2010, May 5   **Perf. 13¼**
143-144 A80   Set of 2   8.00 8.00
Souvenir Sheet
Perf. 14x14¼
145 A81   €2 multi   5.25 5.25

2010 World Cup Soccer Championships, South Africa — A82

Designs: €1, Map of Kosovo and emblem of Kosovo Soccer Federation, map of Africa with soccer field. €2, Map of Kosovo and emblem of Kosovo Soccer Federation, map of Africa on soccer ball.
No. 148: a, Soccer ball as pendant on multicolored ribbon. b, Flag of South Africa on soccer ball.

2010, June 29   **Perf. 13¼**
146-147 A82   Set of 2   8.00 8.00
Souvenir Sheet
Perf. 14¼x14
148 A82 50c Sheet of 2, #a-b   3.00 3.00

Azem (1889-1924) and Shota (1895-1927) Galica, Fighters for Albanian Independence A83

2010, July 14   **Perf. 13¼**
149 A83   €2 multi   5.25 5.25

National Parks — A84

Scenery from: 20c, Mirusha National Park. 50c, Rugova National Park. 70c, Gjeravica National Park. €1, Sharri National Park.

2010, Aug. 2   **Litho.**
150-153 A84   Set of 4   6.50 6.50

Mother Teresa (1910-97), Humanitarian A85

2010, Aug. 26   **Perf. 13**
154 A85   €1 multi   2.75 2.75
See Albania No. 2889, Macedonia No. 529.

A86

Traffic in the Pathways of Integration — A87

2010, Sept. 9   Litho.   Perf. 13¼
155 A86   70c multi   2.00 2.00
Souvenir Sheet
Perf. 14¼x14
156 A87   €1 multi   3.00 3.00

A88   A89

A90   A91

Birds — A92

No. 161: a, 30c, Brown bird on branch. b, 30c, Blue and red bird on wire. c, 70c, Bird in flight. d, 70c, Blue and red bird on wire, bird in flight.

2010, Sept. 23   **Perf. 14x14¼**
157 A88 30c multi   .85 .85
158 A89 50c multi   1.50 1.50
159 A90 70c multi   2.00 2.00
160 A91 €1 multi   3.00 3.00
      Nos. 157-160 (4)   7.35 7.35
Souvenir Sheet
161 A92   Sheet of 4, #a-d   6.25 6.25

Local Foods — A93

Designs: 70c, Beehive, honeycombs, jar of honey. €1, Plates of food.

2010, Nov. 8   **Perf. 14¼x14**
162-163 A93   Set of 2   4.75 4.75

Campaign Against Violence Towards Women A94

2010, Nov. 25
164 A94 €1 multi   3.00 3.00

Historical Photographs of Basare — A95

Various street scenes: 50c, 70c, €1.

2010, Dec. 6
165-167 A95   Set of 3   6.50 6.50

A96

Independence, 3rd Anniv. — A97

2011, Feb. 27   **Perf. 14¼x14**
168 A96 €1 multi   2.50 2.50
169 A97 €2 multi   5.50 5.50

Elena Gjika (Dore D'Istria, 1828-88), Writer — A98

2011, Mar. 8   **Perf. 14x14¼**
170 A98 €1 multi   2.75 2.75

Prizren — A99

Designs: 20c, Houses on hillside. 50c, House and benches. 70c, View of city.

2011, Mar. 15
171-173 A99 Set of 3   4.00 4.00

A100

A101

Intl. Year of Forests — A102

2011, May 9   *Perf. 14¼x14*
174 A100 €1 multi   0.00 0.00
175 A101 €2 multi   5.75 5.75
Souvenir Sheet
176 A102 €2 multi   5.75 5.75

Archaeology
A103

Designs: 10c, Building ruins. 15c, Building ruins, diff. €1, Bas-relief head.

2011, June 7   *Perf. 14x14¼*
177-179 A103 Set of 3   3.75 3.75

A104

Traditional Costumes of Hasit
Region — A105

Designs: 30c, Shoes. 50c, Women's dress. 70c, Pouch. €1, Vest. €2, Kerchief.

2011, Oct. 19
180-183 A104 Set of 4   7.00 7.00
Souvenir Sheet
184 A105 €2 multi   5.50 5.50

A106

A107

A108

Mills — A109

2011, Nov. 2
185 A106 50c multi   1.40 1.40
186 A107 70c multi   2.00 2.00
187 A108 €1 multi   2.75 2.75
    Nos. 185-187 (3)   6.15 6.15
Souvenir Sheet
Perf. 14¼x14
188 A109 €2 multi   5.50 5.50

A110

Caves
A111

2011, Nov. 15   *Perf. 14x14¼*
189 A110 70c multi   1.90 1.90
190 A111 €1 multi   2.75 2.75

Rooster
A112

Rooster facing: 70c, Right. €1, Left.

2011, Nov. 21
191-192 A112 Set of 2   4.75 4.75

Esat Mekuli
(1916-93),
Poet — A113

2011, Dec. 17   *Perf. 14¼x14*
193 A113 €1 multi   2.60 2.60

Enver Zymeri
(1979-2011),
Police
Officer — A114

2011, Dec. 26
194 A114 €1 multi   2.60 2.60

Mitrovica
A115

Designs: €1, Monument, workers, street, aerial view of city. €2, Old and new street scenes.

2012, Jan. 20   *Perf. 14¼x14*
195-196 A115 Set of 2   8.00 8.00

A116

Freedom
Fighters — A117

2012, Jan. 27
197 A116 €1 multi   2.60 2.60
198 A117 €1 multi   2.60 2.60

Rexho Mulliqi
(1923-82),
Composer
A118

2012, Feb. 23
199 A118 €1 multi   2.75 2.75

Butterflies
A119

Various butterflies: 10c, 70c, €1. €2, Butterflies and orchids.

2012, Mar. 9   *Perf. 14x14¼*
200-202 A119 Set of 3   4.75 4.75
Souvenir Sheet
203 A119 €2 multi   5.25 5.25

A120

Europa — A121

Designs: €1, Cliff and valley. No. 205, €2, House. No. 206, €2, Buildings and bridge.

2012, Apr. 12   *Perf. 14¼x14*
204-205   A120   Set of 2   8.00 8.00
Souvenir Sheet
206   A121   €2 multi   5.25 5.25

Lakes A122

Designs: 20c, Badovac Lake. 50c, Gazivoda Lake. 70c, Lake Licenat.

2012, May 3   *Perf. 14x14¼*
207-209   A122   Set of 3   3.75 3.75

Isa Boletini (1864-1916), Kosovar Freedom Fighter — A123

Hasan Prishtina (1873-1933), Prime Minister of Albania — A124

2012, May 21   *Perf. 14¼x14*
210   A123   70c multi   1.75 1.75
211   A124   €1 multi   2.50 2.50

Bride in Archway — A125

2012, June 18
212   A125   €1 multi   2.50 2.50

Mejlinda Kelmendi, Kosovar Judoka Competing for Albania at 2012 Summer Olympics — A126

No. 213: a, 70c, Three images of Kelmendi. b, €1, Two images of Kelmendi.

2012, July 25   *Perf. 14x14¼*
213   A126   Pair, #a-b   4.25 4.25
Printed in sheets containing two pairs.

A127

A128

Myths and Legends — A129

2012, Sept. 5   *Perf. 14¼x14*
214   A127   70c multi   1.90 1.90
215   A128   €1 multi   2.60 2.60
Souvenir Sheet
Perf. 14x14¼
216   A129   €2 multi   5.25 5.25

Traditional Dances — A130

Various dancers: 50c, 70c, €1.

2012, Oct. 25   *Perf. 14¼x14*
217-219   A130   Set of 3   5.75 5.75

Albanian Independence, Cent. — A131

2012, Nov. 27
220   A131   €1 multi   2.60 2.60

Marin Barleti (c.1450-c. 1512), Historian A132

2012, Dec. 26
221   A132   €1 multi   2.75 2.75

Independence, 5th Anniv. — A133

2013, Feb. 17   *Perf. 14x14¼*
222   A133   €2 multi   5.25 5.25

Pristina — A134

Designs: 50c, Old and modern photographs of Pristina. 70c, Drawing of Pristina buildings. €1, People near building, Pristina skyline.

2013, Mar. 20   *Perf. 14¼x14*
223-225   A134   Set of 3   5.75 5.75

A135

A136

Museum Exhibits — A137

No. 228 — Table with window and small wall niche at: a, Left. b, Right.

2013, Apr. 5   *Perf. 14x14¼*
226   A135   70c multi   1.90 1.90
227   A136   €1 multi   2.60 2.60
Souvenir Sheet
Perf. 14¼x14
228   A137   €1 Sheet of 2, #a-b   5.25 5.25

A138

A139

Postal Transportation — A140

No. 231: a, Horse-drawn wagon. b, Postman on scooter.

2013, May 2   *Litho.*   *Perf. 14x14¼*
229   A138   €1 multi   2.60 2.60
230   A139   €2 multi   5.25 5.25
Souvenir Sheet
Perf. 14¼x14
231   A140   €1 Sheet of 2, #a-b   5.25 5.25

Mountain Scenery — A141

Designs: 50c, Mt. Gjeravica. 70c Rugova Canyon (Gryka e Rugoves). €1, Mt. Gjeravica, diff.

2013, June 14   *Litho.*   *Perf. 14¼x14¼*
232-234   A141   Set of 3   6.00 6.00

Villages
A142

Designs: 50c, Stublla e Eperme. 70c, Opoja. €1, Lluka e Eperme.

2013, July 18   Litho.   Perf. 14x14¼
235-237 A142   Set of 3   6.00 6.00

Famous Women — A143

No. 238: a, 50c, Hyrije Hana (1929-2004), radio broadcaster. b, 70c, Xheve Lladrovici (1955-98), freedom fighter. c, €1, Katarina Josipi (1923-69), actress.

2013, Aug. 15   Litho.   Perf. 14¼x14
238 A143   Horiz. strip of 3, #a-c   6.00 6.00

Bajram Curri (1862-1925), Albanian Politician — A144

2013, Sept. 9   Litho.   Perf. 14x14¼
239 A144   €1 multi   2.75 2.75

Paintings by Adem Kastrati (1930-2000) — A145

Various paintings depicting: a, 70c, Buildings on hill. b, €1, Sheep and shepherds. c, €2, Musicians.

2013, Spet. 26   Litho.   Perf. 14x14¼
240 A145   Vert. strip of 3, #a-c   10.00 10.00

Pristina University A146

2014, Oct. 28   Litho.   Perf. 14x14¼
241 A146   €1 multi   2.75 2.75

Singers
A147

No. 242: a, 20c, Qamili i Vogel (1923-91). b, 30c, Sali Krasniqi (1919-87). c, 50c, Dervish Shaqa (1912-85).

2013, Nov. 15   Litho.   Perf. 14x14¼
242 A147   Vert. strip of 3, #a-c   2.75 2.75

Bekim Fehmiu (1936-2010), Actor — A148

2013, Dec. 5   Litho.   Perf. 14¼x14
243 A148   €1 multi   2.75 2.75

Paintings by Muslim Mulliqi (1934-98) A149

Various paintings.

2014, Jan. 13   Litho.   Perf. 14¼x14
244   Horiz. strip of 4   7.75 7.75
  a. A149 30c multi   .80 .80
  b. A149 60c multi   1.60 1.60
  c. A149 90c multi   2.50 2.50
  d. A149 €1 multi   2.75 2.75

Souvenir Sheet

Mountaineering — A151

2014, Feb. 7   Litho.   Perf. 14x14¼
246 A151   €2 multi   5.50 5.50

Pec
A152

Buildings in Pec: €1, Color photograph. €2, Sepia-toned photograph.

2014, Mar. 10   Litho.   Perf. 14x14¼
247-248 A152   Set of 2   8.25 8.25

World Shotokan Karate Championships, Pristina — A153

No. 249 — Two karateka and: a, 80c, Colored belts and "5." b, 90c, Map of Kosovo and world.
€2, Karateka and map of Kosovo and world.

2014, Apr. 3   Litho.   Perf. 14x14¼
249 A153   Pair, #a-b   4.75 4.75
Souvenir Sheet
250 A153   €2 multi   5.50 5.50

No. 249 was printed in sheets containing two pairs + label.

Ibrahim Rugova Highway — A154

No. 251: a, €1, Bridge and interchange. b, €2, Entrance and exit ramps.

2014, Apr. 25   Litho.   Perf. 14x14¼
251 A154   Pair, #a-b   8.25 8.25

Europa — A155

Musical instruments: €1, Two instruments. No. 253, €2, Lakuta.
No. 254, €2, Four instruments, horiz.

2014, May 8   Litho.   Perf. 14¼x14
252-253 A155   Set of 2   8.25 8.25
Souvenir Sheet
Perf. 14x14¼
254 A155   €2 multi   5.50 5.50

Flowers — A156

Designs: 80c, Liliaceae. 90c, Gladiolus illyricus. €1, Tulipa kosovarica.

2014, June 12   Litho.   Perf. 14¼x14
255-257 A156   Set of 3   7.50 7.50

Jeronim de Rada (1814-1903), Writer — A157

2014, July 3   Litho.   Perf. 14¼x14
259 A157   €1 multi   2.75 2.75

Woven Items — A158

Various woven items.

2014, Aug. 8   Litho.   Perf. 14¼x14
260   Horiz. strip or block of 4,
       #a-d   8.75 8.75
  a. A158 60c multi   1.60 1.60
  b. A158 80c multi   2.10 2.10
  c. A158 90c multi   2.40 2.40
  d. A158 €1 multi   2.60 2.60

Fehmi (1950-98) and Xheve (1955-98) Lladrovci, Freedom Fighters A159

2014, Sept. 22   Litho.   Perf. 14x14¼
261 A159   €2 multi   5.00 5.00

Adrian Krasniqi (1972-97), Freedom Fighter — A160

2014, Oct. 16   Litho.   Perf. 14¼x14
262 A160   €1 multi   2.50 2.50

Tringe Smajli (1880-1917), Freedom Fighter — A161

2014, Nov. 2   Litho.   Perf. 14¼x14
263 A161   €1 multi   2.50 2.50

Intl. Year of Crystallography — A162

Various mineral crystals: €1, €2.

2014, Nov. 20   Litho.   Perf. 14x14¼
264-265 A162   Set of 2   7.50 7.50

Granting of Intl. Olympic Committee Membership to Kosovo Olympic Committee — A163

2014, Dec. 5   Litho.   Perf. 14¼x14
266 A163 €2 multi   5.00 5.00

No. 266 was printed in sheets of 6 + 3 labels.

KUWAIT

ku-'wāt

LOCATION — Northwestern coast of the Persian Gulf
GOVT. — Sheikdom
AREA — 7,000 sq. mi.
POP. — 1,991,115 (1999 est.)
CAPITAL — Kuwait

Kuwait was under British protection until June 19, 1961, when it became a fully independent state.

16 Annas = 1 Rupee
100 Naye Paise = 1 Rupee (1957)
1000 Fils = 1 Kuwaiti Dinar (1961)

> Catalogue values for unused stamps in this country are for Never Hinged items, beginning with Scott 72 in the regular postage section, Scott C5 in the air post section, and Scott J1 in the postage due section.

There was a first or trial setting of the overprint with the word "Koweit." Twenty-four sets of regular and official stamps were printed with this spelling. Value for set, $10,000.

> Catalogue values for Nos. 1-71 used, are for postally used examples. Stamps with telegraph cancellations are worth less.

Iraqi Postal Administration
Stamps of India, 1911-23, Overprinted

a   b

1923-24		**Wmk. 39**	**Perf. 14**	
1	A47(a)	½a green	4.75	13.50
2	A48(a)	1a dk brn	7.00	5.00
3	A58(a)	1½a choc	5.00	10.00
4	A49(a)	2a violet	5.00	8.00
5	A57(a)	2a6p ultra	3.75	8.00
6	A51(a)	3a brn org	5.00	25.00
7	A51(a)	3a ultra ('24)	12.50	4.00
8	A52(a)	4a ol green	11.50	25.00
9	A53(a)	6a bister	13.00	16.00
10	A54(a)	8a red vio	12.00	50.00
11	A55(a)	12a claret	16.00	55.00
12	A56(b)	1r grn & red brn	45.00	55.00
13	A56(b)	2r brn & car rose	60.00	115.00
14	A56(b)	5r vio & ultra	140.00	275.00

15	A56(b)	10r car & grn	250.00	525.00
	Nos. 1-15 (15)		590.50	*1,189.*

Overprint "a" on India No. 102 is generally considered unofficial.
Nos. 1-4, 6-7 exist with inverted overprint. None of these are believed to have been sold at the Kuwait post office.
For overprints see Nos. O1-O13.

Stamps of India, 1926-35, Overprinted Type "a"

1929-37			**Wmk. 196**	
17	A47	½a green	10.00	2.25
18	A71	½a green ('34)	8.00	2.00
19	A48	1a dark brown	7.00	3.50
20	A72	1a dk brown ('34)	14.00	1.25
21	A60	2a dk violet	7.00	1.75
22	A60	2a vermilion	27.50	95.00
23	A49	2a ver ('34)	17.50	6.75
a.	Small die		6.50	2.50
24	A51	3a ultramarine	6.00	3.00
25	A51	3a car rose ('34)	9.00	4.50
26	A61	4a olive green	40.00	100.00
27	A52	4a ol green ('34)	14.00	14.50
28	A53	6a bister ('37)	27.50	65.00
29	A54	8a red violet	42.50	15.00
30	A55	12a claret	35.00	50.00

Overprinted — c

31	A56	1r grn & brn	80.00	50.00
32	A56	2r buff & car rose	25.00	72.50
33	A56	5r dk vio & ultra ('37)	130.00	325.00
34	A56	10r car & grn ('34)	275.00	525.00
35	A56	15r ol grn & ultra ('37)	900.00	1,150.
	Nos. 17-35 (19)		1,675.	*2,487.*

For overprints see Nos. O15-O25.

Stamps of India, 1937, Overprinted Type "a" (A80, A81) or "c" (A82)

1939		**Wmk. 196**	**Perf. 13½x14**	
45	A80	½a brown	4.25	3.50
46	A80	1a carmine	4.25	3.50
47	A81	2a scarlet	4.50	5.00
48	A81	3a yel green	6.00	3.25
49	A81	4a dark brown	25.00	30.00
50	A81	6a peacock blue	16.00	20.00
51	A81	8a blue violet	17.50	35.00
52	A81	12a car lake	12.00	85.00
53	A82	1r brown & slate	16.00	8.75
a.	Elongated "T"		650.00	675.00
54	A82	2r dk brn & dk vio	5.00	27.50
a.	Elongated "T"		650.00	1,125.
55	A82	5r dp ultra & dk green	12.00	30.00
a.	Elongated "T"		950.00	
56	A82	10r rose car & dk violet	50.00	100.00
a.	Double overprint		500.00	—
b.	Elongated "T"		1,525.	
57	A82	15r dk grn & dk brn	75.00	225.00
a.	Elongated "T"		3,000.	
	Nos. 45-57 (13)		247.50	*576.50*
	Set, never hinged		400.00	

The elongated "T" variety was corrected in later printings.

Indian Postal Administration

From May 24, 1941, until August 1947, the Kuwaiti postal service was administered by India, and during 1941-45 unoverprinted Indian stamps were used in Kuwait.
Kuwait postal services were administered by Pakistan from August 1947 through March 1948. Control was transferred to Great Britain on April 1, 1948.

Stamps of India 1940-43, Overprinted in Black

1945		**Wmk. 196**	**Perf. 13½x14**	
59	A83	3p slate	2.75	10.00
60	A83	3a rose violet	1.75	5.50
61	A83	9p lt green	2.75	18.50
62	A83	1a car rose	2.00	2.50

63	A84	1½a dark purple	2.75	11.00
64	A84	2a scarlet	3.00	8.50
65	A84	3a violet	4.00	16.00
66	A84	3½a ultramarine	3.75	17.50
67	A85	4a chocolate	4.00	4.75
68	A85	6a peacock blue	11.00	22.50
69	A85	8a blue violet	5.75	15.00
70	A85	12a car lake	6.00	9.00
71	A81	14a rose violet	11.00	24.00
	Nos. 59-71 (13)		60.50	*164.75*
	Set, never hinged		110.00	

> Catalogue values for unused stamps in this section, from this point to the end of the section, are for Never Hinged items.

British Postal Administration

See Oman (Muscat) for similar stamps with surcharge of new value only.

Great Britain Nos. 258 to 263, 243 and 248 Surcharged in Black

1948-49		**Wmk. 251**	**Perf. 14½x14**	
72	A101	½a on ½p grn	3.50	4.00
73	A101	1a on 1p ver	3.50	2.50
74	A101	1½a on 1½p lt red brown	4.50	2.50
75	A101	2a on 2p lt org	3.50	2.50
76	A101	2½a on 2½p ultra	4.00	1.25
77	A101	3a on 3p violet	3.50	1.10
a.	Pair, one without surcharge		6,250.	
78	A102	6a on 6p rose lil	3.50	1.00
79	A103	1r on 1sh brown	7.50	2.50

Great Britain Nos. 249A, 250 and 251A Surcharged in Black

		Wmk. 259	**Perf. 14**	
80	A104	2r on 2sh6p yel grn	8.50	9.00
81	A104	5r on 5sh dull red	11.00	9.00
81A	A105	10r on 10sh ultra	60.00	11.50
	Nos. 72-81A (11)		113.00	*46.85*

Issued: Nos. 72-81, 4/48; 10r, 7/4/49.
Bars of surcharge at bottom on No. 81A.

Silver Wedding Issue

Great Britain Nos. 267 and 268 Surcharged in Black

		Perf. 14½x14, 14x14½		
1948			**Wmk. 251**	
82	A109	2½a on 2½p brt ul-tra	3.00	3.00
83	A110	15r on £1 deep chalky blue	42.50	42.50

Three bars obliterate the original denomination on No. 83.

Olympic Games Issue

Great Britain Nos. 271 to 274 Surcharged "KUWAIT" and New Value in Black

1948			**Perf. 14½x14**	
84	A113	2½a on 2½p brt ultra	1.75	3.25
85	A114	3a on 3p dp violet	2.00	3.50
86	A115	6a on 6p red violet	2.10	4.00
87	A116	1r on 1sh dk brown	2.50	4.50
	Nos. 84-87 (4)		8.35	*15.25*

A square of dots obliterates the original denomination on No. 87.

UPU Issue

Great Britain Nos. 276 to 279 Surcharged "KUWAIT", New Value and Square of Dots in Black

1949, Oct. 10			**Photo.**	
89	A117	2½a on 2½p brt ul-tra	1.25	2.50
90	A118	3a on 3p brt vio	1.50	3.00

91	A119	6a on 6p red vio	1.60	3.00
92	A120	1r on 1sh brown	1.75	1.75
	Nos. 89-92 (4)		6.10	*10.25*

Great Britain Nos. 280-285 Surcharged Like Nos. 72-79 in Black

1950-51		**Wmk. 251**	**Perf. 14½x14**	
93	A101	½a on ½p lt org	2.75	1.50
94	A101	1a on 1p ultra	2.75	1.60
95	A101	1½a on 1½p green	2.75	2.25
96	A101	2a on 2p lt red brown	2.75	1.50
97	A101	2½a on 2½p ver	2.75	2.75
98	A102	4a on 4p ultra ('50)	2.75	1.50

Great Britain Nos. 286-288 Surcharged in Black

		Perf. 11x12		
		Wmk. 259		
99	A121	2r on 2sh6p green	24.00	8.75
100	A121	5r on 5sh dl red	30.00	10.00
101	A122	10r on 10sh ultra	50.00	11.00
	Nos. 93-101 (9)		120.50	*40.85*

Longer bars, at lower right, on No. 101.
Issued: 4a, 10/2/50; others, 5/3/51.

Stamps of Great Britain, 1952-54 Surcharged "KUWAIT" and New Value in Black or Dark Blue

1952-54		**Wmk. 298**	**Perf. 14½x14**	
102	A126	½a on ½p red org ('53)	.30	1.25
103	A126	1a on 1p ultra ('53)	.30	.25
104	A126	1½a on 1½p green ('53)	.25	1.75
105	A126	2a on 2p red brn ('53)	.35	.25
106	A127	2½a on 2½p scarlet	.40	1.75
107	A127	3a on 3p dk pur (Dk Bl) ('54)	.55	.25
108	A128	4a on 4p ultra ('53)	1.60	1.00
109	A129	6a on 6p lilac rose ('54)	2.25	.25
111	A132	12a on 1sh3p dk green ('53)	6.00	2.50
112	A131	1r on 1sh6p dk blue ('53)	4.75	.25
	Nos. 102-112 (10)		16.75	*9.50*

Coronation Issue

Great Britain Nos. 313-316 Surcharged "KUWAIT" and New Value in Black

1953, June 3				
113	A134	2½a on 2½p scarlet	3.75	2.00
114	A135	4a on 4p brt ultra	3.25	2.00
115	A136	12a on 1sh3p dk grn	5.00	3.50
116	A137	1r on 1sh6p dk blue	4.00	1.00
	Nos. 113-116 (4)		16.00	*8.50*

Squares of dots obliterate the original denominations on Nos. 115 and 116.

Great Britain Stamps of 1955-56 Surcharged "KUWAIT" and New Value in Black

1955		**Wmk. 308 Engr.**	**Perf. 11x12**	
117	A133	2r on 2sh6p dk brown	10.00	3.00
118	A133	5r on 5sh crimson	11.00	8.00
119	A133	10r on 10sh dp ultra	12.00	6.00
	Nos. 117-119 (3)		33.00	*17.00*

The surcharge on Nos. 117-119 exists in two types.

1956		**Photo.**	**Perf. 14½x14**	
120	A126	½a on ½p red org	.35	1.75
121	A126	1a on 1p ultra	.50	3.25
122	A126	1½a on 1½p green	.40	.75
123	A126	2a on 2p red brown	.40	.50
124	A127	2½a on 2½p scar	.85	3.75
125	A128	4a on 4p ultra	4.75	3.50
126	A129	6a on 6p lil rose	2.25	.40
127	A132	12a on 1sh3p dk grn	10.00	8.00
128	A131	1r on 1sh6p dk bl	12.00	.35
	Nos. 120-128 (9)		31.50	*22.25*

Great Britain Nos. 317-325, 328 and 332 Surcharged "KUWAIT" and New Value in Black

1957-58		**Wmk. 308**	**Perf. 14½x14**	
129	A129	1np on 5p lt brown	.35	.70
130	A126	3np on ½p red org	.75	3.00
131	A126	6np on 1p ultra	.75	1.25

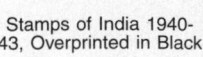

132	A126	9np on 1½p green	.75	3.25
133	A126	12np on 2p red brn	.75	4.25
134	A127	15np on 2½p scar, type I	.75	5.50
a.		Type II ('58)	50.00	110.00
135	A127	20np on 3p dk pur	.80	.45
136	A128	25np on 4p ultra	2.75	3.25
137	A129	40np on 6p lilac rose	1.00	.30
138	A130	50np on 9p dp ol grn	5.75	4.00
139	A132	75np on 1sh3p dk grn	6.00	5.00
		Nos. 129-139 (11)	20.40	30.95

The arrangement of the surcharge varies on different values; there are three bars through value on No. 138.

Sheik Abdullah A1   Dhow A2

Oil Derrick A3

Designs: 50np, Pipe lines. 75np, Main square, Kuwait. 2r, Dhow, derrick and Sheik. 5r, Mosque and Sheik. 10r, Oil plant at Burgan and Sheik.

Perf. 12½

1959, Feb. 1   Unwmk.   Engr.

140	A1	5np green	1.00	.25
141	A1	10np rose brown	.70	.25
142	A1	15np yellow brown	.45	.25
143	A1	20np gray violet	.45	.25
144	A1	25np vermilion	.75	.25
145	A1	40np rose claret	4.25	1.25

Perf. 13½x13

146	A2	40np dark blue	.80	.25
147	A2	50np carmine	.80	.25
148	A2	75np olive green	.85	.45

Perf. 14x13½

149	A3	1r claret	1.50	.55
150	A3	2r red brn & dp bl	3.75	1.00
151	A3	5r green	7.50	2.75
152	A3	10r purple	22.50	6.50
		Nos. 140-152 (13)	45.30	14.25

No. 140-141 and 145 were issued in 1958 for local use. They became valid for international mail on Feb. 1, 1959, but No. 145 was withdrawn after two weeks.

Sheik Abdullah and Flag — A4

1960, Feb. 25   Engr.   Perf. 14

153	A4	40np olive grn & red	.65	.25
154	A4	60np blue & red	.95	.30

10th anniv. of the accession of Sheik Sir Abdullah As-Salim As-Sabah.

Types of 1959, Redrawn

Designs: 20f, 3d, Mosque and Sheik. 25f, 100f, Vickers Viscount. 30f, 75f, Dhow, derrick and Sheik. 35f, 90f, Shuwaikh secondary school. 45f, 1d, Wara Hill, Burgan oil field.

1961   Perf. 12½

155	A1	1f green	.35	.25
156	A1	2f rose brown	.35	.25
157	A1	4f yellow brown	.35	.25
158	A1	5f gray violet	.35	.25
159	A1	8f salmon pink	.35	.25
160	A1	15f rose claret	.35	.25

Perf. 14x13½, 13½ (40f, 250f)

161	A3	20f green	.35	.25
162	A3	25f blue	.55	.25
163	A3	30f red brn & dp bl	.65	.25
164	A3	35f ver & black	.75	.30
165	A2	40f dark blue	.80	.30
166	A3	45f violet brown	.95	.30
167	A3	75f green & sepia	1.50	.75
168	A3	90f ultra & brown	1.25	.65
169	A3	100f rose red	2.50	.30
170	A2	250f olive green	10.00	1.50

171	A3	1d orange	18.00	5.00
172	A3	3d brick red	50.00	30.00
		Nos. 155-172 (18)	89.40	41.35

Nos. 165 and 170 are 32x22mm.
Issued: 75f, 90f, 4/27; 35f, 5/8; others, 4/1.

Symbols of Telecommunications — A5

Perf. 11½

1962, Jan. 11   Unwmk.   Photo.
Granite Paper

173	A5	8f blue & black	.45	.25
174	A5	20f rose & black	1.00	.55

4th Arab Telecommunications Union Conference.

Mubarakiya School and Sheiks Abdullah and Mubarak — A6

1962, Apr. 15   Unwmk.   Perf. 11½

175	A6	8f gldn brn, blk, org & gold	.45	.25
176	A6	20f lt blue, blk, org & gold	.90	.45

50th anniversary of Mubarakiya School.

Arab League Building, Cairo, and Emblem — A7

1962, Apr. 23   Perf. 13½x13

177	A7	20f purple	.30	.25
178	A7	45f brown	1.00	.55

Arab Publicity Week, Mar. 22-28.

Flag of Kuwait — A8

1962, June 19   Perf. 11½
Flag in Green, Black & Red

179	A8	8f black & tan	.30	.25
180	A8	20f black & yellow	.45	.30
181	A8	45f black & lt blue	.90	.45
182	A8	90f black & lilac	1.40	1.00
		Nos. 179-182 (4)	3.05	2.00

Issued for National Day, June 19.

Malaria Eradication Emblem — A9

1962, Aug. 1   Perf. 13½x13

183	A9	4f slate green & yel grn	.30	.25
184	A9	25f green & gray	.60	.30

WHO drive to eradicate malaria. No. 184 has laurel leaves added and inscription rearranged.

Cogwheel, Oil Wells, Camels and Modern Building — A10

Perf. 11x13

1962, Dec. 8   Unwmk.   Litho.

185	A10	8f multicolored	.35	.25
186	A10	20f multicolored	.60	.25
187	A10	45f multicolored	1.00	1.00
188	A10	75f multicolored	1.75	1.00
		Nos. 185-188 (4)	3.70	2.00

Bicentenary of the Sabah dynasty.

Mother and Child — A11

1963, Mar. 21   Photo.   Perf. 14½x14

189	A11	8f yel, red, blk & green	.30	.25
190	A11	20f blue, red, blk & grn	.40	.25
191	A11	45f lt ol, red, blk & grn	.90	.50
192	A11	75f gray, red, blk & grn	1.10	.60
		Nos. 189-192 (4)	2.70	1.60

Issued for Mother's Day, Mar. 21, 1963.

Wheat Emblem, Date Palm, Cow and Sheep — A12

1963, Mar. 21   Perf. 14x14½

193	A12	4f red brn, lt blue & grn	.50	.25
194	A12	8f brown, yel & green	.60	.25
195	A12	20f red brn, pale vio & green	.90	.60
196	A12	45f red brn, rose & green	1.75	1.25
		Nos. 193-196 (4)	3.75	2.35

FAO "Freedom from Hunger" campaign.

Test Tube, Oil Drops and Ship — A13

1963, Apr. 15   Photo.   Perf. 14½x14

197	A13	4f brown, yel & blue	.30	.25
198	A13	20f green, yel & blue	.45	.25
199	A13	45f brt mag, yel & blue	1.00	.50
		Nos. 197-199 (3)	1.75	1.00

Issued for Education Day.

Sheik Abdullah, Flags and Map of Kuwait A14

1963, June 19   Perf. 14x13
Flags in Black, Bright Green & Red; Denominations in Black

200	A14	4f ultramarine	1.00	.50
201	A14	5f ocher	1.25	.80
202	A14	20f bright lilac	4.50	3.00
203	A14	50f olive	9.00	6.00
		Nos. 200-203 (4)	15.75	10.30

Second anniversary of National Day.

Lungs and Emblems of World Health Organization and Kuwait Tuberculosis Society A15

1963, July 27   Perf. 13x13½
Design in Yellow, Black, Emerald & Red

204	A15	2f ocher	.30	.25
205	A15	4f dark green	.35	.25
206	A15	8f lt violet blue	.50	.25
207	A15	20f rose brown	1.10	.60
		Nos. 204-207 (4)	2.25	1.35

Issued to publicize tuberculosis control.

Sheik Abdullah, Scroll and Scales of Justice — A16

1963, Oct. 29   Photo.   Perf. 11x13
Center in Gray

208	A16	4f dp red & red brn	.35	.25
209	A16	8f dk green & red brn	.50	.25
210	A16	20f vio brn & red brn	.75	.30
211	A16	45f brn org & red brn	1.25	.65
212	A16	75f purple & red brown	1.90	1.25
213	A16	90f ultra & red brown	2.50	1.60
		Nos. 208-213 (6)	7.25	4.30

Promulgation of the constitution.

Soccer — A17

Sports: 4f, Basketball. 5f, Swimming, horiz. 8f, Track. 15f, Javelin, horiz. 20f, Pole vault, horiz. 35f, Gymnast on rings, horiz. 45f, Gymnast on parallel bars.

1963, Nov. 8   Unwmk.   Perf. 14½x14

214	A17	1f multicolored	.30	.25
215	A17	4f multicolored	.30	.25
216	A17	5f multicolored	.30	.25
217	A17	8f multicolored	.40	.25
218	A17	15f multicolored	.70	.25
219	A17	20f multicolored	1.00	.30
220	A17	35f multicolored	1.75	.75
221	A17	45f multicolored	3.00	1.40
		Nos. 214-221 (8)	7.75	3.70

Arab School Games of 1963.

UNESCO
Emblem, Scales
and
Globe — A18

1963, Dec. 10   Litho.   Perf. 13x12½
222	A18	8f violet, blk & pale grn	.30	.25
223	A18	20f gray, black & yel	.60	.45
224	A18	25f blue, black & tan	1.25	.80
		Nos. 222-224 (3)	2.15	1.50

15th anniv. of the Universal Declaration of
Human Rights.

Sheik
Abdullah — A19

Perf. 12½x13
1964, Feb. 1   Unwmk.   Photo.
Portrait in Natural Colors
225	A19	1f gray & silver	.25	.25
a.		Booklet pane of 6 ('66)	2.25	
226	A19	2f brt blue & silver	.25	.25
227	A19	4f ocher & silver	.30	.25
228	A19	5f fawn & silver	.30	.25
229	A19	8f dk brown & sil	.30	.25
230	A19	10f citron & sil	.40	.25
a.		Booklet pane of 6 ('66)	2.25	
231	A19	15f brt green & sil	.75	.25
a.		Booklet pane of 6 ('66)	6.00	
232	A19	20f blue gray & sil	.55	.25
a.		Booklet pane of 6 ('66)	3.75	
233	A19	25f green & silver	.65	.30
234	A19	30f gray grn & sil	.75	.30
235	A19	40f brt vio & sil	1.10	.45
236	A19	45f violet & silver	1.20	.55
237	A19	50f olive & silver	1.25	.55
238	A19	70f red lilac & sil	1.50	.65
239	A19	75f rose red & sil	2.00	.75
240	A19	90f ultra & silver	3.00	.75
241	A19	100f pale lilac & sil	3.50	.65

Perf. 14x14½
Size: 25x30mm
242	A19	250f brown & sil	10.00	2.75
243	A19	1d brown vio & sil	35.00	10.00
		Nos. 225-243 (19)	63.05	19.70

Ramses II
Battling the
Hittites (from
Abu
Simbel) — A20

Engr. & Litho.
1964, Mar. 8   Perf. 13x12½
244	A20	8f buff, ind & maroon	.30	.25
245	A20	20f lt blue, indigo & vio	.75	.55
246	A20	30f bluish grn, ind & vio	1.10	.65
		Nos. 244-246 (3)	2.15	1.45

UNESCO world campaign to save historic
monuments in Nubia.

Mother and
Child — A21

1964, Mar. 21   Litho.   Perf. 14x13
247	A21	8f green, gray & vio blk	.30	.25
248	A21	20f green, red & vio blk	.45	.25
249	A21	30f grn, ol bis & vio blk	.60	.40
250	A21	45f grn, saph & vio blk	.75	.60
		Nos. 247-250 (4)	2.10	1.50

Issued for Mother's Day, Mar. 21.

Nurse
Giving TB
Test, and
Thorax
A22

Perf. 13x13½
1964, Apr. 7   Photo.   Unwmk.
251	A22	8f brown & green	.50	.25
252	A22	20f green & rose red	1.40	.35

Issued for World Health Day (fight against
tuberculosis), Apr. 7, 1964.

Microscope and
Dhow — A23

1964, Apr. 15   Perf. 12½x13
253	A23	8f multicolored	.25	.25
254	A23	15f multicolored	.30	.25
255	A23	20f multicolored	.50	.30
256	A23	30f multicolored	.75	.60
		Nos. 253-256 (4)	1.80	1.40

Issued for Education Day.

Doves and State Seal — A24

1964, June 19   Litho.   Perf. 13½
**Seal in Blue, Brown, Black, Red &
Green**
257	A24	8f black & bister brn	.35	.25
258	A24	20f black & green	.55	.30
259	A24	30f black & gray	1.10	.50
260	A24	45f black & blue	1.25	.75
		Nos. 257-260 (4)	3.25	1.80

Third anniversary of National Day.

Arab Postal Union
Emblem — A25

1964, Nov. 21   Photo.   Perf. 11x11½
261	A25	8f lt blue & brown	.35	.25
262	A25	20f yellow & ultra	.70	.25
263	A25	45f olive & brown	1.25	.70
		Nos. 261-263 (3)	2.30	1.20

Permanent Office of the APU, 10th anniv.

Conference
Emblem
A26

1965, Feb. 8   Litho.   Perf. 14
264	A26	8f black, org brn & yel	.45	.25
265	A26	20f multicolored	.75	.30

First Arab Journalists' Conference.

Oil Derrick, Dhow,
Sun and
Doves — A27

1965, Feb. 25   Perf. 13½
266	A27	10f lt green & multi	.35	.25
267	A27	15f pink & multi	.75	.25
268	A27	20f gray & multi	1.10	.45
		Nos. 266-268 (3)	2.20	.95

Fourth anniversary of National Day.

Mother and
Children — A28

1965, Mar. 21   Unwmk.   Perf. 13½
269	A28	8f multicolored	.35	.25
270	A28	15f multicolored	.50	.35
271	A28	20f multicolored	.75	.60
		Nos. 269-271 (3)	1.60	1.20

Mother's Day, Mar. 21.

Weather
Balloon
A29

1965, Mar. 23   Photo.   Perf. 11½x11
272	A29	4f deep ultra & yellow	.55	.25
273	A29	5f blue & dp orange	.65	.25
274	A29	20f dk blue & emerald	1.25	1.00
		Nos. 272-274 (3)	2.45	1.50

Fifth World Meteorological Day.

Census
Chart,
Map and
Family
A30

1965, Mar. 28   Litho.   Perf. 13½
275	A30	8f multicolored	.30	.25
276	A30	20f multicolored	.75	.25
277	A30	50f multicolored	1.90	.85
		Nos. 275-277 (3)	2.95	1.35

Issued to publicize the 1965 census.

ICY
Emblem
A31

1965, Mar. 7   Engr.
278	A31	8f red & black	.30	.25
279	A31	20f lt ultra & black	.65	.30
280	A31	30f emerald & black	1.25	.55
		Nos. 278-280 (3)	2.20	1.10

International Cooperation Year.

Dagger in Map of
Palestine — A31a

Perf. 11x11½
1965, Apr. 9   Photo.   Unwmk.
281	A31a	4f red & ultra	2.25	.35
282	A31a	45f red & emerald	4.75	1.00

Deir Yassin massacre, Apr. 9, 1948. See
Iraq Nos. 372-373 and Jordan No. 499.

Tower of
Shuwaikh
School and
Atom Symbol
A32

1965, Apr. 15   Litho.   Perf. 14x13
283	A32	4f multicolored	.30	.25
284	A32	20f multicolored	.65	.40
285	A32	45f multicolored	1.25	1.00
		Nos. 283-285 (3)	2.20	1.65

Issued for Education Day.

ITU Emblem, Old and New
Communication Equipment — A33

1965, May 17   Perf. 13½x14
286	A33	8f dk blue, lt bl & red	.40	.30
287	A33	20f green, lt grn & red	1.50	.40
288	A33	45f red, pink & blue	2.75	1.25
		Nos. 286-288 (3)	4.65	1.95

ITU, centenary.

Library
Aflame
and Lamp
A33a

1965, June 7   Photo.   Perf. 11
289	A33a	8f black, green & red	.70	.25
290	A33a	15f black, red & green	1.40	.45

Burning of Library of Algiers, June 7, 1962.

Falcon — A34

1965, Dec. 1   Engr.   Perf. 13
Center in Sepia
291	A34	8f red lilac	2.25	.30
292	A34	15f olive green	2.00	.30
293	A34	20f dark blue	3.00	.55
294	A34	25f orange	3.25	.70
295	A34	30f emerald	4.00	.80
296	A34	45f blue	8.00	1.25
297	A34	50f claret	9.00	1.40
298	A34	90f carmine	16.00	2.75
		Nos. 291-298 (8)	47.50	8.05

Book and Wreath
Emblem — A35

1966, Jan. 10   Photo.   Perf. 14x15
299	A35	8f lt violet & multi	.35	.25
300	A35	20f brown red & multi	.70	.40
301	A35	30f blue & multi	1.25	.65
		Nos. 299-301 (3)	2.30	1.30

Issued for Education Day.

Sheik Sabah as-
Salim as-
Sabah — A36

1966, Feb. 1   Photo.   Perf. 14x13
302 A36   4f lt blue & multi   .30   .25
303 A36   5f pale rose & multi   .30   .25
304 A36 20f multicolored   .50   .25
305 A36 30f lt violet & multi   .75   .35
306 A36 40f salmon & multi   .90   .50
307 A36 45f lt gray & multi   1.00   .60
308 A36 70f yellow & multi   2.00 1.00
309 A36 90f pale green & multi   3.00 1.50
        Nos. 302-309 (8)   8.75 4.70

Wheat and Fish — A37

1966, Feb. 15   Perf. 11x11½
310 A37 20f multicolored   2.25   .90
311 A37 45f multicolored   3.50 1.60
    "Freedom from Hunger" campaign.

Eagle, Banner, Scales and Emblems — A38

1966, Feb. 25   Litho.   Perf. 12½x13
312 A38 20f tan & multi   1.25   .40
313 A38 25f lt green & multi   1.25   .55
314 A38 45f gray & multi   3.00 1.25
        Nos. 312-314 (3)   5.50 2.20
    Fifth anniversary of National Day.

Wheel of Industry and Map of Arab Countries A39

1966, Mar. 1   Perf. 14x13½
315 A39 20f brt blue, brt grn & blk   .75   .25
316 A39 50f lt red brn, brt grn & black 1.25   .75
    Issued to publicize the conference on industrial development in Arab countries.

Mother and Children — A40

1966, Mar. 21   Perf. 11½x11
317 A40 20f pink & multi   .75   .25
318 A40 45f multicolored   1.60   .75
    Mother's Day, Mar. 21.

Medical Conference Emblem — A41

1966, Apr. 1   Photo.   Perf. 14½x14
319 A41 15f blue & red   .60   .75
320 A41 30f red & blue   1.20   .75
    Fifth Arab Medical Conference, Kuwait.

Composite View of a City — A42

1966, Apr. 7   Litho.   Perf. 12½x13
321 A42   8f multicolored   .75   .25
322 A42 10f multicolored   1.25   .30
    Issued for World Health Day, Apr. 7.

Inauguration of WHO Headquarters, Geneva — A43

1966, May 3   Litho.   Perf. 11x11½
323 A43   5f dull sal, ol grn & vio bl   .70   .25
324 A43 10f lt grn, ol grn & vio blue   1.40   .25

Traffic Signal at Night — A44

1966, May 4
325 A44 10f green, red & black   1.00   .25
326 A44 20f green, red & black   1.25   .40
    Issued for Traffic Day.

"Blood Transfusion" — A45

1966, May 5   Perf. 13½
327 A45   4f multicolored   .70   .25
328 A45   8f multicolored   1.10   .50
    Blood Bank Day, May 5.

Sheik Ahmad and Ship Carrying First Crude Oil Shipment A46

1966, June 30   Perf. 13½
329 A46 20f multicolored   1.25   .55
330 A46 45f multicolored   2.50 1.10
    20th anniv. of the first crude oil shipment, June 30, 1946.

Ministry of Guidance and Information — A47

1966, July 25   Photo.   Perf. 11½x11
331 A47   4f rose & brown   .25   .25
332 A47   5f yel brn & brt grn   .30   .25
333 A47   8f brt green & purple   .45   .25
334 A47 20f salmon & ultra   .85   .30
        Nos. 331-334 (4)   1.85 1.05
    Opening of Ministry of Guidance and Information Building.

Fishing Boat, Lobster, Fish, Crab and FAO Emblem A48

1966, Oct. 10   Litho.   Perf. 13½
335 A48   4f buff & multi   .80   .25
336 A48 20f lt lilac & multi   2.10   .95
    Fisheries' Conference of Near East Countries under the sponsorship of the FAO, Oct. 1966.

United Nations Flag — A49

1966, Oct. 24   Perf. 13x14
337 A49 20f blue, dk blue & pink 1.00   .30
338 A49 45f blue, dk bl & pale grn 2.25 1.25
    Issued for United Nations Day.

UNESCO Emblem — A50

1966, Nov. 4   Litho.   Perf. 12½x13
339 A50 20f multicolored   1.00   .30
340 A50 45f multicolored   2.25 1.10
    20th anniversary of UNESCO.

Kuwait University Emblem — A51

1966, Nov. 27   Photo.   Perf. 14½
Emblem in Yellow, Bright Blue, Green and Gold
341 A51   8f lt ultra, vio & gold   .35   .25
342 A51 10f red, brown & gold   .45   .25
343 A51 20f lt yel grn, slate & gold 1.00   .30
344 A51 45f buff, green & gold   2.00 1.25
        Nos. 341-344 (4)   3.80 2.05
    Opening of Kuwait University.

Jabir al-Ahmad al-Jabir and Sheik Sabah A52

1966, Dec. 11   Perf. 14x13
345 A52   8f yel green & multi   .40   .25
346 A52 20f yellow & multi   .80   .30
347 A52 45f pink & multi   1.90 1.10
        Nos. 345-347 (3)   3.10 1.65
    Appointment of the heir apparent, Jabir al-Ahmad al-Jabir.

Scout Badge and Square Knot — A52a

1966, Dec. 21   Litho.   Perf. 14x13
347A A52a   4f ol green & fawn   1.40   .45
347B A52a 20f yel brn & blue grn 3.75 1.50
    Kuwait Boy Scouts, 30th anniversary.

"Symbols of Science and Peace" — A53

1967, Jan. 15   Litho.   Perf. 13x14
348 A53 10f multicolored   .40   .25
349 A53 45f multicolored   1.20   .55
    Issued for Education Day.

Fertilizer Plant — A54

1967, Feb. 19   Unwmk.   Perf. 13
350 A54   8f lt blue & multi   .55   .25
351 A54 20f cream & multi   1.40   .45
    Opening of Chemical Fertilizer Plant.

Sun, Dove and Olive Branch — A55

1967, Feb. 25   Litho.   Perf. 13
352 A55   8f salmon & multi   .50   .25
353 A55 20f yellow & multi   1.10   .45
    Sixth anniversary of National Day.

Map of Arab States and Municipal Building A56

1967, Mar. 11   Perf. 14½x13
354 A56 20f gray & multi   1.50   .55
355 A56 30f lt brown & multi   2.75 1.40
    1st conf. of the Arab Cities Org., Kuwait.

Family — A57

1967, Mar. 21   Litho.   Perf. 13x13½
356 A57 20f pale rose & multi   1.50   .55
357 A57 45f pale green & multi   2.75 1.40
Issued for Family Day, Mar. 21.

Arab League
Emblem — A58

1967, Mar. 27   Perf. 13x14
358 A58 8f gray & dk blue   .45   .25
359 A58 10f bister & green   .85   .25
Issued for Arab Publicity Week.

Sabah
Hospital and
Physicians at
Work — A59

1967, Apr. 7   Perf. 14x13
360 A59 8f dull rose & multi   1.20   .25
361 A59 20f gray & multi   1.60   .55
Issued for World Health Day.

Two Heads
of Ramses
II — A60

1967, Apr. 17   Perf. 13½
362 A60 15f citron, green & brn   .90   .30
363 A60 20f chalky blue, grn &
        pur   1.60   .55
Arab Week to Save the Nubian Monuments.

Traffic
Policeman
A61

1967, May 4   Litho.   Perf. 14x13
364 A61 8f lt green & multi   1.00   .35
365 A61 20f rose lilac & multi   2.25   .75
Issued for Traffic Day.

ITY
Emblem — A62

1967, June 4   Photo.   Perf. 13
366 A62 20f Prus blue, lt bl & blk   1.00   .30
367 A62 45f rose lilac, lt bl & blk   2.00 1.10
International Tourist Year.

Arab League
Emblem and
Hands Reaching
for
Knowledge — A63

1967, Sept. 8   Litho.   Perf. 13x14
368 A63 8f blue & multi   1.25   .25
369 A63 20f dull rose & multi   2.25   .65
Issued to publicize the literacy campaign.

Map of Palestine and
UN Emblem — A64

1967, Oct. 24   Litho.   Perf. 13
370 A64 20f blue & pink   2.25   .30
371 A64 45f orange & pink   3.25 1.00
Issued for United Nations Day.

Factory and Cogwheels — A65

1967, Nov. 25   Photo.   Perf. 13
372 A65 20f crimson & yellow   1.00   .30
373 A65 45f gray & yellow   2.00 1.25
3rd Conf. of Arab Labor Ministers, Kuwait.

Flag and Open
Book — A66

1968, Jan. 15   Litho.   Perf. 14
374 A66 20f brt blue & multi   .65   .30
375 A66 45f yel orange & multi   2.00 1.10
Issued for Education Day.

Map of Kuwait
and Oil
Derrick — A67

1968, Feb. 23   Litho.   Perf. 12
376 A67 10f multicolored   1.00   .35
377 A67 20f multicolored   2.25 1.10
30th anniv. of the discovery of oil in the
Greater Burgan Field.

Sheik
Sabah and
Sun — A68

1968, Feb. 25   Litho.   Perf. 14x15
378 A68 8f red lilac & multi   .45   .25
379 A68 10f lt blue & multi   .50   .25
380 A68 15f violet & multi   .60   .25
381 A68 20f vermilion & multi   .80   .35
    Nos. 378-381 (4)   2.35 1.10
Seventh anniversary of National Day.

Open Book and
Emblem — A69

1968, Mar. 2   Perf. 14
382 A69 8f yellow & multi   .40   .25
383 A69 20f lilac rose & multi   .90   .25
384 A69 45f orange & multi   1.75 1.10
    Nos. 382-384 (3)   3.05 1.60
Issued for Teachers' Day.

Family
Picnic
A70

1968, Mar. 21   Perf. 13½x13
385 A70 8f blue & multi   .30   .25
386 A70 10f red & multi   .45   .25
387 A70 15f lilac & multi   .50   .25
388 A70 20f dk brown & multi   .90   .25
    Nos. 385-388 (4)   2.15 1.00
Issued for Family Day.

Sheik Sabah, Arms of WHO and
Kuwait — A71

1968, Apr. 7   Photo.   Perf. 12
389 A71 20f brt lilac & multi   .95   .55
390 A71 45f multicolored   2.25 1.30
20th anniv. of WHO.

Dagger in Map of Palestine — A72

1968, Apr. 9   Litho.   Perf. 14
391 A72 20f lt blue & vermilion   3.00   .60
392 A72 45f lilac & vermilion   5.25 1.25
Deir Yassin massacre, 20th anniv.

Map of Palestine
and Torch — A75

1968, May 15   Litho.   Perf. 13½x12½
398 A75 10f lt ultra & multi   1.10   .45
399 A75 20f yellow & multi   2.75   .55
400 A75 45f aqua & multi   4.75 1.75
    Nos. 398-400 (3)   8.60 2.75
Issued for Palestine Day.

Palestinian Refugees — A76

1968, June 5   Litho.   Perf. 13x13½
401 A76 20f pink & multi   .55   .25
402 A76 30f ultra & multi   .90   .45
403 A76 45f green & multi   1.50   .55
404 A76 90f lilac & multi   3.00 1.60
    Nos. 401-404 (4)   5.95 2.85
International Human Rights Year.

Museum of
Kuwait — A77

Perf. 12½
1968, Aug. 25   Unwmk.   Engr.
405 A77 1f dk brown & brt grn   .30   .25
406 A77 2f dp claret & grn   .30   .25
407 A77 5f black & orange   .30   .25
408 A77 8f dk brown & grn   .30   .25
409 A77 10f Prus blue & cl   .45   .25
410 A77 20f org brown & blue   .75   .25
411 A77 25f dk blue & orange   .85   .25
412 A77 30f Prus blue & yel grn   1.10   .30
413 A77 45f plum & vio black   1.75   .60
414 A77 50f green & carmine   2.00 1.00
    Nos. 405-414 (10)   8.10 3.65

Man
Reading
Book, Arab
League,
UN and
UNESCO
Emblems
A78

1968, Sept. 8   Litho.   Perf. 12½x13
415 A78 15f blue gray & multi   .40   .25
416 A78 20f pink & multi   1.10   .30
Issued for International Literacy Day.

Map of Palestine on UN Building and
Children with Tent — A79

1968, Oct. 25   Litho.   Perf. 13
417 A79 20f multicolored   .50   .25
418 A79 30f gray & multi   .75   .45
419 A79 45f salmon pink & multi   1.10   .55
    Nos. 417-419 (3)   2.35 1.25
Issued for United Nations Day.

Street
Crossing
A74

1968, May 4   Photo.   Perf. 14x14½
395 A74 10f dk brown & multi   1.00   .55
396 A74 15f brt violet & multi   1.50   .70
397 A74 20f green & multi   2.60   .90
    Nos. 395-397 (3)   5.10 2.10
Issued for Traffic Day.

Kuwait Chamber of Commerce A80

1968, Nov. 6   Litho.   Perf. 13½x12½
420 A80 10f dp orange & dk brn .40 .25
421 A80 15f rose claret & vio bl .45 .25
422 A80 20f brown org & dk green .65 .45
Nos. 420-422 (3) 1.50 .95

Opening of the Kuwait Chamber of Commerce Building.

Conference Emblem — A81

1968, Nov. 10   Litho.   Perf. 13
Emblem in Ocher, Blue, Red and Black
423 A81 10f dk brown & blue .50 .25
424 A81 15f dk brown & orange .60 .25
425 A81 20f dk brown & vio blue .75 .45
426 A81 30f dk brown & org brn 1.00 .55
Nos. 423-426 (4) 2.85 1.50

14th Conference of the Arab Chambers of Commerce, Industry and Agriculture.

Shuaiba Refinery — A82

1968, Nov. 18   Perf. 13½
Emblem in Red, Black and Blue
427 A82 10f black & lt blue grn .65 .25
428 A82 20f black & gray 1.10 .40
429 A82 30f black & salmon 1.25 .60
430 A82 45f black & emerald 2.10 1.10
Nos. 427-430 (4) 5.10 2.35

Opening of Shuaiba Refinery.

Koran, Scales and People A83

1968, Dec. 19   Photo.   Perf. 14x14½
431 A83 8f multicolored .45 .25
432 A83 20f multicolored 1.00 .60
433 A83 30f multicolored 1.60 .85
434 A83 45f multicolored 1.90 1.25
Nos. 431-434 (4) 4.95 2.95

The 1400th anniversary of the Koran.

Boeing 707 — A84

1969, Jan. 1   Litho.   Perf. 13½x14
435 A84 10f brt yellow & multi .75 .25
436 A84 20f green & multi 1.00 .50
437 A84 25f multicolored 1.50 .75
438 A84 45f lilac & multi 2.75 1.00
Nos. 435-438 (4) 6.00 2.50

Introduction of Boeing 707 service by Kuwait Airways.

Globe, Retort and Triangle — A85

1969, Jan. 15   Perf. 13
439 A85 15f gray & multi .80 .30
440 A85 20f multicolored .90 .60

Issued for Education Day.

Kuwait Hilton Hotel — A86

1969, Feb. 15   Litho.   Perf. 14x12½
441 A86 10f brt blue & multi .45 .25
442 A86 20f pink & multi .95 .30

Opening of the Kuwait Hilton Hotel.

Teachers' Society Emblem, Father and Children — A87

1969, Feb. 15   Perf. 13
443 A87 10f violet & multi .45 .25
444 A87 20f rose & multi .95 .40

Issued for Education week.

Wreath, Flags and Dove — A88

1969, Feb. 25   Photo.   Perf. 14½x14
445 A88 15f lilac & multi .40 .25
446 A88 20f blue & multi .60 .30
447 A88 30f ocher & multi .90 .55
Nos. 445-447 (3) 1.90 1.10

Eighth anniversary of National Day.

Emblem, Teacher and Students — A89

1969, Mar. 8   Litho.   Perf. 13x12½
448 A89 10f multicolored .45 .25
449 A89 20f deep red & multi .75 .55

Issued for Teachers' Day.

Family A90

1969, Mar. 21   Perf. 13½
450 A90 10f dark blue & multi .55 .25
451 A90 20f deep car & multi 1.10 .30

Issued for Family Day.

Avicenna, WHO Emblem, Patient and Microscope — A91

1969, Apr. 7   Litho.   Perf. 13½
452 A91 15f red brown & multi 1.00 .25
453 A91 20f lt green & multi 1.75 .30

Issued for World Health Day, Apr. 7.

Motorized Traffic Police A92

1969, May 4   Litho.   Perf. 12½x13
454 A92 10f multicolored 1.40 .25
455 A92 20f multicolored 3.00 .60

Issued for Traffic Day.

ILO Emblem A93

1969, June 1   Perf. 11½
456 A93 10f red, black & gold .45 .25
457 A93 20f lt blue grn, blk & gold .95 .30

50th anniv. of the ILO.

S.S. Al Sabahiah A94

1969, June 10   Litho.   Perf. 13½
458 A94 20f multicolored 1.10 .55
459 A94 45f multicolored 2.75 1.50

4th anniversary of Kuwait Shipping Co.

UNESCO Emblem, Woman, Globe and Book — A95

1969, Sept. 8   Litho.   Perf. 13½
460 A95 10f blue & multi .45 .25
461 A95 20f rose red & multi .90 .45

International Literacy Day, Sept. 8.

Sheik Sabah — A96

1969-74   Litho.   Perf. 14
462 A96 8f lt blue & multi .40 .25
463 A96 10f pink & multi .45 .25
464 A96 15f gray & multi .50 .25
465 A96 20f yellow & multi .55 .25
466 A96 25f violet & multi .75 .30
467 A96 30f sal & multi 1.00 .35
468 A96 45f tan & multi 1.50 .50
469 A96 50f yel grn & multi 1.60 .50
470 A96 70f multicolored 1.90 .75
471 A96 75f ultra & multi 2.50 .90
472 A96 90f pale rose & multi 2.50 1.00
a. 90f brownish rose & multi 2.50 1.00
473 A96 250f lilac & multi 7.50 2.75
473A A96 500f gray green & multi 15.00 10.00
473B A96 1d lilac rose & multi 27.50 16.00
Nos. 462-473B (14) 63.65 34.05

Issued: Nos. 473A-473B, 1/12/74; others 10/5/69.

UN Emblem and Scroll — A97

1969, Oct. 24   Litho.   Perf. 13
474 A97 10f emer & multi .50 .25
475 A97 20f bister & multi 1.00 .25
476 A97 45f rose red & multi 2.50 .90
Nos. 474-476 (3) 4.00 1.40

Issued for United Nations Day.

Radar, Satellite Earth Station, Kuwait A98

Design: 45f, Globe and radar, vert.

1969, Dec. 15   Photo.   Perf. 14½
477 A98 20f silver & multi 1.25 .50
478 A98 45f silver & multi 2.75 1.10

Inauguration of the Kuwait Earth Station for Satellite Communications.

Globe with Science Symbols, and Education Year Emblem — A99

1970, Jan. 15   Photo.   Perf. 13½x13
479 A99 20f brt lilac & multi .75 .30
480 A99 45f blue & multi 1.50 .95

International Education Year.

Shoue A100

Old Kuwaiti Vessels: 10f, Sambook. 15f, Baghla. 20f, Batteel. 25f, Boom. 45f, Bakkara. 50f, Shipbuilding.

1970, Feb. 1   *Perf. 14½x14*
481 A100 8f multicolored   .55   .30
482 A100 10f multicolored   .60   .40
483 A100 15f multicolored   1.00   .50
484 A100 20f multicolored   1.50   .65
485 A100 25f multicolored   1.75   .75
486 A100 40f multicolored   2.75   1.40
487 A100 50f multicolored   3.25   1.60
       Nos. 481-487 (7)   11.40   5.60

Refugee Father and
Children — A101

1970   Photo.   *Perf. 14x12½*
488 A101 20f red brown & multi 2.00   .65
489 A101 45f olive & multi   4.00 2.00

Issued for Universal Palestinian Refugees
Week, Dec. 16-22, 1969.

Kuwait Flag,
Emblem and
Sheik
Sabah — A102

1970, Feb. 25   *Perf. 13½x13*
490 A102 15f silver & multi   .85   .25
491 A102 20f gold & multi   1.10   .25

Ninth anniversary of National Day.

Dome of the Rock, Jerusalem, and
Boy Commando — A103

Designs: 20f, Dome and man commando.
45f, Dome and woman commando.

1970, Mar. 4   Litho.   *Perf. 13*
492 A103 10f pale violet & multi 1.40   .85
493 A103 20f lt blue & multi   2.75 1.75
494 A103 45f multicolored   5.75 3.75
       Nos. 492-494 (3)   9.90 6.35

Honoring Palestinian commandos.

Parents
and
Children
A104

1970, Mar. 21   *Perf. 14*
495 A104 20f multicolored   .55   .25
496 A104 30f pink & multi   .95   .35

Issued for Family Day.

Map of
Arab
League
Countries,
Flag and
Emblem
A104a

1970, Mar. 22   *Perf. 11½x11*
497 A104a 20f lt blue, grn & lt
                 brn   .70   .25
498 A104a 45f sal, grn & dk pur 1.25   .60

25th anniversary of the Arab League.

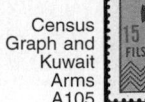

Census
Graph and
Kuwait
Arms
A105

1970, Apr. 1   Litho.   *Perf. 13½x13*
499 A105 15f dull orange & multi .45   .25
500 A105 20f yellow & multi   .50   .35
501 A105 30f pink & multi   .75   .40
       Nos. 499-501 (3)   1.70 1.00

Issued to publicize the 1970 census.

"Fight Cancer,"
Kuwait Arms,
WHO
Emblem — A106

1970, Apr. 7   *Perf. 13½x13*
502 A106 20f blue, vio bl & rose
                 lil   1.10   .50
503 A106 30f dl yel, vio bl & lil
                 rose   1.40   .70

World Health Organization Day, Apr. 7, and
to publicize the fight against cancer.

Traffic Signs
A107

1970, May 4   Photo.   *Perf. 13½*
504 A107 20f multicolored   1.50   .50
505 A107 30f multicolored   2.10 1.10

Issued for Traffic Day.

Red
Crescent
A108

1970, May 8   Litho.   *Perf. 12½x13½*
506 A108 10f yellow & multi   .50   .25
507 A108 15f emerald & multi   1.10   .45
508 A108 30f tan & multi   2.25   .75
       Nos. 506-508 (3)   3.85 1.45

Intl. Red Crescent and Red Cross Day.

Opening of UPU Headquarters,
Bern — A109

1970, May 25 Photo.   *Perf. 12x11½*
509 A109 20f multicolored   .95   .30
510 A109 30f multicolored   1.40   .75

Sheik
Sabah
A110

1970, June 15   Photo.   *Perf. 14*
511 A110 20f silver & multi   1.50   .50
512 A110 45f gold & multi   3.00 1.00
   a.   Miniature sheet of 2   8.50 5.00

Nos. 511-512 have circular perforation
around vignette set within a white square of
paper, perforated on 4 sides. No. 512a contains 2 imperf. stamps similar to Nos. 511-512.

UN Emblem,
Symbols of
Peace, Progress,
Justice — A111

1970, July 1   Litho.   *Perf. 13½x12½*
513 A111 20f lt green & multi   .55   .25
514 A111 45f multicolored   1.10   .50

25th anniversary of the United Nations.

Tanker
Loading
Crude
Oil from
Sea
Island
A112

1970, Aug. 1   *Perf. 13½x13*
515 A112 20f multicolored   1.75   .50
516 A112 45f multicolored   2.25 1.10

Issued to publicize the artificial "Sea Island"
loading facilities in Kuwait.

"Writing,"
Kuwait and
UN
Emblems
A113

1970, Sept. 8   Photo.   *Perf. 13½*
517 A113 10f brt blue & multi   1.10   .25
518 A113 15f brt green & multi 1.30   .50

International Literacy Day, Sept. 8.

National
Guard and
Emblem
A114

1970, Oct. 20   Photo.   *Perf. 13x13½*
519 A114 10f gold & multi   1.00   .25
520 A114 20f silver & multi   1.60   .50

First National Guard graduation.

Flag of Kuwait,
Symbols of
Development
A115

1971, Feb. 25   Litho.   *Perf. 12*
521 A115 20f gray & multi   1.10   .40
522 A115 30f multicolored   1.60   .55

Tenth anniversary of National Day.

Charles
H. Best,
Frederick
G.
Banting
A116

1971, Apr. 7   Litho.   *Perf. 14*
523 A116 20f multicolored   1.40   .25
524 A116 45f multicolored   3.00   .75

World Health Day; discoverers of insulin.

Globe with
Map of
Palestine
A117

1971, May 3   Litho.   *Perf. 12½x13*
525 A117 20f yel green & multi 2.00 1.10
526 A117 45f lilac & multi   3.75 2.25

International Palestine Week.

ITU
Emblem
and Waves
A118

1971, May 17   Photo.   *Perf. 13x13½*
527 A118 20f silver, dk red & blk 1.10 .30
528 A118 45f gold, dk red & blk   2.40 .85

3rd World Telecommunications Day.

Men of 3
Races — A119

1971, June 5   Litho.   *Perf. 11½x11*
529 A119 15f red brown & multi   .75   .30
530 A119 30f ultra & multi   1.25   .60

Intl. Year against Racial Discrimination.

Arab Postal
Union
Emblem
A120

1971, Aug. 30   *Perf. 13x12½*
531 A120 20f brown & multi   .90   .30
532 A120 45f blue & multi   1.60   .70

25th anniv. of the Conf. of Sofar, Lebanon,
establishing the Arab Postal Union.

Symbols of
Learning,
UNESCO and
Kuwait
Emblems
A121

1971, Sept. 8 *Perf. 12*
533 A121 25f dull yellow & multi   .90   .25
534 A121 60f lt blue & multi   2.10 1.00
International Literacy Day, Sept. 8.

Soccer
A122

Design: 30f, Soccer, different.

1971, Dec. 10 *Perf. 13*
535 A122 20f green & multi   1.75   .55
536 A122 30f ultra & multi   2.40   .95
Regional Sports Tournament, Kuwait, Dec.

UNICEF Emblem and Arms of
Kuwait — A123

Litho. & Engr.
1971, Dec. 11 *Perf. 11x11½*
537 A123 25f gold & multi   .60   .30
538 A123 60f silver & multi 1.50   .75
25th anniv. of UNICEF.

Book Year
Emblem
A124

1972, Jan. 2 **Litho.** *Perf. 14x13*
539 A124 20f black & buff   .70   .45
540 A124 45f black & lt blue grn 1.60 .95
International Book Year.

Kuwait
Emblem
with 11
Rays, Olive
Branch
A125

1972, Feb. 25 **Litho.** *Perf. 13x13½*
541 A125 20f pink, gold & multi 1.10   .30
542 A125 45f lt blue, gold & multi 1.90 1.00
11th anniversary of National Day.

Telecommunications Center — A126

1972, Feb. 28 *Perf. 13½*
543 A126 20f lt blue & multi 1.40   .50
544 A126 45f multicolored   3.75 1.40
Opening of Kuwait Telecommunications
Center.

"Your Heart is
your
Health" — A127

1972, Apr. 7 **Photo.** *Perf. 14½x14*
545 A127 20f red & multi   1.75   .60
546 A127 45f red & multi   4.50 1.40
World Health Day.

Nurse and
Child — A128

1972, May 8 **Litho.** *Perf. 12½x13*
547 A128 8f vio blue, red & em-
er   1.00   .30
548 A128 40f pink & multi   4.00 1.25
Red Cross and Red Crescent Day.

Soccer, Olympic Emblems — A129

1972, Sept. 2 **Litho.** *Perf. 14½*
549 A129 2f shown   .35   .25
550 A129 4f Running   .35   .25
551 A129 5f Swimming   .40   .25
552 A129 8f Gymnastics   .45   .25
553 A129 10f Diooug   .70   .30
554 A129 15f Equestrian   1.00   .35
555 A129 20f Basketball   1.10   .40
556 A129 25f Volleyball   1.25   .55
     Nos. 549-556 (8)   5.60 2.60
20th Olympic Games, Munich, 8/26-9/11.

FAO Emblem,
Vegetables, Fish
and Ship — A130

1972, Sept. 9 **Litho.** *Perf. 14x13½*
557 A130 5f blue & multi   .50   .40
558 A130 10f emerald & multi 1.50 1.10
559 A130 20f orange & multi 3.00 2.25
     Nos. 557-559 (3)   5.00 3.75
11th FAO Regional Conference in the Near
East, Kuwait, Sept.

National
Bank
Emblem
A131

1972, Nov. 15 **Photo.** *Perf. 13x14*
560 A131 10f green & multi   .50   .25
561 A131 35f dull red & multi 1.75 .90
20th anniversary of Kuwait National Bank.

Capitals
A132

Relics of Failaka: 5f, View of excavations.
10f, Acanthus leaf capital. 15f, Excavations.

1972, Dec. 4 **Litho.** *Perf. 12*
562 A132 2f lilac rose & multi   .30   .25
563 A132 5f bister & multi   .40   .25
564 A132 10f lt blue & multi   1.25   .30
565 A132 15f green & multi   1.75   .40
     Nos. 562-565 (4)   3.70 1.20

Flower and Kuwait
Emblem — A133

1973, Feb. 25 **Litho.** *Perf. 13½x13*
566 A133 10f lt olive & multi   .45   .25
567 A133 20f multicolored   .90   .40
568 A133 30f yellow & multi   1.40   .85
     Nos. 566-568 (3)   2.75 1.50
12th anniversary of National Day.

INTERPOL
Emblem
A134

1973, June 3 **Litho.** *Perf. 12*
569 A134 10f emerald & multi 1.00   .75
570 A134 15f red orange & multi 1.75 1.00
571 A134 20f blue & multi   2.75 1.25
     Nos. 569-571 (3)   5.50 3.00
50th anniv. of Intl. Criminal Police Org.
(INTERPOL).

I.C.M.S.
Emblem and
Flag of
Kuwait — A135

1973, June 24 *Perf. 13*
572 A135 30f gray & multi   1.10   .55
573 A135 40f brown & multi 1.75   .75
Intl. Council of Military Sports, 25th anniv.

Kuwait Airways
Building — A136

1973, July 1 **Litho.** *Perf. 12½x14*
574 A136 10f lt green & multi   .65   .25
575 A136 15f lilac & multi   .85   .30
576 A136 20f lt ultra & multi 1.00   .50
     Nos. 574-576 (3)   2.50 1.05
Opening of Kuwait Airways Corporation
Building.

Weather Map of Suez Canal and
Persian Gulf Region — A137

1973, Sept. 4 **Photo.** *Perf. 14*
577 A137 5f red & multi   .65   .25
578 A137 10f green & multi   .90   .30
579 A137 15f multicolored   1.25   .60
     Nos. 577-579 (3)   2.80 1.15
Intl. meteorological cooperation, cent.

Sheiks Ahmad and Sabah — A138

1973, Nov. 12 **Photo.** *Perf. 14*
580 A138 10f lt green & multi   .60   .25
581 A138 20f yel orange & multi 1.25 .40
582 A138 70f lt blue & multi   3.75 1.50
     Nos. 580-582 (3)   5.60 2.15
Stamps overprinted "Kuwait," 50th anniv.

Mourning Dove, Eurasian Hoopoe,
Rock Dove, Stone Curlew — A139

Designs: Birds and traps.

1973, Dec. 1 **Litho.** *Perf. 14*
Size (single stamp): 32x32mm
583 A139 Block of 4   5.50   5.50
  a.   5f Mourning dove   .70   .25
  b.   5f Eurasian hoopoe   .70   .25
  c.   5f Rock dove   .70   .25
  d.   5f Stone curlew   .70   .25
584 A139 Block of 4   7.25   7.25
  a.   8f Great gray shrike .90   .35
  b.   8f Red-backed shrike .90   .35
  c.   8f Rufous-backed shrike .90 .35
  d.   8f Black-naped oriole .90   .35
585 A139 Block of 4   8.00   8.00
  a.   10f Willow warbler   1.00   .45
  b.   10f Great reed warbler 1.00 .45
  c.   10f Blackcap   1.00   .45
  d.   10f Common (barn) swal-
       low   1.00   .45
586 A139 Block of 4   11.50 11.50
  a.   15f Common rock thrush 1.50 1.50
  b.   15f European redstart 1.50 1.50
  c.   15f Wheatear   1.50 1.50
  d.   15f Bluethroat   1.50 1.50
587 A139 Block of 4   13.50 13.50
  a.   20f Houbara bustard 1.60 1.60
  b.   20f Pin-tailed sandgrouse 1.60 1.60
  c.   20f Ypecaha wood rail 1.60 1.60
  d.   20f Spotted crake   1.60 1.60
Size (single stamp): 35x35mm
588 A139 Block of 4   17.50 17.50
  a.   25f American sparrow
       hawk   2.00 2.00
  b.   25f Great black-backed
       gull   2.00 2.00
  c.   25f Purple heron   2.00 2.00
  d.   25f Wryneck   2.00 2.00

589	A139	Block of 4	25.00	25.00
a.		30f European bee-eater	3.00	3.00
b.		30f Goshawk	3.00	3.00
c.		30f Gray wagtail	3.00	3.00
d.		30f Pied wagtail	3.00	3.00
590	A139	Block of 4	32.50	32.50
a.		45f Crossbows	4.25	4.25
b.		45f Tent-shaped net	4.25	4.25
c.		45f Hand net	4.25	4.25
d.		45f Rooftop trap	4.25	4.25
		Nos. 583-590 (8)	120.75	120.75

Human Rights
Flame — A141

1973, Dec. 10　　Litho.　　Perf. 12

594	A141	10f red & multi	.60	.25
595	A141	40f lt green & multi	1.50	.55
596	A141	75f lilac & multi	2.75	1.50
		Nos. 594-596 (3)	4.85	2.30

25th anniv. of the Universal Declaration of Human Rights.

Promoting Animal
Resources
A142

1974, Feb. 16　　Litho.　　Perf. 12½

| 597 | A142 | 30f violet blue & multi | .95 | .40 |
| 598 | A142 | 40f rose & multi | 1.20 | .90 |

4th Congress of the Arab Veterinary Union, Kuwait.

Stylized Wheat
and Kuwaiti
Flag — A143

1974, Feb. 25　　　　　　Perf. 13½x13

599	A143	20f lemon & multi	.45	.25
600	A143	30f bister brn & multi	.85	.40
601	A143	70f silver & multi	1.75	.90
		Nos. 599-601 (3)	3.05	1.55

13th anniversary of National Day.

Conference Emblem and Sheik
Sabah — A144

1974, Mar. 8　　　　　　Perf. 12½

| 602 | A144 | 30f multicolored | 1.90 | .55 |
| 603 | A144 | 40f yellow & multi | 3.00 | 1.10 |

12th Conf. of the Arab Medical Union and 1st Conf. of the Kuwait Medical Soc.

Tournament
Emblem — A145

1974, Mar. 15

| 604 | A145 | 25f multicolored | 1.25 | .50 |
| 605 | A145 | 45f multicolored | 2.25 | 1.10 |

Third Soccer Tournament for the Arabian Gulf Trophy, Kuwait, Mar. 1974.

Scientific Research Institute — A146

1974, Apr. 3　　Photo.　　Perf. 12½

| 606 | A146 | 15f magenta & multi | 1.50 | .40 |
| 607 | A146 | 20f green & multi | 2.00 | .65 |

Opening of Kuwait Scientific Research Institute.

Arab
Postal
Union,
Kuwait
and UPU
Emblems
A147

1974, May 1　　　　　　Perf. 13x14

608	A147	20f gold & multi	.60	.25
609	A147	30f gold & multi	.75	.45
610	A147	60f gold & multi	1.40	.80
		Nos. 608-610 (3)	2.75	1.50

Centenary of Universal Postal Union.

Telephone Dial
with
Communications
Symbols and
Globe — A148

1974, May 17　　　　　　Perf. 14x13½

611	A148	10f blue & multi	.70	.25
612	A148	30f multicolored	1.60	.60
613	A148	40f black & multi	2.25	.80
		Nos. 611-613 (3)	4.55	1.65

World Telecommunications Day, May 17.

Emblem of Unity
Council and Flags
of Member
States — A149

1974, June 25　　Litho.　　Perf. 13½

| 614 | A149 | 20f red, black & green | .85 | .45 |
| 615 | A149 | 30f green, black & red | .90 | .45 |

17th anniversary of the signing of the Arab Economic Unity Agreement.

WPY Emblem, Embryo,
"Growth" — A150

1974, Aug. 19　　Litho.　　Perf. 14x14½

| 616 | A150 | 30f black & multi | 1.00 | .40 |
| 617 | A150 | 70f violet blue & multi | 2.25 | 1.50 |

World Population Year.

Development Building and
Emblem — A151

1974, Oct. 30　　Litho.　　Perf. 13x13½

| 618 | A151 | 10f pink & multi | .70 | .25 |
| 619 | A151 | 20f ultra & multi | 1.10 | .45 |

Kuwait Fund for Arab Economic Development.

Emblem of Shuaiba Industrial
Area — A152

1974, Dec. 17　　Litho.　　Perf. 12½x12

620	A152	10f lt blue & multi	.60	.25
621	A152	20f salmon & multi	1.50	.45
622	A152	30f lt green & multi	2.00	.95
		Nos. 620-622 (3)	4.10	1.65

Shuaiba Industrial Area, 10th anniversary.

Arms of
Kuwait and
"14" — A153

1975, Feb. 25　　Litho.　　Perf. 13x13½

623	A153	20f multicolored	.50	.30
624	A153	70f yel green & multi	1.50	.85
625	A153	75f rose & multi	2.50	1.00
		Nos. 623-625 (3)	4.50	2.15

14th anniversary of National Day.

Male and Female Symbols — A154

1975, Apr. 14　　Photo.　　Perf. 11½x12

626	A154	8f lt green & multi	.35	.25
627	A154	20f rose & multi	.40	.25
628	A154	30f blue & multi	.65	.45
629	A154	70f yellow & multi	1.75	1.10
630	A154	100f black & multi	3.00	1.40
		Nos. 626-630 (5)	6.15	3.45

Kuwaiti census 1975.

IWY and Kuwaiti Women's Union
Emblems — A155

1975, June 10　　Litho.　　Perf. 14½

631	A155	15f brown org & multi	.90	.40
632	A155	20f olive & multi	1.10	.40
633	A155	30f violet & multi	1.60	.65
		Nos. 631-633 (3)	3.60	1.30

International Women's Year.

Classroom
and
UNESCO
Emblem
A156

1975, Sept. 8　　Litho.　　Perf. 12½x12

| 634 | A156 | 20f green & multi | .80 | .25 |
| 635 | A156 | 30f multicolored | 1.40 | .65 |

International Literacy Day.

Symbols of
Measurements
A157

1975, Oct. 14　　Photo.　　Perf. 14x13

| 636 | A157 | 10f green & multi | .70 | .25 |
| 637 | A157 | 20f purple & multi | 1.00 | .45 |

World Standards Day.

UN Flag, Rifle
and Olive
Branch — A158

1975, Oct. 24　　Litho.　　Perf. 12x12½

| 638 | A158 | 20f multicolored | .60 | .25 |
| 639 | A158 | 45f orange & multi | 1.40 | .75 |

United Nations, 30th anniversary.

Sheik
Sabah — A159

1975, Dec. 22　　Litho.　　Perf. 12½x12

640	A159	8f yellow & multi	.95	.25
641	A159	20f lilac & multi	1.25	.40
642	A159	30f buff & multi	1.50	.50
643	A159	50f salmon & multi	2.25	.75
644	A159	90f lt blue & multi	4.00	1.25
645	A159	100f multicolored	5.00	1.50
		Nos. 640-645 (6)	14.95	4.65

"Progress" — A160

1976, Feb. 25   Litho.   Perf. 12
646 A160 10f multicolored   .70   .25
647 A160 20f multicolored   1.25   .30
15th anniversary of National Day.

Medical Equipment, Emblem and Surgery — A161

1976, Mar. 1   Litho.   Perf. 14½
648 A161   5f dull green & multi   .40   .25
649 A161 10f blue & multi   1.20   .45
650 A161 30f gray & multi   3.00   1.50
      Nos. 648-650 (3)   4.60   2.20
Kuwait Medical Assoc., 2nd annual conference.

Telephones, 1876 and 1976 — A162

1976, Mar. 10   Litho.   Perf. 12
651 A162   5f orange & black   .50   .25
652 A162 15f lt blue & black   1.10   .30
Centenary of first telephone call by Alexander Graham Bell, Mar. 10, 1876.

Human Eye — A163

Photo. & Engr.

1976, Apr. 7   Perf. 11½
653 A163 10f multicolored   .70   .25
654 A163 20f black & multi   1.10   .30
655 A163 30f multicolored   1.40   .85
      Nos. 653-655 (3)   3.20   1.40
World Health Day: "Foresight prevents blindness."

Red Crescent Emblem A164

1976, May 8   Litho.   Perf. 12x11½
656 A164 20f brt green, blk & red   .50   .30
657 A164 30f vio blue, blk & red   .90   .55
658 A164 45f yellow, blk & red   1.50   .85
659 A164 75f lilac rose, blk & red 3.25   2.00
      Nos. 656-659 (4)   6.15   3.70
Kuwait Red Crescent Society, 10th anniv.

Modern Suburb of Kuwait A165

1976, June 1   Photo.   Perf. 13x13½
660 A165 10f light green & multi   .65   .25
661 A165 20f salmon & multi   1.10   .30
Habitat, UN Conference on Human Settlements, Vancouver, Canada, May 31-June 11.

Basketball, Kuwait Olympic Emblem — A166

Designs: 8f, Running. 10f, Judo. 15f, Fieldball. 20f, Gymnastics. 30f, Water polo. 45f, Soccer. 70f, Swimmers at start.

1976, July 17   Litho.   Perf. 14½
662 A166   4f black & multi   .30   .25
663 A166   8f red & multi   .30   .25
664 A166 10f green & multi   .35   .25
665 A166 15f lemon & multi   .45   .25
666 A166 20f blue & multi   .55   .30
667 A166 30f lilac & multi   .90   .55
668 A166 45f multicolored   1.25   .75
669 A166 70f brown & multi   1.75   1.10
      Nos. 662-669 (8)   5.85   3.70
21st Olympic Games, Montreal, Canada, July 17-Aug. 1.

Various Races, Map of Sri Lanka — A167

1976, Aug. 16   Photo.   Perf. 14
670 A167 20f dk blue & multi   .50   .25
671 A167 30f purple & multi   .70   .45
672 A167 45f green & multi   1.10   .65
      Nos. 670-672 (3)   2.30   1.35
5th Summit Conf. of Non-aligned Countries, Colombo, Sri Lanka, Aug. 9-19.

"UNESCO," Torch and Kuwait Arms — A168

1976, Nov. 4   Litho.   Perf. 12x11½
673 A168 20f yel green & multi   .65   .25
674 A168 45f scarlet & multi   1.50   .60
30th anniversary of UNESCO.

Blindman's Buff A169

Popular games. 5f, 15f, 30f, vertical.

Perf. 14½x14, 14x14½

1977, Jan. 10   Litho.
675 A169   5f Pot throwing   .35   .25
676 A169   5f Kite flying   .35   .25
677 A169   5f Balancing sticks   .35   .25
678 A169   5f Spinning tops   .35   .25
  a.   Block of 4, #675-678   2.00   2.00
679 A169 10f shown   .65   .25
680 A169 10f Rowing   .65   .25
681 A169 10f Hoops   .65   .25
682 A169 10f Ropes   .65   .25
  a.   Block of 4, #679-682   3.00   3.00
683 A169 15f Rope skipping   1.10   .35
684 A169 15f Marbles   1.10   .35
685 A169 15f Cart steering   1.10   .35
686 A169 15f Teetotum   1.10   .35
  a.   Block of 4, #683-686   5.00   5.00
687 A169 20f Halma   1.25   .55
688 A169 20f Model boats   1.25   .55
689 A169 20f Pot and candle   1.25   .55
690 A169 20f Hide and seek   1.25   .55
  a.   Block of 4, #687-690   6.00   6.00
691 A169 30f Throwing bones   1.50   .75
692 A169 30f Mystery gifts   1.50   .75
693 A169 30f Hopscotch   1.50   .75
694 A169 30f Catch as catch
                 can   1.50   .75
  a.   Block of 4, #691-694   7.00   7.00
695 A169 40f Bowls   2.75   1.00
696 A169 40f Sword fighting   2.75   1.00
697 A169 40f Mother and child   2.75   1.00
698 A169 40f Fivestones   2.75   1.00
  a.   Block of 4, #695-698   12.00 12.00
699 A169 60f Hiding a cake   3.50   1.75
700 A169 60f Chess   3.50   1.75
701 A169 60f Dancing   3.50   1.75
702 A169 60f Treasure hunt   3.50   1.75
  a.   Block of 4, #699-702   16.00 16.00
703 A169 70f Hobby-horses   4.25   1.90
704 A169 70f Hide and seek   4.25   1.90
705 A169 70f Catch   4.25   1.90
706 A169 70f Storytelling   4.25   1.90
  a.   Block of 4, #703-706   19.00 19.00
      Nos. 675-706 (32)   61.40 27.10

Diseased Knee — A170

1977, Feb. 15   Perf. 13x13½
707 A170 20f yellow & multi   .75   .25
708 A170 30f multicolored   1.25   .45
709 A170 45f red & multi   1.50   .70
710 A170 75f black & multi   2.50   1.25
      Nos. 707-710 (4)   6.00   2.65
World Rheumatism Year.

Sheik Sabah A171

1977, Feb. 25   Photo.   Perf. 13½x13
711 A171 10f multicolored   .50   .25
712 A171 15f multicolored   .65   .30
713 A171 30f multicolored   1.25   .55
714 A171 80f multicolored   1.50   1.10
      Nos. 711-714 (4)   3.90   2.20
16th National Day.

Kuwait Tower — A172

1977, Feb. 26   Perf. 14x13½
715 A172 30f multicolored   .85   .25
716 A172 80f multicolored   2.25   1.10
Inauguration of Kuwait Tower.

APU Emblem — A173

1977, Apr. 12   Litho.   Perf. 13½x14
717 A173   5f yellow & multi   .35   .25
718 A173 15f pink & multi   .40   .25
719 A173 30f lt blue & multi   .80   .30
720 A173 80f lilac & multi   1.90   .90
      Nos. 717-720 (4)   3.45   1.70
Arab Postal Union, 25th anniversary.

Electronic Tree — A174

1977, May 17   Litho.   Perf. 12x12½
721 A174 30f brown & red   1.00   .40
722 A174 80f green & red   2.10   1.50
World Telecommunications Day.

Sheik Sabah — A175

1977, June 1   Photo.   Perf. 11½x12
723 A175   15f blue & multi   1.25   1.10
724 A175   25f yellow & multi   2.00   1.10
725 A175   30f red & multi   2.50   1.60
726 A175   80f violet & multi   6.75   2.75
727 A175 100f dp org & multi   8.00   3.50
728 A175 150f ultra & multi   12.00   6.00
729 A175 200f olive & multi   16.00   9.00
      Nos. 723-729 (7)   48.50 25.05

Games Emblem — A176

1977, Oct. 1   Litho.   Perf. 12
730 A176 30f multicolored   .90   .50
731 A176 80f multicolored   1.90   1.10
4th Asian Basketball Youth Championship, Oct. 1-15.

Dome of the Rock, Bishop Capucci, Fatima Bernawi, Sheik Abu Tair — A177

1977, Nov. 1   *Perf. 14*
732 A177 30f multicolored   2.50 1.25
733 A177 80f multicolored   5.75 3.00
Struggle for the liberation of Palestine.

Children and Houses A178

Children's Paintings: No. 735, Women musicians. No. 736, Boats. No. 737, Women preparing food, vert. No. 738, Women and children, vert. No. 739, Seated woman, vert.

1977, Nov.   Photo.   Perf. 13½x13
734 A178 15f lt green & multi   .40   .30
735 A178 15f yellow & multi   .40   .30
736 A178 30f brt yellow & multi .85   .60
737 A178 30f lt violet & multi   .85   .60
738 A178 80f black & multi   2.00 1.60
739 A178 80f rose & multi   2.00 1.60
     Nos. 734-739 (6)   6.50 5.00

Dentist Treating Patient A179

1977, Dec. 3
740 A179 30f green & multi   1.40   .75
741 A179 80f violet & multi   2.60 1.40
10th Arab Dental Union Congress, Kuwait, Dec. 3-6.

Ships Unloading Water A180

Kuwait water resources. 30f, 80f, 100f, vert.

Perf. 14x13½, 13½x14

1978, Jan. 25   Litho.
742   Block of 4   1.50 1.50
  a. 5f shown   .30   .25
  b. 5f Home delivery by camel   .30   .25
  c. 5f Man with water bags   .30   .25
  d. 5f Man with wheelbarrow   .30   .25
743   Block of 4   2.50 2.50
  a. 10f Well   .50   .25
  b. 10f Trough   .50   .25
  c. 10f Water hole   .50   .25
  d. 10f Irrigation   .50   .25
744   Block of 4   3.00 3.00
  a. 15f Sheep drinking   .60   .25
  b. 15f Laundresses   .60   .25
  c. 15f Sheep and camels drinking .60 .25
  d. 15f Water stored in skins   .60   .25
745   Block of 4   3.50 3.50
  a. 20f Animals at well   .75   .25
  b. 20f Water in home   .75   .25
  c. 20f Water pot   .75   .25
  d. 20f Communal fountain   .75   .25
746   Block of 4   4.25 4.25
  a. 25f Distillation plant   .85   .30
  b. 25f Motorized delivery   .85   .30
  c. 25f Water trucks   .85   .30
  d. 25f Water towers   .85   .30
747   Block of 4   6.00 6.00
  a. 30f Shower bath   1.25   .30
  b. 30f Water tower   1.25   .30
  c. 30f Gathering rain water   1.25   .30
  d. 30f 2 water towers   1.25   .30
748   Block of 4   13.50 13.50
  a. 80f Donkey with water bags 2.75   .90
  b. 80f Woman with water can   2.75   .90
  c. 80f Woman with water skin 2.75   .90
  d. 80f Loading tank car   2.75   .90
749   Block of 4   17.50 17.50
  a. 100f Truck delivering water 3.50 1.10
  b. 100f Barnyard water supply 3.50 1.10
  c. 100f Children at water basin 3.50 1.10
  d. 100f Well in courtyard   3.50 1.10
     Nos. 742-749 (8)   51.75 51.75

Radar, Torch, Minarets A181

1978, Feb. 25   Litho.   Perf. 14x14½
750 A181 30f multicolored   .60   .25
751 A181 80f multicolored   1.50   .75
17th National Day.

Man with Smallpox, Target — A182

1978, Apr. 17   Litho.   Perf. 12½
752 A182 30f violet & multi   1.00   .50
753 A182 80f green & multi   2.50 1.10
Global eradication of smallpox.

Antenna and ITU Emblem A183

1978, May 17   *Perf. 14*
754 A183 30f silver & multi   .50   .30
755 A183 80f silver & multi   1.50   .85
10th World Telecommunications Day.

Sheik Sabah — A184

1978, June 28   Litho.   Perf. 13x14
          Portrait in Brown
          Size: 21½x27mm
756 A184 15f green & gold   .40   .25
757 A184 30f orange & gold   .65   .45
758 A184 80f rose lilac & gold 1.50 1.10
759 A184 100f lt green & gold   1.75 1.25
760 A184 130f lt brown & gold   2.00 1.75
761 A184 180f violet & gold   3.50 2.75
          Size: 23½x29mm
762 A184   1d red & gold   15.00 12.50
763 A184   4d blue & gold   62.50 57.50
     Nos. 756-763 (8)   87.30 77.55

Mt. Arafat, Pilgrims, Holy Kaaba A185

1978, Nov. 9   Photo.   Perf. 11½
764 A185 30f multicolored   1.00 .50
765 A185 80f multicolored   2.50 1.25
Pilgrimage to Mecca.

UN and Anti-Apartheid Emblems — A186

1978, Nov. 27   Litho.   Perf. 12
766 A186 30f multicolored   .50   .30
767 A186 80f multicolored   1.10 1.00
768 A186 180f multicolored   2.50 2.00
     Nos. 766-768 (3)   4.10 3.30
Anti-Apartheid Year.

Refugees, Human Rights Emblems A187

1978, Dec. 10   Photo.   Perf. 13x13½
769 A187 30f multicolored   .65   .35
770 A187 80f multicolored   1.60   .80
771 A187 100f multicolored   2.25 1.50
     Nos. 769-771 (3)   4.50 2.65
Declaration of Human Rights, 30th anniv.

Information Center — A188

1978, Dec. 26   Photo.   Perf. 13
772 A188   5f multicolored   .30   .25
773 A188 15f multicolored   .40   .25
774 A188 30f multicolored   .70   .35
775 A188 80f multicolored   1.60   .95
     Nos. 772-775 (4)   3.00 1.80
New Kuwait Information Center.

Kindergarten A189

1979, Jan. 24   Photo.   Perf. 13½x14
776 A189 30f multicolored   .75   .50
777 A189 80f multicolored   1.90 1.10
International Year of the Child.

Flag and Peace Doves — A190

1979, Feb. 25   *Perf. 14½x14*
778 A190 30f multicolored   .75   .45
779 A190 80f multicolored   1.50 1.10
18th National Day.

Modern Agriculture in Kuwait — A191

1979, Mar. 13   Photo.   Perf. 14
780 A191 30f multicolored   .60   .45
781 A191 80f multicolored   1.50 1.10
4th Congress of Arab Agriculture Ministers of the Gulf and Arabian Peninsula.

World Map, Book, Symbols of Learning A192

1979, Mar. 22
782 A192 30f multicolored   .75   .45
783 A192 80f multicolored   1.75 1.10
Cultural achievements of the Arabs.

Children with Balloons — A193

Children's Paintings: No. 785, Boys flying kites. No. 786, Girl and doves. No. 787, Children and houses, horiz. No. 788, Four children, horiz. No. 789, Children sitting in circle, horiz.

1979, Apr. 18   Photo.   Perf. 14
784 A193 30f yellow & multi   .90   .55
785 A193 30f buff & multi   .90   .55
786 A193 30f pale yel & multi   .90   .55
787 A193 80f lt blue & multi   2.00 1.25
788 A193 80f yel green & multi 2.00 1.25
789 A193 80f lilac & multi   2.00 1.25
     Nos. 784-789 (6)   8.70 5.40

Cables, ITU Emblem, People A194

1979, May 17
790 A194 30f multicolored   .60   .40
791 A194 80f multicolored   1.60 1.10
World Telecommunications Day.

Military Sports Council Emblem — A195

1979, June 1   Photo.   Perf. 14
792 A195 30f multicolored   .60   .40
793 A195 80f multicolored   1.75 1.25
29th Intl. Military Soccer Championship.

Child, Industrial Landscape, Environmental Emblems — A196

1979, June 5   *Perf. 12x11½*
794 A196 30f multicolored   .85   .60
795 A196 80f multicolored   2.10 1.60
World Environment Day, June 5.

Children Holding Globe, UNESCO Emblem A197

1979, July 25   Litho.   Perf. 11½x12
796 A197 30f multicolored   .50   .40
797 A197 80f multicolored   1.25 1.00
798 A197 130f multicolored   2.25 1.50
     Nos. 796-798 (3)   4.00 2.90
Intl. Bureau of Education, Geneva, 50th anniv.

Kuwait Kindergartens, 25th Anniversary
A198

Children's Drawings: 80f, Children waving flags.

1979, Sept. 15   Litho.   Perf. 12½
799 A198 30f multicolored   .60   .40
800 A198 80f multicolored   1.60 1.00

Pilgrims at Holy Ka'aba, Mecca Mosque
A199

1979, Oct. 29   Perf. 14x14½
801 A199 30f multicolored   1.00   .50
802 A199 80f multicolored   2.50 1.00
Hegira (Pilgrimage Year).

International Palestinian Solidarity Day — A200

1979, Nov. 29   Photo.   Perf. 11½x12
803 A200 30f multicolored   2.00   .95
804 A200 80f multicolored   4.75 1.90

Kuwait Airways 25th Anniversary
A201

1979, Dec. 24   Photo.   Perf. 13x13½
805 A201 30f multicolored   1.10   .60
806 A201 80f multicolored   2.75 1.75

19th National Day
A202

1980, Feb. 25   Litho.   Perf. 14x14½
807 A202 30f multicolored   .75   .40
808 A202 80f multicolored   1.75 1.00

1980 Population Census
A203

1980, Mar. 18   Perf. 13½x14
809 A203 30f multicolored   .70   .35
810 A203 80f multicolored   1.60   .95

World Health Day
A204

1980, Apr. 7
811 A204 30f multicolored   1.25   .35
812 A204 80f multicolored   2.75 1.25

Kuwait Municipality, 50th Anniversary
A205

1980, May 1   Photo.   Perf. 14
813 A205 15f multicolored   .40   .25
814 A205 30f multicolored   .85   .50
815 A205 80f multicolored   2.00 1.25
     Nos. 813-815 (3)   3.25 2.00

Citizens of Kuwait
A206

Future Kuwait (Children's Drawings): 80f, Super highway.

1980, May 14   Litho.   Perf. 14x14½
816 A206 30f multicolored   .85   .50
817 A206 80f multicolored   2.40 1.50

World Environment Day — A207

1980, June 5   Litho.   Perf. 12x11½
818 A207 30f multicolored   .85   .45
819 A207 80f multicolored   2.25 1.10

Swimming, Moscow '80 and Kuwait Olympic Committee Emblems — A208

1980, July 19   Litho.   Perf. 12x12½
820 A208 15f Volleyball   .40   .25
821 A208 15f Tennis   .40   .25
 a.   Vert. pair, #820-821   1.00 1.00
822 A208 30f shown   .60   .30
823 A208 30f Weight lifting   .60   .30
824 A208 30f Basketball   .60   .30
825 A208 30f Judo   .60   .30
 a.   Block of 4, #822-825   4.00 4.00
826 A208 80f Gymnast   1.50   .80
827 A208 80f Badminton   1.50   .80
828 A208 80f Fencing   1.50   .80
829 A208 80f Soccer   1.50   .80
 a.   Block of 4, #826-829   8.50 8.50
     Nos. 820-829 (10)   9.20 4.90
22nd Summer Olympic Games, Moscow, July 19-Aug. 3.

20th Anniversary of OPEC
A209

1980, Sept. 16   Litho.   Perf. 14x14½
830 A209 30f multicolored   1.00   .50
831 A209 80f multicolored   2.00 1.10

Hegira (Pilgrimage Year)
A210

1980, Nov. 9   Photo.   Perf. 12x11½
832 A210 15f multicolored   .60   .25
833 A210 30f multicolored   1.00   .45
834 A210 80f multicolored   2.25 1.25
     Nos. 832-834 (3)   3.85 1.95

Dome of the Rock, Jerusalem — A211

1980, Nov. 29   Perf. 12x11½
835 A211 30f multicolored   1.75   .85
836 A211 80f multicolored   4.50 2.40
International Palestinian Solidarity Day.

Avicenna (980-1037), Philosopher and Physician
A212

1980, Dec. 7   Perf. 12x12½
837 A212 30f multicolored   1.25   .35
838 A212 80f multicolored   2.50 1.20

Conference Emblem — A213

1981, Jan. 12   Photo.   Perf. 13½x13
839 A213 30f multicolored   .90   .65
840 A213 80f multicolored   2.50 1.60
First Islamic Medical Conference.

Girl in Wheelchair
A214

International Year of the Disabled: 30f, Man in wheelchair playing billiards, vert.

Perf. 13½x13, 13x13½
1981, Jan. 26   Photo.
841 A214 30f multicolored   .90   .40
842 A214 80f multicolored   2.10 1.40

20th National Day
A215

1981, Feb. 25   Litho.   Perf. 13x13½
843 A215 30f multicolored   .85   .40
844 A215 80f multicolored   2.00 1.40

First Kuwait Dental Association Conference
A216

1981, Mar. 14   Perf. 11½x12
845 A216 30f multicolored   1.75 1.00
846 A216 80f multicolored   4.75 2.25

A217

1981, May 8   Photo.   Perf. 14
847 A217 30f multicolored   1.75 1.25
848 A217 80f multicolored   4.75 3.50
Intl. Red Cross day.

A218

1981, May 17   Litho.   Perf. 14½x14
849 A218 30f multicolored   1.50   .75
850 A218 80f multicolored   3.25 2.25
13th World Telecommunications day.

World Environment Day — A219

1981, June 5   Photo.   Perf. 12
851 A219 30f multicolored   1.00   .60
852 A219 80f multicolored   2.75 1.75

Sief Palace
A220

A221

1981, Sept. 16   Litho.   Perf. 12

853	A220	5f	multicolored	.25	.25
854	A220	10f	multicolored	.25	.25
855	A220	15f	multicolored	.25	.25
856	A220	25f	multicolored	.25	.25
857	A220	30f	multicolored	.25	.25
858	A220	40f	multicolored	.40	.25
859	A220	60f	multicolored	.65	.25
860	A220	80f	multicolored	.85	.45
861	A220	100f	multicolored	1.10	.65
862	A220	115f	multicolored	1.25	.80
863	A220	130f	multicolored	1.40	1.00
864	A220	150f	multicolored	1.75	1.00
865	A220	180f	multicolored	2.10	1.10
866	A220	250f	multicolored	3.00	1.25
867	A220	500f	multicolored	6.00	2.25
868	A221	1d	multicolored	11.00	3.75
869	A221	2d	multicolored	24.00	8.50
870	A221	3d	multicolored	35.00	14.00
871	A221	4d	multicolored	45.00	17.50

Nos. 853-871 (19)   134.75 54.00

Islamic
Pilgrimage
A222

1981, Oct. 7   Photo.   Perf. 13x13½

872	A222	30f	multicolored	.80	.60
873	A222	80f	multicolored	2.75	1.50

World Food
Day
A223

1981, Oct. 16   Litho.   Perf. 13

874	A223	30f	multicolored	.90	.60
875	A223	80f	multicolored	2.50	1.50

A224

1981, Dec. 30   Photo.   Perf. 14

876	A224	30f	multicolored	1.00	.50
877	A224	80f	multicolored	3.00	1.50

20th anniv. of national television.

A225

1982, Jan. 16   Photo.   Perf. 14

878	A225	30f	multicolored	1.10	1.10
879	A225	80f	multicolored	3.50	1.75

First Intl. Pharmacology of Human Blood
Vessels Symposium, Jan. 16-18.

21st Natl.
Day — A226

1982, Feb. 25   Perf. 13½x13

880	A226	30f	multicolored	.65	.45
881	A226	80f	multicolored	1.90	1.25

Scouting
Year
A227

1982, Mar. 22   Photo.   Perf. 12x11½

882	A227	30f	multicolored	.80	.60
883	A227	80f	multicolored	2.25	1.50

Arab Pharmacists' Day — A228

1982, Apr. 2   Litho.   Perf. 12x11½

884	A228	30f	lt green & multi	1.00	.60
885	A228	80f	pink & multi	3.00	1.60

World Health
Day — A229

1982, Apr. 7   Litho.   Perf. 13½x13

886	A229	30f	multicolored	1.25	.90
887	A229	80f	multicolored	3.75	2.75

Arab Postal
Union, 30th
Anniv. — A230

1982, Apr. 12   Photo.   Perf. 13½x13

888	A230	30f	multicolored	1.00	.50
889	A230	80f	multicolored	3.25	1.50

TB Bacillus
Centenary
A231

1982, May 24   Litho.   Perf. 11½x12

890	A231	30f	multicolored	2.00	.90
891	A231	80f	multicolored	5.50	2.50

1982
World Cup
A232

1982, June 17   Photo.   Perf. 14

892	A232	30f	multicolored	1.00	.50
893	A232	80f	multicolored	3.50	1.50

10th Anniv. of
Science and
Natural History
Museum
A233

1982, July 14   Perf. 14

894	A233	30f	multicolored	4.50	2.00
895	A233	80f	multicolored	11.00	5.00

6th
Anniv. of
United
Arab
Shipping
Co.
A234

Designs: Freighters.

1982, Sept. 1   Perf. 13

896	A234	30f	multicolored	1.00	.40
897	A234	80f	multicolored	2.75	1.25

Arab Day of the
Palm
Tree — A235

1982, Sept. 15   Perf. 14

898	A235	30f	multicolored	.75	.45
899	A235	80f	multicolored	1.75	1.25

Islamic
Pilgrimage
A236

1982, Sept. 26   Litho.

900	A236	15f	multicolored	.50	.30
901	A236	30f	multicolored	1.10	.50
902	A236	80f	multicolored	3.00	1.50

Nos. 900-902 (3)   4.60 2.30

Desert
Flowers &
Plants — A237

Frame colors: No. 903a, green. b, violet. c,
deep salmon. d, rose red. e, pale brown. f,
deep green. g, pale orange. h, brown red. i,
tan. j, violet blue.
No. 904: a, yellow green. b, pink. c, pale
blue. d, dark blue. e, pale gray green. f, lake.

g, pale orange. h, blue. i, red lilac. j, red
orange.
No. 905: a, brown. b, pink. c, blue. d, olive
green. e, orange red. f, dark blue. g, green. h,
rose. i, bister. j, pale orange.
No. 906: a, yellow green. b, dark blue. c,
pale orange. d, rose red. e, green. f, gray violet. g, gray blue. h, violet. i, yellow brown. j,
orange red.
No. 907: a, lilac. b, blue green. c, pale
orange. d, pale brown. e, violet blue. f, yellow.
g, green blue. h, purple. i, pale brown. j, pale
orange.

1983, Jan. 25   Litho.   Perf. 12

903			Strip of 10	3.50	2.00
	a.-j.		A237 10f any single	.30	.25
904			Strip of 10	4.50	2.75
	a.-j.		A237 15f any single	.35	.25
905			Strip of 10	7.50	4.50
	a.-j.		A237 30f any single	.55	.45
906			Strip of 10	9.00	5.50
	a.-j		A237 40f any single, horiz.	.70	.55
907			Strip of 10	20.00	12.00
	a.-j.		A237 80f any single, horiz.	1.50	.85

Nos. 903-907 (5)   44.50 26.75

22nd Natl.
Day
A238

1983, Feb. 25   Litho.   Perf. 12½

908	A238	30f	multicolored	.75	.35
909	A238	80f	multicolored	2.00	1.25

25th
Anniv. of
Intl.
Maritime
Org.
A239

1983, Mar. 17   Photo.   Perf. 14

910	A239	30f	multicolored	.50	.30
911	A239	80f	multicolored	1.40	.85

Map of Middle East and Africa,
Conference Emblem — A240

1983, Mar. 19   Perf. 13

912	A240	15f	multicolored	.40	.25
913	A240	30f	multicolored	.85	.50
914	A240	80f	multicolored	2.50	1.50

Nos. 912-914 (3)   3.75 2.25

3rd Intl. Conference on the Impact of Viral
Diseases on the Development of the Middle
East and Africa, Mar. 19-27.

World
Health
Day
A241

1983, Apr. 7   Perf. 12x11½

915	A241	15f	multicolored	.45	.30
916	A241	30f	multicolored	.90	.70
917	A241	80f	multicolored	2.50	1.90

Nos. 915-917 (3)   3.85 2.90

World Communications Year — A242

1983, May 17 Photo. *Perf. 13x13½*
918 A242 15f multicolored   .50   .30
919 A242 30f multicolored   1.00   .70
920 A242 80f multicolored   2.75 1.90
  Nos. 918-920 (3)   4.25 2.90

World Environment Day — A243

1983, June 5 Litho. *Perf. 12½*
921 A243 15f multicolored   .50   .30
922 A243 30f multicolored   1.00   .70
923 A243 80f multicolored   3.50 1.90
  Nos. 921-923 (3)   5.00 2.90

Wall of Old Jerusalem A244

1983, July 25 Litho. *Perf. 12*
924 A244 15f multicolored   .70   .25
925 A244 30f multicolored   1.50   .55
926 A244 80f multicolored   3.50 1.60
  Nos. 924-926 (3)   5.70 2.40

World Heritage Year.

Islamic Pilgrimage A245

1983, Sept. 15 Photo. *Perf. 11½*
927 A245 15f multicolored   .55   .25
928 A245 30f multicolored   1.25   .55
929 A245 80f multicolored   3.00 1.60
  Nos. 927-929 (3)   4.80 2.40

Intl. Palestinian Solidarity Day — A246

1983, Nov. 29 Photo. *Perf. 14*
930 A246 15f multicolored   .50   .25
931 A246 30f multicolored   1.25   .65
932 A246 80f multicolored   3.50 1.75
  Nos. 930-932 (3)   5.25 2.65

21st Pan Arab Medical Congress, Jan. 30-Feb. 2 — A247

1984, Jan. 30 Litho. *Perf. 14½x14*
933 A247 15f purple & multi   .50   .25
934 A247 30f blue grn & multi   1.25   .65
935 A247 80f pink & multi   3.25 1.75
  Nos. 933-935 (3)   5.00 2.65

Key, Natl. Emblem, and Health Establishments Emblem A248

1984, Feb. 20 Photo. *Perf. 13x13½*
936 A248 15f multicolored   .55   .25
937 A248 30f multicolored   .95   .45
938 A248 80f multicolored   3.00 1.50
  Nos. 936-938 (3)   4.50 2.20

Inauguration of Amiri and Al-Razi Hospitals, Allergy Center and Medical Stores Center.

23rd National Day — A249

1984, Feb. 25 Litho. *Perf. 13½*
939 A249 15f multicolored   .40   .25
940 A249 30f multicolored   1.00   .45
941 A249 80f multicolored   2.75 1.50
  Nos. 939-941 (3)   4.15 2.20

2nd Kuwait Intl. Medical Science Conf., Mar. 4-8 — A250

1984, Mar. 4 Photo. *Perf. 12*
Granite Paper
942 A250 15f multicolored   .50   .25
943 A250 30f multicolored   1.10   .65
944 A250 80f multicolored   2.75 1.70
  Nos. 942-944 (3)   4.35 2.60

30th Anniv. of Kuwait Airways Corp. A251

1984, Mar. 15 *Perf. 13½*
946 A251 30f multicolored   .80   .80
947 A251 80f multicolored   2.25 1.75

Al-Arabi Magazine, 25th Anniv. — A252

1984, Mar. 20 *Perf. 14½x14*
948 A252 15f multicolored   .40   .25
949 A252 30f multicolored   .85   .50
950 A252 80f multicolored   2.25 1.40
  Nos. 948-950 (3)   3.50 2.15

World Health Day — A253

1984, Apr. 7 *Perf. 12*
951 A253 15f multicolored   .40   .25
952 A253 30f multicolored   .80   .45
953 A253 80f multicolored   2.40 1.50
  Nos. 951-953 (3)   3.60 2.20

Hanan Kuwaiti Orphan Village, Sudan A254

1984, May 15 Litho. *Perf. 12*
954 A254 15f multicolored   .50   .25
955 A254 30f multicolored   .90   .45
956 A254 80f multicolored   2.60 1.50
  Nos. 954-956 (3)   4.00 2.20

Intl. Civil Aviation Org., 40th Anniv. A255

1984, June 12
957 A255 15f multicolored   .55   .30
958 A255 30f multicolored   1.00   .65
959 A255 80f multicolored   2.75 1.75
  Nos. 957-959 (3)   4.30 2.70

Arab Youth Day — A256

1984, July 5 *Perf. 13½*
960 A256 30f multicolored   .75   .55
961 A256 80f multicolored   2.25 1.60

1984 Summer Olympics A257

1984, July 28 *Perf. 15x14*
962 A257 30f Swimming   .55   .55
963 A257 30f Hurdles   .55   .55
  a.   Pair, #962-963   1.40 1.40
964 A257 80f Judo   1.60 1.60
965 A257 80f Equestrian   1.60 1.60
  a.   Pair, #964-965   4.00 4.00
  Nos. 962-965 (4)   4.30 4.30

10th Anniv. of the Science Club A258

1984, Aug. 11 Photo. *Perf. 13½x13*
966 A258 15f multicolored   .45   .30
967 A258 30f multicolored   1.00   .65
968 A258 80f multicolored   2.60 1.80
  Nos. 966-968 (3)   4.05 2.75

Islamic Pilgrimage — A259

1984, Sept. 4 Photo. *Perf. 12x11½*
969 A259 30f multicolored   1.25   .75
970 A259 80f multicolored   3.25 2.00

INTELSAT '84, 20th Anniv. A260

1984, Oct. 1 Litho. *Perf. 13½x14*
971 A260 30f multicolored   1.00   .70
972 A260 80f multicolored   2.50 1.75

G.C.C. Supreme Council, 5th Session A261

1984, Nov. 24 Litho. *Perf. 15x14*
973 A261 30f multicolored   .75   .55
974 A261 80f multicolored   2.25 1.60

Map of Israel, Fists, Shattered Star of David — A262

1984, Nov. 29 Photo. *Perf. 12*
975 A262 30f multicolored   1.75   .75
976 A262 80f multicolored   4.50 2.00

Intl. Palestinian Solidarity Day.

Globe, Emblem A263

1984, Dec. 24 *Perf. 12x11½*
Granite Paper
977 A263 30f multicolored   1.00   .60
978 A263 80f multicolored   2.50 1.50

Kuwait Oil Co., 50th anniv.

Intl. Youth Year — A264

1985, Jan. 15 *Perf. 13½*
979 A264 30f multicolored   .50   .25
980 A264 80f multicolored   1.50 1.20

24th Natl.
Day — A265

1985, Feb. 25　Litho.　*Perf. 14x15*
981　A265　30f multicolored　　　　.65　.40
982　A265　80f multicolored　　　　2.50　1.25

Intl. Program for the Development of
Communications — A266

1985, Mar. 4　Photo.　*Perf. 11½*
Granite Paper
983　A266　30f multicolored　　　　.75　.45
984　A266　80f multicolored　　　　2.25　1.50

1st Arab Gulf
Week for Social
Work — A267

1985, Mar. 13　Photo.　*Perf. 13½x13*
985　A267　30f multicolored　　　　1.00　.45
986　A267　80f multicolored　　　　2.25　1.50

Kuwait
Dental
Assoc. 3rd
Conference
A268

1985, Mar. 23　Litho.　*Perf. 13½*
987　A268　30f multicolored　　　　1.00　.70
988　A268　80f multicolored　　　　2.25　1.75

1985
Census — A269

1985, Apr. 1　　　*Perf. 14x13½*
989　A269　30f multicolored　　　　1.00　.45
990　A269　80f multicolored　　　　2.50　1.50

World Health
Day — A270

1985, Apr. 7　Photo.　*Perf. 13½x13*
991　A270　30f multicolored　　　　1.10　.55
992　A270　80f multicolored　　　　2.50　1.60

Names of Books, Authors and Poets in
Arabic — A271

1985, May 20　　　*Perf. 12*
Granite Paper
993　A271　Block of 4　　　　　6.75　4.00
 a.-d.　　30f any single　　　　　1.40　.75
994　A271　Block of 4　　　　16.50　10.00
 a.-d.　　80f any single　　　　　3.50　1.40

Central Library, 50th anniv.

World Environment Day — A272

1985, June 5　　　*Perf. 11½*
995　A272　30f multicolored　　　　1.40　.75
996　A272　80f multicolored　　　　3.25　2.00

Org. of
Petroleum
Exporting
Countries,
25th Anniv.
A273

1985, Sept. 1　　　*Perf. 13x13½*
997　A273　30f multicolored　　　　1.10　.55
998　A273　80f multicolored　　　　2.75　1.60

Inauguration of Civil Information
System — A274

1985, Oct. 1　Photo.　*Perf. 12x11½*
999　A274　30f multicolored　　　　1.00　.45
1000　A274　80f multicolored　　　　2.50　1.50

Intl. Day of
Solidarity with
Palestinian
People
A275

1985, Nov. 29　Photo.　*Perf. 12*
1001　A275　15f multicolored　　　　1.00　.45
1002　A275　30f multicolored　　　　1.75　.90
1003　A275　80f multicolored　　　　4.00　2.50
　Nos. 1001-1003 (3)　　　　　6.75　3.85

25th Natl.
Day
A276

1986, Feb. 25　Litho.　*Perf. 15x14*
1004　A276　15f multicolored　　　　.40　.25
1005　A276　30f multicolored　　　　1.10　.60
1006　A276　80f multicolored　　　　2.75　1.75
　Nos. 1004-1006 (3)　　　　　4.25　2.60

Natl. Red
Crescent
Soc., 20th
Anniv.
A277

1986, Mar. 26　Photo.　*Perf. 13½*
1007　A277　20f multicolored　　　　.75　.40
1008　A277　25f multicolored　　　　1.00　.60
1009　A277　70f multicolored　　　　2.75　1.75
　Nos. 1007-1009 (3)　　　　　4.50　2.75

World Health
Day — A278

1986, Apr. 7　　　*Perf. 13½x13*
1010　A278　20f multicolored　　　　.85　.65
1011　A278　25f multicolored　　　　1.25　.80
1012　A278　70f multicolored　　　　3.00　2.00
　Nos. 1010-1012 (3)　　　　　5.10　3.45

Intl. Peace
Year
A279

1986, June 5　Litho.　*Perf. 13½*
1013　A279　20f multicolored　　　　.75　.45
1014　A279　25f multicolored　　　　1.25　.70
1015　A279　70f multicolored　　　　2.75　1.60
　Nos. 1013-1015 (3)　　　　　4.75　2.75

United
Arab
Shipping
Co., 10th
Anniv.
A280

1986, July 1　Photo.　*Perf. 12x11½*
1016　A280　20f Al Mirqab　　　　.75　.50
1017　A280　70f Al Mubarakiah　　　3.50　2.00

Gulf Bank,
25th Anniv.
A281

1986, Oct. 1　Photo.　*Perf. 12½*
1018　A281　20f multicolored　　　　.65　.50
1019　A281　25f multicolored　　　　1.10　.60
1020　A281　70f multicolored　　　　3.25　1.75
　Nos. 1018-1020 (3)　　　　　5.00　2.85

Sadu
Art — A282

Various tapestry weavings.

1986, Nov. 5　Photo.　*Perf. 12x11½*
Granite Paper
1021　A282　20f multicolored　　　　.75　.40
1022　A282　70f multicolored　　　　2.50　1.50
1023　A282　200f multicolored　　　6.00　3.75
　Nos. 1021-1023 (3)　　　　　9.25　5.65

Intl. Day of Solidarity with the
Palestinian People — A283

1986, Nov. 29　　　*Perf. 14*
1024　A283　20f multicolored　　　　1.50　.85
1025　A283　25f multicolored　　　　2.00　1.10
1026　A283　70f multicolored　　　　5.25　3.25
　Nos. 1024-1026 (3)　　　　　8.75　5.20

5th Islamic Summit
Conference — A284

1987, Jan. 26　Litho.　*Perf. 14½*
1027　A284　25f multicolored　　　　.85　.45
1028　A284　50f multicolored　　　　1.60　.80
1029　A284　150f multicolored　　　4.75　2.25
　Nos. 1027-1029 (3)　　　　　7.20　3.50

26th Natl.
Day
A285

1987, Feb. 25　　　*Perf. 13½x14*
1030　A285　50f multicolored　　　　1.40　.60
1031　A285　150f multicolored　　　4.25　2.00

Natl.
Health
Sciences
Center
A286

1987, Mar. 15　Photo.　*Perf. 12x11½*
Granite Paper
1032　A286　25f multicolored　　　　.75　.35
1033　A286　150f multicolored　　　3.50　2.00

3rd Kuwait Intl. Medical Sciences Conference on Infectious Diseases in Developing
Countries.

World Health Day — A287

1987, Apr. 7   Photo.   Perf. 13x13½
1034 A287 25f multicolored   .75   .40
1035 A287 50f multicolored   1.40   .70
1036 A287 150f multicolored   4.75 2.00
     Nos. 1034-1036 (3)   6.90 3.10

Day of Ghods (Jerusalem) — A288

1987, June 7   Photo.   Perf. 12x11½
1037 A288 25f multicolored   .75   .30
1038 A288 50f multicolored   1.50   .65
1039 A288 150f multicolored   4.25 2.25
     Nos. 1037-1039 (3)   6.50 3.20

Islamic Pilgrimage to Miqat Wadi
Mihrim — A289

1987, Aug.   Photo.   Perf. 13½x14½
1040 A289 25f multicolored   .75   .30
1041 A289 50f multicolored   1.50   .80
1042 A289 150f multicolored   4.00 2.25
     Nos. 1040-1042 (3)   6.25 3.35

Arab Telecommunications Day — A290

1987, Sept. 9   Litho.   Perf. 14x13½
1043 A290 25f multicolored   .60   .30
1044 A290 50f multicolored   1.25   .80
1045 A290 150f multicolored   3.50 1.25
     Nos. 1043-1045 (3)   5.35 2.35

World
Maritime
Day
A291

1987, Sept. 24   Perf. 12x11½
Granite Paper
1046 A291 25f multicolored   .85   .35
1047 A291 50f multicolored   1.75   .75
1048 A291 150f multicolored   5.00 2.00
     Nos. 1046-1048 (3)   7.60 3.10

Al Qurain
Housing
Project — A292

1987, Oct. 5   Perf. 13x13½
1049 A292 25f multicolored   .60   .35
1050 A292 50f multicolored   1.25   .60
1051 A292 150f multicolored   3.50 1.75
     Nos. 1049-1051 (3)   5.35 2.70

Port Authority, 10th Anniv. — A293

1987, Nov. 16   Litho.   Perf. 14½
1052 A293 25f multicolored   .75   .25
1053 A293 50f multicolored   1.25   .65
1054 A293 150f multicolored   4.00 2.00
     Nos. 1052-1054 (3)   6.00 2.90

A294

1987, Nov. 29   Perf. 14x13½
1055 A294 25f multicolored   .65   .30
1056 A294 50f multicolored   1.25   .60
1057 A294 150f multicolored   4.00 2.00
     Nos. 1055-1057 (3)   5.90 2.90

Intl. Day of Solidarity with the Palestinian
People

A295

1988, Feb. 3   Photo.   Perf. 14
1058 A295 25f multicolored   .55   .30
1059 A295 50f multicolored   1.00   .50
1060 A295 150f multicolored   2.75 1.25
     Nos. 1058-1060 (3)   4.30 2.05

Women's Cultural and Social Soc., 25th
anniv.

A296

1988, Feb. 25
1061 A296 25f multicolored   .55   .25
1062 A296 50f multicolored   .90   .50
1063 A296 150f multicolored   2.50 1.10
     Nos. 1061-1063 (3)   3.95 1.85

National Day, 27th anniv.

A297

1988, Apr. 7   Litho.   Perf. 14x15
1064 A297 25f multicolored   .75   .30
1065 A297 50f multicolored   1.25   .65
1066 A297 150f multicolored   3.75 1.25
     Nos. 1064-1066 (3)   5.75 2.20

World Health Day, WHO 40th anniv.

A298

1988, Apr. 24   Photo.   Perf. 12
Granite Paper
1067 A298 35f multicolored   .80   .35
1068 A298 50f multicolored   1.25   .55
1069 A298 150f multicolored   4.25 1.75
     Nos. 1067-1069 (3)   6.30 2.65

Regional Marine Environment Day. Kuwait
Regional Convention on the Marine Environment, 10th anniv. See Iraq Nos. 1333-1336.

A299

1988, July 10   Photo.   Perf. 14
1070 A299 25f multicolored   .85   .25
1071 A299 50f multicolored   1.25   .60
1072 A299 150f multicolored   4.25 1.75
     Nos. 1070-1072 (3)   6.35 2.60

Kuwait Teachers Soc., 25th anniv.

Pilgrimage
to Mecca
A300

1988, Sept. 12   Litho.   Perf. 13½x14
1073 A300 25f multicolored   .85   .25
1074 A300 50f multicolored   1.50   .55
1075 A300 150f multicolored   4.50 1.75
     Nos. 1073-1075 (3)   6.85 2.55

Palestinian
"Children of
Stone" Fighting
Israelis — A301

1988, Sept. 15   Photo.   Perf. 13x13½
1076 A301 50f multicolored   2.00   .70
1077 A301 150f multicolored   7.00 2.50

Palestinian Uprising. Dated 1987.

Arab Housing
Day — A302

1988, Oct. 3
1078 A302 50f multicolored   1.10   .60
1079 A302 100f multicolored   2.25 1.25
1080 A302 150f multicolored   3.75 1.75
     Nos. 1078-1080 (3)   7.10 3.60

Intl. Day for
Solidarity with
the
Palestinian
People
A303

1988, Nov. 29   Litho.   Perf. 14x13
1081 A303 50f multicolored   1.10   .60
1082 A303 100f multicolored   2.25 1.25
1083 A303 150f multicolored   4.00 1.75
     Nos. 1081-1083 (3)   7.35 3.60

A304

1988, Dec. 5   Perf. 13x14
1084 A304 50f multicolored   .90   .50
1085 A304 100f multicolored   2.00 1.00
1086 A304 150f multicolored   3.25 1.50
     Nos. 1084-1086 (3)   6.15 3.00

Intl. Volunteers Day.

A305

1989, Feb. 18   Litho.   Perf. 14x13½
1087 A305 50f multicolored   1.00   .50
1088 A305 100f multicolored   2.00 1.00
1089 A305 150f multicolored   3.50 1.50
     Nos. 1087-1089 (3)   6.50 3.00

18th Arab Engineering Conference.

28th Natl.
Day
A306

1989, Feb. 25   Perf. 13x13½
1090 A306 50f multicolored   1.00   .50
1091 A306 100f multicolored   2.00 1.00
1092 A306 150f multicolored   3.50 1.50
     Nos. 1090-1092 (3)   6.50 3.00

5th Natl. Dental
Assoc.
Conference
A307

1989, Mar. 30   Litho.   Perf. 13½x13
1093 A307 50f multicolored   1.00   .50
1094 A307 150f multicolored   3.00 1.25
1095 A307 250f multicolored   4.50 2.00
     Nos. 1093-1095 (3)   8.50 3.75

World
Health Day
A308

1989, Apr. 7   *Perf. 13x13½*
1096 A308 50f multicolored   .80   .40
1097 A308 150f multicolored   2.50 1.25
1098 A308 250f multicolored   4.25 2.00
    Nos. 1096-1098 (3)   7.55 3.65

A309

1989, May 10   *Perf. 13x14*
1099 A309 50f multicolored   .80   .40
1100 A309 150f multicolored   2.50 1.25
1101 A309 250f multicolored   4.25 2.00
    Nos. 1099-1101 (3)   7.55 3.65

Arab Board for Medical Specializations, 10th
anniv.

A310

1989, June 10 Litho.   *Perf. 14x15*
1102 A310 50f multicolored   .90   .50
1103 A310 200f multicolored   3.50 2.25
1104 A310 250f multicolored   4.50 2.75
    Nos. 1102-1104 (3)   8.90 5.50

Natl. Journalists Assoc., 25th anniv.

Al-Taneem Mosque — A311

1989, July 9 Litho.   *Perf. 13½x14½*
1105 A311 50f multicolored   1.00   .50
1106 A311 150f multicolored   3.00 1.50
1107 A311 200f multicolored   4.00 2.00
    Nos. 1105-1107 (3)   8.00 4.00

Pilgrimage to Mecca.

Arab Housing
Day — A312

1989, Oct. 2   *Perf. 13½*
1108 A312 25f multicolored   .65   .25
1109 A312 50f multicolored   1.50   .50
1110 A312 150f multicolored   4.75 1.50
    Nos. 1108-1110 (3)   6.90 2.25

Annual Greenery
Week Celebration
A313

1989, Oct. 15   *Perf. 13½x13*
1111 A313 25f multicolored   .75   .25
1112 A313 50f multicolored   1.75   .50
1113 A313 150f multicolored   5.00 1.50
    Nos. 1111-1113 (3)   7.50 2.25

Dhow — A314

**Numbers in Black, Moon and Dhow
in Gold**

1989, Nov. 1   *Perf. 14x15*
Coil Stamps
1114 A314 50f brt apple grn   *2.25 2.25*
1115 A314 100f brt blue   *4.00 4.00*
1116 A314 200f vermilion   *8.50 8.50*
    Nos. 1114-1116 (3)   *14.75 14.75*

Nos. 1114-1116 available only at two post
office locations, where they were dispensed
from machines. Printed in rolls of 3000 con-
secutively numbered stamps. Stamps with
overprinted asterisks but lacking printed numbers are from the ends of coil rolls.

Gulf
Investment
Corp., 5th
Anniv. — A315

1989, Nov. 4   *Perf. 15x14*
1117 A315 25f multicolored   .80   .25
1118 A315 50f multicolored   1.50   .50
1119 A315 150f multicolored   4.50 1.50
    Nos. 1117-1119 (3)   6.80 2.25

Declaration of
Palestinian State,
1st
Anniv. — A316

1989, Nov. 15 Litho.   *Perf. 14x15*
1120 A316 50f multicolored   1.00   .50
1121 A316 150f multicolored   3.00 1.75
1122 A316 200f multicolored   4.25 2.25
    Nos. 1120-1122 (3)   8.25 4.50

Zakat House,
Orphan
Sponsorship
Program — A317

1989, Dec. 10   *Perf. 13½x13*
1123 A317 25f multicolored   .50   .30
1124 A317 50f multicolored   1.10   .75
1125 A317 150f multicolored   3.50 2.00
    Nos. 1123-1125 (3)   5.10 3.05

Kuwait Police,
50th
Anniv. — A318

1989, Dec. 30 Litho.   *Perf. 15x14*
1126 A318 25f gray & multi   .50   .30
1127 A318 50f lt ultra & multi   1.10   .75
1128 A318 150f lt violet & multi   3.50 2.00
    Nos. 1126-1128 (3)   5.10 3.05

National Day,
29th
Anniv. — A319

1990, Feb. 25   *Perf. 14x13½*
1129 A319 25f multicolored   .55   .30
1130 A319 50f multicolored   1.00   .75
1131 A319 150f multicolored   3.25 1.75
    Nos. 1129-1131 (3)   4.80 2.80

World Meteorological Day — A320

1990, Mar. 23 Litho.   *Perf. 13½x14*
1132 A320 50f multicolored   1.00   .50
1133 A320 100f multicolored   2.25 1.25
1134 A320 200f multicolored   3.25 2.00
    Nos. 1132-1134 (3)   6.50 3.75

World Health
Day — A321

1990, Apr. 7   *Perf. 14x15*
1135 A321 50f multicolored   1.10   .50
1136 A321 100f multicolored   2.25 1.25
1137 A321 150f multicolored   3.00 2.00
    Nos. 1135-1137 (3)   6.35 3.75

Hawk — A322

1990, July 7 Litho.   *Perf. 14½*
1138 A322 50f blue & gold   6.00 6.00
1139 A322 100f maroon & gold   8.00 8.00
1140 A322 150f green & gold   11.00 11.00
    Nos. 1138-1140 (3)   25.00 25.00

Liberation of
Kuwait — A323

1991   **Litho.**   *Perf. 14½*
1141 A323 25f multicolored   .75   .40
1142 A323 50f multicolored   1.50   .80
1143 A323 150f multicolored   4.00 2.50
    Nos. 1141-1143 (3)   6.25 3.70

Peace — A324

1991, May   *Perf. 13½x14*
1144 A324 50f multicolored   1.25   .75
1145 A324 100f multicolored   2.50 1.50
1146 A324 150f multicolored   4.00 2.25
    Nos. 1144-1146 (3)   7.75

Reconstruction
A325

1991, May
1147 A325 50f multicolored   1.25   .85
1148 A325 150f multicolored   3.25 2.00
1149 A325 200f multicolored   4.00 2.75
    Nos. 1147-1149 (3)   8.50 5.60

Liberation of Kuwait — A326

Flags of forces joining international coalition
for liberation of Kuwait: a, Sweden. b, USSR.
c, U.S. d, Kuwait. e, Saudi Arabia. f, UN. g,
Singapore. h, France. i, Italy. j, Egypt. k,
Morocco. l, UK. m, Philippines. n, UAE. o,
Syria. p, Poland. q, Australia. r, Japan. s, Hungary. t, Netherlands. u, Denmark. v, New Zealand. w, Czechoslovakia. x, Bahrain. y, Honduras. z, Turkey. aa, Greece. ab, Oman. ac,
Qatar. ad, Belgium. ae, Sierra Leone. af,
Argentina. ag, Norway. ah, Canada. ai, Germany. aj, South Korea. ak, Bangladesh. al,
Bulgaria. am, Senegal. an, Spain. ao, Niger.
ap, Pakistan.

No. 1151, Flags of all forces of coalition.

1991, July 25 Litho.   *Perf. 14½*
1150 A326 50f Sheet of 42   *50.00 50.00*
a.-ap.   Any single   1.00 1.00
     Size: 87x134mm
     Imperf
1151 A326 1d multicolored   *27.50 27.50*

Invasion of
Kuwait, 1st
Anniv. — A327

50f, Human terror. 100f, Invasion of Kuwait.
150f, Environmental terrorism, horiz. 250f,
Desert Storm.

1991, Aug. 2   *Perf. 14½*
1152 A327 50f multi   *1.50 1.00*
1153 A327 100f multi   *2.75 1.50*
1154 A327 150f multi   *4.25 2.50*
     Size: 90x65mm
     Imperf
1155 A327 250f multi   *10.00 10.00*
    Nos. 1152-1155 (4)   *18.50 15.00*

12th Gulf Cooperation Council Summit A328

Design: 150f, Tree of flags.

1991, Dec. 23   Litho.   Perf. 14½
1156	A328	25f multicolored	.75	.55
a.		see footnote	.80	.55
1157	A328	150f multicolored	4.25	3.25
a.		Sheet, 2 ea #1156-1157	10.00	10.00
b.		Sheet, 2 ea #1156a, 1157	10.00	10.00

No. 1156a has tree with inscriptions (country names in Arabic) in colors of flags shown on No. 1157.

Intl. Literacy Year — A329

1992, Feb. 12   Litho.   Perf. 13½x13
1158	A329	50f dark blue & buff	1.00	.75
1159	A329	100f dark blue & cit	2.00	1.50
1160	A329	150f dk blue & pale lil	3.00	2.00
		Nos. 1158-1160 (3)	6.00	4.25

Dated 1990.

OPEC, 30th Anniv. (in 1990) — A330

1992, Oct. 29   Perf. 14½x13½
1161	A330	25f red & multi	.75	.50
1162	A330	50f yellow & multi	1.50	1.00
1163	A330	150f green & multi	4.00	3.00
		Nos. 1161-1163 (3)	6.25	4.50

31st Natl. Day A331

1992   Perf. 14½
1164	A331	50f Flag, doves	.75	.50
1165	A331	150f Flags	2.25	1.50
a.		Min. sheet, 2 ea #1164-1165	7.50	7.50

Liberation Day (No. 1165). Issue dates, 50f, Feb. 25; 150f, Feb. 26.

Don't Forget Our P.O.W.'s — A332

50f, Flag, chains. 150f, Cell bars, chains.

1991, Nov. 16
1166	A332	50f multicolored	1.25	.75
1167	A332	150f multicolored	4.00	2.25
a.		Min. sheet, 2 each #1166-1167	14.00	14.00

Dated 1991. Issued: 50f, 2/25; 150f, 2/26.

Camels A333

1991, Nov. 16   Perf. 12½
1168	A333	25f pink & multi	.60	.60
1169	A333	50f beige & multi	1.00	1.00
1170	A333	150f lt violet & multi	2.50	2.50
1171	A333	200f blue & multi	3.00	3.00
1172	A333	350f orange & multi	6.00	6.00
		Nos. 1168-1172 (5)	13.10	13.10

Environmental Terrorism, by Jafar Islah — A334

Designs: No. 1174, Snake, flag, map. No. 1175, Skull, dead fish. No. 1176, Dying camel.

1992, June   Perf. 14½
1173	A334	150f multicolored	2.00	1.50
1174	A334	150f multicolored	2.00	1.50
1175	A334	150f multicolored	2.00	1.50
1176	A334	150f multicolored	2.00	1.50
a.		Block of 4, #1173-1176	13.00	10.00
b.		Miniature sheet of 4, #1173-1176	15.00	15.00

Earth Summit, Rio De Janeiro. No. 1176a printed in continuous design.

EXPO '92, Seville A335

Designs: No. 1177, Kuwaiti Pavilion, La Giralda Tower, Seville. No. 1178, Dhows. No. 1179, Dhow. No. 1180, Pavilion, dhow.
Flags of Spain or Kuwait and: No. 1181, Pavilion. No. 1182, La Giralda Tower. No. 1183, La Giralda Tower, dhow. No. 1184, Pavilion, dhow.

1992, June 19
1177	A335	50f multicolored	.60	.60
1178	A335	50f multicolored	.60	.60
1179	A335	50f multicolored	.60	.60
1180	A335	50f multicolored	.60	.60
a.		Block of 4, #1177-1180	2.75	2.75
1181	A335	150f multicolored	1.90	1.90
1182	A335	150f multicolored	1.90	1.90
1183	A335	150f multicolored	1.90	1.90
1184	A335	150f multicolored	1.90	1.90
a.		Block of 4, #1181-1184	9.00	9.00
b.		Miniature sheet of 8, #1177-1184	16.50	16.50
		Nos. 1177-1184 (8)	10.00	10.00

Nos. 1180a, 1184a have continuous designs.

Palace of Justice A336

1992, July 4   Perf. 12½
1185	A336	25f lilac & multi	.40	.30
1186	A336	50f lil rose & multi	.80	.50
1187	A336	100f yel grn & multi	1.25	.90
1188	A336	150f yel org & multi	2.00	1.25
1189	A336	250f blue grn & multi	3.00	2.25
		Nos. 1185-1189 (5)	7.45	5.20

1992 Summer Olympics, Barcelona — A337

Olympic flag, Fahed Al Ahmed Al Sabah, member of the Intl. Olympic committee and: 50f, Swimmer, soccer player. 100f, Runner, basketball player. 150f, Judo, equestrian.

1992, July 25   Perf. 14½
1190	A337	50f multicolored	1.00	.65
1191	A337	100f multicolored	2.25	1.25
1192	A337	150f multicolored	3.25	2.00
		Nos. 1190-1192 (3)	6.50	3.90

Invasion by Iraq, 2nd Anniv. A338

Children's paintings: No. 1193, Tanks, people holding signs, two people being tortured. No. 1194, Truck, Iraqi soldiers looting. No. 1195, Iraqi soldiers killing civilians, tanks. No. 1196, Houses ablaze. No. 1197, Tanks, civilians, soldiers. No. 1198, Planes bombing in attack on fort. No. 1199, Tank, civilians holding flags, signs. No. 1200, Battlefield.

1992, Aug. 2   Litho.   Perf. 14x14½
1193	A338	50f multicolored	.60	.60
1194	A338	50f multicolored	.60	.60
1195	A338	50f multicolored	.60	.60
1196	A338	50f multicolored	.60	.60
a.		Block of 4, #1193-1196	2.75	2.75
1197	A338	150f multicolored	1.90	1.90
1198	A338	150f multicolored	1.90	1.90
1199	A338	150f multicolored	1.90	1.90
1200	A338	150f multicolored	1.90	1.90
a.		Block of 4, #1197-1200	9.50	9.50
b.		Min. sheet of 8, #1193-1200	15.00	15.00
		Nos. 1193-1200 (8)	10.00	10.00

Extinguishing of Oil Well Fires, 1st Anniv. — A339

Various scenes showing oil well fire being extinguished.

1992   Litho.   Perf. 14½
1201	A339	25f multi, vert.	.35	.35
1202	A339	50f multi, vert.	.70	.70
1203	A339	150f multi, vert.	2.00	2.00
1204	A339	250f multicolored	3.50	3.50
		Nos. 1201-1204 (4)	6.55	6.55

Kuwait Tower — A340

1993, Jan. 16   Litho.   Perf. 14x15
Background Color
1205	A340	25f lilac	.35	.35
1206	A340	100f blue	1.25	1.25
1207	A340	150f salmon	2.00	1.75
		Nos. 1205-1207 (3)	3.60	3.35

A341

1993, Feb. 25   Litho.   Perf. 13½x14
1208	A341	25f green & multi	.35	.35
1209	A341	50f blue & multi	.75	.70
1210	A341	150f pink & multi	2.00	1.75
		Nos. 1208-1210 (3)	3.10	2.80

National Day, 32nd anniv.

Liberation Day, 2nd Anniv. — A342

1993, Feb. 26   Perf. 15x14
1211	A342	25f org yel & multi	.35	.35
1212	A342	50f green & multi	.75	.75
1213	A342	150f red lilac & multi	2.00	1.75
		Nos. 1211-1213 (3)	3.10	2.85

Remembering Prisoners of War — A343

Designs: 50f, Prisoner shackled in cell, vert. 150f, Shackled hand pointing to cell window, bird. 200f, Cell, prisoner's face, vert.

Perf. 13½x14, 14x13½
1993, May 15   Litho.
1214	A343	50f multicolored	.75	.75
1215	A343	150f multicolored	2.00	2.00
1216	A343	200f multicolored	2.50	2.50
		Nos. 1214-1216 (3)	5.25	5.25

A344

1993, Apr. 20   Litho.   Perf. 11½x12
Granite Paper
1217	A344	25f gray & multi	.35	.35
1218	A344	50f green & multi	.75	.75
1219	A344	150f yellow & multi	2.60	2.00
1220	A344	350f blue & multi	4.75	4.00
		Nos. 1217-1220 (4)	8.45	7.10

18th Deaf Child Week.

A345

1993, Aug. 2   Litho.   Perf. 13½x14
1221	A345	50f green & multi	.60	.60
1222	A345	150f orange & multi	2.00	1.75

Invasion by Iraq, 3rd anniv.

Kuwait
Airforce,
40th Anniv.
A346

1993, Dec. 9   Litho.   *Perf. 13x13½*
1223 A346 50f blue & multi   .60   .60
1224 A346 150f green & multi   2.00   1.75

Natl. Day, 33rd
Anniv. — A347

1994, Feb. 25   Litho.   *Perf. 13½x14*
1225 A347 25f salmon & multi   .40   .40
1226 A347 50f yellow & multi   .75   .75
1227 A347 150f green & multi   2.00   1.75
     Nos. 1225-1227 (3)   3.15   2.90

Liberation Day,
3rd
Anniv. — A348

1994, Feb. 26
1228 A348 25f yellow & multi   .40   .40
1229 A348 50f blue & multi   .75   .75
1230 A348 150f gray green &
              multi   2.10   1.90
     Nos. 1228-1230 (3)   3.25   3.05

Central Bank of
Kuwait, 25th
Anniv. — A349

1994, Apr. 20   Litho.   *Perf. 13½x13*
1231 A349 25f salmon & multi   .40   .40
1232 A349 50f green & multi   .75   .75
1233 A349 150f blue violet &
              multi   2.25   2.00
     Nos. 1231-1233 (3)   3.40   3.15

A350

A351

**Intl. Year of
the Family
A352**

1994, May 15   Litho.   *Perf. 13*
1234 A350 50f multicolored   .75   .75
1235 A351 150f multicolored   2.25   2.25
1236 A352 200f multicolored   3.25   3.00
     Nos. 1234-1236 (3)   6.25   6.00

A353

1994, June 5   Litho.   *Perf. 14*
1237 A353 50f yellow & multi   .65   .65
1238 A353 100f blue & multi   1.25   1.25
1239 A353 150f green & multi   2.00   1.75
     Nos. 1237-1239 (3)   3.90   3.65

Industrial Bank of Kuwait, 20th anniv.

A354

1994, June 15   Litho.   *Perf. 13*
1240 A354 50f Whirlpool   .75   .50
1241 A354 100f Shifting sands   1.50   1.00
1242 A354 150f Finger print   2.25   2.25
1243 A354 250f Clouds   2.75   2.50
  a.   Min. sheet of 4, #1240-1243 9.00   9.00
     Nos. 1240-1243 (4)   7.25   6.25

Martyr's Day.

A355

1994, June 25   Litho.   *Perf. 14*
1244 A355 50f vio & multi   .75   .75
1245 A355 150f pink & multi   2.00   2.00
1246 A355 350f blue & multi   4.75   4.25
     Nos. 1244-1246 (3)   7.50   7.00

ILO, 75th anniv.

A356

1994, Aug. 2   Litho.   *Perf. 12½x13½*
1247 A356 50f green blue &
              multi   .75   .75
1248 A356 150f blue & multi   2.00   2.00
1249 A356 350f lilac & multi   4.75   4.25
     Nos. 1247-1249 (3)   7.50   7.00

Invasion by Iraq, 4th anniv.

Port
Authority — A357

1994, Aug. 31   Litho.   *Perf. 12½x14*
1250 A357 50f pink & multi   .75   .75
1251 A357 150f blue & multi   2.00   2.00
1252 A357 350f green & multi   4.75   4.25
     Nos. 1250-1252 (3)   7.50   7.00

Science Club, 20th
Anniv. — A358

1994, Sept. 11   *Perf. 14*
1253 A358 50f blue & multi   .75   .75
1254 A358 100f green & multi   1.50   1.50
1255 A358 150f red & multi   2.00   1.75
     Nos. 1253-1255 (3)   4.25   4.00

A359

Designs showing emblem and: 50f, Map of
Arab countries, building. 100f, Windows, building. 150f, Doors below portico.

1994, Nov. 12   *Perf. 11½*
1256 A359 50f multicolored   .75   .75
1257 A359 100f multicolored   1.25   1.25
1258 A359 150f multicolored   2.50   2.25
     Nos. 1256-1258 (3)   4.50   4.25

Arab Towns Organization, opening of
headquarters.

A360

Designs: 100f, Emblems, sailing ship. 150f,
Emblems, co-operation, co-ordination. 350f,
Emblem, airplane in flight.

1994, Dec. 7   *Perf. 14½*
1259 A360 100f silver, gold &
              multi   1.50   1.50
1260 A360 150f silver, gold &
              multi   2.25   2.25
1261 A360 350f gold & multi   5.00   4.00
     Nos. 1259-1261 (3)   8.75   7.75

ICAO, 50th anniv.

A361

1994, Dec. 20   *Perf. 13x14*
1262 A361 50f lake & multi   .75   .75
1263 A361 100f green & multi   1.25   1.25
1264 A361 150f slate & multi   2.50   2.25
     Nos. 1262-1264 (3)   4.50   4.25

Kuwait Airways, 40th anniv.

A362

1995, Feb. 6   Litho.   *Perf. 14*
1265 A362 50f yellow & multi   .75   .75
1266 A362 100f green & multi   1.25   1.25
1267 A362 150f brown & multi   2.50   2.25
     Nos. 1265-1267 (3)   4.50   4.25

1995 Census.

National Day,
34th
Anniv. — A363

1995, Feb. 25   *Perf. 13*
1268 A363 25f blue & multi   .40   .40
1269 A363 50f yellow & multi   .75   .75
1270 A363 150f lilac & multi   2.25   1.75
     Nos. 1268-1270 (3)   3.40   2.90

Liberation Day,
4th
Anniv. — A364

1995, Feb. 26
1271 A364 25f blue & multi   .40   .40
1272 A364 50f green & multi   .75   .75
1273 A364 150f rose lilac &
              multi   2.25   1.75
     Nos. 1271-1273 (3)   3.40   2.90

Medical
Research
A365

1995, Mar. 20   *Perf. 14*
1274 A365 50f Medical building   .75   .75
1275 A365 100f Classroom in-
              struction   1.25   1.25
1276 A365 150f Map of Kuwait   2.25   2.00
     Nos. 1274-1276 (3)   4.25   4.00

Arab
League,
50th Anniv.
A366

Designs: 50f, Kuwaiti, league flags over
emblems, map, vert. 100f, Flags over "50,"
emblem. 150f, Flags as clasping hands, vert.

1995, Mar. 22   *Perf. 13*
1277 A366 50f multicolored   .75   .75
1278 A366 100f multicolored   1.25   1.25
1279 A366 150f multicolored   2.25   2.00
     Nos. 1277-1279 (3)   4.25   4.00

A367

1995, Apr. 7   Litho.   Perf. 13½x13
1280 A367 50f blue & multi   .75   .75
1281 A367 150f pink & multi   2.25   2.00
1282 A367 200f yellow & multi   2.75   2.50
  Nos. 1280-1282 (3)   5.75   5.25
   World Health Day.

A368

1995, June 5   Litho.   Perf. 14
1283 A368 50f shown   .75   .75
1284 A368 100f multicolored   1.25   1.25
1285 A368 150f multicolored   2.25   2.00
  Nos. 1283-1285 (3)   4.25   4.00
   Volleyball, cent.

Designs: 50f, One gold ball. 100f, Gold "1,"
one gold ball. 150f, "1," both balls in gold.

Invasion by Iraq,
5th
Anniv. — A369

1995, Aug. 2   Litho.   Perf. 13
1286 A369 50f purple & multi   .75   .75
1287 A369 100f red & multi   1.25   1.25
1288 A369 150f green & multi   2.25   2.00
  Nos. 1286-1288 (3)   4.25   4.00

UN, 50th
Anniv.
A370

1995, Aug. 12   Perf. 13x13½
1289 A370 25f multi   .50   .50
1290 A370 50f orange & multi   1.00   1.00
1291 A370 150f bl grn & multi   2.00   1.75
  Nos. 1289-1291 (3)   3.50   3.25

FAO, 50th
Anniv. — A371

People in traditional dress with: 50f, Cattle,
camels, sheep. 100f, Fish, boat. 150f, Poultry,
fruits, vegetables.

1995, Sept. 21   Perf. 13½x13
1292 A371 50f multicolored   .75   .75
1293 A371 100f multicolored   1.25   1.25
1294 A371 150f multicolored   2.25   2.00
 a. Min. sheet of 3, #1292-1294   5.00   5.00
  Nos. 1292-1294 (3)   4.25   4.00

A372

World Standards Day — A373

1995, Oct. 14   Perf. 13
1295 A372 50f multicolored   .75   .75
1296 A373 100f green & multi   1.25   1.25
1297 A373 150f violet & multi   2.25   2.00
  Nos. 1295-1297 (3)   4.25   4.00

Flowers — A374

Designs: 5f, Onobrychis ptolemaica. 15f,
Convolvulus oxyphyllus. 25f, Papaver rhoeas.
50f, Moltkiopsis ciliata. 150f, Senecio
desfontainei.

1995, Nov. 15   Litho.   Perf. 14½
1298 A374 5f multicolored   .30   .30
1299 A374 15f multicolored   .40   .40
1300 A374 25f multicolored   .75   .75
1301 A374 50f multicolored   1.25   1.25
1302 A374 150f multicolored   2.50   2.00
  Nos. 1298-1302 (5)   5.20   4.70

Natl. Day, 35th
Anniv. — A375

1996, Feb. 25   Perf. 14
1303 A375 25f lil rose & multi   .40   .40
1304 A375 50f blue green &
    multi   .75   .75
1305 A375 150f salmon & multi   2.25   2.00
  Nos. 1303-1305 (3)   3.40   3.15

Liberation
Day, 5th
Anniv.
A376

1996, Feb. 26
1306 A376 25f violet & multi   .40   .40
1307 A376 50f brown & multi   .75   .75
1308 A376 150f blue green &
    multi   2.25   2.00
  Nos. 1306-1308 (3)   3.40   3.15

Arab City
Day — A377

1996, Mar. 1   Perf. 13½
1309 A377 50f yel grn & multi   .75   .75
1310 A377 100f pink & multi   1.50   1.50
1311 A377 150f blue green &
    multi   2.25   2.00
  Nos. 1309-1311 (3)   4.50   4.25

A378

1996, Jan. 27   Perf. 14
1312 A378 50f blue & multi   .75   .75
1313 A378 100f gray & multi   1.25   1.25
1314 A378 150f rose lilac &
    multi   2.25   2.00
  Nos. 1312-1314 (3)   4.25   4.00

Scouting in
Kuwait, 60th
Anniv. — A379

50f, On top of watchtower. 100f, Drawing
water from well. 150f, Planting seedling.

1996, Jan. 14   Perf. 13½
1315 A379 50f yellow & multi   1.00   1.00
1316 A379 100f lilac & multi   2.25   2.25
1317 A379 150f blue green &
    multi   3.50   3.00
  Nos. 1315-1317 (3)   6.75   6.25

Kuwait Money
Show — A380

1996, Jan. 2   Perf. 14
1318 A380 25f gold & multi   .40   .40
1319 A380 100f blue & multi   1.50   1.25
1320 A380 150f dk gray & multi   2.25   2.00
  Nos. 1318-1320 (3)   4.15   3.65

7th Kuwait Dental
Assoc.
Conference — A381

1996, Mar. 27   Litho.   Perf. 14x13½
1321 A381 25f orange & multi   .40   .40
1322 A381 50f violet & multi   .75   .75
1323 A381 150f blue & multi   2.25   2.00
  Nos. 1321-1323 (3)   3.40   3.15

UNESCO, 50th
Anniv. — A382

1996, Apr. 10   Perf. 13½x14
1324 A382 25f violet & multi   .40   .40
1325 A382 100f green & multi   1.25   1.25
1326 A382 150f orange & multi   2.25   2.00
  Nos. 1324-1326 (3)   3.90   3.65

1st Oil Exports,
50th
Anniv. — A383

1996, June 30   Litho.   Perf. 13
1327 A383 25f multicolored   .40   .40
1328 A383 100f gray & multi   1.50   1.50
1329 A383 150f bister & multi   2.25   2.00
  Nos. 1327-1329 (3)   4.15   3.90

Rule of Al-Sabah
Family,
Cent. — A384

1996, Aug. 12
1330 A384 25f shown   .40   .40
1331 A384 50f Shiek, flags   .75   .75
1332 A384 150f like #1330   2.25   2.00
  Nos. 1330-1332 (3)   3.40   3.15

1996 Summer
Olympic Games,
Atlanta — A385

1996, Oct. 5   Perf. 13½
1333 A385 25f Shooting   .40   .40
1334 A385 50f Running   .75   .75
1335 A385 100f Weight lifting   1.50   1.50
1336 A385 150f Fencing   2.50   2.25
  Nos. 1333-1336 (4)   5.15   4.65

A 750f souvenir sheet exists. Value $100.

Kuwait University,
30th
Anniv. — A386

1006, Nov. 27   Litho.   Perf. 13½x14
1337 A386 25f green & multi   .40   .40
1338 A386 100f blue & multi   1.50   1.50
1339 A386 150f yellow & multi   2.25   2.00
  Nos. 1337-1339 (3)   4.15   3.90

1st Children's
Cultural
Festival — A387

1996, Nov. 20   Perf. 14x13½
1340 A387 25f brn gray & multi   .40   .40
1341 A387 100f multicolored   1.50   1.50
1342 A387 150f yel grn & multi   2.25   2.00
  Nos. 1340-1342 (3)   4.15   3.90

3rd Al-Qurain
Cultrual
Festival — A388

1996, Nov. 20   Perf. 14
1343 A388 50f orange & multi   .75   .75
1344 A388 100f blue & multi   1.50   1.50
1345 A388 150f green & multi   2.25   2.00
  Nos. 1343-1345 (3)   4.50   4.25

Liberation
Tower — A389

1996, Dec. 10   **Perf. 13x13½**

1346	A389	5f red & multi	.25	.25
1347	A389	10f yel bis & multi	.25	.25
1348	A389	15f brt rose & multi	.40	.30
1349	A389	25f pale pink & multi	.50	.45
a.	Booklet pane of 4		—	
	Complete booklet, #1349a		—	
1350	A389	50f violet & multi	1.10	.90
a.	Booklet pane of 4		—	
	Complete booklet, #1350a		—	
1351	A389	100f brt yel & multi	2.00	1.25
1352	A389	150f blue & multi	3.25	2.00
a.	Booklet pane of 4		—	
	Complete booklet, #1352a		—	
1353	A389	200f pink & multi	4.50	3.25
1354	A389	250f dp blue & multi	5.50	4.00
1355	A389	350f blue & multi	7.50	5.00
	Nos. 1346-1355 (10)		25.25	17.65
	Set of 3 booklets, #1349a-1350a, 1352a		31.00	

National Day, 36th Anniv. A390

1997, Feb. 25   **Litho.**   **Perf. 14½**

1356	A390	25f blue & multi	.40	.40
1357	A390	50f lilac & multi	.75	.75
1358	A390	150f orange & multi	2.25	2.00
	Nos. 1356-1358 (3)		3.40	3.15

Liberation Day, 6th Anniv. A391

1997, Feb. 26   **Perf. 13x13½**

1359	A391	25f tan & multi	.40	.40
1360	A391	50f lilac & multi	.75	.75
1361	A391	150f blue & multi	2.25	2.00
	Nos. 1359-1361 (3)		3.40	3.15

Marine Life — A392

No. 1368: Various views of a school of shrimp: a, b, c, d, 25f. e, f, g, h, 50f. i, j, k, l, 100f. m, n, o, p, 150f.

1997, Jan. 15   **Perf. 14½**

1362	A392	25f Maid	.40	.40
1363	A392	50f Sheim	.75	.75
1364	A392	100f Hamoor	1.50	1.50
1365	A392	150f Sobaity	2.25	2.25
1366	A392	200f Nagroor	3.25	3.25
1367	A392	350f Zobaidy	5.50	5.50
	Nos. 1362-1367 (6)		13.65	13.65

Sheet of 16

1368	A392	Sheet of 16, #a.-p.	19.00	19.00

Montreal Protocol on Substances that Deplete Ozone Layer, 10th Anniv. — A393

1997, Sept. 16   **Litho.**   **Perf. 13½x13**

1369	A393	25f blue & multi	.40	.40
1370	A393	50f violet & multi	.75	.75
1371	A393	150f bl grn & multi	2.25	2.00
	Nos. 1369-1371 (3)		3.40	3.15

Industries Exhibition A394

1997, Oct. 1

1372	A394	25f brt pink & multi	.40	.40
1373	A394	50f green & multi	.75	.75
1374	A394	150f blue & multi	2.25	2.00
	Nos. 1372-1374 (3)		3.40	3.15

22nd Kuwait Arabic Book Exhibition A395

1997, Nov. 19   **Litho.**   **Perf. 13½x13**
Border Color

1375	A395	25f pink	.40	.40
1376	A395	50f blue	.75	.75
1377	A395	150f blue green	2.25	2.00
	Nos. 1375-1377 (3)		3.40	3.15

Cultural History A396

a, 50f, Qibliya Girls School, 1937. b, 50f, Scissors cutting ribbon, Fine Arts Exhibition, 1959. c, 150f, Folk Theatre Group, 1956. d, 25f, 1st Book Fair, 1975. e, 25f, Kuwait Magazine, 1928. f, 50f, Mubarakiya School, 1912. g, 50f, Kuwait Natl. Museum, 1958. h, 150f, Academy of Music, 1972. i, 25f, A'lam Al-Fikr (periodical), 1970. j, 25f, Al'Bitha Magazine, 1946. k, 50f, Building complex, 1953 (Al-Arabi Magazine). l, 50f, Building, 1959. m, 150f, Al-Sharqiya Cinema, 1955. n, 25f, Al'Lam Al Ma'rifa (periodical), 1978. o, 25f, Dalil Almohtar Fi Alaam al-Bihar (boat), 1923. p, 50f, Alma'had Aldini (arabesques), 1947. q, 50f, Folklore Center, 1956. r, 150f, Theatrical Academy, 1967. s, 25f, Al-Arabi Magazine, 1958. t, 25f, Public Library (book), 1923. u, 50f, Al Ma'Arif Printing Press (Arabic writing), 1947. v, 50f, Literary Club, 1924. w, 150f, Bas Ya Bahar (1st Kuwaitii feature film), 1970. x, 25f, Al Thaqafa Al-Alamiya (periodical), 1981. y, 25f, The World Theatre (periodical), 1969.

1997, Nov. 30

1378	A396	Sheet of 25, #a.-y.	25.00 25.00

Nos. 1378a-1378y each contain year date of event depicted.

Educational Science Museum, 25th Anniv. A397

Designs: 25f, Whale, quadrant, vert. 50f, Space exploration, whale, dinosaur. No. 1381, Astronaut, dinosaur, satellite dish, airplane, globe, skeleton encircling whale, vert. No. 1382, Coelacanth.

Perf. 13½x13, 13x13½

1997, Nov. 1   **Litho.**

1379	A397	25f multicolored	.40	.40
1380	A397	50f multicolored	.75	.75
1381	A397	150f multicolored	2.75	2.25
	Nos. 1379-1381 (3)		3.90	3.40

Souvenir Sheet

1382	A397	150f multicolored	15.00 15.00

No. 1382 is a continuous design and sold for 1d.

18th Summit of Gulf Cooperation Countries — A398

Designs: 25f, Flags of member countries, doves, vert. 50f, Map, birds with flag colors. 150f, Doves perched atop flags, vert.

1997, Dec. 20   **Perf. 13½x14**

1383	A398	25f multicolored	.50	.50
1384	A398	50f multicolored	1.00	1.00
1385	A398	150f multicolored	3.25	2.75
a.	Bklt. pane of 3, #1383-1385		14.00	
	Complete booklet, #1385a		14.00	
	Nos. 1383-1385 (3)		4.75	4.25

National Day, 37th Anniv. A399

1998, Feb. 25   **Litho.**   **Perf. 13x13½**

1386	A399	25f yellow & multi	.50	.50
1387	A399	50f pink & multi	1.00	1.00
1388	A399	150f blue & multi	3.25	2.75
	Nos. 1386-1388 (3)		4.75	4.25

Liberation Day, 7th Anniv. A400

1998, Feb. 26

1389	A400	25f yellow & multi	.50	.50
1390	A400	50f orange & multi	1.00	1.00
1391	A400	150f green & multi	3.25	2.75
	Nos. 1389-1391 (3)		4.75	4.25

A401

1998, Mar. 16   **Litho.**   **Perf. 13½x13**

1392	A401	25f tan & multi	.50	.50
1393	A401	50f blue & multi	1.00	1.00
1394	A401	150f white & multi	3.25	2.75
	Nos. 1392-1394 (3)		4.75	4.25

Say No to Drugs.

A402

1997, May 2   **Litho.**   **Perf. 13½x14**

1395	A402	25f orange & multi	.50	.50
1396	A402	50f blue & multi	1.00	1.00
1397	A402	150f red & multi	3.25	2.75
	Nos. 1395-1397 (3)		4.75	4.25

Chernobyl disaster, 10th anniv.

Martyrs — A403

25f, Dates, 1/17, 2/25, 2/26, flowers. 50f, Stylized tree. 150f, Lines, inscriptions. No. 1401: a, Man with hands in dirt. b, Three boys emptying basket of dirt.

1998, Mar. 31   **Litho.**   **Perf. 14**

1398	A403	25f multicolored	.50	.50
1399	A403	50f multicolored	1.00	1.00
1400	A403	150f multicolored	3.50	3.00
a.	Bklt. pane, 2 ea #1398-1400		16.00	
	Complete booklet, #1400a		16.00	

Perf. 14½ Between
Size: 31x54mm

1401	A403	500f Pair, a.-b.	17.50	17.50
	Nos. 1398-1401 (4)		22.50	22.00

Ban Land Mines — A405

Stylized amputees using crutches for support: 25f, Two people. 50f, One person. 150f, Two people, nurse. 500f, Three people, nurse.

1998, Aug. 2   **Perf. 14½**

1402	A405	25f multicolored	.50	.50
1403	A405	50f multicolored	1.00	1.00
1404	A405	150f multicolored	2.50	2.50

Size: 89x82mm
Imperf

1405	A405	500f multicolored	11.00	11.00
	Nos. 1402-1405 (4)		15.00	15.00

Life in Pre-Oil Kuwait — A406

Designs: 25f, Seated at ceremonial meal. 50f, Building boat. 100f, Weaving. 150f, Loading boat. 250f, Pouring water from water skin into bowl. 350f, Man with pigeons.

1998, Apr. 14   **Litho.**   **Perf. 14**
Booklet Stamps

1406	A406	25f multicolored	.50	.50
1407	A406	50f multicolored	1.00	1.00
1408	A406	100f multicolored	2.00	2.00
1409	A406	150f multicolored	3.00	3.00
1410	A406	250f multicolored	5.00	5.00
1411	A406	350f multicolored	7.00	7.00
a.	Booklet pane, #1406-1411		27.50	
	Complete booklet, #1411a		27.50	

1998, Sept. 1   **Litho.**   **Perf. 14**

25f, Man shaving another man's head. 50f, Woman using grindstone. 100f, Man pulling thread through cloth. 150f, Man gluing artifacts together. 250f, Potter. 350f, Veiled woman holding rope.

Booklet Stamps

1412	A406	25f multicolored	.50	.50
1413	A406	50f multicolored	1.00	1.00
1414	A406	100f multicolored	2.00	2.00
1415	A406	150f multicolored	3.00	3.00
1416	A406	250f multicolored	5.00	5.00
1417	A406	350f multicolored	7.00	7.00
a.	Booklet pane, #1412-1417		27.50	
	Complete booklet, #1417a		27.50	

Emblem of
Kuwait Post
A407

1998, Oct. 3   Litho.   Perf. 13x13½
1418 A407 25f green & multi   .40   .40
1419 A407 50f blue & multi   .80   .80
1420 A407 100f brt pink &
                multi   1.25   1.25
1421 A407 150f orange & multi   2.25   2.25
1422 A407 250f brick red &
                multi   3.50   3.00
      Nos. 1418-1422 (5)   8.20   7.70

Intl. Year of the Ocean — A408

1998, June 1   Litho.   Perf. 13½
1423 A408 25f green & multi   .50   .50
1424 A408 50f blue & multi   1.00   1.00
1425 A408 150f lilac & multi   3.25   3.00
      Nos. 1423-1425 (3)   4.75   4.50

No. 1424 is 27x37mm.

Union of
Consumer Co-
operative
Societies, 25th
Anniv. — A409

1998, July 1   Litho.   Perf. 13½x13
1426 A409 25f buff & multi   .50   .50
1427 A409 50f blue & multi   1.00   1.00
1428 A409 150f multicolored   3.25   3.00
      Nos. 1426-1428 (3)   4.75   4.50

Children's Cultural House — A410

1998, Nov. 28   Litho.   Perf. 13½x13
1429 A410 25f yellow & multi   .50   .50
1430 A410 50f grn, yel & multi   1.00   1.00
1431 A410 150f green & multi   3.00   2.75
      Nos. 1429-1431 (3)   4.50   4.25

A411

1998, Dec. 10   Perf. 14x14½
1432 A411 25f multicolored   .50   .50
1433 A411 50f multicolored   1.00   1.00
1434 A411 150f multicolored   3.00   2.75
      Nos. 1432-1434 (3)   4.50   4.25

Universal Declaration of Human Rights,
50th anniv.

A412

1998   Litho.   Perf. 14x14½
1435 A412 25f orange & multi   .40   .40
1436 A412 50f violet & multi   .80   .80
1437 A412 150f green & multi   2.50   2.25
      Nos. 1435-1437 (3)   3.70   3.45

The Public Authority for Applied Education
and Training, 25th anniv.

Organ Transplantation in Kuwait, 20th
Anniv. — A413

1999   Litho.   Perf. 13x13½
1438 A413 50f Liver   .75   .75
1439 A413 150f Heart   2.25   2.00

Liberation
Day, 8th
Anniv.
A414

1999, Feb. 26
1440 A414 50f Building   .75   .75
1441 A414 150f Building, diff.   2.25   2.00

Sief Palace Complex — A415

Various buildings in complex.

1999   Perf. 15x14
1442 A415 25f multicolored   .30   .30
1443 A415 50f multicolored   .50   .50
1444 A415 100f multicolored   1.25   1.25
1445 A415 150f multicolored   2.00   2.00
1446 A415 250f multicolored   3.75   3.75
1447 A415 350f multicolored   5.00   5.00
  a.   Booklet pane, #1442-1447   16.00
       Complete booklet, #1447a   16.00
      Nos. 1442-1447 (6)   12.80 12.80

Al Arabi
Magazine
A416

1999   Perf. 13½x13
1448 A416 50f violet & multi   .75   .75
1449 A416 150f green & multi   2.25   2.00

Natl. Day,
38th Anniv.
A417

1999   Perf. 13x13½
1450 A417 50f brown & multi   .75   .75
1451 A417 150f blue & multi   2.25   2.00

Hawk   Sailing Ship
A418   A419

50f, Camel. 100f, Traditional Boat.

1999(?)-2003   Litho.   Perf. 14½x14
1452 A418 25f multicolored   .75   .75
1453 A418 50f multicolored   1.50   1.50
              Coil Stamp
1453A A419 100f multicolored   2.00   2.00
1454 A419 150f multicolored   4.50   4.50
      Nos. 1452-1454 (4)   8.75   8.75

Issued: 100f, Jan. 2003.

Science
Club, 25th
Anniv.
A420

Background color: 50f, Blue. 150f, Green.
350f, Red.

1999, Oct. 20   Litho.   Perf. 13x13¼
1455-1457 A420 Set of 3   8.50   8.50

Intl. Civil Aviation Day — A421

1999, Dec. 7   Litho.   Perf. 13x13¼
1458 A421 50f multi   1.00   1.00
1459 A421 150f multi   2.75   2.75
1460 A421 250f multi   4.50   4.00
      Nos. 1458-1460 (3)   8.25   7.75

UPU, 125th
Anniv. — A421a

Panel colors: 50f, Orange. 150f, Purple.
350f, Green.
1d, Two hemispheres.

1999   Litho.   Perf. 13¼x13
1460A-1460C A421a Set of 3   8.50   8.50
1460Ce   Booklet pane, #1460A-
            1460C + label   8.50
          Booklet, #1460Ce   8.50
            Size: 100x75mm
            Imperf
1460D A421a 1d multi   14.50 14.50

Kuwait Intl.
Airport — A422

2000, Jan. 2   Perf. 13¼x13
1461 A422 50f multi   .75   .75
1462 A422 150f multi   1.75   1.75
1463 A422 250f multi   4.00   3.75
      Nos. 1461-1463 (3)   6.50   6.25

National Day,
39th
Anniv. — A423

2000
1464 A423 25f multi   .50   .50
1465 A423 50f multi   1.00   1.00
1466 A423 150f multi   3.25   3.00
      Nos. 1464-1466 (3)   4.75   4.50

Liberation Day,
9th
Anniv. — A424

2000
1467 A424 25f multi   1.00   1.00
1468 A424 50f multi   2.75   2.75
1469 A424 150f multi   3.75   3.75
      Nos. 1467-1469 (3)   7.50   7.50

Kuwait Conference for Autism and
Communication Deficits — A425

Designs: 25f, Puzzle pieces, three children,
Kuwait Tower. 50f, Puzzle pieces, children.
150f, Children, Kuwait Tower, flowers.

2000   Perf. 13x13¼
1470 A425 25f multi   .50   .50
1471 A425 50f multi   1.00   1.00
1472 A425 150f multi   3.25   3.00
      Nos. 1470-1472 (3)   4.75   4.50

Kuwait
City — A425a

Background colors: 50f, Blue. 150f, Green.
350f, Red violet.

2000, Apr. 24   Litho.   Perf. 14x14½
1472A-1472C A425a Set of 3   6.50   6.50

Third Special
Education
Week — A425b

Background color: 50f, Yellow. 150f,
Salmon. 350f, Blue.

2000, May 10   Perf. 13¼x13
1472D-1472F A425b Set of 3   6.50   6.50

2000
Summer
Olympics,
Sydney
A425c

Emblems of 2002 Olympics, Kuwait Olympic Committee and: 25f, Judo. 50f, Shooting. 150f, Swimming. 200f, Weight lifting. 250f, Hurdles. 350f, Soccer.

No. 1472M, Emblems of 2002 Olympics, Kuwait Olympic Committee and judo, swimming, shooting, weight lifting, hurdles and soccer.

2000		Litho.		Perf. 13x13¼
1472G-1472L	A425c	Set of 6	15.00	15.00

Souvenir Sheet
Size: 98x69mm

1472M	A425c	1d multi	65.00	65.00

Sixth Gulf
Cooperation
Council
Countries Joint
Stamp
Exhibition,
Kuwait
A425d

Denomination color: 25f, Blue. 50f, Red. 150f, Green.
1d, Emblems of previous exhibitions.

2000		Litho.		Perf. 14¼
1472N-1472P	A425d	Set of 3	4.50	4.50

Size: 146x112mm
Imperf

1472Q	A425d	1d multi	17.00	17.00

Intl.
Investment
Forum
A426

Background colors: 25f, Gray. 50f, White. 150f, Black.

2000, Mar. 4		Litho.		Perf. 13x13¼
1473-1475	A426	Set of 3	4.50	4.50

National
Committee
for Missing
and
Prisoner of
War Affairs
A426a

Designs: 25f, Emblem. 50f, Emblem and chains. 150f, Emblem and years.

2000, Aug. 2		Litho.		Perf. 13x13¼
1475A-1475C	A426a	Set of 3	3.25	3.25

Kuwaiti Dental
Association, 25th
Anniv. — A426b

Frame color: 50f, Pink. 150f, Light blue. 350f, Lilac.

2000, Oct. 15			Perf. 13¼x13
1475D-1475F	A426b	Set of 3	6.50 6.50

World Environment Day — A427

Denominations, 50f, 150f, 350f.

2000		Litho.		Perf. 13x13¼
1476-1478	A427	Set of 3	7.00	7.00

Gulf Investment Corporation, 15th
Anniv. — A428

New Gulf Investment Corporation headquarters, emblem, "15" and frame color of: 25f, Green. 50f, Blue. 150f, Red.

2000, Oct. 31		Litho.		Perf. 13x13¼
1479-1481	A428	Set of 3	4.75	4.75

General Administration of Customs,
Cent. — A429

Denominations: 50f, 150f, 350f.

2000		Litho.		Perf. 13¼x14
1482-1484	A429	Set of 3	6.75	6.75
a.		Booklet pane, #1482-1484	15.00	
		Complete booklet, #1484a	15.00	

Imperf
Size: 100x75mm

1485	A429	1d multi	13.50	13.50

No. 1485 contains one 47x28mm perf. 13¼x14 non-denominated label.

Hala
Fibrayar — A430

Panel colors: 25f, Purple. 50f, Red violet. 150f, Blue.

2001		Litho.		Perf. 13¼x13
1486-1488	A430	Set of 3	4.75	4.75

Prisoners of
War — A431

Background colors: 25f, White. 50f, Blue & blue green. 150f, Multicolored.

2001			Perf. 13x13¼
1489-1491	A431	Set of 3	4.25 4.25

UN High Commissioner for Refugees,
50th Anniv. — A432

Various depictions of anniversary emblem: 25f, 50f, 150f.

2001			
1492-1494	A432	Set of 3	4.75 4.75

Kuwait,
2001 Arab
Cultural
Capital
A433

Background colors: 25f, Yellow. 50f, Green. 150f, Blue.

2001			
1495-1497	A433	Set of 3	4.75 4.75

Liberation Day,
10th
Anniv. — A434

Frame color: 25f, Lilac. 50f, Blue. 150f, Yellow.

2001			Perf. 13¼x13
1498-1500	A434	Set of 3	4.75 4.75

National Day, 40th
Anniv. — A435

Frame color: 25f, Orange. 50f, Yellow. 150f, Blue green.

2001			
1501-1503	A435	Set of 3	4.75 4.75

Kuwait
Diving
Team, 10th
Anniv.
A436

"10" and: 25f, Fish. 50f, Divers. 150f, Shark, turtle, vert.

2001			Perf. 13x13¼, 13¼x13
1504-1506	A436	Set of 3	4.75 4.75

Radio
Kuwait, 50th
Anniv.
A437

Frame color: 25f, Yellow brown. 50f, Blue, vert. 150f, Red, vert.

2001			Perf. 13x13¼, 13¼x13
1507-1509	A437	Set of 3	4.75 4.75

Intifada
A438

Dome of the Rock, Jerusalem: 25f, 50f, 150f.

2001			Perf. 13x13¼
1510-1512	A438	Set of 3	5.00 5.00

Year of Dialogue
Among
Civilizations
A439

Background colors: 25f, Orange & yellow. 50f, Dark & light green. 150f, Rose & pink.

2001			Perf. 13¼x13
1513-1515	A439	Set of 3	4.75 4.75

Human
Rights
A440

Designs: 25f, Hands covering man's face, vert. 50f, Barbed wire, clock, man's face. 150f, Chains, globe, child, woman.

2001			Perf. 13¼x13, 13x13¼
1516-1518	A440	Set of 3	4.75 4.75

A441

A442

AWQAF
Foundation
A443

2001			Perf. 14x13
1519	A441	25f multi	.50 .50
1520	A442	50f multi	1.00 1.00
1521	A443	150f multi	3.25 3.25
		Nos. 1519-1521 (3)	4.75 4.75

Kuwait Fund for
Arab Economic
Development, 40th
Anniv. — A444

Background colors: 25f, Yellow. 50f, Green & gray.

2001
1522-1523 A444 Set of 2 1.75 1.75

Touristic Enterprises Company, 25th Anniv. — A445

Stylistic flora: 25f, 50f, 100f, 150f. 250f, Combined designs of four stamps.

2001 *Perf. 13¼x13*
1524-1527 A445 Set of 4 7.50 7.50
Size: 60x80mm
Imperf
1528 A445 250f multi 6.00 6.00

National Bank of Kuwait, 50th Anniv. A447

Emblem and: 25f, Facade of old building. 50f, Modern building. 150f, Camels.

2002, Jan. 16 Litho. Perf. 13x13¼
1532-1534 A447 Set of 3 4.75 4.75

Liberation Day, 11th Anniv. — A448

Background color: 25f, Light blue. 50f, Light yellow. 150f, White.

2002, Feb. 26 *Perf. 13¼x13*
1535-1537 A448 Set of 3 4.75 4.75

Social Development Office, 10th Anniv. — A449

Background color: 25f, Light yellow. 50f, Light blue.

2002, Apr. 21
1538-1539 A449 Set of 2 1.75 1.75

41st National Day — A450

Frame color: 25f, Orange. 50f, Green. 150f, Purple.

2002, Feb. 25 Litho. Perf. 13¼x13
1540-1542 A450 Set of 3 4.50 4.50

Nomadism From the Hejaz to Africa — A451

Top panel color: 25f, Pale orange. 50f, Blue. 150f, Purple.

2002, Mar. 11
1543-1545 A451 Set of 3 5.00 5.00

Rehabilitation of Al-Qurain Landfill Site — A452

Panel color: 25f, Blue. 50f, Purple. 150f, Green.

2002, Apr. 1
1546-1548 A452 Set of 3 4.50 4.50

Kuwait Scientific Center — A453

Designs; Nos. 1549a, 1550e, Lapwing. Nos. 1549b, 1550d, Spur-winged plover. Nos. 1549c, 1550c, Eurasian river otter. Nos. 1549d, 1550b, Saltwater crocodile. Nos. 1549e, 1550i, Fennec fox. Nos. 1549f, 1550h, Caracal. Nos. 1549g, 1550g, Cushion sister starfish. Nos. 1549h, 1550f, Cuttlefish. Nos. 1549i, 1550m, Sand tiger shark. Nos. 1549j, 1550l, Lionfish. Nos. 1549k, 1550k, Kestrel. Nos. 1549l, 1550j, Egyptian fruit bat. Nos. 1549m, 1550a, Science center.

Perf. 13¼x13¾, 14x13¼ (#1550k)
2002, Apr. 17
1549 Sheet of 13 24.00 24.00
a.-l. A453 25f Any single .25 .25
m. A453 50f multi .30 .30
1550 Booklet of 13 panes 40.00
a.-m. A453 50f Any single pane .30 .30
Imperf
Size: 80x60mm
1551 A453 250f shown 12.00 12.00

Stamp sizes: Nos. 1549a-1549l, 30x25mm; No. 1549m, 45x27mm. Nos. 1550a-1550j, 1550l-1550m, 50x36mm; No. 1550k, 32x48mm.

Kuwait Foundation for the Advancement of Sciences, 25th Anniv. (in 2001) — A454

Foundation emblem and: 25f, 25th anniversary emblem. 50f, 25th anniversary emblem and building. 150f, Map of Kuwait, vert.

Perf. 13x13¼, 13¼x13
2002 ? Litho.
1552-1554 A454 Set of 3 4.75 4.75

Intl. Volunteers Year (in 2001) — A455

Background colors: 25f, White. 50f, Lilac. 150f, Yellow.

2002 ? *Perf. 13¼x13*
1555-1557 A455 Set of 3 4.50 4.50

National Council for Culture, Arts and Letters, 25th Anniv. — A456

Panel color: 25f, Lilac. 50f, Olive green. 150f, Bright blue. 500f, Lilac.

2002 ? *Perf. 13¼x13*
1558-1560 A456 Set of 3 4.50 4.50
Souvenir Sheet
Imperf
1561 A456 500f multi 10.00 10.00

No. 1561 contains one 42x58mm stamp.

Kuwait Society of Engineers, 40th Anniv. A457

Panel color at LR: 25f, Brown. 50f, Bright green. 150f, Yellow green.

2002 *Perf. 13x13¼*
1562-1564 A457 Set of 3 4.50 4.50

Public Authority for Applied Education and Training, 20th Anniv. — A458

"20," "1982-2002" and: 25f, Men at work. 50f, Surgeon. 100f, Man with machine. 150f, Building and Kuwait flag. 250f, Ironworkers.

2002 *Perf. 13¼x13*
1565-1569 A458 Set of 5 10.00 10.00

42nd National Day — A459

Frame color: 25f, Green. 50f, Red. 150f, Blue.

2003, Feb. 25 Litho. Perf. 13x13¼
1570-1572 A459 Set of 3 6.00 6.00

Martyr's Bureau A460

Emblem and: 25f, Ship. 50f, Flag on Qarow Island. 150f, Fingerprint. 350f, Map of Kuwait.

2003
1573-1576 A460 Set of 4 14.00 14.00
1576a Booklet pane, #1573-1576 14.00 —
Complete booklet, #1576a 14.00

Intl. Day Against Desertification A461

Designs: 25f, Dead tree. 50f, Log. 150f, Palm trees.

2003 Litho. Perf. 13¼x13
1577-1579 A461 Set of 3 4.75 4.75

Commercial Bank of Kuwait, 43rd Anniv. — A462

"43" and: 25f, Geometric design. 50f, Old bank building. 150f, New bank building.

2003 *Perf. 13*
1580-1582 A462 Set of 3 4.50 4.50

Kuwait Awqaf Public Foundation, 10th Anniv. A463

Emblem, "10," and: 50f, Building, family. 100f, Fingers. 150f, Man, minaret.

2004, Jan. 19
1583-1585 A463 Set of 3 5.50 5.50

A464

A465

Ministry of Information, 50th
Anniv. — A466

2003
1586	A464	25f multi	.60	.60
1587	A465	100f multi	2.00	2.00
1588	A466	150f multi	3.25	3.25
	Nos. 1586-1588 (3)		5.85	5.85

43rd National
Day — A467

Designs: 25f, Palm tree. 50f, Pearl in shell.
150f, Fortress, flags. 350f, Buildings, dhow.

2004, Feb. 25   *Perf. 13¼x13*
1589-1592	A467	Set of 4	10.00	10.00

Kuwait
Airways,
50th Anniv.
A468

Various airplanes: 25f, 50f, 75f, 100f, 125f,
150f.

2004, Dec. 18   *Litho.*   *Perf. 13x13¼*
1593-1598	A468	Set of 6	8.00	8.00

Kuwait Petroleum Corporation, 25th
Anniv. — A469

Headquarters: 50f, In daytime. 75f, With sun
on horizon. 125f, At night.

2005, Jan. 1   *Perf. 14½*
1599-1601	A469	Set of 3	5.00	5.00

44th National
Day — A470

Sheikhs, dhow, eagle and: 75f, Towers.
125f, Truck at port.

2005, Feb. 25   *Perf. 14*
1602-1603	A470	Set of 2	3.00	3.00

Liberation Day,
14th
Anniv. — A471

Sheikhs, flag and: 50f, Airplane, satellite
dish. 150f, Tower.

2005, Feb. 26
1604-1605	A471	Set of 2	4.00	4.00

Technical
Education, 50th
Anniv. — A472

Background color: 25f, Purple. 50f, Red.
75f, Orange. 125f, Green.

2005, Mar. 15
1606-1609	A472	Set of 4	4.25	4.25

Flags and
Emblems
A473

Designs: No. 1610, Triangular 1961 ship
and harbor flag. No. 1611, 1940 official flag.
No. 1612, 1903 special event flag. No. 1613,
1940-50 ruling family flag. No. 1614, Two 1914
right triangle flags. No. 1615, 1921-40, 1956-
62 and 1962 emblems.
No. 1616, 1962-56 emblem. No. 1617,
1921-40 emblem.
No. 1618, Right triangle flag of 1914 with
Arabic script and emblem in center and script
along short side like that on #1613. No. 1619,
Right triangle flag of 1914 with Arabic script in
center. No. 1620, Right triangle flag of 1914
with Arabic script in center and script along
short side.
No. 1621, Triangular 1921 ship and harbor
flag. No. 1622, Like #1610. No. 1623, Rectangular 1961 ship and harbor flag. No. 1624,
Rectangular 1921 ship and harbor flag.
No. 1625, 1914-61 official flag. No. 1626,
1871-1914 official flag. No. 1627, 1746-1871
official flag. No. 1628, Like #1611. No. 1629,
1921-61 official flag.
No. 1630, 1903 special event flag. No. 1631,
1866 special event flag. No. 1632, 1921 special event flag.
No. 1633, 1921-40 ruling family flag with two
white stripes. No. 1634, Like #1613, with
colored background. No. 1635, 1921-40 ruling
family flag with one white stripe.

2005, Oct. 15   *Litho.*   *Perf. 14x13¾*
1610	A473	200f multi	2.25	2.25
1611	A473	250f multi	3.25	3.25

Perf. 14
Size: 40x30mm
1612	A473	350f multi	4.00	4.00
1613	A473	500f multi	6.50	6.50

Perf. 14x13¾
Size: 60x30mm
1614	A473	1d multi	11.00	11.00
1615	A473	1d multi	11.00	11.00
	Nos. 1610-1615 (6)		38.00	38.00

Booklet Stamps
Self-Adhesive
Die Cut Perf. 13
Size:40x34mm
1616	A473	100f multi	2.00	2.00
1617	A473	100f multi	2.00	2.00
a.	Booklet pane, #1616-1617		4.00	

Die Cut Perf. 13x13¼
Size: 40x30mm
1618	A473	175f multi	3.75	3.75
1619	A473	175f multi	3.75	3.75
1620	A473	175f multi	3.75	3.75
a.	Booklet pane, #1618-1620		11.50	

Die Cut Perf. 10x10¾
Size: 30x20mm
1621	A473	200f multi	3.75	3.75
1622	A473	200f multi	3.75	3.75
1623	A473	200f multi	3.75	3.75
1624	A473	200f multi	3.75	3.75
a.	Booklet pane, #1621-1624		15.00	
1625	A473	250f multi	3.75	3.75
1626	A473	250f multi	3.75	3.75
1627	A473	250f multi	3.75	3.75
1628	A473	250f multi	3.75	3.75
1629	A473	250f multi	3.75	3.75
a.	Booklet pane, #1625-1629		19.00	

Die Cut Perf. 13x13¼
Size: 40x30mm
1630	A473	350f multi	5.75	5.75
1631	A473	350f multi	5.75	5.75
1632	A473	350f multi	5.75	5.75
a.	Booklet pane, #1630-1632		17.50	
1633	A473	500f multi	9.50	9.50
1634	A473	500f multi	9.50	9.50
1635	A473	500f multi	9.50	9.50
a.	Booklet pane, #1633-1635		28.50	
	Complete booklet, #1617a,			
	1620a, 1624a, 1629a,			
	1632a, 1635a		97.50	
	Nos. 1616-1635 (20)		94.75	94.75

Civil
Defense
A474

Designs: 50f, Civil defense workers and
emergency vehicles. 75f, Civil defense workers and children. 125f, Civil defene workers.

2005, Nov. 15   *Litho.*   *Perf. 14½*
1636-1638	A474	Set of 3	3.75	3.75

Al-Arabi Al-
Saghir
Children's
Magazine,
20th Anniv.
A475

Background colors: 100f, Blue. 200f, Yellow.
350f, Red.

2006, Feb. 1   *Litho.*   *Perf. 14¼x13¾*
1639-1641	A475	Set of 3	11.50	11.50

45th National
Day — A476

Frame color: 75f, Purple. 200f, Green. 250f,
Black. 350f, Red.

2006, Feb. 25   *Perf. 13¼*
1642-1645	A476	Set of 4	13.00	13.00

A477

Gulf Cooperation Council, 25th
Anniv. — A478

Litho. With Foil Application
2006, May 25   *Perf. 14*
1646	A477	50f multi	4.00	4.00

Imperf
Size: 165x105mm
1647	A478	500f multi	14.00	14.00

See Bahrain Nos. 628-629, Oman Nos. 477-
478, Qatar Nos. 1007-1008, Saudi Arabia No.
1378, and United Arab Emirates Nos. 831-
832.

Emblem
A479

A480

A481

A482

A483

A484

A485

A486

A487

A488

A489

A490

A491

A492

A493

A494

A495

A496

A497

A498

A499

A500

A501

A502

A503

A504

A505

A506

A507

A508

A509

A510

A511

A512

A513

A514

A515

A516

A517

A518

A519

A520

Coins — A521

2006, May 30   Litho.   Perf. 13¼

1648	Sheet of 28, #1648b- 1648v, 7#1648a	20.00	20.00
a.	A479 50f lt blue & multi	.60	.60
b.	A480 50f multi	.60	.60
c.	A481 50f multi	.60	.60
d.	A482 50f multi	.60	.60
e.	A483 50f multi	.60	.60
f.	A484 50f multi	.60	.60
g.	A485 50f multi	.60	.60
h.	A486 50f multi	.60	.60
i.	A487 50f multi	.60	.60
j.	A488 50f multi	.60	.60
k.	A489 50f multi	.60	.60
l.	A490 50f multi	.60	.60
m.	A491 50f multi	.60	.60
n.	A492 50f multi	.60	.60
o.	A493 50f multi	.60	.60
p.	A494 50f multi	.60	.60
q.	A495 50f multi	.60	.60
r.	A496 50f multi	.60	.60
s.	A497 50f multi	.60	.60
t.	A498 50f multi	.60	.60
u.	A499 50f multi	.60	.60
v.	A500 50f multi	.60	.60
1649	Sheet of 28, #1649b- 1649v, 7#1649a	55.00	55.00
a.	A479 150f pink & multi	1.75	1.75
b.	A501 150f multi	1.75	1.75
c.	A502 150f multi	1.75	1.75
d.	A503 150f multi	1.75	1.75
e.	A504 150f multi	1.75	1.75
f.	A505 150f multi	1.75	1.75
g.	A506 150f multi	1.75	1.75
h.	A507 150f multi	1.75	1.75
i.	A508 150f multi	1.75	1.75
j.	A509 150f multi	1.75	1.75
k.	A510 150f multi	1.75	1.75
l.	A511 150f multi	1.75	1.75
m.	A512 150f multi	1.75	1.75
n.	A513 150f multi	1.75	1.75
o.	A514 150f multi	1.75	1.75
p.	A515 150f multi	1.75	1.75
q.	A516 150f multi	1.75	1.75
r.	A517 150f multi	1.75	1.75
s.	A518 150f multi	1.75	1.75
t.	A519 160f multi	1.75	1.75
u.	A520 150f multi	1.75	1.75
v.	A521 150f multi	1.75	1.75

Islamic Development Bank Group annual meeting.

15th Asian Games, Doha, Qatar
A522

Designs: 25f, Tennis. 50f, Bowling. 150f, Shooting. 250f, Equestrian. 350f, Fencing.

2006   Litho.   Perf. 14½
1650-1654 A522 Set of 5   13.00 13.00

Campaign Against Hypertension
A523

Frame colors: 50f, Green. 150f, Red. 350f, Brown.

2007, Jan. 15   Perf. 13¼x13
1655-1657 A523 Set of 3   9.25 9.25

46th National Day — A524

Sky color: 25f, Dark blue. 50f, Blue. 150f, Orange brown.

2007, Feb. 25
1658-1660 A524 Set of 3 4.00 4.00

Liberation Day, 16th Anniv. A525

Frame color: 25f, Red. 50f, Dark blue. 150f, Purple.

2007, Feb. 26 Litho. Perf. 13x13¼
1661-1663 A525 Set of 3 4.00 4.00

Kuwait University, 40th Anniv. (in 2006) A526

Color behind emblem: 25f, Blue. 50f, Yellow. 150f, Green. 350f, Red.

2007, Mar. 20
1664-1667 A526 Set of 4 10.00 10.00

Kuwait Oil Tanker Company, 50th Anniv. A527

Background colors: 25f, Pale blue. 50f, Pale green. 150f, Gray.

Litho. & Embossed With Foil Application
2007, Nov. 25 Perf. 13
1668-1670 A527 Set of 3 5.25 5.25

Kuwait Philatelic & Numismatic Society, 1st Anniv. — A528

2007, Dec. 5 Litho. Perf. 13¼
1671 A528 Horiz. strip of 3 5.25 5.25
  a.   25f Coin .70 .70
  b.   50f Kuwait #146 1.10 1.10
  c.   150f Society emblem 3.00 3.00
  No. 1671c is 60x35mm.

47th National Day — A529

Designs: 25f, Women voting. 150f, Stylized people, dhows, fish, towers, horiz.

Perf. 13¼x13, 13x13¼
2008, Feb. 25 Litho.
1672-1673 A529 Set of 2 3.75 3.75

Liberation Day, 17th Anniv. A530

Hand holding map of Kuwait with background color of: 25f, Dull rose. 50f, Purple.

2008, Feb. 26 Litho. Perf. 13x13¼
1674-1675 A530 Set of 2 2.00 2.00

First Gulf Cooperation Council Women's Sports Tournament A531

No. 1676 — Emblem and: a, Gymnastics. b, Running. c, Shooting. d, Basketball. e, Tennis. No. 1677, horiz. — Emblem, five sports with background color of: a, Orange. b, Red. c, Purple. d, Olive green. e, Red violet.

2008, Mar. 5 Litho. Perf. 13¼x13
1676 Vert. strip of 5 2.50 2.50
  a.-e. A531 25f Any single .40 .40
Perf. 13x13¼
1677 Horiz strip of 5 8.00 8.00
  a.-e. A531 150f Any single 1.25 1.25

Diplomatic Relations Between Kuwait and Romania, 45th Anniv. — A532

No. 1678: a, Kuwaiti man building ship model. b, Romanian woman weaving. 500f, Flags of Romania and Kuwait, handshake, vert.

2008, June 21 Perf. 13¼x13
1678 Horiz. pair + 2 labels 10.00 10.00
  a.-b. A532 150f Either single + label 4.75 4.75
  c. Miniature sheet, 4 #1678 40.00 —

Souvenir Sheet
Perf. 13x13¼
1679 A532 500f multi 20.00 20.00

Labels of Nos. 1678a and 1678b are separated from stamps by a partial row of perforations. The labels, which have different designs, are to the left of No. 1678a and to the right of No. 1678b. The labels are adjacent to each other on half of the pairs on No. 1678c. No. 1678 was also printed in sheets containing 6 pairs, two of which have the labels adjacent. Value, $60.
  See Romania Nos. 5053-5054.

Old Kuwait A533

Designs: 25f, Drummer and swordsmen. 50f, Drummers and boat painter. 100f, Street with thatched roof. 150f, Fair. 200f, Man and minarets. 250f, Donkey riders at town gate. 350f, Boats in harbor. 500f, People at town gate.

2008, Aug. 1 Perf. 13
1680 A533 25f multi .25 .25
1681 A533 50f multi .40 .40
1682 A533 100f multi .75 .75
1683 A533 150f multi 1.10 1.10
1684 A533 200f multi 1.50 1.50
1685 A533 250f multi 1.90 1.90
1686 A533 350f multi 2.75 2.75
1687 A533 500f multi 3.75 3.75
  Nos. 1680-1687 (8) 12.40 12.40

48th National Day — A534

Frame color: 25f, Black. 50f, Green. 150f, Red. 250f, No frame.

2009, Feb. 25 Litho. Perf. 13¼
1688-1690 A534 Set of 3 3.00 3.00
  Size: 100x66mm
  Imperf
1691 A534 250f multi 3.00 3.00

Liberation Day, 18th Anniv. — A535

Denomination color: 25f, Green. 50f, Red. 150f, Black.

2009, Feb. 26 Perf. 13¾
1692-1694 A535 Set of 3 3.00 3.00

Kuwait Finance House A536

Denomination color: 25f, White. 50f, Silver. 150f, Gold.

Litho. & Embossed
2009, June 21 Perf. 13¾
1695-1697 A536 Set of 3 2.75 2.75

Kuwait Chamber of Commerce and Industry, 50th Anniv. — A537

Designs: 25f, Building. 50f, Dhow. 150f, Cogwheels.

2009 Granite Paper Litho.
1698-1700 A537 Set of 3 2.75 2.75

49th National Day — A538

Designs: 25f, Buildings and falcon. 50f, Sheikhs and falcon. 150f, Sheikhs and buildings.

2010, Feb. 25 Litho. Perf. 13¼x13
1701-1703 A538 Set of 3 4.25 4.25

Liberation Day, 19th Anniv. A539

Designs: 25f, Children's drawing of people waving flags in car and on side of road. 50f, Child waving flags. 150f, Fabric art of girls wearing dresses in colors of Kuwait flag.

2010, Feb. 26 Perf. 13x13¼
1704-1706 A539 Set of 3 4.25 4.25

Jerusalem, Capital of Arab Culture — A540

Denomination color: 25f, Green. 50f, Red.

2010, Mar. 26 Perf. 13¼x13
1707-1708 A540 Set of 2 2.00 2.00

Kuwait E-Gate A541

Frame color: 25f, Pink. 50f, Yellow. 150f, Light green.

2010, Apr. 20 Perf. 14x13¼
1709-1711 A541 Set of 3 4.00 4.00

Organization of the Petroleum Exporting Countries, 50th Anniv. A542

Background color: 25f, Gray. 50f, Light blue. 150f, White.

Litho. & Embossed With Foil Application
2010, May 23 Perf. 13¾
1712-1714 A542 Set of 3 3.75 3.75

A543

Liberation Day, 20th Anniv. and
National Day, 50th Anniv. — A544

No. 1715: a, Flag, shiekh, "20." b, Dove,
sheikhs, flag, "20." c, Flag, sheikh, "50." d,
Flag, sheikh, "50," diff.

**Litho. & Embossed With Foil
Application**

2011, Feb. 25		Perf. 13¼	
1715	Horiz. strip of 4	1.00	1.00
a.	A543 25f silver & multi	.25	.25
b.	A544 25f silver & multi	.25	.25
c.	A543 25f gold & multi	.25	.25
d.	A544 25f gold & multi	.25	.25

A souvenir sheet with a lithographed 250f
stamp was produced in limited quantities.

A545

A546

A547

A548

Commercial
Bank of Kuwait,
50th Anniv. (in
2010) — A549

2011, Sept.	Litho.	Perf. 13¼	
1716	Horiz. strip of 5	2.50	2.50
a.	A545 50f multi	.50	.50
b.	A546 50f multi	.50	.50
c.	A547 50f multi	.50	.50
d.	A548 50f multi	.50	.50
e.	A549 50f multi	.50	.50

15th General Assembly of Arab Towns
Organization, Kuwait (in 2010) — A550

No. 1717 — Stylized tree and man emblem,
Arab Towns Organization emblem, and back-
ground color of: a, Rose brown. b, Yellow. c,
Chocolate. d, Yellow green. e, Blue. f, Gray
green. g, Gray. h, Tan. i, Orange brown. j,
Brown.

2011, Nov. 5		Perf. 13½	
1717	Block of 10	5.00	5.00
a.-j.	A550 50f Any single	.50	.50

Miniature Sheet

Kuwait Fund for Arab Economic
Development, 50th Anniv. — A551

No. 1718: a, 50th anniversary emblem, red
background. b, Airport terminal with overhanging roof. c, Airport runway. d, Airplane at
Banjul Intl. Airport, Gambia. e, Pipeline. f, Offshore oil rig. g, Workers examining produce. h,
Farm. i, Well. j, Water works. k, Dump truck on
hill. l, Culvert, hill in background. m, Electrical
station. n, Ships in harbor. o, Highway bridge
in populated area. p, Highway interchange. q,
Elevated highway near hill. r, Culvert with
three round holes. s, Elevated highway, diff.

2011, Dec.		Perf. 14¼	
1718	A551 150f Sheet of 20, 2 #1718a, 1 each #1718b-1/18s	22.00	22.00

Emir Abdullah III
(1895-1965)
A552

Emir Sabah III
(1913-77)
A553

Emir Jaber III
(1926-2006)
A554

Emir Saad
(1930-2008)
A555

Crown Prince
Nawaf — A556

Emir Sabah
IV — A557

Sheikh Ahmad
(1885-1950)
A558

Sheikh Salim
(1864-1921)
A559

Sheikh Jaber II
(1860-1917)
A560

Sheikh Mubarak
(1840-1915)
A561

Independence, 51st Anniv. — A562

No. 1720 — Flags and scenes of of Kuwait
and: a, Sheikh Mubarak (40x30mm). b, Sheikh
Jaber II (40x30mm). c, Emir Abdullah III
(80x30mm). d, Emir Sabah III (40x30mm). e,
Emir Jaber III (40x30mm). f, Sheikh Salim
(40x30mm). g, Sheikh Ahmad (40x30mm). h,
Nine ruling sheikhs and emirs (80x30mm). i,
Emir Saad (40x30mm). j, Emir Sabah IV
(40x30mm).

2012, Feb. 25		Perf. 13	
1719	Sheet of 10	25.00	25.00
a.	A552 100f multi	2.50	2.50
b.	A553 100f multi	2.50	2.50
c.	A554 100f multi	2.50	2.50
d.	A555 100f multi	2.50	2.50
e.	A556 100f multi	2.50	2.50
f.	A557 100f multi	2.50	2.50
g.	A558 100f multi	2.50	2.50
h.	A559 100f multi	2.50	2.50
i.	A560 100f multi	2.50	2.50
j.	A561 100f multi	2.50	2.50

Perf. 13x13¼

1720	A562	Sheet of 10	25.00	25.00
a.-j.		150f Any single	2.50	2.50

A563

A564

A565

A566

A567

A568

A569

A570

A571

Liberation Day,
21st
Anniv. — A572

2012, Feb. 26		Perf. 13¼x13	
1721	Sheet of 10	12.50	12.50
a.	A563 50f multi	1.25	1.25
b.	A564 50f multi	1.25	1.25

484

KUWAIT

c.	A565 50f multi		1.25	1.25
d.	A566 50f multi		1.25	1.25
e.	A567 50f multi		1.25	1.25
f.	A568 50f multi		1.25	1.25
g.	A569 50f multi		1.25	1.25
h.	A570 50f multi		1.25	1.25
i.	A571 50f multi		1.25	1.25
j.	A572 50f multi		1.25	1.25

Miniature Sheet

Membership in UNESCO, 50th Anniv.
(in 2010) — A573

No. 1722 — UNESCO membership 50th anniv. emblem and: a, Kuwaiti flag, emblems of Intangible Cultural Heritage, Intl. Festival of Cultural Diversity, Italian National UNESCO Commission, and UNESCO Associated Schools, white background. b, Emblem of Italian National UNESCO Commission, bister and olive background, denomination 3mm tall at UR. c, Intl. Festival of Cultural Diversity emblem, lilac background. d, Stylized "U" and "O", green and red stripes at bottom. e, Stylized figure of man with arms raised, dull orange background. f, Intl. Astronomical Union emblem, orange and green background. g, Man and Biosphere (MaB) emblem, blue and white background. h, Intangible Cultural Heritage emblem, gray and white background. i, Global Geoparks Network emblem, orange background with blue and white concentric circles. j, Multicolored squares below UNESCO emblem, blue and lilac background. k, UNESCO Associated Schools emblem, blue background with brown stripe at bottom. l, Kuwaiti flag, emblems of Global Geoparks Network, Intl. Festival of Cultural Diversity (with French inscription) and Intl. Bureau of Education, white background. m, UNESCO Institute for Lifelong Learning emblem, red, white and blue background. n, Intl. Bureau of Education (IBE) emblem, white background in blue frame. o, World Heritage emblem, orange background with yellow circle. p, Stylized dove, olive and bister background, denomination 2½mm tall at UR. q, Circle and blue stripes, light blue background. r, UNESCO Chair in Sustainable Mountain Development emblem, UHI Millennium Institute emblem, pink and white background with brown stripes at top and bottom. s, Intl. Festival of Cultural Diversity emblem with French inscription, gray background. t, UNESCO spiral emblem, blue and dull orange background.

2012, June 6   **Perf. 14**
1722 A573 150f Sheet of 20,
     #a-t   38.00 38.00

A574

A575

A576

A577

A578

A579

A580

A581

A582

A583

A584

A585

A586

A587

A588

A589

A590

A591

A592

Children's Art — A593

2012, Nov.
1723   Sheet of 20   16.00 16.00
a.	A574 50f multi	.80	.80
b.	A575 50f multi	.80	.80
c.	A576 50f multi	.80	.80
d.	A577 50f multi	.80	.80
e.	A578 50f multi	.80	.80
f.	A579 50f multi	.80	.80
g.	A580 50f multi	.80	.80
h.	A581 50f multi	.80	.80
i.	A582 50f multi	.80	.80
j.	A583 50f multi	.80	.80
k.	A584 50f multi	.80	.80
l.	A585 50f multi	.80	.80
m.	A586 50f multi	.80	.80
n.	A587 50f multi	.80	.80
o.	A588 50f multi	.80	.80
p.	A589 50f multi	.80	.80
q.	A590 50f multi	.80	.80
r.	A591 50f multi	.80	.80
s.	A592 50f multi	.80	.80
t.	A593 50f multi	.80	.80

Kuwait Society for the Handicapped.

Miniature Sheet

Partnership Between Kuwait and
United Nations, 50th Anniv. — A594

No. 1724 — 50th anniversary emblem and: a, United Nations Headquarters, flags of United Nations and member nations, emblem of Kuwait (60x30mm). b, United Nations House, Kuwait, emblems of various United Nations ororganizations (60x30mm). c, United Nations Secretary General Ban Ki-moon and Sheikh Sabah (30x40mm). d, Emblems of Kuwait and United Nations, national flags (30x40mm). e, Hoisting of Kuwaiti flag at United Nations Headquarters (30x40mm). f, Sheikh Sabah at podium at United Nations (30x40mm). g, United Nations House, and United Nations flag (30x40mm). h, Dhow (30x40mm). i, Kuwait Towers (30x40mm). j, Emblem at United Nations House (30x40mm).

Perf. 13¼x13¼x14x13¼ (#1724a-1724b), 14

2013, Dec. 1   **Litho.**
1724 A594 50f Sheet of 10, #a-j   7.50 7.50

AIR POST STAMPS

Air Post Stamps of India, 1929-30, Overprinted type "c"
1933-34	**Wmk. 196**	*Perf. 14*	
C1	AP1 2a dull green	24.00	27.50
C2	AP1 3a deep blue	5.00	3.50
C3	AP1 4a gray olive	160.00	225.00
C4	AP1 6a bister ('34)	8.00	4.50
	Nos. C1-C4 (4)	197.00	260.50

Counterfeits of Nos. C1-C4 exist.

> Catalogue values for unused stamps in this section, from this point to the end of the section, are for Never Hinged items.

Dakota and Comet Planes AP1

Perf. 11x11½
1964, Nov. 29	**Litho.**	**Unwmk.**	
C5	AP1 20f multicolored	1.00	.30
C6	AP1 25f multicolored	1.10	.40
C7	AP1 30f multicolored	1.25	.60
C8	AP1 45f multicolored	2.00	.80
	Nos. C5-C8 (4)	5.35	2.10

10th anniversary of Kuwait Airways.

POSTAGE DUE STAMPS

> Catalogue values for unused stamps in this section are for Never Hinged items.

D1

KUWAIT

Perf. 14x15

1963, Oct. 19   Unwmk.   Litho.
Inscriptions in Black

J1	D1	1f ocher	.60	.30
J2	D1	2f lilac	.70	.45
J3	D1	5f blue	1.00	.30
J4	D1	8f pale green	1.60	.55
J5	D1	10f yellow	2.00	1.00
J6	D1	25f brick red	3.25	3.25
		Nos. J1-J6 (6)	9.15	5.85

D2

1965, Apr. 1   Perf. 13

J7	D2	4f rose & yellow	.50	.30
J8	D2	15f dp rose & blue	1.75	.55
J9	D2	40f blue & brt yel grn	3.00	1.25
J10	D2	50f green & pink	3.75	1.75
J11	D2	100f dk blue & yel	5.50	3.25
		Nos. J7-J11 (5)	14.50	7.10

OFFICIAL STAMPS

Stamps of India, 1911-23, Overprinted

Nos. O1-O9

Nos. O10-O14

1923-24   Wmk. 39   Perf. 14

O1	A47	½a green	6.50	50.00
O2	A48	1a brown	5.50	27.50
O3	A58	1½a chocolate	5.00	65.00
O4	A49	2a violet	11.00	50.00
O5	A57	2a6p ultra	7.00	80.00
O6	A51	3a brown org	7.50	75.00
O7	A61	3a ultra ('24)	7.75	75.00
O8	A52	4a olive grn	6.25	75.00
O9	A54	8a red violet	9.50	110.00
O10	A56	1r grn & brn	35.00	190.00
O11	A50	2r brn & car rose	37.50	275.00
O12	A56	5r vio & ultra	125.00	475.00
O13	A56	10r car & grn	250.00	440.00
O14	A56	15r ol grn & ultra	400.00	675.00
		Nos. O1-O14 (14)	913.50	2,662.

Stamps of India, 1926-30, Overprinted

Nos. O15-O20

Nos. O21-O25

1929-33   Wmk. 196

O15	A48	1a dk brown	6.50	42.50
O16	A60	2a violet	70.00	250.00
O17	A51	3a blue	6.00	55.00
O18	A61	4a ol green	6.75	90.00
O19	A54	8a red violet	9.00	130.00
O20	A55	12a claret	45.00	225.00
O21	A56	1r green & brn	14.00	275.00
O22	A56	2r buff & car rose	18.00	400.00
O23	A56	5r dk vio & ultra	50.00	500.00
O24	A56	10r car & green	85.00	850.00
O25	A56	15r olive grn & ultra	300.00	1,450.
		Nos. O15-O25 (11)	610.25	4,267.

KYRGYZSTAN

ˌkir-gi-ˈstan

(Kirghizia)

LOCATION — Bounded by Kazakhstan, Uzbekistan, Tadjikistan and China.
GOVT. — Independent republic, member of the Commonwealth of Independent States.
AREA — 77,180 sq. mi.
POP. — 4,546,055 (1999 est.)
CAPITAL — Bishkek

With the breakup of the Soviet Union on Dec. 26, 1991, Kyrgyzstan and ten former Soviet republics established the Commonwealth of Independent States.
In 2013, the Universal Postal Union announced that a second postal organization, Kyrgyz Express Post, was granted permission to provide unrestricted postal services throughout the country. This allowed for competition between the state corporation, Kyrgyz Pochtasy, the original UPU-designated postal operator in Kyrgyzstan having post offices nationwide, and Kyrgyz Express Post for postal business. Listings for stamps issued by Kyrgyz Express Post follow those of the listings for stamps from Kyrgyz Pochtasy.

100 Kopecks = 1 Ruble
100 Tyiyn = 1 Som

Catalogue values for all unused stamps in this country are for Never Hinged items.

ISSUES OF KYRGYZ POCHTASY

Sary-Chelek Nature Preserve — A1

Unwmk.
1992, Feb. 4   Litho.   Perf. 12

1	A1	15k multicolored	.55	.55

Hawk — A2

1992, Aug. 31   Litho.   Perf. 12½x12

2	A2	50k multicolored	.55	.55

Man with Cattle, by G.A. Aytiev — A3

1992, Aug. 31

3	A3	1r multicolored	.35	.35

Handicrafts A4

1992, Dec. 1   Litho.   Perf. 12x11½

4	A4	1.50r multicolored	.55	.55

Sites and Landmarks A5

Designs: 10k, Petroglyphs. 50k, 11th Cent. tower, vert. 1r + 25k, Mausoleum, vert. 2r + 50k, 12th Cent. mausoleum. 3r, Yurt. 5r + 50k, Statue of epic hero Manas, Pishpek. 9r, Commercial complex, Pishpek. 10r, Native jewelry.

1993, Mar. 21   Litho.   Perf. 12

5	A5	10k multicolored	.25	.25
6	A5	50k multicolored	.25	.25
7	A5	1r +25k multi	.25	.25
8	A5	2r +50k multi	.25	.25
9	A5	3r multicolored	.25	.25
10	A5	5r +50k multi	.30	.30
11	A5	9r multi	.50	.50
		Nos. 5-11 (7)	2.05	2.05

Souvenir Sheet

12	A5	10r multicolored	1.00	1.00

Independence and Admission to UN, 2nd Anniv. — A6

No. 15a, 120t, like #13. No. 15b, 130t, like #14.

Perf. 13x12½, 12½x13
1993, Aug. 31   Litho.

13	A6	50t Map	.80	.80
14	A6	60t UN emblem, flag, building, vert.	.95	.95

Souvenir Sheet
Imperf

15	A6	Sheet of 2, #a.-b.	6.00	6.00

Nos. 15a-15b have simulated perforations.

Russia Nos. 4598, 5838, 5984 Surcharged in Violet Blue, Prussian Blue or Black

Methods and Perfs as Before
1993, Apr. 6

16	A2765	10r on 1k #5838 (VB)	.25	.25
17	A2765	20r on 2k #5984 (PB)	.30	.30
18	A2139	30r on 3k #4598 (Blk)	.35	.30
		Nos. 16-18 (3)	.90	.80

Russia Nos. 4599-4600 Surcharged in Blue or Red

Methods and Perfs as Before
1993, June 29

19	A2138	20t on 4k #4599 (Bl)	.70	.70
20	A2139	30t on 6k #4600 (R)	1.00	1.00

New Year 1994 (Year of the Dog) — A7

1994, Feb. 10   Litho.   Perf. 12x12½

26	A7	60t multicolored	.80	.80

Musical Instrument — A8

1993, Dec. 30   Litho.   Perf. 13x12½

27	A8	30t Komuz	.35	.35

Souvenir Sheet
Perf. 13

28	A8	140t multi	16.00	16.00

No. 28 exists imperf. Value $45.
Issued: No. 27, 12/30; No. 28, 4/4/94.

Panthera Uncia A9

1994, Mar. 21   Litho.   Perf. 12½x12

29	A9	10t shown	.40	.40
30	A9	20t Lying down	.50	.50
31	A9	30t Seated	.75	.75
32	A9	40t Up close	.95	.95
		Nos. 29-32 (4)	2.60	2.60

World Wildlife Fund.

Flowers — A10

Perf. 12x12½, 12½x12
1994, Aug. 31   Litho.
Color of Flower

33	A10	1t violet & white	.25	.25
34	A10	3t white & yellow, horiz.	.25	.25
a.		Miniature sheet of 6	1.40	1.40
35	A10	10t red & yellow	.30	.30
36	A10	16t white & yellow	.30	.30
37	A10	20t pink & yellow	.40	.40
38	A10	30t white & yellow	.45	.45
39	A10	40t yellow & brown	.55	.55
a.		Miniature sheet of 6, #33, #35-39	5.75	5.75
b.		Strip of 7, #33-39	4.00	4.00

Souvenir Sheet

40	A10	50t yellow & orange	1.40	1.40

For surcharge see No. 141.

Minerals — A11

1994, Dec. 1   Litho.   Perf. 13½x13
41	A11	80t Fluorite-Cinnabar	.50	.50
42	A11	90t Calcite	.55	.55
43	A11	100t Getchellite	.60	.60
45	A11	110t Barite	.65	.65
45	A11	120t Orpiment	.70	.70
46	A11	140t Stibnite	1.00	1.00
		Nos. 41-46 (6)	4.00	4.00

Souvenir Sheet
47	A11	200t Cinnabar	3.50	3.50
a.		Miniature sheet of 6	9.00	9.00

No. 47a contains Nos. 42-46 and single from No. 47.

Fish — A12

Designs: 110t, Glyptosternum reticulatum. 120t, Leuciscus schmidti. 130t, Piptychus dybowskii. 140t, Nemachilus strauchi. 200t, Cyprinus carpio.

1994, Dec. 1   Perf. 13x13½
48	A12	110t multicolored	.40	.40
49	A12	120t multicolored	.45	.45
50	A12	130t multicolored	.50	.50
51	A12	140t multicolored	.60	.60
a.		Miniature sheet, #48-51	2.50	2.50
		Nos. 48-51 (4)	1.95	1.95

Souvenir Sheet
52	A12	200t multicolored	1.75	1.75

Wild Animals — A13

No. 60: a, 130t, Raptor, diff. b, 170t, Bighorn sheep.

Perf. 12x12½, 12½x12

1995, Apr. 21   Litho.
53	A13	110t Bear	.30	.30
54	A13	120t Snow leopard, horiz.	.30	.30
55	A13	130t Raptor	.35	.35
56	A13	140t Woodchuck, horiz.	.40	.40
57	A13	150t Raptor, horiz.	.45	.45
58	A13	160t Vulture	.50	.50
59	A13	190t Fox, horiz.	.65	.65
		Nos. 53-59 (7)	2.95	2.95

Souvenir Sheet
60	A13	Sheet of 2, #a.-b.	1.50	1.50

Nos. 53-60 exist imperf. Value $7.

Natl. Costumes — A14

1995, Mar. 24   Perf. 12x12½
61	A14	50t shown	.30	.30
62	A14	50t Man with mandolin	.30	.30
63	A14	100t Man with falcon	.45	.45
64	A14	100t Woman seated	.45	.45
		Nos. 61-64 (4)	1.50	1.50

Nos. 61-64 exist imperf. Value, set $2.50.

Traffic Safety — A15

1995, Mar. 24   Perf. 12
65	A15	200t multicolored	.75	.75

Souvenir Sheet

End of World War II, 50th Anniv. — A16

1995, May 4   Litho.   Perf. 12x12½
66	A16	150t multicolored	1.40	1.40

UPU Intl. Letter Week A17

1995, Oct. 3   Litho.   Perf. 12x12½
67	A17	200t multicolored	1.10	1.10

Natl. Arms — A18

1995, Oct. 13   Perf. 12
68	A18	20t purple	.35	.35
69	A18	50t blue	.35	.35
70	A18	100t brown	.45	.45
71	A18	500t green	1.50	1.50
		Nos. 68-71 (4)	2.65	2.65

Compare with design A37.

Horses A19

Various adult, juvenile horses.

1995, Oct. 16   Perf. 12½x12, 12x12½
Background Color
72	A19	10t olive brown	.25	.25
73	A19	50t light brown, vert.	.25	.25
74	A19	100t tan, vert.	.25	.25
75	A19	140t yellow brown, vert.	.30	.30
76	A19	150t lilac	.40	.40
77	A19	200t gray	.45	.45
78	A19	300t yellow green	.65	.65
		Nos. 72-78 (7)	2.55	2.55

Souvenir Sheet
79	A19	600t Herd of horses, vert.	2.50	2.50

Raptors — A20

1995, Sept. 12   Perf. 12x12½
80	A20	10t Pandion haliaetus	.25	.25
81	A20	50t Aquila rapax	.25	.25
82	A20	100t Gyps himalayensis	.30	.30
83	A20	140t Falco cherrug	.35	.35
84	A20	150t Circaetus gallicus	.40	.40
85	A20	200t Gypaetus barbatus	.45	.45
86	A20	300t Aquila chrysaetos	.65	.65
		Nos. 80-86 (7)	2.65	2.65

Souvenir Sheet
87	A20	600t Halliaeetus albicilla	2.50	2.50

"Aquila" spelled wrong on No. 86.
Nos. 80-87 exist imperf. Value: Nos. 80-86, $4.25; No. 87, $2.75.

Souvenir Sheet

UN, 50th Anniv. — A21

Designs: a, UN headquarters, NYC. b, Mountains, rainbow.

1995, Oct. 24   Litho.   Perf. 12½x12
88	A21	100t Sheet of 2, #a.-b.	1.60	1.60

Natural Wonders of the World — A22

10t, Nile River. 50t, Kilimanjaro. 100t, Sahara Desert. 140t, Amazon River, vert. 150t, Grand Canyon, vert. 200t, Victoria Falls, vert. 350t, Mount Everest. 400t, Niagara Falls. Issyk-Kul Lake, Kyrgyzstan: No. 97, Raptor, row boat, sail boats. No. 98, Water bird, motor boat, row boat.

1995, Dec. 29   Perf. 11½
89	A22	10t multicolored	.30	.30
90	A22	50t multicolored	.35	.35
91	A22	100t multicolored	.45	.45
92	A22	140t multicolored	.50	.50
93	A22	150t multicolored	.55	.55
94	A22	200t multicolored	.70	.70
95	A22	350t multicolored	.90	.90
96	A22	400t multicolored	1.25	1.25
		Nos. 89-96 (8)	5.00	5.00

Souvenir Sheets
97	A22	600t multicolored	1.75	1.75
98	A22	600t multicolored	1.75	1.75

Reptiles A23

Designs: 20t, Psammophis lineolatum. No. 100, Natrix tessellata. No. 101, Eublepharis macularius. 100t, Agkistrodon halys. 150t, Eremias arguta. 200t, Elaphe dione. 250t, Asymblepharus. 500t, Lacerta agilis.

1996, Feb. 2   Perf. 12½x12
99	A23	20t multicolored	.25	.25
100	A23	50t multicolored	.25	.25
101	A23	100t multicolored	.25	.25
102	A23	100t multicolored	.30	.30
103	A23	150t multicolored	.40	.40
104	A23	200t multicolored	.50	.50
105	A23	250t multicolored	.65	.65
		Nos. 99-105 (7)	2.60	2.60

Souvenir Sheet
106	A23	500t multicolored	2.25	2.25

Souvenir Sheet

Save the Aral Sea — A24

Designs: a, Felis caracal. b, Salmo trutta aralensis. c, Hyaena hyaena. d, Pseudoscaphirhynchus kaufmanni. e, Aspiolucius esocinus.

1996, Apr. 29   Litho.   Perf. 14
107	A24	100t Sheet of 5, #a.-e.	4.00	4.00

See Kazakhstan No. 145. Tadjikistan No. 91, Turkmenistan No. 52, Uzbekistan No. 113.

Fauna — A27

a, Aquila chrysaetos. b, Capra falconeri. c, Ovis ammon. d, Gyps himalayensis. e, Equus hemionus. f, Canis lupus. g, Ursus arctor. h, Saiga tatarica.

1997, Aug. 29   Litho.   Perf. 12x12½
114	A27	600t Sheet of 8, #a.-h.	7.00	7.00

See No. 117.

New Year 1998 (Year of the Tiger) A28

1998, June 5   Litho.   Perf. 13½x14
115	A28	600t multicolored	1.40	1.40

Butterflies — A29

Designs: a, Parnasius actius. b, Colias christophi. c, Papilio machaon. d, Colias thisoa. e, Parnassius delphius. f, Panassius tianschanicus.

1998, June 5
116	A29	600t Sheet of 6, #a.-f.	3.75	3.75

Fauna Type of 1997

a, 600t, Capreolus capreolus. b, 1000t, Oriolus oriolus. c, 600t, Pandion haliaetus. d, 1000t, Uncia uncia. e, 600t, Upupa epops. f, 600t, Ciconia ciconia. g, 1000t, Alcedo atthis. h, 1000t, Falco tinnunculus.

1998, June 5 Litho. Perf. 12x12½
117 A27 Sheet of 8, #a-h 9.00 9.00

Dinosaurs — A31

Designs: a, Saurolophus, vert. b, Euoplocephalus. c, Velociraptor. d, Tyrannosaurus, vert. e, Gallimimus. f, Protoceratops.

Perf. 14x13½, 13½x14
1998, Dec. 4 Litho.
118 A31 10s Sheet of 6, #a.-f. 6.00 6.00

Universal Declaration of Human Rights, 50th Anniv. — A32

a, Andrei Sakharov (1921-89). b, Crowd of people raising their arms. c, Martin Luther King, Jr. d, Mahatma Gandhi. e, Eleanor Roosevelt.

1998, Dec. 4 Perf. 14x13½
119 A32 10s Sheet of 5, #a.-e. + label 5.00 5.00

No. 119 exists with 2 different inscriptions on label.

Constitution, 5th Anniv. — A33

1998, Dec. Perf. 12
120 A33 1000t multi 1.60 1.60

Imperf
Size: 120x90mm
120A A33 10,000t multi 65.00 65.00

No. 120A, issued 2/5/99.

Fauna A34

Designs: a, 600t, Fish, denomination UR. b, 1000t, Duck standing beside rocks. c, 1000t, Two birds. d, 1000t, Duck standing beside water. e, 1000t, Duck swimming. f, 1000t, Rodent. g, 1000t, Bird. h, 600t, Fish, denomination UL.

1998, Dec. Litho. Perf. 12
121 A34 Sheet of 8, #a.-h. 9.00 9.00

Corsac Fox (Vulpes Corsac) A35

World Wildlife Fund: Nos. 122a, 123a, 10s, Adult sitting. Nos. 122b, 123b, 10s, Adult sleeping. Nos. 122c, 123c, 30s, Two standing. Nos. 122d, 123d, 50s, Adult with young.

1999, Apr. 27 Litho. Perf. 12½x12
122 A35 Block of 4, #a.-d. 5.50 5.50
Size: 48x34mm
Perf. 13½
123 A35 Block of 4, #a.-d. 6.00 6.00

Nos. 123a-123d each contain a holographic image. Soaking in water may affect the hologram. IBRA '99, World Philatelic Exhibition, Nuremberg (No. 123). No. 123 was issued in sheets of 8 stamps.

For overprints and surcharges, see Nos. 175, 384.

Aleksandr Pushkin (1799-1837), Poet — A36

No. 124: a, 36t, Knight, giant. b, 6s, Man, woman, fish. c, 10s, Archer, angel. d, 10s, King in carriage.
20s, Portrait of Pushkin.

1999, June Litho. Perf. 12x12½
124 A36 Strip of 4, #a.-d. 4.75 4.75
Souvenir Sheet
125 A36 20s multicolored 4.25 4.25

No. 124 printed in sheets of 8 stamps.

Natl. Arms — A37

1999, July Litho. Perf. 11¼x11½
126 A37 20t dark blue .95 .95

Souvenir Sheet

China 1999 World Philatelic Exhibition — A38

No. 131: a, 10s, Ailuropoda melanoleuca. b, 15s, Strix leptogrammica.

1999, Aug. 21 Litho. Perf. 13x12½
131 A38 Sheet of 2, #a.-b. 2.50 2.50

Exists imperf. Value $3.75.

12th World Kickboxing Championships, Bishkek — A39

Emblem, globe and: No. 132, White background. No. 133, Blue panel. c, No. 134, Green, red, and black panels.
No. 135: a, Black background. b, Yellow and brown panels.

1999, Oct. 7 Litho. Perf. 13¼
132 A39 3s multi .70 .70
133 A39 3s multi .70 .70
134 A39 3s multi .70 .70
 Nos. 132-134 (3) 2.10 2.10
Souvenir Sheet
Perf. 12½
135 A39 6s Sheet of 2, #a.-b., + label 2.00 2.00

No. 135 contains 37x26mm stamps.

UPU, 125th Anniv. A40

1999, Oct. Perf. 14x14¼
136 A40 3s shown .50 .50
137 A40 6s Airplane, man on horse 1.00 1.00

Dogs — A41

No. 138: a, 3s, Taigan. b, 6s, Tasy. c, 6s, Afghan hound. d, 10s, Saluki. e, 15s, Mid-Asian shepherd. f, 15s, Akbash dog. g, 20s, Chow chow. h, 25s, Akita.

2000, Mar. 18 Litho. Perf. 12¼x12
138 A41 Sheet of 8, #a-h 6.75 6.75

Exists imperf. Value $10.

Kyrgyzstan postal officials have declared as "not authentic and not valid" stamps with a face value of 20s depicting the Beatles, Madonna, Pop music stars, Tiger Woods, 2000 French Olympic gold medal winners, Mushrooms, American Political Cartoons concerning the 2000 Presidential election, The Simpsons, Superman, and Warner Brothers cartoon characters.

Bulat Minzhilkiev(1940-98), Opera Singer — A42

2000, Apr. 20 Litho. Perf. 14x14¼
139 A42 5s multi .60 .60

Victory in World War II, 55th Anniv. A43

Heroes: a, Cholponbay Tuleberdiev (1922-42). b, I. V. Panfilov (1893-1941), vert. c, Duyshenkul Shopokov (1915-41).

Perf. 14x14¼ (#140a, 140c), 14¼x14 (#140b)
2000, May 20 Litho.
140 A43 6s Vert. strip of 3, #a-c 3.25 3.25

Issued in sheets of 2 each Nos. 140a-140c.

No. 33 Surcharged

2000, Sept. 22 Litho. Perf. 12x12½
141 A10 36t on 1t multi .30 .30

No. 141 exists with bar obliterators with smaller numerals and with thinner numerals and rosette obliterators in magenta. Value: each, $11.

2000 Summer Olympics, Sydney A44

Designs: 1s, Wrestling. 3s, Hurdles, vert. 6s, Boxing. 10s, Weight lifting, vert.

Perf. 14x14¼, 14¼x14
2000, Sept.
142-145 A44 Set of 4 4.25 4.25

Kyrgyzstan postal officials have declared as "not authentic and not valid" a sheet of nine 20s stamps depicting the History of Golf.

488

KYRGYZSTAN

Atay Ogunbaev, Composer
A45

2000, Oct. 28 Litho. Perf. 14x14¼
146 A45 6s multi .80 .80

Butterflies — A46

Designs: No. 147, 3s, Aglais urticae. No. 148, 3s, Argynnis aglaja. No. 149, 3s, Colias thisoa. No. 150, 3s, Inachis io. No. 151, 3s, Papilio machaon. No. 152, 3s, Parnassius apollo.

2000, Nov. 18 Perf. 13½
147-152 A46 Set of 6 4.50 4.50

Kyrgyzstan postal officials have declared as "not authentic and not valid" stamps with a face value of 20s in sheets of 6 depicting Jennifer Aniston and Tennis, and sheets of 9 depicting Backstreet Boys, Beverly Hills 90210, Minerals, Penguins, Tom and Jerry, Prince William, Babylon 5 and the End of Mir.

Intl. Year of Mountains (in 2002) — A47

Designs: No. 153, 10s, Khan-Tengri Mountain, 7,010 meters. No. 154, 10s, Victory Peak, 7,439 meters. No. 155, 10s, Lenin Peak, 7,134 meters.

2000, Dec. 23 Litho. Perf. 13½
153-155 A47 Set of 3 3.00 3.00
a. Souvenir sheet, #153-155 + label 3.00 3.00

Medals — A48

No. 156: a, 36t, Dank. b, 48t, Baatyr Jene. c, 1s, Manas (third class). d, 2s, Manas (second class). e, 3s, Manas (first class). f, 6s, Danaker. g, 10s, Ak Shumkar.

2001, Jan. 20 Litho. Perf. 14¼x14
156 A48 Sheet of 7, #a-g, + label 4.00 4.00

UN High Commissioner for Refugees — A49

2001, Mar. 10 Litho. Perf. 14x14¼
157 A49 10s multi .85 .85

New Year 2002 (Year of the Snake) A50

2001, Mar. 17
158 A50 6s multi .75 .75

Exists imperf. Value $2.

Year of Dialogue Among Civilizations A51

2001, Apr. 14 Perf. 13½
159 A51 10s multi 1.25 1.25

Intl. Year of Mountains A52

Mountains and: Nos. 160, 163a, 10s, Horses crossing stream. Nos. 161, 163b, 10s, Grazing animals, yurt. Nos. 162, 163c, 10s, Valley.

2001, July 7 Perf. 14x14¼
With White Frame
160-162 A52 Set of 3 3.00 3.00
Souvenir Sheet
Without White Frame
163 A52 10s Sheet of 3, #a-c, + label 3.50 3.50

Bishkek Buildings — A53

Designs: 48t, Communications Building. 1s, Town Hall. 3s, Opera House.

2001, July 7 Perf. 14x13¼
164 A53 48t slate gray .30 .25
165 A53 1s olive gray .30 .25
166 A53 3s violet brown .35 .30
a. Horiz. strip, #164-166 .95 .95

2001, Jan. 20 Litho. Perf. 14¼x14

Intl. Year of Ecotourism (in 2002) A54

Designs: No. 167, 10s, Mountains, lake. No. 168, 10s, Mountains, field of flowers. No. 169, 10s, Sailboat on lake. No. 170, Mosque, vert.

2001, July 21 Perf. 14x14¼
167-169 A54 Set of 3 4.00 4.00
Souvenir Sheet
Imperf (Simulated Perfs)
170 A54 10s multi 1.75 1.75

Independence, 10th Anniv. — A55

Designs: 1.50s, Eagle, mountain. 7s, Pres. Askar Akaev, flag. 11.50s, Governmental building.

2001, Aug. 29 Perf. 14x14¼
171-172 A55 Set of 2 3.50 3.50
Souvenir Sheet
173 A55 11.50s Sheet of 1 + 8 labels 4.25 4.25

Kurmanbek Baatyr, 500th Anniv. of Birth — A56

2001, Sept. 8 Perf. 14¼x14
174 A56 1.50s multi .50 .50

Nos. 123a-123b Surcharged and Nos. 123c-123d Overprinted With Text Only

No. 175: a, 25s on 10s #123a. b, 25s on 10s, #123b. c, 30s #123c. d, 50s #123d.

Litho. With Hologram
2001 Perf. 13½
175 A35 Block of 4, #a-d 7.00 7.00

Regional Communications Accord, 10th Anniv. — A57

2001, Oct. 20 Litho. Perf. 14¼x14
176 A57 7s multi 1.00 1.00

Commonwealth of Independent States, 10th Anniv. — A58

2001, Dec. 8
177 A58 6s Prus bl & yel .85 .85

Kyrgyzstan postal officials have declared as "illegal:"

Stamps with a face value of 20s in sheets of nine depicting Shrek, Harry Potter, Concorde, Dogs, Tigers, Formula 1 racing, Mother Teresa, and The Beatles;

Stamps with various face values in sheets of nine depicting Defenders of Peace and Freedom, Superman, Green Lantern, Flash, Ironman, Legends of Baseball;

Stamps with various values in sheets of three depicting Princess Diana and Elvis Presley;

Stamps with a face value of 20s in sheets of six depicting Harley Davidson motorcycles;

Souvenir sheets of one 100s stamp depicting Harry Potter and Penguins.

2002 Winter Olympics, Salt Lake City — A59

Designs: 50t, Speed skating. 1.50s, Biathlon. 7s, Ice hockey. 10s, Ski jumping. 50s, Downhill skiing.

2002, Feb. 23 Litho. Perf. 14x14¼
178-181 A59 Set of 4 1.75 1.75
Souvenir Sheet
182 A59 50s multi + label 4.75 4.75

New Year 2002 (Year of the Horse) A60

2002, Mar. 23 Perf. 14x14¼
183 A60 1s multi 1.00 1.00

2002 World Cup Soccer Championships, Japan and Korea — A61

No. 184: a, 1.50s. b, 3s. c, 7.20s. d, 12s. e, 24s. f, 60s.

2002, Apr. 13 Perf. 14¼x14
184 A61 Sheet of 6, #a-f 11.00 11.00

No. 184 exists with an overprint in silver or gold with scores of the final and third place matches of the tournament. Value: each, $25.

Kyrgyzstan/Pakistan Diplomatic Relations, 10th Anniv. — A62

2002, Apr. 18 Perf. 14¼x14
185 A62 12s multi 1.75 1.75

Kyrgyzstan postal officials have declared as "illegal:"

Stamps with a face value of 20s in sheets of nine depicting Pandas, Dinosaurs, Marine Life, Cats and Scouting Emblem, and the Beatles.

Stamps with various face values in sheets of nine depicting Caricatures of World Cup Soccer Players (3 sheets).

Summer Olympics — A63

No. 186: a, 1s, Discus, Greece #125 (Athens, 1896). b, 2s, Boxing, France #113 (Paris, 1900). c, 3s, Diving, US #324 (St. Louis, 1904). d, 5s, Weight lifting, Great Britain #127 (London, 1908). e, 7s, Rowing, Sweden #97 (Stockholm, 1912). f, 7s, Hurdles, Belgium #B48 (Antwerp, 1920).

No. 187: a, 1s, Rhythmic gymnastics, France #201 (Paris, 1924). b, 2s, Diving, Netherlands #B25 (Amsterdam, 1928). c, 3s, Table tennis, US #718 (Los Angeles, 1932). d, 5s, Running, Germany #B86 (Berlin, 1936). e, 7s, Fencing, Great Britain #274 (London, 1948). f, 7s, Men's gymnastics (pommel horse), Finland #B112 (Helsinki, 1952).

No. 188: a, 1.50s, Volleyball, Australia #277 (Melbourne, 1956). b, 3s, Tennis, Italy #799 (Rome, 1960). c, 5s, Swimming, Japan #B12 (Tokyo, 1964). d, 5s, Judo, Mexico #990 (Mexico City, 1968). e, 7.20s, Kayaking, Germany #B490e (Munich, 1972). f, 12s, Yachting, Canada #B11 (Montreal, 1976).

No. 189: a, 1.50s, Men's gymnastics (rings), Russia #B99 (Moscow, 1980). b, 3s, Synchronized swimming, US #2085a (Los Angeles, 1984). c, 5s, Cycling, South Korea #B54 (Seoul, 1988). d, 5s, High jump, Spain #B197 (Barcelona, 1992). e, 7.20s, Sailboarding, US #3068a (Atlanta, 1996). f, 12s, Women's gymnastics, Australia #1779 (Sydney, 2000).

2002, Aug. 28   Litho.   **Perf. 13x13¼**
Sheets of 6, #a-f, + 3 labels
186-189   A63   Set of 4   12.00   12.00

Jalal-Abad
A64

Talas
A65

Osh — A66

2002, Dec. 7   **Perf. 13½**
190   A64   20t claret   .35   .35
191   A65   50t claret   .35   .35
192   A66   60t claret   .35   .35
193   A64   1s Prussian bl   .35   .35
194   A65   1.50s Prussian bl   .35   .35
195   A66   2s blue gray   .35   .35
196   A64   3s blue gray   .55   .55
197   A65   7s blue gray   .90   .90
198   A66   10s Prussian bl   1.25   1.25
    Nos. 190-198 (9)   4.80   4.80

Kyrgyzstan postal officials have declared as "illegal:"

Sheets of 9 with various denominations depicting Looney Tunes Characters (Merry Cristmas! (sic)) (2 different), Harry Potter, 71st Academy Awards, MTV Video Awards.

Sheets of 9 with 20s denominations depicting 20th Century Dreams (5 different), Chess, Teddy bears, MTV Video Awards.

Sheet of 6 with various denominations depicting Dinosaurs.

Sheet of 3 with various denominations depicting Pope John Paul II.

Nos. 33, 35
Surcharged in
Red or Black

No. 34 Surcharged

Methods and Perfs As Before
2002, Dec. 28
199   A10   1.50s on 1t multi (R)   .25   .25
200   A10   3.60s on 3t multi   .35   .35
201   A10   7s on 10t multi   .75   .75
    Nos. 199-201 (3)   1.35   1.35

New denomination is at left on No. 201.
Nos. 199-201 exist imperf. Value, set $1.75.

Olmoskhan
Atabekova (1922-
87) — A67

2003, Jan. 11   Litho.   **Perf. 14¼x14**
202   A67   7.20s multi   .80   .80

Intl. Association of Academies of Science, 10th Anniv. A68

Emblem and: 1.50s, Atom model. 7.20s, Circles.

2003, Mar. 8   **Perf. 14x14¼**
203-204   A68   Set of 2   1.00   1.00

Gold and Bronze Artifacts From Sakov — A69

No. 205: a, 1.50s, Two figurines of people. b, 3s, Coin. c, 3.60s, Lion. d, 5s, Idol with horns. e, 7s, Rooster. f, 10s, Goats. g, 20s, Bird on coin. h, 42s, Animal's head.

No. 206, Mask.

2003, May 10   **Perf. 14x14¼**
205   A69   Sheet of 8, #a-h   8.00   8.00
Souvenir Sheet
Imperf. (With Simulated Perforations)
206   A69   42s multi   5.50   5.50

No. 205 exists imperf. with simulated perforations. Value $13.

Bishkek Post Office, 125th Anniv. A70

Bishkek Post Office, emblem, dove and: 1s, Airplane. 3s, Covered wagon and Jeep. 7s, Covered wagon. 50s, "1878-2003."

2003, May 31   **Perf. 14x14¼**
207-209   A70   Set of 3   1.50   1.50
Souvenir Sheet
Imperf. (With Simulated Perforations)
210   A70   50s multi   5.25   5.25

Famous Men — A71

Various men: a, 1.50s. b, 3s. c, 3.60s. d, 5s. e, 7.20s. f, 10s. g, 18s. h, 20s. i, 25s. j, 30s.

2003, June 20   **Perf. 14x14¼**
211   A71   Sheet of 10, #a-j   13.00   13.00

Issyk Kul — A72

No. 212: a, 1s, Rahat. b, 1.50s, Raduga. c, 2s, Teltoru. d, 3s, Kyrgyzskoe Vzmorije. e, 3.60s, Tamga. f, 5s, Solnyshko. g, 7s, Vityaz. h, 8s, Ak Bermet. i, 12s, Royal Beach. j, 20s, Luchezarnoe Poberejie.

2003, Aug. 15   **Perf. 13½x13¾**
212   A72   Sheet of 10, #a-j, + 10 labels   6.25   6.25

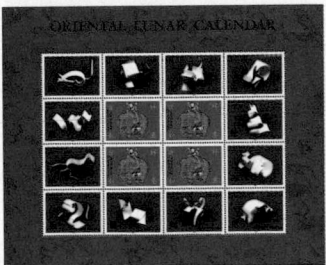

Lunar New Year Animals — A73

No. 213: a, 1.50s, Rat. b, 3s, Ox. c, 5s, Tiger. d, 7s, Hare. e, 12s, Dragon. f, 12s, Snake. g, 15s, Horse. h, 15s, Sheep. i, 20s, Monkey. j, 20s, Cock. k, 25s, Dog. l, 25s, Pig.

2003, Aug. 25   **Perf. 13x13¼**
213   A73   Sheet of 12, #a-l,
  +4 labels   14.00   14.00

National Symbols A74

History of Syma Chan — A75

Designs: No. 214, 3s, Flag. No. 215, 3s, National anthem. 5s, Coat of arms.

2003, Oct. 4   Litho.   **Perf. 13½**
214-216   A74   Set of 3   1.00   1.00
216a   Souvenir sheet, #214-216   1.00   1.00
Souvenir Sheet
217   A75   12s multi   1.25   1.25

New Year 2003 (Year of the Sheep) A76

2003, Dec. 30   Litho.   **Perf. 14x14¼**
218   A76   1.50s multi   .40   .40

Meerim Fund, 10th Anniv. A77

Designs: 1.50s, Fund emblem, buildings. 7s, Fund emblem, buildings, diff. 20s, Fund emblem.

2004, Feb. 17   Litho.   **Perf. 14x14¼**
219-220   A77   Set of 2   1.50   1.50
Souvenir Sheet
Perf. 13½
221   A77   20s multi   3.00   3.00

No. 221 contains one 37x51mm stamp.

New Year 2004 (Year of the Monkey) A78

2004, Apr. 3   Litho.   **Perf. 14x14¼**
222   A78   3s multi   .60   .60

Automobiles — A79

No. 223: a, 3.60s, 1913 Peugeot. b, 3.60s, 1999 Mercedes-Benz. c, 10s, 1996 Volvo S40. d, 10s, 1908 Ford. e, 15s, 1932 Alfa-Romeo. f, 15s, 1972 VAZ 2101. g, 25s, 1998 Nissan. h, 25s, 1950 ZIS-110.

2004, May 1   Litho.   Perf. 14x13½
223 A79   Sheet of 8, #a-h   9.00 9.00
No. 223 exists imperf. Value $15.

Insects — A80

No. 224: a, 3.60s, Insect with red wings. b, 3.60s, Grasshopper. c, 10s, Cricket. d, 10s, Ladybugs. e, 15s, Dragonfly. f, 15s, Praying mantis. g, 25s, Moth with red wings. h, 25s, Bee.

2004, May 15
224 A80   Sheet of 8, #a-h   10.00 10.00
2004 Singapore World Stamp Championship.
No. 224 exists imperf. Value $15.

FIFA (Fédération Internationale de Football Association), Cent. — A81

No. 225: a, 5s, Soccer ball. b, 6s, FIFA emblem, soccer ball, athletic shoes. c, 7s, Soccer player with red shirt. d, 10s, Soccer player with white shirt.

2004, May 21   Litho.   Perf. 14x14¼
225 A81   Block of 4, #a-d   3.00 3.00

2004, June 19   Litho.   Perf. 12
226 A5   20s on 10r #12   3.00 3.00
Peace and Respect Intl. Festival of Arts.

Karakol Region A82   Naryn Region A83

Tokmok Region — A84

2004, July 6   Litho.   Perf. 13½x13¾
227 A82   10t indigo   .25   .25
228 A83   20t dark green   .25   .25
229 A84   50t dark brown   .25   .25
230 A82   60t blue   .25   .25
231 A83   1s blue green   .25   .25
232 A84   2s brown   .25   .25
233 A82   3s violet   .50   .50
234 A83   5s green   .75   .75
235 A84   7s light brown   1.00 1.00
         Nos. 227-235 (9)   3.75 3.75

Chynykei Biy (1788-1874) — A85

2004, Sept. 18   Litho.   Perf. 14x14¼
236 A85   3s multi   .45   .45

National Academy of Sciences, 50th Anniv. A86

Emblem and: 1.50s, Old building. 3.60s, New building.

2004, Nov. 6
237-238 A86   Set of 2   .90   .90

Basketball A87

Basketball player and: 1.50s, Coach Nikolay Zvenchukov. 3.60s, Coach Kubat Karabekov.

2004, Dec. 4
239-240 A87   Set of 2   1.00 1.00

Falcon — A88

2004-05   Litho.   Perf. 13¼x14
241 A88   10t green   .35   .35
242 A88   50t blue   .35   .35
243 A88   1s brown   .50   .50
         Nos. 241-243 (3)   1.20 1.20
Issued: 1s, 12/28/04. 50t, 2/12/05. 10t, 6/16/05.

New Year 2005 (Year of the Rooster) A89

2005, Mar. 21   Litho.   Perf. 14
244 A89   3s multi   1.25 1.25

Souvenir Sheet

Salizhan Sharipov, Astronaut — A90

2005, Apr. 20   Litho.   Perf. 13¾
245 A90   100s multi   13.50 13.50

Folk Art — A91

Various folk art objects.

2005, Apr. 23   Perf. 14¼x14
246   Strip of 6   4.50 4.50
  a. A91 2s orange panel   .25   .25
  b. A91 3.60s light blue panel .25   .25
  c. A91 7s green panel   .55   .55
  d. A91 12s green panel   .85   .85
  e. A91 15s bright pink panel 1.10 1.10
  f. A91 20s orange panel   1.50 1.50
         Souvenir Sheet
247 A91   40s multi   4.50 4.50

End of World War II, 60th Anniv. A92

2005, May 6   Perf. 14x14¼
248 A92   5s multi   .50   .50

End of World War II, 60th Anniv. — A93

World War II personalities: No. 249, 5s, Gen. Tito. No. 250, 5s, Cervi Brothers. No. 251, 5s, Ferruccio Parri. No. 252, 10s, Air Marshal Sir Hugh Dowding. No. 253, 10s, Gen. George S. Patton. No. 254, 10s, Gen. Konstantin Rokossovsky. No. 255, 10s, Gen. Harold Alexander. No. 256, 10s, Gen. Omar N. Bradley. No. 257, 10s, Gen. Charles de Gaulle. No. 258, 10s, Gen. Jean Leclerc. No. 259, 10s, Field Marshal Bernard Montgomery. No. 260, 10s, Gen. Ivan Konev. No. 261, 10s, Marshal Georgy Zhukov. No. 262, 10s, Gen. Dwight D. Eisenhower. No. 263, 10s, Marshal Semyon Timoshenko. No. 264, 10s, Gen. Vasily Chuikov. No. 265, 15s, Pres. Franklin D. Roosevelt. No. 266, 15s, Prime Minister Winston Churchill. No. 267, 15s, King George VI. No. 268, 15s, Joseph Stalin.

Embossed on Metal
2005, June 18   Die Cut Perf 12½
                   Self-Adhesive
249-268 A93   Set of 20   35.00 35.00

National Games — A94

2005, Aug. 6   Litho.   Perf. 14¼x14
269 A94   3s multi   .45   .45

World Summit on the Information Society, Tunis A95

2005, Sept. 10   Perf. 14x14¼
270 A95   3.60s multi   .45   .45

Falcon — A96

2005, Sept. 14   Litho.   Perf. 13¼x14
271 A96   60t violet   .35   .35
No. 271 exists imperf. Value $5.25.

Souvenir Sheet

Lakes — A97

No. 272: a, 7s, Lake Chatyrkul. b, 20s, Lake Sonkul. c, 25s, Lake Sarychelek. d, 30s, Lake Issyk-Kul.

2005, Dec. 10   Perf. 14x14¼
272 A97   Sheet of 4, #a-d   6.75 6.75

Europa Stamps, 50th Anniv. (in 2006) — A98

Designs: 15s, Uzgen Minaret, Kyrgyzstan. 20s, Acropolis, Athens, Greece. 25s, Buran Tower, Kyrgyzstan. 45s, Kolossi Castle, Limassol, Cyprus. 60s, Tash Rabat, Kyrgyzstan. 85s, St. Mark's Basilica, Venice, Italy.

2005, Dec. 29   Perf. 13¼x13
273-278 A98   Set of 6   17.50 17.50
278a   Souvenir sheet, #273-278   17.50 17.50
     Nos. 273-278 and 278a exist imperf. Values: set, $22.50; sheet, $22.50.

Tugolbai Sydykbekov (1912-97), Writer A99

2006, Jan. 7   Perf. 14x14¼
279 A99 10s multi   1.00 1.00

New Year 2006 (Year of the Dog) A100

2006, Feb. 4
280 A100 3s multi   1.00 1.00

2006 Winter Olympics, Turin A101

2006, Mar. 11
281 A101 5s multi   .80 .80

Falcon — A102

2006   Litho.   Perf. 13¼x14
282 A102 50t Prus blue   .30 .30
283 A102 1s car lake   .25 .25
284 A102 3s black   .45 .45
     Nos. 282-284 (3)   1.00 1.00
     Issued: 50t, 4/15; 1s, 5/6; 3s, 8/5.
     Nos. 282-284 exist imperf. Value, each $6.

2006 World Cup Soccer Championships, Germany — A103

2006, June 9   Litho.   Perf. 14x14¼
285 A103 15s multi   1.25 1.25

Miniature Sheet

Commemorative Coins — A104

No. 286: a, 1.50s, 1995 100-som gold coin. b, 3s, 1995 10-som silver coin. c, 16s, 2000 100-som gold coin. d, 20s, 2001 10-som silver coin. e, 24s, 2002 10-som silver coin depicting flower. f, 28s, 2002 10-som silver coin depicting ram. g, 30s, 2003 10-som silver and gold coin depicting other coins. h, 40s, 2003 10-som silver and gold coin depicting national symbols. i, 45s, 2005 10-som silver coin. j, 50s, 2005 10-som silver and gold coin.

2006, June 24
286 A104 Sheet of 10, #a-j   17.50 17.50

Regional Communications Commonwealth, 15th Anniv. — A105

2006, Sept. 23   Litho.   Perf. 14x14¼
287 A105 12s multi   1.25 1.25

Souvenir Sheet

Public Buildings in Bishkek — A106

No. 288: a, Sports arena (two word inscription, large tree at left). b, Theater (three word inscription). c, Philharmonic hall (one word inscription). d, Museum (two word inscription, no tree).

2006, Sept. 30   Perf. 12¾x13¼
288 A106 12s Sheet of 4, #a-d   4.25 4.25

Intl. Telecommunications Union Plenipotentiary Conference, Antalya, Turkey — A107

2006, Oct. 7   Litho.   Perf. 13x13½
289 A107 25s multi   2.25 2.25

Defense of Moscow in World War II, 65th Anniv. A108

2006, Nov. 11   Perf. 14x14¼
290 A108 7s multi   .65 .65

Miniature Sheet

Kyrgyz Cinema, 65th Anniv. — A109

No. 291: a, S. Chokmorov (on horse). b, B. Bejshenaliev (man wearing hat). c, T. Tursunbaeva (woman wearing headdress). d, B. Kydykeeva (two women).

2006, Dec. 9
291 A109 12s Sheet of 4, #a-d   4.00 4.00

New Year 2007 (Year of the Pig) A110

2007, Jan. 27   Litho.   Perf. 14x14¼
292 A110 3s multi   .40 .40

Miniature Sheet

Paintings — A111

No. 293: a, Chingiz Aitmatov (seated man with striped shirt). b, Syimenkul Chokmorov (seated man with clasped hands). c, Kurmangazy Azykbaev (man playing flute). d, Omor Sultanov (seated man wearing light gray suit). e, Zhylkychy Zhakypov (man with dark blue shirt).

2007, Mar. 3   Litho.   Perf. 14x14¼
293 A111 12s Sheet of 5, #a-e, + label   5.00 5.00

Kyrgyz National Games A112

2007, May 5   Litho.   Perf. 14x14¼
294 A112 7s multi   .65 .65

Miniature Sheet

Bishkek-Osh Highway, 50th Anniv. — A113

No. 295: a, Tunnel. b, Road turning to left. c, Road turning to right. d, Straight road.

2007, May 19   Perf. 13x13¼
295 A113 25s Sheet of 4, #a-d   8.00 8.00

Aigul — A114

Flower and: 1s, Solid blue background. 100s, Mountains in background.

2007, June 23   Perf. 13¼x14
296 A114 1s multi   .25 .25
Souvenir Sheet   Perf. 13¼x13
297 A114 100s multi   8.25 8.25
     No. 297 contains one 30x40mm stamp.

Miniature Sheet

Seventh Conference of Shanghai Cooperation Organization — A115

No. 298 — Flags of: a, Kazakhstan. b, Kyrgyzstan. c, People's Republic of China. d, Russia. e, Tajikistan. f, Uzbekistan.

2007, Aug. 16   Perf. 13¾x14½
298 A115 12s Sheet of 6, #a-f   6.00 6.00

Miniature Sheet

Birds of Prey — A116

No. 299: a, Haliaeetus albicilla. b, Falco rusticolus. c, Aquila chrysaetus. d, Accipiter gentilis. e, Milvus migrans. f, Falco peregrinus.

2007, Nov. 30   Litho.   Perf. 14¼
299 A116 25s Sheet of 6, #a-f   11.00 11.00

Santa Claus — A117

2007, Dec. 1
300 A117 3s multi   .45   .45

New Year 2008 (Year of the Rat) — A118

2008, Jan. 19   *Perf. 14¼x14*
301 A118 7s multi   1.10 1.10

Mammals — A119

Designs: Nos. 302, 310a, 7s, Uncia uncia. Nos. 303, 310b, 7s, Ailuropoda melanoleuca. Nos. 304, 310c, 12s, Panthera tigris. Nos. 305, 310d, 12s, Ailurus fulgens. Nos. 306, 310e, 16s, Hystrix cristata. Nos. 307, 310f, 16s, Pygathrix roxellana. Nos. 308, 310g, 25s, Otocolobus manul. Nos. 309, 310h, 25s, Ovis ammon.

2008, Jan. 19   *Perf. 14x13½*
Stamps With White Frames
302-309 A119 Set of 8   9.00 9.00
Souvenir Sheet
Stamps With Colored Frames
310 A119 Sheet of 8, #a-h   9.75 9.75

Kyrgyz National Games — A120

2008, Mar. 1   *Perf. 14¼x14*
311 A120 5s multi   .60   .60

2008 Summer Olympics, Beijing — A121

No. 312: a, Soccer. b, Wrestling. c, Javelin. d, Basketball.

2008, Mar. 1   *Perf. 12½x13*
312 A121 20s Block of 4, #a-d   5.75 5.75

Souvenir Sheet

Mountains — A122

No. 313: a, Khan-Tengri, Kyrgyzstan. b, Sabalan Peak, Iran.

2008, Mar. 8   *Perf. 13x13¼*
313 A122 16s Sheet of 2, #a-b, +
            central label   3.25 3.25
See Iran No. 2964.

Outlines of Stamps, Mountain, Kyrgyz Post Emblem — A123

2008   Litho.   *Perf. 14x13¼*
314 A123 50t multi   .25   .25
315 A123 1s multi   .25   .25
316 A123 3s multi   .25   .25
317 A123 7s multi   .65   .65
        Nos. 314-317 (4)   1.40 1.40
Issued: 1s, 3s, 4/2. 50t, 7s, 5/10.

Heroes of the Kyrgyz Republic and Medals A124

Designs: 10s, Sabira Kumushalieva (1917-2007), actress. 15s, Absamat Masaliev (1933-2004), politician.

2008, Apr. 5 Litho. *Perf. 14x14¼*
318-319 A124 Set of 2   2.50 2.50

Miniature Sheets

Civil Aircraft — A125

No. 320: a, JAK-12. b, MI-2. c, AN-2. d, TU-154. e, IL-14. f, IL-18. g, AN-24. h, MI-4.
No. 321: a, AN-28. b, JAK-40. c, AN-26. d, TU-134. e, IL-76. f, A-320. g, MI-8.
No. 322: a, Sopwith. b, Air-6. c, P5. d, Po-2. e, Ju-52/3. f, ANT-9. g, Mi-1. h, Li-2.

2008   *Perf. 14x13¼*
320 A125 20s Sheet of 8, #a-
            h, + central la-
            bel   13.50 13.50
                           Perf. 13x13½
321 A125 20s Sheet of 7, #a-
            g, + label   12.00 12.00
322 A125 20s Sheet of 8, #a-
            h, + label   12.00 12.00
Issued: No. 320, 5/24; No. 321, 9/20; No. 322, 11/1.

Hats — A126

Various hats: 6s, 7s, 12s, 50s.

2008, June 28 Litho. *Perf. 14¼x14*
323-326 A126 Set of 4   6.00 6.00

Yaks — A127

No. 325: a, Buka yak (denomination on cloud). b, Mamalak yak (denomination on light blue sky and mountain). c, Inek yak facing right (denomination on purple mountain). d, Inek yak facing left (denomination on dark blue sky and mountain).

2008, July 26   *Perf. 13x13¼*
327 A127 25s Block of 4, #a-d   7.50 7.50

Isa Akhunbaev (1908-75), Surgeon — A128

2008, Aug. 30   *Perf. 14¼x14*
328 A128 12s multi   1.10 1.10

No. 312 Overprinted in Red

No. 329: a, #312a (Soccer) with overprint at bottom. b, #312b (Wrestling) with overprint at bottom. c, #312c (Javelin) with overprint at top. d, #312d (Basketball) with overprint at top. e, #312d with overprint at bottom. f, #312c with overprint at bottom. g, #312b with overprint at top. h, #312a with overprint at top.

2008, Nov. 22 Litho. *Perf. 12½x13*
329 A121 20s Sheet of 8, #a-h 21.00 21.00

Campaign Against Drug Abuse — A129

2008, Dec. 6   *Perf. 14¼x14*
330 A129 12s multi   1.25 1.25

New Year 2009 (Year of the Ox) — A130

2009, Feb. 1   *Perf. 14x14¼*
331 A130 25s multi   2.00 2.00

Ishembai Abdraimov (1914-2001), Soviet Pilot — A131

2009, Feb. 26   *Perf. 14¼x14*
332 A131 10s multi   .95   .95

Kok-boru (Buzkashi) A132

2009, Apr. 25   *Perf. 14x14¼*
333 A132 25s multi   1.75 1.75

Miniature Sheet

Horses — A133

No. 334 — Various horses: a, 16s. b, 42s. c, 50s. d, 60s.

2009, May 30   *Perf. 13x13½*
334 A133 Sheet of 4, #a-d   11.00 11.00

Worldwide Fund for Nature (WWF) A134

Saker falcon: 10s, Head. 15s, On nest. 25s, In flight. 50s, On nest, with chicks.

2009, June 20   *Perf. 13½x14*
335-338 A134 Set of 4   5.50 5.50
338a   Sheet, 4 each #335-338 22.00 22.00

Miniature Sheet

Scenes From Writings of Chynghyz Aitmatov (1928-2008) — A135

No. 339: a, 7s, Woman, horse, cart and farmer in field. b, 12s, Man and horse. c, 16s, Woman and truck. d, 21s, Women near train. e, 28s, Man carrying boy. f, 30s, Boy with binoculars, buck. g, 45s, Birds flying above horse and rider. h, 60s, Men in canoe.

2009, Aug. 13   Litho.   Perf. 13x13¼
339 A135   Sheet of 8, #a-h, + label   13.00 13.00

Barpy Alykulov (1884-1949), Poet — A136

2009, Aug. 22   Litho.   Perf. 14x13½
340 A136 16s multi   1.10 1.10

Horses Type of 2009

Designs: 16s, Like #334a. 42s, Like #334b. 50s, Like #334c. 60s, Like #334d.

2009, Sept. 19   Litho.   Perf. 14x14¼
341-344 A133   Set of 4   11.00 11.00
Nos. 041-044 were each printed in sheets of 6.

National Library, 75th Anniv. A137

2009, Sept. 30   Perf. 13½x14
345 A137 12s multi   .90 .90

Miniature Sheet

Glaciers — A138

No. 346: a, 12s, Ak-Sai Glacier. b, 16s, Kotur Glacier. c, 21s, Semenovsky Glacier. d, 28s, Zvezdochka Glacier. e, 45s, North Inylchek Glacier. f, 60s, South Inylchek Glacier.

2009, Dec. 12   Perf. 13x13¼
346 A138   Sheet of 6, #a-f   12.50 12.50

Railways of Kyrgyzstan A139

Designs: 16s, Station. 42s, Train on bridge. 50s, Train leaving tunnel. 60s, Train on bridge over highway.

2009, Dec. 19   Perf. 14x14¼
347-350 A139   Set of 4   12.00 12.00

United Nations Declaration of the Rights of the Child, 50th Anniv. (in 2009) — A140

2010, Feb. 6
351 A140 21s multi   1.50 1.50

New Year 2010 (Year of the Tiger) A141

2010, Feb. 6
352 A141 25s multi   1.75 1.75

2010 Winter Olympics, Vancouver — A142

Designs: 21s, Cross-country skiing. 28s, Biathlon. 45s, Giant slalom. 60s, Snowboarding.

2010, Feb. 12   Perf. 14¼x14
353-356 A142   Set of 4   10.50 10.50

Peonies — A143

No. 357: a, 25s, Flowers. b, 30s, Flower.

2010, Mar. 30   Perf. 12½
357 A143   Horiz. pair, #a-b   3.75 3.75
   c.   Souvenir sheet, #357b   2.10 2.10

Victory in World War II, 65th Anniv. A144

2010, Apr. 10   Perf. 14x14¼
358 A144 12s multi   .75 .75

Miniature Sheet

Kyrgyz National Museum of Fine Arts, 75th Anniv. — A145

No. 359 — Paintings: a, 12s, Portrait of Y. M. Vengerov, by Ilya E. Repin, 1916. b, 16s, Cabbage Field, by Robert R. Falk, 1910. c, 21s, Dishes on a Red Cloth, by Pyotr P. Konchalovsky, 1916. d, 24s, Seascape in the Crimea, by Ivan K. Ayvazovsky, 1866. e, 28s, Autumn Djailoo, by Semen A. Chuykov, 1945. f, 30s, Evening in the South of Kyrgyzstan, by Gapar A. Aitiev, 1967. g, 42s, Autumn Garden, by A. Ignatev, 1989. h, 45s, By Night, by D. N. Deymant, 1971.

2010, Apr. 24   Perf. 13x13¼
359 A145   Sheet of 8, #a-h, + central label   13.00 13.00

2010 World Cup Soccer Championships, South Africa — A146

Players and: 24s, Emblem. 30s, World Cup. 42s, Emblem, diff. 60s, World Cup, diff.

2010, June 26   Litho.   Perf. 14x14¼
360-363 A146   Set of 4   10.00 10.00

Ancient Silver Jewelry A147

Designs: 16s, Earrings. 24s, Buttons. 58s, Bangles. 66s, Hair ornaments.

2010, July 31   Perf. 13½
364-367 A147   Set of 4   11.00 11.00

Souvenir Sheet

Kambar-Ata 2 Hydroelectric Station — A148

No. 368: a, 28s, Explosion. b, 42s, Station under construction. c, 60s, Station under construction, diff.

2010, Aug. 31   Perf. 13x13¼
368 A148   Sheet of 3, #a-c   7.75 7.75

Souvenir Sheet

Intl. Telecommunications Union Plenipotentiary Conference, Guadalajara, Mexico — A149

2010, Sept. 25   Perf. 13
369 A149 100s multi   6.50 6.50

Famous Men — A150

Designs: 12s, Togolok Moldo (1860-1942), poet. 16s, Murataly Kurenkeev (1860-1949), composer. 21s, Zhenizhok Coco Uulu (1860-1918), poet. 28s, Itzhak Razzakov (1910-79), statesman.

2010   Perf. 14¼x14
370-373 A150   Set of 4   4.50 4.50
Issued: 28s, 10/25; others, 10/23.

Turtles A151

Designs: 16s, Agrionemys horstieldi. 24s, Pseudemys scripta. 48s, Geochelone elegans. 72s, Testudo kleinmanni.

2010, Dec. 11   Perf. 14x14¼
374-377 A151   Set of 4   10.00 10.00

New Year 2011 (Year of the Rabbit) A152

2011, Jan. 29
378 A152 24s multi   1.45 1.45

Miniature Sheet

Animals and National Reserves — A153

No. 379: a, 7s, Eagle, Ala-Archa Reserve. b, 12s, Bear, Chon-Kemin Reserve. c, 16s, Buck, Naryn Reserve. d, 21s, Ram, Sary-Chelek Reserve. e, 24s, Fish, Issyk-Kul Reserve. f, 28s, Duck, Karatal-Zhapryk Reserve. g, 42s, Falcon, Besh-Tash Reserve. h, 45s, Cat,

Sarychat-Ertash Reserve. i, 60s, Pheasant, Padysha-Ata Reserve.

2011, Feb. 25   *Perf. 13x13¼*
379 A153   Sheet of 9, #a-i   15.00 15.00

Souvenir Sheet

First Man in Space, 50th
Anniv. — A154

No. 380: a, 60s, Vostok 1. b, Yuri Gagarin (1934-68), first cosmonaut.

2011, Apr. 2   *Perf. 13¼x13*
380 A154   Sheet of 2, #a-b   8.50 8.50

2011 Intl. Ice Hockey Federation Championships, Slovakia — A155

Intl. Ice Hockey Federation emblem and: 28s, Player approaching goalie with puck. 42s, Two players and puck.

2011, May 14   *Perf. 14x14¼*
381-382 A155   Set of 2   4.50 4.50
382a   Miniature sheet of 6, 3   13.50 13.50
      each #381-382

Miniature Sheet

Bishkek Bus Station, 30th
Anniv. — A156

No. 383 — Vehicles: a, 12s, PAZ-672 bus, RAF-22038 van. b, 16s, Ikarus-256 bus, GAZ-M24 Volga taxi. c, 21s, LAZ 697R Tourist bus, UAZ-2206 van. d, 24s, Ford E series van, Volvo B12B bus. e, 30s, Volkswagen Transporter T4 van, Setra S 431 dt bus. f, 42s, Mercedes Sprinter 313 van, Mitsubishi Fuso Aero Queen bus.

2011, July 21   *Perf. 13x13¼*
383 A156   Sheet of 6, #a-f +   9.00 9.00
      central label

**No. 123 Overprinted in Gold with
Nos. 123c and 123d Surcharged in
Metallic Red**

No. 384: a, Overprint on #123a. b, Overprint on #123b. c, 60s on 20s #123c. d, 90s on 50s #123d.

Litho. With Hologram
2011, Aug. 5   *Perf. 13½*
384 A35   Block of 4, #a-d   42.50 42.50

Plum Blossoms — A157

No. 385: a, 16s, Denomination at UL. b, 60s, Denomination at UR.

2011, Aug. 15   **Litho.**   *Perf. 13*
385 A157   Horiz. pair, #a-b   5.00 5.00

Regional Communications
Commonwealth, 20th Anniv. — A158

2011, Oct. 1   *Perf. 14x14¼*
386 A158   28s multi   1.90 1.90

Souvenir Sheet

Independence, 20th Anniv. — A159

2011, Oct. 1   *Perf. 14*
387 A159   100s multi   6.50 6.50

Commonwealth of Independent States,
20th Anniv. — A160

2011, Oct. 8   *Perf. 14x14¼*
388 A160   42s multi   3.00 3.00

Mushrooms
A161

Designs: 16s, Agaricus. 28s, Pleurotus. 42s, Marasmius oreades. 72s, Lycoperdon.

2011, Nov. 12   **Litho.**   *Perf. 14¼x14*
389-392 A161   Set of 4   9.50 9.50

Musical
Instruments
A162

Designs: 16s, Surnai (wind instrument). 24s, Dobulbas (drum). 48s, Kyl kayak (stringed instrument with bow). 60s, Ooz komuz (mouth harp).

2011, Nov. 26
393-396 A162   Set of 4   8.75 8.75

Airships
A163

Designs: 12s, Dirigible of Henri Giffard. 28s, LZ-127 Graf Zeppelin. 45s, AU-30 Argus dirigible. 48s, Dirigible of the future.

2011, Dec. 17   *Perf. 14x14¼*
397-400 A163   Set of 4   8.25 8.25

New Year
2012 (Year of
the Dragon)
A164

2012, Jan. 14   *Perf. 13¼*
401 A164   36s multi   2.25 2.25
     Printed in sheets of 4.

Miniature Sheet

Oriental Lunar Calendar
Animals — A165

No. 402: a, Dog. b, Boar. c, Rat. d, Ox. e, Rooster. f, Tiger. g, Monkey. h, Rabbit. i, Sheep. j, Horse. k, Snake. l, Dragon.

2012, Jan. 14   *Perf. 13¾x13½*
402 A165   25s Sheet of 12, #a-   18.00 18.00
     l, + central label

Women's
Headdresses
A166

Various headdresses: 16s, 28s, 45s, 60s.

2012, Feb. 25   *Perf. 13*
403-406 A166   Set of 4   9.00 9.00

Helianthus
A167

2012, Mar. 29   *Perf. 14¼x14*
407 A167   42s multi   2.75 2.75

Bolot Beishenaliev
(1937-2002),
Actor — A168

Gapar Aitiev
(1912-84),
Artist — A169

2012, Apr. 28   **Litho.**
408 A168   23s multi   1.40 1.40
409 A169   49s multi   3.00 3.00

Miniature Sheet

Inventions — A170

No. 410: a, 21s, Writing. b, 23s, Bread. c, 45s, Wheel. d, 49s, Money.

2012, June 2   *Perf. 14*
410 A170   Sheet of 4, #a-d   8.75 8.75
    2012 World Stamp Championship, Jakarta, Indonesia.

United Nations Environment Program,
40th Anniv. — A171

2012, June 5   *Perf. 14x14¼*
411 A171   45s multi   3.00 3.00

National
Games
A172

2012, Aug. 4   **Litho.**   *Perf. 14x14¼*
412 A172   28s multi   1.75 1.75

Battle of Borodino, Bicent. — A173

No. 413: a, 12s, Battlefield Monument, Borodino. b, 45s, Triumphal Arch, Moscow.

2012, Aug. 25   **Perf. 14¼x14**
413 A173   Pair, #a-b   3.50   3.50

Snow Leopard A174

Designs: 17s, Leopard. 20s, Leopard, diff. 23s, Head of leopard. 30s, Three leopards.

2012, Sept. 15   **Perf. 14x14¼**
414-417 A174   Set of 4   5.75   5.75

Man and Woman in Traditional Costumes and Emblem of Regional Communications Commonwealth A175

2012, Oct. 20   **Perf. 14¼x14**
418 A175   30s multi   2.00   2.00

Inscribed Tablets — A176

No. 419 — Tablet from: a, 35s, 8th cent. b, 40s, 9th cent.

2012, Nov. 3
419 A176   Horiz. pair, #a-b   4.75   4.75

Gen. Ysakbek Monuev (1902-49) — A177

Ormon Khan (1792-1854), Kyrgyz Tribal Leader — A178

2012, Nov. 24
420 A177   35s multi   2.25   2.25
421 A178   40s multi   2.50   2.50

Prehistoric Animals A179

Designs: 23s, Kyrgyzsaurus. 30s, Xenacanthidae. 40s, Longisquama. 52s, Mammoth.

2012, Dec. 8   **Perf. 14x14¼**
422-425 A179   Set of 4   9.50   9.50

Souvenir Sheet

Mayan Calendar — A180

No. 426: a, 29s, Mayan calendar. b, 52s, Mayan pyramid.

2012, Dec. 21   **Perf. 14**
426 A180   Sheet of 2, #a-b   5.00   5.00

New Year 2013 (Year of the Snake) A181

2013, Feb. 16   **Perf. 14x14¼**
427 A181   30s multi   1.90   1.90

2012 Universal Postal Congress International Stamp Exhibition, Doha, Qatar — A182

No. 428: a, 28s, Gold medal diploma awarded to Kyrgyzstan. b, 43s, Exhibition emblem.

2013, Feb. 23
428 A182   Pair, #a-b   4.25   4.25
No. 428 was printed in sheets containing three pairs.

Miniature Sheet

Walnuts — A183

No. 429: a, 17s, Cluster of walnuts on tree branch. b, 20s, Walnuts with opened husks. c, 23s, Walnut in husk, walnuts in shell, opened walnut, jar of product containing walnuts. d, 29s, Walnut in shell, kernels. e, 35s, Basket of walnuts. f, 40s, Walnut grove, mountains.

2013, Mar. 9
429 A183   Sheet of 6, #a-f   10.00   10.00

National Horse Games A184

2013, Mar. 23
430 A184   35s multi   2.25   2.25

Spaceflight of Valentina Tereshkova, First Woman in Space, 50th Anniv. A185

2013, Apr. 13
431 A185   50s multi   3.25   3.25

Introduction of Som Currency, 20th Anniv. A186

2013, Apr. 27
432 A186   28s multi   1.75   1.75

Marco Polo Argali (Mountain Sheep) A187

Design: 29s, Head of ram. 35s, Adult and juveniles grazing. 40s, Ram on mountain ledge. 52s, Ram in winter.

2013, May 18
433-436 A187   Set of 4   11.00   11.00
436a   Souvenir sheet of 4, #433-436   11.00   11.00

Kozhomkul (1888-1955), Wrestler — A188

2013, June 8
437 A188   30s multi   2.10   2.10

Sulayman Mountain A189

2013, June 22
438 A189   45s multi   3.25   3.25

Miniature Sheet

Worldwide Fund for Nature (WWF) — A190

No. 439 — Snow leopard: a, 29s, Resting on rock. b, 35s, Leaping. c, 43s, Standing on rock. d, 52s, Kittens.

2013, July 13
439 A190   Sheet of 4, #a-d   10.50   10.50
Intl. Forum on Snow Leopard Conservation, Bishkek.

Regional Communications Commonwealth Emblem, Train, Airplane, Satellite Dish, Cover and Tablet — A191

2013, Aug. 17   **Litho.**   **Perf. 14x14¼**
440 A191   36s multi   1.90   1.90

Miniature Sheet

13th Shanghai Cooperation Organization Council of Heads of State Session, Bishkek — A192

No. 441 — Emblems or coat of arms of: a, 12s, Kazakhstan. b, 17s, Kyrgyzstan. c, 20s, People's Republic of China. d, 23s, Russia. e, 30s, Tajikistan. f, 35s, Uzbekistan.

Litho. With Foil Application
2013, Sept. 13   **Perf. 13½x13¼**
441 A192   Sheet of 6, #a-f   6.50   6.50

Nasirdin Isanov (1943-91), First Prime Minister of Kyrgyzstan A193

2013, Oct. 1   **Litho.**   **Perf. 14x14¼**
442 A193   17s multi   1.10   1.10

Kyrgyz Khaganate, 1170th
Anniv. — A194

No. 443: a, 20s, Kyrgyz soldier wearing helmet, map of Khaganate. b, 23s, Mounted
soldiers. c, 30s, Mounted soildier and
petroglyphs.

2013, Nov. 16   Litho.   Perf. 14¼x14
443 A194   Horiz. strip of 3, #a-c 4.25 4.25
Printed in sheets of 6 containing two of each
stamp.

Medicinal
Plants — A195

Designs: 20s, Capparis spinosa. 30s, Aconi-
tum leucostomum. 35s, Hippophae rhamnoides. 52s, Glycyrrhiza glabra.

2013, Dec. 14   Litho.   Perf. 14¼x14
444-447 A195   Set of 4   9.25 9.25

New Year
2014 (Year
of the
Horse)
A196

2014, Feb. 16   Litho.   Perf. 14x14¼
448 A196 35s multi   2.25 2.25

2014
Winter
Olympics,
Sochi,
Russia
A197

Designs: 12s, Speed skating. 21s, Cross-
country skiing. 52s, Freestyle skiing. 74s,
Bobsledding.

2014, Feb. 22   Litho.   Perf. 14x14¼
449-452 A197   Set of 4   8.25 8.25

Jousting
Horsemen
A198

2014, Mar. 22   Litho.   Perf. 14x14¼
453 A198 30s multi   1.90 1.90

Children on
Sleds
A200

2014, May 10   Litho.   Perf. 14x14¼
459 A200 40s multi   2.25 2.25

Medicinal
Plants — A201

Designs: 20s, Tussilago farfara. 23s, Ferula
foetida. 35s, Ziziphora clinopodioides. 40s,
Helichrysum maracandicum.

2014, May 31   Litho.   Perf. 12¼x12
460-463 A201   Set of 4   7.00 7.00

Worldwide
Fund for
Nature
(WWF)
A202

Aegypius monachus: 29s, Head. 35s, In
flight. 62s, Adult and chick in nest. 74s, On
ground.

2014, June 21   Litho.   Perf. 14x14¼
464-467 A202   Set of 4   11.00 11.00
467a   Block of 4, #464-467   11.00 11.00

Miniature Sheet

Soccer Players — A203

No. 468: a, 29s, Five players. b, 35s, Three
players. c, 40s, Two players. d, 52s, Four
players.

2014, July 1   Litho.   Perf. 12x12¼
468 A203   Sheet of 4, #a-d   9.00 9.00

Dooronbek Sadyrbaev (1939-2008),
Film Director, and Medal — A204

2014, July 26   Litho.   Perf. 14x14¼
469 A204 35s multi   1.90 1.90

Carpets
A205

UNESCO emblem and: 35s, Ala-kiyiz. 45s,
Shyrdak.

2014, Aug. 16   Litho.   Perf. 12x12¼
470-471 A205   Set of 2   4.75 4.75
Nos. 470-471 each were printed in sheets of
5 + label.

Communist
Leaders — A206

Designs: 20s, Imanaly Aidarbekov (1884-
1938). 29s, Abdykerim Sydykov (1889-1938).
35s, Abdykadyr Orozbekov (1889-1938).

2014, Aug. 31   Litho.   Perf. 14¼x14
472-474 A206   Set of 3   4.75 4.75

Souvenir Sheet

Kyrgyz State Technical University, 60th
Anniv. — A207

No. 475: a, 52s, University building and
statue. b, 62s, University building, no statue.

2014, Sept. 18   Litho.   Perf. 12x12¼
475 A207   Sheet of 2, #a-b   6.75 6.75

Souvenir Sheet

International Telecommunication Union
Plenipotentiary Conference, Busan,
South Korea — A208

2014, Oct. 11   Litho.   Perf. 12x12¼
476 A208 30s multi   1.90 1.90

Toktogul   Suimenkul
Satylganov   Chokmorov
(1864-1933),   (1939-92), Film
Poet — A209   Actor — A210

2014, Nov. 1   Litho.   Perf. 12¼x12
477 A209 35s multi   2.00 2.00
478 A210 40s multi   2.25 2.25

Kyrgyz Flag and People — A211

2014, Dec. 6   Litho.   Perf. 13x13½
479 A211 30s multi   1.90 1.90

Souvenir Sheet

Cotton — A212

No. 480: a, 35s, Cotton bolls and leaves. b,
52s, Cotton bolls.

2014, Dec. 13   Litho.   Perf. 12x12¼
480 A212   Sheet of 2, #a-b   4.75 4.75

Endangered Animals — A213

Designs: 23s, Ursus arctos. 30s,
Otocolobus manul. 40s, Cuon alpinus. 52s,
Lynx lynx linnaeus.

2014, Dec. 20   Litho.   Perf. 14x14¼
481-484 A213   Set of 4   7.75 7.75

SEMI-POSTAL STAMPS

Natl. Epic
Poem, Manas,
Millennium
SP1

SP2

Designs: 10t+5t, Woman with bird in hand.
20t+10t, Bird on man's wrist. No. B3, Women
watching as baby held up. No. B4, Woman
with spear, leading horse. 40t+15t, Warrior
looking at dead dragon. No. B6, Warrior on
horse holding axe. No. B7, Man wearing tall
hat on horseback. No. B8, Warrior with sword
on horseback.
No. B9, Man in red cradling fallen warrior.
No. B10, Man in black seated in desert,
tornado.

Perf. 12, Imperf

1995, June 16   Litho.

B1	SP1	10t +5t blue & bis	.35 .35
B2	SP1	20t +10t blue & bis	.35 .35
B3	SP1	30t +10t blue & bis	.35 .35
B4	SP1	30t +10t blue & bis	.35 .35
B5	SP1	40t +15t blue & bis	.35 .35
B6	SP1	50t +15t blue & bis	.35 .35
B7	SP1	50t +15t blue & bis	.35 .35
B8	SP1	50t +15t blue & bis	.35 .35
a.		Sheet of 8, #B1-B8 + label	3.75 3.75

Souvenir Sheets

B9	SP2	2s +50t multi	2.00 2.00
B10	SP2	2s +50t multi	2.00 2.00

1996 Summer Olympic Games, Atlanta SP3

Designs: 100t+20t, Equestrian events. 140t+30t, Boxing. 150t+30t, Archery. 300t+50t, Judo, hot air balloon, sailing, water skiing.

1996, July 10   Litho.   Perf. 12½x12

B11	SP3	100t +20t multi	.30 .30
B12	SP3	140t +30t multi	.60 .60
B13	SP3	150t +30t multi	.80 .80
B14	SP3	300t +50t multi	1.25 1.25
		Nos. B11-B14 (4)	2.95 2.95

Town of Osh, 3000th Anniv. — SP4

No. B15. a, Globe, mountains, mosque, "Osh" and "3000." b, Mosque with three arches, mountains (green panel at UR). c, Solomon's Throne (mosque on mountain). d, Mausoleum of Asaf ibn Burkiya (denomination at LL).
Illustration reduced.

2000, Feb. 19   Litho.   Perf. 13½

B15	SP4	6s +25t Sheet of 4, #a-d	3.50 3.50

Exists imperf. Value $5.

Kurmanzhan Datka, 190th Anniv. of Birth — SP5

2001, Oct. 13   Litho.   Perf. 14x14¼

B16	SP5	10s +70t ind & gray	1.50 1.50

KYRGYZ EXPRESS POST

On May 21, 2013, Kyrgyz Express Post was declared a designated postal operator by the Universal Postal Union, marking the first time the UPU has had two designated postal operators in one country. Kyrgyz Express Post company was created in March 2012 and granted a license from the Kyrgyzstan Ministry of Transport and Communications on Dec. 7, 2012 to offer all types of postal services to customers and to compete with the state corporation Kyrgyz Pochtasy, which has post offices across the country. At the time Kyrgyz Express Post issued its first stamps, it had two post offices and a philatelic bureau in Bishkek.

A1

Methods of Postal Conveyance — A2

Designs: 500s, Jet airplane. No. 2: a, 25s, Post rider. b, 50s, Locomotive. c, 250s, Mail van. 700s, Dove carrying letter, Universal Postal Union emblem.

2014, Nov. 18   Litho.   Perf. 14x14½

1	A1	500s multi	24.00 24.00
2	A1	Sheet of 4, #1, 2a-2c	42.50 42.50

Souvenir Sheet of 1 + 8 Labels
Perf. 13 Syncopated

3	A2	700s multi	37.50 37.50

No. 1 was printed in panes of 4.

Wild Animals — A3

Designs: 250s, Panthera uncia. No. 5: a, 15s, Falco cherrug. b, 25s, Bos grunniens. c, 125s, Capra sibirica alaiana.

2014, Nov. 19   Litho.   Perf. 14x14¾

4	A3	250s multi	13.00 13.00
5	A3	Sheet of 4, #4, 5a-5c	22.00 22.00

No. 4 was printed in sheets of 4.

LABUAN

lə-ˈbü-ən

LOCATION — An island in the East Indies, about six miles off the northwest coast of Borneo.
GOVT. — A British possession, administered as a part of the North Borneo Colony
AREA — 35 sq. mi.
POP. — 8,963 (estimated)
CAPITAL — Victoria

The stamps of Labuan were replaced by those of Straits Settlements in 1906.

100 Cents = 1 Dollar

Watermark

Wmk. 46 — C A over Crown

Queen Victoria — A1

On Nos. 1, 2, 3, 4 and 11 the watermark is 32mm high. It is always placed sideways and extends over two stamps.

1879, May   Engr.   Wmk. 46   Perf. 14

1	A1	2c green	1,625. 975.00
2	A1	6c orange	240.00 225.00
3	A1	12c carmine	1,925. 850.00
4	A1	16c blue	77.50 200.00
		Nos. 1-4 (4)	3,867. 2,250.

See Nos. 5-10, 16-24, 33-39, 42-48. For surcharges see Nos. 12-15, 25, 31, 40-41.

1880-82   Wmk. 1

5	A1	2c green	30.00 50.00
6	A1	6c orange	145.00 160.00
7	A1	8c carmine ('82)	135.00 135.00
8	A1	10c yel brown	205.00 100.00
9	A1	12c carmine	330.00 400.00
10	A1	16c blue ('81)	100.00 125.00
		Nos. 5-10 (6)	945.00 970.00

A2

A3

1880-83   Wmk. 46

11	A2	6c on 16c blue (with additional "6" across original value) (R)	4,200. 1,325.

   Wmk. 1

12	A2	8c on 12c carmine	1,825. 1,000.
a.		Original value not obliterated	3,600. 2,000.
b.		Additional surcharge "8" across original value	2,300. 1,450.
c.		"8" inverted	2,100. 1,200.
d.		As "a," "8" inverted	4,200. —
13	A3	8c on 12c car ('81)	475.00 525.00
14	A3a	8c on 12c car ('81)	160.00 170.00
a.		"Eighr"	22,500.
b.		Inverted surcharge	16,000.
c.		Double surcharge	2,900. 2,400.
15	A4	$1 on 16c blue (R) ('83)	4,800.

On No. 12 the original value is obliterated by a pen mark in either black or red.

A3a

A4

Types of 1879 Issue
1883-86   Wmk. 2

16	A1	2c green	30.00 50.00
a.		Horiz. pair, imperf. btwn.	18,500.
17	A1	2c rose red ('85)	4.25 20.00
18	A1	8c carmine	325.00 120.00
19	A1	8c dk violet ('85)	50.00 9.25
20	A1	10c yellow brn	57.50 57.50
21	A1	10c black brn ('86)	35.00 70.00
22	A1	16c blue	115.00 215.00
23	A1	16c gray blue ('86)	175.00
24	A1	40c ocher	30.00 145.00
		Nos. 16-24 (9)	821.75 686.75

Nos. 1-10, 16-24 are in sheets of 10. For surcharges see Nos. 26-30, 32.

A5

A6

A7

1885   Wmk. 1

25	A5	2c on 16c blue	1,150. 1,100.

   Wmk. 2

26	A5	2c on 8c car	275.00 550.00
a.		Double surcharge	
27	A6	2c on 16c blue	135.00 200.00
a.		Double surcharge	7,500.
28	A7	2c on 8c car	80.00 145.00

A8

1891   Black or Red Surcharge

29	A8	6c on 8c violet	16.50 15.00
a.		6c on 8c dark violet	210.00 190.00
b.		Double surcharge	390.00 —
c.		As "a," "Cents" omitted	550.00 550.00
d.		Inverted surcharge	90.00 85.00
e.		Dbl. surch., one inverted	1,100. —
f.		Dbl. surch., both inverted	1,100. —
g.		"6" omitted	625.00
h.		Pair, one without surcharge	2,000. 2,000.
30	A8	6c on 8c dk vio (R)	1,325. 825.00
a.		Inverted surcharge	1,850. 925.00

   Wmk. 46

31	A8	6c on 16c blue	2,800. 2,300.
a.		Inverted surcharge	15,500. 8,250.

   Wmk. 2

32	A8	6c on 40c ocher	14,000. 5,750.
a.		Inverted surcharge	12,000. 9,000.

Types of 1879 Issue

			Engr.	Unwmk.
1892				
33	A1	2c rose	7.25	4.25
34	A1	6c yellow green	13.50	5.75
35	A1	8c violet	12.50	18.50
36	A1	10c brown	30.00	9.50
37	A1	12c deep ultra	14.50	8.00
38	A1	16c gray	22.00	45.00
39	A1	40c ocher	27.50	45.00
		Nos. 33-39 (7)	127.25	136.00

The 2c, 8c and 10c are in sheets of 30; others in sheets of 10.

Nos. 39 and 38 Surcharged

1893

40	A1	2c on 40c ocher	200.00 110.00
a.		Inverted surcharge	500.00 675.00
41	A1	6c on 16c gray	450.00 180.00
a.		Inverted surcharge	675.00 350.00
b.		Surcharge sideways	675.00 375.00
c.		"Six" omitted	— —
d.		"Cents" omitted	— —
e.		Handstamped "Six Cents"	2,275.

Surcharges on Nos. 40-41 each exist in 10 types. Counterfeits exist.
No. 41e was handstamped on examples of No. 41 on which the surcharge failed to print or was printed partially or completely albino.

From Jan. 1, 1890, to Jan. 1, 1906, Labuan was administered by the British North Borneo Co. Late in that period, unused remainders of Nos. 42-83, 53a, 63a, 64a, 65a, 66a, 68a, 85-86, 96-118, 103a, 107a, J1-J9, J3a and J6a were canceled to order by bars forming an oval. Values for these stamps used are for those with this form of cancellation, unless described as postally used, which are for stamps with dated town cancellations. Nos. 63b, 64b, 65b, 104a, J6a, and possibly others, only exist c.t.o.

For detailed listings of Labuan, see the *Scott Classic Specialized Catalogue.*

Types of 1879 Issue

			Litho.
1894, Apr.			
42	A1	2c bright rose	2.00	.65
43	A1	6c yellow green	27.50	.65
a.		Horiz. pair, imperf. btwn.	11,250.
44	A1	8c bright violet	27.00	.65
45	A1	10c brown	60.00	.65
46	A1	12c light ultra	37.50	.80
47	A1	16c gray	40.00	.65
48	A1	40c orange	60.00	.65
		Nos. 42-48 (7)	254.00	4.70

Counterfeits exist.

Dyak Chieftain — A9

Malayan Sambar — A10

Sago Palm A11

Argus Pheasant A12

Arms of North Borneo — A13

Dhow — A14

Saltwater Crocodile — A15

Mt. Kinabalu — A16

Arms of North Borneo — A17

Perf. 12 to 16 and Compound

				Engr.
1894				
49	A9	1c lilac & black	2.00	.65
a.		Vert. pair, imperf. between	1,300.	575.00
50	A10	2c blue & black	3.00	.65
a.		Imperf., pair	725.00
51	A11	3c bister & black	4.50	.65
52	A12	5c green & black	38.50	1.10
a.		Horiz. pair, imperf. between	1,800.
53	A13	6c brn red & blk	3.00	.65
a.		Imperf., pair	725.00	350.00
54	A14	8c rose & black	10.00	.65
55	A15	12c orange & black	27.50	.65
56	A16	18c ol brn & blk	26.50	.65
b.		Vert. pair, imperf. between		2,500.
57	A17	24c lilac & blue	20.00	1.30
		Nos. 49-57 (9)	135.00	6.95

A18

				Perf. 14
1895, June		Litho.		
58	A18	4c on $1 red	3.00	.50
59	A18	10c on $1 red	11.00	.50
60	A18	20c on $1 red	50.00	.50
61	A18	30c on $1 red	52.50	1.50
62	A18	40c on $1 red	52.50	1.50
		Nos. 58-62 (5)	169.00	4.50

A19

A20

A21

1896				
63	A19	25c blue green	40.00	.80
a.		Imperf., pair		72.50
b.		Without overprint	35.00	2.00
c.		As "b," imperf, pair	60.00
64	A20	50c claret	42.50	.80
a.		Imperf., pair		72.50
b.		Without overprint	32.50	2.00
c.		As "b," imperf, pair	52.50
65	A21	$1 dark blue	82.50	1.25
a.		Imperf., pair		72.50
b.		Without overprint	50.00	3.00
c.		As "b," imperf, pair	60.00
		Nos. 63-65 (3)	165.00	2.85

For surcharges and overprint see Nos. 93-95, 116-118, 120.

Nos. 49-54 Overprinted

Dyak Chieftain A22

Malayan Sambar A23

1896		**Perf. 12 to 15 and Compound**		
66	A9	1c lilac & black	24.00	1.75
a.		"JEBILEE"	1,450.	360.00
b.		"JUBILE"	3,000.
c.		Orange overprint	325.00	24.00
e.		Double overprint	450.00	—
67	A10	2c blue & black	52.50	1.75
a.		Vert. pair, imperf. btwn.	1,525.
b.		"JUBILE"	1,850.	—
c.		"JUBILE"	3,500.
d.		Vert. strip of 3, imperf between	8,000.
68	A11	3c bister & black	50.00	1.50
a.		"JEBILEE"	2,250.	850.00
b.		"JUBILE"		—
g.		Double overprint	925.00	—
h.		Triple overprint	775.00	—
69	A12	5c green & black	72.50	1.50
a.		Double overprint	975.00
70	A13	6c brown red & blk	47.50	1.00
a.		Double overprint	975.00	—
b.		"JUBILE"	3,600.	—
71	A14	8c rose & black	57.50	1.00
a.		Double overprint		3,000.
		Nos. 66-71 (6)	304.00	8.50

Cession of Labuan to Great Britain, 50th anniv.

Sago Palm A24

Argus Pheasant A25

A26

Dhow — A27

Saltwater Crocodile — A28

Mt. Kinabalu "Postal Revenue" — A29

Coat of Arms — A30

Perf. 13½ to 16 and Compound

				Engr.
1897-1900				
72	A22	1c lilac & black	6.75	.60
72A	A22	1c red brn & blk	3.75	.80
73	A23	2c blue & black	32.50	.90
a.		Vert. pair, imperf between		1,125.
b.		Horiz. pair, imperf between		1,550.
74	A23	2c grn & blk ('00)	4.50	.35
a.		Horiz. pair, imperf between	3,100.	1,550.
75	A24	3c bister & blk	10.00	.60
a.		Vert. pair, imperf between	1,325.	675.00
76	A25	5c green & blk	62.50	.85
77	A25	5c lt bl & blk ('00)	27.50	.80
78	A26	6c brn red & blk	14.50	.60
a.		Vert. pair, imperf between		850.00
79	A27	8c red & black	25.00	
80	A28	12c red & black	40.00	2.50
81	A29	18c ol bis & blk	125.00	2.40
a.		Vert. pair, imperf between		3,750.
82	A30	24c gr lilac & bl	14.50	.60
		Nos. 72-82 (12)	366.50	11.00

"Postage & Revenue" — A31

"Postage & Revenue" — A32

Perf. 13½ to 16 and Compound

1897				
83	A31	18c bister & black	95.00	2.40
84a	A32	24c ocher & blue	—	4.75

"Postage & Revenue" — A33

"Postage & Revenue" — A34

1898				
85	A33	12c red & black	—	4.00
86a	A34	18c bister & black	42.50	3.75

No. 85a cto is always perf. 13½x14.
For surcharges see Nos. 90-91, 113-114.

Regular Issue Surcharged in Black

1899				
87	A25	4c on 5c grn & blk	55.00	30.00
88	A26	4c on 6c brn red & blk	30.00	22.50
89	A27	4c on 8c red & blk	72.50	52.50
90	A33	4c on 12c red & blk	60.00	42.50
91	A34	4c on 18c bis & blk	40.00	21.50
a.		Double surcharge	575.00	675.00
92a	A32	4c on 24c lil & bl	32.50	36.00
93	A19	4c on 25c blue grn	7.25	8.00
94	A20	4c on 50c claret	8.75	8.00
95	A21	4c on $1 dk blue	8.75	8.00
		Nos. 87-95 (9)	314.75	229.00

Orangutan A35

Sun Bear A36

Railroad Train — A37

Perf. 12 to 16 and Compound

1899-1901				
96	A35	4c yel brown & blk	10.00	.75
a.		Vert. pair, imperf. btwn.	1,350.
97a	A35	4c car & blk ('00)	6.00	.60
98	A36	10c gray vio & dk brn ('01)	60.00	.75
99	A37	16c org brn & grn (G) ('01)	60.00	3.00
		Nos. 96-99 (4)	136.00	5.10

Crown — A38

Perf. 12½ to 16 and Compound

				Engr.
1902-03				
99A	A38	1c vio & black	6.75	.60
100	A38	2c green & blk	5.00	.35
100A	A38	3c sepia & blk	4.00	.35
101	A38	4c car & black	4.00	.35

102	A38	8c org & black	15.00	.80
103	A38	10c sl blue & brn	4.00	.35
a.		Vert. pair, imperf. between		925.00
104	A38	12c yel & black	13.50	.35
a.		Vert. strip of 3, imperf. horiz.		4,000.
105	A38	16c org brn & grn	5.75	.35
a.		Vert. pair, imperf. between	—	2,300.
106	A38	18c bis brn & blk	4.00	.35
107	A38	25c grnsh bl & grn	9.00	.60
a.		25c greenish blue & black		625.00
108	A38	50c gray lil & vio	12.00	2.75
109	A38	$1 org & red brn	10.00	2.75
		Nos. 99A-109 (12)	93.00	9.95

There are 3 known examples of No. 104a, all cto. A 16c vertical pair, imperf between has been reported. The editors would like to receive evidence of the existence of this item.

Regular Issue of 1896-97 Surcharged in Black

1904

110	A25	4c on 5c green & blk	57.50	17.00
111	A26	4c on 6c brown red & black	14.50	17.00
112	A27	4c on 8c red & blk	30.00	17.00
113	A33	4c on 12c red & blk	40.00	17.00
114	A34	4c on 18c bis & blk	30.00	17.00
115	A32	4c on 24c brn lil & bl	19.25	17.00
116	A19	4c on 25c blue green	10.00	17.00
117	A20	4c on 50c claret	10.00	17.00
a.		Double surcharge	400.00	
118	A21	4c on $1 dark blue	12.50	17.00
		Nos. 110-118 (9)	223.75	153.00

Stamps of North Borneo, 1893, and Labuan No. 65a Overprinted in Black

a

b

c

1905

119	A30(a)	25c slate blue	1,325.	1,100.
120	A21(c)	$1 blue		1,050.
121	A33(b)	$2 gray green	4,000.	
122	A34(c)	$5 red violet	7,250.	1,850.
a.		$5 dull purple	7,000.	1,800.
123	A35(c)	$10 brown	55,000.	14,500.

POSTAGE DUE STAMPS

Regular Issues Overprinted

1901		Unwmk.	Perf. 14	
J1	A23	2c grn & blk	25.00	1.10
a.		Double overprint	425.00	
J2	A24	3c bis & blk	32.50	1.00
J3b	A35	4c car & black	60.00	.60
a.		Double overprint		875.00
J4	A25	5c lt blue & blk	52.50	1.50
J5	A26	6c brn red & blk	50.00	1.10
J6	A27	8c red & black	110.00	3.00
a.		Center inverted, ovpt. reading down		12,000.
J7	A33	12c red & black	170.00	6.75
a.		Overprint reading down		1,125.
J8	A34	18c ol bis & blk	40.00	1.75
J9	A32	24c brn lil & bl	77.50	7.75
		Nos. J1-J9 (9)	617.50	24.55

See note after No. 41.

The stamps of Labuan were superseded by those of Straits Settlements in 1906.

LAGOS

'lā-ˌgäs

LOCATION — West Africa, bordering on the former Southern Nigeria Colony
GOVT. — British Crown Colony and Protectorate
AREA — 3,460 sq. mi. (approx.)
POP. — 1,500,000 (1901)
CAPITAL — Lagos

This territory was purchased by the British in 1861 and placed under the Governor of Sierra Leone. In 1874 it was detached and formed part of the Gold Coast Colony until 1886 when the Protectorate of Lagos was established. In 1899 Lagos and the territories of the Royal Niger Company were surrendered to the Crown of Great Britain and formed into the Northern and Southern Nigeria Protectorates. In 1906 Lagos and Southern Nigeria were united to form the Colony and Protectorate of Southern Nigeria.

12 Pence = 1 Shilling

Queen Victoria — A1

1874-75		Typo.	Wmk. 1	Perf. 12½
1	A1	1p lilac	80.00	50.00
2	A1	2p blue	80.00	42.50
3	A1	3p red brown ('75)	130.00	42.50
4	A1	4p rose	145.00	50.00
5	A1	6p blue green	150.00	17.50
6	A1	1sh orange ('75)	425.00	70.00
a.		Value 15½mm instead of 16½mm long	700.00	160.00
		Nos. 1-6 (6)	1,010.	272.50

1876				Perf. 14
7	A1	1p lilac	50.00	21.00
8	A1	2p blue	80.00	15.00
9	A1	3p red brown	120.00	30.00
10	A1	4p rose	225.00	12.50
11	A1	6p green	130.00	7.00
12	A1	1sh orange	950.00	95.00
		Nos. 7-12 (6)	1,555.	180.50

The 4p exists with watermark sideways.

1882-1902				Wmk. 2
13	A1	½p green ('86)	2.25	.95
14	A1	1p lilac	32.50	25.00
15	A1	1p car rose	2.25	.95
16	A1	2p blue	200.00	8.50
17	A1	2p gray	100.00	9.50
18	A1	2p lil & bl ('87)	8.50	3.25
19	A1	2½p ultra ('91)	8.00	2.00
a.		2½p blue	90.00	57.50
20	A1	3p orange brn	30.00	8.00
21	A1	3p lil & brn org ('91)	3.00	3.75
22	A1	4p rose	225.00	14.00
23	A1	4p violet	160.00	9.50
24	A1	4p lil & blk ('87)	2.50	2.00
25	A1	5p lil & grn ('94)	3.00	12.50
26	A1	6p olive green	9.00	55.00
27	A1	6p lil & red vio ('87)	5.50	3.50
28	A1	6p lilac & car rose ('02)	5.75	13.50
29	A1	7½p lilac & car rose ('94)	4.50	35.00

30	A1	10p lil & yel ('94)	4.50	15.00
31	A1	1sh org ('85)	17.00	22.50
32	A1	1sh yel grn & blk ('87)	6.50	32.50
33	A1	2sh6p ol brn ('86)	375.00	325.00
34	A1	2sh6p green & car rose ('87)	27.50	92.50
35	A1	5sh blue ('86)	750.00	550.00
36	A1	5sh brn & ultra ('87)	47.50	175.00
37	A1	10sh brn vio ('86)	2,750.	2,000.
38	A1	10sh grn & brn ('87)	120.00	275.00

Excellent forgeries exist of Nos. 33, 35 and 37 on paper with genuine watermark.

No. 24 Surcharged in Black

1893				
39	A1	½p on 4p lilac & blk	10.00	3.00
a.		Double surcharge	70.00	62.50
b.		Triple surcharge	175.00	
c.		½p on 2p lilac & blue (#18)		27,500.

Four settings of surcharge.
Only one used example is known of No. 39c. The two unused examples are in museums.

King Edward VII — A3

1904, Jan. 22				
40	A3	½p grn & bl grn	2.50	6.25
41	A3	1p vio & blk, red	1.25	.25
42	A3	2p violet & ultra	6.75	7.00
43	A3	2½p vio & ultra, bl	1.50	1.75
44	A3	3p vio & org brn	3.25	2.00
45	A3	6p vio & red vio	40.00	11.50
46	A3	1sh green & blk	40.00	47.50
47	A3	2sh6p grn & car rose	160.00	325.00
48	A3	5sh grn & ultra	150.00	350.00
49	A3	10sh green & brn	350.00	975.00
		Nos. 40-49 (10)	755.25	1,726.

1904-05				Wmk. 3
Ordinary or Chalky Paper				
50	A3	½p grn & bl grn	14.50	3.00
51a	A3	1p vio & blk, red	1.75	.25
52	A3	2p violet & ultra	4.50	3.50
53a	A3	2½p vio & ultra, bl	2.00	18.50
54	A3	3p vio & org brn	4.00	1.50
55a	A3	6p vio & red vio	5.00	1.75
56	A3	1sh green & blk	20.00	27.50
57	A3	2sh6p grn & car rose	27.50	75.00
58	A3	5sh grn & ultra	27.50	110.00
59	A3	10sh green & brn	100.00	275.00
		Nos. 50-59 (10)	206.75	516.00

See *Scott Classic Specialized Catalogue of Stamps & Covers* for detailed listings of ordinary and chalky paper varieties.

The stamps of Lagos were superseded by those of Southern Nigeria.

LAOS

'laus

LOCATION — In northwestern Indo-China
GOVT. — Republic
AREA — 91,400 sq. mi.
POP. — 5,407,453 (1999 est.)
CAPITAL — Vientiane

Before 1949, Laos was part of the French colony of Indo-China and used its stamps until 1951. The kingdom was

replaced by the Lao Peoples Democratic Republic Dec. 2, 1975.

100 Cents = 1 Piaster
100 Cents = 1 Kip (1955)

Imperforates

Most Laos stamps issued during 1951-75 exist as imperforate proofs in issued and trial colors, and also as proofs in small presentation sheets in issued colors. Many post-1975 issues exist imperforate.

Paper

Most Laos stamps issued before 1976 exist on both white and yellowish papers in approximately equal quantities. Souvenir sheets from this period were printed primarily on yellowish paper. Souvenir sheets printed on white paper are scarce.

Catalogue values for all unused stamps in this country are for Never Hinged items.

Boat on Mekong River — A1

King Sisavang-Vong A2

Laotian Woman A3

Designs: 50c, 60c, 70c, Luang Prabang. 1pi, 2pi, 3pi, 5pi, 10pi, Temple at Vientiane.

1951-52		Unwmk.	Engr.	Perf. 13	
1	A1	10c dk grn & emer		.60	.25
2	A1	20c dk car & car		.60	.25
3	A1	30c ind & dp ultra		2.00	1.25
4	A3	30c ind & pur ('52)		1.00	.30
5	A1	50c dark brown		.50	.50
6	A1	60c red & red org		.50	.50
7	A1	70c ultra & bl grn		1.25	.50
8	A3	80c brt grn & dk bl green ('52)		1.25	.60
9	A1	1pi dk pur & pur		1.25	.50
10	A3	1.10pi dark plum & carmine ('52)		1.25	1.25
11	A2	1.50pi blk brn & vio brown		1.60	1.25
12	A3	1.90pi indigo & dp blue ('52)		1.50	1.25
13	A1	2pi dk grn & gray green		20.00	9.00
14	A1	3pi dk scar & red		2.50	1.50
15	A3	3pi choc & black brown ('52)		1.75	1.50
16	A1	5pi ind & dp ultra		3.25	1.75
17	A1	10pi blk brn & vio brown		4.25	2.00
		Nos. 1-17 (17)		45.05	24.15
		Set, hinged		25.00	

A booklet containing 26 souvenir sheets was issued in 1952 on the anniversary of the first issue of Laos stamps. Each sheet contains a single stamp in the center (Nos. 1-17, C2-C4, J1-J6). Value $300.
See No. 223.

UPU Monument and King Sisavang-
Vong — A4

1952, Dec. 7
18	A4	80c ind, blue & pur	.90	.80
19	A4	1pi dk car, car & org brown	.90	.80
20	A4	1.20pi dk pur, purple & ultra	1.00	.90
21	A4	1.50pi dk grn, bl grn & dk brn	1.25	1.00
22	A4	1.90pi blk brn, vio brn & dk Prus grn	1.50	1.25
		Nos. 18-22,C5-C6 (7)	16.55	14.75

Laos' admission to the UPU, May 13, 1952.

Court of
Love — A5

1953, July 14
23	A5	4.50pi indigo & bl grn	.85	.55
24	A5	6pi gray & dark brn	1.25	.55

Composite of Laotian Temples — A6

1954, Mar. 4
25	A6	2pi indigo & purple	35.00	25.00
26	A6	3pi blk brn & dk red	35.00	25.00
		Nos. 25-26,C13 (3)	255.00	235.00

Accession of King Sisavang-Vong, 50th
anniv.

Buddha Statue and Monks — A7

1956, May 24   Engr.   Perf. 13
27	A7	2k reddish brown	3.00	2.00
28	A7	3k black	3.50	2.50
29	A7	5k chocolate	5.50	3.50
		Nos. 27-29,C20-C21 (5)	72.00	59.00

2500th anniversary of birth of Buddha.

UN Emblem — A8

1956, Dec. 14   Perf. 13½x13
30	A8	1k black	.65	.45
31	A8	2k blue	.90	.70
32	A8	4k bright red	1.25	.95
33	A8	6k purple	1.40	1.10
		Nos. 30-33,C22-C23 (6)	15.20	14.20

Admission of Laos to the UN, 1st anniv.

Khouy Player — A9

Khene
Player — A10

Musical Instrument: 8k, Ranat.

1957, Mar. 25   Unwmk.   Perf. 13
34	A9	2k multicolored	1.75	1.10
35	A10	4k multicolored	2.00	1.25
36	A9	8k org, bl & red brn	2.50	2.00
		Nos. 34-36,C24-C26 (6)	15.50	11.35

See No. 224.

Harvesting Rice — A11

Drying
Rice — A12

1957, July 22   Engr.   Perf. 13
37	A11	3k shown	.90	.60
38	A12	5k shown	1.25	.75
39	A12	16k Winnowing rice	2.00	1.50
40	A11	26k Polishing rice	4.00	2.00
		Nos. 37-40 (4)	8.15	4.85

Elephants — A13

Various Elephants: 30c, 5k, 10k, 13k, vert.

1958, Mar. 17
41	A13	10c multi	1.00	.50
42	A13	20c multi	1.00	.50
43	A13	30c multi	1.00	.50
44	A13	2k multi	1.50	.90
45	A13	5k multi	2.75	1.50
46	A13	10k multi	3.00	2.00
47	A13	13k multi	5.00	2.50
		Nos. 41-47 (7)	15.25	8.40

For surcharge see No. B5.

Globe and Goddess — A14

UNESCO
Building and
Mother with
Children — A15

Designs: 70c, UNESCO building, globe and
mother with children. 1k, UNESCO building
and Eiffel tower.

1958, Nov. 3   Engr.   Perf. 13
48	A14	50c multicolored	.50	.25
49	A15	60c emer, vio & maroon	.65	.25
50	A15	70c ultra, rose red & brn	.65	.25
51	A14	1k ol bis, cl & grnsh bl	1.00	.60
		Nos. 48-51 (4)	2.80	1.35

UNESCO Headquarters in Paris opening,
Nov. 3.

King Sisavang-Vong — A16

1959, Sept. 16   Unwmk.
52	A16	4k rose claret	.35	.35
53	A16	6.50k orange red	.35	.35
54	A16	9k bright pink	.35	.35
55	A16	13k green	.75	.60
		Nos. 52-55 (4)	1.80	1.65

For surcharges see Nos. 112-113, B4.

Dancers
A17

Student and
Torch of
Learning — A18

Education and Fine Arts: 3k, Globe, key of
knowledge and girl student. 5k, Dancers and
temple.

1959, Oct. 1   Engr.   Perf. 13
56	A17	1k vio blk, ol & bl	.50	.30
57	A18	2k maroon & black	.55	.30
58	A17	3k slate grn & vio	.85	.30
59	A18	5k rose vio, yel & brt grn	1.10	.60
		Nos. 56-59 (4)	3.00	1.50

Portal of Wat
Phou,
Pakse — A19

Historic Monuments: 1.50k, That Inghang,
Savannakhet, horiz. 2.50k, Phou Temple,
Pakse, horiz. 7k, That Luang, Vientiane. 11k,
That Luang, Vientiane, horiz. 12.50k, Phousi,
Luang Prabang.

1959, Nov. 2   Unwmk.   Perf. 13
60	A19	50c sepia, grn & org	.25	.25
61	A19	1.50k multi	.35	.25
62	A19	2.50k pur, vio bl & ol	.50	.40
63	A19	7k vio, olive & claret	.75	.50
64	A19	11k brn, car & grn	.90	.75
65	A19	12.50k bl, vio & bister	1.25	.80
		Nos. 60-65 (6)	4.00	2.95

Funeral Urn and
Monks — A20

King Sisavang-
Vong — A21

Designs: 6.50k, Urn under canopy. 9k, Cat-
afalque on 7-headed dragon carriage.

1961, Apr. 29   Engr.   Perf. 13
66	A20	4k black, bis & org	.70	.50
67	A20	6.50k black & bister	.70	.50
68	A20	9k black & bister	.70	.50
69	A21	25k black	3.00	2.00
		Nos. 66-69 (4)	5.10	3.50

King Sisavang-Vong's (1885-1959) funeral,
Apr. 23-29, 1961.

King Savang
Vatthana — A22

1962, Apr. 16   Perf. 13
Portrait in Brown and Carmine
70	A22	1k ultramarine	.25	.25
71	A22	2k lilac rose	.25	.25
72	A22	5k greenish blue	.35	.30
73	A22	10k olive	.90	.40
		Nos. 70-73 (4)	1.75	1.20

Boy and Malaria Eradication Emblem — A23

9k, Girl. 10k, Malaria eradication emblem.

1962, July 19   Engr.
74	A23	4k bluish grn, blk & buff	.60	.25
75	A23	9k lt bl, blk & lt brn	.80	.40
76	A23	10k ol, bis & rose red	1.25	.45
		Nos. 74-76 (3)	2.65	1.10

WHO drive to eradicate malaria.
Nos. 74-76 exist imperf.
An imperf. souvenir sheet on white paper with light blue inscription exists. Value, $300. Three other varieties of this sheet also exist: off white paper with light blue inscription, value, $500; white paper with dark blue inscription, value, $350; and off white paper with dark blue inscription, value, $650.

A24

A25

Designs: 50c, Modern mail service (truck, train, plane). 70c, Globe, stamps, dancer. 1k, Ancient mail service (messenger on elephant). 1.50k, Royal Messenger

1962, Nov. 15   Unwmk.   Perf. 13
77	A24	50c multicolored	.60	.60
78	A24	70c multicolored	.60	.60
79	A25	1k dp claret, grn & blk	1.25	1.25
80	A25	1.50k multicolored	1.00	1.00
		Nos. 77-80 (4)	3.45	3.45

Souvenir sheets exist. One contains the 50c and 70c; the other, the 1k and 1.50k. The sheets exist both perf and imperf in a souvenir booklet of four sheets. Value intact booklet, $200.

Fishermen with Nets — A26

Threshing Rice — A27

Designs: 5k, Plowing and planting in rice paddy. 9k, Woman with infant harvesting rice.

1963, Mar. 21   Perf. 13
81	A26	1k grn, bister & pur	.35	.30
82	A27	4k bister, bl & grn	.45	.35
83	A26	5k grn, bis & indigo	.65	.45
84	A27	9k grn, vio bl & ocher	1.00	.50
a.		Min. sheet of 4, #81-84, imperf.	5.00	5.00
b.		As "a," left panel of No. 83 green instead of brown	100.00	100.00
		Nos. 81-84 (4)	2.45	1.60

FAO "Freedom from Hunger" campaign.
No. 84a exists on yellowish and white papers; No. 84b exists only on yellowish paper.

Queen Khamphouy Handing out Gifts — A28

1963, Oct. 10   Engr.
85	A28	4k brn, dp car & blue	.50	.40
86	A28	6k grn, red, yel & bl	.60	.50
87	A28	10k bl, dp car & dk brn	.90	.65
a.		Miniature sheet of 3, #85-87	4.00	4.00
		Nos. 85-87 (3)	2.00	1.55

Centenary of the International Red Cross.

Man Holding UN Emblem A29

1963, Dec. 10   Unwmk.   Perf. 13
88	A29	4k dk bl, dp org & vio brn	1.50	.80

15th anniv. of the Universal Declaration of Human Rights.
No. 88 also was issued imperf. Value, $15.

Temple of That Luang, Map of Nubia and Ramses II — A30

1964, Mar. 8   Engr.
89	A30	4k multicolored	.40	.40
90	A30	6k multicolored	.60	.60
91	A30	10k multicolored	.75	.75
a.		Miniature sheet of 3, #89-91	3.00	3.00
		Nos. 89-91 (3)	1.75	1.75

UNESCO world campaign to save historic monuments in Nubia. No. 91a sold for 25k.

Ceremonial Chalice A31

Designs: 15k, Buddha. 20k, Soldier leading people through Mekong River Valley. 40k, Royal Palace, Luang Prabang.

1964, July 30   Unwmk.   Perf. 13
92	A31	10k multicolored	.40	.30
93	A31	15k multicolored	.60	.40
94	A31	20k multicolored	.80	.60
95	A31	40k multicolored	1.25	.75
a.		Miniature sheet of 4, #92-95	3.50	3.50
		Nos. 92-95 (4)	3.05	2.05

"Neutral and Constitutional Laos." When the stamps are arranged in a block of four with 40k and 15k in first row and 10k and 20k in second row, the map of Laos appears.
A souvenir booklet containing No. 95a exists. Value, $45.

Prince Vet and Wife Mathie — A32

Scenes from Buddhist Legend of Phra Vet Sandone: 32k, God of the Skies sending his son to earth. 45k, Phaune's daughter with beggar husband. 55k, Beggar cornered by guard and dogs.

1964, Nov. 17   Photo.   Perf. 13x12½
96	A32	10k multicolored	.50	.50
97	A32	32k multicolored	.75	.75
98	A32	45k multicolored	1.00	1.00
99	A32	55k multicolored	1.25	1.25
a.		Miniature sheet of 4	5.00	3.75
		Nos. 96-99 (4)	3.50	3.50

No. 99a contains 4 imperf. stamps similar to Nos. 96-99.
A souvenir booklet containing No. 99a exists. Value, $100.

Lao Women — A33

1964, Dec. 15   Engr.   Perf. 13
100	A33	25k blk, org brn & pale ol	.75	.75
		Nos. 100,C43-C45 (4)	3.45	2.35

Butterflies A34

1965, Mar. 13   Unwmk.   Perf. 13
Size: 36x36mm
101	A34	10k Cethosia biblis	2.25	1.25
102	A34	25k Precis cebrene	4.50	1.75

Size: 48x27mm
103	A34	40k Dysphania militaris	11.50	2.50
		Nos. 101-103,C46 (4)	24.25	8.00

Teacher and School, American Aid — A35

Designs: 25k, Woman at Wattay Airport, French aid, horiz. 45k, Woman bathing child and food basket, Japanese aid. 55k, Musicians broadcasting, British aid, horiz.

1965, Mar. 30   Engr.   Perf. 13
104	A35	25k bl grn, brn & car rose	.45	.30
105	A35	45k ol grn & brn	.95	.50
106	A35	55k brt bl & bister	1.25	.65
107	A35	75k multicolored	1.75	.80
		Nos. 104-107 (4)	4.40	2.25

Issued to publicize foreign aid to Laos.

Hophabang Temple A36

1965, Apr. 23   Unwmk.   Perf. 13
108	A36	10k multicolored	.75	.35

Telewriter, Map of Laos and Globe A37

30k, Communication by satellite & map of Laos. 50k, Globe, map of Laos & radio.

1965, June 15   Engr.   Perf. 13
109	A37	5k vio bl, brn & red lil	.25	.25
110	A37	30k bl, org brn & sl grn	.65	.50
111	A37	50k crim, lt bl & bis	1.25	.90
a.		Miniature sheet of 3, #109-111	4.75	4.75
		Nos. 109-111 (3)	2.15	1.65

ITU, centenary.
A souvenir booklet containing No. 111a exists. Value, $35.

Nos. 52-53 Surcharged in Dark Blue with New Value and Bars

1965, July 5   Unwmk.   Perf. 13
112	A16	1k on 4k rose claret	.70	.25
113	A16	5k on 6.50k org red	.70	.25

Mother and Child, UNICEF and WHO Emblems — A38

1965, Sept. 1   Engr.   Perf. 13
114	A38	35k lt ultra & dk red	.85	.70
a.		Miniature sheet	4.75	4.75

Mother and Child Protection movement, 6th anniv.

Map of Laos and
UN
Emblem — A39

1965, Nov. 3   Perf. 12½x13
115 A39 5k emer, gray & vio bl   .30   .25
116 A39 25k lil rose, gray & vio
          bl   .45   .35
117 A39 40k bl, gray & vio bl   .70   .50
      Nos. 115-117 (3)   1.45 1.10

UN, 20th anniv. Although first day covers were canceled "Oct. 24," the actual day of issue is reported to have been Nov. 3.

Tikhy
(Hockey)
A40

Pastimes: 10k, Two bulls fighting. 25k, Canoe race. 50k, Rocket festival.

1965, Dec. 23   Engr.   Perf. 13
118 A40 10k org, brn & gray   .30   .25
119 A40 20k grn, ver & dk bl   .40   .30
120 A40 25k brt blue & multi   .40   .35
121 A40 50k orange & multi   .90   .50
      Nos. 118-121 (4)   2.00 1.40

Slaty-headed Parakeet — A41

Birds: 15k, White-crested laughing thrush. 20k, Osprey. 45k, Bengal roller.

1966, Feb. 10   Engr.   Perf. 13
122 A41 5k car rose, ol & brn   .85   .50
123 A41 15k bluish grn, brn & blk 1.25   .60
124 A41 20k dl bl, sep & bister   2.10 1.00
125 A41 45k vio, Prus bl & sepia   4.25 2.40
      Nos. 122-125 (4)   8.45 4.50

WHO Headquarters, Geneva — A42

1966, May 3   Engr.   Perf. 13
126 A42 10k bl grn & indigo   .25   .25
127 A42 25k car & dk green   .40   .30
128 A42 50k ultra & black   .85   .70
   a. Miniature sheet of 3, #126-
       128   19.00 19.00
      Nos. 126-128 (3)   1.50 1.25

Inauguration of the WHO Headquarters, Geneva. No. 128a sold for 150k.

Ordination of Buddhist Monk — A43

Folklore: 25k, Women building ceremonial sand hills. 30k, Procession of the Wax Pagoda, vert. 40k, Wrist-tying ceremony (3 men, 3 women), vert.

1966, May 20   Perf. 13
129 A43 10k multicolored   .30   .25
130 A43 25k multicolored   .45   .30
131 A43 30k multicolored   .75   .50
132 A43 40k multicolored   1.00   .70
      Nos. 129-132 (4)   2.50 1.75

UNESCO
Emblem
A44

1966, July 7   Engr.   Perf. 13
133 A44 20k ocher & gray   .25   .25
134 A44 30k brt blue & gray   .40   .30
135 A44 40k brt green & gray   .55   .30
136 A44 60k crimson & gray   .80   .45
   a. Miniature sheet, #133-136   6.00 6.00
      Nos. 133-136 (4)   2.00 1.30

UNESCO, 20th anniv. No. 136a sold for 250k.

Addressed Envelope Carrier Pigeon, Globe and Hand with Quill Pen — A45

1966, Sept. 7   Engr.   Perf. 13
137 A45 5k red, brn & bl   .25   .25
138 A45 20k bl grn, blk & lil   .45   .30
139 A45 40k bl, red brn & dk ol
          bister   .55   .35
140 A45 45k brt rose lil, bl grn &
          black   .75   .50
   a. Min. sheet of 4, #137-140   6.00 6.00
      Nos. 137-140 (4)   2.00 1.40

Intl. Letter Writing Week, Oct. 6-12. No. 140a sold for 250k.

Sculpture from Siprapouthbat Temple — A46

Sculptures: 20k, from Visoun Temple. 50k, from Xiengthong Temple. 70k, from Visoun Temple.

1967, Feb. 21   Engr.   Perf. 12½x13
141 A46 5k olive grn & grn   .30   .25
142 A46 20k brn ol & gray bl   .70   .40
143 A46 50k dk brn & dp claret   1.25   .50
144 A46 70k dk brn & dk magen-
          ta   1.50   .80
      Nos. 141-144 (4)   3.75 1.95

General
Post Office
A47

1967, Apr. 6   Engr.   Perf. 13
145 A47 25k brn, grn & vio brn   .35   .25
146 A47 50k ind, brt blue & grn   .55   .40
147 A47 70k dk red, grn & brn   1.25   .75
      Nos. 145-147 (3)   2.15 1.40

Inauguration of the new Post and Telegraph Headquarters.

Snakehead
A48

Fish: 35k, Giant catfish. 45k, Spiny eel. 60k, Knifefish.

1967, June 8   Engr.   Perf. 13x12½
148 A48 20k dl bl, bis & blk   1.25   .50
149 A48 35k aqua, bis & gray   1.50   .60
150 A48 45k pale grn, bis & ol
          brn   2.50   .70
151 A48 60k sl grn, bis & blk   3.75   .80
      Nos. 148-151 (4)   9.00 2.60

Drumstick Tree
Flower — A49

Blossoms: 55k, Turmeric. 75k, Peacock flower. 80k, Pagoda tree.

1967, Aug. 10   Engr.   Perf. 12½x13
152 A49 30k red lil, yel & grn   .60   .35
153 A49 55k org, mag & lt grn   .90   .45
154 A49 75k bl, red & lt grn   1.25   .65
155 A49 80k brt grn, mag & yel   1.50   .75
      Nos. 152-155 (4)   4.25 2.20

Banded Krait — A50

Reptiles: 40k, Marsh crocodile. 100k, Malayan moccasin. 200k, Water monitor.

1967, Dec. 7   Engr.   Perf. 13
156 A50 5k emer, ind & yel   .85   .40
157 A50 40k sep, lt grn & yel   1.75   .60
158 A50 100k lt grn, brn &
          ocher   3.50 1.75
159 A50 200k grn, blk & bister   8.50 5.00
      Nos. 156-159 (4)   14.60 7.75

Human Rights Flame — A51

1968, Feb. 8   Engr.   Perf. 13
160 A51 20k brt grn, red & grn   .30   .25
161 A51 30k brn, red & grn   .40   .30
162 A51 50k brt bl, red & grn   .80   .60
   a. Souv. sheet of 3, #160-162   5.00 5.00
      Nos. 160-162 (3)   1.50 1.15

Intl. Human Rights Year. No. 162a sold for 250k.

WHO
Emblem — A52

1968, July 5   Engr.   Perf. 12½x13
163 A52 15k rose vio, ver &
          ocher   .25   .25
164 A52 30k brt bl, brt grn &
          ocher   .25   .25
165 A52 70k ver, plum & ocher   .55   .40
166 A52 110k brn, brt rose lil &
          ocher   .90   .55
167 A52 250k brt grn, brt bl &
          ocher   2.40 1.50
   a. Souv. sheet of 5, #163-167   6.50 6.50
      Nos. 163-167 (5)   4.35 2.95

WHO, 20th anniv. No. 167a sold for 500k.

Parade and
Memorial
Arch — A53

Designs: 20k, Armored Corps with tanks. 60k, Three soldiers with Laotian flag.

1968, July 15   Perf. 13
168 A53 15k multicolored   .35   .25
169 A53 20k multicolored   .45   .35
170 A53 60k multicolored   .90   .45
      Nos. 168-170,C52-C53 (5)   5.95 3.15

Laotian Army. For souvenir sheet see No. C53a.

Chrysochroa
Mnizechi — A54

Insects: 50k, Aristobia approximator. 90k, Eutaenia corbetti.

1968, Aug. 28   Engr.   Perf. 13
171 A54 30k vio bl, grn & yel   .90   .35
172 A54 50k lil, blk & ocher   1.50   .50
173 A54 90k bis, blk & org   2.25 1.25
      Nos. 171-173,C54-C55 (5)   8.40 4.20

Mangoes — A55

Fruits: 50k, Tamarind. 180k, Jackfruit, horiz. 250k, Watermelon, horiz.

1968, Oct. 3   Engr.   Perf. 13
174 A55 20k ind, lt bl & emer   .40   .25
175 A55 50k lt bl, emer & brn   .70   .40
176 A55 180k sep, org & yel grn   2.00 1.10
177 A55 250k sep, bis & emer   2.75 1.60
      Nos. 174-177 (4)   5.85 3.35

Hurdling — A56

1968, Nov. 15   Engr.   Perf. 13
178 A56 15k shown .50 .50
179 A56 80k Tennis 1.00 .50
180 A56 100k Soccer 1.00 .50
181 A56 110k High jump 1.50 1.00
Nos. 178-181 (4) 4.00 2.50
19th Olympic Games, Mexico City, 10/12-27.

Wedding of Kathanam and Nang Sida A57

Design: 200k, Thao Khathanam battling the serpent Ngou Xouang and the giant bird Phanga Houng. Design from panels of the central gate of Ongtu Temple, Vientiane. Design of 150k is from east gate.

1969, Feb. 28   Photo.   Perf. 12x13
182 A57 150k blk, gold & red 2.00 1.25
183 A57 200k blk, gold & red 2.75 1.75

Soukhib Ordered to Attack — A58

Scenes from Royal Ballet: 15k, Pharak pleading for Nang Sita. 20k, Thotsakan reviewing his troops. 30k, Nang Sita awaiting punishment. 40k, Pharam inspecting troops. 60k, Hanuman preparing to rescue Nang Sita.

1969   Photo.   Perf. 14
184 A58 10k multicolored .50 .25
185 A58 15k blue & multi .70 .40
186 A58 20k lt bl & multi .70 .50
187 A58 30k salmon & multi 1.00 .55
188 A58 40k salmon & multi 1.60 .70
189 A58 60k pink & multi 2.00 1.10
Nos. 184-189,C56-C57 (8) 17.00 8.50
For surcharges see Nos. B12-B17, CB1-CB2.

ILO Emblem and Basket Weavers at Vientiane Vocational Center A59

1969, May 7   Engr.   Perf. 13
190 A59 30k claret & violet .50 .40
191 A59 60k slate grn & vio brn 1.00 .75
Nos. 190-191,C58 (3) 7.00 4.40
ILO, 50th anniv.

Chinese Pangolin — A60

1969, Nov. 6   Photo.   Perf. 13x12
192 A60 15k multicolored .60 .25
193 A60 30k multicolored 1.00 .50
Nos. 192-193,C59-C61 (5) 7.85 3.85

That Luang, Luang Prabang A61

King Sisavang-Vong — A62

1969, Nov. 19   Engr.   Perf. 13
194 A61 50k dk brn, bl & bister .80 .60
195 A62 70k maroon & buff 1.40 1.00
a. Pair, #194-195 + label 3.50 3.50
Death of King Sisavang-Vong, 10th anniv.

Carved Capital from Wat Xiengthong A63

1970, Jan. 10   Photo.   Perf. 12x13
196 A63 70k multicolored 1.75 1.25
Nos. 196,C65-C66 (3) 5.15 2.90

Kongphene (Midday) Drum — A64

Designs: 55k, Kongthong (bronze) drum.

1970, Mar. 30   Engr.   Perf. 13
197 A64 30k gray, ol & org 1.00 .60
198 A64 55k ocher, blk & yel grn 1.75 1.35
Nos. 197-198,C67 (3) 5.75 3.45

Lenin Explaining Electrification Plan, by L. Shmatko — A65

1970, Apr. 22   Litho.   Perf. 12½x12
199 A65 30k blue & multi 1.10 .55
200 A65 70k rose red & multi 1.40 .75
Lenin (1870-1924), Russian communist leader.

Silk Weaver and EXPO Emblem A66

1970, July 7   Engr.   Perf. 13
201 A66 30k shown .70 .30
202 A66 70k Woman winding thread 1.00 .80
Nos. 201-202,C69 (3) 3.45 2.35
Laotian silk industry; EXPO '70 Intl. Exposition, Osaka, Japan, Mar. 15-Sept. 13.

Wild Boar A67

1970, Sept. 7   Engr.   Perf. 13
203 A67 20k green & dp brn .55 .25
204 A67 60k dp brn & ol bis 1.00 .45
Nos. 203-204,C70-C71 (4) 9.30 4.45

Buddha, UN Headquarters and Emblem — A68

1970, Oct. 24   Size: 22x36mm
205 A68 30k ultra, brn & rose red .70 .40
206 A68 70k brt grn, sep & vio 1.40 .60
Nos. 205-206,C75 (3) 4.50 2.10
UN, 25th anniv.

Nakhanet, Symbol of Arts and Culture — A69

1971, Feb. 5
207 A69 30k shown 1.00 .60
208 A69 85k Rahu swallowing the moon 1.40 .85
Nos. 207-208,C76 (3) 4.80 2.45

Silversmithing — A70

1971, Apr. 12   Engr.   Perf. 13
Size: 36x36mm
209 A70 30k shown .35 .25
210 A70 50k Pottery .55 .35

Size: 47x36mm
211 A70 70k Boat building 1.10 .40
Nos. 209-211 (3) 2.00 1.00

Laotian and African Children, UN Emblem — A71

60k, Women musicians, elephants, UN emblem.

1971, May 1   Engr.   Perf. 13
212 A71 30k lt grn, brn & blk .50 .30
213 A71 60k yel, pur & dull red 1.10 .50
Intl. year against racial discrimination.

Miss Rotary, Wat Ho Phrakeo — A72

Design: 30k, Monk on roof of That Luang and Rotary emblem, horiz.

1971, June 28   Engr.   Perf. 13
214 A72 30k purple & ocher .60 .40
215 A72 70k gray ol, dk bl & rose 1.25 .55
Rotary International, 50th anniversary.

Dendrobium Aggregatum A73

50k, Asocentrum ampullaceum, horiz. 70k, Trichoglottis fasciata, horiz.

Perf. 12½x13, 13x12½
1971, July 7   Photo.
Size: 26x36, 36x26mm
216 A73 30k shown 1.00 .50
217 A73 50k multicolored 1.40 .95
218 A73 70k multicolored 2.00 1.25
Nos. 216-218,C79 (4) 8.90 4.20
See Nos. 230-232, C89.

Palm Civet A74

Animals: 40k, like 25k. 50k, Lesser mouse deer. 85k, Sika deer.

1971, Sept. 16   Engr.   Perf. 13
219 A74 25k pur, dk bl & blk .80 .45
220 A74 40k grn, ol bis & blk 1.00 .60
221 A74 50k brt grn & ocher 1.50 .70
222 A74 85k sl grn, grn & brn orange 2.50 1.25
Nos. 219-222,C83 (5) 10.05 5.75

Types of 1952-57 with Ornamental Panels and Inscriptions
Designs: 30k, Laotian woman. 40k, So player (like #C25). 50k, Rama (like #C19).

1971, Oct. 31

223	A3	30k brn vio & brn	.50	.30
a.		Souvenir sheet of 3	6.00	6.00
224	A10	40k sepia, blk & ver	.70	.50
225	AP7	50k ultra, blk & salmon	1.00	.70
		Nos. 223-225,C84 (4)	4.20	2.90

20th anniv. of Laotian independent postal service. All stamps inscribed: "Vingtième Anniversaire de la Philatélie Lao," "Postes" and "1971." No. 223a contains No. 223 and 60k and 85k in design of 30k, sold for 250k.

Children Learning to Read A75

1972, Jan. 30   Engr.   Perf. 13
Size: 36x22mm

226	A75	30k shown	.35	.30
227	A75	70k Scribe writing on palm leaves	.70	.50
		Nos. 226-227,C87 (3)	2.80	1.80

Intl. Book Year.

Nam Ngum Hydroelectric Dam, Monument and ECAFE Emblem — A76

1972, Mar. 28   Engr.   Perf. 13

228	A76	40k grn, ultra & lt brn	.35	.25
229	A76	80k grn, brn ol & dk bl	.70	.40
		Nos. 228-229,C88 (3)	2.45	1.45

25th anniv. of the Economic Commission for Asia and the Far East (ECAFE), which helped build the Nam Ngum Hydroelectric Dam.

Orchid Type of 1971

Orchids: 40k, Hynchostylis giganterum. 60k, Paphiopedilum exul. 80k, Cattleya, horiz.

1972, May 5   Photo.   Perf. 13
Size: 26x36mm, 36x26mm

230	A73	40k lt bl & multi	.95	.35
231	A73	60k multicolored	1.60	.45
232	A73	80k lt bl & multi	2.00	.50
		Nos. 230-232,C89 (4)	8.55	2.80

Woman Carrying Water, UNICEF Emblem — A77

Children's drawings: 80k, Child learning bamboo-weaving, UNICEF emblem.

1972, July 20   Engr.   Perf. 13

233	A77	50k blue & multi	.70	.50
234	A77	80k brown & multi	1.00	.65
		Nos. 233-234,C90 (3)	3.10	2.15

25th anniv. (in 1971) of UNICEF.

Attopeu Costume, Religious Ceremony — A78

Design: 90k, Phongsaly festival costume.

1973, Feb. 16   Engr.   Perf. 13

235	A78	40k maroon & multi	.50	.30
236	A78	90k multicolored	1.10	.50
		Nos. 235-236,C101-C102 (4)	4.90	2.60

Lion from Wat That Luang and Lions Emblem — A79

1973, Mar. 30   Engr.   Perf. 13

237	A79	40k vio bl, rose cl & lil	.70	.25
238	A79	80k pur, org brn & yel	1.10	.40
		Nos. 237-238,C103 (3)	3.70	1.40

Lions International of Laos.

Dr. Hansen, Map of Laos, "Dok Hak" Flowers — A80

1973, June 28   Engr.   Perf. 13

239	A80	40k multicolored	.60	.30
240	A80	80k multicolored	1.25	.45

Centenary of the discovery by Dr. Armauer G. Hansen of the Hansen bacillus, the cause of leprosy.

Wat Vixun, Monk Blessing Girl Scouts — A81

1973, Sept. 1   Engr.   Perf. 13

241	A81	70k ocher & brown	.90	.40
		Nos. 241,C106-C107 (3)	3.25	1.10

25th anniv. of Laotian Scout Movement.

INTERPOL Headquarters — A82

1973, Dec. 22   Engr.   Perf. 13x12½

242	A82	40k greenish bl	.45	.25
243	A82	80k brown	.75	.60
		Nos. 242-243,C110 (3)	2.60	1.45

Intl. Criminal Police Org., 50th anniv.

Boy Mailing Letter — A83

1974, Apr. 30   Engr.   Perf. 13

244	A83	70k bl, lt grn & ocher	1.00	.25
245	A83	80k lt grn, bl & ocher	1.20	.40
		Nos. 244-245,C114-C115 (4)	11.95	3.65

UPU, cent.

Blue Sage — A84

1974, May 17
Size: 26x36mm, 36x26mm

246	A84	30k grn & vio	.55	.40
247	A84	50k Water lilies, horiz.	.90	.50
248	A84	80k Scheffler's kapokier, horiz.	1.25	.75
		Nos. 246-248,C116 (4)	8.20	4.65

Mekong River Ferry — A85

90k, Samlo (passenger tricycle), vert.

1974, July 31   Engr.   Perf. 13

249	A85	25k red brn & choc	.40	.40
250	A85	90k brown ol & lt ol	1.25	1.25
		Nos. 249-250,C117 (3)	4.15	3.15

Marconi, Indigenous Transmission Methods, Transistor Radio — A86

1974, Aug. 28   Engr.   Perf. 13

251	A86	60k multicolored	.50	.50
252	A86	90k multicolored	.75	.75
		Nos. 251-252,C118 (3)	3.50	2.35

Guglielmo Marconi (1874-1937), Italian electrical engineer and inventor.

Diastocera Wallichi Tonkinensis A87

90k, Macrochenus isabellunus. 100k, Purpuricenus malaccensis.

1974, Oct. 23   Engr.   Perf. 13

253	A87	50k shown	.90	.60
254	A87	90k multicolored	1.40	.85
255	A87	100k multicolored	1.75	.90
		Nos. 253-255,C119 (4)	5.80	3.35

Temple, Houeisai, and Sapphire A88

1975, Feb. 12   Engr.   Perf. 13x12½

256	A88	100k bl, brn & grn	1.50	.50
257	A88	110k Sapphire panning at Attopeu	1.75	.75

King Sisavang-Vong, Princes Souvanna Phouma and Souphanou-Vong — A89

1975, Feb. 21   Engr.   Perf. 13

258	A89	80k olive & multi	1.00	.40
259	A89	300k multicolored	1.75	.90
260	A89	420k multicolored	2.00	1.25
		Nos. 258-260 (3)	4.75	2.55

1st anniv. of Peace Treaty of Vientiane. A souvenir sheet exists, embossed on paper with a foil application. Value, $10.

Fortuneteller Working on Forecast for New Year (Size of pair: 100x27mm) — A90

New Year Riding Rabbit, and Tiger (Old Year) — A92

Designs: 40k, Chart of New Year symbols. 200k, Fortune teller. 350k, As shown.

1975, Apr. 14   Engr.   Perf. 13

261		40k bister & red brn	.50	.25
262		200k bis, red brn & sl	1.40	.80
a.		A90 Pair, #261-262	2.25	1.75
263	A92	350k blue & multi	2.50	1.60
		Nos. 261-263 (3)	4.40	2.65

New Year 1975, Year of the Rabbit.

UN Emblem, "Equality" — A93

200k, IWY emblem, man and woman.

1975, June 19   Engr.

264	A93	100k dl bl & vio bl	.55	.40
265	A93	200k multi	1.20	.85
a.		Miniature sheet of 2, #264-265	5.50	5.50

International Women's Year.

UPU, Cent. — A93a

Designs: 15k, Runner, rocket reaching orbit, vert. 30k, Docked Soyuz capsules, chariot, vert. 40k, Biplane, Concorde. 1000k, Apollo spacecraft in orbit. 1500k, Apollo spacecraft, astronaut, vert. No. 266F, stagecoach. No. 266G, Mail truck, Concorde. No. 266H, Wagon train, Lunar Rover. No. 266I, Zeppelin, locomotive.

Perf. 13x14, 14x13
1975, July 7   **Litho.**

266	A93a	10k multi	.30	.25
b.		Souvenir sheet of 1	12.50	12.50
266A	A93a	15k multi	.50	.25
b.		Souvenir sheet of 1	12.50	12.50
266B	A93a	30k multi	.70	.35
a.		Souvenir sheet of 1	12.50	12.50
266C	A93a	40k multi	.90	.60
a.		Souvenir sheet of 1	12.50	12.50
266D	A93a	1000k multi	2.75	2.00
a.		Souvenir sheet of 1	12.50	12.50
266E	A93a	1500k multi	4.75	3.00
a.		Souvenir sheet of 1	12.50	12.50
		Nos. 266-266E (6)	9.90	6.45

Litho. & Embossed
Perf. 13½

266F	A93a	2500k gold & multi	11.00	11.00
a.		Souvenir sheet of 1	95.00	95.00
266G	A93a	3000k gold & multi	11.00	11.00
a.		Souvenir sheet of 1	90.00	90.00

Souvenir Sheets

266H	A93a	2500k gold & multi	35.00	35.00
266I	A93a	3000k gold & multi	30.00	30.00

Nos. 266D-266E, 266G-266I are airmail.
Nos. 266-266E also exist imperf. Value, set of six pairs $150. Nos. 266b, 266Ab and 266Ba-266Ea also exist imperf. Value, set of six sheets $375. Nos. 266Fa, 266Ga and 266H-266I also exist imperf. Value, set of four sheets $550.
No. 266H exists perf and imperf. in sheets of 4. Single stamps from these sheets are indistinguishable from the stamp in No. 266H.

Apollo-Soyuz Mission — A93b

Designs: 125k, Astronauts, Thomas Stafford, Vance D. Brand, Donald Slayton. 150k, Cosmonauts Alexei Leonov, Valery Koubasov. 200k, Apollo-Soyuz link-up. 300k, Handshake in space. 450k, Preparation for re-entry. 700k, Apollo splashdown.

1975, July 7   **Litho.**   **Perf. 14x13**

267	A93b	125k multicolored	.80	.75
267A	A93b	150k multicolored	.95	.75
267B	A93b	200k multicolored	1.50	1.00
267C	A93b	300k multicolored	2.00	1.50
267D	A93b	450k multicolored	3.25	1.75
267E	A93b	700k multicolored	3.75	1.50
		Nos. 267-267E (6)	12.25	7.25

Nos. 267D-267E are airmail.
Nos. 267-267E exist imperf. Value, set $55.00
Nos. 267-267E exist in souvenir sheets of 1. Value, set perf. $75., set imperf. $150.

Scene from Vet Sandone Legend — A94

Designs: Scenes from Buddhist legend of Prince Vet Sandone.

1975, July 22   **Photo.**   **Perf. 13**

268	A94	80k multicolored	.65	.30
268A	A94	110k multicolored	.70	.40
268B	A94	120k multicolored	.90	.50
268C	A94	130k multicolored	1.50	.60
		Nos. 268-268C (4)	3.75	1.80

American Revolution, Bicent. — A94a

Presidents: 10k, Washington, J. Adams, Jefferson, Madison. 15k, Monroe, J.Q. Adams, Jackson, Van Buren. 40k, Harrison, Tyler, Polk, Taylor. 1000k, Truman, Eisenhower, Kennedy. 1500k, L. Johnson, Nixon, Ford.

1975, July 30   **Litho.**   **Perf. 13½**

269	A94a	10k multicolored	—	
269A	A94a	15k multicolored	—	
269B	A94a	40k multicolored	—	
269C	A94a	1000k multicolored	—	
269D	A94a	1500k multicolored	—	

Nos. 269C-269D are airmail. Stamps of similar design in denominations of 50k, 100k, 125k, 150k, and 200k exist but were not available in Laotian post offices. Value for set of 10, $60. Also exists imperf., set of 10, $225.00.

Buddha, Stupas of Borobudur — A95

Design: 200k, Borobudur sculptures and UNESCO emblem.

1975, Aug. 20   **Engr.**   **Perf. 13**

270	A95	100k indigo & multi	.85	.40
271	A95	200k multicolored	1.60	.85
a.		Miniature sheet of 2, #270-271	2.50	2.50

UNESCO campaign to save Borobudur Temple, Java.

Coat of Arms of Republic — A96

1976, Dec. 2   **Litho.**   **Perf. 14**

272	A96	1k blue & multi	.30	.25
273	A96	2k rose & multi	.30	.25
274	A96	5k brt grn & multi	.30	.25
275	A96	10k lilac & multi	.50	.40
276	A96	200k orange & multi	3.50	2.25
a.		Min. sheet of 5, #272-276	10.00	10.00
		Nos. 272-276 (5)	4.90	3.40

Miniature sheets of 1 exist. Value $100.
Nos. 272-276 exist imperf. Value, set $70.
For overprints, see Nos. 426A, 426V, 508C, 676H.

Thathiang Pagoda, Vientiane — A97

Designs: 2k, 80k, 100k, Phonsi Pagoda, Luang Prabang. 30k, 300k, like 1k.

1976, Dec. 18   **Perf. 13½**

277	A97	1k multicolored	.25	.25
278	A97	2k multicolored	.40	.25
279	A97	30k multicolored	.85	.50
280	A97	80k multicolored	1.75	1.00
281	A97	100k multicolored	2.50	1.40
a.		Souv. sheet of 3, #278, 280-281	5.25	
b.		As a, imperf.	12.00	
282	A97	300k multicolored	4.00	2.50
a.		Souv. sheet of 3, #277, 279, 282	5.25	
b.		As a, imperf.	12.00	
		Nos. 277-282 (6)	9.75	5.90

Nos. 277-282 exist imperf. Value, set $45.

Silversmith — A98

Perf. 13x12½, 12½x13
1977, Apr. 1   **Litho.**

283	A98	1k shown	.25	.25
284	A98	2k Weaver	.25	.25
285	A98	20k Potter	.65	.25
286	A98	50k Basket weaver, vert.	1.25	.40
		Nos. 283-286 (4)	2.40	1.15

Miniature sheets of 2 exist, perf. and imperf. Values: perf, $13; imperf. $16.
For overprints, see Nos. 426B, 426C, 426D, 426E, 426R, 676B.

Cosmonauts A.A. Gubarev, G.M. Grechko A99

Government Palace, Vientiane, Kremlin, Moscow — A100

20k, 50k, Lenin speaking on Red Square.

Perf. 12x12½, 12½x12
1977, Oct. 25   **Litho.**

287	A99	5k multicolored	.25	.25
288	A99	20k multicolored	.40	.25
289	A99	50k multicolored	.70	.30
290	A99	60k multicolored	.90	.40
291	A100	100k multicolored	1.40	.65
a.		Souv. sheet of 3, #288, 290-291	6.00	6.00
292	A100	250k multicolored	2.25	1.50
a.		Souv. sheet of 3, #287, 289, 292	6.00	6.00
		Nos. 287-292 (6)	5.90	3.35

60th anniv. of Russian October Revolution.
Nos. 287-292 exist imperf. Value, set $15.
For overprints, see Nos. 426F, 426N, 676C, 676F, 676I.

Natl. Arms — A101

1978, May 26   **Litho.**   **Perf. 12½**

293	A101	5k dull org & blk	.30	.25
294	A101	10k tan & black	.35	.25
295	A101	50k brt pink & blk	.50	.25
296	A101	100k yel grn & blk	1.25	.45
297	A101	250k violet & blk	2.00	.85
		Nos. 293-297 (5)	4.40	2.05

For overprints, see Nos. 426G, 676J.

A102

Army Day: 20k, Soldiers with flag. 40k, Fighters and burning house, horiz. 300k, Anti-aircraft battery.

Perf. 12½x12¼, 12½x12¾
1978, Sept. 15   **Litho.**

298	A102	20k multicolored	.30	.25
299	A102	40k multicolored	.55	.25
300	A102	300k multicolored	2.10	1.00
		Nos. 298-300 (3)	2.95	1.50

Nos. 298-300 exist imperf. Value, set $55.
For overprints see No. 426O, 426Q, 676A, 676L.

Marchers with Banner A103

1978, Dec. 2   **Litho.**   **Perf. 11½**

301	A103	20k shown	.50	.25
302	A103	50k Women with flag	.70	.25
303	A103	400k Dancer	2.25	1.40
a.		Sheet of 3, #301-303, imperf.	4.25	
		Nos. 301-303 (3)	3.45	1.90

National Day. A second printing in slightly different colors and with rough perforation exists; values the same. Stamps in souvenir sheet are in reverse order.

Electronic Tree, Map of Laos, ITU Emblem — A104

Design: 250k, Electronic tree, map of Laos and broadcast tower.

1979, Jan. 18   **Litho.**   **Perf. 12½**

304	A104	30k multicolored	.30	.25
305	A104	250k multicolored	2.50	1.00

World Telecommunications Day, 1978.
Nos. 304-305 exist imperf. Value, set $10.
For overprints, see Nos. 426P, 426W, 676K.

Woman Mailing Letter A105

10k, 80k, Processing mail. 100k, like 5k.

1979, Jan. 18

306	A105	5k multicolored	.25	.25
307	A105	10k multicolored	.25	.25
308	A105	80k multicolored	1.00	.30
309	A105	100k multicolored	1.40	.40
		Nos. 306-309 (4)	2.90	1.20

Asian-Oceanic Postal Union, 15th anniv.
Nos. 306-309 exist imperf. Value, set $12.50.
For overprints, see Nos. 426H, 426J, 426K, 426T, 426U, 676E, 676G.

Intl.
Year
of the
Child
A106

No. 310, Playing with ball, vert. No. 311,
Studying. No. 312, Playing musical instru-
ments. No. 313, Breast-feeding, vert. No. 314,
Map, globe, vert. No. 315, Immunization, vert.
No. 316, Girl dancing, vert.

1979   **Litho.**   **Perf. 11**
Without Gum

310	A106	20k multicolored	.25	.25
311	A106	50k multicolored	.40	.25
312	A106	100k multicolored	1.00	.35
313	A106	200k multicolored	2.00	.65
314	A106	200k multicolored	1.75	.65
315	A106	500k multicolored	6.00	1.50
316	A106	600k multicolored	4.00	1.50
		Nos. 310-316 (7)	15.40	5.15

Issued: Nos. 310-311, 313, 315, 8/1; others,
12/25.
Imperf sheets of 4 containing Nos. 310-311,
313, 315 and of 3 containing Nos. 312, 314,
316 exist. Value for both sheets $25.
Two varieties of imperf sheet of 3 exist:
inscribed "1979" or "1975" on No. 314
vignette. Sheet with "1975" imprint is very
scarce.

Traditional Modes of
Transportation — A107

1979, Oct. 9   **Perf. 12½x13**

317	A107	5k Elephants, buffa-lo, pirogues	.25	.25
318	A107	10k Buffalo, carts	.30	.35
319	A107	70k like 10k	.65	1.50
320	A107	500k like 5k	2.50	2.00
		Nos. 317-320 (4)	3.70	4.10

Nos. 317-320 exist imperf. Value, set $15.
For overprints, see Nos. 426I, 426L, 426M,
426S, 676D.

5th Anniv. of the Republic — A108

30c, Agriculture, vert. 50c, Education, health
services. 1k, Three women, vert. 2k, Hydro-
lectric energy.

1980, May 30   **Perf. 11**

321	A108	30c multicolored	.35	.25
322	A108	50c multicolored	.60	.25
323	A108	1k multicolored	.75	.40
324	A108	2k multicolored	1.75	1.10
		Nos. 321-324 (4)	3.45	2.00

Imperf. souvenir sheet of 4 exists in three
types. Values: vowel missing above first Lao
word at top of sheet, $20; vowel 9mm above
first Lao word, $10; vowel 7.5mm above first
Lao word, $10.

Lenin,
110th Birth
Anniv.
A109

1980, July 5   **Perf. 12x12½, 12½x12**

325	A109	1k Lenin reading	.25	.25
326	A109	2k Writing	.45	.25
327	A109	3k Lenin, red flag, vert.	.65	.40
328	A109	4k Orating, vert.	1.25	.55
		Nos. 325-328 (4)	2.60	1.45

Nos. 325-328 exist imperf. Value, set $12.50.
Imperf. souvenir sheet of 4 exists. Value $5.

> **From this point to No. 1365,**
> **used values are for CTO stamps.**
> **For Nos. 426A-426W, 676A-676L,**
> **1318A-1318C, 1359, used values**
> **are for postally used stamps.**

5th Anniv. of the Republic — A110

50c, Threshing rice. 1.60k, Logging. 4.60k,
Veterinary medicine. 5.40k, Rice paddy.

1980, Dec. 2   **Perf. 11**
Without Gum

329	A110	50c multicolored	.30	.25
330	A110	1.60k multicolored	.70	.30
331	A110	4.60k multicolored	1.40	.50
332	A110	5.40k multicolored	1.75	.80
		Nos. 329-332 (4)	4.15	1.85

Imperf. souvenir sheet of 4 exists. Value $10.

26th
Communist
Party
(PCUS)
Congress
A111

4.60k, Globe, broken chains. 5.40k, Grain,
cracked bomb.

1981, June 26   **Perf. 12x12½**
Without Gum

333	A111	60c shown	.30	.25
334	A111	4.60k multicolored	1.75	.80
335	A111	5.40k multicolored	2.00	.85
a.		Souv. sheet of 3, #333-335, im-perf.	7.00	7.00
		Nos. 333-335 (3)	4.05	1.90

No. 335a sold for 15k.

Souvenir Sheet

PHILATOKYO '81 — A112

1981, Sept. 20   **Perf. 13**
Without Gum

336	A112	10k Pandas	6.00	4.00

1982 World Cup
Soccer
Championships,
Spain — A113

1981, Oct. 15   **Perf. 12½**
Without Gum

337	A113	1k Heading ball	.25	.25
338	A113	2k Dribble	.40	.25
339	A113	3k Kick	.55	.25
340	A113	4k Goal, horiz.	.75	.25
341	A113	5k Dribble, diff.	1.00	1.00
342	A113	6k Kick, diff.	1.40	.80
		Nos. 337-342 (6)	4.35	2.80

Intl. Year of the
Disabled
A114

1981   **Without Gum**   **Perf. 13**

343	A114	3k Office worker	1.60	.40
344	A114	5k Teacher	2.00	.80
345	A114	12k Weaver, fishing net	4.00	2.00
		Nos. 343-345 (3)	7.60	3.20

Wildcats — A115

1981   **Without Gum**   **Perf. 12½**

346	A115	10c Felis silvestris ornata	.25	.25
347	A115	20c Felis viverrinus	.25	.25
348	A115	30c Felis caracal	.35	.25
349	A115	40c Neofelis nebulosa	.40	.25
350	A115	50c Felis planiceps	.45	.25
351	A115	9k Felis chaus	3.50	1.25
		Nos. 346-351 (6)	5.20	2.50

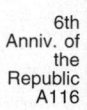

6th
Anniv. of
the
Republic
A116

1981, Dec.   **Without Gum**   **Perf. 13**

352	A116	3k Satellite dish, flag	65.00	.30
353	A116	4k Soldier, flag	80.00	.40
354	A116	5k Map, flag, wo-men, soldier	110.00	.50
		Nos. 352-354 (3)	255.00	1.20

Indian
Elephants
A117

1k, Head. 2k, Carrying log in trunk. 3k,
Transporting people. 4k, In trap. 5k, Adult and
young. 5.50k, Herd.

1982, Jan. 23   **Perf. 12½x13**
Without Gum

355	A117	1k multicolored	.30	.25
356	A117	2k multicolored	.60	.25
357	A117	3k multicolored	.80	.30
358	A117	4k multicolored	1.10	.30
359	A117	5k multicolored	1.50	.55
360	A117	5.50k multicolored	2.25	.70
		Nos. 355-360 (6)	6.55	2.35

Laotian
Wrestling
A118

Various moves.

1982, Jan. 30   **Perf. 13**
Without Gum

361	A118	50c multicolored	.25	.25
362	A118	1.20k multi, diff.	.25	.25
363	A118	2k multi, diff.	.30	.25
364	A118	2.50k multi, diff.	.35	.25
365	A118	4k multi, diff.	.60	.35
366	A118	5k multi, diff.	1.00	.55
		Nos. 361-366 (6)	2.75	1.90

Water Lilies
A119

30c, Nymphaea zanzibariensis. 40c,
Nelumbo nucifera gaertn rose. 60c,
Nymphaea rosea. 3k, Nymphaea nouchali. 4k,
Nymphaea white. 7k, Nelumbo nucifera gaertn
white.

1982, Feb. 10   **Perf. 12½x13**
Without Gum

367	A119	30c multicolored	.25	.25
368	A119	40c multicolored	.25	.25
369	A119	60c multicolored	.25	.25
370	A119	3k multicolored	.65	.25
371	A119	4k multicolored	1.00	.25
372	A119	7k multicolored	1.75	.30
		Nos. 367-372 (6)	4.15	1.55

Birds
A120

50c, Hirundo rustica, vert. 1k, Upupa epops,
vert. 2k, Alcedo atthis, vert. 3k, Hypothymis
azurea. 4k, Motacilla cinerea. 10k,
Orthotomus sutorius.

1982, Mar. 9   *Perf. 13*
Without Gum

373	A120	50c multicolored	.25	.25
374	A120	1k multicolored	.25	.25
375	A120	2k multicolored	.50	.25
376	A120	3k multicolored	.65	.25
377	A120	4k multicolored	1.25	.25
378	A120	10k multicolored	2.75	.80
		Nos. 373-378 (6)	5.65	2.05

A121

1982 World Cup Soccer
Championships, Spain — A122

Various match scenes.

1982, Apr. 7   **Without Gum**

379	A121	1k multicolored	.25	.25
380	A121	2k multicolored	.40	.25
381	A121	3k multicolored	.55	.30
382	A121	4k multicolored	.70	.40
383	A121	5k multicolored	1.00	.45
384	A121	6k multicolored	1.25	.55
		Nos. 379-384 (6)	4.15	2.20

Souvenir Sheet

| 385 | A122 | 15k multicolored | 4.00 | 4.00 |

Nos. 379-384 exist imperf.

Butterflies
A123

1k, Herona marathus. 2k, Neptis paraka. 3k,
Euripus halitherses. 4k, Lebadea martha. 5k,
Iton semamora. 6k, Elymnias hypermnestra.

1982, May 5   *Perf. 12½x13*
Without Gum

386	A123	1k multicolored	.25	.25
387	A123	2k multicolored	.60	.25
388	A123	3k multicolored	.75	.30
389	A123	4k multicolored	1.25	.30

Size: 42x26mm
Perf. 12½

| 390 | A123 | 5k multicolored | 2.00 | .70 |

Size: 54x36½mm
Perf. 13x12½

| 391 | A123 | 6k multicolored | 2.50 | .70 |
| | | Nos. 386-391 (6) | 7.35 | 2.50 |

Souvenir Sheet

PHILEXFRANCE '82 — A124

1982, June 9   *Perf. 13*
Without Gum

| 392 | A124 | 10k Temple, Vientiane | 2.75 | 2.75 |

River
Vessels
A125

50c, Raft. 60c, River punt. 1k, Houseboat.
2k, Passenger steamer. 3k, Ferry. 8k, Self-
propelled barge.

1982, June 24   **Without Gum**

393	A125	50c multicolored	.25	.25
394	A125	60c multicolored	.25	.25
395	A125	1k multicolored	.25	.25
396	A125	2k multicolored	.35	.25
397	A125	3k multicolored	.55	.40
398	A125	8k multicolored	1.50	.70
		Nos. 393-398 (6)	3.15	2.10

Pagodas
A126

1982, Aug. 2   **Without Gum**

399	A126	50c Chanh	.25	.25
400	A126	60c Inpeng	.25	.25
401	A126	1k Dong Mieng	.25	.25
402	A126	2k Ho Tay	.35	.25
403	A126	3k Ho Pha Keo	.60	.30
404	A126	8k Sisaket	1.60	.65
		Nos. 399-404 (6)	3.30	1.95

Dogs
A127

1982, Oct. 13   **Without Gum**

405	A127	50c Poodle	.25	.25
406	A127	60c Samoyed	.25	.25
407	A127	1k Boston terrier	.25	.25
408	A127	2k Cairn terrier	.40	.25
409	A127	3k Chihuahua	.75	.40
410	A127	8k Bulldog	2.50	.65
		Nos. 405-410 (6)	4.40	2.05

World Food
Day — A128

1982, Oct. 16   **Without Gum**

| 411 | A128 | 7k Watering seedlings | 1.75 | .65 |
| 412 | A128 | 8k Planting rice | 2.00 | .80 |

Classic Automobiles — A129

1982, Nov. 7   **Without Gum**

413	A129	50c 1925 Fiat	.25	.25
414	A129	60c 1925 Peugeot	.25	.25
415	A129	1k 1925 Berliet	.25	.25
416	A129	2k 1925 Ballot	.40	.25
417	A129	3k 1926 Renault	.75	.40
418	A129	8k 1925 Ford	2.00	.90
		Nos. 413-418 (6)	3.90	2.05

7th
Anniv. of
the
Republic
A130

50c, Kaysone Phomvihan, vert. 1k, Tractors,
field, industry. 2k, Cows, farm. 3k, Truck,
microwave dish. 4k, Nurse, child, vert. 5k,
Education. 6k, Folk dancer, vert.

1982, Dec. 2   **Without Gum**

419	A130	50c multicolored	.25	.25
420	A130	1k multicolored	.25	.25
421	A130	2k multicolored	.45	.25
422	A130	3k multicolored	.65	.25
423	A130	4k multicolored	.90	.40
424	A130	5k multicolored	1.10	.40
425	A130	6k multicolored	1.40	.50
		Nos. 419-425 (7)	5.00	2.30

Nos. 419-425 exist imperf.

Bulgarian Flag, Coat of Arms and
George Dimitrov (1882-1949),
Bulgarian Statesman — A131

1982, Dec. 15   *Perf. 12½*
Without Gum

| 426 | A131 | 10k multicolored | 1.90 | 1.10 |

Nos. 272, 276,
283, 284, 286-
288, 293, 298,
299, 304-309,
317-319 Ovptd.
in Red or Black

Methods and Perfs as before

1982

426A	A96	1k multi	70.00	70.00
426B	A98	1k multi (Bk)	75.00	75.00
a.		"I" instead of "1" in overprint	—	
b.		"à" instead of "2" in overprint	—	
c.		Inverted "8" in overprint	—	
426C	A98	1k multi	55.00	55.00
a.		"I" instead of "1" in overprint	—	
b.		"9" in overprint omitted	—	
c.		Inverted "8" in overprint	—	
426D	A98	2k multi	50.00	50.00
426E	A98	2k multi (Bk)	65.00	65.00
426F	A99	5k multi	85.00	85.00
a.		Double overprint	—	
426G	A101	5k dull org & blk	75.00	75.00
426H	A105	5k multi	55.00	55.00
a.		Inverted "8" in overprint	—	
b.		Inverted "1" in overprint	—	
426I	A107	5k multi	35.00	35.00
426J	A105	10k multi (Bk)	70.00	70.00
a.		Inverted "8" in overprint	—	
b.		Double overprint, one inverted	—	
426K	A105	10k multi	70.00	70.00
426L	A107	10k multi (Bk)	65.00	65.00
a.		Inverted "8" in overprint	—	
426M	A107	10k multi	175.00	175.00
426N	A99	20k multi	—	
426O	A102	20k multi	175.00	175.00
a.		Small "2" in overprint	—	
426P	A104	30k multi	75.00	75.00
a.		Small "2" in overprint	—	
426Q	A102	40k multi	85.00	85.00
a.		Inverted "8" in overprint	—	
426R	A98	50k multi	85.00	85.00
a.		Inverted "8" in overprint	—	
426S	A107	70k multi	115.00	115.00
a.		Inverted "8" in overprint	—	
426T	A105	80k multi (Bk)	125.00	125.00
a.		Inverted "8" in overprint	—	
426U	A105	100k multi	175.00	175.00
a.		Inverted "8" in overprint	—	
426V	A96	200k org & multi (Bk)	275.00	275.00
a.		Inverted "8" in overprint	—	
b.		Double overprint, one inverted	—	
426W	A104	250k multi (Bk)	450.00	450.00
		Nos. 426A-426W (23)	2,505.	2,505.

Constitution of
the USSR, 60th
Anniv. — A132

1982, Dec. 30   **Without Gum**

| 427 | A132 | 3k Kremlin | .65 | .40 |
| 428 | A132 | 4k Maps | .90 | .55 |

Souvenir Sheet
Perf. 13½x13

428A		Sheet of 2	3.75	2.00
b.		A132 5k like 3k	1.25	.65
c.		A132 10k like 4k	2.50	1.75

Nos. 428Ab-428Ac not inscribed in Laotian
at top; buff and gold decorative margin contains the inscription.

1984 Summer
Olympics, Los
Angeles
A133

1983, Jan. 25   *Perf. 13*
Without Gum

429	A133	50c Hurdling	.25	.25
430	A133	1k Women's javelin	.25	.25
431	A133	2k Basketball	.35	.25
432	A133	3k Diving	.55	.25
433	A133	4k Gymnastics	.75	.40
434	A133	10k Weight lifting	2.10	.80
		Nos. 429-434 (6)	4.25	2.20

Souvenir Sheet

| 435 | A133 | 15k Soccer | 3.25 | 2.00 |

No. 435 contains one stamp 32x40mm.
Nos. 429-434 exist imperf.

Horses
A134

Various breeds.

1983, Feb. 1   **Without Gum**

436	A134	50c multicolored	.25	.25
437	A134	1k multi, diff.	.25	.25
438	A134	2k multi, diff.	.40	.25
439	A134	3k multi, diff.	.65	.25
440	A134	4k multi, diff.	.80	.30
441	A134	10k multi, diff.	2.75	.80
		Nos. 436-441 (6)	5.10	2.10

Nos. 436-441 exist imperf.

A135

Raphael, 500th Birth Anniv. — A136

Paintings (details) by Raphael: 50c, St. Catherine of Alexandra, Natl. Gallery, London. 1k, Adoration of the Kings (spectators), Vatican. 2k, Granduca Madonna, Pitti Gallery, Florence. 3k, St. George and the Dragon, The Louvre, Paris. 4k, Vision of Ezekiel, Pitti Gallery. No. 447, Adoration of the Kings (Holy Family), Vatican. No. 448, Coronation of the Virgin, Vatican.

1983, Mar. 9   **Perf. 12½x13**
Without Gum
442 A135 50c multicolored   .25   .25
443 A135 1k multicolored   .25   .25
444 A135 2k multicolored   .35   .25
445 A135 3k multicolored   .60   .25
446 A135 4k multicolored   .75   .30
447 A135 10k multicolored   2.50   .80
    Nos. 442-447 (6)   4.70 2.10
Souvenir Sheet
Perf. 13x13½
448 A136 10k multicolored   2.50 1.50

INTERCOSMOS
Space
Cooperation
Program — A137

Cosmonaut and flags of USSR and participating nations.

1983, Apr. 12   **Perf. 12½**
449 A137 50c Czechoslovakia   .25   .25
450 A137 50c Poland   .25   .25
451 A137 1k East Germany   .25   .25
452 A137 1k Bulgaria   .25   .25
453 A137 2k Hungary   .40   .25
454 A137 3k Mongolia   .65   .25
455 A137 4k Romania   .80   .25
456 A137 6k Cuba   1.25   .40
457 A137 10k France   2.25   .80
    Nos. 449-457 (9)   6.35 2.95
Souvenir Sheet
Perf. 13½x13
458 A137 10k Vietnam   2.75 1.50
    No. 458 contains one stamp 32x40mm. Date of issue: 7/24/83.

A138

First Manned Balloon Flight, Bicent. — A139

Various balloons.

1983, May 4   **Perf. 12½x13**
459 A138 50c shown   .25   .25
460 A138 1k multi, diff.   .25   .25
461 A138 2k multi, diff.   .35   .25
462 A138 3k multi, diff.   .50   .25
463 A138 4k multi, diff.   .65   .40
464 A138 10k multi, diff.   2.25   .80
    Nos. 459-464 (6)   4.25 2.20
Souvenir Sheet
Perf. 13½x13
465 A139 10k shown   2.40 1.50
    Nos. 459-464 exist imperf.

Souvenir Sheet

TEMBAL '83, Basel — A140

1983, May 21   **Perf. 13x13½**
Without Gum
466 A140 10k German Maybach   3.00 1.60
    No. 466 exists imperf.

Flora
A141

1k, Dendrobium sp. 2k, Aerides odoratum. 3k, Dendrobium aggregatum. 4k, Dendrobium. 5k, Moschatum. 6k, Dendrobium sp., diff.

1983, June 10   **Perf. 13**
Without Gum
467 A141 1k multicolored   .25   .25
468 A141 2k multicolored   .40   .25
469 A141 3k multicolored   .60   .25
470 A141 4k multicolored   .75   .25
471 A141 5k multicolored   1.10   .30
472 A141 6k multicolored   1.40   .50
    Nos. 467-472 (6)   4.50 1.80
    Nos. 467-472 exist imperf.

1984 Winter Olympics, Sarajevo — A142

1983, July 2   **Without Gum**
473 A142 50c Downhill skiing   .25   .25
474 A142 1k Slalom   .25   .25
475 A142 2k Ice hockey   .40   .25
476 A142 3k Speed skating   .70   .25
477 A142 4k Ski jumping   .85   .30
478 A142 10k Luge   2.25   .80
    Nos. 473-478 (6)   4.70 2.10

Souvenir Sheet
Perf. 13x13½
479 A142 15k 2-Man bobsled   3.50 1.50
    No. 479 contains one 40x32mm stamp.
    Nos. 473-478 exist imperf.

Souvenir Sheet

BANGKOK '83 — A143

1983, Aug. 4   **Perf. 13½x13**
480 A143 10k Boats on river   2.25 1.50
    No. 480 exists imperf. Value, $60.

Mekong River Fish — A144

1k, Notopterus chitala. 2k, Cyprinus carpio. 3k, Pangasius sp. 4k, Catlocarpio siamensis. 5k, Morulius sp. 6k, Tilapia nilotica.

1983, Sept. 5   **Perf. 12½**
Without Gum
481 A144 1k multicolored   .25   .25
482 A144 2k multicolored   .40   .25
483 A144 3k multicolored   .65   .25
484 A144 4k multicolored   .75   .25
485 A144 5k multicolored   1.10   .30
486 A144 6k multicolored   1.50   .50
    Nos. 481-486 (6)   4.65 1.80
    Nos. 481-486 exist imperf.

Explorers and Their Ships — A145

1k, Victoria, Magellan. 2k, Grand Hermine, Cartier. 3k, Santa Maria, Columbus. 4k, Cabral and caravel. 5k, Endeavor, Capt. Cook. 6k, Pourquoi-Pas, Charcot.

1983, Oct. 8   **Perf. 13x12½**
Without Gum
487 A145 1k multicolored   .25   .25
488 A145 2k multicolored   .40   .25
489 A145 3k multicolored   .65   .25
490 A145 4k multicolored   .75   .25
491 A145 5k multicolored   1.10   .30
492 A145 6k multicolored   1.50   .50
    Nos. 487-492 (6)   4.65 1.80
    No. 492 incorrectly inscribed "CABOT."

Domestic
Cats
A146

1983, Nov. 9   **Perf. 12½x13**
Without Gum
493 A146 1k Tabby   .25   .25
494 A146 2k Long-haired Persian   .60   .25
495 A146 3k Siamese   .75   .25
496 A146 4k Burmese   .85   .25
497 A146 5k Persian   1.25   .30
498 A146 6k Tortoiseshell   1.75   .50
    Nos. 493-498 (6)   5.45 1.80
    Nos. 493-498 exist imperf.

Karl Marx (1818-1883) — A147

1983, Nov. 30   **Perf. 13**
Without Gum
499 A147 1k multicolored   .25   .25
500 A147 4k Marx, 3 flags, diff., vert.   1.00   .40
501 A147 6k Marx, flag of Laos   1.60   .55
    Nos. 499-501 (3)   2.85 1.05

8th Anniv. of the Republic — A148

1983, Dec. 2   **Perf. 12½x13, 13x12½**
Without Gum
502 A148 1k Elephant dragging log, vert.   .25   .25
503 A148 4k Oxen, pig   1.00   .25
504 A148 6k Produce, vert.   1.60   .55
    Nos. 502-504 (3)   2.85 1.05
    Nos. 502-504 exist imperf.

World Communications Year — A149

1983, Dec. 15   **Perf. 13**
505 A149 50c Teletype   .25   .25
506 A149 1k Telephone   .25   .25
507 A149 4k Television   .65   .30
508 A149 6k Satellite, dish receiver   1.00   .55
    Nos. 505-508 (4)   2.15 1.35

Nos. 275, 306
Overprinted in Red

1983   **Method and Perf. As Before**
508B A105 5k multi   450.00 —
508C A96 10k lilac & multi   575.00 —

1984 Winter Olympics, Sarajevo — A150

1984, Jan. 16

509	A150	50c	Women's figure skating	.25 .25
510	A150	1k	Speed skating	.25 .25
511	A150	2k	Biathlon	.40 .25
512	A150	4k	Luge	.80 .30
513	A150	5k	Downhill skiing	1.00 .30
514	A150	6k	Ski jumping	1.25 .50
515	A150	7k	Slalom	1.50 .55

Nos. 509-515 (7) 5.45 2.40

Souvenir Sheet
Perf. 13½x13

516 A150 10k Ice hockey 2.25 1.50

Nos. 509-511, 514-515 vert. No. 516 contains one stamp 32x40mm.

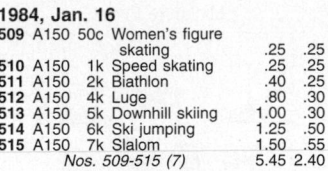

World Wildlife Fund A151

Panthera tigris.

1984, Feb. 1 *Perf. 13*
517	A151	25c	Adult, vert.	.50 .25
518	A151	25c	shown	.50 .25
519	A151	3k	Nursing cubs	5.00 1.25
520	A151	4k	Two cubs, vert.	8.00 1.75

Nos. 517-520 (4) 14.00 3.50

1984 Summer Olympics, Los Angeles A152

Gold medals awarded during previous games, and athletes. 50c, Athens 1896, women's diving. 1k, Paris 1900, women's volleyball. 2k, St. Louis 1904, running. 4k, London 1908, basketball. 5k, Stockholm 1912, judo. 6k, Antwerp 1920, soccer. 7k, Paris 1924, gymnastics. 10k, Moscow 1980, wrestling.

1984, Mar 26
521	A152	50c	multicolored	.25 .25
522	A152	1k	multicolored	.25 .25
523	A152	2k	multicolored	.60 .25
524	A152	4k	multicolored	1.10 .25
525	A152	5k	multicolored	1.25 .30
526	A152	6k	multicolored	1.60 .40
527	A152	7k	multicolored	1.90 .50

Nos. 521-527 (7) 6.95 2.20

Souvenir Sheet
Perf. 12½

528 A152 10k multicolored 2.75 1.50

No. 528 contains one stamp 32x40mm.

Musical Instruments — A153

1984, Mar. 27 *Perf. 13*
529	A153	1k	Tuned drums	.25 .25
530	A153	2k	Xylophone	.40 .25
531	A153	3k	Pair of drums	.65 .25
532	A153	4k	Hand drum	.90 .30
533	A153	5k	Barrel drum	1.10 .30
534	A153	6k	Pipes, string instrument	1.25 .50

Nos. 529-534 (6) 4.55 1.85

Natl. Day — A154

1984, Mar. 30 *Perf. 12½*
535	A154	60c	Natl. flag	.35 .25
536	A154	1k	Natl. arms	.50 .25
537	A154	2k	like 1k	.75 .25

Nos. 535-537 (3) 1.60 .75

For surcharges, see Nos. 1884-1886.

Chess A155

Illustrations of various medieval and Renaissance chess games.
10k, Royal game, human chessmen.

1984, Apr. 14 *Perf. 12½x13*
538	A155	50c	multi	.25 .25
539	A155	1k	multi, diff.	.25 .25
540	A155	2k	multi, red brn board, diff.	.50 .25
541	A155	2k	multi, blk board, diff.	.50 .25
542	A155	3k	multi, diff.	.70 .30
543	A155	4k	multi, diff.	1.25 .30
544	A155	8k	multi, diff.	2.25 .50
a.			Souv. sheet of 6, #538-540, 542-544, with gutter between	— —

Nos. 538-544 (7) 5.70 2.10

Souvenir Sheet
Perf. 13½x13

545 A155 10k multi 3.25 2.50

World Chess Federation, 60th anniv. No. 545 contains one stamp 32x40mm.

ESPANA '84, Madrid — A156

Paintings: 50c, Cardinal Nino de Guevara, by El Greco. 1k, Gaspar de Guzman, Duke of Olivares, on Horseback, byVelazquez. No. 548, The Annunciation, by Murillo. No. 549, Portrait of a Lady, by Francisco de Zurburan (1598-1664). 3k, The Family of Charles IV, by Goya. 4k, Two Harlequins, by Picasso. 8k, Abstract, by Miro. 10k, Burial of the Count of Orgaz, by El Greco.

1984, Apr. 27 *Perf. 12½*
546	A156	50c	multicolored	.25 .25
547	A156	1k	multicolored	.25 .25
548	A156	2k	multicolored	.45 .25
549	A156	2k	multicolored	.45 .25
550	A156	3k	multicolored	.65 .30
551	A156	4k	multicolored	.90 .30
552	A156	8k	multicolored	1.75 .50

Nos. 546-552 (7) 4.70 2.10

Souvenir Sheet
Perf. 13½x13

553 A156 10k multicolored 4.75 2.50

No. 553 contains one stamp 32x40mm and also exists imperf.

Woodland Flowers — A157

50c, Adonis aestivalis. 1k, Alpinia speciosa. No. 556, 2k, Aeschynanthus speciosus. No. 557, 2k, Cassia lechenaultiana. 3k, Datura meteloides. 4k, Quamoclit pennata. 8k, Commelina benghalensis.

1984, May 11 *Perf. 13*
554	A157	50c	multicolored	.25 .25
555	A157	1k	multicolored	.25 .25
556	A157	2k	multicolored	.45 .25
557	A157	2k	multicolored	.45 .25
558	A157	3k	multicolored	.65 .30
559	A157	4k	multicolored	.90 .30
560	A157	8k	multicolored	1.75 .50

Nos. 554-560 (7) 4.70 2.10

Nos. 554-560 exist imperf.

A158

19th UPU Congress, Hamburg — A159

Classic sport and race cars.

1984, June 19
561	A158	50c	Nazzaro	.25 .25
562	A158	1k	Daimler	.25 .25
563	A158	2k	Delage	.35 .25
564	A158	2k	Fiat S 57/14B	.35 .25
565	A158	3k	Bugatti	.50 .30
566	A158	4k	Itala	.65 .30
567	A158	8k	Blitzen Benz	1.40 .50

Nos. 561-567 (7) 3.75 2.10

Souvenir Sheet
Perf. 12½

568 A159 10k Winton Bullet 1.90 1.25

Paintings by Correggio (1494-1534) A160

Designs: 50c, Madonna and Child (Holy Family). 1k, Madonna and Child (spectators). No. 571, Madonna and Child (Holy Family, diff.). No. 572, Mystical Marriage of St. Catherine (Catherine, child, two women). 3k, The Four Saints. 4k, Noli Me Tangere. 8k, Christ Bids Farewell to the Virgin Mary. 10k, Madonna and Child, diff.

1984, June 26 *Perf. 13*
569	A160	50c	multicolored	.25 .25
570	A160	1k	multicolored	.25 .25
571	A160	2k	multicolored	.45 .25
572	A160	2k	multicolored	.45 .25
573	A160	3k	multicolored	.65 .30
574	A160	4k	multicolored	.75 .30
575	A160	8k	multicolored	1.40 .50

Nos. 569-575 (7) 4.20 2.10

Souvenir Sheet
Perf. 13½x13

576 A160 10k multicolored 3.25 1.75

No. 576 contains one stamp 32x40mm.

Space Exploration A161

No. 577, Luna 1. No. 578, Luna 2. No. 579, Luna 3. No. 580, Sputnik 2, Kepler, horiz. No. 581, Lunokhod 2, Newton, horiz. No. 582, Luna 13, Jules Verne, horiz. No. 583, Space station, Copernicus, horiz.

1984, July 12 *Perf. 13*
577	A161	50c	multicolored	.25 .25
578	A161	1k	multicolored	.25 .25
579	A161	2k	multicolored	.35 .25
580	A161	2k	multicolored	.35 .25
581	A161	3k	multicolored	.75 .25
582	A161	4k	multicolored	1.00 .40
583	A161	8k	multicolored	1.75 .65

Nos. 577-583 (7) 4.70 2.30

Reptiles A162

No. 584, Malaclemys terrapin. No. 585, Bungarus fasciatus. No. 586, Python reticulatus. No. 587, Python molurus, vert. No. 588, Gekko gecko. No. 589, Natrix subminiata. No. 590, Eublepharis macularius.

1984, Aug. 20
584	A162	50c	multicolored	.25 .25
585	A162	1k	multicolored	.25 .25
586	A162	2k	multicolored	.40 .25
587	A162	2k	multicolored	.40 .25
588	A162	3k	multicolored	.75 .25
589	A162	4k	multicolored	1.00 .40
590	A162	8k	multicolored	1.90 .65

Nos. 584-590 (7) 4.95 2.30

Marsupials — A163

No. 591, Schoinobates volans. No. 592, Ornithorhynchus anatinus. No. 593, Sarcophilus harrisii. No. 594, Lasiorhinus latifrons. No. 595, Thylacinus cynocephalus. No. 596, Dasyurops maculatus. No. 597, Wallabia isabelinus.
10k, Macropus rufus.

1984, Sept. 21
591	A163	50c	multicolored	.25 .25
592	A163	1k	multicolored	.25 .25
593	A163	2k	multicolored	.40 .25
594	A163	2k	multicolored	.40 .25
595	A163	3k	multicolored	.75 .25
596	A163	4k	multicolored	1.00 .40
597	A163	8k	multicolored	1.90 .65

Nos. 591-597 (7) 4.95 2.30

Souvenir Sheet
Perf. 12½

598 A163 10k multicolored 2.75 1.50

AUSIPEX '84, Melbourne. No. 598 contains one stamp 32x40mm and also exists imperf.

Stop Polio Campaign — A164

1984, Sept. 29   *Perf. 13*
599	A164	5k shown	1.10	.55
600	A164	6k Vaccinating child	1.20	.55

Art
A165

1984, Oct. 26
601	A165	50c Dragon (hand rail)	.25	.25
602	A165	1k Capital	.25	.25
603	A165	2k Oval panel	.40	.25
604	A165	2k Deity	.40	.25
605	A165	3k Leaves	.80	.25
606	A165	4k Floral pattern	1.25	.40
607	A165	8k Lotus flower (round panel)	2.50	.65
		Nos. 601-607 (7)	5.85	2.30

Nos. 601-604 and 607 vert.

9th Anniv. of the Republic — A166

1984, Dec. 17
608	A166	1k River boats	.50	.25
609	A166	2k Aircraft	.70	.25
610	A166	4k Bridge building	1.20	.65
611	A166	10k Surveying, construction	2.50	.95
		Nos. 608-611 (4)	4.90	2.10

1986 World Cup Soccer
Championships, Mexico — A167

Various match scenes and flag of Mexico.

1985, Jan. 18
612	A167	50c multicolored	.25	.25
613	A167	1k multi, diff.	.25	.25
614	A167	2k multi, diff.	.50	.25
615	A167	3k multi, diff.	.65	.25
616	A167	4k multi, diff.	.85	.25
617	A167	5k multi, diff.	1.10	.40
618	A167	6k multi, diff.	1.40	.65
		Nos. 612-618 (7)	5.00	2.35

Souvenir Sheet
Perf. 12½
619	A167	10k multi, diff.	2.25	1.50

No. 619 contains one stamp 32x40mm.
Nos. 612-618 exist imperf.

Motorcycle, Cent. — A168

1985, Feb. 25   *Perf. 12½*
620	A168	50c shown	.25	.25
621	A168	1k 1920 Gnome Rhone	.25	.25
622	A168	2k 1928 F.N. M67C	.40	.25
623	A168	3k 1930 Indian Chief	.60	.25
624	A168	4k 1914 Rudge Multi	.80	.30
625	A168	5k 1953 Honda Benly J	1.10	.40
626	A168	6k 1938 CZ	1.25	.65
		Nos. 620-626 (7)	4.65	2.35

Nos. 620-626 exist imperf.

Mushrooms —
A169

1985, Apr. 8   *Perf. 13*
627	A169	50c Amanita muscaria	.25	.25
628	A169	1k Boletus edulis	.25	.25
629	A169	2k Coprinus comatus	.50	.25
630	A169	2k Amanita rubescens	.50	.25
631	A169	3k Xerocomus subtomentosus	.75	.30
632	A169	4k Lepiota procera	1.00	.40
633	A169	8k Paxillus involutus	1.00	.60
		Nos. 627-633 (7)	5.25	2.30

Nos. 627-633 exist imperf.

End of
World War
II, 40th
Anniv.
A169a

1k, Battle of Kursk. 2k, Red Army parade, Moscow. 4k, Battle of Stalingrad. 5k, Battle for Berlin. 6k, Victory parade through Brandenburg Gate.

1985, May   **Litho.**   *Perf. 12½x12*
633A	A169a	1k multicolored	1.40	.25
633B	A169a	2k multicolored	2.50	.25
633C	A169a	4k multicolored	4.00	.40
633D	A169a	5k multicolored	5.00	.50
633E	A169a	5.5k multicolored	5.50	.55
		Nos. 633A-633E (5)	18.40	1.95

Lenin, 115th
Birth
Anniv. — A170

1k, Reading Pravda, horiz. 10k, Addressing revolutionaries.

1985, June 28   *Perf. 12½*
634	A170	1k multicolored	.35	.25
635	A170	2k shown	2.00	.30
636	A170	10k multicolored	2.00	.30
		Nos. 634-636 (3)	4.35	.85

Orchids — A171

50c, Cattleya percivaliana. 1k, Odontoglossum luteo-purpureum. No. 639, Cattleya lueddemanniana. No. 640, Maxillaria sanderiana. 3k, Miltonia vexillaria. 4k, Oncidium varicosum. 8k, Cattleya dowiana aurea. 10k, Catasetum fimbriatum.

1985, July 5   *Perf. 13*
637	A171	50c multicolored	.25	.25
638	A171	1k multicolored	.25	.25
639	A171	2k multicolored	.45	.25
640	A171	2k multicolored	.45	.25
641	A171	3k multicolored	.70	.25
642	A171	4k multicolored	1.00	.30
643	A171	8k multicolored	2.25	.65
		Nos. 637-643 (7)	5.35	2.20

Souvenir Sheet
Perf. 13½x13
644	A171	10k multicolored	2.75	1.50

ARGENTINA '85, Buenos Aires. No. 644 contains one stamp 32x40mm.

Fauna — A172

2k, Macaca mulatta. 3k, Bos sauveli. 4k, Hystrix leucura, horiz. 5k, Selenarctos thibotanus, horiz. 10k, Manis pentadactyla.

1985, Aug. 15   *Perf. 13*
645	A172	2k multicolored	.35	.25
646	A172	3k multicolored	.55	.25
647	A172	4k multicolored	.80	.30
648	A172	5k multicolored	1.00	.30
649	A172	10k multicolored	2.00	.65
		Nos. 645-649 (5)	4.70	1.75

Nos. 645-49 exist imperf.

Apollo-Soyuz Flight, 10th
Anniv. — A173

50c, Apollo launch pad, vert. 1k, Soyuz launch pad, vert. No. 652, Apollo approaching Soyuz. No. 653, Soyuz approaching Apollo. 3k, Apollo, astronauts. 4k, Soyuz, cosmonauts. 8k, Docked spacecrafts.

1985, Sept. 6
650	A173	50c multicolored	.25	.25
651	A173	1k multicolored	.25	.25
652	A173	2k multicolored	.40	.25
653	A173	2k multicolored	.65	.25
654	A173	3k multicolored	.80	.25
655	A173	4k multicolored	1.00	.30
656	A173	8k multicolored	1.60	.65
		Nos. 650-656 (7)	4.95	2.20

Nos. 650-656 exist imperf.

Aircraft
A174

1985, Oct. 25
657	A174	50c Fiat	.25	.25
658	A174	1k Cant z.501	.25	.25
659	A174	2k MF-5	.40	.25
660	A174	3k Macchi Castoldi	.65	.25
661	A174	4k Anzani	.80	.25
662	A174	5k Ambrosini	1.00	.30
663	A174	6k Piaggio	1.10	.35
		Nos. 657-663 (7)	4.45	1.90

Souvenir Sheet
Perf. 13x13½
664	A174	10k MF-4	4.50	2.40

ITALIA '85, Rome. No. 664 contains one stamp 40x32mm and also exists imperf.
Nos. 657-663 exist imperf.

Miniature Sheet

Columbus's Fleet — A175

1985, Oct. 25   *Perf. 13*
665	A175	Sheet of 5 + 4 labels	15.00	7.50
a.		1k Pinta	.50	.25
b.		2k Nina	.75	.25
c.		3k Santa Maria	1.25	.30
d.		4k Columbus	1.50	.40
e.		5k Map of 1st voyage	2.00	1.50

ITALIA '85.

UN, 40th
Anniv. — A176

1985, Oct.
666	A176	2k UN and natl. flag	.55	.25
667	A176	3k Coats of arms	.80	.30
668	A176	10k Map, globe	2.50	1.00
		Nos. 666-668 (3)	3.85	1.55

Health — A177

1k, Mother feeding child. 3k, Immunization, horiz. 4k, Hospital care, horiz. 10k, Breastfeeding.

1985, Nov. 15
669	A177	1k multicolored	.40	.25
670	A177	3k multicolored	.80	.25
671	A177	4k multicolored	.95	.30
672	A177	10k multicolored	2.00	.80
		Nos. 669-672 (4)	4.15	1.60

10th
Anniv. of
the
Republic
A178

1985, Dec. 2
673	A178	3k shown	.65	.25
674	A178	10k multi, diff.	2.50	1.00

People's Revolutionary Party, 30th
Anniv. — A179

1985, Dec. 30
675	A179	2k shown	.95	.25
676	A179	8k multi, diff.	2.50	.65

Nos. 276, 286, 289, 291-292, 297, 299-300, 305, 308-309, 319 Overprinted in Red

Methods and Perfs As Before
1985

676A	A102	40k multi	40.00	40.00
m.		Inverted "8" in overprint		
676B	A98	50k multi	40.00	40.00
n.		Inverted overprint	—	
o.		"1895" instead of "1985"	—	
676C	A99	50k multi	100.00	100.00
676D	A107	70k multi	40.00	40.00
676E	A105	80k multi	50.00	50.00
676F	A100	100k multi	120.00	120.00
676G	A105	100k multi	50.00	50.00
676H	A96	200k org & multi	110.00	110.00
676I	A100	250k multi	150.00	150.00
676J	A101	250k vio & blk	170.00	170.00
676K	A104	300k multi	120.00	120.00
p.		Inverted overprint	—	
676L	A102	300k multi	120.00	120.00
		Nos. 676A-676L (12)	1,110.	1,110.

1986 World Cup Soccer Championships, Mexico — A180

Various match scenes.

1986, Jan. 20

677	A180	50c multicolored	.25	.25
678	A180	1k multi, diff.	.25	.25
679	A180	2k multi, diff.	.40	.25
680	A180	3k multi, diff.	.50	.25
681	A180	4k multi, diff.	.70	.25
682	A180	5k multi, diff.	.80	.30
683	A180	6k multi, diff.	1.10	.40
		Nos. 677-683 (7)	4.00	1.95

Souvenir Sheet
Perf. 13x13½

684	A180	10k multi, diff.	2.00	.90

No. 684 contains one stamp 40x32mm.

27th Congress of the Communist Party of the Soviet Union A180a

1986, Jan. Litho. Perf. 12x12½

684A	A180a	4k Cosmonaut, spacecraft	2.50	.30
684B	A180a	20k Lenin	7.50	1.00

Flowering Plants — A181

1986, Feb. 28 Perf. 13

685	A181	50c Pelargonium grandiflorum	.25	.25
686	A181	1k Aquilegia vulgaris	.25	.25
687	A181	2k Fuchsia globosa	.45	.25
688	A181	3k Crocus aureus	.65	.25
689	A181	4k Althaea rosea	.80	.30
690	A181	5k Gladiolus purpureo	1.00	.40
691	A181	6k Hyacinthus orientalis	1.25	.55
		Nos. 685-691 (7)	4.65	2.25

Butterflies A182

1986, Mar. 30

692	A182	50c Aporia hippia	.25	.25
693	A182	1k Euthalia irrubescens	.25	.25
694	A182	2k Japonica lutea	.45	.25
695	A182	3k Pratapa ctesia	.65	.25
696	A182	4k Kallina inachus	.80	.30
697	A182	5k Ixias pyrene	1.00	.40
698	A182	6k Parantica sita	1.25	.55
		Nos. 692-698 (7)	4.65	2.25

A183

First Man in Space, 25th Anniv. — A184

Designs: 50c, Launch, Baikonur Space Center, vert. 1k, Interkosmos communications satellite, vert. 2k, Salyut space station. 3k, Yuri Gagarin, Sputnik 1 disengaging stage. 4k, Luna 3, the Moon, vert. 5k, Leonov on first space walk, vert. 6k, Luna 16 lifting off Moon, vert. 10k, Spacecrafts docking.

1986, Apr. 12

699	A183	50c multicolored	.25	.25
700	A183	1k multicolored	.25	.25
701	A183	2k multicolored	.40	.25
702	A183	3k multicolored	.65	.25
703	A183	4k multicolored	.80	.25
704	A183	5k multicolored	1.00	.40
705	A183	6k multicolored	1.10	.50
		Nos. 699-705 (7)	4.45	2.15

Souvenir Sheet
Perf. 13x13½

706	A184	10k multicolored	2.50	1.00

No. 706 exists imperf.

Fauna — A185

50c, Giraffa camelopardalis. 1k, Panthera leo. 2k, Loxodonta africana africana. 3k, Macropus rufus. 4k, Gymnobelideus leadbeateri. 5k, Phoenicopterus ruber. 6k, Ailuropoda melanoleucus.

10k, Bison, vert.

1986, May 22 Perf. 12½x13, 13x12½

707	A185	50c multicolored	.25	.25
708	A185	1k multicolored	.25	.25
709	A185	2k multicolored	.40	.25
710	A185	3k multicolored	.70	.25
711	A185	4k multicolored	1.00	.25
712	A185	5k multicolored	1.25	.30
713	A185	6k multicolored	1.50	.55
		Nos. 707-713 (7)	5.35	2.10

Souvenir Sheet
Perf. 13½x13

714	A185	10k multicolored	3.00	1.50

Nos. 707-712 vert. No. 714 has the Ameripex '86 stamp exhibition logo in the margin.

Pheasants — A187

50c, Argusianus argus. 1k, Cennaeus nycthemerus. 2k, Phasianus colchicus. 3k, Chrysolophus amherstiae. 4k, Symaticus reevesii. 5k, Chrysolophus pictus. 6k, Syrmaticus soemmerringii.

1986, June 29 Perf. 12½x13

715	A187	50c multicolored	.25	.25
716	A187	1k multicolored	.25	.25
717	A187	2k multicolored	.45	.25
718	A187	3k multicolored	.60	.25
719	A187	4k multicolored	.80	.25
720	A187	5k multicolored	1.00	.30
721	A187	6k multicolored	1.25	.40
		Nos. 715-721 (7)	4.60	1.95

Snakes — A188

1986, July 21 Perf. 12½x13, 13x12½

722	A188	50c Elaphe guttata	.25	.25
723	A188	1k Thalerophis richardi	.30	.25
724	A188	1k Lampropeltis doliata annulata	.35	.25
725	A188	2k Diadophis amabilis	.40	.25
726	A188	4k Boiga dendrophila	.70	.25
727	A188	5k Python molurus	1.00	.30
728	A188	8k Naja naja	1.25	.40
		Nos. 722-728 (7)	4.25	1.95

Nos. 722-723 and 728 vert.

Halley's Comet — A189

50c, Acropolis, Athens. #730a, 1k, Bayeux Tapestry. #730b, 2k, Edmond Halley. #731a, 3k, Vega space probe. #731b, 4k, Galileo. #732a, 5k, Comet. #732b, 6k, Giotto probe.

1986, Aug. 22 Perf. 12½x13

729	A189	50c multi	.25	.25
730	A189	Pair, #a.-b.	.75	.40
731	A189	Pair, #a.-b.	1.25	.50
732	A189	Pair, #a.-b.	2.25	.70
		Nos. 729-732 (4)	4.50	1.85

Souvenir Sheet
Perf. 13x13½

733	A189	10k Comet, diff.	2.50	1.25

Nos. 730-732 printed in continuous designs. Sizes of Nos. 730a, 731a, 732a: 46x25mm; Nos. 730b, 731b, 732b: 23x25mm. No. 733 contains one 40x32mm stamp.

Dogs — A190

1986, Aug. 28 Perf. 13

737	A190	50c Keeshond	.25	.25
738	A190	1k Elkhound	.25	.25
739	A190	2k Bernese	.45	.25
740	A190	3k Pointing griffon	.65	.25
741	A190	4k Sheep dog (border collie)	.85	.25
742	A190	5k Irish water spaniel	1.00	.30
743	A190	6k Briard	1.25	.55
		Nos. 737-743 (7)	4.70	2.10

Souvenir Sheet
Perf. 13x13½

744	A190	10k Brittany spaniels	2.10	1.10

STOCKHOLMIA '86. Nos. 738-743 horiz. No. 744 contains one 40x32mm stamp. Nos. 737-743 exist imperf.

Cacti — A191

Designs: 50c, Mammillaria matudae. 1k, Mammillaria theresae. 2k, Ariocarpus trigonus. 3k, Notocactus crassigibbus. 4k, Astrophytum asterias hybridum. 5k, Melocactus manzanus. 6k, Astrophytum ornatum hybridum.

1986, Sept. 28 Perf. 13

745	A191	50c multicolored	.25	.25
746	A191	1k multicolored	.25	.25
747	A191	2k multicolored	.40	.25
748	A191	3k multicolored	.65	.25
749	A191	4k multicolored	.80	.25
750	A191	5k multicolored	1.00	.30
751	A191	6k multicolored	1.10	.40
		Nos. 745-751 (7)	4.45	1.95

Nos. 745-751 exist imperf.

Intl. Peace Year — A192

3k, Natl. arms, dove, globe. 5k, Dove, shattered bomb. 10k, Emblem held aloft.

1986, Oct. 24

752	A192	3k multicolored	.75	.25
753	A192	5k multicolored	1.10	.40
754	A192	10k multicolored	2.25	1.00
		Nos. 752-754 (3)	4.10	1.65

UNESCO Programs in Laos — A193

3k, Vat Phu Champasak ruins. 4k, Satellite dish, map, globe. 9k, Laotians learning to read, horiz.

1986, Nov. 4
755	A193	3k multicolored	.70	.25
756	A193	4k multicolored	1.00	.30
757	A193	9k multicolored	1.75	.65
		Nos. 755-757 (3)	3.45	1.20

1988 Winter Olympics,
Calgary — A194

1987, Jan. 14
758	A194	50c Speed skating	.25	.25
759	A194	1k Biathlon	.25	.25
760	A194	2k Pairs figure skating	.40	.25
761	A194	3k Luge	.60	.25
762	A194	4k 4-Man bobsled	.75	.25
763	A194	5k Ice hockey	1.00	.30
764	A194	6k Ski jumping	1.10	.40
		Nos. 758-764 (7)	4.35	1.95

Souvenir Sheet
Perf. 13½x13
765	A194	10k Slalom	2.25	1.10

Nos. 758-760 vert. No. 765 contains one stamp 32x40mm.

1988 Summer Olympics,
Seoul — A195

1987, Feb. 2   **Perf. 12½x13, 13x13½**
766	A195	50c Women's gymnastics	.25	.25
767	A195	1k Women's discus	.25	.25
768	A195	2k Running	.40	.25
769	A195	3k Equestrian	.65	.25
770	A195	4k Women's javelin	.75	.25
771	A195	5k High jump	1.00	.30
772	A195	6k Wrestling	1.10	.40
		Nos. 766-772 (7)	4.40	1.95

Souvenir Sheet
Perf. 12½
773	A195	10k Runners leaving start	2.00	1.00

Nos. 766, 768, 770 and 772 vert. No. 773 contains one 40x32mm stamp.
Nos. 766-772 exist imperf.

Dogs
A196

1987, Mar. 5   **Perf. 12½x13**
774	A196	50c Great Dane	.25	.25
775	A196	1k Labrador retriever	.25	.25
776	A196	2k St. Bernard	.40	.25
777	A196	3k Schippercke	.65	.25
778	A196	4k Alsatian (German shepherd)	.75	.25
779	A196	5k Beagle	1.00	.30
780	A196	6k Spaniel	1.25	.55
		Nos. 774-780 (7)	4.55	2.10

Space
Flight,
30th
Anniv.
A197

1987, Apr. 12   **Perf. 13**
781	A197	50c Sputnik 1	.25	.25
782	A197	1k Sputnik 2	.25	.25
783	A197	2k Cosmos 87	.40	.25
784	A197	3k Cosmos	.50	.25
785	A197	4k Mars	.65	.25
786	A197	5k Luna 1	.80	.30
787	A197	9k Luna 3, vert.	1.25	.50
		Nos. 781-787 (7)	4.10	2.05

Packet Ships and Stampless Packet
Letters — A198

Canada No. 282 — A199

50c, "Montreal". 1k, "Paid Montreal". 2k, "Paid" and "Montreal Nov 24". 3k, "Williamsbvrg" and "Forwarded". 4k, "Montreal Fe 18 1844". 5k, "Paid" and "Montreal Jy 10 1848". 6k, "Paid" and "Montreal Paid Ap 16 1861 Canada".

1987, May 12
788	A198	50c multicolored	.25	.25
789	A198	1k multicolored	.25	.25
790	A198	2k multicolored	.35	.25
791	A198	3k multicolored	.55	.25
792	A198	4k multicolored	.75	.25
793	A198	5k multicolored	.85	.30
794	A198	6k multicolored	1.10	.40
		Nos. 788-794 (7)	4.10	1.95

Souvenir Sheet
Perf. 12½
795	A199	10k multicolored	2.50	1.25

CAPEX '87.

Orchids — A200

3k, Vanda teres. 7k, Laeliocattleya. 10k, Paphiopedilum hibrido. 39k, Sobralia. 44k, Paphiopedilum hibrido, diff. 47k, Paphiopedilum hibrido, diff. 50k, Cattleya trianaei. 95k, Vanda tricolor.

1987, Aug. 10   **Litho.**   **Perf. 13**
796	A200	3k multicolored	.25	.25
796A	A200	7k multicolored	.25	.25
796B	A200	10k multicolored	.40	.25
796C	A200	39k multicolored	.75	.25
796D	A200	44k multicolored	.80	.30
796E	A200	47k multicolored	1.00	.40
796F	A200	50k multicolored	1.10	.40
		Nos. 796-796F (7)	4.55	2.10

Souvenir Sheet
Perf. 12½
796G	A200	95k multicolored	2.25	1.10

No. 796G contains one 32x40mm stamp.
Nos. 796, 796A-796G exist imperf.

Automobiles — A201

1987, July 2   **Litho.**   **Perf. 12½**
797	A201	50c Toyota 480	.25	.25
798	A201	1k Alfa 33	.25	.25
799	A201	2k Ford Fiesta	.40	.25
800	A201	3k Datsun	.65	.25
801	A201	4k Vauxhall Cavalier	.80	.25
802	A201	5k Renault 5	1.00	.30
803	A201	6k Rover-800	1.25	.55
		Nos. 797-803 (7)	4.60	2.10

Miniature Sheet
Perf. 13
804	A201	10k Talbot	2.10	1.00

HAFNIA
'87,
Denmark
A202

Various Indian elephants.

1987, Sept. 2   **Perf. 13**
805	A202	50c Adult, calf	.25	.25
806	A202	1k Two adults, calf	.25	.25
807	A202	2k Adult eating grass	.40	.25
808	A202	3k Adult, diff.	.60	.25
809	A202	4k Adult, calf drinking	.75	.25
810	A202	5k Adult, diff.	.90	.30
811	A202	6k Adult, vert.	1.10	.40
		Nos. 805-811 (7)	4.25	1.95

Souvenir Sheet
812	A202	10k Herd, diff.	2.25	1.10

No. 812 contains one stamp 40x32mm.

Horses — A203

Perf. 13x12½, 12½x13
1987, June 3   **Litho.**
813	A203	50c multicolored	.25	.25
814	A203	1k multi, diff.	.25	.25
815	A203	2k multi, diff.	.40	.25
816	A203	3k multi, diff.	.60	.25
817	A203	4k multi, diff.	.75	.25
818	A203	5k multi, diff.	1.00	.30
819	A203	6k multi, diff.	1.10	.40
		Nos. 813-819 (7)	4.35	1.95

Nos. 814-819 vert.

Fish
A204

Designs: 3k, Botia macracantha. 7k, Oxymocanthus longirostris. 10k, Adioryx caudimaculatus. 39k, Synchiropus splendidus. 44k, Cephalopolis miniatus. 47k, Dendrochirus zebra. 50k, Pomacantus semicirculatus.

1987, Oct. 14   **Litho.**   **Perf. 13x12½**
820	A204	3k multicolored	.25	.25
821	A204	7k multicolored	.25	.25
822	A204	10k multicolored	.40	.25
823	A204	39k multicolored	.70	.25
824	A204	44k multicolored	.80	.30
825	A204	47k multicolored	1.00	.40
826	A204	50k multicolored	1.10	.40
		Nos. 820-826 (7)	4.50	2.10

World
Food
Day
A205

1987, Oct. 16   **Perf. 13**
827	A205	1k Tending crops	.25	.25
828	A205	3k Harvesting corn, vert.	.25	.25
829	A205	5k Harvesting wheat	.30	.25
830	A205	63k Youths, fish, vert.	1.25	.50
831	A205	142k Tending pigs, chickens	2.40	1.00
		Nos. 827-831 (5)	4.45	2.25

Cultivation of Rice in Mountainous
Regions — A206

1987, Nov. 9   **Perf. 13**
832	A206	64k Tilling soil	1.25	.30
833	A206	100k Rice paddy	1.90	.80

October
Revolution,
Russia, 70th
Anniv.
A207

Paintings: 1k, Wounded soldier on battlefield. 2k, Mother and child. 4k, Storming the Winter Palace. 8k, Lenin and revolutionaries. 10k, Rebuilding Red Square.

1987, Nov.   **Perf. 12x12½**
834	A207	1k multicolored	.25	.25
835	A207	2k multicolored	.40	.25
836	A207	4k multicolored	.70	.25
837	A207	8k multicolored	1.25	.50
838	A207	10k multicolored	1.75	.65
		Nos. 834-838 (5)	4.35	1.90

For surcharges, see Nos. 1882-1883.

Women
Wearing
Regional
Costumes
A208

1987, Dec. 2
839	A208	7k Mountain	.25	.25
840	A208	38k Urban	.80	.25
841	A208	144k Mountain, diff.	2.75	1.10
		Nos. 839-841 (3)	3.80	1.60

Nos. 839-841 exist imperf.

A209

1988 Winter Olympics,
Calgary — A210

1988, Jan.10			Perf. 13x12½	
842	A209	1k Bobsled	.25	.25
843	A209	4k Biathlon	.25	.25
844	A209	20k Skiing	.45	.25
845	A209	42k Ice hockey	.75	.30
846	A209	63k Speed skating	1.10	.50
847	A209	70k Slalom	1.25	.55
		Nos. 842-847 (6)	4.05	2.10

Souvenir Sheet
Perf. 13

848	A210	95k Slalom, diff.	2.25	1.10

No. 848 contains one stamp 40x32mm.

ESSEN
'88 — A211

Locomotives: 6k, Nonpareil, vert. 15k,
Rocket, vert. 20k, Royal George. 25k,
Trevithick. 30k, Novelty. 100k, Tom Thumb.
95k, Locomotion.

1988			Perf. 12½x13, 13x12½	
849	A211	6k multicolored	.25	.25
850	A211	15k multicolored	.25	.25
851	A211	20k multicolored	.45	.25
852	A211	25k multicolored	.55	.25
853	A211	30k multicolored	.65	.25
854	A211	100k multicolored	1.90	.80
		Nos. 849-854 (6)	4.05	2.05

Souvenir Sheet
Perf. 13

855	A211	95k multicolored	2.25	1.10

No. 855 contains one stamp 40x32mm.
Nos. 849-854 exist imperf.

Intl. Year of Shelter for the
Homeless — A212

1988		Litho.	Perf. 13	
856	A212	1k Building frame of house	.25	.25
857	A212	27k Cutting lumber	.55	.25
858	A212	46k Completed house	1.00	.30
859	A212	70k Community	1.60	.65
		Nos. 856-859 (4)	3.40	1.45

Dinosaurs — A213

3k, Tyrannosaurus. 7k, Ceratosaurus
nasicornis. 39k, Iguanodon bernissartensis.
44k, Scolosaurus. 47k, Phororhacus. 50k,
Trachodon.
95k, Pteranodon.

Perf. 13x12½, 12½x13

1988, Mar. 3			Litho.	
860	A213	3k multicolored	.25	.25
861	A213	7k multicolored	.25	.25
862	A213	39k multicolored	.75	.25
863	A213	44k multicolored	.80	.40
864	A213	47k multicolored	1.00	.40
865	A213	50k multicolored	1.10	.40
		Nos. 860-865 (6)	4.15	1.95

Souvenir Sheet
Perf. 12½

866	A213	95k multicolored	2.25	1.10

JUVALUX '88. Nos. 861-864 vert.
Identifications on Nos. 860 and No. 865 are
switched.
No. 866 contains one 40x32mm stamp.

WHO,
40th
Anniv.
A214

1988, Apr. 8			Perf. 12½	
867	A214	5k Students, teacher	.25	.25
868	A214	27k Pest control	.50	.25
869	A214	164k Public water supply, vert.	3.00	1.25
		Nos. 867-869 (3)	3.75	1.75

Flowers — A215

8k, Plumieria rubra. 9k, Althaea rosea. 15k,
Ixora coccinea. 33k, Cassia fistula. 64k, Dahlia
coccinea (pink). 69k, Dahlia coccinea (yellow).
95k, Plumieria, Althaea, Ixora.

1988			Perf. 13x12½	
870	A215	8k multicolored	.25	.25
871	A215	9k multicolored	.25	.25
872	A215	15k multicolored	.40	.25
873	A215	33k multicolored	.75	.25
874	A215	64k multicolored	1.25	.50
875	A215	69k multicolored	1.50	.55
		Nos. 870-875 (6)	4.40	2.05

Souvenir Sheet
Perf. 13

876	A215	95k multicolored	2.50	1.25

FINLANDIA '88. No. 876 contains one
32x40mm stamp.

Birds — A216

1988			Perf. 13	
877	A216	6k Pelargopsis capensis	.25	.25
878	A216	10k Coturnix japonica	.25	.25
879	A216	13k Psittacula roseata	.40	.25
880	A216	44k Treron bicincta	.85	.25
881	A216	63k Pycnonotus melanicterus	1.10	.50
882	A216	64k Ducula badia	1.10	.55
		Nos. 877-882 (6)	3.95	2.05

1988 Summer Olympics,
Seoul — A217

1988			Perf. 12½x12	
883	A217	2k Javelin	.25	.25
884	A217	5k Long jump	.25	.25
885	A217	10k Horizontal bar	.40	.25
886	A217	12k Canoeing	.50	.25
887	A217	38k Balance beam	.80	.25
888	A217	46k Fencing	1.00	.30
889	A217	100k Wrestling	2.00	.70
		Nos. 883-889 (7)	5.20	2.25

Souvenir Sheet
Perf. 13

889A	A217	95k Horizontal bar, diff.	2.10	1.00

No. 889A contains one 40x32mm stamp.
Nos. 883-889 exist imperf.

Decorative Stencils — A218

1988			Perf. 13	
890	A218	1k Scarf	.25	.25
891	A218	2k Pagoda entrance, vert.	.25	.25
892	A218	3k Pagoda wall, vert.	.35	.25
893	A218	25k Pagoda pillar	.50	.25
894	A218	163k Skirt	3.00	1.50
		Nos. 890-894 (5)	4.35	2.50

Completion of the 5-Year Plan (1981-
85) — A219

1988		Litho.	Perf. 13	
895	A219	20k Health care	.40	.25
896	A219	40k Literacy	.80	.40
897	A219	50k Irrigation	1.00	.55
898	A219	100k Communication, transport	1.75	1.00
		Nos. 895-898 (4)	3.95	2.20

Intl. Red Cross and Red Crescent
Organizations, 125th Annivs. — A220

Designs: 4k, Dove, 3 stylized figures representing mankind, vert. 52k, Giving aid to the
handicapped, vert. 144k, Child immunization.

1988				
899	A220	4k multi	.25	.25
900	A220	52k multi	1.10	.55
901	A220	144k multi	2.75	1.50
		Nos. 899-901 (3)	4.10	2.30

Chess Champions — A220a

1988		Litho.	Perf. 13	
901A	A220a	1k R. Segura	.25	.25
901B	A220a	2k Adolph Anderssen	.25	.25
901C	A220a	3k P. Morphy	.25	.25
901D	A220a	6k W. Steinitz	.25	.25
901E	A220a	7k E. Lasker	.30	.25
901F	A220a	12k J.R. Capablanca	.40	.25
901G	A220a	172k A. Alekhine	3.00	1.10
		Nos. 901A-901G (7)	4.70	2.60

Nos. 901C is incorrectly inscribed "Murphy."

1990 World Cup Soccer
Championships, Italy — A221

Various plays.

1989			Perf. 13x12½	
902	A221	10k multi	.25	.25
903	A221	15k multi, diff.	.25	.25
904	A221	20k multi, diff.	.40	.25
905	A221	25k multi, diff.	.55	.25
906	A221	45k multi, diff.	.80	.30
907	A221	105k multi, diff.	2.00	.80
		Nos. 902-907 (6)	4.25	2.10

Souvenir Sheet
Perf. 13

907A	A221	95k multi, diff.	2.10	1.00

No. 907A contains one 40x32mm stamp.

INDIA
'89
A222

Cats.

1989, Jan. 7			Perf. 12½	
908	A222	5k multi	.25	.25
909	A222	6k multi, diff.	.25	.25
910	A222	10k multi, diff.	.40	.25
911	A222	20k multi, diff.	.60	.25
912	A222	50k multi, diff.	1.10	.40
913	A222	172k multi, diff.	3.25	1.00
		Nos. 908-913 (6)	5.85	2.40

Souvenir Sheet
Perf. 13

914	A222	95k multi, diff.	2.10	1.00

No. 914 contains one 32x40mm stamp.

1992 Winter Olympics,
Albertville — A223

Various figure skaters.

1989, May 1 — Perf. 13

915	A223	9k multi, vert.		.25	.25
916	A223	10k shown		.25	.25
917	A223	15k multi, diff., vert.		.35	.25
918	A223	24k multi, diff., vert.		.50	.25
919	A223	29k multi, diff., vert.		.65	.25
920	A223	114k multi, diff., vert.		2.00	1.00
		Nos. 915-920 (6)		4.00	2.25

Souvenir Sheet
Perf. 12½

921	A223	95k Pairs figure skating	2.10	1.10

No. 921 contains one 32x40mm stamp.

People's Army, 40th Anniv. A224

1989, Jan. 20 — Perf. 13

922	A224	1k shown		.25	.25
923	A224	2k Military school, vert.		.25	.25
924	A224	3k Health care		.25	.25
925	A224	250k Ready for combat		6.00	1.00
		Nos. 922-925 (4)		6.75	1.75

1992 Summer Olympics, Barcelona — A225

Perf. 12x12½, 12½x12
1989, June 1 — Litho.

926	A225	5k Pole vault, vert.		.25	.25
927	A225	15k Gymnastic rings, vert.		.25	.25
928	A225	20k Cycling		.30	.25
929	A225	25k Boxing		.40	.30
930	A225	70k Archery, vert.		1.10	.55
931	A225	120k Swimming, vert.		1.75	.65
		Nos. 926-931 (6)		4.05	2.25

Souvenir Sheet
Perf. 13

932	A225	95k Baseball	2.10	1.10

No. 932 contains one 32x40mm stamp.

PHILEXFRANCE '89 — A226

Paintings by Picasso: 5k, *Beggars by the Edge of the Sea*. 7k, *Maternity*. 8k, *Portrait of Jaime S. Le Bock*. 9k, *Harlequins*. 105k, *Dog with Boy*. 114k, *Girl Balancing on Ball*. 95k *Woman in Hat*.

1989, July 17 — Perf. 12½x13

933	A226	5k multi		.25	.25
934	A226	7k multi		.25	.25
935	A226	8k multi		.25	.25
936	A226	9k multi		.35	.25
937	A226	105k multi		1.75	.65
938	A226	114k multi		2.00	.80
		Nos. 933-938 (6)		4.85	2.45

Souvenir Sheet
Perf. 12½

939	A226	95k multicolored	2.10	1.10

No. 939 contains one 32x40mm stamp.

Cuban Revolution, 30th Anniv. — A227

1989, Apr. 20 — Litho. — Perf. 13

940	A227	45k shown	1.10	.40
941	A227	50k Flags	1.25	.40

Fight the Destruction of Forests — A228

1989, Mar. 30 — Litho. — Perf. 13

942	A228	4k Planting saplings		.25	.25
943	A228	10k Fight forest fires		.25	.25
944	A228	12k Do not chop down trees		.25	.25
945	A228	200k Map of woodland		3.25	1.00
		Nos. 942-945 (4)		4.00	1.75

Nos. 944-945 are vert.

Jawaharlal Nehru (1889-1964), Indian Statesman A229

1989, Nov. 9 — Litho. — Perf. 12½

946	A229	1k multicolored		.25	.25
947	A229	60k multi, horiz.		1.10	.50
948	A229	200k multi, diff.		3.50	1.10
		Nos. 946-948 (3)		4.85	1.85

Mani Ikara Zapota — A230

1989, Sept. 18 — Perf. 12½x13

949	A230	5k shown		.25	.25
950	A230	20k Psidium guajava		.40	.25
951	A230	20k Annona sguamosa		.40	.25
952	A230	30k Durio zibethinus		.55	.25
953	A230	50k Punica granatum		.90	.50
954	A230	172k Moridica charautia		3.00	1.00
		Nos. 949-954 (6)		5.50	2.50

A231

Historic Monuments: No. 955, That Sikhotabong, Khammouane. No. 956, That Dam, Vientiane. No. 957, That Ing Hang, Savannakhet. No. 958, Ho Vay Phra Thatluang, Vientiane.

1989, Oct. 19 — Litho. — Perf. 12½

955	A231	5k multicolored		.25	.25
956	A231	15k multicolored		.30	.25
957	A231	61k multicolored		1.10	.55
958	A231	161k multicolored		2.75	1.25
		Nos. 955-958 (4)		4.40	2.30

1992 Summer Olympics, Barcelona A232

1990, Mar. 5 — Litho. — Perf. 12½x13

959	A232	10k Basketball		.25	.25
960	A232	30k Hurdles		.45	.25
961	A232	45k High jump		.65	.25
962	A232	50k Cycling		.75	.30
963	A232	60k Javelin		.90	.50
964	A232	90k Tennis		1.40	.80
		Nos. 959-964 (6)		4.40	2.35

Souvenir Sheet

965	A232	95k Rhythmic gymnastics	2.00	1.00

Nos. 959-964 exist imperf.

1992 Winter Olympics, Albertville — A233

1990, June 20 — Perf. 13

966	A233	10k Speed skating		.25	.25
967	A233	25k Cross country skiing, vert.		.40	.25
968	A233	30k Slalom skiing		.45	.25
969	A233	35k Luge		.55	.25
970	A233	80k Ice dancing, vert.		1.25	.55
971	A233	90k Biathlon		1.40	.65
		Nos. 966-971 (6)		4.30	2.20

Souvenir Sheet

972	A233	95k Hockey, vert.	2.00	1.00

New Zealand Birds A234

Designs: 10k, Prosthemadera novaeseelandie. 15k, Alauda arvensis. 20k, Haemotopus unicolor. 50k, Phalacrocorax carbo. 60k, Demigretta sacra. 100k Apteryx australis mantelli. 95k, Phalacrocorax corunculatus.

1990, Aug. 24 — Perf. 12½

973	A234	10k multicolored		.25	.25
974	A234	15k multicolored		.35	.25
975	A234	20k multicolored		.45	.25
976	A234	50k multicolored		.90	.30
977	A234	60k multicolored		1.10	.50
978	A234	100k multicolored		1.90	.80
		Nos. 973-978 (6)		4.95	2.35

Souvenir Sheet

979	A234	95k multicolored	2.25	1.10

World Stamp Expo, New Zealand '90. No. 979 contains one 32x40mm stamp and also exists imperf.

That Luang Temple, 430th Anniv. A235

1990, July 25 — Perf. 13x12½, 12½x13

980	A235	60k 1867		1.50	.50
981	A235	70k 1930		1.75	.65
982	A235	130k 1990, vert.		3.25	1.25
		Nos. 980-982 (3)		6.50	2.40

Ho Chi Minh (1890-1969), Vietnamese Leader — A236

40k, Addressing people. 60k, With Laotian President. 160k, Waving, vert.

1990, May 11 — Perf. 13

983	A236	40k multicolored		.90	.30
984	A236	60k multicolored		1.40	.45
985	A236	160k multicolored		3.75	1.25
		Nos. 983-985 (3)		6.05	2.00

UN Development Program, 40th Anniv. — A237

1990, Oct. 24 — Litho. — Perf. 13

986	A237	30k Surgeons		.75	.25
987	A237	45k Fishermen		1.25	.30
988	A237	80k Flight controller, vert.		2.00	.75
989	A237	90k Power plant		2.25	.90
		Nos. 986-989 (4)		6.25	2.20

15th Anniv. of the Republic A238

Designs: 15k, Placing flowers at monument. 20k, Celebratory parade. 80k, Visiting sick. 120k, Women marching with banner.

1990, Dec. 2 — Litho. — Perf. 13

990	A238	15k multicolored		.40	.25
991	A238	20k multicolored		.60	.25
992	A238	80k multicolored		2.00	.90
993	A238	120k multicolored		3.00	1.25
		Nos. 990-993 (4)		6.00	2.65

New Year's Day A239

1990, Nov. 20

994	A239	5k shown		.25	.25
995	A239	10k Parade		.30	.25
996	A239	50k Ceremony		.90	.40

Size: 40x29mm

997	A239	150k Ceremomy, diff.		2.50	1.25
		Nos. 994-997 (4)		3.95	2.15

World Cup Soccer Championships, Italy — A240

Designs: Various soccer players in action.

1990		Litho.		Perf. 13	
998	A240	10k multicolored	.25	.25
999	A240	15k multicolored	.30	.25
1000	A240	20k multicolored	.45	.25
1001	A240	25k multicolored	.55	.25
1002	A240	45k multicolored	.85	.30
1003	A240	105k multicolored	1.90	.80
	Nos. 998-1003 (6)		4.30	2.10

Souvenir Sheets
Perf. 12½

1004	A240	95k multi, horiz.	2.00	1.00

Perf. 13

1004A	A240	95k multi	2.00	1.00

No. 1004 contains one 39x31mm stamp; No. 1004A one 32x40mm stamp.

Intl. Literacy Year A241

50k, Woman with child, vert. 60k, Monk teaching class. 150k, Two women, man reading.

1990, Feb. 27		Litho.		Perf. 12½	
1005	A241	10k shown	.25	.25
1006	A241	50k multicolored	1.00	.75
1007	A241	60k multicolored	1.25	.90
1008	A241	150k multicolored	3.00	1.25
	Nos. 1005-1008 (4)		5.50	3.15

Stamp World London '90 — A242

Stamps, modes of mail transport: 15k, Great Britain #1, stagecoach. 20k, US #1, train. 40k, France #3, balloons. 50k, Sardinia #1, post rider. 60k, Indo-China #3, elephant. 95k, Laos #272, jet. 100k, Spain #1, sailing ship.

1990, Apr. 26		Litho.		Perf. 13x12½	
1009	A242	15k multicolored	.25	.25
1010	A242	20k multicoloroed	.40	.25
1011	A242	40k multicolored	.70	.25
1012	A242	50k multicolored	1.00	.30
1013	A242	60k multicolored	1.10	.50
1014	A242	100k multicolored	1.90	.75
	Nos. 1009-1014 (6)		5.35	2.30

Souvenir Sheet
Perf. 13

1015	A242	95k multicolored	2.00	1.00

No. 1015 contains one 40x32mm stamp.
Nos. 1009-1014 exist imperf.

Endangered Animals — A242a

10k, Brow-antlered deer. 20k, Gaur. 40k, Wild water buffalo. 45k, Kouprey. 120k, Javan rhinoceros.

1990, Sept. 15		Litho.		Perf. 12½	
1015A	A242a	10k multicolored	.25	.25
1015B	A242a	20k multicolored	.40	.25
1015C	A242a	40k multicolored	.70	.25
1015D	A242a	45k multicolored	.75	.30
1015E	A242a	120k multicolored	1.75	1.00
	Nos. 1015A-1015E (5)		3.85	2.05

A243

1992 Olympics, Barcelona and Albertville — A244

Perf. 12½x12, 12x12½, 13 (A244)
1991, Jan. 25

1016	A243	22k 2-man canoe	.25	.25
1017	A243	32k 1-man kayak	.30	.25
1018	A244	32k Bobsled, vert.	.30	.25
1019	A244	135k Cross country skiing	.50	.50
1020	A243	250k Ski jumping	.85	.25
1021	A244	275k Biathlon	1.00	.30
1022	A243	285k Diving, vert.	1.00	.30
1023	A244	330k Sailing, vert.	1.20	.35
1024	A244	900k Speed skating	2.75	1.00
1025	A243	1000k Swimming	2.50	1.00
	Nos. 1016-1025 (10)		10.65	4.20

Souvenir Sheets
Perf. 12½, 13½x13

1026	A243	700k 2-man kayak	2.75	1.00
1027	A244	700k Slalom skiing, vert.	2.75	1.00

No. 1026 contains one 40x32mm stamp. No. 1027 contains one 32x40mm stamp.

Tourism — A245

Designs: 155k, Rapids, Champassak. 220k, Vangvieng. 235k, Waterfalls, Saravane, vert. 1000k Plain of Jars, Xieng Khouang, vert.

1991				Perf. 13x12½, 12½x13	
1028	A245	155k multicolored	.55	.25
1029	A245	220k multicolored	.80	.30
1030	A245	235k multicolored	1.00	.35
1031	A245	1000k multicolored	3.25	1.10
	Nos. 1028-1031 (4)		5.60	2.00

1994 World Cup Soccer Championships — A246

Designs: Various players in action.

1991		Litho.		Perf. 13	
1032	A246	32k multicolored	.25	.25
1033	A246	330k multicolored	.75	.35
1034	A246	340k multi, vert.	.85	.40
1035	A246	400k multicolored	1.00	.45
1036	A246	500k multicolored	1.25	.65
	Nos. 1032-1036 (5)		4.10	2.10

Souvenir Sheet
Perf. 13½x13

1037	A246	700k multi, vert.	2.00	1.00

No. 1037 contains one 32x40mm stamp.

Espamer '91, Buenos Aires — A247

25k, Mallard 4-4-2. 32k, Pacific 231 4-6-2. 285k, American style 4-8-4. 650k, Canadian Pacific 4-6-2. 750k, Beyer-Garrant 4-8-2 2-8-4. 700k, Inter-city diesel.

1991, June 30		Litho.		Perf. 12½x12	
1038	A247	25k multicolored	.25	.25
1039	A247	32k multicolored	.25	.25
1040	A247	285k multicolored	.90	.35
1041	A247	650k multicolored	2.00	.75
1042	A247	750k multicolored	2.25	1.10
	Nos. 1038-1042 (5)		5.65	2.70

Souvenir Sheet
Perf. 12½

1043	A247	700k multicolored	2.00	1.00

Espamer '91, Buenos Aires. No. 1039 does not show denomination or country in Latin characters. Size of Nos. 1038, 1040-1042: 44x28mm.

Musical Celebrations — A248

Designs: 220k, Man playing mong, vert. 275k, Man, woman singing Siphandone, vert. 545k, Man, woman singing Khapngum. 690k, People dancing.

1991, July 10		Litho.		Perf. 13	
1044	A248	20k multicolored	.25	.25
1045	A248	220k multicolored	.55	.25
1046	A248	275k multicolored	.75	.30
1047	A248	545k multicolored	1.25	.65
1048	A248	690k multicolored	1.75	1.00
	Nos. 1044-1048 (5)		4.55	2.45

Butterflies — A248a

55k, Sasakia charonda. 90k, Luendorfia puziloi. 255k, Papilio bianor. 285k, Papilio machaon. 900k, Graphium doson. 700k, Cyrestis thyodamas.

1991, Oct. 15		Litho.		Perf. 12½x12	
1048A	A248a	55k multicolored	.25	.25
1048B	A248a	90k multicolored	.30	.25
1048C	A248a	255k multicolored	.90	.25
1048D	A248a	285k multicolored	1.00	.30
1048E	A248a	900k multicolored	2.50	1.10
	Nos. 1048A-1048E (5)		4.95	2.15

Souvenir Sheet
Perf. 13

1048F	A248a	700k multicolored	3.25	1.25

No. 1048F contains one 40x32mm stamp. Phila Nippon '91.

Arbor Day A249

700k, 6 people planting trees. 800k, Nursery.

1991, June 1				Perf. 12½	
1049	A249	250k multicolored	.70	.35
1050	A249	700k multicolored	1.60	.80
1051	A249	800k multicolored	2.00	1.10
	Nos. 1049-1051 (3)		4.30	2.25

1992 Winter Olympics, Albertville A250

Perf. 12½x12, 12x12½

1992, Jan. 12				Litho.	
1052	A250	200k Bobsled	.50	.25
1053	A250	220k Skiing	.60	.25
1054	A250	250k Skiing, horiz.	.70	.25
1055	A250	500k Luge	1.25	.30
1056	A250	600k Figure skater	1.50	.80
	Nos. 1052-1056 (5)		4.55	1.85

Souvenir Sheet
Perf. 12½

1057	A250	700k Speed skater	2.00	1.00

No. 1057 contains one 32x40mm stamp.

1992 Summer Olympics, Barcelona A251

1992, Feb. 21		Litho.		Perf. 12½	
1058	A251	32k Women's running	.25	.25
1059	A251	245k Baseball	.70	.25
1060	A251	275k Tennis	.80	.25
1061	A251	285k Basketball	.90	.30
1062	A251	900k Boxing, horiz.	2.25	1.00
	Nos. 1058-1062 (5)		4.90	2.05

Souvenir Sheet

1062A	A251	700k Diving	2.00	1.00

No. 1062A contains one 40x32mm stamp.

World Health Day A252

Designs: 200k, Spraying for mosquitoes. 255k, Campaign against smoking. 330k, Receiving blood donation. 1000k, Immunizing child, vert.

1992, Apr. 7					
1063	A252	200k multicolored	.50	.25
1064	A252	255k multicolored	.70	.30
1065	A252	330k multicolored	.90	.65
1066	A252	1000k multicolored	2.25	1.25
	Nos. 1063-1066 (4)		4.35	2.45

A253

516

LAOS

Flags, ball and players: 260k, Argentina, Italy. 305k, Germany, Great Britain. 310k, US, World Cup trophy (no players). 350k, Italy, Great Britain. 800k, Germany, Argentina.

1992, May 1   Litho.   Perf. 13
1067 A253 260k multicolored   .60 .25
1068 A253 305k multicolored   .65 .25
1069 A253 310k multicolored   .70 .30
1070 A253 350k multicolored   .80 .50
1071 A253 800k multicolored   1.90 1.00
   Nos. 1067-1071 (5)   4.65 2.30
Souvenir Sheet
Perf. 12½
1072 A253 700k Goalie   3.25 1.65
1994 World Cup Soccer Championships, US.

A254

Children playing.

1992, Nov. 8   Litho.   Perf. 13
1073 A254 220k Playing drum   .85 .25
1074 A254 285k Jumping rope, horiz.   1.10 .25
1075 A254 330k Walking on stilts   1.25 .30
1076 A254 400k Escape from line, horiz.   1.60 .65
   Nos. 1073-1076 (4)   4.80 1.45

Poisonous Snakes — A255

280k, Naja naja kaouthia. 295k, Naja naja atra. 420k, Trimeresurus wagleri. 700k, Ophiophagus hannah, vert.

Perf. 12½x13, 13x12½
1992, July 10   Litho.
1078 A255 280k multicolored   .85 .25
1079 A255 295k multicolored   .85 .25
1080 A255 420k multicolored   1.25 .35
1081 A255 700k multicolored   2.25 1.00
   Nos. 1078-1081 (4)   5.20 1.85

Restoration of Wat Phou — A256

Different views of Wat Phou.

Perf. 13x12½, 12½x13
1992, Aug. 22   Litho.
1082 A256 185k multicolored   .50 .30
1083 A256 220k multicolored   .60 .30
1084 A256 1200k multi, horiz.   3.75 1.40
   Nos. 1082-1084 (3)   4.85 2.00

Genoa '92 — A257

Sailing ships and maps by: 100k, Juan Martinez. 300k, Piri Reis, vert. 350k, Paolo del Pozo Toscanelli. 400k, Gabriel de Vallseca. 455k, Juan Martinez, diff. 700k, Juan de la Cosa.

Perf. 13x12½, 12½x13
1992, Sept. 12
1085 A257 100k multicolored   .25 .25
1086 A257 300k multicolored   .85 .25
1087 A257 350k multicolored   1.10 .25
1088 A257 400k multicolored   1.20 .50
1089 A257 455k multicolored   1.60 .65
   Nos. 1085-1089 (5)   5.00 1.90
Souvenir Sheet
Perf. 13
1090 A257 700k multicolored   2.75 1.00

Traditional Costumes of the Montagnards A258

Various costumes.

1992, Oct. 2   Litho.   Perf. 13
1091 A258 25k multicolored   .25 .25
1092 A258 55k multicolored   .25 .25
1093 A258 400k multicolored   1.25 .50
1094 A258 1200k multicolored   4.00 1.25
   Nos. 1091-1094 (4)   5.75 2.25

A259

UN, UNESCO emblems, stylized faces and: 330k, Drum. 1000k, Traditional flute.

1991, Nov. 1   Litho.   Perf. 13
1095 A259 285k shown   .85 .35
1096 A259 330k multicolored   1.00 .35
1097 A259 1000k multicolored   3.00 1.25
   Nos. 1095-1097 (3)   4.85 1.95

Cultural Development Decade, 1988-1997.

A260

Designs: Apes.

1992, Dec. 22
1098 A260 10k Black gibbon   .25 .25
1099 A260 100k Douc langur   .25 .25
1100 A260 250k Pileated gibbon   .75 .35
1101 A260 430k Francois langur   1.10 .50
1102 A260 800k Pygmy loris   2.00 .80
   Nos. 1098-1102 (5)   4.35 2.15

Natl. Customs A261

Designs: 100k, Woman praying before Buddha, vert. 160k, Procession. 1500k, People giving food to monks.

1992, Dec. 2   Perf. 12½
1103 A261 100k multicolored   .30 .25
1104 A261 140k multicolored   .40 .25
1105 A261 160k multicolored   .45 .25
1106 A261 1500k multicolored   4.50 2.25
   Nos. 1103-1106 (4)   5.65 3.00

First Subway System, 130th Anniv. A262

1993, Jan. 9   Litho.   Perf. 13
1107 A262 15k New York   .25 .25
1108 A262 50k Berlin   .25 .25
1109 A262 100k Paris   .30 .25
1110 A262 200k London   .75 .35
1111 A262 900k Moscow   2.75 1.40
   Nos. 1107-1111 (5)   4.30 2.50
Souvenir Sheet
Perf. 13x13½
1112 A262 700k Antique engine, vert.   3.00 1.25
No. 1112 contains one 32x40mm stamp.

Frogs A263

55k, Kaloula pulchra. 90k, Xenopus muelleri. 100k, Centrolenella vireovittata, vert. 185k, Bufo marinus. 1200k, Hyla arborea, vert.

1993, Feb. 1   Litho.   Perf. 12½
1113 A263 55k multicolored   .25 .25
1114 A263 90k multicolored   .30 .25
1115 A263 100k multicolored   .35 .25
1116 A263 185k multicolored   .70 .35
1117 A263 1200k multicolored   3.50 1.25
   Nos. 1113-1117 (5)   5.10 2.35

Animals A264

45k, Tupaia glis. 60k, Cynocephalus volans. 120k, Loris grasilis. 500k, Tarsium spectrum. 600k, Symphalangus syndactylus.

1993, Mar. 13   Litho.   Perf. 13
1118 A264 45k multicolored   .25 .25
1119 A264 60k multicolored   .25 .25
1120 A264 120k multicolored   .45 .25
1121 A264 500k multicolored   1.60 .75
1122 A264 600k multicolored   1.90 1.25
   Nos. 1118-1122 (5)   4.45 2.75

Native Houses A265

Various houses.

1993, July 12   Litho.   Perf. 13
1123 A265 32k multi, vert.   .50 .40
1124 A265 200k multicolored   1.50 .60
1125 A265 650k multicolored   5.00 1.00
1126 A265 750k multicolored   6.75 1.75
   Nos. 1123-1126 (4)   13.75 3.75

Campaign Against Illegal Drugs — A266

Designs: 200k, Drugs, skull smoking cigarette. 430k, Burning confiscated drugs. 900k, Instructor showing danger of drugs to audience.

1993, June 26   Perf. 12½
1127 A266 200k multicolored   .65 .35
1128 A266 430k multicolored   1.50 .75
1129 A266 900k multicolored   3.25 1.40
   Nos. 1127-1129 (3)   5.40 2.50

A267

Shells: 20k, Chlamys senatorius nobilis. 30k, Epitonium prestiosum. 70k, Lambis rugosa. 500k, Conus aulicus. 1000k, Lambis millepeda.

1993, May 29   Litho.   Perf. 12x12½
1130 A267 20k multicolored   .25 .25
1131 A267 30k multicolored   .25 .25
1132 A267 70k multicolored   .30 .25
1133 A267 500k multicolored   1.60 .75
1134 A267 1000k multicolored   3.00 1.40
   Nos. 1130-1134 (5)   5.40 2.90

A268

Birds of prey: 10k, Aquila clanga. 100k, Athene brama. 330k, Circus melanoluecos. 1000k, Circaetus gallicus.

1993, Aug. 10   Litho.   Perf. 13
1135 A268 10k multicolored   .25 .25
1136 A268 100k multicolored   .50 .25
1137 A268 330k multicolored   1.50 .50
1138 A268 1000k multicolored   4.00 1.40
   Nos. 1135-1138 (4)   6.25 2.40
No. 1137 is horiz.

Environmental Protection — A269

Designs: 32k, Fighting forest fire. 40k, Animals around clean river. 260k, Rice paddies. 1100k, Water buffalo, people in water.

1993, Sept. 25   Litho.   Perf. 13
1139 A269 32k multicolored   .25 .25
1140 A269 40k multicolored   .25 .25
1141 A269 260k multicolored   1.00 .35
1142 A269 1100k multicolored   4.25 1.40
   Nos. 1139-1142 (4)   5.75 2.25

Butterflies: 35k, Narathura atosia. 80k, Parides philoxenus. 150k, Euploea harrisi. 220k, Ixias pyrene. 500k, Elymnias hypermnestra. 700k, Stichopthalma louisa.

1993, Oct. 1   Litho.   Perf. 13
1143 A270 35k multicolored   .25 .25
1144 A270 80k multicolored   .25 .25
1145 A270 150k multicolored   .45 .25
1146 A270 220k multicolored   .75 .35
1147 A270 500k multicolored   2.00 .85
Nos. 1143-1147 (5)   3.70 1.95

Souvenir Sheet
1148 A270 700k multicolored   3.00 1.50

No. 1148 contains one 40x32mm stamp.

1994 World Cup Soccer Championships, US — A271

Various soccer players.

1993, Nov. 3   Perf. 13
1149 A271 10k multicolored   .25 .25
1150 A271 20k multicolored   .25 .25
1151 A271 285k multicolored   1.10 .25
1152 A271 400k multicolored   1.60 .50
1153 A271 800k multicolored   3.25 1.25
Nos. 1149-1153 (5)   6.45 2.50

Souvenir Sheet
Perf. 12½
1154 A271 700k multicolored   2.75 1.40

Nos. 1154 contains one 32x40mm stamp.

Prehistoric Birds — A272

1994, Jan. 20   Litho.   Perf. 13
1155 A272 10k Hesperornis   .25 .25
1156 A272 20k Dronte   .25 .25
1157 A272 150k Archaeopterix   .60 .25
1158 A272 600k Phororhachos   2.00 .50
1159 A272 700k Dinornis maximus   2.25 1.00
Nos. 1155-1159 (5)   5.35 2.25

Souvenir Sheet
1160 A272 700k Teratornis, horiz. 2.50 1.25

Intl. Olympic Committee, Cent. — A273

100k, Flag, flame. 250k, Ancient Olympians. 1000k, Baron de Coubertin, Olympic runner.

Perf. 12x12½, 12½x12
1994, Mar. 15   Litho.
1161 A273 100k multi, vert.   .25 .25
1162 A273 250k multi   .75 .25
1163 A273 1000k multi, vert.   3.25 1.50
Nos. 1161-1163 (3)   4.25 2.00

1994 World Cup Soccer Championships, U.S. — A274

Various soccer plays.

1994, June 15   Litho.   Perf. 12½
1164 A274 40k multicolored   .25 .25
1165 A274 50k multicolored   .25 .25
1166 A274 60k multicolored   .25 .25
1167 A274 320k multicolored   1.10 .35
1168 A274 900k multicolored   3.25 1.00
Nos. 1164-1168 (5)   5.10 2.10

Souvenir Sheet
Perf. 13
1169 A274 700k multicolored   3.75 1.65

No. 1169 contains one 32x40mm stamp and is also known imperf.

Pagodas A275

Various ornate gables.

1994, July 1   Litho.   Perf. 12½
1170 A275 30k multicolored   .25 .25
1171 A275 150k multicolored   .55 .25
1172 A275 380k multicolored   1.25 .40
1173 A275 1100k multicolored   3.75 1.65
Nos. 1170-1173 (4)   5.80 2.55

Nos. 1170-1173 exist imperf.

Ursus Malayanus — A276

1994, July 23
1174 A276 50k shown   .75 .25
1175 A276 90k Adult   1.00 .40
1176 A276 200k Cub, adult   2.25 1.00
1177 A276 220k Adult standing   3.25 1.25
Nos. 1174-1177 (4)   7.25 2.90

World Wildlife Fund.

Reptiles — A277

70k, Natrix natrix. 80k, Natrix tessellata. 90k, Salamandra salamandra. 600k, Triturus alpestris. 700k, Triturus cristatus. 800k, Lacerta viridis.

1994, Aug. 1   Litho.   Perf. 12½
1178 A277 70k multi, horiz.   .30 .25
1179 A277 80k multi, horiz.   .35 .25
1180 A277 90k multi, horiz.   .40 .25
1181 A277 600k multi, horiz.   2.50 .50
1182 A277 800k multicolored   3.25 1.25
Nos. 1178-1182 (5)   6.80 2.50

Souvenir Sheet
1183 A277 700k multi, horiz.   3.25 1.25

No. 1183 contains one 40x32mm stamp.

Intl. Year of the Family — A278

Designs: 500k, Mother taking child to school, horiz. No. 1186, Mother walking with children. No. 1187, Family.

1994, Sept. 24
1184 A278 200k multicolored   .85 .35
1185 A278 500k multicolored   2.10 .75
1186 A278 700k multicolored   3.25 1.25
Nos. 1184-1186 (3)   6.20 2.35

Souvenir Sheet
1187 A278 700k multicolored   3.25 1.25

No. 1187 contains one 32x40mm stamp.

Drums A279

Designs: 440k, Two people with hanging drum. 450k, Barrel shaped drum. 600k, Hanging drum.

Perf. 12½, 13x12½ (#1189)
1994, Oct. 20   Litho.
1188 A279 370k multicolored   1.60 .40
1189 A279 440k multicolored   1.75 .50
1190 A279 450k multicolored   1.75 .50
1191 A279 600k multicolored   2.40 .75
Nos. 1188-1191 (4)   7.50 2.15

No. 1189 is 40x29mm.

Elephants — A280

1994, Nov. 25
1192 A280 140k shown   .55 .25
1193 A280 400k Beside railing   1.60 .80
1194 A280 890k Being ridden, vert.   3.25 1.40
Nos. 1192-1194 (3)   5.40 2.45

Peace Bridge Between Laos and Thailand — A281

1994, Apr. 8   Litho.   Perf. 14x14½
1195 A281 500k multicolored   2.50 1.25

Buddha — A282

15k, Phra Xayavoraman 7. 280k, Phra Thong Souk. 390k, Phra Monolom. 800k, Phra Ongtu.

1994, Aug. 25   Litho.   Perf. 13
1196 A282 15k multicolored   .25 .25
1197 A282 280k multicolored   1.25 .35
1198 A282 390k multicolored   1.60 .50
1199 A282 800k multicolored   3.50 1.40
Nos. 1196-1199 (4)   6.60 2.50

Dinosaurs A283

1994, Dec. 8
1200 A283 50k Theropod   .25 .25
1201 A283 380k Iguanodon   1.75 .65
1202 A283 420k Sauropod   2.00 .75
Nos. 1200-1202 (3)   4.00 1.65

World Tourism Organization, 20th Anniv. — A284

1995, Jan. 2   Litho.   Perf. 12½
1203 A284 60k Traditional music .25 .25
1204 A284 250k Traditional dance   1.00 .25
1205 A284 400k Traditional food 1.75 .50
1206 A284 650k Waterfalls, vert.   2.75 .90
Nos. 1203-1206 (4)   5.75 1.90

Souvenir Sheet
Perf. 13
1207 A284 700k like #1206, vert. 4.00 2.40

No. 1207 contains one 32x44mm stamp.

Dinosaurs A285

1995, Feb. 20   Perf. 12½
1208 A285 50k Tracodon   .25 .25
1209 A285 70k Protoceratops   .30 .25
1210 A285 300k Brontosaurus   1.25 .35
1211 A285 400k Stegosaurus   1.75 .50
1212 A285 600k Tyranosaurus   2.50 .75
Nos. 1208-1212 (5)   6.05 2.10

Birds A286

50k, Acridotheres javanicus. 150k, Starnus burmannicus. 300k, Acridotheres tristis. 700k, Gracula religiosa.

1995, Mar. 10
1213 A286 50k multicolored   .25 .25
1214 A286 150k multicolored   .65 .25
1215 A286 300k multicolored   1.25 .40
1216 A286 700k multicolored   3.00 .90
Nos. 1213-1216 (4)   5.15 1.80

Nos. 1213-1216 exist imperf.

Francophonie, 25th Anniv. — 1216A

Designs: 50k, People with arms linked. 380k, Temple. 420k, Map of Laos.

1995, Mar. 20   Litho.   Perf. 13
1216A A286a 50k multi   .25 .25
1216B A286a 380k multi   1.50 .65
1216C A286a 420k multi   1.75 .75
    Nos. 1216A-1216C (3)   3.50 1.65

Antique Containers A287

1995, May 1   Litho.   Perf. 12½
1217 A287 70k "Hanche" cup,
            vert.   .30 .25
1218 A287 200k Resin bowl   .85 .25
1219 A287 450k Button design
            bowl   1.90 .55
1220 A287 600k Loving cup   2.50 .75
    Nos. 1217-1220 (4)   5.55 1.80

1996 Atlanta Pre-Olympics A288

1995, Apr. 5
1221 A288 60k Pole vault   .25 .25
1222 A288 80k Javelin   .35 .25
1223 A288 200k Hammer throw .85 .25
1224 A288 350k Long jump   1.60 .40
1225 A288 700k High jump   3.25 .90
    Nos. 1221-1225 (5)   6.30 2.05
        Souvenir Sheet
1226 A288 700k Baseball   3.25 1.90
No. 1226 contains one 40x32mm stamp.

Rocket Festival A289

Designs: 80k, Launching rocket from scaffolding, vert. 160k, Carrying rocket in procession led by monk. 500k, Man carrying rocket on shoulder. 700k, People looking at rockets on tripods.

1995, June 1   Litho.   Perf. 13
1227 A289 80k multicolored .30 .25
1228 A289 160k multicolored .65 .25
1229 A289 500k multicolored 1.90 .55
1230 A289 700k multicolored 2.50 .90
    Nos. 1227-1230 (4)   5.35 1.95

Domestic Cats A290

Designs: 40k, Red tabby longhair. 50k, Siamese seal point. 250k, Red tabby longhair. 400k, Tortoise-shell shorthair. 650k, Tortoiseshell shorthair, vert. 700k, Tortoise-shell shorthair.

1995, July 25   Litho.   Perf. 12½
1231 A290 40k multicolored .25 .25
1232 A290 50k multicolored .25 .25
1233 A290 250k multicolored .80 .25
1234 A290 400k multicolored 1.20 .30
1235 A290 650k multicolored 1.40 .75
    Nos. 1231-1235 (5)   3.90 1.80
        Souvenir Sheet
1236 A290 700k multicolored 2.50 1.90
No. 1236 contains one 40x32mm stamp.

Insect-Eating Plants — A291

Designs: 90k, Nepenthes villosa. 100k, Dionaea muscipula. 350k, Sarracenia flava. 450k, Sarracenia purpurea. 500k, Nepenthes ampullaria.
1000k, Nepenthes gracilis.

1995, Aug. 24
1237 A291 90k multicolored .30 .25
1238 A291 100k multicolored .40 .25
1239 A291 350k multicolored 1.20 .35
1240 A291 450k multicolored 1.60 .35
1241 A291 500k multicolored 2.00 .75
    Nos. 1237-1241 (5)   5.50 1.95
        Souvenir Sheet
1242 A291 1000k multicolored 4.50 2.00
No. 1242 contains one 40x32mm stamp.

Insects A292

Designs: 40k, Lucanus cervus. 50k, Melolontha melolontha. 500k, Xylocopa violacea. 800k, Tettigonia viridissima.

1995, Sept. 20
1243 A292 40k multicolored .25 .25
1244 A292 50k multicolored .25 .25
1245 A292 500k multicolored 2.00 .50
1246 A292 800k multicolored 2.75 .90
    Nos. 1243-1246 (4)   5.25 1.90

FAO, 50th Anniv. A293

Designs: 80k, Cattle grazing. 300k, Farmer tilling rice paddy. 1000k, Planting, irrigating rice paddies, stocking pond with fish.

1995, Oct. 16   Litho.   Perf. 12½
1247 A293 80k multicolored .25 .25
1248 A293 300k multicolored 1.00 .50
1249 A293 1000k multicolored 3.50 1.70
    Nos. 1247-1249 (3)   4.75 2.45

Traditional Culture — A294

Designs: 50k, Man with musical instrument, two women. 280k, Dance. 380k, Playing game with bamboo poles. 420k, Woman, man with musical instruments.

1996, Jan. 10
1250 A294 50k multicolored .25 .25
1251 A294 280k multicolored 1.40 .35
1252 A294 380k multicolored 2.00 .50
1253 A294 420k multicolored 2.25 .50
    Nos. 1250-1253 (4)   5.90 1.60

1996 Summer Olympics, Atlanta — A295

1996, Feb. 20
1254 A295 30k Cycling   .25 .25
1255 A295 150k Soccer   .75 .25
1256 A295 200k Basketball,
            vert.   1.00 .25
1257 A295 300k Running, vert. 1.50 .30
1258 A295 500k Shooting   2.50 .65
    Nos. 1254-1258 (5)   6.00 1.70
        Souvenir Sheet
1259 A295 1000k Pole vault   3.50 1.70
No. 1259 contains one 38x30mm stamp.

Fauna — A296

Designs: 40k, Helarctos malayanus. 60k, Pelecanus philippensis. 200k, Panthera pardus. 250k, Papilio machaon. 700k, Python molurus.

1996, Feb. 26   Litho.   Perf. 13
1260 A296 40k multicolored .25 .25
1261 A296 60k multicolored .35 .25
1262 A296 200k multicolored 1.10 .35
1263 A296 250k multicolored 1.25 .30
1264 A296 700k multicolored 3.00 .90
    Nos. 1260-1264 (5)   5.95 1.95

Intl. Women's Day A297

20k, Weaving textile. 290k, Instructing calisthenics. 1000k, Feeding infant, vert.

1996, Mar. 8
1265 A297 20k multicolored .25 .25
1266 A297 290k multicolored 1.10 .30
1267 A297 1000k multicolored 3.50 1.70
    Nos. 1265-1267 (3)   4.85 2.25

A298

Various soccer plays.

1996, May 3   Litho.   Perf. 13
1268 A298 20k multicolored .25 .25
1269 A298 50k multicolored .25 .25
1270 A298 300k multicolored .60 .30
1271 A298 400k multicolored .75 .50
1272 A298 500k multicolored 1.00 .60
    Nos. 1268-1272 (5)   2.85 1.90
        Souvenir Sheet
1273 A298 1000k multicolored 2.50 1.50
1998 World Soccer Cup Championships, France.
No. 1273 contains one 32x40mm stamp.

A299

Various rats.

1996, Apr. 15   Litho.   Perf. 13½x13
1274 A299 50k purple & multi .25 .25
1275 A299 340k blue & multi   1.40 .65
1276 A299 350k green & multi 1.40 .65
1277 A299 370k red & multi   1.50 .75
    Nos. 1274-1277 (4)   4.55 2.30
New Year 1996 (Year of the Rat).

Laos Rural Development Program, 20th Anniv. — A300

50k, Instruction for giving medical care. 280k, Irrigation system. 600k, Bridge over waterway.

1995, Dec. 2   Perf. 13
1278 A300 50k multicolored .25 .25
1279 A300 280k multicolored .55 .50
1280 A300 600k multicolored 1.50 1.00
    Nos. 1278-1280 (3)   2.30 1.75

UN, 50th Anniv. A301

Designs: 290k, Men seated at round table. 310k, Men playing game, checkers. 440k, Boys in swing, playing ball.

1995, Oct. 24
1281 A301 290k multicolored 1.00 .40
1282 A301 310k multicolored 1.10 .50
1283 A301 440k multicolored 1.50 .75
    Nos. 1281-1283 (3)   3.60 1.65

Antique Aircraft A302

1996, July 5   Litho.   Perf. 13
1284 A302 25k Morane   .25 .25
1285 A302 60k Sopwith Camel .25 .25
1286 A302 150k De Haviland
            DH-4   .65 .25
1287 A302 250k Albatros   1.10 .35
1288 A302 800k Caudron   2.50 1.00
    Nos. 1284-1288 (5)   4.75 2.10

Capex '96.

Carts
A303

1996, Aug. 21
1289	A303	50k shown	.25	.25
1290	A303	100k Cart, diff.	.40	.25
1291	A303	440k Pulled by oxen	1.50	.65
		Nos. 1289-1291 (3)	2.15	1.15

Flowers — A304

Designs: 50k, Dendrobium secundum. 200k, Ascocentrum miniatum. 500k, Aerides multiflorum. 520k, Dendrobium aggregatum.

1996, Oct. 25   Litho.   Perf. 13
1292	A304	50k multicolored	.25	.25
1293	A304	200k multicolored	.75	.25
1294	A304	500k multicolored	1.90	.65
1295	A304	520k multicolored	2.00	.65
		Nos. 1292-1295 (4)	4.90	1.80

Draft
Horses — A305

Various breeds.

1996, Nov. 5   Litho.   Perf. 13
1296	A305	50k yellow & multi	.25	.25
1297	A305	80k green & multi	.25	.25
1298	A305	200k pink & multi	.55	.25
1299	A305	400k blue & multi	1.25	.50
1300	A305	600k yellow & multi	1.75	.75
		Nos. 1296-1300 (5)	4.05	2.00

Souvenir Sheet
1301	A305	1000k pink & multi	3.00	1.50

No. 1301 contains one 32x40mm stamp.

UNICEF,
50th
Anniv.
A306

200k, Children in school. 500k, Child breastfeeding, vert. 600k, Woman pumping water.

1996, Dec. 11   Litho.
1302	A306	200k multicolored	.80	.30
1303	A306	500k multicolored	2.00	.90
1304	A306	600k multicolored	2.40	1.25
		Nos. 1302-1304 (3)	5.20	2.45

Greenpeace, 25th Anniv. — A306a

Turtles: 150k, Dermochelys coriacea on sand. 250k, Dermochelys coriacea in surf. 400k, Erethochelys imbricata. 450k, Chelonia agassizi.

1996, Dec. 27   Litho.   Perf. 13
1304A	A306a	150k multicolored	.80	.25
1304B	A306a	250k multicolored	1.25	.50
1304C	A306a	400k multicolored	2.00	.80
1304D	A306a	450k multicolored	2.25	.90
	e.	Souvenir sheet, #1304A-1304D	6.50	4.75
		Nos. 1304A-1304D (4)	6.30	2.45

Steam Locomotives — A307

Designs: 100k, Kinnaird, 1846. 200k, Pioneer, 1836, portrait of George Stephenson. 300k, Portrait of Robert Stephenson, Long Boiler Express, 1848. 400k, Adler, 1835. 500k, Lord of the Isles, 1851-84. 600k, The Columbine, 1845.
2000k, Best friend of Charleston, 1830.

Perf. 12½x12, 12x13 (#1306-1309)
1997   Litho.
1305	A307	100k multicolored	.25	.25
1306	A307	200k multicolored	.40	.25
1307	A307	300k multicolored	.60	.35
1308	A307	400k multicolored	.75	.50
1309	A307	500k multicolored	1.00	.65
1310	A307	600k multicolored	1.25	.75
		Nos. 1305-1310 (6)	4.25	2.75

Souvenir Sheet
Perf. 12½
1311	A307	2000k multicolored	3.25	3.00

Nos. 1306-1309 are 42x21mm.
No. 1311 contains one 40x32mm stamp.

Parrots — A308

Designs: 50k, Agapornis personata. 150k, Agapornis cana. 200k, Agapornis lilianae. 400k, Agapornis fischeri. 500k, Agapornis nigregenis. 800k, Agapornis roseicollis. 2000k, Agapornis taranta.

1997   Perf. 12½
1312	A308	50k multicolored	.25	.25
1313	A308	150k multicolored	.45	.25
1314	A308	200k multicolored	.60	.25
1315	A308	400k multicolored	1.00	.50
1316	A308	500k multicolored	1.10	.65
1317	A308	800k multicolored	1.75	1.00
		Nos. 1312-1317 (6)	5.15	2.90

Souvenir Sheet
1318	A308	2000k multicolored	5.00	4.00

No. 1318 contains one 32x40mm stamp.

Year of the
Ox — A308a

Designs: 300k, Ox, rider with flag, vert. 440k, Ox, rider with umbrella.

1997   Litho.   Perf. 13x13½, 13½x13
1318A	A308a	50k multi	.25	.25
1318B	A308a	300k multi	1.60	1.40
1318C	A308a	440k multi	2.25	1.75
		Nos. 1318A-1318C (3)	4.10	3.40

Cooking
Utensils
A309

50k, Cooking over open fire, vert. 340k, Traditional food containers. 370k, Traditional meal setting.

1997
1319	A309	50k multicolored	.25	.25
1320	A309	340k multicolored	1.00	.55
1321	A309	370k multicolored	1.00	.60
		Nos. 1319-1321 (3)	2.25	1.40

Orchids
A310

Designs: 50k, Roeblingiana. 100k, Findlayanum. 150k, Crepidatum. 250k, Sarcanthus birmanicus. 400k, Cymbidium lowianum. 1000k, Dendrobium gratiossissimum. 2000k, Chamberlainianum.

1997   Litho.   Perf. 12½
1322	A310	50k multicolored	.25	.25
1323	A310	100k multicolored	.35	.25
1324	A310	150k multicolored	.45	.25
1325	A310	250k multicolored	.60	.35
1326	A310	400k multicolored	.90	.50
1327	A310	1000k multicolored	1.75	1.25
		Nos. 1322-1327 (6)	4.30	2.85

Souvenir Sheet
1328	A310	2000k multicolored	4.25	3.50

No. 1328 contains one 32x40mm stamp.

Elephants — A311

Elephas maximus: 100k, Adult, vert. 250k, Adult holding log. 300k, Adult, calf.
Loxodonta africana: 350k, Adult. 450k, Adult in water. 550k, Adult, vert. 2000k, Head of adult.

1997   Litho.   Perf. 12½
1329	A311	100k multicolored	.30	.25
1330	A311	250k multicolored	.60	.35
1331	A311	300k multicolored	.65	.35
1332	A311	350k multicolored	.70	.40
1333	A311	450k multicolored	.85	.55
1334	A311	550k multicolored	1.20	.65
		Nos. 1329-1334 (6)	4.30	2.55

Souvenir Sheet
1335	A311	2000k multicolored	4.25	3.00

No. 1335 contains one 32x40mm stamp.

Head
Pieces
and
Masks
A312

Various designs.

1997   Litho.   Perf. 12½
1336	A312	50k multi, vert.	.25	.25
1337	A312	100k multi, vert	.25	.25
1338	A312	150k multi	.40	.25
1339	A312	200k multi, vert.	.55	.25
1340	A312	350k multi, vert.	1.25	.40
		Nos. 1336-1340 (5)	2.70	1.40

1998 World Cup
Soccer
Championships,
France — A313

Various soccer plays.

1997   Litho.   Perf. 12½
1341	A313	100k multicolored	.25	.25
1342	A313	200k multicolored	.50	.25
1343	A313	250k multicolored	.55	.30
1344	A313	300k multicolored	.55	.30
1345	A313	350k multicolored	.65	.40
1346	A313	700k multicolored	.95	.80
		Nos. 1341-1346 (6)	3.45	2.30

Souvenir Sheet
1347	A313	2000k multicolored	3.50	2.50

Sailing
Ships
A314

50k, Phoenician. 100k, 13th cent. ship. 150k, 15th cent. vessel. 200k, Portuguese caravel, 16th cent. 400k, Dutch, 17th cent. 900k, HMS Victory.
2000k, Grand Henry, 1514.

1997   Perf. 13
1348	A314	50k multicolored	.25	.25
1349	A314	100k multicolored	.25	.25
1350	A314	150k multicolored	.35	.25
1351	A314	200k multicolored	.40	.25
1352	A314	400k multicolored	.80	.40
1353	A314	900k multicolored	1.40	.80
		Nos. 1348-1353 (6)	3.45	2.20

Souvenir Sheet
1354	A314	2000k multicolored	3.50	2.50

No. 1354 contains one 40x28mm stamp.

Canoe
Races
A315

Designs: 50k, Team in red shirts, team in yellow shirts rowing upward. 100k, Crowd cheering on teams. 300k, Teams rowing left. 500k, People standing in canoe cheering on teams.

1997   Litho.   Perf. 12½
1355	A315	50k multicolored	.25	.25
1356	A315	100k multicolored	.25	.25
1357	A315	300k multicolored	.75	.30
1358	A315	500k multicolored	1.25	.55
		Nos. 1355-1358 (4)	2.50	1.35

Admission of
Laos to
ASEAN — A316

Central flag: a, Brunei. b, Indonesia. c, Laos. d, Malaysia. e, Taiwan. f, Philippines. g, Singapore. h, Thailand. i, Viet Nam.

1997, July 23   Litho.   Perf. 14x14½
1359	A316	550k Strip of 9, #a.-i.	9.50	9.50
	j.	Sheet of 9, #1359a-1359i + label		

Nos. 1359a-1359i also exist in souvenir sheets of 1. No. 1359 was not available in the philatelic market until 8/98.

Vaccination Day — A317

Design: 50k, Child receiving oral vaccination. 340k, Child receiving shot. 370k, Child in wheelchair.

1997, Jan. 3   **Litho.**   **Perf. 13x13¼**
1363 A317 50k multi   .25 .25
1364 A317 340k multi   1.50 .65
1365 A317 370k multi   1.60 .75
   Nos. 1363-1365 (3)   3.35 1.65

> **Beginning with No. 1366, used values are for postally used stamps.**

Pseudoryx Saola — A319

Various views of Pseudoryx saola.

1997, Feb. 10   **Perf. 13x13¼, 13¼x13**
1366 A319 350k multi   1.60 1.60
1367 A319 380k multi, vert.   1.75 1.75
1368 A319 420k multi   2.00 2.00
   Nos. 1366-1368 (3)   5.35 5.35

ASEAN (Assoc. of South East Asian Nations), 30th Anniv. — A321

1997, Aug. 8   **Litho.**   **Perf. 13**
1373 A321 150k Headquarters   .90 .65
1374 A321 600k Map of Laos   3.50 2.75

Fishing A322

Designs: 50k, Holding large net with a pole, vert. 100k, Casting net. 450k, Woman using small net, vert. 600k, Placing fish traps in water.

1997
1375 A322 50k multicolored   .30 .25
1376 A322 100k multicolored   .60 .30
1377 A322 450k multicolored   2.00 1.60
1378 A322 600k multicolored   2.75 2.00
   Nos. 1375-1378 (4)   5.65 4.15

New Year 1998 (Year of the Tiger) A323

1998
1379 A323 150k green & multi   .90 .70
1380 A323 350k gray & multi   1.75 1.60
1381 A323 400k pale lilac & multi   1.90 1.75
   Nos. 1379-1381 (3)   4.55 4.05

Canoes — A325

Designs: 1100k, Barque. 1200k, Covered pirogue. 2500k, Motorized pirogue.

1998   **Litho.**   **Perf. 14½x14**
1387 A325 1100k multicolored   2.50 2.50
1388 A325 1200k multicolored   2.75 2.75
1389 A325 2500k multicolored   6.25 6.25
   Nos. 1387-1389 (3)   11.50 11.50

A326

Various wind musical instruments.

1998   **Perf. 14x14½**
1390 A326 900k multicolored   2.25 2.25
1391 A326 1200k multicolored   3.25 3.25
1392 A326 1500k multicolored   4.00 4.00
   Nos. 1390-1392 (3)   9.50 9.50

A327

Buddha Luang, Phabang.

1998
1393 A327 3000k multicolored   7.50 7.50

Orchids — A328

Designs: 900k, Paphiopedilum callosum. 950k, Paphiopedilum concolor. 1000k, Dendrobium thyrsiflorum, vert. 1050k, Dendrobium lindleyi, vert.

1998   **Perf. 14½x14, 14x14½**
1394 A328 900k multicolored   2.75 2.75
1395 A328 950k multicolored   3.00 3.00
1396 A328 1000k multicolored   3.00 3.00
1397 A328 1050k multicolored   3.25 3.25
   Nos. 1394-1397 (4)   12.00 12.00

Universal Declaration of Human Rights, 50th Anniv. — A329

Designs: 170k, Women voting. 300k, Children in classroom.

1998   **Perf. 14½x14**
1398 A329 170k multicolored   2.25 2.25
1399 A329 300k multicolored   3.75 3.75

Historic Sites — A330

Designs: 10,000k, Hotay Vat Sisaket, vert. 25,000k, Vat Phou. 45,000k, That Luong.

Perf. 14x14¼, 14¼x14
1998, Sept. 1   **Litho.**
1400-1402 A330 Set of 3   120.00 120.00

People's Army, 50th Anniv. — A331

Designs: 1300k, Soldiers, flag, flowers. 1500k, Soldiers, cave, jungle, vert.

1999, Jan. 20   **Litho.**   **Perf. 13¼**
1403 A331 1300k multi   4.00 1.40
1404 A331 1500k multi   5.00 1.50

Souvenir Sheet

Visit Laos Year (in 2000) — A331a

Various temples: b, 2500k. c, 4000k, d, 5500k, e, 8000k.

1999, Aug. 1   **Typo.**   **Perf. 13¼**
     Gold Stamps
1404A A331a   Sheet of 4, #b-e   25.00 25.00
   f.   As 1404A, with larger margins with Thaipex 99 and China Stamp Exhibition 99 emblems   30.00 30.00
   g.   As 1404A, with larger margins with China 1999 Philatelic Exhibition emblem   30.00 30.00

No. 1404Af issued 8/2; No. 1404Ag issued 8/4.

Luang Prabang World Heritage Site — A332

Designs: 400k, Commemorative marker, vert. 1150k, Building. 1250k, Vat Xiengthong (building with curved roof).

1999, Feb. 2
1405 A332 400k multi   2.50 .80
1406 A332 1150k multi   5.50 1.50
1407 A332 1250k multi   6.50 2.00
   Nos. 1405-1407 (3)   14.50 4.30

Tourism — A333

Designs: 200k, Yaos, Muong Sing. 500k, Phadeang, Vangvieng District. 1050k, That Makmo, Luang Prabang. 1300k, Patuxay, Vientiane, vert.

Perf. 14¾x14, 14x14¾
1999, Mar. 2   **Litho.**
1408 A333 200k multi   1.00
1409 A333 500k multi   1.50
1410 A333 1050k multi   2.50
1411 A333 1300k multi   3.50
   Nos. 1408-1411 (4)   8.50

Nocturnal Creatures A334

Designs: 900k, Glaucidium brodiei. 1600k, Otus lempiji. 2100k, Tyto alba. 2800k, Chironax melanocephalus.

1999, July 2   **Litho.**   **Perf. 14x14½**
1412 A334 900k multi   1.50 1.00
1413 A334 1600k multi   3.00 2.00
1414 A334 2100k multi   3.50 3.00
1415 A334 2800k multi   5.00 4.00
   Nos. 1412-1415 (4)   13.00 10.00

New Year 1999 (Year of the Rabbit) — A335

1500k, Rabbit, other animals of calendar cycle. 1600k, Rabbit.

1999, Apr. 15   **Litho.**   **Perf. 14x14¼**
1416 A335 1500k multi, vert.   7.00 5.00
   Perf. 14¾x14
1417 A335 1600k multi, horiz.   8.00 6.00

Farming Implements — A336

1999, May 1   **Litho.**   **Perf. 14¾x14**
1418 A336 1500k Plow   2.50 1.50
1419 A336 2000k Yoke   3.00 2.00
1420 A336 3200k Plow, diff.   4.00 3.00
   Nos. 1418-1420 (3)   9.50 6.50

UPU, 125th Anniv. A337

1999, Oct. 9
1421 A337 2600k shown   5.00 3.00
1422 A337 3400k Postman   7.00 4.00

Wildlife — A338

700k, Rhinoceros sondaicus. 900k, Bubalus bubalis. 1700k, Prionodon pardicolor. 1800k, Cervus unicolor. 1900k, Panthera leo.

Perf. 14¾x14, 14x14¾

1999, Nov. 10
1423	A338	700k multi	1.50	.60
1424	A338	900k multi, vert.	1.75	.80
1425	A338	1700k multi	3.00	1.50
1426	A338	1800k multi	3.25	1.75
1427	A338	1900k multi, vert.	3.50	1.90
		Nos. 1423-1427 (5)	13.00	6.55

Expo '99, Kunming, China — A339

Designs: 300k, Carved tree stump. 900k, China Hall. 2300k, Science and Technology Hall. 2500k, Laos traditional wooden house.

1999, Oct. 15   **Perf. 14¾x14**
1428	A339	300k multi	.70	.25
1429	A339	900k multi	1.50	.75
1430	A339	2300k multi	3.25	1.90
1431	A339	2500k multi	4.50	2.00
		Nos. 1428-1431 (4)	9.95	4.90

Millennium — A340

No. 1432, 2000k: a, Airport, bus, hospital. b, Temple, tractor, elephant. c, Building, truck. d, River, waterfalls.

2000, Jan. 1   **Litho.**   **Perf. 13½**
1432	A340	Block of 4, #a-d	10.00	5.50
e.		Souvenir sheet, #1432	12.00	6.75

No. 1432e sold for 10,000k. No. 1432e exists imperf. Value, $30.

New Year 2000 (Year of the Dragon) — A341

Dragons: 1800k, And other zodiac animals. 2300k, In water.

2000, Apr. 1   **Perf. 14½x14**
1433-1434	A341	Set of 2	5.50	1.25

Wedding Costumes A342

Designs: 800k, Lao Theung. 2300k, Lao Lum. 3400k, Lao Sung.

2000, Oct. 30   **Perf. 14x14½**
1435-1437	A342	Set of 3	4.50	3.00

Children's Drawings — A343

Designs: 300k, Waterfall. 400k, Forest fire. 2300k, Animals at river. 3200k, Animals at river, vert.

2000, June 1   **Perf. 14½x14, 14x14½**
1438-1441	A343	Set of 4	7.50	3.00

Bangkok 2000 Stamp Exhibition — A344

Orchids: 500k, Dendrobium draconis. 900k, Paphiopedilum hirsutissimum. 3000k, Dendrobium sulcatum. 3400k, Rhynchostylis gigantea.

2000, Mar. 25   **Perf. 14x14½**
1442-1445	A344	Set of 4	10.00	3.00
1445a		Souv. sheet, #1442-1445, perf. 13½	15.00	15.00

No. 1445a sold for 10,000k. No. 1445a exists imperf. Value, $80.

Peacocks A345

700k, Male with feathers down, vert., 1000k, Male with feathers up, vert., 1800k, Female. 3500k, Male and female.

10,000k, Male with feathers up, vert.

2000, July 10   **Perf. 14x14½, 14½x14**
1446-1449	A345	Set of 4	4.50	2.50

Souvenir Sheet
Perf. 13½
Litho. With Foil Application
1450	A345	10,000k multi	7.50	7.50

2000 Summer Olympics, Sydney — A346

Designs: 500k, Cycling. 900k, Boxing. 2600k, Judo. 3600k, Kayaking.

2000, Sept. 15   **Litho.**   **Perf. 14½x14**
1451-1454	A346	Set of 4	6.00	3.00
1454a		Souvenir sheet, #1451-1454, perf. 13½	10.00	10.00

No. 1454a sold for 10,000k. No. 1454a exists imperf. Value, $40.

Laotian postal officials have declared as "illegal" a sheet of stamps for Great People of the 20th Century (Elvis Presley, Roberto Clemente, Marilyn Monroe, Dr. Martin Luther King, Jr., Pope John Paul II, Frank Sinatra, Albert Einstein, Princess Diana and Walt Disney) and stamps depicting Tiger Woods, Payne Stewart, Arnold Palmer, Elvis Presley, Marilyn Monroe, John Lennon and the Beatles.

Women's Costumes — A347

2000, Mar. 8   **Litho.**   **Perf. 14¼x14½**
1455	A347	100k Kor Loma	.30	.25
1456	A347	200k Kor Pchor	.40	.25
1457	A347	500k Nhuan Krom	.50	.25
1458	A347	900k Taidam	2.00	.40
1459	A347	2300k Yao	3.00	1.00
1460	A347	2500k Meuy	3.00	1.10
1461	A347	2600k Sila	1.50	1.10
1462	A347	2700k Hmong	3.50	1.25
1463	A347	2800k Yao, diff.	3.50	1.25
1464	A347	3100k Kor Nukkuy	3.50	1.40
1465	A347	3200k Kor Pouxang	3.50	1.40
1466	A347	3300k Yao Lanten	2.00	1.40
1467	A347	3400k Khir	2.25	1.50
1468	A347	3500k Kor	4.00	1.50
1469	A347	3900k Hmong, diff.	4.00	1.75
		Nos. 1455-1469 (15)	36.95	15.80

Laotian-Japanese Bridge Project — A348

Flags, various views of bridge: 900k, 2700k, 3200k.

2000, Aug. 2   **Perf. 14½x14**
1470-1472	A348	Set of 3	5.00	2.75

Souvenir Sheet

No. 1472A: b, 4000k, Similar to #1470. c, 7500k, Similar to #1471. d, 8500k, Similar to #1472.

2000   **Typo.**   **Perf. 13¼x13½**
1472A	A348	Sheet of 3, #b-d	15.00 15.00

No. 1472A contains three 48x33mm stamps in gold. No. 1472A exists imperf. Value, $40.

Tourism — A349

Designs: 300k, Phousy Stupa, Luang Prabang. 600k, Than Chang Cave. 2800k, Inhang Stupa. 3300k, Buddha, Phiawat Temple.

2000, Nov. 20   **Perf. 14x14½**
1473-1476	A349	Set of 4	6.00	3.00

Lao People's Democratic Republic, 25th Anniv. — A350

2000, Dec. 2   **Perf. 13¼**
1477	A350	4000k multi	2.75	1.50

Mekong River at Twilight A351

Various views: 900k, 2700k, 3400k.

2000, June 20   **Perf. 14½x14**
1478-1480	A351	Set of 3	5.00	2.50

Anti-Drug Campaign — A352

Designs: 100k, Poppy field. 4000k, Burning of seized drugs.

2000, June 26   **Litho.**
1481-1482	A352	Set of 2	3.50	1.50

Souvenir Sheet

Route 13 Bridge Reconstruction Project — A353

Bridge in: a, Savannakhet. b, Saravane. c, Pakse.

2000, Feb. 14   **Perf. 13¼**
1483	A353	4000k Sheet of 3, #a-c	9.00	9.00

Souvenir Sheet

Anti-Polio Campaign — A354

No. 1484: a, 900k, People receiving vaccine. b, 2500k, Family, map of Laos.

2000, June 1
1484 A354   Sheet of 2, #a-b   3.50 3.50

Millennium
A355

Designs: 3200k, Satellite, telecommunication dishes, map of Laos, student. 4000k, High tension lines, dam.

2001, Jan. 1   *Perf. 14x14½*
1485-1486 A355   Set of 2   4.00 2.50

New Year 2001 (Year of the Snake) A356

Designs: 900k, Snake coiled around branch. 3500k, Snake, other zodiac animals.

2001, Apr. 15   *Perf. 14½x14*
1487-1488 A356   Set of 2   4.00 2.00

Cockfighting — A357

Pair of cocks fighting: 500k, 900k, 3300k, 3500k.
10,000k, Single cock, vert.

2001, Mar. 10   *Perf. 14½x14*
1489-1492 A357   Set of 4   5.50 3.25
Souvenir Sheet
Perf. 13¼
1493 A357   10,000k multi   7.50 7.50

No. 1493 contains one 36x50mm stamp. No. 1493 exists imperf. Value, $40.

Laos-People's Republic of China Diplomatic Relations, 40th Anniv. — A358

2001, Apr. 25   *Perf. 14¼x14½*
1494 A358   1000k multi   1.25 .40

Phila Nippon '01 A359

Birds: Nos. 1495, 1499a, 700k, Egretta intermedia. Nos. 1496, 1499b, 800k, Bubulcus ibis (36x50mm). Nos. 1497, 1499c, 3100k, Ardea cinera (36x50mm). Nos. 1498, 1499d, 3400k, Egretta alba.

Perf. 14½x14, 13¼ (#1496-1497)
2001, Aug. 1   With White Frames
1495-1498 A359   Set of 4   6.00 3.00
Souvenir Sheet
Without White Frames
Perf. 13¼
1499 A359   Sheet of 4, #a-d   7.50 7.50

No. 1499 sold for 10,000k. No. 1499 exists imperf. Value, $50.

Mortars and Pestles — A360

Designs: 900k, Two women using large hand-held pestle, vert. 2600k, Water-driven mortar and pestle. 3500k, Woman operating mechanical mortar and pestle, vert.

Perf. 14x14½, 14½x14
2001, Nov. 15
1500-1502 A360   Set of 3   4.50 2.25

Ceremonies — A361

Designs: 300k, Pou Nyer and Nya Nyer, vert. 600k, Hae Nang Sangkhan, vert. 1000k, Sand Stupa. 2300k, Hae Prabang, vert. 4000k, Takbat, vert.

2001, Apr. 13 *Perf. 14x14½, 14½x14*
1503-1507 A361   Set of 5   7.50 3.50

Buddhist Art — A362

Designs: 200k, Himavanta. 900k, Vanapavesa. 3200k, Kumarakanda. 3600k, Sakkapabba.

2001, Dec. 5   *Perf. 13¼*
1508-1511 A362   Set of 4   6.00 3.25
1511a   Souvenir sheet, #1508-1511   7.00 7.00

No. 1511a exists imperf. Value, $50.

Men's Costumes — A363

Designs: 100k, Yao Mane. 200k, Gnaheun. 500k, Katou. 2300k, Hmong Dam. 2500k, Harlak. 2600k, Kui. 2700k, Krieng. 3100k, Khmu Nhuan. 3200k, Ta Oy. 3300k, Tai Theng. 3400k, Hmong Khao. 3500k, Gnor. 3600k, Phouthai Na Gnom. 4000k, Yao. 5000k, Hmong.

2001, Feb. 20   *Perf. 14¼x14½*
1512 A363   100k multi   .25   .25
1513 A363   200k multi   .25   .25
1514 A363   200k multi   .30   .25
1515 A363   2300k multi   1.25   .80
1516 A363   2500k multi   1.40   .85
1517 A363   2600k multi   1.40   .85
1518 A363   2700k multi   1.50   .90
1519 A363   3100k multi   1.60   1.00
1520 A363   3200k multi   1.75   1.10
1521 A363   3300k multi   1.75   1.10
1522 A363   3400k multi   1.75   1.25

1523 A363   3500k multi   2.00   1.25
1524 A363   3600k multi   2.00   1.25
1525 A363   4000k multi   2.25   1.50
1526 A363   5000k multi   2.75   1.90
   Nos. 1512-1526 (15)   22.20 14.50

Buddhist Temple Doors — A364

Various doors: 600k, 2300k, 2500k, 2600k.

2001, Sept. 17 Litho. *Perf. 14x14½*
1527-1530 A364   Set of 4   6.00 3.00

Frangipani Flowers — A365

Designs: 1000k, White flowers. 2500k, Pink flowers, vert. 3500k, Red flowers.

2001, Oct. 2 *Perf. 14x14½, 14x14½*
1531-1533 A365   Set of 3   4.50 2.50
a.   Souvenir sheet, #1531-1533, perf. 13¼   6.00 4.00

Intl. Volunteers Year — A366

2001, Dec. 29   *Perf. 13¼*
1534 A366   1000k multi   2.50   .40

Women's Costumes — A367

Designs: 200k, Meuy. 300k, Leu. 500k, Tai Kouane. 700k, Tai Dam. 1000k, Tai Men. 1500k, Lanten. 2500k, Hmong. 3000k, Phouxang. 3500k, Taitheng. 4000k, Tai O. 5000k, Tai Dam, diff.

2002, Jan. 10   *Perf. 14x14½*
1535 A367   200k multi   .25   .25
1536 A367   300k multi   .25   .25
1537 A367   500k multi   .25   .25
1538 A367   700k multi   .30   .25
1539 A367   1000k multi   .50   .30
1540 A367   1500k multi   .70   .45
1541 A367   2500k multi   1.25   .75
1542 A367   3000k multi   1.50   .95
1543 A367   3500k multi   1.75   1.10
1544 A367   4000k multi   2.00   1.25
1545 A367   5000k multi   2.25   1.60
   Nos. 1535-1545 (11)   11.00   7.40

Intl. Year of Mountains — A368

Designs: No. 1546, 1500k, Pha Tang. No. 1547, 1500k, Phou Phamane.

2002, Mar. 30   *Perf. 14½x14*
1546-1547 A368   Set of 2   2.50 1.10

Nos. 1546-1547 are a corrected printing. The first printing, which was erroneously inscribed "LAO PRD" instead of "LAO PDR," was removed from sale after a few panes had been sold. Value, set of 2 $100.

New Year 2002 (Year of the Horse) A369

Designs: 1500k, Horse, zodiac animals. 3500k, Galloping horse.

2002, Apr. 14
1548-1549 A369   Set of 2   3.00 1.60

Laos - Viet Nam Cooperation A370

Designs: 2500k, Musical instruments. 3500k, Laotian leader with Ho Chi Minh, horiz.

2002, July 18   *Perf. 13*
1550-1551 A370   Set of 2   3.25 1.90

Phila Korea 2002 World Stamp Exhibition, Seoul — A371

Insects: Nos. 1552a, 1553a, Sagra femorata. Nos. 1552b, 1552b, Cerambycidae. Nos. 1552c, 1552c, Chrysochroa mniszechii. Nos. 1552d, 1553d, Anoplophora sp. Nos. 1552e, 1553e, Chrysochroa sandersi. Nos. 1552f, 1553f, Mouhotia batesi. Nos. 1552g, 1553g, Megaloxantha assamensis. Nos. 1552h, 1553h, Eupaturus gracillicornis.

2002, Aug. 1   *Perf. 14½x14*
Insects and Colored Backgrounds
1552   Vert. strip of 8   5.00 5.00
a.-h. A371 1000k Any single   .50   .30
Souvenir Sheet
Insects On Vegetation
1553 A371 1000k Sheet of 8,
              #a-h   5.00 5.00

No. 1553 exists imperf. Value, $45.

Admission to UPU, 50th Anniv. A372

2002, May 20 Litho. *Perf. 13x13¼*
1554 A372   3000k black   2.00 2.00

Goldfish — A373

No. 1555: a, Pearlscale goldfish. b, Moor. c, Bubble eyes goldfish. d, Red-capped oranda. e, Lionhead goldfish. f, Pom pom. g, Ranchu. h, Fantail goldfish. i, Celestial goldfish. j, Ryukin. k, Brown oranda. l, Veiltail goldfish.

2002, Oct. 2   ***Perf. 13¼***
1555 A373 1000k Sheet of 12,
      #a-l   6.00 6.00
  No. 1555 exists imperf. Value, $25.

Buffalo Fighting A374

Various buffalo: 200k, 300k, 3000k, 4000k.

2002, Dec. 15   ***Perf. 13x13¼***
1556-1559 A374   Set of 4   4.50 3.00

Souvenir Sheet

National Route 9 Improvement Project — A375

No. 1560: a, Curve. b, Interchange. c, Curve and building.

2002, Dec. 18   **Litho.**   ***Perf. 13¼***
1560 A375 1500k Sheet of 3,
      #a-c   6.00 6.00

Vat Phou World Heritage Site — A376

Designs: 1500k, Temple, vert. 3000k, Temple, diff. 4000k, Statue of Buddha, vert. 10,000k, Stone carving.

2003, Feb. 14   ***Perf. 14x14½, 14½x14***
1561-1563 A376   Set of 3   4.50 2.60

Souvenir Sheet
           Perf. 13¼
1564 A376 10,000k multi   6.00 6.00
  No. 1564 contains one 93x27mm stamp.

Butterflies — A377

No. 1565: a, Hasora schoenherr. b, Spindasis lohita. c, Graphium sarpedon. d, Polyura schreiber. e, Castalius rosimon. f, Dalias pasithoe. g, Pachliopta aristolochiae. h, Papilio memnon.

10,000k, Danaus genutia.

2003, Mar. 8   ***Perf. 14½x14***
1565 A377   Block of 8   6.00 6.00
a.-h.   1000k Any single   .60 .35

Souvenir Sheet
           Perf. 13¼
1566 A377 10,000k multi   6.00 6.00
  No. 1566 exists imperf. Value, $30.

New Year 2003 (Year of the Goat) A378

Designs: 2500k, Two goats. 5000k, Goat, zodiac animals.

2003, Apr. 15   ***Perf. 14½x14***
1567-1568 A378   Set of 2   5.00 2.25

Orchids — A379

Designs: 200k, Phalaenopsis Paifang's Golden Lion. 300k, Coelogyne lentiginosa. 500k, Phalaenopsis sumatrana. 1000k, Phalaenopsis bellina. 1500k, Paphiopedilum appletonianum. 2000k, Vanda bensonii. 2500k, Dendrobium harveyanum. 3000k, Paphiopedilum glaucophyllum. 3500k, Paphiopedilum gratrixianum. 4000k, Vanda roeblingiana. 5000k, Phalaenopsis Lady Sakhara.

2003, Apr. 25   ***Perf. 14½x14¼***
1569 A379   200k multi   .30 .25
1570 A379   300k multi   .40 .25
1571 A379   500k multi   .60 .25
1572 A379   1000k multi   .70 .30
1573 A379   1500k multi   .80 .45
1574 A379   2000k multi   1.00 .60
1575 A379   2500k multi   1.25 .75
1576 A379   3000k multi   1.40 .90
1577 A379   3500k multi   1.75 1.00
1578 A379   4000k multi   1.75 1.25
1579 A379   5000k multi   2.25 1.50
    Nos. 1569-1579 (11)   12.20 7.50

Wood Handicrafts — A380

Designs: 500k, Bowl. 1500k, Pitcher and goblets. 2500k, Fluted bowl. 3500k, Bowl, vert.

2003, May 10   ***Perf. 13***
1580-1583 A380   Set of 4   4.75 2.40

Traditional Games A381

Designs: 1000k, Walking on stringed coconut shells. 3000k, Top spinning. 4000k, Field hockey.

2003, June 1
1584-1586 A381   Set of 3   3.50 2.40

Stop Hunting Campaign A382

Designs: 1500k, Deer. 2000k, Gun. 4500k, Wild animals.

2003, July 25   **Litho.**   ***Perf. 13***
1587-1589 A382   Set of 3   3.75 2.50

Fruit A383

Designs: 500k, Mango. 1500k, Watermelon. 2500k, Custard apple. 4000k, Pineapple.

2003, Aug. 8   ***Perf. 14½x14***
1590-1593 A383   Set of 4   4.50 2.60

Palm Leaf Manuscripts A384

Designs: 500k, Monk writing palm leaf manuscript. 1500k, Palm leaf manuscript. 2500k, Manuscript casket. 3000k, Ho Tai.

2003, Sept. 12   ***Perf. 14x14½***
1594-1597 A384   Set of 4   4.00 3.00

Bangkok 2003 Intl. Philatelic Exhibition — A385

Buddhas of Luang Prabang: 500k, Pha Sene Souk. 1500k, Pha Gnai. 3000k, Pha Ong Luang. 3500k, Pha Ong Sene. 10,000k, Pha Attharatsa.

2003, Oct. 4   ***Perf. 14x14½***
1598-1601 A385   Set of 4   5.00 3.25

Souvenir Sheet
           Perf. 13½
1602 A385 10,000k multi   6.00 6.00
  No. 1602 contains one 30x95mm stamp. No. 1602 exists imperf. Value, $30.

Textiles — A386

Various textiles with panel colors of: 500k, Blue. 1000k, Red brown. 3000k, Green. 4000k, Yellow brown.

2003, Dec. 1   ***Perf. 14x14½***
1603-1606 A386   Set of 4   5.00 3.00

Installed Emerald Buddha — A387

2004, Feb. 5   **Litho.**   ***Perf. 14½x14***
1607 A387 5500k multi   3.00 1.90

Birds — A388

Designs: 2000k, Buceros bicornis. 2500k, Pycnonotus jocosus. 3000k, Ploceus hypoxanthus. 3500k, Alcedo atthis. 4000k, Magalaima incognita. 4500k, Serilophus lunatus. 5000k, Lacedo pulchella. 5500k, Eurylaimus ochromalus.

2004, Feb. 20   ***Perf. 14¼x14½***
1608-1615 A388   Set of 8   13.50 11.00

Dolphins — A389

Two dolphins: 1500k With heads above water. 2500k, Leaping out of water. 3500k, Underwater.

2004, Mar. 29   ***Perf. 14½x14***
1616-1618 A389   Set of 3   3.50 2.50

New Year 2004 (Year of the Monkey) — A390

Designs: 500k, Two monkeys. 4500k, Monkey, zodiac animals.

2004, Apr. 15
1619-1620 A390   Set of 2   2.75 1.75

FIFA (Fédération Internationale de Football Association), Cent. — A391

No. 1621 — FIFA emblem and: a, Flags of various countries. b, Soccer players.

2004, May 21   ***Perf. 13½***
1621 A391 12,000k Pair, #a-b   12.00 10.00
  Values are for stamps with surrounding selvage.

Children's Day — A392

Designs: 3500k, Four children. 4500k, Children, globe, school.

2004, June 1   **Perf. 14½x14**
1622-1623   A392   Set of 2   3.50   2.60

11th ASEAN Postal Business Meeting — A393

2004, July 5   **Litho.**   **Perf. 14x14½**
1624   A393   5000k multi   3.00   1.75

Worldwide Fund for Nature (WWF) — A394

No. 1625 — Cuora amboinensis: a, 5000k, In water. b, 5500k, On rock near water. c, 6000k, Pair. d, 7000k, Head, feet and shell.

2004, Aug. 16   **Litho.**   **Perf. 13½x14**
1625   A394   Block of 4, #a-d   6.00   5.00

Dances — A395

Designs: 1000k, Tangwai. 1500k, Khabthoume Luangprabang. 2000k, Lao Lamvong. 2500k, Salavan.

2004, Aug. 23   **Perf. 14x14¾**
1626-1629   A395   Set of 4   3.25   2.10
1629a   Souvenir sheet, #1626-1629, perf. 13¼   5.00   5.00

No. 1629a sold for 10,000k. No. 1629a exists imperf. Value, $40.

Marigolds A396

Designs: 3500k, Yellow, orange marigolds. 5000k, Red and orange marigolds. 5500k, Decorations made with marigolds.

2004, Sept. 28   **Perf. 13¼x13**
1630-1632   A396   Set of 3   4.75   4.75

Scenes From Ramakian — A397

Various scenes: 3500k, 4500k, 5500k, 6500k.

2004, Oct. 10   **Perf. 13¼**
1633-1636   A397   Set of 4   9.00   6.75

Naga Fireball — A398

Designs: 2000k, Figure above river, serpent in river. 3000k, Buildings, serpent, horiz. 3500k, Fireball in serpent's mouth, horiz. 4000k, Fireballs above serpent.

2004, Oct. 28   **Perf. 13 Syncopated**
1637-1640   A398   Set of 4   4.25   4.25

Betel Tray A399

Designs: 2000k, Betel nuts, bowls and containers. 4000k, Betel nut and leaf. 6000k, Betel tray.

2004, Nov. 11   **Litho.**   **Perf. 13**
1641-1643   A399   Set of 3   4.00   4.00

Laos — Sweden Diplomatic Relations, 40th Anniv. — A400

2004, Dec. 12   **Litho.**   **Perf. 13x13½**
1644   A400   8500k multi   4.00   2.75

Handicrafts — A401

Designs: 1000k, Short, round basket. 2000k, Paddle. 2500k, Basket with handle, vert. 5500k, Basket with handle and lid, vert.

2005, Mar. 10   **Perf. 14½x14, 14x14½**
1645-1648   A401   Set of 4   5.25   3.25

New Year 2005 (Year of the Rooster) — A402

Rooster and: 2000k, Hen. 7500k, Zodiac animals.

2005, Apr. 13   **Perf. 14½x14**
1649-1650   A402   Set of 2   5.00   3.50

Daily Buddhas — A403

Buddha for: 500k, Sunday. 1000k, Monday. 1500k, Tuesday, horiz. 2000k, Wednesday. 2500k, Thursday. 3000k, Friday. 3500k, Saturday.

Perf. 14x14½, 14½x14
2005, May 15   **Litho.**
1651-1657   A403   Set of 7   6.50   4.50

Rice — A404

Designs: 1500k, Rice plants. 3000k, Cooked rice on plate, horiz. 6500k, Bundles of rice plants, horiz.

Perf. 13 Syncopated
2005, June 1   **Litho.**
1658-1660   A404   Set of 3   5.25   3.25

Mekong River Giant Catfish — A405

Designs: 3500k, Shown. 6500k, Catfish, diff.

2005, July 13   **Litho.**   **Perf. 14½x14**
1661-1662   A405   Set of 2   4.75   3.25

Gold Panning — A406

Designs: 2000k, Pan. 7500k, Woman panning for gold, vert.

Perf. 13 Syncopated
2005, Aug. 1   **Litho.**
1663-1664   A406   Set of 2   4.00   3.00

Folk Songs — A407

Designs: 1000k, Two musicians standing. 3500k, Two musicians seated. 5500k, Four musicians, horiz.

2005, Sept. 2
1665-1667   A407   Set of 3   4.50   3.00

Europa Stamps, 50th Anniv. (in 2006) A408

Designs: 6000k, Stonehenge, England, and Plain of Jars, Laos. No. 1669, 7000k, Knossos Palace, Greece, and Patuxay, Laos. No. 1670, 7000k, Colosseum, Rome, and Wat Phu, Laos. No. 1671, 7500k, Stave Church, Lom, Norway, and Wat Xieng Thong, Laos. No. 1672, 7500k, Notre Dame Cathedral, Paris, and That Luang, Laos. 8000k, Trier Cathedral, Germany, and Wat Phra Keo, Laos.

2005, Oct. 24   **Litho.**   **Perf. 14¾x14**
1668-1673   A408   Set of 6   15.00   12.50
1673a   Souvenir sheet, #1668-1673   30.00   30.00

No. 1673a exists imperf. Value, $60.

People's Democratic Republic, 30th Anniv. — A409

Designs: 500k, Flag and building. 1000k, Flag and people. 2000k, Flag and coat of arms. 5000k, People and coat of arms.

2005, Dec. 2   **Perf. 13**
1674-1677   A409   Set of 4   4.50   2.50

Diplomatic Relations with Thailand, 55th Anniv. — A410

2005, Dec. 19
1678   A410   7500k multi   4.50   2.25

Laos-United Nations Cooperation, 50th Anniv. — A411

Designs: No. 1679, 3000k, Rice harvesters. No. 1679A, 3000k, Children at school gate. No. 1679B, 3000k, Infant health care.

2005, Oct. 24   **Litho.**   **Perf. 13x13¼**
1679-1679B   A411   Set of 3   4.50   3.50
1679Bc   Souvenir sheet, #1679-1679B   15.00   15.00

No. 1679Bc sold for 15,000k.

Lao People's Democratic Republic, 30th Anniv. — A411a

Designs: 500k, Buildings and flag. 1000k, Map, people and flag. 2000k, Flag, coat of arms. 5000k, Arms, people.

2005, Dec. 2   **Litho.**   **Perf. 13**
1679D-1679G   A411a   Set of 4   4.50   4.50

Lao People's Democratic Republic, 30th Anniv. — A411b

2005, Dec. 16 Litho. Perf. 13¼x13
1679H A411b 15,500k multi 9.00 5.50

Souvenir Sheet
1679I A411b 20,000k multi 10.00 7.00

Diplomatic Relations Between Laos and Japan, 50th Anniv. — A411c

Designs: 7000k, Flowers. 20,000k, Temples.

2005, Dec. 30 Perf. 13
1679J A411c 7000k multi 4.50 2.60

Size: 170x130mm
Imperf
1679K A411c 20,000k multi 15.00 15.00

Statue of King Phangum Lenglathorany A412

2006, Mar. 9 Litho. Perf. 14x14½
1680 A412 8500k multi 3.50 2.60

A souvenir sheet containing one perf. 13½ example of No. 1680 sold for 20,000k.

New Year 2006 (Year of the Dog) A413

Designs: 2000k, Dog. 6500k, Dog, zodiac animals.

2006, Apr. 14 Perf. 14½x14
1681-1682 A413 Set of 2 6.50 3.50

AGL Insurance in Laos, 15th Anniv. — A414

AGL Insurance emblem and: 8000k, Car, minivan and motorcycle. 8500k, Map of Laos. 9500k, Family.

2006, May 1 Perf. 13
1683-1685 A414 Set of 3 11.00 7.75

Friendship Between Vientiane and Moscow — A415

Laotian and Russian: 7500k, Women. 8500k, Sculptures and houses of worship.

2006, May 1
1686-1687 A415 Set of 2 8.00 4.75
1687a Souvenir sheet, #1686-1687 10.00 10.00

No. 1687a sold for 20,000k.

Diplomatic Relations Between Laos and People's Republic of China, 45th Anniv. — A416

2006, July 7 Perf. 13x12¾
1688 A416 8500k multi 5.00 5.00

No. 1688 exists imperf. Value, $20.

Shrimp A417

Various depictions of shrimp: 1000k, 2000k, 4000k, 6000k.

2006, July 10 Perf. 13
1689-1692 A417 Set of 4 7.00 4.00
1692a Souvenir sheet, #1689-1692 8.50 8.50

No. 1692a sold for 15,000k.

Léopold Sédar Senghor (1906-2001), First President of Senegal — A418

2006, Sept. 4
1693 A418 8500k multi 5.00 3.00

Bronze Drums A419

Various drums with background colors of: 2000k, Red brown. 3500k, Blue. 7500k, Olive green.

2006, Oct. 9
1694-1696 A419 Set of 3 7.00 4.00
1696a Souvenir sheet, #1694-1696 9.00 9.00

No. 1696a sold for 15,000k.

Xieng Khouane Temple — A420

Various views of temple and sculptures: 1000k, 2500k, 3000k, 5000k.

2006, June 10 Litho. Perf. 13
1697-1700 A420 Set of 4 6.50 4.00

Bananas A421

Designs: 1000k, Pisang Masak Hijau. 2000k, Pisang Mas. 4000k, Pisang Ambon. 8000k, Pisang Awak.

2006, Nov. 1
1701-1704 A421 Set of 4 7.50 5.00

Opening of Second Thai-Lao Friendship Bridge — A422

Designs: No. 1705, 7500k, Bridge in daylight. No. 1706, 7500k, Bridge at night.

2006, Dec. 20
1705-1706 A422 Set of 2 8.00 5.00

Jewelry — A423

Designs: 2000k, Pins. 5000k, Bracelet. 7000k, Earrings. 7500k, Necklace and pendant.

2007, Jan. 15 Litho. Perf. 13¼x13
1707-1710 A423 Set of 4 11.00 8.00
1710a Souvenir sheet, #1707-1710 14.00 12.00

No. 1710a sold for 25,000k.

Crabs A424

Various crabs: 1000k, 2000k, 7000k, 7500k.

2007, Feb. 20 Perf. 13x13¼
1711-1714 A424 Set of 4 9.00 6.50
1714a Souvenir sheet, #1711-1714, perf. 13½x13¾ 10.00 9.00

No. 1714a sold for 20,000k.

New Year 2007 (Year of the Pig) A425

Designs: No. 1715, 7500k, Pig and piglets. No. 1716, 7500k, Pig, zodiac animals.

2007, Apr. 15 Perf. 13x13¼
1715-1716 A425 Set of 2 8.00 5.75

Takbat Festival — A425a

Designs: 2000k, Monks standing, women placing items on ground. 5000k, Woman reaching into monk's bowl. 7500k, Women holding bowls.

2007, July 10 Litho. Perf. 13
1716A-1716C A425a Set of 3 7.00 5.50

Association of South East Asian Nations (ASEAN), 40th Anniv — A426

Designs: 7000k, Typical house, Laos. No. 1718: a, Like 7000k. b, Secretariat Building, Bandar Seri Begawan, Brunei. c, National Museum of Cambodia. d, Fatahillah Museum, Jakarta, Indonesia. e, Malayan Railway Headquarters Building, Kuala Lumpur, Malaysia. f, Yangon Post Office, Myanmar. g, Malacañang Palace, Philippines. h, National Museum of Singapore. i, Vimanmek Mansion, Bangkok, Thailand. j, Presidential Palace, Hanoi, Viet Nam.

2007, Aug. 8 Litho. Perf. 13
1717 A426 7000k multi 3.00 3.00
1718 Sheet of 10 7.00 7.00
a.-j. A426 700k Any single .50 .40

See Brunei No. 607, Burma No. 370, Cambodia No. 2339, Indonesia Nos. 2120-2121, Malaysia No. 1170, Philippines Nos. 3103-3105, Singapore No. 1265, Thailand No. 2315, and Viet Nam Nos. 3302-3311.

Transportation — A426a

Designs: 2000k, Airplanes. 5000k, Ferry. 7500k, Trucks.

2007, Sept. 1 Litho. Perf. 13
1718K-1718M A426a Set of 3 7.00 6.00

That Luang Festival — A426b

Designs: 2000k, Monks leading procession. 5000k, Procession with temple in background. 8000k, Temple at night.

2007, Nov. 13
1718N-1718P A426b Set of 3 7.50 5.75

Traditional Foods — A426c

Designs: 2000k, Sticky rice cooked in bamboo tubes. 5500k, Green papaya salad. 7500k, Grilled chicken.

2007, Dec. 30
1718Q-1718S A426c Set of 3 7.50 5.75

Worldwide Fund for Nature (WWF) A427

Hylobates lar: 6000k, Head. 7000k, Adult and juvenile. 8000k, With open mouth. 9000k, Two adults.

2008 **Litho.** **Perf. 13½x14**
1719-1722 A427 Set of 4 12.00 7.25
1722a Miniature sheet, 4 each #1719-1722 120.00 120.00

Nos. 1719-1722, 1722a exist imperf. Value, Nos. 1719-1722 imperf. block of 4 $40.

2008 Summer Olympics, Beijing A428

Designs: No. 1723, 5000k, Taekwondo. No. 1724, 5000k, High jump. No. 1725, 5000k, Cycling. No. 1726, 5000k, Soccer.

2008, Apr. 17 **Perf. 12½x13**
1723-1726 A428 Set of 4 8.00 4.75

Nos. 1723-1726 each were printed in sheets of 16. Two sheet varieties exist: English inscriptions in the top and bottom selvage, and a combination of English (right and bottom selvage) and Ukrainian (top and left selvage) inscriptions. Sheets with the English and Ukrainian inscriptions are scarce. Value, set of four singles of Nos. 1723-1726 each with attached Ukrainian selvage $20.

Elephant Festival — A429

Designs: 1000k, Tuskless elephant and rider. 2000k, Two elephants and riders. 3000k, Man in crowd holding rope. 5000k, Tusked elephant with rider. 7500k, Woman decorating elephant. 8500k, Elephants moving logs. 20,000k, Elephants, riders and guides.

2008 **Litho.** **Perf. 13**
1727-1732 A429 Set of 6 12.00 11.00
Size: 146x110mm
Imperf
1733 A429 20,000k multi + label 12.50 8.50

Coffee — A430

Designs: Nos. 1734, 1737a, 3000k, Mug and roasted coffee beans. Nos. 1735, 1737b, 5000k, Coffee berries. Nos. 1736, 1737c, 6000k, Roasted coffee beans.

2008, Feb. 11 **Litho.** **Perf. 13**
Size: 30x45mm
1734-1736 A430 Set of 3 8.00 6.25
Souvenir Sheet
Perf. 13¼x13
1737 A430 Sheet of 3, #a-c 10.00 8.00

No. 1737 contains three 32x43mm stamps and sold for 18,000k.

Cotton A432

Designs: Nos. 1739, 1742a, 1000k, Woman at cotton gin. Nos. 1740, 1742b, 5000k, Cotton plant. Nos. 1741, 1742c, 5500k, Cotton plant, diff.

2008, Apr. 10 **Perf. 13**
Size: 45x30mm
1739-1741 A432 Set of 3 7.50 5.25
Souvenir Sheet
Perf. 13½x13¾
1742 A432 Sheet of 3, #a-c 8.50 6.75

No. 1742 contains three 42x32mm stamps and sold for 15,000k.

Bees A434

Designs: 1000k, Bees and honeycomb. 4000k, Bees on flower. 6000k, Beehive. 8500k, Bee in flight.

2008, June 23 **Perf. 13**
1747-1750 A434 Set of 4 11.00 8.75

Waterfalls A435

Designs: Nos. 1751, 1755a, 500k, Taat Fan Waterfall. Nos. 1752, 1755b, 2000k, Tad Sae Waterfall, horiz. Nos. 1753, 1755c, 5000k, Kuang Si Waterfall. Nos. 1754, 1755d, 6500k, Khonphapheng Waterfall, horiz.

2008, July 28 **Perf. 13**
Sizes: 30x45mm, 45x30mm (Horiz. Stamps)
1751-1754 A435 Set of 4 9.00 6.25
Souvenir Sheet
Perf. 13¾x13½, 13½x13¾
1755 A435 Sheet of 4, #a-d 9.50 7.25

No. 1755 contains two 32x42mm stamps and two 42x32mm stamps and sold for 16,000k.

Eggplants — A436

Designs: Nos. 1756, 1760a, 1000k, White eggplants. Nos. 1757, 1760b, 2000k, Green eggplants. Nos. 1758, 1760c, 4000k, Green, striped eggplants. Nos. 1759, 1760d, 5500k, Purple eggplants.

2008, Oct. 1 **Perf. 13**
Size: 45x30mm
1756-1759 A436 Set of 4 8.00 5.75
Souvenir Sheet
1760 A436 Sheet of 4, #a-d 9.00 6.75

No. 1760 contains four 42x32mm stamps and sold for 15,000k.

Hmong New Year — A437

Designs: Nos. 1761, 1765a, 1000k, Woman. Nos. 1762, 1765b, 5500k, Two oxen, horiz. Nos. 1763, 1765c, 6000k, Musician. Nos. 1764, 1765d, 7500k, Two women holding umbrellas, horiz.

2008, Dec. 1 **Perf. 13**
Size: 30x45mm, 45x30mm (Horiz. Stamps)
1761-1764 A437 Set of 4 12.00 9.00
Souvenir Sheet
Perf. 13¾x13½, 13½x13¾
1765 A437 Sheet of 4, #a-d 12.50 9.00

No. 1765 contains two 32x42mm stamps and two 42x32mm stamps.

Antiquities of Laos — A438

Designs: Nos. 1766, 1770a, 1000k, Haw Phra Kaew. Nos. 1767, 1770b, 2000k, Plain of Jars. Nos. 1768, 1770c, 4000k, Phat That Luang. Nos. 1769, 1770d, 7500k, Temple.

2009, Jan. 3 **Perf. 13**
Stamps With White Frames
1766-1769 A438 Set of 4 8.50 5.00
Souvenir Sheet
Stamps With Colored Frames
1770 A438 Sheet of 4, #a-d 8.50 5.25

No. 1770 sold for 15,000k.

A439

A440

A441

Army, 60th Anniv. A442

2009, Jan. 20
1771 A439 2000k multi 2.00 1.25
1772 A440 2000k multi 2.00 1.25
1773 A441 2000k multi 2.00 1.25
1774 A442 2000k multi 2.00 1.25
a. Souvenir sheet of 4, #1771-1774 6.00 6.00
Nos. 1771-1774 (4) 8.00 5.00

No, 1774a sold for 10,000k.

A443

A444

Opening of Laos-Thailand Rail Link — A445

2009, Mar. 5
1775 A443 3000k multi 2.00 1.50
1776 A444 3000k multi 2.00 1.50
1777 A445 3000k multi 2.00 1.50
a. Souvenir sheet of 3, #1775-1777 12.00 12.00
Nos. 1775-1777 (3) 6.00 4.50

No. 1777a sold for 15,000k.

China 2009
World Stamp
Exhibition
A446

Color of flower: No. 1778, 7500k, White. No. 1779, 7500k, Red.

2009, Mar. 20
1778-1779 A446   Set of 2   8.00   6.50
1779a   Souvenir sheet of 2,
                #1778-1779   12.00 12.00

No. 1779a sold for 20,000k, and exists imperf.

Flowers
A447

Designs: 500k, Mari flower. 2000k, Ixora. 4000k, White Vuddish flowers (Calotropis gigantea). 7500k, Lilac Vuddish flowers (Calotropis gigantea).

2009, May 15
1780-1783 A447   Set of 4   6.00   5.00
1783a   Souvenir sheet of 4,
                #1780-1783   8.00   6.00

No. 1783a sold for 15,000k.

Rice
Alcohol — A448

Designs: 1000k, Pots with sticks. 2000k, Horn and pot. 5500k, Man and pot.

2009, Aug. 11
1784-1786 A448   Set of 3   5.00   5.00

A souvenir sheet containing Nos. 1784-1786 sold for 18,000k.

Postmarks
A449

No. 1787 — Postmark of: a, R. P. Vientiane. b, Centre de Tri. c, Phongsaly. d, Luangnamtha. e, Oudomxay. f, Bokeo. g, Luangpabang. h, Huaphan. i, Sayaboury. j, Xiengkhouang. k, Vientiane. l, Bolikhamxay. m, Khammouane. n, Savannakhet. o, Saravan. p, Sekong. q, Champasack. r, Attapeu.

2009, Oct. 9   *Perf. 13½*
1787   Sheet of 18   17.50 17.50
a.-r. A449 2000r Any single   .75   .50

25th South East Asian Games,
Vientiane — A450

Mascots and: 5000k, Red background. 7000k, Flag, blue background.

2009, Nov. 16   *Perf. 14½x14*
1788-1789 A450   Set of 2   6.50   6.50
1789a   Souvenir sheet of 2,
                #1788-1789   9.00   9.00

No. 1789a sold for 15,000k.
Nos. 1788-1789 exist in a souvenir sheet of 4 containing 2 each, along with 4 labels that could be personalized.

Wat Simuong
A451

Designs: 4000k, Statue. 5000k, Stone temple. 6000k, Temple.

2009, Dec. 7   *Perf. 13*
1790-1792 A451   Set of 3   9.00   9.00
1792a   Souvenir sheet of 3,
                #1790-1792   11.00 11.00

No. 1792a sold for 18,000k.

Flora
A452

Designs: 1000k, Litsea cubeba. 3000k, Orthosiphon stamineus, vert. 4000k, Strychnos nux-vomica, vert. 5000k, Zingiber sp. 8000k, Styrax tonkinensis, vert. 9000k, Aquilaria crassna, vert.

2010   *Litho.*
1793-1798 A452   Set of 6   25.00 25.00

Rural
Life
A453

Designs: 1000k, Huts and people near stream. 6000k, Weavers. 12,000k, Woman and children winnowing rice.

2010, Feb. 15
1799-1801 A453   Set of 3   10.00 10.00
1801a   Souvenir sheet of 3,
                #1799-1801   12.00 12.00

No. 1801a sold for 20,000k.

Laotian Landscapes — A454

Designs: 1000k, Cave entrance. 3000k, Lake. 4000k, Boat on river. 10,000k, Canyon.

2010, Apr. 1
1802-1805 A454   Set of 4   10.00 10.00
1805a   Souvenir sheet of 4,
                #1802-1805   12.00 12.00

No. 1805a sold for 20,000k.

Rice Blessing
Festival — A455

Designs: 4000k, Boy placing stick in clay pot. 5000k, Offering. 11,000k, People looking at burning candles.

2010, July 26
1806-1808 A455   Set of 3   12.00 12.00
1808a   Souvenir sheet of 3,
                #1806-1808   11.00 11.00
1808b   Souvenir sheet of 1 #1808 11.00 11.00

No. 1808b sold for 15,000k.

Wild
Fruit — A456

Color of fruit: 500k, Brown. 1500k, Red. 8000k, Yellow orange. 9000k, Green.

2010. Sept. 1
1809-1812 A456   Set of 4   12.00 12.00
1812a   Souvenir sheet of 4,
                #1809-1812   12.50 12.50

No. 1812a sold for 20,000k.

Vientiane, 450th Anniv. — A457

Emblem and Pha That Luang Stupa, Vientiane, in: 1000k, 1889. 3000k, 1910. 5000k, 1935. 6000k, 2010.
20,000k, Golden Stupa and statue, vert.

2010, Nov. 15   Litho.   *Perf. 14½x14*
1813-1816 A457   Set of 4   8.50   8.50
        Souvenir Sheet
   **Litho. & Embossed With Foil
        Application**
1817 A457 20,000k gold &
                multi   12.00 12.00

No. 1817 contains one 48x60mm stamp.

People's Democratic Republic of Laos,
35th Anniv. — A458

Designs: 5000k, Army officer pointing. 6000k, Soldiers and large gun, vert. 10,000k, Laotian leaders and soldiers. No. 1821a, Like 10,000k.

2010, Dec. 2   Litho.   *Perf. 13*
1818-1820 A458   Set of 3   11.00 11.00
1821 A458   Souvenir sheet of
                3, #1818, 1819,
                1821a   18.00 18.00
a.   9000k multi   5.00   5.00

Selection of Luang Prabang as
UNESCO World Heritage Site, 15th
Anniv. — A459

Various views of Luang Prabang festivals: 2000k, 3000k, 5000k, 10,000k.

2010, Dec. 2
1822-1825 A459   Set of 4   12.00 12.00
1825a   Souvenir sheet of 4,
                #1822-1825   12.00 12.00

Traditional
Women's
Costumes
A460

Various women in traditional costumes: 1000k, 3000k, 4000k, 5000k, 8000k.

2011, Jan. 31
1826-1830 A460   Set of 5   12.00 12.00

Potters and
Pottery — A461

Designs: 1000k, Potter. 3000k, Clay pot. 5000k, Decorated clay pot. 6000k, Potter, diff.

2011, Mar. 14
1831-1834 A461   Set of 4   10.00 10.00

Peonies — A462

No. 1835: a, 7000k, Pink peonies. b, 8000k, White peonies.

2011, Apr. 2   *Perf. 12½*
1835 A462   Pair, #a-b   10.00 10.00
c.   Souvenir sheet of 1 #1835b 7.00   7.00

Diplomatic
Relations
Between Laos
and Thailand,
60th
Anniv. — A463

Designs: No. 1836, 8000k, Laotian woman with black skirt. No. 1837, 8000k, Thai woman with yellow dress. No. 1838, 8000k, White frangipani flowers. No. 1839, 8000k, Yellow Cassia fistula flowers.

2011, Apr. 22   Perf. 13
1836-1839 A463 Set of 4   20.00 20.00
1839a   Souvenir sheet of 4,
              #1836-1839   25.00 25.00

No. 1839a sold for 35,000k. See Thailand No. 2602.

Dipmomatic Relations Beween Laos and People's Republic of China, 50th Anniv. — A464

2011, Apr. 25
1840 A464 9000k multi   5.00 5.00

A souvenir sheet containing one No. 1840 sold for 20,000k.

Orchids — A465

Paphiopedilum barbigerum var. sulivongii: 1000k, One flower. 9000k, Three flowers. 11,000k, One flower, with leaves.

2011, May 22
1841-1843 A465 Set of 3   20.00 20.00
1843a   Souvenir sheet of 3,
              #1841-1843   30.00 30.00

No. 1843a sold for 25,000k. Imperforate examples of No. 1843a sold for 35,000k.

Forest Products A466

Products harvested from trees: 3000k, Lac resin. 4000k, Cinnamon. 5000k, Malva nuts. 6000k, Gurjum balsam. 11,000k, Dammar gum. 12,000k, Beeswax, horiz.

2011, June 1   Perf. 13
1844-1849 A466 Set of 6   25.00 25.00

Wildlife Conservation — A467

Designs: 1000k, Asian elephant. 3000k, Tiger. 5000k, Saola. 8000k, Red-shanked douc langur.

2011, July 13
1850-1853 A467 Set of 4   12.00 12.00
1853a   Souvenir sheet of 4,
              #1850-1853   15.00 15.00

No. 1853a sold for 20,000k.

Lotus Flowers — A468

No. 1854: a, 7000k, Lotus flower. b, 8000k, Lotus flower, diff.

2011, Aug. 12
1854 A468 Horiz. pair, #a-b   9.00 9.00

A469

A470

City Pillar, Vientiane — A471

2011, Nov. 10
1855 A469 9000k multi   6.00 6.00
1856 A470 9000k multi   6.00 6.00
1857 A471 9000k multi   6.00 6.00
  a.   Souvenir sheet of 3, #1855-
        1857   20.00 20.00
  Nos. 1855-1857 (3)   18.00 18.00

No. 1857a sold for 30,000k.

Miniature Sheet

Architecture in Vientiane and Moscow — A472

No. 1858: a, 6000k, Pha That Luang, Vientiane. b, 7000k, St. Basil's Cathedral, Moscow.

c, 8000k, Temple, Vientiane. d, 9000k, Egg House, Moscow.

2011, Dec.   Perf. 14¼x14
1858 A472 Sheet of 4, #a-d   25.00 25.00

No. 1858 exists imperforate. For overprint, see No. 1873.

New Year 2012 (Year of the Dragon) A473

2012, Jan. 10 Litho.   Perf. 13¼
1859 A473 8000k multi   4.50 4.50

No. 1859 was printed in sheets of 4.

Laos Pres. Kaysone Phomvihane (1920-92), North Viet Nam Pres. Ho Chi Minh (1890-1969), Flags of Laos and Viet Nam — A474

Buildings in Laos and Viet Nam — A475

2012, July 18 Litho.   Perf. 13x12¾
1860 A474 4000k multi   2.50 2.50
1861 A475 12,000k multi   6.50 6.50

See Viet Nam Nos. 3458-3459.

Asia-Europe Summit Meeting, Vientiane — A476

Emblems for summit and: 9000k, Laotian temple. 11,000k, Map with Europe and Southeast Asis highlighted.

2012, Nov. 5 Litho.   Perf. 13x12¾
1862-1863 A476 Set of 2   9.00 9.00

An imperforate souvenir sheets containing No. 1862 sold for 20,000k. A souvenir sheet containing No. 1863 sold for 20,000k.

Silk Processing — A477

Designs: 2000k, Boiling of silk cocoons. 3000k, Spinning of silk. 4000k, Collection of cocoons. 5000k, Mulberries on tree.

2013, Apr. 22 Litho.   Perf. 13
1864-1867 A477 Set of 4   7.25 7.25
1867a   Souvenir sheet of 4,
              #1864-1867   13.00 13.00

No. 1867a sold for 25,000k and exists imperforate.

Miniature Sheet

Cultural Cooperation Between Laos and Russia — A478

No. 1868: a, 6000k, Patuxai Gate, Vientiane. b, 7000k, Triumphal Arch, Moscow. c, 8000k, Pagoda, Laos. d, 9000k, Tower, Russia.

2013, July 5 Litho.   Perf. 14¼x14
1868 A478 Sheet of 4, #a-d   22.00 22.00

No. 1868 exists imperforate.

Fish A479

Designs: 2000k, Clupisoma sinense. 4000k, Hemibarus filamentus. 6000k, Great white catfish. 9000k, Bagarius yarrelli.

2013, July 6 Litho.   Perf. 13
1869-1872 A479 Set of 4   11.00 11.00
1872a   Souvenir sheet of 4,
              #1869-1872   13.00 13.00

No. 1872a sold for 25,000k and exists imperforate.

No. 1858 Overprinted in Red and Blue

Methods and Perfs. As Before
2013, July 10
1873 A472 Sheet of 4, #a-d   57.50 57.50

Nos. 1873a-1873d are Nos. 1858a-1858d with a different part of the overprint covering the sheet.

Stupas A480

Designs: 1000k, Xiengkhoeng Stupa, Huaphanh. 2000k, Wat That Noi Stupa, Luang Prabang. 3000k, Makmo Stupa, Luang Prabang. 4000k, Phonphao Stupa, Luang

Prabang. 10,000k, Phousi Stupa, Luang Prabang.

2013, Nov. 11   Litho.   Perf. 13
1874-1878 A480 Set of 5   9.75 9.75

Perforate and imperforate souvenir sheets containing one example of No. 1874 exist. Each sheet sold for 25,000k.

Fourth International Mekong Bridge — A481

Designs: No. 1879, 8000k, Border checkpoint and parking lot. No. 1880, 8000k, Bridge.

2013, Dec. 11   Litho.   Perf. 13
1879-1880 A481 Set of 2   7.50 7.50
1880a   Souvenir sheet of 2,   12.50 12.50
             #1879-1880

No. 1880a sold for 25,000k and exists imperforate.

First Laos-Thailand Friendship Bridge, 20th Anniv. — A482

No. 1881 — Bridge and: a, Sai Buddha Image Procession Festival, Nong Khai, Thailand, and Wax Candle Procession Festival, Vientiane. b, Pho Chai Temple, Nong Khai, and On Teu Temple, Vientiane.

2014, Apr. 8   Litho.   Perf. 14½x14
1881 A482 9000k Horiz. pair, #a-
            b   8.00 8.00
   c.   Souvenir sheet of 2, #1881a-
             1881b   9.00 9.00

No. 1881c sold for 20,00k and exists imperforate.

Nos. 535-537, 834-835 Handstamp Surcharged

Methods and Perfs. As Before
2014, July 22
1882 A207 5000k on 1k
            #834   3.00 3.00
1883 A207 8000k on 2k
            #835   4.75 4.75
1884 A154 10,000k on 60c
            #535   6.00 6.00
1885 A154 11,000k on 1k
            #536   6.50 6.50
1886 A154 12,000k on 2k
            #537   7.00 7.00
      Nos. 1882-1886 (5) 27.25 27.25

SEMI-POSTAL STAMPS

Laotian Children — SP1

Unwmk.
1953, July 14   Engr.   Perf. 13
B1 SP1 1.50pi + 1pi multi   2.50 2.00
B2 SP1 3pi + 1.50pi multi   2.50 2.00
B3 SP1 3.90pi + 2.50pi multi 2.50 2.00
    Nos. B1-B3 (3)   7.50 6.00

The surtax was for the Red Cross.

Nos. 52 and 46 Surcharged: "1k ANNEE MONDIALE DU REFUGIE 1959-1960"
1960, Apr. 7
B4 A16 4k + 1k rose claret   3.00 3.00
B5 A13 10k + 1k multicolored 4.50 4.50

World Refugee Year, July 1, 1959-June 30, 1960. The surcharge was for aid to refugees.

Flooded Village SP2

40k+10k, Flooded market place and truck. 60k+15k, Flooded airport and plane.

1967, Jan. 18   Engr.   Perf. 13
B6 SP2 20k + 5k multi   .50 .25
B7 SP2 40k + 10k multi   .75 .50
B8 SP2 60k + 15k multi 1.25 1.00
  a. Miniature sheet of 3 6.00 6.00
      Nos. B6-B8 (3)   2.50 1.75

The surtax was for victims of the Mekong Delta flood. No. B8a contains one each of Nos. B6-B8. Size: 148x99mm. Sold for 250k.

Women Working in Tobacco Field — SP3

1967, Oct. 5   Engr.   Perf. 13
B9   SP3 20k + 5k multi   .50 .50
B10 SP3 50k + 10k multi   .90 .90
B11 SP3 60k + 15k multi 1.25 1.25
  a. Souv. sheet of 3, #B9-B11 4.50 4.50
      Nos. B9-B11 (3)   2.65 2.65

Laotian Red Cross, 10th anniv. No. B11a sold for 250k+30k.

Nos. 184-189 Surcharged: "Soutien aux Victimes / de la Guerre / + 5k"
1970, May 1   Photo.   Perf. 14
B12 A58 10k + 5k multi   .50 .25
B13 A58 15k + 5k multi   .50 .25
B14 A58 20k + 5k multi   .50 .25
B15 A58 30k + 5k multi   .50 .25
B16 A58 40k + 5k multi   .75 .50
B17 A58 60k + 5k multi   1.00 .50
     Nos. B12-B17,CB1-CB2 (8) 9.75 6.50

AIR POST STAMPS

Weaving — AP1

Design: 3.30pi, Wat Pra Koo.

Unwmk.
1952, Apr. 13   Engr.   Perf. 13
C1 AP1 3.30pi dk pur & pur   1.50 1.00
C2 AP1 10pi ultra & bl grn   3.00 2.00
C3 AP1 20pi deep cl & red   4.50 3.00
C4 AP1 30pi blk brn & dk
         brn violet   5.00 4.00
    Nos. C1-C4 (4)   14.00 10.00

See note following No. 17.

UPU Monument and King Sisavang-Vong — AP2

1952, Dec. 7
C5 AP2 25pi vio bl & indigo 5.00 4.50
C6 AP2 50pi dk brn & vio brn 6.00 5.50

Laos' admission to the UPU, May 13, 1952.

AP3

AP4

Designs: Various Buddha statues.

1953, Nov. 18
C7   AP3 4pi dark green   1.25 .60
C8   AP4 6.50pi dk bl green   1.25 .60
C9   AP4 9pi blue green   1.75 .90
C10 AP3 11.50pi red, yel & dk
          vio brn   2.75 1.25
C11 AP4 40pi purple   4.50 1.75
C12 AP4 100pi olivo   8.00 4.50
     Nos. C7-C12 (6)   19.50 9.60

Great Oath of Laos ceremony.

Accession Type of Regular Issue
1954, Mar. 4   Unwmk.
C13 A6 50pi indigo & bl
         grn   185.00 185.00
     Hinged   100.00

Ravana — AP6

Sita and Rama — AP7

Scenes from the Ramayana: 4k, Hanuman, the white monkey. 5k, Ninh Laphath, the black monkey. 20k, Lucy with a friend of Ravana. 30k, Rama.

1955, Oct. 28   Engr.   Perf. 13
C14 AP6 2k bl grn, emer &
          ind   1.00 .50
C15 AP6 4k red brn, dk red
          brn & ver   1.50 1.00

C16 AP6 5k scar, sep & olive   2.50 1.50
C17 AP7 10k blk, org & brn   5.00 1.75
C18 AP7 20k vio, dk grn & ol-
          ive   7.00 3.00
C19 AP7 30k ultra, blk & salm-
          on   9.00 4.50
     Nos. C14-C19 (6)   26.00 12.25

See No. 225.

Buddha Type of Regular Issue, 1956
1956, May 24
C20 A7 20k carmine rose   30.00 23.50
C21 A7 30k olive & olive bister 30.00 27.50

2500th anniversary of birth of Buddha.

UN Emblem AP8

1956, Dec. 14
C22 AP8 15k light blue   4.50 4.50
C23 AP8 30k deep claret   6.50 6.50

Admission of Laos to the UN, 1st anniv.

Types of Regular Issue, 1957

Musical Instruments: 12k, Khong vong. 14k, So. 20k, Kong.

1957, Mar. 25   Unwmk.   Perf. 13
C24 A9   12k multicolored   2.75 1.75
C25 A10 14k multicolored   3.00 2.25
C26 A10 20k bl grn, yel grn &
          pur   3.50 3.00
     Nos. C24-C26 (3)   9.25 7.00

Monk Receiving Alms — AP9

Monks Meditating in Boat — AP10

18k, Smiling Buddha. 24k, Ancient temple painting (horse and mythological figures.)

1957, Nov. 5
C27 AP9   10k dk pur, pale brn &
           dk grn   1.25 1.25
C28 AP10 15k dk vio brn, brn
           org & yel   1.25 1.25
C29 AP9   18k slate grn & ol   1.50 1.50
C30 AP10 24k claret, org yel &
           blk   3.25 3.25
     Nos. C27-C30 (4)   7.25 7.25

No. C28 measures 48x27mm. No. C30, 48x36mm. See No. C84.

Mother Nursing Infant — AP11

1958, May 2   Cross in Red
C31 AP11 8k lil gray & dk gray   1.50   .75
C32 AP11 12k red brn & brn   1.75   1.00
C33 AP11 15k sl grn & bluish
     green   2.00   1.00
C34 AP11 20k bister & vio   2.50   1.50
    Nos. C31-C34 (4)   7.75   4.25

3rd anniversary of Laotian Red Cross.

Plain of Stones,
Xieng Khouang
AP12

Papheng Falls, Champassak — AP13

Natl. Tourism Industry: 15k, Buffalo cart.
19k, Buddhist monk and village.

1960, July 1   Engr.   Perf. 13
C35 AP12 9.50k bl, ol & claret   .50   .50
C36 AP13 12k vio bl, red brn &
     gray   .50   .50
C37 AP13 15k yel grn, ol gray
     & cl   .75   .75
C38 AP12 19k multicolored   1.00   1.00
    Nos. C35-C38 (4)   2.75   2.75

Pou Gneu Nha
Gneu
Legend — AP14

Garuda — AP15

Hanuman, the
White
Monkey — AP16

Nang Teng
One
Legend
AP17

1962, Feb. 19   Unwmk.   Perf. 13
C39 AP14 11k grn, car & ocher   .60   .60
C40 AP15 14k ultra & org   .60   .60
C41 AP16 20k multicolored   .80   .80
C42 AP17 25k multicolored   .90   .90
    Nos. C39-C42 (4)   2.90   2.90

Makha Bousa festival.

Yao
Hunter — AP18

1964, Dec. 15   Engr.   Perf. 13
C43 AP18 5k shown   .55   .25
C44 AP18 10k Kha hunter   .55   .35
C45 AP18 50k Meo woman   1.60   1.00
   a.   Min. sheet of 4, #100, C43-C45   7.50   6.50
    Nos. C43-C45 (3)   2.70   1.60

No. C45a exists imperf in a booklet. Value,
intact booklet $75.

Butterfly Type of 1965
1965, Mar. 13   Size: 48x27mm
C46 A34 20k Attacus atlas   6.00   2.50

Phayre's Flying
Squirrel — AP19

Designs: 25k, Leopard cat. 75k, Javan mongoose. 100k, Crestless porcupine. 200k,
Binturong.

1965, Oct. 7   Engr.   Perf. 13
C47 AP19 25k dk brn, yel grn &
     ocher   .50   .25
C48 AP19 55k brown & blue   .75   .35
C49 AP19 75k brt grn & brn   1.00   .50
C50 AP19 100k ocher, brn & blk   1.75   1.10
C51 AP19 200k red & black   3.50   2.50
    Nos. C47-C51 (5)   7.50   4.70

Army Type of Regular Issue
Design: 200k, 300k, Parading service flags
before National Assembly Hall.

1968, July 15   Engr.   Perf. 13
C52 A53 200k multicolored   1.75   .85
C53 A53 300k multicolored   2.50   1.25
   a.   Souv. sheet of 5, #168-170,
     C52-C53   6.00   6.00

No. C53a sold for 600k.

Insect Type of Regular Issue
Insects: 120k, Dorysthenes walkeri, horiz.
160k, Megaloxantha bicolor, horiz.

1968, Aug. 28   Engr.   Perf. 13
C54 A54 120k brn, org & blk   1.50   .85
C55 A54 160k rose car, Prus bl
     & yel   2.25   1.25

Ballet Type of Regular Issue
Designs: 110k, Sudagnu battling Thotsakan. 300k, Pharam dancing with Thotsakan.

1969   Photo.   Perf. 14
C56 A58 110k multicolored   3.50   1.75
   a.   Souv. sheet of 4, #187-189,
     C56, imperf.   24.00   24.00
C57 A58 300k multicolored   7.00   3.25
   a.   Souv. sheet of 4, #184-186,
     C57, imperf.   24.00   24.00

No. C56a sold for 480k; No. C57a for 650k.
For surcharges see Nos. CB1-CB2.

Timber
Industry,
Paksane
AP20

1969, May 7   Engr.   Perf. 13
C58 AP20 300k olive bister & blk   5.50   3.25
    ILO, 50th anniversary.

Animal Type of Regular Issue
Animals: 70k, Malaysian black bear. 120k,
White-handed gibbon, vert. 150k, Indochinese
tiger.

1969, Nov. 6   Photo.   Perf. 12x13
C59 A60 70k multicolored   1.10   .60
C60 A60 120k multicolored   2.40   1.10
C61 A60 150k multicolored   2.75   1.40
    Nos. C59-C61 (3)   5.85   3.10

Hairdressing, by Marc Leguay — AP21

Paintings: No. C63, Village Market, by Marc
Leguay, horiz. No. C64, Tree on the Bank of
the Mekong, by Marc Leguay, horiz.

1969-70   Photo.   Perf. 12x13, 13x12
C62 AP21 120k multicolored   1.00   .40
C63 AP21 150k multicolored   2.00   .65
C64 AP21 150k multi ('70)   2.00   .65
    Nos. C62-C64 (3)   5.00   1.70

See Nos. C72-C74.

Wat Xiengthong, Luang
Prabang — AP22

1970, Jan. 10   Perf. 12x13, 13x12
C65 AP22 100k Library, Wat
     Sisaket, vert.   1.40   .65
C66 AP22 120k shown   2.00   1.00

Drum Type of 1970
1970, Mar. 30   Engr.   Perf. 13
C67 A64 125k Pong wooden
     drum, vert.   3.00   1.50

Franklin D. Roosevelt (1882-
1945) — AP23

1970, Apr. 12
C68 AP23 120k olive & slate   1.60   1.10

EXPO '70 Type of Regular Issue
Design: 125k, Woman boiling cocoons in
kettle, and spinning silk thread.

1970, July 7   Engr.   Perf. 13
C69 A66 125k olive & multi   1.75   1.25
    See note after No. 202.

Animal Type of Regular Issue
1970, Sept. 7   Engr.   Perf. 13
C70 A67 210k Leopard   2.75   1.25
C71 A67 500k Gaur   5.00   2.50

Painting Type of 1969-70
Paintings by Marc Leguay: 100k, Village
Foot Path. 120k, Rice Field in Rainy Season,
horiz. 150k, Village Elder.

Perf. 11½x13, 13x11½
1970, Dec. 21   Photo.
C72 AP21 100k multicolored   1.10   1.10
C73 AP21 120k multicolored   1.40   1.40
C74 AP21 150k multicolored   1.60   1.60
    Nos. C72-C74 (3)   4.10   4.10

UN Type of Regular Issue
125k, Earth Goddess Nang Thorani wring-
ing her hair; UN Headquarters and emblem.

1970, Oct. 24   Perf. 13
Size: 26x36mm
C75 A68 125k brt bl, pink & dk
     grn   2.40   1.10

Hanuman and Nang Matsa — AP24

1971, Feb. 5   Perf. 13
C76 AP24 125k multicolored   2.40   1.00

Orchid Type of Regular Issue
Design: 125k, Brasilian cattleya.

1971, July   Photo.   Perf. 13x12½
Size: 48x27mm
C79 A73 125k Brasilian cattleya   4.50   1.50

Laotian and
French
Women,
That Luang
Pagoda
and Arms
AP25

1971, Aug. 6   **Engr.**   *Perf. 13*
C80 AP25 30k brn & dull red   .25 .25
C81 AP25 70k vio & lilac   .50 .40
C82 AP25 100k slate grn & grn   .70 .55
Nos. C80-C82 (3)   1.45 1.20

Kinship between the cities Keng Kok, Laos, and Saint Astier, France.

Animal Type of Regular Issue
1971, Sept. 16
C83 A74 300k Javan rhinoceros   4.25 2.75

Type of 1957 with Ornamental Panel and Inscription
Design: Monk receiving alms (like No. C27).

1971, Oct. 31   **Engr.**   *Perf. 13*
C84 AP9 125k dk pur, pale brn & dk grn   2.00 1.40

20th anniv. of Laotian independent postal service. No. C84 inscribed: "Vingtième Anniversaire de la Philatélie Lao," "Poste Aerienne" and "1971."

Sunset Over the Mekong, by Chamnane Prisayane — AP26

Design: 150k, "Quiet Morning" (village scene), by Chamnane Prisayane.

1971, Dec. 20   **Photo.**   *Perf. 13x12*
C85 AP26 125k black & multi   1.00 1.00
C86 AP26 150k black & multi   1.25 1.25

Book Year Type of Regular Issue
Design: 125k, Father teaching children to read palm leaf book.

1972, Jan. 30   **Engr.**   *Perf. 13*
Size: 48x27mm
C87 A75 125k bright purple   1.75 1.00

Dam Type of Regular Issue
Design: 145k, Nam Ngum Hydroelectric Dam and ECAFE emblem.

1972, Mar. 28   **Engr.**   *Perf. 13*
C88 A76 145k brown, bl & grn   1.40 .80

Orchid Type of Regular Issue
1972, May 5   **Photo.**   *Perf. 13x12½*
Size: 48x27mm
C89 A73 150k Vanda teres, horiz.   4.00 1.50

UNICEF Type of Regular Issue
Design: 120k, Boy riding buffalo to water hole (child's drawing).

1972, July   **Engr.**   *Perf. 13*
C90 A77 120k multicolored   1.40 1.00

Nakharath, Daughter of the Dragon King AP27

Wood carvings from Wat Sikhounvieng Dongmieng, Vientiane: 120k, Nang Kinnali, Goddess from Mt. Kailath. 150k, Norasing, Lion King from Himalayas.

1972, Sept. 15   **Engr.**   *Perf. 13*
C91 AP27 100k blue green   .70 .70
C92 AP27 120k violet   .80 .80
C93 AP27 150k brn orange   1.10 1.10
Nos. C91-C93 (3)   2.60 2.60

That Luang Religious Festival — AP28

1972, Nov. 18   **Engr.**   *Perf. 13*
C94 AP28 110k Presentation of wax castles   .90 .90
C95 AP28 125k Procession   1.10 1.10

Workers in Rice Field, by Leguay AP29

Paintings by Mark Leguay: No. C97, Women and water buffalo in rice field. Nos. C98, Rainy Season in Village (Water buffalo in water). No. C99, Rainy Season in Village (Water buffalo on land). 120k, Mother and Child.

1972, Dec. 23   **Photo.**   *Perf. 13*
C96 AP29 50k multicolored   .45 .45
C97 AP29 50k multicolored   .45 .45
C98 AP29 70k multicolored   .65 .65
C99 AP29 70k multicolored   .65 .65
C100 AP29 120k yel & multi   1.25 1.25
Nos. C96-C100 (5)   3.45 3.45

Nos. C97, C99 have denomination and frame at right.

Costume Type of Regular Issue
Women's Costumes: 120k, Luang Prabang marriage costume. 150k, Vientiane evening costume.

1973, Feb. 16   **Engr.**   *Perf. 13*
C101 A78 120k multicolored   1.40 .80
C102 A78 150k brown & multi   1.90 1.00

Lions Club Emblems, King Sayasettha-Thirath — AP30

1973, Mar. 30   **Engr.**   *Perf. 13*
C103 AP30 150k rose & multi   1.90 .75

Lions Club of Vientiane.

Rahu with Rockets and Sputnik — AP31

Space achievements: 150k, Laotian festival rocket and US lunar excursion module.

1973, May 11   **Engr.**   *Perf. 13*
C104 AP31 80k ultra & multi   .55 .35
C105 AP31 150k buff & ultra   1.00 .45

Dancing Around Campfire — AP32

Design: 125k, Boy Scouts helping during Vientiane Flood, 1966.

1973, Sept. 1   **Engr.**   *Perf. 13*
C106 AP32 110k vio & orange   1.10 .30
C107 AP32 125k Prus grn & bis   1.25 .40

Laotian Scout Movement, 25th anniv.

Sun Chariot and WMO Emblem — AP33

Design: 90k, Nang Mékhala, the weather goddess, and WMO emblem, vert.

1973, Oct. 24   **Engr.**   *Perf. 13*
C108 AP33 90k vio, red & ocher   .75 .35
C109 AP33 150k ocher, red & brn ol   .85 .50

Intl. meteorological cooperation, cent.

Woman in Poppy Field, INTERPOL Emblem — AP34

1973, Dec. 22   **Engr.**   *Perf. 13*
C110 AP34 150k vio, yel grn & red   1.40 .60

Intl. Criminal Police Org., 50th anniv.

Phra Sratsvady, Wife of Phra Phrom AP35

Designs: 110k, Phra Indra on 3-headed elephant Erawan. 150k, Phra Phrom, the Creator, on phoenix. Designs show giant sculptures in park at Thadeua.

1974, Mar. 23   **Engr.**   *Perf. 13*
C111 AP35 100k lilac, red & blk   .80 .40
C112 AP35 110k car, vio & brn   1.00 .50
C113 AP35 150k ocher, vio & sepia   1.25 .70
Nos. C111-C113 (3)   3.05 1.60

UPU Emblem, Women Reading Letter — AP36

1974   **Engr.**   *Perf. 13*
C114 AP36 200k lt brn & car   3.75 1.00
C115 AP36 500k lilac & red   6.00 2.00
   a.   Souvenir sheet   5.50 5.50

Centenary of Universal Postal Union. Issue dates: 200k, Apr. 30; 500k, Oct. 9.

Flower Type of 1974
1974, May 17   **Size: 36x36mm**
C116 A84 500k Pitcher plant   5.50 3.00

Transportation Type of Regular Issue
1974, July 31   **Engr.**   *Perf. 13*
C117 A85 250k Sampan   2.50 1.50

Marconi Type of 1974
Old & new means of communications.

1974, Aug. 28   **Engr.**   *Perf. 13*
C118 A86 200k vio bl & brn   2.25 1.10

Insect Type of 1974
1974, Oct. 23   **Engr.**   *Perf. 13*
C119 A87 110k Sternocera multipunctata   1.75 1.00

Boeing 747 — AP37

1986, June 2   **Litho.**   *Perf. 12½*
C120 AP37 20k shown   3.50
C121 AP37 50k IL86   8.00

AIR POST SEMI-POSTAL STAMPS

Nos. C56-C57 Surcharged: "Soutien aux Victimes / de la Guerre / + 5k"
1970, May 1   **Photo.**
CB1 A58 110k + 5k multi   2.00 1.50
CB2 A58 300k + 5k multi   4.00 3.00

The surtax was for war victims.

POSTAGE DUE STAMPS

Vat-Sisaket Monument D1   Boat and Raft D2

Perf. 13½x13
1952-53   **Unwmk.**   **Engr.**
J1 D1 10c dark brown   .40 .25
J2 D1 20c purple   .40 .25
J3 D1 50c carmine   .50 .25
J4 D1 1pi dark green   .55 .25
J5 D1 2pi deep ultra   .65 .25
J6 D1 5pi rose violet   1.00 1.00
J7 D2 10pi indigo ('53)   1.50 1.25
Nos. J1-J7 (7)   5.00 3.50

Serpent — D3

1973, Oct. 31   **Photo.**   *Perf. 13*
J8 D3 10k yellow & multi   .40 .25
J9 D3 15k emerald & multi   .40 .25
J10 D3 20k blue & multi   .40 .25
J11 D3 50k scarlet & multi   .60 .50
Nos. J8-J11 (4)   1.80 1.25

PARCEL POST STAMPS

Wat Ong Theu PP1

2000, June 7　Litho.　Die Cut
Self-Adhesive
Serial Number in Black

Q1	PP1	5000k orange	5.00	5.00
Q2	PP1	40,000k milky		
		blue	30.00	30.00
Q3	PP1	60,000k gray blue	32.50	32.50
Q4	PP1	80,000k cerise	55.00	55.00
Q5	PP1	100,000k carmine	65.00	65.00
Q6	PP1	250,000k ultra	160.00	160.00
	Nos. Q1-Q6 (6)		347.50	347.50

Phra That Luang — PP2

2003, Aug. 14　　　　Die Cut
Self-Adhesive
Serial Number in Black

Q7	PP2	5000k vio bl & bl	5.00	5.00
Q8	PP2	40,000k claret &		
		red	30.00	30.00
Q9	PP2	60,000k grn &		
		claret	45.00	45.00
Q10	PP2	90,000k red & blue	70.00	70.00
	Nos. Q7-Q10 (4)		150.00	150.00

Pha That Luang, Vientiane — PP7

2013, July 3　Litho.　Imperf.
Self-Adhesive
Frame Color

Q17	PP7	50,000k blue	25.00	25.00
Q18	PP7	100,000k red	45.00	45.00
Q19	PP7	200,000k green	85.00	85.00
	Nos. Q17-Q19 (3)		155.00	155.00

LATAKIA

ˌla-tə-ˈkē-ə

LOCATION — A division of Syria in Western Asia
GOVT. — French Mandate
AREA — 2,500 sq. mi.
POP. — 278,000 (approx. 1930)
CAPITAL — Latakia

This territory, included in the Syrian Mandate to France under the Versailles Treaty, was formerly known as Alaouites. The name Latakia was adopted in 1930. See Alaouites and Syria.

100 Centimes = 1 Piaster

Stamps of Syria Overprinted in Black or Red

Perf. 12x12½, 13½

1931-33 **Unwmk.**

1	A6	10c red violet	1.25	1.25
2	A6	10c vio brn ('33)	1.60	1.60
3	A7	20c dk blue (R)	1.25	1.25
4	A7	20c brn org ('33)	1.60	1.60
5	A8	25c gray grn (R)	1.25	1.25
6	A8	25c dk bl gray		
		(R) ('33)	1.60	1.60
7	A9	50c violet	2.00	2.00
8	A15	75c org red ('32)	3.25	3.25
9	A10	1p green (R)	2.40	2.40
10	A11	1.50p bis brn (R)	3.25	3.25
11	A11	1.50p dp grn ('33)	4.00	4.00
12	A12	2p dk vio (R)	4.00	4.00
13	A13	3p yel grn (R)	6.00	6.00
14	A14	4p orange	5.50	5.50
15	A15	4.50p rose car	5.75	5.75
16	A16	6p grnsh blk (R)	5.75	5.75
17	A17	7.50p dl blue (R)	5.50	5.50
a.		Inverted overprint	650.00	
18	A18	10p dp brown (R)	9.50	9.50
a.		Inverted overprint	650.00	
19	A19	15p dp green (R)	11.00	11.00
20	A20	25p violet brn	24.00	24.00
21	A21	50p dk brown (R)	22.50	22.50
a.		Inverted overprint	650.00	
22	A22	100p red orange	55.00	55.00
	Nos. 1-22 (22)		177.95	177.95

AIR POST STAMPS

Air Post Stamps of Syria, 1931, Overprinted in Black or Red

1931-33 **Unwmk.** **Perf. 13½**

C1	AP2	50c ocher	1.25	1.25
a.		Inverted overprint	1,200.	1,200.
C2	AP2	50c blk brn (R)		
		('33)	2.50	2.50
C3	AP2	1p ches brn	2.50	2.50
C4	AP2	2p Prus blue		
		(R)	4.00	4.00
C5	AP2	3p blue grn		
		(R)	5.50	5.50
C6	AP2	5p red violet	7.00	7.00
C7	AP2	10p sl grn (R)	8.75	8.75
C8	AP2	15p orange red	12.50	12.50
C9	AP2	25p orange brn	24.00	24.00
C10	AP2	50p black (R)	40.00	40.00
C11	AP2	100p magenta	42.50	42.50
	Nos. C1-C11 (11)		150.50	150.50

POSTAGE DUE STAMPS

Postage Due Stamps of Syria, 1931, Overprinted like Regular Issue

1931 **Unwmk.** **Perf. 13½**

J1	D7	8p blk, *gray bl* (R)	24.00	24.00
J2	D8	15p blk, *dl rose* (R)	24.00	24.00

Stamps of Latakia were superseded in 1937 by those of Syria.

LATVIA

ˈlat-vē-ə

(Lettonia, Lettland)

LOCATION — Northern Europe, bordering on the Baltic Sea and the Gulf of Riga
GOVT. — Independent Republic
AREA — 25,395 sq. mi.
POP. — 2,353,874 (1999 est.)
CAPITAL — Riga

Latvia was created a sovereign state following World War I and was admitted to the League of Nations in 1922. In 1940 it became a republic in the Union of Soviet Socialist Republics. Latvian independence was recognized by the Soviet Union on Sept. 6, 1991.

100 Kapeikas = 1 Rublis
100 Santims = 1 Lat (1923, 1993)
100 Kopecks = 1 Ruble (1991)
100 Cents = 1 Euro (2014)

> **Catalogue values for unused stamps in this country are for Never Hinged items, beginning with Scott 300 in the regular postage section, Scott B150 in the semi-postal section, and Scott 2N45 in the Russian Occupation section.**

Watermarks

Wmk. 108
Honeycomb

Wmk. 145 — Wavy Lines

Wmk. 181 Wavy Lines

Wmk. 197 — Star and Triangles

Wmk. 212 Multiple Swastikas

Wmk. 265 — Multiple Waves

Wmk. 387 — Squares and Rectangles

Arms — A1

Printed on the Backs of German Military Maps
Unwmk.

1918, Dec. 18　Litho.　Imperf.

1	A1	5k carmine	1.00	2.00

Perf. 11½

2	A1	5k carmine	1.00	2.00

Values given are for stamps where the map on the back is printed in brown and black. Maps printed only in black are valued at: No. 1 unused $2.00; used $6; No. 2 unused $1.20, used $2.50. Stamps with no map at all valued: No. 1 unused $1.50, used $3.28; No. 2 unused $1.20, used $2.50. Stamps with no printing on the back are from the outer rows of some sheets.

Redrawn
Paper with Ruled Lines

1919 **Imperf.**

3	A1	5k carmine	.25	.25
4	A1	10k dark blue	.25	.25
5	A1	15k green	.50	.50

Perf. 11½

6	A1	5k carmine	2.40	4.00
7	A1	10k dark blue	2.40	4.00
8	A1	15k deep green	7.25	9.50
	Nos. 3-8 (6)		13.05	18.50

In the redrawn design the wheat heads are thicker, the ornament at lower left has five points instead of four, and there are minor changes in other parts of the design.

The sheets of this and subsequent issues were usually divided in half by a single line of perforation gauging 10. Thus stamps are found with this perforation on one side.

1919 **Pelure Paper** **Imperf.**

9	A1	3k lilac	4.75	4.50
10	A1	5k carmine	.25	.25
11	A1	10k deep blue	.25	.25
12	A1	15k dark green	.25	.25
13	A1	20k orange	.25	.25
13A	A1	25k gray	40.00	40.00
14	A1	35k dark brown	.25	.25
15	A1	50k purple	.25	.25
16	A1	75k emerald	2.50	2.50
	Nos. 9-16 (9)		48.75	48.50

Perf. 11½, 9½

17	A1	3k lilac	35.00	35.00
18	A1	5k carmine	.80	.80
19	A1	10k deep blue	4.00	4.00
20	A1	15k dark green	3.00	3.00
21	A1	20k orange	3.75	3.75
22	A1	35k dark brown	4.50	4.50
23	A1	50k purple	5.50	5.50
24	A1	75k emerald	8.00	8.00
	Nos. 17-24 (8)		64.55	64.55

Values are for perf 11½. Examples Perf 9½ sell for more.

Nos. 17-24 are said to be unofficially perforated varieties of Nos. 9-16.

1919   **Wmk. 108**   *Imperf.*
25	A1	3k lilac	.30	.25
26	A1	5k carmine	.30	.25
27	A1	10k deep blue	.30	.25
28	A1	15k deep green	.30	.25
29	A1	20k orange	.35	.25
30	A1	25k gray	.40	.35
31	A1	35k dark brown	.35	.25
32	A1	50k purple	.35	.25
33	A1	75k emerald	.35	.25
		Nos. 25-33 (9)	3.00	2.35

The variety "printed on both sides" exists for 3k, 10k, 15k, 20k and 35k. Value, $20 each.
See Nos. 57-58, 76-82. For surcharges and overprints see Nos. 86, 132-133, 2N1-2N8, 2N12-2N19.

Liberation of Riga — A2

1919   **Wmk. 108**
43	A2	5k carmine	.25	.25
44	A2	15k deep green	.25	.25
45	A2	35k brown	.35	.80
		Nos. 43-45 (3)	.85	1.30

Unwmk.
Pelure Paper
49	A2	5k carmine	9.50	16.00
50	A2	15k deep green	9.50	16.00
51	A2	35k brown	21.00	16.00
		Nos. 49-51 (3)	40.00	48.00

For surcharge and overprints see Nos. 87, 2N9-2N11, 2N20-2N22.

Rising Sun — A4

1919   *Imperf.*
55	A4	10k gray blue	.85	.60

Perf. 11½
56	A4	10k gray blue	1.00	1.50

Type of 1918
1919 Laid Paper   *Perf. 11½*
57	A1	3r slate & org	1.00	1.00
58	A1	5r gray brn & org	1.00	1.00

Independence Issue

Allegory of One Year of Independence A5

1919, Nov. 18   **Unwmk.**
Wove Paper
Size: 33x45mm
59	A5	10k brown & rose	1.75	1.75

Laid Paper
60	A5	10k brown & rose	1.75	1.75

Size: 28x38mm
61	A5	10k brown & rose	.40	.40
a.		Imperf.	50.00	
62	A5	35k indigo & grn	.40	.40
a.		Vert. pair, imperf. btwn.	50.00	45.00

Wmk. 197
Thick Wove Paper
Blue Design on Back
63	A5	1r green & red	.55	.55
		Nos. 59-63 (5)	4.85	4.85

There are two types of Nos. 59 and 60. In type I the trunk of the tree is not outlined. In type II it has a distinct white outline.
No. 63 was printed on the backs of unfinished 5r bank notes of the Workers and Soldiers Council, Riga.

For surcharges see Nos. 83-85, 88, 94.

Warrior Slaying Dragon — A6

1919-20   **Unwmk.**   *Perf. 11½*
Wove Paper
64	A6	10k brown & car	.50	.50
a.		Horiz. pair, imperf. btwn.	55.00	45.00
65	A6	25k ind & yel grn	.50	.50
a.		Pair, imperf. btwn.	55.00	45.00
66	A6	35k black & bl ('20)	.50	.50
a.		Horiz. pair, imperf. btwn.	55.00	45.00
67	A6	1r dk grn & brn ('20)	.50	.50
a.		Horiz. pair, imperf. vert.	50.00	40.00
b.		Horiz. pair, imperf. btwn.	50.00	40.00
		Nos. 64-67 (4)	2.00	2.00
		Set, never hinged	5.75	

Issued in honor of the liberation of Kurzeme (Kurland). The paper sometimes shows impressed quadrille lines.
For surcharges see Nos. 91-93.

Latgale Relief Issue

Latvia Welcoming Home Latgale Province — A7

1920, Mar.
Brown and Green Design on Back
68	A7	50k dk green & rose	1.00	.50
a.		Horiz. pair, imperf. vert.	50.00	
69	A7	1r slate grn & brn	.50	.50
a.		Horiz. pair, imperf. vert.	50.00	
		Set, never hinged	10.00	

No. 68-69 were printed on the backs of unfinished bank notes of the government of Colonel Bermondt-Avalov and on the so-called German "Ober-Ost" money.
For surcharges see Nos. 95-99.

First National Assembly Issue

Latvia Hears Call to Assemble — A8

1920
70	A8	50k rose	.50	.30
a.		Imperf., pair	5.00	5.00
71	A8	1r blue	.50	.30
a.		Vert. pair, imperf. btwn.	45.00	45.00
b.		Imperf., pair	20.00	15.00
72	A8	3r dk brn & grn	.50	.75
73	A8	5r slate & vio brn	.80	.80
		Nos. 70-73 (4)	2.30	2.15
		Set, never hinged	10.00	

For surcharges see Nos. 90, 134.

Type of 1918 Issue
Wove Paper
1920-21   **Unwmk.**   *Perf. 11½*
76	A1	5k carmine	.25	.25
78	A1	20k orange	.25	.25
79	A1	40k lilac ('21)	.30	.25
80	A1	50k violet	.35	.25
81	A1	75k emerald	.35	.25
82	A1	5r gray brn & org ('21)	1.50	1.00
		Nos. 76-82 (6)	3.00	2.25
		Set, never hinged	6.00	

No. 63 Surcharged in Black, Brown or Blue

1920, Sept. 1
83	A5	10r on 1r grn & red (Bk)	1.60	1.60
84	A5	20r on 1r grn & red (Br)	4.00	4.00
85	A5	30r on 1r grn & red (Bl)	5.50	4.00
		Nos. 83-85 (3)	11.10	9.60
		Set, never hinged	20.00	

Types of 1919 Surcharged

1920-21   **Wmk. 108**   *Perf. 11½*
86	A1	2r on 10k dp blue	2.00	7.25
87	A2	2r on 35k brown	.75	5.50
		Set, never hinged	5.00	

No. 62 Surcharged in Red

Unwmk.
88	A5	2r on 35k ind & grn	.40	.50
		Never hinged		.75

No. 70 Surcharged in Blue

1921
90	A8	2r on 50k rose	.50	.60
		Never hinged		1.00

Nos. 64-66 Surcharged in Red or Blue

1920-21
91	A6	1r on 35k blk & bl (R)	.35	.35
92	A6	2r on 10k brn & rose (Bl)	.70	.75
93	A6	2r on 25k ind & grn (R)	.40	.40
a.		Imperf.	—	
		Nos. 91-93 (3)	1.45	1.50
		Set, never hinged	3.50	

On Nos. 92 and 93 the surcharge reads "DIVI 2 RUBLI."

No. 83 with Added Surcharge

1921   **Wmk. 197**
94	A5	10r on 10r on 1r	1.50	1.00
		Never hinged	5.00	

Latgale Relief Issue of 1920 Surcharged in Black or Blue

1921, May 31   **Unwmk.**
95	A7	10r on 50k	1.25	1.00
a.		Imperf.		
96	A7	20r on 50k	3.50	4.00
97	A7	30r on 50k	5.00	4.00
98	A7	50r on 50k	7.50	5.00
99	A7	100r on 50k (Bl)	17.50	16.00
		Nos. 95-99 (5)	34.75	30.00
		Set, never hinged	60.00	

Excellent counterfeits exist.

Arms and Stars for Vidzeme, Kurzeme & Latgale — A10

Type I, slanting cipher in value.
Type II, upright cipher in value.

Perf. 10, 11½ and Compound
Wmk. Similar to 181
1921-22   **Typo.**
101	A10	50k violet (II)	.50	.30
102	A10	1r orange yel	.50	.50
103	A10	2r deep green	.25	.25
104	A10	3r brt green	.65	.45
105	A10	5r rose	1.40	.40
106	A10	6r dp claret	2.00	.80
107	A10	9r orange	1.25	.55
108	A10	10r blue (I)	1.25	.25
109	A10	15r ultra	3.25	.50
a.		Printed on both sides	50.00	
110	A10	20r dull lilac (II)	20.00	2.00

Coat of Arms — A11

1922, Aug. 21   *Perf. 11½*
111	A11	50r dk brn & pale brn (I)	30.00	4.50
112	A11	100r dk bl & pale bl (I)	35.00	4.50
		Nos. 101-112 (12)	96.05	15.00
		Set, never hinged	200.00	

Nos. 101-131 sometimes show letters and numerals of the paper maker's watermark "PACTIEN LIGAT MILLS 1858." Stamps showing part of the inscription command a 100 percent premium. Pairs with the complete year "1858" command a 300 percent premium.
See Nos. 126-131, 152-154.

A12

2 SANTIMS
Type A, tail of "2" ends in an upstroke.
Type B, tail of "2" is nearly horizontal.

1923-25   *Perf. 10, 11, 11½*
113	A12	1s violet	.40	.25
114	A12	2s org yel (A)	.60	.35
115	A12	4s dark green	.60	.25
a.		Horiz. pair, imperf. btwn.	55.00	50.00
116	A12	5s lt green ('25)	2.50	.65
117	A12	6s grn, yel ('25)	3.50	.25
118	A12	10s rose red (I)	1.50	.25
a.		Horiz. pair, imperf. btwn.	55.00	50.00
119	A12	12s claret	.25	.40
120	A12	15s brn, sal	3.50	.25
a.		Horiz. pair, imperf. btwn.	55.00	50.00
121	A12	20s dp blue (II)	1.50	.25
122	A12	25s ultra ('25)	.50	.25
123	A12	30s pink (I) ('25)	5.00	.25
124	A12	40s lilac (I)	2.00	.25
125	A12	50s lil gray (II)	3.75	.35
126	A11	1 l dk brn & pale brn	12.50	1.00
127	A11	2 l dk blue & blue	20.00	1.60
130	A11	5 l dp grn & pale grn	60.00	5.00
131	A11	10 l car rose & pale rose (I)	3.00	6.00
		Nos. 113-131 (17)	121.10	17.60
		Set, never hinged	250.00	

Value in "Santims" (1s); "Santimi" (2s-6s) or "Santimu" (others).
See note after No. 110.
See Nos. 135-151, 155-157. For overprints and surcharges see Nos. 164-167, B21-B23.

Nos. 79-80 Surcharged   No. 72 Surcharged

1927   **Unwmk.**   *Perf. 11½*
132	A1	15s on 40k lilac	.45	.45
133	A1	15s on 50k violet	1.40	1.60
134	A8	1 l on 3r brn & grn	11.00	8.00
		Nos. 132-134 (3)	12.85	10.05
		Set, never hinged	25.00	

Types of 1923-25 Issue

1927-33   **Wmk. 212**   *Perf. 10, 11½*
135	A12	1s dull violet	.25	.25
136	A12	2s org yel (A)	.35	.25
137	A12	2s org yel (B) ('33)	.30	.25
138	A12	3s org red ('31)	.25	.25
139	A12	4s dk green ('29)	3.50	2.21
140	A12	5s lt green ('31)	.50	.25
141	A12	6s grn, yel	.25	.25
142	A12	7s dk green ('31)	.50	.25
143	A12	10s red (I)	2.50	.70
144	A12	10s grn, yel (I) ('32)	10.00	.25
145	A12	15s brn, sal	3.50	.45
146	A12	20s pink (I)	5.00	.25
147	A12	20s pink (II)	6.00	.25
148	A12	30s lt blue (I)	1.25	.40
149	A12	35s dk blue ('31)	1.50	.25
150	A12	40s dl lil (I) ('29)	2.25	.25
151	A12	50s gray (II)	2.50	.45
152	A11	1 l dk brn & pale brn	8.00	.30
153	A11	2 l dk bl & bl ('31)	30.00	2.25
154	A11	5 l grn & pale grn ('33)	140.00	30.00
		Nos. 135-154 (20)	218.40	39.80
		Set, never hinged	400.00	

The paper of Nos. 141, 144 and 145 is colored on the surface only.
See note above No. 113 for types A and B, and note above No. 101 for types I and II.

Type of 1927-33 Issue
Paper Colored Through

1931-33   *Perf. 10*
155	A12	6s grn, yel	.25	.25
156	A12	10s grn, yel (I) ('33)	15.00	.25
157	A12	15s brn, salmon	3.00	.25
		Nos. 155-157 (3)	18.25	.75
		Set, never hinged	37.50	

View of Rezekne — A13

Designs (Views of Cities): 15s, Jelgava. 20s, Cesis (Wenden). 30s, Liepaja (Libau). 50s, Riga. 1 l, Riga Theater.

1928, Nov. 18   **Litho.**   *Perf. 10, 11½*
158	A13	6s dp grn & vio	1.00	.40
159	A13	15s dk brn & ol grn	1.00	.40
160	A13	20s cerise & bl grn	1.25	.45
161	A13	30s ultra & vio brn	1.50	.40
162	A13	50s dk gray & plum	1.50	1.00
163	A13	1 l blk brn & brn	3.75	1.75
		Nos. 158-163 (6)	10.00	4.40
		Set, never hinged	20.00	

10th anniv. of Latvian Independence.

Riga Exhibition Issue

Stamps of 1927-33 Overprinted

Latvijas ražojumu izstāde Rīgā, 1932.g. 10.—18.IX.

1932, Aug. 30   *Perf. 10, 11*
164	A12	3s orange	.95	.50
165	A12	10s green, yel	.95	.50
166	A12	20s pink (I)	1.90	1.00
167	A12	35s dark blue	4.25	2.00
		Nos. 164-167 (4)	8.05	4.00
		Set, never hinged	30.00	

Riga Castle — A19   Arms and Shield — A20

Allegory of Latvia — A21   Ministry of Foreign Affairs — A22

1934, Dec. 15   **Litho.**   *Perf. 10½, 10*
174	A19	3s red orange	.25	.25
175	A20	5s yellow grn	.25	.25
176	A20	10s gray grn	1.00	.25
177	A21	20s deep rose	1.00	.25
178	A22	35s dark blue	.35	.25
179	A19	40s brown	.35	.25
		Nos. 174-179 (6)	3.20	1.50
		Set, never hinged	6.00	

Atis Kronvalds A23   A. Pumpurs A24

Juris Maters A25   Mikus Krogzemis (Auseklis) A26

1936, Jan. 4   **Wmk. 212**   *Perf. 11½*
180	A23	3s vermilion	3.00	4.75
181	A24	10s green	3.00	4.75
182	A25	20s rose pink	3.00	6.00
183	A26	35s dark blue	3.00	6.00
		Nos. 180-183 (4)	12.00	21.50
		Set, never hinged	40.00	

President Karlis Ulmanis — A27

1937, Sept. 4   **Litho.**   *Perf. 10, 11½*
184	A27	3s org red & brn org	.25	.25
185	A27	5s yellow grn	.25	.25
186	A27	10s dk sl grn	.75	.60
187	A27	20s rose lake & brn lake	1.50	.60
188	A27	25s black vio	2.25	1.25
189	A27	30s dark blue	2.25	1.25
190	A27	35s indigo	1.00	1.00
191	A27	40s lt brown	2.00	1.25
192	A27	50s olive blk	2.25	1.50
		Nos. 184-192 (9)	12.50	7.95
		Set, never hinged	25.00	

60th birthday of President Ulmanis.

Independence Monument, Rauna (Ronneburg) A28

Monument Entrance to Cemetery at Riga A29

Independence Monument, Jelgava — A30

War Memorial, Valka — A31

Independence Monument, Iecava — A32

Independence Monument, Riga — A33

Tomb of Col. Kalpaks — A34

Unwmk.
1937, July 12   **Litho.**   *Perf. 10*
Thick Paper
193	A28	3s vermilion	.60	.90
194	A29	5s yellow grn	.60	.90
195	A30	10s deep grn	.60	.50
196	A31	20s carmine	1.50	1.00
197	A32	30s lt blue	2.00	2.00

Wmk. 212
Engr.   *Perf. 11½*
Thin Paper
198	A33	35s dark blue	2.00	2.00
199	A34	40s brown	3.25	3.00
		Nos. 193-199 (7)	10.55	10.30
		Set, never hinged	22.50	

View of Vidzeme — A35

General J. Balodis A37

President Karlis Ulmanis A38

Views: 5s, Latgale. 30s, Riga waterfront. 35s, Kurzeme. 40s, Zemgale.

1938, Nov. 17   *Perf. 10, 10½x10*
200	A35	3s brown org	.25	.25
a.		Booklet pane of 4	40.00	
201	A35	5s yellow grn	.25	.25
a.		Booklet pane of 4	40.00	
202	A37	10s dk green	.25	.25
a.		Booklet pane of 2	40.00	
203	A38	20s red lilac	.25	.25
a.		Booklet pane of 2	40.00	
204	A35	30s deep blue	.90	.25
205	A35	35s indigo	.90	.25
a.		Booklet pane of 2	40.00	
206	A35	40s rose violet	1.25	.25
		Nos. 200-206 (7)	4.05	1.75
		Set, never hinged	9.00	

The 20th anniversary of the Republic.

School, Riga — A42

Independence Monument, Riga — A45

President
Karlis Ulmanis
A49

Designs: 5s, Castle of Jelgava. 10s, Riga Castle. 30s, Symbol of Freedom. 35s, Community House Daugavpils. 40s, Powder Tower and War Museum, Riga.

1939, May 13   Photo.   Perf. 10

207	A42	3s brown orange	.25	.80
208	A42	5s deep green	.50	.80
209	A42	10s dk slate grn	.75	.80
210	A45	20s dk car rose	1.50	1.60
211	A42	30s brt ultra	1.00	.80
212	A42	35s dark blue	1.50	1.60
213	A45	40s brown violet	2.00	1.00
214	A49	50s grnsh black	3.00	1.00
		Nos. 207-214 (8)	10.50	8.40
		Set, never hinged	20.00	

5th anniv. of National Unity Day.

Harvesting Wheat — A50   Apple — A51

1939, Oct. 8

215	A50	10s slate green	.90	.60
216	A51	20s rose lake	.90	.65
		Set, never hinged	3.00	

8th Agricultural Exposition held near Riga.

Arms and Stars for Vidzeme, Kurzeme and Latgale — A52

1940

217	A52	1s dk vio brn	.30	.30
218	A52	2s ocher	.40	.30
219	A52	3s red orange	.25	.25
220	A52	5s dk olive brn	.25	.25
221	A52	7s dk green	.30	.30
222	A52	10s dk blue grn	.75	.25
224	A52	20s rose brown	.75	.25
225	A52	30s dp red brn	1.25	.30
226	A52	35s brt ultra	.25	.80
228	A52	50s dk slate grn	1.75	.80
229	A52	1 l olive green	3.50	2.40
		Nos. 217-229 (11)	9.75	6.20
		Set, never hinged	20.00	

Catalogue values for unused stamps in this section, from this point to the end of the section, are for Never Hinged items.

Natl. Arms — A70

1991, Oct. 19   Litho.   Perf. 13x12½

300	A70	5k multicolored	5.50	5.50
301	A70	10k multicolored	.40	.40
302	A70	15k multicolored	.50	.50
303	A70	20k multicolored	.65	.65
304	A70	40k multicolored	1.40	1.40
305	A70	50k multicolored	1.90	1.90

Size: 28x32mm
Perf. 13½x14

306	A70	100k silver & multi	3.00	3.00
307	A70	200k gold & multi	5.50	5.50
		Nos. 300-307 (8)	18.85	18.85

Most issues, Nos. 300-342, have one blocked value that was not freely available at Latvian post offices.

Russia Nos. 5984, 5985a Ovptd. "LATVIJA" and Srchd. in Red Lilac, Orange, Green, Violet

1991, Dec. 23   Photo.   Perf. 12x11½

308	A2765	100k on 7k (RL)	.50	.50
a.		Vert. pair, one without ovpt.	9.50	
b.		Litho., perf. 12x12½	.50	.50

Perf. 12x12½
Litho.

309	A2765	300k on 2k (O)	.85	.85
a.		Vert. pair, one without ovpt.	9.50	
310	A2765	500k on 2k (G)	1.25	1.25
a.		Vert. pair, one without ovpt.	9.50	
311	A2765	1000k on 2k (V)	2.40	2.40
a.		Vert. pair, one without ovpt.	9.50	
		Nos. 308-311 (4)	5.00	5.00

On Nos. 308-311 the sixth row of the sheet was not surcharged.
Forgeries exist.

Liberty Monument, Riga — A71

1991, Dec. 28   Perf. 12½x13

312	A71	10k ol brn & multi	.25	.25
313	A71	15k violet & multi	1.00	1.00
314	A71	20k bl grn & multi	.80	.80
315	A71	30k ol grn & multi	.90	.90
316	A71	50k choc & multi	1.25	1.25
317	A71	100k dp blue & multi	2.00	1.25
		Nos. 312-317 (6)	6.20	5.45

A72   A73

Monuments — A74

1992, Feb. 29   Perf. 14

318	A72	10k black	.25	.25
319	A73	20k violet black	.50	.25
320	A73	30k brown	.70	.25
321	A73	30k purple	.70	.25
322	A74	40k violet blue	.95	.25
323	A73	50k green	1.10	.25
324	A73	50k olive green	1.10	.25
325	A74	100k red brown	2.25	.60
326	A72	200k blue	3.50	1.10
		Nos. 318-326 (9)	11.05	3.45

Russia Nos. 4599, 5984, 5985a Ovptd. "LATVIJA" and Srchd. in Red, Brown, Emerald and Violet

1992, Apr. 4   Photo.   Perf. 12x11½

327	A2765	1r on 7k (R)	.25	.25

Perf. 12x12½
Litho.

328	A2765	3r on 2k (Br)	.40	.25
329	A2765	5r on 2k (E)	.65	.35
330	A2765	10r on 2k (V)	1.10	.75
331	A2138	25r on 4k	2.25	1.75
		Nos. 327-331 (5)	4.65	3.35

Surcharged denominations expressed in rubles (large numerals) and kopecks (small zeros).

Birds of the Baltic Shores — A75

Litho. & Engr.
1992, Oct. 3   Perf. 12½x13
Booklet Stamps

332	A75	5r Pandion haliaetus	.30	.30
333	A75	5r Limosa limosa	.30	.30
334	A75	5r Mergus merganser	.30	.30
335	A75	5r Tadorna tadorna	.30	.30
a.		Booklet pane of 4, #332-335	2.25	

See Estonia Nos. 231-234a, Lithuania Nos. 427-430a, and Sweden Nos. 1975-1978a.

Christmas
A76

2r, 10r Angels with children around Christmas tree. 3r, Angels with musical instruments, Christmas tree. 15r, Nativity scene.

1992, Nov. 21   Litho.   Perf. 13½x13

336	A76	2r silver & multi	1.00	1.00
337	A76	3r multicolored	.30	.25
338	A76	10r gold & multi	1.00	.60
339	A76	15r multicolored	1.50	1.00
		Nos. 336-339 (4)	3.80	2.85

Russia Nos. 4728, 5107, 5109 Surcharged in Brown or Blue

Perfs. & Printing Methods as Before
1993, Feb. 26

340	A2229	50r on 6k #4728 (Br)	.75	.55
341	A2435	100r on 6k #5109	1.60	1.00
342	A2435	300r on 6k #5107	4.25	3.00
		Nos. 340-342 (3)	6.60	4.55

Traditional Costumes — A77

1993, Apr. 29   Litho.   Perf. 13x13½

343	A77	5s Kuldiga	.25	.25
344	A77	10s Alsunga	.30	.25
345	A77	20s Lielvarde	.55	.30
346	A77	50s Rucava	1.50	.80
347	A77	100s Zemgale	3.00	1.50
348	A77	500s Ziemellatgale	15.00	12.00
a.		Miniature sheet of 6, #343-348	25.00	25.00
		Nos. 343-348 (6)	20.60	15.10

See Nos. 400-401, 415-416, 440-441, 466-467.

21st Natl. Song Festival
A78   A79

1993, July 3   Litho.   Perf. 12½x13

349	A78	3s rose brn, gold & black	1.00	.50
350	A78	5s purple, gold & black	1.50	.80
351	A79	15s multicolored	2.00	1.25
		Nos. 349-351 (3)	4.50	2.55

A80

1993, Aug. 28   Litho.   Perf. 14

352	A80	15s Pope John Paul II	1.25	1.00

A81

1993, Nov. 11   Litho.   Perf. 12½x13

353	A81	5s silver, black & red	.75	.30
354	A81	15s gold, black & red	1.40	.45

Independence, 75th anniv.

A82

1994, Apr. 2   Litho.   Perf. 14

355	A82	15s multicolored	1.40	.35

Evalds Valters, actor, 100th birthday.

A83

1994, Apr. 20   Litho.   Perf. 12½x13

356	A83	5s Biathlon	.40	.40
357	A83	10s 2-man bobsled	.85	.40
358	A83	15s Luge	1.00	.65
359	A83	100s Men's figure skating	6.00	3.25
		Nos. 356-359 (4)	8.25	4.70

Souvenir Sheet

360	A83	200s like #357	12.00	9.50

1994 Winter Olympics, Lillehammer.

Ethnographical Open Air Museum — A84

1994, Apr. 30   Litho.   Perf. 13x12½

361	A84	5s multicolored	1.40	.35

1994 Basketball Festival, Riga — A85

1994, June 4   Litho.   Perf. 12½x13
362 A85 15s multicolored   1.60   .45

Provincial Municipal Arms — A86

Nos. 363-377A are inscribed with the year date of issue below the design. The year noted in each description is the date that appears on the stamp.

Perf. 13x12½, 14x14¼ (#373)
1994-2007
363 A86 1s Kurzeme, "1994"   .25   .25
  a.   "1996"   .25   .25
  b.   "1997"   .75   .25
  c.   "1998"   .25   .25
  d.   Perf 14x14¼, "1999"   1.25   .50
  e.   As "d," "2002"   .25   .25
  f.   Perf. 13¼x13¾, "2006"   .25   .25
  g.   As "f," "2007"   .25   .25
  h.   As "d," "2011"   .25   .25
  i.   As "d," "2012"   .25   .25
364 A86 2s Auce, "1996"   .40   .25
  a.   "1997"   .40   .25
  b.   "1998"   .30   .25
  c.   Perf 14x14¼, "1999"   1.25   1.25
  d.   As "c," "2000"   .40   .25
  e.   As "c," "2002"   .25   .25
  f.   Perf 13¼x13¾, "2005"   .25   .25
  g.   As "f," "2006"   .25   .25
  h.   As "f," "2007"   .25   .25
  i.   As "c," "2011"   .25   .25
  j.   As "c," "2012"   .25   .25
  k.   As "c," "2013"   .25   .25
365 A86 3s Zemgale, 1994   .55   .35
  a.   Perf 14x14¼, "1999"   .55   .35
  b.   As "a," "2000"   .55   .35
  c.   As "a," "2002"   .25   .25
  d.   Perf 13¼x13¾, "2005"   .25   .25
  e.   As "d," "2006"   .25   .25
  f.   As "d," "2007"   .25   .25
  g.   Perf. 14x14¼, "2010"   .25   .25
  h.   As "g," "2011"   .25   .25
  i.   As "g," "2012"   .25   .25
  j.   As "g," "2013"   .25   .25
366 A86 5s Vidzeme, "1994"   .55   .25
  a.   "1996"   .50   .50
  b.   Perf 14x14¼, "1999"   .50   .50
  c.   As "b," "2000"   .50   .50
367 A86 8s Livani, "1995"   .50   .40
  a.   "1996"   .50   .40
368 A86 10s Latgale, "1994"   .50   .50
  a.   "1997"   1.60   1.00
  b.   "1998"   .50   .50
369 A86 13s Preili, "1996"   .70   .70
  a.   Perf 14x14¼, "2010"   .50   .50
370 A86 16s Ainazi, "1995"   .80   .80
  a.   "1996"   1.00   1.00
371 A86 20s Grobina, "1995"   1.00   1.00
  a.   "1996"   1.00   1.00
372 A86 24s Tukums, "1995"   1.10   1.10
  a.   "1996"   1.10   1.10
373 A86 28s Madona, "1996"   1.75   1.50
374 A86 30s Riga, "1994"   1.50   1.50
375 A86 36s Priekule, "1996"   2.25   1.50
376 A86 50s Natl. arms,
                "1994"   2.25   2.25
Size: 29x24mm
Perf. 14
377   A86 100s Riga   4.25   2.50
377A A86 200s Natl. arms   8.75   4.75
      Nos. 363-377A (16)   27.10 19.60

Issued: No. 363, 6/21/94; No. 363a, 1/30/96; No. 363b, 2/5/97; No. 363c, 1/12/98; No. 363d, 1/20/99; No. 363e, 2/6/02; No. 363f, 9/9/06; No. 363g, 6/8/97; No. 363h, 6/8/11; No. 363i, 3/15/12. No. 364, 4/12/96; No. 364a, 2/5/97; No. 364b, 2/11/98; No. 364c, 1/20/99; No. 364d, 4/26/00; No. 364e, 2/6/02; No. 364f, 9/10/05; No. 364g, 9/9/06; No. 364h, 6/8/07. No. 364i, 6/8/11; No. 364j, 3/15/12. No. 364k, 3/3/13. No. 365, 6/21/94; No. 365a, 3/16/99; No. 365b, 4/26/00; No. 365c, 2/6/02; No. 365d, 9/10/05; No. 365e, 9/9/06; No. 365f, 6/8/07; No. 365g, 2/15/10; No. 365h, 6/8/11; No. 365i, 3/15/12. No. 365j, 3/3/13. No. 366, 6/21/94; No. 366a, 1/30/96; No. 366b, 1/20/99; No. 366c, 4/26/00. No. 367, 6/1/95; No. 367a, 1/30/96. No. 368, 6/21/94; No. 368a, 8/28/97; No. 368b, 8/4/98. No. 369, 4/12/96; No. 369a, 3/12/10 No. 370, 6/1/95; No. 370a, 4/8/96. No. 371, 6/1/95; No. 371a, 9/6/96. No. 372, 6/1/95; No. 372a, 4/8/96. No. 373, 11/5/96. No. 374, 12/21/94. No. 375, 11/5/96. Nos. 376, 377, 378, 12/21/94.
See Nos. 450-451, 472-473, 482-483, 506-507, 525-526.

A87

1994, Sept. 24   Litho.   Perf. 14
378 A87 5s multicolored   .60   .30
    University of Latvia, 75th anniv.

A88

Items balanced on scales (Europa): 10s, Latvian coins. 50s, Locked chest, money card.

1994, Oct. 29   Litho.   Perf. 14x13½
379 A88 10s multicolored   .65   .25
  a.   Tete-beche pair   1.75   1.75
380 A88 50s multicolored   2.75   1.50
  a.   Tete-beche pair   7.00   6.00

Dormouse A89

1994, Nov. 19   Litho.   Perf. 13½x13
381 A89 5s shown   .45   .35
382 A89 10s Among leaves   .75   .35
383 A89 10s Eating berries   .75   .35
384 A89 15s Berry, large mouse 1.50   .50
      Nos. 381-384 (4)   3.45   1.55

World Wildlife Fund.

A90

Christmas: 3s, Angel. 8s, Angels playing flute & violin. 13c, Angels singing. 100s, Candles.

1994, Dec. 3   Perf. 14
385 A90 3s multicolored   .30   .25
386 A90 8s multicolored   .55   .25
387 A90 13s multicolored   1.00   .30
388 A90 100s multicolored   5.00   2.10
      Nos. 385-388 (4)   6.85   2.90

A91

Children's Fairy Tales, by Margarita Staraste: 5s, Elf with candle. No. 390, Small bear in snow. No. 391, Boy on sled.

Perf. 13x12½ on 3 Sides
1994, Dec. 17   Booklet Stamps
389 A91 5s multicolored   .25   .25
390 A91 10s multicolored   .50   .25
391 A91 10s multicolored   .50   .25
  a.   Booklet pane, 2 each #389-391   2.75
        Complete booklet, #391a + label 3.50
      Nos. 389-391 (3)   1.25   .75

A92

1995, Feb. 18   Perf. 14
392 A92 10s multicolored   1.00   .35
    European safe driving week.

A93

1995, Mar. 4   Litho.   Perf. 14
393 A93 15s silver, blue & red 1.25   .55
    UN, 50th anniv.

A94

Via Baltica Highway Project: 8s, No. 395b, Castle, Bauska, Latvia. No. 395a, Beach Hotel, Parnu, Estonia. c, Kaunas, Lithuania.

1995, Apr. 20   Litho.   Perf. 14
394 A94 8s multicolored   .40   .25
Souvenir Sheet
395 A94 18s Sheet of 3, #a.-c. 2.75   2.00
    See Estonia Nos. 288-289, Lithuania Nos. 508-509.

A95

8s, Dendrocopos leucotos. 20s, Crex crex. 24s, Chlidonias leucopterus.

1995, July 8   Litho.   Perf. 12½
396 A95 8s multicolored   .35   .25
397 A95 20s multicolored   .85   .40
398 A95 24s multicolored   1.10   .50
      Nos. 396-398 (3)   2.30   1.15

European nature conservation year.

Julian Cardinal Vaivods, Birth Cent. — A96

1995, Aug. 18   Litho.   Perf. 14
399 A96 8s multicolored   .50   .25

Traditional Costume Type of 1993
1995, Sept. 8   Litho.   Perf. 13x13½
400 A77 8s Nica   .45   .25
Souvenir Sheet
401 A77 100s Like #400   4.75   4.75

Friendly Appeal, by Karlis Ulmanis, 60th Anniv. — A97

1995, Sept. 8   Perf. 14
402 A97 8s multicolored   .50   .25

Riga, 800th Anniv. — A98

1995, Sept. 23   Perf. 13½
403 A98 8s Natl. Opera   .40   .25
404 A98 16s Natl. Theatre   .80   .40
Size: 45x27mm
405 A98 24s Academy of Arts   1.00   .60
406 A98 36s State Art Museum   1.50   .90
      Nos. 403-406 (4)   3.70   2.15
    See Nos. 508-511, 529-531, 529-531.

Peace and Freedom — A99

Heroes from national epic, Lacplesis, dates of independence: 16s, Spidola with sword and shield, 1918. 50s, Lacplesis with leaves and banner, 1991.

1995, Nov. 15   Litho.   Perf. 13½
407 A99 16s multicolored   .75   .30
  a.   Tete beche pair   2.50   2.50
408 A99 50s multicolored   2.25   .95
  a.   Tete beche pair   5.00   5.00
    Europa.

Christmas A100

Designs: No. 409, Characters surrounding Christmas tree at night. No. 410, Santa gliding through sky holding candle. 15s, Characters outside snow-covered house. 24s, Santa standing between dog and cat.

1995, Dec. 2
409 A100 6s multicolored   .55   .25
410 A100 6s multicolored   .55   .25
411 A100 15s multicolored   .30   .60
412 A100 24s multicolored   2.25   1.00
      Nos. 409-412 (4)   3.65   2.10

Pauls Stradins (1896-1958), Physician — A101

1996, Jan. 17   Litho.   Perf. 14
413 A101 8s multicolored   .40   .25

Zenta Maurina (1897-1978) A102

1996, May 10 Litho. Perf. 13½x14
414 A102 36s multicolored   1.60 .95
a.   Tete beche pair   3.25 3.25
    Europa.

Traditional Costume Type of 1993
1996, May 18 Litho. Perf. 13x13½
415 A77 8s Barta   .50 .25
Souvenir Sheet
416 A77 100s like No. 415   4.00 3.00

Souvenir Sheet

Children's Games — A103

1996, June 8 Litho. Perf. 14x13½
417 A103 48s Sheet of 1   2.25 1.50

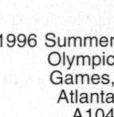

1996 Summer Olympic Games, Atlanta A104

Perf. 14x13½, 13½x14
1996, June 19
418 A104 8s Cycling,vert.   .40 .25
419 A104 16s Basketball, vert .70 .40
420 A104 24s Walking, vert.   .80 .50
421 A104 36s Canoeing   1.50 .80
    Nos. 418-421 (4)   3.40 1.95
Souvenir Sheet
422 A104 100s Javelin   4.50 3.50

Nature Museum, 150th Anniv. A105

Butterflies: 8s, Papilio machaon. 24s, Catocala fraxini. 80s, Pericallia matronula.

1996, Aug. 30 Perf. 13
423 A105 8s multicolored   .35 .25
424 A105 24s multicolored   .90 .45
425 A105 80s multicolored   3.75 1.90
    Nos. 423-425 (3)   5.00 2.60

Car Production in Latvia — A106

Designs: 8s, 1912 Russo-Balt fire truck. 24s, 1899 Leutner-Russia. 36s, 1939 Ford-Vairogs.

1996, Oct. 25 Litho. Perf. 13x12½
426 A106 8s multicolored   .35 .25
427 A106 24s multicolored   1.20 .55
428 A106 36s multicolored   1.75 .85
    Nos. 426-428 (3)   3.30 1.65

City of Riga, 800th Anniv. — A107

1996, Dec. 5 Litho. Perf. 13½
429 A107 8s Building front   .40 .25

Size: 30x26mm
430 A107 16s Stained glass window   .85 .40
Size: 37x26mm
431 A107 24s Buildings   1.40 .55
432 A107 30s Art figures   1.50 .70
    Nos. 429-432 (4)   4.15 1.90

Christmas A108

Designs: 6s, Santa's elves, presents. 14s, Santa on skis, dog, children in animal costumes. 20s, Child in front of Christmas tree, santa in chair, pets.

1996, Dec. 7 Perf. 14
433 A108 6s multicolored   .30 .25
434 A108 14s multicolored   .70 .35
435 A108 20s multicolored   1.00 .50
    Nos. 433-435 (3)   2.00 1.10

See Nos. 458-460.

Birds — A109

Designs: 10s, Caprimulgus eurpaeus. 20s, Aquila clanga. 30s, Acrocephalus paludicola.

1997, Feb. 8 Perf. 13x12½
436 A109 10s multicolored   .50 .25
437 A109 20s multicolored   .90 .45
438 A109 30s multicolored   1.40 .70
    Nos. 436-438 (3)   2.80 1.40

Turn of the Epochs — A110

1997, Mar. 25 Litho. Perf. 14
439 A110 10s multicolored   .70 .35

Traditional Costume Type of 1993
1997, Apr. 3 Perf. 13x13½
440 A77 10s Rietumvidzeme   1.25 .80
Souvenir Sheet
441 A77 100s like #440   4.50 3.50

Stamp Day.

Legend of Rozi Turaidas — A111

1997, Apr. 26 Litho. Perf. 12½x13
442 A111 32s multicolored   1.50 .70
a.   Tete beche pair   3.50 3.50
    Europa.

Old Baltic Ships — A112

Designs: 10s, Linijkugis, 17th cent.

No. 444: a, Linijkugis, 17th cent., diff. b, Kurenas 16th cent. c, Maasilinn ship, 16th cent.

1997, May 10 Perf. 14x14½
443 A112 10s multicolored   .50 .40
Souvenir Sheet
444 A112 20s Sheet of 3, #a.-c. 3.00 2.75
    See Estonia Nos. 322-323, Lithuania Nos. 571-572.

Port of Ventspils, Cent. — A113

1997, May 21 Litho. Perf. 13½x14
445 A113 20s Hermes, Poseidon .90 .50

Children's Activities A114

Designs: 10s, Stamp collecting. 12s, Riding dirt bike, vert. 20s, Boy in hockey uniform, girl in skiwear, vert. 30s, Tennis, soccer, basketball.

1997, June 7 Perf. 13½x13
446 A114 10s multicolored   .45 .25
447 A114 12s multicolored   .60 .30
448 A114 20s multicolored   1.00 .45
449 A114 30s multicolored   1.50 .75
    Nos. 446-449 (4)   3.55 1.75

Municipal Arms Type of 1994
1997-2005 Litho. Perf. 13x12½
Date imprint below design
450 A86 10s Valmiera, "1997"   1.00 .40
a.   "1998"   1.00 .40
b.   Perf 14x14¼, "1999"   1.00 .40
c.   "2000"   1.00 .40
d.   Perf. 13¼x13¾, "2001"   1.00 .40
e.   "2005"   1.00 .30
451 A86 20s Rezekne, "1997"   2.25 .85

    Issued: No. 450, 9/6/97; No. 450a, 1/12/98; No. 450b, 1/20/99; No. 450c, 4/26/00; No. 450d, 9/12/01; No. 450e, 9/10/05. No. 451, 9/6/97.

Nature Preserves A115

1997, Oct. 18 Litho. Perf. 13x12½
452 A115 10s Moricsala, 1912   .50 .25
453 A115 30s Slitere, 1921   1.50 .80

See Nos. 464-465.

City of Riga, 800th Anniv. A116

10s, Woman, house, 12th cent. 20s, Monument to Bishop Albert, seal of the bishop, rosary, writing tool, 13th-16th cent. 30s, Riga castle, weapons used during Middle Ages. 32s, Houses, arms of Riga, statue of St. John.

1997, Nov. 27 Litho. Perf. 13x14
454 A116 10s multicolored   .40 .25
455 A116 20s multicolored   .75 .40
456 A116 30s multicolored   1.10 .60
Size: 27x26mm
457 A116 32s multicolored   1.25 .70
    Nos. 454-457 (4)   3.50 1.95

See Nos. 468-471, 488-491, 508-511, 529-531.

Christmas Type of 1996

People dressed in masks, costumes for mummery: 8s, Santa, bear. 18s, Two goats. 28s, Horse.

1997, Nov. 29 Perf. 14
458 A108 8s multicolored   .45 .25
459 A108 18s multicolored   1.00 .40
460 A108 28s multicolored   1.50 .60
    Nos. 458-460 (3)   2.95 1.25

A117

1998, Jan. 31 Litho. Perf. 14x13½
461 A117 20s multicolored   1.00 .50

1998 Winter Olympic Games, Nagano.

A118

Statue at Spridisi, museum home of Anna Brigadere(1861-1933), writer.

1998, Feb. 21 Litho. Perf. 13½
462 A118 10s multicolored   .55 .25

National Song Festival — A119

1998, Mar. 28 Litho. Perf. 13x14
463 A119 30s multicolored   2.50 1.25
a.   Tete beche pair   5.50 5.50
    Europa.

Nature Preserves Type of 1997
1998, Apr. 30 Perf. 13x12½
464 A115 10s Grini, 1936   .50 .25
465 A115 30s Teici, 1982   1.40 1.00

Traditional Costume Type of 1993

No. 467, Krustpils, man wearing crown of leaves.

1998, May 9 Perf. 13x13½
466 A77 10s Krustpils region   .75 .30
Souvenir Sheet
467 A77 100s multicolored   4.25 4.00

City of Riga, 800th Anniv., Type of 1997

10s, Dannenstern House, 16th and 17th cent. coins issued by kings of Poland and Sweden, 17th cent. wooden sculpture. 20s, City Library, monument to G. Herder, poet, philosopher, teacher. 30s, 18th cent. arsenal, column celebrating defeat of Napoleon's troops, octant, compass. 40s, Sculpture of Mother Latvia at Warriors' Cemetery, entrance to Cemetery, obv. & rev. of 5 lat coin, 1930.

1998, May 29 Perf. 13x14
468 A116 10s multicolored   .50 .25
469 A116 20s multicolored   1.10 .45
470 A116 30s multicolored   1.50 .60
471 A116 40s multicolored   2.00 .85
    Nos. 468-471 (4)   5.10 2.15

No. 468 is 30x26mm.

Municipal Arms Type of 1994
1998-2004 Litho. Perf. 13¼x13¾
Date imprint below design
472 A86 15s Bauska, "1998"   .55 .35
473 A86 30s Liepaja, "1998"   1.25 .75
a.   Perf 13½x14, "2004"   1.35 .85

    Issued: No. 472, 473, 9/26/98; No. 473a, 9/7/04.

World Stamp
Day — A120

1998, Oct. 20   Litho.   Perf. 14
474 A120 30s #2, various stamps   1.50   .60

Dome Church,
Riga,
1211 — A121

1998, Oct. 23
475 A121 10s multicolored   .55   .30

Pres. Janis Cakste
(1859-1927)
A122

1998, Nov. 11   Perf. 14x13½
476 A122 10s multicolored   .55   .30
See No. 497, 515, 524.

Independence,
80th
Anniv. — A123

1998, Nov. 14   Perf. 13x12½
477 A123 10s shown   .50   .25
478 A123 30s Arms, flags   1.60   .75

Christmas
A124

Christmas elves: 10s, Rolling snow balls.
20s, Decorating tree, preparing presents. 30s,
Pulling sled over snow.

1998, Nov. 28   Perf. 13½x14
479 A124 10s multicolored   .55   .30
480 A124 20s multicolored   1.30   .65
481 A124 30s multicolored   1.75   .85
    Nos. 479-481 (3)   3.60   1.80

Municipal Arms Type of 1994
1999-2004   Litho.   Perf. 13¼x13¾
Date imprint below design
482 A86 15s Ogre, "1999"   .80   .40
a.   "2000"   .90   .50
483 A86 40s Jelgava, "1999"   2.00   1.00
a.   "2004"   1.50   .75
    Issued: No. 482, 2/12/99; No. 482a,
2/25/00. No. 483, 4/10/99; No. 483a, 9/7/04.

Nature Parks
and Reserves
A125

Europa: 30s, Krustkalnu Nature Reserve.
60s, Gauja Natl. Nature Park.

1999, Mar. 20   Perf. 13x12½
484 A125 30s multicolored   1.75   .85
485 A125 60s multicolored   4.00   1.75

Council of
Europe, 50th
Anniv. — A126

1999, Apr. 24
486 A126 30s multicolored   1.50   .80

Rudolfs
Blaumanis
(1863-1908),
Writer — A127

1999, Apr. 24   Perf. 14x13
487 A127 110s multicolored   5.00   2.40

City of Riga, 800th Anniv. Type
10s, Streetcar. 30s, Schooner "Widwud."
40s, Airplane. 70s, TK-type locomotive.

Perf. 13¼x13¾
1999, June 26   Litho.
488 A116 10s multicolored   .45   .25
489 A116 30s multicolored   1.40   .70
490 A116 40s multicolored   1.90   .95
491 A116 70s multicolored   3.00   1.60
    Nos. 488-491 (4)   6.75   3.50
    No. 488 is 30x27mm.

Aglona
Basilica — A129

1999, July 10   Litho.   Perf. 14x14½
492 A129 15s multicolored   .80   .35
    Complete booklet, 6 #492   12.00

"Baltic Chain,"
10th
Anniv. — A130

Families and flags: 15s, No. 494a, Latvian.
No. 494: b, Lithuanian. c, Estonian.

1999, Aug. 23   Litho.   Perf. 12½x13
493 A130 15s multicolored   1.25   .50
Souvenir Sheet
494 A130 30s Sheet of 3, #a.-c.   4.50   4.00
    See Estonia Nos. 366-367, Lithuania Nos.
639-640.

Rundâle
Palace — A131

1999, Sept. 25   Litho.   Perf. 14
495 A131 20s multicolored   1.20   .50
    See Nos. 512, 536, 578.

Landscape, by Julijs Feders (1838-
1909) — A132

1999, Oct. 13   Litho.   Perf. 13½
496 A132 15s multi   .85   .45

Presidents Type of 1998
15s, Pres. Gustavs Zemgals (1871-1939).

1999, Nov. 16   Litho.   Perf. 14x13½
497 A122 15s multicolored   .75   .45

A134

1999, Nov. 25   Perf. 14x14½
498 A134 40s multi   2.00   .85
    UPU, 125th anniv.

A135

Christmas and Millennium: 12s, Santa,
tree, candle. 15s, Santa, tree, children. 40s,
Santa, tree with ornaments.

1999, Nov. 27   Perf. 14¼
499 A135 12s multi   .65   .25
500 A135 15s multi   .80   .35
501 A135 40s multi   2.00   .85
    Nos. 499-501 (3)   3.45   1.45

Nude, by J.
Rozentals
A136

Perf. 14½x14¼
2000, Feb. 26   Litho.
502 A136 40s multi   2.25   1.50

Aleksandrs
Caks (1901-50),
Poet — A137

2000, Apr. 8   Litho.   Perf. 14x13½
503 A137 40s multi   2.00   .90
    Booklet, 6 #503   12.50

Europa, 2000
Common Design Type
2000, May 9
504 CD17 60s multi   5.00   2.40
a.   Tete beche pair   10.00   10.00

Ice Hockey — A138

Wmk. 387
2000, June 21   Litho.   Perf. 14
505 A138 70s multi + label   3.00   1.40

Issued in sheets of 8 + 8 labels. Vertical
columns of four labels, which depict players
Helmut Balderis, Vitalijs Samoilovs, Sandis
Ozolinsh and Arturs Irbe, flank a central block
of eight stamps. Color photos of the players
appear at left or right of the labels.

Municipal Arms Type of 1994
2000-05   Unwmk.   Perf. 13¼x13¾
Date imprint below design
506 A86 15s Daugavpils, "2000"   .75   .40
a.   "2005"   .65   .35
507 A86 15s Jūrmala, "2000"   .75   .40
a.   "2001"   .75   .40
b.   "2002"   .75   .40
c.   "2005"   .65   .35

Issued: No. 506, 7/6/00; No. 506a, 8/5/05.
No. 507, 7/6/00; No. 507a, 9/12/01; No. 507b,
1/12/02; No. 507c, 8/5/05.

**City of Riga, 800th Anniv. Type of
1995**
Designs: 20s, Central Market. No. 509, Riga
Zoo. No. 510, Riga Dome Organ. 70s, Powder
Tower.

2000, July 22   Perf. 13¼x14
Size: 40x28mm
508 A98 20s multi   1.00   .50
Size: 47x28mm
509 A98 40s multi   2.00   1.00
    Complete booklet, 6 #509   12.00
Perf. 14x13¼
Size: 28x32mm
510 A98 40s multi   2.00   1.00
511 A98 70s multi   3.25   1.25
    Nos. 508-511 (4)   8.25   3.75

Palace Type of 1999
2000, Aug. 12   Perf. 13¼x14
512 A131 40s Jelgava Palace   2.00   1.00
    Booklet, 6 #512   13.00

2000 Summer Olympics,
Sydney — A139

2000, Sept. 15   Perf. 14¼x14
513 A139 70s multi + label   3.00   2.00
    See No. 518.

Millennium — A140

No. 514: a, 15s, Freedom Monument, Riga.
b, House of Blackheads, Riga.

Perf. 14x13¼
2000, Sept. 28   Litho.   Wmk. 387
514 A140 Pair + label   3.00   2.75
a.   15s multi   .80   .40
b.   50s multi   2.00   1.10

President Type of 1998
Perf. 13¾x13¼
2000, Nov. 11   Unwmk.
515 A122 15s Alberts Kveisis
    (1881-1936)   1.25   .40

LATVIA									539

Orthodox Cathedral — A141

2000, Nov. 17   **Perf. 14**
516 A141 40s multi   1.90 1.00
See Nos. 537, 559, 573.

Red Cross — A142

2000, Nov. 22
517 A142 15s multi   .95 .40

Olympics Type of 2000
2000, Nov. 22
518 A139 40s multi   1.75 .85
Issued in sheets of 4 + 2 different labels depicting gold medal winner Igors Vihrovs.

Christmas — A143

Designs: 12s, Watch. No. 520, 15s, Angels. No. 521, 15s, Madonna and child.

2000, Nov. 25
519-521 A143 Set of 3   1.90 1.00

International Recognition of Latvia, 80th Anniv. — A144

2001, Jan. 13   Litho.   **Perf. 14**
522 A144 40s multi   2.25 1.00

Kad Silavas Mostas, by Vilhelmis Purvitis A145

Perf. 14¼x14½
2001, Feb. 1   Litho.   **Unwmk.**
523 A145 40s multi   3.00 1.50
Booklet, 6 #523   18.00

President Type of 1998
2001, Feb. 17   **Perf. 13¾x13¼**
524 A122 15s Karlis Ulmanis (1877-1942)   1.25 .35

Municipal Arms Type of 1994
2001-06   **Perf. 13¼x13¾**
   Date imprint below design
525 A86 5s Smiltene, "2001"   .50 .25
a.   "2002"   .50 .25
b.   "2005"   .25 .25
c.   "2006"   .25 .25
d.   Perf. 14x14¼, "2011"   .25 .25
e.   As "d," "2012"   .25 .25
f.   As "d," "2013"   .25 .25
526 A86 15s Kuldiga, "2001"   .60 .30
a.   "2002"   .60 .30

Issued: No. 525, 3/5/01; No. 525a, 9/16/02; No. 525b, 9/10/05; No. 525c, 9/9/06. No.

525d, 6/8/11; No. 525e, 3/15/12; No. 525f, 3/3/13. No. 526, 3/5/01; No. 526a, 9/16/02.

Narrow Gauge Locomotive A146

2001, Mar. 24   **Perf. 14**
527 A146 40s multi   2.50 1.00

Europa — A147

2001, Apr. 14
528 A147 60s multi   3.50 1.75
a.   Tete beche pair   4.50 4.50

Riga, 800th Anniv. Type of 1995
Riga in: No. 529a, 20th cent. No. 529b, 21st cent. 60s, 16th cent. 70s, 17th cent.

2001, May 24   Litho.   **Perf. 13¾x13½**
   Size: 29x33mm (each stamp)
529 A98 15s Horiz. pair, #a-b   1.50 .75
   Size: 47x28mm
   Perf. 13½x13¾
530 A98 60s multi   2.50 1.25
531 A98 70s multi   2.75 1.40
Nos. 529-531 (3)   6.75 3.40

Kakisa Dzirnavas, by Karlis Skalbe — A148

2001, June 9   **Perf. 13¾**
532 A148 40s multi   2.00 1.00
Booklet, 6 #532   12.00

Souvenir Sheet

Mikhail Tal (1936-92), Chess Champion — A149

2001, Aug. 18   Litho.   **Perf. 14**
533 A149 100s multi   4.25 3.50

Baltic Coast Landscapes A150

Designs: 15s, No. 535a, Vidzeme. No. 535b, Palanga. No. 535c, Lahemaa.

2001, Sept. 15   **Perf. 13½**
534 A150 15s multi   1.50 .75
Booklet, 6 #534   10.00

Souvenir Sheet
535   Sheet of 3   4.25 3.50
a.-c.   A150 30s Any single   1.25 .75
See Estonia Nos. 423-424, Lithuania Nos. 698-699.

Palace Type of 1999
2001, Oct. 24   **Perf. 14½x14**
536 A131 40s Cesvaines Palace   2.00 1.25
a.   Perf. 13¼x14   2.00 1.25
b.   Booklet pane, 6 #536a   12.00
   Booklet, #536b   12.00

House of Worship Type of 2000
2001, Nov. 3   **Perf. 13¾x14**
537 A141 70s Riga Synagogue   3.00 1.50
Booklet, 6 #537   24.00

Latvian Seamen — A151

Designs: 15s, Krisjanis Valdemars (1825-91), founder of Naval College. 70s, Duke Jekabs Ketlers (1610-82), shipbuilder.

2001, Nov. 14   **Perf. 13¼x14**
538-539 A151 Set of 2   3.25 2.00

Christmas A152

Designs: 12s, Rabbits. No. 541, 15s, Dog, rabbit. No. 542, 15s, Lambs.

2001, Nov. 22   **Perf. 13¼**
540-542 A152 Set of 3   2.25 1.25

Town Arms — A153

2002, Jan. 29   Litho.   **Perf. 13¼x13¾**
543 A153 5s Ludza   .40 .35
544 A153 10s Dubele   .60 .50
a.   Perf. 14x14¼, dated "2012"   .50 .50
b.   As "a," "2013"   .40 .40
545 A153 15s Sigulda   .80 .50
Nos. 543-545 (3)   1.80 1.35

See Nos. 565-567, 585-587, 609-611, 638-640, 670-672, 696-698, 726-728, 753-755, 776-777, 798-800, 824-826.
Issued: No. 544a, 3/15/12; No. 544b, 3/3/13.

2002 Winter Olympics, Salt Lake City — A154

2002, Feb. 8   **Perf. 13¼x13¾**
546 A154 40s multi   1.75 1.00
a.   Booklet pane of 6, perf. 13¼x13¾ on 3 sides   15.00 —
   Booklet, #546a   15.00

2002 Winter Paralympics, Salt Lake City — A155

2002, Mar. 5   **Perf. 14¼x13¾**
547 A155 15s multi   1.00 .70

Refugees, by Jekabs Kazaks — A156

2002, Apr. 20   Litho.   **Perf. 14½x14¼**
548 A156 40s multi   2.50 1.25

Europa — A157

2002, May 4   **Perf. 14**
549 A157 60s multi   2.50 1.75
a.   Tete-beche pair   6.00 6.00

Endangered Plants — A158

Designs: 15s, Cypripedium calceolus. 40s, Trapa natans.

2002, May 25   **Perf. 13¾**
550-551 A158 Set of 2   2.50 1.50
See Nos. 568-569, 589-590, 612-613.

Latvian Armed Forces — A159

2002, June 15   **Perf. 13¾x13¼**
552 A159 40s multi   1.50 1.00

Janis Jaunsudrabins (1877-1962), Writer — A160

2002, July 6   **Perf. 13¾x13½**
553 A160 40s multi   1.75 1.10
a.   Booklet pane of 6, perf. 13¾x13½ on 3 sides   12.00
   Booklet, #553a   12.00

Kristians Johans Dals (1839-1904) and Ship — A161

2002, July 20   **Perf. 13¼x13¾**
554 A161 70s multi   3.00 1.75

Fish — A162

Designs: 15s, Gadus morhua callarias. 40s, Siluris glanis.

2002, Aug. 10   Litho.   Perf. 14
555-556 A162   Set of 2   2.50 1.75
  a.   Booklet pane, perf. 14 on 3
       sides   15.00
       Booklet, #556a   15.00

Souvenir Sheet

Venta River Bridge — A163

2002, Aug. 24   Perf. 12¾x12½
557 A163 100s multi   4.25 3.50

Jaunmoku
Palace — A164

2002, Sept. 14   Perf. 14¼x13¾
558 A164 40s multi   1.90 1.25

House of Worship Type of 2000
  70s, Grebenschikov Old Belief Praying
House.

2002, Oct. 12   Perf. 13¾x14
559 A141 70s multicolored   3.00 1.75
  a.   Booklet pane of 6, perf.
       13¾x14 on 3 sides   20.00
       Booklet, #559a   20.00

Mittens
A165

2002, Nov. 2   Perf. 13¼x13¾
560 A165 15s multi   1.00 .50
       See Nos. 579, 604, 629.

Christmas — A166

  Designs: 12s, Elf on sack, Christmas tree.
No. 562, 15s, Angel, Christmas tree. No. 563,
15s, Elves on gift.

2002, Nov. 23   Perf. 13¾x13¼
561-563 A166   Set of 3   2.00 1.25

A Man Entering
a Room, by
Niklavs Strunke
(1894-1966)
A167

2003, Jan. 25   Litho.   Perf. 13¼x14
564 A167 40s multi   2.00 1.25

Town Arms Type of 2002

2003, Feb. 15   Perf. 13¼x13¾
565 A153 10s Balvi   .50 .25
566 A153 15s Gulbene   .65 .40
567 A153 20s Ventspils   .90 .60
       Nos. 565-567 (3)   2.05 1.25

Endangered Plants Type of 2002
  Designs: 15s, Ophrys insectifera. 30s,
Taxus baccata.

2003, Mar. 21   Perf. 13¾
568 A158 15s multi   .75 .50
569 A158 30s multi   1.75 1.00
  a.   Perf. 14½x14¼ on 3 sides 2.00 1.00
  b.   Booklet pane, 6 #569a   12.00 —
       Complete booklet, #569b 12.00

Straumeni, by
Edvarts Virza
(1883-1940)
A168

2003, Apr. 12   Perf. 13¾x13¼
570 A168 40s multi   2.00 1.25

Europa — A169

2003, May 3   Litho.   Perf. 13¼x13¾
571 A169 60s multi   2.75 1.75
  a.   Tete beche pair   6.00 6.00

Kolka
Lighthouse — A170

2003, May 17   Perf. 13¾x13¼
572 A170 60s multi   2.50 1.75
       See Nos. 602, 626, 662, 676, 709, 746.

House of Worship Type of 2000
2003, June 6   Perf. 13¼x13¾
573 A141 70s Salvation Temple,
          horiz.   3.00 1.75

Souvenir Sheet

Gauja River Bridge, Sigulda — A171

2003, July 19
574 A171 100s multi   4.75 3.75

Fish — A172

  Designs: 15s, Thymallus thymallus. 30s,
Salmo salar.

2003, Aug. 2   Perf. 14x13¾
575 A172 15s multi   .75 .50
576 A172 30s multi   1.75 1.25
  a.   Booklet pane of 6, perf.
       14x13¾ on 3 sides   13.00 —
       Complete booklet, #576a 13.00

Motacilla
Alba — A173

2003, Aug. 30   Perf. 14¾x14
577 A173 15s multi   1.00 .50

Palace Type of 1999
2003, Sept. 27   Perf. 14¼x13¾
578 A131 40s Birini Palace 1.75 1.25
  a.   Booklet pane of 6   11.00
       Complete booklet, #578a 11.00

Mittens Type of 2002
2003, Oct. 11   Perf. 14x13¾
579 A165 15s Libiesi mittens .80 .45

Motorcycle
Racing
A174

2003, Oct. 31   Perf. 13¼x13¾
580 A174 70s multi   3.00 1.75
  a.   Booklet pane of 6   20.00 —
       Complete booklet, #580a 20.00

Christmas — A175

  Designs: 12s, Madonna and Child with two
angels. No. 582, 15s, The Annunciation
(golden brown frame). No. 583, 15s, Nativity
(gray frame).

2003, Nov. 22   Perf. 13¾x14¼
581-583 A175   Set of 3   2.25 1.25

Still Life with
Triangle, by
Romans
Suta — A176

2004, Jan. 25   Litho.   Perf. 13¼x14
584 A176 40s multi   2.00 1.00

Town Arms Type of 2002
2004, Feb. 14   Perf. 13¼x13¾
585 A153 5s Valka   .30 .30
586 A153 15s Cesis   .70 .50
587 A153 20s Saldus   .90 .50
       Nos. 585-587 (3)   1.90 1.30

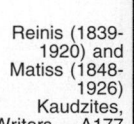

Reinis (1839-
1920) and
Matiss (1848-
1926)
Kaudzites,
Writers — A177

2004, Mar. 20   Perf. 13¾
588 A177 40s multi   1.75 1.00

Endangered Plants Type of 2002
  Designs: 15s, Gentiana cruciata. 30s,
Onobrychis arenaria.

2004, Apr. 3
589-590 A158   Set of 2   2.00 1.25

2006 World Ice Hockey
Championships, Riga — A178

2004, Apr. 17 Litho. Perf. 13¼x13¾
591 A178 30s multi   1.50 .80
  a.   Booklet pane of 4, perf.
       13¼x13¾ on 3 sides   7.00 —
       Complete booklet, #591a 7.00

Admission to European Union — A179

  Designs: No. 592, 30s, Stars, map of
Europe, flags of newly-added countries. No.
593, 30s, Seven stars.

2004, May 1   Perf. 13x13¼
592-593 A179   Set of 2   2.50 1.75

Europa — A180

2004, May 8   Litho.   Perf. 13¼x13¾
594 A180 60s multi   2.50 1.75
  a.   Tete beche pair   5.50 5.50

European Soccer Championships,
Portugal — A181

2004, June 3   Perf. 14x13½
595 A181 30s multi   1.75 1.60

Fish — A182

  Designs: 15s, Oncorhynchus mykiss. 30s,
Psetta maxima.

2004, June 26   Perf. 13¼x14
596 A182 15s multi   .60 .40
597 A182 30s multi   1.50 .90
  a.   Booklet pane of 6, perf.
       13¼x14 on 3 sides   11.00 —
       Complete booklet, #597a 11.00
       See Nos. 620-621.

Visit of Pres. Bill Clinton to Latvia, 10th Anniv. — A183

2004, July 6   *Perf. 13¾x13¼*
598 A183 40s multi   1.75 1.25

Souvenir Sheet

Dzelzcela Bridge, Riga — A184

2004, July 24   *Perf. 13¼x13¾*
599 A184 100s multi   4.25 4.25

2004 Summer Olympics, Athens A185

2004, Aug. 14   Litho.   *Perf. 14*
600 A185 30s multi   1.25 .90

St. Jacob's Cathedral — A186

Perf. 13¾x13¼
2004, Aug. 28   Litho.
601 A186 40s multi   2.00 1.25

Lighthouse Type of 2003
2004, Sept. 18
602 A170 60s Mikelbaka   2.50 1.50
a. Booklet pane of 4, perf. 13¾x13¼ on 3 sides   11.00 —
Complete booklet, #602a   11.00

Jaunpils Palace — A187

2004, Oct. 15   *Perf. 14¼x13¾*
603 A187 40s multi   1.75 1.25
a. Booklet pane of 6, perf. 14¼x13¾ on 3 sides   11.00 —
Complete booklet, #603a   11.00

See Nos. 628, 678.

Mittens Type of 2002
2004, Nov. 6   *Perf. 13¼x13¾*
604 A165 15s Piebalga mittens   .90 .50

Christmas — A188

Designs: 12s, Children, rabbit, bird, heart. No. 606, 15s, Snowman, birds. No. 607, 15s, Angel.

2004, Dec. 4   *Perf. 13¾x13¼*
605-607 A188   Set of 3   1.90 1.20

1905 Revolution, Cent. A189

2005, Jan. 13   Litho.   *Perf. 13¾x13¼*
608 A189 15s multi   1.00 .75

Town Arms Type of 2002
2005, Feb. 11   *Perf. 13¼x13¾*
609 A153 15s Aluksne   .60 .40
610 A153 15s Talsi   .60 .40
611 A153 40s Jekabpils   1.75 1.25
Nos. 609-611 (3)   2.95 2.05

Endangered Plants Type of 2002
Designs: 20s, Pulsatilla patens. 30s, Allium ursinum.

2005, Mar. 5   *Perf. 13¼*
612-613 A158   Set of 2   2.00 1.25
613a Booklet pane of 6 #613, perf. 13¼ on 3 sides   12.00 —
Complete booklet, #613a   12.00

Krimuldas Church, 800th Anniv. A190

2005, Mar. 19   *Perf. 13¼x13¾*
614 A190 40s multi   1.60 1.00

The Adventures of Baron Munchausen, by Rudolph Erich Raspe A191

2005, Apr. 1   Litho.   *Perf. 13¼x13¾*
615 A191 30s multi   1.25 .90

Europa — A192

2005, Apr. 23
616 A192 60s multi   2.50 1.50
a. Tete beche pair   6.00 6.00

Mother and Child, by Janis Rozentals A193

2005, May 8   *Perf. 14x13¼*
617 A193 40s multi   1.60 1.00
a. Booklet pane of 4, perf. 14x13¼ on 3 sides   7.25
Complete booklet, #617a   7.25

Baumanu Karlis (1835-1905), Composer of National Anthem — A194

2005, May 21   *Perf. 13¾x13¼*
618 A194 20s multi   .80 .50

Kaive Oak — A195

Serpentine Die Cut 14
2005, June 11   Self-Adhesive
619 A195 15s multi   1.10 .75

Printed in sheets of 8.

Fish Type of 2004
Designs: 15s, Lampetra fluviatilis. 40s, Clupea harengus membras.

2005, Aug. 13   Litho.   *Perf. 13¼x14*
620-621 A182   Set of 2   2.25 1.50

Pope John Paul II (1920-2005) A196

2005, Aug. 14   *Perf. 14¼x13½*
622 A196 15s multi   .80 .50

Souvenir Sheet

Latvian National Library — A197

2005, Aug. 27   *Perf. 13¼x12¾*
623 A197 100s multi   4.25 3.75

Janis Plieksans (Rainis), (1865-1929), Writer — A198

2005, Sept. 10   *Perf. 14¼*
624 A198 40s multi   1.60 1.00
a. Booklet pane of 6, perf. 14¼ on 3 sides   11.00 —
Complete booklet, #624a   11.00

Souvenir Sheet

Bridge Over Railroad Tracks, Riga — A199

2005, Sept. 24   *Perf. 13¼x13¾*
625 A199 100s multi   5.00 4.00

Lighthouse Type of 2003
2005, Oct. 8   Litho.   *Perf. 14x13¼*
626 A170 40s Daugavgrivas   1.75 1.00
a. Booklet pane of 4, perf. 14x13¼ on 3 sides   8.50 —
Complete booklet, #626a   8.50

Gunars Astra (1931-88), Human Rights Activist in Soviet Union — A200

2005, Oct. 22   *Perf. 13½x14¼*
627 A200 15s multi   .60 .40

Palace Type of 2004
2005, Nov. 5   *Perf. 13¼x14*
628 A187 40s Durbes Palace, horiz.   1.60 1.00

Mittens Type of 2002
2005, Nov. 26   *Perf. 13¼x13¾*
629 A165 20s Dienvidlatgale mittens   .80 .50

Christmas A201

Designs: 12s, Goat riding on wolf's back. No. 631, 15s, Woman, dog near tree, vert. No. 632, 15s, Cat, woman carrying rooster, vert.

2005, Dec. 3   *Serpentine Die Cut 15*
Self-Adhesive
630-632 A201   Set of 3   1.70 1.25

Europa Stamps, 50th Anniv. A202

Latvian Europa stamps: Nos. 633, 637a, 10s, #414. Nos. 634, 637b, 15s, #463. Nos. 635, 637c, 15s, #442. Nos. 636, 637d, 20s, #484-485.

2006, Jan. 7   Litho.   *Perf. 13¾x13¼*
633-636 A202   Set of 4   2.50 1.50
Souvenir Sheet
Perf. 13½ Syncopated
637 A202   Sheet of 4, #a-d   2.50 2.50
No. 637 contains four 45x28mm stamps.

Town Arms Type of 2002
2006, Jan. 11   *Perf. 13¼x13¾*
638 A153 7s Aizkraukle   .30 .25
639 A153 22s Kraslava   .80 .60
640 A153 31s Limbazi   1.25 .90
Nos. 638-640 (3)   2.35 1.75

2006 Winter
Olympics,
Turin — A203

2006, Feb. 4   ***Perf. 14***
641 A203 45s multi   1.75 1.00

Stamerienas
Palace — A204

2006, Feb. 25   ***Perf. 14¼x13¾***
642 A204 95s multi   3.75 2.25

Zvartes
Iezis — A205

Serpentine Die Cut 14
2006, Mar. 11   **Self-Adhesive**
643 A205 22s multi   .85 .55
     Printed in sheets of 8.

Souvenir Sheet

Raunu Railroad Bridge — A206

2006, Mar. 25   ***Perf. 13½x14***
644 A206 100s multi   3.75 3.25

2006 World Ice Hockey
Championships, Riga — A207

Perf. 13½x14¼
2006, Mar. 31   **Litho.**
645 A207 55s multi + label   2.00 1.25
   a.   Booklet pane of 4, perf.
      13½x14¼ on 3 sides, without
      labels   10.00
      Complete booklet, #645a   10.00

Cesis, 800th
Anniv. — A208

     Various sites in Cesis: 22s, 31s, 45s, 55s.
45s and 55s are horiz.

Perf. 13¼x13¾, 13¾x13¼
2006, Apr. 7
646-649 A208   Set of 4   6.00 4.00

Traditional Jewelry — A209

     No. 650: a, Brooch, Latvia. b, Bracelet,
Kazakhstan.

2006, Apr. 19   ***Perf. 14x13¾***
650 A209 22s Horiz. pair, #a-b   1.75 1.00
     See Kazakhstan No. 509.

Europa — A210

2006, May 3   ***Perf. 13½x14¼***
651 A210 85s multi   3.25 2.50
   a.   Tete beche pair   7.00 7.00

Ciganiete ar
Tamburinu, by
Karlis
Huns — A211

2006, May 13   ***Perf. 13¼x14***
652 A211 40s multi   1.50 1.00
   a.   Booklet pane of 4, perf. 13¼x14
      on 3 sides   7.00
      Complete booklet, #652a   7.00

A212

Personalizable
Stamps
A213

2006, June 9   ***Perf. 13¾***
653 A212 31s yel bister   1.25 1.00
654 A213 31s yel bister   1.25 1.00
     Stamp vignettes could be personalized by
customers, presumably for an extra fee.

"Big Christopher"
Statue — A214

2006, June 16   ***Perf. 14x13½***
655 A214 36s multi   1.40 1.00

Art by Anna
Koshkina — A215

Booklet Stamp
Die Cut Perf. 14½x13 on 3 Sides
2006, Aug. 11   **Self-Adhesive**
656 A215 22s multi   .90 .60
   a.   Booklet pane of 8   7.25

Volunteer
Army, 15th
Anniv. — A216

2006, Aug. 23   ***Perf. 13½x14***
657 A216 22s multi   .90 .60

Staburags — A217

2006, Sept. 9   Litho.   ***Perf. 14¼x13¾***
658 A217 58s multi   2.25 1.50
   a.   Tete beche pair   5.00 5.00

Wild Animals and
Their
Tracks — A218

     Designs: 45s, Lynx lynx. 55s, Cervus
elaphus.

2006, Sept. 23   ***Perf. 14¼x13½***
659-660 A218   Set of 2   3.75 2.50
659a   Booklet pane of 4 #659, perf.
       14¼x13½ on 3 sides   7.50 —
       Complete booklet, #659a   7.50
659b   Tete beche pair   4.00 4.00
660a   Tete beche pair   4.50 4.50
     See Nos. 691-692, 719-720, 744-745.

Pansija Pili,
Novel by
Anslavs Eglitis
(1906-93)
A219

2006, Oct. 14   Litho.   ***Perf. 13¼x13½***
661 A219 67s multi   2.50 1.50

Lighthouse Type of 2003
2006, Oct. 27   ***Perf. 14¼x13½***
662 A170 40s Mersraga Light-
       house   1.50 1.00
   a.   Booklet pane of 4, perf.
      14¼x13½ on 3 sides   7.00 —
      Complete booklet, #662a   7.00

NATO
Summit,
Riga
A220

2006, Nov. 17   ***Perf. 13¾x13¼***
663 A220 55s multi   2.25 1.25

Christmas
A221

     Cookies in shape of: 18s, Christmas tree.
22s, Star. 31s, Crescent moon. 45s, Bell.

Serpentine Die Cut 14
2006, Nov. 17   **Self-Adhesive**
664-667 A221   Set of 4   4.50 3.25

Oskars Kalpaks (1882-1919), First
Commander-in-chief of Latvian
Army — A222

2007, Jan. 6   ***Perf. 14¼x14***
668 A222 22s multi   .85 .60

Mobile Telecommunications in Latvia,
15th Anniv. — A223

2007, Jan. 19
669 A223 22s multi   .85 .60
   a.   Tete beche pair   2.00 2.00

Town Arms Type of 2002
2007, Feb. 3   ***Perf. 13¼x13¾***
670 A153   5s Staicele   .25 .25
   a.   Perf. 14x14¼, "2010"   .25 .25
671 A153   10s Sabile   .35 .25
672 A153   22s Vecumnieki   .80 .65
     Nos. 670-672 (3)   1.40 1.15
     Issued: No. 670a, 3/12/10.

Tilts Tornkalna,
Painting by
Ludolfs Liberts
(1895-1959)
A224

2007, Feb. 17   ***Perf. 14¼x14***
673 A224 58s multi   2.25 1.50

Pauls
Stradins
Museum of
the History
of
Medicine,
Riga, 50th
Anniv.
A225

2007, Mar. 9   ***Perf. 14x14¼***
674 A225 22s multi   .85 .60

Baltic
Coast — A226

Serpentine Die Cut 14
2007, Mar. 24   **Self-Adhesive**
675 A226 22s multi   .85 .60

Lighthouse Type of 2003
2007, Apr. 14   **Perf. 13¾x13½**
676 A170 67s Papes Lighthouse   2.50 1.75
    a.   Booklet pane of 4, perf.
       13¾x13½ on 3 sides   12.00 —
       Complete booklet, #676a   12.00

Europa — A227

2007, Apr. 28   Litho.   **Perf. 13½x14¼**
677 A227 85s multi   3.25 2.50
    a.   Tete beche pair   7.50 7.50
      Scouting, cent.

Palace Type of 2004
2007, June 8   Litho.   **Perf. 13½x14¼**
678 A187 22s Krustpils, horiz.   .85 .60

UNESCO World Heritage
Sites — A228

Designs: 36s, Historic Center of Riga. 45s,
Historic Centers of Straslund and Wismar,
Germany.

2007, July 12   Litho.   **Perf. 14x13¾**
679-680 A228   Set of 2   3.25 2.25
     See Germany Nos. 2449-2450.

Sigulda, 800th
Anniv. — A229

Designs: 22s, New Sigulda Castle. 31s,
Bobsled course. 40s, Sigulda Castle ruins.

Serpentine Die Cut 15¼
2007, Aug. 10   **Self-Adhesive**
681-683 A229   Set of 3   3.75 2.50

Berries and
Mushrooms
A230

Designs: 22s, Vaccinium vitis-idaea. 58s,
Cantharellus cibarius.

2007, Aug. 25   **Perf. 14x13½**
684 A230 22s multi   .80 .55
    a.   Tete beche pair   2.00 2.00

---

685 A230 58s multi   2.25 1.50
    a.   Booklet pane of 4, perf.
       14x13½ on 3 sides   10.00 —
       Complete booklet, #685a   10.00
    b.   Tete beche pair   5.00 5.00
     See Nos. 715-716, 742-743, 767-768.

Organized Soccer in Latvia,
Cent. — A231

2007, Sept. 8   **Perf. 13¾**
686 A231 45s multi   1.75 1.75
    Values are for stamps with surrounding
selvage.

Souvenir Sheet

Aivieksti Railroad Bridge — A232

2007, Oct. 13   **Perf. 14**
687 A232 100s multi   4.00 3.50

Latvia Post,
375th Anniv.
A233

Designs: 22s, Postrider. 31s, Postal worker
and van.

Serpentine Die Cut 15
2007, Oct. 20   **Litho.**
        Self-Adhesive
688-689 A233   Set of 2   2.00 1.50

13th Century
Decorations
A234

2007, Nov. 3   **Perf. 13¼x14**
690 A234 60s multi   2.50 1.75

Wild Animals and Their Tracks Type
of 2006
Designs: 45s, Vulpes vulpes. 55s, Alces
alces.

2007, Nov. 16   **Perf. 14¼x13½**
691 A218 45s multi   1.75 1.25
    a.   Tete beche pair   3.50 3.50
692 A210 55s multi   2.25 1.50
    a.   Tete beche pair   5.00 5.00

Christmas — A235

Christmas tree and children with: 22s, Musical instruments. 31s, Cookies. 45s, Skis and
sled.

Serpentine Die Cut 15
2007, Nov. 24   **Self-Adhesive**
693-695 A235   Set of 3   3.75 3.00

Town Arms Type of 2002 With
Country Name at Top
2008, Feb. 9   **Perf. 13¼x13¾**
696 A153 22s Salaspils   .80 .60
697 A153 28s Plavinas   1.00 .75
698 A153 45s Saulkrasti   1.75 1.25
     Nos. 696-698 (3)   3.55 2.60

Easter
A236

2008, Feb. 23   **Perf. 13¼x13**
699 A236 22s multi   .85 .75

Augli, by
Leo
Svemps
A237

2008, Mar. 8   Litho.   **Perf. 13x13¼**
700 A237 63s multi   2.40 2.40

State Awards of the
Baltic
Countries — A238

Designs: Nos. 701, 702a, Order of Three
Stars, Latvia. No. 702b, Order of Vytautas the
Great, Lithuania. No. 702c, Order of the
National Coat of Arms, Estonia.

2008, Mar. 15   **Perf. 13½x13¾**
701 A238 31s multi   1.25 1.25

Souvenir Sheet
702 A238 31s Sheet of 3, #a-c   3.75 3.75

    On No. 701, the second line of type above
the medal is 18mm wide, while it is 15mm
wide on No. 702a.
    See Estonia Nos. 592-593, Lithuania Nos.
862-863.

Worldwide Fund
for Nature
(WWF) — A239

Bats: 22s, Barbastella barbastellus. 31s,
Myotis dasycneme. 45s, Barbastella barbastellus, vert. 55s, Myotis dasycneme, vert.

Perf. 13½x14¼, 14¼x13½
2008, Apr. 12
703 A239 22s multi   .90 .90
    a.   Tete beche pair   2.00 2.00
704 A239 31s multi   1.25 1.25
    a.   Tete beche pair   3.00 3.00
705 A239 45s multi   1.75 1.75
    a.   Tete beche pair   4.00 4.00
706 A239 55s multi   2.00 2.00
    a.   Tete beche pair   5.00 5.00
     Nos. 703-706 (4)   5.90 5.90

Europa — A240

Designs: 45s, Letters and postcards. 85s,
Person writing letter.

2008, Apr. 22   **Perf. 13½**
707 A240 45s multi   1.75 1.75
    a.   Tete beche pair   4.00 4.00
708 A240   multi   3.25 3.25
    a.   Tete beche pair   7.50 7.50

Lighthouse Type of 2003
2008, May 5   **Perf. 14¼x13½**
709 A170 63s Akmenraga Light-
       house   2.25 2.25
    a.   Booklet pane of 4, perf.
       14¼x13½ on 3 sides   12.00 —
       Complete booklet, #709a   12.00

European
Orienteering
Championships,
Ventspils — A241

2008, May 23   Litho.   **Perf. 13x13¼**
710 A241 45s multi   1.75 1.75
    a.   Tete beche pair   4.25 4.25

Nature
Protection
A242

Serpentine Die Cut 12½
2008, June 7   **Self-Adhesive**
711 A242 22s multi   .85 .85

Riga Museum Foundations — A243

2008, June 26   **Perf. 13x13½**
712 A243 22s multi   .85 .85

2008 Summer
Olympics,
Beijing — A244

2008, Aug. 8   **Perf. 13½x13**
713 A244 63s multi   2.25 2.25

Sudraba Fairy Tale — A245

Perf. 14¼x13½

2008, Aug. 23   **Litho.**
714 A245 22s multi   .85 .85
    a.   Tete beche pair   1.90 1.90

Berries and Mushrooms Type of 2007

Designs: 22s, Vaccinium myrtillus. 58s, Leccinum aurantiacum.

2008, Sept. 6   **Perf. 14x13½**
715 A230 22s multi   .80 .80
    a.   Tete beche pair   2.00 2.00
716 A230 58s multi   2.00 2.00
    a.   Perf. 13½x14 on 3 sides   2.25 2.25
    b.   Booklet pane of 4 #716a   9.00 —
       Complete booklet, #716b   9.00
    c.   Tete beche pair   4.50 4.50

Souvenir Sheet

Kandavas Bridge — A246

2008, Sept. 27   **Perf. 14**
717 A246 100s multi   3.75 3.75

Tautas Fronte Newspaper, 20th Anniv. — A247

2008, Oct. 8   **Perf. 13½**
718 A247 22s multi   .85 .85
    a.   Tete beche pair   1.75 1.75

Wild Animals and Their Tracks Type of 2006

Designs: 45s, Martes martes. 55s, Castor fiber.

2008, Oct. 10   **Perf. 14¼x13½**
719 A218 45s multi   1.75 1.75
    a.   Tete beche pair   3.50 3.50
720 A218 55s multi   2.25 2.25
    a.   Tete beche pair   5.00 5.00

Maris Strombergs, 2008 BMX Cycling Olympic Gold Medalist — A248

2008, Oct. 24   **Perf. 13½**
721 A248 22s multi   .85 .85

Plate, Bow and Tablecloth A249

2008, Oct. 25   **Perf. 13½x13¾**
722 A249 28s multi   1.00 1.00

Latvian Republic, 90th Anniv. — A250

2008, Nov. 7   **Perf. 13¼x13**
723 A250 31s multi   1.25 1.25

Mezotnes Palace A251

2008, Nov. 8   **Perf. 13½x14¼**
724 A251 63s multi   2.40 2.40

Christmas — A252

2008, Nov. 28   **Perf. 14¼x13¾**
725 A252 25s multi   .90 .90

Town Arms Type of 2002 With Country Name at Top

2009, Jan. 10   **Litho.**   **Perf. 14x14¼**
726 A153 33s Dagda   1.25 1.25
727 A153 35s Balozi   1.40 1.40
728 A153 60s Stende   2.00 2.00
    Nos. 726-728 (3)   4.65 4.65

Brooch, 8th Cent. A. D. — A253

2009, Jan. 24   **Perf. 14**
729 A253 98s multi   3.50 3.50
    a.   Tete beche pair   7.50 7.50

Dancing Boy and Animals Folktale A254

2009, Feb. 21   **Perf. 13¼**
730 A254 40s multi   1.50 1.50

Souvenir Sheet

Preservation of Polar Regions and Glaciers — A255

No. 731: a, 35s, Polar bear. b, 55s, Penguins.

2009, Mar. 18   **Litho.**   **Perf. 13¼**
731 A255 Sheet of 2, #a-b   3.75 3.75

Europa — A256

Designs: 50s, Janis Ikaunieks, astronomer, and Baldone Observatory telescope. 55s, Map of solar system, asteroid, University of Latvia Institute of Astronomy, radio telescope, five astronomers.

2009, Apr. 2   **Perf. 14x13¾**
732 A256 50s multi   2.25 2.25
    a.   Tete beche pair   4.75 4.75
733 A256 55s multi   2.50 2.50
    a.   Tete beche pair   5.25 5.25

Intl. Year of Astronomy.

Natl. Museum of History A257

2009, May 14   **Perf. 13½**
734 A257 35s multi   1.30 1.30

Basketball A258

Player from opposing team and: 35s, Male Latvian team player, 1935. 40s, Female TTT Riga player. 60s, Male ASK Riga player. 120s, Latvian player in 2009 Women's European Basketball Championships.

2009, June 6
735-737 A258   Set of 3   5.25 5.25
Souvenir Sheet
738 A258 120s multi   4.50 4.50

Nos. 735-737 each were printed in sheets of 9 + label.

Bauska, 400th Anniv. A259

2009, July 10   **Litho.**   **Perf. 13½x14**
739 A259 38s multi   1.25 1.25

Steam Locomotive — A260

2009, Aug. 5   **Litho.**   **Perf. 13½**
740 A260 35s multi   1.40 1.40

Souvenir Sheet

Dienvidu Bridge, Riga — A261

2009, Aug. 22
741 A261 100s multi   4.00 4.00

Berries and Mushrooms Type of 2007

Designs: 55s, Fragaria vesca. 60s, Russula paludosa.

2009, Sept. 12
742 A230 55s multi   2.25 2.25
    a.   Tete beche pair   5.00 5.00
743 A230 60s multi   2.50 2.50
    a.   Tete beche pair   5.50 5.50
    b.   Perf. 13½ on 3 sides   2.50 2.50
    c.   Booklet pane of 4 #743b   11.00 —
       Complete booklet, #743c   11.00

Wild Animals and Their Tracks Type of 2006

Designs: 35s, Canis lupus. 98s, Lepus europaeus.

2009, Oct. 21   **Perf. 13½x14¼**
744 A218 35s multi   1.25 1.25
    a.   Tete beche pair   2.75 2.75
745 A218 98s multi   4.00 4.00
    a.   Tete beche pair   8.25 8.25

Lighthouse Type of 2003
2009, Nov. 5   **Litho.**   **Perf. 13¼**
746 A170 63s Liepaja Lighthouse   2.40 2.40

Republic of Latvia, 91st Anniv. — A262

Designs: 35s, Formation of Latvian People's Council, Nov. 17, 1918. 40s, Proclamation of Latvian Republic, Nov. 18, 1918. 100s, First meeting of Constitutional Assembly, May 1, 1920.

2009, Nov. 14   **Litho.**   **Perf. 14**
747-749 A262   Set of 3   6.50 6.50

Christmas A263

Designs: 35s, Horse Christmas ornament, building. 55s, Fish Christmas ornament, building. 60s, Snowflake Christmas ornament.

2009, Nov. 27   **Perf. 13¼**
750-752 A263   Set of 3   5.50 5.50

Town Arms Type of 2002 With Country Name at Top

2010, Jan. 16 Litho. Perf. 14x14¼
753	A153	35s Viesite	1.25 1.25
754	A153	40s Ligatne	1.40 1.40
755	A153	55s Iecava	2.00 2.00
	Nos. 753-755 (3)		4.65 4.65

2010 Winter Olympics, Vancouver — A264

2010, Feb. 5 Perf. 13¼x13¾
756	A264	55s multi	1.90 1.90

Peonies A265

2010, Mar. 26 Perf. 13¼
757	A265	35s multi	1.25 1.25
a.		Tete beche pair	2.75 2.75

Europa A266

Designs: 55s, Girl holding books, characters from children's books. 120s, Boy reading book, ship, castle, mountain.

2010, Apr. 9 Litho. Perf. 13½x13¼
758	A266	55s multi	2.00 2.00
a.		Tete beche pair	4.25 4.25
759	A266	120s multi	4.50 4.50
a.		Tete beche pair	9.25 9.25

Expo 2010, Shanghai A267

2010, Apr. 23 Perf. 13¼
760	A267	150s multi	5.75 5.75

Declaration of May 4, 1990, 20th Anniv. A268

2010, May 4
761	A268	35s multi	1.40 1.40
a.		Tete beche pair	3.00 3.00

Fire Fighting Museum A269

2010, May 21
762	A269	98s multi	3.75 3.75
a.		Tete beche pair	7.75 7.75

Birds — A270

Designs: 35s, Coracias garrulus. 98s, Bubo bubo, vert.

Perf. 14x13¾, 13¾x14
2010, June 18
763-764	A270	Set of 2	5.00 5.00
		See Nos. 790-791.	

Talsos Sports Hall — A271

2010, July 16 Perf. 13¼
765	A271	150s multi	5.75 5.75

RP Series Locomotive — A272

2010, Aug. 5 Perf. 13¼x13½
766	A272	40s multi	1.50 1.50

Berries and Mushrooms Type of 2007

Designs: 55s, Rubus ideus. 120s, Leccinum scabrum.

2010, Sept. 10 Perf. 13½x13¼
767	A230	55s multi	2.00 2.00
a.		Tete beche pair	4.50 4.50
768	A230	120s multi	4.75 4.75
a.		Tete beche pair	9.75 9.75

Lighthouse Type of 2003

2010, Oct. 15 Litho. Perf. 13½x13¼
769	A170	98s Uzavas Lighthouse	3.75 3.75
a.		Booklet pane of 4, perf. 13½x13¼ on 3 sides	16.00 —
		Complete booklet, #769a	16.00

Republic of Latvia, 92nd Anniv. — A273

National symbols: 35s, Flag. 38s, Arms. 98s, Anthem.

2010, Nov. 12 Litho. Perf. 14
770-772	A273	Set of 3	6.50 6.50

Christmas A274

Designs: 35s, Girl, cat, Christmas tree. 60s, Boy with gift, bird in tree.

2010, Dec. 3 Perf. 13½x13¼
773	A274	35s multi	1.35 1.35
a.		Tete beche pair	3.00 3.00
774	A274	60s multi	2.40 2.40
a.		Tete beche pair	5.00 5.00

New Year 2011 (Year of the Rabbit) A275

2011, Jan. 14 Litho. Perf. 13½x13¼
775	A275	35s multi	1.40 1.40

Town Arms Type of 2002 With Country Name at Top

2011, Feb. 25 Litho. Perf. 14x14¼
776	A153	35s Ikskiles	1.35 1.35
777	A153	98s Carnikavas	5.25 5.25

Rose — A276

2011, Mar. 25 Perf. 13½x13¼
778	A276	35s multi	1.35 1.35
a.		Tete beche pair	3.00 3.00

Europa — A277

Animals in forest: 55s, Deer. 120s, Wolf.

2011, Apr. 8 Perf. 14x13¾
779	A277	55s multi	2.10 2.10
a.		Tete beche pair	4.50 4.50
780	A277	120s multi	4.50 4.50
a.		Tete beche pair	9.50 9.50
		Intl. Year of Forests.	

Souvenir Sheet

Struve Geodetic Arc — A278

No. 781: a, 35s, Map of arc and stone. b, 55s, Map and Friedrich Georg Wilhelm von Struve (1793-1864), astronomer.

2011, May 5 Perf. 13¼x13½
781	A278	Sheet of 2, #a-b	3.50 3.50

First Coin of Riga, 800th Anniv. A279

2011, May 23 Perf. 13½x13¼
782	A279	98s multi	3.75 3.75
a.		Tete beche pair	8.00 8.00

Johanna (1904-90) and Zanis Lipke (1900-87), Rescuers of Jews During World War II — A280

2011, July 4 Perf. 14x13¾
783	A280	60s multi	2.25 2.25
a.		Tete beche pair	5.00 5.00

Phoenix III Passenger Coach — A281

2011, Aug. 5 Perf. 13¼x13½
784	A281	33s multi	1.25 1.25

A282

A283

Personalized Stamps — A284

2011, Aug. 22 Perf. 13¾
785	A282	35s yel bis & blk	1.30 1.30
786	A283	55s yel bis & blk	2.10 2.10
787	A284	60s yel bis & blk	2.25 2.25
	Nos. 785-787 (3)		5.65 5.65

The generic vignettes shown for Nos. 785-787 could be personalized by customers for an extra fee.

Latvian Cycling Federation, 125th Anniv. — A285

2011, Aug. 25 Perf. 14x13¾
788	A285	35s multi	1.40 1.40

Port of Riga A286

2011, Sept. 2 Litho. Perf. 13¼x13½
789	A286	60s multi	2.25 2.25

Birds Type of 2010

Designs: 35s, Hippolais icterina. 98s, Circaetus gallicus, vert.

2011, Sept. 23 Litho. Perf. 14x13¾
790	A270	35s multi	1.25 1.25
a.		Perf. 13¾x14 on 3 sides, granite paper	1.25 1.25
b.		Booklet pane of 4 #790a	8.50 —

Complete booklet, #790b   8.50

Perf. 13¾x14

791 A270 98s multi   3.75 3.75
a. Perf. 13¾x14 on 3 sides, granite paper   3.75 3.75
b. Booklet pane of 4 #791a   15.00 —
Complete booklet, #791b   15.00

Parventa Library, Ventspils
A287

2011, Oct. 14   Perf. 13½x13¼
792 A287 100s multi   4.00 4.00

Republic of Latvia, 93rd Anniv. — A288

Designs: 35s, Merchant fleet ships and their captains. 60s, Krisjanis Valdemars, founder of Latvian Naval School, Ainazi. 100s, Admiral Teodors Spade, Navy emblem, ships and sailors.

2011, Nov. 11   Perf. 14
Granite Paper
793-795 A288   Set of 3   7.50 7.50

Christmas
A289

Designs: 35s, Reindeer with clothesline between antlers, Santa Claus with ripped bag. 60s, Santa Claus pushing reindeer and bag on dragon's back.

2011, Dec. 2   Perf. 13¼
Granite Paper
796-797 A289   Set of 2   3.75 1.90

Town Arms Type of 2002 With Country Name At Top
2012, Jan. 7   Perf. 13¼x13¾
798 A153 33s Piltene   1.25 .90
799 A153 35s Riga   1.40 1.00
800 A153 38s Lielvardes Novads   1.50 1.10
Nos. 798-800 (3)   4.15 3.00

Nos. 798-800 are dated "2011."

Library No. 1 Restaurant, Riga
A290

2012, Jan. 27   Perf. 13¼
801 A290 35s multi   1.40 1.40

Lilies — A291

2012, Feb. 11
802 A291 35s multi   1.40 1.40
a. Tete beche pair   3.00 3.00

Europa — A292

Designs: 55s, Dancers. 120s, National Opera House.

2012, Mar. 17   Perf. 14
803 A292 55s multi   2.10 2.10
a. Tete beche pair   4.50 4.50
804 A292 120s multi   4.50 4.50
a. Tete beche pair   9.50 9.50

Riga Zoo, Cent. — A293

2012, Apr. 14   Perf. 13¼
805 A293   Block or horiz. strip of 3 + label   6.00 6.00
a. 35s Lion   1.40 1.40
b. 55s Horse   2.10 2.10
c. 60s Frog   2.25 2.25
d. Booklet pane of 4 #805c, perf. 13¼ on 3 sides   9.50 —
Complete booklet, #805d   9.50

Janis Misins (1862-1945), Librarian — A294

2012, Apr. 25   Perf. 13¼
806 A294 98s multi   3.75 3.75
a. Tete beche pair   8.00 8.00

Port of Ventspils — A295

2012, May 11   Perf. 13¼x13½
807 A295 35s multi   1.25 1.25

Birds — A296

Designs: 35s, Hirundo rustica. 98s, Carduelis carduelis.

2012, June 16   Litho.   Perf. 13¾x14
808-809 A296   Set of 2   4.75 4.75

2012 Summer Olympics, London — A297

2012, July 14   Perf. 13¼x13½
810 A297 60s multi   2.25 2.25
a. Tete beche pair   5.00 5.00

Ungurmuiza Manor
A298

2012, Aug. 18
811 A298 98s multi   3.75 3.75

Friedrich Zander (1887-1933), Rocketry Pioneer — A299

2012, Aug. 23   Perf. 13¼
812 A299 60s multi   2.25 2.25
a. Tete beche pair   5.00 5.00

Souvenir Sheet

Duchy of Courland and Semigallia, 450th Anniv. — A300

No. 813: a, 35s, Duke Ernsts Johans Birons (1690-1772). b, 55s, Duke Jekabs Kettlers (1610-82).

Granite Paper
2012, Sept. 21   Perf. 13¼x13½
813 A300   Sheet of 2, #a-b   3.50 3.50

Riga Technical University, 150th Anniv. — A301

2012, Oct. 8   Perf. 13¼
814 A301 98s multi   3.75 3.75

Railway Bridges
A302

Train and: Nos. 815, 816a, Carnikava Bridge, Latvia. No. 816b, Lyduvenai Bridge, Lithuania. No. 816c, Narva Bridge, Estonia.

2012   Perf. 13¼
815 A302 35s multi   1.40 1.40
Souvenir Sheet
816 A302 55s Sheet of 3, #a-c   6.00 6.00

Issued: No. 815, 10/8; No. 816, 10/25. See Estonia Nos. 713-714, Lithuania Nos. 985-986.

Republic of Latvia, 94th Anniv. — A303

Composers: 35s, Emils Darzins (1875-1910). 60s, Jazeps Vitols (1863-1948). 100s, Talivaldis Kenins (1919-2008).

2012, Nov. 10   Litho.   Perf. 14
817-819 A303   Set of 3   7.25 7.25

Latvian Medalists at 2012 Summer Olympics, London — A304

Designs: No. 820, 35s, Martins Plavins and Janis Smedins, beach volleyball bronze medalists. No. 821, 35s, Maris Strombergs, BMX cycling gold medalist.

2012, Nov. 23   Perf. 13¼
820 A304 35s multi   1.30 1.30
a. Tete beche pair   2.75 2.75
821 A304 35s multi   1.30 1.30
a. Tete beche pair   2.75 2.75

Christmas
A305

Designs: 35s, Girl, gifts, Christmas tree. 60s, Snow-covered house.

2012, Nov. 30   Perf. 14x13¾
822 A305 35s multi   1.25 1.25
a. Tete beche pair   2.75 2.75
823 A305 60s multi   2.50 2.50
a. Tete beche pair   5.25 5.25

Town Arms Type of 2002 With Country Name at Top
2013, Jan. 13   Perf. 14
824 A153 35s Varaklani   1.40 1.40
825 A153 60s Strencu Novads   2.40 2.40
826 A153 98s Varkavas Novads   3.75 3.75
Nos. 824-826 (3)   7.55 7.55

Janis Uzraugs, Cyclist
A306

2013, Jan. 30   Perf. 13¾x13½
827 A306 35s multi   1.40 1.40

Starting with Nos. 827, 2013 stamps also have euro denominations, in anticipation of a change to the euro currency in 2014.

Dailes Theater, Riga
A307

2013, Feb. 15   Perf. 13¼x13½
828 A307 100s multi   3.75 3.75

Irises — A308

2013, Mar. 8   **Perf. 13¼**
829 A308 35s multi   1.40 1.40
   a.   Tete beche pair   3.00 3.00

Europa — A309

Postal vehicles: 55s, Horse-drawn carriage, rail car. 120s, Airplane, truck, van, bicycle.

2013, Apr. 19   **Perf. 14x13¾**
    Granite Paper
830 A309 55s multi   2.10 2.10
   a.   Tete beche pair   4.50 4.50
   b.   Booklet pane of 4, perf. 14x13¼
      on 3 sides   8.50 —
      Complete booklet, #830b   8.50
831 A309 120s multi   4.50 4.50
   a.   Tete beche pair   9.50 9.50

Souvenir Sheet

Paul Walden (1863-1957), Chemist — A310

2013, May 14   **Perf. 13¼**
    Granite Paper
832 A310 100s multi   4.00 4.00

Birds — A311

Designs: 35s, Clangula hyemalis. 98s, Merops apiaster, vert.

    Perf. 14x13¾, 13¾x14
2013, June 7   **Litho.**
833-834 A311   Set of 2   5.25 5.25

Souvenir Sheet

25th Latvian Song and Dance Festival — A312

No. 835: a, Singers. b, Dancers.

2013, June 28   **Litho.**   **Perf. 13¼**
835 A312 35s Sheet of 2, #a-b   2.60 2.60

Cover With Russia (Wenden) No. L2 — A313

2013, July 12   **Litho.**   **Perf. 13¼**
    Granite Paper
836 A313 100s multi   3.75 3.75

First postage stamp issued in Latvia, 150th anniv.

Cats — A314

Designs: 35s, Kittins in basket. 98s, Cats in doorway,vert.

    Perf. 14x13¾, 13¾x14
2013, July 29   **Litho.**
837-838 A314   Set of 2   5.00 5.00

Port of Liepaja A315

2013, Aug. 23   **Litho.**   **Perf. 13½**
839 A315 98s multi   3.75 3.75

Latvia University of Agriculture, 150th Anniv. A316

2013, Sept. 16   **Litho.**   **Perf. 13¼**
840 A316 40s multi   1.60 1.60

Mark Rothko (1903-70), Painter — A317

2013, Sept. 25   **Litho.**   **Perf. 13¾x14**
841 A317 60s multi   2.40 2.40

Latvian Popular Front, 25th Anniv. — A318

2013, Oct. 5   **Litho.**   **Perf. 13¾x14**
842 A318 35s multi   1.40 1.40

Printing in Latvia, 425th Anniv. — A319

2013, Oct. 22   **Litho.**   **Perf. 13¼**
    Granite Paper
843 A319 60s multi   2.40 2.40

No. 843 was printed in sheets of 8 + 4 labels.

Pink Ribbon and Flower — A320

2013, Oct. 30   **Litho.**   **Perf. 14**
844 A320 4s multi   .25 .25

Breast cancer awareness.

Republic of Latvia, 95th Anniv. — A321

Writers: 35s, Rainis (1865-1929). 60s, Rudolfs Blaumanis (1863-1908). 98s, Zenta Maurina (1897-1978).

2013, Nov. 8   **Litho.**   **Perf. 13¾**
845-847 A321   Set of 3   7.50 7.50

Christmas A322

Falling snow and: 35s, Girl on rocking horse, Christmas gifts. 60s, Girl and cats on building's roof.

2013, Nov. 22   **Litho.**   **Perf. 14x13¾**
    Granite Paper
848-849 A322   Set of 2   3.75 3.75

    100 Cents = 1 Euro

Flowers — A323

Designs: 3c, Narcissi. 47c, Crocuses. 57c, Pansies. 78c, Cornflowers. 85c, Poppies. €1.39, Asters.

2014, Jan. 2   **Litho.**   **Perf. 14**
850 A323   3c multi   .25 .25
851 A323   47c multi   1.25 .65
852 A323   57c multi   1.60 .80
853 A323   78c multi   2.10 1.10
854 A323   85c multi   2.40 1.25
855 A323   €1.39 multi   3.75 1.90
   a.   Souvenir sheet of 6, #850-855   11.50 6.00
     Nos. 850-855 (6)   11.35 5.95

See Nos. 867-870, 895-899.

Imants Ziedonis (1933-2013), Poet — A324

2014, Jan. 6   **Litho.**   **Perf. 13¼x13¾**
856 A324 50c multi   1.40 .70

Bildmuseet, Umea, Sweden A325

National Library, Riga, Latvia A326

2014, Jan. 16   **Litho.**   **Perf. 13¼**
    Granite Paper
857 A325 50c multi   1.40 1.40
858 A326 78c multi   2.10 2.10

Selection of Umea and Riga as European Capitals of Culture. See Sweden Nos. 2720-2721.

2014 Winter Olympics, Sochi, Russia — A327

2014, Feb. 7   **Litho.**   **Perf. 13¼x13½**
    Granite Paper
859 A327 85c multi   2.40 1.25

Personalized Stamp With Horizontal Orientation — A328

Personalized Stamp With Vertical Orientation A329

    Perf. 13¼x13½, 13½x13¾
2014, Feb. 28   **Litho.**
860 A328 50c multi   1.40 .70
861 A329 50c multi   1.40 .70
862 A328 78c multi   2.25 1.10
863 A329 78c multi   2.25 1.10
864 A328 85c multi   2.40 1.25
865 A329 85c multi   2.40 1.25
     Nos. 860-865 (6)   12.10 6.10

Stamps with generic images of museums and their displays were made available on Nos. 860, 863 and 865. Stamps with generic images of airplanes were made available on Nos. 861, 862 and 864.

Tulips — A330

2014, Mar. 7   **Litho.**   **Perf. 13¼**
866 A330 50c multi   1.40 .70

Flowers Type of 2014

Designs: 1c, Daisies. 4c, Hepatica. 7c, Marigolds. 50c, Lily of the valley.

2014, Mar. 22		Litho.	Perf. 14	
867	A323	1c multi	.25	.25
868	A323	4c multi	.25	.25
869	A323	7c multi	.25	.25

Granite Paper

870	A323	50c multi	1.40	.70
	Nos. 867-870 (4)		2.15	1.45

Diplomatic Relations With Georgia, 20th Anniv. — A331

Perf. 13¼x13½

2014, Mar. 28			Litho.
Granite Paper			
871	A331	85c multi	2.40 1.25

Europa — A332

Musical instruments: 78c, Kokle (zither). €1.71, Dudas (bagpipe).

2014, Apr. 11		Litho.	Perf. 14x13¾
Granite Paper			
872-873	A332	Set of 2	7.00 3.50
872a	Booklet pane of 4 #872, perf.		
	14x13¾ on 3 sides	8.75	—
	Complete booklet, #872a	8.75	

Emblem of *Te!* Television Show — A333

2014, Apr. 17	Litho.	Perf. 13¼x13¾
Granite Paper		
874	A333	50c multi	1.40 .70

Birds — A334

Designs: 50c, Lymnocryptes minimus. €1.39, Upupa epops, vert.

Perf. 13¾x14, 14x13¾

2014, May 16			Litho.
875-876	A334	Set of 2	5.25 2.60

Latvian Medalists at 2014 Winter Olympics A335

Designs: No. 877, 50c, Martin Dukurs, silver medalist in skeleton. No. 878, 50c, Daumants Dreiskens, Oskars Melbardis, Janis Strenga, Arvis Vilkaste, silver medalists in four-man bobsled. No. 879, 50c, Juris Sics, Andris Sics, bronze medalists in men's doubles luge. No. 880, 50c, Juris Sics, Andris Sics, Martins

Rubenis, Eliza Tiruma, bronze medalists in Mixed team relay luge.

2014, May 27		Litho.	Perf. 13¼
Granite Paper			
877-880	A335	Set of 4	5.50 2.75

Nos. 877-880 each were printed in sheets of 4.

Janis Cimze (1814-81), Collector and Publisher of Folk Songs — A336

2014, July 3	Litho.	Perf. 13¼x13½
Granite Paper		
881	A336	57c multi	1.60 .80

Turaida Castle, 800th Anniv. — A337

2014, July 11	Litho.	Perf. 13¼x13½
882	A337	50c multi	1.40 .70

Baltic Chain Demonstration, 25th Anniv. — A338

Designs: 50c, Three women. No. 884: a, Five adults and one child. b, Like #883. c, Man and child.

2014, Aug. 23		Litho.	Perf. 13¼
883	A338	50c multi	1.40 .70

Souvenir Sheet

884	A338	78c Sheet of 3, #a-c	6.25 3.25

See Estonia Nos. 764-765; Lithuania No. 1031.

Gothards Fridrihs Stenders (1714-96), Lexicographer A339

2014, Aug. 24		Litho.	Perf. 13¼
885	A339	€1.39 multi	3.75 1.90

No. 885 was printed in sheets of 8 + 4 labels.

Ainazu Lighthouse A340

2014, Sept. 12		Litho.	Perf. 13¼
886	A340	71c multi	1.90 .95

Republic of Latvia, 96th Anniv. — A342

Designs: 57c, Painter. 64c, Graphic artist. 78c, Sculptor.

2014, Nov. 7		Litho.	Perf. 14
888-890	A342	Set of 3	5.00 2.50

SEMI-POSTAL STAMPS

"Mercy" Assisting Wounded Soldier — SP1

1920		Unwmk. Typo.	Perf. 11½
Brown and Green Design on Back			
B1	SP1	20(30)k dk brn & red	.50 *1.00*
B2	SP1	40(55)k dk bl & red	.50 *1.00*
B3	SP1	50(70)k dk grn & red	.50 *1.00*
B4	SP1	1(1.30)r dl sl & red	.50 *1.50*

Wmk. 197

Blue Design on Back

B5	SP1	20(30)k dk brn & red	.70 *1.00*
B6	SP1	40(55)k dk bl & red	.70 *1.00*
a.		Vert. pair, imperf. btwn.	40.00
B7	SP1	50(70)k dk grn & red	.70 *1.25*
B8	SP1	1(1.30)r dk sl & red	.70 *2.00*

Wmk. Similar to 145

Pink Paper   Imperf.

Brown, Green and Red Design on Back

B9	SP1	20(30)k dk brn & red	1.00 *2.50*
B10	SP1	40(55)k dk bl & red	1.00 *2.50*
B11	SP1	50(70)k dk grn & red	1.00 *2.50*
B12	SP1	1(1.30)r dk sl & red	2.00 *4.25*
	Nos. B1-B12 (12)		9.80 *21.50*
	Set, never hinged		17.50

These semi-postal stamps were printed on the backs of unfinished bank notes of the Workers and Soldiers Council, Riga, and the Bermondt-Avalov Army. Blocks of stamps showing complete banknotes on reverse are worth approximately three times the catalogue value of the stamps.

Nos. B1-B8 Surcharged

1921		Unwmk.	Perf. 11½
Brown and Green Design on Back			
B13	SP1	20k + 2r dk brn & red	2.50 *4.00*
B14	SP1	40k + 2r dk bl & red	2.50 *4.00*
B15	SP1	50k + 2r dk grn & red	2.50 *4.00*
B16	SP1	1r + 2r dk sl & red	2.50 *4.00*

Wmk. 197

Blue Design on Back

B17	SP1	20k + 2r dk brn & red	10.00 *40.00*
B18	SP1	40k + 2r dk bl & red	10.00 *40.00*
B19	SP1	50k + 2r dk grn & red	10.00 *40.00*
B20	SP1	1r + 2r dk sl & red	10.00 *40.00*
	Nos. B13-B20 (8)		50.00 *176.00*
	Set, never hinged		140.00

Regular Issue of 1923-25 Surcharged in Blue

1923		Wmk. Similar to 181	Perf. 10
B21	A12	1s + 10s violet	.75 *1.75*
B22	A12	2s + 10s yellow	.75 *1.75*
B23	A12	4s + 10s dk green	.75 *1.75*
	Nos. B21-B23 (3)		2.25 *5.25*
	Set, never hinged		5.00

The surtax benefited the Latvian War Invalids Society.

Lighthouse and Harbor, Liepaja (Libau) SP2

Church at Liepaja — SP5

Coat of Arms of Liepaja — SP6

Designs: 15s (25s), City Hall, Liepaja. 25s (35s), Public Bathing Pavilion, Liepaja.

1925, July 23			Perf. 11½
B24	SP2	6s (12s) red brn & dp blue	2.50 *5.50*
B25	SP2	15s (25s) dk bl & brn	1.50 *4.00*
B26	SP2	25s (35s) vio & dk grn	2.50 *4.00*
B27	SP5	30s (40s) dk blue & lake	4.50 *12.00*
B28	SP6	50s (60s) dk grn & vio	6.50 *16.00*
	Nos. B24-B28 (5)		17.50 *41.50*
	Set, never hinged		40.00

Tercentenary of Liepaja (Libau). The surtax benefited that city. Exist imperf. Value, unused set $500.

President Janis Cakste — SP7

1928, Apr. 18			Engr.
B29	SP7	2s (12s) red orange	2.50 *3.25*
B30	SP7	6s (16s) deep green	2.50 *3.25*
B31	SP7	15s (25s) red brown	2.50 *3.25*
B32	SP7	25s (35s) deep blue	2.50 *3.25*
B33	SP7	30s (40s) claret	2.50 *3.25*
	Nos. B29-B33 (5)		12.50 *16.25*
	Set, never hinged		27.50

The surtax helped erect a monument to Janis Cakste, 1st pres. of the Latvian Republic.

Venta River — SP8

Allegory, "Latvia" — SP9

View of Jelgava SP10

National Theater, Riga — SP11

View of Cesis (Wenden) SP12

Riga Bridge and Trenches SP13

Perf. 11½, Imperf.
1928, Nov. 18   Wmk. 212   Litho.

B34	SP8	6s (16s) green	2.50	2.75
B35	SP9	10s (20s) scarlet	2.50	2.75
B36	SP10	15s (25s) maroon	2.50	2.75
B37	SP11	30s (40s) ultra	2.50	2.75
B38	SP12	50s (60s) dk gray	2.50	2.75
B39	SP13	1 l (1.10 l) choc	3.75	2.75
	Nos. B34-B39 (6)		16.25	16.50
	Set, never hinged		35.00	

The surtax was given to a committee for the erection of a Liberty Memorial.

Z. A. Meierovics SP14

1929, Aug. 22   Perf. 11½, Imperf.

B46	SP14	2s (4s) orange	3.50	2.75
B47	SP14	6s (12s) dp grn	3.50	2.75
B48	SP14	15s (25s) red brown	3.50	2.75
B49	SP14	25s (35s) deep blue	3.50	2.75
B50	SP14	30s (40s) ultra	3.50	2.75
	Nos. B46-B50 (5)		17.50	13.75
	Set, never hinged		35.00	

The surtax was used to erect a monument to Z. A. Meierovics, Latvian statesman.

Tuberculosis Cross — SP15

Allegory of Hope for the Sick — SP16

Gustavs Zemgals — SP17

Riga Castle — SP18

Daisies and Double-barred Cross — SP20

Tuberculosis Sanatorium, near Riga — SP22

Cakste, Kviesis and Zemgals SP23

Designs: No. B61, Janis Cakste, 1st pres. of Latvia. No. B63, Pres. Alberts Kviesis.

1930, Dec. 4   Typo.   Perf. 10, 11½

B56	SP15	1s (2s) dk vio & red orange	.75	.85
B57	SP15	2s (4s) org & red orange	.75	.85
a.		Cliché of 1s (2s) in plate of 2s (4s)	700.00	700.00
B58	SP16	4s (8s) dk grn & red	.75	.85
B59	SP17	5s (10s) brt grn & dk brown	1.50	1.75
B60	SP18	6s (12s) ol grn & bister	1.50	1.75
B61	SP17	10s (20s) dp red & black	2.20	2.25
B62	SP20	15s (30s) mar & dl green	2.25	2.25
B63	SP17	20s (40s) rose lake & ind	2.25	2.25
B64	SP22	25s (50s) multi	3.00	3.50
B65	SP23	30s (60s) multi	3.50	5.00
	Nos. B56-B65 (10)		18.45	21.30
	Set, never hinged		45.00	

Surtax for the Latvian Anti-Tuberculosis Soc. For surcharges see Nos. B72-B81.

J. Rainis and New Buildings, Riga SP24

Character from Play and Rainis SP25

Characters from Plays — SP26

Rainis and Lyre SP27

Flames, Flag and Rainis SP28

1930, May 23   Wmk. 212   Perf. 11½

B66	SP24	1s (2s) dull violet	.75	3.25
B67	SP25	2s (4s) yellow org	.75	3.25
B68	SP26	4s (8s) dp green	.75	3.25
B69	SP27	6s (12s) yel grn & red brown	.75	3.25
B70	SP28	10s (20s) dark red	22.50	47.50
B71	SP27	15s (30s) red brn & yel grn	22.50	47.50
	Nos. B66-B71 (6)		48.00	108.00
	Set, never hinged		95.00	

Sold at double face value, surtax going to memorial fund for J. Rainis (Jan Plieksans, 1865-1929), writer and politician.

Exist imperf. Value twice that of perf. stamps.

Nos. B56 to B65 Surcharged in Black With Bars

Nos. B56 to B65 Surcharged in Black Without Bars

1931, Aug. 19   Perf. 10, 11½

B72	SP18	9s on 6s (12s)	1.00	2.00
B73	SP15	16s on 1s (2s)	12.50	24.00
B74	SP15	17s on 2s (4s)	1.25	2.00
B75	SP16	19s on 4s (8s)	3.75	8.50
B76	SP17	20s on 5s (10s)	2.50	8.50
B77	SP20	23s on 15s (30s)	1.00	1.50
B78	SP17	25s on 10s (20s)	2.50	4.50
B79	SP17	35s on 20s (40s)	3.75	7.00
B80	SP22	45s on 25s (50s)	10.00	20.00
B81	SP23	55s on 30s (60s)	12.50	32.50
	Nos. B72-B81 (10)		50.75	110.50
	Set, never hinged		110.00	

The surcharge replaces the original total price, including surtax.

Nos. B73-B81 have no bars in the surcharge. The surtax aided the Latvian Anti-Tuberculosis Society.

Lacplesis, the Deliverer SP29

Designs: 1s, Kriva telling stories under Holy Oak. 2s, Enslaved Latvians building Riga

under knight's supervision. 4s, Death of Black Knight. 5s, Spirit of Lacplesis over freed Riga.

Inscribed: "AIZSARGI" (Army Reserve)
1932, Feb. 10   Perf. 10½, Imperf.

B82	SP29	1s (11s) vio brn & bluish	2.50	2.50
B83	SP29	2s (17s) ocher & ol green	2.50	2.50
B84	SP29	3s (23s) red brn & org brown	2.50	2.50
B85	SP29	4s (34s) dk green & green	2.50	2.50
B86	SP29	5s (45s) green & emerald	2.50	2.50
	Nos. B82-B86 (5)		12.50	12.50
	Set, never hinged		22.00	

Surtax aided the Militia Maintenance Fund.

Marching Troops SP30

Infantry in Action SP31

Nurse Binding Soldier's Wound — SP32

Army Soup Kitchen — SP33

Gen. J. Balodis — SP34

1932, May   Perf. 10½, Imperf.

B87	SP30	6s (25s) ol brn & red violet	4.50	6.50
B88	SP31	7s (35s) dk bl grn & dark blue	4.50	6.50
B89	SP32	10s (45s) ol green & black brown	4.50	6.50
B90	SP33	12s (55s) lake & ol green	4.50	6.50
B91	SP34	15s (75s) red org & brown violet	4.50	6.50
	Nos. B87-B91 (5)		22.50	32.50
	Set, never hinged		45.00	

The surtax aided the Latvian Home Guards.

Symbolical of Unified Latvia — SP35

Symbolical of the Strength of the Latvian Union — SP36

Aid to the Sick SP37

"Charity" SP38

Wmk. 212
1936, Dec. 28   **Litho.**   **Perf. 11½**

B92	SP35	3s orange red	1.50	3.50
B93	SP36	10s green	1.50	3.50
B94	SP37	20s rose pink	1.50	4.50
B95	SP38	35s blue	1.50	4.50
	Nos. B92-B95 (4)		6.00	16.00
	Set, never hinged		12.00	

Souvenir Sheets

SP39

1938, May 12   **Wmk. 212**   **Perf. 11**

B96	SP39	Sheet of 2	12.00	20.00
	Never hinged		22.50	
a.	35s Justice Palace, Riga		2.00	5.00
b.	40s Power Station, Kegums		2.00	5.00

Sold for 2 l. The surtax of 1.25 l was for the National Reconstruction Fund.
No. B96 exists imperf.

Overprinted in Blue with Dates 1934 1939 and "15" over "V"
1939

B97	SP39	Sheet of 2	15.00	55.00
	Never hinged		45.00	

5th anniv. of Natl. Unity Day. Sold for 2 lats.
Surtax for the Natl. Reconstruction Fund.

Natl. Olympic Committee
SP50

1992, Feb. 8   **Litho.**   **Perf. 13½x13**
Background Color

B150	SP50	50k +25k gray	.60	.60
B151	SP50	50k +25k buff	1.25	1.25
B152	SP50	100k +50k bister	.80	.80
	Nos. B150-B152 (3)		2.65	2.65

No. B150 inscribed "Berlin 18.09.91."

AIR POST STAMPS

Blériot
XI — AP1

Wmk. Wavy Lines Similar to 181
1921, July 30   **Litho.**   **Perf. 11½**

C1	AP1	10r emerald	3.00	4.50
a.	Imperf.		6.00	35.00
C2	AP1	20r dark blue	3.00	4.50
a.	Imperf.		6.00	35.00
	Set, perf, never hinged		12.00	
	Set, imperf, never hinged		25.00	

1928, May 1

C3	AP1	10s deep green	4.50	1.60
C4	AP1	15s red	2.00	1.60
C5	AP1	25s ultra	3.75	2.50
a.	Pair, imperf. btwn.		35.00	
	Nos. C3-C5 (3)		10.25	5.70
	Set, never hinged		16.00	

Nos. C1-C5 sometimes show letters of a paper maker's watermark "PACTIEN LIGAT MILLS."

1931-32   **Wmk. 212**   **Perf. 11½**

C6	AP1	10s deep green	1.00	.90
a.	Perf. 11		12.00	14.50
C7	AP1	15s red	1.50	1.00
a.	Perf. 11		120.00	32.50

C8	AP1	25s deep blue ('32)	8.50	1.25
a.	Perf. 11		28.00	14.50
	Nos. C6-C8 (3)		11.00	3.15
	Set, never hinged		22.50	

Type of 1921 Overprinted or Surcharged in Black

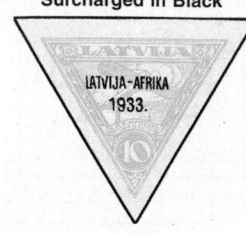

1933, May 26   **Wmk. 212**   **Imperf.**

C9	AP1	10s deep green	40.00	80.00
C10	AP1	15s red	40.00	80.00
C11	AP1	25s deep blue	40.00	80.00
C12	AP1	50s on 15s red	200.00	525.00
C13	AP1	100s on 25s dp blue	200.00	525.00
	Nos. C9-C13 (5)		520.00	1,290.
	Set, never hinged		800.00	

Honoring and financing a flight from Riga to Bathurst, Gambia. The plane crashed at Neustettin, Germany.
Counterfeits exist of Nos. C1-C13.

AIR POST SEMI-POSTAL STAMPS

Durbes Castle, Rainis Birthplace — SPAP1

Wmk. 212
1930, May 26   **Litho.**   **Perf. 11½**

CB1	SPAP1	10s (20s) red & olive green	6.50	14.50
CB2	SPAP1	15s (30s) dk yel green & copper red	6.50	14.50
	Set, never hinged		25.00	

Surtax for the Rainis Memorial Fund.

Imperf.

CB1a	SPAP1	10s (20s)	10.00	27.50
CB2a	SPAP1	15s (30s)	10.00	27.50
	Set, never hinged		40.00	

Nos. C6-C8 Surcharged in Magenta, Blue or Red

1931, Dec. 5

CB3	AP1	10s + 50s dp grn (M)	6.50	7.50
CB4	AP1	15s + 1 l red (Bl)	6.50	7.50
CB5	AP1	25s + 1.50 l dp blue	6.50	7.50
	Nos. CB3-CB5 (3)		19.50	22.50
	Set, never hinged		40.00	

Surtax for the Latvian Home Guards.

Imperf.

CB3a	AP1	10s + 50s	10.00	11.00
CB4a	AP1	15s + 1 l	10.00	11.00
CB5a	AP1	25s + 1.50 l	10.00	11.00
	Nos. CB3a-CB5a (3)		30.00	33.00
	Set, never hinged		55.00	

SPAP2

1932, June 17   **Perf. 10½**

CB6	SPAP2	10s (20s) dk sl grn & grn	12.50	25.00
CB7	SPAP2	15s (30s) brt red & buff	12.50	25.00
CB8	SPAP2	25s (50s) dp bl & gray	12.50	25.00
	Nos. CB6-CB8 (3)		37.50	75.00
	Set, never hinged		75.00	

Surtax for the Latvian Home Guards.

Imperf.

CB6a	SPAP2	10s (20s)	12.50	25.00
CB7a	SPAP2	15s (30s)	12.50	25.00
CB8a	SPAP2	25s (50s)	12.50	25.00
	Nos. CB6a-CB8a (3)		37.50	75.00
	Set, never hinged		75.00	

Icarus — SPAP3   Leonardo da Vinci — SPAP4

Charles Balloon — SPAP5

Wright Brothers Biplane SPAP6

Bleriot Monoplane SPAP7

1932, Dec.   **Perf. 10, 11½**

CB9	SPAP3	5s (25s) ol bis & grn	17.50	20.00
CB10	SPAP4	10s (50s) ol brn & gray grn	17.50	20.00
CB11	SPAP5	15s (75s) red brn & gray grn	17.50	20.00
CB12	SPAP6	20s (1 l) gray grn & lil rose	17.50	20.00
CB13	SPAP7	25s (1.25 l) brn & bl	17.50	20.00
	Nos. CB9-CB13 (5)		87.50	100.00
	Set, never hinged		150.00	

Issued to honor pioneers of aviation. The surtax of four times the face value was for wounded Latvian aviators.

Imperf.

CB9a	SPAP3	5s (25s)	17.50	20.00
CB10a	SPAP4	10s (50s)	17.50	20.00
CB11a	SPAP5	15s (75s)	17.50	20.00
CB12a	SPAP6	20s (1 l)	17.50	20.00
CB13a	SPAP7	25s (1.25 l)	17.50	20.00
	Nos. CB9a-CB13a (5)		87.50	100.00
	Set, never hinged		150.00	

Icarus Falling SPAP8   Monument to Aviators SPAP9

Proposed Tombs for Aviators
SPAP10   SPAP11

1933, Mar. 15   **Perf. 11½**

CB14	SPAP8	2s (52s) blk & ocher	14.00	20.00
CB15	SPAP9	3s (53s) blk & red org	14.00	20.00
CB16	SPAP10	10s (60s) blk & dk yel green	14.00	20.00
CB17	SPAP11	20s (70s) blk & cerise	14.00	20.00
	Nos. CB14-CB17 (4)		56.00	80.00
	Set, never hinged		125.00	

50s surtax for wounded Latvian aviators.

Imperf.

CB14a	SPAP8	2s (52s)	15.00	21.00
CB15a	SPAP9	3s (53s)	15.00	21.00
CB16a	SPAP10	10s (60s)	15.00	21.00
CB17a	SPAP11	20s (70s)	15.00	21.00
	Nos. CB14a-CB17a (4)		60.00	84.00
	Set, never hinged		135.00	

Biplane Taking Off SPAP12

Designs: 7s (57s), Biplane under fire at Riga. 35s (1.35 l), Map and planes.

1933, June 15   **Wmk. 212**   **Perf. 11½**

CB18	SPAP12	3s (53s) org & sl blue	19.00	40.00
CB19	SPAP12	7s (57s) sl bl & dk brn	19.00	40.00
CB20	SPAP12	35s (1.35 l) dp ultra & ol blk	19.00	40.00
	Nos. CB18-CB20 (3)		57.00	120.00
	Set, never hinged		125.00	

Surtax for wounded Latvian aviators. Counterfeits exist.

Imperf.

CB18a	SPAP12	3s (53s)	22.50	42.50
CB19a	SPAP12	7s (57s)	22.50	42.50
CB20a	SPAP12	35s (1.35 l)	22.50	42.50
	Nos. CB18a-CB20a (3)		67.50	127.50
	Set, never hinged		130.00	

American Gee-Bee
SPAP13

English Seaplane S6B
SPAP14

Graf
Zeppelin
over Riga
SPAP15

DO-X
SPAP16

1933, Sept. 5   *Perf. 11½*

CB21	SPAP13	8s (68s) brn & gray blk	40.00	85.00
CB22	SPAP14	12s (1.12 l) brn car & ol grn	40.00	85.00
CB23	SPAP15	30s (1.30 l) blue & gray blk	50.00	90.00
CB24	SPAP16	40s (1.90 l) brn vio & indigo	40.00	85.00
	Nos. CB21-CB24 (4)		170.00	345.00
	Set, never hinged		275.00	

Surtax for wounded Latvian aviators.

Imperf.

CB21a	SPAP13	8s (68s)	40.00	85.00
CB22a	SPAP14	12s (1.12 l)	40.00	85.00
CB23a	SPAP15	30s (1.30 l)	50.00	95.00
CB24a	SPAP16	40s (1.90 l)	40.00	90.00
	Nos. CB21a-CB24a (4)		170.00	355.00
	Set, never hinged		275.00	

OCCUPATION STAMPS

Issued under German Occupation

German Stamps of
1905-18 Handstamped

1919   **Wmk. 125**   *Perf. 14, 14½*

Red Overprint

1N1	A22	2½pf gray	275.00	325.00
1N2	A16	5pf green	225.00	100.00
1N3	A22	15pf dk vio	375.00	100.00
1N4	A16	20pf blue vio	135.00	65.00
1N5	A16	25pf org & blk, yel	475.00	325.00
1N6	A16	50pf pur & blk, buff	475.00	325.00

Blue Overprint

1N7	A22	2½pf gray	275.00	325.00
1N8	A16	5pf green	225.00	120.00
1N9	A16	10pf carmine	190.00	47.50
1N10	A22	15pf dk vio	325.00	325.00
1N11	A16	20pf bl vio	135.00	65.00
1N12	A16	25pf org & blk, yel	675.00	525.00
1N13	A16	50pf pur & blk, buff	675.00	525.00
	Nos. 1N1-1N13 (13)		4,460.	3,172.

Inverted and double overprints exist, as well as counterfeit overprints.
Some experts believe that Nos. 1N1-1N7 were not officially issued. All used examples are canceled to order.

Russian Stamps
Overprinted

1941, July

1N14	A331	5k red (#734)	1.00	4.25
1N15	A109	10k blue (#616)	1.00	4.25
1N16	A332	15k dk grn (#735)	32.50	72.50
1N17	A97	20k dull grn (#617)	1.00	4.25
1N18	A333	30k dp blue (#736)	1.00	4.25

1N19	A111	50k dp brn (#619A)	3.50	10.00
	Nos. 1N14-1N19 (6)		40.00	99.50
	Set, never hinged		77.50	

Issued: 20k, 30k, 7/17; 5k, 10k, 7/18; 15k, 7/19; 50k, 7/23.
Nos. 1N14-1N19 were replaced by German stamps in mid-October. On Nov. 4, 1941, German stamps overprinted "Ostland" (Russia Nos. N9-N28) were placed into use.
The overprint exists on imperf examples of the 10k and 50k stamps. Value, each $800.
Counterfeit overprints exist.

KURLAND

German Stamps
Surcharged

1945, Apr. 20

1N20	A115	6pf on 5pf dp yel grn (#509)	37.50	72.50
	Never hinged		72.50	
1N21	A115	6 pf 10pf dk brn (#511A)	15.00	30.00
	Never hinged		27.50	
a.	Inverted surcharge		100.00	175.00
	Never hinged		175.00	
b.	Double surcharge		85.00	150.00
	Never hinged		150.00	
1N22	A115	6 pf on 20pf blue	8.50	14.50
	Never hinged		16.00	
a.	Inverted surcharge		100.00	175.00
	Never hinged		175.00	
b.	Double surcharge		85.00	150.00
	Never hinged		150.00	

Germany Nos.
MQ1 & MQ1a
Surcharged

Perf 13½

1N23	MPP1	12pf on (-) red brn, (#MQ1)	42.50	72.50
	Never hinged		82.50	
a.	Inverted surcharge		150.00	275.00
	Never hinged		275.00	
b.	Double surcharge		150.00	275.00
	Never hinged		275.00	

Rouletted

1N24	MPP1	12pf on (-) red brn, (#MQ1a)	6.50	16.00
	Never hinged		16.00	
a.	Inverted surcharge		75.00	135.00
	Never hinged		135.00	
b.	Double surcharge		67.50	120.00
	Never hinged		120.00	
	Nos. 1N20-1N24 (5)		110.00	205.50
	Set, never hinged		200.00	

Nos. 1N20-1N24 were used in the German-held enclave of Kurland (Courland) from April 20-May 8, 1945.
Counterfeit surcharges are plentiful.

ISSUED UNDER RUSSIAN OCCUPATION

Fake overprints/surcharges exist on Nos. 2N1-2N36.

The following stamps were issued at Mitau during the occupation of Kurland by the West Russian Army under Colonel Bermondt-Avalov.

Stamps of Latvia
Handstamped

1919   **Wmk. 108**   *Imperf.*
On Stamps of 1919

2N1	A1	3k lilac	40.00	52.50
2N2	A1	5k carmine	40.00	52.50
2N3	A1	10k dp blue	140.00	240.00
2N4	A1	20k orange	40.00	52.50
2N5	A1	25k gray	40.00	52.50
2N6	A1	35k dk brown	40.00	52.50
2N7	A1	50k purple	40.00	52.50
2N8	A1	75k emerald	40.00	80.00

On Riga Liberation Stamps

2N9	A2	5k carmine	40.00	52.50
2N10	A2	15k dp green	20.00	40.00
2N11	A2	35k brown	20.00	40.00

Stamps of Latvia
Overprinted

On Stamps of 1919

2N12	A1	3k lilac	6.00	9.50
2N13	A1	5k carmine	6.00	9.50
2N14	A1	10k dp blue	120.00	200.00
2N15	A1	20k orange	12.00	20.00
2N16	A1	25k gray	27.50	60.00
2N17	A1	35k dk brown	20.00	27.50
2N18	A1	50k purple	20.00	27.50
2N19	A1	75k emerald	20.00	27.50

On Riga Liberation Stamps

2N20	A2	5k carmine	4.00	8.00
2N21	A2	15k dp green	4.00	8.00
2N22	A2	35k brown	4.00	8.00
a.	Inverted overprint		200.00	
	Nos. 2N1-2N22 (22)		743.50	1,173.

The letters "Z. A." are the initials of "Zapadnaya Armiya"-i.e. Western Army.

Russian Stamps of 1909-
17 Surcharged

Perf. 14, 14½x15
Unwmk.
On Stamps of 1909-12

2N23	A14	10k on 2k grn	6.00	8.00
a.	Inverted surcharge		30.00	
2N24	A15	30k on 4k car	8.00	8.00
2N25	A14	40k on 5k cl	8.00	9.50
2N26	A15	50k pn 10k dk bl	6.00	8.00
2N27	A11	70k on 15k red brn & bl	6.00	8.00
a.	Inverted surcharge		200.00	
2N28	A8	90k on 20k bl & car	12.00	16.00
2N29	A11	1r on 25k grn & vio	6.00	8.00
2N30	A11	1½r on 35k red brn & grn	47.50	65.00
2N31	A8	2r on 50k vio & grn	12.00	16.00
a.	Inverted surcharge		120.00	
2N32	A11	4r on 70k brn & org	20.00	27.50

Perf. 13½

2N33	A9	6r on 1r pale brn, brn & org	27.50	40.00

On Stamps of 1917
Imperf

2N34	A14	20k on 3k red	6.00	8.00
2N35	A14	40k on 5k claret	95.00	100.00
2N36	A12	10r on 3.50r mar & lt grn	80.00	80.00
a.	Inverted surcharge		300.00	
	Nos. 2N23-2N36 (14)		340.00	402.00

Eight typographed stamps of this design were prepared in 1919, but never placed in use. They exist both perforated and imperforate. Value, set, imperf. $1, perf. $2.
Reprints and counterfeits exist.

> **Catalogue values for unused stamps in this section, from this point to the end of the section, are for Never Hinged items.**

Arms of Soviet
Latvia — OS1

1940   **Typo.**   **Wmk. 265**   *Perf. 10*

2N45	OS1	1s dk violet	.25	.25
2N46	OS1	2s orange yel	.25	.25
2N47	OS1	3s orange ver	.25	.25
2N48	OS1	5s dk olive grn	.25	.25
2N49	OS1	7s turq green	.25	.80
2N50	OS1	10s slate green	2.00	.40
2N51	OS1	20s brown lake	1.20	.25
2N52	OS1	30s light blue	2.40	.40
2N53	OS1	35s brt ultra	.25	.40
2N54	OS1	40s chocolate	2.00	1.20
2N55	OS1	50s lt gray	2.50	1.20
2N56	OS1	1 l lt brown	3.25	1.20
2N57	OS1	5 l brt green	24.00	13.50
	Nos. 2N45-2N57 (13)		38.85	20.65

Used values of Nos. 2N45-2N57 are for CTOs. Commercially used examples are worth three times as much.

LEBANON

'le-bə-nən

(Grand Liban)

LOCATION — Asia Minor, bordering on the Mediterranean Sea
GOVT. — Republic
AREA — 4,036 sq. mi.
POP. — 3,562,699 (1999 est.)
CAPITAL — Beirut

Formerly a part of the Syrian province of Turkey, Lebanon was occupied by French forces after World War I. It was mandated to France after it had been declared a separate state. Limited autonomy was granted in 1927 and full independence achieved in 1941. The French issued two sets of occupation stamps (with T.E.O. overprint) for Lebanon in late 1919. The use of these and later occupation issues (of 1920-24, with overprints "O.M.F." and "Syrie-Grand Liban") was extended to Syria, Cilicia, Alaouites and Alexandretta. By custom, these are all listed under Syria.

100 Centimes = 1 Piaster
100 Piasters = 1 Pound

Watermark

Wmk. 400

Catalogue values for unused stamps in this country are for Never Hinged items, beginning with Scott 177 in the regular postage section, Scott B13 in the semipostal section, Scott C97 in the airpost section, Scott CB5 in the airpost semi-postal section, Scott J37 in the postage due section, and Scott RA11 in the postal tax section.

Issued under French Mandate

Stamps of France 1900-21 Surcharged

GRAND LIBAN 10 CENTIMES

1924		**Unwmk.**	**Perf.**	**14x13½**
1	A16	10c on 2c vio brn	1.60	1.60
a.		Inverted surcharge	45.00	45.00
2	A22	25c on 5c orange	1.60	1.60
3	A22	50c on 10c green	1.60	1.60
4	A20	75c on 15c sl grn	2.75	2.40
5	A22	1p on 20c red brn	1.60	1.60
a.		Double surcharge	45.00	45.00
b.		Inverted surcharge	45.00	45.00
6	A22	1.25p on 25c blue	4.50	2.40
a.		Double surcharge	40.00	40.00
7	A22	1.50p on 30c org	2.75	2.00
8	A22	1.50p on 30c red	2.75	2.40
9	A20	2.50p on 50c dl bl	2.40	2.00
a.		Inverted surcharge	35.00	35.00

Surcharged

GRAND LIBAN 2 PIASTRES

10	A18	2p on 40c red & pale bl	5.50	3.75
a.		Inverted surcharge	27.50	27.50
11	A18	3p on 60c violet & ultra	8.00	6.75
12	A18	5p on 1fr cl & ol grn	10.00	7.50
13	A18	10p on 2fr org & pale bl	15.00	12.00
a.		Inverted surcharge	50.00	50.00

14	A18	25p on 5fr dk bl & buff	22.50	19.00
a.		Inverted surcharge	85.00	85.00
		Nos. 1-14 (14)	82.55	66.60

Broken and missing letters and varieties of spacing are numerous in these surcharges.
For overprints see Nos. C1-C4.

Stamps of France, 1923, (Pasteur) Surcharged "GRAND LIBAN" and New Values

15	A23	50c on 10c green	3.50	1.10
a.		Inverted surcharge	35.00	25.00
16	A23	1.50p on 30c red	4.50	2.25
17	A23	2.50p on 50c blue	3.75	1.10
a.		Inverted surcharge	30.00	17.50
		Nos. 15-17 (3)	11.75	4.45

Commemorative Stamps of France, 1924, (Olympic Games) Surcharged "GRAND LIBAN" and New Values

18	A24	50c on 10c gray grn & yel grn	32.50	32.50
19	A25	1.25p on 25c rose & dk rose	32.50	32.50
a.		Inverted surcharge	350.00	
20	A26	1.50p on 30c brn red & blk	32.50	32.50
a.		Inverted surcharge	350.00	
21	A27	2.50p on 50c ultra & dk bl	32.50	32.50
a.		Inverted surcharge	350.00	
		Nos. 18-21 (4)	130.00	130.00

Stamps of France, 1900-24, Surcharged

Gᵈ Liban 0, P. 25 لبنان الكبير ¼ الغرش

1924-25				
22	A16	10c on 2c vio brn	1.00	.50
23	A22	25c on 5c orange	1.25	.75
24	A22	50c on 10c green	2.00	1.40
25	A20	75c on 15c gray grn	1.75	1.10
26	A22	1p on 20c red brn	1.50	.95
27	A22	1.25p on 25c blue	1.60	1.60
28	A22	1.50p on 30c red	2.00	1.25
29	A22	1.50p on 30c orange	62.50	57.50
30	A22	2p on 35c vio ('25)	2.25	1.60
31	A20	3p on 60c lt vio ('25)	3.00	2.10
32	A20	4p on 85c ver	3.50	2.50

Surcharged

Grand Liban 2 Piastres لبنان الكبير REPVBLIQVE FRANÇAISE

33	A18	2p on 40c red & pale bl	2.25	1.60
a.		2nd line of Arabic reads "2 Piastre" (singular)	2.50	.50
34	A18	2p on 45c grn & blue ('25)	27.50	22.50
35	A18	3p on 60c violet & ultra	3.50	2.50
36	A18	5p on 1fr cl & ol grn	4.25	3.25
37	A18	10p on 2fr org & pale bl	9.75	8.50
38	A18	25p on 5fr dk bl & buff	15.00	13.50
		Nos. 22-38 (17)	145.25	123.10

Last line of surcharge on No. 33 has four characters, with a 9-like character between the third and fourth in illustration. Last line on No. 33a is as illustrated.
The surcharge may be found inverted on most of Nos. 22-38, and double on some values.
For overprints see Nos. C5-C8.

Stamps of France 1923-24 (Pasteur) Surcharged as Nos. 22-32

39	A23	50c on 10c green	2.00	.85
a.		Inverted surcharge	35.00	25.00
b.		Double surcharge	40.00	21.00
40	A23	75c on 15c green	2.25	1.40
41	A23	1.50p on 30c red	2.75	1.40
a.		Inverted surcharge	35.00	25.00
42	A23	2p on 45c red	5.00	3.50
a.		Inverted surcharge	35.00	21.00
43	A23	2.50p on 50c blue	2.00	.95
a.		Inverted surcharge	35.00	21.00
b.		Double surcharge	40.00	21.00
44	A23	4p on 75c blue	5.00	3.50
		Nos. 39-44 (6)	19.00	11.60

France Nos. 198 to 201 (Olympics) Surcharged as Nos. 22-32

Gᵈ Liban 2, Pˢ 50 لبنان الكبير ٢/½ الغرش 50 PARIS 1924 RF

45	A24	50c on 10c	32.50	32.50
46	A25	1.25p on 25c	32.50	32.50
47	A26	1.50p on 30c	32.50	32.50
48	A27	2.50p on 50c	32.50	32.50
		Nos. 45-48 (4)	130.00	130.00

France No. 219 (Ronsard) Surcharged

Gᵈ Liban 4 Piastres لبنان الكبير غروش ٤

49	A28	4p on 75c bl, *bluish*	3.50	3.50
a.		Inverted surcharge	65.00	50.00

Cedar of Lebanon — A1

Crusader Castle, Tripoli — A3

View of Beirut — A2

Designs: 50c, Crusader Castle, Tripoli. 75c, Beit-ed-Din Palace. 1p, Temple of Jupiter, Baalbek. 1.25p, Mouktara Palace. 1.50p, Harbor of Tyre. 2p, View of Zahle. 2.50p, Ruins at Baalbek. 3p, Square at Deir-el-Kamar. 5p, Castle at Sidon. 25p, Square at Beirut.

1925		**Litho.**	**Perf. 12½, 13½**	
50	A1	10c dark violet	.50	.25
		Photo.		
51	A2	25c olive black	.95	.25
52	A2	50c yellow grn	.75	.25
53	A2	75c brn orange	.75	.25
54	A2	1p magenta	2.00	.80
55	A2	1.25p deep green	2.25	1.40
56	A2	1.50p rose red	1.00	.25
57	A2	2p dark brown	1.25	.25
58	A2	2.50p peacock bl	2.00	.80
59	A2	3p orange brn	2.75	1.10
60	A2	5p violet	3.00	1.40
61	A3	10p violet brn	7.50	2.10
62	A2	25p ultramarine	20.00	12.00
		Nos. 50-62 (13)	44.70	21.10

For surcharges and overprints see Nos. 63-107, B1-B12, C9-C38, CB1-CB4.

Stamps of 1925 with Bars and Surcharged

3ᴾ·50 ٣ ½

1926				
63	A2	3.50p on 75c brn org	1.50	1.50
64	A2	4p on 25c ol blk	2.50	2.50
65	A2	6p on 2.50p pck bl	2.00	2.00
66	A2	12p on 1.25p dp grn	1.40	1.40
67	A2	20p on 1.25p dp grn	6.75	6.75

Stamps of 1925 with Bars and Surcharged

4ᴾ·50 ٤ ½

68	A2	4.50p on 75c brn org	2.75	2.75
69	A2	7.50p on 2.50p pck bl	2.75	2.75
70	A2	15p on 25p ultra	2.75	2.75
		Nos. 63-70 (8)	22.40	22.40

No. 51 with Bars and Surcharged

4ᴾ· ٤

1927				
71	A2	4p on 25c ol blk	2.50	2.50

Issues of Republic under French Mandate

Stamps of 1925 Issue Overprinted in Black or Red

République Libanaise

1927				
72	A1	10c dark vio (R)	.55	.25
a.		Black overprint	35.00	
73	A2	50c yellow grn	.55	.25
74	A2	1p magenta	.55	.25
75	A2	1.50p rose red	.80	.60
76	A2	2p dark brown	1.10	.90
77	A2	3p orange brn	.90	.25
78	A2	5p violet	1.75	1.00
79	A3	10p violet brn	2.25	1.10
80	A2	25p ultramarine	19.00	9.00
		Nos. 72-80 (9)	27.45	12.60

On Nos. 72 and 79 the overprint is set in two lines. On all stamps the double bar obliterates GRAND LIBAN.

Same Overprint on Provisional Issues of 1926-27

15 PIASTERS ON 25 PIASTERS
TYPE I — "République Libanaise" at foot of stamp.
TYPE II — "République Libanaise" near top of stamp.

81	A2	4p on 25c ol blk	.75	.25
82	A2	4.50p on 75c brn org	.85	.25
83	A2	7.50p on 2.50p pck bl	1.10	.25
84	A2	15p on 25p ultra (I)	7.50	5.25
a.		Type II	11.50	8.00
		Nos. 81-84 (4)	10.20	6.00

Most of Nos. 72-84 are known with overprint double, inverted or on back as well as face.

Stamps of 1927 Overprinted in Black or Red

الجمهورية اللبنانية République Libanaise

1928				
86	A1	10c dark vio (R)	.80	.60
a.		French overprint omitted, on #50		
87	A2	50c yel grn (Bk)	2.00	1.50
a.		Arabic overprint inverted	35.00	25.00
88	A2	1p magenta (Bk)	1.00	.70
a.		Inverted overprint	35.00	25.00
89	A2	1.50p rose red (Bk)	2.00	1.50
90	A2	2p dk brn (R)	2.75	2.10
90A	A2	2p dk brn (Bk+R)	110.00	110.00
91	A2	3p org brn (Bk)	1.90	1.40
92	A2	5p violet (Bk+R)	3.50	2.75
93	A2	5p violet (R)	3.00	2.40
a.		French opt. below Arabic	30.00	14.00
94	A3	10p vio brn (Bk)	4.00	4.25
a.		Double overprint	100.00	90.00
b.		Double overprint inverted		
c.		Inverted overprint	100.00	70.00
95	A2	25p ultra (Bk+R)	11.50	10.50
95A	A2	25p ultra (R)	13.00	13.00
		Nos. 86-95A (12)	156.45	150.70

On all stamps the double bar with Arabic overprint obliterates Arabic inscription.

Same Overprint on Nos. 81-84

96	A2	4p on 25c ol blk (Bk+R)	2.00	1.50
97	A2	4.50p on 75c (Bk)	2.00	1.50
98	A2	7.50p on 2.50p (Bk+R)	4.50	3.50
99	A2	7.50p on 2.50p (R)	7.00	6.00

100 A2 15p on 25p (II)
(Bk+R)   11.00 9.50
  a. Arabic overprint inverted
101 A2 15p on 25p (I) (R) 14.00 12.00
  Nos. 96-101 (6)   40.50 34.00

The new values are surcharged in black. The initials in ( ) refer to the colors of the overprints.

Stamps of 1925 Srchd. in Red or Black

1928-29   **Perf. 13½**
102 A2 50c on 75c brn org
(Bk) ('29) 1.50 1.90
103 A2 2p on 1.25p dp grn 1.50 1.90
104 A2 4p on 25c ol blk 1.50 1.90
  a. Double surcharge 35.00 25.00
105 A2 7.50p on 2.50p pck bl 2.50 2.75
  a. Double surcharge 40.00 25.00
  b. Inverted surcharge 55.00 25.00
106 A2 15p on 25p ultra 22.50 10.00
  Nos. 102-106 (5) 29.50 18.45

On Nos. 103, 104 and 105 the surcharged numerals are 3¼mm high, and have thick strokes.

No. 86 Surcharged in Red

1928
107 A1 5c on 10c dk vio 1.75 .30

Silkworm, Cocoon and Moth — A4

1930, Feb. 11 **Typo.** **Perf. 11**
108 A4 4p black brown 15.00 15.00
109 A4 4½p vermilion 15.00 15.00
110 A4 7½p dark blue 15.00 15.00
111 A4 10p dk violet 15.00 15.00
112 A4 15p dark green 15.00 15.00
113 A4 25p claret 15.00 15.00
  Nos. 108-113 (6) 90.00 90.00

Sericultural Congress, Beirut. Presentation imperfs exist.

Pigeon Rocks, Ras Beirut — A5

View of Bickfaya A8

Beit-ed-Din Palace A10

Crusader Castle, Tripoli A11

Ruins of Venus Temple, Baalbek A12

Ancient Bridge, Dog River A13

Belfort Castle A14

Afka Falls — A19

20c, Cedars of Lebanon. 25c, Ruins of Bacchus Temple, Baalbek. 1p, Crusader Castle, Sidon Harbor. 5p, Arcade of Beit-ed-Din Palace. 6p, Tyre Harbor. 7.50p, Ruins of Sun Temple, Baalbek. 10p, View of Hasbeya. 25p, Government House, Beirut. 50p, View of Deir-el-Kamar. 75c, 100p, Ruins at Baalbek.

1930-35 **Litho.** **Perf. 12½, 13½**
114 A5 10c brn org .60 .25
115 A5 20c yellow brn .60 .25
116 A5 25c deep blue .75 .45
        Photo.
117 A8 50c orange brn 3.00 1.50
118 A11 75c ol brn ('32) 1.50 1.00
119 A8 1p deep green 1.75 1.25
120 A8 1p brn vio ('35) 3.00 1.00
121 A10 1.50p violet brn 3.25 1.90
122 A10 1.50p dp grn ('32) 3.50 1.50
123 A11 2p Prussian bl 4.50 1.60
124 A12 3p black brown 4.50 1.60
125 A13 4p orange brn 4.75 1.60
126 A14 4.50p carmine 5.00 1.60
127 A13 5p greenish blk 3.00 1.50
128 A13 6p brn violet 5.25 2.75
129 A10 7.50p deep blue 5.00 1.60
130 A10 10p dk ol grn 9.00 1.60
131 A19 15p blk violet 11.50 3.50
132 A19 25p blue green 20.00 6.00
133 A8 50p apple grn 60.00 15.00
134 A11 100p black 65.00 19.00
  Nos. 114-134 (21) 215.45 66.45

See Nos. 135, 144, 152-155. For surcharges see Nos. 147-149, 161, 173-174.

Pigeon Rocks Type of 1930-35 Redrawn
1934 **Litho.** **Perf. 12½x12**
135 A5 10c dull orange 6.75 4.00

Lines in rocks and water more distinct. Printer's name "Hélio Vaugirard, Paris," in larger letters.

Cedar of Lebanon A23

President Emile Eddé A24

Dog River Panorama A25

1937-40 **Typo.** **Perf. 14x13½**
137 A23 10c rose car .50 .25
137A A23 20c carmine .50 .25
137B A23 25c pale rose lilac ('40) .50 .25
138 A23 50c magenta .50 .25
138A A23 75c brown ('40) .50 .25
        Engr.
        Perf. 13
139 A24 3p dk violet 4.00 .75
140 A24 4p black brown .75 .25
141 A24 4.50p carmine 1.00 .25
142 A25 10p brn carmine 2.25 .25
142A A25 12½p dp ultra ('40) 1.00 .25
143 A25 15p dk grn ('38) 4.00 .75
143A A25 20p chestnut ('40) 1.00 .25
143B A25 25p crimson ('40) 1.50 .60
143C A25 50p dk vio ('40) 5.00 1.60
143D A25 100p sepia ('40) 3.50 2.25
  Nos. 137-143D (15) 26.50 8.45

Nos. 137A, 137B, 138A, 142A, 143A, 143B, 143C, and 143D exist imperforate.

For surcharges see Nos. 145-146A, 150-151, 160, 162, 175-176.

View of Bickfaya A26

Type A8 Redrawn
1935 (?) **Photo.** **Perf. 13½**
144 A26 50c orange brown 17.50 9.75

Arabic inscriptions more condensed.

Stamps of 1930-37 Surcharged in Black or Red

1937-42   **Perf. 13, 13½**
145 A24 2p on 3p dk vio 1.50 1.50
146 A24 2½p on 4p blk brn 1.50 1.50
146A A24 2½p on 4p black brown (R) ('42) 1.50 1.50
147 A10 6p on 7.50p dp bl (R) 4.00 4.00

Stamps of 1930-35 and Type of 1937-40 Surcharged in Black or Red

Perf. 13½, 13
148 A8 7.50p on 50p ap grn 2.50 2.50
149 A11 7.50p on 100p blk (R) 2.50 2.50
150 A25 12.50p on 7.50p dk bl (R) 5.00 5.00

Type of 1937-40 Srchd. in Red

1939 **Engr.** **Perf. 13**
151 A25 12½p on 7.50p dk bl 2.00 2.00
  Nos. 145-151 (8) 20.50 20.50

Type of 1930-35 Redrawn
Imprint: "Beiteddine-Imp.-Catholique-Beyrouth-Liban."
1939 **Litho.** **Perf. 11½**
152 A10 1p dk slate grn 2.25 .25
153 A10 1.50p brn violet 2.25 .75
154 A10 7.50p carmine lake 2.25 1.10
  Nos. 152-154 (3) 6.75 2.10

Bridge Type of 1930-35
Imprint: "Degorce" instead of "Hélio Vaugirard"
1940 **Engr.** **Perf. 13**
155 A13 5p grnsh blue 1.50 .25

Exists imperforate.

Independent Republic

Amir Beshir Shehab — A27

1942, Sept. 18 **Litho.** **Perf. 11½**
156 A27 50c emerald 3.75 3.75
157 A27 1.50p sepia 3.75 3.75
158 A27 6p rose pink 3.75 3.75
159 A27 15p dull blue 3.75 3.75
  Nos. 156-159 (4) 15.00 15.00

1st anniv. of the Proclamation of Independence, Nov. 26, 1941.
Nos. 156-159 exist imperforate.

Nos. 140, 154 and 142A Surcharged in Blue, Green or Black

1943   **Perf. 13, 11½**
160 A24 2p on 4p (Bl) 6.75 7.25
161 A10 6p on 7.50p (G) 3.00 1.00
162 A25 10p on 12½p (Bk) 3.00 1.00
  Nos. 160-162 (3) 12.75 9.25

The surcharge is arranged differently on each value.

Parliament Building A28

Government House, Beirut — A29

1943 **Litho.** **Perf. 11½**
163 A28 25p salmon rose 15.00 6.00
164 A29 50p bluish green 15.00 6.00
165 A28 150p light ultra 15.00 6.00
166 A29 200p dull vio brn 15.00 6.00
  Nos. 163-166 (4) 60.00 24.00
  Nos. 163-166,C82-C87 (10) 149.25 97.00

2nd anniv. of Proclamation of Independence. Nos. 163-166 exist imperforate. For overprints see Nos. 169-172.

Quarantine Station, Beirut A30

Black Overprint
1943, July 8   **Photo.**
167 A30 10p cerise 7.00 4.00
168 A30 20p light blue 7.00 4.00
  Nos. 167-168,C88-C90 (5) 28.00 18.75

Arab Medical Congress, Beirut.

Nos. 163 to 166 Overprinted in Blue, Violet, Red or Black

1944

169	A28	25p sal rose (Bl)	16.00	13.50
170	A29	50p bluish grn (V)	16.00	13.50
171	A28	150p lt ultra (R)	16.00	13.50
172	A29	200p dull vio brn (Bk)	22.50	19.00
		Nos. 169-172,C91-C96 (10)	226.25	207.75

Return to office of the president and his ministers, Nov. 22, 1943.

Type of 1930 and No. 142A Surcharged in Violet, Black or Carmine

1945 Unwmk. Engr. Perf. 13

173	A13	2p on 5p dk bl grn (V)	1.50	.25
174	A13	3p on 5p dk bl grn (Bk)	1.50	.25
175	A25	6p on 12½p deep ultra (Bk)	2.00	.35
176	A25	7½p on 12½p deep ultra (C)	3.00	.95
		Nos. 173-176 (4)	8.00	1.80

Trees at bottom on Nos. 175 and 176.

> Catalogue values for unused stamps in this section, from this point to the end of the section, are for Never Hinged items.

Citadel of Jubayl (Byblos) A31

Crusader Castle, Tripoli A32

1945 Litho. Perf. 11½

177	A31	15p violet brown	5.50	4.00
178	A31	20p deep green	5.50	4.00
179	A32	25p deep blue	5.50	4.00
180	A32	50p dp carmine	9.50	4.50
		Nos. 177-180,C97-C100 (8)	77.00	37.10

See Nos. 229-233.

Soldiers and Flag of Lebanon A33

1946 Litho.

Stripes of Flag in Red Orange

181	A33	7.50p red & pale lil	1.75	.25
182	A33	10p lil & pale lilac	3.00	.25
183	A33	12.50p choc & yel grn	4.00	.25
184	A33	15p sepia & pink	5.00	.25
185	A33	20p ultra & pink	4.25	.30
186	A33	25p dk grn & yel grn	7.00	.35
187	A33	50p dk bl & pale bl	15.00	1.50
188	A33	100p gray blk & pale bl	20.00	3.00
		Nos. 181-188 (8)	60.00	6.15

Type of 1946 Ovptd. in Red

1946, May 8

Stripes of Flag in Red

189	A33	7.50p choc & pink	1.50	.25
190	A33	10p dk vio & pink	1.75	.25
191	A33	12.50p brn red & pale lilac	2.00	.45
192	A33	15p lt grn & yel grn	3.25	.65
193	A33	20p sl grn & yel grn	3.00	.70
194	A33	25p sl bl & pale bl	5.00	.95
195	A33	50p ultra & gray	7.50	.90
196	A33	100p blk & pale bl	11.00	2.25
		Nos. 189-196 (8)	35.00	6.40

See Nos. C101-C106, note after No. C106.

Cedar of Lebanon — A34

Night Herons over Mt. Sanin A35

1946-47 Unwmk. Perf. 10½

197	A34	50c red brn ('47)	1.50	.25
198	A34	1p purple ('47)	1.50	.25
199	A34	2.50p violet	2.75	.25
200	A34	5p red	4.00	.25
201	A34	6p gray ('47)	4.00	.25
		Perf. 11½		
202	A35	12.50p deep car	30.00	.25
		Nos. 197-202,C107-C110 (10)	121.25	10.85

For surcharge see No. 246.

A36

Crusader Castle, Tripoli A37

1947 Litho. Perf. 14x13½

203	A36	50c dark brown	2.00	.25
204	A36	2.50p bright green	3.25	.25
205	A36	5p car rose	4.00	.25
		Perf. 11½		
206	A37	12.50p rose pink	10.50	.50
207	A37	25p ultramarine	12.50	.55
208	A37	50p turq green	32.50	1.10
209	A37	100p violet	45.00	5.75
		Nos. 203-209 (7)	109.75	8.65

A38

Zubaida Aqueduct — A39

1948 Perf. 14x13½

210	A38	50c blue	.75	.25
211	A38	1p yel brown	.90	.25
212	A38	2.50p rose violet	1.10	.25
213	A38	3p emerald	2.75	.25
214	A38	5p crimson	3.25	.25
		Perf. 11½		
215	A39	7.50p rose red	7.00	.25
216	A39	10p dl violet	5.00	.25
217	A39	12.50p blue	10.50	.40
218	A39	25p blue vio	18.00	.90
219	A39	50p green	32.50	4.75
		Nos. 210-219 (10)	81.75	7.80

See Nos. 227A-228A, 234-237. For surcharge see No. 245.

Europa A40

Avicenna — A41

1948 Litho.

220	A40	10p dk red & org red	6.00	1.40
221	A40	12.50p pur & rose	7.00	1.90
222	A40	25p ol grn & pale green	8.00	1.50
223	A41	30p org brn & buff	9.00	1.50
224	A41	40p Prus grn & buff	13.00	1.50
		Nos. 220-224 (5)	43.00	7.80

UNESCO. Nos. 220 to 224 exist imperforate (see note after No. C145).

Camel Post Rider A42

1949, Aug. 16 Unwmk. Perf. 11½

225	A42	5p violet	2.00	.40
226	A42	7.50p red	3.00	.60
227	A42	12.50p blue	4.00	1.00
		Nos. 225-227,C148-C149 (5)	29.00	10.50

UPU, 75th anniv. See note after No. C149.

Cedar Type of 1948 Redrawn and Jubayl Type of 1945

1949		Litho.	Perf. 14x13½	
227A	A38	50c blue	2.75	.25
228	A38	1p red orange	2.75	.25
228A	A38	2.50p rose lilac	13.00	.35
		Perf. 11½		
229	A31	7.50p rose red	4.00	.25
230	A31	10p violet brn	7.00	.25
231	A31	12.50p deep blue	14.00	.25
232	A31	25p violet	25.00	.40
233	A31	50p green	47.50	1.90
		Nos. 227A-233 (8)	116.00	3.90

On No. 227A in left numeral tablet, top of "P" stands higher than flag of the 1¼mm high "5." On No. 210, tops of "P" and the 2mm "5" are on same line.

On No. 228, "1 P." is smaller than on No. 211, and has no line below "P."

On No. 228A, the "O" does not touch tablet frame; on No. 212, it does. No. 228A exists on gray paper.

Cedar Type of 1948 Redrawn and

Ancient Bridge across Dog River — A43

1950 Litho. Perf. 14x13½

234	A38	50c rose red	1.25	.25
235	A38	1p salmon	1.75	.25
236	A38	2.50p violet	2.50	.25
237	A38	5p claret	4.00	.25

Cedar slightly altered and mountains eliminated.

		Perf. 11½		
238	A43	7.50p rose red	5.50	.25
239	A43	10p rose vio	6.00	.25
240	A43	12.50p light blue	9.00	.25
241	A43	25p deep blue	2.25	1.25
242	A43	50p emerald	35.00	5.00
		Nos. 234-242 (9)	67.25	8.00

See Nos. 251-255, 310-312.

Flags and Building A44

1950, Aug. 8 Perf. 11½

243	A44	7.50p gray	2.75	.25
244	A44	12.50p lilac rose	2.75	.25
		Nos. 243-244,C150-C153 (6)	21.00	4.20

Conf. of Emigrants, 1950. See note after No. C153.

Nos. 213 and 201 Surcharged with New Value and Bars in Carmine

1950		Unwmk.	Perf. 14x13½, 10½	
245	A38	1p on 3p emerald	1.50	.25
246	A34	2.50p on 6p gray	2.50	.25

Cedar — A45

1951 Litho. Perf. 14x13½

247	A45	50c rose red	1.75	.25
248	A45	1p light brown	2.50	.25
249	A45	2.50p slate gray	5.50	.25
250	A45	5p rose lake	5.50	.25

Bridge Type of 1950, Redrawn

		Typo.	Perf. 11½	
251	A43	7.50p red	6.50	.25
252	A43	10p dl rose vio	9.00	.25
253	A43	12.50p blue	15.00	.25
254	A43	25p dull blue	19.00	.50
255	A43	50p green	40.00	3.75
		Nos. 247-255 (9)	104.75	6.00

Nos. 238-242 are lithographed from a fine-screen halftone; "P" in the denomination has serifs. Nos. 251-255 are typographed and much coarser; "P" without serifs.

Cedar — A46

Ruins at Baalbek A47

Design: 50p, 100p, Beaufort Castle.

1952 Litho. Perf. 14x13½

256	A46	50c emerald	1.50	.25
257	A46	1p orange brn	1.75	.25
258	A46	2.50p grnsh blue	2.75	.25
259	A46	5p car rose	3.75	.25
		Perf. 11½		
260	A47	7.50p red	5.00	.25
261	A47	10p brt violet	7.00	.70
262	A47	12.50p blue	7.75	.70
263	A47	25p violet bl	8.50	1.40
264	A47	50p dk blue grn	24.00	2.75
265	A47	100p chocolate	47.50	7.50
		Nos. 256-265 (10)	109.50	14.30

Cedar of Lebanon A48

Postal Administration Building A49

1953 Perf. 14x13½

266	A48	50c blue	2.25	.25
267	A48	1p rose lake	2.25	.25
268	A48	2.50p lilac	2.50	.25

269	A48	5p emerald	2.50	.25
		Perf. 11½		
270	A49	7.50p car rose	5.00	.25
271	A49	10p dp yel grn	5.50	.65
272	A49	12.50p aquamarine	6.50	.75
273	A49	25p ultra	9.50	1.40
274	A49	50p violet brn	15.00	3.00
		Nos. 266-274 (9)	51.00	7.05

See No. 306.

A50

Gallery, Beit-ed-Din Palace — A51

1954			**Perf. 14x13½**	
275	A50	50c blue	1.75	.25
276	A50	1p dp orange	2.00	.25
277	A50	2.50p purple	2.25	.25
278	A50	5p blue green	3.75	.25
		Perf. 11½		
279	A51	7.50p dp carmine	5.50	.25
280	A51	10p dl ol grn	6.50	.35
281	A51	12.50p blue	8.50	1.00
282	A51	25p vio blue	12.50	2.75
283	A51	50p aqua	20.00	5.00
284	A51	100p black brn	40.00	9.00
		Nos. 275-284 (10)	102.75	19.35

Arab Postal Union Issue

Globe — A52

1955, Jan. 1	Litho.		**Perf. 13½x13**	
285	A52	12.50p blue green	1.50	.25
286	A52	25p violet	1.75	.25
		Nos. 285-286,C197 (3)	4.75	.75

Founding of the APU, July 1, 1954.

Cedar A53

Jeita Cave A54

1955			**Perf. 14x13½**	
287	A53	50c violet blue	2.00	.25
288	A53	1p vermilion	2.00	.25
289	A53	2.50p purple	2.00	.25
290	A53	5p emerald	2.50	.25
		Perf. 11½		
291	A54	7.50p deep orange	3.00	.25
292	A54	10p yellow grn	3.25	.25
293	A54	12.50p blue	3.50	.25
294	A54	25p dp vio blue	4.75	.25
295	A54	50p dk gray grn	6.25	.45
		Nos. 287-295 (9)	29.25	2.45

See Nos. 308-309, 315-318, 341-343A. For overprint see No. 351.

Cedar of Lebanon A55

Globe and Columns A56

1955	Unwmk.		**Perf. 13x13½**	
296	A55	50c dark blue	1.75	.25
297	A55	1p deep orange	1.75	.25
298	A55	2.50p deep violet	2.00	.25
299	A55	5p green	2.25	.25
300	A56	7.50p yel org & cop red	2.75	.25
301	A56	10p emer & sal	2.50	.25
302	A56	12.50p ultra & bl grn	3.00	.25
303	A56	25p dp ultra & brt pink	4.50	.25
304	A56	50p dk grn & lt bl	6.00	.25
305	A56	100p dk brn & sal	7.50	.50
		Nos. 296-305 (10)	33.00	2.75

For surcharge see No. 333.

Cedar Type of 1953 Redrawn

1956	Litho.		**Perf. 13x13½**	
306	A48	2.50p violet	10.00	1.75

No. 306 measures 17x20½mm. The "2p.50" is in Roman (upright) type face.

Cedar Type of 1955 Redrawn & Bridge Type of 1950, Second Redrawing

1957	Litho.		**Perf. 13x13½**	
308	A53	50c light ultra	1.50	.25
309	A53	2.50p claret	2.00	.25
		Perf. 11½		
310	A43	7.50p vermilion	2.25	.40
311	A43	10p brn orange	3.00	.50
312	A43	12.50p blue	4.00	.75
		Nos. 308-312 (5)	12.75	2.15

On Nos. 308 and 309 numerals are slanted and clouds slightly changed.
Nos. 310-312 inscribed "Liban" instead of "Republique Libanaise," and different Arabic characters.

Runners — A57

1957, Sept. 12	Litho.		**Perf. 13**	
313	A57	2.50p shown	1.75	.25
314	A57	12.50p Soccer players	2.25	.35
		Nos. 313-314,C243-C244 (4)	11.25	4.35

Second Pan-Arab Games, Beirut.
A souvenir sheet of 4 contains Nos. 313-314, C243-C244.

Cedar Type of 1955 Redrawn and

Workers — A58

Ancient Potter — A59

1957	Unwmk.		**Perf. 13x13½**	
315	A53	50c light blue	1.75	.25
316	A53	1p light brown	1.75	.25
317	A53	2.50p bright vio	2.00	.25
318	A53	5p light green	2.50	.25
		Perf. 11½, 13½x13 (A59)		
319	A58	7.50p crim rose	2.50	.25
320	A58	10p dull red brn	2.50	.25
321	A58	12.50p bright blue	2.75	.25

322	A59	25p dull blue	2.75	.25
323	A59	50p yellow grn	4.50	.30
324	A59	100p sepia	5.50	.75
		Nos. 315-324 (10)	28.50	3.05

The word "piaster" is omitted on No. 315; on Nos. 316 and 318 there is a line below "P"; on No. 317 there is a period between "2" and "50."

Nos. 315-318 are 16mm wide and have three shading lines above tip of cedar. See No. 343A and footnote.
For surcharges see Nos. 334-335, 339.

Cedar of Lebanon A60

Soldier and Flag A61

1958	Litho.		**Perf. 13**	
325	A60	50c blue	1.75	.25
326	A60	1p dull orange	1.75	.25
327	A60	2.50p violet	1.75	.25
328	A60	5p yellow grn	2.00	.25
329	A61	12.50p bright blue	2.25	.25
330	A61	25p dark blue	2.50	.25
331	A61	50p orange brn	2.75	.25
332	A61	100p black brn	4.00	.40
		Nos. 325-332 (8)	18.75	2.15

For surcharges see Nos. 336-338.

No. 304 Surcharged

1959, Sept. 1				
333	A56	30p on 50p dk grn & lt bl	2.50	.25

Arab Lawyers Congress. See No. C265.

No. 323 Surcharged

1959			**Perf. 13½x13**	
334	A59	30p on 50p yel grn	2.25	.25
335	A59	40p on 50p yel grn	2.50	.35

Convention of the Assoc. of Arab Emigrants in the United States.

Nos. 329-330 and 323 Surcharged with New Value and Bars

1959			**Perf. 13, 13½x13**	
336	A61	7.50p on 12.50p brt bl	1.25	.25
337	A61	10p on 12.50p brt bl	1.50	.25
338	A61	15p on 25p dark blue	1.60	.25
339	A59	40p on 50p yel grn	2.25	.25
		Nos. 336-339,C271 (5)	9.60	1.30

Arab League Center, Cairo A62

			Perf. 13x13½	
1960, May 23	Unwmk.		Litho.	
340	A62	15p lt blue green	1.75	.25

Opening of the Arab League Center and the Arab Postal Museum in Cairo.

For overprint see No. 352.

Cedar Type of 1955, Second Redrawing

1960	Litho.		**Perf. 13x13½**	
341	A53	50c light violet	1.25	.25
342	A53	1p rose claret	1.25	.25
343	A53	2.50p ultramarine	1.50	.25
343A	A53	5p light green	1.75	.25
		Nos. 341-343A (4)	5.75	1.00

Nos. 341-343A are 16½-17mm wide and have two shading lines above cedar. In other details they resemble the redrawn A53 type of 1957 (Nos. 315-318).

President Fuad Chehab — A63

1960	Photo.		**Perf. 13½**	
344	A63	50c deep green	1.25	.25
345	A63	2.50p olive	1.25	.25
346	A63	5p green	1.25	.25
347	A63	7.50p rose brown	1.50	.25
348	A63	15p bright blue	1.75	.25
349	A63	50p lilac	2.00	.25
350	A63	100p brown	2.50	.25
		Nos. 344-350 (7)	11.50	1.75

Nos. 343A and 340 Overprinted in Red

1960, Nov.	Litho.		**Perf. 13x13½**	
351	A53	5p light green	1.25	.25
352	A62	15p lt blue green	1.75	.25

Arabian Oil Conference, Beirut.

President Fuad Chehab — A64

1961, Feb.	Litho.		**Perf. 13½x13**	
353	A64	2.50p blue & light bl	1.25	.25
354	A64	7.50p dark vio & pink	1.25	.25
355	A64	10p red brn & yel	1.25	.25
		Nos. 353-355 (3)	3.75	.75

Cedar — A65

Post Office, Beirut A66

1961	Unwmk.	Litho.	**Perf. 13**	
356	A65	2.50p green	2.50	.25
		Redrawn		
357	A65	2.50p orange	2.50	.25
358	A65	5p maroon	1.25	.25
359	A65	10p black	1.75	.25

Nos. 357-359 have no clouds.

		Perf. 11½		
361	A66	2.50p rose carmine	1.25	.25
362	A66	5p bright green	2.00	.25
363	A66	15p dark blue	2.75	.25
		Nos. 356-363 (7)	14.00	1.75

Cedars — A67

10p, 15p, 50p, 100p, View of Zahle.

1961		Litho.	Perf. 13	
365	A67	50c yellow green	1.50	.25
366	A67	1p brown	1.50	.25
367	A67	2.50p ultramarine	1.50	.25
368	A67	5p carmine	1.75	.25
369	A67	7.50p violet	2.00	.25
370	A67	10p dark brown	2.25	.25
371	A67	15p dark blue	2.50	.25
372	A67	50p dark green	2.75	.25
373	A67	100p black	3.25	.35
		Nos. 365-373 (9)	19.00	2.35

See Nos. 381-384.

Unknown Soldier
Monument — A68

1961, Dec. 30		Unwmk.	Perf. 12	
374	A68	10p shown	3.00	.25
375	A68	15p Soldier & flag	3.75	.25

Anniv. of Lebanon's independence; evacuation of foreign troops, Dec. 31, 1946.
See Nos. C329-C330.

Bugler — A69

Scout
Carrying
Flag and
Scout
Emblem
A70

Designs: 2.50p, First aid. 6p, Lord Baden-Powell. 10p, Scouts building campfire.

1962, Mar. 1		Litho.	Perf. 12	
376	A69	50c yel grn, blk & yel	1.50	.25
377	A70	1p multicolored	1.50	.25
378	A70	2.50p dk red, blk & grn	1.50	.25
379	A69	6p multicolored	1.50	.25
380	A70	10p dp bl, blk & yel	1.50	.25
		Nos. 376-380,C331-C333 (8)	10.75	2.15

50th anniversary of Lebanese Boy Scouts.

Type of 1961
Redrawn

Designs as before.

1962		Unwmk.	Perf. 13	
381	A67	50c yellow green	1.50	.25
382	A67	1p brown	1.50	.25
383	A67	2.50p ultramarine	1.60	.25
384	A67	15p dark blue	4.00	.25
		Nos. 381-384,C341-C342 (6)	15.95	1.65

Temple of
Nefertari, Abu
Simbel — A71

1962, Aug. 1		Unwmk.	Perf. 13	
390	A71	5p light ultra	1.25	.25
391	A71	15p brn lake & mar	1.75	.25

Campaign to save the historic monuments in Nubia. See Nos. C351-C352.

Cherries — A72

Designs: 50c, 2.50p, 7.50p, Cherries. 1p, 5p, Figs. 10p, 17.50p, 30p, Grapes. 50p, Oranges. 100p, Pomegranates.

1962		Vignette Multicolored	Litho.	
392	A72	50c violet blue	1.50	.25
393	A72	1p gray blue	1.50	.25
394	A72	2.50p brown	1.50	.25
395	A72	5p bright blue	1.50	.25
396	A72	7.50p lilac rose	1.50	.25
397	A72	10p chocolate	1.75	.25
398	A72	17.50p slate	2.50	.25
399	A72	30p slate grn	2.75	.25
400	A72	50p green	3.00	.25
401	A72	100p brown blk	5.00	.50
		Nos. 392-401,C359-C366 (18)	31.65	5.05

Elementary
Schoolboy — A73

1962, Oct. 1		Litho.	Perf. 12	
404	A73	30p multicolored	1.50	.25

Students' Day, Oct. 1. See No. C355.

Cedar of Lebanon
A74   A75

1963-64		Unwmk.	Perf. 13x13½	
405	A74	50c green	7.00	.25
406	A75	50c gray grn ('64)	1.50	.25
407	A75	2.50p ultra ('64)	1.50	.25
408	A75	5p brt pink ('64)	1.60	.25
409	A75	7.50p orange ('64)	1.75	.25
410	A75	17.50p rose lil ('64)	2.25	.25
		Nos. 405-410 (6)	15.60	1.50

Bicyclist — A76

1964, Feb. 11		Litho.	Perf. 13	
415	A76	2.50p shown	1.50	.25
416	A76	5p Basketball	1.50	.25
417	A76	10p Track	1.50	.25
		Nos. 415-417,C385-C387 (6)	6.70	1.50

4th Mediterranean Games, Naples, Sept. 21-29, 1963.

Hyacinth — A77

1964		Unwmk.	Perf. 13x13½	
		Size: 26x27mm		
418	A77	50c shown	1.50	.25
419	A77	1p Hyacinth	1.50	.25
420	A77	2.50p Hyacinth	1.50	.25
421	A77	5p Cyclamen	1.50	.25
422	A77	7.50p Cyclamen	1.50	.25
		Perf. 13		
		Size: 26x37mm		
423	A77	10p Poinsettia	1.50	.25
424	A77	17.50p Anemone	2.50	.25
425	A77	30p Iris	3.50	.25
426	A77	50p Poppy	7.00	.45
		Nos. 418-426,C391-C397 (16)	29.20	4.25

See Nos. C391-C397.

Temple of
the Sun,
Baalbek
A78

1965, Jan. 11		Litho.	Perf. 13x13½	
429	A78	2.50p blk & red org	2.00	.25
430	A78	7.50p black & blue	2.75	.25
		Nos. 429-430,C420-C423 (6)	9.10	1.85

International Festival at Baalbek.

Swimmer
A79

1965, Jan. 23		Engr.	Perf. 13	
431	A79	2.50p shown	2.50	.25
432	A79	7.50p Fencer	2.75	.25
433	A79	10p Basketball, vert.	4.00	.25
		Nos. 431-433,C424-C426 (6)	11.10	1.50

18th Olympic Games, Tokyo, Oct. 10-25, 1964.

Golden
Oriole
A80

5p, Bullfinch. 10p, European goldfinch. 15p, Hoopoe. 17.50p, Rock partridge. 32.50p, European bee-eater.

1965		Engr.	Perf. 13	
434	A80	5p multicolored	8.00	.25
435	A80	10p multicolored	13.00	.25
436	A80	15p multicolored	10.00	.25
437	A80	17.50p multicolored	12.00	.25
438	A80	20p shown	15.00	.25
439	A80	32.50p multicolored	20.00	.25
		Nos. 434-439 (6)	78.00	1.50

For surcharge see No. 459.

Cow and
Calf — A81

1965		Photo.	Perf. 11x12	
440	A81	50c shown	2.00	.25
441	A81	1p Rabbit	2.25	.25
442	A81	2.50p Ewe & lamb	2.50	.25
		Nos. 440-442 (3)	6.75	.75

Hippodrome,
Beirut — A82

1p, Pigeon Rocks. 2.50p, Tabarja. 5p, Ruins, Beit-Méry. 7.50p, Statue and ruins, Anjar.

1966		Unwmk.	Perf. 12x11½	
443	A82	50c gold & multi	1.75	.25
444	A82	1p gold & multi	2.00	.25
445	A82	2.50p gold & multi	2.25	.25
446	A82	5p gold & multi	2.50	.25
447	A82	7.50p gold & multi	2.75	.25
		Nos. 443-447 (5)	11.25	1.25

See Nos. C486-C492. For surcharge see No. 460.

ITY Emblem
and Cedars
A83

1967		Photo.	Perf. 11x12	
448	A83	50c lem, blk & brt bl	4.00	.25
449	A83	1p sal, blk & brt bl	4.00	.25
450	A83	2.50p gray, blk & brt bl	4.00	.25
451	A83	5p lt rose lil, blk & brt bl	4.00	.25
452	A83	7.50p yel, blk & brt bl	4.00	.25
		Nos. 448-452 (5)	20.00	1.25

Intl. Tourist Year; used as a regular issue. See Nos. C515-C522. For surcharge see No. 461.

Goat and
Kid
A84

1968, Feb.		Photo.	Perf. 12x11½	
453	A84	50c shown	3.00	.25
454	A84	1p Cattle	4.00	.25
455	A84	2.50p Sheep	5.00	.25
456	A84	5p Camels	6.00	.25
457	A84	10p Donkey	7.00	.25
458	A84	15p Horses	9.00	.25
		Nos. 453-458 (6)	34.00	1.50

See Nos. C534-C539.

No. 439 Srchd.

1972, Apr.		Engr.	Perf. 13	
459	A80	25p on 32.50p multi	22.50	.25

Nos. 447 and 452 Surcharged with
New Value and Bars
Perf. 12x11½, 11x12

1972, May			Photo.	
460	A82	5p on 7.50p multi	4.50	.25
461	A83	5p on 7.50p multi	4.50	.25

Cedar — A85

1974 **Litho.** **Perf. 11**
462 A85 50c orange & olive .25 .25

Army Badge — A86

1980, Dec. 28 **Litho.** **Perf. 11½**
463 A86 25p multicolored 2.50 .25
Army Day. See Nos. C792-C793.

Pres. Elias Sarkis — A87

1981, Sept. 23 Photo. **Perf. 14x13½**
464 A87 125p multicolored 2.75 .80
465 A87 300p multicolored 2.75 1.60
466 A87 500p multicolored 7.50 2.40
Nos. 464-466 (3) 13.00 4.80

World Food Day, Oct. 16, 1981 A88

1982, Nov. 23 Photo. **Perf. 12x11½**
467 A88 50p Stork carrying food packages 1.75 .30
468 A88 75p Wheat, globe 2.00 .50
469 A88 100p Produce 2.25 .65
Nos. 467-469 (3) 6.00 1.45

World Communications Year — A89

1983, Dec. 19 Photo. **Perf. 14**
470 A89 300p multicolored 6.00 1.75

Illustrations from Khalil Gibran's The Prophet A90

1983, Dec. 19 **Perf. 13½x14**
471 A90 200p The Soul Is Back 2.75 1.00
472 A90 300p The Family 4.25 1.75
473 A90 500p Self-portrait 7.50 2.40
474 A90 1000p The Prophet 15.00 4.75
a. Souvenir sheet, #471-474 37.50 37.50
Nos. 471-474 (4) 29.50 9.90
No. 474a sold for £25.

Scouting Year — A91

1983, Dec. 19 **Perf. 14**
475 A91 200p Rowing 3.50 .65
476 A91 300p Signaling 4.00 .80
477 A91 500p Camp 7.25 1.25
Nos. 475-477 (3) 14.75 2.70

Cedar of Lebanon — A93

1984, Dec. Photo. **Perf. 14½x13½**
481 A93 5p multicolored 2.00 .25

Flowers — A94

1984, Dec. Photo. **Perf. 14½x13½**
482 A94 10p Iris of Sofar 2.00 .25
483 A94 25p Periwinkle 3.00 .30
484 A94 50p Flowering thorn 4.00 .40
Nos. 482-484 (3) 9.00 .95
For surcharges see Nos. 531-532.

Defense — A95

1984, Dec. Photo. **Perf. 14½x13½**
485 A95 75p Dove over city 3.50 .90
486 A95 150p Soldier, cedar 4.75 1.90
487 A95 300p Olive wreath, cedar 6.25 3.50
Nos. 485-487 (3) 14.50 6.30

Temple Ruins A96

1985 **Photo.** **Perf. 13½x14½**
488 A96 100p Fakra 3.00 .55
489 A96 200p Bziza 3.50 1.10
490 A96 500p Tyre 6.50 2.75
Nos. 488-490 (3) 13.00 4.40

Pres. Gemayel, Map of Lebanon, Dove, Text — A97

1988, Feb. 1 Litho. **Perf. 14**
491 A97 £50 multicolored 5.00 2.00

Pres. Gemayel, Military Academy Graduate — A98

1988, Mar. 9
492 A98 £25 multicolored 5.50 1.50

Arab Scouts, 75th Anniv. A99

1988, Mar. 9 **Perf. 13½x14½**
493 A99 £20 multicolored 5.50 1.25

UN Child Survival Campaign A100

1988, Mar. 9 **Perf. 14½x13½**
494 A100 £15 multicolored 3.50 .75

Prime Minister Rashid Karame (1921-1987), Satellite, Flags, Earth A101

1988, Mar. 9 **Perf. 13½x14½**
495 A101 £10 multicolored 2.50 .60

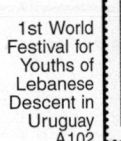
1st World Festival for Youths of Lebanese Descent in Uruguay A102

1988, Mar. 9
496 A102 £5 multicolored 3.25 .50

Cedar — A103

1989 **Photo.** **Perf. 13x13½**
497 A103 £50 dk grn & vio 3.00 .35
498 A103 £70 dk grn & brn 3.50 .50
499 A103 £100 dk grn & brt yel 4.00 .50
500 A103 £200 dk grn & bluish grn 6.00 1.25
501 A103 £500 dk grn & brt yel grn 11.00 3.00
Nos. 497-501 (5) 27.50 5.60

Independence, 50th Anniv. — A104

Designs: £200, Al Muntazah Restaurant, Zahle, 1883. £300, Sea Castle, Sidon, vert. £500, Presidential Palace, Baabda. £1000, Army graduation ceremony, vert. £3000, Beirut 2000, architectural plan. £5000, Pres. Elias Harawi, Lebanese flag, vert.

1993 **Litho.** **Perf. 14**
502 A104 £200 multi 1.75 .25
503 A104 £300 multi 2.25 .55
504 A104 £500 multi 3.50 .85
505 A104 £1000 multi 5.00 1.75
506 A104 £3000 multi 9.25 3.00
507 A104 £5000 multi 17.50 8.25
Nos. 502-507 (6) 39.25 14.65
For overprints, see Nos. 533B, 533C, 533G.

Size: 126x150mm
Imperf
508 A104 £10,000 multi 57.50 57.50

A105

Environmental Protection: £100, Stop polluting atmosphere. £200, Stop fires. £500, Trees, building. £1000, Birds, trees in city. £2000, Mosaic of trees. £5000, Green tree in middle of polluted city.

1994, May 7 Litho. **Perf. 13½x13**
509 A105 £100 multicolored 1.75 .25
510 A105 £200 multicolored 2.00 .45
511 A105 £500 multicolored 3.25 .95
512 A105 £1000 multicolored 5.25 1.60
513 A105 £2000 multicolored 8.75 2.75
514 A105 £5000 multicolored 20.00 6.50
Nos. 509-514 (6) 41.00 12.50
For overprints see Nos. 533D, 533H, 537.

A106

1995, May 6 Litho. **Perf. 13½x13**
515 A106 £1500 Martyr's Day 7.00 3.00
For overprint see No. 534.

Anniversaries and Events — A107

£500, UNICEF, 50th anniv., horiz. £1000, Intl. Year of the Family (1994), horiz. £2000, ILO, 75th anniv. (in 1994), horiz. £3000, Bar Association (Berytus Nutrix Legum), 75th anniv.

1996, Feb. 21   Litho.   Perf. 14
516 A107 £500 multi, horiz.   4.25 1.10
517 A107 £1000 multi, horiz.   6.75 2.25
518 A107 £2000 multi, horiz. 12.00 4.25
519 A107 £3000 multicolored   17.50 6.75
  Nos. 516-519 (4)   40.50 14.35
For overprints, see Nos. 533E, 534A, 535A.

Anniversaries and Events of 1995 — A108

£100, Opening of Museum of Arab Postage Stamps. £500, FAO, 50th anniv. £1000, UN, 50th anniv. £2000, Arab League, 50th anniv. £3000, Former Pres. René Moawad (1925-89).

1996, Feb. 21   Perf. 13½x13
520 A108 £100 multicolored   2.75   .25
521 A108 £500 multicolored   4.25 1.10
522 A108 £1000 multicolored   7.00 2.10
523 A108 £2000 multicolored 11.50 4.00
524 A108 £3000 multicolored 17.50 6.50
  Nos. 520-524 (5)   43.00 13.95
For overprints see Nos. 533A, 533F, 533I, 535-536.

Massacre at Cana A109

1997, Oct. 13   Litho.   Perf. 14
525 A109 £1100 multicolored 11.00 2.75
For overprint, see No. 533J.

1997 Visit of Pope John Paul II to Lebanon A110

1997   Litho.   Perf. 13½x13
526 A110 £10,000 multi   100.00 32.50
For overprint see Nos. 533O, 538.

Fakhr al-Din Palace, Deir-el-Kamar — A111

£100, Chehab Palace, Hasbaya, vert. £300, ESCWA Building, Beirut, vert. £1100, Grand Seraglio, Beirut.

1999   Litho.   Perf. 12
527 A111 £100 multicolored   1.50   .25
528 A111 £300 multicolored   2.50   .45
529 A111 £500 shown   3.00   .80
530 A111 £1100 multicolored 6.00 1.75
  Nos. 527-530 (4)   13.00 3.25

Nos. 484, 485 and C775 Surcharged in Silver and Black

Methods and Perfs. as before
1999
531 A94 £100 on 50p (#484)   1.75   .25
532 A95 £300 on 75p (#485)   2.50   .45
533 AP154 £1100 on 70p (#C775) 6.00 1.75
  Nos. 531-533 (3)   10.25 2.45

Nos. 502, 504-505, 511-512, 516, 518-522, 525 Overprinted in Gold

Similar to Nos. 534-538 but with Symbol Oriented as a Cross
Methods and Perfs As Before
1999
533A A108 £100 multi   15.00
533B A104 £200 multi   15.00
533C A104 £500 multi   25.00
533D A105 £500 multi   25.00
533E A107 £500 multi   25.00
533F A108 £500 multi   25.00
533G A104 £1000 multi   50.00
533H A105 £1000 multi   47.50
533I A108 £1000 multi   30.00
533J A109 £1100 multi   300.00
533K A106 £1500 multi   40.00
533L A107 £2000 multi   75.00
533M A107 £3000 multi   115.00
533N A105 £5000 multi   225.00
533O A110 £10,000 multi 425.00
  Nos. 533A-533O (15) 1,437.

Nos. 514, 515, 523, 524 and 526 Overprinted in Gold or Silver

Methods and Perfs As Before
1999
534 A106 £1500 multi   7.50   5.00
535 A108 £2000 multi   11.50   9.00
536 A108 £3000 multi (S) 15.00 12.50
537 A105 £5000 multi   20.00 17.50
538 A110 £10,000 multi   40.00 40.00
  Nos. 534-538 (5)   94.00 84.00

Cedar of Lebanon — A112

Perf. 13x13¼, 11x11¼ (£500, £1000, £1100)
2000 ?   Litho.   Unwmk.
539 A112 £100 dark red   .50 .25
540 A112 £300 Prus blue 1.00 .35

Wmk. 400
541 A112 £500 green   1.50   .65
  a. Perf. 13x13¼   1.50   .65
  b. Booklet pane, 10 #541a 15.00
     Booklet, #541b   15.00
542 A112 £1000 blue   3.50 1.25
543 A112 £1100 olive brn   3.75 1.40
  a. Perf. 13x13¼   3.75 1.40
  b. Booklet pane, 10 #543a 37.50
     Booklet, #543b   37.50
544 A112 £1500 vio blue   4.50 1.90
  a. Booklet pane, 10 #544 45.00
     Booklet, #544a   45.00
  b. Perf. 11x11¼   4.50 1.90
  Nos. 539-544 (6)   14.75 5.80

Cedar of Lebanon Type of 2000 Redrawn
Perf. 11x11¼, 13x13¼ (£1000)
2001 ?   Litho.   Unwmk.
Numerals 1½mm Tall
544C A112 £500 olive grn   —
544D A112 £1000 blue   —
544E A112 £1100 brown   —
544F A112 £1500 purple   —
  g. Perf. 13x13¼
On Nos. 539-544, numerals are 2mm tall.

A113

2001   Litho.   Perf. 11¼x11
545 A113 £1100 multi   4.00 1.50

Geneva Conventions, 50th Anniv. (in 1999) — A114

Red Cross/Red Crescent A115

2001   Litho.   Perf. 11x11½
546 A114 £500 shown   2.00   .70
547 A114 £1100 "50," fist 4.00 1.50
548 A115 £1500 shown   5.00 2.10
  Nos. 546-548 (3)   11.00 4.30

SOS Children's Villages A116

2001
549 A116 £300 multi   1.25   .40

Prisoners in Israel A117

2001
550 A117 £500 multi   2.00   .70

Ibrahim Abd el Al (1908-59), Hydrologist A118

2001
551 A118 £1000 multi   3.50 1.40

Abdallah Zakher (1680-1748), Printer — A119

2001
552 A119 £1000 multi   3.50 1.40

Elias Abu Chabke (1904-49), Poet — A120

2001   Perf. 11½x11
553 A120 £1500 multi   5.00 2.10

Saint Joseph University, 125th Anniv. (in 2000) A121

2001   Perf. 11x11½
554 A121 £5000 multi   15.00 7.00

Economic & Social Commission for Western Asia, 25th Anniv. (in 1999) — A122

2001   Perf. 11½x11
555 A122 £10,000 multi 32.50 20.00

Arab Woman's Day — A123

2002, Feb. 1   Litho.   Perf. 13¼x13½
556 A123 £1000 multi   3.25 2.60

Arab League Summit Conference, Beirut — A124

Arab League member flags and: £2000, Emblem. £3000, Cedar tree, Lebanese Pres. Emile Lahoud.

2002, Mar. 27
557-558 A124 Set of 2   11.00 9.25

Souvenir Sheet

Israeli Withdrawal From Southern Lebanon, 2nd Anniv. — A125

No. 559: a, Pres. Emile Lahoud, flag. b, Pres. Lahoud holding book. c, Pres. Lahoud and map. d, Pres. Lahoud receiving sword.

2002, Mar. 27   *Perf. 13¼*
559 A125 £1100 Sheet of 4, #a-d   10.50 9.50

Souvenir Sheet

Martyrs of Justice — A126

2002, June 14   *Perf. 13¼x13½*
560 A126 £3000 multi   7.00 5.75

UPU, 125th Anniv. (in 1999) A127

2002, Oct. 11 Litho. *Perf. 13½x13¼*
561 A127 £2000 multi   7.00 5.75

City Views — A128

Ruins — A129

Paleontonlogy — A130

Designs: £100 Old souk, Zouk Mikael. £300, Old souk, Sidon. £500, Byblos. £1000, Souk, Tripoli. £1100, Bziza. £1500, Arqa. £2000, Niha. £3000, Mousailaha Citadel. £5000, Libanobythus milkii in amber. £10,000, Nematonotus longispinus fossil.

Perf. 13¼x13½, 13½x13¼
2002-03   Litho.
562 A128 £100 multi   .50 .25
563 A128 £300 multi   .90 .50
564 A128 £500 multi   1.75 .90
565 A128 £1000 multi   2.50 1.75
566 A129 £1100 multi   3.00 2.00
567 A129 £1500 multi   3.50 2.75
568 A129 £2000 multi   4.50 3.75
569 A129 £3000 multi   7.25 5.75
570 A130 £5000 multi   10.50 9.25
571 A130 £10,000 multi   21.00 18.00
    Nos. 562-571 (10)   55.40 44.90

Issued: £100, £300, 10/11; £1000, £1500, £2000, £3000, £10,000, 11/20; £500, £1100, 12/20; £5000, 1/8/03.

Ninth Francophone Summit, Beirut — A131

Summit emblem and: No. 572, £1500, Mountains. No. 573, £1500, Pres. Emile Lahoud.

2002, Oct. 23   *Perf. 13¼x13½*
572-573 A131 Set of 2   7.00 5.50

Beirut, 1999 Arab Cultural Capital — A132

2002, Nov. 13
574 A132 £2000 multi   5.00 4.00

Independence, 60th Anniv. (in 2001) — A133

Stylized flag and: No. 575, £1250, Crowd viewing horse and rider. No. 576, £1250, Men

and flag on staff. No. 577, £1750, Arabic text. No. 578, £1750, Soldier saluting group of men. £6000, Vignettes of Nos. 575-578.

2003, Dec. 5 Litho. *Perf. 12¾x13*
575-578 A133 Set of 4   14.00 14.00
    Imperf
    Size: 160x110mm
579 A133 £6000 multi   14.00 14.00

Faqra Ski Resort A134

2004 Litho. *Perf. 11x11¼*
580 A134 £500 multi   1.25 1.25

General Post Office, Beirut — A135

Post office in: £100, 1953. £300, 2002.

2004 *Perf. 11¼x11*
581-582 A135 Set of 2   1.00 1.00

Al Bustan Festival A136

2004 Litho. *Perf. 11x11¼*
583 A136 £1000 multi   2.50 2.50

St. George's Hospital, Beirut, 125th Anniv. (in 2003) — A137

2004, Oct. 28 Litho. *Perf. 11x11¼*
584 A137 £3000 multi   4.00 4.00

Ski Resorts A138

2004 Litho. *Perf. 11x11¼, 11¼x11*
585 A138 £100 Kamouaa
586 A138 £100 Aayoun Siman   .25 .25
587 A138 £250 Laklouk, vert.   .35 .35
588 A138 £300 Zaarour
589 A138 £300 Kanat Bakish   .40 .40
590 A138 £1000 Cedres   1.40 1.40
    Nos. 585-590 (5)   2.40 2.40

Issued: No. 585, 10/28; £250, 11/26; No. 588, 10/28; Nos. 586, 589, £1000, 12/10.

Baalbeck Intl. Festival A139

Tyre Festival — A140

Beiteddine Festival — A141

Byblos Intl. Festival — A142

Perf. 11x11¼, 11¼x11
2004, Nov. 26   Litho.
591 A139 £500 multi   .70 .70
592 A140 £1250 multi   1.75 1.75
593 A141 £1400 multi   1.90 1.90
594 A142 £1750 multi   2.40 2.40
    Nos. 591-594 (4)   6.75 6.75

Rotary International, Cent. — A143

2005, Feb. 23   *Perf. 11¼x11*
595 A143 £3000 multi   4.00 4.00

Beirut Buildings A144

Designs: £100, Rafiq Hariri Intl. Airport. £250, Parliament. £300, Camille Chamoun Sports Center. £500, National Museum. £1000, Governmental Palace. £1250, Bank of Lebanon. £1400, St. Paul's Cathedral. £1750, Bahaeddine Hariri Mosque. £2000, Presidential Palace.

2005 Litho. *Perf. 13x13½*
596-604 A144 Set of 9   15.00 15.00

Issued: £100, £300, £500, £1000, 10/11; others, 11/11.

Pres. Rafiq Hariri (1944-2005) — A145

Designs: No. 605, £1250, Pres. Hariri, flag.
No. 606, £1250, Pres. Hariri, mosque, church
and statues. No. 607, £1750, Pres. Hariri,
mosque. No. 608, £1750, Child kissing picture
of Pres. Hariri.

2006, Feb. 13   **Perf. 13¼x13**
605-608 A145   Set of 4   10.50 10.50
608a   Souvenir sheet, #605-608,
   imperf.   10.50 10.50
No. 608a has embossed margin and simulated perforations between stamps.

Arabic Book
Exhibition
A146

2007, Apr. 18   **Litho.**   **Perf. 13x13¼**
609 A146 £1000 multi   1.40 1.40

Basil Fuleihan (1963-2005), Economy
Minister — A147

Fuleihan: £500, Wearing cap and gown, suit
and tie. £1500, With flags of Lebanon and
European Union. £2000, With flag of Lebanon.
£4000, Vignettes of Nos. 610-612, map and
flag of Lebanon.

2007, Apr. 18   **Perf. 13¼x13**
610-612 A147   Set of 3   5.75 5.75
Size: 160x100mm
Imperf
613 A147 £4000 multi   5.75 5.75

Pres. Fouad Chehab (1902-
73) — A148

2007, June 4   **Perf. 13¼x13**
614 A148 £1400 multi   1.90 1.90

World
Summit on
the
Information
Society,
Tunis (in
2005)
A149

2007, July 2   **Perf. 13x13¼**
615 A149 £100 multi   .25 .25

Léopold Sédar Senghor (1906-2001),
First President of Senegal — A150

2007, July 2   **Perf. 13¼x13**
616 A150 £300 multi   .45 .45

Intl. Year of
Sports and
Physical
Education
(in 2005)
A151

2007, July 2   **Perf. 13¼x13**
617 A151 £500 multi   .70 .70

OPEC Development Fund, 30th
Anniv. — A152

2007, July 2
618 A152 £1400 multi   1.90 1.90

Baalbeck Intl. Festival, 50th
Anniv. — A153

50th anniv. emblem and: £1000, Names of
performers. £5000, Female performers.

2007, July 2   **Perf. 13¼x13**
619-620 A153   Set of 2   7.50 7.50

Islamic Makassed Association of
Sidon, 125th Anniv. (in 2004) — A154

Emblem and: £1400, Pres. Rafiq Hariri.
£1750, Prime Minister Riad El Solh.

2007, July 2
621-622 A154   Set of 2   4.00 4.00

Islamic Makassed Association of
Beirut, 125th Anniv. (in 2003) — A155

Emblem and: £250, "125" in Arabian script.
£500, Prime Minister Saeb Salam. £1400,
Pres. Rafiq Hariri. £1750, Omar El Daouk.

2007, July 2
623-626 A155   Set of 4   5.00 5.00

Souvenir Sheet

2006 Ascent of Mt. Everest by Maxime
Chaya — A156

2007, July 2
627 A156 £3000 multi   3.75 3.75

2004 Return of Freed
Prisoners — A157

2007, July 2   ***Imperf.***
628 A157 £5000 multi   6.25 6.25

Souvenir Sheet

Hills, by Nizar Daher — A158

2007, July 2   **Litho.**   **Perf. 13¼x13**
629 A158 £5000 multi   6.25 6.25

Rotary International District 2450
Conference, Beirut — A159

2008, Apr. 30   **Litho.**   **Perf. 13¼x13**
630 A159 £2000 multi   3.00 3.00

Kahlil Gibran (1883-1931), Writer and
Artist — A160

Designs: £100, Mother and Her Child. £500,
Sultana. £1400, Gibran Museum, Bsharri.
£2000, Gibran.
£4000, Gibran and vignettes of Nos. 631-
634, horiz.

2008, Apr. 30   **Perf. 13x13¼**
631-634 A160   Set of 4   5.75 5.75
Imperf
Size: 160x110mm
635 A160 £4000 multi   5.75 5.75

Army
Day
A161

Emblem and: £500, Soldier and flag of Lebanon. £1000, Stylized flag of Lebanon. £1250,
Soldier holding wheat stalks. £1750, Eye.
£4500, Soldiers and vignettes of Nos. 636-
639.

2008   **Litho.**   **Perf. 13¼x13**
636-639 A161   Set of 4   6.00 6.00
Size: 160x110mm
Imperf
640 A161 £4500 multi   6.00 6.00

Souvenir Sheet

Arab Postal Day — A162

No. 641 — Emblem and: a, World map and
pigeon. b, Camel caravan.

Perf. 13¼ Vert. Through Center
2008
641 A162 £5000 Sheet of 2,
      #a-b   13.50 13.50
Stamps have simulated perforations on
three sides.

Lebanon Post, 10th Anniv. — A163

Simulated postmarks, Lebanon Post emblem, streamers, airplane and: £1250, "10" in Arabian script. £1750, Open envelope and "10th anniversary."
£3000, Simulated postmarks, Lebanon Post emblem, streamers, airplane and vignettes of Nos. 642-643.

2008   *Perf. 13¼x13*
642-643 A163   Set of 2   4.00 4.00
            Size: 160x110mm
               Imperf
644 A163 £3000 multi   4.00 4.00

Trees and Map of Mediterranean Area — A164

2008, Nov. 20   *Perf. 13*
645 A164 £1750 multi   2.40 2.40
         See France No. 3569.

Gen. François El Hajj (1953-2007) — A165

2009, Jan. 8   *Perf. 13x13¼*
646 A165 £1750 multi   2.60 2.60

Universal Declaration of Human Rights, 60th Anniv. — A166

2009, Jan. 8   *Perf. 13¼x13*
647 A166 £2000 multi   3.00 3.00
            Dated 2008.

Beirut, World Book Capital A167

2009, Sept. 17 *Litho.* *Perf. 13x13¼*
648 A167 £750 multi   1.25 1.25

Jerusalem, Capital of Arab Culture — A168

2009, Sept. 17   *Perf. 13¼x13*
649 A168 £1000 multi   1.60 1.60

Pierre Deschamps (1873-1958), Founder of French Lay Mission — A169

2009, Sept. 17
650 A169 £500 blue & black   .85 .85

Sixth Francophone Games, Beirut — A170

2009, Sept. 28
651 A170 £1000 multi   1.60 1.60

Fire Fighters A171

Fire fighters with panel color of: £100, Green. £250, Red.

2010, Aug. 2 *Litho.* *Perf. 13¼x13*
652-653 A171 Set of 2   .50 .50

Nature Reserves A172

2010, Aug. 2
654 A172 £300 multi   .45 .45

Architecture A173

Various buildings with frame color of: £500, Red. £1000, Blue. £1200, Red.

2010, Aug. 2   *Perf. 13¼x13*
655-657 A173 Set of 3   3.75 3.75

Soap Production A174

2010, Aug. 2   *Perf. 13x13¼*
658 A174 £1400 multi   1.90 1.90

Soldier, Map of Lebanon A175

2010, Aug. 2
659 A175 £1750 multi   2.40 2.40

Lungs and Cigarette Butts A176

2010, Aug. 2
660 A176 £2000 multi   2.75 2.75

Syringe and Arrows — A177

2010, Aug. 2   *Perf. 13¼x13*
661 A177 £5000 black & red   7.00 7.00

Imam Al Ouzaai (707-74) — A178

2010, Oct. 9
662 A178 £1000 multi   1.40 1.40

Grand Mufti Hassan Khaled (1921-89) — A179

Musa as-Sadr (1929-78), Religious Leader A180

2010, Oct. 9   *Perf. 13¼x13*
663 A179 £1400 multi   2.00 2.00
                              Perf. 13x13¼
664 A180 £1400 multi   2.00 2.00

Assassinated Political Leaders — A181

Designs: No. 665, £1400, Kamal Jumblatt (1917-77). No. 666, £1400, Prime Minister Rashid Karami (1921-87). No. 667, £1400, President René Moawad (1925-89). No. 668, £1400, President Bachir Gemayel (1947-82), horiz.

2010, Oct. 9 *Perf. 13x13¼, 13¼x13*
665-668 A181 Set of 4   8.00 8.00

World Tourism Day A182

2010, Oct. 9   *Perf. 13x13¼*
669 A182 £2000 multi   3.00 3.00

Dove and
Flowers
A183

2010, Oct. 9
670 A183 £3000 multi   4.25 4.25

Source of
the
Alphabet
A184

Arab Permanent Postal
Commission — A185

Famous
People
A186

Designs: £1750, Sabah, singer and actress.
£2250, Nabih Abou El-Hossn, actor. £2750,
Hassan Alaa Eddine (1939-75), comedian.
£3000, Caracalla Dance Ensemble. £5000,
Alfred (1924-2006), Michel (1921-1981) and
Youssef (1926-2001) Basbous, sculptors.
£10,000, Saïd Akl, poet.

2011, May 23 Litho. Perf. 13x13¼
671 A184 £250 multi   .35   .35
672 A185 £500 multi   .70   .70
673 A186 £1750 multi   2.50   2.50
674 A186 £2250 multi   3.25   3.25
675 A186 £2750 multi   4.00   4.00
676 A186 £3000 multi   4.25   4.25
677 A186 £5000 multi   7.00   7.00
678 A186 £10,000 multi   14.00 14.00
　　　Nos. 671-678 (8)   36.05 36.05

Famous People Type of 2011 and

Ehden
Reserve
A187

Pres. Suleiman
Franjieh (1910-
92)
A188

Designs: £1500, Fayrouz, singer. £2000,
Wadih El-Safi, singer.

Perf. 13x13¼, 13¼x13 (£1000)
2011, June 27
679 A187 £750 multi   1.10   1.10
680 A188 £1000 multi   1.40   1.40
681 A186 £1500 multi   2.10   2.10
682 A186 £2000 multi   3.00   3.00
　　　Nos. 679-682 (4)   7.60   7.60

Pres. Michel Suleiman — A189

Pres. Suleiman and: £750, Cedar trees.
£1750, People at President's Summer Residence, Beiteddine. £2500, Dove with flags of
Syria and Lebanon on wings. £2750, United
Nations emblem.

2011, Nov. 5 Perf. 13¼x13
683-686 A189 Set of 4   12.00 12.00

Mother's
Day
A190

2012, Mar. 12 Perf. 13x13¼
687 A190 £2000 multi   72.50 72.50

Lions International in Lebanon, 60th
Anniv. — A191

2012, Apr. 2
688 A191 £750 multi   1.60   1.60

Pope Benedict XVI and Pres. Michel
Suleiman — A192

2012, Sept. 15 Perf. 13¼x13
689 A192 £1250 multi   2.10   2.10
Visit of Pope Benedict XVI to Lebanon.

Beirut Marathon,
10th
Anniv. — A193

2012, Nov. 12
690 A193 £750 multi   1.25   1.25

Christmas
A194

2012, Nov. 13 Perf. 13x13¼
691 A194 £2000 multi   3.25   3.25

World Map
and Statue
of Lebanese
Man
A195

2012, Nov. 21 Litho. Perf. 13x13¼
692 A195 £500 multi   16.00 16.00

Adel Osseiran (1905-98),
Politician — A196

2012, Nov. 21 Litho. Perf. 13¼x13
693 A196 £1000 multi   1.60   1.60

National Scientific Research Council,
50th Anniv. — A197

2012, Dec. 10
694 A197 £250 multi   .45   .45

Pres.
Michel
Suleiman
A198

2012, Dec. 13 Perf. 13x13¼
695 A198 £250 multi   37.50 37.50

Ghassan Tueni (1926-2012), Journalist
and Politician — A199

2012, Dec. 14
696 A199 £750 multi   1.25   1.25

100th Birthday (in 2011) of Saïd Akl,
Poet — A200

2012, Dec. 26 Perf. 13¼x13
697 A200 £500 multi   .80   .80

Mother's
Day
A201

2013, Mar. 20 Perf. 13x13¼
698 A201 £2000 multi   7.00   7.00

Lebanon
Post, 15th
Anniv.
A202

2013, Nov. 11 Litho. Perf. 13x13¼
699 A202 £3000 multi   4.75   4.75

Amin Maalouf, Member of French
Academy — A203

2013, Nov. 19 Litho. Perf. 13¼x13
700 A203 £100 multi   1.75   1.75

Independence, 70th Anniv. — A204

2013, Nov. 27 Litho. Perf. 13x13¼
701 A204 £1000 multi   1.75   1.75

Christmas
A205

2013, Dec. 16 Litho. Perf. 13¼x13
702 A205 £2000 multi   3.50   3.50

Armenian Genocide Monument, Bikfaya — A206

2014, Apr. 15   **Litho.**   *Perf. 13¼x13*
703   A206   £2000 multi   4.75   4.75

Medicine, Law and Engineering Faculties of St. Joseph University, Cent. A207

2014, Apr. 29   **Litho.**   *Perf. 13x13¼*
704   A207   £500 multi   .85   .85

Famous Women — A208

Designs: No. 705, £2000, Laure Moughhaizel (1929-97), women's rights advocate. No. 706, £2000, Mounira el Solh (1911-2010), advocate for women's rights and the disabled. No. 707, £2000, Alexandra Issa el Khoury, President of Lebanese Red Cross. No. 708, £2000, Anissa Najjar, founder of Al Ahlia Magazine.

2014, May 22   **Litho.**   *Perf. 13¼x13*
705-708   A208   Set of 4   14.00   14.00

Bank of Lebanon, 50th Anniv. A209

2014, June 2   **Litho.**   *Perf. 13x13¼*
709   A209   £1750 multi   3.00   3.00

Father's Day — A210

2014, June 17   **Litho.**   *Perf. 13¼x13*
710   A210   £1750 multi   3.00   3.00

Euromed Postal Emblem and Mediterranean Sea — A211

2014, July 9   **Litho.**   *Perf. 13x13¼*
711   A211   £1000 multi   1.90   1.90

2014 World Cup Soccer Championships, Brazil — A212

Designs: £1750, Mascot. £2000, Emblem.

2014, July 12   **Litho.**   *Perf. 13¼x13*
712-713   A212   Set of 2   7.25   7.25

Monsignor Germanos Mouakkad (1853-1912), Missionary A213

2014, Sept. 5   **Litho.**   *Perf. 13¼x13*
714   A213   £250 multi   .60   .60

Youssef Bey Karam (1823-89), Leader of 1866-67 Rebellion Against Ottoman Rule — A214

2014, Nov. 10   **Litho.**   *Perf. 13¼x13*
715   A214   £1750 multi   3.25   3.25

Writers — A215

Designs: No. 716, £1750, Kamal Youssef El-Hage (1917-76). No. 717, £1750, Ounsi El-Hage (1937-2014). No. 718, £1750, Joseph Harb (1941-2014).

2014, Nov. 10   **Litho.**   *Perf. 13¼x13*
716-718   A215   Set of 3   8.75   8.75

Independence, 71st Anniv. — A216

2014, Nov. 22   **Litho.**   *Perf. 13¼x13*
719   A216   £2750 multi   5.00   5.00

SEMI-POSTAL STAMPS

Stamps of 1925 Srchd. in Red or Black

1926		**Unwmk.**	**Perf. 14x13½**	
B1	A2	25c + 25c ol blk	4.25	4.25
B2	A2	50c + 25c yel grn (B)	4.25	4.25
B3	A2	75c + 25c brn org	4.25	4.25
B4	A2	(B)	4.25	4.25
B4	A2	1p + 50c mag	4.25	4.25
B5	A2	1.25p + 50c dp grn	4.75	4.75
B6	A2	1.50p + 50c rose red	4.75	4.75
		(B)	4.75	4.75
a.		Double surcharge	40.00	30.00
B7	A2	2p + 75c dk brn	4.25	4.25
B8	A2	2.50p + 75c pck bl	4.75	4.75
B9	A2	3p + 1p org brn	4.75	4.75
B10	A2	5p + 1p vio (B)	4.75	4.75
B11	A3	10p + 2p vio brn (B)	4.75	4.75
B12	A2	25p + 5p ultra	4.75	4.75
		Nos. B1-B12 (12)	54.50	54.50

On No. B11 the surcharge is set in six lines to fit the shape of the stamp. All values of this series exist with inverted surcharge. Value each, $14.

See Nos. CB1-CB4.

> Catalogue values for unused stamps in this section, from this point to the end of the section, are for Never Hinged items.

Boxing — SP1

1961, Jan. 12   **Litho.**   *Perf. 13*
B13   SP1   2.50p + 2.50p shown   .50   .25
B14   SP1   5p + 5p Wrestling   .50   .25
B15   SP1   7.50p + 7.50p Shot put   .50   .25
   Nos. B13-B15,CB12-CB14 (6)   13.50   5.55

17th Olympic Games, Rome, Aug. 25-Sept. 11, 1960.

Nos. B13-B15 with Arabic and French Overprint in Black, Blue or Green and two Bars through Olympic Inscription: "CHAMPIONNAT D'EUROPE DE TIR, 2 JUIN 1962"

1962, June 2
B16   SP1   2.50p + 2.50p blue & brn (Bk)   .50   .25
B17   SP1   5p + 5p org & brn (G)   .90   .25
B18   SP1   7.50p + 7.50p vio & brn (Bl)   1.00   .40
   Nos. B16-B18,CB15-CB17 (6)   9.40   4.35

European Marksmanship Championships held in Lebanon.

Red Cross SP2

No. B20, Stylized profile. No. B21, Globe, emblems, dove.

1988, June 8   **Litho.**   *Perf. 14*
B19   SP2   £10 + £1 shown   1.75
B20   SP2   £20 + £2 multi   2.75
B21   SP2   £30 + £3 multi   3.75
   Nos. B19-B21 (3)   8.25

AIR POST STAMPS

Nos. 10-13 with Additional Overprint

1924		**Unwmk.**	**Perf. 14x13½**	
C1	A18	2p on 40c	13.00	13.00
a.		Double surcharge	52.50	52.50
C2	A18	3p on 60c	13.00	13.00
a.		Invtd. surch. and ovpt.	87.50	87.50
C3	A18	5p on 1fr	13.00	13.00
a.		Dbl. surch. and ovpt.	72.50	72.50
b.		"5" omitted	300.00	
C4	A18	10p on 2fr	13.00	13.00
a.		Invtd. surch. and ovpt.	110.00	110.00
b.		Dbl. surch. and ovpt.	60.00	60.00
		Nos. C1-C4 (4)	52.00	52.00

Nos. 33, 35-37 Overprinted

C5	A18	2p on 40c	13.00	13.00
a.		Overprint reversed	45.00	
C6	A18	3p on 60c	13.00	13.00
a.		Overprint reversed	45.00	
C7	A18	5p on 1fr	13.00	13.00
a.		Overprint reversed	45.00	
C8	A18	10p on 2fr	13.50	13.50
a.		Overprint reversed	45.00	
b.		Double surcharge	45.00	
		Nos. C5-C8 (4)	52.50	52.50

Nos. 57, 50 61 Overprinted in Green

1925				
C9	A2	2p dark brown	4.50	4.50
C10	A2	3p orange brown	4.50	4.50
C11	A2	5p violet	4.50	4.50
a.		Inverted overprint		
C12	A2	10p violet brown	4.50	4.50
		Nos. C9-C12 (4)	18.00	18.00

Nos. 57, 59-61 Ovptd. in Red — c

1926				
C13	A2	2p dark brown	4.75	4.75
C14	A2	3p orange brown	4.75	4.75
C15	A2	5p violet	4.75	4.75
C16	A3	10p violet brown	4.75	4.75
		Nos. C13-C16 (4)	19.00	19.00

Airplane pointed down on No. C16. Exist with inverted overprint. Value, each $45.

Issues of Republic under French Mandate

Nos. C13-C16 Overprinted — d

1927				
C17	A2	2p dark brown	5.50	5.50
C18	A2	3p orange brown	5.50	5.50
C19	A2	5p violet	5.50	5.50
C20	A3	10p violet brown	5.50	5.50
		Nos. C17-C20 (4)	22.00	22.00

On No. C19 "Republique Libanaise" is above the bars. Overprint set in two lines on No. C20.

Nos. C17-
C20 with
Additional
Ovpt. — e

1928　　　　　Black Overprint

C21	A2	2p brown	12.50	10.00
a.		Double overprint	65.00	65.00
b.		Inverted overprint	65.00	65.00
C22	A2	3p orange brown	12.50	10.00
a.		Double overprint	65.00	65.00
C23	A2	5p violet	12.50	10.00
a.		Double overprint	65.00	65.00
C24	A3	10p violet brown	12.50	10.00
a.		Double overprint	65.00	65.00
		Nos. C21-C24 (4)	50.00	40.00

On Nos. C21-C24 the airplane is always in red.

Nos. 52,
54, 57, 59-
62 Ovptd.
in Red or
Black — f

1928

C25	A2	2p dark brown	4.50	4.50
C26	A2	3p orange brown	3.00	3.00
C27	A2	5p violet	4.50	4.50
C28	A3	10p violet brown	4.50	4.50

1929

C33	A2	50c yellow green	1.25	1.25
a.		Inverted overprint	45.00	45.00
C34	A2	1p magenta (Bk)	1.00	1.00
a.		Inverted overprint	45.00	45.00
C35	A2	25p ultra	190.00	160.00
a.		Inverted overprint	525.00	525.00
		Nos. C25-C34 (6)	18.75	18.75
		Nos. C25-C35 (7)	208.75	178.75

On Nos. C25-C28 the airplane is always in red.

On No. C28 the overprinted orientation is horizontal. The bars covering the old country names are at the left.

The red overprint of a silhouetted plane and "Republique Libanaise," as on Nos. C25-C27, was also applied to Nos. C9-C12. These are believed to have been essays, and were not regularly issued.

No. 62 with
Surcharge
Added in
Red

Two types of surcharge:

I — The "5" of "15 P." is italic. The "15" is 4mm high. Arabic characters for "Lebanese Republic" and for "15 P." are on same line in that order.

II — The "5" is in Roman type (upright) and smaller; "15" is 3½mm high. Arabic for "Lebanese Republic" is centered on line by itself, with Arabic for "15 P." below right end of line.

C36	A2	15p on 25p ultra (I)	225.00	175.00
a.		Type II (#106)	800.00	800.00

Nos. 102 Overprinted Type "c" in Blue

C37	A2	50c on 75c	1.00	1.00
a.		Airplane inverted	45.00	
b.		French and Arabic surch. invtd.		
c.		"P" omitted		
d.		Airplane double	50.00	

No. 55 Surcharged in Red

1930

C38	A2	2p on 1.25p dp green	1.75	1.25
a.		Inverted surcharge	72.50	45.00

Airplane
over
Racheya
AP2

Designs: 1p, Plane over Broumana. 2p, Baalbek. 3p, Hasroun. 5p, Byblos. 10p, Kadicha River. 15p, Beirut. 25p, Tripoli. 50p, Kabeljas. 100p, Zahle.

1930-31　　　Photo.　　Perf. 13½

C39	AP2	50c dk violet ('31)	.50	.50
C40	AP2	1p yellow grn ('31)	.80	.80
C41	AP2	2p dp orange ('31)	2.50	2.50
C42	AP2	3p magenta ('31)	2.50	2.50
C43	AP2	5p indigo	2.50	2.50
C44	AP2	10p orange red	3.25	3.25
C45	AP2	15p orange brn	3.25	3.25
C46	AP2	25p gray vio ('31)	4.75	4.75
C47	AP2	50p dp claret	9.00	9.00
C48	AP2	100p olive brown	12.00	12.00
		Nos. C39-C48 (10)	41.05	41.05

Nos. C39-C48 exist imperforate. Value, set $200.

Tourist Publicity Issue

Skiing in
Lebanon
AP12

Bay of
Jounie
AP13

1936, Oct. 12

C49	AP12	50c slate grn	3.00	3.00
C50	AP13	1p red orange	3.75	3.75
C51	AP12	2p black violet	3.75	3.75
C52	AP13	3p yellow grn	4.00	4.00
C53	AP12	5p brown car	4.00	4.00
C54	AP13	10p orange brn	4.00	4.00
C55	AP13	15p dk carmine	37.50	37.50
C56	AP12	25p green	125.00	125.00
		Nos. C49-C56 (8)	185.00	185.00

Nos. C49-C56 exist imperforate. Value, set $650.

Lebanese
Pavilion at
Exposition
AP14

1937, July 1　　　　　Perf. 13½

C57	AP14	50c olive black	1.50	1.50
C58	AP14	1p yellow green	1.50	1.50
C59	AP14	2p dk red orange	1.50	1.50
C60	AP14	3p dk olive grn	1.50	1.50
C61	AP14	5p deep green	2.00	2.00
C62	AP14	10p carmine lake	9.00	9.00
C63	AP14	15p rose lake	10.00	10.00
C64	AP14	25p orange brn	17.50	17.50
		Nos. C57-C64 (8)	44.50	44.50

Paris International Exposition.

Arcade of
Beit-ed-Din
Palace
AP15

Ruins of
Baalbek
AP16

1937-40　　　Engr.　　Perf. 13

C65	AP15	50c ultra ('38)	.35	.25
C66	AP15	1p henna brn ('40)	.35	.25
C67	AP15	2p sepia ('40)	.35	.25
C68	AP15	3p rose ('40)	3.25	1.25
C69	AP15	5p lt green ('40)	.35	.25
C70	AP16	10p dull violet	.35	.25
C71	AP16	15p turq bl ('40)	2.75	1.75
C72	AP16	25p violet ('40)	6.00	5.00
C73	AP16	50p yel grn ('40)	11.00	7.00
C74	AP16	100p brown ('40)	6.00	3.50
		Nos. C65-C74 (10)	30.75	19.75

Nos. C65-C74 exist imperforate.

Medical
College of
Beirut
AP17

1938, May 9　　　Photo.　　Perf. 13

C75	AP17	2p green	3.00	3.50
C76	AP17	3p orange	3.00	3.50
		Never hinged	6.00	
C77	AP17	5p lilac gray	5.50	6.50
C78	AP17	10p lake	10.50	12.00
		Nos. C75-C78 (4)	22.00	25.50

Medical Congress.

Maurice Noguès and View of
Beirut — AP18

1938, July 15　　　　　Perf. 11

C79	AP18	10p brown carmine	4.00	1.50
a.		Souv. sheet of 4, perf. 13½	35.00	20.00
b.		Perf. 13½	7.50	4.00

10th anniversary of first Marseille-Beirut flight, by Maurice Noguès.

No. C79a has marginal inscriptions in French and Arabic. Exists imperf.; value $250.

Independent Republic

Plane Over
Mt.
Lebanon
AP19

1942, Sept. 18　　Litho.　　Perf. 11½

C80	AP19	10p dk brown vio	7.00	7.00
C81	AP19	50p dk gray grn	7.00	8.00

1st anniv. of the Proclamation of Independence, Nov. 26, 1941.

Nos. C80 and C81 exist imperforate.

Bechamoun
AP20

Rachaya
Citadel
AP21

Air View of
Beirut
AP22

1943, May 1　　　　　Perf. 11½

C82	AP20	25p yellow grn	4.75	4.75
C83	AP20	50p orange	6.50	5.50
C84	AP21	100p buff	6.50	5.50
C85	AP21	200p blue vio	8.00	7.25
C86	AP22	300p sage green	21.00	17.50
C87	AP22	500p sepia	42.50	32.50
		Nos. C82-C87 (6)	74.25	59.50

2nd anniv. of the Proclamation of Independence. Nos. C82-C87 exist imperforate.

See Nos. 163-166. For overprints see Nos. C91-C96.

Bhannes
Sanatorium
AP23

1943, July 8　　　　　Photo.

Black Overprint

C88	AP23	20p orange	3.75	2.75
C89	AP23	50p steel blue	4.25	3.50
C90	AP23	100p rose violet	6.00	4.50
		Nos. C88-C90 (3)	14.00	8.25

Arab Medical Congress, Beirut.

Nos. C82
to C87
Overprinted
in Red,
Blue or
Violet

1944, Nov. 23

C91	AP20	25p yel grn (R)	7.25	7.25
C92	AP20	50p orange (Bl)	12.00	12.00
C93	AP21	100p buff (V)	14.00	14.00
C94	AP21	200p blue vio (R)	25.00	25.00
C95	AP22	300p sage grn (R)	32.50	30.00
C96	AP22	500p sepia (Bl)	65.00	60.00
		Nos. C91-C96 (6)	155.75	148.25

Return to office of the President and his ministers, Nov. 22, 1943.

> Catalogue values for unused stamps in this section, from this point to the end of the section, are for Never Hinged items.

Falls of
Litani — AP24

The
Cedars
AP25

1945, July　　Unwmk.　　Litho.

C97	AP24	25p gray brown	3.50	2.10
C98	AP24	50p rose violet	5.00	2.75
C99	AP25	200p violet	15.00	5.25
C100	AP25	300p brown black	27.50	10.50
		Nos. C97-C100 (4)	51.00	20.60

Lebanese
Soldiers at
Bir
Hacheim
AP26

1946, May 8

C101	AP26	15p bl blk, org & red org	1.00	.25
C102	AP26	20p red, lil & bl	1.00	.60
C103	AP26	25p brt bl, org & red	1.25	.25
C104	AP26	50p gray blk, bl & red	1.75	.50
C105	AP26	100p pur, pink & red	5.00	1.25
C106	AP26	150p brn, pink & red	6.00	3.75
		Nos. C101-C106 (6)	16.00	6.60

Victory of the Allied Nations in WWII, 1st anniv.

Three imperf. souvenir sheets of 14 exist. They contain one each of Nos. C101-C106 and 189-196 in changed colors. One has sepia inscriptions, and one on thin white card has blue inscriptions. Value $30 each. The third, with blue inscriptions, is on thick honeycombed chamois card. Value $110.

Night Herons Type

1946, Sept. 11

C107	A35	10p orange	7.00	1.00
C108	A35	25p ultra	8.00	2.00
C109	A35	50p blue green	25.00	1.60
C110	A35	100p dk vio brn	37.50	6.50
		Nos. C107-C110 (4)	77.50	9.30

Symbols of Communications — AP28

1946, Nov. 22
C111	AP28	25p deep blue	1.75	.70
C112	AP28	50p green	2.50	.80
C113	AP28	75p orange red	4.25	1.75
C114	AP28	150p brown black	6.00	2.75
	Nos. C111-C114 (4)		14.50	6.00

Arab Postal Congress, Sofar, 1946.

Stone Tablet, Dog River and Pres. Bechara el-Khoury AP29

1947, Feb. 11
C115	AP29	25p ultra	7.00	.35
C116	AP29	50p dull rose	9.00	.60
C117	AP29	75p gray black	11.00	.65
C118	AP29	150p blue green	17.50	1.40
	Nos. C115-C118 (4)		44.50	3.00

Evacuation of foreign troops from Lebanon, Dec. 31, 1946.

Bay of Jounie AP30

Government House, Beirut — AP31

1947, Feb. 11   Grayish Paper
C119	AP30	5p dp blue grn	60	.25
C120	AP30	10p rose vio	.90	.25
C121	AP30	15p vermilion	2.25	.25
C122	AP30	20p orange	2.50	.25
a.		20p red orange, white paper	2.25	.25
C123	AP30	25p deep blue	3.00	.25
C124	AP30	50p henna brn	5.00	.25
C125	AP30	100p chocolate	10.50	.30
C126	AP31	150p dk vio brn	18.00	.50
C127	AP31	200p slate	27.50	2.40
C128	AP31	300p black	45.00	6.00
	Nos. C119-C128 (10)		115.25	10.70

See Nos. C145A-C147B.

Post Horn and Letter — AP32

Phoenician Galley AP33

1947, June 17   Litho.
C129	AP32	10p brt ultra	1.75	.50
C130	AP32	15p rose car	2.00	.50
C131	AP32	25p bright blue	2.50	.80
C132	AP33	50p dk slate grn	5.75	.90
C133	AP33	75p purple	7.00	1.90
C134	AP33	100p dark brown	9.00	2.50
	Nos. C129-C134 (6)		28.00	7.10

Lebanon's participation in the 12th UPU congress, Paris.

Lebanese Village AP34

1948, Sept. 1   Perf. 11½
C135	AP34	5p dp orange	.75	.25
C136	AP34	10p rose lilac	1.75	.25
C137	AP34	15p orange brn	3.50	.25
C138	AP34	20p slate	4.50	.25
C139	AP34	25p Prus blue	10.50	1.00
C140	AP34	50p gray black	17.50	1.40
	Nos. C135-C140 (6)		38.50	3.40

Apollo — AP35

Minerva AP36

1948, Nov. 23   Unwmk.
C141	AP35	7.50p blue & lt blue	4.00	1.00
C142	AP35	15p black & gray	5.00	1.25
C143	AP35	20p rose brn & rose	5.25	1.90
C144	AP36	35p car rose & rose	8.00	2.50
C145	AP36	75p bl grn & lt green	15.00	5.00
	Nos. C141-C145 (5)		37.25	11.65

UNESCO. Nos. C141-C145 exist imperforate, and combined with Nos. 220-224 in an imperforate souvenir sheet on thin buff cardboard, with black inscriptions in top margin in Arabic and at bottom in French. Value $275.

Bay Type of 1947 Redrawn
1949   White Paper
C145A	AP30	10p rose lilac	9.00	1.00
C146	AP30	15p dark green	11.00	1.25
C147	AP30	20p orange	25.00	9.00
C147A	AP30	25p dark blue	65.00	3.25
C147B	AP30	50p brick red	275.00	35.00
	Nos. C145A-C147B (5)		385.00	49.50

In the redrawn designs, Nos. C145A, C147 and C147B have zeros with broader centers than in the 1947 issue (Nos. C120, C122 and C124).

Helicopter Mail Delivery — AP37

1949, Aug. 16   Unwmk.   Perf. 11½
C148	AP37	25p deep blue	8.00	4.00
C149	AP37	50p green	12.00	4.50
a.		Souvenir sheet of 5, #225-227, C148-C149	75.00	35.00

UPU, 75th anniv. No. 149a exists on thin cardboard. Value $250.

Homing Birds AP38

Pres. Bechara el-Khoury AP39

1950, Aug. 8   Litho.
C150	AP38	5p violet blue	3.75	.65
C151	AP38	15p rose vio	4.25	.70
C152	AP39	25p chocolate	3.00	.95
C153	AP39	35p gray green	4.50	1.40
a.		Souvenir sheet of 6, #243-244, C150-C153, chamois paper	70.00	55.00
	Nos. C150-C153 (4)		15.50	3.70

Conference of Emigrants, 1950.

Crusader Castle, Sidon Harbor AP40

1950, Sept. 7
C154	AP40	10p chocolate	1.00	.25
C155	AP40	15p dark green	2.00	.25
C156	AP40	20p crimson	4.00	.25
C157	AP40	25p ultra	7.00	.80
C158	AP40	50p gray black	10.00	2.25
	Nos. C154-C158 (5)		24.00	3.80

1951, June 9   Redrawn   Typo.
C159	AP40	10p grnsh black	2.00	.25
C160	AP40	15p black brown	3.00	.25
C161	AP40	20p vermilion	3.00	.25
C162	AP40	25p deep blue	4.00	.25
C163	AP40	35p lilac rose	8.00	2.40
C164	AP40	50p indigo	11.00	2.40
	Nos. C159-C164 (6)		31.00	5.80

Nos. C154-C158 are lithographed from a fine-screen halftone; Nos. C159-C164 are typographed and much coarser, with larger plane and many other differences.

Khaldé International Airport, Beirut — AP41

Design: 50p to 300p, Amphitheater, Byblos.

1952   Litho.   Perf. 11½
C165	AP41	5p crimson	1.50	.25
C166	AP41	10p dull green	1.50	.25
C167	AP41	15p rose lilac	1.75	.25
C168	AP41	20p brown org	2.00	.25
C169	AP41	25p grnsh blue	2.00	.25
C170	AP41	35p violet bl	2.75	.25
C171	AP41	50p blue green	14.00	.60
C172	AP41	100p deep blue	55.00	2.40
C173	AP41	200p dk blue grn	35.00	3.50
C174	AP41	300p black brn	52.50	7.50
	Nos. C165-C174 (10)		168.00	15.50

Lockheed Constellation — AP42

1953, Oct. 1
C175	AP42	5p yellow green	.90	.25
C176	AP42	10p deep plum	1.25	.25
C177	AP42	15p scarlet	1.75	.25
C178	AP42	20p aqua	2.25	.25
C179	AP42	25p blue	4.00	.25
C180	AP42	35p orange brn	5.75	.25
C181	AP42	50p violet blue	11.00	.30
C182	AP42	100p black brown	16.00	2.40
	Nos. C175-C182 (8)		42.90	4.20

Ruins at Baalbek AP43

Irrigation Canal, Litani AP44

1954, Mar.
C183	AP43	5p yel green	.75	.25
C184	AP43	10p dull purple	.90	.25
C185	AP43	15p carmine	1.50	.25
C186	AP43	20p brown	2.00	.25
C187	AP43	25p dull blue	2.50	.25
C188	AP43	35p black brn	3.00	.25
C189	AP44	50p dk olive grn	10.00	.25
C190	AP44	100p dp car	19.00	.35
C191	AP44	200p dark brown	27.50	.70
C192	AP44	300p dk gray blue	50.00	1.50
	Nos. C183-C192 (10)		117.15	4.30

Khaldé International Airport, Beirut — AP45

1954, Apr. 23   Perf. 11½
C193	AP45	10p pink & rose red	1.25	.25
C194	AP45	25p dp bl & gray bl	2.75	.50
C195	AP45	35p dl brn & yel brn	4.25	.90
C196	AP45	65p dp grn & grn	6.25	1.60
	Nos. C193-C196 (4)		14.50	3.25

Opening of Beirut's Intl. Airport. Exist imperf.

Arab Postal Union Type of Regular Issue, 1955
1955, Jan. 1   Perf. 13½x13
C197	A52	2.50p yellow brn	1.50	.25

Rotary Emblem AP47

1955, Feb. 23   Perf. 11½
C198	AP47	35p dull green	1.50	.40
C199	AP47	65p dull blue	2.50	.55

Rotary International, 50th anniversary.

Skiing Among the Cedars AP48

1955, Feb. 24   Litho.
C200	AP48	5p blue green	2.00	.25
C201	AP48	15p crimson	2.25	.25
C202	AP48	20p lilac	2.75	.25
C203	AP48	25p blue	5.00	.25
C204	AP48	35p olive brn	6.50	.25
C205	AP48	50p chocolate	11.00	.70
C206	AP48	65p deep blue	17.50	2.10
	Nos. C200-C206 (7)		47.00	4.05

See Nos. C233-C235. For surcharge see No. C271.

Tourist — AP49

1955, Sept. 10 Unwmk. Perf. 13

C207	AP49	2.50p brn vio & lt bl	.50	.25
C208	AP49	12.50p ultra & lt bl	.65	.25
C209	AP49	25p indigo & lt bl	1.50	.25
C210	AP49	35p ol grn & lt bl	1.75	.25
a.		Sheet of 4, #C207-C210, imperf.	22.50	7.75
		Nos. C207-C210 (4)	4.40	1.00

Tourist Year. No. C210a is printed on cardboard.

Oranges AP50

Designs: 25p, 35p, 50p, Grapes, vert. 65p, 100p, 200p, Apples.

1955, Oct. 15

C211	AP50	5p yel grn & yel	1.10	.25
C212	AP50	10p dk grn & dp orange	1.25	.25
C213	AP50	15p yel grn & red orange	1.40	.25
C214	AP50	20p olive & yel org	2.00	.25
C215	AP50	25p blue & vio bl	2.75	.25
C216	AP50	35p green & cl	3.25	.25
C217	AP50	50p blk brn & dl yel	3.25	.25
C218	AP50	65p green & lemon	6.50	.25
C219	AP50	100p yel grn & dp orange	8.50	.85
C220	AP50	200p green & car	15.00	4.25
		Nos. C211-C220 (10)	45.00	7.10

For surcharge see No. C265.

United Nations Emblem AP52

1956, Jan. 23 Perf. 11½

C221	AP52	35p violet blue	5.25	1.90
C222	AP52	65p green	6.50	2.25

UN, 10th anniv. (in 1955).
An imperf. souvenir sheet contains one each of Nos. C221 and C222. Value $90.

Temple of the Sun Colonnade, Masks and Lion's Head — AP53

Temple of Bacchus, Baalbek AP54

Design: 35p, 65p, Temple of the Sun colonnade, masks and violincello.

1956, Dec. 10 Litho. Perf. 13

C223	AP53	2.50p dark brown	.85	.25
C224	AP53	10p green	1.10	.25
C225	AP54	12.50p light blue	1.10	.25
C226	AP54	25p brt vio bl	1.60	.35
C227	AP53	35p red lilac	3.00	.45
C228	AP53	65p slate blue	4.25	.90
		Nos. C223-C228 (6)	11.90	2.45

International Festival at Baalbek.

Skiing Type of 1955 Redrawn and

Irrigation Canal, Litani AP55

1957 Litho. Perf. 11½

C229	AP55	10p brt violet	.65	.25
C230	AP55	15p orange	.90	.25
C231	AP55	20p yel green	1.00	.25
C232	AP55	25p slate blue	1.10	.25
C233	AP48	35p gray green	2.50	.25
C234	AP48	65p dp claret	4.00	.25
C235	AP48	100p brown	6.00	.65
		Nos. C229-C235 (7)	16.15	2.15

Different Arabic characters used for the country name; letters in "Liban" larger.
For surcharge see No. C271.

Pres. Camille Chamoun and King Saud AP56

King Saud, Pres. Chamoun, King Hussein, Pres. Kouatly, King Faisal, Pres. Nasser — AP57

Pres. Chamoun and: No. C237, King Hussein. No. C238, Pres. Kouatly. No. C239, King Faisal. No. C240, Pres. Nasser. 25p, Map of Lebanon.

1957, July 15 Litho. Perf. 13

C236	AP56	15p green	.75	.25
C237	AP56	15p blue	.75	.25
C238	AP56	15p red lilac	.75	.25
C239	AP56	15p red orange	.75	.25
C240	AP56	15p claret	.75	.25
C241	AP56	25p blue	.75	.25
C242	AP57	100p dl red brn	6.00	1.50
		Nos. C236-C242 (7)	10.50	3.00

Congr. of Arab Leaders, Beirut, 11/12-15/56.

Fencing AP58

50p, Pres. Chamoun and stadium with flags.

1957, Sept. 12 Unwmk. Perf. 13

C243	AP58	35p claret	3.25	1.50
C244	AP58	50p lt green	4.00	2.25

2nd Pan-Arab Games, Beirut. See note on souvenir sheet below No. 314.

Symbols of Communications — AP59

Power Plant, Chamoun AP60

1957 Perf. 13x13½, 11½ (AP60)

C245	AP59	5p brt green	.55	.25
C246	AP59	10p yel orange	.60	.25
C247	AP59	15p brown	.60	.25
C248	AP59	20p maroon	.80	.25
C249	AP59	25p violet blue	1.10	.25
C250	AP60	35p violet brn	1.40	.25
C251	AP60	50p green	1.60	.25

C252	AP60	65p sepia	2.25	.25
C253	AP60	100p dark gray	3.00	.55
		Nos. C245-C253 (9)	11.90	2.55

Plane at Airport AP61

Cogwheel AP62

1958-59 Unwmk. Perf. 13

C254	AP61	5p green	.55	.25
C255	AP61	10p magenta	.75	.25
C256	AP61	15p dull violet	.90	.25
C257	AP61	20p orange ver	1.10	.25
C258	AP61	25p dk vio bl	1.40	.25
C259	AP62	35p grnsh gray	1.60	.25
C260	AP62	50p aquamarine	2.25	.25
C261	AP62	65p pale brown	3.75	.25
C262	AP62	100p brt ultra	4.25	.25
		Nos. C254-C262 (9)	16.55	2.30

Nos. C259 and C261 Srchd. in Black or Dark Blue

1959 Unwmk. Litho. Perf. 13

C263	AP62	30p on 35p grnsh gray	1.00	.25
C264	AP62	40p on 65p pale brn (Bl)	1.40	.45

Arab Engineers Congress.

No. C217 Surcharged

1959, Sept. 1

C265	AP50	40p on 50p blk brn & dull yel	1.50	.50

Arab Lawyers Congress.

Myron's Discobolus — AP63

Wreath and Hand Holding Torch AP64

1959, Oct. 11 Litho. Perf. 11½

C266	AP63	15p shown	1.00	.25
C267	AP63	30p Weight lifter	1.25	.30
C268	AP64	40p shown	1.90	.40
		Nos. C266-C268 (3)	4.15	.95

3rd Mediterranean Games, Beirut. A souvenir sheet on white cardboard contains one each of Nos. C266-C268, imperf. Sold for 100p. Value $67.50.

Soldiers and Flag — AP65

1959, Nov. 25 Perf. 13½x13

C269	AP65	40p sep, brick red & sl	1.50	.30
C270	AP65	60p sep, dk grn & brick red	2.00	.35

Lebanon's independence, 1941-1959.

No. C234 Surcharged with New Value and Bars

1959, Dec. 15 Perf. 11½

C271	AP48	40p on 65p dp claret	3.00	.30

Hands Planting Tree — AP66

1960, Jan. 18 Litho. Perf. 11½

C272	AP66	20p rose vio & grn	1.00	.25
C273	AP66	40p dk brn & green	1.25	.40

Friends of the Tree Society, 25th anniv.

Postal Administration Building — AP67

1960, Feb. Unwmk. Perf. 13

C274	AP67	20p green	.90	.25

President Fuad Chehab — AP68

1960, Mar. 12 Photo. Perf. 13½

C275	AP68	5p green	.50	.25
C276	AP68	10p Prus blue	.50	.25
C277	AP68	15p orange brn	.50	.25
C278	AP68	20p brown	.55	.25
C279	AP68	30p olive	.80	.25
C280	AP68	40p dull red	.90	.25
C281	AP68	50p blue	1.10	.25
C282	AP68	70p red lilac	1.10	.25
C283	AP68	100p dark green	2.00	.40
		Nos. C275-C283 (9)	7.85	2.40

Uprooted Oak Emblem — AP69

1960, Apr. 7   Litho.   *Perf. 13½x13*
Size: 20½x36½mm

C284	AP69	25p yellow brn	1.00	.25
C285	AP69	40p green	1.25	.30
a.		Souv. sheet of 2, #C284-C285, imperf.	45.00	19.00

Size: 20x36mm

C284b	AP69	25p yellow brown	1.00	.40
C285b	AP69	40p green	1.75	.65

World Refugee Year, 7/1/59-6/30/60. No. C285a sold for 150p.

Nos. C284b-C285b appear fuzzy and pale when compared to the bolder, clear-cut printing of Nos. C284-C285. Issue date: July 18.

Nos. C284b-C285b exist with carmine surcharges of "30P.+15P." (on C284b) and "20P.+10P." (on C285b), repeated in Arabic, with ornaments covering original denominations.

Martyrs' Monument — AP70

Martyrs of May 6th: 70p, Statues from Martyrs' monument, vert.

1960, May 6   *Perf. 13x13½, 13½x13*

C286	AP70	20p rose lilac & grn	.80	.25
C287	AP70	40p Prus grn & dk grn	1.00	.30
C288	AP70	70p gray olive & blk	2.00	.50
		Nos. C286-C288 (3)	3.80	1.05

Pres. Chehab and King of Morocco AP71

1960, June 1   *Perf. 13x13½*

C289	AP71	30p choc & dk brn	1.00	.30
C290	AP71	70p blk, dk brn & buff	2.00	.35

Visit of King Mohammed V of Morocco. A souvenir sheet of 2 on white cardboard contains Nos. C289-C290, imperf. Value $72.50.

Child Learning to Walk — AP72

1960, Aug. 16   Litho.   *Perf. 13½x13*

C291	AP72	20p shown	1.00	.25
C292	AP72	60p Mother & child	2.00	.40
		Nos. C291-C292,CB10-CB11 (4)	6.50	1.50

Day of Mother and Child, Mar. 21-22.

Bird, Ribbon of Flags and Map of Beirut — AP73

40p, Cedar & birds. 70p, Globes & cedar, horiz.

Perf. 13½x13, 13x13½
1960, Sept. 20   Unwmk.

C293	AP73	20p multicolored	.50	.25
C294	AP73	40p vio, bl & grn	.75	.25
C295	AP73	70p multicolored	1.00	.25
		Nos. C293-C295 (3)	2.25	.75

Union of Lebanese Emigrants in the World. A souvenir sheet of 3 contains Nos. C293-C295, imperf., printed on cardboard. Sold for 150p. Value $22.50.

Pres. Chehab and Map of Lebanon — AP74

1961, Feb.   Litho.   *Perf. 13½x13*

C296	AP74	5p bl grn & yel grn	.50	.25
C297	AP74	10p brown & bister	.50	.25
C298	AP74	70p vio & rose lilac	1.25	.35

Casino, Maameltein Lebanon AP75

1961   *Perf. 13x13½*

C299	AP75	15p rose claret	.60	.25
C300	AP75	30p greenish blue	1.00	.25
C301	AP75	40p brown	1.25	.25
C302	AP75	200p bis brn & dl bl	5.25	1.40
		Nos. C296-C302 (7)	10.35	3.00

On Nos. C299-C301, the denomination, inscription and trees differ from type AP75.

UN, 15th Anniv. (in 1960) — AP76

20p, UN Emblem & map of Lebanon, vert. 30p, UN Emblem & symbolic building, vert. 50p, UN Headquarters, New York.

1961, May 5   *Perf. 13½x13, 13x13½*

C306	AP76	20p lake & lt blue	.70	.25
C307	AP76	30p green & beige	.85	.25
C308	AP76	50p vio bl & grnoh bl	1.40	.25
a.		Souvenir sheet of 3	9.00	9.00
		Nos. C306-C308 (3)	2.95	.75

No. C308a contains one each of Nos. C306-C308, imperf., against a light blue background showing UN emblem. Sold for 125p.

Pottery Workers AP77

1961, July 11   Litho.   *Perf. 13x13½*

C309	AP77	30p shown	2.75	.25
C310	AP77	70p Weaver	1.60	.25

Issued for Labor Day, 1961.

Fireworks AP78

Water Skiing AP79

70p, Tourists on boat ride through cave.

1961, Aug. 8   *Perf. 13½x13, 13x13½*

C311	AP78	15p lt pur & dk bl	1.50	1.00
C312	AP79	40p blue & pink	2.10	1.25
C313	AP79	70p dull brn & pink	.90	.50
		Nos. C311-C313 (3)	4.50	2.75

Issued to publicize tourist month.

Highway Circle at Dora, Beirut Suburb AP80

1961, Aug.   *Perf. 11½*

C314	AP80	35p yellow green	1.00	.30
C315	AP80	50p orange brown	1.25	.45
C316	AP80	100p gray	1.25	.55
		Nos. C314-C316 (3)	3.50	1.30

Beach at Tyre — AP81

Afka Falls — AP82

1961, Sept.   Litho.   *Perf. 13*

C317	AP81	5p carmine rose	.50	.25
C318	AP81	10p brt violet	.75	.25
C319	AP81	15p bright blue	.80	.25
C320	AP81	20p orange	1.00	.25
C321	AP81	30p brt green	1.25	.25
C322	AP82	40p dp claret	1.00	.25
C323	AP82	50p ultramarine	1.10	.25
C324	AP82	70p yellow green	1.50	.25
C325	AP82	100p dark brown	2.00	.35
		Nos. C317-C325 (9)	9.90	2.35

See Nos. C341-C342.

Entrance to UNESCO Building AP83

"UNESCO" and Cedar — AP84

Design: 50p, UNESCO headquarters, Paris.

1961, Nov. 20   Unwmk.   *Perf. 12*

C326	AP83	20p bl, buff & blk	.65	.25
C327	AP84	30p lt grn, blk & mag	.80	.25
C328	AP83	50p multicolored	1.25	.25
		Nos. C326-C328 (3)	2.70	.75

UNESCO, 15th anniv.

Emir Bechir and Fakhr-el-Din El Maani — AP85

Design: 25p, Cedar emblem.

1961, Dec. 30   Litho.

C329	AP85	25p Cedar emblem	.65	.25
C330	AP85	50p shown	1.00	.30

See note after No. 375.

Scout Types of Regular Issue, 1962

15p, Trefoil & cedar emblem. 20p, Hand making Scout sign. 25p, Lebanese Scout emblem.

1962, Mar. 1   Unwmk.   *Perf. 12*

C331	A70	15p grn, blk & red	.80	.25
C332	A69	20p lil, blk & yel	.95	.25
C333	A70	25p multicolored	1.50	.40
		Nos. C331-C333 (3)	3.25	.80

Arab League Building, Cairo — AP86

1962, Mar. 20   *Perf. 13*

C334	AP86	20p ultra & lt bl	.60	.25
C335	AP86	30p red brn & pink	.75	.25
C336	AP86	50p grn & grnsh bl	1.00	.30
		Nos. C334-C336 (3)	2.35	.80

Arab League Week, Mar. 22-28. See Nos. C372-C375.

Blacksmith AP87

Farm Tractor AP88

Perf. 13½x13, 13x13½
1962, May 1   Litho.

C337	AP87	5p green & lt blue	.50	.25
C338	AP87	10p blue & pink	.50	.25
C339	AP88	25p brt vio & pink	.75	.25
C340	AP88	35p car rose & blue	1.00	.25
		Nos. C337-C340 (4)	2.75	1.00

Issued for Labor Day.

Types of 1961 Redrawn with Large Numerals Similar to Redrawn Regular Issue of 1962

1962   *Perf. 13*

C341	AP81	5p carmine rose	1.10	.25
C342	AP82	40p deep claret	6.25	.40

Hand Reaching for Malaria Eradication Emblem — AP89

Design: 70p, Malaria eradication emblem.

1962, July 2   Litho.   *Perf. 13½x13*

C349	AP89	30p tan & brown	1.00	.25
C350	AP89	70p bluish lil & vio	1.25	.50

WHO drive to eradicate malaria.

Bas-relief of Isis, Kalabsha Temple, Nubia — AP90

1962, Aug. 1   Unwmk.   Perf. 13
C351 AP90 30p yellow green   2.00   .25
C352 AP90 50p slate   4.00   .60
Campaign to save historic monuments in Nubia.

Spade, Heart, Diamond, Club — AP91

1962, Sept.
C353 AP91 25p car rose, blk & red   3.25 1.25
C354 AP91 40p multicolored   4.50 1.25
European Bridge Championship Tournament.

College Student — AP92

1962, Oct. 1   Perf. 12
C355 AP92 45p multicolored   .90   .25
Issued for Students' Day, Oct. 1.

Sword Severing Chain — AP93

1962, Nov. 22   Litho.   Perf. 13
C356 AP93 25p vio, lt bl & red   1.00   .25
C357 AP93 25p bl, lt bl & red   1.00   .25
C358 AP93 25p grn, lt bl & red   1.00   .25
   Nos. C356-C358 (3)   3.00   .75
19th anniversary of independence.

Fruit Type of Regular Issue, 1962

5p, Apricots. 10p, 30p, Plums. 20p, 40p, Apples. 50p, Pears. 70p, Medlar. 100p, Lemons.

1962   Vignette Multicolored
C359 A72 5p orange brown   .50   .25
C360 A72 10p black   .55   .25
C361 A72 20p brown   .60   .25
C362 A72 30p gray   .75   .25
C363 A72 40p dark gray   1.00   .25
C364 A72 50p light brown   1.25   .25
C365 A72 70p gray olive   1.50   .30
C366 A72 100p blue   3.00   .50
   Nos. C359-C366 (8)   9.15 2.00

Harvest — AP94

Design: 15p, 20p, UN Emblem and hand holding Wheat Emblem, horiz.

1963, Mar. 21   Litho.   Perf. 13
C367 AP94 2.50p ultra & yel   .50   .25
C368 AP94 5p gray grn & yel   .50   .25
C369 AP94 7.50p rose lil & yel   .50   .25
C370 AP94 15p rose brn & pale grn   .80   .25
C371 AP94 20p rose & pale grn   1.00   .25
   Nos. C367-C371 (5)   3.30 1.25
FAO "Freedom from Hunger" campaign.

Redrawn Type of 1962, Dated "1963"

Design: Arab League Building, Cairo.

1963, Mar.   Unwmk.   Perf. 12
C372 AP86 5p violet & lt blue   .50   .25
C373 AP86 10p green & lt blue   .50   .25
C374 AP86 15p claret & lt blue   .55   .25
C375 AP86 20p gray & lt blue   .70   .25
   Nos. C372-C375 (4)   2.25 1.00
Issued for Arab League Week.

Blood Transfusion AP95

Design: 35p, 40p, Nurse and infant, vert.

1963, Oct. 5   Unwmk.   Perf. 13
C376 AP95 5p green & red   .50   .25
C377 AP95 20p grnsh bl & red   .55   .25
C378 AP95 35p org, red & blk   .70   .25
C379 AP95 40p purple & red   1.00   .25
   Nos. C376-C379 (4)   2.75 1.00
Centenary of International Red Cross.

Lyre Player and Columns — AP96

1963, Nov. 7   Unwmk.   Perf. 13
C380 AP96 35p lt bl, org & blk   1.50   .30
International Festival at Baalbek.

Lebanon Flag, Rising Sun — AP97

1964, Jan. 8   Litho.
C381 AP97 5p bluish grn, ver & yel   .50   .25
C382 AP97 10p yel grn, ver & yel   .55   .25
C383 AP97 25p ultra, ver & yel   .75   .25
C384 AP97 40p gray, ver & yel   1.10   .35
   Nos. C381-C384 (4)   2.90 1.10
20th anniversary of Independence.

Sports Type of Regular Issue, 1964
1964, Feb. 11   Unwmk.   Perf. 13
C385 A76 15p Tennis   .55   .25
C386 A76 17.50p Swimming, horiz.   .65   .25
C387 A76 30p Skiing, horiz.   1.00   .25
  a.   Souvenir sheet of 3   13.50 10.50
   Nos. C385-C387 (3)   2.20   .60
No. C387a contains three imperf. stamps similar to Nos. C385-C387 with simulated orange brown perforations and green marginal inscription. Sold for 100p.

Anemone AP98

1964, June 9   Unwmk.   Perf. 13
C391 AP98 5p Lily   .50   .25
C392 AP98 10p Ranunculus   .60   .25
C393 AP98 20p shown   .75   .25
C394 AP98 40p Tuberose   1.00   .25
C395 AP98 45p Rhododendron   1.10   .25
C396 AP98 50p Jasmine   1.25   .25
C397 AP98 70p Yellow broom   2.00   .30
   Nos. C391-C397 (7)   7.20 1.50

Girls Jumping Rope AP99

Children's Day: 20p, 40p, Boy on hobby-horse, vert.

1964, Apr. 8
C398 AP99 5p emer, org & red   .50   .25
C399 AP99 10p yel brn, org & red   .55   .25
C400 AP99 20p dp ultra, lt bl & org   .60   .25
C401 AP99 40p lil, lt bl & yel   1.00   .30
   Nos. C398-C401 (4)   2.65 1.05

Flame and UN Emblem — AP100

40p, Flame, UN emblem and broken chain.

1964, May 15   Litho.   Unwmk.
C402 AP100 20p sal, org & brn   .50   .25
C403 AP100 40p lt bl, gray bl & org   .75   .25
15th anniv. (in 1963) of the Universal Declaration of Human Rights.

Arab League Conference — AP101

1964, Apr. 20   Perf. 13x13½
C404 AP101 5p blk & pale sal   1.00   .25
C405 AP101 10p black   1.25   .35
C406 AP101 15p green   1.75   .50
C407 AP101 20p dk brn & pink   2.25   .65
   Nos. C404-C407 (4)   6.25 1.75
Arab League meeting.

Child in Crib — AP102

Beit-ed-Din Palace and Children — AP103

1964, July 20   Perf. 13½x13, 13½
C408 AP102 2.50p multicolored   .50   .25
C409 AP102 5p multicolored   .50   .25
C410 AP102 15p multicolored   .60   .25
C411 AP103 17.50p multicolored   .80   .25
C412 AP103 20p multicolored   .90   .25
C413 AP103 40p multicolored   1.00   .25
   Nos. C408-C413 (6)   4.30 1.50
Ball of the Little White Beds, Beirut, for the benefit of children's hospital beds.

Clasped Hands and Map of Lebanon AP104

1964, Oct. 16   Litho.   Perf. 13½x13
C414 AP104 20p yel grn, yel & gray   .65   .25
C415 AP104 40p slate, yel & gray   1.10   .40
Congress of the Intl. Lebanese Union.

Rocket Leaving Earth — AP105

Battle Scene — AP106

1964, Nov. 24   Unwmk.   Perf. 13½
C416 AP105 5p multicolored   .50   .25
C417 AP105 10p multicolored   .50   .25
C418 AP106 40p sl blue & blk   1.00   .30
C419 AP106 70p dp claret & blk   2.00   .50
   Nos. C416-C419 (4)   4.00 1.30
21st anniversary of independence.

Woman in Costume AP107

Design: 10p, 15p, Man in costume.

1965, Jan. 11   Litho.   Perf. 13½

C420	AP107	10p multicolored	.70	.25
C421	AP107	15p multicolored	.90	.25
C422	AP107	25p green & multi	1.25	.35
C423	AP107	40p brown & multi	1.50	.50
		Nos. C420-C423 (4)	4.35	1.25

International Festival at Baalbek.

Equestrian AP108

25p, Target shooting, vert. 40p, Gymnast on rings.

1965, Jan. 23   Engr.   Perf. 13

C424	AP108	15p shown	.50	.25
C425	AP108	25p multicolored	.60	.25
C426	AP108	40p multicolored	.75	.25
a.		Souvenir sheet of 3, #C424-C426, imperf.	18.00	9.25
		Nos. C424-C426 (3)	1.85	.60

18th Olympic Games, Tokyo, Oct. 10-25, 1964. No. 426a sold for 100p.

Heliconius Cybria AP109

30p, Pericallia matronula. 40p, Red admiral. 45p, Satyrus semele. 70p, Machaon. 85p, Aurore. 100p, Morpho cypris. 200p, Erasmia sanguiflua. 300p, Papilio crassus. 500p, Charaxes ameliae.

1965   Unwmk.   Perf. 13

Size: 36x22mm

C427	AP109	30p multi	2.75	.25
C428	AP109	35p multi	4.00	.35
C429	AP109	40p multi	5.00	.35
C430	AP109	45p multi	5.50	.50
C431	AP109	70p multi	6.75	.75
C432	AP109	85p multi	7.50	.90
C433	AP109	100p multi	11.00	1.00
C434	AP109	200p multi	18.00	1.25
C435	AP109	300p multi	24.50	3.50

Engr. and Litho.

Perf. 12

Size: 35x25mm

C436	AP109	500p lt ultra & blk	50.00	7.00
		Nos. C427-C436 (10)	135.00	15.85

For surcharges see Nos. C654-C656.

Pope Paul VI and Pres. Charles Helou — AP110

1965, June 28   Photo.   Perf. 12

C437	AP110	45p gold & brt vio	5.25	1.00
a.		Souv. sheet of 1, imperf.	52.50	32.50

Visit of Pope Paul VI to Lebanon. No. C437a sold for 50p.

Cedars of Friendship AP111

1965, Oct. 16   Photo.   Perf. 13x12½

C438	AP111	40p multicolored	1.50	.25

Cocoon, Spindle and Silk — AP112

15p, 30p, 40p, 50p, Silk weaver at loom.

1965, Oct. 16   Perf. 12½x13

Design in Buff and Bright Green

C439	AP112	2.50p brown	1.25	.25
C440	AP112	5p dk olive grn	1.25	.25
C441	AP112	7.50p Prus blue	1.25	.25
C442	AP112	15p deep ultra	1.25	.25
C443	AP112	30p deep claret	1.50	.25
C444	AP112	40p brown	2.40	.25
C445	AP112	50p rose brown	3.50	.60
		Nos. C439-C445 (7)	12.40	2.10

Parliament Building AP113

1965, Oct. 26   Perf. 13x12½

C446	AP113	35p red, buff & brn	.80	.25
C447	AP113	40p emer, buff & brn	1.00	.25

Centenary of the Lebanese parliament.

UN Headquarters, NYC, UN Emblem and Lebanese Flags — AP114

1965, Nov. 10   Engr.   Perf. 12

C448	AP114	2.50p dull blue	.50	.25
C449	AP114	10p magenta	.50	.25
C450	AP114	17.50p dull violet	.50	.25
C451	AP114	30p green	.60	.25
C452	AP114	40p brown	.85	.25
		Nos. C448-C452 (5)	2.95	1.25

UN, 20th anniv. A souvenir sheet contains one 40p imperf. stamp in bright rose lilac. Sold for 50p. Value $15.

Playing Card King, Laurel and Cedar — AP115

1965, Nov. 15   Photo.   Perf. 12½x13

C453	AP115	2.50p multicolored	.70	.25
C454	AP115	15p multicolored	1.10	.25
C455	AP115	17.50p multicolored	1.25	.25
C456	AP115	40p multicolored	1.40	.25
		Nos. C453-C456 (4)	4.45	1.00

Intl. Bridge Championships. A souvenir sheet contains two imperf. stamps similar to Nos. C454 and C456. Sold for 75p. Value $22.50.

Dagger in Map of Palestine — AP116

1965, Dec. 12   Perf. 12½x11

C457	AP116	50p multicolored	4.50	.55

Deir Yassin massacre, Apr. 9, 1948.

ITU Emblem, Old and New Communication Equipment and Early Bird Satellite — AP117

1966, Apr. 15   Perf. 13x12½

C458	AP117	2.50p multi	.50	.25
C459	AP117	15p multi	.55	.25
C460	AP117	17.50p multi	.60	.25
C461	AP117	25p multi	1.00	.25
C462	AP117	40p multi	1.25	.25
		Nos. C458-C462 (5)	3.90	1.25

ITU, centenary (in 1965).

Folk Dancers Before Temple of Bacchus — AP118

Designs: 7.50p, 15p, Dancers before Temple of Jupiter, vert. 30p, 40p, Orchestra before Temple of Bacchus.

1966, July 20   Unwmk.   Perf. 12

Gold Frame

C463	AP118	2.50p brn vio, bl & orange	.50	.25
C464	AP118	5p mag, bl & org	.50	.25
C465	AP118	7.50p vio bl, bl & pink	.50	.25
C466	AP118	15p pur, bl & pink	.60	.25
C467	AP118	30p dk grn, org & blue	.65	.25
C468	AP118	40p vio, org & bl	1.10	.25
		Nos. C463-C468 (6)	3.85	1.50

11th International Festival at Baalbek.

Opening of WHO Headquarters, Geneva — AP119

1966, Aug. 25   Engr.   Perf. 12

C469	AP119	7.50p dp yel grn	.50	.25
C470	AP119	17.50p car rose	.60	.25
C471	AP119	25p blue	1.00	.25
		Nos. C469-C471 (3)	2.10	.75

Skier AP120

Designs: 5p, Children on toboggan. 17.50p, Cedar in snow. 25p, Ski lift.

1966, Sept. 15   Photo.   Perf. 12x11½

C472	AP120	2.50p multi	.50	.25
C473	AP120	5p multi	.50	.25
C474	AP120	17.50p multi	.75	.25
C475	AP120	25p multi	1.00	.25
		Nos. C472-C475 (4)	2.75	1.00

International Festival of Cedars.

Sarcophagus of King Ahiram with Early Alphabet — AP121

15p, Phoenician ship. 20p, Map of the Mediterranean Sea showing Phoenician travel routes, and ship. 30p, Phoenician with alphabet tablet.

Litho. & Engr.

1966, Sept. 25   Perf. 12

C476	AP121	10p dl grn, blk & lt brn	.50	.25
C477	AP121	15p rose lil, brn & ocher	.50	.25
C478	AP121	20p tan, dk brn & bl	.60	.25
C479	AP121	30p org, dk brn & yel	1.00	.25
		Nos. C476-C479 (4)	2.60	1.00

Invention of alphabet by Phoenicians.

Child in Bathtub and UNICEF Emblem AP122

5p, Boy in rowboat. 7.50p, Girl skier. 12p, Girl feeding bird. 20p, Boy doing homework. 50p, Children of various races, horiz.

1966, Oct. 10   Photo.   Perf. 11½x12

C480	AP122	2.50p multi	.50	.25
C481	AP122	5p multi	.50	.25
C482	AP122	7.50p multi	.60	.25
C483	AP122	15p multi	.75	.25
C484	AP122	20p multi	1.00	.25
		Nos. C480-C484 (5)	3.35	1.25

Miniature Sheet

Imperf

C485	AP122	50p dl yellow & multi	7.50	3.50

UNICEF; World Children's Day. No. C485 contains one horizontal stamp 43x33mm.

Scenic Type of Regular Issue, 1966

Designs: 10p, Waterfall, Djezzine. 15p, Castle of the Sea, Saida. 20p, Amphitheater, Jubayl (Byblos). 30p, Temple of the Sun, Baalbek. 50p, Beit-ed-Din Palace. 60p, Church of Christ the King, Nahr-el-Kalb. 75p, Abu Bakr Mosque, Tripoli.

1966, Oct. 12   Perf. 12x11½

C486	A82	10p gold & multi	.50	.25
C487	A82	15p gold & multi	.60	.25
C488	A82	20p gold & multi	.75	.25
C489	A82	30p gold & multi	1.00	.25
C490	A82	50p gold & multi	1.75	.25
C491	A82	60p gold & multi	2.00	.25
C492	A82	75p gold & multi	3.00	.25
		Nos. C486-C492 (7)	9.60	1.75

Symbolic Water Cycle — AP123

15p, 20p, Different wave pattern without sun.

1966, Nov. 15   Photo.   Perf. 12½
C493	AP123	5p red, bl & vio bl	.50	.25
C494	AP123	10p org, bl & brn	.50	.25
C495	AP123	15p org, emer & dk brn	.60	.25
C496	AP123	20p org, emer & grnsh blue	.75	.25
		Nos. C493-C496 (4)	2.35	1.00

Hydrological Decade (UNESCO), 1965-74.

Daniel Bliss — AP124

Designs: 30p, Chapel, American University, Beirut. 50p, Daniel Bliss, D.D., and American University, horiz.

1966, Dec. 3
C497	AP124	20p grn, yel & brn	.50	.25
C498	AP124	30p red brn, grn & blue	.60	.25

Souvenir Sheet
Imperf
C499	AP124	50p grn, brn & org brown		2.50 1.00

Cent. of American University, Beirut, founded by the Rev. Daniel Bliss (1823-1916). Nos. C497-C498 are printed each with alternating labels showing University emblem. No. C499 contains one stamp 59x37mm.

Flags of Arab League Members, Hand Signing Scroll — AP125

1967, Aug. 2   Photo.   Perf. 12½x11½
C500	AP125	5p brown & multi	.50	.25
C501	AP125	10p multicolored	.50	.25
C502	AP125	15p black & multi	.55	.25
C503	AP125	20p multicolored	.65	.25
		Nos. C500-C503 (4)	2.20	1.00

Signing of Arab League Pact in 1945.

Veteran's War Memorial Building, San Francisco — AP126

10p, 20p, 30p, Scroll, flags of Lebanon & UN.

1967, Sept. 1   Photo.   Perf. 12x11½
C504	AP126	2.50p blue & multi	.50	.25
C505	AP126	5p multicolored	.50	.25
C506	AP126	7.50p multicolored	.50	.25
C507	AP126	10p blue & multi	.50	.25
C508	AP126	20p multicolored	.60	.25
C509	AP126	30p multicolored	.75	.25
		Nos. C504-C509 (6)	3.35	1.50

San Francisco Pact (UN Charter), 22nd anniv.

Ruins at Baalbek — AP127

Intl. Tourist Year: 10p, Ruins at Anjar. 15p, Bridge over Ibrahim River and ruins. 20p, Boat on underground lake, Jaita cave. 50p, St. George's Bay, Beirut.

1967, Sept. 25   Perf. 12½
C510	AP127	5p multicolored	.50	.25
C511	AP127	10p multicolored	.60	.25
C512	AP127	15p violet & multi	.80	.25
C513	AP127	20p brn & multi	.95	.25
		Nos. C510-C513 (4)	2.85	1.00

Souvenir Sheet
Imperf
C514	AP127	50p multicolored		27.50 20.00

View of Tabarja AP128

Views: 15p, Pigeon Rock and shore, Beirut. 17.50p, Beit-ed-Din Palace. 20p, Ship at Sidon. 25p, Tripoli. 30p, Beach at Byblos. 35p, Ruins, Tyre. 40p, Temple of Bacchus, Baalbek.

1967, Oct.   Perf. 12x11½
C515	AP128	10p multi	.50	.25
C516	AP128	15p multi	1.00	.25
C517	AP128	17.50p multi	1.50	.25
C518	AP128	20p multi	1.50	.25
C519	AP128	25p multi	1.50	.25
C520	AP128	30p multi	2.00	.25
C521	AP128	35p multi	2.50	.25
C522	AP128	40p multi	3.50	.25
		Nos. C515-C522 (8)	14.00	2.00

Intl. Tourist Year; used as a regular airmail issue.

India Day — AP129

1967, Oct. 30   Engr.   Perf. 12
C523	AP129	2.50p orange	.50	.25
C524	AP129	5p magenta	.50	.25
C525	AP129	7.50p brown	.50	.25
C526	AP129	10p blue	.55	.25
C527	AP129	15p green	.60	.25
		Nos. C523-C527 (5)	2.65	1.25

Globe and Arabic Inscription — AP130

Design: 10p, 20p, 30p, UN emblem.

1967, Nov. 25   Engr.   Perf. 12
C528	AP130	2.50p rose	.50	.25
C529	AP130	5p gray blue	.50	.25
C530	AP130	7.50p green	.50	.25
C531	AP130	10p brt carmine	.50	.25
C532	AP130	20p violet blue	.60	.25
C533	AP130	30p dark green	.80	.25
		Nos. C528-C533 (6)	3.40	1.50

Lebanon's admission to the UN. A 100p rose red souvenir sheet in the globe design exists. Value $6.25.

Basking Shark AP131

Fish: 30p, Needlefish. 40p, Pollack. 50p, Cuckoo wrasse. 70p, Red mullet. 100p, Rainbow trout.

1968, Feb.   Photo.   Perf. 12x11½
C534	AP131	20p multi	1.90	.25
C535	AP131	30p multi	1.90	.25
C536	AP131	40p multi	2.75	.25
C537	AP131	50p multi	4.00	.25
C538	AP131	70p multi	7.00	.25
C539	AP131	100p multi	9.00	.25
		Nos. C534-C539 (6)	26.55	1.50

Ski Jump — AP132

5p, 7.50p, 10p, Downhill skiers (various). 25p, Congress emblem (skis and cedar).

1968   Perf. 12½x11½
C540	AP132	2.50p multicolored	.50	.25
C541	AP132	5p multicolored	.50	.25
C542	AP132	7.50p multicolored	.50	.25
C543	AP132	10p multicolored	.50	.25
C544	AP132	25p multicolored	.75	.25
		Nos. C540-C544 (5)	2.75	1.25

26th Intl. Ski Congress, Beirut. A 50p imperf. souvenir sheet exists in design of the 25p. Value $7.25.

Emir Fakhr al-Din II — AP133

2.50p, Emira Khaskiah. 10p, Citadel of Sidon, horiz. 15p, Citadel of Chekif & grazing sheep, horiz. 17.50p, Citadel of Beirut & harbor, horiz.

Perf. 11½x12, 12x11½
1968, Feb. 20   Litho.
C546	AP133	2.50p multicolored	.50	.25
C547	AP133	5p multicolored	.50	.25
C548	AP133	10p multicolored	.50	.25
C549	AP133	15p multicolored	.75	.25
C550	AP133	17.50p multicolored	.75	.25
		Nos. C546-C550 (5)	3.00	1.25

In memory of the Emir Fakhr al-Din II. A 50p imperf. souvenir sheet exists showing the Battle of Anjar. Value $11.50.

Roman Bust AP134

Ruins of Tyre: 5p, Colonnade, horiz. 7.50p, Arch, horiz. 10p, Banquet, bas-relief.

Litho. & Engr.
1968, Mar. 20   Perf. 12
C552	AP134	2.50p pink, brn & buff	.50	.25
C553	AP134	5p yel, brn & lt bl	.60	.25
C554	AP134	7.50p lt grnsh bl, brn & yel	.80	.25
C555	AP134	10p sal, brn & lt bl	.95	.25
a.		Souvenir sheet	22.50	17.50
		Nos. C552-C555 (4)	2.85	1.00

No. C555a contains one dark brown and light blue stamp, perf. 10½x11½. Sold for 50p. Exists imperf. Value $22.50.
For surcharge see No. C657.

Emperor Justinian AP135

Design: 15p, 20p, Justinian and map of the Mediterranean, horiz.

Perf. 11½x12, 12x11½
1968, May 10   Photo.
C556	AP135	5p blue & multi	.50	.25
C557	AP135	10p blue & multi	.50	.25
C558	AP135	15p red & multi	.55	.25
C559	AP135	20p blue & multi	.60	.25
		Nos. C556-C559 (4)	2.15	1.00

Beirut, site of one of the greatest law schools in antiquity; Emperor Justinian (483-565), who compiled and preserved the Roman law.

Arab League Emblem AP136

1968, June 6   Photo.   Perf. 12x11½
C560	AP136	5p orange & multi	.50	.25
C561	AP136	10p multicolored	.50	.25
C562	AP136	15p pink & multi	.60	.25
C563	AP136	20p multicolored	.75	.25
		Nos. C560-C563 (4)	2.35	1.00

Issued for Arab League Week.

Cedar and Globe Emblem — AP137

1968, July 10
C564 AP137 2.50p sal pink, brn
& green .50 .25
C565 AP137 5p gray, brn & .55 .25
grn
C566 AP137 7.50p brt bl, brn & .60 .25
grn
C567 AP137 10p yel grn, brn & .75 .25
grn
Nos. C564-C567 (4) 2.40 1.00

3rd Congress of Lebanese World Union.

Temple
of
Jupiter,
Baalbek
AP138

Designs: 10p, Fluted pilasters, cella of
Bacchus Temple. 15p, Corniche, south peristyle of Jupiter Temple, horiz. 20p, Gate,
Bacchus Temple. 25p, Ceiling detail, south
peristyle of Bacchus Temple.

1968, Sept. 25   Photo.   Perf. 12½
C568 AP138 5p gold & multi .50 .25
C569 AP138 10p gold & multi .50 .25
C570 AP138 15p gold & multi .60 .25
C571 AP138 20p gold & multi .76 .26
C572 AP138 25p gold & multi 1.00 .25
Nos. C568-C572 (5) 3.35 1.25

13th Baalbek International Festival.

Broad Jump and Phoenician
Statue — AP139

Designs: 10p, High jump and votive stele,
Phoenician, 6th century B.C. 15p, Fencing
and Olmec jade head, 500-400 B.C. 20p,
Weight lifting and axe in shape of human
head, Vera Cruz region. 25p, Aztec stone calendar and Phoenician ship.

1968, Oct. 19   Photo.   Perf. 12x11½
C573 AP139 5p lt ultra, yel &
gray .50 .25
C574 AP139 10p mag, lt ultra &
blk .50 .25
C575 AP139 15p cit, ocher & brn .50 .25
C576 AP139 20p dp org, brn &
ocher .60 .25
C577 AP139 25p light brown 1.00 .25
Nos. C573-C577 (5) 3.10 1.25

19th Olympic Games, Mexico City, 10/12-27.

Human Rights
Flame and
Tractor
AP140

Human Rights Flame and: 15p, People.
25p, Boys of 3 races placing hands on globe.

1968, Dec. 10   Litho.   Perf. 11½
C578 AP140 10p multicolored .50 .25
C579 AP140 15p yellow & multi .60 .25
C580 AP140 25p lilac & multi 1.00 .25
Nos. C578-C580 (3) 2.10 .75

International Human Rights Year.

Minshiya Stairs,
Deir El-Kamar
AP141

Views in Deir El-Kamar: 15p, The Seraglio
Kiosk. 25p, Old paved city road.

1968, Dec. 26
C581 AP141 10p multicolored .50 .25
C582 AP141 15p multicolored .60 .25
C583 AP141 25p multicolored .80 .25
Nos. C581-C583 (3) 1.90 .75

1st Municipal Council in Lebanon, established in Deir El-Kamar by Daoud Pasha, cent.

Nurse Treating Child, and UN
Emblem — AP142

Designs: 10p, Grain, fish, grapes and jug.
15p, Mother and children. 20p, Reading girl
and Phoenician alphabet. 25p, Playing
children.

1969, Jan. 20   Litho.   Perf. 12
C584 AP142 5p blk, lt bl & se-
pia .50 .25
C585 AP142 10p blk, brt yel &
grn .50 .25
C586 AP142 15p blk, red lil & ver .50 .25
C587 AP142 20p blk, citron & bl .50 .25
C588 AP142 25p blk, pink & bis
brn .70 .25
Nos. C584-C588 (5) 2.70 1.25

UNICEF, 22nd anniversary.

Silver Coin from Byblos, 5th Century
B.C. — AP143

National Museum, Beirut: 5p, Gold dagger,
Byblos, 18th cent. B.C. 7.50p, King Dining in
the Land of the Dead, sarcophagus of Ahiram,
13-12th cent. B.C. 30p, Breastplate with car-
touche of Amenemhat III (1849-1801 B.C.).
40p, Phoenician bird vase from Khalde, 8th
cent. B.C.

Photogravure; Gold Impressed
Perf. 12
C589 AP143 2.50p grn, yel & lt bl .50 .25
C590 AP143 5p vio, brn & yel .60 .25
C591 AP143 7.50p dl yel, brn &
pink .80 .25
C592 AP143 30p blue & multi 1.00 .25
C593 AP143 40p multicolored 1.10 .25
Nos. C589-C593 (5) 4.00 1.25

Intl. Congress of Museum Councils; 20th
anniv. of the Intl. Council of Museums.

Water Skier
AP144

Designs: 5p, Water ballet. 7.50p, Parachutist, vert. 30p, Yachting, vert. 40p, Regatta.

1969, Mar. 3   Litho.   Perf. 11½
C594 AP144 2.50p multicolored .50 .25
C595 AP144 5p multicolored .50 .25
C596 AP144 7.50p multicolored .50 .25
C597 AP144 30p multicolored 1.00 .25
C598 AP144 40p multicolored 1.25 .25
Nos. C594-C598 (5) 3.75 1.25

Tomb of Unknown Soldier at Military
School — AP145

2.50p, Frontier guard. 7.50p, Soldiers doing
forestry work. 15p, Army engineers building
road. 30p, Ambulance and helicopter. 40p, Ski
patrol.

1969, Aug. 1   Litho.   Perf. 12x11½
C599 AP145 2.50p multicolored .50 .25
C600 AP145 5p multicolored .50 .25
C601 AP145 7.50p multicolored .50 .25
C602 AP145 15p multicolored .50 .25
C603 AP145 30p multicolored .60 .25
C604 AP145 40p multicolored .75 .25
Nos. C599-C604 (6) 3.35 1.50

25th anniversary of independence.

Crosses and
Circles
AP146

1971, Jan. 6   Photo.   Perf. 11½x12
C605 AP146 15p shown .50 .25
C606 AP146 85p Crosses, cedar 1.75 .45

Lebanese Red Cross, 25th anniversary.

Foil
Fencing
AP147

10p, Flags of participating Arab countries.
15p, Flags of participating non-Arab countries.
40p, Sword fencing. 50p, Saber fencing.

1971, Jan. 15   Litho.   Perf. 12
C607 AP147 10p yellow & multi .50 .25
C608 AP147 15p yellow & multi .50 .25
C609 AP147 35p yellow & multi .60 .25
C610 AP147 40p yellow & multi .80 .25
C611 AP147 50p yellow & multi .95 .25
Nos. C607-C611 (5) 3.35 1.25

10th World Fencing Championships, held in
Lebanon.

Agricultural Workers, Arab Painting,
12th Century — AP148

1971, Feb. 1
C612 AP148 10p silver & multi 1.00 .25
C613 AP148 40p gold & multi 1.75 .25

International Labor Organization.

UPU Building and Monument,
Bern — AP149

1971, Feb. 15   Litho.   Perf. 12
C614 AP149 15p yel, blk & dp
org 1.00 .25
C615 AP149 35p dp org, yel &
blk 1.75 .35

Opening of new UPU Headquarters in Bern,
Switzerland.

Ravens
Burning
Owls — AP150

Children's Day: 85p, Jackal and lion.
Designs of the 15p and 85p are after 13th-
14th century paintings, illustrations for the
"Kalila wa Dumna."

1971, Mar. 1   Photo.   Perf. 11
Size: 30x30mm
C616 AP150 15p gold & multi .25 .25
Perf. 12x11½
Size: 38½x29mm
C617 AP150 85p gold & multi 2.75 .70

Map and
Flag of
Arab
League
AP151

1971, Mar. 20   Perf. 12x11½
C618 AP151 30p orange & multi .55 .25
C619 AP151 70p yellow & multi 1.25 .35

Arab League, 25th anniv.

Bechara
el Khoury
AP152

Famous Lebanese Men: No. C620, Sym-
bolic design for Imam al Ouzai. No. C622,
Hassan Kamel al Sabbah. No. C623, Kahlil
Gibran.

1971, Apr. 10
C620 AP152 25p lt grn, gold &
brn .25 .25
C621 AP152 25p yel, gold & brn .40 .25
C622 AP152 25p yel, gold & brn .40 .25

C623 AP152 25p lt grn, gold &
brn .40 .25
Nos. C620-C623 (4) 1.45 1.00

Education Year
Emblem,
Computer
Card — AP153

1971, Apr. 30 Photo. Perf. 11½x12
C624 AP153 10p blk, vio & bl .35 .25
C625 AP153 40p blk, org & yel .70 .25

Intl. Education Year.

Maameltein Bridge — AP154

5p, Jamhour Substation. 15p, Hotel Management School. 20p, Litani Dam. 25p, Television set wiring. 35p, Temple of Bziza. 40p,
Jounieh Port. 45p, Airport radar. 50p, Flower.
70p, New School of Sciences. 85p, Oranges.
100p, Arbanieh earth satellite station.

1971, May Litho. Perf. 12
C626 AP154 5p multicolored .25 .25
C627 AP154 10p multicolored .25 .25
C628 AP154 15p multicolored .45 .25
C629 AP154 20p multicolored .85 .25
C630 AP154 25p multicolored 1.25 .25
C631 AP154 35p multicolored 1.60 .25
C632 AP154 40p multicolored 1.60 .25
C633 AP154 45p multicolored 1.75 .25
C634 AP154 50p multicolored 2.75 .25
C635 AP154 70p multicolored 4.00 .25
C636 AP154 85p multicolored 5.50 .25
C637 AP154 100p multicolored 7.00 .40
Nos. C626-C637 (12) 27.25 3.15

For overprints and surcharges see Nos.
C771, C775, C779, 533.

Dahr-el-Bacheq
Sanatorium
AP155

1971, June 1
C638 AP155 50p shown 1.25 .25
C639 AP155 100p multi, diff. 1.75 .60

Campaign against tuberculosis.

Solar Wheel
(Festival
Emblem)
AP156

1971, July 1 Photo. Perf. 11
C640 AP156 15p ultra & org .25 .25
C641 AP156 85p Corinthian capi-
tal 1.25 .35

16th Baalbek International Festival.

Mirage
Fighters
Flying
Over
Baalbek
Ruins
AP157

Army Day: 15p, 155mm Cannon. 40p, Army
Headquarters. 70p, Naval patrol boat.

1971, Aug. 1 Perf. 12x11½
C642 AP157 15p gold & multi 3.25 .25
C643 AP157 25p gold & multi 5.75 .25
C644 AP157 40p gold & multi 7.75 .25
C645 AP157 70p gold & multi 13.00 .25
Nos. C642-C645 (4) 29.75 1.00

Wooden
Console, Al
Aqsa Mosque
AP158

1971, Aug. 21 Perf. 12
C646 AP158 15p dk brn & ocher .75 .25
C647 AP158 35p dk brn & ocher 1.25 .25

2nd anniversary of the burning of Al Aqsa
Mosque in Jerusalem.

Lenin (1870-1924) — AP159

1971, Oct. 1 Perf. 12x11½
C648 AP159 30p gold & multi .60 .25
C649 AP159 70p multicolored 1.40 .30

UN
Emblem,
World Map
AP160

1971, Oct. 24 Perf. 13x12½
C650 AP160 15p multicolored .35 .25
C651 AP160 85p multicolored 1.25 .35

UN, 25th anniv. (in 1970).

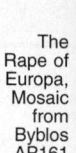

The
Rape of
Europa,
Mosaic
from
Byblos
AP161

1971, Nov 20 Litho. Perf. 12
C652 AP161 10p slate & multi .50 .25
C653 AP161 40p gold & multi 2.50 .25

Publicity for World Lebanese Union (ULM).

Nos. C435-C436 Surcharged

Engr.; Engr. & Litho.
1972, May Perf. 13, 12
C654 AP109 100p on 300p 20.00 .40
C655 AP109 100p on 500p 20.00 .40
C656 AP109 200p on 300p 35.00 .80
Nos. C654-C656 (3) 75.00 1.60

The numerals on No. C655 are taller (5mm)
and bars spaced 1½mm apart.

No. C554 Surcharged

1972, June Litho. & Engr. Perf. 12
C657 AP134 5p on 7.50p multi 3.00 .25

Hibiscus — AP162

1973 Litho. Perf. 12
C658 AP162 2.50p shown .25 .25
C659 AP162 5p Roses .25 .25
C660 AP162 15p Tulips .35 .25
C661 AP162 25p Lilies 1.00 .25
C662 AP162 40p Carnations 1.10 .25
C663 AP162 50p Iris 1.60 .25
C664 AP162 70p Apples 1.25 .25
C665 AP162 75p Grapes 1.40 .25
C666 AP162 100p Peaches 1.90 .25
C667 AP162 200p Pears 6.75 .25
C668 AP162 300p Cherries 7.25 .55
C669 AP162 500p Oranges 12.00 .90
Nos. C658-C669 (12) 35.10 4.05

For overprints see Nos. C758-C759, C763,
C766, C769, C772, C776, C778, C782, C785-
C787.

Lebanese
House
AP163

Designs: Old Lebanese houses.

1973 Perf. 14
C670 AP163 35p yel & multi 2.50 .25
C671 AP163 50p lt bl & multi 3.50 .25
C672 AP163 85p buff & multi 5.75 .30
C673 AP163 100p multicolored 7.75 .40
Nos. C670-C673 (4) 19.50 1.20

For overprints see Nos. C768, C773, C780,
C783.

Woman with
Rose — AP164

Lebanese Costumes: 10p, Man. 20p, Man
on horseback. 25p, Woman playing mandolin.

1973, Sept. 1 Litho. Perf. 14
C674 AP164 5p yellow & multi 1.25 .25
C675 AP164 10p yellow & multi 3.75 .25
C676 AP164 20p yellow & multi 5.75 .25
C677 AP164 25p yellow & multi 8.25 .25
Nos. C674-C677 (4) 19.00 1.00

For overprints see Nos. C760-C761, C764,
C767.

Swimming, Temple at
Baalbek — AP165

Designs: 10p, Running and portal. 15p,
Woman athlete and castle. 20p, Women's volleyball and columns. 25p, Basketball and
aqueduct. 50p, Women's table tennis and
buildings. 75p, Handball and building. 100p,
Soccer and cedar.

1973, Sept. 25 Photo. Perf. 11½x12
C678 AP165 5p multicolored .25 .25
C679 AP165 10p multicolored .25 .25
C680 AP165 15p grn & multi .35 .25
C681 AP165 20p multicolored .35 .25
C682 AP165 25p ultra & multi .50 .25
C683 AP165 50p org & multi 1.25 .30
C684 AP165 75p vio & multi 1.50 .40
C685 AP165 100p multicolored 2.75 .80
 a. Souvenir sheet 3.75 1.75
Nos. C678-C685 (8) 7.20 2.75

5th Pan-Arabic Scholastic Games, Beirut.
No. C685a contains one stamp with simulated
perforations similar to No. C685; gold inscription and denomination.

View of Brasilia — AP166

20p, Old Salvador (Bahia). 25p, Lebanese
sailing ship enroute from the Old World to
South America. 50p, Dom Pedro I & Emir
Fakhr al-Din II.

1973, Nov. 15 Litho. Perf. 12
C686 AP166 5p gold & multi .40 .25
C687 AP166 20p gold & multi 2.25 .35
C688 AP166 25p gold & multi 2.25 .35
C689 AP166 50p gold & multi 4.75 .65
Nos. C686-C689 (4) 9.65 1.60

Sesquicentennial of Brazil's independence.

Inlay
Worker
AP167

1973, Dec. 1
C690 AP167 10p shown .80 .25
C691 AP167 20p Weaver 1.25 .25
C692 AP167 35p Glass blower 2.00 .35
C693 AP167 40p Potter 2.75 .50
C694 AP167 50p Metal worker 3.00 .50
C695 AP167 70p Cutlery mak-
er 5.00 .65
C696 AP167 85p Lace maker 7.00 1.00
C697 AP167 100p Handicraft
Museum 8.00 1.40
Nos. C690-C697 (8) 29.80 4.90

Lebanese handicrafts.
For overprints see Nos. C762, C765, C770,
C774, C777, C781, C784.

Camp Site, Log Fire and Scout
Emblem — AP168

Designs: 5p, Lebanese Scout emblem and
map. 7½p, Lebanese Scout emblem and map
of Middle East. 10p, Lord Baden-Powell, ruins
of Baalbek. 15p, Girl Guide, camp and
emblem. 20p, Lebanese Girl Guide and Scout
emblems. 25p, Scouts around camp fire. 30p,

Symbolic globe with Lebanese flag and Scout emblem. 35p, Flags of participating nations. 50p, Old man, and Scout chopping wood.

1974, Aug. 24   Litho.   Perf. 12

C698	AP168	2.50p multi	.75	.25
C699	AP168	5p multi	.75	.25
C700	AP168	7.50p multi	1.40	.25
C701	AP168	10p multi	1.40	.25
C702	AP168	15p multi	1.75	.55
a.		Vert. strip of 5, #C698-C702	7.00	
C703	AP168	20p multi	2.50	.65
C704	AP168	25p multi	3.50	.65
C705	AP168	30p multi	4.75	.65
C706	AP168	35p multi	5.75	.90
C707	AP168	50p multi	7.00	1.40
a.		Vert. strip of 5, #C703-C707	25.00	
		Nos. C698-C707 (10)	29.55	5.80

11th Arab Boy Scout Jamboree, Smar-Jubeil, Aug. 1974. Nos. C702-C703 are for the 5th Girl Guide Jamboree, Deir-el-Kamar.

Mail Train and Postman Loading Mail, UPU Emblem — AP169

UPU Emblem and: 20p, Postal container hoisted onto ship. 25p, Postal Union Congress Building, Lausanne, and UPU Headquarters, Bern. 50p, Fork-lift truck loading mail on plane.

1974, Nov. 4   Photo.   Perf. 11½x12

C708	AP169	5p multicolored	.45	.25
C709	AP169	20p multicolored	2.00	.25
C710	AP169	25p multicolored	3.00	.25
C711	AP169	50p ultra & multi	6.25	.70
		Nos. C708-C711 (4)	11.70	1.45

Centenary of Universal Postal Union.

Congress Building, Sofar — AP170

Arab Postal Union Emblem and: 20p, View of Sofar. 25p, APU Headquarters, Cairo. 50p, Ministry of Post, Beirut.

1974, Dec. 4   Litho.   Perf. 13x12½

C712	AP170	5p orange & multi	.35	.25
C713	AP170	20p yellow & multi	.60	.25
C714	AP170	25p blue & multi	.90	.25
C715	AP170	50p multicolored	4.25	1.00
		Nos. C712-C715 (4)	6.10	1.75

Arab Postal Union, 25th anniversary.

Mountain Road, by Omar Onsi — AP171

Paintings by Lebanese artists: No. C717, Clouds, by Moustapha Farroukh. No. C718, Woman, by Gebran Kahlil Gebran. No. C719, Embrace, by Cesar Gemayel. No. C720, Self-portrait, by Habib Serour. No. C721, Portrait of a Man, by Daoud Corm.

1974, Dec. 6   Litho.   Perf. 13x12½

C716	AP171	50p lilac & multi	2.00	.50
C717	AP171	50p blue & multi	2.00	.50
C718	AP171	50p green & multi	2.00	.50
C719	AP171	50p lt vio & multi	2.00	.50
C720	AP171	50p brown & multi	2.00	.50
C721	AP171	50p gray brn & multi	2.00	.50
		Nos. C716-C721 (6)	12.00	3.00

Hunter Spearing Lion — AP172

Excavations at Hermel: 10p, Statue of Astarte. 25p, Dogs hunting boar, tiled panel. 35p, Greco-Roman tomb.

1974, Dec. 13

C722	AP172	5p blue & multi	.40	.25
C723	AP172	10p lilac & multi	.90	.25
C724	AP172	25p multicolored	2.25	.25
C725	AP172	35p multicolored	2.75	.40
		Nos. C722-C725 (4)	6.30	1.15

UNESCO Emblems and Globe AP173

1974, Dec. 16   Perf. 12½x13

C726	AP173	5p violet & multi	.40	.25
C727	AP173	10p bister & multi	.85	.25
C728	AP173	25p blue & multi	2.00	.30
C729	AP173	35p multicolored	2.50	.40
		Nos. C726-C729 (4)	5.75	1.20

International Book Year.

Symbolic Stamp under Magnifying Glass — AP174

Designs (Symbolic): 10p, Post horns. 15p, Stamp printing. 20p, Mounted stamp.

1974, Dec. 20   Perf. 13x12½

C730	AP174	5p blue & multi	.25	.25
C731	AP174	10p olive & multi	.40	.25
C732	AP174	15p brown & multi	.80	.25
C733	AP174	20p lilac & multi	1.00	.25
		Nos. C730-C733 (4)	2.45	1.00

Georgina Rizk — AP175

5p, 25p, Georgina Rizk in Lebanese costume.

1974, Dec. 21

C734	AP175	5p multicolored	.25	.25
C735	AP175	20p violet & multi	.55	.25
C736	AP175	25p yellow & multi	.75	.25
C737	AP175	50p blue & multi	1.50	.25
a.		Souvenir sheet of 4	8.00	4.25
		Nos. C734-C737 (4)	3.05	1.00

Georgina Rizk, Miss Universe 1971. No. C737a contains 4 stamps similar to Nos. C734-C737 with simulated perforations.

UNICEF Emblem, Helicopter, Camel, Supplies — AP176

UNICEF Emblem and: 25p, Child welfare clinic. 35p, Kindergarten class. 70p, Girls in chemistry laboratory.

1974, Dec. 28   Litho.   Perf. 12½x13

C738	AP176	20p multicolored	.25	.25
C739	AP176	25p multicolored	.25	.25
C740	AP176	35p blue & multi	.75	.25
C741	AP176	70p blue & multi	1.75	.25
a.		Souvenir sheet of 4	5.75	3.00
		Nos. C738-C741 (4)	3.00	1.00

UNICEF, 25th anniv. No. C741a contains 4 stamps similar to Nos. C738-C741 with simulated perforations. Sold for 200p.

Discus and Olympic Rings — AP177

1974, Dec. 30   Perf. 13x12½

C742	AP177	5p shown	.25	.25
C743	AP177	10p Shot put	.30	.25
C744	AP177	15p Weight lifting	.40	.25
C745	AP177	35p Running	.85	.25
C746	AP177	50p Wrestling	1.25	.25
C747	AP177	85p Javelin	2.00	.35
a.		Souvenir sheet of 6	8.00	5.25
		Nos. C742-C747 (6)	5.05	1.60

20th Olympic Games, Munich, Aug. 26-Sept. 11, 1972. No. C747a contains 6 stamps similar to Nos. C742-C747 with simulated perforations.

Clouds and Environment Emblem AP178

1975

C748	AP178	5p shown	.25	.25
C749	AP178	25p Landscape	.55	.25
C750	AP178	30p Flowers and tree	.55	.25
C751	AP178	40p Waves	.85	.25
a.		Souvenir sheet of 4	7.00	4.75
		Nos. C748-C751 (4)	2.20	1.00

UN Conf. on Human Environment, Stockholm, June 5-16, 1972. No. C751a contains four stamps similar to Nos. C748-C751 with simulated perforations. Sold for 150p.

Archaeology — AP179

Symbols of: 25p, Science & medicine. 35p, Justice & commerce. 70p, Industry & commerce.

1975, Aug.   Litho.   Perf. 12½x13

C752	AP179	20p multicolored	.90	.25
C753	AP179	25p multicolored	1.25	.25
C754	AP179	35p blue & multi	1.75	.40
C755	AP179	70p buff & multi	4.00	.70
		Nos. C752-C755 (4)	7.90	1.60

Beirut, University City.

Stamps of 1971-73 Ovptd. with Various Overall Patterns Including Cedars in Blue, Red, Orange, Lilac, Brown or Green

1978   Litho.   Perf. 12, 14

C758	AP162	2.50p (#C658;B)	.25	.25
C759	AP162	5p (#C659;R)	.25	.25
C760	AP164	5p (#C674;R)	.25	.25
C761	AP164	10p (#C675;B)	.25	.25
C762	AP167	10p (#C690;O)	.25	.25
C763	AP164	15p (#C660;R)	1.00	.25
C764	AP164	20p (#C676;B)	.70	.25
C765	AP167	20p (#C691;B)	.70	.25
C766	AP162	25p (#C661;L)	.70	.25
C767	AP164	25p (#C677;B)	1.40	.25
C768	AP163	35p (#C670;Br)	1.60	.25
C769	AP162	40p (#C662;L)	1.60	.25
C770	AP167	40p (#C693;G)	1.60	.25
C771	AP154	45p (#C633;L)	1.60	.25
C772	AP162	50p (#C663;L)	2.50	.25
C773	AP163	50p (#C671;L)	2.50	.25
C774	AP167	50p (#C694;Rr)	2.50	.25
C775	AP154	70p (#C635;R)	2.75	.55
C776	AP162	70p (#C664;L)	2.75	.55
C777	AP167	70p (#C695;B)	2.75	.55
C778	AP167	75p (#C665;B)	4.50	.55
C779	AP154	85p (#C636;R)	3.25	.60
C780	AP163	85p (#C672;B)	3.25	.60
C781	AP167	85p (#C696;B)	3.25	.60
C782	AP162	100p (#C666;O)	5.00	.80
C783	AP163	100p (#C673;B)	5.00	.80
C784	AP167	100p (#C697;L)	5.00	.80
C785	AP162	200p (#C667;O)	10.00	2.75
C786	AP162	300p (#C668;O)	14.50	5.25
C787	AP162	500p (#C669;O)	21.00	7.50
		Nos. C758-C787 (30)	102.65	26.15

Heart and Arrow — AP180

1978, Apr. 7   Litho.   Perf. 12

C788	AP180	50p blue, blk & red	1.00	.80

World Health Day; drive against hypertension.

Poet Mikhail Naimy and Sannine Mountains — AP181

Designs: 50p, Naimy and view of Al Chakhroub Baskinta. 75p, Naimy portrait in sunburst, vert.

1978, May 17

C789	AP181	25p gold & multi	.90	.25
C790	AP181	50p gold & multi	1.60	.55
C791	AP181	75p gold & multi	2.50	.80
		Nos. C789-C791 (3)	5.00	1.60

Mikhail Naimy Festival.

Army Day Type of 1980

Designs: 50p, Emir Fakhr al-Din statue, vert. 75p, Soldiers and flag.

1980, Dec. 28   Litho.   Perf. 11½

C792	A86	50p multicolored	1.50	.25
C793	A86	75p multicolored	2.00	.40

28th UPU Congress, Rio de Janeiro, 1979 — AP182

1981, Feb. 17 Photo. Perf. 12x11½
C794	AP182	25p multicolored	1.10	.25
C795	AP182	50p multicolored	2.40	.70
C796	AP182	75p multicolored	3.50	1.00
		Nos. C794-C796 (3)	7.00	1.95

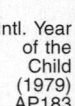

Intl. Year of the Child (1979) AP183

1981, Mar. 25 Litho. Perf. 12x11½
C797	AP183	100p multicolored	4.50	1.40

1974 Chess Championships — AP184

Various chess pieces. Nos. C799-C802 vert.

Perf. 12x11½, 11½x12
			Photo.	
1980-81				
C798	AP184	50p multicolored	1.90	.65
C799	AP184	75p multicolored	2.25	.85
C800	AP184	100p multicolored	2.75	1.25
C801	AP184	150p multicolored	4.50	2.40
C802	AP184	200p multicolored	5.75	3.25
		Nos. C798-C802 (5)	17.15	8.40

Makassed Islamic Institute Centenary (1978) AP185

1981 Photo. Perf. 13½x14
C803	AP185	50p Children	1.00	.25
C804	AP185	75p Institute	1.50	.25
C805	AP185	100p Makassed	1.75	.40
		Nos. C803-C805 (3)	4.25	.90

AIR POST SEMI-POSTAL STAMPS

Nos. C13-C16 Surcharged Like Nos. B1-B12
			Perf. 13½	
1926				
CB1	A2	2pi + 1pi dk brn	15.00	8.00
CB2	A2	3pi + 2pi org brn	15.00	8.00
CB3	A2	5pi + 3pi violet	15.00	8.00
CB4	A3	10pi + 5pi vio brn	15.00	8.00
		Nos. CB1-CB4 (4)	60.00	32.00

These stamps were sold for their combined values, original and surcharged. The latter represented their postal franking value and the former was a contribution to the relief of refugees from the Djebel Druze War.

Catalogue values for unused stamps in this section, from this point to the end of the section, are for Never Hinged items.

Independent Republic

Natural Bridge, Faraya SPAP1

Bay of Jounie SPAP2

Perf. 11½
1947, June 27 Unwmk. Litho.
Cross in Carmine
CB5	SPAP1	12.50 + 25pi brt bl grn	12.50	3.75
CB6	SPAP1	25 + 50pi blue	15.00	4.50
CB7	SPAP2	50 + 100pi choc	17.50	5.25
CB8	SPAP2	75 + 150pi brt pur	35.00	10.00
CB9	SPAP2	100 + 200pi sl	65.00	14.00
		Nos. CB5-CB9 (5)	145.00	37.50

The surtax was for the Red Cross.

Mother & Child Type of Air Post Stamps, 1960
1960, Aug. 16 Perf. 13½x13
CB10	AP72	20p + 10p dk red & buff	1.00	.25
CB11	AP72	60p + 15p bl & lt bl	2.50	.60

Olympic Games Type of Semi-Postal Issue, 1961
1961, Jan. 12 Unwmk. Perf. 13
CB12	SP1	15p + 15p Fencing	4.00	1.60
CB13	SP1	25p + 25p Bicycling	4.00	1.60
CB14	SP1	35p + 35p Swimming	4.00	1.60
		Nos. CB12-CB14 (3)	12.00	4.80

An imperf. souvenir sheet exists, containing one each of Nos. CB12-CB14. Value $32.50.

Nos. CB12-CB14 with Arabic and French Overprint in Green, Red or Maroon

1962, June 2
CB15	SP1	15p + 15p (G)	1.50	.60
CB16	SP1	25p + 25p (M)	2.50	1.25
CB17	SP1	35p + 35p (R)	3.00	1.60
		Nos. CB15-CB17 (3)	7.00	3.45

European Marksmanship Championships held in Lebanon.

POSTAGE DUE STAMPS

Postage Due Stamps of France, 1893-1920, Surcharged like Regular Issue
1924 Unwmk. Perf. 14x13½
J1	D2	50c on 10c choc	6.75	4.25
J2	D2	1p on 20c ol grn	6.75	4.25
J3	D2	2p on 30c red	6.75	4.25
J4	D2	3p on 50c vio brn	6.75	4.25
J5	D2	5p on 1fr red brn, straw	6.75	4.25
		Nos. J1-J5 (5)	33.75	21.25

Gᵈ Liban 2 Piastres

Postage Due Stamps of France, 1893-1920, Surcharged
1924
J6	D2	50c on 10c choc	7.25	4.00
J7	D2	1p on 20c ol grn	7.25	4.00
J8	D2	2p on 30c red	7.25	4.00
J9	D2	3p on 50c vio brn	7.25	4.00
J10	D2	5p on 1fr red brn, straw	7.25	4.00
		Nos. J6-J10 (5)	36.25	20.00

Ancient Bridge across Dog River — D3

Designs: 1p, Village scene. 2p, Pigeon Rocks, near Beirut. 3p, Belfort Castle. 5p, Venus Temple at Baalbek.

1925 Photo. Perf. 13½
J11	D3	50c brown, yellow	.95	.45
J12	D3	1p violet, rose	1.35	.65
J13	D3	2p black, blue	2.25	.90
J14	D3	3p black, red org	3.50	2.00
J15	D3	5p black, bl grn	5.75	3.75
		Nos. J11-J15 (5)	13.80	7.75
		Set, never hinged	42.50	

Nos. J11 to J15 Overprinted

1927
J16	D3	50c brown, yellow	1.50	.40
J17	D3	1p violet, rose	2.50	.85
J18	D3	2p black, blue	3.50	1.25
J19	D3	3p black, red org	7.25	3.00
J20	D3	5p black, bl grn	9.50	4.50
		Nos. J16-J20 (5)	24.25	10.00
		Set, never hinged	35.00	

Nos. J16-J20 with Additional Ovpt.

1928
J21	D3	50c brn, yel (Bk+R)	1.75	1.25
J22	D3	1p vio, rose (Bk)	1.75	1.25
J23	D3	2p blk, bl (Bk+R)	3.00	2.00
J24	D3	3p blk, red org (Bk)	6.00	3.50
J25	D3	5p blk, bl grn (Bk+R)	6.75	4.25
		Nos. J21-J25 (5)	19.25	12.25
		Set, never hinged	65.00	

No. J23 has not the short bars in the upper corners.

Postage Due Stamps of 1925 Overprinted in Red like Nos. J21-J25
1928
J26	D3	50c brn, yel (R)	1.00	.50
J27	D3	2p blk, bl (R)	4.25	3.50
J28	D3	5p blk, bl grn (R)	11.50	7.50
		Nos. J26-J28 (3)	16.75	11.50
		Set, never hinged	32.50	

No. J28 has not the short bars in the upper corners.

Bas-relief of a Ship — D5

D6

D7

D8

Bas-relief from Sarcophagus of King Ahiram — D9

D10

1930-40 Photo.; Engr. (No. J35)
J29	D4	50c black, rose	.75	.50
J30	D5	1p blk, gray bl	1.25	1.00
J31	D6	2p blk, yellow	1.75	1.25
J32	D7	3p blk, bl grn	1.75	1.25
J33	D8	5p blk, orange	7.25	5.50
J34	D9	8p blk, lt rose	5.00	3.50
J35	D8	10p dk green ('40)	7.75	4.50
J36	D10	15p black	6.25	2.75
		Nos. J29-J36 (8)	31.75	20.25
		Set, never hinged	65.00	

Nos. J29-J36 exist imperf.

Catalogue values for unused stamps in this section, from this point to the end of the section, are for Never Hinged items.

Independent Republic

National Museum, Beirut D11

1945 Unwmk. Litho. Perf. 11½
J37	D11	2p brn black, yel	8.25	2.00
J38	D11	5p ultra, rose	10.00	2.50
J39	D11	25p blue, bl green	14.00	4.00
J40	D11	50p dark bl, blue	17.50	6.00
		Nos. J37-J40 (4)	49.75	14.50

D12

1947
J41	D12	5p black, green	6.00	1.25
J42	D12	25p blk, yellow	60.00	3.50
J43	D12	50p black, blue	30.00	6.00
		Nos. J41-J43 (3)	96.00	10.75

Hermel Monument D13

1948

J44	D13	2p blk, *yellow*	4.75	3.75
J45	D13	3p black, *pink*	9.00	3.00
J46	D13	10p black, *blue*	22.50	5.50
		Nos. J44-J46 (3)	36.25	12.25

D14

1950

J47	D14	1p carmine rose	3.50	.25
J48	D14	2p violet blue	13.00	.60
J49	D14	10p gray green	27.50	1.50
		Nos. J47-J49 (3)	44.00	2.35

D15

1952

J50	D15	1p dp rose lilac	.75	.25
J51	D15	2p bright violet	.75	.25
J52	D15	3p dk blue green	1.50	.25
J53	D15	5p blue	2.00	.35
J54	D15	10p chocolate	2.75	.55
J55	D15	25p black	20.00	1.25
		Nos. J50-J55 (6)	27.75	2.90

D16

1953

J56	D16	1p carmine rose	.35	.25
J57	D16	2p blue green	.35	.25
J58	D16	3p orange	.35	.25
J59	D16	5p lilac rose	.60	.30
J60	D16	10p brown	.95	.35
J61	D16	15p deep blue	2.00	.75
		Nos. J56-J61 (6)	4.60	2.15

D17

1955　　Unwmk.　　Perf. 13

J62	D17	1p orange brown	.35	.25
J63	D17	2p yellow green	.35	.25
J64	D17	3p blue green	.35	.25
J65	D17	5p carmine lake	.35	.25
J66	D17	10p gray green	.60	.25
J67	D17	15p ultramarine	.70	.30
J68	D17	25p red lilac	1.50	.80
		Nos. J62-J68 (7)	4.20	2.35

Cedar of
Lebanon — D18

1966　　Photo.　　Perf. 11½

J69	D18	1p bright green	.55	.25
J70	D18	5p rose lilac	.55	.25
J71	D18	15p ultramarine	.65	.25
		Nos. J69-J71 (3)	1.75	1.05

Emir Fakhr al-Din
II — D19

1968　　Litho.　　Perf. 11

J72	D19	1p dk & lt gray	.65	.25
J73	D19	2p dk & lt blue grn	.65	.25
J74	D19	3p deep org & yel	.65	.25
J75	D19	5p brt rose lil & pink	.65	.25
J76	D19	10p olive & lemon	.65	.25

J77	D19	15p vio & pale violet	.95	.50
J78	D19	25p brt & lt blue	1.50	1.25
		Nos. J72-J78 (7)	5.70	3.00

POSTAL TAX STAMPS

Fiscal Stamp
Surcharged in
Violet

Wmk. A T 39 Multiple

1945　　　　　　　　Perf. 13½
RA1	R1	5pi on 30c red brn	350.00	1.50

The tax was for the Lebanese Army.

No. RA1
Overprinted in
Black

1948
RA2	R1	5pi on 30c red brn	17.50	1.40

Fiscal Stamps
Surcharged in
Various Colors

RA3	R1	5pi on 15pi dk vio bl (П)	15.00	1.60
a.		Brown surcharge	18.00	2.25
RA4	R1	5pi on 25c dk blue green (R)	15.00	1.60
RA5	R1	5pi on 30c red brn (Bl)	17.50	1.60
RA6	R1	5pi on 60c lt ultra (Br)	24.00	1.60
RA7	R1	5pi on 3pi salmon rose (Ult)	15.00	1.60

No RA4 exists with watermarks "AT37" or
"AT38."

Same With
Additional Overprint

RA8	R1	5pi on 10pi red	70.00	5.00

Fiscal Stamp
Surcharged Like
Nos. RA3-RA7 with
Top Arabic
Characters
Replaced by

RA9	R1	5pi on 3pi rose (Bk+V)	18.00	1.40

Fiscal Stamp
Surcharged in
Black and Violet

RA10	R1	5pi on 3pi sal rose	200.00	15.00

The tax was to aid the war in Palestine.

> **Catalogue values for unused
> stamps in this section, from this
> point to the end of the section, are
> for Never Hinged items.**

Family among
Ruins — R2

1956　　Unwmk.　　Litho.　　Perf. 13
RA11	R2	2.50pi brown	5.00	.25

The tax was for earthquake victims. These
stamps were obligatory on all inland mail and
all mail going to Arab countries.

Building a
House — R3

1957-58　　　　　　Perf. 13½x13
RA12	R3	2.50p brown	4.25	.25
RA13	R3	2.50p dk blue grn ('58)	2.50	.25

Type of 1957 Redrawn

1959
RA14	R3	2.50p light brown	2.75	.25

On No. RA14 the denomination is on top
and the Arabic lines are at the bottom of
design.

R4

1961　　Unwmk.　　Perf. 13½x13
RA15	R4	2.50p yellow brown	2.50	.25

Building a
House — R5

1962　　　　　　Perf. 13½x14
RA16	R5	2.50p blue green	4.00	.25

The tax was for the relief of earthquake
victims.

LEEWARD ISLANDS

ˈlē-wərd ˈī-lənds

LOCATION — A group of islands in the
West Indies, southeast of Puerto
Rico
GOVT. — British Colony
AREA — 423 sq. mi.
POP. — 108,847 (1946)
CAPITAL — St. John

While stamps inscribed "Leeward
Islands" were in use, 1890-1956, the
colony consisted of the presidencies
(now colonies) of Antigua, Montserrat,

St. Christopher (St. Kitts) with Nevis
and Anguilla, the British Virgin Islands
and Dominica (which became a separate colony in 1940).

Each presidency issued its own
stamps, using them along with the Leeward Islands general issues. The Leeward Islands federation was abolished
in 1956.

　12 Pence = 1 Shilling
　20 Shillings = 1 Pound
　100 Cents = 1 Dollar

> **Catalogue values for unused
> stamps in this country are for
> Never Hinged items, beginning
> with Scott 116.**

Queen Victoria — A1

1890　　Typo.　　Wmk. 2　　Perf. 14
1	A1	½p lilac & green	3.75	1.40
2	A1	1p lilac & car	8.00	.25
3	A1	2½p lilac & ultra	8.50	.30
4	A1	4p lilac & org	10.00	9.50
5	A1	6p lilac & brown	12.50	14.00
6	A1	7p lilac & slate	11.00	18.50
7	A1	1sh green & car	24.00	55.00
8	A1	5sh green & ultra	140.00	300.00
		Nos. 1-8 (8)	217.75	398.95

Denomination of Nos. 7-8 are in color on
plain tablet: "ONE SHILLING" or "FIVE
SHILLINGS."

For overprints and surcharges see Nos. 9-
19.

Jubilee Issue

Regular Issue of 1890
Handstamp Overprinted

1897, July 22
9	A1	½p lilac & green	7.75	24.00
10	A1	1p lilac & car	8.75	24.00
11	A1	2½p lilac & ultra	9.25	24.00
12	A1	4p lilac & org	55.00	80.00
13	A1	6p lilac & brown	60.00	130.00
14	A1	7p lilac & slate	60.00	130.00
15	A1	1sh green & car	130.00	275.00
16	A1	5sh green & ultra	525.00	850.00
		Nos. 9-16 (8)	855.75	1,537.

Double Overprints
9a	A1	½p		1,400.
b.		Triple overprint		9,000.
10a	A1	1p		1,150.
b.		Triple overprint		5,750.
11a	A1	2½p		1,350.
12a	A1	4p		1,350.
13a	A1	6p	1,700.	4,500.
14a	A1	7p	1,700.	2,100.
15a	A1	1sh		2,250.
16a	A1	5sh		6,000.

60th year of Queen Victoria's reign.
Excellent counterfeits of Nos. 9-16 exist.

Stamps of 1890 Surcharged in
Black or Red

b　　　　　　　c

1902, Aug.
17	A1(b)	1p on 4p lilac & org	6.00	10.00
a.		Tall narrow "O" in "One"	40.00	77.50
18	A1(b)	1p on 6p lilac & brn	8.00	16.50
a.		Tall narrow "O" in "One"	60.00	125.00
19	A1(c)	1p on 7p lilac & sl	6.25	11.00
		Nos. 17-19 (3)	20.25	37.50

King Edward VII — A4

Numerals of ¼p, 2p, 3p and 2sh6p of type A4 are in color on plain tablet. The 1sh and 5sh denominations are expressed as "ONE SHILLING" and "FIVE SHILLINGS" on plain tablet.

1902

20	A4	½p violet & green	6.00	1.10
21	A4	1p vio & car rose	8.75	.25
22	A4	2p violet & bister	3.00	4.50
23	A4	2½p violet & ultra	6.00	2.50
24	A4	3p violet & black	9.50	8.00
25	A4	6p violet & brown	2.75	8.50
26	A4	1sh grn & car rose	9.50	27.50
27	A4	2sh6p green & blk	29.00	80.00
28	A4	5sh green & ultra	65.00	95.00
		Nos. 20-28 (9)	139.50	227.35

1905-11   **Wmk. 3**
Chalky Paper (Ordinary Paper #29, 33)

29	A4	½p vio & grn ('06)	4.00	2.25
a.		Chalky paper ('08)	32.50	20.00
30	A4	1p vio & car rose	10.00	.90
31	A4	2p violet & bis ('08)	12.00	24.00
32	A4	2½p vio & ultra	80.00	50.00
33	A4	3p violet & black	22.50	55.00
a.		Chalky paper ('08)	60.00	95.00
34	A4	3p violet, yel ('10)	3.75	8.00
35	A4	6p vio & brn ('08)	55.00	95.00
36	A4	6p violet & red violet ('11)	9.00	8.25
37	A4	1sh grn & car rose ('08)	47.50	130.00
38	A4	1sh blk, grn ('11)	7.00	22.50
39	A4	2sh6p blk & red, blue ('11)	42.50	55.00
40	A4	5sh grn & red, yel ('11)	47.50	70.00
		Nos. 29-40 (12)	340.75	520.90

1907-11   **Ordinary Paper**

41	A4	¼p brown ('09)	3.00	1.90
42	A4	½p green	4.50	1.40
43	A4	1p red	12.50	.85
a.		1p rose carmine	47.50	3.75
44	A4	2p gray ('11)	4.75	11.00
45	A4	2½p ultramarine	8.00	4.50
		Nos. 41-45 (5)	32.75	19.65

King George V — A5

For description of dies I and II, see "Dies of British Colonial Stamps" in Table of Contents. The ½p, 1p, 2½p and 6p denominations of type A5 show the numeral on horizontally-lined tablet. The 1sh and 5sh denominations are expressed as "ONE SHILLING" and "FIVE SHILLINGS" on plain tablet.

Die I

1912   **Ordinary Paper**

46	A5	¼p brown	1.90	1.10
47	A5	½p green	5.50	2.00
48	A5	1p carmine	5.25	1.10
a.		1p scarlet	12.50	1.10
49	A5	2p gray	4.25	5.75
50	A5	2½p ultramarine	3.50	7.25

1912-22   **Chalky Paper**

51	A5	3p violet, yel	2.75	22.50
52	A5	4p blk & red, yel (Die II) ('22)	7.00	22.50
53	A5	6p vio & red vio	3.75	8.50
54	A5	1sh blk, bl grn, ol back	15.00	8.50
a.		1sh black, green	3.25	8.50
55	A5	2sh vio & ultra, bl (Die II) ('22)	18.00	65.00
56	A5	2sh6p black & red, blue ('14)	20.00	55.00
57	A5	5sh grn & red, yel ('14)	65.00	120.00
a.		5sh green & red, lemon ('15)	50.00	85.00
		Nos. 46-57 (12)	151.90	319.20

1913, Nov.   **Surface-colored Paper**

58	A5	3p violet, yel	95.00	180.00
59	A5	1sh black, green	90.00	40.00
60	A5	5sh green & red, yel	55.00	90.00
		Nos. 58-60 (3)	240.00	310.00

King George V — A6

Die II

1921-32   **Wmk. 4**   **Ordinary Paper**

61	A5	¼p dk brn ('22)	2.50	1.10
a.		¼p dark brown (I) ('32)	15.50	21.00
62	A5	½p green	1.25	.80
a.		½p green (I) ('32)	27.50	65.00
63	A5	1p carmine	2.50	.60
a.		1p rose red (I) ('32)	45.00	1.00
b.		1p bright scarlet (II) ('29)	15.00	2.50
64	A5	1p dp violet ('22)	2.50	1.10
65	A5	1½p rose red ('26)	7.00	1.50
66	A5	1½p red brn ('29)	1.50	.25
a.		1½p red brown (I) ('32)	4.50	3.00
68	A5	2p gray ('22)	2.75	.85
69	A5	2½p orange ('23)	12.00	60.00
70	A5	2½p ultra ('27)	3.75	1.40
a.		Die I ('32)	7.50	3.75
71	A5	3p ultra ('23)	16.00	32.50
a.		3p deep ultramarine ('25)	65.00	65.00

Chalky Paper

72	A5	3p violet, yel	7.00	6.75
73	A5	4p blk & red, yel ('23)	3.25	22.50
74	A5	5p vio & ol grn ('22)	2.75	4.50
75	A5	6p vio & red vio ('23)	17.50	45.00
a.		Die I ('32)	32.50	95.00
76	A5	1sh blk, emerald ('23)	11.00	8.50
a.		1sh black, green (I) ('32)	60.00	85.00
77	A5	2sh vio & ultra, bl ('22)	22.50	45.00
a.		2sh red purple & blue, blue ('26)	11.00	52.50
78	A5	2sh6p blk & red, bl ('23)	11.00	24.00
79	A5	3sh green & vio	12.50	40.00
80	A5	4sh black & scar	18.00	42.50
81	A5	5sh grn & red, yel	50.00	85.00
82	A6	10sh red & grn, emer ('28)	80.00	140.00

Wmk. 3

83	A6	£1 black & vio, red ('28)	240.00	325.00
		Nos. 61-66,68-83 (22)	527.25	888.85

Common Design Types pictured following the introduction.

Silver Jubilee Issue
Common Design Type
Perf. 11x12

1935, May 6   **Engr.**   **Wmk. 4**

96	CD301	1p car & dk blue	1.75	3.25
97	CD301	1½p blk & ultra	2.75	1.60
98	CD301	2½p ultra & brn	4.75	4.75
99	CD301	1sh brn vio & ind	26.50	40.00
		Nos. 96-99 (4)	35.75	49.60
		Set, never hinged	42.50	

Coronation Issue
Common Design Type

1937, May 12   *Perf. 13½x14*

100	CD302	1p carmine	.50	1.00
101	CD302	1½p brown	.50	1.50
102	CD302	2½p bright ultra	.55	1.50
		Nos. 100-102 (3)	1.55	4.00
		Set, never hinged	3.00	

A7   A8

King George VI

1938-51   **Typo.**   *Perf. 14*

103	A7	¼p brown	.40	1.50
a.		¼p deep brown, chalky paper ('49)	.25	1.75
104	A7	½p green	.75	.75
105	A7	1p carmine	1.25	1.75
a.		1p scarlet ('42)	1.40	12.50
b.		1p red ('48)	3.75	6.75
106	A7	1½p red brown	.80	.50
107	A7	2p gray	2.00	2.25
a.		2p slate gray ('42)	4.00	3.75
108	A7	2½p ultramarine	.60	4.00
a.		2½p bright blue	18.00	1.20
109	A7	3p dl org ('42)	.40	.90
a.		3p brown orange	22.50	2.75

110	A7	6p vio & red vio	6.00	3.50
a.		6p deep dull purple & bright purple	16.00	7.00
b.		6p purple & deep magenta ('47)	9.00	5.50
111	A7	1sh blk, emerald ('42)	3.50	1.50
a.		1sh black, emerald, chalky paper	10.00	5.50
112	A7	2sh vio & ultra, bl	7.75	2.25
a.		2sh reddish purple & blue, blue, chalky paper	17.00	3.00
113	A7	5sh grn & red, yel	21.00	18.00
a.		5sh green & red, yel, chalky paper	30.00	22.50
114	A8	10sh dp ver & dp grn, emer, ordinary paper ('47)	82.50	100.00
a.		10sh dp red & bluish grn, green, chalky paper	125.00	140.00
b.		10sh dull red & pale grn, green, ordinary paper ('44)	475.00	375.00
c.		10sh red & green, green, ordinary paper ('45)	100.00	90.00

Two dies were used for the 1p, differing in thickness of shading line at base of "1."

Wmk. 3   *Perf. 13*

115	A8	£1 blk & vio, scar ('51)	22.50	37.50
a.		£1 black & brown purple, red, perf. 14	225.00	375.00
		Never hinged	375.00	
b.		£1 black & purple, carmine, perf. 14 ('41)	55.00	55.00
		Never hinged	90.00	
c.		£1 black & brown purple, salmon, perf. 14 ('43)	27.50	29.00
		Never hinged	45.00	
d.		Wmkd. sideways (as #115, perf. 13)	4,000.	
		Never hinged	7,000.	
		Nos. 103-115 (13)	149.45	174.40
		Set, never hinged	240.00	

The 3p-£1 were issued on chalky paper in 1938 and on ordinary paper in 1942. Values are for the most common varieties.
Issued: #115, 12/13/51; others, 11/25/38.
See Nos. 120-125.

> **Catalogue values for unused stamps in this section, from this point to the end of the section, are for Never Hinged items.**

Peace Issue
Common Design Type
Perf. 13½x14

1946, Nov. 1   **Wmk. 4**   **Engr.**

116	CD303	1½p brown	.25	.75
117	CD303	3p deep orange	.25	.75

Silver Wedding Issue
Common Design Types

1949, Jan. 2   **Photo.**   *Perf. 14x14½*

118	CD304	2½p bright ultra	.25	.25

Perf. 11½x11
Engr.; Name Typographed

119	CD305	5sh green	6.75	8.00

George VI Type of 1938

1949, July 1   **Typo.**   *Perf. 13½x14*

120	A7	½p gray	2.00	1.50
121	A7	1p green	.55	.25
122	A7	1½p orange & black	1.75	.40
123	A7	2p crimson rose	1.40	1.25
124	A7	2½p black & plum	1.00	.25
125	A7	3p ultramarine	1.00	.25
		Nos. 120-125 (6)	7.70	3.90

UPU Issue
Common Design Types
Engr.; Name Typo. on 3p and 6p

1949, Oct. 10   *Perf. 13½, 11x11½*

126	CD306	2½p slate	.25	2.40
127	CD307	3p indigo	2.00	2.40
128	CD308	6p red lilac	.40	2.40
129	CD309	1sh blue green	.40	2.40
		Nos. 126-129 (4)	3.05	9.60

University Issue
Common Design Types
Perf. 14x14½

1951, Feb. 16   **Engr.**   **Wmk. 4**

130	CD310	3c gray black & org	.35	2.00
131	CD311	12c lilac & rose car	1.00	2.00

Coronation Issue
Common Design Type

1953, June 2   *Perf. 13½x13*

132	CD312	3c dk green & black	1.00	2.25

A9   Queen Elizabeth II — A10

1954, Feb. 22   **Typo.**   *Perf. 14*

133	A9	½c brown	.25	.60
134	A9	1c gray	1.25	1.50
135	A9	2c green	1.75	.25
136	A9	3c orange & blk	2.50	1.50
137	A9	4c rose red	1.75	.25
138	A9	5c blk & claret	2.25	1.50
139	A9	6c orange	2.25	.65
140	A9	8c deep ultra	2.75	.25
141	A9	12c rose vio & mag	2.00	.25
142	A9	24c black & green	2.00	.30
143	A9	48c rose vio & ultra	8.00	4.00
144	A9	60c brown & green	6.00	3.25
145	A9	$1.20 yel grn & rose red	7.00	4.50

Perf. 13

146	A10	$2.40 red & blue grn	12.00	7.75
147	A10	$4.80 black & claret	16.00	11.00
		Nos. 133-147 (15)	67.75	37.55

LESOTHO

lə-'sō-ˌtō

LOCATION — An enclave within the Republic of South Africa
GOVT. — Independent state in British Commonwealth
AREA — 11,720 sq. mi.
POP. — 2,128,950 (1999 est.)
CAPITAL — Maseru

Basutoland, the British Crown Colony, became independent, October 4, 1966, taking the name Lesotho.

100 Cents = 1 Rand
100 Lisente (s) = 1 Maloti (1979)

Catalogue values for all unused stamps in this country are for Never Hinged items.

Watermark

Wmk. 362 — Basotho Hat Multiple

Moshoeshoe I and II — A1

Perf. 12½x13

			Unwmk.	
1966, Oct. 4		**Photo.**		
1	A1	2½c red brn, blk & red	.25	.25
2	A1	5c red brn, blk & brt bl	.25	.25
3	A1	10c red brn, blk & brt green	.25	.25
4	A1	20c red brn, blk & red lilac	.40	.40
		Nos. 1-4 (4)	1.15	1.15

Lesotho's independence, Oct. 4, 1966.

Basutoland Nos. 72-74, 76-82 Overprinted

Perf. 13½

			Wmk. 4	Engr.
1966, Nov. 1				
5	A7	½c dk brown & gray	.25	.25
6	A7	1c dp grn & gray blk	.25	.25
7	A7	2c orange & dp blue	.70	.25
8	A7	3½c dp blue & indigo	.35	.25
9	A7	5c dk grn & org brn	.25	.25
10	A7	10c rose vio & dk ol	.30	.25
11	A7	12½c aqua & brown	5.00	.40
12	A7	25c lil rose & dp ultra	.50	.25
13	A7	50c dp car & black	1.00	.80

Perf. 11½

14	A8	1r dp claret & blk	1.25	3.00
a.		"Lseotho"	80.00	
		Nos. 5-14 (10)	9.85	5.95

Same Overprint on Nos. 87-91 and Type of 1954

			Wmk. 314	Perf. 13½
15	A7	1c green & gray blk	.25	.25
16	A7	2½c car & ol green	.80	.25
17	A7	5c dk grn & org brn	.40	.25
18	A7	12½c aqua & brown	.60	.40
19	A7	50c dp car & black	1.25	.75

Perf. 11½

20	A8	1r dp claret & blk	1.25	1.25
a.		"Lseotho"	50.00	60.00
		Nos. 15-20 (6)	4.55	3.15

UNESCO Emblem, Microscope, Book, Violin and Retort — A2

			Unwmk.	
1966, Dec. 1		**Litho.**	**Perf. 14**	
21	A2	2½c green & ocher	.25	.25
22	A2	5c olive & brt green	.25	.25
23	A2	12½c ver & lt blue	.30	.25
24	A2	25c dull blue & orange	.50	.60
		Nos. 21-24 (4)	1.30	1.35

20th anniv. of UNESCO.

King Moshoeshoe II and Corn — A3

King Moshoeshoe II — A4

Designs: 1c, Bull. 2c, Aloes. 2½c, Basotho hat. 3½c, Merino sheep. 5c, Basotho pony. 10c, Wheat. 12½c, Angora goat. 25c, Maletsunyane Falls. 50c, Diamonds. 1r, Coat of Arms.

Perf. 13½x14½

				Unwmk.
1967, Apr. 1		**Photo.**		
25	A3	½c violet & green	.25	.25
26	A3	1c dk red & brown	.25	.25
27	A3	2c green & yellow	.25	.25
28	A3	2½c yel bister & blk	.25	.25
29	A3	3½c yellow & black	.25	.25
30	A3	5c brt blue & yel bis	.25	.25
31	A3	10c gray & ocher	.35	.25
32	A3	12½c orange & blk	.40	.45
33	A3	25c ultra & blk	.80	.85
34	A3	50c Prus green & blk	5.75	2.00
35	A3	1r gray & multi	1.10	1.75

Perf. 14½x13½

36	A4	2r mag, blk & gold	1.50	2.50
		Nos. 25-36 (12)	11.40	9.30

See Nos. 47-59.

University Buildings and Graduates — A4a

				Perf. 14x14½
1967, Apr. 7				
37	A4a	1c yel, sep & dp blue	.25	.25
38	A4a	2½c blue, sep & dp bl	.25	.25
39	A4a	12½c dl rose, sep & dp bl	.25	.25
40	A4a	25c lt vio, sep & dp bl	.25	.25
		Nos. 37-40 (4)	1.00	1.00

1st conferment of degrees by the Univ. of Botswana, Lesotho and Swaziland at Roma, Lesotho.

Statue of Moshoeshoe I — A5

1st Anniv. of Independence: 12½c, Flag of Lesotho. 25c, Crocodile.

				Perf. 14
1967, Oct. 4		**Photo.**		
41	A5	2½c apple green & black	.25	.25
42	A5	12½c multicolored	.50	.50
43	A5	25c tan, blk & dp green	.90	.90
		Nos. 41-43 (3)	1.65	1.65

Boy Scout and Lord Baden-Powell — A6

1967, Nov. 1		**Unwmk.**	**Perf. 14x14½**	
44	A6	15c lt ol grn, dk grn & brn	.35	.25

60th anniv. of the Boy Scouts.

World Map and WHO Emblem — A7

20th anniv. of WHO: 25c, Nurse and child, arms of Lesotho and WHO emblem.

1968, Apr. 8		**Photo.**	**Perf. 14x14½**	
45	A7	2½c dp bl, car rose & gold	.25	.25
46	A7	25c gold, gray grn & redsh brown	.50	.40

Types of 1967

Design: 3c, Sorghum. Others as before.

			Perf. 13½x14½	
1968-69		**Photo.**	**Wmk. 362**	
47	A3	½c violet & green	.25	.25
48	A3	1c dk red & brown	.25	.25
49	A3	2c green & yellow	.25	.25
50	A3	2½c yel bister & blk	.25	.25
51	A3	3c lt brn, dk brn & green	.25	.25
52	A3	3½c yellow & black	.25	.25
53	A3	5c brt bl & yel bis	.35	.25
54	A3	10c gray & ocher	.70	.60
55	A3	12½c org & blk ('69)	1.10	1.00
56	A3	25c ultra & blk ('69)	2.10	1.60
57	A3	50c Prussian grn & black ('69)	14.00	3.50
58	A3	1r gray & multi	4.00	4.00

Perf. 14½x13½

59	A4	2r magenta, blk & gold ('69)	11.50	15.00
		Nos. 47-59 (13)	35.25	27.45

Hunters, Rock Painting — A8

Rock Paintings: 3½c, Baboons. 5c, Javelin thrower, vert. 10c, Archers. 15c, Cranes, vert. 20c, Eland. 25c, Hunting scene.

			Perf. 14½x14, 14x14½	
1968, Nov. 1		**Photo.**	**Wmk. 362**	
60	A8	3c dk & lt green & brn	.35	.25
61	A8	3½c dk brown & yel	.45	.25
62	A8	5c sepia, yel & red brn	.50	.25
63	A8	10c black, brt rose & org	.65	.30
64	A8	15c olive brn & buff	1.00	.50
65	A8	20c black, yel & lt grn	1.25	.70
66	A8	25c dk brown, yel & org	1.40	1.10
		Nos. 60-66 (7)	5.60	3.35

Protection for Lesotho's rock paintings.

Queen Elizabeth II Hospital — A9

Designs: 10c, Radio Lesotho. 12½c, Leabua Jonathan Airport. 25c, Royal Palace.

			Perf. 14x13½	
1969, Mar. 11		**Litho.**		
67	A9	2½c multicolored	.25	.25
68	A9	10c multicolored	.25	.25
69	A9	12½c multicolored	.25	.25
70	A9	25c multicolored	.25	.25
		Nos. 67-70 (4)	1.00	1.00

Centenary of Maseru, capital of Lesotho.

Mosotho Horseman and Car — A10

Designs: 12½c, Car on mountain pass. 15c, View from Sani Pass and signal flags. 20c, Map of Lesotho and Independence Trophy.

			Perf. 14½x14	
1969, Sept. 26		**Photo.**		
71	A10	2½c brown & multi	.25	.25
72	A10	12½c multicolored	.25	.25
73	A10	15c multicolored	.30	.30
74	A10	20c yellow & multi	.35	.35
		Nos. 71-74 (4)	1.15	1.15

Roof of Africa Auto Rally, Sept. 19-20.

Gryponyx A11

Prehistoric Reptile Footprints, Moyeni: 3c, Dinosaur. 10c, Plateosauravus and Footprints. 15c, Tritylodon. 25c, Massospondylus.

			Perf. 14½x14	
1970, Jan. 5			**Wmk. 362**	
		Size: 60x23mm		
75	A11	3c brown, yel & black	.90	.75
		Perf. 15x14		
		Size: 40x23mm		
76	A11	5c maroon, blk & pink	1.25	.40
77	A11	10c sepia, blk & yel	1.60	.45
78	A11	15c slate grn, blk & yel	2.50	3.00
79	A11	25c gray blue, blk & bl	3.50	3.00
		Nos. 75-79 (5)	9.75	7.60

Moshoeshoe I — A12

Design: 25c, Moshoeshoe I with top hat.

			Perf. 14x13½	
1970, Mar. 11		**Litho.**	**Wmk. 362**	
80	A12	2½c brt grn & car rose	.25	.25
81	A12	25c lt blue & org brn	.25	.25

Cent. of the death of Moshoeshoe I, chief of the Bakoena clan of the Basothos.

UN Headquarters, New York — A13

2½c, UN emblem. 12½c, UN emblem, people. 25c, UN emblem, peace dove.

			Perf. 14½x14	
1970, June 26		**Litho.**		
82	A13	2½c pink, red brn & bl	.25	.25
83	A13	10c blue & multi	.25	.25
84	A13	12½c olive, ver & lt blue	.25	.25
85	A13	25c tan & multi	.25	.25
		Nos. 82-85 (4)	1.00	1.00

25th anniversary of the United Nations.

Basotho Hat Gift Shop, Maseru A14

Tourism: 5c, Trout fishing. 10c, Horseback riding. 12½c, Skiing, Maluti Mountains. 20c, Holiday Inn, Maseru.

1970, Oct. 27   Perf. 14x14½
86	A14	2½c multicolored	.25	.25
87	A14	5c multicolored	.25	.25
88	A14	10c multicolored	.30	.30
89	A14	12½c multicolored	.30	.30
90	A14	20c multicolored	.40	.40
		Nos. 86-90 (5)	1.50	1.50

Corn — A15

Designs: 1c, Bull. 2c, Aloes. 2½c, Basotho hat. 3c, Sorghum. 3½c, Merino sheep. 4c, National flag. 5c, Basotho pony. 10c, Wheat. 12½c, Angora goat. 25c, Maletsunyane Falls. 50c, Diamonds. 1r, Coat of Arms. 2r, Statue of King Moshoeshoe I in Maseru, vert.

1971   Litho.   Wmk. 362   Perf. 14
91	A15	½c lilac & green	.25	.25
92	A15	1c brn red & brn	.25	.25
93	A15	2c yel brn & yel	.25	.25
94	A15	2½c dull yel & blk	.25	.25
95	A15	3c bis, brn & grn	.25	.25
96	A15	3½c yellow & black	.25	.25
97	A15	4c ver & multi	.25	.25
98	A15	5c blue & brown	.25	.25
99	A15	10c gray & ocher	.35	.30
100	A15	12½c orange & brn	.40	.35
101	A15	25c ultra & black	.70	.60
102	A15	50c lt bl grn & blk	6.00	4.00
103	A15	1r gray & multi	2.25	2.00
104	A15	2r ultra & brown	2.25	3.00
a.		Unwmkd. ('80)	1.75	2.00
		Nos. 91-104 (14)	13.95	12.25

Issue dates: 4c, Apr. 1; others, Jan. 4.
For overprints and surcharges see Nos. 132-135, 245, 312.

Lammergeier A16

Birds: 5c, Bald ibis. 10c, Rufous rock jumper. 12½c, Blue korhaan (bustard). 15c, Painted snipe. 20c, Golden-breasted bunting. 25c, Ground woodpecker.

1971, Mar. 1   Perf. 14
105	A16	2½c multicolored	3.00	.25
106	A16	5c multicolored	4.00	2.10
107	A16	10c multicolored	4.00	1.60
108	A16	12½c multicolored	4.50	3.25
109	A16	15c multicolored	5.25	4.25
110	A16	20c multicolored	5.25	4.25
111	A16	25c multicolored	6.25	4.25
		Nos. 105-111 (7)	32.25	19.95

Lionel Collett Dam A17

Designs: 10c, Contour farming. 15c, Earth dams. 25c, Beaver dams.

1971, July 15   Litho.   Wmk. 362
112	A17	4c multicolored	.25	.25
113	A17	10c multicolored	.25	.25
114	A17	15c multicolored	.25	.25
115	A17	25c multicolored	.30	.30
		Nos. 112-115 (4)	1.05	1.05

Soil conservation and erosion control.

Diamond Mining A18

10c, Potter. 15c, Woman weaver at loom. 20c, Construction worker and new buildings.

1971, Oct. 4
116	A18	4c olive & multi	1.10	.40
117	A18	10c ocher & multi	.45	.25
118	A18	15c red & multi	.70	.60
119	A18	20c dk brown & multi	.90	1.40
		Nos. 116-119 (4)	3.15	2.65

Mail Cart, 19th Century A19

Designs: 10c, Postal bus. 15c, Cape of Good Hope No. 17, vert. 20c, Maseru Post Office.

1972, Jan. 3
120	A19	5c pink & black	.25	.25
121	A19	10c lt blue & multi	.25	.25
122	A19	15c gray, black & blue	.30	.25
123	A19	20c yellow & multi	.40	.60
		Nos. 120-123 (4)	1.20	1.35

Centenary of mail service between Maseru and Aliwal North in Cape Colony.

Runner and Olympic Rings — A20

1972, Sept. 1
124	A20	4c shown	.25	.25
125	A20	10c Shot put	.25	.25
126	A20	15c Hurdles	.40	.35
127	A20	25c Broad jump	.60	.60
		Nos. 124-127 (4)	1.50	1.45

20th Olympic Games, Munich, 8/26-9/11.

Adoration of the Shepherds, by Matthias Stomer — A21

1972, Dec. 1   Litho.   Perf. 14
128	A21	4c blue & multi	.25	.25
129	A21	10c red & multi	.25	.25
130	A21	25c emerald & multi	.25	.25
		Nos. 128-130 (3)	.75	.75

Christmas.

WHO Emblem — A22

1973, Apr. 7   Litho.   Perf. 13½
131	A22	20c blue & yellow	.50	.50

WHO, 25th anniversary.

Nos. 94, 97-99 ovptd. "O.A.U. / 10th Anniversary / Freedom in Unity"
1973, May 25   Wmk. 362   Perf. 14
132	A15	2½c dull yellow & black	.25	.25
133	A15	4c vermilion & multi	.25	.25
134	A15	5c blue & brown	.25	.25
135	A15	10c gray & ocher	.25	.25
		Nos. 132-135 (4)	1.00	1.00

Basotho Hat, WFP/FAO Emblem — A23

Designs: 15c, School lunch. 20c, Child drinking milk and cow. 25c, Map of mountain roads and farm workers.

1973, June 1   Perf. 13½
136	A23	4c ultra & multi	.25	.25
137	A23	15c buff & multi	.25	.25
138	A23	20c yellow & multi	.25	.25
139	A23	25c violet & multi	.25	.25
		Nos. 136-139 (4)	1.00	1.00

World Food Program, 10th anniversary.

Christmas Butterfly A24

Designs: Butterflies of Lesotho.

1973, Sept. 3   Perf. 14x14½
140	A24	4c Mountain Beauty	1.25	.25
141	A24	5c shown	1.40	.60
142	A24	10c Painted lady	2.10	.60
143	A24	15c Yellow pansy	3.50	2.10
144	A24	20c Blue pansy	3.50	2.25
145	A24	25c African monarch	4.25	3.00
146	A24	30c Orange tip	4.25	4.25
		Nos. 140-146 (7)	20.25	13.05

Map of Northern Lesotho and Location of Diamond Mines — A25

Designs: 15c, Kimberlite (diamond-bearing) rocks. 20c, Diagram of Kimberlite volcano, vert. 30c, Diamond prospector, vert.

Perf. 13½x14, 14x13½
1973, Oct. 1   Litho.   Wmk. 362
147	A25	10c gray & multi	2.25	.50
148	A25	15c multicolored	2.50	2.25
149	A25	20c multicolored	2.50	2.50
150	A25	30c multicolored	4.25	7.00
		Nos. 147-150 (4)	11.50	12.25

International Kimberlite Conference.

Nurses' Training and Medical Care — A26

Designs: 10c, Classroom, student with microscope. 20c, Farmers with tractor and bullock team and crop instruction. 25c, Potter and engineers with lathe. 30c, Boy scouts and young bricklayers.

1974, Feb. 18   Litho.   Perf. 13½x14
151	A26	4c lt blue & multi	.25	.25
152	A26	10c ocher & multi	.25	.25
153	A26	20c multicolored	.25	.25
154	A26	25c bister & multi	.25	.25
155	A26	30c yellow & multi	.30	.30
		Nos. 151-155 (5)	1.30	1.30

Youth and development.

Open Book and Wreath — A27

Designs: 15c, Flags of Botswana, Lesotho and Swaziland; cap and diploma. 20c, Map of Africa and location of Botswana, Lesotho and Swaziland. 25c, King Moshoeshoe II, Chancellor of UBLS, capping graduate.

1974, Apr. 7   Litho.   Perf. 14
156	A27	10c multicolored	.25	.25
157	A27	15c multicolored	.25	.25
158	A27	20c multicolored	.25	.25
159	A27	25c multicolored	.25	.50
		Nos. 156-159 (4)	1.00	1.25

10th anniversary of the University of Botswana, Lesotho and Swaziland.

Senqunyane River Bridge, Marakabei — A28

5c, Tsoelike River Bridge. 10c, Makhaleng River Bridge. 15c, Seaka Bridge, Orange/Senqu River. 20c, Masianokeng Bridge, Phuthiatsana River. 25c, Mahobong Bridge, Hlotse River.

1974, June 26   Wmk. 362   Perf. 14
160	A28	4c multicolored	.25	.25
161	A28	5c multicolored	.25	.25
162	A28	10c multicolored	.25	.25
163	A28	15c multicolored	.50	.40
164	A28	20c multicolored	.55	.55
165	A28	25c multicolored	.60	.60
		Nos. 160-165 (6)	2.40	2.30

Bridges and rivers of Lesotho.

UPU Emblem A29

1974, Sept. 6   Litho.   Perf. 14x13
166	A29	4c shown	.25	.25
167	A29	10c Map of Lesotho	.25	.25
168	A29	15c GPO, Maseru	.25	.40
169	A29	20c Rural mail delivery	.80	1.00
		Nos. 166-169 (4)	1.55	1.90

Centenary of Universal Postal Union.

Siege of Thaba-Bosiu — A30

King
Moshoeshoe I
A31

5c, King Moshoeshoe II laying wreath at grave of Moshoeshoe I. 20c, Makoanyane, warrior hero.

Perf. 12½x12, 12x12½
1974, Nov. 25
170	A30	4c multicolored	.25	.25
171	A30	5c multicolored	.25	.25
172	A31	10c multicolored	.25	.25
173	A31	20c multicolored	.60	.40
		Nos. 170-173 (4)	1.35	1.15

Sesquicentennial of Thaba-Bosiu becoming the capital of Basutoland and Lesotho.

Mamokhorong — A32

Musical Instruments of the Basotho: 10c, Lesiba. 15c, Setolotolo. 20c, Meropa (drums).

Perf. 14x14½
1975, Jan. 25   **Wmk. 362**
174	A32	4c multicolored	.25	.25
175	A32	10c multicolored	.25	.25
176	A32	15c multicolored	.30	.30
177	A32	20c multicolored	.50	.50
a.		Souvenir sheet of 4, #174-177	1.75	2.00
		Nos. 174-177 (4)	1.30	1.30

View, Sehlabathebe National
Park — A33

5c, Natural arch. 15c, Mountain stream. 20c, Lake and mountains. 25c, Waterfall.

1975, Apr. 8   **Litho.**   **Perf. 14**
178	A33	4c multicolored	.35	.25
179	A33	5c multicolored	.35	.25
180	A33	15c multicolored	.70	.70
181	A33	20c multicolored	.70	.70
182	A33	25c multicolored	.90	.90
		Nos. 178-182 (5)	3.00	2.80

Sehlabathebe National Park.

Moshoeshoe I (1824-1870) A34   Mofumahali Mantsebo Seeiso (1940-1960) A35

Leaders of Lesotho: 4c, Moshoeshoe II. 5c, Letsie I (1870-1891). 6c, Lerotholi (1891-1905). 10c, Letsie II (1905-1913). 15c, Griffith (1913-1939). 20c, Seeiso Griffith Lerotholi (1939-1940).

1975, Sept. 10   **Litho.**   **Wmk. 362**
183	A34	3c dull blue & black	.25	.25
184	A34	4c lilac rose & black	.25	.25
185	A34	5c pink & black	.25	.25
186	A34	6c brown & black	.25	.25

187	A34	10c rose car & black	.25	.25
188	A34	15c orange & black	.25	.25
189	A34	20c olive & black	.25	.30
190	A35	25c lt blue & black	.25	.40
		Nos. 183-190 (8)	2.00	2.20

No. 190 issued for Intl. Women's Year.

Mokhibo, Women's Dance A36

Traditional Dances: 10c, Ndlamo, men's dance. 15c, Raleseli, men and women. 20c, Mohobelo, men's dance.

1975, Dec. 17   **Perf. 14x14½**
191	A36	4c blue & multi	.25	.25
192	A36	10c black & multi	.25	.25
193	A36	15c black & multi	.30	.40
194	A36	20c blue & multi	.40	.70
a.		Souvenir sheet of 4, #191-194	5.00	5.00
		Nos. 191-194 (4)	1.20	1.60

Enrollment in Junior Red Cross — A37

Designs: 10c, First aid team and truck. 15c, Red Cross nurse on horseback in rural area. 25c, Supplies arriving by plane.

1976, Feb. 20   **Litho.**   **Perf. 14**
195	A37	4c red & multi	.55	.40
196	A37	10c red & multi	.80	.60
197	A37	15c red & multi	1.05	1.00
198	A37	25c red & multi	1.60	2.00
		Nos. 195-198 (4)	4.00	4.00

Lesotho Red Cross, 25th anniversary.

Mosotho Horseman — A38

King
Moshoeshoe II
A39

2c, Tapestry (weavers and citation). 4c, Map of Lesotho. 5c, Hand holding Lesotho brown diamond. 10c, Lesotho Bank. 15c, Flags of Lesotho and Organization of African Unity. 25c, Sehlabathebe National Park. 40c, Pottery. 50c, Pre-historic rock painting.

1976, June 2   **Perf. 14**
199	A38	2c multicolored	.25	.25
200	A38	3c multicolored	.25	.25
201	A38	4c multicolored	1.25	.25
202	A38	5c multicolored	.50	.80
203	A38	10c multicolored	.30	.30
204	A38	15c multicolored	1.60	.80
205	A38	25c multicolored	.80	.60
206	A38	40c multicolored	1.00	1.60
207	A38	50c multicolored	2.50	1.90
208	A39	1r multicolored	1.00	2.00
		Nos. 199-208 (10)	9.45	8.75

For surcharges see Nos. 302-311.

Soccer — A40

Olympic Rings and: 10c, Weight lifting. 15c, Boxing. 25c, Discus.

1976, Aug. 9   **Litho.**   **Wmk. 362**
209	A40	4c citron & multi	.25	.25
210	A40	10c lilac & multi	.25	.25
211	A40	15c salmon & multi	.30	.30
212	A40	25c blue & multi	.65	.65
		Nos. 209-212 (4)	1.45	1.45

21st Olympic Games, Montreal, Canada, July 17-Aug. 1.

Rising Sun of Independence
A41

Designs: 10c, Opening gates. 15c, Broken chain. 25c, Plane over Molimo Restaurant.

1976, Oct. 4   **Perf. 14**
213	A41	4c yellow & multi	.25	.25
214	A41	10c pink & multi	.25	.25
215	A41	15c blue & multi	.50	.25
216	A41	25c dull blue & multi	.60	.50
		Nos. 213-216 (4)	1.60	1.25

Lesotho's independence, 10th anniversary.

Telephones, 1876 and 1976 — A42

Designs: 10c, Woman using telephone, and 1895 telephone. 15c, Telephone operators and wall telephone. 25c, A.G. Bell and 1905 telephone.

Perf. 13x13½
1976, Dec. 6   **Wmk. 362**
217	A42	4c multicolored	.25	.25
218	A42	10c multicolored	.30	.30
219	A42	15c multicolored	.40	.40
220	A42	25c multicolored	.60	.60
		Nos. 217-220 (4)	1.55	1.55

Centenary of first telephone call by Alexander Graham Bell, Mar. 10, 1876.

Aloe
Striatula — A43

Aloes and Succulents: 4c, Aloe aristata. 5c, Kniphofia caulescens. 10c, Euphorbia pulvinata. 15c, Aloe saponaria. 20c, Caralluma lutea. 25c, Aloe polyphylla.

1977, Feb. 14   **Litho.**   **Perf. 14**
221	A43	3c multicolored	.30	.25
222	A43	4c multicolored	.35	.25
223	A43	5c multicolored	.40	.25
224	A43	10c multicolored	.55	.25
225	A43	15c multicolored	1.75	.40
226	A43	20c multicolored	1.75	.60
227	A43	25c multicolored	1.90	.80
		Nos. 221-227 (7)	7.00	2.80

Rock
Rabbits
A44

Perf. 14x14½
1977, Apr. 25   **Wmk. 362**
228	A44	4c shown	7.25	.55
229	A44	5c Porcupine	7.25	.75
230	A44	10c Polecat	7.25	.90
231	A44	15c Klipspringers	21.00	3.75
232	A44	25c Baboons	26.00	5.00
		Nos. 228-232 (5)	68.75	10.95

Man with Cane,
Concentric
Circles — A45

Man with Cane: 10c, Surrounded by flames of pain. 15c, Surrounded by chain. 25c, Man and globe.

1977, July 4   **Litho.**   **Perf. 14**
233	A45	4c red & yellow	.25	.25
234	A45	10c dk blue & lt blue	.25	.25
235	A45	15c blue green & yellow	.40	.25
236	A45	25c black & orange	.50	.60
		Nos. 233-236 (4)	1.40	1.35

World Rheumatism Year.

Small-mouthed Yellow-fish — A46

Fresh-water Fish: 10c, Orange River mud fish. 15c, Rainbow trout. 25c, Oreodaimon quathlambae.

1977, Sept. 28   **Wmk. 362**   **Perf. 14**
237	A46	4c multicolored	.45	.25
238	A46	10c multicolored	.85	.25
239	A46	15c multicolored	1.60	.60
240	A46	25c multicolored	1.75	1.25
		Nos. 237-240 (4)	4.65	2.35

White and Black
Equal — A47

Designs: 10c, Black and white jigsaw puzzle. 15c, White and black cogwheels. 25c, Black and white handshake.

1977, Dec. 12   **Litho.**   **Perf. 14**
241	A47	4c lilac rose & black	.25	.25
242	A47	10c brt blue & black	.25	.25
243	A47	15c orange & black	.25	.25
244	A47	25c lt green & black	.30	.30
		Nos. 241-244 (4)	1.05	1.05

Action to Combat Racism Decade.

No. 99
Surcharged

1977, Dec. 7
245	A15	3c on 10c gray & ocher	1.75	1.50

Poppies — A48

Flowers of Lesotho: 3c, Diascia integerrima. 4c, Helichrysum trilineatum. 5c, Zaluzianskya maritima. 10c, Gladioli. 15c, Chironia krebsii. 25c, Wahlenbergia undulata. 40c, Brunsvigia radulosa.

1978, Feb. 13   Litho.   Wmk. 362
246	A48	2c multicolored	.25	.30
247	A48	3c multicolored	.25	.30
248	A48	4c multicolored	.25	.25
249	A48	5c multicolored	.25	.25
250	A48	10c multicolored	.25	.30
251	A48	15c multicolored	.25	.45
252	A48	25c multicolored	.80	1.00
253	A48	40c multicolored	1.40	2.00
		Nos. 246-253 (8)	3.70	4.85

Edward Jenner Vaccinating Child — A49

Global Eradication of Smallpox: 25c, Child's head and WHO emblem.

1978, May 8   Litho.   Perf. 13½x13
254	A49	5c multicolored	.40	.25
255	A49	25c multicolored	1.40	1.50

Tsoloane Falls — A50

Lesotho Waterfalls: 10c, Qiloane Falls. 15c, Tsoelikana Falls. 25c, Maletsunyane Falls.

1978, July 28   Litho.   Perf. 14
256	A50	4c multicolored	.25	.25
257	A50	10c multicolored	.35	.35
258	A50	15c multicolored	.60	.60
259	A50	25c multicolored	.90	.90
		Nos. 256-259 (4)	2.10	2.10

Flyer 1 A51

25c, Orville and Wilbur Wright, Flyer 1.

1978, Oct. 9   Wmk. 362   Perf. 14½
260	A51	5c multicolored	.25	.25
261	A51	25c multicolored	1.00	1.00

75th anniversary of 1st powered flight.

Dragonflies — A52

Insects: 10c, Winged grasshopper. 15c, Wasps. 25c, Praying mantis.

1978, Dec. 18   Litho.   Perf. 14
262	A52	4c multicolored	.25	.25
263	A52	10c multicolored	.30	.30
264	A52	15c multicolored	.45	.45
265	A52	25c multicolored	.75	.75
		Nos. 262-265 (4)	1.75	1.75

Trees — A53

1979, Mar. 26   Litho.   Perf. 14
266	A53	4c Leucosidea Sericea	.25	.25
267	A53	10c Wild olive	.25	.25
268	A53	15c Blinkblaar	.40	.40
269	A53	25c Cape holly	.65	.65
		Nos. 266-269 (4)	1.55	1.55

Reptiles A54

1979, June 4   Wmk. 362   Perf. 14
270	A54	4s Agama Lizard	.25	.25
271	A54	10s Berg adder	.35	.30
272	A54	15s Rock lizard	.50	.40
273	A54	25s Spitting snake	.85	.75
		Nos. 270-273 (4)	1.95	1.75

A55

1979, Oct. 22   Litho.   Perf. 14½
274	A55	4s Basutoland No. 2	.25	.25
275	A55	15s Basutoland No. 72	.35	.35
276	A55	25s Penny Black	.50	.50
		Nos. 274-276 (3)	1.10	1.10

Souvenir Sheet
277	A55	50s Lesotho No. 122	1.00	1.00

Sir Rowland Hill (1795-1879), originator of penny postage.

A56

Children's Games, by Brueghel the Elder, and IYC emblem: 4s, Children Climbing Tree. 10s, Follow the leader. 15s, Three cup montie. 25s, Entire painting.

1979, Dec. 10   Wmk. 362   Perf. 14½
278	A56	4s multicolored	.25	.25
279	A56	10s multicolored	.25	.25
280	A56	15s multicolored	.25	.25
		Nos. 278-280 (3)	.75	.75

Souvenir Sheet
281	A56	25s multicolored	.80	.80

International Year of the Child.

Beer Strainer, Brooms and Mat A57

1980, Feb. 18   Litho.   Perf. 14½
282	A57	4s shown	.25	.25
283	A57	10s Winnowing basket	.25	.25
284	A57	15s Basotho hat	.30	.30
285	A57	25s Grain storage pots	.50	.50
		Nos. 282-285 (4)	1.30	1.30

Qalabane Ambush A58

Gun War Centenary: 4s, Praise poet, text. 5s, Basotho army commander Lerotholi. 15s, Snider and Martini-Henry rifles. 25s, Map of Basutoland showing battle sites.

1980, May 6   Litho.   Perf. 14
286	A58	4s multicolored	.25	.25
287	A58	5s multicolored	.25	.25
288	A58	10s multicolored	.30	.30
289	A58	15s multicolored	.65	.40
290	A58	25s multicolored	.80	.65
		Nos. 286-290 (5)	2.25	1.85

St. Basil's, Moscow, Olympic Torch A59

No. 292, Torch and flags. No. 293, Soccer. No. 294, Running. No. 295, Misha and stadium. No. 296,

1980, Sept. 20   Litho.   Perf. 14½
291	A59	25s shown	.35	.35
292	A59	25s multicolored	.35	.35
293	A59	25s multicolored	.35	.35
294	A59	25s multicolored	.35	.35
295	A59	25s multicolored	.35	.35
a.		Strip of 5, #291-295	2.25	2.25

Souvenir Sheet
296	A59	1.40m multicolored	2.00	2.00

22nd Summer Olympic Games, Moscow, July 19-Aug. 3.

Beer Mug and Man Drinking A60

Prince Philip — A61

Wmk. 362
1980, Oct. 1   Litho.   Perf. 14
297	A60	4s shown	.25	.25
298	A60	10s Beer brewing pot	.25	.25
299	A60	15s Water pot	.25	.25
300	A60	25s Pots and jugs	.30	.25
		Nos. 297-300 (4)	1.05	1.00

Souvenir Sheet
Perf. 14x14½
301		Sheet of 4	1.25	1.25
a.		A61 40s shown	.30	.30
b.		A61 40s Queen Elizabeth	.30	.30
c.		A61 40s Prince Charles	.30	.30
d.		A61 40s Princess Anne	.30	.30

Traditional pottery; 250th birth anniversary of Josiah Wedgewood, potter.

Nos. 104, 199-208 Surcharged
Wmk. 362
1980, Oct. 20   Litho.   Perf. 14
302	A38	2s on 2c multi	.25	.25
303	A38	3s on 3c multi	.25	.25
304	A38	5s on 5c multi	.25	.25
a.		5s on 6s on 5c multi		
305	A38	6s on 4c multi	.25	.25
306	A38	10s on 10c multi	.25	.25
307	A38	25s on 25c multi	.35	.35
308	A38	40s on 40c multi	.55	.55
309	A38	50s on 50c multi	.80	.80
310	A38	75s on 15c multi	2.00	2.00
311	A39	1m on 1r multi	2.40	2.40
312	A15	2m on 2r multi	4.50	4.50
		Nos. 302-312 (11)	11.85	11.85

Numerous surcharge errors exist (double triple, inverted, etc.).

Queen Mother Elizabeth and Prince Charles — A62

Basutoland No. 36, Flags of Lesotho and Britain — A63

1980, Dec. 1   Unwmk.   Perf. 14½
313		Sheet of 9	3.50	3.50
a.		A62 5s shown	.25	.25
b.		A62 10s Portrait	.25	.25
c.		A63 1m shown	1.00	1.00

Queen Mother Elizabeth, 80th birthday. No. 313 contains 3 each Nos. 313a-313c.

St. Agnes' Anglican Church, Teyateyaneng — A63a

Nativity — A64

4s, Lesotho Evangelical Church, Morija. 25s, Our Lady's Victory Cathedral, Maseru. 75s, University Chapel, Roma.

1980, Dec. 8   Perf. 14x14½
314	A63a	4s multicolored	.25	.25
315	A63a	15s shown	.25	.25
316	A63a	25s multicolored	.25	.25
317	A63a	75s multicolored	.25	.25
		Nos. 314-317 (4)	1.00	1.00

Souvenir Sheet
318	A64	1.50m shown	1.00	1.00

Christmas.

LESOTHO

Voyager Satellite and Saturn — A65

1981, Mar. 15   Litho.   Perf. 14
319   Strip of 5   2.75 2.75
  a.   A65 25s Voyager, planet   .45   .40
  b.   A65 25s shown   .45   .40
  c.   A65 25s Voyager, Saturn's rings   .45   .40
  d.   A65 25s Columbia space shuttle   .45   .40
  e.   A65 25s Columbia, diff.   .45   .40

Souvenir Sheet
320   A65 1.40m Saturn   2.25 2.25
Voyager expedition to Saturn and flight of Columbia space shuttle.

Rock Pigeons — A66

1s, Greater kestrel, vert. 3s, Crowned cranes, vert. 5s, Bokmakierie, vert. 6s, Cape robins, vert. 7s, Yellow canary, vert. 10s, Red-billed teal. 25s, Malachite kingfisher, vert. 40s, Malachite sunbirds. 60s, Orange-throated longclaw. 75s, African hoopoe. 1m, Red bishops. 2m, Egyptian goose. 5m, Lilac-breasted rollers.

1981, Apr. 20   Unwmk.   Perf. 14½
321   A66   1s multicolored   .25   .25
322   A66   2s shown   .25   .25
323   A66   3s multicolored   .25   .25
324   A66   5s multicolored   .25   .25
325   A66   6s multicolored   .40   .25
326   A66   7s multicolored   .40   .25
327   A66   10s multicolored   .40   .25
328   A66   25s multicolored   1.00   .60
329   A66   40s multicolored   1.25   1.00
330   A66   60s multicolored   1.60   1.50
331   A66   75s multicolored   2.00   1.75
332   A66   1m multicolored   2.50   2.50
333   A66   2m multicolored   4.75   4.75
334   A66   5m multicolored   9.00   9.00
    Nos. 321-334 (14)   24.30 22.85
For surcharges see Nos. 558A, 561-563, 598A, 599, 600B, 600C.

1981   Perf. 13
321a   A66   1s   1.40   .70
322a   A66   2s   1.60   .70
324a   A66   5s   2.00   .70
327a   A66   10s   2.00   .70
    Nos. 321a-327a (4)   7.00 2.80

1982, June 14   Wmk. 373   Perf. 14½
321b   A66   1s   .25   .40
322b   A66   2s   .25   .40
323a   A66   3s   .35   .40
324b   A66   5s   .35   .45
325a   A66   6s   .35   .25
326a   A66   7s   .35   .25
327b   A66   10s   .35   .25
328a   A66   25s   1.00   .45
329a   A66   40s   1.10   .50
330a   A66   60s   1.50   .90
331a   A66   75s   2.00   .90
332a   A66   1m   2.40   2.75
333a   A66   2m   3.00   4.00
334a   A66   5m   6.00   10.00
    Nos. 321b-334a (14)   19.25 21.90

Common Design Types pictured following the introduction.

Royal Wedding Issue
Common Design Type and

Royal Wedding — A66a

Unwmk.
1981, July 22   Litho.   Perf. 14
335   CD331 25s Bouquet   .25   .25
  a.   Booklet pane of 3 + label   .80
336   CD331 50s Charles   .35   .35
  a.   Booklet pane of 3 + label   1.40
337   CD331 75s Couple   .50   .50
  b.   Booklet pane of 3 + label   1.60
  c.   Bklt. pane of 3, #335-337 + label   1.25
    Nos. 335-337 (3)   1.10 1.10

1981   Litho.   Perf. 14½
337A   A66a 1.50m Couple   1.75 1.75
Nos. 335-337A exist imperf. Value, set $6.75.

Tree Planting A67

1981, Oct. 30   Litho.   Perf. 14½
338   A67   6s Duke of Edinburgh   .25   .25
339   A67   7s shown   .25   .25
340   A67   25s Digging   .25   .25
341   A67   40s Mountain climbing   .45   .45
342   A67   75s Emblem   .80   .80
    Nos. 338-342 (5)   2.00 2.00

Souvenir Sheet
343   A67 1.40m Duke of Edinburgh, diff.   1.90 1.90
Duke of Edinburgh's Awards, 25th anniv. No. 343 contains 1 45x29mm stamp, perf. 13½.

Santa Claus at Globe, by Norman Rockwell A68

The Mystic Nativity, by Botticelli — A69

Christmas: Saturday Evening Post covers by Norman Rockwell.

1981, Oct. 5   Perf. 13½x14
344   A68   6s multicolored   .25   .25
345   A68   10s multicolored   .25   .25
346   A68   15s multicolored   .25   .25
347   A68   20s multicolored   .35   .35
348   A68   25s multicolored   .40   .40
349   A68   60s multicolored   .75   .75
    Nos. 344-349 (6)   2.25 2.25

Souvenir Sheet
350   A69 1.25m multicolored   2.00 2.00

Chacma Baboons A70

Perf. 14x13½, 14½ (20s, 40s, 50s)
1982, Jan. 15   Litho.
351   A70   6s African wild cat   3.00   .45
352   A70   20s shown   4.00   1.10
353   A70   25s Cape eland   5.00   1.60

---

354   A70   40s Porcupine   6.00   2.10
355   A70   50s Oribi   6.25   2.75
    Nos. 351-355 (5)   24.25 8.00

Souvenir Sheet
Perf. 14
356   A70 1.50m Black-backed jackal   10.00 8.00
6s, 25s; 50x37mm. No. 356 contains one stamp 48x31mm.

Scouting Year — A71

1982, Mar. 5   Litho.   Perf. 14x13½
357   A71   6s Bugle call   .25   .25
358   A71   30s Hiking   .50   .50
359   A71   40s Drawing   .70   .70
360   A71   50s Holding flag   .90   .90
361   A71   75s Salute   1.30   1.30
  a.   Booklet pane of 10 + sheet   11.00
    Nos. 357-361 (5)   3.65 3.65

Souvenir Sheet
362   A71 1.50m Baden-Powell   2.40 2.40
No. 361a contains 2 each Nos. 357-361 with gutter and No. 362.
Nos. 357-361 issued in sheets of 8 with gutter.

1982 World Cup Soccer A72

Championships, 1930-1978: a, Uruguay, 1930. b, Italy, 1934. c, France, 1938. d, Brazil, 1950. e, Switzerland, 1954. f, Sweden, 1958. g, Chile, 1962. h, England, 1966. i, Mexico, 1970. j, Germany, 1974. k, Argentina, 1978. l, World Cup.

1982, Apr. 14   Perf. 14½
363   Sheet of 12   4.00 4.00
  a.-l.   A72 15s any single   .25   .25

Souvenir Sheet
364   A72 1.25m Stadium   2.00 2.00
Nos. 363b, 363c, 363f, 363g, 363j, 363k exist se-tenant in sheets of 72.

George Washington's Birth Bicentenary — A73

Paintings: 6s, Portrait. 7s, With children. 10s, Indian Chief's Prophecy. 25s, With troops. 40s, Arriving at New York. 1m, Entry into New York.
1.25m, Crossing Delaware.

1982, June 7
365   A73   6s multicolored   .25   .25
366   A73   7s multicolored   .25   .25
367   A73   10s multicolored   .25   .25
368   A73   25s multicolored   .35   .35
369   A73   40s multicolored   .50   .50
370   A73   1m multicolored   1.10   1.10
    Nos. 365-370 (6)   2.70 2.70

Souvenir Sheet
371   A73 1.25m multicolored   2.00 2.00

Princess Diana Issue
Common Design Type
Wmk. 373
1982, July 1   Litho.   Perf. 14
372   CD333 30s Arms   .75   .75
373   CD333 50s Diana   .75   .75
374   CD333 75s Wedding   1.00   1.00
375   CD333 1m Portrait   1.50   1.50
    Nos. 372-375 (4)   4.00 4.00

Sesotho Bible Centenary A74

1982, Aug. 20   Litho.   Perf. 14½
376   A74   6s Man reading bible   .25   .25
377   A74   15s Angels, bible   .25   .25

Size: 59½x40½mm
378   A74   1m Bible, Maseru Cathedral   .50   .50
    Nos. 376-378 (3)   1.00 1.00
Issued in sheets of 9 (3 each Nos. 376-378).

Birth of Prince William of Wales, June 21 — A75

1982, Sept. 30
379   A75   6s Congratulation   3.25 3.25
380   A75   60s Diana, William   1.75 1.75
Issued in sheets of 6 (No. 379, 5 No. 380).

Christmas — A76

Designs: Scenes from Walt Disney's The Twelve Days of Christmas. Stamps of same denomination se-tenant.

1982, Dec. 1   Litho.   Perf. 11
381   A76   2s multicolored   .25   .25
382   A76   2s multicolored   .25   .25
383   A76   3s multicolored   .25   .25
384   A76   3s multicolored   .25   .25
385   A76   4s multicolored   .25   .25
386   A76   4s multicolored   .25   .25
387   A76   75s multicolored   1.25   2.00
388   A76   75s multicolored   1.25   2.00
    Nos. 381-388 (8)   4.00 5.50

Souvenir Sheet
Perf. 14x13½
389   A76 1.50m multicolored   4.25 4.25

Local Mushrooms — A77

10s, Lepista caffrorum. 30s, Broomexia congregate. 50s, Afroboletus luteolus. 75s, Lentinus tuberregium.

1983, Jan. 11   *Perf. 14½*
390	A77	10s multicolored	.25	.25
391	A77	30s multicolored	.50	.40
a.		Booklet pane of 2, #390, 391	1.05	
392	A77	50s multicolored	.90	.80
393	A77	75s multicolored	1.25	1.10
a.		Booklet pane of 4, #390-393	4.00	
		Nos. 390-393 (4)	2.90	2.55

Commonwealth Day — A78

1983, Mar. 14   **Litho.**   *Perf. 14½*
394	A78	5s Ba-Leseli dance	.25	.25
395	A78	25s Tapestry weaving	.25	.25
396	A78	60s Elizabeth II	.35	.35
397	A78	75s Moshoeshoe II	.40	.40
		Nos. 394-397 (4)	1.25	1.25

Trance Dancers A79

Hunters — A79a

Rock Paintings: 25s, Baboons, Sehonghong Thaba Tseka. 60s, Hunter attacking mountain reedbuck, Makhetha Berera. 75s, Eland, Leribe.

1983, May 20   **Litho.**   *Perf. 14½*
398	A79	6s multicolored	.40	.40
399	A79	25s multicolored	.80	.80
400	A79	60s multicolored	.90	.90
401	A79	75s multicolored	1.00	1.00
		Nos. 398-401 (4)	3.10	3.10

Souvenir Sheet
402		Sheet of 5, #398-401, 402a	3.25	3.25
a.		A79a 10s multicolored	.35	.25

Manned Flight Bicentenary — A80

1983, July 11   **Litho.**   *Perf. 14½*
403	A80	7s Montgolfier, 1783	.25	.25
404	A80	30s Wright brothers	.45	.35
405	A80	60s 1st airmail plane	.85	.75
406	A80	1m Concorde	2.50	2.50
		Nos. 403-406 (4)	4.05	3.85

Souvenir Sheet
407		Sheet of 5	3.25	3.25
a.		A80 6s Dornier 228	.35	.35

No. 407 contains Nos. 403-406, 407a (60x60mm).

Sesquicentennial of French Missionaries' Arrival — A81

6s, Rev. Eugene Casalis, flags. 25s, Morija, 1833. 40s, Baptism of Libe. 75s, Map of Basutoland, 1834.

1983, Sept. 5   **Litho.**   *Perf. 13½x14*
408	A81	6s multicolored	.35	.35
409	A81	25s multicolored	.35	.35
410	A81	40s multicolored	.35	.35
411	A81	75s multicolored	.70	.70
		Nos. 408-411 (4)	1.75	1.75

Christmas — A82

Scenes from Disney's Old Christmas, from Washington Irving's Sketch Book: 2s, Christmas Eve, diff. 3s, Christmas Day. 4s, Christmas Day, diff. 5s, Christmas dinner. 6s, Christmas dinner, diff. 75s, Christmas games. 1m, Christmas dancers.
1.75m, Christmas Eve.

1983, Dec.   **Litho.**   *Perf. 14*
412	A82	1s shown	.25	.25
413	A82	2s multicolored	.25	.25
414	A82	3s multicolored	.25	.25
415	A82	4s multicolored	.25	.25
416	A82	5s multicolored	.25	.25
417	A82	6s multicolored	.25	.25
418	A82	75s multicolored	2.25	2.25
419	A82	1m multicolored	2.50	2.50
		Nos. 412-419 (8)	6.25	6.25

Souvenir Sheet
420	A82	1.75m multicolored	5.00	5.00

African Monarch A83

Butterflies.

1984, Jan. 20   **Litho.**
421	A83	1s shown	.50	.35
422	A83	2s Mountain Beauty	.50	.35
423	A83	3s Orange Tip	.60	.40
424	A83	4s Blue Pansy	.60	.40
425	A83	5s Yellow Pansy	.60	.40
426	A83	6s African Migrant	.60	.40
427	A83	7s African Leopard	.60	.40
428	A83	10s Suffused Acraea	.70	.50
429	A83	15s Painted Lady	1.10	1.10
430	A83	20s Lemon Traveller	1.50	1.25
431	A83	30s Foxy Charaxes	1.75	1.75
432	A83	50s Broad-Bordered Grass Yellow	1.75	1.75
433	A83	60s Meadow White	1.75	1.75
434	A83	75s Queen Purple Tip	1.90	2.00
435	A83	1m Diadem	1.90	2.00
436	A83	5m Christmas Butterfly	3.00	4.50
		Nos. 421-436 (16)	19.35	19.30

For surcharges see Nos. 559-560, 561A, 564-566, 600, 600A, 600D, 617A-617B.

Easter A84

Designs: Nos. 437a-437j, The Ten Commandments. 1.50m, Moses holding tablets.

1984, Mar. 30   **Litho.**   *Perf. 14*
437		Sheet of 10 + 2 labels	6.50	6.50
a.-j.		A84 20s any single	.30	.30

Souvenir Sheet
438	A84	1.50m multicolored	2.00	2.00

No. 438 contains one stamp 45x29mm.

1984 Summer Olympics — A85

1984, May 5   **Litho.**   *Perf. 13½*
439	A85	10s Torch bearer	.25	.25
440	A85	30s Equestrian	.25	.25
441	A85	50s Swimming	.30	.30
442	A85	75s Basketball	.40	.40
443	A85	1m Running	.50	.50
		Nos. 439-443 (5)	1.70	1.70

Souvenir Sheet
444	A85	1.50m Flags, flame, stadium	1.60	1.60

Prehistoric Footprints — A86

1984, July 2   **Litho.**   *Perf. 13½*
445	A86	10s Sauropodomorph	.30	.30
446	A86	30s Lesothosaurus	.90	.90
447	A86	50s Carnivorous dinosaur	1.60	1.60
		Nos. 445-447 (3)	2.80	2.80

Mail Coach Bicentenary and Ausipex '84 — A87

6s, Wells Fargo, 1852. 7s, Basotho mail cart, 1900. 10s, Bath mail coach, 1784. 30s, Cobb coach, 1853. 50s, Exhibition buildings. 1.75m, Penny Black, Basutoland #O4, Western Australia #3.

1984, Sept. 5   **Litho.**   *Perf. 14*
448	A87	6s multicolored	.25	.25
a.		Sheet of 4 #448, 1 #451A	1.00	1.00
449	A87	7s multicolored	.25	.25
a.		Sheet of 4 #449, 1 #451A	1.00	1.00
450	A87	10s multicolored	.25	.25
a.		Sheet of 4 #450, 1 #451A	1.00	1.00
451	A87	30s multicolored	.25	.25
b.		Sheet of 4 #451, 1 #451A	1.00	1.00

Size: 82x26mm
451A	A87	50s multicolored	.45	.45
		Nos. 448-451A (5)	1.45	1.45

Souvenir Sheet
452	A87	1.75m multicolored	3.25	3.25

No. 452 contains one stamp 82x26mm.

Trains — A88

6s, Orient Express, 1900. 15s, 05.001, Class 5, 1935. 30s, Cardean, Caledonian, 1906. 60s, Santa Fe, Super Chief, 1940. 1m, Flying Scotsman, 1934.
2m, The Blue Train, 1972.

1984, Nov. 5   **Litho.**   *Perf. 13½*
453	A88	6s multicolored	.25	.25
454	A88	15s multicolored	.30	.30
455	A88	30s multicolored	.40	.40
456	A88	60s multicolored	.90	1.25
457	A88	1m multicolored	1.75	2.00
		Nos. 453-457 (5)	3.60	4.20

Souvenir Sheet
Perf. 14x13½
458	A88	2m multicolored	2.25	2.25

Indigenous Young Animals — A89

1984, Dec. 20   *Perf. 14½*
459	A89	15s Cape Eland calf	.25	.25
460	A89	20s Chacma baboons	.30	.30
461	A89	30s Oribo calf	.45	.45
462	A89	75s Red rock hares	1.00	1.25

Size: 47x28mm
Perf. 13½
463	A89	1m Black-backed jackals	1.40	1.75
		Nos. 459-463 (5)	3.40	4.00

King Moshoeshoe II — A90

1985, Jan. 30   **Litho.**   *Perf. 15*
464	A90	6s Royal crown, 1974	.25	.25
465	A90	30s Moshoeshoe II, 1966	.25	.25
466	A90	75s In Basotho dress	.45	.45
467	A90	1m In military uniform	.65	.65
		Nos. 464-467 (4)	1.60	1.60

25th anniversary of reign.

Miniature Sheet

Easter — A91

Stations of the Cross: a, Condemned to death. b, Bearing cross. c, Falls the first time. d, Meets his mother. e, Cyrenean helps carry cross. f, Veronica wipes His face. g, Second fall. h, Consoles women of Jerusalem. i, Third fall. j, Stripped. k, Nailed to cross. l, Dies on cross. m, Taken down from cross. n, Laid in sepulchre.
No. 469, The Crucifixion, detail, by Mathias Grunewald (c. 1460-1528).

1985, Mar. 8		**Perf. 11**	
468	Sheet of 14 + label	6.50	6.50
a.-n.	A91 20s any single	.25	.25

Souvenir Sheet
Perf. 14

469	A91 2m multicolored	2.50	2.50

Queen Mother, 85th Birthday — A92

Photographs: 10s, Queen Mother, Princess Elizabeth, 1931. 30s, 75th birthday portrait. 60s With Queen Elizabeth II and Princess Margaret, 80th birthday. No. 473, With Queen Elizabeth II, Princess Diana, Princes Henry and Charles, christening of Prince Henry.
No. 474, like No. 473, with Prince William.

1985, May 30		**Perf. 13½x14**	
470	A92 10s multicolored	.25	.25
471	A92 30s multicolored	1.00	1.00
472	A92 60s multicolored	1.10	1.10
473	A92 2m multicolored	1.90	1.90
	Nos. 470-473 (4)	4.25	4.25

Souvenir Sheet

474	A92 2m multicolored	2.00	2.00

No. 474 contains one stamp 38x51mm.

Automobile Centenary — A93

Luxury cars: 6s, BMW 732i. 10s, Ford LTD Crown Victoria. 30s, Mercedes-Benz 500SE. 90s, Cadillac Eldorado Biarritz. No. 479, Rolls Royce Silver Spirit.
No. 480, 1907 Rolls Royce Silver Ghost Tourer, vert.

1985, June 10		**Perf. 14**	
475	A93 6s multicolored	.35	.25
476	A93 10s multicolored	.50	.25
477	A93 30s multicolored	.80	.60
478	A93 90s multicolored	1.50	1.50
479	A93 2m multicolored	3.00	3.00
	Nos. 475-479 (5)	6.15	5.60

Souvenir Sheet

480	A93 2m multicolored	5.50	5.50

No. 480 contains one stamp 38x51mm.

Audubon Birth Bicentenary — A94

Illustrations of North American bird species by artist and naturalist John J. Audubon.

1985, Aug. 5		**Perf. 14½**	
481	A94 5s Cliff swallow, vert.	.55	.45
482	A94 6s Great crested grebe	.70	.45
483	A94 10s Vesper sparrow	1.25	.60
484	A94 30s Greenshank	1.75	1.75
485	A94 60s Stilt sandpiper	2.25	2.25
486	A94 2m Glossy ibis	3.50	3.50
	Nos. 481-486 (6)	10.00	9.00

Nos. 481-486 printed in sheets of 5 with labels picturing various birds.

Intl. Youth Year, Girl Guides 75th Anniv. — A95

1985, Sept. 26		**Perf. 15**	
487	A95 10s Mountain climbing	.25	.25
488	A95 30s Medical research	.60	.60
489	A95 75s Guides on parade	1.25	1.25
490	A95 2m Guide saluting	2.50	2.50
	Nos. 487-490 (4)	4.60	4.60

Souvenir Sheet

491	A95 2m Lady Baden-Powell, World Chief Guide	3.50	3.50

UN, 40th Anniv. — A96

Designs: 10s, UN No. 1, flag, horiz. 30s, Dish satellite, Ha Sofonia Earth Satellite Station, ITU emblem. 50s, Aircraft, Maseru Airport, ICAO emblem, horiz. 2m, Maimonides (1135-1204), medieval Jewish scholar, WHO emblem.

1985, Oct. 15	**Litho.**	**Perf. 15**	
492	A96 10s multicolored	.30	.30
493	A96 30s multicolored	.55	.55
494	A96 50s multicolored	1.00	1.00
495	A96 2m multicolored	5.00	5.00
	Nos. 492-495 (4)	6.85	6.85

Wildflowers — A97

1985, Nov. 11		**Perf. 11**	
496	A97 6s Cosmos	.45	.25
497	A97 10s Small agapanthus	.60	.25
498	A97 30s Pink witchweed	1.10	.75
499	A97 60s Small iris	1.75	1.75
500	A97 90s Wild geranium	2.25	2.25
501	A97 1m Large spotted orchid	3.00	3.00
	Nos. 496-501 (6)	9.15	8.25

Mark Twain, Author, Jacob and Wilhelm Grimm, Fabulists A98

Disney characters acting out Mark Twain quotes or portraying characters from The Wishing Table, by the Grimm Brothers.

1985, Dec. 2		**Perf. 11**	
502	A98 6s multicolored	.25	.25
503	A98 10s multicolored	.25	.25
504	A98 50s multicolored	1.40	1.40
505	A98 60s multicolored	1.90	1.90
506	A98 75s multicolored	2.25	2.25
507	A98 90s multicolored	2.75	2.75
508	A98 1m multicolored	3.00	3.00
509	A98 1.50m multicolored	5.00	5.00
	Nos. 502-509 (8)	16.80	16.80

Souvenir Sheets
Perf. 14

510	A98 1.25m multicolored	6.00	6.00
511	A98 1.50m multicolored	6.00	6.00

Christmas. Nos. 505, 507 printed in sheets of 8.

World Wildlife Fund — A99

Lammergeier vulture.

1986, Jan. 20		**Perf. 15**	
512	A99 7s Male	2.00	.75
513	A99 15s Male, female	3.75	1.00
514	A99 50s Male in flight	5.50	2.00
515	A99 1m Adult, young	7.00	3.50
	Nos. 512-515 (4)	18.25	7.25

Flora and Fauna — A100

1986, Jan. 20			
516	A100 9s Prickly pear	.50	.25
517	A100 12s Stapelia	.50	.25
518	A100 35s Pig's ears	.75	.50
519	A100 2m Columnar cereus	2.75	2.50
	Nos. 516-519 (4)	4.50	3.50

Souvenir Sheet

520	A100 2m Black eagle	10.00	10.00

1986 World Cup Soccer Championships, Mexico — A101

Various soccer plays.

1986, Mar. 17		**Perf. 14**	
521	A101 35s multicolored	1.25	1.25
522	A101 50s multicolored	1.75	1.75
523	A101 1m multicolored	3.50	3.50
524	A101 2m multicolored	7.00	7.00
	Nos. 521-524 (4)	13.50	13.50

Souvenir Sheet

525	A101 3m multicolored	10.00	10.00

New Currency, 1st Anniv. (in 1980) A101a

No. 525A — Both sides of: b, 1979 Intl. Year of the Child gold coin. c, Five-maloti banknote. d, 1979 50-lisente coin. e, Ten-maloti banknote. f, 1979 1-sente coin.

1986, Apr. 1	**Litho.**	**Perf. 13¾x14**	
525A	Horiz. strip of 5	30.00	32.50
b.-f.	A101a 30s Any single	6.00	6.50

A102

Halley's Comet — A103

Designs: 9s, Hale Telescope, Mt. Palomar, Galileo. 15s, Pioneer Venus 2 probe, 1985 sighting. 70s, 684 sighting illustration, Nuremberg Chronicles. 3m, 1066 sighting, Norman conquest of England. 4m, Comet over Lesotho.

1986, Apr. 5			
526	A102 9s multicolored	.65	.25
527	A102 15s multicolored	.90	.25
528	A102 70s multicolored	2.00	.75
529	A102 3m multicolored	5.50	6.00
	Nos. 526-529 (4)	9.05	7.25

Souvenir Sheet

530	A103 4m multicolored	9.00	9.00

Queen Elizabeth II, 60th Birthday
Common Design Type

Designs: 90s, In pantomime during youth. 1m, At Windsor Horse Show, 1971. 2m, At Royal Festival Hall, 1971. 4m, Age 8.

1986, Apr. 21			
531	CD339 90s lt yel bis & black	.55	.55
532	CD339 1m pale grn & multi	.65	.65
533	CD339 2m dull vio & multi	1.30	1.30
	Nos. 531-533 (3)	2.50	2.50

Souvenir Sheet

534	CD339 4m tan & black	3.00	3.00

For overprints see Nos. 636-639.

Statue of Liberty, Cent. A104

Statue and famous emigrants: 15s, Bela Bartok (1881-1945), composer. 35s, Felix Adler (1857-1933), philosopher. 1m, Victor Herbert (1859-1924), composer. No. 538, David Niven (1910-1983), actor. No. 539, Statue, vert.

1986, May 1

535	A104	15s multicolored	1.00	.25
536	A104	35s multicolored	1.00	.35
537	A104	1m multicolored	3.50	1.75
538	A104	3m multicolored	5.50	3.00
		Nos. 535-538 (4)	11.00	5.35

Souvenir Sheet

539	A104	3m multicolored	7.00	7.00

AMERIPEX '86 — A105

Walt Disney characters.

1986, May 22   *Perf. 11*

540	A105	15s Goofy, Mickey	1.10	.25
541	A105	35s Mickey, Pluto	1.40	.45
542	A105	1m Goofy	3.00	1.90
543	A105	2m Donald, Pete	3.50	2.50
		Nos. 540-543 (4)	9.00	5.10

Souvenir Sheet

Perf. 14

544	A105	4m Goofy, Chip'n'Dale	11.00	11.00

Royal Wedding Issue, 1986

Common Design Type

Designs: 50s, Prince Andrew and Sarah Ferguson. 1m, Andrew. 3m, Andrew at helicopter controls. 4m, Couple, diff.

1986, July 23   *Perf. 14*

545	CD340	50s multicolored	.50	.50
546	CD340	1m multicolored	.95	.95
547	CD340	3m multicolored	2.50	2.50
		Nos. 545-547 (3)	3.95	3.95

Souvenir Sheet

548	CD340	4m multicolored	4.00	4.00

Natl. Independence, 20th Anniv. — A106

1986, Oct. 20   *Litho.*   *Perf. 15*

549	A106	9s Basotho pony, rider	.25	.25
550	A106	15s Mohair spinning	.25	.25
551	A106	35s River crossing	.25	.25
552	A106	3m Thaba Tseka P.O.	2.25	2.25
		Nos. 549-552 (4)	3.10	3.10

Souvenir Sheet

553	A106	4m Moshoeshoe I	7.00	7.00

Christmas A107

Walt Disney characters.

1986, Nov. 4   *Litho.*   *Perf. 11*

554	A107	15s Chip'n'Dale	.85	.25
555	A107	35s Mickey, Minnie	1.25	.40
556	A107	1m Pluto	1.75	1.60
557	A107	2m Aunt Matilda	2.50	2.50
		Nos. 554-557 (4)	6.35	4.75

Souvenir Sheet

Perf. 14

558	A107	5m Huey and Dewey	10.00	10.00

Butterfly and Bird Type of 1981-84 SURCHARGED

1986   *Litho.*   *Perf. 14, 14½*

558A	A66	9s on 10s #327b		
b.		9s on 10s #327		
559	A83	9s on 30s No. 431	.25	.25
a.		9s on 30s #431 (surcharge smaller & sans serif)		
560	A83	9s on 60s No. 433	.25	.25
561	A66	15s on 1s No. 321	.25	.25
b.		15s on 1s #321a		
c.		15s on 1s #321b		
561A	A83	15s on 1s No. 421	2.00	2.00
562	A66	15s on 2s No. 322	.25	.25
563	A66	15s on 60s No. 330	.25	.25
		15s on 60s #330a		
564	A83	15s on 2m No. 422	.25	.25
565	A83	15s on 3s No. 423	.25	.25
566	A83	35s on 75s No. 434	.35	.35
a.		35s on 75s #434, small "s"		
		Nos. 558A-566 (10)	4.10	4.10

Issued: Nos. 559-560, July 1. Nos. 561-563, Aug. 22. Nos. 561A, 564-566, June 25. See Nos. 617A-617B.

Roof of Africa Rally — A108

1987, Apr. 28   *Litho.*   *Perf. 14*

567	A108	9s White car	.45	.25
568	A108	15s Motorcycle #26	.55	.25
569	A108	35s Motorcycle #25	.75	.35
570	A108	4m Red car	3.50	3.50
		Nos. 567-570 (4)	5.25	4.35

1988 Summer Olympics, Seoul — A109

1987, May 29   *Perf. 14*

571	A109	9s Tennis	.80	.25
572	A109	15s Judo	.80	.25
573	A109	20s Running	.90	.25
574	A109	35s Boxing	1.00	.45
575	A109	1m Diving	1.25	1.10
576	A109	3m Bowling	3.00	3.00
		Nos. 571-576 (6)	7.75	5.30

Souvenir Sheet

577	A109	2m Tennis, diff.	2.75	2.75
577A	A109	4m Soccer	5.25	5.25

See Nos. 606-611.
No. 577A shows green at lower left diagonal half of the flag.

Inventors and Innovators A110

Designs: 5s, Sir Isaac Newton, reflecting telescope. 9s, Alexander Graham Bell, telephone. 75s, Robert H. Goddard, liquid fuel rocket. 4m, Chuck Yeager (b. 1923), test pilot. No. 582, Mariner 10 spacecraft.

1987, June 30   *Perf. 15*

578	A110	5s multicolored	.45	.25
579	A110	9s multicolored	.45	.25
580	A110	75s multicolored	1.00	.75
581	A110	4m multicolored	3.50	3.50
		Nos. 578-581 (4)	5.40	4.75

Souvenir Sheet

582	A110	4m multicolored	5.00	5.00

Fauna and Flora A111

5s, Gray rhebuck. 9s, Cape clawless otter. 15s, Cape gray mongoose. 20s, Free state daisy. 35s, River bells. 1m, Turkey flower. 2m, Sweet briar. 3m, Mountain reedbuck. No. 591, Pig-lily. No. 592, Cape wildebeest.

1987, Aug. 14

583	A111	5s multicolored	.50	.25
584	A111	9s multicolored	.50	.25
585	A111	15s multicolored	.70	.25
586	A111	20s multicolored	.80	.25
587	A111	35s multicolored	.90	.25
588	A111	1m multicolored	2.00	1.00
589	A111	2m multicolored	2.50	2.00
590	A111	3m multicolored	3.00	3.00
		Nos. 583-590 (8)	10.90	7.35

Souvenir Sheet

591	A111	2m multicolored	3.25	3.25
592	A111	4m multicolored	5.75	5.75

Nos. 586-589 and 591 vert.

16th World Scout Jamboree, Australia, 1987-88 — A112

1987, Sept. 10   *Litho.*   *Perf. 14*

593	A112	9s Orienteering	.25	.25
594	A112	15s Playing soccer	.25	.25
595	A112	35s Kangaroos	.65	.65
596	A112	75s Salute, flag	1.25	1.25
597	A112	4m Windsurfing	6.25	6.25
		Nos. 593-597 (5)	8.65	8.65

Souvenir Sheet

598	A112	4m Map, flag of Australia	5.50	5.50

Nos. 324, 425, 424, 328 and 427 Surcharged

1987   *Litho.*   *Perf. 14½, 14*

598A	A66	9s on 5s No. 324	.75	.25
599	A66	15s on 5s No. 324	2.00	.25
600	A83	15s on 5s No. 425	.25	.25
600A	A83	20s on 4s No. 424	.25	.25
600B	A66	35s on 25s No. 328	1.50	.60
e.		35s on 25s #328, small "s"		
f.		35s on 25s #328a		
g.		35s on 25s #328a, small "s"		
600C	A66	35s on 75s #331		
h.		35s on 75s #331, small "s"		
600D	A83	40s on 7s No. 427	.40	.40

Issued: Nos. 599-600, 11/16; No. 600B, 12/15; Nos. 598A, 600A, 600D, 12/30.

A113

A114

Religious paintings (details) by Raphael: 9s, Madonna and Child. 15s, Marriage of the Virgin. 35s, Coronation of the Virgin. 90s, Madonna of the Chair. 3m, Madonna and Child Enthroned with Five Saints.

1987, Dec. 21   *Perf. 14*

601	A113	9s multicolored	.25	.25
602	A113	15s multicolored	.25	.25
603	A113	35s multicolored	1.25	1.25
604	A113	90s multicolored	3.00	3.00
		Nos. 601-604 (4)	4.75	4.75

Souvenir Sheet

605	A114	3m multicolored	4.50	4.50

Christmas.

Summer Olympics Type of 1987

1987, Nov. 30   *Litho.*   *Perf. 14*

606	A109	5s like 9s	.25	.25
607	A109	10s like 15s	.25	.25
608	A109	25s like 20s	.25	.25
609	A109	40s like 35s	.35	.35
610	A109	50s like 1m	.50	.50
611	A109	3.50m like 3m	3.25	3.25
		Nos. 606-611 (6)	4.85	4.85

Souvenir Sheet

612	A109	4m Soccer	4.00	4.00

No. 612 shows green at lower right diagonal half of the flag.

Discovery of America, 500th Anniv. (in 1992) A115

Columbus's fleet and marine life: 9s, Spotted trunkfish. 15s, Green sea turtle. 35s, Common dolphin. 5m, White-tailed tropicbird. 4m, Ship.

1987, Dec. 14   *Litho.*   *Perf. 14*

613	A115	9s multicolored	.25	.25
614	A115	15s multicolored	.25	.25
615	A115	35s multicolored	.60	.60
616	A115	5m multicolored	8.00	8.00
		Nos. 613-616 (4)	9.10	9.10

Souvenir Sheet

617	A115	4m multicolored	6.50	6.50

Nos. 328, 559 Surcharged

1988

Methods and Perfs as Before

617A	A83	3s on 9s on 30s		
617B	A83	7s on 9s on 30s		
617C	A66	16s on 25s No. 328	—	—

Issued: Nos. 617A, 617B, 2/2/88; No. 617C, 3/88.

Birds
A116

2s, Pied kingfisher. 3s, Three-banded plover. 5s, Spurwing goose. 10s, Clapper lark. 12s, Red-eyed bulbul. 16s, Cape weaver. 20s, Red-headed finch. 30s, Mountain chat. 40s, Stone chat. 55s, Pied barbet. 60s, Cape glossy starling. 75s, Cape sparrow. 1m, Cattle egret. 3m, Giant kingfisher. 10m, Crowned guinea fowl.

1988, Apr. 5	Litho.	Perf. 15		
618	A116	2s multicolored	.25	.25
619	A116	3s multicolored	.25	.25
620	A116	5s multicolored	.25	.25
621	A116	10s multicolored	.25	.25
622	A116	12s multicolored	.25	.25
623	A116	16s multicolored	.25	.25
624	A116	20s multicolored	.25	.25
625	A116	30s multicolored	.30	.30
626	A116	40s multicolored	.40	.40
627	A116	55s multicolored	.55	.55
628	A116	60s multicolored	.60	.60
629	A116	75s multicolored	.75	.75
630	A116	1m multicolored	.85	.85
631	A116	3m multicolored	2.50	2.50
632	A116	10m multicolored	9.00	9.00
		Nos. 618-632 (15)	16.70	16.70

For surcharges see Nos. 755, 805-806.

1989, Sept. 18			Perf. 14	
620a	A116	5s multicolored	.25	.25
622a	A116	12s multicolored	.25	.25
623a	A116	16s multicolored	.25	.25
624a	A116	20s multicolored	.25	.25
630a	A116	1m multicolored	.80	.80
631a	A116	3m multicolored	2.40	2.40
632a	A116	10m multicolored	8.00	8.00
		Nos. 620a-632a (7)	12.20	12.20

Dated 1989.

1990			Perf. 12½x12	
620b	A116	5s multicolored	.25	.25
622b	A116	12s multicolored	.25	.25
623b	A116	16s multicolored	.25	.25
624b	A116	20s multicolored	.25	.25
630b	A116	1m multicolored	.80	.80
631b	A116	3m multicolored	2.40	2.40
632b	A116	10m multicolored	8.00	8.00
		Nos. 620b-632b (7)	12.20	12.20

Dated 1989.

1991 (?)			Perf. 11½x13	
620c	A116	5s multicolored	.25	.25
622c	A116	12s multicolored	.25	.25
623c	A116	16s multicolored	.25	.25
624c	A116	20s multicolored	.25	.25
630c	A116	1m multicolored	.80	.80
631c	A116	3m multicolored	2.40	2.40
632c	A116	10m multicolored	8.00	8.00
		Nos. 620c-632c (7)	12.20	12.20

Dated 1989.

Nos. 531-534 Ovptd. "40th WEDDING ANNIVERSARY / H.M. QUEEN ELIZABETH II / H.R.H. THE DUKE OF EDINBURGH" in Silver

1988, May 3			Perf. 14	
636	CD339	90s lt yel bis & blk	.90	.90
637	CD339	1m pale grn & multi	1.00	1.00
638	CD339	2m dull vio & multi	2.00	2.00
		Nos. 636-638 (3)	3.90	3.90

Souvenir Sheet

| 639 | CD339 | 4m tan & black | 4.25 | 4.25 |

FINLANDIA '88, Helsinki, June 1-12 — A117

Disney animated characters and Helsinki sights: 1s, Touring President's Palace. 2s, Sauna. 3s, Lake Country fishing. 4s, Finlandia Hall. 5s, Photographing Sibelius Monument. 10s, Pony trek, youth hostel. 3m, Olympic Stadium. 5m, Santa Claus, Arctic Circle.
No. 648, Market Square. No. 649, Lapp encampment, vert.

1988, June 2	Litho.	Perf. 14x13½		
640	A117	1s multicolored	.25	.25
641	A117	2s multicolored	.25	.25
642	A117	3s multicolored	.25	.25
643	A117	4s multicolored	.25	.25
644	A117	5s multicolored	.25	.25
645	A117	10s multicolored	.30	.30
646	A117	3m multicolored	4.50	3.50
647	A117	5m multicolored	5.75	4.75
		Nos. 640-647 (8)	11.80	9.80

Souvenir Sheets
Perf. 14x13½, 13½x14

| 648 | A117 | 4m multicolored | 4.50 | 4.50 |
| 649 | A117 | 4m multicolored | 4.50 | 4.50 |

Mickey Mouse, 60th anniv.

A118

55s, Pope giving communion. 2m, Leading procession. 3m, Walking in garden. 4m, Wearing scullcap.
5m, Pope, Archbishop Morapeli of Lesotho, horiz.

1988, Sept. 1	Litho.	Perf. 14		
650	A118	55s multicolored	.50	.50
651	A118	2m multicolored	1.75	1.75
652	A118	3m multicolored	2.75	2.75
653	A118	4m multicolored	3.75	3.75
		Nos. 650-653 (4)	8.75	8.75

Souvenir Sheet

| 654 | A118 | 5m multicolored | 8.00 | 8.00 |

Visit of Pope John Paul II, Sept. 14-16.

A119

Small indigenous mammals.

1988, Oct. 13	Litho.	Perf. 14		
655	A119	16s Rock hyrax	.25	.25
656	A119	40s Honey badger	.85	.85
657	A119	75s Genet	1.50	1.50
658	A119	3m Yellow mongoose	5.75	5.75
		Nos. 655-658 (4)	8.35	8.35

Souvenir Sheet

| 659 | A119 | 4m Meerkat | 5.50 | 5.50 |

Birth of Venus, 1480, by Botticelli
A120

Paintings: 25s, View of Toledo, 1608, by El Greco. 40s, Maids of Honor, 1656, by Diego Velazquez. 50s, The Fifer, 1866, by Manet. 55s, The Starry Night, 1889, by Van Gogh. 75s, Prima Ballerina, 1876, by Degas. 2m, Bridge over Water Lilies, 1899, by Monet. 3m, Guernica, 1937, by Picasso. No. 668, The Presentation of the Virgin in the Temple, c. 1534, by Titian. No. 669, The Miracle of the Newborn Infant, 1511, by Titian.

1988, Oct. 17	Litho.	Perf. 13½x14		
660	A120	15s multicolored	.40	.25
661	A120	25s multicolored	.55	.25
662	A120	40s multicolored	.65	.40
663	A120	50s multicolored	.75	.50
664	A120	55s multicolored	.80	.55
665	A120	75s multicolored	.90	.90
666	A120	2m multicolored	2.00	2.00
667	A120	3m multicolored	2.50	2.50
		Nos. 660-667 (8)	8.55	7.35

Souvenir Sheets

| 668 | A120 | 4m multicolored | 3.50 | 3.50 |
| 669 | A120 | 4m multicolored | 3.50 | 3.50 |

1988 Summer Olympics, Seoul — A121

1988, Nov. 11	Litho.	Perf. 14		
670	A121	12s Wrestling, horiz.	.25	.25
671	A121	16s Equestrian	.25	.25
672	A121	55s Shooting, horiz.	.40	.40
673	A121	3.50m like 16s	2.40	2.40
		Nos. 670-673 (4)	3.30	3.30

Souvenir Sheet

| 674 | A121 | 4m Olympic flame | 4.75 | 4.75 |

Intl. Tennis Federation, 75th Anniv. — A122

Tennis champions, views of cities or landmarks: 12s, Yannick Noah, Eiffel Tower, horiz. 20s, Rod Laver, Sydney Opera House and Harbor Bridge, horiz. 30s, Ivan Lendl, Prague, horiz. 65s, Jimmy Connors, Tokyo. 1m, Arthur Ashe, Barcelona. 1.55m, Althea Gibson, NYC. 2m, Chris Evert, Vienna. 2.40m, Boris Becker, London. 3m, Martina Navratilova, Golden Gate Bridge, horiz. 4m, Steffi Graf, Berlin, West Germany.

1988, Nov. 18				
675	A122	12s multi	.70	.25
676	A122	20s multi	.90	.25
677	A122	30s multi	.80	.35
678	A122	65s multi	.95	.80
679	A122	1m multi	1.25	1.25
680	A122	1.55m multi	1.50	1.50
681	A122	2m multi	2.25	2.25
682	A122	2.40m multi	2.50	2.50
683	A122	3m multi	3.00	3.00
		Nos. 675-683 (9)	13.85	12.15

Souvenir Sheet

| 684 | A122 | 4m multi | 4.50 | 4.50 |

No. 676 has "Sidney" instead of "Sydney." No. 679 has "Ash" instead of "Ashe."

Paintings by Titian A123

Designs: 12s, The Averoldi Polyptych. 20s, Christ and the Adulteress (Christ). 35s, Christ and the Adulteress (adultress). 45s, Angel of the Annunciation. 65s, Saint Dominic. 1m, The Vendramin Family. 2m, Mary Magdalen. 3m, The Tribute Money. No. 693, Christ and the Woman Taken in Adultery. No. 694, The Mater Dolorosa.

1988, Dec. 1			Perf. 14x13½	
685	A123	12s multicolored	.40	.25
686	A123	20s multicolored	.50	.25
687	A123	35s multicolored	.60	.35
688	A123	45s multicolored	.70	.45
689	A123	65s multicolored	.70	.65
690	A123	1m multicolored	.90	.90
691	A123	2m multicolored	1.75	1.75
692	A123	3m multicolored	2.50	2.50
		Nos. 685-692 (8)	8.05	7.10

Souvenir Sheets

| 693 | A123 | 5m multicolored | 4.50 | 4.50 |
| 694 | A123 | 5m multicolored | 4.50 | 4.50 |

Birth of Titian, 500th anniv. Nos. 685-693 inscribed "Christmas 1988."

Intl. Red Cross, 125th Anniv. A124

Anniv. emblem, supply and ambulance planes: 12s, Pilatus PC-6 Turbo Porter. 20s, Cessna Caravan. 55s, De Havilland DHC-6 Otter. 3m, Douglas DC-3 in thunderstorm. 4m, Douglas DC-3, diff.

1989, Jan. 30	Litho.	Perf. 14		
695	A124	12s multicolored	.25	.25
696	A124	20s multicolored	.25	.25
697	A124	55s multicolored	1.25	1.25
698	A124	3m multicolored	5.25	5.25
		Nos. 695-698 (4)	7.00	7.00

Souvenir Sheet

| 699 | A124 | 4m multi, vert. | 9.00 | 9.00 |

Landscapes by Hiroshige — A125

Designs: 12s, Dawn Mist at Mishima. 16s, Night Snow at Kambara. 20s, Wayside Inn at Mariko Station. 35s, Shower at Shono. 55s, Snowfall on the Kisokaido Near Oi. 1m, Autumn Moon at Seba. 3.20m, Evening Moon at Ryogaku Bridge. 5m, Cherry Blossoms, Arashiyama. No. 708, Listening to the Singing Insects at Dokanyama. No. 709, Moonlight, Nagakubo.

1989, June 19	Litho.	Perf. 14x13½		
700	A125	12s multi	.40	.25
701	A125	16s multi	.45	.25
702	A125	20s multi	.45	.25
703	A125	35s multi	.45	.30
704	A125	55s multi	.70	.45
705	A125	1m multi	1.00	.80
706	A125	3.20m multi	2.25	2.25
707	A125	5m multi	3.75	3.75
		Nos. 700-707 (8)	9.45	8.30

Souvenir Sheets

| 708 | A125 | 4m multi | 4.25 | 4.25 |
| 709 | A125 | 4m multi | 4.25 | 4.25 |

Hirohito (1901-1989) and enthronement of Akihito as emperor of Japan.

PHILEXFRANCE '89, French Revolution Bicent. — A126

Disney characters wearing insurgent uniforms.

1989, July 10		Perf. 13½x14, 14x13½		
710	A126	1s General	.25	.25
711	A126	2s Infantry	.25	.25
712	A126	3s Grenadier	.25	.25
713	A126	4s Cavalry	.25	.25
714	A126	5s Hussar	.25	.25
715	A126	10s Marine	.25	.25
716	A126	3m Natl. guard	3.25	3.25
717	A126	5m Admiral	5.00	5.00
		Nos. 710-717 (8)	9.75	9.75

Souvenir Sheets

718	A126	4m Natl. guard, royal family, horiz.	5.00	5.00
719	A126	4m La Marseillaise	5.00	5.00

Maloti Mountains — A127

No. 720: a, Sotho thatched dwellings. b, Two trees, cliff edge. c, Waterfall. d, Tribesman.

1989, Sept.   Litho.   Perf. 14

720		Strip of 4	4.00	4.00
a.-d.	A127	1m any single	.75	.75

Souvenir Sheet

721	A127	4m Flora	4.25	4.25

Mushrooms A128

12s, Paxillus involutus. 16s, Ganoderma applanatum. 55s, Suillus granulatus. 5m, Stereum hirsutum.
4m, Scleroderma flavidum.

1989, Sept. 8   Litho.   Perf. 14

722	A128	12s multicolored	.35	.35
723	A128	16s multicolored	.35	.25
723A	A128	55s multicolored	.65	.55
724	A128	5m multicolored	4.50	4.50
		Nos. 722-724 (4)	5.85	5.55

Souvenir Sheet

725	A128	4m multicolored	6.25	6.25

Birds A129

1989, Oct. 23   Litho.   Perf. 14

726	A129	12s Marsh sandpipers	.25	.25
727	A129	65s Little stints	1.10	1.10
728	A129	1m Ringed plovers	1.75	1.75
729	A129	4m Curlew sandpipers	6.25	6.25
		Nos. 726-729 (4)	9.35	9.35

Souvenir Sheet

730	A129	5m Ruff, vert.	11.00	11.00

1st Moon Landing, 20th Anniv. A130

Highlights of the Apollo 11 mission.

1989, Nov. 6   Perf. 14

731	A130	12s Liftoff	.25	.25
732	A130	16s Eagle landing	.25	.25
733	A130	40s Astronaut on ladder	.40	.40
734	A130	55s Buzz Aldrin	.60	.60
735	A130	1m Solar wind experiment	1.00	1.00
736	A130	2m Eagle lifting off	2.00	2.00

737	A130	3m Columbia in orbit	2.75	2.75
738	A130	4m Splashdown	4.00	4.00
		Nos. 731-738 (8)	11.25	11.25

Souvenir Sheet

739	A130	5m Astronaut, Eagle	7.25	7.25
		Nos. 731, 733, 738-739 vert.		

World Stamp Expo '89 A131

Cathedral Church of Sts. Peter and Paul, Washington, DC — A132

No. 740: a, Postal marking, England, 1680. b, Wax seal and feather, Germany, 1807. c, Crete #1. d, Perot postmaster's provisional, Bermuda, 1848. e, Pony Express handstamp, US, 1860. f, Finland #1. g, Fiji #1. h, Swedish newspaper handstamp, 1823. i, Bhor #1.

1989, Nov. 17   Litho.   Perf. 14

740		Sheet of 9	8.25	8.25
a.-i.	A131	75s any single	.35	.35

Souvenir Sheet

741	A132	4m shown	4.25	4.25

Christmas — A133

Religious paintings by Velazquez: 12s, The Immaculate Conception. 20s, St. Anthony Abbot and St. Paul the Hermit. 35s, St. Thomas the Apostle. 55s, Christ in the House of Martha and Mary. 1m, St. John Writing the Apocalypse on Patmos. 3m, The Virgin Presenting the Chasuble to St. Ildephonsus. 4m, The Adoration of the Magi. 5m, The Coronation of the Virgin.

1989, Dec. 18

742	A133	12s multicolored	.25	.25
743	A133	20s multicolored	.25	.25
744	A133	35s multicolored	.35	.35
745	A133	55s multicolored	.55	.55
746	A133	1m multicolored	.90	.90
747	A133	3m multicolored	2.50	2.50
748	A133	4m multicolored	3.25	3.25
		Nos. 742-748 (7)	8.05	8.05

Souvenir Sheet

749	A133	5m multicolored	9.00	9.00

1990 World Cup Soccer Championships, Italy — A134

Various athletes, emblem and name of previous championship host nations.

1989, Dec. 27

750	A134	12s England, 1966	.25	.25
751	A134	16s Mexico, 1970	.25	.25
752	A134	55s West Germany, 1974	1.00	1.00
753	A134	5m Spain, 1982	6.50	6.50
		Nos. 750-753 (4)	8.00	8.00

Souvenir Sheet

754	A134	4m Diego Maradona, Argentina	7.50	7.50

No. 622a Surcharged

1990   Litho.   Perf. 14

755	A116	16s on 12s multi		

Orchids A135

12s, Satyrium princeps. 16s, Huttonaea pulchra. 55s, Herschelia graminifolia. 1m, Ansellia gigantea. 1.55m, Polystachya pubescens. 2.40m, Penthea filicornis. 3m, Disperis capensis. 4m, Disa uniflora.
5m,

1990, Mar. 12   Litho.   Perf. 14

756	A135	12s multicolored	.25	.25
757	A135	16s multicolored	.25	.25
758	A135	55s multicolored	.90	.90
759	A135	1m multicolored	1.60	1.60
760	A135	1.55m multicolored	2.25	2.25
761	A135	2.40m multicolored	3.50	3.50
762	A135	3m multicolored	4.25	4.25
763	A135	4m multicolored	6.00	6.00
		Nos. 756-763 (8)	19.00	19.00

Souvenir Sheet

764	A135	5m multicolored	10.00	10.00
		Expo '90.		

Butterflies — A136

1990, Feb. 26   Litho.   Perf. 14

765	A136	12s Pseudo ergolid	.95	.25
766	A136	16s Painted lady	1.10	.25
767	A136	55s Ringed pansy	1.60	.55
768	A136	65s False acraea	1.75	.65
769	A136	1m Eyed pansy	2.40	1.10
770	A136	2m Golden pansy	3.75	2.25
771	A136	3m African monarch	5.25	3.25
772	A136	4m African giant swallowtail	6.50	5.50
		Nos. 765-772 (8)	23.30	13.80

Souvenir Sheet

773	A136	5m Citrus swallowtail	11.00	11.00

Queen Mother, 90th Birthday — A137

1990, July 5   Litho.   Perf. 14

774		1.50m In hat	1.25	1.25
775		1.50m Two children	1.25	1.25
776		1.50m Young woman	1.25	1.25
a.	A137	Strip of 3, #774-776	4.50	4.50
		Nos. 774-776 (3)	3.75	3.75

Souvenir Sheet

777	A137	5m Child	5.50	5.50

A139

Designs: 12s, King Moshoeshoe II, Prince Mohato wearing blankets. 16s, Prince Mohato in Seana-Marena blanket. 1m, Pope John Paul II in Seana-Marena blanket. 3m, Basotho men on horses.
5m, Pope with blanket and hat.

1990, Aug. 17   Litho.   Perf. 14

778	A139	12s multicolored	.25	.25
779	A139	16s multicolored	.25	.25
780	A139	1m multicolored	1.40	1.40
781	A139	3m multicolored	3.50	3.50
		Nos. 778-781 (4)	5.40	5.40

Souvenir Sheet

782	A139	5m multi, horiz.	7.50	7.50

A140

Highland Water Project: 16s, Moving gravel. 20s, Fuel truck. 55s, Piers for bridge construction. 2m, Road construction.
5m, Drilling blasting holes.

1990, Aug. 24

783	A140	16s multicolored	.25	.25
784	A140	20s multicolored	.25	.25
785	A140	55s multicolored	.90	.90
786	A140	2m multicolored	2.75	2.75
		Nos. 783-786 (4)	4.15	4.15

Souvenir Sheet

787	A140	5m multicolored	7.50	7.50

A141

1990, Sept. 26   Litho.   Perf. 14

788	A141	12s Breastfeeding	.25	.25
789	A141	55s Oral rehydration	1.75	1.75
790	A141	1m Baby being weighed	2.50	2.50
		Nos. 788-790 (3)	4.50	4.50

UNICEF Save the Children campaign.

A142

1990, Oct. 5

791	A142	16s Triple jump	.25	.25
792	A142	55s 200-meter race	1.00	1.00
793	A142	1m 5000-meter race	1.50	1.50
794	A142	4m Equestrian show jumping	5.50	5.50
		Nos. 791-794 (4)	8.25	8.25

Souvenir Sheet

795	A142	5m Lighting Olympic flame	8.50	8.50

1992 Summer Olympics, Barcelona.

Christmas
A143

Different details from paintings by Rubens: 12s, 1m, 3m, Virgin and Child. 16s, 80s, 2m, 4m, Adoration of the Magi. 55s, Head of One of the Three Kings, diff. 5m, Assumption of the Virgin.

1990, Dec. 5   Litho.   Perf. 13½x14

796	A143	12s multicolored	.25	.25
797	A143	16s multicolored	.25	.25
798	A143	55s multicolored	.55	.55
799	A143	80s multicolored	.85	.85
800	A143	1m multicolored	1.00	1.00
801	A143	2m multicolored	2.10	2.10
802	A143	3m multicolored	2.75	2.75
803	A143	4m multicolored	3.75	3.75
		Nos. 796-803 (8)	11.50	11.50

Souvenir Sheet

804	A143	5m multicolored	7.25	7.25

Nos. 625-626 Surcharged

1991, Jan. 18   Litho.   Perf. 15

805	A116	16s on 30s #625	—	—
806	A116	16s on 40s #626	—	—

Phila Nippon '91 — A144

Walt Disney characters visit Japan: 20s, Mickey at Nagasaki Peace Park. 30s, Mickey at Kamakura Beach. 40s, Mickey, Donald entertain at Bunraku Puppet Theater. 50s, Mickey, Donald eat soba at noodle shop. 75s, Minnie, Mickey at tea house. 1m, Mickey, Bullet Train. 3m, Mickey, deer at Todaiji Temple. 4m, Mickey, Minnie before Imperial Palace. No. 815, Mickey skiing at Happo-One, Nagano. No. 816, Mickey, Minnie at Suizenji Park.

1991, June 10   Litho.   Perf. 14x13½

807	A144	20s multicolored	.25	.25
808	A144	30s multicolored	.25	.25
809	A144	40s multicolored	.50	.50
810	A144	50s multicolored	.70	.70
811	A144	75s multicolored	1.40	1.40
812	A144	1m multicolored	1.40	1.40
813	A144	3m multicolored	3.75	3.75
814	A144	4m multicolored	5.00	5.00
		Nos. 807-814 (8)	13.25	13.25

Souvenir Sheets

815	A144	6m multicolored	5.50	5.50
816	A144	6m multicolored	5.50	5.50

Entertainers in Films About Africa — A145

Designs: 12s, Stewart Granger, King Solomon's Mines. 16s, Johnny Weissmuller, Tarzan, the Ape Man. 30s, Clark Gable, Grace Kelly, Mogambo. 55s, Sigourney Weaver, Gorillas in the Mist. 70s, Humphrey Bogart, Katharine Hepburn, The African Queen. 1m, John Wayne, Hatari. 2m, Meryl Streep, Out of Africa. 4m, Eddie Murphy, Arsenio Hall, Coming to America. 5m, Elsa, Born Free.

1991, June 20   Litho.   Perf. 14

817	A145	12s multicolored	.65	.25
818	A145	16s multicolored	.65	.25
819	A145	30s multicolored	.80	.25
820	A145	55s multicolored	.95	.70
821	A145	70s multicolored	1.25	.90
822	A145	1m multicolored	1.60	1.25
823	A145	2m multicolored	2.50	2.50
824	A145	4m multicolored	4.25	4.25
		Nos. 817-824 (8)	12.65	10.35

Souvenir Sheet

825	A145	5m multicolored	6.75	6.75

Butterflies
A146

2s, Satyrus aello. 3s, Erebia medusa. 5s, Melanargia galathea. 10s, Erebia aethiops. 20s, Coenonympha pamphilus. 25s, Pyrameis atalanta. 30s, Charaxes jasius. 40s, Colias palaeno. 50s, Colias cliopatra. 60s, Colias philodice. 70s, Rhumni gonepterix. 1m, Colias caesonia. 2m, Pyrameis cardui. 3m, Danaus chrysippus. 10m, Apatura iris.

No date inscription below design

1991, Aug. 1   Litho.   Perf. 13½

827	A146	2s multicolored	.25	.25
828	A146	3s multicolored	.25	.25
829	A146	5s multicolored	.25	.25
830	A146	10s multicolored	.25	.25
831	A146	20s multicolored	.30	.25
832	A146	25s multicolored	.30	.25
833	A146	30s multicolored	.45	.30
834	A146	40s multicolored	.45	.35
835	A146	50s multicolored	.50	.45
836	A146	60s multicolored	.60	.55
837	A146	70s multicolored	.60	.60
838	A146	1m multicolored	.90	.90
839	A146	2m multicolored	1.75	1.75
840	A146	3m multicolored	2.50	2.50
840A	A146	10m multicolored	8.75	8.75
		Nos. 827-840A (15)	18.10	17.65

For surcharge see No. 1062.

1992, Apr.   Inscribed "1992"

827a	A146	2s multicolored	.25	.25
828a	A146	3s multicolored	.25	.25
829a	A146	5s multicolored	.25	.25
830a	A146	10s multicolored	.25	.25
831a	A146	20s multicolored	.30	.25
832a	A146	25s multicolored	.30	.25
833a	A146	30s multicolored	.45	.30
834a	A146	40s multicolored	.50	.35
835a	A146	50s multicolored	.65	.45
836a	A146	60s multicolored	.70	.70
837a	A146	70s multicolored	1.00	1.00
838a	A146	1m multicolored	1.25	1.25
839a	A146	2m multicolored	2.75	2.75
840a	A146	3m multicolored	4.00	4.00
840Aa	A146	10m multicolored	8.75	8.75
		Nos. 827a-840Aa (15)	21.65	21.05

SADCC, 10th Anniv. A147

Tourism: 12s, Wattled cranes. 16s, Butterfly, flowers in national parks. 25s, Tourist bus and Mukurub, the Finger of God. 3m, People in traditional dress.

1991, Oct. 10   Litho.   Perf. 14x13½

841	A147	12s multicolored	1.75	1.75
842	A147	16s multicolored	1.75	1.75
843	A147	25s multicolored	1.75	1.75
		Nos. 841-843 (3)	5.25	5.25

Souvenir Sheet

844	A147	3m multicolored	5.50	5.50

Say No to Drugs
A148

1991, Oct. 10

845	A148	16s multicolored	2.25	2.25

Charles de Gaulle, Birth Cent. — A149

DeGaulle: 40s, Wearing brigadier general's kepi. 50s, Facing left. 60s, Facing right. 4m, In later years.

1991, Dec. 6   Litho.   Perf. 14

846	A149	20s black & brown	.25	.25
847	A149	40s black & violet	.65	.65
848	A149	50s black & olilve	.85	.85
849	A149	60s black & dk blue	1.00	1.00
850	A149	4m black & brn org	6.75	6.75
		Nos. 846-850 (5)	9.50	9.50

Christmas
A150

Engravings by Albrecht Durer: 20s, St. Anne with Mary and the Child Jesus. 30s, Mary on the Grass Bench. 50s, Mary with the Crown of Stars. 60s, Mary with Child beside a Tree. 70s, Mary with Child beside the Wall. 1m, Mary in a Halo on the Crescent Moon. 2m, Mary Breastfeeding Her Child. 4m, Mary with the Infant in Swaddling Clothes. No. 859, Holy Family with the Dragonfly. No. 860, The Birth of Christ.

1991, Dec. 13   Litho.   Perf. 12

851	A150	20s rose & black	.25	.25
852	A150	30s blue & black	.50	.50
853	A150	50s green & black	.80	.80
854	A150	60s red & black	1.00	1.00
855	A150	70s yellow & black	1.10	1.10
856	A150	1m yel org & black	1.60	1.60
857	A150	2m violet & black	2.75	2.75
858	A150	4m dk blue & black	5.75	5.75
		Nos. 851-858 (8)	13.75	13.75

Souvenir Sheets
Perf. 14½

859	A150	5m blue & black	5.00	5.00
860	A150	5m pink & black	5.00	5.00

Games
A151

Walt Disney characters playing games: 20s, Mickey, Pluto playing pin the tail on the donkey. 30s, Mickey enjoying board game, Mancala. 40s, Mickey hoop rolling. 50s, Minnie with hula hoops. 70s, Mickey throwing Frisbee to Pluto. 1m, Donald trying to play Diabolo. 2m, Huey, Dewey and Louie playing marbles. 3m, Donald frustrated by Rubik's cube. No. 869, Donald and Mickey's nephews in tug-of-war. No. 870, Mickey, Donald stick fighting.

1991, Dec. 16   Perf. 13½x14

861	A151	20s multicolored	.25	.25
862	A151	30s multicolored	.55	.55
863	A151	40s multicolored	.65	.65
864	A151	50s multicolored	.90	.90
865	A151	70s multicolored	1.25	1.25
866	A151	1m multicolored	1.75	1.75
867	A151	2m multicolored	3.25	3.25
868	A151	3m multicolored	5.00	5.00
		Nos. 861-868 (8)	13.60	13.60

Souvenir Sheets

869	A151	5m multicolored	6.00	6.00
870	A151	5m multicolored	6.00	6.00

Royal Family Birthday, Anniversary
Common Design Type

1991, Dec. 9   Litho.   Perf. 14

871	CD347	50s multicolored	.70	.70
872	CD347	70s multicolored	.95	.95
873	CD347	1m multicolored	1.40	1.40
874	CD347	3m multicolored	4.25	4.25
		Nos. 871-874 (4)	7.30	7.30

Souvenir Sheet

875	CD347	4m Charles, Diana, sons	6.25	6.25

Charles and Diana, 10th wedding anniversary.

Queen Elizabeth II's Accession to the Throne, 40th Anniv.
Common Design Type

1992, Feb. 6   Litho.   Perf. 14

881	CD348	20s multicolored	.25	.25
882	CD348	30s multicolored	.40	.40
883	CD348	1m multicolored	1.25	1.25
884	CD348	4m multicolored	4.00	4.00
		Nos. 881-884 (4)	5.90	5.90

Souvenir Sheet

885	CD348	5m multicolored	6.00	6.00

Birds — A152

Designs: a, Lanner falcon. b, Bateleur. c, Red-headed finch. d, Lesser-striped swallow. e, Alpine swift. f, Diederik cuckoo. g, Malachite sunbird. h, Crimson-breasted shrike. i, Pin-tailed whydah. j, Lilac-breasted roller. k, Black korhaan. l, Black-collared barbet. m, Secretary bird. n, Red-billed quelea. o, Rod bishop. p, Ring-necked dove. q, Yellow canary. r, Orange-throated longclaw. s, Blue waxbill. t, Golden bishop.

1992, Feb. 10   Perf. 14½

886	A152	30s Sheet of 20, #a.-t.	16.00	16.00

World Columbian Stamp Expo '92, Chicago
A153

Walt Disney characters depicting native Americans: 30s, Donald Duck making arrowheads. 40s, Goofy playing lacrosse. 1m, Mickey, Donald planting corn. 3m, Minnie Mouse mastering art of beading. No. 891, Mickey as "Blackhawk" hunting for moose.

1992, Apr.   Litho.   Perf. 13½x14
887	A153	30s multicolored	.55	.55
888	A153	40s multicolored	.65	.65
889	A153	1m multicolored	1.75	1.75
890	A153	3m multicolored	4.50	4.50
		Nos. 887-890 (4)	7.45	7.45

Souvenir Sheet
891	A153	5m multicolored	7.75	7.75

Granada
'92 — A154

Walt Disney characters in Spanish costumes: 20s, Minnie Mouse as Lady of Rank, 1540-1660. 50s, Mickey as conqueror of Lepanto, 1571. 70s, Donald Duck from Galicia, 1880. 2m, Daisy Duck from Aragon, 1880. No. 901, Goofy as bullfighter.

1992, Apr. 13   Litho.   Perf. 13½x14
897	A154	20s multicolored	.25	.25
898	A154	50s multicolored	1.25	1.25
899	A154	70s multicolored	1.60	1.60
900	A154	2m multicolored	4.00	4.00
		Nos. 897-900 (4)	7.10	7.10

Souvenir Sheet
901	A154	5m multicolored	7.75	7.75

Dinosaurs
A155

20s, Stegosaurus. 30s, Ceratosaurus. 40s, Procompsognathus. 50s, Lesothosaurus. 70s, Plateosaurus. 1m, Gasosaurus. 2m, Massospondylus. 3m, Archaeopteryx.
No. 915, Archaeopteryx, diff. No. 916, Lesothosaurus, diff.

1992, June 9   Perf. 14
907	A155	20s multicolored	.25	.25
908	A155	30s multicolored	.65	.65
909	A155	40s multicolored	.75	.75
910	A155	50s multicolored	1.00	1.00
911	A155	70s multicolored	1.40	1.40
912	A155	1m multicolored	2.00	2.00
913	A155	2m multicolored	3.50	3.50
914	A155	3m multicolored	5.25	5.25
		Nos. 907-914 (8)	14.80	14.80

Souvenir Sheet
915	A155	5m multicolored	7.75	7.75
916	A155	5m multicolored	7.75	7.75

No. 915 printed in continuous design.

1992 Olympics,
Barcelona and
Albertville — A156

Designs: 20s, Discus. 30s, Long jump. 40s, Women's 4x100-meter relay. 70s, Women's 100-meter dash. 1m, Parallel bars. 2m, Two-man luge, horiz. 3m, Women's cross-country skiing, horiz. 4m, Biathlon.
No. 925, Ice hockey, horiz. No. 926, Women's figure skating.

1992, Aug. 5   Litho.   Perf. 14
917	A156	20s multicolored	.25	.25
918	A156	30s multicolored	.25	.25
919	A156	40s multicolored	.30	.30
920	A156	50s multicolored	.65	.65
921	A156	1m multicolored	.95	.95
922	A156	2m multicolored	1.75	1.75
923	A156	3m multicolored	2.50	2.50
924	A156	4m multicolored	3.50	3.50
		Nos. 917-924 (8)	10.15	10.15

Souvenir Sheet
925	A156	5m multicolored	5.50	5.50
926	A156	5m multicolored	5.50	5.50

Christmas
A158

Details or entire paintings: 20s, Virgin and Child, by Sassetta. 30s, Coronation of the Virgin, by Master of Bonastre. 40s, Virgin and Child, by Master of Saints Cosmas and Damian. 70s, The Virgin of Great Panagia, by Russian School, 12th cent. 1m, Madonna and Child, by Vincenzo Foppa. 2m, Madonna and Child, by School of Lippo Memmi. 3m, Virgin and Child, by Barnaba da Modena. 4m, Virgin and Child, by Simone Dei Crocifissi.
No. 935, Virgin & Child Enthroned & Surrounded by Angels, by Cimabue. No. 936, Virgin and Child with Saints (entire triptych), by Dei Crocifissi.

1992, Nov. 2   Litho.   Perf. 13½x14
927	A158	20s multicolored	.25	.25
928	A158	30s multicolored	.45	.45
929	A158	40s multicolored	.55	.55
930	A158	70s multicolored	1.10	1.10
931	A158	1m multicolored	1.50	1.50
932	A158	2m multicolored	2.75	2.75
933	A158	3m multicolored	4.25	4.25
934	A158	4m multicolored	5.75	5.75
		Nos. 927-934 (8)	16.60	16.60

Souvenir Sheets
935	A158	5m multicolored	6.50	6.50
936	A158	5m multicolored	6.50	6.50

Souvenir Sheet

World Trade Center, New York
City — A159

1992, Oct. 28   Litho.   Perf. 14
937	A159	5m multicolored	10.00	10.00

Postage Stamp Mega Event '92, NYC.

Anniversaries and Events — A160

Designs: 20s, Baby harp seal. 30s, Giant panda. 40s, Graf Zeppelin, globe. 70s, Woman grinding corn. 4m, Zeppelin shot down over Cuffley, UK by Lt. Leefe Robinson flying BE 2c, WWI. No. 943, Valentina Tereshkova, first woman in space. No. 944, West African crowned cranes. No. 945, Dr. Ronald McNair.

1993, Jan.   Litho.   Perf. 14
938	A160	20s multicolored	.25	.25
939	A160	30s multicolored	.40	.40
940	A160	40s multicolored	.50	.50
941	A160	70s multicolored	.90	.90
942	A160	4m multicolored	4.75	4.75
943	A160	5m multicolored	5.75	5.75
		Nos. 938-943 (6)	12.55	12.55

Souvenir Sheets
944	A160	5m multicolored	6.50	6.50
945	A160	5m multicolored	6.50	6.50

Earth Summit, Rio de Janeiro (Nos. 938-939, 944). Count Zeppelin, 75th death anniv. (Nos. 940, 942). Intl. Conference on Nutrition, Rome (No. 941). Intl. Space Year (Nos. 943, 945).

Louvre
Museum,
Bicent.
A161

No. 947 — Details or entire paintings, by Nicolas Poussin: a, Orpheus and Eurydice. b-c, Rape of the Sabine Women (left, right). d-e, The Death of Sapphira (left, right). f-g, Echo and Narcissus (left, right). h, Self-portrait.
No. 948, The Moneychanger and His Wife, by Quentin Metsys.

1993, Mar. 19   Litho.   Perf. 12
947	A161	70s Sheet of 8, #a.-		
		h. + label	8.75	8.75

Souvenir Sheet
Perf. 14½
948	A161	5m multicolored	7.25	7.25

No. 948 contains one 55x88mm stamp.

Flowers — A162

1993, June   Litho.   Perf. 14
949	A162	20s Healing plant	.25	.25
950	A162	30s Calla lily	.25	.25
951	A162	40s Bird of Paradise	.30	.30
952	A162	70s Belladonna	.75	.75
953	A162	1m African lily	1.00	1.00
954	A162	2m Veldt lily	2.00	2.00
955	A162	4m Watsonia	3.75	3.75
956	A162	5m Gazania	4.50	4.50
		Nos. 949-956 (8)	12.80	12.80

Souvenir Sheets
957	A162	7m Leadwort	5.75	5.75
958	A162	7m Desert rose	5.75	5.75

Miniature Sheet

Coronation of Queen Elizabeth II, 40th
Anniv. — A163

No. 959: a, 20s, Official coronation photograph. b, 40s, St. Edward's Crown, Scepter with the Cross. c, 1m, Queen Mother. d, 5m, Queen, family.
7m, Conversation Piece at Royal Lodge, Windsor, by Sir James Gunn, 1950.

1993, June 2   Litho.   Perf. 13½x14
959	A163	Sheet, 2 each,		
		#a.-d.	8.00	8.00

Souvenir Sheet
Perf. 14
960	A163	7m multicolored	15.00	15.00

Butterflies
A164

1993, June 30   Litho.   Perf. 14
961	A164	20s Bi-colored pansy	.25	.25
962	A164	40s Golden pansy	.35	.35
963	A164	70s Yellow pansy	.55	.55
964	A164	1m Pseudo ergolid	.90	.90
965	A164	2m African giant swallowtail	1.75	1.75
966	A164	5m False acraea	3.75	3.75
		Nos. 961-966 (6)	7.55	7.55

Souvenir Sheets
967	A164	7m Seasonal pansy	5.50	5.50
968	A164	7m Ringed pansy	5.50	5.50

African
Trains
A165

Designs: 20s, East African Railways Vulcan 2-8-2, 1929. 30s, Zimbabwe Railways Class 15A, 1952. 40s, South African Railways Class 25 4-8-4, 1953. 70s, East African Railways A58 Class Garratt. 1m, South Africa Class 9E Electric. 2m, East African Railways Class 87, 1971. 3m, East African Railways Class 92, 1971. 5m, South Africa Class 26 2-D-2, 1982.
No. 977, Algeria 231-132BT Class, 1937. No. 978, South African Railway Class 6E Bo-Bo, 1969.

1993, Sept. 24   Litho.   Perf. 14
969	A165	20s multicolored	.25	.25
970	A165	30s multicolored	.40	.40
971	A165	40s multicolored	.45	.45
972	A165	70s multicolored	.90	.90
973	A165	1m multicolored	1.25	1.25
974	A165	2m multicolored	2.40	2.40
975	A165	3m multicolored	3.25	3.25
976	A165	5m multicolored	5.25	5.25
		Nos. 969-976 (8)	14.15	14.15

Souvenir Sheets
977	A165	7m multicolored	6.75	6.75
978	A165	7m multicolored	6.75	6.75

Taipei '93 — A166

Disney characters in Taiwan: 20s, Chung Cheng Park, Keelung. 30s, Chiao-Tienkung Temple Festival. 40s, Procession. 70s, Temple Festival. 1m, Queen's Head Rock Formation, Yehliu, vert. 1.20m, Natl. Concert Hall, Taiwan, vert. 2m, C.K.S. Memorial Hall, Taiwan, vert. 2.50m, Grand Hotel, Taipei.
No. 987, 5m, Natl. Palace Museum, Taipei. No. 988, 6m, Presidential Palace Museum, Taipei, vert.

1993   Litho.   Perf. 14x13½, 13½x14
979-986	A166	Set of 8	13.00	13.00

Souvenir Sheets
987-988	A166	Set of 2	11.00	11.00

Domestic
Cats — A167

Various cats: 20s, 30s, 70s, 5m.
No. 992A, Brown cat eating mouse, vert.

1993, Oct. 29   Litho.   Perf. 14
989-992	A167	Set of 4	6.50	6.50

Souvenir Sheet
992A	A167	5m multicolored	5.50	5.50

Traditional
Houses
A168

Designs: 20s, Khoaling, Khotla. 30s, Lelapa le seotloana morao ho, 1833. 70s, Thakaneng, Baroetsana. 4m, Mohlongoafatse pele ho, 1833.

No. 996A, Lelapa litema le mekhabiso.

1993, Sept. 24
993-996 A168 Set of 4 7.25 7.25

Souvenir Sheet
996A A168 4m multicolored 5.50 5.50

A169

Players, country: 20s, Khomari, Lesotho. 30s, Mohale, Lesotho. 40s, Davor, Yugoslavia; Rincon, Colombia. 50s, Lekhotla, Lesotho. 70s, Khali, Lesotho. 1m, Milla, Cameroun. 1.20m, Platt, England. 2m, Rummenigge, Germany; Lerby, Denmark.

No. 1005, Stejskal & Hasek, Czechoslovakia; Baresi, Italy, horiz. No. 1006, Lindenberger, Czechoslovakia; Schillaci, Italy.

1993 Litho. Perf. 13½x14
997-1004 A169 Set of 8 9.50 9.50

Souvenir Sheets
Perf. 13
1005-1006 A169 6m Set of 2 11.00 11.00

1994 World Cup Soccer Championships, US.

A170

New Democratic Government: 20s, King Letsie III signs oath of office under new constitution. 30s, Parliament building. 50s, Dr. Ntsu Mokhehle sworn in as prime minister. 70s, Transfer of power from Major Gen. P. Ramaema to Dr. Mokhehle.

30s, 50s, 70s are horizontal.

1994, Apr. 2 Litho. Perf. 14
1007 A170 20s multicolored .25 .25
1008 A170 30s multicolored .45 .45
1009 A170 50s multicolored .65 .65
1010 A170 70s multicolored .90 .90
    Nos. 1007-1010 (4) 2.25 2.25

A171

PHILAKOREA '94 — A172

Frogs: 35s, Aquatic river. 50s, Bubbling kassina. 1m, Guttural toad. 1.50m, Common river. No. 1015, Green frog statue. No. 1016, 5m, Black spotted frog, oriental white-eye bird, vert.

1994, Aug. 16 Litho. Perf. 14
1011-1014 A171 Set of 4 3.25 3.25

Souvenir Sheets
1015-1016 A172 Set of 2 11.00 11.00

ICAO, 50th Anniv. A173

Designs: 35s, Airplane, passengers on ground. 50s, Airplane, control tower. 1m, Airplane banking, terminal, control tower. 1.50m, Airplane ascending.

1994 Litho. Perf. 14
1017 A173 35s multicolored .25 .25
1018 A173 50s multicolored .65 .65
1019 A173 1m multicolored 1.25 1.25
1020 A173 1.50m multicolored 2.00 2.00
    Nos. 1017-1020 (4) 4.15 4.15

Medicinal Plants — A174

Designs: 35s, Tagetes minuta. 50s, Plantago lanceolata. 1m, Amaranthus spinosus. 1.50m, Taraxacum officinale. 5m, Datura stramonium.

1995, May 22 Litho. Perf. 14
1021-1024 A174 Set of 4 2.25 2.25

Souvenir Sheet
1025 A174 5m multicolored 2.75 2.75

Pius XII Natl. University, 50th Anniv. A175

Designs: 35s, Pius XII College, 1962. 50s, Univ. of Basutoland, Bechuanaland Protectorate & Swaziland, 1965. 70s, Univ. of Botswana, Lesotho & Swaziland, 1970. 1m, Univ. of Bostswana, Lesotho & Swaziland, 1975. 1.50m, Natl. Univ. of Lesotho, 1988. 2m, Natl. Univ. of Lesotho, procession of vice-chancellors at celebration.

1995, July 26 Litho. Perf. 14
1026-1031 A175 Set of 6 4.25 4.25

A176

Designs: 35s, Qiloane Pinnacle, Thaba-Bosiu, horiz. 50s, Rock Formation, Ha Mohalenyane, horiz. 1m, Botsoela Falls, Malealea. 1.50m, Backpacking, Makhaleng River Gorge, horiz.

4m, Red hot pokers.

1995, Aug. 28 Litho. Perf. 14
1032-1035 A176 Set of 4 2.75 2.75

Souvenir Sheet
1036 A176 4m multicolored 2.50 2.50

No. 1036 contains one 38x58mm stamp. World Tourism Organization, 20th anniv.
No. 1036 withdrawn 9/15 because "Pokers" was misspelled "Porkers."

A177

UN emblem and: 35s, Peace dove. 50s, Scales of justice. 1.50m, Handshake of reconciliation, horiz.

1995, Sept. 26
1037-1039 A177 Set of 3 2.25 2.25
    UN, 50th anniv.

Christmas A178

Roses: 35s, Sutter's Gold. 50s, Michele Meilland. 1m, J. Otto Thilow. 2m, Papa Meilland.

1995, Nov. 1 Litho. Perf. 14
1040-1043 A178 Set of 4 2.75 2.75

A179

UNICEF, 50th Anniv.: 35s, Using iodized salt. 50s, Taking care of livestock, horiz. 70s, Children in classroom. horiz. 1.50m, Children learning traditional dance, singing, horiz.

1996, July 30 Litho. Perf. 14
1044-1047 A179 Set of 4 2.50 2.50

A180

1996 Summer Olympic Games, Atlanta: 1m, US Basketball team, 1936, horiz. 1.50m, Olympic Stadium, Brandenburg Gate, Berlin, horiz. 2m, Jesse Owens, 1936. 3m, Motor boating, horiz.

Past Olympic medalists: No. 1052a, Glen Morris, long jump, decathlon, 1936. b, Said Aouita, 5000-meters, 1984. c, Arnie Robinson, long jump, 1976. d, Hans Woellke, shot put, 1936. e, Renate Stecher, 100-meters, 1972. f, Evelyn Ashford, 100-meters, 1984. g, Willie Davenport, 110-meter hurdles, 1968. h, Bob Beamon, long jump, 1968. i, Heidi Rosenthal, long jump, 1972.

No. 1053, 8m, Michael Gross, swimming, 1984. No. 1054, 8m, Kornelia Ender, swimming, 1976.

1996, Aug. 1
1048-1051 A180 Set of 4 4.00 4.00
1052 A180 1.50m Sheet of 9,
    #a.-i. 10.50 10.50

Souvenir Sheets
1053-1054 A180 Set of 2 11.50 11.50

Maps of Lesotho — A181

No. 1055 — 1911 map: a, Lephaqlioa. b, Maqaleng. c, Molapo. d, Nkeu. e, No area specified. f, Rafanyane. g, No area specified

---

(7800). h, Madibomatso River. i, Konyani. j, Semena River.

No. 1056 — 1978 map: a, No area specified. b, Lepaqoa. c, Mamoha (name). d, Ha Nkisi. e, Ha Rafanyan, Ha Thoora. f, Ha Mikia, Ha Ntseli. g, Ha Kosetabole, Ha Mpeli. h, Ha Selebeli, Ha Theko. i, Ha Rapooane, Ha Ramabotsa. j, Ha Ramani, Khohlontso (Kolberg).

No. 1057 — Locations on 1994 Map: a, Mafika-Lisiu Pass. b, Rampai's Pass, Ha Lesaoana. c, Ha Masaballa. d, Ha Nkisi, Ha Molotanyan. e, Ha Rafanyane, Kobong. f, Laitsoka Pass. g, Katse Reservoir. h, Seshote. i, Ha Rapoeea, Ha Kennan. j, Katse (i, name), Ha Mense.

1996 Sheets of 10, #a-j
1055-1057 A181 35s Set of 3 15.00 15.00

Trains A182

No. 1058, 1.50m: a, ETR 450, Italy. b, TGV, France. c, XPT, Australia. d, Blue Train, South Africa. e, IC 255, Great Britain. f, Bullet Train, Japan.

No. 1059, 1.50m: a, WP Streamlined 4-6-2, India. b, Canadian Pacific 2471, Canada. c, The Caledonian 4-2-2, Scotland. d, Wllllam Mason 4-4-0, US. e, Trans-Siberian Express, Russia. f, Swiss Federal 4-6-0, Switzerland.

No. 1060, 8m, 52 Class, Germany. No. 1061, 8m, ICE, Germany.

1996, Sept. 1 Litho. Perf. 14
Sheets of 6, #a-f
1058-1059 A182 Set of 2 11.50 11.50

Souvenir Sheets
1060-1061 A182 Set of 2 11.00 11.00

Nos. 1060-1061 each contain one 56x42mm stamp.

No. 833 Surcharged

1996 Litho. Perf. 13½
1062 A146 20s on 30s multi — —

Christmas — A183

Women from Mother's Unions: 35s, Methodist Church. 50s, Roman Catholic Church. 1m, Lesotho Evangelical Church. 1.50m, Anglican Church.

1996, Dec. 10 Litho. Perf. 14
1063-1066 A183 Set of 4 2.75 2.75

Highlands Water Project A184

Designs: 35s, "Cooperation for Development." 50s, "Nature and Heritage." 1m, "An Engineering Feat." 1.50m, "LHDA 10th Anniv., 1986-1996."

1997, Apr. 21 Litho. Perf. 14
1067-1070 A184 Set of 4 3.25 3.25

No. 1070 is 72x25mm.

Environmental
Protection —
A184a

Emblem of National Environment Secretariat and: 35s, Animals grazing on reclaimed land. 50s, Person throwing trash in can. 1m, Hands holding globe with tree. 1.20m, Trash and recycling emblem. 1.50m, Collection of rainwater.

1997, June 30
1070A-1070E A184a Set of 5   —   —

1998 World Cup Soccer
Championships, France — A185

Players: 1m, Schmeichel, Denmark. 1.50m, Bergkamp, Holland. 2m, Southgate, England. 2.50m, Asprilla, Colombia. 3m, Gascoigne, England. 4m, Giggs, Wales.
No. 1077: Various action scenes of Argentina vs. Holland, 1978.
No. 1078, 8m, Littbarski, W. Germany, horiz. No. 1079, 8m, Shearer, England.

1997, Oct. 31   *Perf. 13½*
1071-1076 A185 Set of 6   6.50   6.50
1077   A185 1.50m Sheet of 6,
                 #a.-f.   11.00 11.00
Souvenir Sheets
1078-1079 A185 Set of 2   9.00   9.00

Butterflies
A186

No. 1080: a, Spialia spio. b, Cyclyrius pirithous. c, Acraea satis. d, Belenois aurota. e, Spindasis natalensis. f, Torynesis orangica. g, Lepidochrysops variabilis. h, Pinacopteryx eriphea. i, Anthene butleri.
No. 1081, 8m, Bematistes aganice. No. 1082, 8m, Papilio demodocus.

1997, Nov. 28   *Perf. 14*
1080 A186 1.50m Sheet of 9,
            #a.-i.   7.75   7.75
Souvenir Sheets
1081-1082 A186 Set of 2   11.00 11.00

Morija
Museum and
Archives,
40th Anniv.
A187

Designs: 35s, Rock paintings, child, vert. 45s, Lower jaw of hippopotamus, hippo walking in water. 50s, Traditional attire, vert. 1m, Traditional musical instruments, vert. 1.50m, Award, Man with ceremonial garb, vert. 2m Boy riding bull.

Perf. 14½ Syncopated Type A
1998, Jan. 30   Litho.
1083-1088 A187 Set of 6   3.25   3.25

Diana, Princess of
Wales (1961-
97) — A188

Designs: No. 1089, Various portaits. No. 1090, Taking flowers from child.

1998, Mar. 16   Litho.   *Perf. 13½*
1089 A188 3m Sheet of 6, #a.-f.   9.00 9.00
Souvenir Sheet
1090 A188 9m multicolored   9.00 9.00

A189

A190

Wildlife — A191

No. 1091 — Cape vulture: a, Head. b, Perched on rock with head down. c, Looking left. d, Looking right.
No. 1092: a, Atitlan grebe. b, Cabot's tragopan. c, Spider monkey. d, Dibatag. e, Right whale. f, Imperial parrot. g, Cheetah. h, Brown-eared pheasant. i, Leatherback turtle. j, Imperial woodpecker. k, Andean condor. l, Barbary deer. m, Grey gentle lemur. n, Cuban parrot. o, Numbat. p, Short-tailed albatross. q, Green turtle. r, White rhinoceros. s, Diademed sifaka. t, Galapagos penguin.
No. 1093: a, Impala. b, Black bear. c, Buffalo. d, Elephant. e, Kangaroo. f, Lion. g, Panda. h, Tiger. i, Zebra.
No. 1094, 8m, Nectarinia talatala. No. 1095, 8m, Psephotus chrysopterygius. No. 1096, 8m, Percina tanasi.
No. 1097, 8m, Monkey.

1998, Apr. 27   Litho.   *Perf. 14*
1091 A189 1m Strip of 4,
            #a.-d.   4.50   4.50
1092 A190 1m Sheet of 20,
            #a.-t.   11.00 11.00
1093 A191 1.50m Sheet of 9,
            #a.-i.   7.00   7.00
Souvenir Sheets
1094-1096 A190 Set of 3   12.00 12.00
1097   A191 8m multicolored 4.00 4.00

No. 1091 was issued in sheets of 12 stamps. World Wildlife Fund (No. 1091).

Cats
A192

Designs: 70s, Siamese. 1m, Chartreux. 2m, Korat. 3m, Egyptian mau. 4m, Bombay. 5m, Burmese.
No. 1104, 2m: a, Japanese bobtail. b, British white. c, Bengal. d, Abyssinian. e, Snowshoe. f, Scottish fold.

No. 1105, 2m: a, Maine coon. b, Balinese. c, Persian. d, Javanese. e, Turkish angora. f, Tiffany.
No. 1106, 8m, Singapura. No. 1107, 8m, Tonkinese.

1998, May 18
1098-1103 A192 Set of 6   7.75   7.75
Sheets of 6, #a-f
1104-1105 A192 Set of 2   16.00 16.00
Souvenir Sheets
1106-1107 A192 Set of 2   10.00 10.00

Mushrooms — A193

Designs: 70s, Laccaria laccata. 1m, Mutinus caninus. 1.50m, Tricholoma lascivum. 2m, Clitocybe geotrapa. 3m, Amanita excelsa. 4m, Red-capped bolete.
No. 1114: a, Parrot wax cap. b, Cortinarius obtusus. c, Volvariella bombycina. d, Continarius caerylescens. e, Laccaria amethystea. f, Tricholoma aurantium. g, Amanita excelsa. h, Clavaria helvola. i, Cortinarius caerylescens. j, Russula queletii. k, Amanita phalloides. l, Lactarius delicious.
No. 1115, 8m, Amanita pantherina. No. 1116, 8m, Boletus satanus.

1998, June 15   Litho.   *Perf. 14*
1108-1113 A193 Set of 6   6.50   6.50
1114 A193 1m Sheet of 12, #a.-l. 6.50 6.50
Souvenir Sheets
1115-1116 A193 Set of 2   9.00   9.00

Japanese
Film Stars
A194

No. 1117: a, Takamine Hideko. b, James Shigeta. c, Miyoshi Umeki. d, May Ishimara. e, Sessue Hayakawa. f, Miiko Taka. g, Mori Masayuki. h, Hara Setsuko. i, Kyo Machiko. 10m, Toshiro Mifune.

1998, July 14   Litho.   *Perf. 14*
1117 A194 2m Sheet of 9, #a.-i. 7.50 7.50
Souvenir Sheet
1118 A194 10m multicolored   4.00 4.00

Prehistoric Animals — A195

No. 1119, 2m: a, Nyctosaurus (b). b, Volcanoes, wings of nyctosaurus, eudimorphodon. c, Eudimorphodon (b). d, Apatosaurus (g). e, Peteinosaurus (d, f, i). f, Tropeognathus. g, Pteranodon ingens (d). h, Ornithodesmus (g). i, Wuerhosaurus.
No. 1120, 2m: a, Ceresiosaurus (b, c, d). b, Rhomaleosaurus (d, e, f). c, Anomalocaris (b, f). d, Mixosaurus (e, g, h). e, Stethacanthus. f, Dunklosteus (c, e, i). g, Tommotia. h, Sanctacaris. i, Ammonites (a, f, h).
No. 1121, 2m: a, Rhamphorhynchus (b, d). b, Brachiosaurus (c, f). c, Mamenchisaurus hochuanensis (a, d, e, f). d, Ceratosaurus nasicornis (e, g, h). e, Archaeopteryx (b). f, Leaellynasaura amicargraphica (e, i). g, Chasmosaurus belli (h). h, Deinonychus. i, Deinonychus (h).
No. 1122, 10m, Woolly rhinoceros. No. 1123, 10m, Tyrannosaurus. No. 1124, 10m, Coelophysis.

1998, Aug. 10   **Sheets of 9, #a-i**
1119-1121 A195 Set of 3   24.00 24.00
Souvenir Sheets
1122-1124 A195 Set of 3   14.00 14.00

Intl. Year
of the
Ocean
A196

Fish: No. 1125, 1m, Treefish. No. 1126, 1m, Tiger barb. No. 1127, 1m, Bandtail puffer. No. 1128, 1m, Cod. No. 1129, 1.50m, Filefish. No. 1130, 1.50m, Clown loach. No. 1131, 1.50m, Sicklefin killie. No. 1132, 1.50m, Christy's lyretail. No. 1133, 2m, Brook trout. No. 1134, 2m, Pacific electric ray. No. 1135, 2m, Bighead searobin. No. 1136, 2m, Emerald betta. 3m, Harlequin tuskfish. 4m, Half-moon angelfish. 5m, Spotted trunkfish. 6m, Wolf-eel. 7m, Cherubfish.
No. 1142, 2m: a, Platy variatus. b, Archerfish. c, Clown knifefish. d, Angelicus. e, Black arowana. f, Spotted scat. g, Kribensis. h, Golden pheasant.
No. 1143, 2m: a, Bluegill. b, Grayling. c, Walleye. d, Brown trout. e, Atlantic salmon. f, Northern pike. g, Large mouth bass. h, Rainbow trout.
No. 1144, 2m: a, Purple firefish. b, Halequin sweetlips. c, Clown wrasse. d, Bicolor angelfish. e, False cleanerfish. f, Mandarinfish. g, Regal tang. h, Clownfish.
No. 1145, 2m: a, Weakfish. b, Red drum. c, Blue marlin. d, Yellowfin tuna. e, Barracuda. f, Striped bass. g, White shark. h, Permit.
No. 1146, 12m, Cyprinus carpio. No. 1147, 12m, Oncorhychus. No. 1148, 12m, Pseudopleuronectes americanus. No. 1149, 12m, Heterodontus francisci.

1998, Oct. 15   Litho.   *Perf. 14*
1125-1141 A196 Set of 17   17.50 17.50
Sheets of 8, #a-h
1142-1145 A196 Set of 4   26.00 26.00
Souvenir Sheets
1146-1149 A196 Set of 4   19.00 19.00

...

Africa in
Films
A197

No. 1150: a, "Simba." b, "Call to Freedom." c, "Cry the Beloved Country." d, "King Solomon's Mines." e, "Flame and the Fire." f, "Cry Freedom." g, "Bopha!" h, "Zulu."
10m "Born Free," horiz.

1998, July 14   Litho.   *Perf. 14*
1150 A197 2m Sheet of 8, #a.-
            h.   7.50   7.50
Souvenir Sheet
1151 A197 10m multicolored   4.00   4.00

Flowers — A198

Designs: 10s, Pelargonium sidoides. 15s, Aponogeton ranunculiflorus. 20s, Sebaea leiostyla. 40s, Sebaea grandis. 50s, Satyrium neglectum. 60s, Massonia jasminiflora. 70s, Ajuga ophrydis. 80s, Nemesia fruticans. 1m, Aloe broomii. 2m, Wahlenbergia androsacea. 2.50m, Phygelius capensis. 3m, Dianthus basuticus. 4.50m, Rhodohypoxis baurii. 5m, Turbina oblongata. 6m, Hibiscus microcarpus. 10m, Lobelia erinus, moraea stricta.

1998   Litho.   *Perf. 14*
1152 A198 10s multicolored   .25   .25
1153 A198 15s multicolored   .25   .25
1154 A198 20s multicolored   .25   .25

1155	A198	40s multicolored	.25	.25
1156	A198	50s multicolored	.25	.25
1157	A198	60s multicolored	.25	.25
1158	A198	70s multicolored	.25	.25
1159	A198	80s multicolored	.40	.40
1160	A198	1m multicolored	.50	.50
1161	A198	2m multicolored	1.00	1.00
1162	A198	2.50m multicolored	1.25	1.25
1163	A198	3m multicolored	1.50	1.50
1164	A198	4.50m multicolored	2.25	2.25
1165	A198	5m multicolored	2.40	2.40
1166	A198	6m multicolored	3.00	3.00
1167	A198	10m multicolored	4.50	4.50
		Nos. 1152-1167 (16)	18.55	18.55

Nos. 1152-1167 are dated 1997.

Coronation of King Letsie III, 1st Anniv. — A199

No. 1168: a, Receiving crown. b, Waving. c, Facing left.

1998, Oct. 31
1168 A199 1m Strip of 3, #a.-c.   2.25 2.25

Dogs
A200

Designs: 70s, Akita. 1m, Canaan. 2m, Eskimo. 4.50m, Norwegian elkhound.
No. 1173, 2m: a, Cirneco dell'etna. b, Afghan hound. c, Finnish spitz. d, Dalmatian. e, Basset hound. f, Shar-pei.
No. 1174, 2m: a, Boxer. b, Catalan sheepdog. c, English toy spaniel. d, Greyhound. e, Keeshond. f, Bearded collie.
No. 1175, 8m, Rough collie. No. 1176, 8m, Borzoi.

1999, May 18   Litho.   Perf. 14
1169-1172 A200   Set of 4   4.00 4.00
Sheets of 6, #a-f
1173-1174 A200   Set of 2   11.00 11.00
Souvenir Sheets
1175-1176 A200   Set of 2   10.00 10.00

Birds
A201

Designs: 70s, Belted kingfisher. 1.50m, Palm cockatoo, vert. 2m, Red-tailed hawk. 3m, Tufted puffin. 4m, Reddish egret. 5m, Hoatzin, vert.
No. 1183, 2m: a, Evening grosbeak. b, Lesser blue-winged pitta. c, Altamira oriole. d, Rose-breasted grosbeak. e, Yellow warbler. f, Akiapolaau. g, American goldfinch. h, Northern flicker. i, Western tanager.
No. 1184, 2m, vert: a, Blue jay. b, Northern cardinal. c, Yellow-headed blackbird. d, Red crossbill. e, Cedar waxwing. f, Vermilion flycatcher. g, Pileated woodpecker. h, Western meadowlark. i, Kingfisher.
No. 1185, 8m, Great egret. No. 1186, 8m, Zosterops erythropleura.

1999, June 28   Litho.   Perf. 14
1177-1182 A201   Set of 6   8.00 8.00
Sheets of 9, #a-i
1183-1184 A201   Set of 2   19.00 19.00
Souvenir Sheets
1185-1186 A201   Set of 2   10.00 10.00
No. 1183c is incorrectly inscribed "Atlamira."

Orchids — A202

Designs: 1.50m, Cattleya dowiana. 3m, Diurus behri. 4m, Ancistrochilus rothchildianus. 5m, Aerangis curnowiana. 7m, Arachnis flos-aerls. 8m, Aspasia principissa.
No. 1193, 2m: a, Dendrobium bellaudum. b, Dendrobium trigonopus. c, Dimerandra emarginata. d, Dressleria eburnea. e, Dracula tubeana. f, Disa kirstenbosch. g, Encyclia alata. h, Epidendrum pseudepidendrum. i, Eriopsis biloba.
No. 1194, 2m: a, Apasia epidendroides. b, Barkaria lindleyana. c, Bifrenaria terragona. d, Bulbophyllum graveolens. e, Brassavola flagellaris. f, Bollea lawrenceana. g, Caladenia carnea. h, Catasetum macrocarpum. i, Cattleya aurantiaca.
No. 1195, 2m: a, Cochleanthes discolor. b, Cischweinfia dasyandra. c, Ceratostylis retisquama. d, Comparettia speciosa. e, Cryptostylis subulata. f, Cycnoches ventricsum. g, Dactylorhiza maculata. h, Cypripedium calceolus. i, Cymbidium finlaysonianum.
No. 1196, 10m, Paphiopedilum tonsum. No. 1197, 10m, Laelia rubescens. No. 1198, 10m, Ansellium africana. No. 1199, 10m, Ophrys apifera.

1999, July 30   Litho.   Perf. 14
1187-1192 A202   Set of 6   13.00 13.00
Sheets of 9, #a-i
1193-1195 A202   Set of 3   22.50 22.50
Souvenir Sheets
1196-1199 A202   Set of 4   15.00 15.00

Chinese Art — A203

No. 1200 — Paintings by Pan Tianshou (1897-1971): a, Water Lily at Night. b, Hen and Chicks. c, Plum Blossom and Orchid. d, Plum Blossom and Banana Tree. e, Crane and Pine. f, Swallows. g, Eagle on the Pine (black eagle). h, Palm Tree. i, Eagle on the Pine (gray eagle). j, Orchids.
No. 1201: a, Sponge Gourd. b, Dragonfly.

1999, Aug. 16   Perf. 13x13¼
1200 A203 1.50m Sheet of 10, #a.-j.   8.50 8.50
Souvenir Sheet
1201 A203 6m Sheet of 2, #a.-b.   6.50 6.50
China 1999 World Philatelic Exhibition. No. 1201 contains two 51x40mm stamps.

UN Rights of the Child Convention, 10th Anniv. — A204

No. 1202: a, Black boy. b, Asian girl. c, Caucasian boy.

1999, Aug. 16   Perf. 14
1202 A204 2m Sheet of 3, #a.-c.   3.00 3.00

Paintings by Hokusai (1760-1849) — A205

No. 1203, 3m: a, Nakamaro Watching the Moon from a Hill. b, Peonies and Butterfly. c, The Blind (bald man, both eyes open). d, The Blind (bald man, one eye shut). e, People Crossing an Arched Bridge (two at crest). f, People Crossing an Arched Bridge (river).
No. 1204, 3m: a, A View of Sumida River in Snow. b, Two Carp. c, The Blind (man with hair, both eyes shut). d, The Blind (man with hair, one eye open). e, Fishing by Torchlight. f, Whaling off the Goto Islands.
No. 1205, 10m, The Moon Above Yodo River and Osaka Castle, vert. No. 1206, 10m, Bellflower and Dragonfly, vert.

1999, Aug. 16   Perf. 13¾
Sheet of 6, #a-f
1203-1204 A205   Set of 2   14.00 14.00
Souvenir Sheets
1205-1206 A205   Set of 2   8.00 8.00

Queen Mother (b. 1900) — A206

No. 1207: a, Wearing hat, 1938. b, With King George VI, 1948. c, Wearing tiara, 1963. d, Wearing hat, 1989.
15m, Waving at Clarence House.

1999, Aug. 16   Perf. 14
1207 A206 5m Sheet of 4, #a.-d., + label   7.50 7.50
Souvenir Sheet
Perf. 13¾
1208 A206 15m multicolored   6.25 6.25
No. 1208 contains one 38x51mm stamp.

Johann Wolfgang von Goethe (1749-1832) — A207

No. 1209: a, Mephistopheles appears as a dog in Faust's study. b, Portraits of Goethe and Friedrich von Schiller. c, Mephistopheles disguised as dog scorching the earth.
12m, Mephistopheles.

1999, Aug. 16   Perf. 14
1209 A207 6m Sheet of 3, #a.-c.   6.25 6.25
Souvenir Sheet
1210 A207 12m multicolored   4.50 4.50

IBRA '99, Nuremberg, Germany — A208

Designs: 7m, Austerity 2-10-10 locomotive, building in Frankfurt am Main. 8m, Adler locomotive, Brandenburg Gate.

1999, Aug. 16   Perf. 14x14½
1211 A208 7m multicolored   2.75 2.75
1212 A208 8m multicolored   3.25 3.25

Ships
A209

No. 1213, 4m: a, James Watt. b, Savannah. c, Amistad. d, Brick. e, Great Briain. f, Sirius.
No. 1214, 4m: a, France. b, Queen Elizabeth II. c, United States. d, Queen Elizabeth I. e, Michelangelo. f, Mauretania.
No. 1215, 4m: a, New Jersey. b, Aquila. c, De Zeven Provincien. d, Formidable. e, Vittorio Veneto. f, Hampshire.
No. 1216, 4m: a, Shearwater. b, British submarine. c, Hovercraft SRN 130. d, Italian submarine. e, Sr. N/3. f, Soucoupe Plongeante.
No. 1217, 15m, E. W. Morrison. No. 1218, 15m, Titanic. No. 1219, 15m, German U-boat. No. 1220, 15m, Enterprise.

1999, Dec. 31   Litho.   Perf. 14
Sheets of 6, #a.-f.
1213-1216 A209   30.00 30.00
Souvenir Sheets
1217-1220 A209   Set of 4   21.00 21.00
Names of ships are only found on sheet margins.

Millennium
A210

No. 1221 — Highlights of the 12th century: a, Chinese make first rocket. b, Burmese temple guardian. c, Troubador. d, Abbé Suger. e, Pope Adrian IV. f, King Henry II of England. g, Holy Roman Emperor Barbarossa. h, Yoritomo establishes shogunate in Japan. i, Crusader monument. j, Ibn Rushd translates Aristotle. k, Archbishop Thomas Becket. l, Leaning Tower of Pisa. m, Pivot windmill. n, Saladin. o, Richard the Lion-Hearted. p, Easter Island statues (60x40mm) q, Third Crusade begins.

1999, Dec. 31   **Perf. 12¾x12½**
1221 A210 1.50m Sheet of 17,
    #a.-q.   11.00 11.00

Wedding of King
Letsie III to
Karabo Anne
Motsoeneng
A211

No. 1222: a, King, bride in Western attire. b,
Bride. c, King. d, King, bride in native attire.

2000, Feb. 18   **Litho.**   **Perf. 14**
1222 A211 1m Sheet of 4, #a.-d.,
    + label   3.75 3.75

Prince William, 18th Birthday — A212

No. 1223: a, Wearing bow tie. b, Wearing
scarf. c, Wearing striped shirt. d, Wearing
sweater, holding car door.
15m, Wearing sweater, diff.

2000, June 21   **Litho.**   **Perf. 14**
1223 A212 4m Sheet of 4, #a-d 6.50 6.50
    Souvenir Sheet
       Perf. 13¾
1224 A212 15m multi   6.50 6.50
No. 1223 contains four 28x42mm stamps.

First Zeppelin Flight, Cent. — A213

No. 1225 — Ferdinand von Zeppelin and: a,
LZ- 127. b, LZ-130. c, LZ-10.
15m, LZ-130, diff.

2000, July 6   **Perf. 14**
1225 A213 8m Sheet of 3, #a-c 8.50 8.50
    Souvenir Sheet
1226 A213 15m multi   6.50 6.50
No. 1225 contains three 42x28mm stamps.

Berlin Film Festival, 50th
Anniv. — A214

No. 1227: a, Gena Rowlands. b, Vlastimil
Brodsky. c, Carlos Saura. d, La Collection-
euse. e, Le Depart. f, Le Diable Probablement.
15m, Stammheim.

2000, July 6
1227 A214 6m Sheet of 6,
       #a-f   12.00 12.00
    Souvenir Sheet
1228 A214 15m multi   6.50 6.50

Souvenir Sheets

2000 Summer Olympics,
Sydney — A215

No. 1229: a, Nedo Nadi. b, Swimming. c,
Aztec Stadium, Mexico City and Mexican flag.
d, Ancient Greek boxers.

2000, July 6
1229 A215 6m Sheet of 4, #a-d 8.50 8.50

Public Railways, 175th Anniv. — A216

No. 1230: a, George Stephenson. b, Stephenson's patent locomotive engine. c, Stephenson's Britannia Tubular Bridge.

2000, July 6
1230 A216 8m Sheet of 3, #a-c 8.50 8.50

Johann Sebastian Bach (1685-
1750) — A217

2000, July 6
1231 A217 15m multi   6.50 6.50

Flowers — A218

Designs: 4m, Moore's crinum. 5m, Flame
lily. 6m, Cape clivia. 8m, True sugarbush.
No. 1236, 3m: a, Spotted leaved arum. b,
Christmas bells. c, Lady Monson. d, Wild
pomegranate. e, Blushing bride. f, Bot River
protea.
No. 1237, 3m: a, Starry gardenia. b, Pink
hibiscus. c, Dwarf poker. d, Coast kaffirboom.
e, Rose cockade. f, Pride of Table Mountain.
No. 1238, 3m: a, Drooping agpanthus. b,
Yellow marsh afrikander. c, Weak stemmed
painted lady. d, Impala lily. e, Beatrice wat-
sonia. f, Pink arum.
No. 1239, 15m, Green arum. No. 1240,
15m, Red hairy erica, horiz.

2000, July 12
1232-1235 A218 Set of 4   9.00 9.00
    Sheets of 6, #a-f
1236-1238 A218 Set of 3   21.00 21.00
    Souvenir Sheets
1239-1240 A218 Set of 2   15.00 15.00

Apollo-Soyuz Mission, 25th
Anniv. — A219

No. 1241: a, Apollo 18 and Soyuz 19
docked. b, Apollo 18. c, Soyuz 19.

2000, July 6   **Litho.**   **Perf. 14**
1241 A219 8m Sheet of 3,
       #a-c   9.00 9.00
    Souvenir Sheet
1242 A219 15m shown   6.50 6.50

Souvenir Sheet

Albert Einstein (1879-1955) — A220

2000, July 6   **Perf. 14¼**
1243 A220 15m multi   6.50 6.50

Endangered Wildlife — A221

No. 1244, 4m, horiz.: a, Alethe. b, Temminck's pangolin. c, Cheetah. d, African elephant. e, Chimpanzee. f, Northern white
rhinoceros.
No. 1245, 4m, horiz.: a, African black rhinoceros. b, Leopard. c, Roseate tern. d,
Mountain gorilla. e, Mountain zebra. f, Zanzibar red colobus monkey.
No. 1246, horiz: a, Wildebeest. b, Tree
hyrax. c, Red lechwe. d, Eland.
No. 1247, 15m, Dugong. No. 1248, 15m,
West African manatee.

2000, Aug. 10   **Litho.**   **Perf. 14**
    Sheets of 6, #a-f
1244-1245 A221 Set of 2   18.00 18.00
1246 A221 5m Sheet of 4, #a-
    d   7.75 7.75
    Souvenir Sheets
1247-1248 A221 Set of 2   16.00 16.00
The Stamp Show 2000, London.

Automobiles — A222

No. 1249, 3m: a, 1960 Cadillac El Dorado
Seville. b, 1955-75 Citroen DS. c, 1961 Ford
Zephyr Zodiac Mk II. d, 1945-55 MG TF. e,
1949-65 Porsche 356. f, 1955 Ford
Thunderbird.
No. 1250, 3m: a, 1948-52 Cisitalia 202
Coupe. b, 1990s Dodge Viper. c, 1968-69,
TVR Vixen Sl. d, 1957-70 Lotus 7. e, 1964-68
Ferrari 275 GTB/4. f, 1951 Pegasus Touring
Spider.
No. 1251, 4m: a, 1913 Fiat Type O. b, 1914
Stutz Bearcat. c, 1924 French Levat. d, 1888

Benz Motorwagen. e, 1925 Isota Fraschini Type 8A. f, 1887 Markus Motor Carriage.
No. 1252, 4m: a, 1951 Morris Minor. b, 1935 Hispano-Suiza Type 68. c, 1949 MG TC. d, 1955 Morgan 4/4. e, 1950 Jaguar XK120. f, 1946-49 Triumph 1800/2000 Roadster.
No. 1253, 15m, 1896 Bersey Electric Car. No. 1254, 15m, 1948-71 Morris Minor 1000. No. 1255, 15m, 1953-63 AC Ace. No. 1256, 15m, Ferrari F40, vert.
Illustration reduced.

2000, Sept. 1   **Sheets of 6, #a-f**
1249-1252 A222   Set of 4   30.00 30.00
Souvenir Sheets
1253-1256 A222   Set of 4   25.00 25.00

Fight Against AIDS
A223

Designs: 70s, "Fight AIDS, not people living with it." 1m, "Speed kills, so does AIDS. Go Slow!" 1.50m, "People with AIDS need friends, not rejection," vert. 2.10m, "Even when you're off duty, protect the nation."

2001, Jan. 22   **Litho.**   **Perf. 14**
1257-1260 A223   Set of 4   5.00 5.00

Butterflies
A224

Designs: 70s, Great orange tip. 1m, Red-banded pereute. 1.50m, Sword grass brown. No. 1264, 2m, Striped blue crow. No. 1265, 3m, Alfalfa. 4m, Doris.
No. 1267, 2m: a, African migrant. b, Large oak blue. c, Wanderer. d, Tiger swallowtail. e, Union jack. f, Saturn. g, Broad-bordered grass yellow. h, Hewitson's uraneis.
No. 1268, 2m: a, Orange-banded sulfur. b, Large wood nymph. c, Postman. d, Palmfly. e, Gulf fritillary. f, Cairns birdwing. g, Common morpho. h, Common dotted border.
No. 1269, 3m: a, Bertoni's antwren (bird). b, Clorinde. c, Iolas blue. d, Mocker swallowtail. e, Common Indian crow. f, Grecian shoemaker. g, Small flambeau. h, Orchid swallowtail.
No. 1270, 15m, Crimson tip. No. 1271, 15m, Forest queen.

2001, Mar. 1   **Litho.**   **Perf. 13¼x13¾**
1261-1266 A224   Set of 6   7.00 7.00
Sheets of 8, #a-h
1267-1269 A224   Set of 3   24.00 24.00
Souvenir Sheets
1270-1271 A224   Set of 2   22.00 22.00

Phila Nippon '01, Japan
A225

Designs: 1.50m, Man in carriage from The Battle of Lepanto and the Map of the World, by unknown artist. 2m, Battle scene from The Battle of Lepanto and the Map of the World. 3m, Crane from Birds and Flowers of the Four Seasons, by Eitoku Kano. 4m, The Four Elegant Pastimes. 7m, Maple Viewing at Mount Takao, by unknown artist. 8m, The Four Accomplishments, by Yusho Kaiho.
No. 1278, 5m: a, Portrait of a Lady, by unknown artist. b, Portrait of Tadakatsu Honda, by unknown artist. c, Portrait of the Wife of Tokujo Goto, by unknown aritst. d, Portrait of Emperor Go-yosei, by Takanobu Kano. e, Portrait of Tenzuiin, Hideyoshi's Mother, by Sochin Hoshuku.
No. 1279, 6m: a, Portrait of Yusai Hosokawa, by Suden Ishin. b, Portrait of Sen No Rikyu, attributed to Tohaku Hasegawa. c, Portrait of Oichi No Kata, by unknown artist. d,

Portrait of Ittetsu Inaba, attributed to Hasegawa. e, Portrait of Nobunaga Oda, by Sochin Kokei.
No. 1280, 15m, Portrait of Ieyasu Tokugawa, by unknown artist. No. 1281, 15m, Portrait of Hideyoshi Toyotomi, by unknown artist.

Perf. 13¾, 14 (#1278-1279)
2001, May 31   **Litho.**
1272-1277 A225   Set of 6   6.00 6.00
Sheets of 5, #a-e
1278-1279 A225   Set of 2   30.00 30.00
Souvenir Sheets
1280-1281 A225   Set of 2   14.50 14.50
Size of stamps on Nos. 1278-1279: 85x28mm.
Nos. 1274-1275 are incorrectly inscribed. No. 1274 actually depicts "Landscape with Flowers and Birds." No. 1275 shows a detail from "The Four Elegant Pastimes," by Eitoku Kano.

Mushrooms
A226

Designs: No. 1282, 5m, Bell-shaped panaeolus. No. 1283, 5m, Golden false pholiota. No. 1284, 5m, Shiny cap. No. 1285, 5m, Sooty brown waxy cap.
No. 1286, 3m: a, Violet cortinarius. b, Angel's wings. c, Collybia velutibes. d, Lentinellus. e, Anthurus aseroiformis. f, Caesar's mushroom.
No. 1287, 4m: a, Pungent cortinarius. b, Peziza sarcosphaera. c, Emetic russula. d, Questionable stropharia. e, Apricot jelly mushroom. f, Anise-scented clitocybe.
No. 1288, 15m, Cone-shaped waxy cap, horiz. No. 1289, 15m, Boletus, horiz.

2001, June 29   **Perf. 14**
1282-1285 A226   Set of 4   9.00 9.00
Sheets of 6, #a-f
1286-1287 A226   Set of 2   19.00 19.00
Souvenir Sheets
1288-1289 A226   Set of 2   14.00 14.00
Belgica 2001 Intl. Stamp Exhibition, Brussels (Nos. 1286-1289).

UN High Commissioner for Refugees, 50th Anniv. — A227

Designs: 70s, Silhouette of woman and child. 1m, Child and animal. 1.50m, Woman, vert. 2.10m, Information technology, vert.

2001, Aug. 20   **Perf. 14**
1290-1293 A227   Set of 4   4.75 4.75

Birds of Prey — A228

Designs: 70s, Black kite. 1m, Martial eagle. 1.50m, Bateleur. 2.10m, African goshawk. 2.50m, Bearded vulture. 3m, Jackal buzzard.

2001, Oct. 1   **Litho.**   **Perf. 14**
1294-1299 A228   Set of 6   5.00 5.00

Southern African Wildlife
A229

Designs: 1m, Grass owl. 2.10m, Klipspringer. 3m, Saddlebacked jackal. 5m, Black wildebeest.
No. 1304, 4m: a, Damara zebra. b, Bontebok. c, Eland. d, Lion. e, Saddlebacked jackal, diff. f, Yellow-billed kite.
No. 1305, 4m: a, Aardvark. b, Rock kestrel. c, Black-footed cat. d, Springhare. e, Aardwolf. f, Rock hyrax.
No. 1306, 15m, black-shouldered kite. No. 1307, 15m, Caracal, vert.

2001, Oct. 15   **Litho.**   **Perf. 14**
1300-1303 A229   Set of 4   6.00 6.00
Sheets of 6, #a-f
1304-1305 A229   Set of 2   21.00 21.00
Souvenir Sheets
1306-1307 A229   Set of 2   15.00 15.00

Reign of Queen Elizabeth II, 50th Anniv. — A230

No. 1308: a, Queen seated. b, Queen with Prince Philip and British flag. c, Queen with man. c, Prince Philip.
20m, Queen wearing black suit.

2002, Feb. 6   **Litho.**   **Perf. 14¼**
1308 A230   8m Sheet of 4,   #a-d   13.00 13.00
Souvenir Sheet
1309 A230   20m multi   10.00 10.00

United We Stand — A231

2002, Aug. 13   **Perf. 14**
1310 A231   7m multi   4.00 4.00
Printed in sheets of 4.

SOS Children's Village, Lithabaneng — A232

2002, Aug. 13
1311 A232   10m multi   4.50 4.50

Rotary International in Lesotho, 25th Anniv. — A233

Designs: 8m, Horner Wood. 10m, Paul Harris.
No. 1314, 25m, Stylized globe and clasped hands. No. 1315, 25m, Golden Gate Bridge, horiz.

2002, Aug. 13
1312-1313 A233   Set of 2   7.00 7.00
Souvenir Sheets
1314-1315 A233   Set of 2   18.00 18.00

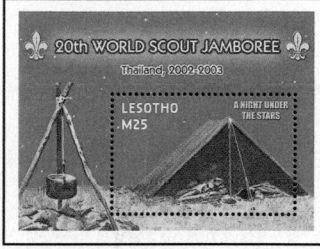

20th World Scout Jamboree, Thailand — A234

No. 1316: a, Sheet bend knots. b, Pup and forester tents. c, Canoeing. d, Water rescue. 25m, A night under the stars.

2002, Aug. 13
1316 A234   9m Sheet of 4,   #a-d   11.50 11.50
Souvenir Sheet
1317 A234   25m multi   11.00 11.00

Intl. Year of Mountains — A235

No. 1318, horiz.: a, Mt. Machache. b, Mt. Thabana Li-Mèle. c, Mt. Qiloane. d, Mt. Thaba Bosiu.
25m, Mt. Rainier, US.

2002, Aug. 13
1318 A235   8m Sheet of 4,   #a-d   11.50 11.50
Souvenir Sheet
1319 A235   25m multi   11.50 11.50

Intl. Year of Ecotourism — A236

No. 1320, horiz.: a, Plant. b, Flowers. c, Man and horses. d, Lion. e, Frog. f, House. 20m, Bird.

2002, Aug. 13
1320 A236   6m Sheet of 6,
                #a-f   13.00 13.00
Souvenir Sheet
1321 A236   20m multi   8.50 8.50

Flowers, Insects and Spiders — A237

No. 1322, 6m — Flowers: a, Angel's fishing rod. b, Marigold. c, Joan's blood. d, Mule pink. e, Tiger lily. f, Comtesse de Bouchaud.
No. 1323, 6m — Orchids: a, Phragmipedium besseae. b, Cypripedium calceolus. c, Cattleya Louise Georgiana. d, Brassocattleya binosa. e, Laelia gouldiana. f, Paphiopedilum maudiae.
No. 1324, 6m, horiz. — Insects: a, Leaf grasshopper. b, Golden-ringed dragonfly. c, Weevil-hunting wasp. d, European grasshopper. e, Thread-waisted wasp. f, Mantid.
No. 1325, 20m, Bleeding heart. No. 1326, 20m, Brassavola tuberculata. No. 1327, 20m, Orb web spider.

2002, Aug. 30   **Perf. 14**
Sheets of 6, #a-f
1322-1324 A237   Set of 3   35.00 35.00
Souvenir Sheets
1325-1327 A237   Set of 3   25.00 25.00

Coronation of Queen Elizabeth II, 50th Anniv. (in 2003) — A238

No. 1328: a, Wearing blue hat. b, Wearing white hat. c, Wearing black hat. 15m, Wearing red hat.

2004, May 17   Litho.   Perf. 14
1328 A238   8m Sheet of 3, #a-c   7.00 7.00
Souvenir Sheet
1329 A238   15m multi   4.50 4.50

Prince William, 21st Birthday (in 2003) — A239

No. 1330: a, Wearing sunglasses. b, Wearing suit and tie c, Wearing sports shirt. 15m, As young boy.

2004, May 17
1330 A239   8m Sheet of 3, #a-c   8.00 8.00
Souvenir Sheet
1331 A239   15m multi   4.75 4.75

Intl. Year of Fresh Water (in 2003) — A240

No. 1332: a, Top of Qiloane Falls (gray water at top). b, Middle portion of Qiloane Falls (narrow at top). c, Bottom portion of Qiloane Falls. 15m, Orange River.

2004, May 17   **Perf. 14¼**
1332 A240   8m Sheet of 3,
                #a-c   12.00 12.00
Souvenir Sheet
1333 A240   15m multi   7.50 7.50

Powered Flight, Cent. (in 2003) — A241

No. 1334: a, Louis Blériot's Canard at Bagatelle, 1906. b, Blériot's Double-winged Libellule, 1907. c, Cross-country flight of Blériot VIII, Toury to Artenay, 1908. d, Blériot XII test flight, 1909. 15m, Blériot XI.

2004, May 17
1334 A241   6m Sheet of 4, #a-d   9.00 9.00
Souvenir Sheet
1335 A241   15m multi   6.75 6.75

Worldwide Fund for Nature (WWF) — A242

No. 1336 — Southern bald ibis: a, On nest, country name in white at LR. b, Flying to right, black denomination. c, Standing on rock, black denomination. d, Facing left.
No. 1337 — Southern bald ibis: a, Standing on rock, red denomination. b, Flying to left, red denomination. c, On nest, country name in black at UR.

2004, May 17   **Perf. 14**
1336   Horiz. strip of 4   4.50 4.50
a.-d.   A242 3m Any single   .90 .90
1337   Horiz. strip of 4,
            #1336d, 1337a-1337c   4.50 4.50
a.-c.   A242 3m Any single   .90 .90
No. 1336 printed in sheets of 4 strips. No. 1337 printed in sheets of 2 strips.

Mammals A243

Designs: 1m, Cape porcupine. 1.50m, Brown rat. 2.10m, Springhare, vert. No. 1341, 5m, South African galago, vert.
No. 1342, 5m: a, Striped grass mouse. b, Greater galago. c, Ground pangolin. d, Banded mongoose.
15m, Egyptian rousette, vert.

2004, May 17
1338-1341 A243   Set of 4   7.00 7.00
1342 A243   5m Sheet of 4, #a-d   9.50 9.50
Souvenir Sheet
1343 A243   15m multi   8.00 8.00

Birds — A244

Designs: 1.50m, Secretary bird. 2.10m, Gray-crowned crane. 3m, Pied avocet. 5m, Common kestrel.
No. 1348: a, European roller. b, Common cuckoo. c, Great spotted cuckoo. d, Pel's fishing owl.
15m, Kori bustard.

2004, May 17
1344-1347 A244   Set of 4   8.00 8.00
1348 A244   6m Sheet of 4,
                #a-d   12.00 12.00
Souvenir Sheet
1349 A244   15m multi   9.50 9.50

Butterflies A245

Designs: 1.50m, Acraea rabbaiae. 2.10m, Alaena margaritacea. 4m, Bematistes aganice. No. 1353, 6m, Acraea quirina.
No. 1354, 6m: a, Bematistes excisa male. b, Bematistes excisa female. c, Bematistes epiprotea. d, Bematistes poggei. 15m, Acraea satis.

2004, May 17
1350-1353 A245   Set of 4   8.00 8.00

1354 A245   6m Sheet of 4,
                #a-d   11.00 11.00
Souvenir Sheet
1355 A245   15m multi   7.50 7.50

Flowers — A246

Designs: 1.50m, Sparaxis grandiflora. 2.10m, Agapanthus africanus. 3m, Protea linearis. No. 1359, 5m, Nerine cultivars.
No. 1360, 5m: a, Kniphofia uvaria. b, Amaryllis belladonna. c, Cazania splendens. d, Erica coronata.
15m, Saintpaulia cultivars.

2004, May 17
1356-1359 A246   Set of 4   6.75 6.75
1360 A246   5m Sheet of 4, #a-d   9.00 9.00
Souvenir Sheet
1361 A246   15m multi   6.00 6.00

Houses A247

Designs: 70s, Mokhoro. 1m, Heisi. 1.50m, Lesotho. 2.10m, Mohlongoa-Fat'se.

2005, Feb. 21   Litho.   Perf. 14
1362-1365 A247   Set of 4   4.00 4.00

Girl Guides A248

Girl Guides: 70s, Dancing. 1m, Marching in parade. 1.50m, Collecting cans, vert. 2.10m, Standing near building.
10m, Leader holding microphone, vert.

2005, May 20   Litho.   Perf. 14
1366-1369 A248   Set of 4   4.75 4.75
Souvenir Sheet
1370 A248   10m multi   6.25 6.25

Pope John Paul II (1920-2005) A249

2005, Aug. 22   **Perf. 12¾**
1371 A249   10m multi   6.25 6.25
Printed in sheets of 4.
Souvenir Sheet

Rotary International, Cent. — A250

No. 1372: a, Alleviating poverty. b, Advancement of literacy. c, Helping at-risk children.

2005, Aug. 22
1372 A250 8m Sheet of 3, #a-c   7.75 7.75

World Cup Soccer Championships,
75th Anniv. — A251

No. 1373, horiz. — Players from final match from: a, 1930. b, 1938. c, 1990.
15m, Bodo Illgner, 1990 goalie for Germany.

2005, Aug. 22   **Perf. 12**
1373 A251 8m Sheet of 3, #a-c   9.50 9.50
Souvenir Sheet
1374 A251 15m multi   6.50 6.50

Hans Christian Andersen (1805-75),
Author — A252

No. 1375: a, Statue of Andersen, Copenhagen. b, Childhood home of Andersen, Odense, Denmark. c, Scene from "The Steadfast Tin Soldier".
15m, Little Mermaid statue, Copenhagen.

2005, Aug. 22   **Perf. 12¾**
1375 A252 8m Sheet of 3, #a-c   9.75 9.75
Souvenir Sheet
1376 A252 15m multi   6.50 6.50

Jules Verne (1828-1905),
Writer — A253

No. 1377, horiz.: a, Journey to the Center of the Earth. b, Verne, without hat. c, 20,000 Leagues Under the Sea.
15m, Verne wearing hat.

2005, Aug. 22
1377 A253 8m Sheet of 3, #a-c   10.00 10.00
Souvenir Sheet
1378 A253 15m multi   6.50 6.50

Albert Einstein (1879-1955),
Physicist — A254

No. 1379, horiz. — Einstein and: a, Country name in black. b, Nikola Tesla, Charles Steinmetz. c, Country name in red violet.
15m, Time Magazine "Person of the Century" cover.

2005, Aug. 22
1379 A254 8m Sheet of 3, #a-c   10.00 10.00
Souvenir Sheet
1380 A254 15m multi   6.50 6.50

Battle of Trafalgar, Bicent. — A255

No. 1381: a, HMS Victory. b, Admiral Horatio Nelson facing left. c, Nelson wounded in battle. d, Ships in battle.
25m, Nelson facing right.

2005, Aug. 22   **Perf. 12¾**
1381 A255 8m Sheet of 4, #a-d   19.00 19.00
Souvenir Sheet
Perf. 12
1382 A255 25m multi   19.00 19.00
No. 1381 contains four 42x28mm stamps.

End of World War II, 60th
Anniv. — A256

No. 1383, 4m — V-E Day: a, U.S. troops land on Omaha Beach, 1944. b, Gen. George C. Marshall. c, German Field Marshal Wilhelm Keitel signing surrender. d, Generals Dwight D. Eisenhower and George S. Patton. e, Soldiers sifting through war damage.
No. 1384, 4m — V-J Day: a, USS Arizona. b, Bunker, Chula Beach, Tinian Island. c, Bockscar flight crew. d, Newspaper announcing Japanese surrender. e, Historic marker commemorating loading of second atomic bomb on Tinian Island.

2005, Aug. 22   **Perf. 12¾**
Sheets of 5, #a-e
1383-1384 A256 Set of 2   13.00 13.00

A257

People and Livestock — A258

Designs: 70 l, Boy riding calf. 1m, Man feeding cattle. 1.50m, Cattle tenders playing game. 2.10m, Shepherd carrying lamb.
10m, Dancers.

2006, Mar. 13   **Litho.**   **Perf. 14**
1385-1388 A257 Set of 4   4.00 4.00
Souvenir Sheet
1389 A258 10m multi   6.50 6.50

A259

Women Balancing Items on
Heads — A260

Women carrying: 70 l, Sticks. 1m, Cooking pot. 1.50m, Water jar. 2.10m, Bowl of fruit.
10m, Bowl of grain.

2006, June 19
1390-1393 A259 Set of 4   4.00 4.00
Souvenir Sheet
1394 A260 10m multi   5.75 5.75

A261

Handicrafts — A262

Designs: 70 l, Baskets. 1m, Artist and drawing, vert. 1.50m, Painted pottery. 2.10m, Figurines of stork and fish, decorated bull's horn.

10m, Boy, native costume.

2006, Oct. 9   **Litho.**   **Perf. 14¼**
1395-1398 A261 Set of 4   4.00 4.00
Souvenir Sheet
1399 A262 10m multi   6.50 6.50

Birds — A263

Designs: 1m, Crested caracara. 1.50m, Wood storks. 2.10m, Tawny-shouldered blackbird. No. 1403, 15m, Jabiru.
No. 1404: a, Great blue heron. b, Anna's hummingbird. c, Gray silky flycatcher. d, Limpkin.
No. 1405, 15m, Western reef heron. No. 1406, 15m, Monk parakeet.

2007, Aug. 20   **Litho.**   **Perf. 14**
1400-1403 A263 Set of 4   24.00 24.00
1404 A263 6m Sheet of 4, #a-d   8.00 8.00
Souvenir Sheets
1405-1406 A263 Set of 2   10.00 10.00

Butterflies — A264

Designs: 1m, Mylothris erlangeri. 1.50m, Papilio nireus. 2.10m, Acraea terpiscore. 10m, Salamio tomora.
No. 1411: a, Danaus chrysippus. b, Myrina silenus. c, Chrysiridia madagascariensis. d, Hypolimnas dexithea.
No. 1412, 15m, P. demodocus. No. 1413, 15m, Amphicallia tigris.

2007, Aug. 20
1407-1410 A264 Set of 4   9.00 9.00
1411 A264 6m Sheet of 4, #a-d   7.00 7.00
Souvenir Sheets
1412-1413 A264 Set of 2   9.00 9.00

Orchids — A265

Designs: 1.50m, Spiranthes laciniata. 2.10m, Triphora craigheadii. 3m, Arethusa bulbosa. 10m, Calypso bulbosa.
No. 1418: a, Encyclia tampensis. b, Prosthechea cochleata. c, Vanilla pompona. d, Cypripedium acaule.
No. 1419, 15m, Vanilla barbellata. No. 1420, 15m, Epidendrum radicans.

2007, Aug. 20
1414-1417 A265 Set of 4   22.50 22.50
1418 A265 6m Sheet of 4, #a-d   7.50 7.50
Souvenir Sheets
1419-1420 A265 Set of 2   10.00 10.00

A266

A267

Mushrooms — A268

Designs: 1m, Amanita pantherina. 1.50m, Agaricus xanthodermus. 2.10m, Amanita rubescens. No. 1424, 15m, Amanita phalloides.

No. 1425: a, Amanita phalloides, diff. b, Amanita pantherina, diff. c, Panaeolus papilionaceus. d, Amanita rubescens, diff.

No. 1426, 15m, Amanite panther. No. 1427, 15m, Podaxis pistillaris.

2007, Aug. 20
1421-1424	A266	Set of 4	12.00	12.00
1425	A267	6m Sheet of 4,	12.00	12.00
		#a-d		

Souvenir Sheets
1426	A267	15m multi	9.00	9.00
1427	A268	15m multi	9.00	9.00

Miniature Sheet

2008 Summer Olympics, Beijing — A269

No. 1428: a, Rowing. b, Softball. c, Wrestling. d, Volleyball.

2008, Aug. 18　Litho.　Perf. 12
1428	A269	3.50m Sheet of 4, #a-d	6.50	6.50

POSTAGE DUE STAMPS

Basutoland Nos. J9-J10 Overprinted

Wmk. 314
1966, Nov. 1　Typo.　Perf. 14
J1	D2	1c carmine	.25	.25
a.		"Lseotho"	42.50	
J2	D2	5c dark purple	.75	.60
a.		"Lseotho"	70.00	

D1

Perf. 13½
1967, Apr. 1　Unwmk.　Litho.
J3	D1	1c dark blue	.25	.25
J4	D1	2c dull rose	.25	.30
J5	D1	5c emerald	.55	.70
		Nos. J3-J5 (3)	1.05	1.25

1976, Nov. 30　Wmk. 362
J7	D1	2c dull rose	3.00	3.00
J8	D1	5c emerald	3.00	3.00

D2

1986　Litho.　Perf. 13x13½
J9	D2	2s green	.55	.55
J10	D2	5s blue	.55	.55
J11	D2	25s purple	.55	.55
		Nos. J9-J11 (3)	1.65	1.65

LIBERIA

lĭ-'bir-ē-ə

LOCATION — West coast of Africa, between Ivory Coast and Sierra Leone
GOVT. — Republic
AREA — 43,000 sq. mi.
POP. — 2,602,100 (1997 est.)
CAPITAL — Monrovia

100 Cents = 1 Dollar

> Catalogue values for unused stamps in this country are for Never Hinged items, beginning with Scott 330 in the regular postage section, Scott B19 in the semipostal section, Scott C67 in the airpost section, and Scott CB4 in the airpost semi-postal section.

Values for unused stamps are for examples with original gum as defined in the catalogue introduction. Any exceptions will be noted. Very fine examples of Nos. 1-3, 13-21 and 157-159 will have perforations just clear of the design due to the narrow spacing of the stamps on the plates and/or imperfect perforating methods.

Watermarks

Wmk. 116 — Crosses and Circles

Wmk. 143

For watermarks 373 and 384 see British Watermark page.

"Liberia" — A1

Thick Paper
1860　Unwmk.　Litho.　Perf. 12
1	A1	6c red	400.00	300.00
a.		Imperf, pair	500.00	
2	A1	12c deep blue	25.00	50.00
a.		Imperf, pair	250.00	
3	A1	24c green	50.00	50.00
a.		Imperf, pair	300.00	
		Nos. 1-3 (3)	475.00	400.00

Stamps set very close together. Examples of the 12c occasionally show traces of a frame line around the design.

Medium to Thin Paper
With a single-line frame around each stamp, about 1mm from the border
1864　　　　Perf. 11, 12
7	A1	6c red	62.50	85.00
a.		Imperf, pair	225.00	
8	A1	12c blue	80.00	95.00
a.		Imperf, pair	225.00	
9	A1	24c lt green	87.50	100.00
a.		Imperf, pair	225.00	
		Nos. 7-9 (3)	230.00	280.00

Stamps set about 5mm apart. Margins large and perforation usually outside the frame line.

1866-69　　Without Frame Line
13	A1	6c lt red	25.00	40.00
14	A1	12c lt blue	25.00	40.00
15	A1	24c lt yellow grn	25.00	40.00
		Nos. 13-15 (3)	75.00	120.00

Stamps set 2-2½mm apart with small margins. Stamps are usually without frame line but those from one transfer show broken and irregular parts of a frame.

1880　With Frame Line　Perf. 10½
16	A1	1c ultra	5.00	8.00
17	A1	2c rose	5.00	5.25
a.		Imperf, pair	175.00	
18	A1	6c violet	5.00	5.25
19	A1	12c yellow	5.00	5.25
20	A1	24c rose red	6.00	5.50
		Nos. 16-20 (5)	26.00	29.25

Unused values for Nos. 16-20 are for stamps without gum.
For surcharges see Nos. 157-159.

Counterfeits
Counterfeits exist of Nos. 1-28, 32 and 64.

From Arms of Liberia — A2

1881
21	A2	3c black	15.00	10.00

Unused value is for a stamp without gum.

A3

A4

1882　　Perf. 11½, 12, 14
22	A3	8c blue	50.00	50.00
23	A4	16c red	8.00	5.00

On No. 22 the openings in the figure "8" enclose a pattern of slanting lines. Compare with No. 32.

Canceled to Order
Beginning with the issue of 1885, values in the used column are for "canceled to order" stamps. Postally used examples sell for much more.

A5

A6

From Arms of Liberia — A7

Perf. 10½, 11, 12, 11½x10½, 14, 14½
1885
24	A5	1c carmine	2.00	2.00
a.		1c rose	2.00	2.00
25	A5	2c green	2.00	2.00
26	A5	3c violet	2.00	2.00
27	A5	4c brown	2.00	2.00
28	A5	6c olive gray	2.00	2.00
29	A6	8c bluish gray	4.00	4.00
a.		8c lilac	7.00	7.00
30	A6	16c yellow	15.00	12.00
31	A7	32c deep blue	35.00	29.00
		Nos. 24-31 (8)	64.00	55.00

In the 1885 printing, the stamps are spaced 2mm apart and the paper is medium. In the 1892 printing, the stamps are 4½mm apart. For surcharges see Nos. J1-J2.

Imperf., Pair
24b	A5	1c		3.00
25a	A5	2c		4.75
26a	A5	3c		5.00
27a	A5	4c		5.00
28a	A5	6c	4.25	4.25
29b	A6	8c		12.50
30a	A6	16c		30.00
31a	A7	32c		50.00

Imperf. pairs with 2mm spacing sell for higher prices.

A8

1889　　Perf. 12, 14
32	A8	8c blue	4.25	4.25
a.		Imperf., pair	20.00	

The openings in the figure "8" are filled with network. See No. 22.

A9

Elephant — A10

Oil Palm — A11

Pres. Hilary R. W. Johnson — A12

Vai Woman in Full Dress — A13

Coat of Arms — A14

Liberian Star — A15

Coat of Arms — A16

Hippopotamus A17

Liberian Star — A18

President Johnson — A19

1892-96   Wmk. 143   Engr.   Perf. 15

33	A9	1c vermilion	.50	.40
a.		1c blue (error)	40.00	
34	A9	2c blue	.50	.40
a.		2c vermilion (error)	40.00	
35	A10	4c green & blk	1.75	1.00
a.		Center inverted	225.00	
36	A11	6c blue green	.70	.50
37	A12	8c brown & blk	.95	.95
a.		Center inverted	500.00	500.00
b.		Center sideways	750.00	
38	A12	10c chrome yel & indigo ('96)	.95	.65
39	A13	12c rose red	.95	.65
40	A13	15c slate ('96)	.95	.65
41	A14	16c lilac	3.50	1.75
a.		16c deep greenish blue (error)	110.00	
42	A14	20c vermilion ('96)	3.50	1.75
43	A15	24c ol grn, yel	2.00	1.10
44	A15	25c yel grn ('96)	2.00	1.40
45	A16	30c steel bl ('96)	6.25	4.50
46	A16	32c grnsh blue	3.50	2.75
a.		32c lilac (error)	110.00	
47	A17	$1 ultra & blk	12.00	9.00
a.		$1 blue & black	13.50	11.00
48	A18	$2 brown, yel	9.00	8.00
49	A19	$5 carmine & blk	10.00	10.00
a.		Center inverted	400.00	400.00
		Nos. 33-49 (17)	59.00	45.45

Many imperforates, part-perforated and mis-perforated varieties exist.

The 1c, 2c and 4c were issued in sheets of 60; 6c, sheet of 40; 8c, 10c, sheets of 30; 12c, 15c, 24c, 25c, sheets of 20; 16c, 20c, 30c, sheets of 15; $1, $2, $5, sheets of 10.

For overprints & surcharges see Nos. 50, 64B-64F, 66, 71-77, 79-81, 85-93, 95-100, 160, O1-O13, O15-O25, O37-O41, O44-O45.

No. 36 Surcharged

5   5   5

Five Cents

Five Cents

a   b

1893

50	A11	(a) 5c on 6c blue grn	1.75	1.10
a.		"5" with short flag	6.00	6.00
b.		Both 5's with short flags	19.00	19.00
c.		"i" dot omitted	19.00	19.00
d.		Surcharge "b"	30.00	30.00

"Commerce," Globe and Krumen — A22

1894   Unwmk.   Engr.   Imperf.

52	A22	5c carmine & blk	5.00	5.00
		Rouletted		
53	A22	5c carmine & blk	10.00	7.50

For overprints see Nos. 69, O26-O27.

Oil Palm A23

Hippopotamus A24

Elephant — A25

Liberty — A26

1897-1905   Wmk. 143   Perf. 14 to 16

54	A23	1c lilac rose	1.00	.65
a.		1c violet	1.00	.65
55	A23	1c dp grn ('00)	1.25	.95
56	A23	1c lt green ('05)	3.00	1.60
57	A24	2c bister & blk	3.00	1.60
58	A24	2c org red & blk ('00)	6.00	2.10
59	A24	2c rose & blk ('05)	3.00	1.60
60	A25	5c lake & black	3.00	1.60
a.		5c lilac rose & black	3.00	1.60
61	A25	5c gray bl & blk ('00)	6.00	5.00
62	A25	5c ultra & blk ('05)	4.25	2.75
a.		Center inverted	1,500.	
63	A26	50c red brn & blk	4.00	3.50
		Nos. 54-63 (10)	34.50	21.35

For overprints & surcharges see Nos. 65, 66A-68. 70, 78, 82-84, M1, O28-O36, O42, O92.

A27

Two types:
I — 13 pearls above "Republic Liberia."
II — 10 pearls.

1897   Unwmk.   Litho.   Perf. 14

64	A27	3c red & green (I)	.25	.60
a.		Type II	20.00	.25

No. 64a is considered a reprint, unissued. "Used" examples are CTO.
For surcharge see No. 128.

Official Stamps Handstamped in Black

1901-02   Wmk. 143

On Nos. O7-O8, O10-O12

64B	A14	16c lilac	525.00	525.00
64C	A15	24c ol grn, yel	575.00	400.00
64D	A17	$1 blue & blk	3,000.	2,000.
64E	A18	$2 brown, yel	—	—
64F	A19	$5 carmine & blk	—	—

On Stamps with "O S" Printed

65	A23	1c green	37.50	40.00
66	A9	2c blue	100.00	100.00
66A	A24	2c bister & blk		150.00
67	A24	2c org red & blk	45.00	40.00
68	A25	5c gray bl & blk	37.50	35.00
69	A22	5c vio & grn (No. O26)	300.00	300.00
70	A25	5c lake & blk	275.00	225.00
71	A12	10c yel & blue blk	37.50	60.00
a.		"O S" omitted		
72	A13	15c slate	40.00	60.00
73	A14	16c lilac	550.00	350.00
74	A14	20c vermilion	42.50	

75	A15	24c ol grn, yel	52.50	50.00
76	A15	25c yellow grn	42.50	50.00
a.		"O S" omitted	750.00	
77	A16	30c steel blue	42.50	40.00
78	A26	50c red brn & blk	100.00	52.50
79	A17	$1 ultra & blk	325.00	275.00
a.		"O S" omitted		
80	A18	$2 brn, yel	2,000.	1,800.
81	A19	$5 car & blk	2,500.	2,000.
a.		"O S" omitted	3,000.	2,750.

On Stamps with "O S" Handstamped

82	A23	1c deep green	62.50	—
83	A24	2c org red & blk	75.00	—
84	A25	5c lake & blk	200.00	—
85	A12	10c yel & bl blk	125.00	—
86	A14	20c vermilion	140.00	—
87	A15	24c ol grn, yel	140.00	—
88	A15	25c yel grn	160.00	—
89	A16	30c steel blue	525.00	—
90	A16	32c grnsh blue	210.00	—

Varieties of Nos. 65-90 include double and inverted overprints.

Nos. 47, O10, O23a Surcharged in Carmine

1902

91	A17	75c on $1 #47	15.00	13.00
a.		Thin "C" and comma	20.00	20.00
b.		Inverted surcharge	62.50	62.50
c.		As "a," inverted		
92	A17	75c on $1 #O10	2,750.	
a.		Thin "C" and comma	4,250.	
93	A17	75c on $1 #O23a	4,000.	
a.		Thin "C" and comma	5,250.	

Liberty — A29

1903   Unwmk.   Engr.   Perf. 14

94	A29	3c black	.30	.25
a.		Printed on both sides	45.00	
b.		Perf. 12	20.00	6.00

For overprint see No. O43.

Stamps of 1892 Surcharged in Blue

TEN Cents.

FIFTEEN Cents.

a   b

1903   Wmk. 143

95	A14	(a) 10c on 16c lilac	3.00	5.00
96	A15	(b) 15c on 24c ol grn, yel	4.50	6.00
97	A16	(b) 20c on 32c grnsh bl	6.25	8.50
		Nos. 95-97 (3)	13.75	19.50

Nos. 50, O3 and 45 Surcharged in Black or Red

One Cent

TWO

2

1904

98	A11	1c on 5c on 6c bl grn	.70	.55
a.		"5" with short flag	4.25	4.25
b.		Both 5's with short flags	8.75	8.75
c.		"i" dot omitted	10.00	10.00
d.		Surcharge on #50d	12.50	12.50
e.		Inverted surcharge	6.75	6.75
99	A10	2c on 4c grn & blk	2.75	4.00
a.		Pair, one without surcharge	35.00	
b.		Double surcharge		
c.		Double surcharge, red and blk	62.50	
d.		Surcharged on back also	19.00	
e.		"Official" overprint missing	30.00	
100	A16	2c on 30c stl bl (R)	9.50	15.00
		Nos. 98-100 (3)	12.95	19.55

African Elephant — A33

Mercury — A34

Chimpanzee A35

Great Blue Touraco — A36

Agama — A37

Egret — A38

Head of Liberty From Coin — A39

A40

Liberian Flag — A41

Pygmy
Hippopotamus
A42

Liberty with Star
of Liberia on
Cap — A43

Mandingos — A44

Executive
Mansion and
Pres. Arthur
Barclay — A45

1906　Unwmk.　Engr.　Perf. 14

101	A33	1c green & blk	1.50	.50
102	A34	2c carmine & blk	.30	.25
103	A35	5c ultra & blk	2.75	.85
104	A36	10c red brn & blk	4.00	.85
105	A37	15c pur & dp grn	14.50	3.00
106	A38	20c orange & blk	8.50	2.50
107	A39	25c dull blue & gray	.85	.25
108	A40	30c deep violet	1.00	.25
109	A41	50c dp grn & blk	1.00	.25
110	A42	75c brown & blk	12.00	2.50
111	A43	$1 rose & gray	3.00	.25
112	A44	$2 dp grn & blk	4.50	.35
113	A45	$5 red brn & blk	9.25	4.50
		Nos. 101-113 (13)	63.15	12.30

For surcharges see Nos. 114, 129, 130, 141, 145-149, 161, M2, M5, O72-O73, O82-O85, O96. For overprints see Nos. O46-O58.

Center Inverted

101a	A33	1c	110.00	55.00
102a	A34	2c	120.00	35.00
103a	A35	5c	175.00	175.00
104a	A36	10c	80.00	80.00
105a	A37	15c	175.00	175.00
106b	A38	20c	175.00	175.00
107a	A39	25c	75.00	75.00
109b	A41	50c	75.00	75.00
110b	A42	75c	125.00	125.00
111a	A43	$1	100.00	100.00
112a	A44	$2	95.00	95.00

Imperf., Pairs

101b	A33	1c	13.50	
102b	A34	2c	5.50	
106a	A38	20c	20.00	
107b	A39	25c	55.00	45.00
109a	A41	50c	20.00	
110a	A42	75c	20.00	
113a	A45	$5	27.00	

No. 104 Surcharged
in Black

1909

114	A36	3c on 10c red brn & blk	6.00	6.00

Coffee
Plantation — A46

Pres.
Barclay — A47

S. S. Pres. Daniel
E. Howard, former
Gunboat
Lark — A48

Commerce with Caduceus — A49

Vai Woman
Spinning
Cotton — A50

Blossom and
Fruit of Pepper
Plants — A51

Circular
House — A52

President
Barclay — A53

Men in
Canoe — A54

Liberian
Village — A55

1909-12　　　　　　　　　Perf. 14

115	A46	1c yel grn & blk	.70	.55
116	A47	2c lake & blk	.70	.55
117	A48	5c ultra & blk	.70	.55
118	A49	10c plum & blk, perf. 12½ ('12)	.70	.55
a.		Imperf., pair	19.00	
b.		Perf 14 ('12)	2.25	2.25
c.		As "b," pair, imperf between	27.50	
d.		Perf 12½x14	2.75	2.25
119	A50	15c indigo & blk	3.50	.60
120	A51	20c rose & grn	4.50	.60
b.		Imperf.		
121	A52	25c dk brn & blk	1.40	.60
a.		Imperf.		
122	A53	30c dark brown	4.50	.60
123	A54	50c green & blk	4.50	.60
124	A55	75c red brn & blk	4.50	.60
		Nos. 115-124 (10)	25.70	5.80

Rouletted

125	A49	10c plum & blk	.75	.45

For surcharges see Nos. 126-127E, 131-133, 136-140, 142-144, 151-156, 162, B1-B2, M3-M4, M6-M7, O70-O1, O74-O81, O86-O91, O97.

For overprints see Nos. O59-O69.

Center Inverted

116a	A47	2c	70.00	60.00
117a	A48	5c	62.50	55.00
119a	A50	15c	100.00	60.00

120a	A51	20c	70.00	55.00
121b	A52	25c	47.50	42.50
123a	A54	50c	95.00	80.00

Stamps and Types of 1909-12
Surcharged in Blue or Red

1910-12　　　　　　　　　Rouletted

126	A49	3c on 10c plum & blk (Bl)	.40	.25
a.		"3" inverted		
126B	A49	3c on 10c blk & ultra (R)	30.00	5.00

No. 126B is roulette 7. It also exists in roulette 13.

Perf. 12½, 14, 12½x14

127	A49	3c on 10c plum & blk (Bl) ('12)	.40	.25
a.		Imperf., pair	22.50	
b.		Double surcharge, one invtd.	22.50	
c.		Double vertical surcharge	25.00	
127E	A49	3c on 10c blk & ultra (R) ('12)	17.00	.55
		Nos. 126-127E (4)	47.80	6.05

Nos. 64, 64a
Surcharged in
Dark Green

1913

128	A27	8c on 3c red & grn (I)	.30	.25
a.		Surcharge on No. 64a	3.00	.25
b.		Double surcharge	6.25	
c.		Imperf., pair	20.00	
d.		Inverted surcharge	25.00	

Stamps of Preceding Issues
Surcharged

a　　　　　　　　　b

1914　　　　　　On Issue of 1906

129	A39	(a)	2c on 25c dl bl & gray	11.50	3.25
130	A40	(b)	5c on 30c dp violet	11.50	3.25

On Issue of 1909

131	A52	(a)	2c on 25c brn & blk	11.50	3.25
132	A53	(b)	5c on 30c dk brown	11.50	3.25
133	A54	(a)	10c on 50c grn & blk	11.50	3.25
			Nos. 129-133 (5)	57.50	16.25

Liberian
House
A57

Providence
Island,
Monrovia
Harbor
A58

1915　Engr.　Wmk. 116　Perf. 14

134	A57	2c red	.25	.25
135	A58	3c dull violet	.25	.25

For overprints see Nos. 196-197, O113-O114, O128-O129.

Nos. 109, 111-113, 119-124
Surcharged in Dark Blue, Black or
Red

c　　　　　　　　　d

e

f　　　　　　　　　g

1915-16　　　　　　　　Unwmk.

136	A50	(c)	2c on 15c (R)	.90	.90
137	A52	(d)	2c on 25c (R)	8.50	8.50
138	A51	(e)	5c on 20c (Bk)	1.10	6.25
139	A53	(f)	5c on 30c (R)	4.50	4.50
a.			Double surcharge	15.00	15.00
140	A53	(g)	5c on 30c (R)	40.00	40.00

h

i

141	A41	(h)	10c on 50c (R)	8.00	8.00
a.			Double surch., one invtd.		
142	A54	(i)	10c on 50c (R)	15.00	15.00
a.			Double surcharge red & blk	35.00	35.00
b.			Blue surcharge	35.00	35.00
143	A54	(i)	10c on 50c (Bk)	20.00	15.00

j

k

144	A55	(j)	20c on 75c (Bk)	4.00	7.50
145	A43	(k)	25c on $1 (Bk)	42.50	42.50

l   m

146 A44 (l) 50c on $2 (R)   12.00 12.00
  a.   "Ceuts"   22.50 22.50
147 A44 (m) 50c on $2 (R)   800.00 800.00

n

148 A45 $1 on $5 (Bk)   65.00 65.00
  a.   Double surcharge   90.00 90.00

o

149 A45 $1 on $5 (R)   52.50 52.50
The color of the red surcharge varies from light dull red to almost brown.

Handstamped Surcharge, Type "i"
150 A54   10c on 50c (Dk Bl)   14.00 14.00

No. 119 Surcharged in Black

151 A50   2c on 15c   650.00 650.00

No. 119 Surcharged in Red

152 A50   2c on 15c   45.00 40.00
  a.   Double surcharge   92.50

Nos. 116-117 Surcharged in Black or Red

a   b

c   d

e   f

g

h

i   j

k

l

m

n

o

p

q

r

s

t

Types A-J are for No. 153. Types K-T are for No. 154.

153 A47   1c on 2c lake & blk   2.50 2.50
  a.   Strip of 10 types   35.00
154 A48   2c on 5c ultra & blk
      (R)   3.50 2.50
  a.   Black surcharge   14.00 14.00
  b.   Strip of 10 types (R)   35.00
  c.   Strip of 10 types (Bk)   175.00

The 10 types of surcharge are repeated in illustrated sequence on 1c on 2c in each horiz. row and on 2c on 5c in each vert. row of sheets of 100 (10x10).

No. 116 and Type of 1909 Surcharged

155 A47   1c on 2c lake & blk   190.00 190.00

No. 117 Surcharged

156 A48   2c on 5c turq & blk   140.00 140.00

Nos. 18-20 Surcharged

1916
157 A1   3c on 6c violet   45.00 45.00
  a.   Inverted surcharge   100.00 75.00
158 A1   5c on 12c yellow   3.00 3.00
  a.   Inverted surcharge   12.50 12.50
  b.   Surcharge sideways   12.50
159 A1   10c on 24c rose red   2.75 3.00
  a.   Inverted surcharge   15.00 15.00
  b.   Surcharge sideways
      Nos. 157-159 (3)   50.75 51.00

Unused values for Nos. 157-159 are for examples without gum.

Nos. 44 and 108 Surcharged

p   r

1917   **Wmk. 143**
160 A15 (p)   4c on 25c yel grn   12.00 12.00
  a.   "OUR"   27.50 27.50
  b.   "FCUR"   27.50 27.50

Unwmk.
161 A40 (r)   5c on 30c dp vio   90.00 90.00

No. 118 Surcharged in Red

1918
162 A49   3c on 10c plum & blk   2.75 4.25
  a.   "3" inverted   9.25 9.25

Bongo Antelope — A59   Symbols of Liberia — A61

Two-spot Palm Civet A60

A62   Palm-nut Vulture — A66

Oil Palm — A63   Mercury — A64

Traveler's Tree — A65

"Mudskipper" or Bommi Fish — A67

Mandingos A68   "Liberia" A71

Coast Scene A69

Liberia College A70

1918   **Engr.**   **Perf. 12½, 14**

163	A59	1c dp grn & blk	.65	.25
164	A60	2c rose & blk	.80	.25
165	A61	5c gray bl & blk	.25	.25
166	A62	10c dark green	.25	.25
167	A63	15c blk & dk grn	3.00	.25
168	A64	20c claret & blk	.35	.25
169	A65	25c dk grn & grn	3.25	.25
170	A66	30c red vio & blk	15.00	.80
171	A67	50c ultra & blk	26.50	3.50
172	A68	75c ol bis & blk	.90	.25
173	A69	$1 yel brn & bl	7.25	.25
174	A70	$2 lt vio & blk	6.50	.25
175	A71	$5 dark brown	7.00	.40
		Nos. 163-175 (13)	71.70	7.20

For surcharges see Nos. 176-177, 228-229, 248-270, B3-B15, O111-O112, O155-O157.

For overprints see Nos. O98-O110.

Nos. 163-164, F10-F14 Surcharged

1920

176	A59	3c on 1c grn & blk	1.10	1.10
a.		"CEETS"	17.00	17.00
b.		Double surcharge	10.00	10.00
c.		Triple surcharge	15.00	15.00
177	A60	4c on 2c rose & blk	1.10	1.10
a.		Inverted surcharge	20.00	20.00
b.		Double surcharge	10.00	10.00
c.		Double surcharge, one invtd.	18.00	
d.		Triple surcharge, one inverted	25.00	25.00
e.		Quadruple surcharge	30.00	30.00
f.		Typewritten surcharge		
g.		Same as "f" but inverted		
h.		Printed and typewritten surcharges, both inverted		
178	R6	5c on 10c bl & blk	2.50	2.75
a.		Inverted surcharge	10.00	10.00
b.		Double surcharge	10.00	10.00
c.		Double surcharge, one invtd.	15.00	15.00
d.		Typewritten surcharge ("five")		100.00
e.		Printed and typewritten surcharges	100.00	
179	R6	5c on 10c org red & blk	2.50	2.75
a.		5c on 10c orange & black	4.00	2.75
b.		Inverted surcharge	15.00	
c.		Double surcharge	15.00	
d.		Double surcharge, one invtd.	18.00	15.00
e.		Typewritten surch. in violet	100.00	100.00
f.		Typewritten surch. in black		
g.		Printed and typewritten surcharges	100.00	
180	R6	5c on 10c grn & blk	2.50	2.75
a.		Double surcharge	10.00	10.00
b.		Double surcharge, one invtd.	18.00	18.00
c.		Inverted surcharge		18.00
d.		Quadruple surcharge	25.00	
e.		Typewritten surcharge		100.00
f.		Printed and typewritten surcharges		
181	R6	5c on 10c vio & blk (Monrovia)	4.00	5.00
a.		Double surcharge, one invtd.	25.00	25.00

182	R6	5c on 10c mag & blk (Robert-sport)	2.25	2.40
a.		Double surcharge	15.00	15.00
b.		Double surcharge, one invtd.	15.00	15.00
c.		Double surcharge, both invtd.	25.00	
		Nos. 176-182 (7)	15.95	17.85

Cape Mesurado A75

Pres. Daniel E. Howard — A76   Arms of Liberia — A77

Crocodile A78

Pepper Plant — A79

Leopard A80

Village Scene — A81

Krumen in Dugout A82

Rapids in St. Paul's River — A83

Bongo Antelope A84

Hornbill A85

Elephant A86

1921   **Wmk. 116**   **Perf. 14**

183	A75	1c green	.25	.25
184	A76	5c dp bl & blk	.25	.25
185	A77	10c red & dl bl	.25	.25
186	A78	15c dl vio & grn	6.50	.55
187	A79	20c rose red & grn	2.75	.25
188	A80	25c org & blk	7.50	.55
189	A81	30c grn & dl vio	.40	.25
190	A82	50c org & ultra	.45	.25
191	A83	75c red & blk brn	.80	.25
a.		Center inverted		70.00
192	A84	$1 red & blk	20.00	1.75
193	A85	$2 yel & ultra	16.00	1.25
194	A86	$5 car rose & vio	32.50	1.50
		Nos. 183-194 (12)	87.65	7.35

For overprints see Nos. 195, 198-208, O115-O127, O130-O140.

Nos. 134-135, 183-194 Ovptd.

195	A75	1c green	22.50	.40
196	A57	2c red	22.50	.40
197	A58	3c dull violet	32.50	.40
198	A76	5c dp bl & blk	3.50	.30
199	A77	10c red & dull bl	50.00	.40
200	A78	15c dull vio & grn	22.50	1.40
201	A79	20c rose red & grn, ovpt. invtd.	7.25	.75
202	A80	25c orange & blk	22.50	1.40
203	A81	30c grn & dull vio	2.50	.30
204	A82	50c orange & ultra	3.50	.30
205	A83	75c red & blk brn	4.75	.30
206	A84	$1 red & blk	62.50	2.10
207	A85	$2 yellow & ultra	22.50	2.10
208	A86	$5 car rose & vio	60.00	2.75
		Nos. 195-208 (14)	339.00	13.30

Overprint exists inverted in Nos. 195-208 and normal on No. 201.

First Settlers Landing at Cape Mesurado from U. S. S. Alligator A87

1923   **Litho.**

209	A87	1c lt blue & blk	18.00	.45
210	A87	2c claret & ol gray	26.00	.45
211	A87	5c ol grn & ind	26.00	.45
212	A87	10c bl grn & vio	1.00	.45
213	A87	$1 rose & brn	3.25	.45
		Nos. 209-213 (5)	74.25	2.25

Centenary of founding of Liberia.

Memorial to J. J. Roberts, 1st Pres. — A88

Hall of Representatives, Monrovia — A89

Liberian Star — A90

A91

Pres. Charles Dunbar Burgess King — A92

Hippopotamus — A93

Antelope A94

West African Buffalo A95

Grebos Making Dumboy A96

Pineapple A97

Carrying
Ivory Tusk
A98

Rubber Planter's House — A99

Stockton Lagoon — A100

Grebo Houses — A101

1923 Perf. 13½x14½, 14½x13½
White Paper

214	A88	1c yel grn & dp grn	7.50	1.25
215	A89	2c claret & brn	7.50	.25
216	A90	3c lilac & blk	.35	.25
217	A91	5c bl vio & blk	115.00	.25
218	A92	10c slate & brn	.35	.25
219	A93	15c bister & bl	35.00	.50
220	A94	20c bl grn & vio	2.50	.35
221	A95	25c org red & brn	160.00	.60
222	A96	30c dk brn & vio	.60	.25
223a	A97	50c dull vio & brn, brnsh	1.00	.25
224	A98	75c gray & bl	1.90	.40
225a	A99	$1 dp red & dk vio, brnsh	4.50	.60
226	A100	$2 orange & blue	7.50	.80
227a	A101	$5 dp grn & brn, brnsh	8.00	.90
		Nos. 214-227a (14)	351.70	6.90

No. 163 Surcharged
in Black

1926 Unwmk. Perf. 14
228	A59	2c on 1c dp grn & blk	3.50	3.50
a.		Surcharge with ornamental design as on #O155	17.00	

No. 163 Surcharged
in Red

1927
229	A59	2c on 1c dp grn & blk	9.50	9.50
a.		"Ceuts"	14.00	
b.		"Vwo"	14.00	
c.		"Twc"	14.00	
d.		Double surcharge	27.50	
e.		Wavy lines omitted	17.50	

Palms
A102

Map of
Africa — A103

President
King — A104

1928 Engr. Perf. 12
230	A102	1c green	.75	.50
231	A102	2c dark violet	.50	.35
232	A102	3c bister brn	.50	.35
a.		Horiz. pair, imperf vert.	—	
233	A103	5c ultra	1.00	.55
234	A103	10c olive gray	1.40	.55
235	A103	15c dull violet	6.25	2.25
236	A103	$1 red brown	77.50	26.50
		Nos. 230-236 (7)	87.90	31.05

For surcharges & overprints see Nos. 288A,
289A, 290A-291, 292A, C1-C3, O158-O165.

Nos. 164-168, 170-175 Surcharged in Various Colors and Styles

No. 248

No. 250

1936 Perf. 12½, 14
248	A60	1c on 2c (Bl)	.55	3.50
249	A61	3c on 5c (Bl)	.25	2.00
250	A62	4c on 10c (Br)	.25	2.00
251	A63	6c on 15c (Bl)	.55	3.50
252	A64	8c on 20c (V)	.25	2.00
253	A66	12c on 30c (V)	1.00	9.75
254	A67	14c on 50c (Bl)	1.10	11.00
255	A68	16c on 75c (Br)	.55	5.50
256	A69	18c on $1 (Bk)	.55	5.50
a.		22c on $1 yellow brown & blue	7.25	
257	A70	22c on $2 (V)	.75	7.75
258	A71	24c on $5 (Bk)	1.00	9.75
		Nos. 248-258 (11)	6.80	62.25

Official Stamps, Nos. O99-O110, Srchd. or Ovptd. in Various Colors & Styles

1936
259	A60	1c on 2c (Bl)	.40	4.00
260	A61	3c on 5c (Bl)	.40	4.00
261	A62	4c on 10c (Bl)	.40	4.00
262	A63	6c on 15c (Bl)	.40	4.00
263	A64	8c on 20c (V)	.40	4.00
264	A66	12c on 30c (V)	1.50	20.00
a.		"193" instead of "1936"	19.00	
265	A67	14c on 50c (Bl)	2.00	21.00
266	A68	16c on 75c (Bl)	1.00	12.00
267	A69	18c on $1 (Bk)	1.00	12.00
268	A70	22c on $2 (Bl)	1.25	15.00
269	A71	24c on $5 (Bk)	1.50	12.00
270	A65	25c (Bk)	2.00	21.00
		Nos. 259-270 (12)	12.25	138.00

Hornbill — A106

Designs: 2c, Bushbuck. 3c, West African
dwarf buffalo. 4c, Pygmy hippopotamus. 5c,
Lesser egret. 6c, Pres. E. J. Barclay.

Perf. Compound of 11½, 12, 12½, 14
1937, Apr. 10 Engr. Unwmk.
271	A106	1c green & blk	1.50	.80
272	A106	2c carmine & blk	1.50	.25
273	A106	3c violet & blk	1.50	.80
274	A106	4c orange & blk	2.25	1.25
275	A106	5c blue & blk	2.25	.95
276	A106	6c green & blk	.80	.25
		Nos. 271-276 (6)	9.80	4.30

Coast
Line of
Liberia,
1839
A107

Seal of
Liberia,
Map
and
Farming
Scenes
A108

Thomas Buchanan and Residence at
Bassa Cove — A109

1940, July 29 Engr. Perf. 12
277	A107	3c dark blue	.35	.35
278	A108	5c dull red brn	.35	.35
279	A109	10c dark green	.35	.35
		Nos. 277-279 (3)	1.05	1.05

100th anniv. of the founding of the Commonwealth of Liberia.
For overprints & surcharges see Nos. 280-
282, B16-B18, C14-C16, CB1-CB3, CE1,
CF1, E1, F35.

Imperforates
Many stamps of Liberia exist imperforate or with various perforation errors, in
issued and trial colors, and also in small
presentation sheets in issued colors.

Nos. 277-279 Overprinted in Red or Blue

1941, Feb. 21
280	A107	3c dk blue (R)	2.50	2.50
281	A108	5c dull red brn (Bl)	2.50	2.50
282	A109	10c dark green (Bl)	2.50	2.50
		Nos. 280-282,C14-C16 (6)	15.75	15.75

Royal
Antelope
A110

Bay-thighed Diana
Monkey — A115

2c, Water chevrotain. 3c, White-shouldered
duiker. 4c, Bushbuck. 5c, Zebra antelope.

1942 Engr.
283	A110	1c violet & fawn	1.10	.25
284	A110	2c brt ultra & yel brn	1.40	.25
285	A110	3c brt grn & yel brn	1.90	.90
286	A110	4c blk & red org	2.40	1.90
287	A110	5c olive & fawn	3.00	1.90
288	A115	10c red & black	5.25	2.40
		Nos. 283-288 (6)	15.05	7.60

Nos. 231, 233-234, 271-276 Srchd. with New Values and Bars or X's in Violet, Black, Red Brown or Blue

Perf. 12, 12x12½, 14
1944-46 Unwmk.
288A	A102	1c on 2c (Bk)	9.25	6.50
289	A102	1c on 4c (Bk)	55.00	47.50
289A	A104	1c on 10c (R Br)	12.50	9.50
b.		Double surcharge, one red brown, one violet	25.00	19.00
290	A106	2c on 3c	62.50	50.00
290A	A103	2c on 5c (Bk)	2.75	2.75
290B	A103	2c on 5c (Bl)	21.00	9.25
291	A102	3c on 5c	30.00	35.00
292	A106	4c on 5c	11.00	7.25
292A	A104	4c on 10c (Bk)	3.25	3.25
b.		Double surch., one inverted		
293	A106	5c on 1c (Bk)	100.00	50.00
294	A106	6c on 2c (Bk)	11.00	9.50
295	A106	10c on 6c	11.00	9.50
		Nos. 288A-295 (12)	329.25	240.00

Surcharges on Nos. 289, 290, 293, 294 are
found double or inverted. Such varieties command a small premium.

Pres. Franklin D. Roosevelt Reviewing
Troops — A116

1945, Nov. 26 Engr. Perf. 12½
Grayish Paper
296	A116	3c brt violet & blk	.25	.25
297	A116	5c dk blue & blk	.45	.45
		Nos. 296-297,C51 (3)	1.95	2.10

In memory of Pres. Franklin D. Roosevelt
(1882-1945).

Monrovia Harbor — A117

1947, Jan. 2
298	A117	5c deep blue	.25	.25

Opening of the Monrovia Harbor Project,
Feb. 16, 1946. See No. C52.

Without Inscription at Top
1947, May 16
299	A117	5c violet	.25	.25

See No. C53.

1st US Postage Stamps and Arms of Liberia — A118

1947, June 6
300 A118 5c carmine rose .25 .25
Nos. 300,C54-C56 (4) 1.20 1.00

Cent. of US postage stamps and the 87th anniv. of Liberian postal issues.

Matilda Newport Firing Cannon — A119

1947, Dec. 1 **Engr. & Photo.**
Center in Gray Black
301 A119 1c brt blue green .25 .25
302 A119 3c brt red violet .25 .25
303 A119 5c brt ultra .60 .25
304 A119 10c yellow 3.25 .80
Nos. 301-304,C57 (5) 5.60 1.85

125th anniv. of Matilda Newport's defense of Monrovia, Dec. 1, 1822.

Liberian Star — A120

Cent. of Independence: 2c, Liberty. 3c, Liberian Arms. 5c, Map of Liberia.

1947, Dec. 22 **Engr.**
305 A120 1c dark green .55 .25
306 A120 2c brt red vio .55 .25
307 A120 3c brt purple .55 .25
308 A120 5c dark blue .55 .25
Nos. 305-308,C58-C60 (7) 3.80 1.95

Centenary of independence.

Natives Approaching Village — A124

Rubber Tapping and Planting A125

Landing of First Colonists — A126

Jehudi Ashmun and Defenders — A127

1949, Apr. 4 **Litho.** **Perf. 11½**
309 A124 1c multicolored .45 .75
310 A125 2c multicolored .45 .75
311 A126 3c multicolored .45 .75
312 A127 5c multicolored .45 .75
Nos. 309-312,C63-C64 (6) 2.50 4.30

Nos. 309-312 exist perf. 12½ and sell at a much lower price. The status of the perf. 12½ set is indefinite.

Stephen Benson — A128

Liberian Presidents: 1c, Pres. Joseph J. Roberts. 3c, Daniel B. Warner. 4c, James S. Payne. 5c, Executive mansion. 6c, Edward J. Roye. 7c, A. W. Gardner and A. F. Russell. 8c, Hilary R. W. Johnson. 9c, Joseph J. Cheeseman. 10c, William D. Coleman. 15c, Garretson W. Gibson. 20c, Arthur Barclay. 25c, Daniel E. Howard. 50c, Charles D. B. King. $1, Edwin J. Barclay.

1948-50 Unwmk. Engr. Perf. 12½
Caption and Portrait in Black
313 A128 1c green ('48) 2.75 7.00
314 A128 2c salmon pink .40 .65
315 A128 3c rose violet .40 .65
a. "1876-1878" added 16.00 40.00
316 A128 4c lt olive grn .90 .90
317 A128 5c ultra .50 .90
318 A128 6c red orange .90 1.75
319 A128 7c lt blue ('50) 1.10 2.10
320 A128 8c carmine 1.10 2.40
321 A128 9c red violet 1.25 2.10
322 A128 10c yellow ('50) .85 .90
323 A128 15c yellow orange 1.00 .70
324 A128 20c blue gray 1.40 1.40
325 A128 25c cerise 2.00 2.10
326 A128 50c aqua 3.75 1.40
327 A128 $1 rose lilac 6.25 1.40
Nos. 313-327,C65 (16) 25.15 26.65

Issued: 1c, 11/18; 7c, 10c, 1950; others, 7/21/49.
See Nos. 328, 371-378, C118.

Pres. Joseph J. Roberts — A129

1950
328 A129 1c green & blk .25 .25

Hand Holding Book — A130

1950, Feb. 14
329 A130 5c deep blue .45 .25

National Literacy Campaign. See No. C66.

Catalogue values for unused stamps in this section, from this point to the end of the section, are for Never Hinged items.

UPU Monument — A131

First UPU Building, Bern — A132

1950, Apr. 21 **Engr.** **Unwmk.**
330 A131 5c green & blk .25 .25
331 A132 10c red vio & blk .25 .25
Nos. 330-331,C67 (3) 3.25 3.25

UPU, 75th anniv. (in 1949).
Exist imperf., same value.

Jehudi Ashmun and Seal of Liberia — A133

John Marshall, Ashmun and Map of Town of Marshall — A134

Designs (Map or View and Two Portraits): 2c, Careysburg, Gov. Lott Carey (1780-1828), freed American slave, and Jehudi Ashmun (1794-1828), American missionary credited as founder of Liberia. 3c, Town of Harper, Robert Goodloe Harper (1765-1825), American statesman, and Ashmun. 5c, Upper Buchanan, Gov. Thomas Buchanan and Ashmun. 10c, Robertsport, Pres. Joseph J. Roberts and Ashmun.

1952, Apr. 10 **Perf. 10½**
332 A133 1c deep green .25 .25
333 A133 2c scarlet & ind .30 .25
334 A133 3c purple & grn .30 .25
335 A134 4c brown & grn .30 .25
336 A133 5c ultra & org red .30 .25
337 A134 10c org red & dk bl .30 .25
Nos. 332-337,C68-C69 (8) 2.70 2.45

Nos. 332-337 exist imperf. Value about two and one-half times that of the perf. set.
No. 334 exists with center inverted. Value $50.
See No. C69a.

UN Headquarters Building A135

Scroll and Flags A136

10c, Liberia arms, letters "UN" and emblem.

1952, Dec. 20 **Unwmk.** **Perf. 12½**
338 A135 1c shown .30 .30
339 A136 4c car & ultra .30 .30
340 A136 10c red brn & yel .30 .30
a. Souvenir sheet of 3, #338-340 2.00 2.00
Nos. 338-340,C70 (4) 1.80 1.55

Nos. 338-340 and 340a exist imperforate.

Pepper Bird — A137

Roller A138

1953, Nov. 18 **Perf. 10½**
341 A137 1c shown 1.00 .25
342 A138 3c shown 1.00 .25
343 A137 4c Hornbill 1.60 .25
344 A137 5c Kingfisher 1.75 .25
345 A138 10c Jacana 1.90 .25
346 A138 12c Weaver 2.50 .25
Nos. 341-346 (6) 9.75 1.50

Exist imperf. Value, set unused $20.

Tennis A139

1955, Jan. 26 **Litho.** **Perf. 12½**
347 A139 3c shown .25 .25
348 A139 5c Soccer .25 .25
349 A139 25c Boxing .40 .25
Nos. 347-349,C88-C90 (6) 1.80 1.65

Callichilia
Stenosepala
A140

Various Native Flowers: 7c, Gomphia sub-cordata. 8c, Listrostachys caudata. 9c, Musaenda isertiana.

1955, Sept. 28   **Unwmk.**
350 A140 6c yel grn, org & yel   .30 .25
351 A140 7c emer, yel & car   .30 .25
352 A140 8c yel grn, buff & bl   .30 .25
353 A140 9c orange & green   .40 .25
   Nos. 350-353,C91-C92 (6)   2.10 1.50

Rubber
Tapping
A141

1955, Dec. 5   **Perf. 12½**
354 A141 5c emerald & yellow   .25 .25
   Nos. 354,C97-C98 (3)   1.20 .75

50th anniv. of Rotary Intl. No. 354 exists printed entirely in emerald.

Statue of
Liberty
A142

Coliseum, New York City — A143

Design: 6c, Globe inscribed FIPEX.

1956, Apr. 28   **Perf. 12**
355 A142 3c brt grn & dk red brn   .25 .25
356 A143 4c Prus grn & bis brn   .25 .25
357 A143 6c gray & red lilac   .25 .25
   Nos. 355-357,C100-C102 (6)   2.15 1.50

Fifth International Philatelic Exhibition (FIPEX), NYC, Apr. 28-May 6, 1956.

Kangaroo and Emu — A144

Discus
Thrower
A145

Designs: 8c, Goddess of Victory and Olympic symbols. 10c, Classic chariot race.

1956, Nov. 15   **Litho.**   **Unwmk.**
358 A144 4c lt ol grn & gldn brn   .25 .25
359 A145 6c emerald & gray   .25 .25
360 A144 8c lt ultra & redsh brn   .25 .25
361 A144 10c rose red & blk   .40 .25
   Nos. 358-361,C104-C105 (6)   2.15 2.00

16th Olympic Games at Melbourne, Nov. 22-Dec. 8, 1956.
Nos. 358-361 exist imperf.

Idlewild
Airport,
New
York
A146

5c, Roberts Field, Liberia, plane & Pres. Tubman.

Lithographed and Engraved
1957, May 4   **Perf. 12**
362 A146 3c orange & dk blue   .25 .25
363 A146 5c red lilac & blk   .25 .25
   Nos. 362-363,C107-C110 (6)   3.15 1.50

1st anniv. of direct air service between Roberts Field, Liberia, and Idlewild (Kennedy), NY.

Orphanage Playground — A147

Orphanage and: 5c, Teacher and pupil. 6c, Singing boys and natl. anthem. 10c, Children and flag.

1957, Nov. 25   **Litho.**   **Perf. 12**
364 A147 4c green & red   .25 .25
365 A147 5c bl grn & red brn   .25 .25
366 A147 6c brt vio & bis   .25 .25
367 A147 10c ultra & rose car   .25 .25
   Nos. 364-367,C111-C112 (6)   2.25 1.50

Founding of the Antoinette Tubman Child Welfare Foundation.

Windmill and Dutch Flag — A148

Designs: No. 369, German flag and Brandenburg Gate. No. 370, Swedish flag, palace and crowns.

Engraved and Lithographed
1958, Jan. 10   Unwmk.   Perf. 10½
Flags in Original Colors
368 A148 5c reddish brn   .25 .25
369 A148 5c blue   .25 .25
370 A148 5c lilac rose   .25 .25
   Nos. 368-370,C114-C117 (7)   2.55 2.55

European tour of Pres. Tubman in 1956. Exist imperf.

Presidential Types of 1948-50
Designs as before.

1958-60   Engr.   Perf. 12
Caption and Portrait in Black
371 A129 1c salmon pink   .45 .25
372 A128 2c brt yellow   .45 .25
373 A128 10c blue gray   .55 .55
374 A128 15c brt bl & blk ('59)   .25 .25
375 A128 20c dark red   .65 .65
376 A128 25c blue   .65 .65
377 A128 50c red lil & blk ('59)   .75 .65
378 A128 $1 bister brn ('60)   5.75 5.75
   Nos. 371-378,C118 (9)   10.75 4.90

Many shades of 1c.

Open Globe Projection — A149

Designs: 5c, UN Emblem and building. 10c, UN Emblem and initials of agencies.

1958, Dec. 10   Litho.   Perf. 12
379 A149 3c gray, bl & blk   .30 .25
380 A149 5c blue & choc   .25 .25
381 A149 10c black & org   .40 .25
382 A149 12c black & car   1.10 1.10
   Nos. 379-382 (4)   2.05 1.85

10th anniv. of the Universal Declaration of Human Rights. See No. C119.

People of Africa on the March — A150

1959, Apr. 15
383 A150 20c orange & brown   .45 .45
African Freedom Day, Apr. 15. Exists imperf. See No. C120.

Symbols of
UNESCO
A151

1959, May 11   **Unwmk.**
384 A151 25c dp plum & emer   .55 .55
Opening of UNESCO Headquarters in Paris, Nov. 3, 1958. Exists imperf. See Nos. C121, C121a.

Abraham
Lincoln — A152

1959, Nov. 20   Engr.   Perf. 12
385 A152 10c ultra & blk   .40 .40
386 A152 15c orange & blk   .40 .40
 a. Souv. sheet of 3, Nos. 385-386,
     C122, imperf.   2.50 4.00
   Nos. 385-386,C122 (3)   1.70 1.70

150th anniv. of the birth of Abraham Lincoln.

Touré,
Tubman
and
Nkrumah
A153

1960, Jan. 27   Litho.   Unwmk.
387 A153 25c crimson & blk   .55 .55

1959 "Big Three" conference of Pres. Sékou Touré of Guinea, Pres. William V. S. Tubman of Liberia and Prime Minister Kwame Nkrumah of Ghana at Saniquellie, Liberia. See No. C123.

World Refugee Year Emblem — A154

1960, Apr. 7   **Perf. 11½**
388 A154 25c emerald & blk   .70 1.00

World Refuge Year, July 1, 1959-June 30, 1960. See No. C124, C124a. Exist imperf.

Map of
Africa — A155

1960, May 11   Litho.   Perf. 11½
389 A155 25c green & black   .00 .00

10th anniv. of the Commission for Technical Cooperation in Africa South of the Sahara (CCTA). See No. C125.

Weight Lifter and Porter — A156

Designs: 10c, Rower and canoeists, horiz. 15c, Walker and porter.

1960, Sept. 6   **Unwmk.**
390 A156 5c dk brn & emer   .25 .25
391 A156 10c brown & red lil   .25 .25
392 A156 15c brown & org   .70 .75
   Nos. 390-392,C126 (4)   2.10 1.95

17th Olympic Games, Rome, 8/25-9/11. Exist imperf.

Liberian Stamps
of 1860 — A157

1960, Dec. 1   Litho.   Perf. 11½
393 A157 5c multicolored   .25 .25
394 A157 20c multicolored   .70 .70
   Nos. 393-394,C128 (3)   1.95 1.95

Liberian postage stamps, cent.

Laurel Wreath — A158

1961, May 19   Unwmk.   Perf. 11½
395 A158 25c red & dk blue   .60 .60
Liberia's membership in the UN Security Council. Exists imperf. See Nos. C130-C131 and note after No. C131.

Anatomy Class A159

1961, Sept. 8   Perf. 11½
396 A159 25c green & brown   .60 .60
15th anniv. of UNESCO. See Nos. C132-C133.

Joseph J. Roberts Monument, Monrovia — A160

Design: 10c, Pres. Roberts and old and new presidential mansions, horiz.

1961, Oct. 25   Litho.
397 A160 5c orange & sepia   .25 .25
398 A160 10c ultra & sepia   .45 .25
    Nos. 397-398,C134 (3)   1.40 1.20
150th anniv. of the birth of Joseph J. Roberts, 1st pres. of Liberia. Exist imperf.

Boy Scout A161

Design: Insignia and Scouts camping.

1961, Dec. 4   Unwmk.   Perf. 11½
399 A161 5c lilac & sepia   .25 .25
400 A161 10c ultra & bister   .50 .50
    Nos. 399-400,C135 (3)   2.15 2.15
Boy Scouts of Liberia. Exist imperf. Value, $5.50.

Dag Hammarskjold and UN Emblem — A162

1962, Feb. 1   Perf. 12
401 A162 20c black & ultra   .45 .45
Dag Hammarskjold, Secretary General of the UN, 1953-61. See Nos. C137-C138.

Malaria Eradication Emblem — A163

1962, Apr. 7   Litho.   Perf. 12½
402 A163 25c dk green & red   .55 .45
WHO drive to eradicate malaria. See Nos. C139-C140.

United Nations Emblem A164

1962, Oct. 22   Perf. 12x12½
403 A164 20c green & yel bister   .35 .35
Issued to mark the observance of United Nations Day, Oct. 24, as a national holiday. See Nos. C144-C145.

Executive Mansion, Monrovia A165

1c, 80c, Executive Mansion, Monrovia. 5c, Treasury Department Building, Monrovia. 10c, Information Service. 15c, Capitol.

1962-64
403A A165 1c vio bl & dp org   .25 .25
                  ('64)
404 A165 5c lt blue & pur   .25 .25
405 A165 10c bister & brn   .25 .25
406 A165 15c salmon & dk bl   .40 .30
406A A165 80c brn & yel ('64)   1.75 1.20
    Nos. 403A-406A,C146-C148 (9)   9.50 8.85

"FAO" Emblem and Food Bowl — A166

1963, Mar. 21   Perf. 12½
407 A166 5c aqua & dk car   .40 .25
FAO "Freedom from Hunger" campaign. See Nos. C149-C150.

Rocket in Space A167

Design: 15c, Space capsule and globe.

1963, May 27   Litho.   Perf. 12½
408 A167 10c dp vio bl & yel   .25 .25
409 A167 15c blue & red brn   .60 .60
    Nos. 408-409,C151 (3)   1.55 1.55
Achievements in space exploration for peaceful purposes.

Red Cross A168

10c, Centenary emblem and torch, vert.

1963, Aug. 26   Unwmk.   Perf. 11½
410 A168 5c blue grn & red   .25 .25
411 A168 10c gray & red   .25 .25
    Nos. 410-411,C153-C154 (4)   1.60 1.60
Intl. Red Cross, cent.

Palm Tree and Scroll — A169

1963, Oct. 28   Perf. 12½
412 A169 20c brown & green   .45 .45
Conference of African heads of state for African Unity, Addis Ababa, May, 1963. See No. C156.

Ski Jump — A170

1963, Dec. 11   Unwmk.   Perf. 12½
413 A170 5c rose red & dk vio bl   .25 .25
    Nos. 413,C157-C158 (3)   1.30 1.30
9th Winter Olympic Games, Innsbruck, Austria, Jan. 29-Feb. 9, 1964. Exist imperf.

John F. Kennedy A171

1964, Apr. 6   Litho.
414 A171 20c blk & brt blue   .35 .35
John F. Kennedy (1917-63). See Nos. C160-C161.

Syncom Satellite A172

Satellites: 15c, Relay I, vert. 25c, Mariner II.

1964, June 22   Unwmk.   Perf. 12½
415 A172 10c orange & emer   .30 .25
416 A172 15c brt car rose & vio   .40 .25
417 A172 25c blue, org & blk   .40 .70
    Nos. 415-417 (3)   1.10 1.20
Progress in space communications and the peaceful uses of outer space. See No. C162. Exist imperf. Value, set $9.

Mt. Fuji A173

Designs: 15c, Torii and Olympic flame. 25c, Cherry blossoms and stadium.

1964, Sept. 15   Litho.
418 A173 10c orange yel & emer   .25 .25
419 A173 15c lt red & purple   .25 .25
420 A173 25c ocher & red   .95 .95
    Nos. 418-420 (3)   1.45 1.45
Issued for the 18th Olympic Games, Tokyo, Oct. 10-25, 1964. See No. C163. Exist imperf. Value, set $9.

Boy Scout Emblem and Scout Sign — A174

10c, Bugle and Liberian Scout emblem, horiz.

1965, Mar. 8   Litho.   Perf. 12½
421 A174 5c lt blue & brown   .30 .25
422 A174 10c dk green & ocher   .40 .25
    Nos. 421-422,C164 (3)   1.50 1.30
Liberian Boy Scouts. Exist imperf. Value, set $8.

"Emancipation" by Thomas Ball — A175

Designs: 20c, Abraham Lincoln and John F. Kennedy, horiz. 25c, Lincoln by Augustus St. Gaudens, Lincoln Park, Chicago.

1965, May 3   Unwmk.   Perf. 12½
423 A175 5c dk gray & brn org   .25 .25
424 A175 20c emer & lt gray   .50 .50
425 A175 25c maroon & blue   .65 .65
    Nos. 423-425 (3)   1.40 1.40
Centenary of the death of Abraham Lincoln. Exist imperf. Value, set $9. See No. C166.

ICY Emblem A176

1965, June 21   Litho.   Perf. 12½
426 A176 12c orange & brn   .40 .25
427 A176 25c vio blue & brn   .75 .40
428 A176 50c emerald & brn   1.50 .85
    Nos. 426-428 (3)   2.65 1.50
Intl. Cooperation Year. See No. C167.

ITU Emblem, Old and New Communication Equipment — A177

1965, Sept. 21   Unwmk.   Perf. 12½
429 A177 25c brt grn & red brn   .40   .40
430 A177 35c black & car rose   .50   .50
   Nos. 429-430,C168 (3)   1.70 1.60
   Cent. of the ITU.

Pres. Tubman and Liberian Flag A178

1965, Nov. 29   Litho.
431 A178 25c red, ultra & brn   .60   .60
   Pres. William V. S. Tubman's 70th birthday. See No. C169, C169a.

Churchill in Admiral's Uniform A179

Designs: 15c, Churchill giving "V" sign, vert.

1966, Jan. 18   Litho.   Perf. 12½
432 A179 15c orange & blk   .40   .40
433 A179 20c black & brt grn   .90   .90
   Nos. 432-433,C170 (3)   2.00 1.70
   Issued in memory of Sir Winston Spencer Churchill (1874-1965), statesman and World War II leader. Exist imperf. Value, set $5.

Pres. Joseph J. Roberts — A180

Presidents: 2c, Stephen Benson. 3c, Daniel Bashiel Warner. 4c, James S. Payne. 5c, Edward James Roye. 10c, William D. Coleman. 25c, Daniel Edward Howard. 50c, Charles Dunbar Burgess King. 80c, Hilary R. W. Johnson. $1, Edwin J. Barclay. $2, Joseph James Cheeseman ("Cheesman" on stamp).

1966-69   Litho.   Perf. 12½
434 A180 1c black & brick red   .25   .25
435 A180 2c black & yellow   .25   .25
436 A180 3c black & lilac   .25   .25
437 A180 4c ap grn & blk ('67)   .25   .25
438 A180 5c black & dull org ('67)   .25   .25
439 A180 10c pale grn & blk ('67)   .25   .25
440 A180 25c black & lt blue   .60   .25
441 A180 50c blk & brt lil rose   1.25   .90
442 A180 80c dp rose & blk ('67)   1.90 1.10
443 A180 $1 black & ocher   2.25   .25
   Perf. 11½x11
443A A180 $2 blk & dp red lil ('69)   4.50 3.00
   Nos. 434-443A,C182 (12)   12.60 7.30

Soccer Players and Globe A181

Designs: 25c, World Championships Cup, ball and shoes, vert. 35c, Soccer player dribbling, vert.

1966, May 3   Litho.   Perf. 12½
444 A181 10c brt green & dk brn   .40   .25
445 A181 25c brt pink & brn   .60   .30
446 A181 35c brown & orange   .80   .45
   Nos. 444-446 (3)   1.80 1.00
   World Cup Soccer Championships, Wembley, England, July 11-30. Exist imperf. See No. C172.

Pres. Kennedy Taking Oath of Office A182

20c, 1964 Kennedy stamps, #414, C160.

1966, Aug. 16   Litho.   Perf. 12½
447 A182 15c red & blk   .35   .35
448 A182 20c brt bl & red lil   .35   .35
   Nos. 447-448,C173-C174 (4)   1.80 1.20
   3rd anniv. of Pres. Kennedy's death (Nov. 22). Exist imperf. Value, set $20.

Children on Seesaw and UNICEF Emblem A183

Design: 80c, Boy playing doctor.

1966, Oct. 25   Unwmk.   Perf. 12½
449 A183 5c brt blue & red   .25   .25
450 A183 80c org brn & yel grn   1.10 1.10
   20th anniv. of UNICEF.

Giraffe — A184

Designs: 3c, Lion. 5c, Olender-nosed crocodile, horiz. 10c, Baby chimpanzees. 15c, Leopard, horiz. 20c, Black rhinoceros, horiz. 25c, Elephant.

1966, Dec. 20
451 A184 2c multicolored   1.25   .25
452 A184 3c multicolored   1.25   .25
453 A184 5c multicolored   1.25   .25
   a. Black omitted ("5¢ LIBERIA" and imprint)   50.00
454 A184 10c multicolored   1.25   .25
455 A184 15c multicolored   1.60   .30
456 A184 20c multicolored   2.25   .55
457 A184 25c multicolored   3.25   .65
   Nos. 451-457 (7)   12.10 2.50

Jamboree Badge — A185

Designs: 25c, Boy Scout emblem and various sports, horiz. 40c, Scout at campfire and vision of moon landing, horiz.

1967, Mar. 23   Litho.   Perf. 12½
458 A185 10c brt lil rose & grn   .25   .25
459 A185 25c brt red & blue   .65   .55
460 A185 40c brt grn & brn org   1.10   .85
   Nos. 458-460 (3)   2.00 1.65
   12th Boy Scout World Jamboree, Farragut State Park, Idaho, Aug. 1-9. Exist imperf. Value, set $9. See No. C176.

A186

Pre-Hispanic Sculpture of Mexico: 25c, Aztec Calendar and Olympic rings. 40c, Mexican pottery, sombrero and guitar, horiz.

1967, June 20   Litho.   Perf. 12½
461 A186 10c ocher & violet   .25   .25
462 A186 25c lt bl, org & blk   .50   .25
463 A186 40c yel grn & car   .75   .50
   Nos. 461-463 (3)   1.50 1.00
   Issued to publicize the 19th Olympic Games, Mexico City. Exist imperf. See No. C177.

A187

Designs: 5c, WHO Office for Africa, horiz. 80c, WHO Office for Africa.

1967, Aug. 28   Litho.   Perf. 12½
464 A187 5c blue & yellow   .25   .25
465 A187 80c brt grn & yel   2.10 2.10
   Inauguration of the WHO Regional Office for Africa in Brazzaville, Congo.

Boy Playing African Rattle A188

Africans Playing Native Instruments: 3c, Tom-tom and soko violin, horiz. 5c, Mang harp, horiz. 10c, Alimilim. 15c, Xylophone drums. 25c, Large tom-toms. 35c, Large harp.

1967, Oct. 16   Litho.   Perf. 14
466 A188 2c violet & multi   .25   .25
467 A188 3c blue & multi   .25   .25
468 A188 5c lilac rose & multi   .25   .25
469 A188 10c yel grn & multi   .25   .25
470 A188 15c violet & multi   .40   .25
471 A188 25c ocher & multi   .90   .40
472 A188 35c dp rose & multi   1.40   .65
   Nos. 466-472 (7)   3.70 2.30

Ice Hockey — A189

Designs: 25c, Ski jump. 40c, Bobsledding.

1967, Nov. 20   Litho.   Perf. 12½
473 A189 10c emer & vio bl   .25   .25
474 A189 25c grnsh bl & dp plum   .40   .25
475 A189 40c ocher & org brn   .70   .50
   Nos. 473-475 (3)   1.35 1.00
   10th Winter Olympic Games, Grenoble, France, Feb. 6-18, 1968. See No. C178.

Pres. William Tubman — A190

1967, Dec. 22   Litho.   Perf. 12½
476 A190 25c ultra & brown   1.00   .50
   Souvenir Sheet
   Imperf
477 A190 50c ultra & brown   2.50 2.50
   Inauguration of President Tubman, Jan. 1, 1968. No. 476 exists imperf. No. 477 contains one stamp with simulated perforations and picture frame.

Human Rights Flame — A191

1968, Apr. 26   Litho.   Perf. 12½
478 A191 3c ver & dp bl   .25   .25
479 A191 80c brown & emer   1.40 1.40
   Intl. Human Rights Year. See No. C179. Exist imperf.

Martin Luther King, Jr. — A192

Designs: 15c, Mule-drawn hearse and Dr. King. 35c, Dr. King and Lincoln monument by Daniel Chester French, horiz.

1968, July 11   Unwmk.   Perf. 12½
480 A192 15c brt bl & brn   .25   .25
481 A192 25c indigo & brn   .40   .25
482 A192 35c olive & blk   .65   .40
   Nos. 480-482 (3)   1.30   .90
   Rev. Dr. Martin Luther King, Jr. (1929-1968), American civil rights leader. See No. C180. Exist imperf.

Javelin and Diana Statue, Mexico City A193

Designs: 25c, Discus, pyramid and serpent god Quetzalcoatl. 35c, Woman diver and Xochicalco from ruins near Cuernavaca.

1968, Aug. 22   Litho.   Perf. 12½
483 A193 15c dp vio & org brn   .40   .25
484 A193 25c red & brt blue   .70   .25
485 A193 35c brown & emer   1.00   .45
   Nos. 483-485 (3)   2.10   .95
   19th Olympic Games, Mexico City, Oct. 12-27. Exist imperf. See No. C181.

Pres. Wm. V. S. Tubman
A194

Unification Monument, Voinjama-Lofa County — A195

1968, Dec. 30   Unwmk.   Perf. 12½
486 A194 25c silver, blk & brn   1.60 1.00

Souvenir Sheet
Imperf
487 A195 80c silver, ultra & red   3.25 3.25
25th anniv. of Pres. Tubman's administration.

"ILO" with Cogwheel and Wreath
A196

1969, Apr. 16   Litho.   Perf. 12½
488 A196 25c lt blue & gold   .70 .40
50th anniv. of the ILO. Exists imperf.
See No. C183.

Red Roofs, by Camille Pissarro — A197

Paintings: 3c, Prince Balthasar Carlos on Horseback, by Velazquez, vert. 10c, David and Goliath, by Caravaggio. 12c, Still Life, by Jean Baptiste Chardin. 15c, The Last Supper, by Leonardo da Vinci. 20c, Regatta at Argenteuil, by Claude Monet. 25c, Judgment of Solomon, by Giorgione. 35c, Sistine Madonna, by Raphael.

1969, June 26   Litho.   Perf. 11
489 A197 3c gray & multi   .25 .25
490 A197 5c gray & multi   .25 .25
491 A197 10c lt blue & multi   .25 .25
492 A197 12c gray & multi   .50 .25
493 A197 15c gray & multi   .50 .25
494 A197 20c gray & multi   .80 .25
495 A197 25c gray & multi   .95 .25
496 A197 35c gray & multi   1.25 .40
       Nos. 489-496 (8)   4.75 2.15

See Nos. 502-509.

African Development Bank Emblem — A198

1969, Aug. 12   Litho.   Perf. 12½
497 A198 25c blue & brown   .60 .50
498 A198 80c yel grn & red   1.90 1.00
5th anniversary of the African Development Bank. Exist imperf.

Moon Landing and Liberia No. C174
A199

15c, Memorial tablet left on moon, rocket, earth & moon, horiz. 35c, Take-off from moon.

1969, Oct. 15   Litho.   Perf. 12½
499 A199 15c blue & bister   .65 .25
500 A199 25c dk vio bl & org   1.00 .25
501 A199 35c gray & red   1.50 .40
       Nos. 499-501 (3)   3.15 .90
Man's 1st landing on the moon, July 20, 1969. US astronauts Neil A. Armstrong and Col. Edwin E. Aldrin, Jr., with Lieut. Col. Michael Collins piloting Apollo 11. Exist imperf.
See No. C184.

Painting Type of 1969
Paintings: 3c, The Gleaners, by Francois Millet. 5c, View of Toledo, by El Greco, vert. 10c, Heads of Negroes, by Rubens. 12c, The Last Supper, by El Greco. 15c, Dancing Peasants, by Brueghel. 20c, Hunters in the Snow, by Brueghel. 25c, Detail from Descent from the Cross, by Rogier van der Weyden, vert. 35c, The Ascension, by Murillo (inscribed "The Conception"), vert.

1969, Nov. 18   Litho.   Perf. 11
502 A197 3c lt blue & multi   .25 .25
503 A197 5c lt blue & multi   .25 .25
504 A197 10c lt blue & multi   .25 .25
505 A197 12c gray & multi   .40 .25
506 A197 15c gray & multi   .55 .25
507 A197 20c lt blue & multi   .70 .25
508 A197 25c gray & multi   .95 .40
509 A197 35c lt blue & multi   1.25 .40
       Nos. 502-509 (8)   4.60 2.30

Peace Dove, UN Emblem and Atom — A200

1970, Apr. 16   Litho.   Perf. 12½
510 A200 5c green & silver   .30 .30
25th anniv. of the UN. Exists imperf.
See No. C185.

Official Emblem — A201

Designs: 10c, Statue of rain god Tlaloc, vert. 25c, Jules Rimet cup and sculptured wall, vert. 35c, Sombrero and soccer ball. 55c, Two soccer players.

1970, June 10   Litho.   Perf. 12½
511 A201 5c pale blue & brn   .25 .25
512 A201 10c emerald & ocher   .25 .25
513 A201 25c dp rose lil & gold   .70 .25
514 A201 35c ver & ultra   1.00 .35
       Nos. 511-514 (4)   2.20 1.10

Souvenir Sheet
Perf. 11½
515 A201 55c brt bl, yel & grn   1.75 1.60
9th World Soccer Championships for the Jules Rimet Cup, Mexico City, May 30-June 21, 1970. Exist imperf.

EXPO '70 Emblem, Japanese Singer and Festival Plaza — A202

Designs (EXPO '70 Emblem and): 3c, Male Japanese singer, EXPO Hall and floating stage. 5c, Tower of the Sun and view of exhibition. 7c, Tanabata Festival. 8c, Awa Dance Festival. 25c, Sado-Okesa Dance Festival. 50c, Ricoh Pavilion with "eye," and Mt. Fuji, vert.

1970, July   Litho.   Perf. 11
516 A202 2c multicolored   .25 .25
517 A202 3c multicolored   .25 .25
518 A202 5c multicolored   .45 .25
519 A202 7c multicolored   .60 .25
520 A202 8c multicolored   .75 .25
521 A202 25c multicolored   1.75 .65
       Nos. 516-521 (6)   4.05 1.90

Souvenir Sheet
522 A202 50c multicolored   3.25 1.00
Issued to publicize EXPO '70 International Exhibition, Osaka, Japan, Mar. 15-Sept. 13.

UPU Headquarters and Monument, Bern — A203

Design: 80c, Like 25c, vert.

1970, Aug. 25   Perf. 12½
523 A203 25c blue & multi   1.25 1.10
524 A203 80c multicolored   3.00 2.50
Inauguration of the new UPU Headquarters in Bern. Exist imperf.

Napoleon as Consul, by Joseph Marie Vien, Sr.
A204

Paintings of Napoleon: 5c, Visit to a School, by unknown painter. 10c, Napoleon Bonaparte, by François Pascal Gerard. 12c, The French Campaign, by Ernest Meissonier. 20c, Napoleon Signing Abdication at Fontainebleau, by François Bouchot. 25c, Napoleon Meets Pope Pius VII, by Jean-Louis Demarne. 50c, Napoleon's Coronation, by Jacques Louis David.

1970, Oct. 20   Litho.   Perf. 11
525 A204 3c blue & multi   .25 .25
526 A204 5c blue & multi   .25 .25
527 A204 10c blue & multi   .55 .25
528 A204 12c blue & multi   .75 .25
529 A204 20c blue & multi   1.10 .25
530 A204 25c blue & multi   2.10 .25
       Nos. 525-530 (6)   5.00 1.50

Souvenir Sheet
Imperf
531 A204 50c blue & multi   3.25 .80
200th anniv. of the birth of Napoleon Bonaparte (1769-1821). No. 531 contains one stamp with simulated perforations.

Pres. Tubman
A205

1970, Nov. 20   Litho.   Perf. 13½
532 A205 25c multicolored   1.10 .55

Souvenir Sheet
Imperf
533 A205 50c multicolored   2.00 1.10
Pres. Tubman's 75th birthday. No. 533 contains one imperf. stamp with simulated perforations.

Adoration of the Kings, by Rogier van der Weyden — A206

Paintings (Adoration of the Kings, by): 5c, Hans Memling. 10c, Stefan Lochner. 12c, Albrecht Altdorfer, vert. 20c, Hugo van der Goes, Adoration of the Shepherds. 25c, Hieronymus Bosch, vert. 50c, Andrea Mantegna (triptych).

Perf. 13½x14, 14x13½
1970, Dec. 21   Litho.
534 A206 3c multicolored   .25 .25
535 A206 5c multicolored   .25 .25
536 A206 10c multicolored   .25 .25
537 A206 12c multicolored   .35 .25
538 A206 20c multicolored   .50 .25
539 A206 25c multicolored   .75 .25
       Nos. 534-539 (6)   2.35 1.50

Souvenir Sheet
Imperf
540 A206 50c multicolored   3.00 .85
Christmas 1970.
No. 540 contains one 60x40mm stamp.

Dogon Tribal Mask
A207

African Tribal Ceremonial Masks: 2c, Bapendé. 5c, Baoulé. 6c, Dédougou. 9c, Dan. 15c, Bamiléké. 20c, Bapendé mask and costume. 25c, Bamiléké mask and costume.

1971, Feb. 24   Litho.   Perf. 11
541	A207	2c lt green & multi	.25	.25
542	A207	3c pink & multi	.25	.25
543	A207	5c lt blue & multi	.25	.25
544	A207	6c lt green & multi	.25	.25
545	A207	9c lt blue & multi	.25	.25
546	A207	15c lt green & multi	.45	.25
547	A207	20c lt green & multi	.85	.55
548	A207	25c pink & multi	.45	.25
		Nos. 541-548 (8)	3.00	2.30

Astronauts on Moon — A208

Designs: 5c, Astronaut and lunar transport vehicle. 10c, Astronaut with US flag on moon. 12c, Space capsule in Pacific Ocean. 20c, Astronaut leaving capsule. 25c, Astronauts Alan B. Shepard, Stuart A. Roosa and Edgar D. Mitchell.

1971, May 20   Litho.   Perf. 13½
549	A208	3c vio blue & multi	.25	.25
550	A208	5c vio blue & multi	.25	.25
551	A208	10c vio blue & multi	.45	.25
552	A208	12c vio blue & multi	.60	.25
553	A208	20c vio blue & multi	.85	.25
554	A208	25c vio blue & multi	1.00	.35
		Nos. 549-554 (6)	3.40	1.60

Apollo 14 moon landing, Jan. 31-Feb. 9. Exist imperf.
See No. C186.

Map, Liberian Women and Pres. Tubman A209

3c, Pres. Tubman & women at ballot box, vert.

1971, May 27   Perf. 12½
555	A209	3c ultra & brn	.25	.25
556	A209	80c green & brn	2.10	2.10

25th anniversary of women's suffrage.

Hall of Honor, Munich, and Olympic Flag — A210

Munich Views and Olympic Flag: 5c, General view. 10c, National Museum. 12c, Max Joseph's Square. 20c, Propylaeum on King's Square. 25c, Liesel-Karlstadt Fountain.

1971, June 28   Litho.   Perf. 11
557	A210	3c multicolored	.25	.25
558	A210	5c multicolored	.25	.25
559	A210	10c multicolored	.25	.25
560	A210	12c multicolored	.25	.25
561	A210	20c multicolored	1.10	.25
562	A210	25c multicolored	1.90	.90
		Nos. 557-562 (6)	4.00	2.15

Publicity for the 20th Summer Olympic Games, Munich, Germany, 1972. Exist imperf.
See No. C187.

Boy Scout, Emblem and US Flag — A211

Boy Scout, Natl. Flag & Boy Scout Emblem of: 5c, German Federal Republic. 10c, Australia. 12c, Great Britain. 20c, Japan. 25c, Liberia.

1971, Aug. 6   Litho.   Perf. 13½
563	A211	3c multicolored	.25	.25
564	A211	5c multicolored	.25	.25
565	A211	10c multicolored	.25	.25
566	A211	12c multicolored	.35	.25
567	A211	20c multicolored	.60	.25
568	A211	25c multicolored	.75	.25
		Nos. 563-568 (6)	2.45	1.50

13th Boy Scout World Jamboree, Asagiri Plain, Japan, Aug. 2-10. Exist imperf.
See No. C188.

Pres. Tubman (1895-1971) A212

1971, Aug. 23   Perf. 12½
569	A212	3c black, ultra & brn	.25	.25
570	A212	25c blk, brt rose lil & brn	1.10	1.10

Zebra and UNICEF Emblem — A213

Animals (UNICEF Emblem and Animals with their Young): 7c, Koala. 8c, Llama. 10c, Red fox. 20c, Monkey. 25c, Brown bear.

1971, Oct. 1   Perf. 11
571	A213	5c multicolored	.25	.25
572	A213	7c multicolored	.50	.25
573	A213	8c multicolored	.50	.25
574	A213	10c multicolored	.65	.25
575	A213	20c multicolored	1.25	.50
576	A213	25c multicolored	1.60	.65
		Nos. 571-576 (6)	4.75	2.15

25th anniv. of UNICEF. See No. C189.

Sapporo 72 Emblem, Long-distance Skiing, Sika Deer — A214

3c, Sledding & black woodpecker. 5c, Ski Jump & brown bear. 10c, Bobsledding & murres. 15c, Figure skating & pikas. 25c, Downhill skiing & Japanese cranes.

1971, Nov. 4   Perf. 13x13½
577	A214	2c multicolored	.25	.25
578	A214	3c multicolored	.25	.25
579	A214	5c multicolored	.25	.25
580	A214	10c multicolored	.30	.25
581	A214	15c multicolored	1.75	.25
582	A214	25c multicolored	3.75	.25
		Nos. 577-582 (6)	6.55	1.50

11th Winter Olympic Games, Sapporo, Japan, Feb. 3-13, 1972. Exist imperf.
See No. C190.

Dove Carrying Letter, APU Emblem A215

1971, Dec. 9   Perf. 12½
583	A215	25c ultra & dp org	.60	.55
584	A215	80c gray & dp brn	2.00	1.60

10th anniversary of African Postal Union.

Pioneer Fathers' Monument, Monrovia — A216

Designs: 3c, 25c, Sailing ship "Elizabeth," Providence Island, horiz. 35c, as 20c.

1972, Jan. 1
585	A216	3c blue & brt grn	.25	.25
586	A216	20c orange & blue	.95	.70
587	A216	25c orange & purple	1.00	.85
588	A216	35c lil rose & brt grn	1.75	1.25
		Nos. 585-588 (4)	3.95	3.05

Founding of Liberia, sesqui. See No. C191.

Pres. William R. Tolbert, Jr. — A217

25c, Pres. Tolbert and map of Liberia, horiz.

1972, Jan. 1
589	A217	25c emerald & brown	.65	.40
590	A217	80c blue & brown	2.25	.70

Inauguration of William R. Tolbert, Jr. as 19th president of Liberia.

Soccer and Swedish Flag — A218

Olympic Rings, "Motion" Symbol and: 5c, Swimmers at start, Italian flag. 10c, Equestrian, British flag. 12c, Bicycling, French flag. 20c, Long jump, US flag. 25c, Running and Liberian flag.

1972, May 19   Litho.   Perf. 11
591	A218	3c lemon & multi	.25	.25
592	A218	5c lt lilac & multi	.25	.25
593	A218	10c multicolored	.75	.25
594	A218	12c gray & multi	1.00	.25
595	A218	20c lt blue & multi	1.40	.60
596	A218	25c pink & multi	1.90	.75
		Nos. 591-596 (6)	5.55	2.35

20th Olympic Games, Munich, Aug. 26-Sept. 10. Exist imperf.
See No. C192.

Y's Men's Club Emblem, Map — A219

Design: 90c, Y's Men's Club emblem and globe; inscribed "fifty and forward."

1972, June 12   Perf. 13½
597	A219	15c purple & gold	.50	.25
598	A219	90c vio bl & emer	2.40	2.00

Intl. Y's Men's Club, 50th anniv.

Astronaut and Lunar Rover — A220

5c, Moon scene reflected in astronaut's helmet. 10c, Astronauts with cameras. 12c, Astronauts placing scientific equipment on moon. 20c, Apollo 16 badge. 25c, Astronauts riding lunar rover.

1972, June 26
599	A220	3c lt blue & multi	.25	.25
600	A220	5c red org & multi	.25	.25
601	A220	10c pink & multi	.50	.25
602	A220	12c yellow & multi	.80	.25
603	A220	20c lt vio & multi	1.00	.25
604	A220	25c emerald & multi	1.40	.25
		Nos. 599-604 (6)	4.20	1.50

Apollo 16 US moon mission, Apr. 15-27, 1972. Exist imperf. Value, set $10.
See No. C193.

Emperor Haile Selassie — A221

1972, July 21   Perf. 14x14½
605	A221	20c olive grn & yel	.70	.70
606	A221	25c maroon & yel	.85	.85
607	A221	35c brown & yel	1.25	1.25
		Nos. 605-607 (3)	2.80	2.80

80th birthday of Emperor Haile Selassie of Ethiopia.

Ajax, 1809, and Figurehead — A222

1972, Sept. 6   Perf. 11
608	A222	3c shown	.25	.25
609	A222	5c Hogue, 1811	.25	.25
610	A222	7c Ariadne, 1816	.55	.25
611	A222	15c Royal Adelaide, 1828	1.00	.25
612	A222	20c Rinaldo, 1860	1.25	.25
613	A222	25c Nymphe, 1888	1.45	.45
		Nos. 608-613 (6)	4.75	1.70

Famous sailing ships and their figureheads.
See No. C194.

Pres. Tolbert Taking Oath, Richard A.
Henries — A223

1972, Oct. 23   Litho.   Perf. 13½

614	A223	15c green & multi	1.10	.95
615	A223	25c vio blue & multi	1.50	1.45

Pres. William R. Tolbert, Jr. sworn in as 19th
President of Liberia, July 23, 1971. See No.
C195.

Klaus Dibiasi, Italy, Diving — A224

8c, Valery Borzov, USSR, running. 10c,
Hideaki Yanagida, Japan, wrestling. 12c, Mark
Spitz, US, swimming. 15c, Kipchoge Keino,
Kenya, 3000-meter steeplechase. 25c, Rich-
ard Meade, Great Britain, equestrian. 55c,
Hans Winkler, Germany, grand prix jumping.

1973, Jan. 5   Litho.   Perf. 11

616	A224	5c lt blue & multi	.25	.25
617	A224	8c violet & multi	.25	.25
618	A224	10c multicolored	.25	.25
619	A224	12c green & multi	.55	.25
620	A224	15c orange & multi	.80	.25
621	A224	25c pale salmon & multi	1.10	.55
		Nos. 616-621 (6)	3.20	1.80

Souvenir Sheet

622	A224	55c multicolored	4.50	2.25

Gold medal winners in 20th Olympic Games.

Astronaut on Moon and Apollo 17
Badge — A225

Designs (Apollo 17 Badge and): 3c, Astronauts on earth in lunar rover. 10c, Astronauts
collecting yellow lunar dust. 15c, Astronauts in
lunar rover exploring moon crater. 20c, Capt.
Eugene A. Cernan, Dr. Harrison H. Schmitt
and Comdr. Ronald E. Evans on launching
pad. 25c, Astronauts on moon with scientific
equipment.

1973, Mar. 28   Litho.   Perf. 11

623	A225	2c blue & multi	.25	.25
624	A225	3c blue & multi	.25	.25
625	A225	10c blue & multi	.25	.25
626	A225	15c blue & multi	.70	.25
627	A225	20c blue & multi	1.00	.50
628	A225	25c blue & multi	1.25	.60
		Nos. 623-628 (6)	3.70	2.10

Apollo 17 US moon mission, Dec. 7-19,
1972. Exist imperf. Value, set $10.
See No. C196.

Locomotive, England — A226

Designs: Locomotives, 1895-1905.

1973, May 4

629	A226	2c shown	.25	.25
630	A226	3c Netherlands	.25	.25
631	A226	10c France	.90	.25
632	A226	15c United States	1.25	.25
633	A226	20c Japan	2.25	.25
634	A226	25c Germany	3.25	.75
		Nos. 629-634 (6)	8.15	2.00

See No. C197.

OAU Emblem and Flags — A227

1973, May 24   Litho.   Perf. 13½

635	A227	3c multicolored	.25	.25
636	A227	4c multicolored	.25	.25
637	A227	10c multicolored	.25	.25
638	A227	15c multicolored	.45	.25
639	A227	25c multicolored	.55	.45
640	A227	50c multicolored	1.25	1.00
		Nos. 635-640 (6)	3.00	2.40

10th anniv. of the Organization for African
Unity.

WHO Emblem, Edward Jenner and
Roses — A228

Designs (WHO Emblem and): 4c, Sigmund
Freud and pansies. 10c, Jonas E. Salk and
chrysanthemums. 15c, Louis Pasteur and scabiosa caucasia. 20c, Emil von Behring and
rhododendron. 25c, Alexander Fleming and
tree mallows.

1973, June 26   Litho.   Perf. 11

641	A228	1c gray & multi	.25	.25
642	A228	4c orange & multi	.25	.25
643	A228	10c lt blue & multi	.25	.25
644	A228	15c rose & multi	.40	.25
645	A228	20c blue & multi	.50	.25
646	A228	25c yel grn & multi	.75	.40
		Nos. 641-646 (6)	2.40	1.65

25th anniv. of WHO. See No. C198.

Stanley Steamer, 1910 — A229

Designs: Classic automobiles.

1973, Sept. 11   Litho.   Perf. 11

647	A229	2c shown	.25	.25
648	A229	3c Cadillac, 1903	.25	.25
649	A229	10c Clement-Bayard, 1904	.40	.25
650	A229	15c Rolls Royce, 1907	.55	.25
651	A229	20c Maxwell, 1905	.80	.25
652	A229	25c Chadwick, 1907	1.00	.50
		Nos. 647-652 (6)	3.25	1.75

See No. C199.

Copernicus, Armillary Sphere, Satellite
Communication — A230

Portraits of Copernicus and: 4c, Eudoxus
solar system. 10c, Aristotle, Ptolemy, Copernicus and satellites. 15c, Saturn and Apollo
spacecraft. 20c, Orbiting astronomical observatory. 25c, Satellite tracking station.

1973, Dec. 14   Litho.   Perf. 13½

653	A230	1c yellow & multi	.25	.25
654	A230	4c lt violet & multi	.25	.25
655	A230	10c lt blue & multi	.25	.25
656	A230	15c yel grn & multi	.50	.25
657	A230	20c bister & multi	.65	.25
658	A230	25c pink & multi	.80	.40
		Nos. 653-658 (6)	2.70	1.65

Nicolaus Copernicus (1473-1543), Polish
astronomer. Exist imperf.
See No. C200.

Radio
Tower, Map
of Africa
A231

15c, 25c, Map of Liberia, Radio tower and
man listening to broadcast. 17c, like 13c.

1974, Jan. 16   Litho.   Perf. 13½

659	A231	13c multicolored	.60	.60
660	A231	15c yellow & multi	.60	.50
661	A231	17c lt gray & multi	.75	.60
662	A231	25c brt green & multi	1.00	.65
		Nos. 659-662 (4)	2.95	2.35

20th anniv. of Radio ELWA, Monrovia.

Thomas Coutts, 1817; Aureal, 1974;
UPU Emblem — A232

Designs (UPU Emblem and): 3c, Jet, satellite, Post Office, Monrovia, ship. 10c, US and
USSR telecommunication satellites. 15c, Mail
runner and jet. 20c, Futuristic mail train and
mail truck. 25c, American Pony Express rider.

1974, Mar. 4   Litho.   Perf. 13½

663	A232	2c ocher & multi	.25	.25
664	A232	3c lt green & multi	.25	.25
665	A232	10c lt blue & multi	.25	.25
666	A232	15c pink & multi	.50	.25
667	A232	20c gray & multi	.65	.25
668	A232	25c lt lilac & multi	.85	.40
		Nos. 663-668 (6)	2.75	1.65

Cent. of UPU. Exist imperf. Value, set $15.
See No. C201.

Fox Terrier — A233

1974, Apr. 16   Litho.   Perf. 13½

669	A233	5c shown	.25	.25
670	A233	10c Boxer	.25	.25
671	A233	16c Chihuahua	.65	.25

672	A233	19c Beagle	.70	.25
673	A233	25c Golden retriever	.80	.25
674	A233	50c Collie	1.75	.40
		Nos. 669-674 (6)	4.40	1.65

Exist imperf. See No. C202.

Soccer Game, West Germany and
Chile — A234

Designs: Games between semi-finalists,
and flags of competing nations: 2c, Australia
and East Germany. 5c, Brazil and Yugoslavia.
10c, Zaire and Scotland. 12c, Netherlands and
Uruguay. 15c, Sweden and Bulgaria. 20c, Italy
and Haiti. 25c, Poland and Argentina.

1974, June 4   Litho.   Perf. 11

675	A234	1c shown	.25	.25
676	A234	2c multicolored	.25	.25
677	A234	5c multicolored	.25	.25
678	A234	10c multicolored	.25	.25
679	A234	12c multicolored	.25	.25
680	A234	15c multicolored	.45	.25
681	A234	20c multicolored	.65	.25
682	A234	25c multicolored	.75	.45
		Nos. 675-682 (8)	3.10	2.20

World Cup Soccer Championship, Munich,
June 13-July 7. Exist imperf. Value, set $20.
See No. C203.

Chrysiridia Madagascariensis — A235

Tropical Butterflies: 2c, Catagramma
sorana. 5c, Erasmia pulchella. 17c, Morpho
cypris. 25c, Agrias amydon. 40c, Vanessa
cardui.

1974, Sept. 11   Litho.   Perf. 13½

683	A235	1c gray & multi	.25	.25
684	A235	2c gray & multi	.25	.25
685	A235	5c gray & multi	.25	.25
686	A235	17c gray & multi	.95	.25
687	A235	25c gray & multi	1.25	.40
688	A235	40c gray & multi	2.40	.65
		Nos. 683-688 (6)	5.35	2.05

See No. C204.

Pres. Tolbert and Medal — A236

$1, Pres. Tolbert, medal & Liberian flag.

1974, Dec. 10   Litho.   Perf. 13½

689	A236	3c multi	.25	.25
690	A236	$1 multi, vert.	2.75	2.75

Pres. William R. Tolbert, Jr., recipient of
1974 Family of Man Award.

Winston Churchill, 1940 — A237

Churchill and: 10c, RAF planes in dog fight. 15c, In naval launch on way to Normandy. 17c, In staff car reviewing troops in desert. 20c, Aboard landing craft crossing Rhine. 25c, In conference with Pres. Roosevelt.

1975, Jan. 17		**Litho.**		**Perf. 13½**
691	A237	3c multicolored	.25	.25
692	A237	10c multicolored	.25	.25
693	A237	15c multicolored	.25	.25
694	A237	17c multicolored	.45	.25
695	A237	20c multicolored	.55	.25
696	A237	25c multicolored	.90	.45
		Nos. 691-696 (6)	2.65	1.70

Sir Winston Churchill (1874-1965), birth centenary. Exist imperf. Value, set $10.
See No. C205.

Women's Year Emblem and Marie Curie — A238

3c, Mahalia Jackson with microphone. 5c, Joan of Arc. 10c, Eleanor Roosevelt and children. 25c, Matilda Newport firing cannon. 50c, Valentina Tereshkova in space suit.

1975, Mar. 14		**Litho.**		**Perf. 14½**
697	A238	2c citron & multi	.25	.25
698	A238	3c dull orange & multi	.25	.25
699	A238	5c lilac rose & multi	.25	.25
700	A238	10c yellow & multi	.25	.25
701	A238	25c yellow grn & multi	.55	.25
702	A238	50c lilac & multi	1.00	.65
		Nos. 697-702 (6)	2.55	1.90

Intl. Women's Year 1975. Exist imperf. Value, set $10.
See No. C206.

Old State House, Boston, US No. 627 — A239

10c, George Washington, US #645. 15c, Town Hall & Court House, Philadelphia, US #798. 20c, Benjamin Franklin, US #835. 25c, Paul Revere's Ride, US #618. 50c, Santa Maria, US #231.

1975, Apr. 25		**Litho.**		**Perf. 13½**
703	A239	5c multicolored	.25	.25
704	A239	10c multicolored	.50	.25
705	A239	15c multicolored	.60	.25
706	A239	20c multicolored	.80	.25
707	A239	25c multicolored	1.25	.25
708	A239	50c multicolored	2.50	.50
		Nos. 703-708 (6)	5.90	1.75

American Revolution Bicentennial. Exist imperf.
See No. C207.

Dr. Schweitzer, Hospital and Baboon Mother — A240

Designs (Dr. Schweitzer and): 3c, Elephant, and tribesmen poling boat. 5c, Water buffalo, egret, man and woman paddling canoe. 6c, Antelope and dancer. 25c, Lioness, woman cooking outdoors. 50c, Zebra and colt, doctor's examination at clinic.

1975, June 26		**Litho.**		**Perf. 13½**
709	A240	1c multicolored	.25	.25
710	A240	3c multicolored	.25	.25
711	A240	5c multicolored	.25	.25
712	A240	6c multicolored	.25	.25
713	A240	25c multicolored	.55	.25
714	A240	50c multicolored	1.25	.65
		Nos. 709-714 (6)	2.80	1.90

Dr. Albert Schweitzer (1875-1965), medical missionary, birth centenary. Exist imperf. Value, set $10.
See No. C208.

American-Russian Handshake in Space — A241

Designs (Apollo-Soyuz Emblem and): 5c, Apollo. 10c, Soyuz. 20c, Flags and maps of US and USSR. 25c, A. A. Leonov, and V. N. Kubasov. 50c, D. K. Slayton, V. D. Brand, T. P. Stafford.

1975, Sept. 18		**Litho.**		**Perf. 13½**
715	A241	5c multicolored	.25	.25
716	A241	10c multicolored	.25	.25
717	A241	15c multicolored	.40	.25
718	A241	20c multicolored	.55	.25
719	A241	25c multicolored	.75	.25
720	A241	50c multicolored	1.40	.45
		Nos. 715-720 (6)	3.60	1.70

Apollo Soyuz space test project (Russo-American cooperation), launching July 15; link-up, July 17. Exist imperf. Value, set $10.
See No. C209.

Presidents Tolbert, Siaka Stevens; Treaty Signing; Liberia and Sierra Leone Maps — A242

1975, Oct. 3		**Litho.**		**Perf. 13½**
721	A242	2c gray & multi	.25	.25
722	A242	3c gray & multi	.25	.25
723	A242	5c gray & multi	.25	.25
724	A242	10c gray & multi	.25	.25
725	A242	25c gray & multi	.65	.40
726	A242	50c gray & multi	1.25	.80
		Nos. 721-726 (6)	2.90	2.20

Mano River Union Agreement between Liberia and Sierra Leone, signed Oct. 3, 1973.

Figure Skating — A243

Designs (Winter Olympic Games Emblem and): 4c, Ski jump. 10c, Slalom. 25c, Ice hockey. 35c, Speed skating. 50c, Two-man bobsled.

1976, Jan. 23		**Litho.**		**Perf. 13½**
727	A243	1c lt blue & multi	.25	.25
728	A243	4c lt blue & multi	.25	.25
729	A243	10c lt blue & multi	.25	.25
730	A243	25c lt blue & multi	.90	.25

731	A243	35c lt blue & multi	1.25	.25
732	A243	50c lt blue & multi	1.75	.90
		Nos. 727-732 (6)	4.65	2.15

12th Winter Olympic Games, Innsbruck, Austria, Feb. 4-15. Exist imperf. Value, set $11.
See No. C210.

Pres. Tolbert Taking Oath of Office — A244

25c, Pres. Tolbert at his desk, vert. $1, Seal & flag of Liberia, $400 commemorative gold coin.

1976, Apr. 5		**Litho.**		**Perf. 13½**
733	A244	3c multicolored	.25	.25
734	A244	25c multicolored	.50	.50
735	A244	$1 multicolored	2.50	2.50
		Nos. 733-735 (3)	3.25	3.25

Inauguration of President William R. Tolbert, Jr., Jan. 5, 1976.

Weight Lifting and Olympic Rings — A245

Designs (Olympic Rings and): 3c, Pole vault. 10c, Hammer and shot put. 25c, Yachting. 35c, Women's gymnastics. 50c, Hurdles.

1976, May 4		**Litho.**		**Perf. 13½**
736	A245	2c gray & multi	.25	.25
737	A245	3c orange & multi	.25	.25
738	A245	10c lt violet & multi	.25	.25
739	A245	25c lt green & multi	.90	.25
740	A245	35c yellow & multi	1.25	.70
741	A245	50c pink & multi	1.75	.70
		Nos. 736-741 (6)	4.65	2.40

21st Olympic Games, Montreal, Canada, July 17-Aug. 1. Exist imperf. Value, set $11.
See No. C211.

A. G. Bell, Telephone and Receiver, 1876, UPU Emblem — A246

UPU Emblem and: 4c, Horsedrawn mail coach and ITU emblem. 5c, Intelsat IV satellite, radar and ITU emblem. 25c, A. G. Bell, ship laying underwater cable, 1976 telephone. 40c, A. G. Bell, futuristic train, telegraph and telephone wires. 50c, Wright brothers' plane, Zeppelin and Concorde.

1976, June 4		**Litho.**		**Perf. 13½**
742	A246	1c green & multi	.25	.25
743	A246	4c ocher & multi	.25	.25
744	A246	5c orange & multi	.25	.25
745	A246	25c green & multi	.90	.25
746	A246	40c lilac & multi	1.25	.25
747	A246	50c blue & multi	1.50	.70
		Nos. 742-747 (6)	4.40	1.95

Cent. of 1st telephone call by Alexander Graham Bell, Mar. 10, 1876. Exist imperf. Value, set $12.
See No. C212.

Gold Nugget on Chain, Gold Panner A247

1c, Mano River Bridge. 5c, "V" ring. 10c, Rubber tire, tree. 15c, Harvesting. 20c, Hydroelectric plant. 25c, Mesurado shrimp. 27c, Woman tie-dying cloth. 55c, Lake Piso, barracuda. $1, Train hauling iron ore.

1976-81		**Litho.**		**Perf. 14½**
749	A247	1c multicolored	.25	.25
750	A247	3c shown	.25	.25
751	A247	5c multicolored	.25	.25
752	A247	7c like 5c ('81)	.25	.25
753	A247	10c multicolored	.45	.25
754	A247	15c multicolored	.75	.60
755	A247	17c like 55c ('81)	.80	.60
756	A247	20c multicolored	1.00	.80
757	A247	25c multicolored	1.25	.25
758	A247	27c multicolored	1.40	1.00
759	A247	55c multicolored	2.75	.75
760	A247	$1 multicolored	5.00	3.50
		Nos. 749-760 (12)	14.40	8.75

See Nos. 945-953.

Rhinoceros — A249

African Animals: 3c, Zebra antelope. 5c, Chimpanzee, vert. 15c, Pigmy hippopotamus. 25c, Leopard. $1, Gorilla, vert.

1976, Sept. 1		**Litho.**		**Perf. 13½**
763	A249	2c orange & multi	.60	.60
764	A249	3c gray & multi	.60	.60
765	A249	5c blue & multi	.60	.60
766	A249	15c brt blue & multi	.60	.60
767	A249	25c ultra & multi	1.00	.75
768	A249	$1 multicolored	3.50	2.25
		Nos. 763-768 (6)	6.90	5.40

See No. C213.

Maps of US and Liberia; Statue of Liberty, Unification Monument, Voinjama and Liberty Bell — A250

$1, George Washington, Gerald R. Ford, Joseph J. Roberts (1st Pres. of Liberia), William R. Tolbert, Jr., Bicentennial emblem, US & Liberian flags.

1976, Sept. 21		**Litho.**		**Perf. 13½**
769	A250	25c multicolored	.55	.40
770	A250	$1 multicolored	1.75	.95

American Bicentennial and visit of Pres. William R. Tolbert, Jr. to the US, Sept. 21-30. See No. C214.

Baluba Masks and Festival Emblem A251

Tribal Masks: 10c, Bateke. 15c, Basshilele. 20c, Igungun. 25c, Masai. 50c, Kifwebe.

1977, Jan. 20			Litho.		Perf. 13½	
771	A251	5c	yellow & multi		.25	.25
772	A251	10c	green & multi		.25	.25
773	A251	15c	salmon & multi		.25	.25
774	A251	20c	lt blue & multi		.65	.25
775	A251	25c	violet & multi		.80	.25
776	A251	50c	lemon & multi		1.50	.65
		Nos. 771-776 (6)			3.70	1.90

FESTAC '77, 2nd World Black and African Festival, Lagos, Nigeria, Jan. 15-Feb. 12. See No. C215.

Latham's Francolin — A252

Birds of Liberia: 10c, Narina trogon. 15c, Rufous-crowned roller. 20c, Brown-cheeked hornbill. 25c, Common bulbul. 50c, Fish eagle. 80c, Gold Coast touraco.

1977, Feb. 18			Litho.		Perf. 14	
777	A252	5c	multicolored		.25	.25
778	A252	10c	multicolored		.55	.25
779	A252	15c	multicolored		.75	.25
780	A252	20c	multicolored		1.10	.25
781	A252	25c	multicolored		1.40	.25
782	A252	50c	multicolored		3.50	.65
		Nos. 777-782 (6)			7.55	1.90

Souvenir Sheet

783	A252	80c	multicolored		4.50	3.00

Edmund Coffin, Combined Training, US — A253

Designs: 15c, Alwin Schockemohle, single jump. Germany, vert. 20c, Christine Stuck-elberger, Switzerland, individual dressage. 25c, Prix de Nations (team), France.

1977, Apr. 22			Litho.		Perf. 13½	
784	A253	5c	ocher & multi		.25	.25
785	A253	15c	ocher & multi		.95	.25
786	A253	20c	ocher & multi		1.10	.25
787	A253	25c	ocher & multi		1.40	.80
		Nos. 784-787,C216 (5)			6.95	3.15

Equestrian gold medal winners in Montreal Olympic Games. Exist imperf. Value, set $10. See No. C217.

Elizabeth II Wearing Crown — A254

Designs: 25c, Elizabeth II Prince Philip, Pres. and Mrs. Tubman. 80c, Elizabeth II, Prince Philip, royal coat of arms.

1977, May 23			Litho.		Perf. 13½	
788	A254	15c	silver & multi		.45	.25
789	A254	25c	silver & multi		.85	.25
790	A254	80c	silver & multi		2.50	.70
		Nos. 788-790 (3)			3.80	1.20

25th anniversary of the reign of Queen Elizabeth II. Nos. 788-790 exist imperf. Value, set $8.
See No. C218.

Jesus Blessing Children A255

Christmas: 25c, The Good Shepherd. $1, Jesus and the Samaritan Woman. Designs after stained-glass windows, Providence Baptist Church, Monrovia.

1977, Nov. 3			Litho.		Perf. 13½	
791	A255	20c	lt blue & multi		.45	.25
792	A255	25c	lt blue & multi		.60	.45
793	A255	$1	lt blue & multi		1.90	1.10
		Nos. 791-793 (3)			2.95	1.80

Dornier DOX, 1928 — A256

Progress of Aviation: 3c, Piggyback space shuttle, 1977. 5c, Eddie Rickenbacker and Douglas DC 3. 25c, Charles A. Lindbergh and Spirit of St. Louis. 35c, Louis Bleriot and Bleriot XI. 50c, Orville and Wilbur Wright and flying machine, 1903. 80c, Concorde landing at night at Dulles Airport, Washington, DC.

1978, Jan. 6			Litho.		Perf. 13½	
794	A256	2c	multicolored		.25	.25
795	A256	3c	multicolored		.25	.25
796	A256	5c	multicolored		.25	.25
797	A256	25c	multicolored		.65	.25
798	A256	35c	multicolored		.90	.55
799	A256	50c	multicolored		1.60	.75
		Nos. 794-799 (6)			3.90	2.30

Souvenir Sheet

800	A256	80c	multicolored		3.50	2.50

Exist imperf. Values, set $10., souvenir sheet $9.

Baladeuse by Santos-Dumont, 1903 — A257

Airships: 3c, Baldwin's, 1908, and US flag. 5c, Tissandier brothers', 1883. 25c, Parseval PL VII, 1912. 40c, Nulli Secundus II, 1908. 50c, R34 rigid airship, 1919.

1978, Mar. 9			Litho.		Perf. 13½	
801	A257	2c	multicolored		.25	.25
802	A257	3c	multicolored		.25	.25
803	A257	5c	multicolored		.25	.25
804	A257	25c	multicolored		.55	.25
805	A257	40c	multicolored		.85	.25
806	A257	50c	multicolored		1.10	.25
		Nos. 801-806 (6)			3.25	1.50

75th anniv. of the Zeppelin. Exist imperf. Value, set $12.
See No. C219.

Soccer, East Germany and Brazil — A258

Soccer Games: 2c, Poland and Argentina, vert. 10c, West Germany and Netherlands. 25c, Yugoslavia and Brazil. 35c, Poland and Italy, vert. 50c, Netherlands and Uruguay.

1978, May 16			Litho.		Perf. 13½	
807	A258	2c	multicolored		.25	.25
808	A258	3c	multicolored		.25	.25
809	A258	10c	multicolored		.25	.25
810	A258	25c	multicolored		.75	.25
811	A258	35c	multicolored		1.00	.50
812	A258	50c	multicolored		1.50	.75
		Nos. 807-812 (6)			4.00	2.25

11th World Cup Soccer Championships, Argentina, June 1-25. Exist imperf. Value, set $12.
See No. C220.

Coronation Chair — A259

Designs: 25c, Imperial state crown. $1, Buckingham Palace, horiz.

1978, June 12						
813	A259	5c	multicolored		.25	.25
814	A259	25c	multicolored		.75	.25
815	A259	$1	multicolored		2.75	1.00
		Nos. 813-815 (3)			3.75	1.50

25th anniversary of coronation of Queen Elizabeth II. Exist imperf. Value, set $9.
See No. C221.

Jinnah, Liberian and Pakistani Flags — A260

1978, June			Litho.		Perf. 13	
816	A260	30c	multicolored		37.50	8.25

Mohammed Ali Jinnah (1876-1948), first Governor General of Pakistan.

Carter and Tolbert Families — A261

Designs: 25c, Pres. Tolbert, Rosalynn Carter and Pres. Carter at microphone, Robertsfield Airport. $1, Jimmy Carter and William R. Tolbert, Jr. in motorcade from airport.

1978, Oct. 26			Litho.		Perf. 13½	
817	A261	5c	multicolored		.25	.25
818	A261	25c	multicolored		.85	.85
819	A261	$1	multicolored		3.50	3.50
		Nos. 817-819 (3)			4.60	4.60

Pres. Carter's visit to Liberia, Apr. 1978.

Soccer Game: Italy-France A262

Soccer Games: 1c, Brazil-Spain, horiz. 10c, Poland-West Germany, horiz. 27c, Peru-Scotland. 35c, Austria-West Germany. 50c, Argentina the victor.

1978, Dec. 8			Litho.		Perf. 13½	
820	A262	1c	multicolored		.25	.25
821	A262	2c	multicolored		.25	.25
822	A262	10c	multicolored		.40	.25
823	A262	27c	multicolored		.95	.65
824	A262	35c	multicolored		1.25	.80
825	A262	50c	multicolored		1.75	1.25
		Nos. 820-825 (6)			4.85	3.45

1978 World Cup Soccer winners. Exist imperf. Value, set $12.
See No. C222.

Liberian Lumbermen — A263

Designs: 10c, Hauling timber by truck, vert. 25c, Felling trees with chain saw. 50c, Moving logs.

1978, Dec. 15			Litho.		Perf. 13½x14	
826	A263	5c	multicolored		.25	.25
827	A263	10c	multicolored		.25	.25
828	A263	25c	multicolored		.85	.25
829	A263	50c	multicolored		1.75	1.25
		Nos. 826-829 (4)			3.10	2.00

8th World Forestry Congress, Djakarta, Indonesia.

"25" and Waves — A264

Design: $1, Radio tower and waves.

1979, Apr. 6			Litho.		Perf. 14x13½	
830	A264	35c	multicolored		.70	.70
831	A264	$1	multicolored		1.90	1.90

25th anniversary of Radio ELWA.

Emblems of IYC, African Child's Decade and SOS Village — A265

Designs: 25c, $1, like 5c, with UNICEF emblem replacing SOS emblem. 35c, like 5c.

1979, Apr. 6					Perf. 13½x14	
832	A265	5c	multicolored		.25	.25
833	A265	25c	multicolored		.25	.25
834	A265	35c	multicolored		.60	.60
835	A265	$1	multicolored		1.40	1.40
		Nos. 832-835 (4)			2.50	2.50

IYC and Decade of the African Child.

Presidents Gardner and Tolbert, and
Post Office, Monrovia — A266

Design: 35c, Anthony W. Gardner, William
R. Tolbert, Jr. and UPU emblem.

1979, Apr. 2   Litho.   Perf. 13½x14
836 A266 5c multicolored   .25   .25
837 A266 35c multicolored   1.10 1.10

Cent. of Liberia's joining UPU.

Unity Problem, Map of Africa,
Torches — A267

Designs: 27c, Masks. 35c, Elephant, giraffe,
lion, antelope, cheetah and map of Africa. 50c,
Huts, pepper birds and map of Africa.

1979, July 6   Litho.   Perf. 14x13½
838 A267 5c multicolored   .25   .25
839 A267 27c multicolored   .75   .75
840 A267 35c multicolored   1.00 1.00
841 A267 50c multicolored   1.50 1.50
      Nos. 838-841 (4)   3.50 3.50

Organization for African Unity, 16th anniversary, and OAU Summit Conference.

Liberia No. 666, Rowland Hill — A268

10c, Pony Express rider, 1860. 15c, British
mail coach, 1800. 25c, Mail steamship John
Penn, 1860. 27c, Stanier Pacific train, 1939.
50c, Concorde. $1, Curtiss Jenny, 1916.

1979, July 20
842 A268 3c multicolored   .25   .25
843 A268 10c multicolored   .25   .25
844 A268 15c multicolored   .45   .45
845 A268 25c multicolored   .85   .65
846 A268 27c multicolored   1.00   .75
847 A268 50c multicolored   1.75 1.40
      Nos. 842-847 (6)   4.55 3.75

Souvenir Sheet

848 A268 $1 multicolored   3.50 2.50

Sir Rowland Hill (1795-1879), originator of
penny postage. Exist imperf. Value, set $20.

Red Cross, Pres. Tolbert Donating
Blood — A269

Design: 50c, Red Cross, Pres. Tolbert.

1979, Aug. 15   Litho.   Perf. 13½
849 A269 30c multicolored   .65   .65
850 A269 50c multicolored   1.25 1.25

National Red Cross, 30th anniversary and
blood donation campaign.

M.S. World Peace — A270

Design: $1, M.S. World Peace, diff.

1979, Aug. 15
851 A270 5c multicolored   .25   .25
852 A270 $1 multicolored   3.25 3.25

2nd World Maritime Day, March 16; Liberia
Maritime Program, 30th anniversary.

A Good
Turn, by
Norman
Rockwell
A271

Paintings — Scouting through the eyes of
Norman Rockwell (1925-76): No. 853: a, Stories. b, 3 branches of Scouts. c, camping. d,
Church. e, Animal care. f, advancements. g,
Scout, Lincoln. h, First aid on puppy. i, Reading with elderly and dog. j, Scout teaching
cubs..
  No. 854: a, "1910." b, Feeding dog. c, Man,
dog, Scout on top of rock. d, Merit badges. e,
Hiking in mountains. f, With explorer and
eagle. g, Wearing new uniform. h, Indian lore.
i, First camping. j, Group saluting.
  No. 855: a, Eagle ceremony. b, Hiking with
compass. c, The Scouting Trail. d, Phyical fit-
ness. e, Prayer. f, Tales of the sea. g, Foreign
and US scouts dancing. h, Building a birdhouse. i, In front of flag. j, Rescueing girl and
kitten.
  No. 856: a, Painting outdoors. b, Scout
saluting in front of flag. c, Scout, Lincoln,
Washington, eagle. d, Starting on hike. e, Knot
tying. f, Reading instructions. g, Scouts of 6
nations. h, Boy, Girl Scouts and leaders. i, "On
my honor..." j, Cooking outdoors.
  No. 857: a, Portaging. b, "Spirit of '76." c,
Saluting flag with astronaut. d, 5 branches of
scouting. e, Planting trees. f, Washington praying. g, First aid on dog. h, Saying grace in
mess tent. i, First time in Scout uniform. j,
Rock climbing.

1979, Sept. 1   Litho.   Perf. 11
853 A271 5c #a.-j, any single   .50   .30
854 A271 10c #a.-j, any single   .50   .30
855 A271 15c #a.-j, any single   .80   .40
856 A271 25c #a.-j, any single 1.40   .45
857 A271 35c #a.-j, any single 2.00   .05
    Nos. 853-857, Set of 50 in 5
    strips of 10   85.00 85.00

Mrs. Tolbert, Children, Children's
Village Emblem — A272

40c, Mrs. Tolbert, children, emblem, vert.

1979, Nov. 14   Litho.   Perf. 14
858 A272 25c multicolored   .60   .60
859 A272 40c multicolored   1.40 1.40

SOS Children's Village in Monrovia, Liberia.

Rotary International Headquarters,
Evanston, Ill., Emblem — A273

Rotary Emblem and: 5c, Vocational services. 17c, Man in wheelchair, nurse, vert.
27c, Flags of several nations. 35c, People of
various races holding hands around globe.
50c, Pres. Tolbert, map of Africa, vert. $1, "Gift
of Life."

1979, Dec. 28   Perf. 11
860 A273 1c multicolored   .25   .25
861 A273 5c multicolored   .25   .25
862 A273 17c multicolored   .40   .40
863 A273 27c multicolored   .85   .85
864 A273 35c multicolored   1.00 1.00
865 A273 50c multicolored   1.75 1.75
      Nos. 860-865 (6)   4.50 4.50

Souvenir Sheet

866 A273 $1 multicolored   3.25 3.25

Rotary International, 75th anniversary. Exist
imperf. Values: set $14.; souvenir sheet $11.

Ski Jump, Lake Placid '80
Emblem — A274

Lake Placid '80 Emblem and: 5c, Figure
skating. 17c, Bobsledding. 27c, Cross-country
skiing. 35c, Women's speed skating. 50c, Ice
hockey. $1, Slalom.

1980, Jan. 21
867 A274 1c multicolored   .25   .25
868 A274 5c multicolored   .25   .25
869 A274 17c multicolored   .05   .05
870 A274 27c multicolored   1.90 1.90
871 A274 35c multicolored   1.90 1.90
872 A274 50c multicolored   2.75 2.75
      Nos. 867-872 (6)   8.00 8.00

Souvenir Sheet

873 A274 $1 multicolored   3.50 3.50

13th Winter Olympic Games, Lake Placid,
NY, Feb. 12-24. Exist imperf. Values: set
$12.50; souvenir sheet $12.50.

Pres. Tolbert, Pres. Stevens, Maps of
Liberia and Sierra Leone, Mano
River — A275

1980, Mar. 6   Litho.   Perf. 14x13½
874 A275 8c multicolored   .25   .25
875 A275 27c multicolored   .80   .80
876 A275 35c multicolored   1.10 1.10
877 A275 80c multicolored   2.40 2.40
      Nos. 874-877 (4)   4.55 4.55

Mano River Agreement, 5th anniversary;
Mano River Postal Union, 1st anniversary.

Sgt. Doe and Soldiers, Clenched
Hands Angel — A276

1981, Feb. 6   Litho.   Perf. 14
878 A276 1c Redemption horn,
                vert.   .25   .25
879 A276 6c like 1c   .25   .25
880 A276 10c shown   .25   .25
881 A276 14c Citizens, map,
                Flag   .25   .25
882 A276 23c like 10c   .30   .30
883 A276 31c like 14c   .45   .45
884 A276 41c like $2   .60   .60
885 A276 $2 Sgt. Samuel Doe,
                vert.   3.00 3.00
      Nos. 878-885 (8)   5.35 5.35

Establishment of new government under the
People's Redemption Council, Apr. 12, 1980.

Soccer Players, World Cup, Flags of
1930 and 1934 Finalists — A277

Soccer Players, Cup, Flags of Finalists
from: 5c, 1938, 1950. 20c, 1954, 1958. 27c,
1962, 1966. 40c, 1970, 1974. 55c. 1978. $1,
Spanish team.

1981, Mar. 4   Litho.   Perf. 14
886 A277 3c multicolored   .25   .25
887 A277 5c multicolored   .25   .25
888 A277 20c multicolored   .55   .55
889 A277 27c multicolored   .90   .90
890 A277 40c multicolored   1.25 1.25
891 A277 55c multicolored   1.75 1.75
      Nos. 886-891 (6)   4.85 4.85

Souvenir Sheet

892 A277 $1 multicolored   3.50 3.50

ESPANA '82 World Cup Soccer
Championship.

Sgt. Samuel Doe and Citizens — A278

1981, Apr. 7   Litho.   Perf. 14
893 A278 22c shown   .70   .70
894 A278 27c Doe, Liberian flag .90   .90
895 A278 30c Clasped arms   1.40 1.40
896 A278 $1 Doe, soldiers, Jus-
                tice   3.50 3.50
      Nos. 893-896 (4)   6.50 6.50

People's Redemption Council government,
first anniversary.

Royal Wedding
A279

1981, Aug. 12   Litho.   Perf. 14x13½
897	A279	31c Couple	.85 .85
898	A279	41c Initials, roses	1.10 1.10
899	A279	62c St. Paul's Cathedral	2.10 2.10
		Nos. 897-899 (3)	4.05 4.05

Souvenir Sheet
900	A279	$1 Couple	3.50 3.50

John Adams,
US
President,
1797-1801
A280

Washington Crossing the
Delaware — A281

1981, July 4   Perf. 11
901	A280	4c shown	.25 .25
902	A280	5c Wm. H. Harrison	.25 .25
903	A280	10c Martin Van Buren	.25 .25
904	A280	17c James Monroe	.50 .40
905	A280	20c John Q. Adams	.60 .50
906	A280	22c James Madison	.70 .55
907	A280	27c Thomas Jefferson	.75 .65
908	A280	30c Andrew Jackson	.85 .70
909	A280	40c John Tyler	1.25 .95
910	A280	80c George Washington	2.40 1.50
		Nos. 901-910 (10)	7.80 6.00

Souvenir Sheet
911	A281	$1 multi	3.50 3.50

1981, Nov. 26   Litho.   Perf. 11
912	A280	6c Rutherford B. Hayes	.25 .25
913	A280	12c Ulysses S. Grant	.25 .25
914	A280	14c Millard Fillmore	.25 .25
915	A280	15c Zachary Taylor	.25 .25
916	A280	20c Abraham Lincoln	.60 .25
917	A280	27c Andrew Johnson	.70 .60
918	A280	31c James Buchanan	.80 .60
919	A280	41c James A. Garfield	1.00 .80
920	A280	50c James K. Polk	1.25 .95
921	A280	55c Franklin Pierce	1.40 1.00
		Nos. 912-921 (10)	6.75 5.20

Souvenir Sheet
922	A281	$1 Washington at Valley Forge	5.50 5.50

1982, Apr. 7   Litho.   Perf. 11
923	A280	4c William H. Taft	.25 .25
924	A280	5c Calvin Coolidge	.25 .25
925	A280	6c Benjamin Harrison	.25 .25
926	A280	10c Warren G. Harding	.25 .25
927	A280	22c Grover Cleveland	.65 .50
928	A280	27c Chester Arthur	.75 .55
929	A280	31c Woodrow Wilson	.80 .65
930	A280	41c William McKinley	1.25 .95
931	A280	80c Theodore Roosevelt	2.25 1.75
		Nos. 923-931 (9)	6.70 5.40

Souvenir Sheet
932	A281	$1 Signing Constitution, horiz.	3.50 3.50

1982, July 15   Litho.   Perf. 11
933	A280	4c Jimmy Carter	.25 .25
934	A280	6c Gerald Ford	.25 .25
935	A280	14c Harry Truman	.25 .25
936	A280	17c F. D. Roosevelt	.25 .25
937	A280	23c L. B. Johnson	.55 .25
938	A280	27c Richard Nixon	.65 .25
939	A280	31c John F. Kennedy	.75 .55
940	A280	35c Ronald Reagan	.90 .65
941	A280	50c Herbert Hoover	1.25 .90
942	A280	55c Dwight D. Eisenhower	1.40 1.00
		Nos. 933-942 (10)	6.50 4.60

Souvenir Sheet
Perf. 14x13½
943	A281	$1 Battle of Yorktown	3.50 3.50
		See No. 1113.	

Type of 1976
1981-83   Litho.   Perf. 14½x13½
Size: 34x20mm
945	A247	1c like #749	.25 .25
946	A247	3c like #750	.25 .25
947	A247	6c like #753	.25 .25
948	A247	15c like #754	.60 .60
949	A247	25c like #757	1.00 1.00
950	A247	31c like #756	1.25 1.25
951	A247	41c like #758	1.75 1.75
952	A247	80c like #759	3.50 3.50
953	A247	$1 like #760	5.00 5.00
		Nos. 945-953 (9)	13.85 13.85

Issued: Nos. 946-947, 949, 950, 11/27/81;
Nos. 945, 953, 10/12/82; Nos. 948, 951,
12/10/82; No. 952, 11/3/83.

Intl. Year of the Disabled
(1981) — A282

Designs: Various disabled people.

1982, Mar. 24   Litho.   Perf. 14
954	A282	23c multi, vert.	.55 .55
955	A282	62c multicolored	1.25 1.25

1982, Mar. 24
956	A283	6c multicolored	.25 .25
957	A283	31c multicolored	1.25 1.25

30th Anniv. of West African
Examinations Council — A283

21st Birthday of
Princess
Diana — A284

31c, 41c, 62c, Diana portraits. $1, Wedding.

1982, July 1   Perf. 14x13½
958	A284	31c multicolored	.85 .85
959	A284	41c multicolored	1.25 1.25
960	A284	62c multicolored	2.25 2.25
		Nos. 958-960 (3)	4.35 4.35

Souvenir Sheet
961	A284	$1 multicolored	3.50 3.50

Nos. 958-961
Overprinted in
Silver

1982, Aug. 30   Litho.   Perf. 14x13½
962	A284	31c multicolored	.85 .85
963	A284	41c multicolored	1.25 1.25
964	A284	62c multicolored	2.25 2.25
		Nos. 962-964 (3)	4.35 4.35

Souvenir Sheet
965	A284	$1 multicolored	3.50 3.50

Birth of Prince William of Wales, June 21.

3rd Natl.
Redemption
Day — A285

1983, Apr. 5   Litho.   Perf. 13½
966	A285	3c Fallah Varney	.25 .25
967	A285	6c Samuel Doe	.25 .25
968	A285	10c Jlatoh N. Podier, Jr.	.25 .25
969	A285	15c Jeffry S. Gbatu	.40 .40
970	A285	31c Thomas G. Quiwonkpa	.95 .95
971	A285	41c Abraham D. Kollie	1.75 1.75
		Nos. 966-971 (6)	3.85 3.85

Souvenir Sheet
972	A285	$1 like 6c	3.50 3.50

Natl. Archives Opening — A286

Building views.

1983, Apr. 5
973	A286	6c multicolored	1.60 1.60
974	A286	31c multicolored	2.75 2.75

Christmas
1983
A287

Raphael Paintings: 6c, Circumcision of
Christ. 15c, Adoration of the Magi. 25c,
Announcement to Mary. 31c, Madonna with
Baldachin. 41c, Holy Family. 62c, Detail of
Madonna with Child Surrounded by Five
Saints. $1.25 Madonna of Foligno.

1983, Dec. 14   Litho.   Perf. 13½
975	A287	6c multicolored	.25 .25
976	A287	15c multicolored	.25 .25
977	A287	25c multicolored	.50 .50
978	A287	31c multicolored	.70 .70
979	A287	41c multicolored	.85 .85
980	A287	62c multicolored	1.10 1.10
		Nos. 975-980 (6)	3.65 3.65

Souvenir Sheet
981	A287	$1.25 multicolored	2.75 2.50

Sheets of 1 showing entire painting exist.

Mano River Union, 10th Anniv.
(1983) — A288

1984, Apr. 6   Litho.   Perf. 14x13½
982	A288	6c Training school graduates	.25 .25
983	A288	25c Emblem	.85 .85
984	A288	31c Maps, leaders	1.10 1.10
985	A288	41c Guinea's accession	1.75 1.75
		Nos. 982-985 (4)	3.95 3.95

Souvenir Sheet
986	A288	75c Guinea's accession, diff.	3.50 3.50

4th Natl. Redemption Day — A289

3c, Hospital, New Kru Town. 10c, Ganta-
Harper Highway construction. 20c, Constitution Assembly opening. 31c, Doe at highway
construction. 41c, Draft Constitution
presentation.

1984, Apr. 12   Perf. 14½
987	A289	3c multicolored	.25 .25
988	A289	10c multicolored	.25 .25
989	A289	20c multicolored	.60 .60
990	A289	31c multicolored	1.10 1.10
991	A289	41c multicolored	1.75 1.75
		Nos. 987-991 (5)	3.95 3.95

Adoration of
the Wise
Men, by
Rubens
(1577-1640)
A290

15c, Crowning of Katharina. 25c, Mother
and Child Adored by Wise Men. 31c, Madonna
and Child with Halo. 41c, Adoration of the
Shepherds. 62c, Madonna and Child with
Saints.
$1.25, Madonna Adored by Saints.

1984, June 1   Litho.   Perf. 13½
992	A290	6c shown	.25 .25
993	A290	15c multicolored	.25 .25
994	A290	25c multicolored	.55 .55
995	A290	31c multicolored	.75 .75
996	A290	41c multicolored	.95 .95
997	A290	62c multicolored	1.50 1.50
		Nos. 992-997 (6)	4.25 4.25

Souvenir Sheet
998	A290	$1.25 multicolored	5.50 5.50

Sheets of 1 showing entire painting exist.

1984
Summer
Olympics
A291

3c, Jesse Owens, 1936. 4c, Rafer Johnson, 1960. 25c, Miruts Yifter, 1980. 41c, Kipchoge Keino, 1968, 1972. 62c, Muhammad Ali, 1960. $1.25, Wilma Rudolph, 1960, horiz.

1984, July 2   **Perf. 13½x14**
999	A291	3c multicolored	.25	.25
1000	A291	4c multicolored	.25	.25
1001	A291	25c multicolored	1.00	1.00
1002	A291	41c multicolored	1.60	1.60
1003	A291	62c multicolored	2.25	2.25
		Nos. 999-1003 (5)	5.35	5.35

Souvenir Sheet
Perf. 14x13½
1004	A291	$1.25 multicolored	5.50	5.50

1984 Louisiana Expo — A292

6c, Water birds. 31c, Ship, Buchanan Harbor. 41c, Fish. 62c, Train carrying iron ore.

1984, July 24   **Perf. 14½**
1005	A292	6c multicolored	.25	.25
1006	A292	31c multicolored	1.25	1.25
1007	A292	41c multicolored	1.50	1.50
1008	A292	62c multicolored	2.50	2.50
		Nos. 1005-1008 (4)	5.50	5.50

Pygmy Hippopotamus, World Wildlife Fund Emblem — A293

Various pygmy hippopotomi.

1984, Nov. 22   **Litho.**   **Perf. 14½**
1009	A293	0c multicolored	.75	.75
1010	A293	10c multicolored	1.00	1.00
1011	A293	20c multicolored	2.75	2.75
1012	A293	31c multicolored	4.00	4.00
		Nos. 1009-1012 (4)	8.50	8.50

Exist imperf.

Indigent Children Home, Bensonville — A294

First Lady Mrs. Nancy Doe and various children.

1984, Dec. 14
1013	A294	6c multicolored	.25	.25
1014	A294	31c multicolored	1.25	1.25

Natl. Redemption Day, Apr. 12 — A295

6c, Army barracks, Monrovia. 31c, Pan-African Plaza, Monrovia.

1985, Apr. 5   **Litho.**   **Perf. 14½**
1015	A295	6c multicolored	.25	.25
1016	A295	31c multicolored	1.25	1.25

Liberian Revolution, fifth anniv.

Audubon Birth Bicentenary — A296

Illustrations by artist/naturalist J. J. Audubon: 1c, Bohemian waxwing. 3c, Bay-breasted warbler. 6c, White-winged crossbill. 31c, Red phalarope. 41c, Eastern bluebird. 62c, Northern cardinal.

1985, Apr. 5
1017	A296	1c multicolored	.25	.25
1018	A296	3c multicolored	.25	.25
1019	A296	6c multicolored	.25	.25
1020	A296	31c multicolored	1.10	1.10
1021	A296	41c multicolored	1.60	1.60
1022	A296	62c multicolored	2.40	2.40
		Nos. 1017-1022 (6)	5.85	5.85

Venus and Mirror — A297

Paintings (details) by Rubens: 15c, Adam & Eve in Paradise. 25c, Andromeda. 31c, The Three Graces. 41c, Venus & Adonis. 62c, The Daughters of Leucippus. $1.25, The Judgement of Paris.

1985, Nov. 14   **Litho.**   **Perf. 14**
1023	A297	6c multicolored	.25	.25
1024	A297	15c multicolored	.70	.70
1025	A297	25c multicolored	1.00	1.00
1026	A297	31c multicolored	1.25	1.25
1027	A297	41c multicolored	1.75	1.75
1028	A297	62c multicolored	3.00	3.00
		Nos. 1023-1028 (6)	7.95	7.95

Souvenir Sheet
1029	A297	$1.25 multicolored	4.50	4.50

Sheets of 1 showing entire painting exist.

1986 World Cup Soccer Championships, Mexico — A298

6c, Germany-Morocco, 1970. 15c, Zaire-Brazil, 1974. 25c, Tunisia-Germany, 1978. 31c, Cameroun-Peru, 1982, vert. 41c, Algeria-Germany, 1982. 62c, 1986 Senegal team. $1.25, Liberia-Nigeria.

1985, Nov. 14
1030	A298	6c multicolored	.25	.25
1031	A298	15c multicolored	.50	.50
1032	A298	25c multicolored	.85	.85
1033	A298	31c multicolored	1.00	1.00
1034	A298	41c multicolored	1.25	1.25
1035	A298	62c multicolored	2.10	2.10
		Nos. 1030-1035 (6)	5.95	5.95

Souvenir Sheet
1036	A298	$1.25 multicolored	4.50	4.50

Queen Mother, 85th Birthday — A299

31c, Elizabeth in garter robes. 41c, At the races. 62c, In garden, waving. $1.25, Wearing diadem.

1985, Dec. 12   **Litho.**   **Perf. 14½**
1037	A299	31c mutlicolored	.80	.80
1038	A299	41c multicolored	1.00	1.00
1039	A299	62c multicolored	1.60	1.60
		Nos. 1037-1039 (3)	3.40	3.40

Souvenir Sheet
1040	A299	$1.25 multicolored	3.00	3.00

World Food Day — A300

1985, Dec. 12
1041	A300	25c multicolored	.70	.70
1042	A300	31c multicolored	1.00	1.00

AMERIPEX '86 — A301

1986, June 10   **Litho.**   **Perf. 14½**
1043	A301	25c The Alamo	1.25	1.25
1044	A301	31c Liberty Bell	1.40	1.40
1045	A301	80c #344, 802, C102	3.75	3.75
		Nos. 1043-1045 (3)	6.40	6.40

Statue of Liberty, Cent. — A302

1986, June 10
1046	A302	20c Unveiling, 1886	.50	.50
1047	A302	31c Frederic A. Bartholdi	.90	.90
1048	A302	$1 Statue close-up	2.75	2.75
		Nos. 1046-1048 (3)	4.15	4.15

1988 Winter Olympics, Calgary — A303

1984 Gold medalists: 3c, Max Julen, Switzerland, men's giant slalom. 6c, Debbie Armstrong, U.S., women's giant slalom. 31c, Peter Angerer, West Germany, biathlon. 60c, Bill Johnson, U.S., men's downhill. 80c, East Germany, 4-man bobsled. $1.25, H. Stangassinger, F. Wembacher, West Germany, 2-man luge.

1987, Aug. 21   **Litho.**   **Perf. 14**
1049	A303	3c multicolored	.25	.25
1050	A303	6c multicolored	.25	.25
1051	A303	31c multicolored	.75	.75
1052	A303	60c multicolored	1.75	1.75
1053	A303	80c multicolored	2.25	2.25
		Nos. 1049-1053 (5)	5.25	5.25

Souvenir Sheet
1054	A303	$1.25 multicolored	2.50	2.50

City of Berlin, 750th Anniv. — A304

6c, State (Royal) Theater in the Gendarmenmarkt, c. 1820, archltect Schlnkel. 31c, Kaiser Friedrich Museum, Museum Is. on River Spree. 60c, Charlottenburg Castle, 17th cent. 80c, Modern church bell tower & Kaiser Wilhelm Gedachtniskirche. $1.50, MIRAK rocket development, Spaceship Society Airfield, Reinickendorf, 1930.

1987, Sept. 4
1055	A304	6c multicolored	.25	.25
1056	A304	31c multicolored	.85	.85
1057	A304	60c multicolored	1.60	1.60
1058	A304	80c multicolored	2.00	2.00
		Nos. 1055-1058 (4)	4.70	4.70

Souvenir sheet
Perf. 11½
1059	A304	$1.50 buff & dk brown	4.50	4.50

No. 1059 contains one 25x61mm stamp.

Shakespearean Plays — A305

1987, Nov. 6   **Litho.**   **Perf. 14**
1060		Sheet of 8	8.50	8.50
a.	A305	3c Othello	.35	.35
b.	A305	6c Romeo & Juliet	.35	.35
c.	A305	10c The Merry Wives of Windsor	.35	.35
d.	A305	15c Henry IV	.35	.35
e.	A305	31c Hamlet	.60	.60
f.	A305	60c Macbeth	.60	.60
g.	A305	80c King Lear	1.50	1.50
h.	A305	$2 Shakespeare and the Globe Theater, 1598	3.50	3.50

Amateur Radio Association, 25th Anniv. — A306

1987, Nov. 23   **Litho.**   **Perf. 14**
1061	A306	10c Emblem	.45	.45
1062	A306	10c Village	.45	.45
1063	A306	35c On-the-Air certificate	1.50	1.50
1064	A306	35c Globe, flags	1.50	1.50
		Nos. 1061-1064 (4)	3.90	3.90

Miniature Sheets

Statue of Liberty, Cent. (in 1986) — A307

No. 1065: a, Torch, southern view of NYC. b, Overhead view of crown and scaffold. c, 4 workmen repairing crown. d, 5 workmen, crown. e, Statue's right foot.
No. 1066: a, Tall ship, statue. b, Bay Queen ferry. c, Statue on poster at a construction site, NYC. d, Tug boat, tall ship. e, Building frieze.
No. 1067: a, Statue flanked by fireworks. b, Lighting of the statue. c, Crown observatory illuminated. d, Statue surrounded by fireworks. e, Crown and torch observatories illuminated.
No. 1068: a, Liberty "Happy Birthday" poster at a construction site. b, Ships in NY Harbor. c, Woman renovating statue nose. d, Man & woman renovating nose. e, Man, nose. #1068a-1068e vert.

1987, Dec. 10   *Perf. 13½*
1065		Sheet of 5 + label	.95	
a.-e.	A307	6c any single	.25	.25
1066		Sheet of 5 + label	3.00	
a.-e.	A307	15c any single	.50	.50
1067		Sheet of 5 + label	5.75	
a.-e.	A307	31c any single	.95	.95
1068		Sheet of 5 + label	10.00	
a.-e.	A307	60c any single	1.75	1.75
		Nos. 1065-1068 (4)	19.70	

Nos. 1065-1068 contain label inscribed "CENTENARY OF THE STATUE OF LIBERTY" in two or five lines.

Second Republic, 2nd Anniv. A308

Design: Natl. flag, coat of arms, hand grip, Pres. Doe and Vice Pres. Moniba.

1988, Jan. 6   *Perf. 14½*
1069	A308	10c multicolored	.60	.60
1070	A308	35c multicolored	1.90	1.90

UN Child Survival Campaign A309

3c, Breast-feeding. 6c, Oral rehydration therapy, vert. 31c, Immunization. $1, Growth monitoring, vert.

1988, Jan. 15   *Perf. 13x13½, 13½x13*
1071	A309	3c multicolored	.25	.25
1072	A309	6c multicolored	.25	.25
1073	A309	31c multicolored	2.00	2.00
1074	A309	$1 multicolored	5.75	5.75
		Nos. 1071-1074 (4)	8.25	8.25

Inauguration of the Second Republic — A310

Design: Pres. Doe greeting Chief Justice Emmanuel N. Gbalazeh.

1988, Jan. 15   *Perf. 13x13½*
1075	A310	6c multicolored	.30	.30

Samuel Kanyon Doe Sports Complex, Opened Apr. 12, 1986 A311

1988, Jan. 15
1076	A311	31c multicolored	.90	.90

Green (Agricultural) Revolution — A312

1988, Apr. 4   *Perf. 15*
1077	A312	10c multicolored	.40	.40
1078	A312	35c multicolored	1.50	1.50

US Peace Corps in Liberia, 25th Anniv. A313

1988, Apr. 4
1079	A313	10c multicolored	.40	.40
1080	A313	35c multicolored	1.50	1.50

Souvenir Sheet

1988 Summer Olympics, Seoul — A314

1988, Apr. 14   *Perf. 14*
1081	A314	$3 multicolored	10.00	10.00

Organization of African Unity, 25th Anniv. — A315

1988, May 25
1082	A315	10c multicolored	.45	.45
1083	A315	35c multicolored	1.50	1.50
1084	A315	$1 multicolored	4.50	4.50
		Nos. 1082-1084 (3)	6.45	6.45

Rail Transport A316

10c, GP10 at Nimba. 35c, Triple-headed iron ore train.
No. 1087, King Edward II, 1930. No. 1088, GWR 57 No. 3697, 1941. No. 1089, GWR 0-4-2T No. 1408, 1932. No. 1090, GWR No. 7034 Ince Castle, 1950.

1988, July 30   *Litho.*   *Perf. 14½*
1085	A316	10c multicolored	.50	.50
1086	A316	35c multicolored	1.25	1.25

Souvenir Sheets
Perf. 11
1087	A316	$2 multicolored	5.50	5.50
1088	A316	$2 multicolored	5.50	5.50
1089	A316	$2 multicolored	5.50	5.50
1090	A316	$2 multicolored	5.50	5.50

Nos. 1087-1090 contain one 64x44mm stamp each.

Nos. 1087-1090 with Added Text

1993, Aug. 3   **Souvenir Sheets**
1087a	With added text in margin	7.50	7.50
1088a	With added text in margin	7.50	7.50
1089a	With added text in margin	7.50	7.50
1090a	With added text in margin	7.50	7.50

Added text on Nos. 1087a-1090a reads: "25th ANNIVERSARY OF THE LAST STEAM TRAIN TO / RUN ON BRITISH RAIL 1968-1993."

1988 Summer Olympics, Seoul — A317

1988, Sept. 13   *Litho.*
1091	A317	10c Baseball	.25	.25
1092	A317	35c Hurdles	.85	.85
1093	A317	45c Fencing	1.00	1.00
1094	A317	80c Synchronized swimming	1.90	1.90
1095	A317	$1 Yachting	2.25	2.25
		Nos. 1091-1095 (5)	6.25	6.25

Souvenir Sheet
1096	A317	$1.50 Tennis	3.00	3.00

Intl. Tennis Federation, 75th anniv. ($1.50).

St. Joseph's Catholic Hospital, 25th Anniv. — A318

No. 1098, Hospital, 4 staff members. No. 1099, St. John of God. No. 1100, Doctor, nurse, map.

1988, Aug. 26   *Litho.*   *Perf. 14½*
1097	A318	10c shown	.25	.25
1098	A318	10c multicolored	.25	.25
1099	A318	35c mutlicolored	.80	.80
1100	A318	$1 multicolored	2.25	2.25
		Nos. 1097-1100 (4)	3.55	3.55

Common Design Types pictured following the introduction.

Lloyds of London, 300th Anniv.
Common Design Type

CD341

Designs: 10c, Royal Exchange destroyed by fire, 1838, vert. 35c, Air Liberia BN2A aircraft. 45c, Supertanker Chevron Antwerp. $1, Lakonia on fire off Madeira, 1963, vert.

1988, Oct. 31   *Litho.*   *Perf. 14*
1101	CD341	10c multicolored	.25	.25
1102	CD341	35c multicolored	1.00	1.00
1103	CD341	45c multicolored	1.25	1.25
1104	CD341	$1 multicolored	2.75	2.75
		Nos. 1101-1104 (4)	5.25	5.25

Sasa Players A319

10c, Monkey bridge, vert. 45c, Snake dancers, vert.

Perf. 14x14½, 14½x14
1988, Sept. 30   *Litho.*
1105	A319	10c multicolored	.50	.50
1106	A319	35c shown	1.40	1.40
1107	A319	45c multicolored	1.90	1.90
		Nos. 1105-1107 (3)	3.80	3.80

Intl. Fund for Agricultural Development, 10th Anniv. — A320

1988, Oct. 7   *Litho.*   *Perf. 14x14½*
1108	A320	10c Crops	.50	.50
1109	A320	35c Spraying crops, livestock	1.90	1.90

3rd Anniv. of the 2nd Republic — A321

10c, Pres. Doe, officials. 50c, Pres. Doe, doctor.

1989, Jan. 6   *Litho.*   *Perf. 14*
1110	A321	10c multicolored	.50	.50
1111	A321	35c like 10c	1.90	1.90
1112	A321	50c multicolored	2.40	2.40
		Nos. 1110-1112 (3)	4.80	4.80

US Presidents Type of 1981-82
1989, Jan. 20   *Perf. 13½x14*
1113	A280	$1 George Bush	4.75	4.75

Rissho Kosei-Kai Buddhist Assoc., Tokyo, 50th Anniv. — A322

Natl. flags and: No. 1114, "Harmony" in Japanese. No. 1115, Organization headquarters, Tokyo. No. 1116, Nikkyo Niwano, founder. 50c, Statue of Buddha in the Great Sacred Hall.

1989, Feb. 28   *Litho.*   *Perf. 14x14½*
1114	A322	10c multicolored	.60	.60
1115	A322	10c multicolored	.60	.60
1116	A322	10c multicolored	.60	.60
1117	A322	50c multicolored	2.50	2.50
		Nos. 1114-1117 (4)	4.30	4.30

Liberian-Japanese friendship.

Souvenir Sheet

Emperor Hirohito of Japan (1901-1989) — A323

Commemorative coins: a, Silver. b, Gold.

1989, Feb. 28   Unwmk.   Perf. 14½
1118 A323 Sheet of 2   8.00 8.00
a.-b.   75c any single   3.25 3.25

For overprint see No. 1147.

Mano River Union, 15th Anniv. A324

Natl. flag, crest and: 10c, Union Glass Factory, Gardnersville, Monrovia. 35c, Pres. Doe, Momoh of Sierra Leone and Conte of Guinea. 45c, Monrovia-Freetown Highway. 50c, Sierra Leone-Guinea land postal services. $1, Communique, 1988 summit.

Unwmk.
1989, May 8   Litho.   Perf. 14
1119 A324 10c multicolored   .25   .25
1120 A324 35c multicolored   1.25 1.25
1121 A324 45c multicolored   1.75 1.75
1122 A324 50c multicolored   1.90 1.90
1123 A324 $1 multicolored   3.75 3.75
      Nos. 1119-1123 (5)   8.90 8.90

World Telecommunications Day — A325

1989, May 17   Litho.   Perf. 12½
1124 A325 50c multicolored   1.40 1.40

Moon Landing, 20th Anniv.
Common Design Type

CD342

Apollo 11: 10c, Recovery ship USS Okinawa. 35c, Buzz Aldrin, Neil Armstrong and Michael Collins. 45c, Mission emblem. $1, Aldrin steps on the Moon. $2, Aldrin preparing to conduct experiments on the Moon's surface.

Perf. 14x13½, 14 (35c, 45c)
1989, July 20   Litho.   Wmk. 384
Size of Nos. 1126-1127: 29x29mm
1125 CD342 10c multicolored   .25   .25
1126 CD342 35c multicolored   .90   .90
1127 CD342 45c multicolored   1.25 1.25
1128 CD342 $1 multicolored   2.75 2.75
       Nos. 1125-1128 (4)   5.15 5.15
Souvenir Sheet
1129 CD342 $2 multicolored   5.50 5.50

Souvenir Sheet

The Women's March on Versailles — A326

1989, July 7   Wmk. 384   Perf. 14
1130 A326 $1.50 multicolored   4.00 4.00
French revolution, bicent., PHILEXFRANCE '89.

Souvenir Sheet

Renovation and Re-dedication of the Statue of Liberty, 1986 — A327

Photographs: a, Workman. b, French dignitary, US flag. c, Dignitaries at ceremony, statue.

Perf. 14x13½
1989, Oct. 2   Litho.   Wmk. 373
1131   Sheet of 3   2.25 2.25
a.-c.   A327 25c any single   .75   .75
World Stamp Expo '89 and PHILEXFRANCE '89.

Souvenir Sheet

A328

1989, Nov. 17   Unwmk.   Perf. 14½
1132 A328 $2 black   5.50 5.50
World Stamp Expo '89, Washington, DC.

Jawaharlal Nehru, 1st Prime Minister of Independent India — A329

1989, Dec. 22   Unwmk.   Perf. 14
1133 A329 45c Nehru, signature, flag   1.50 1.50
1134 A329 50c Nehru, signature   3.25 3.25

New Standard-A Earth Satellite Station — A330

1990, Jan. 5
1135 A330 10c shown   .25   .25
1136 A330 35c multi, diff.   1.25 1.25

US Educational & Cultural Foundation in Liberia, 25th Anniv. (in 1989) — A331

1990, Jan. 5
1137 A331 10c multicolored   .25   .25
1138 A331 45c multicolored   1.40 1.40

Pan-African Postal Union, 10th Anniv. — A332

1990, Jan. 18   Perf. 13x12½
1139 A332 35c multicolored   1.00 1.00

Flags of Liberian Counties — A333

Designs: a, Bomi. b, Bong. c, Grand Bassa. d, Grand Cape Mount. e, Grand Gedeh. f, Grand Kru. g, Lofa. h, Margibi. i, Maryland. j, Montserrado. k, Nimba. l, Rivercess. m, Sinoe.

Perf. 14x13½
1990, Mar. 2   Litho.   Unwmk.
1140   Strip of 13   5.00 5.00
a.-m.   A333 10c any single   .30   .30
1141   Strip of 13   17.00 17.00
a.-m.   A333 35c any single   1.00 1.00
1142   Strip of 13   22.50 22.50
a.-m.   A333 45c any single   1.50 1.50
1143   Strip of 13   25.00 25.00
a.-m.   A333 50c any single   1.60 1.60
1144   Strip of 13   50.00 50.00
a.-m.   A333 $1 any single   3.00 3.00
       Nos. 1140-1144 (5)   119.50 119.50

Queen Mother, 90th Birthday
Common Design Types
Designs: 10c, At age 6. $2, At age 22.

Perf. 14x15
1991, Oct. 28   Wmk. 384
1145 CD343 10c multicolored   .25   .25
Perf. 14½
1146 CD344 $2 brn & blk   4.00 4.00
For overprints see Nos. 1162-1163.

No. 1118 Overprinted

Perf. 14½
1991, Nov. 16   Litho.   Unwmk.
1147 A323 Sheet of 2   4.50 4.50
a.-b.   75c any single   2.25 2.25

National Unity — A334

Designs: 35c, Hands clasp over map of Liberia. 45c, Liberian flag, hands, African map. 50c, All Liberia conference, March 1991, conferees, flag, map.

1991, Dec. 30   Perf. 13½
1148 A334 35c multicolored   1.10 1.10
1149 A334 45c multicolored   1.60 1.60
1150 A334 50c multicolored   1.75 1.75
      Nos. 1148-1150 (3)   4.45 4.45

1992 Summer Olympics, Barcelona — A335

1992, Aug. 7   Litho.   Perf. 14
1151 A335 45c Boxing   2.00 2.00
1152 A335 50c Soccer   2.25 2.25
1153 A335 $1 Weight lifting   4.50 4.50
1154 A335 $2 Water polo   8.25 8.25
      Nos. 1151-1154 (4)   17.00 17.00
Souvenir Sheet
1155 A335 $1.50 Running   6.00 6.00

Disarmament — A336

Designs: 50c, Disarm today. $1, Join your parents & build Liberia. $2, Peace must prevail in Liberia.

1993, Feb. 10   Litho.   Perf. 13½x14
1156 A336 50c multicolored   1.90 1.90
1157 A336 $1 multicolored   3.75 3.75
1158 A336 $2 multicolored   7.25 7.25
      Nos. 1156-1158 (3)   12.90 12.90

See Nos. 1237-1239.

Miniature Sheets

FLORA OF LIBERIA

Flora and Fauna — A337

No. 1159 — Flora: a, Papaya. b, Sausage tree. c, Angraecum eichlerianum. d, Arachnis flos-aeris. e, Screw pine. f, African tulip tree. g, Coffee tree. h, Bolusiella talbotii. i, Bulbophyllum lepidum. j, Oeceoclades maculata. k, Plectrelminthus caudatus. l, Diaphananthe rutila.

No. 1160 — Fauna: a, Diana monkey. b, Flying squirrel. c, Egyptian rousette. d, Serval. e, Potto. f, Chimpanzee. g, African horned chameleon. h, Royal python. i, Golden cat. j, Banded duiker. k, Pygmy hippopotamus. l, Water chevrotain.

No. 1161 — Birds: a, Grey heron. b, Bat hawk. c, Martial eagle. d, Little sparrow hawk. e, Hoopoe. f, Red bishop. g, Purple-throated sunbird. h, African fish eagle. i, African grey parrot. j, Black-crowned night heron. k, Swallow. l, Great white egret.

1993-94		Litho.		Perf. 14
1159	A337	70c Sheet of 12,		
		#a.-l.	35.00	35.00
1160	A337	90c Sheet of 12,		
		#a.-l.	37.50	37.50
1161	A337	$1 Sheet of 12,		
		#a.-l.	37.50	37.50
	Nos. 1159-1161 (3)		110.00	110.00

Issued: 70c, 10/14; 90c, 11/18; $1, 1/14/94.

Nos. 1145-1146
Ovptd. with Hong Kong '94 Emblem

	Perf. 14x15		
1994, Feb. 18	Litho.	Wmk. 384	
1162 CD343	10c multicolored	.25	.25
	Perf. 14½		
1163 CD344	$2 multicolored	7.75	7.75

Miniature Sheet

Roberts Field, Monrovia, 50th Anniv. — A338

No. 1164: a, Vickers Supermarine Spitfire Mk IX. b, Boeing B-17G. c, Douglas A-20 Boston. d, North American B-25J Mitchell. e, Beech C-45 Expeditor. f, Douglas C-54. g, Piper L4 Cub. h, Martin PBM-3C.

1994, July 11	Litho.	Perf. 13½x13	
1164 A338	35c Sheet of 8,		
	#a.-h. + label	11.00	11.00

Souvenir Sheets

Locomotives — A339

Designs: No. 1165, $1, Class A3 #60044 Melton, Class A4 #60017 Silver Fox. No. 1166, $1, GWR 2-6-2 Prairie Tank #4561. No. 1167, $1, GWR 2-6-2 Small Prairie. No. 1168, $1, GWR Castle Class 4-6-0 No. Kinswear Castle. No. 1169, $1, GWR 0-6-0 Pannier Tank. No. 1170, $1, Bong Mining Company diesel hauling iron ore.

1994, Aug. 16	Litho.	Perf. 14	
1165-1170 A339	Set of 6	18.00	18.00

See Nos. 1194-1199, 1205.

LIBERIA 70c

The Liberia National Red Cross Society 1919 - 1994

Liberian Natl. Red Cross, 75th Anniv. — A340

Designs: 70c, No. 1172, Globe. No. 1173, $2, Jean-Henri Dunant.

1994, Oct. 3	Litho.	Perf. 14½x14	
1171 A340	70c multicolored	2.50	2.50
1172 A340	$1 multicolored	3.50	3.50
1173 A340	$1 multicolored	3.50	3.50
1174 A340	$2 multicolored	7.25	7.25
Nos. 1171-1174 (4)		16.75	16.75

End of World War II, 50th Anniv.
Common Design Types

Designs: 70c, Sunderland on U-boat patrol. 90c, US Army Engineer Task Force. $1, MV Abosso sunk off Liberia, 1942. No. 1178, MV Adda sunk off Liberia, 1941.

No. 1179, Obverse of U.S. Victory Medal depicting Liberty.

1995, May 8	Litho.	Perf. 13½	
1175 CD351	70c multicolored	2.10	2.10
1176 CD351	90c multicolored	2.75	2.75
1177 CD351	$1 multicolored	3.00	3.00
1178 CD351	$2 multicolored	5.75	5.75
Nos. 1175-1178 (4)		13.60	13.60

Souvenir Sheet
Perf. 14

1179 CD352	$2 multicolored	6.00	6.00

Wild Animals A341

1995, June 1		Perf. 14	
1180 A341	70c Cheetah	2.50	2.50
1181 A341	70c Giraffe	2.50	2.50
1182 A341	90c Rhinoceros	3.25	3.25
1183 A341	$1 Elephant	3.75	3.75
1184 A341	$2 Lion	7.50	7.50
Nos. 1180-1184 (5)		19.50	19.50

Souvenir Sheet

1995 IAAF World Track & Field Championships, Gothenburg — A342

No. 1185: a, Merlene Ottey. b, Heike Drechsler.

1995, Aug. 4	Litho.	Perf. 14	
1185 A342	$1 Sheet of 2, #a.-b.	8.50	8.50

Miniature Sheet

Orchids — A343

No. 1186: a, Ancistrochilus rothschildianus. b, Disa uniflora. c, Polystachya ottoniana. d, Aerangis brachycarpa. e, Plectrelminthus caudatus. f, Polystachya bella. g, Ansellia africana. h, Bulbophyllum cochleatum.

1995, Sept. 1		Perf. 13	
1186 A343	70c Sheet of 8, #a.-h. + label	24.00	24.00

Singapore '95.

UN, 50th Anniv.
Common Design Type

Designs: 25c, UN Land Rovers. 50c, Delivering food supplies. $1, Ilyushin IL-76 freighter airlifting supplies. $2, MIL MI-8 helicopter.

1995, Oct. 24	Litho.	Perf. 14	
1187 CD353	25c multicolored	1.00	1.00
1188 CD353	50c multicolored	2.00	2.00
1189 CD353	$1 multicolored	4.00	4.00
1190 CD353	$2 multicolored	8.00	8.00
Nos. 1187-1190 (4)		15.00	15.00

Economic Community of West African States, 20th Anniv. — A344

Designs: 25c, Map, Liberian flag, soldiers, civilians. 50c, Soldier carrying child, vert. $1, Logo, vert.

	Perf. 13½x13, 13½x13		
1995, Nov. 10		Litho.	
1191 A344	25c multicolored	1.00	1.00
1192 A344	50c multicolored	2.00	2.00
1193 A344	$1 multicolored	4.00	4.00
Nos. 1191-1193 (3)		7.00	7.00

Train Type of 1994
Souvenir Sheets

Designs: No. 1194, $1, 4-4-0 locomotive 11 "The Reno," galloping horses. No. 1195, $1, Halwill station, Southern Region T9 class locomotive #30719. No. 1196, $1, GWR 0-4-2T "1400" class locomotive #1408, cricket match. No. 1197, $1, LMS Jubilee class 4-6-0 #45684 "Jutland," Kettering station. No. 1198,

$1, GWR 2-6-2 "Prairie" locomotive #4547, Lustleigh station. No. 1199, $1, Wainwright "H" class 0-4-4T locomotive, winter countryside.

1996, Feb. 29	Litho.	Perf. 14x15	
1194-1199 A339	Set of 6	18.00	18.00

LIBERIA 20c

Modern Olympic Games, Cent. — A345

1996, Apr. 22	Litho.	Perf. 13	
1200 A345	20c Runners	.70	.70
1201 A345	35c Boxing	1.25	1.25
1202 A345	50c Javelin	1.75	1.75
1203 A345	$1 Hurdles	3.50	3.50
Nos. 1200-1203 (4)		7.20	7.20

Butterflies A346

No. 1204: a, Papilio zalmoxis. b, Papilio dardanus. c, Charaxes varanes. d, Acraea natalica. e, Euphaedra neophron. f, Craphium antheus. g, Salamis anacardii. h, Kallima cymodoce. i, Precis hierta.

1996, May 22	Litho.	Perf. 13½	
1204 A346	70c Sheet of 9, #a.-i.	18.00	18.00

Train Type of 1994
Souvenir Sheet

Design: G4a Class Pacific locomotive, Canadian Pacific Railroad.

1996, June 1		Perf. 14x15	
1205 A339	$1 multi	3.00	3.00

CAPEX '96.

90c Atlantic Sailfish Istiophorus albicans

Fish A347

No. 1206: a, Atlantic Sailfish. b, Guinean flyingfish. c, Blue marlin. d, Little tunny (e). e, Common dolphinfish (f). f, Guachanche barracuda. g, Guinean parrotfish. h, Cadenat's chromis (g). i, Dusky grouper (h). j, Hoefler's butterflyfish (k). k, African hind (l). l, West African Angelfish.

1996, July 15	Litho.	Perf. 14	
1206 A347	90c Sheet of 12, #a.-l.	32.50	32.50

LIBERIA 20¢

Butterflies — A348

No. 1207: a, Euphaedra judith. b, Euphaedra eleus. c, Acraea encedon. d, Euphaedra neophron. e, Liptena praestans. f, Neptis exalenca. g, Palla decius. h, Salamis cytora. i, Pseudacraea dolomena. j, Anaphaeis eriphia. k, Euphaedra themis. l, Hadrodontes varanes.

No. 1208: a, Papilio mnestheus. b, Papilio nobilis. c, Graphium antheus. d, Asterope benguelae. e, Graphium illyris. f, Emphaedra eupalus. g, Charaxes protoclea. h, Cymothoe beckeri. i, Euphaedra cyparissa. j, Coliades chalybe. k, Mimacraea neokoton. l, Charaxes ethalion.

$2, Charaxes pelias.

1996 Litho. *Perf. 14*
1207 A348 20c Sheet of 12, #a.-l. 7.00
1208 A348 25c Sheet of 12, #a.-l. 9.00
Souvenir Sheet
1209 A348 $2 multicolored 6.00

Birds — A349

Designs, horiz: 35c, African jacana. 50c, Pel's fishing owl. $1, Paradise whydah.
No. 1213: a, Turtle dove. b, Bee-eater. c, Golden oriole. d, Pied flycatcher. e, Sardinian warbler. f, Goliath heron. g, Rock thrush. h, Kestrel. i, Cattle egret. j, Woodchat shrike. k, Hoopoe. l, Great egret.
No. 1214, horiz: a, Red faced crimsonwing. b, Egyptian goose. c, African pitta. d, Paradise flycatcher. e, Garganey. f, Southern carmine bee-eater. g, Fulvous whistling duck. h, Village weaver. i, Martial eagle.
$2, Pintail duck, horiz.

1996
1210-1212 A349 Set of 3 5.50
1213 A349 25c Sheet of 12, #a.-l. 9.50
1214 A349 35c Sheet of 9, #a.-i. 9.50
Souvenir Sheet
1215 A349 $2 multicolored 6.00

Marilyn Monroe (1926-62) A350

1996
1216 A350 20c multicolored .70
No. 1216 was issued in sheets of 16.

UNICEF, 50th Anniv. — A351

Designs: 35c, Education for all. 70c, Health care. $1, Children first.
1996, Sept. 16 *Perf. 13½x13*
1217-1219 A351 35c Set of 3 7.00

1996 Summer Olympic Games, Atlanta A352

Designs: No. 1220, 20c, Cricket (discontinued sport), vert. No. 1221, 20c, Babe Didrikson, vert. No. 1222, 35c, Vitaly Scherbo, winner of 6 gold medals, 1992, vert. No. 1223, 35c, Betty Robinson, vert. No. 1224, 50c, Cuban baseball team, gold medal, 1992. No. 1225, 50c, Ancient Greek wall painting of boxers, vert. No. 1226, $1, Stadium, Barcelona, 1992. No. 1227, $1, Stadium, Amsterdam, 1928, vert.
No. 1228, 35c, vert. — Olympic events: a, Men's athletics. b, Men's gymnastics. c, Weight lifting. d, Women's volleyball. e, Women's diving. f, Women's gymnastics. g, Women's track. h, Women's tennis. i, Discus.

No. 1229, 35c, vert. — Boxing gold medalists, boxing: a, Tyrell Biggs, U.S. b, Isan Gura, Tanzania (no medal). c, Mark Breland, U.S. d, Teofilo Stevenson, Cuba. e, Ray Leonard, U.S. f, Michael Spinks, U.S. g, Joe Frazier, U.S. h, Floyd Patterson, US. i, George Foreman, US. $2, Evelyn Ashford.

1996 Litho. *Perf. 14*
1220-1227 A352 Set of 8 14.00
Sheets of 9, #a-i
1228-1229 A352 Set of 2 22.50
Souvenir Sheet
1230 A352 $2 multicolored 7.00

Flowers and Flowering Trees — A353

No. 1231: a, Olive tree. b, Olive flower. c, Fig tree. d, Almond tree. e, Almug tree. f, Cedar. g, Pomegranate (b). h, Citron. i, Date palm (d, e, j). j, Date palm (fruit). k, Cedar of Lebanon. l, Rock rose. m, Narcissus. n, Oleander (i). o, Date palm (flower). p, Shittah tree. q, Hyacinth. r, Barley, flax (s). s, Grape vine. t, Lily of the field. u, Mandrake. v, Caper desire. w, Madonna lily. x, Aloe (s). y, Date palm tree.

1996
1231 A353 25c Sheet of 25, #a.-y. 30.00

History of Rock and Roll A354

No. 1232: a, Wilson Pickett. b, Bill Haley. c, Otis Redding. d, Fats Domino. e, Buddy Holly. f, Chubby Checker. g, Marvin Gaye. h, Jimi Hendrix.

1996 *Perf. 13½x14*
1232 A354 35c Sheet of 8, #a.-h. + label 10.00

Kingfisher A355

No. 1233 — Kingfishers: a, Striped. b, Grey-headed. c, Pied. d, Giant. e, Shining-blue.
1996, Oct. 7 Litho. *Perf. 13½*
1233 A355 75c Strip of 5, #a.-e. 11.00
See No. 1236.

Mao Zedong, 20th Anniv. of Death — A356

1996, Nov. 1 Litho. *Perf. 14½x14*
1234 A356 $1 shown 3.25
1235 A356 $1 As older man 3.25

Kingfisher Type of 1996
Souvenir Sheet
1997, Feb. 3 Litho. *Perf. 14*
1236 A355 $1 Like #1233b 3.00
Hong Kong '97. No. 1236 contains one 29x43mm stamp.

Disarmament Type of 1993
Inscribed "PEACE TODAY"
1997 Litho. 13½x14
1237 A336 $1 Like #1157 4.00
1238 A336 $2 Like #1158 8.25
1239 A336 $3 Like #1156 12.50
Nos. 1237-1239 (3) 24.75
Nos. 1237-1239 are dated 1996.

Wildlife — A357

No. 1240: a, Olive baboon. b, Leopard. c, African tree pangolin. d, Vervet. e, Aardvark. f, Spotted hyena. g, Hunting dog. h, Thomson's gazelle. i, Warthog. j, African civet. k, Nile crocodilo. l, African polecat.

1997, Apr. 2 Litho. *Perf. 14*
1240 A357 50c Sheet of 12, #a.-l. 18.00

Deng Xiaoping (1904-97), British Transfer of Hong Kong — A358

Different portraits of Deng Xiaoping, "July 1, 1997," Hong Kong: 70c, In daylight, vert. $1, At night.
No. 1243: a, 50c. b, 70c. c, $1.20.
1997 *Perf. 14*
1241 A358 70c multicolored 2.00
1242 A358 $1 multicolored 3.25
1243 A358 Sheet of 3, #a.-c. 7.75
No. 1241 is 28x44mm, and was issued in sheets of 4. No. 1242 was issued in sheets of 3.

UNESCO, 50th Anniv. — A359

No. 1244, 50c, vert.: a, Canals, Venice, Italy. b, Mosque of Badshahi, Gardens of Shalamar, Lahore, Pakistan. c, Palace of

Orando, Spain. d, Grounds of Temple of Hera, Greece. e, Church and Monastery of Daphni, Greece. f, Fraser Island, Australia. g, Canadian Rocky Mountains Park, Canada. h, Church of Santo Domingo Puebla, Mexico.
No. 1245, 50c, vert.: a, City of Ohrid and lake, Macedonia. b, Thracian Tomb of Sveshtari, Bulgaria. c, Monastery of Hossios Luckas, Greece. d, Church of Santa Cristina of Lena, Spain. e, Church of Santa Maria Della Salute, Venice, Italy. f, Center of Puebla, Mexico. g, Bagrati Cathedral, Georgia. h, Quebec City, Canada.
No. 1246: a, Ngorongoro Conservation Area, Tanzania. b, Garamba Natl. Park, Zaire. c, Canaima Natl. Park, Venezuela. d, Simien Natl. Park, Ethiopia. e, Mana Pools Natl. Park, Zimbabwe.
No. 1247, $2, Palace of Diocletian, Split, Croatia. No., 1248, $2, Monument of Nubia at Abu Simbel, Egypt. No. 1249, $2, Quedlinberg, Germany.

Perf. 13½x14, 14x13½
1997, June 17 Litho.
Sheets of 8, #a-h + Label
1244-1245 A359 Set of 2 27.50
1246 A359 70c Sheet of 5, #a-e, + label 12.50
Souvenir Sheets
1247-1249 A359 Set of 3 21.00

Queen Elizabeth II, Prince Philip, 50th Wedding Anniv. — A360

No. 1250: a, Queen holding umbrella. b, Royal arms. c, Prince in white uniform, Queen. d, Queen waving, Prince. e, Windsor Castle. f, Prince Philip.
No. 1251, $2, Queen seated on sofa. No. 1252, $2, Queen, Prince wearnig robes of Order of the Garter.

1997, June 17 *Perf. 14*
1250 A360 50c Sheet of 6, #a.-f. 11.00
Souvenir Sheet
1251-1252 A360 $2 Set of 2 14.00

Grimm's Fairy Tales A361

Mother Goose — A362

No. 1253 — Scenes from Rapunzel: a, Girl. b, Wicked person, raven. c, Prince.
No. 1254, Prince rescuing girl.
No. 1255, Little Bo Peep, sheep.

1997, June 17   Perf. 13½x14
1253 A361 $1 Sheet of 3, #a.-c. 10.00
Souvenir Sheets
1254 A361 $2 multicolored   7.00
Perf. 14
1255 A362 $2 multicolored   7.00

1998 Winter Olympics, Nagano — A363

Designs: 50c, Olympic Stadium, Lillehammer, 1994. 70c, Johann Koss, speed skating. $1, Katarina Witt, figure skating. $1.50, Sonia Henie, figure skating.
No. 1260: a, K. Seizinger, Alpine downhill skiing. b, J. Weissflog, 120-m ski jump. c, T. Kono, Nordic combined. d, G. Hackl, luge.
No. 1261: a, E. Bredesen, 90-m ski jump. b, L. Kjus, downhill skiing. c, B. Daehlie, cross-country skiing. d, P. Wiberg, combined Alpine skiing. e, S.L. Hattestad, freestyle skiing. f, G. Weder, D. Acklin, 2-man bobsled. g, Swedish hockey player. h, T. Alsgaard, cross-country skiing.
No. 1262, $2, German biathlete, 1994. No. 1263, $2, M. Wasmeier, giant slalom. No. 1264, $2, J. Koss, speed skating, diff. No. 1265, $2, V. Schneider, slalom.

1997, June 23   Perf. 14
1256-1259 A363   Set of 4   13.00
1260 A363 50c Strip or block
      of 4, #a.-d.   7.00
1261 A363 50c Sheet of 8,
      #a.-h.   14.00
Souvenir Sheets
1262-1265 A363   Set of 4   27.50

No. 1260 was issued in sheets of 8 stamps.

Flowers — A364

No. 1266, 50c: a, Sugar cane dahlia. b, Windsor tall phlox. c, Creative art daylily. d, Columbine. e, Infinite Grace bearded iris. f, Fairy lilies mini amaryllis.
No. 1267, 50c: a, White coneflower. b, Peggy Lee hybrid tea rose. c, Daffodil. d, Bowl of Beauty peony. e, Hardy lily. f, Windflower.
No. 1268, $2, Lily-flowered tulip. No. 1269, $2, Chrysanthemum Potomac.

1997, July 1   Litho.   Perf. 14
Sheets of 6, #a-f
1266-1267 A364   Set of 2   20.00 20.00
Souvenir Sheets
1268-1269 A364   Set of 2   16.00 16.00

Flora and Fauna A365

No. 1270: a, Lovebirds. b, Genet. c, Leopard, crowned night heron. d, Gorilla. e, Giant wild boar. f, Elephant. g, Sterculia flower, skink. h, Ladybugs, bush baby. i, Cape primroses, ground hornbill.
No. 1271, $2, Rufus-crowned roller. No. 1272, $2, Gray heron.

1997, July 1
1270 A365 50c Sheet of 9,
      #a.-i.   13.00 13.00
Souvenir Sheets
1271-1272 A365   Set of 2   12.00 12.00

Chernobyl Disaster, 10th Anniv. A366

1997, June 17   Litho.   Perf. 13½x14
1273 A366 $1 UNESCO   3.25 3.25

Marcello Mastroianni (1923-96), Actor — A367

No. 1274 — Scenes from motion pictures: a, Casanova, 1970. b, Divorce Italian Style. c, 8½. d, La Dolce Vita.

1997, Sept. 3
1274 A367 75c Sheet of 4,
      #a.-d.   10.00 10.00

Contemporary Artists and Paintings — A368

No. 1275, 50c: a, Andy Warhol (1927-87). b, "Multicolored Retrospective," by Warhol, 1979. c, "The Three Muscians," by Picasso, 1921. d, Pablo Picasso (1881-1973). e, Henri Matisse (1869-1954). f, "The Dance," by Matisse, 1910. g, "Lavender Mist," by Pollock, 1950. h, Jackson Pollock (1912-56).
No. 1276, 50c: a, Piet Mondrian (1872-1944). b, "Broadway Boogie Woogie," by Mondrian, 1942-43. c, "Persistence of Memory," by Dali, 1931. d, Salvador Dali (1904-89). e, Roy Lichtenstein (1923-97). f, "Artist's Studio: The Dance," by Lichtenstein, 1974. g, "Europe After the Rain," by Ernst, 1940-42. h, Max Ernst (1891-1976).

1997, Sept. 3   Perf. 14
Sheets of 8, #a-h
1275-1276 A368   Set of 2   27.50 27.50

Nos. 1275b-1275c, 1275f-1275g, 1276b-1276c, 1276f-1276g are 53x38mm.

Owls — A369

No. 1277: a, Akun eagle owl. b, Shelley's eagle owl. c, African wood owl. d, Rufous fishing owl. e, Maned owl. f, Sandy scops owl.

1997
1277 A369 50c Sheet of 6, #a.-f.   9.00 9.00

Birds — A370

Designs: 1c, Black bee-eater. 2c, Yellow-billed barbet. 3c, Carmine bee-eater. 4c, Malachite kingfisher. 5c, Emerald cuckoo. 10c, Blue-throated roller. 15c, Blue-headed bee-eater. 20c, Black-collared lovebird. 25c, Broad-billed roller. 50c, Blue-breasted kingfisher. 70c, Little bee-eater. 75c, Yellow spotted barbet. 90c, White-throated bee-eater. $1, Double-toothed barbet. $2, Blue-cheeked bee-eater. $3, Narina's trogon.

1997
1278	A370	1c multicolored	.25	.25
1279	A370	2c multicolored	.25	.25
1280	A370	3c multicolored	.25	.25
1281	A370	4c multicolored	.25	.25
1282	A370	5c multicolored	.25	.25
1283	A370	10c multicolored	.25	.25
1284	A370	15c multicolored	.40	.40
1285	A370	20c multicolored	.50	.50
1286	A370	25c multicolored	.65	.65
1287	A370	50c multicolored	1.25	1.25
1288	A370	70c multicolored	1.90	1.90
1289	A370	75c multicolored	2.00	2.00
1290	A370	90c multicolored	2.40	2.40
1291	A370	$1 multicolored	2.75	2.75
1292	A370	$2 multicolored	5.25	5.25
1293	A370	$3 multicolored	7.75	7.75
Nos. 1278-1293 (16)			26.35	26.35

1998 World Cup Soccer — A371

Players, country, vert: 50c, Salenko, Russia. 70c, Schillaci, Italy. $1, Lineker, England. $1.50, Pele, Brazil. $2, Fontaine, France. $2, Rahn, W. Germany.
No. 1300, 50c, vert: a, Ardiles, Argentina. b, Romario, Brazil. c, Rummenigge, Germany. d, Charlton, England. e, Villa, Argentina. f, Matthäus, Germany. g, Maradona, Argentina. h, Lineker, England.
No. 1301, 50c: a, Paulo Rossi, Italy. b, Ademir, Brazil. c, Grzegorz Lato, Poland. d, Gary Lineker, England. e, Gerd Muller, W. Germany. f, Johan Cruyff, Holland. g, Karl-Heinz Rummenigge, Germany. h, Mario Kempes, Argentina.
No. 1302, $6, Beckenbauer, W. Germany, vert. No. 1303, $6, Maier, W. Germany, vert.

Perf. 13½x14, 14x13½
1997, Oct. 1   Litho.
1294-1299 A371   Set of 6   18.00 18.00
Sheets of 8, #a-h, + Label
1300-1301 A371   Set of 2   27.50 27.50
Souvenir Sheets
1302-1303 A371   Set of 2   40.00 40.00

Marine Life A372

No. 1304: a, Flamingoes (beach, palm trees). b, Six flamingoes. c, Sailfish (d). d, Egret. e, Yellow-tail snapper. f, Manatee. g, Clown coris. h, White-collar butterflyfish. i, Royal angelfish. j, Titan triggerfish. k, Three-striped wrasse. l, Pacific blue-eye. m, Wobbegono. n, Jellyfish. o, Sea urchin, red sea triggerfish. p, Harlequin fish.
No. 1305, $2, Seahorses, vert. No. 1306, $2, Anemone fish.

1998, Mar. 9   Litho.   Perf. 14
1304 A372 20c Sheet of 16,
      #a.-p.   9.50 9.50
Souvenir Sheets
Perf. 13½x14, 14x13½
1305-1306 A372   Set of 2   12.00 12.00

No. 1305 contains one 38x51mm stamp. No. 1306 contains one 51x38mm stamp.

Butterflies — A373

Designs: No. 1307, 50c, Orange tip. No. 1308, 50c, Saturn. No. 1309, 50c, Queen of Spain fritillary. No. 1310, 50c, Plain tiger. No. 1311, 50c, Doris. No. 1312, 50c, Forest queen. No. 1313, 50c, Figure-of-eight. No. 1314, 50c, Orange-barred sulphur.
No. 1315, 50c: a, Alfalfa. b, Orange-barred sulphur, diff. c, Union jack. d, Mocker swallowtail. e, Large green-banded blue. f, Common dotted border.
No. 1316, 50c: a, Cairns birdwing. b, Leafwing. c, Banded kin shoemaker. d, Tiger swallowtail. e, Adonis blue. f, Palmfly.
No. 1317, $2, Great orange tip. No. 1318, $2, Japanese emperor.

1998, Apr. 6   Litho.   Perf. 14
1307-1314 A373   Set of 8   12.00 12.00
Sheets of 6, #a-f
1315-1316 A373   Set of 2   18.00 18.00
Souvenir Sheets
1317-1318 A373   Set of 2   12.00 12.00

Noah's Ark — A374

No. 1319: a, Condors. b, Giraffes, skunks. c, Mallard ducks. d, Snowy owl. e, Snowy owl (face forward). f, Noah. g, Noah's wife. h, Polar bears. i, Elephants. j, Zebras. k, Rhinoceros. l, Sheep. m, Ruby-throated hummingbird. n, Wives of Noah's sons. o, Bats. p, Ring-necked pheasant. q, Tiger. r, Deer. s, Kangaroos. t, Camels. u, Red-eyed frogs. v, Raccoons. w, Rooster, hen. x, Marmosets. y, Lions.
$2, Black-legged kittiwake gull, ark on top of mountain, horiz.

1998, May 4   Litho.   Perf. 14
1319 A374 15c Sheet of 25,
      #a.-y.   11.00 11.00
Souvenir Sheet
1320 A374 $2 multicolored   6.00 6.00

World Wildlife Fund — A375

No. 1321 — Liberian Mongoose: a, Looking straight ahead. b, Holding object between front paws. c, With front legs on branch. d, With mouth wide open.

1998, June 16   Litho.   Perf. 14
1321 A375 32c Block or strip of
4, #a.-d.   5.50 5.50
Issued in sheets of 12 stamps.

Mushrooms
A376

Designs: 10c, Lepiota cristata. 15c, Russula emetica. 20c, Coprinus comatus. 30c, Russula cyanoxantha. 50c, Cortinarius violaceus. 75c, Amanita cothurnata. $1, Stropharia cyanea. $1.20, Panaeolus semiovatus.

No. 1330, 40c: a, Collybia butyracea. b, Asterophora parasitica. c, Tricholomopsis rutilans. d, Marasmius alliaceus. e, Mycena crocata. f, Mycena polygramma. g, Oudemansiella mucida. h, Entoloma conferendum. i, Entoloma serrulatum.

No. 1331, 40c: a, Cordyceps militaris. b, Xylaria hypoxlon. c, Sarcoscypha austriaca. d, Auriscalpium. e, Fomitopsis pinicola. f, Pleurotus ostreatus. g, Lepista flaccida. h, Clitocybe metachroa. i, Hygrocybe conica.

No. 1332, $2, Gomphidus roseus. No. 1333, $2, Paxillus atrotomentosus. No. 1334, $2, Russula occidentalis. No. 1335, $2, Cantharellus cibarius.

1998, July 1
1322-1329   Set of 8   14.00 14.00
Sheets of 9, #a-i
1330-1331   Set of 2   24.00 24.00
Souvenir Sheets
1332-1335 A376   Set of 4   27.50 27.50

Monarchs
A377

No. 1336, 50c: a, Kaiser Wilhelm II, Germany. b, Qabus Bin Said, Oman. c, King Albert, Belgium. d, Haile Selassie, Ethiopia. e, King Hussein, Jordan. f, Sheik Jaber Al-Ahmad Al-Sabah, Kuwait.

No. 1337, 50c: a, Alexander the Great, Greece. b, Charlemagne, France. c, Cleopatra, Egypt. d, Henry VIII, England. e, Peter the Great, Russia. f, Frederick the Great, Prussia.

No. 1338, 50c: a, Queen Beatrix, Netherlands. b, King Juan Carlos, Spain. c, Queen Elizabeth II, England. d, Franz Joseph I, Austria-Hungary. e, Princess Grace, Monaco. f, King Carl XVI Gustaf, Sweden.

No. 1339, $2, Empress Michiko, Japan. No. 1340, $2, Emperor Akihito, Japan. No. 1341, $2, Kublai Khan, China.

1998, July 27   Litho.   Perf. 14
Sheets of 6, #a-f
1336-1338   Set of 3   24.00 24.00
Souvenir Sheets
1339-1341   Set of 3   21.00 21.00

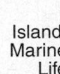

Diana, Princess of Wales (1961-
97) — A378

Various portraits of Diana in black outfit.

1998   **Imperf.**
1342 A378 50c Sheet of 4, #a.-d. 4.00 4.00

Birds
A379

No. 1343, 32c, Great green macaw. No. 1344, 32c, Crowned pigeon, vert. No. 1345, 32c, Blue-gray tanager. No. 1346, 32c, Roseate spoonbill, vert. No. 1347, 32c, Red-capped manakin. No. 1348, 32c, Groove-billed ani. No. 1349, 32c, South African crowned crane, vert.

No. 1350, vert: a, African sunbird. b, Seven-colored tanager. c, Red-throated bee-eater. d, Blue-crowned motmot. e, Duvaucel's trogon. f, Green bulbul. g, Grass-green tanager. h, Turaco. i, Hammer-head. j, Sarus crane. k, Limpkin. l, Ground hornbill.

No. 1351, $2, Red-crested touraco. No. 1352, $2, Flamingo, vert.

1998, Aug. 31   Litho.   Perf. 14
1343-1349 A379   Set of 7   7.00 7.00
1350 A379 32c Sheet of 12,
#a.-l.   12.00 12.00
Souvenir Sheets
1351-1352 A379   Set of 2   12.00 12.00

Children's
Stories
A380

No. 1354: a, Tom Sawyer, by Mark Twain. b, Peter Rabbit, by Beatrix Potter. c, The Nutcracker, by E.T.A. Hoffman. d, Hansel & Gretel, by The Brothers Grimm. e, The Princess and the Pea, by Hans Christian Andersen. f, Oliver Twist, by Charles Dickens. g, Little Red Riding Hood, by The Brothers Grimm. h, Rumpelstiltskin, by The Brothers Grimm. i, The Wind & the Willows, by Kenneth Grahame.

$2, Rapunzel, by Brothers Grimm.

1998, Sept. 16   Litho.   Perf. 14½
1354 A380 40c Sheet of 9,
#a.-i.   12.00 12.00
Souvenir Sheet
Perf. 13½
1355 A380 $2 multicolored   7.00 7.00
No. 1355 contains one 38x51mm stamp.

Island,
Marine
Life
A381

No. 1356: a, Litoria peronii. b, Volcano, denomination UL. c, Volcano, denomination UR. d, Egretta alba. e, Graphium antiphates itamputi. f, Rhododendron zoelleri. g, Boat. h, Lava flow. i, Cormorants. j, Vaccinium. k, Caranx latus. l, Dugongs. m, Underwater lava flow. n, Cetocarus bicolor. o, Chilomycterus spilostylus. p, Lienardella fasliatus. q, Aerobatus. r, Gray reef shark. s, Acanthurus leucosternon, denomination UR. t, Hippocampus kuda. u, Coral, denomination UR. v, Chelonia. w, Myripristis hexogona. x, Coral, denomination UL. y, Acanthurus leucosternon, denonination UL.

No. 1357: a, Sperm whale (b, c). b, Lollipop tang. c, Bottlenose dolphin (b, f). d, Jackass penguin (e). e, Harlequin tuskfish. f, Manta ray (a, b, e, j). g, Sealion (a, g, l). i, Hammerhead shark (m). j, Butterfly fish. k, Garibaldi (g). l, Marine iguana (p). m, Loggerhead turtle (n). n, Seahorse. o, Horseshow crab (n, p). p, Moray eel.

No. 1358, 32c: a, Walrus. b, Pockfish-harlequin. c, Striped marlin. d, Whale shark. e, Spiny boxfish. f, Porcupine fish. g, Octopus. h, Dragonfish. i, Sea krait.

No. 1359, 32c: a, Snapping turtle. b, Atlantic spadefish. c, Bottlenose dolphin. d, Humpback whale. e, Whitetip shark. f, Twilight and deep seafish. g, Moorish idol. h, American lobster. i, Stingrays.

No. 1360, $2, Great white shark. No. 1361, $2, Banner fish. No. 1362, $2, Killer whale. No. 1363, $2, Surgeon fish.

1998, Oct. 15   Perf. 14
1356 A381 15c Sheet of 25,
#a.-y.   12.00 12.00
1357 A381 20c Sheet of 16,
#a.-p.   10.00 10.00
Sheets of 9, #a-i
1358-1359 A381   Set of 2   18.00 18.00
Souvenir Sheets
1360-1363 A381   Set of 4   22.50 22.50
International Year of the Ocean.

Diana, Princess
of Wales (1961-
97)
A382

Design: a, 50c, Inscription panel on left. b, 50c, panel on right.

1998, Oct. 26   Litho.   Perf. 14½x14
1364 A382 50c Pair, a.-b.   3.25 3.25
No. 1364 was issued in sheets of 6.

Pablo Picasso (1881-1973) — A383

Entire paintings or details: 50c, Woman Throwing a Stone, 1931. 70c, Man with Sword and Flower, 1969, vert. $1, Large Bather with a Book, 1937, vert.
$2, French Cancan, 1901.

1998, Oct. 26   Perf. 14½
1365-1367 A383   Set of 3   7.50 7.50
Souvenir Sheet
1368 A383 $2 multicolored   7.00 7.00

Mahatma Gandhi
(1869-1948)
A384

1998, Oct. 26   Perf. 14
1369 A384 50c shown   1.75 1.75
Souvenir Sheet
1370 A384 $2 Portrait, diff.   7.00 7.00
No. 1369 was issued in sheets of 4.

1998 World Scout Jamboree,
Chile — A385

No. 1371: a, Daniel Carter Beard, Ernest Thompson Seton, award scouts, 1912. b, Robert Baden-Powell in Matabeleland, 1896. c, Scout repairing small girl's wagon.

1998, Oct. 26
1371 A385 $1 Sheet of 3, #a.-
c.   10.00 10.00

Enzo Ferrari (1898-1988), Automobile
Manufacturer — A386

No. 1372: a, King Leopold Cabriolet. b, 195 S. c, 250 GTO 64.
$2, 250MM Cabriolet.

1998, Oct. 26   Litho.   Perf. 14
1372 A386 $1 Sheet of 3, #a.-c.   9.00 9.00
Souvenir Sheet
1373 A386 $2 multicolored   8.50 8.50
No. 1373 contains one 91x35mm stamp.

Royal
Air
Force,
80th
Anniv.
A387

No. 1374: a, Hawker Hurricane XII. b, Avro Lancaster in flight. c, Avro Lancaster B2. d, Supermarine Spitfire HG Mk 1XB.
No. 1375, $2, Bristol F2B fighter, Eurofighter. No. 1376, $2, Hawk, biplane.

1998, Oct. 26
1374 A387 70c Sheet of 4,
#a.-d.   9.50 9.50
Souvenir Sheet
1375-1376 A387   Set of 2   14.00 14.00

Famous People
and Events of the
Twentieth
Cent. — A388

No. 1380, 40c: a, Mao Tse-tung. b, Cultural Revolution begins. c, Promoting Third World unity. d, Zhou Enlai. e, Deng Xiaoping. f, Hong Kong returns to China, 1997. g, Shanghai, an Asian metropolis. h, Jiang Zemin.
No. 1381, 40c: a, Robert E. Peary. b, Expedition to the North Pole. c, Climbing Mt. Everest. d, Sir Edmund Hillary. e, Neil Armstrong. f, Walking on the moon. g, Expedition to the South Pole. h, Roald Amundsen.
$2, Matthew Henson.

1998, Dec. 1   Litho.   Perf. 14
Sheets of 8, #a-h
1380-1381 A388   Set of 2   22.50 22.50

Souvenir Sheet
1382 A388 $2 multicolored   6.50 6.50

Nos. 1380b-1380c, 1380f-1380g, 1381b-1381c, 1380f-1381g are each 53x38mm.

Classic Cars A389

Designs: No. 1383, 32c, 1966-72 Lamborghini Miura. No. 1384, 32c, 1966-93 Alfa Romeo Spider. No. 1385, 32c, 1948-61 Jaguar XK140. No. 1386, 32c, 1959-63 Lotus Elite.
No. 1387, 50c: a, 1949-53 Bristol 401. b, 1952-55 Bentley Continental R. c, 1973-75 Lancia stratos. d, 1963-67 Chevrolet Corvette Stingray. e, 1948-52 Austin A90 Atlantic. f, 1969-90 Aston Martin V8.
No. 1388, 50c: a, 1961-75 Jaguar E-Type. b, 1955-57 Ford Thunderbird. c, 1964-73, Ford Mustang GT350. d, 1957-77 Fiat 500. e, 1955-59 BMW 507. f, 1963-65 Buick Riviera.
No. 1389, $2, 1945-55 MG TD. No. 1390, $2, 1959-65 Rolls Royce Silver Cloud.

1998, Dec. 24
1383-1386 A389   Set of 4   4.00 4.00

Sheets of 6, #a-f
1387-1388 A389   Set of 2   20.00 20.00

Souvenir Sheets
1389-1390 A389   Set of 2   13.00 13.00

New Year 1999 (Year of the Rabbit) — A390

Paintings, by Liu Jiyou (1918-83): No. 1391, Two rabbits. No. 1392, Three rabbits. No. 1393, Two rabbits, flowers, vert.

1999, Jan. 5
1391 A390 50c multicolored   1.75 1.75
1392 A390 50c multicolored   1.75 1.75

Souvenir Sheet
1393 A390 $2 multicolored   6.50 6.50

Nos. 1391-1392 were issued in sheets of 2 each. No. 1393 contains one 43x52mm stamp.

US Presidents A391

No. 1394, 75c, Various portraits of Abraham Lincoln. No. 1395, 75c, Various portraits of Bill Clinton.

1998, Dec. 1   Litho.   Perf. 14
Sheets of 4, #a-d
1394-1395 A391   Set of 2   20.00 20.00

Zhou Enlai (1898-1976), Chinese Premier — A392

Various portraits.

1999   Litho.   Perf. 14
1396 A392 50c Sheet of 6,
   #a.-f.   10.00 10.00

Souvenir Sheet
1397 A392 $2 multicolored   7.00 7.00

Raptors — A393

Designs: 50c, Snowy owl. 70c, Barn owl. $1, American kestrel $1.50, Golden eagle.
No. 1402, 50c: a, Eurasian eagle owl. b, Osprey. c, Egyptian vulture. d, Lizard buzzard. e, Pale chanting goshawk. f, Bald eagle.
No. 1403, 50c: a, Goshawk. b, Laughing falcon. c, Oriental bay-owl. d, Swallow-tailed kite. e, Secretary bird. f, Brown falcon.
No. 1404, $2, Northern harrier. No. 1405, $2, Peregrine falcon.

1999, Jan. 4
1398-1401 A393   Set of 4   11.00 11.00

Sheets of 6, #a-f
1402-1403 A393   Set of 2   20.00 20.00

Souvenir Sheets
1404-1405 A393   Set of 2   13.00 13.00

Dinosaurs — A395

No. 1406, 50c, Pachyrinosaur. No. 1407, 50c, Centrosaurus, vert. No. 1408, 70c, Pentaceratops, vert. No. 1409, 70c, Oviraptor, vert. No. 1410, 70c, Corythosaur. $1.50, Stegosaurus, vert.
No. 1412, 40c: a, Baryonyx (e). b, Pachycephalosaur (a, c). c, Homalocephale. d, Pterodustro (c, g). e, Pycnosteroides. f, Giant nautiloid. g, Kronosaur (e, f). h, Giant cephalopod (g).
No. 1413, 40c: a, Camarasaur. b, Albertosaur (c, f, g). c, Eudimorphodon (b, d). d, Dimorphodon (c). e, Compsognathus. f, Torosaurus. g, Nodosaurid (h). h, Probactrosaurus.
No. 1414, $2, Tarbosaurus, vert. No. 1415, $2, Shunosaurus, vert.

1999, Jan. 18
1406-1411 A395   Set of 6   12.00 12.00

Sheets of 8, #a-h
1412-1413 A395   Set of 2   22.50 22.50

Souvenir Sheets
1414-1415 A395   Set of 2   13.00 13.00

Dinosaurs — A396

Designs: 50c, Brachiosaurus, vert. 70c, Tyrannosaurus, vert. $1, Mosasaurus. $1.50, Triceratops.
No. 1420: a, Albertosaurus. b, Parasaurolophus. c, Styracosaurus. d, Struthiomimus. e, Ankylosaurus. f, Chasmosaurus.
No. 1421, $2, Deinonychus. No. 1422, $2, Stegosaurus.

1999
1416-1419 A396   Set of 4   9.00 9.00
1420 A396 50c Sheet of 6,
   #a.-f.   10.00 10.00

Souvenir Sheets
1421-1422 A396   Set of 2   13.00 13.00

Flowers — A397

Designs: No. 1423, 50c, Tecophilaea cyanocrocus. 70c, Nymphoides peltata. $1, Angraecum scottianum. $1.50, Grevillea dielsiana.
No. 1427, 50c: a, Cyrtopodium parvilflorum. b, Catharanthus roseus. c, Acacia acuminata. d, Herbertia lahue. e, Protea venusta. f, Clianthus formosus.
No. 1428, 50c: a, Dendrobium rarum. b, Cyrtorchis arcuata. c, Zygopetalum intermedium. d, Cassia fistula. e, Saintpaulia ionantha. f, Heliconia collinsiana.
No. 1429, $2, Hibiscus tilliaceus. No. 1430, $2, Rhododendron thomsonii.

1999, Feb. 8
1423-1426 A397   Set of 4   11.00 11.00

Sheets of 6, #a-f
1427-1428 A397   Set of 2   20.00 20.00

Souvenir Sheets
1429-1430 A397   Set of 2   13.00 13.00

Orchids — A398

Designs: No. 1431, 50c, Tridactyle bicaudata. No. 1432, 50c, Angraecum infundibulare. No. 1433, 70c, Oeceoclades maculata. No. 1434, 70c, Ophyrs fusca. No. 1435, $1, Sobennikoffia robusta. No. 1436, $1, Stenoglottis fimbriata. No. 1437, $1.50, Plectrelminthus caudatus. No. 1438, $1.50, Satyrium erectum.
No. 1439, 50c: a, Angraecrum eichlerianum. b, Ansellia africana. c, Cymbidiella pardalina. d, Angraecum eburnium. e, Ancistrochilus rothchildianus. f, Aerangis luteoalba.
No. 1440, 50c: a, Dis cardinalis. b, Cytorchus arcuata. c, Cynorkis compacta. d, Disa kewensis. e, Eulophia guineensis. f, Eulophia speciosa.
No. 1441, Angraecum compactum. No. 1442, Calanthe vestita.

1999, Mar. 13
1431-1438 A398   Set of 8   22.50 22.50

Sheets of 6, #a-f
1439-1440 A398   Set of 2   19.00 19.00

Souvenir Sheets
1441-1442 A398   Set of 2   13.00 13.00

Orchids — A399

Designs: No. 1443, 50c, Calypso bulbosa. No. 1444, 50c, Maclellanara pagan lovesong. No. 1445, 70c, Masdevallia chimaera. No. 1446, 70c, Yamadara midnight. $1, Cleistes divaricata. $1.50, Oncidium golden sunset.
No. 1449: a, Trichopilia tortilis. b, Stenoglottis longifolia. c, Telipogon pulcher. d, Esmeralda clarkei. e, Papilionanthe teres. f, Mormodes rolfeanum. g, Cypripedium acaule. h, Serapias lingua.

1999, Mar. 13
1443-1448 A399   Set of 6   15.00 15.00
1449 A399 30c Sheet of 8,
   #a.-h.   9.00 9.00

Wildlife — A400

No. 1450: a, Mink. b, Arctic fox. c, Lynx. d, Snowy owl. e, Polar bear. f, Golden eagle. $2, Big horn sheep.

1999, Feb. 24   Litho.   Perf. 14
1450 A400 50c Sheet of 6, #a.-f. 7.00 7.00

Souvenir Sheet
1451 A400 $2 multicolored   5.00 5.00

Flora and Fauna A401

No. 1452: a, Madagascan red fody. b, Indri (e). c, Coral-billed nuthatch. d, Safaka (g, j). e, Golden piper. f, Aye aye (i). g, Croad-bordered grass yellowy. h, Ring-tailed lemur (g, j, k). i, Parson's chameleon. j, Madagascar day gecko. k, Leaf-tailed gecko. l, Orchid.
No. 1453, $2, Wattled false sunbird. No. 1454, $2, Parson's chameleon. No. 1455, $2, Ring-tailed lemur.

1999, Apr. 1
1452 A401 20c Sheet of 12,
   #a.-l.   7.00 7.00

Souvenir Sheets
1453-1455 A401   Set of 3   15.00 15.00

Seabirds — A402

Designs: No. 1456, 50c, Harlequin duck. No. 1457, 50c, Eleonor's falcon, vert. No. 1458, 70c, Wilson's plover. No. 1459, 70c, Common eider. No. 1460, $1, Little tern. No. 1461, $1, American oystercatcher. No. 1462, $1.50, Herring gull, vert. No. 1463, $1.50, Brown pelican, vert.
No. 1464, 30c, vert: a, Great cormorant. b, Crested cormorant. c, Red faced cormorant. d, Whimbrel. e, Tufted puffin. f, Ivory gull. g, Common murre. h, Shelduck. i, Razorbill.
No. 1465, 30c: a, Common tern. b, Black-legged kittiwake. c, Bernacle goose. d, Black-headed gull. e, Semipalmated plover. f, Northern gannet. g, King eider. h, Iceland gull. i, Ring-billed gull.

No. 1466, $2, Arctic loon. No. 1467, $2, Atlantic puffin. No. 1468, $2, California gull, vert.

1999, Apr. 1   Litho.   Perf. 14
1456-1463 A402   Set of 8   17.00 17.00
Sheets of 9, #a-i
1464-1465 A402   Set of 2   13.00 13.00
Souvenir Sheets
1466-1468 A402   Set of 3   15.00 15.00

Queen Mother (b. 1900) — A404

No. 1475: a, With King George VI at wedding, 1923. b, In Nairobi, 1959. c, Wearing tiara, 1953. d, Wearing hat, 1990. $2, Wearing hat, 1990, diff.

1999, Aug. 4   Perf. 14
1475 A404 $1 Sheet of 4, #a.-d., + label   9.00 9.00
Souvenir Sheet
Perf. 13¾
1476 A404 $2 multicolored   5.00 5.00
No. 1476 contains one 38x51mm stamp.

Trains A405

Designs: 32c, Nozomi Train, Japan. 40c, 401 Intercity Express, Germany. 50c, C53, Japan Railways. 70c, Beuth 2-2-2, Germany.
No. 1481, 40c: a, "Adler," Germany. b, Suburban EMU, Japan. c, Class 01, 4-6-2, Germany. d, Class 120 Bo-Bo, Germany. e, Class P8, 4-6-0, Germany. f, Fujikawa Express, Japan. g, Class 081, Germany. h, Kodama 8-car train, Japan. i, Class C62, 4-6-4, Japan.
No. 1482, 40c: a, KF Type, 4-8-4, China. b, Minobu Line train, Japan. c, Class S34-40, Germany. d, Class EF81, Bo-Bo, Japan. e, V200, B-B, Germany. f, SVT 877 "Flying Hamburger," Japan. g, C51, 4-6-2 Japan Railways. h, AEO Single rail car, Germany. i, Class D51, Japan.
No. 1483, $2, Yamonote Line train, Japan. No. 1484, $2, Class B8, Germany.

1999, Aug. 25   Litho.   Perf. 14
1477-1480 A405   Set of 4   4.50 4.50
Sheets of 9, #a-i
1481-1482 A405   Set of 2   17.00 17.00
Souvenir Sheets
1483-1484 A405   Set of 2   10.00 10.00

Dogs A406

No. 1485, Lhasa apso. 70c, Samoyed.
No. 1487, vert.: a, Dalmatian. b, Pyrennean Mountain dog. c, Golden retriever. d, Bearded collie. e, Basset hound. f, Bernese Mountain dog.
No. 1488, Beagle, vert.

1999, Aug. 30   Perf. 14
1485 A406 50c multicolored   1.25 1.25
1486 A406 70c multicolored   1.75 1.75
1487 A406 50c Sheet of 6, #a.-f.   7.50 7.50
Souvenir Sheet
1488 A406 $2 multicolored   5.00 5.00

During 1999-2004 Liberia was torn by a brutal and chaotic civil war that reduced the nation to a state of anarchy. Government services, including postal operations, functioned erratically, if at all, for months at a time. During this period, overseas stamp agents continued to produce stamps under pre-war contracts, and a large number of issues appeared that were marketed to overseas collectors. It appears that some of these stamps have been released in Liberia since the end of hostilities. These will be listed when their sale and postal use has been confirmed.

Paintings by Norman Rockwell A580

Paintings: $15, Playing Party Games. $30, Saturday Night Out. $35, The Portrait. No. 2328, $50, Grandpa's Little Ballerina.
No. 2329, $50: a, The Cave of the Winds. b, Redhead Loves Hatty. c, The Rivals. d, Three's Company.
No. 2330, $50: a, Distortion. b, Summer Vacation. c, Runaway Pants. d, Tumble.
No. 2331, $50: a, Daydreams. b, A Patient Friend. c, Lands of Enchantment. d, The Little Spooners.
No. 2332, $50: a, The Skating Lesson. b, The Fortune Teller. c, God Bless You. d, Knowledge is Power.

2005, Jan. 10   Litho.   Perf. 14¼
2325-2328 A580   Set of 4   7.00 7.00
Sheets of 4, #a-d
2329-2332 A580   Set of 4   40.00 40.00

Jules Verne (1828-1905), Writer — A581

No. 2333, $30: a, The Adventures of Captain Hatteras. b, The Mysterious Island (deflated balloon). c, The Mysterious Island (Men looking at ape). d, 20,000 Leagues Under the Sea (spotlights on ship).
No. 2334, $30: a, Around the World in Eighty Days. b, From the Earth to the Moon (people watching man on space capsule ladder). c, Paris in the Twentieth Century. d, Master of the World (ship captain at wheel).
No. 2335, $30: a, The Chase of the Golden Meteor. b, Master of the World (flying machine, country name in white). c, Five Weeks in a Balloon. d, From the Earth to the Moon (rocket in space).
No. 2336, $30: a, The Mysterious Island (People in balloon basket). b, Robur the Conqueror. c, Round the Moon. d, Master of the World (flying machine, country name in black).
No. 2337, $30: Scenes from 20,000 Leagues Under the Sea: a, Ships on water. b, Shark and octopus attacking ship. c, Shark attacking diver. d, Squid attacking ship.
No. 2338, $100, Deep sea divers. No. 2339, $100, Admiral Richard E. Byrd. No. 2340, $100, Radio satellite communication. No. 2341, $100, Long range ballistic missile. No. 2342, $100, Extravehicular satellite repair.

2005, Jan. 11   Perf. 13¼x13½
Sheets of 4, #a-d
2333-2337 A581   Set of 5   32.50 32.50
Souvenir Sheets
2338-2342 A581   Set of 5   27.50 27.50

Marilyn Monroe (1926-62), Actress — A582

2005, Jan. 26   Perf. 14
2343 A582 $12 multi   .70 .70

Prehistoric Animals — A583

No. 2344, $50: a, Torosaurus. b, Tyrannosaurus. c, Polacanthus. d, Stegosaurus.
No. 2345, $50: a, Smilodon. b, Brontothere. c, Doedicurus. d, Moeritherium.
No. 2346, $50: a, Cymbospondylus. b, Archelon. c, Xiphactinus. d, Dunkleosteus.
No. 2347, $120, Stegosaurus, diff. No. 2348, $120, Woolly rhinoceros. No. 2349, $120, Odobenoceptops.

2005, Jan. 26   Perf. 13¼x13½
Sheets of 4, #a-d
2344-2346 A583   Set of 3   32.50 32.50
Souvenir Sheet
2347-2349 A583   Set of 3   18.00 18.00

Battle of Trafalgar, Bicent. — A584

Various ships: $10, $20, $40, $50. $100, Death of Admiral Horatio Nelson.

2005, May 4   Perf. 14¼
2350-2353 A584   Set of 4   6.00 6.00
Souvenir Sheet
2354 A584 $100 multi   5.50 5.50

Hans Christian Andersen (1805-75), Author — A585

No. 2355: a, Medal. b, Open book. c, Andersen. $100, Sketch of Little Mermaid.

2005, May 4   Perf. 14¼
2355 A585 $50 Sheet of 3, #a-c   7.50 7.50
Souvenir Sheet
2356 A585 $100 multi   5.50 5.50

Friedrich von Schiller (1759-1805), Writer — A586

No. 2357: a, Bust of Schiller on round pedestal. b, Bust and foliage. c, Bust on monument. $100, Statue of Schiller, Chicago.

2005, May 4   Perf. 14¼
2357 A586 $50 Sheet of 3, #a-c   7.50 7.50
Size: 48x67mm
Imperf
2358 A586 $100 multi   5.50 7.50
No. 2357 contains three 28x42mm stamps.

Miniature Sheets

Elvis Presley (1935-77) — A587

No. 2359, $35 — Presley in: a, 1956. b, 1969. c, 1969 (country name in yellow). d, 1969 (country name in pink). e, 1970.
No. 2360, $35 — Presley wearing: a, Red suit and white shirt. b, Yellow sweater. c, Red shirt. d, Brown suit. e, Gray suit.

2005, May 19   Perf. 13½x13¼
Sheets of 5, #a-e
2359-2360 A587   Set of 2   19.00 19.00

Pope John Paul II (1920-2005) A588

2005, Aug. 22   Perf. 12¾
2361 A588 $50 multi   2.50 2.50
Printed in sheets of 4.

World Cup Soccer Championships, 75th Anniv. — A589

No. 2362: a, Norbert Eder. b, Paul Breitner. c, Thomas Helmer.
$100, Manfred Kaltz.

2005, Aug. 22   *Perf. 13¼*
2362 A589 $60 Sheet of 3, #a-c   10.00 10.00
Souvenir Sheet
Perf. 12
2363 A589 $100 multi   5.50 5.50

Albert Einstein (1879-1955), Physicist — A590

No. 2364 — Einstein and: a, Charlie Chaplin. b, Max Planck. c, William Allen White.
$100, J. Robert Oppenheimer

2005, Aug. 22   *Perf. 12¾*
2364 A590 $60 Sheet of 3, #a-c   9.00 9.00
Souvenir Sheet
2365 A590 $100 multi   5.00 5.00

End of World War II, 60th Anniv. — A591

No. 2366, $40 — V-E Day: a, Gen. Dwight D. Eisenhower. b, Prime Minister Winston Churchill. c, Gen. George Patton. d, Field Marshal Bernard Montgomery.
No. 2367, $40 — V-E Day: a, Air Marshal Sir Arthur "Bomber" Harris. b, Gen. Douglas MacArthur. c, Field Marshal Alan Brooke. d, Pres. Franklin D. Roosevelt.
No. 2368, $40 — V-J Day: a, RAF Wellington bomber. b, Mitsubishi A6M Zero. c, RAF Hudson bomber. d, B-17 bomber.
No. 2369, $40 — V-J Day: a, P-51 Mustang. b, RAF Hamilcar glider. c, P-38 Lightning. d, RAF Supermarine Spitfire.

2005, Aug. 22   *Perf. 13¼x13½*
Sheets of 4, #a-d
2366-2369 A591 Set of 4   26.00 26.00

Worldwide Fund for Nature (WWF) — A592

No. 2370: a, Jentink's duiker. b, Head of Ogilby's duiker. c, Ogilby's duiker. d, Head of Jentink's duiker.

2005, Aug. 31   *Perf. 14*
2370 A592 $20 Block or vert. strip of 4, #a-d   4.00 4.00
e. Miniature sheet, 2 each #2370a-2370d   6.50 6.50

Rotary International, Cent. — A593

Emblem: $10, $25, $35, $50.
$100, Mother Teresa.

2005, Sept. 22   *Perf. 14*
2371-2374 A593 Set of 4   5.00 5.00
Souvenir Sheet
2375 A593 $100 multi   5.00 5.00

Christmas — A594

Paintings: $20, Glory to God, by Kim Kichang. $25, Flight Into Egypt, by Fra Angelico. $30, Christmas Mom, by Will Hickock Low. $50, The Nativity, by Bernadino Luini.
$100, Adoration of the Magi, by Nicolas Poussin.

2005, Dec. 1
2376-2379 A594 Set of 4   6.00 6.00
Souvenir Sheet
2380 A594 $100 multi   5.00 5.00

Elvis Presley (1935-77) — A595

Variable Serpentine Die Cut
2006, Jan. 17   **Litho. & Embossed**
Without Gum
2381 A595 $350 gold & multi   20.00 20.00

African Antelopes — A596

No. 2382: a, Gemsbok. b, Kudu. c, Sable antelope. d, Impala.
$100, Springbok.

2006, Jan. 17   **Litho.**   *Perf. 13½*
2382 A596 $45 Sheet of 4, #a-d   9.00 9.00
Souvenir Sheet
2383 A596 $100 multi   5.00 5.00

Mammals — A597

No. 2384: a, Jackal. b, Fox. c, Wolf. d, Coyote.
$100, Hyena.

2006, Jan. 17
2384 A597 $45 Sheet of 4, #a-d   9.00 9.00
Souvenir Sheet
2385 A597 $100 multi   5.00 5.00

Wild Cats — A598

No. 2386: a, Jaguar. b, Lion. c, Puma. d, Cheetah.
$100, Siberian tiger.

2006, Jan. 17
2386 A598 $45 Sheet of 4, #a-d   9.00 9.00
Souvenir Sheet
2387 A598 $100 multi   5.00 5.00

Animals of the Bible — A599

No. 2388, $45: a, Lions. b, Camels. c, Doves. d, Donkey.
No. 2389, $45: a, Foxes. b, Vultures. c, Turtles. d, Ducks.
No. 2390, $45: a, Goat. b, Bear. c, Ravens. d, Sheep.
No. 2391, $120, Pig. No. 2392, $120, Whale. No. 2393, $120, Snake.

2006, Jan. 17   **Sheets of 4, #a-d**
2388-2390 A599 Set of 3   25.00 25.00
Souvenir Sheets
2391-2393 A599 Set of 3   20.00 20.00

Snakes — A600

No. 2394: a, Rough green snake. b, Speckled king snake. c, Garter snake. d, Brown snake.
$100, Red milk snake.

2006, Jan. 27
2394 A600 $45 Sheet of 4, #a-d   9.00 9.00
Souvenir Sheet
2395 A600 $100 multi   5.00 5.00

2006 Winter Olympics, Turin — A601

Designs: $20, Austria #B337. $25, Poster for 1976 Innsbruck Winter Olympics, vert. $35, Austria #B338. $50, Austria #B335. $70, US #3555. $100, Poster for 2002 Salt Lake City Winter Olympics, vert.

2006, Apr. 6   *Perf. 13½*
2396-2399 A601 Set of 4   8.00 8.00
2399A A601 $70 multi   4.00 4.00
2399B A601 $100 multi   6.00 6.00
Nos. 2399A-2399B were not made available until 2007.

Souvenir Sheet

Benjamin Franklin (1706-90), Statesman — A602

2006, May 27   *Perf. 13½*
2400 A602 $120 multi   7.50 7.50
Washington 2006 World Philatelic Exhibition.

Queen Elizabeth II, 80th Birthday — A603

No. 2401 — Hat color: a, Green. b, Blue. c, Beige. d, Black.
$120, Queen wearing tiara.

2006, June 13   *Perf. 14¼*
2401 A603 $40 Sheet of 4, #a-d   9.00 9.00
Souvenir Sheet
2402 A603 $120 multi   7.00 7.00

Rembrandt (1606-69), Painter A604

Artwork: $15, Young Man in a Turban. $30, Man Leaning on a Windowsill. $40, Officer with a Gold Chain. $45, The Art Dealer Clement de Jonghe.

No. 2407, $60: a, Self-portrait, 1633. b, Self-portrait, 1634. c, Self-portrait, 1639. d, Self-portrait, 1640.

No. 2408, $60: a, Christ and the Canaanite Woman. b, The Mocking of Christ. c, Head of an Old Man (Three-quarters view). d, Head of an Old Man (profile).

No. 2409, $60: a, David and Jonathan. b, Nude Woman with a Snake. c, The Abduction of Europa. d, Daniel and Cyrus Before the Idol Bel.

No. 2410, $60: a, Shah Jahan and Dara Shikoh. b, Farm Building Surrounded by Trees. c, Two Thatched Cottages with Figures at Window. d, A Sailing Boat on Wide Expanse of Water.

No. 2411, $120, Bearded Old Man with a Gold Chain. No. 2412, $120, A Scholar in His Study. No. 2413, $120, Rembrandt's Mother. No. 2414, $120, Portrait of Jan Six.

2006, June 13   **Litho.**
2403-2406 A604   Set of 4   7.00   7.00
Sheets of 4, #a-d
2407-2410 A604   Set of 4   50.00   50.00
Imperf
Size: 76x103mm
2411-2414 A604   Set of 4   30.00   30.00

Souvenir Sheet

Wolfgang Amadeus Mozart (1756-91), Composer — A605

2006, July 25   **Perf. 12¾**
2415 A605 $120 multi   7.50   7.50

Miniature Sheet

Chinese Ceramics — A606

No. 2416: a, Bowl with red, black and white exterior, brown interior. b, Bowl with blue and white exterior, blue, red and white interior. c, Bowl with green on white exterior, square opening. d, Bowl with red, white and blue exterior, brown interior. e, Bowl with green on white exterior, circular opening. f, Bowl with red, white and green exterior, square opening.

2006, Aug. 16   **Perf. 12x12¼**
2416 A606 $35 Sheet of 6, #a-
   f   12.00   12.00

Inauguration of Pres. Ellen Johnson-Sirleaf — A607

Designs: $10, Pres. Johnson-Sirleaf and flag. $25, Certification by National Election Commission, horiz. $30, Casting of ballots. $40, Pres. Johnson-Sirleaf holding child, horiz.
$100, Pres. Johnson-Sirleaf at microphone.

2006, Aug. 22   **Perf. 13¼**
2417-2420 A607   Set of 4   6.00   6.00
Souvenir Sheet
2421 A607 $100 multi   6.00   6.00

Millennium Development Goals — A608

Goals: No. 2422, $10, Achieve universal primary education (graduates). No. 2423, $10, Promote gender equality and empower women. No. 2424, $25, Eradicate extreme hunger and poverty. No. 2425, $25, Reduce child mortality. No. 2426, $30, Develop a global partnership for development (map). No. 2427, $30, Develop a global partnership for development (ships and airplane). $40, Improve maternal health. $50, Achieve universal primary education (classroom). No. 2430, $100, Ensure environmental sustainability. No. 2431, $100, Combat HIV/AIDS, malaria and other diseases.

No. 2432, Achieve universal primary education (classroom), vert.

2006, Sept. 22
2422-2431 A608   Set of 10   25.00   25.00
Souvenir Sheet
2432 A608 $100 multi   6.00   6.00

Space Achievements — A609

No. 2433, $40 — Intl. Space Station: a, Country name and denomination in black, at top. b, Country name in black, denomination in white. c, Country name and denomination in white, at top. d, Country name and denomination in black, at bottom. e, Space shuttle (country name and denomination in white, at bottom). f, Astronaut (country name and denomination in white, at bottom.

No. 2434, $40, vert. — Apollo 11: a, Lunar module. b, Rocket on launch pad. c, Nose cone of rocket. d, Astronaut on moon. e, Command module. f, Astronauts and rocket.

No. 2435, $55, vert. — First Flight of Space Shuttle Columbia: a, Astronaut Bob Crippen. b, Front of space shuttle. c, Astronaut John Young. d, Tail of space shuttle.

No. 2436, $55 — Space Shuttle returns to space: a, Wing. b, Fuselage, reflection of sunlight. c, Wing inscribed "Discovery." d, Fuselage and Earth.

No. 2437, $120, Apollo-Soyuz. No. 2438, $120, Mars Reconnaissance Orbiter. No. 2439, $120, Venus Express. No. 2440, $120, Deep Impact Probe.

2006, Oct. 3   **Litho.**   **Perf. 12¾**
Sheets of 6, #a-f
2433-2434 A609   Set of 2   30.00   30.00
Sheets of 4, #a-d
2435-2436 A609   Set of 2   25.00   25.00
Souvenir Sheets
2437-2440 A609   Set of 4   25.00   25.00

Christopher Columbus (1451-1506), Explorer — A610

Designs: $25, Columbus, drawings of ships. $50, Columbus, ships, horiz. $70, Columbus and Santa Maria, horiz. $100, Ship, crew encountering natives, horiz. $120, Men on shore.

2006, Nov. 15
2441-2444 A610   Set of 4   12.50   12.50
Souvenir Sheet
2445 A610 $120 multi   7.00   7.00

Souvenir Sheet

Christmas — A611

No. 2446 — Details from The Adoration of the Magi, by Peter Paul Rubens: a, Man and boy. b, Mary. c, Man with headcovering. d, Infant Jesus.

2006, Dec. 21   **Litho.**   **Perf. 14**
2446 A611 $40 Sheet of 4, #a-d   9.00   9.00

A612

Concorde — A613

No. 2447, $30 — Concorde: a, G-BOAF. b, G-BOAB.
No. 2448, $35 — Concorde: a, F-BVFA on runway. b, G-BOAA taking off.

2007, Mar. 1   **Litho.**   **Perf. 13½**
Horiz. Pairs, #a-b
2447-2448 A612   Set of 2   7.50   7.50
Litho. & Embossed
Without Gum
Irregular Serpentine Die Cut
2449 A613 $350 gold & multi   20.00   20.00

Souvenir Sheet

Ludwig Durr (1878-1956), Engineer — A614

No. 2450: a, Durr and Zeppelin. b, Interior cabin plan for LZ-127. c, Count Ferdinand von Zeppelin.

2007, Mar. 1   **Litho.**   **Perf. 13¼**
2450 A614 $60 Sheet of 3, #a-
   c   10.00   10.00

Souvenir Sheet

Marilyn Monroe (1926-62), Actress — A615

Various portraits.

2007, Mar. 1
2451 A615 $50 Sheet of 4, #a-
   d   12.00   12.00

Pres. John F. Kennedy (1917-62) — A616

No. 2452, $45: a, Signing executive order establishing the Peace Corps. b, With Sargent Shriver. c, Peace Corps volunteers in Tanganyika. d, Jack Hood Vaughn, second director of Peace Corps.

No. 2453, $45 — Kennedy: a, And Eleanor Roosevelt. b, Delivering Alliance for Progress speech. c, With Mrs. Kennedy in Venezuela. d, And Secretary of State Dean Rusk.

2007, Mar. 1   **Litho.**
Sheets of 4, #a-d
2452-2453 A616   Set of 2   20.00   20.00

Mushrooms A617

Designs: $25, Boletus edulis. $35, Begriipt russula. No. 2456, $45, Lactarius helvus. $50, Amanita pantherina.

No. 2458, $45: a, Russula cyanoxantha. b, Cantharellus subalbidus. c, Leccinum oxydalile. d, Boletus badius.

No. 2459, $45: a, Amanita bingensis. b, Chlorophyllum molybdites. c, Calvatia utriformis. d, Amanita loosii.

No. 2460, $100, Amanita muscaria. No. 2461, $100, Chlorophyllum molybdites, diff. No. 2462, $100, Agaricus silvaticus.

2007, Mar. 1

| 2454-2457 | A617 | Set of 4 | 9.00 | 9.00 |

Sheets of 4, #a-d

| 2458-2459 | A617 | Set of 2 | 20.00 | 20.00 |

Souvenir Sheets

| 2460-2462 | A617 | Set of 3 | 18.00 | 18.00 |

Scouting, Cent. A618

Designs: $50, Scouts and 2006 World Jamboree emblem. $150, Scouts, horiz.

2007, Mar. 15

| 2463 | A618 | $50 multi | 3.00 | 3.00 |

Souvenir Sheet

| 2464 | A618 | $150 multi | 9.00 | 9.00 |

No. 2463 was printed in sheets of 4.

Pope Benedict XVI — A619

2007, Nov. 30　　Litho.　　Perf. 13¼

| 2465 | A619 | $30 multi | 1.75 | 1.75 |

Miniature Sheet

New Year 2007 (Year of the Boar) — A620

No. 2466 — Wild Boar, by Liu Jiyou with text "Year of the Boar" in: a, Red. b, Green. c, Brown. d, Blue.

2007, Nov. 30

| 2466 | A620 | $30 Sheet of 4, #a-d | 7.00 | 7.00 |

Miniature Sheet

Wedding of Queen Elizabeth II and Prince Philip, 60th Anniv. — A621

No. 2467: a, Couple, denomination in white. b, Queen, denomination in yellow. c, Couple, denomination in lilac. d, Queen, denomination in white. e, Couple, denomination in yellow. f, Queen, denomination in lilac.

2007, Nov. 30

| 2467 | A621 | $35 Sheet of 6, #a-f | 12.00 | 12.00 |

Princess Diana (1961-97) — A622

No. 2468 — Various depictions of Diana with denomination in: a, Red violet. b, Blue. c, Green. d, Red. $125, Red denomination.

2007, Nov. 30

| 2468 | A622 | $45 Sheet of 4, #a-d | 10.00 | 10.00 |

Souvenir Sheet

| 2469 | A622 | $125 multi | 7.50 | 7.50 |

Souvenir Sheets

Pres. Ellen Johnson-Sirleaf and Foreign Dignitaries — A623

Pres. Johnson-Sirleaf meeting with: No. 2470, $100, Chinese Pres. Hu Jintao. No. 2471, $100, U.S. Pres. George W. Bush.

2007, Nov. 30

| 2470-2471 | A623 | Set of 2 | 12.00 | 12.00 |

Miniature Sheet

Elvis Presley (1935-77) — A624

No. 2472 — Presley: a, Wearing red and white sweater, country name in white. b, Holding guitar, country name in blue. c, Wearing cap, country name in white. d, Holding guitar, country name in purple. e, Wearing cap, country name in red violet. f, Wearing red and white sweater, country name in yellow.

2007, Nov. 30

| 2472 | A624 | $35 Sheet of 6, #a-f | 12.00 | 12.00 |

Souvenir Sheet

Japanese Prime Minister Junchiro Koizumi, U.S. Pres. George W. Bush and Wife at Graceland — A625

2007, Nov. 30

| 2473 | A625 | $100 multi | 6.00 | 6.00 |

New Year 2008 (Year of the Rat) A626

2007, Dec. 26　　Litho.　　Perf. 11½x12

| 2474 | A626 | $25 multi | 1.50 | 1.50 |

Printed in sheets of 4.

Birds — A627

Designs: $20, Pin-tailed whydahs. $30, Lesser honeyguides. $40, African jacanas. $50, Malachite sunbirds.

No. 2479, $45, horiz.: a, White-brown sparrow weavers. b, Parasitic weavers. c, Black-winged orioles. d, Crested guineafowl.

No. 2480, $45, horiz.: a, Red-billed francolins. b, Rufous-crowned rollers. c, African golden orioles. d, Black-crowned tchagras.

No. 2481, $100, Kori bustard. No. 2482, $100, Ostrich. No. 2483, $100, Great white pelican, horiz.

2007, Dec. 26　　　　　Perf. 14

| 2475-2478 | A627 | Set of 4 | 8.00 | 8.00 |

Sheets of 4, #a-d

| 2479-2480 | A627 | Set of 2 | 20.00 | 20.00 |

Souvenir Sheets

| 2481-2483 | A627 | Set of 3 | 18.00 | 18.00 |

Butterflies — A628

Designs: $20, Appias epaphia. $30, Papilio bromius. $40, Charaxes jasius. $50, Mimacraea marshalli dohertyi.

No. 2488, $45: a, Belenois thysa. b, Papilio pelodorus. c, Cymothoe sangaris. d, Colotis aurigineus.

No. 2489, $45: a, Junonia hierta. b, Myrina silenus. c, Byblia ilithyia. d, Argyrogrammana attsonii.

No. 2490, $100, Iolaus menas. No. 2491, $100, Leptomyrina hirundo. No. 2492, $100, Pinacopteryx eriphia.

2007, Dec. 26

| 2484-2487 | A628 | Set of 4 | 8.00 | 8.00 |

Sheets of 4, #a-d

| 2488-2489 | A628 | Set of 2 | 20.00 | 20.00 |

Souvenir Sheets

| 2490-2492 | A628 | Set of 3 | 18.00 | 18.00 |

Orchids — A629

Designs: $20, Neobenthamia gracilis. $30, Eulophia guineensis. $40, Aerangis curnowiana. $50, Cymbidiella pardalina.

No. 2497, $45: a, Ophrys lutea. b, Ophrys holoserica. c, Ophrys fusca. d, Ophrys scolopax.

No. 2498, $45: a, Disa veitchii. b, Disa racemosa. c, Disa kewensis. d, Disa diores.

No. 2499, $100, Disa crassicornis. No. 2500, $100, Aerangis citrata. No. 2501, $100, Angraecum sororium.

2007, Dec. 26

| 2493-2496 | A629 | Set of 4 | 8.00 | 8.00 |

Sheets of 4, #a-d

| 2497-2498 | A629 | Set of 2 | 20.00 | 20.00 |

Souvenir Sheets

| 2499-2501 | A629 | Set of 3 | 18.00 | 18.00 |

Christmas A630

Designs: $30, Madonna and Child. $40, Holy Family. $45, Flight into Egypt. $50, The Three Magi, horiz.

2007, Dec. 26　　Perf. 14x14¾, 14¾x14

| 2502-2505 | A630 | Set of 4 | 10.00 | 10.00 |

Miniature Sheet

2008 Summer Olympics, Beijing — A631

No. 2506: a, Babe Didrikson. b, 1932 Summer Olympics poster. c, Helene Madison. d, Chuhei Nambu.

2008, Apr. 8　　　　　Perf. 12¾

| 2506 | A631 | $30 Sheet of 4, #a-d | 7.00 | 7.00 |

National Basketball Association Players — A632

No. 2507 — NBA and Boston Celtics emblems and Kevin Garnett: a, Wearing white uniform, not holding basketball. b, Wearing green uniform. c, Wearing white uniform, holding basketball.

No. 2508 — NBA and Boston Celtics emblems and Paul Pierce: a, Wearing white uniform, hands at side. b, Wearing green uniform. c, Wearing white uniform, pointing.

No. 2509 — NBA and Washington Wizards emblems and Gilbert Arenas: a, Wearing white uniform, hands on hips. b, Wearing blue uniform. c, Wearing white uniform, with basketball.

No. 2510 — NBA and Milwaukee Bucks emblems and Yi Jianlian: a, Wearing white uniform, basketball at left. b, Wearing blue green uniform. c, Wearing white uniform, basketball at right.

2008, Apr. 30   **Perf. 13½x13¼**

2507		Vert. strip of 3	7.00	7.00
a.-c.	A632	$40 Any single	1.25	1.25
2508		Vert. strip of 3	7.00	7.00
a.-c.	A632	$40 Any single	1.25	1.25
2509		Vert. strip of 3	7.00	7.00
a.-c.	A632	$40 Any single	1.25	1.25
2510		Vert. strip of 3	7.00	7.00
a.-c.	A632	$40 Any single	1.25	1.25
		Nos. 2507-2510 (4)	28.00	28.00

Nos. 2507-2510 each printed in sheets of 6 containing 2 of each stamp in strip.

Souvenir Sheet

Meeting of Liberian Pres. Ellen Johnson-Sirleaf and US Pres. George W. Bush. — A633

No. 2511: a, Pres. Bush. b, Pres. Johnson-Sirleaf.

2008, June 12   **Perf. 13¼**

2511	A633	$125 Sheet of 2, #a-b	12.00	12.00

Elvis Presley (1935-77) — A634

No. 2512: a, Presley: a, Holding microphone, red background. b, Holding microphone, "Elvis" in lights. c, Holding microphone, blue background. d, Wearing glasses.

2008, June 12   **Perf. 13¼**

2512	A634	$60 Sheet of 4, #a-d	12.00	12.00

Space Achievements — A635

No. 2513, $40 — International Space Station with denomination at: a, UR. b, UL. c, LR.

No. 2514, $40 — Chandra X-ray Observatory: a, Observatory below nebula. b, Interior of Observatory. c, Observatory above nebula.

No. 2515: a, Calisto, Europa, Voyager I, Jupiter and Io. b, Lift-off of Voyager I. c, Voyager I record cover. d, Voyager I, Titan and Saturn.

No. 2516, $150, International Space Station, horiz. No. 2517, $150, Chandra X-ray Observatory, horiz. No. 2518, $150, Voyager I and rings of Saturn, horiz.

Illustration reduced.

2008, June 12   **Perf. 13¼**
Horiz. Strips of 3, #a-c

2513-2514	A635	Set of 2	18.00	18.00

Miniature Sheet

2515	A635	$60 Sheet of 4, #a-d	18.00	18.00

Souvenir Sheets

2516-2518	A635	Set of 3	24.00	24.00

Nos. 2513-2514 were each printed in sheets of 6 containing 2 of each stamp in strip.

Pope Benedict XVI — A636

2008, June 30   **Litho.**

2519	A636	$45 multi	2.00	2.00

Printed in sheets of 4.

County Flags A637

Flag of: No. 2520, $10, Maryland County. No. 2521, $10, Montserrado County. No. 2522, $25, Gbarpolu County. No. 2523, $25, Grand Bassa County. No. 2524, $30, Grand Cape Mount County. No. 2525, $30, Nimba County. No. 2526, $40, Lofa County. No. 2527, $40, Sinoe County. No. 2528, $50, Bong County. No. 2529, $50, Margibi County. No. 2530, $100, Bomi County. No. 2531, $100, Grand Gedeh County. No. 2532, $100, Grand Kru County. No. 2533, $100, River Cess County. No. 2534, $100, River Gee County.

2008, June 30

2520-2534	A637	Set of 15	26.00	26.00

Miniature Sheet

Ferrari F2008 — A638

No. 2535: a, "F" under "E" of "Liberia." b, "F" under "B" of Liberia. c, Side view of car. d, Car straddling yellow line on track.

2008, Sept. 5   **Litho.**   **Perf. 13½**

2535	A638	$60 Sheet of 4, #a-d	12.00	12.00

A639

Election of Barack Obama as US President — A640

Inscriptions: No. 2537, Joseph Biden. No. 2539a, Joseph Robinette Biden, Jr. No. 2539B: c, Barack Obama. d, Joseph Biden.

Perf. 14¼x14¾, 12¼x11¾ (#2538)
2008, Nov. 5

2536	A639	$45 shown	1.50	1.50
2537	A639	$45 multi	1.50	1.50
2538	A640	$65 shown	2.10	2.10
		Nos. 2536-2538 (3)	5.10	5.10

Souvenir Sheet

2539		Sheet of 2, #2536, 2539a	3.00	3.00
a.	A639	$45 multi	1.50	1.50
2539B		Sheet of 2	17.00	17.00
c.-d.	A639	$160 Either single	8.50	8.50

No. 2536 was printed in sheets of 9 and in No. 2539. No. 2537 was printed in sheets of 9. No. 2538 was printed in sheets of 4.

A641

Solo Aerial Circumnavigation of the World by Wiley Post, 75th Anniv. — A642

No. 2540: a, Post arriving in Cleveland. b, Harold Gatty, navigator. c, Post wearing pressure suit. d, Post atop plane. e, Post and wife Mae. f, The Winnie Mae.

$100, Post and map of flight.

2008, Nov. 24   **Perf. 13¼**

2540	A641	$40 Sheet of 6, #a-f	12.00	12.00

Souvenir Sheet

2541	A642	$100 multi	6.00	6.00

Christmas A643

Paintings: $10, The Nativity, by Martin Schongauer. $25, Birth of Christ, by Robert Campin. $30, Adoration of the Magi, by Geertgen tot Sint Jans. $40, The Birth of Christ, by Sandro Botticelli.

2008, Dec. 1   **Litho.**   **Perf. 14¼x14¾**

2542-2545	A643	Set of 4	3.50	3.50

New Year 2009 (Year of the Ox) A644

2009, Jan. 2   **Perf. 12**

2546	A644	$60 multi	1.90	1.90

Printed in sheets of 4.

Blindness A645

Designs: $10, Blind student reading Braille. $30, Blind man in crosswalk. $45, Blind man, map of Liberia. $100, Sighted man leading blind man.

2009, Jan. 4   **Perf. 14¾x14¼**

2547-2550	A645	Set of 4	5.75	5.75

Miniature Sheets

Star Trek — A646

No. 2551: a, Captain Kirk. b, USS Enterprise. c, Scotty. d, Uhura. e, Spock. f, Spock, Rand and Kirk.

No. 2552: a, Scotty. b, Spock and Kirk. c, Dr. McCoy. d, Sulu.

2009, Jan. 14   **Perf. 11½**

2551	A646	$35 Sheet of 6, #a-f	6.75	6.75

     Perf. 13½x13¼

2552	A646	$60 Sheet of 4, #a-d	7.50	7.50

No. 2552 contains four 38x51mm stamps.

Miniature Sheet

Abraham Lincoln (1809-65), US President — A647

No. 2553: a, US #1282. b, US #555. c, US #367. d, US #222.

2009, Feb. 2   *Perf. 13¼x13½*
2553 A647 $60 Sheet of 4, #a-d   7.50 7.50

Miniature Sheet

John F. Kennedy (1917-63), US President — A648

No. 2554 — Kennedy: a, Greeting Cuban-exile Bay of Pigs invasion force, with wife Jackie, shaking hand. b, Standing with Jackie. c, In White House. d, With Jackie at stadium.

2009, Feb. 25   *Perf. 11¼x11½*
2554 A648 $50 Sheet of 4, #a-d   6.25 6.25

A649

Peonies — A650

No. 2556: a, White peony, tan background. b, Pink peony, white background.

2009, Apr. 10   *Perf. 13¼*
2555 A649 $32 multi   1.00 1.00
Souvenir Sheet
2556 A650 $65 Sheet of 2, #a-b   4.00 4.00
No. 2555 was printed in sheets of 6.

Miniature Sheets

A651

A652

China 2009 World Stamp Exhibition, Luoyang — A653

No. 2557: a, Panda, Chengdu. b, West Lake, Hangzhou. c, Bonsai Garden, Suzhou. d, Fuzi Miao and Qinhuai River, Nanjing.
No. 2558: a, Ornamental plaque (770-476 B.C.). b, Vessel (206 B.C.-A.D. 8). c, Covered jar (1279-1368). d, Head of a Bodhisattva (618-907).
No. 2559: a, Wheel of mountain bike. b, Hand holding tennis racquet. c, Hand holding water polo ball. d, Hand holding handball.

2009, Apr. 10   *Perf. 12½*
2557 A651 $35 Sheet of 4, #a-d   4.50 4.50
Perf. 12
2558 A652 $35 Sheet of 4, #a-d   4.50 4.50
2559 A653 $35 Sheet of 4, #a-d   4.50 4.50
Nos. 2557-2559 (3)   13.50 13.50

Pope Benedict XVI — A654

2009, May 4   *Perf. 11¼x11½*
2560 A654 $60 multi   1.75 1.75
Printed in sheets of 4.

Miniature Sheet

Felix Mendelssohn (1809-47), Composer — A655

No. 2561: a, Portrait of young Mendelssohn, by Carl Begas. b, Fanny Mendelssohn, sister of Felix. c, Mendelssohn's sketch of Thomasschule, Leipzig. d, Leipzig Conservatory. e, Portrait of Mendelssohn, by James Warren Childe. f, Mendelssohn drawing made during visit to Scotland.

2009, May 4   *Perf. 11¼x11½*
2561 A655 $50 Sheet of 6, #a-f   8.75 8.75

A656

A657

A658

A659

Elvis Presley (1935-77) — A660

No. 2562 — Background color: a, Red brown. b, Tan. c, Gray green. d, Black.

2009, May 4   *Perf. 13¼*
2562 A656 $65 Sheet of 4, #a-d   7.50 7.50
Souvenir Sheets
Perf. 14¼
2563 A657 $160 multi   4.75 4.75
2564 A658 $160 multi   4.75 4.75
2565 A659 $160 multi   4.75 4.75
2566 A660 $160 multi   4.75 4.75
Nos. 2563-2566 (4)   19.00 19.00

US Presidents — A661

No. 2567, $20, vert.: a, George Washington. b, John Adams. c, Thomas Jefferson. d, James Madison. e, James Monroe. f, John Quincy Adams. g, Andrew Jackson. h, Martin Van Buren. i, William Henry Harrison. j, John Tyler. k, James K. Polk. l, Zachary Taylor. m, Millard Fillmore. n, Franklin Pierce. o, James Buchanan.
No. 2568, $20, vert.: a, Abraham Lincoln. b, Andrew Johnson. c, Ulysses S. Grant. d, Rutherford B. Hayes. e, James A. Garfield. f, Chester A. Arthur. g, Grover Cleveland (1885-89). h, Benjamin Harrison. i, Grover Cleveland (1893-97). j, William McKinley. k, Theodore Roosevelt. l, William Howard Taft. m, Woodrow Wilson. n, Warren G. Harding. o, Calvin Coolidge.
No. 2569, $20, vert.: a, Herbert Hoover. b, Franklin D. Roosevelt. c, Harry S Truman. d, Dwight D. Eisenhower. e, John F. Kennedy. f, Lyndon B. Johnson. g, Richard M. Nixon. h, Gerald R. Ford. i, Jimmy Carter. j, Ronald Reagan. k, George H. W. Bush (1989-93). l, William J. Clinton. m, George W. Bush (2001-09). n, Barack H. Obama. o, Presidential seal.
$320, Barack Obama.

2009, May 4   *Perf. 13¼*
Sheets of 15, #a-o
2567-2569 A661 Set of 3   26.00 26.00
2568p   Sheet of 9 #2568a   5.25 5.25
2569p   Miniature sheet, #2569o, 14 #2569n   8.50 8.50
Souvenir Sheet
Perf. 14¼
2570 A661 $320 multi   9.25 9.25
Nos. 2567-2569 each contain fifteen 28x42mm stamps. Issued: No. 2568p, 3/23/10. 2569p, 9/4.

Famous People — A662

Designs: No. 2571, $50, Madame Suakoko (1816-1927), first female paramount chief. No. 2572, $50, Chief Flomo Doughba Barwulor.

2009, Aug. 2 Litho. *Perf. 11¼x11½*
2571-2572 A662 Set of 2   2.75 2.75

Masks — A663

Designs: $10, Korkpor mask. $25, Landa mask. $35, Borwhoo mask. $45, Zoba mask. $100, Kote mask.

2009, Aug. 2			*Perf. 13¼*	
2573-2577	A663	Set of 5	6.00	6.00

Dance — A664

Designs: $30, Traditional dancers. $40, Traditional dancers, diff. $45, Poro dancers.

2009, Aug. 2				
2578-2580	A664	Set of 3	3.25	3.25

Souvenir Sheet

Monkey Bridge — A665

2009, Aug. 2				
2581	A665	$100 multi	2.75	2.75

Miniature Sheets

Players in 2009 National Basketball Association All-Star Game — A666

No. 2582, $30 — Eastern All-stars: a, Ray Allen. b, Kevin Garnett. c, Danny Granger. d, Devin Harris. e, Dwight Howard. f, Allen Iverson. g, LeBron James. h, Joe Johnson. i, Rashard Lewis. j, Paul Pierce. k, Dwayne Wade. l, Mo Williams.

No. 2583, $30 — Western All-stars: a, Chauncey Billups. b, Kobe Bryant. c, Tim Duncan. d, Pau Gasol. e, Yao Ming. f, Dirk Nowitzki. g, Shaquille O'Neal. h, Tony Parker. i, Chris Paul. j, Brandon Roy. k, Amar'e Stoudemire. l, David West.

2009, Aug. 2	*Perf. 11¼x11½*	
Sheets of 12, #a-l		
2582-2583	A666	Set of 2	20.00	20.00

Liberian Presidents — A667

Designs: $10, Ellen Johnson-Sirleaf. $25, Moses Z. Blah. $35, Charles M.G. Taylor. $45, Samuel K. Doe. $50, William Richard Tolbert. $70, William V.S. Tubman.

Nos. 2590, 2611, Joseph Jenkins Roberts. Nos. 2591, 2612, Stepehen Allen Benson. Nos. 2592, 2613, Daniel Bashiel Warner. Nos. 2593, 2614, James Spriggs Payne. Nos. 2594, 2615, Edward James Roye. Nos. 2595, 2616, Anthony Williams Gardiner. Nos. 2596, 2617, Alfred Francis Russell. Nos. 2597, 2618, Hilary R.W. Johnson. Nos. 2598, 2619, Joseph James Cheeseman. Nos. 2599, 2620, William David Coleman. Nos. 2600, 2621, Garretson W. Gibson. Nos. 2601, 2622, Arthur Barclay. Nos. 2602, 2623, Daniel E. Howard. Nos. 2603, 2624, Charles D.B. King. Nos. 2604, 2625, Edwin James Barclay. No. 2605, Tubman. No. 2606, Tolbert. No. 2607, Doe. No. 2608, Taylor. No. 2609, Blah. No. 2610, Johnson-Sirleaf.

2009, Aug. 22			*Perf. 12¾*	
2584	A667	$10 multi	.30	.30
2585	A667	$25 multi	.70	.70
2586	A667	$35 multi	1.00	1.00
2587	A667	$45 multi	1.25	1.25
2588	A667	$50 multi	1.40	1.40
2589	A667	$70 multi	2.00	2.00
2590	A667	$100 multi	2.75	2.75
2591	A667	$100 multi	2.75	2.75
2592	A667	$100 multi	2.75	2.75
2593	A667	$100 multi	2.75	2.75
2594	A667	$100 multi	2.75	2.75
2595	A667	$100 multi	2.75	2.75
2596	A667	$100 multi	2.75	2.75
2597	A667	$100 multi	2.75	2.75
2598	A667	$100 multi	2.75	2.75
2599	A667	$100 multi	2.75	2.75
2600	A667	$100 multi	2.75	2.75
2601	A667	$100 multi	2.75	2.75
2602	A667	$100 multi	2.75	2.75
2603	A667	$100 multi	2.75	2.75
2604	A667	$100 multi	2.75	2.75
2605	A667	$100 multi	2.75	2.75
2606	A667	$100 multi	2.75	2.75
2607	A667	$100 multi	2.75	2.75
2608	A667	$100 multi	2.75	2.75
2609	A667	$100 multi	2.75	2.75
2610	A667	$100 multi	2.75	2.75
2611	A667	$500 multi	14.00	14.00
2612	A007	$500 multi	14.00	14.00
2613	A667	$500 multi	14.00	14.00
2614	A667	$500 multi	14.00	14.00
2615	A667	$500 multi	14.00	14.00
2616	A667	$500 multi	14.00	14.00
2617	A667	$500 multi	14.00	14.00
2618	A667	$500 multi	14.00	14.00
2619	A667	$500 multi	14.00	14.00
2620	A667	$500 multi	14.00	14.00
2621	A667	$500 multi	14.00	14.00
2622	A667	$500 multi	14.00	14.00
2623	A667	$500 multi	14.00	14.00
2624	A667	$500 multi	14.00	14.00
2625	A667	$500 multi	14.00	14.00
Nos. 2584-2625 (42)			274.40	274.40

Chinese Aviation, Cent. — A668

No. 2626: a, H-2 missiles. b, H-2B missiles. c, H-12 missiles on trucks. d, H-12 missiles on truck.
$150, H-9 missiles.

2009, Nov. 12			*Perf. 14*	
2626	A668	$50 Sheet of 4, #a-d	6.00	6.00
Souvenir Sheet				
Perf. 14¼				
2627	A668	$150 multi	4.50	4.50

No. 2626 contains four 42x32mm stamps.

Miniature Sheet

Charles Darwin (1809-82), Naturalist — A669

No. 2628: a, Rhea darwinii. b, Proctotretus fitzingerii. c, Vespertilio chiloensis. d, Geospiza fortis.

2009, Dec. 10			*Perf. 12x11½*	
2628	A669	$60 Sheet of 4, #a-d	7.50	7.50

Miniature Sheet

The Three Stooges — A670

No. 2629: a, Stooges with open book. b, Moe sticking drill into Curly's mouth. c, Stooges at table looking at book. d, Curly pointing stick at man.

2009, Dec. 10			*Perf. 11½x12*	
2629	A670	$60 Sheet of 4, #a-d	7.50	7.50

Miniature Sheet

Pres. John F. Kennedy and Wife, Jacqueline — A671

No. 2630: a, Pres. Kennedy with Jacqueline, wearing cape. b, Pres. Kennedy. c, Pres. Kennedy with Jacqueline in limousine. d, Jacqueline Kennedy and crowd. e, Pres. Kennedy and wife (Jacqueline holding arm of husband). f, Jacqueline Kennedy.

2009, Dec. 10			*Perf. 11¼x11½*	
2630	A671	$60 Sheet of 6, #a-f	11.00	11.00

Intl. Year of Astronomy — A672

No. 2631, horiz.: a, Sergei Korolev and Luna 9. b, Luna 9 horizontal on transporter. c, Lift-off of Luna 9. d, Luna 9 over Moon. e, Luna 9 open, with antennae erect. f, Luna 9 open, antennae not erect.
$160, Lift-off of Apollo 11.

2009, Dec. 10			*Perf. 13½*	
2631	A672	$40 Sheet of 6, #a-f	7.50	7.50
Souvenir Sheet				
2632	A672	$160 multi	5.00	5.00

Nos. 2631a, 2631b and 2631d have country name misspelled as "Libeira."

Christmas — A673

Paintings: $25, Nativity (Holy Night), by Correggio. $40, Adoration of the Magi, by Bartolomé Esteban Murillo. $50, Adoration of the Magi, by Vicente Gil. $100, Adoration of the Magi, by Peter Paul Rubens.

2009, Dec. 10			*Perf. 13¼x13*	
2633-2636	A673	Set of 4	6.50	6.50

Miniature Sheet

Awarding of Nobel Peace Prize to US Pres. Barack Obama — A674

No. 2637 — Pres. Obama wearing: a, Red tie, facing right. b, Red tie, facing forward. c, Blue tie, facing forward. d, Blue tie, facing left.

2009, Dec. 30	Litho.		*Perf. 12x11½*	
2637	A674	$60 Sheet of 4, #a-d	7.00	7.00

628 LIBERIA

Miniature Sheet

Chinese Zodiac Animals — A675

No. 2638: a, Dragon. b, Snake. c, Horse. d, Goat. e, Monkey. f, Rooster. g, Dog. h, Pig. i, Rat. j, Ox. k, Tiger. l, Rabbit.

2010, Jan. 4   **Perf. 12½**
2638 A675 $15 Sheet of 12, #a-l   6.00 6.00

Souvenir Sheet

New Year 2010 (Year of the Tiger) — A676

No. 2639: a, Tiger. b, Tiger and Chinese characters.

2010, Jan. 4   **Perf. 14¾x14¼**
2639 A676 $130 Sheet of 2, #a-b   7.50 7.50

Miniature Sheets

Dogs — A677

No. 2640, $65 — German shorthaired pointer: a, At duckpond. b, With trees and building in background. c, On rocks. d, Sniffing flowers.
No. 2641, $65 — Chihuahua: a, On pink dog bed. b, Standing. c, At pond. d, In small pot.

2010, Jan. 19   **Perf. 11½x12**
Sheets of 4, #a-d
2640-2641 A677   Set of 2   15.00 15.00

Miniature Sheets

A678

Visit of Pope Benedict XVI to Great Synagogue of Rome — A679

No. 2642: a, Great Synagogue. b, Pope Benedict XVI and Rome's Chief Rabbi Riccardo Di Segni. c, Pope Benedict XVI and Cardinal. d, Rabbi Di Segni and man wearing white yarmulke.
No. 2643: a, Pope Benedict XVI and Rabbi Di Segni seated. b, Rome's former Chief Rabbi Elio Toaff. c, Pope Benedixt XVI, standing and reaching for Toaff. d, Pope Benedict XVI with hands clasped.

2010, Mar. 23   **Perf. 12x11½**
2642 A678 $110 Sheet of 4, #a-d   12.50 12.50
    Perf. 11½
2643 A679 $110 Sheet of 4, #a-d   12.50 12.50

Miniature Sheets

Boy Scouts of America, Cent. — A680

No. 2644, $55 — Merit badges: a, Swimming, First Aid. b, Environmental Science, Family Life. c, Citizenship in the Community, Personal Management. d, Camping, Lifesaving. e, Citizenship in the Nation, Communications. f, Personal Fitness, Citizenship in the World.
No. 2645, $55 — Merit badges: a, Aviation, Fishing. b, Engineering, Electronics. c, Medicine, Music. d, Graphic Arts, Soil and Water Conservation. e, Cinematography, Oceanography. f, Animal Science, Art.

2010, Mar. 23   **Perf. 13¼**
Sheets of 6, #a-f
2644-2645 A680   Set of 2   19.00 19.00

Whales and Dolphins — A681

No. 2646: a, Harbor porpoise. b, Killer whale. c, Sowerby's beaked whale. d, Atlantic spotted dolphin. e, Atlantic hump-backed dolphin. f, Clymene dolphin.
$180, Gervais beaked whale.

2010, Apr. 26   **Perf. 14¾x14¼**
2646 A681 $60 Sheet of 6, #a-f   10.50 10.50
    Souvenir Sheet
2647 A681 $180 multi   5.25 5.25

US Pres. Barack Obama and Wife, Michelle — A682

No. 2648: a, Pres. Obama. b, Pres Obama with arm around wife's waist. c, Pres. Obama and wife dancing. d, Michelle Obama.
No. 2649, Head of Michelle Obama. No. 2650, Michelle Obama (30x81mm).

2010, Apr. 26   **Perf. 14¼x14¾**
2648 A682 $60 Sheet of 4, #a-d 7.00 7.00
    Souvenir Sheets
2649 A682 $100 multi   3.00 3.00
2650 A682 $100 multi   3.00 3.00

Miniature Sheets

A683

Pres. Abraham Lincoln (1809-65) — A684

No. 2651, $80 — Lincoln: a, Facing right, hand visible at LR. b, Facing left. c, Facing right, no hand visible. d, Facing right, hand visible at center bottom.
No. 2652, $80 — Lincoln: a, Photograph without hat. b, Photograph with hat. c, Lincoln Memorial sculpture. d, Mount Rushmore sculpture.

2010, June 25   **Perf. 12x11½**
2651 A683 $80 Sheet of 4, #a-d 9.00 9.00
2652 A684 $80 Sheet of 4, #a-d 9.00 9.00

Girl Guides, Cent. — A685

No. 2653, horiz.: a, Three Girl Guides, one wearing cap. b, Three Girl Guides wearing neckerchiefs. c, Three Girl Guides. d, Five Girl Guides in uniform.
$160, Girl Guide wearing cap.

2010, June 25   **Perf. 13x13¼**
2653 A685 $65 Sheet of 4, #a-d 7.25 7.25
    Souvenir Sheet
    Perf. 13¼x13
2654 A685 $160 multi   4.50 4.50

Lech Kaczynski (1949-2010), President of Poland — A686

2010, Aug. 27   **Perf. 11½**
2655 A686 $75 multi   2.10 2.10
Printed in sheets of 4.

Paintings by Michelangelo Merisi da
Caravaggio (1573-1610) — A687

No. 2656, horiz.: a, The Beheading of St.
John the Baptist. b, Judith Beheading Holofernes. c, Abraham's Sacrifice. d, Medusa.
$180, The Penitent Mary Magdalene.

2010, Aug. 27   **Perf. 11½x11¼**
2656 A687 $80 Sheet of 4, #a-d 9.00 9.00
        Souvenir Sheet
        Perf. 11¼x11½
2657 A687 $180 multi 5.25 5.25

Henri Dunant (1828-1910), Founder of
the Red Cross — A688

No. 2658 — Red Cross, Florence Nighting-
gale, depictions of war casualties and nurses,
and portrait of Dunant in: a, Gray green. b,
Brown. c, Purple. d, Gray blue.
$180, Red Cross, Nightingale, war casual-
ties at Red Cross station, Dunant in purple.

2010, Aug. 27   **Perf. 11½x12**
2658 A688 $80 Sheet of 4, #a-d 9.00 9.00
        Souvenir Sheet
        Perf. 11½x11¼
2659 A688 $180 multi 5.25 5.25

Miniature Sheets

A689

A690

Princess Diana (1961-97) — A691

No. 2660 — Princess Diana with: a, Bare
shoulders and single-stand pearl necklace. b,
Pink and white hat. c, White dress, earrings,
no hat. d, White hat, dark blue and white
dress.
No. 2661 — Princess Diana with: a, Tiara.
b, Pink hat and dress. c, Green sweater, white
blouse. d, Red and white jacket, white blouse.
No. 2662 — Princess Diana with: a, Red
dress and flower bouquet. b, White dress,
pendant earrings, no hat. c, Bare shoulders
and multi-strand pearl necklace. d, White
dress, pearl necklace, no hat.

2010, Aug. 27   **Perf. 13¼**
2660 A689 $75 Sheet of 4, #a-
     d 8.50 8.50
2661 A690 $75 Sheet of 4, #a-
     d 8.50 8.50
2662 A691 $75 Sheet of 4, #a-
     d 8.50 8.50
  Nos. 2660-2662 (3) 25.50 25.50

Miniature Sheets

A692

A693

Elvis Presley (1935-77) — A694

No. 2663 — Presley: a, With hands pointing
left. b, Holding microphone. c, With guitar,
holding microphone.
No. 2664 — Paintings of Presley with backgrounds of: a, Green and black. b, Orange and
bister. c, Black and red.
No. 2665: a, Presley's face in orange and
yellow. b, Presley's face in light blue and

white. c, Presley's face in blue and gray. d,
Silhouette of Presley.

2010, Aug. 27   **Perf. 11½x11¼**
2663 A692 $90 Sheet of 3, #a-
     c 7.75 7.75
        Perf. 11¼x11½
2664 A693 $90 Sheet of 3, #a-
     c 7.75 7.75
        Perf. 13
2665 A694 $90 Sheet of 4, #a-
     d 10.00 10.00
  Nos. 2663-2665 (3) 25.50 25.50

Cats — A695

No. 2666, vert.: a, Siberian. b, Turkish
Angora. c, British shorthair. d, Maine coon. e,
Abyssinian. f, Scottish fold.
$180, Bluepoint Himalayan.

2010, Oct. 27   **Perf. 11¼x11½**
2666 A695 $60 Sheet of 6,
     #a-f 10.50 10.50
        Souvenir Sheet
        Perf. 11½x11¼
2667 A695 $180 multi 5.25 5.25
Nos. 2666-2667 exist imperf. Value, set $25.

Miniature Sheets

Pres. John F. Kennedy (1917-
63) — A696

No. 2668, $80 — Olive bister frames with
Kennedy: a, Walking with Vice-president Lyndon B. Johnson. b, On telephone. c, At lectern. d, Looking upwards.
No. 2669, $80 — Blue frames with Kennedy:
a, At lectern. b, Walking with McGeorge
Bundy. c, Campaigning in New York City. d,
With hands clasped.
No. 2670, $80 — Red frames with Kennedy:
a, With Dr. Wernher von Braun. b, With wife,
Jacqueline, watching space flight on television. c, At lectern. d, Viewing Friendship 7
space capsule.

2010, Oct. 27   **Perf. 12x11½**
        Sheets of 4, #a-d
2668-2670 A696 Set of 3 28.00 28.00

Christmas — A697

Paintings: $25, The Annunciation, by Fra
Angelico. $40, The Angelic Announcement to
the Shepherds, by Taddeo Gaddi. $50, Adora-
tion of the Shepherds, by Guido Reni. $100,
Virgin and Child with Angels and Saints, by
Felice Torelli.

2010, Oct. 27   **Litho.**   **Perf. 11½**
2671-2674 A697 Set of 4 6.25 6.25

Liberian
Politicians
A698

Designs: $25, Pres. Ellen Johnson-Sirleaf
receiving gift. $45, Pres. Johnson Sirleaf
standing with Chinese Pres. Hu Jintao, vert.
No. 2677, $50, Pres. Johnson-Sirleaf reading.
No. 2678, $50, Vice-president Joseph N.
Boakai. No. 2679, $100, Pres. Johnson-Sirleaf
sitting with Pres. Hu. No. 2680, $100, Pres.
Johnson-Sirleaf shaking hands with Vice-president Boakai. No. 2681, $100, Pres. Johnson-
Sirleaf wearing sash of office, vert. No. 2682,
$500, Pres. Johnson-Sirleaf meeting with
international investors. No. 2683, $500, Pres.
Johnson-Sirleaf with Vice-president Boakai
and cabinet.

2010, Dec. 16   **Perf. 12**
2675-2683 A698 Set of 9 5.00 5.00
Nos. 2675-2683 were sold to the philatelic
trade at prices well below that indicated by
currency exchange rates at the date of issue.

Mother Teresa
(1910-97),
Humanitarian
A699

Various photos with frame color of: No.
2684, $80, Olive bister. No. 2685, $80, Blue.

2010, Dec. 16
2684-2685 A699 Set of 2 4.50 4.50
Nos. 2684-2685 each were printed in sheets
of 4.

Pope John
Paul II
(1920-2005)
A700

No. 2686 — Red background: a, Without
crucifix. b, With crucifix.
No. 2687 — Purple background: a, With crucifix. b, Without crucifix.

2010, Dec. 16
2686 A700 $80 Pair, #a-b 4.50 4.50
2687 A700 $80 Horiz. pair, #a-b 4.50 4.50
Nos. 2686-2687 each were printed in sheets
containing two pairs.

Paintings of Sandro Botticelli (1455-
1510) — A701

No. 2688 — Details from The Birth of
Venus: a, Head of Venus. b, Reversed image
of torso of winged zephyrs. c, Reversed image
of heads of winged zephyrs. d, Nymph.
$160, Portrait of St. Augustine, vert.

2010, Dec. 16   **Perf. 12**
2688 A701 $80 Sheet of 4, #a-d   9.00 9.00

Souvenir Sheet
Perf. 12½x12¾
2689 A701 $160 multi   4.50 4.50
No. 2689 contains one 38x50mm stamp.

A702

Michael Jackson (1958-2009),
Singer — A703

No. 2690 — Jackson: a, With arched back,
holding microphone. b, Moving hat to cover
face. c, Wearing white glove and hat. d, With
arched back, arms stretched outward.
No. 2691 — Jackson: a, Wearing red shirt.
b, Holding microphone. c, With arm outstretched. d, With spotlights in background,
holding microphone.
$180, Jackson singing.

2010, Dec. 16   **Perf. 12**
2690 A702 $80 Sheet of 4, #a-d   9.00 9.00
2691 A703 $80 Sheet of 4, #a-d   9.00 9.00

Souvenir Sheet
2692 A703 $180 multi   5.00 5.00

Miniature Sheets

Mao Zedong (1893-1976), Chairman
of People's Republic of China — A704

Hu Jintao, President of People's
Republic of China — A705

No. 2693 — Mao: a, Without cap, no pockets shown on jacket. b, Wearing cap, pockets
shown on jacket. c, Without cap, pockets
shown on jacket. d, With cap, no pockets
shown on jacket.
No. 2694 — Pres. Hu: a, Ear at left visible,
tie over jacket. b, Both ears visible. c, Ear at
right visible. d, Ear at left visible, tie under
jacket.

2010, Nov. 7   Litho.   Perf. 12
2693 A704 $90 Sheet of 4,
                    #a-d   10.50 10.50
2694 A705 $90 Sheet of 4,
                    #a-d   10.50 10.50
Beijing 2010 Intl. Philatelic Exhibition.

Miniature Sheet

Anti-Apartheid Activists of South
Africa — A706

No. 2695: a, Helen Suzman (1917-2009). b,
Eli Weinberg (1908-81). c, Hymie Barsel
(1920-87). c, Esther Barsel (1924-2008), and
South African Pres. Nelson Mandela.

2011, Mar. 1
2695 A706 $75 Sheet of 4, #a-d   8.50 8.50

Chinese Zodiac Animals — A707

New Year 2011 (Year of the
Rabbit) — A708

No. 2696: a, Rat. b, Ox. c, Tiger. d, Rabbit.
e, Dragon. f, Snake. g, Horse. h, Sheep. i,
Monkey. j, Rooster. k, Dog. l, Pig.

2011, Mar. 28
2696 A707 $25 Sheet of 12, #a-l 8.50 8.50

Souvenir Sheet
2697 A708   Sheet of 2
                    #2697a   5.75 5.75
a. $100 Single stamp   2.75 2.75

British Monarchs
A709

Designs: No. 2698, $80, King George V
(1865-1936). No. 2699, $80, King Edward VIII
(1894-1972). No. 2700, $80, King George VI
(1895-1952). No. 2701, $80, Queen Elizabeth
II.

Perf. 13 Syncopated, 12 (#2700)
2011, Mar. 28
2698-2701 A709 Set of 4   9.00 9.00
Nos. 2698-2701 each were printed in sheets
of 4.

Princess Diana (1961-97) in
India — A710

No. 2702, vert. — Princess Diana: a, Greeting girl with hands together, red background.
b, Touching woman on cot, red background. c,
Talking with Mother Teresa, red background.
d, Shaking hands with seated man, purple
background. e, With woman and small boy,
purple background. f, At Taj Mahal, purple
background.

$360, Princess Diana talking with seated
people.

2011, Mar. 28   Perf. 13 Syncopated
2702 A710 $60 Sheet of 6,
                    #a-f   10.00 10.00

Souvenir Sheet
2703 A710 $360 multi   10.00 10.00
Indipex 2011 Intl. Philatelic Exhibition, New
Delhi.

Engagement of
Prince William
and Catherine
Middleton
A711

Deisgns: No. 2704, $65, Couple, dull green
background. No. 2705, $65, Couple, gray
background.
No. 2706, $100: a, Catherine Middleton. b,
Prince William.
No. 2707, $100, horiz.: a, Couple, Middleton
touching hat. b, Couple, Middleton not touching hat.

Perf. 12, 13 Syncopated (#2707)
2011, Mar. 28
2704-2705 A711 Set of 2   3.75 3.75

Sheets of 2, #a-b
2706-2707 A711 Set of 2   11.50 11.50

Pres. John F. Kennedy (1917-
63) — A712

No. 2708 — Kennedy: a, Oval portrait. b,
Close-up of head. c, Wearing patterned tie. d,
Wearing pinstripe suit and solid tie.
$180, Kennedy, diff.

2011, Mar. 28   **Perf. 12**
2708 A712 $80 Sheet of 4, #a-d   9.00 9.00

Souvenir Sheet
2709 A712 $180 multi   5.00 5.00

Miniature Sheets

U.S. Civil War, 150th Anniv. — A713

No. 2710, $80 — Lieutenant Colonel John
B. Baylor, Major Isaac Lynde and Battle of
Mesilla image: a, Town and valley of Mesilla. b,
Fort Fillmore. c, Confederates near the Organ
Mountains. d, Union soldiers firing at long
range.
No. 2711, $80 — Colonel Martin E. Green,
Colonel David Moore and Battle of Athens
image: a, Confederates near the Fabius River.
b, Col. Moore leads Union troops. c, Cavalries
clash at Athens encounter. d, Col. Green's
Missouri State Guard.
No. 2712, $80 — Major General Sterling
Price, Captain Nathaniel Lyon and Battle of

Wilson's Creek image: a, Missouri State Guardsmen on Bloody Hill. b, Confederate battery in action. c, Lt. Omar Weaver is wounded. d, 2nd Kansas Infantry on Bloody Hill.

No. 2713, $80 — Brigadier General John B. Floyd, Colonel Erastus Tyler and Battle of Kessler's Cross Lanes image: a, Confederate forces in the Kanawha Valley. b, 7th Ohio Regiment at Kessler's Cross Lanes. c, The Union forces surprised and routed. d, Confederate forces near the Gauley River.

No. 2714, $80 — Captain Samuel Barron, Major General Benjamin F. Butler and Battle of Hatteras Inlet image: a, Capture of Fort Hatteras. b, Union Atlantic blockading squadron. c, USS Harriet Lane. d, USS Cumberland.

2011, Mar. 28   Perf. 13 Syncopated
Sheets of 4, #a-d
2710-2714 A713   Set of 5   45.00 45.00

Mushrooms — A714

No. 2715: a, Penny bun. b, Ola'h. c, The miller. d, False ink cap. e, The blusher. f, Glistening ink cap.
No. 2716: a, Death cap. b, Panther cap.

2011, Mar. 28   Perf. 12
2715 A714 $65 Sheet of 6,
            #a-f   11.00 11.00
Souvenir Sheet
2716 A714 $65 Sheet of 2,
            #a-b   3.75 3.75

Birds — A715

No. 2717: a, Red-faced cisticola. b, Orange-cheeked waxbill. c, Zebra waxbill. d, African firefinch.
No. 2718, $180, Guinea turaco. No. 2719, $180, Lavender waxbill, vert.

Perf. 12, 13 Syncopated (#2718)
2011, Mar. 28
2717 A715 $80 Sheet of 4,
            #a-d   9.00 9.00
Souvenir Sheets
2718-2719 A715   Set of 2   10.00 10.00

Miniature Sheets

Zodiac Constellations — A716

No. 2720, $100: a, Aries. b, Leo. c, Sagittarius.
No. 2721, $100: a, Gemini. b, Libra. c, Aquarius.
No. 2722, $100: a, Cancer. b, Scorpio. c, Pisces.
No. 2723, $100: a, Virgo. b, Taurus. c, Capricorn.

2011, Mar. 28   Perf. 12
Sheets of 3, #a-c
2720-2723 A716   Set of 4   34.00 34.00

Souvenir Sheets

Pres. Ellen Johnson-Sirleaf — A717

Designs: $45, Pres. Johnson-Sirleaf and Chinese President Hu Jintao. No. 2725, $100, Pres. Johnson-Sirleaf. No. 2726, $100, Pres. Johnson-Sirleaf and Pres. Hu, horiz.

2011, Mar. 28   Perf. 13¼x13, 13x13¼
2724-2726 A717   Set of 3   7.00 7.00

Souvenir Sheets

Popes and Their Arms — A718

No. 2727, $250: a, Pope Pius XII (1876-1958). b, Arms of Pope Pius XII.
No. 2728, $250: a, Pope John XXIII (1881-1963). b, Arms of Pope John XXIII.

2011, Mar. 28   Imperf.
Sheets of 2, #a-b
Without Gum
2727-2728 A718   Set of 2   28.00 28.00

Visit of Chinese President Hu Jintao to Washington, D.C. — A719

No. 2729 — Presidents Hu Jintao and Barack Obama: a, Shaking hands. b, Standing near lectern. c, Greeting crowd. d, Walking outside of White House.
$180, Reviewing troops.

2011, Mar. 28   Litho.   Perf. 12
2729 A719 $75 Sheet of 4, #a-d 8.50 8.50
Souvenir Sheet
2730 A719 $180 multi   5.25 5.25

Back to the
Soil — A720

Inscriptions: $25, Invest in the Soil Rubber Farm. $45, Women scratching rice, horiz. $50, Rice nursery in Bong County. $70, The soil is a bank. $100, President Ellen Johnson-Sirleaf harvesting rice, horiz. No. 2736, $500, Fresh fruits and vegetables. No. 2737, $500, Harvesting rice, horiz.

Perf. 12¾x12½, 12½x12¾
2011, Mar. 28
2731-2737 A720   Set of 7   37.50 37.50

Worldwide Fund for Nature (WWF) — A721

No. 2738 — Water chevrotain: a, Standing in foliage. b, In water. c, Eating. d, Pair in foliage.

2011, June 30   Perf. 13¼
2738   Strip of 4   5.75 5.75
a.-d. A721 $50 Any single   1.40 1.40
e.   Souvenir sheet of 8, 2 each
     #2738a-2738d   11.50 11.50

Miniature Sheet

A.C. Milan Soccer Team — A722

No. 2739 — Team emblem and photographs of: a, 2003 UEFA Champions League match. b, Centennial emblem, 1999. c, 2001 6-0 A.C. Milan- Milan Inter match. d, Carlo Ancellotti. e, 2010-11 team. f, Paolo Maldini. g, 2007 UEFA Champions League match. h, Team members with 2007 FIFA Club World Cup. i, Team owner Italian Prime Minister Silvio Berlusconi.

2011, June 30   Perf. 13½
2739 A722 $35 Sheet of 9, #a-i   8.75 8.75

Miniature Sheets

A723

Chocolate Candy — A724

No. 2740: a, Cacao pods. b, Sun. c, Ship. d, Fires. e, Mound of cocoa powder. f, Milk and butter. g, Chocolate bar and wrapped candy. h, Cash register and chocolate bar. i, Mouth and chocolate bar.
No. 2741 — Piece of candy with: a, Chocolate coating with white chocolate swirls. b, Dark chocolate coating with walnut. c, White chocolate coating with dark chocolate swirls. d, White chocolate coating with chocolate swirls. e, Chocolate coating with dark chocolate ribbons. f, Dark chocolate coating with chocolate sprinkles. g, Chocolate coating with chocolate rosette. h, Dark chocolate coating with almond. i, White chocolate coating with candy heart.

2011, June 30   Perf. 13 Syncopated
2740 A723 $30 Sheet of 9, #a-i   7.50 7.50
2741 A724 $30 Sheet of 9, #a-i   7.50 7.50

Nos. 2740-2741 each are impregnated with a chocolate aroma.

A725

U.S. Civil War, 150th Anniv. — A726

No. 2742: a, Union General Ulysses S. Grant. b, Drum, rifles, Union and Confederate flags. c, Confederate General Robert E. Lee. d, Pres. Abraham Lincoln. e, Cannons.
No. 2743 — Paintings depicting Lincoln: a, Abraham Lincoln, by William F. Cogswell. b, The Peacemakers, by George Healy. c, President Lincoln Writing the Proclamation of Freedom, by David Gilmour Blythe.

2011, June 30   Perf. 12¾x13
2742 A725 $70 Sheet of 5, #a-e   9.75 9.75
Perf. 13¼x13
2743 A726 $100 Sheet of 3, #a-c 8.25 8.25

Jane Goodall's Roots and Shoots, 25th Anniv. — A727

No. 2744: a, Adult showing group of children how to plant seedlings. b, Two children planting seedlings. c, Children holding sign. d, Children and teachers in classroom.
$180, Children.

2011, June 30   Perf. 13x13¼
2744 A727 $90 Sheet of 4,
            #a-d   10.00 10.00
Souvenir Sheet
2745 A727 $180 multi   5.00 5.00

A728

A729

A730

A731

A732

A733

Elvis Presley (1935-77) — A734

No. 2746: a, Face in color. b, Face in black and white, microphone cord above "E." c, As "b," microphone between "I" and "S." d, As "b," microphone cord above "L." e, As "b," microphone cord above "S." f, As "b," microphone cord between "V" and "I."
No. 2747: a, Head of microphone above shoulder. b, Head of microphone even with edge of guitar. c, Head of microphone at right. d, Head of microphone even with tip of chin.
No. 2748 — Presley: a, On motorcycle. b, Wearing white tie. c, Wearing white shirt open at neck. d, Playing guitar.

2011, June 30   **Perf. 12¾x13**

| 2746 | A728 | $60 | Sheet of 6, #a-f | 10.00 | 10.00 |

Perf. 13¼x13

| 2747 | A729 | $80 | Sheet of 4, #a-d | 8.75 | 8.75 |

Perf. 13 Syncopated

| 2748 | A730 | $90 | Sheet of 4, #a-d | 10.00 | 10.00 |
| | | | Nos. 2746-2748 (3) | 28.75 | 28.75 |

Souvenir Sheets
Perf. 12¾

2749	A731	$180	multi	5.00	5.00
2750	A732	$180	multi	5.00	5.00
2751	A733	$180	multi	5.00	5.00
2752	A734	$180	multi	5.00	5.00
			Nos. 2749-2752 (4)	20.00	20.00

Beatification of Pope John Paul II — A735

No. 2753 — Pope John Paul II facing: a, Right, gray area at LR. b, Left, gray area at top. c, Right, no gray area at LR. d, Left, no gray area at top.
$180, Pope John Paul II wearing miter and green stole.

2011, Aug. 5   **Litho.**   **Perf. 12**

| 2753 | A735 | $80 | Sheet of 4, #a-d | 9.00 | 9.00 |

Souvenir Sheet

| 2754 | A735 | $180 | multi | 5.00 | 5.00 |

Statue of Liberty, 125th Anniv. — A736

No. 2755 — Inscription at right: a, National Monument. b, Lighting the Night Sky. c, Liberty Island, New York Harbor. d, Designed by Frédéric Auguste Bartholdi. e, Enlightening the World, 1886, by Edward Moran. f, Under Construction in Paris, France.
$180, Statue of Liberty and Manhattan buildings, horiz.

2011, Aug. 5   **Perf. 12**

| 2755 | A736 | $60 | Sheet of 6, #a-f | 10.00 | 10.00 |

Souvenir Sheet
Perf. 12½

| 2756 | A736 | $180 | multi | 5.00 | 5.00 |

No. 2756 contains one 51x38mm stamp.

A738

Princess Diana (1961-97) — A739

No. 2759: a, Wearing hat with veil. b, Wearing dark hat and winter jacket. c, Without hat. d, Wearing dark hat and white dress.
No. 2760: a, Wearing blue dress and necklace. b, Wearing blue hat. c, Wearing blue jacket, no necklace. d, Wearing white hat.

2011, Aug. 5   **Perf. 13 Syncopated**

| 2759 | A738 | $75 | Sheet of 4, #a-d | 8.25 | 8.25 |
| 2760 | A739 | $75 | Sheet of 4, #a-d | 8.25 | 8.25 |

First Man in Space, 50th Anniv. — A740

No. 2761, $80: a, Statue of Yuri Gagarin. b, American astronaut John Glenn. c, Gagarin on medal. d, Vostok spacecraft in orbit.
No. 2762, $80, horiz.: a, Gagarin souvenir medal. b, Mosaic of Gagarin. c, Vostok rocket on train. d, American astronauts Virgil Grissom and John Young.
No. 2763, $180, Gagarin. No. 2764, $180, Vostok spacecraft, horiz.

2011, Aug. 5   **Perf. 13 Syncopated**
Sheets of 4, #a-d

| 2761-2762 | A740 | Set of 2 | 18.00 | 18.00 |

Souvenir Sheets

| 2763-2764 | A740 | Set of 2 | 10.00 | 10.00 |

Orchids — A741

No. 2765: a, Polystachya longiscapa. b, Vanilla polylepis. c, Ansellia africana. d, Bolusiella maudiae.
No. 2766, $180, Polystachya zambesiaca.
No. 2767, $180, Polystachya bella.

2011, Aug. 5   **Perf. 12**

| 2765 | A741 | $80 | Sheet of 4, #a-d | 9.00 | 9.00 |

Souvenir Sheets

| 2766-2767 | A741 | Set of 2 | 10.00 | 10.00 |

Miniature Sheets

Butterflies — A737

No. 2757: a, Gaudy commodore. b, Yellow pansy. c, White lady swallowtail. d, Broad-bordered grass yellow. e, Blue pansy. f, Citrus swallowtail.
No. 2758: a, Mimic female. b, Wandering donkey acaea.

2011, Aug. 5   **Perf. 12**

| 2757 | A737 | $65 | Sheet of 6, #a-f | 11.00 | 11.00 |

Souvenir Sheet

| 2758 | A737 | $100 | Sheet of 2, #a-b | 5.50 | 5.50 |

Sept. 11, 2001 Terrorist Attacks, 10th Anniv. — A742

No. 2768: a, World Trade Center. b, September 11 Memorial, New York. c, Tribute in Light. d, The Pentagon.
$200, World Trade Center and Brooklyn Bridge, vert.

2011, Sept. 11   Perf. 13 Syncopated
2768 A742 $75 Sheet of 4, #a-d 8.25 8.25
Souvenir Sheet
2769 A742 $200 multi 5.50 5.50

Chinese Civil Engineering A743

Designs: $40, Qingdao Cross-sea Bridge. No. 2771 — Qingdao Jiaozhouwan Undersea Tunnel: a, Entrance. b, Cross-sectional diagram.

2011, Oct. 11   Litho.
2770 A743 $40 multi 1.10 1.10
2771 A743 $25 Sheet of 6, 3 each #2771a-2771b 4.25 4.25

No. 2770 was printed in sheets of 4.

A744

Wedding of Prince William and Catherine Middleton — A745

No. 2772 — Red frames: a, Bride facing right. b, Couple kissing. c, Couple holding hands. d, Groom. e, Bride facing left. f, Couple in coach.
No. 2773 — Blue frames: a, Couple holding hands. b, Groom waving. c, Bride facing left. d, Couple in coach, groom waving. e, Couple standing, bride waving. f, Groom facing right.
$180, Couple in coach, bride waving.

2011, Oct. 11   Perf. 12
2772 A744 $80 Sheet of 6, #a-f 13.50 13.50
2773 A745 $80 Sheet of 6, #a-f 13.50 13.50
Souvenir Sheet
2774 A745 $180 multi 5.00 5.00

Christmas A746

Paintings: $25, Madonna with Members of the Pesaro Family, by Titian. $40, The Nativity, by Prero della Francesca. $50, The Virgin of the Rocks, by Leonardo da Vinci. $100, Madonna with Child, by Fra Filippo Lippi.

2011, Oct. 11   Perf. 13 Syncopated
2775-2778 A746 Set of 4 6.00 6.00

Chinese Zodiac Animals — A747

New Year 2012 (Year of the Dragon) — A748

No. 2779: a, Rat. b, Ox. c, Tiger. d, Rabbit. e, Dragon. f, Snake. g, Horse. h, Sheep. i, Monkey. j, Rooster. k, Dog. l, Boar.

Litho. With Foil Application
2011, Oct. 11   Perf. 13 Syncopated
2779 A747 $18 Sheet of 12, #a-l 6.00 6.00

Souvenir Sheet
Litho.
Perf. 13¼
2780 A748 $200 multi 5.75 5.75

China 2011 World Philatelic Exhibition, Wuxi (No. 2780).

Binhai New Area, People's Republic of China — A749

No. 2781: a, Dove, city. b, Highway cloverleaf interchange. c, City at nightfall. d, Ship at dock.
$160, City, ship, airplanes, rocket.

Perf. 13 Syncopated
2011, Oct. 26   Litho.
2781 A749 $40 Sheet of 4, #a-d 4.50 4.50
Souvenir Sheet
2782 A749 $160 multi 4.50 4.50
No. 2782 contains one 119x40mm stamp.

Peking Opera — A750

No. 2783 — Character with: a, Two sharp teeth, (gray, red and pink face). b, Beard (black and red face). c, Heart-shaped nose (pink, red and black face). d, Ten teeth (red, black and gray face). $180, Character with red, dark red and black face.

2011, Oct. 26   Perf. 13¼
2783 A750 $50 Sheet of 4, #a-d 5.75 5.75
Souvenir Sheet
2784 A750 $180 multi 5.00 5.00
China 2011 Intl. Philatelic Exhibition, Wuxi. No. 2784 contains one 44x44mm stamp.

Pres. Ronald Reagan (1911-2004) A751

Flags and Pres. Reagan wearing suit: No. 2785, $100, Without handkerchief in suit pocket. No. 2786, $100, With handkerchief in suit pocket.

2011, Dec. 16   Perf. 13 Syncopated
2785-2786 A751 Set of 2 5.50 5.50
Nos. 2785-2786 each were printed in sheets of 3.

Awarding of Nobel Peace Prize to Pres. Ellen Johnson-Sirleaf A752

Designs: $75, Shown. $250, Pres. Johnson-Sirleaf, horiz.

2011, Dec. 5   Perf. 12
2787 A752 $75 multi 2.10 2.10
Souvenir Sheet
2788 A752 $250 multi 7.00 7.00
No. 2787 was printed in sheets of 6. No. 2788 contains one 50x30mm stamp.

Reptiles — A753

No. 2789: a, Natal green snake. b, African tree snake. c, African python.
No. 2790: a, African spiny-tailed lizard. b, Western Cape crag lizard. c, Eastern Cape crag lizard. d, Armadillo lizard.
No. 2791: a, African tent tortoise. b, Serrated tortoise.
No. 2792: a, Underside of Nile crocodile. b, Top of Nile crocodile.

2011, Dec. 16   Perf. 12
2789 A753 $90 Sheet of 3, #a-c 7.50 7.50
2790 A753 $90 Sheet of 4, #a-d 10.00 10.00
Souvenir Sheets
2791 A753 $180 Sheet of 2, #a-b 10.00 10.00
2792 A753 $180 Sheet of 2, #a-b 10.00 10.00

No. 2790 contains four 50x30mm stamps. No. 2792 contains two 80x30mm stamps.

Completion of St. Paul's Cathedral, London, 300th Anniv. — A754

No. 2793: a, Plan of Cathedral. b, Building St. Paul's by J. Seymour Lucas. c, Architect Sir Christopher Wren. d, Pope Clement XI. e, St. Paul's Cathedral. f, Pope Benedict XVI.
No. 2794: a, Pope Clement XI, diff. b, Pope Benedict XVI, diff.

2011, Dec. 16 *Perf. 13 Syncopated*
2793 A754 $50 Sheet of 6, #a-f 8.25 8.25
Souvenir Sheet
2794 A754 $150 Sheet of 2, #a-b 8.25 8.25
St. Paul's Cathedral is an Anglican cathedral and was not visited by Pope Benedict XVI in his travels to the United Kingdom.

Sinking of the Titanic, Cent. — A755

No. 2795: a, Titanic Captain Edward J. Smith. b, Cross-section of the Titanic. c, Iceberg. d, Titanic sinking. $250, Titanic sinking, vert.

2012, Jan. 1 *Perf. 13¼*
2795 A755 $90 Sheet of 4, #a-d 10.00 10.00
Souvenir Sheet
Perf. 12
2796 A755 $250 multi 7.00 7.00
No. 2796 contains one 38x50mm stamp.

Souvenir Sheet

Pope Benedict XVI, 85th Birthday — A756

No. 2797: a, Joseph Ratzinger as young boy (44x25mm). b, Pope Benedict XVI, vert. (30x44mm). c, Birthplace of Pope Benedict XVI (44x25mm).

2012, Feb. 22 *Imperf.*
2797 A756 $250 Sheet of 3, #a-c 21.00 21.00

Mao Zedong (1893-1976), Chairman of People's Republic of China — A757

Photograph of Mao Zedong: No. 2798, $25, No. 2802a, $90, With blue background. No. 2799, $25, No. 2802b, $90, Reading in library. No. 2800, $25, No. 2802c, $90, Waving. No. 2801, $25, No. 2802d, $90, Seated.

2012, Feb. 22 *Litho.* *Perf. 14*
2798-2801 A757 Set of 4 2.75 2.75
2802 A757 $90 Sheet of 4, #a-d 9.75 9.75

Premiere of *The Three Stooges* Movie — A758

No. 2803: a, Chris Diamantopolous as Moe, denomination in yellow. b, Diamantopolous as Moe, denomination in orange. c, Sean Hayes as Larry, denomination in yellow. d, Hayes as Larry, denomination in orange. e, Will Sasso as Curly, denomination in yellow. f, Sasso as Curly, denomination in orange.
No. 2804: a, Stooges, denomination in blue. b, Stooges, denomination in red violet.

2012, Mar. 13 *Perf. 13 Syncopated*
2803 A758 $75 Sheet of 6, #a-f 12.50 12.50
Souvenir Sheet
2804 A758 $125 Sheet of 2, #a-b 7.00 7.00

Meeting of U.S. Pres. Barack Obama and Xi Jinping, Vice-President of People's Republic of China — A759

No. 2805: a, Xi Jinping. b, Temple, Beijing. c, Pres. Obama. d, Washington Monument.
No. 2806: a, Xi Jinping, diff. b, Pres. Obama, diff.

2012, Apr. 4 *Perf. 12*
2805 A759 $90 Sheet of 4, #a-d 10.00 10.00
Souvenir Sheet
2806 A759 $125 Sheet of 2, #a-b 7.00 7.00

African Wildlife — A760

No. 2807: a, West African giraffe (30x80mm). b, Dorcas gazelle (30x40mm). c, Blue duiker (30x40mm). d, Red river hog (30x40mm). e, Hartebeest (30x40mm).
No. 2808, horiz.: a, Spotted hyena. b, Side-striped jackal. c, Serval.
No. 2809, African bush elephant. No. 2810, Patas monkey.

2012, May 3 *Perf. 14*
2807 A760 $75 Sheet of 5, #a-e 10.50 10.50
Perf. 12
2808 A760 $100 Sheet of 3, #a-c 8.25 8.25
Souvenir Sheets
2809 A760 $250 multi 7.00 7.00
2810 A760 $250 multi 7.00 7.00

Miniature Sheet

2012 Summer Olympics, London — A761

No. 2811: a, Track and field. b, Swimming. c, Weight lifting. d, Kayaking.

2012, May 30 *Perf. 14*
2811 A761 $60 Sheet of 4, #a-d 6.50 6.50

Dinosaurs — A762

No. 2812, horiz.: a, Albertaceratops. b, Zuniceratops. c, Prestosaurus. d, Saurolophus. e, Ampelosaurus. f, Euoplocephalus.
No. 2813: a, Pachyrhinosaurus. b, Hypsilophodon.

2012, June 27 *Perf. 13 Syncopated*
2812 A762 $75 Sheet of 6, #a-f 12.50 12.50
Souvenir Sheet
2813 A762 $125 Sheet of 2, #a-b 7.00 7.00

Dogs — A763

No. 2814, $120: a, Afghan hound. b, Dalmatian. c, Greyhound.
No. 2815, $120: a, English bulldog. b, Bichon Frise. c, Dachshund.
No. 2816, $250, Scottish terrier. No. 2817, $250, Poodle.

2012, June 27 *Perf. 14, 12 (#2816)*
Sheets of 3, #a-c
2814-2815 A763 Set of 2 20.00 20.00
Souvenir Sheets
2816-2817 A763 Set of 2 14.00 14.00

SOS Children's Village, Liberia, 30th Anniv. (in 2011) A764

SOS Children's Village emblem, map of Liberia and: $45, Inscription and slogan. $55, Inscription and palm tree.

2012, Feb. 14 *Perf. 14*
2818-2819 A764 Set of 2 2.75 2.75
Miniature Sheet

Apes — A765

No. 2820: a, Barbary macaque. b, Bonobo. c, Silverback gorilla. d, Chacma baboon.

2012, Aug. 9 *Perf. 12*
2820 A765 $90 Sheet of 4, #a-d 9.75 9.75

Souvenir Sheets

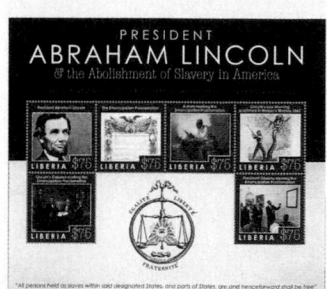

Elvis Presley (1935-77) — A766

Designs: No. 2821, $250, Presley with guitar, light blue frame. No. 2822, $250, Presley behind microphone, light blue frame. No. 2823, $250, Two black-and white photographs of Presley, dull red frame. No. 2824, $250, Color and black-and-white photographs of Presley, red frame. No. 2825, $250, Presley in army uniform, red frame.

2012, Aug. 9 *Perf. 12½*
2821-2825 A766 Set of 5 35.00 35.00

First Draft of the Emancipation Proclamation, 150th Anniv. — A767

No. 2826: a, Pres. Abraham Lincoln. b, Printed copy of Emancipation Proclamation. c, Man reading Emancipation Proclamation. d, Lincoln's Last Warning, political cartoon from Harper's Weekly, 1862. e, First Reading of the Emacipation Proclamation of President Lincoln, by Francis Bicknell Carpenter. f, Pres. Barack Obama viewing Emancipation Proclamation.
$250, President Lincoln Writing the Proclamation of Freedom, by David Gilmour Blythe, horiz.

2012, Sept. 21 *Perf. 13¾*
2826 A767 $75 Sheet of 6, #a-f 12.50 12.50
Souvenir Sheet
Perf. 12½
2827 A767 $250 multi 7.00 7.00
No. 2827 contains one 51x38mm stamp.

Chinese Zodiac Animals — A768

Designs: No. 2828, $15, Monkeys. No. 2829. $15, Cock.

2012, Sept. 27   *Perf. 13¼x13*
2828-2829 A768   Set of 2   .85   .85

Christmas A769

Paintings: $25, Adoration of the Shepherds, by Guido Reni. $35, Adoration of the Shepherds, by Correggio. $40, Holy Family with St. John the Baptist, by Michelangelo. $45, Tempi Madonna (detail), by Raphael. $50, The Annunciation, by Francisco Goya. $100, Virgin and Child Before an Archway, by Albrecht Dürer.

2012, Oct. 1   *Perf. 12½*
2830-2835 A769   Set of 6   8.25   8.25

Giant Pandas — A770

No. 2836 — Giant Panda: a, On tree, facing left. b, Eating. c, Walking, foliage at right. d, With log at right.
$220, Panda on tree, vert.

2012, Nov. 15   *Perf. 13 Syncopated*
2836 A770 $85 Sheet of 4, #a-d   7.00   7.00
    Souvenir Sheet
2837 A770 $220 multi   6.00   6.00
    Beijing 2012 Intl. Stamp Exhibition.

Aircraft Carriers — A771

No. 2838: a, Admiral Gorshkov, Russia. b, Dédalo, Spain. c, Foch (R99), France. d, USS Philippine Sea. e, USS Intrepid. f, HTMS Chakri Naruebet, Thailand.
$250, USS Ticonderoga, horiz.

2012, Nov. 28   *Perf. 13¾*
2838 A771 $75 Sheet of 6, #a-f   12.50   12.50
    Souvenir Sheet
    Perf. 12½
2839 A771 $250 multi   6.75   6.75
    No. 2839 contains one 51x38mm stamp.

Flowers — A772

No. 2840: a, Nymphaea lotus. b, Papaver somniferum. c, Protea repens. d, Liparia splendens. e, Tulipa florenskyi. f, Gladiolus carmineus.
$280, Zantedeschia aethiopica, vert.

2013, Jan. 8   *Perf. 13¾*
2840 A772 $70 Sheet of 6, #a-f   11.50   11.50
    Souvenir Sheet
    Perf. 12½
2841 A772 $280 multi   7.75   7.75
    No. 2841 contains one 38x51mm stamp.

World Radio Day — A773

No. 2842: a, Hindenburg disaster reporting, 1937. b, Winston Churchill's "We Shall Fight on the Beaches" broadcast, 1940. c, Pres. John F. Kennedy's Cuban Missile Crisis address, 1962. d, Dr. Martin Luther King, Jr.'s "I Have a Dream" speech, 1963.
$250, Orson Welles' "War of the Worlds" broadcast, 1938.

2013, Jan. 8   *Perf. 12½*
2842 A773 $90 Sheet of 4, #a-d   9.75   9.75
    Souvenir Sheet
    Perf.
2843 A773 $250 multi   6.75   6.75
    No. 2843 contains one 38mm diameter stamp.

Gems and Rocks — A774

No. 2844, $100: a, Aquamarine. b, Euclase. c, Rainbow garnet.
No. 2845, $100: a, Rhodochrosite. b, Opal. c, Tanzanite.
Mo. 2846: a, Agate with red inner rings, small hole. b, Agate with white inner rings, large hole.

2013, Jan. 8   *Perf. 13¾*
    Sheets of 3, #a-c
2844-2845 A774   Set of 2   16.50   16.50
    Souvenir Sheet
    Perf. 12½
2846 A774 $140 Sheet of 2, #a-b   7.75   7.75
    Nos. 2844-2845 each contain three 35x35mm stamps.

American Civil Rights Leaders — A775

No. 2847, $85: a, Harriet Tubman (c. 1820-1913), abolitionist (without head covering). b, Frederick Douglass (1818-95), abolitionist. c, John Brown (1800-59), abolitionist. d, Martha Coffin Wright (1806-75), abolitionist.
No. 2848, $85: a, Union Major General David Hunter (1802-86). b, Pres. Abraham Lincoln (1809-65). c, Susan B. Anthony (1820-1906), suffragist. d, Tubman (with head covering).
No. 2849, $280, Tubman and slave capture reward notice. No. 2850, $280, Tubman, daughter Gertie and husband Nelson Davis, horiz.

2013, Mar. 20   *Perf. 12½*
    Sheets of 4, #a-d
2847-2848 A775   Set of 2   18.50   18.50
    Souvenir Sheets
    Perf. 12
2849-2850 A775   Set of 2   15.50   15.50
    No. 2849 contains on 30x40mm stamp. No. 2850 contains one 40x30mm stamp.

African Wildlife — A776

No. 2851: a, Acionyx jubatus. b, Aepyceros melampus. c, Diceros bicornis. d, Equus grevyi. e, Panthera leo. f, Phacochoerus africanus.
No. 2852, vert.: a, Giraffa camelopardalis. b, Loxodonta africana. c, Connochaetes taurinus.
$280, Panthera pardus pardus, horiz.

2013, Apr. 3   *Perf. 13¾*
2851 A776 $70 Sheet of 6, #a-f   11.50   11.50
    Perf. 12
2852 A776 $100 Sheet of 3, #a-c   8.25   8.25
    Souvenir Sheet
    Perf. 12½
2853 A776 $280 multi   7.75   7.75
    No. 2852 contains three 30x50mm stamps. No. 2853 contains one 51x38mm stamp.

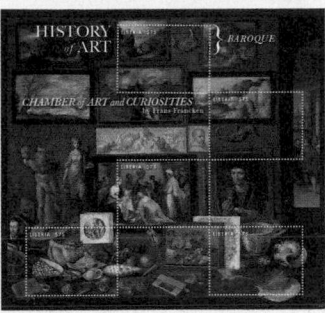

History of Art — A777

No. 2854 — Chamber of Art and Curiosities, by Frans Francken (details) with: a, Fish at UR. b, Seahorse at L. c, Religious painting and tasselled cord. d, Shells, book at LL. e, Shells, bowl at top.
No. 2855, $100, vert.: a, Girl with a Pearl Earring, by Johannes Vermeer. b, A Commander Being Armed for Battle, by Peter Paul Rubens. c, David with the Head of Goliath, by Caravaggio.
No. 2856, $100, vert.: a, Still-life with Flowers, by Rachel Ruysch. b, Maddalena Penitente, by Artemisia Gentileschi. c, The Fruit and Vegetable Costermonger, by Louise Moillon.
$280, La Gamme d'Amour, by Jean-Antoine Watteau.

2013, Apr. 4   *Litho.*   *Perf. 12½*
2854 A777 $75 Sheet of 5, #a-e   10.50   10.50
    Sheets of 3, #a-c
2855-2856 A777   Set of 2   16.50   16.50
    Souvenir Sheet
2857 A777 $280 multi   7.75   7.75

Pope Benedict XVI — A778

No. 2858, $85 — Pope Benedict XVI at Beatification Ceremony for Pope John Paul II: a, Wearing miter, with two assistants. b, Wearing miter, waving. c, Kissing glass object. d, Holding censer.
No. 2859, $85 — Pope Benedict XVI visiting Germany: a, Meeting Chancellor Angela Merkel. b, Waving. c, With German President Christian Wulff and wife. d, Facing left.
No. 2860, $280, Pope Benedict XVI seated at beatification ceremony. No. 2861, $280, Pope Benedict XVI with Wulff and Merkel.

2013, Apr. 30   *Perf. 12*
    Sheets of 4, #a-d
2858-2859 A778   Set of 2   18.50   18.50
    Souvenir Sheets
2860-2861 A778   Set of 2   15.50   15.50

Lady Margaret Thatcher (1925-2013), British Prime Minister — A779

No. 2862 — Thatcher: a, At microphone. b, Wearing black dress, facing left. c, With Pres. Ronald Reagan. d, With hand on chin.
$280, Thatcher, vert.

2013, June 1   *Perf. 12*
2862 A779 $85 Sheet of 4, #a-d 9.25 9.25
Souvenir Sheet
Perf. 12½
2863 A779 $280 multi   7.50 7.50
No. 2863 contains one 38x51mm stamp.

Pres. John F. Kennedy (1917-63) — A780

No. 2864 — Pres Kennedy: a, On telephone. b, Sitting in rocking chair. c, Standing behind microphone. d, Signing document. e, Wearing sunglasses. f, Standing in crowd.
$280, Pres. Kennedy on yacht.

Perf. 13 Syncopated
2013, June 25   Litho.
2864 A780 $70 Sheet of 6, #a-f   11.00 11.00
Souvenir Sheet
2865 A780 $280 multi   7.50 7.50

Medicinal Plants — A781

No. 2866: a, Acacia. b, Rooibos. c, Buchu. d, Caralluma. e, Common myrrh. f, Shea tree.
$280, Aloe, vert.

2013, June 25   Litho.   *Perf. 13¾*
2866 A781 $70 Sheet of 6, #a-f   11.00 11.00
Souvenir Sheet
Perf. 12¾
2867 A781 $280 multi   7.50 7.50
No. 2867 contains one 38x51mm stamp.

Birds — A782

No. 2868, $85: a, Barnacle geese. b, Brown pelican. c, Long-billed curlew. d, Eurasian griffon.
No. 2869, $85: a, Eastern great egret. b, Red and green macaw. c, Roseate spoonbill. d, Mute swan.
No. 2870, $280, Blue peafowl. No. 2871, $280, Crowned crane, vert.

Perf. 14, 12 (#2871)
2013, July 30   Litho.
Sheets of 4, #a-d
2868-2869 A782 Set of 2   17.50 17.50
Souvenir Sheets
2870-2871 A782 Set of 2   14.50 14.50

Birth of Prince George of Cambridge — A783

No. 2872: a, Duchess of Cambridge handing Prince George to Duke of Cambridge. b, Duke of Cambridge holding Prince George. c, Duchess of Cambridge holding Prince George. d, Duke and Duchess of Cambridge, Prince George.
$280, Duke and Duchess of Cambridge, Prince George.

2013, Sept. 17   Litho.   *Perf. 12x12½*
2872 A783 $85 Sheet of 4, #a-d 8.50 8.50
Souvenir Sheet
Perf. 13¼
2873 A783 $280 multi   7.00 7.00
No. 2873 contains one 38x51mm stamp.

Coronation of Queen Elizabeth II, 60th Anniv. — A784

No. 2874 — Queen Elizabeth II wearing: a, Pink jacket and hat. b, Pink jacket, pink and white hat, fur coat. c, Gray hat and dress. d, Black hat and coat.
$280, Queen Elizabeth II wearing black feathered hat.

2013, Oct. 7   Litho.   *Perf. 13¾*
2874 A784 $85 Sheet of 4, #a-d 8.50 8.50
Souvenir Sheet
2875 A784 $280 multi   7.00 7.00

Miniature Sheet

2014 Intl. Horiticultural Exposition, Qingdao, People's Republic of China — A785

No. 2876: a, Exposition emblem. b, Mascot waving. c, Mascot with watering can. d, Mascot snorkeling. e, Mascot surfing. f, Mascot teaching.

2013, Jan. 1   Litho.   *Perf. 14*
2876 A785 $50 Sheet of 6, #a-f   8.25 8.25

Miniature Sheet

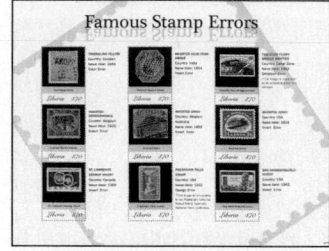

Famous Stamp Errors — A786

No. 2877: a, Sweden #1a. b, India #6c. c, Canal Zone #157a. d, Belgium #139a. e, Western Australia #3a. f, United States #C3a. g, Canada #387a. h, Philippines #357. i, United States #1204.

2013, Jan. 1   Litho.   *Perf. 14*
2877 A786 $70 Sheet of 9, #a-i   17.50 17.50

New Year 2014 (Year of the Horse) — A787

No. 2878 — Six steeds of Zhaoling from the Mausoleum of Tang Emperor Taizong: a, Horse and attendant. b, Horse facing left, galloping. c, Horse facing left, walking. d, Horse facing right, galloping, diagonal crack running from denomination to horse's head. e, Horse facing right, walking. f, Horse facing right, galloping, vertical crack behind horse's head running to bottom.
$280, Horse's head.

2013, Nov. 25   Litho.   *Perf. 14*
2878 A787 $70 Sheet of 6, #a-f   10.50 10.50
Souvenir Sheet
Perf. 12
2879 A787 $280 multi   7.00 7.00

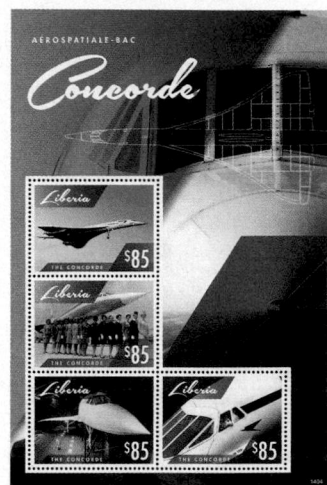

Intl. Red Cross, 150th Anniv. — A788

No. 2880: a, Horse-drawn ambulances at Red Cross site. b, Red Cross equipment bag. c, Red Cross volunteer tending to prisoners near train. d, Red Cross stenciled on wall.
$280, Jean-Henri Dunant, Red Cross founder.

2013, Dec. 2   Litho.   *Perf. 14*
2880 A788 $85 Sheet of 4, #a-d 8.50 8.50
Souvenir Sheet
2881 A788 $280 multi   7.00 7.00

Trains — A789

No. 2882: a, 20th Century Limited, United States. b, Ghan, Australia. c, Flying Scotsman, Great Britain. d, Indian Pacific, Australia.
$280, Super Chief, United States, vert.

2013, Dec. 2   Litho.   *Perf. 14*
2882 A789 $85 Sheet of 4, #a-d 8.50 8.50
Souvenir Sheet
2883 A789 $280 multi   7.00 7.00

Concorde — A790

No. 2884: a, Concorde in flight. b, Concorde and flight attendants. c, Nose of Concorde. d, Pilot in cockpit window of Concorde.
$280, Concorde in flight in front of clouds.

2013, Dec. 2   Litho.   *Perf. 14*
2884 A790 $85 Sheet of 4, #a-d 8.50 8.50
Souvenir Sheet
Perf. 12
2885 A790 $280 multi   7.00 7.00
No. 2885 contains one 50x30mm stamp.

Miniature Sheets

Zodiac Constellations — A791

No. 2886, $70: a, Aries. b, Leo. c, Virgo. d, Cancer. e, Taurus. f, Pisces.
No. 2887, $70: a, Gemini. b, Libra. c, Sagittarius. d, Scorpio. e, Aquarius. f, Capricorn.

2013, Dec. 2   Litho.   *Perf. 12*
Sheets of 6, #a-f
2886-2887 A791 Set of 2   21.00 21.00

Military Vehicles — A792

No. 2888: a, Light utility vehicle. b, Armored personnel carrier. c, Half-track armored personnel carrier. d, Amphibious vehicle. $280, Amphibious transport.

2013, Dec. 23   Litho.   Perf. 14
2888 A792 $85 Sheet of 4, #a-d   8.50 8.50

Souvenir Sheet
Perf. 12
2889 A792 $280 multi   7.00 7.00

Christmas
A793

Paintings: $25, Madonna and Child, by Taddeo di Bartolo. $40, Madonna and Saints, by Giovanni Bellini. $50, Nativity, by Lorenzo Lotto. $175, San Marco Altarpiece, by Fra Angelico.

2013, Dec. 2   Litho.   Perf. 12½
2890-2893 A793 Set of 4   7.25 7.25

A794

A795

Nelson Mandela (1918-2013),
President of South Africa — A796

No. 2894 — Mandela: a, Wearing green and red shirt, denomination in black. b, Close-up of head. c, With clenched fist, two people in background. d, Wearing flowered shirt, brick wall in background. e, With fist raised, crowd in background. f, Sitting in chair, flag in background.
No. 2895 — Mandela: a, Wearing gray blue shirt, pen in breast pocket. b, Wearing suit and tie, curtains in background. c, Wearing shirt with gray squares, black background. d, Wearing blue and white shirt with red AIDS ribbon under collar button. e, Wearing brown and red shirt. f, Wearing suit and tie, with fist raised.
$280, Mandela in suit and tie, diff. $765, Mandela waving.

2013, Dec. 15   Litho.   Perf. 14
2894 A794 $70 Sheet of 6,
              #a-f   10.50 10.50
2895 A795 $70 Sheet of 6,
              #a-f   10.50 10.50

Souvenir Sheets
Perf. 12
2896 A795 $280 multi   7.00 7.00

Litho., Margin Embossed With Foil Application
Without Gum
Imperf
2897 A796 $765 multi   19.00 19.00

The Christening of Prince George   10/23/2013

Christening of Prince George of
Cambridge — A797

No. 2898: a, Prince George. b, Duchess of Cambridge holding Prince George. c, Duke of Cambridge holding Prince George. d, Duke and Duchess of Cambridge, Prince George. $280, Prince George, diff.

2013, Dec. 31   Litho.   Perf. 14
2898 A797 $85 Sheet of 4, #a-d 8.50 8.50

Souvenir Sheet
Perf. 12
2899 A797 $280 multi   7.00 7.00

Poems by
Mao
Zedong
A798

A799

Mao Zedong (1893-1976), Chinese
Communist Leader — A800

No. 2900 — Poem with: a, 13 vertical columns of characters. b, 12 vertical columns of characters. c, 11 vertical columns of characters.
No. 2901 — Mao Zedong: a, With other people, building's roof visible. b, With Jawaharlal Nehru. c, With Kwame Nkrumah at dinner table. d, Surrounded by people from different countries.
No. 2902: a, Painting of Mao Zedong carrying scroll. b, Black-and-white photograph of Mao Zedong without hat. c, Painting of Mao Zedong with cap. d, Black-and-white photograph of Mao Zedong with cap. e, Painting of Mao Zedong without cap. f, Great Wall of China.

2013, Mar. 7   Litho.   Perf. 14
2900   Horiz. strip of 3   1.25 1.25
  a.-c. A798 $15 Any single   .40   .40
2901 A799 $15 Sheet of 4, #a-d 1.60 1.60
2902 A800 $15 Sheet of 6, #a-f 2.50 2.50

No. 2900 was printed in sheets of 6, containing two of each stamp.

Souvenir Sheet

Elvis Presley (1935-77) — A801

Litho., Sheet Margin Embossed
2014, Jan. 1   Imperf.
2903 A801 $740 multi   18.50 18.50

Yosemite National Park — A802

No. 2904: a, Cathedral Rocks. b, Yosemite Falls. c, Giant sequoias. d, Tenaya Lake. e, Hetch Hetchy Reservoir. f, Half Dome. $280, El Capitan.

2014, Jan. 2   Litho.   Perf. 14
2904 A802 $70 Sheet of 6,
              #a-f   10.50 10.50

Souvenir Sheet
Perf. 12¾
2905 A802 $280 multi   7.00 7.00
  Yosemite Grant, 150th anniv. No. 2905 contains one 51x38mm stamp.

Miniature Sheets

Winter Games — A803

No. 2906, $85: a, Snowboarding. b, Alpine skiing. c, Curling. d, Freestyle skiing. e, Figure skating.
No. 2907, $85: a, Ski jumping. b, Ice hockey. c, Bobsled. d, Cross-country skiing. e, Speed skating.

2014, Mar. 5   Litho.   Perf. 13¾
Sheets of 5, #a-e
2906-2907 A803 Set of 2   20.00 20.00

Paintings — A804

No. 2908, $125: a, Portrait of a Man Aged 32, by Frans Pourbus the Younger. b, Apricot Branch, by Georg Flegel. c, Meu Taporo, by Paul Gauguin.
No. 2909, $125: a, Portrait of a Woman, by Antonio del Pollaiuolo. b, A World, by Maximilian Lenz. c, Woman Carrying a Pitcher on Her Head, by Camille Pissarro.
No. 2910, $350, The Piano Lesson, by Pierre-Auguste Renoir. No. 2911, $350, The Japanese Bridge, by Claude Monet.

2014, Mar. 10   Litho.   Perf. 12¾
Sheets of 3, #a-c
2908-2909 A804 Set of 2   17.50 17.50
Size: 100x100mm
Imperf
2910-2911 A804 Set of 2   16.50 16.50

A805

Pope Francis

A806

Pope Francis

A807

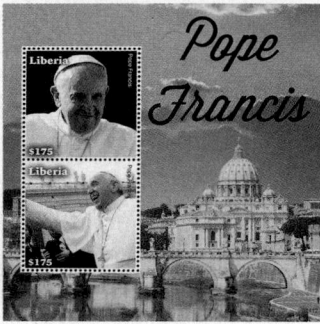

Pope Francis

Pope Francis — A808

No. 2912 — Pope Francis: a, Waving. b, Looking up. c, Hugging boy. d, Smiling.

No. 2913 — Pope Francis: a, Looking left. b, Waving, diff. c, Waving, with other hand over heart. d, Waving in front of building.

No. 2914 — Pope Francis, denominations with large numerals: a, Looking right. b, Talking to young girl.

No. 2915 — Pope Francis, denominations with small numerals: a, Smiling, diff. b, With arm extended.

2014, Mar. 24   Litho.   Perf. 13¾
| 2912 | A805 | $100 Sheet of 4, #a-d | 9.50 | 9.50 |
| 2913 | A806 | $100 Sheet of 4, #a-d | 9.50 | 9.50 |

Souvenir Sheets
| 2914 | A807 | $175 Sheet of 2, #a-b | 8.25 | 8.25 |
| 2915 | A808 | $175 Sheet of 2, #a-b | 8.25 | 8.25 |

Mythical Creatures — A809

No. 2916, $100: a, Dragon. b, Minotaur. c, Centaur. d, Phoenix.

No. 2917, $100, vert.: a, Vampire. b, Leprechaun. c, Mermaid. d, Angel.

No. 2918, $175, vert.: a, Werewolf. b, Unicorn.

No. 2919, $175, vert.: a, Mermaid, with arms above head. b, Mermaid, swimming.

Perf. 14 (#2916), 12¾
2014, Apr. 2   Litho.
Sheets of 4, #a-d
| 2916-2917 | A809 | Set of 2 | 19.00 | 19.00 |

Souvenir Sheets of 2, #a-b
| 2918-2919 | A809 | Set of 2 | 16.50 | 16.50 |

No. 2917 contains four 38x51mm stamps. Nos. 2918-2919 each contain two 38x51mm stamps.

A810

World War I, Cent. — A811

No. 2920: a, Battle of Vimy Ridge, 1915. b, Battle of Gallipoli, 1915. c, Battle of the Somme, 1916. d, Battle of St. Mihiel, 1918.

No. 2921 — Battleships: a, Voltaire. b, Slava. c, Kaiser Barbarossa. d, Asahi.

No. 2922: a, Battle of Verdun, 1916. b, Third Battle of Ypres, 1917.

No. 2923 — Battleships: a, USS Alabama. b, SMS Helgoland.

2014, May 19   Litho.   Perf. 12
| 2920 | A810 | $100 Sheet of 4, #a-d | 9.50 | 9.50 |
| 2921 | A811 | $100 Sheet of 4, #a-d | 9.50 | 9.50 |

Souvenir Sheets
| 2922 | A810 | $175 Sheet of 2, #a-b | 8.25 | 8.25 |

Perf. 14
| 2923 | A811 | $175 Sheet of 2, #a-b | 8.25 | 8.25 |

Korean Food — A812

No. 2924: a, Boneless ribs and Kimchi. b, Cucumber kimchi and Gyeongdan. c, Seafood pancake and Japchae.

$350, Soft tofu stew.

2014, June 17   Litho.   Perf. 13
| 2924 | A812 | $125 Sheet of 3, #a-c, + central label | 8.25 | 8.25 |

Souvenir Sheet
Perf.
| 2925 | A812 | $350 multi | 7.75 | 7.75 |

Philakorea 2014 World Stamp Exhibition, Seoul

2014 World Cup Soccer Championships, Brazil — A813

Team photographs: No. 2926, $30, Algeria. No. 2927, $30, Argentina. No. 2928, $30, Australia. No. 2929, $30, Belgium. No. 2930, $30, Bosnia & Herzegovina. No. 2931, $30, Brazil. No. 2932, $30, Cameroun. No. 2933, $30, Chile. No. 2934, $30, Colombia. No. 2935, $30, Costa Rica. No. 2936, $30, Cote d'Ivoire (Ivory Coast). No. 2937, $30, Croatia. No. 2938, $30, Ecuador. No. 2939, $30, England. No. 2940, $30, France. No. 2941, $30, Germany. No. 2942, $30, Ghana. No. 2943, $30, Greece. No. 2944, $30, Honduras. No. 2945, $30, Iran. No. 2946, $30, Italy. No. 2947, $30, Japan. No. 2948, $30, South Korea. No. 2949, $30, Mexico. No. 2950, $30, Netherlands. No. 2951, $30, Nigeria. No. 2952, $30, Portugal. No. 2953, $30, Russia. No. 2954, $30, Spain. No. 2955, $30, Switzerland. No. 2956, $30, United States. No. 2957, $30, Uruguay.

2014, June 17   Litho.   Perf. 14
| 2926-2957 | A813 | Set of 32 | 21.50 | 21.50 |

Nos. 2926-2957 each were printed in sheets of 6. See No. 2980.

Orchids — A814

No. 2958, $100: a, Disa racemosa. b, Eulophia nutans. c, Eulophia hians. d, Eulophia ensata.

No. 2959, $100: a, Satyrium erectum. b, Satyrium coriifolium. c, Eulophia buchanani. d, Disa gladioflora.

No. 2960, $175: a, Habenaria bonatea. b, Polystachya pubescens.

No. 2961, $175: a, Eulophia reichenbachiana. b, Disa uniflora.

2014, June 23   Litho.   Perf. 14
Sheets of 4, #a-d
| 2958-2959 | A814 | Set of 2 | 18.00 | 18.00 |

Souvenir Sheets of 2, #a-b
| 2960-2961 | A814 | Set of 2 | 15.50 | 15.50 |

Bats — A815

No. 2962, $100: a, Lissonycteris angolensis. b, Epomophorus gambianus. c, Nanonycteris veldkampii. d, Epomops buettikoferi.

No. 2963, $100: a, Coleura afrea. b, Epomophorus wahlbergi. c, Miniopterus africanus. d, Rhinolophus ferrumequinum.

No. 2964, $175: a, Miniopterus inflatus. b, Taphozous mauritianus.

No. 2965, $175: a, Micropteropus pusillus. b, Rousettus aegyptiacus.

2014, Aug. 14   Litho.   Perf. 12x12½
Sheets of 4, #a-d
| 2962-2963 | A815 | Set of 2 | 17.50 | 17.50 |

Souvenir Sheets of 2, #a-b
| 2964-2965 | A815 | Set of 2 | 15.50 | 15.50 |

Mongooses — A816

No. 2966, $100: a, Dwarf mongoose. b, Selous's mongoose. c, Kusimanse. d, Long-nosed mongoose.

No. 2967, $100: a, Angolan slender mongoose. b, Yellow mongoose. c, Ethiopian dwarf mongoose. d, Banded mongoose.

No. 2968, $175: a, Meerkat. b, Alexander's kusimanse.

No. 2969, $175: a, Slender mongoose. b, Somalian slender mongoose.

2014, Aug. 27   Litho.   Perf. 14
Sheets of 4, #a-d
| 2966-2967 | A816 | Set of 2 | 17.50 | 17.50 |

Souvenir Sheets of 2, #a-b
| 2968-2969 | A816 | Set of 2 | 15.50 | 15.50 |

Paintings by Henri de Toulouse-Lautrec (1864-1901) — A817

No. 2970, $100: a, Party in the Moulin Rouge. b, Count Alphonse de Toulouse-Lautrec Driving a Four-Horse Hitch. c, Equestrienne. d, Two Girls in Bed.

No. 2971, $100, vert.: a, Moulin Rouge La Goulue. b, Babylone d'Allemagne. c, Portrait of Madame la Comtesse de Toulouse-Lautrec. d, Portrait of Vincent van Gogh.

No. 2972, $200, vert.: a, La Clownesse Assise. b, La Clownesse.

No. 2973, $200, vert.: a, The Stage Manager Behind the Scenes. b, Portrait of Louis Pascal.

2014, Aug. 27   Litho.   Perf. 14
Sheets of 4, #a-d
| 2970-2971 | A817 | Set of 2 | 17.50 | 17.50 |

Souvenir Sheets of 2, #a-b
| 2972-2973 | A817 | Set of 2 | 17.50 | 17.50 |

National Parks of Africa — A818

No. 2974: a, Serengeti National Park, Tanzania (single tree). b, Victoria Falls, Zambia. c, Mt. Kilimanjaro, Kenya (view from mountain). d, Drakensberg Mountains, South Africa. e, Matopos National Park, Zimbabwe. f, Serengeti National Park (trees and vehicle path). g, Mt. Kilimanjaro (view of mountain). h, Sapo National Park, Liberia. i, Golden Gate Highlands National Park, South Africa.
$350, Namib-Naukluft National Park, Namibia.

2014, Sept. 3	**Litho.**	**Perf. 13¾**	
2974	A818	$85 Sheet of 9, #a-i	16.50 16.50
		Souvenir Sheet	
2975	A818	$350 multi	7.50 7.50

Race Horses — A819

No. 2976, $100: a, Flying Childers. b, Highflyer. c, Regulus. d, Sceptre.
No. 2977, $100: a, Cherimoya. b, American Eclipse. c, Bay Middleton. d, Crucifix.
No. 2978, $175: a, Kincsem. b, Eclipse. $350, Goldfinder.

2014, Sept. 3	**Litho.**	**Perf. 14**	
		Sheets of 4, #a-d	
2976-2977	A819	Set of 2	17.50 17.50
		Perf. 12½	
2978	A819	$175 Sheet of 2, #a-b	7.50 7.50
		Souvenir Sheet	
2979	A819	$350 multi	7.50 7.50

No. 2978 contains two 51x38mm stamps; No. 2979 contains one 51x38 stamp.

No. 2941 With Inscription Added in Yellow

and

German Soccer Team, 2014 World Cup Champions — A820

2014, Sept. 4	**Litho.**	**Perf. 14**	
2980	A813	$30 multi	.65 .65
		Souvenir Sheet	
		Perf. 12½	
2981	A820	$350 multi	7.50 7.50

SEMI-POSTAL STAMPS

No. 127 Surcharged in Red

1915	**Unwmk.**	**Perf. 14**	
B1	A40	2c + 3c on 10c	1.00 3.50
a.		Double red surcharge	
b.		Double blue surcharge	
c.		Both surcharges double	
d.		Pair, one without "2c"	

Same Surcharge On Official Stamp of 1912

B2	A49	2c + 3c on 10c blk & ultra	1.00 3.50
a.		Double surcharge	

Regular Issue of 1918 Surcharged in Black and Red

1918		**Perf. 12½, 14**	
B3	A59	1c + 2c dp grn & blk	1.40 10.50
B4	A60	2c + 2c rose & blk	1.40 10.50
a.		Double surch., one inverted	
b.		Invtd. surch., cross double	
c.		Invtd. surch., cross omitted	17.00
B5	A61	5c + 2c gray bl & blk	.65 3.00
a.		Imperf., pair	19.00
B6	A62	10c + 2c dk green	1.25 3.00
a.		Inverted surcharge	5.75 27.50
B7	A63	15c + 2c blk & dk grn	5.25 10.50
B8	A64	20c + 2c claret & blk	2.10 8.50
B9	A65	25c + 2c dk grn & grn	4.25 15.00
B10	A66	30c + 2c red vio & blk	10.00 10.50
B11	A67	50c + 2c ultra & blk	8.50 16.00
B12	A68	75c + 2c ol bis & blk	3.75 30.00
B13	A69	$1 + 2c yel brn & bl	6.25 57.50
B14	A70	$2 + 2c lt vio & blk	8.50 80.00
B15	A71	$5 + 2c dk brown	20.00 200.00
		Nos. B3-B15 (13)	73.30 455.00

Used values are for postally canceled stamps.

Nos. 277-279 Surcharged in Red or Blue

1941	**Unwmk.**	**Perf. 12**	
B16	A107	3c + 2c dk blue (R)	2.25 2.25
B17	A108	5c + 2c dull red brn	2.25 2.25
B18	A109	10c + 2c dk grn (R)	2.25 2.25
		Nos. B16-B18 (3)	6.75 6.75

> **Catalogue values for unused stamps in this section, from this point to the end of the section, are for Never Hinged items.**

Research — SP1

Lithographed and Engraved		
1954	**Unwmk.**	**Perf. 12½**
B19	SP1 5c + 5c rose lilac & blk	.25 .25
	Nos. B19,CB4-CB6 (4)	1.40 1.00

The surtax was for the Liberian Government Hospital. No. B19 exists imperforate.

Remember the African Child SP2

Designs: 25c + 10c, Village life. 70c + 20c, Mr. Sean feeding children. 75c + 15c, Fleeing conflict. 80c + 20c, Nuns teaching children. No. B24, Nuns killed in Oct. 1992, vert. No. B25, Sean Devereux (1964-93), vert.

	Perf. 13½x14	
1994, Jan. 6	**Unwmk.**	**Litho.**
B20	SP2 25c +10c multi	1.00 1.00
B21	SP2 70c +20c multi	3.25 3.25
B22	SP2 75c +15c multi	3.25 3.25
B23	SP2 80c +20c multi	3.50 3.50
	Nos. B20-B23 (4)	11.00 11.00
	Souvenir Sheets	
B24	SP2 $1.50 +50c multi	7.50 7.50
B25	SP2 $1.50 +50c multi	7.50 7.50

Surtax for Sean Devereux Liberian Children's Fund.

Charities — SP3

Designs: 25c+10c, No. B30, Natl. map in flag colors, blind man with cane. No. B27, Logo depicting children. No. B28, Blind man crossing street. No. B29, Dr. Herman Gmeiner, children.

1995	**Litho.**	**Perf. 14**
B26	SP3 25c +10c multi	1.25 1.25
B27	SP3 80c +20c multi	3.50 3.50
B28	SP3 80c +20c multi	3.50 3.50

B29	SP3 $1.50 +50c multi	6.75 6.75
B30	SP3 $1.50 +50c multi	6.75 6.75
	Nos. B26-B30 (5)	21.75 21.75

Christian Assoc. of the Blind, 10th anniv. (Nos. B26, B28, B30). SOS Children's Village (Nos. B27, B29).
Issued: Nos. B27, B29, 4/26; others, 4/28.

George Weah, Soccer Player — SP4

Designs: 50c+20c, In AC Milan strip. 75c+25c, In Liberia Natl. strip. 80c+20c, With 1989 Golden Ball Award. $1.50+50c, Two-time Golden Ball Winner.

1995, Oct. 6	**Litho.**	**Perf. 13x13½**
B31	SP4 50c +20c multi	2.50 2.50
B32	SP4 75c +25c multi	3.50 3.50
B33	SP4 80c +20c multi	3.50 3.50
B34	SP4 $1.50 +50c multi	7.25 7.25
a.	Souvenir sheet of 1, perf. 13	7.25 7.25
	Nos. B31-B34 (4)	16.75 16.75

Issued: No. B34a, 6/24/96. Surcharge for Liberian charities supported by George Weah.

AIR POST STAMPS

Regular Issue of 1928 Srchd. in Black

1936, Feb. 28	**Unwmk.**	**Perf. 12**
C1	A102 6c on 2c violet	250.00 275.00
C2	A102 6c on 3c bis brn	250.00 275.00

Same Srch. on Official Stamp of 1928

C3	A102 6c on 1c green	250.00 275.00
m.	On No. 230 (error)	750.00
	Nos. C1-C3 (3)	750.00 825.00

Values are for stamps with disturbed gum. Many counterfeits exist.

Waco Plane — AP1

1936, Sept. 30	**Engr.**	**Perf. 14**
C3A	AP1 1c yellow grn & blk	.25 .25
C3B	AP1 2c carmine & blk	.25 .25
C3C	AP1 3c purple & blk	.25 .25
C3D	AP1 4c orange & blk	.25 .25
C3E	AP1 5c blue & blk	.25 .25
C3F	AP1 6c green & blk	.25 .25
	Nos. C3A-C3F (6)	1.50 1.50

Liberia's 1st air mail service of Feb. 28, 1936.
Nos. C3A-C3F exist in pairs imperf. between (value, $50 each) and in pairs imperf. (value $15 each).

Eagle in Flight — AP2

Trimotor Plane AP3

Egrets — AP4

Sikorsky Amphibian — AP5

Designs: 3c, 30c, Albatross.

		1938, Sept. 12	**Photo.**	**Perf. 12½**	
C4	AP2	1c green		.25	.25
C5	AP3	2c red orange		.40	.25
C6	AP3	3c olive green		.50	.25
C7	AP4	4c orange		.60	.25
C8	AP4	5c brt blue grn		1.00	.25
C9	AP3	10c violet		1.00	.25
C10	AP5	20c magenta		1.25	.25
C11	AP3	30c gray black		2.25	.25
C12	AP2	50c brown		3.00	.25
C13	AP5	$1 blue		5.25	.25
		Nos. C4-C13 (10)		*15.50*	*2.50*

For surcharges see Nos. C17-C36, C45-C46, C47-C48, C49-C50.

Nos. 280-282 Overprinted in Red or Dark Blue

		1941, Feb. 25		**Perf. 12**	
C14	A107	3c dark blue (R)		2.75	2.75
C15	A108	5c dull red brn (DB)		2.75	2.75
C16	A109	10c dark green (R)		2.75	2.75
		Nos. C14-C16 (3)		*8.25*	*8.25*

Nos. C4-C13 Surcharged in Black

		1941		**Perf. 12½**	
C17	AP2	50c on 1c green		*3,000.*	325.00
C18	AP3	50c on 2c red org		175.00	105.00
C19	AP3	50c on 3c ol grn		175.00	105.00

C20	AP4	50c on 4c org		80.00	60.00
C21	AP4	50c on 5c brt bl grn		80.00	60.00
C22	AP3	50c on 10c vio		80.00	50.00
C23	AP5	50c on 20c mag		*2,500.*	70.00
C24	AP3	50c on 30c gray blk		65.00	40.00
C25	AP2	50c brown		65.00	40.00
C26	AP5	$1 blue		80.00	40.00

Nos. C17 to C26 with Additional Overprint

		1942			
C27	AP2	50c on 1c green		6.75	6.75
C28	AP3	50c on 2c red org		6.75	5.75
C29	AP3	50c on 3c ol grn		6.00	5.75
C30	AP4	50c on 4c orange		4.75	6.00
C31	AP4	50c on 5c brt bl grn		3.00	3.00
C32	AP3	50c on 10c violet		4.25	4.25
C33	AP5	50c on 20c mag		4.25	4.25
C34	AP3	50c on 30c gray blk		4.75	4.75
C35	AP2	50c brown		4.75	4.75
C36	AP5	$1 blue		4.25	4.25
		Nos. C27-C36 (10)		*49.50*	*49.50*

Plane and Air Route from United States to South America and Africa AP6

Plane over House AP7

		1942-44	**Engr.**	**Perf. 12**	
C37	AP6	10c rose		.25	.25
C38	AP7	12c brt ultra ('44)		.25	.25
C39	AP7	24c turq grn ('44)		.25	.25
C40	AP6	30c brt green		.25	.25
C41	AP6	35c red lilac ('44)		.25	.25
C42	AP6	50c violet		.25	.25
C43	AP6	70c olive gray ('44)		.60	.25
C44	AP6	$1.40 scarlet ('44)		1.50	.60
		Nos. C37-C44 (8)		*3.60*	*2.35*

No. C3A-C3C, C5-C8, C12 Srchd. with New Values and Large Dot, Bar or Diagonal Line in Violet, Blue, Black or Violet and Black

No. C45

No. C46

No. C46A

No. C48

No. C48B

No. C49

No. C50

		1944-45		**Perf. 12½**	
C45	AP3	10c on 2c (V+Bk)		35.00	25.00
C46	AP4	10c on 5c (V+Bk) ('45)		12.00	12.00
C46A	AP1	30c on 1c (Bk)		140.00	70.00
C47	AP3	30c on 3c (V)		150.00	65.00
C48	AP4	30c on 4c (V+Bk)		12.00	12.00
C48A	AP1	50c on 3c (Bk)		32.50	32.50
C48B	AP1	70c on 3c (Bk)		60.00	60.00
C49	AP3	$1 on 3c (Bl)		22.50	22.50
C50	AP2	$1 on 50c (V)		35.00	26.50
		Nos. C45-C50 (9)		*499.00*	*325.50*

These surcharges were handstamped with the possible exception of the large "10 CTS." of No. C46 and the "30 CTS." of No. C48. On No. C47, the new value was created by handstamping a small, violet, broken "O" beside the large "3" of the basic stamp.

Surcharges on Nos. C46A, C48A, C48B are found inverted. Values same as normal.

Roosevelt Type of Regular Issue

		1945, Nov. 26	**Engr.**		
C51	A116	70c brn & blk, *grysh*		1.25	1.40

Examples on thick white paper appeared later on the stamp market at reduced prices.

Monrovia Harbor Type

		1947, Jan. 2			
C52	A117	24c brt bluish grn		1.50	1.25

Without Inscription at Top

		1947, May 16			
C53	A117	25c dark carmine		.90	.45

1st US Postage Stamps Type

		1947, June 6			
C54	A118	12c green		.25	.25
C55	A118	25c brt red violet		.30	.25
C56	A118	50c brt blue		.40	.25
a.		Souv. sheet of 4, #300, C54-C56		50.00	
		Nos. C54-C56 (3)		*.60*	*.60*
		Set, never hinged		2.10	

No. C56a exists imperf. Values: hinged $65; never hinged $160.

Matilda Newport Firing Cannon — AP11

		1947, Dec. 1	**Engr. & Photo.**		
C57	AP11	25c scar & gray blk		1.25	.30

See note after No. 304.

Monument to Joseph J. Roberts — AP12

Centenary Monument AP14

Design: 25c, Flag of Liberia.

		1947, Dec. 22	**Engr.**		
C58	AP12	12c brick red		.30	.25
C59	AP12	25c carmine		.50	.25
C60	AP14	50c red brown		.80	.45
		Nos. C58-C60 (3)		*1.60*	*.85*
		Set, never hinged		5.50	

Centenary of independence.

L. I. A. Plane in Flight AP15

		1948, Aug. 17		**Perf. 11½**	
C61	AP15	25c red		1.50	1.50
C62	AP15	50c deep blue		1.00	1.00
		Set, never hinged		5.00	

1st flight of Liberian Intl. Airways, Aug. 17, 1948. Exist imperf.

Map and Citizens — AP16

Farm Couple, Arms and Agricultural Products — AP17

		1949, Apr. 12	**Litho.**	**Perf. 11½**	
C63	AP16	25c multicolored		.35	.65
C64	AP17	50c multicolored		.35	.65
		Set, never hinged		2.00	

Nos. C63-C64 exist perf. 12½. Definite information concerning the status of the perf. 12½ set has not reached the editors. The set also exists imperf.

Type of Regular Issue of 1948-50
Design: William V. S. Tubman.

1949, July 21   **Engr.**   **Perf. 12½**
C65 A128 25c blue & black   .60 .65
  Set, never hinged   1.60
   See No. C118.

Sun and Open Book — AP18

1950, Feb. 14   **Engr.**   **Perf. 12½**
C66 AP18 25c rose carmine   1.00 .50
  Set, never hinged   2.75
a.   Souv. sheet of 2, #329, C66, imperf.   1.75 1.75
  Set, never hinged   4.75

Campaign for National Literacy.

> Catalogue values for unused stamps in this section, from this point to the end of the section, are for Never Hinged items.

UPU Monument AP19

1950, Apr. 21
C67 AP19 25c orange & vio   2.75 2.75
a.   Souv. sheet of 3, #330-331, C67, imperf.   24.00 24.00
  UPU, 75th anniv. (in 1949).
  No. C67 exists imperf.

Map of Monrovia, James Monroe and Ashmun — AP20

50c, Jehudi Ashmun, President Tubman & map.

1952, Apr. 1   **Perf. 10½**
C68 AP20 25c lilac rose & blk   .25 .25
C69 AP20 50c dk blue & car   .70 .70
a.   Souvenir sheet of 8   24.00
  Nos. C68-C69 exist imperf. Value about two and one half times that of the perf. set.
  Nos. C68-C69 exist with center inverted. Value $50 each.
  No. C69a contains one each of Nos. 332 and 333, and types of Nos. 333-337 and C69 with centers in black; imperf.
  The 25c exists in colors of the 50c and vice versa. Value, each $8.

Flags of Five Nations — AP21

1952, Dec. 10   **Perf. 12½**
C70 AP21 25c ultra & carmine   .90 .65
a.   Souvenir sheet   2.25 2.25
  Nos. C70 and C70a exist imperforate.
  Value, No. C70a, imperf., $4.50.

Road Building — AP22

Designs: 25c, Ships in Monrovia harbor. 35c, Diesel locomotive. 50c, Free port, Monrovia. 70c, Roberts Field. $1, Wm. V. S. Tubman bridge.

1953, Aug. 3   **Litho.**
C71 AP22 12c orange brown   .25 .25
C72 AP22 25c lilac rose   .25 .25
C73 AP22 35c purple   1.00 .25
C74 AP22 50c orange   1.00 .25
C75 AP22 70c dull green   1.75 .25
C76 AP22 $1 blue   2.25 1.00
  Nos. C71-C76 (6)   6.50 2.25
  Exist imperf. See Nos. C82-C87.

Flags, Emblem and Children — AP23

1954, Sept. 27   **Size: 51x39mm**
C77 AP23 $5 bl, red, vio bl & blk   40.00 40.00
  A reproduction of No. C77, size 63x49mm, was prepared for presentation purposes. Value $35.
  Half the proceeds from the sale of No. C77 was given to the UNICEF.

UN Technical Assistance Agencies — AP24

Designs: 15c, Printing instruction. 20c, Sawmill maintenance. 25c, Geography class.

1954, Oct. 25
C78 AP24 12c black & blue   .25 .25
C79 AP24 15c dk brown & yel   .25 .25
C80 AP24 20c black & yel grn   .25 .25
C81 AP24 25c vio blue & red   .80 .25
  Nos. C78-C81 (4)   1.55 1.00
  UN Technical Assistance program.
  Nos. C78-C81 exist imperf.

Type of 1953 Inscribed: "Commemorating Presidential Visit U. S. A.-1954"
Designs as before.

1954, Nov. 19
C82 AP22 12c vermilion   .25 .25
C83 AP22 25c blue   .80 .25
C84 AP22 35c carmine rose   3.50 2.00
C85 AP22 50c rose violet   .95 .30
C86 AP22 70c orange brown   1.25 .55
C87 AP22 $1 dull green   1.90 .80
  Nos. C82-C87 (6)   8.65 4.15
  Visit of Pres. William V.S. Tubman to the US. Exist imperforate.

Baseball AP25

1955, Jan. 26   **Litho.**   **Perf. 12½**
C88 AP25 10c shown   .30 .30
C89 AP25 12c Swimming   .30 .30
C90 AP25 25c Running   .30 .30
a.   Souvenir sheet   18.00 18.00
  Nos. C88-C90 (3)   .90 .90
  No. C90a contains 1 each of Nos. 349, C90 with colors transposed. Exists imperf.; same value.

Costus AP26

Design: 25c, Barteria nigritiana.

1955, Sept. 28   **Unwmk.**   **Perf. 12½**
C91 AP26 20c violet, grn & yel   .40 .25
C92 AP26 25c green, red & yel   .40 .25

UN Emblem — AP27

UN Charter AP28

15c, General Assembly. 25c, Gabriel L. Dennis signing UN Charter for Liberia.

1955, Oct. 24   **Unwmk.**   **Perf. 12**
C93 AP27 10c ultra & red   .25 .25
C94 AP27 15c violet & blk   .25 .25
C95 AP27 25c green & red brn   .60 .25
C96 AP28 50c brick red & grn   1.50 .25
  Nos. C93-C96 (4)   2.60 1.00
  10th anniv. of the UN, Oct. 24, 1955.

Rotary International Headquarters, Evanston, Ill. — AP29

Design: 15c, View of Monrovia.

1955, Dec. 5   **Litho.**   **Perf. 12½**
C97 AP29 10c deep ultra & red   .25 .25
C98 AP29 15c redsh brn, red & bis   .70 .25
  Souvenir Sheet
C99 AP29 50c deep ultra & red   1.75 1.75
  Nos. C97-C99 (3)   2.70 2.25
  No. C99 design as No. C97, but redrawn and with leaves omitted.
  50th anniversary of Rotary International.
  Nos. C97-C99 exist without Rotary emblem; No. C97 printed entirely in deep ultramarine; No. C98 with bister impression omitted.

FIPEX Type of Regular Issue
10c, New York Coliseum. 12c, Globe inscribed FIPEX. 15c, 50c, Statue of Liberty.

1956, Apr. 28   **Unwmk.**   **Perf. 12**
C100 A143 10c rose red & ultra   .25 .25
C101 A143 12c orange & purple   .25 .25
C102 A142 15c aqua & red lilac   .90 .25
  Nos. C100-C102 (3)   1.40 .75
  Souvenir Sheet
C103 A142 50c lt green & brn   1.75 1.75

Olympic Park, Melbourne — AP32

20c, 40c, Map of Australia & Olympic torch.

1956, Nov. 15   **Unwmk.**   **Perf. 12**
C104 AP32 12c emerald & vio   .50 .50
C105 AP32 20c multicolored   .50 .50
  Souvenir Sheet
C106 AP32 40c multicolored   7.50 7.50
  Nos. C104-C106 (3)   8.50 8.50
  16th Olympic Games, Melbourne, 11/22-12/8.
  Nos. C104-C105 exist imperf.

Type of Regular Issue, 1957.
12c, 25c, Idlewild airport, NYC. 15c, 50c, Roberts Field, Liberia, plane & Pres. Tubman.

Lithographed and Engraved
1957, May 4   **Perf. 12**
C107 A146 12c brt grn & dk bl   .25 .25
C108 A146 15c red brn & blk   .25 .25
C109 A146 25c carmine & dk bl   .75 .25
C110 A146 50c lt ultra & blk   1.40 .25
  Nos. C107-C110 (4)   2.65 1.00

Type of Regular Issue, 1957
Orphanage and. 15c, Nurse inoculating boy. 35c, The Kamara triplets. 70c, Children and flag.

1957, Nov. 25   **Litho.**   **Perf. 12**
C111 A147 15c lt blue & brn   .25 .25
C112 A147 35c maroon & lt gray   1.00 .25
  Souvenir Sheet
C113 A147 70c ultra & rose car   1.50 1.25
  Nos. C111-C113 (3)   2.75 1.75

Type of Regular Issue, 1958
10c, Italian flag & Colosseum. #C115, French flag & Arc de Triomphe. #C116, Swiss flag & chalet. #C117, Vatican flag & St. Peter's.

Engr. and Litho.
1958, Jan. 10   **Perf. 10½**
Flags in Original Colors
C114 A148 10c dark gray   .45 .45
C115 A148 15c dp yellow grn   .45 .45
C116 A148 15c ultra   .45 .45
C117 A148 15c purple   .45 .45
  Nos. C114-C117 (4)   1.80 1.80

Type of Regular Issue, 1948-50
Design: William V. S. Tubman.

1958   **Engr.**   **Perf. 12**
C118 A128 25c lt green & blk   1.25 .90

  Souvenir Sheet

Preamble to Declaration of Human Rights — AP33

1958, Dec. 17   **Litho.**   **Perf. 12**
C119 AP33 20c blue & red   2.75 2.75
  10th anniv. of the signing of the Universal Declaration of Human Rights. Exists imperf.

Liberians Reading
Proclamation
AP34

1959, Apr. 15   Unwmk.
C120 AP34 25c blue & brown   .60 .60
African Freedom Day, Apr. 15.

UNESCO
Building,
Paris
AP35

1959, May 1
C121 AP35 25c ultra & red   .60 .50
a.   Souvenir sheet   1.75 1.75
Opening of UNESCO Headquarters in
Paris, Nov. 3, 1958.

Lincoln Type of Regular Issue
1959, Nov. 20   Engr.   Perf. 12
C122 A152 25c emerald & black   .90 .90
For souvenir sheet see No. 386a.

Touré,
Tubman
and
Nkrumah
AP36

1960, Jan. 27   Litho.   Unwmk.
C123 AP36 25c beige, vio bl &
            blk   .60 .80
See note after No. 387.

WRY Type of Regular Issue, 1960
1960, Apr. 7   Perf. 11½
C124 A154 25c ultra & black   .80 .70
a.   Souv. sheet of 2, #388, C124,
       imperf.   3.50 2.75

Map of
Africa — AP37

1960, May 11   Perf. 11½
C125 AP37 25c ultra & brown   .80 .80
See note after No. 389.

Olympic Games Type of 1960
Designs: 25c, Javelin thrower and hunter,
horiz. 50c, Runner and stadium, horiz.
1960, Sept. 6   Perf. 11½
C126 A156 25c brown & brt ultra   .90 .70
Souvenir Sheet
Imperf
C127 A156 50c lilac & brown   3.50 3.50

Stamp Centenary Type of 1960
1960, Dec. 1   Litho.   Perf. 11½
C128 A157 25c multicolored   1.00 1.00
Souvenir Sheet
C129 A157 50c multicolored   1.75 1.75
No. C129 exists imperf.

Globe,
Dove and
UN
Emblem
AP38

Design: 50c, Globe and dove.

1961, May 19   Unwmk.   Perf. 11½
C130 AP38 25c indigo & red   .50 .50
Souvenir Sheet
C131 AP38 50c red brn & emer-
            ald   2.25 2.25
Liberia's membership in the UN Security
Council.
    A second souvenir sheet contains one each
of Nos. 395, C130 and the 50c from No. C131,
imperf. Size: 133x83mm. Value $8.
No. C130 exists imperf.

Science
Class
AP39

Design: 50c, Science class, different
design.

1961, Sept. 8   Litho.
C132 AP39 25c purple & brown   .50 .25
Souvenir Sheet
C133 AP39 50c blue & brown   1.75 1.75
15th anniv. of UNESCO.

Joseph J. Roberts and Providence
Island — AP40

1961, Oct. 25   Litho.   Perf. 11½
C134 AP40 25c emerald & sepia   .70 .70
a.   Souvenir sheet of 3   1.75 1.75
150th anniv. of the birth of Joseph J. Roberts, 1st pres. of Liberia.
No. C134a contains three imperf. stamps
similar to Nos. 397-398 and C134, but printed
in different colors; 5c, emerald & sepia. 10c,
orange & sepia. 25c, ultramarine & sepia.

Scout Type of Regular Issue and

Boy
Scout — AP41

1961, Dec. 4   Unwmk.   Perf. 11½
C135 AP41 25c emerald & sepia   1.40 1.40
Souvenir Sheet
Design: Like No. 399.
C136 A161 35c dull blue & sepia   5.00 5.00
No. C136 exists imperf.

Dag Hammarskjold Type of 1962
1962, Feb. 1   Unwmk.   Perf. 12
C137 A162 25c black & red lilac   .60 .60
Souvenir Sheet
Imperf
C138 A162 50c black & ultra   1.75 1.75

Malaria
Eradication
Emblem
AP42

1962, Apr. 7   Perf. 12½
C139 AP42 25c purple & orange   .60 .50
Souvenir Sheet
Imperf
C140 AP42 50c dark red & ultra   2.00 1.50

Pres. Tubman, Statue of Liberty, New
York Skyline and Flags of US and
Liberia
AP43

1962, Sept. 17   Litho.   Perf. 11½x12
C141 AP43 12c multicolored   .25 .25
C142 AP43 25c multicolored   .60 .50
C143 AP43 50c multicolored   1.25 .85
      Nos. C141-C143 (3)   2.10 1.60
Pres. Tubman's visit to the US in 1961.

United
Nations
Emblem
and Flags
AP44

Design: 50c, UN emblem.

1962, Oct. 22   Perf. 12x12½
C144 AP44 25c lt ultra & dk bl   .50 .50
Souvenir Sheet
Imperf
C145 AP44 50c brt grnsh bl & blk   2.00 1.25
Observance of UN Day, Oct. 24, as a
national holiday.

Building Type of Regular Issue
12c, 70c, Capitol. 50c, Information Service.
$1, Treasury Department Building, Monrovia.
1962-63   Perf. 12x12½, 12 (70c)
C146 A165 12c brt yel grn &
                mar   .25 .25
C147 A165 50c orange & ultra   1.50 1.50
C147A A165 70c brt pink & dk bl
                ('63)   2.10 2.10
C148 A165 $1 sal & blk ('63)   2.75 2.75
      Nos. C146-C148 (4)   6.55 6.55

"FAO" Emblem
and
Globe — AP45

Design: 50c, "FAO" and UN Emblems.

1963, Mar. 21   Unwmk.   Perf. 12½
C149 AP45 25c dk green & yel   .70 .70
Souvenir Sheet
Perf. 12
C150 AP45 50c emerald & ultra   2.00 1.75
FAO "Freedom from Hunger" campaign.

Type of Regular Issue, 1963
Designs: 25c, Telstar satellite, vert. 50c,
Telstar and rocket, vert.
1963, May 27   Litho.   Perf. 12½
C151 A167 25c Prus blue & org   .70 .70

Souvenir Sheet
Perf. 12
C152 A167 50c dp violet & yel   3.00 1.60
No. C152 exists imperf. Value $12.50.

Red Cross Type of Regular Issue
Design: 25c, Red Cross and globe. 50c,
Centenary emblem and globe.
1963, Aug. 26   Unwmk.   Perf. 12
C153 A168 25c purple & red   .40 .40
C154 A168 50c deep ultra & red   .70 .70

Map of
Africa — AP46

1963, Oct. 28   Perf. 12½
C156 AP46 25c red orange & grn   .40 .40
See note after No. 412.

Olympic Type of Regular Issue
10c, Torch and mountains. 25c, Mountains,
horiz. 50c, Torch, background like No. 413.
1963, Dec. 11   Litho.   Perf. 12½
C157 A170 10c vio blue & red   .25 .25
C158 A170 25c green & orange   .80 .80
Souvenir Sheet
Perf. 12
C159 A170 50c gray & red   1.75 1.75
No. C159 exists imperf. Value $12.

Kennedy Type of Regular Issue,
1964
Designs: 25c, John F. Kennedy, vert. 50c,
John F. Kennedy (like No. 414).
1964, Apr. 6   Unwmk.   Perf. 12½
C160 A171 25c blk & red lil   .60 .50
Souvenir Sheet
Perf. 12
C161 A171 50c blk & red lil   1.75 1.40
An imperf. miniature sheet containing one of
No. C160 exists. No marginal inscription.
Value $15.

Satellite Type of Regular Issue
Souvenir Sheet
Design: Launching rocket separating from
booster in space, vert.
1964, June 22   Litho.
C162 A172 50c vio bl & red   3.00 3.00
Exists imperf. Value $12.50.

Olympic Type of Regular Issue
Souvenir Sheet
Design: 50c, Runner and Olympic rings.
1964, Sept. 15   Unwmk.   Perf. 12
C163 A173 50c grnsh bl & red   3.00 1.25
Exists imperf. Value $6.

Scout Type of Regular Issue, 1965
Designs: 25c, Liberian flag and fleur-delis.
50c, Globe and Scout emblem.
1965, Mar. 8   Litho.   Perf. 12½
C164 A174 25c crimson & ultra   .80 .80
Souvenir Sheet
C165 A174 50c yellow & lilac   4.00 4.00
No. C165 exists imperf. Value $7.

Lincoln Type of Regular Issue
Souvenir Sheet
50c, Lincoln and John F. Kennedy, horiz.
1965, May 3   Unwmk.   Perf. 12
C166 A175 50c dp plum & lt gray   1.75 1.75
Exists imperf. Value $5.50.

ICY Type of Regular Issue, 1965
Souvenir Sheet
1965, June 21   **Litho.**
C167 A176 50c car rose & brn   1.75 1.75

ITU Type of Regular Issue, 1965
1965, Sept. 21   **Unwmk.**   **Perf. 12½**
C168 A177 50c red org & vio bl   .80 .70

Tubman Type of Regular Issue
25c, Pres. Tubman and coat of arms.

1965, Nov. 29   **Litho.**   **Perf. 12½**
C169 A178 25c ultra, red & brn   .70 .70
  a.   Souv. sheet of 2, #431, C169,
      imperf.   1.75 1.75

Churchill Type of Regular Issue
25c, "Angry Lion" portrait by Karsh & Parliament, London. 50c, "Williamsburg Award Dinner" portrait by Karsh & map of Europe.

1966, Jan. 18   **Litho.**   **Perf. 12½**
C170 A179 25c blk & vio bl   .70 .55
Souvenir Sheet
Perf. 12
C171 A179 50c blk & red lil   1.75 1.75
  No. C171 exists imperf.

Soccer Type of Regular Issue
Souvenir Sheet
Design: 50c, Soccer match in stadium.

1966, May 3   **Litho.**   **Perf. 11½**
C172 A181 50c ultra & red brn   2.50 2.50
  Exists imperf. Value $15.

Kennedy Type of Regular Issue
25c, UN General Assembly & Pres. Kennedy. 35c, Pres. Kennedy & rocket on launching pad, Cape Kennedy. 40c, Flame on grave at Arlington.

1966, Aug. 16   **Litho.**   **Perf. 12½**
C173 A182 25c ultra, blk & ocher   .50 .25
C174 A182 35c dk vio bl & pink   .60 .25
Souvenir Sheet
Perf. 11½
C175 A182 40c dk vio bl & multi   2.50 2.50
  No. C175 exists imperf. Value $20.

Boy Scout Type of Regular Issue
Souvenir Sheet
50c, Scout at campfire & vision of moon landing.

1967, Mar. 23   **Litho.**   **Perf. 12½**
C176 A185 50c brt red lil & scar   5.00 5.00
  Exists imperf. Value $9.

Olympic Type of Regular Issue
Souvenir Sheet
Design: 50c, Pre-Hispanic sculpture, serape and Olympic rings, horiz.

1967, June 20   **Litho.**   **Perf. 12½**
C177 A186 50c vio & car   3.75 1.60
  Exists imperf. Value $15.

Winter Olympic Games Type of Regular Issue
Souvenir Sheet
Design: 50c, Woman skater.

1967, Nov. 20   **Litho.**   **Perf. 11½**
C178 A189 50c ver & blk   2.25 .70
  Exists imperf. Value $15.

Human Rights Type of Regular Issue
Souvenir Sheet
1968, Apr. 26   **Litho.**   **Perf. 11½**
C179 A191 80c bl & red   3.00 1.10
  No. C179 exists imperf.

M. L. King Type of Regular Issue
Souvenir Sheet
55c, Pres. Kennedy congratulating Dr. King.

1968, July 11   **Litho.**   **Perf. 11½**
C180 A192 55c brn & blk   3.75 1.00

Olympic Type of Regular Issue
Souvenir Sheet
Design: 50c, Steeplechase and ancient sculpture.

1968, Aug. 22   **Litho.**   **Perf. 11½**
C181 A193 50c brt bl & org brn   2.25 1.10
  Exists imperf. Value $15.

President Type of Regular Issue 1966-69
Design: 25c, Pres. William V. S. Tubman.

1969, Feb. 18   **Litho.**   **Perf. 11½x11**
C182 A180 25c blk & emer   .60 .30

ILO Type of Regular Issue
Design: 80c, "ILO" surrounded by cogwheel and wreath, vert.

1969, Apr. 16   **Litho.**   **Perf. 12½**
C183 A196 80c emer & gold   2.50 1.10
  No. C183 exists imperf.

Apollo 11 Type of Regular Issue
Souvenir Sheet
65c, Astronauts Neil A. Armstrong, Col. Edwin E. Aldrin, Jr., & Lieut. Col. Michael Collins, horiz.

1969, Oct. 15   **Litho.**   **Perf. 11½**
C184 A199 65c dk vio bl & brt red   2.50 1.10
  Exists imperf. Value $20.

UN Type of 1970
Design: $1, UN emblem, olive branch and plane as symbols of peace and progress, vert.

1970, Apr. 16   **Litho.**   **Perf. 12½**
C185 A200 $1 ultra & sil   2.40 1.40
  Exists imperf.

Apollo 14 Type of Regular Issue
Souvenir Sheet
Design: 50c, Moon, earth and star.

1971, May 20   **Litho.**   **Imperf.**
C186 A208 50c multi   3.50 3.50

Souvenir Sheet

Olympic Yachting Village, Kiel, and Yachting — AP47

1971, June 28   **Litho.**   **Perf. 14½x14**
C187 AP47   Sheet of 2   3.50 3.50
  a.   25c multi   .50 .50
  b.   30c multi   .60 .60
  Publicity for the 20th Summer Olympic Games, and the yachting races in Kiel, Germany, 1972. Exists imperf.

Boy Scout Type of Regular Issue
Souvenir Sheet
Boy Scouts of various nations cooking, horiz.

1971, Aug. 6   **Litho.**   **Perf. 15**
C188 A211 50c multi   4.25 4.25
  Exists imperf.

UNICEF Type of Regular Issue
Souvenir Sheet
UNICEF emblem & Bengal tigress with cubs.

1971, Oct. 1   **Imperf.**
C189 A213 50c multi   3.00 3.00

Souvenir Sheet

Japanese Royal Family — AP48

1971, Nov. 4   **Perf. 15**
C190 AP48 50c multi   4.25 4.25
  11th Winter Olympic Games, Sapporo, Japan, Feb. 3-13, 1972. Exists imperf. Value $15.

Sesquicentennial Type of Regular Issue
Souvenir Sheet
Design: 50c, Sailing ship "Elizabeth" between maps of America and Africa, horiz.

1972, Jan. 1   **Litho.**   **Imperf.**
C191 A216 50c car & vio bl   3.00 3.00

Olympic Type of Regular Issue
Souvenir Sheet
Design: 55c, View of Olympic Stadium and symbol of "Motion."

1971, May 19   **Litho.**   **Perf. 15**
C192 A218 55c multi   5.50 5.50
  Exists imperf.

Apollo 16 Type of Regular Issue
Souvenir Sheet
Lt. Comdr. Thomas K. Mattingly, 2nd, Capt. John W. Young & Lt. Col. Charles M. Duke, Jr.

1972, June 26   **Litho.**
C193 A220 55c pink & multi   2.50 2.50
  Exists imperf. Value $10.

Ship Type of 1972
Souvenir Sheet
Design: Lord Nelson's flagship Victory, and her figurehead (1765).

1972, Sept. 6   **Litho.**   **Perf. 15**
C194 A222 50c multi   3.00 3.00

Pres. Tolbert Type of 1972.
Souvenir Sheet
1972, Oct. 23   **Litho.**   **Perf. 15**
C195 A223 55c multi   2.00 2.00

Apollo 17 Type of Regular Issue
Souvenir Sheet
55c, Apollo 17 badge, moon and earth.

1973, Mar. 28   **Litho.**   **Perf. 11**
C196 A225 55c bl & multi   2.50 2.50
  Exists imperf. Value $10.

Locomotive Type of Regular Issue
Souvenir Sheet
Design: 55c, Swiss locomotive.

1973, May 4   **Litho.**   **Perf. 11**
C197 A226 55c multi   4.00 4.00

WHO Type of Regular Issue 1973
Souvenir Sheet
Design: 55c, WHO emblem, Paul Ehrlich and poppy anemones.

1973, June 26   **Litho.**   **Perf. 11**
C198 A228 55c lt vio & multi   2.50 2.50

Automobile Type of Regular Issue
Souvenir Sheet
Franklin 10 HP cross-engined 1904-05 models.

1973, Sept. 11   **Litho.**   **Perf. 11**
C199 A229 55c multi   2.50 2.50

Copernicus Type of Regular Issue
Souvenir Sheet
Design: 55c, Copernicus and concept of orbiting station around Mars.

1973, Dec. 14   **Litho.**   **Perf. 13½**
C200 A230 55c gray & multi   2.25 2.25
  Exists imperf. Value $15.

UPU Type of Regular Issue
Souvenir Sheet
55c, UPU emblem and English coach, 1784.

1974, Mar. 4   **Litho.**   **Perf. 13½**
C201 A232 55c multi   3.00 3.00
  Exists imperf. Value $15.

Dog Type of Regular Issue
Souvenir Sheet
Design: Hungarian sheepdog (kuvasz).

1974, Apr. 16   **Litho.**   **Perf. 13½**
C202 A233 75c multi   4.50 4.50
  Exists imperf.

Soccer Type of Regular Issue
Souvenir Sheet
Design: 60c, World Soccer Championship Cup and Munich Stadium.

1974, June 4   **Litho.**   **Perf. 11**
C203 A234 60c multi   2.50 2.50
  Exists imperf. Value $12.

Butterfly Type of Regular Issue
Souvenir Sheet
Tropical butterfly: 60c, Pierella nereis.

1974, Sept. 11   **Litho.**   **Perf. 13½**
C204 A235 60c gray & multi   4.50 4.50

Churchill Type of 1974
Souvenir Sheet
60c, Churchill at easel painting landscape.

1975, Jan. 17   **Litho.**   **Perf. 13½**
C205 A237 60c multi   2.00 2.00
  Exists imperf. Value $10.

Women's Year Type of 1975
Souvenir Sheet
Design: 75c, Vijaya Lakshmi Pandit, Women's Year emblem and dais of UN General Assembly.

1975, Mar. 14   **Litho.**   **Perf. 13**
C206 A238 75c gray & multi   1.50 1.50
  Exists imperf. Value $10.

American Bicentennial Type
Souvenir Sheet
Design: 75c, Mayflower and US No. 548.

1975, Apr. 25   **Litho.**   **Perf. 13½**
C207 A239 75c multi   3.50 3.50
  Exists imperf. Value $11.

Dr. Schweitzer Type, 1975
Souvenir Sheet
Schweitzer as surgeon in Lambarene Hospital.

1975, June 26   **Litho.**   **Perf. 13½**
C208 A240 60c multi   3.00 3.00
  Exists imperf. Value $11.

Apollo-Soyuz Type, 1975
Souvenir Sheet
75c, Apollo-Soyuz link-up and emblem.

1975, Sept. 18   **Litho.**   **Perf. 13½**
C209 A241 75c multi   2.50 2.50

Winter Olympic Games Type, 1976
Souvenir Sheet
Downhill skiing & Olympic Games emblem.

1976, Jan. 23   **Litho.**   **Perf. 13½**
C210 A243 75c multi   2.00 2.00
  Exists imperf. Value $9.

Olympic Games Type, 1976
Souvenir Sheet
Design: 75c, Dressage and jumping.

1976, May 4	Litho.	Perf. 13½
C211 A245 75c multi		2.50 2.50

Exists imperf. Value $9.

Bell Type
Design: 75c, A. G. Bell making telephone call, UPU and ITU emblems.

1976, June 4	Litho.	Perf. 13½
C212 A246 75c ocher & multi		3.00 3.00

Exists imperf. Value $11.

Animal Type of 1976
Souvenir Sheet
Design: 50c, Elephant, vert.

1976, Sept. 1	Litho.	Perf. 13½
C213 A249 50c org & multi		4.00 4.00

Bicentennial Type of 1976
Souvenir Sheet
Design: 75c, Like No. 770.

1976, Sept. 21	Litho.	Perf. 13½
C214 A250 75c multi		3.00 3.00

Mask Type of 1977
Souvenir Sheet
75c, Ibo mask and Festival emblem.

1977, Jan. 20	Litho.	Perf. 13½
C215 A251 75c lil & multi		2.25 2.25

Equestrian Type of 1977
Designs: 55c, Military dressage (team), US. 80c, Winners receiving medals, vert.

1977, Apr. 22	Litho.	Perf. 13½
C216 A253 55c ocher & multi		3.25 1.60

Souvenir Sheet
C217 A253 80c ocher & multi		3.00 3.00

No. C217 exists imperf. Value $9.

Elizabeth II Type of 1977
Souvenir Sheet
75c, Elizabeth II, laurel and crowns.

1977, May 23	Litho.	Perf. 13½
C218 A254 75c sil & multi		1.75 1.25

Exists imperf. Value $9.

Zeppelin Type of 1978
Souvenir Sheet
75c, Futuristic Goodyear aerospace airship.

1978, Mar. 9	Litho.	Perf. 13½
C219 A257 75c multi		2.50 2.50

Exists imperf. Value $10.

Soccer Type of 1978
Souvenir Sheet
Soccer game Netherlands & Uruguay, vert.

1978, May 16	Litho.	Perf. 13½
C220 A258 75c multi		2.50

Exists imperf. Value $14.

Coronation Type of 1978
Souvenir Sheet
Design: 75c, Coronation coach, horiz.

1978, June 12		
C221 A259 75c multi		3.25

Exists imperf. Value $14.

Soccer Winners' Type of 1978
Souvenir Sheet
Design: 75c, Argentine team, horiz.

1978, Dec. 8	Litho.	Perf. 13½
C222 A262 75c multi		3.25

Exists imperf. Value $12.50.

AIR POST SEMI-POSTAL STAMPS

Nos. C14-C16 Overprinted in Red or Blue Like Nos. B16-B18

1941	Unwmk.	Perf. 12
CB1 A107 3c +2c dk bl (R)		4.00 4.00
CB2 A108 5c +2c dl red brn (Bl)		4.00 4.00
CB3 A109 10c +2c dk grn (R)		4.00 4.00
Nos. CB1-CB3 (3)		12.00 12.00

> Catalogue values for unused stamps in this section, from this point to the end of the section, are for Never Hinged items.

Nurses Taking Oath — SPAP1

Designs: 20c+5c, Liberian Government Hospital. 25c+5c, Medical examination.

1954, June 21	Litho. & Engr.
Size: 39½x28½mm	
CB4 SPAP1 10c +5c car & blk	.30 .25
CB5 SPAP1 20c +5c emer & blk	.40 .25
Size: 45x34mm	
CB6 SPAP1 25c +5c ultra, car & blk	.45 .25
Nos. CB4-CB6 (3)	1.15 .75

Surtax for the Liberian Government Hospital. Nos. CB4-CB6 exist imperf. No. CB6 exists with carmine omitted.

AIR POST SPECIAL DELIVERY STAMP

No. C15 Overprinted in Dark Blue Like No. E1

1941	Unwmk.	Perf. 12
CE1 A108 10c on 5c dl red brn		2.00 2.00

AIR POST REGISTRATION STAMP

No. C15 Overprinted in Dark Blue

1941	Unwmk.	Perf. 12
CF1 A108 10c on 5c dl red brn		2.00 2.00

SPECIAL DELIVERY STAMP

No. 278 Surcharged in Dark Blue

1941	Unwmk.	Perf. 12
E1 A108 10c on 5c dl red brn		2.00 2.00

REGISTRATION STAMPS

R1

1893 Unwmk. Litho. Perf. 14, 15		
Without Value Surcharged		
F1 R1 (10c) blk (Buchanan)	250.	250.
F2 R1 (10c) blk (Greenville)	2,500.	—
F3 R1 (10c) blk (Harper)	2,500.	—
F4 R1 (10c) blk (Monrovia)	30.	30.
F5 R1 (10c) blk (Roberts-port)	1,000.	1,000.

Types of 1893 Surcharged in Black

1894		Perf. 14
F6 R1 10c bl, pink (Buchanan)	5.50	5.50
F7 R1 10c grn, buff (Harper)	5.50	5.50
F8 R1 10c red, yel (Monrovia)	5.50	5.50
F9 R1 10c rose, blue (Roberts-port)	5.50	5.50
Nos. F6-F9 (4)	22.00	22.00

Exist imperf or missing one 10. Value, each $10.

President Garretson W. Gibson — R6

1903	Engr.	Perf. 14
F10 R6 10c bl & blk (Buchanan)	1.75	.25
a. Center inverted	100.00	
F11 R6 10c org red & blk ("Grenville")	1.75	
a. Center inverted	100.00	
b. 10c orange & black	1.90	.25
F12 R6 10c grn & blk (Harper)	1.75	.25
a. Center inverted	100.00	
F13 R6 10c vio & blk (Monrovia)	1.75	.25
a. Center inverted	100.00	
b. 10c lilac & black	1.90	
F14 R6 10c magenta & blk (Robertsport)	1.75	.25
a. Center inverted	100.00	
Nos. F10-F14 (5)	8.75	
Nos. F10, F11b, F12-F14		.75

For surcharges see Nos. 178-182.

S.S. Quail on Patrol — R7

1919	Litho.	Serrate Roulette 12
F15 R7 10c blk & bl (Buchanan)	1.40	2.75
Serrate Roulette 12, Perf. 14		
F16 R7 10c ocher & blk ("Grenville")	1.40	2.75
F17 R7 10c grn & blk (Harper)	1.40	2.75
F18 R7 10c vio & bl (Monrovia)	1.40	2.75
F19 R7 10c rose & blk (Robertsport)	1.40	2.75
Nos. F15-F19 (5)	7.00	13.75

Gabon Viper — R8

Wmk. Crosses and Circles (116)
1921	Engr.	Perf. 13x14
F20 R8 10c cl & blk (Buchanan)	90.00	3.50
F21 R8 10c red & blk (Greenville)	22.50	3.50
F22 R8 10c ultra & blk (Harper)	22.50	3.50
F23 R8 10c org & blk (Monrovia)	22.50	3.50
F24 R8 10c grn & blk (Robertsport)	22.50	3.50
a. Imperf., pair	225.00	
Nos. F20-F24 (5)	180.00	17.50

Nos. F-20-F24 Overprinted in Black

F25 R8 10c (Buchanan)	25.00	6.25
F26 R8 10c (Greenville)	25.00	6.25
F27 R8 10c (Harper)	70.00	6.25
F28 R8 10c (Monrovia)	25.00	6.25
F29 R8 10c (Robertsport)	25.00	6.25
Nos. F25-F29 (5)	170.00	31.25

Nos. F20-F24 are printed tete-beche. Thus, the "1921" overprint appears upright on half the stamps in a sheet and inverted on the other half. Values are the same for either variety.

Passengers Going Ashore from Ship — R9

Designs: No. F31, Transporting merchandise, shore to ship (Greenville). No. F32, Sailing ship (Harper). No. F33, Ocean liner (Monrovia). No. F34, Canoe in surf (Robertsport).

1924	Litho.	Perf. 14
F30 R9 10c gray & carmine	7.00	.60
F31 R9 10c gray & blue grn	7.00	.60
F32 R9 10c gray & orange	7.00	.60
F33 R9 10c gray & blue	7.00	.60
F34 R9 10c gray & violet	7.00	.60
Nos. F30-F34 (5)	35.00	3.00

No. 278 Surcharged in Dark Blue

1941	Unwmk.	Perf. 12
F35 A108 10c on 5c dull red brn		2.00 2.00

POSTAGE DUE STAMPS

Nos. 26, 28
Surcharged

1892   Unwmk.   Perf. 11
J1 A5 3c on 3c violet 6.50 4.25
  a. Imperf., pair 30.00
  b. Inverted surcharge 45.00 45.00
  c. As "a," inverted surcharge 110.00

Perf. 12
J2 A5 6c on 6c olive gray 15.00 13.50
  a. Imperf., pair 40.00
  b. Inverted surcharge 52.50 35.00

D2

**Engr.; Figures of Value
Typographed in Black**
1893   Wmk. 143   Perf. 14, 15
J3 D2 2c org, *yel* 2.00 1.00
J4 D2 4c rose, *rose* 2.00 1.00
J5 D2 6c brown, *buff* 2.00 1.25
J6 D2 8c blue, *blue* 2.00 1.25
J7 D2 10c grn, *lil rose* 2.25 1.50
J8 D2 20c vio, *gray* 2.25 1.50
  a. Center inverted 110.00 110.00
J9 D2 40c ol brn, *grnsh* 4.50 3.00
Nos. J3-J9 (7) 17.00 10.50

All values of the above set exist imperforate. Each value also exists with center inverted.

MILITARY STAMPS

"LFF" are the initials of "Liberian Frontier Force." Nos. M1-M7 were issued for the use of troops sent to guard the frontier.

Issues of 1905, 1906 and 1909 Surcharged

1916   Wmk. 143
M1 A23 1c on 1c lt grn 190.00 190.00
  a. 2nd "F" inverted 250.00 250.00
  b. "FLF" 250.00 250.00
  c. Inverted surcharge 250.00 250.00

Unwmk.
M2 A33 1c on 1c grn & blk 600.00 550.00
  a. 2nd "F" inverted 700.00 600.00
  b. "FLF" 700.00 600.00
M3 A46 1c on 1c yel grn & blk 4.00 4.75
  a. 2nd "F" inverted 7.50 7.50
  b. "FLF" 7.50 7.50
M4 A47 1c on 2c lake & blk 4.00 4.75
  a. 2nd "F" inverted 7.50 7.50
  b. "FLF" 7.50 7.50

Surcharge exists sideways on Nos. M2, M5; double on Nos. M1-M4; inverted on Nos. M2-M4.

Nos. O46, O59-O60 Surcharged

M5 A33 1c on 1c 500.00 475.00
  a. 2nd "F" inverted 700.00 650.00
  b. "FLF" 700.00 650.00
M6 A46 1c on 1c 4.75 5.50
  a. 2nd "F" inverted 9.00 9.00
  b. "FLF" 9.00 9.00
  c. "LFF 1c" inverted 12.50 12.50

  d. As "a" and "1c" inverted 15.00
  e. "FLF 1c" inverted 15.00
M7 A47 1c on 2c 3.25 4.00
  a. 2nd "F" inverted 6.50 6.50
  b. "FLF" 6.50 6.50
  c. Pair, one without "LFF 1c"

OFFICIAL STAMPS

Types of Regular Issues Overprinted in Various Colors

Perf. 12½ to 15 and Compound
1892   Wmk. 143
O1 A9 1c vermilion .80 .80
O2 A9 2c blue .80 .80
O3 A10 4c grn & blk .80 .80
O4 A11 6c bl grn .80 .80
O5 A12 8c brn & blk .80 .80
O6 A13 12c rose red 2.00 2.00
O7 A14 16c red lilac 2.00 2.00
O8 A15 24c ol grn, yel 2.00 2.00
O9 A16 32c grnsh bl 2.00 2.00
O10 A17 $1 bl & blk 40.00 16.00
O11 A18 $2 brn, yel 16.00 11.50
O12 A19 $5 car & blk 24.00 9.00
Nos. O1-O12 (12) 92.00 48.50

a   "5" With Short Flag

1893 A11 5c on 6c bl grn
(a) (No. 50) 1.20 1.20
  a. "5" with short flag 6.00 6.00
  b. Both 5's with short flags 6.00 6.00
  c. "i" dot omitted 20.00 20.00
  d. Overprinted on #50d 45.00 45.00

Overprinted in Various Colors

1894
O15 A9 1c vermilion .70 .35
O16 A9 2c blue .85 .40
  a. Imperf.
O17 A10 4c grn & blk 1.00 .55
O18 A12 8c brn & blk 1.00 .55
O19 A13 12c rose red 1.40 .60
O20 A14 16c red lilac 1.40 .60
O21 A15 24c ol grn, yel 1.40 .70
O22 A16 32c grnsh bl 2.75 .80
O23 A17 $1 bl & blk 27.50 21.00
  a. $1 ultra & black 27.50 21.00
O24 A18 $2 brn, yel 27.50 21.00
O25 A19 $5 car & blk 125.00 87.50
Nos. O15-O25 (11) 190.50 134.05

Unwmk.
Imperf
O26 A22 5c vio & grn 3.50 2.25

Rouletted
O27 A22 5c vio & grn 3.50 2.25

Regular Issue of 1896-1905 Overprinted in Black or Red

1898-1905   Wmk. 143   Perf. 14, 15
O28 A23 1c lil rose .90 .90
O29 A23 1c dp grn ('00) .90 .90
O30 A23 1c lt grn (R) ('05) .90 .90
O31 A24 2c bis & blk 1.75 .60
  a. Pair, one without overprint 900.00
O32 A24 2c org red & blk ('00) 2.75 1.50
O33 A24 2c rose & blk ('05) 4.50 2.75
O34 A25 5c lake & blk 3.00 1.50

O35 A25 5c gray bl & blk ('00) 3.50 1.50
O36 A25 5c ultra & blk (R) ('05) 6.00 3.75
O37 A12 10c chr yel & ind 1.75 1.75
O38 A13 15c slate 1.75 1.75
O39 A14 20c vermilion 3.00 2.10
O40 A15 25c yel grn 1.75 1.75
O41 A16 30c steel blue 4.50 2.75
O42 A26 50c red brn & blk 4.50 2.75
Nos. O28-O42 (15) 41.45 27.15

For surcharge see No. O92.

Official stamps overprinted "ORDINARY" or with a bar with an additional surcharge are listed as Nos. 64B-90, 92-93, 99.

Red Overprint

1903   Unwmk.   Perf. 14
O43 A29 3c green .25 .25
  a. Overprint omitted 5.00
  b. Inverted overprint

Two overprint types: I — Thin, sharp, dark red. II — Thick, heavier, orange red. Same value.

On No. 50   O3

1904   Black Surcharge   Wmk. 143
O44 A11 1c on 5c on 6c bl grn 1.60 2.00
  a. "5" with short flag 4.25
  b. Both "5s" with straight flag 8.00 8.00

Red Surcharge
O45 O3 2c on 30c steel blue 9.50 9.50
  a. Double surcharge, red and black
  b. Surcharge also on back

Types of Regular Issue Overprinted in Various Colors

a

1906   Unwmk.
O46 A33 1c grn & blk (R) .65 .40
O47 A34 2c car & blk (Bl) .25 .25
  a. Center and overprint inverted 30.00 3.00
  b. Inverted overprint 6.00
O48 A35 5c ultra & blk (Bk) .65 .40
  a. Inverted overprint 15.00 15.00
  b. Center and overprint invtd. 50.00
O49 A36 10c dl vio & blk (R) .75 .55
  a. Inverted overprint 10.00 10.00
  b. Center and overprint invtd. 50.00
O50 A37 15c brn & blk (Bk) 3.00 .55
  a. Inverted overprint 4.50
  b. Overprint omitted 12.00 6.00
  c. Center and overprint invtd. 60.00
O51 A38 20c dp grn & blk (R) .75 .55
  a. Inverted overprint 15.00
O52 A39 25c plum & gray (Bl) .50 .25
  a. With 2nd ovpt in blue, invtd. 15.00
O53 A40 30c dk brn (Bk) .55 .25
O54 A41 50c org brn & dp grn (G) .75 .25
  a. Inverted overprint 5.00 4.00
O55 A42 75c ultra & blk (Bl) 1.40 .95
  a. Inverted overprint 9.50 5.75
  b. Overprint omitted 22.50
O56 A43 $1 dp grn & gray (R) .90 .25
  a. Inverted overprint
O57 A44 $2 plum & blk (Bl) 2.75 .25
  a. Inverted overprint 22.50 15.00
O58 A45 $5 org & blk (Bk) 5.50 .25
  a. Overprint omitted 11.00
  b. Inverted overprint 12.00 8.00
Nos. O46-O58 (13) 18.40 5.15

Nos. O52, O54, O55, O56 and O58 are known with center inverted.
For surcharges see Nos. O72, O82-O85, O96.

b

1909-12
O59 A46 1c emer & blk (R) .40 .25
O60 A47 2c car rose & brn (Bl) .40 .25
  a. Overprint omitted 7.50
O61 A48 5c turq & blk (Bk) .45 .25
O62 A49 10c blk & ultra (R) ('12) .60 .25
O63 A50 15c cl & blk (Bl) .60 .45
O64 A51 20c bis & grn (Bk) 1.10 .55
O65 A52 25c ultra & grn (Bk) 1.10 .55
  a. Double overprint 4.75 4.75
O66 A53 30c dk bl (R) .85 .25
O67 A54 50c brn & grn (Bk) 1.40 .40
  a. Center inverted 27.50
  b. Inverted overprint 4.00 2.75
O68 A55 75c pur & blk (R) 1.50 .25
Nos. O59-O68 (10) 8.40 3.45

Nos. O63, O64, O67 and O68 are known without overprint and with center inverted.
For surcharges see Nos. O74-O81, O86-O90, O97.

Rouletted
O69 A49 10c blk & ultra (R) 1.00 .95

Nos. 126B and 127E Overprinted type "a" ("OS") In Red
1910-12   Rouletted
O70 A49 3c on 10c blk & ultra .70 1.25

Perf. 12½, 14, 12½x14
O71 A49 3c on 10c blk & ultra ('12) .70 .40
  a. Pair, one without srch., the other with dbl. srch., one invtd.
  b. Double surcharge, one inverted 4.00

Stamps of Preceding Issues Srchd. with New Values like Regular Issue and — c

1914   On Nos. O52 and 110
O72 A39 (a) 2c on 25c plum & gray 25.00 10.50
O73 A42 (c) 20c on 75c brn & blk 8.75 5.25

On Nos. O66 and O68
O74 A53 (b) 5c on 30c dk bl 8.75 5.25
O75 A55 (c) 20c on 75c pur & blk (R) 13.00 5.25
Nos. O72-O75 (4) 55.50 26.25

Official Stamps of 1906-09 Surcharged Like Regular Issues of Same Date
1915-16
O76 A50 (c) 2c on 15c (Bk) .95 .50
O77 A52 (d) 2c on 25c (Bk) 5.25 5.25
O78 A51 (e) 5c on 20c (Bk) .95 .65
O79 A53 (g) 5c on 30c (R) 8.50 8.50
O80 A54 (i) 10c on 50c (Bk) 5.50 3.25
O81 A55 (j) 20c on 75c (R) 2.75 2.75
O82 A43 (k) 25c on $1 (R) 20.00 20.00
  a. "25" double 25.00
  b. "OS" inverted 25.00
O83 A44 (l) 50c on $2 (Bk) 50.00 50.00
  a. "Ceuts" 70.00 70.00
O84 A44 (m) 50c on $2 (Br) 22.50 22.50
O85 A45 (n) $1 on $5 (Bk) 21.00 21.00

Handstamped Surcharge
O86 A54 (i) 10c on 50c (Bk) 11.00 11.00

Nos. O60-O61 Surcharged like Nos. 153-154 in Black or Red

a1, b1

c1, d1

e1, f1

g1, h1

i1, j1

O87 A47	1c on 2c	2.75	2.75
	Strip of 10 types	30.00	
O88 A48	2c on 5c (R)	2.75	2.75
a.	Black surcharge	10.00	10.00
	Strip of 10 types (Bk)	140.00	

See note following Nos. 153-154.

Nos. O60-O61
Surcharged

O90 A47	1c on 2c	125.00	125.00
O91 A48	2c on 5c	100.00	100.00

No. O42 Surcharged

O92 A26	10c on 50c (Bk)	11.00	11.00

No. O53 Surcharged

1917

O96 A40	5c on 30c dk brn	21.00	21.00
a.	"FIV"	35.00	35.00

The editors consider the 1915-17 issues unnecessary and speculative.

No. O62 Surcharged in Red like No. 162

1918

O97 A49	3c on 10c blk & ultra	2.40	2.40

Types of Regular
Issue of 1918 Ovptd.
Type "a" in Black,
Blue or Red

1918	**Unwmk.**	**Perf. 12½, 14**	
O98 A59	1c dp grn & red brn (Bk)	.60	.25
O99 A60	2c red & blk (Bl)	.60	.25
O100 A61	5c ultra & blk (R)	1.10	.25
O101 A62	10c ultra (R)	.60	.25
O102 A63	15c choc & dk grn (Bl)	2.75	.60
O103 A64	20c gray lil & blk (R)	.85	.25
O104 A65	25c choc & grn (Bk)	5.25	.65
O105 A66	30c brt vio & blk (R)	6.50	.65
O106 A67	50c mar & blk (Bl)	7.75	.65
a.	Overprint omitted	11.00	
O107 A68	75c car brn & blk (Bl)	3.00	.25
O108 A69	$1 ol bis & turq bl (Bk)	6.00	.25
O109 A70	$2 ol bis & blk (R)	9.25	.25
O110 A71	$5 yel grn (Bk)	12.00	.40
	Nos. O98-O110 (13)	56.25	4.95

For surcharges see Nos. 259-269, O111-O112, O155-O157. For overprint see No. 270.

Official Stamps of 1918 Surcharged like Regular Issue

1920

O111 A59	3c on 1c grn & red brn	1.10	.70
a.	"CEETS"	15.00	15.00
b.	Double surcharge	8.00	8.00
c.	Double srch., one invtd.	15.00	15.00
d.	Triple surcharge	20.00	20.00
O112 A60	4c on 2c red & blk	.70	.70
a.	Inverted surcharge	12.00	12.00
b.	Double surcharge	12.00	12.00
c.	Double srch., one invtd.	10.00	10.00
d.	Triple surcharge	15.00	15.00

Types of
Regular
Issues of
1915-21
Overprinted

1921	**Wmk. 116**	**Perf. 14**	
O113 A57	2c rose red	8.25	.25
O114 A58	3c brown	1.75	.25
O115 A79	20c brn & ultra	2.25	.40

Same, Overprinted "O S"

O116 A75	1c dp grn	1.75	.25
O117 A76	5c dp bl & brn	1.75	.25
O118 A77	10c red vio & blk	.85	.25
O119 A78	15c blk & grn	4.75	.60
a.	Double overprint		
O120 A80	25c org & grn	6.50	.60
O121 A81	30c brn & red	1.75	.25
O122 A82	50c grn & blk	1.75	.25
a.	Overprinted "S" only		
O123 A83	75c bl & vio	3.25	.25
O124 A84	$1 bl & blk	22.50	.65
O125 A85	$2 grn & org	12.00	.95
O126 A86	$5 grn & bl	13.50	2.10
	Nos. O113-O126 (14)	82.60	7.30

Preceding Issues Overprinted "1921"

1921

O127 A75	1c dp grn	7.50	.25
O128 A57	2c rose red	7.50	.25
O129 A58	3c brown	7.50	.25
O130 A76	5c dp bl & brn	4.50	.25
O131 A77	10c red vio & blk	7.50	.25
O132 A78	15c blk & grn	8.50	.25
O133 A79	20c brn & ultra	8.50	.40
O134 A80	25c org & grn	8.25	.80
O135 A81	30c brn & red	7.50	.25
O136 A82	50c grn & blk	8.75	.25
O137 A83	75c bl & vio	5.50	.25
O138 A84	$1 bl & blk	15.00	2.00
O139 A85	$2 org & grn	19.00	2.25
O140 A86	$5 grn & bl	15.00	3.25
	Nos. O127-O140 (14)	130.50	10.95

Types of
Regular Issue
of 1923 Ovptd.

1923	**Perf. 13½x14½, 14½x13½**		
	White Paper		
O141 A88	1c bl grn & blk	8.75	.25
O142 A89	2c dl red & yel brn	8.75	.25
O143 A90	3c gray bl & blk	8.75	.25
O144 A91	5c org & dk grn	8.75	.25
O145 A92	10c ol bis & dk vio	8.75	.25
O146 A93	15c yel grn & bl	1.10	.40
O147 A94	20c vio & ind	1.10	.40
O148 A95	25c brn & red brn	32.50	.40
	White, Buff or Brownish Paper		
O149a A96	30c dp ultra & brn	1.10	.30
b.	Overprint omitted	2.00	
O150a A97	50c dl bis & red brn	2.25	.45
O151 A98	75c gray & grn	2.25	.25
O152a A99	$1 red org & grn	2.25	.65
b.	Overprint omitted	11.00	
O153 A100	$2 red lil & ver	6.00	.25
O154a A101	$5 bl & brn vio	4.50	2.25
	Nos. O141-O154a (14)	96.80	6.25

Nos. O149-154 exist on white, buff or brownish paper. Values are for the most common varieties. For detailed listings, see the *Scott Classic Specialized Catalogue.*

No. O98
Surcharged in Red
Brown

1926	**Unwmk.**	**Perf. 14**	
O155 A59	2c on 1c	2.25	2.25
a.	"Gents"	15.00	
b.	Surcharged in black	5.75	
c.	As "b," "Gents"	15.00	

No. O98
Surcharged in Black

1926

O156 A59	2c on 1c	1.00	1.00
a.	Inverted surcharge	20.00	
b.	"Gents"	10.00	

No. O98
Surcharged in Red

1927

O157 A59	2c on 1c	35.00	35.00
a.	"Ceuts"	55.00	
b.	"Vwo"	55.00	
c.	"Twc"	55.00	

Regular
Issue of
1928
Overprinted
in Red or
Black

1928		**Perf. 12**	
O158 A102	1c grn (R)	1.10	.55
O159 A102	2c gray vio (R)	3.50	2.10
O160 A102	3c bis brn (Bk)	3.75	4.25
O161 A103	5c ultra (R)	1.10	.55
O162 A103	10c ol gray (R)	3.50	1.75
O163 A103	15c dl vio (R)	3.50	1.00
O164 A103	$1 red brn (Bk)	77.50	22.50
	Nos. O158-O164 (7)	93.95	32.70

For surcharges see Nos. C3, O165.

No. O162 Surcharged with New Value and Bar in Black

1945	**Unwmk.**	**Perf. 12**	
O165 A104	4c on 10c (Bk)	12.00	12.00

LIBYA

'li-bē-ə

(Libia)

LOCATION — North Africa, bordering on the Mediterranean Sea
GOVT. — Republic
AREA — 679,358 sq. mi.
POP. — 4,992,838 (1999 est.)
CAPITAL — Tripoli

In 1939, the four northern provinces of Libya, a former Italian colony, were incorporated in the Italian national territory. Included in the territory is the former Turkish Vilayet of Tripoli, annexed in 1912. Libya became a kingdom on Dec. 24, 1951. The Libyan Arab Republic was established Sept. 1, 1969. "People's Socialist . . ." was added to its name in 1977. See Cyrenaica and Tripolitania.

100 Centesimi = 1 Lira
Military Authority Lira (1951)
Franc (1951)
1,000 Milliemes = 1 Pound (1952)
1,000 Dirhams = 1 Dinar (1972)

Watermarks

Wmk. 140 —
Crown

Wmk. 195 —
Multiple Crown
and Arabic F

Wmk. 310 —
Multiple
Crescent
and Star

Catalogue values for unused stamps in this country are for Never Hinged items, beginning with Scott 102 in the regular postage section, Scott C51 in the airpost section, Scott E13 in the special delivery section, Scott J25 in the postage due section, Scott O1 in the official section, Scott N1 in the Fezzan-Ghadames section, Scott 2N1 in the Fezzan section, Scott 2NB1 in the Fezzan semipostal section, Scott 2NC1 in the Fezzan airpost section, Scott 2NJ1 in the Fezzan postage due section, Scott 3N1 in the Ghadames section, and Scott 3NC1 in the Ghadames airpost section.

Used values in italics are for postally used stamps. CTO's sell for about the same as unused, hinged stamps.

Stamps of Italy Overprinted in Black

1912-22		**Wmk. 140**		**Perf. 14**
1	A42	1c brown ('15)	1.40	.85
a.		Double overprint	225.00	225.00
2	A43	2c orange brn	1.40	.50
3	A48	5c green	1.50	.35
a.		Double overprint	85.00	85.00
b.		Imperf., pair	300.00	
c.		Inverted overprint		—
d.		Pair, one without overprint	425.00	425.00
4	A48	10c claret	14.00	.35
a.		Pair, one without overprint	425.00	425.00
b.		Double overprint	160.00	160.00
5	A48	15c slate ('22)	5.50	8.50
6	A45	20c orange ('15)	5.50	.35
a.		Double overprint	175.00	175.00
b.		Pair, one without overprint	750.00	750.00
7	A50	20c brn org ('18)	4.25	5.50
8	A49	25c blue	5.50	.35
b.		Double overprint	175.00	
9	A49	40c brown	14.00	1.00
10	A45	45c ol grn ('17)	37.50	30.00
a.		Inverted overprint	675.00	
11	A49	50c violet	35.00	1.40
12	A49	60c brn car ('18)	19.00	25.00
13	A46	1 l brn & grn ('15)	62.50	1.75
14	A46	5 l bl & rose ('15)	425.00	500.00
15	A51	10 l gray grn & red ('15)	35.00	190.00
		Nos. 1-15 (15)	667.05	765.90

Two types of overprint were applied to this issue. Type I has bold letters, with dots close within "i"; type II has thinner letters, with dots further away within "i." All values, along with Nos. E1 and E2, received the type I overprint, and values shown are for this type. Nos. 1, 3-4, 6, 8, 11, 13-15 and E1-E2 also received the type II overprint. For detailed listings, see the *Scott Classic Specialized Catalogue of Stamps and Covers*.
For surcharges see Nos. 37-38.

Overprinted in Violet

1912				**Unwmk.**
16	A58	15c slate	260.00	1.75
a.		Blue black overprint	21,000.	42.50

No. 16 Surcharged

1916, Mar.				**Unwmk.**
19	A58	20c on 15c slate	55.00	10.00

Roman
Legionary — A1

Diana of
Ephesus — A2

Ancient Galley
Leaving
Tripoli — A3

"Victory" — A4

1921	**Engr.**	**Wmk. 140**		**Perf. 14**
20	A1	1c blk & gray brn	2.75	7.00
21	A1	2c blk & red brn	2.75	7.00
22	A1	5c blk & grn	3.50	.70
a.		5c black & red brown (error)	1,900.	

b.		Center inverted	50.00	77.50
c.		Imperf., pair	525.00	525.00
23	A2	10c blk & rose	3.50	.70
a.		Center inverted	50.00	77.50
24	A2	15c blk brn & brn org	85.00	2.75
a.		Center inverted	125.00	240.00
25	A2	25c dk bl & bl	3.50	.25
a.		Center inverted	17.50	24.50
b.		Imperf., pair	775.00	775.00
26	A3	30c blk & blk brn	35.00	.70
a.		Center inverted	2,750.	3,000.
27	A3	50c blk & ol grn	16.00	.25
a.		50c black & brown (error)	625.00	
b.		Center inverted		4,750.
28	A3	55c black & vio	16.00	24.00
29	A4	1 l dk brn & brn	47.50	.25
30	A4	5 l blk & dk blue	27.50	21.00
31	A4	10 l dk bl & ol grn	300.00	160.00
		Nos. 20-31 (12)	543.00	224.60

Nos. 20-31 also exist perf. 14x13. Values substantially higher.
See No. 47-61. For surcharges see No. 102-121.

20d	A1	1c blk & gray brn	5.50	11.00
21d	A1	2c blk & red brn	5.50	11.00
		Never hinged	14.00	
22d	A1	5c blk & red green	7.00	1.40
23d	A2	10c blk & rose	7.00	1.40
		Never hinged	17.50	
24d	A2	15c blk & brn org	160.00	5.50
		Never hinged	390.00	
25d	A2	25c dk bl & bl	7.00	.35
		Never hinged	17.50	
26d	A3	30c blk & blk brn	70.00	1.40
		Never hinged	175.00	
27d	A3	50c blk & ol grn	32.50	.35
		Never hinged	80.00	
28d	A3	55c blk & vio	32.50	55.00
		Never hinged	80.00	
29d	A4	1 l dk brn & brn	95.00	.35
		Never hinged	240.00	
30d	A4	5 l blk& dk blue	55.00	30.00
		Never hinged	140.00	
31d	A4	10 l blk& ol grn	625.00	190.00
		Never hinged	1,600.	

Italy Nos. 136-139
Overprinted

1922, Apr.				
33	A64	5c olive green	1.75	6.25
a.		Double overprint	450.00	450.00
34	A64	10c red	1.75	6.25
a.		Double overprint	450.00	450.00
b.		Inverted overprint	950.00	950.00
35	A64	15c slate green	1.75	9.75
36	A64	25c ultramarine	1.75	9.75
		Nos. 33-36 (4)	7.00	32.00

3rd anniv. of the victory of the Piave.

Nos. 11, 8 Surcharged

1922, June 1				
37	A49	40c on 50c violet	3.50	2.10
38	A49	80c on 25c blue	3.50	8.50

Libyan Sibyl — A6

1924-31		**Unwmk.**		**Perf. 14½x14**
39	A6	20c deep green	.70	.25
c.		Vert. pair, imperf between and top	1,400.	
d.		Horiz. pair, imperf between and at right	1,400.	
e.		Horiz. pair, imperf between and at left	1,400.	
40	A6	40c brown	2.10	.70
b.		Imperf single	275.00	425.00
41	A6	60c deep blue	.70	.70
b.		Imperf single	275.00	
42	A6	1.75 l orange ('31)	1.40	.25
43	A6	2 l carmine	4.25	1.00
b.		Imperf single	275.00	425.00
44	A6	2.55 l violet ('31)	8.50	17.50
		Nos. 39-44 (6)	17.65	19.95

1926-29				**Perf. 11**
39a	A6	20c	42.50	.30
40a	A6	40c	30.00	2.40
41a	A6	60c	30.00	.45
43a	A6	2 l ('29)	14.00	5.00
		Nos. 39a-43a (4)	116.50	8.15

Type of 1921

1924-40		**Unwmk.**		**Perf. 13½ to 14**
47	A1	1c blk & gray brown	2.75	5.50
48	A1	2c blk & red brn	2.75	5.50
49	A1	5c blk & green	3.50	.70
50	A1	7½c blk & brown ('31)	1.40	14.00
51	A2	10c blk & dl red	2.75	.30
b.		10c blk & carmine		.30
c.		As "b," center inverted	175.00	
52	A2	15c blk brn & org	8.50	1.00
b.		Center inverted, perf. 11	4,500.	6,500.
53	A2	25c dk bl & bl	42.50	.50
a.		Center inverted	240.00	350.00
54	A3	30c blk & blk brn	2.75	.50
55	A3	50c blk & ol grn	2.75	.30
b.		Center inverted	4,500.	
56	A3	55c black & vio	625.00	825.00
57	A4	75c violet & red	6.50	.25
58	A4	1 l dk brn & brn	10.00	.35
59	A3	1.25 l indigo & ultra ('31)	1.40	.25
60	A4	5 l blk & dark blue ('40)	150.00	175.00
		Nos. 47-60 (14)	862.55	1,029.

				Perf. 11
47a	A1	1c	375.00	
48a	A1	2c	375.00	
49a	A1	5c	70.00	17.50
51a	A2	10c	35.00	7.00
52a	A2	15c	475.00	45.00
54a	A3	30c	140.00	2.10
55a	A3	50c	775.00	.25
58a	A4	1 l	350.00	.35
60a	A4	5 l ('37)	2,400.	450.00
61	A4	10 l dk bl & olive grn ('37)	625.00	500.00

Nos. 47a and 48a were not sent to the colony. A few philatelically inspired covers exist.

Italy Nos. 197 and 88 Overprinted Like Nos. 1-15

1929		**Wmk. 140**		**Perf. 14**
62	A86	7½c light brown	10.00	55.00
a.		Double overprint		
63	A46	1.25 l blue & ultra	60.00	21.00
a.		Inverted overprint	3,750.	

Italy No. 193 Overprinted Like Nos. 33-36

1929		**Unwmk.**		**Perf. 11**
64	A85	1.75 l deep brown	75.00	2.10
h.		Perf 13¾	12,000.	

Water
Carriers
A7

Man of Tripoli — A8

Designs: 25c, Minaret. 30c, 1.25 l, Tomb of Holy Man near Tagiura. 50c, Statue of Emperor Claudius at Leptis. 75c, Ruins of gardens.

1934, Feb. 17		**Photo.**		**Perf. 14**
64A	A7	10c brown	4.25	17.50
64B	A8	20c car rose	4.25	15.00
64C	A8	25c green	4.25	15.00
64D	A7	30c dark brown	4.25	15.00
64E	A8	50c purple	4.25	15.00
64F	A7	75c rose	4.25	27.50
64G	A7	1.25 l blue	55.00	95.00
		Nos. 64A-64G (7)	80.50	200.00
		Nos. 64A-64G,C14-C18 (12)	508.50	980.00

8th Sample Fair, Tripoli.

Bedouin
Woman — A15

1936, May 11   Wmk. 140   *Perf. 14*
65	A15	50c purple	1.75	2.75
66	A15	1.25 l deep blue	1.75	7.75

10th Sample Fair, Tripoli.

Highway Memorial
Arch — A16

1937, Mar. 15
67	A16	50c copper red	2.75	5.50
68	A16	1.25 l sapphire	2.75	12.50
		Nos. 67-68,C28-C29 (4)	11.00	36.00

Coastal road to the Egyptian frontier,
opening.

Nos. 67-68
Overprinted in Black

1937, Apr. 24
69	A16	50c copper red	14.00	35.00
70	A16	1.25 l sapphire	14.00	35.00
		Nos. 69-70,C30-C31 (4)	56.00	140.00

11th Sample Fair, Tripoli.

Roman
Wolf and
Lion of St.
Mark
A17

View of Fair
Buildings
A18

1938, Feb. 20
71	A17	5c brown	.30	1.00
72	A18	10c olive brown	.30	.70
73	A17	25c green	.55	1.25
74	A18	50c purple	.55	.55
75	A17	75c rose red	1.40	2.75
76	A18	1.25 l dark blue	1.40	7.00
		Nos. 71-76,C32-C33 (8)	7.30	21.50

12th Sample Fair, Tripoli.

Augustus   Goddess
Caesar   Abundantia
(Octavianus)   A20
A19

1938, Apr. 25
77	A19	5c olive brown	.25	1.40
78	A20	10c brown red	.25	1.40
79	A19	25c dk yel green	.50	.70
80	A20	50c dk violet	.50	.45

81	A19	75c orange red	1.40	1.75
82	A20	1.25 l dull blue	1.40	2.75
		Nos. 77-82,C34-C35 (8)	5.65	13.95

Birth bimillenary of Augustus Caesar
(Octavianus), first Roman emperor.

Desert
City — A21

View of
Ghadames
A22

1939, Apr. 12   Photo.
83	A21	5c olive brown	.70	1.00
84	A22	20c red brown	.70	1.00
85	A21	50c rose violet	.70	1.00
86	A22	75c scarlet	.70	3.50
87	A21	1.25 l gray blue	1.40	4.25
		Nos. 83-87,C36-C38 (8)	6.60	17.70

13th Sample Fair, Tripoli.

Modern
City — A23

Oxen and
Plow
A24

Mosque — A25

1940, June 3   Wmk. 140   *Perf. 14*
88	A23	5c brown	.70	1.00
89	A24	10c red orange	.70	.70
90	A25	25c dull green	.70	1.00
91	A23	50c dark violet	.70	.70
92	A24	75c crimson	.70	3.50
93	A25	1.25 l ultramarine	1.40	5.50
94	A24	2 l + 75c rose lake	1.40	16.00
		Nos. 88-94,C39-C42 (11)	9.70	50.50

Triennial Overseas Exposition, Naples.

"Two
Peoples,
One War,"
Hitler and
Mussolini
A26

1941, May 16
95	A26	5c orange	2.10	7.00
96	A26	10c brown	2.10	7.00
97	A26	20c dull violet	3.50	7.00
98	A26	25c green	3.50	7.00
99	A26	50c purple	3.50	7.00
100	A26	75c scarlet	3.50	19.00
101	A26	1.25 l sapphire	3.50	19.00
		Nos. 95-101,C43 (8)	24.45	115.50
		Set, never hinged	42.50	

The Rome-Berlin Axis.

> **Catalogue values for unused stamps in this section, from this point to the end of the section, are for Never Hinged items.**

United Kingdom of Libya

Stamps of Cyrenaica
1950 Surcharged in
Black

For Use in Tripolitania

1951, Dec. 24   Unwmk.   *Perf. 12½*
102	A2	1mal on 2m rose car	.25	.25
103	A2	2mal on 4m dk grn	.25	.25
104	A2	4mal on 8m red org	.25	.25
105	A2	5mal on 10m pur	.45	.45
106	A2	6mal on 12m red	.45	.45
a.		Inverted surcharge	30.00	30.00
107	A2	10mal on 20m dp bl	.85	.85
a.		Arabic "20" for "10"	25.00	25.00
108	A3	24mal on 50m choc & ultra	3.25	3.25
109	A3	48mal on 100m bl blk & car rose	13.50	13.50
110	A3	96mal on 200m vio & pur	30.00	30.00
111	A3	240mal on 500m dk grn & org	75.00	75.00
		Nos. 102-111 (10)	124.25	124.25

The surcharge is larger on Nos. 108 to 111.

For Use in Fezzan
Same Surcharge in Francs
112	A2	2fr on 2m rose car	.25	.50
113	A2	4fr on 4m dk grn	.25	.50
114	A2	8fr on 8m red org	.35	.70
115	A2	10fr on 10m pur	.50	1.00
116	A2	12fr on 12m red	.90	1.75
117	A2	20fr on 20m dp bl	2.00	4.50
118	A3	48fr on 50m choc & ultra	42.50	45.00
119	A3	96fr on 100m bl blk & car rose	42.50	240.00
120	A3	192fr on 200m vio & pur	120.00	240.00
121	A3	480fr on 500m dk grn & org	225.00	260.00
		Nos. 112-121 (10)	434.25	793.95

The surcharge is larger on Nos. 118-121.
A second printing of Nos. 118-121 has an elongated first character in second line of Arabic surcharge.

Cyrenaica Nos. 65-77
Overprinted in Black

For Use in Cyrenaica
122	A2	1m dark brown	.25	.40
123	A2	2m rose carmine	.30	.40
124	A2	3m orange	.30	.50
125	A2	4m dark green	35.00	55.00
126	A2	5m gray	.30	.50
127	A2	8m red orange	.75	1.25
128	A2	10m purple	1.25	1.90
129	A2	12m red	1.40	2.25
130	A2	20m deep blue	2.00	3.75
131	A3	50m choc & ultra	9.50	19.00
132	A3	100m bl blk & car rose	17.50	24.00
133	A3	200m violet & pur	55.00	70.00
134	A3	500m dk grn & org	180.00	190.00
		Nos. 122-134 (13)	303.55	368.95

Wider spacing between the two lines on Nos. 131-134.

King Idris

A27   A28

1952, Apr. 15   Engr.   *Perf. 11½*
135	A27	2m yellow brown	.25	.25
136	A27	4m gray	.25	.25
137	A27	5m blue.green	20.00	.65
138	A27	8m vermilion	.85	.55
139	A27	10m purple	20.00	.40
140	A27	12m lilac rose	1.75	.40

141	A27	20m deep blue	22.50	.90
142	A27	25m chocolate	22.50	.90
143	A28	50m brown & blue	3.00	1.40
144	A28	100m gray blk & car rose	5.25	3.00
145	A28	200m dk blue & pur	11.00	6.00
146	A28	500m dk grn & brn orange	37.50	21.00
		Nos. 135-146 (12)	144.85	35.70

For surcharge and overprints see Nos. 168,
O1-O8.

Globe — A29

Perf. 13½x13
1955, Jan. 1   Photo.   Wmk. 195
147	A29	5m yellow brown	2.00	1.30
148	A29	10m green	3.00	2.00
149	A29	30m violet	5.50	3.50
		Nos. 147-149 (3)	10.50	6.80

Arab Postal Union founding, July 1, 1954.

Nos. 147-149
Overprinted

1955, Aug. 1
150	A29	5m yellow brn	1.00	.65
151	A29	10m green	2.00	1.10
152	A29	30m violet	3.75	2.00
		Nos. 150-152 (3)	6.75	3.75

Arab Postal Congress, Cairo, Mar. 15.

Emblems of Tripolitania,
Cyrenaica and Fezzan
with Royal
Crown — A30

1955   Engr.   Wmk. 310   *Perf. 11½*
153	A30	2m lemon	2.00	.70
154	A30	3m slate blue	.25	.25
155	A30	4m gray green	2.75	1.25
156	A30	5m light blue grn	.85	.25
157	A30	10m violet	1.50	.25
158	A30	18m crimson	.25	.25
159	A30	20m orange	.50	.25
160	A30	30m blue	.85	.25
161	A30	35m brown	1.25	.25
162	A30	40m rose carmine	2.00	.60
163	A30	50m olive	1.25	.60

Size: 27½x32½mm
164	A30	100m dk green & pur	2.75	1.20
165	A30	200m ultra & rose car	13.00	2.50
166	A30	500m grn & orange	20.00	12.00

Size: 26½x32mm
167	A30	£1 ocher, brn & grn, yel	30.00	18.00
		Nos. 153-167 (15)	79.20	38.60

See Nos. 177-179, 192-206A.

No. 136 Surcharged

1955, Aug. 25   Unwmk.
168	A27	5m on 4m gray	2.00	.90

Tomb of
El
Senussi,
Jagbub
A31

Perf. 13x13½
1956, Sept. 14 Photo. Wmk. 195
169 A31 5m green .50 .50
170 A31 10m bright violet .60 .50
171 A31 15m rose carmine 1.40 1.25
172 A31 30m sapphire 2.25 1.40
Nos. 169-172 (4) 4.75 3.65

Death centenary of the Imam Seyyid
Mohammed Aly El Senussi (in 1859).

Map, Flags and UN
Headquarters — A32

1956, Dec. 14 Litho. Perf. 13½x13
173 A32 15m bl, ocher & ol bis .75 .35
174 A32 35m bl, ocher & vio brn 1.60 .75

Libya's admission to the UN, 1st anniv.

Globe and Postal
Emblems — A33

1957 Wmk. 195 Perf. 13½x13
175 A33 15m blue 1.50 1.50
176 A33 500m yellow brown 22.00 12.00

Arab Postal Congress, Tripoli, Feb. 9.

Emblems Type of 1955
1957 Wmk. 310 Engr. Perf. 11½
177 A30 1m black, yellow .25 .25
178 A30 2m bister brown .25 .25
179 A30 4m brown carmine .35 .35
Nos. 177-179 (3) .85 .85

UN Emblem and
Broken
Chain — A34

Unwmk.
1958, Dec. 10 Photo. Perf. 14
180 A34 10m bluish violet .35 .25
181 A34 15m green .60 .35
182 A34 30m ultramarine 1.50 .85
Nos. 180-182 (3) 2.45 1.45

Universal Declaration of Human Rights,
10th anniv.

Date Palms
and FAO
Emblem
A35

1959, Dec. 5 Unwmk. Perf. 14
183 A35 10m pale vio & black .40 .25
184 A35 15m bluish grn & blk .60 .45
185 A35 45m light blue & blk 1.50 1.20
Nos. 183-185 (3) 2.50 1.90

1st Intl. Dates Conf., Tripoli, Dec. 5-11.

Arab
League
Center,
Cairo, and
Arms of
Libya
A36

Perf. 13x13½
1960, Mar. 22 Wmk. 328
186 A36 10m dull grn & blk .60 .35

Opening of the Arab League Center and the
Arab Postal Museum in Cairo.

Emblems of WRY
and UN, Arms of
Libya — A37

1960, Apr. 7 Unwmk. Perf. 14
187 A37 10m violet & black .60 .35
188 A37 45m blue & black 1.75 1.25

World Refugee Year, 7/1/59-6/30/60.

Palm Tree and
Radio
Mast — A38

1960, Aug. 4 Engr. Perf. 13x13½
189 A38 10m violet .35 .25
190 A38 15m blue green .50 .25
191 A38 45m dk carmine rose 1.80 1.25
Nos. 189-191 (3) 2.65 1.75

3rd Arab Telecommunications Conf., Tripoli,
Aug. 4.

Emblems Type of 1955
1960 Wmk. 310 Engr. Perf. 11½
Size: 18x21½mm
192 A30 1m black, gray .25 .25
193 A30 2m bis brn, buff .25 .25
194 A30 3m blue, bluish .25 .25
195 A30 4m brn car, rose .25 .25
196 A30 5m grn, greenish .25 .25
197 A30 10m vio, pale vio .25 .25
198 A30 15m brown, buff .25 .25
199 A30 20m orange, buff .50 .25
200 A30 30m red, pink .50 .25
201 A30 40m rose car, rose .75 .25
202 A30 45m blue, bluish .85 .25
203 A30 50m olive, buff .85 .25
Size: 27½x32½mm
204 A30 100m dk grn & pur,
  gray 1.50 .70
205 A30 200m bl & rose car,
  bluish 4.25 1.40
206 A30 500m green & org,
  greenish 30.00 9.00
Size: 26½x32mm
206A A30 £1 ocher, brn &
  grn, brn 35.00 18.00
Nos. 192-206A (16) 75.95 32.10

Watchtower and
Broken
Chain — A39

1961, Aug. 9 Photo. Unwmk.
207 A39 5m lt yel grn & brn .50 .25
208 A39 15m light blue & brn .85 .35

Issued for Army Day, Aug. 9, 1961.

Map of Zelten
Oil Field and
Tanker at
Marsa
Brega — A40

1961, Oct. 25 Perf. 11½
209 A40 15m ol grn & buff .50 .25
210 A40 50m red brn & pale vio 1.50 1.00
211 A40 100m ultra & blue 3.50 1.25
Nos. 209-211 (3) 5.50 2.50

Opening of first oil pipe line in Libya.

Hands Breaking Chain, Tractor and
Cows — A41

Designs: 50m, Modern highways and buildings. 100m, Machinery.

1961, Dec. 24 Perf. 11½
Granite Paper
212 A41 15m pale grn, grn &
  brown .25 .25
213 A41 50m buff & brown .90 .60
214 A41 100m sal, vio & brn 3.25 1.25
Nos. 212-214 (3) 4.40 2.10

10th anniversary of independence.

Camel Riders — A42

15m, Well. 50m, Oil installations in desert.

1962, Feb. 20 Photo. Perf. 12
215 A42 10m choc & org brn .85 .25
216 A42 15m plum & yel grn 1.00 .60
217 A42 50m emer & ultra 2.75 2.10
a. Souv. sheet of 3, #215-217,
  imperf. 65.00 30.00
Nos. 215-217 (3) 4.60 2.95

Intl. Fair, Tripoli, Feb. 20-Mar. 20.
Nos. 215-217 exist imperf. Value about
twice that of perf.

Malaria Eradication
Emblem and
Palm — A43

1962, Apr. 7 Unwmk. Perf. 11½
218 A43 15m multicolored .60 .50
219 A43 50m grn, yel & brn 1.50 1.20

WHO drive to eradicate malaria.
Exist imperf. Value $10.
Two imperf. souvenir sheets exist, one containing the 15m, the other the 50m. Sold for
20m and 70m respectively. Value for both,
$34.

Ahmed Rafik El
Mehdawi (1898-
1961),
Poet — A44

1962, July 6 Engr. Perf. 13x14
220 A44 15m green .40 .25
221 A44 20m brown .85 .50

El Mehdawi, 1st death anniv.

Clasped Hands
and Scout
Emblem — A45

Designs: 10m, 30m, Boy Scouts. 15m,
50m, Scout emblem and tents.

1962, July 13 Photo. Perf. 12
222 A45 5m yel, blk & red .25 .25
223 A45 10m bl, blk & yel .50 .25
224 A45 15m multicolored .60 .50
Nos. 222-224 (3) 1.35 1.00

Souvenir Sheet
Imperf
225 Sheet of 3 20.00 20.00
a. A45 20m yellow, black & red 5.00 5.00
b. A45 30m blue, black & yellow 5.00 5.00
c. A45 50m blue gray, yel, blk &
  grn 5.00 5.00

Third Libyan Scout meeting (Philia).
Nos. 222-224 exist imperf. Value for set, $3.

Drop of Oil with New
City, Desert, Oil
Wells and Map of
Coast Line — A46

1962, Nov. 25 Perf. 11x11½
226 A46 15m grn & vio blk .50 .25
227 A46 50m brn org & ol 1.40 .75

Opening of the Essider Terminal Sidrah
pipeline system.

Centenary
Emblem — A47

Litho. & Photo.
1963, Jan. 1 Perf. 11½
228 A47 10m rose, blk, red & bl .75 .40
229 A47 15m citron, blk, red & bl .85 .60
230 A47 20m gray, blk, red & bl 1.60 .85
Nos. 228-230 (3) 3.20 1.85

Centenary of the International Red Cross.

Rainbow and Arches over Map of
Africa and Libya — A48

1963, Feb. 28 Litho. Perf. 13½
231 A48 15m multicolored .50 .35
232 A48 30m multicolored .85 .35
233 A48 50m multicolored 1.80 1.00
Nos. 231-233 (3) 3.15 1.70

Tripoli Intl. Fair "Gateway of Africa," Feb. 28-
Mar. 28. Every other horizontal row inverted in
sheet of 50 (25 tête bêche pairs). Value, set of
tête bêche pairs, $6.50.

Date Palm and Well — A49

Designs: 15m, Camel and flock of sheep. 45m, Sower and tractor.

1963, Mar. 21   Photo.   *Perf. 11½*
234 A49 10m green, lt bl & bis   .50 .25
235 A49 15m pur, lt grn & bis   .60 .50
236 A49 45m dk bl, sal & sep   1.60 1.00
   Nos. 234-236 (3)   2.70 1.75

FAO "Freedom from Hunger" campaign.

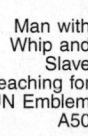

Man with Whip and Slave Reaching for UN Emblem A50

1963, Dec. 10   Unwmk.   *Perf. 11½*
237 A50 5m red brown & bl   .25 .25
238 A50 15m deep claret & bl   .50 .25
239 A50 50m green & blue   1.25 .75
   Nos. 237-239 (3)   2.00 1.25

Universal Declaration of Human Rights, 15th anniv.

Exhibition Hall and Finger Pointing to Libya — A51

1964, Feb. 28   Photo.   *Perf. 11½*
240 A51 10m red brn, gray grn & brn   1.00 .25
241 A51 15m pur, gray grn & brn   1.40 .60
242 A51 30m dk bl, gray grn & brn   2.00 1.40
   Nos. 240-242 (3)   4.40 2.25

3rd Intl. Fair, Tripoli, Feb. 28-Mar. 20.

Child Playing with Blocks — A52

Design: 15m, Child in bird's nest.

1964, Mar. 22   *Perf. 11½*
243 A52 5m multicolored   .25 .25
244 A52 15m multicolored   .60 .25
245 A52 45m multicolored   1.75 .85
  a. Souvenir sheet of 3, #243-245, imperf.   5.00 5.00
   Nos. 243-245 (3)   2.60 1.35

Children's Day. Exist imperf. Value about 1½ times that of perf.
No. 245a sold for 100m.

Lungs and Stethoscope — A53

1964, Apr. 7   Photo.   *Perf. 13½x14*
246 A53 20m deep purple   1.25 .60

Campaign against tuberculosis.

Map of Libya A54

1964, Apr. 27   Unwmk.   *Perf. 11½*
247 A54 5m emerald & org   .25 .25
248 A54 50m blue & yellow   1.50 .60

First anniversary of Libyan union.

Moth Emerging from Cocoon, Veiled and Modern Women — A55

1964, June 15   Litho. & Engraved
249 A55 10m vio bl & lt grn   .35 .25
250 A55 20m vio blue & yel   .75 .60
251 A55 35m vio bl & pink   1.25 1.10
  a. Souv. sheet of 3, #249-251   5.50 5.50
   Nos. 249-251 (3)   2.35 1.95

To honor Libyan women in a new epoch. No. 251a sold for 100m.

Hand Giving Scout Sign, Scout and Libyan Flags — A56

Design: 20m, Libyan Scout emblem and hands.

1964, July 24   Photo.   *Perf. 12x11½*
252 A56 10m lt bl & multi   .85 .35
253 A56 20m multicolored   1.75 .85
  a. Souvenir sheet of 2, #252-253, imperf.   11.50 11.50

Opening of new Boy Scout headquarters; installation of Crown Prince Hassan al-Rida el Senussi as Chief Scout. No. 253a sold for 50m.
Nos. 252-253 exist imperf. Value about 1½ times that of perf.

Bayonet, Wreath and Map — A57

1964, Aug. 9   Litho.   *Perf. 14x13½*
254 A57 10m yel grn & brn   .25 .25
255 A57 20m org & blk   .75 .35

Founding of the Senussi Army.

Ahmed Bahloul el-Sharef — A58

1964, Aug. 11   Engr.   *Perf. 11½*
256 A58 15m lilac   .50 .25
257 A58 20m greenish blue   .85 .50

Poet Ahmed Bahloul el-Sharef, died 1953.

Soccer A59

1964, Oct. 1   Litho.   *Perf. 14*
Black Inscriptions and Gold Olympic Rings
258 A59 5m shown   .75 .50
259 A59 10m Bicycling   .75 .50
260 A59 20m Boxing   .75 .50
261 A59 30m Sprinter   .75 .60
262 A59 35m Woman diver   .75 .60
263 A59 50m Hurdling   .75 .60
  a. Block of 6, #258-263   5.00 5.00

18th Olympic Games, Tokyo, Oct. 10-25. No. 263a printed in sheet of 48. The two blocks in each double row are inverted in relation to the two blocks in the next row, providing various tete beche and se-tenant arrangements.
Nos. 258-263 exist imperf. Value for set, $27.50.
Perf. and imperf. souvenir sheets exist containing six 15m stamps in the designs and colors of Nos. 258-263. Sheets sold for 100m. Value for both, $32.50.

Arab Postal Union Emblem — A59a

1964, Dec. 1   Photo.   *Perf. 11x11½*
264 A59a 10m yellow & blue   .25 .25
265 A59a 15m pale vio & org brn   .50 .25
266 A59a 30m lt yel grn & brn   1.40 .85
   Nos. 264-266 (3)   2.15 1.35

Permanent Office of the APU, 10th anniv.

International Cooperation Year Emblem — A60

1965, Jan. 1   Litho.   *Perf. 14½x14*
267 A60 5m vio bl & gold   .50 .25
268 A60 15m rose car & gold   1.50 .70

Imperfs. exist. Value about twice that of perfs.
See Nos. C51-C51a.

European Bee Eater — A61

Birds: 5m, Long-legged buzzard, vert. 15m, Chestnut-bellied sandgrouse. 20m, Houbara bustard. 30m, Spotted sandgrouse. 40m, Libyan Barbary partridge, vert.

1965, Feb. 10   Photo.   *Perf. 11½*
Granite Paper
Birds in Natural Colors
269 A61 5m gray & black   1.25 .50
270 A61 10m lt bl & org brn   2.00 .55
271 A61 15m lt green & blk   2.25 .60
272 A61 20m pale lil & blk   3.75 .85
273 A61 30m tan & dark brn   4.75 1.50
274 A61 40m dull yel & blk   5.50 1.90
   Nos. 269-274 (6)   19.50 5.90

Map of Africa with Libya A62

1965, Feb. 28   Photo.   *Perf. 11½*
Granite Paper
275 A62 50m multicolored   1.00 .55

4th Intl. Tripoli Fair, Feb. 28-Mar. 20.

Compass Rose, Rockets, Balloons and Stars — A63

1965, Mar. 23   Litho.
276 A63 10m multicolored   .25 .25
277 A63 15m multicolored   .50 .25
278 A63 50m multicolored   1.50 1.00
   Nos. 276-278 (3)   2.25 1.60

Fifth World Meteorological Day.

ITU Emblem, Old and New Communication Equipment — A64

1965, May 17   Unwmk.
279 A64 10m sepia   .25 .25
280 A64 20m red lilac   .35 .25
281 A64 50m lilac rose   1.25 .90
   Nos. 279-281 (3)   1.85 1.40

ITU, centenary.

Library Aflame and Lamp — A65

1965, June   Litho.   *Perf. 11½*
282 A65 15m multicolored   .50 .25
283 A65 50m multicolored   1.25 .55

Burning of the Library of Algiers, June 7, 1962.

Rose — A66

1965, Aug.   Litho.   *Perf. 14*
284 A66 1m shown   .25 .25
285 A66 2m Iris   .25 .25
286 A66 3m Opuntia   .35 .25
287 A66 4m Sunflower   .75 .25
   Nos. 284-287 (4)   1.60 1.00

Jet Plane and Globe — A67

1965, Oct.   Photo.   Perf. 11½
288 A67 5m multicolored   .25 .25
289 A67 10m multicolored   .50 .25
290 A67 15m multicolored   1.00 .25
Nos. 288-290 (3)   1.75 .75
Issued to publicize Libyan Airlines.

Forum, Cyrene — A68

Designs: 100m, Arch of Trajan. 200m, Temple of Apollo, Cyrene. 500m, Antonine Temple of Jupiter, Sabratha, horiz. £1, Theater, Sabratha.

Perf. 12x11½, 11½x12
1965, Dec. 24   Engr.   Wmk. 310
291 A68 50m vio blue & olive   2.00 .60
292 A68 100m Prus bl & dp org   2.75 .85
293 A68 200m pur & Prus bl   6.50 1.50
294 A68 500m car rose & grn   15.00 4.00
295 A68 £1 grn & dp org   32.50 10.00
Nos. 291-295 (5)   58.75 16.95
Nos. 293-295 with "Kingdom of Libia" in both Arabic and English blocked out with a blue felt-tipped pen were issued June 21, 1970, by the Republic.

Mausoleum at Germa — A69

Perf. 11½
1966, Feb. 10   Unwmk.   Litho.
296 A69 70m purple & salmon   3.00 1.00
"POLIGRAFICA & CARTEVALORI-NAPLES" and Libyan Coat of Arms printed on back in yellow green. See No. E13.
Booklet pane containing 4 No. 296 and 4 No. E13 exists. Value $30.

Globe in Space, Satellites — A70

1966, Feb. 28   Perf. 12
297 A70 15m multicolored   .50 .25
298 A70 45m multicolored   1.00 .45
299 A70 55m multicolored   1.25 .65
Nos. 297-299 (3)   2.75 1.35
5th Intl. Fair at Tripoli, Feb. 28-Mar. 20.

Arab League Center, Cairo, and Emblem — A71

Litho. & Photo.
1966, Mar. 22   Perf. 11
300 A71 20m car, emer & blk   .35 .35
301 A71 55m brt bl, ver & blk   1.50 .65
Issued to publicize the Arab League.

Souvenir Sheet

WHO Headquarters, Geneva, and Emblem — A72

1966, May 3   Litho.   Imperf.
302 A72 50m multicolored   9.50 15.00
Inauguration of the WHO headquarters. See Nos. C55-C57.

Tuareg and Camel — A73

A74

Three Tuareg Riders — A75

Design: 20m, like 10m, facing left.

1966, June 20   Unwmk.   Perf. 10
303 A73 10m bright red   1.25 .80
304 A73 20m ultramarine   2.75 1.50
305 A74 50m multicolored   6.00 4.00
a.   Strip of 3, Nos. 303-305   11.00 8.50

Imperf
306 A75 100m multicolored   16.00 16.00

Gazelle — A76

Emblem — A77

Perf. 13x11, 11x13
1966, Aug. 12   Litho.
307 A76 5m lt grn, blk & red   .50 .25
308 A77 25m multicolored   .90 .35
309 A77 65m multicolored   2.50 .65
Nos. 307-309 (3)   3.90 1.25
1st Arab Girl Scout Camp (5m); 7th Arab Boy Scout Camp, Good Daim, Libya, Aug. 12 (25m, 60m).

UNESCO Emblem A78

1967, Jan.   Litho.   Perf. 10x10½
310 A78 15m multicolored   .50 .25
311 A78 25m multicolored   1.10 .45
UNESCO, 20th anniv. (in 1966).

Castle of Columns, Tolemaide — A79

Design: 55m, Sebha Fort, horiz.

Perf. 13x13½, 13½x13
1966, Dec. 24   Engr.
312 A79 25m lil, red brn & blk   .65 .35
313 A79 55m blk, lil & red brn   1.25 .65

Fair Emblem — A80

1967, Feb. 28   Photo.   Perf. 11½
314 A80 15m multicolored   .65 .25
315 A80 55m multicolored   1.00 .55
6th Intl. Fair, Tripoli, Feb. 28-Mar. 20.

Oil Tanker, Marsa Al Hariga Terminal — A81

1967, Feb. 14   Litho.   Perf. 10
316 A81 60m multicolored   2.25 .75
Opening of Marsa Al Hariga oil terminal.

Tourist Year Emblem — A82

1967, May 1   Litho.   Perf. 10½x10
317 A82 5m gray, blk & brt bl   .25 .25
318 A82 10m lt bl, blk & brt bl   .25 .25
319 A82 45m pink, blk & brt bl   .75 .35
Nos. 317-319 (3)   1.25 .85
International Tourist Year.

Map of Mediterranean and Runners — A83

1967, Sept. 8   Litho.   Perf. 10½
320 A83 5m shown   .25 .25
321 A83 10m Javelin   .25 .25
322 A83 15m Bicycling   .25 .25
323 A83 45m Soccer   .75 .55
324 A83 75m Boxing   1.10 .75
Nos. 320-324 (5)   2.60 2.05
5th Mediterranean Games, Tunis, Sept. 8-17.

A84

Arab League emblem and hands reaching for knowledge.

1967, Oct. 1   Litho.   Perf. 12½x13
325 A84 5m orange & dk pur   .25 .25
326 A84 10m brt grn & dk pur   .25 .25
327 A84 15m lilac & dk pur   .25 .25
328 A84 25m blue & dk pur   .50 .25
Nos. 325-328 (4)   1.25 1.00
Literacy campaign.

A85

Human rights flame.

1968, Jan. 15   Litho.   Perf. 13½x14
329 A85 15m grn & vermilion   .35 .25
330 A85 60m org & vio bl   .90 .55
International Human Rights Year.

Map, Derrick, Plane and Camel Riders — A86

1968, Feb. 28   Photo.   Perf. 11½
331 A86 55m car rose, brn & yel   1.25 .75
7th Intl. Fair, Tripoli, Feb. 28-Mar. 20.

Arab League Emblem A87

1968, Mar. 22   Engr.   Perf. 13½
332 A87 10m blue gray & car   .25 .25
333 A87 45m fawn & green   .90 .65
Issued for Arab League Week.

Children,
Statuary
Group
A88

Children's Day: 55m, Mother and children.

1968, Mar. 21   Litho.   Perf. 11
334 A88 25m gray, blk & mag   .65   .35
335 A88 55m gray & multi   1.25   .65

Hands Reaching for
WHO
Emblem — A89

1968, Apr. 7   Photo.   Perf. 13½x14½
336 A89 25m rose cl, dk bl & gray bl   .60   .25
337 A89 55m bl, blk & gray   .90   .55

WHO, 20th anniversary.

From Oil
to
Tanker
A90

1968, Apr. 23   Litho.   Perf. 11
338 A90 10m multicolored   .50   .25
339 A90 60m multicolored   1.50   .80

Opening of the Zueitina oil terminal.

Teacher
and Crowd
A91

1968, Sept. 8   Litho.   Perf. 13½
340 A91 5m bright pink   .25   .25
341 A91 10m orange   .25   .25
342 A91 15m blue   .25   .25
343 A91 20m emerald   .50   .50
Nos. 340-343 (4)   1.25   1.25

Literacy campaign.

Arab Labor
Emblem
A92

1968, Nov. 3   Photo.   Perf. 14x13½
344 A92 10m multicolored   .25   .25
345 A92 15m multicolored   .50   .25

4th session of the Arab Labor Ministers' Conf., Tripoli, Nov. 3-10.

Wadi el Kuf
Bridge and
Road
Sign — A93

1968, Dec. 25   Litho.   Perf. 11x11½
346 A93 25m ultra & multi   .40   .35
347 A93 60m emer & multi   1.00   .90

Opening of the Wadi el Kuf Bridge.

Television
Screen and
Chart
A94

1968, Dec. 25   Photo.   Perf. 14x13½
348 A94 10m yellow & multi   .25   .25
349 A94 30m lilac & multi   .90   .45

Inauguration of television service, Dec. 24.

Melons — A95

**1969, Jan.   Photo.   Perf. 11½
Granite Paper**
350 A95 5m shown   .25   .25
351 A95 10m Peanuts   .25   .25
352 A95 15m Lemons   .25   .25
353 A95 20m Oranges   .40   .25
354 A95 25m Peaches   .65   .35
355 A95 35m Pears   1.25   .55
Nos. 350-355 (6)   3.05   1.90

Nos. 350-355 with "Kingdom of Libya" in both English and Arabic blocked out with a blue felt-tipped pen were issued in December, 1971, by the Republic.

Tripoli Fair
Emblem
A96

1969, Apr. 8   Granite Paper
356 A96 25m silver & multi   .40   .25
357 A96 35m bronze & multi   .65   .35
358 A96 40m gold & multi   .75   .45
Nos. 356-358 (3)   1.80   1.05

8th Intl. Fair, Tripoli, Mar. 6-26.

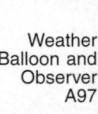

Weather
Balloon and
Observer
A97

1969, Mar. 21   Photo.   Perf. 14x13
359 A97 60m gray & multi   1.50   .80

World Meteorological Day, Mar. 23.

Cogwheel
and
Workers
A98

1969, Mar. 29   Litho.   Perf. 13½
360 A98 15m blue & multi   .25   .25
361 A98 55m salmon & multi   .75   .55

10th anniversary of Social Insurance.

ILO
Emblem — A99

1969, June 1   Photo.   Perf. 14
362 A99 10m bl grn, blk & lt ol   .25   .25
363 A99 60m car rose, blk & lt ol   .90   .65

ILO, 50th anniversary.

African Tourist Year Emblem — A100

**1969, July   Perf. 11½
Emblem in Emerald, Light Blue & Red**
364 A100 15m emer & silver   .45   .25
365 A100 30m blk & gold   .90   .65

Issued to publicize African Tourist Year.

Libyan Arab Republic

Soldiers, Tanks and
Planes — A101

1969, Dec. 7   Photo.   Perf. 12x12½
366 A101 5m org & multi   .45   .25
367 A101 10m ultra & multi   .70   .40
368 A101 15m multicolored   1.00   .50
369 A101 25m multicolored   1.50   .70
370 A101 45m brt bl & multi   1.75   1.10
371 A101 60m multicolored   3.00   1.50
Nos. 366-371 (6)   8.40   4.45

Establishment of the Libyan Arab Republic, Sept. 1, 1969. See Nos. 379-384.

Radar, Flags and
Carrier
Pigeon — A102

**1970, Mar. 1   Photo.   Perf. 11½
Granite Paper**
372 A102 15m multicolored   .70   .25
373 A102 20m multicolored   1.10   .40
374 A102 25m multicolored   1.50   .50
375 A102 40m multicolored   2.10   1.10
Nos. 372-375 (4)   5.40   2.25

Map of
Arab
League
Countries,
Flag and
Emblem
A102a

1970, Mar. 22
376 A102a 10m lt bl, brn & grn   .35   .25
377 A102a 15m org, brn & grn   .60   .25
378 A102a 20m ol, brn & grn   1.00   .45
Nos. 376-378 (3)   1.95   .95

25th anniversary of the Arab League.

Type A101
Redrawn — A103

1970, May 2   Photo.   Perf. 12x12½
379 A103 5m org & multi   .40   .25
380 A103 10m ultra & multi   .70   .60
381 A103 15m multicolored   1.00   .50
382 A103 25m multicolored   1.50   1.40
383 A103 45m brt bl & multi   1.75   1.10
384 A103 60m multicolored   3.00   1.50
Nos. 379-384 (6)   8.35   5.35

On Nos. 379-384 the numerals are in black, the bottom inscription is in 2 lines and several other changes.

Inauguration of UPU Headquarters,
Bern — A104

1970, May 20   Photo.   Perf. 11½x11
385 A104 10m multicolored   .25   .25
386 A104 25m multicolored   .60   .25
387 A104 60m multicolored   1.25   .65
Nos. 385-387 (3)   2.10   1.15

Arms of Libyan Arab
Republic — A105

1970, June 20   Photo.   Perf. 11
388 A105 15m black & brt rose   .25   .25
389 A105 25m vio bl, yel & brt rose   .50   .25
390 A105 45m emer, yel & brt rose   1.75   .45
Nos. 388-390 (3)   2.50   .95

Evacuation of US military base in Libya.

Flags, Soldiers and
Tank — A106

1970, Sept. 1   Photo.   Perf. 11x11½
391 A106 20m multicolored   .75   .25
392 A106 25m multicolored   1.00   .55
393 A106 30m blue & multi   1.60   .75
Nos. 391-393 (3)   3.35   1.55

Libyan Arab Republic, 1st anniv.

UN Emblem, Dove and Scales — A107

1970, Oct. 24   Photo.   Perf. 11x11½
394 A107 5m org & multi   .60   .35
395 A107 10m olive & multi   .90   .45
396 A107 60m multicolored   2.50   .90
     Nos. 394-396 (3)   4.00 1.70

25th anniversary of the United Nations.

Map and Flags of UAR, Libya, Sudan A107a

1970, Dec. 27   Photo.   Perf. 11½
397 A107a 15m lt grn, car & blk 7.00 2.25

Signing of the Charter of Tripoli affirming the unity of UAR, Libya and the Sudan, Dec. 27, 1970.

UN Emblem, Dove and Globe — A108

1971, Jan. 10   Litho.   Perf. 12x11½
398 A108 15m multicolored   .60   .25
399 A108 20m multicolored   .90   .45
400 A108 60m lt vio & multi   2.50   .90
     Nos. 398-400 (3)   4.00 1.60

UN declaration on granting of independence to colonial countries and peoples, 10th anniv.

Education Year Emblem — A109

1971, Jan. 16
401 A109 5m red, blk & ocher   .25   .25
402 A109 10m red, blk & emer   .60   .55
403 A109 20m red, blk & vio bl 1.60   .80
     Nos. 401-403 (3)   2.45 1.60

International Education Year.

Al Fatah Fighter — A110

1971, Mar. 14   Photo.   Perf. 11
404 A110 5m ol & multi   .50   .25
405 A110 10m yel & multi   .80   .25
406 A110 100m multicolored   1.90   .25
     Nos. 404-406 (3)   3.20   .75

Fight for the liberation of Palestine.

Tripoli Fair Emblem — A111

1971, Mar. 18   Litho.   Perf. 14
407 A111 15m multicolored   .35   .25
408 A111 30m org & multi   .90   .45

9th International Fair at Tripoli.

10th Anniv. of OPEC — A112

1971, May 29   Litho.   Perf. 12
409 A112 10m yellow & brown   .25   .25
410 A112 70m pink & vio bl   1.60   .65

Globe and Waves A113

1971, June 10   Perf. 14½x13½
411 A113 25m brt grn, blk & vio bl   .50   .25
412 A113 35m gray & multi   1.25 1.00

3rd World Telecommunications Day, May 17, 1971.

Map of Africa and Telecommunications Network — A114

1971, June 10
413 A114 5m yel, blk & grn   .25   .25
414 A114 15m dl bl, blk & grn   .40   .25

Pan-African telecommunications system.

Torchbearer and Banner — A115

1971, June 15   Photo.   Perf. 11½x12
415 A115 5m yel & multi   .25   .25
416 A115 10m org & multi   .35   .35
417 A115 15m multicolored   .50   .45
     Nos. 415-417 (3)   1.10 1.05

Evacuation of US military base, 1st anniv.

Ramadan Suehli — A116

1971, Aug. 24   Perf. 14x14½
418 A116 15m multicolored   .25   .25
419 A116 55m bl & multi   1.00   .55

Ramadan Suehli (1879-1920), freedom fighter.
See Nos. 422-423, 426-427, 439-440, 479-480.

Date Palm — A117

1971, Sept. 1
420 A117 5m multicolored   .25   .25
421 A117 15m multicolored   1.25 1.25

Sept. 1, 1969 Revolution, 2nd anniv.

Portrait Type of 1971

Portrait: Omar el Mukhtar (1858-1931), leader of the Martyrs.

1971, Sept. 16   Perf. 14x14½
422 A116 5m lt grn & multi   .25   .25
423 A116 100m multicolored   2.50 1.50

Gamal Abdel Nasser (1918-1970), President of Egypt — A118

1971, Sept. 28   Photo.   Perf. 11x11½
424 A118 5m lil, grn & blk   .35   .25
425 A118 15m grn, lil & blk   1.25   .25

Portrait Type of 1971

Ibrahim Usta Omar (1908-50), patriotic poet.

1971, Oct. 8   Litho.   Perf. 14x14½
426 A116 25m vio bl & multi   .60   .60
427 A116 30m multicolored   1.10   .45

Racial Equality Emblem A119

1971, Oct. 24   Perf. 13½x14½
428 A119 25m multicolored   .60   .25
429 A119 35m multicolored   1.10   .45

Intl. Year Against Racial Discrimination.

Arab Postal Union Emblem — A120

1971, Nov. 6   Litho.   Perf. 14½
Emblem in Black, Yellow and Blue
430 A120 5m red   .25   .25
431 A120 10m violet   .40   .25
432 A120 15m bright rose lilac .40   .25
     Nos. 430-432 (3)   1.05   .75

Conference of Sofar, Lebanon, establishing Arab Postal Union, 25th anniv.

Postal Union Emblem and Letter A121

25m, 55m, APU emblem, letter and dove.

1971, Dec.   Photo.   Perf. 11½x11
433 A121 10m org brn, bl & blk   .35   .25
434 A121 15m org, lt bl & blk   .50   .35
435 A121 25m lt grn, org & blk   .75   .55
436 A121 55m lt brn, yel & blk 1.60   .70
     Nos. 433-436 (4)   3.20 1.85

10th anniversary of African Postal Union.
Issued: 25m, 55m, 12/2; 10m, 15m, 12/12.

Despite the change from milliemes to dirhams in 1972, both currencies appear on stamps until August.

Book Year Emblem — A122

1972, Jan. 1   Litho.   Perf. 12½x13
437 A122 15m ultra, brn, gold & blk   .35   .35
438 A122 20m gold, brn, ultra & blk   .60   .60

International Book Year.

Portrait Type of 1971

Ahmed Gnaba (1898-1968), poet of unity.

1972, Jan. 12   Perf. 14x14½
439 A116 20m red & multi   .60   .25
440 A116 35m olive & multi   .85   .45

Coat of Arms — A123

1972, Feb. 10   Photo.   Perf. 14½
Size: 19x23mm
441 A123 5m gray & multi   .25   .25
442 A123 10m lt ol & multi   .25   .25
443 A123 15d lilac & multi   .25   .25
445 A123 25m lt bl & multi   .25   .25
446 A123 30m rose & multi   .35   .25
447 A123 35m lt ol & multi   .45   .25
448 A123 40m dl yel & multi   .60   .25
449 A123 45m lt grn & multi   .75   .35
451 A123 55m multicolored   1.00   .50
452 A123 60m bister & multi   1.90   .65
453 A123 65d multicolored   .75   .55
454 A123 70d lt vio & multi   1.00   .65
455 A123 80d ocher & multi   1.50   .80
456 A123 90m bl & multi   1.90   .90

Size: 27x32mm
Perf. 14x14½
457 A123 100d multicolored   2.25 1.20
458 A123 200d multicolored   3.75 2.25
459 A123 500d multicolored   9.50 6.50
460 A123 £1 multicolored   17.50 11.00
     Nos. 441-460 (18)   44.20 27.10

During the transition from milliemes and pounds to dirhams and dinars, stamps were issued in both currencies.

A124

A124a

A124b

Coil Stamps

1972, July 27   Photo.   Perf. 14½x14
461 A124   5m sl bl, ocher & black   2.75 2.25
462 A124a 20m bl, lil & blk   12.00 2.25
463 A124b 50m bl, ol & blk   27.50 5.50
     Nos. 461-463 (3)   42.25 10.00

See Nos. 496-498, 575-577.

Tombs at Ghirza — A125

Designs: 10m, Kufic inscription, Agedabia, horiz. 15m, Marcus Aurelius Arch, Tripoli. 25m, Exchange of weapons, mural from Wan Amil Cave. 55m, Garamanthian (Berber) chariot, petroglyph, Wadi Zigza. 70m, Nymph Cyrene strangling a lion, bas-relief, Cyrene.

1972, Feb. 15   Litho.   Perf. 14
464 A125 5m lilac & multi   .50 .50
465 A125 10m multicolored   .50 .50
466 A125 15m dp org & multi   1.00 .35
467 A125 25m emer & multi   1.50 .90
468 A125 55m scar & multi   3.50 .90
469 A125 70m ultra & multi   7.00 1.25
           Nos. 464-469 (6)   14.00 4.40

Fair Emblem A126

1972, Mar. 1
470 A126 25d gray & multi   .60 .25
471 A126 35d multicolored   .65 .25
472 A126 50d multicolored   1.40 .35
473 A126 70d multicolored   1.60 .60
           Nos. 470-473 (4)   4.25 1.45

10th International Fair at Tripoli.

Dissected Arm, and Heart — A127

1972, Apr. 7   Perf. 14½
474 A127 15d multicolored   1.50 .45
475 A127 25d multicolored   3.25 1.00

"Your heart is your health," World Health Day.

"Arab Unity" — A128

Litho. & Engr.
1972, Apr. 17   Perf. 13½x13
476 A128 15d bl, yel & blk   .25 .25
477 A128 20d lt grn, yel & blk   .60 .25
478 A128 25d lt ver, yel & blk   1.25 .80
           Nos. 476-478 (3)   2.10 1.30

Fed. of Arab Republics Foundation, 1st anniv.

Portrait Type of 1971

Suleiman el Baruni (1870-1940), patriotic writer.

1972, May 1   Litho.   Perf. 14x14½
479 A116 10m yellow & multi   1.25 .80
480 A116 70m dp org & multi   2.00 1.00

Environment Emblem — A129

1972, Aug. 15   Litho.   Perf. 14½
481 A129 15m red & multi   .60 .25
482 A129 55m green & multi   1.40 .40

UN Conference on Human Environment, Stockholm, June 5-16.

Olympic Emblems — A130

1972, Aug. 26
483 A130 25d brt bl & multi   2.00 .60
484 A130 35d red & multi   3.00 1.25

20th Olympic Games, Munich, 8/26-9/11.

Emblem and Broken Chain — A131

1972, Oct. 1   Litho.   Perf. 14x13½
485 A131 15d blue & multi   .40 .25
486 A131 25d yellow & multi   .90 .35

Libyan Arab Republic, 3rd anniv.

Dome of the Rock, Jerusalem — A132

1972   Perf. 12½x13
487 A132 10d multicolored   .40 .25
488 A132 25d multicolored   .60 .25

Nicolaus Copernicus (1473-1543), Polish Astronomer — A133

Design: 25d, Copernicus in Observatory, by Jan Matejko, horiz.

Perf. 14½x13½, 13½x14½
1973, Feb. 26
489 A133 15d yellow & multi   .40 .25
490 A133 25d blue & multi   .60 .35

Eagle and Fair Buildings A134

1973, Mar. 1   Perf. 13½x14½
491 A134 5d dull red & multi   .40 .25
492 A134 10d blue grn & multi   .60 .25
493 A134 15d vio blue & multi   1.25 .25
           Nos. 491-493 (3)   2.25 .75

11th International Fair at Tripoli.

Blind Person, Books, Loom and Basket — A135

1973, Apr. 18   Photo.   Perf. 12x11½
494 A135 20d gray & multi   8.25 1.60
495 A135 25d dull yel & multi   12.00 5.25

Role of the blind in society.

Numeral Type of 1972
Denominations in Dirhams

A135a

A135b

A135c

Coil Stamps
1973, Apr. 26   Photo.   Perf. 14½x14
496 A135a 5d sl bl, ocher & blk 1.00 1.00
497 A135b 20d blue, lilac & blk 1.50 1.50
498 A135c 50d blue, olive & blk 5.50 5.50
            Nos. 496-498 (3)   8.00 8.00

Map of Africa — A136

1973, May 25   Photo.   Perf. 11x11½
499 A136 15d yel, green & brown   .50 .25
500 A136 25d lt yel grn, grn &
           blk   1.00 .50

"Freedom in Unity" (Org. for African Unity).

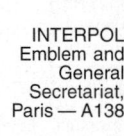

INTERPOL Emblem and General Secretariat, Paris — A138

Perf. 13½x14½
1973, June 30   Litho.
501 A138 10d lilac & multi   .25 .25
502 A138 15d ocher & multi   .50 .25
503 A138 25d lt grn & multi   .75 .25
           Nos. 501-503 (3)   1.50 .75

50th anniv. of Intl. Criminal Police Org.

Map of Libya, Houses, People, Factories, Tractor A139

1973, July 15   Photo.   Perf. 11½
504 A139 10d rose red, black &
           ultra   4.25 .85
505 A139 25d ultra, blk & grn   6.00 1.90
506 A139 35d grn, blk & org   11.50 3.75
           Nos. 504-506 (3)   21.75 6.50

General census.

UN Emblem — A140

1973, Aug. 1   Perf. 12½x11
507 A140 5d ver, blk & bl   .25 .25
508 A140 10d yel grn, blk & bl   .50 .50

Intl. meteorological cooperation, cent.

Soccer — A141

1973, Aug. 10   Photo.   Perf. 11½
509 A141 5d yel grn & dk brn   .50 .25
510 A141 25d orange & dk brn   1.10 .70

2nd Palestinian Cup Soccer Tournament.

Torch and Grain — A142

1973, Sept. 1   Litho.   Perf. 14
511 A142 15d brown & multi   .50 .25
512 A142 25d emer & multi   1.40 .25

4th anniv. of Sept. 1 Revolution.

Writing Hand, Lamp and Globe — A143

1973, Sept. 8
513 A143 25d multicolored   .60 .60

Literacy campaign.

Gate of First City Hall — A144

1973, Sept. 18   Perf. 13
514 A144 10d not shown   .50 .50
515 A144 25d Khondok fountain   .60 .60
516 A144 35d Clock tower   .90 .35
           Nos. 514-516 (3)   2.00 1.45

Centenary of Tripoli as a municipality.

Militia, Flag and Factories — A145

1973, Oct. 7   Photo.   Perf. 11½x11
517 A145 15d yel, blk & red   .50 .25
518 A145 25d green & multi   .75 .35

Libyan Militia.

Revolutionary Proclamation by
Khadafy — A146

70d, as 25d, with English inscription.

1973, Oct. 15   Litho.   Perf. 12½
519 A146 25d orange & multi   .50   .50
520 A146 70d green & multi   1.50   .75
Proclamation of People's Revolution by
Pres. Muammar Khadafy.

FAO
Emblem,
Camel
Pulling
Plow
A147

1973, Nov. 1   Photo.   Perf. 11
521 A147 10d ocher & multi   .25   .25
522 A147 25d dk brn & multi   .50   .50
523 A147 35d black & multi   .75   .35
　　　Nos. 521-523 (3)   1.50   1.10
World Food Org., 10th anniv.

Human Rights
Flame — A148

1973, Dec. 20   Photo.   Perf. 11x11½
524 A148 25d pur, car & dk bl   .05   .05
525 A148 70d lt grn, car & dk bl   1.50   .65
Universal Declaration of Human Rights,
25th anniv.

Fish
A149

Designs: Various fish from Libyan waters.

1973, Dec. 31   Photo.   Perf. 14x13½
526 A149 5d light blue & multi   .65   .50
527 A149 10d light blue & multi   1.25   .45
528 A149 15d light blue & multi   1.90   .55
529 A149 20d light blue & multi   2.75   .60
530 A149 25d light blue & multi   5.25   1.50
　　　Nos. 526-530 (5)   11.80   3.60

1975, Jan. 5
526a A149 5d greenish blue &
　　　　　multi   2.25   1.50
527a A149 10d greenish blue &
　　　　　multi   4.50   1.50
528a A149 15d greenish blue &
　　　　　multi   4.50   1.50
529a A149 20d greenish blue &
　　　　　multi   6.50   .75
530a A149 25d greenish blue &
　　　　　multi   8.50   2.75
　　　Nos. 526a-530a (5)   26.25   8.00

Scout, Sun and
Scout
Signs — A150

Fair Emblem, Flags of
Participants — A151

1974, Feb. 1   Litho.   Perf. 11½
531 A150 5d blue & multi   1.25   .40
532 A150 20d light lilac & multi   3.50   .65
533 A150 25d lt grn & multi   5.75   2.60
　　　Nos. 531-533 (3)   10.50   3.65
Libyan Boy Scouts.

1974, Mar. 1   Litho.   Perf. 12x11½
534 A151 10d lt ultra & multi   .65   .40
535 A151 25d tan & multi   1.00   .55
536 A151 35d lt green & multi   1.90   .25
　　　Nos. 534-536 (3)   3.55   1.20
12th Tripoli International Fair.

Protected Family,
WHO
Emblem — A152

1974, Apr. 7   Litho.   Perf. 12½
537 A152 5d lt green & multi   .35   .25
538 A152 25d red & multi   .60   .60
World Health Day.

Minaret and
Star — A153

1974, Apr. 16   Perf. 11½x11
539 A153 10d pink & multi   .50   .50
540 A153 25d yellow & multi   1.00   .60
541 A153 35d orange & multi   1.40   .50
　　　Nos. 539-541 (3)   2.90   1.60
City University of Bengazi, inauguration.

UPU Emblem
and
Star — A154

1974, May 22   Litho.   Perf. 13½x14½
542 A154 25d multicolored   7.50   1.10
543 A154 70d multicolored   14.00   2.25
Centenary of Universal Postal Union.

Traffic Signs — A156

1974, June 8   Photo.   Perf. 11
547 A156 5d gold & multi   .25   .25
548 A156 10d gold & multi   .40   .25
549 A156 25d gold & multi   .50   .25
　　　Nos. 547-549 (3)   1.15   .75
Automobile and Touring Club of Libya.

Tank, Oil Refinery,
Book — A157

Symbolic "5" — A158

1974, Sept. 1   Litho.   Perf. 14
550 A157 5d red & multi   .25   .25
551 A157 20d violet & multi   .40   .40
552 A157 25d vio bl & multi   .40   .40
553 A157 35d green & multi   .50   .50
　　　Nos. 550-553 (4)   1.55   1.55

Souvenir Sheet
Perf. 13
554 A158 55d yel & maroon   9.50   9.50
Revolution of Sept. 1, 5th anniv. English
inscription on No. 553.

WPY Emblem and
Crowd — A159

1974, Oct. 19   Perf. 14
555 A159 25d multicolored   .35   .25
556 A159 35d lt brn & multi   .75   .60
World Population Year.

Libyan
Woman — A160

Libyan Costumes: 10d, 15d, Women. 20d,
Old man. 25d, Man riding camel. 50d, Man on
horseback.

1975, Mar. 1   Litho.   Perf. 13x12½
557 A160 5d org yel & multi   .25   .25
558 A160 10d org yel & multi   .25   .25
559 A160 15d org yel & multi   .50   .25
560 A160 20d org yel & multi   .75   .25
561 A160 25d org yel & multi   1.50   .75
562 A160 50d org yel & multi   2.75   .75
　　　Nos. 557-562 (6)   6.00   2.50

Congress
Emblem — A161

1975, Mar. 4   Litho.   Perf. 12x12½
563 A161 10d brown & multi   .25   .25
564 A161 25d vio & multi   .40   .40
565 A161 35d gray & multi   .75   .25
　　　Nos. 563-565 (3)   1.40   .90
Arab Labor Congress.

Teacher
Pointing to
Blackboard
A162

1975, Mar. 10   Perf. 11½
566 A162 10d gold & multi   .25   .25
567 A162 25d gold & multi   .50   .25
Teacher's Day.

Bodies, Globe,
Proclamation
A163

1975, Apr. 7   Litho.   Perf. 12½
568 A163 20d lilac & multi   .40   .40
569 A163 25d emer & multi   .50   .25
World Health Day.

Woman and Man
in Library — A164

1975, May 25   Litho.   Perf. 12½
570 A164 10d bl grn & multi   .25   .25
571 A164 25d olive & multi   .50   .50
572 A164 35d lt vio & multi   .60   .60
　　　Nos. 570-572 (3)   1.35   1.35
Libyan Arab Book Exhibition.

Festival
Emblem — A165

1975, July 5   Litho.   Perf. 13x12½
573 A165 20d lt bl & multi   .40   .40
574 A165 25d orange & multi   .50   .50
2nd Arab Youth Festival.

**Redrawn Type of 1973 Without
"LAR"**
Coil Stamps

1975, Aug. 15   Photo.   Perf. 14½x14
575 A124 5d blue, org & blk   .50   .50
576 A124 20d blue, yel & blk   1.00   1.00
577 A124 50d blue, grn & blk   2.00   2.00
　　　Nos. 575-577 (3)   3.50   3.50

Games Emblem
and Arms — A166

1975, Aug. 23   *Perf. 13x12½*
578 A166 10d salmon & multi   .25   .25
579 A166 25d lilac & multi   .50   .50
580 A166 50d yellow & multi   1.40   .40
    Nos. 578-580 (3)   2.15 1.15

7th Mediterranean Games, Algiers, 8/23-9/6.

Peace Dove,
Symbols of
Agriculture and
Industry — A167

Khadafy's Head Over Desert — A168

Design: 70d, Peace dove, diff.

1975, Sept.   Litho.   Perf. 13x12½
581 A167 25d multicolored   .40   .25
582 A167 70d multicolored   1.40   .50

Souvenir Sheet
Imperf
Litho. & Embossed
583 A168 100d multicolored   6.00 6.00

6th anniversary of Sept. 1 revolution. No. 583 contains one stamp with simulated perforations.

Khalil Basha   Al Kharruba
Mosque — A169   Mosque — A170

Mosques: 10d, Sidi Abdulla El Shaab. 15d, Sidi Ali El Fergani. 25d, Katikhtha. 30d, Murad Agha. 35d, Maulai Mohammed.

1975, Dec. 13   Litho.   Perf. 12½
584 A169 5d gray & multi   .25   .25
585 A169 10d purple & multi   .25   .25
586 A169 15d green & multi   .25   .25
587 A170 20d ocher & multi   .40   .25
588 A170 25d multicolored   .40   .25
589 A170 30d multicolored   .50   .25
590 A170 35d lilac & multi   .75   .60
    Nos. 584-590 (7)   2.80 2.10

Mohammed's 1405th birthday.

Arms of Libya
and
People — A171

1976, Jan. 15   Photo.   Perf. 13
591 A171 35d blue & multi   .50   .25
592 A171 40d multicolored   .60   .25
    General National (People's) Congress.

Islamic - Christian
Dialogue
Emblem — A172

1976, Feb. 5   Litho.   Perf. 13x12½
593 A172 40d gold & multi   .60   .25
594 A172 115d gold & multi   1.90   .90

Seminar of Islamic-Christian Dialogue, Tripoli, Feb. 1-5.

Woman Blowing
Horn — A173

National Costumes: 20d, Lancer. 30d, Drummer. 40d, Bagpiper. 100d, Woman carrying jug on head.

1976, Mar. 1   Litho.   Perf. 13x12½
595 A173 10d multicolored   .25   .25
596 A173 20d multicolored   .50   .40
597 A173 30d pink & multi   1.00   .25
598 A173 40d multicolored   1.25   .25
599 A173 100d yel & multi   3.00   .50
    Nos. 595-599 (5)   6.00 1.65

14th Tripoli International Fair.

Telephones, 1876 and 1976, ITU and
UPU Emblems — A174

70d, Alexander Graham Bell, telephone, satellites, radar, ITU & UPU emblems.

1976, Mar. 10   Photo.   Perf. 13
600 A174 40d multicolored   2.50   .80
  a.   Souvenir sheet of 4   10.00 10.00
601 A174 70d multicolored   4.00   .80
  a.   Souvenir sheet of 4   16.50 8.50

Centenary of first telephone call by Alexander Graham Bell, Mar. 10, 1876.
    Nos. 600a and 601a exist imperf. Value, both sheets $100.

Mother and
Child — A175

1976, Mar. 21   Perf. 12
602 A175 85d gray & multi   1.50 1.25
603 A175 110d pink & multi   1.60 1.50
    International Children's Day.

Hands, Eye and
Head — A176

1976, Apr. 7   Photo.   Perf. 13½x13
604 A176 30d multicolored   .35   .35
605 A176 35d multicolored   .50   .50
606 A176 40d multicolored   .60   .60
    Nos. 604-606 (3)   1.45 1.45

"Foresight prevents blindness;" World Health Day.

Little
Bittern
A177

Birds of Libya: 10d, Great gray shrike. 15d, Songbird. 20d, European bee-eater, vert. 25d, Hoopoe.

Perf. 13x13½, 13½x13
1976, May 1   Litho.
607 A177 5d orange & multi   .65   .50
608 A177 10d ultra & multi   1.40 1.10
609 A177 15d rose & multi   2.75 1.40
610 A177 20d yellow & multi   4.75 1.50
611 A177 25d blue & multi   9.50 2.75
    Nos. 607-611 (5)   19.05 7.25

Al Barambekh
A178

Designs: 15d, Whale, horiz. 30d, Lizard (alwaral), horiz. 40d, Mastodon skull, horiz. 70d, Hawk. 115d, Wild mountain sheep.

1976, June 20   Litho.   Perf. 12½
612 A178 10d multicolored   1.40 1.10
613 A178 15d multicolored   2.50 1.90
614 A178 30d multicolored   3.00 2.40
615 A178 40d multicolored   5.00 4.25
616 A178 70d multicolored   8.75 7.25
617 A178 115d multicolored   14.50 12.25
    Nos. 612-617 (6)   35.15 29.15

Museum of Natural History.

Bicycling — A179

1976, July 17   Litho.   Perf. 12x11½
Granite Paper
618 A179 15d shown   .25   .25
619 A179 25d Boxing   .50   .50
620 A179 70d Soccer   1.50 1.50
    Nos. 618-620 (3)   2.25 2.25

Souvenir Sheet
621 A179 150d Symbolic of
              various sports   16.00 16.00

21st Olympic Games, Montreal, Canada, July 17-Aug. 1.

Tree Growing
from
Globe — A180

1976, Aug. 9   Perf. 13
622 A180 115d multicolored   1.25   .90

5th Conference of Non-Aligned Countries, Colombo, Sri Lanka, Aug. 9-19.

Beginning with No. 622 numerous issues are printed with multiple coats of arms in pale green on back of stamps.

Symbols of
Agriculture and
Industry — A181

Drummer and Pipeline — A182

1976, Sept. 1   Perf. 14½x14
623 A181 30d yel & multi   .40   .25
624 A181 40d multicolored   .50   .25
625 A181 100d multicolored   1.25   .90
    Nos. 623-625 (3)   2.15 1.40

Souvenir Sheet
Perf. 13
626 A182 200d multicolored   6.00 6.00

Sept. 1 Revolution, 7th anniv.

Sports, Torch
and Emblems
A183

145d, Symbolic wrestlers and various emblems.

1976, Oct. 6   Litho.   Perf. 13
627 A183 15d multicolored   .25   .25
628 A183 30d multicolored   .35   .35
629 A183 100d multicolored   1.60   .90
    Nos. 627-629 (3)   2.20 1.50

Souvenir Sheet
630 A183 145d multi, horiz.   4.50 4.50

5th Arab Games, Damascus, Syria.

Chess Board, Rook,
Knight,
Emblem — A184

1976, Oct. 24   Photo.   Perf. 11½
631	A184	15d pink & multi	2.10	.45
632	A184	30d buff & multi	3.50	1.00
633	A184	100d multicolored	10.50	2.00
		Nos. 631-633 (3)	16.10	3.45

The "Against" (protest) Chess Olympiad, Tripoli, Oct. 24-Nov. 15.

A185

Designs: Various local flowers.

1976, Nov. 1   Photo.   Perf. 11½
Granite Paper
634	A185	15d lilac & multi	.35	.35
635	A185	20d multicolored	.35	.35
636	A185	35d yellow & multi	.80	.25
637	A185	40d salmon & multi	1.25	.35
638	A185	70d multicolored	3.00	.50
		Nos. 634-638 (5)	5.75	1.80

International Archives Council Emblem and Document — A186

1976, Nov. 10   Litho.   Perf. 13x13½
639	A186	15d brown, org & buff	.25	.25
640	A186	35d brn, brt grn & buff	.35	.35
641	A186	70d brown, blue & buff	.75	.75
		Nos. 639-641 (3)	1.35	1.35

Arab Regional Branch of International Council on Archives, Baghdad.

Holy Ka'aba and Pilgrims — A187

1976, Dec. 12   Litho.   Perf. 14
642	A187	15d multicolored	.25	.25
643	A187	30d multicolored	.25	.25
644	A187	70d multicolored	.80	.80
645	A187	100d multicolored	1.00	1.00
		Nos. 642-645 (4)	2.30	2.30

Pilgrimage to Mecca.

Numeral — A188

Coil Stamps

1977, Jan. 15   Photo.   Perf. 14½x14
646	A188	5d multicolored	.25	.25
647	A188	20d multicolored	.35	.35
648	A188	50d multicolored	.90	.90
		Nos. 646-648 (3)	1.50	1.50

Covered Basket — A189

Designs: 20d, Leather bag. 30d, Vase. 40d, Embroidered slippers. 50d, Ornate saddle. 100d, Horse with saddle and harness.

1977, Mar. 1   Litho.   Perf. 12½x12
649	A189	10d multicolored	.25	.25
650	A189	20d multicolored	.25	.25
651	A189	30d multicolored	.35	.25
652	A189	40d multicolored	.60	.35
653	A189	50d multicolored	1.00	.35
		Nos. 649-653 (5)	2.45	1.45

Souvenir Sheet
Imperf
| 654 | A189 | 100d multicolored | 4.50 | 4.50 |

15th Tripoli International Fair. No. 654 contains one stamp 49x53mm with simulated perforations.

Girl and Flowers, UNICEF Emblem A190

Children's drawings, UNICEF Emblem and: 30d, Clothing store. 40d, Farm yard.

1977, Mar. 28   Litho.   Perf. 13x13½
655	A190	10d multicolored	.35	.25
656	A190	30d multicolored	.60	.35
657	A190	40d multicolored	.75	.50
		Nos. 655-657 (3)	1.70	1.10

Children's Day.

Gun, Fighters, UN Headquarters A191

1977, Mar. 13   Perf. 13½
658	A191	15d multicolored	.25	.25
659	A191	25d multicolored	.25	.25
660	A191	70d multicolored	1.25	1.25
		Nos. 658-660 (3)	1.75	1.75

Battle of Al-Karamah, 9th anniversary.

Child, Raindrop, WHO Emblem — A192

1977, Apr. 7   Litho.   Perf. 13x12½
| 661 | A192 | 15d multicolored | .25 | .25 |
| 662 | A192 | 30d multicolored | .50 | .50 |

World Health Day.

Arab Postal Union, 25th Anniv. — A193

1977, Apr. 12   Perf. 13½
663	A193	15d multicolored	.25	.25
664	A193	30d multicolored	.35	.35
665	A193	40d multicolored	.50	.50
		Nos. 663-665 (3)	1.10	1.10

Maps of Africa and Libya A194

1977, May 8   Litho.   Perf. 14x13½
| 666 | A194 | 40d multicolored | 1.50 | 1.25 |
| 667 | A194 | 70d multicolored | 2.25 | 1.90 |

African Labor Day.

Map of Libya and Heart — A195

1977, May 10   Perf. 14½x14
668	A195	5d multicolored	.35	.25
669	A195	10d multicolored	.50	.35
670	A195	30d multicolored	1.40	.60
		Nos. 668-670 (3)	2.25	1.20

Libyan Red Crescent Society.

Electronic Tree, ITU Emblem, Satellite and Radar A196

Electronic Tree, ITU Emblem and: 115d, Communications satellite, Montreal Olympics emblem, boxer on TV screen. 200d, Spacecraft over earth. 300d, Solar system.

1977, May 17   Litho.   Perf. 13½x13
671	A196	60d multicolored	.80	.80
672	A196	200d multicolored	2.00	2.00
673	A196	200d multicolored	3.75	3.75
		Nos. 671-673 (3)	6.55	6.55

Souvenir Sheet
| 674 | A196 | 300d multicolored | 8.50 | 6.50 |

9th World Telecommunications Day. No. 674 contains one stamp 52x35mm.
Nos. 671-673 exist imperf. Value, set $45. They also exist in miniature sheets of 4, perf and imperf. Values: set perf, $100; set imperf, $135.

Plane over Tripoli, Messenger — A197

UPU Emblem and: 25d, Concorde, messenger on horseback. 150d, Loading transport plane and messenger riding camel. 300d, Graf Zeppelin LZ127 over Tripoli.

1977, May 17   Litho.   Perf. 13½
675	A197	20d multicolored	.80	.80
676	A197	25d multicolored	1.75	1.75
677	A197	150d multicolored	3.50	3.50
		Nos. 675-677 (3)	6.05	6.05

Souvenir Sheet
| 678 | A197 | 300d multicolored | 8.50 | 6.50 |

UPU centenary (in 1974). No. 678 contains one stamp 52x35mm.
Nos. 675-678 exist imperf. Values: set $45; souvenir sheet, $50. Nos. 675-677 also exist in miniature sheets of 4, perf and imperf. Values: set perf, $60; set imperf, $125.

Mosque A198

Various Mosques. 50d, 100d, vertical.

1977, June 1   Photo.   Perf. 14
679	A198	40d multicolored	.55	.55
680	A198	50d multicolored	.80	.80
681	A198	70d multicolored	1.10	1.10
682	A198	90d multicolored	1.40	1.40
683	A198	100d multicolored	1.60	1.60
684	A198	115d multicolored	2.10	2.10
		Nos. 679-684 (6)	7.55	7.55

Palestinian Archbishop Hilarion Capucci, Jailed by Israel in 1974, Map of Palestine — A199

1977, Aug. 18   Litho.   Perf. 13½
687	A199	30d multicolored	.40	.40
688	A199	40d multicolored	.55	.55
689	A199	115d multicolored	2.10	1.00
		Nos. 687-689 (3)	3.05	1.95

Raised Hands, Pylons, Wheel, Buildings — A200

Star and Ornament — A201

1977, Sept. 1   Litho.   Perf. 13½x12½
690	A200	15d multicolored	.25	.25
691	A200	30d multicolored	.35	.35
692	A200	85d multicolored	1.25	.60
		Nos. 690-692 (3)	1.85	1.20

Souvenir Sheet
Perf. 12½
| 693 | A201 | 100d gold & multi | 5.00 | 3.50 |

8th anniversary of Sept. 1 Revolution.

Team Handball — A202

1977, Oct. 8   *Perf. 13½*
694 A202 5d Swimmers, vert.   .25 .25
695 A202 10d shown   .25 .25
696 A202 15d Soccer, vert.   .25 .25
697 A202 25d Table tennis   .75 .75
698 A202 40d Basketball, vert. 1.60 .90
    Nos. 694-698 (5)   3.10 2.40

7th Arab School Games.

Steeplechase — A203

Show Emblem and: 10d, Bedouin on horse-back. 15d, Show emblem (Horse and "7"), vert. 45d, Steeplechase. 100d, Hurdles. 115d, Bedouins on horseback.

1977, Oct. 10   *Perf. 14½*
699 A203 5d multicolored   .25 .25
700 A203 10d multicolored   .25 .25
701 A203 15d multicolored   .35 .35
702 A203 45d multicolored   .90 .90
703 A203 115d multicolored   2.00 2.00
    Nos. 699-703 (5)   3.75 3.75

Souvenir Sheet

704 A203 100d multicolored   4.50 4.50

7th Intl. Turf Championships, Tripoli, Oct. 1977.

Dome of the Rock, Jerusalem — A204

1977, Oct. 14   *Perf. 14½x14*
705 A204 5d multicolored   .30 .25
706 A204 10d multicolored   .45 .25

Palestinian fighters and their families.

"The Green Book" — A205

35d, Hands with broken chain holding hook over citadel. 40d, Hands above chaos. 115d, Dove and Green Book rising from Africa, world map.

1977   **Litho.**   *Perf. 14*
707 A205 Strip of 3   2.75 2.75
    a. 35d multicolored   .35 .35
    b. 40d multicolored   .50 .50
    c. 115d multicolored   1.75 1.75

The Greek Book, by Khadafy outlines Libyan democracy. Green descriptive inscription on back beneath gum, in English on 35d, French on 40d, Arabic on 115d.

Emblems A206

1977   *Perf. 12½x13*
708 A206 5d multicolored   .60 .25
709 A206 15d multicolored   .80 .25
710 A206 30d multicolored   1.10 .35
    Nos. 708-710 (3)   2.50 .85

Standardization Day.

Elephant hunt. A207

Rock Carvings, Wadi Mathendous, c. 8000 B.C.: 10d, Crocodile and Young. 20d, Giraffe, vert. 30d, Antelope. 40d, Trumpeting elephant.

1978, Jan. 1   *Perf. 12½x13, 13x12½*
711 A207 10d multicolored   .25 .25
712 A207 15d multicolored   .25 .25
713 A207 20d multicolored   .35 .35
714 A207 30d multicolored   .60 .60
715 A207 40d multicolored   1.00 1.00
    Nos. 711-715 (5)   2.45 2.45

Silver Pendant — A208

Silver Jewelry: 10d, Ornamental plate. 20d, Necklace with pendants. 25d, Crescent-shaped brooch. 115d, Armband.

1978, Mar. 1   **Litho.**   *Perf. 13x12½*
716 A208 5d multicolored   .25 .25
717 A208 10d multicolored   .25 .25
718 A208 20d multicolored   .25 .25
719 A208 25d multicolored   .25 .25
720 A208 115d multicolored   1.50 1.50
    Nos. 716-720 (5)   2.50 2.50

Tripoli International Fair.

Emblem, Compass and Lightning — A209

1978, Mar. 10   *Perf. 13½*
721 A209 30d multicolored   .50 .50
722 A209 115d multicolored   2.00 2.00

Arab Cultural Education Organization.

Children's Drawings and UNICEF Emblem — A210

a, Dancing. b, Children with posters. c, Shopping street. d, Playground. e, Bride and attendants.

1978, Mar. 21
723 A210 40d Strip of 5, #a.-e. 7.25 7.25

Children's Day.

Clenched Fist, Made of Bricks A211

1978, Mar. 22
728 A211 30d multicolored   .65 .40
729 A211 115d multicolored   1.50 .70

Determination of Arab people.

Blood Pressure Gauge, WHO Emblem — A212

1978, Apr. 7   *Perf. 13x12½*
730 A212 30d multicolored   .35 .35
731 A212 115d multicolored   1.75 .90

World Health Day, drive against hypertension.

Antenna and ITU Emblem A213

1978, May 17   **Photo.**   *Perf. 13½*
732 A213 30d silver & multi   .35 .25
733 A213 115d gold & multi   1.50 .65

10th World Telecommunications Day.

Games Emblem — A214

1978, July 13   **Litho.**   *Perf. 12½*
734 A214 15d multicolored   .25 .25
735 A214 30d multicolored   .35 .35
736 A214 115d multicolored   1.50 1.50
    Nos. 734-736 (3)   2.10 2.10

3rd African Games, Algiers, 1978.

Inauguration of Tripoli International Airport — A215

1978, Aug. 10   **Litho.**   *Perf. 13½*
737 A215 40d shown   .50 .50
738 A215 115d Terminal   2.00 .90

View of Ankara — A216

1978, Aug. 17
739 A216 30d multicolored   .50 .25
740 A216 35d multicolored   .60 .35
741 A216 115d multicolored   1.60 1.60
    Nos. 739-741 (3)   2.70 2.20

Turkish-Libyan friendship.

Soldiers, Jet, Ship — A217

35d, Tower, Green Book, oil derrick. 100d, View of Tripoli with mosque and modern buildings. 115d, View of Tripoli within cogwheel.

1978, Sept. 1   *Perf. 14½*
742 A217 30d multicolored   .50 .50
743 A217 35d org & multi   .35 .35
744 A217 115d blue & multi   1.50 1.25
    Nos. 742-744 (3)   2.35 2.10

Souvenir Sheet

745 A217 100d multicolored   2.75 2.75

9th anniversary of Sept. 1 Revolution. No. 745 contains one 50x41mm stamp.

Quarry and Symposium Emblem — A218

Designs: 40d, Oasis lake. 115d, Crater.

1978, Sept. 16   *Perf. 13½*
746 A218 30d multicolored   .50 .50
747 A218 40d multicolored   .60 .60
748 A218 115d multicolored   2.00 2.00
    Nos. 746-748 (3)   3.10 3.10

2nd Symposium on Libyan Geology.

Green Book and Three Races A219

1978, Oct. 18   *Perf. 12½*
749 A219 30d multicolored   .25 .25
750 A219 40d multicolored   .50 .50
751 A219 115d multicolored   1.25 1.25
    Nos. 749-751 (3)   2.00 2.00

International Anti-Apartheid Year.

Pilgrims, Minarets, Holy Kaaba A220

1978, Nov. 9   Photo.   Perf. 12
752	A220 5d multicolored	.25	.25
753	A220 10d multicolored	.25	.25
754	A220 15d multicolored	.25	.25
755	A220 20d multicolored	.25	.25
	Nos. 752-755 (4)	1.00	1.00

Pilgrimage to Mecca.

Handclasp over Globe — A221

1978, Nov. 10   Litho.   Perf. 13½
756	A221 30d multicolored	.40	.30
757	A221 40d multicolored	.50	.40
758	A221 115d multicolored	1.50	1.25
	Nos. 756-758 (3)	2.40	1.95

Technical Cooperation Among Developing Countries Conf., Buenos Aires, Argentina, Sept. 1978.

Fists, Guns, Map of Israel — A222

40d, 115d, Map of Arab countries and Israel, eagle and crowd. 145d, like 30d.

1978, Dec. 5   Litho.   Perf. 13½
759	A222 30d multi	.35	.35
760	A222 40d multi, horiz.	.50	.40
761	A222 115d multi, horiz.	1.25	1.25
762	A222 145d multi	1.50	.90
	Nos. 759-762 (4)	3.60	3.00

Anti-Israel Summit Conf., Baghdad, Dec. 2-8.

Scales, Globe and Human Rights Flame — A223

1978, Dec. 10
763	A223 15d multicolored	.25	.25
764	A223 30d multicolored	.50	.50
765	A223 115d multicolored	1.25	1.25
	Nos. 763-765 (3)	2.00	2.00

Universal Declaration of Human Rights, 30th anniv.

Libyan Fort and Horse Racing — A224

1978, Dec. 11
766	A224 20d multicolored	.40	.25
767	A224 40d multicolored	.50	.50
768	A224 115d multicolored	1.50	1.50
	Nos. 766-768 (3)	2.40	2.25

Libyan Study Center.

Lilienthal's Glider, 1896 A225

25d, Spirit of St. Louis, 1927. 30d, Adm. Byrd's Polar flight, 1929. 50d, Graf Zeppelin, 1934, hydroplane and storks. 115d, Wilbur and Orville Wright and Flyer A. No. 774, Icarus falling. No. 775, Eagle and Boeing 727.

1978, Dec. 26   Litho.   Perf. 14
769	A225 20d multicolored	.25	.25
770	A225 25d multicolored	.45	.45
771	A225 30d multicolored	1.40	1.40
772	A225 50d multicolored	1.60	1.60
773	A225 115d multicolored	1.40	1.40
	Nos. 769-773 (5)	5.10	5.10

Souvenir Sheets
774	A225 100d multicolored	3.00	3.00
775	A225 100d multicolored	3.00	3.00

75th anniversary of 1st powered flight. Nos. 769-773 issued also in sheets of 4. Value, set perf. $45. Also exists imperf. Nos. 774-775 exist imperf. Value, pair $50.

Mounted Stag's Head — A226

Coil Stamps

1979, Jan. 15   Photo.   Perf. 14½x14
776	A226 5d multicolored	.35	.35
777	A226 20d multicolored	.75	.75
778	A226 50d multicolored	1.50	1.50
	Nos. 776-778 (3)	2.60	2.60

Carpobrotus Acinaciformis A227

Flora of Libya: 15d, Caralluma europaea. 20d, Arum cirenaicum. 35d, Lavatera arborea. 40d, Capparis spinosa. 50d, Ranunculus asiaticus.

1979, May 15   Litho.   Perf. 14
779	A227 10d multicolored	.25	.25
780	A227 15d multicolored	.25	.25
781	A227 20d multicolored	.25	.25
782	A227 35d multicolored	.60	.60
783	A227 40d multicolored	.60	.60
784	A227 50d multicolored	.75	.75
	Nos. 779-784 (6)	2.70	2.70

People, Torch, Olive Branches — A228

1979   Litho.   Perf. 13x12½
Size: 18x23mm
785	A228 5d multi	.25	.25
786	A228 10d multi	.25	.25
787	A228 15d multi	.25	.25
788	A228 30d multi	.35	.25
789	A228 50d multi	.50	.25
790	A228 60d multi	.60	.35
791	A228 70d multi	.75	.35
792	A228 100d multi	1.25	.60
793	A228 115d multi	1.25	.60

Perf. 13½
Size: 26½x32mm
794	A228 200d multi	1.90	1.25
795	A228 500d multi	4.75	2.50
796	A228 1000d multi	10.00	6.25
	Nos. 785-796 (12)	22.10	13.15

See Nos. 1053-1055.

Tortoise A229

Animals: 10d, Antelope. 15d, Hedgehog. 20d, Porcupine. 30d, Arabian camel. 35d, African wildcat. 45d, Gazelle. 115d, Cheetah. 10d, 30d, 35d, 45d, vert.

1979, Feb. 1   Litho.   Perf. 14½
797	A229 5d multicolored	.25	.25
798	A229 10d multicolored	.25	.25
799	A229 15d multicolored	.65	.65
800	A229 20d multicolored	.65	.65
801	A229 30d multicolored	1.10	.65
802	A229 35d multicolored	1.50	.65
803	A229 45d multicolored	1.75	.80
804	A229 115d multicolored	3.50	1.25
	Nos. 797-804 (8)	9.65	5.15

Rug and Tripoli Fair Emblem — A230

Tripoli Fair emblem and various rugs.

1979, Mar. 1   Litho.   Perf. 11
805	A230 10d multicolored	.25	.25
806	A230 15d multicolored	.25	.25
807	A230 30d multicolored	.35	.35
808	A230 45d multicolored	.50	.50
809	A230 115d multicolored	1.25	1.25
	Nos. 805-809 (5)	2.60	2.60

17th Tripoli Fair. Exist imperf. Value, set $30.

Children's Drawings and IYC Emblem A231

a, Families and planes. b, Shepherd, sheep and dog. c, Beach umbrellas. d, Boat in storm. e, Traffic policeman.

1979, Mar. 20   Perf. 13½
810	A231 20d Strip of 5, #a.-e.	5.00	3.50

Intl. Year of the Child. Exists imperf. Value $30.

Book, World Map, Arab Achievements A232

1979, Mar. 22   Perf. 13
815	A232 45d multicolored	.50	.50
816	A232 70d multicolored	.75	.75

WMO Emblem, Weather Map and Tower — A233

1979, Mar. 23
817	A233 15d multicolored	.25	.25
818	A233 30d multicolored	.35	.35
819	A233 60d multicolored	.60	.60
	Nos. 817-819 (3)	1.20	1.20

World Meteorological Day.

Medical Services, WHO Emblem — A234

1979, Apr. 7
820	A234 40d multicolored	.60	.60

Farmer Plowing and Sheep — A235

1979, Sept. 1   Litho.   Perf. 14½
821	A235 Block of 4	1.00	1.00
a.	15d Harvester, sheep	.25	.25
b.	15d Men holding Green Book	.25	.25
c.	15d Oil field	.25	.25
d.	15d Oil refinery	.25	.25
822	A235 Block of 4	2.00	2.00
a.	30d Dish antenna	.40	.40
b.	30d Hospital	.40	.40
c.	30d Doctor examining patient	.40	.40
d.	30d Surgery	.40	.40
823	A235 Block of 4	3.00	3.00
a.	40d Street, Tripoli	.50	.50
b.	40d Steel mill	.50	.50
c.	40d Tanks	.50	.50
d.	40d Tuareg horsemen	.50	.50
824	A235 Block of 4	4.00	4.00
a.	70d Revolutionaries, Green Book	.90	.90
b.	70d Crowd, map of Libya	.90	.90
c.	70d Mullah	.90	.90
d.	70d Student	.90	.90
	Nos. 821-824 (4)	10.00	10.00

Souvenir Sheets
Imperf
825	A235 50d Revolution symbols, Green Book	2.50	2.50
826	A235 50d Monument	2.50	2.50

Sept. 1st revolution, 10th anniversary.

Volleyball
A236

1979, Sept. 10
827 A236 45d shown   .50 .50
828 A236 115d Soccer   1.25 1.25

Universiade '79 World University Games, Mexico City, Sept.
Exists imperf. Value, set $17.50.

Mediterranean Games, Split, Yugoslavia — A237

1979, Sept. 15 Litho.   Perf. 12x11½
829 A237 15d multicolored   .50 .50
830 A237 30d multicolored   1.40 .50
831 A237 70d multicolored   3.50 1.00
     Nos. 829-831 (3)   5.40 2.00

Exhibition
Emblem — A238

1979, Sept. 25 Photo.   Perf. 11½x11
832 A238 45d multicolored   .50 .50
833 A238 115d multicolored   1.50 1.50

TELECOM '79, 3rd World Telecommunications Exhibition, Geneva, Sept. 20-26.

A239

No. 834: a, 10d, Seminar emblem, Green Book, crowd. b, 35d, Meeting hall (Size: 67x43½mm). c, 100d, Col. Khadafy.
No. 835, Central portion of #834c.

1979, Oct. 1
834 A239   Strip of 3, #a.-c.   2.50 2.50
     Size: 87x114mm
         Imperf
835 A239 100d multicolored   3.50 3.50

Intl. Seminar of the Green Book, Benghazi, Oct. 1-3. No. 834 has continuous design.

Evacuation of Foreign Forces — A240

1979, Oct. 7
837 A240 30d shown   .60 .40
838 A240 40d Tuareg horsemen   .90 .50

Souvenir Sheet
Imperf
839 A240 100d Vignettes   3.00 3.00

Cyclist, Championship Emblem — A241

1979, Nov. 21
840 A241 15d shown   .25 .25
841 A241 30d Cyclists, emblem,
              diff.   .50 .50

Junior Cycling Championships, Tripoli, Nov. 21-23. Issued in sheetlets of 4.

Hurdles, Olympic Rings, Moscow '80 Emblem — A242

1979, Nov. 21
842 A242 45d Equestrian   .50 .50
843 A242 60d Javelin   .75 .75
844 A242 115d Hurdles   1.50 1.50
845 A242 160d Soccer   1.75 1.75
     Nos. 842-845 (4)   4.50 4.50

Souvenir Sheets
846 A242 150d shown   3.75 3.75
847 A242 150d like #845   3.75 3.75

Pre-Olympics (Moscow '80 Olympic Games). Nos. 842-845 issued in sheetlets of 4 and sheets of 20 (4x5) with silver Moscow '80 Emblem covering background of every 20 stamps. Value, set of sheetlets of 4, $45.
Nos. 842-847 exist imperf. Values: set $55; souvenir sheets, $90.

Intl. Day of Cooperation with Palestinian People — A242a

1979, Nov. 29 Photo.   Perf. 12
847A A242a 30d multicolored   .25 .25
847B A242a 115d multicolored   1.75 1.75

Tug of War, Jumping — A243

National Games: No. 848, Polo, leap frog. No. 849, Racing, ball game, No. 850, Wrestling, log rolling. No. 852, Horsemen.

1980, Feb. 15
848 A243 Block of 4, #a.-d.   1.00 1.00
849 A243 Block of 4, #a.-d.   1.00 1.00
850 A243 Block of 4, #a.-d.   1.00 1.00
851 A243 Block of 4, #a.-d.   2.00 2.00
852 A243 Block of 4, #a.-d.   3.50 3.50
     Nos. 848-852 (5)   8.50 8.50

Battles — A244

No. 853: a, 20d, Gardabia, 1915. b, 35d, same. No. 854: a, 20d, Shoghab, 1913. b, 35d, same. No. 855: a, 20d, Fundugh Al-Shibani, 1922. b, 35d, same. No. 856: a, 20d, Ghira. b, 35d, same.
Pairs have continuous design.

1980   Litho.   Perf. 14½
853 A244 Pair, #a.-b.   1.25 1.25
854 A244 Pair, #a.-b.   1.25 1.25
855 A244 Pair, #a.-b.   1.25 1.25
856 A244 Pair, #a.-b.   1.25 1.25
     Nos. 853-856 (4)   5.00 5.00

Issued: No. 853, 4/28; No. 854, 5/25; No. 855, 6/1; No. 856, 8/15.
See Nos. 893-896, 921-932, 980-991, 1059-1070.

Girl Guides Examining Plant — A245

1980, Aug. 22   Perf. 13½
861 A245 15d shown   .25 .25
862 A245 30d Guides cooking   .35 .35
863 A245 50d Scouts at camp-
              fire   .60 .60
864 A245 115d Scouts reading
              map   1.50 1.50
     Nos. 861-864 (4)   2.70 2.70

Souvenir Sheets
865 A245 100d like #861   2.25 2.25
866 A245 100d like #863   2.25 2.25

8th Pan Arab Girl Guide and 14th Pan Arab Scout Jamborees, Aug.

Men Holding OPEC Emblem A246

1980, Sept. 15   Perf. 14½
867 A246 45d Emblem, globe   .50 .50
868 A246 115d shown   1.50 1.50

20th anniversary of OPEC.

Martyrdom of Omar Muktar, 1931 — A247

1980, Sept. 16
869 A247 20d multicolored   .25 .25
870 A247 35d multicolored   .50 .50

Souvenir Sheet
870A A247 100d multicolored   2.50 2.50

UNESCO Emblem and Avicenna A248

1980, Sept. 20
871 A248 45d Scientific symbols   .50 .50
872 A248 115d shown   1.50 1.50

School Scientific Exhibition, Sept. 20-24 and birth millenium of Arab physician Avicenna (115d).

18th Tripoli Fair A249

Various musical instruments. 15d vert.

1980   Litho.   Perf. 13½
873 A249 5d multicolored   .25 .25
874 A249 10d multicolored   .25 .25
875 A249 15d multicolored   .25 .25
876 A249 20d multicolored   .25 .25
877 A249 25d multicolored   .40 .40
     Nos. 873-877 (5)   1.40 1.40

Souvenir Sheet
878 A249 100d Musicians   2.50 2.50

World Olive Oil Year A250

1980, Jan. 15 Litho.   Perf. 13½
879 A250 15d multicolored   .25 .25
880 A250 30d multicolored   .35 .35
881 A250 45d multicolored   .50 .50
     Nos. 879-881 (3)   1.10 1.10

Intl. Year of the Child (1979) — A251

Children's drawings: a, Riding horses. b, water sports. c, Fish. d, Gift sale. e, Preparing feast.

1980, Mar. 21
882   Strip of 5   5.00 5.00
a.-e. A251 20d any single   .50 .40

The Hegira, 1500th Anniv. A252

1980, Apr. 1
883 A252 50d multicolored   .60 .60
884 A252 115d multicolored   1.50 1.50

Operating Room, Hospital — A253

1980, Apr. 7   Litho.   Perf. 13½
885 A253 20d multicolored   .40 .40
886 A253 50d multicolored   .75 .75

World Health Day.

Sheik Zarruq Festival, Misurata, June 16-20 — A254

1980, June 16
887 A254 40d multicolored   .50 .50
888 A254 115d multicolored   1.50 1.50

Souvenir Sheet
889 A254 100d multicolored   2.75 2.75

Arabian Towns Organization A255

1980, July 1   Perf. 11½x12
890 A255 15d Ghadames   .25 .25
891 A255 30d Derna   .35 .35
892 A255 50d Tripoli   .60 .60
    Nos. 890-892 (3)   1.20 1.20

Battles Type of 1980

No. 893: a, 20d, Yefren, 1915, b, 35d, same.
No. 894: a, 20d, El Hani, 1911, b, 35d, same.

No. 895: a, 20d, Sebha, 1914, b, 35d, same.
No. 896: a, 20d, Sirt, 1912, b, 35d, same.
Pairs have continuous design.

1980   Perf. 13½
893 A244 Pair, #a.-b.   1.25 1.25
894 A244 Pair, #a.-b.   1.25 1.25
895 A244 Pair, #a.-b.   1.25 1.25
896 A244 Pair, #a.-b.   1.25 1.25
    Nos. 893-896 (4)   5.00 5.00

Issued: No. 893, 7/16; No. 894, 10/23; No. 895, 11/27; No. 896, 12/31.

Sept. 1 Revolution, 11th Anniv. — A256

Achievements of the Revolution.

1980, Sept. 1
901 A256 5d Oil industry   .25 .25
902 A256 10d Youth festival   .25 .25
903 A256 15d Agriculture   .50 .50
904 A256 25d Transportation   1.25 .50
905 A256 40d Education   1.25 .50
906 A256 115d Housing   3.00 1.25
    Nos. 901-906 (6)   6.50 3.25

Souvenir Sheet
907 A256 100d Montage of
              achievements   2.75 2.75

No. 907 contains one stamp 30x50mm.

World Tourism Conference A257

1980, Sept. 10
908 A257 45d multicolored   .50 .50
909 A257 115d multicolored   1.50 1.50

Intl. Year of the Disabled — A258

Intl. Year of the Disabled emblem and: 20d, Eye, man on crutches. 45d, Stylized globe. 115d, Eye, man on crutch, hands.

1981, Jan. 1   Perf. 15
910 A258 20d multicolored   .25 .25
911 A258 45d multicolored   .35 .25
912 A258 115d multicolored   1.50 .50
    Nos. 910-912 (3)   2.10 1.00

No. 911 Redrawn with Arabic Writing and "Arab League" Above Emblem

1981, Nov. 21   Litho.   Perf. 15
913 A258 45d blue & multi   .35 .25
914 A258 115d rose & multi   1.10 1.10

UPA Disabled Persons Campaign. Design redrawn to include Arab League Emblem.

Mosaics — A259

1981, Jan. 15   Perf. 13½
915 A259 10d Horse   1.00 .25
916 A259 20d Sailing ship   1.00 .50
917 A259 30d Peacocks   2.00 .50
918 A259 40d Panther   2.00 .50
919 A259 50d Musician   2.50 .50
920 A259 115d Fish   6.50 1.00
    Nos. 915-920 (6)   15.00 3.25

Battles Type of 1980

No. 921: a, 20d, Dernah, 1912, b, 35d, same. No. 922: a, 20d, Bir Tagreft, 1928. b, 35d, same. No. 923: a, 20d, Tawargha, 1923. b, 35d, same. No. 924: a, 20d, .Funduk El-Jamel Misurata, 1915 b, 35d, same. No. 925: a, 20d, Zuara, 1912. b, 35d, same. No. 926: a, 20d, Sidi El-Khemri, 1915. b, 35d, same. No. 927: a, 20d, El-Khoms, 1913. b, 35d, same. No. 928: a, 20d, Roghdalin, 1912. b, 35d, same. No. 929: a, 20d, Rughbat El-Naga, 1925. b, 35d, same. No. 930: a, 20d, Tobruk. 1911. 1922, b, 35d, same. No. 931: a, 20d, Bir Ikshadia, 1924. b, 35d, same. No. 932: a, 20d, Ain Zara, 1924. b, 35d, same.
Pairs have continuous design.

1981   Perf. 13½, 14½ (#926, 932)
921 A244 Pair, #a.-b.   1.25 1.25
922 A244 Pair, #a.-b.   1.25 1.25
923 A244 Pair, #a.-b.   1.25 1.25
924 A244 Pair, #a.-b.   1.25 1.25
925 A244 Pair, #a.-b.   1.25 1.25
926 A244 Pair, #a.-b.   1.25 1.25
927 A244 Pair, #a.-b.   1.25 1.25
928 A244 Pair, #a.-b.   1.25 1.25
929 A244 Pair, #a.-b.   1.25 1.25
930 A244 Pair, #a.-b.   1.25 1.25
931 A244 Pair, #a.-b.   1.25 1.25
932 A244 Pair, #a.-b.   1.25 1.25
    Nos. 921-932 (12)   15.00 15.00

Issued: No. 921, 1/17; No. 922, 2/25; No. 923, 3/20; No. 924, 4/13; No. 925, 5/26; No. 926, 6/4; No. 927, 7/27; No. 928, 8/15; No. 929, 9/16; No. 930, 10/27; No. 931, 11/19; No. 932, 12/4.

Tripoli Intl. Fair — A260

Ceramicware.

1981, Mar. 1   Perf. 13½
945 A260 5d Bowls, horiz.   .25 .25
946 A260 10d Lamp   .25 .25
947 A260 15d Vase   .25 .25
948 A260 45d Water jar, horiz.   .60 .25
949 A260 115d Spouted water
              jar, horiz.   1.75 .60
    Nos. 945-949 (5)   3.10 1.60

No. 707b, Crowd — A261

1981, Mar. 2   Perf. 15
950 A261 50d multicolored   .35 .35
951 A261 115d multicolored   1.50 .50

People's Authority Declaration, The Green Book.

Children's Day, IYC — A262

Children's illustrations: a, Desert camp. b, Women doing chores. c, Village scene. d, Airplane over playground. e, Minaret, camel, man.

1981, Mar. 21   Litho.   Perf. 13½
952   Strip of 5   5.00 5.00
a.-e. A262 20d any single   .50 .40

Bank of Libya, 25th Anniv. — A263

1981, Apr. 1   Litho.   Perf. 13½
953 A263 45d multicolored   .50 .35
954 A263 115d multicolored   1.75 1.10

Souvenir Sheet
955 A263 50d multicolored   1.50 1.50

World Health Day A264

1981, Apr. 7   Perf. 14
956 A264 45d multicolored   .50 .50
957 A264 115d multicolored   1.50 .75

Intl. Year for Combating Racial Discrimination A265

1981, July 1   Perf. 15
958 A265 45d multicolored   1.10 .65
959 A265 50d multicolored   1.50 .75

September 1 Revolution, 12th Anniv. — A266

No. 960: a-b, Helicopter and jets; c-d, Paratroopers. No. 961: a-b, Tanks; c-d, Frogman parade. No. 962: a-b, Twelve-barrel rocket launchers; c-d, Trucks with rockets. No. 963: a-b, Sailor parade; c-d, Jeep and trucks with twelve-barrel rocket launchers. No. 964: a-b, Wheeled tanks and jeeps; c-d, Tank parade. Nos. 960-962 vert. Pairs have continuous designs.

1981, Sept. 1   Perf. 14½
960 A266 5d Block of 4, #a.-
              d.   1.40 1.40
961 A266 10d Block of 4, #a.-
              d.   1.40 1.40

962 A266 15d Block of 4, #a.-
d.   1.40 1.40
963 A266 20d Block of 4, #a.-
d.   1.40 1.40
964 A266 25d Block of 4, #a.-
d.   2.75 2.75
      Nos. 960-964 (5)   8.35 8.35

Souvenir Sheet
Perf. 11

965 A266 50d Naval troop marching   7.00 7.00

No. 965 contains one 63x38mm stamp.

Miniature Sheet

Butterflies — A267

1981, Oct. 1   **Perf. 14½**
966 A267 Sheet of 16   11.00
 a.-d.   5d, any single   .25 .25
 e.-h.   10d, any single   .45 .25
 i.-l.   15d, any single   .50 .40
 m.-p.   25d, any single   1.00 .60

No. 966 printed in a continuous design, stamps of same denomination in blocks of 4. Sheetlets exist containing blocks of 4 for each denomination. Value, set of 4 sheets, $20.

A268

1981, Oct. 16   **Perf. 15**
967 A268 45d multicolored   .50 .50
968 A268 200d multicolored   2.50 2.50

World Food Day.

A269

1981, Nov. 17   **Perf. 13½**
969 A269 5d Grapes   .25 .25
970 A269 10d Dates   .25 .25
971 A269 15d Lemons   .25 .25
972 A269 20d Oranges   .40 .25
973 A269 35d Cactus fruit   .80 .35
974 A269 55d Pomegranates   1.50 .60
     Nos. 969-974 (6)   3.45 1.95

Miniature Sheet

A270

Mosaics: a, Animals facing right. b, Orpheus playing music. c, Animals facing left. d, Fish. e, Fishermen. f, Fish in basket. g, Farm yard. h, Birds eating fruit. i, Milking a goat.

1982, Jan. 1   **Perf. 13½**
975 A270 Sheet of 9   9.00 9.00
 a.-i.   45d any single   .75 .75

Nos. 975a-975c, shown in illustration, printed in continuous design.

3rd Intl. Koran
Reading
Contest — A271

Designs: 10d, Stone tablets, Holy Ka'aba, Mecca. 35d, Open Koran, creation of the world. 115d, Scholar, students.

1982, Jan. 7
976 A271 10d multicolored   .25 .25
977 A271 35d multicolored   .50 .25
978 A271 115d multicolored   1.50 .75
     Nos. 976-978 (3)   2.25 1.25

Souvenir Sheet

979 A271 100d like 115d   3.50 3.50

Battles Type of 1980

No. 980: a, 20d, Hun Gioffra, 1915; b, 35d, same. No. 981: a, 20d, Gedabia, 1914; b, 35d, same. No. 982: a, 20d, El-Asaba, 1913; b, 35d, same. No. 983: a, 20d, El-Habela, 1917; b, 35d, same. No. 984: a, 20d, Suk El-Ahad, 1915; b, 35d, same. No. 985: a, 20d, El-Tangi, 1913; b, 35d, same. No. 986: a, 20d, Sokna, 1913; b, 35d, same. No. 987: a, 20d, Wadi Smalus, 1925; b, 35d, same. No. 988: a, 20d, Sidi Abuagela, 1917; b, 35d, same. No. 989: a, 20d, Sidi Surur, 1914; b, 35d, same. No. 990: a, 20d, Kuefia, 1911; b, 35d, same. No. 991: a, 20d, Abunjeim, 1940; b, 35d, same.
Pairs have continuous design.

1982   *Perf. 13½, 14½ (#985-988)*
980 A244 Pair, #a.-b.   1.25 1.25
981 A244 Pair, #a.-b.   1.25 1.25
982 A244 Pair, #a.-b.   1.25 1.25
983 A244 Pair, #a.-b.   1.25 1.25
984 A244 Pair, #a.-b.   1.25 1.25
985 A244 Pair, #a.-b.   1.25 1.25
986 A244 Pair, #a.-b.   1.25 1.25
987 A244 Pair, #a.-b.   1.25 1.25
988 A244 Pair, #a.-b.   1.25 1.25
989 A244 Pair, #a.-b.   1.25 1.25
990 A244 Pair, #a.-b.   1.25 1.25
991 A244 Pair, #a.-b.   1.25 1.25
    Nos. 980-991 (12)   15.00 15.00

Issued: No. 980, 1/26; No. 981, 3/8; No. 982, 3/23; No. 983, 4/24; No. 984, 5/15; No. 985, 6/19; No. 986, 7/23; No. 987, 8/11; No. 988, 9/4; No. 989, 10/14; No. 990, 11/28; No. 991, 12/13.

Tripoli Intl.
Fair — A272

1982, Mar. 1   **Perf. 13x12½**
1004 A272 5d Grinding stone   .25 .25
1005 A272 10d Ox-drawn plow   .25 .25
1006 A272 25d Pitching hay   .25 .25
1007 A272 35d Tapestry weaving   .50 .25
1008 A272 45d Traditional cooking   .75 .35
1009 A272 100d Grain harvest   1.50 .75
    Nos. 1004-1009 (6)   3.50 2.10

People's Authority Declaration, The
Green Book — A273

1982, Mar. 2   **Perf. 13½**
1010   Strip of 3   8.00 8.00
 a. A273 100d Harvester combine   1.25 .80
 b. A273 200d Khadafy, scholar, rifles   2.50 2.25
 c. A273 300d Govt. building, citizens   3.25 2.25

Scouting
Movement, 75th
Anniv. — A274

1982, Mar. 2
1011   Strip of 4   22.50 22.50
 a. A274 100d Cub scout, blimp   1.75 .90
 b. A274 200d Scouts, dog   3.25 1.60
 c. A274 300d Scholar, scout   4.75 2.00
 d. A274 400d Boy scout, rocket   7.25 3.75

Souvenir Sheets

1012 A274 500d Green Book   8.00 8.00
1013 A274 500d Khadafy,
scouts   8.00 8.00

Nos. 1012-1013 each contain one stamp 39x42mm.
Nos. 1011-1013 exist imperf.

13th African
Soccer Cup
Championships
A275

1982, Mar. 5
1014 A275 100d multi   1.50 .75
1015 A275 200d multi   3.00 1.50

1982 World Cup Soccer
Championships, Spain — A276

World Cup trophy and various soccer plays.

1982, Mar. 15   **Perf. 14½**
1016 A276 45d multi   .60 .60
1017 A276 100d multi   1.50 1.50
1018 A276 200d multi   2.75 2.75
1019 A276 300d multi   3.25 3.25
    Nos. 1016-1019 (4)   8.10 8.10

Souvenir Sheets

1020 A276 500d like 45d   7.50 7.50
1021 A276 500d like 100d   7.50 7.50

Nos. 1016-1019 issued in sheets of 8 over-printed in silver with soccer ball in motion. Value $75. Sheetlets of 4 in each denomination exist without overprint.
Nos. 1020-1021 have Arabic text in green on reverse. Value $35.
Nos. 1016-1019 exist imperf. Value $15. Nos. 1020-1021 also exist imperf.

Palestinian
Children's
Day — A277

Designs: a, Two children. b, Girl with bowl. c, Girl with kaffiyeh. d, Girl hiding. e, Boy.

1982, Mar. 7   **Perf. 13½**
1022   Strip of 5   2.75 2.75
 a.-e. A277 20d, any single   .40 .40

Miniature Sheet

Birds — A278

1982, Apr. 1   **Perf. 14½**
1023 A278 Sheet of 16   20.00 20.00
 a.-d.   15d, any single   .50 .45
 e.-h.   25d, any single   .75 .60
 i.-l.   45d, any single   1.10 1.00
 m.-p.   95d, any single   2.40 1.80

No. 1023a-1023p printed se-tenant in a continuous design; stamps of same denomination in blocks of 4.
Each denomination was also printed in a sheet of 16, each sheet containing four se-tenant blocks of the same denomination. Value, set of four sheets, $75.

Teaching
Hospitals
Anniv.
A279

1982, Apr. 7   **Perf. 13x12½**
1024 A279 95d multi   1.25 1.25
1025 A279 100d multi   1.25 1.25
1026 A279 205d multi   2.75 2.75
    Nos. 1024-1026 (3)   5.25 5.25

Arab Postal
Union,
30th — A280

1982, Apr. 12   **Perf. 13½**
1027 A280 100d multi   1.50 .75
1028 A280 200d multi   2.75 1.50

1982 World Chess Championships — A281

Board positions and chessmen: a, Chinese piece. b, African piece. c, Modern piece. d, European piece.
500d, Overhead view of chessboard.

1982, May 1
1029	A281	Block of 4	10.00	10.00
a.-d.		100d, any single	2.25	1.10

Souvenir Sheet
1030	A281	500d multicolored	10.00	10.00

No. 1030 contains one stamp 39x42mm.
Nos. 1029 and 1030 exist imperf.

World Telecommunications Day — A282

1982, May 17
1031	A282	100d multi	1.25	1.25
1032	A282	200d multi	2.50	2.50

Map of Libya, Green Book A283

1982, June 11
1033	A283	200d multi	2.50	1.50

Souvenir Sheet
1034	A283	300d multi	5.00	5.00

Post Day, FIP 51st anniv.

Organization of African Unity, 19th Summit A284

50d, OAU flag, Arab family. 100d, Map of Africa, emblem. 200d, Khadafy, Green Book. 300d, Fist, map.

1982, Aug. 5 — *Perf. 14*
1035	A284	50d multicolored	.75	.75
1036	A284	100d multicolored	1.25	1.25

Size: 69x40mm
1037	A284	200d multicolored	2.50	2.50
		Nos. 1035-1037 (3)	4.50	4.50

Souvenir Sheet — *Perf. 13x13½*
1038	A284	300d multicolored	5.00	5.00

No. 1038 contains one stamp 29x42mm.

September 1 Revolution, 13th Anniv. — A285

Khadafy in uniforms and various armed forces' exercises.

1982, Sept. 1 — *Perf. 11½*
1039	A285	15d multi	.25	.25
1040	A285	20d multi	.25	.25
1041	A285	30d multi	1.00	1.00
1042	A285	45d multi	.60	.60
1043	A285	70d multi	1.00	1.00
1044	A285	100d multi	1.50	1.50
		Nos. 1039-1044 (6)	4.60	4.60

Souvenir Sheet
Imperf
1045	A285	200d multi	4.00	4.00

Libyan Red Crescent, 25th Anniv. — A286

1982, Oct. 5 — *Perf. 13½*
1046	A286	100d Palm tree	1.75	1.25
1047	A286	200d "25," crescents	3.50	2.50

Intl. Day of Cooperation with Palestinian People — A287

1982, Nov. 29
1048	A287	100d gray grn & blk	1.50	.75
1049	A287	200d brt bl, gray grn & blk	2.75	1.50

Al-Fateh University Symposium on Khadafy's Green Book — A288

100d, Khadafy in uniform. 200d, Khadafy, map, Green Book.

1982, Dec. 1 — *Perf. 12*
1050	A288	100d multicolored	1.25	1.10
1051	A288	200d multicolored	2.50	2.50

Miniature Sheet

Flowers — A289

Designs: a, Philadelphus. b, Hypericum. c, Antinhinum. d, Lily. e, Capparis. f, Tropaeolum. g, Rose. h, Chrysanthemum. i, Nigella damascena. j, Gaillardia lanceolata. k, Dahlia. l, Dianthus carophyllus. m, Notobasis syriaca. n, Nerium oleander. o, Iris histriodes. p, Scolymus hispanicus.

1983, Jan. 1 — *Perf. 14½*
1052	A289	Sheet of 16	10.00	10.00
a.-p.		25d, any single	.50	.40

Torch Type of 1979

1983, Jan. 2 — *Perf. 13½*
Size: 26½x32mm
1053	A228	250d multi	3.25	2.00
1054	A228	1500d multi	20.00	12.50
1055	A228	2500d multi	37.50	25.00
		Nos. 1053-1055 (3)	60.75	39.50

Customs Cooperation Council, 30th Anniv. — A290

1983, Jan. 15 — *Perf. 14½x14*
1056	A290	25d Arab riding horse	.25	.25
1057	A290	50d Riding camel	.60	.60
1058	A290	100d Drawing sword	1.50	1.50
		Nos. 1056-1058 (3)	2.35	2.35

Battles Type of 1980

No. 1059, Ghaser Ahmed, 1922. No. 1060, Sidi Abuarghub, 1923. No. 1061, Ghar Yunes, 1913. No. 1062, Bir Otman, 1926. No. 1063, Sidi Sajeh, 1922. No. 1064, Ras El-Hamam, 1915. No. 1065, Zawiet Ishghefa, 1913. No. 1066, Wadi Essania, 1930. No. 1067, El-Meshiashta, 1917. No. 1068, Gharara, 1925. No. 1069, Abughelan, 1922. No. 1070, Mahruka, 1913.
Pairs have continuous design.

1983 — *Perf. 13½*
1059	A244	50d Pair, #a.-b.	2.00	2.00
1060	A244	50d Pair, #a.-b.	2.00	2.00
1061	A244	50d Pair, #a.-b.	2.00	2.00
1062	A244	50d Pair, #a.-b.	2.00	2.00
1063	A244	50d Pair, #a.-b.	2.00	2.00
1064	A244	50d Pair, #a.-b.	2.00	2.00
1065	A244	50d Pair, #a.-b.	2.00	2.00
1066	A244	50d Pair, #a.-b.	2.00	2.00
1067	A244	50d Pair, #a.-b.	2.00	2.00
1068	A244	50d Pair, #a.-b.	2.00	2.00
1069	A244	50d Pair, #a.-b.	2.00	2.00
1070	A244	50d Pair, #a.-b.	2.00	2.00
		Nos. 1059-1070 (12)	24.00	24.00

Issued: No. 1059, 1/26; No. 1060, 2/2; No. 1061, 3/26; No. 1062, 4/9; No. 1063, 5/2; No. 1064, 6/24; No. 1065, 7/13; No. 1066, 8/8; No. 1067, 9/9; No. 1068, 10/22; No. 1069, 11/17; No. 1070, 12/24.

Miniature Sheet

Farm Animals — A291

Designs: a, Camel. b, Cow. c, Horse. d, Bull. e, Goat. f, Dog. g, Sheep. h, Ram. i, Goose. j, Turkey hen. k, Rabbit. l, Pigeon. m, Turkey. n, Rooster. o, Hen. p, Duck.

1983, Feb. 15 — *Perf. 14½*
1083	A291	Sheet of 16	10.00	10.00
a.-p.		25d any single	.50	.40

Tripoli Intl. Fair A292

Libyans playing traditional instruments.

1983, Mar. 5 — *Perf. 14½x14, 14x14½*
1084	A292	40d multi, vert.	.60	.40
1085	A292	45d multicolored	.75	.50
1086	A292	50d multi, vert.	.75	.50
1087	A292	55d multicolored	1.00	.60
1088	A292	75d multi, vert.	1.25	.90
1089	A292	100d multi, vert.	1.60	1.10
		Nos. 1084-1089 (6)	5.95	4.00

Intl. Maritime Organization, 25th Anniv. — A293

Early sailing ships.

1983, Mar. 17 — *Perf. 14½*
1090	A293	100d Phoenician	2.00	.75
1091	A293	100d Viking	2.00	.75
1092	A293	100d Greek	2.00	.75
1093	A293	100d Roman	2.00	.75
1094	A293	100d Libyan	2.00	.75
1095	A293	100d Pharoah's ship	2.00	.75
		Nos. 1090-1095 (6)	12.00	4.50

Children's Day (1983) A294

Children's illustrations: a, Car. b, Tractor towing trailer. c, Children, dove. d, Boy Scouts. e, Dinosaur.

1983, Mar. 21 — *Perf. 14x14½*
1096		Strip of 5	2.75	2.75
a.-e.	A294	20d, any single	.40	.30

1st Intl. Symposium on Khadafy's Green Book — A295

50d, Khadafy, Green Book, map. 70d, Lecture hall, emblem. 80d, Khadafy, Green Book, emblem.
100d, Khadafy, Green Books.

1983, Apr. 1			**Perf. 13½**	
1097	A295	50d multicolored	.60	.40
1098	A295	70d multicolored	1.00	.50
1099	A295	80d multicolored	1.10	.75
		Nos. 1097-1099 (3)	2.70	1.65

Souvenir Sheet
Perf. 12½

1100	A295	100d multicolored	3.00	3.00

No. 1100 contains one stamp 57x48mm.

World Health Day A296

25d, Healthy children, vert. 50d, Man in wheelchair, vert. 100d, Girl in hospital bed.

1983, Apr. 7			**Perf. 12½**	
1101	A296	25d multicolored	.25	.25
1102	A296	50d multicolored	.60	.40
1103	A296	100d multicolored	1.25	.75
		Nos. 1101-1103 (3)	2.10	1.40

Pan-African Economic Committee, 25th Anniv. — A297

1983, Apr. 20			**Perf. 13½**	
1104	A297	50d multi	.60	.40
1105	A297	100d multi	1.25	.75
1106	A297	250d multi	3.00	2.00
		Nos. 1104-1106 (3)	4.85	3.15

Miniature Sheet

Fish — A298

Designs: a, Labrus bimaculatus. b, Trigloporus lastoviza. c, Thalassoma pavo. d, Apogon imberbis. e, Scomber scombrus. f, Spondyliosoma cantharus. g, Trachinus draco. h, Blennius pavo. i, Scorpaena notata. j, Serranus scriba. k, Lophius piscatorius. l, Uranoscopus scaber. m, Auxis thazard. n, Zeus faber. o, Dactylopterus volitans. p, Umbrina cirrosa.

1983, May 15			**Perf. 14½**	
1107	A298	Sheet of 16	10.00	10.00
a.-p.		25d any single	.40	.30

Still-life by Gauguin (1848-1903) — A299

Paintings: No. 1108b, Abstract, unattributed. c, The Conquest of Tunis by Charles V, by Rubens. d, Arab Musicians in a Carriage, unattributed.
No. 1109a, Khadafy Glorified on Horseback, unattributed, vert. b, Triumph of David over the Syrians, by Raphael, vert. c, Laborers, unattributed, vert. d, Flower Vase, by van Gogh, vert.

1983, June 1			**Perf. 11**	
1108		Strip of 4	3.00	3.00
a.-d.	A299	50d, any single	.50	.35
1109		Strip of 4	3.00	3.00
a.-d.	A299	50d, any single	.50	.35

Souvenir Sheet

Ali Siala — A300

Scientists: No. 1110b, Ali El-Najar.

1983, June 1				
1110	A300	Sheet of 2	3.50	3.50
a.-b.		100d, any single	1.50	1.50

World Communications Year — A302

1983, July 1			**Perf. 13**	
1119	A302	10d multicolored	.40	.30
1120	A302	50d multicolored	.90	.60
1121	A302	100d multicolored	2.00	1.25
		Nos. 1119-1121 (3)	3.30	2.15

The Green Book, by Khadafy A303

Ideologies: 10d, The House is to be served by its residents. 15d, Power, wealth and arms are in the hands of the people. 20d, Masters in their own castles, vert. 35d, No democracy without popular congress. 100d, The authority of the people, vert. 140d, The Green Book is the guide of humanity for final release.
200d, Khadafy in uniform.

1983, Aug. 1			**Perf. 13½**	
1122	A303	10d multi	.25	.25
1123	A303	15d multi	.25	.25
1124	A303	20d multi	.25	.25
1125	A303	35d multi	.40	.25
1126	A303	100d multi	1.25	.75
1127	A303	140d multi	1.75	1.25
		Nos. 1122-1127 (6)	4.15	3.00

Souvenir Sheet
Litho. & Embossed

1128	A303	200d multi	4.50	4.50

No. 1128 contains one gold embossed stamp 36x51mm.

2nd African Youth Sports Festival — A304

Designs: a, Team Handball. b, Basketball. c, Javelin. d, Running. e, Soccer.

1983, Aug. 22			**Litho.**	
1129		Strip of 5	7.50	4.00
a.-e.	A304	100d, any single	1.25	.75

September 1 Revolution, 14th Anniv. — A305

Women in the Armed Forces.

1983, Sept. 1			**Perf. 11½**	
1130	A305	65d multi	.75	.75
1131	A305	75d multi	.90	.90
1132	A305	90d multi	1.00	1.00
1133	A305	100d multi	1.25	1.25
1134	A305	150d multi	1.75	1.75
1135	A305	250d multi	3.25	3.25
		Nos. 1130-1135 (6)	8.90	8.90

Souvenir Sheet
Perf. 11

1136	A305	200d multi	4.50	4.50

No. 1136 contains one stamp 63x38mm.

2nd Islamic Scout Jamboree — A306

1983, Sept. 2			**Perf. 12½**	
1137	A306	50d Saluting	.75	.75
1138	A306	100d Camping	2.00	2.00

Souvenir Sheet

1139		Sheet of 2	4.50	4.50
a.	A306	100d like 50d	2.00	2.00

No. 1139 contains Nos. 1138 and 1139a.

Traffic Day — A307

30d, Youth traffic monitors. 70d, Traffic officer. 200d, Motorcycle police.

1983, Oct. 1			**Perf. 14½x14**	
1140	A307	30d multicolored	1.25	.75
1141	A307	70d multicolored	2.50	1.00
1142	A307	200d multicolored	8.00	3.50
		Nos. 1140-1142 (3)	11.75	5.25

Saadun (1893-1923) A308

1983, Oct. 11			**Perf. 13½**	
1143	A308	100d multicolored	1.50	.75

1st Manned Flight, Bicent. — A309

Early aircraft and historic flights: a, Americana, 1910. b, Nulli Secundus, 1907. c, J. B. Meusnier, 1785. d, Blanchard and Jeffries, 1785, vert. e, Pilatre de Rozier, 1784, vert. f, Montgolfiere, Oct. 19, 1783, vert.

1983, Nov. 1				
1144		Strip of 6	11.00	11.00
a.-f.	A309	100d, any single	1.60	.85

Intl. Day of Cooperation with Palestinian People — A310

1983, Nov. 29			**Perf. 14½x14**	
1145	A310	30d pale vio & lt bl grn	.50	.30
1146	A310	70d lil & lt yel grn	1.40	.55
1147	A310	200d lt ultra & grn	3.75	2.00
		Nos. 1145-1147 (3)	5.65	2.85

1984 Summer Olympic Games, Los Angeles — A301

1983, June 15			**Perf. 13½**	
1111	A301	10d Basketball	.25	.25
1112	A301	15d High jump	.25	.25
1113	A301	25d Running	.25	.25
1114	A301	50d Gymnastics	.50	.40
1115	A301	100d Wind surfing	1.25	.75
1116	A301	200d Shot put	2.50	1.60
		Nos. 1111-1116 (6)	5.00	3.50

Souvenir Sheets

1117	A301	100d Equestrian	3.00	3.00
1118	A301	100d Soccer	3.00	3.00

Nos. 1111-1116 exist imperf. Value, set $22.50. Nos. 1117-1118 also exist imperf.
Nos. 1111-1116 exist printed together in a miniature sheet of 6. Values: perf $35; imperf $50. Each value was also printed in a miniature sheet of 4. Value, set of 6 sheets, $45.

Miniature Sheet

Roman Mosaic — A311

Designs: Nos. 1148a-1148c, Gladiators. Nos. 1148d-1148f, Musicians, Nos. 1148g-1148i, Hunters.

1983, Dec. 1   **Perf. 12**
1148	A311	Sheet of 9	7.00 7.00
a.-i.		50d, any single	.75 .35

Nos. 1148a-1148c, 1148d-1148f and 1148g-1148i se-tenant in a continuous design.

Achievements of the Sept. 1 Revolution — A312

1983, Dec. 15   **Perf. 13½**
1149	A312	10d Mosque	.25 .25
1150	A312	15d Agriculture	.25 .25
1151	A312	20d Industry	.40 .25
1152	A312	35d Office building	.50 .25
1153	A312	100d Health care	1.50 .60
1154	A312	140d Airport	2.25 1.10
		Nos. 1149-1154 (6)	5.15 2.70

Souvenir Sheet
Litho. & Embossed
1155	A312	200d Khadafy	4.50 4.50

No. 1155 contains one gold embossed stamp 36x51mm.

Khadafy, Irrigation Project Survey Map A313

1983, Dec. 15
1156	A313	150d multicolored	2.25 1.25

A314

A315

Famous men: No. 1157a, Mahmud Burkis. No. 1157b, Ahmed El-Bakbak. No. 1157c, Mohamed El-Misurati. No. 1157d, Mahmud Ben Musa. No. 1157e, Abdulhamid Ben Ashiur. No. 1158a, Hosni Fauzi El-Amir. No. 1158b, Ali Haidar El-Saati. No. 1159, Mahmud Mustafa Dreza. No. 1160, Mehdi El-Sherif. No. 1161a, Ali El-Gariani. No. 1161b, Muktar Shakshuki. No. 1161c, Abdurrahman El-Busayri. No. 1161d, Ibbrahim Bakir. No. 1161e, Mahmud El-Janzuri. No. 1162a, Ahmed El-Feghi Hasan. No. 1162b, Bashir El Jawab.

1984   **Litho.**   **Perf. 13½**
1157		Strip of 5	6.00 6.00
a.-e.	A314	100d single	1.10 1.10
1158		Pair	3.50 1.50
a.-b.	A314	100d single	1.50 .60
1159	A314	100d multi	1.75 .60
1160	A315	100d multi	1.75 .60
1161		Strip of 5	15.00 15.00
a.-e.	A314	200d single	2.50 2.50
1162		Pair	6.00 6.00
a.-b.	A315	200d single	2.50 2.50
		Nos. 1157-1162 (6)	34.00 29.70

Issued: Nos. 1157, 1161-1162, 1/1; No. 1158-1160, 2/20.

Miniature Sheet

Water Sports — A316

Designs: a, Two windsurfers. b, Two-man craft. c, Two-man craft, birds. d, Wind sailing, skis. e, Water skier facing front. f, Fisherman in boat. g, Power boating. h, Water skier facing right. i, Fisherman in surf. j, Kayaking. k, Surfing. l, Water skier wearing life jacket. m, Scuba diver sketching underwater. n, Diver. o, Snorkel diver removing fish from harpoon. p, Scuba diver surfacing.

1984, Jan. 10   **Perf. 14½**
1164	A316	Sheet of 16	8.50 8.50
a.-p.		25d any single	.50 .50

African Children's Day — A317

Designs: a, Khadafy, girl scouts. b, Khadafy, children. c, Map, Khadafy, children (size: 63x44mm).

1984, Jan. 15   **Litho.**   **Perf. 14½**
1165	A317	Strip of 3	3.50 3.50
a.-b.		50d, any single	.80 .80
c.		100d multi	2.00 2.00

Women's Emancipation — A318

70d, Women, diff., vert. 100d, Soldiers, Khadafy.

1984, Jan. 20   **Perf. 12**
1166	A318	55d multicolored	.75 .40
1167	A318	70d multicolored	1.25 .45
1168	A318	100d multicolored	1.50 .75
		Nos. 1166-1168 (3)	3.50 1.60

Irrigation — A319

No. 1169: a, Desert, water. b, Produce, sheep grazing. c, Khadafy, irrigation of desert (size: 63x44mm). Nos. 1170-1171, Khadafy, map.

1984, Feb. 1   **Perf. 14½**
1169	A319	Strip of 3	2.50 2.50
a.-b.		50d any single	.50 .25
c.		100d multicolored	1.50 .60

Size: 72x36mm
Perf. 13½
1170	A319	100d multicolored	1.50 .60

Souvenir Sheet
1171	A319	300d multicolored	7.00 7.00

World Heritage — A320

Architectural ruins: 50d, Theater, Sabratha. 60d, Temple, Cyrene. 70d, Monument, Sabratha, vert. 100d, Arena, Leptis Magna. 150d, Temple, Cyrene, diff. 200d, Basilica, Leptis Magna.

1984, Feb. 10   **Perf. 12**
1172	A320	50d multicolored	.60 .25
1173	A320	60d multicolored	.75 .30
1174	A320	70d multicolored	.90 .35
1175	A320	100d multicolored	1.50 .60
1176	A320	150d multicolored	2.00 .90
1177	A320	200d multicolored	2.75 1.40
		Nos. 1172-1177 (6)	8.50 3.80

Silver Dirhams Minted A.D. 671-757 — A321

Designs: a, Hegira 115. b, Hegira 93. c, Hegira 121. d, Hegira 49. e, Hegira 135.

Litho. & Embossed
1984, Feb. 15   **Perf. 13½**
1178		Strip of 5	15.00 15.00
a.-e.	A321	200d, any single	2.75 1.25

Tripoli Intl. Fair A322

Tea served in various settings.

1984, Mar. 5   **Litho.**   **Perf. 12½**
1179	A322	25d multicolored	.25 .25
1180	A322	35d multicolored	.40 .25
1181	A322	45d multicolored	.75 .25
1182	A322	55d multicolored	.90 .40
1183	A322	75d multicolored	1.10 .40
1184	A322	100d multicolored	1.75 .95
		Nos. 1179-1184 (6)	5.15 2.50

Musicians — A323

Designs: a, Muktar Shiaker Murabet. b, El-Aref El-Jamal. c, Ali Shiaalia. d, Bashir Fehmi.

1984, Mar. 15   **Perf. 14½**
1185		Strip of 4 + label	9.00 9.00
a.-d.	A323	100d, any single	1.90 1.00

Children's Day, IYC A324

Children's drawings: a, Recreation. b, Rainy day. c, Military strength. d, Playground. e, Porch swing, children, motorcycle.

1984, Mar. 21   **Perf. 14**
1186		Strip of 5	2.75 2.75
a.-e.	A324	20d, any single	.45 .25

Arab League Constitution, 39th Anniv. A325

1984, Mar. 22   **Perf. 13½**
1187	A325	30d multicolored	.60 .60
1188	A325	40d multicolored	.70 .70
1189	A325	50d multicolored	1.00 1.00
		Nos. 1187-1189 (3)	2.30 2.30

Miniature Sheet

Automobiles, Locomotives — A326

1984, Apr. 1
1190	A326	Sheet of 16	30.00 30.00
a.-h.		100d, Car, any single	1.75 .90
i.-p.		100d, Locomotive, any single	1.75 .90

No. 1190 pictures outline of two camels in gold. Size: 214x135mm.

World Health Day A327

1984, Apr. 7   **Perf. 14½**
1191	A327	20d Stop Polio	.25 .25
1192	A327	30d No. 910	.40 .25
1193	A327	40d Arabic text	.90 .40
		Nos. 1191-1193 (3)	1.55 .90

**Crafts
A328**

Designs: a, Shoemaker. b, Saddler. c,
Women, wool. d, Spinner. e, Weaver. f, Tapestry weavers.

1984, May 1   **Perf. 12½**
1194   Strip of 6   15.00 15.00
a.-f. A328 150d, any single   2.25 1.25

**Postal and Telecommunications Union
Congress — A329**

Designs: a, Telephones, mail. b, Computer
operators. c, Emblem.

1984, May 15   **Perf. 14½**
1195   A329   Strip of 3   3.50 3.50
a.-b.   50d, any single   .75   .40
c.   100d multicolored   1.50   .75

**Armed
Crowd — A330**

A331

No. 1197a, Map, Fire, Military. No. 1197b,
Soldiers. No. 1197c, Khadafy. No. 1198,
Khadafy giving speech.

1984, May 17   Perf. 12, 14½ (#1197)
1196 A330 50d multi   .90   .40
1197 A331 Strip of 3   3.00 3.00
a.-b.   50d, any single   .75   .25
c.   100d multi   1.75   .90
1198 A330 100d multi   1.50   .75
        Nos. 1196-1198 (3)   5.40 4.15

Abrogation of the May 17 Treaty. Size of No.
1197c: 63x45mm.

**Youth War
Casualties
A332**

1984, June 4   **Perf. 10**
1199 A332 70d Damaged flag   1.00   .40
1200 A332 100d Children impris-
              oned   1.50   .75

Miniature Sheet

Green Book Quotations — A333

Designs: a, The Party System Aborts
Democracy. b, Khadafy. c, Partners Not
Wage-Workers. d, No Representation in Lieu
of the People . . . e, Green Book. f, Commit-
tees Everywhere. g, Forming Parties Splits
Societies. h, Party building, text on track. i, No
Democracy without Popular Congresses.

1984, June 20   **Perf. 14**
1201 A333 Sheet of 9   14.00 14.00
a.-i.   100d, any single   1.50   .75
        See No. 1270.

**Folk
Costumes — A334**

Background colors: a, Green. b, Beige. c,
Violet. d, Pale greenish blue. e, Salmon rose.
f, Blue.

1984, July 1   **Perf. 14½x14**
1202   Strip of 6   12.50 12.50
a.-f. A334 100d, any single   1.75 1.00

Miniature Sheet

Natl. Soccer Championships — A335

Stadium, star, world cup and various action
scenes.

1984, July 15   **Perf. 13½**
1203 A335 Sheet of 16   20.00 20.00
a.-p.   70d, any single   1.10   .60

**1984 Los
Angeles
Olympics — A336**

1984, July 28
1204 A336 100d Soccer   2.00 1.10
1205 A336 100d Basketball   2.00 1.10
1206 A336 100d Swimming   2.00 1.10
1207 A336 100d Sprinting   2.00 1.10
1208 A336 100d Windsurfing   2.00 1.10
1209 A336 100d Discus   2.00 1.10
        Nos. 1204-1209 (6)   12.00 6.60

Souvenir Sheets
1210 A336 250d Equestrian   6.25 6.25
1211 A336 250d Arab equestri-
              an   6.25 6.25

**World Food
Day — A337**

1984, Aug. 1   **Perf. 12**
1212 A337 100d Forest scenes 1.75   .75
1213 A337 200d Men riding cam-
              els, oasis   3.50 1.25

Miniature Sheet

**Sept. 1 Revolution, 15th
Anniv. — A338**

Designs: a, Green books, building at right
angle. b, Green book, building, minaret. c,
Minaret, party building and grounds. d,
Revolution leader. e, Eight-story building. f,
Construction, dome. g, Highway, bridge. h,
Green book, building at left angle. i, Shepherd,
sheep. j, Harvester. k, Tractors. l, Industry. m,
Khadafy. n, Irrigation pipe, man drinking. o,
Silos, factory. p, Shipping.

1984, Sept. 15   **Perf. 14½**
1214 A338 Sheet of 16   9.00 9.00
a.-p.   25d any single   .50   .25

A339

Evacuation Day — A340

No. 1215: b, Warrior facing left; c, Khadafy
leading battle (size: 63x45mm). No. 1216,
Female rider. No. 1217, Battle scene. No.
1218, Italian whipping Libyan.

1984, Oct. 7
1215 A339 Strip of 3   3.50 3.50
a.-b.   50d, any single   .75   .40
c.   100d multi   1.50   .60

                                Perf. 11½
1216 A340 100d multicolored   1.50   .60
1217 A340 100d multicolored   1.50   .60
1218 A340 100d multicolored   1.50   .60
        Nos. 1215-1218 (4)   8.00 5.30

Miniature Sheet

Equestrians — A341

Various jumping, racing and dressage exercises printed in a continuous design.

1984, Oct. 15   **Perf. 13½**
1219 A341 Sheet of 16   9.00   .90
a.-p.   25d any single   .50   .50

PHILAKOREA '84.

**Agricultural
Traditions — A342**

Designs: a, Farmer. b, Well, man, ox. c,
Basket weaver. d, Shepherd, ram. e, Tanning
hide. f, Coconut picker.

1984, Nov. 1   **Perf. 13½**
1220   Strip of 6   12.50 12.50
a.-f. A342 100d, any single   1.75 1.00

**Union of Arab Pharmacists, 9th
Congress — A343**

1984, Nov. 6   **Perf. 12**
1221 A343 100d multicolored   1.75 1.75
1222 A343 200d multicolored   3.50 3.50

Arab-African Union — A344

1984, Nov. 15   **Perf. 12**
1223 A344 100d Map, banner,
              crowd   1.75 1.75
1224 A344 100d Men, flags   1.75 1.75

**Nos.
1046,
1147
A345**

1984, Nov. 29   **Perf. 12½**
1225 A345 100d pink & multi   3.75 3.75
1226 A345 150d brt yel grn &
              multi   4.75 4.75

Intl. Day of Cooperation with the Palestinian
People.

Miniature Sheet

Intl. Civil Aviation Organization, 40th Anniv. — A346

Aircraft: a, Boeing 747 SP, 1975. b, Concorde, 1969. c, Lockheed L1011-500 Tristar, 1978. d, Airbus A310, 1982. e, Tupolev TU-134A, 1962. f, Shorts 360, 1981. g, Boeing 727, 1963. h, Caravelle 10, 1965. i, Fokker F27, 1955. j, Lockheed 749A Constellation, 1946. k, Martin 130, 1955. l, Douglas DC-3, 1936. m, Junkers JU-52, 1932. n, Lindbergh's Spirit of St. Louis, 1927 Ryan. o, De Havilland Moth, 1925. p, Wright Flyer, 1903.

1984, Dec. 7   *Perf. 13½*
1227 A346   Sheet of 16   27.50 27.50
  a.-p.   70d any single   1.50   .75

African Development Bank, 20th Anniv. — A347

"20" in different configurations and: 70d, Map, symbols of industry, education and agriculture. 100d, Symbols of research and development.

1984, Dec. 15
1228 A347   50d multicolored   .90   .90
1229 A347   70d multicolored   1.25 1.25
1230 A347   100d multicolored   1.75 1.75
  Nos. 1228-1230 (3)   3.90 3.90

UN Child Survival Campaign A348

1985, Jan. 1   *Perf. 12*
1231 A348   70d Mother, child   1.50   .75
1232 A348   70d Children   1.50   .75
1233 A348   70d Boys at military school   1.50   .75
1234 A348   70d Khadafy, children   1.50   .75
  Nos. 1231-1234 (4)   6.00 3.00

Irrigation — A349

Drop of Water, Map — A350

1985, Jan. 15   *Perf. 14½x14*
1235 A349   100d shown   2.00 1.00
1236 A349   100d Flowers   2.00 1.00
1237 A349   100d Map, water   2.00 1.00
  Nos. 1235-1237 (3)   6.00 3.00

Souvenir Sheet
Perf. 14x14½
1238 A350   200d shown   4.00 4.00

Musicians — A351

No 1239: a, Kamel El-Ghadi; b, Lute. No. 1240: a, Ahmed El-Khogia; b, Violin. No 1241: a, Mustafa El-Fallah; b, Zither. No 1242: a, Mohamed Hamdi; b, Mask.

1985, Feb. 1   *Perf. 14½*
1239 A351   Pair   5.00 3.75
  a.-b.   100d, any single   2.25 1.75
1240 A351   Pair   5.00 3.75
  a.-b.   100d, any single   2.25 1.75
1241 A351   Pair   5.00 3.75
  a.-b.   100d, any single   2.25 1.75
1242 A351   Pair   5.00 3.75
  a.-b.   100d, any single   2.25 1.75
  Nos. 1239-1242 (1)   20.00 15.00

Nos. 1239-1242 printed in sheets of 20, four strips of 5 consisting of two pairs each musician flanking center stamps picturing instruments.

Gold Dinars Minted A.D. 699-727 — A352

No. 1243: a, Hegira 105. b, Hegira 91. c, Hegira 77. No. 1244, Dinar from Zuela.

Litho. and Embossed
1985, Feb. 15   *Perf. 13½*
1243   Strip of 3   12.50 12.50
  a.-c.   A352 200d, any single   4.00 2.50

Souvenir Sheet
1244 A352   300d multi   7.50 7.50

Fossils A353

1985, Mar. 1   Litho.   *Perf. 13½*
1245 A353   150d Frog   6.00 3.00
1246 A353   150d Fish   6.00 3.00
1247 A353   150d Mammal   6.00 3.00
  Nos. 1245-1247 (3)   18.00 9.00

People's Authority Declaration A354

Khadafy wearing: a, Folk costume. b, Academic robe. c, Khaki uniform. d, Black uniform. e, White uniform.

1985, Mar. 2   Litho.   *Perf. 14½*
1248   Strip of 5   10.00 10.00
  a.-e.   A354 100d, any single   2.00 1.50

Tripoli Intl. Fair — A355

Musicians playing: a, Cymbals. b, Double flute, bongo. c, Wind instrument, drum. d, Drum. e, Tambourine.

1985, Mar. 5   *Perf. 14*
1249   Strip of 5   10.00 10.00
  a.-e.   A355 100d, any single   1.90 1.75

Children's Day, IYC A356

Children's drawings, various soccer plays: a, Goalie and player. b, Four players. c, Players as letters of the alphabet. d, Goalie save. e, Player heading the ball.

1985, Mar. 21   *Perf. 12*
1250   Strip of 5   7.50 7.50
  a.-e.   A356 20d, any single   .40   .25

Intl. Program for Development of Telecommunications A357

1985, Apr. 1
1251 A357   30d multicolored   .40   .40
1252 A357   70d multicolored   1.00 1.00
1253 A357   100d multicolored   2.00 2.00
  Nos. 1251-1253 (3)   3.40 3.40

World Health Day — A358

1985, Apr. 7
1254 A358   40d Invalid, nurses   1.00   .60
1255 A358   60d Nurse, surgery   1.50 1.00
1256 A358   100d Nurse, child   2.50 1.60
  Nos. 1254-1256 (3)   5.00 3.20

Miniature Sheet

Sea Shells — A359

Designs: a, Mytilidae. b, Muricidae (white). c, Cardiidae. d, Corallophilidae. e, Muricidae. f, Muricacea. g, Turridae. h, Argonautidae. i, Tonnidae. j, Aporrhaidae. k, Trochidae. l, Cancellariidae. m, Epitoniidae. n, Turbnidae. o, Mitridae. p, Pectinidae.

1985, Apr. 20
1257 A359   Sheet of 16   13.00 13.00
  a.-p.   25d, any single   .60   .25

Tripoli Intl. Book Fair — A360

1985, Apr. 28   *Perf. 13½*
1258 A360   100d multi   2.00 1.50
1259 A360   200d multi   4.00 3.00

Intl. Youth Year — A361

Games: No. 1260a, Jump rope. No. 1260b, Board game. No. 1260c, Hopscotch. No. 1260d, Stickgame. No. 1260e, Tops. No. 1261a, Soccer. No. 1261b, Basketball.

1985, May 1
1260   Strip of 5   6.00 6.00
  a.-e.   A361 20d, any single   .40   .25

Souvenir Sheet
1261   Sheet of 2   9.00 9.00
  a.-b.   A361 100d, any single   3.00 3.00

No. 1261 contains 2 stamps 30x42mm.

Miniature Sheet

Mosque Minarets and Towers — A362

Mosques: a, Abdussalam Lasmar. b, Zaoviat Kadria. c, Zaoviat Amura. d, Gurgi. e, Mizran. f, Salem. g, Ghat. h, Ahmed Karamanli. i, Atya. j, El Kettani. k, Benghazi. l, Derna. m, El Derug. n, Ben Moussa. o, Ghadames. p, Abdulwahab.

1985, May 15 — Perf. 12
1262 A362 Sheet of 16   15.00 15.00
 a.-p.   50d, any single   .75   .60

Hamida El-Anezi — A363

1985, June 1   Litho.   Perf. 13½
1263 A363 100d multicolored   2.00 1.50
1264 A363 100d Jamila Zemerli   2.00 1.50
Teachers' Day.

A364

Battle of the Philadelphia: a, Ship sinking. b, Militia. c, Hand-to-hand combat.

1985 June 12
1265 A364 Strip of 3   4.00 4.00
 a.-b.   50d, any single   1.00 1.00
 c.   100d multicolored   1.75 1.75

Size of No. 1265c: 60x48mm. Continuous design with No. 1265c in middle.

A365

Khadafy's Islamic Pilgrimage — A366

"The Holy Koran is the Law of Society" and Khadafy: a, Writing. b, Kneeling. c, With Holy Kaaba. d, Looking in window. e, Praying at pilgrimage ceremony.

1985, June 16
1266 Strip of 5   22.50 22.50
 a.-e.   A365 200d, any single   4.00 2.50
Souvenir Sheet
1267 A366 300d multicolored   6.50 6.50

Miniature Sheet

Mushrooms — A367

Designs: a, Leucopaxillus lepistoides. b, Amanita caesarea. c, Coriolus hirsutus. d, Cortinarius subfulgens. e, Dermocybe pratensis. f, Macrolepiota excoriata. g, Amanita curtipes. h, Trametes ljubarskyi. i, Pholiota aurivella. j, Boletus edulis. k, Geastrum sessile. l, Russula sanguinea. m, Cortinarius herculeus. n, Pholiota lenta. o, Amanita rubenscens. p, Scleroderma polyrhizum.

1985, July 15
1268 A367 Sheet of 16   17.50 17.50
 a.-p.   50d, any single   1.00   .40

No. 1268 exists imperf. Value $50.

Women's Folk Costumes — A368

Designs: a, Woman in violet. b, In white. c, In brown and blue. d, In blue. e, In red.

1985, Aug. 1   Perf. 14½x14
1269 Strip of 5   10.00 10.00
 a.-e.   A368 100d, any single   1.75 1.50

Green Book Quotations Type of 1984
Miniature Sheet

Designs: a, In Need Freedom Is Latent. b, Khadafy reading. c, To Make A Party You Split Society. d, Public Sport Is for All the Masses. e, Green Books, doves. f, Wage-Workers Are a Type of Slave . . . g, People Are Only Harmonious with Their Own Arts and Heritages. h, Khadafy orating. i, Democracy Means Popular Rule Not Popular Expression.

1985, Aug. 15   Perf. 14
1270 Sheet of 9   17.50 17.50
 a.-i.   A333 100d, any single   1.75 1.50

A369

September 1 Revolution, 16th Anniv. — A370

Designs: a, Food. b, Oil pipeline, refinery. c, Capital, olive branch. d, Mosque, modern buildings. e, Flag, mountains. f, Telecommunications apparatus.

1985, Sept. 1   Perf. 12½
1271 Strip of 6   12.50 12.50
 a.-f.   A369 100d, any single   2.00 1.50
Souvenir Sheet
1272 A370 200d multi   4.50 4.50

Mosque Entrances A371

Designs: a, Zauiet Amoura, Janzour. b, Shiaieb El-ain, Tripoli. c, Zauiet Abdussalam El-asmar, Zliten. d, Karamanli, Tripoli. e, Gurgi, Tripoli.

1985, Sept. 15   Perf. 14
1273 Strip of 5   10.00 10.00
 a.-e.   A371 100d, any single   2.00 1.50

Miniature Sheet

Basketball A372

Various players in action.

1985, Oct. 1   Litho.   Perf. 13x12½
1274 Sheet of 16   9.00 9.00
 a.-p.   A372 25d any single   .50   .40

Evacuation — A373

Designs: a, Man on crutches, web, tree. b, Man caught in web held by disembodied hands. c, Three men basking in light.

1985, Oct. 7   Perf. 15
1275 A373 Strip of 3   7.00 7.00
 a.-c.   100d any single   1.75 1.50

Stamp Day — A374

Italia 85: a, Man sitting at desk, Type A228, Earth. b, Magnifying glass, open stock book, Type A228. c, Stamps escaping envelope.

1985, Oct. 25   Perf. 12
1276 A374 Strip of 3   4.00 4.00
 a.-c.   50d, any single   1.00   .60

1986 World Cup Soccer Championships — A375

No. 1277, Block, heading the ball. No. 1278, Kick, goalie catching ball. No. 1279, Goalie, block, dribble. No. 1280, Goalie, dribble, sliding block. No. 1281, Goalie catching the ball. No. 1282, Block. No. 1283, Four players.

1985, Nov. 1   Perf. 13½
1277 A375 100d multicolored   2.00 1.50
1278 A375 100d multicolored   2.00 1.50
1279 A375 100d multicolored   2.00 1.50
1280 A375 100d multicolored   2.00 1.50
1281 A375 100d multicolored   2.00 1.50
1282 A375 100d multicolored   2.00 1.50
 Nos. 1277-1282 (6)   12.00 9.00
Souvenir Sheet
1283 A375 200d multicolored   8.50 8.50

Intl. Day of Cooperation with the Palestinian People A376

1985, Nov. 29   Litho.   Perf. 12½
1284 A376 100d multi   1.75 1.50
1285 A376 150d multi   3.25 2.25

Khadafy

A377   A377a

Perf. 12½x13, 13¼x13
1986, Jan. 1   Engr.
1286 A377 50d vermilion   45.00 45.00
1287 A377 60d blue   45.00 45.00
1288 A377 70d carmine   45.00 45.00
1289 A377 80d violet   45.00 45.00
1290 A377 90d brown   45.00 45.00
1291 A377 100d dk grn   50.00 50.00
1292 A377 200d dk rose   50.00 50.00
1293 A377 250d brt grn   50.00 50.00
1294 A377a 300d grysh blue   50.00 50.00
1295 A377a 500d redsh brn   50.00 50.00
1296 A377a 1500d grysh grn   60.00 60.00
1297 A377a 2500d purple   70.00 70.00
 Nos. 1286-1297 (12)   605.00 605.00

Supposedly Nos. 1286-1297 were on sale for two hours. Value on first day cover, $350.

Importation Prohibited
Importation of the stamps of Libya was prohibited as of Jan. 7, 1986.

General Post and Telecommunications Co. — A378

1986, Jan. 15   *Perf. 12*
1298 A378 100d yel & multi   2.25 1.50
1299 A378 150d yel grn & multi   2.75 2.00

Peoples Authority Declaration — A379

Designs: b, Hand holding globe and paper. c, Dove, Khadafy's Green Book (size: 53x37mm).

1986, Mar. 2   *Perf. 12½x13*
1300   Strip of 3   4.50 4.50
   a.-b.   A379 50d, any single   1.00 .60
   c.   A379 100d multicolored   2.00 1.25

Musical Instruments — A380

Designs: a, Flute. b, Drums. c, Horn. d, Cymbals. e, Hand drum.

1986, Mar. 5
1301   Strip of 5   10.00 10.00
   a.-e.   A380 100d any single   2.00 1.50

Tripoli International Fair.

Intl. Children's Day — A381

Designs: a, Boy Scout fishing. b, Riding camel. c, Chasing butterflies. d, Beating drum. e, Soccer game.

1986, Mar. 21   *Perf. 13½*
1302   Strip of 5   8.50 8.50
   a.-e.   A381 50d any single   1.25 .75

World Health Day — A382

1986, Apr. 7
1303 A382 250d sil & multi   5.00 3.00
1304 A382 250d gold & multi   5.00 3.00

Government Programs — A383

Designs: a, Medical examinations. b, Education. c, Farming (size: 63x42mm).

1986, May 1   *Perf. 14½*
1305 A383   Strip of 3   3.75 3.75
   a.-b.   50d any single   .85 .60
   c.   100d multicolored   1.75 1.25

Miniature Sheet

World Cup Soccer Championships, Mexico — A384

Designs: No. 1306a, 2 players. No. 1306b, 3 players in red and white shirts, one in green. No. 1306c, 2 players, referee. No. 1306d, Shot at goal. No. 1306e, 2 players with striped shirts. No. 1306f, 2 players with blue shirts, one with red.
No. 1307, 7 players. No. 1308, 1st Libyan team, 1931.

1986, May 31   *Perf. 13½*
1306 A384   Sheet of 6   7.50 7.50
   a.-f.   50d any single   1.10 .75

Souvenir Sheets
1307 A384 200d multicolored   6.50 6.50
1308 A384 200d multicolored   6.50 6.50

Nos. 1307-1308 each contain one 52x37mm stamp.

Miniature Sheet

Vegetables A385

Designs: a, Peas. b, Zucchini. c, Beans. d, Eggplant. e, Corn. f, Tomato. g, Red pepper. h, Cucumbers. i, Garlic. j, Cabbage. k, Cauliflower. l, Celery. m, Onions. n, Carrots. o, Potato. p, Radishes.

1986, June 1   *Perf. 13x12½*
1309   Sheet of 16   15.00 15.00
   a.-p.   A385 50d any single   .85 .75

No. 1309 has a continuous design.

Miniature Sheet

Khadafy and Irrigation Project A386

Khadafy and: a, Engineer reviewing plans, drill rig. b, Map. c, Well. d, Drought conditions. e, Water pipe. f, Pipes, pulleys, equipment. g, Lowering water pipe. h, Construction workers, trailer. i, Hands holding water. j, Opening water valve. k, Laying pipeline. l, Trucks hauling pipes. m, Khadafy holding green book, city. n, Giving vegetables to people. o, Boy drinking, man cultivating field. p, Men in prayer, irrigation. (Khadafy not shown on Nos. 1310h, 1310i, 1310k, 1310 l, 1310o.)

1986, July 1   *Perf. 13½*
1310   Sheet of 16   35.00 35.00
   a.-p.   A386 100d any single   2.00 1.40

A387

A388

American Attack on Libya, Apr. 15 — A389

Designs: Nos. 1311a-1311p, Various scenes in Tripoli during and after air raid. No. 1312a. F14 aircraft. No. 1312b, Aircraft carrier, people. No. 1312c, Sinking of USS *Philadelphia*, 1801.

1986, July 13
1311 A387   Sheet of 16, #a.-p.   26.00 26.00
1312 A388   Strip of 3   3.50 3.50
   a.-b.   50d multicolored   .85 .65
   c.   100d multicolored   1.75 1.25
1313 A389 100d multicolored   2.10 1.50

No. 1312 has a continuous design. Size of No. 1312b: 60x38mm.

Khadafy's Peace Methods A390

Khadafy: b, Reading Green Book. c, With old woman. d, Praying with children. e, Visiting sick. f, Driving tractor.

1986, July 13
1314   Sheet of 6   12.50 12.50
   a.-f.   A390 100d any single   2.00 1.40

Miniature Sheet

Green Book Quotations A391

Designs: a, The House Must be Served by its Own Tenant. b, Khadafy. c, The Child is Raised by His Mother. d, Democracy is the Supervision of the People by the People. e, Green Books. f, Representation is a Falsification of Democracy. g, The Recognition of Profit is an Acknowledgement of Exploitation. h, Flowers. i, Knowledge is a Natural Right of Every Human Being...

1986, Aug. 1   *Perf. 14*
1315   Sheet of 9   19.00 19.00
   a.-i.   A391 100d any single   2.00 1.40

Sept. 1st Revolution, 17th Anniv. A392

a, Public health. b, Agriculture. c, Sunflowers by Vincent Van Gogh. d, Defense. e, Oil industry.

1986, Sept. 1
1316   Strip of 5   22.50 22.50
   a.-e.   A392 200d any single   4.00 2.75

A393

Arab-African Union, 1st Anniv. — A394

No. 1317, Libyan, Arab horsemen. No. 1318, Women in native dress.

1986, Sept. 15   *Perf. 12*
1317 A393 250d multicolored   5.00 4.00
1318 A394 250d multicolored   5.00 4.00

Evacuation Day — A395

Designs: a, Mounted warrior. b, Two horsemen, infantry. c, Cavalry charge.

1986, Oct. 7   *Perf. 13½*
1319 A395   Strip of 3   6.00 6.00
   a.   50d multicolored   1.00 .60
   b.   100d multicolored   2.00 1.10
   c.   150d multicolored   2.75 2.40

Intl. Peace Year A396

1986, Oct. 24   *Perf. 14½*
1320 A396 200d bl & multi   4.00 3.00
1321 A396 200d grn & multi   4.00 3.00

Solidarity with the Palestinians — A397

1986, Nov. 29   *Perf. 12½*
1322 A397 250d pink & multi   5.00 4.00
1323 A397 250d blue & multi   5.00 4.00

Music and Dance — A398

Designs: a, Man beating drum. b, Masked dancer. c, Woman dancing with jugs on her head. d, Man playing bagpipe. e, Man beating hand drum.

1986, Dec. 1   *Perf. 12*
1324   Strip of 5   8.00 8.00
   a.-e.   A398 70d any single   1.50 1.25

Gazella Leptoceros — A399

1987, Mar. 2   **Perf. 13½**
1325 A399 100d Two adults   3.00 2.00
1326 A399 100d Fawn nursing   3.00 2.00
1327 A399 100d Adult sleeping   3.00 2.00
1328 A399 100d Adult drinking   3.00 2.00
      Nos. 1325-1328 (4)   12.00 8.00
World Wildlife Fund.
Nos. 1325-1328 exist imperf. Value, set $27.50.

A400

Crowd of People and: a, Oilfields. b, Buildings. c, Khadafy, buildings, globe.

1987, Mar. 2   **Perf. 13½**
1329 A400 Strip of 3   40.00 40.00
a.-b.   500d multicolored   10.00 8.00
c.   1000d multicolored   20.00 15.00
People's Authority declaration.
No. 1329 has a continuous design. Size of No. 1329c: 42x37mm.

Miniature Sheet

A401

Sept. 1st Revolution, 18th Anniv.: a, Shepherd, sheep. b, Khadafy. c, Mosque. d, Irrigation pipeline. e, Combine in field. f, Khadafy at microphones. g, Harvesting grain. h, Irrigation. i, Soldier. j, Militiaman. k, Fountain. l, Skyscrapers. m, House, women. n, Children. o, Assembly hall. p, Two girls.

1987, Sept. 1   **Perf. 13½**
1330 A401 Sheet of 16   70.00 70.00
a.-p.   150d any single   3.00 2.25
No. 1330 has a continuous design.

Libyan Freedom Fighters — A402

No. 1331: a, Omer Abed Anabi Al Mansuri. b, Ahmed Ali Al Emrayd. c, Khalifa Said Ben Asker. d, Mohamed Ben Farhat Azawi. e, Mohamed Souf Al Lafi Al Marmori.

1988, Feb. 15
1331 A402 Strip of 5   29.00 29.00
a.   100d multicolored   2.00 1.25
b.   200d multicolored   5.75 4.25

c.   A402 300d multicolored   8.00 4.50
d.   A402 400d multicolored
e.   A402 500d multicolored   9.00 6.50

Freedom Festival Day — A403

1988, June 1
1332 A403 100d yel & multi   1.75 1.25
1333 A403 150d grn & multi   3.00 2.00
1334 A403 250d brn org &
                  multi   5.00 3.50
      Nos. 1332-1334 (3)   9.75 6.75

Miniature Sheet

American Attack on Libya, 2nd Anniv. — A404

Khadafy: a, With woman and children. b, Playing chess. c, Fleeing from bombing with children. d, Praying in desert. e, Praying with children. f, Visiting wounded child. g, With infants and children, horiz. h, Delivering speech, horiz. i, With family, horiz.
No. 1336, In desert, vert. No. 1337, Making speech.

1988, July 13
1335 A404 Sheet of 9   25.00 25.00
a.-i.   150d any single   2.75 2.00

Souvenir Sheets
Litho. & Embossed
1336 A404 500d gold & multi   10.00 10.00
1337 A404 500d gold & multi   10.00 10.00
No. 1335 exists imperf.

September 1st Revolution, 19th Anniv. — A405

1988, Sept. 19   **Litho.**
1338 A405 100d brt bl & multi 1.75 1.25
1339 A405 250d gray & multi   4.50 3.00
1340 A405 300d cit & multi   5.00 4.25
1341 A405 500d bl grn & multi 10.00 7.00
      Nos. 1338-1341 (4)   21.25 15.50

1988 Summer Olympics, Seoul — A406

1988, Sept. 17
1342 A406 150d Tennis   2.75 2.00
1343 A406 150d Equestrian   2.75 2.00
1344 A406 150d Relay race   2.75 2.00
1345 A406 150d Soccer   2.75 2.00

1346 A406 150d Distance race 2.75 2.00
1347 A406 150d Cycling   2.75 2.00
      Nos. 1342-1347 (6)   16.50 12.00
Souvenir Sheet
1348 A406 750d Soccer, diff. 13.00 13.00
No. 1348 contains one 30x42mm stamp. Exists imperf. Nos. 1342-1347 exist in miniature sheets of 1. Value, set $37.50.

Miniature Sheet

1988 Summer Olympics, Seoul — A407

1988, Sept 17
1350   Sheet of 3   8.50 8.50
a.   A407 100d Bedouin rider   2.00 2.00
b.   A407 200d shown   3.00 3.00
c.   A407 200d Show jumping, diff. 3.00 3.00
Olymphilex '88, Seoul.

A408

Design: Libyan Palm Tree.

1988, Nov. 1
1351 A408 500d Fruit   10.00 6.50
1352 A408 1000d Palm tree   18.00 12.00

A409

1988
1353 A409 Strip of 3   11.50 11.50
a.   100d shown   2.00 1.40
b.   200d Boy with rocks 3.50 2.75
c.   300d Flag, map   5.75 4.25
Palestinian uprising. No. 1353b, size: 45x39mm.

People's Authority Declaration — A410

1989
1354 A410 260d dk grn & multi 5.00 3.00
1355 A410 500d gold & multi   10.00 6.00

Miniature Sheet

September 1 Revolution, 20th Anniv. — A411

Designs: a, Crowd, Green Books, emblem. b, Soldiers, Khadafy, irrigation pipeline. c, Military equipment, Khadafy, communication and transportation. d, Mounted warriors. e, Battle scenes.

1989   **Perf. 13½**
1356 A411 Sheet of 5   14.00 14.00
a.-e.   150d any single   2.75 2.00

f.   Bklt. pane of 5, perf. 13½
      horiz.   14.00 14.00
Souvenir Sheet
1357 A411 250d Khadafy   4.00 4.00
No. 1357 contains one 36x51mm stamp. Stamps from No. 1356f have gold border at right.

Libyans Deported to Italy — A412

No. 1359, Libyans in boats. No. 1360, Khadafy, crescent moon. No. 1361, Khadafy at left, in desert. No.1362, Khadafy at right, soldiers. No. 1363, Khadafy in center, Libyans.

1989
1358 A412 100d shown   1.75 1.25
1359 A412 100d multicolored   1.75 1.25
1360 A412 100d multicolored   1.75 1.25
1361 A412 100d multicolored   1.75 1.25
1362 A412 100d multicolored   1.75 1.25
      Nos. 1358-1362 (5)   8.75 6.25
Souvenir Sheet
1363 A412 150d multicolored   3.00 3.00
No. 1363 contains one 72x38mm stamp.

A413

1989   **Perf. 12**
1364 A413 150d multicolored   2.75 2.75
1365 A413 200d multicolored   4.25 4.25
Demolition of Libyan-Tunisian border fortifications.

A414

1989   **Perf. 12x11½**
1366 A414 100d shown   2.25 2.25
1367 A414 300d Man, flag,
                  crowd   6.50 6.50
1368 A414 500d Emblem   10.00 10.00
      Nos. 1366-1368 (3)   18.75 18.75
Solidarity with the Palestinians.

Ibn Annafis, Physician A415

1989   **Perf. 12**
1369 A415 100d multicolored   2.75 2.75
1370 A415 150d multicolored   4.00 4.00

A416

1990, Oct. 18   **Litho.**   *Perf. 14*
Granite Paper
1371 A416 100d multicolored   1.75 1.75
1372 A416 300d multicolored   8.00 8.00
Intl. Literacy Year.

A417

1990, Oct. 18   **Granite Paper**
1373 A417 100d multicolored   1.75 1.75
1374 A417 400d multicolored   5.25 5.25
Organization of Petroleum Exporting Countries (OPEC), 30th anniv.

A410

1990, June 28   *Perf. 11½x12*
1375 A418 100d brt org & multi   1.75 1.75
1376 A418 400d grn & multi   8.00 8.00
Evacuation of US military base, 20th anniv.

A419

1990, Apr. 24
1377 A419 300d bl & multi   5.00 5.00
1378 A419 500d vio & multi   10.00 10.00
People's authority declaration.

A420

Plowing Season in Libya: 2000d, Man on tractor plowing field.

1990, Dec. 4   *Perf. 14*
Granite Paper
1379 A420 500d multicolored   11.00 11.00
1380 A420 2000d multicolored   37.50 37.50

A421

1990, Nov. 5   *Perf. 14*
Granite Paper
1381 A421 100d grn & multi   1.75 1.75
1382 A421 400d vio & multi   8.00 8.00
1383 A421 500d bl & multi   9.25 9.25
   Nos. 1381-1383 (3)   19.00 19.00
Souvenir Sheet
Perf. 11½
1384 A421 500d Trophy, map, horiz.   11.00 11.00
World Cup Soccer Championships, Italy. No. 1384 contains one 38x33mm stamp.

Sept. 1st
Revolution,
21st Anniv.
A422

1990, Sept. 3   *Perf. 14*
Granite Paper
1385 A422 100d multicolored   2.00 2.00
1386 A422 400d multicolored   8.50 8.50
1387 A422 1000d multicolored   21.00 21.00
   Nos. 1385-1387 (3)   31.50 31.50
Imperf
Size: 120x90mm
1388 A422 200d multi, diff.   8.50 8.50

Maghreb Arab
Union, 2nd
Anniv. — A423

1991, Mar. 10   **Litho.**   *Perf. 13½*
1389 A423 100d multicolored   2.00 2.00
1390 A423 300d gold & multi   5.75 5.75

People's Authority Declaration — A424

1991, Mar. 10
1391 A424 300d multicolored   5.00 5.00
1392 A424 400d silver & multi   10.00 10.00

Children's
Day — A425

1991, Mar. 22
1393 A425 100d Butterflies, girl   2.75 2.75
1394 A425 400d Bird, boy   10.00 10.00

World Health
Day — A426

1991, Apr. 7
1395 A426 100d blue & multi   1.75 1.75
1396 A426 200d green & multi   3.50 3.50

Scenes
from Libya
A427

1991, June 20
1397 A427 100d Wadi el Hayat, vert.   1.75 1.75
1398 A427 250d Mourzuk   5.00 5.00
1399 A427 500d Ghadames   10.00 10.00
   Nos. 1397-1399 (3)   16.75 16.75

Irrigation Project — A428

a, Laborers, heavy equipment. b, Khadafy, heavy equipment. c, Livestock, fruit & vegetables.

1991, Aug. 28   *Perf. 12*
1400 A428 50d Strip of 3, #a.- c.   3.50 3.50
No. 1400 has a continuous design. Size of No. 1400b: 60x36mm.

Sept. 1st Revolution, 22nd
Anniv. — A429

1991, Sept. 1   *Perf. 13½*
1401 A429 300d Chains, roses & "22"   5.75 5.75
1402 A429 400d Chains, "22"   7.25 7.25
   a. Souv. sheet of 2, #1401-1402   16.00 16.00

Telecom
'91
A430

1991, Oct. 7   **Litho.**   *Perf. 13½*
1403 A430 100d Emblems, vert.   1.75 1.75
1404 A430 500d Buildings, satillite dish   9.25 9.25

Libyans
Deported
to Italy
A431

100d, Monument, soldier. 400d, Ship, refugees, soldiers.

Arab Unity
A432

1991, Oct. 26   **Litho.**   *Perf. 13½*
1405 A431 100d multicolored   1.75 1.75
1406 A431 400d multicolored   7.25 7.25
   a. Souv. sheet of 2, #1405-1406   10.00 10.00

1991, Nov. 15   *Perf. 12*
1407 A432 50d tan & multi   1.00 1.00
1408 A432 100d blue & multi   2.00 2.00

Miniature Sheet

Trucks,
Automobiles and
Motorcycles
A433

Designs: a-d, Various trucks. e-h, Various off-road race cars. i-p, Various motorcycles.

1991, Dec. 28   *Perf. 14*
1409 A433 50d Sheet of 16, #a.-p.   17.50 17.50

Eagle — A434

Col.
Khadafy — A434a

1992   *Perf. 11½*
Granite Paper (#1412-1419)
Background Colors
1412 A434 100d yellow   1.40 .85
1413 A434 150d blue gray   2.25 1.25
1414 A434 200d brt blue   2.75 1.75
1415 A434 250d orange   3.75 2.00
1416 A434 300d purple   4.25 2.50
1418 A434 400d brt pink   5.75 3.50
1419 A434 450d brt grn   7.25 3.75
Perf. 13½
1420 A434a 500d yel grn   6.50 3.50
1421 A434a 1000d rose   13.00 7.00
1422 A434a 2000d blue   26.00 14.00
1423 A434a 5000d violet   65.00 37.50
1424 A434a 6000d yel brn   80.00 45.00
   Nos. 1412-1424 (12)   217.90 122.60
Issued: No 1412-1416, 1418-1419, 1/1; Nos. 1420-1424, 9/1.

People's Authority
Declaration
A435

1992, Mar.   **Litho.**   *Perf. 12*
1425 A435 100d yellow & multi   1.50 1.50
1426 A435 150d blue & multi   2.25 2.25

African Tourism Year (in 1991)
A436

1992, Apr. 5 *Perf. 14½*

Granite Paper

1427 A436 50d purple & multi .75 .75
1428 A436 100d pink & multi 1.40 1.40

1992 Summer Olympics, Barcelona
A437

1992, June 15 *Perf. 12*

1429 A437 50d Tennis .75 .75
1430 A437 50d Long jump .75 .75
1431 A437 50d Discus .75 .75
Nos. 1429-1431 (3) 2.25 2.25

Size: 106x82mm

Imperf

1432 A437 100d Olympic torch, rings 1.50 1.50

Revolutionary Achievements — A438

Designs: 100d, Palm trees. 150d, Steel mill. 250d, Cargo ship. 300d, Libyan Airlines. 400d, Natl. Assembly, Green Books. 500d, Irrigation pipeline, Khadafy.

1992, June 30 *Perf. 14*

Granite Paper

1433 A438 100d multicolored 1.40 1.40
1434 A438 150d multicolored 2.25 2.25
1435 A438 250d multicolored 3.75 3.75
1436 A438 300d multicolored 4.25 4.25
1437 A438 400d multicolored 5.75 5.75
1438 A438 500d multicolored 7.25 7.25
Nos. 1433-1438 (6) 24.65 24.65

Tripoli Intl. Fair — A439

1992, Mar. *Perf. 12*

1439 A439 50d Horse & buggy
1440 A439 100d Horse & sulky

Mahgreb Arab Union Philatelic Exhibition — A440

1992, Feb. 17 *Perf. 14½*

1441 A440 75d blue green & multi 2.50 1.75
1442 A440 80d blue & multi 2.50 1.75

Miniature Sheet

Fish
A441

Designs: a, Fish with spots near eye. b, Thin fish. d, Brown fish, currents. e, Fish, plants at LR. f, Fish, plants at LL.

1992, Apr. 15 *Perf. 14*

1443 A441 100d Sheet of 6, #a.-f. 14.00 14.00

Miniature Sheet

Horsemanship — A442

Designs: a, Woman rider with gun. b, Man on white horse. c, Mongol rider. d, Roman officer. e, Cossack rider. f, Arab rider. 250d, Two Arab riders.

1992, Apr. 25 *Perf. 13½x14*

1444 A442 100d Sheet of 6, #a.-f. 9.50 9.50

Souvenir Sheet

1445 A442 250d multicolored 5.00 5.00

Khadafy — A443

Designs: No. 1450a, like No. 1446. b, like No. 1447. c, like No. 1448. d, like No. 1449.

1992, Jan. 1 *Perf. 14x13½*

1446 A443 100d blue green & multi 2.00 2.00
1447 A443 100d gray & multi 2.00 2.00
1448 A443 100d rose lake & multi 2.00 2.00
1449 A443 100d yellow & multi 2.00 2.00
Nos. 1446-1449 (4) 8.00 8.00

Souvenir Sheet

1450 A443 150d Sheet of 4, #a.-d. 11.00 11.00

Evacuation of Foreign Forces — A444

75d, Horse, broken chain. 80d, Flag, broken chain.

1992, Oct. 7 **Litho.** *Perf. 14*

1451 A444 75d multicolored 1.00 1.00
1452 A444 80d multicolored 1.00 1.00

Costumes — A445

Women wearing various traditional costumes.

Denomination color: a, green. b, black. c, violet blue. d, sky blue. e, yellow brown.

1992, Dec. 15 **Litho.** *Perf. 12*

1453 A445 50d Strip of 5, #a.-e. 4.00 4.00

Sept. 1st Revolution, 23rd Anniv. — A446

1992, Sept. 1

1454 A446 50d Torch, "23" .75 .75
1455 A446 100d Flag, "23" 1.40 1.40

Souvenir Sheet

1456 A446 250d Eagle, "23" 3.50 3.50

No. 1456 contains one 50x40mm stamp.

Libyans Deported to Italy — A447

1992, Oct. 26

1457 A447 100d tan & multi 1.40 1.40
1458 A447 250d blue & multi 3.00 3.00

Oasis
A448

Designs: 100d, Gazelle drinking. 200d, Camels, palm trees, vert. 300d, Palm trees, camel and rider.

1992, Oct. 1 *Perf. 14*

1459 A448 100d multicolored 1.50 1.50
1460 A448 200d multicolored 3.00 3.00
1461 A448 300d multicolored 5.00 5.00
Nos. 1459-1461 (3) 9.50 9.50

Palestinian Intifada — A449

Designs: 100d, Palestinian holding rock and flag. 300d, Map of Israel and Palestine, Dome of the Rock, Palestinian flag, olives, hand holding rock, vert.

1992, Nov. 26 **Litho.** *Perf. 12*

1462-1463 A449 Set of 2 4.50 4.50

Doctors — A450

Designs: 40d, Dr. Mohamed Ali Imsek (1883-1945). 60d, Dr. Aref Adhani Arif (1884-1935).

1993, Feb. 1

1464-1465 A450 Set of 2 1.25 1.25

Intl. Conference on Nutrition, Rome — A451

Background colors: 70d, Blue. 80d, Green.

1993, Feb. 15

1466-1467 A451 Set of 2 1.75 1.75

People's Authority Declaration — A452

Col. Khadafy, map of Libya, crowd, eagle, oil rig, pipeline and tanker: 60d, 65d, 75d.

1993, Mar. 2 *Perf. 14¾*

1468-1470 A452 Set of 3 2.25 2.25

Tripoli Intl. Fair
A453

Various Fair participants, Fair emblem and panel color of: No. 1471, 60d, Pink. No. 1472, 60d, Yellow green. No. 1473, 60d, Blue, vert. No. 1474, 60d, Orange, vert.

100d, People on horses.

1993, Mar. 15 *Perf. 14*

1471-1474 A453 Set of 4 2.50 2.50

Souvenir Sheet

Perf. 11¾

1475 A453 100d multi 1.50 1.50

No. 1475 contains one 38x32mm stamp.

World Health Day
A454

Designs: 75d, Doctor and three nurses examining child. 85d, Doctor and two nurses examining woman.

1993, Apr. 7   **Perf. 13¼**
1476-1477 A454   Set of 2   1.60 1.60

Children's
Day — A455

No. 1478 — Various girls with background of: a, Gray green (red headdress). b, Red curtains. c, Gray. d, Home furnishings. e, Beige.

1993, May 1   **Perf. 13¾**
1478   Horiz. strip of 5   4.25 4.25
   a.-e. A455 75d Any single   .80 .80

Miniature Sheet

Watercraft — A456

No. 1479: a, Ship with swan's head figurehead. b, Ship with triangular sail and oars. c, Ship with one large white sail. d, Ship with rectangular sail and oars. e, Ship with three triangular sails. f, Sailboat, map of Western Mediterranean area. g, Sailboat, map of Eastern Mediterranean area. h, Ship with two red triangular sails. i, Ship with four sails, red flag. j, Sailboat, map of Western Libya. k, Sailboat, map of Eastern Libya. l, Ship with three sails on main mast. m, Ocean liner with black hull. n, Ship with six tan sails. o, Ship with furled sails. p, Ocean liner with white hull.

1993, July 15   **Perf. 13¼**
1479 A456 50d Sheet of 16,
     #a-p   10.00 10.00

Miniature Sheet

Sept. 1 Revolution, 24th
Anniv. — A457

No. 1480: a, Grain combine. b, Col. Khadafy. c, Cows, man with feed bucket. d, Shepherd and sheep. e, Oil platform, map of Western Libya. f, Eagle, man on camel, map of Eastern Libya. g, Cranes lifting large tanks. h, Water pipeline. i, Man picking dates. j, Man in field, crates of vegetables. k, Crates of vegetables. l, Man picking vegetables. m, Three

children. n, Building, women at typewriter and microscope. o, Man in field, tractor. p, Tractors in field.

1993, Dec. 10   **Perf. 14**
1480 A457 50d Sheet of 16,
     #a-p   12.00 12.00

Miniature Sheet

Libyans Deported to Italy — A458

No. 1481: a, Guard tower, soldier with gun, woman tending to sick man. b, Soldier with gun and bayonet guarding Libyans. c, Col. Khadafy with headdress. d, Man holding box and walking stick. e, Soldiers whipping man. f, Man on horse. g, Four men. h, Soldier guarding people looking at hanged man. i, Soldier standing near wooden post, soldier guarding Libyans. j, Woman on camel, soldiers. k, Soldiers on horses among Libyans. l, Boat with deportees. m, Col. Khadafy without headdress. n, Libyan with arm raised, hand of Col. Khadafy. o, Soldier pointing gun at horseman with sword. p, Horseman carrying gun.

1993, Dec. 15   **Perf. 14½**
1481 A458 50d Sheet of 16,
     #a-p   12.00 12.00

Miniature Sheet

Items Made of Silver — A459

No. 1482: a, Medallion with five-pointed star and tassels. b, Wristband. c, Medallion with star with ten rays and tassels. d, Rod with tassels. e, Necklace. f, Slippers.

**Litho. & Embossed With Foil
Application**
1994, Aug. 10   **Perf. 13¼**
1482 A459 55d Sheet of 6, #a-f   4.25 4.25

A460

Sept. 1 Revolution, 25th
Anniv. — A461

No. 1483: a, Jet, Col. Khadafy in robe (40x40mm). b, Warriors on horseback, mother and child, Col. Khadafy in military uniform (60x40mm). c, Ship, shepherd, man and woman, man on camel (40x40mm).

1994, Sept. 1   **Litho.**   **Perf. 12**
1483 A460   100d Horiz. strip
    of 3, #a-c   4.25 4.25

Souvenir Sheet
1484 A461 1000d multi   13.50 13.50

1994 World Cup
Soccer
Championships,
United
States — A462

World Cup, and various soccer players with horizontal stripes in: No. 1485, 100d, Red and brown. No. 1486, 100d, Red violet, purple, and green. No. 1487, 100d, Green and purple. No. 1488, 100d, Green, black and yellow. No. 1489, 100d, Orange, brown and red. No. 1490, 100d, Yellow orange, brown and orange. No. 1491, 500d, Soccer players, World Cup, red violet background. No. 1492, 500d, Soccer player, ball, "1990," horiz.

1994, Oct. 15   **Perf. 13¼**
1485-1490 A462   Set of 6   8.50 8.50

Souvenir Sheets
1491-1492 A462   Set of 2   14.00 14.00
No. 1491 contains one 42x51mm stamp; No. 1492 contains one 51x42mm stamp.

Miniature Sheet

Libyans Deported to Italy — A463

No. 1493: a, Col. Khadafy. b, Airplane, man with rifle. c, Two men, one with rifle, nose of airplane. d, Tail of airplane, man with rifle. e, Soldier with bayoneted rifle, Libyans looking at dead animal. f, Libyans with rifles, camel. g, Nose of camel, horsemen and soldiers. h, Man carrying child, drawn swords, horsemen. i, Soldier with whip. j, Man with open mouth. k, Tank and soldiers. l, Soldiers on horseback, women. m, Woman tending to injured man, man with bound hands, rifles. n, Soldier bayoneting man. o, Building, women, soldiers on horseback. p, Deportees in boats.

1994, Oct. 26   **Perf. 12**
1493 A463 95d Sheet of 16,
     #a-p   22.50 22.50

Mosques — A464

No. 1494 — Mosques in: a, Darghut. b, Benghazi. c, Kabao. d, Gouzgu. e, Siala. f, El Kettani.

1994, Nov. 15   **Litho.**
1494   Horiz. strip of 6   11.50 11.50
   a.-f. A464 70d Any single   1.50 1.50

Miniature Sheet

People's Authority Declaration — A465

No. 1495: a, Navy ship, jet, women soldiers. b, Wheat, hand holding Green Book, tractor trailer cab. c, Family, water pipeline, tractor trailers. d, Fruit, vegetables, people holding Green Book. e, Col. Khadafy, butterfly, flowers. f, Young men, fruit and vegetables.

1994, Dec. 1   **Perf. 14¾**
1495 A465 80d Sheet of 6, #a-
    f   12.00 12.00

Evacuation of
Foreign
Forces — A466

Denomination in: 65d, Blue. 95f, Green.

1994, Dec. 15   **Perf. 14**
1496-1497 A466   Set of 2   2.75 2.75

Miniature Sheet

Khadafy Prize for Human
Rights — A467

No. 1498: a, Helmeted soldiers, men with sticks, South African flag. b, Men with sticks, South African flag. c, South African Pres. Nelson Mandela. d, Col. Khadafy. e, Indian at fire, crescent moon. f, Armed Indians on horses. g, Indian chief. h, Indian dancer. i, Men with rifles, jets. j, Women, jet, open book. k, Open book. l, Surgeons. m, Palestinians with flag, denomination at left. n, Palestinians with flag, denomination at right. o, Palestinians throwing rocks. p, Palestinians, soldiers.

1994, Dec. 31   **Perf. 13¼**
1498 A467 95d Sheet of 16,
     #a-p   95.00 95.00

No. 1498 was first issued with marginal inscription with incorrect spelling of "Prize" as "Price." Value is for sheet with corrected spelling. Value, sheet with incorrect spelling $250.

People's Authority Declaration
A468

Background color: No. 1499, 100d, Green. No. 1500, 100d, Blue. No. 1501, 100d, Yellow.

1995, July 1   **Perf. 12**
1499-1501 A468 Set of 3   2.25 2.25

Arab League, 50th Anniv. A469

Background color: No. 1502, 200d, Green. No. 1503, 200d, Blue.

No. 1504: a, Emblem in silver. b, Emblem in gold.

1995, July 20 Litho. Perf. 13¼
1502-1503 A469 Set of 2   7.50 7.50
Litho. & Embossed With Foil Application
1504 A469 1000d Sheet of 2,
#a-b   13.00 13.00

Miniature Sheet

Libyan Soccer Players — A470

No. 1505: a, Messaud Zentuti. b, Salem Shermit. c, Ottoman Marfua. d, Ghaleb Siala. e, 1935 Libyan Team. f, Senussi Mresila.

1995, Aug. 1   Litho.
1505 A470 100d Sheet of 6, #a-f 9.50 9.50

Miniature Sheet

Zoo Animals — A471

No. 1506: a, Camel. b, Secretary bird. c, African wild dog. d, Oryx. e, Baboon. f, Golden jackal. g, Crowned eagle. h, Eagle owl. i, Desert hedgehog. j, Sand gerbil. k, Addax. l, Fennec. m, Lanner falcon. n, Desert wheatear. o, Pintailed sandgrouse. p, Jerboa.

1995, Aug. 15   Perf. 13¾x14
1506 A471 100d Sheet of 16,
#a-p   25.00 25.00

Miniature Sheet

Fruit — A472

No. 1507: a, Grapefruit. b, Wild cherries. c, Mulberries. d, Strawberry tree fruit (arbutus). e, Plums. f, Pears. g, Apricots. h, Almonds. i, Prickly pears. j, Lemons. k, Peaches. l, Dates. m, Olives. n, Oranges. o, Figs. p, Grapes.

1995, Aug. 20
1507 A472 100d Sheet of 16,
#a-p   24.00 24.00

Miniature Sheet

Sept. 1 Revolution, 26th Anniv. — A473

No. 1508: a, Students and chemist. b, Minaret, fist of Col. Khadafy. men. c, Col. Khadafy. d, Scientists and buildings. e, Nurses, doctor and patients. f, Surgeons. g, Woman at keyboard, shoemakers. h, Audio technicians, musician. i, Crane, bulldozer and buildings. j, Grain elevator. k, Offshore oil rig, nose of airplane. l, Tail of airplane, ship. m, Goats and sheep. n, Water pipeline. o, Camels, vegetables, water. p, Fruit, grain combine.

1995, Sept. 1
1508 A473 100d Sheet of 16,
#a-p   22.50 22.50

Scouts — A474

No. 1509 — Scouting emblem and: a, Antelope, Scout and butterflies (40x40mm). b, Scouts, butterflies, antelope and cat (60x40mm). c, Scouts, wheat, butterfly, flower.

1995, Sept. 10   Perf. 12
1509 A474 250d Horiz. strip of 3, #a-c   17.00 17.00

American Attack on Libya, 9th Anniv. — A475

No. 1510: a, Ships and people (40x50mm). b, Airplanes, helicopters and people, hand holding Green Book (60x50mm). c, Airplane, mother and child (40x50mm).

1995, Sept. 15
1510 A475 100d Horiz. strip of 3, #a-c   4.50 4.50

Tripoli Intl. Fair — A476

Horsemen with background colors of: No. 1511, 100d, Light blue. No. 1512, 100d, Blue. No. 1513, 100d, Violet. No. 1514, 100d, Blue green, vert. No. 1515, 100d, Blue green with black stripes, vert. No. 1516, 100d, Orange, vert.

1000d, Col. Khadafy on horse.

1995, Sept. 20
1511-1516 A476 Set of 6   9.00 9.00
Souvenir Sheet
1517 A476 1000d multi   14.00 14.00

No. 1517 contains one 80x50mm stamp.

Miniature Sheet

City of Ghadames — A477

No. 1518: a, Camel, woman with water jugs. b, Woman with bread on wooden board. c, Seated woman with vase. d, Woman feeding chickens. e, Woman at spinning wheel. f, Woman standing. g, Woman cooking. h, Woman milking goat. i, Shoemaker. j, Man at loom. k, Metalworker with hammer. l, Date picker. m, Men at religious school. n, Potter. o, Tanner. p, Man picking tomatoes.

Perf. 14½x14¼
1995, Sept. 30   Litho.
1518 A477 100d Sheet of 16,
#a-p   21.00 21.00

Evacuation of Foreign Forces — A478

Panel color: 50d, Pink. 100d, Green. 200d, Lilac.

1995, Oct. 7 Litho. Perf. 14¾x14¼
1519-1521 A478 Set of 3   5.00 5.00

Bees and Flowers A479

Panel color: No. 1522, 100d, Green. No. 1523, 100d, Pink. No. 1524, 100d, Purple.

1995, Oct. 10   Perf. 14¼x13¾
1522-1524 A479 Set of 3   4.50 4.50

Dr. Mohamed Feituri — A480

1995, Oct. 20   Perf. 14¾x14¼
1525 A480 200d multi   2.75 2.75

Campaign Against Smoking — A481

Color of central stripe: No. 1526, 100d, Orange. No. 1527, 100d, Yellow.

1995, Oct. 20
1526-1527 A481 Set of 2   3.25 3.25

Miniature Sheet

Libyans Deported to Italy — A482

No. 1528: a, Col. Khadafy. b, Horsemen. c, Battle scene with blue sky, denomination at LR. d, Battle scene with blue sky, airplane, denomination at LL. e, Battle scene, arch. f, Battle scene, red building at UR. g, Battle scene with red sky, soldier holding pistol. h, Battle scene with red sky, building at UR. i, Three Libyans in foreground. j, Battle scene with running soldiers. k, Battle scene of horsemen and riflemen facing right. l, Soldiers, Libyan man in foreground at LR. m, Two horsemen with arms raised. n, Man in foreground shooting at horsemen. o, Children. p, Child, deportees in boats.

1995, Oct. 26   *Perf. 12*
1528 A482 100d Sheet of 16,
    #a-p   22.00 22.00

Miniature Sheet

Musical Instruments — A483

No. 1529: a, Rababa. b, Nouba (drum). c,
Clarinet. d, Drums. e, Magruna. f, Zukra. g, Zii
(cymbals). h, Kaman (violin). i, Guitar. j, Trumpet. k, Tapla (drum). l, Gonga (drum). m, Saxophone. n, Piano. o, Gandon (zither). p, Ood.

1995, Nov. 1   *Perf. 13¾x14*
1529 A483 100d Sheet of 16,
    #a-p   21.00 21.00

Doors of
Mizda — A484

No. 1530: a, Blue door. b, Door with arched
design in rectangular doorway. c, Log door. d,
Door with rounded top in archway. e, Door of
planks in rectangular doorway.

1995, Nov. 10   *Perf. 13¼*
1530   Horiz. strip of 5   3.50 3.50
    a.-e. A484 100d Any single   .65 .65

Intl. Olympic Committee,
Cent. — A485

Denomination color: No. 1531, 100d, Red.
No. 1532, 100d, Black.

1995, Nov. 15   *Perf. 13½*
1531-1532 A485   Set of 2   1.40 1.40

Prehistoric Animals — A486

No. 1533: a, Baryonyx. b, Oviraptor. c,
Stenonychosaurus. d, Tenontosaurus. e,
Yangchuanosaurus. f, Stegotetrabelodon,
denomination at LR. g, Stegotetrabelodon,
denomination at LL. h, Psittacosaurus. i,
Heterodontosaurus. j, Loxodonta atlantica. k,
Mammuthus. l, Erlikosaurus. m, Cynognathus.
n, Plateosaurus. o, Staurikosaurus. p,
Lystrosaurus.
   500d, Stegotetrabelodon, horiz.

1995, Nov. 20   *Perf. 13½*
1533   Miniature sheet of 16 12.50 12.50
    a.-p. A486 100d Any single   .75 .70

Souvenir Sheet
Perf. 13¼
1534 A486 500d multi   4.25 4.25

No. 1534 contains one 53x49mm stamp.

Children's
Day
A487

No. 1535: a, Boy, dinosaur with cane. b, Boy
on elephant. c, Boy, Scout emblem, turtle and
mushroom. d, Dinosaur and soccer ball. e,
Boy with gun, pteranodon.

1995, Nov. 25   *Perf. 13½*
1535   Horiz. strip of 5   15.00 15.00
    a.-e. A487 100d Any single   2.75 2.75

Palestinian Intifada — A488

No. 1536: a, Boy throwing object at helicopter. b, Dome of the Rock, Palestinian with flag.
c, People, Palestinian flag.

1995, Nov. 29   *Perf. 14*
1536 A488 100d Horiz. strip of 3,
    #a-c   4.50 4.50

Intl. Civil Aviation Organization, 50th
Anniv. — A489

Denomination color: No. 1537, 100d, Black.
No. 1538, 100d, Blue.

1995, Dec. 7   *Perf. 13½x13¼*
1537-1538 A489   Set of 2   1.40 1.40

United Nations,
50th
Anniv. — A490

Background color: No. 1539, 100d, Dark red
lilac. No. 1540, 100d, Light red lilac.

1995, Dec. 20   *Perf. 13½*
1539-1540 A490   Set of 2   1.40 1.40

Miniature Sheet

Flowers — A491

No. 1541: a, Iris germanica. b, Canna edulis. c, Nerium oleander. d, Papaver rhoeas. e,
Strelitzia reginae. f, Amygdalus communis.

1995, Dec. 31   *Perf. 14¾*
1541 A491 200d Sheet of 6,
    #a-f   11.00 11.00

People's
Authority
Declaration
A492

Panel color: 100d, Pink. 150d, Light blue.
200d, Light green.

1996, Mar. 2   *Perf. 13¼*
1542-1544 A492   Set of 3   5.00 5.00

1996 Summer Olympics,
Atlanta — A493

No. 1545: a, Soccer. b, Long jump. c, Ten-
nis. d, Cycling. e, Boxing. f, Equestrian.
   No. 1546, 500d, Runner. No. 1547, 500d,
Equestrian, diff.

1996, Aug. 15   *Perf. 14½*
1545 A493 100d Sheet of 6,
    #a-f   6.75 6.75
    Souvenir Sheets
1546-1547 A493   Set of 2   11.00 11.00

Miniature Sheet

Sept. 1 Revolution, 27th
Anniv. — A494

No. 1548: a, Camel, man, fruits, water. b,
Water pipeline, fruit. c, Tractor, water, women.
d, Oil worker. e, Tailor. f, Seamstress. Col.
Khadafy's fist. g, Col. Khadafy. h, Building,
women with microscope. i, Nurses at anatomy
lesson, man with microscope. j, School child.
k, Woman with open book. l, Man playing
zither. m, Airplanes. n, Dish antenna, ship,
man on camel. o, Ship, television camera. p,
Television actress, woman at microphone.

1996, Sept. 1   *Perf. 13¾x14*
1548 A494 100d Sheet of 16,
    #a-p   20.00 20.00

Miniature Sheet

American Attack on Libya, 10th
Anniv. — A495

No. 1549: a, Left side of missile, explosion.
b, Right side of missile, man with raised arms.
c, Casualties, airplanes. d, Airplane at left,
man on ground. e, Firefighter spraying burning
car. f, Damaged vehicles. g, Col. Khadafy. h,
Casualties, airplane at top. i, Rescuers assisting casualties. j, Man with extended hand. k,
Woman with hands to face. l, Stretcher bearers. m, Three men and casualty. n, Man with
bloody hand. o, Woman and child casualties.
p, Burning car, rescuers attending to bleeding
casualty.

1996, Sept. 15   *Perf. 13¾*
1549 A495 100d Sheet of 16,
    #a-p   20.00 20.00

Miniature Sheet

Crustaceans — A496

No. 1550: a, Necora puber. b, Lissa chiragra. c, Palinurus elephas. d, Scyllarus arctus. e, Carcinus maenas. f, Calappa granulata. g, Parapenaeus longirostris. h, Nephrops norvegicus. i, Eriphia verrucosa. j, Cancer pagurus. k, Penaeus kerathurus. l, Squilla mantis. m, Maja squinado. n, Pilumnus hirtellus. o, Pagurus alatus. p, Macropodia tenuirostris.

1996, Oct. 1   **Perf. 14x13¾**
1550 A496 100d Sheet of 16,
     #a-p   20.00 20.00

Miniature Sheet

THE INTERNATIONAL DAY OF MAGHREB HANDICRAFTS

Intl. Day of Maghreb Handicrafts — A497

Various handicrafts.

1996, Oct. 15   **Perf. 13¾x14**
1551 A497 100d Sheet of 16,
     #a-p   20.00 20.00

Miniature Sheet

LIBYAN DEPORTEES

Libyans Deported to Italy — A498

No. 1552: a, Guard tower, soldier with gun, woman tending to sick man. b, Soldier with gun and bayonet, soldier on horseback. c, Col. Khadafy with headdress. d, Man holding box and walking stick. e, Soldiers whipping man. f, Man on horse. g, Four men. h, Soldier guarding people looking at hanged man. i, Soldier standing near wooden post, soldier guarding Libyans. j, Woman on camel, soldiers. k, Soldiers on horses among Libyans. l, Boat with deportees. m, Col. Khadafy without headdress. n, Libyan with arm raised, hand of Col. Khadafy. o, Soldier pointing gun at horseman with sword. p, Horseman carrying gun.

1996, Oct. 26   **Litho.**
1552 A498 100d Sheet of 16,
     #a-p   20.00 20.00

Miniature Sheet

HORSES

Horses — A499

No. 1553: a, Brown horse, lake at right. b, Brown horse in front of lake, tree at right. c, Brown horse in front of lake, tree at left. d, Dark brown horse, trees in background. e, Dark brown horse with raised leg. f, Horse at base of tree. g, Gray horse galloping. h, Piebald horse. i, Gray horse, palm tree at left. j, Head of black horse and tail of brown horse. k, Brown horse, palm fronds at upper right. l, Brown horse with gray mane, palm tree at right. m, Head of black horse, body of gray horse, tail of brown horse. n, Head of brown horse, body of black horse, hindquarters of two brown horses. o, Head of brown horse, parts of three other brown horses. p, Head of brown horse, chest of another brown horse, palm tree at right.

1996, Oct. 30   **Perf. 14x13¾**
1553 A499 100d Sheet of 16,
     #a-p   20.00 20.00

Miniature Sheet

CAMELS

Camels — A500

No. 1554: a, Camelus dromedarius with head at right. b, Head of Camelus dromedarius. c, Camelus dromedarius with head at left. d, Camelus ferus bactrianus with head at right. e, Camelus ferus ferus. f, Camelus ferus bactrianus with head at left.

1996, Nov. 15   **Perf. 12**
1554 A500 200d Sheet of 6,
     #a-f   13.50 13.50

Press and Information A501

Designs: 100d, Photographer, newspapers, computer. 200d, Musicians, video technician, computer, dish antenna.

1996, Nov. 20
1555-1556 A501   Set of 2   3.25 3.25

Miniature Sheet

FOSSILS IN LIBYA

Fossils and Prehistoric Animals — A502

No. 1557: a, Mene rhombea fossil. b, Mesodon macrocephalus fossil. c, Eyron arctiformis fossil. d, Stegosaurus. e, Pteranodon. f, Allosaurus.

1996, Nov. 25
1557 A502 200d Sheet of 6,
     #a-f   16.00 16.00

Palestinian Intifada — A503

Frame color: 100d, Yellow. 150d, Green. 200d, Blue.

1996, Nov. 29
1558-1560 A503   Set of 3   5.00 5.00

African Children's Day — A504

Designs: 50d, Child, beige frame. 150d, Child, blue frame. 200d, Mother, child, dove.

1996, Dec. 5   **Perf. 13¼**
1561-1563 A504   Set of 3   2.50 2.50

Children's Day — A505

No. 1564 — Various cats with background colors of: a, Rose. b, Blue green. c, Blue. d, Yellow green. e, Gray green.

1996, Dec. 5
1564   Horiz. strip of 5   5.50 5.50
a.-e.   A505 100d Any single   1.00 1.00

Intl. Family Day — A506

No. 1565 — Family and: a, 150d, Building (21x27mm). b, 150d, Automobile (21x27mm). c, 200d, Stylized globe (46x27mm).

1996, Dec. 10   **Perf. 13x13¼**
1565 A506   Horiz. strip of 3, #a-c   3.00 3.00

Miniature Sheet

LIBYAN TEACHERS

Teachers — A507

No. 1566: a, Mohamed Kamel El-Hammali. b, Mustafa Abdulla Ben-Amer. c, Mohamed Messaud Fesheka. d, Kairi Mustafa Serraj. e, Muftah El-Majri. f, Mohamed Hadi Arafa.

1996, Dec. 15   **Perf. 13¼**
1566 A507 100d Sheet of 6, #a-f   3.75 3.75

Miniature Sheet

LIBYAN SINGERS

Singers — A508

No. 1567: a, Mohamed Salim and zither. b, Mohamed M. Sayed Bumedyen and flute. c, Otman Najim and ood. d, Mahmud Sherif and tapla. e, Mohamed Ferjani Marghani and piano. f, Mohamed Kabazi and violin.

1996, Dec. 15
1567 A508 100d Sheet of 6, #a-f   3.75 3.75

Miniature Sheet

REPTILES

Reptiles — A509

No. 1568: a, Snake, leaves and building at top. b, Snake, building at top. c, Turtle, water and part of snake. d, Snake on tree branch. e, Brown lizard on rock. f, Cobra with head at left. g, Cobra and water. h, Turtle, water, tail of cobra. i, Green lizard on rock. j, Snake, foliage at bottom. k, Snake, foliage at bottom and right. l, Lizard with curled tail. m, Turtle on rock. n, Cobra with head at right. o, Turtle on grass. p, Gray lizard on rock.

1996, Dec. 20   **Perf. 13¾x14**
1568 A509 100d Sheet of 16,
     #a-p   18.50 18.50

Miniature Sheet

TRIPOLI INTERNATIONAL FAIR

Tripoli Intl. Fair — A510

No. 1569: a, Mirror and brush. b, Container and plate. c, Two containers with rounded bases. d, Two containers on pedestals. e, Oval ornament. f, Brushes.

Litho. & Embossed with Foil Application
1996, Dec. 30   **Perf. 13¾**
1569 A510 100d Sheet of 6, #a-f   6.75 6.75

A511

People's Authority Declaration, 20th Anniv. — A512

Frame color: 100d, Yellow. 200d, Blue. 300d, Green.

1997, Mar. 2   Litho.   Perf. 12
1570-1572 A511   Set of 3   7.75 7.75

Souvenir Sheet
Imperf

1573 A512 10,000d multi   90.00 90.00
No. 1573 has a perforated label that bears the denomination but lacks the country name.

Scouts and Philately — A513

No. 1574: a, 50d, Group of scouts, open album, wheat, flag. b, 50d, Two scouts, two albums, wheat. c, 100d, Butterflies, books, scouts and flags.

1997, Mar. 15   Perf. 14
1574 A513   Horiz. strip of 3, #a-
c   2.75 2.75

Health Care — A514

No. 1575: a, 50d, Doctor looking at test tube. b, 50d, Doctor, microscope. c, 100d, Doctor and nurse examining baby.

1997, Apr. 7
1575 A514   Horiz. strip of 3, #a-
c   2.25 2.25

Buildings
A515

Designs: 50d, Shown. 100d, Building with attached tower, vert. 200d, Tower, vert.

Perf. 14¼x14¾, 14¾x14¼
1997, Apr. 15
1576-1578 A515   Set of 3   5.00 5.00

Campaign Against Smoking — A516

Frame color: 100d, Blue. 150d, Green. 200d, Pink.

1997, Apr. 30   Perf. 14¾x14¼
1579-1581 A516   Set of 3   2.75 2.75

Arab National Central Library — A517

Building, map, open book, and olive branches with background in: 100d, Blue. 200d, Green.
1000d, Building, map, books, computer and Col. Khadafy, horiz.

1997, Aug. 10   Perf. 13¼
1582-1583 A517   Set of 2   1.75 1.75

Souvenir Sheet
1584 A517 1000d multi   6.00 6.00
No. 1584 contains one 116x49mm stamp.

Arab Tourism Year — A518

Perf. 13¼x13½
1997, Aug. 20   Litho.
1585 A518   Horiz. strip of 3   10.50 10.50
a.   100d Black denomination   2.00 2.00
b.   200d Red denomination   3.75 3.75
c.   250d Blue denomination   4.75 4.75

Miniature Sheet

A519

Sept. 1 Revolution, 28th Anniv. — A520

No. 1586: a, 100d, Mother and child. b, 100d, Col. Khadafy as student. c, 100d, Khadafy at microphone. d, 100d, People on tank. e, 100d, Khadafy and man in suit. f, 100d, Khadafy with fist raised. g, 100d, Woman, child, corner of Green Book. h, 100d, Three people, corner of Green Book. i, 100d, Khadafy with pen. j, 100d, Man and child. k, 100d, Government buildings, helicopters. l, 100d, Khadafy in military uniform. m, 500d, Khadafy on horse. Size of Nos. 1586a-1586l: 28x43mm. Size of No. 1586m: 56x86mm.

Litho., Litho with Foil Application (#1586m)
1997, Sept. 1   Perf. 14
1586 A519   Sheet of 13, #a-
m   17.50 17.50

Souvenir Sheet
Perf. 13¾
1587 A520 500d multi   6.00 6.00

Miniature Sheet

Intl. Day of Maghreb Handicrafts — A521

No. 1588 — Various shoes with toes pointing to: a, LR corner. b, Bottom. c, LL corner. d, UR corner. e, Top. f, UL corner.

Litho. With Foil Application
1997, Sept. 20   Perf. 13¾
1588 A521 300d Sheet of 6,
#a-f   18.00 18.00

Miniature Sheet

Tripoli Intl. Fair — A522

No. 1589 — Items made of silver: a, Medallion with tassels. b, Round medallion. c, Diamond-shaped medallion with tassels. d, Curved medallion. e, Necklace. f, Ring.

Litho. & Embossed With Foil Application
1997, Sept. 20
1589 A522 500d Sheet of 6,
#a-f   19.00 19.00

Evacuation of Foreign Forces — A523

Denominations: 100d, 150d, 250d.

1997, Oct. 7   Litho.   Perf. 14¾x14¼
1590-1592 A523   Set of 3   2.75 2.75

Miniature Sheet

Libyans Deported to Italy — A524

No. 1593: a, Person carrying water jug. b, Col. Khadafy with headdress. c, Man, soldier on horse. d, Soldier and Libyans. e, Soldier whipping man. f, Soldier, man on horse. g, Libyan man and man in uniform. h, People at hanging. i, Man with purple fez, woman with red headdress. j, People, horse and camel. k, Col. Khadafy without headdress. l, Deportees on boats. m, Hand of Khadafy above pillars. n, Horsemen and pillars. o, Horsemen. p, Horsemen and hand of Khadafy.

1997, Oct. 26   Perf. 14
1593 A524 200d Sheet of 16,
#a-p   32.50 32.50

Worldwide Fund for Nature (WWF) A525

No. 1594 — Felis lybica: a, With prey at water. b, Adult and kittens. c, Under tree. d, Two adults.

1997, Nov. 1   Perf. 13¼
1594   Horiz. strip of 4   7.50 7.50
a.-d.   A525 200d Any single   1.75 1.75
Printed in sheets containing two strips.

Souvenir Sheet

Natl. Society for Wildlife Conservation — A526

No. 1595: a, Antelope facing forward. b, Ram. c, Antelope facing left.

1997, Nov. 1   Perf. 13¼
1595 A526 100d Sheet of 3,
#a-c   14.00 14.00

Miniature Sheet

American Attack on Libya, 11th
Anniv. — A527

No. 1596: a, Explosion. b, Green Book, Libyan airplanes. c, Minarets, hand of Col.
Khadafy. d, Col. Khadafy without headdress.
e, Wing of American airplane. f, Nose of American airplane. g, Libyan airplanes. h, People
looking at tail of American airplane. i, Rockets
hitting American airplane. j, Arm of Col.
Khadafy. k, Col. Khadafy with headdress. l,
Man, fist of Col. Khadafy. m, Rockets and people. n, Col. Khadafy visiting injured person. o,
Col. Khadafy kissing girl's hand. p, People
with fists raised.

1997, Nov. 15   Perf. 14
1596 A527 200d Sheet of 16,
         #a-p   34.00 34.00

Miniature Sheet

Great Man-Made River — A528

No. 1597: a, Fist, outline map of Libya. b,
Col. Khadafy pointing to pipeline. c, Technicians reading paper, equipment. d, Col.
Khadafy pointing to map. e, Col. Khadafy. f,
Pipe, crane lifting cylinders. g, Col. Khadafy,
pipe, vertical cylinder. h, Col. Khadafy, vertical
cylinder. i, Col. Khadafy, construction trailer. j,
Technician and equipment. k, Col. Khadafy,
pipes lifted by crane. l, Col. Khadafy, line of
trucks carrying pipe. m, Man with hand on
spigot. n, Col. Khadafy with clasped hands. o,
Hands under faucet, crops. p, Woman, child,
flowers and fruit.

1997, Dec. 1   Perf. 14
1597 A528 200d Sheet of 16,
         #a-p   34.00 34.00

People's Authority Declaration — A529

Panel color: 150d, Blue green. 250d, Purple.
300d, Blue.

1998, Mar. 2   Perf. 13¼
1598-1600 A529   Set of 3   10.50 10.50

Miniature Sheet

Tripoli Intl. Fair — A530

No. 1601 — Items made of silver: a,
Container with two spouts. b, Bowl on pedestal. c, Amphora. d, Container on tray. e, Lidded
bowl. f, Three-legged container.

**Litho. & Embossed With Foil
Application**
1998, Mar. 5   Perf. 13¾
1601 A530 400d Sheet of 6,
         #a-f   24.00 24.00

Children's
Day — A531

No. 1602 — Various girls in native dress
with background colors of: a, Light blue. b,
Yellow green. c, Red orange. d, Lilac. e, Yellow
brown.

1998, Mar. 21   Litho.   Perf. 13¼
1602   Horiz. strip of 5   5.50 5.50
a.-e. A531 100d Any single   1.00 1.00

World Health
Day — A532

Panel color: 150d, Buff. 250d, Light blue.
300d, Lilac.

1998, Apr. 7
1603-1605 A532   Set of 3   7.75 7.75

American Attack on Libya, 12th
Anniv. — A533

No. 1606 — Airplanes, ships and: a, Heli-
copters, people with raised fists (28x48mm). b,
Mother and child, Col. Khadafy (60x48mm). c,
Man, boy and birds (28x48mm).

1998, Apr. 15
1606 A533 100d Horiz. strip of 3,
         #a-c   3.50 3.50

Libyan Blind Association, 35th
Anniv. — A534

Designs: 150d, Eye, hand with cane, raised
hand. 250d, Blind people, stringed instrument,
books.

1998, May 1   Perf. 12
1607-1608 A534   Set of 2   4.75 4.75

Arab Bee
Union — A535

Frame color: 250d, Blue. 300d, Yellow.
400d, Light green.

1998, June 1
1609-1611 A535   Set of 3   13.50 13.50

1998 World Cup Soccer
Championships, France — A536

No. 1612 — Soccer player with: a, Ball at
LR, orange and white lines at bottom. b, Top of
World Cup. c, Ball at left, orange and white
lines at bottom. d, No visible uniform number,
left part of stadium at bottom. e, Bottom of
World Cup, stadium. f, Uniform No. 5, right
part of stadium at bottom.
No. 1613, 1000d, Player, World Cup,
denomination at LL. No. 1614, 1000d, Player,
World Cup, denomination at LR.

1998, June 10   Perf. 13¼
1612 A536 200d Sheet of 6,
         #a-f   15.00 15.00
Souvenir Sheets
1613-1614 A536   Set of 2   24.00 24.00
Nos. 1613-1614 each contain one
42x51mm stamp.

Miniature Sheet

World Book Day — A537

No. 1615: a, Man, boy, mosque. b, Gymnasts. c, Science teacher at blackboard, student, ear. d, Men picking vegetables. e, Men at
blackboard, man with machinery. f, Man with
headset microphone, world map. g, Teacher
with compass, student. h, Scientists with
microscope. i, Girl writing, horseman. j,
Teacher, student, map of Libya, globe. k,
Music teacher at blackboard, student. l,
Woman at sewing machine. m, Chemistry
teacher and student. n, Teacher and women at
typewriters. o, Cooks. p, Woman at computer
keyboard, computer technician.

1998, June 23
1615 A537 100d Sheet of 16,
         #a-p   17.50 17.50

Map of
the Great
Man-Made
River
A538

Denomination color: 300d, Green. 400d,
Blue.
2000d, Bister.

**Litho. & Embossed With Foil
Application**
1998, July 1
1616-1617 A538   Set of 2   8.50 8.50
Souvenir Sheet
1618 A538 2000d gold & multi   22.00 22.00

Miniature Sheet

Great Man-Made River and
Vegetables — A539

No. 1619: a, Garlic. b, Peas. c, Potatoes. d,
Corn. e, Leeks. f, Tomatoes. g, Carrots. h,
Radishes. i, Beans. j, Peppers. k, Eggplant. l,
Lettuce. m, Squash. n, Cucumbers. o, Onions,
p, Cauliflower.

1998, Sept. 1   Litho.   Perf. 14
1619 A539 100d Sheet of 16,
         #a-p   21.00 21.00

Miniature Sheet

Children's Day — A540

No. 1620 — Scouting trefoil and: a, Scouts,
dog. b, Scouts saluting, birds. c, Scouts saluting, flags, tents. d, Scouts, sheep. e, Scouts

playing musical instruments, tying down tent. f, Scouts at campfire, bird, boat.

1998, Aug. 1 — *Perf. 14¼*
1620 A540 400d Sheet of 6, #a-f — 55.00 55.00

A541

Sept. 1 Revolution, 29th Anniv. — A542

No. 1621: a, Col. Khadafy. b, Horseman, pipeline, vegetables. c, Fruit, pipeline, head of eagle. d, Tail of eagle, minaret. e, Surgeons, students. f, Book, map of Northwestern Africa. g, Book, men, map of Northeastern Africa and Arabian Peninsula. h, Mosque. i, People with flags, grain combine. j, Ship. k, Apartment buildings, l, Boy. m, People, irrigation rig, building. n, Building with flagpole at right. o, Building with flagpole at right, irrigation rig. p, Building, irrigation rig.

1998, Sept. 1 **Litho.** *Perf. 14¼*
1621 A541 200d Sheet of 16, #a-p — 37.50 37.50

Souvenir Sheet
Litho. & Embossed
Perf. 13½x13¾
1622 A542 200d shown — 2.50 2.50

Evacuation of Foreign Forces — A543

Panel color: 100d, Pink. 150d, Light green. 200d, Light blue.

1998, Oct. 7 **Litho.** *Perf. 13¼*
1623-1625 A543 Set of 3 — 5.00 5.00

Stamp Day — A544

Panel color: 300d, Buff. 400d, Blue.

1998, Oct. 9 *Perf. 12*
1626-1627 A544 Set of 2 — 10.00 10.00

Miniature Sheet

Libyans Deported to Italy — A545

No. 1628: a, Ship, trucks. b, Bound woman, barbed wire. c, Man, barbed wire. d, Soldiers marching Libyans at gunpoint. e, Airplane, battle scene. f, Barbed wire, line of Libyans. g, Barbed wire, soldier and Libyan. h, Soldiers aiming rifles at Libyans, man with camel. i, Horsewoman, man ladling water. j, Soldier in boat. k, Boats with deportees. l, Boats with deportees, ships. m, Horsemen, man carrying woman. n, Horsemen raising rifles. o, Horseman and flag. p, Mother and child.

1998, Oct. 26 *Perf. 13¼*
1628 A545 150d Sheet of 16, #a-p — 26.00 26.00

Miniature Sheet

Leadership of Islam — A546

No. 1629: a, 100d, White mosque, minaret at left. b, 100d, White mosque, minaret at right. c, 100d, Modern mosque. d, 100d, Mosque seen through arch. e, 100d, Mosque and palm tree, minaret at left. f, 100d, Mosque with blue dome. g, 100d, Mosque with brown dome, six minarets. h, 100d, Mosque, five minarets. i, 500d, Koran, Holy Kaaba. j, 500d, Col. Khadafy on horse. Sizes: 100d stamps, 28x42mm; 500d stamps, 56x84mm.

Litho., Litho. With Foil Application (#1629j)
1998, Nov. 1 *Perf. 14*
1629 A546 Sheet of 10, #a-j — 22.00 22.00

Miniature Sheet

Scouts and the Handicapped — A547

No. 1630: a, Scout reading to boy in wheelchair, butterfly. b, Scout leader instructing group of Scouts. c, Scout photographing bird, boy in wheelchair. d, Scout raising flag, boy in wheelchair. e, Scout sawing log, boy in wheelchair. f, Scout near campfire, boy in wheelchair. g, Scouts with pots in fire, crutches. h, Scouts with pad of paper and pencil. i, Wheelchair basketball player in purple uniform. j, Wheelchair basketball player making shot. k, Handicapped runners. l, Man in wheelchair playing table tennis. m, Man in wheelchair playing hockey. n, Man in wheelchair throwing shot put. o, Handicapped cyclist. p, Handicapped javelin thrower.

1998, Nov. 15 **Litho.** *Perf. 13¼*
1630 A547 100d Sheet of 16, #a-p — 27.50 27.50

Miniature Sheet

A548

Sept. 1 Revolution, 30th Anniv. — A549

No. 1631: a, 100d, Antelopes and "30." b, 100d, Mosque. c, 100d, Woman playing stringed instrument. d, 100d, Horsemen in desert. e, 100d, Grain combine. f, 100d, Ship. g, 100d, Ship, horsemen, flag. h, 100d, Horsemen, flag. i, 100d, Water pipeline, fruit. j, 100d, Butterflies, shepherd and sheep. k, 100d, Building, ship, horse's legs. l, 100d, Dates. m, 200d, Col. Khadafy on horse. Sizes: 100d stamps; 28x42mm, 200d, 56x84mm.

Litho., Litho. With Foil Application (#1631m, 1632)
1999, Sept. 1 *Perf. 14*
1631 A548 Sheet of 13, #a-m — 12.00 12.00
Souvenir Sheet
Perf. 13¾
1632 A549 200d shown — 2.00 2.00

A550

Organization of African Unity Assembly of Heads of State and Government, Tripoli — A551

No. 1633: a, Pipeline worker, musicians, minarets. b, Surgeons, woman carrying jug. c, Artisan, camel rider, satellite. d, Col. Khadafy, butterflies. e, Pipeline worker, fruit picker. f, Fruit picker, grain combine.

1999, Sept. 8 **Litho.** *Perf. 14¼x14½*
1633 A550 300d Sheet of 6, #a-f — 12.50 12.50
Souvenir Sheet
Perf. 13¾x14
1634 A551 500d shown — 4.00 4.00

Evacuation of Foreign Forces — A552

Frame color: 150d, Pink. 250d, Beige. 300d, Light blue.

1999, Oct. 7 *Perf. 12*
1635-1637 A552 Set of 3 — 8.25 8.25

A553

People's Authority Declaration — A554

No. 1638: a, Col. Khadafy with fist raised, man on camel. b, People looking at book. c, Airplane, building, dish antenna. d, Antelope, weaver, tractor. e, Open faucet, pipeline. f, Pipeline, fruit pickers.
No. 1639, 300d, Map of Libya, Col. Khadafy with raised fist, building. No. 1640, 300d, Dove, people, Col. Khadafy.

2000, Mar. 2   Litho.   Perf. 14½x14¼
1638   A553   100d   Sheet of 6, #a-f   4.75   4.75
Souvenir Sheets
Perf. 13¾
Litho. & Embossed with Foil Application
1639-1640   A554   Set of 2   5.00   5.00

A555

Sept. 1 Revolution, 31st Anniv. — A556

No. 1641: a, Man walking, camel rider. b, Tea drinkers, camels. c, Col. Khadafy. d, Men with raised fists. e, Machinist with torch. f, Boy reading. g, Classroom. h, Scientist. i, Mother and child. j, People attending speech. k, Man and palm tree. l, Patient in X-ray machine. m, Mosque. n, Bulldozer, crane and building. o, Oil workers. p, Bulldozer.
No. 1642, 300d, Col. Khadafy, minaret. No. 1643, 300d, Col. Khadafy, boy and palm tree.

2000, Sept. 1   Litho.   Perf. 14
1641   A555   100d   Sheet of 16, #a-p   12.50   12.50
Souvenir Sheets
Litho. With Foil Application
Perf. 13¾
1642-1643   A556   Set of 2   5.00   5.00

El-Mujahed Mohamed Abdussalam Ahmeda Abouminiar El-Gaddafi — A557

No. 1644: a, Man holding box. b, Palm tree and horsemen. c, Horsemen and soldiers on horseback. d, Soldiers and armed horsemen. e, Horseman raising rifle above head. f, Men raising rifles, Col. Khadafy.
300d, Man reading book.

2000, Sept. 9   Litho.   Perf. 13¼
1644   A557   200d   Sheet of 6, #a-f   9.50   9.50
Souvenir Sheet
Litho. & Embossed With Foil Application
1645   A557   300d   multi   2.50   2.50

Souvenir Sheet

España 2000 Intl. Philatelic Exhibition — A558

No. 1646: a, A. Castellano (1926-97). b, M. B. Karamanli (1922-95).

2000, Oct. 6   Litho.   Imperf.
1646   A558   250d   Sheet of 2, #a-b   4.00   4.00

People's Authority Declaration A559

Denomination color: 150d, Pink. 200d, Blue.

2001, Mar. 2   Perf. 14
1647-1648   A559   Set of 2   2.75   2.75

Miniature Sheet

Organization of African Unity Assemby of Heads of State and Government — A560

No. 1649: a, Heads of various states. b, Heads of state, horsemen. c, Men on camels. d, People with hands raised. e, Man holding picture of Col. Khadafy. f, Col. Khadafy at microphone.

2001, Mar. 2   Litho.   Perf. 13½x13¼
1649   A560   200d   Sheet of 6, #a-f   9.50   9.50

Souvenir Sheets

Organization of African Unity Assembly of Heads of State and Government — A561

Background colors: No. 1650, 500d, Gold. No. 1651, 500d, Silver.

Litho. & Embossed With Foil Application
2001, Mar. 2   Perf. 13¼
1650-1651   A561   Set of 2   8.50   8.50

Miniature Sheet

Tripoli Intl. Fair — A562

No. 1652: a, Rear view of saddle. b, Side view of saddle. c, Front view of saddle. d, Stirrup. e, Four pieces of tack. f, Two pieces of tack.

Litho. & Embossed with Foil Application
2001, Apr. 2   Perf. 13¾
1652   A562   300d   Sheet of 6, #a-f   22.00   22.00

Miniature Sheet

Fight Against American Aggression — A563

No. 1653: a, Exploding jet. b, American jet. c, Pilot. d, American plane shooting missile. e, Parachute. f, Airplanes. g, Child crying. h, Palm tree, explosion. i, Missiles. j, Broken egg. k, Teddy bear. l, Clock. m, Explosion in city. n, Man rescuing casualty. o, Man holding child casualty. p, Family fleeing.

2001, Apr. 15   Litho.   Perf. 13¼
1653   A563   100d   Sheet of 16, #a-p   13.00   13.00

Desertification Project — A564

No. 1654: a, Man with hoe (30x39mm). b, Men near stream (60x39mm). c, Camels (30x39mm).

2001, June 26   Litho.   Perf. 13¼
1654   A564   250d   Horiz. strip of 3, #a-c   12.00   12.00

Miniature Sheet

Great Man-Made River — A565

No. 1655: a, Smokestack. b, Pipeline and flags. c, Palm tree, fruit. d, Grapes. e, Clothed boy, rainbow. f, Bathing boy, rainbow. g, Woman carrying fruit. h, Woman holding jug. i, Woman with red and black headdress. j, Woman with green striped headdress. k, Duck, rainbow. l, Boy running. m, Drummer hitting drum with hand. n, Horn player. o, Drummer hitting drum with stick. p, Tractors in field.

2001, Sept. 15   Litho.   Perf. 11¾
1655   A565   200d   Sheet of 16, #a-p   29.00   29.00

A566

Sept. 1 Revolution, 32nd Anniv. — A567

No. 1656: a, Col. Khadafy in headdress. b, Buildings, water pipeline, helicopters, tank, horsemen. c, Ship, airplane, camel rider. d, Tea drinkers. e, Children. f, Pillars, antelopes, woman. g, Man walking, camel rider. h, Camels, birds. i, Woman with container. j, Sword fight. k, Man and camel rider. l, Camels, pipeline worker, fruit. m, Potter. n, Musicians and weaver. o, Artisan. p, Col. Khadafy with clasped hands.

No. 1657, 300d, Col. Khadafy, pipeline and fruit (gold background). No. 1658, 300d, Col. Khadafy, pipeline and fruit (silver background).

Litho. and Hologram

2001, Sept. 1			**Perf. 13¼**
1656	A566	100d Sheet of 16, #a-p	27.50 27.50
q.	Booklet pane, #a-p, litho.		27.50 —
	Complete booklet, #1656q		27.50

Souvenir Sheets

Litho. & Embossed With Foil Application

1657-1658	A567	Set of 2	5.50 5.50

Intl. Day of the Orphan — A568

Panel color: 100d, Blue. 200d, Red violet. 300d, Olive green.

2001, Oct. 1	Litho.	**Perf. 14¾x14½**
1659-1661	A568	Set of 3	9.00 9.00

Health Care — A569

Arabic inscription color: 200d, Green. 300d, Yellow orange.

2001, Dec. 1	Litho.	**Perf. 14**
1662-1663	A569	Set of 2	6.50 6.50

Miniature Sheet

Tourism — A570

Various tourist attractions.

2002, May 1		**Perf. 11¾**
1664	A570 200d Sheet of 16, #a-p	52.50 52.50

Intl. Customs Day — A571

Designs: 200d, 400d.

2002, July 1		**Perf. 14**
1665-1666	A571	Set of 2	8.25 8.25

A572

Sept. 1 Revolution, 33rd Anniv. — A573

No. 1667: a, Col. Khadafy. b, Airplanes. c, Camel rider, woman pouring tea. d, Artisans. e, Bulldozer, building. f, Chemist, oil rig. g, Ships. h, Doctors and patients. i, Technician at industrial plant. j, Man at computer. k, Man, spigot, water pipeline, crane. l, Chemist, man at microscope. m, Television camera and technician. n, Fruit, vegetables, grain combine. o, Spear carriers, musician. p, Map of Africa, musicians.

No. 1668, 300d, Col. Khadafy, map of Africa (gold background). No. 1669, 300d, Col. Khadafy, map of Africa (silver background).

Litho. & Hologram

2002, Sept. 1			**Perf. 13¼**
1667	A572	100d Sheet of 16, #a-p	22.50 22.50
q.	Booklet pane, #a-p, litho.		40.00
	Complete booklet, #1667q		50.00

Souvenir Sheets

Litho. & Embossed With Foil Application

1668-1669	A573	Set of 2	8.00 8.00

Universal Declaration of Human Rights, 50th Anniv. — A576

Panel color: 250d, Red orange. 500d, Blue green.

2002, Nov. 1	Litho.	**Perf. 14**
1672-1673	A576	Set of 2	9.50 9.50

Universal Postal Union, 125th Anniv. — A577

Panel color: 200d, Blue. 250d, Red violet.

2002, Dec. 1		
1674-1675	A577	Set of 2	5.50 5.50

A580

September 1 Revolution, 34th Anniv. — A581

No. 1679: a, 300d, Doctors and microscope (30x40mm). b, 300d, Nurses studying anatomy (30x40mm). c, 300d, Mother and child (30x40mm). d, 300d, Soldiers, white flag (30x40mm). e, 500d, Teachers, students, building (60x40mm). f, 500d, Helicopter, pilot, women, nurse and patients (60x40mm). g, 500d, Marching band, soldiers in vehicle (60x40mm). h, 1000d, Col. Khadafy, airplane, satellite dish.

2003, May 20	Litho.	**Perf. 12**
1679	A580	Sheet of 8, #a-h	22.50 22.50

Souvenir Sheet

Litho. & Embossed With Foil Application

1680	A581	2000d multi	17.00 17.00

September 1 Revolution, 35th Anniv. A582

Background color: 750d, Gray green. 1000d, Yellow green.

2004	Litho.	**Perf. 13**
1681-1682	A582	Set of 2	4.50 4.50

Khairi Khaled Nuri (1943-2004), Philatelist — A583

2004	Litho. & Hologram	**Perf. 13¼**
1683	A583	500d multi	2.00 2.00

People's Authority Declaration, 27th Anniv. A584

Color of rays: 400d, Yellow brown. 1000d, Blue green.

2004	Litho.	**Perf. 13**
1684-1685	A584	Set of 2	12.00 12.00

1st Communication and Information Technology Exhibition — A585

2005, July 29		**Perf. 13**
1686	A585 750d multi	5.00 5.00

Souvenir Sheet

Imperf

1687	A585 1000d multi	6.00 6.00

People's Authority Declaration, 28th Anniv. — A586

Delegates: 300d, Seated. 1000d, Voting.

2005		**Perf. 13**
1688-1689	A586	Set of 2	12.00 12.00

September 1 Revolution, 36th Anniv. — A587

Background color: 750d, Yellow orange. 1000d, Blue.

2005		
1690-1691	A587	Set of 2	15.00 15.00

Miniature Sheet

Total Solar Eclipse of March 29, 2006 — A588

No. 1692 — Eclipse and: a, Band of totality over map of Libya. b, Buildings, map of Libya. c, Altitude and duration figures. d, Stylized fish, camel, cactus, palm tree and Libyan. e, Saddled camel. f, Camels and riders.

2006, Mar. 29
1692 A588 250d Sheet of 6,
        #a-f   12.50 12.50

People's Authority Declaration, 29th Anniv. A589

Wheat ear, flag, fist and torch with background color of: 400d, Yellow. 1000d, Blue.

2006, Nov. 1
1693-1694 A589 Set of 2   11.00 11.00

September 1 Revolution, 37th Anniv. — A590

2006
1695 A590 1000d multi   8.00 8.00

Famous African Leaders — A591

Map of Africa and: No. 1696, 500d, Gamal Abdel Nasser (1918-70), Egyptian President. No. 1697, 500d, Kwame Nkrumah (1909-72), President of Ghana. No. 1698, 500d, Ahmed Ben Bella, President of Algeria. No. 1699, 500d, Patrice Lumumba (1925-61), Congolese Prime Minister. No. 1700, 500d, Kenneth Kaunda, President of Zambia. No. 1701, 500d, Julius Nyerere (1922-99), President of Tanzania. No. 1702, 500d, Modibo Keita (1915-77), President of Mali.
1000d, Map of Africa, Nasser, Nkrumah, Ben Bella, Lumumba, Kaunda, Nyerere and Keita, horiz.

2007, Mar. 6   **Perf. 12¾**
1696-1702 A591 Set of 7   32.50 32.50
1702a   Miniature sheet of 7,
            #1696-1702   32.50 32.50

Size: 98x75mm
Imperf
1703 A591 1000d multi   8.00 8.00

Third Communication and Information Technology Exhibition — A592

2007, May 27   **Perf. 13**
1704 A592 750d multi   6.50 6.50

Tripoli, Capital of Islamic Culture A593

2007, June 16   **Litho.**
1705 A593 500d multi   4.50 4.50

Intl. Day Against Drug Abuse and Illicit Trafficking A594

2007, June 26
1706 A594 750d multi   6.50 6.50

People's Authority Declaration, 30th Anniv. A595

2007, July 4
1707 A595 750d multi   6.50 6.50

36th Tripoli Intl. Fair — A596

No. 1708: a, Ring (orange background). b, Pendant (green background). c, Ring (purple background).
Illustration reduced.

2007, July 4   **Perf. 13x13x13¼**
1708   Strip of 3   16.00 16.00
 a.-c.   A596 500d Any single 3.50   3.00
Printed in sheets containing 2 strips + 2 labels. Value, $32.50.

Mosque
A597

2007, Aug. 24   **Litho.   Perf. 13**
1709 A597 500d multi   5.00 5.00
 a.   Souvenir sheet of 1   5.00 5.00

African Soccer Federation, 50th Anniv. A598

2007, Aug. 25
1710 A598 750d multi   6.50 6.50
Values are for stamps with surrounding selvage.

September 1 Revolution, 38th Anniv. — A599

2007, Sept. 1   **Litho.   Perf. 13**
1711 A599 1000d multi   8.00 8.00
 a.   Souvenir sheet of 1   8.00 8.00

Khadafy Project for African Women, Children and Youth A600

2007, Sept. 9
1712 A600 500d multi   4.25 4.25

Libyan Red Crescent Society, 50th Anniv. A601

Red Crescent emblem and: 500d, Red Crescent volunteers. 1000d, 50th anniversary emblem.

2007   **Perf. 13**
1713-1714 A601 Set of 2   12.50 12.50

People's Authority Declaration, 31st Anniv. — A602

Type I — Two dots and vertical line in Arabic inscription directly above second "A" in "Jamahiriya."
Type II — No dots or vertical line in Arabic inscription directly above second "A" in "Jamahiriya."

2008, Mar. 2   **Litho.   Perf. 13**
1715 A602 500d multi, type I 50.00 50.00
 a.   Type II   4.50   4.50

37th Tripoli International Fair — A603

No. 1716: a, Emblems, colored rectangles. b, Emblems. c, Emblems, buildings, displays.
Illustration reduced.

2008, Apr. 2   **Perf. 13x12¾**
1716 A603 500d Horiz. strip of
              3, #a-c   13.00 13.00
Printed in sheets of 6 containing two of each stamp.

Worldwide Fund for Nature (WWF) A604

Rueppell's fox: No. 1717, Head. No. 1718, Walking. No. 1719, Curled up. No. 1720, Sitting.

2008, May 1   **Perf. 12**
1717 A604 750f multi   1.50   1.50
 a.   Imperf.   6.00   6.00
1718 A604 750f multi   1.50   1.50
 a.   Imperf.   6.00   6.00
1719 A604 750f multi   1.50   1.50
 a.   Imperf.   6.00   6.00
1720 A604 750f multi   1.50   1.50
 a.   Imperf.   6.00   6.00
 b.   Horiz. strip of 4, #1717-
         1720   8.00   8.00
 c.   Horiz. strip of 4, #1717a-
         1720a   35.00 35.00

Fourth Telecommunications and Information Technology Exhibition — A605

2008, May 25   **Perf. 13**
1721 A605 1000d multi   6.75 6.75

Gamal Abdel Nasser (1918-70), Egyptian President A606

2008, July 23
1722 A606 500d multi   5.00 5.00

Egyptian Revolution, 56th anniv.

Khadafy 6+6 Mediterranean Project — A607

2008, July 27
1723 A607 750d multi   5.00 5.00

Tenth Meeting of Leaders and Heads of State of Community of Sahel-Sahara Countries — A608

2008, Aug. 3
1724 A608 1000d multi   6.00 6.00

Libyan Participation in 2008 Summer Olympics, Beijing A609

2008, Aug. 18
1725 A609 1000d multi   8.00 8.00

September 1 Revolution, 39th Anniv. — A610

Col. Khadafy with denomination in: No. 1726, White. No. 1727, Green.

2008, Sept. 1   **Perf. 13x12¾**
1726 A610 1000d multi   8.00 8.00
          Souvenir Sheet
1727 A610 1000d multi   8.00 8.00

Total Mobile Phone Penetration in Libya A611

2008, Sept. 11   **Perf. 13**
1728 A611 750d multi   6.00 6.00

Fourth Intl. Waatasemu Women's Competition for Koran Memorization — A612

2008, Sept. 23
1729 A612 750d multi   5.00 5.00

Koran Exhibition A613

2008, Sept. 26
1730 A613 500d multi   3.50 3.50

People's Authority Declaration, 32nd Anniv. — A614

2009, Mar. 9
1731 A614 500d multi   3.00 3.00

Support for Gaza Palestinians A615

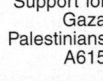

2009, May 7
1732 A615 1000d multi   5.00 5.00

American Aggression Against Libya — A616

2009, May 14   **Litho.**   **Perf. 13**
1733 A616 500d multi   4.00 4.00

Fifth Telecommunications and Information Technology Exhibition — A617

2009, May 30
1734 A617 500d multi   3.00 3.00

Omar Bongo (1935-2009), President of Gabon A618

2009, June 20   **Litho.**   **Perf. 13**
1735 A618 750d multi   3.00 3.00

16th Mediterranean Games, Pescara, Italy — A619

2009, June 26
1736 A619 500d multi   3.00 3.00

Jerusalem, Capital of Arab Culture — A620

2009, Aug. 3
1737 A620 1000d multi   4.50 4.50

25th African Men's Basketball Championships, Libya — A621

2009
1738 A621 500d multi   3.00 3.00

Souvenir Sheet

September 1 Revolution, 40th Anniv. — A622

No. 1739 — Col. Khadafy and background color of: a, 400d, Yellow. b, 600d, White. c, 750d, Green.

2009
1739 A622 Sheet of 3, #a-c   7.50 7.50

Col. Khadafy, Map of Africa and African Union Emblem — A623

Litho. & Embossed With Foil Application
2009   **Serpentine Die Cut 11**
          Self-Adhesive
1740 A623 1000d multi   4.50 4.50
          Souvenir Sheet
1741 A623 2000d multi   9.00 9.00

First Al Fateh Futsal (Indoor Soccer) Contintental Cup Tournament A624

2009, Oct. 12   Litho.   Perf. 13
1742 A624 500d multi   1.50 1.50

Pan-African Postal Union, 30th Anniv. — A625

2010, Jan. 18
1743 A625 500d multi   1.50 1.50

People's Authority Declaration, 33rd Anniv. — A626

Litho. With Foil Application
2010, Mar. 2   Serpentine Die Cut 10
Self-Adhesive
1744 A626 500d multi   1.50 1.50

22nd Session of the Council of the League of Arab States, Sirt — A627

Serpentine Die Cut 10
2010, Mar. 27   Self-Adhesive
1745 A627 500d multi   1.50 1.50

Organization of Petroleum Exporting Countries, 50th Anniv. — A628

2010, June 1   Litho.   Perf. 13
1746 A628 1000d multi   2.75 2.75

Evacuation of US Forces From Bases in Libya, 40th Anniv. A629

2010, June 9
1747 A629 1000d multi   3.00 3.00

Libyan Revolution After 40 Years — A630

No. 1748: a, Nationalization of banks and insurance companies. b, Nationalization of the oil sector. c, Declaration of the People's Revolution, 1973 d, Arab Republics Union. e, Italian evacuation from Libyan soil. f, Evacuation of American troops from Libyan soil. g, Evacuation of British troops from Libyan soil. h, Dawn of Great A-Fatah, 1969. i, Al-Fatah, an industrial revolution. j, Huge residential projects. k, Al-Fatah, an agricultural revolution. l, Establishment of the largest electricity networks. m, Establishment of roads network in Great Jamahiriya. n, Al-Fatah scientific revolution. o, Comprehensive health welfare. p, Al-Fatah, an Islamic revolution. q, Defining death line. r, The great Man-made River builder. s, Wajda City Agreement, 1984. t, Producer's revolution, 1978. u, The Green Book. v, The birth of first Jamahiriya in history, 1977. w, Student's revolution, 1976. x, Tunisia-Libya Jerba Unity Agreement. y, The African Arab Union, Sept. 9, 1999. z, By the Community of Sahel and Saharan States. aa, Break of the injustice embargo against Great Jamahiriya. ab, Demolition of borders. ac, The Arab Magreb Union, 1989. ad, Great Green Charter for Human Rights. ae, Demolition of jails. af, Courageous response to the failed NATO aggression. ag, The 40th anniversary of the 1st September Revolution. ah, Moammar Khadafy, heart of the world. ai, The return of the political hostage A. B. Almagrahi. aj, Italian apology to Libya about the Colonial period. ak, Moammar Khadafy, the king of Africa kings. al, Revolution of telecommunication and technology. am, The establishment of huge fleet maritime transports. an, Emancipation of women lost by the Great Al-Fatah Revolution.

Litho. With Foil Application
Serpentine Die Cut 10
2010, Aug. 23   Self-Adhesive
1748   Sheet of 40   57.50
a.-an.   A630 400d Any single   1.40 1.40

Great Green Document of Human Rights, 22nd Anniv. — A631

Dr. Martin Luther King, Jr., civil rights marchers, and scroll with: 1500d, Arabic text. 2000d, English text.

2010, Aug. 28   Litho.   Perf. 13
1749-1750 A631 Set of 2   15.00 15.00

Miniature Sheets

Sept. 23, 2009 Speech of Col. Khadafy to United Nations Security Council, 1st Anniv. — A633

No. 1753, 1000d — Map of world, Col. Khadafy, U.N. emblem, text of speech in Arabic with: a, First line of text 53mm, second line of text 47mm. b, First line of text 68mm. c, First line of text 53mm, second line of text 52mm. d, First line of text 44mm, second line of text 42mm. e, First line of text 61mm. f, First line of text 45mm, second line of text 58mm.
No. 1754, 1000d — Map of world, Col. Khadafy, U.N. emblem, text of speech in English starting with: a, "Brothers, you can in our political life . . ." b, "In order that colonization is not repeated . . ." c, "The solution to achieve democracy . . ." d, "The International Court of Justice . . ." e, "Africa as of now . . ." f, "The International Atomic Energy Agency . . ."
No. 1755, 1000d — Map of world, Col. Khadafy, U.N. emblem, text of speech in French starting with: a, "Vous voyez, mes frères . . ." b, "Pour eviter une nouvelle colonisation . . ." c, "Donc la solution . . ." d, "La Cour Internationale de Justice . . ." e, "L'Afrique a besoin . . ." f, "L'Agence Internationale de l'Energie . . ."

2010, Sept. 23   Litho.   Perf. 13
Sheets of 6, #a-f
1753-1755 A633 Set of 3   60.00 60.00

February 17, 2011 Revolution A635

Denominations: 250d, 500d, 750d, 1000d, 5000d.

2011   Litho.   Perf. 13¼
1757-1761 A635 Set of 5   22.50 22.50

February 17 Revolution, 1st Anniv. A636

No. 1762: a, Woman in burqa, man waving flag. b, Crowd with flag. c, Flowers and emblem. No. 1763, Map of Libya, flag in circle.

2012, Feb. 17   Perf. 13
1762   Horiz. strip of 3   6.00 6.00
a.-b.   A636 500d Either single   1.50 1.50
c.   A636 1000d multi   3.00 3.00
Souvenir Sheet
1763 A636 1000d multi   3.00 3.00

Children's Drawings A637

No. 1764: a, Tree with colors of Libyan flag, flowers. b, Flowers and trees. c, People and various animals. d, Child with flag, house. e, Boat with flag, palm tree.

2012, Sept. 12   Perf. 12¾
1764   Horiz. strip of 5   8.25 8.25
a.   A637 100d multi   .40 .40
b.   A637 200d multi   .80 .80
c.   A637 250d multi   1.00 1.00
d.   A637 500d multi   2.00 2.00
e.   A637 1000d multi   4.00 4.00

Independence, 61st Anniv. — A638

National colors, "61," and: 500d, Crescent and star. 1000d, Olive branch, crescent and star.

2012, Dec. 24   Perf. 13¼
1765-1766 A638 Set of 2   16.50 16.50

Monument to the Foundation of the Libyan Army — A639

2013, Feb. 17
1767 A639 500d multi   6.50 6.50

A640

A641

February 17 Revolution, 2nd Anniv. A642

2013, Feb. 17   Perf. 13
1768   Horiz. strip of 3   19.50 19.50
a.   A640 250d multi   2.75 2.75
b.   A641 500d multi   5.50 5.50
c.   A642 1000d multi   11.00 11.00

Miniature Sheet

Tripoli International Fair — A643

No. 1769: a, Necklace and pendants. b, Fair emblem. c, Triangular pendant. d, Semi-circular pendant. e, Pin. f, Earrings.

2013, Apr. 2
1769 A643 500d Sheet of 6, #a-f   19.50 19.50

Intl. Letter Writing Competition for Young People A644

2013, May 4   Litho.   *Perf. 13*
1770 A644 1000d multi   6.75 6.75

February 17 Revolution, 2nd Anniv. — A645

Libyan flag with background color of: 5000d, Light blue. 10,000d, Light orange.

Litho. & Embossed With Foil Application
2013, May 27 *Serpentine Die Cut 10*
Self-Adhesive
1771 A645 5000d multi   24.00 24.00
1772 A645 10,000d multi   47.50 47.50

Campaign Against Desertification A646

2013, June 17   Litho.   *Perf. 13¼*
1773 A646 500d multi   10.00 10.00

Libyan Parliament Building, Al Bayda, 50th Anniv. (in 2014) — A647

2013, Aug. 20   Litho.   *Perf. 13¼*
1774 A647 500d multi   4.25 4.25

Benghazi Lighthouse A648

2013, Aug. 20   Litho.   *Perf. 13*
1775 A648 1000d multi   11.00 11.00

Miniature Sheet

Dinosaurs — A651

No. 1779: a, Triceratops. b, Head of dinosaur, building ruins. c, Tyrannosaurus, sky in background. d, Tyrannosaurus, head upright, building ruins in background, no sky. e, Dinosaurs and flowers. f, Tyrannosaurus, head lowered, building ruins in background, no sky.

2013, Dec. 11   Litho.   *Perf. 12¾*
1779 A651 250d Sheet of 6, #a-f   19.00 19.00

Independence, 62nd Anniv. — A652

No. 1780: a, King Idris, Libyan flag. b, Emblem. c, Horseman carrying flag, King Idris, Omar Mukhtar, map of Libya.

2013, Dec. 24   Litho.   *Perf. 13*
1780   Horiz. strip of 3   13.00 13.00
  a. A652 250d multi   1.75 1.75
  b. A652 750d multi   5.00 5.00
  c. A652 1000d multi   6.50 6.50

National Post Day — A653

2013, Dec. 24   Litho.   *Perf. 13¼*
1781 A653 100d multi   7.75 7.75

2013 National Stamp Exhibition A654

2013, Dec. 25   Litho.   *Perf. 13*
1782 A654 100d multi   4.25 4.25

February 17th Revolution, 3rd Anniv. A655

No. 1783: a, Stylized people and emblem. b, Libyan people and flags. c, Torch and map of Libya.

2014, Feb. 17   Litho.   *Perf. 13*
1783   Horiz. strip of 3   16.50 16.50
  a. A655 500d multi   3.75 3.75
  b. A655 750d multi   5.50 5.50
  c. A655 1000d multi   7.25 7.25

Libya, Champions of 2014 African Nations Soccer Championships — A656

No. 1784: a, 500d, Libyan team, trophy. b, 750d, Trophy, Libyan Soccer Federation emblem, map of Libya.

2014, Feb. 17   Litho.   *Perf. 13*
1784 A656   Horiz. pair, #a-b   7.75 7.75

Miniature Sheet

Vegetables — A657

No. 1786: a, Garlic. b, Onions. c, Tomatoes. d, Peppers. e, Eggplants. f, Potatoes.

2014, Feb. 24   Litho.   *Perf. 12¾*
1786 A657 500d Sheet of 6, #a-f   19.00 19.00

Scouting in Libya, 60th Anniv. — A658

No. 1787: a, 500d, Scouts. b, 1000d, Ali Khalefa Zaidi (1909-66), scouting leader.

2014, Feb. 27   Litho.   *Perf. 13*
1787 A658   Horiz. pair, #a-b 19.00 19.00

Miniature Sheet

2014 Tripoli International Fair — A659

No. 1788: a, Bazin with meat. b, Fair emblem, map of Libya. c, Couscous with meat. d, Bazin with fish. e, Fair emblems. f, Couscous with fish.

2014, Apr. 2   Litho.   *Perf. 13*
1788 A659 500d Sheet of 6, #a-f   19.00 19.00

SEMI-POSTAL STAMPS

Many issues of Italy and Italian Colonies include one or more semipostal denominations. To avoid splitting sets, these issues are generally listed as regular postage, semipostals or airmails, etc.

Semi-Postal Stamps of Italy Overprinted

1915-16   Wmk. 140   *Perf. 14*
B1 SP1 10c + 5c rose   3.50 14.00
  a. Double overprint   825.00
B2 SP2 15c + 5c slate   30.00 24.00
B3 SP2 20c + 5c org ('16)   4.25 30.00
  Nos. B1-B3 (3)   37.75 68.00

No. B2 with Additional Surcharge

1916, Mar.
B4 SP2 20c on 15c + 5c slate   30.00 30.00
  a. Double surcharge   850.00

View of Port, Tripoli SP1

Designs: B5, B6, View of port, Tripoli. B7, B8, Arch of Marcus Aurelius. B9, B10, View of Tripoli.

1927, Feb. 15   Litho.
B5 SP1 20c + 5c brn vio & black   3.50 15.00
B6 SP1 25c + 5c bl grn & black   3.50 15.00
B7 SP1 40c + 10c blk brn & black   3.50 15.00
B8 SP1 60c + 10c org brn & black   3.50 15.00
B9 SP1 75c + 20c red & black   3.50 15.00
B10 SP1 1.25 l + 20c bl & blk   24.00 42.50
  Nos. B5-B10 (6)   41.50 117.50

First Sample Fair, Tripoli. Surtax aided fair. See Nos. EB1-EB2.

View of Tripoli — SP2

Knights of Malta Castle SP3

Designs: 50c+20c, Date palm. 1.25 l+20c, Camel riders. 2.55 l+50c, View of Tripoli. 5 l+1 l, Traction well.

1928, Feb. 20   Wmk. 140   *Perf. 14*
B11 SP2 30c + 20c mar & blk   3.50 15.00
B12 SP2 50c + 20c bl grn & blk   3.50 15.00
B13 SP2 1.25 l + 20c red & blk   3.50 15.00
B14 SP3 1.75 l + 20c bl & blk   3.50 15.00
B15 SP3 2.55 l + 50c brn & blk   7.00 22.50
B16 SP3 5 l + 1 l pur & blk   9.50 25.00
  Nos. B11-B16 (6)   30.50 107.50

2nd Sample Fair, Tripoli, 1928. The surtax was for the aid of the Fair.

Olive Tree — SP4

Herding
SP5

Designs: 50c+20c, Dorcas gazelle. 1.25 l+20c, Peach blossoms. 2.55 l+50c, Camel caravan. 5 l+1 l, Oasis with date palms.

1929, Apr. 7

B17	SP4	30c + 20c mar & blk	14.00	27.50
B18	SP4	50c + 20c bl grn & blk	14.00	27.50
B19	SP4	1.25 l + 20c scar & blk	14.00	27.50
B20	SP5	1.75 l + 20c bl & blk	14.00	27.50
B21	SP5	2.55 l + 50c yel brn & blk	14.00	27.50
B22	SP5	5 l + 1 l pur & blk	125.00	300.00
		Nos. B17-B22 (6)	195.00	437.50

3rd Sample Fair, Tripoli, 1929. The surtax was for the aid of the Fair.

Harvesting Bananas — SP6

Water Carriers SP7

Designs: 50c, Tobacco plant. 1.25 l, Venus of Cyrene. 2.55 l+45c, Black bucks. 5 l+1 l, Motor and camel transportation. 10 l+2 l, Rome pavilion.

1930, Feb. 20   **Photo.**

B23	SP6	30c dark brown	4.25	17.50
B24	SP6	50c violet	4.25	17.50
B25	SP6	1.25 l deep blue	4.25	17.50
B26	SP6	1.75 l + 20c scar	7.00	26.00
B27	SP7	2.55 l + 45c dp grn	16.00	37.50
B28	SP7	5 l + 1 l dp org	16.00	50.00
B29	SP7	10 l + 2 l dk vio	16.00	62.50
		Nos. B23-B29 (7)	67.75	228.50

4th Sample Fair at Tripoli, 1930. The surtax was for the aid of the Fair.

Statue of Ephebus — SP8

Exhibition Pavilion SP9

Designs: 25c, Arab musician. 50c, View of Zeughet. 1.25 l, Snake charmer. 1.75 l+45c, Windmill. 2.75 l+45c, "Zaptie." 5 l+1 l, Mounted Arab.

1931, Mar. 8

B30	SP8	10c black brown	5.50	9.75
B31	SP8	25c green	5.50	9.75
B32	SP8	50c purple	5.50	9.75
B33	SP8	1.25 l blue	5.50	14.00
B34	SP8	1.75 l + 25c car rose	5.50	16.00
B35	SP8	2.75 l + 45c org	5.50	24.00
B36	SP8	5 l + 1 l dl vio	15.00	35.00
B37	SP9	10 l + 2 l brn	50.00	70.00
		Nos. B30-B37 (8)	98.00	188.25
		Nos. B30-B37,C3,EB3 (10)	104.90	229.75

Fifth Sample Fair, Tripoli. Surtax aided fair.

Papaya Tree SP10

Dorcas Gazelle SP12

Ar Tower, Mogadiscio SP11

Designs: 10c, 50c, Papaya tree. 20c, 30c, Euphorbia abyssinica. 25c, Fig cactus. 75c, Mausoleum, Ghirza. 1.75 l+25c, Lioness. 5 l+1 l, Bedouin with camel.

1932, Mar. 8

B38	SP10	10c olive brn	7.00	16.00
B39	SP10	20c brown red	7.00	16.00
B40	SP10	25c green	7.00	16.00
B41	SP10	30c olive blk	7.00	16.00
B42	SP10	50c dk violet	7.00	16.00
B43	SP10	75c carmine	8.50	16.00
B44	SP11	1.25 l dk blue	8.50	24.00
B45	SP11	1.75 l + 25c ol brn	27.50	77.50
B46	SP11	5 l + 1 l dp bl	27.50	190.00
B47	SP12	10 l + 2 l brn violet	125.00	350.00
		Nos. B38-B47 (10)	232.00	737.50
		Nos. B38-B47,C4-C7 (14)	416.00	1,167.

Sixth Sample Fair, Tripoli. Surtax aided fair.

Ostrich — SP13

Arab Musician SP14

Designs: 25c, Incense plant. 30c, Arab musician. 50c, Arch of Marcus Aurelius. 1.25 l, African eagle. 5 l+1 l, Leopard. 10 l+2.50 l, Tripoli skyline and fasces.

1933, Mar. 2   **Photo.**   **Wmk. 140**

B48	SP13	10c dp violet	37.50	42.50
B49	SP13	25c dp green	21.00	42.50
B50	SP14	30c orange brn	21.00	42.50
B51	SP13	50c purple	21.00	42.50
B52	SP13	1.25 l dk blue	50.00	77.50
B53	SP14	5 l + 1 l ol brn	110.00	175.00
B54	SP13	10 l + 2.50 l car	110.00	300.00
		Nos. B48-B54 (7)	370.50	722.50
		Nos. B48-B54,C8-C13 (13)	484.00	1,102.

Seventh Sample Fair, Tripoli. Surtax aided fair.

Pomegranate Tree — SP15

Designs: 50c+10c, 2 l+50c, Musician. 75c+15c, 1.25 l+25c, Tribesman.

1935, Feb. 16

B55	SP15	10c + 10c brn	1.75	5.00
B56	SP15	20c + 10c rose red	1.75	5.00
B57	SP15	50c + 10c pur	1.75	5.00
B58	SP15	75c + 15c car	1.75	5.00
B59	SP15	1.25 l + 25c dl blue	1.75	5.00
B60	SP15	2 l + 50c ol grn	1.75	12.50
		Nos. B55-B60 (6)	10.50	37.50
		Nos. B55-B60,C19-C24 (12)	27.00	108.00

Ninth Sample Fair, Tripoli. Surtax aided fair.

AIR POST STAMPS

Italy Nos. C3 and C5 Overprinted

1928-29   **Wmk. 140**   **Perf. 14**

C1	AP2	50c rose red	14.00	27.50
C2	AP2	80c brn vio & brn ('29)	55.00	77.50

Airplane AP1

1931, Mar. 8   **Photo.**   **Wmk. 140**

C3	AP1	50c blue	1.40	14.00

See note after No. B37.

Seaplane over Bedouin Camp AP2

Designs: 50c, 1 l, Seaplane over Bedouin camp. 2 l+1 l, 5 l+2 l, Seaplane over Tripoli.

1932, Mar. 1   **Perf. 14**

C4	AP2	50c dark blue	15.00	42.50
C5	AP2	1 l org brown	15.00	42.50
C6	AP2	2 l + 1 l dk gray	29.00	120.00
C7	AP2	5 l + 2 l car	125.00	225.00
		Nos. C4-C7 (4)	207.50	495.00

See note after No. B47.

Seaplane Arriving at Tripoli AP3

Designs: 50c, 2 l+50c, Seaplane arriving at Tripoli. 75c, 10 l+2.50 l, Plane over Tagiura. 1 l, 5 l+1 l, Seaplane leaving Tripoli.

1933, Mar. 1

C8	AP3	50c dp green	11.00	22.50
C9	AP3	75c carmine	11.00	22.50
C10	AP3	1 l dk blue	11.00	22.50
C11	AP3	2 l + 50c pur	18.00	52.50
C12	AP3	5 l + 1 l org brn	30.00	85.00
C13	AP3	10 l + 2.50 l gray blk	32.50	175.00
		Nos. C8-C13 (6)	125.00	390.00

See note after No. B54.

Seaplane over Tripoli Harbor AP4

Airplane and Camel — AP5

Designs: 50c, 5 l+1 l, Seaplane over Tripoli harbor. 75c, 10 l+2 l, Plane and minaret.

1934, Feb. 17   **Photo.**   **Wmk. 140**

C14	AP4	50c slate bl	14.00	30.00
C15	AP4	75c red org	14.00	30.00
C16	AP4	5 l + 1 l dp grn	125.00	210.00
C17	AP4	10 l + 2 l dl vio	125.00	210.00
C18	AP5	25 l + 3 l org brn	150.00	300.00
		Nos. C14-C18 (5)	487.00	900.00

Eighth Sample Fair, Tripoli. Surtax aided fair. See Nos. CE1-CE2.

Plane and Ancient Tower — AP6

Camel Train AP7

Designs: 25c+10c, 3 l+1.50 l, Plane and ancient tower. 50c+10c, 2 l+30c, Camel train. 1 l+25c, 10 l+5 l, Arab watching plane.

1935, Apr. 12

C19	AP6	25c + 10c green	1.40	5.50
C20	AP7	50c + 10c slate bl	1.40	5.50
C21	AP7	1 l + 25c blue	1.40	5.50
C22	AP7	2 l + 30c rose red	1.40	9.50
C23	AP6	3 l + 1.50 l brn	1.40	9.50
C24	AP7	10 l + 5 l dl vio	9.50	35.00
		Nos. C19-C24 (6)	19.00	81.50

See note after No. B60.

Cyrenaica No. C6 Overprinted in Black

1936, Oct.

C25	AP2	50c purple	24.00	.35

Same on Tripolitania Nos. C8 and C12

1937

C26	AP1	50c rose carmine	.70	.25
C27	AP2	1 l deep blue	2.10	.85
		Set, never hinged	7.00	

See Nos. C45-C50.

Ruins of Odeon Theater, Sabrata AP8

1937, Mar. 15   **Photo.**

C28	AP8	50c dark violet	2.75	7.00
C29	AP8	1 l vio black	2.75	11.00
		Set, never hinged	13.50	

Opening of a coastal road to the Egyptian frontier.

Nos. C28-C29 Overprinted "XI FIERA DI TRIPOLI"

1937, Mar. 15

C30	AP8	50c dark violet	14.00	35.00
C31	AP8	1 l violet blk	14.00	35.00
		Set, never hinged	70.00	

11th Sample Fair, Tripoli.

View of Tripoli — AP9

1938, Mar. 12   *Perf. 14*

C32	AP9	50c dk olive grn	1.40	2.75
C33	AP9	1 l slate blue	1.40	5.50
		Set, never hinged	7.00	

12th Sample Fair, Tripoli.

Eagle Attacking Serpent — AP10

1938, Apr. 25   *Wmk. 140*

C34	AP10	50c olive brown	.35	1.75
C35	AP10	1 l brn violet	1.00	3.75
		Set, never hinged	3.25	

Birth bimillenary Augustus Caesar (Octavianus), first Roman emperor.

Arab and Camel AP11

Design: 50c, Fair entrance.

1939, Apr. 12   *Photo.*

C36	AP11	25c green	.70	2.10
C37	AP11	50c olive brown	.70	2.10
C38	AP11	1 l rose violet	1.00	2.75
		Nos. C36-C38 (3)	1.90	6.70
		Set, never hinged	6.00	

13th Sample Fair, Tripoli.

Plane Over Modern City AP12

Design: 1 l, 5 l+2.50 l, Plane over oasis.

1940, June 3

C39	AP12	50c brn blk	.70	.85
C40	AP12	1 l brn vio	.70	1.75
C41	AP12	2 l + 75c indigo	1.00	7.00
C42	AP12	5 l + 2.50 l copper brn	1.00	12.50
		Nos. C39-C42 (4)	4.10	25.50
		Set, never hinged	8.50	

Triennial Overseas Exposition, Naples.

Hitler, Mussolini and Inscription "Two Peoples, One War" AP13

1941, Apr. 24

C43	AP13	50c slate green	2.75	42.50
		Never hinged	7.00	

Rome-Berlin Axis.

Cyrenaica No. C9 Overprinted in Black Like No. C25

1941

C44	AP3	1 l black	12.50	70.00
		Never hinged	30.00	

Same Overprint on Tripolitania Nos. C9-C11, C13-C15

C45	AP1	60c red orange	.70	
C46	AP1	75c deep blue	.70	47.50
C47	AP1	80c dull violet	.70	100.00
C48	AP2	1.20 l dark brown	.70	140.00
C49	AP2	1.50 l orange red	.70	175.00
C50	AP2	5 l green	.70	
		Nos. C45-C50 (6)	4.20	
		Set, never hinged	10.00	

> Catalogue values for unused stamps in this section, from this point to the end of the section, are for Never Hinged items.

United Kingdom of Libya
ICY Type of Regular Issue

Perf. 14½x14

1965, Jan. 1   *Litho.*   *Unwmk.*

C51	A60	50m dp lil & gold	1.90	.90
a.		Souvenir sheet	5.00	5.00

No. C51a exists Imperf.; same value.

Hands Holding Facade of Abu Simbel — AP14

1966, Jan. 1   *Photo.*   *Perf. 11½*
Granite Paper

C52	AP14	10m bis & dk brn	.40	.25
a.		Souvenir sheet of 4	2.00	3.75
C53	AP14	15m gray grn & dk grn	.50	.25
a.		Souvenir sheet of 4	2.50	5.00
C54	AP14	40m dl sal & dk brn	1.60	.65
a.		Souvenir sheet of 4	6.50	13.00
		Nos. C52-C54 (3)	2.50	1.15

UNESCO world campaign to save historic monuments in Nubia.

Inauguration of WHO Headquarters, Geneva — AP15

Perf. 10x10½

1966, May 3   *Litho.*   *Unwmk.*

C55	AP15	20m blk, yel & bl	.25	.25
C56	AP15	50m blk, yel grn & red	.90	.65
C57	AP15	65m blk, sal & brn red	1.40	1.40
		Nos. C55-C57 (3)	2.55	2.30

Flag and Globe — AP16

1966, Oct. 1   *Photo.*   *Perf. 11½*
Granite Paper

C58	AP16	25m multicolored	.50	.40
C59	AP16	60m multicolored	1.40	1.00
C60	AP16	85m gray & multi	1.90	1.40
		Nos. C58-C60 (3)	3.80	2.80

Inauguration of Kingdom of Libya Airlines, 1st anniv.

AIR POST SPECIAL DELIVERY STAMPS

APSD1

Wmk. 140

1934, Feb. 17   *Photo.*   *Perf. 14*

CE1	APSD1	2.25 l olive blk	55.00	70.00
CE2	APSD1	4.50 l + 1 l gray blk	55.00	70.00
		Set, never hinged	280.00	

8th Sample Fair at Tripoli. The surtax was for the aid of the Fair.

SPECIAL DELIVERY STAMPS

Special Delivery Stamps of Italy Overprinted

Two types of overprint. See note preceding No. 1 for descriptions.

1915-16.   *Wmk. 140*   *Perf. 14*

E1	SD1	25c rose red, ovpt. type I	77.50	30.00
E2	SD2	30c blue & rose, ovpt type I	19.00	30.00
		Set, never hinged	217.50	

Issued: Nos. E1, E2, Nov. 1915. For surcharges see Nos. E7-E8.

"Italia" SD3

1921-23   *Engr.*   *Perf. 13½*

E3	SD3	30c blue & rose	2.10	7.00
E4	SD3	50c rose red & brn	4.25	10.00
E5	SD3	60c dk red & brn ('23)	7.00	15.00
E6	SD3	2 l dk bl & red ('23)	14.00	27.50
		Nos. E3-E6 (4)	27.35	59.50
		Set, never hinged	65.00	

30c, 2 l inscribed "EXPRES." For surcharges see Nos. E9-E12.

Nos. E1-E2 Surcharged

1922, June 1

E7	SD1	60c on 25c rose red	12.50	17.50
E8	SD2	1.60 l on 30c bl & rose	15.00	35.00
		Set, never hinged	67.50	

Nos. E5-E6 Surcharged in Blue or Red

No. E9

Nos. E10, E12

No. E11

1926-36

E9	SD3	70c on 60c	7.50	15.00
E10	SD3	2.50 l on 2 l (R)	14.00	27.50

Perf. 11

E11	SD3	1.25 l on 60c	5.50	1.75
a.		Perf. 14 ('36)	21.00	3.50
		Never hinged	52.50	
b.		Black surcharge	105,000.	18,000.
E12	SD3	2.50 l on 2 l (R)	240.00	850.00
		Nos. E9-E12 (4)	267.00	894.25
		Set, never hinged	625.00	

Issued: Nos. E9-E10, July 1926; Nos. E11-E12, 1927.

> Catalogue values for unused stamps in this section, from this point to the end of the section, are for Never Hinged items.

United Kingdom of Libya

Zuela Saracen Castle SD4

Perf. 11½

1966, Feb. 10   *Unwmk.*   *Litho.*

E13	SD4	90m car rose & lt grn	3.00	1.60

Coat of Arms of Libya and "POLIGRAFICA & CARTEVALORI — NAPLES" printed on back in yellow green.

SEMI-POSTAL SPECIAL DELIVERY STAMPS

Camel Caravan SPSD1

Wmk. 140

1927, Feb. 15   *Litho.*   *Perf. 14*

EB1	SPSD1	1.25 l + 30c pur & blk	8.50	42.50
EB2	SPSD1	2.50 l + 1 l yel & blk	8.50	42.50
		Set, never hinged	42.00	

See note after No. B10.
No. EB2 is inscribed "EXPRES."

War Memorial SPSD2

1931, Mar. 8   **Photo.**
EB3 SPSD2 1.25 l + 20c car
     rose   5.50   *27.50*
     Never hinged   14.00
     See note after No. B37.

AUTHORIZED DELIVERY STAMPS

Italy No. EY1
Overprinted in Black

1929, May 11 **Wmk. 140** *Perf. 14*
EY1 AD1 10c dull blue   30.00 *70.00*
     Never hinged   77.50
  a. Perf. 11   125.00 *275.00*
     Never hinged   300.00

Italy No. EY2
Overprinted in Black

1941, May   *Perf. 14*
EY2 AD2 10c dark brown 11.00 *47.50*
     Never hinged   27.50
     A variety of No. EY2, with larger "LIBIA" and yellow gum, was prepared in 1942, but not issued. Value 85 cents, never hinged $2.10.

AD1

1942   **Litho.**   **Wmk. 140**
EY3 AD1 10c sepia   .85
     Never hinged   2.10
     No. EY3 was not issued.

POSTAGE DUE STAMPS

Italian Postage Due
Stamps, 1870-1903
Overprinted in Black

1915, Nov. **Wmk. 140** *Perf. 14*
J1 D3 5c buff & mag   2.10 *10.00*
J2 D3 10c buff & mag   2.10 *5.50*
J3 D3 20c buff & mag   2.75 *8.50*
  a. Double overprint 500.00 *500.00*
  b. Inverted overprint 500.00
J4 D3 30c buff & mag   7.00 *10.00*
J5 D3 40c buff & mag 10.00 *12.50*
  a. "40" in black   4,500.
J6 D3 50c buff & mag   7.00 *8.50*
J7 D3 60c buff & mag 10.00 *19.00*
J8 D3 1 l blue & mag   7.00 *19.00*
  a. Double overprint 10,500. *16,000.*
J9 D3 2 l blue & mag 55.00 *110.00*
J10 D3 5 l blue & mag 77.50 *190.00*
  Nos. J1-J10 (10) 180.45 *393.00*

1926
J11 D3 60c buff & brown 175.00 *325.00*

Postage Due Stamps
of Italy, 1934,
Overprinted in Black

1934
J12 D6 5c brown   .35 *2.75*
J13 D6 10c blue   .35 *2.75*
J14 D6 20c rose red   1.40 *1.40*
J15 D6 25c green   1.40 *1.40*
J16 D6 30c red orange 1.40 *5.50*
J17 D6 40c black brn   1.40 *3.50*
J18 D6 50c violet   1.75 *.35*
J19 D6 60c black   1.75 *17.50*
J20 D7 1 l red orange 1.40 *.35*
J21 D7 2 l green   42.50 *17.50*

J22 D7 5 l violet   95.00 *37.50*
J23 D7 10 l blue   12.50 *52.50*
J24 D7 20 l carmine 12.50 *70.00*
  Nos. J12-J24 (13) 173.70 *213.00*

> In 1942 a set of 11 "Segnatasse" stamps, picturing a camel and rider and inscribed "LIBIA," was prepared but not issued. Values for set: hinged $12; never hinged $30.

> Catalogue values for unused stamps in this section, from this point to the end of the section, are for Never Hinged items.

United Kingdom of Libya

Postage Due Stamps
of Cyrenaica, 1950
Surcharged in Black

For Use in Tripolitania

1951   **Unwmk.**   *Perf. 12½*
J25 D1 1mal on 2m dk
     brown   9.00 *18.00*
J26 D1 2mal on 4m dp grn 15.00 *30.00*
J27 D1 4mal on 8m scar 25.00 *50.00*
J28 D1 10mal on 20m org
     yel   50.00 *100.00*
  a. Arabic "20" for "10"   —
J29 D1 20mal on 40m dp bl 80.00 *160.00*
  Nos. J25-J29 (5) 179.00 *358.00*

Cyrenaica Nos. J1-J7
Overprinted in Black

For Use in Cyrenaica
Overprint 13mm High

1952   **Unwmk.**   *Perf. 12½*
J30 D1 2m dark brown 10.00 *20.00*
J31 D1 4m deep green 10.00 *20.00*
J32 D1 8m scarlet   15.00 *30.00*
J33 D1 10m vermilion 20.00 *4.00*
J34 D1 20m orange yel 30.00 *60.00*
J35 D1 40m deep blue 42.50 *85.00*
J36 D1 100m dk gray 92.50 *180.00*
  Nos. J30-J36 (7) 220.00 *399.00*

D1

1952   **Litho.**   *Perf. 11½*
J37 D1 2m chocolate   1.00 *.35*
J38 D1 5m blue green 1.60 *.90*
J39 D1 10m carmine   3.00 *1.50*
J40 D1 50m violet blue 11.00 *4.00*
  Nos. J37-J40 (4) 16.60 *6.75*

Castle at
Tripoli — D2

1964, Feb. 1 **Photo.** *Perf. 14*
J41 D2 2m red brown   .25 *.25*
J42 D2 6m Prus green   .50 *.50*
J43 D2 10m rose red   1.00 *1.00*
J44 D2 50m brt blue   2.00 *2.00*
  Nos. J41-J44 (4) 3.75 *3.75*

Men in Boat, Birds,
Mosaic — D3

Ancient Mosaics: 10d, Head of Medusa. 20d, Peacock. 50d, Fish.

1976, Nov. 15 **Litho.** *Perf. 14*
J45 D3 5d bister & multi   .25 *.25*
J46 D3 10d orange & multi .25 *.25*
J47 D3 20d blue & multi   .35 *.35*
J48 D3 50d emerald & multi .80 *.80*
  Nos. J45-J48 (4)   1.65 *1.65*
     Nos. J45-J48 have multiple coat of arms printed on back in pale green beneath gum.

OFFICIAL STAMPS

> Catalogue values for unused stamps in this section are for Never Hinged items.

United Kingdom of Libya

Nos. 135-142
Overprinted in Black

1952   **Unwmk.**   *Perf. 11½*
O1 A27 2m yel brn   .90 *.60*
O2 A27 4m gray   1.50 *.90*
O3 A27 5m bl grn   7.50 *3.00*
O4 A27 8m vermilion 5.50 *2.50*
O5 A27 10m purple   7.00 *3.00*
O6 A27 12m lil rose 11.00 *6.25*
O7 A27 20m dp bl   19.00 *9.50*
O8 A27 25m chocolate 25.00 *12.50*
  Nos. O1-O8 (8) 77.40 *38.25*

PARCEL POST STAMPS

These stamps were used by affixing them to the way bill so that one half remained on it following the parcel, the other half staying on the receipt given the sender. Most used halves are right halves. Complete stamps were obtainable canceled, probably to order. Both unused and used values are for complete stamps.

Italian Parcel Post
Stamps, 1914-22,
Overprinted

1915-24 **Wmk. 140** *Perf. 13½*
Q1 PP2 5c brown   7.00 *14.00*
  a. Double overprint 375.00
Q2 PP2 10c deep blue 7.00 *14.00*
Q3 PP2 20c blk ('18)   8.50 *14.00*
Q4 PP2 25c red   8.50 *14.00*
Q5 PP2 50c orange   10.00 *14.00*
Q6 PP2 1 l violet   10.00 *21.00*
Q7 PP2 2 l green   14.00 *21.00*
Q8 PP2 3 l bister   21.00 *21.00*
Q9 PP2 4 l slate   21.00 *21.00*
Q10 PP2 10 l rose lil
     ('24)   70.00 *125.00*
Q11 PP2 12 l red brn
     ('24)   140.00 *260.00*
Q12 PP2 15 l ol grn
     ('24)   140.00 *425.00*
Q13 PP2 20 l brn vio
     ('24)   210.00 *510.00*
  Nos. Q1-Q13 (13) 667.00 *1,474.*

Halves Used

Q1   1.00
Q2   1.50
Q3   1.50
Q4   1.50
Q5   1.50
Q6   1.50
Q7   1.50
Q8   1.50
Q9   1.50
Q10   10.00
Q11   11.00
Q12   25.00
Q13   65.00

Same Overprint on Parcel Post Stamps of Italy, 1927-36

1927-38
Q14 PP3 10c dp bl ('36) 7.00 *10.00*
Q15 PP3 25c red ('36)   7.00 *10.00*
Q16 PP3 30c ultra ('29) 3.50 *7.00*
Q17 PP3 50c orange   50.00 *350.00*
  a. Overprint 8¾x2mm
     ('31)   87.50 *450.00*
Q18 PP3 60c red ('29)   3.50 *7.00*
Q19 PP3 1 l lilac ('36) 37.50 *140.00*
Q20 PP3 2 l grn ('38) 45.00 *140.00*
Q21 PP3 3 l bister   4.25 *14.00*
Q22 PP3 4 l gray   4.25 *21.00*

Q23 PP3 10 l rose lil
     ('36)   275.00 *625.00*
Q24 PP3 20 l brn vio
     ('36)   300.00 *850.00*
  Nos. Q14-Q24 (11) 737.00 *2,174.*

Halves Used

Q14   .50
Q15   .50
Q16   .50
Q17   12.50
Q17a   22.50
Q18   .50
Q19   7.50
Q20   7.50
Q21   1.50
Q22   2.50
Q23   30.00
Q24   35.00
     The overprint measures 10x1½mm on No. Q17.

Same Overprint on Italy No. Q24
1939
Q25 PP3 5c brown   *15,000.*
     Never hinged   *22,500.*
     The overprint was applied to the 5c in error. Few examples exist.

OCCUPATION STAMPS

> Catalogue values for unused stamps in this section are for Never Hinged items.

Issued under French Occupation

     Stamps of Italy and Libya were overprinted in 1943: "FEZZAN Occupation Française" and "R. F. FEZZAN" for use in this region when General Leclerc's forces 1st occupied it.

Fezzan-Ghadames

Sebha Fort — OS1

Mosque
and Fort
Turc
Murzuch
OS2

Map of Fezzan-Ghadames, Soldier and Camel — OS3

1946 **Unwmk.** **Engr.** *Perf. 13*
1N1 OS1 10c black   .35 *.35*
1N2 OS1 50c rose   .35 *.35*
1N3 OS1 1fr brown   .45 *.45*
1N4 OS1 1.50fr green   .55 *.55*
1N5 OS1 2fr ultramarine .70 *.70*
1N6 OS2 2.50fr violet   .90 *.90*
1N7 OS2 3fr rose carmine 1.20 *1.20*
1N8 OS2 5fr chocolate 1.20 *1.20*
1N9 OS2 6fr dark green 1.10 *1.10*
1N10 OS2 10fr blue   1.20 *1.20*
1N11 OS3 15fr violet   1.50 *1.50*
1N12 OS3 20fr red   1.75 *1.75*
1N13 OS3 25fr sepia   1.75 *1.75*
1N14 OS3 40fr dark green 2.25 *2.25*
1N15 OS3 50fr deep blue 2.50 *2.50*
  Nos. 1N1-1N15 (15) 17.75 *17.75*

FEZZAN

> Catalogue values for unused stamps in this section are for Never Hinged items.

Monument, Djerma Oasis — OS1

Tombs of the Beni-Khettab — OS2

Well at Gorda OS3

Col. Colonna d'Ornano and Fort at Murzuch OS4

Philippe F. M. de Hautecloque (Gen. Jacques Leclerc) — OS5

1949   Unwmk.   Engr.   Perf. 13

2N1	OS1	1fr black	1.20	1.20
2N2	OS1	2fr lil pink	1.25	1.25
2N3	OS2	4fr red brn	2.10	2.10
2N4	OS3	5fr emerald	2.10	2.10
2N5	OS3	8fr blue	2.75	2.75
2N6	OS3	10fr brown	4.50	4.50
2N7	OS3	12fr dk grn	7.00	7.00
2N8	OS4	15fr sal red	10.00	10.00
2N9	OS4	20fr brn blk	5.00	5.00
2N10	OS5	25fr dk bl	5.50	5.50
2N11	OS5	50fr cop red	10.00	10.00
		Nos. 2N1-2N11 (11)	51.40	51.40

Camel Raising OS6

Well Drilling — OS8

Ahmed Bey — OS9

1951

2N12	OS6	30c brown	1.40	1.40
2N13	OS6	1fr dp bl	1.40	1.40
2N14	OS6	2fr rose car	1.40	1.40
2N15	OS7	4fr red	2.10	2.10
2N16	OS7	5fr green	2.10	2.10
2N17	OS7	8fr dp bl	2.10	2.10

2N18	OS8	10fr sepia	5.50	5.50
2N19	OS8	12fr dp grn	6.25	6.25
2N20	OS8	15fr brt red	7.00	7.00
2N21	OS9	20fr blk brn & vio brn	7.00	7.00
2N22	OS9	25fr dk bl & bl	7.75	7.75
2N23	OS9	50fr ind & brn org	8.50	8.50
		Nos. 2N12-2N23 (12)	52.50	52.50

OCCUPATION SEMI-POSTAL STAMPS

> Catalogue values for unused stamps in this section are for Never Hinged items.

"The Unhappy Ones"
OSP1   OSP2

1950   Unwmk.   Engr.   Perf. 13

2NB1	OSP1	15fr + 5fr red brn	3.25	3.25
2NB2	OSP2	25fr + 5fr blue	3.25	3.25

The surtax was for charitable works.

OCCUPATION AIR POST STAMPS

> Catalogue values for unused stamps in this section are for Never Hinged items.

Airport in Fezzan OAP1

Plane over Fezzan — OAP2

1948   Unwmk.   Engr.   Perf. 13

2NC1	OAP1	100fr red	7.00	7.00
2NC2	OAP2	200fr indigo	10.00	10.00

Oasis OAP3

Murzuch OAP4

1951

2NC3	OAP3	100fr dark blue	9.75	9.75
2NC4	OAP4	200fr vermilion	14.00	14.00

OCCUPATION POSTAGE DUE STAMPS

> Catalogue values for unused stamps in this section are for Never Hinged items.

Oasis of Brak — D1

1950   Unwmk.   Engr.   Perf. 13

2NJ1	D1	1fr brown black	1.40	1.40
2NJ2	D1	2fr deep green	1.40	1.40
2NJ3	D1	3fr red brown	2.10	2.10
2NJ4	D1	5fr purple	2.10	2.10
2NJ5	D1	10fr red	4.25	4.25
2NJ6	D1	20fr deep blue	6.25	6.25
		Nos. 2NJ1-2NJ6 (6)	17.50	17.50

GHADAMES

> Catalogue values for unused stamps in this section are for Never Hinged items.

Cross of Agadem — OS1

1949   Unwmk.   Engr.   Perf. 13

3N1	OS1	4fr sep & red brn	1.75	1.75
3N2	OS1	5fr pck bl & dk grn	1.75	1.75
3N3	OS1	8fr sep & org brn	4.50	4.50
3N4	OS1	10fr blk & dk ultra	4.50	4.50
3N5	OS1	12fr vio & red vio	12.00	12.00
3N6	OS1	15fr brn & red brn	8.50	8.50
3N7	OS1	20fr sep & emer	10.00	10.00
3N8	OS1	25fr sepia & blue	12.50	12.50
		Nos. 3N1-3N8 (8)	55.50	55.50

OCCUPATION AIR POST STAMPS

> Catalogue values for unused stamps in this section are for Never Hinged items.

Cross of Agadem — OAP1

1949   Unwmk.   Engr.   Perf. 13

3NC1	OAP1	50fr pur & rose	16.00	16.00
3NC2	OAP1	100fr sep & pur brn	19.00	19.00

LIECHTENSTEIN

'lik-tən-‚shtin

LOCATION — Central Europe southeast of Lake Constance, between Austria and Switzerland
GOVT. — Principality
AREA — 61.8 sq. mi.
POP. — 31,320 (1997)
CAPITAL — Vaduz

The Principality of Liechtenstein is a sovereign state consisting of the two counties of Schellenberg and Vaduz. Since 1921 the post office has been administered by Switzerland.

100 Heller = 1 Krone
100 Rappen = 1 Franc (1921)

> **Catalogue values for unused stamps in this country are for Never Hinged items, beginning with Scott 368 in the regular postage section, Scott B22 in the semi-postal section, Scott C24 in the air post section, and Scott O30 in the offical section.**

Watermarks

Greek Cross — Wmk. 183

Crown and Initials — Wmk. 296

Austrian Administration of the Post Office

Prince Johann II — A1

Perf. 12½x13

1912, Feb. 1   Unwmk.   Typo.
Thick Chalky Paper

1	A1	5h yellow green	42.50	17.50
2	A1	10h rose	85.00	17.50
3	A1	25h dark blue	85.00	55.00
		Nos. 1-3 (3)	212.50	90.00
		Set, never hinged	900.00	

1915   Thin Unsurfaced Paper

1a	A1	5h yellow green	14.00	21.00
2a	A1	10h rose	85.00	32.50
3a	A1	25h dark blue	600.00	200.00
b.		25h ultramarine	350.00	425.00
		Never hinged	1,550.	
		#1a-3a, never hinged	2,500.	

Coat of Arms — A2   Prince Johann II — A3

1917-18

4	A2	3h violet	2.00	2.00
5	A2	5h yellow green	2.00	2.00
6	A3	10h claret	2.00	2.00
7	A3	15h dull red	2.00	2.00
8	A3	20h dark green	2.00	2.00
9	A3	25h deep blue	2.00	2.00
		Nos. 4-9 (6)	12.00	12.00
		Set, never hinged	51.00	

Exist imperf. Value set unused original gum, $525; never hinged, $1,150.
For surcharges see Nos. 11-16.

Prince Johann II — A4

1918, Nov. 12
Dates In Upper Corners

10	A4	20h dark green	.70	2.75
		Never hinged	5.50	

Accession of Prince Johann II, 60th anniv.
Exists imperf. Value, unused original gum, $225; never hinged, $560.

National Administration of the Post Office
Stamps of 1917-18 Overprinted or Surcharged

a   b

c

1920

11	A2(a)	5h yellow green	2.75	8.75
a.		Inverted overprint	70.00	175.00
		Never hinged	140.00	
b.		Double overprint	14.00	85.00
		Never hinged	35.00	
12	A3(a)	10h claret	2.75	9.50
a.		Inverted overprint	70.00	175.00
		Never hinged	140.00	
b.		Double overprint	14.00	105.00
		Never hinged	35.00	
c.		Overprint type "c"	14.00	105.00
		Never hinged	27.50	
13	A3(a)	25h deep blue	2.75	9.50
a.		Inverted overprint	70.00	175.00
		Never hinged	140.00	
b.		Double overprint	14.00	105.00
		Never hinged	27.50	
14	A2(b)	40h on 3h violet	2.75	9.50
a.		Inverted surcharge	70.00	175.00
		Never hinged	140.00	
15	A3(c)	1k on 15h dull red	2.75	9.50
a.		Inverted surcharge	70.00	175.00
		Never hinged	140.00	
b.		Overprint type "a"	87.50	350.00
		Never hinged	315.00	
16	A3(c)	2½k on 20h dk grn	2.75	9.50
a.		Inverted surcharge	70.00	175.00
		Never hinged	140.00	
		Nos. 11-16 (6)	16.50	56.25
		Set, never hinged	71.00	

Coat of Arms A5   Chapel of St. Mamertus A6

Coat of Arms with Supporters A15

Designs: 40h, Gutenberg Castle. 50h, Courtyard, Vaduz Castle. 60h, Red Tower, Vaduz. 80h, Old Roman Tower, Schaan. 1k, Castle at Vaduz. 2k, View of Bendern. 5k, Prince Johann I. 7½k, Prince Johann II.

		1920	**Engr.**	**Imperf.**
18	A5	5h olive bister	.35	5.75
19	A5	10h deep orange	.35	5.75
20	A5	15h dark blue	.35	5.75
21	A5	20h deep brown	.35	5.75
22	A5	25h dark green	.35	5.75
23	A5	30h gray black	.35	5.75
24	A5	40h dark red	.35	5.75
25	A6	1k blue	.35	5.75

		Perf. 12½		
32	A5	5h olive bister	.35	.70
33	A5	10h deep orange	.35	.70
34	A5	15h deep blue	.35	.70
35	A5	20h red brown	.35	.70
36	A6	25h olive green	.35	.70
37	A6	30h dark gray	.35	.70
38	A6	40h claret	.35	.70
39	A6	50h yellow green	.35	.70
40	A6	60h red brown	.35	.70
41	A6	80h rose	.35	.70
42	A6	1k dull violet	.70	1.00
43	A6	2k light blue	.70	1.25
44	A6	5k black	.70	1.50
45	A6	7½k slate	.70	1.75
46	A15	10k ocher	.70	3.00
		Nos. 18-46 (23)	9.80	61.50
		Set, never hinged	41.00	

No. 25 perf. 12½ was not officially issued. It is known mint, used and on cover.
Used values for Nos. 18-46 are for canceled to order stamps. Value with postal cancels approximately $95.
Many denominations of Nos. 32-46 are found imperforate, imperforate vertically and imperforate horizontally.
For surcharges see Nos. 51-52.

Madonna and Child — A16

1920, Oct. 5

47	A16	50h olive green	1.00	2.10
48	A16	80h brown red	1.00	2.10
49	A16	2k dark blue	1.00	2.75
		Nos. 47-49 (3)	3.00	6.95
		Set, never hinged	10.50	

80th birthday of Prince Johann II.

Imperf., Singles

47a	A16	50h	7.00	1,400.
48a	A16	80h	7.00	1,400.
49a	A16	2k	7.00	1,400.
		Set, never hinged	63.00	

On 1/31/21 the Swiss took over the Post Office administration. Previous issues were demonetized and remainders of Nos. 4-49 were sold.

Swiss Administration of the Post Office
No. 19 Surcharged

No. 51   No. 52

1921   Unwmk.   Engr.   Imperf.

51	A5	2rp on 10h dp org	1.40	50.00
		Never hinged	7.00	
a.		Double surcharge	105.00	140.00
		Never hinged	140.00	

---

b.		Inverted surcharge	105.00	160.00
		Never hinged	140.00	
c.		Double surch., one inverted	105.00	175.00
		Never hinged	140.00	
52	A5	2rp on 10h dp org	.70	50.00
		Never hinged	5.50	
		First day cover (2/27/21)		875.00
a.		Double surcharge	72.50	160.00
		Never hinged	105.00	
b.		Inverted surcharge	72.50	160.00
		Never hinged	105.00	
c.		Double surch., one inverted	87.50	190.00
		Never hinged	140.00	

Arms with Supporters A19   Chapel of St. Mamertus A20

View of Vaduz A21

Designs: 25rp, Castle at Vaduz. 30rp, View of Bendern. 35rp, Prince Johann II. 40rp, Old Roman Tower at Schaan. 50rp, Gutenberg Castle. 80rp, Red Tower at Vaduz.

1921   Perf. 12½, 9½ (2rp, 10rp, 15rp)
Surface Tinted Paper (#54-61)

54	A19	2rp lemon	1.40	14.00
55	A19	2½rp black	2.10	17.50
a.		Perf. 9½	1.40	70.00
		Never hinged	3.50	
56	A19	3rp orange	2.10	17.50
a.		Perf. 9½	140.00	5,000.
		Never hinged	425.00	
57	A19	5rp olive green	14.00	2.10
a.		Perf. 9½	70.00	27.50
		Never hinged	225.00	
58	A19	7½rp dark blue	7.00	42.50
a.		Perf. 9½	275.00	1,050.
		Never hinged	675.00	
59	A19	10rp yellow green	27.50	17.50
a.		Perf. 12½	27.50	14.00
		Never hinged	140.00	
60	A19	13rp brown	10.50	90.00
a.		Perf. 9½	100.00	2,450.
		Never hinged	250.00	
b.		Perf. 12½x9½	210.00	—
		Never hinged	425.00	
61	A19	15rp dark violet	25.00	70.00
a.		Perf. 12½	27.50	27.50
		Never hinged	50.00	
62	A20	20rp dull vio & blk	70.00	2.10
63	A20	25rp rose red & blk	3.50	5.00
64	A20	30rp dp grn & blk	85.00	21.00
65	A20	35rp brn & blk, straw	7.00	17.50
66	A20	40rp dk blue & blk	10.50	17.50
67	A20	50rp dk grn & blk	17.50	10.50
68	A20	80rp gray & blk	32.00	85.00
69	A21	1fr dp claret & blk	55.00	55.00
		Nos. 54-69 (16)	370.10	474.20
		Set, never hinged	1,039.	

Nos. 54-69 exist imperforate; Nos. 54-61, partly perforated. See Nos. 73, 81. For surcharges see Nos. 70-71.

Nos. 58, 60a Surcharged in Red

1924   Perf. 12½, 9½

70	A19	5rp on 7½rp	1.40	3.50
		Never hinged	4.25	
a.		Perf. 9½	19.00	17.50
		Never hinged	50.00	
71	A19	10rp on 13rp	1.75	3.50
		Never hinged	5.25	
a.		Perf. 12½	20.00	52.50
		Never hinged	60.00	

Type of 1921
Granite Paper

1924   Wmk. 183   Perf. 11½

73	A19	10rp green	21.00	3.50
		Never hinged	85.00	

Peasant
A28

Government Palace
and Church at Vaduz
A30

10rp, 20rp, Courtyard, Vaduz Castle.

1924-28 Typo. Perf. 11½
74	A28	2½rp ol grn & red vio ('28)	1.40	5.50
75	A28	5rp brown & blue	2.75	.75
76	A28	7½rp bl grn & brn ('28)	2.10	5.50
77	A28	15rp red brn & bl grn ('28)	10.50	35.00

Engr.
78	A28	10rp yellow grn	11.25	.70
79	A28	20rp deep red	42.50	.70
80	A30	1½fr blue	85.00	110.00
	Nos. 74-80 (7)		155.50	158.15
	Set, never hinged		503.00	

Bendern Type of 1921

1925
81	A20	30rp blue & blk	17.50	3.50
	Never hinged		55.00	

Prince Johann
II — A31

Prince
Johann II
as Boy
and Man
A32

1928, Nov. 12 Typo. Wmk. 183
82	A31	10rp lt brn & ol grn	7.00	7.00
83	A31	20rp org red & ol grn	10.50	14.00
84	A31	30rp sl bl & ol grn	35.00	25.00
85	A31	60rp red vio & ol grn	70.00	70.00

Engr.
Unwmk.
86	A32	1.20fr ultra	50.00	87.50
87	A32	1.50fr black brown	87.50	210.00
88	A32	2fr deep car	87.50	210.00
89	A32	5fr dark green	87.50	245.00
	Nos. 82-89 (8)		435.00	868.50
	Set, never hinged		1,040.	

70th year of the reign of Prince Johann II.

Prince Francis I,
as a
Child — A33

Prince Francis I
as a
Man — A34

Princess
Elsa — A35

Prince Francis
and Princess
Elsa — A36

1929, Dec. 2 Photo.
90	A33	10rp olive green	.55	4.25
91	A34	20rp carmine	.85	7.00
92	A35	30rp ultra	1.40	17.50
93	A36	70rp brown	25.00	110.00
	Nos. 90-93 (4)		27.80	138.75
	Set, never hinged		77.00	

Accession of Prince Francis I, Feb. 11, 1929.

Grape Girl — A37

Chamois
Hunter — A38

Mountain
Cattle — A39

Courtyard, Vaduz
Castle — A40

Mt.
Naafkopf — A41

Chapel at
Steg — A42

Rofenberg
Chapel — A43

Chapel of St.
Mamertus — A44

Alpine Hotel,
Malbun — A45

Gutenberg
Castle — A46

Schellenberg
Monastery — A47

Castle at
Vaduz — A48

Mountain
Cottage — A49

Prince Francis
and Princess
Elsa — A50

1930 Perf. 10½, 11½, 11½x10½
94	A37	3rp brown lake	1.10	2.80
95	A38	5rp deep green	2.80	7.00
96	A39	10rp dark violet	2.50	7.00
a.		Perf. 11½x10½	11.00	120.00
		Never hinged	28.00	
97	A40	20rp dp rose red	42.50	7.00
98	A41	25rp black	8.50	45.00
a.		Perf. 11½	105.00	350.00
		Never hinged	350.00	
99	A42	30rp dp ultra	8.50	10.50
a.		Perf. 11½x10½	1,050.	2,500.
		Never hinged	2,175.	
		Never hinged	27.50	
100	A43	35rp dark green	11.00	21.00
a.		Perf. 11½	8,750.	14,000.
		Never hinged	13,500.	
101	A44	40rp lt brown	11.00	11.00
102	A45	50rp black brown	105.00	21.00
a.		Perf. 11½	165.00	245.00
		Never hinged	600.00	
103	A46	60rp olive blk	105.00	42.50
104	A47	90rp violet brn	105.00	350.00
105	A48	1.20fr olive brn	125.00	375.00
a.		Perf. 11½x10½	8,750.	14,000.
		Never hinged	13,500.	
106	A49	1.50fr black violet	70.00	77.50
107	A50	2fr gray grn & red brn	85.00	140.00
a.		Perf. 11½x10½	3,850.	7,750.
		Never hinged	6,750.	
	Nos. 94-107 (14)		681.90	1,116.
	Set, never hinged		1,600.	

For overprints see Nos. O1-O8.

Mt. Naafkopf
A51

Gutenberg
Castle
A52

Vaduz Castle — A53

1933, Jan. 23 Perf. 14½
108	A51	25rp red orange	200.00	87.50
109	A52	90rp dark green	10.50	105.00
110	A53	1.20fr red brown	85.00	300.00
	Nos. 108-110 (3)		295.50	492.50
	Set, never hinged		840.00	

For overprints see Nos. O9-O10.

Prince Francis I
A54

A55

Prince Francis I

1933, Aug. 28 Perf. 11
111	A54	10rp purple	21.00	42.50
112	A54	20rp brown car-mine	21.00	42.50
113	A54	30rp dark blue	21.00	42.50
	Nos. 111-113 (3)		63.00	127.50
	Set, never hinged		180.00	

80th birthday of Prince Francis I.

1933, Dec. 15 Engr. Perf. 12½
114	A55	3fr violet blue	125.00	250.00
	Never hinged		250.00	

See No. 152.

Agricultural Exhibition Issue
Souvenir Sheet

Arms of Liechtenstein — A56

1934, Sept. 29   *Perf. 12*
Granite Paper

115	A56 5fr brown	1,400.	2,500.
	Never hinged	2,250.	
	Single stamp	1,000.	1,750.
	Never hinged	1,400.	

See No. 131.

 Coat of Arms A57

 "Three Sisters" (Landmark) A58

 Church of Schaan A59

Bendern A60

 Rathaus, Vaduz — A61

 Samina Valley — A62

 Samina Valley in Winter A63

 Ruin at Schellenberg — A64

 Government Palace — A65

 Vaduz Castle A66

 Gutenberg Castle A68

 Alpine Hut — A69

 Princess Elsa — A70

 Coat of Arms — A71

60rp, Vaduz castle, diff. 1.50fr, Valuna.

1934-35		**Photo.**		**Perf. 11½**
116	A57	3rp copper red	.35	.70
117	A58	5rp emerald	5.50	2.10
118	A59	10rp deep violet	2.75	1.40
119	A60	15rp red org	.35	1.40
120	A61	20rp red	.70	1.40
121	A62	25rp brown	28.00	65.00
122	A63	30rp dk blue	5.50	2.10
123	A64	35rp gray grn	2.75	8.50
124	A65	40rp brown	1.75	7.00
125	A66	50rp lt brown	25.00	21.00
126	A66	60rp claret	2.10	9.00
127	A68	90rp deep green	8.50	32.00
128	A69	1.20fr deep blue	3.50	32.00
129	A69	1.50fr brn car	4.25	35.00
		Nos. 116-129 (14)	91.00	218.60
		Set, never hinged	275.00	

Engr.
Perf. 12½

130	A70	2fr henna brn ('35)	85.00	250.00
		Never hinged	140.00	
131	A71	5fr dk vio ('35)	425.00	1,050.
		Never hinged	700.00	

No. 131 has the same design as the 5fr in the souvenir sheet, No. 115. See No. 226, B14. For overprints see Nos. O11-O20.

 Bridge at Malbun A72

Labor: 20rp, Constructing Road to Triesenberg. 30rp, Binnen Canal. 50rp, Bridge near Planken.

1937, June 30				**Photo.**
132	A72	10rp brt violet	1.75	2.10
133	A72	20rp red	1.75	2.75
134	A72	30rp brt blue	1.75	3.50
135	A72	50rp yellow brown	1.75	4.25
		Nos. 132-135 (4)	7.00	12.60
		Set, never hinged	21.00	

 Ruin at Schalun — A76

 Peasant in Rhine Valley A77

 Ruin at Schellenberg — A78

 Knight and Gutenberg Castle A79

 Baron von Brandis and Vaduz Castle A80

Designs: 5rp, Chapel at Masescha. 10rp, Knight and Vaduz Castle. 15rp, Upper Valüna Valley. 20rp, Wooden Bridge over Rhine, Bendern. 25rp, Chapel at Steg. 90rp, "The Three Sisters". 1fr, Frontier stone. 1.20fr, Gutenberg Castle and Harpist. 1.50fr, Alpine View of Lawena and Schwartzhorn.

1937-38

136	A76	3rp yellow brown	.35	.70
		Pale Buff Shading		
137	A76	5rp emerald	.35	.35
138	A76	10rp violet	.35	.35
139	A76	15rp dk slate grn	.35	.70
140	A76	20rp brn org	.35	.70
141	A76	25rp chestnut	.70	3.50
142	A77	30rp blue & gray	3.50	1.40
144	A78	40rp dark green	2.10	2.75
145	A79	50rp dark brown	1.40	7.00
146	A80	60rp dp claret ('38)	2.75	3.50
147	A80	90rp gray vio ('38)	7.00	42.50
148	A80	1fr red brown	2.10	17.50
149	A80	1.20fr dp brn ('38)	7.00	32.00
150	A80	1.50fr slate bl ('38)	4.25	32.50
		Nos. 136-150 (14)	32.55	145.45
		Set, never hinged	97.00	

For overprints see Nos. O21-O29.

Souvenir Sheet

FÜRSTENTUM LIECHTENSTEIN

geb. Vaduz, 17. März 1839.
gest. München, 25. November 1901.

DRITTE LIECHTENSTEINISCHE BRIEFMARKEN-AUSSTELLUNG
VADUZ, 30. JULI BIS 8. AUGUST 1938

Josef Rheinberger — A91

1938, July 30   **Engr.**   *Perf. 12*

151		Sheet of 4	27.50	27.50
		Never hinged	70.00	
a.		A91 50rp slate gray	3.50	5.25
		Never hinged	7.00	

Third Philatelic Exhibition of Liechtenstein. Sheet size: 99¾x135mm. See No. 153.

Francis Type of 1933
Thick Wove Paper

1938, Aug. 15   *Perf. 12½*

152	A55	3fr black, *buff*	10.50	100.00
		Never hinged	21.00	

Issued in memory of Prince Francis I, who died July 25, 1938. Sheets of 20.

 Josef Gabriel Rheinberger (1839-1901), German Composer and Organist — A92

1939, Mar. 31

153	A92	50rp slate green	1.10	6.25
		Never hinged	2.40	

Issued in sheets of 20. See No. 151.

 Scene of Homage, 1718 — A93

1939, May 29

154	A93	20rp brown lake	1.40	2.75
155	A93	30rp slate blue	1.40	2.75
156	A93	50rp gray green	1.40	2.75
		Nos. 154-156 (3)	4.20	8.25
		Set, never hinged	14.00	

Honoring Prince Franz Joseph II. Sheets of 20.

 Cantonal Coats of Arms — A94

 Prince Franz Joseph II — A96

Design: 3fr, Arms of Principality.

1939

157	A94	2fr dk green, *buff*	7.00	42.50
158	A94	3fr indigo, *buff*	4.50	42.50
159	A96	5fr brown, *buff*	14.00	27.50
a.		Sheet of 4	90.00	140.00
		Never hinged	175.00	
		Nos. 157-159 (3)	25.50	112.50
		Set, never hinged	63.00	

2fr, 3fr issued in sheets of 12; 5fr in sheets of 4.

 Prince Johann as a Child A100

Memorial
Tablet
A101

Prince Johann
II — A102

30rp, Prince Johann and Tower at Vaduz.
50rp, Prince Johann and Gutenberg Castle.
1fr, Prince Johann in 1920 and Vaduz Castle.

1940   **Photo.**   **Perf. 11½.**

160	A100	20rp henna brown	.70	2.75
161	A100	30rp indigo	.70	4.25
162	A100	50rp dk slate grn	1.40	10.50
163	A100	1fr brown vio	10.50	70.00
164	A101	1.50fr violet blk	14.00	62.50
165	A102	3fr brown	5.00	21.00
	Nos. 160-165 (6)		32.30	171.00
	Set, never hinged		66.00	

Birth centenary of Prince Johann II.
Nos. 160-164 issued in sheets of 25; No.
165 in sheets of 12.
Issue dates: 3fr, Oct. 5; others Aug. 10.

Gathering
Corn
A103

Wine
Press
A104

Sharpening Scythe — A105

Milkmaid
and Cow
A106

Native
Costume
A107

1941, Apr. 7

166	A103	10rp dull red brown	.75	.45
167	A104	20rp lake	.75	1.10
168	A105	30rp royal blue	.75	2.50
169	A106	50rp myrtle green	2.40	14.00
170	A107	90rp deep claret	2.40	14.00
	Nos. 166-170 (5)		7.05	32.05
	Set, never hinged		14.00	

Madonna and
Child — A108

1941, July 7   **Engr.**

171	A108	10fr brown car	42.50	97.50
	Never hinged		80.00	

Issued in sheets of 4.

Johann Adam
Andreas — A109

Designs: 30rp, Wenzel. 100rp, Anton
Florian. 150rp, Joseph Adam.

1941, Dec. 18   **Photo.**

172	A109	20rp brown car	.50	1.25
173	A109	30rp royal blue	.70	2.50
174	A109	100rp violet blk	1.90	13.00
175	A109	150rp slate green	1.90	13.00
	Nos. 172-175 (4)		5.00	29.75
	Set, never hinged		11.00	

Saint
Lucius
A113

Designs: 30rp, Reconstruction of Vaduz
Castle. 50rp, Signing the Treaty of May 3,
1342. 1fr, Battle of Gutenberg. 2fr, Scene of
Homage, 1718.

1942, Apr. 22   **Engr.**   **Perf. 11½**

176	A113	20rp brn org, *buff*	1.40	.95
177	A113	30rp steel bl, *buff*	1.40	1.40
178	A113	50rp dk grn, *buff*	1.90	5.50
179	A113	1fr dull brn, *buff*	2.50	13.50
180	A113	2fr vio blk, *buff*	2.75	14.00
	Nos. 176-180 (5)		9.95	35.35
	Set, never hinged		20.00	

600th anniversary of the separation of
Liechtenstein from the House of Monfort.

Johann
Karl — A118

30rp, Franz Joseph I. 1fr, Alois I. 1.50fr,
Johann I.

1942, Oct. 5   **Photo.**

181	A118	20rp rose	.50	1.25
182	A118	30rp brt blue	.50	3.00
183	A118	1fr rose lilac	1.75	16.00
184	A118	1.50fr deep brown	2.00	16.00
	Nos. 181-184 (4)		4.75	36.25
	Set, never hinged		11.00	

Prince Franz
Joseph II — A122   Countess
Georgina von
Wilczek — A123

Prince and Princess — A124

1943, Mar. 5

185	A122	10rp dp rose violet	.45	1.10
186	A123	20rp henna brown	.45	1.10
187	A124	30rp slate blue	.45	1.10
	Nos. 185-187 (3)		1.35	3.30
	Set, never hinged		3.25	

Marriage of Prince Franz Joseph II and
Countess Georgina von Wilczek.

Prince Johann
II — A126

Princes: 20rp, Alois II. 100rp, Franz Joseph
I. 150rp, Franz Joseph II.

Perf. 11½

1943, July 5   **Unwmk.**   **Photo.**

188	A126	20rp copper brown	.35	.60
189	A126	30rp deep ultra	.60	1.10
190	A126	100rp olive gray	1.10	7.00
191	A126	150rp slate green	1.25	7.00
	Nos. 188-191 (4)		3.30	15.70
	Set, never hinged		7.25	

Sheets of 20.

Terrain before
Reclaiming
A129

30rp, Draining the Canal. 50rp, Plowing
Reclaimed Land. 2fr, Harvesting Crops.

1943, Sept. 6

192	A129	10rp violet black	.30	.55
193	A129	30rp deep blue	.85	2.00
194	A129	50rp slate green	1.10	8.50
195	A129	2fr olive brown	2.00	12.50
	Nos. 192-195 (4)		4.25	23.55
	Set, never hinged		8.75	

Vaduz
A133   Gutenberg
A134

1943, Dec. 27

196	A133	10rp dark gray	.45	.45
197	A134	20rp chestnut brown	.50	1.00
	Set, never hinged		2.00	

Planken — A135

Designs: 10rp, Triesen. 15rp, Ruggell. 20rp,
Vaduz. 25rp, Triesenberg. 30rp, Schaan. 40rp,
Balzers. 50rp, Mauren. 60rp, Schellenberg.
90rp, Eschen. 1fr, Vaduz Castle. 120rp,
Valuna Valley. 150rp, Lawena.

1944-45

198	A135	3rp dk brn & buff	.25	.25
199	A136	5rp sl grn & buff	.25	.25
200	A136	10rp gray & buff	.25	.25
201	A136	15rp bl gray & buff	.30	.60
202	A136	20rp org red & buff	.30	.40
203	A136	25rp dk rose vio & buff	.30	.80
204	A136	30rp blue & buff	.35	.40
205	A136	40rp brown & buff	.55	1.00
206	A136	50rp bluish blk & pale gray	.70	1.60
207	A136	60rp green & buff	3.75	5.00
208	A136	90rp ol grn & buff	3.75	5.00
209	A136	1fr dp cl & buff	2.25	5.00

210	A136	120rp red brown	2.25	5.75
211	A136	150rp royal blue	2.25	5.75
	Nos. 198-211 (14)		17.50	32.05
	Set, never hinged		37.50	

Issue years: 10rp, 15rp, 40rp-1fr, 1945;
others, 1944. See No. 239. For surcharge and
overprints see No. 236, O30-O36.

Crown and
Rose — A149

1945, Apr. 9

212	A149	20rp multicolored	.85	.55
213	A149	30rp multicolored	.85	1.40
214	A149	1fr multicolored	1.00	4.50
	Nos. 212-214 (3)		2.70	6.45
	Set, never hinged		4.25	

Birth of Prince Johann Adam Pius, Feb. 14,
1945. Sheets of 20.

Prince Franz
Joseph II — A150

Arms of
Liechtenstein
and Vaduz
Castle — A152

Design: 3fr, Princess Georgina.

1944-45   **Photo.**

215	A150	2fr brown, *buff*	6.00	16.00
216	A150	3fr dark green	3.50	11.50

Engr.

217	A152	5fr bl gray, *cr* ('45)	10.50	32.50
	Nos. 215-217 (3)		20.00	60.00
	Set, never hinged		40.00	

Nos. 215-217 were issued in sheets of 8.
See Nos. 222, 259-260.

Saint Lucius — A153

1946, Mar. 14   **Unwmk.**   **Perf. 11½**

218	A153	10fr gray blk, *cr*	22.50	30.00
	Never hinged		42.50	
	Sheet of 4		160.00	200.00
	Never hinged		190.00	

Issued in sheets measuring 105x130mm.

Red
Deer — A154

Varying
Hare — A155

Capercaillie
A156

1946, Dec. 10   **Photo.**

219	A154	20rp henna brown	1.50	2.50
220	A155	30rp grnsh blue	1.50	3.25
221	A156	150rp olive brown	3.00	11.50
		Nos. 219-221 (3)	6.00	17.25
		Set, never hinged	12.00	

Arms Type of 1945

1947, Mar. 20   **Engr.**

222	A152	5fr henna brn, cream	12.50	37.50
		Never hinged	25.00	

Issued in sheets of 8.

Chamois — A157

Alpine
Marmot — A158

Golden
Eagle — A159

1947, Oct. 15   **Photo.**   **Unwmk.**

223	A157	20rp henna brown	1.60	1.90
224	A158	30rp grnsh blue	2.25	3.25
225	A159	150rp dark brown	4.25	19.00
		Nos. 223-225 (3)	8.10	24.15
		Set, never hinged	16.00	

Elsa Type of 1935

1947, Dec. 10   **Engr.**   **Perf. 14½**

226	A70	2fr black, yelsh	2.25	12.50
		Never hinged	4.25	

Issued in memory of Princess Elsa, who died Sept. 28, 1947. Sheets of 20.

Portrait of
Ginevra dei
Benci by
Leonardo da
Vinci — A160

Designs: 20rp, Girl, Rubens. 30rp, Self-portrait, Rembrandt. 40rp, Canon, Massys. 50rp, Madonna, Memling. 60rp, French Painter, 1456, Fouquet. 80rp, Lute Player, Gentileschi. 90rp, Man, Strigel. 120rp, Man, Raphael.

1949, Mar. 15   **Photo.**   **Perf. 11½**

227	A160	10rp dark green	.25	.35
228	A160	20rp henna brown	.70	.80
229	A160	30rp sepia	1.40	.90
230	A160	40rp blue	3.50	.90
231	A160	50rp violet	2.75	6.75
232	A160	60rp grnsh gray	6.25	6.25
233	A160	80rp brown orange	1.40	4.25
234	A160	90rp olive bister	6.25	5.75
235	A160	120rp claret	1.40	5.25
		Nos. 227-235 (9)	23.90	31.20
		Set, never hinged	47.50	

Issued in sheets of 12.
See No. 238.

**No. 198 Surcharged with New Value
and Bars in Dark Brown**

1949, Apr. 14

236	A135	5rp on 3rp dk brn & buff	.30	.45
		Never hinged	.65	

Map, Post
Horn and
Crown
A161

1949, May 23

237	A161	40rp blue & indigo	2.00	4.75
		Never hinged	3.75	

75th anniversary of the UPU.
For surcharge see No. 246.

**Portrait Type of 1949
Souvenir Sheet**

1949, Aug. 6   **Unwmk.**   **Imperf.**

238		Sheet of 3	65.00	110.00
		Never hinged	110.00	
a.	A160	10rp dull green	5.25	11.00
b.	A160	20rp lilac rose	32.50	65.00
c.	A160	40rp blue	5.25	11.00

5th Philatelic Exhibition.
Sheet size: 121½x69½mm. Sold for 3fr.

Scenic Type of 1944

1949, Dec. 1   **Perf. 11½**

239	A136	5rp dk brown & buff	12.00	1.00
		Never hinged	26.00	

Rossauer
Castle,
Vienna
A163

Church at
Bendern
A164

Prince Johann
Adam
Andreas — A165

1949, Nov. 15   **Engr.**   **Perf. 14½**

240	A163	20rp dark violet	1.00	2.00
241	A164	40rp blue	3.50	6.25
242	A165	150rp brown red	5.50	9.25
		Nos. 240-242 (3)	10.00	17.50
		Set, never hinged	20.00	

250th anniv. of the purchase of the former dukedom of Schellenberg. Sheets of 20.
For surcharge see No. 265.

Roe
Deer — A166

Black
Grouse — A167

Badger — A168

1950, Mar. 7   **Photo.**   **Perf. 11½**

243	A166	20rp red brown	4.75	4.50
244	A167	30rp Prus green	4.75	6.50
245	A168	80rp dark brown	19.00	45.00
		Nos. 243-245 (3)	28.50	56.00
		Set, never hinged	62.50	

Issued in sheets of 20.

**No. 237 Surcharged with New Value
and Bars Obliterating
Commemorative Inscriptions**

1950, Nov. 7

246	A161	1fr on 40rp bl & ind	14.00	45.00

Boy Cutting
Bread — A169

Designs: 10rp, Laborer. 15rp, Cutting hay. 20rp, Harvesting corn. 25rp, Load of hay. 30rp, Wine grower. 40rp, Farmer and scythe. 50rp, Cattle raising. 60rp, Plowing. 80rp, Woman with potatoes. 90rp, Potato cultivation. 1fr, Tractor with potatoes.

       Perf. 11½

1951, May 3   **Unwmk.**   **Photo.**

247	A169	5rp claret	.25	.25
248	A169	10rp green	.25	.45
249	A169	15rp yellow brown	2.50	5.00
250	A169	20rp olive brown	.50	.65
251	A169	25rp rose brown	2.50	5.00
252	A169	30rp grnsh gray	1.25	.55
253	A169	40rp deep blue	4.00	6.50
254	A169	50rp violet brown	3.75	3.25
255	A169	60rp brown	3.75	3.00
256	A169	80rp henna brown	4.00	6.75
257	A169	90rp olive green	7.50	6.75
258	A169	1fr indigo	30.00	6.75
		Nos. 247-258 (12)	60.25	44.90
		Set, never hinged	125.00	

Types of 1944, Redrawn
       Perf. 12½x12

1951, Nov. 20   **Wmk. 296**

259	A150	2fr dark blue	9.00	37.50
a.		Perf. 14½	450.00	160.00
260	A150	3fr dk red brown	80.00	110.00
a.		Perf. 14½	50.00	210.00
		Set, never hinged	175.00	
		Set, perf. 14½, never hinged	900.00	

Issued in sheets of 20.

Portrait,
Savolodo — A170

Madonna,
Botticelli — A171

Design: 40rp St. John, Del Sarto.

       Perf. 11½

1952, May 27   **Unwmk.**   **Photo.**

261	A170	20rp violet brown	19.00	2.75
262	A171	30rp brown olive	12.50	7.00
263	A170	40rp violet blue	6.25	5.75
		Nos. 261-263 (3)	37.75	15.50
		Set, never hinged	75.00	

Issued in sheets of 12.

Vaduz
Castle — A172

Wmk. 296

1952, Sept. 25   **Engr.**   **Perf. 14½**

264	A172	5fr deep green	92.50	150.00
		Never hinged	160.00	

Issued in sheets of 9.

**No. 241 Surcharged with New Value
and Wavy Lines in Red**

1952, Sept. 25   **Unwmk.**

265	A164	1.20fr on 40rp blue	12.50	50.00
		Never hinged	24.00	

Portrait of a Young
Man — A173

St. Nicholas by
Zeitblom — A174

Designs: 30rp, St. Christopher by Cranach. 40rp, Leonhard, Duke of Hag, by Kulmbach.

       Perf. 11½

1953, Feb. 5   **Unwmk.**   **Photo.**

266	A173	10rp dk olive green	.50	.90
267	A174	20rp olive brown	8.25	2.40
268	A174	30rp violet brown	16.00	7.75
269	A173	40rp slate blue	18.00	45.00
		Nos. 266-269 (4)	42.75	56.05
		Set, never hinged	80.00	

Issued in sheets of 12.

Lord Baden-
Powell
A175

1953, Aug. 4   **Engr.**   **Perf. 13x13½**

270	A175	10rp deep green	.70	.90
271	A175	20rp dark brown	6.75	2.25
272	A175	25rp red	5.75	18.00
273	A175	40rp deep blue	5.50	6.00
		Nos. 270-273 (4)	18.70	27.15
		Set, never hinged	35.00	

Intl. Scout Conf. Sheets of 20.

Alemannic Disc,
600 A.
D. — A176

Prehistoric
Settlement of
Borscht
A177

Design: 1.20fr, Rössen jug.

1953, Nov. 26   **Perf. 11½**

274	A176	10rp orange brown	4.50	11.50
275	A177	20rp deep gray green	4.75	11.50
276	A176	1.20fr dark blue gray	24.00	32.50
		Nos. 274-276 (3)	33.25	55.50
		Set, never hinged	65.00	

Opening of National Museum, Vaduz.

Soccer
Players — A178

Designs: 20rp, Player kicking ball. 25rp, Goalkeeper. 40rp, Two opposing players.

1954, May 18   **Photo.**
277 A178 10rp dull rose & brn   .95   .90
278 A178 20rp olive green   3.75   1.40
279 A178 25rp orange brown   10.50   30.00
280 A178 40rp lilac gray   8.50   9.00
    Nos. 277-280 (4)   23.70   41.30
    Set, never hinged   42.50

    See Nos. 289-292, 297-300, 308-311, 320-323.

Nos. B19-B21 Surcharged with New Value and Bars in Color of Stamp
1954, Sept. 28   **Unwmk.**   **Perf. 11½**
281 SP15 35rp on 10rp+10rp   2.00   2.25
282 SP16 65rp on 20rp+10rp   10.00   10.50
283 SP15 65rp on 40rp+10rp   3.00   7.25
    Nos. 281-283 (3)   15.00   20.00
    Set, never hinged   27.50

Madonna in Wood, 14th Century — A179

1954, Dec. 16   **Engr.**
284 A179 20rp henna brown   1.50   1.90
285 A179 40rp gray   8.50   17.50
286 A179 1fr dark brown   8.50   17.00
    Nos. 284-286 (3)   18.50   36.40
    Set, never hinged   37.50

Prince Franz Joooph II A180   Princess Georgina — A181

1955, Apr. 5   **Perf. 14½**
    Cream Paper
287 A180 2fr dark brown   47.50   47.50
288 A181 3fr dark green   47.50   47.50
    Set, never hinged   160.00

    Issued in sheets of 9.

Sports Type of 1954
Designs: 10rp, Slalom. 20rp, Mountain climbing. 25rp, Skiing. 40rp, Resting on summit.

1955, June 14   **Photo.**   **Perf. 11½**
289 A178 10rp aqua & brn vio   .45   .80
290 A178 20rp green & ol bis   3.25   .80
291 A178 25rp lt ultra & sep   9.75   16.00
292 A178 40rp olive & pink   9.75   6.00
    Nos. 289-292 (4)   23.20   23.60
    Set, never hinged   42.50

Prince Johann Adam — A183

Portraits: 20rp, Prince Philipp. 40rp, Prince Nikolaus. 60rp, Princess Nora.

Granite Paper
1955, Dec. 14   **Cross in Red**
293 A183 10rp dull violet   .75   .70
294 A183 20rp slate green   3.00   1.60
295 A183 40rp olive brown   3.00   7.25
296 A183 60rp rose brown   3.25   4.00
    Nos. 293-296 (4)   10.00   13.55
    Set, never hinged   18.00

Liechtenstein Red Cross, 10th anniversary.

Sports Type of 1954
Designs: 10rp, Javelin thrower. 20rp, Hurdling. 40rp, Pole vaulting. 1fr, Sprinters.

1956, June 21   **Unwmk.**   **Photo.**
    Granite Paper
297 A178 10rp lt red brn & ol grn   .45   .40
298 A178 20rp lt ol grn & pur   1.90   .45
299 A178 40rp blue & vio brn   2.75   2.75
300 A178 1fr org ver & ol brn   6.50   9.75
    Nos. 297-300 (4)   11.60   13.35
    Set, never hinged   22.50

Eagle, Crown and Oak Leaves — A184

1956, Aug. 21   **Granite Paper**
301 A184 10rp dk brown & gold   1.10   1.00
302 A184 120rp slate blk & gold   5.75   5.00
    Set, never hinged   14.00

150th anniversary of independence.

Prince Franz Joseph II — A185   Prince Johann Adam — A186

1956, Aug. 21
303 A185 10rp dark green   .95   .45
304 A185 15rp bright ultra   1.40   3.00
305 A185 25rp purple   1.40   3.00
306 A185 60rp dark brown   4.75   2.75
    Nos. 303-306 (4)   8.50   9.20
    Set, never hinged   17.50

50th birthday of Prince Franz Joseph II.

1956, Aug. 21   **Granite Paper**
307 A186 20rp olive green   1.25   .70
    Never hinged   3.00

Issued to publicize the 6th Philatelic Exhibition, Vaduz, Aug. 25-Sept. 2. Sheets of 9.

Sports Type of 1954
Designs: 10rp, Somersault on bar. 15rp, Jumping over vaulting horse. 25rp, Exercise on rings. 1.50fr, Somersault on parallel bars.

1957, May 14   **Photo.**   **Perf. 11½**
308 A178 10rp pale rose & ol grn   .95   .95
309 A178 15rp pale grn & dl grn   2.75   7.00
310 A178 25rp ol bis & Prus blu pur   3.75   8.25
311 A178 1.50fr lemon & sepia   11.00   19.00
    Nos. 308-311 (4)   18.45   35.20
    Set, never hinged   32.50

Pine A187   Lord Baden-Powell A188

Designs: 20rp, Wild roses. 1fr, Birches.

1957, Sept. 10   **Perf. 11½**
    Granite Paper
312 A187 10rp dark violet   1.90   2.25
313 A187 20rp brown carmine   1.90   .95
314 A187 1fr green   3.25   8.00
    Nos. 312-314 (3)   7.05   11.20
    Set, never hinged   16.00

    See Nos. 326-328, 332-334, 353-355.

1957, Sept. 10   **Unwmk.**
Design: 10rp, Symbolical torchlight parade.
315 A188 10rp blue black   .75   1.50
316 A188 20rp dark brown   .75   1.50
   a. Sheet, 6 each #315-316   12.00   21.00
     Never hinged   21.00
    Set, never hinged   3.00

Cent. of the birth of Lord Baden-Powell and the 60th anniv. of the Boy Scout movement.

Chapel of St. Mamertus — A189

40rp, Madonna and saints. 1.50fr, Pieta.

1957, Dec. 16   **Perf. 11½**
317 A189 10rp dark brown   .35   .35
318 A189 40rp dark blue   1.10   5.50
319 A189 1.50fr brown lake   6.50   9.50
    Nos. 317-319 (3)   7.95   15.35
    Set, never hinged   15.00

Issued in sheets of 20. Sheet inscribed: "Furstentum Liechtenstein" and "Weihnacht 1957" (Christmas 1957).

Sports Type of 1954
Designs: 15rp, Girl swimmer. 30rp, Fencers. 40rp, Tennis. 90rp, Bicyclists.

1958, Mar. 18   **Photo.**
    Granite Paper
320 A178 15rp lt blue & pur   .65   1.00
321 A178 30rp pale rose lil & ol grn   3.25   6.00
322 A178 40rp sal pink & sl bl   3.25   6.00
323 A178 90rp lt ol grn & vio brn   1.65   4.00
    Nos. 320-323 (4)   8.80   17.00
    Set, never hinged   12.50

Relief Map of Liechtenstein A190

1958, Mar. 18
324 A190 25rp bister, vio & red   .35   .75
325 A190 40rp blue, vio & red   .35   .75
    Set, never hinged   1.50

World's Fair, Brussels, Apr. 17-Oct. 19. Sheets of 25. For surcharges see Nos. B22-B23.

Tree-Bush Type of 1957
Designs: 20rp, Maples at Lawena. 50rp, Holly at Schellenberg. 90rp, Yew at Maurerberg.

1958, Aug. 12   **Perf. 11½**
    Granite Paper
326 A187 20rp chocolate   1.75   .75
327 A187 50rp olive green   7.00   4.50
328 A187 90rp violet blue   1.75   2.75
    Nos. 326-328 (3)   10.50   8.00
    Set, never hinged   19.00

Sts. Moritz and Agatha — A191

Christmas: 35rp, St. Peter. 80rp, Chapel of St. Peter, Mals-Balzers.

1958, Dec. 4   **Photo.**   **Unwmk.**
    Granite Paper
329 A191 20rp dk dark violet   1.90   2.50
330 A191 35rp dk blue violet   1.90   2.50
331 A191 80rp dark brown   1.90   2.50
    Nos. 329-331 (3)   5.70   7.50
    Set, never hinged   9.50

    Issued in sheets of 20.

Tree-Bush Type of 1957
Designs: 20rp, Larch in Lawena. 50rp, Holly on Alpila. 90rp, Linden in Schaan.

1959, Apr. 15   **Perf. 11½**
332 A187 20rp dark violet   2.50   2.00
333 A187 50rp henna brown   2.50   2.00
334 A187 90rp dark green   2.50   2.00
    Nos. 332-334 (3)   7.50   6.00
    Set, never hinged   14.00

"The Good Shepherd" — A192

1959, Apr. 15   **Unwmk.**
335 A192 30rp rose violet & gold   .50   .85
    Never hinged   .85

Issued in memory of Pope Pius XII.

Flags and Rhine Valley — A193

Man Carrying Hay — A194

Apple Harvest A195

Designs: 5rp, Church at Bendern and sheaves. 20rp, Rhine embankment. 30rp, Gutenberg Castle. 40rp, View from Schellenberg. 50rp, Vaduz Castle. 60rp, Naafkopf, Falknis Range. 75rp, Woman gathering sheaves. 90rp, Woman in vineyard. 1fr, Woman in kitchen. 1.30fr, Return from the field. 1.50fr, Family saying grace.

1959-64   **Granite Paper**
336 A193 5rp gray olive ('61)   .25   .25
337 A193 10rp dull violet   .25   .25
338 A193 20rp lilac rose   .25   .25
339 A193 30rp dark red   .25   .25
340 A193 40rp olive grn ('61)   1.10   .55
341 A193 50rp deep blue   .30   .55
342 A193 60rp brt grnsh bl   .45   .55
343 A194 75rp deep ocher ('60)   1.10   1.00
344 A194 80rp olive grn ('61)   .90   .90
345 A194 90rp red lilac ('61)   .90   .90
346 A194 1fr chestnut ('61)   .90   .90
347 A195 1.20fr orange ver ('60)   1.40   1.10
348 A195 1.30fr brt green ('64)   1.10   .90
349 A195 1.50fr brt blue ('60)   1.40   1.40
    Nos. 336-349 (14)   10.55   9.55
    Set, never hinged   12.50

Belfry, Bendern Church — A196

Christmas: 60rp, Sculpture, bell, St. Theodul's church. 1fr, Sculpture, tower of St. Lucius' church.

1959, Dec. 2   Unwmk.   Perf. 11½
350 A196 5rp dk slate green   .55   .25
351 A196 60rp olive   3.50 4.25
352 A196 1fr deep claret   2.75 2.50
     Nos. 350-352 (3)   6.80 7.00
     Set, never hinged   11.00
        Issued in sheets of 20.

Tree-Bush Type of 1957

Designs: 20rp, Beech tree on Gafadura.
30rp, Juniper on Alpila. 50rp, Pine on Sass.

1960, Sept. 19
353 A187 20rp brown   4.50 6.00
354 A187 30rp deep plum   4.50 6.00
355 A187 50rp Prus green   15.00 6.00
     Nos. 353-355 (3)   24.00 18.00
     Set, never hinged   40.00

Europa Issue

Honeycomb
A197

1960, Sept. 19   Perf. 14
356 A197 50rp multicolored   45.00 45.00
     Never hinged   90.00

   Issued to promote the idea of a united
Europe. Sheets of 20.

Princess
Gina — A198

Portraits: 1.70fr, Prince Johann Adam Pius.
3fr, Prince Franz Joseph II.

1960-64   Engr.   Perf. 14
356A A198 1.70fr violet ('64)   1.00 1.50
   b.   Imperf., pair   1,750. 1,750.
357 A198 2fr dark blue   2.25 2.00
   a.   Imperf., pair   1,750. 1,750.
358 A198 3fr deep brown   2.25 2.00
     Nos. 356A-358 (3)   5.50 5.50
     Set, never hinged   7.00
        Issued in sheets of 16.

Heinrich von
Frauenberg — A199

Minnesingers: 20rp, King Konradin. 25rp,
Ulrich von Liechtenstein. 30rp, Kraft von Tog-
genburg. 35rp, Ulrich von Gutenberg. 40rp,
Heinrich von Veldig. 1fr, Konrad von Alstetten.
1.50fr, Walther von der Vogelweide. 2fr, Tann-
häuser. (Designs from 14th century Manesse
manuscript.)

1961-62   Photo.   Perf. 11½
359 A199 15rp multi   .60   .75
360 A199 20rp multi ('62)   .30   .30
361 A199 25rp multi   1.25 1.65
362 A199 30rp multi ('62)   .40   .40
363 A199 35rp multi   1.50 2.00
364 A199 40rp multi ('62)   .65   .65
365 A199 1fr multi   2.50 2.00
366 A199 1.50fr multi   9.25 15.00
367 A199 2fr multi ('62)   1.65 1.65
     Nos. 359-367 (9)   18.10 24.40
     Set, never hinged   22.50

   Issued in sheets of 20. See Nos. 381-384,
471.

┌─────────────────────────────────┐
│ **Catalogue values for unused**   │
│ **stamps in this section, from this** │
│ **point to the end of the section, are** │
│ **for Never Hinged items.**   │
└─────────────────────────────────┘

Europa Issue, 1961

Cogwheels
A200

1961, Oct. 3   Unwmk.   Perf. 13½
368 A200 50rp multicolored   .35   .25
     Printed in sheets of 20.

Souvenir Sheet

Prince Johann II — A201

Portraits: 10rp, Francis I. 25rp, Franz
Joseph II.

1962, Aug. 2   Photo.   Perf. 11½
369   Sheet of 3   7.00 5.00
   a. A201 5rp gray green   1.40 1.25
   b. A201 10rp deep rose   1.40 1.25
   c. A201 25rp blue   1.40 1.25

   50th anniv. of Liechtenstein's postage
stamps and in connection with the Anniv.
Stamp Exhib., Vaduz, Aug. 4-12. No. 369 sold
for 3fr.

Hands
A202

1962, Aug. 2
370 A202 50rp indigo & red   .45   .45
   Europa. Issued in sheets of 20.

Malaria
Eradication
Emblem — A203

1962, Aug. 2   Engr.
371 A203 50rp turquoise blue   .35   .35
   WHO drive to eradicate malaria. Sheets of
20.

Pietà — A204

Designs: 50rp, Angel with harp, fresco.
1.20fr, View of Mauren.

1962, Dec. 6   Photo.
372 A204 30rp magenta   .60   .60
373 A204 50rp deep orange   .85   .85
374 A204 1.20fr deep blue   1.10 1.10
     Nos. 372-374 (3)   2.55 2.55
        Issued in sheets of 20.

Prince
Franz
Joseph II
A205

1963, Apr. 3   Engr.   Perf. 13½x14
375 A205 5fr dull green   4.00 3.00
   Accession of Prince Franz Joseph II, 25th
anniv.
   Sheets of 8. Exists imperf. Value $1,500.

Angel of the
Annunciation
A206

Perf. 11½
1963, Aug. 26   Unwmk.   Photo.
376 A206 20rp shown   .30   .30
377 A206 80rp Three Kings   .70   .70
378 A206 1fr Family   .70   .70
     Nos. 376-378 (3)   1.70 1.70
   Centenary of the International Red Cross.

Europa Issue

Greek
Architectural
Elements
A207

1963, Aug. 26
379 A207 50rp multicolored   1.00 1.00

Bread and
Milk — A208

1963, Aug. 26
380 A208 50rp dk red pur & brn   .40   .40
   FAO "Freedom from Hunger" campaign.

Minnesinger Type of 1961-62

Minnesingers: 25rp, Heinrich von Sax. 30rp,
Kristan von Hamle. 75rp, Werner von Teufen.
1.70fr, Hartmann von Aue.

Perf. 11½
1963, Dec. 5   Unwmk.   Photo.
381 A199 25rp multicolored   .30   .30
382 A199 30rp multicolored   .30   .30
383 A199 75rp multicolored   .75   .75
384 A199 1.70fr multicolored   1.25 1.25
     Nos. 381-384 (4)   2.60 2.60
        Issued in sheets of 20.

Olympic
Rings, Flags
of Austria and
Japan
A209

1964, Apr. 15   Perf. 11½
385 A209 50rp Prus bl, red & blk .40   .40
   Olympic Games 1964. Sheets of 20.

Arms of Counts of
Werdenberg-Vaduz
A210

Coats of Arms: 30rp, Barons of Brandis.
80rp, Counts of Sulz. 1.50fr, Counts of
Hohenems.

1964, Sept. 1   Photo.
386 A210 20rp multicolored   .25   .25
387 A210 30rp multicolored   .25   .25
388 A210 80rp multicolored   .45   .45
389 A210 1.50fr multicolored   .70   .70
     Nos. 386-389 (4)   1.65 1.65
        See Nos. 396-399.

Europa Issue

Roman
Castle,
Schaan
A211

1964, Sept. 1   Perf. 13x14
390 A211 50rp multicolored   2.00   .80

Masescha
Chapel — A212

Peter
Kaiser — A213

40rp, Mary Magdalene, altarpiece. 1.30fr,
Madonna with Sts. Sebastian & Roch,
altarpiece.

1964, Dec. 9   Photo.   Perf. 11½
391 A212 10rp violet black   .25   .25
392 A212 40rp dark blue   .40   .40
393 A212 1.30fr deep claret   1.00 1.00
     Nos. 391-393 (3)   1.65 1.65
        Issued in sheets of 20.

1964, Dec. 9   Engr.
394 A213 1fr dk grn, buff   .55   .55
   Kaiser (1793-1864), historian. Sheets of 20.

Madonna, Wood
Sculpture, 18th
Century — A214

Perf. 11½
1965, Apr. 22   Unwmk.   Engr.
395 A214 10rp orange red   7.00 6.00
        Issued in sheets of 4.

Arms Type of 1965

Lords of: 20rp, Schellenberg. 30rp,
Gutenberg. 80rp, Frauenberg. 1fr,
Ramschwag.

Perf. 11½
1965, Aug. 31   Unwmk.   Photo.
396 A210 20rp multicolored   .25   .25
397 A210 30rp multicolored   .25   .25
398 A210 80rp multicolored   .50   .50
399 A210 1fr multicolored   .55   .55
     Nos. 396-399 (4)   1.55 1.55

Alemannic Ornament A215

Europa: The design is from a belt buckle, about 600 A.D., found in a man's tomb near Eschen.

1965, Aug. 31
400 A215 50rp vio bl, gray & brn .45 .35

The Annunciation by Ferdinand Nigg — A216

Princess Gina and Prince Franz Josef Wenzel — A217

Paintings by Nigg: 30rp, The Three Kings. 1.20fr, Jesus in the Temple, horiz.

1965, Dec. 7 Photo. Perf. 11½
401 A216 10rp yel grn & dk grn .25 .25
402 A216 30rp orange & red brn .25 .25
403 A216 1.20fr ultra & grnsh bl .50 .50
Nos. 401-403 (3) 1.00 1.00

Ferdinand Nigg (1865-1949), painter.

1965, Dec. 7
404 A217 75rp gray, buff & gold .40 .40

Communication Symbols — A218

1965, Dec. 7
405 A218 25rp multicolored .25 .25

Centenary of the ITU.

Soil Conservation, Tree — A219

20rp, Clean air, bird. 30rp, Unpolluted water, fish. 1.50fr, Nature preservation, sun.

1966, Apr. 26 Photo. Perf. 11½
406 A219 10rp brt yellow & grn .25 .25
407 A219 20rp blue & dk blue .25 .25
408 A219 30rp brt green & ultra .25 .25
409 A219 1.50fr yellow & red .60 .60
Nos. 406-409 (4) 1.35 1.35

Issued to publicize nature conservation.

Prince Franz Joseph II — A220

1966, Apr. 26
410 A220 1fr gray, gold, buff & dk brn .50 .50

60th birthday of Prince Franz Joseph II.

Arms of Barons of Richenstein A221

Coats of Arms: 30rp, Vaistli knights. 60rp, Lords of Trisun. 1.20fr, von Schiel.

Light Gray Background

1966, Sept. 6 Photo. Perf. 11½
411 A221 20rp multicolored .25 .25
412 A221 30rp multicolored .25 .25
413 A221 60rp multicolored .25 .25
414 A221 1.20fr multicolored .45 .45
Nos. 411-414 (4) 1.20 1.20

Common Design Types pictured following the introduction.

Europa Issue, 1966
Common Design Type
1966, Sept. 6 Photo. Perf. 14x13
Size: 25x32mm
415 CD9 50rp ultra, dp org & lt grn .40 .35

Vaduz Parish Church — A222

St. Florin — A223

30rp, Madonna. 1.70fr, God the Father.

1966, Dec. 6 Photo. Perf. 11½
416 A222 5rp orange red & cit .25 .25
417 A223 20rp lemon & magenta .25 .25
418 A223 30rp dull rose & dp bl .25 .25
419 A223 1.70fr gray & red brown .65 .65
Nos. 416-419 (4) 1.40 1.40

Restoration of the Vaduz Parish Church.

Europa Issue, 1967
Common Design Type
1967, Apr. 20 Photo. Perf. 11½
420 CD10 50rp multicolored .45 .40

The Man from Malans and his White Horse — A225

Fairy Tales of Liechtenstein: 30rp, The Treasure of Gutenberg. 1.20fr, The Giant of Guflina slaying the Dragon.

1967, Apr. 20
421 A225 20rp multicolored .25 .25
422 A225 30rp multicolored .25 .25
423 A225 1.20fr green & multi .70 .65
Nos. 421-423 (3) 1.20 1.15

See Nos. 443-445, 458-460.

Souvenir Sheet

Prince Hans Adam and Countess Kinsky — A226

1967, June 26 Engr. Perf. 14x13½
424 A226 Sheet of 2 2.00 2.00
a. 1.50fr slate blue (Prince) 1.00 1.00
b. 1.50fr red brown (Countess) 1.00 1.00

Wedding of Prince Hans Adam of Liechtenstein and Marie Aglae Countess Kinsky of Wichnitz and Tettau, July 30, 1967.

EFTA Emblem A227

1967, Sept. 28 Photo. Perf. 11½
425 A227 50rp multicolored .45 .45

European Free Trade Association. See note after Norway No. 501.

A228

A229

Christian Symbols: 20rp, Alpha and Omega. 30rp, Trophaeum (The Victorious Cross). 70rp, Chrismon.

1967, Sept. 28
426 A228 20rp rose cl, blk, & gold .25 .25
427 A228 30rp multicolored .25 .25
428 A228 70rp dp ultra, blk & gold .55 .45
Nos. 426-428 (3) 1.05 .95

1967, Sept. 28 Engr. & Litho.
429 A229 1fr rose claret & pale grn .75 .55

Johann Baptist Büchel (1853-1927), priest, educator, historian and poet. Printed on fluorescent paper.

Peter and Paul, Patron Saints of Mauren — A230

Patron Saints: 5rp, St. Joseph, Planken. 10rp, St. Laurentius, Schaan. 30rp, St. Nicholas, Balzers. 40rp, St. Sebastian, Nendeln. 50rp, St. George, Schellenberg Chapel. 60rp, St. Martin, Eschen. 70rp, St. Fridolin, Ruggell. 80rp, St. Gallus, Triesen. 1fr, St. Theodul, Triesenberg. 1.20fr, St. Ann, Vaduz Castle. 1.50fr, St. Mary, Bendern-Gamprin. 2fr, St. Lucius, patron saint of the Principality.

1967-71 Photo. Perf. 11½
430 A230 5rp multi ('68) .25 .25
431 A230 10rp multi ('68) .25 .25
432 A230 20rp blue & multi .25 .25
433 A230 30rp dark red & multi .25 .25
433A A230 40rp multi ('71) .45 .35
434 A230 50rp multi ('68) .40 .30
435 A230 60rp multi ('68) .45 .35
436 A230 70rp multi .50 .40
437 A230 80rp multi ('68) .55 .50
438 A230 1fr multi ('68) .75 .55
439 A230 1.20fr violet bl & multi .80 .90
440 A230 1.50fr multi ('68) 1.10 .95
441 A230 2fr multi ('68) 1.25 1.25
Nos. 430-441 (13) 7.25 6.55

Issued: 20rp, 30rp, 70rp, 1.20fr, 12/7/67; 5rp, 1.50fr, 8/29/68; 40rp, 6/11/71; 2fr, 12/5/68; others 4/25/68.

Europa Issue, 1968
Common Design Type
1968, Apr. 25
Size: 32½x23mm
442 CD11 50rp crimson, gold & ultra .45 .40

Fairy Tale Type of 1967

30rp, The Treasure of St. Mamerten. 50rp, The Goblin from the Bergerwald. 80rp, The Three Sisters. (Denominations at right.)

1968, Aug. 29
443 A225 30rp Prus blue, yel & red .25 .25
444 A225 50rp green, yel & bl .35 .30
445 A225 80rp brt bl, yel & lt bl .55 .55
Nos. 443-445 (3) 1.15 1.10

Arms of Liechtenstein and Wilczek A231

1968, Aug. 29
446 A231 75rp multicolored .65 .65

Silver wedding anniversary of Prince Franz Joseph II and Princess Gina.

Sir Rowland Hill — A232

Portraits: 30rp, Count Philippe de Ferrari. 80rp, Carl Lindenberg. 1fr, Maurice Burrus. 1.20fr, Théodore Champion.

1968-69 Engr. Perf. 14x13½
447 A232 20rp green .25 .25
448 A232 30rp red brown .25 .25
449 A232 80rp dark brown .55 .45
450 A232 1fr black .70 .65
451 A232 1.20fr dark blue .90 .70
Nos. 447-451 (5) 2.65 2.30

Issued to honor "Pioneers of Philately." Issued: 80rp, 1.20fr, 8/28/69; others, 12/5/68.
See Nos. 509-511.

Coat of Arms — A233

1969, Apr. 24 Engr. Perf. 14x13½
452 A233 3.50fr dark brown 2.50 1.60

Sheets of 16.

Europa Issue, 1969
Common Design Type
1969, Apr. 24 Photo. *Perf. 14*
Size: 33x23mm
453 CD12 50rp brn red, yel & grn .45 .45

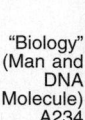

"Biology" (Man and DNA Molecule) A234

30rp, "Physics" (man and magnetic field). 50rp, "Astronomy" (man and planets). 80rp, "Art" (artist and Prince Franz Joseph II and Princess Gina).

1969, Aug. 28 Photo. *Perf. 11½*
454 A234 10rp grn, dk bl & dp cl .25 .25
455 A234 30rp brown & multi .25 .25
456 A234 50rp ultra & green .45 .30
457 A234 80rp brn, dk brn & yel .70 .50
Nos. 454-457 (4) 1.65 1.30

250th anniv. of the Duchy of Liechtenstein.

Fairy Tale Type of 1967
20rp, The Cheated Devil. 50rp, The Fiery Red Goat. 60rp, The Grafenberg Treasure (toad). (Denominations at right.)

1969, Dec. 4 Photo. *Perf. 11½*
458 A225 20rp multicolored .25 .25
459 A225 50rp yellow & multi .40 .35
460 A225 60rp red & multi .55 .45
Nos. 458-460 (3) 1.20 1.05

"T" and Arms of Austria-Hungary, Liechtenstein and Switzerland — A235

1969, Dec. 4 *Perf. 13½*
461 A235 30rp gold & multi .30 .25
Cent. of the Liechtenstein telegraph system.

Arms of St. Lucius Monastery, Chur — A236

Prince Wenzel — A237

Arms of Ecclesiastic Patrons: 50rp, Pfäfers Abbey (dove). 1.50fr, Chur Bishopric (stag).

1969, Dec. 4 *Perf. 11½*
462 A236 30rp multicolored .25 .25
463 A236 50rp multicolored .40 .35
464 A236 1.50fr multicolored 1.00 1.00
Nos. 462-464 (3) 1.65 1.60

See Nos. 475-477, 486-488.

1970, Apr. 30 Photo. *Perf. 11½*
465 A237 1fr sepia & multi .80 .80
25th anniv. of the Liechtenstein Red Cross.

Orange Lily — A238

Native Flowers: 30rp, Bumblebee orchid. 50rp, Glacier crowfoot. 1.20fr, Buck bean.

1970, Apr. 30
466 A238 20rp multicolored .25 .25
467 A238 30rp green & multi .25 .25
468 A238 50rp olive & multi .55 .55
469 A238 1.20rp multicolored 1.10 1.10
Nos. 466-469 (4) 2.15 2.15

Issued to publicize the European Conservation Year 1970. See Nos. 481-484, 500-503.

Europa Issue, 1970
Common Design Type
1970, Apr. 30 Litho. *Perf. 14*
Size: 31½x20½mm
470 CD13 50rp emerald, dk bl & yel .45 .45

Minnesinger Type of 1961-62
Souvenir Sheet
Minnesingers: 30rp, Wolfram von Eschenbach. 50rp, Reinmar der Fiedler. 80rp, Hartmann von Starkenberg. 1.20fr, Friedrich von Hausen.

1970, Aug. 27 Photo. *Perf. 11½*
471 Sheet of 4 2.25 2.25
a. A199 30rp multicolored .25 .25
b. A199 50rp multicolored .30 .30
c. A199 80rp multicolored .50 .50
d. A199 1.20fr multicolored .65 .65

Wolfram von Eschenbach (1170-1220), German minnesinger (poet). Sold for 3fr.

Prince Franz Joseph II A239

Mother & Child, Sculpture by Rudolf Schädler A240

Portrait: 2.50fr, Princess Gina.

1970-71 Engr. *Perf. 14x13½*
472 A239 2.50fr violet blue ('71) 1.90 1.10
473 A239 3fr black 2.00 1.25
Issued: 2.50fr, 6/11; 3fr, 12/3. Sheets of 16.

1970, Dec. 3 Photo. *Perf. 11½*
474 A240 30rp dark red & multi .30 .30
Christmas.

Ecclesiastic Arms Type of 1969
Arms of Ecclesiastic Patrons: 20rp, Abbey of St. John in Thur Valley (Lamb of God). 30rp, Ladies' Abbey, Schänis (crown). 75rp, Abbey of St. Gallen (bear rampant).

1970, Dec. 3
475 A236 20rp lt blue & multi .25 .25
476 A236 30rp gray, red & gold .25 .25
477 A236 75rp multicolored .60 .60
Nos. 475-477 (3) 1.10 1.10

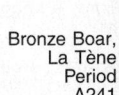

Bronze Boar, La Tène Period A241

30rp, Peacock, Roman, 2nd cent. 75rp, Decorated copper bowl, 13th cent.

1971, Mar. 11 Photo. *Perf. 11½*
478 A241 25rp dp ultra & bluish blk .25 .25
479 A241 30rp dk brown & green .25 .25
480 A241 75rp green, yel & brn .60 .60
Nos. 478-480 (3) 1.10 1.10

Opening of the National Museum, Vaduz.

Flower Type of 1970
Flowers: 10rp, Cyclamen. 20rp, Moonwort. 50rp, Superb pink. 1.50fr, Alpine columbine.

1971, Mar. 11
481 A238 10rp multicolored .25 .25
482 A238 20rp multicolored .25 .25
483 A238 50rp multicolored .45 .45
484 A238 1.50fr multicolored 1.25 1.10
Nos. 481-484 (4) 2.20 2.05

Europa Issue, 1971
Common Design Type
1971, June 11 Photo. *Perf. 13½*
Size: 31x21mm
485 CD14 50rp grnsh bl, yel & blk .45 .45

Ecclesiastic Arms Type of 1969
Arms of Ecclesiastic Patrons: 30rp, Knights of St. John, Feldkirch (Latin and moline crosses). 50rp, Weingarten Abbey (grapes). 1.20fr, Ottobeuren Abbey (eagle and cross).

1971, Sept. 2 Photo. *Perf. 11½*
486 A236 30rp bister & multi .25 .25
487 A236 50rp multicolored .35 .35
488 A236 1.20fr gray & multi .90 .90
Nos. 486-488 (3) 1.50 1.50

Princely Crown A242

Design: 70rp, Page from constitution.

1971, Sept. 2
489 A242 70rp grn, gold, blk & cop .55 .55
490 A242 80rp dk bl, gold, red & plum .65 .65

50th anniversary of the constitution.

Madonna, by Andrea della Robbia — A243

Long-distance Skiing — A244

1971, Dec. 9
491 A243 30rp multicolored .30 .25
Christmas 1971.

1971, Dec. 9
Olympic Rings and: 40rp, Ice hockey. 65rp, Downhill skiing, women's. 1.50fr, Figure skating, women's.
492 A244 15rp lemon & dk brn .25 .25
493 A244 40rp multicolored .35 .30
494 A244 65rp multicolored .55 .55
495 A244 1.50fr multicolored 1.25 1.10
Nos. 492-495 (4) 2.40 2.20

11th Winter Olympic Games, Sapporo, Japan, Feb. 3-13, 1972.

1972, Mar. 16 Photo. *Perf. 11*
10rp, Gymnast. 20rp, High jump. 40rp, Running, women's. 60rp, Discus. All horiz.
496 A244 10rp claret, brn & gray .25 .25
497 A244 20rp olive, brn & yel .25 .25
498 A244 40rp red, brn & gray .30 .30
499 A244 60rp brn, dk brn & bl .65 .50
Nos. 496-499 (4) 1.45 1.30

20th Olympic Games, Munich, Aug. 26-Sept. 10.

Flower Type of 1970
Flowers: 20rp, Anemone. 30rp, Turk's cap. 60rp, Alpine centaury. 1.20fr, Reed mace.

1972, Mar. 16
500 A238 20rp dk blue & multi .25 .25
501 A238 30rp olive & multi .25 .25
502 A238 60rp multicolored .55 .55
503 A238 1.20fr multicolored 1.00 1.00
Nos. 500-503 (4) 2.05 2.05

Europa Issue, 1972
Common Design Type
1972, Mar. 16
504 CD15 40rp dk ol, bl grn & rose red .45 .45

Souvenir Sheet

Bendern and Vaduz Castle — A246

1972, June 8 Engr. *Perf. 13½*
505 A246 Sheet of 2 2.75 2.75
a. 1fr violet blue .90 .90
b. 2fr carmine 1.75 1.75

8th Liechtenstein Philatelic Exhibition, LIBA 1972, Vaduz, Aug. 18-27.

Faun, by Rudolf Schädler — A247

1972, Sept. 7 Photo. *Perf. 11½*
506 A247 20rp shown .25 .25
507 A247 30rp Dancer .25 .25
508 A247 1.10fr Owl .85 .80
Nos. 506-508 (3) 1.35 1.30

Sculptures made of roots and branches by Rudolf Schädler.

Portrait Type of 1968-69
Portraits: 30rp, Emilio Diena. 40rp, André de Cock. 1.30fr, Theodore E. Steinway.

1972, Sept. 7 Engr. *Perf. 14x13½*
509 A232 30rp Prus green .25 .25
510 A232 40rp dk violet brn .30 .25
511 A232 1.30fr violet blue 1.00 .90
Nos. 509-511 (3) 1.55 1.40

Pioneers of Philately.

Madonna with Angels, by Ferdinand Nigg — A248

1972, Dec. 7 Photo. *Perf. 11½*
512 A248 30rp black & multi .30 .25
Christmas 1972.

Silum — A249

Landscapes: 10rp, Lawena Springs. 15rp, Ruggell Marsh. 25rp, Steg, Kirchlispitz. 30rp, Fields, Schellenberg. 40rp, Rennhof, Mauren. 50rp, Tidrüfe Vaduz. 60rp, Eschner Riet. 70rp, Mittagspitz. 80rp, Three Sisters, Schaan Forest. 1fr, St. Peter's and Tower House, Mäls. 1.30fr, Road, Frommenhaus. 1.50fr, Ox Head Mountain. 1.80fr, Hehlawangspitz. 2fr, Saminaschlucht.

1972-73 Engr. & Litho. *Perf. 11½*
513 A249 5rp brown, yel & mag .25 .25
514 A249 10rp slate grn & cit .25 .25
515 A249 15rp red brn & citron .25 .25
516 A249 25rp dk vio & pale grn .25 .25
517 A249 30rp purple & buff .25 .25
518 A249 40rp vio & pale salmon .30 .25
519 A249 50rp vio bl & rose .40 .35
520 A249 60rp green & yellow .50 .45

521	A249	70rp dk & lt blue	.60	.50
522	A249	80rp Prus grn & cit	.65	.55
523	A249	1fr red brn & lt grn	.85	.65
524	A249	1.30fr ultra & lt grn	1.10	1.00
525	A249	1.50fr brn & lt blue	1.25	1.00
526	A249	1.80fr brown & buff	1.50	1.25
527	A249	2fr sepia & pale grn	1.65	1.40
		Nos. 513-527 (15)	10.05	8.65

Issued: 10rp, 15rp, 80rp, 1fr, 1.50fr, 12/7; 30rp, 1.30fr, 1.80fr, 3/8/73; 50rp, 60rp, 70rp, 6/7/73; 5rp, 25rp, 40rp, 2fr, 12/6/73.

Europa Issue, 1973
Common Design Type
1973, Mar. 8   Photo.   Perf. 11½
Size: 33x23mm

| 528 | CD16 | 30rp purple & multi | .25 | .25 |
| 529 | CD16 | 40rp blue & multi | .35 | .35 |

Nautilus Cup — A250

70rp, Ivory tankard. 1.10fr, Silver goblet.

1973, June 7   Photo.   Perf. 11½

530	A250	30rp gray & multi	.25	.25
531	A250	70rp multicolored	.50	.50
532	A250	1.10fr dk blue & multi	.90	.90
		Nos. 530-532 (3)	1.65	1.65

Drinking vessels from the Princely Treasury.

Arms of Liechtenstein and Municipalities A251

Engraved & Photogravure
1973, Sept. 6   Perf. 14x13½

| 533 | A251 | 5fr black & multi | 4.00 | 3.00 |

Coenonympha Oedippus A252

Designs: 15rp, Alpine newt. 25rp, European viper (adder). 40rp, Common curlew. 60rp, Edible frog. 70rp, Dappled butterfly. 80rp, Grass snake. 1.10fr, Three-toed woodpecker.

1973-74   Photo.   Perf. 11½

534	A252	15rp multicolored	.25	.25
535	A252	25rp multicolored	.30	.25
536	A252	30rp orange & multi	.25	.25
537	A252	40rp brown & multi	.35	.35
538	A252	60rp multicolored	.60	.60
539	A252	70rp multicolored	.65	.60
540	A252	80rp multicolored	.70	.70
541	A252	1.10fr multicolored	1.00	1.00
		Nos. 534-541 (8)	4.10	4.00

Issue dates: 30rp, 40rp, 60rp, 80rp, Dec. 6. Others, June 6, 1974.

Virgin and Child, by Bartolomeo di Tommaso — A253

The Vociferant Horseman, by Andrea Riccio — A254

Engraved & Lithographed
1973, Dec. 6   Perf. 13½

| 542 | A253 | 30rp gold & multi | .40 | .30 |

Christmas 1973.

1974, Mar. 21   Photo.   Perf. 11½

Europa: 40rp, Kneeling Venus, by Antonio Susini.

| 543 | A254 | 30rp tan & multi | .35 | .30 |
| 544 | A254 | 40rp ultra & multi | .50 | .45 |

Chinese Vase, 19th Century — A255

Chinese vases from Princely Treasury.

1974, Mar. 21

545	A255	30rp shown	.30	.25
546	A255	50rp from 1740	.45	.40
547	A255	60rp from 1830	.55	.55
548	A255	1fr circa 1700	.95	.95
		Nos. 545-548 (4)	2.25	2.15

Soccer A256

1974, Mar. 21

| 549 | A256 | 80rp lemon & multi | .80 | .75 |

World Soccer Championships, Munich June 13-July 7.

Post Horn and UPU Emblem A257

1974, June 6   Perf. 13½

| 550 | A257 | 40rp gold, green & blk | .35 | .30 |
| 551 | A257 | 60rp gold, red & blk | .55 | .40 |

Centenary of Universal Postal Union.

Bishop F. A. Marxer — A258

Photogravure and Engraved
1974, June 6   Perf. 14x13½

| 552 | A258 | 1fr multicolored | .85 | .85 |

Bicentenary of the death of Bishop Franz Anton Marxer (1703-1775).

Prince Constantin A259

Prince Hans Adam — A260

Princess Gina and Prince Franz Joseph II — A261

80rp, Prince Maximilian. 1.20fr, Prince Alois.

1974-75   Photo.   Perf. 11½

553	A259	70rp dk green & gold	.70	.55
554	A259	80rp dp claret & gold	.75	.65
555	A259	1.20fr bluish blk & gold	1.10	1.00

Engr.
Perf. 14x13½

| 556 | A260 | 1.70fr slate green | 1.40 | 1.25 |

Photogravure and Engraved
Perf. 13½x14

| 557 | A261 | 10fr gold & choc | 8.00 | 8.00 |
| | | Nos. 553-557 (5) | 11.95 | 11.45 |

No. 557 printed in sheets of 4.
Issued: 1.70fr, 12/5; 10fr, 9/5/74; others, 3/13/75.

St. Florian — A262

50rp, St. Wendelin. 60rp, Virgin Mary with Sts. Anna and Joachim. 70rp, Nativity.

1974, Dec. 5   Photo.   Perf. 12

560	A262	30rp multicolored	.30	.25
561	A262	50rp multicolored	.40	.35
562	A262	60rp multicolored	.50	.50
563	A262	70rp multicolored	.65	.65
		Nos. 560-563 (4)	1.85	1.75

Designs are from 19th century devotional glass paintings. Christmas 1974.

"Cold Sun," by Martin Frommelt A263

Europa: 60rp, "Village," by Louis Jaeger.

1975, Mar. 13   Perf. 11½

| 564 | A263 | 30rp multicolored | .25 | .25 |
| 565 | A263 | 60rp multicolored | .50 | .45 |

Red Cross Activities — A264

1975, June 5   Photo.   Perf. 11½

| 566 | A264 | 60rp dk blue & multi | .55 | .55 |

30th anniv. of the Liechtenstein Red Cross.

Coronation Robe — A265

Imperial Crown — A266

1975   Engr. & Photo.   Perf. 14

567	A266	30rp Imperial cross	.45	.40
568	A266	60rp Imperial sword	.70	.70
569	A266	1fr Orb	1.40	1.25
570	A265	1.30fr shown	2.75	2.75
571	A266	2fr shown	3.50	2.75
		Nos. 567-571 (5)	8.80	7.85

Treasures of the Holy Roman Empire from the Treasury of the Hofburg in Vienna, Austria. Issue dates: 1.30fr, Sept. 4; others, June 5. See Nos. 617-620.

St. Mamerten, Triesen A267

Designs: 50rp, Red House, Vaduz, 14th century. 70rp, Prebendary House, Eschen, 14th century. 1fr, Gutenberg Castle.

1975, Sept. 4   Photo.   Perf. 11½

572	A267	40rp multicolored	.40	.35
573	A267	50rp multicolored	.45	.35
574	A267	70rp plum & multi	.85	.85
575	A267	1fr dk blue & multi	1.10	1.10
		Nos. 572-575 (4)	2.80	2.65

European Architectural Heritage Year 1975.

Speed Skating A268

Designs (Olympic Rings and): 25rp, Ice hockey. 70rp, Downhill skiing. 1.20fr, Slalom.

1975, Dec. 4   Photo.   Perf. 11½

576	A268	20rp multicolored	.25	.25
577	A268	25rp multicolored	.25	.25
578	A268	70rp multicolored	.60	.50
579	A268	1.20fr yellow & multi	1.10	.95
		Nos. 576-579 (4)	2.20	1.95

12th Winter Olympic Games, Innsbruck, Austria, Feb. 4-15, 1976.

Daniel in the Lions' Den — A269

Designs: 60rp, Virgin and Child. 90rp, St. Peter. All designs are after Romanesque sculptured capitals in Chur Cathedral, c. 1208.

Photogravure and Engraved
1975, Dec. 4   **Perf. 14**
580	A269	30rp gold & purple	.25	.25
581	A269	60rp gold & green	.40	.40
582	A269	90rp gold & claret	.75	.75
	Nos. 580-582 (3)		1.40	1.40

Christmas and Holy Year 1975.

River Crayfish — A270

World Wildlife Fund: 40rp, European pond turtle. 70rp, Old-world otter. 80rp, Lapwing.

1976, Mar. 11   Photo.   Perf. 11½
583	A270	25rp multicolored	.75	.75
584	A270	40rp multicolored	1.10	1.10
585	A270	70rp multicolored	1.60	1.60
586	A270	80rp multicolored	2.75	2.75
	Nos. 583-586 (4)		6.20	6.20

Mouflon — A271

Europa: 80rp, Pheasant family. Ceramics by Prince Hans von Liechtenstein.

1976, Mar. 11
587	A271	40rp multicolored	*.40*	*.35*
588	A271	80rp violet & multi	*.80*	*.75*

Roman Fibula, 3rd Century A272

1976, Mar. 11
589	A272	90rp vio bl, grn & gold	1.00	.80

Historical Association of Liechtenstein, 75th anniversary.

Souvenir Sheet

Franz Josef II 50fr-Memorial Coin — A273

1976, June 10   Photo.   Imperf.
590	A273	Sheet of 2	1.75	1.75
a.		1fr blue & multi	.85	.85
b.		1fr red & multi	.85	.85

70th birthday of Prince Franz Joseph II of Liechtenstein.

Judo and Olympic Rings — A274

Rubens' Sons, Albrecht and Nikolas — A275

Designs (Olympic Rings and): 50rp, volleyball. 80rp, Relay race. 1.10fr, Long jump, women's.

1976, June 10   Perf. 11½
591	A274	35rp multicolored	.25	.25
592	A274	50rp multicolored	.45	.45
593	A274	80rp multicolored	.65	.65
594	A274	1.10fr multicolored	.90	.90
	Nos. 591-594 (4)		2.25	2.25

21st Olympic Games, Montreal, Canada, July 17-Aug. 1.

1976, Sept. 9   Engr.   Perf. 13½x14

Rubens Paintings: 50rp, Singing Angels. 1fr, The Daughters of Cecrops, horiz. (from Collection of Prince of Liechtenstein).

Size: 24x38mm
595	A275	50rp gold & multi	1.40	1.40
596	A275	70rp gold & multi	2.00	2.00

Size: 48x38mm
597	A275	1fr gold & multi	5.50	5.50
	Nos. 595-597 (3)		8.90	8.90

400th anniversary of the birth of Peter Paul Rubens (1577-1640), Flemish painter. Sheets of 8 (2x4).

Zodiac Signs — A276

1976-78   Photo.   Perf. 11½
598	A276	20rp Pisces	.25	.25
599	A276	40rp Aries	.35	.35
600	A276	40rp Cancer ('77)	.40	.35
601	A276	40rp Scorpio ('78)	.45	.45
602	A276	50rp Sagittarius ('78)	.50	.45
603	A276	70rp Leo ('77)	.65	.65
604	A276	80rp Taurus	.75	.70
605	A276	80rp Virgo ('77)	.75	.75
606	A276	80rp Capricorn ('78)	.75	.70
607	A276	90rp Gemini	1.00	.75
608	A276	1.10fr Libra ('77)	1.10	1.10
609	A276	1.50fr Aquarius ('78)	1.25	1.25
	Nos. 598-609 (12)		8.20	7.75

Flight into Egypt — A277

Monastic Wax Works: 20rp, Holy Infant of Prague, horiz. 80rp, Holy Family and Trinity. 1.50fr, Holy Family, horiz.

1976, Dec. 9   Photo.   Perf. 11½
610	A277	20rp multicolored	.25	.25
611	A277	50rp multicolored	.40	.40
612	A277	80rp multicolored	.55	.55
613	A277	1.50fr multicolored	1.25	1.25
	Nos. 610-613 (4)		2.45	2.45

Christmas 1976.

Ortlieb von Brandis, Sarcophagus A278

Photogravure and Engraved
1976, Dec. 9   Perf. 13½x14
614	A278	1.10fr gold & dk brown	.90	.70

Ortlieb von Brandis, Bishop of Chur (1458-1491).

Map of Liechtenstein, by J. J. Heber, 1721 — A279

Europa: 80rp, View of Vaduz, by Ferdinand Bachmann, 1815.

1977, Mar. 10   Photo.   Perf. 12½
615	A279	40rp multicolored	*.40*	*.40*
616	A279	80rp multicolored	*.80*	*.80*

Treasure Type of 1975

40rp, Holy Lance and Particle of the Cross. 50rp, Imperial Evangel of St. Matthew. 80rp, St. Stephen's Purse. 90rp, Tabard of Imperial Herald.

Engraved and Photogravure
1977, June 8   Perf. 14
617	A266	40rp gold & multi	.40	.30
618	A266	50rp gold & multi	.50	.45
619	A266	80rp gold & multi	.70	.65
620	A266	90rp gold & multi	1.00	.90
	Nos. 617-620 (4)		2.60	2.30

Treasures of the Holy Roman Empire from the Treasury of the Hofburg in Vienna.

Emperor Constantius II Coin — A280

Coins: 70rp, Lindau bracteate, c. 1300. 80rp, Ortlieb von Brandis, 1458-1491.

1977, June 8   Photo.   Perf. 11½
Granite Paper
621	A280	35rp gold & multi	.35	.30
622	A280	70rp silver & multi	.60	.55
623	A280	80rp silver & multi	.80	.65
	Nos. 621-623 (3)		1.75	1.50

Frauenthal Castle A281

Castles: 50rp, Gross Ullersdorf. 80rp, Liechtenstein Castle near Mödling, Austria. 90rp, Liechtenstein Palace, Vienna.

Engraved and Photogravure
1977, Sept. 8   Perf. 13½x14
624	A281	20rp slate grn & gold	.25	.25
625	A281	50rp magenta & gold	.50	.50
626	A281	80rp dk violet & gold	.80	.80
627	A281	90rp dk blue & gold	.90	.90
	Nos. 624-627 (4)		2.45	2.45

Children — A282

Traditional Costumes: 70rp, Two girls. 1fr, Woman in festival dress.

1977, Sept. 8   Photo.   Perf. 11½
Granite Paper
628	A282	40rp multicolored	.50	.40
629	A282	70rp multicolored	.75	.70
630	A282	1fr multicolored	1.25	1.10
	Nos. 628-630 (3)		2.50	2.20

Princess Tatjana A283

1977, Dec. 7   Photo.   Perf. 11½
631	A283	1.10fr brown & gold	.90	.85

Angel — A284

Sculptures by Erasmus Kern: 50rp, St. Rochus. 80rp, Virgin and Child. 1.50fr, God the Father.

1977, Dec. 7
632	A284	20rp multicolored	.25	.25
633	A284	50rp multicolored	.45	.45
634	A284	80rp multicolored	.75	.75
635	A284	1.50fr multicolored	1.50	1.50
	Nos. 632-635 (4)		2.95	2.95

Christmas 1977.

Liechtenstein Palace, Vienna A285

Europa: 80rp, Feldsberg Castle.

Photogravure and Engraved
1978, Mar. 2   Perf. 14
636	A285	40rp gold & slate blue	*.35*	*.30*
637	A285	80rp gold & claret	*.75*	*.70*

Farmhouse, Triesen — A286

Designs: 20rp, Houses, Upper Village, Triesen. 35rp, Barns, Balzers. 40rp, Monastery, Bendern. 50rp, Residential Tower, Balzers-Mäls. 70rp, Parish house. 80rp, Farmhouse, Schellenberg. 90rp, Parish house, Balzers. 1fr, Rheinberger House, Music School, Vaduz. 1.10fr, Street, Mitteldorf, Vaduz. 1.50fr, Town Hall, Triesenberg. 2fr, National Museum and Administrator's Residence, Vaduz.

1978   Photo.   Perf. 11½
638	A286	10rp multicolored	.25	.25
639	A286	20rp multicolored	.25	.25
640	A286	35rp multicolored	.30	.30
641	A286	40rp multicolored	.30	.30
642	A286	50rp multicolored	.40	.40

643	A286	70rp multicolored	.55	.55
644	A286	80rp multicolored	.60	.60
645	A286	90rp multicolored	.70	.70
646	A286	1fr multicolored	.75	.75
647	A286	1.10fr multicolored	.90	.90
648	A286	1.50fr multicolored	1.10	1.10
649	A286	2fr multicolored	1.50	1.50
		Nos. 638-649 (12)	7.60	7.60

Vaduz Castle A287

Vaduz Castle: 50rp, Courtyard. 70rp, Staircase. 80rp, Triptych from High Altar, Castle Chapel.

Engraved and Photogravure
1978, June 1   Perf. 13½x14

650	A287	40rp gold & multi	.45	.45
651	A287	50rp gold & multi	.60	.60
652	A287	70rp gold & multi	.85	.85
653	A287	80rp gold & multi	1.10	1.10
		Nos. 650-653 (4)	3.00	3.00

40th anniversary of reign of Prince Franz Joseph II. Sheet of 8.

Prince Karl I, Coin, 1614 A288

Adoration of the Shepherds A289

Designs: 50rp, Prince Johann Adam, medal, 1694. 80rp, Prince Josef Wenzel, medal, 1773.

1978, Sept. 7   Photo.   Perf. 11½

654	A288	40rp multicolored	.35	.35
655	A288	50rp multicolored	.50	.50
656	A288	80rp multicolored	.95	.95
		Nos. 654-656 (3)	1.80	1.80

1978, Dec. 7   Photo.   Perf. 11½

Stained-glass Windows, Triesenberg: 50rp, Holy Family. 80rp, Adoration of the Kings.

657	A289	20rp multicolored	.25	.25
658	A289	50rp multicolored	.50	.50
659	A289	80rp multicolored	.80	.80
		Nos. 657-659 (3)	1.55	1.55

Christmas 1978.

Piebald, by Hamilton and Faistenberger A290

Golden Carriage of Prince Joseph Wenzel, by Martin von Meytens — A291

Design: 80rp, Black stallion, by Johann Georg von Hamilton.

Photo. & Engr.
1978, Dec. 7   Perf. 13½x14

660	A290	70rp multicolored	.60	.60
661	A290	80rp multicolored	.70	.70
		Perf. 12		
662	A291	1.10fr multicolored	.95	.95
		Nos. 660-662 (3)	2.25	2.25

Sheets of 8.

Mail Plane over Schaan A292

Europa: 80rp, Zeppelin over Vaduz Castle.

1979, Mar. 8   Photo.   Perf. 11½

663	A292	40rp multicolored	.50	.45
664	A292	80rp multicolored	.65	.60

First airmail service, St. Gallen to Schaan, Aug. 31, 1930, and first Zeppelin flight to Liechtenstein, June 10, 1931.

Child Drinking — A293

90rp, Child eating. 1.10fr, Child reading.

1979, Mar. 8

665	A293	80rp silver & multi	.75	.70
666	A293	90rp silver & multi	.85	.85
667	A293	1.10fr silver & multi	.95	.95
		Nos. 665-667 (3)	2.55	2.50

International Year of the Child.

Ordered Wave Fields A294

Sun over Continents A296

Council of Europe A295

1979, June 7   Litho.   Perf. 11½
668 A294 50rp multicolored   .35 .35

Photo.

669	A295	80rp multicolored	.75	.75
670	A296	100rp multicolored	.75	.75
		Nos. 668-670 (3)	1.85	1.85

Intl. Radio Consultative Committee (CCIR) of the Intl. Telecommunications Union, 50th anniv. (50rp); Entry into Council of Europe (80rp); aid to developing countries (100rp).

Heraldic Panel of Carl Ludwig von Sulz — A297

Heraldic Panels of: 70rp, Barbara von Sulz, née zu Staufen. 1.10fr, Ulrich von Ramschwag and Barbara von Hallwil.

Photogravure and Engraved
1979, June 1   Perf. 13½

671	A297	40rp multicolored	.30	.30
672	A297	70rp multicolored	.50	.50
673	A297	1.10fr multicolored	.95	.95
		Nos. 671-673 (3)	1.75	1.75

Sts. Lucius and Florin, Fresco in Waltensburg-Vuorz Church — A298

Photogravure and Engraved
1979, Sept. 6   Perf. 13½
674 A298 20fr multicolored   14.00 13.00

Patron saints of Liechtenstein. Printed in sheets of 4.

Annunciation, Embroidery — A299

Christmas (Ferdnand Nigg Embroideries): 50rp, Christmas. 80rp, Blessed Are the Peacemakers.

1979, Dec. 6   Engr.   Perf. 13½

675	A299	20rp multicolored	.25	.25
676	A299	50rp multicolored	.40	.35
677	A299	80rp multicolored	.60	.50
		Nos. 675-677 (3)	1.25	1.10

Cross-Country Skiing A300

Olympic Rings and: 70rp, Oxhead Mountain. 1.50fr, Ski lift.

1979, Dec. 6   Photo.   Perf. 12

678	A300	40rp multicolored	.30	.25
679	A300	70rp multicolored	.50	.45
680	A300	1.50fr multicolored	1.10	1.00
		Nos. 678-680 (3)	1.90	1.70

13th Winter Olympic Games, Lake Placid, NY, Feb. 12-24, 1980.

Arms of Bailiff Andreas Buchel, 1690 — A301

Designs: Various arms.

1980, Mar. 10   Photo.   Perf. 11½
Granite Paper

681	A301	40rp shown	.30	.25
682	A301	70rp Georg Marxer, 1745	.50	.45
683	A301	80rp Luzius Frick, 1503	.55	.50
684	A301	1.10fr Adam Oehri, 1634	.75	.70
		Nos. 681-684 (4)	2.10	1.90

See Nos. 704-707, 729-732.

Princess Maria Leopoldine Esterhazy, by Antonio Canova — A302

Europa: 80rp, Maria Theresa, Duchess of Savoy, by Martin van Meytens.

1980, Mar. 10

685	A302	40rp multicolored	.40	.35
686	A302	80rp multicolored	.60	.50

Milking Pail — A303

Liechtenstein No. 94 — A304

Old Alpine Farm Tools: 50rp, Wooden heart, ceremonial cattle decoration. 80rp, Butter churn.

1980, Sept. 8

687	A303	20rp multicolored	.25	.25
688	A303	40rp multicolored	.40	.35
689	A303	80rp multicolored	.65	.55
		Nos. 687-689 (3)	1.30	1.15

1980, Sept 8
690 A304 80rp multicolored   .65 .60

Postal Museum, 50th anniversary.

Crossbow with Spanning Device A305

1980, Sept. 8   Engr.   Perf. 13½x14

691	A305	80rp shown	.60	.55
692	A305	90rp Spear, knife	.65	.60
693	A305	1.10fr Rifle, powderhorn	.75	.65
		Nos. 691-693 (3)	2.00	1.80

Triesenberg Family In Traditional Costumes A306

1980, Sept. 8   Photo.   Perf. 12
Granite Paper

694	A306	40rp shown	.30	.25
695	A306	70rp Folk dancers, Schellenberg	.55	.50
696	A306	80rp Brass band, Mauren	.65	.60
		Nos. 694-696 (3)	1.50	1.35

Green Beeches, Matrula Forest — A307

Photogravure and Engraved
1980, Dec. 9   Perf. 14

697	A307	40rp shown	.35	.35
698	A307	50rp White firs, Valorsch Valley	.45	.45

699 A307 80rp Beech forest,
                    Schaan   .65 .65
700 A307 1.50fr Forest, Ober-
                    planken   1.25 1.25
     Nos. 697-700 (4)   2.70 2.70

Glad
Tidings — A308

1980, Dec. 9   Photo.   Perf. 11½
Granite Paper
701 A308 20rp shown   .25 .25
702 A308 50rp Creche   .45 .45
703 A308 80rp Epiphany   .70 .70
     Nos. 701-703 (3)   1.40 1.40

Christmas 1980.

Bailiff Arms Type of 1980
1981, Mar. 9   Photo.   Perf. 11½
Granite Paper
704 A301 40rp Anton Meier,
                    1748   .30 .30
705 A301 70rp Kaspar Kindle,
                    1534   .50 .50
706 A301 80rp Hans Adam
                    Negele, 1600   .60 .60
707 A301 1.10fr Peter Matt, 1693 .90 .90
     Nos. 704-707 (4)   2.30 2.30

Fireworks at Vaduz
Castle — A309

Europa: 80rp, National Day procession.

1981, Mar. 9   Perf. 12½
Granite Paper
708 A309 40rp multicolored   .35 .30
709 A309 80rp multicolored   .65 .60

Souvenir Sheet

Prince Alois, Princess Elisabeth and
Prince Franz Joseph II — A310

1981, June 9   Photo.   Perf. 13
Granite Paper
710 A310 Sheet of 3   2.50 2.50
a.   70rp shown   .50 .50
b.   80rp Princes Alois and Franz Jo-
                    seph II   .55 .55
c.   150rp Prince Franz Joseph II 1.00 1.00
     75th birthday of Prince Franz Joseph II.

Scout Emblems   Man in
A311   Wheelchair
                         A312

1981, June 9
711 A311 20rp multicolored   .25 .25
     50th anniversary of Boy Scouts and Girl
Guides.

1981, June 9
712 A312 40rp multicolored   .25 .25
     International Year of the Disabled.

St. Theodul,
1600th Birth
Anniv. — A313

1981, June 9
713 A313 80rp multicolored   .55 .55

Mosses and
Lichens
A314

Photogravure and Engraved
1981, Sept. 7   Perf. 13½
714 A314 40rp Xanthoria parie-
                    tina   .30 .30
715 A314 50rp Parmelia
                    physodes   .35 .35
716 A314 70rp Sphagnum palus-
                    tre   .50 .50
717 A314 80rp Amblystegium   .60 .60
     Nos. 714-717 (4)   1.75 1.75

Gutenberg
Castle
A315

1981, Sept. 7
718 A315 20rp shown   .25 .25
719 A315 40rp Castle yard   .30 .30
720 A315 50rp Parlor   .35 .35
721 A315 1.10fr Great Hall   .85 .85
     Nos. 718-721 (4)   1.75 1.75

St. Charles
Borromeo
(1538-1584)
A316

Famous Visitors to Liechtenstein (Paintings): 70rp, Goethe (1749-1832), by Angelica
Kauffmann. 80rp, Alexander Dumas (1824-
1895). 1fr, Hermann Hesse (1877-1962), by
Cuno Amiet.

Lithographed and Engraved
1981, Dec. 7   Perf. 14
722 A316 40rp multicolored   .35 .35
723 A316 70rp multicolored   .60 .60
724 A316 80rp multicolored   .70 .70
725 A316 1fr multicolored   .80 .80
     Nos. 722-725 (4)   2.45 2.45
     See Nos. 747-750.

St. Nicholas — A317

1981, Dec. 7   Photo.   Perf. 11½
Granite Paper
726 A317 20rp shown   .25 .25
727 A317 50rp Adoration of the
                    Kings   .45 .45
728 A317 80rp Holy Family   .70 .70
     Nos. 726-728 (3)   1.40 1.40

Christmas 1981.

Bailiff Arms Type of 1980
1982, Mar. 8   Photo.
Granite Paper
729 A301 40rp Johann Kaiser,
                    1664   .35 .35
730 A301 70rp Joseph Anton
                    Kaufmann,
                    1748   .55 .55
731 A301 80rp Christoph Wal-
                    ser, 1690   .70 .70
732 A301 1.10fr Stephan Banzer,
                    1658   1.00 1.00
     Nos. 729-732 (4)   2.60 2.60

Europa
1982 — A318

1982, Mar. 8   Granite Paper
733 A318 40rp Peasants' Uprising,
                    1525   .35 .30
734 A318 80rp Imperial Direct
                    Rule, 1396   .65 .60

Hereditary Prince
Hans
Adam — A319

1982, June 7   Granite Paper
735 A319 1fr shown   .75 .75
736 A319 1fr Princess Marie Aglae .75 .75
     LIBA '82, 10th Liechtenstein Philatelic Exhi-
bition, Vaduz, July 31-Aug. 8.

1982 World
Cup — A320

Designs: Sports arenas.

1982, June 7   Granite Paper
737 A320 15rp Triesenberg   .25 .25
738 A320 25rp Mauren   .25 .25
739 A320 1.80fr Balzers   1.25 1.25
     Nos. 737-739 (3)   1.75 1.75

Farming
A321

1982, Sept. 20 Photo.   Perf. 11½
Granite Paper
740 A321 30rp shown   .25 .25
741 A321 50rp Horticulture   .40 .40
742 A321 70rp Forestry   .50 .50
743 A321 150rp Dairy farming   1.10 1.10
     Nos. 740-743 (4)   2.25 2.25

View of Neu-Schellenberg, 1861, by
Moriz Menzinger (1832-1914) — A322

Photogravure and Engraved
1982, Sept. 20   Perf. 13½x14
744 A322 40rp shown   .30 .30
745 A322 50rp Vaduz, 1860   .35 .35
746 A322 100rp Bendern, 1868   .85 .85
     Nos. 744-746 (3)   1.50 1.50

Visitor Type of 1981
     Paintings: 40rp, Emperor Maximilian I
(1459-1519), by Bernhard Strigel. 70rp, Georg
Jenatsch (1596-1639). 80rp, Angelika Kaufmann (1741-1807), self portrait. 1fr, Fidelis
von Sigmaringen (1577-1622).

1982, Dec. 6   Perf. 14
747 A316 40rp multicolored   .30 .30
748 A316 70rp multicolored   .50 .50
749 A316 80rp multicolored   .60 .60
750 A316 1fr multicolored   .75 .75
     Nos. 747-750 (4)   2.15 2.15

Christmas   Europa
1982 — A323   1983 — A324

Designs: Chur Cathedral sculptures.

1982, Dec. 6   Photo.   Perf. 11½
Granite Paper
751 A323 20rp Angel playing lute .25 .25
752 A323 50rp Virgin and Child   .40 .40
753 A323 80rp Angel playing or-
                    gan   .65 .65
     Nos. 751-753 (3)   1.30 1.30

1983, Mar. 7   Photo.
     Designs: 40rp, Notker Balbulus of St. Gall
(840-912), Benedictine monk, poet and liturgi-
cal composer. 80rp, St. Hildegard of Bingen
(1098-1179).
754 A324 40rp multicolored   .40 .30
755 A324 80rp multicolored   .65 .55

A325   A326

     Shrovetide and Lenten customs: 40rp, Last
Thursday before Lent. 70rp, Begging for eggs
on Shrove Tuesday. 180fr, Bonfire, first Sunday in Lent.

Photogravure and Engraved
1983, Mar. 7   **Perf. 14**
756 A325 40rp multicolored   .35   .35
757 A325 70rp multicolored   .60   .60
758 A325 1.80fr multicolored   1.50 1.50
    Nos. 756-758 (3)   2.45 2.45
    See Nos. 844-846, 915-917, 952-954.

1983, June 6   **Photo.**   **Perf. 12**
Landscapes by Anton Ender (b. 1898).
759 A326 40rp Schaan, on the
                Zollstrasse   .35   .35
760 A326 50rp Balzers with
                Gutenberg Cas-
                tle   .40   .40
761 A326 2fr Stag by the Res-
                ervoir   1.75 1.75
    Nos. 759-761 (3)   2.50 2.50

Protection of
Shores and
Coasts — A327

1983, June 6
762 A327 20rp shown   .25   .25
763 A327 40rp Manned flight bi-
                centenary   .35   .35
764 A327 50rp World communi-
                cations year   .45   .45
765 A327 80rp Humanitarian aid   .70   .70
    Nos. 762-765 (4)   1.75 1.75

Pope John
Paul II
A328

1983, Sept. 5   **Photo.**
766 A328 80rp multicolored   1.00 1.00

Princess
Gina — A329

1983, Sept. 5   **Perf. 12x11½**
767 A329 2.50fr shown   2.25 2.25
768 A329   3fr Prince Franz Jo-
                seph II   2.75 2.75

Christmas
1983 — A330

1983, Dec. 5   **Photo.**   **Perf. 12**
Granite Paper
769 A330 20rp Seeking shelter   .25   .25
770 A330 50rp Child Jesus   .40   .40
771 A330 80rp The Three Magi   .70   .70
    Nos. 769-771 (3)   1.35 1.35

1984 Winter
Olympics,
Sarajevo — A331

Snowflakes.

1983, Dec. 5   Photo.   Perf. 11½x12
Granite Paper
772 A331 40rp multicolored   .40   .40
773 A331 80rp multicolored   .80   .80
774 A331 1.80fr multicolored   1.65 1.65
    Nos. 772-774 (3)   2.85 2.85

Famous Visitors
to Liechtenstein
A332

Paintings: 40rp, Count Alexander Was-
siljewitsch Suworow-Rimnikski (1730-1800),
Austro-Russian Army general. 70rp, Karl
Rudolf Count von Buol-Schauenstein (1760-
1833). 80rp, Carl Zuckmayer (1896-1977),
playwright. 1fr, Curt Goetz (1888-1960), actor
and playwright.

Photogravure and Engraved
1984, Mar. 12   **Perf. 14**
775 A332 40rp multicolored   .40   .40
776 A332 70rp multicolored   .70   .70
777 A332 80rp multicolored   .80   .80
778 A332 1fr multicolored   1.00 1.00
    Nos. 775-778 (4)   2.90 2.90

A333

1984, Mar. 12   Photo.   Perf. 12
Granite Paper
779 A333 50rp multicolored   .45   .40
780 A333 80rp multicolored   .65   .60
    Europa (1959-1984).

A334

The Destruction of Trisona Fairy Tale Illustrations: Root Carvings by Beni Gassner.

Photogravure and Engraved
1984, June 12   **Perf. 14**
781 A334 35rp Warning messen-
                ger   .35   .35
782 A334 50rp Buried town   .50   .50
783 A334 80rp Spared family   .80   .80
    Nos. 781-783 (3)   1.65 1.65

1984 Summer
Olympics
A335

1984, June 12   Photo.   Perf. 11½
Granite Paper
784 A335 70rp Pole vault   .65   .65
785 A335 80rp Discus   .75   .75
786 A335 1fr Shot put   1.00 1.00
    Nos. 784-786 (3)   2.40 2.40

Industries and Occupations — A336

1984, Sept. 10   Photo.   Perf. 11½
787 A336 5rp Banking & trad-
                ing   .25   .25
788 A336 10rp Construction,
                plumbing   .25   .25
789 A336 20rp Production, fac-
                tory worker   .25   .25
790 A336 35rp Contracting,
                draftswoman   .35   .35
791 A336 45rp Manufacturing,
                sales rep   .45   .45
792 A336 50rp Catering   .50   .50
793 A336 60rp Carpentry   .60   .60
794 A336 70rp Public health   .70   .70
795 A336 80rp Industrial re-
                search   .80   .80
796 A336 1fr Masonry   1.00 1.00
797 A336 1.20fr Industrial man-
                agement   1.25 1.25
798 A336 1.50fr Post & communi-
                cations   1.50 1.50
    Nos. 787-798 (12)   7.90 7.90

Princess Marie   Christmas
Aglae — A337   1984 — A338

Photogravure and Engraved
1984, Dec. 10   **Perf. 14x13½**
799 A337 1.70fr shown   1.50 1.50
800 A337   2fr Prince Hans Ad-
                am   1.90 1.90

1984, Dec. 10   Photo.   Perf. 11
801 A338 35rp Annunciation   .35   .35
802 A338 50rp Holy Family   .55   .55
803 A338 80rp Three Kings   .80   .75
    Nos. 801-803 (3)   1.70 1.65

Europa 1985
A339

1985, Mar. 11   Photo.   Perf. 11½
804 A339 50rp Three Muses   .45   .40
805 A339 80rp Pan and Muses   .70   .65

Orders and
Monestaries
A340

Photogravure and Engraved
1985, Mar. 11   **Perf. 13½x14**
806 A340 50rp St. Elisabeth   .55   .55
807 A340 1fr Schellenberg
                Convent   1.10 1.10
808 A340 1.70fr Gutenberg Mis-
                sion   1.90 1.90
    Nos. 806-808 (3)   3.55 3.55

Cardinal
Virtues — A341

1985, June 10   Photo.   Perf. 11½x12
809 A341 35rp Justice   .35   .35
810 A341 50rp Temperance   .50   .50
811 A341 70rp Prudence   .70   .70
812 A341 1fr Fortitude   1.00 1.00
    Nos. 809-812 (4)   2.55 2.55

Princess
Gina,
President of
Natl. Red
Cross, 40th
Anniv.
A342

Portrait and: 20rp, Helping refugees, 1945.
50rp, Rescue service. 1.20fr, Child refugees,
1979.

1985, June 10   **Perf. 12x11½**
813 A342 20rp multicolored   .25   .25
814 A342 50rp multicolored   .55   .55
815 A342 1.20fr multicolored   1.40 1.40
    Nos. 813-815 (3)   2.20 2.20

Souvenir Sheet

State Visit of Pope John Paul
II — A343

Designs: 50rp, Papal coat of arms. 80rp,
Chapel of St. Maria zum Trost, Dux, Schaan.
1.70fr, Our Lady of Liechtenstein, St. Mary the
Comforter.

1985, Feb. 2   **Perf. 11½**
816 A343   Sheet of 3   4.25 4.25
    a. 50rp multi   1.40 1.40
    b. 80rp multi   1.40 1.40
    c. 1.70fr multi   1.40 1.40

Paintings from
the Princely
Collections
A344

50rp, Portrait of a Canon, by Quintin Massys
(1466-1530). 1fr, Portrait of Clara Serena
Rubens, by Peter Paul Rubens (1577-1640).
1.20fr, Portrait of the Duke of Urbino, by
Raphael (1483-1520).

Photogravure and Engraved
1985, Sept. 2   **Perf. 14**
817 A344 50rp multicolored   .50   .50
818 A344 1fr multicolored   1.10 1.10
819 A344 1.20fr multicolored   1.40 1.40
    Nos. 817-819 (3)   3.00 3.00

Christmas
1985 — A345

1985, Dec. 9   Photo.   Perf. 11½x12
820 A345 35rp Frankincense   .35   .35
821 A345 50rp Gold   .50   .50
822 A345 80rp Myrrh   .85   .85
    Nos. 820-822 (3)   1.70 1.70

Kirchplatz
Theater, 15th
Anniv. — A346

Photogravure and Engraved

1985, Dec. 9   *Perf. 14*
823 A346 50rp Tragedy   .40 .40
824 A346 80rp Commedia
     dell'arte   .55 .55
825 A346 1.50rp Opera buffa   1.75 1.75
    Nos. 823-825 (3)   2.70 2.70

Weapons from the Prince's Armory
A347

Designs: 35rp, Halberd, bodyguard of Prince Charles I. 50rp, German morion, 16th cent. 80rp, Halberd, bodyguard of Prince Carl Eusebius.

1985, Dec. 9   *Perf. 13½x14½*
826 A347 35rp multicolored   .35 .35
827 A347 50rp multicolored   .50 .50
828 A347 80rp multicolored   .85 .85
    Nos. 826-828 (3)   1.70 1.70

A348   A349

1986, Mar. 10   Photo.   *Perf. 12*
829 A348 50rp Swallows   .45 .40
830 A348 90rp Robin   .95 .90

Europa 1986.

1986-89   Photo.   *Perf. 11½x12*

Views of Vaduz Castle.

Granite Paper

832 A349 20rp Outer courtyard   .25 .25
833 A349 25rp View from the
     south ('89)   .35 .35
835 A349 50rp Castle, moun-
     tains   .40 .40
838 A349 90rp Inner gate ('87)   1.10 1.10
840 A349 1.10fr Back view   .90 .90
841 A349 1.40fr Inner courtyard
     ('87)   1.75 1.75
    Nos. 832-841 (6)   4.75 4.75

Fasting Sacrifice — A350

1986, Mar. 10   Photo.   *Perf. 12*
843 A350 1.40fr multicolored   1.40 1.40

Customs Type of 1983
Photogravure and Engraved

1986, June 9   *Perf. 13½*
844 A325 35rp Palm Sunday pro-
     cession   .40 .40
845 A325 50rp Wedding   .60 .60
846 A325 70rp Rogation Day pro-
     cession   .80 .80
    Nos. 844-846 (3)   1.80 1.80

A352

Karl Freiherr Haus von Hausen (1823-89), founder.

1986, June 9   Photo.   *Perf. 11½*
847 A352 50rp multicolored   .55 .55

Natl. Savings Bank, Vaduz, 125th anniv.

A353

Photogravure and Engraved

1986, June 9   *Perf. 13½*
848 A353 3.50fr multicolored   4.50 4.50

Prince Franz Joseph II, 80th birthday.

Hunting — A354

1986, Sept. 9   *Perf. 13x13½*
849 A354 35rp Roebuck, Rug-
     geller Riet   .40 .40
850 A354 50rp Chamois in win-
     ter, Rappen-
     stein   .60 .60
851 A354 1.70fr Rutting stag,
     Lawena   2.00 2.00
    Nos. 849-851 (3)   3.00 3.00

Crops A355

1986, Sept. 9   Photo.   *Perf. 12x11½*
852 A355 50rp White cabbage,
     beets   .65 .65
853 A355 80rp Red cabbage   1.10 1.10
854 A355 90rp Potatoes, onions,
     garlic   1.25 1.25
    Nos. 852-854 (3)   3.00 3.00

Christmas   Trees
A356   A357

Archangels.

1986, Dec. 9   *Perf. 11½*
855 A356 35rp Michael   .45 .40
856 A356 50rp Gabriel   .65 .65
857 A356 90rp Raphael   1.25 1.25
    Nos. 855-857 (3)   2.35 2.30

1986, Dec. 9
858 A357 25rp Silver fir   .30 .30
859 A357 90rp Spruce   1.10 1.10
860 A357 1.40fr Oak   1.65 1.65
    Nos. 858-860 (3)   3.05 3.05

Europa 1987 — A358

Modern architecture: 50rp, Primary school, 1980, Gamprin. 90rp, Parish church, c. 1960, Schellenburg.

1987, Mar. 9   Photo.   *Perf. 11½x12*
Granite Paper
861 A358 50rp multicolored   .60 .55
862 A358 90rp multicolored   1.25 1.00

Nicholas Among the Thorns — A359

1987, Mar. 9   *Perf. 11½*
Granite Paper
863 A359 1.10fr multicolored   1.50 1.50

Nicholas von der Flue (1417-1487), canonized in 1947.

Hereditary Prince Alois — A360

Photo. & Engr.

1987, June 9   *Perf. 14*
864 A360 2fr multicolored   2.50 2.50

No. 864 printed in sheets of 8.

Fish — A361

1987, June 9   Photo.   *Perf. 11½*
865 A361 50rp Cottus gobio   .60 .60
866 A361 90rp Salmo trutta
     fario   1.10 1.10
867 A361 1.10fr Thymallus
     thymallus   1.40 1.40
    Nos. 865-867 (3)   3.10 3.10

A362   A363

Liechtenstein City Palace, Vienna.

1987, Sept. 7   Photo.   *Perf. 11½*
Granite Paper
868 A362 35rp Arch   .45 .45
869 A362 50rp Entrance   .60 .60
870 A362 90rp Staircase   1.10 1.10
    Nos. 868-870 (3)   2.15 2.15

1987, Sept. 7   *Perf. 11½*
871 A363 1.40fr House of Liech-
     tenstein coat of
     arms   1.90 1.90

Purchase of County of Vaduz, 275th anniv.

Diet, 125th Anniv. A364

1987, Sept. 7   *Perf. 11½*
872 A364 1.70fr Constitution of
     1862   2.25 2.25

Christmas — A365

The Evangelists, illuminated codices from the Golden Book, c. 1100, Abbey of Pfafers, purportedly made under the direction of monks from Reichenau Is.

Photo. & Engr.

1987, Dec. 7   *Perf. 14*
873 A365 35rp St. Matthew   .30 .30
874 A365 40rp St. Mark   .40 .40
875 A365 60rp St. Luke   .50 .50
876 A365 90rp St. John   .75 .75
    Nos. 873-876 (4)   1.95 1.95

1988 Winter Olympics, Calgary A366

Humorous drawings by illustrator Paul Flora of Austria: 25rp, The Toil of the Cross-country Skier. 90rp, Courageous Pioneer of Skiing. 1.10fr, As Grandfather Used to Ride on a Bobsled.

1987, Dec. 7   *Perf. 14x13½*
877 A366 25rp multicolored   .30 .30
878 A366 90rp multicolored   1.10 1.10
879 A366 1.10fr multicolored   1.40 1.40
    Nos. 877-879 (3)   2.80 2.80

See Nos. 888-891.

Europa 1988 — A367

Modern communication & transportation.

1988, Mar. 7   Photo.   *Perf. 11½x12*
Granite Paper
880 A367 50rp Satellite dish   .60 .55
881 A367 90rp High-speed mon-
     orail   1.00 .90

European Campaign to Protect Undeveloped and Developing Lands — A368

1988, Mar. 7   *Perf. 12*
Granite Paper

882	A368	80rp	Forest preservation	1.00	1.00
883	A368	90rp	Layout for village development	1.10	1.10
884	A368	1.70rp	Traffic planning	2.00	2.00
			Nos. 882-884 (3)	4.10	4.10

Balancing nature conservation with natl. development.

Souvenir Sheet

Succession to the Throne — A369

Portraits: a, Crown Prince Hans Adam. b, Prince Alois, successor to the crown prince. c, Prince Franz Josef II, ruler.

Photo. & Engr.
1988, June 6   *Perf. 14½x13½*

885	A369	Sheet of 3	4.00	4.00
a.		50rp black, gold & bright blue	.65	.65
b.		50rp black, gold & sage green	.65	.65
c.		2fr black, gold & deep rose	2.50	2.50

North and South Campaign A370

1988, June 6   **Photo.**   *Perf. 12x11½*
Granite Paper

886	A370	50rp	Public radio	.65	.65
887	A370	1.40fr	Adult education	1.75	1.75

Cultural cooperation with Costa Rica. See Costa Rica Nos. 401-402.

Olympics Type of 1988

Humorous drawings by illustrator Paul Flora of Austria: 50rp, Cycling. 80rp, Gymnastics. 90rp, Running. 1.40fr, Equestrian.

Photo. & Engr.
1988, Sept. 5   *Perf. 14x13½*

888	A366	50rp	multicolored	.65	.65
889	A366	80rp	multicolored	1.00	1.00
890	A366	90rp	multicolored	1.10	1.10
891	A366	1.40fr	multicolored	1.75	1.75
			Nos. 888-891 (4)	4.50	4.50

Roadside Shrines — A371   Christmas — A372

1988, Sept. 5   **Photo.**   *Perf. 11½x12*
Granite Paper

892	A371	25rp	Kaltweh Chapel, Balzers	.35	.35
893	A371	35rp	Oberdorf, Vaduz, c. 1870	.45	.45
894	A371	50rp	Bangstrasse, Ruggell	.65	.65
			Nos. 892-894 (3)	1.45	1.45

1988, Dec. 5   **Photo.**   *Perf. 11½x12*
Granite Paper

895	A372	35rp	Joseph, Mary	.40	.40
896	A372	50rp	Christ child	.55	.55
897	A372	90rp	Adoration of the Magi	1.00	1.00
			Nos. 895-897 (3)	1.95	1.95

The Letter — A373   Europa 1989 — A374

Details of Portrait of Marie-Therese de Lamballe (The Letter), by Anton Hickel (1745-1798): 90rp, Handkerchief and writing materials in open desk. 2fr, Entire painting.

Photo. & Engr.
1988, Dec. 5   *Perf. 13x13½*

898	A373	50rp	shown	.65	.65
899	A373	90rp	multicolored	1.10	1.10
900	A373	2fr	multicolored	2.50	2.50
			Nos. 898-900 (3)	4.25	4.25

1989, Mar. 6   **Photo.**   *Perf. 11½x12*

Traditional children's games.

Granite Paper

901	A374	50rp	Cat and Mouse	.70	.65
902	A374	90rp	Stockleverband	1.40	1.25

Josef Gabriel Rheinberger (1839-1901), Composer, and Score — A375

Photo. & Engr.
1989, Mar. 6   *Perf. 14x13½*

903	A375	2.90fr multicolored	3.50	3.50

Fish — A376

1989, June 5   **Photo.**   *Perf. 12x11½*
Granite Paper

904	A376	50rp	Esox lucius	.65	.65
905	A376	1.10fr	Salmo trutta lacustris	1.40	1.40
906	A376	1.40fr	Noemacheilus barbatulus	1.75	1.75
			Nos. 904-906 (3)	3.80	3.80

World Wildlife Fund — A377

1989, June 5   *Perf. 12*
Granite Paper

907	A377	25rp	Charadrius dubuis	.65	.65
908	A377	35rp	Hyla arborea	1.10	1.10
909	A377	50rp	Libelloides coccajus	1.50	1.50
910	A377	90rp	Putorius putorius	2.75	2.75
			Nos. 907-910 (4)	6.00	6.00

Mountains A378

1989, Sept. 4   **Photo.**   *Perf. 11½*
Granite Paper

911	A378	50rp	Falknis	.60	.60
912	A378	75rp	Plassteikopf	.90	.90
913	A378	80rp	Naafkopf	.95	.95
914	A378	1.50fr	Garselliturm	1.75	1.75
			Nos. 911-914 (4)	4.20	4.20

See Nos. 930-939.

Customs Type of 1983

Autumn activities: 35rp, Alpine herdsman and flock return from pasture. 50rp, Shucking corn. 80rp, Cattle market.

Photo. & Engr.
1989, Sept. 4   *Perf. 14*

915	A325	35rp	multicolored	.40	.40
916	A325	50rp	multicolored	.60	.60
917	A325	80rp	multicolored	.95	.95
			Nos. 915-917 (3)	1.95	1.95

Christmas A379

Details of the triptych *Adoration of the Magi*, by Hugo van der Goes (50rp) and student (35rp, 90rp), late 15th cent.: 35rp, Melchior and Balthazar. 50rp, Caspar and holy family. 90rp, Donor with St. Stephen.

1989, Dec. 4   *Perf. 13½*
Size of 35rp and 90rp: 23x41mm

918	A379	35rp	multicolored	.45	.45
919	A379	50rp	shown	.60	.60
920	A379	90rp	multicolored	1.10	1.10
			Nos. 918-920 (3)	2.15	2.15

Minerals A380

1989, Dec. 4   *Perf. 13½x13*

921	A380	50rp	Scepter quartz	.55	.55
922	A380	1.10fr	Pyrite ball	1.25	1.25
923	A380	1.50fr	Calcite	1.65	1.65
			Nos. 921-923 (3)	3.45	3.45

Europa 1990 — A381   Postage Stamps, 150th Anniv. — A382

Post offices.

1990, Mar. 5   **Photo.**   *Perf. 11½x12*
Granite Paper

924	A381	50rp	shown	.70	.60
925	A381	90rp	Modern p.o.	1.25	1.10

1990, Mar. 5   *Perf. 11½*
Granite Paper

926	A382	1.50fr	Penny Black	1.65	1.65

1990 World Cup Soccer Championships, Italy — A383

1990, Mar. 5   **Granite Paper**   *Perf. 12*

927	A383	2fr	multicolored	2.50	2.50

Princess Gina A384

1990, June 5   **Litho.**   *Perf. 11½*
Granite Paper

928	A384	2fr	shown	2.75	2.75
929	A384	3fr	Prince Franz Joseph II	4.00	4.00

1st anniv of death.

Mountains Type of 1989

1990-93   **Granite Paper**

930	A378	5rp	Augstenberg	.25	.25
931	A378	10rp	Hahnenspiel	.25	.25
933	A378	35rp	Nospitz	.50	.50
933A	A378	40rp	Ochsenkopf	.50	.50
934	A378	45rp	Drei Schwestern	.60	.60
935	A378	60rp	Kuhgrat	.90	.90
936	A378	70rp	Galinakopf	.95	.95
938	A378	1fr	Schonberg	1.25	1.25
939	A378	1.20fr	Bleikaturm	1.75	1.75
940	A378	1.60fr	Schwarzhorn	2.00	2.00
941	A378	2fr	Scheienkopf	2.50	2.50
			Nos. 930-941 (11)	11.45	11.45

Issued: 5, 45, 70rp, 1fr, 6/5; 10, 35, 60rp, 1.20fr, 9/3; 40rp, 6/3/91; 1.60fr, 3/2/92; 2fr, 3/1/93.

A385

Paintings by Benjamin Steck (1902-1981).

Photo. & Engr.
1990, June 5   *Perf. 14*

942	A385	50rp	shown	.65	.65
943	A385	80rp	Fruit, dish	1.00	1.00
944	A385	1.50fr	Basket, fruit, stein	2.00	2.00
			Nos. 942-944 (3)	3.65	3.65

A386

Game birds.

Photo. & Engr.
1990, Sept. 3   *Perf. 13x13½*

945	A386	25rp	Pheasant	.35	.35
946	A386	50rp	Blackcock	.65	.65
947	A386	2fr	Mallard duck	2.75	2.75
			Nos. 945-947 (3)	3.75	3.75

European Postal Communications, 500th Anniv. — A387

1990, Dec. 3   *Perf. 13½x14*

948	A387	90rp	multicolored	1.25	1.25

A388　　　A389

Christmas (Lenten Cloth of Bendern): 35rp, The Annunciation. 50rp, Birth of Christ. 90rp, Adoration of the Magi.

1990, Dec. 3　Photo.　Perf. 12
Granite Paper
949	A388	35rp multicolored	.50	.50
950	A388	50rp multicolored	.70	.70
951	A388	90rp multicolored	1.25	1.25
		Nos. 949-951 (3)	2.45	2.45

Photo. & Engr.
1990, Dec. 3　　　Perf. 14
Holiday Customs: 35rp, St. Nicholas Visiting Children on Feast of St. Nicholas. 50rp, Waking "sleepyheads" on New Year's Day. 1.50fr, Good wishes on New Year's Day.
952	A389	35rp multicolored	.45	.45
953	A389	50rp multicolored	.65	.65
954	A389	1.50fr multicolored	2.00	2.00
		Nos. 952-954 (3)	3.10	3.10

Europa — A390

Designs: 50rp, Telecommunications satellite, Olympus I. 90rp, Weather satellite, Meteosat.

1991, Mar. 4　Photo.　Perf. 11½
Granite Paper
955	A390	50rp multicolored	.80	.60
956	A390	90rp multicolored	1.25	1.10

St. Ignatius of Loyola (1491-1556), Founder of Jesuit Order — A391

90rp, Wolfgang Amadeus Mozart.

1991, Mar. 4　　　Perf. 11½
Granite Paper
957	A391	80rp multicolored	1.10	1.10
958	A391	90rp multicolored	1.25	1.25

A392　　　A393

1991, Mar. 4　　　Perf. 11½
Granite Paper
959	A392	2.50fr multicolored	3.50	3.50
		UN membership, 1990.		

1991, June 3　Photo.　Perf. 11½
Paintings: 50rp, Maloja, by Giovanni Giacometti. 80rp, Rheintal, by Ferdinand Gehr. 90rp, Bergell, by Augusto Giacometti. 1.10fr, Hoher Kasten, by Hedwig Scherrer.

Granite Paper
960	A393	50rp multicolored	.60	.60
961	A393	80rp multicolored	.95	.95
962	A393	90rp multicolored	1.00	1.00
963	A393	1.10fr multicolored	1.40	1.40
		Nos. 960-963 (4)	3.95	3.95
		Swiss Confederation, 700th anniv.		

Military Uniforms A394

Designs: 50rp, Non-commissioned officer, private. 70rp, Uniform tunic, trunk. 1fr, Sharpshooters, officer and private.

Photo. & Engr.
1991, June 3　　　Perf. 13½x14
964	A394	50rp multicolored	.60	.60
965	A394	70rp multicolored	.85	.85
966	A394	1fr multicolored	.95	.95
		Nos. 964-966 (3)	2.40	2.40

Last action of Liechtenstein's military, 1866 (70rp).

Princess Marie — A395

Photo. & Engr.
1991, Sept. 2　　　Perf. 13x13½
967	A395	3fr shown	3.75	3.75
968	A395	3.40fr Prince Hans Adam II	4.25	4.25

LIBA 92, Natl. Philatelic Exhibition A396

1991, Sept. 2　Photo.　Perf. 11½
Granite Paper
969	A396	90rp multicolored	1.10	1.10

A397　　　A398

Christmas (Altar of St. Mamertus Chapel, Triesen): 50rp, Mary. 80rp, Madonna and Child. 90rp, Angel Gabriel.

Photo. & Engr.
1991, Dec. 2　　　Perf. 13½x14
970	A397	50rp multicolored	.70	.70
971	A397	80rp multicolored	1.10	1.10
972	A397	90rp multicolored	1.25	1.25
		Nos. 970-972 (3)	3.05	3.05

1991, Dec. 2　Photo.　Perf. 11½x12
1992 Winter Olympics, Albertville: 70rp, Cross-country skiers, doping check. 80rp, Hockey players, good sportsmanship. 1.60rp, Downhill skier, safety precautions.

Granite Paper
973	A398	70rp multicolored	.95	.95
974	A398	80rp multicolored	1.10	1.10
975	A398	1.60fr multicolored	2.25	2.25
		Nos. 973-975 (3)	4.30	4.30

1992, Mar. 2　Photo.　Perf. 11½
1992 Summer Olympics, Barcelona: 50rp, Women's relay, drugs, broken medal. 70rp, Cycling, safety precautions. 2.50fr, Judo, good sportsmanship.

Granite Paper
976	A398	50rp multicolored	.65	.65
977	A398	70rp multicolored	.90	.90
978	A398	2.50fr multicolored	3.25	3.25
		Nos. 976-978 (3)	4.80	4.80

Discovery of America, 500th Anniv. A400

1992, Mar. 2　　　Granite Paper
979	A400	80rp shown	1.10	1.00
980	A400	90rp New York skyline	1.40	1.25
		Europa.		

Postillion Blowing Horn — A401

Clown in Envelope A402

Designs: No. 982, Postillion delivering valentine. No. 984, Wedding violinist.

Photo. & Engr.
1992, June 1　　　Perf. 14x13½
981	A401	50rp multicolored	.65	.65
982	A401	50rp multicolored	.65	.65

Photo.
Perf. 12½
Granite Paper
983	A402	50rp multicolored	.65	.65
984	A402	50rp multicolored	.65	.65
		Nos. 981-984 (4)	2.60	2.60

Souvenir Sheet

Prince Hans-Adam and Princess Marie, 25th Wedding Anniv. — A403

Designs: a, 2fr, Coat of Arms of Liechtenstein-Kinsky Alliance. b, 2.50fr, Prince Hans-Adam and Princess Marie.

1992, June 1　　　Perf. 11½
Granite Paper
985	A403	Sheet of 2, #a.-b.	5.75	5.75

Ferns — A404

40rp, Blechnum spicant. 50rp, Asplenium trichomanes. 70rp, Phyllitis scolopendrium. 2.50fr, Asplenium ruta-muraria.

Photo. & Engr.
1992, Sept. 7　　　Perf. 14
986	A404	40rp multicolored	.65	.65
987	A404	70rp multicolored	.75	.75
988	A404	1.10fr multicolored	1.10	1.10
989	A404	2.50fr multicolored	4.00	4.00
		Nos. 986-989 (4)	6.50	6.50

Creation of Vaduz County, 650th Anniv. A405

1992, Sept. 7　　　Perf. 13½x14
990	A405	1.60fr multicolored	2.50	2.50

Christmas A406　　Hereditary Prince Alois A407

Scenes in Triesen: 50rp, Chapel, St. Mamertus. 90rp, Nativity scene, St. Gallus Church. 1.60fr, St. Mary's Chapel.

1992, Dec. 7　Photo.　Perf. 11½
Granite Paper
991	A406	50rp multicolored	.60	.60
992	A406	90rp multicolored	1.10	1.10
993	A406	1.60fr multicolored	2.00	2.00
		Nos. 991-993 (3)	3.70	3.70

Photo. & Engr.
1992, Dec. 7　　　Perf. 13x13½
994	A407	2.50fr multicolored	3.50	3.50

A408

Europa (Contemporary paintings): 80rp, 910805, by Bruno Kaufmann. 1fr, The Little Blue, by Evi Kliemand.

1993, Mar. 1　Photo.　Perf. 11½x12
Granite Paper
995	A408	80rp multicolored	.90	.75
996	A408	1fr multicolored	1.10	.90

A409

Paintings by Hans Gantner (1853-1914): 50rp, Chalets in Steg and Naafkopf. 60rp, Sass Mountain with Hunting Lodge. 1.80fr, Red House in Vaduz.

1993, Mar. 1　　　Perf. 11½
Granite Paper
997	A409	50rp multicolored	.65	.65
998	A409	60rp multicolored	.75	.75
999	A409	1.80fr multicolored	2.25	2.25
		Nos. 997-999 (3)	3.65	3.65

Tibetan Art — A410

60rp, Detail from Thangka painting, Tale of the Ferryman. 80rp, Religious dance mask. 1fr, Detail from Thangka painting, The Tale of the Fish.

1993, June 7   Photo.   Perf. 11½
Granite Paper
1000	A410	60rp multicolored	.75	.75
1001	A410	80rp multicolored	1.00	1.00
1002	A410	1fr multicolored	1.25	1.25
	Nos. 1000-1002 (3)		3.00	3.00

A411   A412

1993, June 7   Perf. 11½x12
Granite Paper
1003	A411	1.80fr Tree of life	2.25	2.25

Church Missionary Work.

Photo. & Engr.
1993, June 7   Perf. 14x13½

Contemporary painting: Black Hatter, by Friedensreich Hundertwasser.
1004	A412	2.80fr multicolored	3.50	3.50

Souvenir Sheet

Marriage of Hereditary Prince Alois and Duchess Sophie of Bavaria, July 3 — A413

1993, June 7   Photo.   Perf. 11½
Granite Paper
1005	A413	4fr multicolored	5.25	5.25

Wild   Meadow
Animals — A414   Plants — A415

Photo. & Engr.
1993, Sept. 6   Perf. 13x13½
1006	A414	60rp Badger	.80	.80
1007	A414	80rp Marten	1.00	1.00
1008	A414	1fr Fox	1.25	1.25
	Nos. 1006-1008 (3)		3.05	3.05

1993, Sept. 6
1009	A415	50rp Origanum vulgare	.65	.65
1010	A415	60rp Salvia pratensis	.80	.80
1011	A415	1fr Seseli annuum	1.25	1.25

1012	A415	2.50fr Prunella grandiflora	3.25	3.25
	Nos. 1009-1012 (4)		5.95	5.95
	See Nos. 1056-1059.			

Christmas — A416

Calligraphic Christmas texts by: 60rp, Rainer Maria Rilke. 80rp, Th. Friedrich. 1fr, Rudolph Alexander Schroder.

1993, Dec. 6   Photo.   Perf. 11½x12
Granite Paper
1013	A416	60rp multicolored	.80	.80
1014	A416	80rp multicolored	1.00	1.00
1015	A416	1fr multicolored	1.25	1.25
	Nos. 1013-1015 (3)		3.05	3.05

A417

1993, Dec. 6   Granite Paper
1016	A417	60rp Ski jump	.80	.80
1017	A417	80rp Slalom skiing	1.00	1.00
1018	A417	2.40fr Bobsled	3.00	3.00
	Nos. 1016-1018 (3)		4.80	4.80

1994 Winter Olympics, Lillehammer.

Anniversaries and Events
A418

A419

A420

1994, Mar. 7   Photo.   Perf. 11½
Granite Paper
1019	A418	60rp multicolored	.75	.75
1020	A419	1.80fr multicolored	2.25	2.25
1021	A420	2.80fr multicolored	3.50	3.50
	Nos. 1019-1021 (3)		6.50	6.50

Principality of Liechtenstein, 275th anniv. (No. 1019). Intl. Olympic Committee, cent. (No. 1020). 1994 World Cup Soccer Championships, US (No. 1021).

Alexander von Humboldt (1769-1859)
A421

Europa: 80rp, Vultur gryphus. 1fr, Rhexia cardinalis.

Photo. & Engr.
1994, Mar. 7   Perf. 13x13½
1022	A421	80rp multicolored	1.10	.90
1023	A421	1fr multicolored	1.40	1.00

Mobile, by Jean Tinguely (1925-91)
A422

Photo. & Engr.
1994, June 6   Perf. 13½x14
1024	A422	4fr multicolored	5.50	5.50

Letter Writing — A423

1994, June 6   Photo.   Perf. 12½
Granite Paper
1025	A423	60rp Elephant	.80	.80
1026	A423	60rp Cherub	.80	.80
1027	A423	60rp Pig	.80	.80
1028	A423	60rp Dog	.80	.80
	Nos. 1025-1028 (4)		3.20	3.20

Life Cycle of Grape Vine
A424

Designs: No. 1029, Spring, vine beginning to flower. No. 1030, Summer, green grapes on vine. No. 1031, Autumn, ripe grapes ready for harvest. No. 1032, Winter, bare vine in snow.

1994, Sept. 5   Photo.   Perf. 11½
Granite Paper
1029	A424	60rp multicolored	.80	.80
1030	A424	60rp multicolored	.80	.80
1031	A424	60rp multicolored	.80	.80
1032	A424	60rp multicolored	.80	.80
a	Block of 4, #1029-1032		3.25	3.25

No. 1032a is continuous design.

Minerals
A425

Photo. & Engr.
1994, Sept. 5   Perf. 13½x12½
1033	A425	60rp Strontianite	.80	.80
1034	A425	80rp Faden quartz	1.10	1.10
1035	A425	3.50fr Ferrous dolomite	4.75	4.75
	Nos. 1033-1035 (3)		6.65	6.65

A426

Christmas contemporary art, by Anne Frommelt: 60rp, The True Light. 80rp, Peace on Earth. 1fr, See the House of God.

1994, Dec. 5   Photo.   Perf. 11½
Granite Paper
1036	A426	60rp multicolored	.90	.90
1037	A426	80rp multicolored	1.25	1.25
1038	A426	1fr multicolored	1.50	1.50
	Nos. 1036-1038 (3)		3.65	3.65

A427

The Four Elements, by Ernst Steiner.

Photo. & Engr.
1994, Dec. 5   Perf. 14
1039	A427	60rp Earth	.90	.90
1040	A427	80rp Water	1.25	1.25
1041	A427	1fr Fire	1.50	1.50
1042	A427	2.50fr Air	4.00	4.00
	Nos. 1039-1042 (4)		7.65	7.65

Peace and Freedom
A428

Europa: 80rp, 1fr, Excerpts from speeches of Prince Franz Josef II.

1995, Mar. 6   Photo.   Perf. 11½
Granite Paper
1043	A428	80rp multicolored	1.10	.90
1044	A428	1fr multicolored	1.40	1.10

A429

Anniversaries and Events
A430   A431

60rp, Princess Marie, Bosnian children.

1995, Mar. 6   Granite Paper
1045	A429	60rp multicolored	.95	.95
1046	A430	1.80fr multicolored	3.00	3.00
1047	A431	3.50fr multicolored	5.50	5.50
	Nos. 1045-1047 (3)		9.45	9.45

Liechtenstein Red Cross, 50th anniv. (No. 1045). UN, 50th anniv. (No. 1046). The Alps, European Landscape of the Year 1995-96 (No. 1047).

Falknis Group, by Anton Frommelt (1895-1975)
A432

Paintings: 80rp, Three Oaks. 4.10fr, Rhine below Triesen.

1995, June 6   Photo.   Perf. 12
Granite Paper
1048	A432	60rp multicolored	1.00	1.00
1049	A432	80rp multicolored	1.40	1.40
1050	A432	4.10fr multicolored	7.25	7.25
	Nos. 1048-1050 (3)		9.65	9.65

Letter Writing — A433

No. 1051, Girl, boy building heart with bricks. No. 1052, Boy, girl bandaging sunflower. No. 1053, Girl, boy & rainbow. No. 1054, Boy in hot air balloon delivering letter to girl.

1995, June 6   *Perf. 12½*
Granite Paper

1051	A433	60rp multicolored	1.00	1.00
1052	A433	60rp multicolored	1.00	1.00
1053	A433	60rp multicolored	1.00	1.00
1054	A433	60rp multicolored	1.00	1.00
a.		Vert. strip of 4, #1051-1054 + label	4.00	4.00

Liechtenstein-Switzerland Postal Relationship — A434

Litho. & Engr.
1995, Sept. 5   *Perf. 13½*

1055	A434	60rp multicolored	1.00	1.00

See Switzerland No. 960.
No. 1055 and Switzerland No. 960 are identical. This issue was valid for postage in both countries.

Plant Type of 1993
Photo. & Engr.
1995, Sept. 5   *Perf. 13x13½*

1056	A415	60rp Arnica montana	1.00	1.00
1057	A415	80rp Urtica dioica	1.40	1.40
1058	A415	1.80fr Valeriana officinalis	3.00	3.00
1059	A415	3.50fr Ranunculus ficaria	6.00	6.00
		Nos. 1056-1059 (4)	11.40	11.40

A435

Paintings by Lorenzo Monaco: 60rp, Angel kneeling, facing right. 80rp, Madonna and Child, two angels at her feet. 1fr, Angel kneeling, facing left.

Photo. & Engr.
1995, Dec. 4   *Perf. 14½x13½*

1060	A435	60rp multicolored	1.00	1.00
1061	A435	80rp multicolored	1.40	1.40
1062	A435	1fr multicolored	1.75	1.75
		Nos. 1060-1062 (3)	4.15	4.15

Christmas.

A436

Painting: 4fr, Lady with Lap Dog, by Paul Wunderlich.

1995, Dec. 4

1063	A436	4fr multicolored	6.75	6.75

Bronze Age in Europe — A437

1996, Mar. 4   **Photo.**   *Perf. 11½*
Granite Paper

1064	A437	90rp Crucible, pin	1.50	1.50

Countess Nora Kinsky (1888-1923), Nurse, Mother of Princess Gina — A438

Profile and: 90rp, Mar. 7, 1917 diary entry. 1.10fr, Feb. 28, 1917 diary entry.

1996, Mar. 4   **Granite Paper**

1065	A438	90rp multicolored	1.75	1.00
1066	A438	1.10fr multicolored	2.25	1.25

Paintings of Village Views, by Marianne Siegl, Based on Sketches by Otto Zeiller A439

10rp, Eschen. 20rp, Farmhouse, St. Joseph's Chapel, Planken. 80rp, Farmhouse, Ruggell. 1fr, Postal auxiliary office, Nendeln. 1.20fr, Buildings, Triesen. 1.30fr, Upper Village, Triesen. 1.70fr, St. Theresa's Church, Schaanwald. 2fr, Rural houses, barns, Gamprin. 4fr, Parish Church, center of village, Triesenberg. 5fr, Vaduz Castle.

1996-99   **Photo.**   *Perf. 12*
Granite Paper

1068	A439	10rp multicolored	.25	.25
1069	A439	20rp multicolored	.40	.30
1070	A439	80rp multicolored	1.50	1.10
1071	A439	1fr multicolored	2.00	1.40
1072	A439	1.20fr multicolored	2.40	1.75
1073	A439	1.30fr multicolored	2.60	1.75
1074	A439	1.70fr multicolored	3.25	2.25
1075	A439	2fr multicolored	4.00	2.70
1076	A439	4fr multicolored	8.00	5.25
1077	A439	5fr multicolored	10.00	8.25
		Nos. 1068-1077 (10)	34.40	25.00

Issued: 10rp, 5fr, 3/4/96; 20rp, 1.30fr, 1.70fr, 3/3/97; 2fr, 4fr, 6/2/98; 80rp, 1fr, 1.20fr, 3/1/99.
See Nos. 1167-1175A.

Modern Olympic Games, Cent. A440

1996, June 3   **Photo.**   *Perf. 11½*
Granite Paper

1079	A440	70rp Gymnastics	1.40	1.10
1080	A440	90rp Hurdles	1.75	1.50
1081	A440	1.10fr Cycling	2.25	1.75
		Nos. 1079-1081 (3)	5.40	4.35

Ferdinand Gehr, 100th Birthday A441

Various paintings of flowers.

1996, June 3   **Granite Paper**

1083	A441	70rp multicolored	1.40	1.10
1084	A441	90rp multicolored	1.75	1.50
1085	A441	1.10fr multicolored	2.25	1.75

Size: 33x23mm

1086	A441	1.80fr multicolored	3.50	3.00
		Nos. 1083-1086 (4)	8.90	7.35

Austria, Millennium A442

Photo. & Engr.
1996, Sept. 2   *Perf. 13½*

1087	A442	90rp multicolored	1.75	1.75

New Constitution, 75th Anniv. — A443

Litho., Engr. & Embossed
1996, Sept. 2   *Perf. 14*

1088	A443	10fr Natl. arms	20.00	20.00

A444

Paintings by Russian Artist, Eugen Zotow (1881-1953): 70rp, "Country Estate in Poltava." 1.10fr, "Three Bathers in a Park in Berlin." 1.40fr, "View of Vaduz."

Photo. & Engr.
1996, Dec. 2   *Perf. 14*

1089	A444	70rp multicolored	1.40	1.10
1090	A444	1.10fr multicolored	2.25	1.75
1091	A444	1.40fr multicolored	2.75	2.25
		Nos. 1089-1091 (3)	6.40	5.10

A445

Christmas: Illuminated manuscripts, symbols of the Evangelists.

1996, Dec. 2

1092	A445	70rp Matthew	1.40	1.10
1093	A445	90rp Mark	1.75	1.40
1094	A445	1.10fr Luke	2.25	1.75
1095	A445	1.80fr John	3.50	3.00
		Nos. 1092-1095 (4)	8.90	7.25

A446

Photo. & Engr.
1997, Mar. 3   *Perf. 13½*

1096	A446	70rp multicolored	1.40	.95

Franz Schubert (1797-1828), composer.

A447

Europa, Liechtenstein Myths: 90rp, Wild Gnomes. 1.10fr, Foal of Planken.

1997, Mar. 3   **Photo.**   *Perf. 12*
Granite Paper

1097	A447	90rp multicolored	*1.75*	*1.00*
1098	A447	1.10fr multicolored	*2.25*	*1.10*

St. Lucius, Virgin Mary Holding Infant Jesus, St. Florin, by Gabriel Dreher A448

Photo. & Engr.
1997, June 2   *Perf. 13½x13*

1099	A448	20fr multicolored	40.00	40.00

A449

Painting, "Jeune Fille en Fleur," by Enrico Baj.

1997, Aug. 22   **Photo.**   *Perf. 11½*
Granite Paper

1100	A449	70rp multicolored	1.40	1.40

A450

Mushrooms: 70rp, Phaeolepiota aurea. 90rp, Helvella silvicola. 1.10fr, Aleuria aurantia.

Photo. & Engr.
1997, Aug. 22   *Perf. 14*

1101	A450	70rp multicolored	1.40	.95
1102	A450	90rp multicolored	1.75	1.20
1103	A450	1.10fr multicolored	2.25	1.50
		Nos. 1101-1103 (3)	5.40	3.65

Railway in Liechtenstein, 125th Anniv. — A451

Train stations: 70rp, Schaanwald. 90rp, Nendeln. 1.80fr, Schaan-Vaduz.

1997, Aug. 22   **Photo.**   *Perf. 11½*
Granite Paper

1104	A451	70rp multicolored	1.40	.95
1105	A451	90rp multicolored	1.75	1.20
1106	A451	1.80fr multicolored	3.50	2.40
		Nos. 1104-1106 (3)	6.65	4.55

Christmas Tree Decorations
A452

Photo. & Engr.
1997, Dec. 1   *Perf. 14*
1107 A452 70rp shown   1.40 1.00
1108 A452 90rp Bell   1.75 1.25
1109 A452 1.10fr Oval with pointed ends   2.25 1.50
     Nos. 1107-1109 (3)   5.40 3.75

A453

Skiing, 1998 Winter Olympic Games, Nagano.

1997, Dec. 1   **Photo.**   *Perf. 12½*
Granite Paper
1110 A453 70rp Cross-country   1.40 1.00
1111 A453 90rp Slalom   1.75 1.25
1112 A453 1.80fr Downhill   3.50 2.50
     Nos. 1110-1112 (3)   6.65 4.75

A454

Contemporary Art, Paintings by Heinz Mack: No. 1113, Verano (Der Sommer) No. 1114, Hommage An Liechtenstein. No. 1115, Zwischen Tag Und Traum. No. 1116, Salute Chirico!.

1998, Mar. 2   *Perf. 12*
Granite Paper
1113 A454 70rp multicolored   1.40 .95
1114 A454 70rp multicolored   1.40 .95
1115 A454 70rp multicolored   1.40 .95
1116 A454 70rp multicolored   1.40 .95
  a.   Block or strip of 4, #1113-1116   6.00 3.80

Festivals
A455

Europa: 90rp, National holiday. 1.10fr, Festival of the Musical Societies.

1998, Mar. 2   **Granite Paper**
1117 A455 90rp multicolored   1.75 1.00
1118 A455 1.10fr multicolored   2.25 1.10

Customs Treaty with Switzerland, 75th Anniv. — A456

1998, Mar. 2   **Granite Paper**
1119 A456 1.70fr multicolored   3.25 2.25

1998 World Cup Soccer Championships, France — A457

1998, Mar. 2   **Granite Paper**
1120 A457 1.80fr multicolored   3.50 2.50

Letter Writing — A458

Clown: No. 1121, With woman. No. 1122, Holding four leaf clovers. No. 1123, Tipping hat. No. 1124, Holding paper with heart.

Photo. & Engr.
1998, June 2   *Perf. 14*
1121 A458 70rp multicolored   1.40 .95
1122 A458 70rp multicolored   1.40 .95
1123 A458 70rp multicolored   1.40 .95
1124 A458 70rp multicolored   1.40 .95
  a.   Strip of 4, #1121-1124   6.00 3.80

1848 Protest March
A459

1998, Sept. 7   **Photo.**   *Perf. 12*
Granite Paper
1125 A459 1.80fr multicolored   3.50 2.50

A460

Traditional Crafts: 90rp, Cooper's tools, tub. 2.20fr, Wooden shoemaker's tools, clog. 3.50fr, Cartwright's tools, wheel.

1998, Sept. 7   **Granite Paper**
1126 A460 90rp multicolored   1.75 1.25
1127 A460 2.20fr multicolored   4.25 3.00
1128 A460 3.50fr multicolored   7.00 4.75
     Nos. 1126-1128 (3)   13.00 9.00

See Nos. 1215-1217.

A461

Christmas (Nativity Scene in high relief): 70rp, Soldier, Virgin Mary. 90rp, Entire nativity scene. 1.10fr, Joseph, donkey.

Photo. & Engr.
1998, Dec. 7   *Perf. 14*
1129 A461 70rp multicolored   1.40 1.00
1130 A461 90rp multicolored   1.75 1.25
1131 A461 1.10fr multicolored   2.25 1.60
     Nos. 1129-1131 (3)   5.40 3.85

No. 1130 is 34x20mm.

Preservation of Historic Sites — A462

Older buildings, Hinterschellengerg: 90rp, Guest house. 1.70fr, St. George's Chapel, vert. 1.80fr, Farmhouse.

1998, Dec. 7   **Photo.**   *Perf. 11½*
Granite Paper
1132 A462 90rp multicolored   1.75 1.25
1133 A462 1.70fr multicolored   3.25 2.50
1134 A462 1.80fr multicolored   3.50 2.50
     Nos. 1132-1134 (3)   8.50 6.25

A463   A464

1998, Dec. 7   **Granite Paper**
1135 A463 2.80fr multicolored   5.50 4.00

Telephone in Liechtenstein, cent.

1999, Mar. 1   **Photo.**   *Perf. 11½x12*
Europa (Conservation Areas): 90rp, Snake, Schwabbrünnen-Aescher marshland. 1.10fr, Bird, Ruggell marsh.

Granite Paper
1136 A464 90rp multicolored   *1.75 1.00*
1137 A464 1.10fr multicolored   *2.25 1.20*

Unterland, 300th Anniv. — A465

Continuous scene of villages: a, Schellenberg, buildings, fortress. b, Mauren, domed steeple on church. c, Eschen,, church, houses. d, Ruggell, road leading into village. e, Gamprin, gray-roofed buildings, church.

1999, Mar. 1   *Perf. 12*
Granite Paper
1138 A465 Sheet of 5 + label   9.00 6.25
  a.-e.   90rp any single   1.75 1.25

Anniversaries
A466

Stylized designs: No. 1139, Council of Europe 50th anniv. emblem. No. 1140, Bird holding letter. No. 1141, Hand holding heart.

1999, May 25   **Photo.**   *Perf. 11½x12*
Granite Paper
1139 A466 70rp multicolored   1.40 .95
1140 A466 70rp multicolored   1.40 .95
1141 A466 70rp multicolored   1.40 .95
     Nos. 1139-1141 (3)   4.20 2.85

No. 1140, UPU, 125th anniv. No. 1141, Caritas Liechtenstein, 75th anniv.

8th Games of the Small European States
A467

1999, May 25   **Granite Paper**
1142 A467 70rp Judo   1.40 .95
1143 A467 70rp Swimming   1.40 .95
1144 A467 70rp Javelin   1.40 .95
1145 A467 90rp Volleyball   1.75 1.25
1146 A467 90rp Squash   1.75 1.25
1147 A467 90rp Tennis   1.75 1.25
1148 A467 90rp Table tennis   1.75 1.25

1149 A467 90rp Cycling   1.75 1.25
1150 A467 90rp Shooting   1.75 1.25
     Nos. 1142-1150 (9)   14.70 10.35

Johann Wolfgang von Goethe (1749-1832), Poet — A468

Quotations and scenes from Faust: 1.40fr, "Grey, dear friend, is all theory and green the golden tree of life." 1.70fr, "I'll take the wager!...Done! And again, and again!"

Photo. & Engr.
1999, Sept. 9   *Perf. 14*
1151 A468 1.40fr multicolored   2.75 1.90
1152 A468 1.70fr multicolored   3.25 2.25

Paintings by Eugen Verling (1891-1968)
A469

Designs: 70rp, Herrengasse. 2fr, Old Vaduz with Castle. 4fr, House in Fürst-Franz-Josef-Strasse, Vaduz.

1999, Sept. 9
1153 A469 70rp multicolored   1.40 .95
1154 A469 2fr multicolored   4.00 2.75
1155 A469 4fr multicolored   8.00 5.50
     Nos. 1153-1155 (3)   13.40 9.20

A470   A471

Walser house identification marks.

1999, Dec. 6   **Photo.**   *Perf. 11¾*
Granite Paper
1156 A470 70rp Door mark   1.40 .90
1157 A470 90rp Picture mark   1.75 1.10
1158 A470 1.80fr Axe mark   3.50 2.40
     Nos. 1156-1158 (3)   6.65 4.40

Photo. & Engr.
1999, Dec. 6   *Perf. 13½*
1159 A471 3.60fr multicolored   4.75 4.75

Johann Gutenberg, inventer of letterpress printing.

Christmas Paintings by Joseph Walser
A472

1999, Dec. 6   *Perf. 13½x14¼*
1160 A472 70rp The Annunciation   1.40 .90
1161 A472 90rp Nativity   1.75 1.10
1162 A472 1.10fr Presentation of
Jesus   2.25 1.40
     Nos. 1160-1162 (3)   5.40 3.40

Souvenir Sheet

Millennium — A473

Designs: 70rp, The Adoration of the Shepherds, by Matthias Stomer. 1.10fr, The Magi, by Ferdinand Gehr.

2000, Jan. 1   Photo.   Perf. 12
Granite Paper

1163		Sheet of 2	4.00	2.25
a.	A473	70rp multi	1.40	.85
b.	A473	1.10fr multi	2.25	1.40

Christianity, 2000th anniv.

Creation of Liechtenstein Post, Ltd. — A474

2000, Jan. 1   Perf. 11¾
Granite Paper

| 1164 | A474 | 90rp multi | | 1.75 | 1.10 |

Village Views Type of 1996

Designs: 50rp, Church and vicarage, Ruggell. 60rp, Chapel of St. Peter, Balzers. 70rp, Parish church, Schellenberg. 1.10fr, Holy Cross Chapel, Eschen. 1.40fr, Farmhouse, parish church, Mauren. 1.80fr, Chapel of Peace, Malbun. 1.90fr, Tower of Church of St. Lawrence, Schaan. 2.20fr, Höfle District, Balzers. 4.50fr, Church mound, Bendern.

2000-01   Photo.   Perf. 11¾
Granite Paper

1167	A439	50rp multi	1.00	.60
1168	A439	60rp multi	1.25	.75
1169	A439	70rp multi	1.40	.85
1171	A439	1.10fr multi	2.25	1.40
1172	A439	1.40fr multi	2.75	1.75
1173	A439	1.80fr multi	3.50	2.25
1174	A439	1.90fr multi	3.75	2.25
1175	A439	2.20fr multi	4.50	2.60
1175A	A439	4.50fr multi	9.00	5.50
		Nos. 1167-1175A (9)	29.40	17.95

Issued: 70rp, 1.80fr, 2.20fr, 4.50fr, 6/5/01.

"Gods Once Walked" Exhibition at Vaduz Museum of Art — A475

Designs: 70rp, Mars and Rhea Silvia, by Peter Paul Rubens. 1.80fr, Cupid With Soap Bubble, by Rembrandt.

Photo. & Engr.
2000, Mar. 6   Perf. 13½x12¾

| 1176 | A475 | 70rp multi | 1.40 | .85 |
| 1177 | A475 | 1.80fr multi | 3.50 | 2.25 |

Europa, 2000
Common Design Type

2000, May 9   Photo.   Perf. 11½x11¾
Granite Paper

| 1178 | CD17 | 1.10fr multi | 2.25 | 1.75 |

Expo 2000, Hanover — A476

Art by Friedensreich Hundertwasser: 70rp, Fragrance of Humus. 90rp, Do Not Wait Houses — Move. 1.10fr, The Car: A Drive Towards Nature and Creation.

Photo. & Engr.
2000, May 9   Perf. 14¼x13½

1179	A476	70rp multi	1.40	.80
1180	A476	90rp multi	1.75	1.00
1181	A476	1.10fr multi	2.25	1.25
		Nos. 1179-1181 (3)	5.40	3.05

Images of Peace A477

Art by mouth and foot painters: 1.40fr, Dove of Peace, by Antonio Martini. 1.70fr, Universal Peace, by Alberto Alvarez. 2.20fr, Rainbow, by Eiichi Minami.

2000, May 9   Photo.   Perf. 11¾x11½

1182	A477	1.40fr multi	2.75	1.60
1183	A477	1.70fr multi	3.25	1.90
1184	A477	2.20fr multi	4.50	2.50
		Nos. 1182-1184 (3)	10.50	6.00

2000 Summer Olympics, Sydney A478

Designs: 80rp, Koalas on rings. 1fr, High jump by kangaroo joey. 1.30fr, Emus racing. 1.80fr, Platypuses swimming.

2000, Sept. 4   Photo.   Perf. 11¾
Granite Paper

1185	A478	80rp multi	1.60	.95
1186	A478	1fr multi	2.00	1.10
1187	A478	1.30fr multi	2.50	1.50
1188	A478	1.80fr multi	3.50	2.10
		Nos. 1185-1188 (4)	9.60	5.65

Organization for Security and Co-operation In Europe, 25th Anniv. A479

2000, Sept. 4   Granite Paper

| 1189 | A479 | 1.30fr multi | 2.50 | 1.50 |

Issued in sheets of 20 stamps and 5 labels.

Opening Of Liechtenstein Art Museum — A480

Designs: 80rp, The Dreaming Bee, by Joan Miró. 1.20fr, Cube by Sol LeWitt. 2fr, A Bouquet of Flowers, by Roelant Savery.

2000, Sept. 4   Photo.   Perf. 11¾
Granite Paper (#1190-1191)

| 1190 | A480 | 80rp multi | 1.60 | .95 |
| 1191 | A480 | 1.20fr multi | 2.40 | 1.40 |

Size: 31x46mm
Photo. & Engr.
Perf. 13¾

| 1192 | A480 | 2fr multi | 4.00 | 2.40 |
| | | *Nos. 1190-1192 (3)* | 8.00 | 4.75 |

Mushrooms A481

90rp, Mycena adonis. 1.10fr, Chalciporus amarellus. 2fr, Hygrocybe caylptriformis.

Photo. & Engr.
2000, Dec. 4   Perf. 14¼

| 1193-1195 | A481 | Set of 3 | 8.00 | 4.50 |

Christmas A482

Various creches: 80rp, 1.30fr, 1.80fr.

2000, Dec. 4   Perf. 13¾x14

| 1196-1198 | A482 | Set of 3 | 7.75 | 4.50 |

Europa — A483

2001, Mar. 5   Photo.   Perf. 11½x11¾
Granite Paper

| 1199 | A483 | 1.30fr multi | 2.50 | 2.25 |

Liechtenstein's Presidency of Council of Europe — A484

2001, Mar. 5   Perf. 11¾
Granite Paper

| 1200 | A484 | 1.80fr multi | 3.50 | 2.10 |

Scratch-off Greetings A485

Postman in: No. 1201, 70rp, Red uniform (hidden flower bouquet). No. 1202, 70rp, Blue uniform (hidden envelope).

2001, Mar. 5   Granite Paper

| 1201-1202 | A485 | Set of 2 unscratched | 3.00 | 1.75 |
| | | Set, scratched | | 1.75 |

Easter Eggs of the Russian Czars — A486

Designs: 1.20fr, Silver egg. 1.80fr, Cloisonné egg. 2fr, Porcelain egg.

Photo. & Engr.
2001, Mar. 5   Perf. 13¾

| 1203-1205 | A486 | Set of 3 | 10.00 | 6.00 |

Liechtenstein Historical Association, Cent. — A487

Designs: No. 1206, 70rp, Mars of Gutenberg. No. 1207, Carolignian cruciform fibula.

2001, June 5   Photo.   Perf. 11¾
Granite Paper

| 1206-1207 | A487 | Set of 2 | 2.75 | 1.75 |

Josef Gabriel Rheinberger (1839-1901), Musician A488

Photo. & Engr.
2001, Sept. 3   Perf. 14

| 1208 | A488 | 3.50fr multi | 7.00 | 4.25 |

Votive Pictures — A489

Designs: 70rp, 1733 picture, Chapel of Our Lady, Dux. 1.20fr, 1802 picture, St. George's Chapel, Schellenberg. 1.30fr, 1718 picture, Chapel of Our Lady, Dux.

2001, Sept. 3   Perf. 13½

| 1209-1211 | A489 | Set of 3 | 6.50 | 4.00 |

Building Preservation A490

Designs: 70rp, St. Theresa's Chapel, Schaanwald. 90rp, St. Johann's winery, Mauren. 1.10fr, Pirsch transformer station, Schaanwald.

2001, Sept. 3   Photo.   Perf. 11¾
Granite Paper

| 1212-1214 | A490 | Set of 3 | 5.25 | 3.25 |

See Nos. 1232-1233, 1251-1252, 1295-1296, 1323-1324, 1361-1362, 1394-1395, 1424.

Traditional Crafts Type of 1998

Designs: 70rp, Blacksmith's tools, horse-shoe, yoke bars. 90rp, Rakemaker's tools, rake. 1.20fr, Saddler's tools, horse collar.

2001, Dec. 3   Photo.   Perf. 11¾
Granite Paper
1215-1217 A460 Set of 3   5.50 3.50

Abstract Art by
Gottfried
Honegger
A491

Untitled works: 1.80fr, 2.20fr.

2001, Dec. 3   Perf. 11½
Granite Paper
1218-1219 A491 Set of 2   8.00 5.00

Christmas — A492

Medallions: 70rp, Annunciation. 90rp, Nativity. 1.30fr, The Presentation of the Lord.

2001, Dec. 3   Perf. 12x11¾
Granite Paper
1220-1222 A492 Set of 3   4.00 3.50

Liechtenstein
Students'
Spice Bees
Experiment
on Space
Shuttle
A493

2002, Mar. 4 Photo. Perf. 13½x14¼
1223 A493 90rp multi   1.75 1.10

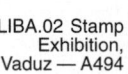

LIBA.02 Stamp
Exhibition,
Vaduz — A494

2002, Mar. 4   Perf. 13¾
1224 A494 1.20fr multi   2.40 1.40

Europa — A495

Designs: 90rp, Tightrope walker. 1.30fr, Juggler.

Photo. & Engr.
2002, Mar. 4   Perf. 14¼x14
1225-1226 A495 Set of 2   4.25 3.75

Intl. Year of
Mountains
A496

Intl. Commision
for Protection of
the Alps
A497

2002, Mar. 4 Photo. Perf. 13¾x13½
1227 A496 70rp multi   1.40 .85
1228 A497 1.20fr multi   2.40 1.40

Paintings by
Friedrich
Kaufmann
(1892-1972)
A498

Views of: 70rp, Schellenberg. 1.30fr, Schaan. 1.80fr, Steg.

2002, Mar. 4   Perf. 13½x13¾
1229-1231 A498 Set of 3   7.50 4.50

Building Preservation Type of 2001

Designs: 70rp, House, Popers, horiz. 1.20fr, House, Weiherring, horiz.

Perf. 13¾x13½
2002, June 3   Photo.
1232-1233 A490 Set of 2   3.75 2.40

2002 World Cup Soccer
Championships, Japan and
Korea — A499

2002, June 3   Perf. 13½x14¼
1234 A499 1.80fr multi   3.50 2.25

Royalty
A500

Designs: 3fr, Princess Marie. 3.50fr, Prince Hans Adam II.

2002, June 3   Perf. 13¾x13½
1235-1236 A500 Set of 2   13.00 8.25

Liba.02 Stamp
Exhibition,
Vaduz — A501

Liechtenstein stamps depicting: 90rp, Various topics. 1.30fr, Royalty.

2002, Aug. 8 Photo. Perf. 13½
1237-1238 A501 Set of 2   4.25 3.00

Royalty Type of 2002

Designs: 2fr, Hereditary Princess Sophie. 2.50fr, Hereditary Prince Alois.

2002, Aug. 8   Perf. 13¾x13½
1239-1240 A500 Set of 2   9.00 6.00

Orchids — A502

Designs: 70rp, Epipogium aphyllum. 1.20fr, Ophrys insectifera. 1.30fr, Nigritella nigra.

2002, Aug. 8   Perf. 13½x13¾
1241-1243 A502 Set of 3   6.25 4.25
See Nos. 1288-1290.

Inn Sign
Art — A503

Designs: 1.20fr, Eagle, Vaduz. 1.80fr, Angel, Balzers. 3fr, Eagle, Bendern.

Photo. & Engr.
2002, Nov. 25   Perf. 13½x14¼
1244-1246 A503 Set of 3   12.00 8.25

Christmas — A504

Batik art by Sister Regina Hassler: 70rp, Search for Shelter. 1.20fr, Nativity. 1.80fr, Flight to Egypt.

Perf. 14¼x13½
2002, Nov. 25   Photo.
1247-1249 A504 Set of 3   7.50 5.25

Europa
A505

2003, Mar. 3 Photo. Perf. 13½x12¾
1250 A505 1.20fr multi   2.40 2.25

Building Preservation Type of 2001

Designs: 70rp, St. Fridolin Church, Ruggell. 2.50fr, House, Spidach, horiz..

Perf. 13½x13¾, 13¾x3½
2003, Mar. 3
1251-1252 A490 Set of 2   6.25 4.75

Viticulture
Throughout the
Year — A506

Designs: 1.30fr, Pruning (February). 1.80fr, Tying vines to arbor (March). 2.20fr, Hoeing soil (April).

2003, Mar. 3   Perf. 14¼
1253-1255 A506 Set of 3   10.50 7.75

2003, June 2 Photo. Perf. 14¼
Designs: 1.20fr, Looping vines (May). 1.80fr, Leaf work (June). 3.50fr, Removing high growth (July).
1256-1258 A506 Set of 3   13.00 10.00

2003, Sept. 1 Photo. Perf. 14¼
Designs: 70rp, Thinning out of vines (August). 90rp, Harvesting grapes (September). 1.10fr, Pressing grapes (October).
1259-1261 A506 Set of 3   5.25 4.00

2003, Nov. 24
Designs: 70rp, First tasting of wine (November). 90rp, Harvest of frozen grapes (December). 1.20fr, Bottling wine (January).
1262-1264 A506 Set of 3   5.50 4.25

Liechtenstein
Association for
the Disabled,
50th
Anniv. — A507

2003, June 2 Photo. Perf. 14¼
1265 A507 70rp multi   1.40 1.10

Reopening of National
Museum — A508

Museum building and: 1.20fr, Ammonite fossil. 1.30fr, Shield of bailiff of Vaduz.

2003, June 2   Perf. 14
1266-1267 A508 Set of 2   5.00 3.75

White Storks and
Nest — A509

Photo. & Engr.
2003, Sept. 1   Perf. 12¾x13½
1268 A509 2.20fr multi   4.50 3.25

Saints — A510

Designs: No. 1269, 1.20fr, St. Blasius. No. 1270, 1.20fr, St. George. No. 1271, 1.30fr, St. Erasmus. No. 1272, 1.30fr, St. Vitus.

2003, Sept. 1   Perf. 13½
1269-1272 A510 Set of 4   10.00 7.25

Stamps of the same denomination were printed in sheets of 20 arranged in blocks of 10 of each stamp separated by a horizontal gutter.
See Nos. 1280-1285, 1308-1311.

Children's
Drawings
A511

Designs: 70rp, Cow, by Laura Beck. No. 1274, 1.80fr, Apple Tree, by Patrick Marxer, vert. No. 1275, 1.80fr, Bee, by Laura Lingg.

Perf. 13½x14¼, 14¼x13½
2003, Nov. 24   Photo.
1273-1275 A511   Set of 3   8.50 6.25

Christmas — A512

Reverse glass paintings: 70rp, Archangel Gabriel. 90rp, Nativity. 1.30fr, Three Magi.

2003, Nov. 24   **Perf. 14¼x13½**
1276-1278 A512   Set of 3   5.75 4.25

AHV Old Age and Survivor's Insurance, 50th Anniv. — A513

2004, Jan. 3   Photo.   **Perf. 14**
1279 A513 85rp multi   1.40 1.40

Saints Type of 2003

Designs: No. 1280, 1fr, St. Achatius. No. 1281, 1fr, St. Margareta. No. 1282, 1.20fr, St. Christophorus. No. 1283, 1.20fr, St. Pantaleon. No. 1284, 2.50fr, St. Aegidius. No. 1285, 2.50fr, St. Cyriakus.

Photo. & Engr.
2004, Mar. 1   **Perf. 13½**
1280-1285 A510   Set of 6   19.00 15.50

Stamps of the same denomination were printed in sheets of 20 arranged in blocks of 10 of each stamp separated by a horizontal gutter.

Europa — A514

2004, Mar. 1   Photo.   **Perf. 13¾x13½**
1286 A514 1.30fr multi   2.50 2.25

2004 Summer Olympics, Athens — A515

2004, June 1   Photo.   **Perf. 14¼**
1287 A515 85rp multi   1.75 1.40

Orchid Type of 2002

Designs: 85rp, Ophrys apifera. 1fr, Orchis ustulata. 1.20fr, Epipactis purpurea.

2004, June 1   **Perf. 13½x13¾**
1288-1290 A502   Set of 3   6.00 4.75

Aerial Views
A516

2004, June 1   **Perf. 13½**
1291 A516 15rp Bendern   .30 .25
1292 A516 85rp Gross-Steg   1.75 1.40
1293 A516 1fr Tuass   2.00 1.60
1294 A516 6fr Gutenberg   12.00 9.25
   Nos. 1291-1294 (4)   16.05 12.50
See No. 1312, 1331-1333, 1340-1341, 1375-1377.

Building Preservation Type of 2001

Designs: 2.20fr, House on Unterdorfstrasse, horiz. 2.50fr, Row of houses, Dorfstrasse, horiz.

Perf. 13¾x13½
2004, Sept. 6   Photo.
1295-1296 A490   Set of 2   9.50 7.50

Sciences — A517

Designs: 85rp, Mathematics. 1fr, Physics. 1.30fr, Chemistry. 1.80fr, Astronomy.

2004, Sept. 6   **Perf. 13¾x14**
1297-1300 A517   Set of 4   10.00 8.00

Digital Palimpsest Research A518

Photo. & Engr.
2004, Nov. 22   **Perf. 14¼**
1301 A518 2.50fr multi   5.00 4.25

Fossils — A519

Designs: 1.20fr, Ammonite. 1.30fr, Sea urchin. 2.20fr, Shark tooth.

2004, Nov. 22
1302-1304 A519   Set of 3   9.50 8.00

Christmas A520

Designs: 85rp, Annunciation. 1fr, Holy Family. 1.80fr, Adoration of the Magi.

2004, Nov. 22   Photo.   **Rouletted 6¾**
1305-1307 A520   Set of 3   7.25 6.25
Punched holes are in stamp frames to give stamps a lace-like appearance.

Saints Type of 2003

Designs: No. 1308, 85rp, St. Eustachius. No. 1309, 85rp, St. Dionysius. No. 1310, 1.80fr, St. Catharine. No. 1311, 1.80fr, St. Barbara.

Photo. & Engr.
2005, Mar. 7   **Perf. 13½**
1308-1311 A510   Set of 4   10.50 9.25

Aerial Views Type of 2004
2005, Mar. 7   Photo.
1312 A516 3.60fr Triesenberg   7.25 6.25

Europa
A521

2005, Mar. 7
1313 A521 1.30fr multi   2.50 2.25

Venus at a Mirror, by Peter Paul Rubens A522

2005, Mar. 7   Photo. & Engr.
1314 A522 2.20fr multi   4.50 4.00
   See Austria No. 1980.

Paintings of Flower Arrangements A523

Designs: No. 1315, 85rp, Magnolia Flowers, by Chen Hongshou (shown). No. 1316, 85rp, Flower Vase in a Windoe Niche, by Ambrosius Bosschaert the Elder.

2005, May 18   Photo.   **Perf. 14**
1315-1316 A523   Set of 2   3.25 3.00
See People's Republic of China Nos. 3433-3434.

Inn Signs — A524

Designs: 1fr, Stallion, Rössle Inn, Schaan. 1.40fr, Edelweiss Inn, Triesenberg. 2.50fr, Lion, Löwen Inn, Bendern.

Photo. & Engr.
2005, June 6   **Perf. 14¼x13½**
1317-1319 A524   Set of 3   10.00 8.25

Postal Museum, 75th Anniv. A525

Designs: 1.10fr, Hermann E. Sieger, museum founder. 1.30fr, Liechtenstein stamps on stock page. 1.80fr, 1930 Zeppelin cover.

Perf. 13½x14¼
2005, June 6   Photo.
1320-1322 A525   Set of 3   8.25 7.00

Building Preservation Type of 2001

Designs: 85rp, Oberbendern. 2.20fr, Church Hill, Bendern.

Perf. 13¾x13½
2005, Sept. 5   Photo.
1323-1324 A490   Set of 2   6.00 5.00

Bats — A526

Designs: 1.80fr, Plecotus auritus. 2fr, Myotis myotis.

2005, Sept. 5   **Perf. 14¼**
1325-1326 A526   Set of 2   7.50 6.25

Pastures A527

Designs: 85rp, Bargälla. 1fr, Pradamee. 1.30fr, Gritsch. 1.80fr, Valüna.

2005, Sept. 5   **Perf. 13½x14¼**
1327-1330 A527   Set of 4   10.00 8.00
See nos. 1356-1358, 1384-1386, 1403-1404.

Aerial Views Type of 2004
2005, Nov. 21   Photo.   **Perf. 13½**
1331 A516 1.50fr Oberland   3.00 2.40
1332 A516 1.60fr Ruggeller Riet   3.25 2.50
1333 A516 3fr Naafkopf   6.00 4.75
   Nos. 1331-1333 (3)   12.25 9.65

2006 Winter Olympics, Turin, Italy — A528

Designs: 1.20fr, Ski jumping. 1.30fr, Biathlon. 1.40fr, Slalom skiing.

2005, Nov. 21   **Perf. 14¼x14**
1334-1336 A528   Set of 3   8.00 6.25

Christmas A529

Wood sculptures by Toni Gstöhl: 85rp, The Annunciation. 1fr, Holy Family. 1.30fr, Adoration of the Shepherds.

Photo. & Engr.
2005, Nov. 21   **Perf. 14¼x13½**
1337-1339 A529   Set of 3   6.25 5.00

Aerial Views Type of 2004
2006, Mar. 6   Photo.   **Perf. 13½**
1340 A516 2.50fr Rhine Canal   5.00 4.00
1341 A516 3.50fr Rhine Valley   7.00 5.50

Lost in Her Dreams, by Friedrich von Amerling A530

2006, Mar. 6   **Photo. & Engr.**
1342 A530 2.20fr multi   4.50 3.50
See Austria No. 2041.

Paintings by Eugen Wilhelm Schüepp (1915-74) A531

Designs: 1fr, Peat Cutters, Ruggell Marsh. 1.80fr, Neugut, Schaan.

2006, Mar. 6   **Photo.**   **Perf. 13½x14¼**
1343-1344 A531   Set of 2   5.50 4.50

Europa A532

Winning designs from stamp design contest: 1.20fr, Bridge, by Nadja Beck. 1.30fr, Face of Integration, by Elisabeth Müssner.

2006, Mar. 6
1345-1346 A532   Set of 2   5.00 4.00

2006 World Cup Soccer Championships, Germany — A533

Perf. 13½x14¼
2006, June 6   **Photo.**
1347 A533 3.30fr multi   6.50 5.50

A534   A535

Designs: 85rp, Woman holding G clef. 1fr, Backpacker. 1.20fr, Restaurant patron. 1.80fr, Skier.

2006, June 6   **Perf. 13¾**
1348-1351 A534   Set of 4   9.75 8.25
Tourism promotion.

2006, June 6   **Litho. & Engr.**
Designs: 85rp, Prince Johann I. 1fr, National flag. 1.30fr, Flag of the Princely House of Liechtenstein. 1.80fr, National arms.
1352-1355 A535   Set of 4   10.00 8.25
Full sovereignty, bicent.

Pastures Type of 2005

Designs: 85rp, Lawena. 1.30fr, Gapfahl. 2.40fr, Gafadura.

Perf. 13½x14¼
2006, Sept. 4   **Photo.**
1356-1358 A527   Set of 3   9.00 7.50

Wolfgang Amadeus Mozart (1756-91), Composer — A536

2006, Sept. 4   **Perf. 13¾x14¼**
1359 A536 1.20fr multi   2.50 2.00

Miniature Sheet

Classical Music — A537

No. 1360: a, The Magic Flute, by Wolfgang Amadeus Mozart. b, Radetzky March, by Johann Strauss. c, Rhapsody in Blue, by George Gershwin. d, Water Music, by George Frideric Handel. e, Pastoral Symphony, by Ludwig van Beethoven. f, Waltz of the Flowers, by Peter Ilich Tchaikovsky. g, The Swan, by Camille Saint-Saens. h, A Midsummer Night's Dream, by Felix Mendelssohn.

2006, Sept. 4   **Perf. 13½x14¼**
1360 A537   Sheet of 8   16.00 13.00
  a.-h.   1fr Any single   2.00 1.60

Building Preservation Type of 2001

Designs: 1.80fr, Governor's residence and Liechtenstein Institute, Bendern. 3.50fr, Bühl House, Gamprin, horiz.

Perf. 13½x13¾, 13¾x13½
2006, Nov. 20   **Photo.**
1361-1362 A490   Set of 2   10.50 8.50

Inventions A538

Designs: 1.30fr, Curta calculator. 1.40fr, Carena film camera. 2.40fr, PAV sliding caliper.

2006, Nov. 20   **Perf. 14¼x14**
1363-1365 A538   Set of 3   10.00 8.25

Christmas A539

Frescos from Chapel of St. Mary, Dux: 85rp, The Annunciation. 1fr, Nativity. 1.30fr, Presentation at the Temple.

Photo. & Engr.
2006, Nov. 20   **Perf. 13½**
1366-1368 A539   Set of 3   6.25 5.00

Scouting, Cent. — A540

2007, Mar. 5   **Photo.**   **Perf. 14¼**
1369 A540 1.30fr multi   2.50 2.10

Portrait of a Lady, by Bernardino Zaganelli da Cotignola A541

Litho. & Engr.
2007, Mar. 5   **Perf. 13¾**
1370 A541 2.40fr multi   4.75 4.00
See Austria No. 2086.

Musical Terms A542

Designs: 85rp, Allegro. 1.80fr, Capriccio. 2fr, Crescendo. 3.50fr, Con fuoco.

2007, Mar. 5   **Photo.**   **Perf. 13½**
1371-1374 A542   Set of 4   16.00 13.50

Aerial Views Type of 2004

2007, June 4   **Photo.**   **Perf. 13½**
1375 A516 1.10fr Nendeln   2.00 2.00
1376 A516 1.80fr Malbun   3.25 3.25
1377 A516 2.60fr Ackerland   4.75 4.75
  Nos. 1375-1377 (3)   10.00 10.00

Greeting Card Art — A543

Designs: 85rp, Boy delivering flower and letter to girl. 1fr, Two children carrying litter with cake, flowers and letter. 1.30fr, Bird carrying letter.

2007, June 4   **Rouletted 6¾**
1378-1380 A543   Set of 3   5.25 5.25
Punched holes are in stamp frames to give stamps a lacelike appearance.

Paintings of Rhine Landscapes by Johann Ludwig Bleuler (1792-1850) A544

Designs: 1fr, Castle and Village of Vaduz. 1.30fr, Rätikon Mountain. 2.40fr, Confluence of the Ill and Rhine.

Perf. 13½x14¼
2007, June 4   **Photo. & Engr**
1381-1383 A544   Set of 3   8.50 8.50

Pastures Type of 2005

Designs: 1fr, Hintervalorsch. 1.40fr, Sücka. 2.20fr, Guschgfiel.

Perf. 13½x14¼
2007, Sept. 3   **Photo.**
1384-1386 A527   Set of 3   8.50 8.50

Technical Innovations From Liechtenstein A545

Designs: 1.30fr, Hilti hammer and drill. 1.80fr, Kaiser mobile walking excavator. 2.40fr, Hoval AluFer composite heating tube.

2007, Sept. 3   **Perf. 14¼**
1387-1389 A545   Set of 3   9.25 9.25
See Nos. 1425-1427.

Beetles A546

Designs: 85rp, Trichodes apiarius. 100rp, Cetania aurata. 130rp, Dytiscus marginalis.

2007, Sept. 3   **Litho.**   **Perf. 13¾x14**
1390-1392 A546   Set of 3   5.75 5.75

Panoramic View of Liechtenstein — A547

2007, Oct. 1   **Litho.**   **Perf. 14**
1393 A547 130rp multi   2.50 2.50

Building Preservation Type of 2001

Designs: 2fr, St. Martin's Church, Eschen. 2.70fr, Mill, Eschen, horiz.

Perf. 13½x13¾, 13¾x13½
2007, Nov. 19   **Photo.**
1394-1395 A490   Set of 2   8.25 8.25

New Parliament Building A548

2007, Nov. 19   **Perf. 13¾**
1396 A548 130rp multi   2.25 2.25

Natural Phenomena A549

Designs: 85rp, Rainbow above Three Sisters Massif. 100rp, Lightning over Bendern.

180rp, Ice crystal halo around Moon over Malbun.

2007, Nov. 19	Litho.	Perf. 14¼
1397-1399	A549	Set of 3	6.50	6.50

Christmas
A550

Designs: 85rp, Chapel of St. Mary, Gamprin-Oberbühl. 1fr, Büel Chapel, Eschen. 1.30fr, Chapel of St. Wolfgang, Triesen.

	Perf. 13½x14¼	Photo.
2007, Nov. 19		
1400-1402	A550	Set of 3	5.75	5.75

Pastures Type of 2005

Designs: 2.60fr, Guschg. 3fr, Güschgle.

2008, Mar. 3	Photo.	Perf. 13½x14¼
1403-1404	A527	Set of 2	11.00	11.00

Europa
A551

2008, Mar. 3	Litho.	Perf. 13½x13¾
1405	A551	130rp multi	2.60	2.60

Volunteer Fire Fighters
A552

2008, Mar. 3		Perf. 13½
1406	A552	1fr multi	2.00	2.00

Sleeping Princess Marie Franziska, by Friedrich von Amerling
A553

2008, Mar. 3	Photo. & Engr.
1407	A553	2.40fr multi	4.75	4.75

See Austria No. 2144.

Spoerry-Areal, Vaduz — A554

Chapel of St. Mamertus, Triesen — A555

Vaduz Castle — A556

2008, Mar. 3	Litho.	Perf. 14
1408	A554	85rp multi	1.75	1.75
1409	A555	1fr multi	2.00	2.00
1410	A556	1.30fr multi	2.60	2.60
	Nos. 1408-1410 (3)		6.35	6.35

Mother and Queen of the Precious Blood with Child, by Unknown Artist — A557

2008, June 2	Litho.	Perf. 12¾x13½
1411	A557	220rp multi	5.00	5.00

Schellenberg Convent, 150th anniv.

2008 Summer Olympics, Beijing — A558

Mascots involved in: 85rp, Martial arts. 100rp, Soccer.

2008, June 2		Perf. 14¼x13½
1412-1413	A558	Set of 2	4.25	4.25

2008 Paralympics, Beijing — A559

Designs: 130rp, Marathon. 180rp, Table tennis.

2008, June 2		Perf. 13½x14¼
1414-1415	A559	Set of 2	7.25	7.25

2008 European Soccer Championships, Austria and Switzerland — A560

Designs: No. 1416, 130rp, St. Stephen's Cathedral, Vienna, soccer player waltzing, violinist. No. 1417, 130rp, Soccer fans holding Liechtenstein flag, wearing Swiss hat, and Austrian scarf. No. 1418, 130rp, Alphorn player, Matterhorn, soccer player.

2008, June 2		Perf. 14
1416-1418	A560	Set of 3	9.00	9.00

Nos. 1416-1418 printed in sheets containing 4 No. 1417 and 6 each Nos. 1416 and 1418.

Hymenopterans
A561

Designs: 85rp, Osmia brevicornis. 1fr, Epeoloides coecutiens. 1.30fr, Odynerus spinipes.

2008, June 2		Perf. 14¼
1419-1421	A561	Set of 3	7.25	7.25

Souvenir Sheet

Prince Karl I (1569-1627) — A562

	Photo. & Engr.	
2008, Sept. 1		Perf. 13¾x13½
1422	A562	5fr multi	11.50	11.50

Princely house of Liechtenstein, 400th anniv.

Miniature Sheet

Drawings by Wilhelm Busch (1832-1908) — A563

No. 1423: a, Schoolmaster Lampel. b, Hans Huckebein. c, Max and Moritz. d, Widow Bolte. e, Pious Helene. f, Fipps the Monkey. g, Tailor Böck. h, Balduin Bählamm.

2008, Sept. 1	Photo.	Perf. 14x13¾
1423	A563	Sheet of 8	24.00	24.00
a.-h.		1.30fr Any single	3.00	3.00

Building Preservation Type of 2001

Design: Schädler Ceramics Building, Nendeln, horiz.

	Perf. 13¾x13½
2008, Nov. 17	Photo.
1424	A490	3.80fr multi	8.75	8.75

Technical Innovations Type of 2007

Designs: 1.20fr, Neutrik NC3MX audio cable connectors. 1.40fr, Ivoclar Vivadent bluephase polymerization unit. 2.20fr, Presta DeltaValveControl variable valve-lift system.

2008, Nov. 17		Perf. 14¼
1425-1427	A545	Set of 3	8.75	8.75

Christmas
A564

Designs: 85rp, Candles, flowers and evergreen branches. 100rp, Children carrying holly, horiz. 130rp, Christmas tree and gifts.

	Perf. 14¼x14½, 14½x14¼
2008, Nov. 17	Litho.
1428-1430	A564	Set of 3	7.25	7.25

Civil Protection Volunteers — A565

2009, Mar. 2	Litho.	Perf. 13¾x13½
1431	A565	1fr multi	2.25	2.25

See Nos. 1471-1472, 1566-1567.

Europa — A566

Litho. With Hologram Affixed

2009, Mar. 2		Perf. 14¼
1432	A566	1.30fr multi	3.00	3.00

Land Registry, 200th Anniv. — A567

2009, Mar. 2	Litho.	Perf. 13¾
1433	A567	330rp multi	7.50	7.50

Liechtenstein Post AG, 10th Anniv. — A568

Designs: 85rp, Counter clerk handling package. 100rp, Mail deliverer. 130rp, Mail sorter.

2009, Mar. 2		Perf. 13¾x13½
1434-1436	A568	Set of 3	7.25	7.25

Linoleum Prints by Stephan Sude — A569

Designs: 1fr, Unfolding. 1.30fr, Awareness. 2.70fr, Fulfillment.

2009, Mar. 2		Perf. 14x13¼
1437-1439	A569	Set of 3	11.50	11.50

Alpine
Association,
Cent.
A570

Crosses on summits of: 100rp, Kuegrat.
130rp, Langspitz, vert. 220rp, Rappastein,
vert. 240rp, Jahn-Turm and Wolan.

Perf. 13¾x13½, 13½x13¾
2009, June 8   Litho.
1440-1443 A570   Set of 4   16.00 16.00

Forests — A571

Designs: 85rp, Ants in forest. 1fr, Path in
forest. 1.40fr, Boulder against tree on hillside.
1.60fr, Cut timber.

2009, June 8   Perf. 13½
1444-1447 A571   Set of 4   11.00 11.00

Vaduz
Castle
A572

Castle in: 130rp, Spring. 180rp, Summer.

2009, June 8   Photo.   Perf. 13¾
1448-1449 A572   Set of 2   7.00 7.00
See Nos. 1488-1489.

Liechtenstein
Philatelic Society,
75th
Anniv. — A573

2009, Sept. 7   Litho.   Perf. 13x13¼
1450 A573 130rp multi   3.00 3.00
Holes are drilled along the map border.

Badminton Cabinet
Ornamentation — A574

Panels with bird and flower designs: 1.30fr,
Bird with blue head. 2fr, Three birds, vert.
(35x50mm). 4fr, Bird with red head.

Perf. 14, 13¾ (2fr)
2009, Sept. 7   Photo. & Engr.
1451-1453 A574   Set of 3   17.00 17.00

Butterflies
A575

Designs: 85rp, Pieris rapae. 100rp, Parnassius apollo. 130rp, Melanargia galathea.
200rp, Vanessa atalanta.

2009, Sept. 7   Litho.   Perf. 12x12½
Self-Adhesive
1454-1457 A575   Set of 4   12.00 12.00
See Nos. 1480-1482, 1515-1516.

Chapel of St. Mamerta,
Triesen — A576

2009, Sept. 16   Perf. 14
1458 A576 130rp multi   3.00 3.00

Contemporary Architecture — A577

Designs: 85rp, University of Applied Sciences, Vaduz. 260rp, Art Museum, Vaduz.
350rp, Border crossing, Rugell.

Perf. 13½x13¾
2009, Nov. 16   Litho.
1459-1461 A577   Set of 3   17.00 17.00
See Nos. 1473-1474.

Lifestyle
Museum,
Schellenberg
A578

Former
Customs
House,
Vaduz — A579

Parish House,
Bendern
A580

2009, Nov. 16   Perf. 12¼
Self-Adhesive
1462 A578 20rp multi   .40   .40
1463 A579 50rp multi   1.00 1.00
1464 A580 60rp multi   1.25 1.25
      Nos. 1462-1464 (3)   2.65 2.65

Christmas — A581

Advent windows by children: 85rp, Annunciation. 100rp, Journey to Bethlehem. 130rp,
Nativity. 180rp, Magi and Star of Bethlehem.

2009, Nov. 16   Perf. 13½x13¾
1465-1468 A581   Set of 4   10.00 10.00

2010 Winter
Olympics,
Vancouver
A582

Designs: 1fr, Downhill skier. 1.80fr, Cross-
country skier, horiz.

2010, Feb. 12   Litho.   Perf. 13¾
1469-1470 A582   Set of 2   5.25 5.25

**Civil Protection Volunteers Type of
2009**

Designs: 85rp, Mountain rescuers. 1.30rp,
Water rescuers.

2010, Mar. 1   Perf. 13¾x13½
1471-1472 A565   Set of 2   4.00 4.00

**Contemporary Architecture Type of
2009**

Designs: 260rp, Natural gas filling station,
Vaduz. 360rp, Liechtenstein Electric Power
Authority transformer station, Schaan.

2010, Mar. 1   Perf. 13½x13¾
1473-1474 A577   Set of 2   11.50 11.50

Agriculture — A583

Designs: 85rp, Fields. 1fr, Flowers, hillside
farmers. 1.10fr, Combine in field. 1.30fr,
Cattle.

2010, Mar. 1   Photo.   Perf. 13½x13¼
1475-1478 A583   Set of 4   8.00 8.00

Souvenir Sheet

Expo 2010, Shanghai — A584

No. 1479: a, Atmospheric View of Vaduz, by
Johann Jakob Schmidt (40x36mm). b, Tidal
Bore on the Qiantang River, by Xu Gu
(32x60mm).

Photo. & Engr.
2010, May 1   Perf. 14
1479 A584   Sheet of 2   6.50 6.50
  a.   1.60fr multi   3.00 3.00
  b.   1.90fr multi   3.50 3.50
  c.   As #1479, imperf.   6.50 6.50
  d.   As "a," imperf.   3.00 3.00
  e.   As "b," imperf.   3.50 3.50

Butterflies Type of 2009
Designs: 140rp, Coenonympha oedippus.
160rp, Gonepteryx rhamni. 260rp, Papilio
machaon.

2010, June 7   Litho.   Perf. 12x12½
Self-Adhesive
1480-1482 A575   Set of 3   9.75 9.75

Liechtenstein
Disability
Insurance, 50th
Anniv. — A585

2010, June 7   Perf. 14x13¼
1483 A585 1fr multi   1.75 1.75

European
Free Trade
Association,
50th Anniv.
A586

2010, June 7   Perf. 12x12½
1484 A586 140rp multi   2.50 2.50

Interpol Vaduz,
50th
Anniv. — A587

2010, June 7   Perf. 12¼
1485 A587 1.90fr multi   3.50 3.50

Ceiling Frescoes in Liechtenstein
Museum, Vienna — A588

Frescoes by Johann Michael Rottmayr: 1fr,
Ariadne Giving Theseus the Thread. 1.40fr,
Surrender of the Golden Fleece to Jason.

Photo. & Engr.
2010, June 7   Perf. 14
1486-1487 A588   Set of 2   4.25 4.25
Values are for stamps with surrounding
selvage.

Vaduz Castle Type of 2009
Castle in: 140rp, Autumn, vert. 190rp, Winter, vert.

2010, Sept. 6   Photo.   Perf. 13¾
1488-1489 A572   Set of 2   6.50 6.50

Europa — A589

2010, Sept. 6   Litho.   Perf. 14
1490 A589 140rp multi   2.75 2.75

Renewable Energy A590

Designs: 100rp, Water. 140rp, Wood. 280rp, Geothermal.

Litho. & Photo.

2010, Sept. 6 ***Perf. 14x13¾***
1491-1493 A590 Set of 3 10.50 10.50

Parts of the designs of Nos. 1491-1493 were printed with thermochromic ink that changes color when warmed. See Nos. 1509-1511.

Rhine Valley Landscape — A591

No. 1494: a, Eschnerberg and Dreischwestern Mountains, cart path, denomination at LL. b, Alvier Mountains, denomination at LR.

2010, Sept. 6 **Litho.** ***Perf. 14x13¼***
1494 Horiz. pair 4.00 4.00
a.-b. A591 1fr Either single 2.00 2.00

Schaan-Vaduz Railroad Station — A592

Red House, Vaduz — A593

St. Joseph Church, Triesenberg A594

2010, Nov. 15 **Litho.** ***Perf. 12¼***

Self-Adhesive

1495 A592 1.10fr multi 2.25 2.25
1496 A593 1.80fr multi 3.75 3.75
1497 A594 1.90fr multi 4.00 4.00
Nos. 1495-1497 (3) 10.00 10.00

Works From Liechtenstein Museum of Art — A595

Designs: 100rp, Normale e Anormale, embroidery by Alighiero Boetti. 220rp, Testa, sculpture by Marisa Merz. 360rp, Untitled sculpture by Jannis Kounellis.

2010, Nov. 15 ***Perf. 13¾x13½***
1498-1500 A595 Set of 3 14.00 14.00

Christmas A596

Ceiling frescoes from Maria-Hilf Chapel, Mäls: 85rp, Annunciation. 1fr, Visitation of Mary. 1.40fr, Presentation of Jesus in the Temple.

2010, Nov. 15 **Photo.** ***Perf. 14***
1501-1503 A596 Set of 3 6.75 6.75

National Library, 50th Anniv — A597

Litho. With Foil Application

2011, Mar. 14 ***Perf. 12½x12***

Self-Adhesive

1504 A597 1fr black & gold 2.25 2.25

Liechtensteinische Landesbank, 150th Anniv. — A598

2011, Mar. 14 **Litho.** ***Perf. 12¼***

Self-Adhesive

1505 A598 1fr multi 2.25 2.25

2011 Games of the Small States, Liechtenstein — A599

Designs: 85rp, Track, volleyball, cycling. 1fr, Judo, shooting, squash. 1.40fr, Table tennis, tennis, swimming.

2011, Mar. 14 **Litho.** ***Perf. 13½***
1506-1508 A599 Set of 3 7.25 7.25

Renewable Energy Type of 2010

Designs: 100rp, Photovoltaics. 110rp, Solar energy. 290rp, Wind energy.

Litho. & Photo.

2011, Mar. 14 ***Perf. 14x13¾***
1509-1511 A590 Set of 3 11.00 11.00

Parts of the designs of Nos. 1509-1511 were printed with thermochromic ink that changes color when warmed.

Decorative Eggs Collected by Adulf Peter Goop — A600

Designs: 1fr, Moscow Workshop Easter egg. 1.40fr, Apple Blossom Egg, by Karl Fabergé, horiz. (47x33mm). 2.60fr, Easter egg, by Pavel Akimovich Ovchinnikov.

Litho. & Engr.

2011, Mar. 14 ***Perf. 13¾***
1512-1514 A600 Set of 3 11.00 11.00

Butterflies Type of 2009

Designs: 220rp, Inachis io. 500rp, Anthocharis cardamines.

2011, June 6 **Litho.** ***Perf. 12x12½***

Self-Adhesive

1515-1516 A575 Set of 2 17.50 17.50

For surcharge, see No. 1556.

Europa — A601

2011, June 6 ***Perf. 12½x12***
1517 A601 1.40fr multi 3.50 3.50

Intl. Year of Forests.

Children of Hereditary Prince Alois and Duchess Sophie — A602

Designs: 1fr, Prince Nikolaus. 1.80fr, Prince Georg. 2fr, Princess Marie Caroline. 2.60fr, Prince Joseph Wenzel.

Photo. & Engr.

2011, June 6 ***Perf. 13½***
1518-1521 A602 Set of 4 18.00 18.00
1521a Souvenir sheet of 4, #1518-1521 18.00 18.00

Fruit, by Shirana Shahbazi A603

2011, Sept. 9 **Litho.** ***Perf. 13¼x13½***
1522 A603 100rp multi 2.25 2.25

See Switzerland No. 1423.

Photographs of Liechtenstein by Xiao Hui Wang — A604

Designs: 1.30fr, Alpine Rhine. 3.70fr, Water Reflections.

2011, Sept. 9 ***Perf. 13¼x14***
1523-1524 A604 Set of 2 11.50 11.50

Miniature Sheet

Worldwide Fund for Nature (WWF), 50th Anniv. — A605

No. 1525 — Endangered birds in Liechtenstein: a, Falco subbuteo. b, Glaucidium passerinum. c, Oriolus oriolus. d, Jynx torquilla. e, Luscinia megarhynchos. f, Phoenicurus phoenicurus. g, Lanius collurio. h, Saxicola rubetra.

2011, Sept. 9 ***Perf. 12½***

Self-Adhesive

1525 A605 Sheet of 8 18.50 18.50
a.-h. 100rp Any single 2.25 2.25

Ruggell Marsh — A606

2011, Sept. 28 ***Perf. 14***
1526 A606 140rp multi 3.25 3.25

Castles A607

Designs: 100rp, Gutenberg Castle. 140rp, Schellenberg Castle. 200rp, Schalun Castle. 260rp, Vaduz Castle.

Photo. & Engr.

2011, Nov. 14 ***Perf. 13½x14¼***
1527-1530 A607 Set of 4 15.50 15.50

Christmas A608

Creche figures from: 85rp, St. Gallus Church, Triesen. 100rp, St. Florin Church, Vaduz (38x32mm). 140rp, Church of the Assumption, Bendern (32x38mm).

Perf. 12¼, 12x12½ (100rp), 12½x12 (140rp)

2011, Nov. 14 **Litho.**

Self-Adhesive

1531-1533 A608 Set of 3 7.25 7.25

New Year 2012 (Year of the Dragon) — A609

Litho. With Foil Application
2011, Nov. 14 *Perf. 12½*
Self-Adhesive
1534 A609 190rp red & gold 4.25 4.25
The dragon vignette was laser cut. Printed in sheets of 4.

Liechtenstein Postage Stamps, Cent. — A610

Princes of Liechtenstein: 1fr, Johann II. 1.40fr, Franz I. 2.20fr, Franz Josef II. 2.80fr, Hans Adam II.

2012, Feb. 1 Litho. *Perf. 13½x13¾*
1535-1538 A610 Set of 4 16.50 16.50
1538a Souvenir sheet of 4,
#1535-1538, imperf. 16.50 16.50

A booklet containing four panes each containing eight examples of each stamp, No. 1538a, a designer-signed and numbered example of No. 1538a in changed colors, examples of Nos. 1535-1538 and their imperforates with first day cancels, and reproductions of Nos. 1-3 was printed in limited quantities and sold for 100fr.

Cattle Moving Past Parliament Building A611

2012, Mar. 5 *Perf. 13¾*
1539 A611 140rp multi 3.25 3.25
Europa.

Liechtenstein Parilament and Constitution, 150th Anniv. — A612

Designs: 1fr, Reverse of 1862 Vereinsthaler, excerpt from first page of Constitutional Charter. 1.40fr, Obverse of 1862 Vereinsthaler, letter authorizing the opening of Parliament.

Litho. & Embossed
2012, Mar. 5 *Perf. 13½x13¾*
1540-1541 A612 Set of 2 5.25 5.25

Pfälzer Hutte Mountain Lodge — A613

2012, June 14 Litho. *Perf. 13¾*
1542 A613 140rp multi 3.00 3.00
See Germany No. 2677.

2012 Summer Olympics, London — A614

Designs: 100rp, Swimming. 140rp, Tennis.

2012, June 14 *Perf. 13¼*
1543-1544 A614 Set of 2 5.00 5.00

Flowers — A615

Designs: 85rp, Dahlie (dahlia). 140rp, Pfingstrose (peony). 500rp, Zinnie (zinnia).

2012, June 14 *Perf. 12½x12*
Self-Adhesive
1545-1547 A615 Set of 3 15.00 15.00
See Nos. 1573-1575.

Mountain Valleys — A616

No. 1548: a, Lawenatal Valley (denomination at LL). b, Valünatal Valley (denomination at LR).

2012, June 14 *Perf. 14x13¼*
1548 Horiz. pair 4.25 4.25
a.-b. A616 1fr Either single 2.10 2.10

Souvenir Sheet

Liechtenstein Oberland, 300th Anniv. — A617

No. 1549 — Stylized flags of: a, Planken and Schaan. b, Vaduz and Tresenberg. c, Triesen and Balzers.

Perf. 14 Vert. on 1 or 2 Sides
2012, June 14
1549 A617 Sheet of 3 11.00 11.00
a. 1fr multi 2.10 2.10
b. 1.40fr multi 3.00 3.00
c. 2.60fr multi 5.50 5.50

Souvenir Sheet

Winning Art in Stamp Design Contest — A618

No. 1550 — Art by: a, N. Schwarz. b, R. Graf. c, G. Rodrigues-Margreiter.

2012, Aug. 16 *Perf. 13¾x13½*
1550 A618 Sheet of 3 13.00 13.00
a. 100rp multi 2.25 2.25
b. 140rp multi 3.00 3.00
c. 360rp multi 7.75 7.75
LIBA 2012 Stamp Exhibition, Schaan.

Antique Automobiles A619

Designs: 85rp, 1908 Brasier. 100rp, 1911 Stanley Steamer. 140rp, 1915 Ford Model T Speedster. 190rp, 1920 Hinstin.

Litho. with Foil Application
2012, Sept. 3 Set of 4
1551-1554 A619 Set of 4 11.00 11.00

Miniature Sheet

Characters From Literature — A620

No. 1555: a, Till Eulenspiegel. b, Sherlock Holmes. c, Don Quixote. d, Hamlet. e, Robin Hood. f, Robinson Crusoe. g, Baron Münchhausen. h, Quasimodo.

2012, Sept. 3 Litho. *Perf. 13¾*
1555 A620 Sheet of 8 18.00 18.00
a.-h. 1fr Any single 2.25 2.25

No. 1516 Surcharged in Purple

Self-Adhesive
2012, Oct. 4 *Perf. 12x12½*
1556 A575 600rp on 500rp
#1516 13.00 13.00

Reliefs by Massimiliano Soldani-Benzi (1656-1740) A621

Designs: 1fr, Christ's Descent from the Cross. 1.40fr, Christ on the Mount of Olives.

Litho. & Engr.
2012, Nov. 12 *Perf. 13¾x14*
1557-1558 A621 Set of 2 5.25 5.25

Art by Hanna Roeckle A622

Designs: 100rp, Crystal B. 140rp, Crystal G.

2012, Nov. 12 Litho. *Perf. 13¾*
1559-1560 A622 Set of 2 5.25 5.25

Christmas A623

Archangels: 85rp, Raphael. 100rp, Michael. 140rp, Gabriel. 190rp, Uriel.

Self-Adhesive
Litho. With Foil Application
2012, Nov. 12 *Perf. 12¼x12½*
1561-1564 A623 Set of 4 11.00 11.00

New Year 2013 (Year of the Snake) A624

Self-Adhesive
Litho. With Foil Application
2012, Nov. 12 *Perf. 12½*
1565 A624 190rp red & gold 4.25 4.25
The snake vignette was laser cut. Printed in sheets of 4.

Civil Protection Volunteers Type of 2009

Designs: 1fr, Avalanche rescue squad. 1.40fr, Civil protection and emergency management workers.

2013, Mar. 4 Litho. *Perf. 13¾x13½*
1566-1567 A565 Set of 2 5.25 5.25

Europa — A625

2013, Mar. 4 *Perf. 14¼x14½*
1568 A625 1.40fr multi 3.00 3.00

Mathematics and Nature — A626

Various leaves and: 100rp, Fibonacci sequence. 260rp, Sum of adjacent Fibonacci numbers. 400rp, Golden ratio.

Litho. With Foil Application
2013, Mar. 4   **Perf. 13¼x13½**
1569-1571 A626   Set of 3   16.50 16.50

Switzerland-Liechtenstein Customs Treaty, 90th Anniv. — A627

No. 1572: a, Rhine Valley, Gonzen, Swiss flag, denomination at UL. b, Liechtenstein Valley, Ellhorn and Liechtenstein flag, denomination at UR.

2013, Mar. 4   **Litho.**   **Perf. 13¼**
1572   Horiz. pair   8.75 8.75
a.-b.   A627 2fr Either single   4.25 4.25

Flowers Type of 2012

Designs: 100rp, Gentiana rhaetica. 190rp, Myosotis alpestris. 400rp, Rhododendrum hirsutum.

2013, June 3   **Perf. 12½x12**
Self-Adhesive
1573-1575 A615   Set of 3   15.00 15.00

Landscapes by Hans Kliemand (1922-76) — A628

Designs: 100rp, View of Vaduz. 190rp, View Into the Rhine Valley.

Litho. & Engr.
2013, June 3   **Perf. 12¾x13**
1576-1577 A628   Set of 2   6.50 6.50

Baby Animals A629

Designs: 85rp, Ibex. 100rp, Chamois. 140rp, Marmot. 190rp, Alpine hare.

2013, June 3   **Litho.**   **Perf. 12x12½**
Self-Adhesive
1578-1581 A629   Set of 4   11.50 11.50

Bridges — A630

No. 1582: a, End of Vaduz-Sevelen Bridge over Rhine River (27x27mm). b, Entire Vaduz-Sevelen Bridge (57x27mm).
No. 1583: a, End of Schaan-Buchs Railway Bridge (27x27mm). b, Entire Schaan-Buchs Bridge (57x27mm).

2013, June 3   **Perf. 14x13¼**
1582 A630   Horiz. pair   4.25 4.25
a.   85rp multi   1.90 1.90
b.   100rp multi   2.25 2.25
1583 A630   Horiz. pair   7.25 7.25
a.   140rp multi   3.00 3.00
b.   190rp multi   4.25 4.25

See Nos. 1600-1601.

Performing Arts — A631

Designs: 100rp, Ballet dancer. 140rp, Actors in theater production. 200rp, Actors in musical theater production. 400rp, Magician.

2013, Sept. 2   **Perf. 12x12½**
Self-Adhesive
1584-1587 A631   Set of 4   18.00 18.00

Automobiles A632

Designs: 85rp, 1954 Aston Martin DB 2/4. 100rp, 1958 Ferrari 250 GT PF. 140rp, 1955 Jaguar XK 140. 190rp, 1956 Mercedes-Benz 300 SL.

Litho. & Embossed With Foil Application
2013, Sept. 2   **Perf. 13¼x13**
1588-1591 A632   Set of 4   11.00 11.00

Paintings by Ivan Myasoyedov (Eugen Zotow) (1881-1953) — A633

No. 1592: a, Voyage of the Argonauts, 1909. b, Silum, 1945.

2013, Sept. 2   **Litho.**   **Perf. 14**
1592   Pair   8.75 8.75
a.   A633 140rp multi   3.00 3.00
b.   A633 260rp multi   5.75 5.75

Printed in sheets of 10 containing 5 each #1592a-1592b, + 2 labels. See Russia No. 7473.

2014 Winter Olympics, Sochi, Russia A634

Litho. & Thermographed With Foil Application
2013, Nov. 11   **Perf. 13¼x13½**
1593 A634 2.60fr multi   5.75 5.75

Portions of the design contain grit from a stone from Sochi.

Souvenir Sheet

Floral-Patterned Silk Wall Covering in Small Courbaril Room of Liechtenstein Palace, Vienna — A635

Litho. & Embossed With Foil Application
2013, Nov. 11   **Perf. 14¼x14½**
Silk-Faced Paper
1594 A635   Sheet of 3   13.00 13.00
a.   1fr multi   2.25 2.25
b.   1.40fr multi   3.00 3.00
c.   3.60fr multi   7.75 7.75

Christmas A636

Designs: 85rp, Annunciation. 1fr, Nativity. 1.40fr, Angel announcing birth of Christ to shepherds and sheep. 1.90fr, Three Kings.

Litho. With Foil Application
2013, Nov. 11   **Perf. 12½x12**
Self-Adhesive
1595-1598 A636   Set of 4   11.50 11.50

New Year 2013 (Year of the Horse) A637

Litho. With Foil Application
2013, Nov. 11   **Perf. 12½**
Self-Adhesive
1599 A637 190rp red & gold   4.25 4.25

The horse vignette was laser cut. Printed in sheets of 4.

In 2014, Liechtenstein began issuing personalizable stamps bearing the inscription "Liechtensteinsche Post AG." Stamps in three different orientations (square, landscape and portrait) could be created for two different frame types, each of which were made available initially in denominations of 55c, 85c, €1, €1.40, €1.90, and €2. These were sold in sheets of 20 stamps. Sheets containing 10 stamps with various non-personalizable images were to be produced and sold for special events.

Bridges Type of 2013

No. 1582: a, End of Buchs-Schaan Footbridge (27x27mm). b, Entire Buchs-Schaan Bridge (57x27mm).
No. 1583: a, End of Bendern-Haag Bridge over the Rhine River (27x27mm). b, Entire Bendern-Haag Bridge (57x27mm).

2014, Mar. 10   **Litho.**   **Perf. 14x13¼**
1600 A630   Horiz. pair   4.25 4.25
a.   85rp multi   1.90 1.90
b.   100rp multi   2.25 2.25
1601 A630   Horiz. pair   7.50 7.50
a.   140rp multi   3.25 3.25
b.   190rp multi   4.25 4.25

Josef Gabriel Rheinberger (1839-1901), Composer — A638

Perf. 13¾x13¼
2014, Mar. 10   **Litho.**
1602 A638 1.40fr multi   3.25 3.25

Europa — A639

2014, Mar. 10   Litho.   Perf. 12½x12
1603 A639 140rp multi   3.25 3.25

Souvenir Sheet

Winged Altarpiece Bequeathed to National Museum — A640

No. 1604 — Details of altarpiece: a, St. Christopher Carrying the Christ Child (33x45mm). b, St. Sebastian (33x45mm). c, St. Anne and St. Mary with the Christ Child (84x44mm).

Perf. 14x13¾, 13½ (600rp)
2014, Mar. 10   **Litho.**
1604 A640   Sheet of 3   20.50 20.50
a.   100rp multi   2.25 2.25
b.   200rp multi   4.50 4.50
c.   600rp multi   13.50 13.50

No. 1640 is sold folded in half, with stamps appearing through the die cut holes in the sheet margin. The top part of the sheet margin, with the holes, is printed on both sides.

Souvenir Sheet

Canonization of Pope John Paul II — A641

Litho. With Foil Application
2014, Apr. 28   **Perf. 14¼x14**
1605 A641 1.40fr multi   3.25 3.25

Ancient Coins Found in
Liechtenstein — A642

Map of Liechtenstein and: 85rp, Roman silver denarius of Julius Caesar, c. 49-48 B.C.
100rp, Florentine golden florin, c. 1360. 130rp,
Silver penny, c. 1360.

**Litho. & Embossed With Foil
Application**
2014, June 2   **Perf. 13½x13¾**
1606-1608 A642   Set of 3   7.00 7.00

Amphibians
A643

Designs: 85rp, Yellow-bellied toad. 2.90fr,
Great crested newt. 3.70fr, Alpine
salamander.

2014, June 2   **Litho.**   **Perf. 12¼**
            Self-Adhesive
1609-1611 A643   Set of 3   17.00 17.00

Flowers — A644

Designs: 100rp, Iris sibirica. 280rp, Parnassia palustris. 360rp, Menyanthes trifoliata.

2014, June 2   **Litho.**   **Perf. 12½x12**
            Self-Adhesive
1612-1614 A644   Set of 3   16.50 16.50

Lindau Messenger Courier
Service — A645

2014, Sept. 1   **Litho.**   **Perf. 14x13¼**
1615 A645 140rp multi   3.00 3.00
   No. 1615 was printed in sheets of 8 + 4
labels.

Etchings by
Brigitte
Hasler — A646

Designs: 100rp, Dust Image A. 140rp, Dust
Image B.

Litho. With Foil Application
2014, Sept. 1   **Perf. 13¼**
1616-1617 A646   Set of 2   5.25 5.25

Intl. Year of Crystallography — A647

Designs: 100rp, Initial crystal metamorpho-
sis sequence. 200rp, Final crystal metamor-
phosis sequence.

Litho. & Embossed
2014, Sept. 1   **Perf. 13½x13¼**
1618-1619 A647   Set of 2   6.50 6.50

Sedans
A648

Designs: 85rp, 1933 Rolls-Royce Phantom
II. 100rp, 1929 Pierce-Arrow Type 133. 140rp,
1935 Studebaker Big Six. 190rp, 1948 Jaguar
Mark IV.

Litho. With Foil Application
2014, Sept. 1   **Perf. 13¼x13**
1620-1623 A648   Set of 4   11.50 11.50
1620a   Inscribed "Rolls-Royce"
       (with hyphen)   1.75 1.75
   Issued: No. 1620a, 11/10. No. 1620 is
inscribed "Rolls Royce" (without hyphen).

Reign of
Prince
Hans
Adam II,
25th
Anniv.
A649

2014, Nov. 10   **Litho. & Engr.**
1624 A649 2fr multi   4.25 4.25

Painting by
Jens W.
Beyrich
A650

Painting by
Hong Sek-
Chern
A651

2014, Nov. 10   **Litho.**   **Perf. 13x13¼**
1625 A650 190rp multi   4.00 4.00
1626 A651 190rp multi   4.00 4.00
        See Singapore Nos.

Chinese
Porcelain in
Princely
Collection
A652

Designs: 1fr, Famille Rose plate, c. 1722-
35. 1.90fr, Kraak kendi, c. 1572-1620
(27x43mm). 2.80fr, Imari baluster vase with
lid, c. 1736-95 (27x43mm). 3.60fr, Imari plate
with lotus blossoms, c. 1736-95.

       **Perf. 13¾x13¼, 12x11¼ (#1628-
                 1629)**
Litho. & Engr. With Foil Application
2014, Nov. 10
1627-1630 A652   Set of 4   19.00 19.00

Christmas
A653

Chapels: 85rp, Freedom Chapel, Malbun.
100rp, St. Wendelin's Chapel, Steg. 140rp, St.
Theodul's Chapel, Masescha.

Litho. With Foil Application
2014, Nov. 10   **Perf. 12¼x12½**
           Self-Adhesive
1631-1633 A653   Set of 3   6.75 6.75

New
Year
2015
(Year of
the
Ram)
A654

Litho. With Foil Application
2014, Nov. 10   **Perf. 12½**
1634 A654 190rp red & gold   4.00 4.00
   The ram vignette was laser cut. Printed in
sheets of 4.

Prince
Hans
Adam II,
70th
Birthday
A655

         Perf. 13¼x13¾
2015, Feb. 14   **Litho. & Engr.**
1635   Pair   6.50 6.50
  a.   A655 1fr green & multi   2.10 2.10
  b.   A655 2fr red & multi   4.25 4.25
   No. 1635 was printed in sheets containing
two pairs.

Liechtenstein
Traditional
Costume
Association,
50th Anniv.
A656

2015, Mar. 2   **Litho.**   **Perf. 12x12½**
           Self-Adhesive
1636 A656 85rp multi   1.75 1.75

Liechtenstein
Development
Service,
50th Anniv.
A657

2015, Mar. 2   **Litho.**   **Perf. 12x12½**
           Self-Adhesive
1637 A657 100rp multi   2.10 2.10

Postage
Stamps, 175th
Anniv. — A658

2015, Mar. 2   **Litho.**   **Perf. 12½x12**
           Self-Adhesive
1638 A658 1.40fr multi   3.00 3.00

Liechtenstein's Admission to United
Nations, 25th Anniv. — A659

2015, Mar. 2   **Litho.**   **Perf. 13½x13**
1639 A659 190rp multi   4.00 4.00

International Year
of Light — A660

2015, Mar. 2   **Litho.**   **Perf. 13¾x13¼**
1640 A660 1.90fr multi   4.00 4.00
   Microperforations are incorporated in the
vignette.

Europa — A661

Toys: No. 1641, 1.40fr, Polar bear in freezer.
No. 1642, 1.40fr, Goat on lemon.

2015, Mar. 2   **Litho.**   **Perf. 13½x13¼**
1641-1642 A661   Set of 2   6.00 6.00

         SEMI-POSTAL STAMPS

Prince   Coat of
Johann   Arms — SP2
II — SP1

           Wmk. 183
1925, Oct. 5   **Engr.**   **Perf. 11½**
B1   SP1 10rp yellow green   42.50 22.50
B2   SP1 20rp deep red   21.00 22.50
B3   SP1 30rp deep blue   7.00 7.00
   Nos. B1-B3 (3)   70.50 52.00
   Set, never hinged   210.00

   85th birthday of the Prince Regent. Sold at a
premium of 5rp each, the excess being
devoted to charities.

1927, Oct. 5   **Typo.**

B4	SP2	10rp multicolored	10.50	25.00
B5	SP2	20rp multicolored	10.50	25.00
B6	SP2	30rp multicolored	5.00	21.00
		Nos. B4-B6 (3)	26.00	71.00
		Set, never hinged	62.00	

87th birthday of Prince Johann II. These stamps were sold at premiums of 5, 10 and 20rp respectively. The money thus obtained was devoted to charity.

Railroad Bridge Demolished by Flood SP3

Designs: 10rp+10rp, Inundated Village of Ruggel. 20rp+10rp, Austrian soldiers rescuing refugees. 30rp+10rp, Swiss soldiers salvaging personal effects.

1928, Feb. 6   **Litho.**   **Unwmk.**

B7	SP3	5rp + 5rp brn vio & brn	17.50	26.00
B8	SP3	10rp + 10rp bl grn & brn	25.00	26.00
B9	SP3	20rp + 10rp dl red & brn	25.00	26.00
B10	SP3	30rp + 10rp dp bl & brn	21.00	26.00
		Nos. B7-B10 (4)	88.50	104.00
		Set, never hinged	220.00	

The surtax on these stamps was used to aid the sufferers from the Rhine floods.

Coat of Arms — SP7   Princess Elsa — SP8

Design: 30rp, Prince Francis I.

1932, Dec. 21   **Photo.**

B11	SP7	10rp (+ 5rp) olive grn	21.00	35.00
B12	SP8	20rp (+ 5rp) rose red	21.00	37.50
B13	SP8	30rp (+ 10rp) ultra	28.00	37.50
		Nos. B11-B13 (3)	70.00	110.00
		Set, never hinged	172.50	

The surtax was for the Child Welfare Fund.

Postal Museum Issue
Souvenir Sheet

SP10

1936, Oct. 24   **Litho.**   **Imperf.**

B14	SP10	Sheet of 4	17.50 50.00
		Never hinged	70.00

Sheet contains 2 each, Nos. 120, 122. Sold for 2fr.

"Protect the Child" — SP11

Designs: No. B16, "Take Care of the Sick." No. B17, "Help the Aged."

Perf. 11½   **Photo.**   **Unwmk.**
1945, Nov. 27

B15	SP11	10rp + 10rp multi	.65	1.75
B16	SP11	20rp + 20rp multi	.65	2.25
B17	SP11	1fr + 1.40fr multi	4.75	20.00
		Nos. B15-B17 (3)	6.05	24.00
		Set, never hinged	11.00	

Souvenir Sheet

Post Coach — SP14

1946, Aug. 10

B18	SP14	Sheet of 2	21.00	32.50
		Never hinged	35.00	
a.		10rp dark violet brown & buff	5.00	15.00
		Never hinged	12.50	

25th anniv. of the Swiss-Liechtenstein Postal Agreement. Sheet, size: 82x60½mm, sold for 3fr.

Canal by Albert Cuyp — SP15

Willem van Huythuysen by Frans Hals — SP16

40rp+10rp, Landscape by Jacob van Ruysdael.

1951, July 24   **Perf. 11½**

B19	SP15	10rp + 10rp olive grn	5.00	7.00
B20	SP16	20rp + 10rp dk vio brn	5.00	14.00
B21	SP15	40rp + 10rp blue	5.00	7.00
		Nos. B19-B21 (3)	15.00	28.00
		Set, never hinged	30.00	

Issued in sheets of 12. For surcharges see Nos. 281-283.

> **Catalogue values for unused stamps in this section, from this point to the end of the section, are for Never Hinged items.**

Nos. 324-325 Surcharged with New Value and Uprooted Oak Emblem
1960, Apr. 7

B22	A190	30rp + 10rp on 40rp	.55	1.00
B23	A190	50rp + 10rp on 25rp	.90	2.00

World Refugee Year, July 1, 1959-June 30, 1960. The surtax was for aid to refugees.

Growth Symbol SP17

1967, Dec. 7   **Photo.**   **Perf. 11½**

B24	SP17	50rp + 20rp multi	.50	.60

Surtax was for development assistance.

AIR POST STAMPS

Airplane over Snow-capped Mountain Peaks — AP1

Airplane above Vaduz Castle — AP2

Airplane over Rhine Valley — AP3

Perf. 10½, 10½x11½
1930, Aug. 12   **Photo.**   **Unwmk.**
Gray Wavy Lines in Background

C1	AP1	15rp dark brown	10.50	17.50
C2	AP1	20rp slate	25.00	25.00
C3	AP2	25rp olive brown	14.00	45.00
C4	AP2	35rp slate blue	21.00	42.50
C5	AP3	45rp olive green	50.00	87.50
C6	AP3	1fr lake	25.00	62.50
		Nos. C1-C6 (6)	175.50	280.00
		Set, never hinged	518.00	

For surcharge see No. C14.

Zeppelin over Naafkopf, Falknis Range AP4

Design: 2fr, Zeppelin over Valüna Valley.

1931, June 1   **Perf. 11½**

C7	AP4	1fr olive black	70.00	125.00
C8	AP4	2fr blue black	140.00	400.00
		Set, never hinged	565.00	

Golden Eagle — AP6

15rp, Golden Eagle in flight, diff. 20rp, Golden Eagle in flight, diff. 30rp, Osprey. 50rp, Eagle.

1934-35

C9	AP6	10rp brt vio ('35)	10.50	55.00
C10	AP6	15rp red org ('35)	28.00	55.00
C11	AP6	20rp red ('35)	28.00	55.00
C12	AP6	30rp brt bl ('35)	28.00	55.00
C13	AP6	50rp emerald	17.50	62.50
		Nos. C9-C13 (5)	112.00	282.50
		Set, never hinged	385.00	

No. C6 Surcharged with New Value
1935, June 24   **Perf. 10½x11½**

C14	AP3	60rp on 1fr lake	42.50	50.00
		Never hinged	160.00	

Airship "Hindenburg" — AP11

Design: 2fr, Airship "Graf Zeppelin."

1936, May 1   **Perf. 11½**

C15	AP11	1fr rose carmine	50.00	105.00
C16	AP11	2fr violet	35.00	105.00
		Set, never hinged	160.00	

AP13

10rp, Barn swallows. 15rp, Black-headed Gulls. 20rp, Gulls. 30rp, Eagle. 50rp, Northern Goshawk. 1fr, Lammergeier. 2fr, Lammergeier.

1939, Apr. 3   **Photo.**

C17	AP13	10rp violet	.70	.70
C18	AP13	15rp red orange	.70	2.50
C19	AP13	20rp dark red	2.75	1.40
C20	AP13	30rp dull blue	1.75	2.75
C21	AP13	50rp brt green	4.25	5.00
C22	AP13	1fr rose car	2.75	17.50
C23	AP13	2fr violet	2.75	17.50
		Nos. C17-C23 (7)	15.65	47.35
		Set, never hinged	48.00	

> **Catalogue values for unused stamps in this section, from this point to the end of the section, are for Never Hinged items.**

AP20

Designs: 10rp, Leonardo da Vinci. 15rp, Joseph Montgolfier. 20rp, Jacob Degen. 25rp, Wilhelm Kress. 40rp, E. G. Robertson. 50rp, W. S. Henson. 1fr, Otto Lilienthal. 2fr, S. A. Andrée. 5fr, Wilbur Wright. 10fr, Icarus.

1948

C24	AP20	10rp dark green	.55	.25
C25	AP20	15rp dark violet	.55	.80
C26	AP20	20rp brown	.90	.25
a.		20rp reddish brown	65.00	2.75
C27	AP20	25rp dark red	1.10	1.25
C28	AP20	40rp violet blue	1.25	1.25
C29	AP20	50rp Prus blue	1.40	1.25
C30	AP20	1fr chocolate	8.00	2.75
C31	AP20	2fr rose lake	4.50	3.50
C32	AP20	5fr olive green	5.75	4.75
C33	AP20	10fr slate black	26.00	14.00
		Nos. C24-C33 (10)	50.00	30.05

Issued in sheets of 9. Exist imperf. Value, set $6,500.

Helicopter, Bell 47-J AP21

Planes: 40rp, Boeing 707 jet. 50rp, Convair 600 jet. 75rp, Douglas DC-8.

1960, Apr. 7   **Unwmk.**   **Perf. 11½**

C34	AP21	30rp red orange	2.25	2.25
C35	AP21	40rp blue black	3.75	2.25
C36	AP21	50rp deep claret	9.50	4.00
C37	AP21	75rp olive green	2.00	2.25
		Nos. C34-C37 (4)	17.50	10.75

30th anniv. of Liechtenstein's air post stamps.

POSTAGE DUE STAMPS

National Administration of the Post Office

D1

1920	Unwmk.	Engr.	Perf. 12½	
J1	D1	5h rose red	.35	.40
J2	D1	10h rose red	.35	.40
J3	D1	15h rose red	.35	.40
J4	D1	20h rose red	.35	.55
J5	D1	25h rose red	.35	.55
J6	D1	30h rose red	.35	.55
J7	D1	40h rose red	.35	.55
J8	D1	50h rose red	.35	.55
J9	D1	80h rose red	.35	.55
J10	D1	1k dull blue	.40	1.40
J11	D1	2k dull blue	.40	1.40
J12	D1	5k dull blue	.40	1.75
	Nos. J1-J12 (12)		4.35	9.05
	Set, never hinged		12.50	

Nos. J1-J12 exist imperf. (value, unused, set $260) and part perf. (value, unused or used, set $7.50).

Swiss Administration of the Post Office

D2

Post Horn — D3

1928	Litho.	Wmk. 183	Perf. 11½	
		Granite Paper		
J13	D2	5rp purple & orange	1.40	3.50
J14	D2	10rp purple & orange	1.40	3.50
J15	D2	15rp purple & orange	2.10	14.00
J16	D2	20rp purple & orange	2.10	3.50
J17	D2	25rp purple & orange	7.00	8.50
J18	D2	30rp purple & orange	7.00	14.00
J19	D2	40rp purple & orange	7.00	14.00
J20	D2	50rp purple & orange	7.00	17.50
	Nos. J13-J20 (8)		35.00	78.50
	Set, never hinged		105.00	

Engraved; Value Typographed in Dark Red

1940		Unwmk.	Perf. 11½	
J21	D3	5rp gray blue	1.75	2.75
J22	D3	10rp gray blue	.70	1.40
J23	D3	15rp gray blue	1.00	5.00
J24	D3	20rp gray blue	1.00	2.00
J25	D3	25rp gray blue	2.00	3.50
J26	D3	30rp gray blue	4.50	5.50
J27	D3	40rp gray blue	4.50	5.50
J28	D3	50rp gray blue	5.25	5.50
	Nos. J21-J28 (8)		20.70	31.15
	Set, never hinged		42.00	

OFFICIAL STAMPS

Regular Issue of 1930 Overprinted in Various Colors

Perf. 10½, 11½, 11½x10½				
1932			Unwmk.	
O1	A38	5rp dk grn (Bk)	10.50	15.50
O2	A39	10rp dark vio (R)	75.00	15.50
O3	A40	20rp dp rose red (Bl)	90.00	15.50
O4	A42	30rp ultra (R)	17.50	21.00
O5	A43	35rp dp grn (Bk)	14.00	35.00
O6	A45	50rp blk brn (Bl)	77.50	21.00
O7	A46	60rp olive blk (R)	14.00	50.00
O8	A48	1.20fr olive brn (G)	150.00	425.00
	Nos. O1-O8 (8)		448.50	598.50
	Set, never hinged		1,763.	

Values are for the most common perf. variety. See Scott Classic Specialized catalogue for detailed listings.

Nos. 108, 110 Overprinted in Black

1933			Perf. 14½	
O9	A51	25rp red orange	42.50	52.50
O10	A53	1.20fr red brown	85.00	350.00
	Set, never hinged		360.00	

Regular Issue of 1934-35 Ovptd. in Various Colors

1934-36			Perf. 11½	
O11	A58	5rp emerald (R)	2.10	3.50
O12	A59	10rp dp vio (Bk)	4.25	3.50
O13	A60	15rp red org (V)	.70	3.50
O14	A61	20rp red (Bk)	.70	3.50
O15	A62	25rp brown (R)	42.50	115.00
O16	A62	25rp brown (Bk)	3.50	21.00
O17	A63	30rp dark bl (R)	5.00	10.50
O18	A66	50rp lt brown (V)	1.40	17.50
O19	A68	90rp dp grn (Bk)	10.50	10.50
O20	A69	1.50fr brown car (Bl)	42.50	280.00
	Nos. O11-O20 (10)		113.15	468.50
	Set, never hinged		358.00	

Regular Issue of 1937-38 Overprinted in Black, Red or Blue

1937-41				
O21	A76	5rp emerald (Bk)	.35	.75
O22	A76	10rp vio & buff (R)	.70	2.00
O23	A76	20rp brn org (Bl)	.70	2.00
O24	A76	20rp brn org (Bk) ('41)	1.40	2.75
O25	A76	25rp chestnut (Bk)	.75	2.75
O26	A77	30rp blue & gray (Bk)	1.75	2.75
O27	A79	50rp dk brn & buff (R)	1.00	2.10
O28	A80	1fr red brown (Bk)	1.00	12.00
O29	A80	1.50fr slate bl (Bk) ('38)	2.75	17.50
	Nos. O21-O29 (9)		10.40	44.60
	Set, never hinged		49.50	

Catalogue values for unused stamps in this section, from this point to the end of the section, are for Never Hinged items.

Stamps of 1944-45 Overprinted in Black

1947				
O30	A136	5rp slate grn & buff	1.25	.75
O31	A136	10rp gray & buff	1.25	.75
O32	A136	20rp org red & buff	1.50	.75
O33	A136	30rp blue & buff	1.90	1.40
O34	A136	50rp bluish blk & pale gray	2.00	3.00
O35	A136	1fr dp cl & buff	9.00	9.00
O36	A136	150rp royal blue	9.00	9.00
	Nos. O30-O36 (7)		25.90	24.65

Crown — O1

Engr.; Value Typo.

1950-68		Unwmk.	Perf. 11½	
		Buff Granite Paper		
		Narrow Gothic Numerals		
O37	O1	5rp red vio & gray	.25	.25
O38	O1	10rp ol grn & mag	.25	.25
O39	O1	20rp org brn & bl	.25	.25
O40	O1	30rp dk red brn & org red	.25	.25
O41	O1	40rp blue & hn brn	.35	.35
O42	O1	55rp dk gray grn & red	.70	1.10
a.		White paper ('68)	45.00	125.00

O43	O1	60rp slate & mag	.70	1.10
a.		White paper ('68)	6.00	22.50
O44	O1	80rp red org & gray	.70	.90
O45	O1	90rp choc & blue	.90	1.25
O46	O1	1.20fr grnsh bl & org	1.10	1.25
	Nos. O37-O46 (10)		5.45	6.95

1968-69			Perf. 11½	
		White Granite Paper		
		Broad Numerals, Varying Thickness		
O47	O1	5rp olive brn & org	.25	.25
O48	O1	10rp violet & car	.25	.25
O49	O1	20rp ver & emer	.25	.25
O50	O1	30rp green & red	.25	.25
O51	O1	50rp ultra & red	.35	.35
O52	O1	60rp orange & ultra	.40	.40
O53	O1	70rp maroon & emer	.50	.50
O54	O1	80rp bl grn & car	.55	.55
O55	O1	95rp slate & red ('69)	.65	.65
O56	O1	1fr rose cl & grn	.70	.70
O57	O1	1.20fr lt red brn & grn	.80	.80
O58	O1	2fr brn & org ('69)	1.25	1.25
	Nos. O47-O58 (12)		6.20	6.20

Government Building, Vaduz — O2

Engr., Value Typo.

1976-89			Perf. 14	
O59	O2	10rp yel brn & vio	.25	.25
O60	O2	20rp car lake & bl	.25	.25
O61	O2	35rp blue & red	.25	.25
O62	O2	40rp dull pur & grn	.30	.30
O63	O2	50rp slate & mag	.40	.40
O64	O2	70rp vio brn & bl grn	.55	.55
O65	O2	80rp green & mag	.60	.60
O66	O2	90rp vio & bl grn	.70	.70
O67	O2	1fr olive & mag	.80	.80
O68	O2	1.10fr brown & ultra	.85	.85
O69	O2	1.50fr dull grn & red	1.25	1.25
O70	O2	2fr orange & blue	1.60	1.60
O75	O2	5fr rose vio & brn org	5.75	5.75
	Nos. O59-O75 (13)		13.55	13.55

Issued: 5fr, 9/4/89; others, 12/9/76.

LITHUANIA

ˌli-thə-ˈwā-nē-ə

(Lietuva)

LOCATION — Northern Europe bordering on the Baltic Sea
GOVT. — Independent republic
AREA — 25,170 sq. mi.
POP. — 3,584,966 (1999 est.)
CAPITAL — Vilnius

Lithuania was under Russian rule when it declared its independence in 1918. The League of Nations recognized it in 1922. In 1940 it became a republic in the Union of Soviet Socialist Republics.

Lithuania declared its independence on March 11, 1990. Lithuanian independence was recognized by the Soviet Union on Sept. 6, 1991.

100 Skatiku = 1 Auksinas
100 Centai = 1 Litas (1922, 1993)
100 Kopecks = 1 Ruble (1991)

Catalogue values for unused stamps in this country are for Never Hinged items, beginning with Scott 371 in the regular postage section.

Nos. 1-26 were printed in sheets of 20 (5x4) which were imperf. at the outer sides, so that only 6 stamps in each sheet were fully perforated. Values are for the stamps partly imperf. The stamps fully perforated sell for at least double these values. There was also a printing of Nos. 19-26 in a sheet of 160, composed of blocks of 20 of each stamp. Pairs or blocks with different values se-tenant sell for considerably more than the values for the stamps singly.
Nos. 1-26 are without gum.

Watermarks

Wmk. 109 — Webbing

Wmk. 144 — Network

Wmk. 145 — Wavy Lines

Wmk. 146 — Zigzag Lines Forming Rectangles

Wmk. 147 — Parquetry

Wmk. 198 — Intersecting Diamonds

Wmk. 209 — Multiple Ovals

Wmk. 238 — Multiple Letters

First Vilnius Printing

A1

Thin Figures
Perf. 11½

1918, Dec. 27   Unwmk.   Typeset

1	A1	10sk black	125.00	100.00
2	A1	15sk black	125.00	100.00

Second Vilnius Printing

1918, Dec. 31   Thick Figures

3	A1	10sk black	70.00	55.00
4	A1	15sk black	70.00	55.00
5	A1	20sk black	30.00	16.00
6	A1	30sk black	35.00	17.50
7	A1	40sk black	50.00	25.00
8	A1	50sk black	40.00	17.50
		Nos. 3-8 (6)	295.00	186.00

First Kaunas Issue

A2

1919, Jan. 29

9	A2	10sk black	8.00	4.50
10	A2	15sk black	8.00	4.50
a.		"5" for "15"	95.00	72.50
11	A2	20sk black	8.00	4.50
12	A2	30sk black	8.00	4.50
		Nos. 9-12 (4)	32.00	18.00

Second Kaunas Issue

A3

1919, Feb. 18

13	A3	10sk black	4.25	2.50
14	A3	15sk black	4.25	2.50
15	A3	20sk black	4.25	2.50
a.		"astas" for "pastas"	80.00	75.00
16	A3	30sk black	4.25	2.50
17	A3	40sk black	4.25	2.50
18	A3	50sk black	4.25	2.50
19	A3	60sk black	4.25	2.50
		Nos. 13-19 (7)	29.75	17.50

Third Kaunas Issue

A4

1919, Mar. 1

20	A4	10sk black	4.25	2.50
21	A4	15sk black	4.25	2.50
22	A4	20sk black	4.25	2.50
23	A4	30sk black	4.25	2.50
24	A4	40sk black	4.25	2.50
25	A4	50sk black	4.25	2.50
26	A4	60sk black	4.25	2.50
		Nos. 20-26 (7)	29.75	17.50

The White Knight "Vytis"
A5   A6

A7   A8

Perf. 10½ to 14 & Compound
1919   Litho.   Wmk. 144
Gray Granite Paper

30	A5	10sk deep rose	1.25	.40
a.		Wmk. vert.	17.50	15.00
31	A5	15sk violet	1.25	.40
a.		Wmk. vert.	17.50	15.00
32	A5	20sk dark blue	1.60	.40
33	A5	30sk deep orange	1.60	.40
a.		Wmk. vert.	17.50	15.00
34	A5	40sk dark brown	1.60	.40
35	A6	50sk blue green	1.60	.50
36	A6	75sk org & dp rose	1.60	.50
37	A7	1auk gray & rose	3.25	.50
38	A7	3auk bis brn & rose	3.25	.50
39	A7	5auk blue grn & rose	3.25	.80
		Nos. 30-39 (10)	20.25	4.80

Nos. 30a, 31a and 33a are from the first printing with watermark vertical showing points to left; various perforations.

Nos. 30-39 exist imperf. Value in pairs, $100.

Issued: Nos. 30a, 31a, 33a, 2/17/19; Nos. 30-36, 3/20/19.

Thick White Paper

1919   Wmk. 145

40	A5	10sk dull rose	.35	.25
41	A5	15sk violet	.35	.25
42	A5	20sk dark blue	.35	.25
43	A5	30sk orange	.35	.25
44	A5	40sk red brown	.35	.25
45	A6	50sk green	.35	.25
46	A6	75sk yel & dp rose	.35	.25
47	A7	1auk gray & rose	.95	.35
48	A7	3auk yellow brn & rose, perf. 12½	.60	.40
49	A7	5auk bl grn & rose	1.00	.40
		Nos. 40-49 (10)	5.00	2.90

Nos. 40-49 exist imperf. Value in pairs, $90.

Perf. 10½ to 14 & Compound
1919, May 8   Thin White Paper

50	A5	10sk red	.40	.25
51	A5	15sk lilac	.40	.25
52	A5	20sk dull blue	.40	.25
53	A5	30sk buff	.40	.25
54	A5	40sk gray brn	.40	.25
55	A6	50sk lt green	.40	.25
56	A6	60sk violet & red	.40	.25
57	A6	75sk bister & red	.40	.25
58	A8	1auk gray & red	.40	.25
59	A8	3auk lt brown & red	.40	.30
60	A8	5auk blue grn & red	.40	.45
		Nos. 50-60 (11)	4.40	3.00

Nos. 50-60 exist imperf. Value, pairs $150.
See Nos. 93-96. For surcharges see Nos. 114-115, 120-139, 149-150.

"Lithuania" Receiving Benediction — A9   The Spirit of Lithuania Rises — A10

"Lithuania" with Chains Broken — A11   White Knight — A12

1920, Feb. 16   Wmk. 146   *Perf. 11½*

70	A9	10sk dp rose	3.75	2.25
71	A9	15sk lt violet	3.75	2.25
72	A9	20sk gray blue	3.75	2.25
73	A10	30sk yellow brn	3.75	2.25
74	A11	40sk brown & grn	3.75	2.25
75	A10	50sk deep rose	3.75	2.25
76	A10	60sk lt violet	3.75	2.25
77	A11	80sk purple & red	3.75	2.25
78	A11	1auk green & red	3.75	2.25
79	A12	3auk green & red	3.75	2.25
80	A12	5auk green & red	3.75	2.25
a.		Right "5" dbl., grn and red	90.00	90.00
		Nos. 70-80 (11)	41.25	24.75

Anniv. of natl. independence. The stamps were on sale only 3 days in Kaunas. The stamps were available in other cities after that. Only a limited number of stamps was sold at post offices but 40,000 sets were delivered to the bank of Kaunas.

All values exist imperforate.

White Knight — A13   Grand Duke Vytautas — A14

Grand Duke Gediminas A15   Sacred Oak and Altar A16

1920, Aug. 25

81	A13	10sk rose	.95	.50
a.		Imperf., pair	40.00	
82	A13	15sk dark violet	.95	.50
83	A14	20sk grn & lt grn	.95	.50
84	A13	30sk brown	.95	.50
		Pair, #82, 84	40.00	
85	A15	40sk gray grn & vio	.95	.50
86	A14	50sk brn & brn org	2.75	1.25
87	A14	60sk red & org	1.50	1.00
88	A15	80sk blk, db & red	1.50	1.00
89	A16	1auk orange & blk	1.75	1.00
90	A16	3auk green & blk	1.75	1.00
91	A16	5auk gray vio & blk	4.50	2.00
		Nos. 81-91 (11)	18.50	9.75

Opening of Lithuanian National Assembly. On sale for three days.

1920

92	A14	20sk green & lilac	150.00	
92A	A15	40sk gray grn, buff & vio	150.00	
92B	A14	50sk brown & gray lil	150.00	
92C	A14	60sk red & green	150.00	
92D	A15	80sk black, grn & red	150.00	
		Nos. 92-92D (5)	750.00	

Nos. 92 to 92D were trial printings. By order of the Ministry of Posts, 2,000 examples of each were placed on sale at post offices.

Type of 1919 Issue

1920   Unwmk.   *Perf. 11½*

93	A5	15sk lilac	5.25	4.00
94	A5	20sk deep blue	5.25	4.00

Wmk. 109

95	A5	20sk deep blue	4.50	4.50
96	A5	40sk gray brown	9.75	7.50
		Nos. 93-96 (4)	24.75	20.00
		Set, never hinged	35.00	

Watermark horizontal on Nos. 95-96.
No. 96 exists perf. 10½x11½.

Imperf., Pairs

93a	A5	15sk	32.00	32.00
94a	A5	20sk	32.00	32.00
95a	A5	20sk	17.00	17.00
96a	A5	40sk	48.00	48.00

Sower A17   Peasant Sharpening Scythe A18

Prince Kestutis A19   Black Horseman A20

Perf. 11, 11½ and Compound
1921-22

97	A17	10sk brt rose	.85	.55
98	A17	15sk violet	.35	.70
99	A17	20sk ultra	.25	.25
100	A18	30sk brown	2.50	1.10
101	A19	40sk red	.25	.25
102	A18	50sk olive	.35	.25
103	A18	60sk grn & vio	2.50	1.65
104	A19	80sk brn org & car	.35	.25
105	A19	1auk brown & grn	.35	.25
106	A19	2auk gray bl & red	.35	.25
107	A20	3auk yel brn & dk bl	1.00	.40
108	A17	4auk yel & dk bl ('22)	.45	.25
109	A20	5auk gray blk & rose	1.00	1.50
110	A17	8auk grn & blk ('22)	.45	.25
111	A20	10auk rose & vio	1.00	.55
112	A20	25auk bis brn & grn	1.25	.85
113	A20	100auk dl red & gray blk	12.50	8.00
		Nos. 97-113 (17)	25.75	17.30
		Set, never hinged	35.00	

Imperf., Pairs

97a	A17	10sk	—
98a	A17	15sk	—
99a	A17	20sk	—
100a	A18	30sk	—
101a	A19	40sk	25.00
102a	A18	50sk	25.00
103a	A18	60sk	—
104a	A19	80sk	—
105a	A19	1auk	—
106a	A19	2auk	120.00
107a	A20	3auk	120.00
109a	A20	5auk	120.00
110a	A17	8auk	10.00 10.00
111a	A20	10auk	50.00
112a	A20	25auk	50.00
113a	A20	100auk	50.00

For surcharges see Nos. 140-148, 151-160.

No. 57 Surcharged

Perf. 12½x11½
1922, May   Wmk. 145

114	A6	4auk on 75sk bis & red	.90	.25
a.		Inverted surcharge	35.00	35.00

Same with Bars over Original Value

115	A6	4auk on 75sk bis & red	4.00	8.00
a.		Double surcharge	30.00	30.00

Povilas Luksis — A20a

Justinas Staugaitis, Antanas Smetona, Stasys Silingas — A20b

Portraits: 40s, Lt. Juozapavicius. 50s, Dr. Basanavicius. 60s, Mrs. Petkeviciute. 1auk, Prof. Voldemaras. 2auk, Pranas Dovidaitis. 3auk, Dr. Slezevicius. 4auk, Dr. Galvanauskas. 5auk, Kazys Grinius. 6auk, Dr. Stulginskis. 8auk, Pres. Smetona.

1922   Litho.   Unwmk.

116	A20a	20s blk & car rose	1.25	.90
116A	A20a	40s bl grn & vio	1.25	.90
116B	A20a	50s plum & grnsh bl	1.25	.90
117	A20a	60s pur & org	1.25	.90
117A	A20a	1auk car & lt bl	1.25	.90
117B	A20a	2auk dp bl & yel brn	1.25	.90
c.		Center inverted	100.00	100.00
118	A20a	3auk mar & ultra	1.25	.90
118A	A20a	4auk dk grn & red vio	1.25	.90
118B	A20a	5auk blk brn & dp rose	1.25	.90
119	A20a	6auk dk bl & grnsh bl	1.25	.90
a.		Cliché of 8auk in sheet of 6auk	175.00	175.00
119B	A20a	8auk ultra & bis	1.25	.90
119C	A20b	10auk dk vio & bl grn	1.25	.90
		Nos. 116-119C (12)	15.00	10.80
		Set, never hinged	24.00	

League of Nations' recognition of Lithuania. Sold only on Oct. 1, 1922.

Forty sheets of the 6auk each included eight examples of the 8auk.

Stamps of 1919-22 Surcharged in Black, Carmine or Green

On Nos. 37-39

1922   Wmk. 144   Perf. 11½x12
Gray Granite Paper

120	A7	3c on 1auk	125.00	225.00
121	A7	3c on 3auk	125.00	225.00
122	A7	3c on 5auk	100.00	140.00
		Nos. 120-122 (3)	350.00	590.00
		Set, never hinged	550.00	

White Paper

Perf. 14, 11½, 12½x11½
Wmk. 145

123	A5	1c on 10sk red	.55	1.50
124	A5	1c on 15sk lilac	.80	1.50
125	A5	1c on 20sk dull bl	.50	1.50
126	A5	1c on 30sk org	250.00	110.00
127	A5	1c on 30sk buff	.25	.40
128	A5	1c on 40sk gray brn	1.60	1.50
129	A6	2c on 50sk green	.70	1.50
130	A6	2c on 60sk vio & red	.25	.25
131	A6	2c on 75sk bis & red	.40	1.50
132	A8	3c on 1auk gray & red	.25	.25
133	A8	3c on 3auk brn & red	.25	.25
134	A8	3c on 5auk bl grn & red	.25	.25
		Nos. 123-125,127-134 (11)	5.80	10.40
		Set, never hinged, Nos. 123-125, 127-134)	24.00	

On Stamps of 1920

1922   Unwmk.   Perf. 11

136	A5	1c on 20sk dp bl (C)	3.75	2.00

Wmk. Webbing (109)
Perf. 11, 11½

138	A5	1c on 20sk dp bl (C)	3.50	2.00
139	A5	1c on 40sk gray brn (C)	7.50	1.25

On Stamps of 1921-22

140	A18	1c on 50sk ol (C)	.25	.25
a.		Imperf., pair	45.00	
b.		Inverted surcharge	40.00	
c.		Double surch., one invtd.		
141	A17	3c on 10sk	11.00	8.00
142	A17	3c on 15sk	.25	.25
143	A17	3c on 20sk	.40	1.50
144	A18	3c on 30sk	18.50	12.00
145	A19	3c on 40sk	.40	.40
a.		Imperf., pair		
146	A18	5c on 50sk	.25	.25
147	A18	5c on 60sk	18.50	18.50
148	A19	5c on 80sk	.55	1.50
a.		Imperf., pair	35.00	15.00

Wmk. Wavy Lines (145)
Perf. 12½x11½

149	A6	5c on 4auk on 75sk (No. 114) (G)		
150	A6	5c on 4auk on 75sk (No. 115) (G)	1.60	10.00
			16.00	17.50

Wmk. Webbing (109)
Perf. 11, 11½

151	A19	10c on 1auk	.80	.25
a.		Inverted surcharge	55.00	
152	A19	10c on 2auk	.25	.25
a.		Inverted surcharge	50.00	
b.		Imperf., pair	45.00	
153	A17	15c on 4auk	.25	.25
a.		Inverted surcharge	45.00	
154	A20	25c on 3auk	18.50	18.50
155	A20	25c on 5auk	11.00	5.00
156	A20	25c on 10auk	2.25	1.50
a.		Imperf., pair	45.00	
157	A17	30c on 8auk (C)	1.15	.35
a.		Inverted surcharge	45.00	25.00
158	A20	50c on 25auk	3.75	2.50
160	A20	1 l on 100auk	4.00	2.50
		Nos. 136-160 (23)	124.40	105.55
		Set, never hinged	140.00	

A21   Ruin — A22

Seminary Church, Kaunas — A23

1923   Litho.   Wmk. 109   Perf. 11

165	A21	10c violet	6.00	.25
166	A21	15c scarlet	2.25	.25
167	A21	20c olive brown	2.25	.25
168	A21	25c deep blue	2.25	.25
169	A22	50c yellow green	2.25	.25
170	A22	60c red	2.25	.25
171	A23	1 l orange & grn	10.00	.25
172	A23	3 l red & gray	13.50	.45
173	A23	5 l brown & blue	21.00	1.00
		Nos. 165-173 (9)	61.75	3.20
		Set, never hinged	85.00	

See Nos. 189-209, 281-282. For surcharges see Nos. B1-B42.

Memel Coat of Arms — A24

Lithuanian Coat of Arms — A25

Biruta Chapel — A26

Kaunas, War Memorial A27

Trakai Ruins A28

Memel Lighthouse — A29

Memel Harbor A30

Perf. 11, 11½, 12

1923, Aug.   Unwmk.

176	A24	1c rose, grn & blk	1.25	1.60
177	A25	2c dull vio & blk	1.25	1.60
178	A26	3c yellow & blk	1.25	1.60
179	A24	5c bl, buff & blk	2.50	1.90
180	A27	10c orange & blk	1.90	1.90
181	A27	15c green & blk	1.90	2.50
182	A28	25c brt vio & blk	1.90	2.50
183	A29	30c red vio & blk	4.00	5.00
184	A29	60c ol grn & blk	2.25	2.75
185	A30	1 l bl grn & blk	2.25	2.75
186	A26	2 l red & black	8.25	7.50
187	A28	3 l blue & black	8.25	7.50
188	A29	5 l ultra & black	8.25	7.50
		Nos. 176-188 (13)	45.20	46.60
		Set, never hinged	85.00	

This series was issued ostensibly to commemorate the incorporation of Memel with Lithuania.

Type of 1923

1923   Unwmk.   Perf. 11

189	A21	5c pale green	3.75	.50
190	A21	10c violet	5.00	.50
a.		Imperf., pair	50.00	
191	A21	15c scarlet	6.00	.50
a.		Imperf., pair	50.00	
193	A21	25c blue	10.00	.50
		Nos. 189-193 (4)	24.75	2.00
		Set, never hinged	60.00	

1923   Wmk. 147

196	A21	2c pale brown	.50	.25
197	A21	3c olive bister	.75	.25
198	A21	5c pale green	.75	.25
199	A21	10c violet	1.50	.25
202	A21	25c deep blue	3.50	.25
a.		Imperf., pair	40.00	
204	A21	36c orange brown	5.50	.75
		Nos. 196-204 (6)	12.50	2.00
		Set, never hinged	26.00	

Perf. 11½, 14½, 11½x14½
1923-25   Wmk. 198

207	A21	25c deep blue	750.00	450.00
208	A22	50c deep green ('25)	25.00	.50
209	A22	60c carmine ('25)	25.00	.50

Double-barred Cross — A31

Dr. Jonas Basanavicius — A32

1927, Jan.   Perf. 11½, 14½

210	A31	2c orange	1.00	.30
211	A31	3c deep brown	1.00	.30
212	A31	5c green	1.50	.30
a.		Imperf., pair	25.00	
213	A31	10c violet	2.25	.30
214	A31	15c red	2.25	.30
a.		Imperf., pair	25.00	
215	A31	25c blue	2.25	.30
		Nos. 210-215 (6)	10.25	1.80
		Set, never hinged	21.00	

1927-29   Wmk. 147   Perf. 14½

216	A31	5c green	30.00	150.00
217	A31	30c blue ('30)	25.00	10.00

See Nos. 233-240, 278-280.

1927   Unwmk.   Perf. 11½, 14½x11½

219	A32	15c claret & blk	2.00	1.25
220	A32	25c dull blue & blk	2.00	1.25
221	A32	50c dk green & blk	2.00	1.25
222	A32	60c dk violet & blk	3.75	2.00
		Nos. 219-222 (4)	9.75	5.75
		Set, never hinged	20.00	

Dr. Jonas Basanavicius (1851-1927), patriot and folklorist.

National Arms — A33

1927, Dec. 23   Wmk. 109   Perf. 14½

223	A33	1 l blue grn & gray	1.25	.75
224	A33	3 l vio & pale grn	3.25	.75
225	A33	5 l brown & gray	4.50	1.25
		Nos. 223-225 (3)	9.00	2.75
		Set, never hinged	21.00	

Pres. Antanas Smetona — A34

Decade of Independence A35

Dawn of Peace — A36

1928, Feb.   Wmk. 109

226	A34	5c org brn & grn	1.00	.30
227	A34	10c violet & blk	1.25	.30
228	A34	15c orange & brn	1.25	.35
229	A34	25c blue & indigo	1.25	.35
230	A35	50c ultra & dl vio	1.50	.45
231	A35	60c carmine & blk	1.75	.55
232	A36	1 l blk brn & drab	.70	.70
		Nos. 226-232 (7)	10.00	3.00
		Set, never hinged	15.00	

10th anniv. of Lithuanian independence.

Type of 1926

1929-31

233	A31	2c orange ('31)	10.00	1.00
234	A31	5c green	2.40	.25
235	A31	10c violet ('31)	7.50	1.00
237	A31	15c red	2.75	.25
a.		Tête bêche pair	45.00	35.00
239	A31	30c dark blue	4.25	.25

Unwmk.

240	A31	15c red ('30)	7.50	.60
		Nos. 233-240 (6)	34.40	3.35
		Set, never hinged	65.00	

Grand Duke Vytautas A37　　　Grand Duke, Mounted A38

1930, Feb. 16　　　Perf. 14

242	A37	2c yel brn & dk brn	.30	.25
243	A37	3c dk brn & vio	.30	.25
244	A37	5c yel grn & dp org	.30	.25
245	A37	10c vio & emer	.30	.25
246	A37	15c dp rose & vio	.30	.25
247	A37	30c dk bl & brn vio	.50	.25
248	A37	36c brn vio & ol blk	.75	.30
249	A37	50c dull grn & ultra	.50	.35
250	A37	60c dk blue & rose	.50	.40
251	A38	1 l bl grn, db & red brn	2.10	1.00
252	A38	3 l dk brn, sal & dk vio	3.25	1.75
253	A38	5 l ol brn, gray & red	7.50	2.75
254	A38	10 l multicolored	20.00	16.00
255	A38	25 l multicolored	42.50	55.00
		Nos. 242-255 (14)	79.10	79.05
		Set, never hinged	200.00	

5th cent. of the death of the Grand Duke Vytautas.

Kaunas, Railroad Station A39

Cathedral at Vilnius — A39a

Designs: 15c, 25c, Landscape on the Neman River. 50c, 60c, Main Post Office, Kaunas.

Perf. 14, Imperf.

1932, July 21　　　Wmk. 238

256	A39	10c dk red brn & ocher	.40	.45
257	A39	15c dk brown & ol	.75	.80
258	A39	25c dk blue & ol	1.15	1.25
259	A39	50c gray blk & ol	2.50	2.50
260	A39a	1 l dk blue & ol	6.50	5.00
261	A39a	3 l red brn & gray grn	6.50	6.50

Wmk. 198

262	A39	5c vio bl & ocher	.40	.45
263	A39a	60c grnsh blk & lil	6.50	5.00
		Nos. 256-263 (8)	24.70	21.95
		Set, never hinged	35.00	

Issued for the benefit of Lithuanian orphans.
In September, 1935, a red overprint was applied to No. 259: "ORO PASTAS / LITUANICA II / 1935 / NEW YORK-KAUNAS." Value, $400.

Vytautas Fleeing from Prison, 1382 A40

Designs: 15c, 25c, Conversion of Ladislas II Jagello and Vytautas (1386). 50c, 60c, Battle at Tannenberg (1410). 1 l, 3 l, Meeting of the Nobles (1429).

1932　　Wmk. 209　　Perf. 14, Imperf.

264	A40	5c red & rose lake	.30	.35
265	A40	10c ol bis & org brn	.35	.35
266	A40	15c rose lil & ol grn	.50	.50
267	A40	25c dk vio brn & ocher	1.10	1.25
268	A40	50c dp grn & bis brn	1.10	1.75
269	A40	60c ol grn & brn car	2.25	2.50
270	A40	1 l ultra & ol grn	2.40	3.00
271	A40	3 l dk brn & dk grn	2.50	4.00
		Nos. 264-271 (8)	10.50	13.70
		Set, never hinged	25.00	

15th anniversary of independence.

A. Visteliauskas A41

Designs: 15c, 25c, Petras Vileisis. 50c, 60c, Dr. John Sliupas. 1 l, 3 l, Jonas Basanavicius.

1933　　　Perf. 14, Imperf.

272	A41	5c yel grn & car	.35	.30
273	A41	10c ultra & car	.45	.40
274	A41	15c orange & red	.55	.50
275	A41	25c dk bl & blk brn	.85	.90
276	A41	50c ol gray & dk bl	1.40	1.50
277	A41	60c org brn & chnt	4.50	4.00
277A	A41	1 l red & vio brn	5.50	4.75
277B	A41	3 l turq grn & vio brn	6.25	6.00
		Nos. 272-277B (8)	19.85	18.35
		Set, never hinged	35.00	

50th anniv. of the 1st newspaper, "Ausra," in lithuanian language.

Mother and Child — A42

Designs: 15c, 25c, Boy reading. 50c, 60c, Boy playing with blocks. 1 l, 3 l, Woman and boy at the Spinning Wheel.

1933, Sept.　　　Perf. 14, Imperf.

277C	A42	5c dp yel grn & org brn	.30	.25
277D	A42	10c rose brn & ultra	.30	.30
277E	A42	15c ol grn & plum	.30	.45
277F	A42	25c org & gray blk	1.10	1.25
277G	A42	50c ol grn & car	1.45	2.00
277H	A42	60c blk & yel org	4.75	3.25
277I	A42	1 l dk brn & ultra	5.50	3.75
277K	A42	3 l rose lil & ol grn	6.50	10.00
		Nos. 277C-277K (8)	20.20	21.25
		Set, never hinged	35.00	

Issued for the benefit of Lithuanian orphans.

Types of 1923-26

1933-34　　Wmk. 238　　Perf. 14

278	A31	2c orange	42.50	6.50
279	A31	10c dark violet	60.00	9.50
280	A31	15c red	42.50	4.50
281	A22	50c green	42.50	9.50
282	A22	60c red	42.50	9.50
		Nos. 278-282 (5)	230.00	39.50
		Set, never hinged	400.00	

Pres. Antanas Smetona, 60th Birthday — A43

1934　　Unwmk.　　Engr.　　Perf. 11½

283	A43	15c red	6.50	.25

Unwmk.

284	A43	30c green	8.25	.35

Unwmk.

285	A43	60c blue	10.00	.50

Unwmk.

	Nos. 283-285 (3)	24.75	1.10
	Set, never hinged	42.50	

A44　　　　Arms — A45

Girl with Wheat — A46

A47

Knight A48

Wmk. 198; Wmk. 209 (35c, 10 l)

1934-35　　　Litho.　　Perf. 14

286	A44	2c rose & dull org	1.50	.25
287	A44	5c bl grn & grn	1.50	.25
288	A45	10c chocolate	3.50	.25
289	A46	25c dk brn & emer	5.50	.25
290	A45	35c carmine	5.50	.25
291	A46	50c dk blue & blue	10.00	.25
292	A47	1 l salmon & mar	92.50	.25
293	A47	3 l grn & gray grn	.45	.25
294	A48	5 l maroon & gray bl	.65	.45
295	A48	10 l choc & yel	4.50	3.75
		Nos. 286-295 (10)	125.60	6.20
		Set, never hinged	260.00	

No. 290 exists imperf. Value, pair $65.
For overprint see No. 2N9.

1936-37　　Wmk. 238　　Perf. 14
Size: 17½x23mm

296	A44	2c orange ('37)	.25	.25
297	A44	5c green	.30	.25

Pres. Smetona A49　　　Arms A50

1936-37　　　　　　Unwmk.

298	A49	15c carmine	5.50	.25
299	A49	30c green ('37)	7.50	.25
300	A49	60c ultra ('37)	6.75	.25
		Nos. 298-300 (3)	19.75	.75
		Set, never hinged	32.00	

Paper with Gray Network

No. 304 exists in two types:
I — "50" is fat and broad, with "0" leaning to right.
II — "50" is thinner and narrower, with "0" straight.

1937-39　　Wmk. 238　　Perf. 14

301	A50	10c green	.85	.25
302	A50	25c magenta	.25	.25
303	A50	35c red	.50	.25
304	A50	50c brown	.30	.25
305	A50	1 l dp vio bl ('39)	.35	.45
		Nos. 301-305 (5)	2.25	1.45
		Set, never hinged	4.50	

For overprint see No. 2N10.

Jonas Basanavicius Reading Act of Independence A51

President Antanas Smetona A52

Perf. 13x13½

1939, Jan. 15　　Engr.　　Unwmk.

306	A51	15c dark red	.25	.30
307	A52	30c deep green	.50	.30
308	A51	35c red lilac	.60	.45
309	A52	60c dark blue	.75	.60
a.		Souvenir sheet of 2, #308-309	5.00	15.00
b.		As "a," imperf.	35.00	72.50
		Nos. 306-309 (4)	2.10	1.65
		Set, never hinged	4.25	

20th anniv. of Independence.
Nos. 309a, 309b sold for 2 l.

Same Overprinted in Blue

1939

310	A51	15c dark red	.40	.90
311	A52	30c deep green	.45	.90
312	A51	35c red lilac	1.00	1.00
313	A52	60c dark blue	1.10	1.00
		Nos. 310-313 (4)	2.95	3.80
		Set, never hinged	6.00	

Recovery of Vilnius.

View of Vilnius A53

Gediminas — A54

Trakai Ruins A55

Unwmk.

1940, May 6　　Photo.　　Perf. 14

314	A53	15c brn & pale brn	.30	.25
315	A54	30c dk grn & lt grn	.60	.85
316	A55	60c dk bl & lt bl	1.10	1.00
a.		Souv. sheet of 3, #314-316, imperf.	8.00	16.00
		Nos. 314-316 (3)	2.00	2.10
		Set, never hinged	4.25	

Return of Vilnius to Lithuania, Oct. 10, 1939.
Exist imperf.
No. 316a has simulated perforations in gold.
Sold for 2 l.

White Knight — A56

Angel — A57

Woman Releasing Dove A58

Mother and Children A59

Liberty Bell — A60

Mythical Animal — A61

1940

317	A56	5c brown carmine	.25	.30
318	A57	10c green	.40	.45
319	A58	15c dull orange	.25	.30
320	A59	25c light brown	.25	.40
321	A60	30c Prussian green	.25	.30
322	A61	35c red orange	.25	.35
		Nos. 317-322 (6)	1.65	2.10
		Set, never hinged	3.00	

Nos. 317-322 exist imperf.
For overprints see Nos. 2N11-2N16.

> Catalogue values for unused stamps in this section, from this point to the end of the section, are for Never Hinged items.

Nos. 371-399 were issued before the Soviet Union recognized the independence of Lithuania on Sept. 6, 1991, but were available and valid for use after that date.

Angel and Map — A66

Colors: 5k, Green. 10k, Brown violet. 20k, Blue. 50k, Red.

1990, Oct. 7   Litho.   Imperf.
Without Gum
371-374 A66 Set of 4   2.50 2.50

Simulated Perforations and Denomination in Brownish Gray
Colors as before.

1990, Dec. 22   Without Gum
375-378 A66 Set of 4   1.60 1.60

White Knight "Vytis" — A67

Hill With Crosses, Siauliai — A68

Design: 200k, Liberty Bell.

1991   Photo.   Perf. 14

379	A67	10k multi	.30	.25
380	A67	15k multi	.30	.25
381	A67	20k multi	.30	.25
382	A67	30k multi	.30	.25
383	A68	50k multi	.30	.25
384	A68	200k multi	.40	.25

Litho.
Imperf
Without Gum

385	A67	15k dl grn & blk	.30	.25
386	A67	25k brn & blk	.30	.25
387	A67	30k plum & blk	.30	.25
		Nos. 379-387 (9)	2.80	2.25

Issued: 10k, 20k, No. 382, 50k, 200k, 1/10; No. 380, 3/15; No. 385, 3/13; 25k, No 387, 7/23.
No. 385 has a simulated outline of a perforated stamp.
See Nos. 411-418.

Liberty Statue — A69

1991, Feb. 16   Photo.   Perf. 13¾x14
388 A69 20k multi   .25 .25

Declaration of Independence from Soviet Union, 1st Anniv. — A70

1991, Mar. 11   Litho.   Perf. 13¼x13
389 A70 20k multi   .25 .25

Religious Symbols — A71

Designs: 40k, Crosses. 70k, Madonna. 100k, Spires, St. Anne's Church, Vilnius.

1991, Mar. 15   Photo.   Perf. 13¾x14
390-392 A71 Set of 3   1.25 .75

Resistance to Soviet and German Occupation, 50th Anniv. — A72

Designs: 20k, Candle, barbed wire. 50k, Heart, daggers. 70k, Sword, wreath.

1991, June 14   Litho.   Perf. 13¼
393-395 A72 Set of 3   1.25 .75

Fourth World Lithuanian Games A73

Emblem and: 20k, Map. 50k+25k, Head.

1991, July 27   Photo.   Perf. 13¼x13
396-397 A73 Set of 2   .85 .50

A74

A75

Denominations: 20k, 70k.

1991, Aug. 20 Litho. Perf. 12½x13
398-399 A74 Set of 2   1.25 .75
Expedition to Mt. Everest.

1991, Sept. 28 Litho. Perf. 13x13½
400 A75 30k Castle   .30 .30
401 A75 50k Grand Duke   .55 .55
402 A75 70k Early view of Vilnius .85 .85
    Nos. 400-402 (3)   1.70 1.70
Grand Duke Gediminas, 650th dath anniv.

Ciconia Nigra — A76

Design: 50k, Grus grus.

1991, Nov. 21   Litho.   Perf. 14
403 A76 30k +15k multi   .65 .55
404 A76 50k multicolored   .75 .65

White Knight Type of 1991
1991, Dec. 20   Photo.   Perf. 14
Background Colors

411	A67	40k black	.25	.25
412	A67	50k purple	.25	.25
415	A67	100k dark green	.25	.25
418	A67	500k blue	1.25	.55
		Nos. 411-418 (4)	2.00	1.30

For surcharges see Nos. 450-452.

A78

1992, Mar. 15   Litho.   Perf. 13x13½
421 A78 100k multicolored   .30 .30
Lithuanian admission to UN.

A79

Emblems.

1992, Mar. 22
422 A79 50k +25k Olympic
             Committee   .30 .30
423 A79 130k Albertville   .45 .45
424 A79 280k Barcelona   1.25 1.25
    Nos. 422-424 (3)   2.00 2.00

Lithuanian Olympic participation. Surtax for Lithuanian Olympic Committee.

A80

1992, July 11   Perf. 12½x13
425 A80 200k Cypripedium   .30 .30
426 A80 300k Eringium mari-
             timum   .50 .50

A81

Birds of the Baltic Shores: No. 427, Pandion haliaetus. No. 428, Limosa limosa. No. 429, Mergus merganser. No. 430, Tadorna tadorna.

Litho. & Engr.
1992, Oct. 3   Perf. 12½x13
Booklet Stamps

427	A81	B grn & grnsh blk	.70	.50
428	A81	B grn & red brn	.70	.50
429	A81	B grn, red brn & brn	.70	.50
430	A81	B grn & red brn	.70	.50
a.		Booklet pane of 4, #427-430	3.50	

Sold for 15r on day of issue.
See Estonia Nos. 231-234a, Latvia Nos. 332-335a and Sweden Nos. 1975-1978a.

Coats of Arms — A82

19th Cent. Costumes — A83

1992, Oct. 11   Litho.   Perf. 14
431 A82 2r Kedainiai   .25 .25
432 A82 3r Vilnius   .25 .25
433 A82 10r National   .55 .55
    Nos. 431-433 (3)   1.05 1.05

See Nos. 454-456, 497-499, 521-522, 554-556, 586-588, 607-609, 642-644, 677-679, 704-706, 716-718, 736-740, 762-764, 788-789, 813-815, 833-835, 879-881, 887-889, 910-912, 945-947, 958-960.

1992, Oct. 18   Perf. 13x13½

Couples in different traditional costumes of the Suwalki region.

434 A83 2r multicolored   .25 .25
435 A83 5r multicolored   .25 .25
436 A83 7r multicolored   .40 .35
    Nos. 434-436 (3)   .90 .85

See Nos. 465-467, 493-495, 511-513, 539-541.

Churches — A84

300k, Zapishkis Church, 16th cent. 1000k, Saints Peter & Paul Church, Vilnius, 17th cent. 1500k, Christ Church of the Resurrection, Kaunas, 1934.

1993, Jan. 15   **Litho.**   *Perf. 12*
437 A84 300k bister & blk   .25 .25
438 A84 1000k blue green & blk   .30 .25
439 A84 1500k gray & blk   .50 .30
    Nos. 437-439 (3)   1.05 .80
     See Nos. 502-504

Independence — A85

Designs: A, Jonas Basanavicius (1851-1927), journalist and politician. B, Jonas Vileisis (1872-1942), lawyer and politician.

1993, Feb. 16
440 A85 (A) red & multi   .25 .25
441 A85 (B) green & multi   .95 .65

   No. 440 sold for 3r and No. 441 sold for 15r on day of issue.
   See Nos. 479-480, 506-507, 536-537, 563-564, 592-593, 622-623, 660-661, 686-687, 711-712.

A86

Grand Duke Vytautas, 600th Birth Anniv. — A87

Designs: 500k, Royal Seal. 1000k, 5000k, Portrait. 1500k, Vytautas in Battle of Grunwald, by Jan Matejko.

1993, Feb. 27
442 A86 500k bister, red & blk   .25 .25
443 A87 1000k citron, blk & red   .40 .30
444 A87 1500k lem, blk & red   .60 .50
    Nos. 442-444 (3)   1.25 1.05

Souvenir Sheet
445 A87 5000k citron, black & red   1.60 1.60

Famous Lithuanians A88

Designs: 1000k, Simonas Daukantas (1793-1864), educator and historian. 2000k, Vydunas (1868-1953), preserver of Lithuanian traditional culture. 4500k, Vincas Mykolaitis Putinas (1893-1967), philosopher and psychologist.

1993, Mar. 13
446 A88 1000k multicolored   .25 .25
447 A88 2000k multicolored   .50 .50
448 A88 4500k multicolored   1.00 .90
    Nos. 446-448 (3)   1.75 1.65

   See Nos. 475-477, 514-516, 533-535, 560-562, 599-601, 624-626.

No. 382, 387 and 411 Surcharged

1993 Photo, Litho. (#451)   *Perf. 14*
450 A67 100k on 30k magenta   .25 .25
451 A67 100k on 30k magenta, imperf, without gum   .25 .25
452 A67 300k on 40k #411   .25 .25
    Nos. 450-452 (3)   .75 .75

   Issued: 300k, 1/19; No. 450, 1/26; No. 451, 3/10.

Coat of Arms Type of 1992
Size: 24x31mm

1993, July 3   **Litho.**   *Perf. 11*
454 A82 5c Skuodas   .25 .25
   a.   Tete-beche pair   .40 .40
455 A82 30c Telsiai   .35 .30
   a.   Tete-beche pair   1.20 .60
456 A82 50c Klaipeda   .55 .45
   a.   Tete-beche pair   1.70 .90
    Nos. 454-456 (3)   1.15 1.00

World Lithuanian Unity Day — A89

5c, The Spring, by M. K. Ciurlionis. 80c, Capts. Steponas Darius and Stasys Girenas.

1993, July 17   *Perf. 13*
457 A89 5c multicolored   .25 .25
   a.   Tete-beche pair   .30
458 A89 80c multicolored   .75 .75
   a.   Tete-beche pair   2.40

   Deaths of Darius and Girenas, 60th anniv. (No. 458).

Natl. Arms — A90

1993, July 21   Litho.   *Perf. 13x12½*
459 A90 (A) bister & multi   .30 .25
460 A90 (B) green & multi   .80 .25

   No. 459 sold for 5c, No. 460 for 80c on day of issue.
   Dated 1992.

Visit of Pope John Paul II — A91

1993, Sept. 3   Litho.   *Perf. 13½x13*
461 A91 60c Kryziu Kalnas   .50 .30
462 A91 60c Siluva   .50 .30
463 A91 80c Vilnius   .70 .35
464 A91 80c Kaunas   .70 .35
    Nos. 461-464 (4)   2.40 1.30

Natl. Costumes Type of 1992
Couples in different traditional costumes of the Dzukai.

1993, Oct. 30   Litho.   *Perf. 12*
Size: 23x36mm
465 A83 60c multicolored   .40 .25
466 A83 80c multicolored   .60 .35
467 A83 1 l multicolored   1.00 .45
    Nos. 465-467 (3)   2.00 1.05

Lithuanian Postal System, 75th Anniv. — A92

Post offices: No. 468, Klaipeda. No. 469, Kaunas. 80c, Vilnius. 1 l, No. 1.

1993, Nov. 16
468 A92 60c multicolored   .40 .25
469 A92 60c multicolored   .40 .25
470 A92 80c multicolored   .60 .30
471 A92 1 l multicolored   .90 .40
    Nos. 468-471 (4)   2.30 1.20

Europa — A93   Endangered Species — A94

80c, The Old Master, by A. Gudaitis, 1939.

1993, Dec. 24   Litho.   *Perf. 12*
472 A93 80c multicolored   1.40 1.40
   a.   Tete-beche pair   3.50 3.50

1993, Dec. 30   Litho.   *Perf. 12*
473 A94 80c Emys orbicularis   .60 .30
474 A94 1 l Bufo calamita   1.00 .40
    See Nos. 500-501, 519-520.

Famous Lithuanians Type of 1993
Designs: 60c, Kristijonas Donelaitis (1714-80), poet. 80c, Vincas Kudirka (1858-99), physician, writer. 1 l, Maironis (1862-1932), poet.

1994, Mar. 26   Litho.   *Perf. 12*
475 A88 60c multicolored   .40 .25
476 A88 80c multicolored   .65 .30
477 A88 1 l multicolored   1.00 .40
    Nos. 475-477 (3)   2.05 .95

1994 Winter Olympics, Lillehammer A95

1994, Feb. 11
478 A95 1.10 l multicolored   .95 .40

Independence Type of 1993
No. 479, Pres. Antanas Smetona (1874-1944). No. 480, Aleksandras Stulginskis.

1994, Feb. 16
479 A85 1 l red brown & multi   .80 .35
480 A85 1 l brown & multi   .80 .35

A96   Natl. Arms — A96a

Perf. 12, 13½ (40c), 13½x13 (50c)
1994-97   **Litho.**
481 A96 5c dark brown   .25 .25
482 A96 10c deep violet   .25 .25
483 A96 20c dark green   .25 .25
484 A96 40c deep rose mag   .25 .25
485 A96 50c green blue   .30 .25
486 A96a 1 l gray & multi   .50 .25
   a.   Souvenir sheet of 4   3.00 3.00
487 A96a 2 l buff & multi   1.90 .50
488 A96a 3 l green & multi   2.50 .75
    Nos. 481-488 (8)   6.20 2.75

   Independence, 5th anniv. (No. 486a).
   Issued: 5c, 10c, 4/9/94; 20c, 11/19/94; 2 l, 3 l, 7/23/94; 1 l, 3/11/95; 40c, 5/4/96; 50c, 4/5/97.

Europa — A97   80ct

1994, May 7   Litho.   *Perf. 12*
491 A97 80c Artillery rockets, 17th cent.   .70 .40

Souvenir Sheet

100th Postage Stamp — A98

1994, May 21   Litho.   *Perf. 12*
492 A98 10 l multicolored   10.00 10.00
    No. 492 sold for 12 l.

Natl. Costumes Type of 1992
Couples in different traditional costumes of Samogitia.

1994, June 25   Litho.   *Perf. 12*
493 A83 5c multicolored   .30 .25
494 A83 80c multicolored   .60 .25
495 A83 1 l multicolored   .70 .30
    Nos. 493-495 (3)   1.60 .80

Lithuanian World Song Festival — A99

1994, July 6
496 A99 10c multicolored   .25 .25

Coat of Arms Type of 1992
1994, Sept. 10   Litho.   *Perf. 12*
Size: 25x32mm
497 A82 10c Punia   .25 .25
498 A82 60c Alytus   .45 .25
499 A82 80c Perloja   .60 .30
    Nos. 497-499 (3)   1.30 .80

Endangered Species Type of 1993
1994, Oct. 22   Litho.   *Perf. 12*
500 A94 20c Nyctalus noctula   .30 .25
501 A94 20c Glis glis   .30 .25

Church Type of 1993
1994, Nov. 12
502 A84 10c Kaunus, 16th cent.   .25 .25
503 A84 60c Kedainiu, 17th cent.   .45 .25
504 A84 80c Vilnius, 18th cent.   .60 .35
    Nos. 502-504 (3)   1.30 .85

Christmas A101

1994, Dec. 3   Litho.   *Perf. 12*
505 A101 20c multicolored   .25 .25

Independence Type of 1993

No. 506, Pranas Dovydaitis. No. 507, Steponas Kairys.

1995, Feb. 16   Litho.   Perf. 12
506 A85 20c multicolored   .25 .25
507 A85 20c multicolored   .25 .25

Via Baltica Highway Project — A102

No. 509: a, Parnu. b, Bauska. c, Like #508.

1995, Apr. 20   Litho.   Perf. 14
508 A102 20c multicolored   .25 .25

Souvenir Sheet
509 A102 1 l Sheet of 3, #a.-c. 2.50 2.50

See Estonia Nos. 288-289, Latvia Nos. 394-395.

Sculpture, Mother's School — A103

1995, Apr. 29   Litho.   Perf. 12
510 A103 1 l multicolored   1.40 1.40

Europa.

Natl. Costumes Type of 1992

Couples in traditional costumes of Aukstaiciai.

1995, May 20   Litho.   Perf. 12
511 A83 20c multicolored   .25 .25
512 A83 70c multicolored   .60 .25
513 A83 1 l multicolored   .75 .30
     Nos. 511-513 (3)   1.60 .80

Famous People Type of 1993

Writers. 30c, Motiejus Valancius (1801-75). 40c, Zemaite (1845-1921). 70c, Kipras Petrauskas (1885-1968).

1995, May 27   Litho.   Perf. 12
514 A88 30c multicolored   .25 .25
515 A88 40c multicolored   .40 .24
516 A88 70c multicolored   .60 .25
     Nos. 514-516 (3)   1.25 .75

A104

1995, June 14   Litho.   Perf. 12
517 A104 20c multicolored   .25 .25

Day of mourning & hope.

A105

1995, July 30   Litho.   Perf. 12
518 A105 30c multicolored   .25 .25

5th World Sports Games.

Endangered Species Type of 1993

1995, Aug. 26   Litho.   Perf. 12
519 A94 30c Arctia villica   .25 .25
520 A94 30c Baptria tibiale   .25 .25

Coat of Arms Type of 1992
Size: 25x32mm

Arms of villages in Suvalkija: 40c, Virbalis. 1 l, Kudirkos Naumiestis, horiz.

1995, Sept. 16   Litho.   Perf. 12
521 A82 40c multicolored   .30 .25
522 A82 1 l multicolored   .90 .30

Valerie Mesalina, by Pranciskus Smuglevicius — A106

1995, Oct. 6   Litho.   Perf. 12½
523 A106 40c multicolored   .35 .25

Castles — A107

1995, Nov. 18   Perf. 11½x12
524 A107 40c Vilnius   .30 .25
525 A107 70c Trakai   .60 .25
526 A107 1 l Birzai   .90 .45
     Nos. 524-526 (3)   1.80 1.00

Christmas A108

1995, Dec. 2   Litho.   Perf. 13
527 A108 40c multicolored   .30 .25
528 A108 1 l multicolored   .90 .45

Bison Bonasus A109

1996, Jan. 20   Perf. 13x13½
529 A109 30c shown   .25 .25
530 A109 40c Two adults   .40 .25
531 A109 70c Adult, calf   .75 .40
532 A109 1 l Two adults, calf   1.00 1.00
  a.   Miniature sheet, 2 each #529-532   4.50 4.50
     Nos. 529-532 (4)   2.40 1.90

World Wildlife Fund.

Famous Lithuanians Type of 1993

Designs: 40c, Kazys Grinius (1866-1950). No. 534, Antanas Zmudzinavicius (1876-1966). No. 535, Balys Sruoga (1896-1947).

1996, Feb. 2   Litho.   Perf. 13x13½
533 A88 40c multicolored   .30 .25
534 A88 1 l multicolored   .85 .30
535 A88 1 l multicolored   .85 .30
     Nos. 533-535 (3)   2.00 .85

Independence Type of 1993

No. 536, Vladas Mironas. No. 537, Jurgis Saulys.

1996, Feb. 16   Litho.   Perf. 13½x13
536 A85 40c gray, blk & buff   .30 .25
537 A85 40c olive, blk & buff   .30 .25

Barbora Radvilaite (1520-51) — A110

1996, Apr. 27   Litho.   Perf. 13½x13
538 A110 1 l multicolored   1.25 1.25

Europa.

19th Cent. Costumes Type of 1992

Couples in different traditional costumes of the Klaipeda region: No. 540, Man in blue coat. No. 541, Man wearing wooden shoes.

1996, May 25   Litho.   Perf. 13½
539 A83 40c multicolored   .35 .25
540 A83 1 l multicolored   .75 .35
541 A83 1 l multicolored   .75 .35
     Nos. 539-541 (3)   1.85 .95

A116

1996, June 14   Litho.   Perf. 13½
547 A116 40c Christ   .35 .25
548 A116 40c Angel   .35 .25

Day of Mourning and Hope.

A117

Designs: No. 549, Greek discus thrower. No. 550, Basketball players.

1996, July 19   Perf. 13½x13
549 A117 1 l multicolored   1.00 .50
550 A117 1 l multicolored   1.00 .50

1996 Summer Olympic Games, Atlanta.

Paintings, by M.K. Ciurlionis — A118

No. 551, Kapines, 1909. No. 552, Auka, 1909. No. 553: a, Andante, 1908. b, Allegro, 1908.

1996, Sept. 21   Litho.   Perf. 13½x13
551 A118 40c multicolored   .35 .25
552 A118 40c multicolored   .35 .25

Souvenir Sheet
Perf. 12½x11½
553 A118 3 l Sheet of 2, #a.-b. 5.00 5.00

No. 553 contains 26x53mm stamps.

Coat of Arms Type of 1992
Size: 25x33mm

1996, Oct. 19   Litho.   Perf. 13½x13
554 A82 50c Seduva   .45 .25
555 A82 90c Panevezys   .70 .35
556 A82 1.20 l Zarasai   1.00 .50
     Nos. 554-556 (3)   2.15 1.10

Souvenir Sheet

Lithuanian Basketball Team, Bronze Medalists, 1996 Summer Olympic Games, Atlanta — A119

1996, Nov. 16   Perf. 12½
557 A119 4.20 l multicolored   3.50 3.50

Christmas A120

1996, Nov. 30   Perf. 13½x13
558 A120 50c Angels   .35 .25
559 A120 1.20 l Santa on horse   1.00 .50

Famous Lithuanians Type of 1993

Designs: 50c, Ieva Simonaityte (1897-1978). 90c, Jonas Sliupas (1861-1944). 1.20 l, Vladas Jurgutis (1885-1966).

1997, Jan. 23   Litho.   Perf. 13x13½
560 A88 50c brown & green   .40 .25
561 A88 90c gray & yellow   .70 .35
562 A88 1.20 l blue green & orange   .90 .45
     Nos. 560-562 (3)   2.00 1.05

Independence Type of 1993

No. 563, Mykolas Birziska. No. 564, Kazimieras Saulys.

1997, Feb. 16   Litho.   Perf. 13½x13
563 A85 50c multicolored   .40 .25
564 A85 50c multicolored   .40 .25

First Lithuanian Book, 450th Anniv. — A121

1997, Feb. 15   Litho.   Perf. 13½x13
565 A121 50c gray & red   .45 .25

Souvenir Sheet
566 A121 4.80 l like #565   4.00 4.00

No. 566 contains one 29x38mm stamp.

Souvenir Sheet

Flag on Mountain Top — A122

1997, Feb. 25   Perf. 11½x12½
567 A122 4.80 l multicolored   4.00 4.00
Expeditions to highest peaks on each continent.

Stories and Legends A123

Children's drawings: No. 568, Girl, horse. No. 569, King, moon, stars, bird, vert.

1997, Apr. 12   Litho.   Perf. 13
568 A123 1.20 l multicolored   1.00 1.00
569 A123 1.20 l multicolored   1.00 1.00
Europa.

A124

1997, May 9   Litho.   Perf. 13
570 A124 50c multicolored   .45 .25
First Lithuanian School, 600th Anniv.

A125

Old Ships of the Baltic Sea: 50c, Kurenas, 16th cent.
No. 572: a, Kurenas, 16th cent., diff. b, Maasilinn ship, 16th cent. c, Linijkugis, 17th cent.

1997, May 10   Perf. 14x14½
571 A125 50c multicolored   .45 .25
572 A125 1.20 l Sheet of 3, #a.-
     c.   3.00 3.00
See Estonia Nos. 322-323, Latvia Nos. 443-444.

Palanga Botanical Park, Cent. — A126

1997, June 1   Litho.   Perf. 13½x13
573 A126 50c multicolored   .45 .25
a.   Tete-beche pair   .90 .90
Numbers 574-577 are unassigned.

2nd Baltic Sea Games — A127

1997, June 25   Litho.   Perf. 13½
578 A127 90c multicolored   .75 .35

Museum Art A128

Designs: 90c, Animal face carved on ritual staff. 1.20 l, Coins, 15th cent.

1997, July 12   Perf. 13½x13
579 A128 90c multicolored   .75 .35
580 A128 1.20 l multicolored   1.00 .50

Double Barred Crosses — A129

1997, Aug. 2   Litho.   Perf. 13½
581 A129 20c olive   .25 .25
582 A129 50c brown   .35 .25
a.   Inscribed "1998"   .35 .25
Nos. 581 and 582 are inscribed "1997."
See Nos. 602, 604, 617-619.

Mushrooms A130

Designs: No. 583, Morchella elata. No. 584, Boletus aereus.

1997, Sept. 20   Litho.   Perf. 13½x13
583 A130 1.20 l multicolored   1.00 .50
a.   Tete-beche pair   2.00 2.00
584 A130 1.20 l multicolored   1.00 .50
a.   Tete-beche pair   2.00 2.00

Letters of Grand Duke Gediminas A131

1997, Oct. 4   Perf. 14
585 A131 50c multicolored   .45 .25

Coat of Arms Type of 1992
Size: 25x33mm

1997, Oct. 18   Litho.   Perf. 13½x13
586 A82 50c Neringa   .45 .25
587 A82 90c Vilkaviskis   .80 .35
588 A82 1.20 l Pasvalys   1.00 .45
Nos. 586-588 (3)   2.25 1.05

Christmas and New Year — A132

1997, Nov. 22   Litho.   Perf. 13
589 A132 50c shown   .40 .25
590 A132 1.20 l Snow on trees   1.00 .50

1998 Winter Olympic Games, Nagano — A133

1998, Jan. 17   Litho.   Perf. 14
591 A133 1.20 l multicolored   1.00 .45
a.   Tete-beche pair   2.00 2.00

Independence Type of 1993 and

Declaration of Independence — A134

Designs: 50c, Alfonsas Petrulis. 90c, Jokubas Sernas.

Perf. 13½x12½
1998, Feb. 16   Litho.
592 A85 50c olive and black   .35 .25
593 A85 90c brown and black   .85 .40
Souvenir Sheet
Perf. 12½x11½
594 A134 6.60 l multicolored   5.50 5.50
Independence, 80th anniv.

Souvenir Sheet

National Anthem, Cent. — A135

1998, Feb. 16   Perf. 12½
595 A135 5.20 l multicolored   4.50 4.50

Antanas Gustaitis, Aviator, Birth Cent. A136

Designs: 2 l, Portrait of Gustaitis, ANBO 41. 3 l, Design drawings, ANBO-VIII.

1998, Mar. 27   Perf. 14
596 A136 2 l multicolored   1.75 .85
597 A136 3 l multicolored   2.50 1.10

Natl. Song Festival — A137

1998, Apr. 18   Perf. 13½
598 A137 1.20 l multicolored   1.25 1.25
a.   Tete-beche pair   3.25 3.25
Europa.

Famous Lithuanians Type of 1993

50c, Tadas Ivanauskas (1882-1971), scientist. No. 600, Jurgis Baltrusaitis (1873-1944), writer, Jurgis Baltrusaitis (1903-88), historian. No. 601, Stasys Lozoraitis (1898-1983), Stasys Lozoraitis (1924-94), politicians.

1998, Apr. 25   Perf. 13x13½
599 A88 50c multicolored   .40 .25
Size: 45x26mm
600 A88 90c multicolored   .70 .35
601 A88 90c multicolored   .70 .35
Nos. 599-601 (3)   1.80 .95

Double-Barred Crosses Type of 1997

1998, June 1   Litho.   Perf. 13½
602 A129 70c yellow bister   .60 .30
a.   Inscribed "1999"   .75 .30
No. 602 is inscribed "1998."

2nd Lithuanian Olympic Games, 6th World Lithuanian Games A138

1998, June 23   Perf. 14
603 A138 1.35 l multicolored   1.10 .55
a.   Tete beche pair   2.25 2.25

Double-Barred Crosses Type of 1997

1998, July 4   Litho.   Perf. 13½
604 A129 35c plum & pink   .30 .25

Red Book of Lithuania A139

Fish: No. 605, Coregonus lavaretus holsatus. No. 606, Salmo salar.

1998, July 11   Perf. 13x13½
605 A139 1.40 l multicolored   1.10 .55
606 A139 1.40 l multicolored   1.10 .55

Coat of Arms Type of 1992
Size: 25x33mm

1998, Sept. 12   Litho.   Perf. 13
607 A82 70c Kernave   .55 .25
608 A82 70c Trakai   .55 .25
609 A82 1.35 l Kaunas   1.10 .55
Nos. 607-609 (3)   2.20 1.05

Vilnius-Cracow Post Route Established, 1562 — A141

1998, Oct. 9   Litho.   Perf. 14
611 A141 70c multicolored   .60 .30

Souvenir Sheet

Lithuanian Post, 80th Anniv. — A142

1998, Oct. 9   Litho.   Perf. 12
612 A142 13 l multicolored   11.00 11.00

No. 612 contains a holographic image. Soaking in water may affect the hologram.

Museum Paintings — A143

70c, "Through the Night," by Antanas Zmuidzinavicius (1876-1966). 1.35 l, "The Garden of Bernardines, Vilnius," by Juozapas Marsevskis (1825-83).

1998, Oct. 17   Litho.   Perf. 13x13
613 A143 70c multicolored   .60   .30
614 A143 1.35 l multicolored   1.00   .50

New Year — A144

Christmas: 1.35 l, Winter scene, people walking through giant tree, village.

1998, Nov. 14   Litho.   Perf. 12
615 A144 70c multicolored   .50   .25
616 A144 1.35 l multicolored   1.10   .55

Double-Barred Crosses Type of 1997

1998, Nov. 14   Litho.   Perf. 13
617 A129 5c lt & dk citron   .25   .25
  a.   Inscribed "1999"   .25   .25
618 A129 10c tan & brown   .25   .25
  a.   Inscribed "1999"   .25   .25
619 A129 20c lt & dk olive green   .25   .25
  a.   Inscribed "1999"   .25   .25
        Nos. 617-619 (3)   .75   .75

Nos. 617-619 inscribed "1998."

Adam Mickiewicz (1798-1855), Poet — A145

1998, Dec. 24   Perf. 14
620 A145 70c multicolored   .60   .30
  a.   Tete beche pair   1.25 1.25

Souvenir Sheet

Publication of "Postile," by M. Dauksa (1527-1613), 400th Anniv. — A146

1999, Jan. 23   Litho.   Perf. 12
621 A146 5.90 l brown & gray   5.00 5.00

Independence Type of 1993

Designs: No. 622, Petras Klimas. No. 623, Donatas Malinauskas.

Perf. 13x12
1999, Feb. 16   Litho.
622 A85 70c red & black   .60   .30
623 A85 70c blue & black   .60   .30

Famous Lithuanians Type of 1993

Designs: No. 624, Juozas Matulis (1899-1993). No. 625, Augustinas Gricius (1899-1972). 1.35 l, Pranas Skardzius (1899-1975).

1999, Mar. 19   Litho.   Perf. 13
624 A88 70c multicolored   .60   .30
625 A88 70c multicolored   .60   .30
626 A88 1.35 l multicolored   1.10   .55
        Nos. 624-626 (3)   2.30 1.15

NATO, 50th Anniv. — A147

1999, Mar. 27   Litho.   Perf. 13x14
627 A147 70c multicolored   .60   .30

National Parks — A148

Europa: No. 628, Traditional homes, lake, islands, Aukotaitija Natl. Park. No. 629, Sand dunes, amber, Curonian Spit Natl. Park.

1999, Apr. 10   Litho.   Perf. 13x13
628 A148 1.35 l multicolored   1.25 1.25
629 A148 1.35 l multicolored   1.25 1.25

Council of Europe, 50th Anniv. — A149

1999, May 1   Litho.   Perf. 14
630 A149 70c multicolored   .60   .30

Melniai Windmill — A150

1999, May 8   Litho.   Perf. 14
631 A150 70c shown   .70   .35
632 A150 70c Pumpenai Windmill   .70   .35

Bees — A151

Designs: 70c, Dasypoda argentata. 2 l, Bombus pomorum.

1999, June 12   Perf. 13x13
633 A151 70c multicolored   .70   .35
634 A151 2 l multicolored   1.60   .80

UPU, 125th Anniv. A152

1999, July 3   Litho.   Perf. 14
635 A152 70c multicolored   .60   .30

Lithuanian Philatelic Society Emblems, No. 1, Pre-independence Stamp — A153

1999, July 31   Litho.   Perf. 14
636 A153 1 l multicolored   1.00   .50
        Complete booklet, 10 #636   11.00

Lithuanian Philatelic Society, 75th Anniv.

Souvenir Sheet

Centenary of First Performance of Play, "America in the Baths" — A154

Designs: a, Producers. b, Theater poster.

1999, Aug. 20   Litho.   Perf. 12
637 A154 4 l Sheet of 2, #a.-b.   7.00 7.00

A155

Baltic Chain, 10th Anniv. — Family and flags: 1 l, No. 640a, Lithuanian.

No. 640: b, Estonian. c, Latvian.

1999, Aug. 23   Litho.   Perf. 12
639 A155 1 l multicolored   .85   .40

Souvenir Sheet
640 A155 2 l Sheet of 3, #a.-c.   5.25 5.25

See Estonia Nos. 366-367, Latvia Nos. 493-494.

A156

1999, Aug. 28   Litho.   Perf. 14
641 A156 70c multicolored   .60   .25

Freedom fight movement, 50th anniv.

Coat of Arms Type of 1992
Size: 25x33mm

1999, Sept. 18   Perf. 13x13
642 A82 70c Marijampole   .50   .25
643 A82 1 l Siaulai   1.00   .35
644 A82 1.40 l Rokiskis   1.25   .45
        Nos. 642-644 (3)   2.75 1.05

Museum Pieces — A157

Designs: 70c, Sword of Gen. S. Zukauskas. 3 l, Hussar armor.

1999, Oct. 9   Perf. 13x13
645 A157 70c multicolored   .65   .25
646 A157 3 l multicolored   2.50 1.00

A158

1999, Oct. 23   Litho.   Perf. 14
647 A158 70c multicolored   .60   .25

Simonas Stanevicius (1799-1848), writer.

A159

Perf. 12x13
1999, Nov. 13   Litho.
648 A159 70c shown   .50   .25
649 A159 1.35 l Buildings, candles 1.25   .50

Christmas and New Year's Day.

Forged Monument
Tops — A160

Designs: 10c, Rietavas. 20c, Andriunal. 1 l,
Veivirzenai. 1.30 l, Vaizgakiemis. 1.70 l,
Baukai.

2000-06   Litho.   Perf. 13½x13¼
Vignettes in Blue
Designs 22mm High

650	A160	10c tan	.30 .25
a.		Perf. 11¼, inscr. "2002"	.30 .25
b.		As "a," inscr. "2003"	.30 .25
c.		As "a," inscr. "2004"	.30 .25
651	A160	20c yellow	.35 .25
a.		Perf. 11¼, inscr. "2002"	.35 .25
b.		As "a," inscr. "2003"	.35 .25
c.		As "a," inscr. "2004"	.35 .25
652	A160	1 l pale rose	.90 .45
a.		Perf. 11¼, inscr. "2002"	1.00 .50
653	A160	1.30 l lt green	1.10 .55
654	A160	1.70 l lt blue	1.40 .70
		Nos. 651-654 (4)	3.75 1.95

Perf. 13x12½
Designs 20mm High

655	A160	10c tan	.25 .25
a.		Inscr. "2006"	.25 .25
656	A160	20c yellow	.25 .25
a.		Inscr. "2006"	.25 .25

Designs 21mm High

657	A160	1 l pale rose	.75 .35
658	A160	1.30 l lt green	1.00 .50
		Nos. 655-658 (4)	2.25 1.35

Issued: Nos. 650-654, 1/3/00; Nos. 650a,
651a, 652a, 5/4/02; Nos. 655-656, 10/8/05;
Nos. 657-658, 5/27/06.

Independence Type of 1993

Designs: 1.30 l, Jonas Vailokaitis (1886-
1994), banker. 1.70 l, Jonas Smilgevicius
(1870-1942), banker.

Perf. 13¼x12¾

2000, Feb. 16			**Litho.**
660	A85	1.30 l multi	1.00 .50
661	A85	1.70 l multi	1.50 .75

Souvenir Sheet

Declaration of Independence From
Soviet Union, 10th Anniv. — A161

Perf. 12¼x11½

2000, Mar. 11			**Litho.**
662	A161	7.40 l multi	6.50 6.50

Famous
Lithuanians
A162

Designs: 1 l, Vincas Pietaris (1850-1902),
writer. 1.30 l, Kanutas Ruseckas (1800-60),
artist. 1.70 l, Povilas Visinskis (1875-1906),
writer.

2000, Mar. 25			**Perf. 13x13¼**
663	A162	1 l multi	.80 .40
664	A162	1.30 l multi	1.00 .50
665	A162	1.70 l multi	1.60 .70
		Nos. 663-665 (3)	3.40 1.60

See Nos. 688-690.

Items From
Klaipeda Clock
Museum — A163

1 l, Sundial. 2 l, Renaissance-style clock.

2000, Apr. 15			**Perf. 12**
666	A163	1 l multi	1.00 .50
667	A163	2 l multi	1.50 .75

Europa, 2000
Common Design Type

2000, May 9			**Perf. 13¼x13**
668	CD17	1.70 l multi	1.50 1.50

Birds of Prey
From Red Book
of
Lithuania — A164

1 l, Pandion haliaetus. 2 l, Milvus migrans.

2000, June 2			**Perf. 13¼x13**
669	A164	1 l multi	.90 .45
670	A164	2 l multi	1.60 .80

Sea Museum of
Lithuania — A165

No. 671, Spheniscus magellanicus. No.
672, Halichoerus grypus.

2000, Aug. 26			**Litho. Perf. 12**
671-672	A165	1 l Set of 2	2.00 1.00
671a		Tete beche pair	2.25 2.25
672a		Tete beche pair	2.25 2.25

2000
Summer
Olympics,
Sydney
A166

Designs: 1 l, Cycling. 3 l, Swimming.

2000, Sept. 2			
673-674	A166	Set of 2	3.50 1.75

Souvenir Sheet

Mikalojus Konstantinas Ciurlionis
(1875-1911), Artist — A167

2000, Sept. 22			**Litho. Perf. 12**
675	A167	4 l multi	3.50 3.50

Reappearance of Lithuanian Postage
Stamps, 10th Anniv. — A168

2000, Oct. 7			**Litho. Perf. 12**
676	A168	1 l multi	.85 .40

Arms Type of 1992

Designs: No. 677, 1 l, Raseiniai. No. 678,
1 l, Taurage. 1.30 l, Utena.

2000, Oct. 21			**Litho. Perf. 12**
		Size: 25x33mm	
677-679	A82	Set of 3	2.75 1.40

Christmas and
New Year's
Day — A169

Roadside shrines: 1 l, 1.70 l.

2000, Nov. 11			
680-681	A169	Set of 2	2.25 1.00

Souvenir Sheet

Holy Year 2000 — A170

No. 682: a, Nativity. b, Jesus and disciples.
c, Crucifixion. d, Resurrection.

2000, Nov. 25			
682	A170	2 l Sheet of 4, #a-d	7.00 7.00

Advent of New
Millennium
A171

2000, Dec. 2			
683	A171	1 l multi	.85 .40

Souvenir Sheet

Medals Won at 2000 Summer
Olympics, Sydney — A172

2000, Dec. 9			**Litho. Perf.**
684	A172	4 l multi	3.50 3.50

Storming of TV Station by Soviet
Troops, 10th Anniv. — A173

2001, Jan. 13			**Perf. 12**
685	A173	1 l multi + label	.85 .40

Independence Type of 1993

Designs: 1 l, Saliamonas Banaitis (1866-
1933), newspaper publisher and politician. 2 l,
Justinas Staugaitis (1863-1943), bishop and
politician.

2001, Feb. 16			**Litho. Perf. 12**
686-687	A85	Set of 2	2.50 1.25

Famous Lithuanians Type of 2000

Designs: No. 688, 1 l, Juozas Mikenas
(1901-64), artist. No. 689, 1 l, Pranas Vaicaitis
(1876-1901), poet. 1.70 l, Petras Vileisis
(1851-1926), civil engineer.

2001, Mar. 24			**Litho. Perf. 12**
688-690	A162	Set of 3	3.25 1.50

Europa
A174

Designs: No. 691, 1.70 l, Neman River. No.
692, 1.70 l, Lake Galve.

2001, Apr. 14			**Perf. 13x13¼**
691-692	A174	Set of 2	3.00 3.00

Flowers From Red
Book of
Lithuania — A175

Designs: 2 l, Nymphoide peltata. 3 l, Erica tetralix.

2001, May 12   **Perf. 13¼x13**
693-694 A175   Set of 2   4.25 2.00

Bridges
A176

Designs: 1 l, Papalauja Bridge. 1.30 l, Pakurojis Dam Bridge.

2001, June 9   **Perf. 12**
695-696 A176   Set of 2   2.00 .95

Souvenir Sheet

Lithuania, 1000th Anniv. (in 2009) — A177

Designs: a, Flag. b, Arms. c, Map of country. d, Map of Europe.

2001, June 23   **Perf. 11**
697 A177 2 l Sheet of 4, #a-d + 2 labels   7.00 7.00

Baltic Coast Landscapes
A178

Designs: 1 l, No. 699a, Palanga. No. 699b, Lahemaa. No. 699c, Vidzeme.

2001, Sept. 15   **Litho.**   **Perf. 13½**
698 A178 1 l multi   .85 .40

Souvenir Sheet
699   Sheet of 3   5.25 5.25
a.-c. A178 2 l Any single   1.60 1.25

See Estonia Nos. 423-424, Latvia Nos. 534-535.

Ethnographic Open Air Museum Exhibits — A179

19th cent. dwellings from: 1 l, Kirdeikiai. 2 l, Darbenai.

2001, Sept. 22   **Perf. 12**
700-701 A179   Set of 2   2.40 1.25

Sculpture by Juozas Zikaras (1881-1944)
A180

2001, Oct. 4
702 A180 3 l multi   2.40 1.25

Postal Regulations Enacted by Stefan Bathory, 1583 — A181

2001, Oct. 6
703 A181 1 l multi   .85 .40

Coat of Arms Type of 1992
Size: 25x33mm

Designs: 1 l, Lazdijai. 1.30 l, Birzai. 1.70 l, Veliuona.

2001, Oct. 27   **Litho.**   **Perf. 12**
704-706 A82   Set of 3   3.50 1.60

Christmas and New Year — A182

Birds on: 1 l, Covered tree. 1.70 l, Christ's cradle.

2001, Nov. 10   **Litho.**   **Perf. 12**
707-708 A182   Set of 2   2.25 1.00

Souvenir Sheet

Dr. Jonas Basanavicius (1851-1927), Patriot, Folklorist — A183

2001, Nov. 17   **Perf. 12x11½**
709 A183 5 l multi   4.25 4.25

2002 Winter Olympics, Salt Lake City — A184

2002, Jan. 26   **Litho.**   **Perf. 12**
710 A184 1.70 l multi   1.40 .70

Independence Type of 1993

Designs: No. 711, 1 l, Kazys Bizauskas (1892-1941), statesman. No. 712, 1 l, Stanislovas Narutavicius (1862-1932), politician.

2002, Feb. 16   Set of 2   1.75 .80
711-712 A85

Famous Lithuanians A185

Designs: 1 l, Antanas Salys (1902-72), linguist. 1.30 l, Satrijos Ragana (1877-1930), writer. 1.70 l, Oskaras Milasius (1877-1939), poet.

2002, Mar. 2   **Litho.**   **Perf. 12**
713-715 A185   Set of 3   3.50 1.50

See Nos. 734-735, 759-761, 782-784, 805-807, 830-832, 858-860, 884-886, 906-908, 934-936, 967-969.

Coat of Arms Type of 1992
Size: 25x33mm

Designs: No. 716, 1 l, Anyksciai. No. 717, 1 l, Birstonas. 1.70 l, Prienai.

2002, Mar. 23   Set of 3   3.25 1.50
716-718 A82

State Historical Archives, 150th Anniv. — A186

2002, Apr. 6
719 A186 1 l multi   .85 .40

Mammals From Red Book of Lithuania
A187

Designs: 1 l, Mustela erminea. 3 l, Lynx lynx.

2002, Apr. 13   **Perf. 13x13¼**
720-721 A187   Set of 2   3.50 1.60

Europa — A188

2002, May 4   **Litho.**   **Perf. 13¼x13**
722 A188 1.70 l multi   1.50 1.50

Vilnius Fire ad Rescue Brigade, Bicent. A189

2002, May 25   **Perf. 12**
723 A189 1 l multi   .85 .40

Narrow-gauge Railways — A190

Designs: 1.30 l, TU2 diesel locomotive. 2 l, PT4 steam engine.

2002, June 8
724-725 A190   Set of 2   2.75 1.40

Souvenir Sheet

Lithuania, 1000th Anniv. (in 2009) — A191

Designs: a, Artifact of first people in Lithuania, 10,000 B.C. b, Roman historian Tacitus mentions Aestii people, 98. c, Vikings attack

---

Apuole Castle, 853. d, First mention of Lithuania in Quedlinburg Annals, 1009.

2002, June 22   **Perf. 11**
726 A191 2 l Sheet of 4, #a-d, + 2 labels   7.00 7.00

Souvenir Sheet

Klaipeda, 750th Anniv. — A192

2002, Aug. 1   **Perf. 11½x12¼**
727 A192 5 l multi   4.25 4.25

Maironis Lithuanian Literature Museum, Kaunas A193

Designs: 1 l, Exhibits. 3 l, Museum exterior.

2002, Sept. 7   **Perf. 12**
728-729 A193   Set of 2   3.50 1.50

Establishment of Postal Service by King Sigismund III Vasa, 1620 — A194

2002, Oct. 5
730 A194 1 l multi   .85 .40

Christmas and New Year's Day — A195

Cross and: 1 l, Clock, candles and holly. 1.70 l, Christmas tree and angels.

2002, Nov. 9
731-732 A195   Set of 2   2.25 1.00

European Children's Day — A196

2002, Nov. 16
733 A196 1 l multi   .85 .40

Famous Lithuanians Type of 2002

Designs: 1 l, Laurynas Stuoka-Gucevicius (1753-98), architect. 1.30 l, Juozas Eretas (1896-1984), author and politician.

2003, Jan. 25   **Perf. 12**
734-735 A185   Set of 2   2.00 .85

Coat of Arms Type of 1992

Designs: No. 736, 1 l, Gargzdai. No. 737, 1 l, Kretinga. No. 738, 1 l, Palanga. No. 739, 1 l, Papile. No. 740, 1 l, Rietavas.

2003, Feb. 15   **Litho.**   **Perf. 12**
Size: 25x33mm
736-740 A82   Set of 5   4.25 2.00

Lighthouses
A198

Designs: 1 l, Pervalka. 3 l, Uostodvaris.

2003, Mar. 15
741-742 A198   Set of 2   3.50 1.50

Europa — A199

2003, Apr. 19   Litho.   Perf. 13½x13
743 A199 1.70 l multi   1.50 1.50
   a.   Tete beche pair   3.25 3.25

Rebuilding of Palace of Lithuania's
Rulers — A200

2003, Apr. 26   Perf. 12
744 A200 1 l multi   .85 .40

Vilnius University
Astronomical
Observatory,
250th
Anniv. — A201

2003, May 10   Perf. 12
745 A201 1 l multi   .85 .40

Insects From
Red Book of
Lithuania
A202

Designs: No. 746, 3 l, Lucanus cervus. No.
747, 3 l, Cerambyx cerdo.

2003, May 24   Perf. 13x13½
746-747 A202   Set of 2   5.25 2.50

Souvenir Sheet

Lithuania, 1000th Anniv. (in
2009) — A203

No. 748: a, Rise of Lithuania, 1183. b, Battle
of Siauliai, 1236. c, Coronation of Mindaugas,
1253. d, Selection of Vilnius as capital of Lithuania, 1323.

2003, June 21   Perf. 11
748 A203 2 l Sheet of 4, #a-d, +
    2 labels   7.00 3.25

Souvenir Sheet

Coronation of Mindaugas, 750th
Anniv. — A204

2003, July 5   Perf. 11½x12¼
749 A204 5 l multi   4.25 2.00

13th European Hot Air Balloon
Championships — A205

2003, Aug. 8   Perf. 12
750 A205 1.30 l multi   1.10 .55

Vincentas
Cardinal
Sladkevicius
(1920-2000)
A206

2003, Aug. 20
751 A206 1 l multi   .85 .40

Panevezys, 500th
Anniv. — A207

2003, Sept. 7
752 A207 1 l multi   .85 .40

Map of Kaunas-Vilnius-Grodno Postal
Route, 1664 — A208

2003, Oct. 4
753 A208 1 l multi   .85 .40

Christmas and
New Year's
Day — A209

Villages at: 1 l, Christmas. 1.70 l, New
Year's Eve.

2003, Nov. 8
754-755 A209   Set of 2   2.25 1.00

Souvenir Sheet

Lithuania, 2003 European Men's
Basketball Champions — A210

2003, Dec. 6   Litho.   Perf. 12x11½
756 A210 5 l multi   4.25 2.00

Gliders in
Lithuanian
Aviation
Museum
A211

Designs: No. 757, 1 l, BK-7. No. 758, 1 l,
BRO-12.

2003, Dec. 17   Perf. 12
757-758 A211   Set of 2   1.75 .80

Famous Lithuanians Type of 2002

Designs: No. 759, 1 l, Jonas Aistis (1904-
73), poet. No. 760, 1 l, Kazimieras Buga
(1879-1924), philologist. No. 761, Adolfas
Jucys (1904-74), physicist.

2004, Jan. 24   Litho.   Perf. 12
759-761 A185   Set of 3   2.50 1.25

Coat of Arms Type of 1992

Designs: 1 l, Mazeikiai. 1.30 l, Radviliskis.
1.40 l, Ukmerge.

2004, Feb. 14
    Size: 25x33mm
762-764 A82   Set of 3   3.25 1.50

Vilnius University,
425th
Anniv. — A213

2004, Mar. 20
765 A213 1 l multi   .85 .40

Europa — A214

Designs: No. 766, 1.70 l, Sailboat. No. 767,
1.70 l, Beach umbrella.

2004, Apr. 10   Litho.   Perf. 12
766-767 A214   Set of 2   3.00 3.00

Return to
Printing
Lithuanian in
Latin Letters,
Cent.
A215

2004, May 1   Litho.   Perf. 12
768 A215 1.30 l multi   1.10 .50

Admission to European Union — A216

No. 769: a, Stars, flags of newly-added
countries, map of Europe. b, Stars and Lithuanian flag, map and arms.

2004, May 1
769 A216 1.70 l Horiz. pair, #a-b   3.00 1.25

FIFA
(Fédération
Internationale
de Football
Association),
Cent.
A217

2004, May 15
770 A217 3 l multi   2.50 1.10

Chiune Sugihara
(1900-86),
Japanese
Diplomat Who
Issued Transit
Visas to Jews in
World War
II — A218

2004, June 19   Litho.   Perf. 12
771 A218 1 l multi   .85 .40

Souvenir Sheet

Lithuania, 1000th Anniv. — A219

No. 772: a, Defense of Pilenai Castle, 1336.
b, Battle at the Blue Waters, 1362. c, Christening of Lithuania, 1387. d, Battle of Zalgiris,
1410.

2004, July 3   Perf. 11
772 A219 2 l Sheet of 4, #a-d, +
    2 labels   7.00 3.00

Exhibits in Tadas Ivanauskas Zoology
Museum, Kaunas — A220

No. 773: a, Aquila chrysaetos. b, Iguana
iguana.

2004, July 10   Perf. 12
773 A220 1 l Horiz. pair, #a-b   1.75 .80

2004 Summer Olympics, Athens A221

2004 Olympic emblem and: 2 l, Pentathlon equestrian event. 3 l, Canoeing.

2004, July 31
774-775 A221 Set of 2   4.25 2.00

Owls From Red Book of Lithuania — A222

Designs: 1.30 l, Bubo bubo. 3 l, Asio flammeus.

2004, Oct. 2   Litho.   Perf. 12
776-777 A222 Set of 2   3.50 1.75

Kaunas Funiculars A223

Designs: 1 l, Aleksotas Funicular. 1.30 l, Zaliakalnis Funicular.

2004, Oct. 16
778-779 A223 Set of 2   2.00 .95

Christmas A224

Stars and: 1 l, Christmas tree. 1.70 l, Bird.

2004, Nov. 6
780-781 A224 Set of 2   2.25 2.25

Famous Lithuanians Type of 2002
Designs: No. 782, 1 l, Kazys Boruta (1905-65), writer. No. 783, 1 l, Petras Kalpokas (1880-1945), painter. No. 784, 1 l, Jonas Puzinas (1905-78), archaeologist.

2005, Jan. 8   Litho.   Perf. 12
782-784 A185 Set of 3   2.50 2.50

Congratulations A225

Designs: No. 785, 1 l, Gerbera daisies, freesias and scroll. No. 786, 1 l, Lilies, freesias and box.

Serpentine Die Cut 6¾
2005, Jan. 29   Litho.
Booklet Stamps
Self-Adhesive
785-786 A225 Set of 2   1.75 1.75
786a Booklet pane, 4 each #785-786 7.00

Sartai Horse Race, Cent. A226

2005, Feb. 5   Perf. 12
787 A226 1 l multi   .85 .85

Coat of Arms Type of 1992
Designs: No. 788, 1 l, Druskininkai. No. 789, 1 l, Vabalninkas.

2005, Mar. 5   Size: 25x33mm
788-789 A82 Set of 2   1.75 1.75

Europa A227

Designs: No. 790, 1.70 l, Cow, cheese. No. 791, 1.70 l, Loaf of black bread.

2005, Apr. 9   Litho.   Perf. 12
790-791 A227 Set of 2   3.00 3.00

National Museum, 150th Anniv. — A228

No. 792: a, Brass jewelry, 1st-2nd cent. b, Illustration of first exhibition in Aula Hall, Vilnius University.

2005, May 7
792 A228 1 l Pair, #a-b   1.75 1.75

Train and Kaunas Railway Tunnel A229

2005, June 11
793 A229 3 l multi   2.50 2.50

Souvenir Sheet

Lithuania, 1000th Anniv. — A230

No. 794: a, Battle of Pabaiskas, 1435. b, Valakai Reform, 1557. c, First Lithuanian statute, 1529. d, Union of Lublin, 1569.

2005, July 2   Perf. 11
794 A230 2 l Sheet of 4, #a-d, + 2 labels   7.00 7.00

90th World Esperanto Congress, Vilnius A231

2005, July 23   Litho.   Perf. 12
795 A231 1 l multi   .85 .85

Churches A232

Designs: 1 l, Vilnius Evangelical Lutheran Church. 1.30 l, St. Casimir Church, Vilnius.

2005, Sept. 3   Perf. 13½
796-797 A232 Set of 2   2.00 2.00

Flora and Fauna from Red Book of Lithuania — A233

No. 798: a, Gavia arctica. b, Trapa natans.

2005, Sept. 10
798 A233 1 l Horiz. pair, #a-b   1.75 1.75

Souvenir Sheet

Mikolajus Konstantinas Ciurlionis (1875-1911), Painter and Composer — A234

No. 799 — Details from Sonata of the Sea triptych: a, Allegro. b, Andante. c, Finale.

2005, Sept. 24   Perf. 14
799 A234 2 l Sheet of 3, #a-c, + label   5.25 5.25

Map of St. Petersburg-Warsaw Post Road, 1830-36 — A235

2005, Oct. 8   Litho.   Perf. 14¼x14
800 A235 1 l multi   .85 .85

Christmas A236

Designs: 1 l, Candle and snow-covered evergreen branch. 1.70 l, Santa Claus in sleigh.

2005, Nov. 5   Perf. 12¾x13
801-802 A236 Set of 2   2.25 2.25

Dr. Jonas Basanavicius, Vilnius City Hall and Commemorative Medal — A237

2005, Dec. 3   Perf. 14¼x14
803 A237 1 l multi   .85 .85
Congress of Lithuanians, cent.

2006 Winter Olympics, Turin — A238

2006, Jan. 28   Litho.   Perf. 14x14¼
804 A238 1.70 l multi   1.45 1.45

Famous Lithuanians Type of 2002
Designs: No. 805, 1 l, Adolfas Sapoka (1906-61), historian. No. 806, 1 l, Petras Rimsa (1881-1961), sculptor. No. 807, 1 l, Antanas Vaiciulaitis (1906-92), writer.

2006, Feb. 11   Perf. 13½
805-807 A185 Set of 3   2.50 2.50

Vilnius Album, by Jonas K. Vilcinskis, 100th Anniv. of Publication A239

2006, Feb. 25   Perf. 13x12¾
808 A239 1 l multi   .85 .85

Social Insurance System, 80th Anniv. A240

2006, Mar. 18   Perf. 14¼x14
809 A240 1 l multi   .85 .85

Lithuanian Theater, Music and Cinema Museum, 80th Anniv. — A241

No. 810: a, Parvo camera, 1930s. b, Music box, 1900.

2006, Mar. 18   Perf. 13½
810 A241 1 l Pair, #a-b   1.75 1.75
Printed in sheets containing 10 of each stamp + 5 labels. Each sheet contains se-tenant pairs of the same stamp.

Europa
A242

Designs: No. 811, 1.70 l, Woman dancing with man in wheelchair. No. 812, 1.70 l, People in wheelchairs being pushed around track.

2006, Apr. 15
811-812 A242 Set of 2 3.00 3.00

Coat of Arms Type of 1992
Designs: No. 813, 1 l, Kupiskis. No. 814, 1 l, Sakiai. No. 815, 1 l, Silute.

2006, May 13 *Perf. 14x14¼*
Size: 25x33mm
813-815 A82 Set of 3 2.50 2.50

Souvenir Sheet

Lithuania, 1000th Anniv. — A243

No. 816: a, Establishment of Vilnius University, 1579. b, Truce of Andrusov, 1667. c, Four-year Sejm, 1788. d, Uprising of 1794.

2006, July 1 *Perf. 11*
816 A243 2 l Sheet of 4, #a-d, + 2 labels 7.00 7.00

Basilicas
A244

Designs: 1 l, Vilnius Basilica. 1.70 l, Kaunas Basilica.

2006, Aug. 5 *Perf. 12¾x13*
817-818 A244 Set of 2 2.25 2.25

Birds and Fish From Red Book of Lithuania
A245

No. 819: a, Polysticta stelleri. b, Acipenser sturio.

2006, Sept. 16 *Perf. 13½*
819 A245 1 l Vert. pair, #a-b 1.75 1.75

Establishment of Lithuania Post and First Postage Stamps, 1918 — A246

2006, Oct. 7 *Perf. 14¼x14*
820 A246 1 l multi .85 .85

Premiere of Opera "Birute," Cent. — A247

2006, Nov. 4 Litho. *Perf. 13¼x12¾*
821 A247 2 l multi 1.75 1.75

Christmas
A248

Designs: 1 l, Birds, triangular window. 1.70 l, Trees, star, berries, straw.

2006, Nov. 18 *Perf. 12¾x13¼*
822-823 A248 Set of 2 2.25 2.25

18th Century Wooden Church Belfries — A249

Belfries from churches in: 10c, Pasvalys. 20c, Rozalimas. 50c, Tryskiai. 1 l, Saukenai. 1.30 l, Vaiguva. 1.70 l, Vajasiskis.

Die Cut Perf. 12½
2007, Jan. 1 **Litho.**
Self-Adhesive
824 A249 10c blue & blk .25 .25
825 A249 20c org & blk .25 .25
826 A249 50c bl grn & blk .40 .40
  a. Dated 2009 .40 .40
  b. Dated 2011 .40 .40
827 A249 1 l brn & blk .80 .80
  a. Dated 2009 .80 .80
  b. Dated 2011 .80 .80
828 A249 1.30 l lil & blk 1.00 1.00
829 A249 1.70 l ol brn & blk 1.40 1.40
  Nos. 824-829 (6) 4.10 4.10

Issued: Nos. 826a, 827a, 2/21/09. Nos. 826b, 827b, 1/8/11.
See Nos. 842-846, 1034.

Famous Lithuanians Type of 2002
Designs: No. 830, 1 l, Bernardas Brazdzionis (1907-2002), writer. No. 831, 1 l, Vytautas Kazimieras Jonynas (1907-97), artist. 3 l, Leonas Sapiega (1557-1633), state chancellor of the Grand Duchy of Lithuania.

2007, Jan. 27 *Perf. 13½*
830-832 A185 Set of 3 4.25 4.25

Coat of Arms Type of 1992
Designs: 1 l, Svencionys. 1.30 l, Kelme. 2 l, Moletai.

2007, Mar. 3 *Perf. 14x14¼*
Size: 25x33mm
833-835 A82 Set of 3 3.75 3.75

Europa
A250

Designs: No. 836, 1.70 l, Scouting flag, musical score. No. 837, 1.70 l, Symbols of Lithuanian Scouts.

2007, Apr. 14 Litho. *Perf. 13½*
836-837 A250 Set of 2 2.75 2.75
Scouting, cent.

Churches
A251

Designs: 1 l, St. Anne's and Bernardine Churches, Vilnius. 1.30 l, Church buildings, Pazaislis.

2007, May 12 *Perf. 12¾x13*
838-839 A251 Set of 2 2.10 2.10

Souvenir Sheet

Lithuania, 1000th Anniv. — A252

No. 840: a, Publication of first Lithuanian newspaper, "Ausra," 1883. b, Abolition of the prohibition on printing in Latin characters, 1904. c, Great Seimas of Vilnius, 1905. d, Lithuanian Declaration of Independence, 1918.

2007, June 23 Litho. *Perf. 11*
840 A252 3 l Sheet of 4, #a-d, + 2 labels 10.00 10.00

Trakai History Museum — A253

No. 841: a, Map of New Trakai in 1600, by J. Kamarauskas. b, Chess pieces, 15th cent.

2007, July 28 Litho. *Perf. 13½*
841 A253 2 l Pair, #a-b 3.50 3.50
Printed in sheets containing 10 of each stamp + 5 labels.

Wooden Church Belfries Type of 2007
Belfries from churches in: 5c, Vabalininkas, 19th cent. 35c, Varputenai, 18th cent. 1.35 l, Deguciai, 19th cent. 1.55 l, Geidziai, 19th cent. 2.15 l, Pavandenes, 17th cent.

Die Cut Perf. 12½
2007, Sept. 1 **Litho.**
Self-Adhesive
842 A249 5c yel grn & blk .25 .25
843 A249 35c gray & blk .30 .30
844 A249 1.35 l yel & blk 1.10 1.10
845 A249 1.55 l brn org & blk 1.25 1.25
846 A249 2.15 l rose lake & blk 1.75 1.75
  Nos. 842-846 (5) 4.65 4.65

Juozas Miltinis (1907-94), Actor and Theater Founder
A254

2007, Sept. 1 Litho. *Perf. 12¾x13*
847 A254 2.45 l multi 2.00 2.00

Birds — A255

No. 848 — Birds of the Cepkeliai Nature Reserve, Lithuania and Katra Sanctuary, Belarus: a, Gallinago media. b, Crex crex.

2007, Oct. 3 *Perf. 14*
848 Horiz. pair + central label 5.00 5.00
  a.-b. A255 2.90 l Either single 2.25 2.25
  See Belarus No. 625.

Stamps and Covers From Establishment of Lithuania Post in 1992 — A256

2007, Oct. 6
849 A256 1.35 l multi 1.25 1.25

Christmas
A257

Conifer sprigs and: 1.35 l, Snowflake, Christmas ornaments. 2.45 l, Stars, globe.

2007, Nov. 10 *Perf. 13x12¾*
850-851 A257 Set of 2 3.25 3.25

Wooden Churches — A258

Churches in: 5c, Antazave, 1794. 10c, Deguciai, 1757. 20c, Inturke, 1855. 35c, Prienai, 1750. 1.35 l, Siaudine, 1775. 1.55 l, Uzventis, 1703.

Die Cut Perf. 12½
2008, Jan. 5 **Litho.**
Self-Adhesive
852 A258 5c multi .25 .25
  a. Dated 2011 .25 .25
853 A258 10c multi .25 .25
  a. Dated 2009 .25 .25
  b. Dated 2011 .25 .25
854 A258 20c multi .25 .25
  a. Dated 2009 .25 .25
  b. Dated 2011 .25 .25
855 A258 35c multi .30 .30
  a. Dated 2011 .30 .30
856 A258 1.35 l multi 1.00 1.00
  a. Dated 2009 1.00 1.00
  b. Dated 2011 1.10 1.10
857 A258 1.55 l multi 1.10 1.10
  Nos. 852-857 (6) 3.15 3.15

Issued: Nos. 853a, 854a, 856a, 2/21/09; Nos. 853b, 856b, 1/8/11. Nos. 852a, 854b, 855a, 10/8/11.

Famous Lithuanians Type of 2002

Designs: 2 l, Martynas Jankus (1858-1946), publisher. 2.15 l, Zenonas Ivinskis (1908-71), historian. 2.90 l, Antanas Maceina (1908-87), philosopher.

2008, Jan. 19   Litho.   Perf. 13½
858-860 A185   Set of 3   6.00 6.00

Restoration of Independence, 90th Anniv. — A259

2008, Feb. 16
861 A259 1.35 l multi   1.25 1.25

State Awards of the Baltic Countries — A260

Designs: Nos. 862, 863a, Order of Vytautas the Great, Lithuania. No. 863b, Order of the National Coat of Arms, Estonia. No. 863c, Order of Three Stars, Latvia.

Perf. 13½x13¾
2008, Mar. 15   Litho.
862 A260 7 l multi   5.50 5.50

Souvenir Sheet
863 A260 5 l Sheet of 3, #a-c,
           + label   13.00 13.00

See Estonia Nos. 592-593, Latvia Nos. 701-702.

Items From Rokiskis Regional Museum — A261

No. 864: a, Wood carving, by Lionginas Sepka. b, 19th cent. women's clothing. Illustration reduced.

2008, Apr. 19   Litho.   Perf. 14
864 A261 1.55 l Horiz. pair, #a-b 2.75 2.75

Europa A262

Designs: No. 865, 2.45 l, Grand Duke Gediminas and his letters of 1323. No. 866, 2.45 l, Vilnius, 2009 European Cultural Capital.

2008, May 3
865-866 A262   Set of 2   4.50 4.50

Sajudis Party, 20th Anniv. A263

2008, May 31
867 A263 1.35 l multi   1.25 1.25

Expo Zaragoza 2008 — A264

2008, June 7   Die Cut Perf. 12½
Self-Adhesive
868 A264 2.45 l multi   2.25 2.25

Miniature Sheet

Lithuania, 1000th Anniv. — A265

No. 869: a, First Lithuanian Cabinet of Ministers, 1918. b, Consitituent Assembly, 1920. c, Opening of Kaunas University, 1922. d, Occupation of Memel (Klaipeda) by Lithuania, 1923. e, Opening of Zemaiciai Road (man signing document, 1939). f, Return of Vilnius to Lithuania from Poland, 1939.

2008, June 28   Perf. 14
869 A265 3 l Sheet of 6, #a-f   15.00 15.00

Crashed Transatlantic Flight of Captains Steponas Darius and Stasys Girenas, 75th Anniv. — A266

2008, July 12
870 A266 2.90 l multi   2.60 2.60

2008 Summer Olympics, Beijing — A267

Designs: 2.15 l, Women's marathon. 2.45 l, Yachting.

2008, July 26
871-872 A267   Set of 2   4.00 4.00

Apparitions of the Virgin Mary at Siluva, 400th Anniv. — A268

2008, Aug. 30   Litho.   Perf. 14
873 A268 1.55 l multi   1.40 1.40

Worldwide Fund for Nature (WWF) A269

Coracias garrulus: Nos. 874, 878a, 1.35 l, On branch with beak closed, denomination at LR. Nos. 875, 878b, 1.35 l, In flight. Nos. 876, 878c, 1.35 l, On branch with beak open, denomination at LL. Nos. 877, 878d, 1.35 l, On branch with beak closed, denomination at LL.

2008, Sept. 6   Perf. 14
Stamps With White Frames
874-877 A269   Set of 4   4.50 4.50
Souvenir Sheet
Stamps Without White Frames
878 A269 1.35 l Sheet of 4, #a-d 4.50 4.50

Arms Type of 1992

Designs: No. 879, 1.35 l, Jurbarkas. No. 880, 1.35 l, Joniskis. 3 l, Sirvintos.

2008, Oct. 4   Litho.
Size: 26x31mm
879-881 A82   Set of 3   5.00 5.00

Christmas and New Year's Day A270

Designs: 1.35 l, Holiday lights. 2.45 l, Snow-covered evergreen branch.

2008, Nov. 8   Perf. 14
882-883 A270   Set of 2   3.25 3.25

Famous Lithuanians Type of 2002

Designs: 1.35 l, Jonas Zemaitas (1909-54), military officer. 2 l, Vaclovas Birziska (1884-1956), educator and library founder. 2.15 l, Mecislovas Reinys (1884-1953), archbishop.

2009, Jan. 17   Litho.   Perf. 14
884-886 A185   Set of 3   4.75 4.75

Arms Type of 1992

Designs: No. 887, 1.35 l, Krekenava. No. 888, 1.35 l, Pakruojis. 3 l, Salcininkai.

2009, Feb. 21   Litho.   Perf. 14
Size: 26x31mm
887-889 A82   Set of 3   5.00 5.00

Souvenir Sheet

Protection of Polar Regions and Glaciers — A271

No. 890 — Glacier with sky in: a, Dark blue. b, Light blue.

2009, Mar. 27
890 A271 2.90 l Sheet of 2, #a-b 5.00 5.00

Vilnius, 2009 European Cultural Capital A272

2009, Apr. 11
891 A272 2.15 l multi   1.75 1.75

Europa — A273

Telescope and: No. 892, Galileo Galilei, Moon. No. 893, Vilnius University Observatory, Sun.

2009, Apr. 25   Litho.   Perf. 14
892 A273 2.45 l multi   2.00 2.00
893 A273 2.45 l multi   2.00 2.00

Intl. Year of Astronomy.

Great Synagogue of Vilnius — A274

2009, May 23
894 A274 1.35 l multi   1.10 1.10

Palanga Amber Museum — A275

No. 895: a, "Sun Stone" (large piece of amber). b, Museum building. Illustration reduced.

2009, June 13
895 A275 1.55 l Pair, #a-b   2.75 2.75

Spindle A276

2009, June 27   Litho.   Perf. 14
896 A276 3.35 l multi   2.75 2.75

Millennium Song Festival, Vilnius.

Miniature Sheet

Lithuania, 1000th Anniv. — A277

No. 897: a, Acceptance of declaration of the Council of the Movement for the Freedom of Lithuania, 1949. b, Illegal production of "Chronicle of the Catholic Church in Lithuania," 1972. c, Lithuanian Reform Movement, 1988. d, Signing of declaration of Lithuanian independence, 1990. e, Entry into European Union, 2004. f, Acceptance into Schengen Area, 2007.

2009, July 4   Litho.   Perf. 14
897 A277 3 l Sheet of 6, #a-f   15.00 15.00

Tall Ships Regatta — A278

Illustration reduced.

Perf. 13½x13¾

2009, Sept. 25   **Litho.**
898 A278 3 l multi + label   2.50 2.50

Railways in
Lithuania,
150th
Anniv. — A279

2009, Aug. 8   **Perf. 14**
899 A279 2.90 l multi   2.40 2.40

Order of the Cross
of Vytis — A280

2009, Sept. 19   **Perf. 13½x13¾**
900 A280 7 l multi   6.00 6.00

Flora and Fauna From Red Book of
Lithuania — A281

No. 901: a, Papilio machaon. b, Gentiana
pneumonanthe.
Illustration reduced.

2009, Oct. 10   **Perf. 14**
901 A281 1.55 l Horiz. pair, #a-b 2.75 2.75

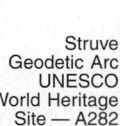

Struve
Geodetic Arc
UNESCO
World Heritage
Site — A282

Designs: No. 902, 2 l, Friedrich Georg Wilhelm von Struve and map of Europe. No. 903, 2 l, Arc post in Meskonys, map of triangulation points.

2009, Oct. 24
902-903 A282   Set of 2   3.50 3.50

Christmas and
New Year's
Day — A283

Designs: 1.35 l, Village church. 2.45 l, Houses.

2009, Nov. 7
904-905 A283   Set of 2   3.50 3.50

Famous Lithuanians Type of 2002

Designs: No. 906, 1.35 l, Jonas Karolis Chodkevicius (Jan Karol Chodkiewicz, 1560-1621), hetman and military leader. No. 907, 1.35 l, Jonas Jablonskis (1860-1930), linguist. 3 l, Mykolas Krupavicius (1885-1970), Minister of Agriculture.

2010, Jan. 16   **Litho.**   **Perf. 14**
906-908 A185   Set of 3   4.75 4.75

2010 Winter
Olympics,
Vancouver
A284

2010, Jan. 30
909 A284 2.45 l multi   2.00 2.00

Arms Type of 1992

Designs: 1.35 l, Silale. 2 l, Jonava. 2.15 l, Varena.

2010, Feb. 20   **Perf. 14**
       Size: 26x31mm
910-912 A82   Set of 3   4.50 4.50

Independence,
20th
Anniv. — A285

2010, Mar. 6   **Litho.**
913 A285 1.35 l multi   1.10 1.10

Easter — A286

2010, Mar. 20   **Perf. 14**
914 A286 1.35 l multi   1.10 1.10

Expo 2010,
Shanghai
A287

2010, Apr. 10
915 A287 2.90 l multi   2.25 2.25

Vladas
Mikenas
(1910-92),
Chess Grand
Master
A288

2010, Apr. 17
916 A288 2 l multi   1.60 1.60

Europa
A289

Half of book and: No. 917, 2.45 l, Rabbit, girl, numerals. No. 918, 2.45 l, Letters, bird, boy.

2010, May 8
917-918 A289   Set of 2   3.50 3.50

       Souvenir Sheet

Oak of Stelmuze — A290

2010, June 5
919 A290 8 l multi   5.75 5.75

Battle of
Grunwald, 600th
Anniv. — A291

2010, July 3
920 A291 2.45 l multi   1.90 1.90

Kretinga Museum, 75th Anniv. — A292

No. 921 — Items in Kretinga Museum: a, Fastener fron 2nd-3rd cent., monument b, St. George slaying the dragon, musuem.

2010, July 10   **Litho.**
921 A292 1.35 l Pair, #a-b   2.10 2.10
Printed in sheets containing 10 pairs and 5 labels.

2010 Youth
Olympics,
Singapore
A293

2010, July 31   **Perf. 14**
922 A293 2.90 l multi   2.25 2.25

Kernave
Archaeological
UNESCO World
Heritage
Site — A294

Designs: No. 923, 3 l, View of town and burial mounds. No. 924, 3 l, Road and burial mound.

2010, Aug. 7
923-924 A294   Set of 2   4.50 4.50

Flora and Fauna from Red Book of
Lithuania — A295

No. 925: a, Columba oenas. b, Anax parthenope and flowers.

2010, Sept. 11
925 A295 1.35 l Horiz. pair, #a-b 2.25 2.25

Cathedrals
A296

Designs: No. 926, 1.35 l, Transfiguration Cathedral, Kaisiadorys. No. 927, 1.35 l, St. Anthony of Padua Cathedral, Telsiai.

2010, Oct. 16   **Perf. 14**
926-927 A296   Set of 2   2.25 2.25
     See Nos. 949-950.

Christmas
A297

New Year
2011
A298

2010, Nov. 6   **Litho.**
928 A297 1.35 l multi   1.10 1.10
929 A298 2.45 l multi   2.00 2.00

Grand Cross of the
Order of the
Lithuanian Grand
Duke
Gediminas — A299

2010, Nov. 20   **Perf. 13½x13¾**
930 A299 7 l multi   5.50 5.50

Defenders of
Freedom
Day — A300

2011, Jan. 8   **Litho.**   **Perf. 14**
931 A300 1.35 l multi   1.10 1.10

37th European Basketball
Championships, Lithuania — A301

2011, Jan. 22   *Perf. 14¼x14*
932 A301 2.45 l multi   1.90 1.90

2011 Census
A302

2011, Feb. 26   *Perf. 14*
933 A302 1.35 l multi   1.10 1.10

Famous Lithuanians Type of 2002

Designs: 1.35 l, Gabriele Petkevicaite-Bite (1861-1943), writer. 2.15 l, Justinas Vienozinskis (1886-1960), artist. 2.90 l, Stasys Salkauskis (1886-1941), philosopher.

2011, Mar. 5
934-936 A185 Set of 3   5.25 5.25

Souvenir Sheet

Kaunas, 650th Anniv. — A303

No. 937 — Buildings in Kaunas: a, Kauno Rotuse (City Hall). b, Kauno Centrinis Pastas (Main Post Office). c, Perkuno Namas Kaune (Perkunas House).

2011, Mar. 19
937 A303 3 l Sheet of 3, #a-c   7.50 7.50

Europa
A304

Tree in foreground, forest and: No. 938, 2.45 l, Field (denomination at LR). No. 939, 2.45 l, River (denomination at LL).

2011, Apr. 23
938-939 A304 Set of 2   4.25 4.25

Intl. Year of Forests.

Pilgrim Route
of Pope John
Paul
II — A305

2011, May 7
940 A305 2.15 l multi   1.75 1.75

Miniature Sheet

Zoo Animals — A306

No. 941: a, Giraffa camelopardalis. b, Pelecanus. c, Cichlasoma octofasciatum. d, Ursus maritimus.

2011, May 21   *Perf. 14¼x13½*
941 A306 4 l Sheet of 4, #a-d   13.50 13.50

Items in Alytus Ethnographic
Museum — A307

No. 942: a, Pot and pitchers. b, Blacksmith's bellows.

2011, June 4   *Perf. 14*
942 A307 2 l Pair, #a-b   3.50 3.50

Czeslaw Milosz (1911-2004), 1980 Nobel Laureate in Literature A308

2011, June 18   *Litho.*
943 A308 3.35 l multi   2.75 2.75

Water Measuring Station, Smalininkai, 200th Anniv. — A309

2011, July 16
944 A309 1.35 l multi   1.10 1.10

Printed in sheets of 4.

Arms Type of 1992

Designs: 1.35 l, Plunge. 2.15 l, Kasiadorys. 2.90 l, Ignalina.

2011, July 30   *Perf. 14*
945-947 A82 Set of 3   5.50 5.50

Souvenir Sheet

Stone of Puntukas — A310

2011, Aug. 20
948 A310 8 l multi   6.50 6.50

Churches
A311

Designs: No. 949, 1.55 l, Church, Trakai. No. 950, 1.55 l, Cathedral, Siaulai.

2011, Sept. 3
949-950 A311 Set of 2   2.50 2.50

Battle of Saule, 775th Anniv. A312

2011, Sept. 17
951 A312 2.45 l multi   2.00 2.00

Vilnius Historic Center UNESCO World Heritage Site — A313

Designs: No. 953, 3 l, Gate of Dawn (Ausros Vartai). No. 954, 3 l, St. John's Church.

2011, Sept. 29   *Litho.*
952-953 A313 Set of 2   4.75 4.75

Haliaeetus
Albicilla
A314

2011, Oct. 8   *Perf. 13½*
954 A314 2.15 l multi   1.75 1.75

Endangered fauna from Red Book of Lithuania.

Christmas
A315

Designs: 1.35 l, Snowman. 2.45 l, Snowflake.

2011, Nov. 5   *Perf. 14*
955-956 A315 Set of 2   3.00 3.00

Grand Cross of the Order for Merits to Lithuania — A316

2011, Nov. 26   *Perf. 13½x13¾*
957 A316 7 l multi   5.50 5.50

Arms Type of 1992

Designs: No. 958, 1.35 l, Kalvarija. No. 959, 1.35 l, Kavarskas. 2.45 l, Naujoji Akmene.

2012, Jan. 7   *Perf. 14*
Size: 26x31mm
958-960 A82 Set of 3   4.00 4.00

Traditional Musical
Instruments — A317

Designs: 10c, Wooden panpipes. 20c, Clay pipes. 35c, Bladderbow bass. 1 l, Alder bark trumpet. 1.35 l, Zither. 2.15 l, Cowhorn reed pipes.

2012, Jan. 7   *Die Cut Perf. 12½*
Self-Adhesive
961 A317 10c multi   .25 .25
  a. Dated "2013"   .25 .25
962 A317 20c multi   .25 .25
  a. Dated "2013"   .25 .25
963 A317 35c multi   .25 .25
  a. Dated "2013"   .25 .25
964 A317 1 l multi   .75 .75
  a. Dated "2013"   .80 .80
965 A317 1.35 l multi   1.00 1.00
  a. Dated "2013"   1.10 1.10
966 A317 2.15 l multi   1.75 1.75
  Nos. 961-966 (6)   4.25 4.25

Issued: Nos. 964a, 965a, 5/11/13.

Famous Lithuanians Type of 2002

Designs: 1.55 l, Mikalojus Radvila Rudasis (Mikolaj Radziwill) (1512-84), Grand Chancellor of Lithuania. 2 l, Domicele Tarabildiene (1912-85), artist. 2.90 l, Stasys Simkus (1887-1943), composer.

2012, Feb. 4   *Perf. 14*
967-969 A185 Set of 3   5.00 5.00

Maironis
(1862-1932),
Poet — A318

2012, Feb. 25
970 A318 3.35 l multi   2.60 2.60

Spiders From Red Book of Lithuania — A319

No. 971: a, Dolomedes plantarius. b, Eresus cinnaberinus.

2012, Mar. 17
971 A319 2.90 l Horiz. pair, #a-b 4.50 4.50

Christianization of Lithuania, 625th Anniv. — A320

2012, Mar. 24 *Perf. 14*
972 A320 1.35 l multi 1.00 1.00

Europa — A321

Designs: No. 973, Hills, trees and river. No. 974, Buildings.

2012, Apr. 28
973 A321 2.45 l multi 1.90 1.90
974 A321 2.45 l multi 1.90 1.90

Souvenir Sheet

Year of Museums — A322

2012, May 12
975 A322 7 l multi 5.25 5.25

Curonian Spit UNESCO World Heritage Site — A323

Designs: No. 976, 3 l, Fisherman's boat and house. No. 977, 3 l, Sand dunes.

2012, May 26
976-977 A323 Set of 2 4.50 4.50

2012 Summer Olympics, London — A324

2012, June 9
978 A324 3.35 l Boxing 2.40 2.40
979 A324 3.55 l Rowing 2.60 2.60

Klaipeda, 760th Anniv. — A325

2012, July 14
980 A325 2 l multi 1.50 1.50

Battle of Blue Waters, 650th Anniv. A326

2012, Aug. 25
981 A326 2.45 l multi 1.90 1.90

Pres. Algirdas Brazauskas (1932-2010) A327

2012, Sept. 22
982 A327 1.35 l multi 1.00 1.00

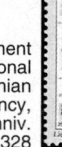

Establishment of Provisional Lithuanian Currency, 20th Anniv. A328

2012, Sept. 29
983 A328 2 l multi 1.50 1.50

Oskar Minkowski (1858-1931), Diabetes Researcher A329

2012, Oct. 20
984 A329 1.35 l multi 1.00 1.00

Railway Bridges A330

Train and: Nos. 985, 986a, Lyduvenai Bridge, Lithuania. No. 986b, Narva Bridge, Estonia. No. 986c, Carnikava Bridge, Latvia.

2012, Oct. 25
985 A330 8 l multi 6.00 6.00

Souvenir Sheet
Perf. 13½

986 A330 4 l Sheet of 3, #a-c 9.00 9.00
See Estonia Nos. 713-714, Latvia Nos. 815-816.

Christmas A331

Designs: 1.35 l, Body of water. 2.45 l, Snow-covered house.

2012, Nov. 10 *Perf. 14*
987-988 A331 Set of 2 3.00 3.00

Christianization of Samogitia, 600th Anniv. — A332

2013, Jan. 5 *Perf. 13x13¼*
989 A332 2.45 l multi 2.00 2.00

Souvenir Sheet

Flora and Fauna of Zuvintas Biosphere Reserve — A333

No. 990: a, Vulpes vulpes. b, Panurus biarmicus. c, Dactylorhiza maculata.

2013, Jan. 19 *Perf. 14¼x14½*
990 A333 3 l Sheet of 3, #a-c 7.25 7.25

New Year 2013 (Year of the Snake) A334

2013, Feb. 9 *Perf. 13x13¼*
991 A334 2.90 l multi 2.25 2.25

Lithuanian Laser Industry — A335

2013, Feb. 23 *Perf. 13¼x13*
992 A335 1.35 l multi 1.00 1.00

Famous Lithuanians A336

Designs: 1.35 l, Antanas Strazdas (1763-1833), poet. 2 l, Pranas Masiotas (1863-1940), writer.

2013, Mar. 9 *Perf. 13¼x13*
993-994 A336 Set of 2 2.50 2.50

Uprising of 1863, 150th Anniv. — A337

2013, Mar. 23 *Perf. 13x13¼*
995 A337 1.35 l multi 1.00 1.00

Ciconia Ciconia A338

2013, Apr. 6 *Perf. 11*
996 A338 7 l multi 5.50 5.50
No. 996 was printed in sheets of 2.

Europa A339

Postal vehicles: No. 997, 2.45 l, Tazzari Zero (yellow vehicle). No. 998, 2.45 l, Moskvitch 401 (blue vehicle).

2013, Apr. 27 *Perf. 13x13¼*
997-998 A339 Set of 2 3.75 3.75

Mother's Day — A340

2013, May 4 *Perf. 13¼x13*
999 A340 1.35 l multi 1.10 1.10

International Red Cross, 150th Anniv. — A341

2013, May 11
1000 A341 2.15 l multi 1.75 1.75

Father's Day — A342

2013, June 1
1001 A342 1.35 l multi 1.10 1.10

Kaunas Cathedral Basilica, 600th Anniv. A343

2013, June 8
1002 A343 1.35 l multi   **Perf. 13x13¼**   1.10 1.10

Lithuanian Presidency of the European Union — A344

2013, June 15   **Perf. 14½x14**
1003 A344 2.45 l multi   1.90 1.90

Souvenir Sheet

Transfer of Klaipeda (Memel) to Lithuanian Control, 90th Anniv. — A345

2013, June 29   **Perf. 14¼x14½**
1004 A345 7 l multi   5.25 5.25

First Lithuanian National Olympics, 75th Anniv. A346

2013, July 13   **Perf. 13x13¼**
1005 A346 1.35 l multi   1.10 1.10

Death of Captains Steponas Darius and Stasys Girenas on New York-Kaunas Flight, 80th Anniv. A347

2013, July 20
1006 A347 2.90 l multi   2.25 2.25

Lighthouses A348

Designs: No. 1007, 2.45 l, Cape Vente Lighthouse. No. 1008, 2.45 l, Kaunas Lighthouse.

2013, July 27   **Perf. 13¼x13**
1007-1008 A348   Set of 2   3.75 3.75

Military Uniforms — A349

2013, Aug. 24   Litho.   Perf. 13¼x13
1009 A349 1.35 l multi   1.10 1.10

Birds From Red Book of Lithuania — A350

Designs: 2.15 l, Acrocephalus paludicola. 2.90 l, Anthus campsetris.

2013, Sept. 7   Litho.   Perf. 13¼x13
1010 A350 2.15 l multi   1.75 1.75
1011 A350 2.90 l multi   2.25 2.25

Postcrossing Post Cards — A351

2013, Oct. 5   Litho.   Perf. 13¼x13
1012 A351 2.45 l multi   2.00 2.00

Christmas and New Year's Day A352

Bear and fox: 1.35 l, Exchanging gifts. 2.45 l, Watching fireworks display.

2013, Nov. 9   Litho.   Perf. 13x13¼
1013-1014 A352   Set of 2   3.00 3.00

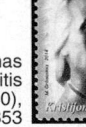

Kristijonas Donelaitis (1714-80), Poet — A353

2014, Jan. 4   Litho.   Perf. 13x13¼
1015 A353 1.55 l multi   1.25 1.25

2014 Winter Olympics, Sochi, Russia A354

Designs: 2.15 l, Two-man bobsled. 2.90 l, Ice hockey.

2014, Jan. 18
1016-1017 A354   Set of 2   4.00 4.00

Souvenir Sheet

New Year 2014 (Year of the Horse) — A355

2014, Feb. 1   Litho.   Perf. 14¼x14½
1018 A355 7 l multi   5.50 5.50

Shrove Tuesday Masks A356

2014. Feb. 15   Litho.   Perf. 13x13¼
1019 A356 2 l multi   1.60 1.60

Re-establishment of Vytautas Magnus University, 25th Anniv. — A357

2014, Mar. 8   Litho.   Perf. 13¼x13
1020 A357 1.55 l multi   1.25 1.25

Admission to NATO, 10th Anniv. — A358

2014, Mar. 29   Litho.   Perf. 13¼x13
1021 A358 2.15 l multi   1.75 1.75

Owls From Red Book of Lithuania — A359

Designs: 2 l, Tyto alba. 3 l, Glaucidium passerinum.

2014, Apr. 5   Litho.   Perf. 13¼x13
1022-1023 A359   Set of 2   4.00 4.00
1023a   Booklet pane of 6, 3 each
    #1022-1023   12.00 —
    Complete booklet, #1023a   12.00

Admission to the European Union, 10th Anniv. A360

2014, Apr. 26   Litho.   Perf. 13c13¼
1024 A360 2.15 l multi   1.75 1.75

Europa A361

Designs: No. 1025, 2.45 l, Goat horn (ozragis), wooden bells (skrabalai). No. 1026, 2.45 l, Reed pipe (birbyne), zither (kankles).

2014, May 3   Litho.   Perf. 13x13¼
1025-1026 A361   Set of 2   4.00 4.00

Protection of the Baltic Sea — A362

2014, May 24   Litho.   Perf. 13¼x13
1027 A362 2.90 l multi   2.40 2.40
a.   Tête-bêche pair   4.80 4.80
b.   Souvenir sheet of 3 #1027a   14.50 —

No. 1027 was printed in sheets of 9, with the central stamp inverted in relation to the others. No. 1027b was sold with, but not attached to, a booklet cover.

Karaite Judaism — A363

No. 1028: a, Seraya Szapszal (1873-1961), leader of Lithuanian Karaite community. b, Kenesa (synagogue), Vilnius.

2014, June 7   Litho.   Perf. 13¼x13
1028 A363 2.15 l Pair, #a-b   3.50 3.50

Lithuanian Song Festival, 90th Anniv. — A364

2014, June 28   Litho.   Perf. 13¼x13
1029 A364 1.35 l multi   1.10 1.10

Lithuanian Term as Non-Permanent Member of United Nations Security Council — A365

2014, July 12   Litho.   Perf. 13¼x13
1030 A365 1.35 l multi   1.10 1.10

In anticipation of Lithuania's official change to Euro currency in January 2015, No. 1030 and stamps issued through the end of 2014 are denominated in litas and the equivalent value in the not-yet-accepted euro currency.

Souvenir Sheet

Baltic Chain Demonstration, 25th Anniv. — A366

No. 1031: a, Five adults and one child. b, Three women. c, Man and child.

2014, Aug. 23   Litho.   Perf. 13¼
1031 A366 7 l Sheet of 3, #a-c 16.00 16.00
See Estonia Nos. 764-765, Latvia Nos. 883-884.

Battle of Orsha, 500th Anniv. — A367

2014, Sept. 6   Litho.   Perf. 13x13¼
1032 A367 2.60 l multi   1.90 1.90

Earth, LituanicaSAT-1 and Litsat-1 A368

2014, Sept. 20   Litho.   Perf. 13x13¼
1033 A368 2.90 l multi   2.25 2.25
  a.   Tete-beche pair   4.50 4.50
  b.   Miniature sheet of 6 + 2 labels   13.50

No. 1033 was printed in sheets of 16 + 4 labels. No. 1033b was sold with, but unattached to, a booklet cover.

Wooden Church Belfries Type of 2007 With Added Euro Denomination

Design: 5c, Belfry from church in Vabalininkas, 19th cent.

Die Cut Perf. 12½
2014, Oct. 11   Litho.
Self-Adhesive
1034 A249 5c multi   .25 .25

Open Heart Surgery, 50th Anniv. — A369

2014, Oct. 11   Litho.   Perf. 13¼x13
1035 A369 2.80 l multi   2.10 2.10

Christmas A370

Designs: 1.35 l, Man holding letter and umbrella. 2.80 l, Santa Claus in balloon.

2014, Nov. 8   Litho.   Perf. 13¼x13
1036-1037 A370   Set of 2   3.00 3.00

SEMI-POSTAL STAMPS

Regular Issue of 1923-24
Surcharged in Blue, Violet or Black

On A21   On A22

On A23

1924, Feb.   Wmk. 147   Perf. 11
B1 A21 2c + 2c pale brn (Bl)   .90 2.25
B2 A21 3c + 3c ol bis (Bl)   .90 2.25
B3 A21 5c + 5c pale grn (V)   .90 2.25
B4 A21 10c + 10c vio (Bk)   2.25 3.25
B5 A21 36c + 34c org brn (V)   4.75 12.00

Wmk. Webbing (109)
B6 A21 10c + 10c vio (Bk)   7.50 20.00
B7 A21 15c + 15c scar (V)   1.10 2.50
B8 A21 20c + 20c ol brn (Bl)   2.25 4.00
B9 A21 25c + 25c bl (Bk)   21.00 55.00
B10 A22 50c + 50c yel grn (V)   5.25 12.00
B11 A22 60c + 60c red (V)   5.25 12.00
B12 A23 1 l + 1 l org & grn (V)   6.00 16.00
B13 A23 3 l + 2 l red & gray (V)   9.00 32.50
B14 A23 5 l + 3 l brn & bl (V)   15.00 40.00

Unwmk.
B15 A21 25c + 25c dp bl (Bk)   4.75 12.00
  Nos. B1-B15 (15)   86.80 228.00
  Set, never hinged   225.00

For War Invalids

Semi-Postal Stamps of 1924 Surcharged in Gold or Copper

1926, Dec. 3   Wmk. 147
B16 A21 1 + 1c on #B1   1.00 1.25
  a.   Inverted surcharge   40.00
B17 A21 2 + 2c on #B2 (C)   1.00 1.25
B19 A21 2 + 2c on #B3   1.00 1.25
  a.   Double surch., one inverted   40.00
B20 A21 5 + 5c on #B4   2.00 2.00
B21 A21 14 + 14c on #B5   6.00 7.00

Wmk. Webbing (109)
B22 A21 5 + 5c on #B6   10.00 10.00
B23 A21 5 + 5c on #B7   2.00 2.00
B24 A21 10 + 10c on #B8   2.00 2.00
B25 A21 10 + 10c on #B9   65.00 65.00

Unwmk.
B26 A21 10 + 10c on #B15   4.00 5.00

Surcharged in Copper or Silver

On A22   On A23

Wmk. Webbing (109)
B27 A22 20 + 20c on #B10   4.00 5.00
B28 A22 25 + 25c on #B11 (S)   6.00 7.00
B29 A23 30 + 30c on #B12 (S)   9.00 11.00
  Nos. B16-B29 (13)   113.00 119.75
  Set, never hinged   225.00

For War Orphans

Surcharged in Gold

1926, Dec. 3   Wmk. 147
B30 A21 1 + 1c on #B1   .90 .90
B31 A21 2 + 2c on #B2   .90 .90
  a.   Inverted surcharge   260.00
B32 A21 2 + 2c on #B3   .90 .90
  a.   Inverted surcharge   30.00
B33 A21 5 + 5c on #B4   2.00 2.25
B34 A21 19 + 19c on #B5   4.00 5.00

Wmk. Webbing (109)
B35 A21 5 + 5c on #B6   10.00 10.00
B36 A21 10 + 10c on #B7   1.75 2.00
B37 A21 15 + 15c on #B8   2.00 2.25
B38 A21 15 + 15c on #B9   65.00 65.00

Unwmk.
B39 A21 15 + 15c on #B15   3.00 3.00

Surcharged in Gold

On A22   On A23

Wmk. 109
B40 A22 25c on #B10   5.00 6.00
B41 A22 30c on #B11   8.00 7.00
B42 A23 50c on #B12   10.00 11.00
  Nos. B30-B42 (13)   113.45 116.20
  Set, never hinged   225.00

Javelin throwing — SP1

Natl. Olympiad, July 15-20: 5c+5c, Archery. 30c+10c, Diving. 60c+15c, Running.

1938, July 13   Photo.   Unwmk.   Perf. 14
B43 SP1 5c + 5c grn & dk grn   2.50 6.50
B44 SP1 15c + 5c org & red org   2.50 6.50
B45 SP1 30c + 10c bl & dk bl   4.50 12.00
B46 SP1 60c + 15c tan & brn   5.75 16.00
  Nos. B43-B46 (4)   15.25 41.00
  Set, never hinged   42.50

Same Overprinted in Red, Blue or Black

Nos. B47, B50   Nos. B48-B49

1938, July 13
B47 SP1 5c + 5c (R)   6.00 7.50
B48 SP1 15c + 5c (Bl)   6.00 7.50
B49 SP1 30c + 10c (R)   7.50 7.50
B50 SP1 60c + 15c (Bk)   10.00 12.50
  Nos. B47-B50 (4)   29.50 35.00
  Set, never hinged   60.00

National Scout Jamboree, July 12-14. Forged cancellations exist.

Basketball Players SP6   SP7

Flags of Competing Nations and Basketball — SP8

1939   Photo.   Perf. 14
B52 SP6 15c + 10c copper brn & brn   3.25 6.50
B53 SP7 30c + 15c myrtle grn & grn   3.25 6.50
B54 SP8 60c + 40c blue vio & gray vio   6.00 12.00
  Nos. B52-B54 (3)   12.50 25.00
  Set, never hinged   25.00

3rd European Basketball Championships held at Kaunas. The surtax was used for athletic equipment. Nos. B52-B54 exist imperf. Value, set pairs, $500.

AIR POST STAMPS

Winged Posthorn AP1

Airplane over Neman River — AP2

Air Squadron AP3

Plane over Gediminas Castle — AP4

1921   Litho.   Wmk. 109   Perf. 11½
C1 AP1 20sk ultra   1.25 .75
C2 AP1 40sk red orange   1.00 .75
C3 AP1 60sk green   1.10 .75
  a.   Imperf., pair   45.00
C4 AP1 80sk lt rose   1.50 .75
  a.   Horiz. pair, imperf. vert.   50.00 40.00
C5 AP2 1auk green & red   1.50 .75
  a.   Imperf., pair   90.00 175.00
C6 AP3 2auk brown & blue   1.60 .75
C7 AP4 5auk slate & yel   2.00 1.75
  Nos. C1-C7 (7)   9.95 6.25
  Set, never hinged   17.50

For surcharges see Nos. C21-C26, C29.

Allegory of
Flight — AP5

1921, Nov. 6
C8	AP5	20sk org & gray bl	1.40	*1.50*
C9	AP5	40sk dl bl & lake	1.40	*1.50*
C10	AP5	60sk vio bl & ol grn	1.40	*1.50*
C11	AP5	80sk ocher & dp grn	1.40	*1.50*
a.		Vert. pair, imperf. btwn.	35.00	35.00
C12	AP5	1auk bl grn & bl	1.40	*1.50*
C13	AP5	2auk gray & brn org	1.40	*1.50*
C14	AP5	5auk dl lil & Prus bl	1.40	*1.50*
		Nos. C8-C14 (7)	9.80	10.50
		Set, never hinged	17.50	

Opening of airmail service.

Plane over Kaunas — AP6

Black Overprint

1922, July 16   *Perf. 11, 11½*
C15	AP6	1auk ol brn & red	1.00	2.75
a.		Imperf., pair	60.00	
C16	AP6	3auk violet & grn	1.00	2.75
C17	AP6	5auk dp blue & yel	1.00	4.00
		Nos. C15-C17 (3)	3.00	9.50
		Set, never hinged	9.75	

Nos. C15-C17, without overprint, were to be
for the founding of the Air Post service but they
were not put in use at that time. Subsequently
the word "ZENKLAS" (stamp) was overprinted
over "ISTEIGIMAS" (founding) and the date
"1921, VI, 25" was obliterated by short vertical
lines.
For surcharge see No. C31.

Plane over
Gediminas
Castle — AP7

1922, July 22
C18	AP7	2auk blue & rose	1.10	.85
C19	AP7	4auk brown & rose	1.10	.85
C20	AP7	10auk black & gray bl	1.25	1.40
		Nos. C18-C20 (3)	3.45	3.10
		Set, never hinged	10.00	

For surcharges see Nos. C27-C28, C30.

Nos. C1-C7, C17-C20 Surcharged like Regular Issues in Black or Carmine

1922
C21	AP1	10c on 20sk	3.25	2.50
C22	AP1	10c on 40sk	1.75	1.50
C23	AP1	10c on 60sk	1.75	1.50
a.		Inverted surcharge	45.00	
C24	AP1	10c on 80sk	1.75	1.50
C25	AP2	20c on 1auk	11.00	6.00
C26	AP3	20c on 2auk	11.00	7.50
a.		Without "CENT"	200.00	140.00
C27	AP7	25c on 2auk	1.00	*1.00*
a.		Inverted surcharge	45.00	40.00
C28	AP7	30c on 4auk (C)	1.00	*1.00*
a.		Double surcharge	50.00	45.00
C29	AP4	50c on 5auk	2.00	1.50
C30	AP7	50c on 10auk	1.00	*1.00*
a.		Inverted surcharge	50.00	45.00
C31	AP6	1 l on 5auk	16.00	15.00
a.		Double surcharge	50.00	
		Nos. C21-C31 (11)	51.50	40.00
		Set, never hinged	92.50	

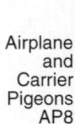

Airplane
and
Carrier
Pigeons
AP8

"Flight"
AP9

1924, Jan. 28   **Wmk. 147**   *Perf. 11*
C32	AP8	20c yellow	1.15	.75
C33	AP8	40c emerald	1.15	.75
a.		Horiz. or vert. pair, imperf. between	60.00	
C34	AP8	60c rose	1.15	.75
a.		Imperf., pair	75.00	
C35	AP9	1 l dk brown	2.50	.75
		Nos. C32-C35 (4)	5.95	3.00
		Set, never hinged	25.00	

Most stamps, if not all, of the
"unwatermarked" varieties show faint traces of
watermark, according to experts.
For surcharges see Nos. CB1-CB4.

Swallow — AP10

1926, June 17   **Wmk. 198**   *Perf. 14½*
C37	AP10	20c carmine rose	1.10	.75
a.		Horiz. or vert. pair, imperf. between	55.00	
C38	AP10	40c violet & red org	1.10	.75
a.		Horiz. or vert. pair, imperf. between	55.00	
C39	AP10	60c blue & black	2.25	.75
a.		Horiz. or vert. pair, imperf. between	55.00	
c.		Center inverted	250.00	160.00
		Nos. C37-C39 (3)	4.45	2.25
		Set, never hinged	6.00	

Juozas
Tubelis — AP11

Vytautas and
Airplane over
Kaunas
AP12

Vytautas and
Antanas
Smetona
AP13

1930, Feb. 16   **Wmk. 109**   *Perf. 14*
C40	AP11	5c blk, bis & brn	.70	.35
C41	AP11	10c dk bl, db & blk	.70	.35
C42	AP11	15c mar, gray & bl	.70	.35
C43	AP12	20c dk brn, org & dl red	.70	.80
C44	AP12	40c dk bl, lt bl & vio	1.25	.80
C45	AP13	60c bl grn, lil & blk	2.00	.85
C46	AP13	1 l dl red, lil & blk	3.75	1.60
		Nos. C40-C46 (7)	9.80	5.10
		Set, never hinged	25.00	

5th cent. of the death of the Grand Duke
Vytautas.

Map of Lithuania, Klaipeda and
Vilnius — AP14

15c, 20c, Airplane over Neman. 40c, 60c,
City Hall, Kaunas. 1 l, 2 l, Church of Vytautas,
Kaunas.

Wmk. Multiple Letters (238)

1932, July 21   *Perf. 14, Imperf.*
C47	AP14	5c ver & ol grn	.25	.65
C48	AP14	10c dk red brn & ocher	.25	.65
C49	AP14	15c dk bl & org yel	.25	.65
C50	AP14	20c sl blk & org	1.40	.90
C51	AP14	40c ultra & ocher	1.90	3.50
C52	AP14	2 l dk bl & yel	2.00	4.50

Wmk. 198
C53	AP14	40c vio brn & yel	1.60	5.00
C54	AP14	1 l vio brn & grn	2.25	5.75
		Nos. C47-C54 (8)	9.90	21.60
		Set, never hinged	40.00	

Issued for the benefit of Lithuanian orphans.

Mindaugas in the Battle of Shauyai,
1236 — AP15

15c, 20c, Coronation of Mindaugas (1253).
40c, Grand Duke Gediminas and his followers.
60c, Founding of Vilnius by Gediminas (1332).
1 l, Gediminas capturing the Russian Fortifications. 2 l, Grand Duke Algirdas before Moscow
(1368).

Perf. 14, Imperf.

1932, Nov. 28   **Wmk. 209**
C55	AP15	5c grn & red lil	.25	.75
C56	AP15	10c emer & rose	.25	.75
C57	AP15	15c rose vio & bis brn	.25	.75
C58	AP15	20c rose red & blk	1.00	1.00
C59	AP15	40c choc & dk gray	1.50	3.50
C60	AP15	60c org & gray blk	1.90	6.50
C61	AP15	1 l rose vio & grn	2.25	5.50
C62	AP15	2 l dp bl & brn	2.50	7.50
		Nos. C55-C62 (8)	9.90	26.25
		Set, never hinged	36.00	

Anniv. of independence.

Nos. C55-C62 exist with overprint "DARIUS
GIRENAS / NEW YORK-1933- KAUNAS"
below small plane. The overprint was applied
in New York with the approval of the Lithuanian
consul general. Lithuanian postal authorities
seem not to have been involved in the creation
or release of these overprints.

Trakai Castle, Home of the Grand
Duke Kestutis — AP16

Designs: 15c, 20c, Meeting of Kestutis and
the Hermit Birute. 40c, 60c, Hermit Birute. 1 l,
2 l, Kestutis and his Brother Algirdas.

1933, May 6   *Perf. 14, Imperf.*
C63	AP16	5c ol gray & dp bl	.50	.45
C64	AP16	10c gray vio & org brn	.50	.45
C65	AP16	15c dp blue & lilac	.80	.60
C66	AP16	20c org brn & lilac	1.75	1.00
C67	AP16	40c lt ultra & lilac	3.50	1.75
C68	AP16	60c brown & lt ultra	5.00	3.50
C69	AP16	1 l ol gray & dp bl	6.00	4.00
C70	AP16	2 l vio gray & yel grn	7.00	8.00
		Nos. C63-C70 (8)	25.05	19.75
		Set, never hinged	35.00	

Reopening of air service to Berlin-Kaunas-
Moscow, and 550th anniv. of the death of
Kestutis.

Joseph Maironis — AP17

Joseph Tumas-Vaizgantas — AP17a

Designs: 40c, 60c, Vincas Kudirka. 1 l, 2 l,
Julia A. Zemaite.

1933, Sept. 15   *Perf. 14, Imperf.*
C71	AP17	5c crim & dp bl	.35	.65
C72	AP17	10c bl vio & grn	.35	.65
C73	AP17a	15c dk grn & choc	.35	.65
C74	AP17a	20c brn car & ultra	.55	.90
C75	AP17	40c red brn & ol grn	1.25	1.50
C76	AP17	60c dk bl & choc	1.50	2.50
C77	AP17	1 l citron & indigo	2.25	3.50
C78	AP17	2 l dp grn & red brn	3.50	5.75
		Nos. C71-C78 (8)	10.10	16.10
		Set, never hinged	30.00	

Issued for the benefit of Lithuanian orphans.

Capts.
Steponas
Darius and
Stasys
Girenas
AP18

Ill-Fated
Plane
"Lituanica"
AP19

The Dark Angel
of
Death — AP20

"Lituanica" over
Globe — AP21

"Lituanica" and
White
Knight — AP22

Perf. 11½

1934, May 18   **Unwmk.**   **Engr.**
C79	AP18	20c scarlet & blk	.25	.25
C80	AP19	40c dp rose & bl	.25	.25
C81	AP18	60c dk vio & blk	.25	.25
C82	AP20	1 l black & rose	.35	.25
C83	AP21	3 l gray grn & org	.45	.50
C84	AP22	5 l dk brn & blk	1.75	3.25
		Nos. C79-C84 (6)	3.30	4.75
		Set, never hinged	5.50	

Death of Capts. Steponas Darius and
Stasys Girenas on their New York-Kaunas
flight of 1933.
No. C80 exists with diagonal overprint: "F.
VAITKUS / nugalejo Atlanta / 21-22-IX-1935."
Value $300.

Felix Waitkus
and Map of
Transatlantic
Flight — AP23

Wmk. 238

1936, Mar. 24	Litho.	*Perf. 14*	
C85	AP23 15c brown lake	2.25	.85
C86	AP23 30c dark green	3.25	.85
C87	AP23 60c blue	4.50	2.50
	Nos. C85-C87 (3)	10.00	4.20
	Set, never hinged	13.75	

Transatlantic Flight of the Lituanica II, Sept. 21-22, 1935.

AIR POST SEMI-POSTAL STAMPS

Nos. C32-C35 Surcharged like Nos. B1-B9 (No. CB1), Nos. B10-B11 (Nos. CB2-CB3), and Nos. B12-B14 (No. CB4) in Red, Violet or Black

1924	Wmk. 147	*Perf. 11*	
CB1	AP8 20c + 20c yellow (R)	12.00	12.00
CB2	AP8 40c + 40c emerald (V)	12.00	12.00
CB3	AP8 60c + 60c rose (V)	12.00	12.00
CB4	AP9 1 l + 1 l dk brown	12.00	12.00
	Nos. CB1-CB4 (4)	48.00	48.00
	Set, never hinged	80.00	

Surtax for the Red Cross. See note following No. C35.

SOUTH LITHUANIA

GRODNO DISTRICT

Russian Stamps of
1909-12 Surcharged in
Black or Red

1919	Unwmk.	*Perf. 14, 14½x15*	
L1	A14 50sk on 3k red	60.00	57.50
a.	Double surcharge	250.00	250.00
L2	A14 50sk on 5k claret	60.00	57.50
a.	Imperf., pair	550.00	475.00
L3	A15 50sk on 10k dk bl (R)	60.00	57.50
L4	A11 50sk on 15k red brn & bl	60.00	57.50
a.	Imperf., pair	650.00	550.00
L5	A11 50sk on 25k grn & gray vio (R)	60.00	57.50
L6	A11 50sk on 35k red brn & grn	60.00	57.50
L7	A8 50sk on 50k vio & grn	60.00	57.50
L8	A11 50sk on 70k brn & org	60.00	57.50
	Nos. L1-L8 (8)	480.00	460.00

Excellent counterfeits are plentiful.
This surcharge exists on Russia No. 119, the imperf. 1k orange of 1917. Value, unused $90, used $60.

OCCUPATION STAMPS

The issue formerly listed as Lithuania 1N1-1N12 is now listed as Russia N1-N12.

Issued under Russian Occupation

Lithuanian Stamps of
1937-40 Overprinted in
Red or Blue

1940	Wmk. 238	*Perf. 14*	
2N9	A44 2c orange (Bl)	.25	.25
	Never hinged	.30	
2N10	A50 50c brown (Bl)	.25	.25
	Unwmk.		
	Never hinged	.75	
2N11	A56 5c brown car (Bl)	.25	.40
	Never hinged	.30	

2N12	A57 10c green (R)	3.75	3.75
	Never hinged	10.00	
2N13	A58 15c dull orange (Bl)	.25	.25
	Never hinged	.30	
2N14	A59 25c lt brown (R)	.25	.25
	Never hinged	.65	
2N15	A60 30c Prus green (R)	.25	.25
	Never hinged	.65	
2N16	A61 35c red orange (Bl)	.35	.35
	Never hinged	.65	
	Nos. 2N9-2N16 (8)	5.60	5.75
	Set, never hinged	13.50	

Values for used stamps are for CTOs. Postally used examples are considerably more.
The Lithuanian Soviet Socialist Republic was proclaimed July 21, 1940.

LOURENCO MARQUES

lə-'ren,t̪-,sō-,mär-'kes

LOCATION — In the southern part of Mozambique in Southeast Africa
GOVT. — Part of Portuguese East Africa Colony
AREA — 28,800 sq. mi. (approx.)
POP. — 474,000 (approx.)
CAPITAL — Lourenço Marques

Stamps of Mozambique replaced those of Lourenço Marques in 1920. See Mozambique No. 360.

1000 Reis = 1 Milreis
100 Centavos = 1 Escudo (1913)

King Carlos — A1

1895	Typo.	Unwmk.	
	Perf. 11½, 12½, 13½		
1	A1 5r yellow	1.00	.25
2	A1 10r redsh violet	1.00	.35
3	A1 15r chocolate	1.50	.50
4	A1 20r lavender	1.50	.50
5	A1 25r blue green	1.50	.30
a.	Perf. 11½	3.50	1.00
6	A1 50r light blue	2.00	1.00
a.	Perf. 13½	15.00	5.00
b.	Perf. 11½		
7	A1 75r rose	3.00	1.25
8	A1 80r yellow grn	4.75	3.00
9	A1 100r brn, *yel*	3.50	1.00
a.	Perf. 12½	5.00	3.25
10	A1 150r car, *rose*	5.00	3.00
11	A1 200r dk bl, *bl*	6.00	3.00
12	A1 300r dk bl, *sal*	7.50	4.00
	Nos. 1-12 (12)	38.25	18.15

For surcharges and overprints see Nos. 29, 58-69, 132-137, 140-143, 156-157, 160.

Saint Anthony of Padua Issue

Regular Issues of
Mozambique, 1886
and 1894,
Overprinted in Black

1895	Without Gum	*Perf. 12½*	
	On 1886 Issue		
13	A2 5r black	20.00	12.00
14	A2 10r green	25.00	12.00
15	A2 20r rose	35.00	14.00
16	A2 25r lilac	40.00	14.00
17	A2 40r chocolate	35.00	15.00
18	A2 50r bl, perf. 13½	30.00	14.00
a.	Perf. 12½	50.00	27.50
19	A2 100r yellow brn	110.00	90.00
20	A2 200r gray vio	42.50	32.50
21	A2 300r orange	70.00	40.00
	On 1894 Issue		
	Perf. 11½		
22	A3 5r yellow	35.00	25.00
23	A3 10r redsh vio	40.00	15.00
24	A3 50r light blue	50.00	32.50
a.	Perf. 12½	275.00	275.00
25	A3 75r rose, perf. 12½	65.00	50.00
26	A3 80r yellow grn	80.00	65.00
27	A3 100r brown, *buff*	350.00	160.00
28	A3 150r car, *rose,* perf. 12½	50.00	40.00
	Nos. 13-28 (16)	1,077.	631.00

No. 12 Surcharged in
Black

1897, Jan. 2			
29	A1 50r on 300r	200.00	150.00

Most examples of No. 29 were issued without gum.

King Carlos — A2

1898-1903	*Perf. 11½*		
	Name, Value in Black except 500r		
30	A2 2½r gray	.35	.30
31	A2 5r orange	.35	.30
32	A2 10r lt green	.35	.30
33	A2 15r brown	1.25	.85
34	A2 15r gray green ('03)	.75	.50
a.	Imperf.		
35	A2 20r gray violet	.65	.40
a.	Imperf.		
36	A2 25r sea green	.70	.40
a.	Perf. 13½	25.00	8.50
b.	25r light green (error)	30.00	30.00
c.	Perf. 12½	40.00	35.00
37	A2 25r car ('03)	.35	.30
a.	Imperf.		
38	A2 50r blue	2.00	.50
39	A2 50r brown ('03)	.90	.75
40	A2 65r dull bl ('03)	30.00	8.50
41	A2 75r rose	2.00	1.50
42	A2 75r lilac ('03)	1.25	.95
a.	Imperf.		
43	A2 80r violet	2.50	1.25
44	A2 100r dk blue, *blue*	1.75	.65
a.	Perf. 13½	14.50	5.00
45	A2 115r org brn, *pink* ('03)	6.00	5.00
46	A2 130r brn, *straw* ('03)	6.00	5.00
47	A2 150r brn, *straw*	2.25	1.40
48	A2 200r red lil, *pnksh*	2.75	1.25
49	A2 300r dk bl, *rose*	3.25	1.50
50	A2 400r dl bl, *straw* ('03)	8.00	5.00
51	A2 500r blk & red, *bl* ('01)	9.00	3.00
52	A2 700r vio, *yelsh* ('01)	15.00	7.00
	Nos. 30-52 (23)	97.40	46.60

For surcharges and overprints see Nos. 57, 71-74, 76-91, 138, 144-155.

Coat of
Arms — A3

Surcharged On Upper and Lower Halves of Stamp

1899		*Imperf.*	
53	A3 5r on 10r grn & brn	20.00	7.00
54	A3 25r on 10r grn & brn	20.00	7.00
55	A3 50r on 30r grn & brn	30.00	11.00
a.	Inverted surcharge		
56	A3 50r on 800r grn & brn	40.00	20.00
	Nos. 53-56 (4)	110.00	45.00

The lower half of No. 55 can be distinguished from that of No. 56 by the background of the label containing the word "REIS." The former is plain, while the latter is formed of white intersecting curved horizontal lines over vertical shading of violet brown.
Values are for undivided stamps. Halves sell for ¼ as much.
Most examples of Nos. 53-56 were issued without gum. Values are for stamps without gum. Values for stamps with gum are two times the values shown.

No. 41 Surcharged in
Black

1899		*Perf. 11½*	
57	A2 50r on 75r rose	6.00	2.50

Most examples of No. 57 were issued without gum. Values are for stamp without gum.

Surcharged in Black

On Issue of 1895

1902		*Perf. 11½, 12½*	
58	A1 65r on 5r yellow	6.00	2.50
59	A1 65r on 15r choc	6.00	2.50
60	A1 65r on 20r lav	7.00	3.00
a.	Perf. 12½	25.00	15.00
61	A1 115r on 10r red vio	7.00	3.00
62	A1 115r on 200r bl, *bl*	7.00	3.00
63	A1 115r on 300r bl, *sal*	7.00	3.00
64	A1 130r on 25r grn, perf. 12½	4.00	2.00
a.	Perf. 11½	30.00	22.50
65	A1 130r on 80r yel grn	4.00	3.00
66	A1 130r on 150r car, *rose*	5.00	3.00
67	A1 400r on 50r lt bl	8.00	6.00
68	A1 400r on 75r rose	8.00	6.00
69	A1 400r on 100r brn, *buff*	7.00	6.00
	On Newspaper Stamp of 1893		
70	N1 65r on 2½ brn	5.00	2.00
	Nos. 58-70 (13)	81.00	44.50

Surcharge exists inverted on Nos. 61, 70.
Nos. 64, 67 and 68 have been reprinted on thin white paper with shiny white gum and clean-cut perforation 13½. Value $6 each.
For overprints see Nos. 132-137, 140-143, 156-157, 160.

Issue of 1898-1903
Overprinted in Black

1903		*Perf. 11½*	
71	A2 15r brown	2.00	.85
72	A2 25r sea green	1.50	.85
73	A2 50r blue	2.50	.85
74	A2 75r rose	3.00	1.40
a.	Inverted overprint	50.00	50.00
	Nos. 71-74 (4)	9.00	3.95

Surcharged in Black

1905			
76	A2 50r on 65r dull blue	4.00	2.00

Regular Issues
Overprinted in
Carmine or Green

1911			
77	A2 2½r gray	.30	.25
78	A2 5r orange	.30	.25
a.	Double overprint	10.00	10.00
b.	Inverted overprint	10.00	10.00
79	A2 10r lt grn	.40	.35
80	A2 15r gray grn	.40	.40
a.	Inverted overprint	10.00	10.00
81	A2 20r dl vio	.40	.40
82	A2 25r car (G)	.90	.50
83	A2 50r brown	.80	.50
84	A2 75r lilac	1.00	.50
85	A2 100r dk bl, *bl*	.80	.55
86	A2 115r org brn, *pink*	9.00	3.50
87	A2 130r brn, *straw*	.80	.60

88	A2	200r red lil, *pnksh*		.85	.60
89	A2	400r dl bl, *straw*		1.25	1.10
90	A2	500r blk & red, *bl*		1.50	1.10
91	A2	700r vio, *yelsh*		1.75	1.25
		Nos. 77-91 (15)		20.45	11.80

Vasco da
Gama Issue of
Various
Portuguese
Colonies
Common
Design Types
Surcharged

1913   Perf. 12½-16
On Stamps of Macao

92	CD20	¼c on ½a bl grn	2.25	2.25
93	CD21	½c on la red	2.25	2.25
94	CD22	1c on 2a red vio	2.25	2.25
95	CD23	2½c on 4a yel grn	2.25	2.25
96	CD24	5c on 8a dk bl	2.25	2.25
97	CD25	7½c on 12a vio brn	4.25	4.25
98	CD26	10c on 16a bis brn	3.50	3.50
a.		Inverted surcharge	40.00	40.00
99	CD27	15c on 24a bister	3.75	3.75
		Nos. 92-99 (8)	22.75	22.75

On Stamps of Portuguese Africa

100	CD20	¼c on 2½ bl grn	1.75	1.75
101	CD21	½c on 5r red	1.75	1.75
102	CD22	1c on 10r red vio	1.75	1.75
103	CD23	2½c on 25r yel grn	1.75	1.75
104	CD24	5c on 50r dk bl	1.75	1.75
105	CD25	7½c on 75r vio brn	4.00	4.00
106	CD26	10c on 100r bis brn	2.75	2.75
107	CD27	15c on 150r bis	2.75	2.75
		Nos. 100-107 (8)	18.25	18.25

On Stamps of Timor

108	CD20	¼c on ½a bl grn	1.75	1.75
109	CD21	½c on 1a red	1.75	1.75
110	CD22	1c on 2a red vio	1.75	1.75
111	CD23	2½c on 4a yel grn	1.75	1.75
112	CD24	5c on 8a dk bl	2.00	1.75
113	CD25	7½c on 12a vio brn	4.00	4.00
114	CD26	10c on 16a bis brn	2.75	2.75
115	CD27	15c on 24a bister	2.75	2.75
		Nos. 108-115 (8)	18.50	18.25
		Nos. 92-115 (24)	59.50	59.25

Ceres — A4

1914   Typo.   Perf. 15x14
Name and Value in Black
Chalky Paper

116	A4	¼c olive brn	.35	.35
117	A4	½c black	.35	.35
118	A4	1c blue grn	.35	.35
119	A4	1½c lilac brn	.75	.75
120	A4	2c carmine	.75	.75
121	A4	2½c lt vio	.75	.75
122	A4	5c dp blue	.75	.75
123	A4	7½c yellow brn	.95	.75
124	A4	8c slate	.95	.75
125	A4	10c orange brn	1.50	.85
126	A4	15c plum	2.00	.70
127	A4	20c yellow grn	2.50	.90
128	A4	30c brown, *green*	4.00	1.00
129	A4	40c brown, *pink*	10.00	4.00
130	A4	50c orange, *sal*	9.00	3.00
131	A4	1e green, *blue*	15.00	3.00
		Nos. 116-131 (16)	39.25	16.00

Glazed Paper

131A	A4	1c blue grn	1.75	1.45
131B	A4	2½c lt vio	1.75	1.45

1918   Ordinary Paper

131C	A4	¼c olive brn	.25	.25
131D	A4	½c black	.25	.25
a.		Value omitted	20.00	
131E	A4	1c blue grn	.25	.25
131F	A4	1½c lilac brn	.25	.25
a.		Imperf.		
131G	A4	2c carmine	.25	.25
131H	A4	2½c lt vio	.25	.25
131I	A4	5c dp blue	.25	.25
131J	A4	7½c yellow brn	.50	.40
131K	A4	8c slate	.50	.40
131L	A4	10c orange brn	25.00	18.50
131M	A4	15c plum	2.00	.70
		Nos. 131C-131M (11)	29.75	21.75

For surcharges see Nos. 139, 159, 161-162, B1-B12.

In 1921 Nos. 131D and 131F were surcharged 10c and 30c respectively, for use in Mozambique as Nos. 230 and 231. These same values, surcharged 5c and 10c respectively, with the addition of the word "PORTEADO," were used in Mozambique as postage dues, Nos. J44 and J45.

Provisional Issue of
1902 Overprinted
Locally in Carmine

1914   Perf. 11½, 12½

132	A1	115r on 10r red vio	1.00	.45
a.		"Republica" inverted	20.00	
133	A1	115r on 200r bl, *bl*	1.00	.45
134	A1	115r on 300r bl, *sal*	1.10	.45
a.		Double overprint	40.00	40.00
135	A1	130r on 25r grn	1.50	.70
a.		Perf. 12½	3.25	1.60
136	A1	130r on 80r yel grn	1.10	.35
137	A1	130r on 150r car, *rose*	1.10	.35
		Nos. 132-137 (6)	6.80	2.75

No. 135a was issued without gum.

Nos. 78 and 117
Perforated Diagonally
and Surcharged in
Carmine

1915   Perf. 11½

138	A2	¼c on half of 5r org, pair	5.00	5.00
a.		Pair without dividing perfs.	20.00	20.00

Perf. 15x14

139	A4	¼c on half of ½c blk, pair	9.00	9.00

The added perforation on Nos. 138-139 runs from lower left to upper right corners, dividing the stamp in two. Values are for pairs, both halves of the stamp.

Provisional Issue of
1902 Overprinted in
Carmine

1915   Perf. 11½, 12½

140	A1	115r on 10r red vio	.55	.40
141	A1	115r on 200r bl, *bl*	.70	.40
142	A1	115r on 300r bl, *sal*	.70	.40
143	A1	130r on 150r car, *rose*	.75	.40
		Nos. 140-143 (4)	2.70	1.60

Nos. 34 and 80
Surcharged

1915   On Issue of 1903

144	A2	2c on 15r gray grn	.90	.80

On Issue of 1911

145	A2	2c on 15r gray grn	.90	.80
a.		New value inverted	22.50	

Regular Issues of
1898-1903
Overprinted Locally
in Carmine

1916

146	A2	15r gray grn	1.50	1.00
147	A2	50r brown	3.50	2.00
a.		Inverted overprint		
148	A2	75r lilac	3.50	2.00
149	A2	100r blue, *bl*	3.00	1.00
150	A2	115r org brn, *pink*	2.50	1.00
151	A2	130r brown, *straw*	10.00	5.00
152	A2	200r red lil, *pnksh*	7.00	2.00
153	A2	400r dull bl, *straw*	12.00	4.00
154	A2	500r blk & red, *bl*	7.00	3.00
155	A2	700r vio, *yelsh*	12.00	5.00
		Nos. 146-155 (10)	62.00	26.00

Same Overprint on Nos. 67-68

1917

156	A1	400r on 50r lt blue	1.25	.65
a.		Perf. 13½	11.50	9.00
157	A1	400r on 75r rose	2.50	1.00

No. 69 exists with this overprint. It was not officially issued.

Type of 1914
Surcharged in Red

1920   Perf. 15x14

159	A4	4c on 2½c violet	1.00	.30

Stamps of 1914 Surcharged in
Green or Black

a   b

1921

160	A1(a)	¼c on 115r on 10r red vio (G)	.80	.80
161	A4(b)	1c on 2½c vio (Bk)	.60	.40
a.		Inverted surcharge	40.00	
162	A4(b)	1½c on 2½c vio (Bk)	.80	.60
		Nos. 160-162 (3)	2.20	1.80

Nos. 159-162 were postally valid throughout Mozambique. No. 162 exists on glazed paper. Value the same as No. 162.

SEMI-POSTAL STAMPS

Regular Issue of 1914 Overprinted
or Surcharged

a

b

c

1918   Perf. 15x14½

B1	A4(a)	¼c olive brn	3.00	3.00
B2	A4(a)	½c black	3.00	4.00
B3	A4(a)	1c bl grn	3.00	4.00
B4	A4(a)	2½c violet	4.00	4.00
B5	A4(a)	5c blue	4.00	6.00

Chalky Paper

B5A	A4(a)	5c blue	4.00	6.00
B6	A4(a)	10c org brn	5.00	7.00
B7	A4(b)	20c on 1½c lil brn	5.00	8.00
B8	A4(b)	30c brn, *grn*	7.00	9.00
B9	A4(b)	40c on 2c car	7.00	10.00
B10	A4(b)	50c on 7½c bis	12.00	12.00
B11	A4(b)	70c on 8c slate	14.00	15.00
B12	A4(c)	$1 on 15c mag	20.00	15.00
		Nos. B1-B12 (13)	91.00	103.00

Nos. B1-B12 were used in place of ordinary postage stamps on Mar. 9, 1918. Nos. B3 and B4 also exist on glazed paper. The unsurfaced paper on which Nos. B1-B5 were printed show a diamond pattern when held to the light. This pattern is used to determine genuine stamps.

NEWSPAPER STAMPS

Numeral of
Value — N1

Perf. 11½

1893, July 28		**Typo.**		**Unwmk.**	
P1	N1	2½r brown		.25	.65
a.		Perf. 12½		20.00	17.50

For surcharge see No. 70.

Saint Anthony of Padua Issue

Mozambique No. P6
Overprinted

1895, July 1				**Perf. 11½, 13½**	
P2	N3	2½r brown		20.00	17.50
a.		Inverted overprint		30.00	30.00

LUXEMBOURG

ˈlək-səm-ˌbərg

LOCATION — Western Europe between southern Belgium, Germany and France
GOVT. — Grand Duchy
AREA — 999 sq. mi.
POP. — 476,200 (2007)
CAPITAL — Luxembourg

12½ Centimes = 1 Silbergroschen
100 Centimes = 1 Franc
100 Cents = 1 Euro (2002)

> Catalogue values for unused stamps in this country are for Never Hinged items, beginning with Scott 321 in the regular postage section, Scott B216 in the semi-postal section.

Watermarks

Wmk. 110 — Octagons

Wmk. 149 — W

Wmk. 213 — Double Wavy Lines

Wmk. 216 — Multiple Airplanes

Wmk. 246 — Multiple Cross Enclosed in Octagons

Wmk. 247 — Multiple Letters

Unused values of Nos. 1-47 are for stamps without gum. Though these stamps were issued with gum, most examples offered are without gum. Stamps with original gum sell for more.

Grand Duke William III — A1

Luxembourg Print
Wmk. 149

1852, Sept. 15   Engr.   Imperf.

1	A1	10c gray black	2,100.	55.00
a.		10c greenish black ('53)	2,250.	55.00
b.		10c intense black ('54)	2,400.	120.00
2	A1	1sg brown red ('53)	1,500.	75.00
a.		1sg brick red	1,500.	80.00
b.		1sg orange red ('54)	1,300.	87.50
c.		1sg blood red	2,750.	475.00
3	A1	1sg rose ('55)	1,350.	87.50
a.		1sg carmine rose ('56)	1,250.	80.00
b.		1sg dark carmine rose, thin paper ('59)	1,400.	240.00
		Nos. 1-3 (3)		217.50

Reprints of both values exist on watermarked paper. Some of the reprints show traces of lines cancelling the plates, but others can be distinguished only by an expert.
See Nos. 278-279, 603.

Coat of Arms
A2   A3

A4   A5

Frankfurt Print

1859-64   Typo.   Unwmk.

4	A2	1c buff ('63)	130.00	450.00
5	A2	2c black ('60)	95.00	550.00
6	A2	4c yellow ('64)	175.00	175.00
a.		4c orange ('64)	190.00	190.00
7	A2	10c blue	175.00	20.00
8	A3	12½c rose	275.00	160.00
9	A3	25c brown	350.00	275.00
10	A3	30c rose lilac	290.00	225.00
11	A3	37½c green	325.00	200.00
12	A3	40c red orange	875.00	240.00

Counterfeits of Nos. 1-12 exist.
See Nos. 13-25, 27-38, 40-47. For surcharges and overprints see Nos. 26, 39, O1-O51.

1865-71   Rouletted

13	A2	1c red brown	200.00	240.00
14	A2	2c black ('67)	20.00	13.50
15	A2	4c yellow ('67)	600.00	175.00
16	A2	4c green ('71)	40.00	24.00
		Nos. 13-16 (4)	860.00	452.50

1865-74   Rouletted in Color

17	A2	1c red brn ('72)	35.00	8.00
18	A2	1c orange ('69)	40.00	8.00
a.		1c brown orange ('67)	120.00	35.00
b.		1c red orange ('69)	1,350.	325.00
19	A3	10c rose lilac	120.00	4.00
a.		10c lilac	100.00	4.00
b.		10c gray lilac	100.00	4.00
20	A3	12½c carmine ('71)	175.00	8.00
a.		12½c rose	175.00	8.00
21	A3	20c gray brown ('72)	120.00	8.00
a.		20c yellow brown ('69)	125.00	8.00
22	A3	25c blue ('72)	1,100.	11.00
22A	A3	25c ultra ('65)	1,100.	11.00
23	A3	30c lilac rose	1,200.	80.00
24	A3	37½c bister ('66)	750.00	240.00
25	A3	40c pale orange ('74)	40.00	80.00
a.		40c orange red ('66)	1,050.	60.00
26	A4	1fr on 37 ½c bis ('73)	875.00	80.00
a.		Surcharge inverted		3,600.

Luxembourg Print

1874   Typo.   Imperf.

27	A2	4c green	110.00	110.00

1875-79   Perf. 13
Narrow Margins

29	A2	1c red brown ('78)	35.00	8.00
30	A2	2c black	125.00	27.50
31	A2	4c green	2.40	9.50
32	A2	5c yellow ('76)	175.00	24.00
a.		5c orange yellow	600.00	125.00
b.		Imperf.	925.00	1,100.
33	A3	10c gray lilac	475.00	2.40
b.		10c lilac	1,350.	29.00
c.		Imperf.	2,700.	3,250.
34	A3	12½c lilac rose ('77)	600.00	20.00
35	A3	12½c car rose ('76)	400.00	27.50
36	A3	25c blue ('77)	800.00	14.00
37	A3	30c dull rose ('78)	750.00	450.00
38	A3	40c orange ('79)	1.60	9.50
39	A5	1fr on 37 ½c bis ('79)	8.00	27.50
a.		"Pranc"	5,250.	6,400.
b.		Without surcharge	475.00	
c.		As "b," imperf.	700.00	
		As "c," pair	1,400.	

In the Luxembourg print the perforation is close to the border of the stamp. Excellent forgeries of No. 39a are plentiful, as well as faked cancellations on Nos. 31, 38 and 39.
Nos. 32b and 33c are said to be essays; Nos. 39b and 39c printer's waste.

Haarlem Print

1880-81   Perf. 11½x12, 12½x12, 13½
Wide Margins

40	A2	1c yel brn ('81)	8.75	6.00
41	A2	2c black	7.25	1.60
42	A2	5c yellow ('81)	200.00	95.00
43	A3	10c gray lilac	160.00	1.60
44	A3	12½c rose ('81)	190.00	190.00
45	A3	20c gray brown ('81)	45.00	20.00
46	A3	25c blue	240.00	4.75
47	A3	30c dull rose ('81)	8.00	24.00

Gray Yellowish Paper
Perf. 12½

42a	A2	5c		7.25
43a	A3	10c		4.00
44a	A3	12½c		9.50
46a	A3	25c		5.50
		Nos. 42a-46a (4)		26.25

Nos. 42a-46a were not regularly issued.

"Industry" and "Commerce"
A6

Grand Duke Adolphe
A7

Perf. 11½x12, 12½x12, 12½, 13½
1882, Dec. 1   Typo.

48	A6	1c gray lilac	.25	.40
49	A6	2c olive gray	.25	.40
50	A6	4c olive bister	.25	2.00
51	A6	5c lt green	.80	.40
52	A6	10c rose	8.00	.40
53	A6	12½c slate	1.25	24.00
54	A6	20c orange	3.25	1.60
55	A6	25c ultra	175.00	1.60
56	A6	30c gray green	24.00	12.00
57	A6	50c bister brown	1.20	12.00
58	A6	1fr pale violet	1.60	24.00
59	A6	5fr brown orange	37.50	160.00
		Nos. 48-59 (12)	253.35	238.80

For overprints see Nos. O52-O64.

Perf. 11, 11½, 11½x11, 12½
1891-93   Engr.

60	A7	10c carmine	.80	.40
a.		Sheet of 25, perf. 11 ½	125.00	
61	A7	12½c slate grn ('93)	1.20	.80
62	A7	20c orange ('93)	8.00	.80
b.		20c brown, perf. 11 ½	160.00	240.00
63	A7	25c blue	.80	.80
a.		Sheet of 25, perf. 11 ½	1,000.	
64	A7	30c olive grn ('93)	1.60	1.25
65	A7	37½c green ('93)	3.25	3.25
66	A7	50c brown ('93)	7.25	4.00
67	A7	1fr dp violet ('93)	14.50	6.50
68	A7	2½fr black ('93)	1.60	20.00
69	A7	5fr lake ('93)	29.00	72.50
		Nos. 60-69 (10)	68.00	110.30

No. 62a was never on sale at any post office, but exists postally used.
Perf. 11 ½ stamps are from the sheets of 25.
For overprints see Nos. O65-O74.

Grand Duke Adolphe — A8

1895, May 4   Typo.   Perf. 12½

70	A8	1c pearl gray	3.25	.40
71	A8	2c gray brown	.40	.25
72	A8	4c olive bister	.40	.90
73	A8	5c green	5.50	.25
74	A8	10c carmine	14.50	.25
		Nos. 70-74 (5)	24.05	2.05

For overprints see Nos. O75-O79.

Coat of Arms — A9   Grand Duke William IV — A10

1906-26   Typo.   Perf. 12½

75	A9	1c gray ('07)	.25	.25
76	A9	2c olive brn ('07)	.25	.25
77	A9	4c bister ('07)	.25	.25
78	A9	5c green ('07)	.25	.25
79	A9	5c lilac ('26)	.25	.25
80	A9	6c violet ('07)	.25	.25
81	A9	7½c orange ('19)	.25	3.25

Engr.
Perf. 11, 11½x11

82	A10	10c scarlet	1.60	.25
a.		Souvenir sheet of 10	450.00	1,200.
83	A10	12½c slate grn ('07)	1.60	.40
84	A10	15c orange brn ('07)	1.60	.65
85	A10	20c orange ('07)	2.75	.55
86	A10	25c ultra ('07)	72.50	.40
87	A10	30c olive grn ('08)	1.20	.55
88	A10	37½c green ('07)	1.20	.80
a.		Perf. 12 ½	16.00	12.00
89	A10	50c brown ('07)	4.00	.80
90	A10	87½c dk blue ('08)	1.60	12.00
91	A10	1fr violet ('08)	4.75	1.60
92	A10	2½fr vermilion ('08)	72.50	80.00
93	A10	5fr claret ('08)	12.00	65.00
		Nos. 75-93 (19)	179.05	167.75

No. 82a for accession of Grand Duke William IV to the throne.
For surcharges and overprints see Nos. 94-96, 112-117, O80-O98.

Nos. 90, 92-93 Surcharged in Red or Black

62½ cts.

1912-15

94	A10	62 ½c on 87 ½c (R)	3.25	2.00
95	A10	62 ½c on 2 ½fr (Bk) ('15)	3.25	4.00
96	A10	62 ½c on 5fr (Bk) ('15)	1.60	2.75
		Nos. 94-96 (3)	8.10	8.75

Grand Duchess Marie Adelaide — A11

1914-17   Engr.   Perf. 11½, 11½x11

97	A11	10c lake	.25	.25
98	A11	12½c dull green	.25	.25
99	A11	15c sepia	.25	.25
100	A11	17½c dp brown ('17)	.25	.40
101	A11	25c ultra	.25	.25
102	A11	30c bister	.25	.40
103	A11	35c dark blue	.25	.40
104	A11	37½c black brn	.25	.40
105	A11	40c orange	.25	.40
106	A11	50c dark gray	.25	.40
107	A11	62½c blue green	.40	2.40
108	A11	87½c orange ('17)	.40	2.40
109	A11	1fr orange brown	2.00	.55

110	A11	2½fr red	.40	2.00
111	A11	5fr dark violet	9.50	47.50
		Nos. 97-111 (15)	15.20	58.25
		Set, never hinged	42.50	

For surcharges and overprints see Nos. 118-124, B7-B10, O99-O113. Nos. 97, 98, 101, 107, 109 and 111 overprinted "Droits de statistique" are revenue stamps.

Stamps of 1906-19 Surcharged with New Value and Bars in Black or Red
1916-24

112	A9	2½c on 5c ('18)	.25	.25
a.		Double surcharge	75.00	
113	A9	3c on 2c ('21)	.25	.25
114	A9	5c on 1c ('23)	.25	.25
115	A9	5c on 4c ('23)	.25	.40
116	A9	5c on 7½c ('24)	.25	.25
117	A9	6c on 2c (R) ('22)	.25	.25
118	A11	7½c on 10c ('18)	.25	.25
119	A11	17½c on 30c	.25	.40
120	A11	20c on 17½c ('21)	.25	.25
121	A11	25c on 37½c ('23)	.25	.25
a.		Double surcharge	90.00	
122	A11	75c on 62½c (R) ('22)	.25	.25
123	A11	80c on 87½c ('22)	.25	.25
124	A11	87½c on 1fr	.55	5.50
		Nos. 112-124 (13)	3.55	8.80

Grand Duchess Charlotte — A12

1921, Jan. 6   Engr.   Perf. 11½

125	A12	15c rose	.25	.25
a.		Sheet of 5, perf 11	150.00	250.00
		Never hinged	350.00	
b.		Sheet of 25, perf. 11½, 11x11½, 12x11½	5.50	17.00

Birth of Prince Jean, first son of Grand Duchess Charlotte, Jan. 5 (No. 125a). No. 125 was printed in sheets of 100.

See Nos. 131-150. For surcharges and overprints see Nos. 154-158, O114-O131, O136.

Vianden Castle — A13

Foundries at Esch — A14

Adolphe Bridge — A15

1921-34   Perf. 11, 11½, 11x11½

126	A13	1fr carmine	.25	.40
127	A13	1fr dk blue ('26)	.25	.45

Perf. 11½x11; 11½ (#129, 130)

128	A14	2fr indigo	.30	.80
129	A14	2fr dk brown ('26)	7.00	2.00
130	A15	5fr dk violet	20.00	9.50
		Nos. 126-130 (5)	27.80	13.15

For overprints see Nos. O132-O135, O137-138, O140. See No. B85.

Charlotte Type of 1921
1921-26   Perf. 11½

131	A12	2c brown	.25	.25
132	A12	3c olive green	.25	.25
a.		Sheet of 25	10.00	25.00
133	A12	6c violet	.25	.25
a.		Sheet of 25	10.00	25.00
134	A12	10c yellow grn	.25	.25
135	A12	10c olive brn ('24)	.25	.25
136	A12	15c brown olive	.25	.25
137	A12	15c pale green ('24)	.25	.25
138	A12	15c dp orange ('26)	.25	.25
139	A12	20c dp orange	.25	.25
a.		Sheet of 25	60.00	110.00
140	A12	20c yellow grn ('26)	.25	.25
141	A12	25c dk green	.25	.25
142	A12	30c carmine rose	.25	.25

143	A12	40c brown orange	.25	.25
144	A12	50c deep blue	.40	.45
145	A12	50c red ('24)	.25	.25
146	A12	75c red	.25	1.20
a.		Sheet of 25	325.00	
147	A12	75c deep blue ('24)	.25	.25
148	A12	80c black	.65	1.25
a.		Sheet of 25	325.00	
		Nos. 131-148 (18)	5.05	6.65

For surcharges and overprints see Nos. 154-158, O114-O131, O136.

Philatelic Exhibition Issue
1922, Aug. 27   Imperf.
Laid Paper

149	A12	25c dark green	2.25	6.00
150	A12	30c carmine rose	2.25	6.00

Nos. 149 and 150 were sold exclusively at the Luxembourg Phil. Exhib., Aug. 1922.

Souvenir Sheet

View of Luxembourg — A16

1923, Jan. 3   Perf. 11

151	A16	10fr dp grn, sheet	1,000.	2,400.

Birth of Princess Elisabeth.

1923, Mar.   Perf. 11½

152	A16	10fr black	9.50	13.50
a.		Perf. 12½ ('34)	8.00	12.00

For overprint see No. O141.

The Wolfsschlucht near Echternach — A17

1923-34   Perf. 11½

153	A17	3fr dk blue & blue	2.75	.80
a.		Perf. 12½ ('34)	2.75	.80

For overprint see No. O139.

Stamps of 1921-26 Surcharged with New Values and Bars
1925-28

154	A12	5c on 10c yel grn	.25	.30
155	A12	15c on 20c yel grn ('28)	.25	.25
a.		Bars omitted		
156	A12	35c on 40c brn org ('27)	.25	.25
157	A12	60c on 75c dp bl ('27)	.25	.25
158	A12	60c on 80c blk ('28)	.40	.35
		Nos. 154-158 (5)	1.40	1.40

Grand Duchess Charlotte — A18

1926-35   Engr.   Perf. 12

159	A18	5c dk violet	.25	.25
160	A18	10c olive grn	.25	.25
161	A18	15c black ('30)	.25	.25
162	A18	20c orange	.40	.40
163	A18	25c yellow grn	.40	.40
164	A18	25c vio brn ('27)	.35	.25
165	A18	30c yel grn ('27)	.35	.50
166	A18	30c gray vio ('30)	.25	.25
167	A18	30c gray vio ('28)	3.00	
168	A18	35c yel grn ('30)	.25	.25
169	A18	40c olive gray	.25	.30
170	A18	50c red brown	.25	.30
171	A18	60c blue grn ('28)	3.00	.25
172	A18	65c black brn	.25	1.10
173	A18	70c blue vio ('35)	.25	.25
174	A18	75c rose	.25	.65
175	A18	75c bis brn ('27)	.25	.25

176	A18	80c bister brn	.35	1.60
177	A18	90c rose ('27)	1.50	1.40
178	A18	1fr black	1.25	.60
179	A18	1fr rose ('30)	.60	.25
180	A18	1¼fr dk blue	.25	.45
181	A18	1¼fr yellow ('30)	15.00	1.60
182	A18	1¼fr blue grn ('31)	.45	.25
183	A18	1¼fr rose car ('34)	22.50	2.00
184	A18	1½fr dp blue ('27)	3.00	1.40
185	A18	1¾fr dk blue ('30)	.75	.25
		Nos. 159-185 (27)	55.95	15.95
		Set, never hinged	90.00	

For surcharges and overprints see Nos. 186-193, N17-N29, O142-O178.

Stamps of 1926-35, Surcharged with New Values and Bars
1928-39

186	A18	10(c) on 30c yel grn ('29)	.50	.40
187	A18	15c on 25c yel grn	.40	.55
187A	A18	30c on 60c bl grn ('39)	.30	1.60
188	A18	60c on 65c blk brn	.25	.40
189	A18	60c on 75c rose	.25	.40
190	A18	60c on 80c bis brn	.35	.65
191	A18	70(c) on 75c bis brn ('35)	12.00	.40
192	A18	75(c) on 90c rose ('29)	2.00	.40
193	A18	1¾(fr) on 1½fr dp bl ('29)	5.50	1.60
		Nos. 186-193 (9)	21.55	6.40
		Set, never hinged	45.00	

The surcharge on No. 187A has no bars.

View of Clervaux A19

1928-34   Perf. 12½

194	A19	2fr black ('34)	1.75	.80
		Never hinged	4.00	
a.		Perf. 11½ ('28)	2.75	.80
		Never hinged	4.00	

See No. B66. For overprint see No. O179.

Coat of Arms — A20

1930, Dec. 20   Typo.   Perf. 12½

195	A20	5c claret	.85	.40
196	A20	10c olive green	1.10	.25
		Set, never hinged	5.50	

View of the Lower City of Luxembourg A21

Gate of "Three Towers" A22

1931, June 20   Engr.

197	A21	20fr deep green	3.50	17.50
		Never hinged	8.00	

For overprint see No. O180.

1934, Aug. 30   Perf. 14x13½

198	A22	5fr blue green	3.00	9.50
		Never hinged	8.50	

For surcharge and overprint see Nos. N31, O181.

Castle From Our Valley A23

1935, Nov. 15   Perf. 12½x12

199	A23	10fr green	3.00	14.00
		Never hinged	6.50	

For surcharge and overprint see Nos. N32, O182.

Municipal Palace — A24

1936, Aug. 26   Photo.   Perf. 11½
Granite Paper

200	A24	10c brown	.25	.45
201	A24	35c green	.35	.90
202	A24	70c red orange	.40	1.40
203	A24	1fr carmine rose	2.00	8.50
204	A24	1.25fr violet	2.50	12.00
205	A24	1.75fr brt ultra	1.60	9.00
		Nos. 200-205 (6)	7.10	32.25
		Set, never hinged	16.00	

11th Cong. of Intl. Federation of Philately. See No. 859.

Arms of Luxembourg A25

William I A26

Designs: 70c, William II. 75c, William III. 1fr, Prince Henry. 1.25fr, Grand Duke Adolphe. 1.75fr, William IV. 3fr, Regent Marie Anne. 5fr, Grand Duchess Marie Adelaide. 10fr, Grand Duchess Charlotte.

1939, May 27   Engr.   Perf. 12½x12

206	A25	35c brt green	.25	.25
207	A26	50c orange	.25	.25
208	A26	70c slate green	.25	.25
209	A26	75c sepia	.65	.95
210	A26	1fr red	1.60	2.00
211	A26	1.25fr brown violet	.25	.25
212	A26	1.75fr dark blue	.25	.25
213	A26	3fr lt brown	.25	.50
214	A26	5fr gray black	.50	8.00
215	A26	10fr copper red	.75	10.00
		Nos. 206-215 (10)	5.00	22.70
		Set, never hinged	8.50	

Centenary of Independence.

Allegory of Medicinal Baths — A35

1939, Sept. 18   Photo.   Perf. 11½

216	A35	2fr brown rose	.50	4.00
		Never hinged	1.25	

Elevation of Mondorf-les-Bains to town status.

See No. B104. For surcharge see No. N30.

1958, Sept. 13   Engr.   Perf. 11x11½
344 A76 2.50fr slate & sepia   .75 .25
345 A77 2.50fr lt grn & sepia   .75 .25

No. 345 issued to publicize 2,000 years of grape growing in Luxembourg region.

Grand Duchess Charlotte — A78

NATO Emblem — A79

1959, Jan. 15   Photo.   Perf. 11½
346 A78 1.50fr pale grn & dk grn   1.00 .50
347 A78 2.50fr pink & dk brn   1.00 .50
348 A78 5fr lt bl & dk bl   1.65 1.25
   Nos. 346-348 (3)   3.65 2.25

40th anniv. of the accession to the throne of the Grand Duchess Charlotte.

1959, Apr. 3   Perf. 12½x12
349 A79 2.50fr brt ol & bl   .25 .25
350 A79 8.50fr red brn & bl   .50 .35

NATO, 10th anniversary.

Flower Type of 1955, Inscribed "1959"
1fr, Iris. 2.50fr, Peonies. 3fr, Hydrangea.

1959, Apr. 3   Perf. 11½
Flowers in Natural Colors
351 A58 1fr dk bl grn   .35 .35
352 A58 2.50fr deep blue   .50 .35
353 A58 3fr deep red lilac   .65 .65
   Nos. 351-353 (3)   1.50 1.35

Flower festival, Mondorf-les-Bains.

Europa Issue, 1959
Common Design Type
Perf. 12½x13½
1959, Sept. 19   Litho.
Size: 22x33mm
354 CD2 2.50fr olive   1.75 .45
355 CD2 5fr dk blue   1.75 .95

Locomotive of 1859 and Hymn — A80

1959, Sept. 19   Engr.   Perf. 13½
356 A80 2.50fr red & ultra   2.00 .35

Centenary of Luxembourg's railroads.

Man and Child Knocking at Door — A81

Holy Family, Flight into Egypt A82

Perf. 11½x11, 11x11½
1960, Apr. 7   Unwmk.
357 A81 2.50fr org & slate   .25 .25
358 A82 5fr pur & slate   .40 .40

World Refugee Year, July 1, 1959-June 30, 1960.

Steel Worker Drawing CECA Initials and Map of Member Countries A83

1960, May 9   Perf. 11x11½
359 A83 2.50fr dk car rose   .70 .25

10th anniv. of the Schumann Plan for a European Steel and Coal Community.

European School and Children A84

1960, May 9
360 A84 5fr bl & gray blk   1.10 .90

Establishment of the first European school in Luxembourg.

Heraldic Lion and Tools A85

1960, June 14   Photo.   Perf. 11½
361 A85 2.50fr gray, red, bl & blk 1.40 .30

Natl. Exhibition of Craftsmanship, Luxembourg-Limpertsberg, July 9-18.

Grand Duchess Charlotte — A86

1960-64   Engr.   Unwmk.
362 A86 10c claret ('61)   .25 .25
363 A86 20c rose red ('61)   .25 .25
363A A86 25c org ('64)   .25 .25
364 A86 30c gray olive   .25 .25
365 A86 50c dull grn   .60 .25
366 A86 1fr vio blue   .75 .25
367 A86 1.50fr rose lilac   .75 .25
368 A86 2fr blue ('61)   .80 .25
369 A86 2.50fr rose vio   1.40 .25
370 A86 3fr vio brn ('61)   1.60 .25
371 A86 3.50fr aqua ('64)   2.25 1.90
372 A86 5fr lt red brn   2.25 .25
373 A86 6fr slate ('64)   2.75 .25
   Nos. 362-373 (13)   14.15 4.90

The 50c, 1fr and 3fr were issued in sheets and in coils. Every fifth coil stamp has control number on back.

Europa Issue, 1960
Common Design Type
1960, Sept. 19   Perf. 11x11½
Size: 37x27mm
374 CD3 2.50fr indigo & emer   .50 .40
375 CD3 5fr maroon & blk   .50 .40

Great Spotted Woodpecker A87

Clervaux and Abbey of St. Maurice and St. Maur A88

Designs: 1.50fr, Cat, horiz. 3fr, Filly, horiz. 8.50fr, Dachshund.

1961, May 15   Photo.   Perf. 11½
376 A87 1fr multicolored   .25 .25
377 A87 1.50fr multicolored   .25 .25
378 A87 3fr gray, buff & red brn   .55 .30
379 A87 8.50fr lt grn, blk & ocher 1.10 .75
   Nos. 376-379 (4)   2.15 1.55

Issued to publicize animal protection.

1961, June 8   Engr.   Perf. 11½x11
380 A88 2.50fr green   .70 .25

General Patton Monument, Ettelbruck A89

1961, June 8   Perf. 11x11½
381 A89 2.50fr dark blue & gray   .70 .25

The monument commemorates the American victory of the 3rd Army under Gen. George S. Patton, Jr., Battle of the Ardennes Bulge, 1944-45.

Europa Issue, 1961
Common Design Type
1961, Sept. 18   Perf. 13x12½
Size: 29½x27mm
382 CD4 2.50fr red   .35 .35
383 CD4 5fr blue   .35 .35

Cyclist Carrying Bicycle — A90

Design: 5fr, Emblem of 1962 championship.

1962, Jan. 22   Photo.   Perf. 11½
384 A90 2.50fr lt ultra, crim & blk .25 .25
385 A90 5fr multicolored   .45 .40

Intl. Cross-country Bicycle Race, Esch-sur-Alzette, Feb. 18.

Europa Issue, 1962
Common Design Type
1962, Sept. 17   Unwmk.   Perf. 11½
Size: 32½x23mm
386 CD5 2.50fr ol bis, yel grn & brn blk   .35 .30
387 CD5 5fr rose lil, lt grn & brn blk   .50 .40

St. Laurent's Church, Diekirch — A91

1962, Sept. 17   Engr.   Perf. 11½x11
388 A91 2.50fr brown & blk   .50 .25

Bock Rock Castle, 10th Century A92

Gate of Three Towers, 11th Century — A93

Designs (each stamp represents a different century): No. 391, Benedictine Abbey, Munster. No. 392, Great Seal of Luxembourg, 1237. No. 393, Rham Towers. No. 394, Black Virgin, Grund. No. 395, Grand Ducal Palace. No. 396, The Citadel of the Holy Ghost. No. 397, Castle Bridge. No. 398, Town Hall. No. 399, Municipal theater, bridge and European Community Center.

Perf. 14x13 (A92), 11½ (A93)
Engr. (A92), Photo. (A93)
1963, Apr. 13
389 A92 1fr slate blue   .25 .25
390 A92 1fr multicolored   .25 .25
391 A92 1.50fr dl red brn   .25 .25
392 A92 1.50fr multicolored   .25 .25
393 A92 2.50fr gray grn   .25 .25
394 A92 2.50fr multicolored   .25 .25
395 A92 3fr brown   .25 .25
396 A93 3fr multicolored   .25 .25
397 A93 5fr brt violet   .25 .25
398 A93 5fr multicolored   .60 .60
399 A92 11fr multicolored   1.40 .65
   Nos. 389-399 (11)   4.25 3.50

Millennium of the city of Luxembourg; MELUSINA Intl. Phil. Exhib., Luxembourg, Apr. 13-21. Set sold only at exhibition. Value of 62fr included entrance ticket. Nos. 390, 392, 394 and 396 however were sold without restriction.

Blackboard Showing European School Buildings — A94

1963, Apr. 13   Photo.   Perf. 11½
400 A94 2.50fr gray, grn & mag   .40 .25

10th anniv. of the European Schools in Luxembourg, Brussels, Varese, Mol and Karlsruhe.

Colpach Castle and Centenary Emblem A95

1963, May 8   Engr.   Perf. 13
401 A95 2.50fr hn brn, gray & red   .35 .25

Centenary of the Intl. Red Cross. Colpach Castle, home of Emile Mayrisch, was donated to the Luxembourg League of the Red Cross for a rest home.

Twelve Stars of Council of Europe — A96

1963, June 25   Perf. 13x14
402 A96 2.50fr dp ultra, gold   .35 .25

10th anniv. of the European Convention of Human Rights.

Europa Issue, 1963
Common Design Type
1963, Sept. 16   Photo.   Perf. 11½
Size: 32½x23mm

403	CD6 3fr bl grn, lt grn & org	.50	.40
404	CD6 6fr red brn, org red & org	.50	.40

Brown Trout Taking Bait — A97

1963, Sept. 16   Engr.   Perf. 13
405	A97 3fr indigo	.30	.25

World Fly-Fishing Championship, Wormeldange, Sept. 22.

Map of Luxembourg, Telephone Dial and Stars — A98   Power House — A99

1963, Sept. 16   Photo.   Perf. 11½
406	A98 3fr ultra, brt grn & blk	.35	.25

Completion of telephone automation.

1964, Apr. 17   Engr.   Perf. 13

3fr, Upper reservoir, horiz. 6fr, Lohmuhle dam.

407	A99 2fr red brn & sl	.25	.25
408	A99 3fr red, sl grn & lt bl	.25	.25
409	A99 6fr choc, grn & bl	.25	.25
	Nos. 407-409 (3)	.75	.75

Inauguration of the Vianden hydroelectric station.

Barge Entering Lock at Grevenmacher Dam — A100

1964, May 26   Unwmk.
410	A100 3fr indigo & brt bl	.35	.25

Opening of Moselle River canal system.

Europa Issue, 1964
Common Design Type
1964, Sept. 14   Photo.   Perf. 11½
Size: 22x38mm

411	CD7 3fr org brn, yel & dk bl	.35	.25
412	CD7 6fr yel grn, yel & dk brn	.55	.30

New Atheneum Educational Center and Students A101

1964, Sept. 14   Unwmk.
413	A101 3fr dk bl grn & blk	.30	.25

Benelux Issue

King Baudouin, Queen Juliana and Grand Duchess Charlotte — A101a

1964, Oct. 12   Size: 45x26mm
414	A101a 3fr dull bl, yel & brn	.30	.25

20th anniv. of the customs union of Belgium, Netherlands and Luxembourg.

Grand Duke Jean and Grand Duchess Josephine Charlotte A102

1964, Nov. 11   Photo.   Perf. 11½
415	A102 3fr indigo	.35	.25
416	A102 6fr dk brown	.50	.30

Grand Duke Jean's accession to throne.

Rotary Emblem and Cogwheels A103   Grand Duke Jean A104

1965, Apr. 5   Photo.   Perf. 11½
417	A103 3fr gold, car, gray & ultra	.40	.25

Rotary International, 60th anniversary.

1965-71   Engr.   Unwmk.
418	A104 25c olive bister ('66)	.25	.25
419	A104 50c rose red	.25	.25
420	A104 1fr ultra	.25	.25
421	A104 1.50fr dk vio brn ('66)	.25	.25
422	A104 2fr magenta ('66)	.25	.25
423	A104 2.50fr orange ('71)	.35	.25
424	A104 3fr gray	.50	.25
425	A104 3.50fr brn org ('66)	.35	.40
426	A104 4fr vio brn ('71)	.30	.25
427	A104 5fr green ('71)	.35	.25
428	A104 6fr purple	.95	.25
429	A104 8fr bl grn ('71)	.80	.25
	Nos. 418-429 (12)	4.85	3.15

The 50c, 1fr, 2fr, 3fr, 4fr, 5fr and 6fr were issued in sheets and in coils. Every fifth coil stamp has control number on back.

See Nos. 570-576.

ITU Emblem, Old and New Communication Equipment — A105

1965, May 17   Litho.   Perf. 13½
431	A105 3fr dk pur, claret & blk	.35	.25

ITU, centenary.

Europa Issue, 1965
Common Design Type
Perf. 13x12½
1965, Sept. 27   Photo.   Unwmk.
Size: 30x23½mm

432	CD8 3fr grn, maroon & blk	.40	.30
433	CD8 6fr tan, dk bl & grn	.40	.30

Inauguration of WHO Headquarters, Geneva — A106

1966, Mar. 7   Engr.   Perf. 11x11½
434	A106 3fr green	.30	.25

Torch and Banner — A107

1966, Mar. 7   Photo.   Perf. 11½
435	A107 3fr gray & brt red	.30	.25

50th anniversary of the Workers' Federation in Luxembourg.

Key and Arms of City of Luxembourg, and Arms of Prince of Chimay — A108

Designs: 2fr, Interior of Cathedral of Luxembourg, painting by Juan Martin. 3fr, Our Lady of Luxembourg, engraving by Richard Collin. 6fr, Column and spandrel with sculptured angels from Cathedral.

1966, Apr. 28   Engr.   Perf. 13x14
436	A108 1.50fr green	.25	.25
437	A108 2fr dull red	.25	.25
438	A108 3fr dk blue	.25	.25
439	A108 6fr red brown	.25	.25
	Nos. 436-439 (4)	1.00	1.00

300th anniv. of the Votum Solemne (Solemn Promise) which made the Virgin Mary Patron Saint of the City of Luxembourg.

Europa Issue, 1966
Common Design Type
Perf. 13½x12½
1966, Sept. 26   Litho.
Size: 25x37mm

440	CD9 3fr gray & vio bl	.40	.30
441	CD9 6fr olive & dk grn	.40	.30

Diesel Locomotive A109

Design: 3fr, Electric locomotive.

1966, Sept. 26   Photo.   Perf. 11½
442	A109 1.50fr multicolored	.40	.25
443	A109 3fr multicolored	.40	.30

5th Intl. Philatelic Exhibition of Luxembourg Railroad Men, Sept. 30-Oct. 3.

Grand Duchess Charlotte Bridge A110

1966, Sept. 26   Engr.   Perf. 13
444	A110 3fr dk car rose	.30	.25

Tower Building, Kirchberg, Seat of European Community — A111

Design: 13fr, Design for Robert Schuman monument, Luxembourg.

1966, Sept. 26
445	A111 1.50fr dk green	.25	.25
446	A111 13fr deep blue	.55	.25

"Luxembourg, Center of Europe."

View of Luxembourg, 1850, by Nicolas Liez — A112

Map of Luxembourg Fortress, 1850, by Theodore de Cederstolpe — A113

1967, Mar. 6   Engr.   Perf. 13
447	A112 3fr bl, vio brn & grn	.25	.25
448	A113 6fr blue, brn & red	.30	.25

Centenary of the Treaty of London, which guaranteed the country's neutrality after the dismantling of the Fortress of Luxembourg.

Europa Issue, 1967
Common Design Type
1967, May 2   Photo.   Perf. 11½
Size: 33x22mm

449	CD10 3fr cl brn, gray & buff	.50	.35
450	CD10 6fr dk brn, vio gray & lt bl	.50	.35

Lion, Globe and Lions Emblem — A115

1967, May 2   Photo.   Perf. 11½
451	A115 3fr multicolored	.30	.25

Lions International, 50th anniversary.

Canceled to Order
Luxembourg's Office des Timbres, Direction des Postes, was offering, at least as early as 1967, to sell commemorative issues canceled to order.

NATO Emblem and European Community Administration Building — A116

1967, June 13   Litho.   Perf. 13x12½
452 A116 3fr lt grn & dk grn .25 .25
453 A116 6fr dp rose & dk car .40 .40
NATO Council meeting, Luxembourg, June 13-14.

Youth Hostel, Ettelbruck A117

Home Gardener A118

1967, Sept. 14   Photo.   Perf. 11½
454 A117 1.50fr multicolored .30 .25
Luxembourg youth hostels.

1967, Sept. 14
455 A118 1.50fr brt grn & org .30 .25
16th Congress of the Intl. Assoc. of Home Gardeners.

Shaving Basin with Wedding Scene, 1819 — A119

Design: 3fr, Ornamental vase, 1820, vert.

1967, Sept. 14
456 A119 1.50fr ol grn & multi .30 .25
457 A119 3fr ultra & lt gray .30 .25
Faience industry in Luxembourg, 200th anniv.

Wormeldange - Moselle River — A120

Mertert, Moselle River Port A121

1967, Sept. 14   Engr.   Perf. 13
458 A120 3fr dp bl, claret & ol .50 .25
459 A121 3fr violet bl & slate .50 .25

Swimming — A122

Sport: 1.50fr, Soccer. 2fr, Bicycling. 3fr, Running. 6fr, Walking. 13fr, Fencing.

1968, Feb. 22   Photo.   Perf. 11½
460 A122 50c bl & grnsh bl .25 .25
461 A122 1.50fr brt grn & emer .25 .25
462 A122 2fr yel grn & lt yel grn .25 .25
463 A122 3fr dp org & dl org .25 .25
464 A122 6fr grnsh bl & pale grn .30 .25
465 A122 13fr rose cl & rose .50 .25
Nos. 460-465 (6) 1.80 1.50
Issued to publicize the 19th Olympic Games, Mexico City, Oct. 12-27.

Europa Issue, 1968
Common Design Type
1968, Apr. 29   Photo.   Perf. 11½
Size: 32½x23mm
466 CD11 3fr ap grn, blk & org brn .40 .35
467 CD11 6fr brn org, blk & ap grn .40 .35

Kind Spring Pavilion A123

1968, Apr. 29   Photo.   Perf. 11½
468 A123 3fr multicolored .30 .25
Issued to publicize Mondorf-les-Bains.

Fair Emblem A124

1968, Apr. 29
469 A124 3fr dp vio, dl bl gold & red .30 .25
20th Intl. Fair, Luxembourg City, May 23-June 2.

Children's Village of Mersch A125

Orphan and Foster Mother — A126

1968, Sept. 18   Engr.   Perf. 13
470 A125 3fr slate grn & dk red brn .25 .25
471 A126 6fr slate bl, blk & brn .45 .25
Mersch children's village. (Modeled after Austrian SOS villages for homeless children.)

Red Cross and Symbolic Blood Transfusion — A127

1968, Sept. 18   Photo.   Perf. 11½
472 A127 3fr lt blue & car .50 .25
Voluntary Red Cross blood donors.

Luxair Plane over Luxembourg — A128

1968, Sept. 18   Engr.   Perf. 13
473 A128 50fr olive, bl & dk bl 3.00 .30
Issued for tourist publicity.

Souvenir Sheet

"Youth and Leisure" — A129

Designs, a, 3fr, Doll. b, 6fr, Ballplayers. c, 13fr, Book, compass rose and ball.

1969, Apr. 3   Photo.   Perf. 11½
Granite Paper
474 A129 Sheet of 3 3.00 3.25
a.-c. any single .90 1.00
1st Intl. Youth Phil. Exhib., JUVENTUS 1969, Luxembourg, Apr. 3-8.
No. 474 was on sale only at the exhibition. Sold only with entrance ticket for 40fr.

Europa Issue, 1969
Common Design Type
1969, May 19   Photo.   Perf. 11½
Size: 32½x23mm
475 CD12 3fr gray, brn & org .50 .35
476 CD12 6fr vio gray, blk & yel .50 .35

Boy on Hobbyhorse, by Joseph Kutter (1894-1941) — A130

Design: 6fr, View of Luxembourg, by Kutter.

1969, May 19   Engr.   Perf. 12x13
477 A130 3fr multicolored .50 .25
a. Green omitted 150.00 150.00
478 A130 6fr multicolored .50 .35

ILO, 50th Anniv. A131

Photo.; Gold Impressed (Emblem)
1969, May 19   Perf. 14x14½
479 A131 3fr brt grn, vio & gold .30 .25

Mobius Strip in Benelux Colors — A131a

1969, Sept. 8   Litho.   Perf. 12½x13½
480 A131a 3fr multicolored .40 .25
25th anniv. of the signing of the customs union of Belgium, Netherlands and Luxembourg.

NATO, 20th Anniv. A132

1969, Sept. 8   Perf. 13½x12½
481 A132 3fr org brn & dk brn .50 .25

Grain and Mersch Agricultural Center — A133

1969, Sept. 8   Photo.   Perf. 11½
482 A133 3fr bl grn, gray & blk .30 .25
Issued to publicize agricultural progress.

St. Willibrord's Basilica and Abbey, Echternach A134

No. 484, Castle and open-air theater, Wiltz.

1969, Sept. 8   Engr.   Perf. 13
483 A134 3fr dark blue & indigo .35 .25
484 A134 3fr slate green & indigo .35 .25

Pasqueflower A135

Design: 6fr, Hedgehog and 3 young.

1970, Mar. 9   Photo.   Perf. 11½
485 A135 3fr multicolored .25 .25
486 A135 6fr green & multi .45 .40
European Conservation Year.

Goldcrest A136

1970, Mar. 9   Engr.   Perf. 13
487 A136 1.50fr org, grn & blk brn .30 .25
Luxembourg Society for the protection and study of birds, 50th anniv.

Traffic Sign and Street Scene A137

1970, May 4   Photo.   Perf. 11½
488 A137 3fr rose mag, red & blk .50 .25
The importance of traffic safety.

Europa Issue, 1970
Common Design Type
1970, May 4   Size: 32½x23mm
489 CD13 3fr brown & multi .40 .40
490 CD13 6fr green & multi .40 .40

Empress Kunigunde and Emperor
Henry II, Window, Luxembourg
Cathedral — A138

1970, Sept. 14   Photo.   Perf. 12
491 A138 3fr multicolored   .30   .25
Centenary of the Diocese of Luxembourg.

Census
Symbol
A139

1970, Sept. 14   Perf. 11½
492 A139 3fr dk grn, grnsh bl &
                red   .30   .25
Census of Dec. 31, 1970.

Lion,
Luxembourg
City
Hall — A140

1970, Sept. 14
493 A140 3fr bister, lt bl & dk brn .30   .25
50th anniversary of the City of Luxembourg
through the union of 5 municipalities.

UN
Emblem
A141

Perf. 12½x13½
1970, Sept. 14   Litho.
494 A141 1.50fr bl & vio bl   .30   .25
25th anniversary of the United Nations.

Monks in Abbey   Olympic Rings,
Workshop   Arms of
A142   Luxembourg
                        A143

Miniatures Painted at Echternach, about
1040: 3fr, Laborers going to the vineyard (Matthew 20:1-6). 6fr, Laborers toiling in vineyard.
13fr, Workers searching for graves of the
saints.

1971, Mar. 15   Photo.   Perf. 12
495 A142 1.50fr gold & multi   .25   .25
496 A142   3fr gold & multi   .25   .25
497 A142   6fr gold & multi   .25   .25
498 A142   13fr gold & multi   .65   .45
        Nos. 495-498 (4)   1.40 1.20

1971, May 3   Photo.   Perf. 12½
499 A143 3fr ultra & multi   .30   .25
Intl. Olympic Committee, 71st session.

Europa Issue, 1971
Common Design Type
1971, May 3   Perf. 12½x13
Size: 34x25mm
500 CD14 3fr ver, brn & blk   .50   .40
501 CD14 6fr brt grn, brn & blk   .50   .40

A145

1971, May 3   Litho.   Perf. 13x13½
502 A145 3fr org, dk brn & yel   .30   .25
Christian Workers Union, 50th anniv.

Artificial
Lake,
Upper Sure
A146

Designs: No. 504, Water treatment plant,
Esch-sur-Sure. 15fr, ARBED Steel Corporation Headquarters, Luxembourg.

1971, Sept. 13   Engr.   Perf. 13
503 A146 3fr ol, grnsh bl & indi-
                go   .40   .25
504 A146 3fr brn, sl grn & grnsh
                bl   .40   .25
505 A146 15fr indigo & blk brn   .80   .25
        Nos. 503-505 (3)   1.60   .75

School Girl with
Coin — A147

1971, Sept. 13   Photo.   Perf. 11½
506 A147 3fr violet & multi   .30   .25
School children's savings campaign.

Coins of   Bronze
Luxembourg and   Mask — A149
Belgium — A148

1972, Mar. 6
507 A148 1.50fr lt grn, sil & blk .30   .25
Economic Union of Luxembourg and
Belgium, 50th anniversary.

1972, Mar. 6
Archaeological Objects, 4th to 1st centuries,
B.C.: 1fr, Earthenware bowl, horiz. 8fr, Limestone head. 15fr, Glass jug in shape of head.

508 A149   1fr lemon & multi   .25   .25
509 A149   3fr multicolored   .30   .25
510 A149   8fr multicolored   .90   .60
511 A149 15fr multicolored   .75   .60
        Nos. 508-511 (4)   2.20 1.70

Europa Issue 1972
Common Design Type
1972, May 2   Photo.   Perf. 11½
Size: 22x33mm
512 CD15 3fr rose vio & multi   .50   .40
513 CD15 8fr gray blue & multi   .50   .40

Archer
A150

1972, May 2
514 A150 3fr crimson, blk & olive .50   .25
3rd European Archery Championships.

Robert Schuman   The Fox
Medal — A151   Wearing
                      Tails — A152

1972, May 2   Engr.   Perf. 13
515 A151 3fr gray & slate green   .60   .25
Establishment in Luxembourg of the European Coal and Steel Community, 20th anniv.

1972, Sept. 11   Photo.   Perf. 11½
516 A152 3fr scarlet & multi   .40   .25
Centenary of the publication of "Renert,"
satirical poem by Michel Rodange.

National
Monument
A153

Court of Justice of European
Communities, Kirchberg — A154

1972, Sept. 11   Engr.   Perf. 13
517 A153 3fr sl grn, olive & vio   .45   .25
518 A154 3fr brn, bl & slate grn   .85   .25

Epona on
Horseback — A155

Archaeological Objects: 4fr, Panther killing
swan, horiz. 8fr, Celtic gold stater inscribed
Pottina. 15fr, Bronze boar, horiz.

1973, Mar. 14   Photo.   Perf. 11½
519 A155   1fr salmon & multi   .25   .25
520 A155   4fr beige & multi   .25   .25
521 A155   8fr multicolored   1.10   .60
522 A155 15fr multicolored   .75   .60
        Nos. 519-522 (4)   2.35 1.70

Europa Issue 1973
Common Design Type
1973, Apr. 30   Photo.   Perf. 11½
Size: 32x22mm
523 CD16 4fr org, dk vio & lt bl   .45   .50
524 CD16 8fr ol, vio blk & yel   .45   .50

Bee on   Nurse Holding
Honeycomb   Child
A156   A157

1973, Apr. 30   Photo.   Perf. 11½
525 A156 4fr ocher & multi   .50   .25
Publicizing importance of beekeeping.

1973, Apr. 30
526 A157 4fr multicolored   .50   .25
Publicizing importance of day nurseries.

Laurel Branch
A158

1973, Sept. 10   Photo.   Perf. 11½
527 A158 3fr violet bl & multi   .30   .25
50th anniv. of Luxembourg Board of Labor.

Jerome de   National Strike
Busleyden   Memorial, Wiltz
A159   A160

1973, Sept. 10   Engr.   Perf. 13
528 A159 4fr black, brn & pur   .40   .25
Council of Mechelen, 500th anniv.

1973, Sept. 10
529 A160 4fr ol bis, sl & sl grn   .50   .25
In memory of the Luxembourg resistance
heroes who died during the great strike of
1942.

Capital,
Byzantine Hall,
Vianden — A161

St. Gregory the
Great — A161a

Designs: No. 534, Sts. Cecilia and Valerian
crowned by angel, Hollenfels Church. No. 535,
Interior, Septfontaines Church. 8fr, Madonna
and Child, St. Irmina's Chapel, Rosport. 12fr,
St. Augustine Sculptures by Jean-Georges
Scholtus from pulpit in Feulen parish church,
c. 1734.

1973-77 Perf. 13x12½, 14 (6fr, 12fr)
533	A161	4fr green & rose vio	.30	.25
534	A161	4fr red brn, grn & lil	.40	.25
535	A161	4fr gray, brn & dk vio	.40	.25
536	A161a	6fr maroon	.25	
537	A161	8fr sepia & vio bl	1.00	.60
538	A161a	12fr slate blue	1.00	.65
		Nos. 533-538 (6)	3.60	2.25

Architecture of Luxembourg: Romanesque, Gothic, Baroque.
Issued: No. 533, 8fr, 9/10/73; Nos. 534-535, 9/9/74; 6fr, 12fr, 9/16/77.

Princess Marie Astrid — A162 · Torch — A163

1974, Mar. 14 Photo. Perf. 11½
540	A162	4fr blue & multi	1.60	.40

Princess Marie-Astrid, president of the Luxembourg Red Cross Youth Section.

1974, Mar. 14
541	A163	4fr ultra & multi	.60	.25

50th anniversary of Luxembourg Mutual Insurance Federation.

Royal Seal of Henri VII — A164

Seals from 13th-14th Centuries: 3fr, Equestrian, seal of Jean, King of Bohemia. 4fr, Seal of Town of Diekirch. 19fr, Virgin and Child, seal of Convent of Marienthal.

1974, Mar. 14
542	A164	1fr purple & multi	.25	.25
543	A164	3fr green & multi	.25	.25
544	A164	4fr multicolored	.35	.25
545	A164	19fr multicolored	1.00	.75
		Nos. 542-545 (4)	1.85	1.50

Hind, by Auguste Trémont — A165 · Winston Churchill, by Oscar Nemon — A166

Europa: 8fr, "Growth," abstract sculpture, by Lucien Wercollier.

1974, Apr. 29 Photo. Perf. 11½
546	A165	4fr ocher & multi	.50	.50
547	A165	8fr brt blue & multi	1.50	1.50

1974, Apr. 29
548	A166	4fr lilac & multi	.50	.25

Sir Winston Churchill (1874-1965), statesman.

Fairground, Aerial View — A167 · Theis, the Blind — A168

1974, Apr. 29
549	A167	4fr silver & multi	.50	.25

Publicity for New International Fairground, Luxembourg-Kirchberg.

1974, Apr. 29
550	A168	3fr multicolored	.50	.25

Mathias Schou, Theis the Blind (1747-1824), wandering minstrel.

UPU Emblem and "100" — A169

1974, Sept. 9 Photo. Perf. 11½
551	A169	4fr multicolored	.30	.25
552	A169	8fr multicolored	.80	.60

Centenary of Universal Postal Union.

"BENELUX" A170

1974, Sept. 9
553	A170	4fr bl grn, dk grn & lt bl	.90	.25

30th anniversary of the signing of the customs union of Belgium, Netherlands and Luxembourg.

View of Differdange A171

1974, Sept. 9 Engr. Perf. 13
554	A171	4fr rose claret	1.00	.25

Bourglinster A172

Designs: 1fr, Fish Market, Old Luxembourg, vert. 4fr, Market Square, Echternach. 19fr, St. Michael's Square, Mersch, vert.

Perf. 14x13½, 13½x14
1975, Mar. 10 Engr.
555	A172	1fr olive green	.55	.25
556	A172	3fr deep brown	1.20	.35
557	A172	4fr dark purple	1.25	.25
558	A172	19fr copper red	1.25	.85
		Nos. 555-558 (4)	4.25	1.70

European Architectural Heritage Year.

Joseph Kutter, Self-portrait A173

Moselle Bridge, Remich, by Nico Klopp — A174

Paintings: 8fr, Still Life, by Joseph Kutter. 20fr, The Dam, by Dominique Lang.

1975, Apr. 28 Photo. Perf. 11½
559	A173	1fr multicolored	.25	.25
560	A174	4fr multicolored	.40	.40
561	A174	8fr multicolored	1.75	1.25
562	A173	20fr multicolored	1.60	.50
		Nos. 559-562 (4)	4.00	2.40

Cultural series. Nos. 560-561 are Europa Issue.

Robert Schuman, Gaetano Martino, Paul-Henri Spaak Medals A175

1975, Apr. 28
563	A175	4fr yel grn, gold & brn	.70	.25

Robert Schuman's declaration establishing European Coal and Steel Community, 25th anniv.

Albert Schweitzer (1875-1965), Medical Missionary — A176

1975, Apr. 28 Engr. Perf. 13
564	A176	4fr bright blue	.70	.25

Civil Defense Emblem — A177 · Figure Skating — A178

1975, Sept. 8 Photo. Perf. 11½
565	A177	4fr multicolored	.70	.25

Civil Defense Org. for protection and rescue.

1975, Sept. 8 Engr. Perf. 13
4fr, Water skiing, horiz. 15fr, Mountain climbing.
566	A178	3fr green, bl & lilac	.45	.25
567	A178	4fr dk brn, grn & lt brn	.60	.25
568	A178	15fr brown, indigo & grn	1.25	.50
		Nos. 566-568 (3)	2.30	1.00

Grand Duke Type of 1965-71
1975-91 Engr. Perf. 11½
Granite Paper (14fr, 22fr)
570	A104	7fr orange	.45	.25
571	A104	9fr yellow green	.65	.25
572	A104	10fr black	.50	.25
573	A104	12fr brick red	1.00	.25
573A	A104	14fr dark blue	.65	.30
574	A104	16fr green	1.00	.25
574A	A104	18fr brown olive	.80	.40
575	A104	20fr blue	.80	.25
576	A104	22fr orange brown	1.10	.80
		Nos. 570-576 (9)	6.95	3.00

Issued: 10fr, 1/9; 9fr, 12fr, 20fr, 12/23; 16fr, 2/25/82; 7fr, 7/1/83; 18fr, 3/3/86; 14fr, 1/2/90; 22fr, 9/23/91.

Grand Duchess Charlotte A179

Design: No. 580, Prince Henri.

1976, Mar. 8 Litho. Perf. 14x13½
579	A179	6fr green & multi	1.25	.30
580	A179	6fr dull blue & multi	1.25	.30

80th birthday of Grand Duchess Charlotte and 21st birthday of Prince Henri, heir to the throne.

Gold Brooch — A180

5fr, Footless beaker, horiz. 6fr, Decorated vessel, horiz. 12fr, Gold coin. All designs show excavated items of Franco-Merovingian period.

Perf. 13½x12½, 12½x13½
1976, Mar. 8
581	A180	2fr blue & multi	.25	.25
582	A180	5fr black & multi	.30	.30
583	A180	6fr lilac & multi	.45	.30
584	A180	12fr multicolored	1.00	1.10
		Nos. 581-584 (4)	2.00	1.95

Soup Tureen A181

Europa: 12fr, Deep bowl. Tureen and bowl after pottery from Nospelt, 19th century.

1976, May 3 Photo. Perf. 11½
585	A181	6fr lt violet & multi	1.00	.30
586	A181	12fr yel grn & multi	1.00	1.00

Independence Hall, Philadelphia — A182

1976, May 3
587	A182	6fr lt blue & multi	.50	.25

American Bicentennial.

Boomerang — A183

1976, May 3
588	A183	6fr brt rose lil & gold	.50	.25

21st Olympic Games, Montreal, Canada, July 17-Aug. 1.

"Vibrations of Sound" A184

1976, May 3
589 A184 6fr red & multi .50 .25

Jeunesses Musicales (Young Music Friends), association to foster interest in music and art.

Alexander Graham Bell — A185 | Virgin and Child with St. Anne — A186

1976, Sept. 9 Engr. Perf. 13
590 A185 6fr slate green .50 .25

Centenary of first telephone call by Alexander Graham Bell, Mar. 10, 1876.

1976, Sept. 9 Photo. Perf. 11½
591 A186 6fr gold & multi .45 .25
592 A186 12fr gold, gray & blk 1.10 .70

Johann Wolfgang von Goethe A187 | Old Luxembourg A188

Portraits: 5fr, J. M. William Turner. 6fr, Victor Hugo. 12fr, Franz Liszt.

1977, Mar. 14 Engr. Perf. 13
593 A187 2fr lake .25 .25
594 A187 5fr purple .35 .25
595 A187 6fr slate green .50 .30
596 A187 12fr violet blue .70 .65
Nos. 593-596 (4) 1.80 1.45

Famous visitors to Luxembourg.

1977, May 3 Photo. Perf. 11½
Europa: 12fr, Adolphe Bridge and European Investment Bank headquarters.
597 A188 6fr multicolored 1.00 .25
598 A188 12fr multicolored 1.00 .80

Esch-sur-Sure A189 | Marguerite de Busbach A190

Design: 6fr, View of Ehnen.

1977, May 3 Engr. Perf. 13
599 A189 5fr Prus blue .60 .25
600 A189 6fr deep brown .50 .25

1977, May 3 Photo. Perf. 11½
No. 602, Louis Braille, by Lucienne Filippi.
601 A190 6fr multicolored .50 .25
602 A190 6fr multicolored .50 .25

Notre Dame Congregation, founded by Marguerite de Busbach, 350th anniversary; Louis Braille (1809-1852), inventor of the Braille system of writing for the blind.

Souvenir Sheet

Luxembourg Nos. 1-2 — A191

Engr. & Photo.
1977, Sept. 15 Perf. 13½
603 A191 40fr gray & red brown 5.25 5.25
125th anniv. of Luxembourg's stamps.

Head of Medusa, Roman Mosaic, Diekirch, 3rd Century A.D. — A192

1977, Sept. 15 Photo. Perf. 11½
604 A192 6fr multicolored .80 .30

Orpheus and Eurydice, by C. W. Gluck A193

1977, Sept. 15 Perf. 11½x12
605 A193 6fr multicolored .80 .25
Intl. Wiltz Festival, 25th anniv.

Europa Tamed, by R. Zilli, and Map of Europe A194

1977, Dec. 5 Photo. Perf. 11½
606 A194 6fr multicolored .60 .30

20th anniversary of the Treaties of Rome, setting up the European Economic Community and the European Atomic Energy Commission.

Souvenir Sheet

Grand Duke and Grand Duchess of Luxembourg — A195

Photogravure and Engraved
1978, Apr. 3 Perf. 13½x14
607 A195 Sheet of 2 2.00 2.00
a. 6fr dark blue & multi .90 .90
b. 12fr dark red & multi .90 .90

Silver wedding anniversary of Grand Duke Jean and Grand Duchess Josephine Charlotte.

Souvenir Sheet

juphilux 78

Youth Fountain, Streamer and Dancers — A196

1978, Apr. 3 Photo. Perf. 11½
608 A196 Sheet of 3 4.25 4.25
a. 5fr ultra & multi 1.40 1.40
b. 6fr orange & multi 1.40 1.40
c. 20fr yellow green & multi 1.40 1.40

Juphilux 78, 5th International Young Philatelists' Exhibition, Luxembourg, Apr. 6-10.

Charles IV, Statue, Charles Bridge, Prague A197 | Emile Mayrisch, by Theo Van Rysselberghe A198

Europa: 12fr, Pierre d'Aspelt, tomb, Mainz Cathedral.

1978, May 18 Engr. Perf. 13½
609 A197 6fr dark violet blue 1.00 .30
610 A197 12fr dull rose lilac 1.00 .80

Charles IV (1316-78), Count of Luxembourg, Holy Roman Emperor. Pierre d'Aspelt (c. 1250-1320), Archbishop of Mainz and Prince-Elector.

1978, May 18 Perf. 11½
611 A190 6fr multicolored .95 .30

Emile Mayrisch (1862-1928), president of International Steel Cartel and promoter of United Europe.

Our Lady of Luxembourg A199 | Trumpeters and Old Luxembourg A200

1978, May 18 Photo. Perf. 11½
612 A199 6fr multicolored .50 .25
613 A200 6fr multicolored .50 .25

Our Lady of Luxembourg, patroness, 300th anniv.; 135th anniv. of Grand Ducal Military Band.

Starving Child, Helping Hand, Millet — A201 | League Emblem, Lungs, Open Window — A202

Open Prison Door — A203

1978, Sept. 11 Photo. Perf. 11½
614 A201 2fr multicolored .25 .25
615 A202 5fr multicolored .30 .25
616 A203 6fr multicolored .30 .30
Nos. 614-616 (3) .85 .80

"Terre des Hommes," an association to help underprivileged children; Luxembourg Anti-Tuberculosis League, 70th anniv.; Amnesty Intl. and 30th anniv. of Universal Declaration of Human Rights.

Squared Stone Emerging from Rock, City of Luxembourg — A204

1978, Sept. 11 Engr. Perf. 13½x13
617 A204 6fr violet blue .50 .25

Masonic Grand Lodge of Luxembourg, 175th anniversary.

Julius Caesar on Denarius, c. 44 B.C. A205 | St. Michael's Church, Mondorf-les-Bains A206

Roman Coins, Found in Luxembourg: 6fr, Empress Faustina I on Sestertius, 141 A.D. 9fr, Empress Helena on Follis, c. 324-330. 26fr, Emperor Valens on Solidus, c. 367-375.

1979, Mar. 5 Photo. Perf. 11½
618 A205 5fr multicolored .25 .25
619 A205 6fr multicolored .60 .25
620 A205 9fr multicolored .90 .40
621 A205 26fr multicolored 1.75 1.00
Nos. 618-621 (4) 3.50 1.90

1979, Mar. 5 Engr. Perf. 13
Design: 6fr, Luxembourg Central Station.
622 A206 5fr multicolored .60 .25
623 A206 6fr rose claret 1.10 .30

Troisvierges Stagecoach A207

Europa: 12fr, Early wall telephone, vert.

1979, Apr. 30 Photo. Perf. 11½
624 A207 6fr multicolored 1.90 .35
625 A207 12fr multicolored 1.90 1.50

Michel Pintz Facing Jury A208

1979, Apr. 30   Engr.   Perf. 13
626   A208   2fr rose lilac   .50   .25
180th anniversary of peasant uprising against French occupation.

Antoine Meyer — A209

Abundance Crowning Work and Thrift, by Auguste Vinet — A210

Design: 6fr, Sidney Gilchrist Thomas.

1979, Apr. 30
627   A209   5fr carmine   .50   .25
628   A209   6fr light blue   .50   .25
629   A210   9fr black   .50   .35
     Nos. 627-629 (3)   1.50   .85
Antoine Meyer (1801-1857), mathematician and first national poet; centenary of acquisition of Thomas process for production of high-quality steel; 50th anniversary of Luxembourg Stock Exchange.

European Parliament A211

1979, June 7   Photo.   Perf. 11½
630   A211   6fr multi   1.40   .90
European Parliament, first direct elections, June 7-10.

Angel with Chalice, by Barthelemy Namur — A212

Rococo Art: 12fr, Angel with anchor, by Namur, from High Altar, St. Michael's Church, Luxembourg.

Engraved and Photogravure
1979, Sept. 10   Perf. 13½
631   A212   6fr multi   .35   .25
632   A212   12fr multi   .65   .50

Road Safety for Children A213

1979, Sept. 10   Photo.   Perf. 11½
633   A213   2fr multi   .30   .25
International Year of the Child.

Radio Tele-Luxembourg Emblem — A214

1979, Sept. 10
634   A214   6fr ultra, blue & red   .60   .25
50 years of broadcasting in Luxembourg.

John the Blind, Silver Coin, 1331 — A215

Ettelbruck Town Hall — A216

14th Century Coins: 2fr, Sts. Gervase and Protais, silver grosso. 6fr, Easter lamb, gold coin. 20fr, Crown and arms, silver grosso.

1980, Mar. 5   Photo.   Perf. 11½
635   A215   2fr multi   .25   .25
636   A215   5fr multi   .25   .25
637   A215   6fr multi   .80   .25
638   A215   20fr multi   1.75   .75
     Nos. 635-638 (4)   3.05   1.50
See Nos. 651-654.

1980, Mar. 5   Engr.   Perf. 13
No. 640, State Archives Building, horiz.
639   A216   6fr brn & dk red   .65   .25
640   A216   6fr multi   .75   .25

Jean Monnet — A217

Sports for All — A218

Europa: 12fr, St. Benedict of Nursia.

1980, Apr. 28   Perf. 13½
641   A217   6fr dark blue   .85   .55
642   A217   12fr olive green   .85   .55

1980, Apr. 28   Photo.   Perf. 11½
Granite Paper
643   A218   6fr multi   .95   .25

Worker Pouring Molten Iron — A219

Design: 6fr, Man, hand, gears, horiz.

1980, Apr. 28
644   A219   2fr multi   .25   .25
645   A219   6fr multi   .50   .25
9th World Congress on Prevention of Occupational Accidents & Diseases, Amsterdam, May 6-9.

Mercury by Jean Mich — A220

Art Nouveau Sculpture by Jean Mich.

1980, Sept. 10   Engr.   Perf. 14
646   A220   8fr shown   .50   .40
647   A220   12fr Ceres   .80   .55

Introduction of Postal Code — A221

1980, Sept. 10   Photo.   Perf. 11½
648   A221   4fr multi   .60   .25

Police Car and Officers A222

1980, Sept. 10
649   A222   8fr multi   .60   .30
State control of police force, 50th anniv.

Grand Duke Jean, Personal Arms — A223

Photo. & Engr.
1981, Jan. 5   Perf. 13½
650   A223   Sheet of 3   2.50   2.50
  a.   8fr multi   .65   .65
  b.   12fr multi   .75   .75
  c.   30fr multi   1.00   1.00
Grand Duke Jean, 60th birthday.

Coin type of 1980
Silver Coins: 4fr, Philip IV patagon, 1635. 6fr, Empress Maria Theresa 12 sol, 1775. 8fr, Emperor Joseph II 12 sol, 1789. 30fr, Emperor Francois II 72 sol, 1795.

1981, Mar. 5   Photo.   Perf. 11½
651   A215   4fr multi   .25   .25
652   A215   6fr multi   .35   .25
653   A215   8fr multi   .35   .30
654   A215   30fr multi   1.25   .75
     Nos. 651-654 (4)   2.20   1.55

National Library A225

1981, Mar. 5   Engr.   Perf. 13
655   A225   8fr shown   .40   .25
656   A225   8fr European Hemicycle, Kirchberg   .40   .25

Hammelsmarsch (Sheep Procession) A226

Europa: 12fr, Bird-shaped whistle, Eimaischen market.

1981, May 4   Photo.   Perf. 13½
657   A226   8fr multi   .85   .35
658   A226   12fr multi   .85   .45

Knight on Chessboard A227

Savings Account Book, State Bank A228

First Bank Note, 1856 — A229

1981, May 4   Perf. 11½
Granite Paper
659   A227   4fr multi   .50   .25
660   A228   8fr multi   .50   .35
661   A229   8fr multi   .50   .35
Luxembourg Chess Federation, 50th anniv.; State Savings Bank, 125th anniv.; Intl. Bank of Luxembourg, 125th anniv. of issuing rights.

Wedding of Prince Henri and Maria Teresa Mestre, Feb. 14 A230

Photo. & Engr.
1981, June 22   Perf. 13½
662   A230   8fr multi   .50   .40
Sheets of 12.

Single-seater Gliders A231

Energy Conservation A232

1981, Sept. 28   **Photo.**   *Perf. 11½*
Granite Paper
663 A231 8fr shown   .40 .30
664 A231 16fr Propeller planes, horiz.   .80 .60
665 A231 35fr Jet, Luxembourg Airport, horiz.   1.60 1.40
Nos. 663-665 (3)   2.80 2.30

1981, Sept. 28   **Granite Paper**
666 A232 8fr multi   .60 .35

Apple Trees in Blossom, by Frantz Seimetz (1858-1914) A233

Landscape Paintings: 6fr, Summer Landscape, by Pierre Blanc (1872-1946). 8fr, The Larger Hallerbach, by Guido Oppenheim (1862-1942). 16fr, Winter Evening, by Eugene Mousset (1877-1941).

1982, Feb. 25   **Engr.**   *Perf. 11½*
667 A233 4fr multi   .25 .25
668 A233 6fr multi   .45 .30
669 A233 8fr multi   .55 .40
670 A233 16fr multi   1.00 .80
Nos. 667-670 (4)   2.25 1.75

World War II Resistance — A234

Design: Cross of Hinzert (Natl. Monument of the Resistance and Deportation) and Political Prisoner, by Lucien Wercollier.

1982, Feb. 25
671 A234 8fr multi   .50 .35

Europa 1982 A235

St. Theresa of Avila (1515-1582) A236

1982, May 4   **Photo.**
Granite Paper
672 A235 8fr Treaty of London, 1867   .90 .25
673 A235 16fr Treaty of Paris, 1951   .90 .65

1982, May 4   **Granite Paper**
Design: 8fr, Raoul Follereau (1903-1977), "Apostle of the Lepers."
674 A236 4fr multi   .30 .25
675 A236 8fr multi   .50 .40

State Museum A237

1982, May 4   **Photo. & Engr.**
676 A237 8fr shown   .45 .35
677 A237 8fr Synagogue of Luxembourg   .45 .35

Bourscheid Castle — A238

Designs: Restored castles.

1982, Sept. 9   **Engr.**   *Perf. 11½*
Granite Paper
678 A238 6fr shown   .35 .25
679 A238 8fr Vianden, horiz.   .55 .25

Intl. Youth Hostel Federation, 50th Anniv. — A239

1982, Sept. 9   **Photo.**
680 A239 4fr shown   .50 .25
681 A239 8fr Scouting year, vert.   .80 .35

Civilian and Military Deportation Monument — A240

1982, Sept. 9
682 A240 8fr multi   .60 .35

Mercury, Sculpture by Auguste Tremont — A241

NATO Emblem, Flags — A242

1983, Mar. 7   **Photo.**   *Perf. 11½*
Granite Paper
683 A241 4fr multi   .30 .25
FOREX '83, 25th Intl. Assoc. of Foreign Exchange Dealers' Congress, June 2-5.

1983, Mar. 7   **Granite Paper**
684 A242 6fr multi   .30 .25
25th anniv. of NAMSA (NATO Maintenance and Supply Agency).

Echternach Cross of Justice, 1236 — A243

Globe, CCC Emblem — A244

1983, Mar. 7   **Granite Paper**
685 A243 8fr multi   .45 .35
30th Cong. of Intl. Union of Barristers, July 3-9.

1983, Mar. 7   **Granite Paper**
686 A244 4fr multi   .45 .35
30th anniv. of Council of Customs Cooperation.

Natl. Federation of Fire Brigades Centenary A245

1983, Mar. 7   **Granite Paper**
687 A245 8fr Fire engine, 1983   .45 .35
688 A245 16fr Hand pump, 1740   .85 .65

Europa 1983 — A246

The Good Samaritan, Codex Aureus Escorialensis Miniatures, 11th Cent., Echternach.

1983, May 3   **Photo.**
689 A246 8fr Highway robbers   1.00 .45
690 A246 16fr Good Samaritan   1.75 .45

Giant Bible, 11th Cent. — A247

World Communications Year — A248

Illuminated Letters.

Photo. & Engr.
1983, May 3   *Perf. 14*
691 A247 8fr "h," Book of Baruch   .45 .05
692 A247 35fr "B," letter of St. Jerome   2.00 1.50

1983, May 3   **Photo.**   *Perf. 11½*
693 A248 8fr Post code   1.00 .25
694 A248 8fr Satellite relay, horiz.   2.00 .30

Town Hall, Dudelange A249

7fr, St. Lawrence Church, Diekirch, vert.

1983, Sept. 7   **Photo. & Engr.**
695 A249 7fr multi   .50 .25
696 A249 10fr multi   .70 .25

Basketball Fed., 50th Anniv. A250

European Working Dog Championship A251

Tourism — A252

1983, Sept. 7   **Photo.**
Granite Paper
697 A250 7fr multi   .60 .25
698 A251 10fr Alsatian sheepdog   .80 .35
699 A252 10fr View of Luxembourg   1.40 .35
Nos. 697-699 (3)   2.80 .95

Environment Protection A253

1984, Mar. 6   **Photo.**   *Perf. 11½*
Granite Paper
700 A253 7fr Pedestrian zoning   .50 .40
701 A253 10fr Water purification   .50 .40

2nd European Parliament Election — A254

1984, Mar. 6   **Granite Paper**
702 A254 10fr Hands holding emblem   .60 .40

A255

A256

1984, Mar. 6   **Engr.**   *Perf. 12½x13*
703 A255 10fr No. 1   .90 .35
704 A255 10fr Union meeting   .90 .35
705 A255 10fr Mail bag   .90 .35
706 A255 10fr Train   .90 .35
Nos. 703-706 (4)   3.60 1.40
Philatelic Federation (1934); Civil Service Trade Union (1909); Postal Workers' Union (1909); Railroad (1859).

1984, May 7   **Photo.**   *Perf. 11½x12*
707 A256 10fr The Race, by Jean Jacoby (1891-1936)   .55 .35
1984 Summer Olympics.

Europa (1959-84) A257

1984, May 7   *Perf. 11½*
Granite Paper
708 A257 10fr green   1.60 .40
709 A257 16fr orange   1.60 .80

Young Turk Caressing His Horse, by Delacroix A258

Paintings: 4fr, The Smoker, by David Teniers the Younger (1610-90). 10fr, Epiphany, by Jan Steen (1626-79). 50fr, The Lacemaker, by Pieter van Slingelandt (1640-91). 4fr, 50fr vert.

Photo. & Engr.
1984, May 7   *Perf. 14*
710 A258 4fr multi .60 .25
711 A258 7fr multi .85 .25
712 A258 10fr multi 1.10 .25
713 A258 50fr multi 4.25 2.00
Nos. 710-713 (4) 6.80 2.75

Marine Life Fossils — A259   Restored Castles — A260

1984, Sept. 10   Photo.   *Perf. 11½*
714 A259 4fr Pecten sp. .40 .25
715 A259 7fr Gryphaea arcuata .60 .25
716 A259 10fr Coeloceras raqy-
    inianum 1.00 .35
717 A259 16fr Daildius 1.40 .60
Nos. 714-717 (4) 3.40 1.45

1984, Sept. 10   Engr.
718 A260 7fr Hollenfels .45 .25
719 A260 10fr Larochette .60 .40

A261   A262

1984, Sept. 10   *Perf. 12x12½*
720 A261 10fr Soldier, US flag 1.25 .35

40th Anniv. of D Day (June 6).

1985, Mar. 4   Photo.   *Perf. 11½*
Portrait medals in the state museum: 4fr, Jean Bertels (1544-1607), Historian, Abbott of Echternach. 7fr, Emperor Charles V (1500-1558). 10fr, King Philip II of Spain (1527-1598). 30fr, Prince Maurice of Orange-Nassau, Count of Vianden (1567-1625).

Granite Paper
721 A262 4fr multi .25 .25
722 A262 7fr multi .40 .25
723 A262 10fr multi .60 .30
724 A262 30fr multi 1.75 .90
Nos. 721-724 (4) 3.00 1.70

See Nos. 739-742.

Anniversaries A263

No. 725, Benz Velo, First automobile in Luxembourg, 1895. No. 726, Push-button telephone, sound waves. No. 727, Fencers.

1985, Mar. 4   *Perf. 12x11½*
Granite Paper
725 A263 10fr multi .70 .40
726 A263 10fr multi .70 .40
727 A263 10fr multi .70 .40
Nos. 725-727 (3) 2.10 1.20

Centenary of the first automobile; Luxembourg Telephone Service, cent.; Luxembourg Fencing Federation, 50th anniv.

Visit of Pope John Paul II — A264

1985, Mar. 4   *Perf. 11½x12*
Granite Paper
728 A264 10fr Papal arms .70 .40

Europa 1985 — A265

Designs: 10fr, Grand-Duke Adolphe Music Federation. 16fr, Luxembourg Music School.

1985, May 8   *Perf. 11½*
729 A265 10fr multi 1.60 .45
730 A265 16fr multi 2.40 1.10

Souvenir Sheet

End of World War II, 40th Anniv. — A266

Designs: a, Luxembourg resistance fighters, Wounded Fighters medal. b, Luxembourg War Cross. c, Badge of the Union of Luxembourg Resistance Movements. d, Liberation of the concentration camps.

1985, May 8   *Perf. 11½x12*
Granite Paper
731 A266 Sheet of 4 2.75 2.75
a.-d. 10fr, any single .60 .40

Endangered Wildlife — A267

1985, Sept. 23   Photo.   *Perf. 12x11½*
732 A267 4fr Athene nocturna,
    vert. .80 .40
733 A267 7fr Felis silvestris 1.60 .40
734 A267 10fr Vanessa atalantica 2.00 .40
735 A267 50fr Hyla arborea, vert. 5.25 1.50
Nos. 732-735 (4) 9.65 2.70

Historic Monuments A268

1985, Sept. 23   Engr.   *Perf. 11½*
736 A268 7fr Echternach Orange-
    ry, 1750 .45 .25
737 A268 10fr Mohr de Waldt
    House, 17th cent. .65 .45

Natl. Art Collection A269

Photo. & Engr.
1985, Sept. 23   *Perf. 14*
738 A269 10fr 18th cent. book cov-
    er, Natl. Library .70 .25

Portrait Medals Type of 1985
1986, Mar. 3   Photo.   *Perf. 11½*
Granite Paper
739 A262 10fr Count of Monte-
    rey, 1675 .65 .40
740 A262 12fr Louis XIV, 1684 .70 .45
741 A262 18fr Pierre de Weyms,
    c. 1700 1.10 .70
742 A262 20fr Duke of Marlbor-
    ough, 1706 1.25 .80
Nos. 739-742 (4) 3.70 2.35

Federation of Luxembourg Beekeepers' Associations, Cent. A270

Mondorf State Spa, Cent. — A271   Natl. Table Tennis Federation, 50th Anniv. — A272

1986, Mar. 3   *Perf. 11½*
743 A270 12fr Bee collecting pol-
    len 1.00 .50
744 A271 12fr Mosaic 1.00 .50
745 A272 12fr Boy playing table
    tennis 1.00 .50
Nos. 743-745 (3) 3.00 1.50

Europa 1986 A273   Fortifications A274

1986, May 5   Photo.   *Perf. 12*
Granite Paper
751 A273 12fr Polluted forest, city 1.75 .25
752 A273 20fr Man, pollution
    sources 1.75 1.00

1986, May 5   **Granite Paper**
753 A274 15fr Ft. Thungen, horiz. 1.60 .60
754 A274 18fr Invalid's Gate 1.60 .70
755 A274 50fr Malakoff Tower 3.00 2.00
Nos. 753-755 (3) 6.20 3.30

Robert Schuman (1886-1963), European Cooperation Promulgator — A275

1986, June 26   *Perf. 12 on 3 Sides*
Granite Paper
756 A275 2fr pink & blk .25 .25
a. Bklt. pane of 4 .30
757 A275 10fr lt bl & blk .50 .40
a. Bklt. pane of 4 2.75
b. Bklt. pane of 2, #756-757 + 2 la-
    bels 1.40

Nos. 756-757 issued in booklets only.

European Road Safety Year — A276

1986, Sept. 15   Photo.   *Perf. 11½*
758 A276 10fr multi .60 .40

Bas-relief, Town Hall, Esch-Sur-Alzette — A277

Design: No. 760, Stairs to the Chapel of the Cross, Grevenmacher.

Photogravure & Engraved
1986, Sept. 15   *Perf. 14x13½*
759 A277 12fr shown .75 .50
760 A277 12fr multi .75 .50

Countess Ermesinde (1186-1247), Ruler of Luxembourg A278

Designs: No. 761, Presentation of the letter of freedom to Echternach inhabitants, 1236, engraving (detail) by P.H. Witkamp, c. 1873. 30fr, Charter seal, Marienthal Convent, 1238.

1986, Sept. 15   *Perf. 13½x14*
761 A278 12fr multi .70 .50
762 A278 30fr multi 1.65 1.20

A279   A280

1987, Mar. 9   Photo.   *Perf. 11½*
763 A279 6fr Eliomys quercinus,
    horiz. .90 .40
764 A279 10fr Calopteryx
    splendens 1.25 .40
765 A279 12fr Cinclus cinclus 1.75 .40
766 A279 25fr Salamandra sala-
    mandra terrestris,
    horiz. 2.75 1.25
Nos. 763-766 (4) 6.65 2.45

Wildlife conservation.

1987, Mar. 9
767 A280 12fr multi .60 .50

Natl. Home Amateur Radio Operators Network, 50th anniv.

A281

1987, Mar. 9
768 A281 12fr multi .60 .50

Luxembourg Intl. Fair, 50th anniv.

Europa
1987 — A282

12fr, Aquatic Sports Center. 20fr, European Communities Court of Justice and abstract sculpture by Henry Moore (1898-1986).

1987, May 4   Photo.   Perf. 11½
769 A282 12fr multi   1.75   .40
770 A282 20fr multi   1.75   .90

St. Michael's Church Millenary
A283

Designs: 12fr, Consecration of the church by Archbishop Egbert of Trier, 987, stained glass window by Gustav Zanter. 20fr, Baroque organ-chest, 17th century.

Photogravure & Engraved
1987, May 4   Perf. 14
771 A283 12fr multi   .75   .50
772 A283 20fr multi   1.25   .80

15th Century Paintings by Giovanni Ambrogio Bevilacqua
A284

Polyptych panels in the State Museum: 10fr, St. Bernard of Sienna and St. John the Baptist. 18fr, St. Jerome and St. Francis of Assisi.

1987, May 4   Perf. 11½
773 A284 10fr multi   .55   .40
774 A284 18fr multi   1.00   .70

Rural Architecture
A285

Photo. & Engr.
1987, Sept. 14   Perf. 13½
775 A285 10fr Hennesbau Bark
          Mill, 1826,
          Niederfeulen   .50   .40
776 A285 12fr Health Center,
          18th cent.,
          Mersch   .60   .50
777 A285 100fr Post Office, 18th
          cent., Bertrange 5.00 4.00
          Nos. 775-777 (3) 6.10 4.90

Chamber of Deputies (Parliament) 139th Anniv. — A286

Designs: 6fr, Charles Metz (1799-1853), first President. 12fr, Parliament, 1860, designed by Antoine Hartmann (1817-1891).

1987, Sept. 14   Engr.   Perf. 14
778 A286 6fr violet brn   .25   .25
779 A286 12fr blue black   .60   .50

Flowers by Botanical Illustrator Pierre-Joseph Redoute (1759-1840)
A287

1988, Feb. 8   Photo.   Perf. 11½x12
780 A287 6fr Orange lily, water
          lily   .80   .40
781 A287 10fr Primula, double
          narcissus   .80   .40
782 A287 12fr Tulip   1.60   .50
783 A287 50fr Iris, gorteria 4.00 2.00
          Nos. 780-783 (4)   7.20 3.30

European Conf. of Ministers of Transport
A288

Eurocontrol, 25th Anniv.
A289

1988, Feb. 8   Perf. 12
784 A288 12fr multi   .70   .70
785 A289 20fr multi   1.25 1.25

Souvenir Sheet

Family of Prince Henri — A290

1988, Mar. 29   Photo.   Perf. 12
786 A290 Sheet of 3   5.50 5.50
  a. 12fr Maria Theresa   .70   .70
  b. 18fr Guillaume, Felix and Louis 1.00 1.00
  c. 50fr Prince Henri   2.75 2.75

JUVALUX '88, 9th intl. youth philatelic exhibition, Mar. 29-Apr. 4.

Europa
1988 — A291

Communication.

1988, June 6   Photo.   Perf. 11½
787 A291 12fr Automatic mail
         handling   1.75   .40
788 A291 20fr Electronic mail 1.75 1.75

Tourism — A292

Designs: 10fr, Wiltz town hall and Cross of Justice Monument, c. 1502. 12fr, Castle, Differdange, 16th cent., vert.

Photo. & Engr.
1988, June 6   Perf. 13½
789 A292 10fr multi   .70   .40
790 A292 12fr multi   .70   .40

See Nos. 824-825, 841-842.

League of Luxembourg Student Sports Associations (LASEL), 50th Anniv.
A293

1988, June 6   Photo.   Perf. 11½
791 A293 12fr multi   .80   .35

Doorways
A294

Architectural drawings by Joseph Wegener (1895-1980) and his students, 1949-1951: 12fr, Septfontaines Castle main entrance, 1785. 25fr, National Library regency north-wing entrance, c. 1720. 50fr, Holy Trinity Church baroque entrance, c. 1740.

Litho. & Engr.
1988, Sept. 12   Perf. 14
792 A294 12fr black & buff   .65   .30
793 A294 25fr blk & citron   1.25   .75
794 A294 50fr blk & yel bister 2.60 1.25
         Nos. 792-794 (3)   4.50 2.30

Jean Monnet (1888-1979), French Economist — A295

1988, Sept. 12   Engr.
795 A295 12fr multi   .70   .35

European Investment Bank, 30th Anniv.
A296

1988, Sept. 12   Litho. & Engr.
796 A296 12fr yel grn & blk   1.10   .35

A297

A298

1988, Sept. 12   Photo.   Perf. 11½
797 A297 12fr multi   .70   .40

1988 Summer Olympics, Seoul.

1989, Mar. 6   Photo.   Perf. 11½x12

Design: 12fr, Portrait and excerpt from his speech to the Chamber of Deputies, 1896.

798 A298 12fr multi   .40   .25

C.M. Spoo (1837-1914), advocate of Luxembourgish as the natl. language.

Book Workers' Fed., 125th Anniv. — A299

Natl. Red Cross, 75th Anniv. — A300

1989, Mar. 6
799 A299 18fr multi   .95   .50

1989, Mar. 6
800 A300 20fr Henri Dunant   2.00 1.00

Independence of the Grand Duchy, 150th Anniv. — A301

Design: 12fr, Lion, bronze sculpture by Auguste Tremont (1892-1980) guarding the grand ducal family vault, Cathedral of Luxembourg.

Photo. & Engr.
1989, Mar. 6   Perf. 14
801 A301 12fr multi   .70   .35

Astra Telecommunications Satollito — A302

1989, Mar. 6   Photo.   Perf. 11½
802 A302 12fr multi   .70   .40

Europa
1989 — A303

Tour de France — A304

Paintings (children at play): 12fr, Three Children in a Park, 19th cent., anonymous. 20fr, Child with Drum, 17th cent., anonymous.

1989, May 8   Photo.   Perf. 11½x12
803 A303 12fr multi   .90   .90
804 A303 20fr multi   .90   .90

1989, May 8   Perf. 11½
805 A304 9fr multi   .90   .50

Start of the bicycle race in Luxembourg City.

A305

A306

1989, May 8   *Perf. 11½x12*
806 A305 12fr multi   .80 .30
Interparliamentary Union, cent.

1989, May 8
807 A306 12fr multi   .80 .50
European Parliament 3rd elections.

Council of Europe, 40th Anniv. A307

1989, May 8   *Perf. 12x11½*
808 A307 12fr multi   .80 .50

Reign of Grand Duke Jean, 25th Anniv. A308   Charles IV (1316-1378) A309

1989, Sept. 18 Photo.   *Perf. 12x11½*
Booklet Stamps
810 A308 3fr black & orange   1.25 1.25
   a.   Bklt. pane of 4   5.00
811 A308 9fr black & blue green   1.25 1.25
   a.   Bklt. pane of 4   5.00
   b.   Bklt. pane, 1 each #810, 811 + 2 labels   2.50
       Booklet, 1 each #810a, 811a, 811b   15.00

Photo. & Engr.
1989, Sept. 18   *Perf. 13½x14*
Stained-glass windows by Joseph Oberberger in the Grand Ducal Loggia, Cathedral of Luxembourg: 20fr, John the Blind (1296-1346). 25fr, Wenceslas II (1361-1419).
821 A309 12fr shown   .45 .45
822 A309 20fr multi   1.25 .95
823 A309 25fr multi   1.25 1.25
    Nos. 821-823 (3)   2.95 2.65
Independence of the Grand Duchy, 150th anniv.

Tourism Type of 1988
Designs: 12fr, Clervaux Castle interior courtyard, circa 12th cent. 18fr, Bronzed wild boar of Titelberg, 1st cent., vert.

Litho. & Engr.
1989, Sept. 18   *Perf. 13½*
824 A292 12fr multi   .65 .30
825 A292 18fr multi   1.25 .65

Views of the Former Fortress of Luxembourg, 1814-1815, Engravings by Christoph Wilhelm Selig (1791-1837) — A310

1990, Mar. 5 Photo.   *Perf. 12x11½*
826 A310 9fr shown   .55 .40
827 A310 12fr multi, diff.   .65 .40
828 A310 20fr multi, diff.   1.50 .95
829 A310 25fr multi, diff.   2.00 1.00
    Nos. 826-829 (4)   4.70 2.75
Congress of Vienna, 1815, during which the Duchy of Luxembourg was elevated to the Grand Duchy of Luxembourg.

Schueberfouer Carnival, 650th Anniv. — A311

1990, Mar. 15   *Perf. 11½x12*
830 A311 9fr Carnival ride   1.00 .45

Batty Weber (1860-1940), Writer — A312   ITU, 125th Anniv. — A313

1990, Mar. 15
831 A312 12fr multi   .70 .30

1990, Mar. 15
832 A313 18fr multicolored   1.20 .45

A314
Europa (Post Offices): 12fr, Luxembourg City. 20fr, Esch-Sur-Alzette, vert.

Litho. & Engr.
1990, May 28   *Perf. 13½*
833 A314 12fr buff & blk   1.75 .30
834 A314 20fr lt bl & blk   1.75 1.20

A315
Prime Ministers: 9fr, Paul Eyschen (1841-1915). 12fr, Emmanuel Servais (1811-1890).

Photo. & Engr.
1990, May 28   *Perf. 14x13½*
835 A315 9fr multicolored   .60 .40
836 A315 12fr multicolored   .70 .40

A316

1990, May 28 Photo.   *Perf. 11½*
837 A316 12fr Psallus Pseudoplatani   .75 .35
Luxembourg Naturalists' Society, cent.

A317
Fountains: 12fr, Sheep's march by Will Lofy. 25fr, Fountain of Doves. 50fr, "Maus Ketty" by Lofy.

Litho. & Engr.
1990, Sept. 24   *Perf. 14*
838 A317 12fr multicolored   .65 .40
839 A317 25fr multicolored   1.50 .90
840 A317 50fr multicolored   3.00 2.00
    Nos. 838-840 (3)   5.15 3.30

Tourism Type of 1988
1990, Sept. 24   *Perf. 13½*
841 A292 12fr Mondercange   .60 .25
842 A292 12fr Schifflange   .60 .25

Souvenir Sheet

Nassau-Weilburg Dynasty, Cent. — A318

Designs: a, Grand Duke Adolphe. b, Grand Duchess Marie-Adelaide. c, Grand Ducal House arms. d, Grand Duchess Charlotte. e, Grand Duke Guillaume. f, Grand Duke Jean.

Photo. & Engr.
1990, Nov. 26   *Perf. 14x13½*
843 A318 Sheet of 6   8.00 8.00
   a.-b.   12fr multicolored   1.00 1.00
   c.-d.   18fr multicolored   1.00 1.00
   e.-f.   20fr multicolored   1.00 1.00

View From the Trier Road by Sosthene Weis (1872-1941) — A319
Paintings: 18fr, Vauban Street and the Via-duct. 25fr, St. Ulric Street.

Perf. 12x11½, 11½x12
1991, Mar. 4   Photo.
844 A319 14fr multicolored   .90 .40
845 A319 18fr multicolored   .90 .70
846 A319 25fr multi, vert.   2.00 1.00
    Nos. 844-846 (3)   3.80 2.10

Fungi — A320

1991, Mar. 4   *Perf. 11½*
847 A320 14fr Geastrum varians   .85 .45
848 A320 14fr Agaricus (Gymnopus) thiebautii   .85 .45
849 A320 18fr Agaricus (lepiota) lepidocephalus   1.25 .90
850 A320 25fr Morchella favosa   2.00 1.10
    Nos. 847-850 (4)   4.95 2.90

Europa A321

1991, May 13 Photo.   *Perf. 12x11½*
851 A321 14fr Astra 1A, 1B satellites   1.75 .50
852 A321 18fr Betzdorf ground station   1.75 1.40

Natl. Miners' Monument, Kayl — A322   Art by Emile Kirscht — A323

Designs: No. 854, Magistrates' Court, Redange-Sur-Attert, horiz.

1991, May 23   *Perf. 11½x12, 12x11½*
853 A322 14fr multicolored   1.00 .40
854 A322 14fr multicolored   1.00 .40

1991, May 23   *Perf. 11½*
No. 856, Edmund de la Fontaine (1823-91), poet.
855 A323 14fr multicolored   1.00 .40
856 A323 14fr multicolored   1.00 .40
Labor Unions, 75th anniv. (No. 855).

Post and Telecommunications Museum — A324

Perf. 11½ on 3 sides
1991, Sept. 23   Photo.
Booklet Stamps
857 A324 4fr Old telephone   1.90 1.40
   a.   Bklt. pane of 1 + 3 labels   2.00
858 A324 14fr Old postbox   .90 .90
   a.   Bklt. pane of 4   3.50

A325   A326

1991, Sept. 23   **Perf. 11½**
859 A325 14fr Stamp of Type
          A24   .90   .40

Stamp Day, 50th anniv.

Photo. & Engr.
1991, Sept. 23   **Perf. 14**
Designs: Gargoyles.
860 A326 14fr Young girl's head   .65   .40
861 A326 25fr Woman's head   1.10 1.00
862 A326 50fr Man's head   2.00 1.60
     Nos. 860-862 (3)   3.75 3.00

See Nos. 874-876.

Jean-Pierre Pescatore Foundation, Cent. A327

Buildings: No. 864, High Technology Institute. No. 865, New Fair and Congress Centre.

1992, Mar. 16   Photo.   Perf. 11½
863 A327 14fr lil rose & multi   1.00   .45
864 A327 14fr grn & multi   1.00   .45
865 A327 14fr brt bl & multi   1.00   .45
     Nos. 863-865 (3)   3.00 1.35

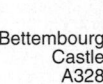

Bettembourg Castle A328

1992, Mar. 16
866 A328 18fr shown   1.00   .65
867 A328 25fr Walferdange station   1.50   .90

Europa A329

Emigrants to US: 14fr, Nicholas Gonner (1835-1892), newspaper editor. 22fr, N. E. Becker (1842-1920), journalist.

Photo. & Engr.
1992, May 18   **Perf. 13½x14½**
868 A329 14fr multicolored   1.75   .50
869 A329 22fr multicolored   1.75 1.25

Lions Clubs Intl., 75th Anniv. — A330   General Strike, 50th Anniv. — A331

1992, May 18   Photo.   Perf. 11½
870 A330 14fr multicolored   1.00   .40
871 A331 18fr sepia & lake   1.00   .70

1992 Summer Olympics, Barcelona A332

1992, May 18   **Perf. 12x11½**
872 A332 14fr multicolored   1.75   .50

Expo '92, Seville A333

1992, May 18   **Perf. 11½**
873 A333 14fr Luxembourg pavilion   .75   .50

Gargoyle Type of 1991
Photo. & Engr.
1992, Oct. 5   **Perf. 14**
874 A326 14fr Ram's head   .75   .45
875 A326 22fr Lion's head   1.25 1.10
876 A326 50fr Satyr's head   2.50 1.75
     Nos. 874-876 (3)   4.50 3.30

Stained Glass Windows, by Auguste Tremont — A334

1992, Oct. 5   Photo.   Perf. 11½x12
877 A334 14fr Post horn, letters   .75   .40
878 A334 22fr Post rider   1.75 1.25
879 A334 50fr Insulators   2.25 1.60
     Nos. 877-879 (3)   4.75 3.25

Luxembourg Post and Telecommunications, 150th anniv.

Single European Market A335

1992, Oct. 5   **Perf. 11½x12**
880 A335 14fr multicolored   .90   .35

Fountain of the Children with Grapes, Schwebsingen — A336

Design: No. 882, Old Ironworks Cultural Center, Steinfort.

1993, Mar. 8   Photo.   Perf. 12x11½
881 A336 14fr multicolored   .80   .50
882 A336 14fr multicolored   .80   .50

Grand Duke Jean — A337

Litho. & Engr.
1993-95   **Perf. 13½x13**
Background Color
883 A337   1fr yellow brown   .25   .25
883A A337   2fr olive gray   .25   .25
884 A337   5fr yellow green   .25   .25
885 A337   7fr brick red   .25   .25
886 A337 10fr blue   .50   .25
887 A337 14fr pink   1.40   .30
888 A337 15fr green   .80   .45
889 A337 16fr orange   .80   .50
890 A337 18fr orange   .70   .35
891 A337 20fr red   1.00   .55
892 A337 22fr dark green   .90   .75
893 A337 25fr gray blue   1.00   .65
894 A337 100fr brown   5.00 2.40
     Nos. 883-894 (13)   13.10 7.20

Issued: 5, 7, 14, 18, 22, 25fr, 3/8/93; 1, 15, 20, 100fr, 3/7/94; 2, 10, 16fr, 1/30/95.
See Nos. 957, 1026.

New Technologies in Surgery A338

1993, May 10   Photo.   Perf. 11½
895 A338 14fr multicolored   .75   .50

Contemporary Paintings — A339

Europa: 14fr, Rezlop, by Fernand Roda. 22fr, So Close, by Sonja Roef.

1993, May 10
896 A339 14fr multicolored   1.25   .40
897 A339 22fr multicolored   1.75   .80

A340

Designs: 14fr, Burgundy Residence. 20fr, Simons House. 50fr, Cassal House.

Photo. & Engr.
1993, May 10   **Perf. 14**
898 A340 14fr multicolored   .80   .35
899 A340 20fr multicolored   1.20   .65
900 A340 50fr multicolored   3.00 1.90
     Nos. 898-900 (3)   5.00 2.90

A341

1993, Sept. 20   Photo.   Perf. 11½
901 A341 14fr multicolored   .70   .35

Environmental protection.

A342   A343

1993, Sept. 20
902 A342 14fr multicolored   .70   .40
903 A343 14fr multicolored   .70   .40

Jean Schortgen (1880-1918), 1st worker elected to Parliament (No. 902); Artistic Circle of Luxembourg, cent.

Museum Exhibits A344

14fr, Electric tram, Tram & Bus Museum, City of Luxembourg. 22fr, Iron ore tipper wagon, Natl. Mining Museum, Rumelange. 60fr, Horse-drawn carriage, Wiltz Museum of Ancient Crafts.

Photo. & Engr.
1993, Sept. 20   **Perf. 14**
904 A344 14fr multicolored   .75   .35
905 A344 22fr multicolored   1.40 1.00
906 A344 60fr multicolored   3.00 1.75
     Nos. 904-906 (3)   5.15 3.10

See Nos. 933-935.

Snow-Covered Landscape, by Joseph Kutter (1894-1941) — A345

Design: No. 908, The Moselle, by Nico Klopp (1894-1930).

1994, Mar. 7   Photo.   Perf. 11½x12
907 A345 14fr multicolored   .80   .40
908 A345 14fr multicolored   .80   .40

4th General Elections to European Parliament A346

1994, May 16   Photo.   Perf. 11½
909 A346 14fr multicolored   .75   .40

European Inventions, Discoveries A347

1994, May 16
910 A347 14fr Armillary sphere   1.00   .40
911 A347 22fr Sail boats, map   1.25 1.00

Europa.

21st Intl. Congress of Genealogy & Heraldry — A348

14th World Congress of Intl. Police Assoc. — A349

Intl. Year of the Family A350

1994, May 16   **Perf. 11½**
912 A348 14fr multicolored   .70   .40
913 A349 18fr multicolored   .80   .60
914 A350 25fr multicolored   1.50   .85
     Nos. 912-914 (3)   3.00 1.85

Europe A351

1994, Sept. 19   **Perf. 11½**
915 A351 14fr Dove, stars   1.25   .35
916 A351 14fr Circle of stars   1.25   .35
917 A351 14fr Bronze Age bowl   2.50   .75
     Nos. 915-917 (3)   5.00 1.45

Western European Union, 40th anniv. (No. 915). Office for Official Publications of European Communities, 25th anniv. (No. 916). European Bronze Age Research Campaign (No. 917).

Liberation, 50th Anniv. A352

1994, Sept. 19   **Photo.**   **Perf. 12x11½**
918 A352 14fr multicolored   .75   .45

Former Refuges in Luxembourg A353

Designs: 15fr, Munster Abbey. 25fr, Holy Spirit Convent. 60fr, St. Maximine Abbey of Trier.

Photo. & Engr.
1994, Sept. 19   **Perf. 14**
919 A353 15fr multicolored   .80   .75
920 A353 25fr multicolored   1.25 1.00
921 A353 60fr multicolored   3.00 1.75
     Nos. 919-921 (3)   5.05 3.50

A354

City of Luxembourg, 1995 European City of Culture — A355

A356

Paintings by Hundertwasser A357

Panoramic view of city showing buildings and: No. 923a, Steeples, trees. b, Gateway through fortress wall. c, Angles in fortress wall. d, Roof of church.
Designs: No. 924, The King of the Antipodes. No. 925, The House with the Arcades and the Yellow Tower. No. 926, Small Path.

Perf. 12x11½, 11½x12
1995, Mar. 6   **Photo.**
922 A354 16fr multicolored   1.00   .60
923   Strip of 4   4.00 4.00
a.-d. A355 16fr any single   .85   .50

Photo. & Engr.
Perf. 14
924 A356 16fr gold, silver & multi   2.00   .80
925 A357 16fr black & multi   2.00   .80
926 A357 16fr yellow & multi   2.00   .80
     Nos. 922-926 (5)   11.00 7.00

No. 923 is a continuous design.

Liberation of the Concentration Camps, 50th Anniv. — A358

Europa: 25fr, Barbed wire, cracked plaster.

1995, May 15   **Photo.**   **Perf. 11½x12**
927 A358 16fr multicolored   1.25   .50
928 A358 25fr multicolored   2.00   .80

European Nature Conservation Year — A359

1995, May 15   **Litho.**   **Perf. 13½**
929 A359 16fr multicolored   .75   .50

A360

1995, May 15   **Photo.**   **Perf. 11½x12**
930 A360 16fr multicolored   .95   .50
Small States of Europe Games, Luxembourg.

European Geodynamics and Seismology Center A361

1995, May 15   **Perf. 11½**
931 A361 32fr multicolored   2.00 1.25

A362

1995, May 15   **Perf. 11½x12**
932 A362 80fr multicolored   4.50 2.50

UN, 50th anniv.

Museum Exhibits Type of 1993

Designs, vert: 16fr, Churn, Country Art Museum, Vianden. 32fr, Wine press, Wine Museum, Ehnen. 80fr, Sculpture of a Potter, by Leon Nosbusch, Pottery Museum, Nospelt.

Photo. & Engr.
1995, Sept. 18   **Perf. 14**
933 A344 16fr multicolored   .75   .40
934 A344 32fr multicolored   2.25   .90
935 A344 80fr multicolored   4.50 2.25
     Nos. 933-935 (3)   7.50 3.55

Luxembourg-Reykjavik, Iceland Air Route, 40th Anniv. — A363

1995, Sept. 18   **Litho.**   **Perf. 13**
936 A363 16fr multicolored   .90   .55

See Iceland No. 807.

Tourism A364

1995, Sept. 18   **Photo.**   **Perf. 11½**
937 A364 16fr Erpeldange   1.00   .65
938 A364 16fr Schengen   1.00   .65

Portrait of Emile Mayrisch (1862-1928), by Théo Van Rysselberghe (1862-1926) — A365

1996, Mar. 2   **Photo.**   **Perf. 11½**
939 A365 (A) multicolored   1.25   .50

On day of issue No. 939 was valued at 16fr. See Belgium No. 1602.

National Railway, 50th Anniv. — A366

Passenger train: a, Cab facing left. b, Hooked together. c, Cab facing right.

1996, Mar. 4   **Photo.**   **Perf. 11½**
940   Strip of 3   3.75 2.75
a.-c. A366 16fr Any single   1.25   .70

No. 940 is a continuous design.

Grand Duchess Charlotte (1896-1985) — A367

Design: Statue, Luxembourg City.

1996, Mar. 4   **Booklet Stamp**
941 A367 16fr multicolored   .95   .75
a.   Booklet pane of 8   7.50
     Complete booklet, #941a   7.50

Mihály Munkácsy (1844-1900), Hungarian Painter — A368

Designs: No. 942, Portrait of Munkácsy, by Edouard Charlemont, 1884. No. 943, Portrait of Marie Munchen, by Munkácsy, 1885, vert.

1996, May 20   **Perf. 11½**
942 A368 16fr multicolored   .70   .50
943 A368 16fr multicolored   .70   .50

Famous Women — A369

Europa: 16fr, Marie de Bourgogne (1457-82), duchess of Luxembourg. 25fr, Empress Maria-Theresa of Austria (1717-80), duchess of Luxembourg.

Photo. & Engr.

1996, May 20			Perf. 14x13½	
944	A369	16fr multicolored	1.00	.70
945	A369	25fr multicolored	1.50	.90

Luxembourg Confederation of Christian Trade Unions, 75th Anniv. A370

Radio, Cent. — A371

Modern Olympic Games, Cent. — A372

Motion Pictures, Cent. — A373

Perf. 12x11½, 11½x12

1996, May 20			Photo.	
946	A370	16fr multicolored	.90	.60
947	A371	20fr multicolored	1.25	.70
948	A372	25fr multicolored	1.60	1.25
949	A373	32fr multicolored	1.90	1.25
		Nos. 946-949 (4)	5.65	3.80

Registration and Property Administration, Bicent. — A374

1996, Sept. 23		Photo.	Perf. 11½	
950	A374	16fr multicolored	1.00	.60

Let Us Live Together A375

No. 951, Four children. No. 952, "L'Abbraccio," bronze statue by M.J. Kerschen, vert.

1996, Sept. 23				
951	A375	16fr multicolored	1.00	.50
952	A375	16fr multicolored	1.00	.50

Mustelidae A376

Litho. & Engr.

1996, Sept. 23			Perf. 13½	
953	A376	16fr Meles meles	1.00	.50
954	A376	20fr Mustela putorius	1.50	.60
955	A376	80fr Lutra lutra	4.00	2.75
		Nos. 953-955 (3)	6.50	3.85

John the Blind (1296-1346), King of Bohemia, Count of Luxembourg A377

Litho. & Engr.

1996, Dec. 9			Perf. 13½	
956	A377	32fr multicolored	1.75	1.00

Grand Duke Jean Type of 1993

Litho. & Engr.

1997, Jan. 2			Perf. 13½x13	
957	A337	8fr green & black	.60	.30

Treaties of Rome, 40th Anniv. A378

Belgian-Luxembourg Economic Union, 75th Anniv. — A379

1997, Mar. 3		Photo.	Perf. 11½	
958	A378	16fr multicolored	1.00	.60
959	A379	20fr multicolored	1.00	.65

Tourism A380

Designs: No. 960, Servais House, Mersch. No. 961, Baroque Church, Koerich, vert.

1997, Mar. 3				
960	A380	16fr multicolored	.85	.60
961	A380	16fr multicolored	.85	.60

11th World Congress of Rose Societies — A381

Roses: 16fr, Grand Duchess Charlotte. 20fr, Beautiful Sultana. 80fr, In Memory of Jean Soupert.

1997, Mar. 3			Perf. 11½	
962	A381	16fr multicolored	1.25	.75

Size: 33x25mm

963	A381	20fr multicolored	1.25	.75
964	A381	80fr multicolored	4.50	3.50
		Nos. 962-964 (3)	7.00	5.00

Stories and Legends — A382

Europa: 16fr, Melusina of Luxembourg. 25fr, Hunter of Hollenfels.

1997, May 12				
965	A382	16fr multicolored	1.25	.60
966	A382	25fr multicolored	2.25	.80

A383   A384

Mondorf Spa, 150th Anniv. A385

1997, May 12				
967	A383	16fr multicolored	.90	.55
968	A384	16fr multicolored	.90	.55
969	A385	16fr multicolored	.90	.55
		Nos. 967-969 (3)	2.70	1.65

Grand-Ducal Gendarmerie, bicent. (No. 967). Union of Small Domestic Animals Farming Societies, 75th anniv. (No. 968).

JUVALUX 98 — A386

1997, May 12				
970	A386	16fr Emblem	.95	.60
971	A386	80fr Postal history	4.00	2.75

Saar-Lorraine-Luxembourg Summit — A387

1997, Oct. 16		Photo.	Perf. 11½	
972	A387	16fr multicolored	1.00	.50

See Germany No. 1982 & France No. 2613.

Mills — A388   Clocks — A389

Litho. & Engr.

1997, Oct. 16			Perf. 13½	
973	A388	16fr Kalborn Mill, horiz.	1.00	.60
974	A388	50fr Ramelli Mill	3.00	2.00

Photo. & Engr.

1997, Oct. 16			Perf. 13x13½	

Designs: 16fr, Oak wall clock, 1816. 32fr, Astronomic clock with walnut case, mid 19th cent. 80fr, Pear tree wood wall clock, 1815.

975	A389	16fr multicolored	1.25	.60
976	A389	32fr multicolored	1.75	1.25
977	A389	80fr multicolored	4.50	3.00
		Nos. 975-977 (3)	7.50	4.85

Henry V, the Blonde (1247-81), Count of Luxembourg A390

1997, Dec. 8		Photo.	Perf. 11½	
978	A390	32fr multicolored	1.60	1.25

Tourism A391

No. 979, Hesperange. No. 980, Rodange Church, vert.

1998, Mar. 23		Photo.	Perf. 11½	
979	A391	16fr multicolored	.95	.60
980	A391	16fr multicolored	.95	.60

See Nos. 1023-1024, 1048-1049.

Freshwater Fish A392

Designs: 16fr, Salmo trutta. 25fr, Cottus gobio. 50fr, Alburnoides bipunctatus.

Litho. & Engr.

1998, Mar. 23			Perf. 13½x13	
981	A392	16fr multicolored	1.00	.50
982	A392	25fr multicolored	2.00	1.40
983	A392	50fr multicolored	3.00	2.00
		Nos. 981-983 (3)	6.00	3.90

NGL (Independent Luxembourg Trade Union), 50th Anniv. — A393

Broom Festival, Wiltz, 50th Anniv. — A394

Jean Antoine Zinnen (1827-98), Composer A395

Abolition of Censorship, 150th Anniv. A396

1998, Mar. 23		Photo.	Perf. 11½	
984	A393	16fr multicolored	1.00	.60
985	A394	16fr multicolored	1.00	.60
986	A395	20fr multicolored	1.00	.80
987	A396	50fr multicolored	2.75	2.00
		Nos. 984-987 (4)	5.75	4.00

King Henri VII (1275?-1313) of
Luxembourg, King of Germany, Holy
Roman Emperor — A397

1998, June 18　Photo.　Perf. 11½
988　A397 (A) multicolored　　　1.25　.60
　Granting of the Right to hold a Luxembourg
Fair, 700th anniv.
　No. 988 was valued at 16fr on the day of
issue.

Natl. Holidays and　　　Juvalux
Festivals — A398　　　　98 — A399

A400

Europa: 16fr, Fireworks over bridge,
National Day. 25fr, Flame, stained glass window, National Remembrance Day.

1998, June 18
989　A398 16fr multicolored　　1.40　.50
990　A398 25fr multicolored　　1.60　.65

1998, June 18　　Photo. & Engr.
　16fr, Town postman, 1880. 25fr, Letter,
1590, horiz. 50fr, Country postman, 1880.
　No. 994, Engraving showing 1861 view of
Luxembourg.
991　A399 16fr multicolored　　1.00　.60
992　A399 25fr multicolored　　1.50　1.00
993　A399 50fr multicolored　　2.50　1.75
　　Nos. 991-993 (3)　　　　　5.00　3.35
　　Souvenir Sheet
994　　　Sheet of 2　　　　6.00　6.00
a.　A400 16fr multicolored　　.90　.90
b.　A400 80fr multicolored　　4.00　4.00

St. Jean de
L'Esperance,
Grand Lodge of
Luxembourg,
150th
Anniv. — A401

1998, Sept. 21　Litho.　Perf. 13½
995　A401 16fr multicolored　　　.90　.50

Abbey of
Echternach,
1300th Anniv.
A402

Various architectural drawings.

1998, Sept 21　Photo.　Perf. 11½
996　A402 16fr multicolored　　1.00　.60
997　A402 48fr multicolored　　2.50　1.90
998　A402 60fr multicolored　　3.50　1.90
　　Nos. 996-998 (3)　　　　　7.00　4.40

Museum
Exhibits
A403

City of Luxembourg History Museum: 16fr,
Spanish army helmet, 16th cent. 80fr, Wayside
Cross, Hollerich, 1718.

Litho. & Engr.
1998, Sept. 21　　　　Perf. 13½
999　A403 16fr multicolored　　1.25　.60
1000　A403 80fr multicolored　　4.25　2.75

NAMSA (NATO Maintenance and
Supply Organization), 40th
Anniv. — A404

1998, Dec. 7　Photo.　Perf. 11½
1001　A404 36fr multicolored　　2.25　1.25

Introduction
of the Euro
A405

1999, Mar. 8　Photo.　Perf. 11½
1002　A405 (A) multicolored　　1.25　.60
　No. 1002 was valued at 16fr on the day of
issue.

Council of Europe, 50th
Anniv. — A406

1999, Mar. 8
1003　A406 16fr multicolored　　　1.25　.65

Owls
A407

1999, Mar. 8　　　　　Perf. 12
1004　A407 (A) Strix aluco, vert.　1.00　.65
1005　A407 32fr Bubo bubo　　2.00　1.75
1006　A407 60fr Tyto alba　　　4.00　2.50
　　Nos. 1004-1006 (3)　　　　7.00　4.90
　No. 1004 was valued at 16fr on the day of
issue.

NATO,
50th
Anniv.
A408

1999, Mar. 8　　　　　Perf. 11½
1007　A408 80fr multicolored　　6.50　3.50

Europa — A409

National Parks: 16fr, Haute-Sûre. 25fr,
Ardennes-Eifel.

1999, May 17　Photo.　Perf. 11½x12
1008　A409 16fr multicolored　　1.25　.50
1009　A409 25fr multicolored　　1.75　.80

Natl. Federation of　　Intl. Year of Older
Mutuality, 75th　　　　Persons — A411
Anniv. — A410

UPU,
125th
Anniv.
A412

A413　　　　　　　A414

1999, May 17　　　　　Perf. 11½
1010　A410 16fr multicolored　　1.00　.65
1011　A411 16fr multicolored　　1.00　.65
1012　A412 16fr multicolored　　1.00　.65
1013　A413 32fr multicolored　　1.75　1.60
1014　A414 80fr multicolored　　4.25　3.25
　　Nos. 1010-1014 (5)　　　　9.00　6.80
　Luxembourg Federation of Amateur Photog-
raphers, 50th anniv. (No. 1013). Luxembourg
Gymnastics Federation, cent. (No. 1014).

18th Birthday of
Prince Guillaume
A415

Photo. & Engr.
1999, Sept. 21　　　　Perf. 13½
1015　A415 16fr multicolored　　1.00　.65

Aline Mayrisch-
de Saint-Hubert
(1874-1947),
President of
Luxembourg
Red
Cross — A416

1999, Sept. 21　　　Litho. & Engr.
1016　A416 20fr multicolored　　1.25　.90

Travelling Into
the Future
A417

1999, Sept. 21　Photo.　Perf. 11¾
1017　A417 16fr Communication
　　　　　　by road　　　　.85　.70
1018　A417 20fr Information age　1.00　1.00
1019　A417 80fr Conquering
　　　　　　space　　　　4.25　3.25
　　Nos. 1017-1019 (3)　　　　6.10　4.95
　　See Nos. 1063-1065.

Johann Wolfgang von Goethe (1749-
1832), German Poet — A418

1999, Nov. 30　Photo.　Perf. 11¾
1020　A418 20fr henna & dk brn　1.25　.90

Year 2000 — A419

No. 1021: a, Large white area under A and
2000. b, Large blue area under A. c, Large
blue area under A and URG. d, Large blue
area under LUX.

Serpentine Die Cut 8 Vert.
2000, Jan. 3　　　　　　Photo.
Self-Adhesive
Booklet Stamps
1021　A419　Booklet pane of 4　4.00
a.-d.　　(A) Any single　　　1.00　.60
　　　Booklet, 2 #1021　　　8.00
Nos. 1021a-1021d sold for 16fr on day of
issue.

Holy Roman
Emperor
Charles V
(1500-58)
A420

Litho. & Engr.
2000, Mar. 7　　　　　Perf. 13½
1022　A420 A multi　　　　1.00　.50
　Sold for 16fr on day of issue.

Tourism Type of 1998
Designs: No. 1023, Walferdange Castle. No.
1024, Wasserbillig railway station, vert.

Perf. 11¾x11½, 11½x11¾
2000, Mar. 7　　　　　　Photo.
Granite Paper
1023　A391 A multi　　　　1.00　.50
1024　A391 A multi　　　　1.00　.50
　Sold for 16fr on day of issue.

World Mathematics Year A421

2000, Mar. 7   **Perf. 11½x11¾**
1025 A421 80fr multi   4.50 2.75

Grand Duke Jean Type of 1993
Litho. & Engr.
2000, Mar. 31   **Perf. 13¼x13**
Background Color
1026 A337 9fr pink   .50 .30

Musical Instruments — A422

Perf. 11½x11¾
2000, Mar. 31   **Photo.**
Granite Paper
1027 A422 3fr French horn   .25 .25
1028 A422 12fr Saxophone   .60 .45
1029 A422 21fr Violin   1.25 .65
1030 A422 30fr Piano   1.50 1.10
    Nos. 1027-1030 (4)   3.60 2.45
    See Nos. 1045-1046.

Ducks A423

Designs: 18fr, Anas platyrhynchos. 24fr, Aythya ferina, vert. 30fr, Aythya fuligula.

2000, May 9   **Perf. 11¾x11½**
Granite Paper
1031 A423 18fr multi   1.00 .60
Perf. 11½x11¾
1032 A423 24fr multi   1.50 .90
1033 A423 30fr multi   2.00 1.25
    Nos. 1031-1033 (3)   4.50 2.75

Esch-sur-Alzette Gas Works, Cent. (in 1999) — A424

2000, May 9   **Perf. 11¾x11½**
Granite Paper
1034 A424 18fr multi   1.25 .60

Europa, 2000
Common Design Type
2000, May 9   **Perf. 11½x11¾**
Granite Paper
1035 CD17 21fr multi   1.40 1.00

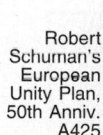

Robert Schuman's European Unity Plan, 50th Anniv. A425

2000, May 9   **Perf. 11½x11¾**
1036 A425 21fr multi   1.25 .75

Art Collection of Luxembourg Posts & Telecommunications — A426

Art by: 21fr, Will Kesseler. 24fr, Joseph Probst, vert. 36fr, Mett Hoffmann.

Perf. 11¾x11½, 11½x11¾
2000, Sept. 27   **Photo.**
Granite Paper
1037 A426 21fr multi   1.25 .50
1038 A426 24fr multi   1.50 .75
1039 A426 36fr multi   2.50 1.25
    Nos. 1037-1039 (3)   5.25 2.50

Towers on Historic Walking Trails A427

Designs: 18fr, Tower of Jacob, Wenzel trail. 42fr, Bons Malades Gate, Vauban trail.

Photo. & Engr.
2000, Sept. 27   **Perf. 13½x14¼**
1040 A427 18fr multi   1.00 .60
1041 A427 42fr multi   2.75 1.75

Blast Furnace "B," Esch-Belval A428

2000, Sept. 27   **Perf. 11¾x11½**
1042 A428 A multi   1.00 .60
    No. 1042 sold for 18fr on day of issue.

Accession of Grand Duke Henri A429

Designs: 18fr, Prince Henri in uniform, Princess Maria Teresa in pink suit. 100fr, Prince in suit, Princess in red blouse.

2000, Sept. 27   **Photo.**   **Perf. 11¾**
Granite Paper (18fr)
1043 A429 18fr multi   1.00 .70
Souvenir Sheet
Photo. (margin Photo. & Engr.)
Perf. 11½
1044 A429 100fr multi   6.00 6.00
    No. 1043 issued in sheets of 12, five of which (positions 6, 8, 9, 10 and 11) have a red and blue "ribbon" running diagonally through stamp margin. No. 1044 contains one 46x35mm stamp.

Musical Instruments Type of 2000
2000, Dec. 5   **Photo.**   **Perf. 11½x11¾**
Granite Paper
1045 A422 9fr Electric guitar   .40 .30
1046 A422 24fr Accordion   1.20 .80

Treaty Establishing European Coal and Steel Community, 50th Anniv. — A430

Perf. 11¼x11½
2001, Mar. 20   **Photo.**
1047 A430 21fr multi   1.25 .75

Tourism Type of 1998
Designs: No. 1048, 18fr, Bestgen Mill, Schifflange. No. 1049, 18fr, Chapel, Wormeldange, and millstone, Ahn, vert.

Perf. 11¾x11½, 11½x11¾
2001, Mar. 20
Granite Paper
1048-1049 A391 Set of 2   2.25 1.25

Writers — A431

Designs: 18fr, Nik Welter (1871-1951). 24fr, André Gide (1869-1951). 30fr, Michel Rodange (1827-76).

Perf. 13½x13¼
2001, Mar. 20   **Litho. & Engr.**
1050-1052 A431 Set of 3   4.25 2.40

Europa A432

Designs: A (18fr), Stream, Mullerthal region. 21fr, Pond and Kaltreis water tower, Luxembourg-Bonnevoie.

Perf. 11¾x11½, 11½x11¾
2001, May 22   **Photo.**
Granite Paper
1053-1054 A432 Set of 2   2.25 1.60

Rescue Workers — A433

Designs: 18fr, Air rescue. 30fr, Rescue divers. 45fr, Fire fighters.

2001, May 22   **Perf. 11½x11¾**
Granite Paper
1055-1057 A433 Set of 3   5.75 4.00

Humanitarian Services — A434

Designs: 18fr, Humanitarian aid. 24fr, Intl. Organization for Migration, 50th anniv.

2001, May 22   **Perf. 11½**
1058-1059 A434 Set of 2   2.50 1.75

Old Postal Vehicles — A435

Designs: 3fr, Citroen 2CV Mini-van, 1960s. 18fr, Volkswagen Beetle, 1970s.

Granite Paper
Serpentine Die Cut 8¼ Vert.
2001, May 22   **Booklet Stamps**
1060 A435 3fr multi   .25 .25
1061 A435 18fr multi   1.10 .75
    a.   Booklet, 6 each #1060-1061   8.00

European Year of Languages A436

2001, Oct. 1   **Photo.**   **Perf. 11¾x11½**
Granite Paper
1062 A436 A multi   1.10 .80

    Luxembourg postal officials state that No. 1062 sold for 45 eurocents on the day of issue, though euro currency was not in circulation on the day of issue. On the day of issue, 45 eurocents was the equivalent of approximately 18fr.

    Nos. 1063-1071, 1074, 1076, 1078, 1080, 1084, and B425-B429 are denominated solely in euro currency though euro currency would not circulate until Jan. 1, 2002. From their date of issue until Dec. 31, 2001, these stamps could be purchased for Luxembourg francs. The official pegged rate of 40.3399 francs to the euro made rounding the franc purchase price a necessity for such purchases. The approximate franc equivalent of the euro denominations is shown in parentheses in the listings.

Traveling Into the Future Type of 1999
Designs: 45c (18fr), Renewable energy. 59c (24fr), Waste recycling. 74c (30fr), Biological research.

2001, Oct. 1   **Perf. 11¾**
Granite Paper
1063-1065 A417 Set of 3   4.50 3.25

Euro Coinage A437

Designs: Coin obverses with values of stamp denominations.

2001, Oct. 1   **Perf. 11½**
1066 A437 5c (2fr) multi   .25 .25
1067 A437 10c (4fr) multi   .25 .25
1068 A437 20c (8fr) multi   .50 .40
1069 A437 50c (20fr) multi   1.25 .90
1070 A437 €1 (40fr) multi   2.50 1.75
1071 A437 €2 (80fr) multi   5.25 3.75
    Nos. 1066-1071 (6)   10.00 7.30

Grand Duke Henri — A438

Photo. & Engr.
2001-03   **Perf. 11¾x11½**
Vignette Color
1072 A438 1c blue   .25 .25
1073 A438 3c green   .25 .25
1074 A438 7c (3fr) blue   .25 .25
1075 A438 22c (9fr) brown   .55 .40

1076	A438	30c (12fr) green		.75	.45
1077	A438	45c (18fr) violet		1.10	.65
1078	A438	52c brown		1.40	.90
1079	A438	59c blue		1.50	.90
1080	A438	74c brown		1.90	1.10
1081	A438	89c red violet		2.25	1.25
		Nos. 1072-1081 (10)		10.20	6.40

Issued: 7c, 22c, 30c, 45c, 10/1/01. 52c, 59c, 74c, 89c, 3/5/02. 1c, 3c, 10/1/03.
See Nos. 1126, 1129-1133A.

Kiwanis International A439

2001, Dec. 6 Photo. Perf. 11½
1084 A439 52c (21fr) multi 1.40 .95

100 Cents = 1 Euro (€)

Art Collection of Luxembourg Posts & Telecommunications — A440

Art by: 22c, Moritz Ney, vert. 45c, Dany Prüm. 59c, Christiane Schmit, vert.

Perf. 14¼x14, 14x14¼
2002, Mar. 5 Photo.
1085-1087 A440 Set of 3 3.25 2.25

European Court Anniversaries A441

Designs: 45c, European Court of Auditors, 25th anniv. 52c, Court of Justice of the European communities, 50th anniv.

2002, Mar. 5 Litho. Perf. 13½
1088-1089 A441 Set of 2 2.50 1.75

Sports — A442

No. 1090: a, Snowboarding. b, Skateboarding. c, Rollerblading. d, Bicycling. e, Volleyball. f, Basketball.

Booklet Stamps
Die Cut Perf. 10 on 3 Sides
2002, Mar. 5 Self-Adhesive
1090 Booklet pane of 6 4.00
a.-c. A442 7c Any single .25 .25
d.-f. A442 45c Any single 1.10 .80
  Booklet, 2 #1090 8.00

Europa — A443

Designs: 45c, Tightrope walker. 52c, Clown.

2002, May 14 Litho. Perf. 13½
1091-1092 A443 Set of 2 3.00 1.75

Cultural Anniversaries — A444

Designs: A, 50th Wiltz Festival. €1.12, Victor Hugo (1802-85), writer.

2002, May 14 Perf. 13¼
1093-1094 A444 Set of 2 4.00 3.00
No. 1093 sold for 45c on day of issue.

Start of Tour de France in Luxembourg A445

Designs: 45c, Stylized bicycle. 52c, François Faber (1887-1915), 1909 champion. €2.45, The Champion, by Joseph Kutter.

Litho. (45c), Litho. & Engr.
Perf. 13¼x13½, 13½x13¼
2002, May 14
1095-1097 A445 Set of 3 9.00 6.25

Grevenmacher Charter of Freedom, 750th Anniv. — A446

2002, Sept. 14 Litho. Perf. 13¼x13
1098 A446 74c multi 1.90 1.50

Nature Museum, Museum of Natural History A447

No. 1099: a, Water drop on spruce needle. b, Butterfly. c, Leaf rosette of *Echeveria* plant. d, Berries.

Serpentine Die Cut 8 Vert.
2002, Sept. 14 Photo.
Self-Adhesive
1099 Booklet pane of 4 4.50
a.-d. A447 A Any single 1.10 .80
  Booklet, 2 #1099 9.00

Nos. 1099a-1099d had franking value of 45c on day of issue, but booklet sold for discounted price of €3.35.

Souvenir Sheet

Luxembourg Stamps, 150th Anniv. — A448

No. 1100: a, Grand Duke William II, man and woman, 1852 (47x27mm). b, Grand Duke Adolphe, woman, 1902 (47x27mm). c, Grand Duchess Charlotte, street scene, 1952 (47x27mm). d, Grand Duke Henri, hot air balloons in street, 2002 (71x27mm).

Photo. & Engr.
2002, Sept. 14 Perf. 11¾
1100 A448 45c Sheet of 4, #a-d 4.75 4.75

The Post in 50 Years A449

Designs: 22c, Postmen in spacecraft, buildings, vert. A, Spacecraft in flight, cell phone, letter and "@" in orbit around planet.

Perf. 14x14½, 14½x14
2002, Oct. 19 Litho.
1101-1102 A449 Set of 2 1.75 1.40
No. 1102 sold for 45c on day of issue.

Grand Duke Jean and Princess Joséphine-Charlotte, 50th Wedding Anniv. — A450

Perf. 14¼x14½
2003, Mar. 18 Litho.
1103 A450 45c multi 1.10 .95

Official Journal of the European Communities, 50th Anniv. — A451

2003, Mar. 18 Perf. 14½x14
1104 A451 52c multi 1.40 1.10

Famous Women A452

Designs: No. 1105, 45c, Catherine Schleimer-Kill (1884-1973), feminist leader. No. 1106, 45c, Lou Koster (1889-1973), composer.

2003, Mar. 18 Photo. Perf. 11½
1105-1106 A452 Set of 2 2.40 1.90

Tourism A453

Designs: 50c, Fontaine Marie Convent, Differdange. €1, Castle, Mamer. €2.50, St. Joseph Church, Esch-sur-Alzette, vert.

Perf. 14½x14, 14x14½
2003, Mar. 18 Litho.
1107-1109 A453 Set of 3 9.50 9.50

Luxembourg Athénée, 400th Anniv. A454

2003, May 20 Litho. Perf. 14¼x14½
1110 A454 45c multi 1.10 1.00

Europa A455

Poster art: 45c, 1952 poster for National Lottery, by Roger Gerson. 52c, 1924 poster for Third Commercial Fair, by Auguste Trémont.

2003, May 20 Perf. 13¼x13
1111-1112 A455 Set of 2 2.25 1.75

Bridges — A456

Designs: 45c, Adolphe Bridge, 1903. 59c, Stierchen Bridge, 14th cent. (36x26mm). 89c, Victor Bodson Bridge, 1994 (36x26mm).

Photo. & Engr.
2003, May 20 Perf. 11½
1113-1115 A456 Set of 3 5.00 4.25

Electrification of Luxembourg, 75th Anniv. — A457

Litho. & Embossed
2003, Sept. 23 Perf. 13¼x13
1116 A457 A multi 1.25 1.25
Sold for 50c on day of issue.

Breastfeeding A458

2003, Sept. 23 Litho. Perf. 13½
1117 A458 A multi 1.25 1.25
Sold for 50c on day of issue.

Gaart an Heem Agricultural Cooperatives, 75th Anniv. — A459

Gardeners with: 25c, Spade. A, Basket and rake. €2, Watering can.

2003, Sept. 23   **Perf. 14½x14**
1118-1120 A459   Set of 3   7.00 6.50

No. 1119 sold for 50c on day of issue.

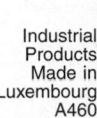

Industrial Products Made in Luxembourg A460

Designs: 60c, Steel. 70c, Industrial valve. 80c, Polyester film.

2003, Oct. 1   **Photo.**   **Perf. 11½**
1121-1123 A460   Set of 3   5.00 5.00

Grand Duke Henri Type of 2001-03
Photo. & Engr.
2004-2010   **Perf. 11¾x11½**
Vignette Color
1124	A438	5c violet brn	.25	.25
1125	A438	10c black	.30	.30
1126	A438	25c claret	.65	.65
1129	A438	50c black	1.25	1.25
1130	A438	60c blue	1.50	1.50
1131	A438	70c purple	1.75	1.75
1132	A438	80c olive black	2.10	2.00
1133	A438	90c brown	2.25	2.25
1133A	A438	€1 blue	2.60	2.60
	Nos. 1126-1133A (7)		12.10	12.00

Issued: 25c, 50c, 60c, 80c, 3/16/04; 70c, 90c, €1, 9/26/06; 5c, 10c, 12/7/10.

Emigrants to the United States A461

Designs: 50c, Edward Steichen (1879-1973), photographer. 70c, Hugo Gernsbach (1884-1967), science fiction writer.

Photo. & Engr.
2004, Mar. 16   **Perf. 11½**
1134-1135 A461   Set of 2   3.25 3.00

Anniversaries of Commercial Events A462

Designs: No. 1136, 50c, Commercial Union of Esch-sur-Alzette, cent. No. 1137, Luxembourg City Annual Street Market, 75th anniv.

2004, Mar. 16   **Litho.**   **Perf. 14¼**
1136-1137 A462   Set of 2   2.60 2.60

Mushrooms — A463

No. 1138: a, Cantharellus tubaeformis. b, Ramaria flava. c, Stropharia cyanea. d, Helvella lacunosa. e, Anthurus archeri. f, Clitopilus prunulus.

Die Cut Perf. 10
2004, Mar. 16   **Litho.**
Self-Adhesive
1138	Booklet pane of 6	4.50	
a.-c.	A463 10c Any single	.25	.25
d.-f.	A463 50c Any single	1.25	1.25
	Complete booklet, 2 #1138	9.00	

European Parliament Elections A464

2004, May 9   **Litho.**   **Perf. 13¼x13**
1139 A464 50c multi   1.25 1.25

2004 Summer Olympics, Athens A465

European Sports Education Year A466

2004, May 9   **Photo.**   **Perf. 11½x11¾**
1140 A465 50c multi   1.25 1.25
1141 A466 60c multi   1.40 1.40

European School, 50th Anniv. A467

2004, May 9   **Litho.**   **Perf. 14¼x14½**
1142 A467 70c multi   1.75 1.75

Europa A468

Designs: 50c, Stone bridge over Schiessen-tuempel. 60c, Bourscheid Beach, Bourscheid Castle.

2004, May 9   **Perf. 13¼x13**
1143-1144 A468   Set of 2   3.00 3.00

Luxembourg Stock Exchange, 75th Anniv. — A469

Perf. 11¼x11½
2004, Sept. 28   **Litho. & Engr.**
1145 A469 50c multi   1.25 1.25

Food Products Made in Luxembourg — A470

Designs: 35c, Baked goods, beer. 60c, Meats, wine. 70c, Dairy products.

Perf. 13½x13¾
2004, Sept. 28   **Litho.**
1146-1148 A470   Set of 3   4.00 4.00

National Museum of History and Art — A471

Designs: 50c, Museum building. €1.10, Young Woman with a Fan, by Luigi Rubio. €3, Charity, by Lucas Cranach the Elder or Lucas Cranach the Younger.

2004, Sept. 28   **Photo.**   **Perf. 11¾**
1149-1151 A471   Set of 3   11.50 11.50

World War II Liberation, 60th Anniv. A472

2004, Dec. 7   **Litho.**   **Perf. 14x13½**
1152 A472 70c multi   1.90 1.90

Luxembourg's Presidency of European Union — A473

No. 1153: a, Building with glass facade. b, Arch, Echternach Basilica. c, Vineyard along Moselle River. d, Rusted iron girder.

Serpentine Die Cut 8¼ Vert.
2005, Jan. 25   **Photo.**
Self-Adhesive
1153	Booklet pane of 4	5.00	
a.-d.	A473 A any single	1.25	1.25
	Complete booklet, 2 #1153	10.00	

On the day of issue, Nos. 1153a-1153d each had a franking value of 50c, but complete booklet sold for €3.80.

Rotary International, Cent. — A474

2005, Mar. 15   **Litho.**   **Perf. 13½x13**
1154 A474 50c multi   1.40 1.40

Ettelbrück Neuro-psychiatric Medical Center, 150th Anniv. — A475

2005, Mar. 15   **Perf. 13½**
1155 A475 50c multi   1.40 1.40

76th Intl. Congress of Applied Mathematics and Mechanics A476

2005, Mar. 15
1156 A476 60c multi   1.60 1.60

Benelux Parliament, 50th Anniv. — A477

2005, Mar. 15   **Perf. 13¼x12¾**
1157 A477 60c multi   1.60 1.60

Tourism A478

Designs: 50c, Shoe factory, Kayl-Tétange. 60c, Village scene and website address of National Tourist Office (44x31mm). €1, Statue of St. Eloi, Rodange, and foundry worker.

Perf. 14x13¼, 12¾ (60c)
2005, Mar. 15
1158-1160 A478   Set of 3   5.50 5.50

Opening of Grand Duchess Joséphine-Charlotte Concert Hall — A479

2005, May 24   **Perf. 13¼x13¾**
1161 A479 50c multi   1.25 1.25

Europa A480

Designs: 50c, Judd mat Gaardebounen (pork and beans). 60c, Feirstengszalot (beef, egg and pickle salad).

2005, May 24   **Perf. 13½**
1162-1163 A480   Set of 2   2.75 2.75

Railways A481

Designs: 50c, Niederpallen Station, CVE 357 car of De Jhangeli narrow-gauge railway. 60c, AL-T3 locomotive. €2.50, PH 408 passenger car.

2005, May 24   **Photo.**   **Perf. 11½**
1164-1166 A481   Set of 3   9.00 9.00

Hand Lifting Self-Adhesive Paper From Backing — A482

Coil Stamps

Serpentine Die Cut 11x11¼

2005, May 24		Self-Adhesive		
1167		Vert. strip of 4	2.50	
a.	A482	25c dark red & multi	.60	.60
b.	A482	25c red orange & multi	.60	.60
c.	A482	25c orange & multi	.60	.60
d.	A482	25c yellow & multi	.60	.60
1168		Vert. strip of 4	5.00	
a.	A482	50c dark green & multi	1.25	1.25
b.	A482	50c green & multi	1.25	1.25
c.	A482	50c emerald & multi	1.25	1.25
d.	A482	50c yellow green & multi	1.25	1.25

Rolls of 100 of the 25c stamps sold for €24, and rolls of 100 of the 50c stamps sold for €48.

Famous People A483

Designs: 50c, Jean-Pierre Pescatore (1793-1855), philanthropist. 90c, Marcel Reuland (1905-56), writer. €1, Marie-Henriette Steil (1898-1930), writer, vert.

Photo. & Engr.

2005, Sept. 27			*Perf. 11½*	
1169-1171	A483	Set of 3	6.00	6.00

Butterflies A484

Designs: 35c, Papilio machaon. 70c, Argynnis paphia, vert. €1.80, Lysandra coridon.

2005, Sept. 27			*Litho.*	
1172-1174	A484	Set of 3	7.25	7.25

Rocks A485

No. 1175: a, Schist. b, Rocks with iron (minerai de fer). c, Luxembourg sandstone. d, Conglomerate rocks.

Serpentine Die Cut 12¾ Vert.

2005, Sept. 27		Self-Adhesive	
1175		Booklet pane of 4	4.75
a.-d.	A485	A any single	1.10 1.10
		Complete booklet, 2 #1175	9.50

The complete booklet sold for €3.80, but each stamp had a franking value of 50c on the day of issue.

Seeing Eye Dog A486

Litho. & Embossed

2005, Dec. 6			*Perf. 13x13¼*	
1176	A486	70c dk blue & lemon	1.75	1.75

25th Wedding Anniversary of Grand Duke Henri and Grand Duchess Maria Teresa — A487

2006, Feb. 7		*Litho.*	*Perf. 13¼x13¾*	
1177	A487	50c multi	1.25	1.25

Souvenir Sheet

Perf. 13¼x13

1178	A487	€2.50 multi	6.25	6.25

No. 1178 contains one 26x37mm stamp.

Blood Donation A488

2006, Mar. 14		*Litho.*	*Perf. 13¼*	
1179	A488	50c multi	1.25	1.25

Tourism A489

Designs: No. 1180, 50c, Parc Merveilleux, Bettembourg. No. 1181, 50c, Birelerhaff Pigeon Tower, Sandweiler, vert.

2006, Mar. 14			*Perf. 11½*	
1180-1181	A489	Set of 2	2.40	1.25

Electrification of Railway Network, 50th Anniv. — A490

Designs: 50c, Train passing station. 70c, Train on bridge. €1, Railway workers repairing electrical wires, vert.

2006, Mar. 14		*Perf. 13¼x13, 13x13¼*		
1182-1184	A490	Set of 3	5.25	5.25

Personalized Stamp Website "meng.post.lu" — A491

2006, May 16		*Litho.*	*Perf. 11½*	
1185	A491	A multi + label	1.40	1.40

No. 1185 sold for 50c on day of issue. Labels could be personalized for a fee.

Esch-sur-Alzette, Cent. — A492

2006, May 16			*Perf. 13½*	
1186	A492	50c multi	1.40	1.40

Soccer Teams in Luxembourg, Cent. — A493

2006 World Cup Soccer Championships, Germany — A494

2006, May 16			*Perf. 13x13¼*	
1187	A493	50c multi	1.40	1.40
1188	A494	90c multi	2.40	2.40

Europa A495

Contest-winning cell phone photos: 50c, Hands making heart. 70c, People holding globe.

2006, May 16			*Perf. 12½*	
1189-1190	A495	Set of 2	3.25	3.25

State Council, 150th Anniv. — A496

Litho. & Embossed

2006, Sept. 26			*Perf. 13½*	
1191	A496	50c multi	1.25	1.25

Luxembourg Chess Federation, 75th Anniv. — A497

2006, Sept. 26				
1192	A497	90c multi	2.25	2.25

Bank Sesquicentenaries — A498

Designs: No. 1193, 50c, State Savings Bank (Spuerkeess). No. 1194, 50c, Dexia-BIL Bank.

2006, Sept. 26		*Litho.*	*Perf. 13¼x13*	
1193-1194	A498	Set of 2	2.60	2.60

Fight Against Drug Addiction A499

Designs: 50c, Children's drawing of man and "No Drugs" sign. €1, Ashtray with vegetables and cheese, vert.

2006, Sept. 26			*Perf. 11½*	
1195-1196	A499	Set of 2	3.75	3.75

Luxembourg Horticultural Federation, 75th Anniv. — A500

No. 1197: a, Flowers. b, Fruits and vegetables.

2006, Dec. 5		*Litho.*	*Perf. 13¼x13¾*	
1197	A500	Horiz. pair	3.75	3.75
a.-b.		70c Either single	1.75	1.75

Luxembourg, 2007 European Cultural Capital — A501

No. 1198 — Silhouettes of deer and men with deer heads with background color of: a, Blue. b, Orange. c, Bright yellow green. d, Red violet.

Serpentine Die Cut 8½ Vert.

2007, Jan. 30			*Litho.*	
1198		Booklet pane of 4	5.25	
a.-d.	A501	A Any single	1.25	1.25
		Complete booklet, 2 #1198	10.50	

Nos. 1198a-1198d each sold for 50c on day of issue.

Luxembourg Caritas, 75th Anniv. A502

2007, Mar. 20		*Litho.*	*Perf. 11½*	
1199	A502	50c multi	1.40	1.40

Luxembourg Automobile Club, 75th Anniv. A503

2007, Mar. 20				
1200	A503	50c multi	1.40	1.40

Treaty of Rome, 50th Anniv. A504

Designs: 70c, Delegates. €1, Text and stars.

2007, Mar. 20   *Perf. 13x13¼*
1201-1202 A504 Set of 2   4.75 4.75

"Postes" A505   Denomination A506

Serpentine Die Cut 11x11¼
2007, Mar. 20   **Photo.**
Self-Adhesive
Coil Stamps
1203 A505 25c pur & multi   .70 .70
1204 A506 25c brn & multi   .70 .70
1205 A505 25c dk bl & multi   .70 .70
1206 A506 25c dk grn & multi   .70 .70
   a.   Vert. strip of 4, #1203-1206   2.80
1207 A505 50c red vio & multi   1.40 1.40
1208 A506 50c red & multi   1.40 1.40
1209 A505 50c bl & multi   1.40 1.40
1210 A506 50c grn & multi   1.40 1.40
   a.   Vert. strip of 4, #1207-1210   5.60
   Nos. 1203-1210 (8)   8.40 8.40

Europa A507

Designs: 50c, Scout campground. 70c, Scouts, globe, knot.

2007, May 22   **Litho.**   *Perf. 13x13¼*
1211-1212 A507 Set of 2   3.25 3.25
   Scouting, cent.

Town Centenaries — A508

Designs: No. 1213, 50c, Differdange. No. 1214, 50c, Dudelenge. No. 1215, 50c, Ettelbruck. No. 1216, 50c, Rumelange.

2007, May 22   **Photo.**   *Perf. 11½*
1213-1216 A508 Set of 4   5.50 5.50

Places of Culture A509

Designs: 50c, Rockhal. 70c, Grand Duke Jean Museum of Modern Art. €1, Neumünster Abbey.

2007, May 22   *Perf. 12½*
1217-1219 A509 Set of 3   6.00 6.00

"Transborderism" A510

2007, Sept. 3   **Photo.**   *Perf. 11½*
1220 A510 50c multi   1.40 1.40

Rotunda of Luxembourg Train Station — A511

2007, Sept. 3   **Photo. & Engr.**
1221 A511 70c multi   1.90 1.90
   See Belgium No. 2253.

Casa Luxemburg, Sibiu, Romania — A512

2007, Sept. 3   **Litho.**   *Perf. 13x13¼*
1222 A512 70c multi   1.90 1.90
   See Romania Nos. 4993-4994.

Luxembourg Army Peace-keeping Missions — A513

2007, Sept. 3   **Photo.**   *Perf. 11½*
1223 A513 70c multi   1.90 1.90

Souvenir Sheet

Roman Mosaic, Vichten — A514

No. 1224: a, Thalia and Euterpe. b, Terpsichore and Melpomene. c, Clio and Urania. d, Polymnia and Erato. e, Calliope and Homer. Nos. 1224a-1224d are 58x29mm octagonal stamps, No. 1224e is a 55x55mm diamond-shaped stamp.

2007, Sept. 3   **Litho.**   *Perf. 14¼*
1224 A514 Sheet of 5   8.25 8.25
   a.-d.   50c Any single   1.40 1.40
   e.   €1 multi   2.60 2.60

Esch-sur-Sure Dam — A515

Uewersauer Stauséi — A516

Serpentine Die Cut 12½x13½
2007, Dec. 4   **Litho.**   **Self-Adhesive**
1225   Horiz. pair   4.25
   a.   A515 70c multi   2.10 2.10
   b.   A516 70c multi   2.10 2.10

St. Willibrord (658-739) A517

2008, Mar. 18   **Litho.**   *Perf. 13*
1226 A517 50c multi   1.60 1.60

European Investment Bank, 50th Anniv. A518

2008, Mar. 18   *Perf. 13x13¼*
1227 A518 70c purple & silver   2.25 2.25

Eurosystem, 10th Anniv. — A519

2008, Mar. 18   *Perf. 13½x13¾*
1228 A519 €1 multi   3.25 3.25

Luxembourg Philharmonic Orchestra, 75th Anniv. — A520

Henri Pensis (1900-58), Conductor — A521

2008, Mar. 18
1229 A520 50c multi   1.60 1.60
1230 A521 70c multi   2.25 2.25

2008 Summer Olympics, Beijing A522

2008, May 20   **Litho.**   *Perf. 14x13½*
1231 A522 70c multi   2.25 2.25

Luxembourg Basketball Federation, 75th Anniv. — A523

Luxembourg Soccer Federation, Cent. — A524

2008, May 20   *Perf. 12½*
1232 A523 A multi   1.60 1.60
1233 A524 A multi   1.60 1.60
   Nos. 1232 and 1233 each sold for 50c on day of issue.

Europa A525

Smiling letter with wings: 50c, Standing on hand. 70c, Flying.

2008, May 20
1234-1235 A525 Set of 2   4.00 4.00

Tourism A526

Designs: No. 1236, A, Bridge, Diekirch, and city arms. No. 1237, A, Building, Leudelange, and city arms. No. 1238, A, Rindschleiden Church, Wahl, vert.

2008, May 20   *Perf. 11½*
1236-1238 A526 Set of 3   4.75 4.75
   Diekirch, 125th anniv., Leudelange, 150th anniv. Nos. 1236-1238 each sold for 50c on day of issue.

Medico-social League, Cent. — A527

2008, Sept. 30   **Litho.**   *Perf. 13¾*
1239 A527 A multi   1.40 1.40
   Sold for 50c on day of issue.

Agricultural Technical School, Ettelbruck, 125th Anniv. A528

2008, Sept. 30
1240 A528 A multi ... 1.40 1.40
Sold for 50c on day of issue.

Federation of Popular Education Associations, Cent. — A529

2008, Sept. 30   **Perf. 13x13¼**
1241 A529 A multi ... 1.40 1.40
Sold for 50c on day of issue.

Natl. League for the Protection of Animals, Cent. A530

2008, Sept. 30
1242 A530 A multi ... 1.40 1.40
Sold for 50c on day of issue.

NATO Maintenance and Supply Agency, 50th Anniv. — A531

2008, Sept. 30
1243 A531 70c multi ... 2.00 2.00

Greetings A532

Winning art from children's stamp design contest by: 70c, A. Wainer. €1, S. Rauschenberger.

2008, Sept. 30   **Perf. 11½**
1244-1245 A532 Set of 2 ... 4.75 4.75

A533   A534

Different shapes of colored background lines with "ATR" at: No. 1246, LR. No. 1247, UL. No. 1248, LL. No. 1249, UR.
Different shapes of colored background lines with "A" at: No. 1250, LL. No. 1251, UL. No. 1252, LR. No. 1253, UR.

Coil Stamps

Serpentine Die Cut 11
2008, Sept. 30   **Self-Adhesive**
1246 A533 ATR blue ... .70 .70
1247 A533 ATR purple ... .70 .70
1248 A533 ATR green ... .70 .70
1249 A533 ATR red ... .70 .70
    a.   Vert. strip of 4, #1246-1249 ... 2.80
1250 A534 A multi ... 1.40 1.40
1251 A534 A multi ... 1.40 1.40
1252 A534 A multi ... 1.40 1.40
1253 A534 A multi ... 1.40 1.40
    a.   Vert. strip of 4, #1250-1253 ... 5.60
    Nos. 1246-1253 (8) ... 8.40 8.40
On day of issue, Nos. 1246-1249 each sold for 25c, Nos. 1250-1253, for 50c.

Happiness — A535

No. 1254: a, Bowling pins, denomination over red violet. b, Gift, denomination over yellow green. c, Wrapped candies, denomination over green. d, Wrapped candies, denomination over blue. e, Gift, denomination over green. f, Bowling pins, denomination over yellow green. g, Dice, "A" over red violet. h, Drum and sticks, "A" over yellow green. i, Four-leaf clovers, "A" over green. j, Four-leaf clovers, "A" over blue. k, Drum and sticks, "A" over green. l, Dice, "A" over yellow green.

Die Cut Perf. 10 on 3 Sides
2008, Sept. 30   **Self-Adhesive**
1254   Booklet pane of 12 ... 12.00
   a.-f.   A535 20c Any single ... .55 .55
   g.-l.   A535 A Any single ... 1.40 1.40
Nos. 1254g-1254l each sold for 50c on day of issue.

New Courthouse of Court of Justice of the European Communities — A536

2008, Dec. 2   **Litho.**   **Perf. 14x13¼**
1255 A536 70c multi ... 1.90 1.90

Election of Holy Roman Emperor Henry VII (c. 1269-1313), 700th Anniv. — A537

2008, Dec. 2   **Perf. 13¼x13**
1256 A537 €1 multi ... 2.60 2.60

Introduction of the Euro, 10th Anniv. — A538

2009, Mar. 17   **Litho.**   **Perf. 12½**
1257 A538 A multi ... 1.25 1.25
No. 1257 sold for 50c on day of issue.

Luxembourg Aero Club, Cent. — A539

New Airport Terminal A540

No. 1258: a, Satellite, airplane, hang glider, left half of balloon. b, Right half of balloon, glider, parachutist, jet plane.

2009, Mar. 17   **Perf. 11½**
1258 A539 50c Horiz. pair, #a-b ... 2.60 2.60
1259 A540 90c multi ... 2.25 2.25

Natl. Federation of Fire Fighters, 125th Anniv. A541

Designs: 20c, Modern fire truck. A, Fire fighter rescuing child. €2, Antique fire truck.

2008, Mar. 17   **Perf. 13¼x13¼**
1260-1262 A541 Set of 3 ... 7.00 7.00
No. 1261 sold for 50c on day of issue.

Postmen's Federation, Cent. A542

General Confederation of the Civil Service, Cent. — A543

Natl. Federation of Railroad and Transportation Workers, Cent. — A544

2009, Mar. 17   **Perf. 14x13¼**
1263 A542 50c multi ... 1.25 1.25
1264 A543 A multi ... 1.25 1.25
1265 A544 A multi ... 1.25 1.25
    Nos. 1263-1265 (3) ... 3.75 3.75
On day of issue, Nos. 1264-1265 each sold for 50c.

June 7 European Elections — A545

2009, May 12   **Litho.**   **Perf. 13**
1266 A545 50c multi ... 1.40 1.40

National Research Fund, 10th Anniv. — A546

2009, May 12   **Perf. 13½**
1267 A546 A multi ... 1.40 1.40
No. 1267 sold for 50c on day of issue.

Children's Houses, 125th Anniv. — A547

2009, May 12   **Perf. 12½**
1268 A547 A multi ... 1.40 1.40
No. 1268 sold for 50c on day of issue.

Europa A548

Designs: 50c, Father and child watching comet. 70c, Galileo, telescope, planets.

2009, May 12   **Perf. 13½**
1269-1270 A548 Set of 2 ... 3.25 3.25
Intl. Year of Astronomy.

Personalized Stamps — A549

Stripe color: A, Red. A Europe, Blue.

2009, May 12   **Perf. 11¾x11½**
    Stamp + Label
1271-1272 A549 Set of 2 ... 3.25 3.25
On day of issue, No. 1271 sold for 50c; No. 1272, 70c. Labels bearing text "PostMusée" and pictures are generic and sold for these prices. Labels could be personalized for an additional fee.

Famous People A550

Designs: 70c, Foni Tissen (1909-75), painter. 90c, Charles Bernhoeft (1859-1933), photographer. €1, Henri Tudor (1859-1928), electrical engineer.

Litho. & Engr.
2009, May 12   **Perf. 13½**
1273-1275 A550 Set of 3 ... 7.00 7.00

Vianden Castle A551

Perf. 13¼x12¾
2009, Sept. 16 Litho.
1276 A551 70c multi 2.00 2.00

Louis Braille (1809-52), Educator of the Blind — A552

Litho. & Embossed
2009, Sept. 16 Perf. 13¼x13
1277 A552 90c multi 2.60 2.60

Railroads in Luxembourg, 150th Anniv. — A553

Designs: 50c, Modern electric train. €1, Older electric train. €3, Steam locomotive.

2009, Sept. 16 Litho. Perf. 12½
1278-1280 A553 Set of 3 13.00 13.00

Souvenir Sheet

Luxembourg Federation of Philatelic Societies, 75th Anniv. — A554

No. 1281: a, Luxembourg #198. b, Gate of Three Towers.

Litho. & Embossed
2009, Sept. 16 Perf. 13¾x14
1281 A554 Sheet of 2 3.50 3.50
a. 50c multi 1.50 1.50
b. 70c multi 2.00 2.00

Johannes Gutenberg (c. 1390-1468), Inventor of Movable Type Presses A555

Website Addresses and Movable Type — A556

2009, Dec. 1 Litho. Perf. 13¼x13½
1282 A555 50c multi 1.50 1.50
1283 A556 70c multi 2.10 2.10

See Switzerland No. 1344.

Schengen Convention, 25th Anniv. — A557

2010, Mar. 16 Litho. Perf. 13½x13
1284 A557 70c multi 1.90 1.90

Luxembourg Pavilion, Expo 2010, Shanghai — A558

2010, Mar. 16 Perf. 14x13½
1285 A558 90c multi 2.50 2.50

Eisch Valley Castles — A559

No. 1286 — Various castles with country name at: a, UL. b, LR.

Serpentine Die Cut 12¼x13¼
2010, Mar. 16 Self-Adhesive
1286 Horiz. pair 4.00
a.-b. A559 A Either single 1.90 1.90
On day of issue, Nos. 1286a-1287a each sold for 70c.

Countdown 2010 — A560

Designs: 70c, Arnica montana. €1, Mussels.

2010, Mar. 16 Perf. 11½
1287-1288 A560 Set of 2 4.75 4.75

A561

Royalty — A562

Designs: 50c, Grand Duke Henri. €1, Grand Duchess Charlotte (1896-1985). €3, Grand Duke Henri and Grand Duchess Maria Teresa.

2010, Mar. 16 Perf. 11½
1289-1290 A561 Set of 2 4.25 4.25
Souvenir Sheet
1291 A562 €3 multi 8.25 8.25
Grand Duke Henri's accession to the throne, 10th anniv. (No. 1289).

Marriage of John of Luxembourg and Elizabeth of Bohemia, 700th Anniv. — A563

Photo. & Engr.
2010, June 16 Perf. 11¾x11¼
1292 A563 70c multi 1.75 1.75
Accession to the throne of Bohemia by the House of Luxembourg. See Czech Republic No. 3457.

Europa — A564

Designs: 50c, Child and dragon reading book. 70c, Girl with lasso riding book.

2010, June 16 Litho. Perf. 13½
1293-1294 A564 Set of 2 3.00 3.00

Outdoor Activities — A565

Designs: No. 1295, A, Motorcycling. No. 1296, A Europe, Camping.

2010, June 16 Perf. 13½x13
1295-1296 A565 Set of 2 3.00 3.00
On day of issue, No. 1295 sold for 50c, and No. 1296 sold for 70c. See Nos. 1337-1338.

Souvenir Sheet

Philalux 2011 Intl. Philatelic Exhibition, Luxembourg — A566

No. 1297 — Various sites in Luxembourg: a, 50c (38x38mm). b, 70c, (38x38mm). c, €3, (60x38mm).

Perf. 13¾, 13¼x13¾ (#1297c)
2010, June 16
1297 A566 Sheet of 3 10.50 10.50
a. 50c multi 1.25 1.25
b. 70c multi 1.75 1.75
c. €3 multi 7.50 7.50

Souvenir Sheet

Superjhemp, Comic Strip by Lucien Czuga — A567

No. 1298: a, Bernie the Dog. b, Man smoking pipe. c, Woman, vert. d, Superjhemp. e, Man with glasses, vert.

Serpentine Die Cut 12¼
2010, June 16 Self-Adhesive
1298 A567 Sheet of 5 6.25 6.25
a.-e. A Any single 1.25 1.25
On day of issue, Nos. 1298a-1298e each sold for 50c.

A568

Winning Art in Children's "Fight Against Poverty" Stamp Design Contest A569

2010, Sept. 27 Litho. Perf. 11½
1299 A568 A multi 1.25 1.25
1300 A569 A Europe multi 1.75 1.75
On day of issue No. 1299 sold for 50c and No. 1300 sold for 70c.

Famous People A570

Designs: 70c, Anne Beffort (1880-1966), educator and writer. 90c, Jean Soupert (1834-1910), rose cultivator. €1, Nicolas Frantz (1899-1985), cyclist.

Litho. & Engr.
2010, Sept. 27 Perf. 13½
1301-1303 A570 Set of 3 6.75 6.75

Bagatelle Rose — A571

Bona Rose — A572

Bordeaux Rose — A573

Reine Marguerite
d'Italie
Rose — A574

Souvenir de
Maria de Zayas
Rose — A575

Clotilde
Rose — A576

Prince Jean de
Luxembourg
Rose — A577

Pierre Watine
Rose — A578

Ivan Misson
Rose — A579

William Notting
Rose — A580

Serpentine Die Cut 9¾
2010, Sept. 27 **Litho.**
Self-Adhesive

1304	Booklet pane of 10		12.50	
a.	A571 A multi		1.25	1.25
b.	A572 A multi		1.25	1.25
c.	A573 A multi		1.25	1.25
d.	A574 A multi		1.25	1.25
e.	A575 A multi		1.25	1.25
f.	A576 A multi		1.25	1.25
g.	A577 A multi		1.25	1.25
h.	A578 A multi		1.25	1.25
i.	A579 A multi		1.25	1.25
j.	A580 A multi		1.25	1.25

Nos. 1304a-1304j each sold for 50c on day
of issue.

Luxembourg Maritime Cluster — A581

No. 1305 — Ships with lion emblem at: a,
Left. b, Right.

2010, Dec. 7 **Litho.** **Perf. 11½**
1305 A581 A Horiz. pair, #a-b   4.75 4.75
Nos. 1305a and 1305b each sold for 85c on
day of issue.

European
Year of
Volunteering
A582

2011, Mar. 15 **Perf. 13¼x13**
1306 A582 A multi   1.75 1.75
No. 1306 sold for 60c on day of issue.

Royalty
A583

Designs: 85c, Prince Guillaume, 30th birthday. €1.10, Grand Duke Jean, 90th birthday.

2011, Mar. 15 **Perf. 11½**
1307-1308 A583   Set of 2   5.50 5.50

Anniversaries
A584

Designs: No. 1309, 60c, Luxembourg Federation of Quilleurs (nine-pin bowling), 50th
anniv. No. 1310, 60c, Amnesty International,
50th anniv. No. 1311, 60c, Stamp Day, 75th
anniv.

2011, Mar. 15
1309-1311 A584   Set of 3   5.00 5.00

Europa
A585

Designs: 60c, Forest. 80c, Hills.

2011, May 17 **Litho.** **Perf. 13½**
1312-1313 A585   Set of 2   4.25 4.25
Intl. Year of Forests.

Viticulture — A586

Designs: 60c, Sun with grapes, wine glass
and bottle. 85c, Cork of Crémant de Luxembourg sparkling wine bottle.

2011, May 17 **Perf. 11½**
1314-1315 A586   Set of 2   4.25 4.25
Federation of Viticulture Associations of
Luxembourg, cent. (No. 1314), Crémant de
Luxembourg, 20th anniv. (No. 1315).

Personalized Stamps — A587

Denominations: 60c, 85c, vert.

Perf. 11¼x11½, 11½x11¼
2011, May 17 **Self-Adhesive**
1316-1317 A587   Set of 2   4.25 4.25
Vignettes showing picture and "Mäi Moment
/ Meng Photo / Meng Post" text are generic
and sold at their face values. Vignettes could
be personalized for an additional fee.

Miniature Sheet

The Last Knight, Comic Strip by
Lucien Czuga and Andy
Genen — A588

No. 1318: a, Dragon. b, Knight wearing sunglasses, horiz. c, Man, horiz. d, Cat.

Serpentine Die Cut 12¼
2011, May 17 **Self-Adhesive**
1318   A588   Sheet of 4   7.00
a.-d.   A Any single   1.75 1.75
On day of issue, Nos. 1318a-1318d each
sold for 60c.

Luxembourg Consumers Union, 50th
Anniv. — A589

2011, Sept. 27 **Perf. 11½**
1319 A589 60c multi   1.75 1.75

Campaign
Against
AIDS, 30th
Anniv.
A590

2011, Sept. 27
1320 A590 60c multi   1.75 1.75

Cercle Cité,
Luxembourg
A591

2011, Sept. 27
1321 A591 A multi   1.75 1.75
No. 1321 sold for 60c on day of issue.

Franz Liszt
(1811-86),
Composer
A592

2011, Sept. 27 **Perf. 14¼x14¾**
1322 A592 85c multi   2.40 2.40

Chemin de la Corniche,
Luxembourg — A593

2011, Sept. 27 **Perf. 11½**
1323 A593 85c multi   2.40 2.40

Post Checks, Cent. — A594

2011, Dec. 6 **Litho.** **Perf. 11½x11¾**
1324 A594 60c multi   1.60 1.60

Souvenir Sheet

Echternacht Hopping Procession
(UNESCO Intangible
Heritage) — A595

No. 1325 — Procession participants and: a,
Left side of scarf. b, Right side of scarf.

2011, Dec. 6 **Perf. 14**
1325 A595   Sheet of 2   4.00 4.00
a.   60c multi   1.60 1.60
b.   85c multi   2.40 2.40

Architecture — A596

No. 1326 — Designs: a, Eislek. b, Réidener
Streech. c, Iechternacher Streech. d, Minett.

Serpentine Die Cut 12½
2011, Dec. 6 **Self-Adhesive**
1326   Booklet pane of 4   6.50
a.-d.   A596 A Any single   1.60 1.60
   Complete booklet, 2 #1326   13.00
Nos. 1326a-1326d each sold for 60c on day
of issue.

Luxembourg Amateur Radio Society,
75th Anniv. — A597

2012, Mar. 13   **Perf. 11½**
1327 A597 60c multi   1.60 1.60

Grand Ducal Institute Arts and Letters Section, 50th Anniv. A598

2012, Mar. 13
1328 A598 60c multi   1.60 1.60

Luxembourg Table Tennis Federation, 75th Anniv. — A599

2012, Mar. 13
1329 A599 60c multi   1.60 1.60

Introduction of Euro Currency, 10th Anniv. A600

Litho. & Embossed
2012, Mar. 13   **Perf. 13**
1330 A600 85c multi   2.25 2.25

Natl. Institute of Statistics and Economic Studies, 50th Anniv. A601

2012, May 15   **Litho.**   **Perf. 12½**
1331 A601 60c multi   1.60 1.60

Luxembourg Olympic Committee, Cent. — A602

2012 Summer Olympics, London A603

2012, May 15   **Perf. 14¼x14¾**
1332 A602   60c multi   1.60 1.60
1333 A603   €1.10 multi   3.00 3.00

Europa A604

Luxembourg tourism website address and various Luxembourg buildings and monuments: 60c, 85c.

2012, May 15   **Perf. 13½**
1334-1335 A604 Set of 2   4.00 4.00

Miniature Sheet

Characters from Mil's Adventures, Comic Strip by Gab Weis — A605

No. 1336 — Various unnamed characters with country name in: a, Red violet (Mil). b, Green. c, Orange. d, Lilac, vert. e, Red violet (2 characters), vert.

Serpentine Die Cut 12¼
2012, May 15   **Self-Adhesive**
1336 A605 Sheet of 5   8.00
  a.-e. A605 A Any single   1.60 1.60
On day of issue, Nos. 1336a-1336e each sold for 60c.

Outdoor Activities Type of 2010
Designs: 60c, Paragliding. 85c, Diving.
2012, Sept. 25   **Perf. 13¼x13**
1337-1338 A565 Set of 2   3.75 3.75

A606

Potable Water A607

2012, Sept. 25   **Perf. 11½**
1339 A606 60c multi   1.50 1.50
1340 A607 85c multi   2.25 2.25

Architecture A608

Paintings by Christian Frantzen of: €1.20, Footbridge, Esch-sur-Alzette. €2.20, Belval-Université Station, Esch-sur-Alzette. €4, Pfaffenthal-Upper Town Link, Luxembourg.

2012, Sept. 25
1341-1343 A608 Set of 3   19.00 19.00

Wedding of Prince Guillaume and Countess Stéphanie de Lannoy A609

Designs: 60c, Couple. 85c, Couple, diff.

2012, Sept. 25   **Perf. 13½**
1344 A609 60c multi   1.50 1.50
    Souvenir Sheet
1345   Sheet of 2, #1344,
           1345a   3.75 3.75
  a. A609 85c multi   2.25 2.25

Souvenir Sheet

Wedding of Prince Guillaume and Countess Stéphanie de Lannoy — A610

2012, Oct. 20   **Perf. 13¼**
1346 A610 €4 multi   10.50 10.50

European Court of Justice, 60th Anniv. A611

2012, Dec. 4   **Perf. 12½**
1347 A611 85c maroon & lt blue 2.25 2.25

European Year of Citizens A612

2013, Mar. 12   **Perf. 13¼x13**
1348 A612 60c multi   1.60 1.60

Grand Duke Adolphe Union, 150th Anniv. A613

2013, Mar. 12   **Perf. 11½**
1349 A613 60c multi   1.60 1.60

Emile Metz Private Technical High School, Cent. A614

2013, Mar. 12
1350 A614 60c multi   1.60 1.60

Round Table Luxembourg, 50th Anniv. — A615

2013, Mar. 12
1351 A615 60c multi   1.60 1.60

Holy Roman Emperor Henry VII (c.1275-1313) — A616

2013, Mar. 12
1352 A616 €1.10 multi   3.00 3.00

Famous Men — A617

Designs: No. 1353, 60c, Nicolas Adames (1813-87), theologian. No. 1354, 60c, Putty Stein (1888-1955), composer.

2013, May 2
1353-1354 A617 Set of 2   3.25 3.25

Europa A618

Postal vehicles: 60c, Citroen 2 CV AZU. 85c, Renault Kangoo.

2013, May 2 **Perf. 13x13¼**
1355-1356 A618 Set of 2 3.75 3.75

15th Games of the Small States of Europe, Luxembourg — A619

2013, May 2 **Perf. 11½**
1357 A619 Horiz. pair 3.25 3.25
a.-b. 60c Either single 1.60 1.60

Souvenir Sheet

100th Tour de France Bicycle Race — A620

2013, May 2 **Perf. 12**
1358 A620 €4 multi 10.50 10.50

Completion of 11th Turbine for Société Electrique de l'Our — A621

2013, Sept. 24 **Perf. 11½**
1359 A621 60c multi 1.60 1.60

Wild Cats A622

Designs: 20c, Panthera tigris sumatrae. 30c, Lynx lynx. 60c, Felis silvestris.

2013, Sept. 24
1360-1362 A622 Set of 3 3.00 3.00

Souvenir Sheet

Selection of "The Family of Man" Photographic Exhibition to UNESCO Memory of the World Register — A623

No. 1363: a, Photograph of crowd. b, Self-portrait of Edward Steichen.

2013, Sept. 24 **Perf. 13¾x14**
1363 A623 Sheet of 2 4.00 4.00
a. 60c blue & black 1.60 1.60
b. 85c blue & black 2.25 2.25

A624   A625

A626   A627

Serpentine Die Cut 11
2013, Sept. 24 **Self-Adhesive**
Coil Stamps
1364 Vert. strip of 4 6.50
a. A624 (60c) multi 1.60 1.60
b. A625 (60c) multi 1.60 1.60
c. A626 (60c) multi 1.60 1.60
d. A627 (60c) multi 1.60 1.60

Moselle Valley — A628

No. 1365 — Various buildings and: a, Bridge over river in foreground. b, Moselle River running through town.

Serpentine Die Cut 12½x13½
2013, Sept. 24 **Self-Adhesive**
1365 A628 Horiz. pair 4.50
a.-b. (85c) Either single 2.25 2.25

Pierre Werner (1913-2002), Prime Minister — A629

2013, Dec. 3 **Litho.** **Perf. 11½**
1366 A629 60c multi 1.75 1.75

Mushrooms A630

Designs: No. 1367, Pezize orangée. No. 1368, Bolet bai. No. 1369, Polypore versicolore. No. 1370, Amanite "tue-mouche." No. 1371, Vesse de loup perlée.

Serpentine Die Cut 12¼
2013, Dec. 3 **Litho.**
Booklet Stamps
Self-Adhesive
1367 A630 (60c) multi 1.75 1.75
1368 A630 (60c) multi 1.75 1.75
1369 A630 (60c) multi 1.75 1.75
1370 A630 (60c) multi 1.75 1.75
1371 A630 (60c) multi 1.75 1.75
a. Booklet pane of 10, 2 each #1367-1371 17.50
Nos. 1367-1371 (5) 8.75 8.75

Scouting in Luxembourg, Cent. — A631

2014, Mar. 11 **Litho.** **Perf. 11½**
1372 A631 60c multi 1.75 1.75

Primary Schools Sports League, 50th Anniv. A632

2014, Mar. 11 **Litho.** **Perf. 11½**
1373 A632 60c multi 1.75 1.75

Ligue HMC, 50th Anniv. A633

2014, Mar. 11 **Litho.** **Perf. 11½**
1374 A633 60c multi 1.75 1.75

Luxembourg Red Cross, Cent. — A634

2014, Mar. 11 **Litho.** **Perf. 11½**
1375 A634 60c multi 1.75 1.75

Souvenir Sheet

Luxembourg Federation of Philatelic Societies, 80th Anniv. — A635

No. 1376: a, Magnifying glass, hand holding stamp tongs, children looking at stamps on stock page. b, Bridge, buildings.

2014, Mar. 11 **Litho.** **Perf. 13¾x14**
Silk-Faced Paper
1376 A635 Sheet of 2 4.00 4.00
a. 60c multi 1.75 1.75
b. 85c multi 2.25 2.25

May 25, 2014 European Elections A636

2014, May 8 **Litho.** **Perf. 13¼x13**
1377 A636 60c multi 1.75 1.75

First Public Recital of Lyrics to National Anthem, 150th Anniv. A637

Independence, 175th Anniv. — A638

2014, May 8 **Litho.** **Perf. 11½**
1378 A637 60c multi 1.75 1.75
1379 A638 60c multi 1.75 1.75

Moselle Commission, 50th Anniv. — A639

2014, May 8 **Litho.** **Perf. 13x13¼**
1380 A639 85c multi 2.40 2.40

Europa A640

Various musicians: 60c, 85c.

2014, May 8 **Litho.** **Perf. 12½**
1381-1382 A640 Set of 2 4.25 4.25

Souvenir Sheet

City of Luxembourg as UNESCO World Heritage Site, 20th Anniv. — A641

No. 1383 — Buildings and fortifications of Old City: a, 60c. b, 85c.

2014, May 8 **Litho.** **Perf. 13¾x14**
1383 A641 Sheet of 2 4.25 4.25
a. 60c multi 1.75 1.75
b. 85c multi 2.40 2.40

German Invasion of Luxembourg, Cent. — A642

2014, Sept. 23 **Litho.** **Perf. 11½**
1384 A642 60c multi 1.50 1.50

World War I, cent.

A643

Winning Designs in Children's Art Contest on Soil and the Environment — A644

2014, Sept. 23   Litho.   Perf. 11½
1385 A643 60c multi   1.50 1.50
1386 A644 85c multi   2.25 2.25

Famous People — A645

Designs: No. 1387, 60c, Samuel Hirsch (1809-89), rabbi. No. 1388, 60c, Nikolaus Hein (1889-1969), writer. No. 1389, 60c, Marie Speyer (1880-1914), educator.

2014, Sept. 23   Litho.   Perf. 11½
1387-1389 A645 Set of 3   4.50 4.50

Vegetables — A646

Designs: 85c, Tragopogon porrifolius. €1, Pisum sativum. €1.10, Cichorium intybus.

2014, Sept. 23   Litho.   Perf. 11½
1390-1392 A646 Set of 3   7.50 7.50

Accession to Throne of Grand Duke Jean, 50th Anniv. — A647

2014, Dec. 2   Litho.   Perf. 13¼x13
1393 A647 (60c) multi   1.50 1.50

Grand Duke Henri — A648

Litho. & Engr.
2015, Mar. 3   Perf. 13½x13
Panel Color
1394 A648 L green   1.40 1.40
1395 A648 E blue   1.90 1.90
1396 A648 M rose carmine   2.50 2.50
      Nos. 1394-1396 (3)   5.80 5.80

On day of issue, Nos. 1394-1396 each sold for 60c, 85c and €1.10 respectively.

Organized Philately in Luxembourg, 125th Anniv. — A649

2015, Mar. 3   Litho.   Perf. 11½
1397 A649 60c multi   1.40 1.40

Order of Architects and Consulting Engineers, 25th Anniv. — A650

2015, Mar. 3   Litho.   Perf. 11½
1398 A650 60c multi   1.40 1.40

Omega 90, 25th Anniv. — A651

2015, Mar. 3   Litho.   Perf. 11½
1399 A651 60c multi   1.40 1.40

Creation of Grand Duchy of Luxembourg, 200th Anniv. — A652

2015, Mar. 3   Litho.   Perf. 11½
1400 A652 60c multi   1.40 1.40

Fruit — A653

No. 1401 — Apple and pear varieties: a, Triumph aus Luxemburg apples. b, Gute Graue pears. c, Luxemburger Renette apples. d, Doppelte Philippsbirne pears. e, Jakob Lebel apples. f, Neue Poiteau pears. g, Porzenapfel apples. h, Saint Remy pears. i,

Eifeler Rambur apples. j, Luxemburger Mostbirne pears.

Serpentine Die Cut 9¾
2015, Mar. 3   Litho.
Self-Adhesive
1401 A653 Booklet pane of 10   14.00
a.-j. L Any single   1.40 1.40

On day of issue, Nos. 1401a-1401j each sold for 60c.

SEMI-POSTAL STAMPS

Clervaux Monastery SP1

Designs: 15c+10c, View of Pfaffenthal. 25c+10c, View of Luxembourg.

Engr.; Surcharge Typo. in Red
1921, Aug. 2   Unwmk.   Perf. 11½
B1 SP1 10c + 5c green   .30   4.50
B2 SP1 15c + 10c org red   .30   6.00
B3 SP1 25c + 10c dp grn   .30   4.50
    Nos. B1-B3 (3)   .90 15.00
    Set, never hinged   2.50

The amount received from the surtax on these stamps was added to a fund for the erection of a monument to the soldiers from Luxembourg who died in World War I.

Nos. B1-B3 with Additional Surcharge in Red or Black

1923, May 27
B4 SP1 25c on #B1 (R)   1.10 14.50
B5 SP1 25c on #B2   1.25 20.00
B6 SP1 25c on #B3   1.10 14.50
    Nos. B4-B6 (3)   3.45 49.00
    Set, never hinged   10.00

Unveiling of the monument to the soldiers who died in World War I.

Regular Issue of 1914-15 Surcharged in Black or Red

1924, Apr. 17   Perf. 11½x11
B7   A11 12½c + 7½c grn   .25   2.75
B8   A11 35c + 10c dk bl (R)   .25   2.75
B9   A11 2½fr + 1fr red   1.75 27.50
B10 A11 5fr + 2fr dk rose   .55 17.50
     Nos. B7-B10 (4)   2.80 50.50
     Set, never hinged   6.25

Nurse and Patient SP4   Prince Jean SP5

1925, Dec. 21   Litho.   Perf. 13
B11 SP4 5c (+ 5c) dl vio   .25   .70
B12 SP4 30c (+ 5c) org   .25   3.00
B13 SP4 50c (+ 5c) red brn   .25   5.50
B14 SP4 1fr (+ 10c) dp bl   .40 14.00
     Nos. B11-B14 (4)   1.15 23.20
     Set, never hinged   1.75

1926, Dec. 15   Photo.   Perf. 12½x12
B15 SP5 5c (+ 5c) vio & blk   .25   .55
B16 SP5 40c (+ 10) grn & blk .25   .90
B17 SP5 50c (+ 15c) lem & blk .25   .95

B18 SP5 75c (+ 20c) lt red & blk   .25 11.00
B19 SP5 1.50fr (+ 30c) gray bl & blk .35 12.00
     Nos. B15-B19 (5)   1.35 25.40
     Set, never hinged   2.50

Grand Duchess Charlotte and Prince Felix — SP6

1927, Sept. 4   Engr.   Perf. 11½
B20 SP6 25c dp vio   1.10 10.00
B21 SP6 50c green   1.50 16.00
B22 SP6 75c rose lake   1.10 10.00
B23 SP6 1fr gray blk   1.10 10.00
B24 SP6 1½fr dp bl   1.10 10.00
     Nos. B20-B24 (5)   5.90 56.00
     Set, never hinged   17.00

Introduction of postage stamps in Luxembourg, 75th anniv. These stamps were sold exclusively at the Luxembourg Philatelic Exhibition, September 4-8, 1927, at a premium of 3 francs per set, which was donated to the exhibition funds.

Princess Elisabeth SP7   Princess Marie Adelaide SP8

1927, Dec. 1   Photo.   Perf. 12½
B25 SP7 10c (+ 5c) turq bl & blk   .25   .55
B26 SP7 50c (+ 10c) dk brn & blk   .25   .95
B27 SP7 75c (+ 20c) org & blk   .25   1.50
B28 SP7 1fr (+ 30c) brn lake & blk .25 11.00
B29 SP7 1½fr (+ 50c) ultra & blk   .25 11.00
     Nos. B25-B29 (5)   1.25 25.00
     Set, never hinged   4.00

The surtax was for Child Welfare societies.

1928, Dec. 12   Perf. 12½x12
B30 SP8 10c (+ 5c) ol grn & brn vio   .25   1.10
B31 SP8 60c (+ 10c) brn & ol grn   .40   2.75
B32 SP8 75c (+ 15c) vio rose & bl grn .70   7.25
B33 SP8 1fr (+ 25c) dk grn & brn   1.75 22.50
B34 SP8 1½fr (+ 50c) cit & bl   1.75 22.50
     Nos. B30-B34 (5)   4.85 56.10
     Set, never hinged   12.00

Princess Marie Gabrielle SP9   Prince Charles SP10

1929, Dec. 14   Perf. 13
B35 SP9 10c (+ 10c) mar & dp grn   .25   1.10
B36 SP9 35c (+ 15c) dk grn & red brn 1.50 7.25
B37 SP9 75c (+ 30c) ver & blk   1.75 9.00
B38 SP9 1¼fr (+ 50c) mag & bl grn   2.25 22.50
B39 SP9 1¾fr (+ 75c) Prus bl & sl   2.75 27.50
     Nos. B35-B39 (5)   8.50 67.35
     Set, never hinged   24.00

The surtax was for Child Welfare societies.

1930, Dec. 10   Perf. 12½
B40 SP10 10c (+ 5c) bl grn & ol brn .25   1.10
B41 SP10 75c (+ 10c) vio brn & bl grn 1.10 4.75

B42	SP10	1fr (+ 25c) car rose & vio	2.50	17.50	
B43	SP10	1¼fr (+ 75c) ol bis & dk brn	4.00	22.50	
B44	SP10	1¾fr (+ 1.50fr) ultra & red brn	4.50	22.50	
		Nos. B40-B44 (5)	12.35	68.35	
		Set, never hinged	40.00		

The surtax was for Child Welfare societies.

Princess Alix SP11   Countess Ermesinde SP12

1931, Dec. 10

B45	SP11	10c (+ 5c) brn org & gray	.30	1.10
B46	SP11	75c (+ 10c) claret & bl grn	4.50	14.50
B47	SP11	1fr (+ 25c) dp grn & gray	9.00	29.00
B48	SP11	1¼fr (+ 75c) dk vio & bl grn	6.00	29.00
B49	SP11	1¾fr (+ 1.50fr) bl & gray	16.00	55.00
		Nos. B45-B49 (5)	35.80	128.60
		Set, never hinged	110.00	

The surtax was for Child Welfare societies.

1932, Dec. 8

B50	SP12	10c (+ 5c) ol bis	.40	1.10
B51	SP12	75c (+ 10c) dp vio	2.75	14.50
B52	SP12	1fr (+ 25c) scar	11.00	32.50
B53	SP12	1¼fr (+ 75c) red brn	11.00	32.50
B54	SP12	1¾fr (+ 1.50fr) dp bl	11.00	32.50
		Nos. B50-B54 (5)	36.15	113.10
		Set, never hinged	92.50	

The surtax was for Child Welfare societies.

Count Henry VII — SP13   John the Blind — SP14

1933, Dec. 12

B55	SP13	10c (+ 5c) yel brn	.40	1.10
B56	SP13	75c (+ 10c) dp vio	4.75	14.50
B57	SP13	1fr (+ 25c) car rose	11.00	35.00
B58	SP13	1¼fr (+ 75c) org brn	14.50	47.50
B59	SP13	1¾fr (+ 1.50fr) brt bl	14.50	50.00
		Nos. B55-B59 (5)	45.15	148.10
		Set, never hinged	125.00	

1934, Dec. 5

B60	SP14	10c (+ 5c) dk vio	.25	1.10
B61	SP14	35c (+ 10c) dp grn	2.50	9.00
B62	SP14	75c (+ 15c) rose lake	2.50	9.00
B63	SP14	1fr (+ 25c) dp rose	14.50	47.50
B64	SP14	1¼fr (+ 75c) org brn	14.50	47.50
B65	SP14	1¾fr (+ 1.50fr) brt bl	14.50	47.50
		Nos. B60-B65 (6)	48.75	161.60
		Set, never hinged	125.00	

Teacher SP15

Sculptor and Painter — SP16

Journalist SP17

Engineer SP18

Scientist SP19

Lawyer — SP20   Savings Bank and Adolphe Bridge — SP21

Surgeon SP22

1935, May 1   Unwmk.   Perf. 12½

B65A	SP15	5c violet	.25	1.10
B65B	SP16	10c brn red	.25	1.10
B65C	SP17	15c olive	.40	1.75
B65D	SP18	20c orange	.55	3.50
B65E	SP19	35c yel grn	.70	3.25
B65F	SP20	50c gray blk	.95	4.75
B65G	SP21	70c dk green	1.40	5.50
B65H	SP22	1fr car red	1.75	7.25
B65J	SP19	1.25fr turq	7.25	50.00
B65K	SP18	1.75fr blue	9.00	52.50
B65L	SP16	2fr lt brown	27.50	110.00
B65M	SP17	3fr dk brown	37.50	150.00
B65N	SP20	5fr lt blue	65.00	275.00
B65P	SP15	10fr red vio	160.00	450.00
B65Q	SP22	20fr dk green	175.00	550.00
		Nos. B65A-B65Q (15)	487.50	1,665.
		Set, never hinged	1,250.	

Sold at double face, surtax going to intl. fund to aid professional people.

Philatelic Exhibition Issue
Type of Regular Issue of 1928
Wmk. 246

1935, Aug. 15   Engr.   Imperf.

B66	A19	2fr (+ 50c) blk	4.75	16.00
		Never hinged	13.00	

Philatelic exhibition held at Esch-sur-Alzette.

Charles I — SP23

Wenceslas I, Duke of Luxembourg — SP24

1935, Dec. 2   Photo.   Unwmk.   Perf. 11½

B67	SP23	10c (+ 5c) vio	.25	.40
B68	SP23	35c (+ 10c) grn	.40	.55
B69	SP23	70c (+ 20c) dk brn	.95	1.50
B70	SP23	1fr (+ 25c) rose lake	14.50	37.50
B71	SP23	1.25fr (+ 75c) org brn	14.50	37.50
B72	SP23	1.75fr (+ 1.50fr) bl	14.50	47.50
		Nos. B67-B72 (6)	45.10	124.95
		Set, never hinged	110.00	

1936, Dec. 1   Perf. 11½x13

B73	SP24	10c + 5(c) blk brn	.25	.25
B74	SP24	35c + 10(c) bl grn	.25	.55
B75	SP24	70c + 20(c) blk	.40	.90
B76	SP24	1fr + 25(c) rose car	2.50	14.50
B77	SP24	1.25fr + 75(c) vio	2.25	29.00
B78	SP24	1.75fr + 75(fr) saph	1.60	17.50
		Nos. B73-B78 (6)	7.25	62.70
		Set, never hinged	37.50	

Wenceslas II — SP25

1937, Dec. 1   Perf. 11½x12½

B79	SP25	10c + 5c car & blk	.25	.40
B80	SP25	35c + 10c red vio & grn	.25	.55
B81	SP25	70c + 20c ultra & red brn	.25	.55
B82	SP25	1fr + 25c dk grn & scar	1.60	17.00
B83	SP25	1.25fr + 75c dk brn & vio	2.25	17.00
B84	SP25	1.75fr + 1.50fr blk & ultra	2.75	17.50
		Nos. B79-B84 (6)	7.35	53.00
		Set, never hinged	23.00	

Souvenir Sheet

SP26

Wmk. 110

1937, July 25   Engr.   Perf. 13

B85	SP26	Sheet of 2	4.00	11.50
		Never hinged	11.00	
a.		2fr red brown, single stamp	1.50	5.50

National Philatelic Exposition at Dudelange on July 25-26.
Sold for 5fr per sheet, of which 1fr was for the aid of the exposition.

Portrait of St. Willibrord — SP28

St. Willibrord, after a Miniature SP29

Abbey at Echternach — SP30

Designs: No, B87, The Rathaus at Echternach. No. B88, Pavilion in Abbey Park, Echternach. No. B91, Dancing Procession in Honor of St. Willibrord.

Perf. 14x13, 13x14

1938, June 5   Engr.   Unwmk.

B86	SP28	35c + 10c dk bl grn	.40	.55
B87	SP28	70c + 10c ol gray	.70	.55
B88	SP28	1.25fr + 25c brn car	1.50	2.50
B89	SP29	1.75fr + 50c sl bl	2.50	2.75
B90	SP30	3fr + 2fr vio brn	5.50	9.00
B91	SP30	5fr + 5fr dk vio	6.50	7.25
		Nos. B86-B91 (6)	17.10	22.60
		Set, never hinged	60.00	

12th centenary of the death of St. Willibrord. The surtax was used for the restoration of the ancient Abbey at Echternach.

Duke Sigismond SP32   Prince Jean SP33

1938, Dec. 1   Photo.   Perf. 11½

B92	SP32	10c + 5c lil & blk	.25	.40
B93	SP32	35c + 10c grn & blk	.25	.55
B94	SP32	70c + 20c buff & blk	.25	.55
B95	SP32	1fr + 25c red org & blk	2.40	14.50
B96	SP32	1.25fr + 75c gray bl & blk	2.40	14.50
B97	SP32	1.75fr + 1.50fr bl & blk	3.50	22.50
		Nos. B92-B97 (6)	9.05	53.00
		Set, never hinged	25.00	

1939, Dec. 1   Litho.   Perf. 14x13

Designs: Nos. B99, B102, Prince Felix. Nos. B100, B103, Grand Duchess Charlotte.

B98	SP33	10c + 5c red brn, *buff*	.25	.40
B99	SP33	35c + 10c sl grn, *buff*	.25	1.10
B100	SP33	70c + 20c blk, *buff*	.95	1.50
B101	SP33	1fr + 25c red org, *buff*	4.00	32.50
B102	SP33	1.25fr + 75c vio brn, *buff*	4.75	50.00
B103	SP33	1.75fr + 1.50fr lt bl, *buff*	5.50	65.00
		Nos. B98-B103 (6)	15.70	150.50
		Set, never hinged	45.00	

See No. 217 (souvenir sheet).

Allegory of Medicinal Baths — SP36

1940, Mar. 1   Photo.   Perf. 11½
B104 SP36 2fr + 50c gray, blk & slate grn   1.25   20.00
Never hinged   4.50

Stamps of 1944, type A37, surcharged "+50C," "+5F" or "+15F" in black, were sold only in canceled condition, affixed to numbered folders. The surtax was for the benefit of Luxembourg evacuees. Value for folder, $15.

Homage to France SP37

Thanks to: No. B118, USSR. No. B119, Britannia. No. B120, America.

1945, Mar. 1   Engr.   Perf. 13
B117 SP37 60c + 1.40fr dp grn   .25   .25
B118 SP37 1.20fr + 1.80fr red   .25   .25
B119 SP37 2.50fr + 3.50fr dp bl   .25   .25
B120 SP37 4.20fr + 4.80fr dp vio   .25   .25
Nos. B117-B120 (4)   1.00   1.00
Set, never hinged   1.25

Issued to honor the Allied Nations. Exist imperf. Value, set $175.

Statue Carried in Procession SP41

Statue of Our Lady "Patrona Civitatis" SP42

"Our Lady of Luxembourg" SP43

Cathedral Façade SP44

Altar with Statue of Madonna — SP45

1945, June 4
B121 SP41 60c + 40c grn   .25   1.10
B122 SP42 1.20fr + 80c red   .25   1.10
B123 SP43 2.50fr + 2.50fr dp bl   .25   5.50

B124 SP44 5.50fr + 6.50fr dk vio   .65   77.50
B125 SP45 20fr + 20fr choc   .65   80.00
Nos. B121-B125 (5)   2.05   165.20
Set, never hinged   4.00
Exist imperf. Value, set $250.

Souvenir Sheet

"Our Lady of Luxembourg" — SP46

1945, Sept. 30   Engr.   Imperf.
B126 SP46 50fr + 50fr blk   1.10   42.50
Never hinged   2.10

Young Fighters — SP47

Refugee Mother and Children — SP48

Political Prisoner — SP49

Executed Civilian — SP50

1945, Dec. 20   Photo.   Perf. 11½
B127 SP47 20c + 30c sl grn & buff   .25   1.10
B128 SP48 1.50fr + 1fr brn red & buff   .25   1.10
B129 SP49 3.50fr + 3.50fr bl, dp bl & buff   .25   10.50
B130 SP50 5fr + 10fr brn, dk brn & buff   .25   10.50
Nos. B127-B130 (4)   1.00   23.20
Set, never hinged   1.40

Souvenir Sheet

1946, Jan. 30   Unwmk.   Perf. 11½
B131 Sheet of 4   8.75   300.00
Never hinged   25.00
a. SP47 2.50fr + 2.50fr sl grn & buff   2.25   50.00
b. SP48 3.50fr + 6.50fr brown red & buff   2.25   50.00
c. SP49 5fr + 15fr bl, dp bl & buff   2.25   50.00
d. SP50 20fr + 20fr brown, dark brown & buff   2.25   50.00

Tribute to Luxembourg's heroes and martyrs. The surtax was for the National Welfare Fund.

Souvenir Sheet

Old Rolling Mill, Dudelange — SP52

1946, July 28   Engr. & Typo.
B132 SP52 50fr brn & dk bl, buff   5.50   35.00
Never hinged   15.00

National Postage Stamp Exhibition, Dudelange, July 28-29, 1946. The sheets sold for 55fr.

Jean l'Aveugle — SP53

1946, Dec. 5   Photo.
B133 SP53 60c + 40c dk grn   .25   1.75
B134 SP53 1.50fr + 50c brn red   .25   3.00
B135 SP53 3.50fr + 3.50fr dp bl   .60   27.50
B136 SP53 5fr + 10fr sepia   .40   22.50
Nos. B133-B136 (4)   1.50   54.75
Set, never hinged   4.00

600th anniv. of the death of Jean l'Aveugle (John the Blind), Count of Luxembourg.

Ruins of St. Willibrord Basilica — SP54

Twelfth Century Miniature of St. Willibrord SP59

Designs: No. B138, Statue of Abbot Jean Bertels. No. B139, Emblem of Echternach Abbey. No. B140, Ruins of the Basilica's Interior. No. B141, St. Irmine and Pepin of Hersta Holding Model of the Abbey.

Perf. 13x14, 14x13
1947, May 25   Engr.
B137 SP54 20c + 10c blk   .25   .25
B138 SP54 60c + 10c dk grn   .40   .55
B139 SP54 75c + 25c dk car   .55   .75
B140 SP54 1.50fr + 50c dk brn   .70   .75
B141 SP54 3.50fr + 2.50fr dk bl   2.25   4.75
B142 SP59 25fr + 25fr dk pur   15.00   25.00
Nos. B137-B142 (6)   19.15   32.05
Set, never hinged   40.00

The surtax was to aid in restoring the Basilica of Saint Willibrord at Echternach.

Michel Lentz — SP60

Edmond de La Fontaine (Dicks) — SP61

1947, Dec. 4   Photo.   Perf. 11½
B143 SP60 60c + 40c sep & buff   .25   1.10
B144 SP60 1.50fr + 50c dp plum & buff   .25   1.10
B145 SP60 3.50fr + 3.50fr dp bl & gray   2.75   17.50
B146 SP60 10fr + 5fr dk grn & gray   2.40   17.50
Nos. B143-B146 (4)   5.65   37.20
Set, never hinged   14.00

1948, Nov. 18
B147 SP61 60c + 40c brn & pale bis   .25   .95
B148 SP61 1.50fr + 50c brn car & buff   .35   .95
B149 SP61 3.50fr + 3.50fr bl & gray   4.50   19.00
B150 SP61 10fr + 5fr dk grn & gray   3.50   19.00
Nos. B147-B150 (4)   8.60   39.90
Set, never hinged   19.00

125th anniversary of the birth of Edmond de La Fontaine, poet and composer.

Type of Regular Issue of 1948
Souvenir Sheet
1949, Jan. 8   Unwmk.   Perf. 11½
B151 Sheet of 3   50.00   55.00
Never hinged   100.00
a. A45 8fr + 3fr blue gray   14.00   17.00
b. A45 12fr + 5fr green   14.00   17.00
c. A45 15fr + 7fr brown   14.00   17.00

30th anniversary of Grand Duchess Charlotte's ascension to the throne. Border and dates "1919-1949" in gray.

Michel Rodange — SP62

1949, Dec. 5
B152 SP62 60c + 40c ol grn & gray   .40   .55
B153 SP62 2fr + 1fr dk vio & rose   2.75   5.00
B154 SP62 4fr + 2fr sl blk & gray   4.50   7.50
B155 SP62 10fr + 5fr brn & buff   4.50   17.50
Nos. B152-B155 (4)   12.15   30.55
Set, never hinged   22.50

Wards of the Nation
SP63   SP64

1950, June 24   Engr.   Perf. 12½x12
B156 SP63 60c + 15c dk sl bl   1.25   1.50
B157 SP64 1fr + 20c dk car rose   3.25   1.50
B158 SP63 2fr + 30c red brn   2.25   1.50
B159 SP64 4fr + 75c dk bl   7.50   17.00
B160 SP63 8fr + 3fr blk   21.00   45.00
B161 SP64 10fr + 5fr lil rose   22.50   45.00
Nos. B156-B161 (6)   57.75   111.50
Set, never hinged   100.00

The surtax was for child welfare.

Jean A. Zinnen
SP65

Laurent
Menager
SP66

1950, Dec. 5   Photo.   *Perf. 11½*
B162	SP65	60c + 10c ind & gray	.35	.25
B163	SP65	2fr + 15c cer & buff	.35	.40
B164	SP65	4fr + 15c vio bl & bl gray	3.25	6.50
B165	SP65	8fr + 5fr dk brn & buff	9.25	25.00
		Nos. B162-B165 (4)	13.20	32.15
		Set, never hinged	27.50	

1951, Dec. 5   Gray Background
B166	SP66	60c + 10c sepia	.25	.40
B167	SP66	2fr + 15c dl ol grn	.25	.40
B168	SP66	4fr + 15c blue	2.50	4.00
B169	SP66	8fr + 5fr vio brn	10.50	30.00
		Nos. B166-B169 (4)	13.50	34.80
		Set, never hinged	29.00	

50th anniversary of the death of Laurent Menager, composer.

J. B.
Fresez — SP67

Traditions — SP68

1952, Dec. 3
B170	SP67	60c + 15c dk bl grn & pale bl	.25	.40
B171	SP67	2fr + 25c chnt brn & buff	.25	.40
B172	SP67	4fr + 25c dk vio bl & gray	1.90	4.00
B173	SP67	8fr + 4.75fr dp plum & lil gray	13.00	35.00
		Nos. B170-B173 (4)	15.40	39.80
		Set, never hinged	32.50	

1953, Dec. 3

Designs: Nos. B174, B177, Candlemas Singing. Nos. B175, B178, Procession with ratchets. Nos. B176, B179, Breaking Easter eggs.

B174	SP68	25c + 15c red org & dp car	.25	.40
B175	SP68	80c + 20c vio brn & bl gray	.25	.40
B176	SP68	1.20fr + 30c bl grn & ol grn	.50	.95
B177	SP68	2fr + 25c brn car & brn	.40	.40
B178	SP68	4fr + 50c grnsh bl & vio bl	3.00	9.00
B179	SP68	7fr + 3.35fr vio & pur	9.00	22.50
		Nos. B174-B179 (6)	13.40	33.65
		Set, never hinged	27.50	

The surtax was for the National Welfare Fund of Grand Duchess Charlotte.

Clay Censer and
Whistle — SP69

Designs: 80c+20c, 4fr+50c, Sheep and bass drum. 1.20fr+30c, 7fr+3.45fr, Merry-go-round horses. 2fr+25c, As No. B180.

1954, Dec. 3
B180	SP69	25c + 5c car lake & cop brn	.25	.45
B181	SP69	80c + 20c dk gray	.25	.45
B182	SP69	1.20fr + 30c dk bl grn & cr	.75	1.25
B183	SP69	2fr + 25c brn & ocher	.35	.55

B184	SP69	4fr + 50c brt bl	3.00	8.00
B185	SP69	7fr + 3.45fr pur	10.00	25.00
		Nos. B180-B185 (6)	14.60	35.70
		Set, never hinged	32.50	

Toys for St.
Nicholas
Day — SP70

Designs: 80c+20c, 4fr+50c, Christ child and lamb (Christmas). 1.20fr+30c, 7fr+3.45fr, Star, crown and cake (Epiphany).

1955, Dec. 5   Unwmk.   *Perf. 11½*
B186	SP70	25c + 5c sal & dk car	.25	.40
B187	SP70	80c + 20c gray & gray blk	.25	.40
B188	SP70	1.20fr + 30c ol grn & sl grn	.35	.95
B189	SP70	2fr + 25c buff & dk brn	.40	.40
B190	SP70	4fr + 50c lt bl & brt bl	3.25	11.00
B191	SP70	7fr + 3.45fr rose vio & claret	6.50	15.00
		Nos. B186-B191 (6)	11.00	28.15
		Set, never hinged	22.50	

Coats of
Arms — SP71

Arms: 25c+5c, 2fr+25c, Echternach. 80c+20c, 4fr+50c, Esch-sur-Alzette. 1.20fr+30c, 7fr+3.45fr, Grevenmacher.

1956, Dec. 5   Photo.
Arms in Original Colors
B192	SP71	25c + 5c blk & sal pink	.25	.40
B193	SP71	80c + 20c ultra & yel	.25	.40
B194	SP71	1.20fr + 30c ultra & gray	.25	1.10
B195	SP71	2fr + 25c blk & buff	.25	.40
B196	SP71	4fr + 50c ultra & lt bl	1.90	5.50
B197	SP71	7fr + 3.45fr ultra & pale vio	3.50	11.50
		Nos. B192-B197 (6)	6.40	19.30
		Set, never hinged	14.50	

1957, Dec. 4   Unwmk.   *Perf. 11½*

25c+5c, 2fr+25c, Luxembourg. 80c+20c, 4fr+50c, Mersch. 1.20fr+30c, 7fr+3.45fr, Vianden.

Arms in Original Colors
B198	SP71	25c + 5c ultra & org	.25	.40
B199	SP71	80c + 20c blk & lem	.25	.40
B200	SP71	1.20fr + 30c ultra & lt bl grn	.25	.70
B201	SP71	2fr + 25c ultra & pale brn	.25	.40
B202	SP71	4fr + 50c blk & pale vio bl	.50	5.50
B203	SP71	7fr + 3.45fr ultra & rose lil	3.25	8.00
		Nos. B198-B203 (6)	4.75	15.40
		Set, never hinged	11.00	

1958, Dec. 3   *Perf. 11½*

30c+10c, 2.50fr+50c, Capellen. 1fr+25c, 5fr+50c, Diekirch. 1.50fr+25c, 8.50fr+4.60fr, Redange.

Arms in Original Colors
B204	SP71	30c + 10c blk & pink	.25	.40
B205	SP71	1fr + 25c ultra & buff	.25	.40
B206	SP71	1.50fr + 25c ultra & pale grn	.25	.55
B207	SP71	2.50fr + 50c blk & gray	.25	.40
B208	SP71	5fr + 50c ultra	2.25	5.50
B209	SP71	8.50fr + 4.60fr ultra & lil	2.50	8.00
		Nos. B204-B209 (6)	5.75	15.25
		Set, never hinged	11.00	

1959, Dec. 2

30c+10c, 2.50fr+50c, Clervaux. 1fr+25c, 5fr+50c, Remich. 1.50fr+25c, 8.50fr+4.60fr, Wiltz.

Arms in Original Colors
B210	SP71	30c + 10c ultra & pink	.25	.40
B211	SP71	1fr + 25c ultra & pale lem	.25	.40
B212	SP71	1.50fr + 25c blk & pale grn	.25	.55
B213	SP71	2.50fr + 50c ultra & pale fawn	.25	.40
B214	SP71	5fr + 50c ultra & lt bl	.65	2.25
B215	SP71	8.50fr + 4.60fr blk & pale vio	2.75	11.00
		Nos. B210-B215 (6)	4.40	15.00
		Set, never hinged	9.25	

> **Catalogue values for unused stamps in this section, from this point to the end of the section, are for Never Hinged items.**

Princess Marie-
Astrid — SP72

1fr+25c, 5fr+50c, Princess in party dress. 1.50fr+25c, 8.50fr+4.60fr, Princess with book.

1960, Dec. 5   Photo.   *Perf. 11½*
B216	SP72	30c + 10c brn & lt bl	.35	.25
B217	SP72	1fr + 25c brn & pink	.35	.25
B218	SP72	1.50fr + 25c brn & lt bl	.65	.50
B219	SP72	2.50fr + 50c brn & yel	.50	.35
B220	SP72	5fr + 50c brn & pale lil	1.00	2.50
B221	SP72	8.50fr + 4.60fr brn & pale ol	9.25	11.50
		Nos. B216-B221 (6)	12.10	15.35

Type of 1960

Prince Henri: 30c+10c, 2.50fr+50c, Infant in long dress. 1fr+25c, 5fr+50c, Informal portrait. 1.50fr+25c, 8.50fr+ 4.60fr, In dress suit.

1961, Dec. 4   Unwmk.   *Perf. 11½*
B222	SP72	30c + 10c brn & brt pink	.35	.25
B223	SP72	1fr + 25c brn & lt vio	.35	.25
B224	SP72	1.50fr + 25c brn & sal	.55	.50
B225	SP72	2.50fr + 50c brn & pale grn	.55	.25
B226	SP72	5fr + 50c brn & cit	2.75	1.75
B227	SP72	8.50fr + 4.60fr brn & gray	4.25	4.50
		Nos. B222-B227 (6)	8.80	7.50

Prince Jean — SP73

Designs: Different portraits of the twins Prince Jean and Princess Margaretha. Nos. B228 and B233 are horizontal.

Inscriptions and Portraits in Dark Brown

1962, Dec. 3   Photo.   *Perf. 11½*
B228	SP73	30c + 10c org yel	.25	.25
B229	SP73	1fr + 25c lt bl	.25	.25
B230	SP73	1.50fr + 25c pale ol	.35	.35
B231	SP73	2.50fr + 50c rose	.35	.25
B232	SP73	5fr + 50c lt yel grn	1.25	2.25
B233	SP73	8.50fr + 4.60fr lil gray	3.25	4.50
		Nos. B228-B233 (6)	5.70	7.85

St. Roch, Patron
of
Bakers — SP74

Three
Towers — SP75

Patron Saints: 1fr+25c, St. Anne, tailors. 2fr+25c, St. Eloi, smiths. 3fr+50c, St. Michael, shopkeepers. 5fr+50c, St. Bartholomew, butchers. St. Theobald, seven crafts.

1963, Dec. 2   Unwmk.   *Perf. 11½*
Multicolored Design
B234	SP74	50c + 10c pale lil	.25	.25
B235	SP74	1fr + 25c tan	.25	.25
B236	SP74	2fr + 25c lt grnsh bl	.25	.25
B237	SP74	3fr + 50c lt bl	.25	.25
B238	SP74	6fr + 50c buff	1.00	1.60
B239	SP74	10fr + 5.90fr pale yel grn	1.60	3.00
		Nos. B234-B239 (6)	3.60	5.60

1964, Dec. 7   Photo.   *Perf. 11½*

Children's paintings: 1fr+25c, 6fr+50c, Grand Duke Adolphe Bridge, horiz. 2fr+25c, 10fr+5.90fr, The Lower City.

B240	SP75	50c + 10c multi	.25	.25
B241	SP75	1fr + 25c multi	.25	.25
B242	SP75	2fr + 25c multi	.25	.30
a.		Value omitted	300.00	
B243	SP75	3fr + 50c multi	.25	.30
B244	SP75	6fr + 50c multi	1.00	1.50
B245	SP75	10fr + 5.90fr multi	1.25	2.50
		Nos. B240-B245 (6)	3.25	5.10

The Roman Lady of
Titelberg — SP76

Fairy Tales of Luxembourg: 1fr+25c, Schäppchen, the Huntsman. 2fr+25c, The Witch of Koerich. 3fr+50c, The Gnomes of Schoenfels. 6fr+50c, Tollchen, Watchman of Hesperange. 10fr+5.90fr, The Old Spinster of Heispelt.

1965, Dec. 6   Photo.   *Perf. 11½*
B246	SP76	50c + 10c multi	.25	.25
B247	SP76	1fr + 25c multi	.25	.25
B248	SP76	2fr + 25c multi	.25	.25
B249	SP76	3fr + 50c multi	.25	.25
B250	SP76	6fr + 50c multi	.50	1.25
B251	SP76	10fr + 5.90fr multi	1.25	3.00
		Nos. B246-B251 (6)	2.75	5.25

Fairy Tale Type of 1965

Fairy Tales of Luxembourg: 50c+10c, The Veiled Matron of Wormeldange. 1.50fr+25c, Jekel, Warden of the Wark. 2fr+25c, The Black Man of Vianden. 3fr+50c, The Gracious Fairy of Rosport. 6fr+1fr, The Friendly Shepherd of Donkolz. 13fr+6.90fr, The Little Sisters of Trois-Vièrges.

1966, Dec. 6   Photo.   *Perf. 11½*
B252	SP76	50c + 10c multi	.25	.25
B253	SP76	1.50fr + 25c multi	.25	.25
B254	SP76	2fr + 25c multi	.25	.25
B255	SP76	3fr + 50c multi	.25	.30
B256	SP76	6fr + 1fr multi	.50	1.00
B257	SP76	13fr + 6.90fr multi	.85	2.25
		Nos. B252-B257 (6)	2.35	4.30

Prince
Guillaume
SP77

Castle of Berg
SP78

Portraits: 1.50fr+25c, Princess Margaretha. 2fr+25c, Prince Jean. 3fr+50c, Prince Henri as Boy Scout. 6fr+1fr, Princess Marie-Astrid.

1967, Dec. 6   Photo.   Perf. 11½

B258	SP77	50c + 10c yel & brn	.25	.25
B259	SP77	1.50fr + 25c gray bl & brn	.25	.25
B260	SP77	2fr + 25c pale rose & brn	.25	.25
B261	SP77	3fr + 50c lt ol & brn	.65	.25
B262	SP77	6fr + 1fr lt vio & brn	.50	1.00
B263	SP78	13fr + 6.90fr multi	.65	3.00
		Nos. B258-B263 (6)	2.55	5.00

Medico-professional Institute at Cap — SP79

Deaf-mute Child Imitating Bird — SP80

Handicapped Children: 2fr+25c, Blind child holding candle. 3fr+50c, Nurse supporting physically handicapped child. 6fr+1fr, Cerebral palsy victim. 13fr+6.90fr, Mentally disturbed child.

1968, Dec. 5   Photo.   Perf. 11½
Designs and Inscriptions in Dark Brown

B264	SP79	50c + 10c lt bl	.25	.25
B265	SP80	1.50fr + 25c lt grn	.25	.25
B266	SP80	2fr + 25c yel	.25	.25
B267	SP80	3fr + 50c bl	.25	.25
B268	SP80	6fr + 1fr buff	.50	1.10
B269	SP80	13fr + 6.90fr pink	1.60	3.00
		Nos. B264-B269 (6)	3.10	5.10

Vianden Castle SP81

Children of Bethlehem SP82

Luxembourg Castles: 1.50fr+25c, Lucilinburhuc. 2fr+25c, Bourglinster. 3fr+50c, Hollenfels. 6fr+1fr, Ansembourg. 13fr+6.90fr, Beaufort.

1969, Dec. 8   Photo.   Perf. 11½

B270	SP81	50c + 10c multi	.25	.25
B271	SP81	1.50fr + 25c multi	.25	.25
B272	SP81	2fr + 25c multi	.25	.25
B273	SP81	3fr + 50c multi	.25	.25
B274	SP81	6fr + 1fr multi	.60	1.25
B275	SP81	13fr + 6.90fr multi	1.00	3.00
		Nos. B270-B275 (6)	2.60	5.25

1970, Dec. 7   Photo.   Perf. 11½

Luxembourg Castles: 50c+10c, Clervaux. 1.50fr+25c, Septfontaines. 2fr+25c, Bourscheid. 3fr+50c, Esch-sur-Sure. 6fr+1fr, Larochette. 13fr+6.90fr, Brandenbourg.

B276	SP81	50c + 10c multi	.25	.25
B277	SP81	1.50fr + 25c multi	.25	.25
B278	SP81	2fr + 25c multi	.25	.25
B279	SP81	3fr + 50c multi	.25	.25
B280	SP81	6fr + 1fr multi	.60	1.25
B281	SP81	13fr + 6.90fr multi	1.00	3.00
		Nos. B276-B281 (6)	2.60	5.25

The surtax on Nos. B180-B281 was for charitable purposes.

1971, Dec. 6   Photo.   Perf. 11½

Wooden Statues from Crèche of Beaufort Church: 1.50fr+25c, Shepherds. 3fr+50c, Nativity. 8fr+1fr, Herdsmen. 18fr+6.50fr, King offering gift.

Sculptures in Shades of Brown

B282	SP82	1fr + 25c lilac	.25	.25
B283	SP82	1.50fr + 25c olive	.25	.25
B284	SP82	3fr + 50c gray	.35	.25
B285	SP82	8fr + 1fr lt ultra	1.10	2.25
B286	SP82	18fr + 6.50fr grn	1.90	4.50
		Nos. B282-B286 (5)	3.85	7.50

The surtax was for various charitable organizations.

Angel — SP83

Sts. Anne and Joachim — SP84

Stained Glass Windows, Luxembourg Cathedral: 1.50fr+25c, St. Joseph. 3fr+50c, Virgin and Child. 8fr+1fr, People of Bethlehem. 18fr+6.50fr, Angel facing left.

1972, Dec. 4

B287	SP83	1fr + 25c multi	.25	.25
B288	SP83	1.50fr + 25c multi	.25	.25
B289	SP83	3fr + 50c multi	.25	.25
B290	SP83	8fr + 1fr multi	1.00	2.25
B291	SP83	18fr + 6.50fr multi	2.75	6.00
		Nos. B287-B291 (5)	4.50	9.00

Surtax was for charitable purposes.

1973, Dec. 5   Photo.   Perf. 11½

Sculptures: 3fr+25c, Mary meeting Elizabeth. 4fr+50c, Virgin and Child and a King. 8fr+1fr, Shepherds. 15fr+7fr, St. Joseph holding candle. Designs from 16th century reredos, Hermitage of Hachiville.

B292	SP84	1fr + 25c multi	.25	.25
B293	SP84	3fr + 25c multi	.25	.25
B294	SP84	4fr + 50c multi	.25	.25
B295	SP84	8fr + 1fr multi	.90	2.25
B296	SP84	15fr + 7fr multi	2.75	6.00
		Nos. B292-B296 (5)	4.40	9.00

Annunciation — SP85

Crucifixion — SP86

Designs: 3fr+25c, Visitation. 4fr+50c, Nativity. 8fr+1fr, Adoration of the King. 15fr+7fr, Presentation at the Temple. Designs of Nos. B297-B301 are from miniatures in the "Codex Aureus Epternacensis" (Gospel from Echternach Abbey). The Crucifixion is from the carved ivory cover of the Codex, by the Master of Echternach, c. 983-991.

1974, Dec. 5   Photo.   Perf. 11½

B297	SP85	1fr + 25c multi	.25	.25
B298	SP85	3fr + 25c multi	.25	.25
B299	SP85	4fr + 50c multi	.25	.25
B300	SP85	8fr + 1fr multi	1.10	3.00
B301	SP85	15fr + 7fr multi	2.00	5.50
		Nos. B297-B301 (5)	3.85	9.25

Souvenir Sheet
Photogravure & Engraved
Perf. 13½

B302	SP86	20fr + 10fr multi	4.00	8.00

50th anniversary of Caritas issues. No. B302 contains one 34x42mm stamp.

Fly Orchid — SP87

Lilies of the Valley — SP88

Flowers: 3fr+25c, Pyramidal orchid. 4fr+50c, Marsh hellebore. 8fr+1fr, Pasqueflower. 15fr+7fr, Bee orchid.

1975, Dec. 4   Photo.   Perf. 11½

B303	SP87	1fr + 25c multi	.25	.25
B304	SP87	3fr + 25c multi	.35	.25
B305	SP87	4fr + 50c multi	.50	.25
B306	SP87	8fr + 1fr multi	1.00	1.60
B307	SP87	15fr + 7fr multi	2.75	5.00
		Nos. B303-B307 (5)	4.85	7.35

The surtax on Nos. B303-B317 was for various charitable organizations.

1976, Dec. 6

Flowers: 2fr+25c, Gentian. 5fr+25c, Narcissus. 6fr+50c, Red hellebore. 12fr+1fr, Late spider orchid. 20fr+8fr, Two-leafed squill.

B308	SP87	2fr + 25c multi	.25	.30
B309	SP87	5fr + 25c multi	.25	.30
B310	SP87	6fr + 50c multi	.30	.30
B311	SP87	12fr + 1fr multi	1.00	2.00
B312	SP87	20fr + 8fr multi	2.75	5.50
		Nos. B308-B312 (5)	4.55	8.40

1977, Dec. 5   Photo.   Perf. 11½

Flowers: 5fr+25c, Columbine. 6fr+50c, Mezereon. 12fr+1fr, Early spider orchid. 20fr+8fr, Spotted orchid.

B313	SP88	2fr + 25c multi	.25	.25
B314	SP88	5fr + 25c multi	.35	.25
B315	SP88	6fr + 50c multi	.60	.25
B316	SP88	12fr + 1fr multi	1.60	2.75
B317	SP88	20fr + 8fr multi	2.75	5.50
		Nos. B313-B317 (5)	5.55	9.00

St. Matthew — SP89

Spring — SP90

Behind-glass Paintings, 19th Century: 5fr+25c, St. Mark. 6fr+50c, Nativity. 12fr+1fr, St. Luke. 20fr+8fr, St. John.

1978, Dec. 5   Photo.   Perf. 11½

B318	SP89	2fr + 25c multi	.25	.25
B319	SP89	5fr + 25c multi	.25	.30
B320	SP89	6fr + 50c multi	.35	.30
B321	SP89	12fr + 1fr multi	1.25	.90
B322	SP89	20fr + 8fr multi	1.90	4.00
		Nos. B318-B322 (5)	4.00	5.75

Surtax was for charitable organizations.

1979, Dec. 5   Photo.   Perf. 12

Behind-glass Paintings, 19th Century: 5fr+25c, Summer. 6fr+50c, Charity. 12fr+1fr, Autumn. 20fr+8fr, Winter.

B323	SP90	2fr + 25c multi	.25	.25
B324	SP90	5fr + 25c multi	.25	.25
B325	SP90	6fr + 50c multi	.35	.25
B326	SP90	12fr + 1fr multi	.85	1.25
B327	SP90	20fr + 8fr multi	1.75	4.50
		Nos. B323-B327 (5)	3.45	6.50

St. Martin — SP91

Behind-glass Paintings, 19th Century: 6fr+50c, St. Nicholas. 8fr+1fr, Madonna and Child. 30fr+1fr, St. George the Martyr.

1980, Dec. 5   Photo.   Perf. 11½

B328	SP91	4fr + 50c multi	.40	.25
B329	SP91	6fr + 50c multi	.40	.25
B330	SP91	8fr + 1fr multi	.40	.45
B331	SP91	30fr + 10fr multi	2.00	1.75
		Nos. B328-B331 (4)	3.20	2.70

Surtax was for charitable organizations.

Arms of Petange SP92

Nativity, by Otto van Veen (1556-1629) SP93

1981, Dec. 4   Photo.
Granite Paper

B332	SP92	4fr + 50c shown	.25	.30
B333	SP92	6fr + 50c Larochette	.30	.35
B334	SP93	8fr + 1fr shown	.50	.60
B335	SP92	16fr + 2fr Stadtbredimus	.90	1.10
B336	SP92	35fr + 12fr Weiswampach	2.25	2.75
		Nos. B332-B336 (5)	4.20	5.10

Surtax was for charitable organizations.

1982, Dec. 6   Photo.   Perf. 11½

Design: 8fr+1fr, Adoration of the Shepherds, stained-glass window, by Gust Zanter, Hoscheid Parish Church.

Granite Paper

B337	SP92	4fr + 50c Bettembourg	.25	.25
B338	SP92	6fr + 50c Frisange	.35	.35
B339	SP93	8fr + 1fr multi	.45	.45
B340	SP92	16fr + 2fr Mamer	.90	.90
B341	SP92	35fr + 12fr Heinerscheid	2.25	2.25
		Nos. B337-B341 (5)	4.20	4.20

Surtax was for charitable organizations.

1983, Dec. 5   Photo.

B342	SP92	4fr + 1fr Winseler	.25	.25
B343	SP92	7fr + 1fr Beckerich	.40	.40
B344	SP93	10fr + 1fr Nativity	.50	.50
B345	SP92	16fr + 2fr Feulen	.85	.85
B346	SP92	40fr + 13fr Mertert	3.00	3.00
		Nos. B342-B346 (5)	5.00	5.00

Surtax was for charitable organizations.

Inquisitive Child — SP94

Children Exhibiting Various Moods.

1984, Dec. 5   Photo.

B347	SP94	4fr + 1fr shown	.40	.25
B348	SP94	7fr + 1fr Daydreaming	.55	.45
B349	SP94	10fr + 1fr Nativity	.80	.55
B350	SP94	16fr + 2fr Sulking	2.00	.95
B351	SP94	40fr + 13fr Admiring	6.50	3.25
		Nos. B347-B351 (5)	10.25	5.45

Surtax was for charitable organizations.

1985, Dec. 5   Photo.

B352	SP94	4fr + 1fr Girl drawing	.40	.25
B353	SP94	7fr + 1fr Two boys	.55	.30
B354	SP94	10fr + 1fr Adoration of the Magi	.95	.40
B355	SP94	16fr + 2fr Fairy tale characters	2.50	1.00
B356	SP94	40fr + 13fr Embarrassed girl	7.50	2.75
		Nos. B352-B356 (5)	11.90	4.70

Surtax was for charitable organizations.

SP95

SP96

Book of Hours,
France, c. 1550,
Natl.
Library — SP97

Christmas: illuminated text.

1986, Dec. 8   Photo.   Perf. 11½

B357	SP95	6fr + 1fr Annunciation	.95	.45
B358	SP95	10fr + 1fr Angel appears to the Shepherds	.55	.55
B359	SP95	12fr + 2fr Nativity	.95	.70
B360	SP95	18fr + 2fr Adoration of the Magi	2.50	1.00
B361	SP95	20fr + 8fr Flight into Egypt	4.75	1.40
		Nos. B357-B361 (5)	9.70	4.10

1987, Dec. 1   Perf. 12

B362	SP96	6fr + 1fr Annunciation	.90	.40
B363	SP96	10fr + 1fr Visitation	1.40	.65
B364	SP96	12fr + 2fr Adoration of the Magi	1.75	.85
B365	SP96	18fr + 2fr Presentation in the Temple	2.75	1.10
B366	SP96	20fr + 8fr Flight into Egypt	5.50	1.60
		Nos. B362-B366 (5)	12.30	4.60

1988, Dec. 5   Perf. 11½

B367	SP97	9fr +1fr Annunciation to the Shepherds	.45	.45
B368	SP97	12fr +2fr Adoration of the Magi	.45	.45
B369	SP97	18fr +2fr Virgin and Child	3.00	3.00
B370	SP97	20fr +8fr Pentecost	3.00	3.00
		Nos. B367-B370 (4)	6.90	6.90

Surtax for charitable organizations.

Christmas
SP98

Chapels: No. B371, St. Lambert and St. Blase, Fennange, vert. No. B372, St. Quirinus, Luxembourg. No. B373, St. Anthony the Hermit, Reisdorf, vert. No. B374, The Hermitage, Hachiville.

1989, Dec. 11   Photo.   Perf. 12x11½

B371	SP98	9fr +1fr multi	.50	.50
B372	SP98	12fr +2fr multi	.70	.70
B373	SP98	18fr +3fr multi	2.75	2.00
B374	SP98	25fr +8fr multi	3.00	3.00
		Nos. B371-B374 (4)	6.95	6.20

Surtax for social work.

1990, Nov. 26   Photo.   Perf. 11½

Chapels: No. B375, Congregation of the Blessed Virgin Mary, Vianden, vert. No. B376, Our Lady, Echternach. No. B377, Our Lady, Consoler of the Afflicted, Grentzingen. B378, St. Pirmin, Kaundorf, vert.

B375	SP98	9fr +1fr multi	.50	.50
B376	SP98	12fr +2fr multi	1.00	1.00
B377	SP98	18fr +3fr multi	2.00	1.50
B378	SP98	25fr +8fr multi	3.50	3.50
		Nos. B375-B378 (4)	7.00	6.50

Surtax for charitable organizations.

1991, Dec. 9   Photo.   Perf. 11½

Chapels: No. B379, St. Donatus, Arsdorf, vert. No. B380, Our Lady of Sorrows,

Brandenbourg. No. B381, Our Lady, Luxembourg. No. B382, The Hermitage, Wolwelange, vert.

B379	SP98	14fr +2fr multi	1.20	1.00
B380	SP98	14fr +2fr multi	1.20	1.00
B381	SP98	18fr +3fr multi	1.75	1.75
B382	SP98	22fr +7fr multi	3.50	3.25
		Nos. B379-B382 (4)	7.65	7.00

Surtax used for philanthropic work.

Endangered
Birds — SP99

Designs: No. B383, Hazel grouse. No. B384, Golden oriole, vert. 18fr+3fr, Black stork. 22fr+7fr, Red kite, vert.

1992, Dec. 7   Photo.   Perf. 11½

B383	SP99	14fr +2fr multi	1.00	1.00
B384	SP99	14fr +2fr multi	1.00	1.00
B385	SP99	18fr +3fr multi	2.75	2.75
B386	SP99	22fr +7fr multi	4.25	3.50
		Nos. B383-B386 (4)	9.00	8.25

Surtax for Luxembourg charitable organizations.

1993, Dec. 6   Photo.   Perf. 11½

Designs: No. B387, Snipe. No. B388, Kingfisher, vert. 18fr+3fr, Little ringed plover. 22fr+7fr, Sand martin, vert.

B387	SP99	14fr +2fr multi	1.25	.90
B388	SP99	14fr +2fr multi	1.25	.90
B389	SP99	18fr +3fr multi	1.60	1.60
B390	SP99	22fr +7fr multi	3.25	2.75
		Nos. B387-B390 (4)	7.35	6.15

Surtax for Luxembourg charitable organizations.

1994, Sept. 19   Photo.   Perf. 11½

Designs: No. B391, Partridge. No. B392, Stonechat, vert. 18fr+3fr, Blue-headed wagtail. 22fr+7fr, Great grey shrike, vert.

B391	SP99	14fr +2fr multi	1.25	1.00
B392	SP99	14fr +2fr multi	1.25	1.00
B393	SP99	18fr +3fr multi	1.75	1.75
B394	SP99	22fr +7fr multi	3.50	2.50
		Nos. B391-B394 (4)	7.75	6.25

Christmas
SP100

Trees
SP101

Design: 16fr + 2fr, Stained glass window, parish church of Alzingen.

1995, Dec. 4   Photo.   Perf. 11½
B395   SP100   16fr +2fr multi   1.25   1.25

Surtax for Luxembourg charitable organizations.

1995, Dec. 4

Designs: No. B396, Tilia platyphyllos. No. B397, Aesculus hippocastanum, horiz. 20fr+3fr, Quercus pedunculata, horiz. 32fr+7fr, Betula pendula.

B396	SP101	16fr +2fr multi	1.25	1.25
B397	SP101	16fr +2fr multi	1.25	1.25
B398	SP101	20fr +3fr multi	1.50	1.50
B399	SP101	32fr +7fr multi	2.75	2.75
		Nos. B396-B399 (4)	6.75	6.75

Surtax for Luxembourg charitable organizations.
See Nos. B400-B403, B405-B408.

1996, Dec. 9

Designs: No. B400, Fraxinus excelsior. No. B401, Salix SSP, horiz. 20fr+3fr, Sorbus domestica, horiz. 32fr+7fr, Fagus silvatica.

B400	SP101	16fr +2fr multi	1.00	1.00
B401	SP101	16fr +2fr multi	1.00	1.00
B402	SP101	20fr +3fr multi	1.75	1.75
B403	SP101	32fr +7fr multi	3.25	2.75
		Nos. B400-B403 (4)	7.00	6.50

Surtax for Luxembourg charitable organizations.

Christmas
SP102

1996, Dec. 9
B404   SP102   16fr +2fr multi   1.50   1.50

Surtax for Luxembourg charitable organizations.

Tree Type of 1995

Designs: No. B405, Ulmus glabra. No. B406, Acer platanoides. 20fr+3fr, Prunus avium. 32fr+7fr, Juglans regia, horiz.

1997, Dec. 8   Photo.   Perf. 11½

B405	SP101	16fr +2fr multi	1.00	1.00
B406	SP101	16fr +2fr multi	1.00	1.00
B407	SP101	20fr +3fr multi	2.00	2.00
B408	SP101	32fr +7fr multi	3.00	3.00
		Nos. B405-B408 (4)	7.00	7.00

Christmas
SP103

1997, Dec. 8
B409   SP103   16fr +2fr multi   1.50   1.50

Christmas
SP104

1998, Dec. 7   Photo.   Perf. 11½
B410   SP104   16fr +2fr multi   1.50   1.50

Charity
Stamps
SP105

Drawings of villages by Abbot Jean Bertels, 16th cent.: No. B411, Bech. No. B412, Ermesturf (Ermsdorf). 20fr+3fr, Itsich (Itzig). 32fr+7fr, Steinhem (Steinheim).

1998, Dec. 7

B411	SP105	16fr +2fr green & multi	1.00	1.00
B412	SP105	16fr +2fr brown & multi	1.00	1.00
B413	SP105	20fr +3fr red & multi	1.25	1.25
B414	SP105	32fr +7fr blue & multi	2.25	2.25
		Nos. B411-B414 (4)	5.50	5.50

See Nos. B415-B418, B420-B423.

Perf. 11¾x11½

1999, Nov. 30   Photo.

Drawings of villages by Abbot Jean Bertels, 16th cent.: No. B415, Oswiler (Osweiler). No. B416, Bettemburch (Bettembourg). 20fr+3fr, Cruchte auf der Alset (Cruchten). 32fr+7fr, Berchem.

B415	SP105	16fr +2fr red vio & multi	1.25	1.25
B416	SP105	16fr +2fr blue & multi	1.25	1.25
B417	SP105	20fr +3fr bl grn & multi	1.25	1.25
B418	SP105	32fr +7fr brown & multi	2.25	2.25
		Nos. B415-B418 (4)	6.00	6.00

Surtax for Luxembourg charitable organizations.

Christmas
SP106

1999, Nov. 30   Perf. 11¾
B419   SP106   16fr +2fr multi   1.25   1.25

Surtax for Luxembourg charitable organizations.

Village Drawings Type of 1998

By Abbot Jean Bertels, 16th cent.: 18fr+2fr, Lorentzwiler (Lorentzweiler). 21fr+3fr, Costurf (Consdorf). 24fr+3fr, Elfingen (Elvange). 36fr+7fr, Sprenckigen (Sprinkange).

2000, Dec. 5   Photo.   Perf. 11¾x11½
Granite Paper

B420	SP105	18fr +2fr grn & multi	.90	.90
B421	SP105	21fr +3fr brn & multi	1.25	1.25
B422	SP105	24fr +3fr red & multi	1.25	1.25
B423	SP105	36fr +7fr bl & multi	2.25	2.25
		Nos. B420-B423 (4)	5.65	5.65

Surtax for Luxembourg charitable organizations.

Christmas
SP107

2000, Dec. 5   Perf. 11¾
Granite Paper
B424   SP107   18fr +2fr multi   2.00   2.00

Surtax for Luxembourg charitable organizations.

Christmas
SP108

2001, Dec. 6   Photo.   Perf. 14
B425   SP108   45c +5c (18fr+2fr) multi   1.25   1.25

See note before No. 1063. A star-shaped hole is found at the UL portion of the design.

Fauna
SP109

Designs: 45c+5c (18fr+2fr), Squirrel. 52c+8c (21fr+3fr), Wild boar. 59c+11c (24fr+4fr), Hare, vert. 89c+21c (36fr+8fr), Wood pigeon, vert.

Perf. 11¾x11½, 11½x11¾
2001, Dec. 6   Granite Paper
B426-B429   SP109   Set of 4   7.00   7.00

Christmas
SP110

2002, Dec. 10 **Photo.** *Perf. 13¾*
B430 SP110 45c +5c multi 1.25 1.25
Surtax for Grand Duchess Charlotte charities.

Fauna
SP111

Designs: 45c+5c, Red fox. 52c+8c, Hedgehog and snail, vert. 59c+11c, Pheasant. 89c+21c, Deer, vert.

2002, Dec. 10 *Perf. 11½*
B431-B434 SP111 Set of 4 7.00 7.00

Christmas — SP112

No. B435: a, Round Church of Ehnen, Christmas tree. b, Wormer Koeppchen Chapel.

2003, Dec. 9 **Litho.** *Perf. 14¼*
B435 SP112 50c +5c Pair, #a-b 2.75 2.75
Surtax for Luxembourg charitable organizations.

Fauna
SP113

Designs: 50c+5c, Roe deer, vert. 60c+10c, Raccoons. 70c+10c, Weasel, vert. €1+25c, Goshawk.

2003, Dec. 9 **Photo.** *Perf. 11½*
B436-B439 SP113 Set of 4 8.00 8.00
Surtax for Luxembourg charitable organizations.

Christmas
SP114

Litho. & Embossed
2004, Dec. 7 *Perf. 13*
B440 SP114 50c +5c multi 1.50 1.50

Sports
SP115

Designs: 50c+5c, Skiing. 60c+10c, Running, vert. 70c+10c, Swimming. €1+25c, Soccer, vert.

Perf. 13x13½, 13½x13
2004, Dec. 7 **Litho.**
B441-B444 SP115 Set of 4 8.75 8.75
See Nos. B446-B449.

Christmas
SP116

2005, Dec. 6 **Litho.** *Perf. 13¼*
B445 SP116 50c +5c multi 1.40 1.40

Sports Type of 2004

Designs: 50c+5c, Figure skating, vert. 70c+10c, Basketball, vert. 90c+10c, Judo, vert. €1+25c, Tennis, vert.

2005, Dec. 6 *Perf. 13½x13*
B446-B449 SP115 Set of 4 8.50 8.50

Christmas
SP117

2006, Dec. 5 **Litho.** *Perf. 12½*
B450 SP117 50c +5c multi 1.40 1.40

Modern Pipe
Organs
SP118

Organ from: 50c+5c, Grand Auditorium of the Luxembourg Music Conservatory. 70c+10c, Bridel. 90c+10c, Mondercange Parish Church. €1+25c, Luxembourg-Grund.

2006, Dec. 5 *Perf. 13¼x13*
B451-B454 SP118 Set of 4 9.25 9.25
See Nos. B456-B459, B461-B464, B466-B469.

Christmas
SP119

2007, Dec. 4 **Litho.** *Perf. 12½*
B455 SP119 50c +5c multi 1.60 1.60

Modern Pipe Organs Type of 2006

Organ from: 50c+5c, Church of Niederwiltz. 70c+10c, Sandweiler, horiz. 90c+10c, Echternach Basilica, horiz. €1+25c, St. Joseph's Church, Esch-sur-Alzette.

2007, Dec. 4 *Perf. 13½x13, 13x13½*
B456-B459 SP118 Set of 4 10.50 10.50

Christmas
SP120

2008, Dec. 2 **Litho.** *Perf. 12½*
B460 SP120 50c +5c multi 1.40 1.40

Modern Pipe Organs Type of 2006

Organ from: 50c+5c, Junglinster. 70c+10c, Church, Mondorf-les-Bains, horiz. 90c+10c, Church, Vianden. €1+25c, Notre Dame Cathedral, Luxembourg.

2008, Dec. 2 *Perf. 13½x13, 13x13½*
B461-B464 SP118 Set of 4 9.25 9.25

Christmas
SP121

2009, Dec. 1 **Litho.** *Perf. 12½*
B465 SP121 50c + 5c multi 1.75 1.75

Modern Pipe Organs Type of 2006

Organ from: 50c+5c, Luxembourg Philharmonic. 70c+10c, St. Martin's Church, Dudelange. 90c+10c, Church, Nommern. 1fr+25c, Saint-Pierre aux Liens Church, Heiderscheid.

2009, Dec. 1 *Perf. 13½x13*
B466-B469 SP118 Set of 4 11.00 11.00

Christmas
SP122

2010, Dec. 7 **Litho.** *Perf. 12½*
B470 SP122 60c + 5c multi 1.90 1.90

Occupations of the Past — SP123

Designs: 60c+5c, Blacksmith. 85c+10c, Basketmaker. €1.10+10c, Grinder, horiz. €1.20+25c, Cooper, horiz.

Litho. & Embossed With Foil Application
2010, Dec. 7 *Perf. 13¼x13, 13x13¼*
B471-B474 SP123 Set of 4 12.00 12.00
See Nos. B476-B479, B482-B485.

Christmas
SP124

2011, Dec. 6 **Litho.** *Perf. 12½*
B475 SP124 60c+5c multi 1.75 1.75
No. B475 is impregnated with a pine scent.

Occupations of the Past Type of 2010

Designs: 60c+5c, Wood joiner (schräiner). 85c+10c, Potter (aulebacker). €1.10+10c, Stonemason (steemetzer), horiz. €1.20+25c, Printer (buchdréker), horiz.

Litho. & Embossed With Foil Application
2011, Dec. 6 *Perf. 13¼x13, 13x13¼*
B476-B479 SP123 Set of 4 11.50 11.50

Christmas
SP125

Stars, Christmas tree and: 60c+5c, Open mailbox. 85c+10c, Open envelope.

Litho. With Foil Application
2012, Dec. 4 *Perf. 13¼*
B480-B481 SP125 Set of 2 4.25 4.25

Occupations of the Past Type of 2010

Designs: 60c+5c, Washerwomen, horiz. 85c+10c, Hatter. €1.10+10c, Farmer. €1.20+25c, Vegetable sellers, horiz.

Litho. & Embossed With Foil Application
2012, Dec. 4 *Perf. 13x13¼, 13¼x13*
B482-B485 SP123 Set of 4 11.00 11.00

Christmas
SP126

Designs: 60c+5c, One Christmas ornament. 85c+10c, Two Christmas ornaments.

2013, Dec. 3 **Litho.** *Perf. 13*
B486-B487 SP126 Set of 2 4.50 4.50
Nos. B486 and B487 have laser-cut holes as part of the design.

Occupations of the Past Type of 2010

Designs: 60c+5c, Miller. 85c+10c, Distiller, horiz. €1.10+10c, Wheelwright. €1.20+25c, Cobbler, horiz.

Litho. & Embossed With Foil Application
2013, Dec. 3 *Perf. 13¼x13, 13x13¼*
B488-B491 SP123 Set of 4 12.00 12.00

Christmas
SP127

Designs: 60c+5c, Fox and rabbit. 85c+10c, Owl and mouse.

2014, Dec. 2 **Litho.** *Perf. 14¼*
Flocked Granite Paper
B492-B493 SP127 Set of 2 4.00 4.00

Automobiles — SP128

Designs: 60c+5c, 1899 De Dion-Bouton Vis-à-vis Type D. 85c+10c, 1904 Peugeot Bébé. €1.10+10c, 1909 Opel 10/20. €1.20+25c, 1910 Renault AX.

Litho. & Embossed With Foil Application

2014, Dec. 2   *Perf. 13x13¼*

B494-B497 SP128 Set of 4 10.50 10.50

AIR POST STAMPS

Airplane over Luxembourg — AP1

1931-33 **Unwmk. Engr.** *Perf. 12½*

C1	AP1	50c green ('33)	.55	1.10
C2	AP1	75c dark brown	.55	1.50
C3	AP1	1fr red	.55	1.50
C4	AP1	1¼fr dark violet	.55	1.50
C5	AP1	1¾fr dark blue	.55	1.50
C6	AP1	3fr gray black ('33)	1.10	6.00
		Nos. C1-C6 (6)	3.85	13.10
		Set, never hinged	8.25	

Aerial View of Moselle River — AP2

Wing and View of Luxembourg AP3

Vianden Castle — AP4

1946, June 7 **Photo.** *Perf. 11½*

C7	AP2	1fr dk ol grn & gray	.25	.25
C8	AP3	2fr chnt brn & buff	.25	.25
C9	AP4	3fr sepia & brown	.25	.25
C10	AP4	4fr dp vio & gray vio	.25	.40
C11	AP3	5fr dp mag & buff	.25	.40
C12	AP4	6fr dk brown & gray	.25	.25
C13	AP3	10fr henna brn & buff	.40	.55
C14	AP3	20fr dk blue & cream	.90	1.50
C15	AP4	50fr dk green & gray	1.75	1.75
		Nos. C7-C15 (9)	4.55	5.90
		Set, never hinged	8.75	

1852 and 1952 AP5

Stamps in Gray and Dark Violet Brown

1952, May 24

C16	AP5	80c olive grn	.25	.45
C17	AP5	2.50fr brt car	.50	1.40
C18	AP5	4fr brt blue	1.60	3.00

C19	AP5	8fr brown red	17.50	55.00
C20	AP5	10fr dull brown	15.00	47.50
		Nos. C16-C20 (5)	34.85	107.35
		Set, never hinged	85.00	

Centenary of Luxembourg's postage stamps. Nos. C16-C18 were available at face, but complete sets sold for 45.30fr, which included admission to the CENTILUX exhibition.

POSTAGE DUE STAMPS

Coat of Arms — D1

1907 **Unwmk.** **Typo.** *Perf. 12½*

J1	D1	5c green & black	.25	.25
J2	D1	10c green & black	.95	.25
J3	D1	12½c green & black	.25	.80
J4	D1	20c green & black	.55	.80
J5	D1	25c green & black	16.00	1.20
J6	D1	50c green & black	.45	3.50
J7	D1	1fr green & black	.25	3.50
		Nos. J1-J7 (7)	18.70	10.30

See Nos. J10-J22.

Nos. J3, J5 Surcharged

1920

J8	D1	15c on 12½c	.50	7.25
J9	D1	30c on 25c	.60	9.00
		Set, never hinged	3.50	

Arms Type of 1907

1921-35

J10	D1	5c green & red	.25	.40
J11	D1	10c green & red	.25	.35
J12	D1	20c green & red	.25	.35
J13	D1	25c green & red	.25	.35
J14	D1	30c green & red	.55	.60
J15	D1	35c green & red ('35)	.55	.35
J16	D1	50c green & red	.55	.60
J17	D1	60c green & red ('28)	.45	.50
J18	D1	70c green & red ('35)	.55	.35
J19	D1	75c green & red ('30)	.55	.25
J20	D1	1fr green & red	.55	1.10
J21	D1	2fr green & red ('30)	.55	6.50
J22	D1	3fr green & red ('30)	1.60	18.00
		Nos. J10-J22 (13)	6.90	29.70
		Set, never hinged	27.50	

D2   D3

1946-48 **Photo.** *Perf. 11½*

J23	D2	5c bright green	.25	.65
J24	D2	10c bright green	.25	.50
J25	D2	20c bright green	.25	.50
J26	D2	30c bright green	.25	.50
J27	D2	50c bright green	.25	.70
J28	D2	70c bright green	.25	.70
J29	D3	75c brt green ('48)	.70	.25
J30	D3	1fr carmine	.25	.25
J31	D3	1.50fr carmine	.25	.25
J32	D3	2fr carmine	.25	.25
J33	D3	3fr carmine	.25	.35
J34	D3	5fr carmine	.55	.45
J35	D3	10fr carmine	.95	4.00
J36	D3	20fr carmine	2.75	22.50
		Nos. J23-J36 (14)	7.45	31.85
		Set, never hinged	22.50	

OFFICIAL STAMPS

Forged overprints on Nos. O1-O64 abound.

Unused values of Nos. O1-O51 are for stamps without gum. Though these stamps were issued with gum, most examples offered are without gum. Stamps with original gum sell for somewhat more.

Regular Issues Overprinted Reading Diagonally Up or Down

Frankfurt Print

Rouletted in Color except 2c

1875   **Unwmk.**

O1	A2	1c red brown	27.50	37.50
O2	A2	2c black	37.50	37.50
O3	A3	10c lilac	2,400.	2,400.
O4	A3	12½c rose	475.00	600.00
O5	A3	20c gray brn	37.50	57.50
O6	A3	25c blue	250.00	140.00
O7	A3	25c ultra	2,100.	1,400.
O8	A3	30c lilac rose	32.50	75.00
O9	A3	40c pale org	160.00	240.00
a.		40c org red, thick paper	250.00	325.00
c.		As "a," thin paper	1,650.	1,400.
O10	A3	1fr on 37½c		
		bis	150.00	22.50

Double overprints exist on Nos. O1-O6, O8-O10.

Overprints reading diagonally down sell for more.

Inverted Overprint

O1a	A2	1c	190.00	225.00
O2a	A2	2c	190.00	225.00
O3a	A3	10c	2,500.	2,500.
O4a	A3	12½c	650.00	925.00
O5a	A3	20c	55.00	75.00
O6a	A3	25c	1,100.	1,300.
O7a	A3	25c	2,100.	1,500.
O8a	A3	30c	650.00	925.00
O9b	A3	40c pale orange	325.00	450.00
O10a		1fr on 37½c	175.00	75.00

Luxembourg Print

1875-76   *Perf. 13*

O11	A2	1c red brown	9.50	27.50
O12	A2	2c black	12.00	32.50
O13	A2	4c green	90.00	160.00
O14	A2	5c yellow	65.00	80.00
a.		5c orange yellow	75.00	110.00
O15	A3	10c gray lilac	92.50	120.00
O16	A3	12½c rose	85.00	120.00
O17	A3	12½c lilac rose	225.00	275.00
O18	A3	25c blue	11.00	32.50
O19	A3	1fr on 37½c bis	35.00	60.00
		Nos. O11-O19 (9)	625.00	907.50

Double overprints exist on Nos. O11-O15.

Inverted Overprint

O11a	A2	1c	92.50	110.00
O12a	A2	2c	150.00	190.00
O13a	A2	4c	160.00	190.00
O14b	A2	5c	500.00	650.00
O15a	A3	10c	500.00	190.00
O16a	A3	12½c	400.00	550.00
O17a	A3	12½c	450.00	525.00
O18a	A3	25c	125.00	175.00
O19a	A3	1fr on 37½c	190.00	250.00
		Nos. O11a-O19a (9)	2,567.	2,830.

Haarlem Print

1880 *Perf. 11½x12, 12½x12, 13½*

O22	A3	25c blue	2.25	2.75

Overprinted

Frankfurt Print

1878   *Rouletted in Color*

O23	A2	1c red brown	140.00	160.00
O25	A3	20c gray brn	190.00	225.00
O26	A3	30c lilac rose	750.00	575.00
O27	A3	40c orange	325.00	400.00
O28	A3	1fr on 37½c bis	550.00	110.00
		Nos. O23-O28 (5)	1,955.	1,520.

Inverted Overprint

O23a	A3	1c	225.00	300.00
O25a	A3	20c	325.00	400.00
O26a	A3	30c	925.00	700.00
O27a	A3	40c	875.00	925.00
O28a	A3	1fr on 37½c	650.00	200.00

Luxembourg Print

1878-80   *Perf. 13*

O29	A2	1c red brown	750.00	925.00
O30	A2	2c black	190.00	225.00
O31	A2	4c green	190.00	225.00
O32	A2	5c yellow	375.00	450.00
O33	A3	10c gray lilac	375.00	400.00
O34	A3	12½c rose	65.00	110.00
O35	A3	25c blue	525.00	550.00
		Nos. O29-O35 (7)	2,470.	2,885.

Inverted Overprint

O29a	A2	1c	140.00	160.00
O30a	A2	2c	14.50	27.50
O31a	A2	4c	150.00	190.00
O32a	A3	5c	1,500.	1,500.
O33a	A3	10c	92.50	110.00
O34a	A3	12½c	525.00	600.00
O35a	A3	25c	850.00	1,000.

Overprinted

Frankfurt Print

1881   *Rouletted in Color*

O39	A3	40c orange	37.50	75.00
a.		Inverted overprint	210.00	275.00

"S.P." are initials of "Service Public."

Luxembourg Print

1881   *Perf. 13*

O40	A2	1c red brown	125.00	160.00
O41	A2	4c green	175.00	200.00
a.		Inverted overprint	250.00	
O42	A2	5c yellow	600.00	750.00
O43	A3	1fr on 37½c bis	32.50	47.50
		Nos. O40-O43 (4)	932.50	1,157.

Haarlem Print

Perf. 11½x12, 12½x12, 13½

O44	A2	1c yellow brn	8.50	9.25
O45	A2	2c black	9.25	9.25
O46	A2	5c yellow	160.00	200.00
a.		Inverted overprint	225.00	
O47	A3	10c gray lilac	160.00	200.00
O48	A3	12½c rose	175.00	240.00
O49	A3	20c gray brown	72.50	92.50
O50	A3	25c blue	72.50	92.50
O51	A3	30c dull rose	75.00	120.00
		Nos. O44-O51 (8)	732.75	963.50

Stamps of the 1881 issue with the overprint of the 1882 issue shown below were never issued.

Overprinted

Perf. 11½x12, 12½x12, 12½, 13½

1882

O52	A6	1c gray lilac	.25	.40
O53	A6	2c ol gray	.25	.40
a.		"S" omitted	110.00	
O54	A6	4c ol bister	.25	.45
O55	A6	5c lt green	.25	.55
O56	A6	10c rose	12.00	16.00
O57	A6	12½c slate	1.60	4.75
O58	A6	20c orange	1.60	4.00
O59	A6	25c ultra	19.00	24.00
O60	A6	30c gray grn	4.00	8.75
O61	A6	50c bis brown	.95	2.75
O62	A6	1fr pale vio	.95	4.00
O63	A6	5fr brown org	16.00	40.00
		Nos. O52-O63 (12)	57.10	106.05

Nos. O52-O63 exist without one or both periods, also with varying space between "S" and "P." Nine denominations exist with double overprint, six with inverted overprint.

Overprinted

1883   *Perf. 13½*

O64	A6	5fr brown org	2,200.	2,200.

Overprinted

1891-93   Perf. 11, 11½, 11½x11, 12½
O65	A7	10c carmine	.25	.50
a.		Sheet of 25	55.00	
O66	A7	12½c slate grn	8.00	7.25
O67	A7	20c orange	13.00	8.50
O68	A7	25c blue	.25	.45
a.		Sheet of 25	65.00	
O69	A7	30c olive grn	8.00	8.00
O70	A7	37½c green	8.00	8.00
O71	A7	50c brown	6.00	8.75
O72	A7	1fr dp vio	8.00	9.50
O73	A7	2½fr black	45.00	72.50
O74	A7	5fr lake	40.00	55.00
		Nos. O65-O74 (10)	136.50	178.45

1895   Perf. 12½
O75	A8	1c pearl gray	1.90	1.90
O76	A8	2c gray brn	1.00	1.60
O77	A8	4c olive bis	1.00	1.60
O78	A8	5c green	4.00	5.00
O79	A8	10c carmine	24.00	35.00
		Nos. O75-O79 (5)	31.90	45.10

Nos. O66-O79 exist without overprint and
perforated "OFFICIEL" through the stamp. Values for set: unused, $12; used, $45.
Nos. O65a and O68a were issued to commemorate the coronation of Grand Duke Adolphe.

Regular Issue of 1906-
26 Overprinted

1908-26   Perf. 11x11½, 12½
O80	A9	1c gray	.25	.40
a.		Inverted overprint	125.00	
O81	A9	2c olive brn	.25	.40
O82	A9	4c bister	.25	.40
a.		Double overprint	140.00	
O83	A9	5c green	.25	.40
O84	A9	5c lilac ('26)	.25	.40
O85	A9	6c violet	.25	.40
O86	A9	7½c org ('19)	.25	.40
O87	A10	10c scarlet	.25	.40
O88	A10	12½c slate grn	.25	.55
O89	A10	15c orange brn	.25	.55
O90	A10	20c orange	.25	.75
O91	A10	25c ultra	.25	.75
O92	A10	30c olive grn	2.75	6.50
O93	A10	37½c green	.45	.75
O94	A10	50c brown	.75	1.50
O95	A10	87½c dk blue	2.00	3.50
O96	A10	1fr violet	2.75	4.00
O97	A10	2½fr vermilion	65.00	65.00
O98	A10	5fr claret	55.00	45.00
		Nos. O80-O98 (19)	131.70	132.05

On Regular Issue of 1914-17

1915-17
O99	A11	10c lake	.25	.75
O100	A11	12½c dull grn	.25	.75
O101	A11	15c olive blk	.25	.75
O102	A11	17½c dp brn ('17)	.25	.75
O103	A11	25c ultra	.25	.75
O104	A11	30c bister	1.40	5.00
O105	A11	35c dk blue	.25	1.20
O106	A11	37½c blk brn	.25	1.60
O107	A11	40c orange	.30	1.20
O108	A11	50c dk gray	.30	.95
O109	A11	62½c blue grn	.30	1.60
O110	A11	87½c org ('17)	.30	1.60
O111	A11	1fr orange brn	.30	1.60
O112	A11	2½fr red	.30	2.50
O113	A11	5fr dk violet	.30	2.50
		Nos. O99-O113 (15)	5.25	23.75

On Regular Issues of 1921-26 in Black

1922-26   Perf. 11½, 11½x11, 12½
O114	A12	2c brown	.25	.25
O115	A12	3c olive grn	.25	.25
O116	A12	6c violet	.25	.40
O117	A12	10c yellow grn	.25	.40
O118	A12	10c ol grn ('24)	.25	.40
O119	A12	15c brown ol	.25	.40
O120	A12	15c pale grn ('24)	.25	.40
O121	A12	15c dp org ('26)	.25	.40
O122	A12	20c dp orange	.25	.40
O123	A12	20c yel grn ('26)	.25	.40
O124	A12	25c dk green	.25	.40
O125	A12	30c car rose	.25	.40
O126	A12	40c brown org	.25	.40
O127	A12	50c dp blue	.25	.45
O128	A12	50c red ('24)	.25	.55
O129	A12	75c red	.25	.55
O130	A12	75c dp bl ('24)	.25	.45
O131	A12	80c black	4.75	8.00
O132	A13	1fr carmine	.40	2.00

O133	A14	2fr indigo	3.00	6.00
O134	A14	2fr dk brn ('26)	1.75	5.00
O135	A15	5fr dk vio	17.50	40.00
		Nos. O114-O135 (22)	31.65	67.90

On Regular Issues of 1921-26 in Red

1922-34   Perf. 11, 11½, 11½x11, 12½
O136	A12	80c blk, perf. 11½	.25	.45
O137	A13	1fr dk bl, perf. 11½ ('26)	.25	1.20
O138	A14	2fr ind, perf. 11½x11	.55	2.00
O139	A17	3fr dk bl & bl, perf. 11	2.75	2.75
a.		Perf. 11½	.60	1.40
b.		Perf. 12½	.50	1.40
O140	A15	5fr dk vio, perf. 11½x11	4.00	9.00
a.		Perf. 12½ ('34)	12.00	20.00
O141	A16	10fr blk, perf. 11½	12.00	24.00
a.		Perf. 12½	12.00	27.50
		Nos. O136-O141 (6)	19.80	39.40

On Regular Issue of 1926-35

1926-27   Perf. 12
O142	A18	5c dk violet	.25	.25
O143	A18	10c olive grn	.25	.25
O144	A18	20c orange	.25	.25
O145	A18	25c yellow grn	.25	.25
O146	A18	25c blk brn ('27)	.35	.55
O147	A18	30c yel grn ('27)	.65	1.20
O148	A18	40c olive gray	.25	.25
O149	A18	50c red brown	.25	.25
O150	A18	65c black brn	.25	.25
O151	A18	75c rose	.25	.25
O152	A18	75c bis brn ('27)	.35	.55
O153	A18	80c bister brn	.25	.40
O154	A18	90c rose ('27)	.35	.55
O155	A18	1fr black	.25	.45
O156	A18	1¼fr dk blue	.25	.45
O157	A18	1½fr dp blue ('27)	.55	1.20
		Nos. O142-O157 (16)	5.00	7.35

Type of Regular
Issue, 1926-35,
Overprinted

1928-35   Wmk. 213
O158	A18	5c dk violet	.25	.40
O159	A18	10c olive grn	.25	.40
O160	A18	15c black ('30)	.25	1.20
O161	A18	20c orange	.45	.75
O162	A18	25c violet brn	.45	.75
O163	A18	30c yellow grn	.50	1.40
O164	A18	30c gray vio ('30)	.25	1.20
O165	A18	35c yel grn ('30)	.25	1.20
O166	A18	35c gray vio	.35	.90
O167	A18	40c olive gray	.35	.75
O168	A18	50c red brown	.35	.75
O169	A18	60c blue grn	.35	.75
O170	A18	70c blue vio ('35)	3.50	7.25
O171	A18	75c bister brn	.35	.75
O172	A18	90c rose	.35	1.20
O173	A18	1fr black	.35	1.20
O174	A18	1fr rose ('30)	.45	2.40
O175	A18	1¼fr yel ('30)	4.00	6.50
O176	A18	1¼fr bl grn ('31)	1.50	4.00
O177	A18	1½fr deep blue	.35	1.40
O178	A18	1¾fr dk blue ('30)	.45	1.60
		Nos. O158-O178 (21)	15.35	36.75

Type of Regular Issues of 1928-31 Overprinted Like Nos. O80-O98

1928-31   Wmk. 216   Perf. 11½
O179	A19	2fr black	.50	1.60

Wmk. 110   Perf. 12½
O180	A21	20fr dp green ('31)	2.25	8.00

No. 198 Overprinted Like Nos. O80-O98

1934   Unwmk.   Perf. 14x13½
O181	A22	5fr blue green	1.50	6.00

Type of Regular Issue of 1935 Overprinted Like Nos. O158-O178 in Red

1935   Wmk. 247   Perf. 12½x12
O182	A23	10fr green	1.60	7.00

OCCUPATION STAMPS

Issued under German Occupation

Stamps of Germany,
1933-36, Overprinted
in Black

1940, Oct. 1   Wmk. 237   Perf. 14
N1	A64	3pf olive bis	.25	.50
N2	A64	4pf dull blue	.25	.55
N3	A64	5pf bright green	.25	.50
N4	A64	6pf dark green	.25	.50
N5	A64	8pf vermilion	.25	.50
N6	A64	10pf chocolate	.25	.50
N7	A64	12pf deep carmine	.25	.50
N8	A64	15pf maroon	.35	.70
a.		Inverted overprint	450.00	1,300.
N9	A64	20pf bright blue	.40	1.10
N10	A64	25pf ultra	.40	1.60
N11	A64	30pf olive green	.40	1.60
N12	A64	40pf red violet	.55	1.60
N13	A64	50pf dk green & blk	.95	3.00
N14	A64	60pf claret & blk	1.10	3.00
N15	A64	80pf dk blue & blk	2.00	6.50
N16	A64	100pf orange & blk	3.50	6.50
		Nos. N1-N16 (16)	11.40	29.15
		Set, never hinged	32.50	

Nos. 159-162, 164, 168-171, 173, 175, 179, 182, 216, 198-199 Surcharged in Black

a

b

c

d

Perf. 12, 14x13½, 12½x12, 11½
1940, Dec. 5   Unwmk.
N17	A18(a)	3rpf on 15c	.25	.35
N18	A18(a)	4rpf on 20c	.25	.35
N19	A18(a)	5rpf on 35c	.25	.35
N20	A18(a)	6rpf on 10c	.25	.35
N21	A18(a)	8rpf on 25c	.25	.35
N22	A18(a)	10rpf on 40c	.25	.35
N23	A18(a)	12rpf on 60c	.25	.35
N24	A18(a)	15rpf on 1fr rose	.25	.35
N25	A18(a)	20rpf on 50c	.25	.60
N26	A18(a)	25rpf on 5c	.25	1.20
N27	A18(a)	30rpf on 70c	.25	.60
N28	A18(a)	40rpf on 75c	.30	1.20
N29	A18(a)	50rpf on 1¼fr	.25	.60
N30	A35(b)	60rpf on 2fr	1.40	9.50
N31	A22(c)	80rpf on 5fr	.40	2.00
N32	A23(d)	100rpf on 10fr	.65	2.75
		Nos. N17-N32 (16)	5.75	21.25
		Set, never hinged	9.00	

OCCUPATION SEMI-POSTAL STAMPS

Semi-Postal
Stamps of
Germany, 1940
Overprinted in
Black

1941, Jan. 12   Unwmk.   Perf. 14
NB1	SP153	3pf + 2pf dk brn	.25	.60
NB2	SP153	4pf + 3pf bluish blk	.25	.60
NB3	SP153	5pf + 3pf yel grn	.25	.60
NB4	SP153	6pf + 4pf dk grn	.25	.60
NB5	SP153	8pf + 4pf dp org	.25	.60
NB6	SP153	12pf + 6pf carmine	.25	.60
NB7	SP153	15pf + 10pf dk vio brn	.30	1.60
NB8	SP153	25pf + 15pf dp ultra	.55	3.50
NB9	SP153	40pf + 35pf red lil	.85	6.00
		Nos. NB1-NB9 (9)	3.20	14.70
		Set, never hinged	8.00	

MACAO

mə-'kau

LOCATION — Off the Chinese coast at the mouth of the Canton River
GOVT. — Special Administrative Area of China (PRC) (as of 12/20/99)
AREA — 8 sq. mi.
POP. — 415,850 (1998)
CAPITAL — Macao

Formerly a Portuguese overseas territory. The territory includes the two small adjacent islands of Coloane and Taipa.

1000 Reis = 1 Milreis
78 Avos = 1 Rupee (1894)
100 Avos = 1 Pataca (1913)

Catalogue values for unused stamps in this country are for Never Hinged items, beginning with Scott 339 in the regular postage section, Scott C16 in the air post section, Scott J50 in the semi-postal section, and Scott RA11 in the postal tax section.

Watermark

Wmk. 232 — Maltese Cross

Portuguese Crown — A1

Perf. 12½, 13½

			Unwmk.	
1884-85		**Typo.**		
1	A1	5r black	13.00	9.00
2	A1	10r orange	25.00	12.00
3	A1	10r green ('85)	30.00	9.00
4	A1	20r bister	32.50	22.50
5	A1	20r rose ('85)	45.00	18.00
6	A1	25r rose	22.50	5.25
7	A1	25r violet ('85)	30.00	13.50
8	A1	40r blue	115.00	40.00
9	A1	40r yellow ('85)	42.50	20.00
10	A1	50r green	250.00	75.00
11	A1	50r blue ('85)	57.50	25.00
12	A1	80r gray ('85)	57.50	30.00
13	A1	100r red lilac	75.00	24.00
a.		100r lilac	75.00	24.00
14	A1	200r orange	70.00	20.00
15	A1	300r chocolate	100.00	25.00
		Nos. 1-15 (15)	965.50	348.25

All values exist both perf 12½ and 13½. The cheaper variety is listed above. For detailed listings, see the Scott Classic Specialized Catalogue of stamps and Covers.
The reprints of the 1885 issue are printed on smooth, white chalky paper, ungummed and on thin white paper with shiny white gum and clean-cut perforation 13½.
For surcharges see Nos. 16-28, 108-109.

No. 13a Surcharged in Black

1884		**Without Gum**	**Perf. 12½**	
16	A1	80r on 100r lilac	90.00	45.00
a.		Inverted surcharge	200.00	75.00
b.		Without accent on "e" of "reis"	80.00	47.50
c.		Perf. 13½	125.00	55.00
d.		As "b," perf. 13½	140.00	62.50

Nos. 6 and 10 Surcharged in Black, Blue or Red

b   c

1885			**Without Gum**	
17	A1(b)	5r on 25r rose, perf. 12½ (Bk)	21.00	6.50
a.		With accent on "e" of "Reis"	35.00	12.00
b.		Double surcharge	225.00	160.00
c.		Inverted surcharge	200.00	125.00
d.		Perf. 13½	125.00	100.00
e.		As "d," inverted surcharge	200.00	140.00
18	A1(b)	10r on 25r rose (Bl)	47.50	18.00
a.		Accent on "e" of "Reis"		
b.		Pair, one without surcharge	—	
19	A1(b)	10r on 50r grn, perf. 13½ (Bl)	625.00	225.00
a.		Perf. 12½	625.00	260.00
20	A1(b)	20r on 50r green, perf. 12½ (Bk)	47.50	10.00
a.		Double surcharge		160.00
b.		Accent on "e" of "Reis"	—	
21	A1(b)	40r on 50r grn, perf. 12½ (R)	175.00	50.00
a.		Perf. 13½	240.00	100.00
		Nos. 17-21 (5)	916.00	309.50

1885			**Without Gum**	
22	A1(c)	5r on 25r rose (Bk)	32.50	18.00
a.		Original value not obliterated		
23	A1(c)	10r on 50r green (Bk)	32.50	18.00
a.		Inverted surcharge		
b.		Perf. 12½	32.50	18.00

Nos. 12, 13a and 14 Surcharged in Black

1887				
24	A1	5r on 80r gray	32.50	9.00
a.		"R" of "Reis" 4mm high	125.00	50.00
b.		Perf. 12½	150.00	45.00
25	A1	10r on 100r lilac	150.00	90.00
a.		Perf. 12½	95.00	60.00
26	A1	10r on 80r gray	65.00	20.00
a.		"R" 4mm high	140.00	47.50
27	A1	10r on 200r orange	160.00	62.50
a.		"R" 4mm high, "e" without accent	200.00	80.00
b.		Perf. 13½	140.00	62.50
28	A1	20r on 80r gray	125.00	35.00
a.		"R" 4mm high	175.00	47.50
b.		Perf. 12½	100.00	50.00
c.		"R" 4mm high, "e" without accent	160.00	47.50
		Nos. 24-28 (5)	532.50	216.50

The surcharges with larger "R" (4mm) have accent on "e." Smaller "R" is 3mm high.
Occasionally Nos. 24, 26 and 28 may be found with original gum. Values the same.

Coat of Arms — A6

Red Surcharge
Without Gum

			Perf. 12½	
1887, Oct. 20				
32	A6	5r green & buff	15.00	7.00
a.		With labels, 5r on 10r	77.50	65.00
b.		With labels, 5r on 20r	90.00	65.00
c.		With labels, 5r on 60r	77.50	65.00
33	A6	10r green & buff	22.50	9.00
a.		With labels, 10r on 10r	95.00	75.00
b.		With labels, 10r on 60r	110.00	75.00

34	A6	40r green & buff	37.50	14.00
a.		With labels, 40r on 20r	150.00	110.00
		Nos. 32-34 (3)	75.00	30.00

Nos. 32-34 were local provisionals, created by perforating contemporary revenue stamps to remove the old value inscriptions and then surcharging the central design portion. The unused portion of the design was normally removed prior to use. For simplicity's sake, we refer to these extraneous portions of the original revenue stamps as "labels."
The 10r also exists with 20r labels, and 40r with 10r labels. Value, $250 each.

King Luiz — A7

Typographed and Embossed
1888, Jan.   Perf. 12½, 13½
Chalk-surfaced Paper

35	A7	5r black	21.00	4.00
36	A7	10r green	21.00	6.00
.		Perf. 13½	75.00	37.50
37	A7	20r carmine	35.00	13.00
38	A7	25r violet	35.00	13.00
39	A7	40r chocolate	35.00	18.00
.		Perf. 13½	60.00	26.00
40	A7	50r blue	60.00	13.50
41	A7	80r gray	95.00	22.50
a.		Imperf., pair	—	
42	A7	100r brown	45.00	22.50
43	A7	200r gray lilac	90.00	45.00
44	A7	300r orange	72.50	45.00
		Nos. 35-44 (10)	509.50	202.50

Nos. 37-44 were issued without gum.
For surcharges and overprints see Nos. 45, 58-66B, 110-118, 164-170, 239.

No. 43 Surcharged in Red

1892		**Without Gum**	**Perf. 13½**	
45	A7	30r on 200r gray lilac	70.00	24.00
a.		Inverted surcharge	275.00	165.00

King Carlos — A9

1894, Nov. 15   Typo.   Perf. 11½

46	A9	5r yellow	8.25	3.75
47	A9	10r redsh violet	8.25	3.75
48	A9	15r chocolate	12.50	5.25
49	A9	20r lavender	14.00	6.00
50	A9	25r green	35.00	11.25
51	A9	50r lt blue	37.50	22.50
.		Perf. 13½	550.00	400.00
52	A9	75r carmine	70.00	30.00
53	A9	80r yellow green	37.50	22.50
54	A9	100r brown, *buff*	40.00	22.50
55	A9	150r carmine, *rose*	45.00	22.50
56	A9	200r dk blue, *blue*	62.50	34.00
57	A9	300r dk blue, *sal*	82.50	45.00
		Nos. 46-57 (12)	453.00	229.00

Nos. 49-57 were issued without gum, No. 49 with or without gum.
For surcharges and overprints see Nos. 119-130, 171-181, 183-186, 240-251, 257-258.

Stamps of 1888 Surcharged in Red, Green or Black

1894		**Without Gum**	**Perf. 12½**	
58	A7	1a on 5r black (R)	11.00	4.50
a.		Short "1"	11.00	4.50
b.		Inverted surcharge	100.00	100.00
c.		Double surcharge	400.00	
d.		Surch. on back instead of face	200.00	200.00

59	A7	3a on 20r carmine (G)	19.00	4.50
a.		Inverted surcharge	—	
60	A7	4a on 25r violet (Bk)	21.00	9.00
a.		Inverted surcharge	60.00	50.00
61	A7	6a on 40r choc (Bk)	25.00	6.75
.		Perf. 13½	19.00	12.00
62	A7	8a on 50r blue (R)	55.00	18.00
a.		Double surch., one inverted	225.00	200.00
b.		Inverted surcharge	125.00	60.00
c.		Perf. 13½	62.50	40.00
d.		As #62, double surch.	150.00	120.00
63	A7	13a on 80r gray (Bk)	30.00	7.00
a.		Double surcharge	150.00	110.00
64	A7	16a on 100r brown (Bk)	60.00	18.00
a.		Inverted surcharge	200.00	125.00
b.		Perf. 13½	115.00	110.00
65	A7	31a on 200r gray lil (Bk)	90.00	25.00
a.		Inverted surcharge	150.00	125.00
b.		Perf. 13½	75.00	25.00
66	A7	47a on 300r orange (G)	72.50	11.00
a.		Double surcharge	160.00	120.00
		Nos. 58-66 (9)	383.50	103.75

The style of type used for the word "PROVISÓRIO" on Nos. 58 to 66 differs for each value.
A 2a on 10r green was unofficially surcharged and denounced by the authorities. Value, $500.

On No. 45

66B	A7	5a on 30r on 200r	150.00	50.00

Common Design Types pictured following the introduction.

Vasco da Gama Issue
Common Design Types

1898, Apr. 1		**Engr.**	**Perf. 12½ to 16**	
67	CD20	½a blue green	7.00	2.25
68	CD21	1a red	7.00	3.75
69	CD22	2a red violet	7.00	5.25
70	CD23	4a yellow green	10.00	7.50
71	CD24	8a dark blue	19.00	12.00
72	CD25	12a violet brown	30.00	22.00
73	CD26	16a bister brown	26.00	22.00
74	CD27	24a bister	30.00	22.00
		Nos. 67-74 (8)	136.00	96.75

For overprints and surcharges see Nos. 187-194.

King Carlos — A11

1898-1903   Typo.   Perf. 11½
Name and Value in Black except #103

75	A11	½a gray	4.50	1.00
a.		Perf. 12½	15.00	7.50
b.		As #75, black ("MACAU" and denom.) inverted	100.00	90.00
76	A11	1a orange	4.50	1.00
a.		Perf. 12½	15.00	7.50
b.		As #76, black ("MACAU" and denom.) inverted	175.00	150.00
77	A11	2a yellow green	5.75	1.50
a.		Black ("MACAU" and denom.) inverted	140.00	110.00
78	A11	2a gray green ('03)	6.25	1.50
79	A11	2½a red brown	7.50	2.25
80	A11	3a gray violet	7.50	2.25
81	A11	3a slate ('03)	6.25	1.65
82	A11	4a sea green	9.00	5.00
83	A11	4a carmine ('03)	6.25	1.50
84	A11	5a gray brn ('00)	15.00	3.75
85	A11	5a pale yel brn ('03)	9.00	2.25
86	A11	6a red brown ('03)	10.00	2.00
87	A11	8a blue	12.50	3.75
88	A11	8a gray brn ('03)	16.00	4.00
89	A11	10a slate blue ('00)	15.00	3.75
90	A11	12a rose	15.00	6.50
91	A11	12a red lilac ('03)	62.50	15.00
92	A11	13a violet	18.00	6.50
93	A11	13a gray lilac ('03)	22.50	6.00
94	A11	13a pale ol grn ('00)	90.00	23.00
95	A11	16a dk blue, *bl*	17.00	7.50
96	A11	18a org brn, *pink* ('03)	32.50	11.50
97	A11	20a brn, *yelsh* ('00)	45.00	11.50
98	A11	24a brown, *buff*	27.50	7.50
99	A11	31a red lilac	27.50	9.00
100	A11	31a red lil, *pink* ('03)	32.50	11.50
101	A11	47a dk blue, *rose*	50.00	11.50
102	A11	47a dull bl, *straw* ('03)	60.00	13.00

103 A11 78a blk & red, *bl*
      ('00)   77.50   17.50
      Nos. 75-103 (29)   712.50   194.65

Issued without gum: Nos. 76a, 77, 79-80, 82, 84, 89, 94, 97 and 103.
For surcharges and overprints see Nos. 104-107, 132-136, 141, 147-157D, 159-161, 182, 195-209, 253-255, 258A.

Nos. 92, 95, 98-99
Surcharged in Black

1900   Without Gum
104 A11   5a on 13a violet   20.00   3.50
105 A11 10a on 16a dk bl, *bl* 22.50   5.00
106 A11 15a on 24a brn, *buff* 22.50   8.25
107 A11 20a on 31a red lilac   25.00   13.50
      Nos. 104-107 (4)   90.00   30.25

Nos. 106-107 were issued with and without gum.

Regular Issues
Surcharged

On Stamps of 1884-85
1902   Black Surcharge   Perf. 11½
108 A1 6a on 10r orange   30.00   9.75
   a.   Double surcharge   300.00 175.00
109 A1 6a on 10r green   21.00   6.00
On Stamps of 1888
Red Surcharge
Perf. 12½, 13½
110 A7 6a on 5r black   10.00   3.50
   a.   Inverted surcharge   110.00   60.00
Black Surcharge
111 A7 6a on 10r green   8.25   3.50
112 A7 6a on 40r choc   8.25   3.50
   a.   Double surcharge   125.00   50.00
   b.   Perf. 13½   30.00   10.00
113 A7 18a on 20r rooo   17.00   4.60
   a.   Double surcharge   160.00   70.00
   b.   Inverted surcharge   175.00
114 A7 18a on 25r violet   200.00   60.00
115 A7 18a on 80r gray   225.00   67.50
   a.   Double surcharge   240.00 175.00
116 A7 18a on 100r brown   42.50   26.00
   a.   Perf. 13½   90.00   35.00
117 A7 18a on 200r gray lil   200.00   67.50
   a.   Perf. 12½   190.00   60.00
118 A7 18a on 300r orange   30.00   10.00
   a.   Perf. 13½   57.50   25.00

Issued without gum: Nos. 110-118.
Nos. 109 to 118 inclusive, except No. 111, have been reprinted. The reprints have white gum and clean-cut perforation 13½ and the colors are usually paler than those of the originals.

On Stamps of 1894
1902-10   Perf. 11½, 13½
119 A9 6a on 5r yellow   7.75   2.75
   a.   Inverted surcharge   82.50   65.00
120 A9 6a on 10r red vio   30.00   5.25
121 A9 6a on 15r choc   26.00   5.25
122 A9 6a on 25r green   7.75   2.75
123 A9 6a on 80r yel grn   7.75   2.75
124 A9 6a on 100r brn,
           buff   15.00   6.00
   a.   Perf. 11½   26.00   10.00
125 A9 6a on 200r bl, *bl*   10.00   2.75
   a.   Vert. half used as 3a on
           cover ('10)   40.00
126 A9 18a on 20r lavender   21.00   6.75
127 A9 18a on 50r lt blue   26.00   6.75
   a.   Perf. 13½   77.50   17.00
128 A9 18a on 75r carmine   21.00   6.75
129 A9 18a on 150r car,
           rose   21.00   7.50
130 A9 18a on 300r bl,
           salmon   26.00   6.75
On Newspaper Stamp of 1893
Perf. 12½
131 N3 18a on 2½r brown   10.00   3.25
   a.   Perf. 13½   27.50   9.00
   b.   Perf. 12½   45.00   14.00
      Nos. 108-131 (24)   1,021.00 327.00

Issued without gum: Nos. 122-130, 131b.

Stamps of 1898-1900
Overprinted in Black

1902   Perf. 11½
132 A11   2a yellow green   21.00   4.00
133 A11   4a sea green   32.50   10.00
134 A11   8a blue   21.00   7.00
135 A11 10a slate blue   26.00   8.00
136 A11 12a rose   70.00   26.00
      Nos. 132-136 (5)   170.50   55.00

Issued without gum: Nos. 133, 135.
Reprints of No. 133 have shiny white gum and clean-cut perforation 13½. Value $1.

No. 91 Surcharged

1905   Without Gum
141 A11 10a on 12a red lilac   30.00   12.50

For overprint see No. 182.

Nos. J1-J3
Overprinted

1910, Oct.   Perf. 11½x12
144 D1 ½a gray green   10.00   6.75
   a.   Inverted overprint   35.00   30.00
   b.   Double overprint   40.00   40.00
   c.   Pair, one without ovpt.
145 D1 1a yellow green   12.00   6.75
   a.   Inverted overprint   35.00   30.00
146 D1 2a slate   20.00   7.50
   a.   Inverted overprint   65.00   45.00
      Nos. 144-146 (3)   42.00   21.00

No. 144 issued without gum, Nos. 145-146 with and without gum.

Stamps of 1898-1903
Overprinted in
Carmine or Green

Overprint 24½mm long. "A" has flattened top.

Lisbon Overprint
1911, Apr. 2   Perf. 11½
147 A11 ½a gray   2.10   .75
   a.   Inverted overprint   20.00   20.00
147B A11 1a orange   2.00   .75
   c.   Inverted overprint   20.00   20.00
148 A11   2a gray green   2.00   .75
   a.   Inverted overprint   12.50   12.50
149 A11   3a slate   6.25   .75
   a.   Inverted overprint   12.50   12.50
150 A11   4a carmine (G)   6.25   2.00
   a.   4a pale yel brn (error) 75.00   50.00
   b.   As No. 150, inverted
           overprint   50.00   50.00
151 A11   5a pale yel brn   6.25   4.00
152 A11   6a red brown   6.25   4.00
153 A11   8a gray brown   6.25   4.00
154 A11 10a slate blue   6.25   4.00
155 A11 13a gray lilac   10.00   5.00
   a.   Inverted overprint   60.00   60.00
156 A11 16a dk blue, *bl*   10.00   5.00
   a.   Inverted overprint   60.00   60.00
157 A11 18a org brn,
           pink   16.00   6.00
157A A11 20a brown,
           straw   16.00   6.00
157B A11 31a red lil, *pink*   30.00   8.00
157C A11 47a dull bl,straw   50.00   10.00
157D A11 78a blk & red, *bl*   82.50   12.00
      Nos. 147-157D (16)   258.10   73.00

Issued without gum: Nos. 151, 153-157D.

Coat of Arms — A14

Red Surcharge
1911   Perf. 11½x12
158 A14 1a on 5r brn & buff   32.50   12.50
   a.   "1" omitted   70.00   60.00
   b.   Inverted surcharge   55.00   55.00

Stamps of 1900-03
Surcharged

Diagonal Halves
Black Surcharge
1911   Without Gum   Perf. 11½
159 A11 2a on half of
           4a car   50.00   32.50
   a.   "2" omitted   100.00   80.00
   b.   Inverted surcharge   150.00   82.50
   d.   Entire stamp   180.00
159C A11 5a on half of
           10a sl bl
           (#89)   750.00 400.00
   e.   Entire stamp   8,500.00 4,000.00
Red Surcharge
160 A11 5a on half of
           10a sl bl
           (#89)   600.00 400.00
   a.   Inverted surcharge   750.00 500.00
   b.   Entire stamp   11,000.00 5,000.00
161 A11 5a on half of
           10a sl bl
           (#135)   150.00 120.00
   a.   Inverted surcharge   350.00 200.00
   b.   Entire stamp   500.00

Nos. 159-161 normally were bisected by the government before being placed on sale.

A15

Laid or Wove Paper
1911   Perf. 12x11½
162 A15 1a black   525.00   —
   a.   "Corrieo"   2,000.00   —
163 A15 2a black   600.00   —
   a.   "Corrieo"   2,000.00   —

The vast majority of used stamps were not canceled.

Surcharged Stamps
of 1902 Overprinted
in Red or Green

Overprint 23mm long. "A" has pointed top.

Local Overprint
1913   Without Gum   Perf. 11½
164 A1 6a on 10r green
           (R)   37.50   12.00
   a.   "REPUBLICA" double   70.00   70.00
Perf. 12½, 13½
165 A7 6a on 5r black (G)   15.00   3.50
166 A7 6a on 10r green
           (R)   31.00   8.00
167 A7 6a on 40r choc (R)   10.50   3.00
   a.   Perf. 13½   50.00   20.00
168 A7 18a on 20r car (G)   21.00   6.00
169 A7 18a on 100r brown
           (R)   82.50   40.00
   a.   Perf. 13½   100.00   50.00
170 A7 18a on 300r org (R)   32.50   9.00
   a.   Perf. 13½   50.00   10.00
      Nos. 164-170 (7)   230.00   81.50

"Republica" overprint exists inverted on Nos. 164-170.

1913   Without Gum   Perf. 11½, 13½
171 A9 6a on 10r red
           vlo (G)   14.50   4.50
172 A9 6a on 10r red
           vio (R)   225.00   26.00
173 A9 6a on 15r choc
           (R)   14.50   5.00
174 A9 6a on 25r green
           (R)   16.00   5.00
175 A9 6a on 80r yel
           grn (R)   14.50   5.00
176 A9 6a on 100r brn,
           buff (R)   30.00   7.00
   a.   Perf. 11½   32.50   8.00
177 A9 18a on 20r lav
           (R)   19.00   5.00
178 A9 18a on 50r lt bl
           (R)   19.00   5.00
   a.   Perf. 13½   21.00   6.00
179 A9 18a on 75r car
           (G)   19.00   5.50
180 A9 18a on 150r car,
           rose (G)   21.00   6.00
181 A9 18a on 300r dk
           bl, *sal* (H)   32.50   10.00
On No. 141
182 A11 10a on 12a red lil
           (R)   13.00   4.50
      Nos. 171-182 (12)   438.00   88.50

"Republica" overprint exists inverted on Nos. 171-181.

Stamps of Preceding Issue Surcharged

1913   Without Gum   Perf. 11½

183	A9	2a on 18a on 20r (R)	10.00	4.00
184	A9	2a on 18a on 50r (R)	10.00	4.00
a.		Perf. 13½	11.00	4.25
185	A9	2a on 18a on 75r (G)	10.00	4.00
186	A9	2a on 18a on 150r (G)	10.00	4.00
		Nos. 183-186 (4)	40.00	16.00

"Republica" overprint exists inverted on Nos. 183-186. Value, each $20.

The 2a surcharge exists inverted or double on Nos. 183-186. For values, see Classic Specialized Catalogue.

Vasco da Gama Issue Overprinted or Surcharged

j

k

187	CD20 (j)	½a blue green	7.75	2.00
188	CD21 (j)	1a red	8.50	2.00
189	CD22 (j)	2a red violet	8.50	2.00
a.		Double ovpt., one inverted	100.00	
190	CD23 (j)	4a yellow grn	7.75	2.00
191	CD24 (j)	8a dk blue	13.00	2.00
192	CD25 (k)	10a on 12a vio brn	24.00	5.00
193	CD26 (j)	16a bister brn	17.00	4.00
194	CD27 (j)	24a bister	27.50	5.00
		Nos. 187-194 (8)	114.00	24.00

Stamps of 1898-1903 Overprinted in Red or Green

1913   Without Gum   Perf. 11½

195	A11	4a carmine (G)	250.00	100.00
a.		Double overprint	175.00	175.00
b.		Inverted overprint	95.00	
196	A11	5a yellow brn	30.00	20.00
a.		Inverted overprint	50.00	40.00
197	A11	6a red brown	77.50	40.00
a.		Inverted overprint	95.00	
198	A11	8a gray brown	625.00	300.00
b.		Inverted overprint	95.00	
198A	A11	10a dull blue		—
199	A11	13a violet	77.50	32.50
a.		Inverted overprint	95.00	
200	A11	13a gray lilac	40.00	20.00
a.		Inverted overprint	95.00	
201	A11	16a blue, *bl*	50.00	20.00
202	A11	18a org brn, *pink*	50.00	20.00
a.		Inverted overprint	95.00	
203	A11	20a brown, *yelsh*	50.00	20.00
204	A11	31a red lil, *pink*	67.50	30.00
a.		Inverted overprint	95.00	
205	A11	47a dull bl, *straw*	100.00	40.00

Only 20 examples of No. 198A were sold by the Post Office.

Stamps of 1911-13 Surcharged

On Stamps of 1911 With Lisbon "Republica"

1913

206	A11	½a on 5a yel brn (R)	15.00	3.00
a.		"½ Avo" inverted	125.00	70.00

207	A11	4a on 8a gray brn (R)	30.00	4.00
a.		"4 Avos" inverted	150.00	70.00

On Stamps of 1913 With Local "Republica"

208	A11	1a on 13a violet (R)	150.00	30.00
209	A11	1a on 13a gray lil (R)	15.00	3.00
a.		Surch. on #155 (error)		
		Nos. 206-209 (4)	210.00	40.00

Issued without gum: Nos. 207-209.

"Ceres" — A16

Name and Value in Black
Chalky Paper

1913   Perf. 15x14

210	A16	½a olive brown	1.75	.25
211	A16	1a black	1.75	.25
212	A16	2a blue green	1.75	.25
213	A16	4a carmine	6.75	1.00
214	A16	5a lilac brown	7.75	3.00
215	A16	6a lt violet	7.75	3.00
216	A16	8a lilac brown	7.75	3.00
217	A16	10a deep blue	7.75	3.00
218	A16	12a yellow brn	11.00	3.00
219	A16	16a slate	20.00	5.00
220	A16	20a orange brn	20.00	5.00
221	A16	40a plum	21.00	5.00
222	A16	58a brown, *grn*	35.00	12.00
223	A16	76a brown, *pink*	60.00	14.00
224	A16	1p orange, *sal*	80.00	20.00
225	A16	3p green, *bl*	200.00	55.00
		Nos. 210-225 (16)	490.00	132.75

Nos. 210, 211 and 212 exist on glazed paper.

Ordinary Paper

1919   Perf. 15x14

226	A16	½a olive brown	5.50	2.25
a.		Inscriptions inverted	50.00	
227	A16	1a black	5.50	2.25
a.		Inscriptions inverted	50.00	
a.		Inscriptions double	50.00	
228	A16	2a blue green	14.50	7.00
a.		Inscriptions inverted	40.00	
229	A16	4a carmine	42.50	21.00
		Nos. 226-229 (4)	68.00	32.50

1922-24   Perf. 12x11½

230	A16	½a olive brown	2.75	1.10
231	A16	1a black	2.75	1.10
232	A16	1½a yellow green ('24)	1.75	.25
233	A16	2a blue green	6.00	3.00
234	A16	3a orange brown	10.00	3.00
235	A16	4a carmine	20.00	5.00
236	A16	4a lemon ('24)	14.00	5.00
237	A16	6a gray ('23)	47.50	7.50
238	A16	8a lilac brown	17.50	5.50
238A	A16	10a pale blue ('23)	27.50	6.00
238B	A16	12a yellow brown	30.00	6.50
238C	A16	14a lilac ('24)	42.50	12.00
238D	A16	16a slate	67.50	20.00
238E	A16	24a slate green ('23)	25.00	7.00
238F	A16	32a orange brown ('24)	25.00	8.00
238G	A16	56a dull rose ('24)	50.00	15.00
238H	A16	72a brown ('23)	67.50	20.00
238I	A16	1p orange ('24)	200.00	30.00

Glazed Paper

238J	A16	3p pale turq ('24)	425.00	95.00
238K	A16	5p carmine rose ('24)	350.00	82.50
		Nos. 230-238K (20)	1,432.	333.45

For surcharges see Nos. 256, 259-267.

Preceding Issues and No. P4 Overprinted in Carmine

On Stamps of 1902
Perf. 11½, 12, 12½, 13½, 11½x12

1915

239	A7	6a on 10r green	14.50	4.00
240	A9	6a on 5r yellow	14.50	4.00
241	A9	6a on 10r red vio	14.50	4.00
242	A9	6a on 15r choc	12.50	3.25
243	A9	6a on 25r green	12.00	4.00

244	A9	6a on 80r yel grn	12.00	4.00
245	A9	6a on 100r brn, *buff*	21.00	4.00
246	A9	6a on 200r bl, *bl*	11.00	6.00
247	A9	18a on 20r lav	21.00	6.00
248	A9	18a on 50r lt bl	45.00	6.75
249	A9	18a on 75r car	40.00	6.75
250	A9	18a on 150r car, *rose*	45.00	8.00
251	A9	18a on 300r bl, *sal*	40.00	10.00
252	N3	18a on 2½r brn	32.50	6.00

With Additional Overprint

253	A11	8a blue	14.50	8.25
254	A11	10a slate blue	14.50	6.00
a.		"Provisorio" double	110.00	

On Stamp of 1905

255	A11	10a on 12a red lilac	19.00	9.75
		Nos. 239-255 (17)	383.50	100.75

Issued without gum: Nos. 243-251 and 255.

No. 217 Surcharged

Without Gum

1919-20   Perf. 15x14

256	A16	½a on 5a lilac brn	100.00	32.50
		Never hinged	125.00	

Nos. 243 and 244 Surcharged

257	A9	2a on 6a on 25r green	500.00	125.00
258	A9	2a on 6a on 80r yel grn	100.00	70.00

No. 152 Surcharged

258A	A11	2a on 6a red brown	175.00	70.00
		Nos. 256-258A (4)	875.00	297.50

Issued without gum: Nos. 256-258A.

Stamps of 1913-24 Surcharged

1931-33   Perf. 12x11½

259	A16	1a on 24a slate green ('33)	14.50	4.00
260	A16	2a on 32a orange brown ('33)	14.50	4.00
261	A16	4a on 12a bister brown ('33)	14.50	4.00
262	A16	5a on 6a light gray ('33)	57.50	35.00
264	A16	7a on 8a lilac brown	24.00	5.00
265	A16	12a on 14a lilac	24.00	5.00
266	A16	15a on 16a dark gray ('33)	24.00	5.00
267	A16	20a on 56a dull rose ('33)	50.00	11.00

Chalky Paper
Perf. 15x14

263	A16	5a on 6a light violet ('33)	30.00	11.00
		Nos. 259-267 (9)	253.00	84.00

"Portugal" and Vasco da Gama's Flagship "San Gabriel" — A17

Wmk. 232

1934, Feb. 1   Typo.   Perf. 11½

268	A17	½a bister	.45	.40
269	A17	1a olive brown	.45	.25
270	A17	2a blue green	1.10	.50
271	A17	3a violet	1.40	.50
272	A17	4a black	1.75	.50
273	A17	5a gray	1.75	.80
274	A17	6a brown	1.75	.80
275	A17	7a brt rose	3.25	1.00
276	A17	8a brt blue	3.25	1.00
277	A17	10a red orange	7.25	2.00
278	A17	12a dark blue	7.25	2.00
279	A17	14a olive green	7.25	2.00
280	A17	15a maroon	7.25	2.00
281	A17	20a orange	7.25	2.00
282	A17	30a apple green	14.00	3.50
283	A17	40a violet	14.00	3.50
284	A17	50a olive bister	21.00	5.00
285	A17	1p lt blue	75.00	20.00
286	A17	2p brown org	90.00	27.50
287	A17	3p emerald	150.00	45.00
288	A17	5p dark violet	225.00	67.50
		Nos. 268-288 (21)	640.40	187.75

See Nos. 316-323. For overprints and surcharges see Nos. 306-315, C1-C6, J43-J49.

Common Design Types
Perf. 13½x13

1938, Aug. 1   Engr.   Unwmk.
Name and Value in Black

289	CD34	1a gray brown	1.00	.35
290	CD34	2a orange brown	1.25	.55
291	CD34	3a dk vio brn	1.25	.55
292	CD34	4a brt green	1.25	.55
293	CD35	5a dk carmine	1.25	.55
294	CD35	6a slate	1.25	.55
295	CD35	8a rose violet	2.10	2.25
296	CD36	10a brt red vio	2.50	2.25
297	CD36	12a red	3.25	2.60
298	CD36	15a orange	3.25	2.60
299	CD37	20a blue	16.50	2.90
300	CD37	40a gray black	16.50	3.50
301	CD37	50a brown	16.50	3.75
302	CD38	1p brown car	50.00	7.25
303	CD38	2p olive green	85.00	17.50
304	CD38	3p blue violet	115.00	25.00
305	CD38	5p red brown	200.00	37.50
		Nos. 289-305 (17)	517.85	110.20

For surcharge see No. 315A.

Stamps of 1934 Surcharged in Black

a   b

1941   Wmk. 232   Perf. 11½x12

306	A17(a)	1a on 6a brown	7.50	3.50
307	A17(b)	2a on 6a brown	3.00	2.00
308	A17(b)	3a on 6a brown	3.00	2.00
309	A17(a)	5a on 7a brt rose	120.00	60.00
310	A17(b)	5a on 7a brt rose	17.50	8.50
311	A17(a)	5a on 8a brt blue	19.50	10.00
312	A17(b)	5a on 8a brt blue	12.00	8.50
313	A17(b)	8a on 30a apple grn	9.50	5.00
314	A17(b)	8a on 40a violet	9.50	5.00
315	A17(b)	8a on 50a olive bis	9.50	5.50
		Nos. 306-315 (10)	211.00	110.00

No. 294 Surcharged
in Black

1941 Unwmk. Perf. 13½x13
315A CD35 3a on 6a slate 75.00 35.00
Counterfeits exist.

"Portugal" Type of 1934
1942 Litho. Rough Perf. 12
Thin Paper Without Gum
316	A17	1a olive brown	2.00	1.25
317	A17	2a blue green	2.00	1.25
318	A17	3a vio, perf. 11	20.00	4.00
a.		Perf. 12	25.00	4.75
319	A17	6a brown	20.00	5.50
a.		Perf. 10	45.00	25.00
b.		Perf. 11	37.50	15.00
320	A17	10a red orange	12.50	4.50
321	A17	20a orange	12.50	4.00
a.		Perf. 11	45.00	17.50
322	A17	30a apple green	15.00	6.50
323	A17	40a violet	30.00	9.50
		Nos. 316-323 (8)	114.00	36.50

Macao
Dwelling
A18

Pagoda of
Barra — A19

Designs: 2a, Mountain fort. 3a, View of
Macao. 8a, Praia Grande Bay. 10a, Leal
Senado Square. 20a, Sao Jeronimo Hill. 30a,
Marginal Ave. 50a, Relief of Goddess Ma. 1p,
Gate of Cerco. 3p, Post Office. 5p, Solidao
Walk.

1948, Dec. 20 Litho. Perf. 10½
324	A18	1a dk brn & org	2.25	.50
325	A19	2a rose brn & rose	1.60	.50
326	A18	3a brn vio & lil	3.75	1.00
327	A18	8a rose car & rose	2.25	1.40
328	A18	10a lilac rose & rose	3.75	1.60
329	A18	20a dk blue & gray	4.75	2.00
330	A18	30a black & gray	15.00	4.00
331	A18	50a brn & pale bis	27.50	9.00
332	A19	1p emer & pale grn	125.00	16.00
333	A19	2p scarlet & rose	100.00	18.00
334	A19	3p dl grn & gray grn	125.00	20.00
335	A18	5p vio bl & gray	200.00	22.50
		Nos. 324-335 (12)	610.85	96.50

See Nos. 341-347A.

Catalogue values for unused
stamps in this section, from this
point to the end of the section, are
for Never Hinged items.

Lady of Fatima Issue
Common Design Type
1949, Feb. 1 Unwmk. Perf. 14½
336 CD40 8a scarlet 40.00 12.00

Symbols of the
UPU — A20

1949, Dec. 24 Litho. Unwmk.
337 A20 32a claret & rose 75.00 27.50
75th anniv. of the formation of the UPU.

Holy Year Issue
Common Design Types
1950, July 26 Perf. 13x13½
339 CD41 32a dk slate gray 27.50 6.00
340 CD42 50a carmine 27.50 6.50

Scenic Types of 1948
Designs as before.

1950-51 Perf. 14
341	A18	1a violet & rose	2.75	1.00
342	A19	2a ol bis & yel	2.75	1.00
343	A18	3a org red & buff	8.50	1.25
344	A18	8a slate & gray	11.00	1.75
345	A18	10a red brn & org	15.00	3.75
346	A18	30a vio bl & bl	19.00	4.50
347	A18	50a ol grn & yel grn	42.50	5.00
347A	A19	1p dk org brn & org brn	115.00	25.00
		Nos. 341-347A (8)	216.50	43.25

A 1p ultra & vio, perf. 11, was not sold in
Macao. Value $110.
Nos. 341-347 issued in 1951, the 1p in
1950.

Dragon — A21

1951 Perf. 11½x12
348 A21 1a org ycl, lemon 2.50 1.25
349 A21 2a dk grn, blue 2.50 1.25
Shaded Background
350 A21 10a vio brn, blue 8.00 2.75
351 A21 10a brt pink, blue 7.00 2.75
Nos. 348-351 (4) 20.00 8.00

Nos. 348-351 were isuued without gum.
For overprints see Nos. J50-J52.

Holy Year Extension Issue
Common Design Type
1951, Dec. 3 Litho. Perf. 14
352 CD43 60a magenta & pink
+ label 37.50 10.00
Stamp without label sells for much less.

Fernao Mendes
Pinto — A22

Portraits: 2a and 10a, St. Francis Xavier. 3a
and 50a, Jorge Alvares. 6a and 30a, Luis de
Camoens.

1951, Aug. 27 Perf. 11½
353	A22	1a steel bl & gray bl	1.00	.50
354	A22	2a dk brown & ol grn	2.00	.60
355	A22	3a deep grn & grn	2.75	.75
356	A22	6a purple	4.00	1.00
357	A22	10a red brn & org	8.00	1.75
358	A22	20a brown car	15.00	3.75
359	A22	30a dk brn & ol grn	30.00	6.00
360	A22	50a red & orange	60.00	14.00
		Nos. 353-360 (8)	122.75	28.25

Sampan — A23   Junk — A24

Design: 5p, Junk.

1951, Nov. 1 Unwmk.
361 A23 1p vio bl & bl 37.50 3.25
362 A24 3p black & vio 130.00 15.00
363 A23 5p henna brown 160.00 32.50
Nos. 361-363 (3) 327.50 50.75

Medical Congress Issue
Common Design Type
Design: Sao Rafael Hospital.
1952, June 16 Unwmk. Perf. 13½
364 CD44 6a black & purple 9.75 4.25

Statue of St.   Statue of Virgin
Francis   Mary — A26
Xavier — A25

St. Francis Xavier Issue
16a, Arm of St. Francis. 40a, Tomb of St.
Francis.

1952, Nov. 28 Litho. Perf. 14
365 A25 3a blk, grnsh gray 4.00 .90
366 A25 16a choc, buff 17.00 3.00
367 A25 40a blk, blue 21.00 5.25
Nos. 365-367 (3) 42.00 9.15

400th anniv. of the death of St. Francis
Xavier.

1953, Apr. 28 Unwmk. Perf. 13½
368 A26 8a choc & dull ol 3.50 1.00
369 A26 10a blue blk & buff 13.50 3.75
370 A26 50a slate grn & ol grn 23.00 5.50
Nos. 368-370 (3) 40.00 10.25

Exhibition of Sacred Missionary Art, held at
Lisbon in 1951.

Stamp of Portugal
and Arms of
Colonies — A27

1954, Mar. 9 Photo. Perf. 13
371 A27 10a multicolored 10.00 2.00
Cent. of Portugal's first postage stamps.

Firecracker
Flower — A28

Flowers: 3a, Forget-me-not. 5a, Dragon
claw. 10a, Nunflower. 16a, Narcissus. 30a,
Peach flower. 39a, Lotus flower. 1p, Chrysanthemum. 3p, Cherry blossoms. 5p, Tangerine
blossoms.

1953, Sept. 22 Perf. 11½
Flowers in Natural Colors
372 A28 1a dark red .60 .35
373 A28 3a dark green .60 .35
374 A28 5a dark brown .75 .40
375 A28 10a dp grnsh blue .75 .40
376 A28 16a yellow brown 1.25 .45

---

377 A28 30a dk olive grn 3.00 1.00
378 A28 39a violet blue 3.25 1.00
379 A28 1p deep plum 7.25 1.25
380 A28 3p dark gray 14.00 2.50
381 A28 5p deep carmine 27.50 4.25
Nos. 372-381 (10) 58.95 11.95
For surcharges see Nos. 443-444.

Sao Paulo Issue
Common Design Type
1954, Aug. 4 Litho. Perf. 13½
382 CD46 39a org, cream & blk 14.00 3.00
Sao Paulo founding, 400th anniversary.
For surcharge see No. 445.

Map of
Colony — A29

**Inscriptions and design in brown,
red, green, ultra & yellow (buff on
10a, 40a, 90a)**
Perf. 12½x13½
1956, May 10				Photo.
383	A29	1a gray	.50	.40
384	A29	3a pale gray	1.10	.50
385	A29	5a pale pink	1.50	.75
386	A29	10a buff	3.00	.90
387	A29	30a lt blue	6.00	1.25
388	A29	40a pale green	9.00	1.75
389	A29	50a pale gray	14.00	3.25
390	A29	1.50p pink	22.50	4.00
		Nos. 383-390 (8)	57.60	12.80

Exhibition Emblems
and View — A30

1958, Nov. 8 Litho. Perf. 14½
391 A30 70a multicolored 6.00 1.75
World's Fair, Brussels, Apr. 17-Oct. 19.

Tropical Medicine Congress Issue
Common Design Type
Design: Cinnamomum camphora.
1958, Nov. 15 Perf. 13½
392 CD47 20a multicolored 8.00 3.00

Armillary
Sphere — A31

1960, June 25 Litho. Perf. 13½
393 A31 2p multicolored 11.50 4.00
500th anniversary of the death of Prince
Henry the Navigator.

Sports Issue
Common Design Type
Sports: 10a, Field hockey. 16a, Wrestling.
20a, Table tennis. 50a, Motorcycling. 1.20p,
Relay race. 2.50p, Badminton.
1962, Feb. 9 Perf. 13½
Multicolored Design
394	CD48	10a blue & yel grn	2.00	.45
395	CD48	16a brt pink	2.50	.90
396	CD48	20a orange	3.50	1.00
397	CD48	50a rose	6.00	1.25
398	CD48	1.20p blue & beige	25.00	3.00
399	CD48	2.50p gray & brown	35.00	8.00
		Nos. 394-399 (6)	74.00	14.60

Anti-Malaria Issue
Common Design Type
Design: Anopheles hyrcanus sinensis.

1962, Apr. 7　　**Litho.**　　*Perf. 13½*
400 CD49 40a multicolored　　6.50 2.00

Bank Building — A32

1964, May 16　**Unwmk.**　*Perf. 13½*
401 A32 20a multicolored　　9.50 2.50
Centenary of the National Overseas Bank of Portugal.

ITU Issue
Common Design Type
1965, May 17　　**Litho.**　　*Perf. 14½*
402 CD52 10a pale grn & multi　　5.00 2.00

National Revolution Issue
Common Design Type
Design: 10a, Infante D. Henrique School and Count de S. Januario Hospital.

1966, May 28　　**Litho.**　　*Perf. 11½*
403 CD53 10a multicolored　　5.00 2.00

Drummer, 1548 — A32a

Designs: 15a, Soldier with sword, 1548. 20a, Harquebusier, 1649. 40a, Infantry officer, 1783. 50a, Infantry soldier, 1783. 60a, Colonial infantry soldier (Indian), 1902. 1p, Colonial infantry soldier (Chinese), 1903. 3p, Colonial infantry soldier (Chinese) 1904.

1966, Aug. 8　　**Litho.**　　*Perf. 13*
404 A32a 10a multicolored　　1.25 .40
405 A32a 15a multicolored　　2.25 .75
406 A32a 20a multicolored　　2.50 .75
407 A32a 40a multicolored　　4.50 .85
408 A32a 50a multicolored　　5.00 1.50
409 A32a 60a multicolored　　12.00 1.75
410 A32a 1p multicolored　　15.00 3.00
411 A32a 3p multicolored　　27.50 7.50
　　Nos. 404-411 (8)　　70.00 16.50

Navy Club Issue, 1967
Common Design Type
Designs: 10a, Capt. Oliveira E. Carmo and armed launch Vega. 20a, Capt. Silva Junior and frigate Dom Fernando.

1967, Jan. 31　　**Litho.**　　*Perf. 13*
412 CD54 10a multicolored　　3.25 1.00
413 CD54 20a multicolored　　6.25 2.75

Arms of Pope Paul VI and Golden Rose — A33　　Cabral Monument, Lisbon — A34

1967, May 13　　　　*Perf. 12½x13*
414 A33 50a multicolored　　5.25 2.00
50th anniversary of the apparition of the Virgin Mary to three shepherd children at Fatima.

Cabral Issue
Design: 70a, Cabral monument, Belmonte.

1968, Apr. 22　　**Litho.**　　*Perf. 14*
415 A34 20a multicolored　　4.25 1.00
416 A34 70a multicolored　　6.00 2.75
500th anniversary of the birth of Pedro Alvares Cabral, navigator who took possession of Brazil for Portugal.

Admiral Coutinho Issue
Common Design Type
Design: 20a, Adm. Coutinho with sextant, vert.

1969, Feb. 17　　**Litho.**　　*Perf. 14*
417 CD55 20a multicolored　　3.75 1.50

Church of Our Lady of the Relics, Vidigueira — A35

Vasco da Gama Issue
1969, Aug. 29　　**Litho.**　　*Perf. 14*
418 A35 1p multicolored　　11.00 1.75
Vasco da Gama (1469-1524), navigator.

Administration Reform Issue
Common Design Type
1969, Sept. 25　　**Litho.**　　*Perf. 14*
419 CD56 90a multicolored　　5.00 1.00

Bishop D. Belchior Carneiro — A36

1969, Oct. 16　　**Litho.**　　*Perf. 13*
420 A36 50a multicolored　　3.25 .75
4th centenary of the founding of the Santa Casa da Misericordia in Macao.

King Manuel I Issue

Portal of Mother Church, Golega — A37

1969, Dec. 1　　**Litho.**　　*Perf. 14*
421 A37 30a multicolored　　5.75 1.00
500th anniversary of the birth of King Manuel I.

Marshal Carmona Issue
Common Design Type
5a, Antonio Oscar Carmona in general's uniform.

1970, Nov. 15　　**Litho.**　　*Perf. 14*
422 CD57 5a multicolored　　2.25 1.25

Dragon Mask — A38

1971, Sept. 30　　　　*Perf. 13½*
423 A38 5a lt blue & multi　　1.10 .50
424 A38 10a Lion mask　　2.25 .75

Portuguese Delegation at Chinese Court — A39

Lusiads Issue

1972, May 25　　**Litho.**　　*Perf. 13*
425 A39 20a citron & multi　　13.00 3.75
4th centenary of publication of The Lusiads by Luiz Camoens.

Olympic Games Issue
Common Design Type
Design: Hockey and Olympic emblem.

1972, June 20　　　　*Perf. 14x13½*
426 CD59 50a multicolored　　3.25 1.00

Lisbon-Rio de Janeiro Flight Issue
Common Design Type
Design: "Santa Cruz" landing in Rio de Janeiro.

1972, Sept. 20　　**Litho.**　　*Perf. 13½*
427 CD60 5p multicolored　　22.50 7.50

Pedro V Theater and Lyre — A42

1972, Dec. 25　　**Litho.**　　*Perf. 13½*
428 A42 2p multicolored　　8.00 2.50
Centenary of Pedro V Theater, Macao.

WMO Centenary Issue
Common Design Type
1973, Dec. 15　　**Litho.**　　*Perf. 13*
429 CD61 20a blue grn & multi　　6.25 1.75

Viscount St. Januario A44

Design: 60a, Hospital, 1874 and 1974.

1974, Jan. 25　　**Litho.**　　*Perf. 13½*
430 A44 15a multicolored　　1.00 .75
431 A44 60a multicolored　　25.00 1.00
Viscount St. Januario Hospital, Macao, cent. For surcharge see No. 457.

George Chinnery, Self-portrait A45

1974, Sept. 23　　**Litho.**　　*Perf. 14*
432 A45 30a multicolored　　3.50 1.50
George Chinnery (1774-1852), English painter who lived in Macao.

Macao-Taipa Bridge — A46

Design: 2.20p, Different view of bridge.

1974, Oct. 7　　**Litho.**　　*Perf. 14x13½*
433 A46 20a multicolored　　1.50 .75
434 A46 2.20p multicolored　　12.50 1.50
Inauguration of the Macao-Taipa Bridge. For surcharge see No. 446.

Man Raising Banner A47

1975, Apr. 25　　　　*Perf. 12*
435 A47 10a ocher & multi　　3.00 1.75
436 A47 1p multicolored　　13.50 4.00
Revolution of Apr. 25, 1974, 1st anniv.

Pou Chai Pagoda — A48

Design: 20p, Tin Hau Pagoda.

1976, Jan. 30　　**Litho.**　　*Perf. 13½x13*
437 A48 10p multicolored　　15.00 3.00
438 A48 20p multicolored　　32.50 5.00

A 1p stamp for the 400th anniv. of the Macao Diocese was prepared but not issued. Some stamps were sold in Lisbon. Value $150.

"The Law" — A50

1978　　　　**Litho.**　　*Perf. 13½*
440 A50 5a blk, dk & lt blue　　3.00 2.75
441 A50 2p blk, org brn & buff　　125.00 10.00
442 A50 5p blk, ol & yel grn　　25.00 12.50
　　Nos. 440-442 (3)　　153.00 25.25
Legislative Assembly, Aug. 9, 1976.

Nos. 376, 378, 382, 434 Surcharged

1979, Nov.
443 A28　10a on 16a　　9.00 3.00
444 A28　30a on 39a (#378)　　11.00 3.00
445 CD46 30a on 39a (#382)　　50.00 15.00
446 A46　2p on 2.20p　　10.00 6.00
　　Nos. 443-446 (4)　　80.00 27.00

Luis de Camoens (1524-80), Poet — A51

1981, June　　**Litho.**　　*Perf. 13½*
447 A51 10a multicolored　　.95 .45
448 A51 30a multicolored　　1.90 .50
449 A51 1p multicolored　　4.25 1.50
450 A51 3p multicolored　　6.25 2.25
　　Nos. 447-450 (4)　　13.35 4.70

Buddha, Macao Cathedral — A52

1981, Sept.
451	A52	15a multicolored	.50	.40
452	A52	40a multicolored	.75	.40
453	A52	50a multicolored	1.25	.50
454	A52	60a multicolored	1.90	.75
455	A52	1p multicolored	2.40	1.00
456	A52	2.20p multicolored	6.00	1.40
		Nos. 451-456 (6)	12.80	4.45

Transcultural Psychiatry Symposium.

No. 431 Surcharged
1981   Litho.   Perf. 13½
| 457 | A44 | 30a on 60a multi | 7.50 | 1.00 |

Health Services Building A53

Designs: Public Buildings and Monuments.

1982, June 10   Litho.   Perf. 12x12½
458	A53	30a shown	.50	.25
459	A53	40a Guia Lighthouse	.65	.25
460	A53	1p Portas do Cerco	1.25	.30
461	A53	2p Luis de Camoes Museum	2.50	.50
462	A53	10p School Welfare Service Building	11.00	3.50
		Nos. 458-462 (5)	15.90	4.80

See Nos. 472-476, 489-493.

Autumn Festivals A54

Designs: Painted paper lanterns.

1982, Oct. 1   Perf. 12x11½
463	A54	40a multicolored	3.25	1.00
464	A54	1p multicolored	8.75	2.25
465	A54	2p multicolored	10.50	4.25
466	A54	5p multicolored	25.00	7.00
		Nos. 463-466 (4)	47.50	14.50

Geographical Position — A55

1982, Dec. 1   Litho.   Perf. 13
| 467 | A55 | 50a Aerial view | 10.00 | 1.75 |
| 468 | A55 | 3p Map | 37.50 | 6.50 |

World Communications Year — A56

No. 469, Telephone operators. No. 470, Mailman, mailbox. No. 471, Globe, satellites.

1983, Feb. 16   Perf. 13½
469	A56	60a multicolored	1.50	.35
470	A56	3p multicolored	3.25	2.00
471	A56	6p multicolored	6.25	3.50
		Nos. 469-471 (3)	11.00	5.85

Architecture Type of 1982
No. 472, Social Welfare Institute. No. 473, St. Joseph's Seminary. No. 474, St. Dominic's Church. No. 475, St. Paul's Church ruins. No. 476, Senate House.

1983, May 12   Litho.   Perf. 13
472	A53	10a multi	.50	.25
473	A53	80a multi	1.00	.40
474	A53	1.50p multi	1.75	.75
475	A53	2.50p multi	2.50	1.40
476	A53	7.50p multi	8.00	3.25
		Nos. 472-476 (5)	13.75	6.05

Medicinal Plants A57

No. 477, Asclepias curassavica. No. 478, Acanthus ilicifolius. No. 479, Melastoma sanguineum. No. 480, Nelumbo nucifera. No. 481, Bombax malabaricum. No. 482, Hibiscus mutabilis.

1983, July 14   Litho.   Perf. 13½x14
477	A57	20a multi	1.00	.70
478	A57	40a multi	1.50	.70
479	A57	60a multi	2.00	1.00
480	A57	70a multi	2.75	1.50
481	A57	1.50p multi	4.25	2.25
482	A57	2.50p multi	8.00	4.25
a.		Souvenir sheet of 6, #477-482	175.00	
		Nos. 477-482 (6)	19.50	10.40

No. 482a sold for 6.50p.

16th Century Discoveries — A58

1983, Nov. 15   Litho.   Perf. 13½x14
483	A58	4p multicolored	5.50	2.00
484	A59	4p multicolored	5.50	2.00
a.		Pair, #483-484	19.50	9.00

A60

1984, Jan. 25   Litho.   Perf. 13½
| 485 | A60 | 60a multicolored | 7.50 | 2.50 |
| a. | | Booklet pane of 5 | 40.00 | |

New Year 1984 (Year of the Rat).
No. 485a has straight edges.
See Nos. 504, 522, 540, 560, 583, 611, 639, 662, 684, 718, 757, 804.

A61

Design of First Stamp Issue, 1884.

1984, Mar. 1   Litho.   Perf. 12½
486	A61	40a orange & blk	1.25	.40
487	A61	3p gray & blk	3.00	1.50
488	A61	5p sepia & blk	6.50	2.50
a.		Souvenir sheet of 3, #486-488	40.00	
		Nos. 486-488 (3)	10.75	4.40

Centenary of Macao postage stamps.

Architecture Type of 1982
No. 489, Holy House of Mercy. No. 490, St. Lawrence Church. No. 491, King Peter V Theater. No. 492, Palace of St. Sancha. No. 493, Moorish barracks.

1984, May 18   Litho.   Perf. 13½
489	A53	20a multicolored	.35	.25
490	A53	60a multicolored	.60	.30
491	A53	90a multicolored	.90	.45
492	A53	3p multicolored	2.10	.60
493	A53	15p multicolored	6.75	2.00
		Nos. 489-493 (5)	10.70	3.60

Birds, Ausipex '84 Emblem A62

1984, Sept. 21   Litho.   Perf. 13
494	A62	30a Kingfishers	.85	.35
495	A62	40a European jay	.90	.40
496	A62	50a White eyes	1.50	.40
497	A62	70a Hoopoe	2.50	.70
498	A62	2.50p Peking nightingale	5.00	2.00
499	A62	6p Wild duck	9.00	3.00
		Nos. 494-499 (6)	19.75	6.85

Philakorea '84 Emblem, Fishing Boats A63

1984, Oct. 22   Litho.
500	A63	20a Hok lou t'eng	.75	.25
501	A63	60a Tai t'ong	1.40	.65
502	A63	2p Tai mei chai	3.50	1.25
503	A63	5p Ch'at pong t'o	7.50	3.00
		Nos. 500-503 (4)	13.15	5.15

New Year Type of 1984
1985, Feb. 13   Litho.   Perf. 13½
| 504 | A60 | 1p Buffalo | 5.00 | 2.75 |
| a. | | Booklet pane of 5 | 25.00 | |

Intl. Youth Year — A65

1985, Apr. 19   Litho.   Perf. 13½
| 505 | A65 | 2.50p shown | 3.75 | .75 |
| 506 | A65 | 3p Clasped hands | 4.75 | 2.25 |

Visit of President Eanes of Portugal A66

1985, May 27   Litho.
| 507 | A66 | 1.50p multicolored | 2.75 | .90 |

Luis de Camoens Museum, 25th Anniv. — A67

Silk paintings by Chen Chi Yun. No. 508, Two travelers, hermit. No. 509, Traveling

merchant. No. 510, Conversation in a garden. No. 511, Veranda of a house.

1985, June 27   Litho.
508	A67	2.50p multi	5.00	1.60
509	A67	2.50p multi	5.00	1.60
510	A67	2.50p multi	5.00	1.60
511	A67	2.50p multi	5.00	1.60
a.		Block or strip of 4, #508-511	30.00	15.00
		Nos. 508-511 (4)	20.00	6.40

Butterflies, World Tourism Assoc. Emblem — A68

No. 512, Euploea midamus. No. 513, Hebomoia glaucippe. No. 514, Lethe confusa. No. 515, Heliophorus epicles. No. 516, Euthalia phemius seitzi. No. 517, Troides helena.

1985, Sept. 27   Litho.
512	A68	30a multi	1.00	.25
513	A68	50a multi	1.25	.35
514	A68	70a multi	2.00	.40
515	A68	2p multi	2.75	1.00
516	A68	4p multi	5.75	1.75
517	A68	7.50p multi	8.00	3.50
a.		Sheet of 6, #512-517	160.00	
		Nos. 512-517 (6)	20.75	7.25

World Tourism Day.

Cargo Boats A69

Designs: 50a, Tou. 70a, Veng Seng Lei motor junk. 1p, Iong Heng Long No. 2 motor junk. 6p, Fong Vong San cargo ship.

1985, Oct. 25   Perf. 14
518	A69	50a multicolored	.75	.25
519	A69	70a multicolored	2.00	.50
520	A69	1p multicolored	3.50	1.10
521	A69	6p multicolored	6.00	3.00
		Nos. 518-521 (4)	12.25	4.85

New Year Type of 1984
1986, Feb. 3   Perf. 13½
| 522 | A60 | 1.50p Tiger | 5.00 | 1.25 |
| a. | | Booklet pane of 5 | 25.00 | |

No. 522a has straight edges.

City of Macau, 400th Anniv. A71

1986, Apr. 10   Litho.   Perf. 13½
| 523 | A71 | 2.20p multicolored | 4.00 | 1.60 |

Musical Instruments A72

1986, May 22
524	A72	20a Suo-na	3.50	.90
525	A72	50a Sheng	4.00	1.25
526	A72	60a Er-hu	5.00	1.50
527	A72	70a Ruan	8.00	2.00
528	A72	5p Cheng	19.00	2.75
529	A72	8p Pi-pa	22.50	5.00
a.		Souvenir sheet of 6, #524-529	225.00	
		Nos. 524-529 (6)	62.00	13.40

AMERIPEX '86.

Ferries
A73

1986, Aug. 28   Litho.   Perf. 13
530 A73 10a Hydrofoil   .50   .35
531 A73 40a Hovermarine   2.25   .65
532 A73 3p   Jetfoil   3.50   1.40
533 A73 7.5p High-speed ferry   8.00   3.00
     Nos. 530-533 (4)   14.25   5.40

Fortresses — A74

No. 534, Taipa. No. 535, Sao Paulo do Monte. No. 536, Our Lady of Guia. No. 537, Sao Francisco.

1986, Oct. 3   Litho.   Perf. 12½
534 A74 2p multi   10.00   2.40
535 A74 2p multi   10.00   2.40
536 A74 2p multi   10.00   2.40
537 A74 2p multi   10.00   2.40
 a. Block or strip of 4, #534-537 80.00 20.00
     Nos. 534-537 (4)   40.00   9.60

Macao Security Forces, 10th anniv. No. 537a has continuous design.

A75

Dr. Sun Yat-sen — A76

1986, Nov. 12   Litho.   Perf. 12½
538 A75 70a multicolored   3.25   2.25
Souvenir Sheet
539 A76 1.30p shown   50.00 30.00

New Year Type of 1984
1987, Jan. 21   Perf. 13½
540 A60 1.50p Hare   5.00   1.25
 a. Booklet pane of 5   25.00

No. 540a has straight edges.

Shek Wan Ceramic Figures in the Luis de Camoens Museum — A78

No. 541, Medicine man (4/1). No. 542, Choi San, god of good fortune (4/2). No. 543, Yi, sun god (4/3). No. 544, Chung Kuei, conqueror of demons (4/4).

1987, Apr. 10   Litho.   Perf. 13½
541 A78 2.20p multi   6.75   2.50
542 A78 2.20p multi   6.75   2.50
543 A78 2.20p multi   6.75   2.50
544 A78 2.20p multi   6.75   2.50
 a. Block or strip of 4, #541-544 40.00 26.50
     Nos. 541-544 (4)   27.00 10.00

Dragon Boat Festival A79

1987, May 29   Litho.   Perf. 13½
545 A79 50a Dragon boat
              race   3.50   .90
546 A79 5p   Figurehead   9.50   3.00

Decorated Fans — A80   Casino Gambling — A81

1987, July 29   Litho.   Perf. 12½
547 A80 30a multicolored   3.50   1.00
548 A80 70a multi, diff.   7.50   1.75
549 A80 1p   multi, diff.   17.50   3.00
550 A80 6p   multi, diff.   24.50   6.50
 a. Souvenir sheet of 4, #547-550 250.00 125.00
     Nos. 547-550 (4)   53.00 12.25

1987, Sept. 30   Perf. 13½
551 A81 20a Fan-tan   9.50   3.00
552 A81 40a Cussec   9.50   3.00
553 A81 4p   Baccarat   9.50   3.00
554 A81 7p   Roulette   9.50   3.00
     Nos. 551-554 (4)   38.00 12.00

Traditional Transportation — A82

1987, Nov. 18   Litho.   Perf. 13½
555 A82 10a Market wagon   .75   .50
556 A82 70a Sedan chair   2.25   .75
557 A82 90a Rickshaw   3.25   .90
558 A82 10p Tricycle rickshaw 10.00   4.00
     Nos. 555-558 (4)   16.25   6.15
Souvenir Sheet
559 A82 7.50p Sedan chair, diff. 47.50 —

New Year Type of 1984
1988, Feb. 10   Litho.   Perf. 13½
560 A60 2.50p Dragon   5.00   2.50
 a. Booklet pane of 5   25.00

No. 560a has straight edges.

Wildlife Protection A84

1988, Apr. 14   Litho.   Perf. 12½x12
561 A84 3p Erinaceus
              europaeus   4.75   1.75
562 A84 3p Meles meles   4.75   1.75
563 A84 3p Lutra lutra   4.75   1.75
564 A84 3p Manis pentadacty-
              la   4.75   1.75
 a. Block or strip of 4, #561-564 27.50 15.00
     Nos. 561-564 (4)   19.00   7.00

World Health Organization, 40th Anniv. — A85

1988, June 1   Litho.   Perf. 13½
565 A85 60a Breast-feeding   2.00   .55
566 A85 80a Immunization   3.50   .65
567 A85 2.40p Blood donation   5.50   2.00
     Nos. 565-567 (3)   11.00   3.20

Modes of Transportation — A86

1988, July 15   Litho.
568 A86 20a Bicycles   .75   .40
569 A86 50a Vespa, Lambret-
              ta   1.50   .80
570 A86 3.30p 1907 Rover 20hp   4.00   1.50
571 A86 5p   1912 Renault
              delivery truck   6.75   3.25
     Nos. 568-571 (4)   13.00   5.95
Souvenir Sheet
572 A86 7.50p 1930s Sedan   52.50

1988 Summer Olympics, Seoul A87

1988, Sept. 19   Litho.
573 A87 40a Hurdles   1.25   .50
574 A87 60a Basketball   2.00   .60
575 A87 1p   Soccer   3.50   1.25
576 A87 8p   Table tennis   6.50   3.00
     Nos. 573-576 (4)   13.25   5.35
Souvenir Sheet
577   Sheet of 5, #573-576,
          577a   55.00
 a. A87 5p Tae kwon do   30.00

World Post Day — A88

1988, Oct. 10   Litho.   Perf. 14
578 A88 13.40p Electronic mail 6.00   1.75
579 A88 40p   Express mail   10.50   5.00

35th Macao Grand Prix — A89

1988, Nov. 24   Litho.   Perf. 12½
580 A89 80a Sedan   1.25   .50
581 A89 2.80p Motorcycle   3.75   1.25
582 A89 7p   Formula 3   10.00   2.75
 a. Souvenir sheet of 3, #580-582 60.00
     Nos. 580-582 (3)   15.00   4.50

New Year Type of 1984
1989, Jan. 20   Litho.   Perf. 13½
583 A60 3p Snake   9.00   2.00
 a. Booklet pane of 5   36.00

No. 583a has straight edges. Value for No. 583 is for stamp perfed on 4 sides.

Occupations A91

1989, Mar. 1   Litho.   Perf. 12x12½
584 A91 50a Water carrier   .75   .25
585 A91 1p   Tan-kya woman   1.50   .50
586 A91 4p   Tin-tin (junk) man 3.00   1.75
587 A91 5p   Tofu peddler   4.00   2.00
     Nos. 584-587 (4)   9.25   4.50

See Nos. 612-615, 640-643.

Watercolors by George Smirnoff in the Luis de Camoens Museum — A92

1989, Apr. 10   Litho.   Perf. 12½x12
588 A92 2p multi (4-1)   2.10   .90
589 A92 2p multi (4-2)   2.10   .90
590 A92 2p multi (4-3)   2.10   .90
591 A92 2p multi (4-4)   2.10   .90
 a. Block or strip of 4, #588-591 12.50 5.75
     Nos. 588-591 (4)   8.40   3.60

Snakes A93

No. 592, Naja naja. No. 593, Bungarus fasciatus. No. 594, Trimeresurus albolabris. No. 595, Elaphe radiata.

1989, July 7   Litho.
592 A93 2.50p multicolored   3.50   1.25
593 A93 2.50p multicolored   3.50   1.25
594 A93 2.50p multicolored   3.50   1.25
595 A93 2.50p multicolored   3.50   1.25
 a. Block or strip of 4, #592-595 16.00 7.00
     Nos. 592-595 (4)   14.00   5.00

Traditional Games — A94

1989, July 31   Litho.   Perf. 13½
596 A94 10a Talu   .75   .40
597 A94 60a Triol   2.25   .50
598 A94 3.30p Chiquia   3.00   1.40
599 A94 5p   Xadrez Chines   4.00   2.50
     Nos. 596-599 (4)   10.00   4.80

Airplanes A95

1989, Oct. 9 — Litho.
600	A95	50a Over church	.50	.30
601	A95	70a American over lighthouse	1.00	.40
602	A95	2.80p Over wharf	1.50	.90
603	A95	4p Over junk	2.75	1.50
		Nos. 600-603 (4)	5.75	3.10

Souvenir Sheet
604	A95	7.50p Over harbor	30.00	15.00

No. 604 contains one 40x30mm stamp.

World Stamp Expo '89, Washington, DC — A96

1989, Nov. 17 — Litho. — Perf. 12½
605	A96	40a Malacca	.45	.25
606	A96	70a Thailand	.90	.30
607	A96	90a India	1.40	.50
608	A96	2.50p Japan	2.25	1.00
609	A96	7.50p China	4.50	2.00
		Nos. 605-609 (5)	9.50	4.05

Souvenir Sheet
610		Sheet of 6, #605-609, 610a	50.00	37.50
a.		A96 3p Macao	18.00	18.00

Influence of the Portuguese in the Far East.

New Year Type of 1984
1990, Jan. 19 — Litho. — Perf. 13½
611	A60	4p Horse	4.00	1.75
a.		Booklet pane of 5	22.00	

No. 611a has straight edges. Value for No. 611 is for stamp perfed on 4 sides.

Occupations Type of 1989
1990, Mar. 1 — Litho. — Perf. 12x12½
612	A91	30a Long chau singer	.90	.45
613	A91	70a Cobbler	1.75	.85
614	A91	1.50p Scribe	2.75	1.00
615	A91	7.50p Net fisherman	8.00	2.50
		Nos. 612-615 (4)	13.40	4.80

Souvenir Sheet

Penny Black, 150th Anniv. — A99

1990, May 3 — Litho. — Perf. 12
616	A99	10p multicolored	30.00	19.00

Stamp World London 90.

Lutianus Malabaricus — A100

Decorative Porcelain A101

1990, June 8 — Perf. 12x12½
617	A100	2.40p shown	2.00	1.10
618	A100	2.40p Epinephelus megachir	2.00	1.10
619	A100	2.40p Macropodus opercularis	2.00	1.10
620	A100	2.40p Ophiocephalus maculatus	2.00	1.10
a.		Block or strip of 4, #617-620	14.00	7.00
		Nos. 617-620 (4)	8.00	4.40

1990, Aug. 24 — Litho. — Perf. 12½
621	A101	3p shown	2.25	1.25
622	A101	3p Furniture	2.25	1.25
623	A101	3p Toys	2.25	1.25
624	A101	3p Artificial flowers	2.25	1.25
a.		Souvenir sheet of 4, #621-624	35.00	15.00
b.		Block or strip of 4, #621-624	16.00	8.00
		Nos. 621-624 (4)	9.00	5.00

Asian Games, Beijing — A102

1990, Sept. 22 — Litho. — Perf. 13½
625	A102	80a Cycling	.70	.40
626	A102	1p Swimming	1.00	.50
627	A102	3p Judo	3.50	1.10
628	A102	4.20p Shooting	5.25	1.75
		Nos. 625-628 (4)	10.45	3.75

Souvenir Sheet
629		Sheet of 5, #625-628, 629a	40.00	20.00
a.		A102 6p Martial arts	13.00	13.00

Compass Roses from Portuguese Charts — A103

Charts by 16th century cartographers: Lazaro Luis, Diogo Homem, Fernao Vaz Dourado, and Luiz Teixeira.

1990, Oct. 9 — Litho. — Perf. 13½
630	A103	50a shown	.90	.45
631	A103	1p multi, diff.	1.50	.50
632	A103	3.50p multi, diff.	3.50	1.25
633	A103	6.50p multi, diff.	7.00	2.00
		Nos. 630-633 (4)	12.90	4.20

Souvenir Sheet
634	A103	5p multi, diff.	55.00	27.50

Games with Animals A104

1990, Nov. 15 — Litho. — Perf. 14
635	A104	20a Cricket fight	.75	.30
636	A104	80a Bird fight	2.00	.55
637	A104	1p Greyhound race	2.75	.75
638	A104	10p Horse race	8.00	2.25
		Nos. 635-638 (4)	13.50	3.85

New Year Type of 1984
1991, Feb. 8 — Litho. — Perf. 13½
639	A60	4.50p Sheep	4.25	1.10
b.		Booklet pane of 5	28.00	

No. 639b has straight edges.

Occupations Type of 1987
1991, Mar. 1 — Perf. 14
640	A91	80a Knife grinder	.75	.45
641	A91	1.70p Flour puppet vender	1.50	.50
642	A91	3.50p Street barber	3.50	1.00
643	A91	4.20p Fortune teller	6.00	2.00
		Nos. 640-643 (4)	11.75	3.95

Shells A106

1991, Apr. 18 — Litho. — Perf. 14
644	A106	3p Murex pecten	2.00	1.40
645	A106	3p Harpa harpa	2.00	1.40
646	A106	3p Chicoreus rosarius	2.00	1.40
647	A106	3p Tonna zonata	2.00	1.40
a.		Strip of 4, #644-647	13.00	9.50
		Nos. 644-647 (4)	8.00	5.60

Chinese Opera — A107

Various performers in costume.

1991, June 5 — Litho. — Perf. 13½
648	A107	60a multicolored	1.25	.35
649	A107	80a multicolored	2.25	.40
650	A107	1p multicolored	3.25	.85
651	A107	10p multicolored	10.00	2.75
		Nos. 648-651 (4)	16.75	4.35

Flowers A108

Designs: 1.70p, Delonix regia. 3p, Ipomoea cairica. 3.50p, Jasminum mesnyi. 4.20p, Bauhinia variegata.

1991, Oct. 9 — Litho. — Perf. 13½
652	A108	1.70p multicolored	1.50	.45
653	A108	3p multicolored	2.25	.90
654	A108	3.50p multicolored	3.75	1.25
655	A108	4.20p multicolored	4.50	2.25
a.		Souvenir sheet of 4, #652-655	52.50	27.50
		Nos. 652-655 (4)	12.00	4.85

Cultural Exchange A109

Namban screen: No. 656, Unloading boat.

1991, Nov. 16 — Litho. — Perf. 12
656	A109	4.20p multicolored	3.00	.95
657	A109	4.20p shown	3.00	.95
a.		Souvenir sheet of 2, #656-657	35.00	20.00

Holiday Greetings A110

1991, Nov. 29 — Litho. — Perf. 14½
658	A110	1.70p Lunar New Year	1.00	.45
659	A110	3p Santa Claus, Christmas	1.75	.65
660	A110	3.50p Old man	2.75	.90
661	A110	4.20p Girl at New Year party	5.75	1.60
		Nos. 658-661 (4)	11.25	3.60

New Year Type of 1984
1992, Jan. 28 — Litho. — Perf. 13½
662	A60	4.50p Monkey	3.75	2.00
a.		Booklet pane of 5	22.50	

No. 662a has straight edges.

Paintings of Doors and Windows A111

1992, Mar. 1 — Perf. 14
663	A111	1.70p multicolored	1.00	.50
664	A111	3p multi, diff.	2.00	1.00
665	A111	3.50p multi, diff.	3.00	1.50
666	A111	4.20p multi, diff.	4.00	2.00
		Nos. 663-666 (4)	10.00	5.00

Mythological Chinese Gods — A112

1992, Apr. 3 — Litho. — Perf. 14
667	A112	3.50p T'it Kuai Lei (4-1)	6.00	3.00
668	A112	3.50p Chong Lei Kun (4-2)	6.00	3.00
669	A112	3.50p Cheong Kuo Lou (4-3)	6.00	3.00
670	A112	3.50p Loi Tong Pan (4-4)	6.00	3.00
a.		Block or strip of 4, #667-670	42.50	24.00
		Nos. 667-670 (4)	24.00	12.00

See Nos. 689-692.

Lion Dance Costume A113

Designs: 2.70p, Lion, diff. 6p, Dragon.

1992, May 18
671	A113	1p multicolored	.90	.40
672	A113	2.70p multicolored	1.50	.60
673	A113	6p multicolored	3.50	1.25
		Nos. 671-673 (3)	5.90	2.25

World Columbian Stamp Expo '92, Chicago.

1992 Summer Olympics, Barcelona — A114

1992, July 1   **Litho.**   *Perf. 13*
674	A114	80a High jump	.75	.30
675	A114	4.20p Badminton	1.60	.75
676	A114	4.70p Roller hockey	2.25	1.10
677	A114	5p Yachting	3.50	1.40
a.		Souvenir sheet of 4, #674-677	18.00	12.00
		Nos. 674-677 (4)	8.10	3.55

Temples
A115

1992, Oct. 9   *Perf. 14*
678	A115	1p Na Cha	.85	.40
679	A115	1.50p Kun Iam	1.10	.55
680	A115	1.70p Hong Kon	1.75	.90
681	A115	6.50p A Ma	3.50	2.00
		Nos. 678-681 (4)	7.20	3.85

See Nos. 685-688.

Portuguese-Chinese
Friendship — A116

1992, Nov. 1   **Litho.**   *Perf. 14*
682	A116	10p multicolored	3.50	2.00
a.		Souv. sheet, perf. 13½	15.00	10.00

Tung Sin Tong Charity Organization,
Cent. — A117

1992, Nov. 27   *Perf. 12x11½*
683	A117	1p multicolored	1.50	.40

New Year Type of 1984

1993, Jan. 18   **Litho.**   *Perf. 13½*
684	A60	5p Rooster	3.25	1.40
a.		Booklet pane of 5	16.00	

No. 684a has straight edges.

Temple Type of 1992

1993, Mar. 1   **Litho.**   *Perf. 14*
685	A115	50a T'am Kong	.30	.25
686	A115	2p T'in Hau	1.00	.35
687	A115	3.50p Lin Fong	1.50	.70
688	A115	8p Pau Kong	2.00	1.50
		Nos. 685-688 (4)	4.80	2.80

Mythological Chinese Gods Type of 1992

Designs: No. 689, Lam Ch'oi Wo seated on crane in flight. No. 690, Ho Sin Ku, seated on peach flower.No. 691, Hon Seong Chi throwing peonies from basket. No. 692, Ch'ou Kuok K'ao seated on gold plate.

1993, Apr. 1   **Litho.**   *Perf. 14*
689	A112	3.50p multi (4-1)	2.25	1.75
690	A112	3.50p multi (4-2)	2.25	1.75
691	A112	3.50p multi (4-3)	2.25	1.75
692	A112	3.50p multi (4-4)	2.25	1.75
a.		Strip of 4, #689-692	11.00	9.00

Chinese
Wedding — A118

No. 693, Three children celebrating. No. 694, Bride. No. 695, Groom. No. 696, Woman with parasol, person being carried. 8p, Bride & groom.

1993, May 19   *Perf. 14*
693	A118	3p multicolored	1.50	1.25
694	A118	3p multicolored	1.50	1.25
695	A118	3p multicolored	1.50	1.25
696	A118	3p multicolored	1.50	1.25
a.		Strip of 4, #693-696	8.00	8.00

Souvenir Sheet
Perf. 14½x14
697	A118	8p multicolored	13.50	11.50

No. 697 contains one 50x40mm stamp.

World
Environment
Day — A119

1993, June 5   **Litho.**   *Perf. 14*
698	A119	1p multicolored	1.75	.55

Birds — A120

No. 699, Falco peregrinus. No. 700, Aquila obrysaetos. No. 701, Asio otus. No. 702, Tyto alba.

1993, June 27
699	A120	3p multicolored	1.50	1.00
700	A120	3p multicolored	1.50	1.00
701	A120	3p multicolored	1.50	1.00
702	A120	3p multicolored	1.50	1.00
a.		Block or strip of 4, #699-702	7.50	6.00
b.		Souvenir sheet of 4, #699-702	14.00	10.00

Union of Portuguese Speaking
Capitals — A121

1993, July 30   **Litho.**   *Perf. 13½*
703	A121	1.50p multicolored	1.10	.50

Portuguese
Arrival in
Japan,
450th
Anniv.
A122

50a, Japanese using musket. 3p, Catholic priests. 3.50p, Exchanging items of trade.

1993, Sept. 22   **Litho.**   *Perf. 12x11½*
704	A122	50a multicolored	.60	.25
705	A122	3p multicolored	1.50	.70
706	A122	3.50p multicolored	1.90	.80
		Nos. 704-706 (3)	4.00	1.75

See Portugal Nos. 1964-1966.

Flowers
A123

Designs: 1p, Spathodea campanulata. 2p, Tithonia diversifolia. 3p, Rhodomyrtus tomentosa. 8p, Passiflora foetida.

1993, Oct. 9   *Perf. 14½*
707	A123	1p multicolored	.65	.25
708	A123	2p multicolored	1.25	.45
709	A123	3p multicolored	1.50	.65
710	A123	8p multicolored	2.50	1.75
a.		Souvenir sheet of 4, #707-710	13.00	12.50
		Nos. 707-710 (4)	5.90	3.10

Portuguese
Ships
A124

1993, Nov. 5   **Litho.**   *Perf. 14*
711	A124	1p Caravel	.60	.30
712	A124	2p Round caravel	1.00	.25
713	A124	3.50p Nau	1.40	.40
714	A124	4.50p Galleon	2.00	1.00
a.		Souvenir sheet of 4, #711-714	8.00	7.00
		Nos. 711-714 (4)	5.00	1.95

Macao
Grand
Prix, 40th
Anniv.
A125

1993, Nov. 16   **Litho.**   *Perf. 13½*
715	A125	1.50p Stock car	.75	.40
716	A125	2p Motorcycle	1.25	.55
717	A125	4.50p Formula 1 race car	2.00	1.40
		Nos. 715-717 (3)	4.00	2.35

New Year Type of 1984

1994, Feb. 3   **Litho.**   *Perf. 13½*
718	A60	5p Dog	3.00	1.25
a.		Booklet pane of 5	20.00	

New Year 1994 (Year of the Dog).
No. 718a has straight edges.

Prince Henry the Navigator (1394-1460) — A126

1994, Mar. 4   **Litho.**   *Perf. 12*
719	A126	3p multicolored	2.25	1.00

See Portugal No. 1987.

Scenes of Macao, by George
Chinnery (1774-1852) — A127

Designs: No. 720, Hut, natives. No. 721, S. Tiago Fortress. No. 722, Overview of Praia Grande. No. 723, S. Francisco Church.

1994, Mar. 21   *Perf. 14*
720	A127	3.50p multi (4-1)	1.40	.90
721	A127	3.50p multi (4-2)	1.40	.90
722	A127	3.50p multi (4-3)	1.40	.90

723	A127	3.50p multi (4-4)	1.40	.90
a.		Block or strip of 4, #720-723	7.00	4.00
b.		Souvenir sheet of 4, #720-723	15.00	10.00

Spring
Festival of
New Lunar
Year
A128

Designs: 1p, Girl, woman shopping. 2p, Celebration. 3.50p, Couple preparing food at table. 4.50p, Old man making decorations.

1994, Apr. 6
724	A128	1p multicolored	.50	.25
725	A128	2p multicolored	1.00	.40
726	A128	3.50p multicolored	1.25	.75
727	A128	4.50p multicolored	1.75	1.10
		Nos. 724-727 (4)	4.50	2.50

Mythological
Chinese
Gods — A129

Statuettes: No. 728, Happiness. No. 729, Prosperity. No. 730, Longevity.

1994, May 9   **Litho.**   *Perf. 12*
728	A129	3p multi (3-1)	2.50	1.50
729	A129	3p multi (3-2)	2.50	1.50
730	A129	3p multi (3-3)	2.50	1.50
a.		Strip of 3, #728-730	9.50	7.00
b.		Souvenir sheet of 3, #728-730	14.00	12.00

A130

1994 World Cup Soccer Championships, US: Various soccer players.

1994, June 1
731	A130	2p multicolored	.65	.40
732	A130	3p multicolored	1.00	.60
733	A130	3.50p multicolored	1.25	.75
734	A130	4.50p multicolored	1.50	1.25
a.		Souvenir sheet of 4, #731-734	12.00	10.00
		Nos. 731-734 (4)	4.40	3.00

A131

Traditional Chinese shops: 1p, Rice shop. 1.50p, Medicinal drink shop. 2p, Salt fish shop. 3.50p, Pharmacy.

1994, June 27   **Litho.**   *Perf. 12*
735	A131	1p multi	.50	.35
736	A131	1.50p multi	.55	.45
737	A131	2p multi	1.25	.65
738	A131	3.50p multi	1.75	.90
		Nos. 735-738 (4)	4.05	2.35

Navigation
Instruments
A132

1994, Sept. 13   Litho.   Perf. 12
739 A132   3p Astrolabe   1.00   .80
740 A132   3.50p Quadrant   1.40 1.10
741 A132   4.50p Sextant   1.60 1.25
   Nos. 739-741 (3)   4.00 3.15

12th Asian
Games,
Hiroshima
1994
A133

1994, Sept. 30   Litho.   Perf. 12
742 A133   1p Fencing   .40   .30
743 A133   2p Gymnastics   .85   .40
744 A133   3p Water polo   1.25   .60
745 A133   3.50p Pole vault   1.50 1.00
   Nos. 742-745 (4)   4.00 2.30

Bridges
A134

1994, Oct. 8
746 A134   1p Nobre de Carvalho   .40   .45
747 A134   8p Friendship   2.60 1.50

Fortune
Symbols — A135

Designs: 3p, Child, carp, water lily. 3.50p, Basket of peaches, child, bats. 4.50p, Flower, child playing mouth organ.

1994, Nov. 7   Litho.   Perf. 12
748 A135   3p multicolored   1.40   .60
749 A135   3.50p multicolored   1.60   .80
750 A135   4.50p multicolored   2.00 1.25
   Nos. 748-750 (3)   5.00 2.65

Religious
Art — A136

Designs: 50a, Stained glass, angel's head. 1p, Stained glass, Holy Ghost. 1.50p, Silver sacrarium. 2p, Silver salver. 3p, Ivory sculpture, Escape to Egypt. 3.50p, Gold & silver chalice.

1994, Nov. 30
751 A136   50a multicolored   .25   .25
752 A136   1p multicolored   .40   .25
753 A136   1.50p multicolored   .60   .30
754 A136   2p multicolored   .85   .45
755 A136   3p multicolored   1.10   .65
756 A136   3.50p multicolored   1.25   .85
   Nos. 751-756 (6)   4.45 2.75

New Year Type of 1984
1995, Jan. 23   Litho.   Perf. 13½
757 A60   5.50p Boar   2.75 1.10
   a.   Booklet pane of 5   18.00

Tourism
A138

Scenes of Macao, by Lio Man Cheong: 50a, Walkway beside pond. 1p, Lighthouse. 1.50p, Temple. 2p, Buildings along coast. 2.50p, Columns, temple. 3p, Ruins on hill overlooking city. 3.50p, Bridge. 4p, Trees in park.

1995, Mar. 1   Litho.   Perf. 12
758 A138   50a multicolored   .25   .25
759 A138   1p multicolored   .45   .30
760 A138   1.50p multicolored   .60   .35
761 A138   2p multicolored   .85   .50
762 A138   2.50p multicolored   .95   .60
763 A138   3p multicolored   1.10   .75
764 A138   3.50p multicolored   1.40   .85
765 A138   4p multicolored   1.75 1.10
   Nos. 758-765 (8)   7.35 4.70

World Day
of the
Consumer
A139

1995, Mar. 15
766 A139   1p multicolored   .85   .40

Asian
Pangolin — A140

No. 767, Facing left (4-1). No. 768, Hanging by tail (4-2). No. 769, On tree limb (4-3). No. 770, On tree stump (4-4).

1995, Apr. 10
767 A140   1.50p multi   1.40   .50
768 A140   1.50p multi   1.40   .50
769 A140   1.50p multi   1.40   .50
770 A140   1.50p multi   1.40   .50
   a.   Block or strip of 4, #767-770   7.50 6.50

World wildlife Fund.
Issued in sheets of 16 stamps.

Legend of
Buddhist
Goddess Kun
Iam — A141

No. 772, Seated atop dragon, holding flower. No. 773, Meditating. No. 774, Holding infant. 8p, Goddess with many faces, hands.

1995, May 5   Litho.   Perf. 12
771 A141   3p multicolored   1.75   .80
772 A141   3p multicolored   1.75   .80
773 A141   3p multicolored   1.75   .80
774 A141   3p multicolored   1.75   .80
   a.   Block or strip of 4, #771-774   10.00 9.00
Souvenir Sheet
775 A141   8p multicolored   18.50 14.00

Senado
Square — A142

Designs: No. 776, Street, bell tower. No. 777, Street, plaza, shops. No. 778, Fountain, plaza. No. 779, Plaza, buildings. 8p, Bell tower, building, horiz.

1995, June 24   Litho.   Perf. 12
776 A142   2p multicolored   .90   .55
777 A142   2p multicolored   .90   .55
778 A142   2p multicolored   .90   .55
779 A142   2p multicolored   .90   .55
   a.   Strip of 4, #776-779   5.00 3.50
Souvenir Sheet
780 A142   8p multicolored   11.00 8.00

Temple Type of 1992
1995, July 17   Litho.   Perf. 12
781 A115   50a Kuan Tai   .25   .25
782 A115   1p Pak Tai   .40   .25
783 A115   1.50p Lin K'ai   .65   .35
784 A115   3p Sek Kam Tong   1.25   .75
785 A115   3.50p Fok Tak   1.40   .90
   Nos. 781-785 (5)   3.95 2.50

Singapore
'95 — A143

Birds: No. 786, Gurrulax canorus. No. 787, Serinus canarius. No. 788, Zosterops japonica. No. 789, Leiothrix lutea. 10p, Copsychus saularis.

1995, Sept. 1   Litho.   Perf. 12
786 A143   2.50p multicolored   1.40   .65
787 A143   2.50p multicolored   1.40   .65
788 A143   2.50p multicolored   1.40   .65
789 A143   2.50p multicolored   1.40   .65
   a.   Strip of 4, #786-789   8.50 4.00
Souvenir Sheet
790 A143   10p multicolored   17.50 11.00

Intl. Music
Festival — A144

1995, Oct. 9   Litho.   Perf. 12
791 A144   1p Pipa (6-1)   .90   .35
792 A144   1p Erhu (6-2)   .90   .35
793 A144   1p Gongo (6-3)   .90   .35
794 A144   1p Sheng (6-4)   .90   .35
795 A144   1p Xiao (6-5)   .90   .35
796 A144   1p Tambor (6-6)   .90   .35
   a.   Block of 6, #791-796   8.50 5.00
Souvenir Sheet
797 A144   8p Musicians, horiz. 10.00 6.00

UN, 50th
Anniv.
A145

1995, Oct. 24   Litho.   Perf. 12
798 A145   4.50p multicolored   1.75 1.10

Macao Intl.
Airport
A146

Designs: 1p, Airplane above terminal. 1.50p, Boeing 747 on ground, terminal. 2p, Hangars, 747 with boarding ramp at door. 3p, Airplane, control tower. 8p, Boeing 747 over runway.

1995, Dec. 8   Litho.   Perf. 12
799 A146   1p multicolored   .50   .25
800 A146   1.50p multicolored   .75   .35
801 A146   2p multicolored   1.00   .45
802 A146   3p multicolored   1.25   .70
   Nos. 799-802 (4)   3.50 1.75
Souvenir Sheet
Perf. 12½
803 A146   8p multicolored   11.50 8.50

No. 803 contains one 51x38mm stamp.

New Year Type of 1984
Miniature Sheet of 12
Designs: a, like #485. b, like #504. c, like #522. d, like #540. e, like #560. f, like #583. g, like #611. h, like #639. i, like #662. j, like #684. k, like #718. l, like #757.

1995, Dec. 15   Litho.   Perf. 13½
804 A60   1.50p #a.-l. + label 17.50 10.00

New Year
1996 (Year
of the Rat)
A147

1996, Feb. 12   Litho.   Perf. 12
805 A147   5p multicolored   3.75 1.75
Souvenir Sheet
806 A147   10p like No. 805   10.00 7.50

Traditional
Chinese Bird
Cages — A148

Various styles.

1996, Mar. 1   Litho.   Perf. 12
807 A148   1p multi (4-1)   .35   .25
808 A148   1.50p multi (4-2)   .55   .35
809 A148   3p multi (4-3)   1.00   .60
810 A148   4.50p multi (4-4)   1.60   .90
   Nos. 807-810 (4)   3.50 2.10
Souvenir Sheet
811 A148   10p purple & multi 12.50 8.50

Paintings,
by
Herculano
Estorninho
A149

Scenes of Macao: 50a, Boats. 1.50p, Street, buildings at night, vert. 3p, Fronts of buildings during day, vert. 5p, Townhouse complex. 10p, Entrance to building, vert.

1996, Apr. 1
812 A149   50a multi (4-1)   .25   .25
813 A149   1.50p multi (4-2)   .65   .45
814 A149   3p multi (4-3)   1.10   .85
815 A149   5p multi (4-4)   2.00 1.40
   Nos. 812-815 (4)   4.00 2.95
Souvenir Sheet
816 A149   10p multi   9.00 5.00

Myths and Legends — A150

Designs: No. 817, Man holding staff. No. 818, Man riding tiger. No. 819, Man on top of fireplace.

1996, Apr. 30   **Litho.**   **Perf. 12**

817	A150	3.50p Tou Tei (3-1)	1.20	.90
818	A150	3.50p Choi San (3-2)	1.20	.90
819	A150	3.50p Chou Kuan (3-3)	1.20	.90
a.		Strip of 3, #817-819	4.50	4.50
b.		Souvenir sheet of 3, #817-819	11.00	8.00

Traditional Chinese Tea Houses A151

Designs: No. 820, Two men seated at table. No. 821, Cook holding steaming tray of food, woman, baby. No. 822, Woman holding up papers. No. 823, Waiter pouring tea, man seated.

8p, Food, serving bowl.

1996, May 17   **Perf. 12**

820	A151	2p multi (4-1)	1.10	.55
821	A151	2p multi (4-2)	1.10	.55
822	A151	2p multi (4-3)	1.10	.55
823	A151	2p multi (4-4)	1.10	.55
a.		Block of 4, #820-823	6.00	4.00

Souvenir Sheet

824	A151	8p multi		11.00	8.00

No. 823a is a continuous design. China '96 (No. 824).

Greetings Stamps A152

Designs: 50a, Get well. 1.50p, Congratulations on new baby. 3p, Happy birthday. 4p, Marriage congratulations.

1996, June 14   **Litho.**   **Perf. 12**

825	A152	50a multi (4-1)	.25	.25
826	A152	1.50p multi (4-2)	.50	.35
827	A152	3p multi (4-3)	1.25	.60
828	A152	4p multi (4-4)	1.50	.90
		Nos. 825-828 (4)	3.50	2.10

1996 Summer Olympic Games, Atlanta A153

1996, July 19

829	A153	2p Swimming (4-1)	.50	.35
830	A153	3p Soccer (4-2)	.80	.55
831	A153	3.50p Gymnastics (4-3)	.90	.60
832	A153	4.50p Sailboarding (4-4)	1.10	.80
		Nos. 829-832 (4)	3.30	2.30

Souvenir Sheet

833	A153	10p Boxing		7.50	5.00

Civil and Military Emblems A154

No. 834, Bird looking left. No. 835, Dragon. No. 836, Bird looking right. No. 837, Leopard.

1996, Sept. 18

834	A154	2.50p bl & multi (4-1)	1.20	.60
835	A154	2.50p grn & multi (4-2)	1.20	.60
836	A154	2.50p grn & multi (4-3)	1.20	.60
837	A154	2.50p pur & multi (4-4)	1.20	.60
a.		Block of 4, #834-837	6.50	4.00

See Nos. 947-951.

Fishing with Nets — A155

Boats, fish in sea: No. 838, Six small nets extended from mast of boat. No. 839, Modern trawler. No. 840, Junk trawling. No. 841, Sailboat with nets extended from both sides.

1996, Oct. 9   **Litho.**   **Perf. 12**

838	A155	3p multi (4-1)	1.20	.60
839	A155	3p multi (4-2)	1.20	.60
840	A155	3p multi (4-3)	1.20	.60
841	A155	3p multi (4-4)	1.20	.60
a.		Strip of 4, #838-841	6.50	5.25

Legislative Assembly, 20th Anniv. — A156

1996, Oct. 15   **Litho.**   **Perf. 12x12½**

842	A156	2.80p multicolored	.95	.60

Souvenir Sheet

843	A156	8p like No. 842		9.00	6.00

Paper Kites A157

No. 844, Dragonfly (4-1). No. 845, Butterfly (4-2). No. 846, Owl in flight (4-3). No. 847, Standing owl (4-4).
No. 848, Dragon.

1996, Oct. 21   **Litho.**   **Perf. 12**

844	A157	3.50p multi	1.50	1.00
845	A157	3.50p multi	1.50	1.00
846	A157	3.50p multi	1.50	1.00
847	A157	3.50p multi	1.50	1.00
a.		Strip or block of 4, #844-847	8.00	8.00

Souvenir Sheet

Perf. 12½

848	A157	8p multi		12.00	9.00

No. 848 contains one 51x38mm stamp.

Traditional Chinese Toys — A158

1996, Nov. 13   **Litho.**   **Perf. 12**

849	A158	50a shown	.40	.25
850	A158	1p Fish	1.00	.60
851	A158	3p Doll	3.00	1.25
852	A158	4.50p Dragon	5.00	1.75
		Nos. 849-852 (4)	9.40	3.90

New Year 1997 (Year of the Ox) A159

1997, Jan. 23   **Litho.**   **Perf. 12**

853	A159	5.50p multicolored		3.00	2.00

Souvenir Sheet

854	A159	10p multicolored		8.00	6.25

No. 854 is a continuous design.

Lucky Numbers A160

1997, Feb. 12   **Litho.**   **Perf. 12**

855	A160	2p "2," Simplicity	.70	.50
856	A160	2.80p "8," Prosperity	.90	.60
857	A160	3p "3," Progress	1.00	.65
858	A160	3.90p "9," Longevity	1.40	1.00
		Nos. 855-858 (4)	4.00	2.75

Souvenir Sheet

859	A160	9p Man outside house		6.00	4.00

Hong Kong '97 (No. 859).

Paintings of Macao, by Kwok Se — A161

2p, Junks. 3p, Fortress on side of mountain. 3.50p, Retreat house. 4.50p, Cerco Gate. 8p, Rooftop of building, horiz.

1997, Mar. 1   **Litho.**   **Perf. 12**

860	A161	2p multicolored	.65	.35
861	A161	3p multicolored	1.10	.55
862	A161	3.50p multicolored	1.25	.75
863	A161	4.50p multicolored	1.80	1.00
		Nos. 860-863 (4)	4.80	2.65

Souvenir Sheet

864	A161	8p multicolored		7.50	6.25

A162

Boat People: 1p, Old woman seated. 1.50p, Woman wearing hat. 2.50p, Woman carrying baby. 5.50p, Man, boy.

1997, Mar. 26   **Litho.**   **Perf. 12**

865	A162	1p multicolored	.60	.40
866	A162	1.50p multicolored	.70	.50
867	A162	2.50p multicolored	1.10	.80
868	A162	5.50p multicolored	2.60	1.75
a.		Block of 4, #865-868	5.00	4.00

A163

Temple A-Ma: No. 869, Steps leading to entrance. No. 870, People strolling past temple, one with umbrella. No. 871, People outside pagoda, pedicab. No. 872, Towers from temple, one emiting smoke.

1997, Apr. 29   **Litho.**   **Perf. 12**

869	A163	3.50p multicolored	.60	.40
870	A163	3.50p multicolored	.60	.40
871	A163	3.50p multicolored	.60	.40
872	A163	3.50p multicolored	.60	.40
a.		Strip of 4, #869-872	3.25	3.25

Souvenir Sheet

873	A163	8p Boat		4.50	4.50

Drunken Dragon Festival — A164

Stylized designs: 2p, Two men, one holding dragon. 3p, Man holding up dragon. 5p, Two men, one holding horn.
9p, Dragon, man, horiz.

1997, May 14

874	A164	2p multicolored	.60	.35
875	A164	3p multicolored	1.00	.55
876	A164	5p multicolored	1.60	1.10
a.		Strip of 3, #874-876	3.50	3.50

Souvenir Sheet

877	A164	9p multicolored		4.25	4.25

Father Luís Fróis, 400th Death Anniv. A165

No. 879, Father Fróis, cathedral, vert.

1997, June 9   **Litho.**   **Perf. 12**

878	A165	2.50p multi (2-1)	.75	.75
879	A165	2.50p multi (2-2)	.75	.75

See Portugal Nos. 2165-2167.

Legends and Myths — A166

Gods of Protection: No. 880, Wat Lot. No. 881, San Su. No. 882, Chon Keng. No. 883, Wat Chi Kong.
10p, Chon Keng and Wat Chi Kong.

1997, June 18   **Litho.**   **Perf. 12**

880	A166	2.50p multicolored	.65	.65
881	A166	2.50p multicolored	.65	.65
882	A166	2.50p multicolored	.65	.65
883	A166	2.50p multicolored	.65	.65
a.		Strip or block of 4, #880-883	3.50	3.50
		Nos. 880-883 (4)	2.60	2.60

Souvenir Sheet

884	A166	10p multicolored		4.00	4.00

No. 884 contains one 40x40mm stamp.

Macao Red Cross, 77th Anniv. — A167

1997, July 12   **Perf. 12½**

885	A167	1.50p multicolored	.40	.40

No. 885 is printed se-tenant with label.

Verandas
A168

Various architectural styles.
8p, Close up of veranda, vert.

1997, July 30   **Litho.**   **Perf. 12**
886	A168	50a multi (6-1)	.25	.25
887	A168	1p multi (6-2)	.25	.25
888	A168	1.50p multi (6-3)	.40	.40
889	A168	2p multi (6-4)	.50	.50
890	A168	2.50p multi (6-5)	.65	.65
891	A168	3p multi (6-6)	.75	.75
a.		Block of 6, #886-891	2.75	2.75

Souvenir Sheet
892	A168	8p multicolored	2.75	2.75

Traditional
Chinese
Fans — A169

1997, Sept. 24   **Litho.**   **Perf. 12**
893	A169	50a Planta (4-1)	.25	.25
894	A169	1p Papel (4-2)	.30	.30
895	A169	3.50p Seda (4-3)	.85	.85
896	A169	4p Pluma (4-4)	1.10	1.10
a.		Strip or block of 4, #893-896	3.00	3.00

Souvenir Sheet
897	A169	9p Sandalo	4.00	3.75

Fong Soi
(Chinese
Geomancy)
A170

Chinese principles of Yin and Yang related to the five elements of the ancient Zodiac.

1997, Oct. 9   **Litho.**   **Perf. 12**
898	A170	50a green & multi	.25	.25
899	A170	1p orange & multi	.30	.30
900	A170	1.50p brown & multi	.45	.45
901	A170	2p yellow & multi	.60	.60
902	A170	2.50p blue & multi	.70	.70
a.		Strip of 5, #898-902	2.50	2.50

Souvenir Sheet
903	A170	10p green & multi	3.75	3.75

Martial
Arts — A171

1997, Nov. 19
904	A171	1.50p Kung Fu	.40	.40
905	A171	3.50p Judo	.90	.60
906	A171	4p Karate	1.00	.80
a.		Strip of 3, #904-906	2.50	2.50

New Year
1998 (Year
of the
Tiger)
A172

1998, Jan. 18   **Litho.**   **Perf. 12**
907	A172	5.50p multicolored	1.75	1.75

Souvenir Sheets
908	A172	10p multicolored	2.75	2.75
a.		Ovptd. in sheet margin	2.75	2.75

No. 908 is a continuous design.
No. 908a overprinted in Gold in Sheet Margin with "Amizade Luso-Chinesa / Festival de Macao" & Chinese Text.

Street
Vendors
A173

Vendors at stands, carts: No. 909, 1p, Frying foods. 1.50p, Food products, eggs. 2p, Clothing items. 2.50p, Balloons. 3p, Flowers. 3.50p, Fruits and vegetables.
6p, Vendor at fruit and vegetable stand, diff.

1998, Feb. 13   **Litho.**   **Perf. 12**
909	A173	1p multi (6-1)	.25	.25
910	A173	1.50p multi (6-2)	.35	.30
911	A173	2p multi (6-3)	.50	.45
912	A173	2.50p multi (6-4)	.60	.50
913	A173	3p multi (6-5)	.75	.65
914	A173	3.50p multi (6-6)	.90	.70
a.		Block of 6, #909-914	3.60	3.60

Souvenir Sheets
915	A173	6p multicolored	1.75	1.75
a.		Ovptd. in sheet margin	2.00	2.00

No. 915a overprinted in Gold in Sheet Margin with "Amizade Luso-Chinesa / Festival de Macao" & Chinese Text.

Traditional
Gates
A174

Inscriptions: 50a, "Beco da Sé." 1p, "Pátio da Ilusao." 3.50p, "Travessa da galinhas." 4p, "Beco das Felicidades."
9p, "Seminário d S. José," vert.

1998, Mar. 1
916	A174	50a multi (4-1)	.25	.25
917	A174	1p multi (4-2)	.25	.25
918	A174	3.50p multi (4-3)	.95	.95
919	A174	4p multi (4-4)	1.10	1.10
		Nos. 916-919 (4)	2.55	2.55

Souvenir Sheets
920	A174	9p multicolored	2.40	2.40
a.		Ovptd. in sheet margin	2.50	2.50

No. 920a overprinted in Gold in Sheet Margin with "Amizade Luso-Chinesa / Festival de Macao" & Chinese Text.

Myths and
Legends — A175

Gods of Ma Chou: No. 921, Holding baby. No. 922, Watching image appear in smoke. No. 923, With cherubs. No. 924, Hovering over junks.
10p, Face.

1998, Apr. 23   **Litho.**   **Perf. 12**
921	A175	4p multi (4-1)	.95	.85
922	A175	4p multi (4-2)	.95	.85
923	A175	4p multi (4-3)	.95	.85
924	A175	4p multi (4-4)	.95	.85
a.		Strip of 4, #921-924	4.25	4.25

Souvenir Sheets
925	A175	10p multicolored	2.50	2.50
a.		Ovptd. in sheet margin	2.60	2.60

No. 925a overprinted in Gold in Sheet Margin with "Amizade Luso-Chinesa / Festival de Macao" & Chinese Text.

Voyage to
India by
Vasco da
Gama,
500th
Anniv.
A176

Designs: 1p, Sailing ship. 1.50p, Vasco da Gama. 2p, Map, sailing ship.
8p, Compass rose.

1998, May 20   **Litho.**   **Perf. 12**
926	A176	1p multi (3-1)	.35	.35
927	A176	1.50p multi (3-2)	.55	.55
928	A176	2p multi (3-3)	.75	.75
a.		Strip of 3, #926-928	2.00	2.00

Souvenir Sheet
929	A176	8p multicolored	3.75	3.75

Nos. 926-929 are inscribed "1598" instead of "1498," and were withdrawn after two days. For corrected version, see Nos. 943-946.

Oceans
A177

Stylized designs: 2.50p, Mermaid, shells, sailing ship, compass rose. 3p, Compass rose, fish, oil derrick.
9p, Sailing ship, seagull, fish, cloud, sun.

1998, May 22
930	A177	2.50p multi (2-1)	.65	.65
931	A177	3p multi (2-2)	.75	.75
a.		Pair, #930-931	2.00	2.00

Souvenir Sheets
932	A177	9p multicolored	2.75	2.75
a.		Ovptd. in sheet margin	3.00	3.00

No. 932a overprinted in Gold in Sheet Margin with "Amizade Luso-Chinesa / Festival de Macao" & Chinese Text.

1998 World Cup Soccer
Championships, France — A178

Various soccer plays.

1998, June 10   **Litho.**   **Perf. 12**
933	A178	3p multicolored	.75	.45
934	A178	3.50p multicolored	.90	.65
935	A178	4p multicolored	.95	.75
936	A178	4.50p multicolored	1.10	.95
		Nos. 933-936 (4)	3.70	2.80

Souvenir Sheet
937	A178	9p multicolored	2.75	2.75
a.		Ovptd. in sheet margin	3.75	3.75

No. 937a overprinted in Gold in Sheet Margin with "Amizade Luso-Chinesa / Festival de Macao" & Chinese Text.

Chinese
Opera
Masks
A179

1998, July 28   **Litho.**   **Perf. 12**
938	A179	1.50p Lio, Seak Chong (4-1)	.35	.25
939	A179	2p Wat, Chi Kong (4-2)	.50	.45
940	A179	3p Kam, Chin Pao (4-3)	.75	.60

941	A179	5p Lei, Kwai (4-4)	1.10	.95
a.		Strip of 4, #938-941	3.25	3.25

Souvenir Sheets
942	A179	8p Masked player	2.25	2.25
a.		Ovptd. in sheet margin	3.75	3.75

No. 942a overprinted in Gold in Sheet Margin with "Amizade Luso-Chinesa / Festival de Macao" & Chinese Text.

**Vasco da Gama Type of 1998
Inscribed "1498"**

1998, Sept. 4   **Litho.**   **Perf. 12**
943	A176	1p like #926	.30	.30
944	A176	1.50p like #927	.60	.60
945	A176	2p like #928	.75	.75
a.		Strip of 3, #943-945	1.90	1.90

Souvenir Sheets
946	A176	8p like #929	2.00	2.00
a.		Ovptd. in sheet margin	3.75	3.75

Issued to correct the error on Nos. 926-929.
No. 946a overprinted in Gold in Sheet Margin with "Amizade Luso-Chinesa / Festival de Macao" & Chinese Text.

**Civil and Military Emblems Type of
1996**

Designs: 50a, Lion. 1p, Dragon. 1.50p, Bird looking right. 2p, Bird looking left.
9p, Bird flying.

1998, Sept. 9
947	A154	50a multi (4-1)	.25	.25
948	A154	1p multi (4-2)	.30	.30
949	A154	1.50p multi (4-3)	.40	.30
950	A154	2p multi (4-4)	.60	.40
a.		Strip of 4, #947-950	1.50	1.50

Souvenir Sheets
951	A154	9p multicolored	2.50	2.50
a.		Ovptd. in sheet margin	3.75	3.75

No. 951a overprinted in Gold in Sheet Margin with "Amizade Luso-Chinesa / Festival de Macao" & Chinese Text.

Kun Iam
Temple
A180

Scenes inside temple compound: No. 952, Buddha figure standing. No. 953, Entrance gate, man running, benches. No. 954, Entrance to building, people. No. 955, People, stream, pagoda, flowers.
10p, Table, chairs, top of incense burner.

1998   **Litho.**   **Perf. 12**
952	A180	3.50p multicolored	.85	.75
953	A180	3.50p multicolored	.85	.75
954	A180	3.50p multicolored	.85	.75
955	A180	3.50p multicolored	.85	.75
a.		Block of 4, #952-955	3.60	3.60

Souvenir Sheets
956	A180	10p multicolored	2.50	2.50
a.		Ovptd. in sheet margin	3.75	3.75

No. 956a overprinted in Gold in Sheet Margin with "Amizade Luso-Chinesa / Festival de Macao" & Chinese Text.

Paintings
of Macao,
by Didier
Rafael
Bayle
A181

Designs: 2p, Street scene, buggy, vert. 3p, People standing outside of buildings. 3.50p, Building atop wall. 4.50p, Buildings, house along street, vert.
8p, Top of building.

1998, Nov. 11   **Litho.**   **Perf. 12**
957	A181	2p multi (4-1)	.50	.40
958	A181	3p multi (4-2)	.75	.60
959	A181	3.50p multi (4-3)	.90	.70
960	A181	4.50p multi (4-4)	1.10	.90
		Nos. 957-960 (4)	3.25	2.60

Souvenir Sheets
961	A181	8p multicolored	2.25	2.25
a.		Ovptd. in sheet margin	3.75	3.75

No. 961a overprinted in Gold in Sheet Margin with "Amizade Luso-Chinesa / Festival de Macao" & Chinese Text.

Tiles
A182

Designs: 1p, Dragon. 1.50p, Sailing ship. 2.50p, Chinese junk. 5.50p, Peacock. 10p, Building, lighthouse.

1998, Dec. 8
962	A182	1p multi (4-1)	.25	.25
963	A182	1.50p multi (4-2)	.35	.30
964	A182	2.50p multi (4-3)	.60	.45
965	A182	5.50p multi (4-4)	1.20	.90
a.		Block of 4, #962-965	2.75	2.75

Souvenir Sheets
966	A182	10p multicolored	3.25	3.25
a.		Ovptd. in sheet margin	4.50	4.50

No. 966a overprinted in Gold in Sheet Margin with "Amizade Luso-Chinesa / Festival de Macao" & Chinese Text.

New Year 1999 (Year of the Rabbit) A183

1999, Feb. 8   Litho.   Perf. 12
967	A183	5.50p multicolored	1.40	1.40

Souvenir Sheet
968	A183	10p multicolored	2.75	2.75
a.		Ovptd. in sheet margin	2.75	2.75

No. 968 is a continuous design.
No. 968a overprinted in gold in sheet margin with "Amizade Luso-Chinesa / Transferencia da Soberania de / MACAU 1999 / Sichuan Chengdu," dates and Chinese text.

Characters from Novel, "Dream of the Red Mansion," by Cao Xuequin — A184

1999, Mar. 1   Litho.   Perf. 12
969	A184	2p Bao Yu (6-1)	.60	.45
970	A184	2p Dayiu (6-2)	.60	.45
971	A184	2p Bao Chai (6-3)	.60	.45
972	A184	2p Xi Feng (6-4)	.60	.45
973	A184	2p San Jie (6-5)	.60	.45
974	A184	2p Qing Wen (6-6)	.60	.45
a.		Block of 6, #969-974	3.60	3.60

Souvenir Sheet
975	A184	8p Bao Yu & Dayiu	2.25	2.25
a.		Ovptd. in sheet margin	2.25	2.25

No. 975a overprinted in gold in sheet margin with "Amizade Luso-Chinesa / Transferencia da Soberania de / MACAU 1999 / Sichuan Chengdu," dates and Chinese text.

Maritime Heritage A185

1999, Mar. 19   Litho.   Perf. 12
976	A185	1.50p Sailing ships	.45	.30
977	A185	2.50p Marine life	.70	.60
a.		Pair, #976-977	1.25	1.25

Souvenir Sheet
978	A185	6p Whale, vert.	2.00	2.00
a.		Ovptd. in sheet margin	2.50	2.50

Australia '99, World Stamp Expo.
No. 978a overprinted in gold in sheet margin with "Amizade Luso-Chinesa / Transferencia da Soberania de / MACAU 1999 / Sichuan Chengdu," dates and Chinese text.

First Portugal-Macao Flight, 75th Anniv. — A186

Airplanes: No. 979, Breguet 16 Bn2, "Patria." No. 980, DH9.

1999, Apr. 19   Litho.   Perf. 12
979	A186	3p multicolored	1.10	1.10
980	A186	3p multicolored	1.10	1.10
a.		Souvenir sheet, #979-980	2.50	2.50
b.		As "a," ovptd. in sheet margin	3.00	3.00

See Portugal Nos. 2289-2290.
No. 980a is a continuous design.
No. 980b overprinted in gold in sheet margin with "Amizade Luso-Chinesa / Transferencia da Soberania de / MACAU 1999 / Sichuan Chengdu," dates and Chinese text.

A187

Traditional Water Carrier: a, 1p, Woman carrying container (4-1). b, 1.50p, Filling container from pump (4-2). c, 2p, Drawing water from well (4-3). d, 2.50p, Filling containers from faucet (4-4).
7p, Woman carrying containers up stairs.

1999, Apr. 28   Perf. 12
Horiz. Strip or Block of 4
981	A187	#a.-d.	2.00	2.00

Souvenir Sheet
982	A187	7p multicolored	2.00	2.00
a.		Ovptd. in sheet margin	2.25	2.25

No. 981 was issued in sheets of 4 strips or blocks, each in a different order.
No. 982a overprinted in gold in sheet margin with "Amizade Luso-Chinesa / Transferencia de Soberania de / MACAU 1999 / China Shanghai," date and Chinese text.

A188

Telecommunications — No. 983: a, 50a, Sea-Me-We cable. b, 1p, Satellite dishes. c, 3.50p, Cellular phones. d, 4p, Television. e, 4.50p, Internet.
8p, Computer mouse.

1999, May 5   Litho.   Perf. 12
983	A188	Strip of 5, #a.-e.	3.50	3.50

Souvenir Sheet
984	A188	8p multi	2.50	2.50
a.		Ovptd. in sheet margin	3.50	3.50

No. 984 has a holographic image. Soaking in water may affect hologram.
No. 984a is overprinted in gold in sheet margin with "Amizade Luso-Chinesa / Transferencia de Soberania de / MACAU 1999 / China Shanghai," date and Chinese text.

Modern Buildings, Construction — A189

1p, Cultural Center. 1.50p, Museum of Macao. 2p, Maritime Museum. 2.50p, Maritime Terminal. 3p, University of Macao. 3.50p, Public Administration Building. 4.50p, World Trade Center. 5p, Coloane Go-kart Track. 8p, Bank of China. 12p, Ultramarine National Bank.

1999, June 2   Litho.   Perf. 12
989	A189	1p multi	.25	.25
990	A189	1.50p multi	.40	.30
991	A189	2p multi	.55	.45
992	A189	2.50p multi	.65	.50
993	A189	3p multi	.75	.55
994	A189	3.50p multi, vert.	.85	.70
995	A189	4.50p multi, vert.	1.10	.90
996	A189	5p multi, vert.	1.25	1.00
997	A189	8p multi, vert.	2.00	1.50
998	A189	12p multi, vert.	2.50	2.00
		Nos. 989-998 (10)	10.30	8.15

TAP SEAC Buildings — A190

No. 999 — Various buildings with enominations in: a, Greenish blue. b, Orange. c, Dull yellow. d, Blue green (blue door).
10p, Orange.

1999, June 24
999	A190	1.50p Strip of 4, #a.-d.	1.60	1.60

Souvenir Sheet
1000	A190	10p multicolored	2.50	2.50
a.		Ovptd. in sheet margin		

No. 1000a overprinted in gold in sheet margin with "Amizade Luso-Chinesa / Transferencia de Soberania de / MACAU 1999 / Guangdong Cantao," date and Chinese text.

Dim Sum — A191

No. 1001 — Table settings with: a, Brown teapot. b, Two food platters. c, Two bamboo steamers. d, Flowered teapot.
9p, Various platters.

1999, Aug. 21
1001	A191	2.50p Strip of 4, #a.-d.	2.50	2.50

Souvenir Sheet
1002	A191	9p multicolored	2.50	2.50
a.		Ovptd. in sheet margin	2.25	2.25

China 1999 World Philatelic Exhibition (No. 1002).
No. 1002a overprinted in gold in sheet margin with "Amizade Luso-Chinesa / Transferencia de Soberania de / MACAU 1999 / Guangdong Cantao," date and Chinese text.

Modern Sculpture A192

Various unidentified sculptures.

1999, Oct. 9   Litho.   Perf. 12
Background Color
1003	A192	1p red violet	.30	.25
1004	A192	1.50p brown, vert.	.45	.25
1005	A192	2.50p gray brn, vert.	.75	.45
1006	A192	3.50p blue grn	1.00	.65
		Nos. 1003-1006 (4)	2.50	1.60

Souvenir Sheet
1007	A192	10p blue gray	2.75	2.75
a.		Ovptd. in sheet margin	2.75	2.75

No. 1007a overprinted in gold in sheet margin with "Amizade Luso-Chinesa / Transferencia da Soberania de / MACAU 1999 / Zhejiang Hangzhou," date and Chinese text.

Meeting of Portuguese and Chinese Cultures — A193

No. 1008: a, 1p, Ships. b, 1.50p, Building. c, 2p, Bridge. d, 3p, Fort.
10p, Fort, diff.

1999, Nov. 19   Litho.   Perf. 12¼
1008	A193	Strip of 4, #a.-d.	2.25	2.25

Souvenir Sheet
1009	A193	10p multi	2.75	2.75
a.		Ovptd. in sheet margin	2.50	2.50

Perforations in corners of stamps on Nos. 1008-1009 are star-shaped.
No. 1009a overprinted in gold in sheet margin with "Amizade Luso-Chinesa / Transferencia da Soberania de / MACAU 1999 / Zhejiang Hangzhou," date and Chinese text.
See Portugal No. 2339.

Retrospective of Macao's Portuguese History — A194

No. 1010: a, 1p, Globe. b, 1.50p, Fort. c, 2p, Chinese, Portuguese people. d, 3.50p, Skyline, Nobre de Carvalho bridge. 9p, Arms.

1999, Dec. 19
1010	A194	Block or strip of 4, #a.-d.	2.75	2.75

Souvenir Sheet
1011	A194	9p multi	2.75	2.75
a.		Ovptd. in sheet margin	2.50	2.50

No. 1011a overprinted in gold in sheet margin with "Amizade Luso-Chinesa / Transferencia de Soberania de / MACAU 1999 / Macau," date and Chinese text.
Perforations in corners of stamps on Nos. 1010-1011 are star-shaped.
See Portugal No. 2340.

Special Administrative Region of People's Republic of China

Establishment of Special Administrative Region — A195

No. 1012: a, 1p, Temple, dragon. b, 1.50p, Friendship Bridge, dragon boats. c, 2p, Cathedral, Santa Claus, Christmas tree. d, 2.50p, Lighthouse, race cars. e, 3p, Building, dragons. f, 3.50p, Building, crowd.
8p, Flower.

1999, Dec. 20   Litho.   Perf. 12
1012	A195	Block of 6, #a.-f.	3.50	3.50

Souvenir Sheet
1013	A195	8p multi	2.75	2.75
a.		Ovptd. in sheet margin	2.75	2.75

No. 1013a overprinted in gold in sheet margin with "Amizade Luso-Chinesa / Transferencia de Soberania de / MACAU 1999 / China

— Macau," dte, "O futuro de Macau será melhor" and Chinese text.

Souvenir Sheet

Millennium — A196

2000, Jan. 1   Litho.   Perf. 12¼
1014 A196 8p multi   2.75 2.75
Perforations in corners of stamp are star-shaped.

New Year 2000 (Year of the Dragon) A197

2000, Jan. 28   Perf. 12¼
1015 A197 5.50p multi   1.60 1.60
Souvenir Sheet
1016 A197 10p multi   2.75 2.75
Perforations in corners of stamps on Nos. 1015-1016 are star-shaped.

Historic Buildings — A198

2000, Mar. 1   Litho.   Perf. 12¼
1017   Strip of 4   2.25 2.25
a.   A198 1p green circles   .25   .25
b.   A198 1.50p pink circles   .40   .40
c.   A198 2p brown circles   .50   .50
d.   A198 3p blue circles   .75   .75
Souvenir Sheet
1018 A198 9p Brown circles   2.50 2.50
Perforations in corners of stamps are star-shaped.

Chinese Calligraphy A199

No. 1019 — Characters: a, Rectangle with bisecting line. b, Rectangle with lines inside. c, 8 horizontal lines, 3 vertical lines. d, 3 spots to left of 6 touching lines.
8p, Characters shown on Nos. 1019a-1019d.

2000, Mar. 23
1019   Block of 4   3.50 3.50
a.-d.   A199 3p any single   .75   .75
Souvenir Sheet
1020 A199 8p multi   2.50 2.50
Bangkok 2000 Stamp Exhibition (No. 1020). Perforations in corners of stamps are star-shaped.

Scenes From "A Journey to the West" — A200

No. 1021: a, 1p, Monkey and tiger. b, 1.50p, Monkey on tree. c, 2p, Monkey and spear carrier. d, 2.50p, Spear carrier and dog. e, 3p, Man in robe. f, 3.50p, Monkey in palm of hand.
9p, Monkey with stick, horiz.

2000, May 5   Litho.   Perf. 12¼
1021   Block of 6, #a-f   3.50 3.50
Souvenir Sheet
1022 A200 9p multi   3.00 3.00
Perforations in corners of stamps are star-shaped.

Board Games A201

Designs: 1p, Chinese chess. 1.50p, Chess. 2p, Go. 2.50p, Parcheesi.

2000, June 8
1023-1026 A201 Set of 4   2.25 2.25
Souvenir Sheet
1027 A201 9p Chinese checkers   2.50 2.50
Perforations in corners of stamps are star-shaped.

Tea Rituals A202

2000, July 7
1028   Horiz. strip of 4   4.00 4.00
a.   A202 2p Square table, 4 people   .50   .40
b.   A202 3p Round table, 5 people   .75   .60
c.   A202 3.50p Round table, 3 people 1.00   .90
d.   A202 4.50p Square table, 3 people 1.25 1.10
Souvenir Sheet
1029 A202 8p Woman pouring tea   2.50 2.50
Perforations in corners are star-shaped. World Stamp Expo 2000, Anaheim (No. 1029).

Tricycle Drivers — A203

No. 1030: a. Driver pointing. b. Driver wearing yellow cap. c. Driver sitting on saddle. d, Driver with feet on saddle. e, Driver with crossed legs. f, Driver repairing tricycle.
8p, Driver standing next to tricycle, vert.

2000, Sept. 1   Granite Paper
1030 A203 2p Block of 6, #a-f   4.00 4.00
Souvenir Sheet
1031 A203 8p multi   2.75 2.75
Perforations in corners of stamps are star-shaped.

Sculpture Type of 1999 Inscribed "Macau, China"
Various unidentified sculptures with background colors of: 1p, Brown. 2p, Green, vert. 3p, Purple, vert. 4p, Purple.
10p, Gray blue.

2000, Oct. 9   Granite Paper
1032-1035 A192 Set of 4   3.00 3.00
Souvenir Sheet
1036 A192 10p multi   3.25 3.25
Perforations in corners of stamps are star-shaped.

Ceramics and Chinaware — A204

No. 1037; a, Style. b, Color. c, Form. d, Function. e, Design. f, Export.

2000, Oct. 31   Granite Paper
1037 A204 2.50p Sheet of 6, #a-f   4.75 4.75
Souvenir Sheet
1038 A204 8p Plate design   2.25 2.25
No. 1038 contains one 38mm diameter stamp. Perforations in corners of No. 1037 are star-shaped.

Jade Ornaments A205

Various ornaments. Colors of country name: 1.50p, Purple. 2p, Green, vert. 2.50p, Red, vert. 3p, Blue.
9p, Red, vert.

2000, Nov. 22   Granite Paper
1039-1042 A205 Set of 4   2.75 2.75
Souvenir Sheet
1043 A205 9p multi   2.75 2.75
Perforations in corners of stamps are star-shaped.

Special Administrative Region, 1st Anniv. — A206

No. 1044: a, 2p, Dancers, flags. b, 3p, Monument, dragon.

2000, Dec. 20   Litho.   Perf. 12¼
Granite Paper (#1044)
1044 A206 Horiz. pair, #a-b   1.75 1.75
Souvenir Sheet
Litho. & Embossed
Perf. 13½x13
1045 A206 18p Flags, monument   5.25 5.25
No. 1045 contains one 60x40mm stamp. Perforations in corners of No. 1044 are star-shaped.

New Year 2001 (Year of the Snake) A207

2001, Jan. 18   Litho.   Perf. 13x13¼
1046 A207 5.50p multi   1.75 1.75
Souvenir Sheet
Granite Paper
1047 A207 10p multi   3.25 3.25

Seng-Yu Proverbs — A208

Designs: No. 1048, Sleeping on a woodpile and tasting gall (4-1). No. 1049, Watching over a stump waiting for a rabbit (4-2). No. 1050, The fox making use of the tiger's fierceness (4-3). No. 1051, Meng Mu moving house three times (4-4).
8p, Man and bell.

2001, Feb. 1   Photo.   Perf. 11¾
Granite Paper
1048 A208 2p multi   .60   .60
a.   Booklet pane of 1, plain paper   3.50
1049 A208 2p multi   .60   .60
a.   Booklet pane of 1, plain paper   3.50
1050 A208 2p multi   .60   .60
a.   Booklet pane of 1, plain paper   3.50
1051 A208 2p multi   .60   .60
a.   Booklet pane of 1, plain paper   3.50
      Booklet, #1048a-1051a   18.00
      Nos. 1048-1051 (4)   2.40 2.40
Souvenir Sheet
1052 A208 8p multi   2.75 2.75
Hong Kong 2001 Stamp Exhibition (No. 1052). Booklet containing Nos. 1048a-1051a sold for 35p.

Traditional Implements A209

Designs: 1p, Abacus. 2p, Plane. 3p, Iron. 4p, Balance scale.
8p, Abacus, plane, iron, balance scale.

2001, Mar. 1   Litho.   Perf. 14½x14
1053-1056 A209 Set of 4   3.00 3.00
Souvenir Sheet
1057 A209 8p multi   2.75 2.75

Religious Beliefs A210

No. 1058: a, Buddha. b, People in prayer. c, Re-enactment of Christ carrying cross. d, People in procession.
8p, Symbols.

2001, Apr. 12   Litho.   Perf. 14½x14
1058   Horiz. strip of 4   2.75 2.75
a.   A210 1p multi   .30   .30
b.   A210 1.50p multi   .50   .45
c   A210 2p multi   .70   .65
d.   A210 2.50p multi   .90   .85
Souvenir Sheet
Photo.
Perf.
1059 A210 8p multi   3.00 3.00
No. 1059 contains one 60mm diameter stamp.

Rescue Workers
A211

No. 1060: a, Fireman. b, Hazardous materials worker. c, Fireman, diff. d, Ambulance crew.
8p, Firemen, diff

2001, May 2   Litho.   Perf. 14½x14
1060   Horiz. strip of 4   4.00 4.00
a. A211 1.50p multi   .55 .45
b. A211 2.50p multi   .85 .80
c. A211 3p multi   .95 .90
d. A211 4p multi   1.30 1.25

Souvenir Sheet
Perf. 14x14½
1061 A211 8p multi   5.00 5.00
No. 1061 contains one 60x40mm stamp.

Internet and E-Commerce — A212

Designs: 1.50p, Keys. 2p, Envelope with "@" symbol. 2.50p, Hand-held computer. 3p, Computer.
6p, Linked computers.

2001, June 30   Litho.   Perf. 14½x14
1062-1065 A212   Set of 4   3.00 3.00
Souvenir Sheet
1066 A212 6p multi   2.50 2.50

Emblem of 2008 Summer Olympics, Beijing — A213

2001, July 14   Photo.   Perf. 13x13¼
1067 A213 1p multi + label   1.00 .60
No. 1067 printed in sheets of 12 stamp + label pairs with one large central label. See People's Republic of China No. 3119, Hong Kong No. 940. No. 1067 with different label is from People's Republic of China No. 3119a.

The Romance of Three Kingdoms — A214

Designs: a, Men praying (4-1). b, Man with spear (4-2). c, Men at outdoors table (4-3). d, Man on horseback (4-4).
7p, Man with sword, horiz.

2001, Aug. 1   Litho.   Perf. 14x14½
1068 A214 3p Block of 4, #a-d   4.00 4.00

Souvenir Sheet
Perf. 14½x14
1069 A214 7p multi   3.00 3.00

2001 Census — A215

Designs: 1p, Buildings, students, child health care. 1.50p, Buildings, street scene. 2.50p, Bridge, people.
6p, Buildings, students, child health care, street scene, bridge, people.

2001, Aug. 23   Litho.   Perf. 14x14½
1070-1072 A215   Set of 3   2.00 2.00
Souvenir Sheet
1073 A215 6p multi   2.00 2.00
No. 1073 contains one 89x39mm stamp.

Stores — A216

No. 1074: a, 1.50p, Municipal market. b, 2.50p, Store with red window frames. c, 3.50p, Store, parked bicycles. d, 4.50p, Store, parked cars.
7p, Store tower and windows.

2001, Sept. 13   Perf. 14½x14
1074 A216 Block of 4, #a-d   3.50 3.50
Souvenir Sheet
Perf. 14x14½
1075 A216 7p multi   2.75 2.75

DNA — A217

Fingerprint and: a, 1p, Guanine. b, 2p, Cytosine. c, 3p, Adenine. d, 4p, Thymine.
8p, Adenine, horiz.

2001, Oct. 9   Photo.   Perf. 14x13½
Granite Paper
1076 A217 Block of 4, #a-d   4.00 4.00
Souvenir Sheet
Perf. 13½x14
1077 A217 8p multi   3.25 3.25
No. 1077 contains one 44x29mm stamp.

Parks and Gardens — A218

No. 1078: a, 1.50p, Comendador Ho Yin Garden. b, 2.50p, Mong Há Hill Municipal Park. c, 3p, City of Flowers Garden. 4.50p, Taipa Grande Nature Park.
8p, Art Garden.

2001, Nov. 30   Litho.   Perf. 13½x14
Granite Paper
1078 A218   Block of 4, #a-d   3.75 3.75
Souvenir Sheet
1079 A218 8p multi   3.00 3.00

I Ching
A219

A219a

No. 1080 — Position of broken bars in trigrams (pa kua): a, No broken bars. b, First and second. c, Second and third. d, Second. e, First and third. f, First. g, Third. h, First, second and third.

2001, Dec. 10   Photo.   Perf. 13
Granite Paper
1080 A219 2p Sheet of 8, #a-h   5.75 5.75
Souvenir Sheet
Perf. 13½x13¼
1081 A219a 8p shown   3.00 3.00
No. 1080 contains eight 39x34mm hexagonal stamps. See Nos. 1111, 1126, 1135, 1203, 1241, 1306, 1360.

New Year 2002 (Year of the Horse) A220

Horse's head: 5.50p, With frame. 10p, With continuous design.

2002, Jan. 28   Litho.   Perf. 14½x14
1082 A220 5.50p multi   2.00 2.00
Souvenir Sheet
1083 A220 10p multi   3.50 3.50

Characters From Novel "Dream of the Red Mansion II," by Cao Xuequin — A221

No. 1084: a, Lao Lao (6/1). b, Jin Chuan (6/2). c, Zi Juan (6/3). d, Xiang Yun (6/4). e, Liu Lang (6/5). f, Miao Yu (6/6).
8d, Woman reading book.

2002, Mar. 1   Perf. 14x14½
1084 A221 2p Block of 6, #a-f   4.25 4.25
Souvenir Sheet
1085 A221 8p multi   3.00 3.00

Tou-tei Festival — A222

No. 1086: a, 1.50p, Opera. b, 2.50p, Dinner in appreciation of the elderly. c, 3.50p, Burning of religious objects. d, 4.50p, Preparing roasted pork.
8p, People watching performance, vert.

2002, Mar. 15   Perf. 14½x14
1086 A222 Block of 4, #a-d   4.25 4.25
Souvenir Sheet
Perf. 14x14½
1087 A222 8p multi   3.00 3.00

Church of St. Paul, 400th Anniv. — A223

Various church statues: 1p, 3.50p.
8p, Statue in niche.

2002, Apr. 12   Perf. 14½x14
1088-1089 A223   Set of 2   1.75 1.75
Souvenir Sheet
Perf. 14x14½
1090 A223 8p multi   3.00 3.00
No. 1090 contains one 30x40mm stamp.

Participation of Chinese Team in 2002 World Cup Soccer Championships — A224

No. 1091: a, 1p, Goalie. b, 1.50p, Two players.

Perf. 12 Syncopated

2002, May 16   **Photo.**
1091 A224   Horiz. pair, #a-b   1.25 1.25

A souvenir sheet containing Nos. 1091a-1091b, People's Republic of China No. 3198 and Hong Kong Nos. 978a-978b exists.

Environmental Protection — A225

Designs: 1p, Conservation of maritime resources. 1.50p, Reforestation. 2p, Recycling. 2.50p, Protection of swamps. 3p, Reuse of resources. 3.50p, Municipal cleaning. 4p, Air purification. 4.50p, Health and hygiene. 8p, Quiet and comfort.

2002, June 5   **Litho.**   **Perf. 13x13¼**
1092-1100 A225   Set of 9   9.00 7.00

Zhong Guanying (1842-1921), Reformer and Author — A226

Zheng and: a, 1p, Another man. b, 2p, Harbor scene. c, 3p, Men at table. d, 3.50p, Chinese text.
6p, Zheng seated at table.

2002, July 24   **Perf. 14**
1101 A226   Strip or block of 4,
           #a-d   3.75 3.75
Souvenir Sheet
1102 A226   6p multi   2.50 2.50

No. 1102 contains one 40x60mm stamp.

Honesty and Equality A227

Various buildings: 1p, 3.50p.

2002, Sept. 13   **Litho.**   **Perf. 14½x14**
1103-1104 A227   Set of 2   1.50 1.50

Macao Snack Food — A228

No. 1105: a, 1p, Bolinhas de peixe (fish balls). b, 1.50p, Carne de vitela seca (dried veal). c, 2p, Bolo (cake). d, 2.50p, Sat Kei Ma.
7p, Pastry.

2002, Sept. 26   **Litho.**   **Perf. 13¼x13**
1105 A228   Block of 4, #a-d   2.00 2.00
Souvenir Sheet
1106 A228   7p multi   2.00 2.00

Portions of Nos. 1105-1106 were applied by a thermographic process, producing a raised, shiny effect. No. 1106 contains one 50x50mm diamond-shaped stamp.

Filial Love — A229

No. 1107: a, 1p, Farmer and elephant (O amor filial comove a Deus). b, 1.50p, Man and woman (Abanar a almofada e aquecer a manta). c, 2p, Man and bamboo plants (Chorar sobre o bambu fez crescer rebentos). d, 2.50p, Man and fish (Pescar para a mae deitado no gelo).
No. 1107E: f, Man with arms extended (Mal agasalhado mas tolerante com a madrasta). g, Man and woman (Saltaram carpas da nascente). h, Man with hat (Quem tem amor filial é também fiel). i, Man (Lealdade de pai, amor filial do filho).
7p, Man wearing deer's head (Dar leite de veado aos pais).

2002, Oct. 9   **Litho.**   **Perf. 14**
1107 A229   Block of 4, #a-d   2.75 2.75
1107E   Souvenir booklet   8.00
   f.-i. A229 4.50p Any booklet pane of
     1   1.60 1.60
Souvenir Sheet
Perf. 13½x13
1108 A229   7p multi   2.50 2.50

Particle Physics — A230

No. 1109: a, Unified electroweak interaction theory developed by Steven Weinberg, Sheldon Lee Glashow and Abdus Salam. b, Discovery of W and Z subatomic particles by Carlo Rubbia, 1983. c, Higgs diagram, developed by Richard Feynman and Peter Higgs. d, CERN large electron positron collider, 1989. e, Classification of particles and prediction of quarks by Murray Gell-Mann and George Zweig. f, Unification theory of Albert Einstein.
8p, Detection of positive and negative W particles, CERN LEP, 1996.

2002, Nov. 22   **Perf. 14x14½**
1109 A230   1.50p Block of 6, #a-f   3.75 3.75
Souvenir Sheet
1110 A230   8p multi   2.75 2.75

I Ching Type of 2001 and

Peace Dance — A231

No. 1111 — Position of broken bars in trigrams (pa kua): a, Fourth. b, First, second and fourth. c, Second, third and fourth. d, Second and fourth. e, First, third and fourth. f, First and fourth. g, Third and fourth. h, First, second, third and fourth.

2002, Dec. 13   **Perf. 14**
Granite Paper
1111 A219   2p Sheet of 8, #a-h   4.75 4.75
Souvenir Sheet
Perf. 11¼x13½
1112 A231   8p multi   2.75 2.75

No. 1111 contains eight 39x34 hexagonal stamps. Stamps from No. 1111 have Roman numeral II below "I Ching" and "Pa Kua."

New Year 2003 (Year of the Ram) A232

2003, Jan. 2   **Perf. 14½x14**
1113   A232 5.50p multi   1.75 1.75
Souvenir Sheet
1113A A232   10p multi   3.00 3.00

Legend of Liang Shanbo and Zhu Yingtai A233

No. 1114: a, People seated and reading. b, People on bridge. c, People, tea pot and cups. d, Man holding red paper.
9p, People with butterfly wings.

2003, Feb. 15   **Litho.**   **Perf. 13x13½**
1114   Horiz. strip of 4   4.25 4.25
   a.-d. A233 3.50p Any single   .90 .90
Souvenir Sheet
1115 A233   9p multi   3.25 3.25

No. 1115 contains one 40x60mm stamp.

The Outlaws of the Marsh — A234

No. 1116: a, Song Jiang. b, Lin Chong. c, Wu Song. d, Lu Zhishen. e, Wu Yong. f, Hua Rong.
8p, Heróis do Monte Liang Shan.

2003, Mar. 1   **Perf. 13½x14**
Granite Paper (#1116)
1116 A234   2p Block of 6, #a-f   4.00 4.00
Souvenir Sheet
Perf. 14x14½
1117 A234   8p multi   2.75 2.75

Basic Law of Macao, 10th Anniv. A235

Designs: 1p, Building, doves, cover of book of laws. 4.50p, Children, dove, flags of Macao and People's Republic of China, law book

2003, Mar. 31   **Perf. 14**
1118-1119 A235   Set of 2   1.75 1.75

Traditional Chinese Medicine — A236

No. 1120 — Various medicines: a, 1.50p. b, 2p. c, 3p. d, 3.50p.
8p, Man holding bowl of medicine, horiz.

2003, May 28
1120 A236   Block of 4, #a-d   2.75 2.75
Souvenir Sheet
1121 A236   8p multi   2.25 2.25

Historic Buildings on Taipa and Coloane Islands — A237

Various buildings.

2003, June 18

1122	Horiz. strip of 4	2.50	2.50
a.	A237 1p multi	.25	.25
b.	A237 1.50p multi	.40	.40
c.	A237 2p multi	.50	.50
d.	A237 3.50p multi	.85	.85

Souvenir Sheet

1123	A237 9p multi	2.50	2.50

Everyday Life in the Past — A238

No. 1124: a, Calligrapher at table. b, Puppet maker. c, Man with food cart. d, Washerwoman. e, Woman with decorative lanterns. f, Man carrying food tray above head, man with baskets. g, Photographer. h, Man in chicken costume playing horn.
8p, Barber.

2003, July 30   **Perf. 13½x13**

1124	Block of 8	3.75	3.75
a.-h.	A238 1.50p Any single	.40	.40

Souvenir Sheet
Perf. 14x14½

1125	A238 8p multi	2.50	2.50

I Ching Type of 2001 and

Woman and Child — A239

No. 1126 — Position of broken bars in trigrams (pa kua): a, Second. b, Second, fifth and sixth. c, Second, fourth and fifth. d, Second and fifth. e, Second, fourth and sixth. f, Second and sixth. g, Second and fourth. h, Second, fourth, fifth and sixth.

2003, Sept. 10   **Perf. 14**
Granite Paper

1126	A219 2p Sheet of 8, #a-h	4.50	4.50

Souvenir Sheet
Perf. 14x13½

1127	A239 8p multi	2.50	2.50

No. 1126 contains eight 39x34mm hexagonal stamps. Stamps from No. 1126 have Roman numeral III below text "Pa Kua" and "I Ching."

Launch of First Manned Chinese Spacecraft A240

No. 1128: a, 1p, Astronaut. b, 1.50p, Ship, Shenzhou spacecraft.

2003, Oct. 16   **Perf. 13x13½**

1128	A240 Pair, #a-b	1.25	1.25

A booklet containing No. 1128, People's Republic of China No. 3314 and Hong Kong No. 1062 exists. The booklet sold for a premium over face value. Value $30.

50th Grand Prix of Macao — A241

No. 1129: a, 1p, Race car #5. b, 1.50p, Yellow race car #11. c, 2p, Red race car #11. d, 3p, Motorcycle #5. e, 3.50p, Race car #15. f, 4.50p, Race car #3.
12p, Race car and motorcycle.

Litho. & Embossed

2003, Oct. 29   **Perf. 14**

1129	A241	Sheet of 6, #a-f	5.00	5.00

Souvenir Sheet
Litho. With Hologram Applied
Perf.

1130	A241 12p multi	5.00	5.00

No. 1129 contains six 36x27mm stamps that have varnish applied to raised portions.

Macao Museum of Art — A242

No. 1131 — Artwork depicting: a, 1p, Man in hooded cloak. b, 1.50p, Hill overlooking harbor. c, 2p, Ruins of St. Paul's Church. d, 2.50p, Two men.
7p, Waterfront buildings, boats in harbor.

2003, Dec. 1   **Litho.**   **Perf. 14½x14**

1131	A242	Block of 4 #a-d	2.25	2.25

Souvenir Sheet

1132	A242 7p multi	2.25	2.25

No. 1132 contains one 57x55mm stamp.

New Year 2004 (Year of the Monkey) A243

2004, Jan. 8   **Perf. 14½x14**

1133	A243 5.50p shown	1.75	1.75

Souvenir Sheet

1134	A243 10p Monkey, diff.	3.00	3.00

I Ching Type of 2001 and

Man Chiseling Stone — A244

No. 1135 — Position of broken bars in trigrams (pa kua): a, Second and third. b, Second, third, fifth and sixth. c, Second, third, fourth and fifth. d, Second, third and fifth. e, Second, third, fourth and sixth. f, Second, third and sixth. g, Second, third and fourth. h, Second, third, fourth, fifth and sixth.

2004, Mar. 1   **Perf. 14**
Granite Paper

1135	A219 2p Sheet of 8, #a-h	5.00	5.00

Souvenir Sheet
Perf. 14x13½

1136	A244 8p multi	3.00	3.00

No. 1135 contains eight 39x34mm hexagonal stamps. Stamps from No. 1135 have Roman numeral IV below text "Pa Kua" and "I Ching."

Li Sao — A245

No. 1137: a, Orientaçao. b, Cultivo. c, Aconselhamento pela Irma. d, Transmissao de esperança pela fénix. e, Viagens e reflexoes. f, Local da vida eterna.
8p, Li Sao, horiz.

2004, May 28   **Perf. 13½x14**
Granite Paper

1137	A245 1.50p Block of 6, #a-f	2.75	2.75

Souvenir Sheet
Perf. 14x13½

1138	A245 8p multi	3.00	3.00

God of Guan Di — A246

2004, June 30   **Perf. 13½x14**
Granite Paper

1139	Horiz. strip of 4	3.25	3.25
a.	A246 1.50p shown	.35	.30
b.	A246 2.50p God, diff.	.65	.60
c.	A246 3.50p God, diff.	.90	.80
d.	A246 4.50p God, diff.	1.10	1.00

Souvenir Sheet
Perf. 14x13½

1140	A246 9p God, diff.	*4.00*	*4.00*

No. 1140 contains one 40x40mm stamp.

2004 Summer Olympics, Athens — A247

Designs: 1p, Woman runner. 1.50p, Long jump. 2p, Discus. 3.50p, Javelin.

2004, July 30   **Perf. 13¼**
Granite Paper

1141-1144	A247 Set of 4	2.25	2.25

Deng Xiaoping (1904-97), Chinese Leader A248

Designs: 1p, Saluting. 1.50p, Wearing white shirt.
8p, As young man.

2004, Aug. 22   **Litho.**   **Perf. 13x13¼**

1145-1146	A248 Set of 2	.65	.65

Souvenir Sheet
Litho. & Embossed
Perf.

1147	A248 8p multi	2.25	2.25

No. 1147 contains one 40mm diameter stamp.

Intl. Fireworks Display Contest — A249

No. 1148 — Various landmarks and fireworks displays: a, 1p, 1.50p, 2p. d, 4.50p.
9p, Statue and fireworks, vert.

Litho. & Silk Screened
2004, Sept. 2   **Perf. 13¼**
Granite Paper

1148	A249 Block of 4, #a-d	2.50	2.50

Souvenir Sheet
Perf. 13x13¼

1149	A249 9p multi	2.50	2.50

No. 1149 contains one 40x60mm stamp.

People's Republic of China, 55th Anniv. — A250

No. 1150 — Buildings and: a, 1p, Flag of People's Republic of China. b, 1.50p, Flag of Macao. c, 2p, Arms of People's Republic of China. d, 3p, Arms of Macao.
7p, Buildings.

2004, Oct. 1   **Litho.**   **Perf. 13x13¼**
Granite Paper

1150	A250 Block of 4, #a-d	2.00	2.00

Souvenir Sheet
Perf. 13¼x13

1151	A250 7p multi	2.50	2.50

No. 1151 contains one 60x40mm stamp.

Cosmology — A251

No. 1152: a, 1p, Expansion and acceleration of the Universe. b, 1.50p, Cosmic radiation. c, 2p, Fluctuations of galaxies. d, 3.50p, What is the Universe?
8p, Big Bang Theory.

2004, Oct. 9   **Perf. 12¼**

1152	A251 Block of 4, #a-d	2.50	2.50

Souvenir Sheet

1153	A251 8p multi	2.50	2.50

Macao Garrison of the People's Liberation Army — A252

No. 1154 — Flag and, in foreground: a, 1p, Soldier holding sword. b, 1p, Soldier in tank. c, 1.50p, Soldiers in car. d, 1.50p, Soldiers giving blood. e, 3.50p, Soldier at attention holding gun. f, 3.50p, Soldier with helmet and rifle with bayonet.
8p, Soldiers in car, vert.

2004, Dec. 1 *Perf. 13x13¼*
1154 A252 Block of 6, #a-f   3.00 3.00
Souvenir Sheet
1155 A252 8p multi   2.25 2.25
No. 1155 contains one 40x60mm stamp.

Establishment of Special Administrative District, 5th Anniv. — A253

Lotus flowers and various buildings.

2004, Dec. 20 Litho. *Perf. 14½x14*
1156   Horiz. strip of 4   2.50 2.50
  a. A253 1.50p multi   .45 .30
  b. A253 2p multi   .55 .40
  c. A253 2.50p multi   .65 .50
  d. A253 3p multi   .80 .65
Souvenir Sheet
Litho. & Embossed
1157 A253 10p multi   3.25 3.25

Souvenir Sheet

Air Macau, 10th Anniv. — A254

2004, Dec. 28 Litho. *Perf. 14*
1158 A254 8p multi   2.25 2.25

New Year 2005 (Year of the Rooster) A255

2005, Jan. 13 Litho. *Perf. 14½x14*
1159 A255 5.50p shown   1.60 1.60
Souvenir Sheet
1160 A255 10p Rooster, diff.   2.75 2.75

Everyday Life in the Past — A256

No. 1161: a, Cook (8/1). b, Man holding pole with hanging bottles (8/2). c, Man at work at small table (8/3). d, Textile worker (8/4). e,

Man cutting coconuts (8/5). f, Cook at cart (8/6). g, Cook under lantern (8/7). h, Seamstress (8/8).
8p, Mailman on bicycle.

2005, Mar. 1 *Perf. 12¼*
1161   Block of 8   3.00 3.00
  a.-h. A256 Any single   .35 .35
Souvenir Sheet
1162 A256 8p multi   2.40 2.40

Sai Van Bridge A257

Designs: 1p, Bridge. 3.50p, Bridge and approaches.
8p, Bridge tower, vert.

2005, Mar. 23 *Perf. 14*
1163-1164 A257 Set of 2   1.10 1.10
Souvenir Sheet
1165 A257 8p multi   2.25 2.25

Libraries A258

2005, Apr. 15
1166   Horiz. strip of 4   2.25 2.25
  a. A258 1p Central Library   .25 .25
  b. A258 1.50p Sir Robert Ho Tung Library   .35 .30
  c. A258 2p Coloane Library   .50 .45
  d. A258 3.50p Mong Há Library   .90 .75
Souvenir Sheet
1167 A258 8p Public Commercial Assoc. Library   2.00 2.00
No. 1167 contains one 60x40mm stamp.

Mothers and Offspring — A259

2005, May 8 *Perf. 14½x14*
1168   Horiz. strip of 4 + 4 alternating labels   2.00 2.00
  a. A259 1p Humans + label   .25 .25
  b. A259 1.50p Kangaroos + label   .35 .30
  c. A259 2p Birds and nest + label   .50 .40
  d. A259 3.50p Ducks + label   .90 .80
Labels could be personalized, with sheets containing 5 strips and 20 labels selling for 60p.

The Romance of the Western Chamber — A260

No. 1169 — Inscriptions: a, Espreitando a Beldade à Luz da Lua (6/1). b, Ying Ying Ouvindo Música (6/2). c, O Amor e Ansiedade de Zhang Sheng (6/3). d, A Interrogaçao da Dama (6/4). e, Sonhando com Ying Ying na Pensao (6/5). f, A Uniao dos Amados (6/6).
8p, A Espera da Lua.

2005, June 10 *Perf. 13¼x14*
Granite Paper
1169 A260 2p Block of 6, #a-f   3.25 3.25
Souvenir Sheet
Perf. 14x13¼
1170 A260 8p multi   3.25 3.25

Voyages of Admiral Zheng He, 600th Anniv. A261

No. 1171: a, Admiral Zheng He. b, Giraffe. c, Ship and map.
8p, Ships.

2005, June 28 Litho. *Perf. 13x13½*
1171   Horiz. strip of 3   3.25 3.25
  a. A261 1p multi   .70 .50
  b.-c. A261 1.50p Either single   .95 .75
Souvenir Sheet
Perf. 13¼
1172 A261 8p multi   3.25 3.25
No. 1172 contains one 50x30mm stamp.

UNESCO World Heritage Sites — A262

Various buildings in Historical Center of Macao World Heritage Site with background colors of: a, 1p, White. b, 1.50p, Red. c, 2p, Orange. d, 3.50p, Dark green.
8p, Green.

2005, July 16 *Perf. 14*
1173 A262 Block of 4, #a-d   2.25 2.25
Souvenir Sheet
1174 A262 8p multi   2.25 2.25

4th East Asian Games, Macao — A263

No. 1175 — Stylized athletes and: a, 1p, Olympic Swimming Pool of Macao. b, 1.50p, Nautical Center, Praia Grande. c, 2p, Tennis Academy. d, 2.50p, IPM Sports Pavilion. e, 3.50p, Macao Stadium. f, 4.50p, Tap Seac Sports Pavilion.
8p, Sports Arena.

2005, Aug. 30 *Perf. 14x13¼*
Granite Paper
1175 A263 Block of 6, #a-f   3.75 3.75
Souvenir Sheet
Perf.
1176 A263 8p multi   2.25 2.25
No. 1176 contains one 55x38mm oval stamp.

Macao Bank Notes, Cent. — A264

Designs: 1p, 1 pataca note. 1.50p, 5 pataca note. 3p, 10 pataca note. 4.50p, 50 pataca note.
8p, 100 pataca note.

2005, Sept. 2 *Perf. 13½x14*
Granite Paper
1177-1180 A264 Set of 4   2.75 2.75
Souvenir Sheet
1181 A264 8p multi   4.00 4.00

Great Chinese Inventions — A265

No. 1182: a, 1p, Textile loom. b, 1.50p, Paper. c, 2p, Metal smelting. d, 4.50p, Calendar.
8p, Seismograph.

2005, Oct. 9 *Perf. 14x13½*
Granite Paper
1182 A265 Block of 4, #a-d   2.50 2.50
Souvenir Sheet
1183 A265 8p multi   2.25 2.25

Chaos and Fractal Mathematics — A266

No. 1184: a, 1p, Hilbert's Curve. b, 1p, Tree Fractal. c, 1.50p, Sierpinski Triangle. d, 1.50p, Chaos Game. e, 2p, Von Koch Curve. f, 2p, Cantor Set.
8p, Julia Set.

2005, Nov. 16 *Perf. 14*
1184 A266 Block of 6, #a-f   2.50 2.50
Souvenir Sheet
1185 A266 8p multi   2.25 2.25

New Year 2006 (Year of the Dog) A267

2006, Jan. 9 Litho. *Perf. 13x13¼*
1186 A267 5.50p multi   1.60 1.60
Souvenir Sheet
1187 A267 10p multi   2.75 2.75

Lanterns — A268

No. 1188 — Various lanterns: a, (4/1). b, (4/2). c, (4/3). d, (4/4).

2006, Feb. 12   **Perf. 13¼x13**
1188	Horiz. strip of 4	1.60	1.60
a.-b.	A268 1p Either single	.30	.25
c.-d.	A268 1.50p Either single	.40	.30

Souvenir Sheet
Perf. 13x13¼
1189	A268 8p multi	2.25	2.25

Everyday Life in the Past — A269

No. 1190: a, Cook (8/1). b, Food vendor (8/2). c, Man holding scissors (8/3). d, Man with small round table (8/4). e, Cobbler (8/5). f, Man with pots (8/6). g, Man hammering pails (8/7). h, Man carrying goods suspended from stick (8/8).

8p, Man looking at kettle.

2006, Mar. 1   **Perf. 14**
1190	Block of 8	3.25	3.25
a.-h.	A269 1.50p Any single	.35	.35

Souvenir Sheet
1191	A269 8p multi	2.25	2.25

Items from Communications Museum — A270

No. 1192: a, Rubber stamp (8/1). b, Scale (8/2). c, Mail box (8/3). d, Mail sorting boxes (8/4). e, Telephone (8/5). f, Telephone switching equipment (8/6). g, Radio (8/7). h, Submarine cable (8/8).

10p, Macao #1, horiz.

2006, May 18   **Perf. 13¼x14**
Granite Paper
1192	Block of 8	3.25	3.25
a.-h.	A270 1.50p Any single	.35	.35

Souvenir Sheet
1193	A270 10p multi	2.50	2.50

2006 World Cup Soccer Championships, Germany — A271

Various soccer players.

Litho. & Embossed
2006, June 9   **Perf. 13¼**
1194	A271 Block of 4	3.00	3.00
a.	1.50p multi	.35	.35
b.	2.50p multi	.65	.65
c.	3.50p multi	.90	.90
d.	4p multi	1.00	1.00

Fans — A272

No. 1195 — Various pictures on fans: a, (5/1). b, (5/2). c, (5/3). d, (5/4). e, (5/5).

10p, Three children.

2006, June 28   Litho.   Perf. 14x13¼
Granite Paper
1195	Vert. strip of 5	3.00	3.00
a.-b.	A272 1.50p Either single	.35	.35
c.-d.	A272 2.50p Either single	.65	.65
e.	A272 3.50p multi	.90	.90

Souvenir Sheet
1196	A272 10p multi	2.50	2.50

No. 1196 contains one 40x30mm stamp.

21st China Adolescents Invention Contest — A273

No. 1197: a, 1.50p, Models of molecules, laboratory equipment (4/1). b, 2p, Dish antenna, Earth, windmills (4/2). c, 2.50p, Gear, compass, pyramid and diagrams (4/3). d, 3.50p, Invention, computer keyboard and mouse (4/4).

10p, Atomic model, contest venue, vert.

2006, July 28   **Perf. 14**
1197	A273 Block of 4, #a-d	2.40	2.40

Souvenir Sheet
1198	A273 10p multi	2.50	2.50

No. 1198 contains one 40x60mm stamp.

Street Scenes — A274

No. 1199: a, Rua de S. Domingos (4/1). b, Rua de Camilo Pessanha (4/2). c, Calcada de S. Francisco Xavier (4/3). d, Travessa da Paixao (4/4).

10p, Largo de Santo Agostinho.

2006, Sept. 13   **Perf. 13½x14**
Granite Paper
1199	Block of 4	2.25	2.25
a.-b.	A274 1.50p Either single	.35	.35
c.	A274 2.50p multi	.65	.65
d.	A274 3.50p multi	.90	.90

Souvenir Sheet
Perf. 14x13½
1200	A274 10p multi	2.50	2.50

University of Macao, 25th Anniv. A275

No. 1201 — Inscriptions for Faculty of: a, Social Sciences and Humanities (5/1). b, Law (5/2). c, Science and Education (5/3). d, Science and Technology (5/4). e, Business Management (5/5).

10p, University emblem.

2006, Sept. 28   **Perf. 13x13½**
1201	Horiz. strip of 5	2.50	2.50
a.-e.	A275 1.50p Any single	.40	.35

Souvenir Sheet
1202	A275 10p multi	2.50	2.50

I Ching Type of 2001 and

Two Women — A276

No. 1203 — Position of broken bars in trigrams (pa kua): a, Sixth. b, First, second and sixth. c, Second, third and sixth. d, Second and sixth. e, First, third and sixth. f, First and sixth. g, Third and sixth. h, First, second, third and sixth.

2006, Oct. 9   **Perf. 13**
1203	A219 2p Sheet of 8, #a-h	4.25	4.25

Souvenir Sheet
1204	A276 10p shown	2.50	2.50

No. 1204 contains eight 39x34mm hexagonal stamps. Stamps from No. 1135 have Roman numeral "V" below text "Pa Kua" and "I Ching."

Jesuits — A277

Designs: No. 1205, 1.50p, Matteo Ricci (1552-1610), missionary, and red Chinese chop. No. 1206, 1.50p, St. Francis Xavier (1506-52), missionary, and cross. No. 1207, 3.50p, Allesandro Valignano (1539-1606), missionary, and capital. No. 1208, 3.50p, Melchior Carneiro (c. 1516-83), in red bishop's stole.

10p, St. Ignatius Loyola (1491-1556), founder of Society of Jesus.

2006, Nov. 30   Litho.   Perf. 13½x14
1205-1208	A277 Set of 4	2.75	2.75

Souvenir Sheet
Perf. 14x13½
1209	A277 10p multi	2.50	2.50

New Year 2007 (Year of the Pig) A278

2007, Jan. 8   Litho.   Perf. 13x13¼
1210	A278 5.50p multi	1.50	1.50

Souvenir Sheet
1211	A278 10p multi	5.00	5.00

Shek Wan Ceramics — A279

No. 1212: a, 1.50p, Lao Zi (4/1). b, 1.50p, Lu Yu (4/2). c, 1.50p, Philosopher (4/3). d, 2.50p, Luo Han Seated (4/4).

8p, Concubine After Bath.

2007, Feb. 3
1212	A279 Block of 4, #a-d	2.00	2.00

Souvenir Sheet
1213	A279 8p multi	2.25	2.25

Everyday Life in the Past — A280

No. 1214: a, Man carrying tray on head (8/1). b, Man pouring tea into bowls (8/2). c, Rickshaw (8/3). d, People around table looking into bowl (8/4). e, Seamstress (8/5). f, Shoemaker (8/6). g, Ceramics artists (8/7). h, Embroiderer at booth (8/8).

10p, Festival dragon.

2007, Mar. 1   **Perf. 14**
1214	Block of 8	3.00	3.00
a.-h.	A280 1.50p Any single	.35	.35

Souvenir Sheet
1215	A280 10p multi	2.50	2.50

Traditional Chinese Shops — A281

No. 1216: a, 1.50p, Seamstress's shop (4/1). b, 1.50p, Acupuncturist and herbalist (4/2). c, 2.50p, Print shop (4/3). d, 3.50p, Restaurant (4/4).

10p, Street scene with man carting sign from shop.

2007, May 8   **Perf. 14½x14**
1216	A281 Block of 4, #a-d	2.40	2.40

Souvenir Sheet
1217	A281 10p multi	2.50	2.50

Seng Yu Proverbs — A282

Designs: Nos. 1218, 1223a, 1.50p, The Foolish Old Man Moved a Mountain (pink frame, 4/1). Nos. 1219, 1223b, 1.50p, The Friendship Between Guan and Bao (blue green frame, 4/2). Nos. 1220, 1223c, 3.50p, Calling Black White (lilac frame, 4/3). Nos. 1221, 1223d, 3.50p, The Quarrel Between Snipe and Clam (orange frame, 4/4).

10p, Horses and riders before riderless horse pulling cart, horiz.

2007, June 1   **Perf. 14**
1218-1221	A282 Set of 4	13.00	13.00

Souvenir Sheet
1222	A282 10p multi	13.00	13.00

Self-Adhesive
Booklet Stamps
Serpentine Die Cut 14
1223	Booklet pane, #1223a-1223d	16.00	16.00
	Complete booklet, 2 #1223	32.00	

No. 1222 contains one 60x40mm stamp.

A Journey to the West — A283

No. 1224: a, 1.50p, King and entourage, sprite with stick on cloud (6/1). b, 1.50p, Sprite on cloud, woman dreaming of horned spirit (6/2). c, 2p, Man with foot pierced by spear tip, woman, sprite without stick on cloud (6/3). d, 2p, Sprite on cloud battling other sprites (6/4). e, 2.50p, Sprite with stick, sprite with rake, sprite with swords (6/5). f, 2.50p, Sprite with rake on cloud, spirit with eight hands, spider (6/6).
10p, Sprite and sun.

2007, June 18   *Perf. 14*
1224 A283   Block of 6, #a-f   3.25   3.25
Souvenir Sheet
1225 A283   10p multi   2.50   2.50

Scouting, Cent. A284

Lord Robert Baden-Powell, Macao Scouting emblem, flag ceremony and: 1.50p, Scout with semaphore flags. 2p, Scouts saluting. 2.50p, Scouts setting up campfire. No. 1229, 3.50p, Scouts lashing sticks together. No. 1230, 3.50p, Scout giving directions to other Scout.
10p, Flag, cannon and buildings, vert.

2007, July 9   *Perf. 13x13¼*
1226-1230 A284   Set of 5   3.25   3.25
Souvenir Sheet
Perf. 13¼x13
1231 A284   10p multi   2.50   2.50

Arrival of Robert Morrison (1782-1834), First Protestant Missionary in China, Bicent. — A285

Morrison and: 1.50p, Lilac panel. 3.50p, Yellow panel.

2007, Sept. 28 Litho.   *Perf. 13x13¼*
1232-1233 A285   Set of 2   1.40   1.40
Souvenir Sheet

Mount Kangrinboqe, Tibet — A286

2007, Oct. 9   *Perf. 14*
1234 A286   10p multi   2.50   2.50

Applications of the Golden Ratio — A287

No. 1235: a, 1.50p, Fibonacci sequence. b, 2p, Sunflower spirals. c, 2.50p, Penrose tiling. d, 3.50p, Nautilus shell.
10p, Phi and equation.

2007, Oct. 26   *Perf. 13¼x13*
1235 A287   Block of 4, #a-d   2.50   2.50
Souvenir Sheet
1236 A287   10p multi   2.50   2.50

Chinese Philosophers — A288

No. 1007 Chinese character and: a, 1.50p, Lao Tzu (Lao Zi). b, 2.50p, Chuang Tzu (Zhuang Zi). c, 3.50p, Confucius (Confúcio). d, 4p, Meng Tzu (Mêncio).
10p, Lao Tzu, Chuang Tzu, Confucius, Meng Tzu.

Litho. & Embossed
2007, Nov. 30   *Perf. 13x13¼*
1237 A288   Block of 4, #a-d   3.00   3.00
Souvenir Sheet
Perf.
1238 A288   10p multi   2.50   2.50
No. 1238 contains one 42mm diameter stamp.

New Year 2008 (Year of the Rat) — A289

No. 1239: a, Metal sculpture of rat. b, Wood carving of rat. c, Watercolor painting of rat. d, Fireworks and laser light image of rat. e, Clay teapot depicting rat.
10p, Clay teapot depicting rat and 2008 Beijing Summer Olympics emblem.

Litho., Litho. & Embossed with Foil and Hologram Application (#1239e, 1240)
2008, Jan. 23   *Perf. 14¼*
1239   Horiz. strip of 5   2.75   2.75
  a.-d.   A289 1.50p Any single   .35   .35
  e.   A289 5p multi   1.25   1.25
Souvenir Sheet
1240 A289   10p multi   2.50   2.50
No. 1240 contains one 50x50mm diamond-shaped stamp.

Man Steering Raft — A290

No. 1241 — Position of broken bars in trigrams (pa kua): a, Fourth and sixth. b, First, second, fourth and sixth. c, Second, third, fourth and sixth. d, Second, fourth and sixth. e, First, third, fourth and sixth. f, First, fourth and sixth. g, Third, fourth and sixth. h, First, second, third, fourth and sixth.

2008, Mar. 1 Litho.   *Perf. 14*
Granite Paper
1241 A219   2p Sheet of 8, #a-h   4.00   4.00
Souvenir Sheet
1242 A290   10p multi   2.50   2.50
No. 1241 contains eight 39x34mm hexagonal stamps. Stamps from No. 1241 have Roman numeral "VI" below text "Pa Kua" and "I Ching."

Olympic Torch Relay A291

Designs: 1.50p, Man holding Olympic torch, Parthenon. 3.50p, Mascot holding Olympic torch, lotus flower.
10p, Olympic torch, doves, vert.

2008, May 3   *Perf. 13x13¼*
1243-1244 A291   Set of 2   1.25   1.25
Souvenir Sheet
Perf. 13
1245 A291   10p multi   2.50   2.50
No. 1245 contains one 40x70mm stamp.

Western Legends — A292

No. 1246: a, The Golden Apple. b, The Gordian Knot. c, The Trojan Horse. d, The Riddle of the Sphinx.
10p, Cupid and Psyche, horiz.

2008, June 2   *Perf. 13¼x14*
Granite Paper
1246   Horiz. strip of 4   3.00   3.00
  a.   A292 1.50p multi   .35   .35
  b.   A292 2.50p multi   .65   .65
  c.   A292 3.50p multi   .90   .90
  d.   A292 5p multi   1.00   1.00
Souvenir Sheet
Perf. 14x13¼
1247 A292   10p multi   2.50   2.50

Native Cuisine of Macao and Singapore A293

No. 1248: a, Panqueca Indiana. b, Arroz de Frango à Hainan. c, Carne de Porco à Alentejana. d, Lombo de Bacalhau Braseado em Lascas. e, Laksa. f, Saté. g, Arroz Frito à Yangzhou. h, Frango Frito.
No. 1249, vert.: a, Arroz no Tacho de Porcelana. b, Caranguejo con Piri-piri.

2008, July 4   *Perf. 13¼x14*
Granite Paper
1248   Block of 8   5.00   5.00
  a.-d.   A293 1.50p Any single   .35   .35
  e.-h.   A293 3.50p Any single   .90   .90
Souvenir Sheet
1249   Sheet of 2   2.50   2.50
  a.-b.   A293 5p Either single   1.25   1.25
See Singapore Nos. 1318-1320.

Historic Center of Macau UNESCO World Heritage Site A294

Designs: 1.50p, Fortaleza do Monte. 2p, Largo do Lilau. 2.50p, Lou Kau House. 3p, Largo do Senado. 3.50p, Sam Kai Vui Kun. 4p, Igreja da Sé. 4.50p, Quartel dos Mouros. 5p, St. Anthony's Church.

2008, July 31 Litho.   *Perf. 13x13½*
1250 A294   1.50p multi   .35   .35
1251 A294   2p multi   .50   .50
1252 A294   2.50p multi   .65   .65
1253 A294   3p multi   .75   .75
1254 A294   3.50p multi   .90   .90
1255 A294   4p multi   1.10   1.10
1256 A294   4.50p multi   1.25   1.25
1257 A294   5p multi   1.40   1.40
  Nos. 1250-1257 (8)   6.90   6.90

2008 Summer Olympics, Beijing A295

Designs: 5p, National Aquatics Center. 10p, National Stadium.

2008, Aug. 8   *Perf. 13x13½*
1258 A295   5p multi   1.40   1.40
Souvenir Sheet
Perf. 13
1259 A295   10p multi   2.75   2.75
No. 1259 contains one 54x74mm irregular, six-sided stamp.

20th Macao Intl. Fireworks Display Contest — A296

No. 1260 — Fireworks displays over various sections of Macao: a, 1.50p. b, 2.50p. c, 3.50p. d, 5p.

2008, Oct. 1 Litho.   *Perf. 14x13½*
Granite Paper
1260 A296   Sheet of 4, #a-d   3.50   3.50
Souvenir Sheet
1261 A296   10p shown   2.75   2.75

Celebration — A297

No. 1262: a, 1.50p, "Celebration" in many languages. b, 3.50p, UPU emblem.

2008, Oct. 9   *Perf. 14*
1262 A297   Horiz. pair, #a-b   1.25   1.25
The images in the frames of Nos. 1262a-1262b could be personalized for an additional fee. The generic images are shown.

Souvenir Sheet

Lijiang, People's Republic of China — A298

2008, Nov. 7
1263 A298 10p multi   2.75 2.75

Traditional Handicrafts A299

Designs: 1.50p, Ivory carving. 2p, Ceramic painting. 2.50p, Basket weaving. 3.50p, Wood carving.
10p, Beaded embroidery.

2008, Dec. 1   *Perf. 13x13¼*
1264-1267 A299   Set of 4   2.50 2.50
Souvenir Sheet
Perf. 13¼x13
1268 A299 10p multi   2.75 2.75
No. 1268 contains one 60x40mm stamp.

Louis Braille (1809-52), Educator of the Blind — A300

2009, Jan. 4   *Litho.*   *Perf. 13¼*
1269 A300 5p black   1.40 1.40

New Year 2009 (Year of the Buffalo) A301

No. 1270: a, Metal sculpture of buffalo head. b, Wood carving of buffalo head. c, Watercolor drawing of buffalo head. d, Fireworks display of buffalo head. e, Clay teapot with buffalo design.
10p, Clay teapot with buffalo design, diff.

Litho. (1.50p), Litho. & Embossed With Foil Application (5p, 10p)
2009, Jan. 8   *Perf. 14¼*
1270   Horiz. strip of 5   3.00 3.00
   a.-d. A301 1.50p Any single   .35   .35
   e. A301 5p multi   1.25 1.25
Souvenir Sheet
1271 A301 10p multi   2.75 2.75
No. 1271 contains one 50x50mm diamond-shaped stamp.

Opening of Kun Iam Treasury — A302

No. 1272 — Crowd of worshipers and holders of incense sticks with red chop at: a, Top. b, Lower left. c, Lower right. d, Left.
10p, Woman praying, horiz.

2009, Feb. 20   *Litho.*   *Perf. 13¼x13*
1272   Horiz. strip of 4   3.25 3.25
   a. A302 1.50p multi   .40   .40
   b. A302 2.50p multi   .65   .65
   c. A302 3.50p multi   .90   .90
   d. A302 4p multi   1.00 1.00
Souvenir Sheet
Perf. 13x13¼
1273 A302 10p multi   2.75 2.75

Traditional Tools A303

Designs: 1.50p, Sand basin for compacting firecrackers. 2.50p, Whetstone. 3.50p, Stone grain mill. 4p, Cake mold.
10p, All four tools.

2009, Mar. 1   *Perf. 14½x14*
1274-1277 A303   Set of 4   3.00 3.00
Souvenir Sheet
Perf. 14x14½
1278 A303 10p multi   2.75 2.75
No. 1278 contains one 60x40mm stamp.

Souvenir Sheet

Buddha, Longmen Cave — A304

2009, Apr. 8   *Perf. 14*
1279 A304 10p multi   2.75 2.75
China 2009 World Stamp Exhibition, Luoyang.

Labor Day A305

"5," "1" and: 1.50p, Construction workers, Macao Tower. 5p, Haulers, ruins of St. Paul's Church.
10p, Men lifting diamond-shaped "5.1." box.

2009, May 1   *Perf. 13x13¼*
1280-1281 A305   Set of 2   1.75 1.75
Souvenir Sheet
1282 A305 10p multi   2.75 2.75

The Mantis Stalking the Cicada — A306

A Fond Dream on Nanke — A307

Songs of Chu on All Sides — A308

Give the Last Measure of Devotion — A309

Design: 10p, Marking the boat to find the sword, horiz.

2009, June 1   *Litho.*   *Perf. 14*
1283 A306 1.50p multi   .40   .40
1284 A307 1.50p multi   .40   .40
1285 A308 3.50p multi   .90   .90
1286 A309 3.50p multi   .90   .90
   Nos. 1283-1286 (4)   2.60 2.60
Souvenir Sheet
1287 A309 10p multi   2.75 2.75
Booklet Stamps
Self-Adhesive
Serpentine Die Cut 14
1288 A306 1.50p multi   .75   .75
1289 A307 1.50p multi   .75   .75
1290 A308 3.50p multi   1.50 1.50
1291 A309 3.50p multi   1.50 1.50
   a. Booklet pane of 8, 2 each
     #1288-1291   9.50
   Nos. 1288-1291 (4)   2.60 2.60
Seng Yu proverbs. No. 1287 contains one 60x40mm stamp.

People's Republic of China, 60th Anniv. — A310

No. 1292 — Lanterns and: a, 1.50p, Archway. b, 2.50p, Soldier in tank. c, 3.50p, Children exercising. d, 4p, Soldiers and flag of People's Republic of China.
10p, Archway, soldiers and flag of People's Republic of China, horiz.

2009, Oct. 1   *Litho.*   *Perf. 13¼x13*
1292 A310   Block of 4, #a-d   3.00 3.00
Souvenir Sheet
Photo.
Perf. 13
1293 A310 10p multi   2.75 2.75
No. 1293 contains one 60x40mm stamp.

Porcelain Plate Paintings by Sou Farong A311

Designs: 1.50p, Bodhisattva Ksitigarbha. 5p, Bodhisattva Avalokitsavara.

2009, Oct. 9   *Litho.*   *Perf. 13x13¼*
1294-1295 A311   Set of 2   1.75 1.75

Pui Ching Middle School, 120th Anniv. — A312

No. 1296: a, 1.50p, Building and basketball court. b, 2p, Building, diff. c, 2.50d, Buildings. d, 3.50p, Bust and fireplace.
10p, Building and fountain.

2009, Nov. 29   *Litho.*   *Perf. 13½x14*
Granite Paper
1296 A312   Block or strip of
    4, #a-d   2.50 2.50
Souvenir Sheet
1297 A312 10p multi   2.75 2.75

Macao Science Center — A313

No. 1298: a, 1.50p, Aerial view of entire complex. b, 2.50p, Exhibition Center and Planetarium. c, 3.50p, Ground-level view of entire complex. d, 4p, Ground-level view of Exhibition Center and Convention Center.
10p, Top of Exhibition Center.

2009, Dec. 19   *Perf. 13½x14*
Granite Paper
1298 A313   Block or strip of
    4, #a-d   3.00 3.00
Souvenir Sheet
1299 A313 10p multi   2.75 2.75

People's Liberation Army Garrison in Macao, 10th Anniv. A314

No. 1300: a, Soldiers with martial arts stances. b, Two women officers. c, Soldiers with gun. d, Soldiers and children with cannon. e, Soldiers and children planting tree. f, Soldiers repairing tank.
10p, Soldiers on parade, vert.

2009, Dec. 20   *Perf. 13x13¼*
1300   Block of 6   2.40 2.40
a.-f. A314 1.50p Any single   .35 .35
Souvenir Sheet
Perf. 13x13½
1301 A314 10p multi   2.75 2.75
No. 1301 contains one 40x60mm stamp.

Return of Macao to China, 10th Anniv. A315

No. 1302: a, Golden Lotus sculpture, flags of People's Republic of China and Macao. b, Senado Square and Macao Tower. c, Macao waterfront.
10p, Golden Lotus, gate, vert.

Perf. 13¼x13 Syncopated
2009, Dec. 20   Photo.
1302   Horiz. strip of 3   1.25 1.25
a.-c. A315 1.50p Any single   .35 .35
Souvenir Sheet
Perf. 13x13½
1303 A315 10p multi   2.75 2.75
No. 1303 contains one 40x60mm stamp.
See People's Republic of China Nos. 3791-3793.

New Year 2010 (Year of the Tiger) — A316

No. 1304: a, Clay sculpture of tiger and cub. b, Fireworks display of tiger's head. c, Water-color drawing of tiger. d, Wood carving of tiger. e, Metal sculpture of tiger.
10p, Metal sculpture of tiger, diff.

Litho. (1.50p), Litho. & Embossed with Hologram and Foil Application (5p, 10p)
2010, Jan. 2   *Perf. 14¼*
1304   Horiz. strip of 5   3.00 3.00
a.-d. A316 1.50p Any single   .35 .35
e. A316 5p multi   1.25 1.25
Souvenir Sheet
1305 A316 10p multi   2.75 2.75
No. 1305 contains one 50x50mm diamond-shaped stamp.

I Ching Type of 2001 and

Child With Toy — A317

No. 1306 — Position of broken bars in trigrams (pa kua): a, First and second. b, First, second, fifth and sixth. c, First, second, fourth and fifth. d, First, second and fifth. e, First, second, fourth and sixth. f, First, second and sixth. g, First, second and fourth. h, First, second, fourth, fifth and sixth.

2010, Mar. 1   Litho.   *Perf. 13*
Granite Paper
1306 A219 2p Sheet of 8, #a-h   4.00 4.00
Souvenir Sheet
Perf. 13½
1307 A317 10p multi   2.75 2.75
No. 1306 contains eight 39x34 hexagonal stamps. Stamps from No. 1306 have Roman numeral "VII" below text "Pa Kua" and "I Ching."

Intl. Women's Day, Cent. — A318

No. 1308 — Women in various costumes: a, 1.50p. b, 2.50p. c, 3.50p. d, 4p.
10p, Three women, vert.

2010, Mar. 8   *Perf. 13¼x14*
Granite Paper
1308 A318 Block of 4, #a-d   3.00 3.00
Souvenir Sheet
1309 A318 10p multi   2.75 2.75
No. 1309 contains one 40x60mm stamp.

Expo 2010, Shanghai — A319

Designs: 3.50p, Rabbits. 4p, Chinese lanterns.
10p, Rabbit and Chinese lanterns.

2010, May 1   *Perf. 13¼x14*
Granite Paper
1310-1311 A319 Set of 2   2.00 2.00
Souvenir Sheet
1312 A319 10p multi   2.75 2.75

Macau Branch of Bank of China, 60th Anniv. — A320

No. 1313 — Yellow ribbons forming "60," Bank of China emblem and: a, 1.50p, Street lamp, ruins of St. Paul's Church. b, 2.50p, Buildings. c, 3.50p, "10" from banknote, 1000-pataca banknote. d, 4p, Child, stylized people, people shaking hands.
10p, Buildings, lotus flower, Bank of China emblem.

2010, June 21   *Perf. 13¼x14*
Granite Paper
1313 A320 Block of 4, #a-d   3.00 3.00
Souvenir Sheet
1314 A320 10p multi   3.00 3.00
No. 1314 contains one 60x40mm stamp.

Historic Center of Macao UNESCO World Heritage Site — A321

No. 1315 — Buildings near St. Augustine's Square: a, 1.50p, Dom Pedro V Theater. b, 2.50p, Sir Robert Ho Tung Library. c, 3.50p,

St. Augustine's Church. d, 4p, Seminary and Church of St. Joseph.
10p, Building on Square.

2010, July 15   *Perf. 14x13¼*
Granite Paper
1315 A321 Block of 4, #a-d   3.50 3.50
Souvenir Sheet
1316 A321 10p multi   3.00 3.00

Stained-Glass Windows — A322

Stained-glass window from St. Lawrence's Church, Macao: 5.50p, Detail. 10p, Entire window, horiz.

2010, Aug. 30   *Perf. 13¼x13*
Granite Paper
1317 A322 5.50p multi   1.50 1.50
Souvenir Sheet
Perf. 13x13¼
1318 A322 10p multi   3.00 3.00
See Aland Islands Nos. 306-307.

Carvings of Religious Figures — A323

No. 1319: a, 1.50p, Buddha. b, 2.50p, Na Tcha. c, 3.50p, Kun Iam. d, 4p, Tin Hau.
10p, The Eight Immortals, horiz.

2010, Sept. 7   *Perf. 14*
1319 A323 Block or strip of 4, #a-d   3.00 3.00
Souvenir Sheet
1320 A323 10p multi   3.00 3.00
No. 1320 contains one 60x30mm stamp.

Old Telephones — A324

No. 1321 — Various old telephones with background color of: a, 1.50p, Green. b, 2.50p, Pink. c, 3.50p, Yellow. d, 4p, Blue.

10p, Old telephone, horiz.

2010, Sept. 1   Litho.   *Perf. 14*
1321 A324 Block or strip of 4, #a-d   3.00 3.00
Souvenir Sheet
1322 A324 10d multi   2.75 2.75
No. 1322 contains one 60x40mm stamp.

Macao Food Festival, 10th Anniv. — A325

Designs: 1.50p, Wonton soup. 2.50p, Xiao Long Bao (steamed buns). 3.50p, Sushi. 4p, Pastel de nata (egg tart).
10p, Portuguese chicken.

2010, Nov. 5   *Perf. 13¼x13*
1323-1326 A325 Set of 4   3.00 3.00
Souvenir Sheet
1327 A325 10p multi   2.75 2.75

Traditional Clothing — A326

★ No. 1328: a, 1.50p, Man in Tang suit. b, 2.50p, Woman in qipao. c, 3.50p, Woman in blouse and long skirt. d, 4p, Man in tunic suit.
10p, Two women, horiz.

2010, Nov. 30
1328 A326 Block of 4, #a-d   3.00 3.00
Souvenir Sheet
1329 A326 10p multi   2.75 2.75
No. 1329 contains one 60x40mm stamp.

Giant Pandas — A327

Panda, domed building and: 1.50p, Chapel of Our Lady of Penha. 5p, Ruins of St. Paul's Church.
10p, Two pandas, domed building, Ruins of St. Paul's Church.

2010, Dec. 18   *Perf. 13¼x13*
1330-1331 A327 Set of 2   2.00 2.00
Souvenir Sheet
Perf. 13x13¼
1332 A327 10p multi   2.75 2.75
No. 1332 contains one 40x60mm stamp.

New Year
2011 (Year of
the Rabbit)
A328

No. 1333: a, Clay sculpture of rabbit. b, Fireworks and laser light image of rabbit. c, Watercolor painting of rabbit. d, Wood carving rabbit. e, Metal sculpture of rabbit.
10p, Metal sculpture of rabbit, diff.

Litho., Litho. & Embossed with Foil and Hologram Application (5p, 10p)

2011, Jan. 5		**Perf. 13¼x13**	
1333	Horiz. strip of 5	2.75	2.75
a.-d.	A328 1.50p Any single	.35	.35
e.	A328 5p multi	1.25	1.25

Souvenir Sheet
Perf. 14¼

1334	A328 10p multi	2.50	2.50

No. 1334 contains one 50x50mm diamond-shaped stamp.

Souvenir Sheet

Ancient City of Fenghuang — A329

2011, Mar. 1	**Litho.**	**Perf. 13x13¼**	
1335	A329 10p multi	3.00	3.00

Public
Buildings
A330

Designs: 1.50p, Government Headquarters. 2.50p, Monetary Authority. 3.50p, Holy House of Mercy Hospice. 4p, Macao Foundation.

2011, Apr. 19		**Perf. 14**	
1336-1339	A330 Set of 4	3.50	3.50

Cantonese Naamyam — A331

No. 1340 — Musician near: a, 1.50p, Building archway. b, 2.50p, Junk with sails up. c, 3.50p, Wall and awning. d, 4p, Harbor.
10p, Musician near wall.

2011, May 30		**Perf. 13¼x13**	
1340	A331 Block of 4, #a-d	3.00	3.00

Souvenir Sheet

1341	A331 10p multi	2.75	2.75

Legend of the White Snake — A332

No. 1342: a, 1.50p, Lady Bai Suzhen and Xu Xian meeting when traveling the lake (6/1). b, 1.50p, Revelation to Xu Xian that Lady Bai is a snake during Dragon Boat Festival (6/2). c, 2p, Lady Bai steals herb to save husband (6/3). d, 2p, Fight between dragon and white snake (6/4). e, 2.50p, Lady Bai captive in pagoda (6/5). f, 2.50p, Flooding of the Jinshan Temple (6/6).
10p, Lacy Bai with sword, horiz.

2011, July 28		**Perf. 13¼x13**	
1342	A332 Block of 6, #a-f	3.00	3.00

Souvenir Sheet
Perf. 13¼

1343	A332 10p multi	2.75	2.75

No. 1343 contains one 60x30mm stamp.

Worldwide Fund for Nature, 50th
Anniv. — A333

No. 1344 — Birds: a, 1.50p, Pycnonotus sinensis. b, 2.50p, Streptopelia chinensis. c, 3.50p, Ixobrychus sinensis. d, 4.50p, Centropus sinensis.

2011, Sept. 11	**Litho.**	**Perf. 14x13¼**	
Granite Paper			
1344	A333 Block of 4, #a-d	3.50	3.50
e.	Souvenir sheet, #1344a-1344d	3.50	3.50

Famous Men — A334

No. 1345: a, 1.50p, Lin Zexu (1785-1850), scholar. b, 2.50p, Ye Ting (1896-1946), military leader. c, 3.50p, Xian Xinghai (1905-45), composer. d, 4p, Ho Yin, industrialist and philanthropist.
10p, Lin Zexu, Ye Ting, Xian Xinghai and Ho Yin, vert.

2011, Oct. 9	**Litho.**	**Perf. 14**	
1345	A334 Block or strip of 4, #a-d	3.00	3.00

Souvenir Sheet
Litho. With Foil Application

1346	A334 10p multi	2.75	2.75

No. 1346 contains one 40x60mm stamp.

25th Macao Intl. Music
Festival — A335

No. 1347 — Musical note, web and: a, 1.50p, Vertical ovals. b, 2.50p, Parabolas. c, 3.50p, Circles. d, 4p, Lines.
10p, Horizontal oval.

2011, Oct. 9		**Perf. 14x13½**	
Granite Paper			
1347	A335 Block or strip of 4, #a-d	3.00	3.00

Souvenir Sheet

1348	A335 10p multi	2.75	2.75

Chinese Revolution, Cent. — A336

No. 1349 — Flags and: a, 1.50p, Gao Jianfu (1879-1951), painter, Macao office of Chinese Revolutionary League. b, 2.50p, Huang Xing (1874-1916), revolutionary leader, Huanghuagang Mausoleum of 72 Martyrs. c, 3.50p, Xiong Bingkun (1885-1969, revolutionary leader, Uprising Gate. d, 4p, Dr. Sun Yat-sen (1866-1925), President of Republic of China, office of Provisional President.
10p, Flags, China #185.

2011, Oct. 10	**Litho.**	**Perf. 13x13¼**	
1349	A336 Block or strip of 4, #a-d	3.00	3.00

Souvenir Sheet
Photo.
Perf. 13¼x13

1350	A336 10p multi	2.75	2.75

No. 1350 contains one 60x40mm stamp.

Kiang Wu Hospital Charitable
Association, 140th Anniv. — A337

Building and: 1.50p, Plaque. 2.50p, Statue of Dr. Sun Yat-sen. 3.50p, Crushing wheel. 4p, Magnetic resonance imaging machine.
10p, Statue of Dr. Sun Yat-sen, scenes from modern hospital.

2011, Oct. 28	**Litho.**	**Perf. 14x13½**	
Granite Paper			
1351-1354	A337 Set of 4	3.00	3.00

Souvenir Sheet

1355	A337 10p multi	2.75	2.75

No. 1355 contains one 40x40mm stamp.

New Year
2012 (Year of
the Dragon)
A338

No. 1356: a, Metal sculpture of dragon. b, Wood carving of dragon. c, Fireworks display of dragon. d, Clay sculpture of dragon. e, Watercolor painting of dragon.
12p, Watercolor painting of dragon, diff.

Litho., Litho. & Embossed with Foil and Hologram Application (5p)

2012, Jan. 5		**Perf. 14¼**	
1356	Horiz. strip of 5	3.00	3.00
a.-d.	A338 1.50p Any single	.40	.40
e.	A338 5p multi	1.25	1.25

Souvenir Sheet
Litho. & Embossed With Foil Application
Perf. 13¼

1357	A338 12p multi	3.00	3.00

No. 1357 contains one 50x50mm diamond-shaped stamp.

Smoke-Free Macao — A339

Macao skyline and: 1.50p, "2012" with "no smoking" symbol replacing zero. 5p, "No smoking" symbol.

2012, Jan. 31	**Litho.**	**Perf. 14**	
1358-1359	A339 Set of 2	1.75	1.75

I Ching Type of 2001 and

Woman and Child — A340

No. 1360 — Position of broken bars in trigrams (pa kua): a, First, second and third. b, First, second, third, fifth and sixth. c, First, second, third, fourth and fifth. d, First, second, third and fifth. e, First, second, third, fourth and sixth. f, First, second, third and sixth. g, First, second, third and fourth. h, First, second, third, fourth and sixth.

2012, Mar. 1		**Perf. 14**	
Granite Paper			
1360	A219 2p Sheet of 8, #a-h	4.00	4.00

Souvenir Sheet
Perf. 14x13¼

1361	A340 10p multi	2.50	2.50

No. 1360 contains eight 39x34mm hexagonal stamps. Stamps from No. 1360 have Roman numeral "VIII" below text "Pa Kuand "I Ching."

Tai Fung
Bank, 70th
Anniv.
A341

Designs: 1.50p, Man, rectangular emblem with Portuguese and Chinese text. 2.50p, Building, emblem with Chinese characters. 3.50p, Building, round emblem with Portuguese and Chinese text. 4p, Emblem with serpents.
10p, 70th anniversary emblem.

2012, Mar. 28		**Perf. 13x13¼**	
Granite Paper			
1362-1365	A341 Set of 4	3.00	3.00

Souvenir Sheet
Perf. 13¼x13

1366	A341 10p multi	2.75	2.75

No. 1366 contains one 60x40mm stamp.

Historic Views of Fishing Harbor A342

Various views of harbor, boats and structures.

2012, May 18   *Perf. 13x13¼*
Granite Paper

1367		Horiz. strip of 4	3.00	3.00
a.	A342	1.50p multi	.40	.40
b.	A342	2.50p multi	.65	.65
c.	A342	3.50p multi	.90	.90
d.	A342	4p multi	1.00	1.00

Souvenir Sheet
Perf. 13½x13

1368	A342	10p multi	2.75	2.75

No. 1368 contains one 60x40mm stamp.

Hou Kong Middle School, 80th Anniv. — A343

No. 1369: a, 1.50p, Students working on models of Chinese junks, students painting and writing Chinese characters. b, 2.50p, Students participating in sporting events. c, 3.50p, Students participating in performing arts. d, 4p, Teacher and student in classroom, student taking piano lesson, child holding artwork, children at play.
10p, Students parading on track with school emblem and banner, school band, vert.

2012, June 10   *Perf. 13x13¼*
Granite Paper

1369	A843	Block of 4, #a-d	3.00	3.00

Souvenir Sheet
Perf. 13½

1370	A343	10p multi	2.50	2.50

No. 1370 contains one 40x40mm stamp.

Tung Sin Tong Charitable Society, 120th Anniv. — A344

No. 1371: a, 1.50p, Woman playing piano, line of children. b, 2.50p, Students in classroom. c, 3.50p, Health care. d, 4p, People of various ages.
10p, Roof of building, fireworks.

2012, Aug. 8   *Perf. 14x13¼*
Granite Paper

1371	A344	Block of 4, #a-d	3.00	3.00

Souvenir Sheet

1372	A344	10p multi	2.50	2.50

Legend of the Cowherd and the Weaving Maid — A345

No. 1373: a, 1.50p, Cowherd and cow, denomination at LR. b, 1.50p, Cowherd taking clothes of bathing maid, denomination at LL. c, 2p, Children playing with cow, cowherd watching maid weaving, denomination at LR. d, 2p, Maid being abducted, denomination at LL. e, 2.50p, Cowherd and cow on knees at edge of sea, denomination at LR. f, 2.50p, Cowherd tossing water, old man and woman, denomination at LL.
10p, Cowherd, maid, children, birds, vert.

2012, Aug. 23   *Perf. 14x13¼*
Granite Paper

1373	A345	Block of 6, #a-f	3.00	3.00

Souvenir Sheet

1374	A345	10p multi	2.50	2.50

No. 1374 contains one 40x60mm stamp.

Safeguarding of Honesty and Transparency, 20th Anniv. — A346

20th anniversary emblem and: 2p, Buildings and bridge. 5p, Buildings.

2012, Sept. 20   *Perf. 14x13¼*
Granite Paper

1375-1376	A346	Set of 2	1.75	1.75

Paintings of Macao Scenes by Lok Cheong — A347

No. 1377: a, 1.50p, Temple, painting of boat on rock. b, 2.50p, Trees. c, 3.50p, People in park. d, 4p, People walking near large trees.
10p, Macao skyline, vert.

2012, Sept. 21   *Perf. 13x13¼*
Granite Paper

1377	A347	Block of 4, #a-d	3.00	3.00

Souvenir Sheet
Perf. 13½

1378	A347	10p multi	2.50	2.50

No. 1378 contains one 40x40mm stamp.

Henrique de Senna Fernandes (1923-2010), Writer — A348

2012, Oct. 9   *Litho.*   *Perf. 14*

1379	A348	5p multi	1.25	1.25

Scenes From *The Peony Pavilion* — A349

No. 1380: a, 1.50p, Du Liniang falls asleep under tree (6/1). b, 1.50p, Du Liniang drawing (6/2). c, 2p, Lord of the Underworld and Du Liniang (6/3). d, 2p, Du Liniang and Liu Mengmei (6/4). e, 2.50p, Du Liniang and Liu Mengmei under tree (6/5). f, 2.50p, Wedding (6/6).
12p, Du Liniang and Liu Mengmei, diff.

2012, Nov. 30   *Perf. 13¼x13*
Granite Paper

1380	A349	Block of 6, #a-f	3.00	3.00

Souvenir Sheet
Perf. 13¼

1381	A349	12p multi	3.00	3.00

No. 1381 contains one 30x60mm stamp.

New Year 2013 (Year of the Snake) A350

No. 1382: a, Metal sculpture of snake. b, Wood carving of snake. c, Fireworks display of snake. d, Clay sculpture of snake. e, Watercolor painting of snake.
12p, Watercolor painting of snake, diff.

Litho., Litho. & Embossed with Foil and Hologram Application (5p)

2013, Jan. 3   *Perf. 14¼*

1382		Horiz. strip of 5	3.00	3.00
a.-d.	A350	1.50p Any single	.40	.40
e.	A350	5p multi	1.25	1.25

Souvenir Sheet
Litho. & Embossed With Foil Application

1383	A350	12p multi	3.00	3.00

No. 1383 contains one 50x50mm diamond-shaped stamp.

Macao Chamber of Commerce, Cent. — A351

No. 1384 — Chamber of Commerce emblem and: a, 1.50p, Chamber of Commerce leader, building, abacus. b, 2.50p, Chamber of Commerce leader, documents, Chamber of Commerce members clapping. c, 3.50p, Chamber of Commerce leader, leaders shaking hands, Chamber of Commerce seal and embosser. d, 4p, Chamber of Commerce members casting ballots, building.
12p, Building.

2013, Jan. 23   *Litho.*   *Perf. 14x13½*
Granite Paper

1384	A351	Block of 4, #a-d	3.00	3.00

Souvenir Sheet

1385	A351	12p multi	3.00	3.00

No. 1385 contains one 40x40mm stamp.

Souvenir Sheet

Diaolou (Watchtower), Kaiping, People's Republic of China — A352

2013, Mar. 1   *Perf. 14x13¼*
Granite Paper

1386	A352	12p multi	3.00	3.00

Basic Law of Macao, 20th Anniv. A353

Various people with denomination in: 1.50p, Green square. 5p, Red square.

2013, Mar. 31   *Perf. 14*

1387-1388	A353	Set of 2	1.75	1.75

First Macao Fire Brigade, 130th Anniv. — A354

No. 1389: a, 1.50p, Manual pump wagon, c. 1877, Central Fire Station (4/1). b, 2.50p, 1955 Ladder truck, Taipa Fire Station (4/2). c, 3.50p, 2008 Aerial ladder truck, Areia Preta Fire Station (4/3). d, 4p, 2007 High Reach Extendable Turret Stinger, Fire Brigade Headquarters and Sai Van Lake Fire Station (4/4).
12p, 19th cent. horse-drawn steam pump, Fire Brigade Command Building, vert.

2013, Apr. 25   *Perf. 14x13¼*
Granite Paper

1389	A354	Block of 4, #a-d	3.00	3.00

Souvenir Sheet

1390	A354	12p multi	3.00	3.00

No. 1390 contains one 40x60mm stamp.

Items in Macao Museum — A355

No. 1391: a, 1.50p, Nativity scene carved in mother-of-pearl (4/1). b, 2.50p, Painted stone sculpture of Madonna and Child (4/2). c, 3.50p, Elephant-shaped Kraak porcelain vessel (4/3). d, 4p, Bronze bell of St. Paul's Church (4/4).

12p, 16th cent. copperplate engraving of Macao, by Theodore de Bry, horiz.

2013, May 10   **Perf. 13¼x13**
1391 A355   Block of 4, #a-d   3.00   3.00
Souvenir Sheet
1392 A355   12p multi   3.00   3.00
No. 1392 contains one 60x40mm stamp.

Na Tcha, Child God of War — A356

No. 1393 — Various depictions of Na Tcha with background color of: a, 2p, Pale orange (4/1). b, 2.50p, Blue black (4/2). c, 3.50p, Red (4/3). d, 4p, Dull blue (4/4).

12p, Na Tcha, orange background.

2013, June 25   **Perf. 13¼x13**
1393 A356   Block of 4, #a-d   3.00   3.00
Souvenir Sheet
1394 A356   12p multi   3.00   3.00

Scenes From *The Romance of the Three Kingdoms* — A357

No. 1395: a, 2p, Rescue of the young prince (4/1). b, 2.50p, Control of Yi Province (4/2). c, 3.50p, Drowning of the Seven Armies (4/3). d, 4p, Zhuge Liang prays to the stars (4/4).

12p, Unification of the Three Kingdoms under the Jin Dynasty, horiz.

2013, Sept. 13   **Litho.**   **Perf. 13¼x13**
Granite Paper
1395 A357   Block of 4, #a-d   3.00   3.00
Souvenir Sheet
Perf. 13x13¼
1396 A357   12p multi   3.00   3.00

Streets of Macao — A358

No. 1397: a, 2p, Avenida de Almeida Ribiero (4/1). b, 2.50p, Calçada dos Quartéis (4/2). c, 3.50p, Calçada do Teatro (4/3). d, 4p, Beco do Lilau (4/4).

12p, Calçada da Igreja de Sao Lázaro, vert.

2013, Oct. 9   **Litho.**   **Perf. 14x13¼**
Granite Paper
1397 A358   Block of 4, #a-d   3.00   3.00
Souvenir Sheet
Perf. 13¼x14
1398 A358   12p multi   3.00   3.00

Christmas — A359

Designs: 3.50p, Church, statue of angel (2/1). 5p, Church, statue of angel, diff. (2/2).
12p, Statue of Madonna and Child.

2013, Oct. 21   **Litho.**   **Perf. 14x13¼**
Granite Paper
1399-1400 A359   Set of 2   2.25   2.25
Souvenir Sheet
1401 A359   12p multi   3.00   3.00

Chinese Calligraphy and Painting — A360

No. 1402: a, Yu Un, by Leong Chong Hin, Guan Wanli, Situ Qi, Chui Tak Kei and Lin Jin (potted plants, 6/1). b, Literary Meeting in Goi Meng House, by Gu Danming (fan, 6/2). c, Blessings of Autumn, by Huang Yunyu, Guan Wanli, U Kuan Wai, Zhou Paiyun, Zhao Wenfeng, Tam Van Iao, Kam Hang, Chan Chi Vai, Chui Tak Kei and Lin Jin (flowers, 6/3). d, Autumn, by Situ Qi, Chui Tak Kei and Huang Haoming (yellow and blue flowers, 6/4). e, Announcement of Spring, by Chui Tak Kei (bird in blossoming tree, 6/5). f, Heroic Kapok, by Chui Tak Kei (tree with red blossoms, 6/6).

12p, Sparrows and Red Leaves, by Deng Fen, Situ Qi and Lin Jin.

2013, Nov. 1   **Litho.**   **Perf. 13x13¼**
Granite Paper
1402 A360   2p Block of 6, #a-f   3.00   3.00
Souvenir Sheet
1403 A360   12p multi   3.00   3.00

60th Macao Grand Prix — A361

No. 1404 — Race cars or motorcycles (#1404c) from: a, 1954 (6/1). b, 1963 (6/2). c, 1973 (6/3). d, 1983 (6/4). e, 1993 (6/5). f, 2003 (6/6).

12p, 2013 race car, older car.

2013, Nov. 8   **Litho.**   **Perf. 14x13¼**
Granite Paper
1404 A361   2p Block of 6, #a-f   3.00   3.00
Souvenir Sheet
Litho. With Foil Application
Perf.
1405 A361   12p multi   3.00   3.00
No. 1405 contains one 55x38mm oval stamp.

Trade and Cooperation Agreement Between Macao and the European Union, 20th Anniv. — A362

Flags of Macao and the European Union, "20" and various symbols with denomination color of: 1.50p, Green (2/1). 5p, Dark blue (2/2).

2013, Nov. 23   **Litho.**   **Perf. 14**
1406-1407 A362   Set of 2   1.75   1.75

New Year 2014 (Year of the Horse) — A363

No. 1408: a, Metal sculpture of horse (5/1). b, Watercolor painting of horse (5/2). c, Horse in fireworks (5/3). d, Clay figurine of horse (5/4). e, Wood carving of horse (5/5).

12p, Wood carving of horse, diff.

Litho., Litho. & Embossed With Foil Application (5p, 12p)
2014, Jan. 3   **Perf. 13¾**
Granite Paper
1408   Horiz. strip of 5   3.25   3.25
   a.-d.   A363 2p Any single   .50   .50
   e.   A363 5p multi   1.25   1.25
Souvenir Sheet
Perf. 14¼
1409 A363   12p multi   3.00   3.00
No. 1409 contains one 50x50mm diamond-shaped stamp.

Conde de Sao Januário General Hospital, 140th Anniv. A364

Designs: 2p, Old hospital building (4/1). 2.50p, Modern hospital building (4/2). 3.50p, Accreditation emblem, surgeons (4/3). 4p, 140th anniversary emblem, doctors examining patient (4/4).

12p, Old and new hospital buildings, 140th anniversary emblem.

2014, Jan. 6   **Litho.**   **Perf. 13x13¼**
Granite Paper
1410-1413 A364   Set of 4   3.00   3.00
Souvenir Sheet
Perf. 13¼x13
1414 A364   12p multi   3.00   3.00
No. 1414 contains one 60x40mm stamp.

Macao Post, 130th Anniv. — A365

No. 1415: a, 2p, Macao Post Headquarters (4/1). b, 2.50p, Arch of post office (4/2). c, 3.50p, Museum of Communications (4/3). d, 4p, Emblems for postal services (4/4).

12p, Macao Post Headquarters (2/1). 50p, Tower and arches of Macao Post Headquarters (2/2), vert.

2014, Mar. 1   **Litho.**   **Perf. 14x13¼**
Granite Paper
1415 A365   Block or strip of 4, #a-d   3.00   3.00
Souvenir Sheets
Litho. With Foil Application
Perf. 13½x14
1416 A365   12p multi   3.00   3.00
Litho.
Perf. 13½
Silk-Faced Granite Paper
1417 A365   50p multi   12.50   12.50
No. 1416 contains one 40x40mm stamp.
No. 1417 contains one 30x60mm stamp.

Animal Protection — A366

No. 1418: a, 2p, Dog (4/1). b, 2.50p, Cat (4/2). c, 3.50p, Cat, diff. (4/3). d, 4p, Dog, diff. (4/4).

12p, Dog and chain-link fence.

2014, Apr. 28   **Litho.**   **Perf. 14x13¼**
Granite Paper
1418 A366   Block or strip of 4, #a-d   3.00   3.00
Souvenir Sheet
Perf. 13½x14
1419 A366   12p multi   3.00   3.00
No. 1419 contains one 60x40mm stamp.

Characters From *The Outlaws of the Marsh* — A367

No. 1420: a, Shi Jin, with tattooed back (6/1). b, Chai Jin, wearing purple robe (6/2). c, Yang Zhi, unsheathing sword (6/3). d, Chao Gai, holding spear (6/4). e, Ruan Xiaoqi, holding oar (6/5). f, Gongsun Sheng, holding leaf (6/6).
12p, Chao Gai and Chai Jin, horiz.

2014, June 26   Litho.   Perf. 13¼x13
Granite Paper
1420 A367 2p Block of 6, #a-f   3.00 3.00
Souvenir Sheet
Perf. 13x13¼
1421 A367 12p multi   3.00 3.00

New Campus of the University of Macao — A368

No. 1422 — Various buildings with stamps numbered as: a, (4/1). b, (4/2). c, (4/3). d, (4/4), diff.

2014, Sept. 5   Litho.   Perf. 13x13¼
Granite Paper
1422 A368 2p Block or strip of 4, #a-d   2.00 2.00
Souvenir Sheet
1423 A368 12p multi   3.00 3.00

Magic Squares — A369

No. 1424: a, 2p, Magic word square (6/1). b, 3p, Bent diagonal square by Benjamin Franklin (6/2). c, 4p, Melancolia I magic square by Albrecht Dürer (6/3). d, 5p, Xuan Ji Tu Chinese palindromic square by Su Hui (6/4). e, 7p, Panmagic square by Lee Sallows (6/5). f, 9p, Magic square construction method by Simon de la Loubère (6/6).
12p, Magic square of dots on turtle shell, by Luo Shu, horiz.

2014, Oct. 9   Litho.   Perf. 13¼x13
Granite Paper
1424 A369 Sheet of 6, #a-f, + 3 labels   7.50 7.50
Souvenir Sheet
1425 A369 12p multi   3.00 3.00
No. 1425 contains one 60x40mm stamp.

General Post Offices — A370

No. 1426 — General Post Office in: a, Macao. b, Bangkok, Thailand.

2014, Nov. 1   Litho.   Perf. 13x13¼
Granite Paper
1426 A370 5.50p Horiz. pair, #a-b   2.75 2.75
See Thailand No.

Lin Zexu Memorial Museum — A371

No. 1427 — Lin Zexu (1785-1850), Qing Dynasty official: a, Wearing robe depicting crane (4/1). b, With Opium War battle in background (4/2). c, Seated with Portuguese naval officer (4/3). d, Meeting Portuguese naval officer at harbor (4/4).
12p, Lin Zexu, diff.

2014, Nov. 5   Litho.   Perf. 13x13¼
Granite Paper
1427 A371 2p Block of 4, #a-d   2.00 2.00
Souvenir Sheet
Perf. 13¼x13
1428 A371 12p multi   3.00 3.00
No. 1428 contains one 60x40mm stamp.

Paintings of Macao by Kam Cheong Ling (1911-91) — A372

No. 1429 — Paintings depicting: a, 2p, Ships (4/1). b, 2p, Fountain and street scene (4/2). c, 3p, Market stalls near building (4/3). d, 5p, Gate near church (4/4).
12p, People on verandah.

2014, Nov. 12   Litho.   Perf. 13x13¼
Granite Paper
1429 A372 Block of 4, #a-d   3.00 3.00
Souvenir Sheet
Perf. 13½
1430 A372 12p multi   3.00 3.00
No. 1430 contains one 40x40mm stamp.

Macao Special Administrative Region, 15th Anniv. — A373

No. 1431: a, Clothing on mannequins in store, building, gears (4/1). b, Buildings, blue sky (4/2). c, Buildings, orange sky (4/3). d, Building and world map (4/4).
12p, Building with flags.

2014, Dec. 20   Litho.   Perf. 13x13¼
Granite Paper
1431 A373 2p Block of 4, #a-d   2.00 2.00
Souvenir Sheet
Perf. 13¼x13
1432 A373 12p multi   3.00 3.00

People's Liberation Army Garrison in Macao, 15th Anniv. — A374

No. 1433: a, Soldiers at flag ceremony (6/1). b, Soldier in camouflage uniform (6/2). c, Soldiers looking at sign (6/3). d, Soldier putting military helmet on child (6/4). e, Musicians (6/5). f, Soldier guiding shooter (6/6).
12p, Soldiers at attention in front of building.

2014, Dec. 20   Litho.   Perf. 13x13¼
1433 A374 2p Block of 6, #a-f   3.00 3.00
Souvenir Sheet
Perf. 13¼x13
1434 A374 12p multi   3.00 3.00
No. 1434 contains one 60x40mm stamp.

SEMI-POSTAL STAMPS

Orbis International, 30th Anniv. — SP1

No. B1: a, 1.50p+1p, Orbis airplane, surgeons. b, 5p+1p, Doctor administering eye examination, eye chart.

2012, Oct. 9   Litho.   Perf. 13x13¼
Granite Paper
B1   SP1   Horiz. pair, #a-b   2.25 2.25

AIR POST STAMPS

Stamps of 1934 Overprinted or Surcharged in Black

| a | b |

1936   Wmk. 232   Perf. 11½
C1	A17 (a)	2a blue green	3.00	1.00
C2	A17 (a)	3a violet	4.50	1.50
C3	A17 (b)	5a on 6a brown	4.50	1.90
C4	A17 (a)	7a brt rose	4.50	1.90
C5	A17 (a)	8a brt blue	12.00	5.00
C6	A17 (a)	15a maroon	29.00	11.50
	Nos. C1-C6 (6)		57.50	22.80

Common Design Type
Name and Value in Black
Perf. 13½x13

1938, Aug. 1   Engr.   Unwmk.
C7	CD39	1a scarlet	.90	.50
C8	CD39	2a purple	1.10	.65
C9	CD39	3a orange	1.60	.90
C10	CD39	5a ultra	3.25	1.25
C11	CD39	10a lilac brn	5.50	1.75
C12	CD39	20a dk green	11.00	3.00
C13	CD39	50a red brown	18.00	4.00
C14	CD39	70a rose car	22.50	5.00
C15	CD39	1p magenta	45.00	18.00
	Nos. C7-C15 (9)		108.85	35.05

No. C13 exists with overprint "Exposicao Internacional de Nova York, 1939-1940" and Trylon and Perisphere. Value $325.

```
Catalogue values for unused
stamps in this section, from this
point to the end of the section, are
for never hinged items.
```

Plane over Bay of Grand Beach — AP1

1960, Dec. 11   Litho.   Perf. 14
C16	AP1	50a shown	2.50	.40
C17	AP1	76a Penha Chapel	5.00	1.25
C18	AP1	3p Macao	14.00	2.00
C19	AP1	5p Bairro de Mong Ha	17.50	2.00
C20	AP1	10p Penha and Bay	28.00	2.25
	Nos. C16-C20 (5)		67.00	7.90
	Set, hinged		37.50	

No. C17 Surcharged
1979, Aug. 3   Litho.   Perf. 14
| C21 | AP1 | 70a on 76a multi | *30.00* | 4.50 |

POSTAGE DUE STAMPS

Numeral of Value — D1

Name and Value in Black
Perf. 11½x12

1904, July   Typo.   Unwmk.
J1	D1	½a gray green	1.50	1.25
a.		Name & value inverted	125.00	60.00
J2	D1	1a yellow grn	2.00	1.25
J3	D1	2a slate	2.00	1.25
J4	D1	4a pale brown	2.75	1.25
J5	D1	5a red orange	3.50	2.00
J6	D1	8a gray brown	4.00	2.00
J7	D1	12a red brown	6.00	2.00
J8	D1	20a dull blue	10.00	4.50
J9	D1	40a carmine	20.00	6.00
J10	D1	50a orange	26.50	12.00
J11	D1	1p gray violet	52.50	25.00
	Nos. J1-J11 (11)		130.75	58.50

Issued with or without gum: No. J4. Others issued with gum.
For overprints see Nos. 144-146, J12-J32.

Issue of 1904 Overprinted in Carmine or Green

Overprint 24½mm long. "A" has flattened top.

1911   Lisbon Overprint
J12	D1	½a gray green	.50	.50
J13	D1	1a yellow green	1.00	1.00
J14	D1	2a slate	1.25	1.40
J15	D1	4a pale brown	1.50	1.50
J16	D1	5a orange	2.00	1.60
J17	D1	8a gray brown	4.00	1.75
J18	D1	12a red brown	7.00	2.00
J19	D1	20a dull blue	9.50	3.00
J20	D1	40a carmine (G)	12.50	6.00
J21	D1	50a orange	16.00	8.50
J22	D1	1p gray violet	30.00	14.00
	Nos. J12-J22 (11)		85.25	41.25

Issued without gum: Nos. J19-J22.

Issue of 1904 Overprinted in Red or Green

Overprint 23mm long. "A" has pointed top.

1914   Local Overprint
J22A	D1	½a gray green	*1,600.*	600.00
J23	D1	1a yellow green	3.00	1.00
J24	D1	2a slate	3.00	1.00
J25	D1	4a pale brown	3.00	1.25
J26	D1	5a orange	4.50	1.25
J27	D1	8a gray brown	5.00	1.50
J28	D1	12a red brown	7.00	2.00
J29	D1	20a dull blue	13.50	5.50

J30	D1	40a car (G)	20.00	7.50
a.		Double ovpt., red and green	100.00	27.50
J31	D1	50a orange	27.50	10.00
J32	D1	1p gray violet	45.00	15.00
		Nos. J23-J32 (10)	131.50	46.00

Issued without gum: Nos. J28, J30-J32.

D2

Name and Value in Black

1947   **Typo.**   **Perf. 11½x12**

J33	D2	1a red violet	1.50	1.25
J34	D2	2a purple	2.00	1.50
J35	D2	4a dark blue	2.50	2.00
J36	D2	5a chocolate	3.50	2.25
J37	D2	8a red violet	4.50	2.50
J38	D2	12a orange brown	7.50	2.50
J39	D2	20a yellow green	8.50	5.00
J40	D2	40a brt carmine	10.00	7.00
J41	D2	50a orange yellow	19.00	8.00
J42	D2	1p blue	25.00	11.00
		Nos. J33-J42 (10)	84.00	44.00

Stamps of 1934 Surcharged "PORTEADO" and New Values in Carmine

1949, May 1   **Wmk. 232**

J43	A17	1a on 4a black	2.75	1.25
J44	A17	2a on 6a brown	2.75	1.25
J45	A17	4a on 8a brt blue	3.00	1.50
J46	A17	5a on 10a red org	3.00	1.75
J47	A17	8a on 12a dk blue	4.25	2.75
J48	A17	12a on 30a apple grn	7.00	3.75
J49	A17	20a on 40a violet	7.50	5.00
		Nos. J43-J49 (7)	30.25	17.25

> Catalogue values for unused stamps in this section, from this point to the end of the section, are for Never Hinged items.

Nos. 348, 349 and 351 Overprinted or Surcharged in Black or Carmine

1951, June 6   **Unwmk.**

J50	A21	1a org yel, *lem*	1.40	.90
J51	A21	2a dk grn, *bl* (C)	1.75	.90
J52	A21	7a on 10a brt pink, *bl*	2.25	1.10
		Nos. J50-J52 (3)	5.40	2.90

Common Design Type

1952   **Photo. & Typo.**   **Perf. 14**
Numeral in Red; Frame Multicolored

J53	CD45	1a violet blue	1.00	.40
J54	CD45	3a chocolate	1.10	.40
J55	CD45	5a indigo	1.10	.50
J56	CD45	10a dark red	2.00	.90
J57	CD45	30a indigo	3.75	1.40
J58	CD45	1p chocolate	8.50	3.25
		Nos. J53-J58 (6)	17.45	6.85

WAR TAX STAMPS

Victory
WT1

1919, Aug. 11   Unwmk.   Perf. 15x14
Overprinted in Black or Carmine

MR1	WT1	2a green	5.50	4.50
MR2	WT1	11a green (C)	10.00	14.00

Nos. MR1-MR2 were also for use in Timor. A 9a value was issued for revenue use. Value $15.

NEWSPAPER STAMPS

Nos. P1-P2   No. P3

Typographed and Embossed
1892-93   **Unwmk.**   **Perf. 12½**
Black Surcharge
Without Gum

P1	A7	2½r on 40r choc	7.00	4.00
a.		Inverted surcharge	70.00	65.00
b.		Perf. 13½	8.00	6.00
P2	A7	2½r on 80r gray	9.00	4.00
a.		Inverted surcharge	70.00	65.00
b.		Double surcharge	70.00	65.00
c.		Perf. 13½	90.00	70.00
P3	A7	2½r on 10r grn ('93)	8.00	4.00
a.		Double surcharge	—	70.00
b.		Perf. 13½	9.00	9.00
		Nos. P1-P3 (3)	24.00	12.00

N3   N4

1893-94   **Typo.**   **Perf. 11½**

P4	N3	2½r brown	7.00	4.25
a.		Perf. 12½	6.00	4.00
b.		Perf. 13½	7.00	4.00
P5	N4	½a on 2½r brn (Bk) ('94)	6.00	4.00
a.		Double surcharge		

For surcharges see Nos. 131, 252.

POSTAL TAX STAMPS

Pombal Commemorative Issue
Common Design Types
Perf. 12½

1925, Nov. 3   **Engr.**   **Unwmk.**

RA1	CD28	2a red org & blk	2.50	1.25
RA2	CD29	2a red org & blk	3.00	1.50
RA3	CD30	2a red org & blk	3.25	1.75
		Nos. RA1-RA3 (3)	8.75	4.50

PT1

Symbolical of Charity
1930, Dec. 25   **Litho.**   **Perf. 11**

RA4	PT1	5a dk brown, *yel*	37.50	17.50

PT2

1945-47   **Perf. 11½, 12, 10**

RA5	PT2	5a blk brn, *yel*	11.00	8.50
RA6	PT2	5a bl, *bluish* ('47)	35.00	20.00
RA7	PT2	10a grn, *citron*	20.00	17.50
RA8	PT2	15a org, *buff*	20.00	15.00
RA9	PT2	20a rose red, *sal*	50.00	17.50

RA10	PT2	50a red vio, *pnksh*	40.00	22.50
		Nos. RA5-RA10 (6)	176.00	101.00

> Catalogue values for unused stamps in this section, from this point to the end of the section, are for Never Hinged items.

1953-56   **Perf. 10½x11½**

RA11	PT2	10a bl, *pale grn* ('56)	2.50	1.75
RA12	PT2	20a chocolate, *yel*	9.00	6.00
RA13	PT2	50a car, *pale rose*	15.00	9.00
		Nos. RA11-RA13 (3)	26.50	16.75

1958   **Perf. 12x11½**

RA14	PT2	1a gray grn, *grnsh*	1.00	.50
RA15	PT2	2a rose lilac, *grysh*	1.50	.85

Type of 1945-47 Redrawn
Imprint: "Lito. Imp. Nac.-Macau"
1961-66   **Perf. 11**

RA16	PT2	1a gray grn, *grnsh*	1.50	1.00
RA17	PT2	2a rose lil, *grysh*	1.50	1.00
RA18	PT2	10a bl, *pale grn* ('62)	1.50	1.00
RA19	PT2	20a brn, *yel* ('66)	1.75	1.10
		Nos. RA16-RA19 (4)	6.25	4.10

Nos. RA16-RA19 have accent added to "E" in "Assistencia."
Nos. RA4-RA19 were issued without gum.

Type of 1945-47 Redrawn and Surcharged

1979   **Litho.**   **Perf. 11x11½**

RA20	PT2	20a on 1p yel grn, *cream*	2.50	2.00

No. RA20 has no accent above "E," no imprint and was not issued without surcharge.

No. RA8
Surcharged

Methods and Perfs As Before
1981

RA20A	PT2	10a on 15a #RA8	3.00	3.00

No. RA17
Surcharged

Methods and Perfs As Before
1981   **Without Gum**

RA21	PT2	20a on 2a #RA17	2.50	2.00

POSTAL TAX DUE STAMPS

Pombal Commemorative Issue
Common Design Types
1925   **Unwmk.**   **Perf. 12½**

RAJ1	CD28	4a red orange & blk	3.25	2.00
RAJ2	CD29	4a red orange & blk	3.25	2.00
RAJ3	CD30	4a red orange & blk	3.25	2.00
		Nos. RAJ1-RAJ3 (3)	9.75	6.00

MACEDONIA

,ma-sə-'dō-nē-ə

LOCATION — Central Balkans, bordered by on the north by Serbia, to the east by Bulgaria, on the south by Greece and by Albania on the west.
GOVT. — Republic
AREA — 9,928 sq. mi.
POP. — 2,022,604 (1999 est.)
CAPITAL — Skopje

Formerly a constituent republic in the Socialist Federal Republic of Yugoslavia. Declared independence on Nov. 21, 1991.

100 Deni (de) = 1 Denar (d)

Catalogue values for all unused stamps in this country are for Never Hinged items.

Watermark

Wmk. 387

Bas
Relief — A1

1992-93   Litho.   Perf. 13½x13
1	A1	30d multicolored	.65 .40

Perf. 10
2	A1	40d multicolored	.60 .30

Issued: 30d, 9/8/92; 40d, 3/15/93.
For surcharges see Nos. 21, 42.

Christmas — A2

Frescoes: 100d, Nativity Scene, 16th cent. 500d, Virgin and Child, 1422.

1992, Dec. 10   Litho.   Perf. 13x13½
3	A2	100d multicolored	1.10 1.10
4	A2	500d multicolored	2.50 2.50

Natl.
Flag — A3

1993, Mar. 15   Perf. 13½x13
5	A3	10d multicolored	.75 .35
6	A3	40d multicolored	2.00 .95
7	A3	50d multicolored	2.25 1.25
		Nos. 5-7 (3)	5.00 2.55

For surcharges see Nos. 23, 40-41.

Fish — A4

Designs: 50d, 1000d, Rutilus macedonicus. 100d, 2000d, Salmothymus achridanus.

1993, Mar. 15   Perf. 10
8	A4	50d multicolored	.35 .25
9	A4	100d multicolored	.45 .25
10	A4	1000d multicolored	4.00 2.00
11	A4	2000d multicolored	5.00 3.00
		Nos. 8-11 (4)	9.80 5.50

Easter — A5

1993, Apr. 16
12	A5	300d multicolored	3.50 2.50

Trans-Balkan Telecommunications Network — A6

1993, May 6
13	A6	500d multicolored	1.30 .80

Admission to the UN, Apr. 8, 1993 — A7

1993, July 28
14	A7	10d multicolored	1.60 .95

A8

1993, Aug. 2
15	A8	10d multicolored	1.60 .95

Souvenir Sheet
Imperf
16	A8	30d multicolored	4.50 4.50

Ilinden Uprising, 90th anniv.

A9

1993, Nov. 4
17	A9	4d multicolored	.65 .60

Size: 85x67mm
Imperf
18	A9	40d multicolored	5.50 5.50

Macedonian Revolutionary Organization, cent.

Christmas — A10

1993, Dec. 31   Perf. 10
19	A10	2d Nativity Scene	.75 .50
20	A10	20d Adoration of the Magi	3.25 2.50

Nos. 1, 5, RA1 Surcharged

1994, Apr. 2   Perfs., Etc. as Before
21	A1	2d on 30d multi	.40 .40
22	PT1	8d on 2.50d multi	1.50 1.50
23	A3	15d on 10d multi	3.25 3.25
		Nos. 21-23 (3)	5.15 5.15

Size and location of surcharge varies.

Easter — A11

1994, Apr. 29   Litho.   Perf. 10
24	A11	2d multicolored	.60 .30

Revolutionaries — A12

Designs: 8d, Kosta Racin (1908-43), writer. 15d, Grigor Prlicev (1830-93), writer. 20d, Nikola Vapzarov (1909-42), poet. 50d, Goce Delchev (1872-1903), politician.

1994, May 23
25	A12	8d multicolored	.75 .50
26	A12	15d multicolored	1.25 1.00
27	A12	20d multicolored	2.50 1.50
28	A12	50d multicolored	3.50 2.50
		Nos. 25-28 (4)	8.00 5.50

Intl. Year of the Family — A13

1994, June 21
29	A13	2d multicolored	.70 .25

Liberation Day, 50th Anniv. — A14

Designs: 5d, St. Prohor Pcinski Monastery, up close. 50d, View of entire grounds.

1994, Aug. 2   Litho.   Perf. 10
30	A14	5d multicolored	.70 .45

Size: 108x73mm
Imperf
31	A14	50d multicolored	4.50 3.50

Swimming Marathon, Ohrid Lake — A15

1994, Aug. 22
32	A15	8d multicolored	.90 .55

Stamp Day — A16

1994, Sept. 12
33	A16	2d multicolored	1.25 .75

Nova Makedonija, Mlad Boretz, & Makedonka Newspapers, 50th Anniv. — A17

1994, Sept. 13   Litho.   Perf. 10
34	A17	2d multicolored	1.30 .65

St. Kliment of Ohrid Library, 50th Anniv. A18

Manuscripts: 2d, 15th cent. 10d, 13th cent.

1994, Sept. 29   Litho.   Perf. 10
35	A18	2d multi	.30 .25
36	A18	10d multi, vert.	1.60 1.30

Macedonian Radio, 50th Anniv. — A19

1994, Dec. 26   Litho.   Perf. 10
37	A19	2d multicolored	.65 .30

Wildlife Conservation — A20

1994, Dec. 26   Litho.   Perf. 10
38	A20	5d Pinus peluse	.55	.45
39	A20	10d Lynx lynx martinoi	1.40	1.10

Nos. 2, 6 Surcharged in Black or Gold

a

b

Perfs., Etc. as Before
1995, Mar. 13   Litho.
40	A3(a)	2d on 40d #6	1.75	1.75
41	A3(b)	2d on 40d #6	1.00	1.00
42	A1(a)	5d on 40d #2 (G)	.75	.75
		Nos. 40-42 (3)	3.50	3.50

Easter — A21

1995, Apr. 23   Litho.   Perf. 10
43	A21	4d multicolored	.60	.35

End of World War II, 50th Anniv. A22

1995, May 9   Litho.   Perf. 10
44	A22	2d multicolored	1.25	.75

Macedonian Red Cross, 50th Anniv. — A23

1995, May 20   Litho.   Perf. 10
45	A23	2d multicolored	1.30	.75

Wilhelm Röntgen (1845-1923), Discovery of the X-Ray, Cent. — A24

1995, May 20
46	A24	2d multicolored	1.40	.75

Vojdan Cernodrinski (1875-1951), Theater Festival, 50th Anniv. — A25

1995, June 8
47	A25	10d multicolored	1.30	.65

Death of Prince Marko Kraljevic, 600th Anniv. A26

1995, June 22
48	A26	20d multicolored	2.40	1.50

Gorgi Puleski (1818-95), Writer A27

1995, July 8
49	A27	2d multicolored	1.25	.65

Writer's Festival, Struga A28

1995, Aug. 23   Litho.   Perf. 10
50	A28	2d multicolored	1.75	1.25

A29

1995, Oct. 4
51	A29	15d Mosque of Tetovo	1.75	1.25

A30

Architecture.

1995, Oct. 4   Litho.   Perf. 10
52	A30	2d Malesevija	.35	.25
53	A30	20d Krakornica	2.25	1.25

See Nos. 81-83 and design A63a.

Motion Pictures, Cent. A31

Film strip of early movie and: No. 54, Auguste and Louis Lumiére. No. 55, Milton and Janaki Manaki, Macedonian cinematographers.

1995, Oct. 6   Perf. 10 on 3 Sides
54	A31	10d multicolored	1.50	1.50
55	A31	10d multicolored	1.50	1.50
a.		Pair, #54-55	4.75	4.75

UN, 50th Anniv. A32

1995, Oct. 24
56	A32	20d Blocks, globe in nest	2.25	1.50
57	A32	50d Blocks, sun	4.50	3.00

Christmas A33

1995, Dec. 13
58	A33	15d multicolored	1.75	1.25

Birds A34

15d, Pelecanus crispus. 40d, Gypaetus barbatus.

1995, Dec. 14
59	A34	15d multicolored	2.00	1.50
60	A34	40d multicolored	4.00	3.00

Reform of Macedonian Language, 50th Anniv. — A35

1995, Dec. 18
61	A35	5d multicolored	.65	.50

St. Bogorodica Church, Ohrid, 700th Anniv. — A36

Designs: 8d, Detail of fresco, exterior view, St. Kliment of Ohrid (840-916). 50d, Portion of fresco inside church, #62.

1995, Dec. 19
62	A36	8d multicolored	1.00	1.00

Size: 80x61mm
Imperf
62A	A36	50d multicolored	50.00	50.00

Macedonia's Admission to UPU, 1st Anniv. — A37

1995, Dec. 27
62B	A37	10d Post office, Skopje	1.25	1.25

Admission to Council of Europe (CE) and Organization for Security and Cooperation in Europe (OSCE) — A37a

1995, Dec. 27
62C	A37a	20d multicolored	2.75	2.75

Modern Olympic Games, Cent., 1996 Summer Olympic Games, Atlanta A38

1996, May 20   Litho.   Perf. 10
63	A38	2d Kayak race	.65	.65
64	A38	8d Basketball, vert.	.85	.85
65	A38	15d Swimming	1.75	1.75
66	A38	20d Wrestling	2.75	2.75
67	A38	40d Boxing, vert.	4.25	4.25
68	A38	50d Running, vert	6.00	6.00
		Nos. 63-68 (6)	16.25	16.25

Intl. Decade to Fight Illegal Drugs — A39

1996, July 11   Litho.   Perf. 10
69	A39	20d multicolored	2.00	2.00

Children's Paintings — A40

1996, July 15
70	A40	2d Boy	.30	.30
71	A40	8d Girl	.85	.85

Peak of Czar Samuel of Bulgaria's Power, 1000th Anniv. A41

1996, July 19
72 A41 40d multicolored — 5.00 5.00

G. Petrov (1865-1921), Revolutionary A42

1996, Aug. 2
73 A42 20d multicolored — 2.00 2.00

Independence, 5th Anniv. — A43

1996, Sept. 8
74 A43 10d multicolored — 1.00 1.00

Vera Ciriviri-Trena (1920-44), Freedom Fighter — A44

Mother Teresa (1910-97) — A45

1996, Nov. 22 Litho. Perf. 13x13½
75 A44 20d multicolored — 6.75 4.00
76 A45 40d multicolored — 10.00 7.50
Europa.

Christmas — A46

Designs: No. 77, Tree, children caroling in snow. No. 78, Candle, nuts, apples.

1996, Dec. 14 Litho. Perf. 10
77 A46 10d multicolored — .75 .60
78 A46 10d multicolored — .75 .60
a. Pair, #77-78 — 2.40 2.40

Terra Cotta Tiles — A47

Nos. 79a, 80a, 4d, Daniel in lions den. Nos. 79b, 80b, 8d, Sts. Christopher & George. Nos. 79c, 80c, 20d, Joshua, Caleb. Nos. 79d, 80d, 50d, Unicorn.

1996, Dec. 19 Blocks of 4, #a.-d.
79 A47 bl grn & multi — 7.50 7.50
80 A47 yel grn & multi — 7.50 7.50

Traditional Architecture Type of 1995
1996
81 A30 2d House, Nistrovo — .25 .25
82 A30 8d House, Brodets — .80 .80
83 A30 10d House, Niviste — .90 .90
Nos. 81-83 (3) — 1.95 1.95
Issued: 8d, 12/20; 2d, 10d, 12/25.
See Nos. 112-116.

Butterflies A49

4d, Pseudochazara cingovskii. 40d, Colias balcanica.

1996, Dec. 21
84 A49 4d multicolored — .35 .35
85 A49 40d multicolored — 4.75 4.75

UNICEF, 50th Anniv A50

1996, Dec. 31 Perf. 14½
86 A50 20d shown — 2.00 2.00
87 A50 40d UNESCO, 50th anniv. — 4.00 4.00

Alpine Skiing Championships, 50th Anniv. — A51

1997, Feb. 7 Perf. 10
88 A51 20d multicolored — 2.00 2.00

Alexander Graham Bell (1847-1922) — A52

1997, Mar. 12
89 A52 40d multicolored — 3.00 3.00

Ancient Roman Mosaics, Heraklia and Stobi A53

1997, Mar. 26 Perf. 10
90 A53 2d Wild dog — .35 .35
91 A53 8d Bull — .60 .60
92 A53 20d Lion — 1.50 1.50
93 A53 40d Leopard with prey — 3.25 3.25
Nos. 90-93 (4) — 5.70 5.70
Size: 79x56mm
Imperf
94 A53 50d Deer, peacocks — 6.00 6.00
No. 94 has simulated perforations within the design.

Cyrilic Alphabet, 1100th Anniv. A54

Cyrillic inscriptions and: No. 95, Gold embossed plate. No. 96, St. Cyril (827-69), St. Methodius (825-84), promulgators of Cyrillic alphabet.

1997, May 2 Perf. 10
95 A54 10d multicolored — .75 .60
96 A54 10d multicolored — .75 .60
a. Pair, #95-96 — 2.10 2.10

A55

Europa (Stories and Legends): 20d, Man kneeling down, another seated in background. 40d, Man, tree, bird dressed as man.

1997, June 6 Perf. 15x14
97 A55 20d multicolored — 2.25 2.00
98 A55 40d multicolored — 5.00 3.50

A56

1997, June 5 Perf. 10
99 A56 15d multicolored — 1.50 1.50
5th Natl. Ecology Day.

St. Naum A57

1997, July 3 Perf. 10
100 A57 15d multicolored — 1.60 1.60

Mushrooms — A58

2d, Cantharellus cibarius. 15d, Boletus aereus. 27d, Amanita caesarea. 50d, Morchella conica.

Week of the Child — A59

1997, Oct. 11
105 A59 27d multicolored — 2.25 2.25

Minerals — A60

1997, Oct. 10
106 A60 27d Stibnite — 2.25 2.25
107 A60 40d Lorandite — 3.75 3.75

1997, Nov. 7 Litho. Perf. 10
101 A58 2d multicolored — .60 .60
102 A58 15d multicolored — 1.25 1.25
103 A58 27d multicolored — 2.00 2.00
104 A58 50d multicolored — 3.50 3.50
Nos. 101-104 (4) — 7.35 7.35

Mahatma Gandhi (1869-1948) A61

1998, Feb. 4 Litho. Perf. 13½
108 A61 30d multicolored — 2.00 2.00

Pythagoras (c. 570-c. 500 BC), Greek Philosopher, Mathematician — A62

1998, Feb. 6
109 A62 16d multicolored — 1.40 1.40

1998 Winter Olympic Games, Nagano — A63

1998, Feb. 7
110 A63 4d Slalom skier + label — .55 .55
111 A63 30d Cross country skiers + label — 3.75 3.75
Nos. 110-111 were each printed with a se-tenant label.

Traditional Architecture A63a

Location of home: 2d, Novo Selo. 4d, Jablanica. 16d, Kiselica. 20d, Konopnica. 30d, Ambar. 50d, Galicnik.

1998

112	A63a	2d multicolored	.25	.25
113	A63a	4d multicolored	.30	.30
113A	A63a	16d multicolored	.80	.80
114	A63a	20d multicolored	.95	.95
115	A63a	30d multicolored	1.50	1.50
116	A63a	50d multicolored	2.50	2.50
	Nos. 112-116 (6)		6.30	6.30

Issued: 2d, 4d, 30d, 2/9; 20d, 50d, 2/12; 16d, 6/10.
See Nos. 146-148.

Painting, "Exodus," by Kole Manev — A64

1998, Feb. 11
117 A64 30d multicolored   3.00 3.00

Exodus from Aegean Macedonia, 50th anniv.

Neolithic Artifacts — A65

Designs: 4d, Water flasks. 18d, Animal-shaped bowl. 30d, Woman figure. 60d, Bowl.

1998, Apr. 29   Litho.   Perf. 13½

118	A65	4d multicolored	.25	.25
119	A65	18d multicolored	.85	.85
120	A65	30d multicolored	1.25	1.25
121	A65	60d multicolored	3.50	3.50
	Nos. 118-121 (4)		5.85	5.85

1998 World Cup Soccer Championships, France — A66

4d, Looking down at soccer field, ball. 30d, Soccer field with world map in center.

1998, Apr. 30

122	A66	4d multicolored	.30	.30
123	A66	30d multicolored	2.25	2.25

Natl. Festivals — A67

Europa: 30d, Dancers, Strumica. 40d, People wearing masks, Vevcani.

1998, May 5   Litho.   Perf. 13½

124	A67	30d multicolored	3.25	1.75
125	A67	40d multicolored	3.75	2.25

Carnival Cities Congress, Strumica — A68

1998, May 10   Litho.   Perf. 13½
126 A68 30d multicolored   2.50 2.50

World Ecology Day — A69

4d, Stylized flower. 30d, Smokestack uprooting tree.

1998, June 5   Litho.   Perf. 13½

127	A69	4d multicolored	.35	.35
128	A69	30d multicolored	2.00	2.00

Dimitri Cupovski, 120th Birth Anniv. — A70

1998, June 30
129 A70 16d multicolored   1.10 1.10

Railroads in Macedonia, 125th Anniv. — A72

30d, Document, building, early steam locomotive, vert. 60d, Locomotive, 1873.

1998, Aug. 9   Litho.   Perf. 13½

130	A72	30d multicolored	2.00	2.00
131	A72	60d multicolored	4.00	4.00

Fossil Skulls Found in Macedonia — A73

Designs: 4d, Ursus spelaeus. 8d, Mesopithecus pentelici. 18d, Tragoceros. 30d, Aceratherium incisivum.

1998, Sept. 17

132	A73	4d multicolored	.30	.30
133	A73	8d multicolored	.50	.50
134	A73	18d multicolored	1.10	1.10
135	A73	30d multicolored	2.00	2.00
	Nos. 132-135 (4)		3.90	3.90

The Liturgy of St. John Chrysostom, Cent. — A74

Design: Atanas Badev, composer.

1998, Sept. 21
136 A74 25d multicolored   1.60 1.60

Children's Day — A75

1998, Oct. 5
137 A75 30d multicolored   2.10 2.10

Beetles — A76

4d, Cerambyx cerdo. 8d, Rosalia alpina. 20d, Oryctes nasicornis. 40d, Lucanus cervus.

1998, Oct. 20

138	A76	4d multicolored	.25	.25
139	A76	8d multicolored	.45	.45
140	A76	20d multicolored	1.10	1.10
141	A76	40d multicolored	2.25	2.25
	Nos. 138-141 (4)		4.05	4.05

A77

Christmas and New Year — A77a

1998, Nov. 20

142	A77	4d multicolored	.25	.25
143	A77a	30d multicolored	2.00	2.00

Universal Declaration of Human Rights, 50th Anniv. — A78

1998, Dec. 10
144 A78 30d multicolored   2.00 2.00

Sharplaninec Dog — A79

1999, Jan. 20   Litho.   Perf. 13¼
145 A79 15d multi   1.25 1.25

Architecture Type of 1998
"Republica Macedonia" in Cyrillic

Location of home: 1d, Bogomila. 4d, Svekani. 5d, Teovo.

1999   Litho.   Perf. 13¼

146	A63A	1d multi	.25	.25
147	A63A	4d multi	.25	.25
148	A63A	5d multi	.30	.30
	Nos. 146-148 (3)		.80	.80

Issued: 4d, 2/1; 5d, 2/25; 1d, 11/5.

Icons — A80

Designs: 4d, 1535 Slepche Monastery Annunciation icon, Demir Hisar, by Dimitar Zograf. 8d, 1862 St. Nicholas Church icon, Ohrid. 18d, 1535 Slepche Monastery Madonna and Child icon, Demir Hisar. 30d, 1393-94 Zrze Monastery Jesus icon, Prilep. 50d, 1626 Lesnovo Monastery Jesus icon, Probishtip.

1999, Mar. 3   Perf. 11¾

149	A80	4d multi	.30	.30
150	A80	8d multi	.50	.50
151	A80	18d multi	1.10	1.10
152	A80	30d multi	1.75	1.75
	Nos. 149-152 (4)		3.65	3.65

Souvenir Sheet
153 A80 50d multi   3.25 3.25

Dimitar A. Pandilov (1899-1963), Painter — A81

1999, Mar. 14   Perf. 13¼
154 A81 4d multi   .40 .40

Telegraphy in Macedonia, Cent. — A82

1999, Apr. 22
155 A82 4d multi   .40 .40

Saints Cyril and Methodius University, Skopje, 50th Anniv. — A83

1999, Apr. 24
156 A83 8d multi   .55 .55

Issued in sheets of 8 + label.

Council of Europe, 50th Anniv. — A84

1999, May 5
157 A84 30d multi   2.00 2.00

Europa
A85

Natl. Parks: 30d, Pelister. 40d, Mavrovo.

1999, May 5
158 A85 30d multi   2.50 1.25
159 A85 40d multi   3.50 1.75

Ecology — A86

1999, June 5
160 A86 30d multi   1.75 1.75

Macedonian Leaders from the Middle
Ages — A87

Designs: a, 30d, Strez (1204-14). b, 8d,
Gorgi Voytech (1072-1073). c, 18d, Dobromir
Hrs (1195-1203). d, 4d, Petar Deljan (1040-
41).

1999, June 25
161 A87 Block of 4, #a.-d.   4.00 4.00

Kuzman Sapkarev (1834-1909),
Folklorist — A88

1999, Sept. 1   Litho.   Perf. 13¼
162 A88 4d multi   .50   .50

Flowers — A89

Designs: 4d, Crocus scardicus. 8d, Astraga-
lus mayeri. 18d, Campanula formanekiana.
30d, Viola kosaninii.

1999, Sept. 16
163 A89 4d multi   .25   .25
164 A89 8d multi   .50   .50
165 A89 18d multi   1.10 1.10
166 A89 30d multi   1.75 1.75
          Nos. 163-166 (4)   3.60 3.60

Children's
Day — A90

1999, Oct. 4
167 A90 30d multi   1.75 1.75

UPU,
125th
Anniv.
A91

1999, Oct. 9
168 A91 5d Post horn, emblem   .30   .30
169 A91 30d Emblem, post horn   1.75 1.75

Krste Petkov
Misirkov (1875-
1926),
Writer — A92

1999, Nov. 18
170 A92 5d multi   .50   .50

Christmas — A93

1999, Nov. 24
171 A93 30d multi   1.60 1.60

New Year's
Day — A94

1999, Nov. 24   Perf. 13¼
172 A94 5d multi   .35   .35

Slavic Presence
in Macedonia,
1400th
Anniv. — A95

1999, Oct. 27   Litho.   Perf. 13¼
173 A95 5d multi   .45   .45

Christianity, 2000th Anniv. — A96

Icons and frescoes: 5d, Altar cross, St. Nik-
ita Monastery, vert. 10d, Fresco of Holy
Mother of God, St. Mark's Monastery. 15d, St.
Clement of Ohrid, vert. 30d, Fresco of Apostle
Paul St. Andrew's Monastery, vert.
50d, St. Sophia's Cathedral, Ohrid, vert.

2000, Jan. 19
174-177 A96 Set of 4   3.25 3.25
Souvenir Sheet
178 A96 50d multi   2.25 2.25
No. 178 contains one 30x31mm stamp.

Millennium
A97

No. 179: a, 5d, "2000." b, 30d, Religious
symbols.

2000, Feb. 16
179 A97 Vert. pair, #a-b   2.25 2.25

Silver
Jewelry — A98

Designs: 5d, Pin with icon, Ohrid, 19th cent.
10d, Bracelet, Bitola, 20th cent. 20d, Earrings,
Ohrid, 18th cent. 30d, Brooch, Bitola, 19th-
20th cent.

2000, Mar. 1   Litho.   Perf. 13¼
180-183 A98 Set of 4   3.75 3.75

Macedonian Philatelic Society, 50th
Anniv. — A99

2000, Mar. 19
184 A99 5d multi   .45   .45

World Meteorological Organization,
50th Anniv. — A100

2000, Mar. 23   Litho.   Perf. 13¼
185 A100 30d multi   1.75 1.75

Easter — A101

2000, Apr. 21   Litho.   Perf. 13¼
186 A101 5d multi   .35   .35

Europa, 2000
Common Design Type
2000, May 9   Perf. 14
187 CD17 30d multi   3.25 3.25

2000
Summer
Olympics,
Sydney
A102

Designs: 5d, Runners. 30d, Wrestlers.

2000, May 17   Perf. 13¼
188-189 A102 Set of 2   2.50 2.50

Ecology — A103

2000, June 5   Litho.   Perf. 13¼
190 A103 5d multi   .45   .45

Architecture Type of 1998
2000, July 28
191 A63a 6d House, Zdunje   .45   .45

Printing
Pioneers — A104

Designs: 6d, Theodosius Sinaitski. 30d,
Johannes Gutenberg.

2000, July 28
192-193 A104 Set of 2   2.00 2.00

Mother
Teresa
(1910-97)
A105

2000, Aug. 26
194 A105 6d multi   .45   .45

Birds — A106

Designs: 6d, Egretta garzeta. 10d, Ardea cinerea. 20d, Ardea purpurea. 30d, Plegadis falcinellus.

2000, Sept. 14
195-198 A106 Set of 4   3.75 3.75

Children's Week
A107

2000, Oct. 2 Litho. Perf. 13¼
199 A107 6d multi   .45 .45

Duke Dimo Hadi Dimov (1875-1924)
A108

2000, Oct. 20
200 A108 6d multi   .45 .45

Economics Faculty of Sts. Cyril & Methodius Univ., 50th Anniv. — A109

2000, Nov. 1
201 A109 6d multi   .45 .45

Joachim Krchovski, 250th Anniv. of Birth
A110

2000, Nov. 8
202 A110 6d multi   .50 .50

Christmas
A111

2000, Nov. 22
203 A111 30d multi   1.90 1.90

UN High Commissioner For Refugees, 50th Anniv. — A112

Designs: 6d, Handprints. 30d, Globe, hands.

2001, Jan. 10 Litho. Perf. 13¼
204-205 A112 Set of 2   2.00 2.00

Worldwide Fund for Nature (WWF) — A113

Imperial eagle: a, 6d, Facing right. b, 8d, With chick. c, 10d, In flight, and close-up of head. d, 30d, Close-up of head.

2001, Feb. 1 Litho. Perf. 14
206 A113 Block of 4, #a-d   3.50 3.50

Partenija Zografski (1818-1876)
A114

2001, Feb. 6 Litho. Perf. 13¼
207 A114 6d multi   .35 .35

A115

Native Costumes — A116

Designs: 6d, Dolmi Polog. 12d, Albanian. 18d, Reka. 30d, Skopska Crna Gora. 50d, Women, men in costumes, house, vegetables.

2001, Mar. 1 Perf. 13¼
208-211 A115 Set of 4   3.50 3.50

Souvenir Sheet
Imperf
Granite Paper
212 A116 50d multi   3.00 3.00

Lazar Licenoski (1901-64), Painter — A117

2001, Mar. 23 Perf. 13¼
213 A117 6d multi   .50 .50

National Archives, 50th Anniv. — A118

2001, Apr. 1
214 A118 6d multi   .35 .35

Easter
A119

2001, Apr. 15
215 A119 6d multi   .50 .50

Europa — A120

No. 216, Boat on lake: a, 18d. b, 36d.

2001, May 16 Granite Paper
216 A120 Horiz. pair, #a-b   3.00 3.00

Revolt Against Ottoman Rule, 125th Anniv.
A121

2001, May 20 Litho. Perf. 13¼
217 A121 6d multi   .45 .45

2nd Individual European Chess Championships
A122

2001, June 1 Litho. Perf. 13¼
218 A122 36d multi   2.00 2.00
a. Booklet pane of 4   10.00
    Booklet, #218a   10.00

Booklet sold for 145d.

Boats in Lake Dojran
A123

2001, June 5 Litho. Perf. 13¼
219 A123 6d multi   .50 .50

Architecture Type of 1998
Perf. 13¼
2001, June 25 Unwmk.
220 A63a 6d House, Mitrasinci   .50 .50

Independence, 10th Anniv. — A124

2001, Sept. 8 Wmk. 387
221 A124 6d multi   .55 .55

Trees
A125

Designs: 6d, Juniperus excelsa. 12d, Quercus macedonica. 24d, Arbutus andrachne. 36d, Quercus coccifera.

Perf. 13¼
2001, Sept. 12 Litho. Unwmk.
222-225 A125 Set of 4   4.75 4.75

Children's Day — A126

Perf. 13¼
2001, Oct. 1 Litho. Unwmk.
226 A126 6d multi   .45 .45

Year of Dialogue Among Civilizations
A127

2001, Oct. 9 Granite Paper
227 A127 36d multi   2.50 2.50

Nature Museum, 75th Anniv.
A128

2001, Oct. 26
228 A128 6d multi   .50 .50

Christmas — A129

2001, Nov. 22
229 A129 6d multi   .45 .45

Nobel Prizes, Cent. A130

2001, Dec. 10   **Litho.**   ***Perf. 13¼***
230 A130 36d multi   2.50 2.50

2002 Winter Olympics, Salt Lake City — A131

Designs: 6d, Skier. 36d, Skier, diff.

2002, Jan. 16   **Litho.**   ***Perf. 14***
231-232 A131   Set of 2   2.50 2.50

Ancient Coins A132

Designs: 6d, King Lykkeios of Paeonia obol, 359-340 B.C. 12d, Alexander III tetradrachm. 24d, Kings of Macedon tetrobol, 185-165 B.C. 36d, Philip II of Macedon gold stater. 50d, Kings of Macedon coin.

2002, Mar. 1
233-236 A132   Set of 4   5.50 5.50
        Souvenir Sheet
237 A132 50d multi   3.50 3.50

Petar Mazev (1927-93), Painter A133

2002, Apr. 15
238 A133 6d multi   .50 .50

Dimitar Kondovski (1927-93), Painter A134

2002, Apr. 15
239 A134 6d multi   .50 .50

Leonardo da Vinci (1452-1519) and Mona Lisa A135

2002, Apr. 15
240 A135 36d multi   2.00 2.00

Easter — A136

2002, Apr. 24
241 A136 6d multi   .50 .50

Europa A137

Designs: 6d, Acrobat, bicycle on wire, seal. 36d, Ball on wire, bicycle.

2002, May 9
242-243 A137   Set of 2   3.00 3.00

2002 World Cup Soccer Championships, Japan and Korea — A138

2002, May 15
244 A138 6d multi   2.00 2.00

Environmental Protection — A139

2002, June 5
245 A139 6d multi   .45 .45

National Arms — A140

Background colors: 10d, Blue. 36d, Greenish blue.

2002, June 18
246-247 A140   Set of 2   3.00 3.00

Architecture A141

Buildings in: 36d, Krushevo. 50d, Bitola.

2002, June 26   ***Perf. 13¼***
248-249 A141   Set of 2   5.00 5.00

Metodija Andonov Cento (1902-57), 1st President of Antifascist Council for the Natl. Liberation of Macedonia A142

2002, Aug. 18   **Litho.**   ***Perf. 13¼***
250 A142 6d multi   .55 .55

Nikola Karev (1877-1905), President of Krushevo Republic, Aug. 1903 — A143

2002, Aug. 18
251 A143 18d multi   1.10 1.10

Fauna — A144

No. 252: a, 6d, Perdix perdix. b, 12d, Sus scrofa. c, 24d, Rupicapra rupicapra. d, 36d, Alectoris graeca.

2002, Sept. 11   ***Perf. 14***
252 A144   Block of 4, #a-d   5.00 5.00

Children's Day — A145

2002, Oct. 1
253 A145 6d multi   .50 .50

Architecture Type of 1998

2002, Nov. 5   ***Perf. 13¼***
254 A63a 3d House, Jachince   .25 .25
255 A63a 9d House, Ratevo   .40 .40

Christmas — A146

2002, Nov. 20
256 A146 9d multi   .50 .50

Andreja Damjanov (1813-78), Builder of Churches A147

2003, Jan. 21
257 A147 36d multi   2.25 2.25

Musical Instruments A148

Designs: 9d, Gajda. 10d, Tambura. 20d, Kemene. 50d, Tapan.

2003, Feb. 19   **Litho.**   ***Perf. 13¼***
258-261 A148   Set of 4   6.00 6.00

Scouting In Macedonia, 50th Anniv. A149

2003, Feb. 22
262 A149 9d multi   .65 .65

Krste Petkov Misirkov Macedonian Language Institute, 50th Anniv. A150

2003, Mar. 5
263 A150 9d multi   .60 .60

Europa — A151

Poster art: No. 264, 36d, 1966 poster. No. 265, 36d, 1994 Intl. Triennial of Graphic Art poster.

2003, May 9   ***Perf. 13¼x13½***
        Granite Paper
264-265 A151   Set of 2   *4.00 3.00*

Ursus Arctos A152

2003, June 5   ***Perf. 13½x13¼***
266 A152 9d multi   .85 .85

Building, Skopje A153

Building, Resen A154

2003, June 16
267 A153 10d multi   .60 .60
268 A154 20d multi   1.10 1.10

Macedonian Arms — A155

Designs: 9d, Latin lettering. 36d, Cyrillic lettering.

2003, June 23   ***Perf. 13¼x13½***
269-270 A155   Set of 2   3.00 3.00

World Youth Handball Championships A156

2003, July 30
271 A156 36d multi   2.25 2.25

Printed in sheets of 8 + label.

Ilinden Uprising, Cent. A157

Uprising participants and: 9d, Seal. 36d, Memorial. 50d, Seal, diff.

2003, Aug. 2   *Perf. 13½x13¼*
272-273 A157   Set of 2   2.50 2.50
Souvenir Sheet
274 A157 50d multi + label   2.50 2.50

Paintings — A158

Paintings by: 9d, Nikola Martinovski (1903-73), vert. 36d, Vincent van Gogh (1853-90)

Perf. 13½x13¼, 13¼x13½
2003, Aug. 18
275-276 A158   Set of 2   2.50 2.50

Flowers — A159

Designs: 9d, Colchicum macedonicum. 20d, Viola allchariensis. 36d, Tulipa mariannae. 50d, Thymus oehmianus.

Perf. 13¼x13½
2003, Sept. 25   Litho.
277-280 A159   Set of 4   6.50 6.50

Writers A160

Designs: No. 281, 9d, Jeronim de Rada (1814-1903). No. 282, 9d, Said Najdeni (1864-1903).

2003, Sept. 30   *Perf. 13½x13¼*
281-282 A160   Set of 2   1.10 1.10

Children's Day — A161

2003, Oct. 6   *Perf. 13¼x13½*
283 A161 9d multi   .60 .60

Kresnensko Uprising, 125th Anniv. A162

2003, Oct. 17   *Perf. 13½x13¼*
284 A162 9d multi   .60 .60

Dimitar Vlahov (1878-1953), Politician — A163

2003, Nov. 8   Litho.   *Perf. 13½x13¼*
285 A163 9d multi   .60 .60

Christmas A164

2003, Nov. 19
286 A164 9d multi   .65 .65

Handicrafts A165

DesignsL 5d, Tassels. 9d, Pitcher. 10d, Kettle. 20d, Ornament.

2003-04   Litho.   *Perf. 13¼x13½*
287 A165 3d multi   .30 .30
288 A165 5d multi   .35 .35
289 A165 9d multi   .55 .55
290 A165 10d multi   .65 .65
291 A165 12d multi   .75 .75
292 A165 20d multi   1.25 1.25
   Nos. 287-292 (6)   3.85 3.85

Issued: 9d, 12/16; 10d, 1/21/04; 5d, 20d, 6/4/04; 3d, 12d, 6/4/04.

Powered Flight, Cent. A166

Perf. 13½x13¼
2003, Dec. 17   Litho.
293 A166 50d multi   3.25 3.25

Paintings Type of 2003

Designs: No. 294, 9d, Street and Buildings, by Tomo Vladimirski (1904-71), vert. No. 295, 9d, Street Scene, by Vangel Kodzoman (1904-94).

Perf. 13½x13¼, 13¼x13½
2004, Feb. 14
294-295 A158   Set of 2   1.10 1.10

Decorated Weapons — A167

Designs: 10d, Sword, 1806. 20d, Saber, 19th cent. 36d, Gun, 18th cent. 50d, Rifle, 18th cent.

2004, Mar. 10   *Perf. 13¼x13½*
Stamps + Labels
296-299 A167   Set of 4   7.00 7.00

Rugs — A168

Various rugs: 36d, 50d.

2004, Mar. 24   Set of 2   5.50 5.50
300-301 A168

Konstandin Kristoforidhi, Publisher of First Albanian Dictionary in Macedonia A169

2004, Apr. 19
302 A169 36d multi   2.00 2.00

House, Kratovo A170

2004, Apr. 23   *Perf. 13½x13¼*
303 A170 20d multi   1.25 1.25

Macedonian Intention to Enter European Union — A171

2004, May 4
304 A171 36d multi   2.00 2.00

Europa — A172

No. 305 — People at beach: a, Denomination at left. b, Denomination at right.

Perf. 13¼x13½   Wmk. 387
2004, May 7
305 A172 50d Horiz. pair, #a-b   5.00 5.00

Prespa Ecopark — A173

Perf. 13¼x13½
2004, June 5   Litho.   Unwmk.
306 A173 36d multi   2.00 2.00

2004 Summer Olympics, Athens — A174

No. 307 — Map of Europe, Olympic rings with flags and 2004 Summer Olympics emblem at: a, Left. b, Right.

Perf. 13½x13¼   Wmk. 387
2004, June 16
307 A174 50d Horiz. pair, #a-b   6.00 6.00

Sami Frasheri (1850-1904), Writer — A175

Perf. 13½x13¼
2004, June 18   Litho.   Unwmk.
308 A175 12d multi   .80 .80

FIFA (Fédération Internationale de Football Association), Cent. — A176

2004, July 3
309 A176 100d multi   5.00 5.00

Marko Cepenkov (1829-1920),
Writer — A177

2004, Sept. 1
310 A177 12d multi .80 .80

Vasil Glavinov
(1869-1929),
Politician — A178

2004, Sept. 1 *Perf. 13¼x13½*
311 A178 12d multi .80 .80

Birds — A179

Designs: 12d, Bombycilla garrulus. 24d,
Lanius senator. 36d, Monticola saxatilis. 48d,
Pyrrhula pyrrhula.
60d, Tichodroma muraria.

Perf. 13¼x13½
2004, Sept. 25 *Litho.*
312-315 A179 Set of 4 7.50 7.50
Souvenir Sheet
Imperf
316 A179 60d multi 4.00 4.00
No. 316 contains one 27x36mm stamp.

Children's
Day
A180

2004, Oct. 4 *Litho.* *Perf. 13½x13¼*
317 A180 12d multi .85 .85

Information
Technology
Society
Summit
A181

2004, Oct. 16
318 A181 36d multi 2.25 2.25

Aseman
Gospel,
1000th
Anniv.
A182

2004, Oct. 27 *Litho.* *Perf. 13½x13¼*
319 A182 12d multi .85 .85

Marco Polo (1254-1324),
Explorer — A183

2004, Nov. 10
320 A183 36d multi 2.25 2.25

Christmas
A184

2004, Nov. 24 *Perf. 13¼x13½*
321 A184 12d multi .85 .85

Konstantin
Miladinov
(1830-62),
Poet
A185

2005, Feb. 4 *Perf. 13½x13¼*
322 A185 36d multi 1.90 1.90

Illuminated
Manuscripts
A186

Designs: 12d, Manuscript from 16th-17th
cent. 24d, Manuscript from 16th cent.

2005, Mar. 9 *Perf. 13¼x13½*
323-324 A186 Set of 2 2.25 2.25

A187

Embroidery — A188

2005, Mar. 23 *Perf. 13½x13¼*
325 A187 36d multi 2.25 2.25
326 A188 50d multi 3.00 3.00

Art — A189

Designs: 36d, Sculpture by Ivan Mestrovic.
50d, Painting by Paja Jovanovic, horiz.

Perf. 13½x13¼, 13¼x13½
2005, Apr. 6
327-328 A189 Set of 2 5.25 5.25

First Book in
Albanian
Language, 450th
Anniv. — A190

2005, Apr. 27 *Perf. 13¼x13½*
329 A190 12d multi .80 .80

Skanderbeg
(1405-68),
Albanian National
Hero — A191

2005, Apr. 27
330 A191 36d multi 2.25 2.25

Europa — A192

Designs: a, 36d, Wheat, bread. b, 60d, Peppers, plate of food.

2005, May 9 *Perf. 13½x13¼*
331 A192 Horiz. pair, #a-b 6.00 6.00

Vlachs'
Day, Cent.
A193

2005, Apr. 27 *Litho.* *Perf. 13½x13¼*
332 A193 12d multi .80 .80

Environmental
Protection — A194

2005, June 4 *Perf. 13¼x13½*
333 A194 36d multi 2.25 2.25

Friezes — A195

Frieze from: 3d, 16th cent. 4d, 15th cent. 6d,
16th cent., diff. 8d, 1883-84. 12d, 16th cent.,
diff.

2005, June 8 *Litho.* *Perf. 13¼x13½*
334-338 A195 Set of 5 2.25 2.25

First Automobile in Macedonia,
Cent. — A196

First Glider in Macedonia, 50th
Anniv. — A197

Perf. 13½x13¼
2005, June 15 *Litho.*
339 A196 12d multi .75 .75
340 A197 36d multi 2.25 2.25

Intl. Year
of Physics
A198

2005, June 30
341 A198 60d multi 4.00 4.00

Fruit
A199

Designs: 12d, Malus Miller (apples). 24d,
Prunus persica (peaches). 36d, Prunus avium
(cherries). 48d, Prunus sp. (plums).
100d, Pyrus sp. (pears), vert.

Perf. 13½x13¼
2005, Sept. 14 *Litho.* *Wmk. 387*
342-345 A199 Set of 4 7.00 7.00
Souvenir Sheet
Perf. 13¼x13½
346 A199 100d multi 6.50 6.50

Smolar Waterfall — A200

2005, Sept. 28   **Unwmk.**
Perf. 13¼x13½
347 A200 24d multi   1.60 1.60

Hans Christian Andersen (1805-75), Author A201

2005, Oct. 3   **Litho.**   **Perf. 13½x13¼**
348 A201 12d multi   .85 .85

Kozjak Dam A202

2005, Oct. 25
349 A202 12d multi   .80 .80

Brsjac Rebellion, 125th Anniv. A203

2005, Oct. 28
350 A203 12d multi   .80 .80

Rila Congress, Cent. — A204

2005, Oct. 28   **Perf. 13¼x13½**
351 A204 12d multi   .80 .80

Europa Stamps, 50th Anniv. (in 2006) — A205

Emblems and Europa stamps: Nos. 352a, 353a, 60d, #243. Nos. 352b, 353b, 170d, #158. Nos. 352c, 353c, 250d, #97. Nos. 352d, 353d, 350d, #76.

2005, Nov. 14   **Perf. 13½x13¼**
352 A205 Block of 4, #a-d   50.00 50.00
       Souvenir Sheet
353 A205 Sheet of 4, #a-d   50.00 50.00
   Stamp sizes: Nos. 352a-352d, 40x30mm; Nos. 353a-353d, 40x29mm.

Whitewater Kayaker A206

2005, Nov. 23
354 A206 36d multi   2.25 2.25

Christmas — A207

2005, Nov. 23   **Perf. 13¼x13½**
355 A207 12d multi   .85 .85

Macedonia Post Emblem — A208

     Perf. 13¼x13½
2005, Dec. 14   **Litho.**
356 A208 12d multi   .80 .80

2006 Winter Olympics, Turin — A209

Designs: 36d, Skiing. 60d, Ice hockey.

2006, Jan. 26
357-358 A209   Set of 2   6.25 6.25

Fresco and Matejce Monastery A210

Isaac Celebi Mosque — A211

2006, Mar. 8
359 A210 12d multi   .65 .65
360 A211 24d multi   1.60 1.60

Léopold Sédar Senghor (1906-2001), First President of Senegal — A212

2006, Mar. 20   **Perf. 13½x13¼**
361 A212 36d multi   2.25 2.25

Handicrafts With Inlaid Mother-of-Pearl A213

Designs: 12d, Wooden shoes. 24d, Decorative objects.

2006, Mar. 22   **Perf. 13¼x13½**
362-363 A213   Set of 2   2.25 2.25

Wood Carving by Makarie Negriev Frckovski A214

Cupola of St. Peter's Basilica, Vatican City, 450th Anniv. A215

2006, Apr. 5   **Perf. 13½x13¼**
364 A214 12d multi   .65 .65
365 A215 36d multi   2.00 2.00

Zivko Firfov (1906-84), Composer A216

2006, Apr. 26   **Perf. 13¼x13½**
366 A216 24d multi   1.50 1.50

Wolfgang Amadeus Mozart (1756-91), Composer A217

2006, Apr. 26
367 A217 60d multi   4.00 4.00

Europa A218

Designs: 36d, Lettered balls. 60d, Lettered blocks.

2006, May 9   **Perf. 13½x13¼**
368-369 A218   Set of 2   6.00 6.00

     Souvenir Sheet

Macedonian Europa Stamps, 10th Anniv. — A219

No. 370: a, Pope John Paul II (1920-2005). b, Mother Teresa (1910-97).

2006, May 9   **Perf. 13¼x13½**
370 A219 60d Sheet of 2, #a-b   7.50 7.50

Fight Against Desertification — A220

2006, June 5   **Litho.**   **Perf. 13½x13¼**
371 A220 12d multi   .80 .80

Grand Prix Racing, Cent. A221

     Perf. 13½x13¼
2006, June 14   **Litho.**
372 A221 36d multi   2.25 2.25

Nikola Tesla (1856-1943), Electrical Engineer — A222

     Perf. 13½x13¼
2006, June 28   **Litho.**
373 A222 24d multi   1.50 1.50

Christopher Columbus (1451-1506), Explorer — A223

2006, June 28
374 A223 36d multi   2.00 2.00

Containers — A224

2006, Aug. 30   Litho.   Perf. 12¾x13
375 A224 3d Carafe   .25 .25
376 A224 6d Pitcher, bowl   .40 .40

Shells — A225

Designs: 12d, Ancylus scalariformis. 24d, Macedopyrgula pavlovici. 36d, Gyraulus trapezoides. 48d, Valvata hirsutecostata. 72d, Ochridopyrgula macedonica.

2006, Sept. 6   Litho.   Perf. 13¼x13½
377-380 A225 Set of 4   7.00 7.00
Souvenir Sheet
381 A225 72d multi   4.25 4.25

UNICEF, 60th Anniv. A226

2006, Oct. 2   Perf. 13½x13¼
382 A226 12d multi   .80 .80

Lynx and Galicica Natl. Park A227

2006, Oct. 2
383 A227 24d multi   1.50 1.50

World Senior Men's and Women's Bowling Championships — A228

2006, Oct. 20
384 A228 36d multi   2.10 2.10

Bishop Frang Bardhi (1606-43) A229

Pres. Boris Trajkovski (1956-2004) A230

Kemal Ataturk (1881-1938), Turkish Statesman A231

Archbishop Dositheus, 100th Anniv. of Birth — A232

2006, Oct. 25   Perf. 13¼x13½
385 A229 12d multi   .60 .60
386 A230 12d multi   .60 .60
387 A231 24d multi   1.40 1.40
388 A232 24d multi   1.40 1.40
    Nos. 385-388 (4)   4.00 4.00

Christmas A233

2006, Nov. 22   Perf. 13½x13¼
389 A233 12d multi   .75 .75

Metal Objects — A234

Designs: 4d, Handled container, Bitola, 19th cent. 5d, Wine flask, Skopje, 20th cent., vert. 10d, Bell, Skopje, 18th cent., vert. 12d, Lidded container, Prilep, 18th-19th cent., vert.

Perf. 13x12¾, 12¾x13
2006, Nov. 30
390 A234 4d multi   .25 .25
391 A234 5d multi   .25 .25
392 A234 10d multi   .55 .55
393 A234 12d multi   .70 .70
    Nos. 390-393 (4)   1.75 1.75

Kokino Megalithic Observatory A235

Designs: 12d, Mold for amulet. 36d, Sunrise over observatory.

2007, Jan. 31   Perf. 13¼x13½
394-395 A235 Set of 2   2.75 2.75
    Nos. 394-395 each were printed in sheets of 8 + label.

Monastery Anniversaries — A236

Designs: 12d, Slivnica Monastery, 400th anniv. 36d, St. Nikita Monastery, 700th anniv., vert.

Perf. 13½x13¼, 13¼x13½
2007, Jan. 31
396-397 A236 Set of 2   3.00 3.00

Handicrafts A237

Designs: 12d, Tepelak, Kicevo, 18th-19th cent. 36d, Casket, Ohrid, 19th cent.

2007, Feb. 14   Perf. 13½x13¼
398-399 A237 Set of 2   2.75 2.75

Fish A238

Designs: 12d, Cobitis vardarensis. 36d, Zingel balcanicus. 60d, Chondrostoma vardarense. No. 403, 100d, Barbus macedonicus. No. 404, 100d, Leuciscus cephalus.

2007, Feb. 28
400-403 A238 Set of 4   11.00 11.00
Souvenir Sheet
404 A238 100d multi   5.25 5.25

Epos of Freedom, Mosaic by Borko Lazeski A239

Head of a Woman, by Pablo Picasso — A240

2007, Mar. 14   Perf. 13½x13¼
405 A239 36d multi   2.00 2.00
Perf. 13¼x13½
406 A240 100d multi   6.00 6.00
    Cubism, cent.

Intl. Francophone Day — A241

2007, Mar. 20   Perf. 13½x13¼
407 A241 12d multi   .70 .70

Cat — A242

2007, Apr. 9   Perf. 13¼x13½
408 A242 12d multi   .75 .75

Europa A243

Macedonian Scouting emblem and: 60d, Scout camp. 100d, Scout, tent, vert.

Perf. 13½x13¼, 13¼x13½
2007, May 9   Litho.
409-410 A243 Set of 2   9.00 9.00

Souvenir Sheet

Europa — A243a

2007, May 9   Litho.   Perf. 13½x13¼
411 A243a 160d multi   40.00 40.00
    Scouting, cent.

Discovery of St. Cyril's Grave, 150th Anniv. — A244

2007, May 23   Perf. 13¼x13½
412 A244 50d multi   2.75 2.75

Smokestacks and Clock — A245

2007, June 5   Litho.   Perf. 13¼x13½
413 A245 12d multi   .75 .75

Carl von Linné
(1707-78),
Botanist — A246

Notes of Dmitri Mendeleev (1834-
1907), Chemist — A247

2007, June 20   **Perf. 13¼x13½**
414 A246 36d multi   2.10 2.10
                           Perf. 13½x13¼
415 A247 36d multi   2.10 2.10

Euro-Atlantic Partnership Council
Security Forum, Ohrid — A248

2007, June 28   **Perf. 13½x13¼**
416 A248 60d multi   3.25 3.25

Intl. Sailing
Federation,
Cent.
A249

2007, July 31 Litho. Perf. 13½x13¼
417 A249 35d multi   2.10 2.10

Maminska River
Waterfall — A250

                           Perf. 13¼x13½
2007, Sept. 19   **Litho.**
418 A250 12d multi   .75   .75

Mitrush Kuteli
(1907-67),
Writer — A251

Fan S. Noli
(1882-1965),
Albanian Prime
Minister — A252

2007, Sept. 25
419 A251 12d multi   .75   .75
420 A252 12d multi   .75   .75

Children's
Day
A253

2007, Oct. 1 Litho. Perf. 13½x13¼
421 A253 12d multi   .75   .75

Launch of
Sputnik 1,
50th Anniv.
A254

2007, Oct. 4 Litho. Perf. 13½x13¼
422 A254 36d multi   2.10 2.10

Petre
Prlicko
(1905-95),
Actor
A255

2007, Oct. 31 Litho. Perf. 13½x13¼
423 A255 12d multi   .75   .75

Jordan Hadzi Konstantinov-Dzinot
(1821-82), Educator — A256

2007, Oct. 31
424 A256 12d multi   .75   .75

Handbag — A257

2007, Nov. 9 Litho. Perf. 12¾x13
425 A257 12d multi   .75   .75

Christmas
A258

                           Perf. 13½x13¼
2007, Nov. 21   **Litho.**
426 A258 12d multi   .75   .75

Tose Proeski
(1981-2007),
Singer — A259

2007, Dec. 15   **Perf. 13¼x13½**
427 A259 12d multi   .75   .75

Earrings
A260

Designs: 12d, Earrings with pigeon design,
2nd cent. B.C. 24d, Earring with lion design,
4th cent. B.C., vert.

Perf. 13½x13¼, 13¼x13½
2008, Jan. 23   **Litho.**
428-429 A260 Set of 2   2.25 2.25

Launch of
Explorer 1
Satellite, 50th
Anniv. — A261

2008, Jan. 31 Litho. Perf. 13¼x13½
430 A261 24d multi   1.60 1.60

High-speed Train — A262

2008, Feb. 27   **Perf. 13½x13¼**
431 A262 100d multi   6.50 6.50

Worldwide Fund for Nature
(WWF) — A263

No. 432 — Upupa epops: a, 12d, In flight. b,
24d, Head. c, 48d, On branch, facing left with
insect in beak. d, 60d, On branch, facing right.

Perf. 13½x13¼
2008, Mar. 28   **Litho.**
432 A263 Block of 4, #a-d   7.50 7.50

Bulldog — A264

2008, Apr. 16 Litho. Perf. 13¼x13½
433 A264 30d multi   2.00 2.00

Europa — A265

No. 434 — Envelopes over: a, 50d, Western
Hemisphere, dark blue panel at top, country
name in yellow. b, 100d, Asia, Eastern Europe
and Africa, dark blue panel at top, country
name in pink.

No. 435, 50d: a, As No. 434a, green panel
at top. b, As No. 434b, green panel at top. c,
As No. 434a, blue panel at top, country name
in orange. d, As No. 434b, blue panel at top,
country name in orange.

2008, May 7 Litho. Perf. 13½x13¼
434 A265 Horiz. pair, #a-b   7.00 7.00
                 Miniature Sheet
435 A265 50d Sheet of 4, #a-d   11.00 11.00

No. 435 was sold with, but not attached to, a
booklet cover.

Robert Schuman,
Macedonian and
European Union
Flags — A266

Macedonian and European Union
Flags, Eiffel Tower, Paris — A267

Macedonian and European Union
Flags, Ljubljana, Slovenia — A268

                 Perf. 13¼x13½, 13½x13¼
2008, May 22
436 A266 36d multi   2.10 2.10
437 A267 50d multi   3.00 3.00
438 A268 50d multi   3.00 3.00
         Nos. 436-438 (3)   8.10 8.10

Environmental Protection — A269

2008, June 5 Litho. Perf. 13½x13¼
439 A269 12d multi   .75   .75

Rudolf Diesel (1858-1918), Inventor — A270

2008, June 18 **Perf. 13¼x13½**
440 A270 30d multi   2.00 2.00

2008 Summer Olympics, Beijing A271

Designs: 12d, Sailing. 18d, Rhythmic gymnastics. 20d, Tennis. 36d, Equestrian.

Perf. 13½x13¼ **Litho.**
441-444 A271   Set of 4   5.50 5.50

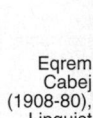

Eqrem Cabej (1908-80), Linguist A272

2008, Aug. 6 Litho. Perf. 13½x13¼
445 A272 12d multi   .75 .75

14th Intl. Congress of Slavists, Ohrid A273

2008, Sept. 10
446 A273 12d multi   .75 .75

Flowers — A274

Designs: 1d, Helichrysum zivojinii. 12d, Pulsatilla halleri, horiz. 50d, Stachys iva, horiz. No. 450, 72d, Fritillaria macedonica. No. 451, 72d, Centaurea grbavacensis.

Perf. 13¼x13½, 13½x13¼
2008, Sept. 10
447-450 A274   Set of 4   8.00 8.00

Souvenir Sheet
451 A274 72d multi   4.25 4.25

Matka Cave A275

2008, Sept. 24 Perf. 13½x13¼
452 A275 12d multi   .75 .75

Children's Day A276

2008, Oct. 6
453 A276 12d multi   .75 .75

European Women's Handball Championships — A277

2008, Oct. 15
454 A277 30d multi   1.40 1.40

Religious Song Lyrics by St. John Kukuzel (c. 1280-1360) A278

2008, Oct. 22 Litho. Perf. 13¼x13½
455 A278 12d multi   .75 .75

Giacomo Puccini (1858-1924), Opera Composer — A279

2008, Oct. 22 Perf. 13½x13¼
456 A279 100d multi   5.25 5.25

Kosta Racin (1908-43), Poet — A280

2008, Nov. 5 Perf. 13¼x13½
457 A280 12d multi   .75 .75

Albanian Language, Cent. — A281

Perf. 13¼x13½
2008, Nov. 14 **Litho.**
458 A281 12d multi   .75 .75

Christmas A282

Perf. 13½x13¼
2008, Nov. 19 **Litho.**
459 A282 12d multi   .65 .65

Cities
A283   A284

Designs: No. 460, Bitola. No. 461, Ohrid. No. 462, Tetovo. No. 463, Skopje. No. 464, Stip.

2008, Dec. 4 Litho. Perf. 12¾x13
Denomination Color
460 A283 12d blue   .70 .70
461 A283 12d black   .70 .70
462 A283 12d red   .70 .70
463 A284 12d gray blue   .70 .70
464 A284 12d gray green   .70 .70
Nos. 460-464 (5)   3.50 3.50
See Nos. 484-485, 499, 500.

Lech Walesa and Solidarity Emblem — A285

2008, Dec. 8 Perf. 13¼x13½
465 A285 50d multi   3.00 3.00
Friendship between Macedonia and Poland. Printed in sheets of 8 + label.

Blacksmithing A286

Designs: 10d, Blacksmiths and anvil. 20d, Horseshoe.

2009, Jan. 21
466-467 A286   Set of 2   1.90 1.90

Yuri Gagarin (1934-68), First Man in Space A287

2009, Feb. 4 Perf. 13½x13¼
468 A287 50d multi   3.00 3.00
Printed in sheets of 8 + label.

Campaign Against Breast Cancer — A288

2009, Mar. 2 Perf. 13¼x13½
469 A288 15d multi   1.00 1.00

Composers — A289

Designs: 12d, Trajko Prokopiev (1909-79) and Todor Skalovski (1909-2004). 60d, George Friedrich Handel (1685-1759) and Joseph Haydn (1732-1809).

2009, Mar. 18 Perf. 13½x13¼
470-471 A289   Set of 2   3.50 3.50
No. 471 was printed in sheets of 8 + label.

A290

Horses — A291

2009, Apr. 15 Litho. Perf. 13¼x13½
Granite Paper
472 A290 20d multi   1.10 1.10
473 A291 50d multi   2.75 2.75

Europa A292

Design: 50d, Hen, chicks, wolf, sheep, Pleiades and Venus. 100d, Cowherd, cows and Orion. 150d, Rooster and Moon, vert.

2009, May 6 Litho. Perf. 13½x13¼
474 A292 50d multi   3.75 3.75
475 A292 100d multi   7.00 7.00

Souvenir Sheet
Perf. 13x13½
476 A292 150d multi   20.00 20.00
Intl. Year of Astronomy.

Prague, Flags of Czech Republic and Macedonia A293

Pippi Longstocking, Flag of Macedonia
A294

2009, May 9 Litho. Perf. 13½x13¼
477 A293 10d multi .65 .65
Perf. 13¼x13½
478 A294 60d multi 3.75 3.75
Macedonia in the European Union. No. 478 was printed in sheets of 8 + label.

Vrelo Cave
A295

2009, June 5 Perf. 13½x13¼
479 A295 12d multi .80 .80

Louis Braille (1809-52), Educator of the Blind
A296

Perf. 13½x13¼
2009, June 17 Litho.
480 A296 18d multi 1.00 1.00

Charles Darwin (1809-82), Naturalist
A297

2009, June 17
481 A297 18d multi 1.25 1.25

Boat and Compass Rose
A298

Boat's Bow — A299

2009, June 24 Perf. 13½x13¼
482 A298 18d multi 1.10 1.10
Perf. 13¼x13½
483 A299 18d multi 1.10 1.10

Cities Type of 2008
Designs: 16d, Strumica. 18d, Prilep.

2009 Perf. 12¾x13
Denomination Color
484 A283 16d brown .90 .90
485 A283 18d blue 1.10 1.10
Issued: 16d, 8/7; 18d, 7/27.

Organized Soccer in Macedonia, Cent. — A300

2009, Aug. 12 Perf. 13¼x13½
486 A300 18d multi 1.10 1.10

Cyclist — A301

Bicycle Pedal
A302

2009, Sept. 2 Litho. Perf. 13¼x13½
487 A301 18d multi 1.00 1.00
Perf. 13½x13¼
488 A302 18d multi 1.00 1.00
Giro d'Italia bicycle race, cent.

Fauna
A303

Dr. Stankos Karaman (1889-1959), Zoologist, and Crustaceans — A304

Designs: 2d, Pelobates syriacus balcanicus. 3d, Salmo letnica. 6d, Austropotamobius torrentium macedonicus. 8d, Triturus macedonicus.

2009, Sept. 9 Litho. Perf. 13½x13¼
489-492 A303 Set of 4 1.40 1.40
Souvenir Sheet
Perf. 13¼x13½
493 A304 100d multi 5.00 5.00

Dimitar Andronov Papardishki (1859-1954), Painter — A305

2009, Sept. 30 Perf. 13½x13¼
494 A305 16d multi .95 .95

Elbasan Normal School and Pedagogical High School, 150th Anniv. — A306

2009, Oct. 14 Perf. 13¼x13½
495 A306 16d multi .95 .95

Filip Shiroka (1859-1935), Poet — A307

Krume Kepeski (1909-88), Linguist — A308

Petre M. Amdreevski (1934-2006), Writer — A309

2009, Nov. 4 Litho. Perf. 13¼x13½
496 A307 16d multi .95 .95
497 A308 16d multi .95 .95
Perf. 13½x13¼
498 A309 16d multi .95 .95
Nos. 496-498 (3) 2.85 2.85

Cities Type of 2008 and

Struga — A309a

Delchevo — A309b

Kumanovo — A309c

Resen — A309d

Designs: No. 499, Gostivar. No. 500, Kichevo.

2009, Nov. 11 Litho. Perf. 12¾x13
Denomination Color
499 A283 16d gray blue .80 .80
500 A283 16d Prus blue .80 .80
501 A309a 16d brown .80 .80
502 A309b 16d brown .80 .80
503 A309c 18d brown .90 .90
504 A309d 18d black .90 .90
Nos. 499-504 (6) 5.00 5.00

Christmas
A310

Perf. 13¼x13½
2009, Nov. 18 Litho.
505 A310 16d multi .95 .95

Helicopter
A311

2010, Feb. 10 Perf. 13½x13¼
506 A311 50d multi 2.75 2.75

2010 Winter Olympics, Vancouver
A312

Olympic rings, Vancouver Olympics emblem, inukshuk and: 50d, Ski jumper. 100d, Ice hockey goalie.

2010, Feb. 12 Perf. 13¼x13½
507-508 A312 Set of 2 7.25 7.25
Nos. 507-508 each were printed in sheets ot 8 + label.

Souvenir Sheet

International Women's Day — A313

No. 509 — Flower with denomination in: a, UL. b, UR.

2010, Mar. 8
509 A313 18d Sheet of 2, #a-b 2.00 2.00

St. Peter's Church, Golem Grad Island, 650th Anniv.
A314

Perf. 13½x13¼

2010, Mar. 25   Litho.
510   A314   18d multi   1.00   1.00

A315

Parrots
A316

2010, Apr. 14   **Perf. 13¼x13½**
511   A315   20d multi   1.25   1.25

Perf. 13½x13¼
512   A316   40d multi   2.25   2.25

Europa
A317

2010, May 5
513   A317   100d multi   8.00   8.00

Macedonian Chairmanship of the
Council of Europe — A318

2010, May 8
514   A318   18d multi   1.00   1.00

Macedonia
in the
European
Union
A319

Buildings: 20d, European Parliament, Brussels. 50d, Main Post Office, Madrid.

2010, May 8
515-516   A319   Set of 2   3.75   3.75

Dobar — A319a

Govgolija —
A319b

Kratovo —
A319c

Veles — A319d

Krusevo — A319e

2010   Litho.   **Perf. 12¾x13**
Denomination Color
517   A319a   16d brown   .70   .70
518   A319b   16d white   .70   .70
519   A319c   16d orange brown   .70   .70
520   A319d   18d olive brown   .75   .75
521   A319e   18d blue   .75   .75
    Nos. 517-521 (5)   3.60   3.60

Issued: No. 520, 5/8; others, 6/2.

Castanea
Sativa
A320

2010, June 5   Litho.   **Perf. 13½x13¼**
522   A320   20d multi   .95   .95

Robert
Schumann
(1810-56),
Composer
A321

Frédéric Chopin
(1810-49),
Composer
A322

2010, June 8   **Perf. 13½x13¼**
523   A321   50d multi   2.75   2.75

Perf. 13¼x13½
524   A322   60d multi   3.25   3.25

2010 World Cup Soccer
Championships, South Africa — A323

Emblem and: 50d, Soccer ball in goal net. 100d, Soccer ball at midfield, vert. 150d, Soccer ball, map of South Africa.

Perf. 13½x13¼, 13¼x13½
2010, June 11
525-526   A323   Set of 2   8.50   8.50
Souvenir Sheet
527   A323   150d multi   8.50   8.50

50th Ohrid
Summer
Festival — A324

2010, June 30   **Perf. 13¼x13½**
528   A324   18d multi   1.00   1.00

Mother Teresa
(1910-97),
Humanitarian
A325

2010, Aug. 26   Litho.   **Perf. 13**
529   A325   60d multi   3.00   3.00

See Albania No. 2889, Kosovo No. 154.

Bayram
Festival — A326

2010, Sept. 9   Litho.   **Perf. 13¼x13½**
530   A326   50d multi   2.40   2.40

Awarding of First Prize in Poetry
Contest to "The Serdar," by Gligor
Prlicev, 150th Anniv.
A327

2010, Sept. 10   **Perf. 10¼**
531   A327   100d multi   4.00   4.00

A328

Flora and
Fauna — A329

Designs: 18d, Chara ohridana. 20d, Gocea ohridana. 44d, Surirella spiralis. 100d, Ochridaspongia rotunda.

Perf. 13¼x13½
2010, Sept. 10   Litho.
532   A328   18d multi   .85   .85
533   A329   20d multi   1.10   1.10
534   A328   44d multi   2.25   2.25
535   A329   100d multi   4.75   4.75
    Nos. 532-535 (4)   8.95   8.95

Henri Dunant
(1828-1910),
Founder of Red
Cross — A330

Robert Koch (1843-1910),
Bacteriologist — A331

Jacques Cousteau (1910-97), Marine
Conservationist — A332

2010, Oct. 20   **Perf. 13¼x13½**
536   A330   10d multi   .50   .50

Perf. 13½x13¼
537   A331   20d multi   .95   .95
538   A332   20d multi   .95   .95
    Nos. 536-538 (3)   2.40   2.40

St. Naum
(c. 830-
910)
A333

Dimitar
Miladinov (1810-
62), Folklorist
A334

2010, Nov. 5   **Perf. 13½x13¼**
539   A333   18d multi   .85   .85

Perf. 13¼x13½
540   A334   18d multi   .85   .85

First
Multiparty
Elections
in
Macedonia
A335

2010, Nov. 11   **Perf. 13½x13¼**
541   A335   16d multi   .75   .75

Marin Barleti (c. 1450-c. 1512), Historian — A336

2010, Nov. 15   *Perf. 13¼x13½*
542 A336 20d multi   .85 .85

Jama, Sculpture by Dimo Todorovski (1910-83) A337

Painting by Dimce Koco (1910-93) A338

2010, Nov. 15   *Perf. 13½x13¼*
543 A337 50d multi   2.50 2.50
544 A338 50d multi   2.50 2.50

Christmas A339

2010, Nov. 22   **Litho.**
545 A339 16d multi   .75 .75

Kavadarci A340

Negotin A342

Kocani — A344

Kriva Palanka A341

Probistip A343

Sveti Nikole — A345

Radovici — A346

2010, Dec. 11   *Perf. 12¾x13*
Denomination Color
546 A340 16d aquamarine   .75 .75
547 A341 16d aquamarine   .75 .75
548 A342 16d purple   .75 .75
549 A343 16d black   .75 .75
550 A344 18d red   .85 .85
551 A345 18d black   .85 .85
    Perf. 13x12¾
552 A346 18d red   .85 .85
   Nos. 546-552 (7)   5.55 5.55

Coin From Reign of Constantine Dragas, c. 1371-95 — A347

2011, Feb. 28   *Perf. 13½x13¼*
553 A347 50d multi   2.50 2.50

First Man in Space, 50th Anniv. — A348

2011, Mar. 4   Litho.   *Perf. 13¼x13½*
554 A348 40d multi   11.00 11.00

Opening of Holocaust Memorial Center of the Jews From Macedonia, Skopje — A349

2011, Mar. 8   *Perf. 13½x13¼*
555 A349 100d multi   5.00 5.00

Macedonian Shepherd A350

2011, Apr. 11   *Perf. 13¼x13½*
556 A350 50d multi   2.50 2.50

Princess Diana (1961-97) A351

2011, Apr. 12
557 A351 100d multi   5.00 5.00

Intl. Year of Chemistry A352

2011, Apr. 13   *Perf. 13½x13¼*
558 A352 60d multi   3.00 3.00

First Automobile, 125th Anniv. — A353

First Automobile in Skopje, Cent. — A354

2011, Apr. 15   *Perf. 13½x13¼*
559 A353 20d multi   1.10 1.10
    Perf. 13¼x13½
560 A354 70d multi   3.50 3.50

Statue of James Watt (1736-1819), Engineer, and Diagram of His Steam Engine — A355

2011, Apr. 20   *Perf. 13½x13¼*
561 A355 60d multi   3.00 3.00

European Capitals A356

Designs: No. 562, 40d, Warsaw, Poland. No. 563, 40d, Budapest, Hungary.

2011, May 4
562-563 A356   Set of 2   4.25 4.25

Europa A357

Designs: 50d, Forest in autumn. No. 565, 100d, Forest in winter. No. 566, 100d, Forest in spring.

2011, May 5   *Perf. 13½x13¼*
564-565 A357   Set of 2   7.25 7.25
    Souvenir Sheet
566 A357 100d multi   4.75 4.75
   Intl. Year of Forests.

Albanian Language Newspaper, Shkupi, Cent. — A358

2011, June 10
567 A358 60d multi   3.00 3.00

Struga Poetry Evenings, 50th Anniv. A359

2011, June 15
568 A359 40d multi   2.00 2.00

Souvenir Sheet

Iustinianus Primus Law Faculty, Saints Cyril and Methodius University, Skopje, 60th Anniv. — A360

2011, July 1
569 A360 100d multi   5.00 5.00

Vinica — A361

2011, July 27   *Perf. 13x12¾*
570 A361 10d multi   .55 .55

Bayram Festival A362

    Perf. 13½x13¼
2011, Aug. 30   **Litho.**
571 A362 50d multi   2.25 2.25

2011 European Basketball Championships, Lithuania — A363

2011, Aug. 31   *Perf. 13¼*
572 A363 70d multi   3.25 3.25
Values are for stamps with surrounding selvage.

Independence, 20th Anniv. — A364

2011, Sept. 5   *Perf. 13½x13¼*
573 A364 20d multi   1.25 1.25

Ljubomir Belogaski (1912-94), Painter A365

2011, Sept. 14
574 A365 20d multi   1.00 1.00

Franz Liszt (1811-86), Composer A366

2011, Sept. 21   *Perf. 13¼x13½*
575 A366 50d black & silver   2.40 2.40

Ernest Hemingway (1899-1961), Writer — A367

2011, Oct. 11   *Perf. 13½x13¼*
576 A367 50d multi   2.40 2.40

Migjeni (Millos Gjergj Nikolla, 1911-38), Writer A368

2011, Oct. 19
577 A368 20d multi   1.00 1.00

Angelarios (1911-86), Archbishop of Ohrid — A369

2011, Oct. 26   *Perf. 13¼x13½*
578 A369 40d multi   2.00 2.00

Buildings
A370   A371

Buildings in: 16d, Demir Hisar. 18d, Dojran.

2011, Nov.   *Perf. 12¾x13*
579 A370 16d multi   .80 .80
580 A371 18d multi   .90 .90

Worldwide Fund for Nature (WWF) — A372

No. 581 — Spermophilus citellus: a, 12d, Two adults and butterfly. b, 24d, Adult and three juveniles. c, 48d, Adult and juvenile. d, 60d, Six adults and den.

2011, Dec. 13   *Perf. 13¼x13½*
581 A372 Block of 4, #a-d   6.50 6.50

Butterflies A373

Designs: 12d, Parnassius apollo. 24d, Zerynthia polyxena. 48d, Parnassius mnemosyne. 60d, Elphinstonia penia.

2011, Dec. 19   *Perf. 13½x13¼*
582-585 A373 Set of 4   6.50 6.50

Christmas A374

2011, Dec. 20   *Litho.*
586 A374 18d multi   1.00 1.00

Gjerasim Qiriazi (1858-94), Founder of Protestant Church of Albania A375

2011, Dec. 28
587 A375 20d multi   1.10 1.10

Tapestry — A376

2012, Feb. 20   *Perf. 13¼x13½*
588 A376 20d multi   1.00 1.00

Turtle A377

2012, Apr. 3   *Perf. 13½x13¼*
589 A377 100d multi   4.25 4.25

A378

Jets A379

2012, Apr. 4
590 A378 40d multi   14.00 14.00
   a.   With corrected spelling of country name (added Cyrillic "E")   2.50 2.50
591 A379 60d multi   2.60 2.60
   Country name is misspelled on No. 590.

Invention of the Telegraph, 175th Anniv. A380

2012, Apr. 5   *Litho.*
592 A380 100d multi   4.50 4.50

European Capitals — A381

Designs: 20d, Nicosia, Cyprus. 40d, Copenhagen, Denmark.

2012, Apr. 9   *Perf. 13¼x13½*
593-594 A381 Set of 2   22.50 22.50
  593a   With corrected spelling of country name (added Cyrillic "E")   1.25 1.25
  594a   With corrected spelling of country name (added Cyrillic "E")   2.40 2.40
   Country name is misspelled on Nos. 593-594.

Europa — A382

Designs: 20d, Building and aerial view of city. No. 596, 100d, Equestrian statue. No. 597, 100d, Bridge, horiz.

2012, Apr. 13   *Perf. 13¼x13½*
595-596 A382 Set of 2   5.25 5.25
Souvenir Sheet
Perf. 13½x13¼
597 A382 100d multi   4.25 4.25

Sinking of the Titanic, Cent. A383

2012, Apr. 17
598 A383 100d multi   4.25 4.25

Introduction of Denar as Currency, 20th Anniv. — A384

2012, Apr. 26
599 A384 50d multi   2.40 2.40

Berovo A385   Valandovo A386

Makedonska Kamenica — A387

2012   *Perf. 12¾x13*
Denomination Color
600 A385 2d gray   .25 .25
601 A386 16d blue   .65 .65
602 A387 18d rose   .75 .75
   Nos. 600-602 (3)   1.65 1.65
   Issued: 2d, 6/4; 16d, 18d, 6/6.

Zani i Maleve Orchestra, Cent. A388

2012, June 12   *Perf. 13½x13¼*
603 A388 40d multi   2.00 2.00

2012 Summer Olympics, London A389

Designs: 50d, Hurdles. 100d, Wrestling.

2012, June 24
604-605 A389 Set of 2   6.50 6.50

Bayram Festival — A390

2012, Aug. 19   Perf. 13¼x13½
606 A390 50d multi   2.40 2.40

Premiere of Opera "Otello," by Giuseppe Verdi, 125th Anniv. A391

2012, Sept. 11   Perf. 13½x13¼
607 A391 40d multi   2.00 2.00

Bats A392

Designs: 10d, Rhinolophus euryale. 20d, Rhinolophus ferrumequinum. 50d, Rhinolophus hipposideros. 100d, Miniopterus schreibersii.

2012, Sept. 18
608-611 A392 Set of 4   7.75 7.75

Kole Nedelkovski (1912-41), Poet A393

2012, Oct. 16
612 A393 50d multi   2.10 2.10

Gabriel II (1912-92), Archbishop of Ohrid — A394

2012, Oct. 16   Perf. 13¼x13½
613 A394 60d multi   2.25 2.25

Grimm's Fairy Tales, 200th Anniv. A395

2012, Dec. 3   Litho.   Perf. 13½x13¼
614 A395 20d multi   .95 .95

Christmas A396

2012, Dec. 11   Litho.
615 A396 50d multi   2.10 2.10

Kitchenware A397

Designs: 40d, Lidded bowl and decorative pattern. 50d, Plate and decorative pattern.

2013, Feb. 27   Perf. 13½x13¼
616-617 A397 Set of 2   4.00 4.00

Rabbit — A398

    Perf. 13¼x13½
2013, Mar. 14   Litho.
618 A398 60d multi   3.00 3.00

Motorcycle A399

    Perf. 13¼x13½
2013, Mar. 21   Litho.
619 A399 50d multi   2.50 2.50

Invention of Pneumatic Tires by John Boyd Dunlop (1840-1921), 125th Anniv. — A400

2013, Apr. 3   Perf. 13½x13¼
620 A400 40d multi   1.75 1.75

Vladimir Zworykin (1888-1982), Inventor, Diagram, and Television — A401

2013, Apr. 3   Litho.   Perf. 13½x13¼
621 A401 50d multi   2.10 2.10

European Capitals A402

Designs: 40d, Dublin, Ireland. 60d, Vilnius, Lithuania.

2013, Apr. 17   Litho.   Perf. 13½x13¼
622-623 A402 Set of 2   4.50 4.50

Europa A403

Designs: 40d, Postal van facing left. 60d, Postal van facing right. 100d, Postal truck and van.

2013, Apr. 22   Litho.   Perf. 13½x13¼
624-625 A403 Set of 2   4.75 4.75
   Souvenir Sheet
    Perf. 13¾x13
626 A403 100d multi   4.75 4.75

Ali Riza Ulqinaku (1855-1913), Writer — A404

    Perf. 13¼x13½
2013, June 10   Litho.
627 A404 16d multi   .85 .85

Rexhep Mitrovica (1887-1967), Prime Minister of Albania — A405

    Perf. 13½x13¼
2013, June 10   Litho.
628 A405 18d multi   .80 .80

Mission of Saints Cyril and Methodius to Slavic Lands, 1150th Anniv. A406

    Perf. 13½x13¼
2013, June 24   Litho.
629 A406 40d multi   1.75 1.75

Building, Demir Kapija — A407   Building, Makedonski Brod — A408

2013   Litho.   Perf. 12¾x13
630 A407 16d multi   .70 .70
631 A408 16d multi   .70 .70
    Issued: No. 630, 7/5; No. 631, 7/18.

Skopje Earthquake, 50th Anniv. — A409

2013, July 26   Litho.   Perf. 13½x13¼
632 A409 100d multi   4.00 4.00

Bayram Festival A410

2013, July 30   Litho.   Perf. 13½x13¼
633 A410 40d multi   1.75 1.75

Vasil Chekalarov (1874-1913), Bulgarian Revolution Leader — A411

    Perf. 13¼x13½
2013, Sept. 10   Litho.
634 A411 16d multi   .70 .70

Gjurchin Kokaleski (1775-1863), Local Chieftain, Writer of First Macedonian Autobiography — A412

    Perf. 13½x13¼
2013, Sept. 10   Litho.
635 A412 18d multi   .80 .80

Ohrid-Debar Rebellion, Cent. — A413

Perf. 13¼x13½
2013, Sept. 19   **Litho.**
636   A413 60d multi   2.75 2.75

2013 Men's European Basketball
Championships, Slovenia — A414

2013, Sept. 20   **Litho.**   *Perf. 13¼*
637   A414 90d multi   4.00 4.00
  Values are for stamps with surrounding
selvage.

Diplomatic Relations Between
Macedonia and People's Republic of
China, 20th Anniv.
A415

2013, Oct. 15   **Litho.**   *Perf. 13½x13¼*
638   A415 100d multi   4.50 4.50

Mushrooms
A416

  No. 639: a, Boletus satanas, butterfly, ladybug. b, Myriostoma coliforme, butterfly, lizard.
c, Caloscypha fulgens, insect. d, Terana
caerulea, insect.

2013, Oct. 16   **Litho.**   *Perf. 13¼x13½*
639   Horiz. strip of 4   8.25 8.25
   a.   A416 10d multi   .45 .45
   b.   A416 20d multi   .90 .90
   c.   A416 50d multi   2.25 2.25
   d.   A416 100d multi   4.50 4.50

Petre Bogdanov-Kocko (1913-88),
Composer — A417

Perf. 13½x13¼
2013, Nov. 13   **Litho.**
640   A417 20d multi   .90 .90

Christmas
A419

Perf. 13½x13¼
2013, Dec. 11   **Litho.**
642   A419 40d multi   1.90 1.90

Calculator   Shopping Cart
A421   A422

2014, Jan. 14   **Litho.**   *Perf. 12¾x13*
645   A421 8d multi   .35 .35
646   A422 8d multi   .35 .35

Decorative
Jewelry
A423

  Various pieces from 19th-20th cent. from
Bitola: 24d, 40d, vert.

Perf. 13½x13¼, 13¼x13½
2014, May 22   **Litho.**
647-648   A423   Set of 2   3.00 3.00

2014 Winter Olympics, Sochi,
Russia — A424

  Designs: 50d, Ice hockey. 100d, Ski
jumping.

2014, May 23   **Litho.**   *Perf. 13¼*
649-650   A424   Set of 2   0.75 0.75
  Values are for stamps with surrounding
selvage.

Michelangelo (1475-1564), Sculptor
and Painter — A425

2014, May 27   **Litho.**   *Perf. 13½x13¼*
651   A425 144d multi   6.50 6.50

Goldfish
A426

  Designs: 21d, Goldfish in water. 60d, Goldfish and air bubbles.

2014, May 28   **Litho.**   *Perf. 13½x13¼*
652-653   A426   Set of 2   3.75 3.75

Galileo Galilei (1564-1642),
Astronomer — A428

2014, May 30   **Litho.**   *Perf. 13½x13¼*
655   A428 20d multi   .90 .90
  No. 655 was printed in sheets of 8 + central
label.

Europa
A431

  Designs: 40d, Zurna. No. 660, 50d, Three-
holed ocarina (light green background).
  No. 661, 50d: a, Tambura (gray green background). b, Two tamburas (pale pink background). c, Kemene and bow (pale orange
background). d, Gajda (pale blue background).
60d, Drum.

2014, June 4   **Litho.**   *Perf. 13½x13¼*
659-660   A431   Set of 2   4.00 4.00
Miniature Sheet
661   Sheet of 4   9.00 9.00
   a.-d.   A431 50d Any single   2.25 2.25
Souvenir Sheet
662   A431 60d multi   2.75 2.75
  No. 661 was sold with but unattached to a
booklet cover.

Battle of
Belasitsa
(Kleidion),
1000th
Anniv.
A436

Perf. 13½x13¼
2014, June 29   **Litho.**
670   A436 50d multi   2.25 2.25

POSTAL TAX STAMPS

Men Blowing
Horns — PT1

1991, Dec. 30   **Litho.**   *Perf. 13½*
RA1   PT1 2.50d multicolored   .90 .90
  No. RA1 was required on mail Dec. 31,
1991-Sept. 8, 1992. For surcharge see No. 22.

Anti-Cancer
Week — PT2

  Designs: Nos. RA2, RA6, Emblems, inscriptions. Nos. RA3, RA7, Magnetic resonance
imaging scanner. Nos. RA4, RA8, Overhead
scanner, examination table. No. RA5, RA9c,
Mammography imager. No. RA9, Ultra sound
computer.

1992, Mar. 1   **Litho.**   *Perf. 10*
RA2   PT2 5d multicolored   .65 .65
RA3   PT2 5d multicolored   .65 .65
RA4   PT2 5d multicolored   .65 .65
RA5   PT2 5d multicolored   .65 .65
   a.   Block of 4, #RA2-RA5   3.75 3.75
RA6   PT2 5d multicolored   .25 .25
RA7   PT2 5d multicolored   .25 .25
RA8   PT2 5d multicolored   .25 .25
RA9   PT2 5d multicolored   .25 .25
   a.   Block of 4, #RA6-RA9   1.25 1.25
   b.   Souv. sheet of 3, #RA7-
      RA9, RA9c   22.50 22.50
   c.   PT2 5d multicolored   .40 .40
    Nos. RA2-RA9 (8)   3.60 3.60

  Inscription at right reads up on No. RA2 and
down on No. RA6. Designs on Nos. RA7-RA8,
RA9c are without red cross symbol.
  Souvenir folders with perf. and imperf.
sheets of RA9b sold for 40d. Value for both
sheets in folder, $50.
  Obligatory on mail Mar. 1-8.
  See Nos. RA28-RA31.

Red Cross
Week
PT3

  Designs: RA10, Slogans. No. RA11, Airplanes dropping supplies. No. RA12, Aiding
traffic accident victim. No. RA13, Evacuating
casualties from building.

1992, May 8   *Perf. 10*
RA10   PT3 10d multicolored   .25 .25
RA11   PT3 10d multicolored   .25 .25
RA12   PT3 10d multicolored   .25 .25
RA13   PT3 10d multicolored   .25 .25
   a.   Block of 4, #RA10-RA13   .65 .65
  Nos. RA10-RA13 exist with silver-colored
borders in perf. and imperf. miniature sheets
that sold for 80d. Value for both sheets $7.50.
  Obligatory on mail May 8-15.

PT4

  Solidarity Week: No. RA14, Skopje earthquake. No. RA15, Woman holding girl. No.
RA16, Mother carrying infant. No. RA17,
Mother, children, airplane.
  130d, Woman, child, airport control tower.

1992, June 1   *Perf. 10*
RA14   PT4 20d multicolored   .25 .25
RA15   PT4 20d multicolored   .25 .25
RA16   PT4 20d multicolored   .25 .25
RA17   PT4 20d multicolored   .25 .25
   a.   Block of 4   .65 .65
Size: 74x97mm
Imperf
RA18   PT4 130d multicolored   3.00 3.00
  No. RA18 also exists with perf. vignette.
Same value.
  Obligatory on mail June 1-7.
  See No. RA55.

PT5

  Anti-Tuberculosis Week: No. RA20, Nurse,
infant. No. RA21, Nurse giving oxygen to
patient. No. RA22, Infant in bed.
  200d, Child being treated by nurse.

1992, Sept. 14   *Perf. 10*
RA19   PT5 20d multicolored   .25 .25
RA20   PT5 20d multicolored   .25 .25
RA21   PT5 20d multicolored   .25 .25

RA22 PT5 20d multicolored   .25 .25
   a.   Block of 4, #RA19-RA22   .65 .65

Size: 74x97mm
Imperf

RA23 PT5 200d vermilion & multi   2.50 2.50

No. RA23 exists with magenta inscriptions, and also with perf. vignette and either magenta or vermilion inscriptions. Obligatory on mail Sept. 14-21.

Red Cross Fund PT6

1993, Feb. 1   Litho.   **Perf. 10**
RA24 PT6 20d Shown   .30 .30
RA25 PT6 20d Marguerites   .30 .30
RA26 PT6 20d Carnations   .30 .30
RA27 PT6 20d Mixed bouquet   .30 .30
   a.   Block of 4, #RA24-RA27   1.25 1.25

Nos. RA24-RA27 exist in perf. or imperf. miniature sheets with either gold or silver backgrounds and inscriptions, that sold for 500d each. Value for both sheets $12. Obligatory on mail Feb. 1-28.

Cancer Therapy Type of 1992

Designs: No. RA28, Nuclear medicine caduceus, inscriptions. No. RA29, Radiographic equipment. No. RA30, Radiology machine. No. RA31, Scanner.

1993, Mar. 1   Litho.   **Perf. 10**
RA28 PT2 20d multicolored   .30 .30
RA29 PT2 20d multicolored   .30 .30
RA30 PT2 20d multicolored   .30 .30
RA31 PT2 20d multicolored   .30 .30
   a.   Block of 4, #RA28-RA31   1.25 1.25

Nos. RA28-RA31 exist in perf. & imperf. miniature sheets with gold background or inscription, that sold for 500d each. Value for both sheets $6.50. Obligatory on mail Mar. 1-8.

Red Cross Week PT7

1993, May 8   Litho.   **Perf. 10**
RA32 PT7 50d Inscriptions   .25 .25
RA33 PT7 50d Man holding baby   .25 .25
RA34 PT7 50d Patient in wheelchair   .25 .25
RA35 PT7 50d Carrying stretcher   .25 .25
   a.   Block of 4, #RA32-RA35   1.20 1.20

Perf. & imperf. miniature sheets of Nos. RA32-RA35 exist with yellow inscription tablets that sold for 700d each. Value for both sheets $7. Obligatory on mail May 8-15.

1993, June 1   **Perf. 10**
RA36 PT7 50de Skopje earthquake   .25 .25
RA37 PT7 50de Unloading boxes   .25 .25
RA38 PT7 50de Labeling boxes   .25 .25
RA39 PT7 50de Boxes, fork lift   .25 .25
   a.   Block of 4, #RA36-RA39   1.20 1.20

Perf. & imperf. miniature sheets of Nos. RA36-RA39 exist with gold inscription tablets that sold for 7d each. Value for both sheets $5. Obligatory on mail June 1-7.

1993, Sept. 14   **Perf. 10**

Designs: Nos. RA40, Inscriptions. Nos. RA41, Children in meadow. No. RA42, Bee on flower. No. RA43, Goat behind rock.

RA40 PT7 50de black, gray & red   .25 .25
RA41 PT7 50de green & multi   .25 .25
RA42 PT7 50de green & multi   .25 .25
RA43 PT7 50de green & multi   .25 .25
   a.   Block of 4, #RA40-RA43   .65 .65

Nos. RA41-RA43 exist in perf. & imperf. miniature sheets that sold for 15d each. Values for both sheets $3.25. Nos. RA40-RA43 exist with yellow omitted, resulting in blue stamps. Value of the blue set $4.25.

Obligatory on mail Sept. 14-21. See Nos. RA52-RA54.

Anti-Cancer Week — PT8

1994, Mar. 1   **Perf. 10**
RA44 PT8 1d Inscription, emblem   .25 .25
RA45 PT8 1d Lily   .25 .25
RA46 PT8 1d Mushroom   .25 .25
RA47 PT8 1d Swans   .25 .25
   a.   Block of 4, #RA44-RA47   .90 .90

Nos. RA44-RA47 without silver color exist in perf. & imperf. miniature sheets and sold for 20d. Value for both sheets $7. Obligatory on mail Mar. 1-8.

Red Cross Type of 1993 and

PT9

1994, May 8   Litho.   **Perf. 10**
RA51 PT9 1d shown   .25 .25
RA52 PT7 1d like #RA41   .25 .25
RA53 PT7 1d like #RA39   .25 .25
RA54 PT7 1d like #RA33   .25 .25
   a.   Block of 4, #RA51-RA54   .65 .65

Nos. RA51-RA54 exist without denomination in perf. & imperf. miniature sheets and sold for 30d each. Value for both sheets $9. Obligatory on mail May 8-15, 1994.

Skopje Earthquake Type of 1993
1994, June 1
RA55 PT4 1d like #RA14   .65 .65

Obligatory on mail June 1-7, 1994.

Red Cross Fund PT10

1994, Dec. 1   Litho.   **Perf. 10**
RA56 PT10 2d shown   .25 .25
RA57 PT10 2d Globe   .25 .25
RA58 PT10 2d AIDS awareness   .25 .25
RA59 PT10 2d Condoms   .25 .25
   a.   Block of 4, Nos. RA56-RA59   1.15 1.15

Size: 80x95mm
Imperf

RA60 PT10 40d like RA57   3.00 3.00

Country name and value omitted from vignette on No. RA60, which also exists with perf. vignette. Obligatory on mail Dec. 1-8.

Anti-Cancer Week — PT11

1995, Mar. 1
RA61 PT11 1d shown   .25 .25
RA62 PT11 1d White lilies   .25 .25
RA63 PT11 1d Red lilies   .25 .25
RA64 PT11 1d Red roses   .25 .25
   a.   Block of 4, Nos. RA61-RA64   1.15 1.15

Size: 97x74mm
Imperf

RA65 PT11 30d like #RA61, RA64   2.25 2.25

Blue inscriptions, country name, and value omitted from vignette on No. RA65, which also exists with perf. vignette. Obligatory on mail Mar. 1-8.

Red Cross Fund — PT12

Designs: No. RA66, Red Cross emblem. No. RA67, Red Cross volunteers holding clipboards. No. RA68, Young volunteers wearing white shirts. No. RA69, RA70, Red Cross, Red Crescent symbols, globe.

1995, May 8
RA66 PT12 1d multicolored   .25 .25
RA67 PT12 1d multicolored   .25 .25
RA68 PT12 1d multicolored   .25 .25
RA69 PT12 1d blue & multi   .25 .25
   a.   Strip of 4, Nos. RA70-RA73   1.15 1.15

Size: 68x85mm
Imperf

RA70 PT12 1d multicolored   2.25 2.25

No. RA70 also exists with perf. vignette. Obligatory on mail May 8-15.

Solidarity Week PT13

1995, June 1
RA71 PT13 1d shown   .45 .45

Size: 85x70
Imperf

RA72 PT13 30d like No. RA75   2.00 2.00

No. RA72 also exists with perf. vignette. Obligatory on mail June 1-7.

Robert Koch (1843-1910), Bacteriologist — PT14

1995, Sept. 14   Litho.   **Perf. 10**
RA73 PT14 1d shown   .60 .60

Size: 90x73mm
Imperf

RA74 PT14 30d like No. RA73   2.00 2.00

No. RA74 exists with perf. vignette. Obligatory on mail Sept. 14-21.

PT15

1995, Oct. 2   Litho.   **Die Cut**
Self-Adhesive
RA75 PT15 2d blue violet & red   .45 .45

Children's Week. Obligatory on mail 10/2-8.

PT16

1995, Nov. 1   Litho.   **Perf. 10**
RA76 PT16 1d multicolored   .40 .40

Size: 90x72mm
Imperf

RA77 PT16 30d like #RA76   2.00 2.00

Red Cross, AIDS awareness. No. RA77 also exists with perf. vignette. Obligatory on mail Nov. 1-7.

Red Cross PT17

1996, Mar. 1   Litho.   **Perf. 10**
RA78 PT17 1d multicolored   .60 .60

Size: 98x76mm
Imperf

RA79 PT17 30d like #RA78   2.25 2.25

No. RA79 also exists with perf. vignette. Obligatory on mail Mar. 1-8.

PT18

Red Cross Week — PT19

Fundamental principles of Red Cross, Red Crescent Societies, inscriptions in: No. RA81, Macedonian. No. RA82, English. No. RA83, French. RA84, Spanish.

1996, May 8   Litho.   **Perf. 10**
RA80 PT18 1d multicolored   .25 .25
RA81 PT19 1d multicolored   .25 .25
RA82 PT19 1d multicolored   .25 .25
RA83 PT19 1d multicolored   .25 .25
RA84 PT19 1d multicolored   .25 .25
   a.   Strip of 5, #RA80-RA84   1.30 1.30

Obligatory on mail May 8-15.

Red Cross, Solidarity Week — PT20

1996, June 1   Litho.   **Perf. 10**
RA86 PT20 1d multicolored   .50 .50

No. RA86 exists without country name or denomination in perf. & imperf. miniature sheets and sold for 30d each. Value for both sheets $5.50. Obligatory on mail June 1-7, 1996.

Red Cross, Fight
Tuberculosis
Week — PT21

1996, Sept. 14   Litho.   Perf. 10
RA87   PT21   1d multicolored   .55   .55
Size: 80x90mm
Imperf
RA88   PT21   30d like #RA87   2.00   2.00
No. RA88 also exists with perf. vignette.
Obligatory on mail Sept. 14-21.

Red Cross,
AIDS
Awareness
PT22

1996, Dec. 6
RA89   PT22   1d multicolored   .55   .55
Size: 90x73mm
Imperf
RA90   PT22   30d like #RA89   2.00   2.00
No. RA90 also exists with perf. vignette.
Obligatory on mail Dec. 1-7.

Red Cross,
Cancer
Week — PT23

1997, Apr. 1
RA91   PT23   1d Cross in pale
            org   .50   .50
  a.   Cross in red   .70   .70
No. RA91 obligatory on mail Apr. 1-8.
No. RA91a issued 5/8.

Red
Cross — PT24

1997, May 8
RA92   PT24   1d multicolored   1.75   1.75
Obligatory on mail May 8-15.

Children's
Day — PT25

1997, June 1
RA93   PT25   1d Cross in deep
            vermilion   .50   .50
  a.   Cross in red   .70   .70
Obligatory on mail June 1-8.

Red Cross, Anti-
Tuberculosis
PT26

1997, Sept. 14
RA94   PT26   1d multicolored   .50   .50
Obligatory on mail, Sept. 14-21.

Red
Cross — PT27

1997, Dec. 1   Litho.   Perf. 10
RA95   PT27   1d multicolored   .50   .50
Obligatory on mail Dec. 1-7.

Red Cross
Fight
Against
Cancer
PT28

1998, Mar. 1   Perf. 13½
RA96   PT28   1d multicolored   .50   .50
Obligatory on mail Mar. 1-8.

Red Cross,
Humanity
PT29

1998, May 8
RA97   PT29   2d multicolored   .50   .50
Obligatory on mail May 8-15.

Red
Cross — PT30

1998, June 1   Litho.   Perf. 13½
RA98   PT30   2d multicolored   .50   .50
Obligatory on mail June 1-7, 1998.

PT31

1998, Sept. 14   Litho.   Perf. 13½
RA99   PT31   2d multicolored   .50   .50
Fight tuberculosis. Obligatory on mail Sept.
14-21, 1998.

PT32

1998, Dec. 1
RA100   PT32   2d multicolored   .50   .50
AIDS awareness. Obligatory on mail Dec. 1-
7, 1998.

PT33

1999, Mar. 1   Litho.   Perf. 13¼
RA101   PT33   2d multi   .50   .50
Red Cross fight against cancer. Obligatory
on mail Mar. 1-7, 1999.

Red Cross
PT34

1999, May 8
RA102   PT34   2d multi   .50   .50
Obligatory on mail May 8-15, 1999.

PT35

1999, June 1
RA103   PT35   2d multi   .50   .50
Red Cross, solidarity week. Obligatory on
mail June 1-7, 1999.

PT36

1999, Sept. 14   Litho.   Perf. 13¼
RA104   PT36   2d multi   .50   .50
Fight tuberculosis. Obligatory on mail Sept.
14-21.

AIDS
Awareness
PT37

1999, Dec. 1
RA105   PT37   2.50d multi   .55   .55
Obligatory on mail Dec. 1-7.

Anti-Cancer
Week — PT38

2000, Mar. 1   Litho.   Perf. 13¼
RA106   PT38   2.50d multi   .50   .50
Obligatory on mail Mar. 1-8.

Red Cross
PT39

2000, May 8
RA107   PT39   2.50d multi   .50   .50
Obligatory on mail May 8-15.

Red
Cross — PT40

2000, June 1
RA108   PT40   2.50d multi   .30   .30
Obligatory on mail June 1-7.

Red
Cross — PT41

2000 Sept. 14   Litho.   Perf. 13¼
RA109   PT41   3d multi   .50   .50
Obligatory on mail Sept. 14-21.

Fight Against
AIDS — PT42

2000 Dec. 1
RA110   PT42   3d multi   .55   .55
Obligatory on mail Dec. 1-7.

Fight Against
Cancer — PT43

2001, Mar. 1   **Litho.**   *Perf. 13¼*
RA111 PT43 3d multi   .50   .50
Obligatory on mail Mar. 1-8.

Red Cross
PT44

2001, May 8
RA112 PT44 3d multi   .50   .50
Obligatory on mail May 8-15.

Red Cross
Solidarity
Week — PT45

2001, June 1
RA113 PT45 3d multi   .50   .50
Obligatory on mail June 1-7.

Fight Against
Tuberculosis
PT46

2001, Sept. 14
RA114 PT46 3d multi   .50   .50
Obligatory on mail Sept. 14-21.

Campaign Against
AIDS — PT47

2001, Dec. 1   **Litho.**   *Perf. 13¼*
RA115 PT47 3d multi   .55   .55
Obligatory on mail Dec. 1-7.

Campaign
Against
Cancer
PT48

2002, Mar. 1
RA116 PT48 3d multi   .50   .50
Obligatory on mail Mar. 1-8.

Red Cross
Week
PT49

2002, May 8   **Litho.**   *Perf. 13¼*
RA117 PT49 3d multi   .50   .50
Obligatory on mail May 8-15.

Red Cross
Solidarity
Week
PT50

2002, June 1
RA118 PT50 3d multi   .50   .50
Obligatory on mail June 1-7.

Tuberculosis
Prevention
PT51

2002, Sept. 14
RA119 PT51 3d multi   .50   .50
Obligatory on mail Sept. 14-21.

Campaign
Against
AIDS
PT52

2002, Dec. 1
RA120 PT52 3d multi   .50   .50

Campaign Against
Cancer — PT53

2003, Mar. 1   **Litho.**   *Perf. 13¼*
RA121 PT53 4d multi   .50   .50
Obligatory on mail Mar. 1-8.

Campaign Against
AIDS — PT54

2003, May 8
RA122 PT54 4d multi   .55   .55
Obligatory on mail May 8-15.

Red Cross
Solidarity — PT55

2003, June 1   *Perf. 13¼x13½*
RA123 PT55 4d multi   .50   .50
Obligatory on mail June 1-7.

Tuberculosis
Prevention
PT56

Perf. 13½x13¼
2003, Sept. 14   **Litho.**
RA124 PT56 4d multi   .50   .50
Obligatory on mail Sept. 14-21.

Campaign
Against
AIDS — PT57

2003, Dec. 1   **Litho.**   *Perf. 13¼x13½*
RA125 PT57 4d multi   .50   .50
Obligatory on mail Dec. 1-7.

Campaign
Against
Cancer — PT58

2004, Mar. 1
RA126 PT58 4d multi   .50   .50
Obligatory on mail Mar. 1-8.

Red Cross
Week — PT59

2004, May 8
RA127 PT59 4d multi   .50   .50
Obligatory on mail May 8-15.

Red Cross
Solidarity
Week — PT60

2004, June 1   **Litho.**   *Perf. 13¼x13½*
RA128 PT60 6d multi   .50   .50
Obligatory on mail June 1-7.

Tuberculosis Week — PT61

2004, Sept. 14   *Perf. 13½x13¼*
RA129 PT61 6d multi   .50   .50
Obligatory on mail Sept. 14-21.

Campaign
Against
AIDS
PT62

2004, Dec. 1   **Litho.**   *Perf. 13½x13¼*
RA130 PT62 6d multi   .60   .60
Obligatory on mail Dec. 1-7.

Campaign
Against
Cancer — PT63

2005, Mar. 1   *Perf. 13¼x13½*
RA131 PT63 6d multi   .60   .60
Obligatory on mail Mar. 1-8.

Red Cross
PT64

2005, May 8   **Litho.**   *Perf. 13½x13¼*
RA132 PT64 6d multi   .60   .60
Obligatory on mail May 8-15.

Campaign Against
Tuberculosis — PT65

Perf. 13½x13¼
2005, Sept. 14   **Litho.**
RA133 PT65 6d multi   .60   .60
Obligatory on mail Sept. 14-21.

Campaign Against AIDS — PT66

2005, Dec. 1   *Perf. 13¼x13½*
RA134 PT66 6d multi   .60   .60
Obligatory on mail Dec. 1-7.

Campaign Against Breast Cancer — PT67

2006, Mar. 1   Litho.   *Perf. 13¼x13½*
RA135 PT67 6d multi   .60   .60
Obligatory on mail Mar. 1-7.

Red Cross Week — PT68

2006, May 18   Litho.   *Perf. 13¼x13½*
RA136 PT68 6d multi   .60   .60
Obligatory on mail May 8-15.

Campaign Against Tuberculosis — PT69

2006, Sept. 14   *Perf. 13½x13¼*
RA137 PT69 6d multi   .60   .60
Obligatory on mail Sept. 14-21.

Campaign Against AIDS PT70

2006, Dec. 1
RA138 PT70 6d multi   .60   .60
Obligatory on mail Dec. 1-7.

Campaign Against Cancer — PT71

2007, Mar. 1   Litho.   *Perf. 13¼x13½*
RA139 PT71 6d multi   .60   .60
Obligatory on mail Mar. 1-8.

Red Cross Week — PT72

2007, May 8
RA140 PT72 6d multi   .60   .60
Obligatory on mail May 8-15.

Campaign Against Tuberculosis PT73

2007, Sept. 14
ПА141 PT70 0d multi   .00   .00
Obligatory on mail Sept. 14-21.

Campaign Against AIDS PT74

2007, Dec. 1   *Perf. 13½x13¼*
RA142 PT74 6d multi   .60   .60
Obligatory on mail Dec. 1-8.

Campaign Against Cancer PT75

2008, Mar. 1   Litho.   *Perf. 13½x13¼*
RA143 PT75 6d multi   .50   .50
Obligatory on mail Mar. 1-8.

Red Cross Week PT76

2008, May 8
RA144 PT76 6d multi   .50   .50
Obligatory on mail May 8-15.

Campaign Against Tuberculosis PT77

2008, Sept. 14   *Perf. 13¼x13½*
RA145 PT77 6d multi   .50   .50
Obligatory on mail Sept. 14-21.

Campaign Against AIDS PT78

2008, Dec. 1   *Perf. 13½x13¼*
RA146 PT78 6d multi   .60   .60
Obligatory on mail Dec. 1-8.

Campaign Against Cancer — PT79

2009, Mar. 1   *Perf. 13¼x13½*
RA147 PT79 6d multi   .50   .50
Obligatory on mail Mar. 1-8.

Red Cross Week PT80

2009, May 8   *Perf. 13½x13¼*
RA148 PT80 6d multi   .50   .50
Obligatory on mail May 8-15.

Campaign Against Tuberculosis — PT81

2009, Sept. 14
RA149 PT81 6d multi   .60   .60
Obligatory on mail Sept. 14-21.

Campaign Against AIDS PT82

2009, Dec. 1
RA150 PT82 8d multi   .60   .60
Obligatory on mail Dec. 1-7.

Campaign Against Cancer — PT83

2010, Mar. 1   *Perf. 13¼x13½*
Granite Paper
RA151 PT83 8d multi   .60   .60
Obligatory on mail Mar. 1-7.

Red Cross Week — PT84

2010, May 8   Litho.
Granite Paper
RA152 PT84 8d multi   .50   .50
Obligatory on mail May 8-15.

Campaign Against Tuberculosis — PT85

     Perf. 13½x13¼
2010, Sept. 14   Litho.
Granite Paper
RA153 PT85 8d multi   .50   .50
Obligatory on mail Sept. 14-21.

Campaign Against AIDS — PT86

2010, Dec. 1   *Perf. 13¼x13½*
Granite Paper
RA154 PT86 8d multi   .50   .50
Obligatory on mail Dec. 1-7.

Campaign Against Cancer — PT87

2011, Mar. 1   **Granite Paper**
RA155 PT87 8d multi   .50   .50
Obligatory on mail Mar. 1-8.

Red Cross
Week — PT88

2011, May 8
RA156 PT88 8d multi   .50   .50
  Obligatory on mail May 8-15.

Campaign
Against
Tuberculosis
PT89

2011, Sept. 14
RA157 PT89 8d multi   .50   .50
  Obligatory on mail Sept. 14-21.

Campaign
Against
AIDS — PT90

2011, Dec. 1
RA158 PT90 8d multi   .50   .50
  Obligatory on mail Dec. 1-7.

Campaign
Against
Cancer — PT91

2012, Mar. 1
RA159 PT91 8d multi   .35   .35
  Obligatory on mail Mar. 1-8.

Red Cross
Week — PT92

2012, May 8
RA160 PT92 8d multi   .35   .35
  Obligatory on mail May 8-15.

Campaign
Against
Tuberculosis
PT93

2012, Sept. 14
RA161 PT93 8d multi   .35   .35
  Obligatory on mail Sept. 14-21.

Campaign
Against
AIDS — PT94

2012, Dec. 1 Litho. Perf. 13¼x13½
RA162 PT94 8d multi   .35   .35
  Obligatory on mail Dec. 1-7.

Campaign
Against
Cancer — PT95

2013, Mar. 1 Litho. Perf. 13¼x13½
RA163 PT95 8d multi   .35   .35
  Obligatory on mail Mar. 1-8.

Red Cross
Week — PT96

2013, May 8 Litho. Perf. 13¼x13½
RA164 PT96 8d multi   .35   .35
  Intl. Red Cross, 150th anniv. Obligatory on
mail May 8-15.

Campaign
Against
Tuberculosis
PT97

Perf. 13¼x13½
2013, Sept. 14   Litho.
RA165 PT97 8d multi   .35   .35
  Obligatory on mail Sept. 14-21.

Campaign
Against
AIDS — PT98

2013, Dec. 1 Litho. Perf. 13¼x13½
RA166 PT98 8d multi   .35   .35
  Obligatory on mail Dec. 1-7.

Campaign
Against
Cancer — PT99

2014, Mar. 1 Litho. Perf. 13¼x13½
RA167 PT99 8d multi   .35   .35
  Obligatory on mail Mar. 1-8.

Red Cross
Week — PT100

2014, May 8 Litho. Perf. 13¼x13½
RA168 PT100 8d multi   .35   .35
  Obligatory on mail May 8-15.

ISSUED UNDER GERMAN OCCUPATION

During World War II, Yugoslav Macedonia was annexed by Bulgaria. From
April 1941 until Sept. 8, 1944, Bulgarian
stamps were used in the region. On
Sept. 8, 1944, Bulgaria signed an
armistace with the Allies, and Macedonia was occupied by German forces. A
puppet state was created, which col-
lapsed upon the German withdrawal on
Nov. 13.

> **Catalogue values for all unused
> stamps in this section are for
> Never Hinged examples. Hinged
> stamps are worth approximately
> 60% of the values shown.**

**Bulgaria Nos 364//413 Overprinted
in Black or Red (R)**

  Ovpt. I   Ovpt. II

Photo., Typo. (#N1, N2)
1944, Oct. 28   Perf. 13
Overprinted I
N1 A177 1 l on 10st red
            org (#364)   6.50   16.00
N2 A178 3 l on 15st blue
            (#365) (R)   6.50   16.00

Overprinted II
N3 A201 6 l on 10st dk
            blue (#398)
            (R)   8.00   26.00
N4 A201 9 l on 15st
            Prus blue
            (#399) (R)   8.00   26.00
N5 A201 9 l on 15st dk
            ol brn
            (#400) (R)   12.00   30.00
N6 A209 15 l on 4 l ol
            gray (#411)
            (R)   40.00   60.00
N7 A210 20 l on 7 l dp
            blue (#412)
            (R)   60.00   60.00
N8 A211 30 l on 14 l fawn
            (#413)   65.00 110.00
  Nos. N1-N8 (8)   206.00 344.00

There are two types of both overprints, differing in the font of the "9" in the year date.
Values for the more common types are given
above.

MADAGASCAR

ˌmad-ə-'gas-kər

British Consular Mail

Postage stamps issued by the British Consulate in Madagascar were in use for a short period until the British relinquished all claims to this territory in favor of France in return for which France recognized Great Britain's claims in Zanzibar.
See Malagasy Republic for stamps inscribed "Madagascar."

12 Pence = 1 Shilling

British Consular Mail stamps of Madagascar were gummed only in one corner. Unused values are for stamps without gum. Examples having the original corner gum will command higher prices. Most used examples of these stamps have small faults and values are for stamps in this condition. Used stamps without faults are scarce and are worth more. Used stamps are valued with the commonly used crayon or pen cancellations.

"B C M" and Arms — A1

Handstamped "British Vice-Consulate"
Black Seal Handstamped

		1884	Unwmk.	Typo.	Rouletted
1	A1	1p violet		550.	450.
b.		Seal omitted		9,500.	9,500.
2	A1	2p violet		375.	325.
3	A1	3p violet		425.	350.
4	A1	4p violet 1 oz.		6,000.	5,250.
a.		"1 oz." corrected to "4 oz." in mss.		1,000.	725.
b.		Seal omitted		8,500.	8,500.
5	A1	6p violet		475.	500.
6	A1	1sh violet		525.	475.
7	A1	1sh6p violet		525.	525.
8	A1	2sh violet		850.	900.
9	A1	1p on 1sh vio			
10	A1	4½ on 1sh vio			
11	A1	6p red		1,325.	825.

		1886	Violet Seal Handstamped	
12	A1	4p violet	1,800.	—
13	A1	6p violet	2,750.	—

Handstamped "British Consular Mail" as on A3
Black Seal Handstamped

14	A1	4p violet	1,850.	—

Violet Seal Handstamped

15	A1	4p violet	7,500.	—

The 1, 2, 3 and 4 pence are inscribed "POSTAL PACKET," the other values of the series are inscribed "LETTER."

"British Vice-Consulate" — A2

Three types of A2 and A3:
I — "POSTAGE" 29½mm. Periods after "POSTAGE" and value.
II — "POSTAGE" 29½mm. No periods.
III — "POSTAGE" 24½mm. Period after value.

		1886	Violet Seal Handstamped	
16	A2	1p rose, I	400.	—
a.		Type II	1,350.	
17	A2	1½p rose, I	1,500.	875.
a.		Type II	3,000.	
18	A2	2p rose, I	400.	—
19	A2	3p rose, I	575.	400.
a.		Type II	1,350.	
20	A2	4p rose, III	500.	—
21	A2	4½p rose, I	725.	350.
a.		Type II	2,250.	
22	A2	6p rose, II	1,700.	—
23	A2	8p rose, I	2,750.	1,900.
a.		Type III	700.	
24	A2	9p rose	1,350.	—
24A	A2	1sh rose, III	22,500.	
24B	A2	1sh6p rose, III	12,500.	—
25	A2	2sh rose, III	6,500.	—

Black Seal Handstamped
Type I

26	A2	1p rose	145.	275.
27	A2	1½p rose	3,000.	1,300.
28	A2	2p rose	200.	
29	A2	3p rose	4,000.	1,450.
30	A2	4½p rose	3,850.	575.
31	A2	8p rose	5,000.	3,150.
32	A2	9p rose	4,750.	2,000.
32A	A2	2sh rose, III		

"British Consular Mail" — A3

		1886	Violet Seal Handstamped	
33	A3	1p rose, II	175.	—
34	A3	1½p rose, II	275.	—
35	A3	2p rose, II	325.	—
36	A3	3p rose, II	210.	—
37	A3	4p rose, III	475.	—
38	A3	4½p rose, II	225.	—
39	A3	6p rose, II	500.	—
40	A3	8p rose, III	1,450.	—
a.		Type I	1,750.	
41	A3	9p rose, I	475.	—
42	A3	1sh rose, III	1,750.	
43	A3	1sh6p rose, III	1,750.	
44	A3	2sh rose, III	1,750.	

Black Seal Handstamped

45	A3	1p rose, II	135.	—
a.		Type II	135.	210.
46	A3	1½p rose, II	170.	300.
a.		Type II	145.	200.
47	A3	2p rose, I	190.	—
a.		Type II	150.	200.
48	A3	3p rose, I	170.	260.
a.		Type II	170.	210.
49	A3	4p rose, III	375.	—
50	A3	4½p rose, I	190.	240.
a.		Type II	160.	200.
51	A3	6p rose, II	170.	260.
52	A3	8p rose, II	200.	—
a.		Type III	2,250.	—
53	A3	9p rose, I	225.	375.
54	A3	1sh rose, III	625.	—
55	A3	1sh6p rose, III	775.	—
56	A3	2sh rose, III	775.	—

Seal Omitted

45b	A3	1p rose, II	5,000.
46b	A3	1½p rose, II	5,250.
48b	A3	3p rose, II	7,750.
49a	A3	4p rose, III	6,250.
50b	A3	4½p rose, II	8,750.
51a	A3	6p rose, II	9,250.
52b	A3	8p rose, II	6,250.
53a	A3	9p rose, I	8,250.
54a	A3	1sh rose, III	8,400.
55a	A3	1sh6p rose, III	7,250.
56a	A3	2sh rose, III	8,500.

Some students of these issues doubt that the 1886 "seal omitted" varieties were regularly issued.

Red Seal Handstamped

57	A3	3p rose, I	20,000.	—
58	A3	4½p rose, I	12,750.	—

MADEIRA

mə-'dir-ə

LOCATION — A group of islands in the Atlantic Ocean northwest of Africa
GOVT. — Part of the Republic of Portugal
AREA — 314 sq. mi.
POP. — 150,574 (1900)
CAPITAL — Funchal

These islands are considered an integral part of Portugal and since 1898 postage stamps of Portugal have been in use. See Portugal for issues also inscribed Madeira, starting in 1980.

1000 Reis = 1 Milreis
100 Centavos = 1 Escudo (1925)

It is recommended that the rare overprinted 1868-81 stamps be purchased accompanied by certificates of authenticity from competent experts.

King Luiz — A1

Stamps of Portugal Overprinted

1868, Jan. 1   Unwmk.   *Imperf.*
Black Overprint

2	A1	20r bister	210.00	120.00
a.		Inverted overprint	—	
b.		Rouletted	—	—
3	A1	50r green	210.00	120.00
4	A1	80r orange	225.00	125.00
a.		Double overprint		
5	A1	100r lilac	225.00	125.00
		Nos. 2-5 (4)	870.00	490.00

The 5r black does not exist as a genuinely imperforate original.
Reprints of 1885 are on stout white paper, ungummed. (Also, 5r, 10r and 25r values were overprinted.) Reprints of 1905 are on ordinary white paper with shiny gum and have a wide "D" and "R." Value, $12 each.

Lozenge Perf.

2c	A1	20r	—
3a	A1	50r	—
4b	A1	80r	—
5a	A1	100r	—

Overprinted in Red or Black

1868-70   *Perf. 12½*

6	A1	5r black (R)	50.00	37.50
8	A1	10r yellow	90.00	80.00
9	A1	20r bister	140.00	110.00
10	A1	25r rose	50.00	12.00
a.		Inverted overprint	—	
11	A1	50r green	200.00	140.00
a.		Inverted overprint	—	
12	A1	80r orange	180.00	140.00
13	A1	100r lilac	190.00	140.00
a.		Inverted overprint	—	
14	A1	120r blue	110.00	80.00
15	A1	240r violet ('70)	500.00	425.00
		Nos. 6-15 (9)	1,510.	1,164.

Two types of 5r differ in the position of the "5" at upper right.
The reprints are on stout white paper, ungummed, with rough perforation 13½, and on thin white paper with shiny white gum and clean-cut perforation 13½. The overprint has the wide "D" and "R" and the first reprints included the 5r with both black and red overprint. Value $10 each.

King Luiz — A2

Overprinted in Red or Black

1871-80   *Perf. 12½, 13½*

16	A2	5r black (R)	11.00	8.00
a.		Inverted overprint	—	
b.		Double overprint	55.00	55.00
c.		Perf. 14	90.00	55.00

18	A2	10r yellow	35.00	22.50
19	A2	10r bl grn ('79)	140.00	110.00
a.		Perf. 13½	160.00	140.00
20	A2	10r yel grn ('80)	65.00	52.50
21	A2	15r brn ('75)	19.00	11.50
22	A2	20r bister	30.00	22.50
23	A2	25r rose	13.50	4.50
a.		Inverted overprint	50.00	40.00
b.		Double overprint	50.00	40.00
24	A2	50r green ('72)	67.50	30.00
a.		Double overprint		
b.		Inverted overprint	200.00	200.00
25	A2	50r blue ('80)	125.00	55.00
26	A2	80r orange ('72)	77.50	67.50
27	A2	100r pale lil ('73)	90.00	60.00
a.		Perf. 14	200.00	85.00
b.		Perf. 13½	160.00	75.00
28	A2	120r blue	110.00	80.00
29	A2	150r blue ('76)	160.00	140.00
a.		Perf. 13½	175.00	150.00
30	A2	150r yel ('79)	300.00	240.00
31	A2	240r vio ('74)	700.00	500.00
32	A2	300r vio ('76)	75.00	67.50
		Nos. 16-32 (16)	2,018.	1,471.

There are two types of the overprint, the second one having a broad "D."
The reprints have the same characteristics as those of the 1868-70 issues.

A3   A4

King Luiz — A5

1880-81

33	A3	5r black	40.00	21.00
34	A4	25r pearl gray	50.00	21.00
a.		Inverted overprint	75.00	75.00
35	A5	25r lilac	50.00	11.00
a.		25r purple brown	32.50	11.00
b.		25r gray	35.00	10.00
		Nos. 33-35 (3)	140.00	53.00

Nos. 33, 34 and 35 have been reprinted on stout white paper, ungummed, and the last three on thin white paper with shiny white gum. The perforations are as previously described.

Common Design Types
pictured following the introduction.

Vasco da Gama Issue
Common Design Types

1898, Apr. 1   Engr.   *Perf. 14-15*

37	CD20	2½r blue grn	2.40	1.25
38	CD21	5r red	2.40	1.25
39	CD22	10r red violet	3.00	1.50
40	CD23	25r yel green	2.75	1.25
41	CD24	50r dk blue	6.00	3.25
42	CD25	75r vio brown	8.00	7.00
43	CD26	100r bister brn	8.00	7.00
44	CD27	150r bister	12.00	11.50
		Nos. 37-44 (8)	44.55	34.00

Nos. 37-44 with "REPUBLICA" overprint and surcharges are listed as Portugal Nos. 199-206.

Ceres — A6

1928, May 1   Engr.   *Perf. 13½*
Value Typographed in Black

45	A6	3c deep violet	.40	.60
46	A6	4c orange	.40	.60
47	A6	5c light blue	.40	.60
48	A6	6c brown	.40	.60
49	A6	10c red	.40	.60
50	A6	15c yel green	.40	.60
51	A6	16c red brown	.40	.60
52	A6	25c violet rose	1.00	.60
53	A6	32c blue grn	1.00	.60
54	A6	40c yel brown	1.50	1.75
55	A6	50c slate	1.50	1.75
56	A6	64c Prus blue	1.50	3.00
57	A6	80c dk brown	1.50	5.00
58	A6	96c carmine rose	5.00	3.00

59	A6	1e black	1.25	3.00
a.		Value omitted	42.50	45.00
60	A6	1.20e light rose	1.25	3.00
61	A6	1.60e ultra	1.25	3.00
62	A6	2.40e yellow	2.00	3.50
63	A6	3.36e dull green	3.00	5.75
64	A6	4.50e brown red	5.00	9.00
65	A6	7e dark blue	6.00	17.50
		Nos. 45-65 (21)	35.55	64.65

It was obligatory to use these stamps in place of those in regular use on May 1, June 5, July 1 and Dec. 31, 1928, Jan. 1 and 31, May 1 and June 5, 1929. The amount obtained from this sale was donated to a fund for building a museum.
Less than very fine examples sell for much less.

NEWSPAPER STAMP

Numeral of
Value — N1

**Newspaper Stamp of Portugal
Overprinted in Black**

Perf. 12½, 13½

1876, July 1   Unwmk.

P1	N1	2½r olive	9.00	4.25
a.		Inverted overprint	30.00	

The reprints have the same papers, gum, perforations and overprint as the reprints of the regular issues.

POSTAL TAX STAMPS

Pombal Commemorative Issue
Common Design Types

1925   Unwmk.   Engr.   *Perf. 12½*

RA1	CD28	15c gray & black	.60	.65
RA2	CD29	15c gray & black	.60	.65
RA3	CD30	15c gray & black	.60	.65
		Nos. RA1-RA3 (3)	1.80	1.95

POSTAL TAX DUE STAMPS

Pombal Commemorative Issue
Common Design Types

1925   Unwmk.   *Perf. 12½*

RAJ1	CD28	30c gray & black	.85	3.50
RAJ2	CD29	30c gray & black	.85	3.50
RAJ3	CD30	30c gray & black	.85	3.50
		Nos. RAJ1-RAJ3 (3)	2.55	10.50

MALAGASY REPUBLIC

ˌmal-lə-ˈgə-sē

Madagascar (French)

Malagasy Democratic Republic

Republic of Madagascar

LOCATION — Large island off the coast of southeastern Africa
GOVT. — Republic
AREA — 226,658 sq. mi.
POP. — 14,062,000 (1995 est.)
CAPITAL — Antananarivo

Madagascar became a French protectorate in 1885 and a French colony in 1896 following several years of dispute among France, Great Britain, and the native government. The colony administered the former protectorates of Anjouan, Grand Comoro, Mayotte, Diego-Suarez, Nossi-Be and Sainte-Marie de Madagascar. Previous issues of postage stamps are found under these individual headings. The Malagasy Republic succeeded the colony in 1958 and became the Democratic

Republic of Malagasy in 1975. The official name was again changed in 1993 to Republic of Madagascar.
For British Consular Mail stamps of 1884-1886, see Madagascar.

100 Centimes = 1 Franc
100 Centimes = 1 Ariary (1976)

See France No. 2767 for stamp inscribed "Madagascar."

Catalogue values for unused stamps in this country are for Never Hinged items, beginning with Scott 241 in the regular postage section, Scott B15 in the semi-postal section, Scott C37 in the airport section, and Scott J31 in the postage due section.

French Offices in Madagascar

The general issues of French Colonies were used in these offices in addition to the stamps listed here.

**Stamps of French Colonies
Surcharged in Black**

a   b

c

Overprint Type "a"

1889   Unwmk.   *Perf. 14x13½*

1	A9	05c on 10c blk, lav	725.	220.
a.		Inverted surcharge	1,950.	1,300.
2	A9	05c on 25c blk, rose	725.	220.
a.		Inverted surcharge	1,950.	1,300.
b.		25c on 10c lav (error)	11,500.	10,000.
3	A9	25c on 40c red, straw	650.	200.
a.		Inverted surcharge	1,700.	1,300.

1891   **Overprint Type "b"**

4	A9	05c on 40c blk, straw	235.00	100.00
5	A9	15c on 25c blk, rose	235.00	110.00
a.		Surcharge vertical	275.00	145.00

Overprint Type "c"

6	A9	5c on 10c blk, lav	275.00	125.00
a.		Double surcharge	1,000.	900.00
7	A9	5c on 25c blk, rose	275.00	125.00

See Senegal Nos. 4, 8 for similar surcharge on 20c, 30c.
Forgeries of Nos. 1-7 exist.

A4

1891   Type-set   *Imperf.*
Without Gum

8	A4	5c blk, green	165.00	32.50
9	A4	10c blk, lt bl	125.00	40.00
10	A4	15c ultra, pale bl	125.00	47.50
11	A4	25c brn, buff	30.00	22.50
12	A4	1fr blk, yellow	1,300.	300.00
13	A4	5fr vio & blk, lil	2,400.	1,275.

Stamps of France 1876-90, Overprinted in Red or Black

POSTE FRANÇAISE
Madagascar

1895   **Perf. 14x13½**

14	A15	5c grn, grnsh (R)	22.50	11.00
15	A15	10c blk, lav (R)	50.00	32.50
16	A15	15c bl (R)	72.50	22.00
17	A15	25c blk, rose (R)	100.00	25.00
18	A15	40c red, straw (Bk)	95.00	45.00
19	A15	50c rose, rose (Bk)	110.00	55.00
20	A15	75c dp vio, org (R)	125.00	62.50
21	A15	1fr brnz grn, straw (Bk)	135.00	72.50
22	A15	5fr vio, lav (Bk)	220.00	100.00
		Nos. 14-22 (9)	930.00	425.50

Majunga Issue
Stamps of France, 1876-86,
Surcharged with New Value

1895

Manuscript Surcharge in Red

22A	A15	0,15c on 25c blk, rose	8,000.
22B	A15	0,15c on 1fr brnz	6,000.

Handstamped in Black

22C	A15	15c on 25c blk, rose	12,750.
22D	A15	15c on 1fr brnz grn, straw	11,750.

On most of No. 22C and all of No. 22D the manuscript surcharge of Nos. 22A-22B was washed off. Three types of "15" were used for No. 22C.

Stamps of France,
1876-84, Surcharged

1896

23	A15	5c on 1c blk, bl	6,400.	2,500.
24	A15	15c on 2c brn, buff	2,600.	1,000.
25	A15	25c on 3c gray, grysh	3,400.	1,100.
26	A15	25c on 4c cl, lav	6,400.	1,950.
27	A15	25c on 40c red, straw	1,650.	875.

The oval of the 5c and 15c surcharges is smaller than that of the 25c, and it does not extend beyond the edges of the stamp as the 25c surcharge does.

Excellent counterfeits of the surcharges on Nos. 22A to 27 exist.

Issues of the Colony

Navigation and
Commerce — A7

1896-1906   **Typo.**   **Perf. 14x13½**
Colony Name in Blue or Carmine

28	A7	1c blk, lil bl	1.50	1.10
29	A7	2c brn, buff	2.25	1.50
a.		Name in blue black	4.25	4.50
30	A7	4c claret, lav	2.50	1.80
31	A7	5c grn, grnsh	8.00	1.50
32	A7	5c yel grn ('01)	1.80	1.10
33	A7	10c blk, lav	8.00	2.25
34	A7	10c red ('00)	3.00	1.10
35	A7	15c blue, quadrille paper	14.00	1.50
36	A7	15c gray ('00)	2.50	1.50
37	A7	20c red, grn	7.25	2.25
38	A7	25c blk, rose	11.00	4.50
39	A7	25c blue ('00)	25.00	32.50
40	A7	30c brn, bis	8.75	3.75
41	A7	35c blk, yel ('06)	45.00	7.25
42	A7	40c red, straw	11.00	6.00
43	A7	50c car, rose	14.50	3.00
44	A7	50c brn, az ('00)	32.50	45.00
45	A7	75c dp vio, org	6.25	4.50
46	A7	1fr brnz grn, straw	14.50	3.75
a.		Name in blue ('99)	30.00	22.00
47	A7	5fr red lil, lav ('99)	37.50	32.50
		Nos. 28-47 (20)	256.80	158.35

Perf. 13½x14 stamps are counterfeits.
For surcharges see Nos. 48-55, 58-60, 115-118, 127-128.

Nos. 32, 43, 44 and 46, affixed to pressboard with animals printed on the back, were used as emergency currency in the Comoro Islands in 1920.

Surcharged in Black   **05**

1902

48	A7	05c on 50c car, rose	7.25	6.00
a.		Inverted surcharge	120.00	120.00
49	A7	10c on 5fr red lil, lav	25.00	22.00
a.		Inverted surcharge	125.00	125.00
50	A7	15c on 1fr ol grn, straw	9.50	8.75
a.		Inverted surcharge	120.00	120.00
b.		Double surcharge	400.00	400.00
		Nos. 48-50 (3)	41.75	36.75

Surcharged in Black   **0,01**

51	A7	0,01 on 2c brn, buff	11.50	11.50
a.		Inverted surcharge	72.50	72.50
b.		"00,1" instead of "0,01"	150.00	155.00
c.		As "b" inverted	—	—
d.		Comma omitted	210.00	210.00
e.		Name in blue black	11.50	11.50
52	A7	0,05 on 30c brn, bis	11.50	11.50
a.		Inverted surcharge	72.50	72.50
b.		"00,5" instead of "0,05"	100.00	100.00
c.		As "b" inverted	2,550.	
d.		Comma omitted	210.00	210.00
53	A7	0,10 on 50c car, rose	9.50	9.50
a.		Inverted surcharge	72.50	72.50
b.		Comma omitted	210.00	210.00
54	A7	0,15 on 75c vio, org	7.25	7.25
a.		Inverted surcharge	72.50	72.50
b.		Comma omitted	210.00	210.00
55	A7	0,15 on 1fr ol grn, straw	14.50	14.50
a.		Inverted surcharge	110.00	110.00
b.		Comma omitted	275.00	275.00
		Nos. 51-55 (5)	54.25	54.25

Surcharged On Stamps of Diego-Suarez

56	A11	0,05 on 30c brn, bis	165.00	145.00
a.		"00,5" instead of "0,05"	1,350.	1,350.
b.		Inverted surcharge	1,450.	1,450.
57	A11	0,10 on 50c car, rose	5,000.	5,000.

Counterfeits of Nos. 56-57 exist with surcharge both normal and inverted.

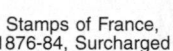

Surcharged in Black   **0,01**

58	A7	0,01 on 2c brn, buff	11.50	11.50
a.		Inverted surcharge	72.50	72.50
b.		Comma omitted	210.00	210.00
59	A7	0,05 on 30c brn, bis	11.50	11.50
a.		Inverted surcharge	72.50	72.50
b.		Comma omitted	210.00	210.00
60	A7	0,10 on 50c car, rose	9.50	9.50
a.		Inverted surcharge	72.50	72.50
b.		Comma omitted	210.00	210.00
		Nos. 58-60 (3)	32.50	32.50

Surcharged On Stamps of Diego-Suarez

61	A11	0,05 on 30c brn, bis	165.00	145.00
a.		Inverted surcharge	1,450.	1,450.
62	A11	0,10 on 50c car, rose	5,000.	5,000.

BISECTS
During alleged stamp shortages at several Madagascar towns in 1904, it is claimed that bisects were used. After being affixed to letters, these bisects were handstamped "Affranchissement - exceptionnel - (faute de timbres)" and other inscriptions of similar import. The stamps bisected were 10c, 20c, 30c and 50c denominations of Madagascar type A7 and Diego-Suarez type A11. The editors believe these provisionals were unnecessary and speculative.

Zebu, Traveler's Tree
and Lemur — A8

1903   **Engr.**   **Perf. 11½**

63	A8	1c dk violet	1.10	1.10
a.		On bluish paper	8.00	6.50
64	A8	2c olive brn	1.10	1.10
65	A8	4c brown	1.45	1.50
66	A8	5c yellow grn	7.25	2.25
67	A8	10c red	13.25	1.50
68	A8	15c carmine	17.00	1.50
a.		On bluish paper	185.00	185.00
69	A8	20c orange	6.50	3.00
70	A8	25c dull blue	30.00	6.00
71	A8	30c pale red	45.00	16.00
72	A8	40c gray vio	30.00	6.50
73	A8	50c brown org	50.00	30.00
74	A8	75c orange yel	65.00	30.00
75	A8	1fr dp green	65.00	30.00
76	A8	2fr slate	87.50	32.50
77	A8	5fr gray black	100.00	105.00
		Nos. 63-77 (15)	520.15	267.95

Nos. 63-77 exist imperf. Value of set, $600.
For surcharges see Nos. 119-124, 129.

Transportation by
Sedan Chair — A9

1908-28   **Typo.**   **Perf. 13½x14**

79	A9	1c violet & ol	.25	.25
80	A9	2c red & ol	.25	.25
81	A9	4c ol brn & brn	.25	.25
82	A9	5c bl grn & ol	1.10	.30
83	A9	5c blk & rose ('22)	.30	.25
84	A9	10c rose & brown	1.10	.35
85	A9	10c bl grn & ol grn ('22)	.65	.45
86	A9	10c org brn & vio ('25)	.35	.35
87	A9	15c dl vio & rose ('16)	.35	.35
88	A9	15c dl grn & lt grn ('27)	.75	.75
89	A9	15c dk bl & rose red ('28)	1.90	1.10
90	A9	20c org & brn	.75	.50
91	A9	25c blue & blk	3.25	1.10
92	A9	25c vio & blk ('22)	.45	.35
93	A9	30c brown & blk	3.25	1.50
94	A9	30c rose red & brn ('22)	.60	.45
95	A9	30c grn & red vio ('25)	.60	.50
96	A9	30c dp grn & yel grn ('27)	1.50	1.10
97	A9	35c red & black	2.25	1.10
98	A9	40c vio brn & blk	1.50	.75
99	A9	45c bl grn & blk	1.10	.75
100	A9	45c red & ver ('25)	.50	.50
101	A9	45c gray lil & mag ('27)	1.45	1.10
102	A9	50c violet & blk	1.10	.75
103	A9	50c blue & blk ('22)	.95	.65
104	A9	50c blk & org ('25)	1.10	.45
105	A9	60c vio, pnksh ('25)	.75	.75
106	A9	65c black & bl ('25)	1.10	.85
107	A9	75c rose red & blk	1.10	.75
108	A9	85c grn & ver ('25)	1.50	.95
109	A9	1fr brown & ol	1.10	.75
110	A9	1fr dull blue ('25)	1.10	1.10
111	A9	1fr rose & grn ('28)	6.25	5.00
112	A9	1.10fr bis & bl grn ('28)	2.25	3.25
113	A9	2fr blue & olive	4.50	1.80
114	A9	5fr vio & vio brn	14.00	6.00
		Nos. 79-114 (36)	61.25	37.45

75c violet on pinkish stamps of type A9 are No. 138 without surcharge.

For surcharges and overprints see Nos. 125-126, 130-146, 178-179, B1, 212-214.

Preceding Issues Surcharged in
Black or Carmine

1912, Nov.   **Perf. 14x13½**

115	A7	5c on 15c gray (C)	1.10	1.10
116	A7	5c on 20c red, grn	1.50	1.50
a.		Inverted surcharge	175.00	
117	A7	5c on 30c brn, bis (C)	1.90	1.90
118	A7	5c on 75c vio, org	10.00	11.50
a.		Double surcharge	310.00	
119	A8	5c on 2c ol brn (C)	1.10	1.10
120	A8	5c on 20c org	1.10	1.10
121	A8	5c on 30c pale red	1.90	1.90
122	A8	10c on 40c gray vio (C)	1.90	1.90
123	A8	5c on 50c brn org	3.75	4.50
124	A8	10c on 75c org yel	6.50	8.00
a.		Inverted surcharge	230.00	
		Nos. 115-124 (10)	30.75	34.50

Two spacings between the surcharged numerals are found on Nos. 115 to 118. For detailed listings, see the *Scott Classic Specialized Catalogue of Stamps and Covers.*

Stamps of Anjouan, Grand Comoro Island, Mayotte and Mohéli with similar surcharges were also available for use in Madagascar and the entire Comoro archipelago.

Preceding Issues Surcharged in
Red or Black

    g   h

1921   **On Nos. 98 & 107**

125	A9 (g)	30c on 40c (R)	2.50	2.50
126	A9 (g)	60c on 75c	3.25	3.25

On Nos. 45 & 47

127	A7	(g) 60c on 75c (R)	12.50	12.50
a.		Inverted surcharge	220.00	220.00
128	A7	(h) 1fr on 5fr	1.10	1.10

On No. 77

129	A8	(h) 1fr on 5fr (R)	100.00	100.00
		Nos. 125-129 (5)	119.35	119.35

Stamps and Type of 1908-16
Surcharged in Black or Red

130	A9	1c on 15c dl vio & rose	1.10	1.10
131	A9	25c on 35c red & blk	6.50	6.50
132	A9	25c on 35c red & blk (R)	32.50	32.50
133	A9	25c on 40c brn & blk	5.00	5.00
134	A9	25c on 45c grn & blk	4.50	4.50
		Nos. 130-134 (5)	49.60	49.60
		Nos. 125-134 (10)	109.45	109.45

Stamps and Type of 1908-28
Surcharged with New Value and
Bars

1922-27

135	A9	25c on 15c dl vio & rose	.35	.35
a.		Double surcharge	95.00	
136	A9	25c on 2fr bl & ol	.50	.50
137	A9	25c on 5fr vio & vio brn	.35	.35
138	A9	60c on 75c vio, pnksh	.60	.60
139	A9	65c on 75c rose red & blk	1.10	1.10
140	A9	85c on 45c bl grn & blk	1.90	1.45
141	A9	90c on 75c dl red & rose red	1.10	1.10
142	A9	1.25fr on 1fr lt bl (R)	.75	.50
143	A9	1.50fr on 1fr dp bl & dl bl	.60	
144	A9	3fr on 5fr grn & vio	2.25	1.45
145	A9	10fr on 5fr org & rose lil	9.50	6.00

146 A9 20fr on 5fr rose & sl
bl   10.00   8.00
Nos. 135-146 (12)   29.15   22.00

Years of issue: No. 138, 1922; Nos. 136, 137, 1924; Nos. 135, 139-140, 1925; No. 142, 1926; Nos. 141, 142-146, 1927.
See Nos. 178-179.

Sakalava Chief — A10

Hova Woman — A12

Hova with Oxen A11

Bétsiléo Woman A13

Perf. 13½x14, 14x13½

1930-44   *Typo.*

147	A11	1c dk bl & bl grn ('33)	.25	.25
148	A10	2c brn red & dk brn	.25	.25
149	A10	4c dk brn & vio	.25	.25
150	A11	5c lt grn & red	.25	.25
151	A12	10c ver & dp grn	.40	.25
152	A13	15c dp red	.25	.25
153	A11	20c yel brn & dk bl	.25	.25
154	A12	25c vio & dk brn	.25	.25
155	A13	30c Prus blue	.65	.45
156	A10	40c grn & red	.75	.50
157	A13	45c dull violet	.90	.55
158	A11	65c brn & vio	1.10	.80
159	A13	75c dk brown	.85	.50
160	A11	90c brn red & dk red	1.40	.90
161	A12	1fr yel brn & dk bl	1.75	1.10
162	A12	1fr dk red & car rose ('38)	.95	.90
163	A12	1.25fr dp bl & dk brn ('33)	1.60	.90
164	A10	1.50fr dk & dp bl	5.50	1.10
165	A10	1.50fr brn & dk red ('38)	.75	.50
165A	A10	1.50fr dk red & brn ('44)	.50	.50
166	A10	1.75fr dk brn & dk red ('33)	4.25	1.60
167	A10	5fr vio & dk brn	1.25	.70
168	A10	20fr yel brn & dk bl	2.00	1.75
		Nos. 147-168 (23)	26.35	14.75

Common Design Types pictured following the introduction.

Colonial Exposition Issue
Common Design Types

1931   *Engr.*   *Perf. 12½*
Name of Country in Black

169	CD70	40c deep green	1.40	1.00
170	CD71	50c violet	2.00	1.25
171	CD72	90c red orange	2.00	1.25
172	CD73	1.50fr dull blue	2.50	1.50
		Nos. 169-172 (4)	7.90	5.00

General Joseph Simon Galliéni — A14

1931   *Engr.*   *Perf. 14*
Size: 21½x34½mm

173	A14	1c ultra	.50	.45
174	A14	50c orange brn	1.40	.35
175	A14	2fr deep red	5.75	4.25
176	A14	3fr emerald	5.50	3.00
177	A14	10fr dp orange	4.00	3.00
		Nos. 173-177 (5)	17.15	11.05

Nos. 113 and 109 Surcharged

1932   *Perf. 13½x14*
178	A9	25c on 2fr bl & ol	.75	.50
179	A9	50c on 1fr brn & ol	.75	.50

No. 178 has numerals in thick block letters.
No. 136 has thin shaded numerals.

Galliéni Type of 1931
1936-40   *Photo.*   *Perf. 13½, 13x13½*
Size: 21x34mm

180	A14	3c sapphire ('40)	.25	.25
181	A14	45c brt green ('40)	.50	.40
182	A14	50c yellow brown	.25	.25
183	A14	60c brt red lil ('40)	.40	.25
184	A14	70c brt rose ('40)	.60	.40
185	A14	90c copper brn ('39)	.50	.40
186	A14	1.40fr org yel ('40)	.90	.50
187	A14	1.60fr purple ('40)	.90	.60
188	A14	2fr dk carmine	.50	.25
189	A14	3fr green	4.50	2.25
190	A14	3fr olive blk ('39)	.90	.70
		Nos. 180-190 (11)	10.20	6.25

Paris International Exposition Issue
Common Design Types

1937, Apr. 15   *Engr.*   *Perf. 13*

191	CD74	20c dp violet	1.90	1.90
192	CD75	30c dk green	1.90	1.90
193	CD76	40c car rose	1.60	1.60
194	CD77	50c dk brn & blk	1.40	1.40
195	CD78	90c red	1.75	1.75
196	CD79	1.50fr ultra	1.75	1.75
		Nos. 191-196 (6)	10.30	10.30

Colonial Arts Exhibition Issue
Common Design Type
Souvenir Sheet

1937   *Imperf.*
197 CD74 3fr orange red   7.25   8.00

Jean Laborde A15

1938-40   *Perf. 13*

198	A15	35c green	.65	.40
199	A15	55c dp purple	.65	.40
200	A15	65c orange red	.90	.40
201	A15	80c violet brn	.65	.40
202	A15	1fr rose car	.90	.40
203	A15	1.25fr rose car ('39)	.40	.25
204	A15	1.75fr dk ultra	1.75	.70
205	A15	2.15fr yel brn	2.50	1.75
206	A15	2.25fr dk ultra ('39)	.60	.50
207	A15	2.50fr blk brn ('40)	.65	.50
208	A15	10fr dk green ('40)	1.25	.90
		Nos. 198-208 (11)	10.90	6.60

New York World's Fair Issue
Common Design Type

1939, May 10   *Engr.*   *Perf. 12½x12*
209	CD82	1.25fr car lake	1.25	1.25
210	CD82	2.25fr ultra	2.50	2.50

Porters Carrying Man in Chair, and Marshal Petain — A15a

1941   *Engr.*   *Perf. 12x12½*
210A	A15a	1fr bister brn	.75
210B	A15a	2.50fr blue	.75

Nos. 210A-210B were issued by the Vichy government in France but were not placed on sale in Madagascar.
For overprints see Nos. B13-B14.

Type of 1930-44 Surcharged in Black with New Value

1942   *Perf. 14x13½*
211 A11 50c on 65c dk brn & mag   2.25   .50

French Explorers de Hell, Passot & Jehenne — A15b

1942   *Engr.*   *Perf. 13x13½*
211A A15b 1.50fr blue & red brn   1.10

Centenary of French colonies of Mayotte and Nossi Bé.
No. 211A was issued by the Vichy government in France, but was not placed on sale in Madagascar.

Nos. 143, 145-146 with Additional Overprint in Red or Black

1942   *Unwmk.*   *Perf. 14x13½*
212	A9	1.50fr on 1fr (R)	1.75	1.75
213	A9	10fr on 5fr (Bk)	10.00	10.00
214	A9	20fr on 5fr (R)	12.50	12.50

Stamps of 1930-40 Overprinted Like Nos. 212-214 in Black or Red or

215	A10	2c brn red & dk brn	1.10	1.10
216	A14	3c sapphire (R)	115.00	115.00
217	A13	15c deep red	10.00	10.00
218	A11	65c dk brn & mag	.80	.80
219	A14	70c brt rose	1.10	1.10
220	A15	80c violet brn	3.25	3.25
221	A14	1.40fr orange yel	1.40	1.40
222	A10	1.50fr dk bl & dp bl (R)	2.50	2.25
223	A10	1.50fr brn & dk red	2.75	2.75
224	A14	1.60fr purple	1.40	1.40
225	A15	2.25fr dk ultra (R)	1.00	1.00
226	A15	2.50fr black brn (R)	5.00	5.000
227	A15	10fr dk green	6.25	6.25
228	A10	20fr yel brn & dk bl (R)	675.00	750.00

Stamps of 1930-40 Surcharged in Black or Red

229	A11	5c on 1c dk bl & bl grn	.65	.65
230	A15	10c on 55c dp pur	1.60	1.60
231	A15	30c on 65c org red	1.00	1.00
232	A14	50c on 90c cop brn	1.00	1.00
233	A12	1fr on 1.25fr dp bl & dk brn	3.25	3.25

234	A15	1fr on 1.25fr rose car	12.50	12.50
235	A10	1.50fr on 1.75fr dk brn & dk red	.95	.95
236	A15	1.50fr on 1.75fr ultra (R)	.95	.95
237	A15	2fr on 2.15fr yel brn	1.60	1.60

No. 211 with additional Overprint Like Nos. 217-218 in Black

239 A11 50c on 65c dk brn & mag   .50   .50

New York World's Fair Stamp Overprinted Like Nos. 217-218 in Red
Perf. 12½x12
240 CD82 2.25fr ultra   1.00   1.00
Nos. 212-227,229-240 (27)   200.80   200.55

> Catalogue values for unused stamps in this section, from this point to the end of the section, are for Never Hinged items.

Traveler's Tree — A16

1943   *Unwmk.*   *Photo.*   *Perf. 14x14½*
241	A16	5c ol gray	.25	.25
242	A16	10c pale rose vio	.25	.25
243	A16	25c emerald	.25	.25
244	A16	30c dp orange	.25	.25
245	A16	40c slate bl	.25	.25
246	A16	80c dk red brn	.25	.25
247	A16	1fr dull blue	.25	.25
248	A16	1.50fr crim rose	.35	.30
249	A16	2fr dull yel	.35	.30
250	A16	2.50fr brt ultra	.35	.30
251	A16	4fr aqua & red	.55	.45
252	A16	5fr green & blk	.55	.45
253	A16	10fr sal pink & dk bl	.95	.75
254	A16	20fr dl vio & brn	1.10	.90
		Nos. 241-254 (14)	5.95	5.20

For surcharges see Nos. 255-256, 261-268.

Types of 1930-44 without "RF"
1943-44
254A	A11	20c yel brn & dk bl	.40
254B	A14	60c lilac rose	.65
254C	A12	1fr dk red & car rose	1.40
254D	A10	1.50fr brn & dk red	.95
254E	A10	5fr vio & dk brn	2.50
		Nos. 254A-254E (5)	5.90

On type A10, the two panels at the top of the frame have been reversed, with the value at the left and a blank (RF removed) panel at right.
Nos. 254A-254E were issued by the Vichy government in France, but were not placed on sale in Madagascar.

Nos. 241 and 242 Surcharged with New Values and Bars in Red or Blue

1944
255	A16	1.50fr on 5c (R)	.65	.55
256	A16	1.50fr on 10c (Bl)	1.00	.85

Nos. 229 and 224 Surcharged with New Values and Bars in Red or Black
Perf. 14x13½, 14
257	A11	50c on 5c on 1c (R)	.85	.70
258	A14	1.50fr on 1.60fr (Bk)	1.10	.95
		Nos. 255-258 (4)	3.60	3.05

Eboue Issue
Common Design Type

1945   *Engr.*   *Perf. 13*
259	CD91	2fr black	.60	.50
260	CD91	25fr Prus green	1.10	.95

Nos. 241, 243 and 250 Surcharged with New Values and Bars in Carmine or Black

1945   *Perf. 14x14½*
261	A16	50c on 5c ol gray (C)	.40	.35
262	A16	60c on 5c ol gray (C)	.60	.50
263	A16	70c on 5c ol gray (C)	.60	.50
264	A16	1.20fr on 5c ol gray (C)	.60	.50
265	A16	2.40fr on 25c emer	.60	.50

266 A16 3fr on 25c emer .60 .50
267 A16 4.50fr on 25c emer .85 .70
268 A16 15fr on 2.50fr brt ultra
(C) .85 .70
Nos. 261-268 (8) 5.10 4.25

Southern Dancer — A17

Gen. J. S. Galliéni — A20

Herd of Zebus A18

Sakalava Man and Woman A19

Betsimisaraka Mother and Child — A21

General Jacques C. R. A. Duchesne A22

Marshal Joseph J. C. Joffre A23

Perf. 13x13½, 13½x13

1946		Photo.	Unwmk.	
269	A17	10c green	.25	.25
270	A17	30c orange	.25	.25
271	A17	40c brown ol	.25	.25
272	A17	50c violet brn	.25	.25
273	A18	60c dp ultra	.25	.25
274	A18	80c blue grn	.40	.25
275	A19	1fr brown	.25	.25
276	A19	1.20fr green	.25	.25
276A	A20	1.50fr dk red	.25	.25
277	A20	2fr slate blk	.25	.25
278	A20	3fr dp claret	.40	.25
278A	A21	3.60fr dk car rose	.85	.65
279	A21	4fr dp ultra	.40	.25
280	A21	5fr red orange	.65	.25
281	A22	6fr dk grnsh bl	.40	.25
282	A22	10fr red brn	.65	.25
283	A23	15fr violet brn	1.00	.30
284	A23	20fr dk vio bl	1.40	.65
285	A23	25fr brown	2.25	1.00
		Nos. 269-285 (19)	10.65	6.35

Military Medal Issue
Common Design Type
Engraved and Typographed
1952, Dec. 1 Unwmk. Perf. 13
286 CD101 15fr multicolored 3.75 2.50
Creation of the French Military Medal, cent.

Tropical Flowers — A24

Long-tailed Ground Roller A25

1954 Engr.
287 A24 7.50fr ind & gray grn 1.25 .25
288 A25 8fr brown carmine .90 .35
289 A25 15fr dk grn & dp ultra 2.25 .35
Nos. 287-289 (3) 4.40 .95

Colonel Lyautey and Royal Palace, Tananarive A26

1954-55
290 A26 10fr vio bl, ind & bl ('55) .90 .25
291 A26 40fr dk sl bl & red brn 1.60 .25

FIDES Issue
Common Design Type
Designs: 3fr, Tractor and modern settlement. 5fr, Gallieni school. 10fr, Pangalanes Canal. 15fr, Irrigation project.

1956, Oct. 22 Engr. Perf. 13x12½
292 CD103 3fr gray vio & vio brn .40 .25
293 CD103 5fr org brn & dk vio brn .40 .35
294 CD103 10fr indigo & lilac .60 .35
295 CD103 15fr grn & bl grn .85 .25
Nos. 292-295 (4) 2.25 1.20

Coffee A26a

1956, Oct. 22 Perf. 13
296 A26a 20r red brn & dk brn .55 .25

Manioc — A27

Vanilla — A28

Design: 4fr, Cloves.

1957, Mar. 12 Unwmk. Perf. 13
297 A27 2fr bl, grn & sepia .25 .25
298 A28 4fr dp grn & red .55 .25
299 A28 12fr dk vio, dl grn & sepia .75 .35
Nos. 297-299 (3) 1.55 .85

Malagasy Republic Human Rights Issue
Common Design Type
1958, Dec. 10 Engr. Perf. 13
300 CD105 10fr brn & dk bl .80 .40
Universal Declaration of Human Rights, 10th anniversary.
"CF" stands for "Communauté française."

Imperforates
Most Malagasy stamps from 1958 onward exist imperforate in issued and trial colors, and also in small presentation sheets in issued colors.

Flower Issue
Common Design Type
Perf. 12½x12, 12x12½
1959, Jan. 31 Photo.
301 CD104 6fr Datura, horiz. .60 .25
302 CD104 25fr Poinsettia .90 .30

Flag and Assembly Building A29

Flag and Map — A30

French and Malagasy Flags and Map — A31

1959, Feb. 28 Engr. Perf. 13
303 A29 20fr brn vio, car & emer .30 .25
304 A30 25fr gray, red & emer .45 .25
Proclamation of the Malagasy Republic.

1959, Feb. 28
305 A31 60fr multi 1.60 .50
Issued to honor the French Community.

Chionaema Pauliani A32

Ylang-ylang — A33

Designs: 30c, 40c, 50c, 3fr, Various butterflies. 5fr, Sisal. 8fr, Pepper. 10fr, Rice. 15fr, Cotton.

1960		Unwmk.	Perf. 13	
306	A32	30c multicolored	.50	.25
307	A32	40c emer, sep & red brn	.50	.25
308	A32	50c vio brn, blk & stl bl	.50	.25
309	A32	1fr ind, red & dl pur	.50	.25
310	A32	3fr ol, vio blk & org	.50	.25
311	A32	5fr red, brn & emer	.50	.25
312	A33	6fr dk grn & brt yel	.55	.25
313	A32	8fr crim rose, emer & blk	.55	.25
314	A33	10fr dk grn, yel grn & lt brn	1.00	.25
315	A32	15fr brown & grn	1.10	.25
		Nos. 306-315 (10)	6.20	2.50

Family Planting Trees — A34

1960, Feb. 1 Engr. Perf. 13
316 A34 20fr red brn, buff & grn .90 .30
Issued for the "Week of the Tree," Feb. 1-7.

C.C.T.A. Issue
Common Design Type
1960, Feb. 22
317 CD106 25fr lt bl grn & plum .60 .30

Pres. Philibert Tsiranana and Map — A36

1960, Mar. 25 Unwmk. Perf. 13
318 A36 20fr green & brn .35 .25

Athletes of Two Races — A37

Pres. Philibert Tsiranana — A38

1060 Engr. Perf. 13
319 A37 25fr choc, org brn & ultra .60 .30
First Games of the French Community, Apr. 13-18, at Tananarive.

1960, July 29 Unwmk. Perf. 13
320 A38 20fr red, blk & brt grn .35 .25
Issued to honor Pres. Tsiranana, "Father of Independence." For surcharge see No. B18.

Gray Lemur — A39

Designs: 4fr, Ruffed lemur, horiz. 12fr, Mongoose lemur.

1961, Dec. 9 Perf. 13
321 A39 2fr brn & grnsh bl .25 .25
322 A39 4fr brn, grn & blk .45 .25
323 A39 12fr grn & red brn 1.10 .25
Nos. 321-323, C67-C69 (6) 16.80 5.20

Pres. Tsiranana Brldge, Sofia River A40

1962, Jan. 4 Unwmk. Perf. 13
324 A40 25fr bright blue 1.00 .25

First Train
Built at
Tananarive
A41

1962, Feb. 1
325 A41 20fr dk grn   1.10 .30

UN and
Malagasy Flags
over Government
Building,
Tananarive
A42

1962, Mar. 14   **Perf. 13**
326 A42 25fr multicolored .45 .25
327 A42 85fr multicolored 1.90 .55
Malagasy Republic's admission to the UN.
For surcharge see No. 409.

Ranomafana Village — A43

Designs: 30fr, Tritriva crater lake. 50fr,
Foulpointe shore. 60fr, Fort Dauphin.

1962, May 7   **Engr.**   **Perf. 13**
328 A43 10fr sl grn, grnsh bl & cl .25 .25
329 A43 30fr sl grn, cl & grnsh bl .65 .25
330 A43 50fr ultra, cl & sl grn .90 .30
331 A43 60fr cl, ultra & sl grn 1.10 .40
     Nos. 328-331,C70 (5) 4.65 1.80

African and Malgache Union Issue
Common Design Type
1962, Sept. 8 Photo. Perf. 12½x12
332 CD110 30fr grn, bluish grn,
     red & gold .80 .80
First anniversary of the African and Malgache Union.

Arms of
Republic
and
UNESCO
Emblem
A44

1962, Sept. 3   **Unwmk.**
333 A44 20fr rose, emer & blk .60 .25
First Conference on Higher Education in
Africa, Tananarive, Sept. 3-12.

Power
Station — A45

Designs: 8fr, Atomic reactor and atom symbol, horiz. 10fr, Oil derrick. 15fr, Tanker, horiz.

Perf. 12x12½, 12½x12
1962, Oct. 18   **Litho.**
334 A45 5fr blue, yel & red .25 .25
335 A45 8fr blue, red & yel .30 .25
336 A45 10fr multicolored .40 .25
337 A45 15fr bl, red brn & blk .50 .25
     Nos. 334-337 (4) 1.45 1.00
Industrialization of Madagascar.

Factory and
Globe
A46

1963, Jan. 7 Typo. Perf. 14x13½
338 A46 25fr dp org & blk .55 .25
International Fair at Tamatave.

Hertzian Cable, Tananarive-
Fianarantsoa — A47

1963, Mar. 7 Photo. Perf. 12½x12
339 A47 20fr multi .55 .25

Madagascar Blue   Gastrorchis
Pigeon — A48   Humblotii — A49

Birds: 2fr, Blue coua. 3fr, Red fody. 6fr,
Madagascar pigmy kingfisher.
Orchids: 10fr, Eulophiella roempleriana.
12fr, Angraecum sesquipedale.

1963   **Unwmk.**   **Perf. 13**
340 A48 1fr multi .45 .30
341 A48 2fr multi .45 .30
342 A48 3fr multi .60 .30
343 A48 6fr multi .75 .30
344 A49 8fr multi 1.00 .30
345 A49 10fr multi 1.90 .45
346 A49 12fr multi 2.10 .50
     Nos. 340-346,C72-C74 (10) 21.50 6.60

Arms — A50

Arms of: 1.50fr, Antsirabe. 5fr, Antalaha.
10fr, Tulear. 15fr, Majunga. 20fr, Fianarantsoa.
25fr, Tananarive. 50fr, Diégo-Suarez.
Imprint: "R. Louis del. So. Ge. Im."
1963-65   **Litho.**   **Perf. 13**
     Size: 23½x35½mm
347 A50 1.50fr multi ('64) .25 .25
348 A50 5fr multi ('65) .25 .25
349 A50 10fr multi ('64) .25 .25
350 A50 15fr multi ('64) .35 .25
351 A50 20fr multi .50 .25
352 A50 25fr multi .55 .25
353 A50 50fr multi ('65) 1.25 .50
     Nos. 347-353 (7) 3.40 2.00
See Nos. 388-390, 434-439.
For surcharge see No. 503.

Map and   Globe and
Centenary   Hands Holding
Emblem — A51   Torch — A52

1963, Sept. 2   **Perf. 12x12½**
354 A51 30fr multi 1.00 .50
Centenary of the International Red Cross.

1963, Dec. 10 Engr. Perf. 12½
355 A52 60fr ol, ocher & car .85 .40
Universal Declaration of Human Rights,
15th anniv.

Scouts and
Campfire
A53

1964, June 6 Engr. Perf. 13
356 A53 20fr dk red, org & car .70 .30
40th anniv. of the Boy Scouts of
Madagascar.

Europafrica Issue

Dove and
Globe
A54

1964, July 20   **Engr.**
357 A54 45fr ol grn, brn red & blk 1.00 .35
First anniversary of economic agreement
between the European Economic Community
and the African and Malgache Union.

Carved Statue of   University
Woman — A55   Emblem — A56

Malagasy Art: 30fr, Statue of sitting man.

1964, Oct. 20 Unwmk. Perf. 13
358 A55 6fr dk bl, brt bl & sepia .45 .25
359 A55 30fr dp grn, ol bis & dk
     brn .80 .30
     Nos. 358-359,C79 (3) 3.50 1.45

Cooperation Issue
Common Design Type
1964, Nov. 7 Engr. Perf. 13
360 CD119 25fr blk, dk brn & org
     brn .60 .25

1964, Dec. 5 Litho. Perf. 13x12½
361 A56 65fr red, blk & grn .70 .35
Founding of the University of Madagascar,
Tannanarive. The inscription reads: "Foolish is
he who does not do better than his father."

Jejy — A57

Valiha
Player
A58

Musical instruments: 3fr, Kabosa (lute). 8fr,
Hazolahy (sacred drum).

1965   **Engr.**   **Perf. 13**
     Size: 22x36mm
362 A57 3fr mag, vio bl & dk brn .50 .25
363 A57 6fr emer, rose lil & dk brn .60 .25
364 A57 8fr brn, grn & blk .90 .25
     Photo.   **Perf. 12½x13**
365 A58 25fr multi 1.75 .60
     Nos. 362-365,C80 (5) 9.25 3.35

PTT
Receiving
Station,
Foulpointe
A59

1965, May 8 Engr. Perf. 13
366 A59 20fr red org, dk grn &
     ocher .50 .25
Issued for Stamp Day, 1965.

ITU Emblem, Old and New
Telecommunication Equipment — A60

1965, May 17
367 A60 50fr ultra, red & grn 1.00 .40
ITU, centenary.

Jean Joseph   Pres. Philibert
Rabearivelo   Tsiranana
A61   A62

1965, June 22 Photo. Perf. 13x12½
368 A61 40fr dk brn & org .60 .30
Issued to honor the poet Jean Joseph
Rabearivelo, pen name of Joseph Casimir,
(1901-37).

1965, Oct. 18   **Perf. 13x12½**
369 A62 20fr multi .25 .25
   a. Souv. sheet of 4 1.00 1.00
370 A62 25fr multi .40 .25
   a. Souv. sheet of 4 2.00 2.00
55th birthday of President Philibert
Tsiranana.

Mail Coach
A63

History of the Post: 3fr, Early automobile. 4fr, Litter. 10fr, Mail runner, vert. 12fr, Mail boat. 25fr, Oxcart. 30fr, Old railroad mail car. 65fr, Hydrofoil.

1965-66   Engr.   Perf. 13
371 A63   3fr vio, dp bis & sky bl ('66)   .40   .25
372 A63   4fr ultra, grn & dk brn ('66)   .35   .25
373 A63 10fr multi   .35   .25
374 A63 12fr multi   .40   .25
375 A63 20fr bis, grn & red brn   .90   .30
376 A63 25fr sl grn, dk brn & org   .85   .30
377 A63 30fr pck bl, red & sep ('66)   2.50   .50
378 A63 65fr vio, brn & Prus bl ('66)   2.00   .50
      Nos. 371-378 (8)   7.75 2.60

Leper's Crippled Hands
A64

1966, Jan. 30
379 A64 20fr dk grn, dk brn & red   .70   .30
Issued for the 13th World Leprosy Day.

Couple Planting Trees
A65

1966, Feb. 21
380 A65 20fr dk brn, pur & bl grn   .60   .25
Reforestation as a national duty.

Tiger Beetle
A66

Insects: 6fr, Mantis. 12fr, Long-horned beetle. 45fr, Weevil.

1966   Photo.   Perf. 12½x12
Insects in Natural Colors
381 A66   1fr brick red   1.25   .25
382 A66   6fr rose claret   1.25   .25
383 A66 12fr Prus blue   3.00   .30
384 A66 45fr lt yel grn   4.25   .50
      Nos. 381-384 (4)   9.75 1.30

Stamp of 1903 — A67

1966, May 8   Engr.   Perf. 13
385 A67 25fr red & sepia   .75   .30
Issued for Stamp Day 1966.

Betsileo Dancers
A68

1966, June 13   Photo.   Perf. 12½x13
Size: 36x23mm
386 A68   5fr multi   .55   .25
See No. C83.

Symbolic Tree and Emblems — A69

1966, June 26
387 A69 25fr multi   .60   .25
Conference of the Organisation Commune Africaine et Malgache (OCAM), Tananarive.
No. 387 dated "JUIN 1966," original date "Janvier 1966" obliterated with bar. Exists without overprint "JUIN 1966" and bar. Value $100.

Arms Type of 1963-65
Imprint: "S. Gauthier So. Ge. Im."
20fr, Mananjary. 30fr, Nossi-Bé. 90fr, Antsohihy.

1966-68   Litho.   Perf. 13
Size: 23½x35½mm
388 A50 20fr multi ('67)   .40   .25
389 A50 30fr multi   .45   .25
390 A50 90fr multi ('68)   1.50   .40
      Nos. 388-390 (3)   2.35   .90
For surcharge see No. 503.

Singers and Map of Madagascar — A70

1966, Oct. 14   Engr.   Perf. 13
392 A70 20fr red brn, grn & dk car rose   .60   .25
Issued in honor of the National Anthem.

UNESCO Emblem
A71

1966, Nov. 4
393 A71 30fr red, yel & slate   .60   .25
UNESCO, 20th anniv.

Lions Emblem — A72

1967, Jan. 14   Photo.   Perf. 13x12½
394 A72 30fr multi   .60   .30
50th anniversary of Lions International.

Rice Harvest
A73

1967, Jan. 27   Perf. 12½x13
395 A73 20fr multi   .60   .25
FAO International Rice Year.

Adventist Temple, Tanambao-Tamatave — A74

Designs: 5fr, Catholic Cathedral, Tananarive, vert. 10fr, Mosque, Tamatave.

1967, Feb. 20   Engr.   Perf. 13
396 A74   3fr lt ultra, grn & bis   .25   .25
397 A74   5fr brt rose lil, grn & vio   .25   .25
398 A74 10fr dp bl, brn & grn   .30   .25
      Nos. 396-398 (3)   .80   .75

Norbert Raharisoa at Piano
A75

1967, Mar. 23   Photo.   Perf. 12½x12
399 A75 40fr citron & multi   .85   .35
Norbert Raharisoa (1914-1963), composer.

Jean Raoult Flying Blériot Plane, 1911
A76

45fr, Georges Bougault and hydroplane, 1926.

1967, Apr. 28   Engr.   Perf. 13
Size: 35½x22mm
400 A76   5fr gray bl, brn & grn   .85   .25
401 A76 45fr brn, stl bl & blk   1.75   .50
      Nos. 400-401,C84 (3)   13.60 3.75
History of aviation in Madagascar.

Ministry of Equipment and Communications — A77

1967, May 8   Engr.   Perf. 13
402 A77 20fr ocher, ultra & grn   .60   .25
Issued for Stamp Day, 1967.

Lutheran Church, Tananarive, Madagascar Map — A78

1967, Sept. 24   Photo.   Perf. 12x12½
403 A78 20fr multi   .70   .25
Lutheran Church in Madagascar, cent.

Map of Madagascar and Emblems — A79

1967, Oct. 16   Engr.   Perf. 13
404 A79 90fr red brn, bl & dk red   1.10   .40
Hydrological Decade (UNESCO), 1965-74.

Dance of the Bilo Sakalavas — A80

Design: 30fr, Atandroy dancers.

1967, Nov. 25   Photo.   Perf. 13x12½
Size: 22x36mm
405 A80   2fr lt grn & multi   .30   .25
406 A80 30fr multi   .60   .25
      Nos. 405-406,C86-C87 (4)   7.65 2.50

Woman's Face, Scales and UN Emblem
A81

1967, Dec. 16   Perf. 12½x13
407 A81 50fr emer, dk bl & brn   .70   .30
UN Commission on the Status of Women.

Human Rights Flame — A82

1968, Mar. 16   Litho.   Perf. 13x12½
408 A82 50fr blk, ver & grn   .70   .30
International Human Rights Year.

No. 327 Surcharged with New value and 3 Bars
1968, June 4   Engr.   Perf. 13
409 A42 20fr on 85fr multi   .70   .40

"Industry"
A83

Designs: 20fr, "Agriculture" (mother and child carrying fruit and grain, and cattle), vert. 40fr, "Communications and Investments," (train, highway, factory and buildings).

1968, July 15
410 A83 10fr rose car, grn & dk pur   .25   .25
411 A83 20fr dp car, grn & blk   .30   .25
412 A83 40fr brn, vio & sl bl   .60   .25
      Nos. 410-412 (3)   1.15   .75
Completion of Five-year Plan, 1964-68.

Church, Translated Bible, Cross and
Map of Madagascar — A84

1968, Aug. 18   Photo.   *Perf. 12½x12*
413 A84 20fr multi   .55   .25
 Sesquicentennial of Christianity in
Madagascar.

Isotry-Fitiavana
Protestant
Church — A85

 12fr, Catholic Cathedral, Fianarantsoa. 50fr,
Aga Khan Mosque, Tananarive.

1968, Sept. 10   Engr.   *Perf. 13*
414 A85 4fr red brn, brt grn &
          dk brn   .25   .25
415 A85 12fr plum, bl & hn brn   .30   .25
416 A85 60fr bl & indigo   .60   .25
     Nos. 414-416 (3)   1.15   .75

President
and Mrs.
Tsiranana
A86

1968, Oct. 14   Photo.   *Perf. 12½x12*
417 A86 20fr car, org & blk   .30   .25
418 A86 30fr car, grnsh bl & blk   .50   .25
  a. Souv. sheet of 4, 2 each #417-
      418   2.00   1.10
 10th anniv. of the Republic.

Madagascar Map
and Cornucopia
with Coins — A87

1968, Nov. 3   Photo.   *Perf. 12x12½*
419 A87 20fr multi   .60   .25
 50th anniversary of the Malagasy Savings
Bank.

Striving
Mankind — A88

 15fr, Mother, child and physician, horiz.

1968, Dec. 3   Photo.   *Perf. 12½x12*
420 A88 15fr ultra, yel & crim   .30   .25
421 A88 45fr vio bl & multi   .55   .25
 Completion of Five-Year Plan, 1964-68.

Queen Adelaide Receiving Malagasy
Delegation, London, 1836 — A89

1969, Mar. 29   Photo.   *Perf. 12x12½*
422 A89 250fr multi   5.75   2.50
 Malagasy delegation London visit, 1836-37.

Cogwheels,
Wrench
and ILO
Emblem
A90

1969, Apr. 11   *Perf. 12½x12*
423 A90 20fr grn & multi   .50   .25
 ILO, 50th anniv.

Telecommunications and Postal
Building, Tananarive — A91

1969, May 8   Engr.   *Perf. 13*
424 A91 30fr bl, brt grn & car
          lake   .60   .25
 Issued for Stamp Day 1969.

Steering Wheel,
Map,
Automobiles — A92

1969, June 1   Photo.   *Perf. 12*
425 A92 65fr multi   1.00   .30
 Automobile Club of Madagascar, 20th anniv.

Pres. Philibert   Banana
Tsiranana — A93   Plants — A94

1969, June 26   Photo.   *Perf. 12x12½*
426 A93 20fr multi   .45   .25
 10th anniversary of the inauguration of Pres.
Philibert Tsiranana.

1969, July 7   Engr.   *Perf. 13*
427 A94 5fr shown   .65   .25
428 A94 15fr Lichi tree   1.25   .25

Runners
A95

1969, Sept. 9   Engr.   *Perf. 13*
429 A95 15fr yel grn, brn & red   .55   .25
 Issued to commemorate the 19th Olympic
Games, Mexico City, Oct. 12-27, 1968.

Malagasy House,
Highlands — A96

 Malagasy Houses: No. 430, Betsileo house,
Highlands. No. 431, Tsimihety house, West
Coast, horiz. 60fr, Malagasy house,
Highlands.

1969-70   Engr.   *Perf. 13*
430 A96 20fr bl, ol & ver   .30   .25
431 A96 20fr sl, brt grn & red   .30   .25
432 A96 40fr blk, bl & dk red   .60   .25
433 A96 60fr vio bl, dp grn & brn   .90   .30
     Nos. 430-433 (4)   2.10   1.05
Issued: 40fr, 60fr, 11/25/69; others, 11/25/70.

Arms Type of 1963-65

 1fr, Maintirano. 10fr, Ambalavao. No. 436,
Morondava. No. 437, Ambatondrazaka. No.
438, Fenerive-Est. 80fr, Tamatave.

1970-72   Photo.   *Perf. 13*
434 A50 1fr multi ('72)   .25   .25
435 A50 10fr multi ('72)   .35   .25
436 A50 25fr multi ('71)   .55   .25
437 A50 25fr multi ('71)   .55   .25
438 A50 25fr multi ('72)   .70   .25
439 A50 80fr pink & multi   1.10   .30
     Nos. 434-439 (6)   3.50   1.55
 The 10fr, 80fr are dated "1970." No. 437 is
dated "1971." Nos. 434, 438 are dated "1972."
 Sizes: Nos. 434, 438, 22x37mm; others,
25½x36mm.
 Imprints: "S. Gauthier" on Nos. 434, 438; "S.
Gauthier Delrieu" on others.

Carnelian — A97

 Semi-precious Stones: 12fr, Yellow calcite.
15fr, Quartz. 20fr, Ammonite.

Perf. 12x12½ (5, 20fr), 13 (12, 15fr)
1970-71   Photo.
440 A97 5fr brn, dl rose & yel   4.25   1.00
441 A97 12fr multi ('71)   4.75   1.00
442 A97 15fr multi ('71)   6.25   1.50
443 A97 20fr grn & multi   17.50   2.00
     Nos. 440-443 (4)   32.75   5.50

UPU Headquarters Issue
Common Design Type
1970, May 20   Engr.   *Perf. 13*
444 CD133 20fr lil rose, brn & ul-
            tra   .55   .25

UN
Emblem
and
Symbols
of
Justice
A98

1970, June 26   Engr.   *Perf. 13*
445 A98 50fr blk, ultra & org   .70   .30
 25th anniversary of the United Nations.

Fruits of Madagascar — A99

1970, Aug. 18   Photo.   *Perf. 13*
446 A99 20fr multi   1.75   .25

Volute Delessertiana — A100

 Shells: 10fr, Murex tribulus. 20fr,
Spondylus.

1970, Sept. 9   Photo.   *Perf. 13*
447 A100 5fr Prus bl & multi   .90   .25
448 A100 10fr vio & multi   1.10   .25
449 A100 20fr multi   3.00   .30
     Nos. 447-449 (3)   5.00   .80

Aye-aye — A101

1970, Oct. 7   Photo.   *Perf. 12½*
450 A101 20fr multi   .45   .25
 Intl. Conference for Nature Conservation,
Tananarive, Oct. 7-10.

Pres. Tsiranana
A102

1970, Dec. 30   Photo.   *Perf. 12½*
451 A102 30fr grn & lt brn   .60   .25
 60th birthday of Pres. Philibert Tsiranana.

Tropical
Soap
Factory,
Tananarive
A103

 Designs: 15fr, Comina chromium smelting
plant, Andriamena. 50fr, Textile mill, Majunga.

1971, Apr. 14   Photo.   *Perf. 12½x12*
452 A103 5fr multi   .30   .25
                   Engr.   *Perf. 13*
453 A103 15fr vio bl, blk & ocher   .35   .25
                   Photo.   *Perf. 13*
454 A103 50fr multi   .65   .25
     Nos. 452-454 (3)   1.30   .75
 Economic development.

Globe, Agriculture, Industry, Science A104

1971, Apr. 22   Photo.   Perf. 12½x12
455 A104 5fr multi   .25   .25
Extraordinary meeting of the Council of the C.E.E.-E.A.M.A. (Communauté Economique Européen-Etats Africains et Malgache Associés).

Mobile Rural Post Office A105

1971, May 8   Perf. 13
456 A105 25fr multi   .55   .25
Stamp Day.

Gen. Charles de Gaulle — A106

1971, June 26   Engr.   Perf. 13
457 A106 30fr ultra, blk & rose   1.00   .35
In memory of Charles de Gaulle (1890-1970), President of France.
For surcharge see No. B24.

Madagascar Hilton, Tananarive A107

Design: 25fr, Hotel Palm Beach, Nossi-Bé.

1971, July 23   Photo.
458 A107 25fr multi   .50   .25
                                Engr.
459 A107 65fr vio bl, brn & lt grn   .85   .30

Trees and Post Horn — A108

1971, Aug. 6   Photo.   Perf. 12½x12
460 A108 3fr red, yel & grn   .30   .25
Forest preservation campaign.

House, South West Madagascar — A109

10fr, House from Southern Madagascar.

1971, Nov. 25   Perf. 13x12½
461 A109 5fr lt bl & multi   .25   .25
462 A109 10fr lt bl & multi   .35   .25

Children Playing, and Cattle A110

1971, Dec. 11   Litho.   Perf. 13
463 A110 50fr grn & multi   1.00   .30
UNICEF, 25th anniv.

Cable-laying Railroad Car, PTT Emblem — A111

1972, Apr. 8   Engr.   Perf. 13
464 A111 45fr slate grn, red & choc   1.50   .40
Coaxial cable connection between Tananarive and Tamatave.

Philibert Tsiranana Radar Station — A112

1972, Apr. 8   Photo.   Perf. 13½
465 A112 85fr bl & multi   1.00   .40

A113   A114

Voters and Pres. Tsiranana.

1972, May 1   Perf. 12½x13
466 A113 25fr yel & multi   .55   .35
Presidential election, Jan. 30, 1972.

1972, May 30   Photo.   Perf. 12x12½
467 A114 10fr Mail delivery   .60   .25
Stamp Day 1972.

Emblem and Stamps of Madagascar A115

Stamps shown are #352, 410, 429, 449.

1972, June 26   Perf. 13
468 A115 25fr org & multi   .50   .25
469 A115 40fr org & multi   .60   .30
470 A115 100fr org & multi   1.50   .50
  a. Souv. sheet of 3, #468-470   3.50 3.50
      Nos. 468-470 (3)   2.60 1.05
2nd Malgache Philatelic Exhibition, Tananarive, June 26-July 9.

Andapa-Sambava Road and Monument — A116

1972, July 6   Perf. 12½x12
471 A116 50fr multi   .60   .30
Opening of the Andapa-Sambava road.

Diesel Locomotive A117

1972, July 6   Engr.   Perf. 13
472 A117 100fr multicolored   4.50   .50

Razafindrahety College — A118

1972, Aug. 6
473 A118 10fr choc, bl & red brn   .25   .25
Razafindrahety College, Tananarive, sesqui.

Volleyball A119

1972, Aug. 6   Typo.   Perf. 12½x13
474 A119 12fr orange, blk & brn   .45   .25
African volleyball championship.

Oil Refinery, Tamatave A120

1972, Sept. 18   Engr.   Perf. 13
475 A120 2fr bl, bister & slate grn   .45   .25

Ravoahangy Andrianavalona Hospital — A121

1972, Oct. 14   Photo.   Perf. 13x12½
476 A121 6fr multi   .25   .25

Plowing A122

1972, Nov. 15   Photo.   Perf. 13½x14
477 A122 25fr gold & multi   .70   .30

Betsimisaraka Costume — A123

Design: 15fr, Merina costume.

1972, Dec. 30   Photo.   Perf. 13x12½
478 A123 10fr blue & multi   .25   .25
479 A123 15fr brown & multi   .45   .25

Farmer and Produce — A124

1973, Feb. 6   Photo.   Perf. 13
480 A124 25fr lt blue & multi   .45   .25
10th anniversary of the Malagasy Committee of "Freedom from Hunger Campaign."
For surcharge see No. 499.

Volva Volva A125

Shells: 10fr, 50fr, Lambis chiragra. 15fr, 40fr, Harpa major. 25fr, Like 3fr.

1973, Apr. 5   Litho.   Perf. 13
481 A125 3fr olive & multi   .35   .25
482 A125 10fr blue grn & multi   .55   .25
483 A125 15fr brt blue & multi   1.00   .25
484 A125 25fr lt blue & multi   1.40   .30
485 A125 40fr multicolored   1.75   .30
486 A125 50fr red lilac & multi   3.00   .40
      Nos. 481-486 (6)   8.05 1.75

Tsimandoa Mail Carrier — A126

1973, May 13   Engr.   Perf. 13
487 A126 50fr ind, ocher & sl grn   .75   .30
Stamp Day 1973.

Lt. Albert
Randriamaromanana — A161

Portrait: No. 578, Avana Ramanantoanina.

1977, Mar. 29
578 A161 25fr multicolored   .25   .25
579 A161 25fr multicolored   .25   .25

National Mausoleum — A162

1977, Mar. 29   Perf. 12½x12
580 A162 100fr multicolored   1.25   .40

Family
A163

1977, Apr. 7   Perf. 12x12½
581 A163 5fr yellow & multi   .25   .25
World Health Day: Immunization protects
the children.

Tananarive Medical School — A164

1977, June 30 Litho.   Perf. 12½x12
582 A164 250fr multicolored   2.50   .80
80th anniversary of Tananarive Medical
School.

Mail Bus — A165

1977, Aug. 18 Litho.   Perf. 12½x12
583 A165 35fr multicolored   .40   .25
Rural mail delivery.

Telegraph Operator — A166

1977, Sept. 13 Litho.   Perf. 12½x12
584 A166 15fr multicolored   .25   .25
Telegraph service Tananarive-Tamatave,
90th anniv.

Malagasy
Art — A167

1977, Sept. 29   Perf. 12x12½
585 A167 10fr multicolored   .25   .25
Malagasy Academy, 75th anniversary.

Lenin and Russian Flag — A168

1977, Nov. 7 Litho.   Perf. 12½x12
586 A168 25fr multicolored   2.00   .35
60th anniversary of Russian October
Revolution.

Raoul
Follereau,
Map of
Malagasy
A169

1978, Jan. 28 Litho.   Perf. 12x12½
587 A169 5fr multicolored   1.10   .30
25th anniversary of Leprosy Day.

Antenna, ITU
Emblem
A170

1978, May 17 Litho.   Perf. 12x12½
588 A170 20fr multicolored   .25   .25
10th World Telecommunications Day.

Black and White
Men Breaking
Chains of
Africa — A171

1978, June 22 Photo.   Perf. 12½x12
589 A171 60fr multicolored   .60   .25
Anti-Apartheid Year.

Boy and Girl,   Farm Workers,
Arch: Pen, Gun   Factory,
and Hoe   Tractor
A172   A173

1978, July 28 Litho.   Perf. 12½x12
590 A172 125fr multicolored   1.00   .40
Youth, the pillar of revolution.

1978, Aug. 24
591 A173 25fr multicolored   .25   .25
Socialist cooperation.

Women — A174

1979, Mar. 8 Litho.   Perf. 12½x12
592 A174 40fr multicolored   .35   .25
Women, supporters of the revolution.

Children
Bringing
Gifts — A175

1979, June 1 Litho.   Perf. 12x12½
593 A175 10fr multicolored   .25   .25
International Year of the Child.

Lemur
Macaco
A176

Fauna: 25fr, Lemur catta, vert. 1000fr,
Foussa.

Perf. 12½x12, 12x12½
1979, July 6   Litho.
594 A176   25fr multi   .70   .25
595 A176   125fr multi   2.75   .35
596 A176 1000fr multi   9.75 2.50
  Nos. 594-596,C172-C173 (5) 15.45 3.60

Jean Verdi
Salomon
A177

1979, July 25   Perf. 12x12½
597 A177 25fr multicolored   .25   .25
Jean Verdi Salomon (1913-1978), poet.

Talapetraka (Medicinal Plant) — A178

1979, Sept. 27 Litho.   Perf. 12½
598 A178 25fr multicolored   .90   .25

Map of Magagascar, Dish
Antenna — A179

1979, Oct. 12
599 A179 25fr multicolored   .25   .25

Stamp
Day
1979
A180

1979, Nov. 9
600 A180 500fr multicolored   4.50 1.40

Jet,
Map
of
Africa
A181

1979, Dec. 12   Perf. 12½
601 A181 50fr multicolored   .60   .25
ASECNA (Air Safety Board), 20th
anniversary.

Lenin Addressing Workers in the Winter Palace A182

1980, Apr. 22   Litho.   Perf. 12x12½
602 A182 25fr multicolored .60 .25
Lenin's 110th birth anniversary.

Bus and Road in Madagascar Colors A183

1980, June 15   Litho.   Perf. 12x12½
603 A183 30fr multicolored .35 .25
Socialist Revolution, 5th anniversary.

Flag and Map under Sun — A184

1980, June 26   Perf. 12½x12
604 A184 75fr multicolored .60 .25
Independence, 20th anniversary.

Armed Forces Day — A185

1980, Aug.   Litho.   Perf. 12½x12
605 A185 50fr multicolored .45 .25

Dr. Joseph Raseta (1886-1979) A186

1980, Oct. 15   Litho.   Perf. 12x12½
606 A186 30fr multicolored .30 .25

Anatirova Temple Centenary — A187

1980, Nov. 27   Litho.   Perf. 12½x12
607 A187 30fr multicolored .35 .25

Hurdles, Olympic Torch, Moscow '80 Emblem — A188

1980, Dec. 29
608 A188 30fr shown .45 .25
609 A188 75fr Boxing .85 .30
   Nos. 608-609,C175-C176 (4) 8.05 2.75
22nd Summer Olympic Games, Moscow, July 19-Aug. 3.

Democratic Republic of Madagascar, 5th Anniversary A189

1980, Dec. 30   Perf. 12x12½
610 A189 30fr multicolored .35 .25

Downhill Skiing — A190

1981, Jan. 26   Litho.   Perf. 12½x12
611 A190 175fr multicolored 1.75 .60
13th Winter Olympic Games, Lake Placid, Feb. 12-24, 1980.

Angraecum Leonis A191

1981, Mar. 23   Litho.   Perf. 11½
612 A191 5fr shown .50 .25
613 A191 80fr Angraecum ramosum 1.75 .30
614 A191 170fr Angraecum sesquipedale 2.75 .65
   Nos. 612-614 (3) 5.00 1.20
For surcharge, see No. 1474B.

A192   A193

1981, June 12   Litho.   Perf. 12
615 A192 25fr Student at desk .30 .25
616 A192 80fr Carpenter .75 .30
Intl. Year of the Disabled.

1981, July 10   Litho.   Perf. 12½x12
617 A193 15fr multi .25 .25
618 A193 45fr multi .55 .25
13th World Telecommunications Day.

Neil Armstrong on Moon (Apollo 11) — A194

Space Anniversaries.

1981, July 23   Perf. 11½
619 A194 30fr Valentina Tereshkova .30 .25
620 A194 80fr shown .80 .25
621 A194 90fr Yuri Gagarin .90 .25
   Nos. 019-021 (3) 2.00 .75

Brother Raphael Louis Rafiringa (1854-1919) A195

1981, Aug. 10   Litho.   Perf. 12
622 A195 30fr multi .35 .25

World Literacy Day — A196

1981, Sept. 8
623 A196 30fr multi .35 .25

World Food Day — A197

1981, Oct. 16   Litho.   Perf. 12x12½
624 A197 200fr multi 1.90 .60
See No. 635.

Oaths of Magistracy Renewal — A198

1981, Oct. 30   Perf. 12½x12
625 A198 30fr blk & lil rose .35 .25

Dove, by Pablo Picasso (1881-1973) — A199

1981, Nov. 18   Photo.   Perf. 11½x12
626 A199 00fr multi 1.00 .30

20th Anniv. of UPU Membership — A200

Design: Nos. C76, C77, emblem.

1981, Nov. 19   Litho.   Perf. 12
627 A200 5fr multi .25 .25
628 A200 30fr multi .35 .25

TB Bacillus Centenary A201

1982, June 21   Litho.   Perf. 12
629 A201 30fr multi .45 .25

Jeannette Mpihira (1903-1981), Actress and Singer — A202

1982, June 24   Perf. 12½
630 A202 30fr multi .35 .25

Haliaeetus Vociferoides
A203

1982, July
631 A203 25fr Vanga curviros-
tris, horiz. 1.10 .25
632 A203 30fr Leptostomus discolor, horiz. 1.40 .25
633 A203 200fr shown 4.75 .70
Nos. 631-633 (3) 7.25 1.20

Pierre Louis Boiteau
(1911-1980),
Educator
A204

1982, Sept. 13
634 A204 30fr multi .35 .25

World Food Day Type of 1981
1982, Oct. 16 Perf. 12x12½
635 A197 80fr multi .75 .25
No. 635 is overprinted "EFA POLO ARIARY"
on the text.

25th Anniv.
of
Launching
of Sputnik
I — A205

1982, Oct. 4 Litho. Perf. 12
636 A205 10fr Sputnik I .25 .25
637 A205 80fr Yuri Gagarin,
Vostok I .80 .25
638 A205 100fr Soyuz-Salyut 1.00 .30
Nos. 636-638 (3) 2.05 .80

1982 World
Cup — A206

Designs: Various soccer players.

1982, Oct. 14 Perf. 12x12½
639 A206 30fr multi .30 .25
640 A206 40fr multi .40 .25
641 A206 80fr multi .80 .25
Nos. 639-641 (3) 1.50 .75

Souvenir Sheet
Perf. 11½x12½
642 A206 450fr multi 4.50 1.60

Scene at a Bar, by Edouard Manet
(1832-1883) — A207

1982, Nov. 25 Perf. 12½x12
643 A207 5fr shown .55 .25
644 A207 30fr Lady in a White
Dress .75 .30
645 A207 170fr Portrait of Mallar-
me 3.50 .70
Nos. 643-645 (3) 4.80 1.25

Souvenir Sheet
Perf. 11½x12½
646 A207 400fr The Fifer, vert. 8.00 2.00
For surcharge, see No. 1475B.

Local
Fish — A208

1982, Dec. 14 Perf. 11½
647 A208 5fr Lutianus sebae .30 .25
648 A208 20fr Istiophorus
platypterus .35 .25
649 A208 30fr Pterois volitans .55 .25
650 A208 50fr Thunnus alba-
cares 1.25 .25
651 A208 200fr Epinephelus fasciatus 3.75 .60
Nos. 647-651 (5) 6.20 1.60

Souvenir Sheet
Perf. 12½x12
652 A208 450fr Latimeria
chalumnae 7.00 2.00
No. 652 contains one stamp 38x26mm.

Fort Mahavelona Ruins — A209

1982, Dec. 22 Perf. 12½x12
653 A209 10fr shown .25 .25
654 A209 30fr Ramena Beach .25 .25
655 A209 400fr Flowering jaca-
randa trees 3.00 1.00
Nos. 653-655 (3) 3.50 1.50

60th Anniv. of USSR — A210

1982, Dec. 29
656 A210 10fr Tractors .25 .25
657 A210 15fr Pylon .25 .25
658 A210 30fr Kremlin, Lenin .25 .25
659 A210 150fr Arms 1.25 .50
Nos. 656-659 (4) 2.00 1.25

World Communications Year — A211

80fr, Stylized figures holding wheel.

1983, May 17 Litho. Perf. 12
660 A211 30fr multi .25 .25
661 A211 80fr multi .80 .30

Organization
of African
Unity, 20th
Anniv.
A212

1983, May 25 Litho. Perf. 12
662 A212 30fr multi .25 .25

Henri Douzon,
Lawyer and
Patriot — A213

1983, June 27 Litho. Perf. 12
663 A213 30fr multi .25 .25

Souvenir Sheet

Manned Flight Bicentenary — A214

1983, July 20 Litho. Perf. 12
664 A214 500fr Montgolfiere balloon 5.75 2.00

Souvenir Sheet

Raphael, 500th Birth Anniv. — A215

1983, Aug. 10 Litho. Perf. 12
665 A215 500fr The Madonna
Connestable 5.75 2.00

Lemur — A216

Various lemurs. Nos. 668-669, 671 vert.

Perf. 12½x12, 12x12½
1983, Dec. 6 Litho.
666 A216 30fr Daubentonia
madagascarien-
sis .55 .25
667 A216 30fr Microcebus
murinus .55 .25
668 A216 30fr Lemur variegatus .55 .25
669 A216 30fr Propithecus verreauxi .55 .25
670 A216 200fr Indri indri 3.50 .80
Nos. 666-670 (5) 5.70 1.80

Souvenir Sheet
671 A216 500fr Perodicticus potto 8.00 2.00

1984 Winter
Olympics
A217

1984, Jan. 20 Litho. Perf. 11½
672 A217 20fr Ski jumping .25 .25
673 A217 30fr Speed skating .25 .25
674 A217 30fr Downhill skiing .25 .25
675 A217 30fr Hockey .25 .25
676 A217 200fr Figure skating 2.00 .60
Nos. 672-676 (5) 3.00 1.60

Souvenir Sheet
677 A217 500fr Cross-country
skiing 4.75 2.00
No. 677 contains one stamp 48x32mm.

Vintage Cars — A218

1984, Jan. 27 Perf. 12½x12
678 A218 15fr Renault, 1907 .25 .25
679 A218 30fr Benz, 1896 .30 .25
680 A218 30fr Baker, 1901 .30 .25
681 A218 30fr Blake, 1901 .30 .25
682 A218 200fr FIAL, 1908 2.40 .60
Nos. 678-682 (5) 3.55 1.60

Souvenir Sheet
Perf. 12½x11½
683 A218 450fr Russo-Baltique,
1909 5.50 2.00

Pastor
Ravelojaona
(1879-1956),
Encyclopedist
A219

1984, Feb. 14 Perf. 12x12½
684 A219 30fr multi .25 .25
See No. 704.

Madonna and Child, by Correggio (1489-1534) A220

Various Correggio paintings.

1984, May 5   Litho.   Perf. 12x12½
685	A220	5fr multi	.25	.25
686	A220	20fr multi	.25	.25
687	A220	30fr multi	.35	.35
688	A220	80fr multi	.75	.30
689	A220	200fr multi	2.10	.60
		Nos. 685-689 (5)	3.70	1.65

Souvenir Sheet
| 690 | A220 | 400fr multi | 5.50 | 2.00 |

A221

1984, July 27
691	A221	5fr Paris landmarks	.25	.25
692	A221	20fr Wilhelm Steinitz	.30	.25
693	A221	30fr Champion, cup	.50	.25
694	A221	30fr Vera Menchik	.50	.25
695	A221	215fr Champion, cup, diff.	3.00	.80
		Nos. 691-695 (5)	4.55	1.80

Souvenir Sheet
| 696 | A221 | 400fr Children playing chess | 5.50 | 2.00 |

World Chess Federation, 60th anniv.

A222

1984, Aug. 10
| 697 | A222 | 100fr Soccer | 1.00 | .35 |

1984 Summer Olympics.

Butterflies A223

1984, Aug. 30   Litho.   Perf. 11½
698	A223	15fr Eudaphaenura splendens	.45	.25
699	A223	50fr Othreis boseae	1.40	.25
700	A223	50fr Pharmacophagus antenor	1.40	.25
701	A223	50fr Acraea hova	1.40	.25
702	A223	200fr Epicausis smithii	5.50	.65
		Nos. 698-702 (5)	10.15	1.65

Miniature Sheet
Perf. 11½x12½
| 703 | A223 | 400fr Papilio delandii | 7.50 | 2.00 |

No. 703 contains one stamp 37x52mm.

Famous People Type
Jean Ralaimongo (1884-1944).

1984, Oct. 4   Perf. 12x12½
| 704 | A219 | 50fr Portrait | .60 | .25 |

Children's Rights A225

1984, Nov. 20   Litho.   Perf. 12½x12
| 705 | A225 | 50fr Youths in school bag | .50 | .25 |

Malagasy Orchids — A226

1984, Nov. 20   Litho.   Perf. 12
706	A226	20fr Disa incarnata	.30	.25
707	A226	235fr Eulophiella roempleriana	3.25	.70
		Nos. 706-707,C180-C182 (5)	6.55	1.70

Miniature Sheet
Perf. 12x12½
| 708 | A226 | 400fr Gastrorchis tuberculosa | 7.50 | 2.00 |

No. 708 contains one stamp 30x42mm.

Cotton Seminar, UN Trade and Development Conference A227

1984, Dec. 15   Litho.   Perf. 13x12½
| 709 | A227 | 100fr UN emblem, cotton bolls | 1.00 | .30 |

Malagasy Language Bible, 150th Anniv. A228

1985, Feb. 11   Litho.   Perf. 12½x12
| 710 | A228 | 50fr multi | .50 | .25 |

1985 Agricultural Census — A229

1985, Feb. 21   Litho.   Perf. 12x12½
| 711 | A229 | 50fr Census taker, farmer | .50 | .25 |

Allied Defeat of Nazi Germany, 40th Anniv. — A230

20fr, Russian flag-raising, Berlin, 1945. 50fr, Normandy-Niemen squadron shooting down German fighter planes. No. 714, Soviet Victory Parade, Red Square, Moscow. No. 715, Victorious French troops marching through Arc de Triomphe, vert.

1985   Perf. 12½x12, 12x12½
712	A230	20fr multi	.30	.25
713	A230	50fr multi	.30	.35
714	A230	100fr multi	.90	.35
715	A230	100fr multi	3.00	.70
		Nos. 712-715 (4)	4.50	1.65

Issue dates: Nos. 712-714, 5/9; No. 715, Oct.

Cats and Dogs A231

1985, Apr. 25   Perf. 12x12½, 12½x12
716	A231	20fr Siamese	.30	.25
717	A231	20fr Bichon	.30	.25
718	A231	50fr Abyssinian, vert.	.75	.25
719	A231	100fr Cocker spaniel, vert.	1.40	.35
720	A231	235fr Poodle	3.50	.80
		Nos. 716-720 (5)	6.25	1.90

Souvenir Sheet
| 721 | A231 | 400fr Kitten | 6.00 | 2.00 |

No. 721 contains one stamp 42x30mm, perf. 12½x12.

Gymnastic Event, Natl. Stadium, Atananarivo — A232

1985, July 9   Perf. 12½x12
| 722 | A232 | 50fr multi | .45 | .25 |

Natl. Socialist Revolution, 10th anniv.

Commemorative Medal, Memorial Stele — A233

1985, July 9
| 723 | A233 | 50fr multi | 1.25 | .25 |

Independence, 25th anniv.

Intl. Youth Year — A234

1985, Sept. 18   Perf. 12
| 724 | A234 | 100fr Emblem, map | 1.00 | .25 |

Natl. Red Cross, 70th Anniv. — A235

1985, Oct. 3   Perf. 12x12½
| 725 | A235 | 50fr multi | .90 | .25 |

Indira Gandhi — A236

1985, Oct. 31   Perf. 13½
| 726 | A236 | 100fr multi | 1.10 | .35 |

22nd World Youth and Student's Festival, Moscow — A237

1985, Nov.   Perf. 12
| 727 | A237 | 50fr multi | .50 | .25 |

Rouen Cathedral at Night, by Monet — A238   UN, 40th Anniv. — A239

Impressionist paintings: No. 729, View of Sea at Sainte-Marie, by van Gogh, horiz. 45fr, Young Women in Black, by Renoir. 50fr, The Red Vineyard at Arles, by van Gogh, horiz. 100fr, Boulevard des Capucines in Paris, by Monet, horiz. 400fr, In the Garden, by Renoir.

1985, Oct. 25   Litho.   Perf. 12
728	A238	20fr multi	.50	.25
729	A238	20fr multi	.50	.25
730	A238	45fr multi	.90	.25
731	A238	50fr multi	1.10	.25
732	A238	100fr multi	2.40	.50
		Nos. 728-732 (5)	5.40	1.50

Souvenir Sheet
Perf. 12x12½
| 733 | A238 | 400fr multi | 6.00 | 2.75 |

No. 733 contains one 30x42mm stamp.

1985, Oct. 31   Perf. 12
| 734 | A239 | 100fr multi | 1.00 | .30 |

Orchids A240

1985, Nov. 8
| 735 | A240 | 20fr Aeranthes grandiflora | 1.00 | .25 |
| 736 | A240 | 45fr Angraecum magdalanae | 1.50 | .25 |

737 A240 50fr Aerangis stylosa 1.75 .30
738 A240 100fr Angraecum
             eburneum
             longicalcar   3.25 .50
739 A240 100fr Angraecum ses-
             quipedale   3.25 .50
   Nos. 735-739 (5)   10.75 1.80
Souvenir Sheet
Perf. 12x12½
740 A240 400fr Angraecum
             aburneum
             superbum   8.00 2.50
   Nos. 735, 737-740 vert. No. 740 contains
one 30x42mm stamp.

INTERCOSMOS — A241

Cosmonauts, natl. flags, rockets, satellites
and probes.

1985, Nov.   *Perf. 12x12½*
741 A241 20fr USSR, Czecho-
             slovakia   .25 .25
742 A241 20fr Soyuz-Apollo em-
             blem   .25 .25
743 A241 50fr USSR, India   .55 .25
744 A241 100fr USSR, Cuba   1.00 .30
745 A241 200fr USSR, France   1.90 .65
   Nos. 741-745 (5)   3.95 1.70
Souvenir Sheet
746 A241 400fr Halley's Comet,
             probe   5.50 1.75
   No. 746 contains one stamp 42x30mm.

Democratic Republic, 10th
Anniv. — A242

1985, Dec. 30   Litho.   *Perf. 12½x12*
747 A242 50fr Industrial symbols   .45 .25

Natl. Insurance
and Securities
Co. (ARO), 10th
Anniv. — A243

1986, Jan. 20   *Perf. 12x12½*
748 A243 50fr dk brn, yel org &
             gray brn   .45 .25

Paintings in the Tretyakov Gallery,
Moscow — A244

Designs: 20fr, Still-life with Flowers and
Fruit, 1839, by I. Chroutzky. No. 750, Portrait
of Alexander Pushkin, 1827, by O. Kiprenski,
vert. No. 751, Portrait of an Unknown Woman,
1883, by I. Kramskoi. No. 752, The Crows
Have Returned, 1872, by A. Sakrassov, vert.
100fr, March, 1895, by I. Levitan. 450fr, Portrait of Pavel Tretyakov, 1883, by I. Repin, vert.

Perf. 12½x12, 12x12½
1986, Apr. 26   Litho.
749 A244 20fr multi   .25 .25
750 A244 50fr multi   .80 .25
751 A244 50fr multi   .80 .25
752 A244 50fr multi   .80 .25
753 A244 100fr multi   2.25 .40
   Nos. 749-753 (5)   4.90 1.40
Souvenir Sheet
754 A244 450fr multi   4.50 2.00

1986 World Cup
Soccer
Championships,
Mexico — A245

1986, May 31   *Perf. 13½*
755 A245 150fr multi   1.40 .45

Paintings in Russian
Museums — A246

No. 756, David and Urie, by Rembrandt,
vert. No. 757, Danae, by Rembrandt. No. 758,
Portrait of the Nurse of the Infant Isabella, by
Rubens, vert. No. 759, The Alliance of Earth
and Water, by Rubens, vert. No. 760, Portrait
of an Old Man in Red, by Rembrandt. No. 761,
The Holy Family, by Raphael.

Perf. 12x12½, 12½x12½
1986, Mar. 24   Litho.
756 A246 20fr multi   .25 .25
757 A246 50fr multi   .70 .25
758 A246 50fr multi   .70 .25
759 A246 50fr multi   .70 .25
760 A246 50fr multi   .75 .25
   Nos. 756-760 (5)   3.10 1.25
Souvenir Sheet
Perf. 11½x12½
761 A246 450fr multi   3.50 2.50

UN Child Survival
Campaign
A247

1986, June 1   Litho.   *Perf. 12x12½*
762 A247 60fr multi   .60 .25

A248

Wildcats — A249

1986, July 17
763 A248 10fr Sable   .25 .25
764 A248 10fr Chaus   .25 .25
765 A248 60fr Serval   .70 .25
766 A248 60fr Caracal   .70 .25
767 A248 60fr Bengal   .70 .25
   Nos. 763-767 (5)   2.60 1.25
Souvenir Sheet
Perf. 12½x12
768 A249 450fr Golden   4.75 2.00

Intl. Peace
Year
A249a

1986, Sept. 12   *Perf. 12*
769 A249a 60fr shown   .55 .25
770 A249a 150fr Hemispheres,
              emblem, vert. 1.25 .40

World Post
Day — A250

1986, Oct. 9   Litho.   *Perf. 13x12½*
771 A250 60fr multi   .60 .25
772 A250 150fr multi   1.40 .40

   No. 772 is airmail.

Birds — A252

Perf. 12x12½, 12½x12
1986, Dec. 23   Litho.
773 A251 60fr Xenopirostris
             daimi, vert.   .80 .25
774 A251 60fr Falculea palliata .80 .25
775 A251 60fr Coua gigas   .80 .25
776 A251 60fr Coua cristata   .80 .25
777 A251 60fr Cianolanius
             madagascarien-
             sis, vert.   .80 .25
   Nos. 773-777 (5)   4.00 1.25
Souvenir Sheet
778 A252 450fr Bubulcus ibis ibis 6.00 2.00

A253

Endangered Species — A254

Perf. 12x12½, 12½x12½
1987, Mar. 13   Litho.
779 A253 60fr Lophotibis cris-
             tata, vert.   1.10 .25
780 A253 60fr Coracopsis nigra 1.10 .25
781 A254 60fr Crocodylus
             niloticus   1.10 .25
782 A254 60fr Geochelone
             yniphora   1.10 .25
   Nos. 779-782 (4)   4.40 1.00
Souvenir Sheet
783 A253 450fr Centropus toulou,
             vert.   6.25 2.00

Anti-Colonial
Revolt, 40th
Anniv. — A255

A256

1987, Mar. 29   *Perf. 12*
784 A255 60fr multi   .50 .25
785 A256 60fr multi   .50 .25

1st Games of
Indian Ocean
Towns
A257

1987, Apr. 15   *Perf. 13½*
786 A257 60fr multi   .55 .25
787 A257 150fr multi   1.25 .40

Le Sarimanok — A258

1987, Apr. 15
788	A258	60fr Port side	.60	.25
789	A258	150fr Starboard side	1.40	.40

African and Madagascar Coffee Organization, 25th Anniv. — A259

1987, Apr. 24   Litho.   Perf. 12
790	A259	60fr Coffee plant	.55	.25
791	A259	150fr Map	1.40	.40

Halley's Comet — A260

Space probes.

1987, May 13   Perf. 13½
792	A260	60fr Giotto, ESA	.40	.25
793	A260	150fr Vega 1, Russia	.90	.25
794	A260	250fr Vega 2, Russia	1.75	.40
795	A260	350fr Planet-A1, Japan	2.50	.60
796	A260	400fr Planet-A2, Japan	2.75	.65
797	A260	450fr ICE, US	3.25	.70
		Nos. 792-797 (6)	11.55	2.85

Souvenir Sheet
798	A260	600fr Halley, Giotto	4.50	1.00

Litho. & Embossed 'Gold Foil' Stamps
These stamps generally are of a different design format than the rest of the issue. Since there is a commemorative inscription tying them to the issue a separate illustration is not being shown.

1988 Calgary Winter Olympics — A261

Men's Downhill — A262

1987, May 13
799	A261	60fr Biathlon	.40	.25
800	A261	150fr shown	.90	.25
801	A261	250fr Luge	1.75	.40

802	A261	350fr Speed skating	2.50	.60
803	A261	400fr Hockey	2.75	.65
804	A261	450fr Pairs figure skating	3.25	.70
		Nos. 799-804 (6)	11.55	2.85

Litho. & Embossed
804A	A261	1500fr Speed skating	11.00

Souvenir Sheets
Litho.
805	A262	600fr shown	4.75	1.25

Litho. & Embossed
805A	A262	1500fr Slalom skiing	7.50

No. 804A exists in souvenir sheet of 1.

Jean-Joseph Rabearivelo (d. 1937), Poet — A263

1987, June 22   Perf. 13½
806	A263	60fr multi	.40	.25

1992 Summer Olympics, Barcelona — A264

Athletes, emblem and art or architecture: 60fr, Equestrian, and the Harlequin, by Picasso. 150fr, Weight lifting, church. 250fr, Hurdles, Canaletas Fountain. 350fr, High jump, amusement park. 400fr, Men's gymnastics, abbey. 450fr, Rhythmic gymnastics, Arc de Triomphe. 600fr, Equestrian, Columbus monument.

1987, Oct. 7   Litho.   Perf. 13½
807	A264	60fr multi	.25	.25
808	A264	150fr multi	.80	.25
809	A264	250fr multi	1.40	.40
810	A264	350fr multi	2.00	.60
811	A264	400fr multi	2.25	.65
812	A264	450fr multi	2.50	.70
		Nos. 807-812 (6)	9.20	2.85

Souvenir Sheet
813	A264	600fr multi	3.75	1.25

Nos. 811-813 are airmail.

A265

Discovery of America, 500th Anniv. (in 1992) — A266

Anniv. emblem and: 60fr, Bartolomeu Dias (c. 1450-1500), Portuguese navigator, departure from De Palos, 1492. 150fr, Henry the Navigator (1394-1460), prince of Portugal, Samana Cay. 250fr, A. De Marchena landing,

1492. 350fr, Paolo Toscanelli dal Pozzo (1397-1482), Italian physician and cosmographer, La Navidad Fort. 400fr, Queen Isabella I, Barcelona, 1493. 450fr, Christopher Columbus, the Nina. 600fr, Landing in New World, 1492.

1987, Sept. 24   Litho.   Perf. 13½
814	A265	60fr multi	.30	.25
815	A265	150fr multi	.80	.30
816	A265	250fr multi	1.25	.55
817	A265	350fr multi	1.90	.85
818	A265	400fr multi	2.25	1.00
819	A265	450fr multi	2.50	1.10
		Nos. 814-819 (6)	9.00	4.05

Souvenir Sheet
820	A266	600fr multi	4.00	1.50

A267   A268

1987, July 27   Perf. 12½x12
821	A267	60fr multi	.40	.25

Natl. telecommunications research laboratory.

1987, Aug. 14
822	A268	60fr lt blue, blk & brt ultra	.40	.25

Rafaravavy Rasalama (d. 1837), Christian martyr.

Antananarivo-Tamatave Telegraph Link, Cent. — A269

1987, Sept. 15   Perf. 12x12½
823	A269	60fr multi	.40	.25

Pasteur Institute, Paris, Cent. A270

1987, Oct. 26   Perf. 13½
824	A270	250fr multi	1.10	.50

City of Berlin, 750th Anniv. — A271

Design: Anniv. emblem, television tower and the Interhotel in East Berlin.

1987, Oct. 18   Litho.   Perf. 12½x12
825	A271	150fr multi	.40	.30

Schools Festival A272

1987, Oct. 23   Perf. 12x12½
826	A272	60fr multi	.25	.25

Paintings in the Pushkin Museum, Moscow — A273

Designs: 10fr, After the Shipwreck (1847), by Eugene Delacroix (1798-1863). No. 828, Still-life with Swan (c. 1620), by Frans Snyders (1579-1647). No. 829, Jupiter and Callisto (1744), by Francois Boucher (1703-1770), vert. No. 830, Chalet in the Mountains (1874), by Jean Desire Gustav Courbet (1819-1877). 150fr, At the Market (1564), by Joachim Bueckelaer. 1000fr, Minerva (1560), by Paolo Veronese (1528-1588), vert.

Perf. 12½x12, 12x12½
1987, Nov. 10
827	A273	10fr multi	.30	.25
828	A273	60fr multi	.45	.25
829	A273	60fr multi	.45	.25
830	A273	60fr multi	.45	.25
831	A273	150fr multi	1.00	.25
		Nos. 827-831 (5)	2.65	1.25

Souvenir Sheet
832	A273	1000fr multi	7.00	2.75

Pan-African Telecommunications Union, 10th Anniv. — A274

1987, Dec. 28   Perf. 13x12½
833	A274	250fr multi	.60	.45

Intl. Year of Shelter for the Homeless A275

1988, Feb. 15   Litho.   Perf. 12
834	A275	80fr shown	.25	.25
835	A275	250fr Family in shelter, rain, vert.	.55	.25

Fauna A276

Designs: 60fr, Hapalemur simus. 150fr, Propithecus diadema diadema. 250fr, Indri indri. 350fr, Varecia variegata variegata. 550fr, Madagascar young heron. No. 841, Nossi-Be chameleon. No. 842, Uratelornis (bird).

1988, Apr. 18   Litho.   Perf. 13½
836	A276	60fr multicolored	1.75	.75
837	A276	150fr multicolored	2.25	.75
838	A276	250fr multicolored	3.25	1.00

839	A276	350fr multicolored	5.00	1.25
840	A276	550fr multicolored	1.50	.60
841	A276	1500fr multicolored	3.50	1.60
		Nos. 836-841 (6)	17.25	5.95

Souvenir Sheet

842	A276	1500fr multicolored	6.50	6.50

Conservation and service organization emblems: World Wildlife Fund (60fr, 150fr, 250fr and 350fr); Rotary Intl. (550fr and No. 842); and Scouting trefoil (No. 841).
Nos. 840-841 exist in souvenir sheet of 2.
For overprints see Nos. 1134, 1154.

October Revolution, Russia, 70th Anniv. A277

1988, Mar. 7　Litho.　Perf. 12x12½

843	A277	60fr Lenin	.60	.25
844	A277	60fr Revolutionaries	.60	.25
845	A277	150fr Lenin, revolutionaries	1.25	.25
		Nos. 843-845 (3)	2.45	.75

1988 Winter Olympics, Calgary A278

1988, May 11　　Perf. 11½

846	A278	20fr Pairs figure skating	.25	.25
847	A278	60fr Slalom	.25	.25
848	A278	60fr Speed skating	.25	.25
849	A278	100fr Cross-country skiing	.30	.25
850	A278	250fr Ice hockey	.70	.30
		Nos. 846-850 (5)	1.75	1.30

Souvenir Sheet

851	A278	800fr Ski jumping	2.50	1.75

Discovery of Radium by Pierre and Marie Curie, 90th Anniv. A279

1988, July 14　Litho.　Perf. 12

852	A279	150fr blk & rose lil	.50	.25

OAU, 25th Anniv. A280

1988, May 25　Litho.　Perf. 13

853	A280	80fr multi	.25	.25

Natl. Telecommunications and Posts Institute, 20th Anniv. — A281

1988, June 22　　Perf. 13½

854	A281	80fr multi	.25	.25

Saint-Michel College, Cent. — A282

1988, July 9

855	A282	250fr multi	.55	.30

Alma-Ata Declaration, 10th Anniv. — A283　　WHO, 40th Anniv. — A284

1988, Aug. 11　Litho.　Perf. 12

856	A283	60fr multi	.30	.25

1988, Aug. 11

857	A284	150fr multi	.30	.25

Tsimbazaza Botanical and Zoological Park, 150th Anniv. — A285

Perf. 12x12½, 12½x12
1988, Aug. 22

858	A285	20fr Lemur habitat	.55	.25
859	A285	80fr Lemur and young	.55	.25
860	A285	250fr shown	1.50	.40
		Nos. 858-860 (3)	2.60	.90

Souvenir Sheet

861	A285	1000fr Lemur and mate	3.50	2.25

Size of No. 859: 25x37mm.

Boy Scouts Studying Birds and Butterflies A286

Designs: 80fr, Upupa epops maginata, Coua caerulea and scout photographing bird. 250fr, Chrysiridia croesus and comparing butterfly to a sketch. 270fr, Nelicurvius nelicourvi, Foudia omissa and constructing bird feeder. 350fr, Papilio dardanus and studying butterflies with magnifying glass. 550fr, Coua critata and tagging bird. No. 867, Argema mittrei and

---

writing observations. No. 868, Merops superciliosus and recording bird calls. No. 868A, Euchloron megaera. No. 868B, Rhynchee.

1988, Sept. 29

862	A286	80fr multi	.25	.25
863	A286	250fr multi	.55	.30
864	A286	270fr multi	.60	.30
865	A286	350fr multi	.80	.40
866	A286	550fr multi	1.25	.60
867	A286	1500fr multi	3.75	1.60
		Nos. 862-867 (6)	7.20	3.45

Souvenir Sheet

868	A286	1500fr multi	3.50	2.25

Litho. & Embossed
Perf. 13½

868A	A286	5000fr gold & multi	8.00

Souvenir Sheet

868B	A286	5000fr gold & multi	8.00

No. 868 contains one stamp 36x51mm. Nos. 868A-868B dated 1989. Nos. 868A-868B exist imperf.

Composers and Entertainers A287

Designs: 80fr, German-made clavier and Carl Philipp Emanuel Bach (1714-1788), organist and composer. 250fr, Piano and Franz Peter Schubert (1797-1828), Austrian composer. 270fr, Scene from opera Carmen, 1875, and Georges Bizet (1838-1875), French composer. 350fr, Scene from opera Pelleas et Melisande, 1902, and Claude Debussy (1862-1918), French composer. 550fr, George Gershwin (1898-1937), American composer. No. 874, Elvis Presley (1935-1977), American entertainer. No. 875, Rimsky-Korsakov (1844-1908), Russian composer, and Le Coq d'Or from the opera of the same name.

1988, Oct. 28　Perf. 12x12½, 12½x12

869	A287	80fr multi	.25	.25
870	A287	250fr multi	.55	.30
871	A287	270fr multi	.60	.30
872	A287	350fr multi	.80	.40
873	A287	550fr multi	1.25	.60
874	A287	1500fr multi	3.50	1.60
		Nos. 869-874 (6)	6.95	3.45

Souvenir Sheet

875	A287	1500fr multi	3.25	3.25

For overprints see Nos. 1135-1136.

Intl. Fund for Agricultural Development (IFAD), 10th Anniv. — A288

1988, Sept. 4　Litho.　Perf. 12

876	A288	250fr multi	.50	.25

School Feast — A289

1988, Nov. 22

877	A289	80fr multi	.25	.25

A290

Ships — A291

Paintings: 20fr, The Squadron of the Sea, Black Feodossia, by Ivan Aivazovski, vert. No. 879, Seascape with Sailing Ships, by Simon de Vlieger, vert. No. 880, The Ship Lesnoie, by N. Semenov, vert. 100fr, The Merchantman, Orel, by N. Golitsine. 250fr, Naval Exercises, by Adam Silo, vert. 550fr, On the River, by Abraham Beerstraten.

1988, Dec. 5　Perf. 12x12½, 12½x12

878	A290	20fr multi	.25	.25
879	A290	80fr multi	.25	.25
880	A290	80fr multi	.25	.25
881	A290	100fr shown	.35	.25
882	A290	250fr multi	.80	.25
		Nos. 878-882 (5)	1.90	1.25

Souvenir Sheet
Perf. 11½x12½

883	A291	550fr shown	2.00	1.00

World Wildlife Fund — A292

Insect species in danger of extinction: 20fr, Tragocephala crassicornis. 80fr, Polybothris symptuosa-gema. 250fr, Euchroea auripigmenta. 350fr, Stellognata maculata.

1988, Dec. 13　　Perf. 12

884	A292	20fr multi	1.00	—
885	A292	80fr multi	6.50	—
886	A292	250fr multi	22.50	—
887	A292	350fr multi	30.00	—
		Nos. 884-887 (4)	60.00	

Intl. Red Cross and Red Crescent Organizations, 125th Annivs. — A293

1988, Dec. 27　Litho.　Perf. 12

888	A293	80fr Globe, stretcher-bearers, vert.	.25	.25
889	A293	250fr Emblems, Dunant	.55	.30

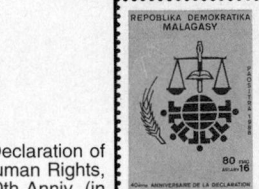

UN Declaration of Human Rights, 40th Anniv. (in 1988) — A294

1989, Jan. 10
890 A294 80fr shown .25 .25
891 A294 250fr Hands, "4" and "0" .60 .30
Dated 1988.

Transportation — A295

Designs: 80fr, 1909 Mercedes-Benz Blitzen Benz. 250fr, Micheline ZM 517 Tsikirity, Tananarive-Moramanga line. 270fr, Bugatti Coupe Binder 41. 350fr, Electric locomotive 1020-DES OBB, Germany. 1500fr, Souleze Autorail 701 DU CFN, Madagascar. No. 897, 1913 Opel race car. No. 898, Bugatti Presidential Autorail locomotive and Bugatti Type 57 Atalante automobile.

1989, Jan. 24 **Perf. 13½**
892 A295 80fr multi .25 .25
893 A295 250fr multi .50 .25
894 A295 270fr multi .60 .25
895 A295 350fr multi 1.00 .35
896 A295 1500fr multi 3.50 1.40
897 A295 2500fr multi 5.50 2.40
Nos. 892-897 (6) 11.35 4.90

Souvenir Sheet
898 A295 2500fr multi 5.00 3.50

Nos. 893-897 exist imperf. Value, set $13.

Dinosaurs — A296

1989, Feb. 1 **Litho.** **Perf. 12½x12**
899 A296 20fr Tyrannosaurus .25 .25
900 A296 80fr Stegosaurus 1.10 .25
901 A296 250fr Arsinoitherium 3.25 .50
902 A296 450fr Triceratops 4.50 1.00
Nos. 899-902 (4) 9.10 2.00

Souvenir Sheet
Perf. 11½x12½
903 A296 600fr Sauralophus, vert. 2.75 1.25

Women as the Subject of Paintings — A297

Designs: 20fr, *Tahitian Pastorales*, by Gauguin. No 905, *Portrait of a Young Woman*, by Titian, vert. No. 906, *Portrait of a Little Girl*, by Jean-Baptiste Greuze (1725-1805), vert. 100fr, *Woman in Black*, by Renoir, vert. 250fr, *Lacemaker*, by Vassili Tropinine, vert. 550fr, *The Annunciation*, by Cima Da Conegliano (c. 1459-1517), vert.

1989, Feb. 10 **Perf. 12½x12, 12x12½**
904 A297 20fr multi .25 .25
905 A297 80fr multi .25 .25
906 A297 80fr multi .25 .25
907 A297 100fr multi .35 .25
908 A297 250fr multi .75 .30
Nos. 904-908 (5) 1.85 1.30

Souvenir Sheet
Perf. 11½x12½
909 A297 550fr multi 1.60 1.00

Orchids
A298

1989, Feb. 28 **Litho.** **Perf. 12**
910 A298 5fr Sobennikoffia robusta, vert. .45 .25
911 A298 10fr Grammangis fallax .45 .25
912 A298 80fr Cymbidiella humblotii, vert. 1.25 .25
913 A298 80fr Angraecum sororium, vert. 1.25 .25
914 A298 250fr Oenia oncidiiflora, vert. 3.00 .35
Nos. 910-914 (5) 6.40 1.35

Souvenir Sheet
915 A298 1000fr Aerangis curnowiana 5.50 2.75

Jawaharlal Nehru (1889-1964), 1st Prime Minister of Independent India — A299

1989, Mar. 7 **Litho.** **Perf. 13**
916 A299 250fr multi .50 .25

Ornamental Mineral Industry A300

1989, Apr. 12 **Litho.** **Perf. 13½**
917 A300 80fr Rose quartz .30 .25
918 A300 250fr Petrified wood .90 .30

Views of Antananarivo A301

Designs: 5fr, Mahamasina Sports Complex, Ampefiloha Quarter. 20fr, Andravoahangy and Anjanahary Quarters. No. 921, Zoma Market and Faravohitra Quarter. No. 922, Andohan'Analakely Quarter and March 29th monument. 250fr, Independence Avenue and Jean Ralaimongo monument. 550fr, Queen's Palace and Andohalo School on Lake Anosy.

1989, Mar. 31 **Litho.** **Perf. 13½**
919 A301 5fr multi .25 .25
920 A301 20fr multi .25 .25
921 A301 80fr multi .25 .25
922 A301 80fr multi .25 .25
923 A301 250fr multi .50 .25
924 A301 550fr multi .90 .35
Nos. 919-924 (6) 2.40 1.60

Visit of Pope John Paul II — A302

1989, Apr. 28 **Perf. 12x12½**
925 A302 80fr shown .30 .25
926 A302 250fr Pope, map 1.00 .25

French Revolution, Bicent. A303

1989, July 7 **Litho.** **Perf. 12½**
927 A303 250fr Storming of the Bastille .60 .25

Phobos Space Program for the Exploration of Mars — A304

1989, Aug. 29 **Litho.** **Perf. 12½x12**
928 A304 20fr Mars 1 .25 .25
929 A304 80fr Mars 3 .25 .25
930 A304 80fr Zond 2 .25 .25
931 A304 250fr Mariner 9 .55 .25
932 A304 270fr Viking 2 .65 .30
Nos. 928-932 (5) 1.95 1.30

Souvenir Sheet
933 A304 550fr Phobos 1.50 .60

PHILEXFRANCE '89 and French Revolution, Bicent. — A305

Exhibition emblems, key people and scenes from the revolution: 250fr, Honore-Gabriel Riqueti (1749-1791), Count of Mirabeau, at the meeting of Estates-General, June 23, 1789. 350fr, Camille Desmoulins (1760-1794), call to arms, July 12, 1789. 1000fr, Lafayette (1757-1834), women's march on Versailles, Oct. 5, 1789. 1500fr, King tried by the National Convention, Dec. 26, 1792. 2500fr, Charlotte Corday (1768-1793), assassination of Marat, July 13, 1793. 3000fr, Bertrand Barere de Vieuzac, Robespierre, Jean-Marie Collot D'Herbois, Lazare Nicolas Carnot, George Jacques Danton, Georges Auguste Couthon, Pierre-Louis Prieur, Antoine Saint-Just and Marc Guillaume Vadier, Committee of Public Safety, July, 1793. No. 939A, Family saying farewell to Louis XVI. No. 939B, Danton and the Club of the Cordeliers.

1989, July 14 **Litho.** **Perf. 13½**
934 A305 250fr multicolored .45 .25
935 A305 350fr multicolored .65 .25
936 A305 1000fr multicolored 1.60 .65
937 A305 1500fr multicolored 2.50 1.00
938 A305 2500fr multicolored 4.25 1.60
Nos. 934-938 (5) 9.45 3.75

Souvenir Sheet
939 A305 3000fr multicolored 4.50 4.50

Litho. & Embossed
939A A305 5000fr gold & multi 8.00

Souvenir Sheet
939B A305 5000fr gold & multi 8.00

Nos. 939A-939B exist imperf.
For overprints see Nos. 1161-1165, 1166A-1166B.

French Revolution, Bicent. — A306

Paintings and sculpture: 5fr, *Liberty Guiding the People*, by Eugene Delacroix. 80fr, "La Marseillaise" from *Departure of the Volunteers in 1792*, high relief on the Arc de Triomphe, 1833-35, by Francois Rude. 250fr, *The Tennis Court Oath*, by David.

1989, Oct. 25 **Perf. 12½x12**
940 A306 5fr multicolored .25 .25
941 A306 80fr multicolored .45 .25
942 A306 250fr multicolored .90 .25
Nos. 940-942 (3) 1.60 .75

No. 942 is airmail.

Rene Cassin (1887-1976), Nobel Peace Prize Winner and Institute Founder — A307

1989, Nov. 21 **Perf. 12**
943 A307 250fr multicolored .40 .25

Intl. Law Institute of the French-Speaking Nations, 25th anniv.

Hapalemur aureus A308

1989, Dec. 5 **Litho.** **Perf. 12**
944 A308 250fr multicolored 1.10 .35

A309

A309a

Various athletes, cup and: 350fr, Cavour Monument, Turin. 1000fr, Christopher Columbus Monument, Genoa, 1903. 1500fr, Michelangelo's *David*. 2500fr, *Abduction of Proserpina*, by Bernini, Rome. 3000fr, Statue of Leonardo da Vinci, 1903. 5000fr, Castel Nuovo, Naples.

1989, Dec. 12 **Litho.** **Perf. 13½**
945 A309 350fr multicolored .65 .25
946 A309 1000fr multicolored 1.60 .65
947 A309 1500fr multicolored 2.25 1.00
948 A309 2500fr multicolored 4.00 1.60
Nos. 945-948 (4) 8.50 3.50

Souvenir Sheet
949 A309 3000fr multicolored 4.25 2.00

Litho. & Embossed
949A A309a 5000fr gold & multi 8.00

1990 World Cup Soccer Championships, Italy.
For overprints see Nos. 1137-1140.

A310

1989, Oct. 7 Litho. Perf. 13½
950 A310 80fr Long jump .25 .25
951 A310 250fr Pole vault .35 .25
952 A310 550fr Hurdles .80 .40
953 A310 1500fr Cycling 2.25 1.10
954 A310 2000fr Baseball 3.00 1.45
955 A310 2500fr Tennis 3.75 1.75
Nos. 950-955 (6) 10.40 5.20

Souvenir Sheet
956 A310 3000fr Soccer 4.50 2.10

1992 Summer Olympics, Barcelona.

Scenic Views and Artifacts
A311

1990, May 29
Size: 47x33mm (#958, 960)
957 A311 70fr Queen Isalo
Rock .25 .25
958 A311 70fr Sakalava pipe .25 .25
959 A311 150fr Sakalava combs .30 .25
960 A311 150fr Lowry Is., Diego
Suarez Bay .30 .25
Nos. 957-960 (4) 1.10 1.00

Fish
A312

1990, Apr. 26 Litho. Perf. 12
961 A312 5fr Heniochus
acuminatus .35 .25
962 A312 20fr Simenhelys
dofleinl .35 .25
963 A312 80fr Rhinobatos
percellens .35 .25
964 A312 250fr Epinephelus fasciatus 1.50 .25
965 A312 320fr Sphyrna zygaena 1.90 .35
Nos. 961-965 (5) 4.45 1.35

Souvenir Sheet
966 A312 550fr Latimeria
chalumnae 3.50 1.50

Nos. 962-963 vert. Nos. 961-966 inscribed 1989.

Moon Landing, 20th Anniv. — A314

Designs: 80fr, Voyager 2, Neptune. 250fr, Hydro 2000 flying boat. 550fr, NOAA satellite. 1500fr, Magellan probe, Venus. 2000fr, Concorde. 2500fr, Armstrong, Aldrin, Collins, lunar module. 3000fr, Apollo 11 astronauts, first step on moon.

1990, June 19 Litho. Perf. 13½
967 A314 80fr multicolored .25 .25
968 A314 250fr multicolored .35 .25
969 A314 550fr multicolored .80 .40
970 A314 1500fr multicolored 2.25 1.10
971 A314 2000fr multicolored 3.00 1.50
972 A314 2500fr multicolored 3.75 1.90
Nos. 967-972 (6) 10.40 5.40

Souvenir Sheet
973 A314 3000fr multicolored 4.75 2.25

For overprint see No. 1304.
Nos. 967-972 exist in souvenir sheets of 1, and se-tenant in a sheet of 6.

A315

1990, July 17
974 A315 350fr Bobsled .50 .25
975 A315 1000fr Speed skating 1.50 .75
976 A315 1500fr Nordic skiing 2.25 1.10
977 A315 2500fr Super giant
slalom 3.75 1.90
Nos. 974-977 (4) 8.00 4.00

Souvenir Sheet
978 A315 3000fr Giant slalom 4.50 2.25

Litho. & Embossed
978A A315 5000fr Pairs figure
skating 8.00

Souvenir Sheet
978B A315 5000fr Ice hockey 8.00

1992 Winter Olympics, Albertville. Nos. 978A-978B exist imperf.
For overprints see Nos. 1141-1145.

A316

1990, June 19 Litho. Perf. 12
979 A316 250fr blk, ultra & bl .45 .25

Intl. Maritime Organization, 30th anniv.

African Development Bank, 25th Anniv. A317

1990, June 19
980 A317 80fr multicolored .30 .25

A318 A319

1990, June 28
981 A318 150fr multicolored .30 .25

Campaign against polio.

1990, Aug. 22
982 A319 100fr multicolored .30 .25

Independence, 30th anniv.

A320 A322

1990, Aug. 24 Perf. 12½x12
983 A320 100fr yellow & multi .35 .25
984 A320 350fr lil rose & multi .65 .30

3rd Indian Ocean Games.

1990, Oct. 19 Litho. Perf. 12
986 A322 350fr multicolored .65 .30

Ho Chi Minh (1890-1969), Vietnamese leader.

Lemurs
A323

1990, Nov. 23 Litho. Perf. 11½
987 A323 10fr Avahi laniger .35 .25
988 A323 20fr Lemur fulvus
sanfordi .35 .25
989 A323 20fr Lemur fulvus al-
bifrons .35 .25
990 A323 100fr Lemur fulvus col-
laris 1.25 .25
991 A323 100fr Lepulemur rufi-
caudatus 1.25 .25
Nos. 987-991 (5) 3.55 1.25

Souvenir Sheet
992 A323 350fr Lemur fulvus
fulvus 3.00 .50

Shells
A324

1990, Dec. 21 Perf. 12½
993 A324 40fr Tridacna
squamosa .80 .25
994 A324 50fr Terebra demidiata,
Terebra subulata .80 .25

Anniversaries and Events
A325

100fr, Charles de Gaulle, liberation of Paris, 1944. 350fr, Galileo probe orbiting Jupiter. 800fr, Apollo 11 crew & Columbia command module, 1st Moon landing, 1969. 900fr, De Gaulle, 1942. 1250fr, Concorde jet, TGV high-speed train. 2500fr, De Gaulle as head of provisional government, 1944. 3000fr, Apollo 11 crew, Eagle lunar module. No. 1001A, De Gaulle with Roosevelt & Churchill. No. 1001B, Charles de Gaulle.

1990, Dec. 28 Litho. Perf. 13½
995 A325 100fr multi .25 .25
996 A325 350fr multi .60 .30
997 A325 800fr multi 1.40 .70
998 A325 900fr multi 1.60 .80
999 A325 1250fr multi 2.25 1.10
1000 A325 2500fr multi 4.50 2.25
Nos. 995-1000 (6) 10.60 5.40

Souvenir Sheet
1001 A325 3000fr multi 5.25 2.75

Litho. & Embossed
1001A A325 5000fr gold & multi 7.50

Souvenir Sheet
1001B A325 5000fr gold & multi 7.50

Nos. 995-1000, 1001A exist in souvenir sheets of 1. A souvenir sheet containing Nos. 996-997 exists.

Mushrooms — A325b

Designs: 25fr, Boletus edulis. 100fr, Suillus luteus. 350fr, Amanita muscaria. 450fr, Boletus calopus. 680fr, Boletus erythropus. 800fr, Leccinum scabrum. 900fr, Leccinum testaceoscabrum.
1500fr, Lycoperdon perlatum.

1990, Dec. 28 Perf. 12
1001C A325b 25fr multi .25 .25
1001D A325b 100fr multi .40 .25
1001E A325b 350fr multi .85 .25
1001F A325b 450fr multi 1.25 .30
1001G A325b 680fr multi 1.75 .45
1001H A325b 800fr multi 1.90 .50
1001I A325b 900fr multi 2.10 .60

Imperf
Size: 71x91mm
1001J A325b 1500fr multi 4.50 4.50
Nos. 1001C-1001J (8) 13.00 7.10

For surcharge, see No. 1478A.

Intl. Literacy Year
A326

1990, Dec. 30 Perf. 12
1002 A326 20fr Book, guiding
hands, vert. .25 .25
1003 A326 100fr Open Book,
hand holding
pencil .25 .25

Dogs — A326a

Designs: 30fr,Greyhound. 50fr, Japanese spaniel. 140fr, Toy terrier. 350fr, Chow. 500fr, Miniature pinscher. 800fr, Afghan. 1140fr, Papillon. 1500fr, Shih tzu.

1991, Mar. 20   Litho.   Perf. 12
1003A	A326a	30fr multi	.25	.25
1003B	A326a	50fr multi	.25	.25
1003C	A326a	140fr multi	.60	.25
1003D	A326a	350fr multi	.90	.25
1003E	A326a	500fr multi	1.25	.30
1003F	A326a	800fr multi	2.10	.50
1003G	A326a	1140fr multi	3.00	.75

Imperf

Size: 70x90mm
1003H	A326a	1500fr multi	4.00	1.40
		Nos. 1003A-1003H (8)	12.35	3.95

Nos. 1003D-1003H are airmail.

Democratic Republic of Madagascar, 15th Anniv. (in 1990) — A327

1991, Apr. 8   Litho.   Perf. 12
1004	A327	100fr multicolored	.25	.25

Dated 1990.

Trees — A328

1991, June 20   Litho.   Perf. 13½
1005	A328	140fr Adansonia fony	.55	.25
1006	A328	500fr Didierea madagascariensis	1.25	.40

Scouts, Insects and Mushrooms A329

Insects: 140fr, Helictopleurus splendidicollis. 640fr, Cocles contemplator. 1140fr, Euchroea oberthurii.
Mushrooms: 500fr, Russula radicans. 1025fr, Russula singeri. 3500fr, Lactariopsis pandani.
4500fr, Euchroea spinnasuta fairmaire and Russula aureotacta.

1991, Aug. 2   Litho.   Perf. 13½
1007	A329	140fr multicolored	.35	.25
1008	A329	500fr multicolored	.90	.30
1009	A329	640fr multicolored	1.00	.40
1010	A329	1025fr multicolored	1.75	.65
1011	A329	1140fr multicolored	2.10	.70
1012	A329	3500fr multicolored	5.25	2.25
		Nos. 1007-1012 (6)	11.35	4.55

Souvenir Sheet
1013	A329	4500fr multicolored	7.00	5.75

Nos. 1007-1012 exist in souvenir sheets of 1.

For overprints see Nos. 1149-1156.

Discovery of America, 500th Anniv. A330

Designs: 15fr, Ship, 9th cent.. 65fr, Clipper ship, 1878. 140fr, Golden Hind. 500fr, Galley, 18th cent. 640fr, Galleon Ostrust, 1721, vert. 800fr, Caravel Amsterdam, 1539, vert. 1025fr, Santa Maria, 1492. 1500fr, Map.

1991, Sept. 10   Litho.   Perf. 12
1014	A330	15fr multicolored	.25	.25
1015	A330	65fr multicolored	.25	.25
1016	A330	140fr multicolored	.55	.25
1017	A330	500fr multicolored	1.25	.30
1018	A330	640fr multicolored	1.50	.40
1019	A330	800fr multicolored	1.60	.50
1020	A330	1025fr multicolored	1.75	.65

Size: 90x70mm
1021	A330	1500fr multicolored	3.50	1.50
		Nos. 1014-1021 (8)	10.65	4.10

No. 1021 contains one 40x27mm perf. 12 label in center of stamp picturing ships and Columbus.

Domesticated Animals A331

Designs: 140fr, Dog. 500fr, Arabian horse. 640fr, House cats. 1025fr, Himalayan cats. 1140fr, Draft horse. 5000fr, German shepherd. 10,000fr, Horse, cat & dog.

1991, Sept. 27   Litho.   Perf. 13½
1022	A331	140fr multicolored	.25	.25
1023	A331	500fr multicolored	.90	.30
1024	A331	640fr multicolored	1.00	.40
1025	A331	1025fr multicolored	1.75	.65
1026	A331	1140fr multicolored	2.25	.70
1027	A331	5000fr multicolored	7.25	3.25
		Nos. 1022-1027 (6)	13.40	5.55

Souvenir Sheet
1028	A331	10,000fr multicolored	13.00	6.50

Nos. 1022-1028 exist imperf. and in souvenir sheets of 1.

Birds — A332

Designs: 40fr, Hirundo rustica. 55fr, Circus melanoluecos, vert. 60fr, Cuculas canorus, vert. 140fr, Threskiornis aethiopicus. 210fr, Porphyrio poliocephalus. 500fr, Coracias garrulus. 2000fr, Oriolus oriolus. 1500fr, Upupa epops.

Perf. 12½x12, 12x12½
1991, Dec. 10   Litho.
1029	A332	40fr multicolored	.25	.25
1030	A332	55fr multicolored	.25	.25
1031	A332	60fr multicolored	.25	.25
1032	A332	140fr multicolored	.45	.25
1033	A332	210fr multicolored	.70	.25
1034	A332	500fr multicolored	1.00	.35
1035	A332	2000fr multicolored	3.00	1.10

Size: 70x90mm

Imperf
1036	A332	1500fr multicolored	3.00	1.40
		Nos. 1029-1036 (8)	8.90	4.10

1992 Winter Olympics, Albertville A333

1991, Dec. 30   Litho.   Perf. 12x12½
1037	A333	5fr Cross-country skiing	.25	.25
1038	A333	15fr Biathlon	.25	.25
1039	A333	60fr Ice hockey	.25	.25
1040	A333	640fr Downhill skiing	.45	.25
1041	A333	640fr Figure skating	1.25	.40
1042	A333	1000fr Ski jumping	1.60	.70
1043	A333	1140fr Speed skating	2.00	.75

Imperf

Size: 90x70mm
1044	A333	1500fr Three hockey players	3.00	1.40
		Nos. 1037-1044 (8)	9.05	4.25

For surcharge see No. 1482.

Paul Minault College, 90th Anniv. A333a

1991   Litho.   Perf. 13½
1044A	A333a	140fr multicolored	.65	.30

Space Program A334

Designs: 140fr, Astronauts repairing space telescope. 500fr, Soho solar observation probe. 640fr, Topex-Poseidon, observing oceans. 1025fr, Hipparcos probe, Galaxy 3C75. 1140fr, Voyager II surveying Neptune. 5000fr, Adeos, ETS VI, earth observation and communications satellites. 7500fr, Crew of Apollo 11.

1992, Apr. 22   Perf. 13½
1045	A334	140fr multi	.25	.25
1046	A334	500fr multi	.70	.30
1047	A334	640fr multi	.90	.40
1048	A334	1025fr multi	1.40	.65
1049	A334	1140fr multi	1.60	.60
1050	A334	5000fr multi	6.75	3.25
a.		Souvenir sheet of 6, #1045-1050	19.00	19.00
		Nos. 1045-1050 (6)	11.60	5.55

Souvenir Sheet
1051	A334	7500fr multi	12.00	9.75

Nos. 1045-1050 exist in souvenir sheets of one.

Entertainers A335

1992, Apr. 29
1052	A335	100fr Ryuichi Sakamoto	.25	.25
1053	A335	350fr John Lennon	.60	.25
1054	A335	800fr Bruce Lee	1.50	.50
1055	A335	900fr Sammy Davis, Jr.	1.75	.60
1056	A335	1250fr John Wayne	1.90	.80
1057	A335	2500fr James Dean	3.50	1.60
		Nos. 1052-1057 (6)	9.50	4.00

Souvenir Sheet
1058	A335	3000fr Clark Gable & Vivien Leigh	5.25	2.00

Nos. 1052-1057 exist in souvenir sheets of one.

Fight Against AIDS — A336

1992, July 29   Litho.   Perf. 12
1059	A336	140fr lll rose & black	.40	.25

Dated 1991.

Reforestation — A337

1992, July 29   Litho.   Perf. 12
1060	A337	140fr black & green	.30	.25

Dated 1991.

1990 Sports Festival — A338

1992, Aug. 20
1061	A338	140fr multicolored	.35	.25

Dated 1991.

Meteorology in Madagascar, Cent. A339

1992, Nov. 10   Litho.   Perf. 12x12½
1062	A339	140fr multicolored	.40	.25

Fruit — A341

Perf. 12½x12, 12x12½

1992, May 27   **Litho.**

1064	A341	10fr Litchis	.30	.25
1065	A341	50fr Oranges	.30	.25
1066	A341	60fr Apples	.35	.25
1067	A341	140fr Peaches	.50	.25
1068	A341	555fr Bananas, vert.	1.25	.45
1069	A341	800fr Avocados, vert.	1.75	.60
1070	A341	1400fr Mangoes, vert.	3.00	1.25

Size: 89x70mm
Imperf

1071	A341	1600fr Mixed fruit	3.25	1.40
		Nos. 1064-1071 (8)	10.70	4.70

For surcharges, see Nos. 1477, 1486.

1992
Summer
Olympics,
Barcelona
A342

1992, June 30   **Perf. 11½**

1072	A342	65fr Women's gymnastics	.25	.25
1073	A342	70fr High jump	.25	.25
1074	A342	120fr Archery	.25	.25
1075	A342	140fr Cycling	.30	.25
1076	A342	675fr Weight lifting	1.10	.45
1077	A342	720fr Boxing	1.10	.50
1078	A342	1200fr Canoeing	1.75	.75

Imperf
Size: 90x70mm

1078A	A342	1600fr Volleyball	3.00	1.40
		Nos. 1072-1078A (8)	8.00	4.10

Litho. & Embossed
Perf. 13½

1079	A342	5000fr Judo	8.00

For surcharge, see No. 1473A.

Butterflies — A344

Designs: 15fr, Eusemia bisma. 35fr, Argema mittrei, vert. 65fr, Alcidis aurora. 140fr, Agarista agricola. 600fr, Trogonoptera croesus. 850fr, Trogonodtera priamus. 1300fr, Pereute leucodrosime. 1500fr, Chrysirridia madagaskariensis.

Perf. 12½x12, 12x12½

1992, June 24   **Litho.**

1080	A344	15fr multicolored	.25	.25
1081	A344	35fr multicolored	.25	.25
1082	A344	65fr multicolored	.45	.25
1083	A344	140fr multicolored	.70	.25
1084	A344	600fr multicolored	1.50	.45
1085	A344	850fr multicolored	2.00	.60
1086	A344	1300fr multicolored	2.50	.85

Imperf
Size: 70x90mm

1087	A344	1500fr multicolored	4.75	1.50
		Nos. 1080-1087 (8)	12.40	4.40

For surcharge, see No. 1485.

Anniversaries and Events — A345

Designs: 500fr, Jean-Henri Dunant, delivery of Red Cross supplies. 640fr, Charles de

Gaulle, battle of Bir Hacheim. 1025fr, Brandenburg Gate, people on Berlin wall. 1500fr, Village health clinic, Rotary, Lions emblems. 3000fr, Konrad Adenauer. 3500fr, Dirigible LZ4, hanger on Lake Constance, Ferdinand von Zeppelin. 7500fr, Wolfgang Amadeus Mozart at piano, palace, cathedral in Salzburg.

1992, Dec. 8   **Litho.**   **Perf. 13½**

1088	A345	500fr multicolored	.70	.30
1089	A345	640fr multicolored	.90	.45
1090	A345	1025fr multicolored	1.50	.75
1091	A345	1500fr multicolored	2.00	1.00
1092	A345	3000fr multicolored	4.25	2.00
1093	A345	3500fr multicolored	5.00	2.50
		Nos. 1088-1093 (6)	14.35	7.00

Souvenir Sheet

1094	A345	7500fr multicolored	10.00	5.00

Intl. Red Cross (No. 1088). Battle of Bir Hacheim, 50th anniv. (No. 1089). Brandenburg Gate, bicent. and destruction of Berlin Wall, 3rd anniv. (No. 1090). Konrad Adenauer, 25th death anniv. (No. 1092). Ferdinand von Zeppelin, 75th death anniv. (No. 1093). Mozart, death bicent. (in 1991) (No. 1094).
For overprint see No. 1146.

1994 World Cup
Soccer
Championships,
U.S. — A346

Soccer players, Georgia landmarks: 140fr, Ficklin Home, Macon. 640fr, Herndon Home, Atlanta. 1025fr, Cultural Center, Augusta. 5000fr, Old Governor's Mansion, Milledgeville. 7500fr, Player, stars, stripes.

1992, Dec. 15   **Litho.**   **Perf. 13½**

1095	A346	140fr multicolored	.25	.25
1096	A346	640fr multicolored	.90	.45
1097	A346	1025fr multicolored	1.40	.75
1098	A346	5000fr multicolored	7.00	3.50
		Nos. 1095-1098 (4)	9.55	4.95

Souvenir Sheet

1099	A346	7500fr multicolored	10.25	5.25

Miniature Sheet

Inventors and Inventions — A347

No. 1100: a, Gutenberg (1394?-1468), printing press. b, Newton (1642-1727), telescope. c, John Dalton (1766-1844), atomic theory. d, Louis-Jacques-Mande Daguerre (1789-1851), photographic equipment. e, Faraday (1791-1867), electric motor. f, Orville (1871-1948), Wilbur Wright (1867-1912), motor-powered airplane. g, Bell (1847-1922), telephone. h, Edison (1847-1931), phonograph. i, Benz (1844-1929), motor-driven vehicle. j, Charles Parsons (1854-1931), steam turbine. k, Diesel (1858-1913), Diesel engine. l, Marconi, radio. m, Auguste-Marie-Louis Lumiere (1862-1954), Louis-Jean Lumiere (1864-1948), motion pictures. n, Oberth (1894-1989), rocketry. o, John W. Mauchly (1907-1980), John P. Eckert, electronic computer. p, Arthur Schawlow, laser.

1993, Apr. 27

1100	A347	500fr Sheet of 16, #a.-p.	11.00	5.50

Dated 1990.

Transportation — A348

No. 1101 — Race cars: a, 20fr, 1956 Bugatti. b, 20fr, 1968 Ferrari. c, 140fr, 1962 Lotus MK25. d, 140fr, 1970 Matra. e, 1250fr, 1963 Porsche. f, 1250fr, 1980 Ligier JS11. g, 3000fr, 1967 Honda. h, 3000fr, 1992 B192 Benetton.

No. 1102 — Locomotives: a, 20fr, C62, Japan, 1948. b, 20fr, SZD, USSR, 1975. c, 140fr, MU A1A-A1A, Norway, 1954. d, 140fr, Series 26 2-D-2, Africa, 1982. e, 1250fr, Amtrak Metroliner, US, 1967. f, 1250fr, VIA, Canada, 1982. g, 3000fr, Diesel, Union Pacific RR, US, 1969. h, 3000fr, Atlantic, TGV, France, 1990.

1993, Mar. 23

1101	A348	Block of 8, #a.-h.	12.00	6.00
1102	A348	Block of 8, #a.-h.	12.00	6.00

Dated 1990.

Wildlife — A349

No. 1103 — Birds: a, 45fr, Coua verreauxi. b, 45fr, Asio helvola hova. c, 60fr, Coua cristata. d, 60fr, Euryceros prevostii. e, 140fr, Coua gigas. f, 140fr, Foudia madagascariensis. g, 3000fr, Falculea palliata. h, 3000fr, Eutriorchis astur.

No. 1104 — Butterflies: a, 45fr, Chrysiridia madagascariensis. b, 45fr, Hypolimnas misippus. c, 60fr, Charaxes antamboulou. d, 60fr, Papilio antenor. e, 140fr, Hypolimnas dexithea. f, 140fr, Charaxes andranodorus. g, 3000fr, Euxanthe madagascariensis. h, 3000fr, Papilio grosesmithi.

1993, May 27

1103	A349	Block of 8, #a.-h.	8.75	4.25
1104	A349	Block of 8, #a.-h.	8.75	4.25

Dated 1991.

Intl. Conference on Nutrition,
Rome — A350

1992, Nov. 3

1105	A350	500fr multicolored	1.00	.40

Automobiles — A351

1993, Jan. 28   **Litho.**   **Perf. 12**

1106	A351	20fr BMW	.25	.25
1107	A351	40fr Toyota	.25	.25
1108	A351	60fr Cadillac	.25	.25
1109	A351	65fr Volvo	.25	.25
1110	A351	140fr Mercedes Benz	.25	.25
1111	A351	640fr Ford	1.00	.50
1112	A351	3000fr Honda	5.00	2.50

Size: 90x70mm
Imperf

1113	A351	2000fr Renault	3.00	1.50
		Nos. 1106-1113 (8)	10.25	5.75

Birds — A352

Designs: 50fr, Anodorhynchus hyacinthinus. 60fr, Nymphicus hollandicus. 140fr, Melopsittacus undulatus. 500fr, Aratinga jandaya. 675fr, Melopsittacus undulatus, diff. 800fr, Cyanoramphus novaezelandiae. 1750fr, Nestor notabilis. 2000fr, Ara militaris.

1993, Feb. 24

1114	A352	50fr multicolored	.40	.25
1115	A352	60fr multicolored	.40	.25
1116	A352	140fr multicolored	.50	.25
1117	A352	500fr multicolored	1.75	.45
1118	A352	675fr multicolored	2.50	.65
1119	A352	800fr multicolored	2.75	.70
1120	A352	1750fr multicolored	6.00	1.50

Size: 71x91mm
Imperf

1121	A352	2000fr multicolored	5.00	2.00
		Nos. 1114-1121 (8)	19.30	6.05

For surcharges, see Nos. 1473B, 1488.

Mollusks
A353

1993, Feb. 3

1122	A353	40fr Turbo marmoratus	.25	.25
1123	A353	60fr Mitra mitra	.25	.25
1124	A353	65fr Argonauta argo	.25	.25
1125	A353	140fr Conus textile	.30	.25
1126	A353	500fr Aplysia depilans	1.10	.45
1127	A353	675fr Harpa amouretta	1.50	.70
1128	A353	2500fr Cypraea tigris	4.50	2.25

Size: 70x90mm
Imperf

1129	A353	2000fr Architectonica maxima	5.00	1.75
		Nos. 1122-1129 (8)	13.15	6.15

For surcharge, see No. 1478.

Boat,
Barges,
Pangalanes
Canal
A354

1993, Jan. 29   **Litho.**   **Perf. 12**

1130	A354	140fr multicolored	.40	.25

Miniature Sheet

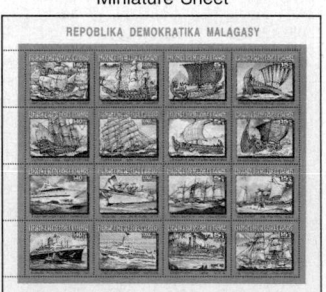

Ships — A355

No. 1131: a, 5fr, Egyptian ship. b, 5fr, Mediterranean galley. c, 5fr, Great Western, England, 1837. d, 5fr, Mississippi River sidewheeler, US, 1850. e, 15fr, Bireme, Phoenicia. f, 15fr, Viking long ship. g, 15fr, Clermont, US, 1806. h, 15fr, Pourquoi-pas, France, 1936. i, 140fr, Santa Maria, Spain, 1492. j, 140fr, HMS Victory, England, 1765. k, 140fr, Fast motor yacht, Monaco. l, 140fr, Bremen, Germany, 1950. m, 10,000fr, Sovereign of the Seas, England, 1637. n, 10,000fr, Cutty Sark, England, 1869. o, 10,000fr, Savannah, US, 1959. p, 10,000fr, Condor, Australia.

1993, Apr. 6   **Litho.**   **Perf. 13½**

1131	A355	Sheet of 16, #a.-p.	50.00	25.00

Miniature Sheet

REPOBLIKA DEMOKRATIKA MALAGASY

Nobel Prize Winners in Physics,
Chemistry and Medicine — A356

No. 1132: a, Albert Einstein, Niels Bohr. b,
Wolfgang Pauli, Max Born. c, Joseph Thomson, Johannes Stark. d, Otto Hahn, Hideki
Yukawa. e, Owen Richardson, William Shockley. f, Albert Michelson, Charles Townes. g,
Wilhelm Wien, Lev Landau. h, Karl Braun, Sir
Edward Appleton. i, Percy Bridgman, Nikolai
Semenov. j, Sir William Ramsay, Glenn Seaborg. k, Otto Wallach, Hermann Staudinger. l,
Richard Synge, Alex Theorell. m, Thomas
Morgan, Hermann Muller. n, Allvar Gullstrand,
Willem Einthoven. o, Sir Charles Sherrington,
Otto Loewi. p, Jules Bordet, Sir Alexander
Fleming.

1993, Mar. 11
1132 A356 500fr Sheet of 16,
#a.-p. 11.00 5.50
Alex misspelled on No. 1132l.

Miniature Sheet

EXPOSITION PHILATELIQUE MALGACHE ANTANANARIVO
Journée Mondiale de la Poste "9 octobre 1992"

Lemurs — A357

No. 1133: a, 60fr, Hapalemur simus. b,
150fr, Propithecus diadema. c, 250fr Indri
indri. d, 350fr, Varecia variegata.

1992, Oct. 9 Litho. Perf. 13½
1133 A357 Sheet of 4, #a.-d. 5.50 2.00
World Post Day.

No. 840
Ovptd. in
Silver

REPOBLIKA DEMOKRATIKA MALAGASY

1993, Sept. 28 Litho. Perf. 13½
1134 A276 550fr multicolored 3.75 1.90
Exists in souvenir sheet of 1.

**No. 874 Ovptd. in Silver Overprint
includes Guitar and reads "THE
ELVIS'S GUITAR / 15th
ANNIVERSARY OF HIS DEATH /
1977-1992" in English or French**

1993, Sept. 28
1135 A287 1500fr English ovpt. 2.50 1.10
1136 A287 1500fr French ovpt. 2.50 1.10
a. Pair, #1135-1136 5.00 2.25
No. 1135 exists in souvenir sheet of 1.

Nos. 945-948
Ovptd. in Gold

1993, Sept. 28
1137 A309 350fr multicolored .50 .30
1138 A309 1000fr multicolored 1.50 .75
1139 A309 1500fr multicolored 2.25 1.25
1140 A309 2500fr multicolored 3.75 1.90
Nos. 1137-1140 (4) 8.00 4.20

Nos. 974-978
Ovptd. in Gold

1993, Sept. 28
1141 A315 350fr multicolored .50 .25
1142 A315 1000fr multicolored 1.50 .75
1143 A315 1500fr multicolored 2.25 1.10
1144 A315 2500fr multicolored 3.75 1.90
Nos. 1141-1144 (4) 8.00 4.00
Souvenir Sheet
1145 A315 3000fr multicolored 4.75 2.50

No. 1088 Overprinted in Red

REPOBLIKA DEMOKRATIKA MALAGASY
130e ANNIVERSAIRE
DE LA CREATION DE LA CROIX-ROUGE
1863-1993

1993, Sept. 28
1146 A345 500fr multicolored 3.50 1.75
Exists in souvenir sheet of 1, overprinted in
red or green.

Miniature Sheet

REPOBLIKA DEMOKRATIKA MALAGASY

Commercial Airlines — A358

No. 1147: a, 10fr, Lufthansa, Germany. b,
10fr, Air France. c, 10fr, Air Canada. d, 10fr,
ANA, Japan. e, 60fr, British Airways. f, 60fr,
DO-X, Germany. g, 60fr, Shinmeiwa, Japan. h,
60fr, Royal Jordanian. i, 640fr, Alitalia, Italy. j,
640fr, Hydro 2000, France-Europe. k, 640fr,
Boeing 314 Clipper, US. l, 640fr, Air Madagascar. m, 5000fr, Emirates Airlines, United Arab
Emirates n, 5000fr, Scandinavian Airways. o,
5000fr, KLM, Netherlands. p, 5000fr, Air
Caledonia.

1993, Nov. 22 Litho. Perf. 13½
1147 A358 Sheet of 16, #a.-p. 30.00 15.00
Dated 1990.

Miniature Sheet

REPOBLIKA DEMOKRATIKA MALAGASY

Painters — A359

No. 1148: a, 50fr, Da Vinci. b, 50fr, Titian. c,
50fr, Rembrandt. d, 50fr, J.M.W. Turner (1775-
1851). e, 640fr, Michelangelo. f, 640fr,
Rubens. g, 640fr, Goya. h, 640fr, Delacroix
(1798-1863). i, 1000fr, Monet. j, 1000fr, Gauguin. k, 1000fr, Toulouse Lautrec (1864-1901).
l, 1000fr, Dali (1904-89). m, 2500fr, Renoir. n,
2500fr, Van Gogh. o, 2500fr, Picasso. p,
2500fr, Andy Warhol.

1993, May 10
1148 A359 Sheet of 16, #a.-p. 22.50 11.50
The local currency on Nos. 1148m-1148p is
obliterated by a black overprint.

Nos. 1007-1013 Ovptd. in Gold

REPOBLIKA DEMOKRATIKA MALAGASY
50ème ANNIVERSAIRE
DE LA MORT DE
BADEN POWEL

No. 841 Ovptd. in Metallic Green

REPOBLIKA DEMOKRATIKA MALAGASY
50ème ANNIVERSAIRE
DE LA MORT DE
BADEN POWEL

1993, Sept. 28 Litho. Perf. 13½
1149 A329 140fr multicolored .25 .25
1150 A329 500fr multicolored .65 .30
1151 A329 640fr multicolored .90 .40
1152 A329 1025fr multicolored 1.25 .60
1153 A329 1140fr multicolored 1.50 .75
1154 A276 1500fr multicolored 2.00 1.00
1155 A329 3500fr multicolored 4.50 2.25
Nos. 1149-1155 (7) 11.05 5.55
Souvenir Sheet
1156 A329 4500fr multicolored 6.00 3.00

REPOBLIKA DEMOKRATIKA MALAGASY

Fauna
A360

No. 1157 — Dogs: a, 40fr, Golden retriever.
b, 140fr, Fox terrier. c, 40fr, Coton de tulear. d,
140fr, Langhaar.
No. 1158 — Cats: a, 40fr, Birman. b, 140fr,
Egyptian. c, 40fr, European creme. d, 140fr,
Rex du Devon.
No. 1159 — Reptiles: a, 1000fr, Phelsuma
madagascariensis. b, 2000fr, Cameleon de
parson. c, 1000fr, Laticauda laticaudate. d,
2000fr, Testudo radiata.
No. 1160 — Beetles: a, 1000fr, Euchroea
spininasuta. b, 2000fr, Orthophagus minnulus
klug. c, 1000fr, Helictopleurus radicollis. d,
2000fr, Euchroea coelestis.

1993, Dec. 7 Litho. Perf. 13½
1157 A360 Block of 4, #a.-d. .50 .25
1158 A360 Block of 4, #a.-d. .50 .25
1159 A360 Block of 4, #a.-d. 8.00 4.00
1160 A360 Block of 4, #a.-d. 8.00 4.00
e. Sheet of 16, #1157-1160 18.00 8.50
Dated 1991.

**Nos. 934-938 Ovptd. in Metallic Blue
Nos. 939-939B Ovptd. in Metallic
Red Lilac**

BICENTENAIRE
DE L'AN I
DE LA REPUBLIQUE
FRANCAISE
REPOBLIKA DEMOKRATIKA MALAGASY

1993, Sept. 28
1161 A305 250fr multicolored .35 .25
1162 A305 350fr multicolored .50 .25
1163 A305 1000fr multicolored 1.50 .75
1164 A305 1500fr multicolored 2.25 1.10
1165 A305 2500fr multicolored 3.75 1.90
Nos. 1161-1165 (5) 8.35 4.25
Souvenir Sheet
1166 A305 3000fr multi 4.50
**Litho. & Embossed
Perf. 13½**
1166A A305 5000fr gold & multi 8.00
Souvenir Sheet
1166B A305 5000fr gold & multi 8.00
Nos. 1161-1165 exist in souvenir sheets of
1, and in a sheet containing Nos. 1161-1165
plus label.
A number has been reserved for an additional value in this set.

REPOBLIKA DEMOKRATIKA MALAGASY

Marine Life — A361

No. 1167 — Shells: a, 15fr, Chicoreus torrefactus. b, 15fr, Fasciolaria filamentosa. c,
30fr, Stellaria solaris. d, 30fr, Harpa ventricosa
lamarck.
No. 1168 — Crustaceans: a, 1250fr, Panulirus. b, 1250fr, Stenopus hispidus. c, 1500fr,
Pagure. d, 1500fr, Bernard l'hermite.
No. 1169 — Fish: a, 15fr, Pigopytes diacanthus. b, 15fr, Coelacanth latimeria
chalumnae. c, 30fr, Ostracion cyanurus. d,
30fr, Coris gaimardi. e, 1250fr, Balistapus
undulatus. f, 1250fr, Forcipiger longirostris. g,
1500fr, Adioryx diadema. h, 1500fr, Pterois
lunulata.

1993, Nov. 26 Perf. 13½
1167 A361 Block of 4, #a.-d. .25 .25
1168 A361 Block of 4, #a.-d. 7.25 3.50
1169 A361 Block of 8, #a.-h. 7.25 3.50
i. Sheet of 16, #1167-1169 16.50 7.50
Dated "1991."

REPOBLIKAN I MADAGASIKARA

Flora — A362

No. 1170 — Orchids: a, 45fr, Oceonia
oncidiflora. b, 60fr, Cymbidella rhodochica. c,
140fr, Vanilla planifolia. d, 3000fr, Phaius
humblotii.
No. 1171 — Fruits: a, 45fr, Artocarpus
altilis. b, 60fr, Eugenia malaceensis. c, 140fr,
Jambosa domestica. d, 3000fr, Papaya.

No. 1172 — Mushrooms: a, 45fr, Russula annulata. b, 60fr, Lactarius claricolor. c, 140fr, Russula tuberculosa. d, 3000fr, Russula fistulosa.

No. 1173 — Vegetables: a, 45fr, Sweet potatoes. b, 60fr, Yams. c, 140fr, Avocados. d, 3000fr, Mangoes.

1993, Dec. 15   **Litho.**   **Perf. 13**
1170 A362   Strip of 4, #a.-d.   4.25   2.25
1171 A362   Strip of 4, #a.-d.   4.25   2.25
1172 A362   Strip of 4, #a.-d.   4.25   2.25
1173 A362   Strip of 4, #a.-d.   4.25   2.25
   e.   Sheet of 16, #1170-1173   18.00   9.00

1994 Winter Olympics, Lillehammer A362a

Designs: 140fr, Biathlon. 1250fr, Ice hockey. 2000fr, Figure skating. 2500fr, Slalom skiing. 5000fr, Downhill skiing. No. 1173K, Ski jumping. No. 1173L, Speed skating.

1994, Jan. 19   **Litho.**   **Perf. 13**
1173F-1173I A362a   Set of 4   18.50   9.25
   Souvenir Sheet
1173J A362a   5000fr multi   7.25   3.50
   Litho. & Embossed
1173K A362a   10,000fr gold & multi   13.00
   Souvenir Sheet
1173L A362a   10,000fr gold & multi   13.00

No. 1173K exists in a souvenir sheet of 1. For overprints see Nos. 1288A-1288E.

1996 Summer Olympics, Atlanta — A362b

Scene in Atlanta, event: 640fr, 1892 Windsor Hotel Americus, dressage. 1000fr, Covington Courthouse, women's shot put. 1500fr, Carolton Community Activities Center, table tennis. 3000fr, Newman Historic Commercial Court Square, soccer.

7500fr, Relay race runner. No. 1173R, Pole vault, vert. No. 1173S, Hurdles, vert.

1994, Jan. 19
1173M-1173P A362b   Set of 4   19.50   9.50
   Souvenir Sheet
1173Q A362b   7500fr multi   27.00   13.50
   Litho. & Embossed
1173R A362b   5000fr gold & multi   7.50
   Souvenir Sheet
1173S A362b   5000fr gold & multi   8.00

Prehistoric Animals — A363

Designs: 35fr, Dinornis maximus, vert. 40fr, Ceratosaurus, vert. 140fr, Mosasavrus, vert. 525fr, Protoceratops. 640fr, Styvacosaurus, vert. 755fr, Smilodon. 1800fr, Uintatherium.

2000fr, Tusks of mammuthus, trees, vert.

1995, Feb. 23   **Litho.**   **Perf. 12**
1174-1180 A363   Set of 7   4.50   4.50
   Souvenir Sheet
1181 A363   2000fr multicolored   3.50   1.50

For surcharge see No. 1474A.

Wild Animals A364

Designs: 10fr, Panthera pardus. 30fr, Martes. 60fr, Vulpes vulpes. 120fr, Canis lupus. 140fr (No. 1186), Fennecus zerda. 140fr (No. 1187), Panthera leo. 3500fr, Uncia uncia.

2000fr, Panthera onca.

1995, Mar. 21
1182-1188 A364   Set of 7   5.00   5.00
1189 A364   2000fr multicolored   3.50   3.50

D-Day Landings, Normandy, 50th Anniv. — A365

No. 1190: a, 3000fr, American troops, flamethrower. b, 1500fr, Coming ashore. c, 3000fr, Explosion, German commander pointing.

No. 1191 — Liberation of Paris, 50th anniv.: a, 3000fr, Notre Dame, resistance fighters, crowd. b, 1500fr, Arch of Triomphe, woman cheering. c, 3000fr, Eiffel Tower, parade, French troops.

1994   **Perf. 13½**
1190 A365   Strip of 3, #a.-c.   6.75   3.50
1191 A365   Strip of 3, #a.-c.   6.75   3.50

Nos. 1190b, 1191b are 30x47mm. Nos. 1190-1191 are continuous design.

Aquarium Fish A366

Designs: 10fr, Pomacanthus imperator. 30fr, Betta splendens. 45fr, Trichogaster leeri. 95fr, Labrus bimaculatus. No. 1196, 140fr, Synodontis nigreventris. No. 1197, 140fr, Cichlasoma biocellatum. 3500fr, Fudulus heteroclitus.

2000fr, Carassius auratus, vert.

1994, June 28   **Litho.**   **Perf. 12½x12**
1192-1198 A366   Set of 7   5.75   5.75
   Souvenir Sheet
   Perf. 12x12½
1199 A366   2000fr multicolored   3.25   3.25

Modern Locomotives — A367

Designs: 5fr, Superviem Odoriko. 15fr, Morrison Knudsen Corporation. 140fr, ER-200. 265fr, General Motors. 300fr, New Jersey Transit. 575fr, Siemens Inter-City Express. 2500fr, Sweden's Fast Train.

2000fr, Alstham T60.

1993, Nov. 10   **Perf. 12**
1200-1206 A367   Set of 7   5.00   4.50
   Souvenir Sheet
1207 A367   2000fr multicolored   3.25   1.50

For surcharge, see Nos. 1475A, 1477A.

Cathedrals A368

Cathedral, location: 10fr, Antwerp, Belgium. 100fr, Cologne, Germany. 120fr, Antsirabe, Masdagascar. 140fr, Kremlin, Moscow. 525fr, Notre Dame, Paris. 605fr, Toledo, Spain. 2500fr, St. Stephens, Vienna.

2000fr, Westminster Abbey, London.

1995, Feb. 14   **Perf. 12x12½**
1208-1214 A368   Set of 7   4.50   4.50
   Souvenir Sheet
1215 A368   2000fr multicolored   2.75   2.75

Dated 1994.
No. 1215 is inscribed with country name only in the sheet margin.
For surcharge, see No. 1472B.

Insects — A369

Designs: 20fr, Necrophorus tomentosus. 60fr, Dynastes tityus. 140fr, Megaloxantha bicolor. 605fr, Calosoma sycophanta. 720fr, Chrysochroa mirabilis. 1000fr, Crioceris asparagi. 1500fr, Cetonia aurata.

2000fr, Goliathus goliathus.

1994, Feb. 2   **Perf. 12**
1216-1222 A369   Set of 7   5.50   5.50
   Size: 85x58mm
   Imperf
1223 A369   2000fr multicolored   2.25   1.25

For surcharge, see No. 1478B.

   Miniature Sheet

PHILAKOREA '94 — A370

No. 1224: a, 100fr, John Lennon, Ella Fitzgerald. b, 140fr, Marilyn Monroe, Elvis Presley. c, 550fr, U.S. Pres. Bill Clinton, Louis Armstrong.

1995, Feb. 23   **Perf. 12**
1224 A370   Sheet of 2 each, #a.- c. + 3 labels   4.75   2.25

Ancient Art & Architecture — A371

Designs: No. 1225, 350fr, Statue of Augustus, vert. No. 1226, 350fr, Statue, Land Surveyor, vert. No. 1227, 350fr, Painting, "Child of Thera," vert. No. 1228, 350fr, Sarcophagous, Cerveteri and Wife, vert. No. 1229, 350fr, Statue, Athena of Fidia, vert. No. 1230, 405fr, Colosseum, Rome. No. 1231, 405fr, Mask of Agamemnon, vert. No. 1232, 405fr, Forum of Caesar. No. 1233, 405fr, She-Wolf suckling

---

Romulus & Remus. No. 1234, 405fr, Parthenon, Athens. No. 1235, 525fr, Carthaginian mask, vert. No. 1236, 525fr, Bust of Emperor Tiberius, vert. No. 1237, 525fr, Statue of Alexandar the Great, vert. No. 1238, 525fr, Detail, Taormina Theater, vert. No. 1239, 525fr, Denarius of Caesar. No. 1240, 605fr, Forum, Pompeii, vert. No. 1241, 605fr, Bronze statue, Riace, vert. No. 1242, 605fr, Venus de Milo, vert. No. 1243, 605fr, Bronze statue, Archer, vert. No. 1244, 605fr, Pont Du Gard Aqueduct, Nimes.

1994   **Litho.**   **Perf. 13½**
1225-1244 A371   Set of 20   6.50   3.25

Elvis Presley (1935-77) A371a

Design: No. 1244B, "The King," "Presley," Elvis wearing black.

   Litho. & Embossed
1994, June 8   **Perf. 13½**
1244A A371a   10,000fr gold & multi   12.00
   Souvenir Sheet
1244B A371a   10,000fr gold & multi   12.00

Exists in sheets of 4.

The Stuff of Heroes, by Philip Kaufman — A372

No. 1245: a, 140fr, Astronaut. b, 140fr, Astronaut up close, walking. c, 5000fr, Spacecraft, astronaut.

1994
1245 A372   Strip of 3, #a.-c.   3.75   1.90

Motion pictures, cent. No. 1245 is a continuous design and exists in souvenir sheet of 1 with scenes from the film "Blade Runner." No. 1245c is 60x47mm.

Intl. Olympic Committee, Cent. — A373

No. 1246: a, 2500fr, Flag. b, 2500fr, Olympic flame. c, 3500fr, Pierre de Coubertin.

1994
1246 A373   Strip of 3, #a.-c.   5.75   2.75

No. 1246 is a continuous design and exists in souvenir sheet of 1. No. 1246c is 60x47mm.

ILO, 75th Anniv. — A374

1994   **Litho.**   **Perf. 13½**
1247 A374   140fr multicolored   .25   .25

A374a

Designs: 30fr, Mahafaly jewelry. 60fr, Sakalava fork and spoon. 140fr, Antandroy jewelry. 430fr, Sakalava jewelry. 580fr, Antaimoro Ambalavao paper. 1250fr Sakalava jewelry, diff. 1500fr, Inlaid cabinet. 2000fr, Ampanihy tapestry.

1995, Feb. 2   Litho.   Perf. 11¼
1247A A374a 30fr multi
1247B A374a 60fr multi
1247C A374a 140fr multi
1247D A374a 430fr multi
1247E A374a 580fr multi
1247F A374a 1250fr multi
1247G A374a 1500fr multi

Souvenir Sheet
Imperf
1247H A374a 2000fr multi

For surcharge, see No. 1472.

Modern Ships — A375

Ships: 45fr, Russian car ferry. 50fr, Australian cargo. 100fr, Japanese cruise. 140fr, US cruise. 300fr, English hovercraft. 350fr, Danish cargo. 3000fr, Korean container ship. 2000fr, Finnish car ferry, vert.

1994   Litho.   Perf. 12
1248-1254 A375 Set of 7   4.50 4.50
Souvenir Sheet
1255 A375 2000fr multicolored   3.25 3.25

1994 World Cup Soccer Championships, U.S. — A375a

Player at: No. 1255A, Left. No. 1255B, Right.

Litho. & Embossed
1994, Aug. 24   Perf. 13½
1255A A375a 10,000fr gold & multi   12.00
Souvenir Sheet
1255B A375a 10,000fr gold & multi   12.00

A377   A378

Sports: 5fr, Hurdles. 140fr, Boxing. 525fr, Gymnastics. 550fr, Weight lifting. 640fr, Swimming. 720fr, Equestrian. 1500fr, Soccer. 2000fr, Running, horiz.

1995, Apr. 4   Litho.   Perf. 12
1264-1270 A377 Set of 7   5.00 2.50
Souvenir Sheet
1271 A377 2000fr multicolored   3.25 1.25

1993, Nov. 10   Litho.   Perf. 12
Orchids: 50fr, Paphiopedilum siamense. 65fr, Cypripedium calceolus. 70fr, Ophrys oestrifera. 140fr, Cephalanthera rubra. 300fr, Cypripedium macranthon. 640fr, Calanthe vestita. 2500fr, Cypripedium guttatum. 2000fr, Oncidium tigrinum.
1272-1278 A378 Set of 7   6.00 2.50
Size: 90x70mm
Imperf
1279 A378 2000fr multicolored   3.25 1.25

Sharks A379

Designs: 10fr, Galeocerdo cuvieri. 45fr, Pristiophorus japonicus. 140fr, Rhincodon typus. 270fr, Sphyrna zygaena. 600fr, Carcharhinus longimanus. 1200fr, Stegostoma tigrinum. 1500fr, Scapanorhynchus owstoni. 2000fr, Galeorhinus zyopterus.

1993, Sept. 22   Perf. 12
1280-1286 A379 Set of 7   5.00 2.50
Size: 70x90mm
Imperf
1287 A379 2000fr multicolored   3.25 1.25

Archaea Workmani A380

1994   Perf. 15
1288 A380 500fr multicolored   1.00 .75

Nos. 1173F-1173J Ovptd. With Names of Winners in Silver or Gold
Overprinted in silver: 140fr, "M. BEDARD / CANADA." 1250fr, "MEDAILLE D'OR / SUEDE." 2000fr, "O. BAYUL / UKRAINE." 2500fr, "M. WASMEIER / ALLEMAGNE." 5000fr,
Overprinted in gold: 5000fr, "D. COMPAGNONI / ITALIE."

1994, Aug. 30   Litho.   Perf. 13
1288A-1288D A362a Set of 4   18.50 9.25
Souvenir Sheet
1288E A362a 5000fr multi   7.25 3.50

Marilyn Monroe (1926-62), Elvis Presley (1935-77) — A381

Scenes from films: No. 1289, 100fr, Gentlemen Prefer Blondes. No. 1290, 100fr, Clambake, Roustabout, Viva Las Vegas. 550fr, Some Like it Hot. 1250fr, Girls, Girls, Girls, King Creole. 5000fr, Niagara. 10,000fr, Double Trouble, Kid Gallahad, Speedway.

1995, Aug. 15   Litho.   Perf. 13½
1289-1294 A381 Set of 6   12.50 12.50
Nos. 1289-1294 exist in souvenir sheets of 1.

Motion Pictures, Cent. A382

Actor, film: No. 1295, 140fr, James Dean, Rebel Without a Cause. No. 1296, 140fr, Burt Lancaster, Vera Cruz. 5000fr, Elvis Presley, Speedway. 10,000fr, Marilyn Monroe, How to Marry a Millionaire.

1995, Aug. 16   Litho.   Perf. 13½
1295-1298 A382 Set of 4   11.00 11.00
  a. Miniature sheet of 4, #1295-1298   17.50 17.50
Nos. 1295-1298 exist in souvenir sheets of 1.

Locusts A383

Designs: No. 1299, Assylidae, natural enemy of the locust. No. 1300, Locust eating corn, vert. No. 1301, Gathering locusts for consumption.

1995, Sept. 26   Litho.   Perf. 13½
1299 A383 140fr multicolored   .90 .25
1300 A383 140fr multicolored   .90 .25
1301 A383 140fr multicolored   .90 .25
  Nos. 1299-1301 (3)   2.70 .75

Malagasyan Bible, 160th Anniv. — A384

1995, June 21   Litho.   Perf. 15
1302 A384 140fr multicolored   .25 .25

World Post Day — A385

1995, Oct. 9   Perf. 13½
1303 A385 500fr multicolored   .80 .35

Nos. 967-972 Ovptd. in Silver

1996, Jan. 21   Litho.   Perf. 13½
1304 A314 2000fr on No. 971   3.50 1.75
1304A A314 Sheet of 6, #b-g, 1304
No. 1304 exists in souvenir sheet of 1, overprinted in gold or silver. No. 1304A exists with gold overprint.

Death of Charles de Gaulle, 25th Anniv. A386

No. 1305: a, 100fr, World War I battle. b, 100fr, As President of France. c, 100fr, Brazzaville, 1940. d, 500fr, Pierre Brossolette, Churchill, De Gaulle. e, 500fr, Young woman. f, 500fr, Yak 9T, Gen. Leclerc. g, 1500fr, Liberation of Paris. h, 1500fr, De Gaulle as younger man. i, 1500fr, Jean Moulin, Free French barricade in Paris. j, 7500fr, Writing Tourbillon de L'Histoire, Colombey Les Deux Eglises. k, 7500fr, Giving speech as older diplomat. l, 7500fr, Doves, French flag, older De Gaulle standing on hilltop.

1996, Apr. 28   Litho.   Perf. 13½
1305 A386 Sheet of 12, #a.-l.   21.50 10.75
See design A390.

Famous People A387

Designs: 1500fr, Wilhelm Steinitz (1836-1900), American chess master. 1750fr, Emmanuel Lasker (1868-1941), German chess master. 2000fr, Enzo Ferrari (1898-1988), automobile designer. 2500fr, Thomas Stafford, American astronaut, A.A. Leonov, Russian cosmonaut. 3000fr, Jerry Garcia (d. 1995), musician. 3500fr, Ayrton Senna (1960-94), race car driver. 5000fr, Paul-Emile Victor (1907-95), polar explorer. 7500fr, Paul Harris (1868-1947), founder of Rotary Intl.

1996, Feb. 20
1306-1313 A387 Set of 8   20.00 10.00
Nos. 1306-1313 exist in souvenir sheets of 1.

UN and UNICEF, 50th Anniv. A388

Designs: No. 1314, 140fr, Hand holding shaft of grain, UN emblem. No. 1315, 140fr, UN building, flags, map, woman feeding child. No. 1316, 140fr, Child holding plate of food, child holding UNICEF emblem. 7500fr, Two children, UNICEF emblem.

1996, Aug. 30
1314-1317 A388 Set of 4   5.25 2.50
Nos. 1314-1317 exist in souvenir sheets of 1.

No. 1491: a, Princess Diana. b, Kwame Nkrumah. c, Gen. Georgy Zhukov. d, Samora Machel. e, Gen. Moshe Dayan. f, Mahatma Gandhi. g, Jacqueline Kennedy. h, Gen. John Pershing.

1999   Litho.   Perf. 13½
1491 A434 1950fr Sheet of 8,
#a.-h.   7.25 7.25

Famous People — A435

Designs: No. 1492, 900fr, Razafindrakotohasina Rahantavololona. No. 1493, 900fr, Gen. Gabriel Ramanantsoa. No. 1494, 900fr, Rasalama. No. 1495, 900fr, Dr. Ralivao Ramiaramanana. No. 1496, 900fr, Jérôme-Henri Cardinal Rakotomalala. No. 1497, 900fr, Rakotovao Razakaboana.

2000, Jan. 12   Litho.   Perf. 14
1492-1497 A435 Set of 6   3.00 3.00

UPU, 125th Anniv. — A436

UPU emblem, postmen of various eras and: 1000fr, Mailbox. 1200fr, Postmen, space shuttle, airplane, cargo. 1800fr, Cable-laying ships. 3200fr, 19th century diligence, modern mail truck. 3500fr, balloon, Apollo 15 astronaut. 5000fr, Stentor satellite, Claude Chappe's semaphore. 5600fr, Micheline ZM 517, Autorail Bouleze 701. 7500fr, Old and modern mail trains.

1999   Litho.   Perf. 13¼
1498-1505 A436 Set of 8   13.00 13.00
Nos. 1498-1505 exist in souvenir sheets of 1.

The Incredible Hulk — A437

No. 1506: a, Hulk with gray skin, wearing white shirt. b, Head of Hulk, red background. c, Hulk with fist raised, blue background. d, Hulk with red violet pants, lilac background. e, Hulk with ripped shirt, orange background. f, Hulk wearing sunglasses. g, Hulk shirtless, orange and red background. h, Hulk holding shirt, red violet and orange background. i, Hulk, multicolored striped background.
12,500fr, Hulk, yellow and orange background.

1999, Apr. 29   Litho.   Perf. 13¼
1506 A437 1800fr Sheet of 9,
#a-i   7.00 7.00
Souvenir Sheet
1507 A437 12,500fr multi   6.00 6.00
No. 1507 contains one 36x42mm stamp.

Silver Surfer — A438

No. 1509: a, Silver Surfer at left, dark blue green background. b, Head of Silver Surfer, red brown background. c, Silver Surfer at right, black background with large star. d, Silver Surfer on surfboard, purple background. e, Head of Silver Surfer, green background. f, Silver Surfer carrying surfboard, purple background. g, Silver Surfer, Earth and outer space in background. h, Silver Surfer, multicolored striped background. i, Silver Surfer on surfboard, outer space background with red and blue spots.
12,500fr, Silver Surfer, diff.

1999, Apr. 29
1508 A438 1800fr Sheet of 9,
#a-i   7.00 7.00
Souvenir Sheet
1509 A438 12,500fr multi   6.00 6.00
No. 1509 contains one 36x42mm stamp.

Spiderman — A439

No. 1510: a, Peter Parker turning into Spiderman. b, Spiderman with fist at upper right. c, Spiderman crouching. d, Spiderman holding silk at top. e, Head of Spiderman. f, Spiderman with rays around head. g, Spiderman with arms together, on silk. h, Spiderman with two strands of silk. i, Spiderman with large black spider on front of costume, and netting under arms.
12,500fr, Spiderman with arms raised.

1999, Apr. 29
1510 A439 3200fr Sheet of
9, #a-i   11.50 11.50
Souvenir Sheet
1511 A439 12,500fr multi   6.00 6.00
No. 1511 contains one 30x42mm stamp.

Garfield — A440

No. 1512: a, Garfield sitting. b, Garfield looking between legs. c, Garfield holding teddy bear. d, Garfield climbing wall. e, Garfield sticking out tongue. f, Garfield with legs crossed. g, Garfield asleep. h, Garfield standing. i, Odie.

1999, Apr. 29
1512 A440 3200fr Sheet of
9, #a-i   11.50 11.50

Miniature Sheets

Trains — A441

No. 1513, 800fr: a, Locomotive PK 102 on Brickaville to Fonavana line. b, Locomotive in Diego-Suarez region, 1904. c, 030T locomotive, 1922. d, BBB Alsthom Diesel-electric, 1937.
No. 1514, 1500fr: a, Locomotive 42104, 1906. b, Decauville 60 gauge locomotive. c, Mallet 020+020T locomotive, 1916. d, Garratt No. 101 locomotive, 1925.
No. 1515, 2000fr: a, Billard ZM 111 rail car, 1938. b, BB AD16 locomotive. c, Brissoneau Diesel-electric rail car, 1958. d, BBB 2nd Series 106-112, 1958.
No. 1516, 3500fr: a, Train at Fianarantsoa Station. b, AD 12 Alsthom locomotive. c, Mallet 131+131 St. Leonard. d, Micheline ZM 514.
No. 1517, 4000fr: a, Decauville 0.20 gauge 1m locomotive. b, BB235 Diesel. c, Baldwin 031 T locomotive. d, BBB Alsthom Diesel locomotive, 1935.
No. 1518, 4400fr: a, Decauville 60 gauge Montagne d'Ambre locomotive. b, Brissoneau & Lotz Diesel, 1938. c, Mallet 120+020 T locomotive, 1902. d, Corpet-Louvet locomotive.
No. 1519, 5200fr: a, Adiz BB229 locomotive. b, 030T Weidnecht locomotive, 1901. c, Jung locomotive, 1922. d, Billard rail car, 1934.
No. 1520, 10,000fr: a, Mallet 020+020 locomotive, 1925. b, Decauville 030 locomotive, 1907. c, Garratt 130+031 locomotive, 1925. d, Nosy Be 030N1, 1868.

2000, July 21   Perf. 13¼
Sheets of 4, #a-d
1513-1520 A441 Set of 8   45.00 45.00

Miniature Sheets

2000 Summer Olympics, Sydney — A442

No. 1521, 500fr: a, Soccer. b, Handball. c, Judo. d, Kayaking.

No. 1522, 1350fr: a, Cycling. b, Swimming. c, Boxing. d, Fencing.
No. 1523, 2500fr: a, Basketball. b, Cycling, diff. c, Equestrian. d, Running.
No. 1524, 3200fr: a, Weight lifting. b, Javelin. c, Equestrian, diff. d, Yachting.
No. 1525, 5000fr: a, Shot put. b, Women's gymnastics. c, Men's tennis. d, High jump.
No. 1526, 7500fr: a, Diving. b, Wrestling. c, Table tennis. d, Pole vault.
12,500fr, Kayaking and equestrian, horiz.

2000, Aug. 2   Litho.
Sheets of 4, #a-d
1521-1526 A442 Set of 6   25.00 25.00
Souvenir Sheet
1527 A442 12,500fr multi   4.00 4.00
No. 1527 contains one 57x51mm stamp and exists imperf.

Space Achievements A443

Launches of: No. 1528, 1500fr, Gemini 1. No. 1529, 1500fr, Saturn 1. No. 1530, 1500fr, Apollo 6. No. 1531, 1500fr, Mariner 3. No. 1532, 1500fr, Mariner 4. No. 1533, 1500fr, Titan IIIC. No. 1534, 1500fr, Discovery. No. 1535, 1500fr, Soyuz 19.
No. 1536, 3500fr — Spacecraft: a, Cassini-Huygens. b, Exosat. c, ICE. d, Solar Mesosphere Explorer. e, Mir Space Station. f, Observer.
No. 1537, 3500fr — Spacecraft: a, Mars 1. b, Solar Max. c, Venera 4. d, Skylab. e, Space Shuttle Challenger. f, Mars 3.
No. 1538, 4400fr — Spacecraft: a, Ranger 1. b, Mariner 4. c, Gemini 9. d, Gemini 2. e, Apollo 15. f, Gemini 12.
No. 1539, 5000fr — Spacecraft: a, Agena. b, Syncom 1. c, Olympus 1. d, FLT Satcom. e, Skynet 4B. f, COBE.
No. 1540, 6800fr, horiz.: a, Skylab. b, Agena 1. c, Agena 2. d, X-36. e, Space Shuttle. f, Dale Gardner spacewalking.
No. 1541, 6800fr, horiz.: a, Hermes prototype. b, Pioneeer 10. c, Venture Star. d, Viking. e, Spacecraft landing on Mars. f, Mars Rover.
No. 1542, 10,000fr, Apollo 1 mission patch. No. 1543, 10,000fr, Apollo 9 mission patch. No. 1544, 10,000fr, Apollo 11 mission patch. No. 1545, 10,000fr, Apollo-Soyuz mission patch. No. 1546, 10,000fr, Columbia Space Shuttle mission patch. No. 1547, 12,500fr, Gemini 4 mission patch. No. 1548, 12,500fr, Gemini 12 mission patch. No. 1549, 12,500fr, Gemini 9 mission patch, horiz. No. 1550, 12,700fr, Huygens Probe approaching Titan. No. 1551, 12,700fr, Space Shuttle at Space Station, horiz.

Perf. 14, 14¾ (#1540-1541, 1550-1551)
2000, Sept. 22
1528-1535 A443 Set of 8   3.75 3.75
Sheets of 6, #a-f
1536-1541 A443 Set of 6   55.00 55.00
Souvenir Sheets
1542-1551 A443 Set of 10   35.00 35.00

June 21, 2001 Solar Eclipse A444

2001, June 21   Perf. 13x13¼
1552 A444 5600fr multi   —   —

Dialogue Among Civilizations — A445

2001, Oct. 12   *Perf. 13½x13¼*
1553 A445 3500fr multi   2.50 2.50

Miniature Sheets

Flora and Fauna — A446

No. 1554, 250fr — Turtles: a, Tortue geante des Seychelles. b, Tortue luth. c, Tortue panthere. d, Caouanne. e, Cistude d'Europe. f, Chelonee.

No. 1555, 400fr — Fish: a, Astronotus ocellatus. b, Cyphotilapia frontosa. c, Bothriolepis. d, Pseudanthias tuka. e, Cleidopus gloriamaris. f, Ablabys taenionotus.

No. 1556, 500fr — Owls: a, Grand duc de Virginie. b, Chouette cheveche Brahmans. c, Grand duc du cap. d, Grand duc d'Afrique. e, Hibou moyen duc. f, Petit duc Choliba.

No. 1557, 1500fr, vert. — Turtles: a, Tortue à cou cache d'Afrique. b, Tortue à dos diamante. c, Tortue d'Hermann. d, Tortue Grecque. e, Tortue caret. f, Geochelone denticulata.

No. 1558, 2500fr, vert. — Parrots: a, Ara militaire. b, Ara vert. c, Ara macao. d, Ara hyacinthe. e, Perroquet de Meyer. f, Ara ararauna.

No. 1559, 3400fr, vert. — Bears and pandas: a, Ours lippu. b, Ours noir. c, Ours polaire. d, Petit panda. e, Ours des cocotiers. f, Ours à collier.

No. 1560, 3500fr — Insects and spiders: a, Xylocopa violacea. b, Triatoma infestans. c, Myrmecia gulosa. d, Mantis religiosa. e, Atrax robustus. f, Euglosse.

No. 1561, 4000fr, vert. — Primates: a, Ouistiti mignon. b, Tamarin lion d'ore. c, Singe de nuit. d, Magot. e, Vervet. f, Ouakari.

No. 1562, 4200fr — Flowers: a, Stapelia wilmaniae. b, Centaurea montana. c, Pagonia suffruticosa. d, Acanthosicyos horrida. e, Erimophila colorhabdos. f, Amaryllis belladonna.

No. 1563, 4400fr — Orchids: a, Cattleya amethystoglossa. b, Vanda coerulea. c, Orchis robusta. d, Orchis papilionacea. e, Orchis fragrans. f, Orchis italica.

Perf. 13½x13¼, 13¼x13½
2001, Oct. 25
    Sheets of 6, #a-f
1554-1563 A446   Set of 10   47.50 47.50

The following items inscribed "Repoblikan'i Madigaskara" have been declared "illegal" by Madagascar postal officials:

Sheets of nine 2000fr stamps: Motorbikes; Concorde; Elephants; Birds (2 different).

Sheets of nine stamps: Dinosaurs.

Sheet of six 5600fr stamps: Mars Exploration.

Sheets of four 5600fr stamps: Chess; Prehistoric horses; Mushrooms and eagles; Mushrooms and cats; Mushrooms and butterflies; Mushrooms and owls (2 different).

Sheet of three 5600fr stamps: Nude females (3 different).

Sheet of four 5000fr stamps: Monet paintings.

Souvenir sheets of one 1750fr stamp: Marilyn Monroe (8 different).

Souvenir sheets of two 7500fr stamps: Marilyn Monroe.

Souvenir sheet of one 12,500fr stamp: J. Baptiste Simeon Chardin.

Souvenir sheet of one: Actors Robert De Niro, Robert Redford and Leonardo DiCaprio; Actress Michelle Pfeiffer; Concorde (2 different); Fire fighting (4 different).

Famous Men — A447

Designs: No. 1564, 1500fr, Rakoto Frah (1925-2001), flutist. No. 1565, 1500fr, Albert Rakoto Ratsimamanga (1907-2001), ambassador.

2002, Oct. 9   **Litho.**   *Perf. 13x12¾*
1564-1565 A447   Set of 2   2.75 2.75

Primates — A448

Design: 1000fr, Verreaux's sifaka (prophiteque de Verreauxi). 2500fr, Lemur catta.

2002, Oct. 9   **Litho.**   *Perf. 13x12¾*
1566 A448 1000fr multi
1567 A448 2500fr multi   1.75 1.75

Furcifer Pardalis — A448a

2002, Oct. 9   **Litho.**   *Perf. 12¾x13*
1568 A448a 3000fr multi   —

Flora A449

Designs: 100fr, Chorisia ventricosa. 350fr, Eichhornia crassipes, vert. 400fr, Didieraceae. 500fr, Palm tree, Nosy Iranja, vert. 900fr, Ravinala, vert. 4400fr, Takhtajania perrieri. 6800fr, Ravinala, diff., vert.

Perf. 12¾x13, 13x12¾
2002, Oct. 9   **Litho.**
1569-1575 A449   Set of 7   12.50 12.50

For surcharge, see No. 1621.

Diplomatic Relations Between Madagascar and People's Republic of China, 30th Anniv. — A450

2002, Nov. 6   *Perf. 12*
1576 A450 2500fr multi   1.90 1.90

5 Iraimbilanja = 1 Ariary

Establishment of Japan International Cooperation Agency Bureau in Madagascar — A451

2003, Dec. 4   **Litho.**   *Perf. 13x13¼*
1577 A451 300a multi   2.25 2.25

The ariary officially replaced the franc on Aug. 1, 2003.

Indri Indri — A452

Denomination color: 500a, Bister. 3000a, White.

2003, Dec. 4   **Litho.**   *Perf. 13¼x13*
1578 A452 500a multi   1.75 1.75
1579 A452 3000amulti

First Catholic Church in Madagascar — A453

House, Falafa A454

House in High Plateaus A455

Pirate Cemetery, Ste. Marie A456

2003, Dec. 4 Litho.   *Perf. 13¼x13½*
1580 A453 800a multi   2.50 2.50
1581 A454 900a multi   3.00 3.00
1582 A455 1100a multi   3.50 3.50
1583 A456 2000a multi   6.25 6.25
   Nos. 1580-1583 (4)   15.25 15.25

Indian Ocean Commission, 20th Anniv. — A457

2003, Dec. 4   **Litho.**   *Perf. 13¼x13*
1584 A457 1200a multi   —

Flowers — A458

Designs: 20a, Xyloolaena perrieri. 100a, Megistostegium microphyllum. 120a, Tambourissa, horiz. 200a, Leptolaena diospyroidea. 300a, Ochna greveanum. 1500a, Schizolaena tampoketsana.

Perf. 13½x13, 13x13½
2003, Dec. 4   **Litho.**
1585 A458 20a multi   —
1586 A458 100a multi   —
1587 A458 120a multi   —
1588 A458 200a multi   —
1589 A458 300a multi   —
1590 A458 1500a multi   —

World Health Day — A459

2004, Oct. 9   **Litho.**   *Perf. 13½x13*
1591 A459 300a multi   1.75 1.75

Isalo Wolf Rock Formation A460

Nosy Mitsio — A461

Fort
Dauphin
A462

Tamatave
A463

Dancers at Rova of
Ambohimanga — A464

Red
Tsingy,
Irodo
A465

Lemur and
Ostriches
A466

Perf. 13¼x13, 13x13¼

2004, Nov. 15   Litho.
1592 A460   400a multi   1.25   .50
1593 A461   600a multi   .60
1594 A462   1000a multi   2.75   1.00
1595 A463   1200a multi   1.25
1596 A464   2000a multi   5.25   1.50
1597 A465   5000a multi   13.00   3.25
1598 A466 10,000a multi   30.00   6.00

Royalty — A467

Designs: 20a, Ranavalona I, 1828-61. 80a,
Ranavalona III, 1883-96. 100a, Radama I,
1810-28. 200a, Radama II, 1861-63. 500a,
Rasoherina, 1863-68. 800a, Andri-
anampoinimerina, 1787-1810. 1500a,
Ranavalona II, 1863-83.

2004, Nov. 15   Litho.   Perf. 13¼x13
1599-1605 A467   Set of 7   15.00 15.00

Rotary International, Cent. — A468

2005, Feb. 23   Perf. 13x13¼
1606 A468   2100a multi   2.60   2.60

Medical Cooperation Between
Madagascar and People's Republic of
China, 30th Anniv. — A469

No. 1607 — Medical workers, patients and
Chinese and Madagascar: a, 1500a, Flags. b,
2300a, Arms.

2005, Dec. 8   Perf. 12
1607 A469   Pair, #a-b   3.50   3.50

Miniature Sheet

Orchids — A470

No. 1608, 1500a: a, Aerangis cryptodon. b,
Aeranthes grandiflora. c, Aeranthes henrici. d,
Aeranthes peyrotii. e, Oeccoclades spathu-
lifera. f, Angraecum sesquipedale. g,
Cynorchis elata. h, Angraecum viguieri. i, Gas-
trochis humblotii. j, Gastrorchis lutea. k, Gas-
trorchis pulcher. l, Jumellea sagittata. m,
Microcoelia gilpinae. n, Angraecum praestans.

2005, Dec. 29   Perf. 13¼x13
1608 A470   Sheet of 14, #a-n,
              + 2 labels   19.50 19.50

Campaign
Against
AIDS — A471

2006, Feb. 10
1609 A471   300a multi   .40   .40

Mpitandrina
Rainimamonjisoa
(1805-82)
A472

2006, Mar. 1
1610 A472   300a blk & lt blue   .40   .40

Madagascar
Philatelists
Association, 20th
Anniv. (in
2004) — A473

2006, Mar. 1
1611 A473   300a multi   .40   .40

Léopold Sédar
Senghor (1906-
2001), First
President of
Senegal — A474

2006, Mar. 20
1612 A474   2000a multi   2.00   2.00

Seventh Indian
Ocean Islands
Games — A475

2007, June 22   Litho.   Perf. 13
1613 A475   300a multi   .40   .40

Ile Sainte
Marie
Whale
Festival
A476

Designs: 1100a, Two whales. 3000a, Whale
and two fish, vert.

Perf. 13x13¼, 13¼x13

2007, Aug. 2   Litho.
1614-1615 A476   Set of 2   8.50   8.50

Régis Rajemisa-Raolison (1913-90),
Linguist, Founder of Havatsa
Upem — A477

2008, May 15   Litho.   Perf. 13
1616 A477   300a red & black   .40   .40

No. 1403E
Surcharged

No. 1600
Surcharged

Methods and Perfs As Before

2008, Sept. 29
1617 A415a 300a on 5600fr
             #1403E   1.10   1.10
1618 A467   300a on 80a #1600 1.10   1.10
      No. 1617 is airmail.

Postman
Delivering
Mail — A478

2008, Oct. 21   Litho.   Perf. 13¼x13
1619 A478   100a multi   .25   .25

"Post For
All" — A479

2009, Oct. 9   Litho.   Perf. 13x13¼
1620 A479   300a multi   —

No. 1573
Surcharged

Method and Perf. As Before

2010, May 14
1621 A449   300a on 900fr #1573   .55   .55

Military
Forces, 50th
Anniv.
A480

Perf. 13¼x13½

2010, June 26   Litho.
1622 A480   300a multi   .65   .65

Flowers
A481

Designs: 100a, Physena sessiliflora. 200a,
Pentachlaena latifolia. 300a, Rhopalocarpus
similis. 500a, Asteropeia amblyocarpa, vert.

2011, Feb. 16 — Perf. 13½

1623	A481 100a multi	— —
1624	A481 200a multi	— —
1625	A481 300a multi	— —
1626	A481 500a multi	— —

Dated 2010.

Antananarivo City Hall — A482

Jean Laborde Blast Furnace A483

Red Cirque of Mahajanga A484

2013, Jan. 30 — Litho. — Perf. 13½

1627	A482 300a multi	1.25	1.25
1628	A483 1600a multi	4.25	4.25
1629	A484 1900a multi	5.25	5.25
	Nos. 1627-1629 (3)	10.75	10.75

SEMI-POSTAL STAMPS

No. 84 Surcharged in Red

1915, Feb. — Unwmk. — Perf. 13½x14

B1	A9 10c + 5c rose & brn	1.50	1.50

Curie Issue
Common Design Type

1938, Oct. 24 — Perf. 13

B2	CD80 1.75fr + 50c brt ultra	11.00	11.00

French Revolution Issue
Common Design Type
Name and Value Typographed in Black

1939, July 5 — Photo.

B3	CD83 45c + 25c grn	9.50	9.50
B4	CD83 70c + 30c brn	9.50	9.50
B5	CD83 90c + 35c red org	9.50	9.50
B6	CD83 1.25fr + 1fr rose pink	9.50	9.50
B7	CD83 2.25fr + 2fr blue	9.50	9.50
	Nos. B3-B7 (5)	47.50	47.50

Common Design Type and

Malgache Sharpshooter — SP1

Tank Corpsman SP2

1941 — Photo. — Perf. 13½

B8	SP1 1fr + 1fr red	1.50
B9	CD86 1.50fr + 3fr maroon	1.50
B10	SP2 2.50fr + 1fr blue	1.75
	Nos. B8-B10 (3)	4.75

Nos. B8-B10 were issued by the Vichy government in France, but were not placed on sale in Madagascar.

Nos. 162, 190 Surcharged "SECOURS +50c NATIONAL"

1942

B11	A12 1fr + 50c dk red & car rose	.40
B12	A14 3fr + 50c olive black	.40

Nos. B11-B12 were issued by the Vichy government in France, but were not placed on sale in Madagascar.

Petain Type of 1941 Surcharged in Black or Blue (Bl)

1944 — Engr. — Perf. 12½x12

B13	50c + 1.50fr on 2.50fr deep blue (Bl)	.80
B14	+ 2.50fr on 1fr bister brown	.80

Colonial Development Fund.
Nos. B13-B14 were issued by the Vichy government in France, but were not placed on sale in Madagascar.

> Catalogue values for unused stamps in this section, from this point to the end of the section, are for Never Hinged items.

Red Cross Issue
Common Design Type

1944 — Unwmk. — Perf. 14½x14

B15	CD90 5fr + 20fr dk grn	.90	.90

The surtax was for the French Red Cross and national relief.

Gen. J. S. Galliéni and Malagasy Plowing — SP3

1946, Nov. — Engr. — Perf. 13

B16	SP3 10fr + 5fr dk vio brn	.60	.60

50th anniv. of Madagascar's as a French Colony.

Tropical Medicine Issue
Common Design Type

1950, May 15

B17	CD100 10fr + 2fr dk Prus grn & brn vio	5.50	5.50

The surtax was for charitable work.

Malagasy Republic
No. 320 Surcharged in Ultramarine with New Value and: "FETES DE L'INDEPENDANCE"

1960, July 29 — Engr. — Perf. 13

B18	A38 20fr + 10fr red, blk & brt grn	.60	.35

Anti-Malaria Issue
Common Design Type

1962, Apr. 7 — Perf. 12½x12

B19	CD108 25fr + 5fr yel grn	.90	.50

Post Office, Tamatave SP4

1962, May 8 — Engr. — Perf. 13

B20	SP4 25fr + 5fr sl grn, bl & lt red brn	.70	.35

Issued for Stamp Day, 1962.

Freedom from Hunger Issue
Common Design Type

1963, Mar. 21 — Perf. 13

B21	CD112 25fr + 5fr red org, plum & brn	.70	.45

FAO "Freedom from Hunger" campaign.

Type of 1962
20fr+5fr, Central Parcel P. O., Tananarive.

1963, May 8 — Engr.

B22	SP4 20fr + 5fr bl grn & red brn	.60	.35

Issued for Stamp Day, 1963.

Postal Savings and Checking Accounts Building, Tananarive — SP5

1964, May 8 — Unwmk. — Perf. 13

B23	SP5 25fr + 5fr bl, bis & dk grn	.90	.50

Issued for Stamp Day, 1964.

No. 457 Surcharged in Violet Blue

1972, June 26 — Engr. — Perf. 13

B24	A106 30fr + 20fr multi	.90	.50

Charles de Gaulle memorial.

SP6	SP7

1989, June 15 — Litho.

B25	SP6 80fr +20fr Torch bearer	.25	.25

Village games.

1990, Aug. 7 — Litho. — Perf. 12

B26	SP7 100fr+20fr on 80fr+20fr	.45	.25
B27	SP7 350fr+20fr on 250fr+20fr	.80	.35

3rd Indian Ocean Games. Nos. B26-B27 were not issued without surcharge. For surcharge see No. 1471.

AIR POST STAMPS

Airplane and Map of Madagascar — AP1

Perf. 13x13½

1935-41 — Photo. — Unwmk.
Map in Red

C1	AP1	50c yellow green	.65	.45
C2	AP1	90c yel grn ('41)	.50	
C3	AP1	1.25fr claret	.50	.50
C4	AP1	1.50fr bright blue	.50	.50
C5	AP1	1.60fr br blue ('41)	.25	.25
C6	AP1	1.75fr orange	8.75	3.75
C7	AP1	2fr Prus blue	.85	.45
C8	AP1	3fr dp org ('41)	.25	.25
C9	AP1	3.65fr ol blk ('38)	.85	.50
C10	AP1	3.90fr turq grn ('41)	.25	.25
C11	AP1	4fr rose	45.00	3.25
C12	AP1	4.50fr black	27.50	2.50
C13	AP1	5.50fr ol blk ('41)	.25	.25
C14	AP1	6fr rose lil ('41)	.35	.25
C15	AP1	6.90fr dl vio ('41)	.25	.25
C16	AP1	8fr rose lilac	1.50	.90
C17	AP1	8.50fr green	1.50	1.10
C18	AP1	9fr ol grn ('41)	.35	.35
C19	AP1	12fr violet brown	.80	.55
C20	AP1	12.50fr dull violet	1.90	.90
C21	AP1	15fr org yel ('41)	.80	.55
C22	AP1	16fr olive green	1.75	1.10
C23	AP1	20fr dark brown	2.50	1.75
C24	AP1	50fr brt ultra ('38)	4.75	4.50
		Nos. C1,C3-C24 (23)	102.05	25.10

According to some authorities the 90c was not placed on sale in Madagascar.

Airplane and Map of Madagascar — AP1a

Type of 1935-41 without "RF"

1942-44
Map in Red, Tablet & Value in Blue (except #C25)

C25	AP1a	50c yel grn	.25
C25A	AP1a	90c yel grn	.55
C25B	AP1a	1.25fr claret	.30
C25C	AP1a	1.50fr bright blue	.50
C25D	AP1a	2fr Prus blue	.50
C25E	AP1a	3.65fr olive black	.65
C25F	AP1a	4fr rose	.65
C25G	AP1a	4.50fr black	.50
C25H	AP1a	5fr red brown	.90
C25I	AP1a	8fr rose lilac	.90
C25J	AP1a	8.50fr green	.90
C25K	AP1a	10fr green	.65
C25L	AP1a	12.50fr dull violet	.70
C25M	AP1a	16fr olive green	.70
C25N	AP1a	20fr dark brown	1.25
C25O	AP1a	50fr brt ultra	1.75
		Nos. C25-C25O (16)	11.65

Nos. C25-C25O were issued by the Vichy government in France, but were not placed on sale in Madagascar.

Airplane Over Farm — AP1b

1942-44 Engr. *Perf. 13*
C26 AP1b 100fr red brown .65

No. C26 was issued by the Vichy government in France, but was not placed on sale in Madagascar.

Air Post Stamps of 1935-38 Overprinted in Black

1942 *Perf. 13x13½*
C27 AP1 1.50fr brt bl & red 6.50 6.50
C28 AP1 1.75fr org & red 92.50 92.50
C29 AP1 8fr rose lil & red 2.10 2.10
C30 AP1 12fr vio brn & red 4.00 4.00
C31 AP1 12.50fr dl vio & red 2.50 2.50
C32 AP1 16fr ol grn & red 6.50 6.50
C33 AP1 50fr brt ultra & red 4.00 4.00

Nos. C3, C9, C17 Surcharged in Black

C34 AP1 1fr on 1.25fr 4.75 4.75
C35 AP1 3fr on 3.65fr 1.25 1.25
C36 AP1 8fr on 8.50fr 1.40 1.40
Nos. C27-C36 (10) 125.50 125.50

Catalogue values for unused stamps in this section, from this point to the end of the section, are for Never Hinged items.

Common Design Type
1943 Photo. *Perf. 14½x14*
C37 CD87 1fr dk orange .25 .25
C38 CD87 1.50fr brt red .25 .25
C39 CD87 5fr brown red .40 .35
C40 CD87 10fr black .40 .35
C41 CD87 25fr ultra .90 .55
C42 CD87 50fr dk green 1.40 .80
C43 CD87 100fr plum 2.00 1.25
Nos. C37-C43 (7) 5.60 3.80

Victory Issue
Common Design Type
Perf. 12½
1946, May 8 Unwmk. Engr.
C44 CD92 8fr brown red .90 .35

European victory of the Allied Nations in World War II.

Chad to Rhine Issue
Common Design Types
1946, June 6
C45 CD93 5fr brt blue 1.50 1.25
C46 CD94 10fr dk car rose 1.60 1.25
C47 CD95 15fr gray grn 1.60 1.25
C48 CD96 20fr brown olive 1.75 1.40
C49 CD97 25fr dk violet 1.75 1.50
C50 CD98 50fr brown org 2.10 1.75
Nos. C45-C50 (6) 10.30 8.40

Tamatave — AP2

Allegory of Air Mail — AP3

Plane over Map of Madagascar — AP4

Perf. 13½x12½, 12½x13½
1946 Photo. Unwmk.
C51 AP2 50fr bl vio & car 1.50 .50
C52 AP3 100fr brn & car 4.00 .90
C53 AP4 200fr bl grn & brn 7.50 2.00
Nos. C51-C53 (3) 13.00 3.40

No. C52 Overprinted in Carmine

1948, Oct. 26 *Perf. 12½x13½*
C54 AP3 100fr brn & car 45.00 65.00

Issued to publicize the French claim to Antarctic Adelie Land, discovered by Jules S. C. Dumont d'Urville in 1840.

UPU Issue
Common Design Type
1949, July 4 Engr. *Perf. 13*
C55 CD99 25fr multi 4.00 2.75

Scene Near Bemananga — AP5

1952, June 30 Unwmk. *Perf. 13*
C56 AP5 500fr brn, blk brn & dk grn 25.00 6.50

Liberation Issue
Common Design Type
1954, June 6
C57 CD102 15fr vio & vio brn 3.25 2.00

Pachypodes — AP6

Designs: 100fr, Antsirabé viaduct, grey-headed gull. 200fr, Ring-tailed lemurs.

1954, Sept. 20
C58 AP6 50fr dk bl grn & dk grn 3.50 .70
C59 AP6 100fr dp ultra, blk & choc 5.75 1.40
C60 AP6 200fr dk grn & sep 19.00 4.50
Nos. C58-C60 (3) 28.25 6.60

Malagasy Republic

Sugar Cane Harvest — AP7

Charaxes Antamboulou — AP8

Designs: 40fr, Tobacco field. 100fr, Chrysiridia Madagascariensis. 200fr, Argema mittrel, vert. 500fr, Mandrare bridge.

1960 Unwmk. Engr. *Perf. 13*
C61 AP7 30fr grn, vio brn & pale brn 2.00 .25
C62 AP7 40fr Prus grn & ol gray 2.25 .25
C63 AP8 50fr multi 4.00 .35
C64 AP8 100fr sl grn, emer & org 6.50 .50
C65 AP8 200fr pur & yel 8.50 1.40
C66 AP7 500fr Prus grn, bis & ultra 16.00 2.50
Nos. C61-C66 (6) 39.25 5.25

Diademed Sifakas — AP9

Lemurs: 85fr, Indri. 250fr, Verreaux's sifaka.

1961, Dec. 9 Unwmk. *Perf. 13*
C67 AP9 65fr slate grn & red brn 2.75 .70
C68 AP9 85fr olive, blk & brn 3.25 1.00
C69 AP9 250fr Prus grn, blk & mar 9.00 2.75
Nos. C67-C69 (3) 15.00 4.45

For surcharge see No. C90.

Plane over Nossi-Bé AP10

1962, May 7 Engr. *Perf. 13*
C70 AP10 100fr red brn, bl & dk grn 1.75 .60
a. Souv. sheet of 5, #328-331, C70 5.00 1.50

1st Malagasy Philatelic Exhibition, Tananarive, May 5-13.

Turbojet Airliner, Emblem — AP11

1963, Apr. 18 Unwmk. *Perf. 13*
C71 AP11 500fr dk bl, red & grn 8.00 3.25

Madagascar commercial aviation.

Helmet Bird — AP12

Birds: 100fr, Pitta-like ground roller. 200fr, Crested wood ibis.

1963, Aug. 12 Photo. *Perf. 13x12½*
C72 AP12 40fr multi 2.25 .65
C73 AP12 100fr multi 4.00 1.25
C74 AP12 200fr multi 8.00 2.25
Nos. C72-C74 (3) 14.25 4.15

African Postal Union Issue
Common Design Type
1963, Sept. 8 *Perf. 12½*
C75 CD114 85fr grn, ocher & red 1.25 .80

Map of Madagascar, Jet Plane and UPU Emblem — AP13

1963, Nov. 2 Engr. *Perf. 13*
C76 AP13 45fr dk car, grnsh bl & ultra .65 .25
C77 AP13 85fr dk car, vio & bl 1.10 .50

Malagasy Republic's admission to the UPU, Nov. 2, 1961.

Meteorological Center, Tananarive and Tiros Satellite — AP14

1964, Mar. 23 Unwmk.
C78 AP14 90fr org brn, ultra & grn 1.50 .90

UN 4th World Meteorological Day, Mar. 23.

Zebu, Wood Sculpture AP15

1964, Oct. 20   Engr.   Perf. 13
C79 AP15 100fr lil rose, dk vio & brn   2.25 .90

Musical Instrument Type of Regular Issue

200fr, Lokanga bara (stringed instrument).

1965, Feb. 16   Unwmk.   Perf. 13
Size: 26x47mm
C80 A57 200fr grn, org & choc   5.50 2.00

Nurse Weighing Infant, and ICY Emblem — AP16

Design: 100fr, Small boy and girl, child care scenes and ICY emblem.

1965, Sept. 20   Engr.   Perf. 13
C81 AP16 50fr multi   .55 .25
C82 AP16 100fr multi   1.10 .55
International Cooperation Year.

Dance Type of Regular Issue

250fr, Dance of a young girl, Sakalava, vert.

1966, June 10   Photo.   Perf. 13
Size: 27x49mm
C83 A68 250fr multi   5.50 2.00

Aviation Type of Regular Issue

Design: 500fr, Dagnaux and his Bréguet biplane, 1927.

1967, Apr. 28   Engr.   Perf. 13
Size: 48x27mm
C84 A76 500fr Prus bl, blk & brn   11.00 3.00
No. C84 for the 40th anniv. of the 1st Majunga-Tananarive flight.

African Postal Union Issue, 1967
Common Design Type

1967, Sept. 9   Engr.   Perf. 13
C85 CD124 100fr ol bis, red brn & brt pink   1.25 .60

Dancer Type of Regular Issue

Designs: 100fr, Tourbillon dance, horiz. 200fr, Male dancer from the South.

1967-68   Photo.   Perf. 11½
Size: 38x23mm
C86 A80 100fr multi ('68)   2.00 .60
Perf. 13
Size: 27x48mm
C87 A80 200fr multi   4.75 1.40
Issue dates: 100fr, Nov. 25; 200fr, Nov. 25.

WHO Emblem, Bull's Head Totem and Palm Fan — AP17

1968, Apr. 7   Photo.   Perf. 12½x13
C88 AP17 200fr bl, yel brn & red   2.00 .90
WHO, 20th anniv.; Intl. Congress of Medical Science, Apr. 2-12.

Tananarive-Ivato International Airport — AP18

1968, May 8   Engr.   Perf. 13
C89 AP18 500fr lt red brn, dl bl & dl grn   6.75 3.00
Issued for Stamp Day.

No. C68 Surcharged in Vermilion with New Value and 2 Bars
1968, June 24   Engr.   Perf. 13
C90 AP9 20fr on 85fr multi   .75 .25

PHILEXAFRIQUE Issue

Lady Sealing Letter, by Jean Baptiste Santerre AP19

1968, Dec. 30   Photo.   Perf. 12½x12
C91 AP19 100fr lilac & multi, with label   3.25 .70
Issued to publicize PHILEXAFRIQUE Philatelic Exhibition in Abidjan, Feb. 14-23. Printed with alternating lilac label.

2nd PHILEXAFRIQUE Issue
Common Design Type

Design: 50fr, Madagascar No. 274, map of Madagascar and Malagasy emblem.

1969, Feb. 14   Engr.   Perf. 13
C92 CD128 50fr gray, brn red & sl grn   1.75 .85

Sunset over Madagascar Highlands, by Henri Ratovo — AP20

Painting: 100fr, On the Seashore of the East Coast of Madagascar, by Alfred Razafinjohany.

1969, Nov. 5   Photo.   Perf. 12x12½
C93 AP20 100fr brn & multi   1.90 .65
C94 AP20 150fr multi   3.75 1.25

Lunar Landing Module and Man on the Moon — AP21

1970, July 20   Engr.   Perf. 13
C95 AP21 75fr ultra, dk gray & sl grn   1.25 .40
1st anniv. of man's 1st landing on the moon.

Boeing 737 — AP22

1970, Dec. 18   Engr.   Perf. 13
C96 AP22 200fr bl, red brn & grn   3.25 .90

Jean Ralaimongo (1884-1944) AP23

Portraits: 40fr, René Rakotobe (1918-71). 65fr, Albert Sylla (1909-67). 100fr, Joseph Ravoahangy Andrianavalona (1893-1970).

1971-72   Photo.   Perf. 12½; 13 (40fr)
C97   AP23 25fr red brn, org & blk   .40 .25
C98   AP23 40fr dp cl, ocher & blk   .60 .25
C99   AP23 65fr grn, lt grn & blk   .50 .25
C100   AP23 100fr vio bl, lt bl & blk   1.25 .35
   Nos. C97-C100 (4)   2.75 1.10
Famous Malagasy men.
Issued: No. C98, 7/25/72; others, 10/14/71.

African Postal Union Issue

"Mpisikidy" by G. Rakotovao and UAMPT Building, Brazzaville, Congo — AP24

1971, Nov. 13   Photo.   Perf. 13x13½
C105 AP24 100fr bl & multi   1.25 .45
10th anniv. of African and Malagasy Posts and Telecommunications Union (UAMPT).

Running, Olympic Village AP25

Design: 200fr, Judo, Olympic Stadium.

1972, Sept. 11   Photo.   Perf. 13½
C106 AP25 100fr multi   1.40 .60
C107 AP25 200fr multi   2.50 .85
20th Olympic Games, Munich, 8/26-9/11.

Mohair Goat AP26

1972, Nov. 15
C108 AP26 250fr multi   5.50 1.60

Adoration of the Kings, by Andrea Mantegna — AP27

Christmas: 85fr, Virgin and Child, Florentine School, 15th century, vert.

1972, Dec. 15   Photo.   Perf. 13
C109 AP27 85fr gold & multi   1.00 .45
C110 AP27 150fr gold & multi   2.25 .70

Landing Module, Astronauts and Lunar Rover AP28

1973, Jan. 25   Engr.   Perf. 13
C111 AP28 300fr dp cl, gray & brn   4.50 1.40
Apollo 17 moon mission, Dec. 7-19, 1972.

The Burial of Christ, by
Grunewald — AP29

Easter: 200fr, Resurrection, by Mattias Grunewald, vert. Both paintings from panels of Issenheim altar.

1973, Mar. 22   Photo.   Perf. 13
C112 AP29 100fr gold & multi   1.25 .45
C113 AP29 200fr gold & multi   2.75 .70

Early Excursion Car — AP30

Design: 150fr, Early steam locomotive.

1973, July 25   Photo.   Perf. 13x12½
C114 AP30 100fr multi   1.90 .70
C115 AP30 150fr multi   3.00 1.00

WMO Emblem,
Radar, Map of
Madagascar,
Hurricane
AP31

1973, Sept. 3   Engr.   Perf. 13
C116 AP31 100fr blk, ultra & org 1.50 .50
Cent. of intl. meteorological cooperation.

Lemur Type of Regular Issue

Designs: 150fr, Lepilemur mustelinus, vert. 200fr, Cheirogaleus major.

1973, Oct. 9   Engr.   Perf. 13
C117 A131 150fr multi   3.00 .90
C118 A131 200fr multi   4.75 1.40

Pres. John F.
Kennedy, US
Flag — AP32

1973, Nov. 22   Photo.   Perf. 13
C119 AP32 300fr multi   9.25 1.40
10th anniv. of the death of John F. Kennedy.

Soccer — AP33

1973, Dec. 20   Engr.   Perf. 13
C120 AP33 500fr lil rose, dk brn
          & org brn   7.00 2.00
World Soccer Cup, Munich, 1974.
For overprint see No. C130.

Copernicus, Ranger and Heliocentric
System — AP34

1974, Jan. 22
C121 AP34 250fr multi   4.00 1.10
500th anniversary of the birth of Nicolaus Copernicus (1473-1543), Polish astronomer.

Scout Type of Regular Issue

Designs (African Scout Emblem and): 100fr, Scouts bringing sick people to Red Cross tent, horiz. 300fr, Scouts fishing and fish, horiz.

1974, Feb. 14   Engr.   Perf. 13
C122 A132 100fr multi   1.10 .35
C123 A132 300fr multi   4.25 1.00

Camellia, Hummingbird, Table Tennis
Player — AP35

100fr, Girl player, flower and bird design.

1974, Mar. 19   Engr.   Perf. 13
C124 AP35 50fr bl & multi   1.00 .30
C125 AP35 100fr multi   1.75 .60
Table Tennis Tournament, Peking.

Autorail Micheline — AP36

Malagasy Locomotives: 85fr, Track inspection trolley. 200fr, Garratt (steam).

1974, June 7   Engr.   Perf. 13
C126 AP36 50fr multi   1.00 .35
C127 AP36 85fr multi   1.40 .45
C128 AP36 200fr multi   3.75 .95
     Nos. C126-C128 (3)   6.15 1.75

Letters and UPU Emblem — AP37

1974, July 9   Engr.   Perf. 13
C129 AP37 250fr multi   4.00 1.10
Centenary of Universal Postal Union.
For overprint see No. C133.

**No. C120 Overprinted: "R.F.A. 2 /
HOLLANDE 1"**

1974, Aug. 20   Engr.   Perf. 13
C130 AP33 500fr multi   6.25 2.00
World Cup Soccer Championship, 1974, victory of German Federal Republic.

Link-up in Space, Globe,
Emblem — AP38

250fr, Link-up, globe and emblem, diff.

1974, Sept. 12
C131 AP38 150fr org, bl & slate
          grn   1.25 .65
C132 AP38 250fr bl, brn & slate
          grn   2.75 .90
Russo-American space cooperation.
For overprints see Nos. C142-C143.

No. C129 Overprinted

1974, Oct. 9   Engr.   Perf. 13
C133 AP37 250fr multi   2.00 .70
100 years of international collaboration.

Adoration
of the
Kings, by J.
L. David
AP39

Christmas: 300fr, Virgin of the Cherries and Child, by Quentin Massys.

1974, Dec. 20   Photo.   Perf. 13
C134 AP39 200fr gold & multi   2.75 .60
C135 AP39 300fr gold & multi   4.00 1.10

UN Emblem and Globe — AP40

1975, June 24   Litho.   Perf. 12½
C136 AP40 300fr grn, bl & blk   3.00 .90
United Nations Charter, 30th anniversary.

American Bicentennial Type, 1975

Designs: 100fr, Count d'Estaing and "Languedoc." 200fr, John Paul Jones, "Bonhomme Richard" and "Serapis." 300fr, Benjamin Franklin, "Millern" and "Montgomery." 500fr, George Washington and "Hanna."

1975, June 30   Litho.   Perf. 11
C137 A144 100fr multi   1.25 .30
C138 A144 200fr multi   2.50 .70
C139 A144 300fr multi   3.75 .90
     Nos. C137-C139 (3)   7.50 1.90
Souvenir Sheet
C140 A144 500fr multi   7.00 1.50
For overprints see Nos. C164-C167.

Flower Type of 1975

Design: 85fr, Turraea sericea.

1975, Aug. 4   Photo.   Perf. 12½
C141 A145 85fr dp grn, yel & org 2.50 .90

Nos. C131-C132 Overprinted

1975, Aug. 5   Engr.   Perf. 13
C142 AP38 150fr multi   1.25 .45
C143 AP38 250fr multi   2.75 .75
Apollo Soyuz link-up in space, July 17, 1975.

Bas-relief and Stupas — AP41

1975, Aug. 10   Engr.   Perf. 13
C144 AP41 50fr bl, car & bister   1.25 .35
UNESCO campaign to save Borobudur Temple, Java.

Exposition Type, 1975

1975, Sept. 16   Litho.   Perf. 14x13½
C145 A147 125fr Deer   1.90 .45
Souvenir Sheet
C146 A147 300fr Jay   4.75 1.00

Hurdling and Olympic Rings — AP42

200fr, Weight lifting and Olympic rings, vert.

1975, Oct. 9   Litho.   Perf. 12½
C147 AP42 75fr multi   1.00 .25
C148 AP42 200fr multi   2.75 .70
Pre-Olympic Year 1975.

12th Winter Olympics Type, 1975

Designs: 200fr, Cross-country skiing. 245fr, Down-hill skiing. 450fr, Figure skating, pairs.

1975, Nov. 19   Perf. 14
C149 A149 200fr multi   2.75 .55
C150 A149 245fr multi   2.75 .65
Souvenir Sheet
C151 A149 450fr multi   4.50 1.40
For overprints see Nos. C161-C163.

Landing Module,
Apollo 14
Emblem — AP43

1976, Jan. 18   Engr.   Perf. 13
C152 AP43 150fr red, grn & ind   1.75 .50
Apollo 14 moon landing, 5th anniversary.
For overprint see No. C157.

21st Summer Olympics Type, 1976

Designs: 100fr, Shot-put and long jump. 200fr, Gymnastics, horse and balance bar. 300fr, Diving, 3-meter and platform. 500fr, Swimming, free-style and breast stroke.

1976, Jan. 21 Litho. Perf. 13½
C153 A151 100fr multi 1.00 .30
C154 A151 200fr multi 2.25 .60
C155 A151 300fr multi 3.25 .90
Nos. C153-C155 (3) 6.50 1.80

Souvenir Sheet
C156 A151 500fr multi 5.25 1.40

For overprints see Nos. C168-C171.

No. C152 Overprinted: "5e Anniversaire / de la mission / APOLLO XIV"

1976, Feb. 5 Engr. Perf. 13
C157 AP43 150fr red, grn & indigo 1.75 .70

Apollo 14 moon landing, 5th anniversary.

Zeppelin Type of 1976

Designs (Count Zeppelin and LZ-127 over): 200fr, Brandenburg Gate, Berlin 300fr, Parliament, London. 450fr, St. Peter's Cathedral, Rome.

1976, Mar. 3 Litho. Perf. 11
C158 A152 200fr multi 3.00 .60
C159 A152 300fr multi 4.25 .90

Souvenir Sheet
C160 A152 450fr multi 5.50 1.40

Nos. C149-C151 Overprinted

(a)

(b)

(c)

1976, June 17
C161 A149 (a) 200fr multi 2.00 .60
C162 A149 (b) 245fr multi 2.50 .80

Souvenir Sheet
C163 A149 (c) 450fr multi 5.25 2.75

12th Winter Olympic games winners.

Nos. C137-C140 Overprinted in Black

1976, July 4
C164 A144 100fr multi 1.00 .30
C165 A144 200fr multi 2.25 .60
C166 A144 300fr multi 2.75 .90
Nos. C164-C166 (3) 6.00 1.80

Souvenir Sheet
C167 A144 500fr multi 5.25 2.75

American Bicentennial.

Nos. C153-C156 Overprinted

(a)

(b)

(c)

(d)

1977, Jan.
C168 A151 (a) 100fr multi 1.00 .30
C109 A151 (b) 200fr multi 2.00 .65
C170 A151 (c) 300fr multi 2.75 .90
Nos. C168-C170 (3) 5.75 1.85

Souvenir Sheet
C171 A151 (d) 500fr multi 5.25 2.75

21st Summer Olympic Games winners.

Fauna Type of 1979

1979, July 6
C172 A176 20fr Tortoises .75 .25
C173 A176 95fr Macaco lemurs 1.50 .25

International
Palestinian
Solidarity
Day — AP44

1979, Nov. 29 Litho. Perf. 12x12½
C174 AP44 60fr multi .50 .25

Olympic Type of 1980

1980, Dec. 29 Litho. Perf. 12½x12
C175 A188 250fr Judo 2.25 .70
C176 A188 500fr Swimming 4.50 1.50

Stamp
Day — AP45

1981, Dec. 17 Litho. Perf. 12x12½
C177 AP45 90fr multi .90 .25

20th Anniv. of
Pan-African
Women's
Org. — AP46

1982, Aug. 6 Litho. Perf. 12
C178 AP46 80fr dk brn & lt brn .70 .25

Hydroelectric Plant,
Andekaleka — AP47

1982, Sept. 13 Perf. 12½x12
C179 AP47 80fr multi .70 .25

Orchid Type of 1984

1984, Nov. 20 Litho. Perf. 12
C180 A226 50fr Eulophiella elisabethae, horiz. 1.00 .25
C181 A226 50fr Grammangis ellisii, horiz. 1.00 .25
C182 A226 50fr Grammangis spectabilis 1.00 .25
Nos. C180-C182 (3) 3.00 .60

Solar
Princess,
by Sadiou
Diouf
AP48

1984, Dec. 22 Litho. Perf. 12
C183 AP48 100fr multi .90 .25

Intl. Civil Aviation Org., 40th anniv.

Halley's
Comet
AP49

1986, Apr. 5 Litho. Perf. 12½x13
C184 AP49 150fr multi 1.25 .50

Admission of
Madagascar
into the
UPU, 25th
Anniv.
AP50

1986, Dec. 23 Litho. Perf. 11½
C185 AP50 150fr multi 1.25 .40

Air Madagascar, 25th Anniv. — AP51

1987, June 17 Litho. Perf. 12x12½
C186 AP51 60fr Piper Aztec .55 .25
C187 AP51 60fr Twin Otter .55 .25
C188 AP51 150fr Boeing 747 1.10 .30
Nos. C186-C188 (3) 2.20 .80

Socialist
Revolution, 15th
Anniv. — AP52

1990, June 16 Litho. Perf. 13½
C189 AP52 100fr Map .25 .25
C190 AP52 350fr Architecture .60 .30

Madagascan Bible Society, 25th
Anniv. — AP53

1990, Sept. 17 Perf. 12½
C191 AP53 25fr lt bl & multi .25 .25
C192 AP53 100fr bl, blk & grn, vert. .25 .25

Stamp Day — AP54

1990, Oct. 9 Litho. Perf. 13x12½
C193 AP54 350fr multicolored 1.25 .30

AP55

1992, June 5 Litho. Perf. 12½
C194 AP55 140fr multicolored .25 .25

World Environment Day.

AP56

1992, Oct. 9　Litho.　Perf. 13½
C195　AP56　500fr multicolored　.70　.35
World Post Day.

Girl Guides,
50th Anniv.
AP57

1993, Aug.　Litho.　Perf. 11½
C196　AP57　140fr multicolored　.25　.25

AP58

1993, Nov. 20　Litho.　Perf. 12
C197　AP58　500fr multicolored　.80　.40
African Industrialization Day.

AP59

1994　Litho.　Perf. 11½x11, 11x11½
C198　AP59　140fr shown　.25　.25
C199　AP59　500fr Logo, vert.　.70　.40
Zone A conference.

Madagascar Hilton, 25th Anniv.—AP60

1995, Oct. 8　Litho.　Perf. 13½
C200　AP60　500fr black, blue & bister　.80　.60

ACCT, 25th
Anniv. — AP60a

1996, Aug. 9　Litho.　Perf. 14¾x15
C200A　AP60a　500fr multi　.60

FAO, 50th Anniv.
— AP60b

Designs: 140fr, Map, FAO emblem, grains.
500fr, FAO emblem, map, grains, diff.

1995, Aug. 16　Litho.　Perf. 15
C200B　AP60b　140fr multi　—　—
C200C　AP60b　500fr multi　—　—
Set of 2　125.00

UN Industrial Development
Organization, 30th Anniv. — AP60c

Perf. 11¾x11½
1996, June 17　　　Litho.
Granite Paper
C200D　AP60c　140fr multi　.25　.25

Souvenir Sheet

Zheng He, Chinese Navigator — AP61

1998　　Litho.　Perf. 13½
C201　AP61　5700fr multicolored　3.00　1.50

AIR POST SEMI-POSTAL STAMPS

French Revolution Issue
Common Design Type
Unwmk.
1939, July 5　Photo.　Perf. 13
Name and Value in Orange
CB1　CD83　4.50fr + 4fr brn blk　18.00　18.00

"Maternity" Statue
at Tannarive City
Hall — SPAP1

Manankavaly Free Milk
Station — SPAP2

Mother & Children — SPAP3

1942, June 22　Engr.　Perf. 13
CB2　SPAP1　1.50fr + 3.50fr lt grn　.65
CB3　SPAP2　2fr + 6fr yel brn　.65
CB4　SPAP3　3fr + 9fr car red　.65
Nos. CB2-CB4 (3)　1.95

Native children's welfare fund.
Nos. CB2-CB4 were issued by the Vichy government in France, but were not placed on sale in Madagascar.

Colonial Education Fund
Common Design Type
1942, June 22
CB5　CD86a　1.20fr + 1.80fr blue & red　.65

No. CB5 was issued by the Vichy government in France, but was not placed on sale in Madagascar.

POSTAGE DUE STAMPS

Postage Due Stamps of
French Colonies
Overprinted in Red or
Blue — D1

1896　Unwmk.　Imperf.
J1　D1　5c blue (R)　12.00　9.50
J2　D1　10c brown (R)　11.00　8.00
J3　D1　20c yellow (Bl)　10.00　8.00
J4　D1　30c rose red (Bl)　11.00　8.00
J5　D1　40c lilac (R)　80.00　50.00
J6　D1　50c gray vio (Bl)　14.50　10.00
J7　D1　1fr dk grn (R)　80.00　65.00
Nos. J1-J7 (7)　218.50　158.50

Governor's
Palace — D2

1908-24　Typo.　Perf. 13½x14
J8　D2　2c vio brn　.25　.25
J9　D2　4c violet　.25　.25
J10　D2　5c green　.25　.25
J11　D2　10c deep rose　.25　.25
J12　D2　20c olive green　.40　.40
J13　D2　40c brn, straw　.45　.45
J14　D2　50c brn, bl　.60　.60
J15　D2　60c orange ('24)　.60　.60
J16　D2　1fr dark blue　1.10　1.10
Nos. J8-J16 (9)　4.15　4.15

Type of 1908 Issue
Surcharged

1924-27
J17　D2　60c on 1fr org　1.90　1.90

Surcharged

J18　D2　2fr on 1fr lil rose ('27)　.90　.90
J19　D2　3fr on 1fr ultra ('27)　.90　.90

Postage Due Stamps
of 1908-27 Ovptd. or
Srchd. in Black

1943　　　Perf. 13½x14
J20　D2　10c dp rose　.95　.95
J21　D2　20c olive grn　.95　.95
J22　D2　30c on 5c green　.95　.95
J23　D2　40c brn, straw　1.00　1.00
J24　D2　50c brn, blue　1.40　1.40
J25　D2　60c orange　.95　.95
J26　D2　1fr dark blue　.95　.95
J27　D2　1fr on 2c vio brn　4.50　4.50
J28　D2　2fr on 1fr lil rose　1.10　1.10
J29　D2　2fr on 4c vio　2.10　2.10
J30　D2　3fr on 1fr ultra　1.25　1.25
Nos. J20-J30 (11)　16.10　16.10

> **Catalogue values for unused stamps in this section, from this point to the end of the section, are for Never Hinged items.**

D3

1947　Photo.　Perf. 13
J31　D3　10c dk violet　.25　.25
J32　D3　30c brown　.25　.25
J33　D3　50c dk bl grn　.25　.25
J34　D3　1fr dp orange　.25　.25
J35　D3　2fr red violet　.45　.45
J36　D3　3fr red brown　.45　.45
J37　D3　4fr blue　.50　.50
J38　D3　5fr henna brown　.55　.55
J39　D3　10fr slate green　.70　.70
J40　D3　20fr vio blue　1.75　1.75
Nos. J31-J40 (10)　5.40　5.40

Malagasy Republic

Independence
Monument — D4

**Engraved; Denomination
Typographed**
1962, May 7　Unwmk.　Perf. 13
J41　D4　1fr brt green　.25　.25
J42　D4　2fr copper brn　.25　.25
J43　D4　3fr brt violet　.25　.25
J44　D4　4fr slate　.25　.25
J45　D4　5fr red　.25　.25
J46　D4　10fr yellow grn　.25　.25
J47　D4　20fr dull claret　.25　.25
J48　D4　40fr blue　.55　.55
J49　D4　50fr rose red　.85　.85
J50　D4　100fr black　1.60　1.60
Nos. J41-J50 (10)　4.75　4.75

MALAWI
mə-'lä-wē

LOCATION — Southeast Africa
GOVT. — Republic in British Commonwealth
AREA — 36,100 sq. mi.
POP. — 10,000,416 (1999 est.)
CAPITAL — Lilongwe

The British Protectorate of Nyasaland became the independent state of Malawi on July 6, 1964, and a republic on July 6, 1966.

12 Pence = 1 Shilling
20 Shillings = 1 Pound
100 Tambalas = 1 Kwacha (1970)

Catalogue values for all unused stamps in this country are for Never Hinged items.

Watermark

Wmk. 357 — Multiple Cockerel

Dr. H. Kamuzu Banda and Independence Monument — A1

Prime Minister Banda and: 6p, Sun rising from lake. 1sh3p, National flag. 2sh6p, Coat of Arms.

Perf. 14½

1964, July 6		**Unwmk.**		**Photo.**
1	A1	3p dk gray & lt ol green	.25	.25
2	A1	6p car rose, red, gold & bl	.25	.25
3	A1	1sh3p dull vio, blk, red & grn	.40	.25
4	A1	2sh6p multicolored	.70	1.00
		Nos. 1-4 (4)	1.60	1.75

Malawi's independence, July 6, 1964.

Mother and Child — A2

Designs: 1p, Chambo fish. 2p, Zebu bull. 3p, Peanuts. 4p, Fishermen in boat. 6p, Harvesting tea. 9p, Tung nut, flower and leaves. 1sh, Lumber and tropical pine branch. 1sh3p, Tobacco drying and Turkish tobacco plant. 2sh6p, Cotton industry. 5sh, Monkey Bay, Lake Nyasa. 10sh, Afzelia tree (pod mahogany). £1, Nyala antelope, vert.

1964, July 6		**Size: 23x19mm**		
5	A2	½p lilac	.30	.30
6	A2	1p green & black	.30	.25
7	A2	2p red brown	.30	.25
8	A2	3p pale brn, brn red & grn	.30	.25
9	A2	4p org yel & indigo	.25	.25
		Size: 41½x25, 25x41½mm		
10	A2	6p bl, vio bl & brt yel grn	1.00	
11	A2	9p grn, yel & brn	.40	.25
12	A2	1sh yel, brn & dk green	.35	.25
13	A2	1sh3p red brn & olive	.65	.70
14	A2	2sh6p blue & brown	1.50	1.10
15	A2	5sh "Monkey Bay-Lake Nyasa"	.90	3.25

16	A2	10sh org brn, grn & gray	2.10	2.25
17	A2	£1 yel & dk brn	9.00	6.25
		Nos. 5-17 (13)	18.20	15.60

See Nos. 26, 41-51. For surcharges see Nos. 27-28.

Star of Bethlehem over World — A3

1964, Dec. 1		**Photo.**		**Perf. 14½**
18	A3	3p brt green & gold	.25	.25
19	A3	6p lilac rose & gold	.25	.25
20	A3	1sh3p lilac & gold	.25	.25
21	A3	2sh6p ultra & gold	.25	.30
a.		Souvenir sheet of 4	1.25	1.50
		Nos. 18-21 (4)	1.00	1.05

Christmas. No. 21a contains Nos. 18-21 with simulated perforations.

Sixpence, Shilling, Florin and Half-Crown Coins — A4

1965, Mar. 1   Unwmk.   Perf. 13x13½
Coins in Silver and Black

22	A4	3p green	.25	.25
23	A4	9p rose	.25	.25
a.		Silver omitted		
24	A4	1sh6p rose violet	.25	.25
25	A4	3sh dark blue	.35	.75
a.		Souvenir sheet of 4	1.75	1.50
		Nos. 22-25 (4)	1.10	1.50

First coinage of Malawi. No. 25a contains Nos. 22-25 with simulated perforations. Sold for 6sh.

Type of 1964 Redrawn

1965, June 1		**Photo.**		**Perf. 14½**
26	A2	5sh "Monkey Bay-Lake Malawi"	8.50	1.25

Nos. 13-14 Surcharged with New Value and Two Bars

1965, June 14				
27	A2	6p on 1sh3p	.30	.25
28	A2	3sh on 2sh6p	.30	.25

John Chilembwe, Rebels and Church at Mbwombwe — A5

1965, Aug. 20		**Photo.**		**Perf. 14½**
29	A5	3p yel grn & purple	.25	.25
30	A5	9p red org & olive	.25	.25
31	A5	1sh6p dk blue & red brn	.25	.25
32	A5	3sh dull bl & green	.25	.25
a.		Souvenir sheet of 4, #29-32	7.00	7.00
		Nos. 29-32 (4)	1.00	1.00

50th anniversary of the revolution of Jan. 23, 1915, led by John Chilembwe (1871-1915), missionary.

Microscope and Open Book — A6

1965, Oct. 6				**Perf. 14**
33	A6	3p emer & slate	.25	.25
34	A6	9p brt rose & slate	.25	.25
35	A6	1sh6p purple & slate	.25	.25
36	A6	3sh ultra & slate	.25	.25
a.		Souvenir sheet of 4, #33-36	4.25	4.25
		Nos. 33-36 (4)	1.00	1.05

Opening of the University of Malawi in temporary quarters in Chichiri secondary school, Blantyre. The University will be located in Zomba.

African Danaine A7

Designs: Various butterflies.

Perf. 13x13½

1966, Feb. 15				**Unwmk.**
37	A7	4p multicolored	1.10	.25
38	A7	9p multicolored	1.90	.25
39	A7	1sh6p lil, blk & blue	2.50	.45
40	A7	3sh blue, dk brn & bis	4.00	6.75
a.		Souvenir sheet of 4, #37-40	25.00	25.00
		Nos. 37-40 (4)	9.50	7.70

See No. 51.

Type of 1964

Designs: 1sh6p, Curing tobacco and Burley tobacco plant. £2, Cyrestis camillus sublineatus (butterfly). Other designs as in 1964.

Wmk. 357

1966-67		**Photo.**		**Perf. 14½**
		Size: 23x19mm		
41	A2	½p lilac	.25	.25
42	A2	1p green & black	.25	.25
43	A2	2p red brown ('67)	.25	.25
44	A2	3p multi ('67)	.25	.25
		Size: 41½x25mm		
45	A2	6p blue, vio bl & brt yel grn ('67)	2.00	.80
46	A2	9p grn, yel & brn ('67)	1.00	.25
47	A2	1sh yel, brn & dk green	.30	.25
48	A2	1sh6p ohoo & emer	.40	.25
49	A2	5sh multi ('67)	8.50	2.75
50	A2	10sh org brn, grn & gray ('67)	16.00	18.50
51	A2	£2 ul vio, yel & blk	32.50	27.50
		Nos. 41-51 (11)	61.70	51.30

British Central Africa Stamp 1891 — A8

President Kamuzu Banda — A9

1966, May 4				**Perf. 14½**
54	A8	4p yel grn & sl blue	.25	.25
55	A8	9p dull rose & sl blue	.25	.25
56	A8	1sh6p lil & slate blue	.25	.25
57	A8	3sh blue & slate blue	.25	.50
a.		Souvenir sheet of 4, #54-57	6.00	3.75
		Nos. 54-57 (4)	1.00	1.00

Postal service, 75th anniv.

Perf. 14x14½

1966, July 6				**Wmk. 357**
58	A9	4p green, sil & brn	.25	.25
59	A9	9p magenta, sil & brn	.25	.25
60	A9	1sh6p violet, sil & brn	.25	.25
61	A9	3sh blue, sil & brn	.25	.25
a.		Souvenir sheet of 4, #58-61	2.50	2.50
		Nos. 58-61 (4)	1.00	1.00

Republic Day, July 6, 1966; 2nd anniv. of Independence.

Star over Bethlehem — A10

1966, Oct. 12	**Photo.**		**Perf. 14½x14**	
63	A10	4p deep green & gold	.25	.25
64	A10	9p plum & gold	.25	.25
65	A10	1sh6p orange & gold	.25	.25
66	A10	3sh deep blue & gold	.25	.50
		Nos. 63-66 (4)	1.00	1.25

Christmas.

Ilala I, 1875 A11

Steamers on Lake Malawi: 9p, Dove, 1892. 1sh6p, Chauncey Maples, 1901. 3sh, Guendolen, 1899.

1967, Jan. 4			**Perf. 14½x14**	
67	A11	4p emer, black & yel	.45	.25
a.		Yellow omitted		650.00
68	A11	9p car rose, blk & yellow	.50	.35
69	A11	1sh6p lt vio, blk & red	.75	.60
70	A11	3sh ultra, black & red	1.50	1.75
		Nos. 67-70 (4)	3.20	2.95

Pseudotropheus Auratus — A12

Fish of Lake Malawi: 9p, Labeotropheus trewavasae. 1sh6p, Pseudotropheus zebra. 3sh, Pseudotropheus tropheops.

1967, May 3	**Photo.**		**Perf. 12½x12**	
71	A12	4p green & multi	.55	.25
72	A12	9p ocher & multi	.80	.25
73	A12	1sh6p multicolored	1.00	.30
74	A12	3sh ultra & multi	2.40	2.40
		Nos. 71-74 (4)	4.75	3.20

Rising Sun and Cogwheel — A13

Perf. 13½x13

1967, July 5	**Litho.**		**Unwmk.**	
75	A13	4p black & brt grn	.25	.25
76	A13	9p black & car rose	.25	.25
77	A13	1sh6p black & brt pur	.25	.25
78	A13	3sh black & brt ultra	.25	.25
a.		Souvenir sheet of 4, #75-78	1.10	1.10
		Nos. 75-78 (4)	1.00	1.00

Malawi industrial development.

Nativity A14

Perf. 14x14½

1967, Oct. 12	**Photo.**		**Wmk. 357**	
79	A14	4p vio blue & green	.25	.25
80	A14	9p vio blue & red	.25	.25
81	A14	1sh6p vio blue & yel	.25	.25

82	A14	3sh bright blue	.25	.25
a.		Souvenir sheet of 4, #79-82, perf. 14x13½	1.25	1.25
		Nos. 79-82 (4)	1.00	1.00

Christmas.

Calotropis Procera — A15

Wild Flowers: 9p, Borreria dibrachiata. 1sh6p, Hibiscus rhodanthus. 3sh, Bidens pinnatipartita.

1968, Apr. 24　Litho.　Perf. 13½x13

83	A15	4p green & multi	.25	.25
84	A15	9p pale green & multi	.25	.25
85	A15	1sh6p lt green & multi	.25	.25
86	A15	3sh brt blue & multi	.25	.80
a.		Souvenir sheet of 4, #83-86	2.50	2.50
		Nos. 83-86 (4)	1.00	1.55

Thistle No. 1, 1902 A16

Locomotives: 9p, G-class steam engine, 1954. 1sh6p, "Zambesi" diesel locomotive No. 202, 1963. 3sh, Diesel rail car No. 1, 1955.

1968, July 24　Photo.　Perf. 14x14½

87	A16	4p gray grn & multi	.25	.25
88	A16	9p red & multi	.55	.50
89	A16	1sh6p cream & multi	.90	.80
90	A16	3sh lt ultra & multi	1.25	2.50
a.		Souv. sheet of 4, #87-90, perf. 14	4.00	4.00
		Nos. 87-90 (4)	2.95	4.05

Nativity, by Piero della Francesca A17

Paintings: 9p, Adoration of the Shepherds, by Murillo. 1sh6p, Adoration of the Shepherds, by Guido Reni. 3sh, Nativity with God the Father and the Holy Ghost, by Giovanni Batista Pittoni.

1968, Nov. 6　Photo.　Wmk. 357

91	A17	4p black & multi	.25	.25
92	A17	9p multicolored	.25	.25
93	A17	1sh6p multicolored	.25	.25
94	A17	3sh blue & multi	.25	.25
a.		Souvenir sheet of 4, #91-94, perf. 14x13½	.70	.70
		Nos. 91-94 (4)	1.00	1.00

Christmas.

Scarlet-chested Sunbird — A18

Nyasa Lovebird — A19

Birds: 2p, Violet-backed starling. 3p, White-browed robin-chat. 4p, Red-billed firefinch. 9p, Yellow bishop. 1sh, Southern carmine bee-eater. 1sh6p, Grayheaded bush shrike. 2sh, Paradise whydah. 3sh, African paradise flycatcher. 5sh, Bateleur. 10sh, Saddlebill. £1, Purple heron. £2, Livingstone's lorie.

1968, Nov. 13　Perf. 14½
Size: 23x19, 19x23mm

95	A18	1p multicolored	.25	.25
96	A18	2p multicolored	.25	.25
97	A18	3p multicolored	.25	.25
98	A18	4p multicolored	.35	.35
99	A19	6p multicolored	.45	.25
100	A19	9p multicolored	.50	.60

Perf. 14
Size: 42x25, 25x42mm

101	A18	1sh multicolored	.55	.25
102	A18	1sh6p multicolored	5.00	6.25
103	A18	2sh multicolored	5.00	6.25
104	A19	3sh multicolored	5.25	4.25
105	A19	5sh multicolored	7.00	4.50
106	A19	10sh multicolored	7.25	8.50
107	A19	£1 multicolored	13.00	18.00
109	A18	£2 multicolored	35.00	47.50
		Nos. 95-109 (14)	80.10	97.45

No. 104 was surcharged "30t Special United Kingdom Delivery Service" in 5 lines and issued Feb. 8, 1971, during the British postal strike. The 30t was to pay a private postal service. Values: unused 50c, used $2.25.

See Nos. 136-137. For overprint see No. 131.

ILO Emblem A20

Photo., Gold Impressed (Emblem)
Perf. 14x14½

1969, Feb. 5　　　Wmk. 357

110	A20	4p deep green	.25	.25
111	A20	9p dk rose brown	.25	.25
112	A20	1sh6p dark gray	.25	.25
113	A20	3sh dark blue	.25	.25
a.		Souvenir sheet of 4, #110-113	1.60	1.60
		Nos. 110-113 (4)	1.00	1.00

ILO, 50th anniversary.

White Fringed Ground Orchid A21

Malawi Orchids: 9p, Red ground orchid. 1sh6p, Leopard tree orchid. 3sh, Blue ground orchid.

1969, July 9　Litho.　Perf. 13½

114	A21	4p gray & multi	.30	.30
115	A21	9p gray & multi	.50	.50
116	A21	1sh6p gray & multi	.70	.70
117	A21	3sh gray & multi	1.50	1.50
a.		Souvenir sheet of 4, #114-117	2.75	2.75
		Nos. 114-117 (4)	3.00	3.00

African Development Bank Emblem — A22

1969, Sept. 10　　　Perf. 14

118	A22	4p multicolored	.25	.25
119	A22	9p multicolored	.25	.25
120	A22	1sh6p multicolored	.25	.25
121	A22	3sh multicolored	.25	.25
a.		Souvenir sheet of 4, #118-121	1.10	1.10
		Nos. 118-121 (4)	1.00	1.00

African Development Bank, 5th anniv.

"Peace on Earth" A23

1969, Nov. 5　Photo.　Perf. 14x14½

122	A23	2p citron & blk	.25	.25
123	A23	4p Prus blue & blk	.25	.25
124	A23	9p scarlet & blk	.25	.25

125	A23	1sh6p purple & blk	.25	.25
126	A23	3sh ultra & blk	.25	.25
a.		Souvenir sheet of 5, #122-126	1.25	1.25
		Nos. 122-126 (5)	1.25	1.25

Christmas.

Bean Blister Beetle — A24

Insects: 4p, Elegant grasshopper. 1sh6p, Pumpkin ladybird. 3sh, Praying mantis.

1970, Feb. 4　Litho.　Perf. 14x14½

127	A24	4p multicolored	.30	.25
128	A24	9p multicolored	.30	.25
129	A24	1sh6p multicolored	.55	.50
130	A24	3sh multicolored	1.00	1.00
a.		Souvenir sheet of 4, #127-130	2.25	2.25
		Nos. 127-130 (4)	2.15	2.00

No. 102 Overprinted in Black

Rand Easter Show MALAWI 1970

1970, Mar. 18　Photo.　Perf. 14

131	A18	1sh6p multicolored	1.00	2.00

75th Anniversary Rand Easter Show, Johannesburg, South Africa, Mar. 24-Apr. 6.

Runner — A25

1970, June 3　Litho.　Perf. 13

132	A25	4p green & dk blue	.25	.25
133	A25	9p rose & dk bl	.25	.25
134	A25	1sh6p dull yel & dk bl	.25	.25
135	A25	3sh blue & dk blue	.25	.25
a.		Souvenir sheet of 4, #132-135	1.10	1.10
		Nos. 132-135 (4)	1.00	1.00

9th Commonwealth Games, Edinburgh, Scotland, July 16-25.

Dual Currency Issue
Bird Type of 1968 with Denominations in Tambalas

Designs: 10t/1sh, Southern carmine bee-eater. 20t/2sh, Paradise whydah.

1970, Sept. 2　Photo.　Perf. 14½
Size: 42x25mm

136	A18	10t/1sh multicolored	1.50	.35
137	A18	20t/2sh multicolored	2.25	1.40

Aegocera Trimenii A26

Moths of Malawi: 9p, Epiphora bauhiniae. 1sh6p, Parasa karschi. 3sh, Teracotona euprepia.

Perf. 11x11½

1970, Sept. 30　　　Wmk. 357

138	A26	4p multicolored	.35	.35
139	A26	9p multicolored	.50	.50
140	A26	1sh6p lt vio & multi	.85	.85

141	A26	3sh multicolored	1.90	1.90
a.		Souvenir sheet of 4, #138-141	7.50	7.50
		Nos. 138-141 (4)	3.60	3.60

Mother and Child A27

1970, Nov. 4　Litho.　Perf. 14½

142	A27	2p black & yel	.25	.25
143	A27	4p black & emer	.25	.25
144	A27	9p black & dp org	.25	.25
145	A27	1sh6p black & red lil	.25	.25
146	A27	3sh black & ultra	.25	.25
a.		Souv. sheet of 5, #142-146 + label	1.40	1.40
		Nos. 142-146 (5)	1.25	1.25

Christmas.

Decimal Currency

Greater Kudu — A28　　　Eland — A29

Antelopes: 2t, Nyala. 3t, Reedbuck. 5t, Puku. 8t, Impala. 15t, Klipspringer. 20t, Livingstone's suni. 30t, Roan antelope. 50t, Waterbuck. 1k, Bushbuck. 2k, Red duiker. 4k, Gray bush duiker.

Perf. 13½x14 (A28), 14x14½ (A29)
1971, Feb. 15　Litho.　Wmk. 357

148	A28	1t dull vio & multi	.25	.25
a.		Perf. 14½x14, coil	.55	.40
b.		Perf. 14 ('74)	.45	1.50
149	A28	2t dp yel & multi	.25	.25
150	A28	3t ap grn & multi	.25	.25
a.		Perf. 14 ('74)	.65	1.25
151	A28	5t multicolored	.25	.25
a.		Perf. 14 ('74)	.65	1.75
152	A28	8t org red & multi	.35	.25
153	A29	10t green & multi	.40	.35
154	A29	15t brt pur & multi	.65	.40
155	A29	20t bl gray & multi	.85	.70
156	A29	30t dull blue & multi	5.75	.70
157	A29	50t multicolored	1.10	.90
158	A29	1k multicolored	4.00	2.00
159	A29	2k gray & multi	8.00	4.00
160	A29	4k multicolored	25.00	22.00
		Nos. 148-160 (13)	47.10	32.30

Decimal Coins A30

1971, Feb. 15　　　Perf. 14½

161	A30	3t multicolored	.25	.25
162	A30	8t dull red & multi	.25	.25
163	A30	15t purple & multi	.30	.30
164	A30	30t brt blue & multi	.40	.40
a.		Souvenir sheet of 4, #161-164	1.60	1.60
		Nos. 161-164 (4)	1.20	1.20

Introduction of decimal currency and coinage.

Engravings by Albrecht Dürer — A31

Design: Nos. 165, 167, 169, 171, Christ on the Cross. Nos. 166, 168, 170, 172, The Resurrection.

1971, Apr. 7   Litho.   Perf. 14x13½
165	3t emerald & black		.25	.25
166	3t emerald & black		.25	.25
a.	A31 Pair, #165-166		.25	.25
167	8t orange & black		.25	.25
168	8t orange & black		.25	.25
a.	A31 Pair, #167-168		.25	.25
169	15t red lilac & black		.25	.25
170	15t red lilac & black		.25	.25
a.	A31 Pair, #169-170		.40	.40
171	30t blue & black		.25	.25
a.	Souv. sheet of 4, #165, 167, 169, 171		1.75	1.75
172	30t blue & black		.25	.25
a.	Souv. sheet of 4, #166, 168, 170, 172		1.75	1.75
b.	A31 Pair, #171-172		.50	.50
	Nos. 165-172 (8)		2.00	2.00

Easter. Printed checkerwise in sheets of 25.

Holarrhena Febrifuga — A32

Flowering Shrubs and Trees: 8t, Brachystegia spiciformis. 15t, Securidaca longepedunculata. 30t, Pterocarpus rotundifolius.

1971, July 14   Litho.   Wmk. 357
173	A32 3t gray & multi	.25	.25
174	A32 8t gray & multi	.25	.25
175	A32 15t gray & multi	.35	.30
176	A32 30t gray & multi	.50	.50
a.	Souvenir sheet of 4, #173-176	2.00	2.00
	Nos. 173-176 (4)	1.35	1.30

Drum Major — A33

1971, Oct. 5   Perf. 14x14½
177	A33 30t lt blue & multi	.90	.90

50th anniversary of Malawi Police Force.

Madonna and Child, by William Dyce — A34

Paintings of Holy Family by: 8t, Martin Schongauer. 15t, Raphael. 30t, Bronzino.

1971, Nov. 10   Perf. 14½
178	A34 3t green & multi	.25	.25
179	A34 8t carmine & multi	.25	.25
180	A34 15t dp claret & multi	.30	.30
181	A34 30t dull blue & multi	.60	.60
a.	Souvenir sheet of 4, #178-181	2.00	2.00
	Nos. 178-181 (4)	1.40	1.40

Christmas.

Vickers Viscount — A35

Airplanes: 8t, Hawker Siddeley 748. 15t, Britten Norman Islander. 30t, B.A.C. One Eleven.

1972, Feb. 9   Litho.   Perf. 13½x14
182	A35 3t brt grn, blk & red	.30	.25
183	A35 8t red org & black	.50	.25
184	A35 15t dp rose lil, red & black	.80	.75
185	A35 30t vio blue & multi	1.40	1.40
a.	Souvenir sheet of 4, #182-185	10.00	10.00
	Nos. 182-185 (4)	3.00	2.65

Publicity for Air Malawi.

Figures, Chencherere Hill — A36

Rock Paintings: 8t, Lizard and cat, Chencherere Hill. 15t, Symbols, Diwa Hill. 30t, Sun behind rain, Mikolongwe Hill.

1972, May 10   Perf. 13½
186	A36 3t black & yel grn	.30	.25
187	A36 8t black & dp car	.35	.25
188	A36 15t black, vio & car	.55	.45
189	A36 30t black, blue & yel	1.00	1.00
a.	Souv. sheet of 4, #186-189, perf. 15	4.50	4.50
	Nos. 186-189 (4)	2.20	1.95

Athlete and Olympic Rings — A37

1972, Aug. 9   Perf. 14x14½
190	A37 3t gray, black & green	.25	.25
191	A37 8t gray, black & scar	.25	.25
192	A37 15t gray, black & lilac	.25	.25
193	A37 30t gray, black & blue	.40	.40
a.	Souvenir sheet of 4, #190-193	2.10	2.10
	Nos. 190-193 (4)	1.15	1.15

20th Olympic Games, Munich, 8/26-9/10.

Malawi Coat of Arms — A38

1972, Oct. 20   Litho.   Perf. 13½x14
194	A38 15t blue & multi	.65	.65

18th Commonwealth Parliamentary Conference, Malawi, Oct. 1972.

Adoration of the Kings, by Orcagna — A39

Paintings of the Florentine School: 8t, Madonna and Child Enthroned, anonymous. 15t, Madonna and Child with Sts. Bonaventura and Louis of Toulouse, by Carlo Crivelli. 30t, Madonna and Child with St. Anne, by Jean de Bruges.

Perf. 14½x14
1972, Nov. 8   Wmk. 357
195	A39 3t lt olive & multi	.25	.25
196	A39 8t carmine & multi	.25	.25
197	A39 15t purple & multi	.25	.25
198	A39 30t blue & multi	.50	.50
a.	Souvenir sheet of 4, #195-198	1.50	1.50
	Nos. 195-198 (4)	1.25	1.25

Christmas.

Charaxes Bohemani — A40

1973   Perf. 13½x14
199	A40 3t shown	.60	.30
200	A40 8t Uranothauma crawshayi	1.00	.80
201	A40 15t Charaxes acuminatus	2.00	1.60
202	A40 30t "Euphaedra zad dachi"	6.00	7.00
a.	Souvenir sheet of 4, #199-202	16.00	15.00
203	A40 30t Amauris ansorgei	5.25	7.00
	Nos. 199-203 (5)	14.85	16.70

Issued: Nos. 199-202, 2/7; No. 203, 4/5.

Dr. Livingstone and Map of West Africa — A41

Livingstone Choosing Site for Mission — A42

1973   Litho.   Perf. 13½x14
204	A41 3t apple grn & multi	.25	.25
205	A41 8t red orange & multi	.25	.25
206	A41 15t multicolored	.25	.25
207	A41 30t blue & multi	.45	.45
a.	Souvenir sheet of 4, #204-207	1.40	1.40
208	A42 50t black & multi	.50	.50
a.	Souvenir sheet of 1	1.25	1.25
	Nos. 204-208 (5)	1.70	1.70

Dr. David Livingstone (1813-73), medical missionary and explorer.

Issued: Nos. 204-207, 207a, 5/1; Nos. 208, 208a, 12/12.

Thumb Dulcitone (Kalimba) A43

African Musical Instruments: 8t, Hand zither (bangwe; vert.). 15t, Hand drum (ng'oma; vert.). 30t, One-stringed fiddle (kaligo).

1973, Aug. 8   Wmk. 357   Perf. 14
209	A43 3t brt green & multi	.25	.25
210	A43 8t red & multi	.25	.25
211	A43 15t violet & multi	.25	.25
212	A43 30t blue & multi	.25	.25
a.	Souvenir sheet of 4, #209-212	3.25	3.25
	Nos. 209-212 (4)	1.00	1.00

The Three Kings A44

1973, Nov. 8   Perf. 13½x14
213	A44 3t blue & multi	.25	.25
214	A44 8t ver & multi	.25	.25
215	A44 15t multicolored	.25	.25
216	A44 30t orange & multi	.25	.25
a.	Souvenir sheet of 4, #213-216	1.25	1.25
	Nos. 213-216 (4)	1.00	1.00

Christmas.

Largemouth Black Bass — A45

Designs: Game fish.

1974, Feb. 20   Litho.   Perf. 14x14½
217	A45 3t shown	.40	.25
218	A45 8t Rainbow trout	.45	.30
219	A45 15t Lake salmon	1.00	.75
220	A45 30t Triggerfish	2.00	2.00
a.	Souvenir sheet of 4, #217-220	5.25	5.25
	Nos. 217-220 (4)	3.85	3.30

30th anniv. of Angling Society of Malawi.

UPU Emblem, Map of Africa with Malawi A46

1974, Apr. 24   Perf. 13½
221	A46 3t green & bistor	.25	.25
222	A46 8t ver & bistor	.25	.25
223	A46 15t lilac & bistor	.25	.25
224	A46 30t gray & bistor	.35	.35
a.	Souvenir sheet of 4, #221-224	1.60	1.60
	Nos. 221-224 (4)	1.10	1.10

Centenary of Universal Postal Union.

Capital Hill, Lilongwe and Pres. Kamuzu Banda A47

1974, July 3   Litho.   Perf. 14
225	A47 3t emerald & multi	.25	.25
226	A47 8t red & multi	.25	.25
227	A47 15t lilac & multi	.25	.25
228	A47 30t vio blue & multi	.25	.25
a.	Souvenir sheet of 4, #225-228	1.10	1.10
	Nos. 225-228 (4)	1.00	1.00

10th anniversary of independence.

Madonna of the Meadow, by Giovanni Bellini — A48

Paintings: 8t, Holy Family, by Jacob Jordaens. 15t, Nativity, by Peter F. de Grebber. 30t, Adoration of the Shepherds, by Lorenzo di Credi.

1974, Dec. 4   Litho.   Perf. 13½x14
229	A48 3t dk green & multi	.25	.25
230	A48 8t multicolored	.25	.25
231	A48 15t purple & multi	.25	.25

232 A48 30t dk blue & multi .25 .25
a. Souvenir sheet of 4, #229-232 1.10 1.10
Nos. 229-232 (4) 1.00 1.00

Christmas.

African Snipe
A49

Double-banded
Sandgrouse
A50

Birds: 3t, Blue quail. 5t, Red-necked francolin. 8t, Harlequin quail. 10t, Spurwing goose. 15t, Denham's bustard. 20t, Knob-billed duck. 30t, Helmeted guinea fowl. 50t, Pigmy goose. 1k, Garganey. 2k, White-faced tree duck. 4k, Green pigeon.

Wmk. 357
1975, Feb. 19   Litho.   Perf. 14
Size: 17x21, 21x17mm

233 A49 1t multicolored .25 .40
234 A50 2t multicolored .35 .40
235 A49 3t multicolored 1.40 1.60
236 A49 5t multicolored 3.75 2.00
237 A50 8t multicolored 5.75 1.60

Perf. 14½
Size: 25x41, 41x25mm

238 A49 10t multicolored 8.00 .80
239 A49 15t multicolored 3.25 5.00
240 A49 20t multicolored 1.10 1.60
241 A49 30t multicolored 1.40 1.25
242 A49 50t multicolored 2.25 2.00
243 A50 1k multicolored 5.75 5.25
244 A49 2k multicolored 13.00 10.50
245 A50 4k multicolored 22.50 20.00
Nos. 233-245 (13) 68.75 52.40

See Nos. 270-279. For overprints see Nos. 263, 294.

Malawi Coat of
Arms — A51

Coil Stamps
1975-84   Perf. 14½x14
246 A51 1t dark violet blue .50 .30
247 A51 5t red ('84) 1.40 1.40

"Mpasa"
A52

Designs: Lake Malawi ships.

1975, Mar. 12   Wmk. 357   Perf. 13½
251 A52 3t shown .35 .30
252 A52 8t "Ilala II" .55 .45
253 A52 15t "Chauncy Maples" 1.00 1.00
254 A52 30t "Nkwazi" 1.75 2.75
a. Souvenir sheet of 4, #251-254, perf. 14½ 4.50 4.50
Nos. 251-254 (4) 3.65 4.50

Habenaria
Splendens — A53

Bush Baby — A54

Orchids of Malawi: 10t, Eulophia cucullata. 20t, Disa welwitschii. 40t, Angraecum conchiferum.

1975, June 6   Litho.   Perf. 14½
255 A53 3t lt green & multi .60 .25
256 A53 10t red orange & multi .70 .50

---

257 A53 20t dull vio & multi 1.20 .90
258 A53 40t multicolored 2.00 2.25
a. Souvenir sheet of 4, #255-258 12.00 12.00
Nos. 255-258 (4) 4.50 3.90

1975, Sept. 3   Litho.   Perf. 14
259 A54 3t shown .25 .25
260 A54 10t Leopard .40 .30
261 A54 20t Roan antelope .80 .80
262 A54 40t Burchell's zebra 1.60 2.00
a. Souvenir sheet of 4, #259-262 6.00 6.00
Nos. 259-262 (4) 3.05 3.35

Animals of Malawi.

No. 242 Overprinted in Black

1975, Dec. 9   Litho.   Perf. 14½
263 A50 50t multicolored 1.75 2.25

10th African, Caribbean and Pacific Ministerial Conference.

Adoration
of the
Kings,
French
A55

Christmas: 10t, Nativity, 16th century, Spanish. 20t, Nativity, by Pierre Raymond, 16th century. 40t, Angel Appearing to the Shepherds, 14th century, English.

1975, Dec. 12   Perf. 13x13½
264 A55 3t multicolored .25 .25
265 A55 10t multicolored .25 .25
266 A55 20t purple & multi .25 .25
267 A55 40t blue & multi .25 .25
a. Souv. sheet of 4, #264-267, perf. 14 2.60 2.60
Nos. 264-267 (4) 1.00 1.00

Bird Types of 1975
1975   Litho.   Unwmk.   Perf. 14
Size: 21x17mm
270 A50 3t multicolored 5.00 3.50

Perf. 14½
Size: 25x41mm
273 A49 10t multicolored 3.00 3.75
274 A49 15t multicolored 3.00 4.25
279 A49 2k multicolored 8.00 15.00
Nos. 270-279 (4) 19.00 26.50

For overprint see No. 293.

Alexander Graham
Bell — A56

Perf. 14x14½
1976, Mar. 24   Litho.   Wmk. 357
281 A56 3t green & black .25 .25
282 A56 10t dp lilac rose & blk .25 .25
283 A56 20t brt purple & blk .25 .25
284 A56 40t brt blue & blk .50 .50
a. Souvenir sheet of 4, #281-284 2.00 2.00
Nos. 281-284 (4) 1.25 1.25

Centenary of first telephone call by Alexander Graham Bell, Mar. 10, 1876.

President
Kamuzu
Banda — A57

1976, July 1   Photo.   Perf. 13
285 A57 3t brt green & multi .25 .25
286 A57 10t multicolored .25 .25
287 A57 20t violet & multi .25 .25
288 A57 40t dull blue & multi .55 .55
a. Souvenir sheet of 4, #285-288 1.75 1.75
Nos. 285-288 (4) 1.30 1.30

10th anniversary of the Republic.

Bagnall
Diesel
No. 100
A58

Diesel Locomotives: 10t, Shire class No. 503. 20t, Nippon Sharyo No. 301. 40t, Hunslet No. 110.

1976, Oct. 1   Litho.   Perf. 14½
289 A58 3t emerald & multi .50 .30
290 A58 10t red & multi 1.00 .40
291 A58 20t lilac & multi 1.75 1.75
292 A58 40t blue & multi 3.00 3.00
a. Souvenir sheet of 4, #289-292 7.00 7.00
Nos. 289-292 (4) 6.25 5.45

Malawi Railways.

Nos. 274 and 241
Overprinted

1976, Oct. 22   Litho.   Unwmk.
293 A49 15t multicolored 2.75 1.40

Wmk. 357
294 A49 30t multicolored 3.25 3.25

Blantyre Mission centenary.

Christ Child on
Straw Bed — A59

Ebony Ancestor
Figures — A60

1976, Dec. 6   Wmk. 357   Perf. 14
295 A59 3t green & multi .25 .25
296 A59 10t magenta & multi .25 .25
297 A59 20t purple & multi .25 .25
298 A59 40t dk blue & multi .25 .25
a. Souvenir sheet of 4, #295-298 2.25 2.25
Nos. 295-298 (4) 1.00 1.00

Christmas.

1977, Apr. 1   Litho.   Wmk. 357

Handicrafts: 10t, Ebony elephant, horiz. 20t, Ebony rhinoceros, horiz. 40t, Wooden antelope.

299 A60 4t yellow & multi .25 .25
300 A60 10t black & multi .25 .25
301 A60 20t ocher & multi .25 .25
302 A60 40t ver & multi .25 .25
a. Souvenir sheet of 4, #299-302 2.00 2.00
Nos. 299-302 (4) 1.00 1.00

Chileka
Airport,
Blantyre,
and
VC10
A61

Transportation in Malawi: 10t, Leyland bus on Blantyre-Lilongwe Road. 20t, Ilala II on Lake Malawi. 40t, Freight train of Blantyre-Nacala line on overpass.

1977, July 12   Litho.   Perf. 14½
303 A61 4t multicolored .45 .25
304 A61 10t multicolored .45 .40
305 A61 20t multicolored 1.10 .95
306 A61 40t multicolored 1.75 3.25
a. Souvenir sheet of 4, #303-306 4.25 4.25
Nos. 303-306 (4) 3.75 4.85

Pseudotropheus Johanni — A62

Lake Malawi Fish: 10t, Pseudotropheus livingstoni. 20t, Pseudotropheus zebra. 40t, Genyochromis mento.

Wmk. 357, Unwmkd.
1977, Oct. 4   Litho.   Perf. 13½x14
307 A62 4t multicolored .40 .25
308 A62 10t multicolored .60 .30
309 A62 20t multicolored 1.40 .60
310 A62 40t multicolored 1.60 1.50
a. Souvenir sheet of 4, #307-310 5.00 5.00
Nos. 307-310 (4) 4.00 2.65

Virgin and Child,
by Bergognone
A63

Entry into
Jerusalem, by
Giotto
A64

Virgin and Child: 10t, with God the Father and Angels, by Ambrogio Bergognone. 20t, detail from Bottigella altarpiece, by Vincenzo Foppa. 40t, with the fountain, by Jan Van Eyck.

Perf. 14x13½
1977, Nov. 21   Unwmk.
311 A63 4t multicolored .25 .25
312 A63 10t red & multi .25 .25
313 A63 20t lilac & multi .25 .25
314 A63 40t vio blue & multi .40 .40
a. Souvenir sheet of 4, #311-314 3.25 3.25
Nos. 311-314 (4) 1.15 1.15

Christmas.

1978, Mar. 1   Litho.   Perf. 12x12½

Giotto Paintings: 10t, Crucifixion. 20t, Descent from the Cross. 40t, Jesus Appearing to Mary.

315 A64 4t multicolored .25 .25
316 A64 10t multicolored .25 .25
317 A64 20t multicolored .30 .25
318 A64 40t multicolored .60 .60
a. Souvenir sheet of 4, #315-318 2.50 2.50
Nos. 315-318 (4) 1.40 1.35

Easter.

Lions,
Wildlife
Fund
Emblem
A65

Animals and Wildlife Fund Emblem: 4t, Nyala, vert. 20t, Burchell's zebras. 40t, Reedbuck, vert.

1978, June 1 Unwmk. *Perf. 13x13½*

319	A65	4t multicolored	4.00	1.00
320	A65	10t multicolored	10.00	2.00
321	A65	20t multicolored	17.50	3.00
322	A65	40t multicolored	25.00	10.00
a.		Souvenir sheet of 4, #319-322, perf. 13½	65.00	50.00
		Nos. 319-322 (4)	56.50	16.00

Malamulo Seventh Day Adventist Church — A66

Virgin and Child and: 10t, Likoma Cathedral. 20t, St. Michael's and All Angel's, Blantyre. 40t, Zomba Catholic Cathedral.

1978, Nov. 15 Wmk. 357 *Perf. 14*

323	A66	4t multicolored	.25	.25
324	A66	10t multicolored	.25	.25
325	A66	20t multicolored	.25	.25
326	A66	40t multicolored	.40	.40
a.		Souvenir sheet of 4, #323-326	1.25	1.25
		Nos. 323-326 (4)	1.15	1.15

Christmas.

Vanilla Polylepis — A67

Orchids of Malawi: 2t, Cirrhopetalum umbellatum. 5t, Calanthe natalensis. 7t, Ansellia gigantea. 8t, Tridactyle bicaudata. 10t, Acampe pachyglossa. 15t, Eulophia quartiniana. 20t, Cyrtorchis arcuata. 30t, Eulophia tricristata. 50t, Disa hamatopetala. 75t, Cynorchis glandulosa. 1k, Aerangis kotschyana. 1.50k, Polystachya dendrobiiflora. 2k, Disa ornithantha. 4k, Cytorchis praetermissa.

1979, Jan. 2 Litho. *Perf. 13½*

327	A67	1t multicolored	.60	.30
328	A67	2t multicolored	.60	.30
329	A67	5t multicolored	.60	.30
330	A67	7t multicolored	.60	.50
331	A67	8t multicolored	.60	.30
332	A67	10t multicolored	.60	.30
333	A67	15t multicolored	.60	.40
334	A67	20t multicolored	.70	.55
335	A67	30t multicolored	1.50	.40
336	A67	50t multicolored	1.25	.60
337	A67	75t multicolored	2.50	4.00
338	A67	1k multicolored	2.25	1.75
339	A67	1.50k multicolored	3.00	4.75
340	A67	2k multicolored	4.00	2.75
341	A67	4k multicolored	9.00	8.50
		Nos. 327-341 (15)	28.40	25.70

Brachystegia Spiciformis A68

Trees: 10t, Widdringtonia nodiflora. 20t, Sandalwood. 40t, African mahogany.

1979, Jan. 21 *Perf. 14x13½*

342	A68	5t multicolored	.30	.25
343	A68	10t multicolored	.40	.35
344	A68	20t multicolored	.70	.75
345	A68	40t multicolored	1.00	2.25
a.		Souvenir sheet of 4, #342-345	3.00	3.00
		Nos. 342-345 (4)	2.40	3.60

National Tree Planting Day.

Railroad Bridge A69

Designs: 10t, Station and train. 20t, 40t, Train passing through man-made pass, diff.

1979, Feb. 17 Litho. *Perf. 14½*

346	A69	5t multicolored	.30	.25
347	A69	10t multicolored	.50	.35
348	A69	20t multicolored	.80	.75
349	A69	40t multicolored	1.40	2.00
a.		Souvenir sheet of 4, #346-349	5.75	5.75
		Nos. 346-349 (4)	3.00	3.35

Inauguration of Salima-Lilongwe Railroad.

Malawi Boy and IYC Emblem — A70

Designs: Malawi children and IYC emblem.

1979, July 10 Wmk. 357 *Perf. 14*

350	A70	5t multicolored	.25	.25
351	A70	10t multicolored	.25	.25
352	A70	20t multicolored	.35	.30
353	A70	40t multicolored	.55	.55
		Nos. 350-353 (4)	1.40	1.35

International Year of the Child.

Malawi No. 1 A71

Stamps of Malawi: 10t, #2. 20t, #3. 40t, #4.

1979, Sept. 17 Litho. *Perf. 13½x14*

354	A71	5t multicolored	.25	.25
355	A71	10t multicolored	.25	.25
356	A71	20t multicolored	.25	.25
357	A71	40t multicolored	.25	.25
a.		Souvenir sheet of 4, #354-357	1.25	1.25
		Nos. 354-357 (4)	1.00	1.00

Sir Rowland Hill (1795-1879), originator of penny postage.

Christmas — A72

Designs: Landscapes.

1979, Nov. 15 Litho. *Perf. 13½x14*

358	A72	5t multicolored	.25	.25
359	A72	10t multicolored	.25	.25
360	A72	20t multicolored	.30	.30
361	A72	40t multicolored	.60	2.00
		Nos. 358-361 (4)	1.40	2.80

Limbe Rotary Club Emblem — A73

Malawi Rotary Club Emblems: 10t, Blantyre. 20t, Lilongwe. 40t, Rotary Intl.

Mangochi District Post Office, 1976, London 1980 Emblem — A74

1980, Feb. 23 Litho. *Perf. 13½*

362	A73	5t multicolored	.25	.25
363	A73	10t multicolored	.25	.25
364	A73	20t multicolored	.25	.25
365	A73	40t multicolored	.70	2.00
a.		Souvenir sheet of 4, #362-365	2.50	2.50
		Nos. 362-365 (4)	1.45	2.75

Rotary International, 75th anniversary.

London 1980 Emblem and: 10t, New Blantyre sorting office, 1979. 20t, Mail transfer hut, Walala. 1k, Nyasaland Post Office, Chiromo, 1891.

1980, May 6 Wmk. 357 *Perf. 14½*

366	A74	5t blue green & blk	.25	.25
367	A74	10t red & black	.25	.25
368	A74	20t dp violet & black	.25	.25
369	A74	1k dk blue & black	.40	.40
a.		Souvenir sheet of 4, #366-369	2.00	2.00
		Nos. 366-369 (4)	1.15	1.15

London 1980 International Stamp Exhibition, May 6-14.

Agate Nodule — A75

1980, Aug. 20 Litho. *Perf. 13½*

370	A75	5t shown	1.00	.25
371	A75	10t Sunstone	1.25	.25
372	A75	20t Smoky Quartz	2.50	.60
373	A75	1k Kyanite crystal	5.50	7.50
		Nos. 370-373 (4)	10.25	8.60

Elephants Drinking (Christmas) A76

1980, Nov. 10 Litho. *Perf. 13*

374	A76	5t shown	.50	.45
375	A76	10t Flowers	.45	.35
376	A76	20t Train	1.10	.90
377	A76	1k Bird	1.75	2.10
		Nos. 374-377 (4)	3.80	3.80

Livingstone's Suni — A77

1981, Feb. 4 Litho. *Perf. 14½*

378	A77	7t shown	.25	.25
379	A77	10t Blue duikers	.30	.25
380	A77	20t African buffalo	.50	.40
381	A77	1k Lichtenstein's hartebeests	1.75	1.75
		Nos. 378-381 (4)	2.80	2.65

Standard A Earth Station A78

1981, Apr. 24 Litho. *Perf. 14½*

382	A78	7t shown	.25	.25
383	A78	10t Blantyre International Gateway Exchange	.25	.25
384	A78	20t Standard B Earth Station	.30	.25
385	A78	1k Satellite and earth	1.50	1.90
a.		Souvenir sheet of 4, #382-385	2.75	2.75
		Nos. 382-385 (4)	2.30	2.65

International communications.

World Food Day A79

1981, Sept. 11 Litho. *Perf. 14*

386	A79	7t Corn	.25	.25
387	A79	10t Rice	.25	.25
388	A79	20t Finger millet	.50	.25
389	A79	1k Wheat	1.40	1.40
		Nos. 386-389 (4)	2.40	2.15

Holy Family, by Lippi A80

Christmas: 7t, Adoration of the Shepherds, by Murillo, vert. 20t, Adoration of the Shepherds, by Louis Le Nain. 1k, Virgin and Child, St. John the Baptist and Angel, by Paolo Morando, vert.

Perf. 13½x13, 13x13½

1981, Nov. 26 Litho.

390	A80	7t multicolored	.25	.25
391	A80	10t multicolored	.30	.25
392	A80	20t multicolored	.60	.55
393	A80	1k multicolored	1.50	1.50
		Nos. 390-393 (4)	2.65	2.55

Wildlife in Natl. Parks A81

1982, Mar. 15 Litho. *Perf. 14½x14*

394	A81	7t Impalas	.25	.25
395	A81	10t Lions	.45	.25
396	A81	20t Kudus	.75	.25
397	A81	1k Flamingos	3.00	3.00
		Nos. 394-397 (4)	4.45	3.75

Kamuzu Academy — A82

Designs: Academy views.

1982, July 1 Litho. *Perf. 14½*

398	A82	7t multicolored	.25	.25
399	A82	20t multicolored	.30	.25
400	A82	30t multicolored	.45	.40
401	A82	1k multicolored	1.50	1.50
		Nos. 398-401 (4)	2.50	2.40

1982 World Cup — A83

1982, Sept.   **Perf. 14x14½**
402 A83 7t Players   1.10 1.00
403 A83 20t World Cup   2.00 2.00
404 A83 30t Stadium   2.50 2.50
    Nos. 402-404 (3)   5.60 5.50
Souvenir Sheet
405 A83 1k Emblem on field   2.50 2.50

Remembrance Day — A84

Designs: War Memorials.

1982, Nov. 5   **Perf. 14½**
406 A84 7t Blantyre   .25 .25
407 A84 20t Zomba   .25 .25
408 A84 30t Chichiri, badges   .30 .30
409 A84 1k Lilongwe   1.00 1.50
    Nos. 406-409 (4)   1.80 2.30

A85

1983, Mar. 14   Wmk. 357   Perf. 14
410 A85 7t Kwacha Intl. Conf.
              Ctr.   .25 .25
411 A85 20t Tea picking, Mulanje .25 .25
412 A85 30t Map   .30 .25
413 A85 1k Pres. Banda, flag   .65 .85
    Nos. 410-413 (4)   1.45 1.60

Commonwealth Day.

The Miraculous Draught of Fishes, by
Raphael (1483-1517) — A86

Designs: 7t, 20t, 30t, Details. 1k, Entire
painting. 7t, 20t vert.

1983, Apr. 4   Litho.   Wmk. 357
414 A86 7t multicolored   .40 .30
415 A86 20t multicolored   1.00 1.00
416 A86 30t multicolored   1.40 1.40
    Nos. 414-416 (3)   2.80 2.70
Souvenir Sheet
417 A86 1k multicolored   3.25 3.25

Fish Eagles — A87

Designs: a, Lakeside sentinel. b, Gull-like,
far-carrying call. c, Diving on its fish prey. d,
Prey captured. e, Feeding on its catch. Nos.
418a-418e in continuous design.

1983, July 11   Wmk. 357   Perf. 14½
418   Strip of 5   17.00 17.00
  a.-e. A87 30t multicolored   1.90 1.90

Manned Flight Bicentenary — A88

Kamuzu Intl. Airport.
1983, Aug. 31   Litho.   Perf. 14
419 A88 7t multicolored   .25 .25
420 A88 20t multi, diff.   .45 .35
421 A88 30t multi, diff.   .60 .60
422 A88 1k multi, diff.   1.75 1.75
  a. Souvenir sheet of 4, #419-422 3.50 3.50
    Nos. 419-422 (4)   3.05 2.95

Christmas — A89

Local flowers.

1983, Nov. 1   Wmk. 357   Perf. 14
423 A89 7t Clerodendrum myri-
              coides   .60 .35
424 A89 20t Gloriosa superba   1.40 1.00
425 A89 30t Gladiolus laxiflorus 1.75 1.40
426 A89 1k Aframomum angus-
              tifolium   4.75 4.75
    Nos. 423-426 (4)   8.50 7.50

Aquarium
Species,
Lake Malawi
A90

Designs: 1t, Melanochromis auratus. 2t,
Haplochromis compressiceps. 5t, Labeotropheus fuelleborni. 7t, Pseudotropheus
lombardoi. 8t, Gold pseudotropheus zebra.
10t, Trematocranus jacobfreibergi. 15t, Melanochromis crabro. 20t, Marbled pseado-
tropheus. 30t, Labidochromis caeruleus. 40t,
Haplochromis venustus. 50t, Aulonacara of
Thumbi. 75t, Melanochromis vermivorus. 1k,
Pseudotropheus zebra. 2k, Trematocranus
spp. 4k, Aulonacara of Mbenje.

Perf. 14½x14
1984, Feb. 2   Wmk. 373
Inscribed "1984" below design
427 A90 1t multicolored   .45 1.00
428 A90 2t multicolored   .45 1.00
429 A90 5t multicolored   .45 1.00
430 A90 7t multicolored   .45 .40
431 A90 8t multicolored   .45 .40
432 A90 10t multicolored   .45 .30
433 A90 15t multicolored   .45 .30
434 A90 20t multicolored   .55 .30
435 A90 30t multicolored   .65 .50
436 A90 40t multicolored   1.10 .65
437 A90 50t multicolored   2.75 2.50
438 A90 75t multicolored   4.00 4.00
439 A90 1k multicolored   4.50 4.50
440 A90 2k multicolored   6.50 6.50
441 A90 4k multicolored   9.25 9.25
    Nos. 427-441 (15)   32.45 32.60

Inscribed "1986" below design
1986
427a A90   1t multicolored   1.75 1.00
430a A90   7t multicolored   1.75 .40
431a A90   8t multicolored   1.75 .40
432a A90   10t multicolored   1.75 .30
433a A90   15t multicolored   1.75 .50
434a A90   20t multicolored   2.25 .30
435a A90   30t multicolored   2.50 .50
436a A90   40t multicolored   4.50 .65
    Nos. 427a-436a (8)   18.00 3.85

Nyika
Red Hare
A91

1984, Feb. 2   Wmk. 357   Perf. 14
442 A91 7t shown   .70 .25
443 A91 20t Sun squirrel   1.40 .45
444 A91 30t Hedgehog   1.90 1.00
445 A91 1k Genet   2.50 3.75
    Nos. 442-445 (4)   6.50 5.45

1984 Summer
Olympics
A92

Local Butterflies
A93

1984, June 1   Litho.   Perf. 14
446 A92 7t Running   .25 .25
447 A92 20t Boxing   .60 .30
448 A92 30t Bicycling   .90 .90
449 A92 1k Long jump   1.60 1.60
  a. Souvenir sheet of 4, #446-449 4.50 4.50
    Nos. 446-449 (4)   3.35 3.05

1984, Aug. 1   Photo.   Perf. 11½
Granite Paper
450 A93 7t Euphaedra ne-
              ophron   1.50 .40
451 A93 20t Papilio dardanus 3.00 .65
452 A93 30t Antanartia
              schaeneia   4.00 1.50
453 A93 1k Spindasis   6.50 9.00
    Nos. 450-453 (4)   15.00 11.55

Christmas — A94

Virgin and Child Paintings.

Wmk. 357
1984, Oct. 15   Litho.   Perf. 14½
454 A94 7t Duccio   .75 .30
455 A94 20t Raphael   2.00 .40
456 A94 30t Lippi   2.50 1.25
457 A94 1k Wilton diptych   5.25 8.00
    Nos. 454-457 (4)   10.50 9.95

Fungi
A94a

1985, Jan. 23   Perf. 14½x14
458 A94a 7t Leucopaxillus
               gracillimus   1.50 .50
459 A94a 20t Limacella guttata 3.50 .65
460 A94a 30t Termitomyces
               eurhizles   4.00 1.75
461 A94a 1k Xerulina asprata 7.75 9.00
    Nos. 458-461 (4)   16.75 11.90

Southern African Development
Coordination Conference — A95

1985, Apr. 1   Litho.   Perf. 14
462 A95 7t Forestry   1.00 .35
463 A95 15t Communications   1.75 .40
464 A95 20t Transportation   4.00 1.50
465 A95 1k Fishing   6.50 6.50
    Nos. 462-465 (4)   13.25 8.75

Ships on
Lake
Malawi
A96

1985, June 3   Perf. 13½x13
466 A96 7t Ufulu   1.00 .40
467 A96 15t Chauncy Maples   2.25 .40
468 A96 20t Mtendere   3.00 1.00
469 A96 1k Ilala   5.75 5.75
  a. Souvenir sheet of 4, #466-469,
      perf. 13x12   12.50 12.50
    Nos. 466-469 (4)   12.00 7.55

Audubon Birth
Bicent. — A97

1985, Aug. 1   Litho.   Perf. 14
470 A97 7t Stierling's wood-
              pecker   1.50 .50
471 A97 15t Lesser seed-
              cracker   2.75 .50
472 A97 20t Gunning's akalat 3.00 1.00
473 A97 1k Boehm's bee-eat-
              er   5.25 5.25
  a. Souvenir sheet of 4, #470-473 12.50 12.50
    Nos. 470-473 (4)   12.50 7.25

Christmas
A98

Halley's Comet
A99

Paintings: 7t, The Virgin of Humility, by
Jaime Serra. 15t, Adoration of the Magi, by
Stefano da Zevio. 20t, Madonna and Child, by
Gerard van Honthorst. 1k, Virgin of Zbraslav,
by a Master of Vissi Brod.

Perf. 11½x12
1985, Oct. 14   Unwmk.
474 A98 7t multicolored   .45 .30
475 A98 15t multicolored   1.10 .35
476 A98 20t multicolored   1.50 .55
477 A98 1k multicolored   4.00 4.75
    Nos. 474-477 (4)   7.05 5.95

1986, Feb. 10   Wmk. 357   Perf. 14½
478 A99 8t Earth, comet and
              Giotto trajectories 1.00 .35
479 A99 15t Comet over Earth 1.10 .35
480 A99 20t Over Malawi   1.75 .45
481 A99 1k Giotto probe   3.25 5.50
    Nos. 478-481 (4)   7.10 6.65

World Cup 86

1986 World Cup Soccer
Championships, Mexico — A100

Various soccer plays.

Perf. 12x11½
1986, May 26   Unwmk.
Granite Paper
482 A100 8t multicolored   1.00 .30
483 A100 15t multicolored   1.50 .35
484 A100 20t multicolored   2.00 .85
485 A100 1k multicolored   5.00 5.50
  a. Souvenir sheet of 4, #482-
      485   14.00 14.00
    Nos. 482-485 (4)   9.50 7.00

Natl. Independence, 20th Anniv. — A101

1986, June 30   Litho.   Perf. 14
486 A101 8t Pres. Banda   2.25   2.25
487 A101 15t Natl. flag   1.25   .25
488 A101 20t Natl. crest   1.40   .35
489 A101 1k Natl. airline   4.75   5.25
       Nos. 486-489 (4)   9.65   8.10

Christmas — A102

Paintings: 8t, Virgin and Child, by Botticelli (1445-1510). 15t, Adoration of the Shepherds, by Guido Reni (1575-1642). 20t, Madonna of the Veil, by Carlo Dolci (1616-86). 1k, Adoration of the Magi, by Jean Bourdichon.

1986, Dec. 15   Litho.   Perf. 11½
490 A102 8t multicolored   .75   .25
491 A102 15t multicolored   1.25   .25
492 A102 20t multicolored   2.00   .50
493 A102 1k multicolored   5.25   8.00
       Nos. 490-493 (4)   9.25   9.00

World Wildlife Fund A103

Bugeranus carunculatus.

1987, Jan. 30   Wmk. 357   Perf. 14½
494 A103 8t Wattled crane   2.75   .45
495 A103 15t Two cranes   4.00   .60
496 A103 20t Nesting   4.75   .90
497 A103 75t Crane in water   8.75   8.75
       Nos. 494-497 (4)   20.25 10.70

1988, Oct.   Wmk. 373
494a A103 8t   7.75   1.75
495a A103 15t   11.00   3.25
496a A103 20t   12.00   3.75
497a A103 75t   16.50 15.00
       Nos. 494a-497a (4) 47.25 23.75

British Steam Locomotives — A104

1987, May 25   Litho.   Perf. 14x13½
498 A104 10t Shamrock No. 2, 1902   3.25   .45
499 A104 25t D Class No. 8, 1914   4.50   .60
500 A104 30t Thistle No. 1, 1902   5.00 1.00
501 A104 1k Kitson No. 6, 1903   9.00 9.00
       Nos. 498-501 (4)   21.75 11.05

Hippopotamus A105

1987, Aug. 24   Photo.   Perf. 12½
Granite Paper
502 A105 10t Feeding   2.00   .35
503 A105 25t Swimming, roaring 3.75   .50
504 A105 30t Mother and young swimming 3.75 .85
505 A105 1k At rest, egret   9.50 8.75
  a. Souvenir sheet of 4, #502-505 19.00 19.00
       Nos. 502-505 (4)   19.00 10.45

Wild Flowers — A106

Unwmk.
1987, Oct. 19   Litho.   Perf. 14
506 A106 10t Stathmostelma spectabile 1.25 .25
507 A106 25t Pentanisia schweinfurthii 2.50 .35
508 A106 30t Chironia krebsii   3.00   .70
509 A106 1k Ochna macrocalyx   5.00 5.00
       Nos. 506-509 (4)   11.75 6.30

Locally Carved and Staunton Chessmen A107

1988, Feb. 8   Wmk. 384   Perf. 14½
510 A107 15t Knights   2.00   .30
511 A107 35t Bishops   3.00   .90
512 A107 50t Rooks   3.50 1.75
513 A107 2k Queens   9.25 9.25
       Nos. 510-513 (4) 17.75 12.20

1988 Summer Olympics, Seoul — A108

1988, June 13   Unwmk.   Perf. 14
514 A108 15t High jump   .60   .25
515 A108 35t Javelin   .90   .40
516 A108 50t Women's tennis 1.25   .70
517 A108 2k Shot put   2.75 2.75
  a. Souvenir sheet of 4, #514-517 6.50 6.50
       Nos. 514-517 (4)   5.50 4.10

Birds — A109

Designs: 1t, Eastern fores scrub-warbler. 2t, Yellow-throated warbler. 5t, Moustached green tinkerbird. 7t, Waller's chestnut-wing starling. 8t, Oriole finch. 10t, No. 533A, Starred robin. 15t, Bar-tailed trogon. 20t, Green twinspot. 30t, Gray cuckoo shrike. 40t, Black-fronted bush shrike. 50t, White-tailed crested flycatcher. 75t, Green barbet. 1k, Cinnamon dove. 2k, Silvery-cheeked hornbill. 4k, Crowned eagle. No. 533, Red and blue sunbird.

Perf. 11½x12, 15x14½ (#533)
1988-94   Photo.
Granite Paper (1t-4k)
518 A109 1t multicolored   .75 .60
519 A109 2t multicolored   .75 .60
520 A109 5t multicolored   .75 .60
521 A109 7t multicolored   .75 .60
522 A109 8t multicolored   .75 .60
523 A109 10t multicolored 1.90 1.00
524 A109 15t multicolored   .75 .25
525 A109 20t multicolored   .75 .25
526 A109 30t multicolored   .75 .25
527 A109 40t multicolored   .80 .40
528 A109 50t multicolored 1.90 1.00
529 A109 75t multicolored 1.40 1.00
530 A109 1k multicolored   1.90 1.10
531 A109 2k multicolored   3.00 2.00
532 A109 4k multicolored   6.50 3.75
533 A109 10k multicolored 16.00 9.75
533A A109 10k multicolored 13.00 5.00
       Nos. 518-533A (17) 52.40 28.75

Issue dates: 10k, Oct. 3, No. 533A, 1994; others, July 25.

Common Design Types pictured following the introduction.

Lloyds of London, 300th Anniv.
Common Design Type
15t, Royal Exchange, 1844. 35t, Opening of the Nkula Falls hydroelectric power station, horiz. 50t, Air Malawi passenger jet, horiz. 2k, Cruise ship Queen Elizabeth (Seawise University) on fire, Hong Kong, 1972.

Wmk. 373
1988, Oct. 24   Litho.   Perf. 14
534 CD341 15t multicolored   .50 .30
535 CD341 35t multicolored 1.00 .50
536 CD341 50t multicolored 3.25 .80
537 CD341 2k multicolored   6.25 6.25
       Nos. 534-537 (4)   11.00 7.85

Christmas — A110

Paintings: 15t, Madonna in the Church, by Jan Van Eyck (d. 1441). 35t, Virgin, Infant Jesus and St. Anne, by Leonardo da Vinci. 50t, Virgin and Angels, by Cimabue (c. 1240-1302). 2k, Virgin and Child, by Alesso Baldovinetti (c. 1425-1499).

1988, Nov. 28   Unwmk.   Perf. 14
538 A110 15t multicolored   .90 .30
539 A110 35t multicolored 1.60 .40
540 A110 50t multicolored 2.00 .90
541 A110 2k multicolored   4.75 4.75
       Nos. 538-541 (4)   9.25 6.35

Angling Soc. of Malawi, 50th Anniv. A111

1989, Apr. 11
542 A111 15t Tsungwa   1.25 .25
543 A111 35t Mpasa   2.25 .40
544 A111 50t Yellow fish 3.00 1.75
545 A111 2k Tiger fish 7.75 7.75
       Nos. 542-545 (4) 14.25 10.15

Natl. Independence, 25th Anniv. — A112

1989, June 26
546 A112 15t Independence Arch 1.25 .30
547 A112 35t Grain silos   2.75 .50
548 A112 50t Capital Hill   3.75 1.75

549 A112 2k Reserve Bank Headquarters 8.75 8.75
       Nos. 546-549 (4)   16.50 11.30

African Development Bank, 25th Anniv. — A113

1989, Oct. 30
550 A113 15t Blantyre Digital Telex Exchange 1.25 .30
551 A113 40t Dzalanyama steer   2.25 .50
552 A113 50t Mikolongwe heifer 2.75 1.75
553 A113 2k Zebu bull   7.25 7.25
       Nos. 550-553 (4)   13.50 9.80

Cooperation with the UN, 25th Anniv. — A114

1989, Dec. 1   Perf. 14
554 A114 15t shown   1.25 .30
555 A114 40t House, diff. 2.25 .45
556 A114 50t Thatched dwelling, house 3.00 1.75
557 A114 2k Tea Plantation 7.00 7.00
       Nos. 554-557 (4) 13.50 9.50

Rural Housing Program.

Christmas A115

Designs: 15t, St. Michael and All Angels Church. 40t, Limbe Cathedral. 50t, Nkhoma CCAP Church. 2k, Likoma Is. Cathedral.

1989, Dec. 15
558 A115 15t multicolored 1.25 .30
559 A115 40t multicolored 2.25 .45
560 A115 50t multicolored 3.00 1.75
561 A115 2k multicolored   7.00 7.00
       Nos. 558-561 (4) 13.50 9.50

Classic Cars A116

Perf. 14x13½
1990, Apr. 2   Litho.   Unwmk.
562 A116 15t Ford Sedan, 1915 1.50 .40
563 A116 40t Two-seater Ford, 1915 3.00 1.00
564 A116 50t Ford, 1915   3.75 2.00
565 A116 2k Chevrolet Luxury Bus, 1930 9.00 9.00
  a. Souvenir sheet of 4, #562-565, perf. 13x12 26.00 26.00
       Nos. 562-565 (4)   17.25 12.40

World Cup Soccer Championships, Italy — A117

1990, June 14 Litho. Perf. 14
566	A117	15t shown	1.25	.30
567	A117	40t Two players	2.75	.75
568	A117	50t Shot on goal	3.75	2.00
569	A117	2k World Cup Trophy	9.00	9.00
a.		Souvenir sheet of 4, #566-569	17.00	17.00
		Nos. 566-569 (4)	16.75	12.05

SADCC, 10th Anniv. A118

1990, Aug. 24 Litho. Perf. 14
570	A118	15t Map	1.25	.40
571	A118	40t Chambo	2.25	.55
572	A118	50t Cedar trees	7.25	2.00
573	A118	2k Nyala	9.00	9.00
a.		Souvenir sheet of 4, #570-573	16.00	16.00
		Nos. 570-573 (4)	19.75	11.95

Christmas A119

Orchids A120

Paintings by Raphael: 15t, Virgin and Child. 40t, The Transfiguration, detail. 50t, St. Catherine of Alexandrie. 2k, The Transfiguration.

1990, Nov. 26 Perf. 13½x14
574	A119	15t multicolored	1.25	.40
575	A119	40t multicolored	2.50	.60
576	A119	50t multicolored	3.50	2.00
577	A119	2k multicolored	8.75	8.75
a.		Souvenir sheet of 4, #574-577, perf. 12x13	18.00	18.00
		Nos. 574-577 (4)	16.00	11.75

1990, Dec. 7
578	A120	15t Aerangis kotschyana	1.75	.40
579	A120	40t Angraecum eburneum	3.50	1.00
580	A120	50t Aerangis luteo alba	3.75	2.00
581	A120	2k Cyrtorchis arcuata	11.50	11.50
a.		Souvenir sheet of 4, #578-581, perf. 12x13	21.00	21.00
		Nos. 578-581 (4)	20.50	14.90

Wild Animals A121

1991, Apr. 23 Litho. Perf. 14x13½
582	A121	20t Buffalo	1.50	.40
583	A121	60t Cheetah	3.50	1.50
584	A121	75t Greater kudu	3.50	1.50
585	A121	2k Black rhinoceros	13.00	10.00
a.		Souvenir sheet of 4, #582-585, perf. 13x12	22.50	22.50
		Nos. 582-585 (4)	21.50	13.40

Malawi Postal Services, Cent. A122

20t, Chiromo Post Office, 1891. 60t, Mail exchange hut, Walala. 75t, Mangochi Post Office. 2k, Standard A Earth station, 1981.

1991, July 2 Perf. 14x13½
586	A122	20t multicolored	1.75	.40
587	A122	60t multicolored	2.50	1.00
588	A122	75t multicolored	2.75	1.25

589	A122	2k multicolored	9.00	7.50
a.		Souvenir sheet of 4, #586-589, perf. 13x12	17.00	17.00
		Nos. 586-589 (4)	16.00	10.15

Insects — A123   Christmas — A124

1991, Sept. 21 Perf. 13½x14
590	A123	20t Red locust	1.75	.40
591	A123	60t Weevil	3.50	1.50
592	A123	75t Cotton stainer bug	3.50	1.75
593	A123	2k Pollen beetle	9.00	7.50
		Nos. 590-593 (4)	17.75	11.15

1991, Nov. 26 Litho. Perf. 13½x14
594	A124	20t Christ Child in manger	.90	.35
595	A124	60t Adoration of the Magi	2.75	.60
596	A124	75t Nativity	3.25	1.00
597	A124	2k Virgin and Child	7.50	7.50
		Nos. 594-597 (4)	14.40	9.45

Birds — A125

Designs: a, Red bishop. b, Lesser striped swallow. c, Long-crested eagle. d, Lilac-breasted roller. e, African paradise flycatcher. f, White-fronted bee-eater. g, White-winged black tern. h, Brown-backed fire-finch. i, White-browed robin-chat. j, African fish eagle. k, Malachite kingfisher. l, Cabani's masked weaver. m, African barn owl. n, Yellow-bellied sunbird. o, Lesser flamingo. p, Crowned crane. q, African pitta. r, African darter. s, White-faced tree duck. t, African pied wagtail.

1992, Apr. 7 Litho. Perf. 14
598	A125	75t Sheet of 20, #a.-t.	60.00	60.00

1992 Summer Olympics, Barcelona — A126

1992, July 28 Litho. Perf. 13½
600	A126	20t Long jump	1.40	.35
601	A126	60t High jump	2.00	.80
602	A126	75t Javelin	2.50	1.10
603	A126	2k Running	5.00	5.00
a.		Souvenir sheet of 4, #600-603	13.00	13.00
		Nos. 600-603 (4)	10.90	7.25

Christmas — A127

Details from paintings: 20t, Angel from The Annunciation, by Philippe de Champaigne.

75t, Virgin and Child, by Bernardino Luini. 95t, Virgin and Child, by Sassoferrato. 2k, Mary from The Annunciation, by Champaigne.

1992, Nov. 9 Litho. Perf. 14
604	A127	20t multicolored	.80	.25
605	A127	75t multicolored	1.90	.50
606	A127	95t multicolored	2.40	.80
607	A127	2k multicolored	5.75	5.50
		Nos. 604-607 (4)	10.85	7.05

Intl. Space Year A128

Designs: 20t, Voyager II, Saturn. 75t, Center of a galaxy. 95t, Kanjedza II ground station. 2k, Communication satellite.

1992, Dec. 7 Litho. Perf. 13½
608	A128	20t multicolored	1.00	.35
609	A128	75t multicolored	2.25	.85
610	A128	95t multicolored	2.50	.50
611	A128	2k multicolored	5.50	5.00
		Nos. 608-611 (4)	11.25	7.20

Fruit — A129

1993, Mar. 21 Litho. Perf. 13½x14
612	A129	20t Strychnos spinosa	1.00	.30
613	A129	75t Adansonia digitata	2.50	1.00
614	A129	95t Ximenia caffra	2.75	1.10
615	A129	2k Uapaca kirkiana	4.75	4.75
		Nos. 612-615 (4)	11.00	7.15

Butterflies A130

1993, June 28 Litho. Perf. 13
616	A130	20t Apaturopsis cleocharis	1.25	.40
617	A130	75t Euryphura achlys	2.75	1.00
618	A130	95t Cooksonia aliciae	3.25	1.60
619	A130	2k Charaxes protoclea azota	4.75	4.50
		Nos. 616-619 (4)	12.00	7.50

A131

Dinosaurs — A132

Designs: No. 623a, Tyrannosaurus Rex. b, Dilophosaurus. c, Brachiosaurus. d, Gallimimus. e, Triceratops. f, Velociraptor.

1993, Dec. 30 Litho. Perf. 13
620	A131	20t Kentrosaurus	1.10	.75
621	A131	75t Stegosaurus	2.50	2.25
622	A131	95t Sauropod	3.00	2.50
		Nos. 620-622 (3)	6.60	5.50

Miniature Sheet
623	A132	2k Sheet of 6, #a.-f.	21.00	21.00

Christmas — A133

1993, Nov. 30 Photo. Perf. 11½
Granite Paper
624	A133	20t Holy family	.45	.45
625	A133	75t Shepherds	.55	.45
626	A133	95t Wise men	.70	.70
627	A133	2k Adoration of the magi	2.00	2.25
		Nos. 624-627 (4)	3.70	3.85

Fish of Lake Malawi — A134

Designs: 20t, Pseudotropheus socolofi. 75t, Melanochromis auratus. 95t, Pseudotropheus lombardoi. 1k, Labeotropheus trewavasae. 2k, Pseudotropheus zebra. 4k, Pseudotropheus elongatus.

1994, Mar. 21 Litho. Perf. 14x15
628	A134	20t multicolored	.45	.35
629	A134	75t multicolored	1.10	.45
630	A134	95t multicolored	1.25	.55
631	A134	1k multicolored	1.25	.90
632	A134	2k multicolored	2.50	2.25
633	A134	4k multicolored	4.25	3.75
		Nos. 628-633 (6)	10.80	8.25

Ships of Lake Malawi — A135

1994, Oct. 19 Litho. Perf. 13x13½
634	A135	20t Ilala	.70	.55
635	A135	75t MV Ufulu	1.10	.55
636	A135	95t The Pioneer	1.40	.65
637	A135	2k Dove	2.25	2.25
		Nos. 634-637 (4)	5.45	4.00

Souvenir Sheet
638	A135	5k Monteith	8.50	8.50

Christmas — A136

Details or entire paintings: 20t, Virgin and Child, by Durer, vert. 75t, Magi Present Gifts to Infant Jesus, Franco-Flemish Book of Hours, vert. 95t, The Nativity, by Fra Filippo Lippi. 2k, Nativity with Magi, by Rogier van der Weyden.

1994, Nov. 30 Litho. Perf. 14½
639	A136	20t multicolored	.55	.55
640	A136	75t multicolored	.65	.55
641	A136	95t multicolored	.80	.55
642	A136	2k multicolored	2.40	2.75
		Nos. 639-642 (4)	4.40	4.40

Pres. Bakili Muluzi — A137

1995, Apr. 10   Litho.   Perf. 11½x12
643	A137	40t red & multi	.45	.45
644	A137	1.40k green & multi	.45	.45
645	A137	1.80k blue & multi	.55	.55
646	A137	2k brn org & multi	.80	.80
		Nos. 643-646 (4)	2.25	2.25

Establishment of COMESA (Common Market for Eastern & Southern African States).

Christmas A138

1995, Nov. 13   Litho.   Perf. 11½
Granite Paper
647	A138	40t Pre-schoolers	.70	.70
648	A138	1.40k Dispensing medicine	.70	.70
649	A138	1.80k Water supply	.90	.90
650	A138	2k Voluntary return	1.25	1.25
		Nos. 647-650 (4)	3.55	3.55

Butterflies A139

1996, Dec. 5   Photo.   Perf. 11½
Granite Paper
651	A139	60t Precis tugela	.60	.60
652	A139	3k Papilo pelodorus	1.40	.75
653	A139	4k Acrea acrita	1.50	.90
654	A139	10k Malantis leda	3.25	3.00
		Nos. 651-654 (4)	6.75	5.25

Christmas — A140

Designs: 10t, Instructor, children raising hands. 20t, Children enacting nativity scene. 30t, Children standing with hands clasped. 60t, Mother and child.

1996, Dec. 12   Granite Paper
655	A140	10t multicolored	.90	.90
656	A140	20t multicolored	.90	.90
657	A140	30t multicolored	1.10	.90
658	A140	60t multicolored	2.25	1.75
		Nos. 655-658 (4)	5.15	4.45

UN, 50th Anniv. A141

40t, Telecommunications & training. 1.40k, Clean water is essential for health. 1.80k, Protecting the environment, Mt. Mulanje. 2k, Food security.

1995, Oct. 30   Litho.   Perf. 11½
659	A141	40t multicolored	.90	.90
660	A141	1.40k multicolored	.90	.90
661	A141	1.80k multicolored	1.10	1.10
662	A141	2k multicolored	1.10	1.10
a.		Souvenir sheet, #659-662	4.75	4.75
		Nos. 659-662 (4)	4.00	4.00

Paul Harris (1868-1947), Founder of Rotary, Intl. — A142

Rotary, Intl. emblem and: 60t, Map of Malawi. 3k, Eagle. 4.40k, Leopard.

1997, Oct. 6   Litho.   Perf. 11½
663	A142	60t multicolored	.65	.65
664	A142	3k multicolored	1.10	1.10
665	A142	4.40k multicolored	1.60	1.60
666	A142	5k shown	1.75	1.75
		Nos. 663-666 (4)	5.10	5.10

UNICEF, 50th Anniv. A143

Designs: 60t, Care and protection. 3k, Education. 4.40k, Nutrition. 5k, Immunization.

1997, Oct. 31   Litho.   Perf. 11¾x11½
667	A143	60t multi	.90	.90
668	A143	3k multi	.90	.90
669	A143	4.40k multi	1.50	1.50
670	A143	5k multi	1.90	1.90
		Nos. 667-670 (4)	5.20	5.20

A144   A145

Christmas: 60t, Holy Night, by Carlo Maratta. 3k, The Nativity, by Bernardino Luini. 4.40k, Adoration of the Magi, by Luini. 5k, Holy Family.

1997, Dec. 15   Perf. 11¾
671	A144	60t multi	1.00	1.00
672	A144	3k multi	1.00	1.00
673	A144	4.40k multi	1.60	1.60
674	A144	5k multi	2.10	2.10
		Nos. 671-674 (4)	5.70	5.70

1998, Nov. 30   Litho.   Perf. 14½
Diana, Princess of Wales (1961-97): Various portraits.
675	A145	60t multicolored	.40	.40
676	A145	6k multicolored	.50	.50
677	A145	7k multicolored	.55	.55
678	A145	8k multicolored	.65	.65
a.		Souvenir sheet, Nos. 675-678	2.50	2.50
		Nos. 675-678 (4)	2.10	2.10

Tourism A146

60t, Tattooed Rock, Mwalawamphini, Cape Maclear, vert. 6k, War Memorial Tower, Zomba, vert. 7k, Mtengatenga Postal hut, Walala. 8k, Original P.I.M. Church, Chiradzulu.

1998, Dec. 2   Litho.   Perf. 13
679	A146	60t multicolored	.60	.60
680	A146	6k multicolored	.70	.70
681	A146	7k multicolored	.85	.85
682	A146	8k multicolored	1.00	1.00
		Nos. 679-682 (4)	3.15	3.15

Universal Declaration of Human Rights, 50th Anniv. A147

Basic rights: 60t, Voting. 6k, Education. 7k, Equal justice. 8k, Owning property.

1998, Dec. 10
683	A147	60t multicolored	.60	.60
684	A147	6k multicolored	.70	.70
685	A147	7k multicolored	.85	.85
686	A147	8k multicolored	1.00	1.00
		Nos. 683-686 (4)	3.15	3.15

Christmas — A148

Design: Madonna and Child.

1998, Dec. 15   Photo.   Perf. 11¾
Granite Paper
687	A148	60t multi	—	—
688	A148	6k multi	—	—
689	A148	7k Angel	—	—
690	A148	8k multi	—	—

Christmas — A149

60t, Madonna & Child. 6k, Nativity. 7k, Adoration of the Magi. 8k, Flight into Egypt.

1999, Dec. 13   Photo.   Perf. 11¾
691	A149	60t multi	.90	.90
692	A149	6k multi	.90	.90
693	A149	7k multi	1.10	1.10
694	A149	8k multi	1.40	1.40
		Nos. 691-694 (4)	4.30	4.30

Southern African Development Community — A150

60t, Map of Africa. 6k, Malambe fruit juice bottles. 7k, Fishing resources research boat R/V Ndunduma. 8k, Locomotive.

Perf. 13¼x13½, 13½x13¼
2000, Feb. 22   Litho.
695	A150	60t multi, vert.	.75	.75
696	A150	6k multi, vert.	.75	.75
697	A150	7k multi	1.00	1.00
698	A150	8k multi	1.25	1.25
		Nos. 695-698 (4)	3.75	3.75

Modern British Commonwealth, 50th Anniv. — A151

African musical instruments: 60t, Ng'oma. 6k, Kaligo. 7k, Kalimba. 8k, Chisekese.

2000, Feb. 22   Perf. 13¼x13½
699	A151	60t multi	.75	.75
700	A151	6k multi	.75	.75
701	A151	7k multi	1.00	1.00
702	A151	8k multi	1.25	1.25
		Nos. 699-702 (4)	3.75	3.75

Christmas — A152

Designs: 5k, Madonna and Child. 18k, Nativity. 20k, Madonna and Child, diff.

2000, Dec. 12   Photo.   Perf. 11¾
| 703-705 | A152 | Set of 3 | 3.25 | 3.25 |

Butterflies — A153

Designs: 1k, Euxanthe wakefieldi. 2k, Psuedacraea boisdurali. 4k, Catacroptera cloanthe. 5k, Myrina silenus ficedula. 10k, Cymothoe zombana. 20k, Charaxes castor. 50k, Charaxes pythoduras ventersi. 100k, Iolaus lalos.

2002 ?   Litho.   Perf. 14½x13¾
706	A153	1k multi	.35	.35
707	A153	2k multi	.35	.35
708	A153	4k multi	.35	.35
709	A153	5k multi	.35	.35
710	A153	10k multi	.35	.35
711	A153	20k multi	.80	.80
712	A153	50k multi	2.40	2.40
713	A153	100k multi	4.50	4.50
		Nos. 706-713 (8)	9.45	9.45

Worldwide Fund for Nature (WWF) A154

Kobus vardonii: a, Male. b, Two males butting heads. c, Male and female. d, Herd.

Perf. 13¼x13½
2003, Nov. 10   Litho.
714		Strip of 4	10.00	10.00
a.-d.	A154	50k Any single	1.25	1.25
e.		Souvenir sheet, 2 #714	20.00	20.00

Butterflies, Birds, Orchids and Mushrooms — A155

No. 715, 50k — Butterflies: a, Bebearia octogramma. b, Charaxes nobilis. c, Cymothoe beckeri. d, Salamis anteva. e,

Charaxes xiphares. f, Bebearia arcadius Fabricius.

No. 716, 50k, vert. — Birds: a, Upupa epops. b, Psittacus erithacus. c, Terathopus ecaudatus. d, Polemaetus bellicosus. e, Agapornis personatus. f, Scotopelia peli.

No. 717, 50k, vert. — Orchids: a, Angraecum eburneum. b, Ancistrochilus rothschildianus. c, Angraecum infundibulare. d, Ansellia africana. e, Disa veitchii. f, Angraecum compactum.

No. 718, 50k — Mushrooms: a, Pleurotus ostreatus. b, Macrolepiota procera. c, Amanita vaginata. d, Cantharellus tubaeformis. e, Hydnum repandum. f, Trametes versicolor.

No. 719, 180k, Carterocephalus palaemon. No. 720, 180k, Ardea cinerea. No. 721, 180k, Aerangis kotschyana. No. 722, 180k, Auricularia auricula, vert.

Perf. 13¼x13½, 13½x13¼

2003, Nov. 10

Sheets of 6, #a-f

715-718 A155 Set of 4 22.50 22.50

Souvenir Sheets

719-722 A155 Set of 4 13.50 13.50

Tour de France Bicycle Race, Cent. (in 2003) — A156

No. 723: a, Joop Zoetemelk, 1980. b, Bernard Hinault, 1981. c, Hinault, 1982. d, Laurent Fignon, 1983.
180k, Miguel Indurain, 1991-95.

2004, Feb. 6   ***Perf. 13¼***

723 A156 75k Sheet of 4, #a-d 5.75 5.75

Souvenir Sheet

724 A156 180k multi 3.50 3.50

Powered Flight, Cent. (in 2003) — A157

No. 725: a, Vickers Vimy. b, D.H. 9A. c, Messerschmidt Bf. d, Mitsubishi A6M3.
180k, Fiat CR-2.

2004, Feb. 6   ***Perf. 14***

725 A157 75k Sheet of 4, #a-d 5.75 5.75

Souvenir Sheet

726 A157 180k multi 3.50 3.50

General Motors Automobiles — A158

No. 727, 75k — Cadillacs: a, 1959 Eldorado. b, 1962 Series 62. c, 1961 Sedan De Ville. d, 1930 V-16.
No. 728, 75k — Corvettes: a, 1965 convertible. b, 1965 Stingray. c, 1979. d, 1998.
No. 729, 180k, 1954 Cadillac Eldorado. No. 730, 180k, 1998 Corvette, diff.

2004, Feb. 6 Litho. *Perf. 14*

Sheets of 4, #a-d

727-728 A158 Set of 2 11.50 11.50

Souvenir Sheets

729-730 A158 Set of 2 6.75 6.75

The following items inscribed "Malawi" have been declared "illegal" by Malawi postal officials:

Souvenir sheets of three 80k stamps depicting Birds of prey; cats; locomotives; Ferrari Formula 1 cars.

A sheetlet of eight hexagonal 15k depicting the national birds of South African Postal Operators Association (SAPOA) countries was produced in limited quantities.

Miniature Sheet

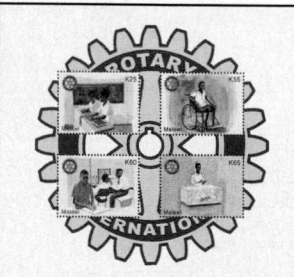

Rotary International, Cent. — A159

No. 731: a, 25k, Boys in classroom. b, 55k, Boy in wheelchair. c, 60k, Doctor examining patient. d, 65k, Nurse monitoring baby in incubator.

2005, July 25 Litho. *Perf. 13¼*

731 A159 Sheet of 4, #a-d 3.50 3.50

Butterflies — A161

Design: 5k, Myrina silenus ficedula. 10k, Cymothoe zombana. 20k, Charaxes castor. 40k, Papilio pelodorus, 50k, Charaxes pythoduras ventersi, 65k, Papilio pelodorus. 75k, Acrita acrita. 100k, Iolaus Ialos. 105k, Acrea acrita. 110k, Euxanthe wakefieldi. 115k, Pseudacraea boisdurali.

2007	**Litho.**		**_Perf. 13¼x12¾_**	
733	A161	5k multi	—	—
734	A161	10k multi	—	—
735	A161	20k multi	—	—
736	A161	40k multi	—	—
736A	A161	50k multi	—	—
737	A161	65k multi	—	—
738	A161	75k multi	—	—
739	A161	100k multi	—	—
740	A161	105k multi	—	—
741	A161	110k multi	—	—
742	A161	115k multi	—	—

Compare with Type A153.

Stop Child Abuse — A162

2008, Nov. 19 Litho. *Perf. 13x13¼*

744 A162 40k multi —

Endangered Animals — A163

No. 745: a, Black rhinoceros. b, Sable antelope. c, Zebra. d, African buffalo.
325k, Roan antelope.

2009, Sept. 30   *Perf. 11½x12*

745 A163 65k Sheet of 4, #a-d 3.75 3.75

Souvenir Sheet

Perf. 11½x11¼

746 A163 325k multi 4.75 4.75

Hippopotamus Amphibius — A164

No. 747 — Hippopotamus: a, Head, facing right. b, Reclining. c, Standing. d, Pair in water.
325k, Hippopotamus, vert.

2009, Sept. 30   *Perf. 11½x12*

747 A164 105k Sheet of 4, #a-d 6.00 6.00

Souvenir Sheet

Perf. 11¼x11½

748 A164 325k multi 4.75 4.75

Wildlife — A166

No. 749: a, Lion. b, Elephant shrew. c, Black-backed jackal. d, Reedbuck. e, African elephant. f, Warthog.
325k, Leopard.

A165

2009, Sept. 30   *Perf. 11½x11¼*

749 A165 110k Sheet of 6, #a-f 9.50 9.50

Souvenir Sheet

750 A166 325k multi 4.75 4.75

Worldwide Fund for Nature (WWF) A167

No. 751 — Lilian's loverbirds: a, Six birds on branches. b, Seven birds in flight. c, Two birds on branch, four in flight. d, Birds on ground and in flight.

2009, Sept. 30   *Perf. 13¼*

751   Strip of 4 10.00 10.00
a.-d. A167 115k Any single 2.00 2.00
e. Sheet of 8, 2 each #751a-751d 20.00 20.00

Numerous items inscribed "Malawi" have been declared illegal by Malawi postal officials, including items with dates of 2007 and 2008 having topics of:

Rugby World Cup, Nelson Mandela, Mahatma Gandhi, Dalai Lama, and Pope John Paul II, Coral, Horses, Minerals, Birds, Bees, Exotic fish, Owls, Dinosaurs, Minerals and Scouts, Space, Automobiles, Mushrooms, Internet and Basketball stars.

Malawi postal officials have also declared "illegal" many other items with dates from 2005-2012 having a variety of topics.

Miniature Sheet

National Animals — A168

No. 752: a, Nyala (Malawi). b, Nyala (Zimbabwe). c, Burchell's zebra (Botswana). d, Oryx (Namibia). e, Buffalo (Zambia).

Litho. With Foil Application

2010, July 7   *Perf. 13¾*

752 A168 55k Sheet of 5, #a-e *3.75 3.75*

See Botswana No. 838, Namibia Nos. 1141-1142, Zambia Nos. 1097-1101, Zimbabwe Nos. 1064-1068.

Miniature Sheet

2010 World Cup Soccer Championships, South Africa — A169

No. 753 — Soccer players, ball, 2010 World Cup mascot and flag of: a, Namibia. b, South

Africa. c, Zimbabwe. d, Malawi. e, Swaziland. f, Botswana. g, Mauritius. h, Lesotho. i, Zambia.

2010, Dec. 20   Litho.   Perf. 13¾
753 A169 105k Sheet of 9, #a-i 12.50 12.50

See Botswana Nos. 896-905, Lesotho No. , Mauritius No. , Namibia No. 1188, South Africa No. 1403, Swaziland Nos. 794-803, Zambia Nos. 1115-1118, and Zimbabwe Nos. 1112-1121.

Christmas
A170

Various creche figures with bottom panel color of: No. 754, 65k, Red. No. 755, 65k, Blue violet. No. 756, 65k, Claret. No. 757, 65k, Green.

2010, Dec. 20   Perf. 13x13¼
754-757 A170   Set of 4   3.50 3.50

Partnership Between Malawi and European Union, 35th Anniv. (in 2010) — A171

Flags of Malawi and European Union and: No. 758, 65k, Partnership projects. No. 759, 65k, Family, 35th anniversary emblem, vert.

2011, Jan. 18   Perf. 14
758-759 A171   Set of 2   1.75 1.75
759a   Souvenir sheet of 2, #758-759   1.75 1.75

Big Game Animals A172

Designs: 80k, Buffalo. 100k, Leopard. 135k, Black rhinoceros. 140k, Elephant. 145k, Lion.

2011, Nov. 3   Perf. 14x13¼
760-764 A172   Set of 5   7.50 7.50
764a   Souvenir sheet of 5, #760-764   7.50 7.50

Christmas A173

Designs: 80k, Angels proclaiming Gospel to shepherds. 100k, Shepherds lauding Jesus. 135k, Wise men following the star. 140k, Wise men giving Jesus gifts. 145k, Simeon blessing baby Jesus.

2011, Dec. 16   Perf. 13¼x14
765-769 A173   Set of 5   7.25 7.25
769a   Souvenir sheet of 5, #765-769   7.25 7.25

Pan-African Tsetse and Trypasonomiasis Eradication Campaign — A174

Stamps with white frames: No. 770, 65k, Man, tsetse fly, zebu, map of Malawi, campaign emblem. No. 771, 105k, Campaign emblem. No. 772, 110k, Tsetse flies, map of Malawi, campaign emblem. No. 773, 115k, Tsetse fly, map of Malawi, campaign emblem. No. 774: a, 65k, Like No. 770, dull brown frame. b, 105k, Like No. 771, orange frame. c, 110k, Like No. 772, blue frame. d, 115k, Like No. 773, brown violet frame.

2012, Jan. 25   Perf. 14
770-773 A174   Set of 4   5.00 5.00
Souvenir Sheet
774 A174   Sheet of 4, #a-d   5.00 5.00

Campaign Against AIDS — A175

Inscriptions: 80k, Stop AIDS keep the promise (red AIDS ribbon, map of Malawi). 100k, Male involvement (man and woman wearing AIDS ribbons). 135k, HTC (man, woman and doctor). 140k, Stop AIDS keep the promise (man and woman wearing AIDS ribbons). 145k, PMTCT (pregnant woman and nurse).

2012, Sept. 5   Perf. 13¼x12¾
775-779 A175   Set of 5   4.50 4.50

One hundred sheetlets of five stamps inscribed "Standard Postage" were created and given to bulk purchasers of Nos. 775-779. The sheet margin is inscribed "Not For Sale" and the individual stamps on the sheet were not valid for postage.

Dances A176

Designs: 165k, Vimbuza. 260k, Uyeni. 270k, Tchopa. 280k, Masewe. 290k, Gule wa Mkulu.

2012, July   Litho.   Perf. 14
780-784 A176   Set of 5   9.50 9.50
784a   Souvenir sheet of 5, #780-784   9.50 9.50

Independence, 50th Anniv. — A178

Flag and: 330k, Independence Ark. 520k, Hastings Kamuzu Banda, first president. 560k, Corn silos. 600k, Parliament. 670k, Zebras.

2014, Oct. 21   Litho.   Perf. 13x13½
795 A178 330k multi   2.10 2.10
  a.   Booklet pane of 1   2.10 —
796 A178 520k multi   3.25 3.25
  a.   Booklet pane of 1   3.25 —
797 A178 560k multi   3.50 3.50
  a.   Booklet pane of 1   3.50 —
798 A178 600k multi   3.75 3.75
  a.   Booklet pane of 1   3.75 —
799 A178 670k multi   4.25 4.25
  a.   Booklet pane of 1   4.25 —
    Complete booklet, #795a, 796a, 797a, 798a, 799a   17.00
  b.   Souvenir sheet of 5, #795-799   17.00 17.00
    Nos. 795-799 (5)   16.85 16.85

POSTAGE DUE STAMPS

D1

Wmk. 357
1967, Sept. 1   Litho.   Perf. 11½
J1 D1 1p deep lilac rose   .25 4.50
J2 D1 2p sepia   .25 4.50
J3 D1 4p lilac   .25 5.00
J4 D1 6p dark blue   .35 5.50
J5 D1 8p emerald   .50 6.00
J6 D1 1sh black   .60 6.00
  Nos. J1-J6 (6)   2.20 31.50

Values in Decimal Currency
1971, Feb. 15   Size: 18x23mm
J7 D1 2t sepia   .30 4.25
J8 D1 4t lilac   .45 4.25
J9 D1 6t dark blue   .75 4.50
J10 D1 8t green   1.00 4.50
J11 D1 10t black   1.25 4.50
  Nos. J7-J11 (5)   3.75 22.00

Type of 1971 Redrawn
1975   Wmk. 357   Perf. 14
Size: 17x21mm
J12 D1 2t brown   1.75 4.00
No. J12 has accent mark over "W."

1977-78   Litho.   Unwmk.   Perf. 14
Size: 18x21mm
J13 D1 2t sepia   9.00 4.50
J14 D1 4t rose lilac   9.00 4.50
J15 D1 8t brt green ('78)   4.00 4.50
J16 D1 10t black   9.00 5.25
  Nos. J13-J16 (4)   31.00 18.75

1982   Wmk. 357, Sideways
J13a D1 2t   .60 4.00
J14a D1 4t   .60 4.00
J16a D1 10t   .60 4.00
  Nos. J13a-J16a (3)   1.00 12.00

1989   Litho.   Unwmk.   Perf. 15x14
Size: 18x20 ½mm
J13b D1 2t   3.75 5.50
J14b D1 4t   3.75 5.50
J15a D1 8t   3.75 5.50
J16b D1 10t   3.75 5.50
  Nos. J13b-J16b (4)   15.00 22.00

MALAYA

mə-ˈlā-ə

Federated Malay States

LOCATION — Malay peninsula
GOVT. — British Protectorate
AREA — 27,585 sq. mi.
CAPITAL — Kuala Lumpur

The Federated Malay States consisted of the sultanates of Negri Sembilan, Pahang, Perak and Selangor.

Stamps of the Federated Malay States replaced those of the individual states and were used until 1935, when individual issues were resumed.

100 Cents = 1 Dollar

Catalogue values for unused stamps in this country are for Never Hinged items, beginning with Scott 80 in the regular postage section, Scott J20 in the postage-due section, Scott 128 in Johore, Scott 55 in Kedah, Scott 44 in Kelantan, Scott 1 in Malacca, Scott 36 in Negri Sembilan, Scott 44 in Pahang, Scott 1 in Penang, Scott 99 in Perak, Scott 1 in Perlis, Scott 74 in Selangor, and Scott 47 in Trengganu.

Watermarks

Wmk. 47 — Multiple Rosettes

Wmk. 71 — Rosette

Wmk. 338 — PTM Multiple

(PTM stands for Persekutuan Tanah Melayu, or Federation of Malaya.)

Stamps of Straits Settlements overprinted "BMA MALAYA" are listed in Straits Settlements.

Stamps and Type of Negri Sembilan Overprinted in Black

FEDERATED MALAY STATES

1900   Wmk. 2   Perf. 14
1 A2 1c lilac & green   3.50 11.00
2 A2 2c lilac & brown   35.00 77.50
3 A2 3c lilac & black   3.25 6.25
4 A2 5c lilac & olive   85.00 200.00
5 A2 10c lilac & org   15.50 47.50
6 A2 20c green & olive   100.00 125.00
7 A2 25c grn & car rose   300.00 425.00
8 A2 50c green & black   110.00 160.00
  Nos. 1-8 (8)   652.25 1,052.

Overprinted on Perak Nos. 51, 53, 57-58, 60-61
1900
9 A9 5c lilac & olive   28.00 72.50
10 A9 10c lilac & org   90.00 80.00
Wmk. 1
11 A10 $1 green & lt grn   210.00 275.00
12 A10 $2 green & car rose   175.00 325.00
13 A10 $5 green & ultra   500.00 800.00
  Revenue cancel   75.00
13A A10 $25 green & org   15,500.
  Revenue cancel   450.00
  Nos. 9-13 (5)   1,003. 1,552.
No. 10 with bar omitted is an essay.

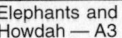
Elephants and Howdah — A3

Tiger — A4

1900   Typo.
14 A3 $1 green & lt green   170. 170.
15 A3 $2 grn & car rose   170. 190.
16 A3 $5 green & ultra   425. 450.
  Revenue cancel   20.
17 A3 $25 grn & orange   4,250. 1,950.
  Revenue cancel   100.
  Nos. 14-17 (4)   5,015. 2,760.

High values with revenue cancellations are plentiful and inexpensive.

1901 — Wmk. 2

Stamps of type A4 are watermarked sideways.

18a	A4	1c green & gray	5.00	1.25
19b	A4	3c brn & gray brn	11.00	.25
20a	A4	4c carmine & gray	10.00	8.25
21	A4	5c scar & grn, yel	3.00	3.75
22a	A4	8c ultra & gray	24.00	9.50
23a	A4	10c violet & gray	90.00	13.50
24	A4	20c black & gray vio	26.00	13.50
25b	A4	50c brn org & gray brn	110.00	50.00
		Nos. 18a-25b (8)	275.50	89.50

1904-10 — Wmk. 3

26a	A4	1c grn & gray brown	45.00	.85
27	A4	3c brown & gray	77.50	1.25
28	A4	4c rose & black	7.75	1.00
29	A4	5c scar & grn, yel	13.00	3.25
30c	A4	8c ultra & gray brn ('07)	11.00	5.75
31c	A4	10c claret & black	40.00	.75
32	A4	20c blk & gray vio ('05)	22.50	1.50
33b	A4	50c orange & gray ('06)	65.00	16.00

The 1c and 4c are on ordinary paper, the other values on both ordinary and chalky papers. The least expensive varieties are shown. For comprehensive listing, see *Scott Classic Specialized Catalogue*.

Chalky Paper

34	A3	$1 green & lt green ('07)	110.00	57.50
35	A3	$2 green & car rose ('06)	120.00	140.00
36	A3	$5 grn & ultra ('06)	325.00	160.00
		Revenue cancellation		25.00
37	A3	$25 grn & org ('10)	2,000.	900.00
		Revenue cancellation		75.00
		Nos. 26a-37 (12)	2,836.	1,287.

High values with revenue cancellations are plentiful and inexpensive.

1906-22 — Ordinary Paper

Two dies for Nos. 38 and 44:
I — Thick line under "Malay."
II — Thin line under "Malay."

38	A4	1c dull grn, die II	12.50	.25
b.		Die I	25.00	.55
39	A4	1c brown ('19)	3.00	1.25
40	A4	2c green ('19)	2.50	.55
41	A4	3c brown	10.50	.25
42	A4	3c carmine ('09)	4.50	.25
43	A4	3c dp gray ('19)	2.50	.25
44	A4	4c scar, die II	2.25	.25
b.		Die I ('19)	3.75	5.50
45	A4	6c orange ('19)	3.25	3.50
46	A4	8c ultra ('09)	16.00	1.40
47	A4	10c ultra ('19)	9.00	2.25
48	A4	35c red, yellow	7.50	15.00
		Nos. 38-48 (11)	73.50	25.20

1922-32 — Wmk. 4 — Ordinary Paper

49	A4	1c brown ('22)	2.25	4.00
50	A4	1c black ('23)	.85	.25
51	A4	2c dk brown ('25)	11.00	12.00
52	A4	2c green ('26)	3.00	.25
53	A4	3c dp gray ('23)	2.50	7.50
54	A4	3c green ('24)	2.75	2.00
55	A4	3c brown ('27)	4.50	.50
56	A4	4c scar (II) ('23)	4.00	.60
57	A4	4c orange ('26)	1.50	.25
c.		Unwatermarked	475.00	300.00
58	A4	5c vio, yel ('22)	1.25	.25
59	A4	5c dk brown ('32)	3.50	.25
60	A4	6c orange ('22)	1.00	.55
61	A4	6c scarlet ('26)	1.50	.25
62	A4	10c ultra ('23)	1.75	8.50
63	A4	10c ultra & blk ('23)	2.50	.80
64	A4	10c vio, yel, chalky paper ('31)	6.00	.55
65	A4	12c ultra ('22)	1.75	.25

Chalky Paper

66	A4	20c blk & vio ('23)	5.00	2.00
a.		Ordinary paper	65.00	4.50
67	A4	25c red vio & ol vio ('29)	3.50	3.00
68	A4	30c yel & dl vio ('29)	4.00	5.00
69	A4	35c red, yel, ordinary paper ('28)	6.00	27.50
70	A4	35c dk vio & car ('31)	17.00	15.00
71	A4	50c org & blk ('24)	17.00	17.50
72	A4	50c blk, bl grn ('31)	5.50	2.50
73	A3	$1 gray grn & yel grn ('26)	24.00	100.00
a.		$1 green & blue green	24.00	100.00
74	A3	$2 grn & car ('26)	37.50	95.00
75	A3	$5 grn & ultra ('25)	190.00	250.00
76	A3	$25 grn & org ('28)	1,850.	1,950.
		Revenue cancel		125.00
		Nos. 49-75 (27)	361.10	556.25

1931-34

77	A4	$1 red & blk, blue	15.00	4.75
78	A4	$2 car & green, yel ('34)	60.00	50.00
79	A4	$5 car & green, emer ('34)	350.00	265.00
		Nos. 77-79 (3)	425.00	319.75

FEDERATION OF MALAYA

GOVT. — Sovereign state in British Commonwealth of Nations
AREA — 50,700 sq. mi.
POP. — 7,139,000 (est. 1961)
CAPITAL — Kuala Lumpur

The Federation comprised the nine states of Johore, Pahang, Negri Sembilan, Selangor, Perak, Kedah, Perlis, Kelantan and Trengganu and the settlements of Penang and Malacca.
Malaya joined the Federation of Malaysia in 1963.

100 Sen (Cents) = 1 Dollar (1957)

> **Catalogue values for unused stamps in this section are for Never Hinged items.**

The Peace Issue of 1946 8c stamp inscribed "MALAYAN UNION" was not issued.

Rubber Tapping — A5

Map of Federation — A6

Designs: 12c, Federation coat of arms. 25c, Tin dredge and flag.

Perf. 13x12½, 12½ — Engr., Litho.

1957, May 5 — Wmk. 314

80	A5	6c blue, red & yel	1.00	.30
a.		Yellow omitted	85.00	
81	A5	12c car & multi	1.75	1.10
82	A5	25c multicolored	3.75	.40
83	A6	30c dp claret & red org	1.50	.30
		Nos. 80-83 (4)	8.00	2.10

Chief Minister Tunku Abdul Rahman and People of Various Races — A7

Perf. 12½

1957, Aug. 31 — Wmk. 4 — Engr.

84	A7	10c brown	.80	.35

Independence Day, Aug. 31.

United Nations Emblem — A8

Design: 30c, UN emblem, vert.

Perf. 13½, 12½

1958, Mar. 5 — Wmk. 314

85	A8	12c rose red	.45	1.00
86	A8	30c plum	.65	1.00

Conf. of the Economic Commission for Asia and the Far East (ECAFE), Kuala Lumpur, Mar. 5-15.

Merdeka Stadium and Flag — A9

Tuanku Abdul Rahman, Paramount Ruler of Malaya — A10

Perf. 13½x14½, 14½x13½

1958, Aug. 31 — Photo. — Wmk. 314

87	A9	10c multicolored	.30	.30
88	A10	30c multicolored	.60	.90

1st anniv. of the Independence of the Federation of Malaya.

A11

Torch of Freedom and Broken Chain — A12

Perf. 12½x13, 13x12½

1958, Dec. 10 — Litho. — Wmk. 314

89	A11	10c multicolored	.25	.25

Photo.

90	A12	30c green	.70	.70

10th anniv. of the signing of the Universal Declaration of Human Rights.

Mace and People — A13

Perf. 12½x13½

1959, Sept. 12 — Photo. — Unwmk.

91	A13	4c rose red	.30	.30
92	A13	10c violet	.30	.30
93	A13	25c yellow green	.60	.40
		Nos. 91-93 (3)	1.20	1.00

1st Federal Parliament of Malaya, inauguration.

WRY Emblem A14

Design: 30c, Similar to 12c, vert.

Perf. 13½, 13

1960, Apr. 7 — Engr. — Wmk. 314

94	A14	12c lilac	.30	.80
95	A14	30c dark green	.30	.30

World Refugee Year, 7/1/59-6/30/60.

Rubber Tree Seedling on Map of Malaya — A15

Tuanku Syed Putra — A16

Perf. 13x13½

1960, Sept. 19 — Litho. — Unwmk.

96	A15	6s red brn, grn & blk	.25	1.25
97	A15	30s ultra, yel grn & blk	.60	.75

15th meeting of the Intl. Rubber Study Group and the Natural Rubber Research Conference, Kuala Lumpur, Sept. 26-Oct. 1.

Perf. 13½x14½

1961, Jan. 4 — Photo. — Wmk. 314

98	A16	10s blue & black	.30	.30

Installation of Tuanku Syed Putra of Perlis as Paramount Ruler (Yang di-Pertuan Agong.)

Colombo Plan Emblem — A17

Malaria Eradication Emblem — A18

1961, Oct. 30 — Unwmk. — Perf. 13½

99	A17	12s rose pink & black	.55	3.25
100	A17	25s brt yellow & black	1.10	2.00
101	A17	30s brt blue & black	.90	1.00
		Nos. 99-101 (3)	2.55	6.25

13th meeting of the Consultative Committee for Technical Co-operation in South and South East Asia, Kuala Lumpur, Oct. 30-Nov. 18.

Wmk. PTM Multiple (338)

1962, Apr. 7 — Perf. 14x14½

102	A18	25s orange brown	.35	.60
103	A18	30s dull violet	.35	.30
104	A18	50s ultramarine	.60	.80
		Nos. 102-104 (3)	1.30	1.70

WHO drive to eradicate malaria.

Palmyra Leaf A19

1962, July 21 — Photo. — Perf. 13½

105	A19	10s violet & gldn brown	.35	.35
106	A19	20s bluish grn & gldn brn	1.00	1.25
107	A19	50s car rose & gldn brn	2.25	2.25
		Nos. 105-107 (3)	3.60	3.85

National Language Month. Watermark inverted on alternating stamps.

Children and their Future Shadows — A20

1962, Oct. 1   Wmk. 338   Perf. 13½

108	A20	10s bright rose lilac	.25 .25
109	A20	25s ocher	.70 1.25
110	A20	30s bright green	3.00 .25
		Nos. 108-110 (3)	3.95 1.75

Free primary education introduced Jan. 1962.

Forms of Food Production and Ears of Wheat — A21

1963, Mar. 21   Unwmk.   Perf. 11½
Granite Paper

111	A21	25s lt ol grn & lilac rose	3.00 4.00
112	A21	30s dk car & lilac rose	3.25 1.75
113	A21	50s ultra & lilac rose	3.25 4.00
		Nos. 111-113 (3)	9.50 9.75

FAO "Freedom from Hunger" campaign.

Cameron Highlands Dam and Pylon — A22

1963, June 26   Wmk. 338   Perf. 14

114	A22	20s purple & brt green	.80 .25
115	A22	30s ultra & brt green	1.25 1.50

Opening of the Cameron Highlands hydroelectric plant.

Check listings for individual states for additional stamps inscribed "Malaya."

POSTAGE DUE STAMPS

D1   D2

Perf. 14½x14

1924-26   Typo.   Wmk. 4

J1	D1	1c violet	4.75 50.00
J2	D1	2c black	2.25 7.00
J3	D1	4c green ('26)	3.25 8.00
J4	D1	8c red	6.00 47.50
J5	D1	10c orange	10.00 17.50
J6	D1	12c ultramarine	10.00 27.50
		Nos. J1-J6 (6)	36.25 157.50

1936-38   Perf. 14½x14

J7	D2	1c dk violet ('38)	17.50 1.10
J8	D2	4c yellow green	40.00 1.40
J9	D2	8c scarlet	20.00 5.00
J10	D2	10c yel orange	25.00 .50
J11	D2	12c blue violet	40.00 17.50
J12	D2	50c black ('38)	30.00 8.00
		Nos. J7-J12 (6)	172.50 33.50

Nos. J7-J12 were also used in Straits Settlements.
For overprints see Nos. NJ1-NJ20, Malacca Nos. NJ1-NJ6.

1945-49

J13	D2	1c reddish violet	5.00 2.25
J14	D2	3c yel green	10.00 6.00
J15	D2	5c org scarlet	6.00 3.50
J16	D2	8c org red ('49)	13.00 16.00
J17	D2	9c yel orange	40.00 50.00
J18	D2	15c blue vio	110.00 35.00
J19	D2	20c dk blue ('48)	10.00 10.00
		Nos. J13-J19 (7)	194.00 122.75

For surcharge see No. J34.

> **Catalogue values for unused stamps in this section, from this point to the end of the section, are for Never Hinged items.**

1951-54   Wmk. 4   Perf. 14

J20	D2	1c dull violet ('52)	.70 1.75
J21	D2	2c dk gray ('53)	1.25 2.25
J22	D2	3c green ('52)	37.50 20.00
J23	D2	4c dk brown ('53)	.70 7.00
J24	D2	5c vermilion	50.00 13.00
J25	D2	8c yel orange	2.50 8.00
J26	D2	12c magenta ('54)	1.25 6.50
J27	D2	20c deep blue	8.00 6.75
		Nos. J20-J27 (8)	101.90 65.25

Nos. J13-J27 were used throughout the Federation and in Singapore, later in Malaysia.

1957-63   Ordinary Paper   Perf. 12½

J21a	D2	2c ('60)	4.50 24.00
b.		2c, chalky paper ('62)	1.75 16.00
J23a	D2	4c ('60)	3.50 25.00
b.		4c, chalky paper ('62)	1.00 20.00
J26a	D2	12c, chalky paper ('62)	5.00 32.50
J27a	D2	20c	8.00 25.00
b.		20c, chalky paper ('63)	10.00 50.00
		Nos. J21a-J27a (4)	21.00 106.50

1965   Wmk. 314   Perf. 12

J28	D2	1c plum	1.50 16.00
J29	D2	2c bluish black	1.10 22.50
J30	D2	4c brown	1.75 16.00
J31	D2	8c yel orange	2.50 22.50
J32	D2	12c magenta	6.50 40.00
J33	D2	20c dark blue	10.00 50.00
		Nos. J28-J33 (6)	23.35 167.00

Nos. J28-J33 were used in Malaysia.

1964, Apr. 14   Perf. 12½

J28a	D2	1c	.50 19.00
J29a	D2	2c	1.75 16.00
J30a	D2	4c	1.00 16.00
J32a	D2	12c	2.25 22.50
J33a	D2	20c	3.00 37.50
		Nos. J28a-J33a (5)	8.50 111.00

No. J16 Surcharged

1965, Jan.   Wmk. 4

J34	D2	10c on 8c yel orange	.60 3.00

OCCUPATION STAMPS

Issued Under Japanese Occupation

Malayan Fruit and Fronds   Tin Dredging
OS1   OS2

Monument to Japanese War Dead   Malayan Plowman
OS3   OS4

1943   Unwmk.   Litho.   Perf. 12½

N30	OS1	2c emerald	1.00 .25
a.		Rouletted	2.25 2.25
b.		Imperf., pair	6.50 6.50
N31	OS2	4c rose red	3.00 .25
a.		Rouletted	2.25 2.25
b.		Imperf., pair	6.50 6.50
N32	OS3	8c dull blue	.50 .25
		Nos. N30-N32 (3)	4.50 .75

1943, Sept. 1

N33	OS4	8c violet	11.00 3.50
N34	OS4	15c carmine red	8.00 3.50

Publicity for Postal Savings which had reached a $10,000,000 total in Malaya.

Rubber Tapping   Seaside Houses
OS5   OS6

Japanese Shrine, Singapore   Sago Palms
OS7   OS8

Johore Bahru and Strait of Johore   Malay Mosque, Kuala Lumpur
OS9   OS10

1943, Oct. 1

N35	OS5	1c gray green	1.75 .70
N36	OS5	3c olive gray	1.00 .25
N37	OS6	10c red brown	1.25 .25
N38	OS7	15c violet	1.75 5.00
N39	OS8	30c olive green	1.50 .50
N40	OS9	50c blue	5.00 5.00
N41	OS10	70c dull blue	27.50 16.00
		Nos. N35-N41 (7)	39.75 27.70

Rice Planting and Map of Malaysia — OS11

1944, Feb. 15

N42	OS11	8c carmine	17.50 4.00
N43	OS11	15c violet	5.00 4.00

Issued on the anniversary of the fall of Singapore to commemorate the "Birth of New Malaya".

OCCUPATION POSTAGE DUE STAMPS

Stamps and Type of Postage Due Stamps of 1936-38 Handstamped in Black, Red or Brown

No. NJ7

1942   Wmk. 4   Perf. 14½x14

NJ1	D2	1c violet	14.00 35.00
a.		Brown overprint	190.00 225.00
b.		Red overprint	200.00 250.00
NJ2	D2	3c yellow green	87.50 97.50
a.		Brown overprint	450.00 475.00
b.		Red overprint	475.00 475.00
NJ3	D2	4c yellow green	95.00 60.00
a.		Brown overprint	220.00 250.00
b.		Red overprint	67.50 60.00
NJ4	D2	8c red	190.00 150.00
a.		Brown overprint	375.00 375.00
b.		Red overprint	175.00 175.00
NJ5	D2	10c yellow orange	40.00 65.00
a.		Brown overprint	110.00 140.00
b.		Red overprint	475.00 475.00
NJ6	D2	12c blue violet	27.50 60.00
a.		Red overprint	475.00 460.00
NJ7	D2	50c black	82.50 125.00
a.		Red overprint	750.00 825.00
		Nos. NJ1-NJ7 (7)	536.50 592.25

Overprinted in Black

1942

NJ8	D2	1c violet	3.50 10.50
NJ9	D2	3c yel green	27.50 35.00
NJ10	D2	4c yel green	25.00 12.50
NJ11	D2	8c red	37.50 27.50
NJ12	D2	10c yel orange	2.00 17.00
NJ13	D2	12c blue violet	2.00 50.00
		Nos. NJ8-NJ13 (6)	97.50 152.50

The 9c and 15c with this overprint were not regularly issued.

Postage Due Stamps of 1936-45 Overprinted

1943

NJ14	D2	1c reddish vio	2.25 5.00
NJ15	D2	3c yel green	2.25 5.00
NJ15A	D2	4c yel green	70.00 52.50
NJ16	D2	5c scarlet	1.50 5.00
NJ17	D2	9c yel orange	.90 8.50
NJ18	D2	10c yel orange	2.25 9.00
NJ19	D2	12c blue violet	2.25 25.00
NJ20	D2	15c blue violet	2.25 10.00
		Nos. NJ14-NJ20 (8)	83.65 120.00

No. NJ15A is said to have been extensively forged.

ISSUED UNDER THAI OCCUPATION

For use in Kedah, Kelantan, Perlis and Trengganu

War Memorial — OS1

Perf. 12½
1943, Dec.   Unwmk.   Litho.

2N1	OS1	1c pale yellow	35.00 37.50
2N2	OS1	2c buff	14.00 24.00
2N3	OS1	3c pale green	22.50 45.00
a.		Imperf., pair		
2N4	OS1	4c dull lilac	16.00 32.50
2N5	OS1	8c rose	16.00 24.00
2N6	OS1	15c lt blue	45.00 72.50
		Nos. 2N1-2N6 (6)	148.50 235.50

These stamps, in cent denominations, were for use only in the four Malayan states ceded to Thailand by the Japanese. The states reverted to British rule in September 1945.

JOHORE

jə-'hōr

LOCATION — At the extreme south of the Malay Peninsula. Linked to Singapore by a causeway.
AREA — 7,330 sq. mi.
POP. — 1,009,649 (1960)
CAPITAL — Johore Bahru

Stamps of the Straits Settlements Overprinted in Black

Overprinted

1876   Wmk. 1   Perf. 14

1	A2	2c brown	21,500. 7,000.
b.		Double overprint	

Overprinted

Overprint 13 to 14mm Wide

1884-86   **Wmk. 2**

1A	A2	2c rose	225.00	225.00
c.		Double overprint		1,100.

Without Period

Overprint 16¾x2mm ("H" & "E" wide)

2	A2	2c rose	3,200.	800.
a.		Double overprint		2,500.

Overprinted

Overprint 11x2½mm

3	A2	2c rose ('86)	130.00	140.00

Overprinted

Overprint 17½x2¾mm

4	A2	2c rose ('85)	9,000.	—

Overprinted

Overprint 12½ to 15x2¾mm

5	A2	2c rose	25.00	22.50

Overprinted

Overprint 9x2½mm

7	A2	2c rose ('86)	80.00	65.00
a.		Double overprint		850.00

Overprinted

Overprint 9x3mm

8	A2	2c rose ('86)	72.50	67.50

Overprinted

Overprint 14 to 15x3mm

9	A2	2c rose	25.00	12.50

Tall "J" 3½mm high

10	A2	2c rose	300.00	200.00

Overprinted

1888   **With Period**

11	A2	2c rose	225.00	75.00
b.		Double overprint		950.00

Overprinted

Overprint 12½ to 13x2½mm

1890-91

12	A2	2c rose	27.50	27.00

Overprint 12x2¾mm

13	A2	2c rose ('91)	10,500.	

Surcharged in Black

a   b

c   d

1891

14	A3(a)	2c on 24c green	47.50	62.50
15	A3(b)	2c on 24c green	150.00	160.00
16	A3(c)	2c on 24c green	30.00	45.00
a.		"CENST"	1,000.	525.00
17	A3(d)	2c on 24c green	140.00	150.00
		Nos. 14-17 (4)	367.50	417.50

Sultan Abubakar — A5

1891-94   **Typo.**   **Unwmk.**

18	A5	1c lilac & vio ('94)	1.00	.60
19	A5	2c lilac & yellow	.75	1.75
20	A5	3c lilac & car rose ('94)	.75	.60
21	A5	4c lilac & black	3.25	22.50
22	A5	5c lilac & green	8.50	22.50
23	A5	6c lilac & blue	9.50	22.50
24	A5	$1 green & car rose	90.00	190.00
		Nos. 18-24 (7)	113.75	260.45

For surcharges and overprints see Nos. 26-36.

Stamps of 1892-94 Surcharged in Black

1894

26	A5	3c on 4c lilac & blk	3.00	.65
a.		No period after "Cents"	125.00	85.00
27	A5	3c on 5c lilac & grn	2.40	4.25
a.		No period after "Cents"	275.00	175.00
28	A5	3c on 6c lilac & bl	4.00	7.50
a.		No period after "Cents"	210.00	240.00
29	A5	3c on $1 green & car	14.50	85.00
a.		No period after "Cents"	500.00	900.00
		Nos. 26-29 (4)	23.90	97.40

Coronation of Sultan Ibrahim
Stamps of 1892-94 Overprinted

Overprinted "KEMAHKOTAAN"

1896

30	A5	1c lilac & violet	.60	1.25
31	A5	2c lilac & yellow	.60	1.25
32	A5	3c lilac & car rose	.65	1.25
33	A5	4c lilac & black	1.00	3.00
34	A5	5c lilac & green	6.00	8.00
35	A5	6c lilac & blue	4.00	7.00
36	A5	$1 green & car rose	60.00	135.00
		Nos. 30-36 (7)	72.85	156.75

Overprinted "KETAHKOTAAN"

30a	A5	1c	5.00	6.00
31a	A5	2c	6.50	8.50
32a	A5	3c	14.50	20.00
33a	A5	4c	3.50	21.00
34a	A5	5c	4.25	8.50
35a	A5	6c	9.00	20.00
36a	A5	$1	42.50	190.00
		Nos. 30a-36a (7)	85.25	274.00

Sultan Ibrahim — A7

1896-99   **Typo.**   **Wmk. 71**

37	A7	1c green	1.00	3.50
38	A7	2c green & blue	.60	1.40
39	A7	3c green & vio	6.00	3.75
40	A7	4c green & car rose	1.25	3.75
41	A7	4c yel & red ('99)	1.75	2.50
42	A7	5c green & brn	2.40	5.00
43	A7	6c green & yel	2.40	7.50
44	A7	10c green & black	8.50	55.00
45	A7	25c green & vio	10.00	50.00
46	A7	50c grn & car rose	19.00	52.50
47	A7	$1 lilac & green	37.50	85.00
48	A7	$2 lilac & car rose	55.00	100.00
49	A7	$3 lilac & blue	50.00	140.00
50	A7	$4 lilac & brn	52.50	100.00
51	A7	$5 lilac & orange	100.00	150.00
		Nos. 37-51 (15)	347.90	759.90

On Nos. 44-46 the numerals are on white tablets. Numerals of Nos. 48-51 are on tablets of solid color.

Stamps of 1896-1926 with revenue cancellations sell for a fraction of those used postally.

For surcharges see Nos. 52-58.

Nos. 40-41 Surcharged in Black

1903

52	A7	3c on 4c yel & red	.80	1.25
a.		Without bars	4.00	27.50
53	A7	10c on 4c grn & car rose	3.00	14.50
a.		Without bars	27.50	85.00

Bars on Nos. 52-53 were handruled with pen and ink.

Surcharged

54	A7	50c on $3 lilac & blue	35.00	87.50

Surcharged

55	A7	$1 on $2 lilac & car rose	75.00	140.00
a.		Inverted "e" in "one"	2,000.	

Surcharged

1904

56	A7	10c on 4c yel & red	25.00	42.50
a.		Double surcharge		8,750.

57	A7	10c on 4c grn & car rose	10.50	72.50
58	A7	50c on $5 lil & org	80.00	175.00
		Nos. 56-58 (3)	115.50	290.00

Sultan Ibrahim — A8

The 10c, 21c, 25c, 50c, and $10 to $500 denominations of type A8 show the numerals on white tablets. The numerals of the 8c, 30c, 40c, and $2 to $5 denominations are shown on tablets of solid colors.

1904-10   **Typo.**   **Wmk. 71**
Ordinary Paper

59	A8	1c violet & green	2.00	.40
a.		Chalky paper ('09)	18.00	12.50
60	A8	2c violet & brn org	3.00	4.25
a.		Chalky paper ('10)	20.00	22.50
61	A8	3c violet & black	5.00	.60
62	A8	4c violet & red	9.25	4.50
63	A8	5c violet & ol grn	2.50	3.00
64	A8	8c violet & blue	4.25	17.50
65	A8	10c violet & black	52.50	11.50
a.		Chalky paper ('10)	120.00	82.50
66	A8	25c violet & green	8.50	42.50
67	A8	50c violet & red	47.50	17.50
68	A8	$1 green & vio	19.00	72.50
69	A8	$2 green & car	32.50	62.50
70	A8	$3 green & blue	45.00	87.50
71	A8	$4 green & brn	45.00	125.00
72	A8	$5 green & org	65.00	100.00
73	A8	$10 green & blk	125.00	210.00
74	A8	$50 green & blue	425.00	575.00
75	A8	$100 green & scar	625.00	1,000.
		Revenue cancel		60.00
		Nos. 59-73 (15)	466.00	759.25

Nos. 74 and 75 were theoretically available for postage but were mostly used for revenue purposes.

For surcharge see No. 86.

1912-19   **Wmk. 47**   **Chalky Paper**

76	A8	1c violet & green	1.25	.25
77	A8	2c violet & orange	6.00	1.00
78	A8	3c violet & black	10.00	.70
79	A8	4c violet & red	30.00	1.00
80	A8	5c violet & ol grn	10.00	2.75
81	A8	8c violet & blue	4.50	14.00
82	A8	10c violet & black	60.00	3.00
83	A8	25c violet & green	27.50	55.00
84	A8	50c violet & red ('19)	77.50	145.00
85	A8	$1 green & vio ('18)	120.00	125.00
		Nos. 76-85 (10)	346.75	347.70

No. 64 Surcharged

1912   **Wmk. 71**

86	A8	3c on 8c vio & blue	15.00	11.50
a.		"T" of "CENTS" omitted	1,750.	

1918-20   **Typo.**   **Wmk. 3**
Chalky Paper

87	A8	2c violet & orange	1.00	7.75
88	A8	2c violet & grn ('19)	1.00	5.50
89	A8	4c violet & red	1.75	.70
90	A8	5c vio & olive grn ('20)	2.00	15.00
91	A8	10c violet & blue	2.00	1.75
92	A8	21c violet & orange ('19)	3.00	3.25
93	A8	25c vio & grn ('20)	9.00	45.00
94	A8	50c vio & red ('19)	25.00	67.50
95	A8	$1 grn & red vio	15.00	77.50
96	A8	$2 green & scar	27.50	67.50
97	A8	$3 green & blue	75.00	145.00
98	A8	$4 green & brn	90.00	210.00
99	A8	$5 green & org	145.00	240.00
100	A8	$10 green & blk	450.00	625.00
		Nos. 87-100 (14)	847.25	1,511.
		Set, ovptd. "SPECIMEN"	750.00	

1921-40   **Wmk. 4**

101	A8	1c violet & black	.30	.25
102	A8	2c violet & brn ('24)	1.25	4.25
103	A8	2c green & dk grn ('28)	.75	.40
104	A8	3c green ('25)	2.25	6.25
105	A8	3c dull vio & brn ('28)	1.40	1.50
106	A8	4c vio & red	2.50	.25
107	A8	5c vio & ol grn	.50	.25
108	A8	6c vio & red brown	.50	.50
109	A8	10c vio & blue	20.00	37.50

No.	Type	Description	Unused	Used
110	A8	10c vio & yel ('22)	.50	.25
111	A8	12c vio & blue	1.25	1.60
111A	A8	12c ultra ('40)	57.50	4.00
112	A8	21c dull vio & org ('28)	2.75	3.50
113	A8	25c vio & green	5.50	1.25
114	A8	30c dull vio & org ('36)	9.50	15.00
115	A8	40c dull vio & brn ('36)	10.50	1.60
116	A8	50c violet & red	3.75	1.60
117	A8	$1 grn & red violet	3.75	1.25
118	A8	$2 grn & red	10.00	5.00
119	A8	$3 grn & blue	85.00	105.00
120	A8	$4 grn & brn ('26)	110.00	190.00
121	A8	$5 grn & org	67.50	52.50
122	A8	$10 grn & blk	325.00	450.00
123	A8	$50 grn & ultra	1,450.	
		Revenue cancel		110.00
124	A8	$100 grn & red	2,000.	
		Revenue cancel		160.00
125	A8	$500 ultra & org brn ('26)	23,000.	
		Revenue cancel		325.00
		Nos. 101-122 (23)	721.95	897.10

Nos. 123, 124 and 125 were available for postage but were probably used only fiscally.

A9   A10

1935, May 15   **Engr.**   **Perf. 12½**
| 126 | A9 | 8c Sultan Ibrahim, Sultana | 6.75 | 3.50 |
| | | Never hinged | 10.00 | |

1940, Feb.   **Perf. 13½**
| 127 | A10 | 8c Sultan Ibrahim | 26.00 | 1.35 |
| | | Never hinged | 40.00 | |

Catalogue values for unused stamps in this section, from this point to the end of the section, are for Never Hinged items.

Silver Wedding Issue
Common Design Types
Inscribed: "Malaya Johore"
Perf. 14x14½
1948, Dec. 1   **Wmk. 4**   **Photo.**
| 128 | CD304 | 10c purple | .25 | .75 |

Perf. 11½x11
Engr.; Name Typo.
| 129 | CD305 | $5 green | 29.00 | 52.50 |

Common Design Types
Pictured following the introduction.

Sultan Ibrahim — A11

1949-55   **Wmk. 4**   **Typo.**   **Perf. 18**
130	A11	1c black	.75	.25
131	A11	2c orange	.40	.30
132	A11	3c green	2.50	1.10
133	A11	4c chocolate	2.00	.25
134	A11	5c rose vio ('52)	3.00	.30
135	A11	6c gray	4.00	.25
a.		Wmk. 4a (error)	3,250.	2,150.
136	A11	8c rose red	5.50	1.40
137	A11	8c green ('52)	10.00	2.25
138	A11	10c plum	1.50	.25
a.		Imperf., pair	5,000.	
139	A11	12c rose red ('52)	11.00	9.00
140	A11	15c ultra	5.00	.45
141	A11	20c dk grn & blk	3.75	1.25
142	A11	20c ultra ('52)	2.00	.30
143	A11	25c org & rose lil	4.00	.25
144	A11	30c plum & rose red ('55)	3.25	2.75
145	A11	35c dk vio & rose red ('52)	12.00	2.25
146	A11	40c dk vio & rose red	8.50	18.00
147	A11	50c ultra & blk	5.50	.30
148	A11	$1 vio brn & ultra	13.00	2.50
149	A11	$2 rose red & emer	32.50	13.50
150	A11	$5 choc & emer	32.50	17.50
		Nos. 130-150 (21)	180.65	74.40

UPU Issue
Common Design Types
Inscribed: "Malaya-Johore"
Engr.; Name Typo. on 15c, 25c
1949, Oct. 10   **Perf. 13½, 11x11½**
151	CD306	10c rose violet	.30	.40
152	CD307	15c indigo	2.00	1.25
153	CD308	25c orange	.80	3.50
154	CD309	50c slate	1.60	3.75
		Nos. 151-154 (4)	4.70	8.90

Coronation Issue
Common Design Type
1953, June 2   **Engr.**   **Perf. 13½x13**
| 155 | CD312 | 10c magenta & black | 1.40 | .30 |

Sultan Ibrahim A12

1955, Nov. 1   **Wmk. 4**   **Perf. 14**
| 156 | A12 | 10c carmine lake | .35 | .35 |

Sultan Ibrahim's Diamond Jubilee.

Sultan Ismail and Johore State Crest Seal — A13

Perf. 11½
1960, Feb. 10   **Unwmk.**   **Photo.**
Granite Paper
| 157 | A13 | 10c multicolored | .35 | .35 |

Coronation of Sultan Ismail.

Types of Kedah 1957 with Portrait of Sultan Ismail
1960   **Wmk. 314**   **Engr.**   **Perf. 13**
158	A8	1c black	.25	.50
159	A8	2c red orange	.25	1.25
160	A8	4c dark brown	.25	.25
161	A8	5c dk car rose	.25	.25
162	A8	8c dark green	2.25	3.50
163	A7	10c violet brown	.35	.70
164	A7	20c blue	2.25	1.00
165	A7	50c ultra & black	.60	.30
166	A8	$1 plum & ultra	4.50	6.00
167	A8	$2 red & green	15.00	22.50
168	A8	$5 ol, grn & brn	35.00	42.50
		Nos. 158-168 (11)	60.95	78.30

Starting in 1965, issues of Johore are listed with Malaysia.

POSTAGE DUE STAMPS

D1

Perf. 12½
1938, Jan. 1   **Typo.**   **Wmk. 4**
J1	D1	1c rose red	22.50	50.00
J2	D1	4c green	45.00	45.00
J3	D1	8c dull yellow	50.00	160.00
J4	D1	10c bister brown	50.00	57.50
J5	D1	12c rose violet	60.00	140.00
		Nos. J1-J5 (5)	227.50	452.50

OCCUPATION POSTAGE DUE STAMPS
Issued under Japanese Occupation

Johore Nos. J1-J5 Overprinted in Black, Brown or Red

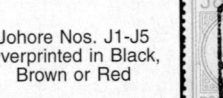

1942   **Wmk. 4**   **Perf. 12½**
NJ1	D1	1c rose red	52.50	85.00
NJ2	D1	4c green	82.50	95.00
NJ3	D1	8c dull yellow	145.00	150.00
NJ4	D1	10c bister brown	52.50	72.50
NJ5	D1	12c rose violet	105.00	115.00
		Nos. NJ1-NJ5 (5)	437.50	517.50

Johore Nos. J1-J5 Overprinted in Black

1943
NJ6	D1	1c rose red	10.00	35.00
NJ7	D1	4c green	8.00	40.00
NJ8	D1	8c dull yellow	10.00	42.50
NJ9	D1	10c bister brown	9.50	50.00
NJ10	D1	12c rose violet	11.00	70.00
		Nos. NJ6-NJ10 (5)	48.50	237.50

Nos. NJ6-NJ10 exist with second character sideways. See Scott Classic Specialized catalogue for listings.

KEDAH
'ke-də

LOCATION — On the west coast of the Malay Peninsula.
AREA — 3,660 sq. mi.
POP. — 752,706 (1960)
CAPITAL — Alor Star

Sheaf of Rice — A1   Native Plowing — A2

Council Chamber — A3

1912-21   **Engr.**   **Wmk. 3**   **Perf. 14**
1	A1	1c green & black	.70	.30
2	A1	1c brown ('19)	.75	.60
3	A1	2c green ('19)	.60	.35
4	A1	3c car & black	5.00	.35
5	A1	3c dk violet ('19)	.75	4.00
6	A1	4c slate & car	12.00	.30
7	A1	4c scarlet ('19)	5.50	1.00
8	A1	5c org brown & grn	2.75	3.50
9	A1	8c ultra & blk	4.25	4.00
10	A2	10c black brn & bl	2.75	1.25
11	A2	20c yel grn & blk	12.50	5.00
12	A2	21c red vio & vio ('19)	6.25	70.00
13	A2	25c red vio & bl ('21)	2.10	37.50
14	A2	30c car & black	3.50	12.00
15	A2	40c lilac & blk	4.00	22.50
16	A2	50c dull bl & brn	10.00	14.00
17	A3	$1 scar & blk, yel	17.50	24.00
18	A3	$2 dk brn & dk grn	25.00	95.00
19	A3	$3 dk bl & blk, bl	135.00	190.00
20	A3	$5 car & black	135.00	200.00
		Nos. 1-20 (20)	385.90	685.65

There are two types of No. 7, one printed from separate plates for frame and center, the other printed from a single plate.
Overprints are listed after No. 45.

Stamps of 1912 Surcharged

1919
21	A3	50c on $2 dk brn & dk grn	80.00	90.00
a.		"C" of ovpt. inserted by hand	1,450.	1,650.
22	A3	$1 on $3 dk bl & blk, blue	22.50	110.00

1921-36   **Wmk. 4**

Two types of 1c:
I — The 1's have rounded corners, small top serif. Small letters "c".
II — The 1's have square-cut corners, large top serif. Large letters "c".

Two types of 2c:
I — The 2's have oval drops. Letters "c" are fairly thick and rounded.
II — The 2's have round drops. Letters "c" thin and slightly larger.

23	A1	1c brown	1.50	.25
24	A1	1c blk (I) ('22)	1.00	.25
a.		1c black (II) ('39)	170.00	5.00
25	A1	2c green (I)	1.50	.25
a.		2c green (II) ('40)	350.00	8.00
26	A1	3c dk violet	1.00	.80
27	A1	3c green ('22)	2.75	1.00
28	A1	4c carmine	7.50	.25
29	A1	4c dull vio ('26)	1.50	.25
30	A1	5c yellow ('22)	3.00	.25
31	A1	6c scarlet ('26)	2.50	.80
32	A1	8c gray ('36)	22.50	.25
33	A2	10c blk brn & bl	3.25	1.00
34	A2	12c dk ultra & blk ('26)	10.00	5.00
35	A2	20c green & blk	8.00	3.00
36	A2	21c red vio & vio	3.25	17.50
37	A2	25c red vio & bl	3.25	9.00
38	A2	30c red & blk ('22)	4.00	11.00
39	A2	35c claret ('26)	22.50	45.00
40	A2	40c red vio & blk	8.00	45.00
41	A2	50c dp blue & brn	4.75	27.50
42	A3	$1 scar & blk, yel ('24)	80.00	85.00
43	A3	$2 brn & green	17.50	125.00
44	A3	$3 dk bl & blk, bl	80.00	110.00
45	A3	$5 car & black	115.00	200.00
		Nos. 23-45 (23)	404.25	708.35

For overprints see Nos. N1-N6.

Stamps of 1912-21 Overprinted in Black: "MALAYA-BORNEO EXHIBITION." in Three Lines
1922   **Wmk. 3**
3a	A1	2c green	5.00	27.50
12a	A2	21c red vio & vio	45.00	95.00
13a	A2	25c red vio & blue	47.50	110.00
b.		Inverted overprint	1,625.	
16a	A2	50c dull blue & brn	50.00	125.00

Wmk. 4
23a	A1	1c brown	7.50	30.00
26a	A1	3c dark violet	5.50	50.00
28a	A1	4c carmine	6.00	25.00
33a	A2	10c blk brn & blue	14.50	50.00
		Nos. 3a-33a (8)	181.00	512.50

Industrial fair at Singapore, Mar. 31-Apr. 15, 1922.
On Nos. 12a, 13a and 16a, "BORNEO" exists both 14mm and 15mm wide.

Sultan of Kedah, Sir Abdul Hamid Halim Shah — A4

1937, July   **Wmk. 4**   **Perf. 12½**
46	A4	10c sepia & ultra	4.00	2.25
47	A4	12c gray vio & blk	42.50	5.50
48	A4	25c brn vio & ultra	10.00	5.50
49	A4	30c dp car & yel grn	10.00	11.50
50	A4	40c brn vio & blk	5.00	16.00
51	A4	50c dp blue & sepia	10.00	5.50
52	A4	$1 dk green & blk	4.00	11.00
53	A4	$2 dk brn & yel grn	90.00	85.00
54	A4	$5 dp car & black	27.50	170.00
		Nos. 46-54 (9)	203.00	312.25
		Set, never hinged	265.00	

For overprints see Nos. N7-N15.

Catalogue values for unused stamps in this section, from this point to the end of the section, are for Never Hinged items.

Silver Wedding Issue
Common Design Types
Inscribed: "Malaya Kedah"
1948, Dec. 1   **Photo.**   **Perf. 14x14½**
| 55 | CD304 | 10c purple | .25 | .25 |

Perf. 11½x11
Engraved; Name Typographed
| 56 | CD305 | $5 rose car | 35.00 | 50.00 |

UPU Issue
Common Design Types
Inscribed: "Malaya-Kedah"

Engr.; Name Typo. on 15c, 25c
1949, Oct. 10   Perf. 13½, 11x11½

57	CD306	10c rose violet	.25	1.75
58	CD307	15c indigo	2.25	1.75
59	CD308	25c orange	.80	3.00
60	CD309	50c slate	1.50	6.00
	Nos. 57-60 (4)		4.80	12.00

Sheaf of
Rice
A5

Sultan
Tungku
Badlishah
A6

1950-55   Wmk. 4   Typo.   Perf. 18

61	A5	1c black	.70	.30
62	A5	2c orange	.50	.25
63	A5	3c green	2.00	1.00
64	A5	4c chocolate	.75	.25
65	A5	5c rose vio ('52)	5.50	3.00
66	A5	6c gray	.70	.25
67	A5	8c rose red	3.75	5.00
68	A5	8c green ('52)	5.50	3.00
69	A5	10c plum	.70	.25
70	A5	12c rose red ('52)	5.50	3.00
71	A5	15c ultramarine	5.00	.70
72	A5	20c dk green & blk	5.00	3.00
73	A5	20c ultra ('52)	2.50	.35
74	A6	25c org & rose lilac	1.50	.50
75	A6	30c plum & rose red ('55)	6.00	1.50
76	A6	35c dk vio & rose red ('52)	6.25	2.00
77	A6	40c dk vio & rose red	7.50	10.00
78	A6	50c ultra & black	6.00	.35
79	A6	$1 vio brown & ultra	7.00	8.00
80	A6	$2 rose red & emer	7.00	8.00
81	A6	$5 choc & emerald	67.50	90.00
	Nos. 61-81 (21)		169.85	177.70

Coronation Issue
Common Design Type
1953, June 2   Engr.   Perf. 13½x13

82	CD312	10c magenta & black	2.25	.60

Fishing Craft — A7

Weaving and
Sultan — A8

Portrait of Sultan Tungku Badlishah and: 1c, Copra. 2c, Pineapples. 4c, Rice field. 5c, Mosque. 8c, East Coast Railway. 10c, Tiger. 50c, Aborigines with blowpipes. $1, Government offices. $2, Bersilat.

Perf. 13x12½, 12½x13
1957   Engr.   Wmk. 314

83	A8	1c black	.35	.60
84	A8	2c red orange	.50	1.75
85	A8	4c dark brown	.35	1.00
86	A8	5c dk car rose	.35	.75
87	A8	8c dark green	3.00	10.00
88	A7	10c chocolate	1.00	.50
89	A7	20c blue	3.50	3.25

Perf. 12½, 13½ ($1)

90	A7	50c ultra & black	3.25	4.25
91	A8	$1 plum & ultra	9.00	15.00
92	A8	$2 red & green	32.50	45.00
	Revenue cancel			.20
93	A8	$5 ol grn & brown	55.00	47.50
	Revenue cancel			.35
	Nos. 83-93 (11)		108.80	129.60

See Nos. 95-105.

Sultan Abdul
Halim — A9

Perf. 14x14½
1959, Feb. 20   Photo.   Wmk. 314

94	A9	10c ultra, red & yellow	.80	.30

Installation of the Sultan of Kedah, Abdul Halim.

Types of 1957

Designs as before with portrait of Sultan Abdul Halim.

Perf. 13x12½, 12½x13, 12½, 13½
1959-62   Engr.   Wmk. 314

95	A8	1c black	.25	.85
96	A8	2c red orange	.25	2.00
97	A8	4c dark brown	.25	.85
98	A8	5c dk car rose	.25	.30
99	A8	8c dark green	4.00	4.00
100	A7	10c chocolate	1.00	.30
101	A7	20c blue	1.00	1.00
102	A7	50c ultra & blk, perf. 12½x13 ('60)	.35	1.75
a.	Perf. 12½		.35	.60
103	A8	$1 plum & ultra	2.50	3.00
104	A8	$2 red & green	15.00	22.50
105	A8	$5 ol grn & brn, perf. 13x12½ ('62)	35.00	19.00
a.	Perf. 12½		20.00	22.50
	Nos. 95-105 (11)		59.85	55.55

Starting in 1965, issues of Kedah are listed with Malaysia.

OCCUPATION STAMPS

Issued Under Japanese Occupation

Stamps of Kedah 1922-36, Overprinted in Red or Black

1942, May 13   Wmk. 4   Perf. 14

N1	A1	1c black (R)	9.50	15.00
N2	A1	2c green (R)	35.00	45.00
N3	A1	4c dull violet (R)	9.50	4.00
N4	A1	5c yellow (R)	5.50	7.50
a.	Black overprint		300.00	325.00
N5	A1	6c scarlet (Bk)	6.00	25.00
N6	A1	8c gray (R)	7.00	5.00

Nos. 46 to 54
Overprinted in Red

Perf. 12½

N7	A4	10c sepia & ultra	18.00	20.00
N8	A4	12c gray vio & blk	42.50	60.00
N9	A4	25c brn vio & ultra	16.00	27.50
a.	Black overprint		450.00	350.00
N10	A4	30c dp car & yel grn	75.00	85.00
N11	A4	40c brn vio & blk	42.50	45.00
N12	A4	50c dp blue & sep	42.50	50.00
N13	A4	$1 dk grn & blk	160.00	160.00
a.	Inverted overprint		875.00	1,000.
N14	A4	2c dk brn & yel green	210.00	190.00
N15	A4	$5 dp car & blk	90.00	125.00
a.	Black overprint		1,600.	1,400.
	Nos. N1-N15 (15)		769.00	869.00

KELANTAN

kə-'lan-ˌtan

LOCATION — On the eastern coast of the Malay Peninsula.
AREA — 5,750 sq. mi.
POP. — 545,620 (1960)
CAPITAL — Kota Bharu

Symbols of
Government — A1

1911-15   Typo.   Wmk. 3   Perf. 14
Ordinary Paper

1	A1	1c gray green	8.00	1.25
a.	1c green		7.25	.35
2	A1	3c rose red	5.00	.25
3	A1	4c black & red	1.90	.25
4	A1	5c grn & red, yel	12.00	1.25
5	A1	8c ultramarine	6.25	1.25
6	A1	10c black & violet	35.00	.90

Chalky Paper

7	A1	30c violet & red	12.50	3.00
8	A1	50c black & org	10.00	3.00
9	A1	$1 green & emer	55.00	45.00
10	A1	$1 grn & brn ('15)	75.00	2.40
11	A1	$2 grn & car rose	1.90	3.75
12	A1	$5 green & ultra	4.75	4.00
13	A1	$25 green & org	55.00	110.00
	Nos. 1-13 (13)		282.30	176.30

For overprints see listings after No. 26. For surcharges see Nos. N20-N22.

1921-28   Wmk. 4
Ordinary Paper

14	A1	1c green	5.00	.75
15	A1	1c black ('23)	1.00	.60
16	A1	2c brown	7.50	4.75
17	A1	2c green ('26)	5.50	.60
18	A1	3c brown ('27)	5.00	1.50
19	A1	4c black & red	3.50	.25
20	A1	5c grn & red, yel	1.75	.25
21	A1	6c claret	3.50	2.00
22	A1	6c rose red ('28)	5.00	5.00
23	A1	10c black & violet	3.00	.25

Chalky Paper

24	A1	30c dull vio & red ('26)	5.00	6.00
25	A1	50c black & orange	7.25	52.50
26	A1	$1 green & brown	35.00	90.00
	Nos. 14-26 (13)		88.00	164.45

Stamps of 1911-21
Overprinted in Black in
Three Lines

1922   Wmk. 3

3a	A1	4c black & red	7.00	50.00
4a	A1	5c green & red, yel	7.50	50.00
7a	A1	30c violet & red	8.00	80.00
8a	A1	50c black & orange	11.00	90.00
10a	A1	$1 green & brown	35.00	125.00
11a	A1	$2 green & car rose	95.00	275.00
12a	A1	$5 green & ultra	275.00	525.00

Wmk. 4

14a	A1	1c green	4.00	55.00
23a	A1	10c black & violet	7.50	75.00
	Nos. 3a-23a (9)		450.00	1,325.

Industrial fair at Singapore. Mar. 31-Apr. 15, 1922.

Sultan Ismail
A2   A2a

1928-33   Engr.   Perf. 12
Size: 21½x30mm

27	A2	$1 ultramarine	17.50	85.00

Perf. 14

28	A2	$1 blue ('33)	75.00	47.50

1937-40   Perf. 12
Size: 22½x34½mm

29	A2a	1c yel & ol green	1.75	.65
30	A2a	2c deep green	5.50	.25
31	A2a	4c brick red	5.50	1.00
32	A2a	5c red brown	3.00	.25
33	A2a	6c car lake	16.00	12.50
34	A2a	8c gray green	3.00	.25
35	A2a	10c dark violet	22.50	3.50
36	A2a	12c deep blue	5.50	8.50
37	A2a	25c vio & red org	6.00	4.75
38	A2a	30c scar & dk vio	40.00	27.50

39	A2a	40c blue grn & org	7.00	45.00
40	A2a	50c org & ol grn	55.00	10.00
41	A2a	$1 dp grn & dk violet	40.00	16.00
42	A2a	$2 red & red brn ('40)	250.00	275.00
43	A2a	$5 rose lake & org ('40)	550.00	950.00
	Nos. 29-43 (15)		1,010.	1,355.
	Set, never hinged		1,000.	

For overprints see Nos. N1-N19.

> **Catalogue values for unused stamps in this section, from this point to the end of the section, are for Never Hinged items.**

Common Design Types pictured following the introduction.

Silver Wedding Issue
Common Design Types
Inscribed: "Malaya Kelantan"
Perf. 14x14½
1948, Dec. 1   Wmk. 4   Photo.

44	CD304	10c purple	.75	2.75

Perf. 11½x11
Engraved; Name Typographed

45	CD305	$5 rose car	35.00	60.00

UPU Issue
Common Design Types
Inscribed: "Malaya-Kelantan"
Engr.; Name Typo. on 15c, 25c
1949, Oct. 10   Perf. 13½, 11x11½

46	CD306	10c rose violet	.40	.40
47	CD307	15c indigo	2.25	2.75
48	CD308	25c orange	.60	6.50
49	CD309	50c slate	1.00	3.00
	Nos. 46-49 (4)		4.25	12.65

Sultan Ibrahim — A3

Perf. 18
1951, July 11   Wmk. 4   Typo.

50	A3	1c black	.50	.40
51	A3	2c orange	1.20	.40
52	A3	3c green	6.75	1.75
53	A3	4c chocolate	2.00	.30
54	A3	6c gray	.80	.30
55	A3	8c rose red	6.00	4.50
56	A3	10c plum	.75	.30
57	A3	15c ultramarine	9.00	.80
58	A3	20c dk green & blk	7.50	15.00
59	A3	25c orange & plum	2.25	.80
60	A3	40c vio brn & rose red	17.50	27.50
61	A3	50c dp ultra & blk	8.00	.60
62	A3	$1 vio brown & ultra	10.00	16.50
63	A3	$2 rose red & emer	47.50	70.00
64	A3	$5 choc & emer	72.50	82.50

1952-55

65	A3	5c rose violet	1.50	.50
66	A3	8c green	7.50	2.25
67	A3	12c rose red	7.50	4.00
68	A3	20c ultramarine	2.00	.25
69	A3	30c plum & rose red ('55)	1.60	6.50
70	A3	35c dk vio & rose red	2.50	1.75
	Nos. 50-70 (21)		214.85	236.90

Compare with Pahang A8, Perak A16, Selangor A15, Trengganu A5.

Coronation Issue
Common Design Type
1953, June 2   Engr.   Perf. 13½x13

71	CD312	10c magenta & black	1.60	1.60

Aborigines
with
Blowpipes
A4

Government Offices
and Sultan
A5

Portrait of Sultan Ibrahim and: 1c, Copra. 2c, Pineapples. 4c, Rice field. 5c, Mosque. 8c, East Coast Railway. 10c, Tiger. 20c, Fishing craft. 50c, Aborigines with blowpipes. $1, Government Offices and Sultan. $2, Bersilat. $5, Weaving.

Perf. 13x12½, 12½x13, 13½ ($1)

			1957-63 Engr.	Wmk. 314	
72	A5	1c black		.25	.45
73	A5	2c red orange		.90	1.50
74	A5	4c dark brown		.45	.25
75	A5	5c dk car rose		.45	.25
76	A5	8c dark green		2.25	3.25
77	A4	10c chocolate		3.00	.25
78	A4	20c blue		2.50	.45
79	A5	50c blue & blk ('60)		1.00	.60
a.		Perf 12½		1.00	1.25
80	A5	$1 plum & ultra		8.00	2.00
81	A5	$2 red & grn ('63)		15.00	32.50
a.		Perf. 12½		19.00	9.00
82	A5	$5 ol grn & brn ('63)		27.50	37.50
a.		Perf. 12½		24.00	14.00
		Nos. 72-82 (11)		61.30	79.00

Sultan Yahya Petra — A6

1961, July 17   Photo.   Perf. 14½x14

83	A6	10s multicolored	.55	1.00

Installation of Sultan Yahya Petra.

Types of 1957 with Portrait of Sultan Yahya Petra

Designs as before.

Perf. 13x12½, 12½x13

			1961-62 Engr.	Wmk. 338	
84	A5	1c black		.25	2.75
85	A5	2c red orange		.60	3.00
86	A5	4c dark brown		1.75	2.00
87	A5	5c dk car rose		1.75	.60
88	A5	8c dark green		14.00	15.00
89	A4	10c violet brown ('61)		1.75	.40
90	A4	20c blue		10.00	2.50
		Nos. 84-90 (7)		30.10	26.25

Starting in 1965, issues of Kelantan are listed with Malaysia.

OCCUPATION STAMPS

Issued Under Japanese Occupation

Kelantan No. 35 Handstamped in Black

1942   Wmk. 4   Perf. 12

N1	A2a	10c dark violet	400.00	500.00

Some authorities believe No. N1 was not regularly issued.

Kelantan Nos. 29-40 Surcharged in Black or Red and Handstamped with Oval Seal "a" in Red

Sunakawa-a   Handa-b

1942

N2		1c on 50c org & ol green	225.00	150.00
a.		With "b" seal	160.00	200.00
N3		2c on 40c bl grn & orange	300.00	200.00
a.		With "b" seal	160.00	200.00
N4		5c on 12c dp bl (R)	200.00	200.00
N5		8c on 5c red brn (R)	175.00	100.00
a.		With "b" seal (R)	110.00	175.00
N6		10c on 6c car lake	475.00	500.00
a.		With "b" seal	120.00	100.00
N7		12c on 8c gray green (R)	60.00	140.00
N8		30c on 4c brick red	2,500.	2,250.
N9		40c on 2c dp grn (R)	70.00	100.00
N10		50c on 1c yel & ol green	1,800.	1,500.

Kelantan Nos. 29-40, 19-20, 22 Surcharged in Black or Red and Handstamped with Oval Seal "b" in Red

50 CENTS $1.00

N10A		1c on 50c org & ol green	350.00	200.00
N11		2c on 40c bl grn & orange	900.00	350.00
N11A		4c on 30c scar & dark vio	2,500.	1,400.
N12		5c on 12c dp bl (R)	350.00	200.00
N13		6c on 25c vio & red org	375.00	200.00
N14		8c on 5c red brown (R)	500.00	150.00
N15		10c on 6c car lake	100.00	125.00
N16		12c on 8c gray grn (R)	225.00	375.00
a.		Seal omitted	70.00	120.00
N17		25c on 10c dk vio	1,600.	1,500.
N17A		30c on 4c brick red	2,500.	2,250.
N18		40c on 2c dp grn (R)	70.00	100.00
N19		50c on 1c yel & ol green	1,800.	1,500.

Perf. 14

N20		$1 on 4c blk & red (R)	60.00	85.00
N21		$2 on 5c grn & red, yel	60.00	85.00
N22		$5 on 6c rose red	60.00	85.00

Examples of Nos. N2-N22 without handstamped seal are from the remainder stocks sent to Singapore after Kelantan was ceded to Thailand. Some authorities believe stamps without seals were used before June 1942.

ISSUED UNDER THAI OCCUPATION

OS1

1943, Nov. 15   Perf. 11

2N1	OS1	1c violet & black	240.00	375.00
2N2	OS1	2c violet & black	300.00	300.00
2N3	OS1	4c violet & black	300.00	375.00
2N4	OS1	5c violet & black	300.00	300.00
2N5	OS1	10c violet & black	450.00	550.00
		Nos. 2N1-2N5 (5)	1,590.	1,900.

Stamps with centers in red are revenues.

MALACCA

mə-'la-kə

Melaka

LOCATION — On the west coast of the Malay peninsula.
AREA — 640 sq. mi.
POP. — 318,110 (1960)

CAPITAL — Malacca

Catalogue values for unused stamps in this section are for Never Hinged items.

Common Design Types pictured following the introduction.

Silver Wedding Issue
Common Design Types
Inscribed: "Malaya Malacca"

Perf. 14x14½

1	CD304	10c purple		.40	2.25

Engraved; Name Typographed
Perf. 11½x11

2	CD305	$5 lt brown		35.00	47.50

Type of Straits Settlements, 1937-41, Inscribed "Malacca"
Perf. 18

			1949, Mar. 1	Wmk. 4	Typo.
3	A29	1c black		.40	.85
4	A29	2c orange		1.00	.60
5	A29	3c green		.40	2.25
6	A29	4c chocolate		.40	.25
7	A29	6c gray		.90	1.10
8	A29	8c rose red		.90	7.50
9	A29	10c plum		.40	.25
10	A29	15c ultramarine		3.50	.85
11	A29	20c dk green & blk		.60	7.00
12	A29	25c org & rose lil		.60	.85
13	A29	40c dk vio & rose red		1.50	13.00
14	A29	50c ultra & black		1.50	1.50
15	A29	$1 vio brn & ultra		15.00	26.00
16	A29	$2 rose red & emer		27.50	27.50
17	A29	$5 choc & emer		60.00	50.00
		Nos. 3-17 (15)		114.60	139.50

See Nos. 22-26.

UPU Issue
Common Design Types
Inscribed: "Malaya-Malacca"

Engr.; Name Typo. on 15c, 25c
Perf. 13½, 11x11½

			1949, Oct. 10	Wmk. 4	
18	CD306	10c rose violet		.35	.55
19	CD307	15c indigo		2.40	2.75
20	CD308	25c orange		.50	8.50
21	CD309	50c slate		1.00	5.50
		Nos. 18-21 (4)		4.25	17.30

Type of Straits Settlements, 1937-41, Inscribed "Malacca"

			1952, Sept. 1	Wmk. 4	Perf. 18
22	A29	5c rose violet		1.25	1.75
23	A29	8c green		6.00	5.25
24	A29	12c rose red		6.00	9.50
25	A29	20c ultramarine		7.50	3.00
26	A29	35c dk vio & rose red		6.00	3.75
		Nos. 22-26 (5)		26.75	23.25

Coronation Issue
Common Design Type

			1953, June 2	Engr.	Perf. 13½x13
27	CD312	10c magenta & black		1.10	1.50

Queen Elizabeth II — A1

			1954-55	Wmk. 4	Typo.	Perf. 18
29	A1	1c black			.25	.75
30	A1	2c orange			.40	1.25
31	A1	4c chocolate			1.50	.25
32	A1	5c rose violet			.40	2.75
33	A1	6c gray			.25	.10
34	A1	8c green			.55	3.00
35	A1	10c plum			2.00	.25
36	A1	12c rose red			.40	3.25
37	A1	20c ultramarine			.25	1.25
38	A1	25c orange & plum			.25	1.75
39	A1	30c plum & rose red ('55)			.25	.40
40	A1	35c vio brn & rose red			.25	1.50
41	A1	50c ultra & black			4.00	2.75
42	A1	$1 vio brn & black			7.50	12.00
43	A1	$2 rose red & grn			29.00	45.00
44	A1	$5 choc & emerald			29.00	47.50
		Nos. 29-44 (16)			76.25	124.05

Types of Kedah with Portrait of Queen Elizabeth II
Perf. 13x12½, 12½x13

			1957 Engr.	Wmk. 314	
45	A8	1c black		.25	.55
46	A8	2c red orange		.25	.55
47	A8	4c dark brown		.50	.25
48	A8	5c dark car rose		.50	.25
49	A8	8c dark green		2.25	3.00
50	A7	10c chocolate		.45	.25
51	A7	20c blue		2.50	1.00

Perf. 12½, 13½ ($1)

52	A7	50c ultra & black		1.00	1.00
53	A8	$1 plum & ultra		6.00	4.75
54	A8	$2 red & green		20.00	27.50
55	A8	$5 olive grn & brn		22.50	47.50
		Nos. 45-55 (11)		56.20	86.60

Types of Kedah, 1957, With Melaka Tree and Mouse Deer Replacing Portrait of Queen Elizabeth II
Perf. 13x12½, 12½x13, 13½ ($1)

			1960, Mar. 15 Engr.	Wmk. 314	
56	A8	1c black		.25	.50
57	A8	2c red orange		.25	.70
58	A8	4c dark brown		.25	.25
59	A8	5c dark car rose		.25	.25
60	A8	8c dark green		3.50	3.75
61	A7	10c violet brown		.45	.25
62	A7	20c blue		2.25	1.00
63	A7	50c ultra & black		1.25	1.00
64	A8	$1 plum & ultra		5.00	3.25
65	A8	$2 red & green		7.50	15.00
66	A8	$5 ol grn & brn		14.00	17.50
		Nos. 56-66 (11)		34.95	43.45

Starting in 1965, issues of Malacca (Melaka) are listed with Malaysia.

OCCUPATION STAMPS

Issued Under Japanese Occupation
Stamps of Straits Settlements, 1937-41 Handstamped in Carmine

The handstamp covers four stamps. Values are for single stamps. Blocks of four showing complete handstamp sell for six times the price of singles.

			1942	Wmk. 4	Perf. 14
N1	A29	1c black		125.00	90.00
N2	A29	2c brown orange		75.00	75.00
N3	A29	3c green		80.00	90.00
N4	A29	5c brown		175.00	175.00
N5	A29	8c gray		300.00	150.00
N6	A29	10c dull violet		125.00	125.00
N7	A29	12c ultramarine		140.00	140.00
N8	A29	15c ultramarine		100.00	125.00
N9	A29	30c org & vio		3,500.	—
N10	A29	40c dk vio & rose red		700.00	700.00
N11	A29	50c blk, emerald		1,100.	1,100.
N12	A29	$1 red & blk, bl		1,350.	1,250.
N13	A29	$2 rose red & gray grn		3,500.	—
N14	A29	$5 grn & red, grn		3,500.	—

Some authorities believe Nos. N9, N13, and N14 were not regularly issued.

OCCUPATION POSTAGE DUE STAMPS

Malaya Postage Due Stamps and Type of 1936-38, Handstamped Like Nos. N1-N14 in Carmine

			1942	Wmk. 4	Perf. 14½x14
NJ1	D2	1c violet		250.00	225.00
NJ2	D2	4c yel green		275.00	275.00
NJ3	D2	8c red		3,500.	2,250.
NJ4	D2	10c yel orange		550.00	525.00

NJ5	D2	12c blue violet	800.00	725.00
NJ6	D2	50c black	3,000.	2,000.
		Nos. NJ1-NJ6 (6)	8,375.	6,000.

Pricing note above No. N1 also applies to Nos. NJ1-NJ6.

NEGRI SEMBILAN

'ne-grē səm-'bē-lən

LOCATION — South of Selangor on the west coast of the Malay Peninsula, bordering on Pahang on the east and Johore on the south.
AREA — 2,580 sq. mi.
POP. — 401,742 (1960)
CAPITAL — Seremban

Stamps of the Straits Settlements Overprinted in Black

1891   **Wmk. 2**   *Perf. 14*
Overprint 14½ to 15mm Wide

1	A2	2c rose	3.50	8.00

Tiger — A1   Tiger Head — A2

1891-94   **Typo.**

2	A1	1c green ('93)	4.00	1.25
3	A1	2c rose	4.00	11.00
4	A1	5c blue ('94)	35.00	47.50
		Nos. 2-4 (3)	43.00	59.75

1895-99

5	A2	1c lilac & green	18.00	8.50
6	A2	2c lilac & brown	42.50	140.00
7	A2	3c lilac & car rose	18.00	1.50
8	A2	5c lilac & olive	10.00	11.50
9	A2	8c lilac & blue	35.00	20.00
10	A2	10c lilac & orange	32.50	17.00
11	A2	15c green & vio	50.00	90.00
12	A2	20c grn & ol ('99)	80.00	45.00
13	A2	25c grn & car rose	85.00	110.00
14	A2	50c green & black	90.00	80.00
		Nos. 5-14 (10)	461.00	523.50

For surcharges see Nos. 15-16, 19-20; Federated Malay States Nos. 1-8.

Stamps of 1891-99 Surcharged

1899   **Blue-green Surcharge**

15	A2	4c on 8c lil & blue	8.50	5.00
a.		Double surcharge	2,750.	2,500.
b.		Pair, one without surcharge	7,250.	4,500.
c.		Double surcharge, 1 green, 1 red	1,000.	1,100.

Black Surcharge

16	A2	4c on 8c lil & blue	1,400.	*1,500.*

Surcharge on No. 16 is thinner and sharper than on No. 15.

Same Surcharge and Bar in Black

17	A1	4c on 1c green	3.00	20.00
18	A1	4c on 5c blue	1.50	17.00
19	A2	4c on 3c lil & car rose	4.00	24.00
a.		Double surcharge	2,750.	1,200.
b.		Pair, one without surcharge	12,000.	6,000.
c.		Bar omitted	1,000.	800.00
g.		Inverted surcharge	2,100.	1,600.

Bar at bottom on Nos. 17-18, at top on No. 19.

No. 11 Surcharged in Black

1900

20	A2	1c on 15c grn & vio	125.00	*350.00*
a.		Inverted period	500.00	*1,300.*

Arms of Negri Sembilan — A4

1935-41   **Typo.**   **Wmk. 4**

21	A4	1c black ('36)	1.40	.25
22	A4	2c dp green ('36)	1.40	.25
22A	A4	2c brown org ('41)	2.25	75.00
22B	A4	3c green ('41)	4.25	11.00
23	A4	4c brown orange	1.25	.25
24	A4	5c chocolate	1.25	.25
25	A4	6c rose red	9.25	.25
25A	A4	6c gray ('41)	3.00	140.00
26	A4	8c gray	1.10	.40
27	A4	10c dull vio ('36)	1.10	.25
28	A4	12c ultra ('36)	1.75	.75
28A	A4	15c ultra ('41)	5.50	75.00
29	A4	25c rose red & dull vio ('36)	2.00	1.00
30	A4	30c org & dull vio ('36)	3.00	2.00
31	A4	40c dull vio & car	2.00	3.00
32	A4	50c blk, *emer* ('36)	5.00	2.25
33	A4	$1 red & blk, *bl* ('36)	3.00	5.00
34	A4	$2 rose red & grn ('36)	30.00	20.00
35	A4	$5 brn red & grn, *emer* ('36)	20.00	100.00
		Nos. 21-35 (19)	98.50	439.40
		Set, never hinged	175.00	

For overprints see Nos. N1-N31.

> **Catalogue values for unused stamps in this section, from this point to the end of the section, are for Never Hinged items.**

Common Design Types
pictured following the introduction.

Silver Wedding Issue
Common Design Types
Inscribed: "Malaya Negri Sembilan"

1948, Dec. 1   **Photo.**   *Perf. 14x14½*

36	CD304	10c purple	.60	.70

Perf. 11½x11
Engraved; Name Typographed

37	CD305	$5 green	27.50	37.50

Arms of Negri Sembilan — A5

1949-55   **Wmk. 4**   **Typo.**   *Perf. 18*

38	A5	1c black	1.25	.25
39	A5	2c orange	1.00	.25
40	A5	3c green	.60	.45
41	A5	4c chocolate	.30	.25
42	A5	5c rose violet	1.00	.45
43	A5	6c gray	2.25	.25
44	A5	8c rose red	.80	.95
45	A5	8c green	5.50	2.25
46	A5	10c plum	.40	.25
47	A5	12c rose red	5.50	3.25
48	A5	15c ultramarine	4.25	.45
49	A5	20c dk green & blk	2.25	2.00
50	A5	20c ultramarine	2.00	.35
51	A5	25c org & rose lilac	1.00	.35
52	A5	30c plum & rose red ('55)	2.00	2.75
53	A5	35c dk vio & rose red	1.50	3.75
54	A5	40c dk vio & rose red	4.75	6.00
55	A5	50c ultra & black	5.00	.45
56	A5	$1 vio brn & ultra	6.00	2.25
57	A5	$2 rose red & emer	18.00	27.50
58	A5	$5 choc & emerald	60.00	75.00
		Nos. 38-58 (21)	125.35	129.45

UPU Issue
Common Design Types
Inscribed: "Malaya-Negri Sembilan"
Engr.; Name Typo. on 15c, 25c

1949, Oct. 10   *Perf. 13½, 11x11½*

59	CD306	10c rose violet	.25	.25
60	CD307	15c indigo	1.40	3.50
61	CD308	25c orange	.75	3.00
62	CD309	50c slate	1.10	4.00
		Nos. 59-62 (4)	3.50	10.75

Coronation Issue
Common Design Type

1953, June 2   **Engr.**   *Perf. 13½x13*

63	CD312	10c magenta & black	1.40	.65

Types of Kedah with Arms of Negri Sembilan
Perf. 13x12½, 12½x13, 13½ ($1)

1957-63   **Engr.**   **Wmk. 314**

64	A8	1c black	.25	.25
65	A8	2c red orange	.25	.25
66	A8	4c dark brown	.25	.25
67	A8	5c dk car rose	.25	.25
68	A8	8c dark green	2.00	1.60
69	A7	10c chocolate	2.00	.25
70	A7	20c blue	1.00	.25
71	A7	50c ultra & blk ('60)	.60	.25
72	A8	$1 plum & ultra	4.50	2.25
a.		Perf. 12½	1.75	1.50
73	A8	$2 red & grn ('63)	20.00	32.50
a.		Perf. 12½	15.00	20.00
74	A8	$5 ol grn & brn ('62)	27.50	25.00
a.		Perf. 12½	20.00	26.00
		Nos. 64-74 (11)	58.60	63.10

Negri Sembilan State Crest and Tuanku Munawir A6

1961, Apr. 17   **Unwmk.**   *Perf. 14x13*

75	A6	10s blue & multi	.45	.70

Installation of Tuanku Munawir as ruler (Yang di-Pertuan Besar) of Negri Sembilan. Starting in 1965, issues of Negri (Negeri) Sembilan are listed with Malaysia.

OCCUPATION STAMPS

Issued under Japanese Occupation

Stamps and Type of Negri Sembilan, 1935-41, Handstamped in Red, Black, Brown or Violet

1942   **Wmk. 4**   *Perf. 14*

N1	A4	1c black	25.00	16.00
N2	A4	2c brown org	16.00	17.50
N3	A4	3c green	21.00	21.00
N4	A4	5c chocolate	29.00	27.50
N5	A4	6c rose red	600.00	600.00
N6	A4	6c gray	150.00	150.00
N7	A4	8c gray	87.50	87.50
N8	A4	8c rose red	55.00	47.50
N9	A4	10c dark violet	110.00	110.00
N10	A4	12c ultramarine	900.00	900.00
N11	A4	15c ultramarine	20.00	11.00
N12	A4	25c rose red & dk vio	35.00	40.00
N13	A4	30c org & dk vio	175.00	190.00
N14	A4	40c dk vio & car	750.00	750.00
N15	A4	$1 red & blk, *bl*	140.00	140.00
N16	A4	$5 brn red & grn, *emerald*	325.00	350.00

The 8c rose red is not known to have been issued without overprint.
Some authorities believe Nos. N5 and N7 were not regularly issued.

Stamps of Negri Sembilan, 1935-41, Overprinted in Black

N17	A4	1c black	1.40	1.40
a.		Inverted overprint	17.00	27.50
b.		Dbl. ovpt., one invtd.	47.50	67.50
N18	A4	2c brown orange	1.60	1.40
N19	A4	3c green	1.40	1.00
N20	A4	5c chocolate	.90	.90
N21	A4	6c gray	2.00	2.00
a.		Inverted overprint		1,000.
N22	A4	8c rose red	2.75	2.75
N23	A4	10c dk violet	5.50	5.50
N24	A4	15c ultramarine	8.00	4.75
N25	A4	25c rose red & dk vio	2.00	6.75
N26	A4	30c org & dk vio	4.00	5.00
N27	A4	$1 red & blk, *bl*	140.00	175.00
		Nos. N17-N27 (11)	169.55	206.45

The 8c rose red is not known to have been issued without overprint.

Negri Sembilan, Nos. 21, 24 and 29, Overprinted or Surcharged in Black

a   b

c

1943

N28	A4	1c black	.65	.65
a.		Inverted overprint	17.00	24.00
N29	A4	2c on 5c choc	.55	.65
N30	A4	6c on 5c choc	.65	.90
a.		"6 cts." inverted	350.00	400.00
N31	A4	25c rose red & dk violet	2.00	2.75
		Nos. N28-N31 (4)	3.85	4.95

The Japanese characters read: "Japanese Postal Service."

PAHANG

pə-'haŋ

LOCATION — On the east coast of the Malay Peninsula, bordering Johore on the south, Parak and Selangor on the west, and Trengganu on the north.
AREA — 13,820 sq. mi.
POP. — 338,210 (1960)
CAPITAL — Kuala Lipis

Stamps of the Straits Settlements Overprinted in Black

Overprinted

Overprint 16x2¾mm

1889   **Wmk. 2**   *Perf. 14*

1	A2	2c rose	140.00	60.00
2	A3	8c orange	2,200.	2,000.
3	A7	10c slate	250.00	300.00

Overprinted

Overprint 12½x2mm

4	A2	2c rose	9.00	10.00

Overprinted

1890   **Overprint 15x2½mm**

5	A2	2c rose	9,000.	2,500.

Overprinted

Overprint 16x2¾mm

6	A2	2c rose	125.00	16.00

Surcharged in Black

a   b

c   d

1891

7	A3 (a) 2c on 24c green	1,100.	1,250.
8	A3 (b) 2c on 24c green	425.00	475.00
9	A3 (c) 2c on 24c green	225.00	275.00
10	A3 (d) 2c on 24c green	1,100.	1,250.
	Nos. 7-10 (4)	2,850.	3,250.

A5   A6

1892-95   **Typo.**

11	A5 1c green	5.00	4.00
12	A5 2c rose	5.50	4.00
13	A5 5c blue	12.50	47.50
	Nos. 11-13 (3)	23.00	55.50

For surcharges see Nos. 21-22.

1895-99

14	A6 3c lilac & car rose	9.75	3.25
14A	A6 4c lil & car rose ('99)	20.00	14.50
15	A6 5c lilac & olive	35.00	25.00
	Nos. 14-15 (3)	64.75	42.75

For surcharge see No. 28.

Stamps of Perak, 1895-99, Overprinted

1898-99

16	A9 10c lilac & orange	25.00	30.00
17	A9 25c green & car rose	95.00	190.00
18	A9 50c green & black	500.00	575.00
18A	A9 50c lilac & black	350.00	425.00

Overprinted

Wmk. 1

19	A10 $1 green & lt grn	425.	600.
20	A10 $5 green & ultra	1,700.	2,700.
	Nos. 16-20 (6)	3,095.	4,520.

No. 13 Cut in Half Diagonally & Srchd. in Red & Initials "JFO" in ms.

1897, Aug. 2   **Wmk. 2**

Red Surcharge

21	A5 2c on half of 5c blue	1,750.	450.
a.	Black surcharge	9,500.	3,500.
22	A5 3c on half of 5c blue	1,750.	450.
a.	Black surcharge	9,500.	3,500.
d.	Se-tenant pair, #21, 22	5,500.	1,200.

Perak No. 52 Surcharged

1898

25	A9 4c on 8c lilac & blue	7.50	7.50
b.	Inverted surcharge	4,250.	1,700.

Surcharged on pieces of White Paper

1898   **Without Gum**   *Imperf.*

26	4c black		4,500.
27	5c black	3,000.	

Pahang No. 15 Surcharged

1899   **Perf. 14**

28	A6 4c on 5c lilac & olive	21.00	70.00

Sultan Abu Bakar — A7

1935-41   **Typo.**   **Wmk. 4**   **Perf. 14**

29	A7 1c black ('36)	.25	.25
30	A7 2c dp green ('36)	1.40	.25
30A	A7 3c green ('41)	10.00	19.00
31	A7 4c brown orange	.70	.25
32	A7 5c chocolate	.70	.25
33	A7 6c rose red ('36)	12.00	3.50
34	A7 6c gray	2.00	.25
34A	A7 8c rose red ('41)	3.00	60.00
35	A7 10c dk violet ('36)	1.75	.25
36	A7 12c ultra ('36)	2.10	2.00
36A	A7 15c ultra ('41)	14.00	65.00
37	A7 25c rose red & pale vio ('36)	3.00	1.50
38	A7 30c org & dk vio ('36)	1.50	1.25
39	A7 40c dk vio & car ('36)	1.25	2.40
40	A7 50c black, emer ('36)	2.50	2.00
41	A7 $1 red & blk, blue ('36)	2.50	8.00
42	A7 $2 rose red & green ('36)	15.00	2.00
43	A7 $5 brn red & grn, emer ('36)	6.00	87.50
	Nos. 29-43 (18)	79.65	303.65

The 3c was printed on both ordinary and chalky paper; the 15c only on ordinary paper; other values only on chalky paper.

Values for Nos. 34A used and 36A used are for stamps with legible postmarks dated in 1941.

A 2c brown orange and 6c gray, type A7, exist, but are not known to have been regularly issued.

For overprints see Nos. N1-N21.

Catalogue values for unused stamps in this section, from this point to the end of the section, are for Never Hinged items.

Common Design Types pictured following the introduction.

Silver Wedding Issue
Common Design Types
Inscribed: "Malaya Pahang"

Perf. 14x14½

1948, Dec. 1   **Photo.**   **Wmk. 4**

44	CD304 10c purple	.50	.55

Perf. 11½x11

Engraved; Name Typopgraphed

45	CD305 $5 green	27.50	37.50

Pahang Four cents

Perak No. 52 Surcharged

Pahang Five cents

Four cents.

UPU Issue
Common Design Types
Inscribed: "Malaya-Pahang"
Engr.; Name Typo. on 15c, 25c

1949, Oct. 10   **Perf. 13½, 11x11½**

46	CD306 10c rose violet	.30	.25
47	CD307 15c indigo	1.10	1.50
48	CD308 25c orange	.60	2.50
49	CD309 50c slate	1.00	3.00
	Nos. 46-49 (4)	3.00	7.25

Sultan Abu Bakar — A8

Perf. 18

1950, June 1   **Wmk. 4**   **Typo.**

50	A8 1c black	.30	.30
51	A8 2c orange	.30	.30
52	A8 3c green	.30	.80
53	A8 4c chocolate	2.25	.35
54	A8 6c gray	.50	.35
55	A8 8c rose red	.50	2.00
56	A8 10c plum	.30	.30
57	A8 15c ultramarine	.75	.35
58	A8 20c dk green & blk	1.00	3.00
59	A8 25c org & rose lilac	.50	.30
60	A8 40c dk vio & rose red	2.25	8.50
61	A8 50c dp ultra & black	1.50	.35
62	A8 $1 vio brn & ultra	3.50	3.50
63	A8 $2 rose red & emer	16.00	30.00
64	A8 $5 choc & emer	65.00	90.00

1952-55

65	A8 5c rose violet	.50	.70
66	A8 8c green	1.25	1.10
67	A8 12c rose red	1.50	1.25
68	A8 20c ultramarine	2.50	.30
69	A8 30c plum & rose red ('55)	2.75	.50
70	A8 35c dk vio & rose red	1.00	.35
	Nos. 50-70 (21)	104.45	144.60

Coronation Issue
Common Design Type

1953, June 2   **Engr.**   **Perf. 13½x13**

71	CD312 10c magenta & black	2.25	.25

Types of Kedah with Portrait of Sultan Abu Bakar

Perf. 13x12½, 12½x13, 13½ ($1)

1957-62   **Engr.**   **Wmk. 314**

72	A8 1c black	.25	.25
73	A8 2c red orange	.25	.25
74	A8 4c dark brown	.25	.25
75	A8 5c dark car rose	.25	.25
76	A8 8c dark green	2.25	2.25
77	A7 10c chocolate	1.25	.25
78	A7 20c blue	2.75	.25
79	A7 50c ultra & blk ('60)	1.00	.25
a.	Perf. 12½	.60	1.00
80	A8 $1 plum & ultra	10.00	2.75
81	A8 $2 red & green ('62)	9.00	22.50
a.	Perf. 12½	7.50	11.00
82	A8 $5 ol grn & brn ('60)	15.00	24.00
a.	Perf. 12½	14.00	17.50
	Nos. 72-82 (11)	42.25	53.25

Starting in 1965, issues of Pahang are listed with Malaysia.

OCCUPATION STAMPS

Issued under Japanese Occupation

Stamps of Pahang, 1935-41, Handstamped in Black, Red, Brown or Violet

1942   **Wmk. 4**   **Perf. 14**

N1	A7 1c black	35.00	40.00
N1A	A7 3c green	125.00	140.00
N2	A7 5c chocolate	15.00	9.50
N3	A7 6c rose red	26.00	11.00
N3A	A7 8c gray	240.00	240.00
N4	A7 10c dk violet	60.00	60.00
N5	A7 12c ultramarine	1,200.	1,200.
N6	A7 15c ultramarine	87.50	87.50
N7	A7 25c rose red & pale vio	21.00	37.50
N8	A7 30c org & dk vio	17.00	32.50
N9	A7 40c dk vio & car	17.50	35.00
N10	A7 50c blk, emerald	300.00	350.00

N11	A7 $1 red & blk, bl	100.00	125.00
N12	A7 $5 brown red & grn, emer	575.00	625.00

Some authorities claim the 2c green, 4c brown orange, 6c rose red and $2 rose red and green were not regularly issued with this overprint.

Stamps of Pahang, 1935-41, Overprinted in Black

N13	A7 1c black	2.00	1.10
N14	A7 5c chocolate	2.00	2.00
N15	A7 8c rose red	35.00	3.75
N16	A7 10c violet brown	20.00	9.00
N17	A7 12c ultramarine	2.00	3.00
N18	A7 25c rose red & pale vio	7.50	10.50
N19	A7 30c org & dk vio	2.75	5.50
	Nos. N13-N19 (7)	71.25	34.85

Pahang No. 32 Overprinted and Surcharged in Black

e   f

1943

N20	A7(e) 6c on 5c chocolate	1.40	1.40
N21	A7(f) 6c on 5c chocolate	2.00	1.50

The Japanese characters read: "Japanese Postal Service."

PENANG

pə-naŋ

LOCATION — An island off the west coast of the Malay Peninsula, plus a coastal strip called Province Wellesley.

AREA — 400 sq. mi.

POP. — 616,254 (1960)

CAPITAL — Georgetown

Catalogue values for unused stamps in this section are for Never Hinged items.

Common Design Types pictured following the introduction.

Silver Wedding Issue
Common Design Types
Inscribed: "Malaya Penang"

Perf. 14x14½

1948, Dec. 1   **Wmk. 4**   **Photo.**

1	CD304 10c purple	.50	.30

Perf. 11½x11

Engraved; Name Typographed

2	CD305 $5 lt brown	40.00	37.50

Type of Straits Settlements, 1937-41, Inscribed "Penang"

1949-52   **Perf. 18**

3	A29 1c black	1.50	.30
4	A29 2c orange	1.50	.30
5	A29 3c green	.60	1.25
6	A29 4c chocolate	.50	.25
7	A29 5c rose vio ('52)	4.25	4.00
8	A29 6c gray	1.50	.30
9	A29 8c rose red	1.25	5.00
10	A29 8c green ('52)	4.00	3.00
11	A29 10c plum	.50	.25
12	A29 12c rose red ('52)	4.50	9.00
13	A29 15c ultramarine	2.00	.40
14	A29 20c dk grn & blk	2.75	1.50
15	A29 20c ultra ('52)	3.25	1.50
16	A29 25c org & rose lilac	3.00	1.25
17	A29 35c dk vio & rose red ('52)	3.25	1.50
18	A29 40c dk vio & rose red	4.25	15.00
19	A29 50c ultra & black	5.50	.30
20	A29 $1 vio brn & ultra	20.00	3.00

Perak No. 45
Overprinted

1894

O10	A7	5c blue	90.00	1.25
a.		Inverted overprint	1,200.	550.00

Same Overprint on No. 51

1897

O11	A9	5c lilac & olive	3.50	.60
a.		Double overprint	700.00	450.00

OCCUPATION STAMPS

Issued under Japanese Occupation

Stamps of Perak, 1938-41, Handstamped in Black, Red, Brown or Violet

1942		**Wmk. 4**		**Perf. 14**
N1	A15	1c black	50.00	35.00
N2	A15	2c brn orange	35.00	21.00
N3	A15	3c green	35.00	37.50
N4	A15	5c chocolate	11.50	11.00
N5	A15	8c gray	55.00	37.50
N6	A15	8c rose red	25.00	35.00
N7	A15	10c dk violet	22.50	27.50
N8	A15	12c ultramarine	150.00	150.00
N9	A15	15c ultramarine	30.00	35.00
N10	A15	25c rose red & pale vio	27.50	30.00
N11	A15	30c org & dk vio	35.00	40.00
N12	A15	40c dk vio & rose red	175.00	190.00
N13	A15	50c blk, emerald	57.50	60.00
N14	A15	$1 red & blk, bl	275.00	300.00
N15	A15	$2 rose red & grn	1,500.	1,500.
N16	A15	$5 red, emerald	750.00	750.00

Some authorities claim No. N6 was not regularly issued. This overprint also exists on No. 85

Stamps of Perak, 1938-41, Overprinted in Black

N16A	A15	1c black	40.00	40.00
N17	A15	2c brn org	1.60	1.60
a.		Inverted overprint	27.50	29.00
N18	A15	3c green	1.25	1.40
a.		Inverted overprint	27.50	30.00
N18B	A15	5c chocolate	40.00	
N19	A15	8c rose red	1.25	.65
a.		Inverted overprint	10.00	10.00
b.		Dbl. ovpt., one invtd.	250.00	275.00
c.		Pair, one without ovpt.	500.00	475.00
N20	A15	10c dk violet	8.50	9.50
N21	A15	15c ultramarine	6.00	6.75
N21A	A15	30c org & dk vio	35.00	35.00
N22	A15	50c blk, emerald	4.00	6.00
N23	A15	$1 red & blk, bl	350.00	375.00
N24	A15	$5 red, emerald	60.00	67.50
a.		Inverted overprint	350.00	400.00

Some authorities claim Nos. N16A, N18B and N21A were not regularly issued.

Overprinted on Perak No. 87 and Surcharged in Black "2 Cents"

N25	A15	2c on 5c chocolate	2.00	1.40

Perak Nos. 84 and 89A
Overprinted in Black

N26	A15	1c black	3.25	4.00
a.		Inverted overprint	35.00	40.00
N27	A15	8c rose red	3.25	2.00
a.		Inverted overprint	20.00	24.00

Overprinted on Perak No. 87 and Surcharged in Black "2 Cents"

N28	A15	2c on 5c chocolate	5.00	5.00
a.		Inverted overprint	35.00	47.50
b.		As "a," "2 Cents" omitted	50.00	57.50

Stamps of Perak, 1938-41, Overprinted or Surcharged in Black

n   No. N31

No. N32

1943

N29	A15	1c black	.65	.65
N30	A15	2c brn orange	35.00	35.00
N31	A15	2c on 5c choc	1.00	1.00
a.		"2 Cents" inverted	35.00	40.00
b.		Entire surcharge inverted	35.00	40.00
N32	A15	2c on 5c choc	1.40	1.40
a.		Vertical characters invtd.	35.00	40.00
b.		Entire surcharge inverted	35.00	40.00
N33	A15	3c green	37.50	37.50
N34	A15	5c chocolate	1.00	1.00
a.		Inverted overprint	50.00	60.00
N35	A15	8c gray	35.00	35.00
N36	A15	8c rose red	1.00	1.00
a.		Inverted overprint	35.00	40.00
N37	A15	10c dk violet	1.25	1.25
N38	A15	30c org & dk vio	2.75	4.00
N39	A15	50c blk, emerald	5.50	9.50
N40	A15	$5 red, emerald	75.00	85.00
		Nos. N29-N40 (12)	197.05	212.30

No. N34 was also used in the Shan States of Burma. The Japanese characters read: "Japanese Postal Service."

Some authorities claim Nos. N30, N33 and N35 were not regularly issued.

PERLIS

'per-ləs

LOCATION — On the west coast of the Malay peninsula, adjoining Siam and Kedah.
AREA — 310 sq. mi.
POP. — 97,645 (1960)
CAPITAL — Kangar

> Catalogue values for unused stamps in this section are for Never Hinged items.

Common Design Types pictured following the introduction.

Silver Wedding Issue
Common Design Types
Inscribed: "Malaya Perlis"

Perf. 14x14½

1948, Dec. 1		**Photo.**	**Wmk. 4**
1	CD304	10c purple	1.00 3.00

Engraved; Name Typographed
Perf. 11½x11

2	CD305	$5 lt brown	32.50 55.00

UPU Issue
Common Design Types
Inscribed: "Malaya-Perlis"
Engr.; Name Typo. on 15c, 25c

1949, Oct. 10			**Perf. 13½, 11x11½**
3	CD306	10c rose violet	.40 2.00
4	CD307	15c indigo	1.40 4.50
5	CD308	25c orange	.65 3.50
6	CD309	50c slate	1.50 4.25
		Nos. 3-6 (4)	3.95 14.25

Raja Syed Putra — A1

Perf. 18			
1951, Mar. 26	**Wmk. 4**		**Typo.**
7	A1	1c black	.25 1.00
8	A1	2c orange	.75 .70
9	A1	3c green	1.75 5.25
10	A1	4c chocolate	1.75 1.50
11	A1	6c gray	1.50 2.50
12	A1	8c rose red	3.75 7.50
13	A1	10c plum	1.25 .50
14	A1	15c ultramarine	5.00 8.50
15	A1	20c dk green & blk	4.50 11.50
16	A1	25c org & rose lilac	2.25 3.75
17	A1	40c dk vio & rose red	5.00 29.00
18	A1	50c ultra & black	4.75 7.00
19	A1	$1 vio brn & ultra	10.00 27.50
20	A1	$2 rose red & emer	20.00 60.00
21	A1	$5 choc & emerald	70.00 125.00
1952-55			
22	A1	5c rose violet	.75 3.75
23	A1	8c green	2.75 4.50
24	A1	12c rose red	2.00 6.25
25	A1	20c ultramarine	1.25 1.75
26	A1	30c plum & rose red ('55)	2.75 15.00
27	A1	35c dk vio & rose red	3.00 8.50
		Nos. 7-27 (21)	145.00 330.95

Coronation Issue
Common Design Type

1953, June 2	**Engr.**	**Perf. 13½x13**
28	CD312	10c magenta & black	1.75 4.00

Types of Kedah with Portrait of Raja Syed Putra
Perf. 13x12½, 12½x13, 12½ ($2, $5), 13½ ($1)

1957-62	**Engr.**	**Wmk. 314**
29	A8	1c black	.25 .40
30	A8	2c red orange	.25 .40
31	A8	4c dark brown	.25 .25
32	A8	5c dk car rose	.25 .25
33	A8	8c dark green	2.50 2.25
34	A7	10c chocolate	1.50 3.00
35	A7	20c blue	3.50 5.00
36	A7	50c ultra & blk ('62)	3.50 4.75
a.		Perf. 12½	1.50 4.00
37	A8	$1 plum & ultra	10.00 14.00
38	A8	$2 red & green	10.00 10.00
39	A8	$5 ol green & brown	15.00 13.00
		Nos. 29-39 (11)	47.00 53.30

Starting in 1965, issues of Perlis are listed with Malaysia.

SELANGOR

sə-'laŋ‑ər

LOCATION — South of Perak on the west coast of the Malay Peninsula.
AREA — 3,160 sq. mi.
POP. — 1,012,891 (1960)
CAPITAL — Kuala Lumpur

Stamps of the Straits Settlements Overprinted

Handstamped in Black or Red

1878		**Wmk. 1**	**Perf. 14**
1	A2	2c brown (Bk)	—
		Wmk. 2	**Perf.**
2	A2	2c brown (R)	600.00

The authenticity of Nos. 1-2 is questioned.

Overprinted in Black

1882			
3	A2	2c brown	— 3,300.

Overprinted

Overprint 16 to 16¾mm Wide

1881			**Wmk. 1**
5	A2	2c brown	140.00 140.00
a.		Double overprint	

Overprint 16 to 17mm Wide

1882-83			**Wmk. 2**
"S" wide, all other letters narrow			
6	A2	2c brown	200.00 160.00
7	A2	2c rose	160.00 125.00

Overprinted

Overprint 14¼x3mm

8	A2	2c rose	11.50	24.00
a.		Double overprint	975.00	850.00

Overprinted

Overprint 14½ to 15½mm Wide

1886-89			
9	A2	2c rose	42.50 55.00

Overprinted

Overprint 16½x1¾mm

9A	A2	2c rose	67.50	72.50
b.		Double overprint		1,000.

Overprinted

Overprint 15½ to 17mm Wide
With Period

10	A2	2c rose	140.00	90.00

Without Period

11	A2	2c rose	14.50	3.25

Same Overprint, but Vertically

12	A2	2c rose	22.50	37.50

Overprinted

12A	A2	2c rose	150.00	3.75

Overprinted

13	A2	2c rose	1,700.	1,850.

Overprint 17mm Wide

Overprinted

14	A2	2c rose	400.00	175.00

Overprinted Vertically

1889
15 A2 2c rose   725.00 40.00

Overprinted Vertically

Overprint 19 to 20¾mm Wide
16 A2 2c rose   325.00 95.00
Similar Overprint, but Diagonally
17 A2 2c rose   3,000.

Overprinted Vertically

18 A2 2c rose   90.00 6.75
Same Overprint Horizontally
18A A2 2c rose   4,500.

Surcharged in Black

a   b

c   d

e

1891
19 A3 (a) 2c on 24c green   40.00   75.00
20 A3 (b) 2c on 24c green 225.00 275.00
21 A3 (c) 2c on 24c green 225.00 250.00
22 A3 (d) 2c on 24c green 125.00 150.00
23 A3 (e) 2c on 24c green 275.00 275.00
      Nos. 19-23 (5)   840.00 1,025.

No. 22a occurred ijn the first printing in one
position (R. 8/3) in the sheet.

A6

1891-95   Typo.   Wmk. 2
24 A6 1c green   1.75   .30
25 A6 2c rose   4.00 1.25
26 A6 2c orange ('95) 3.00 1.00
27 A6 5c blue   27.50 5.25
      Nos. 24-27 (4)   36.25 7.80

Type of 1891
Surcharged

3 CENTS

1894
28 A6 3c on 5c rose   5.00   .70

A8

A9

1895-99   Wmk. 2   Perf. 14
29 A8 3c lilac & car rose   7.00   .35
30 A8 5c lilac & olive   8.50   .35
31 A8 8c lilac & blue   55.00 8.50
32 A8 10c lilac & orange   13.50 2.50
33 A8 25c grn & car rose   90.00 60.00
34 A8 50c lilac & black   80.00 29.00
35 A8 50c green & black   475.00 140.00

Wmk. 1
36 A9 $1 green & lt grn   65.00 150.00
37 A9 $2 grn & car rose   250.00 300.00
38 A9 $3 green & olive   600.00 500.00
39 A9 $5 green & ultra   300.00 400.00
40 A9 $10 grn & brn vio   800.00 1,000.
41 A9 $25 green & org   4,000. 4,000.
      Nos. 29-39, Ovpt. "SPECI-
      MEN"   450.00

High values with revenue cancellations are
plentiful and inexpensive.

Surcharged in Black

One cent.   Three cents.

1900   Wmk. 2
42 A8 1c on 5c lilac & olive 75.00 125.00
43 A8 1c on 50c grn & blk   3.50   29.00
a.   Surcharge reading "cent
     One cent."   3,500.
44 A8 3c on 50c grn & blk   6.00   26.00
      Nos. 42-44 (3)   84.50 180.00

Mosque at   Sultan
Klang   Sulaiman
A12   A13

1935-41   Typo.   Wmk. 4   Perf. 14
45 A12 1c black ('36)   .30   .25
46 A12 2c dp green ('36)   .55   .25
46A A12 2c org brn ('41)   2.25   1.25
46B A12 3c green ('41)   1.25   8.00
47 A12 4c orange brown   .30   .25
48 A12 5c chocolate   .70   .25
49 A12 6c rose red ('37)   4.00   .35
50 A12 8c gray   .35   .25
51 A12 10c dk violet ('36)   .35   .25
52 A12 12c ultra ('36)   .90   .25
52A A12 15c ultra ('41)   7.00   35.00
53 A12 25c rose red &
        pale vio ('36)   .60   .80
54 A12 30c dk vio &
        dk vio ('36)   .60   1.10
55 A12 40c dk vio & car   1.50   1.25
56 A12 50c blk, emer ('36)   1.00   .50
57 A13 $1 red & black,
        blue ('36)   6.00   1.10
58 A13 $2 rose red &
        green ('36)   17.50 9.50
59 A13 $5 brn red & grn,
        emer ('36)   55.00 30.00
      Nos. 45-59 (18)   100.15 90.50
      Set, never hinged   170.00

Nos. 46A-46B were printed on both ordinary
and chalky paper; 15c only on ordinary paper;
other values only on chalky paper.
   An 8c rose red was prepared but not issued.
   For overprints see Nos. N1-N15, N18A-N24,
N26-N39.

Sultan Hisam-ud-Din
Alam Shah — A14

1941
72 A14 $1 red & blk, blue   11.50 7.00
73 A14 $2 car & green   30.00 40.00
      Set, never hinged   70.00

A $5 stamp of type A14, issued during the
Japanese occupation with different overprints

(Nos. N18, N25A, N42), also exists without
overprint. The unoverprinted stamp was not
issued. Value $125.
   For overprints see Nos. N16-N17, N24A,
N25, N40-N41.

Catalogue values for unused
stamps in this section, from this
point to the end of the section, are
for Never Hinged items.

Common Design Types
pictured following the introduction.

Silver Wedding Issue
Common Design Types
Inscribed: "Malaya Selangor"
Perf. 14x14½
1948, Dec. 1   Photo.   Wmk. 4
74 CD304 10c purple   .25   .30
Perf. 11½x11
Engraved; Name Typographed
75 CD305 $5 green   30.00 25.00

UPU Issue
Common Design Types
Inscribed: "Malaya-Selangor"
Engr.; Name Typo. on Nos. 77 & 78
1949, Oct. 10   Perf. 13½, 11x11½
76 CD306 10c rose violet   .40   .30
77 CD307 15c indigo   2.50   2.50
78 CD308 25c orange   .50   4.50
79 CD309 50c slate   1.50   5.00
      Nos. 76-79 (4)   4.90   12.30

Sultan Hisam-ud-Din
Alam Shah — A15

1949, Sept. 12   Typo.   Perf. 18
80 A15 1c black   .25   .60
81 A15 2c orange   .30   1.50
82 A15 3c green   4.00   2.00
83 A15 4c chocolate   .50   .35
84 A15 6c gray   .35   .35
85 A15 8c rose red   2.00   1.25
86 A15 10c plum   .25   .25
87 A15 15c ultramarine   8.00   .35
88 A15 20c dk grn & black   5.00   .50
89 A15 25c orange & rose lil 2.00   .35
90 A15 40c dk vio & rose red 11.00 8.00
91 A15 50c ultra & black   3.50   .35
92 A15 $1 vio brn & ultra   4.00   .60
93 A15 $2 rose red & emer   15.00 1.10
94 A15 $5 choc & emerald   55.00 3.00

1952-55
95 A15 5c rose violet   1.00   2.75
96 A15 8c green   1.00   1.75
97 A15 12c rose red   1.25   3.50
98 A15 20c ultramarine   1.25   .35
99 A15 30c plum & rose red
        ('55)   2.25   2.25
100 A15 35c dk vio & rose
        red   1.50   1.50
      Nos. 80-100 (21)   119.40 32.65

Coronation Issue
Common Design Type
1953, June 2   Engr.   Perf. 13½x13
101 CD312 10c magenta & black 1.75 .25

A16

Sultan Hisam-
ud-Din Alam
Shah — A17

Designs as in Kelantan, 1957.

Perf. 13x12½, 12½x13, 13½ ($1)
1957-60   Engr.   Wmk. 314
102 A17 1c black   .25   2.50
103 A17 2c red orange   .50   1.00
104 A17 4c dark brown   .25   .25
105 A17 5c dark car rose   .25   .25
106 A17 8c dark green   3.00   4.00
107 A16 10c chocolate   2.50   .25
108 A16 20c blue   3.25   .25
109 A16 50c ultra & blk ('60) 1.00 .25
a.   Perf. 12½   .40   .25
110 A17 $1 plum & ultra   4.50   .25
111 A17 $2 red & grn ('60)   5.50   3.00
a.   Perf. 12½   4.00   3.00
112 A17 $5 ol grn & brn ('60) 12.00 2.40
a.   Perf. 12½   12.00 3.00
      Nos. 102-112 (11)   33.00 14.40
      See Nos. 114-120.

Sultan
Salahuddin
Abdul Aziz
Shah — A18

1961, June 28 Photo.   Perf. 14½x14
113 A18 10s multicolored   .30   .25

Sultan Salahuddin Abdul Aziz Shah,
installation.

**Types of 1957 with Portrait of
Sultan Salahuddin Abdul Aziz Shah**

Designs as before.
Perf. 13x12½, 12½x13
1961-62   Engr.   Wmk. 338
114 A17 1c black   .40   2.75
115 A17 2c red orange   .40   3.00
116 A17 4c dark brown   1.00   .25
117 A17 5c dark car rose   1.00   .25
118 A17 8c dark green   4.75   6.00
119 A16 10c vio brown ('61) .90   .25
120 A16 20c blue   8.00   1.50
      Nos. 114-120 (7)   16.45 14.00

Starting in 1965, issues of Selangor are
listed with Malaysia.

OCCUPATION STAMPS

Issued under Japanese Occupation

Stamps of Selangor
1935-41 Handstamped
Vertically or Horizontally
in Black, Red, Brown or
Violet

1942, Apr. 3   Wmk. 4   Perf. 14
N1 A12 1c black   15.00 21.00
N2 A12 2c deep green   600.00 600.00
N3 A12 2c orange brown   55.00 55.00
N4 A12 3c green   35.00 17.00
N5 A12 5c chocolate   10.00 10.00
N6 A12 6c rose red   200.00 200.00
N7 A12 8c gray   27.50 27.50
N8 A12 10c dark violet   22.50 27.50
N9 A12 12c ultramarine   47.50 47.50
N10 A12 15c ultramarine   17.00 20.00
N11 A12 25c rose red &
        pale vio   80.00 95.00
N12 A12 30c org & dk vio   15.00 30.00
N13 A12 40c dk vio & car   100.00 140.00
N14 A12 50c blk, emerald   40.00 47.50
N15 A13 $5 brn red & grn,
        emer   275.00 275.00

Some authorities believe No. N15 was not
issued regularly.

**Handstamped Vertically on Stamps
and Type of Selangor 1941 in Black
or Red**
N16 A14 $1 red & blk, bl   67.50 80.00
N17 A14 $2 car & green   80.00 110.00
N18 A14 $5 brn red & grn,
        emer   110.00 110.00

Stamps and Type of
Selangor, 1935-41,
Overprinted in Black

1942, May
N18A A12 1c black   110.00 110.00
N19 A12 3c green   1.00   1.00
N19A A12 5c chocolate   110.00 110.00
N20 A12 10c dark violet   35.00 35.00

N21	A12	12c ultramarine	2.75	5.00
N22	A12	15c ultramarine	5.50	4.00
N23	A12	30c org & dk vio	35.00	35.00
N24	A12	40c dk vio & car	4.00	4.00
N24A	A14	$1 red & blk, *bl*	35.00	35.00
N25	A14	$2 car & green	24.00	30.00
N25A	A14	$5 red & grn, *emer*	55.00	55.00
		Nos. N18A-N25A (11)	417.25	424.00

Overprint is horizontal on $1, $2, $5.
On Nos. N18A and N19 the overprint is known reading up, instead of down.
Some authorities claim Nos. N18A, N19A, N20, N23, N24A and N25A were not regularly issued.

Selangor No. 46B
Overprinted in Black

1942, Dec.

N26	A12	3c green	400.00	400.00

Stamps and Type of Selangor, 1935-41, Ovptd. or Srchd. in Black or Red

i   k

l   m

1943

N27	A12(i)	1c black	1.40	1.40
N28	A12(k)	1c black (R)	.90	.90
N29	A12(l)	2c on 5c choc (R)	.90	.90
N30	A12(i)	3c green	1.00	1.00
N31	A12(l)	3c on 5c choc	.65	1.00
N32	A12(k)	5c choc (R)	.65	1.00
N33	A12(l)	6c on 5c choc	.25	.90
N34	A12(m)	6c on 5c choc	.25	1.00
N35	A12(i)	12c ultra	1.40	1.60
N36	A12(i)	15c ultra	6.75	10.00
N37	A12(k)	15c ultra	13.50	13.50
N38	A12(m)	$1 on 10c dk vio	.50	1.40
N39	A12(m)	$1.50 on 30c org & dk vio	.50	1.40
N40	A14(i)	$1 red & blk, *blue*	6.75	8.50
N41	A14(i)	$2 car & grn	24.00	24.00
N42	A14(i)	$5 brn red & grn, *em-er*	50.00	55.00
		Nos. N27-N42 (16)	109.40	123.50

The "i" overprint is vertical on Nos. N40-N42 and is also found reading in the opposite direction on Nos. N30, N35 and N36.
The overprint reads: "Japanese Postal Service."

Singapore is listed following Sierra Leone.

SUNGEI UJONG

ˈsuŋ-ü-juŋ

Formerly a nonfederated native state on the Malay Peninsula, which in 1895 was consolidated with the Federated State of Negri Sembilan.

Stamps of the Straits Settlements
Overprinted in Black

Overprinted

1878   **Wmk. 1**   *Perf. 14*

2	A2	2c brown	3,600.	3,900.

Overprinted

4	A2	2c brown	400.00	
5	A2	4c rose	1,950.	2,000.

No. 5 is no longer recognized by some experts.

Overprinted

			S.U.	

1882-83   **Wmk. 2**

6	A2	2c brown	375.00	—
7	A2	4c rose	4,250.	4,800.

This overprint on the 2c brown, wmk. 1, is probably a trial printing.

Overprinted   **SU**

11	A2	2c brown	325.00	400.00

Overprinted

1881-84

14	A2	2c brown	1,200.	550.00
15	A2	2c rose	140.00	140.00
a.		"Ujong" printed sideways		
b.		"Sungei" printed twice		
16	A2	4c brown	325.00	425.00
17	A3	8c orange	2,250.	1,700.
18	A7	10c slate	725.00	625.00

Overprinted

19	A2	2c brown	57.50	160.00

Overprinted

1885-90   **Without Period**

20	A2	2c rose	45.00	77.50

With Period

21	A2	2c rose	125.00	90.00
a.		"UNJOG"	5,750.	4,000.

Overprinted

22	A2	2c rose	95.00	110.00
a.		Double overprint	775.00	775.00

Overprinted

23	A2	2c rose	125.00	150.00

Overprinted

24	A2	2c rose	30.00	47.50
a.		Double overprint		

Overprinted

25	A2	2c rose	110.00	125.00

Overprinted

26	A2	2c rose	175.00	175.00
c.		Double overprint		

Overprint 14-16x3mm

26A	A2	2c rose	12.00	16.00

Overprinted

26B	A2	2c rose	50.00	21.00

Stamp of 1883-91 Surcharged

a   b

c   d

1891

27	A3 (a)	2c on 24c green	240.	275.
28	A3 (b)	2c on 24c green	1,100.	1,200.
29	A3 (c)	2c on 24c green	425.	500.
30	A3 (d)	2c on 24c green	1,100.	1,200.
		Nos. 27-30 (4)	2,865.	3,175.

On Nos. 27-28, SUNGEI is 14½mm, UJONG 12¾x2½mm.

A3

1891-94   **Typo.**   *Perf. 14*

31	A3	2c rose	40.00	35.00
32	A3	2c orange ('94)	2.25	5.50
33	A3	5c blue ('93)	6.50	7.75
		Nos. 31-33 (3)	48.75	48.25

Type of 1891
Surcharged in Black

1894

34	A3	1c on 5c green	1.40	.90
35	A3	3c on 5c rose	3.25	6.00

A4

1895

36	A4	3c lilac & car rose	15.00	4.75

Stamps of Sungei Ujong were superseded by those of Negri Sembilan in 1895.

TRENGGANU

treŋ-ˈgä-ˌnü

LOCATION — On the eastern coast of the Malay Peninsula.
AREA — 5,050 sq. mi.
POP. — 302,171 (1960)
CAPITAL — Kuala Trengganu

Sultan Zenalabidin
A1   A2

1910-19   **Typo.**   **Wmk. 3**   *Perf. 14*
Ordinary Paper

1a	A1	1c blue green	2.10	1.25
2	A1	2c red vio & brn ('15)	1.25	1.10
3	A1	3c rose red	2.75	2.75
4	A1	4c brn orange	4.25	6.75
5	A1	4c grn & org brn ('15)	2.50	5.75
6	A1	4c scarlet ('19)	1.50	2.10
7	A1	5c gray	1.75	4.50
8	A1	5c choc & gray ('15)	3.00	2.40
9	A1	8c ultramarine	1.75	11.00
10	A1	10c red & grn, *yel* ('15)	1.75	2.75

Chalky Paper

11a	A1	10c violet, *pale yel*	4.00	9.00
12	A1	20c red vio & vio	4.25	5.75
13	A1	25c dl vio & grn ('15)	9.75	42.50
14	A1	30c blk & dl vio ('15)	8.50	65.00
15	A1	50c blk & sep, *grn*	5.75	11.50
16	A1	$1 red & blk, *blue*	22.50	29.00

17	A1	$3 red & grn, *grn* ('15)		225.00	500.00
18	A2	$5 lil & blue grn		225.00	675.00
19	A2	$25 green & car		1,200.	2,750.
		Revenue Cancel			300.00
		Nos. 1a-19 (19)		1,727.	4,128.

On No. 19 the numerals and Arabic inscriptions at top, left and right are in color on a colorless background.

Overprints are listed after No. 41. For surcharges see Nos. B1-B4.

Sultan Badaru'l-alam
A3   A4

1921-38   Wmk. 4   Perf. 14
Chalky Paper

20	A3	1c black ('25)		2.75	1.75
21	A3	2c deep green		1.75	2.40
22	A3	3c dp grn ('25)		3.00	1.10
23	A3	3c lt brn ('38)		32.50	22.50
24	A3	4c rose red		2.40	2.00
25	A3	5c choc & gray		3.25	8.00
26	A3	5c vio, *yel* ('25)		2.75	2.00
27	A3	6c orange ('24)		6.00	.85
28	A3	8c gray ('38)		42.50	9.50
29	A3	10c ultramarine		3.25	1.50
30	A3	12c ultra ('25)		7.00	7.25
31	A3	20c org & dl vio		3.50	2.40
32	A3	25c dk vio & grn		3.75	5.00
33	A3	30c blk & dl vio		5.50	6.00
34	A3	35c red, *yel* ('25)		7.75	12.50
35	A3	50c car & green		11.50	5.25
36	A3	$1 ultra & vio, *bl* ('29)		15.00	6.00
37	A3	$3 red & green, *emer* ('25)		87.50	240.00
38	A4	$5 red & grn, *yel* ('38)		500.00	2,800.
39	A4	$25 blue & lil		750.00	1,250.
40	A4	$50 org & green		1,850.	3,200.
41	A4	$100 red & green		5,750.	7,500.
		Nos. 20-37 (18)		241.65	336.00

On Nos. 39 to 41 the numerals and Arabic inscriptions at top, left and right are in color on a colorless background.

A 2c orange, 6c gray, 8c rose red and 16c ultramarine, type A3, exist, but are not known to have been regularly issued.

For surcharges and overprints see Nos. 45-46, N1-N60.

Stamps of 1910-21
Overprinted in Black

1922, Mar.   Wmk. 3

8a	A1	5c chocolate & gray		4.75	37.50
10a	A1	10c red & green, *yel*		4.75	37.50
12a	A1	20c red vio & violet		4.25	50.00
13a	A1	25c dull vio & green		4.25	50.00
14a	A1	30c black & dull vio		4.25	50.00
15a	A1	50c blk & sepia, *grn*		4.25	50.00
16a	A1	$1 red & blk, *blue*		20.00	95.00
17a	A1	$3 red & grn, *green*		210.00	575.00
18a	A2	$5 lil & blue green		300.00	575.00
			Wmk. 4		
21a	A3	2c deep green		2.75	47.50
24a	A3	4c rose red		7.75	47.50
		Nos. 8a-24a (11)		567.00	1,615.

Industrial fair at Singapore, Mar. 31-Apr. 15.

1921   Wmk. 3   Chalky Paper

42	A3	$1 ultra & vio, *bl*		20.00	40.00
43	A3	$3 red & grn, *emer*		140.00	160.00
44	A4	$5 red & green, *yel*		140.00	150.00
		Nos. 42-44 (3)		300.00	350.00

Types of 1921-25
Surcharged in Black

1941, May 1   Wmk. 4   Perf. 13½x14

45	A3	2c on 5c magenta, *yel*		5.50	6.50
46	A3	8c on 10c lt ultra		9.50	6.50

For overprints see Nos. N30-N33, N46-N47, N59-N60.

> **Catalogue values for unused stamps in this section, from this point to the end of the section, are for Never Hinged items.**

Common Design Types pictured following the introduction.

Silver Wedding Issue
Common Design Types
Inscribed: "Malaya Trengganu"
1948, Dec. 1   Photo.   Perf. 14x14½

47	CD304	10c purple		.25	.25

Engraved; Name Typographed
Perf. 11½x11

48	CD305	$5 rose car		35.00	62.50

UPU Issue
Common Design Types
Inscribed: "Malaya-Trengganu"
Engr.; Name Typo. on 15c, 25c
Perf. 13½, 11x11½
1949, Oct. 10   Wmk. 4

49	CD306	10c rose violet		.65	.65
50	CD307	15c indigo		.80	2.10
51	CD308	25c orange		1.40	3.50
52	CD309	50c slate		2.10	3.50
		Nos. 49-52 (4)		4.95	9.75

Sultan Ismail
Nasiruddin Shah — A5

1949, Dec. 27   Typo.   Perf. 18

53	A5	1c black		.40	.45
54	A5	2c orange		.40	.50
55	A5	3c green		1.25	1.50
56	A5	4c chocolate		.00	.50
57	A5	6c gray		1.25	1.25
58	A5	8c rose red		1.60	1.90
59	A5	10c plum		.60	.50
60	A5	15c ultramarine		1.75	1.60
61	A5	20c dk grn & black		2.40	5.00
62	A5	25c org & rose lilac		2.25	3.25
63	A5	40c dk vio & rose red		4.50	27.50
64	A5	50c dp ultra & black		2.75	2.75
65	A5	$1 vio brn & ultra		5.50	10.00
66	A5	$2 rose red & emer		30.00	24.50
67	A5	$5 choc & emerald		80.00	67.50
		1952-55			
68	A5	5c rose violet		.40	.50
69	A5	8c green		1.60	3.25
70	A5	12c rose red		1.60	6.75
71	A5	20c ultramarine		1.60	1.50
72	A5	30c plum & rose red ('55)		3.00	6.75
73	A5	35c dk vio & rose red		3.50	6.75
		Nos. 53-73 (21)		146.95	174.20

Coronation Issue
Common Design Type
1953, June 2   Engr.   Perf. 13½x13

74	CD312	10c magenta & blk		1.50	1.00

Types of Kedah with Portrait of Sultan Ismail
Perf. 13x12½, 12½x13, 13½ ($1), 12½ ($2)
1957-63   Engr.   Wmk. 314

75	A8	1c black		.30	.50
76	A8	2c red orange		1.00	.50
77	A8	4c dark brown		.30	.50
78	A8	5c dark car rose		.30	.50
79	A8	8c dark green		9.00	.50
80	A7	10c chocolate		.40	.50
81	A7	20c bluo		.85	.50
82	A7	50c blue & blk		.40	2.40
a.		Perf. 12½		.50	2.25
83	A8	$1 plum & ultra		9.50	9.50
84	A8	$2 red & green		18.00	12.00
85	A8	$5 ol grn & brn, perf. 12½		27.50	25.00
a.		Perf. 13x12½		32.50	30.00
		Nos. 75-85 (11)		67.55	52.50

Issued: 20c, No. 85, 6/26/57; 2c, 5c, 8c, $1, 7/25/57; 10c, 8/4/57; 1c, 4c, 5c, 8c, $2, 8/21/57; No. 82a, 5/17/60; No. 85a, 8/13/63.

Starting in 1965, issues of Trengganu are listed with Malaysia.

SEMI-POSTAL STAMPS

Nos. 3, 4 and 9
Surcharged

1917, Oct.   Wmk. 3   Perf. 14

B1	A1	3c + 2c rose red		1.50	8.00
a.		"CSOSS"		65.00	100.00
b.		Comma after "2c"		4.00	10.50
c.		Pair, one without surcharge		2,900.	2,900.
B2	A1	4c + 2c brn org		2.25	12.50
a.		"CSOSS"		275.00	275.00
b.		Comma after "2c"		16.00	42.50
B3	A1	8c + 2c ultra		3.50	24.00
a.		"CSOSS"		175.00	210.00
b.		Comma after "2c"		13.00	45.00
		Nos. B1-B3 (3)		7.25	44.50

Same Surcharge on No. 5

1918

B4	A1	4c + 2c grn & org brn		4.25	11.50
a.		Pair, one without surcharge		2,300.	

POSTAGE DUE STAMPS

D1

Perf. 14
1937, Aug. 10   Typo.   Wmk. 4

J1	D1	1c rose red		8.25	65.00
J2	D1	4c green		9.00	72.50
J3	D1	8c lemon		47.50	400.00
J4	D1	10c light brown		92.50	115.00
		Nos. J1-J4 (4)		157.25	652.50
		Set, never hinged		275.00	

For overprints see Nos. NJ1-NJ4.

OCCUPATION STAMPS

Issued under Japanese Occupation

No. N6   No. N17A

Stamps of Trengganu, 1921-38, Handstamped in Black or Brown

1942   Wmk. 4   Perf. 14

N1	A3	1c black		110.00	110.00
N2	A3	2c deep green		190.00	275.00
N3	A3	3c lt brown		140.00	110.00
N4	A3	4c rose red		275.00	190.00
N5	A3	5c violet, *yel*		17.50	19.00
N6	A3	6c orange		13.50	20.00
N7	A3	8c gray		17.50	25.00
N8	A3	10c ultramarine		13.50	27.50
N9	A3	12c ultramarine		15.00	25.00
N10	A3	20c org & dl vio		15.00	22.50
N11	A3	25c dk vio & grn		13.50	27.50
N12	A3	30c blk & dl vio		13.50	25.00
N13	A3	35c red, *yel*		22.50	27.50
N14	A3	50c car & grn		125.00	95.00
N15	A3	$1 ultra & vio, *blue*		1,650.	1,750.
N16	A3	$3 red & grn, *emerald*		125.00	140.00
N17	A4	$5 red & grn, *yellow*		240.00	240.00
N17A	A4	$25 blue & lil		1,500.	
N17B	A4	$50 org & grn		8,800.	
N17C	A4	$100 red & grn		950.00	
		Handstamped in Red			
N18	A3	1c black		275.00	225.00
N19	A3	2c dp green		140.00	160.00
N20	A3	5c violet, *yel*		35.00	20.00
N21	A3	6c orange		20.00	20.00
N22	A3	8c gray		275.00	240.00

N23	A3	10c ultramarine		275.00	275.00
N24	A3	12c ultramarine		55.00	55.00
N25	A3	20c org & dl vio		35.00	35.00
N26	A3	25c dk vio & grn		40.00	40.00
N27	A3	30c blk & dl vio		35.00	35.00
N28	A3	35c red, *yellow*		35.00	20.00
N29	A3	$3 red & grn, *emerald*		100.00	40.00
N29A	A3	$25 blue & lil		500.00	500.00

Handstamped on Nos. 45 and 46 in Black or Red

N30	A3	2c on 5c (Bk)		140.00	140.00
N31	A3	2c on 5c (R)		140.00	140.00
N32	A3	8c on 10c (Bk)		25.00	35.00
N33	A3	8c on 10c (R)		35.00	40.00

Stamps of Trengganu, 1921-38, Overprinted in Black

1942

N34	A3	1c black		15.00	17.00
N35	A3	2c deep green		100.00	140.00
N36	A3	3c light brown		16.00	29.00
N37	A3	4c rose red		15.00	20.00
N38	A3	5c violet, *yel*		10.00	20.00
N39	A3	6c orange		10.00	17.00
N40	A3	8c gray		67.50	20.00
N41	A3	12c ultramarine		10.00	13.50
N42	A3	20c org & dl vio		13.50	20.00
N43	A3	25c dk vio & grn		13.50	17.00
N44	A3	30c blk & dl vio		13.50	17.00
N45	A3	$3 red & grn, *emer*		100.00	140.00

Overprinted on Nos. 45 and 46 in Black

N46	A3	2c on 5c mag, *yel*		13.50	17.00
N47	A3	8c on 10c lt ultra		11.50	20.00
		Nos. N34-N47 (14)		409.00	515.50

Stamps of Trengganu, 1921-38, Overprinted in Black

1943

N48	A3	1c black		13.50	19.00
N49	A3	2c deep green		13.50	27.50
N50	A3	5c violet, *yel*		11.50	27.50
N51	A3	6c orange		15.00	27.50
N52	A3	8c gray		95.00	67.50
N53	A3	10c ultramarine		100.00	175.00
N54	A3	12c ultramarine		19.00	35.00
N55	A3	20c org & dl vio		20.00	35.00
N56	A3	25c dl vio & grn		19.00	35.00
N57	A3	30c blk & dl vio		20.00	35.00
N58	A3	35c red, *yellow*		20.00	40.00

Overprinted on Nos. 45 and 46 in Black

N59	A3	2c on 5c mag, *yel*		11.00	35.00
N60	A3	8c on 10c lt ultra		27.50	25.00
		Nos. N48-N60 (13)		385.00	584.00

The Japanese characters read: "Japanese Postal Service."

OCCUPATION POSTAGE DUE STAMPS

Trengganu Nos. J1-J4 Handstamped in Black or Brown

1942   Wmk. 4   Perf. 14

NJ1	D1	1c rose red		67.50	95.00
NJ2	D1	4c green		125.00	125.00
NJ3	D1	8c lemon		25.00	67.50
NJ4	D1	10c light brown		25.00	50.00
		Nos. NJ1-NJ4 (4)		242.50	337.50

The handstamp reads: "Seal of Post Office of Malayan Military Department."

MALAYSIA

mə-'lā-zh͟ē-ˌə

LOCATION — Malay peninsula and northwestern Borneo
GOVT. — Federation within the British Commonwealth
AREA — 127,317 sq. mi.
POP. — 21,376,066 (1999 est.)
CAPITAL — Putrajaya (administrative); Kuala Lumpur (financial)

The Federation of Malaysia was formed Sept. 16, 1963, by a merger of the former Federation of Malaya, Singapore, Sarawak, and North Borneo (renamed Sabah), totaling 14 states. Singapore withdrew in 1965.

Sabah and Sarawak, having different rates than mainland Malaysia, continued to issue their own stamps after joining the federation. The system of individual state issues was extended to Perak in Oct. 1963, and to the 10 other members in Nov. 1965.

100 Cents (Sen) = 1 Dollar (Ringgit)

Catalogue values for all unused stamps in this country are for Never Hinged items.

Watermarks

Wmk. 233 — "Harrison & Sons, London" in Script

Wmk. 338 — PTM Multiple

Wmk. 378 — Multiple POS in Octagonal Frame

Wmk. 380 — "POST OFFICE"

Wmk. 388 — Multiple "SPM"

Map of Malaysia and 14-point Star — A1

Wmk. PTM Multiple (338)
1963, Sept. 16   Photo.   Perf. 14
1	A1	10s violet & yellow	.30	.25
a.		Yellow omitted	250.00	
2	A1	12s green & yellow	1.90	.60
3	A1	50s dk red brown & yel	1.40	.30
		Nos. 1-3 (3)	3.60	1.15

Formation of the Federation of Malaysia.

Orchids — A2

1963, Oct. 3   Unwmk.   Perf. 13x14
4	A2	6s red & multi	1.25	1.25
5	A2	25s black & multi	2.25	1.00

4th World Orchid Conf., Singapore, Oct. 8-11.

Parliament and Commonwealth Parliamentary Association Emblem — A4

1963, Nov. 4   Perf. 13½
7	A4	20s dk car rose & gold	.50	.40
8	A4	30s dk green & gold	1.50	.50

9th Commonwealth Parliamentary Assoc. Conf.

Globe, Torch, Snake and Hands — A5

1964, Oct. 10   Photo.   Perf. 14x13
9	A5	25s Prus grn, red & blk	.25	.25
10	A5	30s lt violet, red & blk	.25	.25
11	A5	50s dull yellow, red & blk	.35	.25
		Nos. 9-11 (3)	.85	.75

Eleanor Roosevelt, 1884-1962.

ITU Emblem and Radar Tower — A6

1965, May 17   Photo.   Perf. 11½
Granite Paper
12	A6	2c violet, blk & org	.50	1.50
13	A6	25c brown, blk & org	2.75	.80
14	A6	50c emerald, blk & brn	2.50	.30
		Nos. 12-14 (3)	5.75	2.60

Cent. of the ITU.

National Mosque, Kuala Lumpur — A7

1965, Aug. 27   Wmk. 338   Perf. 14½
15	A7	6c dark car rose	.25	.25
16	A7	15c dark red brown	.25	.25
17	A7	20c Prussian green	.35	.30
		Nos. 15-17 (3)	.85	.80

Natl. Mosque at Kuala Lumpur, opening.

Control Tower and Airport — A8

1965, Aug. 30   Perf. 14½x14
18	A8	15c blue, blk & grn	.30	.25
a.		Green omitted	35.00	
19	A8	30c brt pink, blk & grn	.85	.30

Intl. Airport at Kuala Lumpur, opening.

Crested Wood Partridge — A9

Birds: 30c, Fairy bluebird. 50c, Blacknaped oriole. 75c, Rhinoceros hornbill. $1, Zebra dove. $2, Argus pheasant. $5, Indian paradise flycatcher. $10, Banded pitta.

1965, Sept. 9   Photo.   Perf. 14½
20	A9	25c orange & multi	.60	.25
21	A9	30c tan & multi	.70	.25
a.		Blue omitted	300.00	
22	A9	50c rose & multi	1.10	.25
a.		Yellow omitted	180.00	
23	A9	75c yel grn & multi	1.25	.25
24	A9	$1 ultra & multi	2.00	.35
25	A9	$2 maroon & multi	4.00	.65
26	A9	$5 dk grn & multi	21.00	2.25
27	A9	$10 brt red & multi	50.00	8.00
		Nos. 20-27 (8)	80.65	12.25

Soccer and Sepak Raga (Ball Game) — A10

1965, Dec. 14   Unwmk.   Perf. 13
28	A10	25c shown	.40	1.25
29	A10	30c Runner	.40	.30
30	A10	50c Diver	.60	.30
		Nos. 28-30 (3)	1.40	1.85

3rd South East Asia Peninsular Games, Kuala Lumpur, Dec. 14-21.

National Monument, Kuala Lumpur — A11

1966, Feb. 8   Wmk. 338   Perf. 13½
31	A11	10c yellow & multi	.25	.25
a.		Blue omitted	150.00	
32	A11	20c ultra & multi	1.15	.45

The National Monument by US sculptor Felix W. de Weldon commemorates the struggle of the people of Malaysia for peace and for freedom from communism.

Tuanku Ismail Nasiruddin — A12

1966, Apr. 11   Unwmk.   Perf. 13½
33	A12	15c yellow & black	.25	.25
34	A12	50c blue & black	.35	.35

Installation of Tuanku Ismail Nasiruddin of Trengganu as Paramount Ruler (Yang di-Pertuan Agong).

Penang Free School — A13

Design: 50c, like 20c with Malayan inscription and school crest added.

Perf. 13x12½
1966, Oct. 21   Photo.   Wmk. 338
35	A13	20c multicolored	.40	.30
36	A13	50c multicolored	1.15	.40

Penang Free School, 150th anniversary.

Mechanized Plowing and Palms — A14

No. 38, Rural health nurse, mother and child, dispensary. No. 39, Communication: train, plane, ship, cars and radio tower. No. 40, School children. No. 41, Dam and rice fields.

1966, Dec. 1   Unwmk.   Perf. 13
37	A14	15c bister brn & multi	.70	.30
38	A14	15c blue & multi	.70	.30
39	A14	15c crimson & multi	.70	.30
40	A14	15c ol green & multi	.70	.30
41	A14	15c yellow & multi	.70	.30
		Nos. 37-41 (5)	3.50	1.50

Malaysia's First Development Plan.

Maps Showing International and South East Asia Telephone Links — A15

1967, Mar. 30   Photo.   Perf. 13
42	A15	30c multicolored	.50	.50
43	A15	75c multicolored	4.25	4.25

Completion of the Hong Kong-Malaysia link of the South East Asia Commonwealth Cable, SEACOM.

Hibiscus and Rulers of Independent Malaysia — A16

1967, Aug. 31   Wmk. 338   Perf. 14
44 A16 15c yellow & multi   .30 .25
45 A16 50c blue & multi   1.15 .80

10th anniversary of independence.

Arms of Sarawak and Council Mace — A17

1967, Sept. 8   Photo.
46 A17 15c yel green & multi   .25 .25
47 A17 50c multicolored   .35 .50

Representative Council of Sarawak, cent.

Straits Settlements No. 13 and Malaysia No. 20 — A18

30c, Straits Settlements #15, Malaysia #21. 50c, Straits Settlements #17, Malaysia #22.

1967, Dec. 2   Unwmk.   Perf. 11½
48 A18 25c brt blue & multi   1.60 3.00
49 A18 30c dull green & multi   1.90 2.50
50 A18 50c yellow & multi   2.75 3.25
        Nos. 48-50 (3)   6.25 8.75

Cent. of the Malaysian (Straits Settlements) postage stamps.

Tapped Rubber Tree and Molecular Unit — A20

Tapped Rubber Tree and: 30c, Rubber packed for shipment. 50c, Rubber tires for Vickers VC 10 plane.

Wmk. 338
1968, Aug. 29   Litho.   Perf. 12
53 A20 25c brick red, blk & org   .30 .25
54 A20 30c yellow, black & org   .40 .30
55 A20 50c ultra, black & org   .50 .30
        Nos. 53-55 (3)   1.20 .85

Natural Rubber Conference, Kuala Lumpur.

Olympic Rings, Mexican Hat and Cloth — A21

75c, Olympic rings & Malaysian batik cloth.

1968, Oct. 12   Wmk. 338   Perf. 12
56 A21 30c rose red & multi   .30 .25
57 A21 75c ocher & multi   .60 .35

19th Olympic Games, Mexico City, 10/12-27.

Tunku Abdul Rahman Putra Al-Haj — A22

Various portraits of Prime Minister Tunku Abdul Rahman Putra Al-Haj with woven pandanus patterns as background. 50c is horiz.

Perf. 13½
1969, Feb. 8   Photo.   Unwmk.
58 A22 15c gold & multi   .35 .25
59 A22 20c gold & multi   .55 1.25
60 A22 50c gold & multi   .65 .30
        Nos. 58-60 (3)   1.55 1.80

Issued for Solidarity Week, 1969.

Malaysian Girl Holding Sheaves of Rice — A23

1969, Dec. 8   Wmk. 338   Perf. 13½
61 A23 15c silver & multi   .30 .25
62 A23 75c gold & multi   1.10 1.40

International Rice Year.

Kuantan Radar Station — A24

Intelsat III Orbiting Earth A25

Perf. 14x13
1970, Apr. 6   Photo.   Unwmk.
63 A24 15c multicolored   .50 .25
64 A25 30c multicolored   1.40 2.50
65 A25 30c gold & multi   1.40 2.50
        Nos. 63-65 (3)   3.30 5.25

Satellite Communications Earth Station at Kuantan, Pahang, Malaysia.
No. 63 was printed tete beche (50 pairs) in sheet of 100 (10x10).

Blue-branded King Crow — A26

ILO Emblem — A27

Butterflies: 30c, Saturn. 50c, Common Nawab. 75c, Great Mormon. $1, Orange albatross. $2, Raja Brooke's birdwing. $5, Centaur oakblue. $10, Royal Assyrian.

1970, Aug. 31   Litho.   Perf. 13x13½
66 A26 25c multicolored   1.10 .25
67 A26 30c multicolored   1.00 .25
68 A26 50c multicolored   1.50 .25
69 A26 75c multicolored   1.25 .25
70 A26 $1 multicolored   2.25 .25
71 A26 $2 multicolored   3.75 .35

72 A26 $5 multicolored   8.00 3.00
73 A26 $10 multicolored   16.00 5.00
        Nos. 66-73 (8)   34.85 9.60

1970, Sept. 7   Perf. 14½x13½
74 A27 30c gray & blue   .25 .25
75 A27 75c rose & blue   .30 .30

50th anniv. of the ILO.

UN Emblem and Doves — A28

Designs: 25c, Doves in elliptical arrangement. 30c, Doves arranged diagonally.

1970, Oct. 24   Litho.   Perf. 13x12½
76 A28 25c lt brown, blk & yel   .35 .30
77 A28 30c lt blue, yel & black   .35 .30
78 A28 50c lt ol green & black   .40 .55
        Nos. 76-78 (3)   1.10 1.15

25th anniversary of the United Nations.

Sultan Abdul Halim — A29

Perf. 14½x14
1971, Feb. 20   Photo.   Unwmk.
79 A29 10c yellow, blk & gold   .40 .35
80 A29 15c purple, blk & gold   .40 .35
81 A29 50c blue, blk & gold   .65 1.50
        Nos. 79-81 (3)   1.45 2.20

Installation of Sultan Abdul Halim of Kedah as Paramount Ruler.

Bank Building and Crescent A30

1971, May 15   Photo.   Perf. 14
82 A30 25c silver & black   2.50 2.00
83 A30 50c gold & brown   4.00 1.50

Opening of Main office of the Negara Malaysia Bank. Nos. 82-83 have circular perforations around vignette set within a white square of paper, perf. on 4 sides.

Malaysian Parliament — A31

Malaysian Parliament, Kuala Lumpur — A32

1971, Sept. 13   Litho.   Perf. 13½
84 A31 25c multicolored   1.50 .50

Perf. 12½x13
85 A32 75c multicolored   3.50 1.75

17th Commonwealth Parliamentary Conference, Kuala Lumpur.

Malaysian Festival — A33

1971, Sept. 18   Perf. 14½
86 A33 Strip of 3   6.25 5.50
 a.   30c Dancing couple   1.75 .75
 b.   30c Dragon   1.75 .75
 c.   30c Flags and stage horse   1.75 .75

Visit ASEAN (Association of South East Asian Nations) Year.

Elephant and Tiger — A34

Children's Drawings: No. 88, Cat and kittens. No. 89, Sun, flower and chick. No. 90, Monkey, elephant and lion in jungle. No. 91, Butterfly and flowers.

1971, Oct. 2   Perf. 12½
                Size: 35x28mm
87 A34 15c pale yellow & multi   2.50 .60
88 A34 15c pale yellow & multi   2.50 .60
                Size: 21x28mm
89 A34 15c pale yellow & multi   2.50 .60
                Size: 35x28mm
90 A34 15c pale yellow & multi   2.50 .60
91 A34 15c pale yellow & multi   2.50 .60
 a.   Strip of 5, #87-91   14.00 13.00

25th anniv. of UNICEF.

Track and Field — A35

30c, Sepak Raga (a ball game). 50c, Hockey.

1971, Dec. 11   Perf. 14½
92 A35 25c orange & multi   1.00 .40
93 A35 30c violet & multi   1.25 .50
94 A35 50c green & multi   1.50 .95
        Nos. 92-94 (3)   3.75 1.85

6th South East Asia Peninsular Games. Kuala Lumpur, Dec. 11-18.

South East Asian Tourist Attractions — A36

Designs include stylized map.

1972, Jan. 31   Litho.   Perf. 14½
95 A36 Strip of 3   9.00 9.00
 a.   30c Flag at left   2.75 1.25
 b.   30c High rise building   2.75 1.25
 c.   30c Horse & rider   2.75 1.25

Pacific Area Tourist Assoc. Conference.

Secretariat Building — A37

50c, Kuala Lumpur Secretariat Building by night.

1972, Feb. 1　　　　**Perf. 14½x14**
96 A37 25c lt blue & multi　　1.10 1.25
97 A37 50c black & multi　　2.75 1.25

Achievement of city status by Kuala Lumpur.

Social Security Emblem — A38　　WHO Emblem — A39

1973, July 2　Litho.　Perf. 14½x13½
98 A38 10c orange & multi　　.25 .25
99 A38 15c yellow & multi　　.25 .25
100 A38 50c gray & multi　　.50 1.40
　　Nos. 98-100 (3)　　1.00 1.90

Introduction of Social Security System.

1973, Aug. 1　　Perf. 13x12½, 12½x13
Design: 30c, WHO emblem, horiz.
101 A39 30c yellow & multi　　.60 .25
102 A39 75c blue & multi　　1.30 2.50

25th anniv. of World Health Org.

Flag of Malaysia, Fireworks, Hibiscus — A40

1973, Aug. 31　Litho.　Perf. 14½
103 A40 10c olive & multi　　.50 .30
104 A40 15c brown & multi　　.55 .30
105 A40 50c gray & multi　　2.10 1.60
　　Nos. 103-105 (3)　　3.15 2.20

10th anniversary of independence.

INTERPOL and Malaysian Police Emblems A41

Design: 75c, "50" with INTERPOL and Malaysian police emblems.

1973, Sept. 15　　Perf. 12½
106 A41 25c brown org & multi　　1.00 .45
107 A41 75c deep violet & multi　　2.50 2.00

50th anniv. of the Intl. Criminal Police Organization (INTERPOL).

MAS Emblem and Plane A42

1973, Oct. 1　Litho.　Perf. 14½
108 A42 15c green & multi　　.25 .25
109 A42 30c blue & multi　　.60 .55
110 A42 50c brown & multi　　1.40 1.60
　　Nos. 108-110 (3)　　2.25 2.40

Inauguration of Malaysian Airline System.

View of Kuala Lumpur — A43

1974, Feb. 1　Litho.　Perf. 12½x13
111 A43 25c multicolored　　.80 .75
112 A43 50c multicolored　　1.60 1.75

Establishment of Kuala Lumpur as a Federal Territory.

Development Bank Emblem and Projects — A44

1974, Apr. 25　Litho.　Perf. 13½
113 A44 30c gray & multi　　.55 .45
114 A44 75c bister & multi　　.90 1.75

7th annual meeting of the Board of Governors of the Asian Development Bank.

Map of Malaysia and Scout Emblem — A45

Scout Saluting, Malaysian and Scout Flags — A46

Design: 50c, Malaysian Scout emblem.

Perf. 14x13½, 13x13½ (15c)
1974, Aug. 1　　　　Litho.
115 A45 10c multicolored　　.55 .90
116 A46 15c multicolored　　.90 .25
117 A45 50c multicolored　　2.50 2.75
　　Nos. 115-117 (3)　　3.95 3.90

Malaysian Boy Scout Jamboree.

Power Installations, NEB Emblem — A47

National Electricity Board Building A48

Perf. 14x14½, 13½x14½
1974, Sept. 1　　　　Litho.
118 A48 30c multicolored　　.65 .45
119 A48 75c multicolored　　1.10 2.25

National Electricity Board, 25th anniversary.

"100," UPU and P.O. Emblems A49

1974, Oct. 9　Litho.　Perf. 14½x13½
120 A49 25c olive, red & yel　　.35 .35
121 A49 30c blue, red & yel　　.35 .35
122 A49 75c ocher, red & yel　　.75 1.60
　　Nos. 120-122 (3)　　1.45 2.30

Centenary of Universal Postal Union.

Gravel Pump Tin Mine A50

Designs: 20c, Open cast mine. 50c, Silver tin ingot and tin dredge.

1974, Oct. 31　Litho.　Perf. 14
123 A50 15c silver & multi　　.45 .30
124 A50 20c silver & multi　　3.25 2.25
125 A50 50c silver & multi　　6.50 5.25
　　Nos. 123-125 (3)　　10.20 7.80

4th World Tin Conference, Kuala Lumpur.

Hockey, Cup and Emblem A51

1975, Mar. 1　Litho.　Perf. 14
126 A51 30c yellow & multi　　1.25 .50
127 A51 75c blue & multi　　2.75 2.00

Third World Cup Hockey Tournament, Kuala Lumpur, Mar. 1-15.

Trade Union Emblem and Workers — A52

1975, May 1　Litho.　Perf. 14x14½
128 A52 20c orange & multi　　.25 .25
129 A52 25c lt green & multi　　.35 .25
130 A52 30c ultra & multi　　.50 .50
　　Nos. 128-130 (3)　　1.10 1.00

Malaysian Trade Union Cong., 25th anniv.

National Women's Organization Emblem and Heads — A53

1975, Aug. 25　Litho.　Perf. 14
131 A53 10c emerald & multi　　.45 .30
132 A53 15c lilac rose & multi　　.45 .30
133 A53 50c blue & multi　　1.40 2.00
　　Nos. 131-133 (3)　　2.30 2.60

International Women's Year.

Ubudiah Mosque, Perak — A54

b, Zahir Mosque, Kedah. c, National Mosque, Kuala Lumpur. d, Sultan Abu Bakar Mosque, Johore. e, Kuching State Mosque, Sarawak.

1975, Sept. 22　Litho.　Perf. 14½x14
134　　　Strip of 5　　14.50 9.50
a.-e.　A54 15c single stamp　　2.40 .40

Koran reading competition 1975, Malaysia.

Rubber Plantation and Emblem A55

Designs: 30c, "50" in form of latex cup and tire with emblem. 75c, Six test tubes showing various aspects of natural rubber.

1975, Oct. 22　Litho.　Perf. 14x14½
135 A55 10c gold & multi　　.45 .30
136 A55 30c gold & multi　　1.25 .60
137 A55 75c gold & multi　　3.00 2.00
　　Nos. 135-137 (3)　　4.70 2.90

Rubber Research Institute of Malaysia, 50th anniversary.

Butterflies — A55a

No. 137A, Hebomoia glaucippe aturia. No. 137B, Precis orithya wallacei.

Coil Stamps

1976, Feb. 6　　　　Perf. 14
137A A55a 10c multicolored　　3.50 7.00
137B A55a 15c multicolored　　3.50 7.00

Scrub Typhus — A56　　Sultan Jahya Petra — A57

Designs: 25c, Malaria (microscope, blood cells, slides). $1, Beri-beri (grain and men).

1976, Feb. 6　Litho.　Perf. 14
138 A56 20c red orange & multi　　.70 .30
139 A56 25c ultra & multi　　.85 .30
140 A56 $1 yellow & multi　　1.60 2.25
　　Nos. 138-140 (3)　　3.15 2.85

Institute for Medical Research, Kuala Lumpur, 75th anniversary.

Perf. 14½x13½
1976, Feb. 28　　　　Photo.
141 A57 10c yel, black & bis　　.35 .25
142 A57 15c lilac, black & bis　　.30 .25
143 A57 50c blue, black & bis　　2.75 2.25
　　Nos. 141-143 (3)　　3.40 2.75

Installation of Sultan Jahya Petra of Kelantan as Paramount Ruler (Yang di-Pertuan Agong).

Council and Administrative Buildings — A58

1976, Aug. 17　Litho.　Perf. 12½
144 A58 15c orange & black　　.45 .25
145 A58 20c brt red lilac & black　　.55 .35
146 A58 50c blue & black　　1.00 1.25
　　Nos. 144-146 (3)　　2.00 1.85

Opening of the State Council Complex and Administrative Building, Sarawak.

Provident
Fund Building
A59

Provident Fund
Emblems — A60

50c, Provident Fund Building at night.

Perf. 13½x14½, 14½ (A60)
1976, Oct. 18   Litho.
147 A59 10c blue & multi   .50   .35
148 A60 25c gray & multi   .45   .60
149 A59 50c violet & multi   .65 1.25
    Nos. 147-149 (3)   1.60 2.20
Employees' Provident Fund, 25th anniv.

Rehabilitation
of the
Blind — A61

75c, Blind man casting large shadow.

1976, Nov. 20   Perf. 13½x14½
150 A61 10c multicolored   .50   .30
151 A61 75c multicolored   1.50 2.25
25th anniv. of the Malaysian Assoc. for the Blind.

Abdul Razak
and
Crowd — A62

Designs: b, Abdul Razak in cap and gown at lectern. c, Abdul Razak pointing to new roads and bridges on map. d, New constitution. e, Abdul Razak addressing Association of Southeast Asian Countries.

1977, Jan. 14   Photo.   Perf. 14x14½
152   Strip of 5   10.00 8.50
a.-e. A62 15c single stamp   1.25   .40
Prime Minister Tun Haji Abdul Razak bi Dato Hussein (1922-1976).

FELDA
Housing
Development
A63

Design: 30c, View of oil palm settlement area and FELDA emblem.

1977, July 7   Litho.   Perf. 13½x14½
153 A63 15c multicolored   .55   .30
154 A63 30c multicolored   .90 1.75
Federal Land Development Authority (FELDA), 21st anniversary.

"10" — A64

ASEAN, 10th anniv.: 75c, Flags of ASEAN members: Malaysia, Philippines, Singapore, Thailand and Indonesia.

1977, Aug. 8   Litho.   Perf. 13½x14½
155 A64 10c multicolored   .50   .25
156 A64 75c multicolored   1.00   .90

SEA Games
Emblems
A65

Designs: 20c, Ball, symbolic of 9 participating nations. 75c, Running.

Perf. 13½x14½
1977, Nov. 19   Litho.
157 A65 10c multicolored   .30   .25
158 A65 20c multicolored   .30   .25
159 A65 75c multicolored   .75 1.60
    Nos. 157-159 (3)   1.35 2.10
9th South East Asia Games, Kuala Lumpur.

Bank
Emblem
A66

1978, Mar. 15   Litho.   Perf. 14
160 A66 30c multicolored   .40   .25
161 A66 75c multicolored   .80   .80
2nd annual meeting of Islamic Development Bank Governors, Kuala Lumpur, Mar. 1978.

Government
Building
A67

Designs: Views of Shah Alam.

1978, Dec. 7   Litho.   Perf. 13½x14½
162 A67 10c multicolored   .25   .25
163 A67 30c multicolored   .30   .25
164 A67 75c multicolored   .85 1.75
    Nos. 162-164 (3)   1.40 2.25
Inauguration of Shah Alam as state capital of Selangor.

Mobile Post
Office in
Village — A68

Designs: 25c, General Post Office, Kuala Lumpur. 50c, Motorcyclist, rural mail delivery.

1978, July 10   Perf. 13
165 A68 10c multicolored   1.10   .40
166 A68 25c multicolored   1.25 1.75
167 A68 50c multicolored   1.50 2.75
    Nos. 165-167 (3)   3.85 4.90
4th Conf. of Commonwealth Postal Administrators.

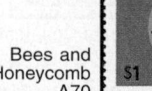

Jamboree
Emblem
A69

Bees and
Honeycomb
A70

1978, July 26   Litho.   Perf. 13½
168 A69 15c multicolored   1.00   .30
169 A70 $1 multicolored   3.75 3.00
4th Boy Scout Jamboree, Sarawak.

Globe, Crest
and WHO
Emblem
A71

1978, Sept. 30   Perf. 13½x14½
170 A71 15c blue, red & black   .45   .35
171 A71 30c green, red & black   .65   .45
172 A71 50c pink, red & black   1.00   .80
    Nos. 170-172 (3)   2.10 1.60
Global eradication of smallpox.

Dome of
the Rock
A72

1978, Aug. 21   Litho.   Perf. 12½
173 A72 15c red & multi   1.00   .35
174 A72 30c blue & multi   2.50 2.50
For Palestinian fighters and their families.

Tiger — A73

Designs: 40c, Cobego. 50c, Chevrotain. 75c, Pangolin. $1, Leatherback turtle. $2, Tapir. $5, Gaur. $10, Orangutan, vert.

Perf. 15x14½, 14½x15
1979, Jan. 4   Litho.   Wmk. 378
175 A73 30c multicolored   .50   .25
176 A73 40c multicolored   .55   .25
177 A73 50c multicolored   .90   .25
178 A73 75c multicolored   1.00   .25
179 A73 $1 multicolored   1.25   .25
180 A73 $2 multicolored   2.00   .75
181 A73 $5 multicolored   5.75 2.00
182 A73 $10 multicolored   10.00 3.00
    Nos. 175-182 (8)   21.95 7.00

1983-87   Unwmk.
175a A73 30c ('84)   1.25   .70
176a A73 40c ('84)   1.40   .55
177a A73 50c ('84)   1.75   .55
178a A73 75c ('87)   10.00 8.50
179a A73 $1   4.75   .55
180a A73 $2   6.25   .85
181a A73 $5 ('85)   18.00 7.00
182a A73 $10 ('86)   29.00 10.50
    Nos. 175a-182a (8)   72.40 29.20

Central Bank of   Year of the Child
Malaysia — A74   Emblem — A75

10c, Central Bank of Malaysia & emblem.

Perf. 13½
1979, Jan. 26   Litho.   Unwmk.
183 A74 10c multicolored, horiz. .30   .30
184 A74 75c multicolored   1.10 1.40
Central Bank of Malaysia, 20th anniv.

1979, Feb. 24   Perf. 14
Intl. Year of the Child: 15c, Children of the world, globe and ICY emblem. $1, Children at play, ICY emblem.
185 A75 10c multicolored   .50   .25
186 A75 15c multicolored   .40   .25
187 A75 $1 multicolored   3.25 3.50
    Nos. 185-187 (3)   4.15 4.00

Symbolic
Rubber
Plant — A76

Designs: 10c, Symbolic palm. 75c, Symbolic rubber products.

1978, Nov. 28   Litho.   Perf. 13
188 A76 10c brt green & gold   .25   .25
189 A76 20c multicolored   .45   .25
190 A76 75c brt green & gold   .60   .90
    Nos. 188-190 (3)   1.30 1.40
Centenary of rubber production (in 1977).

Rafflesia
Hasseltii
A77

Flowers: 2c, Pterocarpus indicus. 5c, Lagerstroemia speciosa. 10c, Durio zibethinus. 15c, Hibiscus. 20c, Rhododendron scortechinii. 25c, Phaeomeria speciosa.

Perf. 15x14½
1979, Apr. 30   Wmk. 378
191 A77 1c multicolored   .25   .25
192 A77 2c multicolored   .25   .25
193 A77 5c multicolored   .25   .25
a.   Unwmkd. ('84)
194 A77 10c multicolored   .25   .25
a.   White flowers, unwmkd. ('84) .25   .25
195 A77 15c multicolored   .25   .25
a.   15c yel & multi, unwmkd. ('83) .25   .25
196 A77 20c multicolored   .30   .25
a.   20c greenish & multi, unwmkd.
     ('83)   .25   .25
197 A77 25c multicolored   .35   .25
a.   Unwmkd. ('85)   5.00
    Nos. 191-197 (7)   1.90 1.75

Temengor
Hydroelectric
Dam — A78

Designs: 25c, 50c, Dam and river, diff.

Perf. 13½x14½
1979, Sept. 19   Litho.   Unwmk.
198 A78 15c multicolored   .30   .30
199 A78 25c multicolored   .70   .50
200 A78 50c multicolored   1.00 1.25
    Nos. 198-200 (3)   2.00 2.05

"TELECOM
79" — A79

Telecom Emblem and: 15c, Telephone receiver and globes. 50c, Modes of communication.

1979, Sept. 20   Perf. 13½
Size: 34x25mm
201 A79 10c multicolored   .35   .50
202 A79 15c multicolored   .25   .25
Perf. 14
Size: 39x28mm
203 A79 50c multicolored   .85 2.25
    Nos. 201-203 (3)   1.45 3.00
3rd World Telecommunications Exhibition, Geneva, Sept. 20-26.

Haji Ahmad
Shah — A80

1980, July 10　Litho.　Perf. 14½
204　A80　10c multicolored　　.25　.40
205　A80　15c multicolored　　.25　.25
206　A80　50c multicolored　　.70　2.00
　　　Nos. 204-206 (3)　　　1.20　2.65

Installation of Sultan Haji Ahmad Shah of Pahang as Paramount Ruler (Yang di-Pertuan Agong).

Pahang-Sarawak Cable — A81

Designs: 15c, Dial with views of Kuantan and Kuching. 50c, Telephone and maps.

1980, Aug. 31　Litho.　Perf. 13½
207　A81　10c shown　　　.25　.35
208　A81　15c multicolored　　.25　.25
209　A81　50c multicolored　　.35　1.75
　　　Nos. 207-209 (3)　　　.85　2.35

National University of Malaysia, 10th Anniversary A82

15c, Jalan Pantai Baru campus. 75c, Great Hall & Tun Haji Abdul Razak (1st chancellor).

1980, Sept. 2　Litho.　Perf. 13½
210　A82　10c shown　　　.25　.25
211　A82　15c multicolored　　.25　.25
212　A82　75c multicolored　　.50　2.75
　　　Nos. 210-212 (3)　　　1.00　3.25

Hegira (Pilgrimage Year) — A83

1980, Nov. 9
213　A83　15c multicolored　　.30　.25
214　A83　50c multicolored　　.45　1.25

International Year of the Disabled A84　　Sultan Mahmud of Trengganu A85

1981, Feb. 14　Litho.　Perf. 13½
215　A84　10c Child learning to walk　　　.50　.25
216　A84　15c Seamstress　　.55　.25
217　A84　75c Athlete　　1.50　3.25
　　　Nos. 215-217 (3)　　　2.55　3.75

1981, Mar. 21　Litho.　Perf. 14½
218　A85　10c multicolored　　.25　.25
219　A85　15c multicolored　　.25　.25
220　A85　50c multicolored　　.90　.30
　　　Nos. 218-220 (3)　　　1.40　.80

Industrial Training Seminar A86

Designs: Various workers.

1981, May 2　Litho.　Perf. 13½
221　A86　10c multicolored　　.35　.25
222　A86　15c multicolored　　.25　.25
223　A86　30c multicolored　　.35　.25
224　A86　75c multicolored　　.60　2.00
　　　Nos. 221-224 (4)　　　1.55　2.75

World Energy Conference, 25th anniv. — A87

1981, June 17　Litho.　Perf. 13½
225　A87　10c "25"　　　.40　.30
226　A87　15c Sources of Energy　　.35　.30
227　A87　75c Non-renewable energy　　1.75　3.25
　　　Nos. 225-227 (3)　　　2.50　3.85

Centenary of Sabah — A88

1981, Aug. 31　Litho.　Perf. 12
228　A88　15c Views, 1881 and 1981　　.60　.30
229　A88　80c Traditional and modern farming　　3.00　4.00

Rain Tree A89

1981, Dec. 16　Litho.　Perf. 14
230　A89　15c shown　　　.50　.25
231　A89　50c Simber tree, vert.　　1.50　1.25
232　A89　80c Borneo camphorwood, vert.　　3.00　4.00
　　　Nos. 230-232 (3)　　　5.00　5.50

Scouting Year and Jamboree, Apr. 9-16 A90

1982, Apr. 10　Litho.　Perf. 13½x13
233　A90　15c Jamboree emblem　　.40　.30
234　A90　50c Flag, emblem　　1.00　.75
235　A90　80c Emblems, knot　　1.75　4.00
　　　Nos. 233-235 (3)　　　3.15　5.05

15th Anniv. of Assoc. of South East Asian Nations (ASEAN) A91

1982, Aug. 8　Litho.　Perf. 14
236　A91　15c Meeting Center　　.50　.25
237　A91　$1 Flags　　2.00　3.25

Dome of the Rock, Jerusalem A92

1982, Aug. 21　Perf. 13½
238　A92　15c multicolored　　1.25　.35
239　A92　$1 multicolored　　6.00　6.00

For the freedom of Palestine.

25th Anniv. of Independence — A93

1982, Aug. 31　Litho.　Perf. 14
240　A93　10c Kuala Lumpur　　.25　.25
241　A93　15c Independence celebration　　.25　.25
242　A93　50c Parade　　.60　.50
243　A93　80c Independence ceremony　　.70　2.00
a.　　Souvenir sheet of 4, #240-243　16.00　16.00
b.　　Souvenir sheet of 4, #240-243　12.00　12.00
　　　Nos. 240-243 (4)　　　1.80　3.50

No. 243a has a narrow silver frame around the center vignette of the 10c value. This frame was removed for the second printing, No. 243b.

Traditional Games — A94

1982, Oct. 30　Perf. 13½
244　A94　10c Shadow play　　1.00　.35
245　A94　15c Cross top　　1.00　.35
246　A94　75c Kite flying　　2.75　4.25
　　　Nos. 244-246 (3)　　　4.75　4.95

Handicrafts — A95

1982, Nov. 26　Litho.　Perf. 13x13½
247　A95　10c Sabah hats　　.40　.45
248　A95　15c Gold-threaded cloth　　.40　.45
249　A95　75c Sarawak pottery　　1.90　3.25
　　　Nos. 247-249 (3)　　　2.70　4.15

Commonwealth Day — A96

1983, Mar. 14　Litho.　Perf. 14
250　A96　15c Flag　　　.30　.25
251　A96　20c Seri Paduka Baginda　　.30　.25
252　A96　40c Oil palm refinery　　.45　.40
253　A96　$1 Globe　　.70　2.25
　　　Nos. 250-253 (4)　　　1.75　3.15

First Shipment of Natural Gas, Bintulu, Sarawak — A97

1983, Jan. 22　Litho.　Perf. 12
254　A97　15c Bintulu Port Authority emblem　　1.10　.35
a.　　Perf. 13½　　30.00　3.25
255　A97　20c LNG Tanker Tenaga Satu　　1.40　1.00
a.　　Perf. 13½　　35.00　3.50
256　A97　$1 Gas plant　　4.50　6.25
a.　　Perf. 13½　　60.00　12.50
　　　Nos. 254-256 (3)　　　7.00　7.60
　　　Nos. 254a-256a (3)　125.00　19.25

Freshwater Fish — A98

1983, June 15　Perf. 12x12½
257　　　Pair　　6.00　3.00
a.　　A98 20c Tilapia nilotica　1.50　.35
b.　　A98 20c Cyprinus carpio　1.50　.35
c.　　As #257, perf. 13½x14　11.00　11.00
258　　　Pair　　7.00　3.50
a.　　A98 40c Puntius gonionotus　1.75　.40
b.　　A98 40c Ctenopharyngodon idellus　1.75　.40
c.　　As #258, perf. 13½x14　11.50　11.50

Opening of East-West Highway — A99

1983, July 1　Perf. 14x13½
259　A99　15c Lower Sungei Pergau Bridge　　1.00　.40
260　A99　20c Sungei Perak Reservoir Bridge　　1.00　.40
261　A99　$1 Map　　5.00　6.00
　　　Nos. 259-261 (3)　　　7.00　7.00

Armed Forces, 50th Anniv. — A100

Designs: 15c, Royal Malaysian Aircraft. 20c, Navy vessel firing missile. 40c, Battle at Pasir Panjang. 80c, Trooping of the Royal colors.

1983, Sept. 16　Litho.　Perf. 13½
262　A100　15c multicolored　　.70　.40
263　A100　20c multicolored　　1.00　.40
264　A100　40c multicolored　　2.00　2.00
265　A100　80c multicolored　　4.50　5.00
a.　　Souvenir sheet of 4, #262-265　13.50　14.00
　　　Nos. 262-265 (4)　　　8.20　7.80

Helmeted Hornbill — A101

1983, Oct. 26　Litho.　Perf. 13½
266　A101　15c shown　　　2.25　.40
267　A101　20c Wrinkled Hornbill　　2.25　.45
268　A101　50c White crested Hornbill　　2.75　1.75
269　A101　$1 Rhinoceros Hornbill　　4.75　5.25
　　　Nos. 266-269 (4)　　12.00　7.85

25th Anniv. of Begara Bank A102

Branch offices.

1984, Jan. 26　Litho.　Perf. 13½x14
270　A102　20c Ipoh　　1.25　.35
271　A102　$1 Alor Setar　　2.25　3.25

10th Anniv. of Federal Territory A103

Views of Kuala Lumpur. 20c, 40c vert.

Perf. 14x13½, 13½x14

1984, Feb. 1   Litho.
272 A103 20c multicolored   1.00 .50
273 A103 40c multicolored   1.40 1.25
274 A103 80c multicolored   4.00 6.00
   Nos. 272-274 (3)   6.40 7.75

Labuan Federal Territory A104

Traditional Weapons A105

1984, Apr. 16   Litho.   Perf. 13½x14
275 A104 20c Development symbols, map, arms   1.50 .40
276 A104 $1 Flag, map   4.75 5.25

1984, May 30   Perf. 13x14
277 A105 40c Keris Semenanjung   1.25 1.50
278 A105 40c Keris Pekakak   1.25 1.50
279 A105 40c Keris Jawa   1.25 1.50
280 A105 40c Tumbuk Lada   1.25 1.50
   a.   Block of 4, #277-280   6.00 7.00

Asia-Pacific Broadcasting Union, 20th Anniv. — A106

1984, June 23   Perf. 14x14½
281 A106 20c Map, waves   1.50 .40
282 A106 $1 "20"   2.50 4.25

Kuala Lumpur Post Office Opening A107

1984, Oct. 29   Perf. 12x11½
283 A107 15c Facsimile transmission   .80 .35
284 A107 20c Building   .80 .35
285 A107 $1 Mail bag conveyor   2.00 4.00
   Nos. 283-285 (3)   3.60 4.70

Installation of Sultan of Johore as 8th Paramount Ruler of Malaysia — A108

Sultan Mahmood, Arms A109

1984, Nov. 15   Litho.   Perf. 12
286 A108 15c multicolored   1.00 .40
287 A108 20c multicolored   1.00 .35
288 A109 40c multicolored   1.40 .90
289 A109 80c multicolored   2.40 4.25
   Nos. 286-289 (4)   5.80 5.90

A110

Malaysian hibiscus.

1984, Dec. 12   Litho.   Perf. 13½
290 A110 10c White hibiscus   1.00 .40
291 A110 20c Red hibiscus   1.00 .35
292 A110 40c Pink hibiscus   2.00 2.00
293 A110 $1 Orange hibiscus   3.25 5.00
   Nos. 290-293 (4)   7.25 7.75

A111

Perf. 13½x14, 14x13½

1985, Mar. 30   Litho.
294 A111 20c Badge, vert.   .80 .30
295 A111 $1 Parliament, Kuala Lumpur   1.75 3.00

Parliament, 25th anniv.

Protected Wildlife A112

1985, Apr. 25   Perf. 14
296 A112 10c Prionodon linsang   1.50 .55
297 A112 40c Nycticebus coucang, vert.   1.75 1.25
298 A112 $1 Petaurista elegans, vert.   4.50 6.00
   Nos. 296-298 (3)   7.75 7.80

Intl. Youth Year — A113

1985, May 15   Perf. 13
299 A113 20c Youth solidarity   1.10 .40
300 A113 $1 Participation in natl. development   4.00 5.00

Malaya Railways Centenary A114

Locomotives.

1985, June 1   Perf. 13
301 A114 15c Steam engine, 1885   2.00 .50
302 A114 20c Diesel-electric, 1957   2.10 .50
303 A114 $1 Diesel, 1963   5.25 6.25
   Nos. 301-303 (3)   9.35 7.25

Souvenir Sheet
Perf. 14x13
304 A114 80c Train leaving Kuala Lumpur Station, 1938   10.50 11.00

No. 304 contains one stamp 48x32mm.

Proton Saga A115

1985, July 9   Perf. 14
305 A115 20c multicolored   1.25 .30
306 A115 40c multicolored   1.75 .80
307 A115 $1 multicolored   3.75 5.75
   Nos. 305-307 (3)   6.75 6.85

Inauguration of natl. automotive industry.

Sultan Salahuddin Abdul Aziz, Selangor Coat of Arms A116

1985, Sept. 5   Perf. 13
308 A116 15c multicolored   .70 .60
309 A116 20c multicolored   .80 .60
310 A116 $1 multicolored   3.75 6.00
   Nos. 308-310 (3)   5.25 7.20

25th anniv. of coronation.

Penang Bridge Opening A117

1985, Sept. 15   Litho.   Perf. 13½x13
311 A117 20c shown   1.40 .45
312 A117 40c Bridge, map   2.75 .75

Size: 44x28mm
Perf. 12½
313 A117 $1 Map   4.00 5.25
   Nos. 311-313 (3)   8.15 6.45

Natl. Oil Industry A118

1985, Nov. 4   Perf. 12½
314 A118 15c Offshore rig, vert.   1.40 .45
315 A118 20c 1st refinery   1.40 .45
316 A118 $1 Map of oil and gas fields   5.00 5.25
   Nos. 314-316 (3)   7.80 6.15

Coronation of Paduka Seri, Sultan of Perak A119

1985, Dec. 9   Perf. 14
317 A119 15c lt blue & multi   .55 .40
318 A119 20c lilac & multi   .80 .40
319 A119 $1 gold & multi   3.75 6.00
   Nos. 317-319 (3)   5.10 6.80

Birds A120

Wmk. 388
1986, Mar. 11   Litho.   Perf. 13¼
320 A120 20c Lophura ignita, vert.   2.50 .40
   a.   Perf. 12   4.75 1.25
321 A120 20c Pavo malacense, vert.   2.50 .40
   a.   Pair, #320-321   5.00 1.50
   b.   Perf. 12   7.50 2.00
   c.   Pair, #320a, 321b   12.50 8.25
322 A120 40c Lophura bulweri   4.00 .50
   a.   Perf. 12   8.25 1.50
323 A120 40c Argusianus argus   5.00 .50
   a.   Pair, #322-323   9.00 1.90
   b.   Perf. 12   7.25 1.50
   c.   Pair, #322a, 323b   15.50 11.50
   Nos. 320-323 (4)   14.00 1.80

PATA '86, Pacific Area Travel Assoc. Conference, Persidangan — A121

No. 324: a, Two women dancing. b, Woman in red. c, Man and woman.
No. 325: a, Woman in gold. b, Woman holding fan. c, Woman in violet.

Perf. 15x14½
1986, Apr. 14   Litho.   Unwmk.
324   Strip of 3   3.00 3.25
   a.-c.   A121 20c any single   .75 1.00
325   Strip of 3   4.00 4.00
   a.-c.   A121 40c any single   1.00 1.25

Malaysia Games A122

Games Emblem — A123

Flags — A124

Wmk. 388
1986, Apr. 14   Litho.   Perf. 12
326 A122 20c multicolored   1.60 .50
327 A123 40c multicolored   4.50 2.00
328 A124 $1 multicolored   6.00 6.50
   Nos. 326-328 (3)   12.10 9.00

Nephelium Lappaceum A125

Averrhoa Carambola A126

Litho. (#329-332), Photo. (#333-336)
Perf. 12 (#329-332)
1986-2000   Wmk. 388
329 A125 40c shown   .40 .25
   a.   Perf. 13½x14   .75
330 A125 50c Ananas comosus   .60 .25
   a.   Perf. 13½x14   .75
331 A125 80c Durio zibethinus   .95 .35
   a.   Perf. 13½x14   1.25
332 A125 $1 Garcinia mangostana   1.00 .35
   a.   Perf. 13½x14   1.25

Perf. 13½x14
332C A125 $5 Musa sapientum ('00)   1.75 .80

Perf. 13½
Wmk. 233
333 A126 $2 shown   2.00 .65
334 A126 $5 Musa sapientum   4.00 1.10
335 A126 $10 Mangifera odorata   6.75 3.75
336 A126 $20 Carica papaya   12.00 5.50
   Nos. 329-336 (9)   29.45 13.00

No. 332C issued 2000; balance of set issued 6/5/86.

Two additional stamps were issued in this set. The editors would like to examine any examples.

Compare with Nos. 766A-766H.

Natl. Assoc. for the Prevention of Drug Abuse, 10th Anniv. A127

1986, June 26   Wmk. 388   Perf. 13
337 A127 20c Skull   1.10   .50
338 A127 40c Dove   1.75   .80
339 A127 $1 Addict, vert.   5.50 4.25
     Nos. 337-339 (3)   8.35 5.55

Malaysian Airlines Kuala Lumpur-Los Angeles Inaugural Flight — A128

1986, July 31   Perf. 14x13½
340 A128 20c Flight routes map   2.25   .50
341 A128 40c MAS emblem, new route   2.75   .70
342 A128 $1 Emblem, stops   6.00 4.25
     Nos. 340-342 (3)   11.00 5.45

Industrial Productivity A129

1986, Nov. 3   Litho.   Perf. 14
343 A129 20c Construction, vert.   .80   .40
344 A129 40c Industry   1.75 1.00
345 A129 $1 Automobile factory   4.75 5.75
     Nos. 343-345 (3)   7.30 7.15

Historic Buildings A130

15c, Istana Lama Seri Menanti, Negri Sembilan. 20c, Istana Kenangan, Perak. 40c, Bangunan Stadthuys, Malacca. $1, Istana Kuching, Sarawak.

1986, Dec. 20   Perf. 13
346 A130 15c multicolored   .90   .30
347 A130 20c multicolored   .90   .30
348 A130 40c multicolored   2.00   .70
349 A130 $1 multicolored   3.00 4.50
     Nos. 346-349 (4)   6.80 5.80

See design A146.

Folk Music Instruments — A131

1987, Mar. 7   Litho.   Perf. 12
350 A131 15c Sompotan   1.00   .65
351 A131 20c Sapih   1.00   .65
352 A131 50c Serunai, vert.   2.40   .65
353 A131 80c Rebab, vert.   4.00 2.25
     Nos. 350-353 (4)   8.40 4.20

Intl. Year of Shelter for the Homeless — A132

1987, Apr. 6   Litho.   Perf. 12
354 A132 20c Model village   .80   .30
355 A132 $1 Symbols of family, shelter   4.00 1.50

UN Anti-Drug Campaign and Congress, Vienna A133

1987, June 8   Litho.   Perf. 13½x13
356   20c Health boy, family, rainbow   .75   .75
357   20c Holding drugs   .75   .75
  a.   A133 Pair, #356-357   3.00 3.00
358   40c Child warding off drugs   1.75   .75
359   40c Drugs, damaged body in capsule 1.75   .75
  a.   A133 Pair, #358-359   7.00 3.00
     Nos. 356-359 (4)   5.00 3.00

Nos. 357a, 359a have continuous designs.

Kenyir Hydroelectric Power Station Inauguration — A134

1987, July 13   Perf. 12
360 A134 20c Power facility, dam   1.60   .40
361 A134 $1 Side view   3.50 1.75

33rd Commonwealth Parliamentary Conference — A135

1987, Sept. 1   Litho.   Perf. 12
362 A135 20c Maces, parliament   .55   .25
363 A135 $1 Parliament, maces, diff.   1.50 1.10

Transportation and Communications Decade in Asia and the Pacific (1985-94) — A136

Designs: 15c, Satellites, Earth, satellite dish. 20c, Car, diesel train, Kuala Lumpur Station. 40c, MISC container ship. $1, Malaysia Airlines jet, Kuala Lumpur Airport.

1987, Oct. 26   Perf. 13½x13
364 A136 15c multicolored   1.25   .60
365 A136 20c multicolored   1.25   .70
366 A136 40c multicolored   2.25 1.25
367 A136 $1 multicolored   4.25 6.00
     Nos. 364-367 (4)   9.00 8.55

Protected Wildcats A137

1987, Nov. 14
368 A137 15c Felis temminckii   3.50   .70
369 A137 20c Felis planiceps   3.50   .70
370 A137 40c Felis marmorata   7.75 1.50
371 A137 $1 Neofelis nebulosa   11.00 6.75
     Nos. 368-371 (4)   25.75 9.65

ASEAN, 20th Anniv. A138

1987, Dec. 14   Litho.   Perf. 13
372 A138 20c "20," flags   .35   .25
373 A138 $1 Flags, Earth   1.60 1.50

Opening of Sultan Salahuddin Abdul Aziz Shah Mosque, Selangor A139

Dome, minarets and: 15c, Arches. 20c, Sultan Abdul Aziz Shah, Selangor crest. $1, Interior, vert.

1988, Mar. 11   Litho.   Perf. 12
374 A139 15c multicolored   .50   .35
375 A139 20c multicolored   .50   .35
376 A139 $1 multicolored   1.40 2.25
     Nos. 374-376 (3)   2.40 2.95

Opening of Sultan Ismail Power Station, Trengganu A140

1988, Apr. 4   Perf. 13
377 A140 20c shown   .40   .30
378 A140 $1 Station, diff.   2.00 1.25

Wildlife Protection — A141

Birds.

1988, June 30   Litho.   Perf. 13
379   20c Hypothymis azurea   .70   .70
380   20c Dicaeum cruentatum   .70   .70
  a.   A141 Pair, #379-380   3.75 3.75
381   50c Aethopyga siparaja   1.40 1.40
382   50c Cymbirhynchus macrorhynchos   1.40 1.40
  a.   A141 Pair, #381-382   6.50 6.50
     Nos. 379-382 (4)   4.20 4.20

Independence of Sabah and Sarawak, 25th Anniv.
       A142   A143

1988, Aug. 31   Litho.   Perf. 13x13½
383 A142 20c Sabah   .65   .70
384 A142 20c Sarawak   .65   .70
  a.   Pair, #383-384   1.40 1.50
385 A143 $1 State and natl. symbols   2.25 3.25
     Nos. 383-385 (3)   3.55 4.65

A144

Marine Life — A145

Nudibranchs: No. 386: a, Glossodoris atromarginata. b, Phyllidia ocellata. c, Chromodoris annae. d, Flabellina macassarana. e, Fryeria ruppelli.

1988, Dec. 17   Litho.   Perf. 12
386   Strip of 5   7.00 7.00
  a.-e. A144 20c any single   .75   .25

Souvenir Sheet
Perf. 14
387 A145 $1 Pomacanthus annularis   5.25 5.25

No. 387 contains one stamp 50x40mm.

Historic Buildings, Malacca A146

No. 388, Perisytiharan Kemerdekaan Memorial. No. 389, Istana Kesultanan. $1, Porta da Santiago.

Perf. 13½x13, 13x13½
1989, Apr. 15   Litho.
388 A146 20c multicolored   .50   .35
389 A146 20c multicolored   .50   .35
390 A146 $1 multicolored, vert.   1.90 1.50
     Nos. 388-390 (3)   2.90 2.20

See design A130.

Crustaceans A147

No. 391, Tetralia nigrolineata. No. 392, Neopetrolisthes maculatus. No. 393, Periclimenes holthuisi. No. 394, Synalpheus neomeris.

Wmk. 388
1989, June 29   Litho.   *Perf. 12*

391	A147	20c multi	.50	.50
392	A147	20c multi	.50	.50
a.		Pair, #391-392	1.60	1.60
393	A147	40c multi	.90	.90
394	A147	40c multi	.90	.90
a.		Pair, #393-394	2.75	2.75
		Nos. 391-394 (4)	2.80	2.80

7th Natl. Scout Jamboree — A148

1989, July 26   *Perf. 13½x13, 13x13½*

395	A148	10c Map, badges	.50	.45
396	A148	20c Scout salute, natl. flag	.50	.45
397	A148	80c Camping out	2.50	3.00
		Nos. 395-397 (3)	3.50	3.90

Nos. 395-396 vert.

15th SEA Games, Kuala Lumpur — A149   Installation of Sultan Azlan as Supreme Ruler — A150

Designs: 10c, Cycling, horiz. 20c, Track events, horiz. 50c, Swimming. $1, Torchbearer, stadium and flags.

Perf. 13½x13, 13x13½
1989, Aug. 20   Litho.   Wmk. 388

398	A149	10c multicolored	.40	.60
399	A149	20c multicolored	.40	.50
400	A149	50c multicolored	1.25	.80
401	A149	$1 multicolored	2.10	0.50
		Nos. 398-401 (4)	4.15	5.40

1989, Sept. 18   *Perf. 13x13½*

402	A150	20c multicolored	.35	.25
403	A150	40c multicolored	.60	.30
404	A150	$1 multicolored	1.40	2.25
		Nos. 402-404 (3)	2.35	2.80

Commonwealth Heads of Government Meeting — A151

1989, Oct. 18   *Perf. 13½x13, 13x13½*

405	A151	20c Conference center	.40	.30
406	A151	50c Folk dancers, vert.	.80	.60
407	A151	$1 Map, flag	1.60	2.50
		Nos. 405-407 (3)	2.80	3.40

Malaysia Airlines Inaugural Non-stop Flight to London, Dec. 2 — A152

No. 408, Passenger jet, Malaysian clock tower, Big Ben. No. 409, Passenger jet, Malaysian skyscraper, Westminster Palace. $1, Map, passenger jet.

1989, Dec. 2   Wmk. 388   *Perf. 13*

408	A152	20c shown	2.00	2.00
409	A152	20c multicolored	2.00	2.00
a.		Pair, #408-409	4.50	4.50
410	A152	$1 multicolored	5.50	5.50
		Nos. 408-410 (3)	9.50	9.50

National Park, 50th Anniv. — A153

1989, Dec. 28   *Perf. 13x13½*

411	A153	20c Map, sloth	1.60	.40
412	A153	$1 Crested arguses	4.50	4.50

Visit Malaysia.

Visit Malaysia Year — A154

1990, Jan. 11   *Perf. 12*

413	A154	20c Map	.60	.50
414	A154	50c Drummers	1.40	1.10
415	A154	$1 Yachts, scuba divers	2.25	3.25
		Nos. 413-415 (3)	4.25	4.85

Wildflowers — A155

1990, Mar. 12

416	A155	15c Dillenia suffruticosa	.30	.30
417	A155	20c Mimosa pudica	.30	.30
418	A155	50c Ipomoea carnea	.80	.80
419	A155	$1 Nymphaea pubescens	1.20	2.25
		Nos. 416-419 (4)	2.60	3.65

Kuala Lumpur — A156

1990, May 14   Wmk. 388   Litho.   *Perf. 12*

420	A156	20c Flag, rainbow, vert.	.40	.40
421	A156	40c shown	.70	.50
422	A156	$1 Cityscape	1.50	2.75
		Nos. 420-422 (3)	2.60	3.65

South-South Consultation and Cooperation Conference — A157

1990, June 1   *Perf. 13*

423	A157	20c shown	.45	.35
424	A157	80c Emblem	1.75	2.25

Alor Setar, 250th Anniv. — A158

1990, June 2   *Perf. 12*

425	A158	20c shown	.40	.30
426	A158	40c Musicians, vert.	.70	.35
427	A158	$1 Government bldg., vert.	1.50	3.00
		Nos. 425-427 (3)	2.60	3.65

Intl. Literacy Year — A159

1990, Sept. 8   *Perf. 12*

428	A159	20c Letters, sign language	.50	.35
a.		Perf. 13	17.50	
429	A159	40c People reading	1.00	.40
430	A159	$1 Globe, pen nib, vert.	2.00	3.00
		Nos. 428-430 (3)	3.50	3.75

Turtles — A160

1990, Nov. 17

431	A160	15c Dermochelys coriacea	1.25	.30
432	A160	20c Chelonia mydas	1.25	.30
433	A160	40c Eretmochelys imbricata	1.50	.65
434	A160	$1 Lepidochelys olivacea	3.25	3.75
		Nos. 431-434 (4)	7.25	5.00

MARA (Council of Indigenous Pooplo), 25th Anniv. — A161

1991, Apr. 25

435	A161	20c Construction	.30	.30
436	A161	40c Education	.50	.35
437	A161	$1 Banking & industry	.70	2.00
		Nos. 435-437 (3)	1.50	2.65

Wasps — A162

Designs: 15c, Eustenogaster calyptodoma. 20c, Vespa affinis indonensis. 50c, Sceliphorn javanum. $1, Ampulex compressa.

1991, July 29

438	A162	15c multicolored	.40	.40
439	A162	20c multicolored	.40	.40
440	A162	50c multicolored	.90	.50
441	A162	$1 multicolored	1.90	2.10
a.		Souvenir sheet of 4, #438-441, perf. 14½x14	5.50	5.50
		Nos. 438-441 (4)	3.60	3.40

Prime Ministers — A163

No. 442, Tunku Abdul Rahman Putra Al-Haj (1903-90). No. 443, Tun Hussein Onn (1922-90). No. 444, Tun Abdul Razak Hussein (1922-76).

1991, Aug. 30

442	A163	$1 multicolored	.90	1.00
443	A163	$1 multicolored	.90	1.00
444	A163	$1 multicolored	.90	1.00
		Nos. 442-444 (3)	2.70	3.00

Historic Buildings — A164

Designs: 15c, Istana Maziah, Trengganu. 20c, Istana Besar, Johore. 40c, Istana Bandar, Kuala Langat, Selangor. $1, Istana Jahar, Kelantan.

1991, Nov. 7

445	A164	15c multicolored	.35	.30
446	A164	20c multicolored	.35	.30
447	A164	40c multicolored	.55	.40
448	A164	$1 multicolored	1.40	2.25
		Nos. 445-448 (4)	2.65	3.25

Sarawak Museum, Cent. — A165

Museum buildings, fabric pattern and: 30c, Brass lamp. $1, Vase.

1991, Dec. 21

449	A165	30c multicolored	.40	.30
450	A165	$1 multicolored	1.40	2.00

Malaysian Postal Service — A166

Designs: No. 451a, Postman on bicycle. b, Postman on motorcycle. c, Mail truck. d, Mail truck, diff., oil tank. e, Globe, airplane.

1992, Jan. 1

451	A166	30c Strip of 5, #a.-e.	3.50	3.50

Malaysian Tropical Forests — A167

Designs: 20c, Hill Dipterocarp Forest, Dyera costulata. 50c, Mangrove Swamp Forest, Rhizophora apiculata. $1, Lowland Dipterocarp Forest, Neobalanocarpus heimii.

1992, Mar. 23

452	A167	20c multicolored	.35	.35
453	A167	50c multicolored	.80	.50
454	A167	$1 multicolored	1.10	2.25
		Nos. 452-454 (3)	2.25	3.10

Installation of Yang di-Pertuan Besar of Negri Sembilan, Silver Jubilee — A168

1992, Apr. 18

455	A168	30c Portrait, arms	.35	.25
456	A168	$1 Building	1.25	2.00

1992 Thomas Cup
Champions in
Badminton — A169

1992, July 25   *Perf. 12*
457 A169 $1 Cup, flag   .90 1.20
458 A169 $1 Players   .90 1.20

Souvenir Sheet
459 A169 $2 multicolored   2.50 2.50
No. 459 contains one 75x28mm stamp.

ASEAN,
25th Anniv.
A170

1992, Aug. 8
460 A170 30c shown   .55 .40
461 A170 50c Flora   1.00 .60
462 A170 $1 Architecture   1.60 2.00
    Nos. 460-462 (3)   3.15 3.00

Postage
Stamps in
Malaysia,
125th Anniv.
A171

No. 463, Straits Settlements #1, Malaya
#84. No. 464, Straits Settlements #2, Malaysia
#2. No. 465, Straits Settlements #11, Malaysia
#421. No. 466, Straits Settlements #14,
Malaysia #467. No. 467, Flag, simulated
stamp.

1992, Sept. 1
463 A171 30c multicolored   .60 .25
464 A171 30c multicolored   .60 .25
  a.   Pair #463-464   1.75 1.75
465 A171 50c multicolored   1.00 .25
466 A171 50c multicolored   1.00 .25
  a.   Pair #465-466   2.25 2.25
    Nos. 463-466 (4)   3.20 1.00

Souvenir Sheet
467 A171 $2 multicolored   2.75 2.75
Kuala Lumpur '92.

A173

Coral — A174

No. 471: a, Acropora. b, Dendronephthya. c,
Dendrophyllia. d, Sinularia. e, Melithaea.
No. 472, Subergorgia.

1992, Dec. 21
471 A173 30c Strip of 5, #a.-e. 5.00 5.00

Souvenir Sheet
472 A174 $2 multicolored   4.50 5.00

16th Asian-
Pacific
Dental
Congress
A175

Children from various countries: No. 473, 4
girls. No. 474, 4 girls, 1 holding koala.
Dentists, flags of: No. 475, Japan, Malaysia,
South Korea. No. 476, New Zealand, Thailand, People's Republic of China, Indonesia.

1993, Apr. 24
473 A175 30c multicolored   .60 .60
474 A175 30c multicolored   .60 .60
  a.   Pair, #473-474   1.50 1.50
475 A175 50c multicolored   .90 .90
476 A175 $1 multicolored   1.75 1.75
  a.   Pair, #475-476   3.50 3.50
    Nos. 473-476 (4)   3.85 3.85

A176   A177

1993, June 24
477 A176 30c Fairway, vert.   .80 .55
478 A176 50c Old, new club
               houses, vert.   1.50 .70
479 A176 $1 Sand trap   2.40 3.00
    Nos. 477-479 (3)   4.70 4.25
Royal Selangor Golf Club, cent.

1993, Aug. 2
Wildflowers.
480 A177 20c Alpinia rafflesiana .65 .50
481 A177 30c Achasma
               megalocheilos   .65 .50
482 A177 50c Zingiber spectabile 1.75 .65
483 A177 $1 Costus speciosus 2.25 3.00
    Nos. 480-483 (4)   5.30 4.65

14th Commonwealth Forestry
Conference — A178

1993, Sept. 13
484 A178 30c Globe, forest   .60 .50
485 A178 50c Hand holding trees 1.10 .60
486 A178 $1 Trees under dome,
               vert.   1.60 2.25
    Nos. 484-486 (3)   3.30 3.35

**Nos. 484-486 with Bangkok '93
Emblem Added**
Wmk. 388
1993, Oct. 1   Litho.   Perf. 12
486A A178 30c multicolored   4.50 4.00
486B A178 50c multicolored   5.50 5.00
486C A178 $1 multicolored   10.00 8.50
    Nos. 486A-486C (3)   20.00 17.50

Kingfishers — A179

1993, Oct. 23
487   30c Halcyon smyrnensis 1.00 1.00
488   30c Alcedo meninting   1.00 1.00
  a.   Pair, #487-488   2.50 2.50
489   50c Halcyon concreta   1.60 1.60
490   50c Ceyx erithacus   1.60 1.60
  a.   A179 Pair, #489-490   4.00 4.00
    Nos. 487-490 (4)   5.20 5.20

A180

1993, Dec. 7
491 A180 30c SME MD3-160 air-
               plane   .60 .40
492 A180 50c Eagle X-TS air-
               plane   1.25 .70
493 A180 $1 Patrol boat KD
               Kasturi   1.75 2.25
    Nos. 491-493 (3)   3.60 3.35

Souvenir Sheet
494 A180 $2 Map of Malaysia 3.00 3.00
Langkawi Intl. Maritime and Aerospace
Exhibition (LIMA '93).

Visit
Malaysia
Year — A181

1994, Jan. 1
495 A181 20c Jeriau Waterfalls .40 .40
496 A181 30c Flowers   .50 .45
497 A181 50c Marine life   1.00 .60
498 A181 $1 Wildlife   1.50 2.00
    Nos. 495-498 (4)   3.40 3.45
See Nos. 527A-527D.

Kuala
Lumpur Natl.
Planetarium
A182

Designs: 30c, Exterior. 50c, Interior displays. $1, Theater auditorium.

1994, Feb. 7
499 A182 30c multicolored   .50 .40
500 A182 50c multicolored   .90 .65
501 A182 $1 multicolored   1.75 2.25
    Nos. 499-501 (3)   3.15 3.30

Orchids — A183

Designs: 20c, Spathoglottis aurea. 30c,
Paphiopedilum barbatum. 50c, Bulbophyllum
lobbii. $1, Aerides odorata. $2, Grammatophyllum speciosum.

1994, Feb. 17
502 A183 20c multicolored   .55 .35
503 A183 30c multicolored   .55 .40
504 A183 50c multicolored   .90 .70
505 A183 $1 multicolored   1.60 2.25
    Nos. 502-505 (4)   3.60 3.70

Souvenir Sheet
506 A183 $2 multicolored   3.75 3.75
Hong Kong '94 (No. 506).

A184   A185

1994, June 17
507 A184 20c Decorative bowl   .35 .30
508 A184 30c Celestial sphere .40 .30
509 A184 50c Dinar coins   .55 .55
510 A184 $1 Decorative tile   1.10 1.25
    Nos. 507-510 (4)   2.40 2.40
World Islamic Civilization Festival '94.
See Nos. 528-531.

1994, July 26
511 A185 30c shown   .60 .40
512 A185 50c Meat processing .80 .60
513 A185 $1 Cattle, laboratory 1.60 2.00
    Nos. 511-513 (3)   3.00 3.00
Veterinary Services, cent.

Electrification, Cent. — A186

1994, Sept. 3
514 A186 30c Laying cable   .55 .40
515 A186 30c Lighted city   .55 .40
  a.   Pair, #514-515   1.40 1.40
516 A186 $1 Futuristic city 1.40 1.75
    Nos. 514-516 (3)   2.50 2.55

North-South
Expressway
A187

1994, Sept. 8
517 A187 30c shown   .40 .30
518 A187 50c Interchange   .55 .45
519 A187 $1 Bridge   1.25 1.60
    Nos. 517-519 (3)   2.20 2.35

A188   A189

1994, Sept. 22
520 A188 30c pink & multi   .45 .30
521 A188 50c yellow & multi   .60 .40
522 A188 $1 green & multi   1.10 1.60
    Nos. 520-522 (3)   2.15 2.30
Installation of 10th Yang Di-Pertuan Agong
(Head of State).

Wmk. 388
1994, Oct. 29   Litho.   Perf. 12
523 A189 $1 shown   1.25 1.25
524 A189 $1 Mascot   1.25 1.25
  a.   Pair, #523-524 + label 2.75 3.25
1998 Commonwealth Games, Kuala Lumpur.

Official
Opening of
Natl. Library
Building
A190

1994, Dec. 16
525 A190 30c Library building .45 .35
526 A190 50c Computer terminal .60 .45
527 A190 $1 Manuscript   1.25 1.00
    Nos. 525-527 (3)   2.30 1.80

Nos. 495-498 with Added Inscription

Wmk. 388

1994, Nov. 8   Litho.   *Perf. 12*

527A	A181	20c multicolored	.75	.85
527B	A181	30c multicolored	1.25	.95
527C	A181	50c multicolored	1.75	1.50
527D	A181	$1 multicolored	3.00	2.75
		Nos. 527A-527D (4)	6.75	6.05

Nos. 507-510 with Added Inscription

Wmk. 388

1994, Aug. 16   Litho.   *Perf. 12*

528	A184	20c multicolored	1.40	1.40
529	A184	30c multicolored	1.10	1.10
530	A184	50c multicolored	2.75	2.75
531	A184	$1 multicolored	5.50	5.50
		Nos. 528-531 (4)	10.75	10.75

A191

1994, Nov. 10   Unwmk.   *Perf. 14½*

532	A191	30c shown	.65	.35
533	A191	$1 Building complex	1.30	1.50

Memorial to Tunku Abdul Rahman Putra Al-Haj (1903-1990), former Prime Minister.

Fungi — A192

1995, Jan. 18   *Perf. 14½x14*

534	A192	20c Bracket fungus	.65	.30
535	A192	30c Cup fungus	.70	.30
536	A192	50c Veil fungus	1.10	.40
537	A192	$1 Coral fungus	2.25	2.75
		Nos. 534-537 (4)	4.70	3.75

Neofelis Nebulosa A193

1995, Apr. 18   Wmk. 373   *Perf. 13½*

538	A193	20c shown	.35	.30
539	A193	30c With young	.55	.40
540	A193	50c With mouth open	.90	.75
541	A193	$1 Lying on rock	1.75	2.00
a.		Strip of 4, #538-541	5.00	5.00

Nos. 538-541 were issued in sheets of 16 stamps.
World Wildlife Fund.

Marine Life — A194

1995, Apr. 10   Wmk. 388   *Perf. 12*
Booklet Stamps

542	A194	20c Feather stars	.90	.90
543	A194	20c Sea fans	.90	.90
a.		Pair, #542-543	2.00	2.00
b.		Booklet pane, 5 each #542-543	9.75	9.75
		Complete booklet, #543b	10.00	
544	A194	30c Soft coral	1.20	1.20
545	A194	30c Cup coral	1.20	1.20
a.		Pair, #544-545	2.60	2.60
b.		Booklet pane, 5 each #544-545	13.00	13.00
		Complete booklet, #543b	14.00	
		Nos. 542-545 (4)	4.20	4.20

X-Ray, Cent. A195

No. 546, Early machine x-raying hand. No. 547, CAT scan machine. $1, Chest x-ray.

1995, May 29

546	A195	30c multicolored	.55	.70
547	A195	30c multicolored	.55	.70
a.		Pair, #546-547	1.25	1.60
548	A195	$1 multicolored	1.50	1.75
		Nos. 546-548 (3)	2.60	3.15

1998 Commonwealth Games, Kuala Lumpur — A196

Various sporting events: No. 549, Badminton, cricket, shooting, tennis, weight lifting, hurdles, field hockey. No. 550, Cycling, lawn bowling, boxing, basketball, rugby, gymnastics.

Wmk. 388
1995, Sept. 10   Litho.   *Perf. 14*

549	A196	$1 multicolored	2.25	2.25
550	A196	$1 multicolored	2.25	2.25
a.		Pair, #549-550 + label	5.00	5.00

Traditional Weapons A197

1995, Sept. 1   Litho.   *Perf. 14*

551	A197	20c Jemblah	.30	.25
552	A197	30c Keris panjang	.30	.25
553	A197	50c Kerambit	.45	.35
554	A197	$1 Keris sundang	.90	1.50
		Nos. 551-554 (4)	1.95	2.35

Souvenir Sheet

555	A197	$2 Lading terus	3.50	3.50

Singapore '95.

UN, 50th Anniv. A198

1995, Oct. 24   *Perf. 13½*

556	A198	30c shown	.40	.30
557	A198	$1 UN emblem	1.10	1.25

Intl. Assoc. of Travel Agents (IATA), 50th Anniv. — A199

Jet, globe and: No. 558, Historic buildings. No. 559, Sydney Opera House, Great Wall of China. No. 560, Eiffel Tower, Tower Bridge. No. 561, Hollywood Walk of Fame, Latin American pyramid.

1995, Oct. 30   *Perf. 14*

558		30c multicolored	.65	.65
559		30c multicolored	.65	.65
a.	A199	Pair, #558-559	1.75	1.75
560		50c multicolored	.90	.90
561		50c multicolored	.90	.90
a.	A199	Pair, #560-561	2.25	2.25
		Nos. 558-561 (4)	3.10	3.10

Turtles A200

Perf. 14x14½
1995, Sept. 26   Litho.   Wmk. 388
Booklet Stamps

562	A200	30c Chelonia mydas	2.00	1.25
563	A200	30c Dermochelys coriacea	2.00	1.25
a.		Booklet pane, 5 each #562-563	22.00	16.00
		Complete booklet, #563a	24.00	

Proton Cars, 10th Anniv. — A201

No. 564, 1985 Saga 1.5. No. 565, 1992 Iswara 1.5 aeroback. No. 566, 1992, Iswara 1.5 sedan. No. 567, 1993 Wira 1.6 sedan. No. 568, 1993 Wira 1.6 aeroback. No. 569, 1994 Rally. No. 570, 1994 Satria 1.6. No. 571, 1995 Perdana 2.0. No. 572, 1995 Wira 1.6 aeroback. No. 573, 1995 Wira 1.8 sedan.

1995, Dec.   Litho.   *Perf. 14*
Booklet Stamps

564	A201	30c multicolored	1.00	1.00
565	A201	30c multicolored	1.00	1.00
566	A201	30c multicolored	1.00	1.00
567	A201	30c multicolored	1.00	1.00
568	A201	30c multicolored	1.00	1.00
569	A201	30c multicolored	1.00	1.00
570	A201	30c multicolored	1.00	1.00
571	A201	30c multicolored	1.00	1.00
572	A201	30c multicolored	1.00	1.00
573	A201	30c multicolored	1.00	1.00
a.		Booklet pane, Nos. 564-573	10.00	10.00
		Complete booklet, No. 573a	10.00	

A202

Malaysia East Asia Satellite: 30c, Ariane 4 being launched. 50c, Satellite in Earth orbit over East Asia. $1, Satellite Control Center, Langkawai.
$5, Satellite entering orbit, horiz.

1996, Jan. 13   *Perf. 13½*

574	A202	30c multicolored	.40	.30
575	A202	50c multicolored	.60	.50
576	A202	$1 multicolored	1.10	1.60
		Nos. 574-576 (3)	2.10	2.40

Souvenir Sheet
Perf. 14

577	A202	$5 multicolored	7.25	7.25

No. 577 contains a holographic image. Soaking in water may affect the hologram.

A203

Pitcher Plants: No. 578, Nepenthes sanguinea. No. 579, Nepenthes macfarlanei. No. 580, Nepenthes rajah. No. 581, Nepenthes lowii.

Perf. 13½, 14½x14 (#580-581)
1996, Apr. 16   Litho.   Wmk. 388

578	A203	30c multicolored	.30	.30
579	A203	30c multicolored	.30	.30
a.		Pair, Nos. 578-579	.75	.90
580	A203	50c multicolored	.45	.40
581	A203	50c multicolored	.45	.40
a.		Pair, Nos. 580-581	1.20	1.40
		Nos. 578-581 (4)	1.50	1.40

Birds of Prey A204

Designs: 20c, Haliastur indus. 30c, Spilornis cheela. 50c, Haliaeetus leucogaster. $1, Spizaetus cirrhatus. $2, Spizaetus alboniger, vert.

Wmk. 388
1996, May 18   Litho.   *Perf. 14*

582	A204	20c multicolored	.40	.40
583	A204	30c multicolored	.45	.45
584	A204	50c multicolored	.65	.65
585	A204	$1 multicolored	1.50	2.00
		Nos. 582-585 (4)	3.00	3.50

Souvenir Sheet

586	A204	$2 multicolored	4.50	4.50

CHINA '96 (No. 586).

Intl. Day Against Drug Abuse and Illicit Drug Trafficking A205

Designs: No. 587, Family, drugs burning. No. 588, Various sporting activities, marajuana plants. $1, Family, rainbow.

Wmk. 388
1996, June 26   Litho.   *Perf. 14*

587	A205	30c multicolored	.40	.30
588	A205	30c multicolored	.40	.30
a.		Pair, #587-588	1.00	1.25
589	A205	$1 multicolored	1.75	1.75
		Nos. 587-589 (3)	2.55	2.35

Butterflies — A206

No. 590, Graphium sarpedon. No. 591, Melanocyma faunula. No. 592, Delias hyparete. No. 593, Trogonoptera brookiana. No. 594, Terinos terpander.

1996, Sept. 27   Litho.   *Perf. 14½x14*
Booklet Stamps

590	A206	30c multicolored	1.75	1.25
591	A206	30c multicolored	1.75	1.25
592	A206	30c multicolored	1.75	1.25
593	A206	30c multicolored	1.75	1.25

594	A206	30c multicolored	1.75	1.25
a.		Pane of 10, 2 each #590-594	17.50	17.50
		Nos. 590-594 (5)	8.75	6.25

Kuala Lumpur Tower A207

30c, Artist's impression. 50c, Tower head diagram. $1, Tower head, city at night. $2, Kuala Lumpur Tower, vert.

Perf. 13½

1996, Oct. 1	Litho.		Unwmk.	
595	A207	30c multicolored	.35	.25
596	A207	50c multicolored	.50	.30
597	A207	$1 multicolored	1.10	1.40
		Nos. 595-597 (3)	1.95	1.95

Souvenir Sheet

598	A207	$2 multicolored	2.50	2.50
a.		With added inscription in sheet margin	2.50	2.50

No. 598a inscribed with TAIPEI '96 emblem, issued 10/16/96.

14th Conference of Confederation of Asian and Pacific Accountants — A208

1996, Oct. 7			Perf. 13½x14	
599	A208	30c CAPA logo	.50	.40
600	A208	$1 Globe	1.10	1.25

Natl. Science Center A209

30c, Model of molecular structure. 50c, Model of atom, Science Center. $1, Natl. Science Center.

		Unwmk.		
1996, Nov. 29	Litho.		Perf. 14	
601	A209	30c multicolored	.45	.35
602	A209	50c multicolored	.60	.40
603	A209	$1 multicolored	1.10	1.25
		Nos. 601-603 (3)	2.15	2.00

Souvenir Sheet

Stamp Week — A210

Wildlife: a, 20c, Nycticebus coucang. b, 30c, Callosciurus prevostil. c, 50c, Attacus atlas. d, $1, Hylobates lar. e, $1, Buceros rhinoceros. f, $2, Hemigalus derbyanus.

1996, Dec. 2				
604	A210	Sheet of 6, #a.-f.	4.25	4.25

No. 604d is 30x60mm. Nos. 605e-605f are 60x30mm.

Birds — A211

Designs: 20c, Muscicapella hodgsoni. 30c, Leiothrix argentauris. 50c, Dicaeum celibicum. $1, Aethopyga mystacalis.

Perf. 13½x14

1997, Jan. 4	Litho.		Unwmk.	
605	A211	20c multicolored	.35	.35
606	A211	30c multicolored	.45	.35
607	A211	50c multicolored	.65	.40
608	A211	$1 multicolored	1.40	1.60
		Nos. 605-608 (4)	2.85	2.70

16th Commonwealth Games, Kuala Lumpur '98 — A212

1996, Dec. 21			Perf. 12	
609	A212	30c Running	.45	.25
610	A212	30c Hurdles	.45	.25
a.		Pair, #609-610	1.10	.90
611	A212	50c High jump	.75	.35
612	A212	50c Javelin	.75	.35
a.		Pair, #611-612	1.75	1.50
		Nos. 609-612 (4)	2.40	1.20

Intl. Cricket Cup Champions A213

1997, Mar. 24	Litho.		Perf. 14	
613	A213	30c shown	.35	.35
614	A213	50c Batsman	.50	.50
615	A213	$1 Wicket keeper	1.25	1.50
		Nos. 613-615 (3)	2.10	2.35

Aviation in Malaysia, 50th Anniv. A214

Designs: 30c, Jet, world map. 50c, Jet approaching Kuala Lumpur. $1, Airplane tailfins of four Malaysian airlines.

Perf. 14, 13½ (#617)

1997, Apr. 2			Wmk. 388	
616	A214	30c multicolored	.55	.40
617	A214	50c multicolored	.95	.75
618	A214	$1 multicolored	2.00	2.25
a.		Perf. 13½	4.00	2.00
		Nos. 616-618 (3)	3.50	3.40

A215　　　A216

Light Rail Transit System: No. 620, Two trains, one on bridge, Kuala Lumpur skyline.

Perf. 14x14½

1997, Mar. 1	Litho.		Unwmk.	
		Booklet Stamps		
619	A215	30c shown	1.60	.80
620	A215	30c multicolored	1.60	.80
a.		Booklet pane, 5 each #619-620	16.00	16.00
		Complete booklet, #620a	16.00	

1997, May 7		Perf. 14½x14	

Highland Flowers: No. 621, Schima wallichii. No. 622, Aeschynanthus longicalyx. No. 623. Aeschynanthus speciosa. No. 624, Phyllagathis tuberculata. No. 625, Didymocarpus quinquevulnerus.

Booklet Stamps

621	A216	30c multicolored	.70	.70
622	A216	30c multicolored	.70	.70
623	A216	30c multicolored	.70	.70
624	A216	30c multicolored	.70	.70
625	A216	30c multicolored	.70	.70
a.		Booklet pane, 2 each #621-625	7.50	7.50
		Complete booklet, #625a	8.00	
		Nos. 621-625 (5)	3.50	3.50

Ruler's Council, Cent. A217

		Unwmk.		
1997, July 31	Litho.		Perf. 14	
626	A217	30c Photo, 1897	.35	.30
627	A217	50c Emblem, arms	.55	.40
628	A217	$1 Emblem	.90	1.40
		Nos. 626-628 (3)	1.80	2.10

ASEAN, 30th Anniv. A218

1997, Aug. 8	Wmk. 388		Perf. 13½	
629	A218	30c shown	.65	.40
630	A218	50c "30," emblem	.85	.50
631	A218	$1 Emblem, color bars	1.50	1.75
		Nos. 629-631 (3)	3.00	2.65

A219　　　A220

Coral: 20c, Tubastrea. 30c, Melithaea. 50c, Aulostomus chinensis. $1, Symphillia.

1997, Aug. 23	Unwmk.		Perf. 14½	
632	A219	20c multicolored	.30	.30
633	A219	30c multicolored	.30	.30
634	A219	50c multicolored	.40	.35
635	A219	$1 multicolored	1.10	1.25
		Nos. 632-635 (4)	2.10	2.20

1997, Aug. 25			Perf. 13x13½	
		Booklet Stamps		
636	A220	30c Career women	.70	.40
637	A220	30c Family	.70	.40
a.		Booklet pane, 5 each #636-637	7.00	7.00
		Complete booklet, #637a	7.00	

20th Intl. Conf. of Pan-Pacific and Southeast Asia Women's Assoc., Kuala Lumpur.

9th World Youth Soccer Championships A221

30c, Mascot. 50c, Soccer ball, players, flag. $1, Map of Malaysia, silhouettes of players, soccer ball.

Perf. 13½x13

1997, June 16			Unwmk.	
638	A221	30c multicolored	.30	.30
639	A221	50c multicolored	.45	.40
		Perf. 13x12½		
640	A221	$1 multicolored	1.00	1.40
		Nos. 638-640 (3)	1.75	2.10

Souvenir Sheet

Chelonia Mydas — A222

1997, Aug. 23	Litho.		Perf. 14½	
641	A222	$2 multicolored	3.00	3.25

Year of the Coral Reef.

7th Summit Level of the Group of 15 — A223

$1, Emblem, natl. flags of member nations.

Perf. 12, 13½ (#643)

1997, Nov. 3	Litho.		Unwmk.	
642	A223	30c shown	.30	.30
643	A223	$1 multicolored	1.25	1.25

Stamp Week A224

Protected wildlife: a, 20c, Tomistoma schlegelli. b, 30c, Tarsius bancanus, vert. c, 50c, Cervus unicolor, vert. d, $2, Rollulus rouloul. e, $2, Scleropages formosus.

1997, Dec. 1			Perf. 14½	
644	A224	Sheet of 5, #a.-e.	3.25	3.25

Philately in Malaysia, 50th Anniv. — A225

Malpex '97: a, 20c, Straits Settlements #7. b, 30c, #605-608. c, 50c, #604. d, $1, Early cover from Straits Settlements.

1997, Sept. 9			Perf. 12½	
645	A225	Sheet of 4, #a.-d.	3.25	3.25
e.		Ovptd. in sheet margin in gold	2.00	2.00

No. 645e is inscribed in sheet margin with INDEPEX '97 exhibition emblem.

Rare Fruit — A226

1998, Jan. 10   *Perf. 13½*
646	A226	20c Bouea macrophylla	.25	.25
647	A226	30c Sandoricum koetjape	.30	.30
648	A226	50c Nephelium ramboutan-ake	.40	.30
649	A226	$1 Garcinia atroviridis	.75	1.25
		Nos. 646-649 (4)	1.70	2.10

Kuala Lumpur '98 Games A227

1998, Feb. 23   *Perf. 12*
650	A227	30c Field hockey	.60	.60
651	A227	30c Women's netball	.60	.60
a.		Pair, #650-651 + label	1.40	1.40
652	A227	50c Cricket	.85	.85
653	A227	50c Rugby	.85	.85
a.		Pair, #652-653 + label	1.90	1.90
		Nos. 650-653 (4)	2.90	2.90

Kuala Lumpur '98 Games — A228

Stadiums for the venues: a, 1r, Utama Bukit Jalil. b, 50c, Tertutup. c, 30c, Hoki. d, 20c, Renang Complex.

Wmk. 388
1998, Feb. 23   **Litho.**   *Perf. 13⅓*
654	A228	Sheet of 4, #a.-d.	2.50	2.50

Early Coins A229

Coin's region, date: 20c, Trengganu, 1793-1808. 30c, Kedah, 1661-87. 50c, Johore, 1597-1615. $1, Kelantan, 1400-1780.

Wmk. 388
1998, Apr. 11   **Litho.**   *Perf. 13½*
655	A229	20c multicolored	.30	.30
a.		Perf. 14¼	3.00	.25
656	A229	30c multicolored	.40	.30
657	A229	50c multicolored	.45	.30
a.		Perf. 14¼	4.25	.35
658	A229	$1 multicolored	.70	1.10
		Nos. 655-658 (4)	1.85	2.00

Kuala Lumpur International Airport — A230

Designs: 30c, Tower, tramway, airplanes. 50c, Tower, airplanes at terminal. $1, Tower, airplane in air, airport below. $2, Tower, globe overhead.

1998, June 27   *Perf. 12*
659	A230	30c multicolored	.35	.30
a.		Perf. 12½	5.00	
660	A230	50c multicolored	.65	.30
661	A230	$1 multicolored	1.00	1.75
a.		Perf. 12½	6.00	3.75
		Nos. 659-661 (3)	2.00	2.35

Souvenir Sheet
Perf. 14
662	A230	$2 multicolored	2.50	2.75

No. 662 contains one 26x36mm stamp.

Malaysian Red Crescent Society, 50th Anniv. — A231

1998, May 8   *Perf. 13½*
663	A231	30c Rescue boat	.45	.40
a.		Perf. 14¼	2.75	2.75
664	A231	$1 Mobile rescue unit	1.25	.60
a.		Perf. 14¼	2.75	2.75

Watermark on No. 664a is inverted. No. 664a also exists with watermark upright. Value $10.

Medicinal Plants — A234

20c, Solanum torvum. 30c, Tinospora crispa. 50c, Jatropha podagrica. $1, Hibiscus rosa-sinensis.

Wmk. 388
1998, July 18   **Litho.**   *Perf. 13¾*
671	A234	20c multicolored	.25	.25
672	A234	30c multicolored	.30	.30

Perf. 14¼
673	A234	50c multicolored	.40	.30
674	A234	$1 multicolored	.60	1.25
		Nos. 671-674 (4)	1.55	2.10

1998 Commonwealth Games, Kuala Lumpur — A235

a, 20c, Weight lifting. b, 20c, Badminton. c, 30c, Field hockey goalie. d, 30c, Field hockey. e, 20c, Netball. f, 20c, Shooting. g, 30c, Cycling. h, 50c, Lawn bowling. i, 50c, Gymnastics. j, 50c, Cricket. k, $1, Swimming. l, $1, Squash. m, 50c, Rugby. n, 50c, Running. o, $1, Boxing. p, $1, Bowling.

Perf. 14½x15
1998, Sept. 11   **Litho.**   **Wmk. 388**
675	A235	Sheet of 16, #a.-p.	7.00	7.50

Modernization of Rail Transport — A236

Designs: 30c, Putra-LRT, 1998. 50c, Star-LRT, 1996. $1, KTM Commuter, 1995.

1998, Oct. 3   *Perf. 13¾, 14¼*
676	A236	30c multicolored	.30	.30
a.		Perf. 14¼	3.25	
677	A236	50c multicolored	.55	.35
a.		Perf. 14¼	1.25	.30

678	A236	$1 multicolored (Perf. 14¼)	1.10	1.25
		Nos. 676-678 (3)	1.95	1.90

1998 APEC (Asia-Pacific Economic Cooperation) Conference A237

Design: $1, Petronas Towers, people working with computers, office workers.

1998, Nov. 14   *Perf. 13½*
679	A237	30c shown	2.25	.35
a.		Perf. 14½	.70	.35
680	A237	$1 multicolored	.85	1.10
a.		Perf. 14½	3.75	3.75

Insects A238

Designs: a, 20c, Xylotrupes gideon, vert. b, 30c, Pomponia imperatoria, vert. c, 50c, Phyllium pulchrifolium, vert. d, $2, Hymenopus coronatus. e, $2, Macrolyristes corporalis.

Wmk. 388
1998, Nov. 28   **Litho.**   *Perf. 12½*
681	A238	Sheet of 5, #a.-e.	3.25	3.75

Stamp Week.
Nos. 681a-681c are each 30x40mm.

Gold Medal Winners at 16th Commonwealth Games — A238a

No. 681F: h, 30c, Air rifle. i, 30c, 48kg boxing. j, 30c, 50km walk. k, 30c, 69kg clean and jerk weight lifting. l, 50c, Men's doubles, bowling. m, 50c, Men's singles, bowling. n, 50c, Men's doubles, badminton. o, 50c, Men's singles, badminton. p, $1, Rhythmic gymnastics (64x26mm).
$2, Team photograph.

Perf. 13¾x14
1998, Dec. 12   **Litho.**   **Wmk. 388**
681F	A238a	Sheet of 9, #h.-p., + 2 labels	10.00	10.00

Souvenir Sheet
681G	A238a	$2 multi	4.25	4.25

No. 681G contains one 128x80mm stamp.

Intl. Year for Older Persons A239

Wmk. 388
1999, Jan. 28   **Litho.**   *Perf. 14*
682	A239	$1 shown	.85	1.00
683	A239	$1 World map, people, diff.	.85	1.00

Fruit — A240

Designs: 20c, Syzygium malaccense. 30c, Garcinia prainiana. 50c, Mangifera caesia. $1, Salacca glabrescens.

1999, Feb. 27   *Perf. 12*
684	A240	20c multicolored	.25	.25
685	A240	30c multicolored	.30	.25
686	A240	50c multicolored	.40	.30
687	A240	$1 multicolored	.70	1.00
a.		Strip of 4, #684-687	1.75	1.75
		Nos. 684-687 (4)	1.65	1.80

Domestic Cats — A241

Designs: 30c, Kucing Malaysia. 50c, Siamese. $1, Abyssinian.
No. 691: a, British shorthair. b, Scottish fold.
No. 692: a, Birman. b, Persian.

1999, Apr. 1   **Litho.**   *Perf. 12*
688	A241	30c multicolored	.35	.30
689	A241	50c multicolored	.55	.30
690	A241	$1 multicolored	.80	1.00
		Nos. 688-690 (3)	1.70	1.60

Sheets of 2
691	A241	$1 #a.-b.	1.30	1.30
692	A241	$1 #a.-b.	1.30	1.30

Protected Mammals A242

Wmk. 388
1999, May 28   **Litho.**   *Perf. 12*
693	A242	20c Rhinoceros	.35	.45
694	A242	30c Panther	.25	.45
695	A242	50c Bear	.40	.55
696	A242	1r Elephant	.80	1.10
697	A242	2r Orangutan	1.50	1.75
a.		Strip of 5, #693-697	3.75	3.75
b.		Souvenir sheet, #697	2.25	2.25

Nos. 693-697 were issued in sheet containing 4 each. No. 697b is a continuous design.

Intl. Congress on AIDS in Asia and the Pacific, Kuala Lumpur A244

Perf. 14, 13½ (#700, 701)
1999, June 19   **Litho.**   **Wmk. 388**
699	A244	30c shown	.35	.35
700	A244	50c Emblems, hearts	.50	.40
701	A244	1r Emblem as heart	.90	1.25
		Nos. 699-701 (3)	1.75	2.00

P. Ramlee (1929-73), Actor, Director — A245

Designs: 20c, Wearing chain around neck. 30c, Wearing bow tie. 50c, Holding gun. No. 705, Behind camera.
No. 706: a, Wearing cap. b, With hands in air. c, Holding microphone. d, Wearing army uniform.
No. 707, Wearing patterned hat. No. 708, Wearing plaid shirt.

Perf. 13½x13¾
1999, July 24   **Litho.**   **Wmk. 388**
702	A245	20c multicolored	.40	.40
703	A245	30c multicolored	.50	.40
704	A245	50c multicolored	.75	.50

705 A245 $1 multicolored   1.30   1.50
a.   Perf. 14¼   1.10   1.30
Nos. 702-705 (4)   2.95   2.80

Strip of 4

706 A245 30c #a.-d.   3.50   3.50

Souvenir Sheets
Perf. 14¼

707 A245 $1 multicolored   10.00   10.00
708 A245 $1 multicolored   10.00   10.00

No. 706 printed in sheets of 16 stamps.

Water Plants and Fish — A246

No. 709, Monochoria hastata. No. 710, Trichopsis vittatus. No. 711, Limnocharis flava. No. 712, Betta imbellis. No. 713, Nymphaea pubescens. No. 714, Trichogaster trichopterus. No. 715, Ipomea aquatica. No. 716, Helostoma temminicki. No. 717, Eichhornia crassipes. No. 718, Sphaerichthys osphronemoides.

Perf. 13¾x14

1999, July 31   Litho.   Wmk. 388

709 A246 10c multi   .40   .40
710 A246 10c multi   .40   .40
a.   Pair, #709-710   .90   .90
711 A246 15c multi   .40   .40
712 A246 15c multi   .40   .40
a.   Pair, #711-712   .90   .90
713 A246 25c multi   .40   .40
714 A246 25c multi   .40   .40
a.   Pair, #713-714   1.00   1.00
715 A246 50c multi   .50   .50
716 A246 50c multi   .50   .50
a.   Pair, #715-716   1.50   1.50
717 A246 50c multi   .50   .50
718 A246 50c multi   .50   .50
a.   Pair, #717-718   1.50   1.50
b.   Block of 10 with bottom row of perforations perf 14½   4.50   4.50
Nos. 709-718 (10)   4.40   4.40

Trees — A247

Designs: No. 719, Dryobalanops aromatica. No. 720, Alstonia angustiloba. No. 721, Fagraea fragrans. No. 722, Lagerstroemia floribunda. No. 723, Elateriospermum tapos.

Perf. 14x13½

1999, Aug. 14   Litho.   Wmk. 388

719 A247 30c multicolored   .60   .60
720 A247 30c multicolored   .60   .60
721 A247 30c multicolored   .60   .60
722 A247 30c multicolored   .60   .60
723 A247 30c multicolored   .60   .60
a.   Strip of 5, #719-723   3.00   3.00
Complete bklt., 4 ea #719-723   12.00

Petronas Towers — A248

Designs: 30c, Daytime view. 50c, Architectural drawing. $1, Nighttime view. $5, Hologram.

Perf. 14x14¼

1999, Aug. 30   Litho.   Unwmk.

724 A248 30c multicolored   .35   .30
725 A248 50c multicolored   .45   .40
726 A248 $1 multicolored   .90   1.10
Nos. 724-726 (3)   1.70   1.80

Souvenir Sheet
Perf. 14½x14¼

727 A248 $5 multicolored   5.00   5.00

No. 727 contains one 30x50mm stamp with a holographic image. Soaking in water may affect hologram. No. 727 exists imperf.

Taiping, 125th Anniv. A249

Designs: 20c, Rickshaw, Peace Hotel. 30c, Automobile, building. 50c, Train, train station. $1, Airplanes, airport building. $2, Building, horse-drawn carriage.

Unwmk.

1999, Sept. 1   Litho.   Perf. 12

728 A249 20c multi   .45   .45
729 A249 30c multi   .45   .45
730 A249 50c multi   .55   .45
731 A249 $1 multi   1.10   1.50
Nos. 728-731 (4)   2.55   2.85

Souvenir Sheet

732 A249 $2 multi   5.00   5.00

Tenaga Nasional, 50th Anniv. A250

Designs: 30c, Power station at night. 50c, High tension wire towers, control room. No. 735, Kuala Lumpur at night. No. 736, Van, vert. No. 737, High tension wire towers, vert.

Perf. 14¼x14½

1999, Sept. 9   Litho.   Unwmk.

733 A250 30c multicolored   .40   .30
734 A250 50c multicolored   .55   .35
735 A250 $1 multicolored   1.05   1.50
Nos. 733-735 (3)   2.00   2.15

Souvenir Sheets
Perf. 13½x13¾

736 A250 $1 multicolored   1.00   1.25
737 A250 $1 multicolored   1.00   1.25

National Theater — A251

Various performers and views of building.

1999   Litho.   Wmk. 388   Perf. 12¼
Panel Colors

738 A251 30c red   .35   .30
739 A251 50c green   .45   .40
740 A251 $1 violet   .80   1.10
Nos. 738-740 (3)   1.60   1.80

Installation of 11th Yang Di-Pertuan Agong (Head of State) A252

Tuanku Salehuddin Abdul Aziz Shah ibni al-Marhum Hisamuddin Alam Shah and: 30c, Flag. 50c, Old building. $1, Modern building. No. 744: a, Purple background. b, Yellow background. c, Blue background.

Perf. 13¾x13½

1999, Sept. 23   Litho.   Wmk. 388

741 A252 30c multicolored   .30   .25

Perf. 14¼

742 A252 50c multicolored   .40   .30
743 A252 $1 multicolored   .80   1.00

Perf. 14x13¾

744 A252 30c Strip of 3, #a.-c.   2.00   2.40
Nos. 741-744 (4)   3.50   3.95

Size of Nos. 744a-744c: 24x30mm.

21st World Road Congress — A253

Unwmk.

1999, Oct. 3   Litho.   Perf. 12

745 A253 30c Entrance ramp   .30   .30
746 A253 50c Bridge   .45   .35
747 A253 $1 Interchange   .90   1.10
Nos. 745-747 (3)   1.65   1.75

A254

1999 Malaysia Grand Prix — A255

Racing helmets and: 20c, Canopy over track's stands. 30c, Stands. 50c, Car on track. $1, side view of car.
No. 752: a, 20c, Stands b, 30c, Race control building. c, 50c, Pits. d, $1, Track.

Unwmk.

1999, Oct. 16   Litho.   Perf. 12

748 A254 20c multi   .40   .35
749 A254 30c multi   .40   .35
750 A254 50c multi   .50   .45
751 A254 $1 multi   .90   1.10
Nos. 748-751 (4)   2.20   2.25

Perf. 12½

752 A255 Strip or block of 4, #a.-d.   2.50   2.75

No. 752 printed in sheets of 16 stamps.

UPU, 125th Anniv. A256

Designs: 20c, Computer, envelopes. 30c, Globe, stamps. 50c, World map, airplane. $1, Malaysian Post Office emblem.

Perf. 13¾x13½

1999, Dec. 18   Litho.   Wmk. 388

753 A256 20c multi   .40   .40
754 A256 30c multi   .40   .40

Perf. 14¼

755 A256 50c multi   .50   .50
756 A256 $1 multi   .90   1.30
Nos. 753-756 (4)   2.20   2.60

Sultan of Pahang, 25th Anniv. of Reign A257

Sultan and: a, Flowers. b, Butterfly, flower, highway. c, Divers, beach. d, Automobile plant. e, Palace.

Wmk. 388

1999, Oct. 23   Litho.   Perf. 14¼

757 A257 30c Strip of 5, #a.-e.   2.50   2.50

Malaysia '99 World Cup Golf Tournament — A258

20c, World Cup. 30c, Ball on tee. 50c, Fairway and green. $1, Clubhouse and flag.

Perf. 14x13¾ Syncopated

1999, Nov. 18

758 A258 20c multi   .40   .40
759 A258 30c multi   .40   .40
760 A258 50c multi   .45   .45
761 A258 $1 multi   .90   1.25
a.   Sheet, 5 each #758-761   10.00   10.00
Nos. 758-761 (4)   2.15   2.50

Flowers — A259

No. 762: a, Strelitzia augusta. b, Heliconia rostrata. c, Heliconia psittacorum (yellow petals). d, Heliconia stricta. e, Musa violescens. f, Strelitzia reginae. g, Heliconia colgantea. h, Heliconia psittacorum (pink and blue petals). i, Heliconia latispatha. j, Phaemoria speciosa.

1999, Nov. 29   Wmk. 388   Perf. 12¼

762 A259 30c Block or strip of 10, #a.-j.   5.00   5.00
k.   Sheet, 2 blocks #762   10.00   10.00

Millennium A260

Stamp number in parentheses.
No. 763: a, Vine, bird (1). b, Pottery, waterfall (2). c, Frog, forest (3). d, People and machine, cultivated land (4). e, Fish, boat and lighthouse (5). f, Chevrotain, house (6). g, Elephant, forest (7). h, Dagger, ship (8). i, Clock tower, archway (9). j, Boat with sail, palm trees (10).
No. 764: a, Man with musical instrument, native people (11). b, Lantern and nautilus shell, native people (12). c, Doctor and patient, native people (13). d, Badminton player, native people (14). e, Dancer, native women (15). f, Motorcycle, automobile and highway (16). g, Butterfly, race car, airplane and tower (17). h, Train, satellite and city buildings (18). i, Computer operator, mosque (19). j, Truck, ship (20).
No. 765, $1, Sailing ship, horiz. No. 766, $1, Airplane, horiz.

1999-2000   Perf. 12¾x12½

763 A260 30c Block of 10, #a.-j.   5.50   5.00
k.   Sheet, 2 #763   11.00   11.00
764 A260 30c Block or strip of 10, #a.-j.   5.50   5.00
k.   Sheet, 2 #764 blocks   11.00   11.00

Perf. 12½x12¾
Wmk. 388

765-766 A260 Set of 2   5.50   5.50

Issued: No. 763, 12/31/99; No. 764, 1/1/00. No. 765, 12/31/99; No. 766, 1/1/00.

Fruit Type of 1986 Redrawn With "Sen" Instead of "C" and "RM" Instead of "$"

Perf. 13¾x14

2002-04   Litho.   Wmk. 388

766A	A125	40sen Like #329	6.00	6.00
766B	A125	50sen Like #330	6.00	6.00
766D	A125	1r Like #332 ('04)	—	—
766E	A126	2r Like #333 ('04)	—	—
766G	A126	10r Like #335	6.00	6.00
766H	A126	20r Like #336	6.00	6.00

New Year 2000 (Year of the Dragon) — A261

No. 767 — Artifacts depicting dragons from: a, New stone age. b, 100 B.C. c, 800. d, 200 B.C. e, 700.

No. 768 — Fish: a, Osteoglossum biorrhosum. b, Scleropages leichardti. c, Scleropages formosus (Prussian blue background). d, Osteoglossum ferreirai. e, Scleropages formosus (bister background).

No. 768G, Dragon on boat prow (square orientation). No. 768H, Dragon in parade (square orientation).

Wmk. 388

2000, Jan. 6   Litho.   Perf. 13¼

767	A261	30c Strip of 5, #a.-e.	2.25	2.25
f.		Sheet, 4 #767	9.00	9.00
768	A261	30c Strip of 5, #a.-e.	2.25	2.25
f.		Sheet, 4 #768	9.00	9.00

Souvenir Sheets

768G	A261	$1 multi	1.50	1.50
768H	A261	$1 multi	1.50	1.50

Dawei 2000 World Team Table Tennis Championships — A262

30c, Paddles, globe. 50c, Tiger mascot playing table tennis. No. 771, Paddles, ball. No. 772: a, Mascot, table and net. b, Paddles and table.

2000, Feb. 19   Perf. 13½

769	A262	30c multi	.35	.35
770	A262	50c multi	.35	.35
771	A262	$1 multi	.85	.95
		Nos. 769-771 (3)	1.55	1.65

Souvenir Sheet

Perf. 14¼

772	A262	$1 Sheet, #a.-b.	1.75	1.75

Souvenir Sheets

Millennium — A263

No. 773, Man, sailboat.
No. 774: a, Mt. Everest climbers with Malaysian flag. b, People with backpacks. c, Parachutist, people with flag, automobile.

2000, Feb. 26   Wmk. 388   Perf. 12

773	A263	50c Sheet of 1	.80	.80
774	A263	50c Sheet of 3, #a.-c.	2.50	2.50

2nd Global Knowledge Conference — A264

No. 775: a, Finger pointing. b, Eye, globe.
No. 776: a, Head facing right. b, Head facing left.

2000, Mar. 7   Perf. 13½

775	A264	30c Pair, a.-b., + central label	.90	.90

Perf. 14x14¼

776	A264	50c Pair, a.-b., + central label	1.30	1.30

Islamic Arts Museum, Kuala Lumpur — A265

20c, Inverted dome. 30c, Main dome. No. 778A, Like No. 778 but with central design element entirely in gold. 50c, Ottoman panel. $1, Art of the mosque.

Perf. 13¾x13½ Syncopated

2000, Apr. 6   Wmk. 388

777	A265	20c multi	.40	.40
778	A265	30c multi	.40	.40
778A	A265	30c multi	.40	.40
779	A265	50c multi	.50	.40
780	A265	$1 multi	1.00	1.40
		Nos. 777-780 (5)	2.70	3.00

Boats — A266

No. 781: a, Perahu Buatan Barat. b, Perahu Payang (red and blue). c, Perahu Burung. d, Perahu Payang (red, white and green).

Perf. 14x13½

2000, Apr. 15   Litho.   Wmk. 388

781	A266	Block of 4	2.00	2.00
a.-d.		30c Any single	.30	.30
e.		Booklet pane, 5 each #a-d	10.50	
		Complete booklet, #781e	10.50	

Unit Trust Investment Week — A267

30c, Emblem, women with flags. 50c, People, Kuala Lumpur skyline. $1, People, globe.

Perf. 13½x13¾

2000, Apr. 20   Litho.   Unwmk.

782	A267	30c multi	.45	.45
783	A267	50c multi	.60	.45
784	A267	$1 multi	1.10	1.40
		Nos. 782-784 (3)	2.15	2.30

Thomas and Uber Cup Badminton Championships — A268

No. 785: a, Male player. b, Flags, Thomas Cup (with handles). c, Mascot. d, Flags, Uber Cup. e, Female player.
$1, Thomas Cup, vert.

Perf. 12½x12¾

2000, May 11   Wmk. 388

785		Horiz. strip of 5	2.00	2.00
a.-e.	A268	30c Any single	.30	.30

Souvenir Sheet

Perf. 12¾x12½x12x12½

786	A268	$1 multi	2.00	2.25

No. 785 printed in sheets of 10 strips and ten labels.

Children's Games — A269

No. 787: a, Hopscotch. b, Tarik Upih. c, Kite flying. d, Marbles. e, Hoops and sticks.

2000, June 24   Perf. 13½x13¾

787		Horiz. strip of 5	3.75	3.75
a.-e.	A269	30c Any single	.50	.50
f.		Miniature sheet, 4 #787	16.50	16.00

Islamic Conference of Foreign Ministers, 27th Session A270

No. 788: a, Red globe, electronic circuitry. b, Blue globe, Islamic design. c, Emblem, flower, butterfly. d, Green globe, Islamic design, diff. e, Purple globe, pens.

2000, June 26   Perf. 13¾x13½

788		Horiz. strip of 5	2.00	2.00
a.-e.	A270	30c Any single	.25	.25

National Census A271

No. 789: a, Family, map. b, Family in house, appliances. c, People on pie chart. d, Map, diplomas, mortarboard, workers. e, Male and female symbols.

2000, July 5   Perf. 14¼

789		Horiz. strip of 5	2.25	2.25
a.-e.	A271	30c Any single	.25	.25

Birds — A272

Designs: 20c, Polyplectron inopinatum. 30c, Rheinardia ocellata. 50c, Argisianus argus. $1, Lophura erythrophthalma. $2, Rheinardia ocellata, diff.

2000, July 22   Perf. 13x13¼

790	A272	20c multi	.55	.55
791	A272	30c multi	.55	.55
a.		Sheet of 20	20.00	
792	A272	50c multi	.70	.55
793	A272	$1 multi	1.50	1.50
		Nos. 790-793 (4)	3.30	3.15

Souvenir Sheet

Perf. 13¾x14

794	A272	$2 multi	3.00	3.00

No. 794 contains one 32x27mm stamp.

A273

Intl. Union of Forestry Research World Congress — A274

No. 795: a, Shorea macrophylla. b, Dyera costulata. c, Alstonia angustiloba. d, Hopea odorata. e, Adenanthera pavonina.

No. 796 — Trees, 10c: a, Fagraea fragrans. b, Dryobalanops aromatica. c, Terminalia catappa. d, Samanea saman. e, Dracontomelon dao.

No. 797 — Leaves, 15c: a, Heritiera javanica. b, Johannesteijsmannia altifrons. c, Macaranga gigantea. d, Licuala grandis. e, Endospermum diadenum.

No. 798 — Tree barks, 25c: a, Pterocymbium javanicum. b, Dryobalanops aromatica. c, Dipterocarpus costulatus. d, Shorea leprosula. e, Ochanostachys amentacea.

No. 799 — Fauna, 50c: a, Muscicapa indigo. b, Nycticebus coucang. c, Felis marmorata. d, Cyprinus carpio. e, Trimerisurus wagleri.

Illustration A274 reduced.

Wmk. 388

2000, Aug. 7   Litho.   Perf. 12

795		Horiz. strip of 5	3.75	3.75
a.-e.	A273	30c Any single	.70	.70
f.		Sheet of 4 each #a-e	15.00	15.00

Sheets of 5, #a-e, + label

796-799	A274	Set of 4	8.00	8.00

Medical Research Institute, Cent. A275

Designs: 30c, Institute in 1901, Brugia malayi, Beri-beri. 50c, Institute in 1953, Clostridium bifermentans malaysia, Anophelese campestris. $1, Institute in 1976, chromatograph of DNA sequence, Eurycoma longifolia.

Perf. 13¾x13½, 14¼ (50c, $1, $2)

2000, Aug. 24   Unwmk.

800-802	A275	Set of 3	2.25	1.25

Souvenir Sheet

Wmk. 388

803	A275	$2 Molecular model	2.40	2.40

Protected Mammals A276

Designs: 20c, Cynogale bennettii (mouth open). No. 805, 30c, Cynogale bennettii (mouth closed). 50c, Arctictis binturong. $1, Arctictis binturong, diff.

No. 808: a, Hemigalus hosei. b, Paradoxurus hermaphroditus. c, Paguma larvata. d, Viverra tangalunga. e, Arctogalidia trivirgata.

No. 809: a, Hemigalus derbyanus. b, Prionodon linsang.

2000, Aug. 26　Wmk. 388　Perf. 13¼
804-807 A276　Set of 4　　1.10　.55
808　　Horiz. strip of 5　1.50　1.50
a.-e. A276 30c Any single　　.25　.25
Souvenir Sheet
809 A276 $1 Sheet of 2, #a-b　2.75 2.75

Rural and Industrial Development Authority, Trust Council for Indiginous People, 50th Anniv. — A277

Designs: 30c, Gear wheels. 50c, Compass, stethoscope. $1, Computer mouse and diskette.

2000, Sept. 14　　　　Perf. 14¼
810-812 A277　Set of 3　　2.25 2.25
810a　　Sheet of 20　　　　2.50 2.50

Children's Games — A278

No. 813, 20c: a, Gasing. b, Baling tin.
No. 814, 30c: a, Letup-letup. b, Sepak raga.
Perf. 14¼, 13¾x13½ (#814)
2000, Sept. 16
Horiz. Pairs, #a-b
813-814 A278　Set of 2　　2.10 1.25

World Heart Day — A279

No. 815: a, People walking, cyclist. b, People jumping rope, playing with hula hoop and ball. c, Boy flying kite, children playing soccer. d, People exercising. e, Man gardening.

2000, Sept. 24　　　　Perf. 12¼
815　　Horiz. strip of 5　2.10 1.25
a.-e. A279 30c Any single　.25　.25

Rhododendrons — A280

No. 816: a, Brookeanum. b, Jasminiflorum. c, Scortechinii. d, Pauciflorum.

No. 817: a, Crassifloium. b, Longiflorum. c, Javanicum. d, Variolosum. e, Acuminatum. f, Praetervisum. g, Himantodes. h, Maxwellii. i, Erocoides. j, Fallacinum.
$1, Malayanum.

2000, Oct. 9
816 A280 30c Block of 4, #a-d　1.40　.80
817 A280 30c Block of 10, #a-j　3.00 1.50
Souvenir Sheet
818 A280 $1 multi　　　　　1.60 1.60

A281

Dragonflies and Damselflies A282

No. 819: a, Vestalis gracilis. b, Crocothemis s. servilia male. c, Trithemis auraora. d, Pseudothemis jorina. e, Diplacodes nebulosa. f, Crocothemis s. servilia female. g, Neurobasis c. chinensis male. h, Burmagomphus divaricatus. i, Ictinogomphus d. melanops. j, Orthetrum testaceum. k, Trithemis festiva. l, Brachythemis contaminata. m, Neurobasis c. chinensis female. n, Neurothemis fluctuans. o, Acisoma panorpoides. p, Orthetrum s. sabina. q, Rhyothemis p. phyllis. r, Rhyothemis obsolescens. s, Neurothemis t. tulia. t, Lathrecista a. asiatica. u, Aethriamanta gracilis. v, Diplacodes trivialis. w, Neurothemis fulvia. x, Rhyothemis triangularis. y, Orthetrum glaucum.

No. 820: a, Neurobasis c. chinensis. b, Aristocypha fenestrella (with blue sky). c, Vestalis gracilis. d, Nannophya pymaea. e, Aristocypha fenestrella (no sky). f, Rhyothemis p. phyllis. g, Crocothemis s. servilia. h, Euphaea ochracea male. i, Euphaea ochracea female. j, Ceriagrion cerinorubellum.

2000, Nov. 25　Perf. 14¼x13¾ Sync.
819　　Sheet of 25　　　11.50 11.50
a.-y. A281 (30c) Any single　　.30　.30
Booklet Stamps
Perf. 13½x14 Syncopated
820　　Block of 10　　　5.25 5.25
a.-j. A282 30c Any single　　.30　.30
k.　　Booklet pane, 2 #820　10.50
　　　Booklet, #820k　　　10.50

Quails and Partridges A283

Designs: 30c, Coturnix chinensis. 50c, Arborophila campbelli. $1, Turnix suscitator.
No. 824: a, Arborophila charltonii. b, Haematortyx sanguiniceps.

Wmk. 388, Unwmkd. (#822-823)
Perf. 13¾x13½, 14¼ (30c)
2001, Jan. 22　　　　Litho.
821-823 A283　Set of 3　　3.50 3.50
Souvenir Sheet
Perf. 14¼x14¼x13¾x14¼
824 A283 $2 Sheet of 2, #a-b　4.75 4.75

Creation of Putrajaya Federal Territory — A284

Designs: 30c, Perdana Putra Building (Prime Minister's office building). $1, Perdana Putra Building, highway, government office buildings.

Perf. 13¾x13½, 14¼ ($1)
2001, Feb. 1　Litho.　Wmk. 388
825-826 A284　Set of 2　　3.25 1.60

Sabah and Sarawak Beads — A285

No. 827: a, Pinakol. b, Mareik Empang. c, Glass beads. d, Orot.

Wmk. 388
2001, Feb. 17　Litho.　Perf. 13¾
827 A285 30c Block of 4, #a-d　2.40 1.25

Flowers — A286

Designs: 30c, Cananga odorata. 50c, Mimusops elengi. $1, Mesua ferrea. $2, Michelia champaca.

2001, Mar. 27　　Perf. 13¾, 14¼ ($1)
828-830 A286　Set of 3　　3.25 1.60
Souvenir Sheet
Perf. 13¾x14¼x13¾x13¾
831 A286 $2 multi　　　　3.25 3.25

Cutltural Items — A287

No. 832, 30c: a, Sireh Junjung. b, Penggendong Anak.
No. 833, 50c: a, Jebak Puyuh. b, Bekas Bara.

2001, June 11　　　　Perf. 13¾
Horiz. pairs, #a-b
832-833 A287　Set of 2　　2.75 1.25

Automobiles A288

No. 834: a, 1995 Perodua Kancil. b, 1995 Proton Tiara. c, 1995 Perodua Rusa. d, 1997 Proton Putra. e, 1999 Inokom Permas. f, 1999 Perodua Kembara. g, 2000 Proton GTi. h, 2000 TD2000. i, 2000 Perodua Kenari. j, 2000 Proton Waja.

2001, July 9
834　　Block of 10　　　6.25 2.75
a.-j. A288 30c Any single　　.30　.30
　　　Booklet, #834　　　6.25

Bantams — A289　21st South East Asia Games — A290

Designs: 30c, Ayam Serama. 50c, Ayam Kapan. $1, Ayam Serama and chicks. $3, Ayam Hutan, horiz.

Perf. 12¾x12½, 12 (50c)
2001, Aug. 1
835-837 A289　Set of 3　　2.75 1.25
Souvenir Sheet
Perf. 12½
838 A289 $3 multi　　　　5.25 5.25
a.　　As #838, with PhilaNippon '01 Emblem in margin　—　—
No. 838 contains one 45x35mm stamp.

2001, Sept. 8　　　Perf. 13½x13¾
Designs: 20c, Diving. 30c, Gymnastics. 50c, Bowling. $1, Weight lifting. $2, Cycling. $5, Running.
839-843 A290　Set of 5　　4.75 2.25
Souvenir Sheet
844 A290 $5 multi　　　　6.75 6.75

2001 World Dental Federation Congress — A291

2001, Sept. 27　　　　Perf. 14¼
845 A291 $1 multi　　　　2.10 1.00

Employees' Provident Fund, 50th Anniv. A292

Designs: 30c, Headquarters. 50c, Bar graph. $1, Emblem, man and woman.

Perf. 14¼, 13¾x13½ ($1)
2001, Oct. 1
846-848 A292　Set of 3　　2.75 1.25

Forestry Dept., Cent. — A293

Designs: 30c, Satellite, map, trees. 50c, Trees, leaf. $1, Seedlings and forest.

2001, Nov. 10　　　　Perf. 14¼
849-851 A293　Set of 3　　2.75 2.00

Stamp Week A294

Marine life: 20c, Tridacna gigas. 30c, Hippocampus sp. 50c, Oreaster occidentalis. $1, Cassis cornuta. $3, Dugong dugon.

2001, Nov. 10　　　Perf. 13¾x13½
852-855 A294　Set of 4　　3.00 1.75

MALAYSIA

Souvenir Sheet
Perf. 14¼

856 A294 $3 multi   3.25 3.25

No. 856 exists imperf. with a slightly larger, numbered margin. Value $5.

2002 KL Field Hockey World Cup — A295

Designs: 30c, Player with ball. 50c, Goaltender. $1, Player with ball, diff. $3, Player, stadium playing field.

Perf. 13½x13¾
2002, Jan. 2   Wmk. 388
857-859 A295   Set of 3   3.00 1.75
Souvenir Sheet
Perf. 12¾x12½x12x12½
860 A295 $3 multi   3.25 3.25

No. 860 exists imperf. with a numbered margin.

Flowers — A296   **Snakes — A297**

Designs: 30c, Couroupita guianensis. No. 862, $1, Camellia nitidissima. No. 863, $1, Couroupita guianensis, diff.
No. 864: a, Schima brevifolia, horiz. b, Schima brevifolia.

2002, Feb. 5   Wmk. 380   Perf. 12¾
861-863 A296   Set of 3   2.75 1.40
Souvenir Sheet
864 A296 $2 Sheet of 2, #a-b   3.25 3.25

See People's Republic of China No. 3180.

2002, Mar. 5   Wmk. 388   Perf. 14¼
Designs: No. 865, 30c, Gonyophis margaritatus. No. 866, 30c, Python reticulatus. 50c, Bungarus candidus. $1, Maticora bivirgata.
No. 869: a, Ophiophagus hannah (brown). b, Ophiophagus hannah (black and white striped).
865-868 A297   Set of 4   3.75 1.75
Souvenir Sheet
Perf. 13¼
869 A297 $2 Sheet of 2, #a-b   4.00 4.00

Nos. 865-868 were each printed in sheets of 20 + 5 labels. No. 869 exists imperf. Value $5.

Express Rail Link A298

Designs: 30c, Kuala Lumpur Central Station.
No. 871: a, Train and station. b, Train, airplane and control tower.
No. 872: a, Train with red violet stripe, train with red stripe. b, Yellow and blue train, train with blue, orange and red stripes.
$2, Train with red violet stripe.

2002, Apr. 13   Wmk. 388   Perf. 12
870 A298 30c multi   1.00 1.00
871 A298 50c Horiz. pair, #a-b   2.75 1.25
Souvenir Sheets
Perf. 12½x12¾
872 A298 $1 Sheet of 2, #a-b   2.75 2.75
Perf. 12½x12¾x12½x12
873 A298 $2 multi   2.75 2.75

17th World Orchid Congress — A299

No. 874: a, Paraphalenopsis labukensis. b, Renanthera bella.
50c, Paphiopedilum sanderianum.
No. 876: a, Coelogyne pandurata. b, Phalaenopsis amabilis.
$5, Cleisocentron merillianum.

2002, Apr. 24   Wmk. 380   Perf. 12¾
874 A299 30c Horiz. pair, #a-b   1.40 .80
875 A299 50c multi   1.10 .80
876 A299 $1 Horiz. pair, #a-b   3.50 1.25
  Nos. 874-876 (3)   6.00 2.85
Souvenir Sheet
Perf. 13
Unwmk.
877 A299 $5 multi   7.00 7.00

No. 877 contains one 45x40mm stamp and exists imperf.

Installation of 12th Yang Di-Pertuan Agong — A300

Yang Di-Pertuan Agongs — A301

Background colors: 30c, Green. 50c, Red violet. $1, Yellow.
No. 881 — Ordinal number of Yang Di-Pertuan Agong: a, 1st. b, 2nd. c, 3rd. d, 4th. e, 5th. f, 6th. g, 7th. h, 8th. i, 9th. j, 10th. k, 11th. l, 12th.

2002, Apr. 25   Wmk. 380   Perf. 12¾
878-880 A300   Set of 3   3.50 3.50
Miniature Sheet
881 A301 $1 Sheet of 12, #a-l   5.25 5.25

Aquatic Plants A302

Designs: 30c, Cryptocoryne purpurea. 50c, Barclaya kunstleri.
No. 884: a, Neptunia oleracea. b, Monochoria hastata.
No. 885: a, $1, Eichhornia crassipes, vert. b, $2, Nymphaea pubescens.

Perf. 12, 12½x12¾ (#884)
2002, May 11   Wmk. 388
882 A302 30c multi   .60 .60
883 A302 50c multi   1.00 .60
884 A302 $1 Horiz. pair, #a-b   3.50 3.25
  Nos. 882-884 (3)   5.10 4.45
Souvenir Sheet
Perf. 12¾x12½x12x12½, 12 (#885b)
885 A302   Sheet of 2, #a-b   7.00 7.00

Tropical Birds — A303

No. 886, 30c: a, Dryocopus javensis. b, Oriolus chinensis.
No. 887, $1: a, Anthreptes rhodolaema. b, Irena puella.
$5, Dicaeum trigonostigma.

2002, June 27   Perf. 12¾x12½
Horiz. Pairs, #a-b
886-887 A303   Set of 2   6.00 3.00
Souvenir Sheet
Perf. 12¾x12½x12x12½
888 A303 $5 multi   7.75 7.75

No. 888 contains one 60x40mm stamp. See Singapore Nos. 1014-1017.

Islands and Beaches — A304

No. 889, 30c: a, Pulau Sibu, Johore. b, Pulau Perhentian, Trengganu.
No. 890, 50c: a, Pulau Manukan, Sabah. b, Pulau Tioman, Pahang.
No. 891, $1: a, Pulau Singa Besar, Kedah. b, Pulau Pangkor, Perak.
No. 892: a, Batu Ferringhi, Penang. b, Port Dickson, Negri Sembilan.

Wmk. 380
2002, July 31   Litho.   Perf. 12¾
Horiz. Pairs, #a-b
889-891 A304   Set of 3   6.50 3.25
Souvenir Sheet
892 A304 $1 Sheet of 2, #a-b   4.25 2.00

Malaysian Unity — A305

No. 893: a, Musicians. b, Children at play. 50c, Seven people (80x29mm).
$2, People pulling rope.

Wmk. 380
2002, Aug. 24   Litho.   Perf. 12¾
893 A305 30c Horiz. pair, #a-b   1.40 .80
894 A305 50c multi   1.00 .80
Souvenir Sheet
895 A305 $2 multi   3.00 1.50

Zainal Abidin bin Ahmad (1895-1973), Academic — A306

Abidin bin Ahmad: 30c, And blackboard.
No. 897: a, And typewriter. b, And building.
$1, In library, vert.

Perf. 13½x13¼
2002, Sept. 17   Wmk. 388
896 A306 30c multi   .75 .75
897 A306 50c Horiz. pair, #a-b   2.00 1.40
Souvenir Sheet
Perf. 13¼x13½
898 A306 $1 multi   2.75 1.40

Clothing — A307

Designs: No. 899, 30c, Green blouse. No. 900, 30c, Red blouse. No. 901, 50c, Yellow blouse. No. 902, 50c, Red blouse, diff.
$2, Blouse and skirt.

Perf. 12¾ (30c), 12¾x13¼ (50c)
2002, Nov. 2
899-902 A307   Set of 4   3.50 1.60
Souvenir Sheet
903 A307 $2 multi   3.50 1.60

No. 903 contains one 35x70mm stamp.

Sultan Idris University, 80th Anniv. A308

Designs: 30c, Suluh Budiman Building.
No. 905: a, Tadahan Selatan. b, Chancellory Building.

2002, Nov. 29   Perf. 12x12x13½x12
904 A308 30c multi   .70 .70
  a.   Perf. 12   .30 .30
Perf. 12
905 A308 50c Horiz. pair, #a-b   2.60 1.10
  c.   As "a," perf. 12x12x13½x12   .40 .25
  d.   As "b," perf. 12x12x13½x12   .40 .25
  e.   Pair, #905c-905d   .85 .40
  f.   As "a," perf. 13½   — —
  g.   As "b," perf. 13½   — —

Wild and Tame Animals — A309

No. 906, 30c: a, Felis bengalensis. b, Felis catus.
No. 907, $1: a, Cacatua sulphurea. b, Ketupa ketupu.
No. 908, $1: a, Ratufa affinis. b, Oryctolagus cuniculus.
No. 909, $1, horiz.: a, Carassius auratus. b, Diodon liturosus.

2002, Dec. 17   Perf. 12½
Horiz. pairs, #a-b
906-907 A309   Set of 2   5.50 2.75
Souvenir Sheets of 2, #a-b
Perf. 13½x12x13¼x13½, 13½x13½x12x13¼ (#909)
908-909 A309   Set of 2   6.50 3.25
Stamp Week.

Endangered Animals — A310

Southern serow: 30c, Head.
No. 911: a, Serow laying down. b, Serow walking.

2003, Jan. 25   Perf. 12¾x12½
910 A310 30c multi   .75 .75
911 A310 50c Horiz. pair, #a-b   2.25 1.00

13th Conference of Heads of State or Government of Non-Aligned Countries — A311

No. 912, 30c — Malaysian flag, world map, conference emblem and: a, Doves, years of previous conferences (1961-1979). b, Hands, years of conferences (1983-2003).
No. 913, 50c — Globe, conference emblem and: a, Map of Malaysia. b, Dove, "2003," Malaysian flag.

2003, Feb. 6   *Perf. 12½x12¾*
Horiz. pairs, #a-b
912-913 A311   Set of 2   3.00 1.50

Roses — A312

Designs: No. 914, Pink Rosa hybrida. No. 915, Red Rosa hybrida.
No. 916: a, Yellow Rosa hybrida. b, Floribunda.
No. 917: a, 1r, Floribunda miniature (29x40mm). b, 2r, Rosa centifolia (29x81mm).

Wmk. 380
2003, Feb. 22   **Litho.**   *Perf. 13¾*
914 A312 30c shown   .60 .50
915 A312 30c multi   .60 .50
916 A312 50c Horiz. pair, #a-b   1.75 1.00
    Nos. 914-916 (3)   2.95 2.00

Souvenir Sheet
Perf. 12¾
917 A312   Sheet of 2, #a-b   3.25 1.60
Nos. 914-917 are impregnated with a rose scent.

Tunku Abdul Rahman Putra Al-Haj (1903-90), Prime Minister — A313

Designs: 30c, Wearing brown hat. 50c, Wearing suit and tie.
No. 920: a, Wearing dark robe. b, Wearing light robe.
No. 921, With arm raised.

Perf. 12¾x12½
2003, Mar. 4   **Wmk. 388**
918 A313 30c multi   .50 .50
919 A313 50c multi   .60 .60
920 A313 $1 Horiz. pair, #a-b   2.75 1.40
    Nos. 918-920 (3)   3.85 2.40

Souvenir Sheet
Perf. 13½
921 A313 $1 multi   2.50 1.25

Fighting Fish A314

Designs: 30c, Red and blue Betta splendens. No. 923, Yellow Betta splendens.
No. 924: a, Blue Betta splendens. b, Red Betta splendens.
No. 925: a, Betta imbellis. b, Betta coccina.

Perf. 12½x12¾, 13½x13¼ (#923)
2003, Apr. 26
922 A314 30c multi   .65 .55
923 A314 50c multi   .80 .55
924 A314 $1 Horiz. pair, #a-b   3.50 1.75
    Nos. 922-924 (3)   4.95 2.85

Souvenir Sheet
Perf. 13½x13¾ Syncopated
925 A314 50c Sheet of 2, #a-b   3.00 1.40
No. 925 contains two 33x28mm stamps.

Clock Towers — A315

Designs: No. 926, 30c, Malacca, 1650. No. 927, 30c, Penang, 1897. No. 928, 30c, Sungai Petani, 1936. No. 929, 30c, Teluk Intan, 1885. No. 930, 30c, Sarawak State Council Monument, 1967.
No. 931: a, Sultan Abdul Samad Building, 1897. b, Taiping Clock Tower, Perak, 1881.

2003, May 24   *Perf. 12¾x12½*
926-930 A315   Set of 5   2.75 1.25
930a   Booklet pane, 2 each #926-930   6.00 —
    Complete booklet, #930a   6.00

Souvenir Sheet
Perf. 12x12½x12¾x12½
931 A315 $1 Sheet of 2, #a-b   2.75 1.50

Beaches and Islands — A316

No. 932, 30c: a, Beach, Ligitan Island, Sabah. b, Map of Ligitan Island.
No. 933, 50c: a, Beach, Sipadan Island, Sabah. b, Map of Sipadan Island.
No. 934, vert.: a, Aerial view of Sipadan Island. b, Map of Ligitan Island.

Litho. (#932a-934a), Litho. & Embossed (#932b-934b)
2003, June 28   **Wmk. 380**   *Perf. 13¼*
Horiz. Pairs, #a-b
932-933 A316   Set of 2   2.75 1.25

Souvenir Sheet
Perf. 12¾
934 A316 50c Sheet of 2, #a-b   2.75 1.25

Independence, Anniv. 46th — A317

Designs: 30c, Flag and clock tower. No. 936, $1, Flag (59x40mm).
No. 937, Tunku Abdul Rahman Putra in motorcade, horiz.

2003, Aug. 19   **Litho.**   *Perf. 12¾*
935-936 A317   Set of 2   2.75 1.25

Souvenir Sheet
937 A317 $1 black   2.75 1.25
No. 937 contains one 59x40mm stamp.

Motorcycles and Scooters Made in Malaysia A318

Designs: 30c, Modenas Jaguh 175.
No. 939: a, Modenas Kriss 2. b, Modenas Kriss SG.
No. 940: a, Modenas Karisma 125. b, Modenas Kriss 1.
No. 941, $1: a, Comel Turbulence RG125. b, Comel Cyclone GP150.

No. 942, $1: a, MZ 125SM. b, MZ Perintis 1205 Classic.
No. 943, $1: a, Caviga Momos 125R. b, Nitro NE150 Windstar.
No. 944, $1: a, Demak Adventurer. b, Demak Beetle.

2003, Aug. 27   *Perf. 12¾*
938 A318 30c multi   .75 .75
939 A318 50c Horiz. pair, #a-b   2.00 .85
940 A318 50c Horiz. pair, #a-b   2.00 .85
    Nos. 938-940 (3)   4.75 2.45
Souvenir Sheets of 2, #a-b
941-944 A318   Set of 4   8.25 4.00
    See Nos. 950-952.

10th Islamic Summit Conference — A319

No. 945, 30c: a, Putrajaya Convention Center. b, Arabic text.
No. 946, 50c: a, Mosque at left, field of flag. b, Mosque at right, flag stripes.

2003, Oct. 3   *Perf. 12¾*
Horiz. Pairs, #a-b
945-946 A319   Set of 2   3.00 1.50

50th World Children's Day — A320

Designs: 20c, World map, children in ring.
No. 948: a, Family, house, car, flag. b, Children with kite, graduate, man at computer, rocket, airplane.
No. 949: a, Text. b, Book, school, flag, kite, rainbow, soccer ball, automobile and flower.

Perf. 13½x13¼
2003, Oct. 11   **Wmk. 388**
947 A320 20c multi   .75 .75
  a.   Perf. 12½x12¾   .30 .30
Perf. 12
948 A320 30c Horiz. pair, #a-b   1.75 1.10
  c.   As "a," perf. 12½x12¾   .35 .35
  d.   As "b," perf. 12½x12¾   .35 .35
949 A320 30c Horiz. pair, #a-b   1.75 1.10
  c.   As "a," perf. 12½x12¾   .35 .35
  d.   As "b" perf. 12½x12¾   .35 .35
  e.   Booklet pane 2 each #947a, 948c, 948d, 949c, 949d   2.75
    Complete booklet, #949e   2.75

Nos. 938-940 with Bangkok 2003 Emblem Added at Upper Right
Wmk. 380
2003, Oct. 4   **Litho.**   *Perf. 12¾*
950 A318 30c Like #938   .70 .50
951 A318 50c Like #939, horiz. pair, #a-b   1.75 .85
952 A318 50c Like #940, horiz. pair, #a-b   1.75 .85
    Nos. 950-952 (3)   4.20 2.20

Monkeys — A321

Designs: No. 953, Red leaf monkey, tail above branch. No. 954, Red leaf monkey, tail below branch.
No. 955: a, Proboscis monkey sitting on branch. b, Proboscis monkey reaching for branch.

2003, Dec. 16
953 A321 30c multi   .60 .60
954 A321 30c multi   .60 .60
955 A321 50c Horiz. pair, #a-b   1.75 1.75
    Nos. 953-955 (3)   2.95 2.95

Lighthouses A322

Designs: No. 956, 30c, Muka Head Lighthouse. No. 957, 30c, One Fathom Bank Lighthouse. No. 958, 30c, Althingsburg Lighthouse. No. 959, 30c, Pulau Undan Lighthouse. $1, Tanjung Tuan Lighthouse.

Perf. 12¾x12½
2004, Jan. 31   **Wmk. 388**
956-959 A322   Set of 4   3.00 1.40
Souvenir Sheet
Perf. 13½
960 A322 $1 multi   3.00 1.40

Convention on Biological Diversity — A323

Designs; 30c, Flora and fauna. No. 962, 50c, DNA molecule, leaf, laboratory equipment, model showing human organs. No. 963, 50c, Convention emblem, world map.

2004, Feb. 9   **Wmk. 380**   *Perf. 12¾*
961-963 A323   Set of 3   3.00 1.50

Commonwealth Tourism Ministers' Meeting — A324

Emblem and: 30c, World map, city skyline, golf ball. 50c, World map, rocky shoreline. $1, Malaysian tourist attractions, vert.

2004, Mar. 19
964-966 A324   Set of 3   3.25 1.60

National Service Program — A325

Designs: 30c, Emblem. 50c, Emblem, people on ropes. $1, Emblem, people with flag. $2, Emblem, man saluting.

2004, May 22   **Wmk. 380**   *Perf. 12¾*
967-969 A325   Set of 3   3.25 1.60
Souvenir Sheet
Perf. 13½
Wmk. 388
970 A325 $2 multi   3.25 1.60

Malaysia - People's Republic of China
Diplomatic Relations, 30th
Anniv. — A326

No. 971, 30c: a, Malaysian flag, ship. b, Chinese flag, ship.
No. 972, $1: a, Ship, handshake. b, Flags, ship, world map.
$2, Malaysian and Chinese buildings, horiz.

Perf. 12¾x12½
2004, May 31   **Wmk. 388**
Horiz. pairs, #a-b
971-972   A326   Set of 2   3.25   1.60
Souvenir Sheet
973   A326 $2 multi   2.75   1.40
   a.   World Stamp Championship emblem added in margin in blue and black   2.75   1.40
No. 973 contains one 60x40mm stamp.
No. 973a issued 8/28.

Mammals — A327

No. 974, 30c: a, Bos javanicus. b, Bos gaurus.
No. 975, $1: a, Panthera tigris. b, Elephas maximusp.
$2, Tapirus indicus, vert.

Perf. 13½x13¼
2004, June 14   **Wmk. 388**
Horiz. pairs, #a-b
974-975   A327   Set of 2   5.00   2.50
Souvenir Sheet
Perf. 12¾
Wmk. 380
976   A327 $2 multi   3.00   1.50
See Nos. 1041-1045.

Multimedia
Super
Corridor
A328

Emblem and: 30c, MSC Building, flags. 50c, Globe, Petronas Towers, binary code. $1, Hand with identity card, people using computers, butterfly, cross-section of brain.
$2, Map of Multimedia Super Corridor, vert.

Horizontal Pairs
2004, July 11   **Wmk. 380**   **Perf. 12¾**
977-979   A328   Set of 3   1.75   .85
Souvenir Sheet
Perf. 12¾x12½
Wmk. 388
980   A328 $2 multi   2.50   1.25

Ports
A329

No. 981: a, Johore. b, Kota Kinabalu.
No. 982: a, Kuantan. b, Penang.
$1, Bintulu. $2, Northport.

12, 13½ (#983)
2004, July 24   **Wmk. 388**
981   A329   30c Horiz. pair, #a-b   1.20   .80
982   A329   50c Horiz. pair, #a-b   1.75   1.75
983   A329 $1 multi   1.75   1.75
   Nos. 981-983 (3)   4.70   4.30
Souvenir Sheet
984   A329 $2 multi   2.75   1.40

Transportation — A330

Designs: 30c, Trishaw. 50c, Rickshaw. $1, Padi horse.
$2, Bullock cart, vert.

Perf. 12, 13½x13¼ (1r)
2004, Aug. 18   **Litho.**   **Wmk. 388**
985-987   A330   Set of 3   2.10   1.00
Souvenir Sheet
Perf. 14
988   A330 $2 multi   2.75   1.40
   a.   Kuala Lumpur Stamp Show emblem in sheet margin   2.75   1.40
No. 988 contains one 40x50mm stamp and exists imperf.
No. 988a issued 9/3/04.

Matang Mangroves, Perak,
Cent. — A331

No. 989, 30c: a, Monkey on mangrove tree root. b, Insect on plant.
No. 990, $1: a, Boat, shells. b, Birds, tree.
$2, Young trees.

2004, Oct. 4   **Wmk. 380**   **Perf. 12¾**
Horiz. pairs, #a-b
989-990   A331   Set of 2   4.00   2.00
Souvenir Sheet
991   A331 $2 multi   2.25   1.10

Marine Life
A332

Designs: 30c, Humpback whale. 50c, Octopus. $1, Bottlenose dolphin.
$2, Thornback ray.

Wmk. 380
2004, Oct. 9   **Litho.**   **Perf. 12¾**
992-994   A332   Set of 3   2.75   1.40
Souvenir Sheet
995   A332 $2 multi   2.25   1.10
   a.   Stamp Week emblem in sheet margin   2.25   1.10

Medicinal
Plants
A333

Designs: 30c, Eurycoma longifolia. 50c, Labisia pumila.
No. 998: a, Pithecellobium bubalinum benth. b, Alleurites moluccana.
$2, Ficus deltoidea jack.

Wmk. 380
2004, Dec. 11   **Litho.**   **Perf. 12¾**
996   A333   30c multi   .40   .25
997   A333   50c multi   .60   .30
998   A333 $1 Horiz. pair, #a-b   2.10   1.00
   Nos. 996-998 (3)   3.10   1.55
Souvenir Sheet
999   A333 $2 multi   2.50   1.25

Rare
Rhododendrons
A334

Designs: No. 1000, 30c, Rhododendron nervulosum. No. 1001, 30c, Rhododendron stenophyllum. 50c, Rhododendron rugosum. $1, Rhododendron stapfianum.
$2, Rhododendron lowii, horiz.

2005, Jan. 11   **Wmk. 380**   **Perf. 12¾**
1000-1003   A334   Set of 4   3.50   1.75
Souvenir Sheet
1004   A334 $2 multi   2.50   1.25

Fifth Minister's Forum on Infrastructure
Development in the Asia-Pacific
Region, Kuala Lumpur — A335

Emblems and: 30c, Kuala Lumpur skyline. 50c, Train and buildings. $1, Train station and airplane.

2005, Jan. 24   **Wmk. 388**   **Perf. 12**
1005-1007   A335   Set of 3   0.00   1.50

Birds
A336

Designs: 30c, Crested honey buzzard. 50c, Purple heron. $1, Lesser crested tern.
$2, Dunlin.

2005, Feb. 3   **Wmk. 388**   **Perf. 13½**
1008-1010   A336   Set of 3   3.00   1.50
Souvenir Sheet
1011   A336 $2 multi   3.00   1.50
   a.   Like #1011, with Pacific Explorer World Stamp Expo emblem in margin   3.00   1.50
No. 1011a issued 4/21.

Proton
Gen-2
Automobile
A337

2005, Feb. 7   **Wmk. 388**   **Perf. 13½**
Color of Automobile
1012   A337   30c beige   .40   .25
   a.   Perf. 12   .40   .25
   b.   Booklet pane, 10 #1012a   4.00
     Complete booklet, #1012b   4.00
1013   A337   50c bright blue   .60   .30
1014   A337 $1 red   1.75   .85
   Nos. 1012-1014 (3)   2.75   1.40
Souvenir Sheet
1015   A337 $2 dark blue, vert.   2.00   1.00

Dances
A338

Designs: 30c, Bharata Natyam and Kathak. 50c, Kipas and Payaung. $1, Zapin and Asyik. $2, Datun Julud and Sumazau.

2005, Apr. 9   **Wmk. 388**   **Perf. 12**
1016   A338   30c multi   .35   .25
   a.   Perf. 13½   .35   .25
1017   A338   50c multi   .50   .25
1018   A338 $1 multi   1.00   .50
   Nos. 1016-1018 (3)   1.85   1.00
Souvenir Sheet
Perf. 13½
1019   A338 $2 multi   2.25   1.10

Songkets
A339

Designs: 30c, Pucuk Rebung Gigi Yu. 50c, Bunga Bertabur Pecah Lapan.
No. 1022: a, Pucuk Rebung Gigi Yu dan Bunga Kayoban. b, Teluk Berantai Bunga Pecah Empat.
$2, Potong Wajik Bertabur.

Perf. 12¾x12½
2005, Apr. 29   **Wmk. 388**
1020   A339   30c multi   .30   .25
1021   A339   50c multi   .50   .25
1022   A339 $1 Horiz. pair, #a-b   1.60   .80
   Nos. 1020-1022 (3)   2.40   1.30
Souvenir Sheet
1023   A339 $2 multi   2.00   1.00

Birds — A340

Designs: 20c, Spotted dove. 30c, Ochraceous bulbul. 40c, Long-tailed parakeet. 50c, White-rumped shama. 75c, Olive-backed sunbird. $1, Green-winged pigeon. $2, Banded pitta. $5, Imperial pigeon.

2005, May 14   **Perf. 13½x14**
1024   A340   20c multi   .35   .25
1025   A340   30c multi   .40   .25
1026   A340   40c multi   .50   .25
1027   A340   50c multi   .60   .30
1028   A340   75c multi   .80   .40
1029   A340 $1 multi   .90   .45
1030   A340 $2 multi   1.75   .85
1031   A340 $5 multi   3.25   1.60
   Nos. 1024-1031 (8)   8.55   4.35

University
of
Malaysia,
Cent.
A341

Designs: 30c, Dewan Tunku Canselor. 50c, Perpustakaan. No. 1034, Pusat Perubatan. No. 1035: a, Rimba Ilmu. b, Koleksi Muzium Seni Asia.

2005, June 9   **Wmk. 388**   **Perf. 12**
1032   A341   30c multi   .30   .25
   a.   Perf. 13½   .30   .25
   b.   Booklet pane, 10 #1032a   3.00   —
     Complete booklet, #1032b   3.00
1033   A341   50c multi   .50   .25
Perf. 13½
1034   A341 $1 multi   .90   .45
   Nos. 1032-1034 (3)   1.70   .95

Souvenir Sheet
Perf. 12½
1035 A341 $1 Sheet of 2, #a-b 1.60 .80

Malaysia — China Relations, 600th Anniv. — A342

Designs: No. 1036, 30c, Chinese chop. No. 1037, 30c, Ship. 50c, Malaysian and Chinese men talking. $1, Decorated plate. $2, Ornament and coin.

Perf. 12¾x12½
2005, July 21   Litho.   Wmk. 388
1036-1039 A342   Set of 4   1.75 .85
Souvenir Sheet
1040 A342 $2 multi   1.50 .75

Mammals Type of 2004
Endangered mammals: No. 1041, 30c, Malay weasel. No. 1042, 30c, Yellow-throated marten. 50c, Hairy-nosed otter. $1, Large spotted civet. $2, Long-tailed porcupine, vert.

Perf. 13½, 12 (50c, $1)
2005, July 27
1041-1044 A327   Set of 4   2.50 1.25
1042a   Perf. 12   .40 .25
Souvenir Sheet
Perf. 12¾x12½
1045 A327 $2 multi   2.00 1.00
  a. As #1045, with Taipei 2005 emblem in sheet margin   2.00 1.00
  No. 1045a issued 8/19.

Water Transport A343

Designs: 30c, Perahu kotak. 50c, Sampan. $1, Rakit buluh. $2, Perahu batang, vert.

2005, Aug. 9   Perf. 13½
1046-1048 A343   Set of 3   1.75 .85
Souvenir Sheet
Perf. 14x13½
1049 A343 $2 multi   2.00 1.00
  No. 1049 contains one 40x55mm stamp.

Malay College, Kuala Kangsar, Cent. A344

Designs: 30c, School building. No. 1051, 50c, Tree. No. 1052, 50c, Prep school. No. 1053, vert.: a, Sultan Idris Murshidul 'Adzam Shah. b, Sultan Alaiddin Sulaiman Shah. c, Yam Tuan Tuanku Muhamad Shah. d, Sultan Ahmad Al-Mu'adzam Shah.

2005, Aug. 30   Perf. 13½
1050-1052 A344   Set of 3   1.50 .75
Souvenir Sheet
Perf. 12x11¾
1053 A344 50c Sheet of 4, #a-d   1.60 .80
  No. 1053 contains four 22x51mm stamps.

Reptiles A345

Designs: No. 1054, 30c, Varanus rudicollis. No. 1055, 30c, Varanus dumerilii. 50c, Gonocephalus grandis. $1, Crocodylus porosus. $2, Draco quinquefasciatus, vert.

2005, Sept. 28   Perf. 13½
1054-1057 A345   Set of 4   2.50 1.25
Souvenir Sheet
Perf. 14x13½
1058 A345 $2 multi   1.75 .85
  No. 1058 contains one 40x50mm stamp.

Kites A346

Designs: 30c, Wau Jala Budi. 50c, Wau Bulan. $1, Wau Kucing. $2, Wau Merak.

2005, Oct. 10   Perf. 13½, 12 ($1)
1059-1061 A346   Set of 3   2.00 1.00
1060a   Perf. 12   .40 .25
Souvenir Sheet
1062 A346 $2 multi   1.60 .80

Batik — A347

Designs: 30c, Binaan Asasi. 50c, Pesona Sutera. $1, Malaysia Bersatu. $2, Penyatuan.

2005, Dec. 2   Perf. 12¾x12½
1063-1065 A347   Set of 3   1.40 .70
Souvenir Sheet
1066 A347 $2 multi   1.40 .70

11th ASEAN Summit, Kuala Lumpur A348

Emblem and: 30c, Flags of participating nations. 50c, Motto. $1, Aerial view of Kuala Lumpur.

2005, Dec. 12   Perf. 12½x12¾
1067-1069 A348   Set of 3   1.40 .70

Islands and Marine Life A349

Designs: No. 1070, 30c, Erica Reef, Nudibranch. No. 1071, 30c, Mariveles Reef, Sea cucumber. No. 1072, $1, Swallow Island, Sea star. No. 1073, $1, Investigator Reef, bivalve. $2, Erica Reef, Mariveles Reef, Swallow Island, Investigator Reef, and Ubi Reef.

Perf. 12½x12¾, 13½ ($1)
2005, Dec. 22
1070-1073 A349   Set of 4   2.00 1.00
Souvenir Sheet
Perf. 14
1074 A349 $2 multi   2.25 1.10
  No. 1074 contains one 50x40mm stamp.

Ducks A350

Designs: No. 1075, 30c, Anas crecca. No. 1076, 30c, Cairina scutulata. No. 1077, 50c, Anas acuta. No. 1078, 50c, Anas clypeata. $2, Phalacrocorax carbo.

Perf. 13½x13¼
2006, Jan. 26   Litho.   Wmk. 388
1075-1078 A350   Set of 4   2.50 1.25
1076a   Perf. 12   .40 .25
Souvenir Sheet
1079 A350 $2 multi   2.75 1.40

Negara Audit Institute, Cent. A351

Designs: 30c, Building. No. 1081, 50c, Documents. No. 1082, 50c, Emblems.

2006, Feb. 14   Perf. 12½x12¾
1080-1082 A351   Set of 3   1.25 .60

Fruits — A352

Designs: 30c, Artocarpus sericicarpus. 50c, Phyllanthus acidus. No. 1085, $1, Garcinia hombroniana. No. 1086, $1: a, Lepisanthes alata. b, Baccaurea polyneura.

Perf. 13¾x13½ Syncopated
2006, Mar. 28
1083-1085 A352   Set of 3   1.60 .80
Souvenir Sheet
Perf. 13¾ Syncopated
1086 A352 $1 Sheet of 2, #a-b   1.60 .80

Mountains — A353

No. 1087, 30c: a, Mt. Kinabalu and orchid. b, Gunung Ledang (Mt. Ophir) and flower. No. 1088, 50c: a, Mt. Jerai and orchid. b, Mt. Mulu. $2, Mt. Tahan.

Litho. & Embossed
Perf. 13½x13¼
2006, Apr. 26   Wmk. 388
Horiz. Pairs, #a-b
1087-1088 A353   Set of 2   2.50 1.25
Souvenir Sheet
Perf. 14
Litho.
1088C A353 $2 multi   1.60 .80
  No. 1088C contains one 50x40mm stamp.

Fish A354

Designs: 30c, Leptobarbus hoevenii. No. 1090, 50c, Hampala macrolepidota. No. 1091, 50c, Pangasius sp. $1, Probarbus jullieni. $5, Clarias batrachus, Mystus nemurus.

Perf. 12½x12¾
2006, May 25   Litho.   Wmk. 388
1089-1092 A354   Set of 4   2.50 1.25
Souvenir Sheet
Litho. With Hologram Applied
Perf. 13¼
1093 A354 $5 multi   3.50 1.75
  No. 1093 contains one 70x33mm stamp.

Dewan Bahasa Dan Pustaka (Malay Language Governing Board), 50th Anniv. A355

Designs: No. 1094, 50c, Emblem and leaf. No. 1095, 50c, Anniversary emblem and people reading. $1, Emblem, books and electronic devices.

2006. June 22   Perf. 12½x12¾
1094-1096 A355   Set of 3   1.90 .95

Federal Land Development Authority, 50th Anniv. — A356

Designs: 30c, Palm plantation, fruit. 50c, Buildings. $1, Globe and buildings.

2006, July 7   Litho.   Perf. 12½x12¾
1097-1099 A356   Set of 3   1.75 .85

Sultan Azlan Shah Gallery A357

Designs: 30c, Gallery emblem, sword and sheath. 50c, Gallery building. $1, Gallery emblem, headdress.

2006, July 18   Perf. 12
1100-1102 A357   Set of 3   1.75 .85

Festivals A358

Designs: 30c, Eid al-Fitr. 50c, Tahun Baru Cina (Chinese New Year). No. 1105, $1, Deepavali. No. 1106, $1, vert.: a, Tadau Kaamatan. b, Pesta Gawai.

2006, Aug. 15   *Perf. 12*
1103-1105 A358   Set of 3   1.75 .85
Souvenir Sheet
Perf. 12½
1106 A358 $1 Sheet of 2, #a-b   1.60 .80

Men's and Women's Traditional Costumes A359

Designs: No. 1107, 50c, Malaysian (blue green background). No. 1108, 50c, Indian (orange background). No. 1109, 50c, Chinese (red background).
No. 1110, $1, vert.: a, Iban (blue background). b, Kadazan (tan background).

2006, Aug. 29   *Perf. 12¾x12½*
1107-1109 A359   Set of 3   1.75 .85
Souvenir Sheet
Perf. 13¼x13½
1110 A359 $1 Sheet of 2, #a-b   2.00 1.00

Semi-aquatic Animals — A360

Designs: 30c, Periophthalmodon schlosseri. 50c, Pagurus bernhardus. No. 1113, $1, Cuora amboinensis.
No. 1114, $1, vert.: a, Polypedates leucomystax. b, Varanus salvator. c, Cynogale bennettii. d, Xenochrophis trianguligera.

Perf. 13½x13¼
2006, Oct. 0   Litho.   Wmk. 300
1111-1113 A360   2.00 1.00
Souvenir Sheet
Perf. 13¾x14¼ Syncopated
1114 A360 $1 Sheet of 4, #a-d   2.75 1.40
Stamp Week. No. 1114 contains four 29x34mm stamps.

18th Intl. Federation of Gynecology and Obstetrics Congress A361

"FIGO" and: 30c, Woman and tree leaves. No. 1116, 50c, Map, woman's torso. No. 1117, 50c, Map, fetus.

2006, Nov. 6   *Perf. 12½x12¾*
1115-1117 A361   Set of 3   1.75 .85

2006 Far East & South Pacific Games for the Disabled, Kuala Lumpur — A362

Designs: 30c, Wheelchair racing. 50c, Swimming. $1, Wheelchair tennis. $2, Wheelchair basketball.

2006, Nov. 25   *Perf. 12¾x12½*
1118-1120 A362   Set of 3   2.00 1.00
Souvenir Sheet
Perf. 13½
1121 A362 $2 multi   2.50 1.25

ASEAN Dialogue with People's Republic of China, 15th Anniv. A363

Designs: 30c, ASEAN emblem, Chinese flag, map with flags. 50c, Great Wall of China, flasks, port, highway, ASEAN emblem and Chinese flag. $1, Bow with ASEAN emblem and Chinese flag.

Perf. 12, 13½x13¼ ($1)
2006, Nov. 30
1122-1124 A363   Set of 3   2.00 2.00

25th General Assembly of World Veterans Federation, Kuala Lumpur A364

Emblem and: 30c, Map. 50c, "25," Kuala Lumpur buildings. $1, Malaysian flag, sculpture of soldiers.

Perf. 13½x13¼, 12 (50c)
2006, Dec. 4   Litho.   Wmk. 388
1125 A364 30c multi   .40 .25
1126 A364 50c multi   .60 .30
1127 A364 $1 multi   1.10 .55
    a.   Perf. 12   1.10 .55
    Nos. 1125-1127 (3)   2.10 1.10

South Pole Expedition A365

Designs: 30c, Mountains, sled, tent. 50c, Man on skis pulling sled. $1, Man on skis pulling sled with parasail.

2006, Dec. 28   *Perf. 13½x13¼*
1128-1130 A365   Set of 3   2.50 1.25

Marine Life — A373

Designs: No. 1139, Leaf scorpionfish. No. 1140, Orange-striped triggerfish. No. 1141: a, Chambered nautilus. b, Spotted boxfish.

Perf. 13½x13¼
2007, Feb. 6   Litho.   Wmk. 388
1139 A373 50c multi   .70 .35
    a.   Perf. 12   .70 .35
1140 A373 50c multi   .70 .35
    a.   Perf. 12   .70 .35
Souvenir Sheet
1141 A373 $1 Sheet of 2, #a-b   2.25 1.10
Dated 2006. See Brunei Nos. 588-590.

Tourism — A374

No. 1142: a, Hornbill, forest and flower. b, Diver and coral reef.
No. 1143: a, Buildings. b, Handicrafts.
No. 1144: a, Woman with red dress, with arms raised. b, Woman with red dress holding fan. c, Woman with blue dress. d, Woman with black dress. e, Woman with red and black dress with geometric patterns. f, Satay, Ketupat dan Aie Sirap. g, Yee Sang. h, Banana leaf rice dan Teh Tarik. i, Hinava. j, Manok Pansuh.

$2, Flag and buildings, vert.

2007, Mar. 19   *Perf. 13½x13¼*
1142 A374 30c Horiz. pair, #a-b   .75 .35
Perf. 12
1143 A374 50c Horiz. pair, #a-b   1.50 .75
Booklet Stamps
Perf. 13½x13¼
1144 A374 30c Booklet pane of 10, #a-j   3.00 1.50
    Compete booklet, #1144   3.00
Souvenir Sheet
Perf. 13¼x13½
1145 A374 $2 multi   2.00 1.00
No. 1145 contains one 30x50mm stamp.

Installation of 13th Yang Di-Pertuan Agong — A375

13th Yang Di-Pertuan Agong and background colors of: 30c, Yellow. 50c, Green. $1, Purple.

2007, Apr. 26   *Perf. 12½*
1146-1148 A375   Set of 3   2.00 1.00

Amphibians A376

Designs: 30c, Pedostibes hosii. No. 1150, 50c, Megophrys nasuta. 50c, Nyctixalus pictus.
$1, Rana laterimaculata

2007, May 3   *Perf. 12*
1149-1151 A376   Set of 3   2.00 1.00
Souvenir Sheet
Perf. 13¼
1152 A376 $1 multi   1.40 .70
No. 1152 contains one 35x33mm stamp.

Airplanes A377

Designs: 30c, Shorts SC-7 Skyvan. No. 1154, 50c, GAF N22 Nomad. No. 1155, 50c, De Havilland Canada DHC 7-110.
No. 1156: a, Airspeed Consul. b, Douglas DC-3.

2007, May 24   *Perf. 12*
1153-1155 A377   Set of 3   1.60 .80
Souvenir Sheet
Perf. 13½x13¼
1156 A377 $1 Sheet of 2, #a-b   1.75 .85

Clock Towers — A378

Designs: 30c, J. W. W. Birch Clock Tower, 1917. 50c, Atkinson Clock Tower, 1905. $1, Alor Setar Clock Tower, 1912.

Perf. 13¼x14x13¼x13½
2007, June 6
1157-1159 A378   Set of 3   2.00 1.00

Children's Folk Tales A379

Designs: Nos. 1160a, 1161a, Bawang Putah Bawang Merah. Nos. 1160b, 1161b, Badang. Nos. 1160c, 1162a, Sang Kancil Dengan Buaya. Nos. 1160d, 1162b, Sang Kancil Menolong Kerbau. No. 1160e, Mat Jenin.
$5, Si Tanggang.

Perf. 13½x13¼
2007, June 26   Litho.   Wmk. 388
1160   Horiz. strip of 5   2.00 2.00
    a.-e.   A379 30c Any single   .40 .30
    f.   Booklet pane, 2 each #1160a-1160e   4.00 —
    Complete booklet, #1160f   4.00
1161   Horiz. pair   1.25 .60
    a.-b.   A379 50c Any single   .60 .30
1162   Horiz. pair   1.25 .60
    a.-b.   A379 50c Any single   .60 .30
Souvenir Sheet
Litho. With Foil Application
Perf. 14
1163 A379 $5 multi   4.00 2.00
No. 1163 contains one 50x38mm stamp.

Insects — A380

No. 1164, 30c: a, Fulgora pyrorhyncha. b, Dysdercus cingulatus.
No. 1165, 50c: a, Valanga nigricornis. b, Rhaphipodus hopei.
$5, Antheraea helferi, horiz.

2007, July 7   *Perf. 12¾x12½*
Horiz. Pairs, #a-b
1164-1165 A380   Set of 2   1.75 .85
Souvenir Sheet
Perf. 14
1166 A380 $5 multi   4.00 2.00
No. 1166 contains one 50x38mm stamp.

Police Force, 200th Anniv. A381

Designs: 30c, Police and building. No. 1168, 50c, Police near jeep and in river, policeman wearing shorts. No. 1169, 50c, Police officers, cars, motorcycles, building and computer operator.

2007, July 24   *Perf. 13½x13¼*
1167-1169 A381   Set of 3   1.75 .85

Association of South East Asian Nations (ASEAN), 40th Anniv. — A382

No. 1170: a, Secretariat Building, Bandar Seri Begawan, Brunei. b, National Museum of Cambodia. c, Fatahillah Museum, Jakarta,

Indonesia. d, Typical house, Laos. e, Malayan Railway Headquarters Building, Kuala Lumpur. f, Yangon Post Office, Myanmar (Burma). g, Malacañang Palace, Philippines. h, National Museum of Singapore. i, Vimanmek Mansion, Bangkok, Thailand. j, Presidential Palace, Hanoi, Viet Nam.

2007, Aug. 8   **Perf. 13¾x14¼**
1170   Block of 10   5.00 5.00
a.-j.   A382 50c Any single   .50   .50

See Brunei No. 607, Burma No. 370, Cambodia No. 2339, Indonesia Nos. 2120-2121, Laos Nos. 1717-1718, Philippines Nos. 3103-3105, Singapore No. 1265, Thailand No. 2315, Viet Nam Nos. 3302-3311.

Malaysian Independence, 50th Anniv. — A383

No. 1171 — Anniversary emblem, flag and: a, Dato' Onn Jaafar. b, Tunku Abdul Rahman Putra Al-Haj. c, Tun Abdul Razak. d, Tun Tan Cheng Lock. e, Tun V. T. Sambanthan.

No. 1172 — Anniversary emblem and: a, Tunku Abdul Rahman Putra Al-Haj, buildings, people, flag, statue. b, Petronas Twin Towers, government building, automobile and bridge.

No. 1173: a, Tunku Abdul Rahman Putra Al-Haj signing declaration of independence and anniversary emblem. b, Anniversary emblem. $5, Flag.

2007, Aug. 31   **Perf. 13½x13¼**
1171   Horiz. strip of 5   2.00 2.00
a.-e. A383 30c any single   .40   .40
1172   Horiz. pair   .80   .80
a.-b. A383 30c any single   .40   .40
1173   Horiz. pair   1.00 1.00
a.-b. A383 50c any single   .50   .50

Souvenir Sheet
Perf. 13¼
1174 A383 $5 multi   4.00 2.00

No. 1174 contains one 70x33mm stamp and has foil application in margin.

Petronas Twin Towers, Kuala Lumpur, 2007 Recipient of Aga Khan Award for Architecture A384

2007, Sept. 4   **Perf. 13¼x13½**
1175 A384 50c multi   3.00 1.50

National and State Arms — A385

No. 1176: a, Malaysia. b, Kedah. c, Negri Sembilan. d, Pahang. e, Kelantan. f, Johore. g, Perak. h, Perlis. i, Selangor. j, Trengganu. k, Sarawak. l, Penang. m, Sabah. n, Malacca.

2007, Sept. 25   **Perf. 13¾x14**
1176   Block of 14   5.75 4.25
a.-n. A385 50c Any single   .40   .30

Vegetables A386

Designs: No. 1177, 50c, Solanum ferox. No. 1178, 50c, Etlingera elatior. No. 1179, 50c, Momordica charantia.

No. 1180: a, Luffa aegyptiaca. b, Psophocarpus tetragonolobus. c, Sesbania grandiflora. d, Solanum torvum.

Perf. 13¾x13½ Syncopated
2007, Nov. 26
1177-1179 A386 Set of 3   1.40   .70

Souvenir Sheet
Perf. 13¾x14 Syncopated
1180 A386 $1 Sheet of 4, #a-d   2.75 1.40

Kuala Lumpur Equestrian Grand Prix — A387

Horses: 30c, Oldenburger. No. 1182, 50c, Dutch Warmblood. No. 1183, 50c, Hanonverian.

2007, Dec. 13   **Perf. 13½**
1181-1183 A387 Set of 3   1.50   .75

Bridges — A388

Designs: 30c, Merdeka Bridge, Kedah. No. 1185, 50c, Kota Bridge, Selangor. No. 1186, 50c, Victoria Bridge, Perak. $1, Sungai Segamat Bridge, Johore.

Perf. 13¾x13¼
2008, Feb. 28   **Litho.**   **Wmk. 388**
1184-1187 A388 Set of 4   2.00 1.00

Nocturnal Animals A389

Designs: No. 1188, 30c, Mydaus javanensis. No. 1189, 30c, Echinosorex gymnurus. 50c, Catopuma temnickii. $1, Pteropas vampyrus.

No. 1192: a, $2, Tarsius bancanus (30x40mm). b, $3, Nycticebus coucang (60x40mm).

2008, Mar. 13   **Perf. 13½x13¼**
1188-1191 A389 Set of 4   1.75   .85

Souvenir Sheet
Perf. 12¾x12½
1192 A389 Sheet of 2, #a-b   3.75 1.75
c.   As #1192, imperf.   3.75 1.75

Butterflies A390

No. 1193: a, Smaller wood nymph. b, Malaysian lacewing.
50c, Malay red harlequin. $1, Glorious begum.
No. 1195A, Common rose. No. 1195B, Blue glassy tiger. No. 1195C, Green dragontail. $5, Five-bar swordtail.

2008, Apr. 24   **Perf. 13½x13¼**
1193 A390 30c Horiz. pair, #a-b   .40   .30
d.   As #1193, perf. 12   .40   .30
e.   As #1193a, perf. 12   .40   .30
f.   As #1193b, perf. 12   .40   .30

1194 A390 50c multi   .40   .30
1195 A390 $1 multi   .65   .40
     Nos. 1193-1195 (3)   1.45 1.00

Booklet Stamps
1195A A390 30c multi   .40   .25
1195B A390 30c multi   .40   .25
1195C A390 30c multi   .40   .25
d.   Booklet pane, 2 each
          #1193a-1193b, 1195A-
          1195C   3.00   —
          Complete booklet, #1195Cd 3.00
     Nos. 1195A-1195C (3)   1.20   .75

Souvenir Sheet
Perf. 14
1196 A390 $5 multi   3.75 1.75

No. 1196 contains one 50x38mm stamp and has die cut slits in the sheet margin.

St. John Ambulance in Malaysia, Cent. A391

Centenary emblem and: 30c, Emergency ambulance service. 50c, First aid. $1, Cardiopulmonary resuscitation.

2008, May 22   **Perf. 13½x13¼**
1197-1199 A391 Set of 3   2.75 1.40

A392

Cultural Items — A393

2008, June 10   **Perf. 13½x13¼**
1200 A392 30c Batu Giling   .30   .25
1201 A392 50c Supu   .45   .45

Perf. 13¼x13¾
1202 A393 50c Kukur Kelapa   .45   .45
     Nos. 1200-1202 (3)   1.20 1.15

Intl. Dragon Boat Federation Club Crew World Championships — A394

Designs: 30c, Boats 6 and 3. 50c, Boats 5 and 2. $1, Boats 4 and 1. $2, Boat 5.

Perf. 13½x13¼
2008, Aug. 1   **Litho.**   **Wmk. 388**
1203-1205 A394 Set of 3   1.75   .85

Souvenir Sheet
1206 A394 $2 multi   1.60   .80
a.   Imperf.   1.60   .80

No. 1206 contains one 80x30mm stamp.

Malaysian Scouting Association, Cent. — A395

Centenary emblem, scouting emblems and: 30c, Scouts reading map, Lord Robert Baden-Powell. No. 1208, 50c, Scout water activities. No. 1209, 50c, Scouts on monkey bridge.

2008, Aug. 14   **Perf. 13½x13¼**
1207-1209 A395 Set of 3   1.50   .75

Art A396

Designs: 30c, Semangat Ledang, by Syed Ahmad Jamal. 50c, Musim Buah, by Chuah Thean Teng, vert. $1, Pago-pago, by Latiff Mohidin.

2008, Aug. 28   **Perf. 12½x12¾**
1210 A396 30c multi   .35   .25

Perf. 12¾x12½
1211 A396 50c multi   .60   .30

Size:35x35mm
Perf. 13¼
1212 A396 $1 multi   .80   .50
     Nos. 1210-1212 (3)   1.75 1.05

Miniature Sheet

Royal Headgear — A397

No. 1213 — Headgear for: a, Leaders of Eight states and Yang Di-Pertuan Agong. b, Yang Di-Pertuan Agong. c, Sultan of Kedah. d, Yang Di-Pertuan Agong of Negri Sembilan. e, Sultan of Pahang. f, Sultan of Kelantan. g, Sultan of Perak. h, Raja of Perlis. i, Sultan of Selangor. j, Sultan of Trengganu.

2008, Sept. 16   **Perf. 13¾x14**
1213 A397 50c Sheet of 10, #a-j   5.50 2.75

Flowers — A398

No. 1214, 30c: a, Goniothalamus tapis. b, Gloriosa superba.
No. 1215, 50c: a, Quisqualis indica. b, Michelia figo.
$5, Epiphyllum oxypetalum, vert.

Wmk. 388
2008, Oct. 9   **Litho.**   **Perf. 13¼**
Horiz. Pairs, #a-b
1214-1215 A398 Set of 2   2.25 1.10

Souvenir Sheet
Perf. 14
1216 A398 $5 multi   3.75 1.90

No. 1216 contains one 39x50mm stamp.

National Space Program — A399

Designs: 30c, Soyuz-TMA II rocket on launch pad. No. 1218, 50c, Malaysian astronaut. No. 1219, 50c, Intl. Space Station.
No. 1220: a, Rocket lifting off from launch pad. b, Rocket above Earth.

2008, Oct. 21   *Perf. 13¼x13¾*
1217-1219 A399   Set of 3   1.60 .80
Souvenir Sheet
1220 A399 $1 Sheet of 2, #a-b   1.75 .85

Shells — A400

Designs: No. 1221, 30c, Burnt murex. No. 1222, 30c, Horned helmet. No. 1223, 50c, Triton's trumpet. No. 1224, 50c, Frog shell.
$2, Venus comb murex.

2008, Nov. 11   *Perf. 11¾*
1221-1224 A400   Set of 4   2.00 1.00
Souvenir Sheet
Perf. 12¾x12½
1224A A400 $2 multi   2.00 1.00
   b.   Imperf.   2.00 1.00
No. 1224A contains one 60x40mm stamp.

The Kampung Boy, Cartoons by Lat — A401

Designs: Nos. 1225a, 1226a, The Kampung Boy (29x33mm). Nos. 1225b, 1226b, Permainan Anak Kampung (58x33mm). Nos. 1225c, 1226c, Guru Sekolah Yang Garang (58x33mm). Nos. 1225d, 1226d, Town Boy (29x33mm). No. 1225e, Kampung Boy drawing picture (29x33mm).
$5, Malaysian daily life (60x40mm).

Perf. 13¾x14 Syncopated
2008, Dec. 1
1225   Horiz. strip of 5   1.50 1.50
  a.-e.   A401 30c Any single   .30 .30
     Complete booklet, 2 #1225   3.00
1226   Horiz. strip of 4   2.25 2.25
  a.-d.   A401 50c Any single   .30 .30
Souvenir Sheet
Perf. 12¾x12½
1227 A401 $5 silver & blk   3.75 1.90

Schools — A402

Designs: No. 1228, 50c, SMK Convent Bukit Nanas, Kuala Lumpur. No. 1229, 50c, SMK St. Thomas, Kuching, Sarawak. No. 1230, 50c, SMK Victoria (Victoria Institution), Kuala Lumpur. No. 1231, 50c, SM All Saints, Kota Kinabalu, Sabah.

2008, Dec. 16   *Perf. 13½x13¼*
1228-1231 A402   Set of 4   2.25 1.10

Birds A403

Designs: 30c, Polyplectron malacense. No. 1233, 50c, Mycteria cinerea. No. 1234, 50c, Myiophonus robinsoni.
$5, Aceros subruficollis.

Perf. 13½x13¼
2009, Jan. 21   Litho.   Wmk. 388
1232-1234 A403   Set of 3   2.00 1.00
Souvenir Sheet
Perf. 12
Litho. & Embossed
1235 A403 $5 multi   4.00 2.00
  a.   With China 2009 World Stamp
    Exhibition emblem in sheet
    margin   4.00 2.00
Nos. 1235 and 1235a each contain one 45x35mm stamp.

Traditional Wedding Costumes A404

No. 1236: a, Bajau. b, Orang Ulu. c, Indian. d, Chinese. e, Malayan.
No. 1237: a, Malayan, diff. b, Chinese, diff. c, Indian, diff. d, Orang Ulu, diff. e, Bajau, diff.

Perf. 13¼x13½
2009, Mar. 23   Litho.
1236   Horiz. strip of 5   1.50 1.50
  a.-e.   A404 30c Any single   .30 .30
     Complete booklet, 2 each
     #1236a-1236e   3.00
1237   Horiz. strip of 5   2.50 2.50
  a.-e.   A404 50c Any single   .50 .50

UNESCO World Heritage Sites — A405

No. 1238, 50c: a, Taman Negara Mulu, Sarawak, and tarsier. b, Taman Kinabalu, Sabah, and bird.
No. 1239, 50c: a, Town Square, Banda Hilir, Malacca, and door. b, Old City Hall, George Town, Penang, and windows.
No. 1240, 50c: a, Building, Banda Hilir, Malacca. b, Lenticular cloud over Taman Kinabalu, Sabah. c, Buildings, George Town, Penang. d, Cave, Taman Negara Mulu.

2009, Apr. 9   *Perf. 13½x13¼*
Horiz. Pairs, #a-b
1238-1239 A405   Set of 2   1.25 .60
Perf. 14x13½
1240 A405 50c Sheet of 4, #a-d   1.25 .60
No. 1240 contains four 60x25mm stamps.

Engineering Projects of the Past and Present — A406

No. 1241, 30c — Transportation and port: a, Past. b, Present.
No. 1242, 30c — Telecommunication and power: a, Past. b, Present.
No. 1243, 50c — Road, bridge and dam: a, Past. b, Present.

Perf. 12½x12¾
2009, Apr. 20   Wmk. 388
Horiz. Pairs, #a-b
1241-1243 A406   Set of 3   2.50 1.25

Palm Trees — A407

Designs: No. 1244, 50c, Licuala grandis. No. 1245, 50c, Caryota mitis. No. 1246, 50c, Livistona saribus.
$3, Livistona endauensis and Johannesteijsmannia altifrons.

2009, May 19   Unwmk.   *Perf. 13¼*
1244-1246 A407   Set of 3   1.50 .75
Souvenir Sheet
Perf. 12
1247 A407 $3 multi   2.25 1.10
No. 1247 contains one 70x50mm L-shaped stamp.

Nature Conservation — A408

Inscriptions: 30c, Clean Water. No. 1249, 50c, Go Green. No. 1250, 50c, Fresh Air.

Perf. 13¾x13½
2009, June 18   Unwmk.
1248-1250 A408   Set of 3   1.75 .85

Miniature Sheet

Traditional Houses — A409

No. 1251 Inscriptions: a, Rumah Traditional Melayu, Selangor. b, Rumah Dusun Lotud, Sabah. c, Rumah Kutai, Perak. d, Rumah Tiang 12, Kelantan. e, Rumah Panjang Iban, Sarawak. f, Rumah Orang Semai, Pahang. g, Rumah Limas, Johor. h, Rumah Panjang, Kedah. i, Rumah Limas Bungkus, Terengganu. j, Rumah Adat Minangkabau, Negeri Sembilan. k, Rumah Serambi Gajah Menyusu, Pulau Pinang. l, Rumah Bumbung Panjang, Perlis. m, Rumah Melayu Melaka, Melaka. n, Rumah Laut Bajau, Sabah. o, Rumah Serambi, Pahang. p, Rumah Ketua Bidayuh, Sarawak.

Perf. 12½x12¾
2009, July 9   Wmk. 388
1251 A409 50c Sheet of 16, #a-p   6.00 3.00

Tubers A410

Designs: No. 1252, 30c, Manihot esculenta crantz. No. 1253, 30c, Ipomoea batatas. No.

1254, 50c, Dioscorea alata. No. 1255, 50c, Pachyrrhizus erosus.
$3, Colocasia esculenta.

Perf. 13¼
2009, July 23   Litho.   Unwmk.
1252-1255 A410   Set of 4   1.50 .75
Souvenir Sheet
Perf. 13¼ Syncopated
1256 A410 $3 multi   2.25 1.10
No. 1256 contains one 45x45mm stamp.

"Malaysia is Number 1" — A411

"1" and: Nos. 1257, 1260, Map of Malaysia. Nos. 1258, 1261, People in ring around Malaysian flag in heart. Nos. 1259, 1262, Lightbulb, seven people. No. 1263, Computer, Kuala Lumpur skyline, gauge, dish antenna, microscope, man at chart, woman with clipboard. No. 1264, Flower, people, gavel, building, traditional hat.
$5, Eight people around "1."

Perf. 13¾x14 Syncopated
2009, Aug. 31   Wmk. 388
1257 A411 30c multi   .40 .30
1258 A411 30c multi   .40 .30
1259 A411 30c multi   .40 .30
   Nos. 1257-1259 (3)   1.20 .90
Booklet Stamps
Perf. 13¾x13½ Syncopated
1260 A411 30c multi   .40 .30
1261 A411 30c multi   .40 .30
1262 A411 30c multi   .40 .30
1263 A411 30c multi   .40 .30
1264 A411 30c multi   .40 .30
  a.   Booklet pane of 10, 2 each
    #1260-1264   4.00 —
    Complete booklet, #1264a   4.00
   Nos. 1260-1264 (5)   2.00 1.50
Souvenir Sheet
Perf. 13¼x13½
1265 A411 $5 multi   3.75 1.90
No. 1265 contains one 30x40mm stamp that has a clear holographic coating.

First Malaysian Submarine — A412

Submarine, flag of Malaysia and Navy crest with denomination at: 30c, LR. No. 1267, 50c, UR. No. 1268, 50c, LR.

2009, Sept. 3   *Perf. 13½x13¼*
1266-1268 A412   Set of 3   1.50 .75

Energy Efficient Buildings — A413

Designs: 30c, Green Energy Office Building, Bangi. 50c, Low Energy Office Building, Putrajaya. $1, Diamond Building, Putrajaya.

2009, Sept. 9   *Perf. 13¼x13½*
1269-1271 A413   Set of 3   1.75 .85
1270a   Perf. 14   .40 .40
1271a   Perf. 14   .75 .35

Declaration of the Rights of the Child, 20th Anniv. A414

No. 1272: a, Girl with pinwheel. b, Boy drinking. c, Boy carrying backpack. d, Girl under umbrella.

2009, Oct. 9   **Litho.**   *Perf. 13½*
1272 A414 30c Block of 4, #a-d   1.50 .75

Litho. & Embossed
1273 A414 $1 shown   1.00 .50

Arachnids — A415

Designs: No. 1274, 30c, Curved spiny spider. No. 1275, 30c, Fighting spider. 50c, St. Andrew's cross spider. $1, Golden orb-web spider. $5, Black scorpion.

Perf. 13¾x13½
2009, Dec. 7   **Litho.**   **Wmk. 388**
1274-1277 A415   Set of 4   2.00 1.00

Souvenir Sheet
Litho. & Embossed
Perf. 13¾x13
1278 A415 $5 multi   3.00 1.50
No. 1278 contains one 64x32mm hexagonal stamp.

Malaysian Currency A416

No. 1279, 50c — 1990 10 sen coin (orange ring): a, Obverse (with date). b, Reverse.
No. 1280, 50c — 1990 20 sen coin (green ring): a, Obverse (with date). b, Reverse.
No. 1281, 50c — 1990 50 sen coin (blue ring): a, Obverse (with date). b, Reverse.
$5, 50 ringgit banknote, horiz.

Perf. 13¼
2010, Jan. 18   **Litho.**   **Unwmk.**
Vertical Pairs, #a-b
1279-1281 A416   Set of 3   1.75 .85

Souvenir Sheet
Litho. With Foil Application
Perf. 14x13½
1282 A416 $5 multi   3.00 1.50
No. 1282 contains one 50x40mm stamp.

A416a

Flag in "1" — A416b

2010   **Litho.**   **Wmk. 388**   *Perf. 13¾*
Stamp and Label Separated By Perforations
1282A A416a 30c multi + label   13.50 13.50

Stamp and Label Not Separated By Perforations
Perf. 14¼
1282B A416b 30c multi   18.00 18.00
1282C A416b 60c multi   24.00 24.00
   Nos. 1282A-1282C (3)   55.50 55.50

Issued: No. 1282A, 2/4; No. 1282B, May. Labels could be personalized. No. 1282A was issued in sheets of 20 + 20 labels that sold for $6. No. 1282B was issued in sheets of 20 that sold for $19. No. 1282C was issued in sheets of 10 that sold for $19.

New Year 2010 (Year of the Tiger) — A417

No. 1283: a, Korean tiger. b, Malayan tiger.

Perf. 13½x14
2010, Feb. 23   **Litho.**   **Wmk. 388**
1283 A417 50c Horiz. pair, #a-b   .60 .30

Ferns — A418

No. 1284: a, Helminthostachys zeylanica. b, Stenochlaena palustris. c, Platycerium coronarium. d, Dicraopteris linearis. e, Diplazium esculentum.
$3, Asplenium nidus, Matonia pectinata, Dipteris conjugata, horiz.

Perf. 13¼x13½
2010, Mar. 10   **Litho.**   **Wmk. 388**
1284 A418 Horiz. strip of 5   1.50 .75
  a.-e. A418 50c Any single   .30 .25

Souvenir Sheet
Perf. 14
1285 A418 $3 multi   1.90 .95
No. 1285 contains one 100x45mm stamp.

A419

Local Markets — A420

No. 1286, 30c: a, Woman with vegetables at Kelantan market. b, Kelantan market.
No. 1287, 50c: a, Fruit at market, Sabah. b, Handicrafts at market, Sabah.
No. 1288 — Market in Sarawak: a, $1, Woman and vegetables. b, $2, Woman and man with potted plants.
No. 1289 — Market in Kedah: a, $1, Man looking at textiles, pile of baskets. b, $2, Man and woman shopping.

2010, Mar. 23   *Perf. 13¼*
Horiz. Pairs, #a-b
1286-1287 A419   Set of 2   1.00 .50

Souvenir Sheets
Perf. 13¼x13½
Sheets of 2, #a-b
1288-1289 A420   Set of 2   3.75 1.90

Medical Excellence in Malaysia A421

Designs: 30c, Limbal stem cell deficiency. 50c, Premaxilla retractor. $1, Arm transplant.

2010, Apr. 26   *Perf. 13¼*
1290-1292 A421   Set of 3   1.25 .60

Fireflies A422

Designs: No. 1293, 30c, Pteroptyx bearni. No. 1294, 30c, Pteroptyx valida. No. 1295, 50c, Lychnuris sp. No. 1296, 50c, Diaphanes sp.
$5, Pteroptyx tener.

2010, May 10   **Litho.**   *Perf. 12¼*
1293-1296 A422   Set of 4   1.00 .50

Souvenir Sheet
Litho. With Hologram
Perf. 12¾x12½
1297 A422 $5 multi   3.00 1.50
No. 1297 contains one 60x40mm stamp.

Malaysian Railways — A423

No. 1298: a, Commuter train. b, ETS train. 50c, Blue Tiger. $1, 56 Class train.
No. 1301, 20 Class train. No. 1302, Commuter and ETS trains. No. 1303, Blue Tiger. No. 1304, 56 Class train. No. 1305, FMSR Class T train.
$3, FMSR Class T train, vert.

2010, June 22   **Litho.**   *Perf. 12*
1298 A423 30c Horiz. pair, #a-b   .40 .25

Size: 70x25mm
1299 A423 50c multi   .35 .25
1300 A423 $1 multi   .65 .30
   Nos. 1298-1300 (3)   1.40 .80

Booklet Stamps
1301 A423 30c multi   .25 .25
1302 A423 30c multi   .25 .25
1303 A423 30c multi   .25 .25

1304 A423 30c multi   .25 .25
1305 A423 30c multi   .25 .25
  a.   Vert. strip of 5, #1301-1305   1.00 1.00
  b.   Booklet pane of 10, 2 each #1301-1305   2.00 —
   Complete booklet, #1305b   2.00

Souvenir Sheet
Perf. 13½
1306 A423 $3 multi   1.90 .95
  a.   As #1306, with Bangkok 2010 emblem in margin   1.90 .95
  b.   As #1306, with PhilaNippon '11 emblem in margin   2.00 1.00
No. 1306 contains one 30x50mm stamp.

Flowers — A424

Designs: 30c, Nelumbium nelumbo. 50c, Hydrangea macrophylla. 60c, Bougainvillea. 70c, Hippeastrum reticulatum. 80c, Hibiscus rosa-sinensis. 90c, Ipomoea indica. $1, Canna orientalis. $2, Allamanda cathartica.

2010, July 1   *Perf. 14x13¾*
1307 A424 30c multi   .25 .25
1308 A424 50c multi   .30 .25
1309 A424 60c multi   .40 .25
1310 A424 70c multi   .45 .25
1311 A424 80c multi   .50 .25
1312 A424 90c multi   .55 .30
1313 A424 $1 multi   .65 .30
1314 A424 $2 multi   1.25 .60
   Nos. 1307-1314 (8)   4.35 2.45

Threatened Habitats — A425

Habitats: 60c, Forest. 70c, Marine. 80c, River.

Perf. 13¾x14 Syncopated
2010, July 15
1315-1317 A425   Set of 3   1.40 .70

Grand Knight of Valor Award — A426

Grand Knight of Valor Award and: 60c, Soldiers, tank. 70c, People, Kuala Lumpur skyline. 80c, Soldiers, building.

2010, July 30   *Perf. 12¾x12½*
1318-1320 A426   Set of 3   1.40 .70

Miniature Sheets

A427

Traditional Festive Food — A428

Nos. 1321 and 1322 — Various foods of people of: a, Malaysia, text at top. b, Malaysia, text at bottom. c, China, text at top. d, China, text at bottom. e, India, text at top. f, India, text at bottom. g, Sabah, text at top. h, Sabah, text at bottom. i, Sarawak, text at top, j, Sarawak, text at bottom. Foods on Nos. 1321 and 1322 are different.

No. 1323: a, Chinese foods. b, Indian foods. c, Malaysian foods.

2010, Aug. 10   **Perf. 13¼**
1321   A427   Sheet of 10   5.25   2.60
  a.-j.   80c Any single   .50   .25

Booklet Stamps
1322   A427   Booklet pane of 10   4.00   —
  a.-j.   60c Any single   .40   .25

Souvenir Sheet
1323   A428   Sheet of 3   2.00   1.00
  a.-c. $1 Any single   .65   .30

Life of Aboriginal People — A429

Designs: 60c. Women holding ketuk buluh (musical instruments). 70c, Man shooting with blowpipe. 80c, Man carving figures.

2010, Sept. 27   **Wmk. 388**
1324-1326   A429   Set of 3   1.40   .70

Old Post Offices — A430

No. 1327: a, Jalan Kelang Lama Post Office, Kuala Lumpur. b, Layang-Layang Post Office. c, Jalan Raja Post Office. d, Temangan Post Office. e, Merlimau Post Office. f, Seremban General Post Office. g, Fraser Hill (Bukit Fraser) Post Office. h, Kuala Kangsar Post Office. i, Kaki Bukit Post Office. j, Jalan Bagan Luar Post Office. k, Kudat Post Office. l, Kuching General Post Office. m, Kajang Post Office. n, Kuala Terengganu Post Office. o, Kuala Lumpur General Post Office, flag of Federal Territory. p, Johor Bahru General Post Office, flag of Johore. q, Sungai Petani Post Office, flag of Kedah. r, Rantau Panjang Post Office, flag of Kelantan. s, Alor Gajah Post Office, flag of Malacca. t, Bandar Baru Serting Post Office, flag of Negri Sembilan. u, Ringlet Post Office, flag of Pahang. v, Tronoh Post Office, flag of Perak. w, Kangar Post Office, flag of Perlis. x, Bukit Mertajam Post Office, flag of Penang. y, Kota Kinabalu General Post Office, flag of Sabah. z, Sarikel Post Office, flag of Sarawak. aa, Bukit Rotan Post Office, flag of Selangor. ab, Jerteh Post Office, flag of Trengganu.

Perf. 13¾x13½ Syncopated
2010, Oct. 9
1327   Sheet of 28   11.00   11.00
  a.-ab.   A430 60c Any single   .35   .25

"Malaysia is Number 1" — A431

Handcrafted products, "Malaysia is Number 1" emblem and: No. 1328, 30c, Computer mouse, satellite dish. No. 1329, 30c, Astronaut and spaceship. No. 1330, 50c, Buildings. No. 1331, 50c, Robot.

2010, Nov. 10   **Perf. 13¼x13½**
1328-1331   A431   Set of 4   1.10   .55

Children's Games — A432

No. 1332, 60c: a, Batu Seremban. b, Congkak.
No. 1333, 60c: a, Galah Panjang. b, Konda-kondi.
No. 1334, 60c: a, Perang-perang. b, Telefon Tin.
$5, Main Bayang-bayang.

Litho. With Glitter Affixed
Perf. 13¾x14¼
2010, Dec. 13   **Unwmk.**
Self-Adhesive
Horiz. Pairs, #a-b
1332-1334   A432   Set of 3   2.40   1.25

Souvenir Sheet
Die Cut Perf. 13½x13¼
1335   A432 $5 multi   3.25   1.60

No. 1335 contains one 75x50mm stamp.

Pets — A433

Child and: 60c, Rabbit. 80c, Cat. $1, Dog. No. 1339, $5, Rabbit. No. 1340, $5, Rabbit, with Indipex 2011 emblem.

2011 Litho. Wmk. 388 Perf. 13¼
1336-1338   A433   Set of 3   1.60   .80

Souvenir Sheets
1339   A433 $5 multi   3.25   1.60
1340   A433 $5 multi   3.50   1.75

Issued: Nos. 1336-1339, 1/18; No. 1340, 2/18. Indipex 2011 World Philatelic Exhibition (No. 1340).

Highlands Tourism — A434

Designs: 50c, Funicular railroad, Bukit Bendera. 60c, Tea picker, Cameron Highlands. 90c, Cable car and station, Mat Cincang Mountain, Langkawi. $1, Cabbage patch, Kundasang.

2011, Feb. 21   **Perf. 13½x13¼**
1341-1344   A434   Set of 4   2.00   1.00

Malaysia, Winners of 2010 Suzuki Cup — A435

Designs: No. 1345, 60c, Medal and emblem of Malaysian soccer team. No. 1346, 60c, Suzuki Cup and tournament emblem, vert. (30x50mm).

Perf. 13¼, 13¼x13½ (#1346)
2011, Feb. 28
1345-1346   A435   Set of 2   .80   .40

Spices A436

Designs: No. 1347, 60c, Cinnamon. 90c, Star anise. $1, Cardamom.

No. 1350, 60c: a, Fennel seed, text at top. b, Fennel seed, text at bottom. c, Turmeric, text at top. d, Turmeric, text at bottom. e, Chili peppers, text at top. f, Chili peppers, text at bottom. g, Coriander, text at top. h, Coriander, text at bottom. i, White pepper, text at top. j, White pepper, text at bottom.

No. 1351: a, $1, Various spice on stone, spice crushing roller. b, $2, Various spices on stone.

2011, Mar. 28   **Perf. 13¼**
1347-1349   A436   Set of 3   1.75   .85
1350   Booklet pane of 10   4.00   —
  a.-j.   A436 60c Any single   .40   .25
    Complete booklet, #1350   4.00

Souvenir Sheet
Perf. 14x13¼
1351   A436   Sheet of 2, #a-b   2.00   1.00

No. 1351 contains two 50x60mm stamps.

National Heritage Artifacts A437

No. 1352: a, Malay belt buckle. b, Gold coin showing deer. c, Sireh set (betel containers) of Sultan Abdul Samad of Selangor. d, Gold coin of Sultan Muzaffar Shah of Johore. e, Arch of sitting Buddha.

No. 1353: a, Royal Trengganu tobacco box. b, Gold Coin of Sultan Alau'uddin Riayat Shah. c, Dong S'on bell. d, Gold coin of Sultan Zainal Abidin II of Trengganu. e, Statue of Avalokitesvara.

2011, Apr. 11   **Perf. 12½x12¾**
1352   Horiz. strip of 5   2.00   1.00
  a.-e.   A437 60c Any single   .40   .25
1353   Horiz. strip of 5   2.00   1.00
  a.-e.   A437 60c Any single   .40   .25

Personalized Stamps — A438

No. 1354: a, Bunga Raya. b, Durian. c, Handicraft. d, Wau Bulan.

2011, Apr. 28   **Perf. 13¾x14**
1354   Block of 4   1.40   .70
  a.-b.   A438 35c Either single   .25   .25
  c.-d.   A438 65c Either single   .45   .25

No. 1354 printed in sheets containing two blocks of 4. The right halves of Nos. 1354a and 1354c and the left halves of Nos. 1354b and 1354d could be personalized. Images showing silver handicrafts are generic images. Compare with No. B1.

Virtues — A439

No. 1355 — Inscriptions in black: a, Love. b, Hardworking. c, Courteous. d, Mutual respect. e, Independent. f, Awareness. g, Kind hearted. h, Thankful ("Thank you" In green in 7 different languages). i, Living in harmony. j, Integrity.

2011, June 13   **Perf. 12¾x12½**
1355   Block of 10   4.00   2.00
  a.-j.   A439 60c Any single   .40   .25
  k.   As "h," "Thank you" in green in 8 different languages   .40   .25
  l.   Block of 10, #1355a-1355g, 1355i-1355k   4.00   2.00

Issued: Nos. 1355k, 1355l, 7/18.

Aviation in Malaysia, Cent. A440

Designs: 60c, Early monoplane. 80c, Airport control tower, passenger airplane and fuel truck. $1, Airport terminal, jets.

Perf. 12½x12¾
2011, July 7 Litho. Wmk. 388
1356-1358   A440   Set of 3   1.60   .80

Miniature Sheet

Royal Palaces — A441

No. 1359 — Palace, arms and map of: a, Kuala Lumpur. b, Negri Sembilan. c, Selangor. d, Perlis. e, Trengganu. f, Kedah. g, Kelantan. h, Pahang. i, Johore. k, Perak.

2011, July 18   **Perf. 14½x14¼**
1359   A441   Sheet of 10   7.00   3.50
  a.-j. $1 Any single   .70   .35

Miniature Sheet

Friendship Between Indonesia and Malaysia — A442

No. 1360: a, National Monument, Malaysia. b, Proclamation Monument, Indonesia. c, 1959 Malaya and North Borneo $1 banknote. d, 1945 5-sen Indonesia banknote. e, Malaya #84. f, Indonesia #1LM1. g, Gallus gallus. h, Gallus varius.

2011, Aug. 8   **Perf. 12½x12¾**
1360   A442   Sheet of 8   5.00   2.40
  a.-h.   90c Any single   .60   .30

See Indonesia Nos. 2284-2285.

Art — A443

Designs: 60c, Datuk Bajau Horseman, North Borneo, by Mohd Hoessein Enas, 1963. 90c, Ayam Jantan, sculpture by Anthony Lau, 1963, horiz. $1, Flag, by Nik Zainal Abidin Nik Salleh, 1970, horiz.

Perf. 12¾x12½, 12½x12¾
2011, Sept. 19
1361-1363	A443	Set of 3	1.60	.80

Mailboxes
A444

No. 1364 — Mailbox, building and postal service emblem with inscription at bottom: a, Bukit Bendera, Pulau Pinang. b, Bukit Fraser, Pahang. c, Melaka Bandaraya Bersejarah. d, Seremban, Negeri Sembilan. e, Pejabat Pos Besar, Kuala Lumpur.

Litho. & Embossed
Perf. 13½x14
2011, Oct. 10   Wmk. 388
1364		Horiz. strip of 5	3.25	1.60
a.-e.	A444	$1 Any single	.65	.30

Mailboxes
A445

Mailbox, buildings and inscription at LL: No. 1365, Bukit Bendera, Pulau Pinang. No. 1366, Bukit Fraser, Pahang. No. 1367, Melaka Bandaraya Bersejarah. No. 1368, Seremban, Negeri Sembilan. No. 1369, Pejabat Pos Besar, Kuala Lumpur.

Serpentine Die Cut 13x12¾
2011, Oct. 10   Litho.   Unwmk.
Booklet Stamps
Self-Adhesive
1365	A445	60c multi	.40	.25
1366	A445	60c multi	.40	.25
1367	A445	60c multi	.40	.25
1368	A445	60c multi	.40	.25
1369	A445	60c multi	.40	.25
a.		Booklet pane of 10, 2 each #1365-1369	4.00	
		Nos. 1365-1369 (5)	2.00	1.25

Tunnel Construction — A446

No. 1370, 60c: a, Tunneling through. b, TBM after breakthrough.
No. 1371, 60c: a, Tunnel breakthrough. b, Construction gantry.

No. 1372, 60c: a, Road tunnel. b, Schematic cross-section.
No. 1373, vert.: a, Vignettes of Nos. 1370a, 1371a, 1371b. b, Vignettes of Nos. 1370b, 1372a, 1372b.

Perf. 13¼x14¼ Syncopated
2011, Nov. 21   Litho.   Unwmk.
Vert. Pairs, #a-b
1370-1372	A446	Set of 3	2.40	1.25

Souvenir Sheet
Self-Adhesive
Litho. With Three-Dimensional Plastic Affixed
Serpentine Die Cut 12x12¾
1373	A446	Sheet of 2	3.25	1.60
a.		$2 multi	1.25	.60
b.		$3 multi	2.00	1.00

No. 1373 contains two 35x40mm stamps.

Regalia — A447

Designs: 60c, Crown (Gandik diraja). 80c, Belt buckle (Pending diraja). 90c, Throne (Singgahsana).

Wmk. 388
2011, Dec. 12   Litho.   Perf. 14
1374-1376	A447	Set of 3	1.50	.75

Women Creating Textiles A448

Dragon on Robe — A449

No. 1377: a, Cindai. b, Songket. c, Pua Kumbu. d, Ci Xiu. e, Rangkit.

Wmk. 388
2012, Jan. 12   Litho.   Perf. 12
1377		Horiz. strip of 5	2.00	1.00
a.-e.	A448	60c Any single	.40	.25

Souvenir Sheets
Variable Perfs. 13½-14
1378	A449	$3 multi	2.00	1.00
a.		With Indonesia 2012 World Stamp Championships emblem in sheet margin, perf. 13½	2.00	1.00

Litho. With Foil Application
1379	A449	$5 gold & multi	3.50	1.75
a.		With Indonesia 2012 World Stamp Championships emblem in sheet margin, variable perfs. 13¼-13½	3.50	1.75

Yes to Life, No to Drugs Campaign — A450

No. 1380: a, Family. b, Children at play.

Perf. 13¾x13
2012, Feb. 27   Litho.   Wmk. 388
1380	A450	60c Horiz. pair, #a-b	.80	.40
1381	A450	$1 shown	.70	.35

Malaysian Antarctic Research Program A451

Design: 60c, Map of Antarctica, flag of Malaysia, scientist, emblem.
No. 1383: a, World map, emblem. b, Penguins, bacteria, scientist, emblem (70x35mm).

2012, Mar. 8   Wmk. 388   Perf. 13¼
1382	A451	60c multi	.40	.25
1383	A451	90c Horiz. pair, #a-b	1.25	.60

Marine Life A452

Designs: No. 1384, Red-spotted coral crab. No. 1385, Leopard moray eel. No. 1386, Mandarinfish. No. 1387, Blue sea star.
$5, Green sea turtle, Robust ghostpipefish, Thorny seahorse.

2012, Mar. 21   Perf. 12
1384	A452	60c multi	.40	.25
1385	A452	60c multi	.40	.25
a.		Perf. 13½	.40	.25
1386	A452	60c multi	.40	.25
a.		Perf. 13½	.40	.25
1387	A452	60c multi	.40	.25
a.		Perf. 13½	.40	.25
		Nos. 1384-1387 (4)	1.60	1.00

Souvenir Sheet
Perf. 12½
1388	A452	$5 multi	3.25	1.60

No. 1388 contains one 90x35mm stamp.

Installation of 14th Yang Di-Pertuan Agong A453

Designs: 60c, 14th Yang Di-Pertuan Agong, yellow green frame. 80c, 14th Yang Di-Pertuan Agong and wife, horiz. $1, 14th Yang Di-Pertuan Agong, red frame.
No. 1392: a, Malaysia #79. b, 14th Yang Di-Pertuan Agong, gold frame.

Wmk. 388
2012, Apr. 11   Litho.   Perf. 14
1389-1391	A453	Set of 3	1.60	.80

Souvenir Sheet
Litho. With Foil Application
1392		Sheet of 2	3.25	1.60
a.		A453 $2 multi	1.25	.60
b.		A453 $3 multi	2.00	1.00
c.		As #1392, with added emblem in gold in sheet margin	3.25	1.60

Issued: No. 1392c, 1/1/13. No. 1392c has added emblem similar to a circular cancel

---

inscribed "100 Tahun Setem Kedah & 125 Tahun Perkhidmatan Pos Di Kedah" and "Pameran Setem."

Aromatic Plants A454

Designs: 60c, Polygonum minus. $1, Mentha piperita. $5, Kaffir lime, vert.

Perf. 14¾x14 Syncopated
2012, May 24   Litho.
1393-1394	A454	Set of 2	1.00	.50

Souvenir Sheet
Perf. 14x14¾ Syncopated
1395	A454	$5 multi	3.25	1.60

No. 1395 is impregnated with a lime scent.

2012 World Gas Conference, Kuala Lumpur — A455

Inscriptions: No. 1396, 60c, Securing Gas Supply. No. 1397, 60c, Enhancing Gas Demand. No. 1398, 60c, A Sustainable Future. No. 1399, 60c, Foundation For Growth.

2012, June 4   Wmk. 388   Perf. 12½
1396-1399	A455	Set of 4	1.50	.75

Miniature Sheet

Yang Di-Pertuan Agongs — A456

No. 1400 — Photograph and Roman numeral of Yang Di-Pertuan Agong: a, XI. b, XII. c, XIII. d, X. e, I. f, IX. g, II. h, VIII. i, III. j, VII. k, VI. l, V. m, IV. n, XIV. Nos. 1400a-1400m are 35x35mm, No. 1400n is 70x70mm.

Litho. With Foil Application
2012, June 21   Wmk. 388   Perf. 13¼
1400	A456	Sheet of 14 + 2 labels	12.00	6.00
a.-m.		$1 Any single	.65	.30
n.		$5 multi	3.25	1.60

Traditional Occupations — A457

No. 1401: a, Tukang seni kertas (artist decorating lanterns). b, Tukang tilik (men with bird and cage).

No. 1402: a, Penjaja satay (satay griller). b, Penjaja nasi kandar (man carrying pot and baskets).

No. 1403: a, Penjaja lemang (woman stirring pot). b, Penjaja manisan (confection vender with bicycle). c, Tukang ubat tradisional (food vendor on mat). d, Penjaja pasembor (juice vendor on bicycle). e, Tukang dobi (laundry men).

2012, June 21   Litho.   Wmk. 388

1401	A457	Horiz. pair	1.00	.50
a.-b.		80c Either single	.50	.25
1402	A457	Horiz. pair	1.30	.65
a.-b.		$1 Either single	.65	.30

Booklet Stamps

1403	A457	Horiz. strip of 5	2.00	1.25
a.-e.		60c Any single	.40	.25
f.		Booklet pane of 10, 2 each #1403a-1403e	4.00	—
		Complete booklet, #1403f	4.00	

Coins — A458

Designs: No. 1404, 60c, Obverse of 5-cent coin (lilac background). No. 1405, 60c, Reverse of 5-cent coin (no numeral on coin, lilac background). No. 1406, 60c, Obverse of 10-cent coin (light blue background). No. 1407, 60c, Reverse of 10-cent coin (no numeral on coin, light blue background). No. 1408, 60c, Obverse of 20-cent coin (light green background). No. 1409, 60c, Reverse of 20-cent coin (no numeral on coin, light green background). No. 1410, 60c, Obverse of 50-cent coin (pink background). No. 1411, 60c, Reverse of 50-cent coin (no numeral on coin, pink background).

Litho. & Embossed With Foil Application

2012, July 16   Unwmk.   Perf. 14

1404-1411	A458	Set of 8	3.25	1.60

Souvenir Sheets

Banknotes — A459

No. 1412: a, 1-ringgit banknote. b, 50-ringgit banknote. c, 20-ringgit banknote.

No. 1413: a, 100-ringgit banknote. b, 5-ringgit banknote. d, 10-ringgit banknote.

Litho. With Foil Application

Perf. 14x13¼

2012, July 16   Unwmk.

1412		Sheet of 3	9.75	5.00
a.-c.		$5 Any single	3.25	1.60
1413	A459	Sheet of 3	9.75	5.00
a.-c.		$5 Any single	3.25	1.60

National Unity — A460

Inscriptions below "Perpaduan": No. 1414, 60c, Bahasa. No. 1415, 60c, Gotong-Royong. No. 1416, 60c, Sukan. No. 1417, 60c, Tarian.

Perf. 13¼x13½

2012, Aug. 30   Litho.   Wmk. 388

1414-1417	A460	Set of 4	1.60	.80

British Royalty A461

Designs: No. 1418, $1.50, Malaya Selangor #101. No. 1419, $1.50, Duke and Duchess of Cambridge.

No. 1420: a, Like No. 1418. b, Like No. 1419.

2012, Sept. 13   Perf. 14

1418-1419	A461	Set of 2	2.00	1.00

Souvenir Sheet

1420		Sheet of 2	3.25	1.60
a.-b.	A461	$2.50 Either single	1.60	.80
c.		As No. 1420, with Thailand 2013 World Stamp Exhibition emblem in sheet margin	3.25	1.60

Reign of Queen Elizabeth II, 60th anniv. (Nos. 1418, 1420a), Wedding of Prince William and Catherine Middleton (Nos. 1419, 1420b).

Issued: No. 1420c, 8/2/13.

Festivals — A462

Inscriptions: No. 1421, 60c, Hari Raya Aidiladha (Eid ul-Adha). No. 1422, 60c, Perayaan Kuih Bulan (Chinese mid-autumn festival). No. 1423, 60c, Pesta Kaul (Kaul Festival). No. 1424, 60c, Regatta Lepa. No. 1425, 60c, Thaipusam.

Litho. With Foil Application

Perf. 13½x14

2012, Sept. 27   Unwmk.

1421-1425	A462	Set of 5	2.00	1.00

Malacca, 750th Anniv. — A463

Anniversary emblem and: 50c, Tokong Cheng Hoon Teng (Cheng Hoon Teng Temple). 90c, Masjid Kampong Hulu (Kampong Hulu Mosque).

750c, Muzium Yang Di-Pertua Negeri Malaka (Malacca Governor's Museum).

Wmk. 388

2012, Oct. 7   Litho.   Perf. 12

1426-1427	A463	Set of 2	.95	.45

Souvenir Sheet

Litho. With Foil Application

Perf. 13¼

1428	A463	750c multi	5.00	2.50

No. 1428 contains one 70x35mm stamp. See No. 1496.

World Post Day A464

Malaysian Postal Service and Universal Postal Union emblems: 60c, Postman with bicycle, 1950. 80c, Postman on scooter, 1970. No. 1431, $1, Postman on scooter, 1990.

No. 1432: a, $1, Postman holding scooter, emblems. b, $2, Five postmen (90x35mm).

Perf. 12½, 12½x12½x12x12½ (#1432b)

2012, Oct. 22   Litho.

1429-1431	A464	Set of 3	1.60	.80

Souvenir Sheet

1432		Sheet of 2	2.00	1.00
a.	A464	$1 multi	.65	.30
b.	A464	$2 multi	1.30	.65

A465

Greetings Stamps — A466

No. 1433 — Inscription: a, Flora & Fauna / Malaysia. b, Bendera Malaysia / Malaysian Flag. c, Batik / Malaysia. d, Latarlangit Malaysia / Malaysian Skyline.

No. 1434 — Inscription: a, Bendera Malaysia / Malaysian Flag (flag in circle). b, Perayaan / Celebration. c, Tulus Ikhlas / Yours Sincerely. d, Salam / Greetings.

Perf. 13½x13¼

2012, Nov. 5   Wmk. 388

1433	A465	Block or vert. strip of 4	1.60	.80
a.-d.		60c Any single	.40	.25
1434	A466	Block or vert. strip of 4	1.60	.80
a.-d.		60c Any single	.40	.25

Children's Hobbies — A467

No. 1435, 60c: a, Girl baking cookies. b, Girl collecting stamps.

No. 1436, 60c: a, Boy playing soccer. b, Robot fishing.

No. 1437, 60c: a, Boy playing drums. b, Boy with camera.

$5, Children reading letters.

Perf. 13½x13¼

2012, Nov. 19   Litho.   Unwmk.

Horiz. Pairs, #a-b

1435-1437	A467	Set of 3	2.40	1.25

Souvenir Sheet

Litho. With Foil Application

Perf. 12

Wmk. 388

1438	A467	$5 multi	3.25	1.60

No. 1438 contains one 70x45mm stamp.

Postal History of Kedah — A468

Designs: No. 1439, 90c, Malaya-Kedah #1. No. 1440, 90c, Malaya-Kedah #16. No. 1441, 90c, Malaya-Kedah #20.

$3, Kedah cancel on postal card from Siam, vert.

Perf. 14 Syncopated

2012, Dec. 20   Litho.   Wmk. 388

1439-1441	A468	Set of 3	1.75	.90

Souvenir Sheet

Perf. 14¼

1442	A468	$3 multi	2.00	1.00

Postage stamps of Kedah, 100th anniv. No. 1442 contains one 28x38mm stamp.

Woodpeckers A469

Designs: 60c, Banded woodpecker. 80c, Common flameback woodpecker. $1, Lesser yellownape woodpecker.

$5, White-bellied woodpecker, horiz.

2013, Jan. 13   Perf. 13¼x13½

1443-1445	A469	Set of 3	1.60	.80

Souvenir Sheet

Perf. 13¾x13½

1446	A469	$5 multi	3.25	1.60

No. 1446 contains one 64x48mm stamp.

Exotic Pets — A470

Designs: 60c, African pygmy hedgehog. 80c, Groon iguana. $1, Sugar glidor. $3, $5, Royal python.

Perf. 13¼x13½

2013, Feb. 5   Litho.   Wmk. 388

1447-1449	A470	Set of 3	1.60	.80
1447a		Perf. 12	.40	.25

Souvenir Sheets

Litho. With Foil Application

1450	A470	$3 multi	2.00	1.00
1451	A470	$5 multi	3.25	1.60

Nos. 1450-1451 each contain one 30x50mm stamp.

National Unity — A471

No. 1452, 60c — Map of Malaysia, "1" and various people with inscription: a, Semangat Kasin Sayang. b, Semangat Keprihatinan.
No. 1453, 60c — Map of Malaysia, "1" and various people with inscription: a, Semangat Kerjasama. b, Semangat Kemasyarakatan.

Wmk. 388
2013, Mar. 26   Litho.   *Perf. 13¼*
Horiz. Pairs, #a-b
1452-1453 A471   Set of 2   1.60   .80

Lighthouses — A472

Designs: 50c, Pulau Rimau Lighthouse, Penang. No. 1455, 60c, Fort Cornwallis Lighthouse, Penang. No. 1456, 60c, Pulau Angsa Lighthouse, Selangor.
$5, One Fathom Bank Lighthouse, Selangor, vert.

Perf. 13½x13¼
2013, Apr. 30   Litho.   Unwmk.
Granite Paper
1454-1456 A472   Set of 3   1.25   .60
Souvenir Sheet
Perf. 13¼x13½
1457 A472 $5 multi   3.25   1.60

Miniature Sheets

Malaysian Forests — A473

No. 1458 — Royal Belum Forest: a, Gould's frogmouth. b, Helmeted hornbill. c, Rafflesia azlanii. d, Trevesia burckii. e, Trilobite larvae.
No. 1459 — Maliau Basin Forest: a, Borneo pygmy elephant (30x40mm). b, Maliau Waterfall (50x40mm). c, Nepenthes veitchii (30x40mm). d, Dead leaf mantis (30x40mm). e, Violin beetle (30x40mm).
No. 1460 — Taman Negara Forest: a, Asian bearcat (30x40mm). b, Berkoh Cascade (30x40mm). c, Heteropoda davidbowie (30x40mm). d, Malayan peacock pheasant (50x40mm). e, Bioluminescent mushrooms (30x40mm).

Serpentine Die Cut 12¾
2013, May 13   Litho.   Unwmk.
Self-Adhesive
1458 A473   Sheet of 5   3.25
a.-e. $1 Any single   .65   .30
1459 A473   Sheet of 5   3.25
a.-e. $1 Any single   .65   .30
1460 A473   Sheet of 5   3.25
a.-e. $1 Any single   .65   .30
Nos. 1458-1460 (3)   9.75

Marine Life — A474

No. 1461, 60c: a, Sea anemone. b, Soft coral.
No. 1462, 60c: Feather stars. b, Sea pen.
$5, Table coral.

Perf. 13½x13¼
2013, June 28   Litho.   Unwmk.
Horiz. Pairs, #a-b
1461-1462 A474   Set of 2   1.50   .75
Souvenir Sheet
1463 A474 $5 multi   3.25   1.60
No. 1463 contains one 75x26mm stamp.

Salad Ingredients A475

No. 1464, 60c: a, Centella asiatica. b, Parkia speciosa.
No. 1465, 60c: a, Psophocarpus tetragonolobus. b, Annacardium occidentale.

Wmk. 388
2013, July 25   Litho.   *Perf. 13¼*
Vert. Pairs, #a-b
1464-1465 A475   Set of 2   1.50   .75

Third Tri-Nation Stamp Exhibition — A476

Exhibition emblem, buildings and flags of Malaysia, Singapore and Thailand with: 90c, Flat flags. $2, Flags blowing in wind.
$3, Exhibition emblem, Hibiscus rosa-sinensis, Vanda Miss Joaquim, Cassia fistula.

Unwmk.
2013, Aug. 23   Litho.   Perf. 14
1466-1467 A476   Set of 2   1.75   .90
Souvenir Sheet
Self-Adhesive
Die Cut Perf. 12
1468 A476 $3 multi   1.90   .95
No. 1468 contains one 54x38mm triangular stamp.

Museums — A477

No. 1469: a, Chimney Museum, Labuan. b, Sungai Lembing Museum, Pahang. c, Adat Museum (Tradition Museum), Jelebu, Negri Sembilan. d, Tekstil Negara Museum (Natl. Textile Museum), Kuala Lumpur.
No. 1470: a, Perak Museum, Taiping, Perak. b, Negara Museum (Natl. Museum), Kuala Lumpur. c, Lembah Bujang Archaeological Museum, Kedah. d, Galeria Perdana, Langkawi, Kedah. e, Kota Kayang Museum, Perlis. f, Labuan Museum, Labuan.

Perf. 14x14¼ Syncopated
2013, Aug. 31   Litho.   Unwmk.
1469   Horiz. strip of 4   1.60   .80
a.-d.   A477 60c Any single   .40   .25
1470   Block of 6   2.40   1.25
a.-f.   A477 60c Any single   .40   .25
The right part of Nos. 1469a-1469d and 1470a-1470f has a rectangle of thermochromic ink, which, when warmed, reveals an item from the museum shown. See Nos. 1494-1495 for stamps dated "2014" without thermochromic ink.

Formation of the Federation of Malaysia, 50th Anniv. — A478

Perf. 13½x13¼
2013, Sept. 16   Litho.   Wmk. 388
1471 A478   60c multi   .40   .25

A479

A480

Art by Diasbled Children — A481

Litho. & Thermography
2013, Oct. 22   Unwmk.   *Perf. 13¼*
Granite Paper
1472 A479   60c multi   .40   .25
1473 A480   60c multi   .40   .25
1474 A481   60c multi   .40   .25
Nos. 1472-1474 (3)   1.20   .75

Fruit — A482

Designs: 60c, Passiflora edulis. 80c, Annona squamosa. $1.20, Cynometra cauliflora.

Perf. 13¼x13½
2013, Oct. 28   Litho.   Wmk. 388
1475-1477 A482   Set of 3   1.60   .80

RHB Bank, Cent. — A483

No. 1478: a, First bank branch building, Old Market Square, Kuala Lumpur. b, First automatic teller machine. c, Launch of Kwong Yik Bank Headquarters. d, RHB Bank Headquarters.

Litho. With Foil Application
2013, Nov. 23   Unwmk.   *Perf. 14¼*
Granite Paper
1478 A483   60c Block of 4, #a-d   1.50   .75

Baba-Nyonya (Peranakan Chinese) Heritage — A484

No. 1479, 60c: a, Nyonyaware. b, Nyonya beaded slippers.
No. 1480, 80c: a, Malacca Peranakan townhouse. b, Baba and Nyonya wedding attire.
$5, Nyonya Kebaya emboridery.

Unwmk.
2013, Nov. 29   Litho.   *Perf. 14*
Horiz. Pairs, #a-b
1479-1480 A484   Set of 2   1.75   .85
Souvenir Sheet
1481 A484 $5 multi   3.25   1.60
No. 1481 contains one 50x60mm stamp with laser-cut holes in the vignette.

Endangered Cats — A485

No. 1482: a, Panthera pardus with spotted fur. b, Panthera pardus with black fur.
No. 1483, Neofelis nebulosa. No. 1484, Neofelis diardi.
$3, Panthera tigris jacksoni, vert.

Perf. 13½x13¼
2013, Dec. 23   Litho.   Wmk. 388
1482   Horiz. pair   .80   .40
a.-b.   A485 60c Either single   .40   .25
1483 A485   80c multi   .50   .25
1484 A485   80c multi   .50   .25
Nos. 1482-1484 (3)   1.80   .90
Souvenir Sheet
Perf. 13¼x13½
1485 A485 $3 multi   1.90   .95

New Year 2014 (Year of the Horse) — A486

No. 1486, 50c — Inscription: a, Sukan Polo. b, Unit Berkuda DBKL.

No. 1487, 80c — Inscription: a, Unit Berkuda PSP PDRM. b, Unit Berkuda Kor Armor Diraja.

$3, Horse and rider, white background. $5, Horse and rider, gold background.

Perf. 13x13¼

2014, Jan. 27   Litho.   Unwmk.
Horiz. Pairs, #a-b
1486-1487 A486   Set of 2   1.60   .80
Souvenir Sheets
1488-1489 A486   Set of 2   4.75   2.40

Roses — A487

Designs: 60c, White hybrid tea roses. 70c, Yellow Grandiflora roses. $1.20, Pink English roses.

$5, Hybrid tea roses.

Unwmk.

2014, Feb. 14   Litho.   *Perf. 13*
1490-1492 A487   Set of 3   1.60   .80
Souvenir Sheet
Perf.
1493 A487 $5 multi   3.25   1.60

No. 1493 contains one 52x50mm heart-shaped stamp and is impregnated with a rose scent.

Museums Type of 2013 Without Thermochromic Ink

No. 1494: a, Chimney Museum, Labuan. b, Sungai Lembing Museum, Pahang. c, Adat Museum (Tradition Museum), Jelebu, Negri Sembilan. d, Tekstil Negara Museum (Natl. Textile Museum), Kuala Lumpur.

No. 1495: a, Perak Museum, Taiping, Perak. b, Negara Museum (Natl. Museum), Kuala Lumpur. c, Lembah Bujang Archaeological Museum, Kedah. d, Galeria Perdana, Langkawi, Kedah. e, Kota Kayang Museum, Perlis. f, Labuan Museum, Labuan.

Perf. 14¼ Syncopated

2014, Mar. 13   Litho.   Unwmk.
Dated "2014"
1494   Horiz. strip of 4   1.60   .80
a.-d. A477 60c Any single   .40   .25
1495   Block of 6   2.40   1.25
a.-f. A477 60c Any single   .40   .25

Nos. 1494a-1494d and 1495a-1495f lack the thermographic ink present on Nos. 1469a-1469d and 1470a-1470f that covers an item from the museum. Stamps with thermographic ink are dated "2013" only.

No. 1427 Redrawn With Added Emblem
Wmk. 388

2014, May 24   Litho.   *Perf. 12*
1496 A463 90c multi   .55   .30

The emblem added to No. 1496 is inscribed "Melaka and Jogja City of Museums 2014" and is to the right of the flag emblem on No. 1427.

Opening of World Scout Bureau, Kuala Lumpur — A488

Scouting tretoil and: 30c, Display at World Scout Bureau. 50c, Malaysian scouting emblem, trefoil made of Scouts. 60c, Malaysian scouting emblem, buildings.

Perf. 13½x13¼

2014, June 18   Litho.   Wmk. 388
1497-1499 A488   Set of 3   .90   .45

Opening of Kuala Lumpur International Airport 2 — A489

Inscriptions: No. 1500, 80c, Main Terminal Building. No. 1501, 80c, Skybridge. No. 1502, 80c, Departure Hall. No. 1503, 80c, Gateway@klia2.

$5, Aerial view of airport.

Perf. 14¼x14

2014, June 24   Litho.   Unwmk.
1500-1503 A489   Set of 4   2.00   1.00
Souvenir Sheet
1504 A489 $5 multi   3.25   1.60

Fruit — A490

Designs: 60c, Artocarpus heterophyllus. 80c, Durio zibethinus. $1.20, Cucumis melo. $1.40, Averrhoa carambola.

Wmk. 388

2014, July 17   Litho.   *Perf. 13¼*
1505-1508 A490   Set of 4   2.50   1.25

Independence, 57th Anniv. — A491

Perf. 13½x13¼

2014, Aug. 31   Litho.   Wmk. 388
1509 A491 60c multi   .40   .25

Local Foods of Malaysia and Hong Kong — A492

Flower and: No. 1510, $1.40, Nasi lemak. No. 1511, $1.40, Satay. No. 1512, $1.40, Egg waffle. No. 1513, $1.40, Poon choi.

Unwmk.

2014, Oct. 19   Litho.   *Perf. 14*
1510-1513 A492   Set of 4   3.50   1.75
1513a   Souvenir sheet of 4, #1510-1513   3.50   1.75

See Hong Kong Nos. 1683-1686.

Folk Tales — A493

No. 1514, 60c: a, Tun Kudu. b, Tun Fatimah. No. 1515, 60c: a, Mahsuri. b, Merong Maha Wangsa.

No. 1516, 60c: a, Hang Tuah. b, Tun Teja.

Perf. 13½x13¼

2014, Oct. 27   Litho.   Wmk. 388
Horiz. Pairs, #a-b
1514-1516 A493   Set of 3   2.25   1.10

Souvenir Sheet

2014 World Youth Stamp Exhibition, Kuala Lumpur — A494

Litho. With Foil Application
2014, Nov. 5   Wmk. 388   *Perf. 14*
1517 A494 $5 multi   3.00   1.50

SEMI-POSTAL STAMPS

Typhoon Haiyan Disaster Relief Fund — SP1

No. B1: a, Bunga Raya. b, Durian. c, Handicraft. d, Wau Bulan.

Perf. 13¾x14

2013, Nov. 14   Litho.   Wmk. 388
B1   Sheet of 8, #B1a, B1b, B1e, B1f, 2 each #B1c, B1d   6.25   6.25
a.-   SP1 35c+65c Either single
b.   .75   .75
c.-   SP1 65c+35c Either single
d.   .75   .75
e.   As "a," perf. 13¾x14x14¼x14   .75   .75
f.   As "b," perf. 13¾x14x14¼x14   .75   .75

No. B1 sold for $10.

POSTAGE DUE STAMPS

Until 1966 Malaysia used postage due stamps of the Malayan Postal Union. See listings under Malaya.

D1   D2

Wmk. 338 Upright

1966, Aug. 15   Litho.   *Perf. 14½x14*
J1   D1   1c pink   .25   4.00
J2   D1   2c slate   .60   4.00
J3   D1   4c lt yellow green   1.00   8.00
J4   D1   8c bright green   2.10   14.00
J5   D1   10c ultramarine   1.50   2.25
J6   D1   12c purple   1.10   4.00
J7   D1   20c brown   1.75   4.00
J8   D1   50c olive bister   3.50   7.00
    Nos. J1-J8 (8)   11.80   45.50

Wmk. 338 Sideways

1972, May 23
J4a   D1   8c bright green   7.75   22.50
J5a   D1   10c ultramarine   7.75   15.00
J7a   D1   20c brown   10.50   15.00
J8a   D1   50c olive bister   11.50   20.00
    Nos. J4a-J8a (4)   37.50   72.50

1980-86   Litho.   Unwmk.
J9   D1   2c slate   .35   3.00
J10   D1   8c bright green   .60   6.00
J11   D1   10c blue   .60   2.75
J11A   D1   12c maroon ('86)   14.00   18.00
J12   D1   20c brown   .80   3.25
J13   D1   50c olive bister   1.25   3.75
    Nos. J9-J13 (6)   17.60   36.75

1986, Sept. 15   Litho.   *Perf. 12x11½*
J14   D2   5c brt rose & lil rose   .25   1.10
J15   D2   10c black & gray   .25   .50
J16   D2   20c deep org & yel org   .40   .65
J17   D2   50c blue grn & lt bl grn   .60   .90
J18   D2 $1 brt blue & lt ultra   1.10   2.00
    Nos. J14-J18 (5)   2.60   5.15

JOHORE

Vanda Hookeriana and Sultan Ismail — A14

Orchids: 2c, Arundina graminifolia. 5c, Paphiopedilum niveum. 6c, Spathoglottis plicata. 10c, Arachnis flosaeris. 15c, Rhyncostylis retusa. 20c, Phalaenopsis violacea.

Wmk. 338
1965, Nov. 15   Photo.   *Perf. 14½*
Flowers in Natural Colors
169   A14   1c blk & lt grnsh bl   .25   .25
a.   Black omitted   375.00
b.   Watermark sideways ('70)   1.60   6.00
170   A14   2c black, red & gray   .25   .80
171   A14   5c black & Prus bl   .25   .25
a.   Yellow omitted   110.00
172   A14   6c black & lt blk   .40   .25
173   A14   10c black & lt ultra   .40   .25
a.   Watermark sideways ('70)   3.00   2.50
174   A14   15c blk, lil rose & grn   1.50   .35
175   A14   20c black & brown   1.50   .65
a.   Purple omitted   300.00
    Nos. 169-175 (7)   4.55   2.80

Malayan Jezebel and Sultan Ismail — A15

Butterflies: 2c, Black-veined tiger. 5c, Clipper. 6c, Lime butterfly. 10c, Great orange tip. 15c, Blue pansy. 20c, Wanderer.

Perf. 13½x13

1971, Feb. 1   Litho.   Unwmk.
176   A15   1c multicolored   .50   1.75
177   A15   2c multicolored   1.40   2.50
178   A15   5c multicolored   1.75   .40
179   A15   6c multicolored   1.75   2.50
180   A15   10c multicolored   1.75   .55
181   A15   15c multicolored   1.75   .50
182   A15   20c multicolored   1.75   1.00
    Nos. 176-182 (7)   10.65   9.20

1977   Photo.
176a   A15   1c   3.00   3.50
177a   A15   2c   3.00   5.25
178a   A15   5c   3.00   .70
180a   A15   10c   4.50   .35
181a   A15   15c   9.25   .35
182a   A15   20c   11.50   1.00
    Nos. 176a-182a (6)   34.25   11.15

Differentiating the lithograph and photogravure printings of the Butterflies issues:

Denominations and inscriptions have straight edges on the lithographed printings and broken edges on the photogravure printings.

Background colors and portrait show prominent screen dots on the lithographed stamps, but these features appear almost solid on the photogravure stamps except under high magnification.

Rafflesia Hasseltii and Sultan Ismail — A16

Flowers: 2c, Pterocarpus indicus. 5c, Lagerstroemia speciosa. 10c, Durio zibethinus. 15c, Hibiscus. 20c, Rhododendron scortechinii. 25c, Phaeomeria speciosa.

Wmk. 378
1979, Apr. 30　Litho.　Perf. 14½

183	A16	1c multicolored	.25	.75
184	A16	2c multicolored	.25	.75
185	A16	5c multicolored	.25	.50
186	A16	10c multicolored	.25	.25
187	A16	15c multicolored	.25	.25
188	A16	20c multicolored	.25	.25
189	A16	25c multicolored	.40	.25
		Nos. 183-189 (7)	1.90	3.00

1984　"Johor" in round type

185a	A16	5c	1.10	1.40
186a	A16	10c	1.10	1.40
187a	A16	15c	.75	.25
188a	A16	20c	1.25	.55
		Nos. 185a-188a (4)	4.20	3.60

Agriculture, State Arms and Sultan Mahmood Iskandar Al-Haj, Regent — A19

Wmk. 388
1986, Oct. 25　Litho.　Perf. 12

190	A19	1c Coffea liberica	.35	.35
191	A19	2c Cocos nucifera	.35	.35
192	A19	5c Theobroma cacao	.35	.35
193	A19	10c Piper nigrum	.35	.35
194	A19	15c Hevea brasiliensis	.35	.35
195	A19	20c Elaeis guineensis	.35	.35
196	A19	30c Oryza sativa	.50	.50
		Nos. 190-196 (7)	2.60	2.60

1994-99?

192a	A19	5c Perf. 14	3.25	.25
192b	A19	5c Perf. 15x14½ ('95)	1.75	
192c	A19	5c Perf. 14x14½ ('98)	19.00	
193a	A19	10c Perf. 14x13	3.25	.25
193b	A19	10c Perf. 14x14½ ('96)	4.25	.25
193c	A19	10c Perf. 15x14½ ('99)	12.50	
195a	A19	20c Perf. 14	2.00	.25
195b	A19	20c Perf. 15x14½	1.60	
195c	A19	20c Perf. 14x14½ ('96)	14.50	.40
196a	A19	30c Perf. 14	3.25	.25
196b	A19	30c Perf. 15x14½	13.50	1.00
196c	A19	30c Perf. 14x14½	3.75	

Flowers, Arms and Sultan Mahmood Iskandar Ibni Al-Marhum Sultan Ismail — A20

Designs: 5c, Nelumbium nelumbo. 10c, Hydrangea macrophylla. 20c, Hippeastrum reticulatum. 30c, Bougainvillea. 40c, Ipomoea indica. 50c, Hibiscus rosa-sinensis.

Perf. 14¾x14½
2007, Dec. 31　Litho.　Wmk. 388

197	A20	5c multi	.35	.25
a.		Perf. 14x13¾	.35	.25
198	A20	10c multi	.35	.25
a.		Perf. 14x13¾	.35	.25

Perf. 14x13¾

199	A20	20c multi	.35	.25
200	A20	30c multi	.35	.25
201	A20	40c multi	.35	.25
202	A20	50c multi	.45	.25
a.		Souvenir sheet of 6, #197a, 198a, 199-202	2.25	1.10
		Nos. 197-202 (6)	2.20	1.50

KEDAH

Orchid Type of Johore, 1965, with Portrait of Sultan Abdul Halim
Wmk. 338
1965, Nov. 15　Photo.　Perf. 14½
Flowers in Natural Colors

106	A14	1c blk & lt grnsh bl	.30	1.25
a.		Black omitted	250.00	
b.		Watermark sideways ('70)	2.50	5.25
107	A14	2c black, red & gray	.30	1.50
108	A14	5c black & Prus bl	.30	.30
109	A14	6c black & lt lil	.30	.50
110	A14	10c black & lt ultra	.50	.30
a.		Watermark sideways ('70)	1.50	4.00
111	A14	15c blk, lil rose & grn	1.75	.30
112	A14	20c black & brown	2.00	.90
		Nos. 106-112 (7)	5.45	5.05

Butterfly Type of Johore, 1971, with Portrait of Sultan Abdul Halim
Perf. 13½x13
1971, Feb. 1　Litho.　Unwmk.

113	A15	1c multicolored	.35	1.50
114	A15	2c multicolored	.45	1.50
115	A15	5c multicolored	1.10	.30
116	A15	6c multicolored	1.10	1.75
117	A15	10c multicolored	1.10	.30
118	A15	15c multicolored	1.10	.30
119	A15	20c multicolored	1.40	.60
		Nos. 113-119 (7)	6.60	6.25

1977　Photo.　Same Designs

114a	A15	2c	22.50	17.00
115a	A15	5c	5.00	1.25
117a	A15	10c	11.00	.70
118a	A15	15c	3.50	.50
119a	A15	20c	5.00	2.25
		Nos. 114a-119a (5)	47.00	21.75

For differentiating the lithograph and photogravure printings of the Butterflies issues, see notes after Johore No. 182a.

Flower Type of Johore, 1979, with Portrait of Sultan Abdul Halim
Wmk. 378
1979, Apr. 30　Litho.　Perf. 14½

120	A16	1c multicolored	.25	.80
121	A16	2c multicolored	.25	.80
122	A16	5c multicolored	.25	.50
123	A16	10c multicolored	.25	.25
a.		Unwmkd. ('85)	22.00	3.25
124	A16	15c multicolored	.25	.25
a.		Unwmkd. ('84)	1.00	1.00
125	A16	20c multicolored	.35	.25
a.		Pale yellow flowers ('84)	.35	.25
126	A16	25c multicolored	.40	.25
		Nos. 120-126 (7)	2.00	3.10

25th Anniv. of Installation of Sultan Abdul Halim — A10

1983, July 15　Litho.　Perf. 13½

127	A10	20c Portrait, vert.	1.10	.35
128	A10	40c View from Mt. Gunung Jerai	2.25	2.25
129	A10	50c Rice fields, Mt. Gunung Jerai	3.00	4.75
		Nos. 127-129 (3)	6.35	7.35

Agriculture and State Arms Type of Johore with Sultan Abdul Halim
Wmk. 388
1986, Oct. 25　Litho.　Perf. 12

130	A19	1c multicolored	.30	.30
131	A19	2c multicolored	.30	.30
132	A19	5c multicolored	.30	.30
133	A19	10c multicolored	.30	.30
134	A19	15c multicolored	.30	.30
135	A19	20c multicolored	.30	.30
136	A19	30c multicolored	.30	.30
		Nos. 130-136 (7)	2.10	2.10

1986?

132a	A19	5c Perf. 15x14½	4.25	.40
132b	A19	5c Perf. 14	1.25	.25
133a	A19	10c Perf. 14	3.00	.30
133b	A19	10c Perf. 14x13¾, unwmk.	8.50	
135a	A19	20c Perf. 14	1.00	.25
136a	A19	30c Perf. 14x14½	2.25	.25
136b	A19	30c Perf. 14x13½	3.00	.25
136c	A19	30c Perf. 15x14½	3.00	.25

Flowers and Arms Type of Johore of 2007 With Portrait of Sultan Abdul Halim
Perf. 14x13¾
2007, Dec. 31　Litho.　Wmk. 388

137	A20	5c multi	.30	.25
138	A20	10c multi	.30	.25
139	A20	20c multi	.30	.25
140	A20	30c multi	.35	.25
141	A20	40c multi	.50	.25
142	A20	50c multi	.65	.30
a.		Souvenir sheet of 6, #137-142	2.25	1.10
		Nos. 137-142 (6)	2.40	1.55

Reign of Sultan Abdul Halim, 50th Anniv. A11

Sultan and: 30c, Buildings, farm field. 50c, Buildings. $1, Buildings and anniversary emblem.

Perf. 13½x13¼x12x13¼
2008, July 15

143-145	A11	Set of 3	1.10	1.10

KELANTAN

Orchid Type of Johore, 1965, with Portrait of Sultan Yahya Petra
Wmk. 338
1965, Nov. 15　Photo.　Perf. 14½
Flowers in Natural Colors

91	A14	1c blk & lt grnsh bl	.35	1.10
a.		Watermark sideways ('70)	1.40	7.50
92	A14	2c black, red & gray	.25	1.50
93	A14	5c black & Prus bl	.25	.25
94	A14	6c black & lt lil	.80	2.00
95	A14	10c black & lt ultra	.40	.25
a.		Watermark sideways ('70)	4.25	4.75
96	A14	15c blk, lil rose & grn	1.75	.25
97	A14	20c black & brown	1.75	1.50
		Nos. 91-97 (7)	5.55	6.85

Butterfly Type of Johore, 1971, with Portrait of Sultan Yahya Petra
Perf. 13½x13
1971, Feb. 1　Litho.　Unwmk.

98	A15	1c multicolored	.30	2.00
99	A15	2c multicolored	.30	2.00
100	A15	5c multicolored	1.25	.50
101	A15	6c multicolored	1.25	2.25
102	A15	10c multicolored	1.40	.25
103	A15	15c multicolored	2.00	.25
104	A15	20c multicolored	2.50	1.25
		Nos. 98-104 (7)	9.00	8.50

1977　Photo.

98a	A15	1c	1.25	4.25
100a	A15	5c	7.75	3.50
102a	A15	10c	8.50	3.00
103a	A15	15c	16.00	1.10
		Nos. 98a-103a (4)	33.50	11.85

For differentiating the lithograph and photogravure printings of the Butterflies issues, see notes after Johore No. 182a.

Flower Type of Johore, 1979, with Portrait of Sultan Yahya Petra
Wmk. 378
1979, Apr. 30　Litho.　Perf. 14½

105	A16	1c multicolored	.25	.90
106	A16	2c multicolored	.25	.90
107	A16	5c multicolored	.25	.70
a.		Unwmkd. ('86)	.75	1.25
108	A16	10c multicolored	.25	.25
a.		White flowers ('84)	.30	.25
109	A16	15c multicolored	.25	.25
110	A16	20c multicolored	.25	.25
a.		Pale yellow flowers ('84)	.35	.25
111	A16	25c multicolored	.45	.55
		Nos. 105-111 (7)	1.95	3.80

Sultan Tengku Ismail Petra, Installation — A7

1980, Mar. 30　Litho.　Perf. 14½

112	A7	10c multicolored	.35	.65
113	A7	15c multicolored	.50	.35
114	A7	50c multicolored	1.25	2.50
		Nos. 112-114 (3)	2.10	3.50

Agriculture and State Arms Type of Johore with Sultan Ismail Petra
Wmk. 388
1986, Oct. 25　Litho.　Perf. 12

115	A19	1c multicolored	.30	.30
116	A19	2c multicolored	.30	.30
117	A19	5c multicolored	.30	.30
118	A19	10c multicolored	.30	.30
119	A19	15c multicolored	.30	.30
120	A19	20c multicolored	.30	.30
121	A19	30c multicolored	.30	.30
		Nos. 115-121 (7)	2.10	2.10

1986?

116a	A19	2c Perf. 15x14½	3.00	.50
118a	A19	10c Perf. 14	3.00	.50
120a	A19	20c Perf. 14	3.25	.50
121a	A19	30c Perf. 14	1.00	.25

Reign of Sultan Tengku Ismail Petra, 25th Anniv. A8

Sultan and various buildings: 30c, 50c, $1.

Perf. 13½, 12 (50c)
2004, Feb. 29　Litho.　Wmk. 388

122-124	A8	Set of 3	.95	.45

Flowers and Arms Type of Johore of 2007 With Portrait of Sultan Ismail Petra
Perf. 14x13¾
2007, Dec. 31　Litho.　Wmk. 388

125	A20	5c multi	.30	.25
126	A20	10c multi	.30	.25
127	A20	20c multi	.30	.25
128	A20	30c multi	.35	.25
129	A20	40c multi	.50	.25
130	A20	50c multi	.65	.30
a.		Souvenir sheet of 6, #125-130	2.25	1.10
		Nos. 125-130 (6)	2.40	1.55

MALACCA
(Melaka)

Orchid Type of Johore, 1965, with State Crest
Wmk. 338
1965, Nov. 15　Photo.　Perf. 14½
Flowers in Natural Colors

67	A14	1c blk & lt grnsh blue	.25	1.50
a.		Watermark sideways ('70)	1.50	7.50
68	A14	2c blk, red & gray	.25	1.25
69	A14	5c black & Prus bl	.25	.25
70	A14	6c black & lt lilac	.40	.90
71	A14	10c black & lt ultra	.30	.25
a.		Watermark sideways ('70)	6.25	7.00
72	A14	15c blk, lil rose & grn	1.75	.30
73	A14	20c black & brown	2.50	.95
		Nos. 67-73 (7)	5.70	5.40

Butterfly Type of Johore, 1971, with State Crest
Perf. 13½x13
1971, Feb. 1　Litho.　Unwmk.

74	A15	1c multicolored	.60	2.00
75	A15	2c multicolored	1.00	1.50
76	A15	5c multicolored	1.50	.90
77	A15	6c multicolored	1.50	2.75
78	A15	10c multicolored	1.50	.65
79	A15	15c multicolored	2.75	.60
80	A15	20c multicolored	2.75	2.25
		Nos. 74-80 (7)	11.60	11.15

1977　Photo.

74a	A15	1c	6.00	9.00
76a	A15	5c	2.75	2.25
78a	A15	10c	7.00	2.25
79a	A15	15c	17.50	.75
80a	A15	20c	6.50	4.25
		Nos. 74a-80a (5)	39.75	18.50

For differentiating the lithograph and photogravure printings of the Butterflies issues, see notes after Johore No. 182a.

Flower Type of Johore, 1979, with State Crest
Wmk. 378
1979, Apr. 30　Litho.　Perf. 14½

81	A16	1c multicolored	.25	1.10
82	A16	2c multicolored	.25	1.10
83	A16	5c multicolored	.25	.90
84	A16	10c multicolored	.25	.30
85	A16	15c multicolored	.25	.25
86	A16	20c multicolored	.35	.25
87	A16	25c multicolored	.45	.70
		Nos. 81-87 (7)	2.05	4.60

1983-86　Unwmk.

84a	A16	10c ('85)	1.25	2.75
85a	A16	15c ('86)	.65	.50
86a	A16	20c	.65	1.10
		Nos. 84a-86a (3)	2.55	

Agriculture and State Arms Type of Johore
Wmk. 388
1986, Oct. 25　Litho.　Perf. 12

88	A19	1c multicolored	.30	.30
89	A19	2c multicolored	.30	.30
90	A19	5c multicolored	.30	.30
91	A19	10c multicolored	.30	.30
92	A19	15c multicolored	.30	.30
93	A19	20c multicolored	.30	.30
94	A19	30c multicolored	.40	.30
		Nos. 88-94 (7)	2.20	2.10

1986?				**Litho.**
90a	A19	5c	Perf. 14	1.25 .25
91a	A19	10c	Perf. 14x13¼	1.00 .25
91b	A19	10c	Perf. 15x14½	1.75 .25
93a	A19	20c	Perf. 14	1.00 .25
94a	A19	30c	Perf. 14	4.50 .25
94b	A19	30c	Perf. 15x14½	6.25 .35

Flowers and Arms Type of Johore of 2007

Perf. 14x13¾, 14¾x14½ (20c)

2007, Dec. 31			**Litho.**		**Wmk. 388**
95	A20	5c	multi	.25	.25
96	A20	10c	multi	.25	.25
97	A20	20c	multi	.25	.25
a.			Perf. 14x13¾	.25	.25
98	A20	30c	multi	.40	.25
99	A20	40c	multi	.50	.30
100	A20	50c	multi	.65	.35
a.			Souvenir sheet of 6, #95, 96, 97a, 98-100	2.25	1.10
			Nos. 95-100 (6)	2.30	1.65

NEGRI SEMBILAN

(Negeri Sembilan)

Orchid Type of Johore, 1965, with State Crest

Wmk. 338

1965, Nov. 15   Photo.   Perf. 14½

Flowers in Natural Colors

76	A14	1c	blk & lt grnsh blue	.25	1.50
a.			Watermark sideways ('70)	3.25	6.00
77	A14	2c	black, red & gray	.25	1.50
78	A14	5c	black & Prus blue	.50	.25
79	A14	6c	black & lt lilac	.50	.60
80	A14	10c	black & lt ultra	.50	.25
81	A14	15c	blk, lil rose & grn	1.00	.25
82	A14	20c	black & brown	1.50	.90
			Nos. 76-82 (7)	4.50	5.25

Tuanku Ja'afar and Crest of Negri Sembilan — A7

1968, Apr. 8		**Photo.**		**Perf. 13½**	
83	A7	15c	brt blue & multi	.25	.60
84	A7	50c	yellow & multi	.40	1.25

Installation of Tuanku Ja'afar ibni Al-Marhum as ruler (Yang di-Pertuan Besar) of Negri Sembilan.

Butterfly Type of Johore, 1971, with State Crest

Perf. 13½x13

1971, Feb. 1		**Litho.**		**Unwmk.**	
85	A15	1c	multicolored	.40	1.75
86	A15	2c	multicolored	.60	1.75
87	A15	5c	multicolored	.90	.30
88	A15	6c	multicolored	1.00	1.75
89	A15	10c	multicolored	1.25	.30
90	A15	15c	multicolored	2.00	.30
91	A15	20c	multicolored	2.00	.45
			Nos. 85-91 (7)	8.15	6.60

1977				**Photo.**	
86a	A15	2c		2.25	4.50
87a	A15	5c		2.25	1.50
89a	A15	10c		11.00	1.25
90a	A15	15c		17.50	.50
91a	A15	20c		5.50	2.00
			Nos. 86a-91a (5)	38.50	9.75

For differentiating the lithograph and photogravure printings of the Butterflies issues, see notes after Johore No. 182a.

Flower Type of Johore, 1979, with State Crest

Wmk. 378

1979, Apr. 30   Litho.   Perf. 14½

92	A16	1c	multicolored	.25	1.10
93	A16	2c	multicolored	.25	1.10
94	A16	5c	multicolored	.25	.30
a.			Unwmkd. ('85)	1.00	1.60
95	A16	10c	multicolored	.25	.25
a.			White flowers ('84)	.25	.25
96	A16	15c	multicolored	.35	.25
a.			Unwmkd. ('84)	.75	.75
97	A16	20c	multicolored	.35	.25
a.			Pale yellow flowers ('84)	.35	.25
98	A16	25c	multicolored	.45	.25
			Nos. 92-98 (7)	2.15	3.50

Agriculture and State Arms Type of Johore

Wmk. 388

1986, Oct. 25   Litho.   Perf. 12

99	A19	1c	multicolored	.30	.30
100	A19	2c	multicolored	.30	.30
101	A19	5c	multicolored	.30	.30

102	A19	10c	multicolored	.30	.30
103	A19	15c	multicolored	.30	.30
104	A19	20c	multicolored	.40	.30
105	A19	30c	multicolored	.30	.30
			Nos. 99-105 (7)	2.20	2.10

1986?					**Litho.**
101a	A19	5c	Perf. 14	1.25	.25
102a	A19	10c	Perf. 14	1.00	.25
102b	A19	10c	Perf. 15x14½	8.25	.35
104a	A19	20c	Perf. 14x13¼	2.50	.25
105a	A19	30c	Perf. 14	3.50	.25
105b	A19	30c	Perf. 14x14½	5.25	.25

Royal Heritage of Negri Sembilan — A8

Designs: 30c, Eight long keris. 50c, Audience Hall. $1, Tuanku Ja'afar Ibni Al-Marhum Tuanku Abdul Rahman, ruler of Negri Sembilan. $2, Tuanku Ja'afar and wife.

Perf. 12¾x12½

2007, Aug. 2				**Wmk. 388**
106-108	A8	Set of 3	1.10	.55

Souvenir Sheet

109	A8	$2 multi		1.25 .60

Flowers and Arms Type of Johore of 2007 With Portrait of Tuanku Jaafar Ibni Al-Marhum Tuanku Abdul Rahman

Perf. 14x13¾, 14¾x14½ (30c)

2007, Dec. 31			**Litho.**		**Wmk. 388**
110	A20	5c	multi	.25	.25
111	A20	10c	multi	.25	.25
112	A20	20c	multi	.25	.25
113	A20	30c	multi	.40	.25
114	A20	40c	multi	.50	.30
a.			Perf. 14¾x14½	.50	.30
115	A20	50c	multi	.65	.35
a.			Perf. 14¾x14½	.65	.40
			Nos. 110-115 (6)	2.30	1.65

Installation of Tuanku Muhriz Ibni Al-Mahrum Tuanku Munawir — A9

Tuanku Muhriz: 30c, Wearing white headdress. 50c, Wearing black hat. $1, With wife, Tuanku Aishah Rohani, horiz. (58x34mm)

Perf. 13¾x14 Syncopated

2009, Oct. 26		**Litho.**		**Wmk. 388**
116-118	A9	Set of 3	1.10	.55

Flowers and Arms Type of Johore of 2007 with Portrait of Tuanku Muhriz Ibni Al-Mahrum Tuanku Munawir

Designs as before.

Perf. 14x13¾

2009, Nov. 24			**Litho.**		**Wmk. 388**
119		Sheet of 6		.95	.45
a.	A20	5c multi		.25	.25
b.	A20	10c multi		.25	.25
c.	A20	20c multi		.25	.25
d.	A20	30c multi		.25	.25
e.	A20	40c multi		.25	.25
f.	A20	50c multi		.30	.25

Tuanku Muhriz's headdress extends well to the left of his ear on Nos. 119a-119f, much like that seen in illustration A9. The headdress of Tuanku Jaafar on Nos. 110-115 does not extend to the left past his ear.

PAHANG

Orchid Type of Johore, 1965, with Portrait of Sultan Abu Bakar

Wmk. 338

1965, Nov. 15   Photo.   Perf. 14½

Flowers in Natural Colors

83	A14	1c	blk & lt grnsh bl	.25	1.10
a.			Watermark sideways ('70)	2.25	6.50

84	A14	2c	black, red & gray	.25	1.10
a.			Unwmkd. ('85)		
85	A14	5c	black & Prus bl	.35	.25
86	A14	6c	black & lt lil	.40	1.10
87	A14	10c	black & lt ultra	.30	.25
a.			Watermark sideways ('70)	1.50	3.25
88	A14	15c	blk, lil rose & grn	1.25	.25
89	A14	20c	black & brown	1.75	.40
			Nos. 83-89 (7)	4.55	4.45

Butterfly Type of Johore, 1971, Portrait of Sultan Abu Bakar

Perf. 13½x13

1971, Feb. 1		**Litho.**		**Unwmk.**	
90	A15	1c	multicolored	.30	1.50
91	A15	2c	multicolored	.40	1.75
92	A15	5c	multicolored	.80	.40
93	A15	6c	multicolored	1.25	2.00
94	A15	10c	multicolored	1.25	.30
95	A15	15c	multicolored	2.00	.30
96	A15	20c	multicolored	2.25	.45
			Nos. 90-96 (7)	8.25	6.70

In 1973 booklet panes of 4 of the 5c, 10c, 15c were made from sheets.

Sultan Haji Ahmad Shah — A9

1975, May 8		**Litho.**		**Perf. 14x14½**	
97	A9	10c	lilac, gold & black	.45	1.10
98	A9	15c	yellow, green & black	.80	.30
99	A9	50c	ultra, dk blue & black	2.00	4.00
			Nos. 97-99 (3)	3.25	5.40

Installation of Sultan Haji Ahmad Shah as ruler of Pahang.

Black-veined Tiger and Sultan Haji Ahmad Shah — A18

1977-78					
100	A18	2c	multi ('78)	65.00	60.00
101	A18	5c	multicolored	.85	1.10
102	A18	10c	multi ('78)	1.25	.85
103	A18	15c	multi ('78)	1.75	1.00
104	A18	20c	multi ('78)	4.50	2.50
			Nos. 100-104 (5)	73.35	65.45

Flower Type of Johore, 1979, with Portrait of Sultan Haji Ahmad Shah

Wmk. 378

1979, Apr. 30   Litho.   Perf. 14½

105	A16	1c	multicolored	.25	.90
106	A16	2c	multicolored	.25	.90
107	A16	5c	multicolored	.25	.25
a.			5c brt rose pink & yel flowers ('84)	.25	.25
108	A16	10c	multicolored	.25	.25
a.			Unwmkd. ('85)	1.25	1.50
109	A16	15c	multicolored	.25	.25
110	A16	20c	multicolored	.30	.25
a.			Unwmkd. ('84)	1.00	.30
111	A16	25c	multicolored	.45	.40
			Nos. 105-111 (7)	2.00	3.20

Agriculture and State Arms Type of Johore with Sultan Haji Ahmad Shah

Wmk. 388

1986, Oct. 25   Litho.   Perf. 12

112	A19	1c	multicolored	.30	.30
113	A19	2c	multicolored	.30	.35
114	A19	5c	multicolored	.30	.30
115	A19	10c	multicolored	.30	.30
116	A19	15c	multicolored	.30	.30
117	A19	20c	multicolored	.30	.30
118	A19	30c	multicolored	.45	.30
			Nos. 112-118 (7)	2.25	2.15

1986?					
112a	A19	1c	Perf. 13½x14	6.50	.35
115a	A19	10c	Perf. 15x14½	8.50	.50
115b	A19	10c	Perf. 14x13½	1.75	.40
117a	A19	20c	Perf. 14	1.00	.25
118a	A19	30c	Perf. 14	3.00	.25
118b	A19	30c	Perf. 15x14½	6.50	.50

Flowers and Arms Type of Johore of 2007 With Portrait of Sultan Haji Ahmad Shah

Perf. 14x13¾

2007, Dec. 31			**Litho.**		**Wmk. 388**
119	A20	5c	multi	.25	.25
120	A20	10c	multi	.25	.25
121	A20	20c	multi	.25	.25
122	A20	30c	multi	.40	.25
123	A20	40c	multi	.50	.25
124	A20	50c	multi	.65	.35
a.			Souvenir sheet of 6, #119-124	2.25	1.10
			Nos. 119-124 (6)	2.30	1.60

Pahang Royalty and Regalia A19

Regalia and: 60c, Sultan Haji Ahmad Shah, Sultana Hajjah Kalson. 80c, Sultan in uniform. $1, Sultan in robe.

		Wmk. 388		
2010, Oct. 24		**Litho.**		**Perf. 14**
125-127	A19	Set of 3	1.60	.80

PENANG

(Pulau Pinang)

Orchid Type of Johore, 1965, with State Crest

Wmk. 338

1965, Nov. 15   Photo.   Perf. 14½

Orchids in Natural Colors

67	A14	1c	black & lt grnsh bl	.25	1.10
a.			Watermark sideways ('70)	1.75	5.50
68	A14	2c	black, red & gray	.25	1.10
69	A14	5c	black & Prus blue	.40	.25
a.			Prussian blue omitted	750.00	
b.			Yellow omitted	75.00	
70	A14	6c	black & lt lilac	.50	1.10
71	A14	10c	black & lt ultra	.30	.25
a.			Watermark sideways ('70)	7.25	3.75
72	A14	15c	black, lil rose & grn	1.10	.25
73	A14	20c	black & brown	1.60	.40
			Nos. 67-73 (7)	4.40	4.45

Butterfly Type of Johore, 1971, with State Crest

Perf. 13½x13

1971, Feb. 1		**Litho.**		**Unwmk.**	
74	A15	1c	multicolored	.40	1.75
75	A15	2c	multicolored	.60	1.75
76	A15	5c	multicolored	1.25	.30
77	A15	6c	multicolored	1.25	1.75
78	A15	10c	multicolored	1.40	.25
79	A15	15c	multicolored	1.50	.25
80	A15	20c	multicolored	1.75	.50
			Nos. 74-80 (7)	8.15	6.55

1977				**Photo.**	
74a	A15	1c		6.00	7.00
76a	A15	5c		3.50	.50
78a	A15	10c		6.00	.50
79a	A15	15c		18.00	.50
80a	A15	20c		8.25	.90
			Nos. 74a-80a (5)	41.75	9.40

For differentiating the lithograph and photogravure printings of the Butterflies issues, see notes after Johore No. 182a.

Flower Type of Johore, 1979, with State Crest

Wmk. 378

1979, Apr. 30   Litho.   Perf. 14½

81	A16	1c	multicolored	.25	.90
82	A16	2c	multicolored	.25	.90
83	A16	5c	multicolored	.25	.25
84	A16	10c	multicolored	.25	.25
85	A16	15c	multicolored	.25	.25
86	A16	20c	multicolored	.30	.25
87	A16	25c	multicolored	.40	.25
			Nos. 81-87 (7)	1.95	3.10

1984-85				**Unwmk.**	
83a	A16	5c		.40	.40
84a	A16	10c	('85)	5.75	2.25
85a	A16	15c		.65	.25
86a	A16	20c		.90	.35

The State arms are larger on Nos. 83a-86a.

Agriculture and State Arms Type of Johore
Wmk. 388

1986, Oct. 25		**Litho.**	**Perf. 12**	
88	A19	1c multicolored	.30	.30
89	A19	2c multicolored	.30	.30
90	A19	5c multicolored	.30	.30
91	A19	10c multicolored	.30	.30
92	A19	15c multicolored	.30	.30
93	A19	20c multicolored	.30	.30
94	A19	30c multicolored	.30	.30
		Nos. 88-94 (7)	2.10	2.10

1986?

90a	A19	5c Perf. 14x13¼	2.50	.25
90b	A19	5c Perf. 15x14½	2.50	.25
91a	A19	10c Perf. 14	1.00	.25
91b	A19	10c Perf. 14x14½	3.00	.25
91c	A19	10c Perf. 15x14½	2.50	.25
93a	A19	20c Perf. 14	1.00	.25
93b	A19	20c Perf. 14x14½	4.00	.25
93c	A19	20c Perf. 15x14½	4.00	.25
94a	A19	30c Perf. 14	1.00	.25
94b	A19	30c Perf. 14x14½	2.50	.25
94c	A19	30c Perf. 15x14½	2.50	.25

Flowers and Arms Type of Johore of 2007
Perf. 14x13¾

2007, Dec. 31		**Litho.**	**Wmk. 388**	
95	A20	5c multi	.25	.25
96	A20	10c multi	.25	.25
97	A20	20c multi	.25	.25
98	A20	30c multi	.40	.25
99	A20	40c multi	.50	.30
100	A20	50c multi	.65	.35
a.		Souvenir sheet of 6, #95-100	2.25	1.10
		Nos. 95-100 (6)	2.30	1.65

PERAK

Sultan Idris Shah — A17

Wmk. 338

1963, Oct. 26		**Photo.**	**Perf. 14**	
138	A17	10c yel, blk, blue & brn	.35	.25

Installation of Idris Shah as Sultan of Perak.

Orchid Type of Johore, 1965, with Portrait of Sultan Idris Shah
1965, Nov. 15   Wmk. 338   Perf. 14½
Flowers in Natural Colors

139	A14	1c blk & lt grnsh bl	.25	.40
a.		Watermark sideways ('70)	2.50	6.50
140	A14	2c black, red & gray	.25	.60
141	A14	5c black & Prus blue	.30	.25
a.		Yellow omitted	80.00	
142	A14	6c black & lt lilac	.30	.30
143	A14	10c black & lt ultra	.30	.25
a.		Watermark sideways ('70)	7.50	3.75
144	A14	15c blk, lil rose & grn	.80	.25
a.		Lilac rose omitted	900.00	
145	A14	20c black & brown	1.25	.25
		Nos. 139-145 (7)	3.45	2.30

Butterfly Type of Johore, 1971, with Portrait of Sultan Idris Shah
Perf. 13½x13

1971, Feb. 1		**Litho.**	**Unwmk.**	
146	A15	1c multicolored	.35	1.75
147	A15	2c multicolored	.90	1.75
148	A15	5c multicolored	1.10	.25
149	A15	6c multicolored	1.10	1.75
150	A15	10c multicolored	1.25	.25
151	A15	15c multicolored	1.25	.35
152	A15	20c multicolored	1.75	.35
		Nos. 146-152 (7)	7.70	6.45

In 1973 booklet panes of 4 of the 5c, 10c, 15c were made from sheets.

1977			**Photo.**	
146a	A15	1c	1.75	3.50
148b	A15	5c	4.00	.65
150b	A15	10c	3.25	.75
151b	A15	15c	11.00	.50
152a	A15	20c	4.50	1.40
		Nos. 146a-152a (5)	24.50	6.80

For differentiating the lithograph and photogravure printings of the Butterflies issues, see notes after Johore No. 182a.

Flower Type of Johore, 1979, with Portrait of Sultan Idris Shah
Wmk. 378

1979, Apr. 30		**Litho.**	**Perf. 14½**	
153	A16	1c multicolored	.25	.75
154	A16	2c multicolored	.25	.75
155	A16	5c multicolored	.25	.25
a.		Brt rose pink & yel flowers ('84)	.25	.25
156	A16	10c multicolored	.25	.25
a.		White flowers ('84)	.25	.25
157	A16	15c multicolored	.30	.25
a.		Unwmkd. ('85)	1.00	.25
158	A16	20c multicolored	.35	.25
a.		Unwmkd. ('84)	.90	.40
159	A16	25c multicolored	.45	.25
		Nos. 153-159 (7)	2.10	2.75

Agriculture and State Arms Type of Johore with Tun Azlan Shah, Raja
Wmk. 388

1986, Oct. 25		**Litho.**	**Perf. 12**	
160	A19	1c multicolored	.25	.25
161	A19	2c multicolored	.25	.30
162	A19	5c multicolored	.25	.30
163	A19	10c multicolored	.25	.25
164	A19	15c multicolored	.25	.25
165	A19	20c multicolored	.25	.25
166	A19	30c multicolored	.35	.25
		Nos. 160-166 (7)	1.85	1.80

1986?

161a	A19	2c Perf. 14x14½	3.00	.30
162a	A19	5c Perf. 14	3.00	.25
162b	A19	5c Perf. 15x14½	4.00	.25
163a	A19	10c Perf. 14x13¼	1.00	.25
165a	A19	20c Perf. 14	1.50	.25
165b	A19	20c Perf. 14x14½	4.00	.35
165c	A19	20c Perf. 14¾x14½	2.75	.45
166a	A19	30c Perf. 14x14½	3.50	.35
166b	A19	30c Perf. 15x14½	7.50	1.00
166c	A19	30c Perf. 14x13½	6.00	.35

Flowers and Arms Type of Johore of 2007 With Portrait of Sultan Azlan Shah
Perf. 14x13¾

2007, Dec. 31		**Litho.**	**Wmk. 388**	
167	A20	5c multi	.25	.25
168	A20	10c multi	.25	.25
169	A20	20c multi	.25	.25
170	A20	30c multi	.40	.25
171	A20	40c multi	.50	.30
172	A20	50c multi	.65	.35
a.		Souvenir sheet of 6, #167-172	2.25	1.10
		Nos. 167-172 (6)	2.30	1.65

Reign of Sultan Azlan Shah, 25th Anniv. — A18

Sultan: 30c, Sultana Tuanku Bainun. 50c, Mosque. $1, Sultana, diff.

Perf. 13½x13¼

2009, Feb. 3	**Litho.**	**Wmk. 388**	
173-175	A18	Set of 3	1.00 .50

PERLIS

Orchid Type of Johore, 1965, with Portrait of Regent Yang Teramat Mulia
Wmk. 338
1965, Nov. 15   Photo.   Perf. 14½
Flowers in Natural Colors

40	A14	1c black & lt grnsh bl	.30	.90
41	A14	2c black, red & gray	.35	1.25
42	A14	5c black & Prus blue	.30	.30
43	A14	6c black & lt lilac	.60	1.25
44	A14	10c black & ultra	.85	.35
45	A14	15c blk, lil rose & grn	1.25	.50
46	A14	20c black & brown	1.25	1.60
		Nos. 40-46 (7)	4.90	6.15

Butterfly Type of Johore, 1971, with Portrait of Sultan Syed Putra
Perf. 13½x13

1971, Feb. 1		**Litho.**	**Unwmk.**	
47	A15	1c multicolored	.25	1.10
48	A15	2c multicolored	.30	1.75
49	A15	5c multicolored	1.10	1.10
50	A15	6c multicolored	1.25	2.75
51	A15	10c multicolored	1.75	1.10
52	A15	15c multicolored	1.75	.50
53	A15	20c multicolored	1.75	2.25
		Nos. 47-53 (7)	8.15	10.55

In 1973 booklet panes of 4 of the 5c, 10c, 15c were made from sheets.

1977			**Photo.**	
51b	A15	10c	190.00	9.50
52b	A15	15c	5.50	2.75
53a	A15	20c	175.00	32.50
		Nos. 51b-53a (3)	370.50	44.75

For differentiating the lithograph and photogravure printings of the Butterflies issues, see notes after Johore No. 182a.

Sultan Syed Putra — A2

1971, Mar. 28		**Litho.**	**Perf. 13½x13**	
54	A2	10c silver, yel & black	.30	2.00
55	A2	15c silver, blue & blk	.35	.65
56	A2	50c silver, lt vio & blk	.90	4.00
		Nos. 54-56 (3)	1.55	6.65

25th anniversary of the installation of Syed Putra as Raja of Perlis. Sold throughout Malaysia on Mar. 28, then only in Perlis.

Flower Type of Johore, 1979, with Portrait of Sultan Syed Putra
Wmk. 378

1979, Apr. 30		**Litho.**	**Perf. 14½**	
57	A16	1c multicolored	.25	.90
58	A16	2c multicolored	.25	.90
59	A16	5c multicolored	.25	.90
60	A16	10c multicolored	.25	.25
61	A16	15c multicolored	.25	.25
62	A16	20c multicolored	.30	.25
a.		Unwmk. ('85)	1.75	1.75
63	A16	25c multicolored	.45	.75
		Nos. 57-63 (7)	2.00	4.20

Agriculture and State Arms Type of Johore with Tuanku Syed Putra, Raja
Wmk. 388

1986, Oct. 25		**Litho.**	**Perf. 12**	
64	A19	1c multicolored	.30	.45
65	A19	2c multicolored	.30	.45
66	A19	5c multicolored	.30	.30
67	A19	10c multicolored	.30	.30
68	A19	15c multicolored	.30	.30
69	A19	20c multicolored	.30	.30
70	A19	30c multicolored	.40	.30
		Nos. 64-70 (7)	2.20	2.40

1986?

67a	A19	10c Perf. 15x14½	4.25	.45
70a	A19	30c Perf. 14	5.25	.25
70b	A19	30c Perf. 15x14½	14.50	

Reign of Tuanku Syed Putra Jamalullail, Raja of Perlis, 50th Anniv. A3

30c, Industry and produce. $1, Palace.

Wmk. 388

1995, Dec. 4		**Litho.**	**Perf. 14**	
71	A3	30c green & multi	.80	.80
72	A3	$1 blue & multi	2.40	2.40

Installation of Raja Tuanku Syed Sirajuddin Putra Jamalullail — A4

Denomination color: 30c, Blue. 50c, Green. $1, Purple.
$2, Raja and wife, horiz.

Perf. 13½x13¾

2001, May 7		**Litho.**	**Wmk. 388**	
73-75	A4	Set of 3	.95	.45

Souvenir Sheet
Perf. 14¼x13½x13¾x13½

76	A4	$2 multi	1.10 1.10

Flowers and Arms Type of Johore of 2007 With Portrait of Raja Tuanku Syed Sirajuddin Putra Jamalullail
Perf. 14x13¾

2007, Dec. 31		**Litho.**	**Wmk. 388**	
77	A20	5c multi	.25	.25
78	A20	10c multi	.25	.25
79	A20	20c multi	.25	.25
80	A20	30c multi	.40	.25
81	A20	40c multi	.50	.30
82	A20	50c multi	.65	.35
a.		Souvenir sheet of 6, #77-82	2.25	1.10
		Nos. 77-82 (6)	2.30	1.65

SABAH

North Borneo Nos. 280-295 Overprinted

On 1c-75c

On $1-$10

Perf. 13x12½, 12½x13

1964, July 1		**Engr.**	**Wmk. 314**	
1	A92	1c lt red brn & grn	.25	.35
2	A92	4c orange & olive	.25	.45
3	A92	5c violet & black	.25	.35
4	A92	6c bluish grn & sl	1.10	.35
5	A92	10c rose red & lt grn	2.00	.35
6	A92	12c dull green & brn	.25	.35
7	A92	20c ultra & blue grn	4.25	.35
8	A92	25c rose red & gray	.90	.80
9	A92	30c gray ol & sepia	.40	.30
10	A92	35c redsh brn & stl bl	.40	.30
11	A92	50c brn org & blue grn	.40	.30
12	A92	75c red vio & sl blue	3.75	.90
13	A93	$1 yel green & brn	9.50	1.75
14	A93	$2 slate & brown	15.00	3.00
15	A93	$5 brown vio & grn	17.00	13.00
16	A93	$10 blue & carmine	17.00	29.00
		Nos. 1-16 (16)	72.70	51.90

Orchid Type of Johore, 1965, with State Crest
Wmk. 338
1965, Nov. 15   Photo.   Perf. 14½
Flowers in Natural Colors

17	A14	1c black & lt grnsh bl	.30	1.10
18	A14	2c black, red & gray	.30	1.50
19	A14	5c black & Prus bl	.45	.25
20	A14	6c black & lt lilac	.45	1.25
21	A14	10c black & lt ultra	.40	.30
a.		Watermark sideways ('70)	5.50	5.50
22	A14	15c black, lil rose & grn	2.00	.30
23	A14	20c black & brown	3.00	.30
		Nos. 17-23 (7)	6.90	5.35

Butterfly Type of Johore, 1971, with State Crest
Perf. 13½x13

1971, Feb. 1		**Litho.**	**Unwmk.**	
24	A15	1c multicolored	.60	2.25
25	A15	2c multicolored	.70	2.25
26	A15	5c multicolored	.70	.40
27	A15	6c multicolored	.90	1.75
28	A15	10c multicolored	1.00	.25
29	A15	15c multicolored	1.25	.25
30	A15	20c multicolored	1.30	1.10
		Nos. 24-30 (7)	6.45	8.25

In 1973 booklet panes of 4 of the 5c, 10c, 15c were made from sheets.

1977			**Photo.**	
24a	A15	1c	1.75	4.25
25a	A15	2c	1.75	4.25
26b	A15	5c	10.00	2.25

28b	A15	10c	2.00	1.00
29b	A15	15c	2.50	.30
30a	A15	20c	225.00	10.00
	Nos. 24a-29b (5)		18.00	12.05

For differentiating the lithograph and photogravure printings of the Butterflies issues, see notes after Johore No. 182a.

Flower Type of Johore, 1979, with State Crest
Wmk. 378

1979, Apr. 30			*Perf. 14½*	
32	A16	1c multicolored	.35	1.50
33	A16	2c multicolored	.35	1.50
34	A16	5c multicolored	.35	.45
35	A16	10c multicolored	.35	.35
36	A16	15c multicolored	.50	.35
37	A16	20c multicolored	.60	.35
38	A16	25c multicolored	.75	.35
	Nos. 32-38 (7)		3.25	4.85

1983-85			Unwmk.	
35a	A16	10c ('85)	5.50	7.25
36a	A16	15c	2.75	.40
37a	A16	20c	17.00	1.75

Agriculture and State Arms Type of Johore
Wmk. 388

1986, Oct. 25			Perf. 12	
39	A19	1c multicolored	.30	.30
40	A19	2c multicolored	.30	.25
41	A19	5c multicolored	.30	.25
42	A19	10c multicolored	.30	.25
43	A19	15c multicolored	.30	.25
44	A19	20c multicolored	.30	.25
45	A19	30c multicolored	.35	.25
	Nos. 39-45 (7)		2.15	1.80

1986?				
40a	A19	2c Perf. 15x14½	3.25	.35
45a	A19	30c Perf. 14	1.00	.25
45b	A19	30c Perf. 15x14½	4.75	.30

Flowers and Arms Type of Johore of 2007
Perf. 14x13¾

2007, Dec. 31			Litho.	Wmk. 388
46	A20	5c multi	.25	.25
47	A20	10c multi	.25	.25
48	A20	20c multi	.25	.25
49	A20	30c multi	.40	.25
50	A20	40c multi	.50	.30
51	A20	50c multi	.65	.35
a.	Souvenir sheet of 6, #46-51		2.25	1.10
	Nos. 46-51 (6)		2.30	1.65

SARAWAK

Types of Sarawak of 1955-57
Perf. 11x11½, 11½x11

1964-65		Engr.	Wmk. 314	
215	A23	1c green	.25	1.00
216	A23	2c red orange	1.00	13.50
217	A24	6c green blue	7.00	5.25
218	A24	10c dark green	2.25	1.40
219	A24	12c purple	3.75	12.00
220	A24	15c ultra	1.50	17.50
221	A24	20c brown & olive	1.00	2.00
222	A24	25c brt grn & brn	4.25	6.00
	Nos. 215-222 (8)		21.00	58.65

Issued: 20c, 6/9/64; 2c, 15c, 8/17/65; others, 9/9/64.

Orchid Type of Johore (Malaysia), 1965, with State Crest
Wmk. 338

1965, Nov. 15		Photo.	*Perf. 14½*	
		Flowers in Natural Colors		
228	A14	1c black & lt grnsh bl	.25	1.25
229	A14	2c black, red & gray	.30	2.50
230	A14	5c black & Prus blue	1.50	.25
231	A14	6c black & lt lilac	.90	2.25
232	A14	10c black & lt ultra	1.25	.25
233	A14	15c black, lil rose & grn	1.75	.25
234	A14	20c black & brown	2.50	.55
	Nos. 228-234 (7)		8.45	7.30

Clipper and State Crest — A26

1c, Delias ninus. 2c, Danaus melanippus. 5c, Parthenos sylvia. 6c, Papilio demoleus. 10c, Hebomnia glaucippe. 15c, Precis orithya. 20c, Valeria valeria.

Perf. 13½x13

1971, Feb. 1		Litho.	Unwmk.	
235	A26	1c multicolored	.85	2.25
236	A26	2c multicolored	.95	2.25
237	A26	5c multicolored	2.00	.25
a.	Booklet pane of 4 ('73)		9.00	
238	A26	6c multicolored	2.00	3.00
239	A26	10c multicolored	2.00	.25
a.	Booklet pane of 4 ('73)		9.00	
240	A26	15c multicolored	3.00	.25
a.	Booklet pane of 4 ('73)		13.00	
241	A26	20c multicolored	3.00	1.50
	Nos. 235-241 (7)		13.80	9.75

Clipper and New State Crest — A27

Changed Colors, Designs as Before

1977-78		Photo.	Unwmk.	
242	A27	1c multi ('78)	8.50	15.00
243	A27	2c multi ('78)	20.00	16.00
244	A27	5c multicolored	2.50	2.00
245	A27	10c multicolored	1.50	.80
246	A27	15c multicolored	3.00	.30
247	A27	20c multi ('78)	7.00	5.75
	Nos. 242-247 (6)		42.50	39.85

Flower Type of Johore, 1979, with State Crest

1979, Apr. 30		Wmk. 47	*Perf. 14½*	
248	A16	1c multicolored	.25	.40
249	A16	2c multicolored	.25	.40
250	A16	5c multicolored	.25	.50
251	A16	10c multicolored	.30	.25
252	A16	15c multicolored	.30	.25
253	A16	20c multicolored	.60	.25
254	A16	25c multicolored	.90	.70
	Nos. 248-254 (7)		2.85	2.75

1983-86			Unwmk.	
250a	A16	5c ('86)	1.00	1.25
251a	A16	10c ('85)	1.00	1.10
253a	A16	20c	1.00	1.10
	Nos. 250a-253a (3)		3.00	3.45

Agriculture and State Arms Type of Johore Shield Divided into 3 Parts of Different Colors
Wmk. 388

1986, Oct. 25		Litho.	Perf. 12	
255	A19	1c multicolored	.25	.25
256	A19	2c multicolored	.25	.25
257	A19	5c multicolored	.30	.25
258	A19	10c multicolored	.40	.25
259	A19	15c multicolored	.55	.25
260	A19	20c multicolored	.55	.25
261	A19	30c multicolored	1.00	.25
	Nos. 255-261 (7)		3.30	1.75

Agriculture and Arms Type of Johore

Yellow Shield Divided by Diagonal Bands of Black and Red

1986-96		Litho.	Wmk. 388	*Perf. 12*
262	A19	1c multicolored	.25	.25
263	A19	2c multicolored	.25	.25
a.	Perf. 15x14½		3.00	
264	A19	5c multicolored	.25	.25
a.	Perf 14 ('96)		.90	.25
265	A19	10c multicolored	.25	.25
a.	Perf. 14 ('95)		2.00	
b.	Perf. 15x14½ ('95)		2.00	
c.	Perf. 14x14½ ('96)		4.50	.35
266	A19	15c multicolored	.25	.25
267	A19	20c multicolored	.30	.25
268	A19	30c multicolored	.40	.25
a.	Perf. 14 ('94)		1.75	.25
b.	Perf. 15x14½ ('94)		4.00	.35
c.	Perf. 14x14½ ('94)		4.25	.45
	Nos. 262-268 (7)		1.95	1.75

Flowers and Arms Type of Johore of 2007

SARAWAK Malaysia 5 sen

Perf. 14x13¾

2007, Dec. 31		Litho.	Wmk. 388	
269	A20	5c multi	.25	.25
270	A20	10c multi	.30	.25
271	A20	20c multi	.35	.25
272	A20	30c multi	.50	.25
273	A20	40c multi	.60	.30
274	A20	50c multi	.75	.35
a.	Souvenir sheet of 6, #269-274		3.00	2.50
	Nos. 269-274 (6)		2.75	1.65

SELANGOR

Orchid Type of Johore, 1965, with Portrait of Sultan Salahuddin Abdul Aziz Shah
Wmk. 338

1965, Nov. 15			*Perf. 14½*	
		Flowers in Natural Colors		
121	A14	1c blk & lt grnsh bl	.25	.25
a.	Watermark sideways ('70)		1.60	7.25
122	A14	2c black, red & gray	.30	1.50
a.	Rose carmine omitted			
123	A14	5c black & Prus blue	.35	.25
124	A14	6c black & lt lilac	.35	.25
125	A14	10c black & lt ultra	.35	.25
a.	Watermark sideways ('70)		5.25	1.75
126	A14	15c blk, lil rose & grn	1.25	.25
127	A14	20c black & brown	2.25	.25
a.	Watermark sideways ('70)		9.25	9.50
	Nos. 121-127 (7)		5.10	3.00

Butterfly Type of Johore, 1971, with Portrait of Sultan Salahuddin Abdul Aziz Shah
Perf. 13½x13

1971, Feb. 1		Litho.	Unwmk.	
128	A15	1c multicolored	.65	1.75
129	A15	2c multicolored	1.25	1.75
130	A15	5c multicolored	1.25	.30
131	A15	6c multicolored	1.25	1.75
132	A15	10c multicolored	1.60	.30
133	A15	15c multicolored	1.25	.30
134	A15	20c multicolored	1.25	.40
	Nos. 128-134 (7)		8.50	6.55

In 1973 booklet panes of 4 of the 5c, 10c, 15c were made from sheets.

1977			Photo.	
128a	A15	1c	.80	4.25
130b	A15	5c	3.75	1.50
132b	A15	10c	7.75	1.50
133b	A15	15c	9.00	.40
134a	A15	20c	25.80	8.90
	Nos. 128a-134a (5)			

For differentiating the lithograph and photogravure printings of the Butterflies issues, see notes after Johore No. 182a.

Flower Type of Johore, 1979, with Portrait of Sultan Salahuddin Abdul Aziz Shah
Wmk. 378

1979, Apr. 30		Litho.	*Perf. 14½*	
135	A16	1c multicolored	.25	.90
136	A16	2c multicolored	.25	.90
137	A16	5c multicolored	.25	.25
a.	brt rose pink & yel flowers ('84)		.65	.80
138	A16	10c multicolored	.25	.25
a.	Unwmkd. ('85)		.85	1.00
139	A16	15c multicolored	.25	.25
a.	Unwmkd. ('84)		.85	.85
140	A16	20c multicolored	.30	.25
a.	pale yellow flowers ('84)		1.00	.50
141	A16	25c multicolored	.40	.25
	Nos. 135-141 (7)		1.95	3.05

Agriculture and State Arms Type of Johore with Sultan Salahuddin Abdul Aziz Shah
Wmk. 388

1986, Oct. 25		Litho.	Perf. 12	
142	A19	1c multicolored	.30	.30
143	A19	2c multicolored	.30	.30
144	A19	5c multicolored	.30	.25
145	A19	10c multicolored	.30	.25
146	A19	15c multicolored	.30	.25
147	A19	20c multicolored	.30	.25
148	A19	30c multicolored	.35	.25
	Nos. 142-148 (7)		2.15	1.85

1986?				
144a	A19	5c Perf. 14x14½	13.00	
144b	A19	5c Perf. 14x14½	4.25	.25
144c	A19	5c Perf. 14x13½	.90	.25
145a	A19	10c Perf. 14	3.25	.25
145b	A19	10c Perf. 15x14½	1.50	.25
147a	A19	20c Perf. 14	1.00	.25
148a	A19	30c Perf. 14	1.00	.25
148b	A19	30c Perf. 14x14½	8.50	.25
148c	A19	30c Perf. 15x14½	5.00	.25

Malaysia 30 sen

Coronation of Sultan Sharafuddin Idris Shah — A19

Designs: 30c, Wearing yellow hat. 50c, Wearing naval uniform. 1r, Wearing crown.

Perf. 12 (30c), 12¾x12½				
2003, Mar. 8		Litho.	Wmk. 388	
149-151	A19	Set of 3	.95	.45

Flowers and Arms Type of Johore of 2007 With Portrait of Sultan Sharafuddin Idris Shah
Perf. 14¾x14½

2007, Dec. 31		Litho.	Wmk. 388	
152	A20	5c multi	.25	.25
a.	Perf. 14x13¾		.25	.25
153	A20	10c multi	.25	.25
a.	Perf. 14x13¾		.25	.25

Perf. 14x13¾				
154	A20	20c multi	.25	.25
155	A20	30c multi	.40	.25
156	A20	40c multi	.50	.30
157	A20	50c multi	.65	.35
a.	Souvenir sheet of 6, #152a, 153a, 154-157		2.25	1.10
	Nos. 152-157 (6)		2.30	1.65

TRENGGANU

Orchid Type of Johore, 1965, with Portrait of Sultan Ismail
Wmk. 338

1965, Nov. 15		Photo.	*Perf. 14½*	
		Flowers in Natural Colors		
86	A14	1c black & lt grnsh bl	.25	1.75
87	A14	2c black, red & gray	.30	1.75
88	A14	5c black & Prus blue	.35	.60
89	A14	6c black & lt lilac	.40	1.75
90	A14	10c black & lt ultra	.35	.25
91	A14	15c blk, lil rose & grn	1.40	.25
92	A14	20c black & brown	1.60	1.25
	Nos. 86-92 (7)		4.55	7.60

malaysia trengganu 10c

Tuanku Ismail Nasiruddin — A6

Perf. 14½x13½				
1970, Dec. 16		Photo.	Unwmk.	
93	A6	10c multicolored	.90	2.25
94	A6	15c brt yellow multi	.70	1.10
95	A6	50c dp plum & multi	1.10	2.75
	Nos. 93-95 (3)		2.70	6.10

Installation of Tuanku Ismail Nasiruddin Shah as Sultan of Trengganu, 25th anniv.

Butterfly Type of Johore, 1971, with Portrait of Sultan Ismail Nasiruddin
Perf. 13½x13

1971, Feb. 1		Litho.	Unwmk.	
96	A15	1c multicolored	.35	2.25
97	A15	2c multicolored	.70	2.25
98	A15	5c multicolored	.90	1.10
99	A15	6c multicolored	1.50	2.50
100	A15	10c multicolored	1.75	.60
101	A15	15c multicolored	2.25	.30
102	A15	20c multicolored	2.25	2.00
	Nos. 96-102 (7)		9.70	11.00

In 1973 booklet panes of 4 of the 5c, 10c, 15c were made from sheets.

1977			Photo.	
98b	A15	5c	24.00	9.50
100b	A15	10c	8.25	3.75
101b	A15	15c	5.25	1.50
	Nos. 98b-101b (3)		37.50	14.75

For differentiating the lithograph and photogravure printings of the Butterflies issues, see notes after Johore No. 182a.

Flower Type of Johore, 1979, with Portrait of Sultan Ismail Nasiruddin

1979, Apr. 30　Litho.　Perf. 14½

103	A16	1c multicolored	.25	1.10
104	A16	2c multicolored	.25	1.10
105	A16	5c multicolored	.25	.50
106	A16	10c multicolored	.25	.25
107	A16	15c multicolored	.30	.25
108	A16	20c multicolored	.35	.25
109	A16	25c multicolored	.45	.40
		Nos. 103-109 (7)	2.10	3.85

1983-86　　　Unwmk.

106a	A16	10c ('86)	13.50	4.25
107a	A16	15c ('85)	.90	1.25
108a	A16	20c	3.00	3.25
109a	A16	25c Pale salmon flowers	.90	1.10
		Nos. 106a-109a (4)	18.30	

The portrait and State arms are smaller.

Agriculture and State Arms Type of Johore with Sultan Mahmud Al Marhum
Wmk. 388

1986, Oct. 25　Litho.　Perf. 12

110	A19	1c multicolored	.30	.30
111	A19	2c multicolored	.30	.30
112	A19	5c multicolored	.30	.30
113	A19	10c multicolored	.30	.30
114	A19	15c multicolored	.30	.30
115	A19	20c multicolored	.30	.30
116	A19	30c multicolored	.40	.30
		Nos. 110-116 (7)	2.20	2.10

1986?

110a	A19	1c Perf. 13½x14	4.25	.35
115a	A19	20c Perf. 14	7.25	.25
116a	A19	30c Perf. 14	7.25	.30

Installation of HRH Sultan Mizan Zainal Abidin
A7

Sultan Abidin and: 30c, Istana Maziah. 50c, Istana Maziah, 1903. $1, Masjid Tengku Tengah Zaharah.

Wmk. 388

1999, Mar. 4　Litho.　Perf. 14¼

117	A7	30c multicolored	.50	.25

Perf. 14½

118	A7	50c multicolored	.75	.50

Perf. 13¾

119	A7	$1 multicolored	1.40	2.50
		Nos. 117-119 (3)	2.65	3.25

Flowers and Arms Type of Johore of 2007 With Portrait of Sultan Mizan Zainal Abidin
Perf. 14x13¾

2007, Dec. 31　Litho.　Wmk. 388

120	A20	5c multi	.25	.25
121	A20	10c multi	.25	.25
122	A20	20c multi	.25	.25
123	A20	30c multi	.40	.25
124	A20	40c multi	.50	.30
125	A20	50c multi	.65	.35
a.		Souvenir sheet of 6, #120-125	2.25	1.10
		Nos. 121-125 (5)	2.05	1.40

WILAYAH PERSEKUTUAN

Agriculture and State Arms Type of Johore
Wmk. 388

1986, Oct. 25　Litho.　Perf. 12

1	A19	1c multicolored	.25	.25
2	A19	2c multicolored	.25	.25
3	A19	5c multicolored	.25	.25
4	A19	10c multicolored	.25	.25
5	A19	15c multicolored	.25	.25
6	A19	20c multicolored	.25	.25
7	A19	30c multicolored	.40	.25
		Nos. 1-7 (7)	1.90	1.75

1986?

3a	A19	5c Perf. 14	3.00	
3b	A19	5c Perf. 15x14½	7.50	
4a	A19	10c Perf. 14	3.00	
4b	A19	10c Perf. 14x14½	7.50	
4c	A19	10c Perf. 14¾x14½	—	—
6a	A19	20c Perf. 14	1.00	—
7a	A19	30c Perf. 14	1.00	
7b	A19	30c Perf. 15x14½	4.00	
7c	A19	30c Perf. 14x14½	—	—

Agriculture and State Arms Type of Johore of 1986 Redrawn With "Sen" Instead of "C"
Designs as before.

Perf. 14¾x14½

2002 ?　　　Litho.　　Wmk. 388

10	A19	5sen multi	—	—

Perf. 14x14¾

11	A19	10sen multi	—	—

Perf. 14x13¾

13	A19	20sen multi	—	
14	A19	30sen multi	—	
a.		Perf. 14x13¾	—	

Additional stamps were released in this set and also for other states. The editors would like to examine any examples.

Flowers and Arms Type of Johore of 2007

2007, Dec. 31　Litho.　Perf. 14x13¾

15	A20	5c multi	.25	.25
a.		Perf. 14¾x14½	.25	.25
16	A20	10c multi	.25	.25
17	A20	20c multi	.25	.25
18	A20	30c multi	.40	.25
19	A20	40c multi	.50	.30
20	A20	50c multi	.65	.35
a.		Souvenir sheet of 6, #15-20	2.25	1.10
		Nos. 15-20 (6)	2.30	1.65

MALDIVE ISLANDS

'mol-,div 'i-lənds

LOCATION — A group of 2,000 islands in the Indian Ocean about 400 miles southwest of Ceylon.
GOVT. — Republic
AREA — 115 sq. mi.
POP. — 300,220 (1999 est.)
CAPITAL — Male

Maldive Islands was a British Protectorate, first as a dependency of Ceylon, then from 1948 as an independent sultanate, except for a year (1953) as a republic. The islands became completely independent on July 26, 1965, and became a republic again on November 11, 1968.

100 Cents = 1 Rupee
100 Larees = 1 Rufiyaa (1951)

Catalogue values for unused stamps in this country are for Never Hinged items, beginning with Scott 20.

Watermarks

Wmk. 47 — Multiple Rosette

Wmk. 200 — "Harrison & Sons, London" in Script

Stamps of Ceylon, 1904-05, Overprinted

Minaret of Juma Mosque, near Male — A1

1906, Sept. 9   Wmk. 3   Perf. 14

1	A36	2c orange brown	22.00	50.00
2	A37	3c green	30.00	50.00
3	A37	4c yellow & blue	50.00	90.00
4	A38	5c dull lilac	5.00	6.50
5	A40	15c ultramarine	100.00	180.00
6	A40	25c bister	110.00	190.00
		Nos. 1-6 (6)	317.00	566.50

1909   Engr.   Wmk. 47

7	A1	2c orange brown	2.25	4.00
8	A1	3c green	.50	.70
9	A1	5c red violet	.50	.35
10	A1	10c carmine	7.50	.80
		Nos. 7-10 (4)	10.75	5.85

Type of 1909 Issue Redrawn
Perf. 14½x14

1933   Photo.   Wmk. 233

11	A1	2c gray	2.75	2.50
12	A1	3c yellow brown	.75	1.75
13	A1	5c brown lake	40.00	10.00
14	A1	6c brown red	1.75	5.50
15	A1	10c green	1.00	.55
16	A1	15c gray black	6.50	22.00
17	A1	25c red brown	6.50	22.00

18	A1	50c red violet	6.50	22.00
19	A1	1r blue black	12.50	5.00
		Nos. 11-19 (9)	78.25	91.30

On the 6c, 15c, 25c and 50c, the right hand panel carries only the word "CENTS."
Nos. 11-19 exist with watermark vert. or horiz. The 5c with vert. watermark sells for twice the price of the horiz. watermark.

Catalogue values for unused stamps in this section, from this point to the end of the section, are for Never Hinged items.

Palm Tree and Seascape — A2

Unwmk.
1950, Dec. 24   Engr.   Perf. 13

20	A2	2 l olive green	2.25	4.00
21	A2	3 l deep blue	12.50	.85
22	A2	5 l dp green	12.50	.85
23	A2	6 l red brown	1.25	1.25
24	A2	10 l red	1.25	1.00
25	A2	15 l orange	1.25	1.00
26	A2	25 l rose violet	1.25	2.75
27	A2	50 l violet blue	1.50	4.00
28	A2	1r dark brown	14.00	37.50
		Nos. 20-28 (9)	47.75	53.20

Maldive Fish — A3

1952

29	A3	3 l shown	2.00	.75
30	A3	5 l Urns	1.10	2.00

Harbor of Male — A4

Fort and Governor's Palace — A5

Perf. 13½ (A4), 11½x11 (A5)
1956   Engr.   Unwmk.

31	A4	2 l lilac	.25	.25
32	A4	3 l gray green	.25	.25
33	A4	5 l reddish brown	.25	.25
34	A4	6 l blue violet	.25	.25
35	A4	10 l light green	.25	.25
36	A4	15 l brown	.25	.25
37	A4	25 l rose red	.25	.25
38	A4	50 l orange	.25	.25
39	A5	1r light green	.40	.30
40	A5	5r ultramarine	1.00	.65
41	A5	10r magenta	2.10	1.25
		Nos. 31-41 (11)	5.50	4.20

Bicyclists and Olympic Emblem A6

Design: 25 l, 50 l, 1r, Basketball, vert.

Perf. 11½x11, 11x11½
1960, Aug. 20   Engr.

42	A6	2 l rose violet & green	.25	.25
43	A6	3 l grnsh gray & plum	.25	.25
44	A6	5 l vio brn & dk blue	.25	.25
45	A6	10 l brt green & brn	.25	.25
46	A6	15 l brown & blue	.25	.25
47	A6	25 l rose red & olive	.25	.25
48	A6	50 l orange & dk vio	.25	.35
49	A6	1r brt green & plum	.40	.75
		Nos. 42-49 (8)	2.15	2.60

17th Olympic Games, Rome, 8/25-9/11.

World Refugee Year Emblem A7

1960, Oct. 15   Perf. 11½x11

50	A7	2 l orange, vio & grn	.25	.25
51	A7	3 l green, brn & red	.25	.25
52	A7	5 l sepia, grn & red	.25	.25
53	A7	10 l dull pur, grn & red	.25	.25
54	A7	15 l gray grn, pur & red	.25	.25
55	A7	25 l redsh brn, ultra & olive	.25	.25
56	A7	50 l rose, olive & blue	.25	.25
57	A7	1r gray, car rose & vio	.35	.50
		Nos. 50-57 (8)	2.10	2.25

WRY, July 1, 1959-June 30, 1960.

Tomb of Sultan — A8

Designs: 3 l, Custom house. 5 l, Cowry shells. 6 l, Old royal palace. 10 l, Road to Minaret, Juma Mosque, Male. 15 l, Council house. 25 l, Government secretariat. 50 l, Prime minister's office. 1r, Tomb and sailboats. 5r, Tomb by the sea. 10r, Port.

1960, Oct. 15   Perf. 11½x11
Various Frames

58	A8	2 l lilac	.45	.45
59	A8	3 l green	.45	.45
60	A8	5 l brown orange	3.75	3.50
61	A8	6 l bright blue	.45	.45
62	A8	10 l carmine rose	.45	.45
63	A8	15 l sepia	.45	.45
64	A8	25 l dull violet	.45	.45
65	A8	50 l slate	.45	.45
66	A8	1r orange	.45	.45
67	A8	5r dark blue	4.00	1.00
68	A8	10r dull green	11.00	2.10
		Nos. 58-68 (11)	22.35	10.20

Stamps in 25r, 50r and 100r denominations were also issued, but primarily for revenue purposes. Value for the three stamps, $350.

Coconuts — A9

Map of Male Showing Population Distribution A10

Perf. 14x14½, 14½x14
1961, Apr. 20   Photo.   Unwmk.
Coconuts in Ocher

69	A9	2 l green	.25	.25
70	A9	3 l ultramarine	.25	.25
71	A9	5 l lilac rose	.25	.25
72	A9	10 l red orange	.25	.25
73	A9	15 l black	.25	.25
74	A10	25 l multicolored	.25	.25
75	A10	50 l multicolored	.25	.25
76	A10	1r multicolored	.50	.70
		Nos. 69-76 (8)	2.25	2.45

Pigeon and 5c Stamp of 1906 A11

Designs: 10 l, 15 l, 20 l, Post horn and 3c stamp of 1906. 25 l, 50 l, 1r, Laurel branch and 2c stamp of 1906.

1961, Sept. 9   Perf. 14½x14

77	A11	2 l violet blue & mar	.25	.25
78	A11	3 l violet blue & mar	.25	.25
79	A11	5 l violet blue & mar	.25	.25
80	A11	6 l violet blue & mar	.25	.25
81	A11	10 l maroon & green	.25	.25
82	A11	15 l maroon & green	.25	.25
83	A11	20 l maroon & green	.25	.25
84	A11	25 l green, mar & blk	.25	.25
85	A11	50 l green, mar & blk	.25	.25
86	A11	1r green, mar & blk	.35	.35
a.		Souvenir sheet of 4	2.40	3.00
		Nos. 77-86 (10)	2.60	2.60

55th anniv. of the 1st postage stamps of the Maldive Islands.
No. 86a contains 4 No. 86, with simulated performations.

Malaria Eradication Emblem — A12

1962, Apr. 7   Engr.   Perf. 13½x13

87	A12	2 l orange brown	.25	.25
88	A12	3 l green	.25	.25
89	A12	5 l blue	.25	.25
90	A12	10 l vermilion	.25	.25
91	A12	15 l black	.25	.25
92	A12	25 l dark blue	.25	.25
93	A12	50 l green	.25	.35
94	A12	1r purple	.35	.45
		Nos. 87-94 (8)	2.10	2.30

WHO drive to eradicate malaria.

Children and Map of Far East and Americas A13

UNICEF, 15th Anniv.: 25 l, 50 l, 1r, 5r, Children and Map of Africa, Europe and Asia.

Perf. 14½x14
1962, Sept. 9   Photo.   Unwmk.
Children in Multicolor

95	A13	2 l sepia	.25	.25
96	A13	6 l violet	.25	.25
97	A13	10 l dark green	.25	.25
98	A13	15 l ultramarine	.25	.25
99	A13	25 l blue	.25	.25
100	A13	50 l bright green	.25	.25
101	A13	1r rose claret	.25	.25
102	A13	5r emerald	.50	.90
		Nos. 95-102 (8)	2.25	2.65

Sultan Mohamed Farid Didi — A14

1962, Nov. 29   Perf. 14x14½
Portrait in Orange Brown and Sepia

103	A14	3 l bluish green	.25	.25
104	A14	5 l slate	.25	.25
105	A14	10 l blue	.35	.35
106	A14	20 l olive	.35	.35
107	A14	50 l dk carmine rose	.35	.35
108	A14	1r dark purple	.65	.65
		Nos. 103-108 (6)	2.20	2.20

9th anniv. of the enthronement of Sultan Mohamed Farid Didi.

Regal Angelfish, Sultan's Crest and Skin Diver — A15

433	A69	2r black & multi	4.50	3.75
434	A69	3r black & multi	5.75	5.75
		Nos. 427-434 (8)	14.00	11.35

Souvenir Sheet

| 435 | A69 | 5r black & multi | 9.50 | *12.50* |

24th Boy Scout World Conference (1st in Africa), Nairobi, Kenya, July 16-21.
For overprints see Nos. 571-574.

Herschel's Marlin A70

Fish and Ships: 2 l, 4r, Skipjack tuna. 3 l, Bluefin tuna. 5 l, 2.50r, Dolphinfish. 60 l, 75 l, Red snapper. 1.50r, Yellow crescent tail. 3r, Plectropoma maculatum. 5r, Like 1 l. 10r, Spanish mackerel.

1973, Aug.   **Perf. 14½**

Size: 38½x24mm

436	A70	1 l lt green & multi	.25	.25
437	A70	2 l dull org & multi	.25	.25
438	A70	3 l brt red & multi	.25	.25
439	A70	5 l multicolored	.25	.25

Size: 28x22mm

| 440 | A70 | 60 l yellow & multi | .80 | .40 |
| 441 | A70 | 75 l purple & multi | 1.00 | .40 |

Size: 38½x24mm

442	A70	1.50r violet & multi	1.60	1.40
443	A70	2.50r blue & multi	2.00	2.00
444	A70	3r multicolored	2.50	2.50
445	A70	10r orange & multi	6.00	6.50
		Nos. 436-445 (10)	14.90	14.20

Souvenir Sheet
Perf. 15

446		Sheet of 2	20.00	20.00
a.	A70 4r carmine & multi		5.50	5.50
b.	A70 5r bright green & multi		6.50	6.50

Nos. 436-445 exist imperf.

Goldenfronted Leafbird — A71

2 l, 3r, Fruit bat. 3 l, 50 l, Indian starred tortoise. 4 l, 5r, Kallima inachus (butterfly).

1973, Oct.   Litho.   Perf. 14½

447	A71	1 l brt pink & multi	.25	.25
448	A71	2 l brt blue & multi	.25	.25
449	A71	3 l ver & multi	.35	.35
450	A71	4 l citron & multi	.50	.35
451	A71	50 l emerald & multi	.90	.50
452	A71	2r lt violet & multi	3.75	4.25
453	A71	3r multicolored	3.00	4.25
		Nos. 447-453 (7)	9.00	10.20

Souvenir Sheet

| 454 | A71 | 5r yellow & multi | 27.50 | 27.50 |

Lantana Camara — A72

Native Flowers: 2 l, Nerium oleander. 3 l, 2r, Rosa polyantha. 4 l, Hibiscus manihot. 5 l, Bougainvillea glabra. 10 l, 3r, Plumera alba. 50 l, Poinsettia pulcherrima. 5r, Ononis natrix.

1973, Dec. 19   Litho.   Perf. 14

455	A72	1 l ultra & multi	.30	.30
456	A72	2 l dp orange & multi	.30	.30
457	A72	3 l emerald & multi	.30	.30
458	A72	4 l blue grn & multi	.30	.30
459	A72	5 l lemon & multi	.30	.30
460	A72	10 l lilac & multi	.30	.30

461	A72	50 l yel grn & multi	.30	.30
462	A72	5r red & multi	2.75	2.75
		Nos. 455-462 (8)	4.85	4.85

Souvenir Sheet

463		Sheet of 2	5.75	6.50
a.	A72 2r lilac & multi		1.25	1.50
b.	A72 3r blue & multi		2.00	2.25

Tiros Weather Satellite A73

Designs: 2 l, 10r, Nimbus satellite. 3 l, 3r, Nomad weather ("weater") station. 4 l, A.P.T. instant weather picture (radar). 5 l, Richard's electrical wind speed recorder. 2r, like 1 l.

1974, Jan. 10   Perf. 14½

464	A73	1 l olive & multi	.25	.25
465	A73	2 l multicolored	.25	.25
466	A73	3 l brt blue & multi	.35	.35
467	A73	4 l ocher & multi	.35	.35
468	A73	5 l ocher & multi	.35	.35
469	A73	2r ultra & multi	2.50	3.50
470	A73	3r orange & multi	4.00	3.00
		Nos. 464-470 (7)	8.05	8.05

Souvenir Sheet

| 471 | A73 | 10r lilac & multi | 9.00 | *11.50* |

World Meteorological Cooperation, cent.

Apollo Spacecraft, John F. Kennedy — A74

Designs: 2 l, 3r, Mercury spacecraft and John Glenn. 3 l, Vostok 1 and Yuri Gagarin. 4 l, Vostok 6 and Valentina Tereshkova. 5 l, Soyuz 11 and Salyut spacecrafts. 2r, Skylab. 10r, Like 1 l.

1974, Feb. 1   Litho.   Perf. 14½

472	A74	1 l multicolored	.25	.25
473	A74	2 l multicolored	.25	.25
474	A74	3 l multicolored	.35	.35
475	A74	4 l multicolored	.35	.35
476	A74	5 l multicolored	.35	.35
477	A74	2r multicolored	3.25	3.25
478	A74	3r multicolored	4.75	4.75
		Nos. 472-478 (7)	9.55	9.55

Souvenir Sheet

| 479 | A74 | 10r multicolored | 13.50 | *14.00* |

Space explorations of US and USSR.

Skylab and Copernicus — A75

Copernicus, Various Portraits and: 2 l, 1.50r, Futuristic orbiting station. 3 l, 5r, Futuristic flight station. 4 l, Mariner 2 on flight to Venus. 5 l, Mariner 4 on flight to Mars. 25 l, like 1 l. 10r, Copernicus Orbiting Observatory.

1974, Apr. 10   Litho.   Perf. 14½

480	A75	1 l multicolored	.25	.25
481	A75	2 l multicolored	.25	.25
482	A75	3 l multicolored	.25	.25
483	A75	4 l multicolored	.30	.30
484	A75	5 l multicolored	.30	.30
485	A75	25 l multicolored	1.00	1.00
486	A75	1.50r multicolored	3.50	3.50
487	A75	5r multicolored	6.75	6.75
		Nos. 480-487 (8)	12.60	12.60

Souvenir Sheet

| 488 | A75 | 10r multicolored | 19.00 | *21.00* |

"Motherhood," by Picasso — A76

Picasso Paintings: 2 l, Harlequin and his Companion. 3 l, Pierrot Sitting. 20 l, 2r, Three Musicians. 75 l, L'Aficionada. 3r, 5r, Still life.

1974, May   Perf. 14

489	A76	1 l multicolored	.30	.30
490	A76	2 l multicolored	.30	.30
491	A76	3 l multicolored	.30	.30
492	A76	20 l multicolored	.50	.30
493	A76	75 l multicolored	1.10	.80
494	A76	5r multicolored	4.75	4.75
		Nos. 489-494 (6)	7.25	6.75

Souvenir Sheet

495		Sheet of 2	9.50	9.50
a.	A76 2r multicolored		2.10	2.10
b.	A76 3r multicolored		3.25	3.25

Pablo Picasso (1881-1973), painter.

UPU Emblem, Old and New Trains A77

UPU Emblem and: 2 l, 2.50r, Old and new ships. 3 l, Zeppelin and jet. 1.50r, Mail coach and truck. 4r, 5r, Like 1 l.

1974, May   Litho.   Perf. 14½, 13½

496	A77	1 l lt green & multi	.30	.30
497	A77	2 l yellow & multi	.30	.30
498	A77	3 l rose & multi	.30	.30
499	A77	1.50r yel green & multi	1.00	1.00
500	A77	2.50r blue & multi	1.75	1.75
501	A77	5r ocher & multi	2.75	2.75
		Nos. 496-501 (6)	6.40	6.40

Souvenir Sheet

| 502 | A77 | 4r ver & multi | 6.75 | 6.75 |

UPU cent. No. 502 exists imperf.
Nos. 496-501 were printed in sheets of 50, perf. 14½, and also in sheets of 5 plus label, perf. 13½. The label shows UPU emblem, post horn, globe and carrier pigeon.

Capricorn A78

Designs: Zodiac signs and constellations.

1974, July 3

503	A78	1 l shown	.25	.25
504	A78	2 l Aquarius	.25	.25
505	A78	3 l Pisces	.25	.25
506	A78	4 l Aries	.25	.25
507	A78	5 l Taurus	.25	.25
508	A78	6 l Gemini	.25	.25
509	A78	7 l Cancer	.25	.25
510	A78	10 l Leo	.30	.30
511	A78	15 l Virgo	.30	.30
512	A78	20 l Libra	.30	.30
513	A78	25 l Scorpio	.30	.30
514	A78	5r Sagittarius	8.50	8.50
		Nos. 503-514 (12)	11.45	11.45

Souvenir Sheet

| 515 | A78 | 10r Sun | 22.50 | 22.50 |

Stamp size of 10r: 50x37mm.

Soccer and Games' Emblem — A79

Various soccer scenes & games' emblem.

1974, July 31   Litho.   Perf. 14½

516	A79	1 l brown & multi	.25	.25
517	A79	2 l green & multi	.25	.25
518	A79	3 l ultra & multi	.25	.25
519	A79	4 l red & multi	.25	.25
520	A79	75 l lt blue & multi	1.25	.75
521	A79	4r olive & multi	2.50	2.50
522	A79	5r lilac & multi	3.00	3.00
		Nos. 516-522 (7)	7.75	7.25

Souvenir Sheet

| 523 | A79 | 10r rose & multi | 12.50 | 12.50 |

World Cup Soccer Championship, Munich, June 13-July 7.

Churchill and WWII Plane A80

Churchill: 2 l, As pilot. 3 l, First Lord of the Admiralty and battleship. 4 l, 10r, Aircraft carrier. 5 l, RAF fighters. 60 l, Anti-aircraft unit. 75 l, Tank. 5r, Seaplane.

1974, Nov. 30   Litho.   Perf. 14½

524	A80	1 l multicolored	.25	.25
525	A80	2 l multicolored	.25	.25
526	A80	3 l multicolored	.30	.30
527	A80	4 l multicolored	.30	.30
528	A80	5 l multicolored	.30	.30
529	A80	60 l multicolored	3.25	3.25
530	A80	75 l multicolored	3.75	3.75
531	A80	5r multicolored	12.50	12.50
		Nos. 524-531 (8)	20.90	20.90

Souvenir Sheet

| 532 | A80 | 10r multicolored | 22.50 | 22.50 |

Sir Winston Churchill (1874-1965).

Cassis Nana — A81   Cypraea Diliculum — A82

1975, Jan. 25   Perf. 14½, 14 (A82)

533	A81	1 l shown	.30	.30
534	A81	2 l Murex triremis	.30	.30
535	A81	3 l Harpa major	.35	.35
536	A81	4 l Lambis chiragra	.35	.35
537	A81	5 l Conus pennaceus	.35	.35
538	A82	60 l shown	3.25	3.25
539	A82	75 l Clanculus pharaonis	3.75	3.75
540	A81	5r Chicoreus ramosus	8.50	8.50
		Nos. 533-540 (8)	17.15	17.15

Souvenir Sheet
Perf. 13½

541		Sheet of 2	14.50	14.50
a.	A81 2r like 3 l		3.75	3.75
b.	A81 3r like 2 l		4.75	4.75

Sea shells, including cowries.

Throne — A83

Eid-Miskith Mosque — A84

Designs: 10 l, Ornamental candlesticks (dul-lisa). 25 l, Tree-shaped lamp. 60 l, Royal umbrellas. 3r, Tomb of Al-Hafiz Abu-al Barakath al-Barubari.

1975, Feb. 22   Litho.   Perf. 14
542	A83	1 l multicolored	.25	.25
543	A83	10 l multicolored	.25	.25
544	A83	25 l multicolored	.25	.25
545	A83	60 l multicolored	.30	.30
546	A84	75 l multicolored	.40	.40
547	A84	3r multicolored	1.60	1.60
		Nos. 542-547 (6)	3.05	3.05

Historic relics and monuments.

Tropical Fruit — A85

1975, Mar.   Litho.   Perf. 14½
548	A85	2 l Guava	.25	.25
549	A85	4 l Maldive mulberry	.25	.25
550	A85	5 l Mountain apples	.25	.25
551	A85	10 l Bananas	.25	.25
552	A85	20 l Mangoes	.25	.25
553	A85	50 l Papaya	.90	.60
554	A85	1r Pomegranates	1.40	.65
555	A85	5r Coconut	7.25	9.50
		Nos. 548-555 (8)	10.80	12.00

Souvenir Sheet
Perf. 13½
556		Sheet of 2	11.00	12.00
a.		A85 2r like 10 l	2.75	3.25
b.		A85 3r like 2 l	3.25	3.75

Phyllangia — A86

Designs: Corals, sea urchins and starfish.

1975, June 6   Litho.   Perf. 14½
557	A86	1 l shown	.25	.25
558	A86	2 l Madrepora ocu-lata	.25	.25
559	A86	3 l Acropora gravida	.25	.25
560	A86	4 l Stylotella	.25	.25
561	A86	5 l Acropora cervicornis	.25	.25
562	A86	60 l Strongylocen-trotus pupuratus	.75	.65
563	A86	75 l Pisaster ochraceus	.90	.75
564	A86	5r Marthasterias glacialis	5.50	6.25
		Nos. 557-564 (8)	8.40	8.90

Souvenir Sheet
Imperf
565	A86	4r shown	14.00	14.00

"10," Clock Tower and Customs House A87

"10" and: 5 l, Government offices. 7 l, North Eastern waterfront, Male. 15 l, Mosque and Minaret. 10r, Sultan Park and Museum.

1975, July 26   Litho.   Perf. 14½
566	A87	4 l salmon & multi	.25	.25
567	A87	5 l lt blue & multi	.25	.25
568	A87	7 l bister & multi	.25	.25
569	A87	15 l lilac & multi	.25	.25
570	A87	10r lt green & multi	3.25	6.00
		Nos. 566-570 (5)	4.25	7.00

10th anniversary of independence.

Nos. 432-435 Overprinted

Overprint reads: "14th Boy Scout Jamboree / July 29-Aug. 7, 1975"

1975, July 26   Litho.   Perf. 14½
571	A69	1r multicolored	.65	.65
572	A69	2r multicolored	1.10	1.10
573	A69	3r multicolored	3.25	3.25
		Nos. 571-573 (3)	5.00	5.00

Souvenir Sheet
574	A69	5r multicolored	8.75	8.75

Nordjamb 75, 14th World Boy Scout Jamboree, Lillehammer, Norway, July 29-Aug. 7.

Madura-Prau Bedang — A88

Sailing ships, except 5r: 2 l, Ganges patile. 3 l, Indian palla, vert. 4 l, "Odhi," vert. 5 l, Maldivian schooner. 25 l, Cutty Sark. 1r, 10r, Maldivian baggala, vert. 5r, Freighter Maldive Courage.

1975, July 26   Perf. 14½
575	A88	1 l multicolored	.25	.25
576	A88	2 l multicolored	.25	.25
577	A88	3 l multicolored	.25	.25
578	A88	4 l multicolored	.25	.25
579	A88	5 l multicolored	.25	.25
580	A88	25 l multicolored	.65	.90
581	A88	1r multicolored	1.25	.75
582	A88	5r multicolored	3.25	6.00
		Nos. 575-582 (8)	6.40	8.30

Souvenir Sheet
Perf. 13½
583	A88	10r multicolored	11.50	13.00

Brahmaea Wallichii A89

Designs: Butterflies.

1975, Sept. 7   Litho.   Perf. 14½
584	A89	1 l shown	.25	.25
585	A89	2 l Teoinopalpus imperialis	.25	.25
586	A89	3 l Cethosia biblis	.30	.30
587	A89	4 l Hestia jasonia	.30	.30
588	A89	5 l Apatura	.30	.30
589	A89	25 l Kallima hor-sfieldi	1.50	1.50
590	A89	1.50r Hebomoia leucippe	4.00	4.00
591	A89	5r Papilio memnon	10.00	10.00
		Nos. 584-591 (8)	16.90	16.90

Souvenir Sheet
Perf. 13½
592	A89	10r like 25 l	25.00	25.00

Dying Slave by Michelangelo A90

Cup and Vase A91

Works by Michelangelo: 2 l, 4 l, 1r, 5r, paintings from Sistine Chapel. 3 l, Apollo. 5 l, Bacchus. 2r, 10r, David.

1975, Oct. 9   Litho.   Perf. 14½
593	A90	1 l blue & multi	.25	.25
594	A90	2 l multicolored	.25	.25
595	A90	3 l red & multi	.25	.25
596	A90	4 l multicolored	.25	.25
597	A90	5 l emerald & multi	.25	.25
598	A90	1r multicolored	.70	.70
599	A90	2r red & multi	1.40	1.40
600	A90	5r multicolored	3.75	3.75
		Nos. 593-600 (8)	7.10	7.10

Souvenir Sheet
Perf. 13½
601	A90	10r multicolored	6.75	7.50

Michelangelo Buonarotti (1475 1564), Italian sculptor, painter and architect.

1975, Dec.   Litho.   Perf. 14

Designs: 4 l, Boxes. 50 l, Vase with lid. 75 l, Bowls with covers. 1r, Worker finishing vases.
602	A91	2 l ultra & multi	.25	.25
603	A91	4 l rose & multi	.25	.25
604	A91	50 l multicolored	.25	.25
605	A91	75 l blue & multi	.35	.35
606	A91	1r multicolored	.45	.45
		Nos. 602-606 (5)	1.55	1.55

Maldivian lacquer ware.

Map of Islands and Atolls A92

Designs: 5 l, Yacht at anchor. 7 l, Sailboats. 15 l, Deep-sea divers and corals. 3r, Hulule Airport. 10r, Cruising yachts.

1975, Dec. 25   Litho.   Perf. 14
607	A92	1 l multicolored	.30	.30
608	A92	4 l multicolored	.30	.30
609	A92	7 l multicolored	.30	.30
610	A92	15 l multicolored	.30	.30
611	A92	3r multicolored	2.60	2.60
612	A92	10r multicolored	7.00	7.50
		Nos. 607-612 (6)	10.80	11.30

Tourist publicity.

Cross-country Skiing — A93

Gen. Burgoyne, by Joshua Reynolds — A94

Winter Olympic Games' Emblem and: 2 l, Speed skating. 3 l, Figure skating, pair. 4 l, Bobsled. 5 l, Ski jump. 25 l, Figure skating, woman. 1.15r, Slalom. 4r, Ice hockey. 10r, Skiing.

1976, Jan. 10   Litho.   Perf. 14½
613	A93	1 l multicolored	.30	.30
614	A93	2 l multicolored	.30	.30
615	A93	3 l multicolored	.30	.30
616	A93	4 l multicolored	.30	.30
617	A93	5 l multicolored	.30	.30
618	A93	25 l multicolored	.40	.30
619	A93	1.15r multicolored	.65	.65
620	A93	4r multicolored	2.00	2.00
		Nos. 613-620 (8)	4.55	4.45

Souvenir Sheet
Perf. 13½
621	A93	10r multicolored	8.00	10.00

12th Winter Olympic Games, Innsbruck, Austria, Feb. 4-15. Exist imperf.

1976, Feb. 15   Perf. 14½

Paintings: 2 l, John Hancock, by John S. Copley. 3 l, Death of Gen. Montgomery, by John Trumbull, horiz. 4 l, Paul Revere, by Copley. 5 l, Battle of Bunker Hill, by Trumbull, horiz. 2r, Crossing of the Delaware, by Thomas Sully, horiz. 3r, Samuel Adams, by Copley. 5r, Surrender of Cornwallis, by Trumbull, horiz. 10r, Washington at Dorchester Heights, by Gilbert Stuart.
622	A94	1 l multicolored	.25	.25
623	A94	2 l multicolored	.25	.25
624	A94	3 l multicolored	.25	.25
625	A94	4 l multicolored	.25	.25
626	A94	5 l multicolored	.25	.25
627	A94	2r multicolored	1.40	1.40
628	A94	3r multicolored	2.00	2.00
629	A94	5r multicolored	3.25	3.25
		Nos. 622-629 (8)	7.90	7.90

Souvenir Sheet
Perf. 13½
630	A94	10r multicolored	17.00	18.00

American Bicentennial.
For overprints see Nos. 639-642.

Thomas Alva Edison A95

Designs: 2 l, Alexander Graham Bell and his telephone. 3 l, Telephones of 1919, 1937 and 1972. 10 l, Cable tunnel. 20 l, Equalizer circuit assembly. 1r, Ships laying underwater cable. 4r, Telephones of 1876, 1890 and 1879 Edison telephone. 10r, Intelsat IV-A over earth station.

1976, Mar. 10   Litho.   Perf. 14½
631	A95	1 l multicolored	.25	.25
632	A95	2 l multicolored	.25	.25
633	A95	3 l multicolored	.25	.25
634	A95	10 l multicolored	.25	.25
635	A95	20 l multicolored	.25	.25
636	A95	1r multicolored	.65	.65
637	A95	10r multicolored	5.50	5.50
		Nos. 631-637 (7)	7.40	7.40

Souvenir Sheet
Perf. 13½
638	A95	4r multicolored	10.50	11.50

Centenary of first telephone call by Alexander Graham Bell, Mar. 10, 1876.

Nos. 627-630 Overprinted in Silver or Black

Overprint reads MAY 29TH-JUNE 6TH "INTERPHIL" 1976

1976, May 29   Litho.   Perf. 14½
639	A94	2r multicolored (S)	1.50	1.50
640	A94	3r multicolored (S)	2.00	2.00
641	A94	5r multicolored (B)	3.25	3.25
		Nos. 639-641 (3)	6.75	6.75

Souvenir Sheet
Perf. 13½
642	A94	10r multicolored (S)	12.00	12.00

Interphil 76 Intl. Philatelic Exhibition, Philadelphia, Pa., May 29-June 6. Overprint on 3r and 10r vertical. Same overprint in one horizontal silver line in margin of No. 642.

Wrestling — A96

Bonavist Beans — A97

Olympic Rings and: 2 l, Shot put. 3 l, Hurdles. 4 l, Hockey. 5 l, Women running. 6 l, Javelin. 1.50r, Discus. 5r, Volleyball. 10r, Hammer throw.

1976, June 1   *Perf. 14½*

643	A96	1 l multicolored	.25	.25
644	A96	2 l multicolored	.25	.25
645	A96	3 l salmon & multi	.25	.25
646	A96	4 l multicolored	.25	.25
647	A96	5 l pink & multi	.25	.25
648	A96	6 l multicolored	.25	.25
649	A96	1.50r bister & multi	1.00	1.00
650	A96	5r lilac & multi	3.00	4.25
		Nos. 643-650 (8)	5.50	6.75

Souvenir Sheet
Perf. 13½

651	A96	10r lemon & multi	8.75	11.00

21st Olympic Games, Montreal, Canada, July 17-Aug. 1.

1976-77   *Litho.*   *Perf. 14*

Designs: 4 l, 20 l, Beans. 10 l, Eggplant. 50 l, Cucumber. 75 l, 2r, Snake gourd. 1r, Balsam pear.

652	A97	2 l green & multi	.25	.25
653	A97	4 l lt blue & multi	.55	.55
654	A97	10 l ocher & multi	.55	.55
655	A97	20 l blue & multi ('77)	.55	.55
656	A97	50 l multicolored	.70	.70
657	A97	75 l bister & multi	.90	.90
658	A97	1r lilac & multi	1.30	1.30
659	A97	2r bis & multi ('77)	2.40	2.40
		Nos. 652-659 (8)	7.20	7.20

1976 stamps issued July 26.

Viking I and Mars — A98

Design: 20r, Landing craft on Mars.

1976, Dec. 2   *Litho.*   *Perf. 14*

660	A98	5r multicolored	2.75	2.75

Souvenir Sheet

661	A98	20r multicolored	16.00	13.00

Viking I US Mars Mission.

Coronation Ceremony — A99

Designs: 2 l, Elizabeth II and Prince Philip. 3 l, Queen, Prince Philip, Princes Edward and Andrew. 1.15r, Queen in procession. 3r, State coach. 4r, Queen, Prince Philip, Princess Anne and Prince Charles. 10r, Queen and Prince Charles.

1977, Feb. 6   *Perf. 14x13½, 12*

662	A99	1 l multicolored	.40	.40
663	A99	2 l multicolored	.40	.40
664	A99	3 l multicolored	.40	.40
665	A99	1.15r multicolored	.60	.60
666	A99	3r multicolored	1.25	1.50
667	A99	4r multicolored	1.25	1.60
		Nos. 662-667 (6)	4.30	4.90

Souvenir Sheet

668	A99	5.75	5.75

25th anniv. of the reign of Elizabeth II.
Nos. 662-667 were printed in sheets of 40 (4x10), perf. 14x13½, and sheets of 5 plus label, perf. 12, in changed colors.
Nos. 662-668 exist imperf. Value, set $12.50.

Beethoven in Bonn, 1785 — A100

Designs: 2 l, Moonlight Sonata and portrait, 1801. 3 l, Goethe and Beethoven, Teplitz, 1811. 4 l, Beethoven, 1815, and his string

instruments. 5 l, Beethoven House, Heiligenstadt, 1817. 25 l, Composer's hands, gold medal. 2r, Missa Solemnis, portrait, 1823. 4r, Piano, room where Beethoven died, death mask. 5r, Portrait, 1825, hearing aids.

1977, Mar. 26   *Litho.*   *Perf. 14*

669	A100	1 l multicolored	.25	.25
670	A100	2 l multicolored	.25	.25
671	A100	3 l multicolored	.35	.35
672	A100	4 l multicolored	.35	.35
673	A100	5 l multicolored	.35	.35
674	A100	25 l multicolored	1.25	1.25
675	A100	2r multicolored	3.50	3.50
676	A100	5r multicolored	7.00	7.00
		Nos. 669-676 (8)	13.30	13.30

Souvenir Sheet

677	A100	4r multicolored	9.50	10.50

Ludwig van Beethoven (1770-1827), composer, 150th death anniversary.

Electronic Tree and ITU Emblem A101

90 l, Central Telegraph Office, Maldives. 5r, Intelsat IV over map. 10r, Parabolic antenna, satellite communications earth station.

1977, May 17   *Litho.*   *Perf. 14*

678	A101	10 l multicolored	.25	.25
679	A101	90 l multicolored	.50	.50
680	A101	10r multicolored	4.50	6.00
		Nos. 678-680 (3)	5.25	6.75

Souvenir Sheet

681	A101	5r multicolored	6.25	6.25

Inauguration of Satellite Earth Station and for World Telecommunications Day.

Portrait by Gainsborough A102   Lesser Frigate Birds A103

Paintings: 2 l, 5 l, 10r, Rubens. 3 l, 95 l, 5r, Titian. 4 l, 1r, Gainsborough.

1977, May 20

682	A102	1 l multicolored	.25	.25
683	A102	2 l multicolored	.25	.25
684	A102	3 l multicolored	.25	.25
685	A102	4 l multicolored	.25	.25
686	A102	5 l multicolored	.25	.25
687	A102	95 l multicolored	.80	.60
688	A102	1r multicolored	.80	.65
689	A102	10r multicolored	4.00	6.00
		Nos. 682-689 (8)	6.85	8.50

Souvenir Sheet

690	A102	5r multicolored	4.75	5.50

Birth annivs. of Thomas Gainsborough; Peter Paul Rubens; Titian.

1977, July 26   *Litho.*   *Perf. 14½*

Birds: 2 l, Crab plovers. 3 l, Long-tailed tropic bird. 4 l, Wedge-tailed shearwater. 5 l, Gray heron. 20 l, White tern. 95 l, Cattle egret. 1.25r, Blacknaped terns. 5r, Pheasant coucals. 10r, Striated herons.

691	A103	2 l multicolored	.25	.25
692	A103	3 l multicolored	.25	.25
693	A103	3 l multicolored	.30	.30
694	A103	4 l multicolored	.30	.30
695	A103	5 l multicolored	.30	.30
696	A103	20 l multicolored	1.25	1.25
697	A103	95 l multicolored	2.50	2.50
698	A103	1.25r multicolored	3.50	3.50
699	A103	5r multicolored	6.50	6.50
		Nos. 691-699 (9)	15.15	15.15

Souvenir Sheet

700	A103	10r multicolored	32.50	32.50

Charles A. Lindbergh — A104

Designs: 2 l, Lindbergh and Spirit of St. Louis. 3 l, Mohawk plane, horiz. 4 l, Lebaudy l airship, 1902, horiz. 5 l, Count Ferdinand von Zeppelin, and Zeppelin in Pernambuco. 1r, Los Angeles, U. S. Navy airship, 1924, horiz. 3r, Henry Ford and Lindbergh, 1942. 5r, Spirit of St. Louis, Statue of Liberty and Eiffel Tower, horiz. 7.50r, German naval airship over battleship, horiz. 10r, Vickers airship, 1917.

Perf. 13x13½, 13½x13

1977, Oct. 31   *Litho.*

701	A104	1 l multicolored	.25	.25
702	A104	2 l multicolored	.25	.25
703	A104	3 l multicolored	.25	.25
704	A104	4 l multicolored	.25	.25
705	A104	5 l multicolored	.25	.25
706	A104	1r multicolored	.60	.30
707	A104	3r multicolored	1.40	1.60
708	A104	10r multicolored	3.25	5.25
		Nos. 701-708 (8)	6.50	8.40

Souvenir Sheet

709		Sheet of 2	16.00	16.00
a.	A104	5r multicolored	3.75	3.75
b.	A104	7.50r multicolored	4.75	4.75

Charles A. Lindbergh's solo transatlantic flight from New York to Paris, 50th anniv., and 75th anniv. of first navigable airship.

Boat Building A105

Maldivian Occupations: 15 l, High sea fishing. 20 l, Cadjan weaving. 90 l, Mat weaving. 2r, Lacemaking, vert.

1977, Dec. 12

710	A105	6 l multicolored	.85	.85
711	A105	15 l multicolored	1.50	1.50
712	A105	20 l multicolored	1.75	1.75
713	A105	90 l multicolored	4.00	4.00
714	A105	2r multicolored	6.50	6.50
		Nos. 710-714 (5)	14.60	14.60

Rheumatic Heart — A106

X-Ray Pictures: 50 l, Shoulder. 2r, Hand. 3r, Knee.

1978, Feb. 9   *Perf. 14*

715	A106	1 l multicolored	.25	.25
716	A106	50 l multicolored	.25	.25
717	A106	2r multicolored	1.00	1.00
718	A106	3r multicolored	1.25	1.25
		Nos. 715-718 (4)	2.75	2.75

World Rheumatism Year.

Otto Lilienthal's Glider, 1890 — A107

Designs: 2 l, Chanute's glider, 1896. 3 l, Wright brothers testing glider, 1900. 4 l, A. V. Roe's plane with paper-covered wings, 1908. 5 l, Wilbur Wright showing his plane to King Alfonso of Spain, 1909. 10 l, Roe's second biplane. 20 l, Alexander Graham Bell and

Wright brothers in Washington D.C., 1910. 95 l, Clifton Hadley's triplane, 1910. 5r, British B.E.2 planes, Upavon Field, 1914. 10r, Wilbur Wright flying first motorized plane, 1903.

1978, Feb. 27   *Litho.*   *Perf. 13x13½*

719	A107	1 l multicolored	.30	.35
720	A107	2 l multicolored	.30	.35
721	A107	3 l multicolored	.30	.35
722	A107	4 l multicolored	.35	.35
723	A107	5 l multicolored	.35	.35
724	A107	10 l multicolored	.90	.90
725	A107	20 l multicolored	2.00	2.00
726	A107	95 l multicolored	4.50	4.50
727	A107	5r multicolored	11.50	11.50
		Nos. 719-727 (9)	20.50	20.65

Souvenir Sheet
Perf. 14

728	A107	10r multicolored	15.00	16.00

75th anniversary of first motorized airplane.

Edward Jenner, Vaccination Discoverer A108

Designs: 15 l, Foundling Hospital, London, where children were first inoculated, 1743, horiz. 50 l, Newgate Prison, London, where first experiments were carried out, 1721.

1978, Mar. 15   *Perf. 14*

729	A108	15 l multicolored	.65	.30
730	A108	50 l multicolored	1.25	.65
731	A108	2r multicolored	2.75	2.75
		Nos. 729-731 (3)	4.65	3.70

World eradication of smallpox.

TV with Maldives Broadcasting Symbol — A109

Designs: 25 l, Circuit pattern. 1.50r, Station control panel, horiz.

1978, Mar. 29

732	A109	15 l multicolored	.55	.55
733	A109	25 l multicolored	.80	.80
734	A109	1.50r multicolored	3.00	3.00
		Nos. 732-734 (3)	4.35	4.35

Inauguration of Maldive Islands television.

Sailing Ship — A110

Ships: 1 l, Phoenician. 2 l, Two-master. 5 l, Freighter Maldive Trader. 1r, Trading schooner. 1.25r, 4r, Sailing boat. 3r, Barque Bangala. (1 l, 2 l, 5 l, 1.25r, 4r, horiz.)

1978, Apr. 27   *Litho.*   *Perf. 14½*

735	A110	1 l multicolored	.25	.25
736	A110	2 l multicolored	.25	.25
737	A110	3 l multicolored	.25	.25
738	A110	5 l multicolored	.25	.25
739	A110	1r multicolored	.50	.50
740	A110	1.25r multicolored	.85	.85
741	A110	3r multicolored	1.40	1.40
742	A110	4r multicolored	1.40	1.40
a.		Souvenir sheet of 2	4.25	4.25
		Nos. 735-742 (8)	5.15	5.15

No. 742a contains No. 742 and a 1r stamp in the design of No. 736.

The Ampulla — A111

Designs: 2 l, Scepter with dove. 3 l, Orb with cross. 1.15r, St. Edward's crown. 2r, Scepter with cross. 5r, Queen Elizabeth II. 10r, Anointing spoon.

1978, May 15   **Perf. 14**
743 A111   1 l multicolored   .25   .25
744 A111   2 l multicolored   .25   .25
745 A111   3 l multicolored   .25   .25
746 A111   1.15r multicolored   .25   .25
747 A111   2r multicolored   .30   .30
748 A111   5r multicolored   .60   .60
      Nos. 743-748 (6)   1.90   1.90

Souvenir Sheet

749 A111   10r multicolored   2.00   2.00

Coronation of Elizabeth II, 25th anniv. Nos. 743-748 were printed in sheets of 40 and in sheets of 3 + label, in changed colors. Labels show coronation regalia.

Capt. James Cook — A112

Designs: 2 l, Kamehameha I statue, Honolulu. 3 l, "Endeavour" and boat. 25 l, Capt. Cook and route of his 3rd voyage. 75 l, "Discovery" and "Resolution," map of Hawaiian Islands, horiz. 1.50r, Capt. Cook's first meeting with Hawaiians, horiz. 5r, "Endeavour." 10r, Capt. Cook's death, horiz.

1978, July 15   Litho.   Perf. 14½
750 A112   1 l multicolored   .25   .25
751 A112   2 l multicolored   .25   .25
752 A112   3 l multicolored   .25   .25
753 A112   25 l multicolored   .50   .35
754 A112   75 l multicolored   1.10   1.10
755 A112   1.50r multicolored   1.50   1.50
756 A112   10r multicolored   6.00   9.00
      Nos. 750-756 (7)   9.85   12.70

Souvenir Sheet

757 A112   5r multicolored   19.00 20.00

Schizophrys Aspera — A113

Maldivian Crabs and Lobster: 2 l, Atergatis floridus. 3 l, Percnon planissimum. 90 l, Portunus granulatus. 1r, Carpilius maculatus. No. 763, Huenia proteus. No. 765, Panulirus longipes, vert. 25r, Etisus laevimanus.

1978, Aug. 30   Litho.   Perf. 14
758 A113   1 l multicolored   .25   .25
759 A113   2 l multicolored   .25   .25
760 A113   3 l multicolored   .25   .25
761 A113   90 l multicolored   .60   .40
762 A113   1r multicolored   .60   .40
763 A113   2r multicolored   .90   1.40
764 A113   25r multicolored   7.00   10.00
      Nos. 758-764 (7)   9.85   12.95

Souvenir Sheet

765 A113   2r multicolored   3.25   3.25

Four Apostles, by Dürer — A114

Paintings by Albrecht Dürer (1471-1528): 20 l, Self-portrait, age 27. 55 l, Virgin and Child with Pear. 1r, Rhinoceros, horiz. 1.80r, Hare. 3r, The Great Piece of Turf. 10r, Columbine.

1978, Oct. 28   Litho.   Perf. 14
766 A114   10 l multicolored   .25   .25
767 A114   20 l multicolored   .25   .25
768 A114   55 l multicolored   .25   .25
769 A114   1r multicolored   .30   .30
770 A114   1.80r multicolored   .60   .60
771 A114   3r multicolored   .90   .90
      Nos. 766-771 (6)   2.55   2.55

Souvenir Sheet

772 A114   10r multicolored   5.25   5.25

Palms and Fishing Boat A115

Designs: 5 l, Montessori School. 10 l, TV tower and ITU emblem, vert. 25 l, Island with beach. 50 l, Boeing 737 over island. 95 l, Walk along the beach. 1.25r, Fishing boat at dawn. 2r, Presidential residence. 3r, Fishermen preparing nets. 5r, Afeefuddin Mosque.

1978, Nov. 11   Litho.   Perf. 14½
773 A115   1 l multicolored   .25   .25
774 A115   5 l multicolored   .25   .25
775 A115   10 l multicolored   .25   .25
776 A115   25 l multicolored   .25   .25
777 A115   50 l multicolored   .25   .25
778 A115   95 l multicolored   .30   .25
779 A115   1.25r multicolored   .50   .50
780 A115   2r multicolored   .65   1.10
781 A115   3r multicolored   1.25   2.25
      Nos. 773-781 (9)   3.95   5.35

Souvenir Sheet

782 A115   3r multicolored   3.00   3.00

10th anniversary of Republic.

Human Rights Emblem A116

1978, Dec. 10   Perf. 14
783 A116   30 l multicolored   .25   .25
784 A116   90 l multicolored   .40   .50
785 A116   1.80r multicolored   .65   1.00
      Nos. 783-785 (3)   1.30   1.75

Universal Declaration of Human Rights, 30th anniversary.

Rare Spotted Cowrie — A117

Bellman Delivering Mail — A118

Sea Shells: 2 l, Imperial cone. 3 l, Green turban. 10 l, Giant spider conch. 1r, Leucodon cowrie. 1.80r, Fig cone. 3r, Glory of the sea. 5r, Top vase.

1979, Jan.   Litho.   Perf. 14
786 A117   1 l multicolored   .25   .25
787 A117   2 l multicolored   .25   .25
788 A117   3 l multicolored   .35   .35
789 A117   10 l multicolored   .55   .55
790 A117   1r multicolored   2.40   2.40
791 A117   1.80r multicolored   3.25   3.25
792 A117   3r multicolored   5.50   5.50
      Nos. 786-792 (7)   12.55 12.55

Souvenir Sheet

793 A117   5r multicolored   14.00 14.00

1979, Feb. 28   Litho.   Perf. 14
Designs: 2 l, Royal mail coach, 1840, horiz. 3 l, First London letter box, 1855. 1.55r, Great Britain No. 1 and post horn. 5r, Maldive Islands No. 5 and carrier pigeon. 10r, Rowland Hill.

794 A118   1 l multicolored   .30   .30
795 A118   2 l multicolored   .30   .30
796 A118   3 l multicolored   .30   .30
797 A118   1.55r multicolored   .45   .45
798 A118   5r multicolored   1.20   1.20
      Nos. 794-798 (5)   2.55   2.55

Souvenir Sheet

799 A118   10r multicolored   2.75   3.25

Sir Rowland Hill (1795-1879), originator of penny postage.
For overprints see Nos. 853-855.

Girl with Teddy Bear — A119

IYC Emblem, Boy and: 1.25r, Model boat. 2r, Rocket launcher. 3r, Blimp. 5r, Train.

1979, May 10   Litho.   Perf. 14
800 A119   5 l multicolored   .25   .25
801 A119   1.25r multicolored   .40   .40
802 A119   2r multicolored   .50   .50
803 A119   3r multicolored   .65   .65
      Nos. 800-803 (4)   1.80   1.80

Souvenir Sheet

804 A119   5r multicolored   1.60   1.60

International Year of the Child.

White Feathers, by Matisse A120

Paintings by Henri Matisse (1869-1954): 25 l, Joy of Life. 30 l, Eggplants. 1.50r, Harmony in Red. 4r, Water Pitcher. 5r, Still-life.

1979, Aug. 20   Litho.   Perf. 14
805 A120   20 l multicolored   .30   .30
806 A120   25 l multicolored   .30   .30
807 A120   30 l multicolored   .30   .30
808 A120   1.50r multicolored   .65   .65
809 A120   5r multicolored   1.75   1.75
      Nos. 805-809 (5)   3.30   3.30

Souvenir Sheet

810 A120   4r multicolored   4.25   4.25

Sari and Mosque — A121

Gloriosa Superba — A122

National Costumes: 75 l, Sashed apron dress. Male Harbor. 90 l, Serape with necklace, radar station. 95 l, Flowered dress, mosque and minaret.

1979, Aug. 22   Litho.   Perf. 14
811 A121   50 l multicolored   .25   .25
812 A121   75 l multicolored   .25   .25
813 A121   90 l multicolored   .30   .30
814 A121   95 l multicolored   .35   .35
      Nos. 811-814 (4)   1.15   1.15

1979, Oct. 29   Litho.   Perf. 14
815 A122   1 l shown   .25   .25
816 A122   3 l Hibiscus   .25   .25
817 A122   50 l Barringtonia asiatica .25 .25
818 A122   1r Abutilon indicum   .40   .40
819 A122   5r Guettarda speciosa   1.60   1.60
      Nos. 815-819 (5)   2.75   2.75

Souvenir Sheet

820 A122   4r Pandanus odoratissimus   2.40   2.40

Maldive wildflowers.

Handicraft Exhibition A123

1979, Nov. 11
821 A123   5 l shown   .25   .25
822 A123   10 l Jar and cup   .25   .25
823 A123   1.30r Tortoise-shell jewelry .55   .55
824 A123   2r Wooden boxes   .75   .75
      Nos. 821-824 (4)   1.80   1.80

Souvenir Sheet

825 A123   5r Bracelets, necklace   1.60   1.60

Postal Scenes A123a

1 l, Goofy delivering package. 2 l, Mickey at mailbox. 3 l, Goofy buried in letters. 4 l, Minnie Mouse, Pluto. 5 l, Mickey Mouse on skates. 10 l, Donald Duck at mailbox. 15 l, Chip and Dale carrying letter. 1.50r, Donald Duck on unicycle. 4r, Pluto at mailbox. 5r, Donald Duck wheeling crate.

1979, Dec.   Litho.   Perf. 11
826 A123a   1 l multicolored   .25   .25
827 A123a   2 l multicolored   .25   .25
828 A123a   3 l multicolored   .25   .25
829 A123a   4 l multicolored   .25   .25
830 A123a   5 l multicolored   .25   .25
831 A123a   10 l multicolored   .25   .25
832 A123a   15 l multicolored   .25   .25
833 A123a   1.50r multicolored   .85   .85
834 A123a   5r multicolored   2.40   2.75
      Nos. 826-834 (9)   5.00   5.35

Souvenir Sheet

835 A123a   4r multicolored   7.50   7.50

National Day A124

Designs: 5 l, Post Ramadan dancing. 15 l, Festival of Eeduu. 95 l, Sultan's ceremonial band. 2r, Music festival. 5r, Sword dance.

1980, Jan. 19   Litho.   Perf. 14
836 A124   5 l multicolored   .25   .25
837 A124   15 l multicolored   .25   .25
838 A124   95 l multicolored   .35   .35
839 A124   2r multicolored   .70   .70
      Nos. 836-839 (4)   1.55   1.55

Souvenir Sheet

840 A124   5r multicolored   2.00   2.00

A157

1984, Feb.   **Perf. 14**
1015	A157	50 l Baseball	.25	.25
1016	A157	1.55r Swimming	.70	.70
1017	A157	3r Judo	1.25	1.25
1018	A157	4r Shot put	1.75	1.75
		Nos. 1015-1018 (4)	3.95	3.95

Souvenir Sheet
| 1019 | A157 | 10r Handball | 4.25 | 4.25 |

23rd Olympic Games, Los Angeles, 7/28-8/12.
For overprints see Nos. 1090-1094.

Nos. 982-984 Overprinted

Overprint reads "19th UPU/CONGRESS HAMBURG"

1984   **Litho.**   **Perf. 14**
| 1020 | A150 | 4r multicolored | 1.75 | 1.75 |
| 1021 | A150 | 5r multicolored | 2.25 | 2.25 |

Souvenir Sheet
| 1022 | A150 | 10r multicolored | 4.75 | 4.75 |

Tourism — A158

1984, Sept. 21   **Litho.**   **Perf. 14½**
1023	A158	7 l Island resorts	.45	.45
1024	A158	15 l Cruising	.45	.45
1025	A158	20 l Snorkelling	.45	.45
1026	A158	2r Wind surfing	1.10	1.10
1027	A158	4r Scuba diving	2.25	2.25
1028	A158	6r Night fishing	3.50	3.50
1029	A158	8r Big game fishing	4.50	4.50
1030	A158	10r Nature (turtle)	5.50	5.50
		Nos. 1023-1030 (8)	18.20	18.20

50th Anniv. of Donald Duck — A160

Scenes from various cartoons and movies.

1984, Nov.   **Litho.**   **Perf. 14**
1040	A160	3 l multi	.25	.25
1041	A160	4 l multi	.25	.25
1042	A160	5 l multi	.25	.25
1043	A160	10 l multi	.25	.25
1044	A160	15 l multi	.25	.25
1045	A160	25 l multi	.25	.25
1045A	A160	5r multi, perf. 12x12 ½	2.00	2.00
1046	A160	8r multi	3.00	3.00
1047	A160	10r multi	4.00	4.00
		Nos. 1040-1047 (9)	10.50	10.50

Souvenir Sheets
| 1048 | A160 | 15r multi | 5.00 | 5.00 |
| 1049 | A160 | 15r multi | 5.00 | 5.00 |

Nos. 952-955, 966-969 Surcharged

1984, July   **Litho.**   **Perf. 14½x14**
1050	CD332	1.45r on 95 l #952	2.50	2.00
1051	CD332	1.45r on 95 l #966	2.50	2.00
1052	CD332	1.45r on 3r #953	2.50	2.00
1053	CD332	1.45r on 3r #967	2.50	2.00
1054	CD332	1.45r on 5r #954	2.50	2.00
1055	CD332	1.45r on 5r #968	2.50	2.00
		Nos. 1050-1055 (6)	15.00	12.00

Souvenir Sheet
| 1056 | CD332 | 1.45r on 8r #955 | 10.00 | 8.00 |
| 1057 | CD332 | 1.45r on 8r #969 | 10.00 | 8.00 |

Namibia Day
A161

1984, Aug. 26   **Perf. 15**
| 1058 | A161 | 6r Breaking chain | 1.50 | 1.50 |
| 1059 | A161 | 8r Family, rising sun | 2.00 | 2.00 |

Souvenir Sheet
| 1060 | A161 | 10r Map, sun | 3.25 | 3.25 |

Ausipex '84
A162

1984, Sept. 21
| 1061 | A162 | 5r Frangipani | 3.00 | 3.00 |
| 1062 | A162 | 10r Cooktown orchid | 6.25 | 6.25 |

Souvenir Sheet
| 1063 | A162 | 15r Sun orchids | 14.00 | 14.00 |

150th Birth Anniv. of Edgar Degas — A163

1984, Oct.   **Litho.**   **Perf. 14**
1064	A163	75 l Portrait of Edmond Duranty	.25	.25
1065	A163	2r Portrait of James Tissot	.55	.55
1066	A163	5r Portrait of Achille Degas	1.25	1.25
1067	A163	10r Lady with Chrysanthemums	2.40	2.40
		Nos. 1064-1067 (4)	4.45	4.45

Souvenir Sheet
| 1068 | A163 | 15r Self-Portrait | 4.75 | 4.75 |

Opening of Islamic Center A164

1984, Nov. 11   **Litho.**   **Perf. 15**
| 1069 | A164 | 2r Mosque | .65 | .65 |
| 1070 | A164 | 5r Mosque, minaret, vert. | 1.50 | 1.50 |

40th Anniv., International Civil Aviation Organization — A165

1984, Nov. 19   **Litho.**   **Perf. 14**
1071	A165	7 l Boeing 737	.35	.35
1072	A165	4r Lockheed L-1011	2.40	2.40
1073	A165	6r McDonnell Douglas DC-10	3.25	3.25
1074	A165	8r Lockheed L-1011	4.00	4.00
		Nos. 1071-1074 (4)	10.00	10.00

Souvenir Sheet
| 1075 | A165 | 15r Shorts SC7 Skyvan | 5.50 | 5.50 |

450th Anniv. of the Death of Correggio — A166

1984, Dec. 10   **Litho.**   **Perf. 14**
| 1076 | A166 | 5r Detail from The Day | 1.25 | 1.25 |
| 1077 | A166 | 10r Detail from The Night | 2.50 | 2.50 |

Souvenir Sheet
| 1078 | A166 | 15r Portrait of a Man | 5.00 | 5.00 |

John J. Audubon A167

Illustrations from Audubon's Birds of America.

1985, Mar. 9   **Litho.**   **Perf. 14**
1079	A167	3r Flesh-footed shearwater, vert.	2.10	1.10
1080	A167	3.50r Little grebe	2.60	1.25
1081	A167	4r Great cormorant, vert.	2.60	1.40
1082	A167	4.50r White-faced storm petrel	2.60	1.50
		Nos. 1079-1082 (4)	9.90	5.25

Souvenir Sheet
| 1083 | A167 | 15r Red-necked phalarope | 6.00 | 6.00 |

See Nos. 1195-1204.

Natl. Security Services — A168

1985, June 6   **Litho.**   **Perf. 14**
1084	A168	15 l Drill	.50	.30
1085	A168	20 l Combat training	.50	.30
1086	A168	1r Fire fighting	2.10	.45
1087	A168	2r Coast guard	2.50	.90
1088	A168	10r Parade, tent	3.25	4.00
		Nos. 1084-1088 (5)	8.85	5.95

Souvenir Sheet
| 1089 | A168 | 10r Badge, cannon | 3.75 | 3.75 |

Nos. 1015-1019 Overprinted

Overprint includes Country or "Gold Medalist," Winner and Nation in 3 Lines

1985, July 17
1090	A157	50 l Japan	.30	.30
1091	A157	1.55r Theresa Andrews	.55	.55
1092	A157	3r Frank Wieneke	1.10	1.10
1093	A157	4r Claudia Loch	1.60	1.60
		Nos. 1090-1093 (4)	3.55	3.55

Souvenir Sheet
| 1094 | A157 | 10r US | 3.00 | 3.00 |

Queen Mother, 85th Birthday A169   Johann Sebastian Bach, Composer A170

1985-86   **Perf. 14, 12 (1r, 4r, 10r)**
1095	A169	1r Wearing tiara	.45	.45
1096	A169	3r like 1r	.55	.55
1097	A169	4r At Middlesex Hospital, horiz.	.65	.65
1098	A169	5r like 4r	.90	.90
1099	A169	7r Wearing fur stole	1.10	1.10
1100	A169	10r like 7r	1.75	1.75
		Nos. 1095-1100 (6)	5.40	5.40

Souvenir Sheet
| 1101 | A169 | 15r With Prince of Wales | 3.50 | 3.50 |

Issued: 1r, 4r, 10r, 1/4/86; 3r, 5r, 7r, 15r, 8/20/85. Nos. 1095, 1097, 1100 printed in sheets of 5 + label.

1985, Sept. 3   **Perf. 14**

Portrait, Invention No. 1 in C Major and: 15 l, Lira da Braccio. 2r, Tenor oboe. 4r, Serpent. 10r, Table organ.
1102	A170	15 l multi	.25	.25
1103	A170	2r multi	.65	.65
1104	A170	4r multi	1.10	1.10
1105	A170	10r multi	2.25	2.25
		Nos. 1102-1105 (4)	4.25	4.25

Souvenir Sheet
| 1106 | A170 | 15r Portrait | 4.25 | 4.25 |

Ships A171

1985, Sept. 23
1107	A171	3 l Masodi	.25	.25
1108	A171	5 l Naalu Baththeli	.25	.25
1109	A171	10 l Addu Odi	.30	.30
1110	A171	2.60r Masdhoni, 2nd generation	1.00	1.00
1111	A171	2.70r Masdhoni	1.00	1.00
1112	A171	3r Baththeli Dhoni	1.10	1.10
1113	A171	5r Inter 1	1.75	1.75
1114	A171	10r Yacht Dhoni	3.50	3.50
		Nos. 1107-1114 (8)	9.15	9.15

For surcharge, see No. 1493B.

World Tourism Org., 10th Anniv. A172

1985, Oct. 2
| 1115 | A172 | 6r Wind surfing | 2.50 | 2.50 |
| 1116 | A172 | 8r Scuba diving | 3.75 | 3.75 |

Souvenir Sheet
| 1117 | A172 | 15r Kuda Hithi Resort | 5.00 | 5.00 |

Maldives Admission to UN, 20th Anniv. — A173

1985, Oct. 24
| 1118 | A173 | 20 l shown | .25 | .25 |
| 1119 | A173 | 15r Flags, UN building | 3.75 | 3.75 |

UN 40th Anniv., Intl. Peace Year A174

1985, Oct. 24   **Litho.**   **Perf. 14**
1120	A174	15 l	UN Building	.25	.25
1121	A174	2r	IPY emblem	.65	.65
1122	A174	4r	Security Council	1.10	1.10
1123	A174	10r	Lion, lamb	1.90	1.90
			Nos. 1120-1123 (4)	3.90	3.90

Souvenir Sheet
1124	A174	15r	UN Building, diff.	3.25	3.25

Nos. 1120-1121, 1123-1124, vert.

Intl. Youth Year A175

1985, Nov. 20   **Perf. 15**
1125	A175	90 l	Culture	.35	.35
1126	A175	6r	Games	1.25	1.25
1127	A175	10r	Community service, vert.	1.75	2.50
			Nos. 1125-1127 (3)	3.35	4.10

Souvenir Sheet
1128	A175	15r	Youth camp, vert.	3.25	3.25

Summit Nations Flags, Dedication by Pres. Maumoon — A176

1985, Dec. 8   **Perf. 14**
1129	A176	3r	multicolored	2.25	2.25

South Asian Regional Cooperation, SARC, 1st Summit, Dec. 7-8, 1985.

Tuna A177

1985, Dec. 10
1130	A177	25 l	Frigate	.45	.45
1131	A177	75 l	Little tuna	.90	.90
1132	A177	3r	Dogtooth	2.75	2.75
1133	A177	5r	Yellowfin	3.25	3.25
			Nos. 1130-1133 (4)	7.35	7.35

Souvenir Sheet
1134	A177	15r	Skipjack	7.00	7.00

Fisherman's Day.

Mark Twain, American Novelist A178

Disney characters and Twain quotes.

1985, Dec. 21
1135	A178	2 l	multicolored	.25	.25
1136	A178	3 l	multicolored	.25	.25
1137	A178	4 l	multicolored	.30	.30
1138	A178	20 l	multicolored	.50	.50
1139	A178	4r	multicolored	1.60	1.60
1140	A178	13r	multicolored	5.00	5.00
			Nos. 1135-1140 (6)	7.90	7.90

Souvenir Sheet
1141	A178	15r	multicolored	7.50	7.50

Intl. Youth Year. 4r issued in sheet of 8.

The Brothers Grimm — A179

Disney characters in Doctor Knowall.

1985, Dec. 21
1142	A179	1 l	multicolored	.25	.25
1143	A179	5 l	multicolored	.25	.25
1144	A179	10 l	multicolored	.30	.30
1145	A179	15 l	multicolored	.30	.30
1146	A179	3r	multicolored	1.40	1.40
1147	A179	14r	multicolored	5.75	5.75
			Nos. 1142-1147 (6)	8.25	8.25

Souvenir Sheet
1148	A179	15r	multicolored	7.00	7.00

3r issued in sheets of 8.

World Disarmament Day — A180

1986, Feb. 10   **Perf. 14½x14**
1149	A180	1.50r shown		40.00	40.00
1150	A180	10r	Dove	40.00	40.00

Halley's Comet A181

Designs: 20 l, NASA space telescope. 1.50r, Giotto space probe. 2r, Plant-A probe, Japan. 4r, Edmond Halley, Stonehenge. 5r, Vega probe, USSR. 15r, Comet over Male.

1986, Apr. 29
1151	A181	20 l	multicolored	.65	.65
1152	A181	1.50r	multicolored	1.40	1.40
1153	A181	2r	multicolored	1.75	1.75
1154	A181	4r	multicolored	2.25	2.25
1155	A181	5r	multicolored	2.25	2.25
			Nos. 1151-1155 (5)	8.30	8.30

Souvenir Sheet
1156	A181	15r	multicolored	8.50	8.50

See Nos. 1210-1215.

Statue of Liberty, Cent. A182

Detail of statue and: 50 l, Walter Gropius (1883-1969), architect. 70 l, John Lennon (1940-1980), musician. 1r, George Balanchine (1904-1983), choreographer. 10r, Franz Werfel (1890-1945), writer. 15r, Close-up of statue, vert.

1986, May 5
1157	A182	50 l	multicolored	.45	.45
1158	A182	70 l	multicolored	1.90	1.90
1159	A182	1r	multicolored	2.00	2.00
1160	A182	10r	multicolored	4.50	4.50
			Nos. 1157-1160 (4)	8.85	8.85

Souvenir Sheet
1161	A182	15r	multicolored	8.50	8.50

AMERIPEX '86 — A183

US stamps and Disney portrayals of American legends: 3 l, #1317, Johnny Appleseed. 4 l, #1122, Paul Bunyan. 5 l, #1381, Casey at the Bat. 10 l, #. 1548, Tales of Sleepy Hollow. 15 l, #922, John Henry. 20 l, #1061, Windwagon Smith. 13r, #1409, Mike Fink. 14r, #993, Casey Jones. No. 1170, Remember the Alamo, #1330. No. 1171, Pocahontas, #328-330.

1986, May 22   **Perf. 11**
1162	A183	3 l	multicolored	.25	.25
1163	A183	4 l	multicolored	.25	.25
1164	A183	5 l	multicolored	.30	.30
1165	A183	10 l	multicolored	.30	.30
1166	A183	15 l	multicolored	.30	.30
1167	A183	20 l	multicolored	.30	.30
1168	A183	13r	multicolored	8.25	8.25
1169	A183	14r	multicolored	9.50	9.50
			Nos. 1162-1169 (8)	19.45	19.45

Souvenir Sheets
Perf. 14
1170	A183	15r	multicolored	8.00	8.00
1171	A183	15r	multicolored	8.00	8.00

Queen Elizabeth II, 60th Birthday
Common Design Type

1986, May 29   **Perf. 14**
1172	CD339	1r	Girl Guides' rally, 1938	.25	.25
1173	CD339	2r	Canada visit, 1985	.50	.50
1174	CD339	12r	At Sandringham, 1970	2.50	2.50
			Nos. 1172-1174 (3)	3.25	3.25

Souvenir Sheet
1175	CD339	15r	Royal Lodge, 1940	3.75	3.75

For overprints see Nos. 1288-1291.

1986 World Cup Soccer Championships, Mexico — A184

Various soccer plays.

1986, June 18   **Litho.**   **Perf. 14**
1176	A184	15 l	multicolored	.85	.85
1177	A184	2r	multicolored	2.50	2.50
1178	A184	4r	multicolored	4.00	4.00
1179	A184	10r	multicolored	7.50	7.50
			Nos. 1176-1179 (4)	14.85	14.85

Souvenir Sheet
1180	A184	15r	multicolored	6.75	6.75

For overprints see Nos. 1205-1209.

Royal Wedding Issue, 1986
Common Design Type

Designs: 10 l, Prince Andrew and Sarah Ferguson. 2r, Andrew. 12r, Andrew on ship's deck in uniform. 15r, Couple, diff.

1986, July 23
1181	CD340	10 l	multi	.25	.25
1182	CD340	2r	multi	.70	.70
1183	CD340	12r	multi	4.00	4.00
			Nos. 1181-1183 (3)	4.95	4.95

Souvenir Sheet
1184	CD340	15r	multi	5.25	5.25

Marine Life A185

Designs: 50 l, Sea fan, moorish idol. 90 l, Regal angelfish. 1r, Anemone fish. 2r, Stinging coral, tiger cowrie. 3r, Emperor angelfish, staghorn coral. 4r, Black-naped tern. 5r, Fiddler crab, staghorn coral. 10r, Hawksbill turtle. No. 1193, Trumpet fish. No. 1194, Long-nosed butterflyfish.

1986, Sept. 22   **Litho.**   **Perf. 15**
1185	A185	50 l	multicolored	1.50	1.50
1186	A185	90 l	multicolored	2.25	2.25
1187	A185	1r	multicolored	2.50	2.50
1188	A185	2r	multicolored	2.75	2.75
1189	A185	3r	multicolored	3.25	3.25
1190	A185	4r	multicolored	2.75	2.75
1191	A185	5r	multicolored	2.75	2.75
1192	A185	10r	multicolored	3.50	3.50
			Nos. 1185-1192 (8)	21.25	21.25

Souvenir Sheets
1193	A185	15r	multicolored	8.50	8.50
1194	A185	15r	multicolored	8.50	8.50

Nos. 1185-1187 and 1189 show the World Wildlife Fund emblem.

Audubon Type of 1985

Birds: 3 l, Little blue heron. 4 l, White-tailed kite, vert. 5 l, Greater shearwater. 10 l, Magnificent frigatebird, vert. 15 l, Eared grebe, vert. 20 l, Common merganser, vert. 13r, Great-footed hawk. 14r, Greater prairie chicken. No. 1203, White-fronted goose. No. 1204, Northern fulmar, vert.

1986, Oct. 9   **Litho.**   **Perf. 14**
1195	A167	3 l	multicolored	.40	.40
1196	A167	4 l	multicolored	.40	.40
1197	A167	5 l	multicolored	.40	.40
1198	A167	10 l	multicolored	.45	.45
1199	A167	15 l	multicolored	.90	.90
1200	A167	20 l	multicolored	.95	.95
1201	A167	13r	multicolored	5.75	5.75
1202	A167	14r	multicolored	5.75	5.75
			Nos. 1195-1202 (8)	15.00	15.00

Souvenir Sheets
1203	A167	15r	multicolored	11.00	11.00
1204	A167	15r	multicolored	11.00	11.00

Nos. 1197, 1199-1201 printed se-tenant with labels picturing a horned puffin, gray kingbird, downy woodpecker and water pipit, respectively.

Nos. 1176-1180 Overprinted in Gold

Overprint reads "WINNERS / Argentina 3 / W. Germany 2"

1986, Oct. 25
1205	A184	15 l	multicolored	.50	.50
1206	A184	2r	multicolored	1.40	1.40
1207	A184	4r	multicolored	2.25	2.25
1208	A184	10r	multicolored	3.75	3.75
			Nos. 1205-1208 (4)	7.90	7.90

Souvenir Sheet
1209	A184	15r	multicolored	5.25	5.25

Nos. 1151-1156 Overprinted with Halley's Comet Symbol in Silver

1986, Oct. 30
1210	A181	20 l	multicolored	.70	.70
1211	A181	1.50r	multicolored	1.40	1.40
1212	A181	2r	multicolored	1.60	1.60
1213	A181	4r	multicolored	2.10	2.10
1214	A181	5r	multicolored	2.10	2.10
			Nos. 1210-1214 (5)	7.90	7.90

Souvenir Sheet
1215	A181	15r	multicolored	6.50	6.50

UNESCO, 40th Anniv. — A186

1986, Nov. 4   **Perf. 15**

1216	A186	1r Aviation	.30	.30
1217	A186	2r Boat-building	.75	.75
1218	A186	3r Education	1.00	1.00
1219	A186	5r Research	1.90	1.90
		Nos. 1216-1219 (4)	3.95	3.95

Souvenir Sheet

| 1220 | A186 | 15r Ocean explora- | | |
| | | tion | 3.75 | 3.75 |

Mushrooms — A187

Designs: 15 l, Hypholoma fasciculare. 50 l, Kuehneromyces mutabilis, vert. 1r, Amanita muscaria, vert. 2r, Agaricus campestris. 3r, Amanita pantherina, vert. 4r, Coprinus comatus vert. 5r, Pholiota spectabilis. 10r, Pluteus cervinus. No. 1229, Armillaria mellea. No. 1230, Stropharia aeruginosa.

1986, Dec. 31   **Litho.**   **Perf. 15**

1221	A187	15 l multicolored	.75	.75
1222	A187	50 l multicolored	1.60	1.60
1223	A187	1r multicolored	2.00	2.00
1224	A187	2r multicolored	2.60	2.60
1225	A187	3r multicolored	2.60	2.60
1226	A187	4r multicolored	2.60	2.60
1227	A187	5r multicolored	2.60	2.60
1228	A187	10r multicolored	3.75	3.75
		Nos. 1221-1228 (8)	18.50	18.50

Souvenir Sheets

| 1229 | A187 | 15r multicolored | 8.00 | 8.00 |
| 1230 | A187 | 15r multicolored | 8.00 | 8.00 |

Flowers — A188

1987, Jan. 29   **Litho.**   **Perf. 15**

1231	A188	10 l Ixora	.25	.25
1232	A188	20 l Frangipani	.25	.25
1233	A188	50 l Crinum	.25	.25
1235	A188	2r Pink rose	.90	.90
1236	A188	4r Flamboyant	1.75	1.75
1238	A188	10r Ground orchid	4.75	4.75
		Nos. 1231-1238 (6)	8.15	8.15

Souvenir Sheet

| 1239 | A188 | 15r Gardenia | 3.50 | 3.50 |
| 1240 | A188 | 15r Oleander | 3.50 | 3.50 |

Girl Guides, 75th Anniv. (in 1985) A189

1987, Apr. 4   **Litho.**   **Perf. 15**

1241	A189	15 l Nature study	.25	.25
1242	A189	2r Guides, rabbits	.65	.65
1243	A189	4r Bird-watching	2.10	2.10
1244	A189	12r Lady Baden-		
		Powell, flag	2.40	2.40
		Nos. 1241-1244 (4)	5.40	5.40

Souvenir Sheet

| 1245 | A189 | 15r Sailing | 3.50 | 3.50 |

Indigenous Trees and Plants — A190

1987, Apr. 22   **Litho.**   **Perf. 14**

1246	A190	50 l Thespesia		
		populnea, vert.	.25	.25
1247	A190	1r Cocos nucifera,		
		vert.	.25	.25

1248	A190	2r Calophyllum		
		mophyllum,		
		vert.	.40	.40
1249	A190	3r Xyanthosoma in-		
		dica	.60	.60
1250	A190	5r Ipomoea batatas	1.00	1.00
1251	A190	7r Artocarpus al-		
		tilis, vert.	1.25	1.25
		Nos. 1246-1251 (6)	3.75	3.75

Souvenir Sheet

| 1252 | A190 | 15r Cocos nucifera, | | |
| | | diff., vert. | 3.50 | 3.50 |

A191

America's Cup — A192

1987, May 4   **Litho.**   **Perf. 15**

1253	A191	15 l Intrepid, 1970	.25	.25
1254	A191	1r France II, 1974	.35	.35
1255	A191	2r Gretel, 1962	.60	.60
1256	A191	12r Volunteer, 1887	2.75	2.75
		Nos. 1253-1256 (4)	3.95	3.95

Souvenir Sheet

1257	A192	15r Defender Vs.		
		Valkyrie III,		
		1895	3.25	3.25

Butterflies — A193   Scientists — A194

1987, Dec. 16   **Litho.**   **Perf. 15**

1258	A193	15 l Precis octavia	.60	.60
1259	A193	20 l Pachliopta		
		hector	.60	.60
1260	A193	50 l Teinopalpus		
		imperialis	1.00	1.00
1261	A193	1r Kallima hor-		
		sfieldi	1.25	1.25
1262	A193	2r Cethosia biblis	2.25	2.25
1263	A193	4r Hestia jasonia	3.00	3.00
1264	A193	7r Papilio mem-		
		non	4.75	4.75
1265	A193	10r Meneris		
		tulbaghia	5.50	5.50
		Nos. 1258-1265 (8)	18.95	18.95

Souvenir Sheets

1266	A193	15r Acraea violae		
		acraeinae	7.50	7.50
1267	A193	15r Hebomoia		
		leucippe	7.50	7.50

1988, Jan. 10   **Perf. 14**

Designs: 1.50r, Sir Isaac Newton using prism to demonstrate his Theory of Light, horiz. 3r, Euclid (c. 300 B.C.), mathematician. 4r, Gregor Johann Mendel (1822-1884), botanist; father of genetics. 5r, Galileo, 1st man to observe 4 moons of Jupiter, horiz. 15r, Apollo spacecraft orbiting the moon.

1268	A194	1.50r multicolored	1.50	1.50
1269	A194	3r multicolored	2.10	2.10
1270	A194	4r multicolored	2.40	2.40
1271	A194	5r multicolored	4.00	4.00
		Nos. 1268-1271 (4)	10.00	10.00

Souvenir Sheet

| 1272 | A194 | 15r multicolored | 7.00 | 7.00 |

Disney Characters, Space Exploration — A195

1988, Feb. 15

1273	A195	3 l Weather satel-		
		lite	.25	.25
1274	A195	4 l Navigation sat-		
		ellite	.25	.25
1275	A195	5 l Communica-		
		tion satellite	.25	.25
1276	A195	10 l Moon rover	.25	.25
1277	A195	20 l Space shuttle	.25	.25
1278	A195	13r Space docking	5.75	5.75
1279	A195	14r Voyager 2	5.75	5.75
		Nos. 1273-1279 (7)	12.75	12.75

Souvenir Sheets

1280	A195	15r 1st Man on		
		Moon	6.25	6.25
1281	A195	15r Space station		
		colony	6.25	6.25
		Nos. 1276-1278 and 1281 vert.		

WHO, 40th Anniv. A196

1988, Apr. 7   **Litho.**   **Perf. 14**

1282	A196	2r Immunization	.60	.60
1283	A196	4r Clean water	1.10	1.10
		For overprints see Nos. 1307-1308.		

World Environment Day — A197

1988, May 9   **Perf. 15**

1284	A197	15 l Save water	.30	.30
1285	A197	75 l Protect the reef	.40	.40
1286	A197	2r Conserve nature	1.00	1.00
		Nos. 1284-1286 (3)	1.70	1.70

Souvenir Sheet

| 1287 | A197 | 15r Banyan tree, vert. | 5.00 | 5.00 |

Nos. 1172-1175 Overprinted in Gold

Overprint reads "40th WEDDING ANNIVERSARY/ H.M. QUEEN ELIZABETH II/ H.R.H. THE DUKE OF EDINBURGH"

1988, July 7   **Litho.**   **Perf. 14**

1288	CD339	1r multicolored	.30	.30
1289	CD339	2r multicolored	.55	.55
1290	CD339	12r multicolored	3.25	3.25
		Nos. 1288-1290 (3)	4.10	4.10

Souvenir Sheet

| 1291 | CD339 | 15r multicolored | 4.75 | 4.75 |

Transportation and Communication Decade for Asia and the Pacific — A198

Globe and: 2r, Postal communications. 3r, Earth satellite telecommunications technology. 5r, Space telecommunications technology. 10r, Automobile, aircraft and ship.

1988, May 31   **Litho.**   **Perf. 14**

1292	A198	2r multicolored	1.25	1.25
1293	A198	3r multicolored	1.75	1.75
1294	A198	5r multicolored	2.75	2.75
1295	A198	10r multicolored	5.50	5.50
		Nos. 1292-1295 (4)	11.25	11.25
		For overprints, see Nos. 1344-1345.		

1988 Summer Olympics, Seoul — A199   Intl. Year of Shelter for the Homeless — A200

1988, July 16

1296	A199	15 l Discus	.25	.25
1297	A199	2r 100-Meter sprint	.50	.50
1298	A199	4r Gymnastics,		
		horiz.	1.00	1.00
1299	A199	12r Steeplechase,		
		horiz.	3.25	3.25
		Nos. 1296-1299 (4)	5.00	5.00

Souvenir Sheet

| 1300 | A199 | 20r Tennis, horiz. | 4.75 | 4.75 |
| | | For overprints see Nos. 1311-1315. | | |

1988, July 20

| 1301 | A200 | 50 l Medical clinic | .35 | .35 |
| 1302 | A200 | 3r Prefab housing | 1.60 | 1.60 |

Souvenir Sheet

| 1303 | A200 | 15r Construction site | 4.00 | 4.00 |

Intl. Fund for Agricultural Development (IFAD), 10th Anniv. — A201

1988, July 30

| 1304 | A201 | 7r Breadfruit | 1.75 | 1.75 |
| 1305 | A201 | 10r Mango, vert. | 2.50 | 2.50 |

Souvenir Sheet

| 1306 | A201 | 15r Coconut palm, | | |
| | | yellowtail tuna | 3.75 | 3.75 |

Nos. 1282-1283 Ovptd.

1988, Dec. 1   **Litho.**   **Perf. 14**

1307	A196	2r multicolored	.55	.55
1308	A196	4r multicolored	1.00	1.00
		Intl. Day for the Fight Against Aids.		

John F. Kennedy (1917-1963), 35th US President — A202

Space achievements: a, Apollo launch. b, 1st Man on the Moon. c, Earth and astronaut driving moon rover. d, Space module and Kennedy. 15r, Kennedy addressing the nation.

1989, Feb. 19

| 1309 | A202 | Strip of 4 | 9.50 | 9.50 |
| a.-d. | | 5r any single | 2.00 | 2.00 |

Souvenir Sheet

| 1310 | A202 | 15r multicolored | 5.00 | 5.00 |

No. 1296 Overprinted | No. 1297 Overprinted

No. 1298 Overprinted

No. 1299 Overprinted

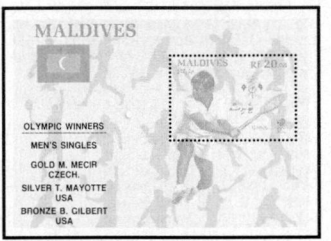

No. 1300 Overprinted

1989, Apr. 29   **Litho.**   **Perf. 14**

1311	A199	15 l multicolored	.25	.25
1312	A199	2r multicolored	.75	.75
1313	A199	4r multicolored	1.40	1.40
1314	A199	12r multicolored	4.50	4.50
		Nos. 1311-1314 (4)	6.90	6.90

Souvenir Sheet

1315	A199	20r multi	7.00	7.00

Paintings by Titian (b. 1489) A203

MALDIVES 15L

Designs: 15 l, Portrait of Benedetto Varchi, c. 1540. 1r, Portrait of a Young Man in a Fur, 1515. 2r, King Francis I of France, 1538. 5r, Portrait of Pietro Aretino, 1545. 15r, The Bravo, c. 1520. 20r, The Concert, 1512. No. 1322, An Allegory of Prudence, c. 1565. No. 1323, Portrait of Francesco Maria Della Rovere.

1989, May 15   **Litho.**   **Perf. 13½x14**

1316	A203	15 l multicolored	.25	.25
1317	A203	1r multicolored	.30	.30
1318	A203	2r multicolored	.70	.70
1319	A203	5r multicolored	1.50	1.50
1320	A203	15r multicolored	4.50	4.50
1321	A203	20r multicolored	5.75	5.75
		Nos. 1316-1321 (6)	13.00	13.00

Souvenir Sheets

1322	A203	20r multicolored	4.50	4.50
1323	A203	20r multicolored	4.50	4.50

"Thirty-six Views of Mt. Fuji" — A204

Prints by Hokusai (1760-1849): 15 l, Fuji from Hodogaya. 50 l, Fuji from Lake Kawaguchi. 1r, Fuji from Owari. 2r, Fuji from Tsukudajima in Edo. 4r, Fuji from a Teahouse at Yoshida. 6r, Fuji from Tagonoura. 10r, Fuji from Mishima-goe. 12r, Fuji from the Sumida River in Edo. No. 1332, Fuji from Fukagawa in Edo. No. 1333, Fuji from Inume Pass.

1989   **Perf. 14**

1324	A204	15 l multicolored	.25	.25
1325	A204	50 l multicolored	.25	.25
1326	A204	1r multicolored	.30	.30
1327	A204	2r multicolored	.55	.55
1328	A204	4r multicolored	1.00	1.00
1329	A204	6r multicolored	1.50	1.50
1330	A204	10r multicolored	2.50	2.50
1331	A204	12r multicolored	3.00	3.00
		Nos. 1324-1331 (8)	9.35	9.35

Souvenir Sheets

1332	A204	18r multicolored	4.75	4.75
1333	A204	18r multicolored	4.75	4.75

Hirohito (1901-1989) and enthronement of Akihito as emperor of Japan.
Issue dates: No. 1332, 10/16, others, 9/2.

Tropical Fish A205

Designs: 20 l, Clown triggerfish. 50 l, Blue surgeonfish. 1r, Bluestripe snapper. 2r, Oriental sweetlips. 3r, Wrasse. 8r, Treadfin butterflyfish. 10r, Bicolor parrotfish. 12r, Saber squirrelfish.
No. 1042, Butterfly perch. No. 1040, Semi circle angelfish.

1989, Oct. 16   **Litho.**   **Perf. 14**

1334	A205	20 l multicolored	.25	.25
1335	A205	50 l multicolored	.30	.30
1336	A205	1r multicolored	.35	.35
1337	A205	2r multicolored	.75	.75
1338	A205	3r multicolored	1.00	1.00
1339	A205	8r multicolored	2.25	2.25
1340	A205	10r multicolored	3.50	3.50
1341	A205	12r multicolored	4.00	4.00
		Nos. 1334-1341 (8)	12.40	12.40

Souvenir Sheet

1342	A205	15r multicolored	7.50	7.50
1343	A205	15r multicolored	7.50	7.50

Nos. 1293-1294 Overprinted in Silver

Overprint reads "ASIA-PACIFIC / TELECOMMUNITY / 10 YEARS"

1989, July 5   **Litho.**   **Perf. 14**

1344	A198	3r multicolored	1.75	1.75
1345	A198	5r multicolored	2.75	2.75

World Stamp Expo '89 Emblem, Disney Characters and Japanese Automobiles — A206

Designs: 15 l, 1907 Takuri Type 3. 50 l, 1917 Mitsubishi Model A. 1r, 1935 Datsun Roadstar. 2r, 1940 Mazda. 4r, 1959 Nissan Bluebird 310. 6r, 1958 Subaru 360. 10r, 1966 Honda S800. 12r, 1966 Daihatsu Fellow. No. 1354, 1981 Isuzu Trooper II. No. 1355, 1985 Toyota Supra.

1989, Nov. 17   **Litho.**   **Perf. 14x13½**

1346	A206	15 l multicolored	.25	.25
1347	A206	50 l multicolored	.25	.25
1348	A206	1r multicolored	.40	.40
1349	A206	2r multicolored	.75	.75
1350	A206	4r multicolored	1.50	1.50
1351	A206	6r multicolored	2.40	2.40
1352	A206	10r multicolored	3.75	3.75
1353	A206	12r multicolored	4.25	4.25
		Nos. 1346-1353 (8)	13.55	13.55

Souvenir Sheets

1354	A206	20r multicolored	6.50	6.50
1355	A206	20r multicolored	6.50	6.50

Souvenir Sheet

The Marine Corps War Memorial, Arlington, VA — A207

1989, Nov. 17   **Litho.**   **Perf. 14**

1356	A207	8r multicolored	3.25	3.25

World Stamp Expo '89.

1st Moon Landing, 20th Anniv. A208

Designs: 1r, Eagle lunar module. 2r, Aldrin taking soil samples. 6r, Solar wind experiment. 10r, Nixon, astronauts.
18r, Armstrong descending ladder.

1989, Nov. 24   **Perf. 14**

1357	A208	1r multicolored	.30	.30
1358	A208	2r multicolored	.60	.60
1359	A208	6r multicolored	1.60	1.60
1360	A208	10r multicolored	2.75	2.75
		Nos. 1357-1360 (4)	5.25	5.25

Souvenir Sheet

1361	A208	18r multicolored	9.00	9.00

Railway Pioneers — A209

Designs: 10 l, Sir William Cornelius Van Horne (1843-1915), chairman of Canadian Pacific Railway, map and locomotive, 1894. 25 l, Matthew Murray, built rack locomotives for Middleton Colliery. 50 l, Louis Favre (1826-1879), built the St. Gotthard (spiral) Tunnel, 1881. 2r, George Stephenson (1781-1848), locomotive, 1825. 1r, Richard Trevithick (1771-1833), builder of 1st rail locomotive, 1804. 8r, George Nagelmackers, Orient Express dining car, 1869. 10r, William Jessop, Surrey horse-drawn cart on rails, 1770. 12r, Isambard Kingdom Brunel (1806-1859), chief engineer of Great Western Railway, introduced broad gauge, 1830's. No. 1370, George Pullman (1831-1897), Pioneer passenger car. No. 1371, Rudolf Diesel (1858-1913), inventor of the diesel engine, 1892, and diesel train.

1989, Dec. 26   **Litho.**   **Perf. 14**

1362	A209	10 l multicolored	.25	.25
1363	A209	25 l multicolored	.25	.25
1364	A209	50 l multicolored	.25	.25
1365	A209	2r multicolored	.65	.65
1366	A209	6r multicolored	1.90	1.90
1367	A209	8r multicolored	2.25	2.25
1368	A209	10r multicolored	3.00	3.00
1369	A209	12r multicolored	3.50	3.50
		Nos. 1362-1369 (8)	12.05	12.05

Souvenir Sheets

1370	A209	18r multicolored	5.00	5.00
1371	A209	18r multicolored	5.00	5.00

Anniversaries and Events (in 1989) — A210

Designs: 20 l, Flag of India, Jawaharlal Nehru, Mahatma Gandhi. 50 l, Syringe, opium poppies, vert. 1r, William Shakespeare, birthplace, Stratford-on-Avon. 2r, Flag of France, storming of the Bastille, Paris, 1789, vert. 3r, Concorde jet, flags of France, Britain. 8r, George Washington, Mount Vernon estate, Virginia. 10r, Capt. William Bligh, the Bounty. 12r, Ships in port. No. 1380, 1st Televised baseball game, 1939, vert. No. 1381, Franz von Taxis (1458-1517), vert.

1990, Feb. 15   **Litho.**   **Perf. 14**

1372	A210	20 l multicolored	.25	.25
1373	A210	50 l multicolored	.25	.25
1374	A210	1r multicolored	.60	.60
1375	A210	2r multicolored	1.10	1.10
1376	A210	3r multicolored	1.75	1.75
1377	A210	8r multicolored	5.50	5.50
1378	A210	10r multicolored	7.00	7.00
1379	A210	12r multicolored	8.50	8.50
		Nos. 1372-1379 (8)	24.95	24.95

Souvenir Sheets

1380	A210	18r multicolored	8.25	8.25
1381	A210	18r multicolored	8.25	8.25

Birth cent. of Nehru (20 l); SAARC Year for Combatting Drug Abuse (50 l); 425th birth anniv. of Shakespeare (1r); French Revolution, bicent. (2r); first test flight of the Concorde supersonic jet, 20th anniv. (3r); American presidency, bicent. (8r); Mutiny on the Bounty, (10r); Hamburg, 800th anniv. (12r); 1st televised baseball game, 50th anniv. (No. 1380); and European postal communications, 500th anniv. (No. 1381).
Johann von Taxis was the first postmaster of Thurn & Taxis in 1489, not Franz, who is credited on No. 1381.

Natl. Independence, 25th Anniv. — A211

Designs: 20 l, Bodu Thakurufaanu Memorial Center, Utheemu. 25 l, Islamic Center, Male. 50 l, Natl. flag, UN, Islamic Conf., Commonwealth and SAARC emblems. 2r, Muleeaage, Male. 5r, Natl. Security Service, Maldives. 10r, Natl. crest, emblem of the Citizens' Majlis (parliament).

1990, Jan. 1   **Litho.**   **Perf. 14**

1382	A211	20 l multicolored	.25	.25
1383	A211	25 l multicolored	.25	.25
1384	A211	50 l multicolored	.25	.25
1385	A211	2r multicolored	.30	.30
1386	A211	5r multicolored	.90	.90
		Nos. 1382-1386 (5)	1.95	1.95

Souvenir Sheet

1387	A211	10r multicolored	4.25	4.25

French Revolution, Bicent. (in 1989) A212

Paintings: 15 l, *Louis XVI in Coronation Robes*, by Duplessis. 50 l, *Monsieur Lavoisier and His Wife*, by David. 1r, *Madame Pastoret*, by David. 2r, *Oath of Lafayette at the Festival of Federation*, by David. 4r, *Madame Trudaine*, by David. 6r, *Chenard Celebrating the Liberation of Savoy*, by Boilly. 10r, *An Officer Swears Allegiance to the Constitution*, artist unknown. 12r, *Self-portrait*, by David. No. 1396, *The Tennis Court Oath, June 20, 1789*, by David, horiz. No. 1397, *Jean-Jacques Rousseau and the Symbols of the Revolution*, by Jeaurat.

1990, Jan. 11   **Litho.**   **Perf. 14**

1388	A212	15 l multicolored	.25	.25
1389	A212	50 l multicolored	.25	.25
1390	A212	1r multicolored	.40	.40
1391	A212	2r multicolored	.85	.85
1392	A212	4r multicolored	1.50	1.50
1393	A212	6r multicolored	2.40	2.40
1394	A212	10r multicolored	4.00	4.00
1395	A212	12r multicolored	4.50	4.50
		Nos. 1388-1395 (8)	14.15	14.15

Souvenir Sheets

1396	A212	20r multicolored	6.50	6.50
1397	A212	20r multicolored	6.50	6.50

Stamp World London '90 — A213

Walt Disney characters demonstrating sports popular in Britain: 15 l, Rugby. 50 l, Curling. 1r, Polo. 2r, Soccer. 4r, Cricket. 6r, Horse racing, Ascot. 10r, Tennis. 12r, Lawn bowling.
No. 1406, Fox hunting. No. 1407, Golf, St. Andrews, Scotland.

1990   **Litho.**   **Perf. 14x13½**

1398	A213	15 l multicolored	.25	.25
1399	A213	50 l multicolored	.25	.25
1400	A213	1r multicolored	.40	.40
1401	A213	2r multicolored	.85	.85
1402	A213	4r multicolored	1.50	1.50
1403	A213	6r multicolored	2.50	2.50
1404	A213	10r multicolored	3.75	3.75
1405	A213	12r multicolored	4.25	4.25
		Nos. 1398-1405 (8)	13.75	13.75

Souvenir Sheets

1406	A213	20r multicolored	8.25	8.25
1407	A213	20r multicolored	8.25	8.25

Penny Black, 150th Anniv. A214

1990, May 3   **Litho.**   **Perf. 15x14**

1408	A214	8r Silhouettes	2.25	2.25
1409	A214	12r Silhouettes, diff.	3.25	3.25

Souvenir Sheet

1410	A214	18r Penny Black	5.50	5.50

Queen Mother 90th Birthday
A215   A216

1990, July 8   **Perf. 14**

1411	A215	6r shown	1.10	1.10
1412	A216	6r shown	1.10	1.10
1413	A215	6r As Lady Bowes-Lyon, diff.	1.10	1.10
		Nos. 1411-1413 (3)	3.30	3.30

Souvenir Sheet

1414	A216	18r On Wedding Day, diff.	3.75	3.75

Nos. 1411-1413 printed in sheets of 9.

A217

A218

A219

Islamic Heritage Year A220

1990, July 22   **Litho.**   **Perf. 14**

1415	A217	1r blue & black	.35	.35
1416	A218	1r blue & black	.35	.35
1417	A218	1r Building, diff.	.35	.35
1418	A219	2r blue & black	.60	.60
1419	A220	2r blue & black	.60	.60
1420	A219	2r Building, diff.	.60	.60
a.		Block of 6, #1415-1420	4.00	4.00

Great Crested Tern A221

Design: 25 l, Great Crested Tern. 50 l, Koel. 1r, White tern. 3.50r, Cinnamon bittern. 6r, Sooty tern. 8r, Audubon's shearwater. 12r, Brown noddy. 15r, Lesser frigatebird.
No. 1429, White-tailed tropicbird. No. 1430, Grey heron.

1990, Aug. 9   **Litho.**   **Perf. 14**

1421	A221	25 l multicolored	.25	.25
1422	A221	50 l multicolored	.25	.25
1423	A221	1r multicolored	.25	.25
1424	A221	3.50r multicolored	.90	.90
1425	A221	6r multicolored	1.50	1.50
1426	A221	8r multicolored	2.00	2.00
1427	A221	12r multicolored	3.00	3.00
1428	A221	15r multicolored	3.75	3.75
		Nos. 1421-1428 (8)	11.90	11.90

Souvenir Sheets

1429	A221	18r multicolored	6.00	6.00
1430	A221	18r multicolored	6.00	6.00

World War II Milestones — A222

Designs: 15 l, US Marines repulse Japanese invasion of Wake Island, Dec. 11, 1941. 25 l, Gen. Stilwell begins offensive in Burma, Mar. 4, 1944. 50 l, US begins offensive in Normandy, July 3, 1944. 1r, US forces secure Saipan, July 9, 1944. 2.50r, D-Day, June 6, 1944. 3.50r, Allied forces land in Norway, Apr. 14, 1940. 4r, Adm. Mountbatten named Chief of Combined Operations, Mar. 18, 1942. 6r, Gen. MacArthur accepts Japanese surrender, Sept. 2, 1945. 10r, Potsdam Conference, July 16, 1945. 12r, Allied invade Sicily, July 10, 1943. 18r, Atlantic convoys.

1990, Aug. 9   **Litho.**   **Perf. 14**

1431	A222	15 l multicolored	.25	.25
1432	A222	25 l multicolored	.30	.30
1433	A222	50 l multicolored	.40	.40
1434	A222	1r multicolored	.55	.55
1435	A222	2.50r multicolored	.90	.90
1436	A222	3.50r multicolored	1.25	1.25
1437	A222	4r multicolored	1.40	1.40
1438	A222	6r multicolored	2.25	2.25
1439	A222	10r multicolored	3.50	3.50
1440	A222	12r multicolored	4.50	4.50
		Nos. 1431-1440 (10)	15.30	15.30

Souvenir Sheet

1441	A222	18r multicolored	10.00	10.00

A223

5th SAARC Summit — A224

Designs: 75 l, Satellite communications. 3.50r, Flags. 20r, Map.

1990, Nov. 21   **Litho.**   **Perf. 14**

1442	A223	75 l multicolored	.50	.50
1443	A223	3.50r multicolored	1.75	1.75

Souvenir Sheet

1444	A224	20r multicolored	8.50	8.50

Flowers — A225

Designs: 20l, Spathoglottis plicata. 75 l, Hippeastrum puniceum. 2r, Tecoma stans. 3.50r, Catharanthus roseus. 10r, Ixora coccinea. 12r, Clitoria ternatea. 15r, Caesalpinia pulcherrima.
No. 1452, Rosa sp. No. 1453, Plumeria obtusa. No. 1454, Jasminum grandiflorum. No. 1455, Hibiscus tiliaceous.

1990, Dec. 9   **Litho.**   **Perf. 14**

1445	A225	20 l multicolored	.25	.25
1446	A225	75 l multicolored	.25	.25
1447	A225	2r multicolored	.65	.65
1448	A225	3.50r multicolored	1.10	1.10
1449	A225	10r multicolored	3.25	3.25
1450	A225	12r multicolored	4.00	4.00
1451	A225	15r multicolored	4.75	4.75
		Nos. 1445-1451 (7)	14.25	14.25

Souvenir Sheets

1452	A225	20r multicolored	4.75	4.75
1453	A225	20r multicolored	4.75	4.75
1454	A225	20r multicolored	4.75	4.75
1455	A225	20r multicolored	4.75	4.75

Expo '90, Intl. Garden and Greenery Exposition, Osaka, Japan.
2r, 3.50r, 10r, 12r are horiz.

Bonsai — A226

Designs: 20 l, Winged Euonymus. 50 l, Japanese black pine. 1r, Japanese five needle pine. 3.50r, Flowering quince. 5r, Chinese elm. 8r, Japanese persimmon. 10r, Japanese wisteria. 12r, Satsuki azalea.

No. 1464, Sargent juniper. No. 1465, Trident maple.

1990-91

1456	A226	20 l multicolored	.25	.25
1457	A226	50 l multicolored	.25	.25
1458	A226	1r multicolored	.30	.30
1459	A226	3.50r multicolored	1.25	1.25
1460	A226	5r multicolored	1.50	1.50
1461	A226	8r multicolored	2.50	2.50
1462	A226	10r multicolored	3.00	3.00
1463	A226	12r multicolored	3.75	3.75
		Nos. 1456-1463 (8)	12.80	12.80

Souvenir Sheets

1464	A226	20r multicolored	7.00	7.00
1465	A226	20r multicolored	7.00	7.00

Expo '90, Intl. Garden and Greenery Exposition, Osaka, Japan.
Issued: 50 l, 1r, 8r, 10r, No. 1464, 12/9/90; 20 l, 3.50r, 5r, 12r, No. 1465, 1/29/91.

Aesop's Fables — A227

Walt Disney characters: 15 l, Tortoise and the Hare. 50 l, Mikado, Sudan Railways. 1r, Town Mouse and Country Mouse. 1r, Fox and the Crow. 3.50r, Travellers and the Bear. 4r, Fox and the Lion. 6r, Mice and the Cat. 10r, Fox and the Goat. 12r, Dog in the Manger. No. 1474, Miller, his Son and the Ass, vert. No. 1475. Miser's Gold, vert.

1990, Dec. 11   **Litho.**   **Perf. 14**

1466	A227	15 l multicolored	.25	.25
1467	A227	50 l multicolored	.25	.25
1468	A227	1r multicolored	.35	.35
1469	A227	3.50r multicolored	1.25	1.25
1470	A227	4r multicolored	1.50	1.50
1471	A227	6r multicolored	2.25	2.25
1472	A227	10r multicolored	3.75	3.75
1473	A227	12r multicolored	4.25	4.25
		Nos. 1466-1473 (8)	13.85	13.85

Souvenir Sheets

1474	A227	20r multicolored	7.50	7.50
1475	A227	20r multicolored	7.50	7.50

Intl. Literacy Year.

A228

Steam Locomotives: 20 l, "31" Class, East African Railways. 50 l, Mikado, Sudan Railways. 1r, Beyer-Garratt GM Class, South African Railways. 3r, "7th" Class, Rhodesia Railways. 5r, Central Pacific 229. 8r, Reading 415. 10r, Porter Narrow-guage. 12r, Great Northern 515. No. 1484, American Standard 315. No. 1485, East African Railways 5950.

1990, Dec. 15

1476	A228	20 l multicolored	.25	.25
1477	A228	50 l multicolored	.25	.25
1478	A228	1r multicolored	.40	.40
1479	A228	3r multicolored	1.25	1.25
1480	A228	5r multicolored	2.00	2.00
1481	A228	8r multicolored	3.25	3.25
1482	A228	10r multicolored	4.00	4.00
1483	A228	12r multicolored	4.75	4.75
		Nos. 1476-1483 (8)	16.15	16.15

Souvenir Sheets

1484	A228	20r multicolored	8.25	8.25
1485	A228	20r multicolored	8.25	8.25

A229

Various players from participating countries: 1r, Holland. 2.50r, England. 3.50r, Argentina. 5r, Brazil. 7r, Italy. 10r, Russia, 15r, West Germany.

No. 1490, Austria. No. 1491, South Korea. No. 1492, Italy (dk blue shirt). No. 1493, Argentina (blue & white shirt).

1990, Dec. 27
1486	A229	1r multicolored	.40	.40
1487	A229	2.50r multicolored	1.00	1.00
1487A	A229	3.50r multicolored	1.60	1.60
1488	A229	5r multicolored	2.10	2.10
1488A	A229	7r multicolored	2.75	2.75
1489	A229	10r multicolored	4.25	4.25
1489A	A229	15r multicolored	6.25	6.25

Nos. 1486-1489A (7) 18.35 18.35

Souvenir Sheets
1490	A229	18r multicolored	4.50	4.50
1491	A229	18r multicolored	4.50	4.50
1492	A229	20r multicolored	5.00	5.00
1493	A229	20r multicolored	5.00	5.00

World Cup Soccer Championships, Italy.

No. 1111 Surcharged

Methods and Perfs As Before
1990
1493B A171 3.50r on 2.70r #1111 —

An additional stamp was issued in this set. The editors would like to examine any examples.

Peter Paul Rubens (1577-1640), Painter — A230

Entire works or details from paintings by Rubens: 20 l, Summer. 50 l, Landscape with Rainbow. 1r, Wreckage of Aeneas. 2.50r, Chateau de Steen. 3.50r, Landscape with Herd of Cows. 7r, Ruins of Palantine. 10r, Landscape with Peasants and Cows. 12r, Wagon Fording a Stream. No. 1502, Landscape with a Sunset. No. 1503, Peasants with Cattle by a Stream in a Woody Landscape. No. 1504, Shepherd with his Flock in a Wooded Landscape. No. 1505, Stuck Wagon.

1991, Feb. 7   Litho.   Perf. 14x13½
1494	A230	20 l multicolored	.25	.25
1495	A230	50 l multicolored	.25	.25
1496	A230	1r multicolored	.35	.35
1497	A230	2.50r multicolored	.80	.80
1498	A230	3.50r multicolored	1.10	1.10
1499	A230	7r multicolored	2.10	2.10
1500	A230	10r multicolored	3.25	3.25
1501	A230	12r multicolored	3.75	3.75

Nos. 1494-1501 (8) 11.85 11.85

Souvenir Sheets
1502-1505 A230 20r each 4.75 4.75

First Marathon Run, 490 B.C. — A231

Events and anniversaries (in 1990): 1r, Anthony Fokker (1890-1939), aircraft builder. 3.50r, Launch of first commercial satellite, 25th anniv. 7r, East, West German foreign ministers sign re-unification documents, Oct. 3, 1990, horiz. 8r, Magna Carta, 775th anniv. 10r, Dwight D. Eisenhower. 12r, Winston Churchill. 15r, Pres. Reagan destroying Berlin Wall, horiz. No. 1514, Brandenburg Gate, horiz. No. 1515, Battle of Britain, 50th anniv., horiz.

1991, Mar. 11   Perf. 14
1506	A231	50 l multicolored	.25	.25
1507	A231	1r multicolored	.30	.30
1508	A231	3.50r multicolored	1.25	1.25
1509	A231	7r multicolored	2.25	2.25
1510	A231	8r multicolored	2.50	2.50
1511	A231	10r multicolored	3.25	3.25
1512	A231	12r multicolored	4.00	4.00
1513	A231	15r multicolored	4.75	4.75

Nos. 1506-1513 (8) 18.55 18.55

Souvenir Sheets
1514	A231	20r multicolored	7.00	7.00
1515	A231	20r multicolored	7.00	7.00

Global Warming A232

1991, Apr. 10
1516	A232	3.50r Dhoni	2.25	2.25
1517	A232	7r Freighter	4.25	4.25

Year of the Girl Child — A233

1991, Apr. 14
1518 A233 7r multicolored 2.25 2.25

Year of the Child A234

Children's drawings: 3.50r, Beach scene. 5r, City scene. 10r, Visualizing fruit. 25r, Scuba diver.

1991, May 10
1519	A234	3.50r multicolored	1.25	1.25
1520	A234	5r multicolored	1.90	1.90
1521	A234	10r multicolored	3.75	3.75
1522	A234	25r multicolored	8.50	8.50

Nos. 1519-1522 (4) 15.40 15.40

Paintings by Vincent Van Gogh — A235

Designs: 15 l, Japanese Vase with Roses and Anemones, vert. 20 l, Still Life: Red Poppies and Daisies, vert. 2r, Vincent's Bedroom in Arles. 3.50r, The Mulberry Tree. 7r, Blossoming Chestnut Branches. 10r, Morning: Peasant Couple Going to Work. 12r, Still Life: Pink Roses. 15r, Child with Orange, vert. No. 1531, Courtyard of the Hospital at Arles. No. 1532, Houses in Auvers, vert.

1991, June 6   Litho.   Perf. 13½
1523	A235	15 l multicolored	.30	.30
1524	A235	20 l multicolored	.30	.30
1525	A235	2r multicolored	.75	.75
1526	A235	3.50r multicolored	1.40	1.40
1527	A235	7r multicolored	2.75	2.75
1528	A235	10r multicolored	4.00	4.00
1529	A235	12r multicolored	4.50	4.50
1530	A235	15r multicolored	5.75	5.75

Nos. 1523-1530 (8) 19.75 19.75

Sizes: 100x75mm, 75x100mm

Imperf
1531	A235	25r multicolored	8.00	8.00
1532	A235	25r multicolored	8.00	8.00

Royal Family Birthday, Anniversary
Common Design Type

1991, July 4   Litho.   Perf. 14
1533	CD347	1r multi	.30	.30
1534	CD347	.60	.60
1535	CD347	3.50r multi	1.10	1.10
1536	CD347	5r multi	1.50	1.50
1537	CD347	7r multi	2.10	2.10
1538	CD347	8r multi	2.50	2.50
1539	CD347	12r multi	3.75	3.75
1540	CD347	15r multi	4.25	4.25

Nos. 1533-1540 (8) 16.10 16.10

Souvenir Sheets
1541	CD347	25r Elizabeth, Philip	6.75	6.75
1542	CD347	25r Charles, Diana, sons	6.75	6.75

1r, 3.50r, 7r, 15r, No. 1542, Charles and Diana, 10th wedding anniversary. Others, Queen Elizabeth II, 65th birthday.

Hummel Figurines — A236

Designs: 10 l, No. 1552a, Child painting. 25 l, No. 1552b, Boy reading at table. 50 l, No. 1552c, Boy with back pack. 2r, No. 1551a, School Girl. 3.50r, No. 1551b, The Bookworm (boy sitting and reading). 8r, No. 1551c, Little Brother's Lesson. 10r, No. 1551d, School Girls. 25r, No. 1552d, Three school boys.

1991, July 25   Litho.   Perf. 14
1543	A236	10 l multicolored	.25	.25
1544	A236	25 l multicolored	.25	.25
1545	A236	50 l multicolored	.25	.25
1546	A236	2r multicolored	.60	.60
1547	A236	3.50r multicolored	1.00	1.00
1548	A236	8r multicolored	2.25	2.25
1549	A236	10r multicolored	2.75	2.75
1550	A236	25r multicolored	6.75	6.75

Nos. 1543-1550 (8) 14.10 14.10

Souvenir Sheets
1551	A236	5r Sheet of 4, #a.-d.	5.50	5.50
1552	A236	8r Sheet of 4, #a.-d.	9.00	9.00

Japanese Steam Locomotives — A237

1991, Aug. 25   Litho.   Perf. 14
1553	A237	15 l C 57, vert.	.25	.25
1554	A237	25 l Series 6250	.25	.25
1555	A237	1r D 51, vert.	.35	.35
1556	A237	3.50r Series 8620	1.25	1.25
1557	A237	5r Class 10	1.90	1.90
1558	A237	7r C 61, vert.	2.60	2.60
1559	A237	10r Series 9600	3.50	3.50
1560	A237	12r D 52	4.50	4.50

Nos. 1553-1560 (8) 14.60 14.60

Souvenir Sheets
1561	A237	20r Class 1080	5.50	5.50
1562	A237	20r C 56	5.50	5.50

Phila Nippon '91.

Butterflies A238

1991, Dec. 2   Litho.   Perf. 14
1563	A238	10 l Blue salamis	.40	.40
1564	A238	25 l Mountain beauty	.55	.55
1565	A238	50 l Lucerne blue	.75	.75
1566	A238	2r Monarch	1.25	1.25
1567	A238	3.50r Common rose	2.00	2.00
1568	A238	5r Black witch	2.75	2.75
1569	A238	8r Oriental swallowtail	4.50	4.50
1570	A238	10r Gaudy commodore	5.50	5.50

Nos. 1563-1570 (8) 17.70 17.70

Souvenir Sheets
1571	A238	20r Pearl crescent	8.50	8.50
1572	A238	20r Friar	8.50	8.50

No. 1570 inscribed "guady."

Japanese Space Program A239

Designs: 15 l, H-11 Launch Vehicle. 20 l, H-II Orbiting plane. 2r, Geosynchronous satellite 5. 3.50r, Marine observation satellite-1. 7r, Communications satellite 3. 10r, Broadcasting satellite-2. 12r, H-1 Launch Vehicle, vert. 15r, Space flier unit, space shuttle. No. 1581, Katsura tracking and data acquisition station. No. 1582, M-3S II Launch vehicle, vert.

1991, Dec. 11
1573	A239	15 l multicolored	.35	.35
1574	A239	20 l multicolored	.35	.35
1575	A239	2r multicolored	.70	.70
1576	A239	3.50r multicolored	1.25	1.25
1577	A239	7r multicolored	2.40	2.40
1578	A239	10r multicolored	3.50	3.50
1579	A239	12r multicolored	4.25	4.25
1580	A239	15r multicolored	5.25	5.25

Nos. 1573-1580 (8) 18.05 18.05

Souvenir Sheets
1581	A239	20r multicolored	8.00	8.00
1582	A239	20r multicolored	8.00	8.00

Miniature Sheet

World War II Leaders of the Pacific Theater — A240

a, Franklin D. Roosevelt. b, Douglas MacArthur. c, Chester Nimitz. d, Jonathan Wainwright. e, Ernest King. f, Claire Chennault. g, William Halsey. h, Marc Mitscher. i, James Doolittle. j, Raymond Spruance.

1991, Dec. 30   Litho.   Perf. 14½x15
1583 A240 3.50r Sheet of 10, #a.-j. 16.00 16.00

Grand Prix Race Cars A241

Designs: 20 l, Williams FW-07. 50 l, Brabham BT50 BMW Turbo. 1r, Williams FW-11 Honda. 3.50r, Ferrari 312 T3. 5r, Lotus Honda 99T. 7r, Benetton Ford B188. 10r, Tyrrell P34 Six-wheeler. 21r, Renault RE-30B Turbo. No. 1592, Ferrari F189. No. 1593, Brabham BT50 BMW Turbo, diff.

1991, Dec. 28   **Litho.**   **Perf. 14**
1584	A241	20 l multicolored	.25	.25
1585	A241	50 l multicolored	.25	.25
1586	A241	1r multicolored	.30	.30
1587	A241	3.50r multicolored	1.10	1.10
1588	A241	5r multicolored	1.60	1.60
1589	A241	7r multicolored	2.10	2.10
1590	A241	10r multicolored	3.00	3.00
1591	A241	21r multicolored	6.25	6.25
		Nos. 1584-1591 (8)	14.85	14.85

Souvenir Sheets
1592	A241	25r multicolored	7.75	7.75
1593	A241	25r multicolored	7.75	7.75

Miniature Sheet

Enzo Ferrari (1898-1988) — A242

Ferrari Race cars: a, 1957 Testa Rossa. b, 1966 275GTB. c, 1951 "Aspirarta". d, Testarossa. f, 1958 Dino 246. g, 1952 Type 375. h, Mansell's Formula One. i, 1975 312T.

1991, Dec. 28
1594	A242	5r Sheet of 9, #a.-i.	17.50	17.50

17th World Scout Jamboree A243

Designs: 10r, Scouts diving on reef. 11r, Hand making scout sign, emblem, vert. 18r, Lord Robert Baden-Powell, vert. 20r, Czechoslovakian scout (local) stamp, vert.

1991, Dec. 30
1595	A243	10r multicolored	2.75	2.75
1596	A243	11r multicolored	3.25	3.25

Souvenir Sheets
1597	A243	18r multicolored	4.75	4.75
1598	A243	20r multicolored	5.25	5.25

Wolfgang Amadeus Mozart, Death Bicent. A244

Portrait of Mozart and: 50 l, Schwarzenberg Palace. 1r, Spa at Baden. 2r, Royal Palace, Berlin. 5r, Viennese Masonic seal. 7r, St. Marx. No. 1604, Josephsplatz, Vienna.

1991, Dec. 30
1599	A244	50 l multicolored	.25	.25
1600	A244	1r multicolored	.25	.25
1601	A244	2r multicolored	.55	.55
1602	A244	5r multicolored	1.25	1.25
1603	A244	7r multicolored	1.75	1.75
1604	A244	20r multicolored	5.00	5.00
		Nos. 1599-1604 (6)	9.05	9.05

Souvenir Sheet
1605	A244	20r Bust of Mozart, vert.	5.00	5.00

Brandenburg Gate, Bicent. — A245

Designs: 20 l, Flag. 1.75 l, Man embracing child, Berlin wall. 4r, Soldiers behind barricade, demonstrator. 15r, World War I Iron Cross. No. 1610, Helmet. No. 1611, 1939 helmet. No. 1612, Studded helmet.

1991, Dec. 30
1606	A245	20 l multicolored	.25	.25
1607	A245	1.75r multicolored	.45	.45
1608	A245	4r multicolored	1.00	1.00
1609	A245	15r multicolored	3.25	3.25
		Nos. 1606-1609 (4)	4.95	4.95

Souvenir Sheets
1610	A245	18r multicolored	4.25	4.25
1611	A245	18r multicolored	4.25	4.25
1612	A245	18r multicolored	4.25	4.25

Anniversaries and Events — A246

Designs: No. 1613, Otto Lilienthal, glider No. 16. No. 1614, "D-Day," Normandy 1944, Charles de Gaulle. 7r, Front of locomotive, vert. 8r, Kurt Schwitters, artist and Landesmuseum. 9r, Map, man in Swiss costume. 10r, Charles de Gaulle in Madagascar, 1958. 12r, Steam locomotive. 15r, Portrait of Charles de Gaulle, vert. 20r, Locomotive and coal car.

1991, Dec. 30   **Litho.**   **Perf. 14**
1613	A246	6r multicolored	2.25	2.25
1614	A246	6r multicolored	1.75	1.75
1615	A246	7r multicolored	2.00	2.00
1616	A246	8r multicolored	2.25	2.25
1617	A246	9r multicolored	2.50	2.50
1618	A246	10r multicolored	2.75	2.75
1619	A246	12r multicolored	3.25	3.25
		Nos. 1613-1619 (7)	16.75	16.75

Souvenir Sheets
1620	A246	15r multicolored	6.00	6.00
1621	A246	20r multicolored	6.50	6.50

First glider flight, cent. (No. 1613). Charles de Gaulle, birth cent. in 1990 (Nos. 1614, 1618, & 1620). Trans-Siberian Railway, cent. (Nos. 1615, 1619 & 1621). Hanover, 750th anniv. (#1616). Swiss Confederation, 700th anniv. (No. 1617).
No. 1621 contains one 58x43mm stamp.

Birds — A247

Designs: 10 l, Numenius phaeopus. 25 l, Egretta alba. 50 l, Ardea cinerea. 2r, Phalacrocorax aristotelis. 3.50r, Sterna dougallii. 5r, Tringa nebularia. 6.50r+50 l, Neophron percnopterus. 8r, Upupa epops. 10r, Elanus caeruleus. 25r, Eudocimus ruber. 30r, Falco peregrinus. 40r, Milvus migrans. 50r, Pluvialis squatarola.

Perf. 14½, 13 (6.50r+50 l, 30r, 40r)
1992-94
1624	A247	10 l multi	.30	.30
1625	A247	25 l multi	.30	.30
1626	A247	50 l multi	.30	.30
1627	A247	2r multi	.70	.70
1628	A247	3.50r multi	1.25	1.25
1629	A247	5r multi	1.75	1.75
1630	A247	6.50r +50 l multi	2.00	2.00
1631	A247	8r multi	2.75	2.75
1632	A247	10r multi	3.50	3.50
1633	A247	25r multi	5.50	5.50
1634	A247	30r multi	7.00	7.00
1635	A247	40r multi	10.00	10.00
1636	A247	50r multi	12.50	12.50
		Nos. 1624-1636 (13)	47.85	47.85

Issued: 10 l, 25 l, 50 l, 2r, 3.50r, 5r, 8r, 10r, 25r, 2/17/92; 6.50r+50 l, 30r, 11/93; 40r, 1994(?).
See No. 2323.

Queen Elizabeth II's Accession to the Throne, 40th Anniv.
Common Design Type

1992, Feb. 6   **Perf. 14**
1637	CD348	1r multicolored	.30	.30
1638	CD348	3.50r multicolored	1.00	1.00
1639	CD348	7r multicolored	2.00	2.00
1640	CD348	10r multicolored	2.75	2.75
		Nos. 1637-1640 (4)	6.05	6.05

Souvenir Sheets
1641	CD348	18r Queen, palm trees	5.75	5.75
1642	CD348	18r Queen, boat	5.75	5.75

This set differs from the common design in that the Queen's portrait and local view are separated by a curved line rather than with a cypher outline.

Disney Characters on World Tour A248

Designs: 25 l, Mickey on Flying Carpet Airways. 50 l, Goofy at Big Ben, London. 1r, Mickey in Holland. 2r, Pluto eating pasta, Italy. 3r, Mickey, Donald do sombrero stomp in Mexico. 3.50r, Mickey, Goofy, and Donald form Miki Tiki, Polynesia. 5r, Goofy's Alpine antics, Austria. 7r, Mickey Maus, Germany. 10r, Donald as Samurai Duck. 12r, Mickey in Russia. 15r, Mickey's Oom-pah Band in Germany. No. 1654, Mickey, globe. No. 1655, Donald in Ireland chasing leprechaun with pot of gold at end of rainbow, horiz. No. 1655A, Pluto, kangaroo with joey, Australia.

1992, Feb. 4   **Perf. 13x13½**
1643	A248	25 l multi	.25	.25
1644	A248	50 l multi	.25	.25
1645	A248	1r multi	.35	.35
1646	A248	2r multi	.65	.65
1647	A248	3r multi	.90	.90
1648	A248	3.50r multi	.90	.90
1649	A248	5r multi	1.25	1.25
1650	A248	7r multi	1.75	1.75
1651	A248	10r multi	2.25	2.25
1652	A248	12r multi	3.00	3.00
1653	A248	15r multi	4.50	4.50
		Nos. 1643-1653 (11)	16.05	16.05

Souvenir Sheets
1654	A248	25r multi	6.00	6.00
1655	A248	25r multi	4.75	4.75
1655A	A248	25r multi	4.75	4.75

While the rest of the set has the same issue date as Nos. 1644-1645, 1647, 1653-1654, their dollar value was lower when they were released.

Fish A249

Designs: 7 l, Blue surgeonfish. 20 l, Bigeye. 50 l, Yellowfin tuna. 1r, two-spot red snapper. 3.50r, Sabre squirrelfish. 5r, Picasso triggerfish. 8r, Bennet's butterflyfish. 10r, Parrotfish. 12r, Grouper. 15r, Skpjack tuna. No. 1666, Clownfish. No. 1667, Sweetlips. No. 1667A, Treadfin butterflyfish. No. 1667B, Clown triggerfish.

1992, Mar. 23   **Litho.**   **Perf. 14**
1656	A249	7 l multicolored	.30	.30
1657	A249	20 l multicolored	.30	.30
1658	A249	50 l multicolored	.30	.30
1659	A249	1r multicolored	.30	.30
1660	A249	3.50r multicolored	1.00	1.00
1661	A249	8r multicolored	1.40	1.40
1662	A249	8r multicolored	2.25	2.25
1663	A249	10r multicolored	3.00	3.00
1664	A249	12r multicolored	3.25	3.25
1665	A249	15r multicolored	4.00	4.00
		Nos. 1656-1665 (10)	16.10	16.10

Souvenir Sheets
1666	A249	20r multicolored	3.75	3.75
1667	A249	20r multicolored	3.75	3.75
1667A	A249	20r multicolored	3.75	3.75
1667B	A249	20r multicolored	3.75	3.75

World Columbian Stamp Expo '92, Chicago A250

Walt Disney characters in Chicago: 1r, Mickey as Indian with Jean Baptiste Pointe du Sable, founder of Chicago. 3.50r, Donald at old Chicago post office, 1831. 7r, Donald in old Fort Dearborn. 15r, Goofy, mastodon at Museum of Science and Industry. 25r, Minnie and Mickey at Ferris wheel midway, Columbian Exposition, 1893, horiz.

1992, Apr. 15   **Perf. 13½x14**
1668	A250	1r multicolored	.30	.30
1669	A250	3.50r multicolored	1.10	1.10
1670	A250	7r multicolored	2.10	2.10
1671	A250	15r multicolored	4.25	4.25
		Nos. 1668-1671 (4)	7.75	7.75

Souvenir Sheet
Perf. 14x13½
1672	A250	25r multicolored	7.00	7.00

No. 1671 identifies Field Museum as Museum of Science and Industry.

Granada '92 — A251

Disney characters in old Alhambra, Granada: 2r, Minnie in Court of Lions. 5r, Goofy bathing in Lions Fountain. 8r, Mickey walking near Gate of Justice. 12r, Donald Duck serenading Daisy in Vermilion Towers. No. 1682, Goofy and Mickey outside Towers of the Alhambra.

1992, Apr. 15   **Perf. 13½x14**
1678	A251	2r multicolored	.60	.60
1679	A251	5r multicolored	1.50	1.50
1680	A251	8r multicolored	2.40	2.40
1681	A251	12r multicolored	3.75	3.75
		Nos. 1678-1681 (4)	8.25	8.25

Souvenir Sheet
1682	A251	25r multicolored	7.00	7.00

A252

Flowers of the World — A253

1992, Apr. 26   **Litho.**   **Perf. 14½**
1688	A252	25 l United States	.25	.25
1689	A252	50 l Australia	.25	.25
1690	A252	2r England	.70	.70
1691	A252	3.50r Brazil	1.25	1.25

1692	A252	5r Holland	1.75	1.75
1693	A252	8r France	2.75	2.75
1694	A252	10r Japan	3.25	3.25
1695	A252	15r Africa	4.75	4.75
		Nos. 1688-1695 (8)	14.95	14.95

Souvenir Sheets
Perf. 14

1696	A253	25r org, yel & red vio flowers	6.25	6.25
1696A	A253	25r red, pink & yel flowers	6.25	6.25

No. 1696 contains one 57x43mm stamp.
No. 1696A contains one 57x34mm stamp.

Natl. Security Service, Cent. A254

1992, Apr. 21   **Perf. 14**

1697	A254	3.50r Coast Guard	1.25	1.25
1698	A254	5r Infantry	2.25	2.25
1699	A254	10r Aakoatey	4.75	4.75
1700	A254	15r Fire department	7.00	7.00
		Nos. 1697-1700 (4)	15.25	15.25

Souvenir Sheet

1701	A254	20r Sultan in procession	7.00	7.00

A255

Mushrooms: 10 l, Laetiporus sulphureus. 25 l, Coprinus atramentarius. 50 l, Gandoderma lucidum. 3.50r, Russula aurata. 5r, Polyporus umbellatus. 8r, Suillus grevillei. 10r, Clavaria zollingeri. No. 1709, Boletus edulis. No. 1710, Irametes cinnabarina. No. 1711, Marasmius oreades.

1992, May 14   **Litho.**   **Perf. 14**

1702	A255	10 l multicolored	.25	.25
1703	A255	25 l multicolored	.25	.25
1704	A255	50 l multicolored	.25	.25
1705	A255	3.50r multicolored	1.00	1.00
1706	A255	5r multicolored	1.25	1.25
1707	A255	8r multicolored	2.25	2.25
1708	A255	10r multicolored	2.50	2.50
1709	A255	25r multicolored	6.50	6.50
		Nos. 1702-1709 (8)	14.25	14.25

Souvenir Sheets

1710	A255	25r multicolored	6.75	6.75
1711	A255	25r multicolored	6.75	6.75

A256

1992, June 1

1712	A256	10 l Hurdles	.25	.25
1713	A256	1r Boxing	.25	.25
1714	A256	3.50r Women's running	.90	.90
1715	A256	5r Discus	1.25	1.25
1716	A256	7r Basketball	1.75	1.75
1717	A256	10r Race walking	2.50	2.50
1718	A256	12r Rhythmic gymnastics	3.00	3.00
1719	A256	20r Fencing	5.00	5.00
		Nos. 1712-1719 (8)	14.90	14.90

Souvenir Sheets

1720	A256	25r Olympic flame	5.00	5.00
1721	A256	25r Olympic rings, flags	5.00	5.00

1992 Summer Olympics, Barcelona.

A256a

1992 Winter Olympics, Albertville: 5r, Two-man bobsled. 8r, Free-style ski jump. 10r, Women's cross-country skiing. No. 1725, Women's slalom skiing, horiz. No. 1726, Men's figure skating.

1992, June 1   **Litho.**   **Perf. 14**

1722	A256a	5r multicolored	1.00	1.00
1723	A256a	8r multicolored	1.60	1.60
1724	A256a	10r multicolored	2.00	2.00
		Nos. 1722-1724 (3)	4.60	4.60

Souvenir Sheets

1725	A256a	25r multicolored	4.75	4.75
1726	A256a	25r multicolored	4.75	4.75

Dinosaurs — A257

Designs: 5 l, Deinonychus. 10 l, Styracosaurus. 25 l, Mamenchisaurus. 50 l, Stenonychosaurus. 1r, Parasaurolophus. 1.25r, Scelidosaurus. 1.75r, Tyrannosaurus. 2r, Stegosaurus. 3.50r, Iguanodon. 4r, Anatosaurus. 5r, Monoclonius. 7r, Tenontosaurus. 8r, Brachiosaurus. 10r, Euoplocephalus. 25r, Triceratops. 50r, Apatosaurus.
No. 1743, Iguanodon, allosaurus. No. 1744, Hadrosaur. No. 1745, Tyrannosaurus, triceratops. No. 1746, Brachiosaurus, iguanodons.

1992, Sept. 15   **Litho.**   **Perf. 14**

1727	A257	5 l multicolored	.25	.25
1728	A257	10 l multicolored	.25	.25
1729	A257	25 l multicolored	.25	.25
1730	A257	50 l multicolored	.25	.25
1731	A257	1r multicolored	.25	.25
1732	A257	1.25r multicolored	.30	.30
1733	A257	1.75r multicolored	.40	.40
1734	A257	2r multicolored	.45	.45
1735	A257	3.50r multicolored	.80	.80
1736	A257	4r multicolored	.90	.90
1737	A257	5r multicolored	1.10	1.10
1738	A257	7r multicolored	1.60	1.60
1739	A257	8r multicolored	1.90	1.90
1740	A257	10r multicolored	2.25	2.25
1741	A257	25r multicolored	5.75	5.75
1742	A257	50r multicolored	11.50	11.50
		Nos. 1727-1742 (16)	28.20	28.20

Souvenir Sheets

1743	A257	25r multicolored	5.00	5.00
1744	A257	25r multicolored	5.00	5.00
1745	A257	25r multicolored	5.00	5.00
1746	A257	25r multicolored	5.00	5.00

Genoa '92.

1992 Summer Olympics, Barcelona A258

10 l, Pole vault, vert.. 25 l, Pommel horse. 50 l, Shot put, vert. 1r, Horizontal bar. 2r, Triple jump. 3.50r, Table tennis, vert. 7r, Wrestling. 9r, Baseball, vert. 12r, Swimming. 25r, Decathlon (high jump).

1992, June 1   **Litho.**   **Perf. 14**

1747	A258	10 l multicolored	.25	.25
1748	A258	25 l multicolored	.25	.25
1749	A258	50 l multicolored	.25	.25
1750	A258	1r multicolored	.25	.25
1751	A258	2r multicolored	.50	.50
1752	A258	3.50r multicolored	.90	.90
1753	A258	7r multicolored	1.90	1.90
1754	A258	9r multicolored	2.10	2.10
1755	A258	12r multicolored	3.00	3.00
		Nos. 1747-1755 (9)	9.40	9.40

Souvenir Sheet

1756	A258	25r multicolored	9.00	9.00

Souvenir Sheets

Mysteries of the Universe — A259

No. 1757, Loch Ness monster. No. 1758, Explosion of the Hindenburg. No. 1759, Crystal skulls. No. 1760, Black holes. No. 1761, UFO near Washington State. No. 1762, UFO near Columbus, Ohio. No. 1763, Explosion at Chernobyl, 1986. No. 1764, Crop circles of Great Britain. No. 1765, Ghosts of English castles and mansions. No. 1766, Drawings of Plain of Nasca, Peru, vert. No. 1767, Stonehenge, England, vert. No. 1768, Bust of Plato, the disappearance of Atlantis. No. 1769, Footprint of Yeti (abominable snowman), vert. No. 1770, Pyramids of Giza. No. 1771, Bermuda Triangle. No. 1772, The Mary Celeste, vert.

1992, Oct. 28

1757-1772	A259	25r each	6.50	6.50

1994 World Cup Soccer Championships, US — A260

Players of 1990 German team: 10 l, Jurgen Klinsmann. 25 l, Pierre Littbarski. 50 l, Lothar Matthaus. 1r, Rudi Voller. 2r, Thomas Hassler. 3.50r, Thomas Berthold. 4r, Jurgen Kohler. 5r, Berti Vogts, trainer. 6r, Bodo Illgner. 7r, Klaus Augenthaler. 8r, Franz Beckenbauer, coach. 10r, Andreas Brehme. 12r, Guido Buchwald.
No. 1786, Team members, horiz. No. 1787, Unidentified player in action, horiz.

1992, Aug. 10   **Litho.**   **Perf. 14**

1773	A260	10 l multicolored	.25	.25
1774	A260	25 l multicolored	.25	.25
1775	A260	50 l multicolored	.25	.25
1776	A260	1r multicolored	.25	.25
1777	A260	2r multicolored	.60	.60
1778	A260	3.50r multicolored	1.00	1.00
1779	A260	4r multicolored	1.10	1.10
1780	A260	5r multicolored	1.50	1.50
1781	A260	6r multicolored	1.75	1.75
1782	A260	7r multicolored	2.00	2.00
1783	A260	8r multicolored	2.25	2.25
1784	A260	10r multicolored	3.00	3.00
1785	A260	12r multicolored	3.50	3.50
		Nos. 1773-1785 (13)	17.70	17.70

Souvenir Sheets

1786	A260	35r multicolored	6.50	6.50
1787	A260	35r multicolored	6.50	6.50

Souvenir Sheet

New York Public Library — A261

1992, Oct. 28   **Litho.**   **Perf. 14**

1788	A261	20r multicolored	7.50	7.50

Postage Stamp Mega Event '92, New York City.

Walt Disney's Goofy, 60th Anniv. — A262

Scenes from Disney cartoon films: 10 l, Father's Weekend, 1953. 50 l, Symphony Hour, 1942. 75 l, Frank Duck Brings 'Em Back Alive, 1946. 1r, Crazy with the Heat, 1947. 2r, The Big Wash, 1948. 3.50r, How to Ride a Horse, 1950. 5r, Two Gun Goofy, 1952. 8r, Saludos Amigos, 1943, vert. 10r, How to Be a Detective, 1952. 12r, For Whom the Bulls Toil, 1953. 15r, Double Dribble, 1946, vert.
No. 1801, Mickey and the Beanstalk, 1947. No. 1802, Double Dribble, 1946, vert., diff. No. 1803, The Goofy Success Story, 1955.

Perf. 14x13½, 13½x14

1992, Dec. 7   **Litho.**

1789	A262	10 l multicolored	.25	.25
1791	A262	50 l multicolored	.25	.25
1792	A262	75 l multicolored	.25	.25
1793	A262	1r multicolored	.25	.25
1794	A262	2r multicolored	.50	.50
1795	A262	3.50r multicolored	.90	.90
1796	A262	5r multicolored	1.25	1.25
1797	A262	8r multicolored	2.00	2.00
1798	A262	10r multicolored	2.25	2.25
1799	A262	12r multicolored	2.75	2.75
1800	A262	15r multicolored	3.50	3.50
		Nos. 1789-1800 (11)	14.15	14.15

Souvenir Sheets

1801	A262	20r multicolored	4.25	4.25
1802	A262	20r multicolored	4.25	4.25
1803	A262	20r multicolored	4.25	4.25

A number has been reserved for an additional value in this set.

A263

Anniversaries and Events — A264

Designs: 1r, Zeppelin on bombing raid over London during World War I. No. 1805, German, French flags, Konrad Adenauer, Charles de Gaulle. No. 1806, Radio telescope. No. 1807, Columbus studying globe. No. 1808, Indian rhinoceros. 7r, WHO, ICN, and FAO emblems. 8r, Green sea turtle. No. 1822, Scarlet macaw. No. 1811, Lion's Intl. emblem and Melvin Jones, founder. No. 1812, Yacht America, first America's Cup winner, 1851. 12r, Columbus claiming San Salvador for Spain. No. 1814, Voyager 1 approaching Saturn. No. 1815, NATO flag, airplanes, Adenauer. 20r, Graf Zeppelin over New York City. No. 1817, Landsat satellite. No. 1818, Count Zeppelin. No. 1819, Santa Maria. No. 1820, Konrad Adenauer. No. 1821, Zubin Mehta, music director, NY Philharmonic, vert. No. 1823, Friedrich Schmiedl (b. 1902), rocket mail pioneer.

1992-93   **Litho.**   **Perf. 14**

1804	A263	1r multicolored	.30	.30
1805	A263	3.50r multicolored	.90	.90
1806	A263	3.50r multicolored	.70	.70
1807	A263	6r multicolored	1.50	1.50
1808	A263	6r multicolored	1.25	1.25
1809	A263	7r multicolored	1.40	1.40
1810	A263	8r multicolored	1.60	1.60
1811	A263	10r multicolored	1.75	1.75
1812	A263	10r multicolored	1.75	1.75
1813	A263	12r multicolored	2.75	2.75
1814	A263	15r multicolored	2.75	2.75
1815	A263	15r multicolored	3.75	3.75
1816	A263	20r multicolored	5.50	5.50
		Nos. 1804-1816 (13)	25.90	25.90

Souvenir Sheets

1817	A263	20r multicolored	6.00	6.00
1818	A263	20r multicolored	6.25	6.25
1819	A263	20r multicolored	6.25	6.25
1820	A263	20r multicolored	6.00	6.00
1821	A264	20r multicolored	6.75	6.75
1822	A263	20r multicolored	6.00	4.60
1823	A263	25r multicolored	6.50	6.50
	Nos. 1817-1823 (7)		43.75	42.35

Count Zeppelin, 75th anniv. of death (Nos. 1804, 1816, 1818). Konrad Adenauer, 25th anniv. of death (Nos. 1805, 1815, 1820). Intl. Space Year (Nos. 1806, 1814, 1817). Columbus' discovery of America, 500th anniversary (Nos. 1807, 1813, 1819). Earth Summit, Rio de Janeiro (Nos. 1808, 1810, 1822). Intl. Conference on Nutrition, Rome (No. 1809). Lions Intl., 75th anniversary (No. 1811). America's Cup yacht race (No. 1812). New York Philharmonic, 150th anniv. (No. 1821).

No. 1823 contains one 27x35mm stamp.

Issue dates: Nos. 1805, 1808, 1810, 1815, 1820, 1822, Jan. 1993. Others, Nov. 1992.

Miniature Sheet

Western Films — A265

Actors and film: No. 1824a, Jimmy Stewart and Marlene Dietrich, Destry Rides Again, 1939. b, Gary Cooper, The Westerner, 1940. c, Henry Fonda, My Darling Clementine, 1940. d, Alan Ladd, Shane, 1953. e, Kirk Douglas and Burt Lancaster, Gunfight at the O.K. Coral, 1957. f, Steve McQueen, The Magnificent Seven, 1960. g, Robert Redford and Paul Newman, Butch Cassidy & The Sundance Kid, 1969. h, Jack Nicholson and Randy Quaid, The Missouri Breaks, 1976.

No. 1825, Clint Eastwood, Pale Rider. No. 1826, John Wayne, The Searchers, 1956.

1992-93		Litho.	**Perf. 13½x14**	
1824	A265	5r Sheet of 8, #a.-h.	11.00	11.00

Souvenir Sheets

1825	A265	20r multicolored	5.25	5.25
1826	A265	20r multicolored	5.25	5.25

Issued: Nos. 1824-1825, 1992; No. 1826, 1/1993.

Miniature Sheet

Opening of Euro Disney Resort, Paris — A266

Disney characters in paintings by French impressionists — No. 1827: a, Minnie on theater balcony. b, Goofy playing cards. c, Mickey and Minnie walking by outdoor cafe. d, Mickey fishing. e, Goofy dancing to music of harp player. f, Mickey and Minnie in boat. g, Minnie on dance floor. h, Mickey strolling through country. i, Minnie standing behind Polynesian woman.

1992, Dec.			**Perf. 14x13½**	
1827	A266	5r Sheet of 9, #a.-i.	15.00	15.00

Souvenir Sheets

1828	A266	20r Goofy	3.75	3.75
1829	A266	20r Minnie	3.75	3.75
1830	A266	20r Mickey	3.75	3.75
		Perf. 13½x14		
1831	A266	20r Donald Duck, vert.	3.75	3.75

SAARC Year of the Environment — A267

Designs: 25 l, Waterfall, drought area. 50 l, Clean, polluted beaches. 5r, Clean, polluted ocean. 10r, Clean island with vegetation, island polluted with trees dying.

1992, Dec. 30		Litho.	**Perf. 14**	
1832	A267	25 l multicolored	.25	.25
1833	A267	50 l multicolored	.25	.25
1834	A267	5r multicolored	.90	.90
1835	A267	10r multicolored	1.75	1.75
	Nos. 1832-1835 (4)		3.15	3.15

Elvis Presley (1935-1977) A268

a, Portrait. b, With guitar. c, With microphone.

1993, Jan. 7				
1836	A268	3.50r Strip of 3, #a.-c.	2.75	2.75

A set of 4 stamps commemorating South Asia Tourism year, formerly listed as Nos. 1837-1840, were prepared but not issued.

Miniature Sheets

Madame Seriziat — A270

Louvre Museum, Bicent.

Details or entire paintings, by Jacques-Louis David (1748-1825):
No. 1841: b, Pierre Seriziat. c, Madame de Verninac. d, Madame Recamier. e, Self-portrait. f, General Bonaparte. g-h, The Lictors Returning to Brutus the Bodies of his Sons (left, right).

Paintings by Jean-Baptiste-Camille Corot (1796-1875):
No. 1842: a, Self-portrait. b, The Woman in Blue. c, The Jeweled Woman. d, Young Girl in her Dressing Room. e, Haydee. f, Chartres Cathedral. g, The Belfry at Douai. h, The Bridge at Mantes.

Paintings by Jean-Honore Fragonard (1732-1806):
No. 1843: a, The Study. b, Denis Diderot. c, Marie-Madeleine Guimard. d, The Inspiration. e, Tivoli Cascades. f, The Music Lesson. g, The Bolt. h, Blindman's Buff.

No. 1844, The Gardens of the Villa D'Este, Tivoli, by Jean-Baptiste-Camille Corot, horiz.

No. 1845, Young Tiger Playing with its Mother, by Delacroix.

1993, Jan. 7		Litho.	**Perf. 12**	
			Sheets of 8	
1841	A270	8r #a.-h. + label	11.00	11.00
1842	A270	8r #a.-h. + label	11.00	11.00
1843	A270	8r #a.-h. + label	11.00	11.00

Souvenir Sheets
Perf. 14½

1844	A270	20r multicolored	6.00	6.00
1845	A270	20r multicolored	6.00	6.00

Nos. 1844-1845 contains one 88x55mm stamp.

Miniature Sheet

Coronation of Queen Elizabeth II, 40th Anniv. — A271

Designs: a, 3.50r, Official coronation photograph. b, 5r, St. Edward's crown. c, 10r, Dignitaries viewing ceremony. d, 10r, Queen, Prince Philip examining banknote.

1993, June 2			**Perf. 13½x14**	
1846	A271	Sheet, 2 ea #a.-d.	13.00	13.00

A number has been reserved for an additional value in this set.

Shells — A272

Designs: 7 l, Precious wentletrap. 15 l, Purple sea snail. 50 l, Arabian cowrie. 3.50r, Major harp. 4r, Royal paper bubble. 5r, Sieve cowrie. 6r, Episcopal miter. 7r, Camp pitarvenus. 8r, Eyed auger. 10r, Onyx cowrie. 12r, Map cowrie. 20r, Caltrop murex.

No. 1856, Scorpion spider conch. No. 1857, Black striped triton. No. 1857A, Bull's-mouth helmet.

1993, July 15		Litho.	**Perf. 14**	
1848	A272	7 l multicolored	.30	.30
1849	A272	15 l multicolored	.30	.30
1850	A272	50 l multicolored	.30	.30
1850A	A272	3.50r multicolored	1.00	1.00
1850B	A272	4r multicolored	1.10	1.10
1851	A272	5r multicolored	1.40	1.40
1852	A272	6r multicolored	1.75	1.75
1852A	A272	7r multicolored	1.90	1.90
1853	A272	8r multicolored	2.25	2.25
1854	A272	10r multicolored	2.75	2.75
1854A	A272	12r multicolored	3.25	3.25
1855	A272	20r multicolored	5.75	5.75
	Nos. 1848-1855 (12)		22.05	22.05

Souvenir Sheets

1856	A272	25r multicolored	8.00	8.00
1857	A272	25r multicolored	8.00	8.00
1857A	A272	25r multicolored	8.00	8.00

Endangered Animals — A273

7 l, Sifaka lemur. 10 l, Snow leopard. 15 l, Numbat. 25 l, Gorilla. 2r, Koalas. 3.50r, Cheetah. 5r, Yellow-footed rock wallaby. 7r, Orangutan. 8r, Black lemur. 10r, Black rhinoceros. 15r, Humpback whale. 20r, Mauritius parakeet.

No. 1866, Asian elephant. No. 1867, Tiger. No. 1867A, Giant panda.

1993, July 20		Litho.	**Perf. 14**	
1857B	A273	7 l multicolored	.30	.30
1858	A273	10 l multicolored	.30	.30
1859	A273	15 l multicolored	.30	.30
1859A	A273	25 l multicolored	.30	.30
1860	A273	2r multicolored	.65	.65
1860A	A273	3.50r multicolored	1.10	1.40
1861	A273	5r multicolored	1.50	1.50
1862	A273	7r multicolored	2.10	2.10
1863	A273	8r multicolored	2.40	2.40
1864	A273	10r multicolored	3.00	3.00
1865	A273	15r multicolored	4.25	4.25
1865A	A273	20r multicolored	5.50	5.50
	Nos. 1857B-1865A (12)		21.70	22.00

Souvenir Sheets

1866	A273	25r multicolored	8.00	8.00
1867	A273	25r multicolored	8.00	8.00
1867A	A273	25r multicolored	8.00	8.00

Miniature Sheets

Fish — A274

No. 1868: b, Black pyramid butterflyfish. c, Bird wrasse. d, Checkerboard wrasse. e, Blue face angelfish. f, Bannerfish. g, Threadfin butterflyfish. h, Picasso triggerfish. i, Pennantfish. j, Grouper. k, Black back butterflyfish. l, Redfin triggerfish. m, Redfin butterflyfish.

No. 1868A: n, Yellow goatfish. o, Emperor angelfish. p, Madagascar butterflyfish. q, Empress angelfish. r, Longnose butterfly. s, Racoon butterflyfish. t, Harlequin filefish. u, Wedgetailed triggerfish. v, Clark's anemonefish. w, Clown triggerfish. x, Zebra lionfish. y, Maldive clownfish.

No. 1869, Goldbelly anemone, vert. No. 1869A, Klein's butterflyfish, vert.

1993, June 30			**Perf. 14x13½**	
			Sheets of 12	
1868	A274	3.50r #b.-m.	10.00	10.00
1868A	A274	3.50r #n.-y.	10.00	10.00

Souvenir Sheets
Perf. 12x13

1869	A274	25r multicolored	6.00	6.00
1869A	A274	25r multicolored	6.00	6.00

Miniature Sheets

Birds — A275

No. 1870: a, Pallid harrier. b, Cattle egret. c, Koel (b). d, Tree pipit. e, Short-ear owl. f, European kestrel. g, Yellow wagtail. h, Common heron. i, Black bittern. j, Common snipe. k, Little egret. l, Little stint.

No. 1871: a, Gull-billed tern. b, Long-tailed tropicbird (a). c, Frigate bird. d, Wilson's petrel. e, White tern. f, Brown booby. g, Marsh harrier. h, Common noddy. i, Little heron. j, Turnstone. k, Curlew. l, Crab plover.

No. 1872, Caspian tern, horiz. No. 1873, Audubon's shearwater, horiz.

1993, July 5			**Perf. 13½x14**	
1870	A275	3.50r Sheet of 12, #a.-l.	9.50	9.50
1871	A275	3.50r Sheet of 12, #a.-l.	9.50	9.50

Souvenir Sheet
Perf. 13x12

1872	A275	25r multicolored	6.00	6.00
1873	A275	25r multicolored	6.00	6.00

No. 1871 is horiz.

Year of Productivity
A276   A277

1993, July 25   Perf. 14
1874 A276 7r multicolored   1.40 1.40
1875 A277 10r multicolored   2.10 2.10

A278   A279

Picasso (1881-1973): 3.50r, Still Life with Pitcher and Apples, 1919. 5r, Bowls and Jug, 1908. 10r, Bowls of Fruit and Loaves, 1908. 20r, Green Still Life, 1914, horiz.

1993, Oct. 11   Litho.   Perf. 14
1876 A278 3.50r multicolored   .80 .80
1877 A278 5r multicolored   1.10 1.10
1878 A278 10r multicolored   2.25 2.25
    Nos. 1876-1878 (3)   4.15 4.15
Souvenir Sheet
1879 A278 20r multicolored   5.00 5.00

1993, Oct. 11
Copernicus (1473-1543): 3.50r, Early astronomical instrument. 15r, Astronaut wearing Manned Maneuvering Unit. 20r, Copernicus.
1880 A279 3.50r multicolored   .90 .90
1881 A279 15r multicolored   4.00 4.00
Souvenir Sheet
1882 A279 20r multicolored   5.00 5.00

Royal Wedding of Crown Prince Naruhito, Princess Masako — A280

3.50r, Crown Prince Naruhito. 10r, Princess Masako, horiz. 25r, Princess Masako.

1993, Oct. 11
1883 A280 3.50r multicolored   .65 .65
1884 A280 10r multicolored   2.00 2.00
Souvenir Sheet
1885 A280 25r multicolored   6.00 6.00

1994 Winter Olympics, Lillehammer, Norway — A281

8r, Marina Kiehl, gold medalist, women's downhill, 1988. 15r, Vegard Ulvang, gold medalist, cross-country skiing, 1992. 25r, Soviet ice hockey goalie, 1980.

1993, Oct. 11
1886 A281 8r multicolored   1.75 1.75
1887 A281 15r multicolored   3.50 3.50
Souvenir Sheet
1888 A281 25r multicolored   6.00 6.00

Polska '93 — A282

Fine arts: 3.50r, Zolte Roze, by Menasze Seidenbeutel, 1932. 5r, Cracow Historical Museum. 18r, Apples and Curtain, by Waclaw Borowski. 25r, Seascape, by Roman Sielski, 1931, horiz.

1993, Oct. 11   Litho.   Perf. 14
1889 A282 3.50r multicolored   .85 .85
1890 A282 5r multicolored   1.10 1.10
1891 A282 8r multicolored   1.90 1.90
    Nos. 1889-1891 (3)   3.85 3.85
Souvenir Sheet
1892 A282 25r multicolored   5.00 5.00

Butterflies
A283

1993, Oct. 25
1893 A283 7 l Commander   .25 .25
1894 A283 20 l Blue tiger   .25 .25
1895 A283 25 l Centaur oak-
                   blue   .25 .25
1896 A283 50 l Common
                   banded pea-
                   cock   .25 .25
1897 A283 5r Glad-eye
                   bushbrown   1.40 1.40
1898 A283 6.50r + 50 l Common tree
                   nymph   2.00 2.00
1899 A283 7r Lemon emi-
                   grant   2.00 2.00
1900 A283 10r Blue pansy   2.75 2.75
1901 A283 12r Painted lady   3.50 3.50
1902 A283 15r Blue mormon   4.25 4.25
1903 A283 18r Tamil yeoman   5.00 5.00
1904 A283 20r Crimson rose   5.50 5.50
    Nos. 1893-1904 (12)   27.40 27.40
Souvenir Sheets
1905 A283 25r Common impe-
                   rial   7.50 7.50
1906 A283 25r Great orange
                   tip   7.50 7.50
1907 A283 25r Black prince   7.50 7.50
    Nos. 1905-1907 are vert.

Aviation Anniversaries — A284

Designs: 3.50r, Zeppelin on bombing raid caught in British search lights, vert. 5r, Homing pigeon. 10r, Dr. Hugo Eckener, vert. 15r,

Airmal service medal, Jim Edgerton's Jenny, mail truck. 20r, USS Macon approaching mooring mast, vert.
    Each 25r: No. 1913, Blanchard's balloon, 1793, vert. No. 1914, Santos-Dumont's flight around Eiffel Tower, 1901, vert.

1993, Nov. 22   Litho.   Perf. 14
1908-1912 A284 Set of 5   14.00 14.00
Souvenir Sheets
1913-1914 A284 Set of 2   9.50 9.50
    Dr. Hugo Eckener, 125th birth anniv. (3.50r, 10r, 20r, No. 1913).

Miniature Sheets

First Ford Engine, First Benz Four-Wheeled Car, Cent. — A285

No. 1915: a, 1915 Model T (b, d-e). b, Henry Ford (e). c, Drawing of 1st Ford engine (b, e-f). d, 1993 Ford Probe GT (e). e, 1947 Ford Sportsman, front (f). f, As "f," rear (e). g, 1915 Ford advertisement (j). h, 1955 Ford Thunderbird (g, i). i, Ford emblem (f, h). j, 1958 Edsel Citation. k, 1941 Ford half-ton pickup. l, Model T.

No. 1916: a, 1937 Daimler-Benz Straight 8 (b). b, Karl Benz (e). c, Mercedes-Benz advertisement (f). d, 1929 Mercedes 38-250SS (e). e, 1893 Benz Viktoria (f, h). f, Mercedes star emblem (i). g, WWI Mercedes engine. h, 1957 Mercedes-Benz 300SL Gullwing (g). i, 1993 Mercedes Benz SL coupe/roadster (h). j, 1906 Benz 4-cylinder car (k). k, Early Benz advertisement. l, Benz Viktoria, 1893.

1993, Nov. 22
1915 A285 3.50r Sheet of 12,
                   #a.-l.   12.00 12.00
1916 A285 3.50r Sheet of 12,
                   #a.-l.   12.00 12.00
Souvenir Sheets
1917 A285 25r 1933 Ford
                   Model Y   6.00 6.00
1918 A285 25r 1955 Mercedes
                   300S   6.00 6.00

Peter and the Wolf — A286

Characters and scenes from Disney animated film: 7 l, 15 l, 20 l, 25 l, 50 l, 1r.
    Nos. 1925a-1925i: Part 1.
    Nos. 1926a-1926i: Part 2.

1993, Dec. 20
1919-1924 A286 Set of 6   1.00 1.00
Miniature Sheets of 9
1925 A286 3.50r #a.-i.   7.50 7.50
1926 A286 3.50r #a.-i.   7.50 7.50
Souvenir Sheets
1927 A286 25r Sonia   5.00 5.00
1928 A286 25r Ivan   5.00 5.00

Fine Art — A287

Paintings by Rembrandt: 50 l, Girl with a Broom. No. 1931, 3.50r, Young Girl at half-open Door. 5r, The Prophetess Hannah (Rembrandt's Mother). 7r, Woman with a Pink Flower. 12r, Lucretia. No. 1939, 15r, Lady with an Ostich Feather Fan.
    Paintings by Matisse: 2r, Girl with Tulips (Jeanne Vaderin). No. 1932, 3.50r. Portrait of Greta Moll. 6.50r, The Idol. 9r, Mme. Matisse in Japanese Robe. 10r, Portrait of MMe Matisse (The Green Line). No. 1940, 15r, The Woman with the Hat.
    Each 25r: No. 1941, Married Couple with 3 Children (A Family Group), by Rembrandt, horiz. No. 1942, The Painter's Family, by Matisse. No. 1942A: The Music Makers, by Rembrandt.

1994, Jan. 11   Litho.   Perf. 13
1929-1940 A287 Set of 12   21.00 21.00
Souvenir Sheets
1941-1942A A287 Set of 3   21.00 21.00
    No. 1942A issued Feb. 2.

1994 World Cup Soccer US — A288

Players, country: 7 l, Windischmann, US; Giannini, Italy. 20 l, Carnevale, Gascoigne. 25 l, Platt & teammates. England. 3.50r, Koeman, Holland; Klinsmann, Germany. 5r, Quinn, Ireland; Maldini, Italy. 7r, Lineker, England. 15r, Hassan, Egypt; Moran, Ireland. 18r, Canniggia, Argentina.
    Each 25r: No. 1951, Conejo, Costa Rica; Mozer, Brazil, horiz. No. 1952, Armstrong & Balboa, US; Ogris, Austria.

1994, Jan. 11   Perf. 14
1943-1950 A288 Set of 8   13.00 13.00
Souvenir Sheets
1951-1952 A288 Set of 2   12.50 12.50

A289

Hong Kong '94 — A290

Stamps, Moon-Lantern Festival, Hong Kong: No. 1953, Hong Kong #416, girls, lanterns. No. 1954, Lanterns, #660.
    Cloisonne Enamel, Qing Dynasty: No. 1955a, Vase. b, Flower holder. c, Elephant

with vase on back. d, Pot (Tibetan-style lama's milk-tea pot. e, Fo-dog. f, Pot with swing handle.

1994, Feb. 18   Litho.   Perf. 14

1953	A289	4r multicolored	.80	.80
1954	A289	4r multicolored	.80	.80
a.		Pair, #1953-1954	1.60	1.60

Miniature Sheet

1955	A290	2r Sheet of 6, #a.-f.	6.75	6.75

Nos. 1953-1954 issued in sheets of 5 pairs. No. 1954a is a continuous design.
New Year 1994 (Year of the Dog) (No. 1955e).

Sierra Club, Cent. A290a

Various animals, each 6.50r:
Nos. 1956a-1956b, Prairie dog. c.-e, Woodland caribou. f, Galapagos penguin.
No. 1957, vert: a, Humpback whale. b.-c, Ocelot. d, Snow monkey. e, Prairie dog. f, Golden lion tamarin.
No. 1958: a.-b, Golden lion tamarin. c.-d, Humpback whale. e, Bengal tiger. f, Ocelot. g.-h, Snow monkey.
No. 1959, vert: a.-b, Galapagos penguin. c.-d, Bengal tiger. e.-g, Philippine tarsier. h, Sierra Club centennial emblem.

1994, May 20   Litho.   Perf. 14
Miniature Sheets of 6, #a-f

1956-1957	A290a	Set of 2	20.00	20.00

Miniature Sheets of 8, #a-h

1958-1959	A290a	Set of 2	24.00	24.00

Dome of the Rock, Jerusalem — A291

1994, June 10   Perf. 13½

1960	A291	8r multicolored	1.60	1.60

A292

Designs: 25 l, Elasmosaurus. 50 l, Dilophosaurus. 1r, Avimimus. 5r, Chasmosaurus. 8r, Edmontonia. 10r, Anatosaurus. 15r, Velociraptor. 20r, Spinosaurus.
No. 1969, each 3r: a, Dimorphodon. b, Megalosaurus. c, Kuehneosaurus. d, Dryosaurus. e, Kentrosaurus. f, Baraposaurus (c). g, Tenontosaurus. h, Elaphrosaurus (i). i, Maiasaura. j, Huayangosaurus. k, Rutiodon. l, Pianitzkysaurus.
No. 1970, each 3r: a, Quetzalcoatlus. b, Daspletosaurus. c, Pleurocoelus. d, Baryonyx. e, Pentaceratops. f, Kritosaurus. g, Microvenator (h). h, Nodosaurus. i, Montanaceratops. j, Dromiceiomimus. k, Dryptosaurus. l, Parkosaurus.
Each 25r: No. 1971, Gallimimus. No. 1972, Plateosaurus, vert.

1994, June 20   Perf. 14

1961-1968	A292	Set of 8	17.00	17.00

Miniature Sheets of 12, #a-l

1969-1970	A292	Set of 2	20.00	20.00

Souvenir Sheets

1971-1972	A292	Set of 2	10.00	10.00

Nos. 1969-1970 are continuous design.

Locomotives A293

Designs: 25 l, 2-6-6-0 Mallet, Indonesia, horiz. 50 l, C62, Japan, horiz. 1r, D51, Japan. 5r, 4-6-0 Steam, India. 8r, Class 485 electric, Japan, horiz. 10r, Class WP Pacific, India. 15r, "People" class RM 4-6-2, China. 20r, C57, Japan, horiz.
No. 1981: a, W Class 0-6-2, India. b, C53 Class, Indonesia. c, C-10, Japan. d, Hanomag 4-8-0, India. e, Hakari bullet train, Japan. f, C-55, Japan.
Each 25r: No. 1982, 4-4-0, Indonesia. No. 1983, Series 8620, Japan.

1994, July 4

1973-1980	A293	Set of 8	12.00	12.00

Miniature Sheet of 6

1981	A293	6.50r +50 l, #a.-f.	8.00	8.00

Souvenir Sheets

1982-1983	A293	Set of 2	11.00	11.00

Domestic Cats — A294

Designs: 7 l, Japanese bobtail, horiz. 20 l, Siamese. 25 l, Persian longhair, horiz. 50 l, Somali. 3.50r, Oriental shorthair, horiz. 5r, Burmese, horiz. 7r, Bombay, horiz. 10r, Turkish van. 12r, Javanese. 15r, Singapura, horiz. 18r, Turkish angora. 20r, Egyptian mau.
Each 25r: No. 1996, Birman. No. 1997, Korat. No. 1998, Abyssinian.

1994, July 11

1984-1995	A294	Set of 12	20.00	20.00

Souvenir Sheets

1996-1998	A294	Set of 3	16.50	16.50

Miniature Sheets of 6

1994 World Cup Soccer Championships, US — A295

No. 1999a, 10 l, Franco Baresi, Italy, Stuart McCall, Scotland. b, 25 l, McCarthy, Great Britain, Lineker, Ireland. c, 50 l, J. Helt, Denmark, R. Gordillo, Spain. d, 5r, Martin Vasquez, Spain, Enzo Scifo, Belgium. e, 10r, Emblem. f, 12f, Tomas Brolin, Sweden, Gordon Durie, Scotland.
No. 2000a, Bebeto, Brazil. b, Lothar Matthaus, Great Britain. c, Diego Maradona, Argentina. d, Stephane Chapuisat, Switzerland. e, George Hagi, Romania. f, Carlos Valderrama, Colombia.
No. 2001, Hossam Hassan, 2nd Egyptian player.

1994, Aug. 4   Litho.   Perf. 14

1999	A295	#a.-f.	5.50	5.50
2000	A295	6.50r #a.-f., vert.	7.50	7.50

Souvenir Sheet

2001	A295	10r multicolored	4.00	4.00

D-Day, 50th Anniv. A296

Designs: 2r, Amphibious DUKW approaches Utah Beach. 4r, Landing craft tank, Sword Beach. 18r, Landing craft infantry damaged at Omaha Beach.
No. 2006, Canadian commandos, Juno Beach.

1994, Aug. 8

2003-2005	A296	Set of 3	4.50	4.50

Souvenir Sheet

2006	A296	25r multicolored	5.75	5.75

A297

Intl. Olympic Committee, Cent. — A298

Designs: 7r, Linford Christie, Great Britain, track 1988. 12r, Koji Gushiken, Japan, gymnastics, 1984.
25r, George Hackl, Germany, single luge, 1994.

1994, Aug. 8

2007	A297	7r multicolored	1.25	1.25
2008	A297	12r multicolored	2.25	2.25

Souvenir Sheet

2009	A298	25r multicolored	5.50	5.50

A299

PHILAKOREA '94 — A300

Designs: 50 l, Suwan Folk Village duck pond. 3.50r, Youngduson Park. 20r, Ploughing, Hahoe Village, Andong region.
Ceramics, Choson & Koryo Dynasties: No. 2013a, Pear-shaped bottle. b, Vase. c, Vase with repaired lip. d, Labed vase, stoneware. e, Vase, celadon-glazed. f, Vase, unglazed stone. g, Ritual water sprinkler. h, Celadonglazed vase.
25r, Hunting (detail from eight-panel screen, Choson Dynasty), vert.

1994, Aug. 8   Perf. 14, 13½ (#2013)

2010-2012	A299	Set of 3	5.25	5.25

Miniature Sheet of 8

2013	A300	3r #a.-h.	5.25	5.25

Souvenir Sheet

2014	A299	25r multicolored	5.50	5.50

First Manned Moon Landing, 25th Anniv. — A301

No. 2015, each 5r: a, Apollo 11 crew. b, Apollo 11 patch, signatures of crew. c, "Buzz" Aldrin, lunar module, Eagle. d, Apollo 12 crew. e, Apollo 12 patch, signatures of crew. f, Alan Bean transporting ALSEP.
No. 2016, each 5r: a, Apollo 16 crew. b, Apollo 16 patch, signatures of crew. c, John Young gives a "Navy salute." d, Apollo 17 crew. e, Apollo 17 patch, signatures of crew. f, Night launch of Apollo 17.
25r, Launch at Baikonur.

1994, Aug. 8   Perf. 14
Miniature Sheets of 6, #a-f

2015-2016	A301		14.00	14.00

Souvenir Sheet

2017	A301	25r multicolored	5.50	5.50

UN Development Plan — A302

1r, Woman, baby, undernourished man, city on island. 8r, Island native, case worker, island, ship.

1994   Litho.   Perf. 14

2018	A302	1r multicolored	.25	.25
2019	A302	8r multicolored	2.00	2.00

Miniature Sheet of 12

Space Exploration — A304

No. 2020: a, Voyager 2. b, Sputnik. c, Apollo-Soyuz. d, Apollo 10 descent. e, Apollo 11 mission insignia. f, Hubble space telescope. g, Buzz Aldrin. h, RCA lunar cam. i, Lunar rover. j, Jim Irwin. k, Apollo 12 lunar module. l, Lunar soil extraction.
Each 25r: No. 2021, David Scott in open hatch of Apollo 9 command module. No. 2022, Alan Shepard, Jr. waving salute from moon, Apollo 14, horiz.

1994, Aug. 8   Litho.   Perf. 14

2020	A304	5r #a.-l.	17.50	17.50

Souvenir Sheets

2021-2022	A304	Set of 2	14.00	14.00

Aminiya School, 50th Anniv. A305

15 l, Discipline. 50 l, Arts. 1r, Emblem, hand holding book, vert. 8r, Girls carrying books,

vert. 10r, Sports. 11r, Girls cheering, vert. 13r, Science.

1994, Nov. 28
| 2023-2029 | A305 | Set of 7 | 8.75 | 8.75 |

ICAO, 50th Anniv. A306

Designs: 50 l, Boeing 747. 1r, De Havilland Comet 4. 2r, Male Intl. Airport, Maldives. 3r, Lockheed 1649 Super Star. 8r, European Airbus. 10r, Dornier Do228. 25r, Concorde.

1994, Dec. 31
| 2030-2035 | A306 | Set of 6 | 8.50 | 8.50 |

Souvenir Sheet
| 2036 | A306 | 25r multicolored | 5.75 | 5.75 |

Miniature Sheets of 9

Water Birds — A307

Designs: No. 2037a, Northern pintail (b, d). b, Comb duck (c). c, Ruddy duck. d, Garganey (a, e, g, h). e, Lesser whistling duck (b, c, f). f, Green winged teal. g, Fulvous whistling duck. h, Northern shoveler (e). i, Cotton pygmy goose (f).

No. 2038, vert.: a, Pochard (b). b, Mallard (c, e, f). c, Wigeon. d, Northern shoveler (e, g). e, Northern pintail (h). f, Garganey (e, i). g, Tufted duck. h, Ferruginous duck (i). i, Red-crested pochard.

Each 25r: No. 2039, Cotton pygmy goose, vert. No. 2040, Garganey, diff.

1995, Feb. 27 Litho. **Perf. 14**
| 2037 | A307 | 5r #a.-i. | 8.25 | 8.25 |
| 2038 | A307 | 6.50r + 50 l #a.-i. | 11.50 | 11.50 |

Souvenir Sheets
| 2039-2040 | A307 | Set of 2 | 11.00 | 11.00 |

Monuments of the World — A308

Designs: 7 l, Taj Mahal. 10 l, Washington Monument. 15 l, Mt. Rushmore Memorial. 25 l, Arc de Triomphe, vert. 50 l, Sphinx, vert. 5r, El Castillo Monument of the Toltec, Chichen Itza, Yucatan, Mexico, vert. 8r, Toltec monument, Tula, Mexico, vert. 12r, Victory Column, Berlin, vert. Each 25r: No. 2049, Moai statues, Easter Island. No. 2050, Stonehenge.

1995, Feb. 28
| 2041-2048 | A308 | Set of 8 | 6.00 | 6.00 |

Souvenir Sheets
| 2049-2050 | A308 | Set of 2 | 9.00 | 9.00 |

No. 2049 contains one 43x57mm stamp, No. 2050 one 85x28mm stamp.

Donald Duck, 60th Birthday (in 1994) — A309

Scenes from "Donald and the Wheel:" 3 l, Racing chariot. 4 l, Standing on log. 5 l, Operating steam locomotive. 10 l, Looking at cave drawing, vert. 20 l, Sitting in "junked" car, vert. 25 l, Listening to phonograph. 5r, Climbing on mammoth. 20r, Pushing old car.

Disney Duck family orchestra, vert, each 5r: No. 2059a, Donald Duck, saxophone. b, Moby Duck, violin. c, Feathry Duck, banjo. d, Daisy Duck, harp. e, Gladstone Gander, clarinet. f, Dewey, Louie, Huey, oboe. g, Gus Goose, flute. h, Ludwig von Drake, trombone.

Donald Duck family portraits, vert, each 5r: No. 2060a, Daisy. b, Donald. c, Grandma. d, Gus Goose. e, Gyro Gearloose, f, Huey, Dewey, Louie. g, Ludwig von Drake. h, Scrooge McDuck.

Each 25r: No. 2061, Dixieland band, vert. No. 2062, Donald conducting symphony orchestra. No. 2063, Donald being photographed, vert. No. 2064, Huey, Dewey, Louie in family portrait.

Perf. 13½x13, 13x13½
| 2051-2058 | A309 | Set of 8 | 6.50 | 6.50 |

Miniature Sheets of 8, #a-h
| 2059-2060 | A309 | Set of 2 | 17.00 | 17.00 |

Souvenir Sheets
| 2061-2064 | A309 | Set of 4 | 18.00 | 18.00 |

EID Greetings — A310

1r, Mosque. 1r, Rose. 8r, Hibiscus. 10r, Orchids.

1995, May 1 Litho. **Perf. 14**
| 2065-2068 | A310 | Set of 4 | 4.25 | 4.25 |

Whales, Dolphins, & Porpoises A311

Nos. 2069-2072: 1r, Killer whale. 2r, Bottlenose dolphin. 8r, Humpback whale. 10r, Common dolphin.

No. 2073, each 3r: a, Hourglass dolphin. b, Bottlenose dolphin. c, Dusky dolphin. d, Spectacled porpoise. e, Fraser's dolphin. f, Commerson's dolphin. g, Spinner dolphin. h, Dalls dolphin. i, Spotted dolphin. j, Indus river dolphin. k, Hector's dolphin. l, Amazon river dolphin.

No. 2074, each 3r: a, Right whale (d). b, Killer whale (a). c, Humpback whale (f). d, Beluga. e, Narwhale. f, Blue whale (e, g). g, Bowhead whale (h, k). h, Fin whale (d, e, g). i, Pilot whale. j, Grey whale. k, Sperm whale (l). l, Goosebeaked whale.

Each 25r: No. 2075, Hourglass dolphin. No. 2076, Sperm whale.

1995, May 16
| 2069-2072 | A311 | Set of 4 | 4.00 | 4.00 |

Miniature Sheets of 12, #a-l
| 2073-2074 | A311 | Set of 2 | 15.50 | 15.50 |

Souvenir Sheets
| 2075-2076 | A311 | Set of 2 | 12.00 | 12.00 |

Singapore '95.

UN, 50th Anniv. A311a

Designs: 30 l, Emblem, security of small states. 8r, Women in development. 11r, Peace keeping, peace making operations. 13r, Disarmament.

1995, July 6 Litho. **Perf. 14**
| 2076A-2076D | A311a | Set of 4 | 5.75 | 5.75 |

UN, 50th Anniv. — A312

No. 2077: a, 6.50r+50 l, Child, dove flying left. b, 8r, Earth from space. c, 10r, Child, Dove flying right. 25r, UN emblem, dove.

1995, July 6 Litho. **Perf. 14**
| 2077 | A312 | Strip of 3, #a.-c. | 4.50 | 4.50 |

Souvenir Sheet
| 2078 | A312 | 25r multicolored | 4.50 | 4.50 |

No. 2077 is a continuous design.

A312a

A313 FAO, 50th Anniv.

1995 Litho. **Perf. 14**
| 2078A | A312a | 7r Food for all | 1.25 | 1.25 |
| 2078B | A312a | 8r Dolphin-friendly fishing | 1.40 | 1.40 |

1995, July 6

No. 2079: a, 6.50r+50 l, Child eating. b, 8r, FAO emblem. c, 10r, Mother, child. 25r, Food emblem, child, horiz.
| 2079 | A313 | Strip of 3, #a.-c. | 6.00 | 6.00 |

Souvenir Sheet
| 2080 | A313 | 25r multicolored | 6.00 | 6.00 |

1995 Boy Scout Jamboree, Holland — A314

No. 2081: a, 10r, Natl. flag, scouts, tents. b, 12r, Scout cooking. c, 15r, Scouts sitting before tents. 25r, Scout playing flute, camp at night, vert.

1995, July 6
| 2081 | A314 | Strip of 3, #a.-c. | 6.75 | 6.75 |

Souvenir Sheet
| 2082 | A314 | 25r multicolored | 4.50 | 4.50 |

No. 2081 is a continuous design.

Queen Mother, 95th Birthday — A315

No. 2083: a, Drawing. b, Blue print dress, pearls. c, Formal portrait. d, Blue outfit. 25r, Pale violet hat, violet & blue dress.

1995, July 6 **Perf. 13½x14**
| 2083 | A315 | 5r Block or strip of 4, #a.-d. | 4.00 | 4.00 |

Souvenir Sheet
| 2084 | A315 | 25r multicolored | 5.75 | 5.75 |

No. 2083 was issued in sheets of 2. Sheets of Nos. 2083-2084 exist overprinted in margin with black frame and text "In Memoriam 1900-2002."

Natl. Library, 50th Anniv. A316

Designs: 2r, Boys seated at library table. 8r, Two people standing, two at table. 10r, Library entrance.

1995, July 12 **Perf. 14**
| 2085 | A316 | 2r multicolored | .30 | .30 |
| 2086 | A316 | 8r multicolored | 1.25 | 1.25 |

Size: 100x70mm
Imperf
| 2087 | A316 | 10r multicolored | 1.60 | 1.60 |

Miniature Sheets of 6 or 8

End of World War II, 50th Anniv. — A317

No. 2088: a, 203mm Red Army howitzer. b, Ruins of Hitler's residence, Berchtesgaden. c, Operation Manna, Allies drop food to starving Dutch. d, Soviet IL-1 fighter. e, Inmates, British troops burn last hut at Belsen. f, Last V1 Buzz Bomb launched against London. g, US 3rd Armored Division passes through ruins of Cologne. h, Gutted Reichstag, May 7, 1946.

No. 2089: a, Grumman F6F-3 Hellcat. b, F4-U1 attacking with rockets. c, Douglas Dauntless. d, Guadalcanal, Aug. 7, 1942. e, US Marines in Alligator landing craft. f, US Infantry landing craft.

Each 25r: No. 2090, Allied soldiers with smiling faces. No. 2091, Corsair fighters.

1995, July 6 Litho. **Perf. 14**
| 2088 | A317 | 5r #a.-h. + label | 7.25 | 7.25 |
| 2089 | A317 | 6.50r +50 l #a.-f. + label | 9.00 | 9.00 |

Souvenir Sheets
| 2090-2091 | A317 | Set of 2 | 10.00 | 10.00 |

Turtles A318

Hawksbill turtle: No. 2092a, Crawling. b, Two in water. c, One crawling out of water. d, Swimming.

No. 2093: a, Spur-thighed tortoise. b, Aldabra turtle. c, Loggerhead turtle. d, Olive ridley. e, Leatherback turtle. f, Green turtle. g, Atlantic ridley. h, Hawksbill turtle.

25r, Chelonia mydas.

1995, Aug. 22
2092 A318 10r Strip of 4, #a.-
            d.   10.00 10.00
Miniature Sheet of 8
2093 A318 3r #a.-h.   10.00 10.00
Souvenir Sheet
2094 A318 25r multicolored   13.00 13.00

World Wildlife Fund (No. 2092). No. 2092 was printed in sheets of 12 stamps.

Fourth World Conference on Women, Beijing — A318a

Designs: 30 l, Woman at computer. 1r, Woman high jumping. 8r, Women dancing. 11r, Woman pilot.

1995, Aug. 24 Litho. Perf. 12¼
2094A-2094D A318a Set of 4   —   —

Miniature Sheets

Singapore '95 — A319

Mushrooms, butterflies, each 2r: No. 2095a, Russula aurata, papilio demodocus. b, Kallimoides rumia, lepista saeva. c, Lapista nuda, hypolimnas salmacis. d, Precis octavia, boletus subtomentosus.
No. 2096: a, 5r, Gyroporus castaneus, hypolimnas salmacis. b, 8r, Papilio dardanus, Gomphidius glutinosus. c, 10r, Russula olivacea, precis octavia. d, 12r, Prepona praeneste, boletus edulis.
Each 25r: No. 2097, Hypolimnas salmacis, boletus rhodoxanthus, vert. No. 2098, Amanita muscaria, kallimoides rumia, vert.

1995, Oct. 18 Litho. Perf. 14
2095 A319 Sheet of 4, #a.-d.   2.00   2.00
2096 A319 Sheet of 4, #a.-d.   10.00 10.00
Souvenir Sheets
2097-2098 A319 Set of 2   10.00 10.00

Flowers
A320

Designs: 1r, Ballade tulip. 3r, White mallow. 5r, Regale trumpet lily. 7r, Lilactime dahlia. 8r, Blue ideal iris. 10r, Red crown imperial.
No. 2105, a, Dendrobium waipahu beauty. b, Brassocattleya Jean Murray "Allan Christenson." c, Cymbidium Fort George "Lewes." d, Paphiopedilum malipoense. e, Cycnoches chlorochilon. f, Rhyncholaelia digbgana. g, Lycaste deppei. h, Masdevallia constricta. i, Paphiopedilum Clair de Lune "Edgard Van Belle."
Each 25r: No. 2106, Psychopsis krameriana. No. 2107, Cockleshell orchid.

1995, Dec. 4 Litho. Perf. 14
2099-2104 A320 Set of 6   7.25   7.25
Miniature Sheet
2105 A320 5r Sheet of 9, #a.-i. 9.25 9.25
Souvenir Sheets
2106-2107 A320 Set of 2   9.00 9.00

Miniature Sheet

Elvis Presley (1935-77) — A321

Various portraits.

1995, Dec. 8   Perf. 13½x14
2108 A321 5r Sheet of 9, #a.-i. 8.00 8.00
Souvenir Sheet
Perf. 14x13½
2109 A321 25r multi, horiz.   4.50 4.50

Miniature Sheets

John Lennon (1940-80), Entertainer — A322

No. 2110, Various portraits.
No. 2111: a, 10r, As young man. b, 8r, Younger man with glasses. c, 3r, With beard. d, 2r, Older picture without beard.
No. 2112, Standing at microphone.

1995, Dec. 8
2110 A322 5r Sheet of 6, #a.-f. 9.00 9.00
2111 A322 Sheet of 4, #a.-d.   7.00 7.00
Souvenir Sheet
2112 A322 25r multicolored   7.25 7.25

Nobel Prize Fund Established, Cent. — A323

Recipients: No. 2113, each 5r: a, Bernardo A. Houssay, medicine, 1947. b, Paul H. Müller, medicine, 1948. c, Walter R. Hess, medicine, 1949. d, Sir MacFarlane Burnet, medicine, 1960. e, Baruch S. Blumberg, medicine, 1976. f, Daniel Nathans, medicine, 1978. g, Glenn T. Seaborg, chemistry, 1951. h, Ilya Prigogine, chemistry, 1977. i, Kenichi Fukui, chemistry, 1981.
No. 2114, each 5r: a, Johannes Van Der Waals, physics, 1910. b, Charles Édouard Guillaume, physics, 1920. c, Sir James Chadwick, physics, 1935. d, Willem Einthoven, medicine, 1924. e, Henrik Dam, medicine, 1943. f, Sir Alexander Fleming, medicine, 1945. g, Hermann J. Muller, medicine, 1946. h, Rodney R. Porter, medicine, 1972. i, Werner Arber, medicine, 1978.
No. 2115, each 5r: a, Dag Hammarskjold, peace, 1961. b, Alva R. Myrdal, peace, 1982. c, Archbishop Desmond M. Tutu, peace, 1984. d, Rudolf C. Eucken, literature, 1908. e, Aleksandr Solzhenitsyn, literature, 1970. f, Gabriel Garcia Márquez, literature, 1982. g, Chen N. Yang, physics, 1957. h, Karl A. Müller, physics, 1987. i, Melvin Schwartz, physics, 1988.
No. 2116, each 5r: a, Niels Bohr, physics, 1922. b, Ben R. Mottelson, physics, 1975. c, Patrick White, literature, 1973. d, Elias Canetti, literature, 1981. e, Theodor Kocher, medicine, 1909. f, August Krogh, medicine, 1920. g, William P. Murphy, medicine, 1934. h, John H. Northrop, chemistry, 1946. i, Luis F. Leloir, chemistry, 1970.
No. 2117, each 5r: a, Carl Spitteler, literatue, 1919. b, Henri Bergson, literature, 1927. c, Johannes V. Jensen, literature, 1944. d, Antoine-Henri Becquerel, physics, 1903. e, Sir William H. Bragg, physics, 1915. f, Sir William L. Bragg, physics, 1915. g, Fredrik Bajer, peace, 1908. h, Léon Bourgeois, peace, 1920. i, Karl Branting, peace, 1921.
No. 2118, each 5r: a, Robert A. Millikan, physics, 1923. b, Louis V. de Broglie, physics, 1929. c, Ernest Walton, physics, 1951. d, Richard Willstätter, chemistry, 1915. e, Lars Onsager, chemistry, 1968. f, Gerhard Herzberg, chemistry, 1971. g, William B. Yeats, literature, 1923. h, George B. Shaw, literature, 1925. i, Eugene O'Neill, literature, 1936.
Each 25r: No. 2119, Eisaku Sato, peace, 1974. No. 2120, Robert Koch, medicine, 1905. No. 2121, Otto Wallach, chemistry, 1910. No. 2122, Konrad Bloch, medicine, 1964. No. 2123, Samuel Beckett, literature, 1969. No. 2124, Hideki Yukawa, physics, 1949.

1995, Dec. 28 Litho. Perf. 14
Miniature Sheets of 9, #a-i
2113-2118 A323 Set of 6   48.00 48.00
Souvenir Sheets
2119-2124 A323 Set of 6   24.00 24.00

1996 Summer Olympics, Atlanta A324

Designs: 1r, Rhythmic gymnastics, Tokyo, 1964. 3r, Archery, Moscow, 1980. 5r, Diving, Stockholm, 1912. 7r, High jump, London, 1948. 10r, Track and field, Berlin, 1936. 12r, Hurdles, Amsterdam 1928.
No. 2131: a, Montreal 1976. b, Decathlon. c, Olympic pin, Moscow, 1980. d, Fencing. e, Olympic medal. f, Equestrian. g, Sydney, 2000. h, Track and field. i, Seoul, 1988.
Each 25r: No. 2132, Olympic torch, vert. No. 2133, Olympic flame, vert.

1996, Jan. 25 Litho. Perf. 14
2125-2130 A324 Set of 6   7.75 7.75
Miniature Sheet
2131 A324 5r Sheet of 9, #a.-i. 9.00 9.00
Souvenir Sheets
2132-2133 A324 Set of 2   10.50 10.50

Paintings from Metropolitan Museum of Art — A325

No. 2134, each 4r: a, Self-portrait, by Degas. b, Andromache & Astyanax, by

Prud'hon. c, René Grenier, by Toulouse-Lautrec. d, The Banks of the Biévre Near Bicetre, by Rousseau. e, The Repast of the Lion, by Rousseau. f, Portrait Yves Gobillard-Morisot, by Degas. g, Sunflowers, by Van Gogh. h, The Singer in Green, by Degas.
No. 2135, each 4r: a, Still Life, by Fantin-Latour. b, Portrait of a Lady in Gray, by Degas. c, Apples & Grapes, by Monet. d, The Englishman, by Toulouse-Lautrec. e, Cypresses, by Van Gogh. f, Flowers in Chinese Vase, by Redon. g, The Gardener, by Seurat. h, Large Sunflowers I, by Nolde.
By Manet: No. 2136, each 4r: a, The Spanish Singer. b, Young Man in Costume of Majo. c, Mademoisselle Victorine. d, Boating. e, Peonies. f, Woman with a Parrot. g, George Moore. h, The Monet Family in Their Garden.
No. 2137, each 4r: a, Goldfish, by Matisse. b, Spanish Woman: Harmony in Blue, by Matisse. c, Nasturtiums & the "Dance" II, by Matisse. d, The House Behind Trees, by Braque. e, Máda Primavesi, by Klimt. f, Head of a Woman, by Picasso. g, Woman in White, by Picasso. h, Harlequin, by Picasso.
Each 25r: No. 2138, Northeaster, by Homer. No. 2139, The Fortune Teller, by Georges de la Tour. No. 2140, Santi (Sanzio), Ritratto di Andrea Navagero E Agostino Beazzano, by Raphael. No. 2141, Portrait of a Woman, by Rubens.

1996, Apr. 22 Litho. Perf. 13½x14
Sheets of 8, #a-h + label
2134-2137 A325 Set of 4   35.00 35.00
Souvenir Sheets
Perf. 14
2138-2141 A325 Set of 4   22.50 22.50

Nos. 2138-2141 each contain one 85x57mm stamp.
Nos. 2140-2141 are not in the Metropolitan Museum.
Nos. 2134-2141 exist imperf. Value, set $100.

Disney Characters Visit China — A326

No. 2142, each 2r: a, Mickey at the Great Wall. b, Pluto's encounter in the Temple Garden. c, Minnie saves the pandas. d, Mickey sails with the junks. e, Goofy at the grottoes. f, Donald, Daisy at the marble boat.
No. 2143, each 2r: a, Mickey leads terra cotta statues. b, Goofy's masks. c, Traditional fishing with Donald, Goofy. d, Mickey, Minnie in dragon boat. e, Donald at Peking Opera. f, Mickey, Minnie, in Chinese Garden.
No. 2144, vert: a, Mickey, Minnie snowballing at ice pagoda. b, Donald, Mickey fly Chinese kites. c, Goofy plays anyiwu. d, Mickey, Goofy, origami. e, Donald, Mickey in dragon dance.
No. 2145, 5r, Mickey viewing Guilin. No. 2146, 7r, Mickey, Minnie at Moon Festival. No. 2147, 8r, Donald enjoying traditional Chinese food.

1996, May 10 Perf. 14x13½, 13½x14
Sheets of 6, #a-f
2142-2143 A326 Set of 2   11.50 11.50
Sheet of 5, #a-e
2144 A326 3r #a.-e. + label   6.00   6.00
Souvenir Sheets
2145 A326 5r multicolored   2.00   2.00
2146 A326 7r multicolored   2.50   2.50
2147 A326 8r multicolored   3.00   3.00

CHINA '96, 9th Asian Intl. Philatelic Exhibition.

1996 Summer Olympic Games, Atlanta A327

Gold medalists: 1r, Stella Walsh, 100-meters, 1932. 3r, Emil Zatopek, 10,000-meters, 1952. vert. 10r, Olga Fikotova, discus throw, 1956. 12r, Joan Benoit, women's marathon, 1984.
No. 2152: a, Ethel Catherwood, high jump, 1928. b, Mildred "Babe" Didrikson, javelin,

1932. c, Francina (Fanny) Blankers-Koen, hurdles, 1948. d, Tamara Press, shot put, 1960. e, Lia Manoliu, discus, 1968. f, Rosa Mota, women's marathon, 1988.

Gold medalists in weight lifting, vert: No. 2153a, Yanko Rusev, lightweight, 1980. b, Peter Baczako, middle heavyweight, 1980. c, Leonid Taranenko, heavyweight, 1980. d, Aleksandr Kurlovich, heavyweight, 1988. e, Assen Zlatev, middleweight, 1980. f, Zeng Guoqiang, flyweight, 1984. g, Yurik Vardanyan, heavyweight, 1980. h, Sultan Rakhmanov, super heavyweight, 1980. i, Vassily Alexeev, super heavyweight, 1972.

Each 25r: No. 2154, Irena Szewinska, gold medal winner, 400-meters, 1976. No. 2155, Naim Suleymanoglu, gold medal winner, weight lifting, 1988, vert.

1996, May 27   Litho.   Perf. 14
2148-2151 A327 Set of 4   5.75   5.75
Miniature Sheets
2152 A327 5r Sheet of 6, #a.-f.   6.50   6.50
2153 A327 5r Sheet of 9, #a.-i.   9.50   9.50
Souvenir Sheets
2154-2155 A327 Set of 2   11.00   11.00

Olymphilex '96 (No. 2155).

Queen Elizabeth II, 70th Birthday A329

Designs: a, Portrait. b, As younger woman wearing hat, pearls. c, Younger picture seated at desk.
25r, On balcony with Queen Mother.

1996, June 21   Litho.   Perf. 13½x14
2164 A329 8r Strip of 3, #a.-c.   5.50   5.50
Souvenir Sheet
2165 A329 25r multicolored   6.25   6.25

No. 2164 was issued in sheets of 9 stamps.

UNICEF, 50th Anniv. — A330

Designs: 5r (No. 2166), 7r (No. 2167), 7r (No. 2167A), girl, blue margin, 10r (No. 2168), Girls of different races.
25r, Baby girl.

1996, July 10   Perf. 14
2166-2168 A330 Set of 4   4.50   4.50
Souvenir Sheet
2169 A330 25r multicolored   4.50   4.50

Butterflies — A331

No. 2170, vert: a, Cymothoe cocccinata. b, Morpho rhetenor. c, Callicore lidwina (b, d). d, Heliconius sara.

No. 2171: a, Epiphora albida. b, Satyrus dryas. c, Satyrus lena. d, Papilio tynderaeus. e, Urota Suraka. f, Satyrus nercis.

No. 2172, vert: a, Spicebush swallowtail. b, Giant swallowtail. c, Lime swallowtail caterpillar (b). d, Painted beauty (c). e, Monarch caterpillar. f, Monarch (e, g). g, Monarch caterpillar & pupa. h, Harris' checkerspot.

Each 25r: No. 2173, Heliconius cydno, vert. No. 2174, Zebra, vert.

1996, July 10
2170 A331 7r Strip of 4, #a.-d.   5.25   5.25
2171 A331 7r Sheet of 6, #a.-f.   8.00   8.00
2172 A331 7r Sheet of 8, #a.-h.   11.00   11.00
Souvenir Sheets
2173-2174 A331 Set of 2   11.00   11.00

No. 2170 was issued in sheets of 8 stamps.

Space Exploration — A332

Designs: No. 2175a, Sputnik I, 1957. b, Apollo 11 Command Module returns to earth, 1969. c, Skylab, 1973. d, Edward White, 1st US astronaut to walk in space, 1965. e, Mariner 9, 1st artificial satellite of Mars, 1971. f, Apollo and Soviet Soyuz dock together, 1975.
25r, Apollo 8 being launched, 1968, vert.

1996, July 10   Perf. 14
2175 A332 6r Sheet of 6, #a.-f.   6.50   6.50
Souvenir Sheet
2176 A332 25r multicolored   5.25   5.25

Trains A333

No. 2177, each 3r: a, Electric container train, Germany. b, John Blenkinsop's rack locomotive. c, DB Diesel electric, West Germany. d, Timothy Hackworth's "Royal George," 1827. e, Robert Stephenson (1803-59) f, Trevithick's "New Castle" locomotive. g, Deltic locomotives, British Rail. h, Stockton No. 5, 1826. i, Passenger shuttle, English Channel Tunnel.

No. 2178, each 3r: a, Southern Pacific's "Daylight," San Francisco, US, 1952. b, Timothy Hackworth's "Sans Pareil." c, Chicago & North Western, US. d, Richard Trevithick's "Pen-Y-Darran" locomotive. e, Isambard Kingdom Brunel (1806-59). f, Great Western engine of 1838. g, Passenger train, Canada. h, Mohawk & Hudson Railroad "Experiment," 1832. i, "The ICE," Germany.

No. 2179, each 3r: a, F4 OPH Diesel locomotives, US. b, Stephenson's "Experiment." c, Indian Pacific Intercontinental, Australia. d, George Stephenson's engine, 1815. e, George Stephenson (1781-1848). f, Stephenson's "Rocket," 1829. g, British Rail 125 HST. h, First rail passenger coach, "Experiment," 1825. i, TOFAC, US.

Each 25r: No. 2180, Tom Thumb, 1830. No. 2181, The DeWitt Clinton, 1831. No. 2182, The General, 1855.

1996, Sept. 2   Litho.   Perf. 14
Sheets of 9, #a-i
2177-2179 A333 Set of 3   24.00   24.00
Souvenir Sheets
2180-2182 A333 Set of 3   16.00   16.00

Fauna A334

Endangered animals:
No. 2183, each 5r: a, Shoebill stork. b, Red-billed hornbill. c, Hippopotamus. d, Gorilla. e, Lion. f, Gray-crowned crane.
No. 2184, each 5r: a, Giant panda. b, Indian elephant. c, Arrow poison frog. d, Mandrill. e, Snow leopard. f, California condor.
Wildlife:
No. 2185, vert, each 5r: a, Yellow baboon. b, Zebra duiker. c, Yellow-backed duiker. d, Pygmy hippopotamus. e, Large-spotted genet. f, African spoonbill. g, White-faced whistling duck. h, Helmeted gunieafowl.
No. 2186, vert, each 5r: a, Bongo. b, Bushback. c, Namaqua dove. d, Hoopoe. e,

African fish eagle. f, Egyptian goose. g, Saddle-billed stork. h, Blue-breasted kingfisher.
Each 25r: No. 2187, Tiger, vert. No. 2188, Leopard.

1996, Sept. 9
Sheet of 6
2183-2184 A334 Set of 2   20.00   20.00
Sheet of 8
2185-2186 A334 Set of 2   26.50   26.50
Souvenir Sheets
2187-2188 A334 Set of 2   12.00   12.00

Motion Pictures, Cent. — A335

Progressive scenes from "Pluto and the Flypaper, each 4r:" Nos. 2189a-2189h, Scenes 1-8. No. 2191a-2191i, Scenes 9-17.
Progressive scenes from "Mickey Mouse in The Little Whirlwind, each 4r." Nos. 2190a-2190h, Scenes 1-8. Nos. 2192a-2192i, Scenes 9-17.
Each 25r: No. 2193, Scene from "Pluto and the Flypaper." No. 2194, Scene from "Mickey Mouse in The Little Whirlwind."

1996, Dec. 2   Litho.   Perf. 13½x14
Sheets of 8, #a-h, + Label
2189-2190 A335 Set of 2   25.00   25.00
Sheets of 9, #a-i
2191-2192 A335 Set of 2   27.50   27.50
Souvenir Sheets
2193-2194 A335 Set of 2   18.50   18.50

Fauna A336

Designs: a, Saguinus oedipus. b, Bison bonasus. c, Panthera tigris. d, Tetrao urogallus. e, Ailuropoda melanoleuca. f, Trogonoptera brookiana. g, Castor canadensis. h, Leiopelma hamiltoni. i, Trichechus manatus latirostris.
25r, Pan troglodytes.

1996   Litho.   Perf. 14
2195 A336 7r Sheet of 9, #a.-i.   12.50   12.50
Souvenir Sheet
2196 A336 25r multicolored   5.00   5.00

Turtle Preservation — A336a

1996 ?   Litho.   Perf. 12¾
2196A Horiz. strip of 3   —   —
   b. A336a 1r Turtle's head   —   —
   c. A336a 7r Turtle's plastron   —   —
   d. A336a 8r Two turtles   —   —

Chinese motifs inside letters: No. 2197a, "H." b, "O." c, "N." d, "G" (birds). e, "K." f, "O," diff. g, "N." h, "G" (junk).
25r, "Hong Kong."

1997, Feb. 12   Litho.   Perf. 14
2197 A337 5r Sheet of 8, #a.-h.   8.50   8.50
Souvenir Sheet
2198 A337 25r multicolored   5.25   5.25

No. 2198 contains one 77x39mm stamp.

Birds — A338

a, Gymnogyps californianus. b, Larus audouinii. c, Fratercula artica. d, Pharomachrus mocinno. e, Amazona vittata. f, Paradisaea minor. g, Nipponia nippon. h, Falco punctatus. i, Strigops habroptilus.
25r, Campephilus principalis.

1997, Feb. 12
2199 A338 5r Sheet of 9, #a.-i.   10.50   10.50
Souvenir Sheet
2200 A338 25r multicolored   6.25   6.25

Eagles
A339   A340

Designs: 1r, Crowned solitary eagle. 2r, African hawk eagle, horiz. 3r, Lesser spotted eagle. 5r, Steller's sea eagle. 8r, Spanish imperial eagle, horiz. 10r, Harpy eagle. 12r, Crested serpent eagle, horiz.
Bald eagles: No. 2208: a, Wings upward in flight. b, Looking backward on limb. c, Up close, head left. d, Up close, head right. e, On limb. f, In flight.
No. 2209, American bald eagle, horiz. No. 2210, Bald eagle.

1997, Mar. 20   Litho.   Perf. 14
2201-2207 A339 Set of 7   8.00   8.00
2208 A340 5r Sheet of 6, #a.-f.   6.00   6.00
Souvenir Sheets
2209 A339 25r multicolored   4.75   4.75
2210 A340 25r multicolored   4.75   4.75

Automobiles — A341

No. 2211, each 5r: a, 1911 Blitzer Benz, Germany. b, 1917 Datsun, Japan. c, 1929 Auburn 8-120, US. d, 1996 Mercedes-Benz C280, Germany. e, Suzuki UR-1, Japan. f, Chrysler Atlantic, US.
No. 2212, each 5r: a, 1961 Mercedes-Benz 190SL, Germany. b, 1916 Kwaishinha DAT, Japan. c, 20/25 Rolls-Royce Roadster, England. d, 1997 Mercedes-Benz SLK, Germany. e, 1996 Toyota Camry, Japan. f, 1959 Jaguar MK2, England.
Each 25r: No. 2213, 1939 VW built by Dr. Porsche. No. 2214, Mazda RX-01.

1997, Mar. 27
Sheets of 6, #a-f
2211-2212 A341 Set of 2   11.50   11.50
Souvenir Sheets
2213-2214 A341 Set of 2   9.50   9.50

1998 Winter Olympics, Nagano — A342

Medalists: 2r, Ye Qiaobo, 1992 speed skating. 3r, Leonhard Stock, 1980 downhill. 8r, Bjorn Daehlie, 1992 cross-country skiing. 12r, Wolfgang Hoppe, 1984 bobsledding.

No. 2219: a, Herma Von Szabo-Planck, 1924 figure skating. b, Katarina Witt, 1988 figure skating. c, Natalia Bestemianova, Andrei Bukin, 1988 ice dancing. d, Jayne Torvill, Christopher Dean, 1984 ice dancing.

Each 25r: No. 2220, Sonja Henie, 1924 figure skating. No. 2221, Andree Joly, Pierre Brunet, 1932 figure skating.

1997, Mar. 13   Litho.   Perf. 14
2215-2218 A342 Set of 4   5.25 5.25
2219 A342 5r Block of 4, #a.-d. 4.25 4.25

Souvenir Sheets
2220-2221 A342 Set of 2   11.00 11.00

No. 2219 was issued in sheets of 8 stamps.

Ships
A343

Designs: 1r, SS Patris II, 1926, Greece. 2r, MV Infanta Beatriz, 1928, Spain. 8r, SS Stavangerjord, 1918, Norway. 12r, MV Baloeran, 1929, Holland.

No. 2226, each 3r: a, SS Vasilefs Constantinos, 1914, Greece. b, SS Cunene, 1911, Portugal. c, MV Selandia, 1912, Denmark. d, SS President Harding, 1921, US. e, MV Ulster Monarch, 1929, Great Britain. f, SS Matsonia, 1913, US. g, SS France, 1911, France. h, SS Campania, 1893, Great Britain. i, SS Klipfontein, 1922, Holland.

No. 2227, each 3r: a, MV Eridan, 1929, France. b, SS Mount Clinton, 1921, US. c, SS Infanta Isabel, 1912, Spain. d, SS Suwa Maru, 1914, Japan. e, SS Yorkshire, 1920, Great Britain. f, MV Highland Chieftan, 1929, Great Britain. g, MV Sardinia, 1920, Norway. h, SS San Guglielmo, 1911, Italy. i, SS Avila, 1927, Great Britain.

Each 25r: No. 2228, SS Mauritania, 1907, Great Britain. No. 2229, SS United States, 1952, US. No. 2230, SS Queen Mary, 1930, Great Britain. No. 2231, Royal Yacht Brittania sailing into Hong Kong harbor.

1997, Apr. 1
2222-2225 A343 Set of 4   6.00 6.00

Sheets of 9, #a-i
2226-2227 A343 Set of 2   12.50 12.50

Souvenir Sheets
2228-2231 A343 Set of 4   22.00 22.00

No. 2231 contains one 57x42mm stamp.

UNESCO, 50th Anniv. — A344

1r, Prayer wheels, Lhasa, vert. 2r, Roman ruins, Temple of Diana, Portugal. 3r, Cathedral of Santa Maria Hildesheim, Germany. 7r, Monument of Nubia at Abu Simbel, Egypt, vert. 8r, Entrance to Port of Mandraki, Rhodes, Greece. 10r, Nature Reserve of Scandola, France. 12r, Temple on the Lake, China.

No. 2232, vert, each 5r: a, Virunga Natl. Park, Zaire. b, Valley of Mai Nature Reserve, Seychelles. c, Kandy, Sri Lanka. d, Taj Mahal, India. e, Istanbul, Turkey. f, Sana'a, Yemen. g, Blenheim Palace, Oxfordshire, England. h, Grand Canyon Natl. Park, US.

No. 2233, vert, each 5r: a, Gondar, Ethiopia. b, Bwindi Natl. Park, Uganda. c, Bemaraha Nature Reserve, Madagascar. d, Buddhist ruins of Takht-i-Bahi, Pakistan. e, Anuradhapura, Sri Lanka. f, Cairo, Egypt. g, Ruins at Petra, Jordan. h, Natl. Park of Ujung Kulon, Indonesia.

Sites in China, vert: No. 2234, each 5r: a-f, Mount Taishan. g-h, Terracotta warriors.

Sites in Japan: No. 2235, each 8r: a-e, Horyu-Ji.

No. 2236, each 8r: a, Monastery of Agios Stefanos Meteora, Greece. b, Taj Mahal, India. c, Cistercian Abbey of Fontenay, France. d, Yakushima, Japan. e, Cloisters of the Convent, San Gonzalo, Portugal.

No. 2237, each 8r: a, Olympic Natl. Park, US. b, Nahanni Waterfalls, Canada. c, Los Glaciares Natl. Park, Argentina. d, Bonfin Salvador Church, Brazil. e, Convent of the Companions of Jesus, Morelia, Mexico.

Each 25r: No. 2238, Temple, Chengde, China. No. 2239, Serengeti Natl. Park, Tanzania. No. 2240, Anuradhapura, Sri Lanka. No. 2241, Monument to Fatehpur Sikri, India.

1997, Apr. 7
2231A-2231G A344 Set of 7   5.75 5.75

Sheets of 8, #a-h, + Label
2232-2234 A344 Set of 3   22.00 22.00

Sheets of 5, #a-e, + Label
2235-2237 A344 Set of 3   22.00 22.00

Souvenir Sheets
2238-2241 A344 Set of 4   18.00 18.00

Queen Elizabeth II, Prince Philip, 50th Wedding Anniv.
A345

No. 2242: a, Queen. b, Royal Arms. c, Queen, Prince seated on thrones. d, Queen, Prince holding baby. e, Buckingham Palace. f, Prince.

25r, Queen wearing crown.

1997, June 12   Litho.   Perf. 14
2242 A345 5r Sheet of 6, #a.-f. 7.75 7.75

Souvenir Sheet
2243 A345 25r multicolored   5.50 5.50

Paintings by Hiroshige (1797-1858)
A346

No. 2244: a, Dawn at Kanda Myojin Shrine. b, Kiyomizu Hall & Shinobazu Pond at Ueno. c, Ueno Yamashita. d, Moon Pine, Ueno. e, Flower Pavilion, Dango Slope, Sendagi. f, Shitaya Hirokoji.

Each 25r: No. 2245, Seido and Kanda River from Shohei Bridge. No. 2246, Hilltop View, Yushima Tenjin Shrine.

1997, June 12   Perf. 13½x14
2244 A346 8r Sheet of 6, #a.-f. 8.50 8.50

Souvenir Sheets
2245-2246 A346 Set of 2   9.00 9.00

Heinrich von Stephan (1831-97)
A347

a, Early mail messenger, India. b, Von Stephan, UPU emblem. c, Autogiro, Washington DC.

1997, June 12   Perf. 14
2247 A347 2r Sheet of 3, #a.-c. 3.25 3.25

PACIFIC 97.
A number has been reserved for a souvenir sheet with this set.

South Asian Assoc. for Regional Cooperation (SAARC) Summit — A348

1997, May 12   Litho.   Perf. 13
2249 A348 3r shown   .60   .60
2250 A348 5r Flags, "SAARC"   1.10 1.10

A349

Birds: 30 l, Anous stolidus. 1r, Spectacled owl. 2r, Buffy fish owl. 3r, Peregrine falcon. 5r, Golden eagle. 8r, Bateleur. No. 2257, 10r, Crested caracara. No. 2258, 10r, Childonias hybrida. 15r, Sula sula.

No. 2260: a, Rueppell's parrot. b, Blue-headed parrot. c, St. Vincent parrot. d, Gray parrot. e, Masked lovebird. f, Sun parakeet.

Each 25r: No. 2261, Secretary bird. No. 2262, Bald eagle.

1997   Perf. 14
2251-2259 A349 Set of 9   9.75 9.75
2260 A349 7r Sheet of 6, #a.-f. 8.25 8.25

Souvenir Sheets
2261-2262 A349 Set of 2   11.50 11.50

A350

Flowers: 1r, Canarina eminii. 2r, Delphinium macrocentron. 3r, Leucadendron discolor. 5r, Nymphaea caerulea. 7r, Rosa multiflora. 8r, Bulbophyllum barbigerum. 12r, Hibiscus vitifolius.

No. 2270, horiz: a, Acacia seyal. b, Gloriosa superba. c, Gnidia subcordata. d, Platycelphium voense. e, Aspilia mossambicensis. f, Adenium obesum.

Each 25r: No. 2271, Aerangis rhodosticta, horiz. No. 2272, Dichrostachys cinerea, horiz.

1997, June 24   Litho.   Perf. 14½x14
2263-2269 A350 Set of 6   7.50 7.50
                 Perf. 14x14½
2270 A350 8r Sheet of 6, #a.-f. 12.00 12.00

Souvenir Sheets
2271-2272 A350 Set of 2   18.00 18.00

No. 2267 is 16x20mm.

Dinosaurs
A352

5r, Archaeopteryx. 8r, Mosasaurus. 12r, Deinonychus. 15r, Triceratops.

No. 2277, each 7r: a, Diplodocus (b, c, d, e, f). b. Tyrannosaurus rex (c, e, f). c, Pteranodon. d, Montanaceratops. e, Dromaeosaurus (d). f, Oviraptor (e).

No. 2278, each 7r: a, Euoplocephalus. b, Compsognathus. c, Herrerasaurus. d, Styracosaurus. e, Baryonyx. f, Lesothosaurus.

No. 2279, each 7r: a, Triceratops. b, Pachycephalosaurus. c, Iguanodon. d, Tyrannosaurus. e, Corythosaurus. f, Stegosaurus.

No. 2280, each 7r: a, Troodon (d). b, Brachiosaurus (c). c, Saltasaurus (a, b, d, e, f). d, Oviraptor. e, Parasaurolophus (f). f, Psittacosaurus.

No. 2281, Tyrannosaurus rex. No. 2282, Archaeopteryx.

1997, Nov. 20   Litho.   Perf. 14
2273-2276 A351 Set of 4   7.25 7.25

Sheets of 6, #a-f
2277 A351 7r #a.-f.   7.50 7.50
2278-2280 A352 Set of 3   22.50 22.50

Souvenir Sheets
2281 A351 25r multicolored   11.50 11.50
2282 A352 25r multicolored   11.50 11.50

1998 World Cup Soccer Championships, France — A353

Past winners: 1r, Brazil, 1994. 2r, West Germany, 1954. 3r, Argentina, 1986. 7r, Argentina, 1978. 8r, England, 1966. 10r, Brazil, 1970.

Various scenes from 1966 finals, England v. West Germany, each 3r: Nos. 2289a-2289h.

Italian tournament winners, each 3r: No. 2290: a, Paulo Rossi, Italy, 1982. b, Zoff & Gentile, Italy, 1982. c, Angelo Schiavio, Italy. d, 1934 team. e, 1934 team entering stadium. f, 1982 team. g, San Paolo Stadium, Italy. h, 1938 team.

Brazilian teams, players, each 3r: No. 2291: a, 1958 team pictue. b, Luis Bellini, 1958. c, 1962 team. d, Carlos Alberto, 1970. e, Mauro, 1962. f, 1970 team. g, Dunga, 1994. h, 1994 team.

Each 25r: No. 2292, Klinsmann, Germany. No. 2293, Ronaldo, Brazil, vert. No. 2294, Schmeichel, Denmark, vert.

Perf. 14x13½, 13½x14
1997, Dec. 10   Litho.
2283-2288 A353 Set of 6   5.75 5.75

Sheets of 8 + Label
2289-2291 A353 Set of 3   13.50 13.50

Souvenir Sheets
2292-2294 A353 Set of 3   15.50 15.50

Diana, Princess of Wales (1961-97) — A354

Various portraits, color of sheet margin, each 7r: No. 2295, Pale pink. No. 2296, Pale yellow. No. 2297, Pale blue.

Each 25r: No. 2298, Diana on ski lift. No. 2299, In polka dot dress. No. 2300, Wearing lei.

1998, Feb. 9   Litho.   Perf. 13½
Sheets of 6, #a-f
2295-2297 A354 Set of 3   20.00 20.00
Souvenir Sheets
2298-2300 A354 Set of 3   13.50 13.50

John F. Kennedy (1917-63)
A355

Various portraits.

1998   Litho.   Perf. 13½x14
2301 A355 5r Sheet of 9, #a.-i.   8.50 8.50

Nelson Mandela, Pres. of South Africa — A356

1998   Perf. 14
2302 A356 4r multicolored   1.60 1.60

Classic Airplanes
A357

No. 2303: a, Yakovlev Yak 18. b, Beechcraft Bonanza. c, Piper Cub. d, Tupolev Tu-95. e, Lockheed C-130 Hercules. f, Piper PA-28 Cherokee. g, Mikoyan-Gurevich MiG-21. h, Pilatus PC-6 Turbo Porter. i, Antonov An-2. 25r, KC-135E.

1998
2303 A357 5r Sheet of 9, #a.-i.   8.50 8.50
Souvenir Sheet
2304 A357 25r multicolored   4.50 4.50
No. 2304 contains one 85x28mm stamp.

Cats
A358

Designs, vert: 5r, White American shorthair. 8r, Sphinx. 10r, Tabby American shorthair. 12r, Scottish fold.
No. 2309, each 7r: a, American curl, Maine coon (d). b, Maine coon (a, d, e). c, Siberian (f). d, Somali. e, European Burmese (d). f, Nebelung.
No. 2310, each 7r: a, Bicolor British shorthair (b, e). b, Manx. c, Tabby American shorthair (b, e, f). d, Silver tabby Persian (e). e, Oriental white. f, Norwegian forest cat (e).
Each 30r: No. 2311, Snowshoe, vert. No. 2312, Norwegian forest cat, vert.

1998, June 1   Litho.   Perf. 14
2305-2308 A358 Set of 4   6.00 6.00
Sheets of 6, #a-f
2309-2310 A358 Set of 2   14.00 14.00
Souvenir Sheets
2311-2312 A358 Set of 2   11.00 11.00

Airplanes
A359

Designs: 2r, Boeing 737 HS. 7r, Boeing 727. 8r, Boeing 747, 1970. 10r, Boeing 737.
No. 2317, each 5r: a, FSW Fighter. b, V-Jet II. c, Pilatus PC-12. d, Citation Exel. e, Stutz Bearcat. f, Cessna T-37 (B). g, Peregrine business jet. h, Beech Baron 53.
No. 2318, each 5r: a, CL-215. b, P-3 Orion. c, Yak 54. d, Cessna float plane. e, CL-215 Amphibian. f, CL-215 SAR Amphibian. g, Twin Otter. h, Rockwell Quail.
Each 25r: No. 2319, Falcon Jet. No. 2320, Beechcraft Model 18.

1998, Aug. 10   Litho.   Perf. 14
2313-2316 A359 Set of 4   4.75 4.75
Sheets of 8, #a-h
2317-2318 A359 Set of 2   14.50 14.50
Souvenir Sheets
2319-2320 A359 Set of 2   10.00 10.00

The Titanic
A360

No. 2321: a, Capt. Edward J. Smith's cap. b, Deck chair. c, Fifth Officer Harold Lowe's coat button. d, Lifeboat. e, Steering wheel. f, Lifejacket.
25r, Newspaper picture of the Titanic at sea.

1998, Sept. 27   Litho.   Perf. 14
2321 A360 7r Sheet of 6, #a.-f.   8.75 8.75
Souvenir Sheet
2322 A360 25r multicolored   5.25 5.25

Bird Type of 1992

1998, Oct. 26   Litho.   Perf. 14½
2323 A247 100r Anas clypeata   14.00 14.00

IFAD, 20th Anniv. — A361

Designs: 1r, Papaya tree. 5r, Fruits. 7r, Fishermen on boat. 8r, Coconut tree. 10r, Vegetables.

1998, Nov. 30   Litho.   Perf. 14
2324-2328 A361 Set of 5   5.50 5.50

Ferrari Automobiles — A361a

No. 2328A: c, 250 TR. d, 1957 250 GT TDF. e, 250 GT.
25r, 365 GTC 2+2.

1998, Dec. 15   Litho.   Perf. 14
2328A A361a 10r Sheet of 3, #c-e   5.25 5.25
Souvenir Sheet
Perf. 13¾x14¼
2328B A361a 25r multi   4.25 4.25
No. 2328A contains three 39x25mm stamps.

1998 World Scout Jamboree, Chile — A362

a, Robert Baden-Powell inspecting Scouts, Amesbury, c. 1909. b, Lord, Lady Baden-Powell, children, South Africa Tour, 1927. c, Robert Baden-Powell pins merit badges on Chicago Scouts, 1926.

1998, Dec. 15
2329 A362 12r Sheet of 3, #a.-c.   6.75 6.75

A363

Diana, Princess of Wales (1961-97) — A364

1998, Dec. 15   Perf. 14½x14
2330 A363 10r multicolored   1.90 1.90
Size: 95x56mm
Litho. & Embossed
Die Cut Perf. 7½
2331 A364 50r shown
2332 A364 50r Rose, Diana
No. 2330 was issued in sheets of 6.

Fish
A365

Designs: No. 2333, 50 l, Threadfin butterfly fish. No. 2334, 50 l, Queen angelfish. 1r, Oriental sweetlips. No. 2336, 7r, Bandit angelfish. No. 2337, 7r, Achilles tang. 8r, Red-headed butterfly fish. 50r, Blue striped butterfly fish.
No. 2340: a, Mandarinfish. b, Copperbanded butterfly fish. c, Harlequin tuskfish. d, Yellow-tailed demoiselle. e, Wimplefish. f, Red emperor snapper. g, Clown triggerfish. h, Common clown. i, Regal tang.
No. 2341: a, Emperor angelfish. b, Common squirrelfish. c, Lemonpeel angelfish. d, Powderblue surgeon. e, Moorish idol. f, Bicolor cherub. g, Scribbled angelfish. h, Two-banded anemonefish. i, Yellow tang.
Each 25r: No. 2342, Porkfish. No. 2343, Long-nosed butterfly fish.

1998, Dec. 10   Litho.   Perf. 14
2333-2339 A365 Set of 7   13.50 13.50
2340 A365 3r Sheet of 9, #a.-i.   4.75 4.75
2341 A365 7r Sheet of 9, #a.-i.   8.25 8.25
Souvenir Sheets
2342-2343 A365 Set of 2   9.00 9.00

Intl. Year of the Ocean
A366

Marine life: No. 2344, Skipjack tuna.

No. 2345: a, 25 l, Triton. b, 50 l, Napoleon wrasse. c, 1r, Whale shark. d, 3r, Gray reef shark. e, 7r, Blue whale.
No. 2346: a, Harp seal. b, Killer whale. c, Sea otter. d, Beluga. e, Narwhal. f, Walrus. g, Sea lion. h, Humpback salmon. i, Emperor penguin.
No. 2347: a, Ocean sunfish. b, Opalescent squid. c, Electric eel. d, Corded neptune.
Each 25r: No. 2348, Horseshoe crab. No. 2349, Blue whale. No. 2350, Triton, diff.

1999, Apr. 1   Litho.   Perf. 14
2344 A366 7r multicolored   1.25 1.25
Sheets of 6, 9, 4
2345 A366 #a.-e. + 1 #2344   3.50 3.50
2346 A366 5r #a.-i.   8.00 8.00
2347 A366 8r #a.-d.   5.75 5.75
Souvenir Sheets
2348-2350 A366 Set of 3   13.50 13.50
No. 2344 was issued in sheets of 6.
No. 2350 incorrectly inscribed Coral Reef.

Mickey Mouse, 70th Anniv. (in 1998) — A367

No. 2351, each 5r: Various pictures of Mickey Mouse.
No. 2352, each 5r: Various pictures of Minnie Mouse.
No. 2353, each 7r: Various pictures of Donald Duck.
No. 2354, each 7r: Various pictures of Daisy Duck.
No. 2355, each 7r: Various pictures of Goofy.
No. 2356, each 7r: Various pictures of Pluto.
Each 25r: No. 2357, Minnie sipping drink. No. 2358, Minnie looking backward. No. 2359, Mickey grabbing Donald's hand, horiz. No. 2360, Minnie wearing pearls. No. 2361, Mickey with hand on head. No. 2362, Mickey after throwing ball.

Perf. 13½x14, 14x13½ (#2359)
1999, May 27   Litho.
Sheets of 6, #a-f
2351-2352 A367 Set of 2   12.00 12.00
2353-2356 A367 Set of 4   31.00 31.00
Souvenir Sheets
2357-2362 A367 Set of 6   30.00 30.00
Stamp in No. 2358 is printed se-tenant with label.
Sheets similar to Nos. 2351-2352 with "5Rs" denomination and Nos. 2353-2356 with "25Rs" exist.

Butterflies
A368

50 l, Great orange tip. 1r, Large green aporandria. 2r, Common mormon. 3r, African migrant. 5r, Common pierrot. 7r, Giant redeye.
No. 2369, vert, each 7r: a, Common red flash. b, Burmese lascar. c, Common peirrot. d, Baron. e, Leaf blue. f, Great orange tip.
No. 2370, vert, each 7r: a, Crimson tip. b, Tawny rajah. c, Leafwing butterfly. d, Great egg-fly. e, Blue admiral. f, African migrant.
Each 25r: No. 2371, Crimson tip. No. 2372, Large oak blue.

1999, June 8   Litho.   Perf. 14
2363-2368 A368 Set of 6   3.75 3.75
Sheets of 6, #a-f
2369-2370 A368 Set of 2   15.00 15.00
Souvenir Sheets
2371-2372 A368 Set of 2   10.00 10.00

Dinosaurs
A369

Designs: 1r, Scelidosaurus. 3r, Yan-sudaurus. 5r, Ornitholestes. 8r, Astrodon.
No. 2377, vert, each 7r: a, Anchisaurus. b, Pterenodon. c, Barosaurus. d, Iguanodon. e, Archaeopteryx. f, Ceratosaurus.
No. 2378, each 7r: a, Stegosaurus. b, Corythosaurus. c, Celiosaurus. d, Avimimus. e, Styracosaurus. f, Massospondylus.
No. 2379, vert, each 7r: a, Dimorphodon. b, Rhamphorhynchus. c, Allosaurus. d, Leaell-lynasaura. e, Troodon. f, Syntarsus.
Each 25r: No. 2380, Brachiosaurus. No. 2381, Megalosaurus.

1999, June 22
2373-2376　A369　Set of 4　　3.25　3.25
Sheets of 6, #a-f
2377-2379　A369　Set of 3　　24.50　24.50
Souvenir Sheets
2380-2381　A369　Set of 2　　10.00　10.00

Marine Environment Wildlife — A370

30 l, Broderip's cowrie. 1r, Fairy tern. 3r, Darker Maldivian green heron. 7r, Blackflag sandperch. 8r, Coral hind. 10r, Olive ridley turtle.
No. 2388, each 5r: a, Brown booby. b, Red-tailed tropicbird. c, Sooty tern. d, Striped dolphin. e, Long-snouted spinner dolphin. f, Crab plover. g, Hawksbill turtle. h, Indo-Pacific sergeant. i, Yellowfin tuna.
No. 2389, each 5r: a, Manta ray. b, Green turtle. c, Pan-tropical spotted dolphin. d, Moor-ish idols. e, Threadfin anthias. f, Goldbar wrasse. g, Palette surgeonfish. h, Three spot angelfish. i, Oriental sweetlips.
Each 25r: No. 2390, Cinnamon bittern. No. 2391, Blue-faced angelfish.

1999, Oct. 26　Litho.　Perf. 14
2382-2387　A370　Set of 6　　6.00　6.00
Sheets of 9, #a-i
2388-2389　A370　Set of 2　　16.50　16.50
Souvenir Sheets
2390-2391　A370　Set of 2　　9.50　9.50

Trains
A371

Designs: 50 l, 2-2-2 locomotive, Egypt. 1r, Le Shuttle, France. 2r, 4-4-0 Gowan & Marx, US. 3r, TGV, France. 5r, Ae 6/6 electric loco-motive, Switzerland. 8r, Stephenson's Long-boiled 2-4-0 locomotive, Great Britain. 10r, The Philadelphia, Austria. 15r. E class, Great Britain.
No. 2400, each 7r: a, Stephenson's Long-boiled locomotive, diff. b, 4-2-2 Cornwall, Great Britain. c, First locomotive, Germany. d, Great Western, Great Britain. e, Standard Stephenson 2-4-0, France. f, 2-2-2 Meteor, Great Britain.
No. 2401, each 7r: a, Type 4 class 4t, Great Britain. b, 1500 horsepower Diesel-electric locomotive, Malaysia. c, Co-Co 7000 Class, France. d, Diesel-hydraulic passenger locomotive, Thailand. e, Diesel-hydraulic locomotive, Burma. f, Hikari, Japan.
Each 25r: No. 2402, 2-2-2, Passenger loco-motive, France. No. 2403, King Arthur class, Great Britain.

1999, Oct. 26
2392-2399　A371　Set of 8　　7.50　7.50
Sheets of 6, #a-f
2400-2401　A371　Set of 2　　14.50　14.50
Souvenir Sheets
2402-2403　A371　Set of 2　　10.00　10.00

A372

Queen Mother (b. 1900) — A373

No. 2404: a, With King George VI, 1936. b, In 1941. c, In 1960. d, In 1981.
25r, At Order of the Garter Service.

Gold Frames

1999, Dec. 1　Litho.　Perf. 14
2404　A372　7r Sheet of 4, #a.-d., + label　6.00　6.00
Souvenir Sheet
Perf. 13¾
2405　A372　25r multi　　6.00　6.00
Litho. & Embossed
Die Cut Perf. 8¾
Without Gum
2406　A373　50r gold & multi
No. 2405 contains one 38x51mm stamp. See Nos. 2605-2606.

Hokusai Paintings — A374

No. 2407, each 7r: a, A Coastal view. b, Bath House by a Lake. c, Drawings (horse). d, Drawings (two birds). e, Evening Cool at Ryogoku. f, Girls Boating.
No. 2408, each 7r: a, Haunted House. b, Juniso Shrine at Yotsuya. c, Drawings (one bird). d, Drawings (two people). e, Lover in the Snow. f, Mountain Tea House.
Each 25r: No. 2409, Girls Gathering Spring Herbs, vert. No. 2410, Scene in the Yoshiwara, vert.

1999, Dec. 23　　Perf. 13¾
Sheets of 6, #a.-f.
2407-2408　A374　Set of 2　　17.00　17.00
Souvenir Sheets
2409-2410　A374　Set of 2　　10.00　10.00

IBRA '99, Nuremberg — A375

Trains (as described): 12r, Drache, 1848. 15r, Der Adler, 1833.

1999, Dec. 23　　Perf. 14x14½
2411-2412　A375　Set of 2　　6.00　6.00
The illustrations of the two stamps were switched.

Souvenir Sheets

PhilexFrance '99 — A376

Trains: No. 2413, Standard Stephenson 2-4-0, 1837. No. 2414, Long-boiled Stephenson, 1841.

1999, Dec. 23　　Perf. 13¾
2413-2414　A376　25r each　　8.00　8.00

Rights of the Child — A377

No. 2415: a, Black denomination in UL. b, White denomination in UL. c, Black denomina-tion in UR.
25r, Peter Ustinov, UNICEF goodwill ambassador.

1999, Dec. 23　　Perf. 14
2415　A377　10r Sheet of 3, #a.-c.　6.25　6.25
Souvenir Sheet
2416　A377　25r multi　　4.50　4.50

Mars Colony of the Future A378

No. 2417, each 5r: a, Phobos and Deimos. b, Improved Hubble Telescope. c, Passenger shuttle. d, Skyscrapers. e, Taxi cab. f, Landing facilities. g, Vegetation. h, Walking on Mars. i, Mars rover.
No. 2418, each 5r: a, Russian Phobos 25. b, Earth and moon. c, Space shuttle. d, Light-house. e, Excursion space liner. f, Inner-city shuttle. g, Viking lander. h, Air and water puri-fication plants. i, Life in a Mars city.
Each 25r: No. 2419, Mars, vert. No. 2420, Astronaut, vert.

2000, Jan. 24　Litho.　Perf. 14
Sheets of 9, #a.-i.
2417-2418　A378　Set of 2　　18.00　18.00
Souvenir Sheets
2419-2420　A378　Set of 2　　10.00　10.00

Millennium — A379

Highlights of 1750-1800: a, American Decla-ration of Independence, 1776. b, Hot air bal-loon flight by Montgolfier brothers, 1783. c, French Revolution begins with storming of the Bastille, 1789. d, James Watt patents steam engine, 1769. e, Wolfgang Amadeus Mozart born, 1756. f, Ts'ao Hsueh-ch'in publishes "Dream of the Red Chamber," 1791. g, Napo-leon conquers Egypt, 1798. h, Catherine the Great becomes Empress of Russia, 1762. i, Joseph Priestley discovers oxygen, 1774. j, Benjamin Franklin publishes studies on elec-tricity, 1751. k, Edward Jenner develops vacci-nation against smallpox, 1796. l, French and Indian War, 1754. m, Jean Honoré Fragonard paints "The Swing," c. 1766. n, Ludwig van Beethoven born, 1770. o, Louis marries Marie Antoinette, 1770. p, Capt. James Cook explores in South Pacific, discovers east coast of Australia, 1770 (60x40mm). q, Luigi Galvani experiments with electricity on nerves and muscles, c. 1780.

2000, Feb. 1　　Perf. 12¾x12½
2421　A379　3r Sheet of 17, #a.-q., + label　10.00　10.00

Destination 2000 Tourism Campaign — A380

Designs: a, Yellow flowers. b, School of fish. c, Airplane, boat prow. d, White flowers. e, Lionfish. f, Windsurfers.

2000, Feb. 1　　Perf. 13¾
2422　A380　7r Sheet of 6, #a.-f.　9.00　9.00

Solar Eclipse, Aug. 11, 1999 — A381

No. 2423 (Sky background), each 7r: a, First contact. b, Second contact. c, Totality. d, Third contact. e, Fourth contact. f, Observatory.
No. 2424 (Outer space background), each 7r: a, First contact. b, Second contact. c, Total-ity. d, Third contact. e, Fourth contact. f, Solar and helisospheric observatory.

2000, Mar. 8　Litho.　Perf. 14
Sheets of 6, #a.-f.
2423-2424　A381　Set of 2　　14.50　14.50

Butterflies — A382

No. 2425, each 5r: a, Red lacewing. b, Large oak blue. c, Yellow coster. d, Great orange tip. e, Common pierrot. f, Cruiser. g, Hedge blue. h, Great egg-fly. i, Common tiger.
No. 2426, each 5r: a, Common wall. b, Koh-i-noor. c, Indian red admiral. d, Tawny rajah. e, Blue triangle. f, Orange albatross. g, Common

rose swallowtail. h, Jeweled nawab. i, Striped blue crow.

Each 25r: No. 2427, Large tree nymph. No. 2428, Blue pansy.

2000, Apr. 10 Litho. *Perf. 13¼x13½*
Sheets of 9, #a-i
2425-2426 A382 Set of 2   18.00 18.00
Souvenir Sheets
2427-2428 A382 Set of 2   10.00 10.00

Paintings of Anthony Van
Dyck — A383

No. 2429, each 5r: a, Martin Rijckaert. b, Frans Snyders. c, Quentin Simons. d, Lucas van Uffel, 1622. e, Nicolaes Rockox. f, Nicholas Lanier.

No. 2430, each 5r: a, Inigo Jones. b, Lucas van Uffel, (actually detail from John, Count of Nassau-Sieger and his Family) c. 1622-25. c, Margaretha de Vos, Wife of Frans Snyders. d, Peter Breughel the Younger. e, Cornelis van der Geest. f, Francois Langlois as a Savoyard.

No. 2431, each 5r: a, Portrait of a Family. b, Earl and Countess of Denby and Their Daughter. c, Family Portrait. d, A Genoese Nobleman with his Children. e, Thomas Howard, Earl of Arundel, and His Grandson. f, The Woman in Gold (Battonia Balbi with her Children).

Each 25r: No. 2432, John, Count of Nassau-Siegen, and His Family. No. 2433, The Lomellini Family. No. 2434, Lucas and Cornelis de Wael. No. 2435, The Painter Jan de Wael and His Wife Gertrude de Jode. No. 2436, Sir Kenelm and Lady Digby with Their Two Eldest Sons. No. 2437, Sir Philip Herbert, 4th Earl of Pembroke, and His Family.

2000, May 1 *Perf. 13¾*
Sheets of 6, #a-f
2429-2431 A383 Set of 3   42.50 42.50
Souvenir Sheets
2432-2437 A383 Set of 6   26.00 26.00

Trains
A384

Designs: 5r, Shinkansen, Japan. 8r, Super Azusa, Japan. No. 2440, 10r, Spacia, Japan. 15r, Nozomi, Japan.

No. 2442, each 10r: a, 1909 Shanghai-Nanking Railway 4-6-2. b, 1910 Shanghai-Nanking Railway 4-2-2. c, 1914 Manchurian Railway 4-6-2. d, 1934 Chinese National Railway Hankow Line 4-8-4. e, 1949 Chinese National Railway 2-8-2. f, 1949 Chinese National Railway 2-10-0.

No. 2443, each 10r: a, 1856 East Indian Railway "Fawn" 2-2-2. b, 1893 East Indian Railway 4-4-0. c, 1909 Bengal-Nagpur Railway 4-4-2. d, 11924 Great Peninsular Railway 4-6-0. e, 1932 North Western Railway 4-6-2. f, 1949 Indian National Railway 4-6-2.

Each 25r: No. 2444, Chinese National Railways Class JS 2-8-2. No. 2445, Indian National Railway Class WP 4-6-2.

2000, June 8 Litho. *Perf. 14*
2438-2441 A384 Set of 4   6.50 6.50
Sheets of 6, #a-f
2442-2443 A384 Set of 2   20.00 20.00
Souvenir Sheets
2444-2445 A384 Set of 2   10.00 10.00
The Stamp Show 2000, London (Nos. 2442-2445). Nos. 2444-2445 each contain one 57x42mm stamp.

Millennium
A385

Designs: 10 l, Republic Monument. 30 l, Bodu Thakurufaanu Memorial Center. 1r, Health services. No. 2449, 7r, Hukuru Miskiiy. No. 2450, 7r, Male Intl. Airport. 10r, Educational development.

No. 2452, 25r, People's Majlis. No. 2453, 25r, Economic development. No. 2454, 25r, Islamic Center.

2000, Aug. 31 Litho. *Perf. 14*
2446-2451 A385 Set of 6   6.25 6.25
Souvenir Sheets
Perf. 13¼
2452-2454 A385 Set of 3   13.50 13.50

Souvenir Sheets

First Public Railways, 175th
Anniv. — A386

No. 2455: a, Locomotion No. 1, George Stephenson. b, William Hedley's Puffing Billy.

2000, Sept. 13 *Perf. 14*
2455 A386 10r Sheet of 2, #a-b   4.75 4.75

2000 Summer Olympics,
Sydney — A387

No. 2456: a, Suzanne Lenglen. b, Fencing. c, Olympic Stadium, Tokyo, and Japanese flag. d, Ancient Greek long jumper.

2000, Sept. 13
2456 A387 10r Sheet of 4, #a-d   7.75 7.75

First Zeppelin Flight, Cent. — A388

No. 2457, horiz.: a, Graf Zeppelin. b, Graf Zeppelin II. c, LZ-9.

2000, Sept. 13 *Perf. 14*
2457 A388 13r Sheet of 3, #a-c   7.00 7.00
Souvenir Sheet
Perf. 13¾
2458 A388 25r LZ-88   6.25 6.25
No. 2457 contains three 39x25mm stamps.

Apollo-Soyuz Mission, 25th
Anniv. — A389

No. 2459, vert.: a, Apollo 18 and Soyuz 19. b, Soyuz 19. c, Apollo 18.

2000, Sept. 13 *Perf. 14*
2459 A389 13r Sheet of 3, #a-c   6.75 6.75
Souvenir Sheet
2460 A389 25r Soyuz 19   5.50 5.50

Orchids — A390

Designs: 50 l, Dendrobium crepidatum. 1r, Eulophia guineensis. 2.50r, Cymbidium finlaysonianum. 3.50r, Paphiopedilum druryi.

No. 2465, 10r: a, Aerides odorata. b, Dendrobium chrysotoxum. c, Dendrobium anosmum. d, Calypso bulbosa. e, Paphiopedilum fairrieanum. f, Cynorkis fastigiata.

No. 2466, 10r: a, Angraecum germinyanum. b, Phalaenopsis amabilis. c, Thrixspermum cantipeda. d, Phaius tankervilleae. e, Rhynchostylis gigantea. f, Papilionanthe teres.

No. 2467, 25r, Cymbidium dayanum. No. 2468, 25r, Spathoglottis plicata.

2000, Sept. 13
2461-2464 A390 Set of 4   1.25 1.25
Sheets of 6, #a-f
2465-2466 A390 Set of 2   22.00 22.00
Souvenir Sheets
2467-2468 A390 Set of 2   10.00 10.00

Birds
A391

Designs: 15 l, White tern. 25 l, Brown booby. 30 l, White-collared kingfisher, vert. 1r, Black-winged stilt, vert.

No. 2473, 10r: a, Great frigatebird. b, Common noddy. c, Common tern. d, Sula sula. e, Sooty tern. f, Phaeton leturus.

No. 2474, 10r, vert.: a, White-collared kingfisher. b, Island thrush. c, Red-tailed tropicbird. d, Peregrine falcon. e, Night heron. f, Great egret.

No. 2475, 13r: a, Ringed plover. b, Turnstone. c, Thicknee. d, Black-bellied plover. e, Crab plover. f, Curlew.

No. 2476, 25r, Great cormorant, vert. No. 2477, 25r, Cattle egret, vert.

2000, Sept. 13 *Perf. 13¾*
2469-2472 A391 Set of 4   2.50 2.50
Sheets of 6, #a-f
2473-2475 A391 Set of 3   32.50 32.50
Souvenir Sheets
2476-2477 A391 Set of 2   10.00 10.00

Motorcycles — A392

No. 2478, 7r: a, 1907 Matchless. b, 1966 Manch 4 1200 TTS. c, 1957 Lambretta LD-150. d, 1990 Yamaha XJP 1200. e, 1885 Daimler. f, 1950-60 John Player Norton.

No. 2479, 7r: a, 1969 Honda CB 750. b, 1913 Harley-Davidson. c, 1925 Bohmerland. d, 1910 American Indian. e, 1993 Triumph Trophy 1200. f, 1928, Moto Guzzi 500S.

No. 2480, 25r, 1960 Electra Glide. No. 2481, 25r, 1950 Harley-Davidson.

2000, Oct. 30 *Perf. 13¼x13½*
Sheets of 6, #a-f
2478-2479 A392 Set of 2   17.00 17.00
Souvenir Sheets
2480-2481 A392 Set of 2   10.00 10.00

A393

Marine Life — A394

No. 2482: a, Longnosed filefish. b, Hawaiian squirrelfish. c, Freckled hawkfish. d, McCosker's flasher wrasse. e, Pygoplites diacanthus. f, Paraeentzopyge venusta.

No. 2483, 5r: a, Chaetodon lunula. b, Stethojulis albovittata. c, Green turtle. d, Jobfish. e, Damsel fish. f, Chaetodon meyeri. g, Cirrhilabrus exquistus. h, Anemonefish.

No. 2484, 5r: a, Coris aygula. b, Snapper. c, Sea bass. d, Chaetodon bennetti. e, Pelagic snapper. f, Cardinalfish. g, Thalassoma hardwicke. h, Surgeonfish.

No. 2485, 5r: a, Grouper. b, Pygoplites diacanthus. c, Forcipiger flavissimus. d, Goatfish. e, Trumpet fish. f, Anthias. g, Centropyge bispinosus. h, Sweetlips.

No. 2486, 25r, H. aberrans. No. 2487, 25r, Angelfish. No. 2488, 25r, Moray eel. No. 2489, 25r, Spiny butterflyfish.

2000, Nov. 15   Litho.   *Perf. 14*
2482 A393 5r Sheet of 6, #a-f   5.50   5.50
Sheets of 8, #a-h
2483-2485 A394 Set of 3   21.00 21.00
Souvenir Sheets
2486 A393 25r multi   4.25   4.25
2487-2489 A394 Set of 3   13.00 13.00

Flowers — A395

No. 2490, 5r: a, Corn lily. b, Clivia. c, Red hot poker. d, Crown of thorns. e, Cape daisy. f, Geranium.
No. 2491, 5r, horiz.: a, Fringed hibiscus. b, Erica vestita. c, Bird-of-paradise. d, Peacock orchid. e, Mesembryanthemums. f, African violets.
No. 2492, 25r, Gladiolus. No. 2493, 25r, Calla lily, horiz.

2000, Nov. 15
Sheets of 6, #a-f
2490-2491 A395 Set of 2   14.00 14.00
Souvenir Sheets
2492-2493 A395 Set of 2   10.00 10.00

Airplanes, Automobiles and
Trains — A396

Designs: 2.50r, Papyrus, vert. 3r, Hiawatha. 12r, Supermarine SGB. 13r, MLX01.
No. 2498, 5r: a, Thrust SSC. b, Curtiss R3C-2. c, Rocket. d, BB-9004. e, Mallard. f, TGV.
No. 2499, 5r: a, Lockheed XP-80. b, Mikoyan MiG-23. c, Tempest. d, Bluebird. e, Blue Flame. f, Thrust 2.
No. 2500, 25r, Bell X-1. No. 2501, 25r, Lockheed SR-71 Blackbird, vert.

2000, Nov. 29
2494-2497 A396 Set of 4   5.25   5.25
Sheets of 6, #a-f
2498-2499 A396 Set of 2   10.00 10.00
Souvenir Sheets
2500-2501 A396 Set of 2   8.50   8.50

Paintings from the Prado — A397

No. 2502, 7r: a, The Nobleman with the Golden Chain, by Tintoretto. b, Triumphal Arch, by Domenichino. c, Don Garcia de Medici, by Bronzino. d, Micer Marsilio from Micer Marsilio and His Wife, by Lorenzo Lotto. e, La Infanta Maria Antoinetta Fernanda, by Jacopo Amigoni. f, Wife from Micer Marsilio and his Wife.
No. 2503, 7r: a, Two women with headdresses. b, Woman in red. c, Men. d, The Duke of Lerma on Horseback, by Rubens. e, The Death of Seneca, by the Workshop of

Rubens. f, Marie de Medici by Rubens. a-c from Achilles Amongst the Daughters of Lycomedes, by Peter Paul Rubens and Anthony Van Dyck.
No. 2504, 7r: a, Self-portrait, by Albrecht Dürer. b, A Woman and Her Daughter, by Adriaen van Cronenburgh. c, Portrait of a man, by Dürer. d, Woman and children. e, Artemisia, by Rembrandt. f, f from The Artist and His Family, by Jacob Jordaens.
No. 2505, 7r: a, The Painter Andrea Sacchi, by Carlo Maratta. b, Two men. c, Charles Cecil Roberts, by Pompeo Girolamo Batoni. d, Francesco Albani, by Sacchi. e, Three men. f, William Hamilton, by Batoni. b, e from The Turkish Ambassador to the Court of Naples, by Giuseppe Bonito.
No. 2506, 7r: a, The Marquesa of Villafranca, by Francisco de Goya. b, Maria Ruthven, by Van Dyck. c, Cardinal-Infante Ferdinand, by Van Dyck. d, Frederik Hendrik, Prince of Orange, by Van Dyck. e, Van Dyck from Self-portrait with Endymion Porter. f, Porter from Self-portrait with Endymion Porter.
No. 2507, 7r: a, Philip V, by Hyacinthe Rigaud. b, Louis XIV, by Rigaud. c, Don Luis, Prince of Asturias, by Michel-Ange Houasse. d, Duke Carlo Emanuele II of Savoy with His Wife and Son, by Charles Dauphin. e, Kitchen Maid by Charles-François Hutin. f, Hurdygurdy Player, by Georges de La Tour.
No. 2508, 25r, Elizabeth of Valois, by Sofonisba Anguisciola. No. 2509, 25r, Camilla Gonzaga, Countess of San Segundo with Her Three Children, by Parmigianino. No. 2510, 25r, The Turkish Ambassador to the Court of Naples. No. 2511, 25r, Duke Carlo Emanuele of Savoy with His Wife and Son. No. 2512, 25r, The Artist and His Family, horiz. No. 2513, 25r, The Devotion of Rudolf I, by Rubens and Jan Wildens, horiz.

Perf. 12x12¼, 12¼x12
2000, Nov. 29
Sheets of 6, #a-f
2502-2507 A397 Set of 6   42.50 42.50
Souvenir Sheets
2508-2513 A397 Set of 6   26.00 26.00
España 2000 Intl. Philatelic Exhibition.

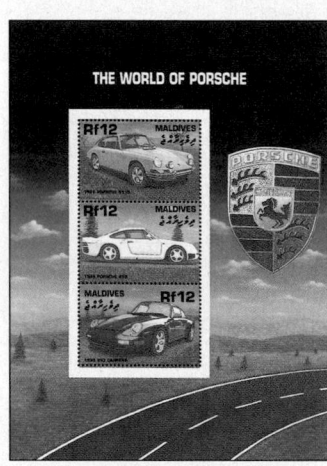

Porsche Automobiles — A398

No. 2514, 12r: a, 1966 911S. b, 1988 959. c, 1995 993 Carrera.
No. 2515, 12r: a, 1963 356 SC. b, 1975 911 Turbo. c, Unidentified.

2000, Nov. 30   Litho.   *Perf. 14*
Sheets of 3, #a-c
2514-2515 A398 Set of 2   12.50 12.50
Souvenir Sheet
2516 A398 25r 2000 Boxter   4.25   4.25
No. 2516 contains one 56x42mm stamp.

Mushrooms
A399

Designs: 30 l, Cortinarius collinitus. 50 l, Russula ochroleuca. 2r, Lepiota acutesquamosa. 3r, Hebeloma radicosum. 13r, Amanita echinocephala. 15r, Collybia iocephala.

No. 2523, 7r: a, Tricholoma aurantium. b, Pholiota spectabilis. c, Russula caerulea. d, Amanita phalloides. e, Mycena strobilinoides. f, Boletus satanas.
No. 2524, 7r: a, Amanita muscaria. b, Mycena lilacifolia. c, Coprinus comatus. d, Morchella crassipes. e, Russula nigricans. f, Lepiota procera.
No. 2525, 25r, Tricholoma aurantium, diff. No. 2526, 25r, Lepiota procera, diff.

2001, Jan. 2
2517-2522 A399 Set of 6   5.75   5.75
Sheets of 6, #a-f
2523-2524 A399 Set of 2   14.50 14.50
Souvenir Sheets
2525-2526 A399 Set of 2   8.50   8.50

Battle of Britain, 60th Anniv. — A400

No. 2527, 5r: a, German commanders look across the English Channel. b, The armorers make ready. c, The German attack begins. d, Germany bombs the British coast. e, Germany bombs British cities. f, Luftwaffe sets St. Paul's Cathedral ablaze. g, Aerial dogfight. h, A British Spitfire is shot down.
No. 2528, 5r: a, Leaders of Great Britain. b, British pilots prepare to confront the Luftwaffe. c, RAF planes take off. d, British aircraft meet the enemy. e, Luftwaffe meets tough resistance. f, Dogfight above English Channel. g, German planes fall short of their objective. h, Many German planes are shot down.
No. 2529, 25r, Hawker Hurricane. No. 2530, 25r, Messerschmitt ME 109.

2001, Jan. 2   *Perf. 14*
Sheets of 8, #a-h
2527-2528 A400 Set of 2   14.50 14.50
Souvenir Sheets
2529-2530 A400 Set of 2   8.50   8.50

Rijksmuseum, Amsterdam, Bicent. (in 2000) — A401

No. 2531, 7r: a, Donkey's head and rider from Donkey Riding on the Beach, by Isaac Lazarus Israels. b, The Paternal Admonition, by Gerard Terborch, the Younger. c, The Sick Woman, by Jan Havicksz Steen. d, Girls with red hats from Donkey Riding on the Beach. e, Pompeius Occo, by Dirck Jacobsz. f, Woman With a Child in a Pantry, by Pieter de Hooch.
No. 2532, 7r: a, The Holy Kinship, by Geertgen tot Sint Jans. b, Sir Thomas Gresham, by Anthonis Mor. c, Self-portrait as St. Paul, by Rembrandt. d, Cleopatra's Banquet, by Gerard Lairesse. e, Still Life With Flowers in a Glass, by Jan Brueghel, the Elder. f, Portrait of a Man, Possibly Nicolaes Hasselaer, by Frans Hals.
No. 2533, 7r: a, Rembrandt's Mother, by Gerard Dou. b, Portrait of a Girl Dressed in Blue, by Jan Cornelisz Verspronck. c, Old Woman at Prayer, by Nicolaes Maes. d, Feeding the Hungry from The Seven Works of Charity, by the Master of Alkmaar. e, The Threatened Swan, by Jan Asselyn. f, The Daydreamer, by Maes.
No. 2534, 7r: a, Woman seated in doorway, from The Little Street, by Jan Vermeer. b, Two women from The Love Letter, by Vermeer. c,

Woman in Blue Reading a Letter, by Vermeer. d, Woman and pillar from The Love Letter. e, The Milkmaid, by Vermeer. f, Arched doorway, from The Little Street.
No. 2535, 25r, Johannes Wtenbogaert, by Rembrandt. No. 2536, 25r, The Staalmeesters (The Syndics), by Rembrandt. No. 2537, 25r, The Night Watch, by Rembrandt. No. 2538, 25r, Shipwreck on a Rocky Coast, by Wijnandus Johannes Joseph Nuyen, horiz.

2001, Jan. 15   *Perf. 13¾*
Sheets of 6, #a-f
2531-2534 A401 Set of 4   30.00 30.00
Souvenir Sheets
2535-2538 A401 Set of 4   17.00 17.00

Ill-fated Ships — A402

No. 2539, 5r: a, Milton Iatrides, 1970. b, Cyclops, 1918. c, Marine Sulphur Queen, 1963. d, Rosalie, 1840. e, Mary Celeste, 1872. f, Atlanta, 1880.
No. 2540, 5r: a, Windfall, 1962. b, Kobenhavn, 1928. c, Pearl, 1874. d, HMS Bulwark, 1914. e, Patriot, 1812. f, Lusitania, 1915.
No. 2541, 25r, La Boussole and L'Astrolabe, 1789. No. 2542, 25r, Titanic, 1912.

2001, Feb. 12   *Perf. 14*
Sheets of 6, #a-f
2539-2540 A402 Set of 2   10.00 10.00
Souvenir Sheets
2541-2542 A402 Set of 2   8.50   8.50

Flower Type of 1997
2001, Mar. 1   *Perf. 14¾x14*
Size: 16x20mm
2543 A350 10r Like #2267   1.75   1.75

Islam in Maldive Islands, 848th Anniv. — A403

No. 2544: a, Dharumavantha Rasgefaanu Mosque. b, Plaque of Hukurumiskiiy. c, Learning the Holy Koran. d, Institute of Islamic Studies. e, Center for the Holy Koran. f, Islamic Center.

2001, July 9   Litho.   *Perf. 13¾*
2544 A403 10r Sheet of 6,
          #a-f   10.00 10.00
Souvenir Sheet
2545 A403 25r Medhu
          Ziyaarath   4.25   4.25

Fish — A404

Designs: No. 2546, 10r, Pterois miles. No. 2547, 10r, Pomacanthus imperator.

2001, July 16   *Perf. 14x14¾*
2546-2547 A404 Set of 2   3.50   3.50

Pontiac Trans-Am Automobiles — A405

No. 2548, 12r: a, 1970. b, 1989. c, 1994.
No. 2549, 12r: a, 1976. b, 1988. c, 1988 Coupe.

2001   **Perf. 14**
Sheets of 3, #a-c
2548-2549 A405   Set of 2   12.50 12.50
Souvenir Sheet
Perf. 14¼
2550 A405 25r 1999   4.25 4.25
Nos. 2548-2549 each contain three 42x28mm stamps.

Automobiles — A406

Designs: 1r, 1930 Pierce-Arrow. 2r, 1938 Mercedes-Benz 540K. 8r, 1934 Duesenberg J. 10r, 1931 Bugatti Royale.
No. 2555, 7r: a, 1931 Auburn convertible sedan. b, 1931 Mercedes SSKL. c, 1929 Packard roadster. d, 1940 Chevrolet. e, 1915 Mercer. f, 1941 Packard sedan.
No. 2556, 7r: a, 1932 Chevrolet roadster. b, 1929 Cadillac Fleetwood roadster. c, 1928 Bentley Speed Six. d, 1930 Cadillac Fleetwood. e, 1936 Ford convertible. f, 1929 Hudson Phaeton.
No. 2557, 25r, 1030 Cord Brougham. No. 2558, 25r, 1931 Rolls-Royce P-1.

2001   **Perf. 14**
2551-2554 A406   Set of 4   3.50 3.50
Sheets of 6, #a-f
2555-2556 A406   Set of 2   14.50 14.50
Souvenir Sheets
2557-2558 A406   Set of 2   8.50 8.50

Phila Nippon '01, Japan — A407

No. 2559, 7r (28x42mm) — Prints of women by Utamaro: a, Reed Blind, Model Young Women Woven in Mist. b, Woman with Parasol. c, High-ranked Courtesan, Five Shades of Ink in the Northern Quarter. d, Comparison of Beauties of the Southern Quarter. e, The Barber.
No. 2560, 7r — Actors by Shunsho Katsukawa: a, Danjuro Ichikawa V (black kimono, 28x85mm). b, Danjuro Ichikawa V (arm raised, 28x85mm). c, Danjuro Ichikawa V (arms crossed on chest, 28x85mm). d, Danjuro Ichikawa V (wrapped in kimono, 28x85mm). e, Tomoeman Otani I and Mitsugaro Bando I (56x85mm).

No. 2561, 25r, The Courtesan Hinazuru of the House Called Keizetsuro, by Utamaro. No. 2562, 25r, Jomyo Tsutsui and the Priest Ichirai on the Uji Bridge, by Kiyomasu Torii.

2001, July 18   **Litho.**   **Perf. 14**
Sheets of 5, #a-e
2559-2560 A407   Set of 2   12.00 12.00
Souvenir Sheets
Perf. 13¾
2561-2562 A407   Set of 2   8.50 8.50

Giuseppe Verdi (1813-1901), Opera Composer — A408

No. 2563: a, Alfred Piccaver. b, Rigoletto costume, Heinrich. c, Rigoletto costume, Cologne. d, Cornell MacNeil.
25r, Matteo Manuguerra.

2001, Aug. 26   **Perf. 14**
2563 A408 10r Sheet of 4, #a-d   6.75 6.75
Souvenir Sheet
2564 A408 25r multi   4.25 4.25

Mao Zedong (1893-1976) — A409

No. 2565: a, Red background. b, Blue background. c, Gray background.
25r, Wearing cap.

2001, Aug. 26   **Perf. 13¾**
2565 A409 15r Sheet of 3, #a-c   7.75 7.75
Souvenir Sheet
2566 A409 25r multi   4.25 4.25

Queen Victoria (1819-1901) — A410

No. 2567: a, Earring at right. b, Earring at left. c, As old woman. d, In black dress.
25r, With hand on chin.

2001, Aug. 26   **Perf. 14**
2567 A410 10r Sheet of 4, #a-d   6.75 6.75
Souvenir Sheet
2568 A410 25r multi   4.25 4.25

Queen Elizabeth II, 75th Birthday — A411

No. 2569: a, Without hat. b, Wearing large crown. c, Wearing tiara. d, Wearing red uniform. e, Wearing black cape and hat. f, Wearing tan hat.
25r, Wearing crown, diff.

2001, Aug. 26
2569 A411 7r Sheet of 6, #a-f   7.25 7.25
Souvenir Sheet
2570 A411 25r multi   4.25 4.25

Nobel Prizes, Cent. — A412

No. 2571 — Economics laureates: a, Simon Kuznets, 1971. b, Wassily Leontief, 1973. c, Lawrence R. Klein, 1980. d, Friedrich A. von Hayek, 1974. e, Leonid V. Kantorovich, 1975.
No. 2572, 7r — Peace laureates: a, Ernesto T. Moneta, 1907. b, Albert J. Luthuli, 1960. c, Henri Dunant, 1901. d, Charles Albert Gobat, 1902. e, Sean MacBride, 1974. f, Elie Ducommun, 1902.
No. 2573, 7r — Peace laureates: a, Adolfo Pérez Esquivel, 1980. b, Mikhail S. Gorbachev, 1990. c, Betty Williams, 1976. d, Alfonso Garcia Robles, 1982. e, Paul D'Estournelles de Constant, 1909. f, Louis Renault, 1907.
No. 2574, 25r, Trygve Haavelmo, Economics, 1989. No. 2575, 25r, Vicente Aleixandre, Literature, 1977. No. 2576, 25r, Octavio Paz, Literature, 1990.

2001, Sept. 29   **Litho.**   **Perf. 14**
2571 A412 7r Sheet of 5, #a-e   6.00 6.00
Sheets of 6, #a-f
2572-2573 A412   Set of 2   14.50 14.50
Souvenir Sheets
2574-2576 A412   Set of 3   13.00 13.00

Mercedes-Benz Automobiles, Cent. — A413

Designs: 2.50r, 1939 W165 Grand Prix. 5r, 1928 460 Nürburg Sport Roadster. 8r, 1928 Boattail Speedster. 15r, 1909 Blitzen Benz.
No. 2581, 7r: a, 1927 680S. b, 1934 150. c, 1936 540K Roadster. d, 1933 770 Grosser Mercedes. e, 1958 220SE. f, 1990 500SL.

No. 2582, 7r: a, 1933 290. b, 1927 Model S. c, 1953 300SL Coupe. d, 1911 Benz Victoria. e, 1968 280SL. f, 1937 W125 Grand Prix.
No. 2583, 25r, 1931 370S. No. 2584, 25r, 1955 300SLR.

2001, Oct. 30   **Litho.**   **Perf. 14**
2577-2580 A413   Set of 4   5.25 5.25
Sheets of 6, #a-f
2581-2582 A413   Set of 2   14.50 14.50
Souvenir Sheets
2583-2584 A413   Set of 2   8.50 8.50

2002 World Cup Soccer Championships, Japan and Korea — A414

World Cup Trophy and: 1r, Eusebio, Portugal, Portuguese flag. 3r, Johan Cruyff, Netherlands, Netherlands flag. 7r, French player and flag. 10r, Japanese player and flag. 12r, Seoul World Cup Stadium, horiz. 15r, 1930 World Cup poster.
25r, Gerd Müller's winning goal for West Germany, 1974, vert.

2001, Nov. 28
2585-2590 A414   Set of 6   8.25 8.25
Souvenir Sheet
2591 A414 25r multi   4.25 4.25
No. 2591 contains one 42x56mm stamp.

Princess Diana (1961-97) — A415

No. 2592: a, Pink rose. b, White rose. c, Yellow rose. d, Beige rose.
25r, Wearing pearl necklace.

2001, Dec. 26
2592 A415 10r Sheet of 4, #a-d   6.75 6.75
Souvenir Sheet
2593 A415 25r multi   4.25 4.25

New Year 2002 (Year of the Horse) — A416

No. 2594 — Paintings by Xu Beihong: a, Running Horse (painting 45mm tall). b, Standing Horse. c, Running Horse (painting 49mm tall). d, Horse (painting 44mm tall). e, Horse (painting 48mm tall).
15r, Horse, horiz.

2001, Dec. 26   **Perf. 14**
2594 A416 5r Sheet of 5, #a-e   5.50 5.50

Souvenir Sheet
Perf. 14x14½
2595 A416 15r multi   2.60 2.60

No. 2594 contains five 31x63mm stamps.

Pres. John F. Kennedy — A417

No. 2596, 5r: a, At Dexter, 1927. b, At Harvard, 1935. c, In Navy, 1943. d, At wedding, 1953. e, With brother Robert, 1956. f, At Presidential inauguration, 1961.

No. 2597, 5r: a, With Nikita Khrushchev, 1961. b, With Harold Macmillan. c, With Charles de Gaulle, 1961. d, With Jawaharlal Nehru, 1962. e, With Konrad Adenauer, 1963. f, With Dr. Martin Luther King, Jr., 1963.

No. 2598, 25r, Portrait. No. 2599, 25r, With wife, 1961.

2001, Dec. 26   **Perf. 14**
Sheets of 6, #a-f
2596-2597 A417   Set of 2   13.00 13.00
Souvenir Sheets
2598-2599 A417   Set of 2   8.50 8.50

Moths — A418

No. 2600, 7r: a, Cymothoe lucasi. b, Milionia grandis. c, Ornithoptera eroesus. d, Hyantis hodeva. e, Ammobiota festiva. f, Blue salamis.

No. 2601, 7r: a, Zygaena occitanica. b, Campyloes desgodinsi. c, Bhutanitis thaidina. d, Six-tailed helicopsis. e, Parnassius charltonius. f, Acraea ecucogiap.

No. 2602: a, Papilio dardanus. b, Baomisa hieroglyphica. c, Troides prattorum. d, Funonia rhadama.

No. 2603, 25r, Hypolera cassotis. No. 2604, 25r, Euphydryas maturna, vert.

2001, Dec. 26   **Litho.**
Sheets of 6, #a-f
2600-2601 A418   Set of 2   14.50 14.50
2602 A418 10r Sheet of 4, #a-d   6.75 6.75
Souvenir Sheets
2603-2604 A418   Set of 2   8.50 8.50

Queen Mother Type of 1999 Redrawn

No. 2605: a, With King George VI, 1936. b, In 1941. c, In 1960. d, In 1981.
25r, At Order of the Garter Service.

2001, Dec.   **Perf. 14**
Yellow Orange Frames
2605 A372 7r Sheet of 4, #a-d, + label   4.75 4.75
Souvenir Sheet
Perf. 13¾
2606 A372 25r multi   4.25 4.25

Queen Mother's 101st birthday. No. 2606 contains one 38x51mm stamp slightly darker than that found on No. 2405. Sheet margins of Nos. 2605-2606 lack embossing and gold arms and frames found on Nos. 2404-2405.

Reign of Queen Elizabeth II, 50th Anniv. — A419

No. 2607: a, With Princess Margaret. b, Wearing white hat. c, Wearing tiara. d, Holding flowers.
25r, At coronation.

2002, Feb. 6   **Litho.**   **Perf. 14¼**
2607 A419 10r Sheet of 4, #a-d   7.75 7.75
Souvenir Sheet
2608 A419 25r multi   4.25 4.25

Cats — A420

Designs: 3r, Havana brown. 5r, American wirehair. 8r, Norwegian forest cat. 10r, Seal point Siamese.

No. 2613, 7r: a, British blue. b, Red mackerel Manx. c, Scottish fold. d, Somali. e, Balinese. f, Exotic shorthair.

No. 2614, 7r, horiz.: a, Persian. b, Exotic shorthair, diff. c, Ragdoll. d, Manx. e, Tonkinese. f, Scottish fold, diff.

25r, Blue mackerel tabby Cornish rex.

2002, Apr. 8   **Perf. 14**
2609-2612 A420   Set of 4   4.75 4.75
Sheets of 6, #a-f
2613-2614 A420   Set of 2   14.50 14.50
Souvenir Sheet
2615 A420 25r multi   4.25 4.25

Birds
A421

Designs: 1r, Swinhoe's snipe. 2r, Oriental honey buzzard. 3r, Asian koel. No. 2619, 5r, Red-throated pipet. No. 2620, 7r, Short-eared owl. 10r, Eurasian spoonbill. 12r, Pied wheatear. 15r, Oriental pratincole.

No. 2624, 5r: a, Lesser noddy. b, Roseate tern. c, Frigate minor. d, Saunder's tern. e, White-bellied storm petrel. f, Red-footed booby.

No. 2625, 5r: a, Cattle egret. b, Barn swallow. c, Osprey. d, Little heron. e, Ruddy turnstone. f, Sooty tern.

No. 2626, 7r: a, Rose-ringed parakeet. b, Common swift. c, Lesser kestrel. d, Golden oriole. e, Asian paradise flycatcher. f, Indian roller.

No. 2627, 7r: a, Pallid harrier. b, Gray heron. c, Blue-tailed bee-eater. d, White-breasted water hen. e, Cotton pygmy goose. f, Maldivian pond heron.

No. 2628, 25r, White-tailed tropicbird. No. 2629, 25r, Greater flamingo. No. 2630, 25r, Cinnamon bittern. No. 2631, 25r, White tern.

2002, Apr. 8
2616-2623 A421   Set of 8   10.00 10.00
Sheets of 6, #a-f
2624-2627 A421   Set of 4   27.50 27.50
Souvenir Sheets
2628-2631 A421   Set of 4   17.00 17.00

Prehistoric Animals — A422

No. 2632, 7r: a, Sivatherium. b, Flat-headed peccary. c, Shasta ground sloth. d, Harlan's ground sloth. e, European woolly rhinoceros. f, Dwarf pronghorn.

No. 2633, 7r: a, Macrauchenia. b, Gyptodon. c, Nesodon. d, Imperial tapir. e, Short-faced bear. f, Mammoth.

No. 2634, 25r, Saber-toothed cat. No. 2635, 25r, Woolly mammoth, vert.

2002, May 21
Sheets of 6, #a-f
2632-2633 A422   Set of 2   15.00 15.00
Souvenir Sheets
2634-2635 A422   Set of 2   8.50 8.50

2002 Winter Olympics, Salt Lake City — A423

Designs: No. 2636, 12r, Freestyle skiing. No. 2637, 12r, Downhill skiing.

2002, July 11   **Litho.**   **Perf. 13½x13¼**
2636-2637 A423   Set of 2   4.50 4.50
   a. Souvenir sheet, #2636-2637   4.50 4.50

Intl. Year of Mountains — A424

No. 2638: a, Mt. Ama Dablam, Nepal. b, Mt. Clements, US. c, Mt. Artesonraju, Peru. d, Mt. Cholatse, Nepal.
25r, Balloon and Mt. Jefferson, US.

2002, July 11   **Perf. 14**
2638 A424 15r Sheet of 4, #a-d   10.50 10.50
Souvenir Sheet
2639 A424 25r multi   4.25 4.25

20th World Scout Jamboree, Thailand — A425

No. 2640, vert.: a, Temple. b, Thailand Scout. c, Merit badges.
25r, Mountain climbing merit badge.

2002, July 11
2640 A425 15r Sheet of 3, #a-c   7.75 7.75
Souvenir Sheet
2641 A425 25r multi   4.25 4.25

Souvenir Sheet

World Customs Organization, 50th Anniv. — A426

2002, Aug. 12   **Perf. 13¾**
2642 A426 50r multi   8.50 8.50

Elvis Presley (1935-77)
A427

2002, Oct. 7
2643 A427 5r multi   1.25 1.25

Printed in sheets of 9.

Flowers and Butterflies — A428

No. 2644, 7r — Flowers: a, Morning glory. b, Wedding bell anemone. c, Barrett Browning narcissus. d, Persian jewel nigella. e, Whirligig pink osteospermum. f, Brown lasso iris.

No. 2645, 7r — Orchids: a, Laelia gouldiana. b, Cattleya Louise Georgiana. c, Laeliocattleya Christopher Gubler. d, Miltoniopsis Bert Field Crimson Glow. e, Lemboglossum bictoniense. f, Derosara Divine Victor.

No. 2646, 7r — Butterflies: a, Morpho menelus. b, Small postman. c, Hewitson's blue hairstreak. d, Green swallowtail. e, Cairns birdwing. f, Queen.

No. 2647, 25r, Little pink beauty aster. No. 2648, 25r, Angraecum veitchii, vert. No. 2649, 25r, Cymothoe lurida butterfly.

2002, Nov. 4   Litho.   *Perf. 14*
Sheets of 6, #a-f
2644-2646 A428 Set of 3   22.50 22.50
Souvenir Sheets
2647-2649 A428 Set of 3   12.00 12.00

2002 World Cup Soccer
Championships, Japan and
Korea — A429

No. 2650, 7r: a, Torsten Frings sliding. b, Roberto Carlos. c, Frings kicking. d, Ronaldo pointing. e, Oliver Neuville. f, Ronaldo with ball.
No. 2651, 7r: a, Eul Yong Lee, Alpay Ozalan. b, Myung Bo Hong, Hakan Sukur. c, Emre Belozoglu, Chong Gug Song. d, Ergun Penbe, Chong Gug Song. e, Ergun Penbe, Ki Hyeon Seol. f, Chong Gug Song, Hakan Unsal.
No. 2652, 15r: a, Cafu and Neuville. b, Hands holding World Cup.
No. 2653, 15r: a, Dietmar Hamann. b, Cafu holding World Cup.
No. 2654, 15r: a, Ilhan Mansiz. b, Young Pyo Lee.
No. 2655, 15r: a, Hakan Sukur. b, Sang Chul Yoo.

2002, Nov. 12   *Perf. 13½*
Sheets of 6, #a-f
2650-2651 A429 Set of 2   13.50 13.50
Souvenir Sheets of 2, #a-b
2652-2655 A429 Set of 4   19.00 19.00

Teddy Bears, Cent. — A430

No. 2656: a, Hairdresser. b, Construction worker. c, Gardener. d, Chef.
No. 2657, 12r: a, Mother. b, Sister and brother. c, Father.
No. 2658, 12r: a, Nurse. b, Doctor. c, Dentist.
No. 2659, 30r, Soccer player. No. 2660, 30r, Golfer. No. 2661, 30r, Snow boarder.

2002, Nov. 18   *Perf. 14*
2656 A430 8r Sheet of 4, #a-d 5.00 5.00
Sheets of 3, #a-c
2657-2658 A430 Set of 2   11.50 11.50
Souvenir Sheets
2659-2661 A430 Set of 3   14.00 14.00

First Non-Stop Solo Transatlantic
Flight, 75th Anniv. — A430a

No. 2661A, 12r — Various photos of Charles Lindbergh and Spirit of St. Louis: c, Blue. d, Brown. e, Gray. f, Red violet.
No. 2661B, 12r: g, Donald Hall, designer of Spirit of St. Louis. h, Charles Lindbergh. i, Lindbergh, Spirit of St. Louis (Lindbergh distorted). j, Lindbergh, Hall and President Mahoney of Ryan Aircraft.

2002, Dec. 2   Litho.   *Perf. 14*
2661A A430a 12r Sheet of 4,
              #c-f   7.50 7.50
2661B A430a 12r Sheet of 4,
              #g-j   7.50 7.50

Princess Diana (1961-97)
A431   A432

2002, Dec. 2   Litho.   *Perf. 14*
2662 A431 12r multi   1.90 1.90
2663 A432 12r multi   1.90 1.90
Nos. 2002-2003 were each printed in sheets of 4.

Pres. John F. Kennedy (1917-
63) — A432a

No. 2663A: b, With father Joseph P., and brother Joseph, Jr. c, At age 11. d, Inspecting Boston waterfront, 1951. e, As Navy Ensign, 1941. f, With sister Kathleen in London, 1939. g, With Eleanor Roosevelt, 1951.

2002, Dec. 2   Litho.   *Perf. 14*
2663A A432a 7r Sheet of 6, #b-g 7.25 7.25

Pres. Ronald
Reagan — A433

Designs: No. 2664, Green background. No. 2665, Blue background.
No. 2666: a, Wearing brown suit. b, Wearing black suit with red tie.

2002, Dec. 2
2664 A433 12r multi   1.90 1.90
2665 A433 12r multi   1.90 1.90
  a.   Horiz. pair, #2664-2665 4.00 4.00
2666 A433 12r Horiz. pair, #a-b 4.00 4.00
       Nos. 2664-2666 (3)   7.80 7.80

Nos. 2664-2665 were printed in sheets containing two of each stamp. No. 2666 was printed in sheets containing two pairs.

Amphilex 2002 Intl. Stamp Exhibition,
Amsterdam — A434

No. 2667, 7r — Life of Queen Mother Juliana and Prince Bernhard: a, Wedding, 1937. b, Birth of Princess Beatrix, 1938. c, Exile in Canada, 1940-45. d, Installation of Juliana as queen, 1948. e, Zeeland flood, 1953. f, Royal couple.
No. 2668, 7r — Portraits depicting Queen Beatrix by: a, Pauline Hille. b, John Klinkenberg. c, Beatrice Filius. d, Will Kellermann. e, Graswinckel. f, Marjolijn Spreeuwenberg.

2002, Dec. 8   *Perf. 14*
Sheets of 6, #a-f
2667-2668 A434 Set of 2   13.50 13.50

Fish
A435

Birds and
Sharks — A436

Designs: 10 l, Flame basslet. 15 l, Teardrop butterflyfish. 20 l, Hamburg damselfish. 25 l, Bridled tern. 50 l, Blue-lined surgeonfish. 1r, Common tern. 2r, Common noddy. No. 2676, Yellow-breasted wrasse. No. 2677, Blue shark. 4r, Harlequin filefish. 5r, Orangespine unicornfish. 10r, Emperor angelfish. 12r, Bullseye. 20r, Scalloped hammerhead shark.

Perf. 14 (A435), 10¾x13 (25 l, 1r, 2r),
13¼x14 (#2677, 20r)
2002, Dec. 24
2669 A435 10 l multi   .25   .25
2670 A435 15 l multi   .25   .25
2671 A435 20 l multi   .25   .25
2672 A436 25 l multi   .25   .25
2673 A435 50 l multi   .25   .25
2674 A436 1r multi   .25   .25
2675 A436 2r multi   .30   .30
2676 A435 2.50r multi   .40   .40
2677 A436 2.50r multi   .40   .40
2678 A435 4r multi   .60   .60
2679 A435 5r multi   .75   .75
2680 A435 10r multi   1.50 1.50
2681 A435 12r multi   1.90 1.90
2682 A436 20r multi   3.00 3.00
       Nos. 2669-2682 (14)   10.35 10.35

Tourism, 30th Anniv. — A437

No. 2683: a, Atolls. b, Sand spit. c, Surfer. d, Underwater scene.

2002, Dec. 25   *Perf. 13½*
2683 A437 12r Sheet of 4, #a-d 7.50 7.50

Popeye — A438

No. 2684, vert: a, Diving. b, Surfing. c, Sailboarding. d, Baseball. e, Hurdles. f, Tennis.
25r, Volleyball.

2003, Jan. 27   *Perf. 14*
2684 A438 7r Sheet of 6, #a-f 6.50 6.50
Souvenir Sheet
2685 A438 25r multi   4.00 4.00

National
Museum,
50th
Anniv.
A439

Various museum items: 3r, 3.50r, 6.50r, 22r.

2003, Jan. 31   Litho.
2686-2689 A439 Set of 4   5.50 5.50

UNICEF — A440

Designs: 2.50r, Father and child. 5r, Mother kissing child. 20r, Child learning to walk.

2003, Jan. 31   *Perf. 15x14*
2690-2692 A440 Set of 3   4.50 4.50

Shells — A441

Designs: No. 2693, 10r, Sundial shell. No. 2694, 10r, Cardita clam. No. 2695, 10r, Corn shell. No. 2696, 10r, Cowrie shell.

2003, Mar. 25   Litho.   *Perf. 13¼*
2693-2696 A441 Set of 4   7.00 7.00

Astronauts Killed in Space Shuttle
Columbia Accident — A442

No. 2697: a, Mission Specialist 1 David M.
Brown. b, Commander Rick D. Husband. c,
Mission Specialist 4 Laurel Blair Salton Clark.
d, Mission Specialist 4 Kalpana Chawla. e,
Payload Commander Michael P. Anderson. f,
Pilot William C. McCool. g, Payload Specialist
4 Ilan Ramon.

2003, Apr. 7		Perf. 13½x13¼	
2697	A442	7r Sheet of 7, #a-g	7.75 7.75

Coronation of Queen Elizabeth II, 50th
Anniv. — A443

No. 2698: a, Wearing hat. b, Wearing crown.
c, Wearing tiara.
25r, Wearing tiara, diff.

2003, May 26		Perf. 14	
2698	A443	15r Sheet of 3, #a-c	6.00 6.00
		Souvenir Sheet	
2699	A443	25r multi	4.00 4.00

Prince William, 21st Birthday — A444

No. 2700: a, As toddler. b, Wearing red and
blue tie. c, Wearing tie with blue squares.
25r, As toddler, wearing cap.

2003, May 26			
2700	A444	15r Sheet of 3, #a-c	6.00 6.00
		Souvenir Sheet	
2701	A444	25r multi	4.00 4.00

Paintings by
Albrecht
Dürer (1471-
1528)
A445

Designs: 3r, Drummer and Piper from wing
of the Jabach Altarpiece. 5r, Portrait of a
Young Man. 7r, Wire-drawing Mill, horiz. 10r,
Innsbruck from the North, horiz.
No. 2706: a, Portrait of Jacob Muffel. b, Por-
trait of Hieronymus Holzschuher. c, Portrait of
Johannes Kleberger. d, Self-portrait.
25r, The Weiden Mill, horiz.

2003, June 17		Perf. 14¼	
2702-2705	A445	Set of 4	4.50 4.50
2706	A445	12r Sheet of 4, #a-d	6.50 6.50
		Souvenir Sheet	
2707	A445	25r multi	4.00 4.00

Japanese
Art — A446

Designs: 2r, Detail from The Actor Sojuro
Nakamura as Mitsukuni, by Yoshitaki Uta-
gawa. 5r, Detail from The Actor Sojuro
Nakamura as Mitsukuni, by Yoshitaki Uta-
gawa, diff. 7r, The Ghost of Koheiji Kohada, by
Hokuei Shunkosai. 15r, Ariwara no Narihira as
Seigen, by Kunisada Utagawa.
No. 2712: a, The Ghost of Mitsumune
Shikibunojo, by Kunisada Utagawa. b, Fuwa
Bansakui, by Yoshitoshi Tsukioka. c, The Lan-
tern Ghost of Oiwa, by Shunkosai. d, The
Greedy Hag, by Tsukioka.
25r, The Spirit of Sogoro Sakura Haunting
Koszuke Hotta.

2003, June 17			
2708-2711	A446	Set of 4	4.75 4.75
2712	A446	10r Sheet of 4, #a-d	5.25 5.25
		Souvenir Sheet	
2713	A446	25r multi	4.00 4.00

Paintings by Joan Miró (1893-
1983) — A447

Designs: 3r, Untitled painting, 1934. 5r,
Hirondelle Amour. 10r, Two Women. 15r,
Women Listening to Music.
No. 2718: a, Woman and Birds. b, Nocturne.
c, Morning Star. d, The Escape Ladder.
No. 2719, 25r, Rhythmic Personages, vert.
No. 2720, 25r, Women Encircled by the Flight
of a Bird, vert.

2003, June 17		Perf. 14¼	
2714-2717	A447	Set of 4	5.25 5.25
2718	A447	12r Sheet of 4, #a-d	6.50 6.50
		Size: 83x104mm	
		Imperf	
2719-2720	A447	Set of 2	7.00 7.00

Tour de France Bicycle Race,
Cent. — A448

No. 2721, 10r: a, Maurice Garin, 1903. b,
Henri Cornet, 1904. c, Louis Trousselier, 1905.
d, René Pottier, 1906.
No. 2722, 10r: a, Lucien Petit-Breton on
Bicycle, 1907. b, Head of Petit-Breton, 1907.
c, François Faber, 1909. d, Octave Lapize,
1910.
No. 2723, 10r: a, Eddy Merckx, 1974. b,
Bernard Thévenet, 1975. c, Lucien Van Impe,
1976. d, Thévenet, 1977.
No. 2724, 25r, Bernard Hinault, 1979. No.
2725, 25r, Henri Desgranges. No. 2726, 25r,
Le Réveil Matin Cafe, Montgeron, France.

2003, July 3		Perf. 13¼	
		Sheets of 4, #a-d	
2721-2723	A448	Set of 3	17.50 17.50
		Souvenir Sheets	
2724-2726	A448	Set of 3	10.00 10.00

Powered Flight, Cent. — A449

No. 2727, 10r — Alberto Santos-Dumont's:
a, Airship No. 1. b, Airship No. 4, c, Airship
with 14bis airplane. d, Airship No. 16.
No. 2728, 10r: a, Santos Dumont with Demoiselle airplane. b, Demoiselle airplane. c, Voi-
sin-Farman No. 1 biplane. d, Gold Bug, built by
Glenn Curtiss.
No. 2729, 25r, Santos-Dumont's Airship No.
6. No. 2730, 25r, Santos-Dumont's 14bis
Airplane.

2003, July 14		Perf. 14	
		Sheets of 4, #a-d	
2727-2728	A449	Set of 2	12.50 12.50
		Souvenir Sheets	
2729-2730	A449	Set of 2	8.00 8.00

Paintings of Paul Klee (1879-
1940) — A450

No. 2731, horiz.: a, Near Taormina, Sci-
rocco. b, Small Town Among the Rocks. c, Still
Life with Props. d, North Room.
25r, Dame Demon.

2003, Dec. 4		Perf. 13½	
2731	A450	10r Sheet of 4, #a-d	6.25 6.25
		Souvenir Sheet	
2732	A450	25r multi	4.00 4.00

Maumoon Abdul Gayoom, 25th Anniv.
as President — A451

	Litho. & Embossed		
2003		**Die Cut Perf. 8**	
		Without Gum	
2733	A451	200r gold & multi	32.50 32.50

Norman Rockwell (1894-1978) — A452

No. 2734 — Four Seasons Calendar: Man
and Boy, 1948: a, Winter (ice skating). b,
Spring (resting amidst flowers). c, Summer
(fishing). d, Autumn (raking leaves).
25r, Illustration for Hallmark Cards, 1937.

2003, Dec. 4		Litho.	Perf. 13¼
2734	A452	10r Sheet of 4, #a-d	6.25 6.25
		Imperf	
2735	A452	25r shown	4.00 4.00

No. 2734 contains four 38x50mm stamps.

Intl. Year of Fresh Water — A453

No. 2736: a, Ari Atoll. b, Fresh water for all.
c, Desalination plant, Malé.
25r, Community rain water tank.

2003, Dec. 22		Perf. 14	
2736	A453	15r Sheet of 3, #a-c	6.00 6.00
		Souvenir Sheet	
2737	A453	25r multi	4.00 4.00

Fish
A454

Designs: 1r, Clown triggerfish. 7r, Sixspot
grouper. 10r, Long-nosed butterflyfish. 15r,
Longfin bannerfish.
No. 2742: a, Goldtail demoiselle. b, Queen
coris. c, Eight-banded butterflyfish. d, Meyer's

butterflyfish. e, Exquisite butterflyfish. f, Yellowstripe snapper. g, Yellowback anthias. h, Black-spotted moray. i, Clown anemonefish.
25r, Chevron butterflyfish.

2003, Dec. 22
2738-2741	A454	Set of 4	5.25	5.25
2742	A454	4r Sheet of 9, #a-i	5.75	5.75
2743	A454	7r Sheet of 6, #a-f	6.75	6.75
		Souvenir Sheet		
2744	A454	25r multi	4.00	4.00

Nos. 2738-2741 were each printed in sheets of four.

Butterflies — A455

Designs: 3r, Yamfly. 5r, Striped blue crow. 8r, Indian red admiral. 15r, Great eggfly.
No. 2749, horiz.: a, Blue triangle. b, Monarch. c, Broad-bordered grass yellow. d, Red lacewing. e, African migrant. f, Plain tiger.
25r, Beak butterfly.

2003, Dec. 22
2745-2748	A455	Set of 4	5.25	5.25
2749	A455	7r Sheet of 6, #a-f	7.25	7.25
		Souvenir Sheet		
2750	A455	25r multi	4.25	4.25

Birds
A456

Designs: 15 l, Great frigatebird. 20 l, Ruddy turnstone. 25 l, Hoopoe. 1r, Cattle egret.
No. 2755: a, Red-billed tropicbird. b, Red-footed booby. c, Common tern. d, Caspian tern. e, Common curlew. f, Black-bellied plover.
25r, Gray heron.

2003, Dec. 22
2751-2754	A456	Set of 4	6.50	6.50
2755	A456	7r Sheet of 6, #a-f	7.25	7.25
		Souvenir Sheet		
2756	A456	25r multi	4.25	4.25

Paintings by Pablo Picasso (1881-1973) — A457

No. 2757: a, Portrait of Jaime Sabartés, 1901. b, Portrait of the Artist's Wife (Olga), 1923. c, Portrait of Olga, 1923. d, Portrait of Jaime Sabartés, 1904.
30r, The Tragedy, 1903.

2003, Dec. 4   Litho.   Perf. 13¼
2757	A457	10r Sheet of 4, #a-d	6.25	6.25
		Imperf		
2758	A457	30r multi	4.75	4.75

No. 2757 contains four 37x50mm stamps.

Flowers — A458

Designs: 30 l, Coelogyne asperata. 75 l, Calanthe rosea. 2r, Eria javanica. 10r, Spathoglottis affinis.
No. 2763, horiz.: a, Bird of paradise. b, Flamingo flower. c, Red ginger. d, Cooktown orchid. e, Vanda tricolor. f, Chinese hibiscus.
25r, Morning glory.

2003, Dec. 22   Perf. 14
2759-2762	A458	Set of 4	2.50	2.50
2763	A458	7r Sheet of 6, #a-f	6.75	6.75
		Souvenir Sheet		
2764	A458	25r multi	4.00	4.00

FIFA (Fédération Internationale de Football Association) Cent. — A459

World Cup winning teams: No. 2765, 5r, Germany, 1974. No. 2766, 5r, Argentina, 1970. No. 2707, 5l, Italy, 1982. No. 2768, 5r, Argentina, 1986. No. 2769, 5r, Germany, 1990. No. 2770, 5r, Brazil, 1994. No. 2771, 5r, France, 1998. No. 2772, 5r, Brazil, 2002.

2004, Mar. 8   Perf. 13½
| 2765-2772 | A459 | Set of 8 | 7.00 | 7.00 |

Paintings by Gao Jian-fu (1879-1951) — A460

No. 2773: a, Landscape. b, Moon Night. c, Fox. d, Spider web. e, Woman with mirror. f, Man sitting on ground.
No. 2774: a, Eagle. b, Sunset.

2004, Mar. 8   Perf. 13¼
| 2773 | A460 | 7r Sheet of 6, #a-f | 5.75 | 5.75 |
| 2774 | A460 | 12r Sheet of 2, #a-b | 3.25 | 3.25 |

2004 Hong Kong Stamp Expo.

Cessation of Concorde Flights — A461

No. 2775: a, F-BVFD, Rio de Janeiro. b, F-BVFC, New York. c, F-BTSD, Honolulu. d, F-BTSD, Lisbon. e, F-BVFA, Washington. f, F-BVFD, Dakar, Senegal. g, G-BOAC, Singapore. h, G-BOAA, Sydney. i, G-BOAD, Hong Kong. j, G-BOAD, Amsterdam. k, G-BOAE, Tokyo. l, G-BOAF, Madrid.
No. 2776, 25r, 214 G-BOAG, Museum of Flight, Seattle. No. 2777, 25r, 214 G-BOAG, horizon. No. 2778, 25r, 204 G-BOAC, British flag.

2004, Mar. 8   Perf. 13¼x13½
2775	A461	1r Sheet of 12, #a-l	1.60	1.60
		Souvenir Sheets		
2776-2778	A461	Set of 3	10.00	10.00

Paintings in the Hermitage, St. Petersburg, Russia A462

Designs: 1r, Self-portrait, by Anthony van Dyck. 3r, Self-portrait, by Michael Sweerts. 7r, Anna Dalkeith, Countess of Morton, by van Dyck. 12r, Lady Anna Kirk, by van Dyck.
No. 2783: a, Portrait of Prince Alexander Kurakin, by Marie-Louise-Elisabeth Vigée-Lebrun. b, Portrait of a Lady in Waiting to the Infanta Isabella, by Peter Paul Rubens. c, Portrait of a Lady in Blue, by Thomas Gainsborough. d, The Actor Pierre Jéliolte in the Role of Apollo, by Louis Tocqué.
No. 2784, 25r, The Stolen Kiss, by Jean-Honoré Fragonard, horiz. No. 2785, 25r, A Scene from Corneille's Tragedy "La Comte d'Essex," by Nicolas Lancret, horiz.

2004, Mar. 29   Perf. 14¼
2779-2782	A462	Set of 4	4.00	4.00
2783	A462	10r Sheet of 4, #a-d	5.25	5.25
		Souvenir Sheets		
2784-2785	A462	Set of 2	6.75	6.75

D-Day, 60th Anniv. — A463

No. 2786, 6r: a, Gen. Dwight Eisenhower. b, Field Marshal Guenther von Kluge. c, Air Marshal Sir Trafford Leigh-Mallory. d, Field Marshal Walter Model. e, Field Marshal Gerd von Rundstedt. f, Sir Arthur Tedder.
No. 2787, 6r: a, Maj. Gen. Clarence Huebner. b, Brig. Gen. Anthony McAuliffe. c, Maj. Gen. Leonard Gerow. d, Gen. Adolf Galland. e, Brig. Gen. W. M. Hoge. f, Maj. Gen. Sir Percy Hobart.
No. 2788, 6r: a, Rear Admiral Kirk. b, Field Marshal Erwin Rommel. c, Gen. George Marshall. d, Gen. Jan Smuts. e, Gen. Lt. Gunther Blumentritt. f, Maj. Gen. J. Lawton Collins.
No. 2789, 6r: a, Winston Churchill. b, Adm. Sir Bertram Ramsay. c, Gen. Lt. Dietrich Kraiss. d, Maj. Gen. Richard Gale. e, Gen. George Patton. f, Maj. Gen. Maxwell Taylor.
No. 2790, 6r, horiz.: a, Lt. Gen. Omar Bradley. b, Rear Admiral Hall. c, Maj. Gen. Huebner, diff. d, Adm. Karl Dönitz. e, Rear Admiral Wilkes. f, Capt. Chauncey Camp.
No. 2791, 30r, Gen. Henry Arnold. No. 2792, 30r, Rear Adm. Donald Moon. No. 2793, 30r, Lt. Gen. Sir Frederick Morgan. No. 2794, 30r, Gen. Sir Bernard Montgomery. No. 2795, 30r, Rear Adm. Carlton Bryant, horiz.

Perf. 13½x13¼, 13¼x13½
2004, May 19   Sheets of 6, #a-f
2786-2790	A463	Set of 5	28.00	28.00
		Souvenir Sheets		
2791-2795	A463	Set of 5	24.00	24.00

Paintings by Paul Cézanne (1839-1906) — A464

No. 2796, horiz.: a, Still Life with Peppermint Bottle and Blue Rug. b, House in Provence. c, Le Château Noir. d, Basket of Apples.
25r, Boy in a Red Waistcoat Leaning on his Elbow.

2004, July 6   Perf. 13¼
2796	A464	10r Sheet of 4, #a-d	6.25	6.25
		Imperf		
2797	A464	25r multi	4.00	4.00

No. 2796 contains four 50x37mm stamps.

Paintings by Henri Rousseau (1844-1910) — A465

No. 2798, horiz.: a, Nègre Attaqué par un Jaguar. b, Paysage Exotique. c. La Cascade. d, Le Repas du Lion.
25r, Le Rêve.

2004, July 6   **Perf. 13¼**
2798 A465 10r Sheet of 4, #a-d   6.25 6.25
Imperf
2799 A465 25r multi   4.00 4.00
No. 2798 contains four 50x37mm stamps.

Paintings by Henri Matisse (1869-1954) — A466

No. 2800, horiz.: a, Conversation. b, Still Life with a Blue Tablecloth. c. Seville Still Life II. d, Woman Before an Aquarium.
25r, Interior at Nice.

2004, July 6   **Perf. 13¼**
2800 A466 10r Sheet of 4, #a-d   6.25 6.25
Imperf
2801 A466 25r multi   4.00 4.00
No. 2800 contains four 50x37mm stamps.

Steam Locomotives, 200th Anniv. — A467

No. 2802, 12r: a, Planet Class 2-2-0. b, American 4-4-0. c, Newmar. d, Class 500 4-6-0.
No. 2803, 12r: a, Firefly Class 2-2-2. b, French "Single." c, Medoc Class 2-4-0. d, German 4-4-0.
No. 2804, 12r: a, Adler 2-2-2. b, Beuth 2-2-2. c, Northumbrian 0-2-2. d, Class 4-6-2.
No. 2805, 12r: a, Woodburning Beyer Garratt 4-8-2+2-8-4. b, Double headed train over Kaaiman River, Africa. c, Garratt 4-8-2+2-8-4. d, Class 15 Garratt.
No. 2806, 12r: a, East African Railways Garratt. b, Rhodesian Railways 12th Class. c, Class 2-6-2. d, Class 19D 4-8-2.
No. 2807, 12r: a, Evening Star. b, Britannia. c, The George Stephenson. d, Sudan Railways 310 2-8-2.
No. 2808, 30r, Claud Hamilton Class 4-4-0. No. 2809, 30r, Class P8 4-6-0. No. 2810, 30r, Vauxhall 2-2-0. No. 2811, 30r, American, diff. No. 2812, 30r, The Lord Nelson. No. 2813, 30r, Flying Scotsman.

2004, July 6   **Perf. 13¼x13½**
Sheets of 4, #a-d
2802-2807 A467 Set of 6   45.00 45.00
Souvenir Sheets
2808-2813 A467 Set of 6   28.00 28.00

Jules Verne (1828-1905), Writer — A468

No. 2814, 12r: a, Archipelago on Fire. b, Clovis Dardentor. c, The Golden Volcano. d, Le Superbe Orénoque.
No. 2815, 12r — Michael Strogoff, Courier of the Czar: a, People (pink background). b, People in grass (green background). c, People (blue background). d, Animal and head in grass (green background).
No. 2816, 12r — Family Without a Name: a, Woman. b, Soldier. c, Crowd. d, Soldiers and Indian with guns.
No. 2817, 12r — César Cascabel: a, Men pushing train car (blue green background). b, Man (brown background). c, Crevasse (blue green background). d, Crowd and sign (pink background).
No. 2818, 12r — The Lighthouse at the End of the World: a, Men on ship. b, Man with arm extended. c, Rocks. d, Fisherman with hat.
No. 2819, 25r, The Survivors of the Chancellor. No. 2820, 25r, Keraban the Inflexible. No. 2821, 25r, Family Without a Name, diff. No. 2822, 25r, César Cascabel, diff. No. 2823, 25r, The Lighthouse at the End of the World, diff.

2004, July 29   **Perf. 13¼x13½**
Sheets of 4, #a-d
2814-2818 A468 Set of 5   37.00 37.00
Souvenir Sheets
2819-2823 A468 Set of 5   19.00 19.00

Marilyn Monroe — A469

2004, Aug. 16   **Perf. 13½x13¼**
2824 A469 7r multi   1.25 1.25
Printed in sheets of 6.

George Herman "Babe" Ruth (1895-1948), Baseball Player — A470

No. 2826: a, Swinging bat. b, Wearing cap, striped uniform. c, Holding two bats. d, Profile of Ruth.

2004
2825 A470   3r shown   .55 .55
2826 A470 10r Sheet of 4, #a-d   6.25 6.25
No. 2825 printed in sheets of 16. World Series, 100th anniv.

Paintings by Salvador Dali (1904-89) — A471

No. 2827: a, The Endless Enigma. b, The Persistence of Memory. c, Soft Construction with Boiled Beans — Premonition of Civil War. d, Still Life — Fast Moving.
25r, Figure on the Rocks.

2004, July 6   **Litho.**   **Perf. 13½**
2827 A471 10r Sheet of 4, #a-d   6.25 6.25
Imperf
2828 A471 25r multi   4.00 4.00
No. 2827 contains four 50x37mm stamps.

2004 Summer Olympics, Athens — A472

Designs: 2r, Gold medal, 1904 St. Louis Olympics. 5r, Krater depicting Olympic athletes. 7r, Count Jean de Beaumont, Intl. Olympic Committee member. 12r, Pommel horse, horiz.

2004, Sept. 30   **Perf. 14¼**
2829-2832 A472   Set of 4   4.25 4.25

Sharks — A473

No. 2833: a, Silvertip shark. b, Silky shark. c, Great white shark. d, Gray reef shark. $25, Starry smoothhound shark.

2004, Nov. 4
2833 A473 10r Sheet of 4, #a-d   6.25 6.25
Souvenir Sheet
2834 A473 25r multi   4.00 4.00

Starfish — A474

Designs: No. 2835, 10r, Fromia monilis (green background). No. 2836, 10r, Linckia laevigata. No. 2837, 10r, Nardoa novae-calidoniae. No. 2838, 10r, Fromia monilis (red background).

2004, Nov. 4   **Perf. 15x14**
2835-2838 A474   Set of 4   6.25 6.25

Worldwide Fund for Nature (WWF) — A475

No. 2839 — Eurypegasus draconis and: a, Country name at LL, denomination at LR. b, Country name at UL, denomination at LR, dark background. c, Country name at LR, denomination at UL. d, Country name at UL, denomination at LR, light background.

2004, Dec. 15   **Litho.**   **Perf. 14**
2839 A475 7r Block of 4, #a-d   4.50 4.50
    e.   Miniature sheet, 2 each
       #2839a-2839d   9.00 9.00

Butterflies — A476

No. 2840, horiz.: a, Red lacewing. b, Amesia sanguiflua. c, Pericallia galactina. d, Limenitis dudu dudu.
25r, Lime butterfly.

2004, Dec. 15
2840 A476 10r Sheet of 4, #a-d   6.25 6.25
Souvenir Sheet
2841 A476 25r multi   4.00 4.00

Dolphins — A477

No. 2842: a, Striped dolphin. b, Amazon River dolphin. c, Bottlenose dolphin. d, Spinner dolphin.
25r, Long-snouted spinner dolphin.

2004, Dec. 15   Litho.   *Perf. 14*
2842 A477 10r Sheet of 4, #a-d   6.25 6.25
Souvenir Sheet
2843 A477 25r multi   4.00 4.00

Reptiles and Amphibians — A478

No. 2844, horiz.: a, Eyelash pit viper. b, Basilisk lizard. c, Calico snake. d, Maki frog.
25r, Naja melanoleuca.

2004, Dec. 15
2844 A478 10r Sheet of 4, #a-d   6.25 6.25
Souvenir Sheet
2845 A478 25r multi   4.00 4.00

Mushrooms — A479

No. 2846, horiz.: a, Parrot mushroom. b, Hygrocybe miniata. c, Aleuria aurantia. d, Thaxterogaster porphyreum.
25r, Galerina autumnalis.

2004, Dec. 15
2846 A479 10r Sheet of 4, #a-d   6.25 6.25
Souvenir Sheet
2847 A479 25r multi   4.00 4.00

Prehistoric Animals — A480

No. 2848, 10r: a, Macroplata. b, Ichthyosaurus. c, Shonisaurus. d, Archelon.

No. 2849, 10r, vert.: a, Albertosaurus. b, Iguanodon. c, Deinonychus, name at right. d, Baryonyx.
No. 2850, 10r, vert.: a, Deinonychus, name at left. b, Styracosaurus. c, Ornitholestes. d, Euoplocephalus.
No. 2851, 10r, vert.: a, Pterodactylus. b, Cearadactylus. c, Pterosaur. d, Sordes.
No. 2852, 25r, Muraeonosaurus. No. 2853, 25r, Styracosaurus, diff. No. 2854, 25r, Leptoceratops. No. 2855, 25r, Archaeopteryx.

2004, Dec. 15   *Perf. 14*
Sheets of 4, #a-d
2848-2851 A480   Set of 4   25.00 25.00
Souvenir Sheets
2852-2855 A480   Set of 4   16.00 16.00

Souvenir Sheet

Deng Xiaoping (1904-97), Chinese Leader — A481

2005, Jan. 26
2856 A481 25r multi   4.00 4.00

2004 European Soccer Championships, Portugal — A482

No. 2857, vert.: a, Jupp Derwall. b, René Vandereycke. c, Horst Hrubesch. d, Stadio Olimpico.
25r, 1980 Germany team.

2005, Jan. 26   Litho.   *Perf. 14*
2857 A482 12r Sheet of 4, #a-d   7.50 7.50
Souvenir Sheet
2858 A482 25r multi   4.00 4.00
No. 2857 contains four 28x42mm stamps.

Rotary International, Cent. — A483

No. 2859 — Chicago skyline: a, Part of Sears Tower at R. b, Sears Tower at L. c, CNA Tower (red brick building) at L.
25r, Telecommunications tower.

2005, July 12   Litho.   *Perf. 12¾*
2859 A483 15r Sheet of 3, #a-c   7.00 7.00
Souvenir Sheet
2860 A483 25r multi   4.00 4.00

Hans Christian Andersen (1805-75), Author — A484

No. 2861: a, Statue of Andersen wearing hat. b, Photograph of Andersen. c, Statue of Andersen without hat.
25r, Little Mermaid Statue, Copenhagen.

2005, Sept. 20
2861 A484 15r Sheet of 3, #a-c   7.00 7.00
Souvenir Sheet
2862 A484 25r multi   4.00 4.00

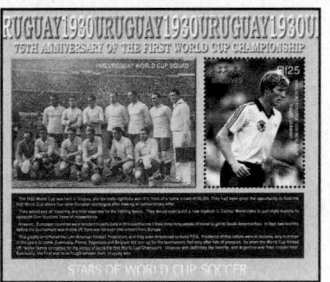

World Cup Soccer Championships, 75th Anniv. — A485

No. 2863: a, Oscar. b, Karl-Heinz Rummenigge. c, Oliver Kahn.
25r, Karlheinz Forster.

2005, Sept. 20   *Perf. 13¼*
2863 A485 15r Sheet of 3, #a-c   7.00 7.00
Souvenir Sheet
Perf. 12¼x12
2864 A485 25r multi   4.00 4.00

Battle of Trafalgar, Bicent. — A486

No. 2865, vert.: a, Admiral Cuthbert Collingwood. b, Napoleon Bonaparte. c, Admiral Horatio Nelson. d, Capt. Thomas Masterman Hardy.
25r, Ships at battle.

2005, Sept. 20   *Perf. 12¾*
2865 A486 10r Sheet of 4, #a-d   7.00 7.00
Souvenir Sheet
2866 A486 25r multi   4.25 4.25

Albert Einstein (1879-1955), Physicist — A487

No. 2867, horiz. — Portraits of Einstein in: a, Red brown (denomination at R). b, Pink & blue (denomination at L). c, Green & pink (denomination at R). d, Brown (denomination at L).
25r, Einstein, diff.

2005, Sept. 20
2867 A487 15r Sheet of 4, #a-d   6.25 6.25
Souvenir Sheet
2868 A487 25r multi   4.00 4.00

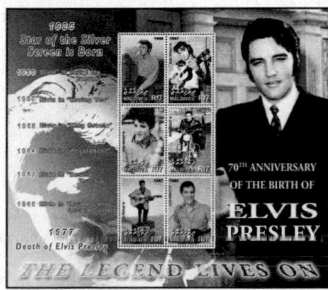

Elvis Presley (1935-77) — A488

No. 2869, 7r — Photographs of Presley from: a, 1956 (sepia). b, 1957. c, 1958. d, 1964. e, 1967. f, 1968.
No. 2870, 7r — Photographs of Presley from: a, 1956 (black and white). b, 1960. c, 1962. d, 1969. e, 1973. f, 1975.

2005, Nov. 15   *Perf. 13¾x13¼*
Sheets of 6, #a-f
2869-2870 A488   Set of 2   13.00 13.00

Elvis Presley (1935-77) — A489

Litho. & Embossed
2006, Jan. 17   *Die Cut Perf 7½*
Without Gum
2871 A489 85r gold & multi   13.50 13.50

Miniature Sheets

Children's Drawings — A490

No. 2872, 10r — Sea Life: a, Bubbles, by Raquel Bobolia. b, Bubble Fish, by Sarah

Bowen. c, Lipfish, by Elsa Fleisher. d, Flounder, by Erica Malchowski.

No. 2873, 10r — Birds: a, Purple Bird, by Anna Badger. b, Parrots, by Nick Abrams. c, Pretty Bird, by Jessie Abrams. d, Royal Parrot, by Ashley Mondfrans.

No. 2874, 10r — Flowers: a, Orange Sunflower, by Brett Walker. b, Red Flower, by Jessica Shutt. c, Flower Pot, by Nick Abrams. d, Blue Flower Vase, by Trevor Nielsen.

2006, Jan. 24   Litho.   Perf. 13¼
Sheets of 4, #a-d
2872-2874 A490 Set of 3   19.00 19.00

Skates and
Rays — A491

Designs: 20 l, Himantura uamak. 1r, Manta birostris. 2r, Taeniura lymma. 20r, Aetobatus narinari.

2006, Feb. 27   Perf. 13¾x14¼
2875-2878 A491 Set of 4   4.00 4.00

Souvenir Sheet

South Asian Association for Regional
Cooperation, 20th Anniv. — A492

2006, Mar. 9   Perf. 13¼
2879 A492 25r multi   4.00 4.00

2006 Winter Olympics, Turin — A493

Designs: 7r, Norway #B52. 8r, Poster for 1952 Oslo Winter Olympics, vert. 10r, Poster for 1936 Garmisch-Partenkirchen Winter Olympics, vert. 12r, Germany #B79, vert.

2006, May 9   Perf. 14¼
2880-2883 A493 Set of 4   5.75 5.75

Miniature Sheet

Wolfgang Amadeus Mozart (1756-91),
Composer — A494

No. 2884: a, Portrait in oval frame. b, Mozart looking left. c, Mozart as child. d, Bust.

2006, June 29   Perf. 12¾
2884 A494 12r Sheet of 4, #a-d   7.50 7.50

Queen Elizabeth II, 80th
Birthday — A495

No. 2885 — Queen and: a, Pres. John F. Kennedy. b, Pres. Ronald Reagan. c, Pres. Gerald R. Ford. d, Pres. George W. Bush.
25r, Portrait of Queen on horse by Chinwe Chukwuogo-Roy.

2006   Perf. 14¼
2885 A495 15r Sheet of 4, #a-d   9.50 9.50
Souvenir Sheet
2886 A495 25r multi   4.00 4.00

Souvenir Sheet

Maldive Islands Postal Service,
Cent. — A496

2006, Nov. 1   Litho.   Perf. 12½
2887 A496 12r multi   1.90 1.90

Souvenir Sheet

Ludwig Durr (1878-1956), Zeppelin
Engineer — A497

No. 2888 — Durr and: a, Zeppelin over Frankfurt. b, Balloons and Festhalle, Frankfurt. c, Hindenburg.

2006, Nov. 15   Perf. 13¼
2888 A497 15r Sheet of 3, #a-c   7.00 7.00

Fish — A498

Designs: No. 2889, 10r, Dascyllus aruanus. No. 2890, 10r, Balistoides conspicillum. No.

2891, 10r, Pomacanthus imperator. No. 2892, 10r, Chaetodon meyeri.

2006, Nov. 1   Litho.   Perf. 12¾
2889-2892 A498 Set of 4   6.25 6.25

Miniature Sheet

Elvis Presley (1935-77) — A499

No. 2893 — Presley with: a, Microphone at left, denomination in pink. b, Microphone at center, denomination in white. c, Microphone at center, denomination in light blue. d, Microphone at left, denomination in light green.

2006, Nov. 15   Perf. 13¼
2893 A499 12r Sheet of 4, #a-d   7.50 7.50

Space Achievements — A500

No. 2894: a, R-7 missile (Sputnik 1 launcher). b, Sputnik 1. c, Inside Sputnik 1. d, Sputnik 2. e, Map of Earth showing Sputnik 1 orbits. f, Sputnik 3.
No. 2895, 12r: a, Calipso satellite. b, CloudSat satellite. c, Aqua satellite. d, Aura satellite.
No. 2896, 12r: a, Nucleus of Halley's Comet. b, Halley's Comet. c, Giotto Space Probe. d, Close-up image of Halley's Comet taken by Giotto.
No. 2897, 25r, Apollo spacecraft. No. 2898, 25r, Giotto. No. 2899, 25r, Stardust satellite.

2006, Nov. 15   Perf. 13¼
2894 A500 8r Sheet of 6, #a-f   7.50 7.50
Sheets of 4, #a-d
2895-2896 A500 Set of 2   15.00 15.00
Souvenir Sheets
2897-2899 A500 Set of 3   12.00 12.00
Nos. 2894-2899 exist imperf. Value, set $75.

Birds
A501

Designs: 1r, Bar-tailed godwit. 2r, Blackheaded gull. No. 2902, 10r, Masked booby, vert. 20r, Kentish plover.
No. 2904, 10r: a, Common swifts. b, Sooty tern. c, Yellow wagtail. d, House sparrow.
No. 2905, 10r: a, Tufted duck. b, Caspian tern. c, Southern giant petrel. d, Glossy ibis.
No. 2906, 30r, Purple herons. No. 2907, 30r, Osprey, vert. No. 2908, 30r, Goldenthroated barbet, vert.

2007, Feb. 8   Perf. 14
2900-2903 A501 Set of 4   5.25 5.25
Sheets of 4, #a-d
2904-2905 A501 Set of 2   12.50 12.50
Souvenir Sheets
2906-2908 A501 Set of 3   14.00 14.00

Fish
A502

Designs: 1r, Ragged-finned lionfish. 2r, Vlaming's unicornfish. 20r, Whitespotted grouper. 20r, Maldive anemonefish.
No. 2913, 10r: a, Bicolor parrotfish. b, Bluebarred parrotfish. c, Bullethead parrotfish. d, Dusky parrotfish.
No. 2914, 10r: a, Imperial angelfish. b, Clown triggerfish. c, Black-saddled coral trout. d, Slender grouper.
No. 2915, 30r, Shadow soldierfish. No. 2916, 30r, Picasso triggerfish. No. 2917, 30r, Blue-faced angelfish.

2007, Feb. 8
2909-2912 A502 Set of 4   5.25 5.25
Sheets of 4, #a-d
2913-2914 A502 Set of 2   12.50 12.50
Souvenir Sheets
2915-2917 A502 Set of 3   14.00 14.00

Flowers
A503

Designs: 1r, Ranunculus eschscholtzii. 2r, Ratibida columnaris. No. 2920, 10r, Mentzelia laevicaulis. 20r, Clintonia uniflora.
No. 2922, 10r: a, Machaeranthera tanacetifolia. b, Aquilegia coerulea. c, Gentiana detonsa. d, Linum perenne.
No. 2923, 10r: a, Ipomopsis aggregata. b, Rosa woodsii. c, Lewisia rediviva. d, Penstemon rydbergii.
No. 2924, 30r, Ipomoea purpurea. No. 2925, 30r, Encelia farinosa. No. 2926, 30r, Epilobium angustifolium.

2007, Feb. 8
2918-2921 A503 Set of 4   5.25 5.25
Sheets of 4, #a-d
2922-2923 A503 Set of 2   12.50 12.50
Souvenir Sheets
2924-2926 A503 Set of 3   14.00 14.00

Orchids — A504

Designs: 1r, Dendrobium formosum. 2r, Bulbophyllum Elizabeth Ann. No. 2929, 10r, Dendrobium bigibbum. 20r, Spathoglottis gracilis.
No. 2931, 10r: a, Bulbophyllum lasiochilum. b, Phaius Microburst. c, Coelogyne mooreana. d, Bulbophyllum nasseri.
No. 2932, 10r: a, Cymbidium erythrostylum. b, Phaius humboldtii x Phaius tuberculosis. c, Dendrobium farmeri. d, Dendrobium junceum.
No. 2933, 30r, Coelogyne cristata, horiz. No. 2934, 30r, Bulbophyllum graveolens, horiz. No. 2935, 30r, Dendrobium crocatum.

2007, Feb. 8
2927-2930 A504 Set of 4   5.25 5.25
Sheets of 4, #a-d
2931-2932 A504 Set of 2   12.50 12.50
Souvenir Sheets
2933-2935 A504 Set of 3   14.00 14.00

Scouting,
Cent.
A505

2007, Feb. 21   *Perf. 13¼*
Color of Denomination
2936 A505 15r purple   2.40 2.40
Souvenir Sheet
2937 A505 25r blue   4.00 4.00

No. 2936 was printed in sheets of 3.

Intl. Polar Year — A506

No. 2938 — King penguins with background color of: a, Light blue. b, Lilac. c, Yellow green. d, Blue green. e, Red violet. f, Green. 25r, African penguin with party hat.

2007, May 1   **Litho.**   *Perf. 13¼*
2938 A506 12r Sheet of 6, #a-f 11.50 11.50
Souvenir Sheet
2939 A506 25r multi   4.00 4.00

Miniature Sheet

Ferrari Automobiles, 60th Anniv. — A507

No. 2940: a, 1979 312 T4. b, 1992 456 GT. c, 1959 250 GT Berlinetta. d, 1989 F1 89. e, 1998 456M GTA. f, 1955 735 LM. g, 1973 Dino 308 GT4. h, 2001 F 2001.

2007, Aug. 12
2940 A507 8r Sheet of 8, #a-h 10.00 10.00

Princess Diana (1961-97) — A508

No. 2941 — Diana with white hat and: a, Gray jacket, close-up. b, Green dress, close-up. c, White striped jacket, close-up. d, Green dress. e, White striped jacket. f, Gray jacket. 25r, Black and white jacket.

2007, Aug. 12
2941 A508 8r Sheet of 6, #a-f   7.50 7.50
Souvenir Sheet
2942 A508 25r multi   4.00 4.00

Fish — A509

Designs: 10 l, Chaetodon triangulum. 50 l, Chaetodon kleinii. 12r, Chaetodon trifasciatus. 15r, Chaetodon madagascariensis. 20r, Chaetodon lunula.

2007, Oct. 9   **Litho.**   *Perf. 13¼*
2943-2947 A509   Set of 5   7.50 7.50

2008 Summer Olympics, Beijing — A510

No. 2948: a, Rie Mastenbroek, swimming gold medalist, 1936. b, Poster for 1936 Summer Olympics. c, Jesse Owens, long jump gold medalist, 1936. d, Jack Beresford, rowing gold medalist, 1936.

2008, Jan. 8   **Litho.**   *Perf. 13¼*
2948   Horiz. strip of 4   4.50 4.50
   a.-d.   A510 7r Any single   1.10 1.10
   e.   Souvenir sheet, #2948a-2948d   4.50 4.50

Miniature Sheet

Elvis Presley (1935-77) — A511

No. 2949 — Presley wearing: a, Brown jacket. b, Blue shirt, holding guitar. c, Red jacket and white shirt. d, Gray jacket and black shirt. e, Blue shirt, holding guitar behind microphone. f, Red shirt, holding microphone.

2008, Jan. 8   **Litho.**   *Perf. 13¼*
2949 A511 8r Sheet of 6, #a-f   7.50 7.50

America's Cup Yachting Championships — A512

No. 2950 — Various yachts with panel colors of: a, Yellow orange. b, Red. c, Dark blue. d, Blue green.

2008, Jan. 8
2950   Strip of 4   9.25 9.25
   a.   A512 10r multi   1.60 1.60
   b.   A512 12r multi   1.90 1.90
   c.   A512 15r multi   2.40 2.40
   d.   A512 20r multi   3.25 3.25

Scouting In Maldive Islands, 50th Anniv. — A513

Scouting, Cent. (in 2007) — A514

No. 2951   Emblems of national jamborees from: a, 5 l, 1986. b, 10 l, 1988. c, 15 l, 1990. d, 20 l, 1992. e, 25 l, 1995. f, 30 l, 1998. g, 95 l, 2002. h, 5r, 2007.

2008, Feb. 19
2951 A513   Sheet of 8, #a-h   1.10 1.10
Souvenir Sheet
2952 A514 8r multi   1.25 1.25

Miniature Sheet

Intl. Day for the Preservation of the Ozone Layer — A515

No. 2953 — Various "Save the Ozone Layer" posters by Maldivian students: a, 5r. b, 12r. c, 15r. d, 18r.

2008, Sept. 10   **Litho.**   *Perf. 12½*
2953 A515   Sheet of 4, #a-d   8.00 8.00

Miniature Sheet

Elvis Presley (1935-77) — A516

No. 2954 — Presley: a, Playing guitar. b, With hand in foreground at right. c, Singing,

---

with legs shown. d, Facing right, holding microphone. e, Singing, with microphone at left. f, Beside car, wearing hat.

2008, Sept. 11   *Perf. 13¼*
2954 A516 8r Sheet of 6, #a-f   7.50 7.50

Miniature Sheet

Royal Air Force, 90th Anniv. — A517

No. 2955: a, Sopwith F-1 Camel. b, Aerospatiale Puma HC1 helicopter. c, Wessex helicopter. d, Armstrong Whitworth Atlas.

2008, Sept. 11   *Perf. 11½*
2955 A517 12r Sheet of 4, #a-d   7.50 7.50

A518

Space Exploration, 50th Anniv. (in 2007) — A519

No. 2956: a, Voyager 2 and rings of Uranus. b, Titan 3E Centaur rocket launching Voyager 2. c, Voyager 2 and Neptune's Great Dark Spot. d, Voyager 2 and Jupiter's Great Red Spot. e, Technician placing gold record into Voyager 2. f, Voyager 2 and rings of Saturn.

No. 2957, 12r — Spitzer Space Telescope: a, Top of telescope pointing to UR corner. b, Top of telescope pointing to top margin. c, Top of telescope pointing to UL corner. d, Solar panels of telescope shown.

No. 2958, 12r — Sputnik 1: a, With black background, denomination at LL. b, With orange background. c, And technician. d, With Moon in background.

No. 2959, 12r — Explorer 1: a, Atop Juno 1 rocket. b, With Earth in background. c, With clouds in background. d, And Dr. James Van Allen.

No. 2960, 12r — Vanguard 1: a, With Earth at top. b, And technicians. c, And rocket. d, With Earth at bottom.

2008, Sept. 11   *Perf. 13¼*
2956 A518 8r Sheet of 6, #a-f   7.50 7.50
Sheets of 4, #a-d
2957-2960 A519   Set of 4   30.00 30.00

Miniature Sheets

End of World War I, 90th
Anniv. — A520

No. 2961, 12r: a, Soldiers in trench. b, Two
soldiers resting in trench. c, Two soldiers aiming guns in trench. d, Soldier carrying
wounded soldier.
No. 2962, 12r, horiz.: a, Soldiers on
motorcycles. b, Soldiers moving up hill. c,
Tank. d, Two soldiers in machine gun nest.

Perf. 11¼x11½, 11½x11¼

2008, Nov. 11   Litho.

Sheets of 4, #a-d

2961-2962 A520 Set of 2   15.00 15.00

Inauguration of U.S. Pres. Barack
Obama — A521

No. 2963, 10r, vert.: a, Pres. Obama waving. b, Obama with dark blue striped tie, facing
right. c, First Lady Michelle Obama. d, Obama
with red striped tie. e, Michelle Obama clapping. f, Obama with light blue tie.
30r, Couple.

2009, Jan. 20   Perf. 11¼x11½

2963 A521 10r Sheet of 6, #a-f   9.50 9.50

Souvenir Sheet

Perf. 13¼

2964 A521 30r multi   4.75 4.75
No. 2963 contains six 30x40mm stamps.

Miniature Sheet

U.S. Pres. Abraham Lincoln (1809-
65) — A522

No. 2965 — Reverse of U.S. $5 banknote
and Lincoln: a, Standing, no suit buttons visible. b, Seated, with hand on arm of chair. c,
Seated, holding paper. d, Standing, with suit
buttons visible.

2009, Feb. 12   Perf. 13¼

2965 A522 12r Sheet of 4, #a-d   7.50 7.50

Fish
A523

Designs: No. 2966, 12r, Black-saddled coral
grouper. No. 2967, 12r, Peacock hind. No.
2968, 12r, Four-saddle grouper. No. 2969,
12r, Six-blotch hind.

2009, Sept. 24   Litho.   Perf. 13¼

2966-2969 A523   Set of 4   7.50 7.50

Miniature Sheet

Visit of Prince Harry to New
York — A524

No. 2970: a, At official naming of the British
Garden. b, At World Trade Center site. c, Head
of Prince Harry. d, Playing polo.

2009, Sept. 29   Perf. 11½

2970 A524 12r Sheet of 4, #a-d   7.50 7.50

Miniature Sheets

A525

Miniature Sheet

Star Trek Characters — A526

No. 2971: a, Fleet crew. b, Lt. Uhura. c, Mr.
Spock. d, Dr. McCoy.
No. 2972: a, Scotty. b, Dr. McCoy, diff. c,
Captain Kirk. d, Mr. Spock, diff.

2009, Sept. 29   Perf. 13¼

2971 A525 12r Sheet of 4, #a-d   7.50 7.50
2972 A526 12r Sheet of 4, #a-d   7.50 7.50

Miniature Sheet

Marilyn Monroe (1926-62),
Actress — A527

No. 2973: a, Face. b, In car. c, Wearing
patterned blouse, in room. d, With hand near
chin.

2009, Oct. 21   Perf. 12½x12¾

2973 A527 16r Sheet of 4, #a-
d   10.00 10.00

Whales — A528

Designs: 10 l, Beluga whale. No. 2975, 12r,
Hector's beaked whale. 16r, Beaked whale.
18r, Baird's beaked whale.
No. 2978, 12r, horiz.: a, Dwarf sperm whale.
b, Pygmy sperm whale. c, Baird's beaked
whale, diff. d, Sperm whale. e, Shepherd's
beaked whale. f, Cuvier's beaked whale.

2009, Oct. 21   Perf. 12½

2974-2977 A528   Set of 4   7.25 7.25
2978 A528 12r Sheet of 6, #a-f 11.50 11.50

Butterflies
A529

Designs: 10 l, Crimson rose. 16r, Common
Mormon. 18r, Common jay. 20r, Common
tiger.
No. 2983, horiz.: a, Small salmon Arab. b,
Lemon pansy. c, Tamil yeoman. d, Dark blue
tiger.
No. 2984: a, Common jezebel. b, Common
gull.

2009, Oct. 21   Perf. 12½

2979-2982 A529   Set of 4   8.50 8.50

Perf. 12

2983 A529 12r Sheet of 4, #a-d 7.50 7.50

Souvenir Sheet

2984 A529 15r Sheet of 2, #a-b 4.75 4.75

Chinese Aviation, Cent. — A530

No. 2985 — Airplanes: a, Y-5. b, Y-7. c, Y-8.
d, Y-12
25r, MA60.

2009, Nov. 12   Litho.   Perf. 14¼

2985 A530   9r Sheet of 4, #a-d 5.75 5.75

Souvenir Sheet

2986 A530 25r multi   4.00 4.00
Aeropex 2009, Beijing. No. 2985 contains
four 42x28mm stamps.

Worldwide Fund for Nature
(WWF) — A531

No. 2987 — Melon-headed whale: a, Pod of
whales underwater. b, Pod of whales at surface, swimming right. c, Whale. d, Pod of
whales at surface, swimming left.

2009, Nov. 18   Perf. 13¼

2987   Block or strip of 4   5.00 5.00
a.-d.   A531 8r Any single   1.25 1.25
e.   Sheet of 8, 2 each #2987a-
          2987d   10.00 10.00

First Man on the Moon, 40th
Anniv. — A532

No. 2988, vert.: a, Apollo 11 Command and
Service Modules. b, Apollo 11 Command, Service and Lunar Modules. c, Neil Armstrong. d,
Apollo 11 Lunar Module.
30r, Crew of Apollo 11.

2009, July 20   Litho.   Perf. 13¼

2988 A532 12r Sheet of 4, #a-d 7.50 7.50

Souvenir Sheet

2989 A532 30r multi   4.75 4.75
Intl. Year of Astronomy.

Miniature Sheets

A533

Mushrooms — A534

No. 2990: a, Copelandia bispora. b, Copelandia cyanescens. c, Psilocybe semilanceata. d, Volvariella volvacea.
No. 2991: Various unnamed mushrooms.

2009, Nov. 18   *Perf. 11½*
2990 A533 8r Sheet of 4, #a-d   5.00 5.00
2991 A534 8r Sheet of 6, #a-f   7.50 7.50

Flowers — A535

No. 2992: a, Nelumbo nucifera. b, Rosa bracteata. c, Freycinetia cumingiata. d, Thespesia lampas. e, Plumeria champa. f, Plumeria cubensis.
No. 2993: a, Lagerstroemia speciosa. b, Plumeria alba.
No. 2994: a, Plumeria rubra. b, Hibiscus tiliaceus.

2009, Dec. 9
2992 A535 10r Sheet of 6, #a-f   9.50 9.50
Souvenir Sheets
2993 A535 15r Sheet of 2, #a-b   4.75 4.75
2994 A535 15r Sheet of 2, #a-b   4.75 4.75

Souvenir Sheet

New Year 2010 (Year of the Tiger) — A536

No. 2995: a, Chinese characters. b, Tiger.

2010, Jan. 4   *Litho.*   *Perf. 12*
2995 A536 25r Sheet of 2, #a-b   8.00 8.00

Shells — A537

Designs: 10 l, Conus abbas. 12r, Conus amadis. 16r, Conus bengalensis. 18r, Pinctada margaritifera.
No. 3000: a, Harpa costata. b, Phalium fimbria. c, Zoila friendii friendii. d, Cyprae leucodon tenuidon.

2010, June 22   *Perf. 11¼x11½*
2996-2999 A537   Set of 4   7.25 7.25
            Perf. 12x11½
3000 A537 15r Sheet of 4, #a-d   9.50 9.50

Miniature Sheets

Election of Pres. John F. Kennedy, 50th Anniv. — A538

No. 3001, 15r: a, Pres. Kennedy at lectern. b, Pulitzer Prize medal. c, Civil Rights Act of 1964. d, Peace Corps emblem.
No. 3002, 15r: a, Vice-president Lyndon B. Johnson. b, Pres. Kennedy. c, Brochures for 1960 presidential election. d, Campaign placard.

2010, June 22   *Perf. 13¼*
     Sheets of 4, #a-d
3001-3002 A538   Set of 2   19.00 19.00

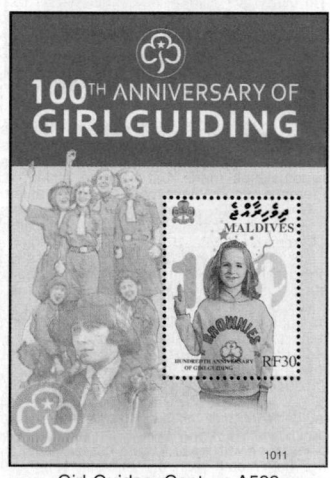

Girl Guides, Cent. — A539

No. 3003, horiz.: a, Three Girl Guides. b, Two Girl Guides, "100." c, Girl Guide climbing rock. d, Two Girl Guides jumping.
30r, Brownie.

2010, June 22   *Perf. 13x13¼*
3003 A539 16r Sheet of 4, #a-d   10.00 10.00
    Souvenir Sheet
     Perf. 13¼x13
3004 A539 30r multi   4.75 4.75

Reptiles — A540

No. 3005: a, Olive ridley turtle. b, Blood sucker lizard. c, Indian wolf snake. d, Green turtle.
No. 3006: a, Common house gecko. b, Loggerhead turtle.

2010, June 22   *Perf. 11½*
3005 A540 16r Sheet of 4, #a-d   9.50 9.50
    Souvenir Sheet
     Perf. 11½x12
3006 A540 15r Sheet of 2, #a-b   4.75 4.75

Birds — A541

No. 3007, horiz.: a, White-tailed tropicbird. b, Common tern. c, Bar-tailed godwit. d, Crab plover. e, Whimbrel. f, Black-winged stilt. 30r, Asian koel.

2010, June 22   *Perf. 11½x12*
3007 A541 8r Sheet of 6, #a-f   7.50 7.50
    Souvenir Sheet
     Perf. 11¼x11½
3008 A541 30r multi   4.75 4.75

Souvenir Sheets

A542

A543

A544

TITLE *GIRLS! GIRLS! GIRLS!*
RELEASED *1962*
CHARACTER *ROSS CARPENTER*

Elvis Presley (1935-77) — A545

2010, June 22   *Perf. 13½*
3009 A542 25r multi   4.00 4.00
3010 A543 25r multi   4.00 4.00
3011 A544 25r multi   4.00 4.00
3012 A545 25r multi   4.00 4.00
    Nos. 3009-3012 (4)   16.00 16.00

Muhammad Ali's Boxing Gold Medal In 1960 Summer Olympics, 50th Anniv.   A596

No. 3013 — Ali: a, Black-and-white photo. b, Sepia photo.
No. 3014 — Silhouette of Ali and photo of Ali: a, Wearing gold medal, country name at top. b, Throwing punch, country name at top. c, As "b," country name at bottom. d, As "a," country name at bottom.

2010, June 22   *Litho.*   *Perf. 12x11½*
3013 A596 15r Vert. pair, #a-b   4.75 4.75
3014 A596 15r Sheet of 4, #a-d   9.50 9.50

Souvenir Sheet

Girl Guides, Cent. — A597

No. 3015: a, Girl Guides emblem and centenary text. b, Maldives Girl Guides 50th anniversary emblem.

2010, June 22   *Perf. 11¾x12¼*
3015 A597 12r Sheet of 2, #a-b   3.75 3.75

King Mohammed V
of Morocco and
Map of Africa — A6

1962, Jan. 4   Photo.   Perf. 12
31   A6   25fr multicolored   .45   .25
32   A6   50fr multicolored   .55   .25

1st anniv. of the conference of African
heads of state at Casablanca.

Patrice
Lumumba
A7

1962, Feb. 12   Unwmk.   Perf. 12
33   A7   25fr choc & brn org   .70   .25
34   A7   100fr choc & emerald   1.00   .45

Issued in memory of Patrice Lumumba, Premier of the Congo (Democratic) Republic.

Pegasus and UPU Monument,
Bern — A8

1962, Apr. 21   Perf. 12½x12
35   A8   85fr red brn, yel & brt grn   1.75   .75

1st anniv. of Mali's admission to the UPU.

Map of Africa and
Post Horn — A8a

1962, Apr. 23   Perf. 13½x13
36   A8a   25fr dk red brn & dp grn   .60   .25
37   A8a   85fr dp green & org   1.10   .40

Establishment of African Postal Union.

Sansanding
Dam — A9

Cotton
Plant
A10

1962, Oct. 27   Photo.   Perf. 12
38   A9   25fr dk gray, ultra & grn   .45   .25
39   A10   45fr multicolored   1.60   .40

Telstar, Earth and Television
Set — A10a

1962, Nov. 24   Engr.   Perf. 13
40   A10a   45fr dk car, vio & brn   1.00   .45
41   A10a   55fr green, vio & ol   1.40   .55

1st television connection of the US and
Europe through the Telstar satellite, 7/11-12.

Bull, Chemical
Equipment,
Chicks — A11

1963, Feb. 23   Unwmk.   Perf. 13
42   A11   25fr red brn & grnsh bl   .50   .25

Sotuba Zootechnical Institute. See No. C15.

Tractor
A12

1963, Mar. 21   Engr.
43   A12   25fr vio bl, dk brn & blk   .65   .25
44   A12   45fr bl grn, red brn & grn   1.10   .30

FAO "Freedom from Hunger" campaign.

High Altitude
Balloon and
WMO
Emblem
A13

1963, June 12   Photo.   Perf. 12½
**Green Emblem; Yellow and Black
Balloon**
45   A13   25fr ultra   .45   .25
46   A13   45fr carmine rose   .80   .35
47   A13   60fr red brown   1.00   .45
       Nos. 45-47 (3)   2.25   1.05

Studies of the atmosphere.

Winners, 800-meter
Race — A14

20fr, Acrobatic dancers. 85fr, Soccer.

1963, Aug. 10   Unwmk.   Perf. 12
48   A14   5fr multi   .25   .25
49   A14   10fr multi   .25   .25
50   A14   20fr multi, horiz.   .60   .25
51   A14   85fr multi, horiz.   1.75   .75
       Nos. 48-51 (4)   2.85   1.50

Issued to publicize Youth Week.

Centenary
Emblem — A15

1963, Sept. 1   Perf. 13½x13
Emblem in Gray, Yellow and Red
52   A15   5fr lt ol grn & blk   .45   .25
53   A15   10fr yellow & blk   .55   .25
54   A15   85fr red & blk   1.30   .75
       Nos. 52-54 (3)   2.30   1.25

Centenary of the International Red Cross.

Kaempferia
Aethiopica — A16

Tropical plants: 70fr, Bombax costatum.
100fr, Adenium Honghel.

1963, Dec. 23   Unwmk.   Perf. 13
55   A16   30fr multicolored   .55   .25
56   A16   70fr multicolored   1.75   .45
57   A16   100fr multicolored   3.75   .60
       Nos. 55-57 (3)   6.05   1.30

Plane
Spraying,
Locust and
Village
A17

Designs (each inscribed "O.I.C.M.A."): 5fr,
Head of locust and map of Africa, vert. 10fr,
Locust in flight over map of Mali, vert.

1964, June 15   Engr.   Perf. 13
58   A17   5fr org brn, dl cl & grn   .50   .25
59   A17   10fr org brn, ol & bl grn   .95   .30
60   A17   20fr bis, org brn & yel
               grn   1.90   .50
       Nos. 58-60 (3)   3.35   1.05

Anti-locust campaign.

Soccer Player and Tokyo
Stadium — A18

Designs (stadium in background): 10fr,
Boxer, vert. 15fr, Runner, vert. 85fr, Hurdler.

1964, June 27   Unwmk.
61   A18   5fr red, brt grn & dk
               pur   .25   .25
62   A18   10fr blk, dl bl & org brn   .35   .25
63   A18   15fr violet & dk red   .45   .25
64   A18   85fr vio, dk brn & sl grn   2.25   1.25
   a.   Min. sheet of 4, #61-64   4.50   4.50
       Nos. 61-64 (4)   3.30   2.00

18th Olympic Games, Tokyo, Oct. 10-25.

IQSY
Emblem
and Eclipse
of
Sun — A19

1964, July 27   Engr.   Perf. 13
65   A19   45fr multicolored   1.00   .40

International Quiet Sun Year, 1964-65.

Map of Viet Nam
A20   Defassa
                   Waterbuck
                   A21

1964, Nov. 2   Photo.   Perf. 12x12½
66   A20   30fr multicolored   .60   .25

Issued to publicize the solidarity of the workers of Mali and those of South Viet Nam.

1965, Apr. 5   Engr.
Designs: 5fr, Cape buffalo, horiz. 10fr,
Scimitar-horned oryx. 30fr, Leopard, horiz.
90fr, Giraffe.

67   A21   1fr choc, brt bl & grn   .25   .25
68   A21   5fr grn, ocher & choc   .25   .25
69   A21   10fr grn, brt pink & bis
               brn   .55   .25
70   A21   30fr dk red, grn & choc   1.00   .35
71   A21   90fr bis brn, sl & yel grn   3.00   .75
       Nos. 67-71 (5)   5.05   1.85

Abraham Lincoln   Denis
A22   Compressed Air
             Transmitter
             A23

1965, Apr. 15   Photo.   Perf. 13x12½
72   A22   45fr black & multi   .75   .50
73   A22   55fr dp green & multi   1.50   .60

Centenary of the death of Lincoln.

1965, May 17   Engr.   Perf. 13
Designs: 30fr, Hughes telegraph system,
horiz. 50fr, Lescurre heliograph.

74   A23   20fr orange, blk & bl   .50   .25
75   A23   30fr org, ocher & sl grn   .75   .30
76   A23   50fr org, dk brn & sl grn   1.10   .50
       Nos. 74-76 (3)   2.35   1.05

Centenary of the ITU.

Mother and
infants — A24

Designs: 5fr, Mobile X-ray Unit and Lungs.
25fr, Examination of patient at Marchoux Institute and slide. 45fr, Biology laboratory.

1965, July 5   Unwmk.   *Perf. 13*

77	A24	5fr lake, red & vio	.25	.25
78	A24	10fr brn ol, red & sl grn	.35	.25
79	A24	25fr dk brn, red & grn	.65	.25
80	A24	45fr dk brn, red & sl grn	1.25	.50
		Nos. 77-80 (4)	2.50	1.25

Issued to publicize the Health Service.

Swimmer
A25

1965, July 19   *Engr.*

| 81 | A25 | 5fr shown | .25 | .25 |
| 82 | A25 | 15fr Judo | .80 | .30 |

1st African Games, Brazzaville, July 18-25.

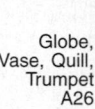

Globe,
Vase, Quill,
Trumpet
A26

55fr, Mask, palette and microphones. 90fr, Dancers, mask and printed cloth.

1966, Apr. 4   *Engr.*   *Perf. 13*

83	A26	30fr black, red & ocher	.45	.25
84	A26	55fr car rose, emer & blk	1.00	.30
85	A26	90fr ultra, org & dk brn	1.60	.45
		Nos. 83-85 (3)	3.05	1.00

International Negro Arts Festival, Dakar, Senegal, Apr. 1-24.

WHO Headquarters, Geneva — A27

1966, May 3   Photo.   *Perf. 12½x13*

| 86 | A27 | 30fr org yel, bl & ol grn | .70 | .25 |
| 87 | A27 | 45fr org yel, bl & dl red | .90 | .30 |

Inauguration of the WHO Headquarters.

Fishermen with Nets — A28

River Fishing: 4fr, 60fr, Group fishing with large net. 20fr, 85fr, Commercial fishing boats.

1966, May 30   *Engr.*   *Perf. 13*

88	A28	3fr ultra & brn	.25	.25
89	A28	4fr Prus bl & org brn	.25	.25
90	A28	20fr dk brn, ultra & grn	.55	.25
91	A28	25fr dk brn, bl & brt grn	.70	.25
92	A28	60fr mag, brn & brt grn	1.10	.30
93	A28	85fr dk pur, dl bl & grn	1.60	.60
		Nos. 88-93 (6)	4.45	1.90

Initiation of Pioneers
A29

Design: 25fr, Dance and Pioneer emblem.

1966, July 25   *Engr.*   *Perf. 13*

| 94 | A29 | 5fr multicolored | .25 | .25 |
| 95 | A29 | 25fr multicolored | .80 | .25 |

Issued to honor the pioneers of Mali.

Inoculation of Zebu
A30

1967, Jan. 16   Photo.   *Perf. 12½x13*

| 96 | A30 | 10fr dp grn, yel grn & brn | .35 | .25 |
| 97 | A30 | 30fr Prus bl, bl & brn | 1.00 | .30 |

Campaign against cattle plague.

View of Timbuktu and Tourist Year Emblem
A31

1967, May 15   *Engr.*   *Perf. 13*

| 98 | A31 | 25fr Prus bl, red lil & org | .70 | .25 |

International Tourist Year, 1967.

Ugada Grandicollis
A32

Insects: 5fr, Chelorrhina polyphemus, vert. 50fr, Phymateus cinctus.

1967, Aug. 14   *Engr.*   *Perf. 13*

99	A32	5fr brt bl, sl grn & brn	.80	.25
100	A32	15fr sl grn, dk brn & red	1.40	.35
101	A32	50fr sl grn, dk brn & dp org	3.25	.75
		Nos. 99-101 (3)	5.45	1.35

Teacher and Adult Class
A33

1967, Sept. 8   Photo.   *Perf. 12½x13*

| 102 | A33 | 50fr black, grn & car | 1.00 | .25 |

International Literacy Day, Sept. 8.

Europafrica Issue

Birds, New Buildings and Map
A34

1967, Sept. 18   *Perf. 12½x12*

| 103 | A34 | 45fr multicolored | 1.25 | .35 |

Lions Emblem and Crocodile — A35

1967, Oct. 16   Photo.   *Perf. 13x12½*

| 104 | A35 | 90fr yellow & multi | 1.75 | .75 |

50th anniversary of Lions International.

Water Cycle and UNESCO Emblem
A36

1967, Nov. 15   Photo.   *Perf. 13*

| 105 | A36 | 25fr multicolored | .70 | .25 |

Hydrological Decade (UNESCO), 1965-74.

WHO Emblem
A37

1968, Apr. 8   *Engr.*   *Perf. 13*

| 106 | A37 | 90fr sl grn, dk car rose & bl | 1.40 | .40 |

20th anniv. of the World Health Organization.

Linked Hearts and People
A38

1968, Apr. 28   *Engr.*   *Perf. 13*

| 107 | A38 | 50fr sl grn, red & vio bl | .90 | .25 |

International Day of Sister Communities.

Books, Student, Chart, and Map of Africa
A39

1968, Aug. 12   *Engr.*   *Perf. 13*

| 108 | A39 | 100fr carmine, ol & blk | 1.25 | .40 |

10th anniv. of the Intl. Assoc. for the Development of Libraries and Archives in Africa.

Michaux bicycle, 1861
A40

Designs: 2fr, Draisienne, 1809. 5fr, De Dion-Bouton automobile, 1894, horiz. 45fr, Panhard & Levassor automobile, 1914, horiz.

1968, Aug. 12

109	A40	2fr grn, olive & magenta	.35	.25
110	A40	5fr lemon, indigo & red	.65	.25
111	A40	10fr brt grn, indigo & brn	1.10	.25
112	A40	45fr ocher, gray grn & blk	2.00	.30
		Nos. 109-112,C60-C61 (6)	7.70	2.05

Tourist Emblem with Map of Africa and Dove
A41

1969, May 12   Photo.   *Perf. 12½x13*

| 113 | A41 | 50fr lt ultra, grn & red | .70 | .25 |

Year of African Tourism.

ILO Emblem and "OIT"
A42

1969, May 12   *Engr.*   *Perf. 13*

| 114 | A42 | 50fr vio, slate grn & brt bl | .50 | .25 |
| 115 | A42 | 60fr slate, red & ol brn | .90 | .25 |

Intl. Labor Organization, 50th anniv.

Panhard, 1897, and Citroen 24, 1969 — A43

30fr, Citroen, 1923, Citroen DS 21, 1969.

1969, May 30   *Engr.*   *Perf. 13*

116	A43	25fr blk, maroon & lemon	.80	.25
117	A43	30fr blk, brt grn & dk grn	1.40	.25
		Nos. 116-117,C71-C72 (4)	5.50	1.45

Play Blocks
A44

Toys: 10fr, Mule on wheels. 15fr, Ducks. 20fr, Racing car and track.

1969   Photo.   *Perf. 12½x13*

118	A44	5fr red, gray & yel	.25	.25
119	A44	10fr red, yel & olive	.25	.25
120	A44	15fr red, salmon & yel grn	.35	.25
121	A44	20fr red, indigo & org	.45	.25
		Nos. 118-121 (4)	1.30	1.00

Intl. Toy Fair in Nuremberg, Germany.

Ram
A45

1969, Aug. 18   *Engr.*   *Perf. 13*

122	A45	1fr shown	.25	.25
123	A45	2fr Goat	.25	.25
124	A45	10fr Donkey	.45	.25
125	A45	35fr Horse	1.25	.30
126	A45	90fr Dromedaries	2.00	.50
		Nos. 122-126 (5)	4.20	1.55

Development Bank Issue
Common Design Type

1969, Sept. 10

| 127 | CD130 | 50fr brt lil, grn & ocher | .40 | .25 |
| 128 | CD130 | 90fr ol brn, grn & ocher | .85 | .25 |

Boy Being Vaccinated
A46

1969, Nov. 10   *Engr.*   *Perf. 13*

| 129 | A46 | 50fr brn, indigo & brt grn | .90 | .25 |

Campaign against smallbox and measles.

ASECNA Issue
Common Design Type

1969, Dec. 12		**Engr.**	**Perf. 13**
130	CD132	100fr dark slate green	1.00 .40

African and Japanese Women
A47

150fr, Flags and maps of Mali and Japan.

1970, Apr. 13		**Engr.**	**Perf. 13**
131	A47	100fr brown, bl & ocher	1.00 .40
132	A47	150fr dk red, yel grn & org	1.50 .50

Issued to publicize EXPO '70 International Exhibition, Osaka, Japan, Mar. 15-Sept. 13.

Satellite Telecommunications, Map of Africa and ITU Emblem — A48

1970, May 17		**Engr.**	**Perf. 13**
133	A48	90fr car rose & brn	1.00 .40

World Telecommunications Day.

UPU Headquarters Issue
Common Design Type

1970, May 20		**Engr.**	**Perf. 13**
134	CD133	50fr dk red, bl grn & ol	.55 .25
135	CD133	60fr red lil, ultra & red brn	.70 .25

Post Office, Bamako
A49

Public Buildings: 40fr, Chamber of Commerce, Bamako. 60fr, Public Works Ministry, Bamako. 80fr, City Hall, Segou.

1970, Nov. 23		**Engr.**	**Perf. 13**
136	A49	30fr brn, brt grn & olive	.40 .25
137	A49	40fr brn, sl grn & dp claret	.50 .25
138	A49	60fr brn red, sl grn & gray	.65 .30
139	A49	80fr brn, brt grn & emer	.90 .40
		Nos. 136-139 (4)	2.45 1.20

Gallet 030T, 1882
A50

Old Steam Locomotives: 40fr, Felou 030T, 1882. 50fr, Bechevel 230T, 1882. 80fr, Type 231, 1930. 100fr, Type 141, 1930.

1970, Dec. 14		**Engr.**	**Perf. 13**
140	A50	20fr brt grn, dk car & blk	1.90 .55
141	A50	40fr blk, dk grn & ocher	2.40 .65
142	A50	50fr bis brn, bl grn & blk	3.25 .90
143	A50	80fr car rose, blk & bl grn	4.50 1.10
144	A50	100fr ocher, bl grn & blk	7.25 1.75
		Nos. 140-144 (5)	19.30 4.95

Scout Sounding Retreat — A51　　Bambara Mask, San — A52

Boy Scouts: 5fr, Crossing river, horiz. 100fr, Canoeing, horiz.

Perf. 13x12½, 12½x13

1970, Dec. 28			**Litho.**
145	A51	5fr multicolored	.25 .25
146	A51	30fr multicolored	.50 .25
147	A51	100fr multicolored	1.25 .40
		Nos. 145-147 (3)	2.00 .90

1971, Jan. 25		**Photo.**	**Perf. 12x12½**

Designs: 25fr, Dogon mask, Bandiagara. 50fr, Kanaga ideogram. 80fr, Bambara ideogram.

148	A52	20fr orange & multi	.25 .25
149	A52	25fr brt green & multi	.45 .25
150	A52	50fr dk purple & multi	.70 .25
151	A52	80fr blue & multi	1.00 .25
		Nos. 148-151 (4)	2.40 1.00

Boy, Medical and Scientific Symbols
A53

1971, Mar. 22		**Engr.**	**Perf. 13**
152	A53	100fr dp car, ocher & grn	1.40 .50

B.C.G. inoculation (Bacillus-Calmette-Guerin) against tuberculosis, 50th anniv.

Boy Scouts, Mt. Fuji, Japanese Print — A54

1971, Apr. 19			
153	A54	80fr lt ultra, dp plum & brt grn	.90 .30

13th Boy Scout World Jamboree, Asagiri Plain, Japan, Aug. 2-10.

UNICEF Emblem, Hands and Rose
A55

60fr, UNICEF emblem, women & children, vert.

1971, May 24		**Engr.**	**Perf. 13**
154	A55	50fr brn org, car & dk brn	.55 .25
155	A55	60fr vio bl, grn & red brn	.70 .25

25th anniv. of UNICEF.

Mali Farmer — A56　　Map of Africa with Communications Network — A57

Costumes of Mali: 10fr, Mali farm woman. 15fr, Tuareg. 60fr, Embroidered robe, Grand Boubou. 80fr, Ceremonial robe, woman.

1971, June 14		**Photo.**	**Perf. 13**
156	A56	5fr gray & multi	.25 .25
157	A56	10fr vio bl & multi	.35 .25
158	A56	15fr yellow & multi	.45 .25
159	A56	60fr gray & multi	.70 .25
160	A56	80fr tan & multi	1.00 .30
		Nos. 156-160 (5)	2.75 1.30

1971, Aug. 16		**Photo.**	**Perf. 13**
161	A57	50fr bl, vio bl & org	.50 .25

Pan-African telecommunications system.

Hibiscus
A58

Flowers: 50fr, Poinsettia. 60fr, Adenium obesum. 80fr, Dogbane. 100fr, Satanocrater berhautii.

1971, Oct. 4		**Litho.**	**Perf. 14x13½**
162	A58	20fr multicolored	.55 .25
163	A58	50fr multicolored	1.00 .30
164	A58	60fr multicolored	1.40 .35
165	A58	80fr multicolored	1.75 .45
166	A58	100fr multicolored	2.25 .55
		Nos. 162-166 (5)	6.95 1.90

For surcharge see No. 204.

Mother, Child and Bird (Sculpture)
A59

1971, Dec. 27		**Engr.**	**Perf. 13x12½**
167	A59	70fr mag, sepia & bl grn	.90 .25

Natl. Institute of Social Security, 15th anniv.

ITU Emblem
A60

1972, May 17		**Photo.**	**Perf. 13x13½**
168	A60	70fr blue, maroon & blk	.90 .25

4th World Telecommunications Day.

Clay Funerary Statuette — A61

Mali Art: 40fr, Female torso, wood. 50fr, Masked figure, painted stone. 100fr, Animals and men, wrought iron.

1972, May 29			**Perf. 12½x13**
169	A61	30fr org red & multi	.35 .25
170	A61	40fr yellow & multi	.55 .25
171	A61	50fr red & multi	.70 .25
172	A61	100fr lt green & multi	1.40 .40
		Nos. 169-172 (4)	3.00 1.15

Morse and Telegraph
A62

1972, June 5		**Engr.**	**Perf. 13**
173	A62	80fr red, emer & choc	1.10 .35

Centenary of the death of Samuel F. B. Morse (1791-1872), inventor of the telegraph.

Weather Balloon over Africa — A63

1972, July 10		**Photo.**	**Perf. 12½x13**
174	A63	130fr multicolored	1.75 .60

12th World Meteorology Day.

Sarakolé Dance, Kayes — A64

Designs: Folk dances.

1972, Aug. 21		**Photo.**	**Perf. 13**
175	A64	10fr shown	.35 .25
176	A64	20fr LaGomba, Bamako	.55 .25
177	A64	50fr Hunters' dance, Bougouni	.70 .25
178	A64	70fr Koré Duga, Ségou	.90 .30
179	A64	90fr Kanaga, Sanga	1.00 .35
180	A64	120fr Targui, Timbuktu	1.60 .45
		Nos. 175-180 (6)	5.10 1.85

People, Book, Pencil — A65

1972, Sept. 8		**Typo.**	**Perf. 12½x13**
181	A65	80fr black & yel grn	.90 .25

World Literacy Day, Sept. 8.

"Edison Classique," Mali Instruments
A66

1972, Sept. 18		**Engr.**	**Perf. 13**
182	A66	100fr multicolored	1.25 .40

First Anthology of Music of Mali.

Aries — A67

Signs of the Zodiac: No. 184, Taurus. No. 185, Gemini. No. 186, Cancer. No. 187, Leo. No. 188, Virgo. No. 189, Libra. No. 190, Scorpio. No. 191, Sagittarius. No. 192, Capricorn. No. 193, Aquarius. No. 194, Pisces.

1972, Oct. 23   Engr.   Perf. 11
183	A67	15fr lilac & bis brn	.40	.25
184	A67	15fr bister brn & blk	.40	.25
	a.	Pair #183-184	.80	.40
185	A67	35fr maroon & indigo	.65	.25
186	A67	35fr emerald & mar	.65	.25
	a.	Pair #185-186	1.40	.40
187	A67	40fr blue & red brn	.70	.25
188	A67	40fr dk pur & red brn	.70	.25
	a.	Pair #187-188	1.40	.40
189	A67	45fr dk blue & mar	.80	.30
190	A67	45fr maroon & brt grn	.80	.30
	a.	Pair #189-180	1.60	.60
191	A67	65fr dk violet & ind	1.00	.35
192	A67	65fr dk vio & gray ol	1.00	.35
	a.	Pair #191-192	2.00	.70
193	A67	90fr brt pink & ind	1.60	.60
194	A67	90fr brt pink & grn	1.60	.60
	a.	Pair #193-194	3.25	1.25
		Nos. 183-194 (12)	10.30	4.00

Arrival of First Locomotive in Bamako, 1906 A68

Designs (Locomotives): 30fr, Thies-Bamako, 1920. 60fr, Thies-Bamako, 1927. 120fr, Two Alsthom BB, 1947.

1972, Dec. 11   Engr.   Perf. 13
195	A68	10fr ind, brn & sl grn	1.90	.60
196	A68	30fr sl grn, ind & brn	3.75	1.25
197	A68	60fr sl grn, ind & brn	5.50	1.75
198	A68	120fr sl grn & choc	7.50	2.50
		Nos. 195-198 (4)	18.65	6.10

2nd African Games, Lagos, Nigeria, Jan. 7-18 — A69

1973, Jan. 15   Photo.   Perf. 12½
199	A69	70fr High jump	.55	.25
200	A69	270fr Discus	1.40	.60
201	A69	280fr Soccer	1.60	.85
		Nos. 199-201 (3)	3.55	1.70

INTERPOL Emblem and Headquarters — A70

1973, Feb. 28   Photo.   Perf. 13
202	A70 80fr multi	.90	.25

50th anniversary of International Criminal Police Organization (INTERPOL).

Blind Man and Disabled Boy — A71

1973, Apr. 24   Engr.   Perf. 12½x13
203	A71 70fr dk car, brick red & blk	.70	.25

Help for the handicapped.

No. 166 Surcharged with New Value, 2 Bars, and Overprinted

Overprint reads "SECHERESSE / SOLIDARITE AFRICAINE".

1973, Aug. 16   Litho.   Perf. 13½
204	A58 200fr on 100fr multi	2.25	.75

African solldarIty in drought emergency.

Cora — A72

Musical Instruments: 10fr, Balafon, horiz. 15fr, Djembe. 20fr, Guitar. 25fr, N'Djarka. 30fr, M'Bolon. 35fr, Dozo N'Goni. 40fr, N'Tamani.

Perf. 12½x13, 13x12½
1973, Dec. 10   Engr.
205	A72	5fr mar, dk grn & brn	.35	.25
206	A72	10fr bl & choc	.45	.25
207	A72	15fr brn, dk red & yel	.55	.25
208	A72	20fr mar & brn ol	.65	.25
209	A72	25fr org, yel & blk	.70	.25
210	A72	30fr vio bl & blk	.80	.25
211	A72	35fr dk red & brn	.90	.35
212	A72	40fr dk red & choc	1.10	.35
		Nos. 205-212 (8)	5.50	2.20

Farmer with Newspaper, Corn — A73

1974, Mar. 11   Engr.   Perf. 12½x13
213	A73 70fr multi	.70	.25

"Kibaru," rural newspaper, 2nd anniv.

Soccer, Goalkeeper, Symbolic Globe and Net — A74

280fr, Games' emblem, soccer and ball.

1974, May 6   Engr.   Perf. 13
214	A74 270fr multi	2.00	.90
215	A74 280fr multi	2.25	.90

World Cup Soccer Championships, Munich, June 13-July 7.
For surcharges see Nos. 219-220.

Old and New Ships, UPU Emblem — A75

90fr, Old and new planes, UPU emblem. 270fr, Old and new trains, UPU emblem.

1974, June 2   Engr.   Perf. 12½x13
216	A75	80fr brn & multir	.55	.25
217	A75	90fr ultra & multi	.80	.35
218	A75	270fr lt grn & multi	2.25	.85
		Nos. 216-218 (3)	3.60	1.45

Centenary of Universal Postal Union.
For surcharges see Nos. 229-230.

Nos. 214-215 Surcharged and Overprinted in Black or Red

Overprint reads "R.F.A. 2 / HOLLANDE 1".

1974, Aug. 28   Engr.   Perf. 13
219	A74	300fr on 270fr multi	2.40	1.00
220	A74	330fr on 280fr multi (R)	2.00	1.10

World Cup Soccer Championship, 1974, victory of German Federal Republic.

Artisans of Mali — A76

1974, Sept. 16   Photo.   Perf. 12½x13
221	A76	50fr Weaver	.55	.25
222	A76	60fr Potter	.65	.25
223	A76	70fr Smiths	.70	.25
224	A76	80fr Sculptor	.80	.30
		Nos. 221-224 (4)	2.70	1.05

Niger River near Gao — A77

Landscapes: 20fr, The Hand of Fatima (rock formation), vert. 40fr, Gouina Waterfall. 70fr, Dogon houses, vert.

Perf. 13x12½, 12½x13
1974, Sept. 23
225	A77	10fr multi	.25	.25
226	A77	20fr multi	.25	.25
227	A77	40fr multi	.55	.25
228	A77	70fr multi	.80	.30
		Nos. 225-228 (4)	1.85	1.05

Nos. 216 and 218 Surcharged and Overprinted in Black or Red

Overprint reads "9 OCTOBRE 1974".

1974, Oct. 9   Engr.   Perf. 13
229	A75	250fr on 80fr multi	2.00	.90
230	A75	300fr on 270fr multi (R)	2.50	1.00

UPU Day.

Mao Tse-tung, Flags, Great Wall — A78

1974, Oct. 21   Engr.   Perf. 13
231	A78 100fr multi	2.75	.65

People's Republic of China, 25th anniv.

Artisans and Lions Emblem — A79

100fr, View of Samanko and Lions emblem.

1975, Feb. 3   Photo.   Perf. 13
232	A79	90fr red & multi	.80	.25
233	A79	100fr blue & multi	1.10	.30

5th anniv. of lepers' rehabilitation village, Samanko, sponsored by Lions Intl.
For surcharges see Nos. 303-304.

Tetrodon Fahaka A80

Designs: Fish.

1975, May 12   Engr.   Perf. 13
234	A80	60fr shown	1.10	.30
235	A80	70fr Malopterurus electricus	1.25	.35
236	A80	80fr Citharinus latus	1.50	.40
237	A80	90fr Hydrocyon forskali	1.75	.45
238	A80	110fr Lates niloticus	2.25	.50
		Nos. 234-238 (5)	7.85	2.00

See Nos. 256-260.

Woman and IWY Emblem — A81

1975, June 9   Engr.   Perf. 13
239	A81 150fr red & grn	1.25	.35

International Women's Year 1975.

Morris "Oxford," 1913 A82

Automobiles: 130fr, Franklin "E," 1907. 190fr, Daimler, 1900. 230fr, Panhard & Levassor, 1895.

1975, June 16
240	A82	90fr blk, ol & lil	.70	.30
241	A82	130fr vio bl, gray & red	1.10	.40
242	A82	190fr bl, grn & indigo	1.60	.55
243	A82	230fr red, ultra & brn ol	1.80	.55
		Nos. 240-243 (4)	5.20	1.80

Carthaginian Tristater, 500 B.C. — A83

Ancient Coins: 170fr, Decadrachma, Syracuse, 413 B.C. 190fr, Acanthe tetradrachma, 400 B.C. 260fr, Didrachma, Eritrea, 480-445 B.C.

1975, Oct. 13　　Engr.　　Perf. 13

244	A83	130fr bl, cl & blk	.70	.25
245	A83	170fr emer, brn & blk	1.00	.50
246	A83	190fr grn, red & blk	1.40	.70
247	A83	260fr dp bl, org & blk	2.00	1.00
		Nos. 244-247 (4)	5.10	2.45

UN Emblem and "ONU" — A84

1975, Nov. 10　　Engr.　　Perf. 13

248	A84	200fr emer & brt bl	1.25	.45

30th anniversary of UN.

A. G. Bell, Waves, Satellite, Telephone — A85

1976, Mar. 8　　Litho.　　Perf. 12x12½

249	A85	180fr brn, ultra & ocher	1.25	.40

Centenary of first telephone call by Alexander Graham Bell, Mar. 10, 1876.

Chameleon A86

1976, Mar. 31　　Litho.　　Perf. 12½

250	A86	20fr shown	.40	.25
251	A86	30fr Lizard	.65	.25
252	A86	40fr Tortoise	.80	.25
253	A86	90fr Python	1.80	.50
254	A86	120fr Crocodile	2.40	.60
		Nos. 250-254 (5)	6.05	1.85

Konrad Adenauer and Cologne Cathedral — A87

1976, Apr. 26　　Engr.　　Perf. 13

255	A87	180fr mag & dk brn	1.40	.50

Konrad Adenauer (1876-1967), German Chancellor.

Fish Type of 1975

1976, June 28　　Engr.　　Perf. 13

256	A80	100fr Heterotis niloticus	.85	.25
257	A80	120fr Synodontis budgetti	1.10	.25
258	A80	130fr Heterobranchus bidorsalis	1.10	.30
259	A80	150fr Tilapia monodi	1.40	.40
260	A80	220fr Alestes macrolepidotus	1.90	.50
		Nos. 256-260 (5)	6.35	1.70

Page from Children's Book — A88

1976, July 19

261	A88	130fr red & multi	.90	.35

Books for children.

"Le Roi de l'Air" — A89

1976, July 26　　Litho.　　Perf. 12½x13

262	A89	120fr multi	1.40	.45

First lottery, sponsored by L'Essor newspaper.

"Do not overload scaffold" — A90

1976, Aug. 16　　Litho.　　Perf. 13

263	A90	120fr multi	.70	.25

National Insurance Institute, 20th anniv.

Letters, UPU and UN Emblems — A91

1976, Oct. 4　　Engr.　　Perf. 13

264	A91	120fr lil, org & grn	.90	.35

UN Postal Administration, 25th anniv.

Moto-Guzzi 254, Italy — A92

Motorcycles: 120fr, BMW 900, Germany. 130fr, Honda-Egli, Japan. 140fr, Motobecane LT-3, France.

1976, Oct. 18　　Engr.　　Perf. 13

265	A92	90fr multi	1.00	.25
266	A92	120fr multi	1.25	.30
267	A92	130fr multi	1.25	.40
268	A92	140fr multi	1.50	.40
		Nos. 265-268 (4)	5.00	1.35

Fishing Boat, Muscat — A93

180fr, Coaster, Cochin China. 190fr, Fireboat, Dunkirk, 1878. 200fr, Nile river boat.

1976, Dec. 6　　Engr.　　Perf. 13

269	A93	160fr multi	.80	.30
270	A93	180fr multi	.90	.30
271	A93	190fr multi	1.00	.35
272	A93	200fr multi	1.00	.45
		Nos. 269-272 (4)	3.70	1.40

Indigo Finch A94

Birds: 25fr, Yellow-breasted barbet. 30fr, Vitelline masked weaver. 40fr, Bee-eater. 50fr, Senegal parrot.

1977, Apr. 18　　Photo.　　Perf. 13

273	A94	15fr multi	.50	.25
274	A94	25fr multi	.90	.25
275	A94	30fr multi	1.10	.25
276	A94	40fr multi	1.40	.30
277	A94	50fr multi	1.80	.35
		Nos. 273-277 (5)	5.70	1.40

See Nos. 298-302.

Braille Statue, Script and Reading Hands — A95

1977, Apr. 25　　Engr.　　Perf. 13

278	A95	200fr multi	1.40	.55

Louis Braille (1809-1852), inventor of the reading and writing system for the blind.

Electronic Tree, ITU Emblem — A96

1977, May 17　　　　　　Photo.

279	A96	120fr dk brn & org	.50	.25

World Telecommunications Day.

Dragonfly A97

Insects: 10fr, Praying mantis. 20fr, Tropical wasp. 35fr, Cockchafer. 60fr, Flying stag beetle.

1977, June 15　　Photo.　　Perf. 13x12½

280	A97	5fr multi	.50	.25
281	A97	10fr multi	.65	.25
282	A97	20fr multi	.80	.25
283	A97	35fr multi	1.25	.25
284	A97	60fr multi	1.50	.30
		Nos. 280-284 (5)	4.70	1.30

Knight and Rook A98

Chess Pieces: 130fr, Bishop and pawn, vert. 300fr, Queen and King.

1977, June 27　　Engr.　　Perf. 13

285	A98	120fr multi	1.60	.45
286	A98	130fr multi	1.75	.55
287	A98	300fr multi	3.75	1.25
		Nos. 285-287 (3)	7.10	2.25

Europafrica Issue

Symbolic Ship, White and Brown Persons — A99

1977, July 18　　Litho.　　Perf. 13

288	A99	400fr multi	2.50	.80

Horse, by Leonardo da Vinci A100

Drawings by Leonardo da Vinci: 300fr, Head of Young Woman. 500fr, Self-portrait.

1977, Sept. 5　　Engr.　　Perf. 13

289	A100	200fr dk brn & blk	1.25	.65
290	A100	300fr dk brn & ol	1.75	.65
291	A100	500fr dk brn & red	2.75	1.10
		Nos. 289-291 (3)	5.75	2.40

Hotel de l'Amitié, Bamako — A101

1977, Oct. 15　　Litho.　　Perf. 13x12½

292	A101	120fr multi	.70	.25

Opening of the Hotel de l'Amitié, Oct. 15.

Dome of the Rock Jerusalem A102

1977, Oct. 17   *Perf. 12½*
293 A102 120fr multi   .90 .25
294 A102 180fr multi   1.10 .40
Palestinian fighters and their families.

Black Man, Chains and UN Emblem A103

130fr, Statue of Liberty, people & UN emblem. 180fr, Black children & horse behind fence.

1978, Mar. 13   **Engr.**   *Perf. 13*
295 A103 120fr multi   .65 .25
296 A103 130fr multi   .70 .25
297 A103 180fr multi   1.10 .35
    Nos. 295-297 (3)   2.45 .85
International Year against Apartheid.

Bird Type of 1977

Birds: 20fr, Granatine bengala. 30fr, Lagonosticta vinacea. 50fr, Lagonosticta. 70fr, Turtle dove. 80fr, Buffalo weaver.

1978, Apr. 10   **Litho.**   *Perf. 13*
298 A94 20fr multi   .90 .25
299 A94 30fr multi   1.10 .25
300 A94 50fr multi   1.40 .30
301 A94 70fr multi   2.10 .40
302 A94 80fr multi   2.75 .50
    Nos. 298-302 (5)   8.25 1.70

Nos. 232-233 Surcharged with New Value, Bar and Overprinted

Overprint reads "XXe ANNIVERSAIRE DU LIONS CLUB DE BAMAKO 1958-1978".

1978, May 8   **Photo.**
303 A79 120fr on 90fr multi   .80 .25
304 A79 130fr on 100fr multi   1.00 .25
20th anniversary of Bamako Lions Club.

Wall and Desert — A105

1978, May 18   **Litho.**   *Perf. 13*
306 A105 200fr multi   1.25 .40
Hammamet Conference for reclamation of the desert.

Mahatma Gandhi and Roses — A106

1978, May 29   **Engr.**
307 A106 140fr blk, brn & red   1.50 .30
Mohandas K. Gandhi (1869-1948), Hindu spiritual leader.

Dermestes — A107

Insects: 25fr, Ground beetle. 90fr, Cricket. 120fr, Ladybird. 140fr, Goliath beetle.

1978, June 12   **Photo.**   *Perf. 13*
308 A107 15fr multi   .60 .25
309 A107 25fr multi   .75 .25
310 A107 90fr multi   1.40 .25
311 A107 120fr multi   1.40 .30
312 A107 140fr multi   1.90 .35
    Nos. 308-312 (5)   6.05 1.40

Bridge — A108

Design: 100fr, Dominoes, vert.

1978, June 26   **Engr.**
313 A108 100fr multi   .90 .25
314 A108 130fr multi   1.25 .30

Aristotle — A109

1978, Oct. 16   **Engr.**   *Perf. 13*
315 A109 200fr multi   1.40 .35
Aristotle (384-322 B.C.), Greek philosopher.

Human Rights and UN Emblems — A110

1978, Dec. 11   **Engr.**   *Perf. 13*
316 A110 180fr red, bl & brn   1.25 .25
Universal Declaration of Human Rights, 30th anniversary.

Manatee — A111

Endangered Wildlife: 120fr, Chimpanzee. 130fr, Damaliscus antelope. 180fr, Oryx. 200fr, Derby's eland.

1979, Apr. 23   **Litho.**   *Perf. 12½*
317 A111 100fr multi   .90 .25
318 A111 120fr multi   1.00 .25
319 A111 130fr multi   1.10 .25
320 A111 180fr multi   1.60 .35
321 A111 200fr multi   1.75 .35
    Nos. 317-321 (5)   6.35 1.45

Boy Praying and IYC Emblem — A112

IYC emblem and: 200fr, Girl and Boy Scout holding bird. 300fr, IYC emblem, boys with calf.

1979, May 7   **Engr.**   *Perf. 13*
322 A112 120fr multi   .70 .25
323 A112 200fr multi   1.00 .35
324 A112 300fr multi   1.75 .50
    Nos. 322-324 (3)   3.45 1.10
International Year of the Child.

Judo and Notre Dame, Paris — A113

1979, May 14   **Engr.**   *Perf. 13*
325 A113 200fr multi   1.40 .45
World Judo Championship, Paris.

Telecommunications A114

Wood Carving A115

1979, May 17   **Litho.**
326 A114 120fr multi   .70 .25
11th Telecommunications Day.

1979, May 18   *Perf. 13x12½*
Sculptures from National Museum: 120fr, Ancestral figures. 130fr, Animal heads, and kneeling woman.

327 A115 90fr multi   .50 .25
328 A115 120fr multi   .65 .25
329 A115 130fr multi   .80 .30
    Nos. 327-329 (3)   1.95 .80
International Museums Day.

Rowland Hill and Mali No. 15 — A116

130fr, Zeppelin & Saxony #1. 180fr, Concorde & France #3. 200fr, Stagecoach & US #2. 300fr, UPU emblem & Penny Black.

1979, May 21   **Engr.**   *Perf. 13*
330 A116 120fr multi   .65 .25
331 A116 130fr multi   .70 .25
332 A116 180fr multi   .90 .30
333 A116 200fr multi   1.00 .30
334 A116 300fr multi   1.75 .55
    Nos. 330-334 (5)   5.00 1.65
Sir Rowland Hill (1795-1879), originator of penny postage.

Cora Players — A117

1979, June 4   **Litho.**   *Perf. 13*
335 A117 200fr multi   1.75 .50

Adenium Obesum and Sankore Mosque — A118

Design: 300fr, Satellite, mounted messenger, globe and letter, vert.

1979, June 8   **Photo.**
336 A118 120fr multi   1.75 .75

       Engr.
337 A118 300fr multi   3.00 1.60
Philexafrique II, Libreville, Gabon, June 8-17. Nos. 336, 337 printed in sheets of 10 and 5 labels showing exhibition emblem.

Map of Mali — A119

Design: 300fr, Men planting trees.

1979, June 18   **Litho.**   *Perf. 13x12½*
338 A119 200fr multi   1.25 .40
339 A119 300fr multi   2.00 .70
Operation Green Sahel.

Lemons — A120

1979, June 25   *Perf. 12½x13*
340 A120 10fr shown   .25 .25
341 A120 60fr Pineapple   .55 .25
342 A120 100fr Papayas   .90 .25
343 A120 120fr Soursops   1.00 .25
344 A120 130fr Mangoes   1.10 .25
    Nos. 340-344 (5)   3.80 1.25

Sigmund Freud — A121

1979, Sept. 17   **Engr.**   *Perf. 13*
345 A121 300fr vio bl & sepia   1.75 .60
Sigmund Freud (1856-1939), founder of psychoanalysis.

Timbuktu, Man and Camel A122

Design: 130fr, Caillié, Map of Sahara.

1979, Sept. 27   Perf. 13x12½
346 A122 120fr multi   .90   .30
347 A122 130fr multi   1.00   .35
René Caillié (1799-1838), French explorer, 180th birth anniversary.

Eurema Brigitta
A123

1979, Oct. 15   Litho.   Perf. 13
348 A123 100fr shown   1.60   .25
349 A123 120fr Papilio pylades   1.75   .30
350 A123 130fr Melanitis leda
             satyridae   2.25   .35
351 A123 180fr Gonimbrasia
             belina oc-
             cidentalis   2.75   .45
352 A123 200fr Bunaea alcinoe   3.00   .50
     Nos. 348-352 (5)   11.35   1.85

Greyhound
A124

Designs: Dogs.

1979, Nov. 12   Litho.   Perf. 12½
353 A124 20fr multi   .50   .25
354 A124 50fr multi   .65   .25
355 A124 70fr multi   .85   .25
356 A124 80fr multi   1.00   .25
357 A124 90fr multi   1.05   .30
     Nos. 353-357 (5)   4.05   1.30

Wild
Donkey — A125

1980, Feb. 4   Litho.   Perf. 13x13½
358 A125 90fr shown   .80   .25
359 A125 120fr Addax   1.05   .25
360 A125 130fr Cheetahs   1.15   .30
361 A125 140fr Mouflon   1.15   .35
362 A125 180fr Buffalo   1.80   .35
     Nos. 358-362 (5)   5.95   1.50

Photovoltaic
Cell
Pumping
Station,
Koni — A126

Solar Energy Utilization: 100fr, Sun shields, Dire. 120fr, Solar stove, Bamako. 130fr, Heliodynamic solar energy generating station, Dire.

1980, Mar. 10   Litho.   Perf. 13
363 A126 90fr multi   .45   .25
364 A126 100fr multi   .55   .25
365 A126 120fr multi   .65   .25
366 A126 130fr multi   .80   .25
     Nos. 363-366 (4)   2.45   1.00

For surcharge see No. 511.

Horse
Breeding,
Mopti
A127

1980, Mar. 17
367 A127 100fr shown   .80   .25
368 A127 120fr Nioro   .90   .25
369 A127 130fr Koro   1.00   .25

370 A127 180fr Coastal zone   1.25   .30
371 A127 200fr Banamba   1.25   .55
     Nos. 367-371 (5)   5.20   1.60

Alexander
Fleming
(Discoverer
of
Penicillin)
A128

1980, May 5   Engr.   Perf. 13
372 A128 200fr multi   1.50   .50

Avicenna
and
Medical
Instruments
A129

Design: 180fr, Avicenna as teacher (12th century manuscript illustration)

1980, May 12   Perf. 13x12½
373 A129 120fr multi   .65   .25
374 A129 180fr multi   .85   .35
Avicenna (980-1037), Arab physician and philosopher, 1000th birth anniversary.

Pilgrim at
Mecca — A130

1980, May 26   Litho.   Perf. 13
375 A130 120fr shown   .55   .25
376 A130 130fr Praying hands,
             stars, Mecca   .55   .25
377 A130 180fr Pilgrims, camels,
             horiz.   .80   .30
     Nos. 375-377 (3)   1.90   .80

Hegira, 1500th Anniversary.

Guavas — A131

1980, June 9
378 A131 90fr shown   .65   .25
379 A131 120fr Cashews   .70   .25
380 A131 130fr Oranges   .80   .25
381 A131 140fr Bananas   1.00   .25
382 A131 180fr Grapefruit   1.10   .30
     Nos. 378-382 (5)   4.25   1.30

League of
Nations,
60th
Anniversary
A132

1980, June 23   Engr.   Perf. 13
383 A132 200fr multi   .90   .30

Festival
Emblem,
Mask,
Xylophone
A133

1980, July 5   Litho.   Perf. 12½
384 A133 120fr multi   .60   .25
6th Biennial Arts and Cultural Festival, Bamako, July 5-15.

Sun Rising over
Map of
Africa — A134

1980, July 7   Engr.   Perf. 13
385 A134 300fr multi   1.25   .45
Afro-Asian Bandung Conference, 25th anniversary.

Market
Place,
Conference
Emblem
A135

1980, Sept. 15   Litho.   Perf. 13
386 A135 120fr View of Mali,
             vert.   .65   .25
387 A135 180fr shown   1.00   .30
World Tourism Conf., Manila, Sept. 27.

Hydro-electric Dam and Power
Station — A136

20th Anniversary of Independence: 120fr, Pres. Traore, flag of Mali, National Assembly building. 130fr, Independence monument, Bamako, Political Party badge, vert.

1980, Sept. 15   Perf. 13x12½
388 A136 100fr multi   .55   .25
389 A136 120fr multi   .70   .25
390 A136 130fr multi   .90   .30
     Nos. 388-390 (3)   2.15   .80

Utetheisa
Pulchella
A137

1980, Oct. 6   Perf. 13½
391 A137 50fr shown   .90   .25
392 A137 60fr Mylothis chloris
             pieridae   1.05   .25
393 A137 70fr Hypolimnas mi-
             shippus   1.25   .30
394 A137 80fr Papilio
             demodocus   1.50   .35
     Nos. 391-394,C402 (5)   8.95   2.15

Fight Against Cigarette
Smoking — A138

1980, Oct. 13   Litho.   Perf. 12½x12
395 A138 200fr multi   1.25   .45

European-African Economic
Convention — A139

1980, Oct. 20   Perf. 12½
396 A139 300fr multi   2.25   .60

Agricultural
Map of West
Africa
A140

West African Economic Council, 5th anniversary (Economic Maps): 120fr, Transportation. 130fr, Industry. 140fr, Communications.

1980, Nov. 5   Perf. 13½x13
397 A140 100fr multi   .55   .25
398 A140 120fr multi   .65   .25
399 A140 130fr multi   .70   .25
400 A140 140fr multi   .80   .30
     Nos. 397-400 (4)   2.70   1.05

African Postal
Union, 5th
Anniv. — A141

1980, Dec. 24   Photo.   Perf. 13½
401 A141 130fr multi   .90   .30

Senuofo Fertility
Statue — A142

Designs: Fertility statues.

1981, Jan. 12   Litho.   Perf. 13
402 A142 60fr Nomo dogon   .35   .25
403 A142 70fr shown   .45   .25
404 A142 90fr Bamanan   .65   .25
405 A142 100fr Spirit   .70   .25
406 A142 120fr Dogon   .90   .25
     Nos. 402-406 (5)   3.05   1.25

Mambi Sidibe — A143

Hegira (Pilgrimage Year) — A144

Designs: Philosophers.

1981, Feb. 16   *Perf. 12½x13*
407 A143 120fr shown .70 .25
408 A143 130fr Amadou
       Hampate .70 .25

1981, Feb. 23   *Perf. 13*
409 A144 120fr multi .65 .25
410 A144 180fr multi 1.10 .35

Maure Zebu A145

Designs: Cattle breeds.

1981, Mar. 9   *Perf. 12½*
411 A145 20fr Kaarta zebu .70 .25
412 A145 30fr Peul du Macina
       zebu .85 .25
413 A145 40fr Maure zebu 1.10 .25
414 A145 80fr Touareg zebu 1.60 .25
415 A145 100fr N'Dama cow 1.75 .30
    Nos. 411-415 (5) 6.00 1.30

See Nos. 433-437.

Hibiscus Double Rose — A146

Designs: Flowers.

1981, Mar. 16
416 A146 50fr Crinum de Moore .45 .25
417 A146 100fr Double Rose Hi-
       biscus .90 .25
418 A146 120fr Pervenche 1.10 .25
419 A146 130fr Frangipani 1.25 .25
420 A146 180fr Orgueil de Chine 1.75 .45
    Nos. 416-420 (5) 5.45 1.45

See Nos. 442-446.

Wrench Operated by Artificial Hand A147

Perf. 13x12½, 12x13
1981, May 4   *Engr.*
421 A147 100fr Heads, vert. .65 .25
422 A147 120fr shown .70 .25

Intl. Year of the Disabled.

13th World Telecommunications Day — A148

1981, May 17   *Litho.*   *Perf. 13x12½*
423 A148 130fr multi 1.00 .25

Pierre Curie, Lab Equipment A149

1981, May 25   *Engr.*
424 A149 180fr multi 2.25 .50

Curie (1859-1906), discoverer of radium.

Scouts at Water Hole — A150

1981, June 8   *Litho.*   *Perf. 13*
425 A150 110fr shown 1.50 .30
426 A150 160fr Sending signals 2.25 .45
427 A150 300fr Salute, vert. 4.00 .70
    Nos. 425-427 (3) 7.75 1.45

Souvenir Sheet
428 A150 500fr Lord Baden-Pow-
       ell 8.50 5.00

4th African Scouting Conf., Abidjan, June.

Nos. 425-428 Overprinted in Red in 2 or 3 Lines

Overprint reads "DAKAR 8 AOUT 1981/28e CONFÉRENCE MONDIALE DU SCOUTISME".

1981, June 29
429 A150 110fr multi 1.50 .30
430 A150 160fr multi 2.25 .45
431 A150 300fr multi 4.00 .70
    Nos. 429-431 (3) 7.75 1.45

Souvenir Sheet
432 A150 500fr multi 8.50 5.00

28th World Scouting Conf., Dakar, Aug. 8.

Cattle Type of 1981

Various goats.

1981, Sept. 14   *Litho.*   *Perf. 13x13½*
433 A145 10fr Maure .25 .25
434 A145 25fr Peul .35 .25
435 A145 140fr Sahel 1.25 .25
436 A145 180fr Tuareg 1.60 .30
437 A145 200fr Djallonke 1.90 .35
    Nos. 433-437 (5) 5.35 1.40

World UPU Day — A151

1981, Oct. 9   *Engr.*   *Perf. 13*
438 A151 400fr multi 3.00 .70

World Food Day — A152

1981, Oct. 16
439 A152 200fr multi 1.50 .40

Europafrica Economic Convention — A153

1981, Nov. 23   *Engr.*   *Perf. 13*
440 A153 700fr multi 4.00 1.05

60th Anniv. of Tuberculosis Inoculation — A154

1981, Dec. 7   *Perf. 13x12½*
441 A154 200fr multi 1.50 .45

Flower Type of 1981

1982, Jan. 18   *Litho.*   *Perf. 13*
442 A146 170fr White water lilies 1.10 .25
443 A146 180fr Red kapok bush 1.10 .25
444 A146 200fr Purple mimosa 1.40 .30
445 A146 220fr Pohego lilies 1.40 .40
446 A146 270fr Satan's chalices 1.75 .50
    Nos. 442-446 (5) 6.75 1.70

Ceremonial Mask — A155

Designs: Various masks.

1982, Feb. 22   *Litho.*   *Perf. 12½*
447 A155 5fr multi .25 .25
448 A155 35fr multi .30 .25
449 A155 180fr multi 1.25 .30
450 A155 200fr multi 1.40 .35
451 A155 250fr multi 1.75 .35
    Nos. 447-451 (5) 4.95 1.50

25th Anniv. of Sputnik I Flight — A156

1982, Mar. 29   *Litho.*   *Perf. 13*
452 A156 270fr multi 1.60 .50

Fight Against Polio — A157

1982, May 3
453 A157 180fr multi 1.10 .35

Lions Intl. and Day of the Blind A158

1982, May 10   *Engr.*
454 A158 260fr multi 1.60 .30

"Good Friends" Hairstyle — A159

Designs: Various hairstyles.

1982, May 24   *Litho.*
455 A159 140fr multi .60 .25
456 A159 150fr multi .80 .25
457 A159 160fr multi 1.10 .30
458 A159 180fr multi 1.50 .35
459 A159 270fr multi 2.25 .60
    Nos. 455-459 (5) 6.25 1.75

Zebu A160

Designs: Various breeds of zebu.

1982, July 5   *Perf. 12½*
460 A160 10fr multi .45 .25
461 A160 60fr multi .90 .25
462 A160 110fr multi 1.25 .25
463 A160 180fr multi 2.00 .35
464 A160 200fr multi 2.25 .40
    Nos. 460-464 (5) 6.85 1.50

Wind Surfing (New Olympic Class) — A161

Designs: Various wind surfers.

1982, Nov. 22   *Litho.*   *Perf. 12½x13*
465 A161 200fr multi 1.25 .35
466 A161 270fr multi 1.75 .50
467 A161 300fr multi 2.00 .60
    Nos. 465-467 (3) 5.00 1.45

Pres. John F. Kennedy — A162

1983, Apr. 4   **Engr.**   **Perf. 13**
468 A162 800fr shown   4.25 1.25
469 A162 800fr Martin Luther King   4.25 1.25

Oua Traditional Hairstyle — A163

1983, Apr. 25   **Litho.**
470 A163 180fr shown   1.25 .25
471 A163 200fr Nation   1.40 .25
472 A163 270fr Rond point   1.75 .35
473 A163 300fr Naamu-Naamu   2.00 .40
474 A163 500fr Bamba-Bamba   3.50 .70
   Nos. 470-474 (5)   9.90 1.95

World Communications Year — A164

1983, May 17   **Litho.**   **Perf. 13**
475 A164 180fr multi   1.25 .40

Bicent. of Lavoisier's Water Analysis — A165

1983, May 27   **Engr.**   **Perf. 13**
476 A165 300fr multi   1.75 .50

Musicians — A166

1983, June 13   **Litho.**   **Perf. 13x13½**
477 A166 200fr Banzoumana Sissoko   1.00 .25
478 A166 300fr Batourou Sekou Kouyate   1.60 .35

Nicephore Niepce, Photography Pioneer, (1765-1833) A167

1983, July 4   **Engr.**   **Perf. 13**
479 A167 400fr Portrait, early camera   2.25 .45

2nd Pan African Youth Festival — A168

Palestinian Solidarity A169

1983, Aug. 22   **Litho.**   **Perf. 12½**
480 A168 240fr multi   1.50 .30
481 A169 270fr multi   1.75 .40

14th World UPU Day — A170

1983, Oct. 10   **Engr.**   **Perf. 12½**
482 A170 240fr multi   1.50 .35
   For surcharge see No. 500.

Sahel Goat A171

1984, Jan. 30   **Litho.**   **Perf. 13**
483 A171 20fr shown   .25 .25
484 A171 30fr Billy goat   .45 .25
485 A171 50fr Billy goat, diff.   .70 .25
486 A171 240fr Kaarta goat   2.25 .30
487 A171 350fr Southern goats   3.25 .45
   Nos. 483-487 (5)   6.90 1.50
   For surcharges see Nos. 497-499, 501-502.

Rural Development A172   Fragrant Trees A173

1984, June 1   **Litho.**   **Perf. 13**
488 A172 5fr Crop disease prevention   .25 .25
489 A172 90fr Carpenters, horiz.   1.00 .25
490 A172 100fr Tapestry weaving, horiz.   1.10 .30
491 A172 135fr Metal workers, horiz.   1.40 .45
   Nos. 488-491 (4)   3.75 1.25

1984, June 1
492 A173 515fr Borassus flabelifer   5.00 1.90
493 A173 1225fr Vitelaria paradoxa   12.00 4.25
   For surcharge see No. 583.

UN Infant Survival Campaign — A174

1984, June 12   **Engr.**
494 A174 120fr Child, hearts   1.25 .40
495 A174 135fr Children   1.50 .45

1984 UPU Congress — A175

1984, June 18
496 A175 135fr Anchor, UPU emblem, view of Hamburg   1.60 .40

Nos. 482-487 Surcharged

1984
497 A171 10fr on 20fr #483   .30 .25
498 A171 15fr on 30fr #484   .30 .25
499 A171 25fr on 50fr #485   .40 .25
500 A170 120fr on 240fr #482   1.60 .30
501 A171 120fr on 240fr #486   2.00 .30
502 A171 175fr on 350fr #487   2.75 .50
   Nos. 497-502 (6)   7.35 1.85

West African Economic Community, CEAO, 10th Anniv. A176

1984, Oct. 22   **Litho.**   **Perf. 13½**
503 A176 350fr multi   3.50 1.75
   For surcharge see No. 588.

Prehistoric Animals A177

1984, Nov. 5   **Litho.**   **Perf. 12½**
504 A177 10fr Dimetrodon   .25 .25
505 A177 25fr Iguanodon, vert.   .55 .25
506 A177 30fr Archaeopteryx, vert.   .80 .25
507 A177 120fr Like 10fr   2.50 .40
508 A177 175fr Like 25fr   4.00 .60
509 A177 350fr Like 30fr   7.50 1.50
510 A177 470fr Triceratops   11.00 2.50
   Nos. 504-510 (7)   26.60 5.75
   For surcharges see Nos. 579, 593.

No. 366 Overprinted "Aide au Sahel 84" and Surcharged

1984   **Litho.**   **Perf. 13**
511 A126 470fr on 130fr   5.25 2.40
   Issued to publicize drought relief efforts.

Mali Horses A178

1985, Jan. 21   **Litho.**   **Perf. 13½**
512 A178 90fr Modern horse   1.25 .35
513 A178 135fr Horse from Beledougou   1.75 .45
514 A178 190fr Horse from Nara   2.75 .70
515 A178 530fr Horse from Trait   7.75 1.90
   Nos. 512-515 (4)   13.50 3.40
   For surcharges see Nos. 586, 591.

Fungi — A179

1985, Jan. 28   **Litho.**   **Perf. 12½**
516 A179 120fr Clitocybe nebularis   1.60 .90
517 A179 200fr Lepiota cortinarius   2.50 1.00
518 A179 485fr Agavicus semotus   6.75 1.75
519 A179 525fr Lepiota procera   7.00 1.75
   Nos. 516-519 (4)   17.85 5.40
   For surcharges see Nos. 589-590.

Health — A180

Designs: 120fr, 32nd World Leprosy Day, Emile Marchoux (1862-1943), Marchoux Institute, 150th anniv. 135fr, Lions Intl., Samanko Convalescence Village, 15th anniv. 470fr, Anti-polio campaign, research facility, victim.

1985, Feb. 18   **Litho.**   **Perf. 13**
520 A180 120fr multi   1.50 .40
521 A180 135fr multi   1.75 .45
522 A180 470fr multi   5.00 1.75
   Nos. 520-522 (3)   8.25 2.60

   For surcharges see Nos. 580, 584. No. 522 is airmail.

Cultural and Technical Cooperation Agency, 15th Anniv. — A181

1985, Mar. 20
523 A181 540fr brn & brt bl grn 5.25 1.75

Intl. Youth Year A182

Youth activities.

1985, May 13 Perf. 12½x13
524 A182 120fr Natl. Pioneers Movement emblem 1.00 .45
525 A182 190fr Agricultural production 2.00 .70
526 A182 500fr Sports 5.00 1.75
Nos. 524-526 (3) 8.00 2.90
For surcharge see No. 587.

PHILEXAFRICA '85, Lome, Togo — A183

1985, June 24 Perf. 13
527 A183 250fr Education, telecommunications 2.75 2.00
528 A183 250fr Road, dam, computers 2.75 2.00
a. Pair, #527-528 + label 7.50 2.75
Nos. 527-528,C517-C518 (4) 10.00 6.50
Nos. 527-528 show the UPU emblem.

Cats A184

1986, Feb. 15 Litho. Perf. 13½
529 A184 150fr Gray 2.75 .55
530 A184 200fr White 3.75 .85
531 A184 300fr Tabby 4.50 1.10
Nos. 529-531 (3) 11.00 2.50
For surcharge see No. 582.

Fight Against Apartheid — A185

1986, Feb. 24 Perf. 13
532 A185 100fr shown 1.50 .35
533 A185 120fr Map, broken chain 1.60 .45

Telecommunications and Agriculture — A186

1986, May 17 Litho. Perf. 13
534 A186 200fr multi 2.50 .70

1986 World Cup Soccer Championships, Mexico — A187

Various soccer plays.

1986, May 24 Litho. Perf. 12½
535 A187 160fr multi 1.50 .50
536 A187 225fr multi 2.50 .75
Souvenir Sheet
537 A187 500fr multi 5.25 2.75
For overprints surcharges see No. 539-541, 585.

James Watt (1736-1819), Inventor, and Steam Engine — A188

1986, May 26 Perf. 12½x12
538 A188 110fr multi 2.00 .40
For surcharge see No. 581.

Nos. 535-537 Ovptd. "ARGENTINE 3 / R.F.A. 2" in Red

1986, July 30 Litho. Perf. 12½
539 A187 160fr multi 2.25 .70
540 A187 225fr multi 3.50 .90
Souvenir Sheet
541 A187 500fr multi 6.50 3.00

World Wildlife Fund — A189

Derby's Eland, Taurotragus derbianus.

1986, Aug. 11 Litho. Perf. 13
542 A189 5fr Adult head 1.40 .25
543 A189 20fr Adult in brush 2.50 .25
544 A189 25fr Adult walking 2.50 .25
545 A189 200fr Calf suckling 22.50 3.50
Nos. 542-545 (4) 28.90 4.25

1987, Feb. 16 Litho. Perf. 13
546 A190 150fr Model A, 1903 2.10 .50
547 A190 200fr Model T, 1923 2.75 1.00
548 A190 225fr Thunderbird, 1968 3.00 1.10
549 A190 300fr Lincoln Continental, 1963 3.25 1.25
Nos. 546-549 (4) 11.10 3.85

Bees A191

1987, May 11 Litho. Perf. 13½
550 A191 100fr Apis florea, Asia 2.00 .55
551 A191 150fr Apis dorsata, Asia 2.40 .65
552 A191 175fr Apis adansonii, Africa 2.50 .85
553 A191 200fr Apis mellifica, worldwide 2.75 1.00
Nos. 550-553 (4) 9.65 3.05

Lions Club Activities — A192

1988, Jan. 13 Litho. Perf. 12½
554 A192 200fr multi 2.50 .85

World Health Organization, 40th Anniv. — A193

1988, Feb. 22 Litho. Perf. 12½x12
555 A193 150fr multi 1.60 .55
For surcharge see No. 557.

John F. Kennedy (1917-1963), 35th US President — A194

1988, June 6 Litho. Perf. 13
556 A194 640fr multi 6.25 2.50
For surcharge see No. 592.

No. 555 Surcharged in Dark Red

1988, June 13 Perf. 12½x12
557 A193 300fr on 150fr multi 3.00 1.60
Mali Mission Hospital in Mopti and World Medicine organization.

Organization of African Unity, 25th Anniv. — A194a

1988, June 27 Litho. Perf. 12½
558 A194a 400fr multi 3.75 1.75

Universal Immunization Campaign — A195

1989, May 2 Litho. Perf. 13½
559 A195 20fr shown .25 .25
560 A195 30fr Inoculating woman .35 .25
561 A195 50fr Emblem, needles, diff. .55 .25
562 A195 175fr Inoculating boy 1.90 .80
Nos. 559-562 (4) 3.05 1.55

Intl. Law Institute of the French-Speaking Nations — A196

1989, May 15 Perf. 12½
563 A196 150fr multi 1.60 .70
564 A196 200fr multi 2.00 .90

World Post Day — A197

1989, Oct. 9 Litho. Perf. 13
565 A197 625fr multicolored 6.50 3.00
For surcharge see No. 594.

Visit of Pope John Paul II — A198

1990, Jan. 28 Litho. Perf. 13x12½
566 A198 200fr multicolored 3.00 .90

Multinational
Postal School,
20th
Anniv. — A199

1990, May 31   Litho.   *Perf. 12½*
567 A199 150fr multicolored   1.60   .65

Independence, 30th Anniv. — A200

1990, Sept. 20   Litho.   *Perf. 13x12½*
568 A200 400fr multicolored   3.75 1.90

Intl.
Literacy
Year
A201

1990, Sept. 24   Litho.   *Perf. 13½*
569 A201 150fr grn & multi   1.40   .65
570 A201 200fr org & multi   2.10   .90

A202

Lions Intl. Water Project, 6th anniv.: No.
572, Rotary Club fight against polio, 30th
anniv.

1991, Feb. 25   Litho.   *Perf. 13x12½*
571 A202 200fr multicolored   2.25 1.00
572 A202 200fr multicolored   2.25 1.00

A203

Designs: Tribal dances of Mali.

1991, Apr. 29   Litho.   *Perf. 12½*
573 A203 50fr Takamba   .50   .30
574 A203 100fr Mandiani   .90   .60
575 A203 150fr Kono   1.40   .90
576 A203 200fr Songho   1.90 1.10
     Nos. 573-576 (4)   4.70 2.90

A204

1991, Dec. 2   Litho.   *Perf. 12½*
577 A204 200fr multicolored   2.00 1.00
Central Fund for Economic Cooperation,
50th anniv.

A205

1992, Mar. 26   Litho.   *Perf. 12½*
578 A205 150fr multicolored   1.60   .75
National Women's Movement.

**Stamps of 1984-89 Srchd. in Black
or Black & Silver**

1992, June   Litho.   *Perfs. as Before*
579 A177 25fr on 470fr #510   .40   .25
580 A180 25fr on 470fr #522   .40   .25
581 A188 30fr on 110fr #538   .50   .25
582 A184 50fr on 300fr #531   .80   .25
583 A173 50fr on 1225fr #493   .80   .25
584 A180 150fr on 135fr #521
             (Bk & S)   2.50   .60
585 A187 150fr on 160fr #535   2.50   .60
586 A178 150fr on 190fr #514   2.50   .60
587 A182 150fr on 190fr #525   2.50   .60
588 A176 150fr on 350fr #503   2.50   .60
589 A179 150fr on 485fr #518   2.50   .60
590 A179 150fr on 525fr #519   2.50   .60
591 A178 150fr on 530fr #515   2.50   .60
592 A194 200fr on 640fr #556   3.25   .80
593 A177 240fr on 350fr #509   3.75 1.00
594 A197 240fr on 625fr #565   3.75 1.00
     Nos. 579-594 (16)   33.65 8.85

No. 580 is airmail. Size and location of
surcharge varies. No. 585 also overprinted
"Euro '92."

New Constitution, 1st
Anniv. — A205a

1993, Jan. 12   Litho.   *Perf. 11½x12*
594A A205a 150fr multi   32.50
594B A205a 225fr multi   52.50

Martyr's Day, 2nd
Anniv. — A206

1993, Mar. 26   Litho.   *Perf. 11½*
595 A206 150fr blue & multi   32.50 32.50
596 A206 160fr yellow & multi   32.50 32.50

Rotary Intl. and World Health
Organization (WHO) — A206a

Designs: 150fr, Polio victims, Rotary
emblem. 200fr, WHO emblem, pregnant
woman receiving vaccination.

1993, Apr. 16   Litho.   *Perf. 14*
596A A206a 150fr multi   37.50
596B A206a 200fr multi   52.50

Lions Club
in Mali,
35th Anniv.
A207

1993, Dec. 20   Litho.   *Perf. 14½*
597 A207 200fr blue & multi   32.50 32.50
598 A207 225fr red & multi   32.50 32.50

Monument, Liberty
Place — A207a

1993, Dec. 20   Photo.   *Perf. 11¾*
Granite Paper
598A A207a 20fr multicolored
598B A207a 25fr multicolored
598C A207a 50fr multicolored
598D A207a 100fr multicolored
598E A207a 110fr multicolored
598F A207a 150fr multicolored
598G A207a 200fr multicolored
598H A207a 225fr multicolored
598I A207a 240fr multicolored
598J A207a 260fr multicolored

1994 Winter
Olympics,
Lillehammer
A208

1994, Feb. 12   Litho.   *Perf. 13*
599 A208 150fr Pairs figure
               skating   .90   .50
600 A208 200fr Giant slalom   1.25   .75
601 A208 225fr Ski jumping   1.75 1.00
602 A208 750fr Speed skating   3.00 1.75
     Nos. 599-602 (4)   6.90 4.00
Souvenir Sheet
603 A208 2000fr Downhill skiing   8.00 8.00
No. 603 contains one 36x36mm stamp.
For overprints see Nos. 671-676.

1994 World Cup
Soccer
Championships,
US — A209

Designs: 200fr, Juan Schiaffino, Uruguay.
240fr, Diego Maradona, Argentina. 260fr,
Paolo Rossi, Italy. 1000fr, Franz Beckenbauer,
Germany. 2000fr, Just Fontaine, France.

1994, Mar. 15   Litho.   *Perf. 13*
604 A209 200fr multicolored   .90   .90
605 A209 240fr multicolored   1.40   .80
606 A209 260fr multicolored   1.60   .90
607 A209 1000fr multicolored   5.00 2.75
     Nos. 604-607 (4)   8.90 5.35
Souvenir Sheet
608 A209 2000fr multicolored   8.00 8.00
For overprints see Nos. 677-681.

Miniature Sheet

Dinosaurs — A210

a, 5fr, Scaphonyx. b, 10fr, Cynognathus. c,
15fr, Lesothosaurus. d, 20fr, Scutellosaurus.
e, 25fr, Ceratosaurus. f, 30fr, Dilophosaurus.
g, 40fr, Dryosaurus. h, 50fr, Heterodontosaurus. i, 60fr, Anatosaurus. j, 70fr,
Saurornithoides. k, 80fr, Avimimus. l, 90fr,
Saltasaurus. m, 300fr, Dromaeosaurus. n,
400fr, Tsintaosaurus. o, 600fr, Velociraptor. p,
700fr, Ouranosaurus.
  2000fr, Daspletosaurus, iguanodon.

1994, Mar. 28
609 A210 Sheet of 16, #a.-p.   13.00 10.00
Souvenir Sheet
610 A210 2000fr multi   10.00 10.00

Insects
A211

Designs: 40fr, Sternuera castanea, vert.
50fr, Eudicella gralli. 100fr, Homoderus mellyi,
vert. 200fr, Kraussaria angulifera.

1994, Mar. 30   Litho.   *Perf. 13*
611 A211 40fr multicolored   .40   .25
612 A211 50fr multicolored   .70   .35
613 A211 100fr multicolored   1.10   .60
614 A211 200fr multicolored   2.00 1.00
     Nos. 611-614 (4)   4.20 2.20

Vaccination Campaign Against
Measles — A212

1994, Apr. 7   Litho.   *Perf. 13½*
615 A212 150fr black & green   .90   .50
616 A212 200fr black & blue   1.60   .90

Birds
A213

1994, Apr. 25
617	A213	25fr Pigeons	.30	.25
618	A213	30fr Turkeys	.30	.25
619	A213	150fr Crowned cranes, vert.	1.40	.70
620	A213	200fr Chickens, vert.	1.50	.80
		Nos. 617-620 (4)	3.50	2.00

Intl. Year of the
Family — A213a

1994, May 2
620A	A213a	220fr multicolored	1.25	.60

Jazz
Musicians
A214

1994, May 23   Litho.   Perf. 13
621	A214	200fr Ella Fitzgerald	.80	.60
622	A214	225fr Lionel Hampton	1.00	.80
623	A214	240fr Sarah Vaughan	1.25	.95
624	A214	300fr Count Basie	1.75	1.40
625	A214	400fr Duke Ellington	2.25	1.75
626	A214	600fr Miles Davis	3.00	2.25
		Nos. 621-626 (6)	10.05	7.75

Souvenir Sheet
627	A214	1500fr Louis Armstrong	8.00	8.00

No. 627 contains one 45x45mm stamp.

Ancient Art — A215

Nos. 628-647: 15fr, Venus of Brassempoury, vert. 25fr, Petroglyphs, Tanum, vert. 45fr, Prehistoric cave drawings, vert. 50fr, Cave paintaings, Lascaux. 55fr, Tomb of Amonherkhopeshef, vert. 65fr, God Anubis and the pharaoh. 75fr, Sphinx. 85fr, Bust of Nefertiti, vert. 95fr, Statue of Shibum, vert. 100fr, Standard of Ur. 130fr, Mesopotamian bull's head harp, vert. 135fr, Mesopotamian scroll. 140fr, Assyrian dignitary, vert. 180fr, Enameled horse, Babylon. 190fr, Assyrian carving of hunters, vert. 200fr, Mona Lisa of Nimrud, vert. 225fr, Carthaginian coin. 250fr, Phoenician sphinx, vert. 275fr, Persian archer, vert. 280fr, Ceramic and glass mask, vert.

1994, Aug. 24   Litho.   Perf. 13½
628-647	A215	Set of 20	15.00 15.00

D-Day Landings, Normandy, 50th
Anniv. — A216

Villiers-Bocage, June 12: No. 648a, Explosion, men being killed. b, Tank firing. c, Tank, men with weapons.
Beaumont-Sur-Sarthe, June 6: No. 649a, Explosion, airplanes. b, British airplanes, tanks. c, German tanks, soldier firing machine gun.
Utah Beach, June 6: No. 650a, Explosion, bow of landing craft. b, Stern of landing craft, soldiers. c, Landing craft filled with troops.
Aerial battle: No. 651a, British planes dropping bombs. b, British, German planes. c, British, German planes, explosion.
Sainte-Mere-Eglise, June 5: No. 652a, German troops firing on paratroopers. b, Church tower. c, Paratroopers, German troops.

1994, June 6   Strips of 3
648	A216	200fr #a.-c.	3.25	2.00
649	A216	300fr #a.-c.	4.00	2.50
650	A216	300fr #a.-c.	4.00	2.50
651	A216	400fr #a.-c.	5.25	3.50
652	A216	400fr #a.-c.	5.25	3.50
		Nos. 648-652 (5)	21.75	14.00

Nos. 648-652 are each continuous designs. Nos. 648b, 649b, 650b, 651b, 652b are each 30x47mm.

Orchids,
Vegetables, &
Mushrooms
A217

Orchids: 25fr, Disa kewensis. 50fr, Angraecum eburneum. 100fr, Ansellia africana.
Vegetables: 140fr, Sorghum. 150fr, Onions. 190fr, Corn.
Mushrooms: 200fr, Lepiota (clitocybe) nebularis. 225fr, Macrolepiota (lepiota) procera. 500fr, Lepiota aspera.

1994, Sept. 12
653	A217	25fr multicolored	.25	.25
654	A217	50fr multicolored	.35	.25
655	A217	100fr multicolored	.65	.35
a.		Souvenir sheet of 3, #653-655	11.00	7.50
656	A217	140fr multicolored	.70	.40
657	A217	150fr multicolored	.80	.45
658	A217	190fr multicolored	1.00	.60
a.		Souvenir sheet of 3, #656-658	11.00	7.50
659	A217	200fr multicolored	1.10	.65
660	A217	225fr multicolored	1.25	.75
661	A217	500fr multicolored	2.75	1.50
a.		Souvenir sheet of 3, #659-661	11.00	7.50
		Nos. 653-661 (9)	8.85	5.20

Moths,
Butterflies &
Insects
A218

Designs: 20fr, Polyptychus roseus. 30fr, Elymniopsis bammakoo. 40fr, Deilephila nerii. 150fr, Utetheisa pulchella. 180fr, Charaxes jasius. 200fr, Mylothris chloris.
Insects: 225fr, Goliath beetle. 240fr, Locust. 350fr, Praying mantis.

1994, Sept. 12
662	A218	20fr multicolored	.25	.25
663	A218	30fr multicolored	.25	.25
664	A218	40fr multicolored	.25	.25
665	A218	150fr multicolored	.90	.50
666	A218	180fr multicolored	1.00	.55
667	A218	200fr multicolored	1.00	.60
a.		Souv. sheet of 6, #662-667	22.50	12.50
668	A218	225fr multicolored	1.10	.65
669	A218	240fr multicolored	1.25	.70
670	A218	350fr multicolored	1.60	.90
a.		Souv. sheet of 3, #668-670	11.00	6.50
		Nos. 662-670 (9)	7.60	4.65

Nos. 599-603 Ovptd. in Silver or Gold with Name of Olympic Medalist, Country

Overprints in silver: No. 671a, "Y. GORDEYEVA / S. GRINKOV / RUSSIE." No. 671b, "O. GRISHCHUK / Y. PLATOV / RUSSIE." No. 672a, "D. COMPAGNONI / ITALIE." No. 672b, "M. WASMEIER / ALLEMAGNE." No. 673a, "E. BREDESEN /NORVEGE." No. 673b, "J. WEISSFLOG / ALLEMAGNE." No. 674a, "B. BLAIR, U.S.A." No. 674b, "J.O. KOSS / NORVEGE."
Overprint in gold: No. 675, "L. KJUS / NORVEGE." No. 676, "P. WIBERG / SUEDE."

1994, Sept. 12   Litho.   Perf. 13
671	A208	150fr Pair, #a.-b.	1.75	1.00
672	A208	200fr Pair, #a.-b.	2.75	1.25
673	A208	225fr Pair, #a.-b.	3.50	2.00
674	A208	750fr Pair, #a.-b.	10.00	5.50
		Nos. 671-674 (4)	18.00	10.00

Souvenir Sheet
675	A208	2000fr multicolored	8.00	6.00
676	A208	2000fr multicolored	8.00	6.00

Nos. 604-608
Ovptd. in Metallic
Red

1994, Sept. 15   Litho.   Perf. 13
677	A209	200fr multicolored	.90	.50
678	A209	240fr multicolored	1.25	.70
679	A209	260fr multicolored	1.40	.80
680	A209	1000fr multicolored	5.25	3.00
		Nos. 677-680 (4)	8.80	5.00

Souvenir Sheet
681	A209	2000fr multicolored	8.00	6.00

Intl. Olympic Committee,
Cent. — A218a

1994, June 23   Litho.   Perf. 13½
681A	A218a	150fr multicolored	1.10	.60
681B	A218a	200fr multicolored	1.60	.90

Exist in imperf souvenir sheets of 1.

Intl. Olympic Committee,
Cent. — A219

Pierre de Coubertin and: 225fr, Woman carrying flame, vert. 240fr, Olympic rings, vert. 300fr, Torch bearer. 500fr, Gold medal of Olympic rings.
600fr, Flame, statue of flag bearer.

1994, June 23   Perf. 13½
682	A219	225fr multicolored	.90	.55
683	A219	240fr multicolored	1.00	.65
684	A219	300fr multicolored	1.60	1.00
685	A219	500fr multicolored	2.75	1.75
		Nos. 682-685 (4)	6.25	3.95

Souvenir Sheet
686	A219	600fr multicolored	3.50	2.25

Anniversaries
& Events
A220

Designs: 150fr, Ernst Julius Opik, Galileo probe, impact of comet on Jupiter. 200fr, Clyde Tombaugh, probe moving toward Pluto. 500fr, Intl. Red Cross, Henri Dunant. 650fr, Crew of Apollo 11, 1st manned moon landing. 700fr, Lions Intl., Rotary Intl. 800fr, Gary Kasparov chess champion.

1995, Apr. 10   Litho.   Perf. 13½
687	A220	150fr multicolored	.50	.30
688	A220	200fr multicolored	.80	.45
689	A220	500fr multicolored	2.25	1.25
690	A220	650fr multicolored	2.50	1.50
691	A220	700fr multicolored	2.75	1.75
692	A220	800fr multicolored	3.25	1.90
		Nos. 687-692 (6)	12.05	7.15

Nos. 687-692 exist in souvenir sheets of 1.

Motion
Picture,
Cent. — A221

Movie star, movie: 100fr, Kirk Douglas, Spartacus. 150fr, Elizabeth Taylor, Cleopatra. 200fr, Clint Eastwood, Sierra Torrid. 225fr, Marilyn Monroe, The River of No Return. 500fr, Arnold Schwarzenegger, Conan the Barbarian. 1000fr, Elvis Presley, Loving You. 1500fr, Charlton Heston, The Ten Commandments.

1994, May 23   Litho.   Perf. 13½
693-698	A221	Set of 6	16.00 8.75

Souvenir Sheet
699	A221	1500fr multicolored	8.25	5.00

No. 695 is airmail.

Fight
Against
AIDS
A222

Designs: 150fr, Woman, man holding condoms. 225fr, Nurse with AIDS patient, researcher looking into microscope.

1994, June 30
700	A222	150fr multicolored	1.10	.60
701	A222	225fr multicolored	1.60	.90

Tourism
A223

Designs: 150fr, Traditional buildings, statue, vert. 200fr, Sphinx, pyramids, ruins.

1994, Dec. 5
702	A223	150fr multicolored	1.10	.60
703	A223	200fr multicolored	1.60	.90

1996 Summer Olympics, Atlanta — A224

Designs: 25fr, Reiner Klimke, dressage. 50fr, Kristin Otto, swimming. 100fr, Hans-Gunther Winkler, equestrian. 150fr, Birgit Fischer-Schmidt, kayak. 200fr, Nicole Uphoff, dressage, vert. 225fr, Renate Stecher, track, vert. 230fr, Michael Gross, swimming. 240fr, Karin Janz, gymnastics. 550fr, Anja Fichtel, fencing, vert. 700fr, Heide Rosendahl-Ecker, track, vert.

1995, Mar. 27
704-713 A224 Set of 10   12.50 8.00
Dated 1994.

Rotary Intl., 90th Anniv. — A225

1995, Oct. 18   Litho.   Perf. 14
714 A225 1000fr Paul Harris, logo   6.50 4.00
Souvenir Sheet
715 A225 1500fr 1905, 1995 Logos   8.00 5.00

Miniature Sheets

Birds, Butterflies — A226

No. 716: a, Campephilus imperialis. b, Momotus momota. c, Ramphastos sulfuratus. d, Halcyon malimbica. e, Trochilus polytmus. f, Cardinalis cardinalis. g, Pharomachrus mocinno. h, Aratinga solstitialis. i, Amazona arausiaca. j, Eudocimus ruber. k, Carduelis cucullatus. l, Anodorhynchus hyacinthinus. m, Passerina leclancherii. n, Pipra mentalis. o, Rupicola rupicola. p, Sicalis flaveola.
No. 717: a, Capito niger. b, Chloroceryle amazona. c, Tersina virdis. d, Momotus momota. e, Campephilus menaloleucos. f, Leistes militaris. g, Sarcoramphus papa. h, Pilherodius pileatus. i, Tityra cayana. j, Tangara chilinsis. k, Amazona ochrocephala. l, Saltator maximus. m, Paroaria dominicana. n, Egretta tricolor. o, Piaya melanogaster. p, Thamnophilus doliatus.
No. 718: a, Paradise whydah (g). b, Red-necked francolin. c, Whale-headed stork (i). d, Ruff (j). e, Marabou stork (k). f, White pelican. g, Western curlew. h, Scarlet ibis. i, Great crested crebe. j, White spoonbill. k, African jacana. l, African pygmy goose.
No. 719: a, Ruby-throated hummingbird. b, Grape shoemaker, blue morpho butterflies. c, Northern hobby. d, Cuvier toucan (g). e, Black-necked red cotinga (h). f, Green-winged

macaws (i). g, Flamingo (j). h, Malachite kingfisher. i, Bushy-crested hornbill (l). j, Purple swamphen (k). k, Striped body (j, l). l, Painted lady butterfly.
Each 1000fr: No. 720, Topaza pella. No. 721, Sporophila lineola.

1995, Oct. 20   Litho.   Perf. 14
Sheets of 16 & 12
716 A226 50fr #a.-p.   6.50 4.00
717 A226 100fr #a.-p.   11.00 6.75
718 A226 150fr #a.-l.   12.00 7.25
719 A226 200fr #a.-l.   16.00 9.25
Nos. 716-719 (4)   45.50 27.25
Souvenir Sheets
720-721 A226 Set of 2   12.00 7.50

John Lennon (1940-80) A227

1995   Litho.   Perf. 14
722 A227 150fr multicolored   1.25 .70
No. 722 was issued in sheets of 16.

Miniature Sheets

Motion Pictures, Cent. — A228

Western actors: No. 723:a, Justus D. Barnes (misidentified as George Barnes). b, William S. Hart. c, Tom Mix. d, Wallace Beery. e, Gary Cooper. f, John Wayne.
Actresses and their directors: No. 724: a, Marlene Dietrich, Josef Von Sternberg. b, Jean Harlow, George Cukor. c, Mary Astor, John Huston (Houston on stamp). d, Ingrid Bergman, Alfred Hitchcock. e, Claudette Colbert, Cecil B. DeMille. f, Marilyn Monroe, Billy Wilder.
Musicals and their stars: No. 725: a, Singin' in the Rain, Gene Kelly. b, The Bandwagon, Anne Miller, Ray Bolger. c, Cabaret, Liza Minnelli, Joel Grey. d, The Sound of Music, Julie Andrews. e, Top Hat, Ginger Rogers, Fred Astaire. f, Saturday Night Fever, John Travolta.
Each 1000fr: No. 726, Robert Redford as the Sundance Kid. No. 727, Liv Ullman, actress, Ingmar Bergman, director. No. 728, Judy Garland in the Wizard of Oz.

1995, Dec. 8   Litho.   Perf. 13½x14
Sheets of 6
723 A228 150fr #a.-f.   5.25 3.50
724 A228 200fr #a.-f.   7.25 4.50
725 A228 240fr #a.-f.   9.00 5.50
Nos. 723-725 (3)   21.50 13.50
Souvenir Sheets
726-728 Set of 3   16.00 10.00
Nos. 723-728 have various styles of lettering.

Miniature Sheet

Stars of Rock and Roll — A229

No. 729: a, Connie Francis. b, The Ronettes. c, Janis Joplin. d, Debbie Harry of Blondie. e, Cyndi Lauper. f, Carly Simon.

No. 730, Bette Midler.

1995, Dec. 8
729 A229 225fr Sheet of 6, #a.-f.   8.00 5.00
Souvenir Sheet
730 A229 1000fr multicolored   5.25 3.50

Traditional Cooking Utensils A230

5fr, Canaris, vert. 50fr, Mortier, calebasse, vert. 150fr, Fourneau. 200fr, Vans, vert. 500fr, Vans.

1995, Nov. 20   Litho.   Perf. 14
731-734 A230 Set of 4   2.75 1.75
Souvenir Sheet
735 A230 500fr multicolored   3.00 2.00

18th World Scout Jamboree, Holland — A231

Scout examining butterfly or mushroom: 150fr, Saturnia pyri. 225fr, Gonepteryx rhamni. 240fr, Myrina silenus. 500fr, Clitocybe nebularis. 650fr, Agaricus semotus. 725fr, Lepiota procera.
1500fr, Morpho cypris.

1995, Aug. 1   Litho.   Perf. 13½
736-741 A231 Set of 6   11.50 5.75
Souvenir Sheet
742 A231 1500fr multicolored   9.25 5.00
Nos. 736-741 exist in souvenir sheets of 1.

UN, 50th Anniv. A232

Designs: 20fr, 170fr, UN emblem, scales of justice, doves, vert. 225fr, 240fr, Doves, UN emblem, four men of different races.

1995, Oct. 24   Litho.   Perf. 13
743 A232 20fr light blue & multi   .25 .25
744 A232 170fr light grn & multi   .80 .60
745 A232 225fr light pur & multi   1.10 .70
746 A232 240fr light org & multi   1.25 .95
Nos. 743-746 (4)   3.40 2.50

Ayrton Senna (1960-94), F-1 Race Car Driver — A233

1000fr, Jerry Garcia (1942-95), entertainer.

1995   Perf. 13½
747 A233 500fr multicolored   2.25 1.25
748 A233 1000fr multicolored   4.50 2.50
Nos. 747-748 exist in souvenir sheets of one.

1945-49 Greenland Expeditions of Paul Emile Victor — A234

1995
749 A234 150fr Charles de Gaulle   .70 .35
750 A234 200fr De Gaulle, liberation of Paris   .90 .50
751 A234 240fr Enzo Ferrari   1.10 .60
752 A234 650fr multicolored   3.00 1.75
753 A234 725fr Paul Harris   3.25 1.80
754 A234 740fr Michael Schumacher   3.50 1.90
Nos. 749-754 (6)   12.45 6.90
Nos. 749-754 exist in souvenir sheets of 1.

A235

Designs: 150fr, Second election party emblems, horiz. 200fr, Pres. Alpha Oumar Konare. 225fr, First election party emblems, horiz. 240fr, Natl. flag, map, party representations.

1995   Litho.   Perf. 13½
755 A235 150fr multicolored   .65 .35
756 A235 200fr multicolored   .80 .45
757 A235 225fr multicolored   .90 .50
758 A235 240fr multicolored   .95 .55
Nos. 755-758 (4)   3.30 1.85
Second Presidential elections.

A236

Economic Community of West African States (ECOWAS): 150fr, Regional integration, horiz. 200fr, Cooperation. 220fr, Prospect of creating one currency, horiz. 225fr, Peace and security, horiz.

1995
759 A236 150fr multicolored   .70 .35
760 A236 200fr multicolored   .90 .45
761 A236 220fr multicolored   1.00 .50
762 A236 225fr multicolored   1.00 .50
Nos. 759-762 (4)   3.60 1.85

Mushrooms — A237

Genus Russula: No. 763: a, Emetica. b, Laurocerasi. c, Rosacea. d, Occidentalis. e, Fragilis. f, Mariae. g, Eeruginea. h, Compacta.
Genus Boletus: No. 764: a, Felleus. b, Elagans. c, Castaneus. d, Edulis. e, Aereus. f, Granulatus. g, Cavipes. h, Badius.
Genus Lactarius: No. 765: a, Deliciosus. b, Luculentus. c, Pseudomucidus. d, Scrobiculatus. e, Deceptivus. f, Indigo. g, Peckii. h, Lignyotus.

Genus Amanita: No. 766a, Caesarea. b, Muscaria. c, Solitaria. d, Verna. e, Malleata. f, Phalloides. g, Citrina. h, Pantherina.

Each 1000fr: No. 767, Coprinus atramentarius. No. 768, Panaeolus subbalteatus.

1996, Mar. 15   Litho.   Perf. 14
763	A237	25fr Sheet of 8, #a.-h.	1.60	.95
764	A237	150fr Sheet of 8, #a.-h.	9.00	5.50
765	A237	200fr Sheet of 8, #a.-h.	12.00	7.25
766	A237	225fr Sheet of 8, #a.-h.	14.00	8.25

Souvenir Sheets
767-768	A237	Set of 2	14.00	9.00

Sites in Beijing — A238

No. 769: a, Bridge, Gateway to Hall of Supreme Harmony. b, Temple of Heaven. c, Great Wall. d, Hall of Supreme Harmony. e, Courtyard, Gate of Heavenly Purity. f, Younghe Gong Temple. g, Lang Ru Ting, Bridge of Seventeen Arches. h, Meridian Gate (Wu Men). i, Corner Tower.

Each 500fr: No. 770, Pagoda, vert. No. 771, Li Peng.

1996, May 13
769	A238	100fr Sheet of 9, #a.-i.	7.50	4.75

Souvenir Sheets
770-771	A238	Set of 2	7.00	4.75

No. 771 contains one 47x72mm stamp. CHINA '96 (Nos. 769, 771).

Trains
A239

Historic: No. 772: a, "Novelty," 1829. b, Premiere class Liverpool & Manchester Line, 1830. c, William Norris, 1843. d, Trevithick, 1808. e, Robert Stephenson "Rocket," 1829. f, "Puffing Billy," William Hedley, 1813.

No. 773: a, Subway Train, London. b, San Francisco cable car. c, Japanese monorail. d, Pantograph car, Stockholm. e, Double-decker tram, Hong Kong. f, Sacre-Coeur Cog Train, Montmartre, France.

No. 774: a, Docklands Light Railway, London. b, British Railway's high-speed diesel train. c, Japanese Bullet Train. d, Germany Inter-City Electric high speed train. e, French TGV high-speed electric train. f, German "Wuppertal" monorail.

Trains of China: No. 775: a, RM Class Pacific. b, Manchurian steam engine. c, SY Class 2-8-2, Tangshan. d, SL Class 4-6-2 Pacific. e, Chengtu-Kunming steam. f, Lanchow passenger train.

Each 500fr: No. 776, Rheingold Express, 1925. No. 777, Matterhorn cable car, vert. No. 778, Superchief, best long-distance diesel, US. No. 779, Shanghai-Nanking Railway.

1996, July 29
772	A239	180fr Sheet of 6, #a.-f.	8.00	5.00
773	A239	250fr Sheet of 6, #a.-f.	12.00	7.00
774	A239	310fr Sheet of 6, #a.-f.	14.00	8.50
775	A239	320fr Sheet of 6, #a.-f.	15.00	9.00

Souvenir Sheets
776-779	A239	Set of 4	13.00	10.00

Nos. 776-779 each contain one 57x43mm stamp.

Express Mail Service, 10th Anniv. A240

Designs: 30fr, Man with package, vert. 40fr, Bird holding package, letter, vert. 90fr, World map, woman with letter holding telephone receiver. 320fr, 320fr, Mail van, hands holding letters, map.

1996, Sept. 1   Litho.   Perf. 14
780	A240	30fr multicolored	.25	.25
781	A240	40fr multicolored	.30	.25
782	A240	90fr multicolored	.55	.30
783	A240	320fr multicolored	1.75	1.00
		Nos. 780-783 (4)	2.85	1.80

Queen Elizabeth II, 70th Birthday A241

Designs: a, Portrait. b, Wearing blue & red hat. c, Portrait as young woman. 1000fr, Portrait as young girl.

1996, Sept. 9   Perf. 13½x14
784	A241	370fr Strip of 3, #a.-c.	4.75	2.50

Souvenir Sheet
785	A241	1000fr multicolored	4.75	2.50

No. 784 was issued in sheets of 9 stamps.

Nanking Bridge — A242

1996   Litho.   Perf. 13½
786	A242	270fr multicolored	2.50	1.25

Mosques A243

1996
787	A243	250fr Djenne	3.50	2.25
788	A243	310fr Sankore	4.50	2.75

Pandas, Dogs, and Cats — A244

Panda, vert: No. 789: a, Climbing on branch. b, On bare limb. c, Closer view. d, Lying in branch with leaves.

Dogs, cats: No. 790: a, Azawakh. b, Basenji. c, Javanais. d, Abyssin.

1996
789	A244	150fr Sheet of 4, #a.-d.	3.25	1.75
790	A244	310fr Sheet of 4, #a.-d.	6.00	3.50

Nos. 789a-789d are 39x42mm.

Marilyn Monroe (1926-62) A245

Various portraits.

1996
791	A245	320fr Sheet of 9, #a.-i.	14.00	8.00

Souvenir Sheet
792	A245	2000fr multicolored	9.50	5.50

No. 792 contains one 42x60mm stamp.

Entertainers — A246

No. 793: a, Frank Sinatra. b, Johnny Mathis. c, Dean Martin. d, Bing Crosby. e, Sammy Davis, Jr. f, Elvis Presley. g, Paul Anka. h, Tony Bennett. i, Nat "King" Cole.

No. 794, Various portraits of John Lennon.

1996   Sheets of 9
793	A246	250fr #a.-l.	10.00	5.50
794	A246	310fr #a.-i.	12.50	7.00

U.S. Space Shuttle, Challenger — A247

Designs: a, Halley's Comet, Andromeda Galaxy. b, Mars. c, Challenger, Saturn. d, Moon, Jupiter. 1000fr, Shuttle Challenger.

1996, Oct. 14   Perf. 14
795	A247	320fr Sheet of 4, #a.-d.	5.75	3.50

Souvenir Sheet
796	A247	1000fr multicolored	5.25	3.50

No. 796 contains one 85x29mm stamp.

Mickey's ABC's A248

Disney characters in various scenes with: No. 797: a, "MICKEY." b, "A." c, "B." d, "C." e, "D." f, "E." g, "F." h, "G." i, "H."

No. 798: a, "I." b, "J." c, "K." d, "L." e, "M." f, "N." g, "O." h, "P." i, "Q."

No. 799: a, "R." b, "S." c, "T." d, "U." e, "V." f, "W." g, "X." h, "Y." i, "Z."

Each 1000fr: No. 800, Mouse child holding "DE MICKEY" sign, horiz. No. 801, Mouse children with various letters.

1996, Oct. 15   Litho.   Perf. 13½x14
797	A248	50fr Sheet of 9, #a.-i.	2.25	1.50
798	A248	100fr Sheet of 9, #a.-i.	4.50	2.75
799	A248	200fr Sheet of 9, #a.-i.	9.00	5.50

Souvenir Sheets
800-801	A248	Set of 2	10.50	6.75

Sites in Beijing A249

No. 802, Hall of Supreme Harmony. No. 803, Great Wall. No. 804, Hall of Prayers for Good Harvests, Temple of Heaven.

1996   Perf. 13½
802	A249	180fr multicolored	1.75	1.00
803	A249	180fr multicolored	1.75	1.00
804	A249	180fr multicolored	1.75	1.00
		Nos. 802-804 (3)	5.25	3.00

Cotton Production A250

Designs: 20fr, Cotton plant, vert. 25fr, People working in cotton fields. 50fr, Holding plant, vert. 310fr, Dumping cotton into cart.

1996   Perf. 13½
805	A250	20fr multicolored	.25	.25
806	A250	25fr multicolored	.25	.25
807	A250	50fr multicolored	.25	.25
808	A250	310fr multicolored	1.40	.70
		Nos. 805-808 (4)	2.15	1.45

Birds and Snakes A251

a, Crowned eagle in flight. b, Tufted eagle. c, Python. d, Gabon viper.

Songbirds: No. 810: a, Choucador splendide. b, Astrid ondulé. c, Martin chasseur. d, Coucou didric.

Butterfies: No. 811a, Salamis parhassus. b, Charaxes bohemani. c, Coeliades forestan. d, Mimacrea marshalli.

1996
809	A251	180fr Sheet of 4, #a.-d.	3.25	1.90
810	A251	250fr Sheet of 4, #a.-d.	4.50	2.75
811	A251	320fr Sheet of 4, #a.-d.	5.75	3.50

No. 1027 — Orchids: a, Epidendrum ellipticum. b, Oncidium macranthum. c, Miltoniopsis roezlii. d, Oncidium barbatum. e, Miltonia warscewiczii. f, Lockhartia oerstedii.

No. 1028 — Birds: a, Amandava subflava. b, Ploceus bojeri. c, Lagonosticta senegala. d, Uraeginthus bengalus. e, Monticola saxatilis. f, Saxicola torquata.

No. 1028G — Birds: a, Tyto alba. b, Pernis apivorus. c, Bubo africanus. d, Gypaetus barbatus meridionalis. e, Strix aluco. f, Milvus migrans.

No. 1029 — Butterflies: a, Cymothoe hypatha. b, Cymothoe sangaris. c, Top view, Charaxes fournierae. d, Male Catopsilia thauruma. e, Bottom view, Charaxes fournierae. f, Female Catopsilia thauruma.

No. 1030 — Mushrooms: a, Amanita muscaria. b, Amanita spissa. c, Helvella acetabulum. d, Pleurotus ostreatus. e, Phallus duplicatus. f, Cortinarius salor.

1999		Sheets of 6		
1026	A313	350fr #a.-f.	10.00	5.00
1027	A313	390fr #a.-f.	11.00	5.50
1028	A313	430fr #a.-f.	12.00	6.00
1028G	A313	460fr #h-m	14.00	7.00
1029	A313	490fr #a.-f.	15.00	7.50
1030	A313	530fr #a.-f.	16.00	8.00
	Nos. 1026-1030 (6)		78.00	39.00

Rocks, Dinosaurs and Volcanoes A314

No. 1031 — Dinosaurs and rocks: a, Edmontonia, Ensisheim meteorite. b, Iguanodon, Saint-Mesmin meteorite. c, Allosaurus, Pallasite meteorite. d, Troodon, Lunar meteorite. e, Lesothosaurus, rock from Bouvant. f, Carnotaurus, Axtell meteorite. g, Deinonychus, Orgueil meteorite. h, Dilophosaurus, rock from Douar Mghila. i, Psittacosaurus, L'Aigle meteorite.

No. 1032 — Volcanic eruptions and rocks: a, Popocatepetl, 1519, Peekskill meteorite. b, Santorin, 1645, Tamentit meteorite. c, Mt. Pelee, 1902, Ouallen meteorite. d, Herculaneum during Vesuvius eruption, 79, Chinguetti meteorite. e, Krakatoa, 1883, Pultush meteorite. f, Soufriere, 1979, rock from Sienne. g, Mt. St. Helens, 1980, Allende meteorite. h, Kilauea, 1984, Parnallee meteorite. i, Mt. Etna, 1986, Tamentit meteorite.

1500fr, Pompeii during Vesuvius eruption, 79.

1999		Sheets of 9	Perf. 13¼	
1031	A314	250fr #a.-i.	11.00	5.50
1032	A314	310fr #a.-i.	15.00	7.50

Souvenir Sheet
Perf. 13½

1033	A314	1500fr multi		7.50	3.75

No. 1033 contains one 39x56mm stamp.

Space A315

No. 1034: a, Hubble Space Telescope. b, Venera 12. c, Space shuttle. d, Ariane 5.

No. 1035: a, Apollo-Soyuz mission. b, Carl Sagan, Viking 1. c, Voyager 1. d, Giotto probe, Edmond Halley.

No. 1036: a, Frank Borman, Apollo 8. b, Neil Armstrong, Apollo 11. c, Luna 16 and Lunokhod 2. d, Surveyor 3.

No. 1037: a, Konstantin Tsiolkovsky. b, Robert H. Goddard. c, Hermann Oberth. d, Theodor von Kármán.

No. 1038: a, Laika, Sputnik 2. b, Yuri Gagarin, Vostok 1. c, Edward White, Gemini 4. d, John Glenn, Friendship 7.

No. 1039: a, Apollo 15 Lunar Rover. b, Pioneer 10. c, Skylab. d, Mariner 10.

1999		Sheets of 4	Perf. 13¼	
1034	A315	250fr #a.-d.	5.50	2.75
1035	A315	310fr #a.-d.	6.00	3.00
1036	A315	320fr #a-d	6.50	3.25
1037	A315	500fr #a-d	11.00	5.50
1038	A315	750fr #a-d	15.00	7.50
1039	A315	900fr #a-d	18.00	9.00
	Nos. 1034-1039 (6)		62.00	31.00

The Malian government declared that sheets of 9 stamps containing 100, 150, 200, 250, 300, 350, 400, 450 and 500fr stamps with the following topics are "illegal": Trains, Chess, Prehistoric Animals, Ferdinand Magellan, Christopher Columbus, Mushrooms, Computers, Wolves, Minerals, International Red Cross, Composers, Horses, and Wild Animals (tiger, lion, eagle, etc.)

I Love Lucy — A318

No. 1045: a, Lucy showing Fred open handcuffs. b, Lucy touching reclining Ricky while handcuffed. c, Fred watching Ricky glare at Lucy. d, Handcuffed Lucy and Ricky trying to go in opposite directions. e, Handcuffed Lucy and Ricky seated. f, Lucy and Ricky handcuffed on bed. g, Lucy trying to get off bed while handcuffed to Ricky. h, Handcuffed Ricky with hand between legs. i, Ricky with arm draped over Lucy.

No. 1046, 1000fr, Fred examining handcuffs on Lucy and Ricky. No. 1047, 1000fr, Lucy and Ricky looking down.

1999, May 20		Litho.	Perf. 13¼	
1045	A318	320fr Sheet of 9,		
		#a-i	16.00	16.00

Souvenir Sheets

1046-1047	A318	Set of 2	12.00	12.00

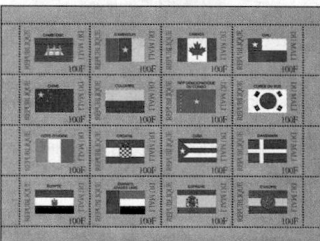

Garfield the Cat — A319

No. 1048: a, With eyes half shut, pink background. b, With eyes open, pink background. c, Touching chin. d, With eyes open and open mouth. e, Showing tongue. f, With eyes open, showing teeth. g, With eyes open, blue background. h, With eyes half shut, blue background. i, Odie.

1000fr, As mailman.

1999, May 20		Litho.	Perf. 13¼	
1048	A319	250fr Sheet of 9,		
		#a-i	12.50	6.25

Souvenir Sheet

1049	A319	1000fr multi		5.50	2.75

No. 1049 contains one 36x42mm stamp.

Miniature Sheet

Millennium — A320

No. 1051: a, Jules Verne, Scene from "20,000 Leagues Under the Sea," 1905. b, Commander William R. Anderson, USS Nautilus, map of Arctic region showing underwater voyage across North Pole, 1958. c, Discovery of tomb of King Tutankhamun, 1922. d, Transatlantic flight of Charles A. Lindbergh, 1927.

No. 1056: a, Mother Teresa holding Nobel diploma, dove. b, Princess Diana, rose, dove. c, Pope John Paul II. d, Fall of the Berlin Wall, doves.

1999, July 2		Litho.	Perf. 13¼	
1051	A320	310fr Sheet of 4, #a-d	—	—
1056	A320	490fr Sheet of 4, #a-d	—	—

Four additional sheets exist in this set. The editors would like to examine any these sheets.

Flags of the World — A321

No. 1058: a, Myanmar. b, Namibia. c, Nepal. d, Niger. e, Nigeria. f, Norway. g, Uganda. h, Pakistan. i, Netherlands. j, Peru. k, Philippines. l, Poland. m, New Zealand. n, Portugal. o, North Korea. p, Romania.

No. 1059: a, Russia. b, Rwanda. c, Singapore. d, Slovakia. e, Sudan. f, Sri Lanka. g, Sweden. h, Switzerland. i, Syria. j, Tanzania. k, Czech Republic. l, Thailand. m, Somalia. n, Tunisia. o, Turkey. p, Ukraine.

No. 1060: a, Finland. b, France. c, Great Britain. d, Greece. e, Guinea. f, Hungary. g, India. h, Indonesia. i, Iran. j, Iraq. k, Ireland. l, Iceland. m, Israel. n, Italy. o, Libya. p, Japan.

No. 1061: a, Cambodia. b, Cameroun. c, Canada. d, Chile. e, People's Republic of China. f, Colombia. g, Democratic Republic of the Congo. h, South Korea. i, Ivory Coast. j, Croatia. k, Cuba. l, Denmark. m, Egypt. n, United Arab Emirates. o, Spain. p, Ethiopia.

No. 1062: a, Afghanistan. b, South Africa. c, Albania. d, Algeria. e, Germany. f, United States. g, Angola. h, Saudi Arabia. i, Argentina. j, Australia. k, Austria. l, Bangladesh. m, Belgium. n, Bolivia. o, Brazil. p, Bulgaria.

No. 1063: a, Jordan. b, Kenya. c, Kuwait. d, Laos. e, Lebanon. f, Lithuania. g, Luxembourg. h, Madagascar. i, Malaysia. j, Mali. k, Viet Nam. l, Morocco. m, Mauritius. n, Mexico. o, Monaco. p, Mongolia.

1999, Aug. 2		Litho.	Perf. 13¼	
1058	A321	20fr Sheet of 16, #a-p	—	—
1059	A321	25fr Sheet of 16, #a-p	—	—
1060	A321	50fr Sheet of 16, #a-p	—	—
1061	A321	100fr Sheet of 16, #a-p	5.00	2.50
q.		Cameroun, flag with green star	—	—
r.		Sheet of 16, #1061a, 1061c-1061q	—	—
1063	A321	100fr Sheet of 16, #a-p	—	—

No. 1061b has a Cameroun flag with a yellow star.

Two additional sheets exist in this set. The editors would like to examine them.

Sikasso Cathedral — A322

No. 1065: a, Photograph. b, Drawing.

1999, Dec. 25		Litho.	Perf. 13¼	
1065	A322	150fr Horiz. pair, #a-b	1.75	.85

Christianity, 2000th Anniv. — A323

No. 1066, 100fr: a, St. Louis. b, Construction of Amiens Cathedral, 13th cent. c, Joan of Arc. d, Pope John Paul II.

No. 1067, 180fr: a, Jesus Christ. b, Persecution of Christians by Nero. c, St. Peter. d, Charlemagne.

1999, Dec. 25
Sheets of 4, #a-d

1066-1067	A323	Set of 2	6.00	3.00

Religious Paintings — A324

No. 1068, 250fr: a, Heller Madonna, by Albrecht Dürer. b, Virgin and Child, by Dürer. c, Madonna with Sts. Francis and Liberale, by Giorgione. d, Virgin and Child, by Giorgione.

No. 1069, 310fr: a, Virgin and Child, by Fra Filippo Lippi. b, Virgin and Child with Two Angels, by Lippi. c, Virgin and Sleeping Child, by Andrea Mantegna. d, Madonna of Victory, by Mantegna.

No. 1070, 320fr: a, Virgin and Child, by Hugo van der Goes. b, Virgin and Child and landscape, by van der Goes. c, Madonna and Child with St. Peter and a Martyred Saint, by Paolo Veronese. d, Adoration of the Magi, by Veronese.

No. 1071, 370fr: a, Madonna and Child Between St. Peter and St. Sebastian, by Giovanni Bellini. b, Madonna and Child with Cherubim, by Bellini. c, Madonna and Child with Two Angels, by Sandro Botticelli. d, Bardi Madonna, by Botticelli.

No. 1072, 390fr: a, Rest During the Flight to Egypt, with St. Francis, by Corregio. b, The Night, by Corregio. c, Senigallia Madonna, by Piero della Francesca. d, Virgin and Child and Four Angels, by della Francesca.

No. 1073, 750fr: a, Virgin and Child (rectangular), by Quentin Massys. b, Virgin and Child (curved top) by Massys. c, Madonna and Saint Sixtus, by Raphael. d, Madonna of the Duke of Alba, by Raphael.

1999, Dec. 25		Sheets of 4, #a-d		
1068-1073	A324	Set of 6	50.00	25.00

2000 Summer Olympics,
Sydney — A325

No. 1074, 150fr — Equestrian events: a, Show jumping. b, Military jumping. c, Dressage, horse facing left. d, Dressage, horse facing right.
No. 1075, 460fr — Tennis: a, Woman with green trim on dress. b, Man with red trim on shirt. c, Woman, diff. d, Man, diff.
No. 1076, 530fr — Table tennis: a, Green and red shirt and shorts. b, White shirt, red shorts. c, White and red shirt, black shorts. d, Yellow and green shirt, black shorts.
No. 1077, 750fr — Basketball: a, Red and yellow uniform. b, Green uniform. c, White and red uniform. d, Yellow and green uniform.
1000fr, Hurdler, horse and rider, horiz.

2000, June 30   Sheets of 4, #a-d
1074-1077 A325   Set of 4   57.50 30.00
Souvenir Sheet
1078 A325 1000fr multi   7.50   3.75
No. 1078 contains one 57x51mm stamp.

2002 World Cup Soccer
Championships, Japan and
Korea — A326

No. 1079, 150fr: a, Pedro Cea. b, Schiavo. c, Luigi Colaussi. d, Juan Schiaffino.
No. 1080, 250fr: a, Fritz Walter. b, Pelé. c, Amarildo. d, Bobby Moore.
No. 1081, 320fr: a, Jairzinho. b, Franz Beckenbauer. c, Mario Kempes. d, Paolo Rossi.
No. 1082, 750fr: a, Diego Maradona. b, Jurgen Klinsmann. c, Romario. d, Zinedine Zidane.

2000, June 30   Sheets of 4, #a-d
1079-1082 A326   Set of 4   42.50 22.50

Fauna, Mushrooms and Prehistoric
Animals — A327

No. 1083, 150fr — Birds: a, Ganga de Liechtenstein. b, Guepier à gorge blanche. c, Moineau domestique. d, Euplecte de feu. e, Irrisor namaquois. f, Pique-boeuf à bec jaune.
No. 1084, 180fr — Dogs: a, Dalmatian. b, Hungarian Kuvasz. c, Swedish shepherd. d, Ibiza dog. e, Golden retriever. f, Dachshund.
No. 1085, 250fr — Cats: a, White cat with orange eyes. b, Somali. c, Himalayan blue tortie point. d, Korat. e, Bombay. f, La Perm.
No. 1086, 310fr — Butterflies: a, Paralethe dendrophilis. b, Papilio ophidicephalus. c, Kallima jacksoni. d, Hypolimnas antevorta. e, Papilio nobilis. f, Euxanthe wakefieldi.
No. 1087, 320fr — Butterflies: a, Euxanthe eurinome. b, Euryphura chalcis. c, Dira mintha. d, Euphaedra zaddachi. e, Euphaedra neophron. f, Euxanthe tiberius.
No. 1088, 370fr — Mushrooms: a, Volvariella acystidiata. b, Leucopricus birnbaumii. c, Cystoderma elegans. d,

Leucoprinus elaidis. e, Leucoprinus discoideus. f, Leucoagaricus carminescens.
No. 1089, 370fr — Birds: a, Pririt du cap. b, Petit duc scops. c, Ouette d'Egypte. d, Rollier d'Europe. e, Promerops du cap. f, Sauteur du cap.
No. 1090, 390fr — Mushrooms: a, Volvariella parvispora. b, Volvariella surrecta. c, Lentinus similis. d, Leucoagaricus holosericeus. e, Leucoagaricus pepinus. f, Agrocybe elegantior.
No. 1091, 460fr — Prehistoric animals: a, Psittacosaurus. b, Phororhacos. c, Coelophysis. d, Saurornithoides. e, Acantholis. f, Varannosaurus.
No. 1092, 490fr — Prehistoric animals: a, Dromiceiomimus. b, Placodus. c, Ceratosaurus. d, Heterodontosaurus. e, Diatryma. f, Ouranosaurus.

2000, Sept. 25   Sheets of 6, #a-f
1083-1092 A327   Set of 10   145.00 75.00

Campaign
Against
Malaria
A328

Designs: No. 1093, 150fr, Doctor, mother and child. No. 1094, 150fr, Man with briefcase, man with crutch, syringe. No. 1095, 150fr, Doctor, syringe. 430fr, Mother, child, syringe, quinine tablets.

2000
1093-1096 A328   Set of 4   4.00   2.00

Intl. Volunteers
Year (in
2001) — A329

2000
1097 A329 250fr multi   1.00   .50

Independence, 40th Anniv. — A330

Designs: 20fr, Provincial map. 375fr, Flag-raising ceremony, front and back of 50-franc banknote, vert.

2001   Litho.   Perf. 13
1099 A330   20fr multi   —   —
1100 A330 375fr multi   —   —
An additional stamp was issued in this set. The editors would like to examine it.

Senegal River Regional
Organization — A331

2001   Litho.   Perf. 12¾
1101 A331   30fr multi, dated "2004"   —   —
1102 A331 100fr multi   —   —
  a.   Dated "2003"
1103 A331 5000fr multi, dated "2002"   —   —

A332

A333

Perf. 13¼ (A332), 13x12¾ (A333)
2002   Litho.
1104 A332 195fr multi   —   —
1105 A333 255fr multi   —   —
1106 A332 385fr multi   —   —
1107 A333 395fr multi   —   —
1108 A333 565fr multi   —   —
1109 A332 975fr multi   —   —
23rd African Cup Soccer Tournament. Dated "2001."

Bobo
Mask — A334

Dogon
Mask — A335

Sénoufo
Sanctuary
Door — A336

Bamanan Fertility
Statue — A337

2001-04   Litho.   Perf. 12¾
1110 A334   5fr multi   —   —
1111 A335   10fr multi   —   —
  a.   Dated "2004"
1112 A336   25fr multi   —   —
  a.   Dated "2004"
1113 A334   40fr multi   —   —
1114 A335   75fr multi   —   —
  a.   Dated "2004"
1115 A334 195fr multi   —   —
1116 A335 195fr multi   1.00   .50
  a.   Dated "2005"
1117 A334 235fr multi   —   —
1118 A335 255fr multi   —   —
1119 A337 255fr multi   1.40   .70
1120 A335 325fr multi   —   —
1121 A336 385fr multi   —   —
1122 A336 400fr multi   —   —
1123 A337 500fr multi   —   —
1124 A337 1000fr multi   —   —
Issued: Nos. 1115, 1117, 1118, 1120, 1121-1123, 2001; Nos. 1110, 1111-1114, 2002. Nos. 1116, 1119, 2003. No. 1124, 2004.

A338

AIDS Prevention
A339

2002, Jan. 10   Litho.   Perf. 12¾
1125 A338 195fr multi   —   —
1127 A338 225fr multi   —   —
1128 A339 225fr multi   —   —
1129 A338 385fr multi   —   —
1130 A339 385fr multi   —   —
An additional stamp was issued in this set. The editors would like to examine any example of it.

Songhoi Woman's
Hairstyle — A340

Peulh
Woman — A341

Badiangara
Cliffs
A342

Perf. 12¾, 13x12¾ (#1131)
2003, Mar. 7   Litho.
1131 A340   50fr multi   .25   .25
1132 A341 385fr multi   2.25   2.25
  a.   Dated "2004"
1133 A342 485fr multi   2.75   2.75

Balaphone
Festival
A343

2003, Mar. 7   Litho.   Perf. 12¾
1134 A343 565fr multi   3.50   3.50

Men Drinking Tea
in Desert — A344

2005, Aug. 18   Litho.   Perf. 12¾
1135 A344   10fr multi   —
See No. 1147.

Djenné
Fair — A345

2005, Aug. 18   Litho.   Perf. 12¾
1136 A345   20fr multi   .50   .50

Map of Africa, Water Drop, Lions International Emblem — A346

2005, Aug. 18　　Litho.　　Perf. 12¾
1137　A346　465fr multi　　　　4.50　4.50

World Summit on the Information Society, Tunis A347

2005, Aug. 18　　Litho.　　Perf. 12¾x13
1138　A347　195fr multi　　　　　　—
1139　A347　255fr multi　　　　　　—
1140　A347　385fr multi　　　　　　—

23rd Summit of Heads of State of Africa and France
A348　　　　　　A349

2005, Aug. 18　　Litho.　　Perf. 13x12¾
1141　A348　195fr multi　　　　　　—
1142　A349　195fr multi　　　　　　—

Three additional stamps were issued in this set. The editors would like to examine any examples.

Men Drinking Tea in Desert Type of 2005

2007　　　Litho.　　　Perf. 12¾
1147　A344　20fr multi　　　　　　—

Mother Nursing Baby — A350

2009　　　Litho.　　　Perf. 13x12¾
1149　A350　195fr multi　　　　　　—

An additional stamp was issued in this set. The editors would like to examine any example.

Independence, 50th Anniv. — A351

50th anniversary emblem with: 5fr, Pale yellow background, orange yellow top panel, green bottom panel. 10fr, White background, orange yellow top panel, red bottom panel. 20fr, White background, orange yellow top and

---

bottom panels. 25fr, Pale yellow background, green top panel, red bottom panel. 40fr, Light blue background, red top panel, orange yellow bottom panel. 100fr, Light blue background, red top panel, green bottom panel. 195fr, White background, red top and bottom panels. 565fr, White background, green top and bottom panels.

2010　　　Litho.　　　Perf. 13
1151-1158　A351　Set of 8　11.50　11.50

Independence, 50th Anniv. — A352

Denomination color: 195fr, Green. 485fr, Red.

2010　　　Litho.　　　Perf. 13
1159-1160　A352　Set of 2　8.00　8.00

SEMI-POSTAL STAMPS

Anti-Malaria Issue
Common Design Type
Perf. 12½x12
1962, Apr. 7　　Engr.　　Unwmk.
B1　CD108　25fr + 5fr pale vio bl　1.25　.60

Algerian Family — SP1

1962, Dec. 24　Photo.　Perf. 12x12½
B2　SP1　25fr + 5fr multi　　.70　.30

Issued for the national campaign to show the solidarity of the peoples of Mali and Algeria.

AIR POST STAMPS

Federation

Composite View of St. Louis, Senegal — AP1

Unwmk.
1959, Dec. 11　　Engr.　　Perf. 13
C1　AP1　85fr multi　　　　2.75　1.00

Founding of St. Louis, Senegal, tercentenary, and opening of the 6th meeting of the executive council of the French Community.

Birds — AP2

100fr, Amethyst starling. 200fr, Bateleur eagle, horiz. 500fr, Barbary shrike.

Perf. 12½x13, 13x12½
1960, Feb. 13　　　　　　Photo.
C2　AP2　100fr multi　　　3.50　2.00
C3　AP2　200fr multi　　　9.00　2.50
C4　AP2　500fr multi　　24.00　11.50
　　Nos. C2-C4 (3)　　36.50　16.00

Republic
Nos. C2-C4 Overprinted or Surcharged "REPUBLIQUE DU MALI" and Bars
1960, Dec. 18
C5　AP2　100fr multi　　　5.25　1.75
C6　AP2　200fr multi　　　8.00　3.00
C7　AP2　300fr on 500fr multi　11.50　6.00
C8　AP2　500fr multi　　20.00　9.00
　　Nos. C5-C8 (4)　　44.75　19.75

Pres. Modibo Keita — AP3

Designs: 200fr, Mamadou Konate.

1961, Mar. 18　　Engr.　　Perf. 13
C9　AP3　200fr claret & gray brn　3.75　.95
C10　AP3　300fr grn & blk　　5.50　1.25

Flag, Map, UN Emblem — AP4

1961, Mar. 18
C11　AP4　100fr multicolored　　2.25　.75
　　a.　Min. sheet of 3, #13, 14, C11　3.00　3.00
Proclamation of independence and admission to UN.

Sankore Mosque, Timbuktu — AP5

200fr, View of Timbuktu. 500fr, Bamako & arms.

1961, Apr. 15　　Unwmk.　　Perf. 13
C12　AP5　100fr Prus bl, red brn
　　　　　　& gray　　　2.75　.60
C13　AP5　200fr grn, brn & red　5.25　1.75
C14　AP5　500fr red brn, Prus bl
　　　　　　& dk grn　　13.50　3.25
　　Nos. C12-C14 (3)　　21.50　5.60

Inauguration of Timbuktu airport and Air Mali.

Bull, Chemical Equipment and Chicks — AP6

1963, Feb. 23　　　　　　　Engr.
C15　AP6　200fr bis, mar & grnsh
　　　　　　bl　　　　　5.00　1.50
Sotuba Zootechnical Institute.

Air Ambulance — AP7

Designs: 55fr, National Line plane loading. 100fr, Intl. Line Vickers Viscount in flight.

1963, Nov. 2　　Unwmk.　　Perf. 13
C16　AP7　25fr dk bl, emer & red
　　　　　　brn　　　　　.45　.25
C17　AP7　55fr bis, bl & red brn　1.10　.35
C18　AP7　100fr dk bl, red brn &
　　　　　　yel grn　　　2.10　.70
　　Nos. C16-C18 (3)　　3.65　1.30
Issued to publicize Air Mali.

Crowned Crane and Giant Tortoise — AP8

1963, Nov. 23　　Unwmk.　　Perf. 13
C19　AP8　25fr sepia, org & ver　1.60　.60
C20　AP8　200fr multi　　　7.00　2.25
Animal protection.

UN Emblem, Flag, Doves — AP9

1963, Dec. 10　　　　　　　Engr.
C21　AP9　50fr lt grn, yel & red　1.40　.50
15th anniversary of the Universal Declaration of Human Rights.

Cleopatra and Ptolemy at Kôm Ombo — AP10

1964, Mar. 9   **Unwmk.**   *Perf. 12*
C22 AP10 25fr dp claret & bister   1.00   .35
C23 AP10 55fr dp claret & lt ol
     grn   2.00   .75
UNESCO world campaign to save historic monuments in Nubia.

Pres. John F. Kennedy — AP11

1964, Oct. 26   **Photo.**   *Perf. 12½*
C24 AP11 100fr sl, red brn &
     blk   2.50   1.25
   a.   Souv. sheet of 4   10.00   10.00

Touracos — AP12

200fr, Abyssinian ground hornbills, vert. 300fr, Egyptian vultures, vert. 500fr, Goliath herons.

1965, Feb. 15   **Engr.**   *Perf. 13*
C25 AP12 100fr grn, dk bl & red   2.75   .90
C26 AP12 200fr blk, red & brt bl   8.00   1.40
C27 AP12 300fr blk, sl grn & yel   12.50   2.50
C28 AP12 500fr sl grn, dk brn &
     claret   20.00   4.00
   Nos. C25-C28 (4)   43.25   8.80

UN Headquarters, New York, and ICY Emblem — AP13

1965, Mar. 15   **Unwmk.**   *Perf. 13*
C29 AP13 55fr bis, dk bl & vio
     brn   1.25   .40
International Cooperation Year.

Pope John XXIII AP14

        Perf. 12½x13
1965, Sept. 14   **Photo.**   **Unwmk.**
C30 AP14 100fr multi   2.50   1.00

Winston Churchill — AP15

1965, Oct. 11   **Engr.**   *Perf. 13*
C31 AP15 100fr brn & indigo   2.50   1.00

Dr. Albert Schweitzer and Sick Child — AP16

1965, Dec. 20   **Photo.**   *Perf. 12½*
C32 AP16 100fr multi   2.75   1.00
   a.   Souv. sheet of 4   11.00   11.00

Major Edward H. White and Gemini 4 — AP17

No. C34, Lt. Col. Alexei A. Leonov. 300fr, Gordon Cooper, Charles Conrad, Alexei Leonov & Pavel Belyayev, Parthenon, Athens, & vase, vert.

1966, Jan. 10
C33 AP17 100fr vio, yel, lt bl &
     blk   1.75   1.10
C34 AP17 100fr bl, red, yel & blk   1.75   1.10
C35 AP17 300fr multi   5.25   3.00
   Nos. C33-C35 (3)   8.75   5.20
Achievements in space research and 16th Intl. Astronautical Congress, Athens, Sept. 12-18, 1965.

Papal Arms and UN Emblem — AP18

1966, July 11   **Engr.**   *Perf. 13*
C36 AP18 200fr brt bl, grnsh bl &
     grn   3.50   1.75
Visit of Pope Paul VI to the UN, NYC, Oct. 4, 1965.

People and UNESCO Emblem — AP19

1966, Sept. 5   **Engr.**   *Perf. 13*
C37 AP19 100fr dk car rose, sl
     grn & ultra   2.50   1.25
20th anniv. of UNESCO.

Soccer Players, Ball, Globe, and Jules Rimet Cup — AP20

1966, Oct. 31   **Photo.**   *Perf. 13*
C38 AP20 100fr multi   2.75   1.40
8th International Soccer Championship Games, Wembley, England, July 11-30.

Crab and Mt. Fuji — AP21

1966, Nov. 30   **Photo.**   *Perf. 13*
C39 AP21 100fr multi   2.25   .90
9th Intl. Anticancer Cong., Tokyo, Oct. 23-29.

UNICEF Emblem and Children — AP22

1966, Dec. 10   **Engr.**
C40 AP22 45fr dp bl, bis brn &
     red lil   1.00   .40
20th anniv. of UNICEF.

Land Cruisers in Hoggar Mountain Pass — AP23

1967, Mar. 20   **Engr.**   *Perf. 13*
C41 AP23 200fr multi   5.75   2.25
"Black Cruise 1924," which crossed Africa from Beni-Abbes, Algeria to the Indian Ocean and on to Tananarive, Madagascar, Oct. 28, 1924-June 26, 1925.

Diamant Rocket and Francesco de Lana's 1650 Flying Boat — AP24

Designs: 100fr, A-1 satellite and rocket launching adapted from Jules Verne. 200fr, D-1 satellite and Leonardo da Vinci's bird-borne flying machine.

1967, Apr. 17   **Engr.**   *Perf. 13*
C42 AP24 50fr brt bl, pur & grn   .90   .25
C43 AP24 100fr dk Prus bl, dk
     car & lil   1.75   .50
C44 AP24 200fr sl bl, ol & pur   3.50   1.00
   Nos. C42-C44 (3)   6.15   1.75
Honoring French achievements in space.

Amelia Earhart and Map of Mali — AP25

1967, May 29   **Photo.**   *Perf. 13*
C45 AP25 500fr bl & multi   11.00   3.50
Amelia Earhart's stop at Gao, West Africa, 30th anniv.

Paul as Harlequin, by Picasso AP26

Picasso Paintings: 50fr, Bird Cage. 250fr, The Flutes of Pan.

1967, June 16   *Perf. 12½*
C46 AP26 50fr multi   1.25   .40
C47 AP26 100fr multi   2.75   .75
C48 AP26 250fr multi   5.75   1.60
   Nos. C46-C48 (3)   9.75   2.75
See Nos. C56, C58, C82.

Jamboree Emblem, Scout Knots and Badges — AP27

Design: 100fr, Scout with portable radio transmitter, tents and Jamboree badge.

1967, July 10   **Engr.**   *Perf. 13*
C49 AP27 70fr dk car, emer &
     bl grn   .90   .25
C50 AP27 100fr dk car lake, sl
     grn & blk   1.25   .30
   a.   Strip of 2, #C49-C50 + label   3.00   1.75
12th Boy Scout World Jamboree, Farragut State Park, Idaho, Aug. 1-9.

Head of Horse, by Toulouse-
Lautrec — AP28

300fr, Cob-drawn gig, by Toulouse-Lautrec.

Perf. 12x12½, 12½x12

1967, Dec. 11   Photo.
C51 AP28 100fr multi   3.25 1.25
C52 AP28 300fr multi, vert.   8.00 2.50

See Nos. C66-C67.

Grenoble
AP29

Design: 150fr, Bobsled course on Huez Alp.

1968, Jan. 8   Engr.   Perf. 13
C53 AP29 50fr bl, yel brn & grn   .90 .25
C54 AP29 150fr brn, vio bl & stl
            bl   2.25 .75

10th Winter Olympic Games, Grenoble,
France, Feb. 6-18.

Painting Type of 1967 and

Roses and Anemones, by Van
Gogh — AP30

Paintings: 150fr, Peonies in Vase, by
Edouard Manet. 300fr, Bouquet, by
Delacroix. 500fr, Daisies in Vase, by Jean
François Millet, horiz.

Perf. 13, 12½x12, 12x12½

1968, June 24   Photo.
C55 AP30 50fr multi   .80 .50
C56 AP26 150fr grn & multi   2.10 .65
C57 AP30 300fr grn & multi   4.00 1.40
C58 AP26 500fr car & multi   6.00 2.00
     Nos. C55-C58 (4)   12.90 4.55

Martin Luther
King, Jr. — AP31

1968, July 22   Perf. 12½
C59 AP31 100fr rose lil, sal pink
            & blk   1.40 .40

Bicycle Type of Regular Issue

Designs: 50fr, Bicyclette, 1918. 100fr, Mercedes Benz, 1927, horiz.

1968, Aug. 12   Engr.   Perf. 13
C60 A40 50fr gray, dk grn &
            brick red   1.10 .30
C61 A40 100fr lemon, indigo &
            car   2.50 .70

Long Jumper and
Satellite — AP32

100fr, Soccer goalkeeper and satellite.

1968, Nov. 25   Photo.   Perf. 12½
C62 AP32 100fr multi, horiz.   1.25 .60
C63 AP32 150fr multi   2.25 .80

19th Olympic Games, Mexico City, 10/12-27.

PHILEXAFRIQUE Issue

Editorial Department, by François
Marius Granet — AP33

1968, Dec. 23   Photo.   Perf. 12½x12
C64 AP33 200fr multi   3.50 1.75

Issued to publicize PHILEXAFRIQUE Philatelic Exhibition in Abidjan, Feb. 14-23. Printed
with alternating light green label.
     See Nos. C85-C87, C110-C112, C205-
C207, C216-C217.

2nd PHILEXAFRIQUE Issue
Common Design Type
100fr, French Sudan #64, sculpture.

1969, Feb. 14   Engr.   Perf. 13
C65 CD128 100fr pur & multi   2.00 1.00

Painting Type of 1967

Paintings: 150fr, Napoleon as First Consul,
by Antoine Jean Gros, vert. 250fr, Bivouac at
Austerlitz, by Louis François Lejeune.

Perf. 12½x12, 12x12½

1969, Feb. 25   Photo.
C66 AP28 150fr multi   4.00 1.25
C67 AP28 250fr multi   5.75 1.75

Napoleon Bonaparte (1769-1821).

Montgolfier's Balloon — AP34

Designs: 150fr, Ferber 5, experimental
biplane. 300fr, Concorde.

1969, Mar. 10   Photo.   Perf. 13
C68 AP34 50fr multi   .70 .30
C69 AP34 150fr multi   2.25 .60
C70 AP34 300fr multi   4.50 1.40
   a. Strip of 3, #C68-C70   9.00 4.50

1st flight of the prototype Concorde plane at
Toulouse, France, Mar. 1, 1969.
For overprints see Nos. C78-C80.

Auto Type of Regular Issue

55fr, Renault, 1898, Renault 16, 1969. 90fr,
Peugeot, 1893, Peugeot 404, 1969.

1969, May 30   Engr.   Perf. 13
C71 A43 55fr rose car, blk & brt
            pink   1.40 .35
C72 A43 90fr blk, dp car & indigo 1.90 .60

Ronald Clarke, Australia, 10,000-meter
Run, 1965 — AP35

World Records: 90fr, Yanis Lusis, USSR,
Javelin, 1968. 120fr, Yoshinobu Miyake,
Japan, weight lifting, 1967. 140fr, Randy Mat-
son, US, shot put, 1968. 150fr, Kipchoge
Keino, Kenya, 3,000-meter run, 1965.

1969, June 23   Engr.   Perf. 13
C73 AP35 60fr bl & ol brn   .40 .25
C74 AP35 90fr car rose & red
            brn   .70 .30
C75 AP35 120fr emer & gray ol   .90 .55
C76 AP35 140fr gray & brn   1.00 .60
C77 AP35 150fr red org & blk   1.10 .65
     Nos. C73-C77 (5)   4.10 2.35

Issued to honor sports world records.

Nos. C68-C70 Overprinted in Red

Overprint includes Lunar Landing Module
and "L'HOMME SUR LA LUNE / JUILLET
1969 / APOLLO 11".

1969, July 25   Photo.   Perf. 13
C78 AP34 50fr multi   .90 .60
C79 AP34 150fr multi   2.25 1.25
C80 AP34 300fr multi   3.50 2.00
   a. Strip of 3, #C78-C80   9.00 4.50

Man's 1st landing on moon, July 20, 1969.
US astronauts Neil A. Armstrong and Col.
Edwin E. Aldrin, Jr., with Lieut. Col. Michael
Collins piloting Apollo 11.

Apollo 8,
Moon and
Earth —
AP35a

Embossed on Gold Foil
1969, July 24   Die-cut perf 10½
C81 AP35a 2000fr gold   25.00 25.00

US Apollo 8 mission, the 1st men in orbit
around the moon, Dec. 21-27, 1968.

Painting Type of 1967
500fr, Mona Lisa, by Leonardo da Vinci.

1969, Oct. 20   Photo.   Perf. 12½
C82 AP26 500fr multi   6.75 3.25

Mahatma
Gandhi — AP36

1969, Nov. 24   Engr.   Perf. 13
C83 AP36 150fr brt bl, ol brn &
            red brn   3.00 .70

Map of West Africa, Post Horns and
Lightning Bolts — AP37

1970, Feb. 23   Photo.   Perf. 12½
C84 AP37 100fr multi   1.00 .40

11th anniversary of the West African Postal
Union (CAPTEAO).

Painting Type of 1968

Paintings: 100fr, Madonna and Child, from
Rogier van der Weyden school. 150fr, Nativity,
by the master of Flemalle. 250fr, Madonna
and Child with St. John, from the Dutch
School.

1970, Mar. 2
C85 AP33 100fr multi   1.00 .40
C86 AP33 150fr multi   1.60 .80
C87 AP33 250fr multi   3.50 1.40
     Nos. C85-C87 (3)   6.10 2.60

Roosevelt
AP38

1970, Mar. 30   Photo.   Perf. 12½
C88 AP38 500fr red, lt ultra & blk 5.00 2.50

Pres. Franklin D. Roosevelt (1882-1945).

Lenin — AP39

1970, Apr. 22
C89 AP39 300fr pink, grn & blk   4.50 1.25

Jules Verne and Firing of Moon
Rockets — AP40

150fr, Jules Verne, rockets, landing modules
& moon. 300fr, Jules Verne & splashdown.

1970, May 4
C90 AP40 50fr multi   .90 .30
C91 AP40 150fr multi   2.25 .80
C92 AP40 300fr multi   4.00 1.60
     Nos. C90-C92 (3)   7.15 2.70

**Nos. C90-C92 Overprinted in Red or
Blue**

Overprint reads "APOLLO XIII / EPOPEE
SPATIALE / 11-17 AVRIL 1970".

1970, June   Photo.   Perf. 12½
C93 AP40 50fr multi (Bl)   .50 .25
C94 AP40 150fr multi (R)   1.50 .80
C95 AP40 300fr multi (B)   3.00 1.60
     Nos. C93-C95 (3)   5.00 2.65

Flight and safe return of Apollo 13, Apr. 11-
13, 1970.

Intelsat III — AP41

Telecommunications Through Space: 200fr, Molniya I satellite. 300fr, Radar. 500fr, "Project Symphony" (various satellites).

1970, July 13   Engr.   Perf. 13
C96 AP41 100fr gray, brt bl & org   .80   .40
C97 AP41 200fr bl, gray & red lil   1.60   .55
C98 AP41 300fr dk brn & gray   2.50   1.60
C99 AP41 500fr org, dk brn, sl & grnsh bl   4.00   2.50
    Nos. C96-C99 (4)   8.90   5.05

For surcharges see Nos. C108-C109.

Auguste and Louis Lumière, Jean Harlow and Marilyn Monroe AP42

1970, July 27   Photo.   Perf. 12½x12
C100 AP42 250fr multi   5.25   2.00

Issued to honor Auguste Lumière (1862-1954), and his brother Louis Jean Lumière (1864-1948), inventors of the Lumière process of color photography and of a motion picture camera.

Soccer — AP43

1970, Sept. 7   Engr.   Perf. 13
C101 AP43 80fr bl, dp car & brn ol   .90   .30
C102 AP43 200fr dp car, bl grn & ol brn   2.25   .80

9th World Soccer Championships for the Jules Rimet Cup, Mexico City, May 30-June 21, 1970.

Rotary Emblem, Map of Mali and Ceremonial Antelope Heads — AP44

1970, Sept. 21   Photo.   Perf. 12½
C103 AP44 200fr multi   2.75   1.25

Issued to honor Rotary International.

Men Holding UN Emblem, and Doves — AP45

1970, Oct. 5   Engr.   Perf. 13
C104 AP45 100fr dk pur, red brn & dk bl   1.25   .50

25th anniversary of the United Nations.

Koran Page, Baghdad, 11th Century AP46

Moslem Art: 200fr, Tree, and lion killing deer, mosaic, Jordan, c. 730, horiz. 250fr, Scribe, miniature, Baghdad, 1287.

1970, Oct. 26   Photo.   Perf. 12½x12
C105 AP46 50fr multi   .80   .30
C106 AP46 200fr multi   1.60   .65
C107 AP46 250fr multi   2.40   .95
    Nos. C105-C107 (3)   4.80   1.90

Nos. C97-C98 Surcharged and Overprinted

Overprint reads "LUNA 16 / PREMIERS PRELEVEMENTS AUTOMATIQUES / SUR LA LUNE / SEPTEMBRE 1970".

1970, Nov. 9   Engr.   Perf. 13
C108 AP41 150fr on 200fr multi   1.25   .65
C109 AP41 250fr on 300fr multi   2.25   .95

Unmanned moon probe of the Russian space ship Luna 16, Sept. 12-24.

Painting Type of 1968

100fr, Nativity, Antwerp School, c. 1530. 250fr, Adoration of the Shepherds, by Hans Memling. 300fr, Adoration of the Kings, Flemish School, 17th cent.

1970, Dec. 1   Photo.   Perf. 12½x12
C110 AP33 100fr brown & multi   1.00   .40
C111 AP33 250fr brown & multi   2.75   .95
C112 AP33 300fr brown & multi   3.50   1.25
    Nos. C110-C112 (3)   7.25   2.60

Christmas 1970.

Gamal Abdel Nasser — AP47

Embossed on Gold Foil
1970, Nov. 25   Perf. 12½
C113 AP47 1000fr gold   15.00   15.00

In memory of Gamal Abdel Nasser (1918-1970), President of Egypt.

Charles de Gaulle AP48

Embossed on Gold Foil
1971, Feb. 8   Die-cut Perf. 10
C114 AP48 2000fr gold, red & dp ultra   70.00   70.00

In memory of Gen. Charles de Gaulle (1890-1970), President of France.

Alfred Nobel — AP49

1971, Feb. 22   Engr.   Perf. 13
C115 AP49 300fr multi   3.50   1.00

Alfred Nobel (1833-1896), inventor of dynamite, sponsor of Nobel Prize.

Tennis, Davis Cup — AP50

Designs: 150fr, Derby at Epsom, horiz. 200fr, Racing yacht, America's Cup.

1971, Mar. 8
C116 AP50 100fr bl, lil & slate   1.75   .60
C117 AP50 150fr brn, brt grn & ol   2.75   .90
C118 AP50 200fr brt bl, ol & brn   3.50   1.25
    Nos. C116-C118 (3)   8.00   2.75

The Arabian Nights — AP51

Designs: 180fr, Ali Baba and the 40 Thieves. 200fr, Aladdin's Lamp.

1971, Apr. 5   Photo.   Perf. 13
C119 AP51 120fr gold & multi   1.75   .60
C120 AP51 180fr gold & multi   2.50   .90
C121 AP51 200fr gold & multi   3.00   1.00
    Nos. C119-C121 (3)   7.25   2.50

Olympic Rings and Sports — AP52

1971, June 28   Photo.   Perf. 12½
C122 AP52 80fr ultra, yel grn & brt mag   .90   .30

Pre-Olympic Year.

Mariner 4 — AP53

Design: 300fr, Venera 5 in space.

1971, Sept. 13   Engr.   Perf. 13
C123 AP53 200fr multi   1.75   .70
C124 AP53 250fr multi   2.75   .95

Space explorations of US Mariner 4 (200fr); and USSR Venera 5 (300fr).

Santa Maria, 1492 — AP54

Famous Ships: 150fr, Mayflower, 1620. 200fr, Potemkin, 1905. 250fr, Normandie, 1935.

1971, Sept. 27
C125 AP54 100fr brn, bluish grn & pur   1.25   .40
C126 AP54 150fr sl grn, brn & pur   2.00   .70
C127 AP54 200fr car, bl & dk ol   2.50   .80
C128 AP54 250fr blk, bl & red   3.25   1.00
    Nos. C125-C128 (4)   9.00   2.90

Symbols of Justice and Maps — AP55

1971, Oct. 18
C129 AP55 160fr mar, ocher & dk brn   1.40   .50

25th anniversary of the International Court of Justice in The Hague, Netherlands.

Statue of Zeus, by Phidias — AP56

The Seven Wonders of the Ancient World: 80fr, Cheops Pyramid and Sphinx. 100fr, Temple of Artemis, Ephesus, horiz. 130fr, Lighthouse at Alexandria. 150fr, Hanging Gardens of Babylon, horiz. 270fr, Mausoleum of Halicarnassus. 280fr, Colossus of Rhodes.

1971, Dec. 13

C130	AP56	70fr ind, dk red & pink	.70	.25
C131	AP56	80fr brn, bl & blk	.90	.25
C132	AP56	100fr org, ind & pur	1.00	.30
C133	AP56	130fr rose lil, blk & grnsh bl	1.25	.40
C134	AP56	150fr brn, brt grn & bl	1.50	.50
C135	AP56	270fr sl, brn & plum	2.50	.70
C136	AP56	280fr sl lil & ol	2.75	.80
		Nos. C130-C136 (7)	10.60	3.20

Nat "King" Cole — AP57

Famous American Black Musicians: 150fr, Erroll Garner. 270fr, Louis Armstrong.

1971, Dec. 6　Photo.　Perf. 13x12½

C137	AP57	130fr blk, brn & yel	2.40	.40
C138	AP57	150fr blk, bl & yel	2.75	.50
C139	AP57	270fr blk, rose car & yel	4.75	.70
		Nos. C137-C139 (3)	9.90	1.60

Slalom and Japanese Child AP58

200fr, Ice hockey & character from Noh play.

1972, Jan. 10　Engr.　Perf. 13

C140	AP58	150fr multicolored	1.25	.50
C141	AP58	200fr multicolored	1.75	.70
a.		Souv. sheet of 2, #C140-C141	3.50	3.50

11th Winter Olympic Games, Sapporo, Japan, Feb. 3-13.

Santa Maria della Salute, by Ippolito Caffi — AP59

Paintings of Venice, by Ippolito Caffi: 270fr, Rialto Bridge. 280fr, St. Mark's Square, vert.

1972, Feb. 21　Photo.　Perf. 13

C142	AP59	130fr gold & multi	1.25	.45
C143	AP59	270fr gold & multi	2.00	.70
C144	AP59	280fr gold & multi	2.10	.75
		Nos. C142-C144 (3)	5.35	1.90

UNESCO campaign to save Venice.

Hands of 4 Races Holding Scout Flag — AP60

1972, Mar. 27　Engr.　Perf. 13

C145	AP60	200fr dk red, ocher & ol gray	2.25	.60

World Boy Scout Seminar, Cotonou, Dahomey, March, 1972.

"Your Heart is your Health" — AP61

1972, Apr. 7　Engr.　Perf. 13

C146	AP61	150fr brt bl & red	1.75	.50

World Health Day.

Soccer Player and Frauenkirche, Munich — AP62

Designs (Sport and Munich Landmarks): 150fr, Judo and TV Tower, vert. 200fr, Steeplechase and Propylaeum, vert. 300fr, Runner and Church of the Theatines.

1972, Apr. 17

C147	AP62	50fr ocher, dk bl & grn	.45	.25
C148	AP62	150fr dk bl, ocher & grn	1.25	.45
C149	AP62	200fr grn, dk bl & ocher	1.60	.60
C150	AP62	300fr dk bl, grn & ocher	2.25	.75
a.		Min. sheet of 4, #C147-C150	5.75	5.75
		Nos. C147-C150 (4)	5.55	2.05

20th Olympic Games, Munich, 8/26-9/10. For overprints see Nos. C165-C166, C168.

Apollo 15, Lunar Rover, Landing Module — AP63

Design: 250fr, Cugnot's steam wagon and Montgolfier's Balloon.

1972, Apr. 27

C151	AP63	150fr multicolored	1.60	.80
C152	AP63	250fr multicolored	3.25	1.50

Development of transportation.

Cinderella AP64

Fairy Tales: 80fr, Puss in Boots. 150fr, Sleeping Beauty.

1972, June 19　Engr.　Perf. 13x12½

C153	AP64	70fr multicolored	1.10	.30
C154	AP64	80fr multicolored	1.25	.35
C155	AP64	150fr multicolored	2.00	.60
		Nos. C153-C155 (3)	4.35	1.25

Charles Perrault (1628-1703), French writer.

Astronauts and Lunar Rover on Moon — AP65

1972, July 24　Engr.　Perf. 13

C156	AP65	500fr multicolored	4.00	1.40

US Apollo 16 moon mission, Apr. 15-27.

Book Year Emblem — AP66

1972, Aug. 7　Litho.　Perf. 12½

C157	AP66	80fr bl, gold & grn	1.75	.60

International Book Year 1972.

Bamako Rotary Emblem with Crocodiles AP67

1972, Oct. 9　Engr.　Perf. 13

C158	AP67	170fr dk brn, red & ultra	1.75	.60

10th anniv. of the Bamako Rotary Club.

Hurdler, Olympic Rings, Melbourne Cathedral, Kangaroo — AP68

Designs (Olympic Rings and): 70fr, Boxing, Helsinki Railroad Station, arms of Finland, vert. 140fr, Running, Colosseum, Roman wolf. 150fr, Weight lifting, Tokyo stadium, phoenix, vert. 170fr, Swimming, University Library, Mexico City; Aztec sculpture. 210fr, Javelin, Munich Stadium, Arms of Munich. Stamps inscribed with name of gold medal winner of event shown.

1972, Nov. 13　Engr.　Perf. 13

C159	AP68	70fr red, ocher & ind	.40	.25
C160	AP68	90fr red brn, bl & sl	.50	.25
C161	AP68	140fr brn, brt grn & ol gray	.80	.30
C162	AP68	150fr dk car, emer & gray ol	.90	.35
C163	AP68	170fr red lil, brn & Prus bl	1.10	.40
C164	AP68	210fr ultra, emer & brick red	1.25	.50
		Nos. C159-C164 (6)	4.95	2.05

Retrospective of Olympic Games 1952-1972. For overprint see No. C167.

Nos. C148-C150, C164 Overprinted

a. JUDO / RUSKA / 2 MEDAILLES D'OR
b. STEEPLE / KEINO / MEDAILLE D'OR
c. MEDAILLE D'OR / 90m. 48
d. 100m.-200m. / BORZOV / 2 MEDAILLES D'OR

1972, Nov. 27　Engr.　Perf. 13

C165	AP62	150fr multi (a)	1.00	.40
C166	AP62	200fr multi (b)	1.40	.50
C167	AP68	210fr multi (c)	1.60	.55
C168	AP62	300fr multi (d)	2.00	.70
		Nos. C165-C168 (4)	6.00	2.15

Gold medal winners in 20th Olympic Games: Wim Ruska, Netherlands, heavyweight judo (No. C165); Kipchoge Keino, Kenya, 3000m. steeplechase (No. C166); Klaus Wolfermann, Germany, javelin (No. C167); Valery Borzov, USSR, 100m., 200m. race (No. C168).

Emperor Haile Selassie AP69

1972, Dec. 26　Photo.　Perf. 12½

C169	AP69	70fr grn & multi	.70	.25

80th birthday of Emperor Haile Selassie of Ethiopia.

Plane, Balloon, Route Timbuktu to Bamako — AP70

300fr, Balloon, jet & route Timbuktu to Bamako.

1972, Dec. 29　　　　　Perf. 13½

C170	AP70	200fr multi	1.25	.50
C171	AP70	300fr bl & multi	2.25	.80

First postal balloon flight in Mali.

Bishop of 14th Century European Chess Set — AP71

Design: 200fr, Knight (elephant), from 18th century Indian set.

1973, Feb. 19　Engr.　Perf. 13

C172	AP71	100fr dk car, bl & ind	1.75	.60
C173	AP71	200fr blk, red & brn	3.50	1.25

World Chess Championship, Reykjavik, Iceland, July-Sept., 1972.

Postal Union Emblem, Letter and Dove AP72

1973, Mar. 9　Photo.　Perf. 11½x11

C174	AP72	70fr bl, blk & org	.70	.25

10th anniv. (in 1971) of African Postal Union. This stamp was to be issued Dec. 8, 1971. It was offered by the agency on Mar. 9, 1973. Copies were sold in Mali as early as July or August, 1972.

No. C20,
Collector's Hand
and Philatelic
Background
AP73

1973, Mar. 12   **Engr.**   *Perf. 13*
C175 AP73 70fr multi   1.75   .50

Stamp Day, 1973.

Astronauts
and Lunar
Rover on
Moon
AP74

1973, Mar. 26
C176 AP74 250fr bl, indigo & bis   2.75 1.00
Souvenir Sheet
C177 AP74 350fr choc, vio bl &
   ultra   2.75 1.60

Apollo 17 US moon mission, 12/7-19/72.

Nicolaus Copernicus — AP75

1973, Apr. 9   **Engr.**   *Perf. 13*
C178 AP75 300fr brt bl & mag   3.50 1.25
500th anniversary of the birth of Nicolaus
Copernicus (1473-1543), Polish astronomer.

Dr. Armauer G. Hansen and Leprosy
Bacillus — AP76

1973, May 7   **Engr.**   *Perf. 13*
C179 AP76 200fr blk, yel grn &
   red   2.25   .85
Centenary of the discovery of the Hansen
bacillus, the cause of leprosy.

Bentley and Alfa Romeo,
1930 — AP77

Designs: 100fr, Jaguar and Talbot, 1953.
200fr, Matra and Porsche, 1972.

1973, May 21   **Engr.**   *Perf. 13*
C180 AP77 50fr bl, org & grn   .50   .25
C181 AP77 100fr grn, ultra & car   .90   .30
C182 AP77 200fr ind, grn & car   2.50   .60
   Nos. C180-C182 (3)   3.90 1.15
50th anniversary of the 24-hour automobile
race at Le Mans, France.

Camp Fire,
Fleur-de-Lis
AP78

Designs (Fleur-de-Lis and): 70fr, Scouts
saluting flag, vert. 80fr, Scouts with flags.
130fr, Lord Baden-Powell, vert. 270fr, Round
dance and map of Africa.

1973, June 4
C183 AP78 50fr dk red, ultra &
   choc   .35   .25
C184 AP78 70fr sl grn, dk brn &
   red   .55   .25
C185 AP78 80fr mag, sl grn &
   ol   .65   .25
C186 AP78 130fr brn, ultra & sl
   grn   1.00   .40
C187 AP78 270fr mag, gray & vio
   bl   2.00   .60
   Nos. C183-C187 (5)   4.55 1.75
Mali Boy and Girl Scouts and International
Scouts Congress.
For surcharges see Nos. C222-C223.

Swimming, US and "Africa"
Flags — AP79

80fr, Discus, javelin, vert. 330fr, Runners.

1973, July 30   **Engr.**   *Perf. 13*
C188 AP79 70fr red, sl grn & bl   .50   .25
C189 AP79 80fr vio bl, dk ol &
   red   .60   .25
C190 AP79 330fr red & vio bl   2.50   .80
   Nos. C188-C190 (3)   3.60 1.30
First African-United States sports meet.

Head and City
Hall, Brussels
AP80

1973, Sept. 17   **Engr.**   *Perf. 13*
C191 AP80 70fr brt ultra, ol & vio   .70   .25
Africa Weeks, Brussels, Sept. 15-30, 1973.

Perseus, by
Benvenuto
Cellini — AP81

Famous Sculptures: 150fr, Pietá, by Michelangelo. 250fr, Victory of Samothrace, Greek
1st century B.C.

1973, Sept. 24
C192 AP81 100fr dk car & sl grn   1.00   .30
C193 AP81 150fr dk car & dp cl   1.60   .50
C194 AP81 250fr dk car & dk ol   2.75   .80
   Nos. C192-C194 (3)   5.35 1.60

Stephenson's Rocket and Buddicom
Engine — AP82

Locomotives: 150fr, Union Pacific, 1890,
and Santa Fe, 1940. 200fr, Mistral and
Tokaido, 1970.

1973, Oct. 8   **Engr.**   *Perf. 13*
C195 AP82 100fr brn, bl & blk   1.10   .40
C196 AP82 150fr red, brt ultra &
   dk car   1.75   .70
C197 AP82 200fr ocher, bl & ind   2.50   .90
   Nos. C195-C197 (3)   5.35 2.00

Apollo XI
on Moon
AP83

75fr, Landing capsule, Apollo XIII. 100fr,
Astronauts & equipment on moon, Apollo XIV.
280fr, Rover, landing module % astronauts on
moon, Apollo XV. 300fr, Lift-off from moon,
Apollo XVII.

1973, Oct. 25
C198 AP83 50fr vio, org & sl
   grn   .35   .25
C199 AP83 75fr slate, red & bl   .55   .25
C200 AP83 100fr slate, bl & ol
   brn   .70   .30
C201 AP83 280fr vio bl, red & sl
   grn   1.75   .55
C202 AP83 300fr slate, red & sl
   grn   2.00   .80
   Nos. C198-C202 (5)   5.35 2.15
Apollo US moon missions.
For surcharges see Nos. C224-C225.

Pablo
Picasso — AP84

1973, Nov. 7   **Litho.**   *Perf. 12½*
C203 AP84 500fr multi   5.50 2.00
Pablo Picasso (1881-1973), painter.

John F.
Kennedy — AP85

1973, Nov. 12
C204 AP85 500fr gold, brt rose lil
   & blk   4.25 1.75

Painting Type of 1968

100fr, Annunciation, by Vittore Carpaccio,
horiz. 200fr, Virgin of St. Simon, by Federico

Barocci. 250fr, Flight into Egypt, by Andrea
Solario.

Perf. 13x12½, 12½x12, 12½x13

1973, Nov. 30   **Litho.**
C205 AP33 100fr blk & multi   .80   .25
C206 AP33 200fr blk & multi   1.50   .60
C207 AP33 250fr blk & multi   2.00   .80
   Nos. C205-C207 (3)   4.30 1.65

Christmas 1973.

Soccer Player
and Ball — AP86

250fr, Goalkeeper & ball. 500fr,
Frauenkirche, Munich, Arms of Munich & soccer ball, horiz.

1973, Dec. 3   **Engr.**   *Perf. 13*
C208 AP86 150fr emer, ol brn &
   red   1.25   .50
C209 AP86 250fr emer, vio bl &
   ol brn   2.25   .70
Souvenir Sheet
C210 AP86 500fr bl & multi   4.00 4.00
World Soccer Cup, Munich.

Musicians, Mosaic from
Pompeii — AP87

Designs (Mosaics from Pompeii): 250fr,
Alexander the Great in battle, vert. 350fr,
Bacchants, vert.

1974, Jan. 21   **Engr.**   *Perf. 13*
C211 AP87 150fr sl bl, ol & rose   1.50   .30
C212 AP87 250fr mag, ol &
   ocher   2.00   .50
C213 AP87 350fr ol, dp brn &
   ocher   2.50   .70
   Nos. C211-C213 (3)   6.00 1.50

Winston
Churchill — AP88

1974, Mar. 18   **Engr.**   *Perf. 13*
C214 AP88 500fr black   3.75 1.25

Chess Game — AP89

1974, Mar. 25   **Engr.**   *Perf. 13*
C215 AP89 250fr multi   5.25 1.75
21st Chess Olympic Games, Nice 1974.

Painting Type of 1968

Paintings: 400fr, Crucifixion, Alsatian School, c. 1380, vert. 500fr, Burial of Christ, by Titian.

Perf. 12½x13, 13x12½

1974, Apr. 12　　　　Photo.
C216 AP33 400fr multi　　　2.40　.90
C217 AP33 500fr multi　　　3.25 1.25

Easter 1974.

Lenin — AP90

1974, Apr. 22　Engr.　Perf. 13
C218 AP90 150fr vio bl & lake　2.40　.60

50th anniversary of the death of Lenin.

Women's Steeplechase — AP91

1974, May 20　Engr.　Perf. 13
C219 AP91 130fr bl, lil & brn　2.25　.60

World Horsewomen's Championship, La Baule, France, June 30-July 7.

Skylab Docking in Space — AP92

250fr, Skylab over globe with Africa.

1974, July 1　Engr.　Perf. 13
C220 AP92 200fr bl, sl & org　1.40　.50
C221 AP92 250fr lil, sl & org　2.40　.70

Skylab's flight over Africa, 1974.

Nos. C184-C185 Surcharged in Violet Blue

(a)

(b)

1974, July 8　Engr.　Perf. 13
C222 AP78 130fr on 70fr (a)　1.50　.50
C223 AP78 170fr on 80fr (b)　1.90　.60

11th Pan-Arab Jamboree and Pan-Arab Congress, Batrun, Lebanon, Aug. 1974.

Nos. C200-C201 Surcharged in Red

(c)

(d)

1974, July 15
C224 AP83 130fr on 100fr (c)　1.00　.40
C225 AP83 300fr on 280fr (d)　3.00 1.25

First manned moon landing, July 20, 1969, and first step on moon, July 21, 1969.

1906 and 1939 Locomotives — AP93

Locomotives: 120fr, Baldwin, 1870, and Pacific, 1920. 210fr, Al., 1925, and Buddicom, 1847. 330fr, Hudson, 1938, and La Gironde, 1839.

1974, Oct. 7　Engr.　Perf. 13
C226 AP93　90fr dk car & multi　.90　.40
C227 AP93 120fr ocher & multi　1.30　.50
C228 AP93 210fr org & multi　2.00　.70
C229 AP93 330fr grn & multi　3.00 1.10
　Nos. C226-C229 (4)　　7.20 2.70

Skier, Winter Sports and Olympic Rings AP94

1974, Oct. 7
C230 AP94 300fr multi　　2.40　.80

Holy Family, by Hans Memling AP95

310fr, Virgin & Child, Bourgogne School. 400fr, Adoration of the Kings, by Martin Schongauer.

1974, Nov. 4　Photo.　Perf. 12½
C231 AP95 290fr multi　　1.75　.60
C232 AP95 310fr multi　　2.00　.70
C233 AP95 400fr multi　　2.75 1.10
　Nos. C231-C233 (3)　　6.50 2.40

Christmas 1974.
See Nos. C238-C240, C267-C269.

Raoul Follereau — AP96

1974, Nov. 18　Engr.　Perf. 13
C234 AP96 200fr brt bl　　2.40　.85

Raoul Follereau (1903-1977), apostle to the lepers and educator of the blind. See No. C468.

Europafrica Issue

Train, Jet, Cogwheel, Grain, Maps of Africa and Europe — AP97

1974, Dec. 27　Engr.　Perf. 13
C235 AP97 100fr brn, grn & indigo　　.80　.30
C236 AP97 110fr ocher, vio bl & pur　1.00　.40

Painting Type of 1974

Designs: 200fr, Christ at Emmaus, by Phillipe de Champaigne, horiz. 300fr, Christ at Emmaus, by Paolo Veronese, horiz. 500fr, Christ in Majesty, Limoges, 13th century.

Perf. 13x12½, 12½x13

1975, Mar. 24　　　　Litho.
C238 AP95 200fr multi　　1.30　.50
C239 AP95 300fr multi　　2.10　.70
C240 AP95 500fr multi　　3.75 1.25
　Nos. C238-C240 (3)　　7.15 2.45

Easter 1975.

"Voyage to the Center of the Earth" — AP99

Jules Verne's Stories: 170fr, "From Earth to Moon" and Verne's portrait. 190fr, "20,000 Leagues under the Sea." 220fr, "A Floating City."

1975, Apr. 7　Engr.　Perf. 13
C241 AP99 100fr multi　　.75　.25
C242 AP99 170fr multi　　1.40　.45
C243 AP99 190fr multi　　1.40　.50
C244 AP99 220fr multi　　1.75　.55
　Nos. C241-C244 (4)　　5.30 1.75

Dawn, by Michelangelo — AP100

Design: 500fr, Moses, by Michelangelo.

1975, Apr. 28　Photo.　Perf. 13
C245 AP100 400fr multi　　2.40　.90
C246 AP100 500fr multi　　3.25 1.25

Michelangelo Buonarroti (1475-1564), Italian sculptor, painter and architect.

Astronaut on Moon — AP101

Designs: 300fr, Constellations Virgo and Capricorn. 370fr, Statue of Liberty, Kremlin, Soyuz and Apollo spacecraft.

1975, May 19　Engr.　Perf. 13
C247 AP101 290fr multi　　1.25　.60
C248 AP101 300fr multi　　1.25　.60
C249 AP101 370fr multi　　2.25　.90
　Nos. C247-C249 (3)　　4.75 2.10

Soviet-American space cooperation.
For overprints see Nos. C264-C266.

Boy Scout, Globe, Nordjamb 75 Emblem AP103

150fr, Boy Scout giving Scout sign. 290fr, Scouts around campfire.

1975, June 23　Engr.　Perf. 13
C251 AP103 100fr claret, brn & bl　.65　.25
C252 AP103 150fr red, brn & grn　1.00　.30
C253 AP103 290fr bl, grn & claret　1.90　.65
　Nos. C251-C253 (3)　　3.55 1.20

Nordjamb 75, 14th Boy Scout Jamboree, Lillehammer, Norway, July 29-Aug. 7.

Battle Scene and Marquis de Lafayette — AP104

300fr, Battle scene & George Washington. 370fr, Battle of Chesapeake Bay & Count de Grasse.

1975, July 7　Engr.　Perf. 13
C254 AP104 290fr lt bl & indigo　1.75　.60
C255 AP104 300fr lt bl & indigo　1.75　.60
C256 AP104 370fr lt bl & indigo　2.25　.90
　a.　Strip of 3, #C254-C256　6.50 3.50

Bicentenary of the American Revolution. No. C256a has continuous design.

Schweitzer, Bach and Score AP105

Designs: No. C257, Albert Einstein (1879-1955), theoretical physicist. No. No. C258, André-Marie Ampère (1775-1836), French physicist. 100fr, Clément Ader (1841-1925), French aviation pioneer. No. C260, Dr. Albert Schweitzer (1875-1965), Medical missionary and musician. No. C261, Sir Alexander Fleming (1881-1955), British bacteriologist, discoverer of penicillin.

1975		**Engr.**	**Perf. 13**	
C257	AP105	90fr multi	1.00	.40
C258	AP105	90fr pur, org & bister	1.00	.40
C259	AP105	100fr bl, red & lilac	1.00	.40
C260	AP105	150fr grn, bl & dk grn	1.40	.60
C261	AP105	150fr lil, bl & brick red	1.10	.45
		Nos. C257-C261 (5)	5.50	2.25

Issued: No. C257, 5/26; No. C258, 9/23; 100fr, 12/8; No. C260, 1/14; No. C261, 7/21. For surcharge see No. C358.

Olympic Rings and Globe — AP106

400fr, Montreal Olympic Games' emblem.

1975, Oct.				
C262	AP106	350fr pur & bl	2.00	.75
C263	AP106	400fr blue	2.50	.85

Pre-Olympic Year 1975.

**Nos. C247-C249 Overprinted:
"ARRIMAGE / 17 Juil. 1975"**

1975, Oct. 20		**Engr.**	**Perf. 13**	
C264	AP101	290fr multi	1.80	.60
C265	AP101	300fr multi	1.90	.65
C266	AP101	370fr multi	2.75	1.00
		Nos. C264-C266 (3)	6.45	2.25

Apollo-Soyuz link-up in space, July 17, 1975.

Painting Type of 1974

Designs: 290fr, Visitation, by Ghirlandaio. 300fr, Nativity, Fra Filippo Lippi school. 370fr, Adoration of the Kings, by Velazquez.

1975, Nov. 24		**Litho.**	**Perf. 12½x13**	
C267	AP95	290fr multi	1.90	.60
C268	AP95	300fr multi	2.00	.70
C269	AP95	370fr multi	3.00	1.10
		Nos. C267-C269 (3)	6.90	2.40

Christmas 1975.

Concorde — AP107

1976, Jan. 12		**Litho.**	**Perf. 13**	
C270	AP107	500fr multi	5.25	1.50

Concorde supersonic jet, first commercial flight, Jan. 21, 1976. For overprint see No. C315.

AP108

1976, Feb. 16		**Litho.**	**Perf. 13**	
C271	AP108	120fr Figure skating	.60	.25
C272	AP108	420fr Ski jump	2.00	.70
C273	AP108	430fr Slalom	2.00	.70
		Nos. C271-C273 (3)	4.60	1.65

12th Winter Olympic Games, Innsbruck, Austria, Feb. 4-15.

AP109

Eye examination, WHO emblem.

1976, Apr. 5		**Litho.**	**Perf. 12½**	
C274	AP109	130fr multi	1.00	.25

World Health Day: "Foresight prevents blindness."

Space Ship with Solar Batteries — AP110

Design: 300fr, Astronaut working on orbital space station, vert.

1976, May 10		**Engr.**	**Perf. 13**	
C275	AP110	300fr org, dk & lt bl	1.75	.60
C276	AP110	400fr mag, dk bl & org	2.75	.90

Futuristic space achievements.

American Eagle, Flag and Liberty Bell — AP111

Designs: 400fr, Revolutionary War naval battle and American eagle. 440fr, Indians on horseback and American eagle, vert.

1976, May 24		**Litho.**	**Perf. 12½**	
C277	AP111	100fr multi	.70	.25
C278	AP111	400fr multi	3.00	.75
C279	AP111	440fr multi	3.00	.80
		Nos. C277-C279 (3)	6.70	1.80

American Bicentennial. Nos. C278-C279 also for Interphil 76, International Philatelic Exhibition, Philadelphia, Pa, May 29-June 6.

Running
AP112

Designs (Olympic Rings and): 250fr, Swimming. 300fr, Field ball. 440fr, Soccer.

1976, June 7		**Engr.**	**Perf. 13**	
C280	AP112	200fr red brn & blk	.90	.30
C281	AP112	250fr multi	1.25	.40
C282	AP112	300fr multi	1.75	.50
C283	AP112	440fr multi	2.50	.75
		Nos. C280-C283 (4)	6.40	1.95

21st Olympic Games, Montreal, Canada, July 17-Aug. 1.

Cub Scout and Leader — AP113

Designs: 180fr, Scouts tending sick animal, horiz. 200fr, Night hike.

1976, June 14		**Engr.**	**Perf. 13**	
C284	AP113	140fr ultra & red brn	.90	.35
C285	AP113	180fr dk brn & multi	1.25	.45
C286	AP113	200fr brn org & vio bl	1.30	.50
		Nos. C284-C286 (3)	3.45	1.30

First African Boy Scout Jamboree, Nigeria.

Mohenjo-Daro, Bull from Wall Relief — AP114

Design: 500fr, Man's head, animals, wall and UNESCO emblem.

1976, Sept. 6		**Engr.**	**Perf. 13**	
C287	AP114	400fr blk, bl & pur	2.40	.60
C288	AP114	500fr dk red, bl & grn	3.25	1.10

UNESCO campaign to save Mohenjo-Daro excavations.

Europafrica Issue

Freighter, Plane, Map of Europe and Africa — AP115

1976, Sept. 20				
C289	AP115	200fr vio brn & bl	2.00	.70

Nativity, by Taddeo Gaddi — AP116

Paintings: 300fr, Adoration of the Kings, by Hans Memling. 320fr, Nativity, by Carlo Crivelli.

1976, Nov. 8		**Litho.**	**Perf. 13x12½**	
C290	AP116	280fr multi	1.60	.50
C291	AP116	300fr multi	1.80	.60
C292	AP116	320fr multi	2.00	.75
		Nos. C290-C292 (3)	5.40	1.85

Christmas 1976.

Viking Flying to Mars — AP117

1000fr, Viking landing craft on Mars.

1976, Dec. 8		**Engr.**	**Perf. 13**	
C293	AP117	500fr red, brn & bl	2.50	1.25
C294	AP117	1000fr multi	4.00	1.75
a.		Miniature sheet of 2	8.50	3.50

Operation Viking, US Mars mission, No. C294a contains 2 stamps similar to Nos. C293-C294 in changed colors.

Pres. Giscard d'Estaing, Village and Bambara Antelope — AP118

1977, Feb. 13		**Photo.**	**Perf. 13**	
C295	AP118	430fr multi	3.50	.90

Visit of Pres. Valéry Giscard d'Estaing of France, Feb. 13-15.

Elizabeth II and Prince Philip — AP119

Designs: 200fr, Charles de Gaulle, vert. 250fr, Queen Wilhelmina, vert. 300fr, King Baudouin and Queen Fabiola. 480fr, Coronation of Queen Elizabeth II, vert.

1977, Mar. 21		**Litho.**	**Perf. 12**	
C296	AP119	180fr multi	1.00	.45
C297	AP119	200fr multi	1.10	.45
C298	AP119	250fr multi	1.40	.55
C299	AP119	300fr multi	1.80	.65
C300	AP119	480fr multi	2.75	1.00
		Nos. C296-C300 (5)	8.05	3.10

Personalities involved in de-colonization.

Newton, Rocket and Apple — AP120

1977, May 7		**Engr.**	**Perf. 13**	
C301	AP120	400fr grn, brn & red	3.25	.90

Isaac Newton (1643-1727), natural philosopher and mathematician, 250th death anniversary.

Charles Lindbergh and Spirit of St. Louis — AP121

430fr, Spirit of St. Louis flying over clouds.

1977, Apr. 4   Litho.   Perf. 12
C302 AP121 420fr org & pur   2.25   .80
C303 AP121 430fr multi   2.25   .80
Charles A. Lindbergh's solo transatlantic flight from New York to Paris, 50th anniversary.

Sassenage Castle, Grenoble — AP122

1977, May 21   Litho.   Perf. 12½
C304 AP122 300fr multi   1.75   .60
Intl. French Language Council, 10th anniv.

Zeppelin No. 1, 1900 — AP123

Designs: 130fr, Graf Zeppelin, 1924. 350fr, Hindenburg aflame at Lakehurst, NJ, 1937. 500fr, Ferdinand von Zeppelin and Graf Zeppelin.

1977, May 30   Engr.   Perf. 13
C305 AP123 120fr multi   .60   .25
C306 AP123 130fr multi   .80   .25
C307 AP123 350fr multi   2.00   .65
C308 AP123 500fr multi   3.00   .75
   Nos. C305-C308 (4)   6.40 1.90
History of the Zeppelin.

Martin Luther King, American and Swedish Flags — AP124

Design: 600fr, Henri Dunant, Red Cross, Swiss and Swedish flags.

1977, July 4   Engr.   Perf. 13
C309 AP124 600fr multi   2.25   .70
C310 AP124 700fr multi   2.75   .75
Nobel Peace Prize recipients.

Soccer — AP125

Designs: 200fr, 3 soccer players, vert. 420fr, 3 soccer players.

1977, Oct. 3   Engr.   Perf. 13
C311 AP125 180fr multi   .70   .30
C312 AP125 200fr multi   .90   .35
C313 AP125 420fr multi   2.00   .75
   Nos. C311-C313 (3)   3.60 1.40
World Soccer Cup Elimination Games.

Mao Tse-tung and COMATEX Hall, Bamako — AP126

1977, Nov. 7   Engr.   Perf. 13
C314 AP126 300fr dull red   5.00   .90
Chairman Mao Tse-tung (1893-1976).

No. C270 Overprinted in Violet Blue:
"PARIS NEW-YORK 22.11.77"
1977, Nov. 22   Litho.   Perf. 13
C315 AP107 500fr multi   11.50 5.50
Concorde, first commerical transatlantic flight, Paris to New York.

Virgin and Child, by Rubens AP127

Rubens Paintings: 400fr, Adoration of the Kings. 600fr, Detail from Adoration of the Kings, horiz.

1977, Dec. 5   Perf. 12½x12, 12x12½
C316 AP127 400fr gold & multi   1.60   .60
C317 AP127 500fr gold & multi   2.00   .80
C318 AP127 600fr gold & multi   2.75 1.00
   Nos. C316-C318 (3)   6.35 2.40
Christmas 1977, and 400th birth anniversary of Peter Paul Rubens (1577-1640).

Battle of the Amazons, by Rubens — AP128

Rubens Paintings: 300fr, Return from the fields. 500fr, Hercules fighting the Nemean Lion, vert.

Perf. 12x12½, 12½x12
1978, Jan. 16   Litho.
C319 AP128 200fr multi   .90   .30
C320 AP128 300fr multi   1.50   .50
C321 AP128 500fr multi   2.50   .80
   Nos. C319-C321 (3)   4.90 1.60
Peter Paul Rubens, 400th birth anniversary.

Schubert Composing "Winterreise" — AP129

Design: 300fr, Schubert and score, vert.

1978, Feb. 13
C322 AP129 300fr multi   1.50   .50
C323 AP129 420fr multi   2.00   .70
Franz Schubert (1797-1828), Austrian composer.

Capt. Cook Receiving Hawaiian Delegation — AP130

Design: 300fr, Cook landing on Hawaii. Designs after sketches by John Weber.

1978, Feb. 27   Engr.   Perf. 13
C324 AP130 200fr multi   1.40   .40
C325 AP130 300fr multi   2.25   .55
Capt. James Cook (1728-1779), bicentenary of his arrival in Hawaii.

Soccer — AP131

250fr, One player. 300fr, Two players, horiz.

1978, Mar. 20
C326 AP131 150fr multi   1.00   .30
C327 AP131 250fr multi   1.60   .50
   a.   "REPUPLIQUE"   3.25   .90
C328 AP131 300fr multi   2.10   .60
   a. Min. sheet of 3, #C326-C328
           + label   6.00 4.00
   b. As "a," #C326, C327a, C328 9.00 6.00
   Nos. C326-C328 (3)   4.70 1.40
World Soccer Cup Championships, Argentina, 1978, June 1-25.
Nos. C327 and C328a were issued in July to correct the spelling error.
For overprints see Nos. C338-C340.

Jesus with Crown of Thorns, by Dürer AP132

430fr, Resurrection, by Albrecht Dürer.

1978, Mar. 28
C329 AP132 420fr multi   2.50   .60
C330 AP132 430fr multi   2.75   .60
Easter 1978. See Nos. C359-C361.

Citroen, C3-Trefle, 1922 — AP133

Citroen Cars: 130fr, Croisiere Noire, 1924, tractor. 180fr, B14G, 1927. 200fr, "11" Tractor Avant, 1934.

1978, Apr. 24   Engr.   Perf. 13
C331 AP133 120fr multi   1.00   .25
C332 AP133 130fr multi   1.10   .25
C333 AP133 180fr multi   1.50   .40
C334 AP133 200fr multi   1.60   .45
   Nos. C331-C334 (4)   5.20 1.35
Andre Citroen (1878-1935), automobile designer and manufacturer.

UPU Emblem, World Map, Country Names — AP133a

Design: 130fr, UPU emblem, globe and names of member countries.

1978, May 15
C334A AP133a 120fr multi   .70   .25
C335 AP133a 130fr red, grn &
               emer   1.00   .25
Centenary of Congress of Paris where General Postal Union became the Universal Postal Union.

Europafrica Issue

Zebra, Miniature by Mansur, Jehangir School, 1620 — AP134

Design: 100fr, Ostrich Incubating Eggs, Syrian Manuscript, 14th Century.

1978, July 24   Litho.   Perf. 13x12½
C336 AP134 100fr multi   2.40   .60
C337 AP134 110fr multi   2.40   .60

Nos. C326-C328a Overprinted in Black

(a)

(c)

b. 2e HOLLANDE

1978, Aug. 7   Engr.   Perf. 13
C338 AP131 150fr multi (a)   1.10   .35
C339 AP131 250fr multi (b)   1.40   .50
C340 AP131 300fr multi (c)   2.00   .60
  a.   Souvenir sheet of 3   6.00 2.50
  Nos. C338-C340 (3)   4.50 1.45
Winners, World Soccer Cup Championship, Argentina. Overprints on No. C340a are green including label overprint: FINALE / ARGENTINA 3 HOLLANDE 1.

Elizabeth II in Coronation Robes AP135

Design: 500fr, Coronation coach.

1978, Sept. 18   Litho.   Perf. 12½x12
C341 AP135 500fr multi   2.10   .65
C342 AP135 1000fr multi   4.50 1.50
Coronation of Queen Elizabeth II, 25th anniv.

US No. C3a and Douglas DC-3 AP136

History of Aviation: 100fr, Belgium No. 252 and Stampe SV-4. 120fr, France No. C48 and Ader's plane No. 3. 130fr, Germany No. C2 and Junker Ju-52. 320fr, Japan No. C25 and Mitsubishi A-6M "Zero."

1978, Oct. 16   Engr.   Perf. 13
C343 AP136 80fr multi   .45   .25
C344 AP136 100fr multi   .55   .25
C345 AP136 120fr multi   .65   .25
C346 AP136 130fr multi   .70   .25
C347 AP136 320fr multi   1.75   .55
  Nos. C343-C347 (5)   4.10 1.55

Annunciation, by Dürer — AP137

Etchings by Dürer: 430fr, Virgin and Child. 500fr, Adoration of the Kings.

1978, Nov. 6
C348 AP137 420fr blk & rose car   1.60   .50
C349 AP137 430fr ol grn & brn   1.75   .60
C350 AP137 500fr blk & red   2.40   .70
  Nos. C348-C350 (3)   5.75 1.80
Christmas 1978 and 450th death anniversary of Albrecht Dürer (1471-1528), German painter.

Rocket and Trajectory Around Moon — AP138

Design: 300fr, Spaceship circling moon.

1978, Nov. 20   Engr.   Perf. 13
C351 AP138 200fr multi   1.50   .60
C352 AP138 300fr multi   2.25   .70
  a.   Pair, #C351-C352 + label   4.75 2.00
10th anniversary of 1st flight around moon.

Ader's Plane and Concorde — AP139

Designs: 130fr, Wright Flyer A and Concorde. 200fr, Spirit of St. Louis and Concorde.

1979, Jan. 25   Litho.   Perf. 13
C353 AP139 120fr multi   .80   .25
C354 AP139 130fr multi   1.00   .30
C355 AP139 200fr multi   1.75   .55
  Nos. C353-C355 (3)   3.55 1.10
1st supersonic commercial flight, 3rd anniv. For surcharges see Nos. C529-C531.

Philexafrique II-Essen Issue
Common Design Types

Designs: No. C356, Dromedary and Mali No. C26. No. C357, Bird and Lubeck No. 1.

1979, Jan. 29   Litho.   Perf. 13x12½
C356 CD138 200fr multi   3.00 1.00
C357 CD139 200fr multi   3.00 1.00
  a.   Pair, #C356-C357 + label   7.50 3.00

No. C257 Surcharged

1979, Mar. 26   Engr.   Perf. 13
C358 AP105 130fr on 90fr multi   1.50   .50
Albert Einstein (1879-1955).

Easter Type of 1978

Dürer Etchings: 400fr, Jesus Carrying Cross. 430fr, Crucified Christ. 480fr, Pietà.

1979, Apr. 9
C359 AP132 400fr bl & blk   2.10   .70
C360 AP132 430fr red & blk   2.25   .75
C361 AP132 480fr ultra & blk   2.40   .85
  Nos. C359-C361 (3)   6.75 2.30
Easter 1979.

Basketball and Cathedral, Moscow AP140

430fr, Soccer and St. Basil's Cathedral.

1979, Apr. 17   Litho.   Perf. 13
C362 AP140 420fr multi   2.25   .80
C363 AP140 430fr multi   2.25   .80
Pre-Olympic Year.

Mali #C92, Apollo Spacecraft AP141

Design: 500fr, Mali No. C176, lift-off.

1979, Oct. 22   Litho.   Perf. 12½x13
C364 AP141 430fr multi   2.00   .70
C365 AP141 500fr multi   2.10   .80
Apollo 11 moon landing, 10th anniversary.

Capt. Cook, Ship, Kerguelen Island — AP142

Design: 480fr, Capt. Cook, Ship, Hawaii.

1979, Oct. 29   Perf. 13x12½
C366 AP142 300fr multi   1.75   .60
C367 AP142 480fr multi   2.40   .85
Capt. James Cook (1728-1779).

David Janowski (1868-1927), Chess Pieces — AP143

Chess Pieces and Grand Masters: 140fr, Alexander Alekhine (1892-1946). 200fr, W. Schlage. 300fr, Effim D. Bogoljubow (1889-1952).

1979, Nov. 30   Engr.   Perf. 13
C368 AP143 100fr red & brn   .90   .25
C369 AP143 140fr multi   1.30   .25
C370 AP143 200fr multi   1.75   .40
C371 AP143 300fr multi   2.50   .55
  Nos. C368-C371 (4)   6.45 1.45
For overprints see Nos. C441-C442.

Adoration of the Kings, by Dürer AP144

Christmas 1979: 400fr, 500fr, Adoration of the Kings by Dürer, diff.

1979, Dec. 10   Perf. 13x13½
C372 AP144 300fr brn org & brn   1.60   .50
C373 AP144 400fr bl & brn   2.25   .70
C374 AP144 500fr dk grn & brn   2.75   .90
  Nos. C372-C374 (3)   6.60 2.10

Jet, Map of Africa AP145

1979, Dec. 27   Litho.   Perf. 12½
C375 AP145 120fr multi   .90   .30
ASECNA (Air Safety Board), 20th anniv.

Train, Globe, Rotary Emblem AP146

Rotary Intl., 75th Anniv.: 250fr, Jet. 430fr, Bamako Club emblem, meeting hall.

1980, Jan. 28   Litho.   Perf. 12½
C376 AP146 220fr multi   1.10   .40
C377 AP146 250fr multi   1.10   .40
C378 AP146 430fr multi   2.00   .70
  Nos. C376-C378 (3)   4.20 1.50

Speed Skating, Lake Placid '80 Emblem, Snowflake AP147

1980, Feb. 11   Perf. 13
C379 AP147 200fr shown   .90   .25
C380 AP147 300fr Ski jump   1.25   .50
  a.   Souvenir sheet of 2   3.00 2.00
13th Winter Olympic Games, Lake Placid, NY, Feb. 12-24. No. C380a contains Nos. C379-C380 in changed colors.

Stephenson's Rocket, Mali No. 196 — AP148

Liverpool-Manchester Railroad, 150th Anniversary: 300fr, Stephenson's Rocket, Mali No. 142.

1980, Feb. 25   Engr.
C381 AP148 200fr multi   1.10   .25
C382 AP148 300fr multi   1.75   .50

Equestrian, Moscow '80 Emblem — AP149

POSTAGE DUE STAMPS

Bambara
Headpiece — D1

Perf. 14x13½

1961, Mar. 18   Engr.   Unwmk.

J1	D1	1fr black	.25	.25
J2	D1	2fr bright ultra	.25	.25
J3	D1	5fr red lilac	.30	.25
J4	D1	10fr orange	.50	.25
J5	D1	20fr bright green	.75	.25
J6	D1	25fr red brown	.95	.25
		Nos. J1-J6 (6)	3.00	1.55

Polyptychus Roseus — D2

No. J8, Deilephila Nerii. No. J9, Gynanisa maja. No. J10, Bunaea alcinoe. No. J11, Teracolus eris. No. J12, Colotis antevippe. No. J13, Charaxes epijasius. No. J14, Manatha microcera. No. J15, Hypokopelates otraeda. No. J16, Lipaphnaeus leonina. No. J17, Gonimbrasia hecate. No. J18, Lobounaea christyi. No. J19, Hypolimnas misippus. No. J20, Catopsilia florella.

1964, June 1   Photo.   Perf. 11
Butterflies and Moths in Natural Colors

J7		1fr olive green	.30	.25
J8		1fr org & brn	.30	.25
a.		D2 Pair, #J7-J8	.60	
J9		2fr emer & brn	.40	.25
J10		2fr emer & brn	.40	.25
a.		D2 Pair, #J9-J10	.80	
J11		3fr rose lil & brn	.40	.25
J12		3fr rose lil & brn	.40	.25
a.		D2 Pair, #J11-J12	.80	
J13		5fr blk & rose	.40	.25
J14		5fr green	.40	.25
a.		D2 Pair, #J13-J14	.80	
J15		10fr yel, org & blk	.85	.35
J16		10fr blue	.85	.35
a.		D2 Pair, #J15-J16	1.75	.70
J17		20fr lt bl & brn	1.60	.70
J18		20fr lt bl & brn	1.60	.70
a.		D2 Pair, #J17-J18	3.25	1.40
J19		25fr grn & yel	2.25	1.00
J20		25fr dp grn & blk	2.25	1.00
a.		D2 Pair, #J19-J20	4.50	2.00
		Nos. J7-J20 (14)	12.40	6.10

Nos. J7-J20 Surcharged

1984   Photo.   Perf. 11

J21		5fr on 1fr #J7	.30	.25
J22		5fr on 1fr #J8	.30	.25
a.		D2 Pair, #J21-J22	.60	
J23		10fr on 2fr #J9	.30	.25
J24		10fr on 2fr #J10	.30	.25
a.		D2 Pair, #J23-J24	.60	
J25		15fr on 3fr #J11	.30	.25
J26		15fr on 3fr #J12	.30	.25
a.		D2 Pair, #J25-J26	.60	
J27		25fr on 5fr #J13	.40	.25
J28		25fr on 5fr #J14	.40	.25
a.		D2 Pair, #J27-J28	.80	
J29		50fr on 10fr #J15	.70	.30
J30		50fr on 10fr #J16	.70	.30
a.		D2 Pair, #J29-J30	1.40	.60
J31		100fr on 20fr #J17	1.60	.70
J32		100fr on 20fr #J18	1.60	.70
a.		D2 Pair, #J31-J32	3.25	1.40
J33		125fr on 25fr #J19	2.00	.85
J34		125fr on 25fr #J20	2.00	.85
a.		D2 Pair, #J33-J34	4.00	1.75
		Nos. J21-J34 (14)	11.20	5.70

OFFICIAL STAMPS

Dogon
Mask — O1

Mali Coat of
Arms — O2

Perf. 14x13½

1961, Mar. 18   Engr.   Unwmk.

O1	O1	1fr gray	.30	.25
O2	O1	2fr red orange	.30	.25
O3	O1	3fr black	.30	.25
O4	O1	5fr light blue	.30	.25
O5	O1	10fr bister brown	.35	.25
O6	O1	25fr brt ultra	.75	.25
O7	O1	30fr car rose	.90	.25
O8	O1	50fr Prus green	1.00	.25
O9	O1	85fr red brown	1.50	.65
O10	O1	100fr emerald	1.50	.65
O11	O1	200fr red lilac	3.75	1.25
		Nos. O1-O11 (11)	10.95	4.55

1964, June 1   Photo.   Perf. 12½
National Colors and Arms in Multicolor, Background in Light Green

O12	O2	1fr green	.30	.25
O13	O2	2fr light vio	.30	.25
O14	O2	3fr gray	.30	.25
O15	O2	5fr lilac rose	.30	.25
O16	O2	10fr bright blue	.30	.25
O17	O2	25fr ocher	.35	.25
O18	O2	30fr dark green	.50	.25
O19	O2	50fr orange	.75	.25
O20	O2	85fr dark brown	.80	.60
O21	O2	100fr red	1.00	.60
O22	O2	200fr dk vio bl	1.80	.75
		Nos. O12-O22 (11)	6.70	3.95

City Coats of
Arms — O3

1981, Sept.   Photo.   Perf. 12½x13

O23	O3	5fr Gao	.30	.25
O24	O3	15fr Timbuktu	.35	.25
O25	O3	50fr Mopti	.45	.25
O26	O3	180fr Segou	1.00	.25
O27	O3	200fr Sikasso	1.25	.35
O28	O3	680fr Koulikoro	3.25	.90
O29	O3	700fr Kayes	3.75	1.10
O30	O3	1000fr Bamako	5.00	1.40
		Nos. O23-O30 (8)	15.35	4.75

Nos. O23-O30 Surcharged

1984   Photo.   Perf. 12½x13

O31	O3	15fr on 5fr	.30	.25
O32	O3	50fr on 15fr	.55	.25
O33	O3	120fr on 50fr	.95	.25
O34	O3	295fr on 180fr	2.50	.60
O35	O3	470fr on 200fr	3.50	.85
O36	O3	515fr on 680fr	3.75	1.00
O37	O3	845fr on 700fr	6.00	1.75
O38	O3	1225fr on 1000fr	10.00	2.25
		Nos. O31-O38 (8)	27.55	7.20

MALTA

ˈmol-tə

LOCATION — A group of islands in the Mediterranean Sea off the coast of Sicily
GOVT. — Republic within the British Commonwealth
AREA — 122 sq. mi.
POP. — 376,513 (1998)
CAPITAL — Valletta

The former colony includes the islands of Malta, Gozo, and Comino. It became a republic Dec. 13, 1974.

4 Farthings = 1 Penny
12 Pence = 1 Shilling
20 Shillings = 1 Pound
10 Mils = 1 Cent (1972)
100 Cents = 1 Pound (1972)
100 Cents = 1 Euro (2008)

> **Catalogue values for unused stamps in this country are for Never Hinged items, beginning with Scott 206 in the regular postage section, Scott B1 in the semipostal section, Scott C2 in the air post section, and Scott J21 in the postage due section.**

Watermark

Wmk. 354 — Maltese Cross, Multiple

Values for unused stamps are for examples with original gum as defined in the catalogue introduction. Very fine examples of Nos. 1-7 will have perforations touching the frameline on one or more sides due to the narrow spacing of the stamps on the plate. Stamps with perfs clear of the frameline are scarce and will command higher prices.

Queen Victoria
A1   A2

A3   A4

1860-61   Unwmk.   Typo.   Perf. 14

1	A1	½p buff ('63)	850.00	400.00
2	A1	½p buff, *bluish*	1,300.	650.00
a.		Imperf. (single)	12,000.	

1863-80   Wmk. 1

3	A1	½p yellow buff ('75)	85.00	65.00
a.		½p buff	120.00	75.00
b.		½p brown orange ('67)	425.00	110.00
c.		½p orange yellow ('80)	250.00	110.00
4	A1	½p golden yel (aniline) ('74)	350.00	400.00

1865   Perf. 12½

5	A1	½p buff	160.00	110.00
a.		½p yellow buff	375.00	190.00

1878   Perf. 14x12½

6	A1	½p buff	200.00	100.00
a.		Perf. 12½x14	—	

No. 6a unused is believed to be unique. It has a small fault.

1882   Wmk. 2   Perf. 14

7	A1	½p reddish orange ('84)	21.00	57.50

1885, Jan. 1

8	A1	½p green	4.50	.60
9	A2	1p car rose	11.00	.40
a.		1p rose	100.00	30.00
10	A3	2p gray	8.50	2.25
11	A4	2½p ultramarine	50.00	1.25
a.		2½p bright ultramarine	50.00	1.25
b.		2½p dull blue	65.00	3.00

12	A3	4p brown	13.00	3.50
a.		Imperf., pair	6,000.	6,000.
13	A3	1sh violet	60.00	22.50
		Nos. 8-13 (6)	147.00	30.50

For surcharge see No. 20.

Queen Victoria within Maltese Cross — A5

1886   Wmk. 1

14	A5	5sh rose	125.00	95.00

Gozo Fishing
Boat — A6   Ancient
Galley — A7

1899, Feb. 4   Engr.   Wmk. 2

15	A6	4½p black brown	24.00	16.00
16	A7	5p brown red	47.50	19.00

See Nos. 42-45.

"Malta" — A8   St. Paul after
Shipwreck — A9

1899   Wmk. 1

17	A8	2sh6p olive gray	47.50	15.00
18	A9	10sh blue black	105.00	75.00

See No. 64. For overprint see No. 85.

Valletta
Harbor — A10

1901, Jan. 1   Wmk. 2

19	A10	1f red brown	1.75	.55

See Nos. 28-29.

No. 11 Surcharged in
Black   **One Penny**

1902, July 4

20	A4	1p on 2½p dull blue	1.50	2.00
a.		"Pnney"	32.50	65.00
b.		Double surcharge	17,500.	4,500.

King Edward VII — A12

1903-04   Typo.

21	A12	½p dark green	10.00	1.00
22	A12	1p car & black	17.50	.50
23	A12	2p gray & red vio	32.50	7.00
24	A12	2½p ultra & brn vio	32.50	5.25
25	A12	3p red vio & gray	2.00	.60
26	A12	4p brown & blk ('04)	30.00	19.00
27	A12	1sh violet & gray	27.50	8.25
		Nos. 21-27 (7)	152.00	41.60

1904-11 — **Wmk. 3**

28	A10	1f red brown ('05)	9.00	2.25
29	A10	1f dk brown ('10)	7.00	.25
30	A12	½p green	6.00	.35
31	A12	1p car & blk ('05)	22.50	.25
32	A12	1p carmine ('07)	3.50	.25
33	A12	2p gray & red vio ('05)	13.00	3.00
34	A12	2p gray ('11)	4.75	6.50
35	A12	2½p ultra & brn vio	32.50	.70
36	A12	2½p ultra ('11)	6.50	4.25
37	A12	4p brn & blk ('06)	13.00	7.50
38	A12	4p scar & blk, yel ('11)	4.75	4.50
39	A12	1sh violet & gray	57.50	2.40
40	A12	1sh blk, grn ('11)	8.75	4.25
41	A12	5sh scar & grn, yel ('11)	75.00	87.50

Engr.

42	A6	4½p black brn ('05)	40.00	7.00
43	A6	4½p orange ('11)	5.25	4.00
44	A7	5p red ('04)	37.50	7.00
45	A7	5p ol green ('10)	5.00	4.00
		Nos. 28-45 (18)	351.50	145.95

A13

A15

1914-21 — **Ordinary Paper** — **Typo.**

49	A13	¼p brown	1.25	.25
50	A13	½p green	2.50	.35
51	A13	1p scarlet ('15)	1.75	.45
a.		1p carmine ('14)	1.75	.25
52	A13	2p gray ('15)	12.00	6.00
53	A13	2½p ultramarine	2.50	.60

Chalky Paper

54	A15	3p vio, yel	3.00	17.50
58	A15	6p dull vio & red vio	13.00	21.00
59	A15	1sh black, green	14.00	22.00
a.		1sh black, bl grn, ol back	22.50	27.50
b.		1sh black, emerald ('21)	37.50	85.00
c.		As "b," olive back	10.00	32.50
60	A16	2sh ultra & dl vio, bl	57.50	37.50
61	A16	5sh scar & grn, yel	105.00	115.00

Surface-colored Paper

62	A13	1sh blk, grn ('15)	16.00	37.50
		Nos. 49-54,58-62 (11)	228.50	258.15

See Nos. 66-68, 70-72. For overprints see Nos. 77-82, 84.

Valletta Harbor — A17

1915 — **Ordinary Paper** — **Engr.**

63	A17	4p black	17.50	7.00

St. Paul A18

George V A19

1919

64	A8	2sh6p olive green	75.00	95.00
65	A18	10sh black	3,500.	4,400.
		Revenue cancel		85.00

For overprint see No. 83.

1921-22 — **Typo.** — **Wmk. 4**
Ordinary Paper

66	A13	¼p brown	6.00	35.00
67	A13	½p green	6.00	32.50
68	A13	1p rose red	6.00	2.50
69	A19	2p gray	8.00	2.00

70	A13	2½p ultramarine	7.00	40.00

Chalky Paper

71	A13	6p dull vio & red vio	35.00	85.00
72	A16	2sh ultra & dull vio, bl	70.00	225.00

Engr.

73	A18	10sh black	400.00	800.00
		Nos. 66-73 (8)	538.00	1,222.

For overprints and surcharge see Nos. 86-93, 97.

Stamps of 1914-19 Overprinted in Red or Black

1922 — **Ordinary Paper** — **Wmk. 3**
Overprint 21mm

77	A13	½p green	1.25	3.00
78	A13	2½p ultra	15.00	45.00

Chalky Paper

79	A15	3p violet, yel	4.50	27.50
80	A13	6p dull lil & red vio	4.50	24.00
81	A15	1sh black, emer	4.75	24.00

Overprint 28mm

82	A16	2sh ultra & dull vio, bl (R)	250.00	525.00

Ordinary Paper

83	A8	2sh6p olive grn	32.50	55.00

Chalky Paper

84	A16	5sh scar & grn, yel	57.50	100.00
		Nos. 77-84 (8)	370.00	803.50

Wmk. 1
Ordinary Paper

85	A9	10sh blue black (R)	225.00	400.00

Same Overprint on Stamps of 1921

1922 — **Ordinary Paper** — **Wmk. 4**
Overprint 21mm

86	A13	¼p brown	.35	.75
87	A13	½p green	4.00	9.50
88	A13	1p rose red	1.10	.25
89	A19	2p gray	4.25	.50
90	A13	2½p ultramarine	1.25	1.75

Chalky Paper

91	A13	6p dull vio & red vio	21.00	50.00

Overprint 28mm

92	A16	2sh ultra & dull vio, bl (R)	50.00	100.00

Ordinary Paper

93	A18	10sh black (R)	160.00	250.00
		Nos. 86-93 (8)	241.95	412.75

No. 69 Surcharged

1922, Apr. 15

97	A19	1f on 2p gray	.85	.50

"Malta" — A20

Britannia and Malta — A21

1922-26 — **Chalky Paper** — **Typo.**

98	A20	¼p brown	3.00	.70
99	A20	½p green	3.00	.25
100	A20	1p buff & plum	4.50	.25
101	A20	1p violet ('24)	4.25	.90
102	A20	1½p org brn ('23)	5.50	.25
103	A20	2p ol brn & turq	3.25	1.40
104	A20	2½p ultra ('26)	4.50	13.00
105	A20	3p ultramarine	5.00	2.00
a.		3p blue	6.00	3.00
106	A20	3p blk, yel ('26)	4.25	20.00
107	A20	4p yel & ultra	3.00	4.25
108	A20	6p ol grn & vio	4.50	3.75

109	A21	1sh ol brn & blue	10.00	3.50
110	A21	2sh ol brn & ol brn	14.00	18.00
111	A21	2sh6p blk & red vio	12.50	16.00
112	A21	5sh ultra & org	24.00	47.50
113	A21	10sh ol brn & gray	65.00	175.00

Engr.
Ordinary Paper

114	A20	£1 car red & blk ('25)	125.00	500.00
a.		£1 rose car & blk ('22)	150.00	350.00
		Nos. 98-114 (17)	295.25	806.75

No. 114a has watermark sideways. For overprints and surcharges see Nos. 115-129.

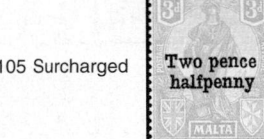

No. 105 Surcharged

1925, Dec.

115	A20	2½p on 3p ultramarine	2.00	4.50

Stamps of 1922-26 Overprinted

1926

116	A20	¼p brown	.80	5.50
117	A20	½p green	.80	.25
118	A20	1p violet	1.10	.25
119	A20	1½p orange brown	1.25	.70
120	A20	2p ol brn & turq	.85	2.00
121	A20	2½p ultramarine	1.40	1.00
122	A20	3p black, yel	.85	.90
a.		Inverted overprint	200.00	550.00
123	A20	4p yel & ultra	17.00	28.00
124	A20	6p ol grn & vio	3.25	5.50
125	A21	1sh ol brn & bl	6.25	6.00
126	A21	2sh ultra & ol brown	100.00	100.00
127	A21	2sh6p blk & red vio	18.50	47.50
128	A21	5sh ultra & org	11.00	47.50
129	A21	10sh ol brn & gray	8.50	21.00
		Nos. 116-129 (14)	131.55	338.10

George V — A22

Valletta Harbor — A23

St. Publius — A24

Notabile (Mdina) — A25

Gozo Fishing Boat — A26

Statue of Neptune — A27

Ruins at Mnaidra — A28

St. Paul — A29

1926-27 — **Typo.** — **Perf. 14½x14**

131	A22	¼p brown	.90	.25
132	A22	½p green	.70	.25
133	A22	1p red	3.50	1.10
134	A22	1½p orange brn	2.25	.25
135	A22	2p gray	5.25	15.00
136	A22	2½p blue	4.50	1.50
137	A22	3p dark violet	5.00	4.00
138	A22	4p org red & blk	3.75	16.00
139	A22	4½p yel buff & vio	4.00	4.50
140	A22	6p red & violet	5.00	6.00

Engr. — **Perf. 12½**
Inscribed: "Postage"

141	A23	1sh black	7.50	8.50
142	A24	1sh6p green & blk	7.50	18.00
143	A25	2sh dp vio & blk	7.50	23.00
144	A26	2sh6p ver & black	19.00	55.00
145	A27	3sh blue & blk	20.00	35.00
146	A28	5sh green & blk	25.00	70.00
147	A29	10sh car & blk	65.00	110.00
		Nos. 131-147 (17)	186.35	368.35

See Nos. 167-183. For overprints see Nos. 148-166.

Stamps and Type of
1926-27 Overprinted in
Black

1928   *Perf. 14½x14*

148	A22	¼p brown	1.75	.25
149	A22	½p green	1.75	.25
150	A22	1p red	2.00	3.75
151	A22	1p orange brown	5.25	.25
152	A22	1½p yel brown	2.25	1.00
153	A22	1½p red	5.00	.25
154	A22	2p gray	5.00	10.50
155	A22	2½p blue	2.25	.25
156	A22	3p dark violet	2.25	1.00
157	A22	4p org red & blk	2.25	2.00
158	A22	4½p yel & violet	2.50	1.10
159	A22	6p red & violet	2.50	1.75

Overprinted in
Red

Perf. 12½

160	A23	1sh black	6.25	3.00
161	A24	1sh6p green & blk	11.00	11.00
162	A25	2sh dp vio & blk	27.50	70.00
163	A26	2sh6p ver & black	20.00	26.00
164	A27	3sh ultra & blk	22.50	35.00
165	A28	5sh yel grn & blk	37.50	75.00
166	A29	10sh car rose & black	70.00	100.00
		Nos. 148-166 (19)	229.50	342.35

Issued: Nos. 151, 153, Dec. 5; others, Oct. 1.

Types of 1926-27 Issue
Inscribed: "Postage & Revenue"

1930, Oct. 20   **Typo.**   *Perf. 14½x14*

167	A22	¼p brown	.70	.25
168	A22	½p green	.70	.25
169	A22	1p yel brown	.70	.25
170	A22	1½p red	.80	.25
171	A22	2p gray	1.40	.60
172	A22	2½p blue	2.25	.25
173	A22	3p dark violet	1.75	.25
174	A22	4p org red & blk	1.40	5.00
175	A22	4½p yel & violet	3.75	1.40
176	A22	6p red & violet	3.25	1.40

Engr.   *Perf. 12½*

177	A23	1sh black	11.00	19.00
178	A24	1sh6p green & blk	9.75	25.00
179	A25	2sh dp vio & blk	12.00	27.00
180	A26	2sh6p ver & black	20.00	60.00
181	A27	3sh ultra & blk	40.00	62.50
182	A28	5sh yel grn & blk	47.50	75.00
183	A29	10sh car rose & blk	100.00	180.00
		Nos. 167-183 (17)	256.95	458.40

Common Design Types
pictured following the introduction.

Silver Jubilee Issue
Common Design Type

1935, May 6   *Perf. 11x12*

184	CD301	½p green & blk	.50	.70
185	CD301	2½p ultra & brn	2.50	4.50
186	CD301	6p ol grn & lt bl	7.00	7.00
187	CD301	1sh brn vio & ind	15.00	22.50
		Nos. 184-187 (4)	25.00	34.70
		Set, never hinged	45.00	

Coronation Issue
Common Design Type

1937, May 12   **Wmk. 4**   *Perf. 13½x14*

188	CD302	½p deep green	.25	.25
189	CD302	1½p carmine	.55	.60
190	CD302	2½p bright ultra	.55	.80
		Nos. 188-190 (3)	1.35	1.65
		Set, never hinged	2.25	

Valletta
Harbor — A30

Fort St.
Angelo — A31

Verdala
Palace — A32

Neolithic
Ruins — A33

Victoria and
Citadel,
Gozo — A34

De l'Isle Adam
Entering
Mdina — A35

St. John's Co-
Cathedral
A36

Mnaidra
Temple — A37

Statue of Antonio
Manoel de
Vilhena — A38

Woman in
Faldetta — A39

St.
Publius — A40

Mdina
Cathedral
A41

Statue of
Neptune — A42

Palace
Square — A43

St. Paul — A44

1938-43   **Wmk. 4**   *Perf. 12½*

191	A30	1f brown	.25	.25
192	A31	½p green	1.75	.30
192A	A31	½p chnt ('43)	.55	.30
193	A32	1p chestnut	3.50	.40
193A	A32	1p grn ('43)	.30	.25
194	A33	1½p rose red	1.00	2.00
194A	A33	1½p dk gray ('43)	.25	.25
195	A34	2p dark gray	1.10	.30
195A	A34	2p rose red ('43)	.40	.25
196	A35	2½p blue	2.00	.60
196A	A35	2½p violet ('43)	.35	.35
197	A36	3p violet	1.25	.80
197A	A36	3p blue ('43)	.40	.25
198	A37	4½p ocher & ol green	.30	.30
199	A38	6p rose red & ol green	1.10	.30
200	A39	1sh black	.90	.55
201	A40	1sh6p sage grn & black	5.00	4.00
202	A41	2sh dk bl & lt grn	2.50	6.00
203	A42	2sh6p rose red & black	5.00	5.50
204	A43	5sh bl grn & blk	4.75	8.00
205	A44	10sh dp rose & blk	15.00	16.00
		Nos. 191-205 (21)	47.65	46.95
		Set, never hinged	75.00	

See No. 236a. For overprints see Nos. 208-222.

> Catalogue values for unused
> stamps in this section, from this
> point to the end of the section, are
> for Never Hinged items.

Peace Issue
Common Design Type
Inscribed: "Malta" and Crosses

Perf. 13½x14

1946, Dec. 3   **Engr.**   **Wmk. 4**

206	CD303	1p bright green	.25	.25
207	CD303	3p dark ultra	.40	1.75

Stamps of 1938-43 Overprinted in Black or Carmine

a

1948, Nov. 25   *Perf. 12½*

208	A30	1f brown	.35	.25
209	A31	½p chestnut	.35	.25
210	A32	1p green	.35	.25
211	A33	1½p dk gray (C)	1.40	.25
212	A34	2p rose red	1.40	.30
213	A35	2½p violet (C)	.90	.25
214	A36	3p blue (C)	3.00	.25
215	A37	4½p ocher & ol grn	2.75	1.75

216	A38	6p rose red & ol green	3.50	.45
217	A39	1sh black	3.75	.70
218	A40	1sh6p sage grn & blk	2.75	1.25
219	A41	2sh dk bl & lt grn	5.75	2.75
220	A42	2sh6p rose red & blk	14.00	2.75
221	A43	5sh bl grn & blk (C)	26.00	5.00
222	A44	10sh dp rose & blk	26.00	25.00
		Nos. 208-222 (15)	92.25	41.50

The overprint is smaller on No. 208. It reads from lower left to upper right on Nos. 209 and 221.

See Nos. 235-240.

Silver Wedding Issue
Common Design Types
Inscribed: "Malta" and Crosses

1949, Jan. 4   **Photo.**   *Perf. 14x14½*

223	CD304	1p dark green	.55	.25

Perf. 11½x11

Engr.

224	CD305	£1 dark blue	40.00	45.00

UPU Issue
Common Design Types
Inscribed: "Malta" and Crosses

Perf. 13½, 11x11½

1949, Oct. 10   **Engr.**   **Wmk. 4**

225	CD306	2½p violet	.30	.25
226	CD307	3p indigo	3.00	1.25
227	CD308	6p dp carmine	.60	1.10
228	CD309	1sh slate	.60	2.75
		Nos. 225-228 (4)	4.50	5.35

Princess
Elizabeth — A45

Madonna and
Child — A46

1950, Dec. 1   **Engr.**   *Perf. 12x11½*

229	A45	1p emerald	.25	.25
230	A45	3p bright blue	.25	.25
231	A45	1sh gray black	1.10	2.00
		Nos. 229-231 (3)	1.60	2.50

Visit of Princess Elizabeth.

1951, July 12

232	A46	1p green	.25	.25
233	A46	3p purple	.55	.25
234	A46	1sh slate black	1.60	1.40
		Nos. 232-234 (3)	2.40	1.90

700th anniv. of the presentation of the scapular to St. Simon Stock.

Types of 1938-43 Overprinted Type "a" in Red or Black

1953, Jan. 8   **Wmk. 4**   *Perf. 12½*

235	A32	1p gray (R)	1.00	.25
236	A33	1½p green	.60	.25
a.		Overprint omitted		18,000.
237	A34	2p ocher	.60	.25
238	A35	2½p rose red	1.10	2.25
239	A36	3p violet (R)	1.10	.25
240	A37	4½p ultra & ol grn (R)	1.10	1.25
		Nos. 235-240 (6)	5.50	4.50

Coronation Issue
Common Design Type
Inscribed: "Malta" and Crosses

1953, June 3   **Engr.**   *Perf. 13½x13*

241	CD312	1½p dk green black	.55	.25

Type of 1938-43 with Portrait of Queen Elizabeth II Inscribed: "Royal Visit 1954."

1954, May 3   *Perf. 12½*

242	A36	3p violet	.35	.25

Visit of Elizabeth II and the Duke of Edinburgh, 1954.

Central Altarpiece,
Collegiate Parish
Church,
Cospicua — A47

Perf. 14½x13½

1954, Sept. 8   Photo.   Wmk. 4

243	A47	1½p bright green	.25	.25
244	A47	3p ultramarine	.25	.25
245	A47	1sh gray black	.30	.25
		Nos. 243-245 (3)	.80	.75

Cent. of the promulgation of the Dogma of the Immaculate Conception.

Monument of the Great Siege, 1565 — A48

Auberge de Castille — A49

Designs: ½p, Wignacourt Aqueduct Horse-trough. 1p, Victory Church. 1½p, War Memorial. 2p, Mosta Dome. 3p, King's Scroll. 4½p, Roosevelt's Scroll. 6p, Neolithic Temples at Tarxien. 8p, Vedette. 1sh, Mdina Gate. 1sh6p, Les Gavroches. 2sh, Monument of Christ the King. 2sh6p, Monument of Nicolas Cottoner. 5sh, Raymond Perellos Monument. 10sh, St. Paul. £1, Baptism of Christ.

1956-57   Engr.   Perf. 11½

246	A48	¼p violet	.25	.25
247	A48	½p yel orange	.45	.25
248	A48	1p black	.45	.25
249	A48	1½p brt green	.30	.25
250	A49	2p brown	1.40	.25
251	A49	2½p orange brown	1.40	.35
252	A48	3p rose red	1.40	.25
253	A48	4½p blue	2.25	.25
254	A49	6p slate blue	.65	.25
255	A48	8p olive bister	3.25	1.10
256	A48	1sh purple	.90	.30
257	A48	1sh6p Prus green	11.00	.40
258	A48	2sh olive green	11.00	2.75

Perf. 13½x13

259	A48	2sh6p cop brown	8.50	2.50
260	A48	5sh emerald	13.50	3.25
261	A48	10sh dk carmine	34.00	14.00
262	A48	£1 yel brn ('57)	34.00	29.00
		Nos. 246-262 (17)	124.70	55.65

See Nos. 296-297.

First George Cross Issue

Symbol of Malta's War Effort — A50

Searchlights over Malta — A51

Design: 1sh, Bombed houses.

Perf. 14x14½, 14½x14

1957, Apr. 15   Photo.

Cross in Silver

263	A50	1½p green	.25	.25
264	A51	3p bright red	.25	.25
265	A50	1sh dark red brown	.25	.25
		Nos. 263-265 (3)	.75	.75

Award of the George Cross to Malta for its war effort.
See Nos. 269-274.

Symbols of Architecture — A52

Designs: 3p, Symbols of Industry, vert. 1sh, Symbols of electronics and chemistry and Technical School, Paola.

Perf. 14½x14, 14x14½

1958, Feb. 15   Wmk. 314

266	A52	1½p dp green & blk	.25	.25
267	A52	3p rose red, blk & gray	.25	.25
268	A52	1sh gray, blk & lilac	.25	.25
		Nos. 266-268 (3)	.75	.75

Technical education on Malta.

Second George Cross Issue
Types of 1957

1½p, Bombed-out family & searchlights. 3p, Convoy entering harbor. 1sh, Searchlight battery.

1958, Apr. 15   Perf. 14½x14, 14x14½

Cross in Silver

269	A51	1½p black & brt green	.25	.25
270	A50	3p black & vermilion	.25	.25
271	A51	1sh black & brt lilac	.25	.25
		Nos. 269-271 (3)	.75	.75

Third George Cross Issue
Types of 1957

Designs: 1½p, Air Raid Precautions Organization helping wounded. 3p, Allegory of Malta. 1sh, Mother and child during air raid.

1959, Apr. 15   Perf. 14x14½, 14½x14

272	A50	1½p gold, green & black	.25	.25
273	A51	3p gold, lilac & black	.25	.25
274	A50	1sh gold, gray & black	.80	1.25
		Nos. 272-274 (3)	1.30	1.75

St. Paul's Shipwreck, Painting in St. Paul's Church, Valletta — A53

Statue of St. Paul, St. Paul's Grotto, Rabat — A54

Designs: 3p, Consecration of St. Publius. 6p, St. Paul leaving Malta; painting, St. Paul's Church, Valletta. 1sh, Angel holding tablet with quotations from Acts of the Apostles. 2sh6p, St. Paul and St. Paul's Bay islets.

Wmk. 314

1960, Feb. 9   Photo.   Perf. 13

275	A53	1½p bister, brt bl & gold	.25	.25
a.		Gold dates & crosses omitted	75.00	65.00
276	A53	3p lt blue, red lil & gold	.30	.25
277	A53	6p car, gray & gold	.40	.25

Perf. 14x14½

278	A54	8p black & gold	.50	.75
279	A54	1sh brt cl & gold	.50	.50
280	A54	2sh6p brt grnsh bl & gold	1.75	2.25
a.		Gold omitted	1,400.	550.00
		Nos. 275-280 (6)	3.70	4.25

19th centenary of St. Paul's shipwreck on Malta.

Stamp of 1860 — A55

Perf. 13x13½

1960, Dec. 1   Engr.   Wmk. 314

281	A55	1½p multi	.25	.25
282	A55	3p multi	.35	.25
283	A55	6p multi	.50	1.10
		Nos. 281-283 (3)	1.10	1.60

Centenary of Malta's first postage stamp.

Fourth George Cross Issue

George Cross A56

Background designs: 3p, Sun and water. 1sh, Maltese crosses.

1961, Apr. 15   Photo.   Perf. 14½x14

284	A56	1½p gray, bister & buff	.25	.25
285	A56	3p ol gray, lt & dk grnsh blue	.30	.25
286	A56	1sh ol green, vio & lil	.70	2.25
		Nos. 284-286 (3)	1.25	2.75

19th anniv. of the award of the George Cross to Malta.

Madonna Damascena — A57

Designs: 3p, Great Siege Monument by Antonio Sciortino and Grand Master La Valette (1557-1568). 1sh, Assault on Fort Elmo (old map).

Perf. 12½x12

1962, Sept. 7   Wmk. 314

287	A57	2p ultramarine	.25	.25
288	A57	3p dark red	.25	.25
289	A57	6p olive green	.25	.25
290	A57	1sh rose lake	.25	.45
		Nos. 287-290 (4)	1.00	1.20

Great Siege of 1565 in which the knights of the Order of St. John and the Maltese Christians defeated the Turks.

Freedom from Hunger Issue
Common Design Type

1963, June 4   Perf. 14x14½

291	CD314	1sh6p sepia	2.25 2.75

Red Cross Centenary Issue
Common Design Type

1963, Sept. 2   Litho.   Perf. 13

292	CD315	2p black & red	.25	.25
293	CD315	1sh6p ultra & red	3.00	4.75

Type of 1956

Designs as before.

1963-64   Engr.   Perf. 11½

296	A48	1p black	1.00	.50
297	A48	2p brown ('64)	2.10	3.50

David Bruce and Themistocles Zammit — A58

1sh6p, Goat and laboratory equipment.

Perf. 14x13½

1964, Apr. 14   Photo.   Wmk. 314

298	A58	2p dl grn, blk & brn	.25	.25
a.		Black omitted	425.00	
299	A58	1sh6p rose lake & blk	1.00	1.00

Anti-Brucellosis (Malta fever) Congress of the UN FAO, Valletta, June 8-13.

Nicola Cottoner Attending Sick Man and Congress Emblem — A59

6p, Statue of St. Luke & St. Luke's Hospital. 1sh6p, Sacra Infermeria, Valletta.

Perf. 13½x14

1964, Sept. 5   Wmk. 354

300	A59	2p multicolored	.25	.25
301	A59	6p multicolored	.55	.55
302	A59	1sh6p multicolored	1.25	2.10
		Nos. 300-302 (3)	2.05	2.90

1st European Cong. of Catholic Physicians, Malta, Sept. 6-10.

Independent State

Dove, Maltese Cross and British Crown — A60

Dove, Maltese Cross and: 3p, 1sh6p, Pope's tiara. 6p, 2sh6p, UN Emblem.

Perf. 14½x13½

1964, Sept. 21   Gold and   Photo.

303	A60	2p gray ol & red	.35	.25
304	A60	3p dk red brn & red	.40	.25
305	A60	6p sl blue & red	.90	.30
306	A60	1sh ultra & red	.90	.40
307	A60	1sh6p bl blk & red	2.50	1.50
308	A60	2sh6p vio bl & red	2.75	3.00
		Nos. 303-308 (6)	7.80	5.70

Malta's independence.

Nativity — A61

Perf. 13x13½

1964, Nov. 3   Wmk. 354

309	A61	2p magenta & gold	.25	.25
310	A61	4p ultra & gold	.25	.25
311	A61	8p dp green & gold	.75	.75
		Nos. 309-311 (3)	1.25	1.25

Cippus, Phoenician and Greek Inscriptions — A62

British Arms, Armory, Valletta A63

Designs (History of Malta): ½p, Neolithic (sculpture of sleeping woman). 1½p, Roman (sculpture). 2p, Proto-Christian (lamp, Roman

Perf. 14 (16x21mm), 2m, 3m, 2c;
Perf. 14½x14 (21x26mm), 5m, 1c, 5c
1972, May 16
439 A101 2m rose red & multi .25 .25
440 A101 3m pink & multi .25 .25
441 A101 5m lilac & multi .25 .25
442 A101 1c multicolored .25 .25
443 A101 2c orange & multi .25 .25
444 A101 5c multicolored .25 .25

Perf. 13½
Size: 27x35mm
445 A101 10c yellow & multi .25 .25
446 A101 50c multicolored 1.50 1.50
Nos. 439-446 (8) 3.25 3.25

Coins to mark introduction of decimal
currency.

**Nos. 319A, 321 and 323 Surcharged
with New Value and 2 Bars**
Perf. 14x14½, 14½
1972, Sept. 30 Photo. Wmk. 354
447 A62 1c3m on 5p multi .25 .25
448 A63 3c on 8p multi .25 .25
449 A63 5c on 1sh3p multi .25 .25
Nos. 447-449 (3) .75 .75

Europa Issue 1972

Sparkles, Symbolic of
Commun-
ications — CD15

1972, Nov. 11 Litho. *Perf. 13x13½*
450 CD15 1c3m yellow & multi .25 .25
451 CD15 3c multicolored .25 .25
452 CD15 5c pink & multi .25 .30
453 CD15 7c5m multicolored .30 .60
Nos. 450-453 (4) 1.05 1.40

Issued in sheets of 10 plus 2 labels (4x3).
Labels are in top row.

Archaeology — A103

1973, Mar. 31 Litho. *Perf. 13½*
Size: 22x24mm
454 A103 2m shown .25 .25
455 A103 4m History
(knights) .25 .25
456 A103 5m Folklore .25 .25
457 A103 8m Industry .25 .25
458 A103 1c Fishing .25 .25
459 A103 1c3m Pottery .25 .25
460 A103 2c Agriculture .25 .25
461 A103 3c Sport .25 .25
462 A103 4c Marina .25 .25
463 A103 5c Fiesta .25 .25
464 A103 7c5m Regatta .30 .30
465 A103 10c Charity (St.
Martin) .45 .25
466 A103 50c Education 2.25 1.00
467 A103 £1 Religion 4.50 3.00

Perf. 13½x14
Size: 32x27mm
468 A103 £2 Arms of Malta 8.75 12.50
Nos. 454-468 (15) 18.75 19.55

Europa Issue 1973
Common Design Type
1973, June 2 Unwmk. *Perf. 14*
Size: 36½x19½mm
469 CD16 3c multicolored .25 .25
470 CD16 5c multicolored .25 .25
471 CD16 7c5m dk bl & multi .40 .60
Nos. 469-471 (3) .90 1.20

Woman with Grain,
FAO Emblem — A104

7c5m, Mother and child, WHO emblem. 10c,
Two heads, Human Rights flame.

1973, Oct. 6 Wmk. 354 *Perf. 13½*
472 A104 1c3m yel grn, blk &
gold .25 .25
473 A104 7c5m ultra, blk & gold .25 .40
474 A104 10c claret, blk & gold .30 .50
Nos. 472-474 (3) .80 1.15

World Food Program, 10th anniv.; WHO,
25th anniv.; Universal Declaration of Human
Rights, 25th anniv.

Girolamo Cassar,
Architect — A105

3c, Giuseppe Barth, opthalmologist. 5c,
Nicolo' Isouard, composer. 7c5m, John Borg,
botanist. 10c, Antonio Sciortino, sculptor.

1974, Jan. 12 Litho. *Perf. 14*
475 A105 1c3m slate green &
gold .25 .25
476 A105 3c indigo & gold .25 .25
477 A105 5c olive gray & gold .25 .25
478 A105 7c5m slate blue & gold .25 .30
479 A105 10c brn vio & gold .25 .45
Nos. 475-479 (5) 1.25 1.50

Prominent Maltese.

Statue of
Goddess,
3rd
Millenium
B.C.
A106

Europa (CEPT Emblem and): 3c, Carved
door, Cathedral, Mdina, 11th cent, vert. 5c,
Silver monstrance, 1689. 7c5m, "Vettina"
(statue of nude woman), by Antonio Sciortino
(1879-1947), vert.

1974, July 13 *Perf. 13½x14, 14x13½*
480 A106 1c3m gray blue, blk &
gold .25 .25
481 A106 3c ol brn, blk & gold .25 .25
482 A106 5c lilac, blk & gold .25 .40
483 A106 7c5m dull grn, blk &
gold .40 .90
Nos. 480-483 (4) 1.15 1.80

Heinrich von
Stephan,
Coach and
Train, UPU
Emblem
A107

UPU Emblem, von Stephan and: 5c, Paddle
steamer and ocean liner. 7c5m, Balloon and
jet. 50c, UPU Congress Building, Lausanne,
and UPU Headquarters, Bern.

Wmk. 354
1974, Sept. Litho. *Perf. 13½*
484 A107 1c3m multicolored .25 .25
485 A107 5c multicolored .30 .30
486 A107 7c5m multicolored .40 .40
487 A107 50c multicolored 1.60 1.60
a. Souvenir sheet of 4, #484-487 5.75 7.00
Nos. 484-487 (4) 2.55 2.55

Centenary of Universal Postal Union.

President, Prime Minister, Minister of
Justice at Microphone — A108

1c3m, President, Prime Minister, Speaker at
Swearing-in ceremony. 5c, Flag of Malta.

1975, Mar. 31 *Perf. 14*
488 A108 1c3m red & multi .25 .25
489 A108 5c gray, red & black .25 .25
490 A108 25c red & multi .90 1.00
Nos. 488-490 (3) 1.40 1.50

Proclamation of the Republic, Dec. 13, 1974.

IWY
Emblem,
Mother and
Child
A109

Designs: 3c, 20c, Secretary (woman in public life), IWY emblem. 5c, Like 1c3m.

Wmk. 354
1975, May 30 Litho. *Perf. 13*
491 A109 1c3m violet & gold .25 .25
492 A109 3c blue gray & gold .25 .25
493 A109 5c olive & gold .25 .25
494 A109 20c red brown & gold 1.75 2.50
Nos. 491-494 (4) 2.50 3.25

International Women's Year.

Allegory of Malta, by Francesco de
Mura — A110

Europa: 15c, Judith and Holofernes, by
Valentin de Boulogne.

1975, July 15 Litho. *Perf. 14*
495 A110 5c multicolored .30 .30
496 A110 15c multicolored .80 .80

Floor Plan of Ggantija Complex, 3000
B.C. — A111

Designs: 3c, View of Mdina. 5c, Typical Maltese town. 25c, Fort St. Angelo.

1975, Sept. 16 *Perf. 14*
497 A111 1c3m black & org .25 .25
498 A111 3c org, pur & black .25 .25
499 A111 5c gray, black & org .45 .35
500 A111 25c org, tan & black 1.75 2.75
Nos. 497-500 (4) 2.70 3.60

European Architectural Heritage Year.

"Right to
Work" — A112

Designs: 5c, Protection of the Environment
(Landscape). 25c, Maltese flags.

1975, Dec. 12 Litho. Wmk. 354
501 A112 1c3m multicolored .25 .25
502 A112 5c multicolored .25 .25
503 A112 25c multicolored .85 1.00
Nos. 501-503 (3) 1.35 1.50

First anniversary of Malta Republic.

Republic Coat
of
Arms — A113

Perf. 13½x14
1976, Jan. 28 Litho. Wmk. 354
504 A113 £2 black & multi 11.00 15.00

Feast of Sts.
Peter and
Paul — A114

Designs: 1c3m, "Festa" (flags and fireworks), vert. 7c5m, Carnival. 10c, Good Friday
(Christ carrying cross), vert.

1976, Feb. 26 Litho. *Perf. 14*
505 A114 1c3m multicolored .25 .25
506 A114 5c multicolored .25 .25
507 A114 7c5m multicolored .35 .60
508 A114 10c multicolored .60 1.10
Nos. 505-508 (4) 1.45 2.20

Maltese folk festivals.

Water Polo,
Olympic
Rings
A115

Olympic Rings and: 5c, Yachting. 30c,
Running.

1976, Apr. 28 Litho. *Perf. 13½x14*
509 A115 1c7m sl green & red .25 .25
510 A115 5c dp blue & red .25 .25
511 A115 30c sepia & red 1.00 1.25
Nos. 509-511 (3) 1.50 1.75

21st Olympic Games, Montreal, Canada,
July 17-Aug. 1.

Europa
A116

1976, July 8 Litho. Wmk. 354
512 A116 7c Lace-making .35 .35
513 A116 15c Stone carving .70 .70

Grandmaster Nicola Cotoner,
Founder — A117

5c, Dissected arm & hand. 7c, Dr. Fra Giuseppe Zammit, 1st professor. 11c, School &
balustrade.

1976, Sept. 14 Litho. *Perf. 13½*
514 A117 2c multicolored .25 .25
515 A117 5c multicolored .25 .25
516 A117 7c multicolored .25 .25
517 A117 11c multicolored .40 .65
Nos. 514-517 (4) 1.15 1.40

School of Anatomy and Surgery, Valletta,
300th anniversary.

Armor of Grand Master
Jean de La
Valette — A118

Suits of Armor: 7c, Grand Master Aloph de
Wignacourt. 11c, Grand Commander Jean
Jacques de Verdelin.

1977, Jan. 20 Litho. Wmk. 354
518 A118 2c green & multi .25 .25
519 A118 7c brown & multi .30 .25
520 A118 11c ultra & multi .35 .40
Nos. 518-520 (3) .90 .90

**No. 318 Surcharged with New Value
and Bar**
1977, Mar. 24 Photo. *Perf. 14x14½*
521 A62 1c7m on 4p multi .40 .25

European Music
Year — A158

Europa: 8c, Nicolo
1971), tenor. 30c, France
1809), composer.

1985, Apr. 25 Li
660 A158 8c multicolored
661 A158 30c multicolo

7c, Karmnu Abela, We
Uprising Memorial Monu

1985, June 7 Perf.
662 A159 3c multicolor
663 A159 7c multicolor
664 A159 35c multicolor
Nos. 662-664 (3

June 7 Uprising,

UN, 40th
Anniv.
A160

1985, July 26
665 A160 4c Stylized b
666 A160 11c Arrows
667 A160 31c Human fi
Nos. 665-667 (3

Portraits: 8c, George M
politician and author, nov
Cause of the People of M
liament. 12c, Pietru Ca
scholar, manuscript.

1985, Oct. 3
668 A161 8c multicolor
669 A161 12c multicolor

Ships Type

1985, Nov. 27
670 A145 3c Scotia pa
steamer,
671 A145 7c Tagliaferro
672 A145 15c Gleneagle
673 A145 23c L'Isle Ada
Nos. 670-673 (4)

Intl.
Peace
Year
A162

Annunciation, Tapestry after
Rubens — A119

Crucifixion — A120

Tapestries after Designs by Rubens: 7c, The
Four Evangelists. 11c, Nativity. 20c, Adoration
of the Kings.
Flemish tapestries commissioned for St.
John's Co-Cathedral, Valletta.

Wmk. 354
1977, Mar. 30 Litho. **Perf. 14**
522 A119 2c multicolored .25 .25
523 A119 7c multicolored .40 .25
524 A120 11c multicolored .55 .45
525 A120 20c multicolored .90 1.00

1978, Jan. 26
Flemish Tapestries: 2c, Jesus' Entry into
Jerusalem, by unknown painter. 7c, Last Supper, by Nicholas Poussin. 11c, Crucifixion, by
Rubens. 25c, Resurrection, by Rubens.
526 A120 2c multicolored .25 .25
527 A120 7c multicolored .40 .25
528 A120 11c multicolored .50 .35
529 A120 25c multicolored 1.10 1.10

1979, Jan. 24
Tapestries after Designs by Rubens (Triumph of): 2c, Catholic Church. 7c, Charity
11c, Faith. 25c, Truth.
530 A119 2c multicolored .25 .25
531 A119 7c multicolored .30 .25
532 A119 11c multicolored .50 .40
533 A119 25c multicolored 1.10 .95
Nos. 522-533 (12) 6.50 5.75

Consecration of St. John's Co-Cathedral,
Valetta, 400th anniv. (Nos. 522-533). Peter
Paul Rubens (1577-1640; Nos. 522-525).
See Nos. 567-569.

Malta Map,
Telecommunication — A121

Designs: 1c, 6c, Map of Italy, Sicily, Malta
and North Africa, telecommunication tower
and waves, vert. 17c, like 8c.

Perf. 14x13½, 13½x14
1977, May 17 Litho. **Wmk. 354**
535 A121 1c green, red & blk .25 .25
536 A121 6c multicolored .25 .25
537 A121 8c multicolored .30 .30
538 A121 17c purple, red & blk .70 .70
Nos. 535-538 (4) 1.50 1.50

World Telecommunication Day.

View of Ta' L-Isperanza — A122

Europa: 20c, Harbor, Is-Salini.

1977, July Litho. **Perf. 13½**
539 A122 7c multicolored .30 .25
540 A122 20c multicolored .60 .90

Issued in sheets of 10.

Help Given
Handicapped
Worker — A123

7c, Stonemason & shipbuilder. 20c, Mother
holding dead son, & Service to the Republic
order, horiz. Sculptures from Workers'
Monument.

1977, Oct. 12 Litho. **Wmk. 354**
541 A123 2c red brown & brn .25 .25
542 A123 7c brown & dk brn .25 .25
543 A123 20c multicolored .65 .65
Nos. 541-543 (3) 1.15 1.15

Tribute to Maltese workers.

Lady on
Horseback and
Soldier, by
Dürer — A124

Dürer Engravings: 8c, Bagpiper. 17c,
Madonna with Long-tailed Monkey.

1978, Mar. 7 **Perf. 14**
544 A124 1c7m dk blue, blk &
red .25 .25
545 A124 8c gray, blk & red .35 .35
546 A124 17c dk grn, blk & red .85 .85
Nos. 544-546 (3) 1.45 1.45

Albrecht Dürer (1471-1528), German
painter and engraver.

Grand Master Nicola
Cotoner
Monument — A125

Europa: 25c, Grand Master Ramon Perellos
monument, by Giusepe Mazzuoli. The monument on 7c is believed to be the work of Giovanni Batista Foggini.

1978, Apr. 26 **Perf. 14x13½**
547 A125 7c multicolored .25 .25
548 A125 25c multicolored 1.00 1.00

Goalkeeper — A126

Argentina '78 Emblem and: 11c, 15c, different soccer scenes.

Perf. 14x13½
1978, June 6 Litho. **Wmk. 354**
549 A126 2c multicolored .25 .25
550 A126 11c multicolored .40 .40
551 A126 15c multicolored .55 .55
a. Souvenir sheet of 3, #549-551 2.40 3.00
Nos. 549-551 (3) 1.20 1.20

11th World Cup Soccer Championship,
Argentina, June 1-25.

Fishing
Boat — A127

Maltese
Speronara and
AirMalta
Fuselage — A128

Designs: 5c, 17c Changing of colors. 7c,
20c, British soldier and oranges. 8c, like 2c.

1979, Mar. 31 **Perf. 14**
552 A127 2c claret & multi .25 .25
553 A127 5c claret & multi .25 .25
554 A127 7c claret & multi .25 .25
555 A127 8c dk blue & multi .30 .30
556 A127 17c dk blue & multi .60 .60
557 A127 20c dk blue & multi .70 .70
Nos. 552-557 (6) 2.35 2.35

End of military agreement between Malta
and Great Britain.

1979, May 9
Europa: 25c, Coastal watch tower and radio
link tower.
558 A128 7c multicolored .25 .25
559 A128 25c multicolored .90 .90

Children and
Globe — A129

Designs: 7c, Children flying kites. 11c, Children in a circle holding hands.

1979, June 13 **Perf. 14x13½, 14**
Size: 20x38mm
560 A129 2c multicolored .25 .25
Size: 27x33mm
561 A129 7c multicolored .25 .25
562 A129 11c multicolored .35 .35
Nos. 560-562 (3) .85 .85

International Year of the Child.

Loggerhead
Turtle — A130

Marine Life: 2c, Gibbula nivosa. 7c,
Dolphinfish. 25c, Noble pen shell.

1979, Oct. 10 Litho. **Perf. 13½**
563 A130 2c multicolored .25 .25
564 A130 5c multicolored .30 .30
565 A130 7c multicolored .40 .40
566 A130 25c multicolored 1.40 1.40
Nos. 563-566 (4) 2.35 2.35

Tapestry Types of 1977-79
Tapestries after Designs by Rubens: 2c, The
Institution of Corpus Domini. 8c, The Destruc-
tion of Idolatry. 50c, Portrait of Grand Master
Perellos, vert.

1980, Jan. 30 **Wmk. 354** **Perf. 14**
567 A127 2c multicolored .25 .25
568 A120 8c multicolored .45 .45
Souvenir Sheet
569 A119 50c multicolored 2.00 2.00

Victoria
Citadel,
Gozo
A131

Monument Restoration (UNESCO Emblem
and): 2c5m, Hal Saflieni Catacombs, Paola,
2500 B.C., vert. 6c, Vilhena Palace, Mdina,
18th century, vert. 12c, St. Elmo Fort, Valletta,
16th century.

1980, Feb. 15
570 A131 2c5m multicolored .25 .25
571 A131 6c multicolored .25 .25
572 A131 8c multicolored .30 .30
573 A131 12c multicolored .45 .45
Nos. 570-573 (4) 1.25 1.25

Don Gorg Preca (1880-
1962), Founder of Soc.
of Christian
Doctrine — A132

1980, Apr. 12 Litho. **Perf. 14x13½**
574 A132 2c5m gray violet .30 .30

Ruzar Briffa (1906-1963), Poet, by
Vincent Apap — A133

Europa (Vincent Apap Sculpture): 30c,
Mikiel Anton Vassalli (1764-1829), freedom
fighter and scholar.

1980, Apr. 29 **Perf. 13½x14**
575 A133 8c slate green & dp
bis .25 .25
576 A133 30c brown red & olive .90 1.10

Chess
Pieces
A134

Designs: Chess pieces. 30c, vert.

1980, Nov. Litho. **Perf. 14**
577 A134 2c5m multicolored .25 .25
578 A134 8c multicolored .45 .45
579 A134 30c multicolored 1.50 1.50
Nos. 577-579 (3) 2.20 2.20

Chess Olympiad, Valletta, Nov. 20-Dec. 8.

Barn Owl — A135

1981, Jan. 20 **Wmk. 354** **Perf. 13½**
580 A135 3c shown .30 .30
581 A135 8c Sardinian warbler .55 .55
582 A135 12c Woodchat shrike .80 .80
583 A135 23c Stormy petrel 1.50 1.50
Nos. 580-583 (4) 3.15 3.15

Europa Issue

Climbing the Gostra
(Greasy
Pole) — A136

1981, Apr. 28 Litho. **Perf. 14**
584 A136 8c Horse race .30 .30
585 A136 30c shown 1.00 1.00

MALTA 4c

1981, June 12
586 A137 4c multic
587 A137 25c multic

Disabled
Artist — A138

1981, July 17
588 A138 3c shown
589 A138 35c Boy o
Intl. Year of

1981, Oct. 16
590 A139 8c multic
591 A139 23c multic

Men Hauling
Building
Stone — A140

1981, Oct. 31 W
592 A140 5m shown
593 A140 1c Growin
594 A140 2c Ship b
595 A140 3c Mintin
596 A140 5c Artistic
ment
597 A140 6c Fishing
598 A140 7c Farmin
599 A140 8c Quarry
600 A140 10c Grape
601 A140 12c Ship r
602 A140 15c Energy
603 A140 20c Comm
604 A140 25c Factor
605 A140 50c Water
606 A140 £1 Sea tra
607 A140 £3 Air tra
Nos. 592-607 (

3c MALTA

S
F
S

1982, Jan. 29 Lit
608 A141 3c Assem
609 A141 8c Ships i
610 A141 13c Tanker
611 A141 27c Tanker
Nos. 608-611

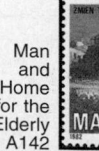

Man
and
Home
for the
Elderly
A142

MALTA

1982, Mar. 16
612 A142 8c shown
613 A142 30c Woman

Globe picturing hemispheres and: 4c, Red Cross, Red Crescent emblems. 18c, Symbolic design dividing world into north and south regions. 19c, Caduceus, EKG readout.

1988, May 25   Litho.   Perf. 14
720 A174 4c multicolored   .45   .45
721 A174 18c multicolored   1.75 1.75
722 A174 19c multicolored   2.00 2.00
Nos. 720-722 (3)   4.20 4.20

Intl. Red Cross and Red Crescent Organizations, 125th annivs. (4c); European Public Campaign on North-South Interdependence and Solidarity (18c); WHO, 40th anniv. (19c).

Military Uniforms Type of 1987

Designs: 3c, Light Infantry private, 1800. 4c, Coast Artillery gunner, 1802. 10c, lst Maltese Provincial Battalion field officer, 1805. 25c, Royal Malta Regiment subaltern, 1809.

1988, July 23   Litho.   Wmk. 354
723 A168 3c multicolored   .40 .40
724 A168 4c multicolored   .45 .45
725 A168 10c multicolored   1.10 1.10
726 A168 25c multicolored   3.00 3.00
Nos. 723-726 (4)   4.95 4.95

A175

Perf. 14x13½
1988, Sept. 17   Wmk. 354
727 A175 4c Running   .35 .35
728 A175 10c Women's diving   .75 .75
729 A175 35c Basketball   2.40 2.40
Nos. 727-729 (3)   3.50 3.50

1988 Summer Olympics, Seoul.

MALTA 2c
INDIPENDENZA 1964-1989
MALTA FIL-COMMONWEALTH

A176

1989, Jan. 28   Litho.   Perf. 13½
730 A176 2c Commonwealth   .35 .35
731 A176 3c Council of Europe   .35 .35
732 A176 4c United Nations   .40 .40
733 A176 10c Labor   .85 .85
734 A176 12c Justice   1.00 1.00
Size: 41x32mm
Perf. 14
735 A176 25c Liberty   2.25 2.25
Nos. 730-735 (6)   5.20 5.20

Natl. independence, 25th anniv.

New Natl. Emblem — A177

1989, Mar. 25   Perf. 14
736 A177 £1 multicolored   6.00 6.00

EUROPA
10c MALTA

Children's
Toys — A178

Europa.

1989, May 6
737 A178 10c Kite   .75 .75
738 A178 35c Dolls   2.75 2.75

Military Uniforms Type of 1987

3c, Officer of the Maltese Veterans, 1815. 4c, Subaltern of the Royal Malta Fencibles, 1839. 10c, Militia private, 1856. 25c, Royal Malta Fencibles Artillery colonel, 1875.

1989, June 24   Litho.   Wmk. 354
739 A168 3c multicolored   .35 .35
740 A168 4c multicolored   .70 .70
741 A168 10c multicolored   1.60 1.60
742 A168 25c multicolored   3.75 3.75
Nos. 739-742 (4)   6.40 6.40

3c
MALTA

Anniversaries and Events — A179

1989, Oct. 17   Litho.   Wmk. 354
743 A179 3c multicolored   .35 .35
744 A179 4c multi, diff.   .55 .55
745 A179 10c multi, diff.   1.10 1.10
746 A179 14c multi, diff.   1.60 1.60
747 A179 25c multi, diff.   2.60 2.60
Nos. 743-747 (5)   6.20 6.20

UN Declaration on Social Progress and Development, 20th anniv. (3c); signing of the European Social Charter by Malta (4c); Council of Europe, 40th anniv. (10c); Natl. Teachers' Union, 70th anniv. (14c); assembly of the Knights of the Sovereign Military Order of Malta (25c).

MALTA
BUSH - GORBACHEV
2-3.XII.1989

10c

Pres. Bush, Map and Gen.-Sec.
Gorbachev — A180

1989, Dec. 2   Litho.   Wmk. 354
748 A180 10c chalky blue, org & brn   1.50 1.50

US-Soviet summit, Malta, Dec. 2-3.

EUROPA   MALTA
POSTA

35c

Europa
1990 — A181

Post offices: 10c, Auberge d'Italie, Valletta, 1574, vert. 35c, Branch P.O., Zebbug, 1987.

1990, Feb. 9
749 A181 10c multicolored   .65 .65
750 A181 35c multicolored   2.40 2.40

4c
Malta

Anniversaries & Events — A182

1990, Apr. 7
751 A182 3c multi, vert.   .45 .45
752 A182 4c shown   .55 .55
753 A182 19c multicolored   2.25 2.25
754 A182 20c multi, vert.   2.25 2.25
Nos. 751-754 (4)   5.50 5.50

UNESCO World Literacy Year (3c); subjection of Malta to Count Roger the Norman and subsequent rulers of Sicily, 900th anniv. (4c); 25th anniv. of Malta's membership in the ITU (19c); and 20th Congress of the Union of European Soccer Associations, Malta (20c).

4c   MALTA
Samuel Taylor Coleridge

British Poets and Novelists — A183

1990, May 3   Perf. 13½
755 A183 4c Samuel Taylor Coleridge   .40 .40
756 A183 10c Lord Byron   .95 .95
757 A183 12c Sir Walter Scott   1.25 1.25
758 A183 25c William Make-peace Thackeray   2.40 2.40
Nos. 755-758 (4)   5.00 5.00

GWANNI PAWLU II
MALTA   4c

Visit of Pope John Paul II, May 25-27 — A184

1990, May 25   Perf. 14
759 A184 4c St. Paul   .30 .30
760 A184 25c Pope John Paul II   2.00 2.00
a. Pair, #759-760   2.50 2.50

5c   Malta
TAZZA TAD-DINJA

World Cup Soccer Championships, Italy — A185

Soccer ball &: 5c, flags. 10c, hands & goal net.

1990, June 8   Wmk. 354
761 A185 5c multicolored   .40 .40
762 A185 10c multicolored   .70 .70
763 A185 14c multicolored   1.10 1.10
a. Souvenir sheet of 3, #761-763   3.25 3.25
Nos. 761-763 (3)   2.20 2.20

Military Uniforms Type of 1987

Designs: 3c, Captain, Royal Malta Militia, 1889. 4c, Field Officer, Royal Malta Artillery, 1905. 10c, Laborer, Malta Labor Corps, 1915. 25c, Lieutenant, King's Own Malta Regiment of Militia, 1918.

1990, Aug. 25   Perf. 14
764 A168 3c multicolored   .55 .55
765 A168 4c multicolored   .95 .95
766 A168 10c multicolored   2.10 2.10
767 A168 25c multicolored   5.00 5.00
Nos. 764-767 (4)   8.60 8.60

SOCJETA FILATELIKA
MALTA   10c

Maltese Philatelic Society, 25th Anniv. A186

1991, Mar. 6   Litho.   Wmk. 354
768 A186 10c multicolored   1.00 1.00

malta

10c

Europa — A187

1991, Mar. 16
769 A187 10c Eurostar   .70 .70
770 A187 35c Ariane 4, space plane   2.40 2.40

IHS
MALTA   SAN INAZJU TA' LOYOLA   3c

St. Ignatius of Loyola (1491-1556), Founder of Jesuit Order — A188

Designs: 4c, Marie Therese Pisani (1806-1865), Benedictine Nun, vert. 30c, St. John of the Cross (1542-1591), Christian mystic.

1991, Apr. 29   Litho.   Perf. 14
771 A188 3c multicolored   .30 .30
772 A188 4c multicolored   .40 .40
773 A188 30c multicoloed   2.40 2.40
Nos. 771-773 (3)   3.10 3.10

Military Uniforms Type of 1987

Colors Officers: 3c, Royal Malta Fencibles, 1860. 10c, Royal Malta Regiment of Militia, 1903. 19c, King's Own Malta Regiment, 1968. 25c, Armed Forces of Malta, 1991.

Wmk. 354
1991, Sept. 23   Litho.   Perf. 14
774 A168 3c multicolored   .35 .35
775 A168 10c multicolored   1.00 1.00
776 A168 19c multicolored   1.75 1.75
777 A168 25c multicolored   2.25 2.25
Nos. 774-777 (4)   5.35 5.35

MALTA
UNION HADDIEMA MAGHQUDIN
4c

Union Haddiema Maghqudin, 25th Anniv. — A189

1991, Sept. 23   Perf. 14x13½
778 A189 4c multicolored   .40 .40

MALTA

Birds of Prey — A190

1991, Oct. 3   Perf. 14
779 A190 4c Pernis apivorus   1.75 1.00
780 A190 4c Circus aerugi-nosus   1.75 1.00
781 A190 10c Falco eleonorae   3.25 1.75
782 A190 10c Falco naumanni   3.25 1.75
a. Strip of 4, #779-782   12.00 12.00

World Wildlife Fund.

MALTA   1c

Tourism A191

Designs: 1c, Ta' Hagrat neolithic temples, Mgarr. 2c, Cottoner Gate. 3c, St. Michael's Bastion, Valletta. 4c, Spinola Palace, St. Julian's. 5c, Old church, Birkirkara. 10c, Wind surfing, Mellieha Bay. 12c, Boat anchored at Wied iz-Zurrieq. 14c, Mgarr Harbor, Gozo. 20c, Yacht Marina. 50c, Gozo Channel. £1, Statue of Arab Horses, by Sciortino. £2, Independence Monument, by Bonnici, vert.

1991, Dec. 9   Perf. 13½
783 A191 1c multicolored   .25 .25
784 A191 2c multicolored   .25 .25
785 A191 3c multicolored   .25 .25
786 A191 4c multicolored   .25 .25
787 A191 5c multicolored   .30 .30
788 A191 10c multicolored   .65 .65
789 A191 12c multicolored   .75 .75
790 A191 14c multicolored   .85 .85
791 A191 20c multicolored   1.25 1.25
792 A191 50c multicolored   3.25 3.25
793 A191 £1 multicolored   6.25 6.25
794 A191 £2 multicolored   12.50 12.50
Nos. 783-794 (12)   26.80 26.80

1997, Apr. 11
911 A229 2c Sug
912 A229 6c Sug
913 A229 16c Sec
914 A229 27c Sec
    ver
Nos. 911-9

A2

Europa (Stories
carrying door, figure
35c, Woman kneel
white horse (St. Dir

1997, May 5
915 A230 16c mult
916 A230 35c mult

1997, July 10
917 A231 1c multi
918 A231 16c multi

Antonio Sciortino

Gozo Cathedral,

1997, July 10
919 A232 6c multi
920 A232 11c multi

Joseph Calle
Actor

1997, July 10
921 A233 6c multi
922 A233 22c multi,

Pioneers of
Education
A234

Designs: 6c, Dr. A
1943). 16c, Sister E
1856). 19c, Msgr. P
26c, Msgr. Tommaso

Malta Intl.
Airport
A192

1992, Feb. 8   *Perf. 14*
795 A192 4c shown   .60 .60
796 A192 10c Flags, airport   1.50 1.50

Discovery of America, 500th
Anniv. — A193

1992, Feb. 20   *Perf. 14x14½*
797 A193 10c Columbus' fleet   .65 .65
798 A193 35c Columbus, map   2.25 2.25
    Europa.

George Cross,
1942 — A194

George Cross and: 4c, Royal Malta Artillery.
10c, Siege Bell. 50c, Santa Maria convoy
entering Grand Harbor.

1992, Apr. 15   *Perf. 14*
799 A194 4c multicolored   .70 .70
800 A194 10c multicolored   1.60 1.60
801 A194 50c multicolored   7.50 7.50
    Nos. 799-801 (3)   9.80 9.80

1992 Summer Olympics,
Barcelona — A195

1992, June 24
802 A195 3c Runners   .30 .30
803 A195 10c High jump   1.05 1.05
804 A195 30c Swimmer   3.25 3.25
    Nos. 802-804 (3)   4.60 4.60

Historic
Buildings
A196

Designs: 3c, Church of the Flight of the Holy
Family into Egypt, vert. 4c, St. John's Co-
Cathedral. 19c, Church of the Madonna del
Pilar, vert. 25c, Auberge de Provence.

1992, July 5
805 A196 3c blk, gray & buff   .50 .50
806 A196 4c blk, salmon & buff   .60 .60
807 A196 19c blk, green & buff   2.40 2.40
808 A196 25c blk, pink & buff   3.00 3.00
    Nos. 805-808 (4)   6.50 6.50

University of Malta, 400th
Anniv. — A197

1992, Nov. 11
809 A197 4c Early building, vert.   .50 .50
810 A197 30c Modern complex   3.50 3.50

Lions Intl.,
75th
Anniv. — A198

1993, Feb. 4
811 A198 4c We serve   .50 .50
812 A198 50c Sight first campaign   4.50 4.50

Europa
A199

Contemporary paintings by: 10c, Pawl Car-
bonaro, vert. 35c, Alfred Chircop.

1993, Apr. 7
813 A199 10c multicolored   .75 .75
814 A199 35c multicolored   2.50 2.50

5th Games
of Small
States of
Europe
A200

1993, May 4   *Perf. 13½x14*
815 A200 3c Torchbearer   .35 .35
816 A200 4c Cycling   .50 .50
817 A200 10c Tennis   1.10 1.10
818 A200 35c Sailing   4.00 4.00
  a.   Souvenir sheet of 4, #815-818   6.50 6.50
    Nos. 815-818 (4)   5.95 5.95

Boy Scouts and
Girl Guides of
Malta — A201

1993, July 21   *Perf. 14*
819 A201 3c Leader bandaging
girl   .30 .30
820 A201 4c Bronze Cross   .30 .30
821 A201 10c Scout at camp fire   1.10 1.10
822 A201 35c Scout recieving
Bronze Cross   3.75 3.75
    Nos. 819-822 (4)   5.45 5.45
Girl Guides in Malta, 70th anniv. (No. 819).
Award of Bronze Cross for Gallantry to Boy
Scouts of Malta, 50th anniv. (Nos. 820-822).

A202

1993, Sept. 23   *Perf. 14½x14*
823 A202 5c Papilio machaon   .60 .60
824 A202 35c Vanessa atalanta   3.00 3.00

A203

1993, Oct. 5   *Perf. 13½*
825 A203 4c multicolored   .50 .50
    General Worker's Union, 50th anniv.

Souvenir Sheet

Local Councils — A204

Designs showing various local coats of
arms with denominations at: a, UL. b, UR. c,
LL. d, LR.

1993, Nov. 20   *Perf. 14½*
826   Sheet of 4   2.00 2.00
  a.-d.   A204 5c any single   .40 .40

Dental Assoc. of
Malta, 50th
Anniv. — A205

Design: 44c, Dental instrument, teeth.

1994, Feb. 12
827 A205 5c multicolored   .75 .75
828 A205 44c multicolored   4.25 4.25

Europa — A206

Designs: 14c, Sir Themistocles Zammit
(1864-1935), discoverer of micro-organism
causing undulant fever. 30c, Marble candela-
brum, 2nd cent. B.C., Natl. Museum of
Archaeology, Valletta.

1994, Mar. 29   *Perf. 14*
829 A206 14c multicolored   1.00 1.00
830 A206 30c multicolored   2.25 2.25

Anniversaries
and
Events — A207

1994, May 10
831 A207 5c shown   .55 .55
832 A207 9c Crosses   .90 .90
833 A207 14c Farm animals   1.40 1.40
834 A207 20c Factory worker   2.10 2.10
835 A207 25c Cathedral, vert.   2.60 2.60
    Nos. 831-835 (5)   7.55 7.55
Intl. Year of the Family (No. 831). Malta Red
Cross Society, 3rd anniv. (No. 832). Agrarian
Society, 150th anniv. (No. 833). ILO, 75th
anniv. (No. 834). St. Paul's Anglican Cathedral, 150th anniv. (No. 835).

1994 World Cup
Soccer
Championships,
U.S. — A208

1994, June 9
836 A208 5c shown   .45 .45
837 A208 14c Ball, net, map   1.25 1.25
838 A208 30c Ball, field, map   2.75 2.75
  a.   Souvenir sheet of 3, #836-838   5.00 5.00
    Nos. 836-838 (3)   4.45 4.45

Aviation Anniversaries &
Events — A209

Aircraft, related objects: 5c, Trophy, map,
Twin Comanche. 14c, Airshow emblem, Phantom jet, demonstration team in silhouette,
Alouette helicopter, flag. 20c, Emblem, Avro
York, old terminal building, DeHavilland Dove.
25c, Emblem, DeHavilland Comet, new terminal, Airbus 320.

1994, July 2
839 A209 5c multicolored   .55 .55
840 A209 14c multicolored   1.50 1.50
841 A209 20c multicolored   2.25 2.25
842 A209 25c multicolored   2.75 2.75
    Nos. 839-842 (4)   7.05 7.05
Intl. Air Rally of Malta, 25th anniv. (No. 839).
Malta Intl. Airshow (No. 840). ICAO, 50th
anniv. (Nos. 841-842).

First Manned
Moon Landing,
25th
Anniv. — A210

1994, July 20
843 A210 14c multicolored   1.50 1.50

Christmas — A211

1994, Oct. 26
844 A211 5c shown   .30 .30
    Size: 28x40mm
845 A211 9c +2c Angel in pink   .75 .75
846 A211 14c +3c Madonna &
child   1.25 1.25
847 A211 20c +3c Angel in green   1.75 1.75
    Nos. 844-847 (4)   4.05 4.05

Antique Mal... Silver — A...

Designs: 5c, ... samina, Pinto ... period. 25c, Sug...

1994, Dec. 1...
848 A212 5c
849 A212 14c
850 A212 20c
851 A212 25c
Nos. 8...

1995, Feb. 27
852 A213 2c
853 A213 5c
854 A213 14c
855 A213 20c
856 A213 25c
Nos. 8...

Natl. Assoc. o... 852). Natl. Youth... (No. 853). 4th W... (No. 854). Malt... Assoc., 50th an... (1822-95) (No. 8...

Peace & Freedom A214

Europa: 14c, ... vert. 30c, Doves...

1995, Mar. 29
857 A214 14c
858 A214 30c

Designs: 5c, ... planes. 14c, For... hands. 35c, FA... wheat, FAO emb...

1995, Apr. 21
859 A215 5c
860 A215 14c
861 A215 35c
Nos. 85...

Europa — A282

Poster art: 16c, Cisk Beer. 46c, 1939 Carnival.

2003, May 9
1123-1124 A282 Set of 2   4.50 4.50

Games of Small European States A283

Designs: 25c, Track and field. 50c, Shooting. 75c, Volleyball. £3, Swimming.

2003, May 21   Litho.   Perf. 14x14¼
1125-1128 A283 Set of 4   30.00 30.00

Coronation of Queen Elizabeth II, 50th Anniv. — A284

Queen Elizabeth II: 12c, With woman. 15c, Seated in limousine. 22c, With Prince Philip, reading book. 60c, With Prince Philip, receiving book from man.
£1, Queen and crowd of people.

2003, June 3
1129-1132 A284 Set of 4   8.00 8.00
Souvenir Sheet
1133 A284 £1 multi   9.00 9.00

Souvenir Sheet

Valletta Bastions — A285

2003, July 1   Litho.   Perf. 14x13¾
1134 A285 £1.50 multi + 4 labels   14.00 14.00
Elton John concert, July 6, 2003.

Shells — A286

No. 1135: a, Chlamys pesfelis. b, Gyroscala lamellosa. c, Phalium granulatum. d, Fusiturris similis. e, Luria lurida. f, Bolinus brandaris. g, Charonia tritonis variegata. h, Clanculus corallinus. i, Fusinus syracusanus. j, Pinna nobilis.

---

k, Acanthocardia tuberculata. l, Aporrhais pespelcani. m, Haliotis tuberculata lamellosa. n, Tonna galea. o, Spondylus gaederopus. p, Mitra zonata.

2003, Aug. 20   Litho.   Perf. 13¾
1135 A286 7c Sheet of 16, #a-p   10.00 10.00

Sailboats A287

Designs: 8c, Malta-Syracuse Race. 22c, Middle Sea Race, vert. 35c, Royal Malta Yacht Club, vert.

2003, Sept. 30   Litho.   Perf. 14
1136-1138 A287 Set of 3   5.50 5.50

Flower Type of 1999

Designs: 7c, Vitex agnus-castus.16c, Crocus longiflorus.

Booklet Stamps
Size: 23x23mm
Serpentine Die Cut 12½ on 2 or 3 Sides

2003, Oct. 22   Self-Adhesive
1139 A253 7c multi   .60 .60
   a.   Booklet pane of 12   7.25
1140 A253 16c multi   1.30 1.30
   a.   Booklet pane of 6   8.00

Windmills — A288

Designs: 11c, Is-Sur ta'San Mikiel, Valletta. 27c, Ta'Kola, Xaghra, vert. 45c, Tax-Xarolla, Zurrieq, vert.

2003, Oct. 29   Perf. 14
1141-1143 A288 Set of 3   7.00 7.00

Christmas — A289

Designs: 7c, The Annunciation, vert. 16c, Holy Family, vert. 22c, Adoration of the Magi. 50c, Adoration of the Magi.

2003, Nov. 12
1144-1147 A289 Set of 4   9.00 9.00

Letter Boxes — A290

Boxes from era of: 1c, Queen Victoria. 16c, King Edward VII. 22c, King George V, King George VI. 37c, Queen Elizabeth II. 76c, Independent Malta (Malta Post).

2004, Mar. 12
1148-1152 A290 Set of 5   14.00 14.00

Cats — A291

Various cats with denominations and country name in: 7c, Golden brown. 27c, Dark brown. 28c, Lilac. 50c, Red brown. 60c, Green.

2004, Mar. 26   Perf. 13¾
1153-1157 A291 Set of 5   14.00 14.00

Souvenir Sheet

Salesians in Malta, Cent. — A292

2004, Apr. 7   Perf. 14
1158 A292 75c multi   6.25 6.25

Fauna — A293

No. 1159: a, Pipistrellus pygmaeus. b, Myotis blythi punicus. c, Mustela nivalis. d, Atelerix algirus fallax. e, Chamaeleo chamaeleon. f, Crocidura sicula. g, Chalcides ocellatus. h, Podarcis filfolensis filfolensis. i, Tarentola mauritanica. j, Hemidactylus turcicus. k, Elaphe situla. l, Coluber viridiflavus. m, Delphinus delphis. n, Stenella coeruleoalba. o, Monachus monachus. p, Chelonia mydas.

2004, Apr. 21   Perf. 13¾
1159 A293 16c Sheet of 16, #a-p   20.00 20.00

Admission to European Union — A294

Stars, map of Europe and: 16c, Flags of newly-admitted countries. 28c, Officials signing treaty.

2004, May 1   Perf. 14
1160-1161 A294 Set of 2   3.25 3.25

Europa — A295

Designs: 16c, Youths jumping into water. 51c, People at archaeological site.

2004, May 19   Perf. 13¾x14
1162-1163 A295 Set of 2   5.00 5.00

Wayside Chapels A296

Designs: 3c, Lunzjata-Hal Milliere, Zurrieq. 7c, San Basilju, Mqabba. 39c, San Cir, Rabat. 48c, Santa Lucija, Mtarfa. 66c, Ta' Santa Marija, Kemmuna.

2004, June 16   Litho.   Perf. 14
1164-1168 A296 Set of 5   14.00 14.00

Trams A297

Designs: 19c, Side view of tram. 37c, Tram and conductor (22x40mm). 50c, Ticket (22x40mm). 75c, Tram and archway.

Perf. 13¾, 14 (37c, 50c)
2004, July 14
1169-1172 A297 Set of 4   10.50 10.50

2004 Summer Olympics, Athens A298

Designs: 11c, Discus thrower. 16c, Doric column, olive wreath. 76c, Javelin thrower.

Perf. 14¼
2004, Aug. 13   Litho.   Unwmk.
1173-1175 A298 Set of 3   7.50 7.50

Religious Festivals — A299

Designs: 5c, Ascension Day. 15c, St. Gregory's Day. 27c, Pilgrimage on First Sunday in Lent. 51c, St. Martin's Day, vert. £1, Feast of Sts. Peter and Paul, vert.

Perf. 14x14¼, 14¼x14
2004, Sept. 15   Wmk. 354
1176-1180 A299 Set of 5   15.00 15.00

Works of Art A300

Designs: 2c, Church of St. Mary, Attard. 20c, Mdina Cathedral organ, music by Benignon Zerafa, vert. 57c, Statue of St. Agatha, vert. 62c, Books, illustration for poem "The Turkish Galleon," by Gian Antonio Vassallo, vert.
72c, Icon of St. Paul, vert.

Perf. 14x14¼, 14¼x14
2004, Oct. 13 Litho. Wmk. 354
1181-1184 A300 Set of 4 14.00 14.00

Souvenir Sheet
1185 A300 72c multi 7.00 7.00

Christmas — A301

Various effigies of Infant Jesus: 7c, 16c, 22c, 50c. Nos. 1187-1189 vert.

Perf. 14x14¼, 14¼x14
2004, Nov. 10 Litho. Wmk. 354
1186-1189 A301 Set of 4 7.50 7.50

Historic Maps A302

Designs: 1c, Map of Malta by Abbé Jean Quintin, 1536. 12c, Map of Malta by Antonio Lafreri, 1551. 37c, Fresco map of Malta, by Matteo Perez d'Aleccio, 1565. £1.02, Map of Gozo, Comino, Cominotto and Marfa Peninsula, by Fr. Luigi Bartolo, 1745.

Wmk. 354
2005, Jan. 19 Litho. Perf. 14
1190-1193 A302 Set of 4 12.00 12.00

Rotary International, Cent. — A303

Rotary emblem and: 27c, Dar il-Kaptan Home, Mtarfa, woman, man. 76c, Map of Malta.

Perf. 14x14¼
2005, Feb. 23 Litho. Wmk. 354
1194-1195 A303 Set of 2 8.50 8.50

Hans Christian Andersen (1805-75), Author A304

Paper Cutting by Andersen, Scissors — A305

Designs: 60c, Pen, inkwell, illustration of duckling, manuscript handwritten by Andersen. 75c, Andersen's drawing of Casino dell'Orologio, Rome, and boots.

Perf. 14x13¾
2005, Mar. 3 Litho. Wmk. 354
1196 A304 7c gray & black .55 .55
1197 A305 22c blue & black 1.75 1.75
1198 A305 60c multi 4.75 4.75
1199 A305 75c multi 6.00 6.00
Nos. 1196-1199 (4) 13.05 13.05
See Denmark Nos. 1323-1326.

Pope John Paul II (1920-2005) A306

2005, Apr. 15 Perf. 14
1200 A306 51c multi 5.50 5.50

Miniature Sheet

Insects — A307

No. 1201: a, Coccinella septempunctata. b, Chrysoperla carnea. c, Apis mellifera. d, Crocothermis erythraea. e, Anax imperator. f, Lampyris pallida. g, Henosepilachna elaterii. h, Forficula decipiens. i, Mantis religiosa. j, Eumenes lunulatus. k, Cerambyx cerdo. l, Gryllus bimaculatus. m, Xylocopa violacea. n, Cicada orni. o, Acrida ungarica. p, Oryctes nasicornis.

2005, Apr. 20 Perf. 14¼
1201 A307 16c Sheet of 16, #a-p 22.50 22.50

Europa — A308

Designs: 16c, Stuffed peppers, zucchini and eggplant. 51c, Fried rabbit in wine and garlic.

2005, May 9 Perf. 14¼x14
1202-1203 A308 Set of 2 5.50 5.50

Paintings Depicting St. Catherine — A309

Designs: No. 1204, 28c, The Beheading of St. Catherine, by unknown artist. No. 1205, 28c, The Martyrdom of St. Catherine, by Mattia Preti, vert. No. 1206, 45c, St. Catherine Disputing the Philosophers, by Francesco Zahra. No. 1207, 45c, Mystic Marriage, by Sahra, vert.

Perf. 14x14¼, 14¼x14
2005, June 15 Litho. Wmk. 354
1204-1207 A309 Set of 4 10.00 10.00

Famous People A310

Designs: 3c, Monsignor Michael Azzopardi (1910-87), religious educator. 19c, Egidio Lapira (1897-1970), dental surgeon. 20c, Petition of Guzeppi Callus (1505-61), doctor executed for taxation opposition. 46c, Hand and quill pen of Geronimo Matteo Abos (1715-60), composer. 76c, Gio Francesco Abela (1592-1655), historian, ambassador.

Wmk. 354
2005, July 13 Litho. Perf. 14¼
1208-1212 A310 Set of 5 11.00 11.00

Flower Type of 1999 Redrawn

Design: 7c, Vitex agnus-castus. 16c, Crocus longiflorus.

2005 Litho. Perf. 14¼
1213 A253 7c multi + label .50 .50
1214 A253 16c multi + label 1.25 1.25

Nos. 1213-1214 have "2005" year date and "Printex Ltd" inscription at lower right. Additionally, No. 1213 has wider distance between denomination and country name than No. 1102, and No. 1214 has denomination and country name in a different font than No. 986. Nos. 1213-1214 were issued in sheets of 10 stamps and 10 labels. Labels could be personalized for an additional fee.

Horses and Mules at Work A311

Designs: 11c, Horse-drawn hearse. 15c, Mule pulling plow. 62c, Mule at grindstone. 66c, Horse pulling cart.

Perf. 14x14¼
2005, Aug. 19 Litho. Wmk. 354
1215-1218 A311 Set of 4 10.00 10.00

End of World War II, 60th Anniv. A312

Scenes from Battle of Malta: 2c, Civilians on food line. 5c, Royal Navy ships under attack. 25c, Anti-aircraft gunners. 51c, Aviators and planes. £1, Tanker "Ohio."

2005, Sept. 23
1219-1223 A312 Set of 5 12.00 12.00

Christmas — A313

Mosaics of paintings by Envin Cremona from National Sanctuary of Our Lady of Ta' Pinu, Gozo: 7c, Nativity. 16c, Annunciation, vert. 28c, Adoration of the Magi. 50c, Flight into Egypt (68x27mm).

Perf. 14¼, 13¾x14 (50c)
2005, Oct. 12 Litho. Wmk. 354
1224-1227 A313 Set of 4 6.50 6.50

Souvenir Sheets

Commonwealth Heads of Governments Meeting — A314

Flags of Malta, British Commonwealth and: 14c, Commonwealth Heads of Government flag. 28c, Doves. 37c, Maltese cross. 75c, People.

Perf. 14x14¼
2005, Nov. 23 Litho. Wmk. 354
1228-1231 A314 Set of 4 11.00 11.00

Souvenir Sheet

Europa Stamps, 50th Anniv. — A315

No. 1232: a, 5c, #677. b, 13c, #628. c, 23c, #540. d, 24c, #738.

2006, Jan. 3 Perf. 13¾x14
1232 A315 Sheet of 4, #a-d 4.50 4.50

Ceramics A316

Designs: 7c, Neolithic terra-cotta female figurine. 16c, Roman terra-cotta head. 28c, Terra-cotta oil lamp holder. 37c, Sicilian maiolica plate. 60c, Stylized figure in traditional Maltese costume, by Ianni Bonnici.

Wmk. 354
2006, Feb. 25 Litho. Perf. 14¼
1233-1237 A316 Set of 5 10.00 10.00

Miniature Sheet

Pets — A317

No. 1238: a, Shetland pony. b, Chihuahua. c, Goldfish. d, Siamese cat. e, Siamese fighting fish. f, Ferret. g, Canary. h, Turtle. i, Chinchilla. j, Parakeet. k, Rabbit. l, Zebra finch. m, Pointer. n, Pigeon. o, Guinea pig. p, House cat.

Wmk. 354

2006, Mar. 14   Litho.   Perf. 14¼

1238	A317	Sheet of 16	17.50	17.50
a.-h.		7c Any single	.50	.50
i.-p.		22c Any single	1.60	1.60

Traditional Holy
Week
Celebrations
A318

Designs: 7c, Men carrying crosses. 15c, Men carrying crucifixion scene. 22c, Float. 27c, Men pulling statue of Jesus. 82c, Decorated altar.

2006, Apr. 12   Perf. 14¼x14

1239-1243	A318	Set of 5	11.00	11.00

Europa
A319

Designs: 16c, Shown. 51c, Stick figures, diff. (28x41mm).

Perf. 14¼, 14¼x14 (51c)
2006, May 9

1244-1245	A319	Set of 2	4.75	4.75

2006 World Cup
Soccer
Championships,
Germany
A320

Designs: 7c, Bobby Charlton. 16c, Pelé. 27c, Franz Beckenbauer. 76c, Dino Zoff.

2006, June 2   Perf. 14¼x14

1246-1249	A320	Set of 4	9.00	9.00
1249a		Souvenir sheet, #1246-1249	9.00	9.00

Stampin' The Future Type of 2000
Souvenir Sheet

2006, June 5   Perf. 14

1250	A261	£1.50 Like #1028	11.00	11.00

Ten percent of the sale went to the Rainforest Foundation.

Naval
Vessels
A321

Designs: 8c, Gran Caracca di Rodi. 29c, Guillaume Tell (HMS Malta). 51c, USS Constitution. 76c, HMS Dreadnought. £1, Slava and USS Belknap.

Wmk. 354

2006, Aug. 18   Litho.   Perf. 14¼

1251-1255	A321	Set of 5	20.00	20.00

Greetings
A322

Inscriptions: 8c, Happy Birthday. 16c, Happy Anniversary. 27c, Congratulations. 37c, Best Wishes.

2006, Sept. 18

1256-1259	A322	Set of 4	6.25	6.25

Castles
and
Towers
A323

Designs: 7c, Wignacourt Tower. 16c, Verdala Castle. 27c, San Lucjan Tower. 37c, Kemmuna Tower. £1, Selmun Castle.

Perf. 14x14¼
2006, Sept. 29   Litho.   Wmk. 354

1260-1264	A323	Set of 5	13.00	13.00

Christmas — A324

Designs: 8c, Paolino Vassallo (1856-1923), composer of "Inno per Natale," Nativity. 16c, Carmelo Pace (1906-93), composer of "They Heard the Angels," Magi on camels. 22c, Paul Nani (1906-86), composer of "Maltese Christmas," angels. 27c, Carlo Diacono (1876-1942), composer of "Notte di Natale," shepherds and angel. 50c, Wolfgang Amadeus Mozart (1756-91), composer of "Alma Dei Creatoris."

2006, Nov. 6   Perf. 14¼

1265-1268	A324	Set of 4	5.25	5.25

Souvenir Sheet
Perf. 13¾

1269	A324	50c multi	3.75	3.75

No. 1269 contains one 40x30mm stamp.

Flower Type of 1999 Redrawn
2006   Litho.   Wmk. 354   Perf. 14¼

1269A	A253	1c Like #1022	.40	.40

No. 1269A has a "2006" year date and "Printex Ltd." inscription at lower right. Additionally, the country name has a different font than No. 1022, with the lines in the lettering being of equal thickness throughout the letter on No. 1269A. Other differences in the vignette exist.

Due to the scheduled conversion to the euro on Jan. 1, 2008, Nos. 1270-1274 and all stamps issued in 2007 will show denominations in pounds and the not-yet-circulating euros.

Crafts
A325

Designs: 8c, Wrought iron window guard, blacksmith and anvil. 16c, Glass ornamental objects, glassblower. 22c, Filigree pendant,

silversmith. 37c, Pottery, potter. 60c, Reed baskets, basket maker.

2006, Dec. 29   Perf. 14¼

1270-1274	A325	Set of 5	10.00	10.00

Sculptures from
3000-2500
B.C. — A326

Designs: 15c, Human head. 29c, Animals, horiz. 60c, Spirals, horiz. £1.50, Headless nude female.

Wmk. 354

2007, Feb. 28   Litho.   Perf. 14¼

1275-1278	A326	Set of 4	16.00	16.00

Miniature Sheet

Fruit — A327

No. 1279: a, Opuntia ficus-indica (prickly pears). b, Viris vinifera (grapes). c, Eriobotrya japonica (loquats). d, Morus nigra (black mulberries). e, Ficus carica (figs). f, Citrus limonum (lemons). g, Pyrus communis (pear). h, Prunus persica (peaches). i, Punica granatum (pomegranates). j, Prunus salicina (plums). k, Citrullus vulgaris (watermelons). l, Citrus sinensis (orange). m, Olea europaea (olives). n, Lycopersicon esculentum (tomatoes). o, Malus domestica (apples). p, Cucumis melo (cantaloupe).

2007, Apr. 16

1279	A327	8c Sheet of 16, #a-p	8.00	8.00

Balconies
A328

Designs: 8c, Wrought iron balcony. 22c, Stone balcony. 27c, Balustraded balcony, National Library. 29c, Closed wooden balcony. 46c, Art Deco balcony by Silvio Mercieca. 51c, Ornamented balcony, Hostel de Verdelin, Valletta, horiz.

Wmk. 354

2007, Apr. 28   Litho.   Perf. 14¼

1280-1284	A328	Set of 5	8.50	8.50

Souvenir Sheet
Perf. 13¾

1285	A328	51c multi	3.25	3.25

No. 1285 contains one 37x28mm stamp.

Europa
A329

Emblems of Scout Association of Malta, Scouting Centenary and: 16c, Lord Robert Baden-Powell. 51c, Maltese scouts at 1957 Jamboree.

2007, May 9   Perf. 14¼

1286-1287	A329	Set of 2	4.75	4.75

Canonization
of St. George
Preca (1880-
1962)
A330

Background color: 8c, Blue. £1, Orange.

Wmk. 354

2007, May 28   Litho.   Perf. 14¼

1288-1289	A330	Set of 2	6.75	6.75

Toys — A331

Photographs of children and: 2c, Rocking horse, tricycle, car. 3c, Baby carriage, drums and tops. 16c, Boats, beach pails and shovel. 22c, Dolls. 50c, Truck, motorcycle and race car.

2007, July 11   Perf. 14¼x14

1290-1294	A331	Set of 5	6.00	6.00

Paintings by Caravaggio — A332

Designs: 5c, St. Jerome. 29c, The Beheading of St. John the Baptist (48x40mm). £2, The Beheading of St. John the Baptist, vert.

2007, July 20   Perf. 14¼

1295-1296	A332	Set of 2	2.25	2.25

Souvenir Sheet

1297	A332	£2 multi	13.00	13.00

Arrival of Caravaggio on Malta, 400th anniv. No. 1297 with an overprint in gold in the sheet margin marking the 400th anniv. of the death of Caravaggio was a limited edtition.

Motorcycles — A333

Designs: 1c, 1954 Royal Enfield. 16c, 1941 Matchless G3/L. 27c, 1903 Minerva. 50c, 1965 Triumph Speed Twin.

Perf. 14x14¼
2007, Sept. 12   Litho.   Wmk. 354
1298-1301 A333 Set of 4   6.25 6.25

Greetings
Stamps
A334

2007, Sept. 28   *Perf. 14¼*
1302 A334 8c Hearts   .55   .55
　a.　　Sheet of 5 + 5 labels   13.50 13.50
1303 A334 8c Stars   .55   .55
　a.　　Sheet of 5 + 5 labels   13.50 13.50
1304 A334 8c Roses   .55   .55
　a.　　Sheet of 5 + 5 labels   13.50 13.50
1305 A334 8c Balloons   .55   .55
　a.　　Sheet of 5 + 5 labels   13.50 13.50
1306 A334 8c Champagne
　　　　　　flutes   .55   .55
　a.　　Sheet of 5 + 5 labels   13.50 13.50
1307 A334 8c Teddy bears   .55   .55
　a.　　Sheet of 5 + 5 labels   13.50 13.50
　　Nos. 1302-1307 (6)   3.30   3.30

Labels on Nos. 1302a-1307a were personalizable, with full sheets each selling for £2, with a minimum purchase of two sheets of any stamp.

Paintings
by John
Martin
Borg
A335

Designs: 11c, Mdina Skyline. 16c, Qrendi. 37c, Vittoriosa Waterfront. 46c, Mgarr Harbor, Gozo. 76c, Xlendi Bay, Gozo.

2007, Oct. 1   *Perf. 14¼*
1308-1312 A335 Set of 5   12.50 12.50

Fruit Type of 2007
Souvenir Sheet
2007, Oct. 18
1313 A327 75c Like #1270m   5.00 5.00

National Tree Planting Weekend. An unspecified portion of the proceeds of the sale went to the 34U Campaign.

Bands
A336

Various bands: 4c, 15c, 21c, 22c, £1.

2007, Nov. 13   Set of 5   11.00 11.00
1314-1318 A336

Christmas
A337

Maltese arms and nave paintings in St. Andrew's Church, Luqa, by Giuseppe Calì: 8c, Madonna and Child. 16c, Holy Family with Women and Young Girl. 21c, Infant Jesus and Young Girl.

2007, Nov. 20
1319-1321 A337 Set of 3   3.50 3.50
　　See Vatican City Nos. 1370-1372.

Youth Soccer
Association, 25th
Anniv. — A338

Society of
Christian
Doctrine
Museum,
Cent. — A339

Religious
Figures — A340

Treaty of Rome, 50th Anniv. — A341

Designs: 16c, Monsignor Frangisk Bonnici (1852-1905), founder of St. Joseph Institute, Hamrun. 43c, Father Manwel Magri (1851-1907), ethnographer and archaeologist. 86c, Carolina Cauchi (1824-1907), founder of Dominican Sisters of Malta.

Wmk. 354
2007, Dec. 1   Litho.   *Perf. 14¼*
1322 A338 4m multi   .25   .25
1323 A339 9c multi   .60   .60
1324 A340 16c multi   1.10   1.10
1325 A340 43c multi   3.00   3.00
1326 A340 86c multi   6.00   6.00
　　Nos. 1322-1326 (5)   10.95 10.95

Souvenir Sheet
Perf. 13¾
1327 A341 76c multi   5.25 5.25
　　No. 1327 contains one 40x30mm stamp.

Souvenir Sheet

Obverse and Reverse of Maltese
Pound Coin — A342

Wmk. 354
2007, Dec. 31   Litho.   *Perf. 14¼*
1328 A342 £1 multi   7.00 7.00
　　Last day of use of pound currency.

100 Cents = 1 Euro
Souvenir Sheet

Introduction of Euro Currency — A343

No. 1329: a, Statue of Aphrodite, map of Cyprus. b, Sleeping Lady statue.

Wmk. 354
2008, Jan. 1   Litho.   *Perf. 14¼*
1329 A343 €1 Sheet of 2, #a-b   6.00 6.00
　　See Cyprus No. 1088.

Souvenir Sheet

Obverse and Reverse of Maltese Euro
Coin — A344

2008, Jan. 1
1330 A344 €1 multi   3.00 3.00

Door Knockers
A345

Various door knockers with background color of: 26c, Blue. 51c, Red. 63c, Brown. €1.77, Green.

2008, Mar. 5   *Perf. 14¼x14*
1331-1334 A345 Set of 4   9.75 9.75

2008 Summer Olympics,
Beijing — A346

Designs: 5c, Shooting. 12c, Swimming. €1.57, Running.

2008, Mar. 7   *Perf. 14x14¼*
1335-1337 A346 Set of 3   5.50 5.50

Europa — A347

Mail room, postman with bicycle in: 37c, Sepia. €1.19, Black.

Wmk. 354
2008, May 9   Litho.   *Perf. 14¼*
1338-1339 A347 Set of 2   5.00 5.00

Birth of St. Paul,
2000th
Anniv. — A348

Statues depicting St. Paul from: 19c, Conversion of St. Paul Church, Safi. 68c, St. Paul's Shipwreck Church, Munxar. €1.08, St. Paul's Shipwreck Church, Rabat.
€3, St. Paul's Shipwreck Church, Valletta.

2008, June 28   Set of 3   6.25 6.25
1340-1342 A348

Souvenir Sheet
1343 A348 €3 multi   9.50 9.50

Intl.
Year of
Planet
Earth
A349

Emblem and: 7c, Sand dune. 86c, Tree in field. €1, Earth. €1.77, Sea coast.

Wmk. 354
2008, Aug. 11   Litho.   *Perf. 14¼*
1344-1347 A349 Set of 4   11.00 11.00

Cruise
Liners
A350

Designs: 63c, MSC Musica. €1.16, M.S. Voyager of the Seas. €1.40, M. S. Westerdam. €3, RMS Queen Elizabeth 2.

Perf. 14x14¼
2008, Nov. 18   Litho.   Wmk. 354
1348-1351 A350 Set of 4   16.00 16.00

Christmas — A351

Paintings: 19c, Madonna and Child with the Infant St. John the Baptist, by Francesco Trevisani. 26c, Nativity, by Master Alberto. 37c, Virgin and Child with the Infant St. John the Baptist, by Carlo Maratta.

2008, Nov. 27   *Perf. 14¼*
1352-1354 A351 Set of 3   2.10 2.10

Mushrooms
A352

Designs: 5c, Laetiorus sulphureus. 12c, Montagnea arenaria. 19c, Pleurotus eryngii. 26c, Inonotus indicus. €1.57, Suillus collinitus.

Wmk. 354

2009, Mar. 27	Litho.		Perf. 14¼
1355-1359	A352	Set of 5	8.00 8.00

Postal Transportation A353

Designs: 9c, Airplane. 35c, Motorcycles. €2.50, Bicycles. €3, Mail boat to Gozo.

2009, Apr. 28			
1360-1363	A353	Set of 4	20.00 20.00

Introduction of Euro Currency, 10th Anniv. — A354

Wmk. 354

2009, Apr. 30	Litho.		Perf. 14¼
1364	A354	€2 multi	7.50 7.50

Europa — A355

Designs: 37c, Galileo Galilei, Sketch of Moon by Galileo, Lunar Module. €1.19, Telescope of William Lassell, M42 nebula.

2009, May 9			Perf. 14¼x14
1365	A355	37c multi	1.10 1.10
a.		Booklet pane of 5	5.50 —
		Complete booklet, #1365a	5.50
1366	A355	€1.19 multi	3.50 3.50

Intl. Year of Astronomy.

13th Games of the Small States of Europe, Cyprus A356

Designs: 10c, Sailing. 19c, Judo. 37c, Shooting. 67c, Swimming. €1.77, Running.

2009, June 1			Perf. 14x14¼
1367-1371	A356	Set of 5	9.75 9.75

Cruise Liners Type of 2008

Designs: 37c, MS Seabourn Pride. 68c, MS Brilliance of the Seas. 91c, Costa Magica and Costa Atlantica. €2, MS MSC Splendida.

2009, July 15			
1372-1375	A350	Set of 4	12.50 12.50

Scenic Views A357

Designs: 2c, Mediterranean coast. 7c, Watchtower. 37c, Salt pans, Qbajjar, Gozo. €1.02, Ggantija Temple ruins.

Perf. 14x14¼

2009, Sept. 16	Litho.	Wmk. 354
1376-1379	A357	Set of 4	6.00 6.00

Christmas A358

Designs: 19c, Mater Admirabilis, in the manner of Botticelli by unknown artist. 37c, Madonna and Child, by Corrado Giaquinto. 63c, Madonna and Child, by Follower of Simone Cantarini.

Perf. 14¼x14

2009, Nov. 30	Litho.	Wmk. 354
1380-1382	A358	Set of 3	4.25 4.25

History of Malta A359

Inscriptions: 1c, Pleistocene Period. 2c, Early Temple Period. 5c, Late Temple Period. 7c, Bronze Period. 9c, Phoenician & Punic Period, vert. 10c, Roman Period. 19c, Byzantine Period, vert. 25c, Arab Period. 37c, Norman & Hohenstaufen Period, vert. 50c, Angevin & Aragaonese, vert. 51c, Knights of St. John. 63c, French Period. 68c, British Period, vert. 86c, Independence, vert. €1, Republic, vert. €1.08, E.U. Accession, vert. €5, Coat of arms, vert.

2009, Dec. 29	Perf. 14x14¼, 14¼x14	
1383	A359	1c multi	.30 .30
1384	A359	2c multi	.30 .30
1385	A359	5c multi	.30 .30
1386	A359	7c multi	.30 .30
1387	A359	9c multi	.30 .30
1388	A359	10c multi	.35 .35
1389	A359	19c multi	.70 .70
1390	A359	25c multi	.95 .95
1391	A359	37c multi	1.40 1.40
1392	A359	50c multi	1.90 1.90
1393	A359	51c multi	1.90 1.90
1394	A359	63c multi	2.50 2.50
1395	A359	68c multi	2.60 2.60
1396	A359	86c multi	3.25 3.25
1397	A359	€1 multi	4.00 4.00
1398	A359	€1.08 multi	4.25 4.25
1399	A359	€5 multi	19.00 19.00
a.		Souvenir sheet, #1383-1399	45.00 45.00
	Nos. 1383-1399 (17)		44.30 44.30

See Nos. 1443-1444.

Miniature Sheet

100-Ton Guns of Malta and Gibraltar — A360

No. 1400 — 100-ton gun from: a, Fort Rinella, Malta, 2010. b, Fort Rinella, 1882. c, Napier of Magdala Battery, Gibraltar, 1880. d, Napier of Magdala Battery, 2010.

Wmk. 354

2010, Feb. 19	Litho.	Perf. 13¾
1400	A360	75c Sheet of 4, #a-d	10.00 10.00

See Gibraltar No. 1221.

Balloons A361

Islands A362

Mortarboard and Diploma — A363

Wedding A364

Champagne Bottle, Bucket and Flutes — A365

Clock Tower and Fireworks A366

Hand Holding Trophy — A367

Map of Malta A368

Wmk. 354

2010, Mar. 17	Litho.	Perf. 14¼
1401	A361	19c multi	.65 .65
1402	A362	19c multi	.65 .65
1403	A363	19c multi	.65 .65
1404	A364	19c multi	.65 .65
1405	A365	19c multi	.65 .65
1406	A366	19c multi	.65 .65

1407	A367	19c multi	.65 .65
1408	A368	37c multi	1.25 1.25
	Nos. 1401-1408 (8)		5.80 5.80

Souvenir Sheet

Visit of Pope Benedict XVI to Malta — A369

2010, Mar. 17			
1409	A369	€3 multi	10.00 10.00

Europa — A370

Characters from children's books: 37c, Puttinu u Toninu, by Dr. Philip Farrugia Randon. €1.19, Meta I-Milied Ma Glex (When Christmas Didn't Come), by Clare Azzopardi.

2010, May 4		Set of 2	4.00 4.00
1410-1411	A370		
1411a		Booklet pane of 5 #1411	4.75
		Complete booklet, #1411a	4.75

2010 World Cup Soccer Championships, South Africa — A371

Designs: 63c, Flags, map of Africa. €2.50, Mascot, flag and map of South Africa.

Wmk. 354

2010, June 11	Litho.		Perf. 14¼
1412-1413	A371	Set of 2	8.50 8.50
1413a		Souvenir sheet, #1412-1413	8.50 8.50

Intl. Year of Biodiversity — A372

Designs: 19c, Maltese wall lizard. 68c, Storm petrel, vert. 86c, Maltese pyramidal orchid, vert. €1.40, Freshwater crab.

Perf. 14x14¼, 14¼x14

2010, Sept. 23	Litho.	Wmk. 354
1414-1417	A372	Set of 4	10.00 10.00

Coastline Features — A373

Designs: 37c, Azure Window, Gozo. 51c, Blue Grotto, Zurrieq, vert. 67c, Ta' Cenc Cliffs, Gozo, vert. €1.16, Filfla.

Perf. 14x14¼, 14¼x14
2010, Oct. 19   Litho.   Wmk. 354
1418-1421 A373   Set of 4   8.50 8.50

Christmas — A374

Designs: 19c, The Adoration of the Magi, by the Studio of Valerio Castello. 37c, The Flight Into Egypt, attributed to Filippo Paladini. 63c, Madonna di Maggio, by Pierre Guillemin, vert.

Perf. 14x14¼, 14¼x14
2010, Nov. 9   Litho.   Wmk. 354
1422-1424 A374   Set of 3   4.00 4.00

Compare with type A358.

Souvenir Sheet

First Malta Stamp, 150th Anniv. — A375

2010, Dec. 1   Perf. 14¼x14
1425 A375   €2.80 multi   9.50 9.50

Maltese Landscape Paintings by Edward Said — A376

Designs: 19c, Valletta. 37c, Manoel Island. €1.57, Cittadella.

Perf. 14x14¼
2011, Mar. 9   Litho.   Wmk. 354
1426-1428 A376   Set of 3   6.00 6.00

Miniature Sheet

Worldwide Fund for Nature (WWF), 50th Anniv. — A377

Various depictions of Chimaera monstrosa: a, 51c. b, 63c. c, 67c. d, 97c.

2011, Apr. 29   Perf. 13¾
1429 A377   Sheet of 4, #a-d   8.00 8.00

Europa — A378

Forest and: 37c, Butterfly and building. €1.19, Building.

2011, May 9   Perf. 14¼x14
1430-1431 A378   Set of 2   4.50 4.50

Intl. Year of Forests.

Miniature Sheets

Buses — A379

No. 1432: a, Reo bus on B'Kara route. b, Dodge T110L bus on Zabbar route. c, Leyland Comet bus on Zurrieq route. d, Ford V8 bus on Zebbug-Siggiewi route. e, Bedford SLD bus on Gudja-Ghaxaq route. f, Maltese Chassis Gozo Mail Bus. g, Federal Bus on Kalafrana route. h, Dodge T110L bus on Siggiewi route. i, Indiana bus on Rabat route. j, Austin CXD bus on Zetjun route.
No. 1433: a, Ford V8 bus on Sliema route. b, Commer Q4 bus on Lija route. c, Fordson BB bus on Mosta-Naxxar route. d, Thornycroft Sturdy ZE bus on Mellieha route. e, Bedford QL bus on Cospicua route. f, Magirus Deutz bus for all routes. g, Commer Q4 bus on Naxxar route. h, Bedford SB8 bus on Gozo route. i, Thames ET7 bus on B'Kara-St. Julians route. j, Bedford QL private hire bus.

2011, July 2   Perf. 14x14¼
1432 A379   20c Sheet of 10, #a-j   5.75 5.75
1433 A379   69c Sheet of 10, #a-j   19.50 19.50

Boats A380

Designs: 26c, Ferry M.V. Ta'Pinu. 37c, Ferry M.V. Jean De La Vallete. 67c, Patrol boat P23. 91c, Tugboat M.V. Spinola.

Perf. 14x14¼
2011, Aug. 10   Litho.   Wmk. 354
1434-1437 A380   Set of 4   6.50 6.50

Souvenir Sheet

Fishing Boat at Mgarr — A381

2011, Sept. 15   Perf. 13¾
1438 A381   €2.07 multi   5.75 5.75

See Iceland No. 1245.

Christmas A382

Paintings: 20c, The Holy Family in an Interior, by Follower of Marcello Venusti. 37c, The Madonna and Child with Infant St. John the Baptist, by the Tuscan School. 63c, The Rest on the Flight to Egypt, attributed to Circle of Pieter van Mol.

2011, Nov. 15   Wmk. 354   Perf. 14¼
1439-1441 A382   Set of 3   3.25 3.25

Souvenir Sheet

Malta No. 114 — A383

2011, Dec. 2
1442 A383   €4.16 multi   11.50 11.50

Malta Senate and Legislative Assembly, 90th anniv.

History of Malta Type of 2009

Inscriptions: 20c, Byzantine Period. 69c, British Period.

Perf. 14¼x14
2012, Mar. 7   Litho.   Wmk. 354
1443 A359   20c multi   .55 .55
1444 A359   69c multi   1.90 1.90

Paintings of Maltese Sites — A384

Designs: 20c, Marsalforn, by H. M. Bateman. 26c, Qala, by Bateman. 37c, Ghajnsielem, by Bateman, vert. 67c, Inquisitor's Palace, by Edward Lear. 97c, Gran Fontana, by Lear.

Wmk. 354
2012, Mar. 23   Litho.   Perf. 14¼
1445-1449 A384   Set of 5   6.50 6.50

Wedding Rings A385

Mortarboard and Diploma — A386

Christmas Ornaments — A387

Comino Shoreline — A388

Auberge de Castille, Painting by Charles Frederick de Brocktorff — A389

St. John's Co-cathedral, Valletta — A390

Trophy — A391

Champagne Bottle and Flutes — A392

2012, Apr. 3

1450	A385	37c multi	1.00	1.00
1451	A386	37c multi	1.00	1.00
1452	A387	37c multi	1.00	1.00
1453	A388	37c multi	1.00	1.00
1454	A389	37c multi	1.00	1.00
1455	A390	37c multi	1.00	1.00
1456	A391	37c multi	1.00	1.00
1457	A392	37c multi	1.00	1.00
	Nos. 1450-1457 (8)		8.00	8.00

Souvenir Sheet

Awarding of George Cross to Malta, 70th Anniv. — A393

2012, Apr. 14

1458	A393	€4.16 multi	11.00	11.00

Europa — A394

No. 1459 — Grand Harbour: a, 37c. b, €1.19.

2012, May 9

1459	A394	Horiz. pair, #a-b	4.25	4.25

Souvenir Sheet

2012 Summer Olympics, London — A395

No. 1460 — 2012 Olympic Games: a, 37c, Emblem. b, €2.11, Mascot.

2012, July 27

1460	A395	Sheet of 2, #a-b	6.25	6.25

Ships Involved in Operation Pedestal — A396

No. 1461: a, S.S. Almeria Lykes. b, H.M.S. Amazon. c, H.M.S. Antelope. d, H.M.S. Ashanti. e, H.M.S. Badsworth. f, H.M.S. Bicester. g, H.M.S. Bramham. h, M.V. Brisbane Star.
No. 1462: a, R.F.A. Brown Ranger. b, H.M.S. Cairo. c, H.M.S. Charybdis. d, M.V. Clan Ferguson. e, H.M.S. Coltsfoot. f, H.M.S. Derwent. g, M.V. Deucalion. h, R.F.A. Dingledale.
No. 1463: a, M.V. Dorset. b, H.M.S. Eagle. c, M.V. Empire Hope. d, H.M.S. Eskimo. e, H.M.S. Foresight. f, H.M.S. Furious. g, H.M.S. Fury. h, H.M.S. Geranium.
No. 1464: a, M.V. Glenorchy. b, H.M.S. Hebe. c, H.M.S. Hythe. d, H.M.S. Icarus. e, H.M.S. Indomitable. f, H.M.S. Intrepid. g, H.M.S. Ithuriel. h, H.M.S. Jaunty.
No. 1465: a, H.M.S. Jonquil. b, H.M.S. Kenya. c, H.M.S. Keppel. d, H.M.S. Laforey. e, H.M.S. Ledbury. f, H.M.S. Lightning. g, H.M.S. Lookout. h, H.M.S. Malcolm.
No. 1466: a, H.M.S. Manchester. b, H.M.S. Matchless. c, M.V. Melbourne Star. d, H.M.S. Nelson. e, H.M.S. Nigeria. f, S.S. Ohio. g, H.M.S. Pathfinder. h, H.M.S. Penn.

No. 1467: a, H.M.S. Phoebe. b, M.V. Port Chalmers. c, H.M.S. Quentin. d, M.V. Rochester Castle. e, H.M.S. Rodney. f, H.M.S. Rye. g, H.M.S. Salvonia. h, S.S. Santa Elisa.
No. 1468: a, H.M.S. Sirius. b, H.M.S. Somali. c, H.M.S. Speedy. d, H.M.S. Spirea. e, H.M.S. Tartar. f, H.M.S. Una. g, H.M.S. Utmost. h, H.M.S. Vansittart.
No. 1469: a, H.M.S. Venomous. b, H.M.S. Victorious. c, H.M.S. Vidette. d, S.S. Waimarama. e, M.V. Wairangi. f, H.M.S. Westcott. g, H.M.S. Wilton. h, H.M.S. Wishart.
No. 1470: a, H.M.S. Wolverine. b, H.M.S. Wrestler. c, H.M.S. Zetland. d, H.M.S. P.34. e, H.M.S. P.42. f, H.M.S. P.44. g, H.M.S. P.46. h, M.L. 321.
No. 1471: a, M.L. 126. b, M.L. 134. c, M.L. 135. d, M.L. 168. e, H.M.S. P.211. f, H.M.S. P.222. g, M.L. 459. h, M.L. 462.

2012, Aug. 10

1461		Sheet of 8, #a-h, + 2 labels	5.75	5.75
a.-h.	A396	26c Any single	.70	.70
1462		Sheet of 8, #a-h, + 2 labels	5.75	5.75
a.-h.	A396	26c Any single	.70	.70
1463		Sheet of 8, #a-h, + 2 labels	5.75	5.75
a.-h.	A396	26c Any single	.70	.70
1464		Sheet of 8, #a-h, + 2 labels	5.75	5.75
a.-h.	A396	26c Any single	.70	.70
1465		Sheet of 8, #a-h, + 2 labels	5.75	5.75
a.-h.	A396	26c Any single	.70	.70
1466		Sheet of 8, #a-h, + 2 labels	5.75	5.75
a.-h.	A396	26c Any single	.70	.70
1467		Sheet of 8, #a-h, + 2 labels	5.75	5.75
a.-h.	A396	26c Any single	.70	.70
1468		Sheet of 8, #a-h, + 2 labels	5.75	5.75
a.-h.	A396	26c Any single	.70	.70
1469		Sheet of 8, #a-h, + 2 labels	5.75	5.75
a.-h.	A396	26c Any single	.70	.70
1470		Sheet of 8, #a-h, + 2 labels	5.75	5.75
a.-h.	A396	26c Any single	.70	.70
1471		Sheet of 8, #a-h, + 2 labels	5.75	5.75
a.-h.	A396	26c Any single	.70	.70
	Nos. 1461-1471 (11)		63.25	63.25

Operation Pedestal, 70th anniv.

Historic Gates A397

Designs: 20c, Notre Dame Gate, Zabbar. 37c, Couvre Port Gate, Victoria, vert. 67c, Lunzjata Valley Gate, Victoria, vert. 69c, Fort Chambray Gate, Ghajnsielem.

2012, Sept. 26

1472-1475	A397	Set of 4	5.00	5.00

Christmas A398

Paintings: 20c, The Adoration of the Magi, by German Follower of Peter Paul Rubens. 37c, The Holy Family, by the Circle of Denys Calvaert. 63c, Holy Family, by the Dutch School.

2012, Oct. 31

1476-1478	A398	Set of 3	3.25	3.25

Souvenir Sheet

Blessed Gerard, by Antoine Favray — A399

2013, Feb. 15

1479	A399	€2.47 multi	6.50	6.50

Papal Bull of Pope Paschal II to Blessed Gerard concerning Hospital of St. John of Jerusalem, 900th anniv.

Souvenir Sheet

Paintings of Mattia Preti (1613-99) — A400

No. 1480: a, 97c, The Baptism of Christ (35x35mm). b, €1.87, Self-portrait (31x44mm).

2013, Feb. 23

1480	A400	Sheet of 2, #a-b	7.50	7.50

Fountains A401

Designs: 6c, Vilhena Fountain, Floriana. 32c, Triton Fountain, Floriana, horiz. €2.62, Spinola Fountain, Valletta.

Perf. 14¼x14, 14x14¼

2013, Mar. 27			**Wmk. 354**	
1481-1483	A401	Set of 3	7.75	7.75

Europa A402

Postal vehicles: 37c, Ford Transit Mark 1 van. €1.19, Lambretta three-wheeled van.

2013, May 9   **Perf. 14x13½**

1484-1485	A402	Set of 2	4.25	4.25

European Maritime Day — A403

Ocean liners: 26c, Riviera. 51c, Costa Deliziosa. 97c, MS Ryndam.

2013, May 20   **Perf. 14x14¼**

1486-1488	A403	Set of 3	4.75	4.75

Mammals — A404

Designs: 37c, Wild rabbit. €2.25, Maltese ox.

2013, June 20

1489-1490	A404	Set of 2	7.00	7.00

Souvenir Sheet

Grand Harbor, Malta — A405

2013, Aug. 20   **Perf. 13½x13¾**

1491	A405	€4.51 multi	12.00	12.00

See Curaçao No. 137.

Buses A406

Designs: 6c, Park Royal-Commer airport bus, 1940s. 10c, Thornycroft bus on Valletta-St. Julian's Route, c. 1903. 37c, Victoria Hire Service bus, c. 1925. 52c, Bedford SB Royal Armed Forces bus, 1950s. €1.16, Thames ET6 police bus, 1970s. €2.25, Magirus-Deutz O3500 bus.

2013, Aug. 27   **Perf. 14x14¼**

1492-1497	A406	Set of 6	12.00	12.00

Souvenir Sheet

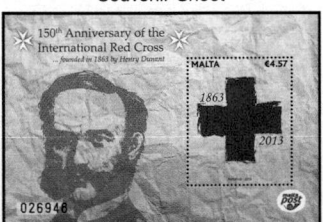

International Red Cross, 150th Anniv. — A407

2013, Oct. 29   **Litho.**   **Wmk. 354**   **Perf. 13¼**

1498	A407	€4.57 multi	12.50	12.50

Christmas A408

Details from creche scene from Jesus of Nazareth Institute, Zejtun: 26c, 37c, 63c.
No. 1502 — Entire creche scene showing: a, Combined designs of 37c and 63c stamps. b, Design of 26c stamp and other creche figures.

Perf. 13¾x14
2013, Nov. 18   Litho.   Wmk. 354
1499-1501 A408   Set of 3   3.50 3.50
Souvenir Sheet
1502 A408   €1 Sheet of 2, #a-b   5.50 5.50
No. 1502 contains two 76x20mm stamps.

Fountains
A409

Fountain at: 42c, Floriana. 59c, San Anton Gardens, Attard, horiz. €1.25, Kercem.

Wmk. 354
2014, Jan. 3   Litho.   Perf. 14¼
1503-1505 A409   Set of 3   6.25 6.25

Halls of the Knights Hospitaller, Acre, Israel and Valletta, Malta — A410

Wmk. 354
2014, Jan. 28   Litho.   Perf. 13¾
1506 A410   51c multi   1.40 1.40
See Israel No. 2000.

Watercraft
A411

Designs: No. 1507, 26c, Police boat at Valletta. No. 1508, 26c, Police boat at Sliema Ferries. No. 1509, €1.55, HMS Alexander. No. 1510, €1.55, HMS London.

Wmk. 354
2014, Mar. 18   Litho.   Perf. 14
1507-1510 A411   Set of 4   10.00 10.00

Malta Police Force, 200th anniv. (Nos. 1507-1508); End of Military Facilities Agreement, 35th anniv. (Nos. 1509-1510).

Souvenir Sheet

Canonization of Popes John XXIII and John Paul II — A412

No. 1511: a, 26c, Pope John XXIII (1881-1963). b, €1.85, Pope John Paul II (1920-2005).

Wmk. 354
2014, Apr. 26   Litho.   Perf. 14¼
1511 A412   Sheet of 2, #a-b   6.00 6.00

Admission to the European Union, 10th Anniv. — A413

Wmk. 354
2014, Apr. 30   Litho.   Perf. 14¼
1512 A413   59c multi   1.75 1.75

Europa — A414

Details from painting by Girolamo Gianni: 59c, Man playing Maltese bagpipe. €2.19, Man playing drum.

Wmk. 354
2014, May 9   Litho.   Perf. 13½
1513-1514 A414   Set of 2   7.75 7.75

Souvenir Sheet

National Anniversaries — A415

No. 1515: a, 59c, #308 redrawn with "50th Anniversary 1964-2014" added (27x33mm). b, €3, #489 redrawn with "40th Anniversary 1974-2014" added (44x31mm).

Perf. 14, 14x14¼ (No. 1515c)
2014, May 15   Litho.   Wmk. 354
1515 A415   Sheet of 2, #a-b   9.75 9.75

Souvenir Sheet

2014 World Cup Soccer Championships, Brazil — A416

No. 1516: a, 59c, Emblem. b, €1.55, Mascot.

Wmk. 354
2014, June 12   Litho.   Perf. 14¼
1516 A416   Sheet of 2, #a-b   6.00 6.00

Flowers — A417

Designs: 26c, Gladiolus italicus. 59c, Verbascum sinuatum. €1.16, Orchis conica.

Perf. 14x13¾
2014, June 27   Litho.   Wmk. 354
1517-1519 A417   Set of 3   5.50 5.50
See Nos. 1532-1534.

Euromed Postal Emblem and Mediterranean Sea — A418

Wmk. 354
2014, July 9   Litho.   Perf. 13¾
1520 A418   €1.85 multi   5.00 5.00

Grand Masters of the Sovereign Military Order of Malta — A419

No. 1521: a, Philippe de Villiers de L'Isle-Adam. b, Pierino del Ponte. c, Didier de Saint-Jaille. d, Jean de Homedes. e, Claude de la Sengle. f, Jean de la Valette-Parisot. g, Pierre de Monte. h, Jean L'Evesque de la Cassière.
No. 1522: a, Hugues Loubenx de Verdala. b, Martin Garzez. c, Alof de Wignacourt. d, Luis Mendez de Vasconcellos. e, Antoine de Paule. f, Jean-Paul de Lascaris-Castellar. g, Martín de Redín. h, Annet de Clermont-Gessant. i, Raphael Cotoner. j, Nicolas Cotoner.
No. 1523: a, Gregorio Carafa. b, Adrien de Wignacourt. c, Ramon Perellos y Roccaful. d, Marc'Antonio Zondadari. e, Antonio Manoel de Vilhena. f, Raymond Despuig. g, Manuel Pinto de Fonseca. h, Francisco Ximenes de Texada. i, Emmanuel de Rohan-Polduc. j, Ferdinand von Hompesch zu Bolheim.

Wmk. 354
2014, Sept. 30   Litho.   Perf. 14¼
1521   Sheet of 8 + 2 labels   5.25 5.25
a.-h. A419 26c Any single   .65   .65
1522   Sheet of 10   6.50 6.50
a.-j. A419 26c Any single   .65   .65
1523   Sheet of 10   6.50 6.50
a.-j. A419 26c Any single   .65   .65
       Nos. 1521-1523 (3)   18.25 18.25

World War I, Cent. A420

Poppy and: 10c, Bighi Hospital. 59c, Floriana Hospital. €2, HMHS Rewa.

Perf. 14x14¼
2014, Nov. 7   Litho.   Wmk. 354
1524-1526 A420   Set of 3   6.75 6.75

Christmas
A421

Actors in live Nativity scene in Ghajnsielem depicting: 26c, Holy Family. 59c, Adoration of the Magi, horiz. 63c, Shepherds, horiz. €1.16, Holy Family, diff.

Perf. 14¼x14, 14x14¼
2014, Nov. 17   Litho.   Wmk. 354
1527-1530 A421   Set of 4   6.50 6.50

Malta and Yalta Conferences, 70th Anniv. — A422

No. 1531: a, Franklin D. Roosevelt and Winston Churchill meeting in Malta. b, Montgomery House, Floriana, Malta. c, Churchill, Roosevelt, Joseph Stalin and other officials at Yalta Conference.

Wmk. 354
2015, Feb. 4   Litho.   Perf. 14¼
1531   Horiz. strip of 3   3.30 3.30
a.-c. A422 €1 Any single   1.10 1.10

Flowers Type of 2014
Designs: 26c, Tragopogon hybridus. 59c, Anemone coronaria. €1.16, Arisarum vulgare.

Perf. 14x13¾
2015, Feb. 14   Litho.   Wmk. 354
1532-1534 A417   Set of 3   4.50 4.50

SEMI-POSTAL STAMPS

All semi-postal issues are for Christmas.

Catalogue values for unused stamps in this section are for Never Hinged items.

Two Peasants with Tambourine and Bagpipe SP1

Star of Bethlehem and: 5p+1p, Angels with Trumpet and Harp, Star of Bethlehem and Mdina Cathedral. 1sh6p+3p, Choir boys singing Christmas carols.
The background of the 3 stamps together shows the Cathedral of Mdina, Malta, and surrounding countryside.

Wmk. 354
1969, Nov. 8   Litho.   Perf. 12½
B1 SP1   1p +1p multi   .25   .25
B2 SP1   5p +1p multi   .25   .25
B3 SP1   1sh6p +3p multi   .25   .45
a.   Triptych, #B1-B3   .50   .50
       Nos. B1-B3 (3)   .75   .95
Nos. B1-B3 were printed each in sheets of 60, and in sheets containing 20 triptychs.

Christmas Eve Procession — SP2

10p+2p, Nativity & Cathedral. 1sh6p+3p, Adoration of the Shepherds & Mdina Cathedral.

1970, Nov. 7　Photo.　Perf. 14x13½
B4	SP2	1p + ½p multi	.25	.25
B5	SP2	10p +2p multi	.25	.25
B6	SP2	1sh6p +3p multi	.25	.45
		Nos. B4-B6 (3)	.75	.95

Surtax for child welfare organizations.

Angel — SP3

No. B8, Madonna & Child. No. B9, Shepherd.

1971, Nov. 8　　　　Perf. 14
B7	SP3	1p + ½p multi	.25	.25
B8	SP3	10p +2p multi	.25	.25
B9	SP3	1sh6p +3p multi	.25	.40
a.		Souv. sheet, #B7-B9, perf. 15	1.00	1.25
		Nos. B7-B9 (3)	.75	.90

1972, Dec.　Litho.　Perf. 13½

Designs: 3c+1c, Angel playing tambourine. 7c5m+1c5m, Angel singing.

B10	SP3	8m +2m dk gray & gold	.25	.25
B11	SP3	3c +1c dk purple & gold	.25	.25
B12	SP3	7c5m +1c5m slate & gold	.30	.50
a.		Souvenir sheet of 3, #B10-B12	2.75	3.75
		Nos. B10-B12 (3)	.80	1.00

1973, Nov. 10　Litho.　Perf. 13½

8m+2m, Singers, organ pipes. 3c+1c, Virgin & Child with star. 7c5m+1c5m, Star, candles, buildings, tambourine.

B13	SP3	8m +2m multi	.25	.25
B14	SP3	3c +1c multi	.30	.30
B15	SP3	7c5m +1c5m multi	.65	1.10
a.		Souvenir sheet of 3, #B13-B15	6.00	7.00
		Nos. B13-B15 (3)	1.20	1.65
		Nos. B7-B15 (9)	3.05	3.05

Star and Holy Family — SP4

Designs: 3c+1c, Star and two shepherds. 5c+1c, Star and three shepherds. 7c5m+1c5m, Star and Three Kings.

1974, Nov. 22　Litho.　Perf. 14
B16	SP4	8m +2m multi	.25	.25
B17	SP4	3c +1c multi	.25	.25
B18	SP4	5c +1c multi	.35	.35
B19	SP4	7c5m +1c5m multi	.35	.50
		Nos. B16-B19 (4)	1.20	1.35

Nativity, by Maestro Alberto — SP5

8m+2m, Shepherds. 7c5m+1c5m, Three Kings.

1975, Nov. 4　　　　Perf. 13½
**Size: 24x23mm (#B20, B22);
49x23mm (#B21)**
B20	SP5	8m +2m multi	.25	.25
B21	SP5	3c +1c multi	.50	.40
B22	SP5	7c5m +1c5m multi	2.00	2.50
a.		Triptych, #B20-B22	3.50	4.00
		Nos. B20-B22 (3)	2.75	3.15

Printed singly and as triptychs. Surtax for child welfare.

SP6

Madonna and Saints, by Domenico di Michelino — SP7

Details of Painting: 5c+1c, Virgin & Child. 7c+1c5m, St. Christopher & Bishop.

1976, Nov. 23　Litho.　Perf. 13½
B23	SP6	1c +5m multi	.25	.25
B24	SP6	5c +1c multi	.35	.30
B25	SP6	7c +1c5m multi	.65	.65

Perf. 13½x14
B26	SP7	10c +2c multi	1.25	1.25
		Nos. B23-B26 (4)	2.50	2.45

Nativity SP8

Crèche Figurines: 1c+5m, Annunciation to the Shepherds. 11c+1c5m, Shepherds.

Perf. 13½x14
1977, Nov. 16　　　Wmk. 354
B27	SP8	1c +5m multi	.25	.25
B28	SP8	7c +1c multi	.45	.45
B29	SP8	11c +1c5m multi	.70	.70
a.		Triptych, #B27-B29	1.50	1.50
		Nos. B27-B29 (3)	1.40	1.40

Nos. B27-B29 printed singly and as triptychs. Surtax was for child welfare.

Christmas Decorations, People and Church — SP9

Designs: 5c+1c, Decorations and angels. 7c+1c5m, Decorations and carolers. 11c+3c, Combined designs of Nos. B30-B32.

1978, Nov. 9　Litho.　Perf. 14
Size: 24x30mm
B30	SP9	1c +5m multi	.25	.25
B31	SP9	5c +1c multi	.35	.35
B32	SP9	7c +1c5m multi	.45	.45

Perf. 13½
Size: 58x22½mm
B33	SP9	11c +3c multi	.70	.70
		Nos. B30-B33 (4)	1.75	1.75

Nativity, by Giuseppe Cali — SP10

Designs (Cali Paintings): 5c+1c, 11c+3c, Flight into Egypt. 7c+1c5m, Nativity.

1979, Nov. 14　Litho.　Perf. 14x13½
B34	SP10	1c +5m multi	.25	.25
B35	SP10	5c +1c multi	.35	.35
B36	SP10	7c +1c5m multi	.45	.45
B37	SP10	11c +3c multi	.70	.70
		Nos. B34-B37 (4)	1.75	1.75

Nativity, by Anton Inglott (1915-1945) — SP11

Details of Painting: 2c+5m, Annunciation. 6c+1c, Angel. 8c+1c5m, Holy Family.

1980, Oct. 7　Litho.　Perf. 14x13½
Size: 20x47mm
B38	SP11	2c +5m multi	.25	.25
B39	SP11	6c +1c multi	.40	.40
B40	SP11	8c +1c5m multi	.50	.50

Perf. 14½x14
Size: 47x39mm
B41	SP11	12c +3c shown	.75	.75
		Nos. B38-B41 (4)	1.90	1.90

SP12

1981, Nov. 18　Wmk. 354　Perf. 14
B42	SP12	2c +1c Children, vert.	.25	.25
B43	SP12	8c +2c Procession	.50	.50
B44	SP12	20c +3c Service, vert.	1.10	1.10
		Nos. B42-B44 (3)	1.85	1.85

SP13

Three Kings Following Star: 2c+1c, Star. 8c+2c, Three Kings. 20c+3c, Entire design.

1982, Oct. 8　Litho.　Perf. 13½
B45	SP13	2c +1c multi	.25	.25
B46	SP13	8c +2c multi	.55	.55

Perf. 14
Size: 45x36mm
B47	SP13	20c +3c multi	1.25	1.25
		Nos. B45-B47 (3)	2.05	2.05

SP14

Illuminated Manuscripts, Book of Hours, 15th Cent.: 2c+1c, Annunciation. 8c+2c, Nativity. 20c+3c, Three Kings bearing gifts. Surtax was for child welfare.

1983, Sept. 6　Litho.　Perf. 14
B48	SP14	2c +1c multi	.25	.25
B49	SP14	8c +2c multi	.60	.60
B50	SP14	20c +3c multi	1.40	1.40
		Nos. B48-B50 (3)	2.25	2.25

SP15

Paintings by Peter-Paul Caruana, Church of Our Lady of Porto Salvo, Valletta, 1850: 2c+1c, Visitation, vert. 8c+2c, Epiphany. 20c+3c, Jesus Among the Doctors.

1984, Oct. 5　Litho.　Perf. 14
B51	SP15	2c +1c multi	.35	.35
B52	SP15	8c +2c multi	.90	.90
B53	SP15	20c +3c multi	2.10	2.10
		Nos. B51-B53 (3)	3.35	3.35

SP16

1985, Oct. 10　Litho.　Perf. 14
B54	SP16	2c +1c Adoration of the Magi	.45	.45
B55	SP16	8c +2c Nativity	1.10	1.10
B56	SP16	20c +3c Trumpeter Angels	2.25	2.25
		Nos. B54-B56 (3)	3.80	3.80

Surtax for child welfare organizations.

SP17

Paintings by Giuseppe D'Arena (1633-1719).

1986, Oct. 10　Wmk. 354　Perf. 14½
B57	SP17	2c +1c The Nativity	.65	.65
B58	SP17	8c +2c The Nativity, detail, vert.	2.00	2.00
B59	SP17	20c +3c The Epiphany	4.75	4.75
		Nos. B57-B59 (3)	7.40	7.40

Surtax for child welfare organizations.

SP18

Illuminated text from choral books of the Veneranda Assemblea of St. John's Conventual Church, Valletta.

1987, Nov. 6　Litho.　Perf. 14
B60	SP18	2c +1c Mary's Visit to Elizabeth	.60	.60
B61	SP18	8c +2c Nativity	1.75	1.75
B62	SP18	20c +3c Adoration of the Magi	4.25	4.25
		Nos. B60-B62 (3)	6.60	6.60

Surtax for child welfare organizations and the handicapped.

SP19

1988, Nov. 5   Litho.   Perf. 14½x14
B63 SP19 3c +1c Shepherd   .40   .40
B64 SP19 10c +2c Nativity   1.00 1.00
B65 SP19 25c +3c Magi   2.25 2.25
    Nos. B63-B65 (3)   3.65 3.65

Surtax for child welfare organizations and the handicapped.

SP20

Various angels from frescoes by Mattia Preti in the vault of St. John's Co-Cathedral, Valletta, 1666.

1989, Nov. 11   Perf. 14
B66 SP20 3c +1c multi   .40   .40
B67 SP20 10c +2c multi   1.40 1.40
B68 SP20 20c +3c multi   2.75 2.75
    Nos. B66-B68 (3)   4.55 4.55

Surtax for child welfare organizations and the handicapped.

SP21   SP22

Creche figures.

1990, Nov. 10
B69 SP21 3c +1c Carrying
            water   .35   .35
B70 SP21 10c +2c Nativity,
            41x27mm   .95   .95
B71 SP21 25c +3c Shepherd   2.10 2.10
    Nos. B69-B71 (3)   3.40 3.40

Surtax for child welfare organizations.

1991, Nov. 6
B72 SP22 3c +1c Wise men   .40   .40
B73 SP22 10c +2c Mary, Joseph,
            Jesus   1.00 1.00
B74 SP22 25c +3c Shepherds   2.50 2.50
    Nos. B72-B74 (3)   3.90 3.90

Surtax for child welfare organizations.

SP23

Paintings from dome spandrels of Mosta Parish Church by Giuseppppe Cali (1846-1930): 3c+1c, Nativity scene. 10c+2c, Adoration of the Magi. 25c+3c, Christ among the Elders in the Temple.

1992, Oct. 22
B75 SP23 3c +1c multi   .40   .40
B76 SP23 10c +2c multi   1.60 1.60
B77 SP23 25c +3c multi   4.00 4.00
    Nos. B75-B77 (3)   6.00 6.00

Surtax for child welfare organizations.

SP24

Designs: 3c+1c, Christ Child in manger. 10c+2c, Christmas tree. 25c+3c, Star.

1993, Nov. 20
B78 SP24 3c +1c multi   .45   .45
B79 SP24 10c +2c multi   .95   .95
B80 SP24 25c +3c multi   2.10 2.10
    Nos. B78-B80 (3)   3.50 3.50

Beginning with No. 845, semi-postal stamps are included with the postage portion of the set.

Christmas — SP25

Children's art: 6c+2c, Man with net chasing star. 15c+2c, People, Chirstmas tree. 16c+2c, People hugging. 19c+3c, Woman with shopping bags.

2001, Nov. 29   Litho.   Perf. 14
B81-B84 SP25 Set of 4   5.25 5.25

Stampin' the Future Type of 2000
Souvenir Sheet
Wmk. 354
2006, Dec. 22   Litho.   Perf. 14
B85 A261 £1.50 + (16c) Like
            #1029   10.00 10.00

Surtax was for the Valletta YMCA.

AIR POST STAMPS

No. 140 Overprinted

Perf. 14½x14
1928, Apr. 1   Typo.   Wmk. 4
C1 A22 6p red & violet   2.00 1.00

Catalogue values for unused stamps in this section, from this point to the end of the section, are for Never Hinged items.

Jet over Valletta AP1

Designs: 3c, 5c, 20c, 35c, Winged emblem. 7c5m, 25c, like 4c.

Wmk. 354
1974, Mar.   Litho.   Perf. 13½
Cross Emblem in Red and Blue
C2 AP1 3c ol brown & gold   .25   .25
C3 AP1 4c dk blue & gold   .25   .25
C4 AP1 5c dk vio bl & gold   .30   .30
C5 AP1 7c5m sl green & gold   .40   .40
C6 AP1 20c vio brn & gold   1.10 1.10
C7 AP1 25c slate & gold   1.40 1.40
C8 AP1 35c brown & gold   2.00 2.00
    Nos. C2-C8 (7)   5.70 5.70

Jet and Megalithic Temple — AP2

Designs: 7c, 20c, Air Malta Boeing 720B approaching Malta. 11c, 75c, Jumbo jet landing at Luqa Airport. 17c, like 5c.

1978, Oct. 3   Litho.   Perf. 13½
C9   AP2 5c multicolored   .30   .30
C10 AP2 7c multicolored   .40   .40
C11 AP2 11c multicolored   .60   .60
C12 AP2 17c multicolored   .95   .95
C13 AP2 20c multicolored   1.10 1.10
C14 AP2 75c multicolored   4.25 4.25
    Nos. C9-C14 (6)   7.60 7.60

Boeing 737, 1984 AP3

1984, Jan. 26   Wmk. 354   Perf. 14
C15 AP3 7c shown   .45   .45
C16 AP3 8c Boeing 720B,
            1974   .50   .50
C17 AP3 16c Vickers Van-
            guard, 1964   .95   .95
C18 AP3 23c Vickers Viscount,
            1958   1.40 1.40
C19 AP3 27c Douglas DC3
            Dakota, 1948   1.60 1.60
C20 AP3 38c AW Atlanta,
            1936   2.40 2.40
C21 AP3 75c Dornier Wal,
            1929   4.50 4.50
    Nos. C15-C21 (7)   11.80 11.80

POSTAGE DUE STAMPS

D1

1925   Typeset   Unwmk.   Imperf.
J1   D1 ½p black, *white*   1.40 8.00
J2   D1 1p black, *white*   3.75 3.50
J3   D1 1½p black, *white*   3.50 4.25
J4   D1 2p black, *white*   12.00 21.00
J5   D1 2½p black, *white*   3.25 3.25
  a. "2" of ½ omitted   1,000. 1,400.
J6   D1 3p black, *gray*   10.50 17.00
J7   D1 4p black, *orange*   5.75 11.00
J8   D1 6p black, *orange*   5.75 22.50
J9   D1 1sh black, *orange*   8.50 25.00
J10 D1 1sh6p black, *orange* 16.00 62.50
    Nos. J1-J10 (10)   70.40 178.00
    Set, never hinged   130.00

These stamps were typeset in groups of 42. In each sheet there were four impressions of a group, two of them being inverted and making tete beche pairs.
Forged examples of No. J5a are known.

Maltese Cross — D2

Wmk. 4 Sideways
1925   Typo.   Perf. 12
J11 D2 ½p blue green   1.40 .70
J12 D2 1p violet   1.40 .50
J13 D2 1½p yellow brown   1.75 1.00
J14 D2 2p gray   12.50 1.25
J15 D2 2½p orange   2.25 1.40
J16 D2 3p dark blue   4.25 1.40
J17 D2 4p olive green   14.00 18.00
J18 D2 6p claret   3.50 4.75

J19 D2 1sh gray black   7.50 14.00
J20 D2 1sh6p deep rose   9.75 42.50
    Nos. J11-J20 (10)   58.30 85.50
    Set, never hinged   85.00

In 1953-57 six values (½p-2p, 3p, 4p) were reissued on chalky paper in slightly different colors.

Catalogue values for unused stamps in this section, from this point to the end of the section, are for Never Hinged items.

1966   Wmk. 314   Perf. 12
J21 D2 2p sepia   22.50 26.00

Wmk. 354 Sideways
1968   Perf. 12½
J22 D2 ½p green   .25   .25
J23 D2 1p rose violet   .25   .25
J24 D2 1½p bister brn   .30   .30
J25 D2 2p brown black   .45   .45
J26 D2 2½p orange   .50   .50
J27 D2 3p Prus blue   .60   .60
J28 D2 4p olive   .90   .90
J29 D2 6p purple   1.50 1.50
J30 D2 1sh black   1.60 1.60
J31 D2 1sh6p rose car   3.75 3.75
    Nos. J22-J31 (10)   10.10 10.10

1967, Nov. 9   Perf. 12
J22a D2 ½p   3.25 3.25
J23a D2 1p   4.50 4.50
J25a D2 2p   6.75 6.75
J28a D2 4p   60.00 110.00
    Nos. J22a-J28a (4)   74.50 124.50

Numeral — D3   Scroll — D4

Perf. 13x13½
1973, Apr. 28   Litho.   Wmk. 354
J32 D3 2m brown   .25   .25
J33 D3 3m brown orange   .25   .25
J34 D3 5m carmine   .25   .25
J35 D3 1c deep green   .30   .35
J36 D3 2c black   .40   .35
J37 D3 3c olive   .40   .35
J38 D3 5c violet blue   .65   .70
J39 D3 10c deep magenta   .85   1.00
    Nos. J32-J39 (8)   3.35 3.50

Wmk. 354
1993, Jan. 4   Litho.   Perf. 14
J40 D4 1c brt pink & lt pink .25   .30
J41 D4 2c brt blue & lt blue .25   .40
J42 D4 5c brt grn & lt grn   .35   .45
J43 D4 10c org yel & brt yel .55   .55
    Nos. J40-J43 (4)   1.40 1.70

WAR TAX STAMPS

Nos. 50, 25 Overprinted

1918   Wmk. 3   Perf. 14
MR1 A13 ½p green   2.00 .30
Wmk. 2
MR2 A12 3p red violet & gray 3.00 12.00

MANCHUKUO
'man-'chü-'kwō

LOCATION — Covering Manchuria, or China's three northeastern provinces —Fengtien, Kirin and Heilung-kiang—plus Jehol province.
GOVT. — Independent state under Japanese influence
AREA — 503,013 sq. mi. (estimated)
POP. — 43,233,954 (est. 1940)
CAPITAL — Hsinking (Changchun)

Manchukuo was formed in 1932 with the assistance of Japan. In 1934 Henry Pu-yi, Chief Executive, was enthroned as Emperor Kang Teh. In 1945, when Japan surrendered to the Allies, the terms included the return of Manchukuo to China. The puppet state was dissolved.

100 Fen = 1 Yuan

Watermarks

Wmk. 141 — Horizontal Zigzag Lines

Wmk. 239 — Curved Wavy Lines

Wmk. 242 — Characters

Pagoda at Liaoyang A1

Chief Executive Henry Pu-yi A2

Five characters in top label.
Inscription reads "Manchu State Postal Administration."

Lithographed
Perf. 13x13½

1932, July 26   Unwmk.
White Paper

1	A1	½f gray brown	1.75	.75
2	A1	1f dull red	2.00	.75
3	A1	1½f lilac	6.50	4.00
4	A1	2f slate	6.50	1.00
5	A1	3f dull brown	8.25	5.00
6	A1	4f olive green	3.00	.50
7	A1	5f green	4.00	.90
8	A1	6f rose	11.00	3.50
9	A1	7f gray	4.75	1.25
10	A1	8f ocher	18.00	11.00
11	A1	10f orange	6.75	1.10
12	A2	13f dull brown	15.00	7.00
13	A2	15f rose	18.00	3.00
14	A2	16f turquoise grn	27.50	9.00
15	A2	20f gray brown	11.00	1.90
16	A2	30f orange	12.00	2.50

17	A2	50f olive green	27.50	3.25
18	A2	1y violet	42.50	12.00
		Nos. 1-18 (18)	226.00	69.65
		Set, never hinged	300.00	

A local provisional overprint of a horizontal line of four characters in red or black, reading "Chinese Postal Administration," was applied to Nos. 1-18 by followers of Gen. Su Ping-wen, who rebelled against the Manchukuo government in September, 1932. Many counterfeits exist.
See Nos. 23-31. For surcharges see Nos. 36, 59-61.
See note on local handstamps at end of the Manchukuo listings.

Flags, Map and Wreath — A3   Old State Council Building — A4

1933, Mar. 1   *Perf. 12½*

19	A3	1f orange	6.50	4.00
20	A4	2f dull green	17.50	12.00
21	A3	4f light red	6.50	4.50
22	A4	10f deep blue	37.50	30.00
		Nos. 19-22 (4)	68.00	50.50
		Set, never hinged	100.00	

1st anniv. of the establishing of the State. Nos. 19-22 were printed in sheets of 100 with a special printing in sheets of 20.

Type of 1932
Perf. 13x13½

1934, Feb.   Engr.   Wmk. 239
Granite Paper

23	A1	½f dark brown	4.00	1.65
24	A1	1f red brown	4.00	2.00
25	A1	1½f dark violet	6.00	3.00
26	A1	2f slate	7.50	2.00
27	A1	3f brown	4.00	.60
28	A1	4f olive brown	32.50	5.00
29	A1	10f deep orange	14.50	2.50
30	A2	15f rose	525.00	225.00
31	A2	1y violet	55.00	14.00
		Nos. 23-31 (9)	652.50	255.75

For surcharge see No. 60.

Emperor's Palace — A5   Phoenix — A6

1934, Mar. 1   *Perf. 12½*

32	A5	1½f orange brown	6.00	5.00
33	A6	3f carmine	5.00	4.00
34	A5	6f green	14.50	10.00
35	A6	10f dark blue	26.00	17.50
		Nos. 32-35 (4)	51.50	36.50
		Set, never hinged	75.00	

Enthronement of Emperor Kang Teh. Nos. 32-35 were printed in sheets of 100, with a special printing in sheets of 20.

No. 6 Surcharged in Black

Perf. 13x13½

1934   Unwmk.   White Paper

36	A1	1f on 4f olive grn	6.00	4.00
		Never hinged	11.00	
a.		Brown surcharge	45.00	45.00
b.		Upper left character of surcharge omitted		
c.		Inverted surcharge	175.00	175.00

Pagoda at Liaoyang A7   Emperor Kang Teh A8

Six characters in top label instead of five as in 1932-34 issues.
Inscription reads "Manchu Empire Postal Administration."

Perf. 13x13½

1934-36   Wmk. 239   Engr.
Granite Paper

37	A7	½f brown	.50	.35
38	A7	1f red brown	1.00	.30
39	A7	1½f dk violet	1.00	.50
a.		Booklet pane of 6	90.00	
41	A7	3f brown ('35)	.75	.35
a.		Booklet pane of 6	80.00	
42	A7	5f dk blue ('35)	10.00	2.00
43	A7	5f gray ('36)	5.00	2.00
44	A7	6f rose ('35)	3.00	.60
45	A7	7f dk gray ('35)	2.50	2.00
47	A7	9f red orange ('35)	2.50	.75
50	A8	15f ver ('35)	2.50	.85
51	A8	18f Prus grn ('35)	25.00	5.00
52	A8	20f dk brown ('35)	4.00	.90
53	A8	30f orange brn ('35)	4.50	.90
54	A8	50f ol grn ('35)	6.00	2.00
55	A8	1y dk violet ('35)	24.00	6.00
a.		1y violet	26.00	8.00
		Nos. 37-55 (15)	92.25	24.50
		Set, never hinged	125.00	

4f and 8f, type A7, were prepared but not issued. Values $45 and $15, respectively.

1935   Wmk. 242   *Perf. 13x13½*

57	A7	10f deep blue	13.00	2.00
58	A8	13f light brown	16.00	8.00
		Set, never hinged	42.00	

Nos. 6 and 28 Surcharged in Black

1935   White Paper   Unwmk.

59	A1	3f on 4f ol grn	70.00	60.00
		Never hinged	100.00	

1935   Granite Paper   Wmk. 239

60	A1	3f on 4f olive brn	9.00	5.50
		Never hinged	16.00	

Similar Surcharge on No. 14

1935   White Paper   Unwmk.

61	A2	3f on 16f turq grn	15.00	10.00
		Never hinged	22.50	
		Nos. 59-61 (3)	94.00	75.50

Orchid Crest of Manchukuo A9

Sacred White Mountains and Black Waters A10

1935, Jan. 1   Litho.   Wmk. 141
Granite Paper

62	A9	2f green	5.50	2.00
63	A10	4f dull ol grn	2.75	1.75
64	A9	8f ocher	4.50	3.25
65	A10	12f brown red	14.00	17.50
		Nos. 62-65 (4)	26.75	24.50
		Set, never hinged	44.00	

Nos. 62-65 exist imperforate.

1935   Wmk. 242

66	A9	2f yellow green	3.50	1.00
68	A9	8f ocher	6.00	4.00
70	A10	12f brown red	12.50	10.00
		Nos. 66-70 (3)	22.00	15.00
		Set, never hinged	30.00	

Nos. 62-70 issued primarily to pay postage to China, but valid for any postal use.

See Nos. 75-78, 113, 115, 158. For surcharges see Nos. 101, 103-104, 106-109, People's Republic of China No. 2L19.

Mt. Fuji — A11

Phoenix — A12

Perf. 11, 12½ and Compound

1935, Apr. 1   Engr.   Wmk. 242

71	A11	1½f dull green	2.50	2.00
72	A12	3f orange	3.50	3.25
a.		3f red orange	6.00	5.00
73	A11	6f dk carmine	5.50	4.75
a.		Horiz. pair, imperf. btwn.	250.00	
b.		Perf. 11x12½	45.00	37.50
74	A12	10f dark blue	7.50	6.00
a.		Perf. 12½x11	50.00	37.50
b.		Perf. 12½	22.50	25.00
		Nos. 71-74 (4)	19.00	16.00
		Set, never hinged	27.50	

Visit of the Emperor of Manchukuo to Tokyo.

Orchid Crest — A13

Types of A9 & A10 Redrawn and Engraved

1936   Wmk. 242   *Perf. 13x13½*

75	A13	2f lt green	1.00	.30
76	A10	4f olive green	3.25	.75
77	A13	8f ocher	3.00	1.25
78	A10	12f orange brn	42.50	32.50
		Nos. 75-78 (4)	49.75	34.80
		Set, never hinged	67.50	

Unbroken lines of shading in the background of Nos. 76 and 78. Shading has been removed from right and left of the mountains. Nearly all lines have been removed from the lake. There are numerous other alterations in the design.
Issued primarily to pay postage to China, but valid for any postal use.
See No. 112. For surcharges see Nos. 102-106.

Wild Goose over Sea of Japan — A14

Communications Building at Hsinking — A15

Perf. 12x12½, 12½x12

1936, Jan. 26   Wmk. 242

79	A14	1½f black brown	4.00	2.50
80	A15	3f rose lilac	4.00	2.00
81	A14	6f carmine rose	8.00	7.00
82	A15	10f blue	10.00	8.50
		Nos. 79-82 (4)	26.00	20.00
		Set, never hinged	42.50	

Postal convention with Japan.

New State
Council
Building
A16

North
Mausoleum at
Mukden
A18

Carting
Soybeans
A17

Summer
Palace at
Chengteh
A19

1936-37 Wmk. 242 Perf. 13x13½
83	A16	½f brown	.40	.25
84	A16	1f red brown	.40	.25
85	A16	1½f violet	4.25	2.75
a.		Booklet pane of 6	85.00	
86	A17	2f lt green ('37)	.40	.25
a.		Booklet pane of 6	20.00	
87	A16	3f chocolate	.40	.25
a.		Booklet pane of 6	200.00	
88	A18	4f lt ol grn ('37)	.45	.25
a.		Booklet pane of 6	25.00	
89	A16	5f gray black	25.00	7.50
90	A17	6f carmine	.45	.25
91	A18	7f brown blk	.75	.30
92	A19	9f red orange	.80	.35
93	A19	10f blue	.70	.25
94	A18	12f dp orange ('37)	.55	.25
95	A18	13f brown	40.00	37.50
96	A18	15f carmine	3.00	.55
97	A18	20f dk brown	1.10	.35
98	A19	30f chestnut brn	1.10	.35
99	A19	50f olive green	1.60	.50
100	A19	1y violet	4.25	.60
		Nos. 83-100 (18)	85.60	52.75
		Set, never hinged	120.00	

Nos. 83, 84, 86, 88 and 93 are known imperforate but were not regularly issued.
See Nos. 159-163. For overprints see Nos. 140-141, 148-151. For surcharges see People's Republic of China Nos. 2L1-2L2, 2L11-2L18, 2L20-2L37, 2L40-2L52.

a

c

d

b

1937 Surcharged on No. 66
101	A9 (a)	2½f on 2f	3.50	3.00

Surcharged on Nos. 75, 76 and 78
102	A13 (a)	2½f on 2f	4.00	2.75
103	A10 (b)	5f on 4f	4.75	4.00
104	A10 (c)	13f on 12f	12.50	11.00

Surcharged in Black on Nos. 75, 76 and 70
Space between bottom characters of surcharge 4½mm
105	A13 (d)	2½f on 2f	2.00	1.90
a.		Inverted surcharge	400.00	425.00
b.		Vert. pair, one without surch.	95.00	
106	A10 (b)	5f on 4f	3.50	2.75
107	A10 (c)	13f on 12f	12.00	10.00

Surcharged on No. 70
Space between characters 6½mm
108	A10 (c)	13f on 12f	225.00	200.00

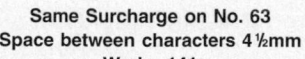

Same Surcharge on No. 63
Space between characters 4½mm
Wmk. 141
109	A10 (b)	5f on 4f	7.25	6.00
		Nos. 101-109 (9)	274.50	241.40
		Set, never hinged	310.00	

Nos. 101-109 were issued primarily to pay postage to China, but were valid for any postal use.

Rising Sun over
Manchurian
Plain — A20

Composite
Picture of
Manchurian
City — A21

Perf. 12½
1937, Mar. 1 Litho. Unwmk.
110	A20	1½f carmine rose	3.50	3.00
111	A21	3f blue green	3.00	2.75
		Set, never hinged	10.00	

5th anniv. of the founding of the State of Manchukuo.

Types of 1936
Perf. 13x13½
1937 Wmk. 242 Engr.
112	A13	2½f dk violet	1.00	.40
113	A10	5f black	.25	.25
115	A10	13f dk red brown	1.00	.60
		Nos. 112-115 (3)	2.25	1.25
		Set, never hinged	2.50	

Issued primarily to pay postage to China, but were valid for any postal use.

Pouter
Pigeon — A22

National Flag
and
Buildings — A23

Perf. 12x12½
1937, Sept. 16 Unwmk.
116	A22	2f dark violet	2.50	1.60
117	A23	4f rose carmine	2.50	1.25
118	A22	10f dark green	5.75	3.25
119	A23	20f dark blue	7.50	5.25
		Nos. 116-119 (4)	18.25	11.35
		Set, never hinged	24.00	

Completion of the national capital, Hsinking, under the first Five-Year Construction Plan.

Map A24

Dept. of Justice
Building — A27

Japanese Residents' Association
Building — A25

Postal Administration Building — A26

Perf. 12x12½, 13
1937, Dec. 1 Litho. Unwmk.
121	A24	2f dark carmine	1.75	.90
122	A25	4f green	2.50	1.10
123	A25	8f orange	5.00	3.50
124	A26	10f blue	6.00	4.00
125	A27	12f lt violet	7.00	5.50
126	A26	20f lilac brown	10.00	6.25
		Nos. 121-126 (6)	32.25	21.25
		Set, never hinged	45.00	

Issued in commemoration of the abolition of extraterritorial rights within Manchukuo.

New Year
Greetings — A28

Map and
Cross — A29

1937, Dec. 15 Engr. Perf. 12x12½
127	A28	2f dk blue & red	2.50	1.00
		Never hinged	3.75	
a.		Double impression of border	12.50	

Issued to pay postage on New Year's greeting cards.

Wmk. 242
1938, Oct. 15 Litho. Perf. 13
128	A29	2f lake & scarlet	1.75	1.25
129	A29	4f slate grn & scar	1.75	1.25
		Set, never hinged	5.00	

Founding of the Red Cross Soc. in Manchukuo.

Network of
State
Railroads in
Manchukuo
A30

Express Train
"Asia"
A31

1939, Oct. 21
130	A30	2f dk org, blk & dp bl	2.00	1.50
131	A31	4f dp blue & indigo	2.00	1.50
		Set, never hinged	6.00	

Attainment of 10,000 kilometers in the railway mileage in Manchuria.

Stork Flying above
Mast of Imperial
Flagship — A32

1940 Photo. Unwmk.
132	A32	2f brt red violet	.80	.80
133	A32	4f brt green	.80	.80
		Set, never hinged	2.00	

Second visit of Emperor Kang Teh to Emperor Hirohito of Japan.

Census Taker
and Map of
Manchukuo
A33

Census Form
A34

1940, Sept. 10 Litho. Wmk. 242
134	A33	2f vio brn & org	.70	.70
135	A34	4f black & green	.75	.75
a.		Double impression of green	50.00	
		Set, never hinged	2.00	

National census starting Oct. 1.

Message of
Congratulation from
Premier Chang Ching-
hui — A35

Dragon
Dance
A36

1940, Sept. 18 Engr. Perf. 13x13½
136	A35	2f carmine	.55	.55

Perf. 13½x13
137	A36	4f indigo	.70	.70
a.		Imperf., pair	100.00	
		Set, never hinged	1.75	

2600th anniversary of the birth of the Japanese Empire.

Soldier — A37

Perf. 13x13½
1941, May 25 Photo. Unwmk.
138	A37	2f deep carmine	.60	.60
139	A37	4f bright ultra	.60	.60
		Set, never hinged	2.00	

Conscription Law, effective June 1, 1941.

Nos. 86 and 88
Overprinted in Red or
Blue

Perf. 13x13½
1942, Feb. 16 Wmk. 242
140	A17	2f lt green (R)	.60	.60
141	A18	4f lt olive grn (Bl)	.60	.60
		Set, never hinged	2.00	

"Return of Singapore to East Asia, 9th year of Kang Teh."

Kengoku Shrine
A38

Map of
Manchukuo
A39

Flag of
Manchukuo
A40

Perf. 12x12½, 12½x12
1942, Mar. 1 Engr.
142	A38	2f carmine	.40	.40
143	A38	4f lilac	.40	.40
144	A39	10f red, yel	1.10	1.50
145	A40	20f indigo, yel	2.50	2.50
		Nos. 142-145 (4)	4.40	4.80
		Set, never hinged	5.00	

"10th anniv. of Manchukuo, Mar. 1, 1942."

Allegory of National Harmony — A41

Women of Five Races, Dancing — A42

1942, Sept. 15
146 A41 3f orange   .50 .40
147 A42 6f light green   .75 1.00
    Set, never hinged   1.75

"10th anniv. of the founding of Manchukuo, Sept. 15, 1942."

Nos. 87 and 90 Overprinted in Green or Blue

1942, Dec. 8   *Perf. 13x13½*
148 A16 3f chocolate (G)   .40 .40
149 A17 6f carmine (Bl)   .40 .40
    Set, never hinged   1.10

1st anniv. of the "Greater East Asia War." The overprint reads "Asiatic Prosperity Began This Day December 8, 1941."

Nos. 87 and 90 Overprinted in Red or Blue

1943, May 1
150 A16 3f chocolate (R)   .40 .40
151 A17 6f carmine (Bl)   .40 .40
    Set, never hinged   1.10

Proclamation of the labor service law.

Red Cross Nurse Carrying Stretcher A43   Smelting Furnace A44

1943, Oct. 1   *Photo.*
152 A43 6f green   .60 .60
    Never hinged   .90

5th anniv. of the founding of the Red Cross Society of Manchukuo, Oct. 1, 1938.

1943, Dec. 8   *Unwmk.*   *Perf. 13*
153 A44 6f red brown   .40 .40
    Never hinged   .55

2nd anniv. of the "Greater East Asia War."

Chinese Characters A45   Japanese Characters A46

Perf. 13x13½
1944   **Wmk. 242**   *Litho.*
154 A45 10f rose   .75 1.25
   a. Imperf., vert. pair #154, 155   15.00
   b. Vert. pair #154, 155   1.50 2.50
155 A46 10f rose   .75 1.25
156 A45 40f gray green   3.50 3.25
   a. Imperf., vert. pair #156, 157   50.00
   b. 40f with 10f vignette, perf.   140.00 140.00
   c. 40f with 10f vignette, imperf.   200.00
   d. Vert. pair #156, 157   6.50 6.50
157 A46 40f gray green   3.50 3.25
    Nos. 154-157 (4)   8.50 9.00
    Set, never hinged   12.00

"Japan's Progress Is Manchukuo's Progress." Issued as propaganda for the close relationship of Japan and Manchukuo.
Frames of the 10f vignettes have rounded corners, those of the 40f vignettes have indented corners.

Types of 1935 and 1936-37
1944-45   *Litho.*
158 A10 5f gray black   1.00 1.75
   a. Imperf., pair   10.00
159 A17 6f crimson rose   2.25 3.50
160 A19 10f light blue   5.00 6.50
161 A17 20f brown   1.75 2.50
162 A19 30f buff ('45)   1.90 2.50
163 A19 1y dull lilac   2.50 2.75
    Nos. 158-163 (6)   14.40 19.50
    Set, never hinged   20.00

For surcharges see People's Republic of China Nos. 2L1, 2L14, 2L19, 2L24, 2L27, 2L30-2L31, 2L35, 2L37, 2L49, 2L52.

"One Heart, One Soul" — A47

1945, May 2
164 A47 10f red   .60 1.50
    Never hinged   .90
   a. Imperf., pair   4.00 5.00

Emperor's edict of May 2, 1935, 10th anniv.

AIR POST STAMPS

Sheep Grazing AP1   Railroad Bridge AP2

Wmk. Characters (242)
1936-37   *Engr.*   *Perf. 13x13½*
Granite Paper
C1 AP1 18f green   15.00 12.50
C2 AP1 19f blue green ('37)   5.00 3.50
C3 AP2 38f blue   16.00 15.00
C4 AP2 39f deep blue ('37)   1.60 1.75
    Nos. C1-C4 (4)   37.60 32.75
    Set, never hinged   50.00

With the end of World War II and the collapse of Manchukuo, the Northeastern Provinces reverted to China. In many Manchurian towns and cities, the Manchukuo stamps were locally handstamped in ideograms: "Republic of China," "China Postal Service" or "Temporary Use for China." A typical example is shown above. Many of these local issues also were surcharged.

MARIANA ISLANDS

ˌmar-ē-ˈa-nə ˈī-ləndz

LOCATION — A group of 14 islands in the West Pacific Ocean, about 1500 miles east of the Philippines.
GOVT. — Possession of Spain, then of Germany
AREA — 246 sq. mi.
POP. — 44,025 (1935)
CAPITAL — Saipan

Until 1899 this group belonged to Spain but in that year all except Guam were ceded to Germany.

    100 Centavos = 1 Peso
    100 Pfennig = 1 Mark (1899)

Values for unused stamps are for examples with original gum as defined in the catalogue introduction. Very fine examples of Nos. 1-6 will have perforations touching or just cutting into the design. Stamps with perfs clear on all sides and well centered are rare and sell for substantially more.

Issued under Spanish Dominion

Philippines Stamps Hstmpd. Vert. in Blackish Violet Reading Up or Down

1899, Sept.   *Unwmk.*   *Perf. 14*
1 A39 2c dark blue green   1,000. 350.
2 A39 3c dark brown   600. 300.
3 A39 5c car rose   900. 300.
4 A39 6c dark blue   5,500. 3,000.
5 A39 8c gray brown   500. 175.
6 A39 15c dull ol grn   1,900. 1,100.

Overprint forgeries of Nos. 1-6 exist.
No. 4 was issued in a quantity of 50 stamps.

Issued under German Dominion

Stamps of Germany, 1889-90, Overprinted in Black at 56 degree Angle

1900, May   *Unwmk.*   *Perf. 13½x14½*
11 A9 3pf dark brown   12.00 30.00
12 A9 5pf green   16.00 32.50
13 A10 10pf carmine   19.00 45.00
14 A10 20pf ultra   25.00 125.00
15 A10 25pf orange   62.50 160.00
   b. Inverted overprint   2,400.
16 A10 50pf red brn   65.00 210.00
    Nos. 11-16 (6)   199.50 602.50

Forged cancellations exist on Nos. 11-16, 17-29.

Stamps of Germany, 1889-90, Overprinted in Black at 48 degree Angle

1899, Nov. 18
11a A9 3pf light brown   2,000. 2,000.
12a A9 5pf green   2,500. 1,700.
13a A10 10pf carmine   190.00 200.00
14a A10 20pf ultra   190.00 200.00
15a A10 25pf orange   2,750. 2,750.
16a A10 50pf red brown   2,750. 2,750.

Kaiser's Yacht "Hohenzollern"
A4   A5

1901, Jan.   *Typo.*   *Perf. 14*
17 A4 3pf brown   1.10 1.75
18 A4 5pf green   1.10 1.90
19 A4 10pf carmine   1.10 4.25
20 A4 20pf ultra   1.25 7.25
21 A4 25pf org & blk, *yel*   1.75 12.50
22 A4 30pf org & blk, *sal*   1.75 13.50
23 A4 40pf lake & blk   1.75 13.50
24 A4 50pf pur & blk, *sal*   2.00 15.00
25 A4 80pf lake & blk, *rose*   2.50 25.00

Engr.
Perf. 14½x14
26 A5 1m carmine   4.00 72.50
27 A5 2m blue   5.50 92.50
28 A5 3m blk vio   8.00 140.00
29 A5 5m slate & car   140.00 500.00
    Nos. 17-29 (13)   171.80 899.65

Wmk. Lozenges (125)
1916-19   *Typo.*   *Perf. 14*
30 A4 3pf brown ('19)   1.00

Engr.
Perf. 14½x14
31 A5 5m slate & carmine, 25x17 holes   30.00

Nos. 30 and 31 were never placed in use.

MARIENWERDER

mä-'rē-ən-,ve̱ə̱rd-ər

LOCATION — Northeastern Germany, bordering on Poland
GOVT. — A district of West Prussia

By the Versailles Treaty the greater portion of West Prussia was ceded to Poland but the district of Marienwerder was allowed a plebiscite which was held in 1920 and resulted in favor of Germany.

100 Pfennig = 1 Mark

Plebiscite Issues

Symbolical of Allied Supervision of the Plebiscite — A1

1920		Unwmk.	Litho.	Perf. 11½	
1	A1	5pf green		.75	2.25
2	A1	10pf rose red		.75	1.75
3	A1	15pf gray		.75	2.00
4	A1	20pf brn org		.75	1.75
5	A1	25pf deep blue		.75	2.25
6	A1	30pf orange		.95	2.25
7	A1	40pf brown		.75	2.75
8	A1	50pf violet		.75	2.00
9	A1	60pf red brown		4.25	3.50
10	A1	75pf chocolate		.95	2.00
11	A1	1m brn & grn		.75	2.00
12	A1	2m dk vio		2.10	4.50
13	A1	3m red		5.00	7.50
14	A1	5m blue & rose		27.50	22.00
		Nos. 1-14 (14)		46.75	58.50
		Set, never hinged		130.00	

These stamps occasionally show parts of two papermakers" watermarks, consisting of the letters "O. B. M." with two stars before and after, or "P. & C. M."
Nos. 1-14 exist imperf.; value for set, $700. Nearly all exist part perf.

Stamps of Germany, 1905-19, Overprinted

1920		Wmk. 125	Perf. 14, 14½	
24	A16	5pf green	15.00	30.00
a.		Inverted overprint	125.00	
		Never hinged	210.00	
26	A16	20pf bl vio	7.25	27.50
a.		Inverted overprint	62.50	
		Never hinged	125.00	
b.		Double overprint	85.00	
		Never hinged	125.00	
28	A16	50pf vio & blk, buff	375.00	850.00
29	A16	75pf grn & blk	4.75	8.75
a.		Inverted overprint	62.50	
		Never hinged	125.00	
30	A16	80pf lake & blk, rose	75.00	120.00
31	A17	1m car rose	85.00	160.00
a.		Inverted overprint	425.00	
		Never hinged	850.00	
		Nos. 24-31 (6)	562.00	1,196.
		Set, never hinged	1,200.	

Trial impressions were made in red, green and lilac, and with 2½mm instead of 3mm space between the lines of the overprint. These were printed on the 75pf and 80pf. The 1 mark was overprinted with the same words in 3 lines of large sans-serif capitals. All these are essays. Some were passed through the post, apparently with speculative intent.

Stamps of Germany, 1905-18, Surcharged

32	A22	1m on 2pf gray	22.50	17.50
33	A22	2m on 2½pf gray	12.00	20.00
a.		Inverted surcharge	55.00	100.00
		Never hinged	100.00	
34	A16	3m on 3pf brown	12.00	20.00
a.		Double surcharge	55.00	100.00
		Never hinged	100.00	

---

b.		Inverted surcharge	55.00	100.00
		Never hinged	100.00	
35	A22	5m on 7½pf org	12.00	21.00
a.		Inverted surcharge	55.00	100.00
		Never hinged	100.00	
b.		Double surcharge	55.00	100.00
		Never hinged	100.00	
		Nos. 32-35 (4)	58.50	108.50
		Set, never hinged	220.00	

There are two types of the letters "M," "C," "i" and "e" and of the numerals "2" and "5" in these surcharges.
Counterfeits exist of Nos. 24-35.

Stamps of Germany, 1920, Overprinted

1920, July			Perf. 15x14½	
36	A17	1m red	2.50	7.25
37	A17	1.25m green	3.25	8.00
38	A17	1.50m yellow brown	4.25	9.75
39	A21	2.50m lilac rose	2.50	8.00
		Nos. 36-39 (4)	12.50	33.00
		Set, never hinged	32.50	

A2

1920		Unwmk.	Perf. 11½	
40	A2	5pf green	3.25	2.00
41	A2	10pf rose red	3.25	2.00
42	A2	15pf gray	11.00	13.50
43	A2	20pf brn org	2.00	2.00
44	A2	25pf dp bl	12.50	17.50
45	A2	30pf orange	1.60	1.60
46	A2	40pf brown	.80	1.60
47	A2	50pf violet	1.60	2.00
48	A2	60pf red brn	6.00	5.50
49	A2	75pf chocolate	6.00	5.50
50	A2	1m brn & grn	1.60	1.60
51	A2	2m dk vio	1.60	1.60
52	A2	3m light red	2.00	2.00
53	A2	5m blue & rose	3.25	2.75
		Nos. 40-53 (14)	56.45	61.15
		Set, never hinged	130.00	

MARSHALL ISLANDS

'mär-shəl 'ī-ləndz

LOCATION — Two chains of islands in the West Pacific Ocean, about 2,500 miles southeast of Tokyo
GOVT. — Republic
AREA — 70 sq. mi.
POP. — 65,507 (1999 est.)
CAPITAL — Dalap-Uliga-Darrit

The Marshall Islands were German possession from 1885 to 1914. Seized by Japan in 1914, the islands were taken by the US in WW II and became part of the US Trust Territory of the Pacific in 1947. By agreement with the USPS, the islands began issuing their own stamps in 1984, with the USPS continuing to carry the mail to and from the islands.
On Oct. 21, 1986 Marshall Islands became a Federation as a Sovereign State in Compact of Free Association with the US.

100 Pfennig = 1 Mark
100 Cents = 1 Dollar

Catalogue values for unused stamps in this country are for Never Hinged items, beginning with Scott 31 in the regular postage section, and Scott C1 in the airpost section.

Watermark

Wmk. 125 — Lozenges

Issued under German Dominion

A1 A2

Stamps of Germany Overprinted "Marschall-Inseln" in Black

1897		Unwmk.	Perf. 13½x14½	
1	A1	3pf dark brown	140.00	725.00
a.		3pf light yellowish brn	4,250.	2,200.
2	A1	5pf green	120.00	550.00
3	A1	10pf carmine	55.00	150.00
4	A2	20pf ultra	50.00	150.00
5	A2	25pf orange	160.00	925.00
6	A2	50pf red brown	140.00	925.00
		Nos. 1-6 (6)	665.00	3,425.

Nos. 5 and 6 were not placed in use, but canceled stamps exist.
A small quantity of the 3pf, 5pf, 10pf and 20pf were issued at Jaluit. These have yellowish, dull gum. Later overprintings of Nos. 1-6 were sold only at Berlin, and have white, smooth, shiny gum. No. 1a belongs to the Jaluit issue. For detailed listings, see the Scott Specialized Catalogue of Stamps and Covers.
Forged cancellations are found on almost all Marshall Islands stamps.

Overprinted "Marshall-Inseln"

1899-1900				
7	A1	3pf dk brn ('00)	4.50	5.50
a.		3pf light brown	275.00	775.00
8	A1	5pf green	9.25	12.50
9	A2	10pf car ('00)	12.00	16.00
a.		Half used as 5pf on postcard		8,000.
10	A2	20pf ultra ('00)	17.00	25.00
11	A2	25pf orange	19.00	42.50
12	A2	50pf red brown	30.00	47.50
a.		Half used as 25pf on cover		35,000.
		Nos. 7-12 (6)	91.75	149.00

Values for Nos. 9a and 12a are for properly used items, addressed and sent to Germany.

Kaiser's Yacht "Hohenzollern"
A3 A4

1901		Unwmk.	Typo.	Perf. 14	
13	A3	3pf brown		.65	1.75
14	A3	5pf green		.65	1.75
15	A3	10pf carmine		.65	5.00
16	A3	20pf ultra		.95	9.25
17	A3	25pf org & blk, yel		1.00	16.00
18	A3	30pf org & blk, sal		1.00	16.00
19	A3	40pf lako & blk		1.00	16.00
20	A3	50pf pur & blk, sal		1.40	25.00
21	A3	80pf lake & blk, rose		2.50	35.00

Engr.
Perf. 14½x14

22	A4	1m carmine	4.00	85.00
23	A4	2m blue	5.50	120.00
24	A4	3m blk vio	8.50	200.00
25	A4	5m slate & car	140.00	500.00
		Nos. 13-25 (13)	167.80	1,030.

Wmk. Lozenges (125)

1916		Typo.	Perf. 14	
26	A3	3pf brown	.85	

Engr.
Perf. 14½x14

27	A4	5m slate & carmine, 25x17 holes	35.00	

Nos. 26 and 27 were never placed in use.
The stamps of Marshall Islands overprinted "G. R. I." and new values in British currency were all used in New Britain and are listed among the issues for that country.

Two unauthorized issues appeared in 1979. The 1st, a set of five for the "Establishment of Government, May 1, 1979," consists of 8c, 15c, 21c, 31c and 75c labels. The 75c is about the size of a postcard. The 2nd, a set of four setenant blocks of four 10c labels for the Intl. Year of the Child. This set also exists imperf. and with specimen overprints.

Catalogue values for unused stamps in this section, from this point to the end of the section, are for Never Hinged items.

Inauguration of Postal Service — A5

1984, May 2		Litho.	Perf. 14x13½	
31	A5	20c Outrigger canoe	.50	.50
32	A5	20c Fishnet	.50	.50
33	A5	20c Navigational stick chart	.50	.50
34	A5	20c Islet	.50	.50
a.		Block of 4, #31-34	2.00	2.00

Mili Atoll, Astrolabe — A6

Maps and Navigational Instruments.

1984-85		Litho.	Perf. 15x14	
35	A6	1c shown	.25	.25
36	A6	3c Likiep, Azimuth compass	.25	.25
37	A6	5c Ebon, 16th cent. compass	.25	.25
38	A6	10c Jaluit, anchor buoys	.25	.25
39	A6	13c Ailinginae, Nocturnal	.25	.25
a.		Booklet pane of 10	8.00	—
40	A6	14c Wotho Atoll, navigational stick chart	.30	.30
a.		Booklet pane of 10	7.50	—
41	A6	20c Kwajalein and Ebeye, stick chart	.40	.40
a.		Booklet pane of 10	10.00	—
b.		Bklt. pane, 5 each 13c, 20c	9.25	—
42	A6	22c Eniwetok, 18th cent. lodestone storage case	.45	.45
a.		Booklet pane of 10	9.50	—
b.		Bklt. pane, 5 each 14c, 22c	8.50	—
43	A6	28c Ailinglaplap, printed compass	.55	.55
44	A6	30c Majuro, navigational stick-chart	.60	.60
45	A6	33c Namu, stick chart	.65	.65
46	A6	37c Rongelap, quadrant	.75	.75
47	A6	39c Taka, map compass, 16th cent. sea chart	.80	.80
48	A6	44c Ujelang, chronograph	.90	.90
49	A6	50c Maloelap and Aur, nocturlabe	1.00	1.00
49A	A6	$1 Arno, 16th cent. sector compass	2.00	2.00
		Nos. 35-49A (16)	9.65	9.65

Issued: 1c, 3c, 10c, 30c, $1, 6/12; 13c, 20c, 28c, 37c, 12/19/84; 14c, 22c, 33c, 39c, 44c, 50c, 6/5/85.
See Nos. 107-109.

No. 7 — A7

1984, June 19　　*Perf. 14½x15*
50	A7	40c shown	.60	.60
51	A7	40c No. 13	.60	.60
52	A7	40c No. 4	.60	.60
53	A7	40c No. 25	.60	.60
a.		Block of 4, #50-53	2.40	2.40

Philatelic Salon, 19th UPU Congress, Hamburg, June 19-26.

Ausipex '84 — A8

Dolphins.

1984, Sept. 5　*Litho.*　*Perf. 14*
54	A8	20c Common	.40	.40
55	A8	20c Risso's	.40	.40
56	A8	20c Spotter	.40	.40
57	A8	20c Bottlenose	.40	.40
a.		Block of 4, #54-57	1.60	1.60

Christmas — A9

1984, Nov. 7　*Litho.*　*Perf. 14*
58		Strip of 4	2.25	2.25
a.-d.		A9 20c any single	.50	.50
e.		Sheet of 16		9.00

Sheet background shows text from Marshallese New Testament, giving each stamp a different background.

Marshall Islands Constitution, 5th Anniv. — A10

1984, Dec. 19　*Litho.*　*Perf. 14*
59	A10	20c Traditional chief	.40	.40
60	A10	20c Amata Kabua	.40	.40
61	A10	20c Chester Nimitz	.40	.40
62	A10	20c Trygve Lie	.40	.40
a.		Block of 4, #59-62	1.60	1.60

Audubon Bicentenary — A11

1985, Feb. 15　*Litho.*　*Perf. 14*
63	A11	22c Forked-tailed Petrel	.60	.60
64	A11	22c Pectoral Sandpiper	.60	.60
a.		Pair, #63-64	1.20	1.20
		Nos. 63-64,C1-C2 (4)	3.00	3.00

Sea Shells — A12

1985, Apr. 17　*Litho.*　*Perf. 14*
65	A12	22c Cymatium lotorium	.45	.45
66	A12	22c Chicoreus cornucervi		.45	.45
67	A12	22c Strombus aurisdanae	.45	.45
68	A12	22c Turbo marmoratus	.45	.45

69	A12	22c Chicoreus palmarosae	.45	.45
a.		Strip of 5, #65-69	2.25	2.25

See Nos. 119-123, 152-156, 216-220.

Decade for Women A13

1985, June 5　*Litho.*　*Perf. 14*
70	A13	22c Native drum	.40	.40
71	A13	22c Palm branches	.40	.40
72	A13	22c Pounding stone	.40	.40
73	A13	22c Ak bird	.40	.40
a.		Block of 4, #70-73	1.65	1.65

Reef and Lagoon Fish A14

1985, July 15　*Litho.*　*Perf. 14*
74	A14	22c Acanthurus dussumieri	.45	.45
75	A14	22c Adioryx caudimaculatus	.45	.45
76	A14	22c Ostracion meleacaris	.45	.45
77	A14	22c Chaetodon ephippium	.45	.45
a.		Block of 4, #74-77	1.80	1.80

Intl. Youth Year A15

IYY and Alele Nautical Museum emblems and: No. 78, Marshallese youths and Peace Corps volunteers playing basketball. No. 79, Legend teller reciting local history, girl listening to recording. No. 80, Islander explaining navigational stick charts. No. 81, Jabwa stick dance.

1985, Aug. 31　*Litho.*　*Perf. 14*
78	A15	22c multicolored	.45	.45
79	A15	22c multicolored	.45	.45
80	A15	22c multicolored	.45	.45
81	A15	22c multicolored	.45	.45
a.		Block of 4, #78-81	1.80	1.80

1856 American Board of Commissions Stock Certificate for Foreign Missions — A16

Missionary ship Morning Star I: 22c, Launch, Jothan Stetson Shipyard, Chelsea, MA, Aug. 7, 1857. 33c, First voyage, Honolulu to the Marshalls, 1857. 44c, Marshall islanders pulling Morning Star I into Ebon Lagoon, 1857.

1985, Oct. 21　*Litho.*　*Perf. 14*
82	A16	14c multicolored	.25	.25
83	A16	22c multicolored	.45	.45
84	A16	33c multicolored	.65	.65
85	A16	44c multicolored	.90	.90
		Nos. 82-85 (4)	2.25	2.25

Christmas.

US Space Shuttle, Astro Telescope, Halley's Comet — A17

Comet tail and research spacecraft: No. 87, Planet A Space Probe, Japan. No. 88, Giotto spacecraft, European Space Agency. No. 89, INTERCOSMOS Project Vega spacecraft, Russia, France, etc. No. 90, US naval tracking ship, NASA observational aircraft, cameo portrait of Edmond Halley (1656-1742), astronomer. Se-tenant in continuous design.

1985, Nov. 21
86	A17	22c multicolored	1.00	1.00
87	A17	22c multicolored	1.00	1.00
88	A17	22c multicolored	1.00	1.00
89	A17	22c multicolored	1.00	1.00
90	A17	22c multicolored	1.00	1.00
a.		Strip of 5, #86-90	5.00	5.00

Medicinal Plants A18

1985, Dec. 31　*Litho.*　*Perf. 14*
91	A18	22c Sida fallax	.45	.45
92	A18	22c Scaevola frutescens	.45	.45
93	A18	22c Guettarda speciosa	.45	.45
94	A18	22c Cassytha filiformis	.45	.45
a.		Block of 4, #91-94	1.90	1.90

Maps Type of 1984

1986-87　　*Perf. 15x14, 14 ($10)*
107	A6	$2 Wotje and Erikub, terrestrial globe, 1571	4.50	4.50
108	A6	$5 Bikini, Stick chart	9.50	9.50

Size: 31x31mm
109	A6	$10 Stick chart of the atolls	16.00	16.00
		Nos. 107-109 (3)	30.00	30.00

Issued: $2, $5, 3/7/86; $10, 3/31/87.

Marine Invertebrates — A19

1986, Mar. 31　*Litho.*　*Perf. 14½x14*
110	A19	14c Triton's trumpet	1.50	1.50
111	A19	14c Giant clam	1.50	1.50
112	A19	14c Small giant clam	1.50	1.50
113	A19	14c Coconut crab	1.50	1.50
a.		Block of 4, #110-113	8.00	8.00

Souvenir Sheet

AMERIPEX '86, Chicago, May 22-June 1 — A20

1986, May 22　*Litho.*　*Perf. 14*
114	A20	$1 Douglas C-54 Globester	2.75	2.75

1st Around-the-world scheduled flight, 40th anniv. No. 114 has multicolored margin continuing the design and picturing US Air Transport Command Base, Kwajalein Atoll and souvenir card.

See Nos. C3-C6.

Operation Crossroads, Atomic Bomb Tests, 40th Anniv. — A21

Designs: No. 115, King Juda, Bikinians sailing tibinal canoe. No. 116, USS Sumner, amphibious DUKW, advance landing. No. 117, Evacuating Bikinians. No. 118, Land reclamation, 1986.

1986, July 1　*Litho.*　*Perf. 14*
115	A21	22c multicolored	.45	.45
116	A21	22c multicolored	.45	.45
117	A21	22c multicolored	.45	.45
118	A21	22c multicolored	.45	.45
a.		Block of 4, #115-118	1.90	1.90

See No. C7.

Seashells Type of 1985

1986, Aug. 1　*Litho.*　*Perf. 14*
119	A12	22c Ramose murex	.45	.45
120	A12	22c Orange spider	.45	.45
121	A12	22c Red-mouth frog shell	.45	.45
122	A12	22c Laciniate conch	.45	.45
123	A12	22c Giant frog shell	.45	.45
a.		Strip of 5, #119-123	2.25	2.25

Game Fish A22

1986, Sept. 10　　　　　*Litho.*
124	A22	22c Blue marlin	.40	.40
125	A22	22c Wahoo	.40	.40
126	A22	22c Dolphin fish	.40	.40
127	A22	22c Yellowfin tuna	.40	.40
a.		Block of 4, #124-127	1.60	1.60

Christmas, Intl. Peace Year — A23

1986, Oct. 28　*Litho.*　*Perf. 14*
128	A23	22c United Nations UR	.60	.60
129	A23	22c United Nations UL	.60	.60
130	A23	22c United Nations LR	.60	.60
131	A23	22c United Nations LL	.60	.60
a.		Block of 4, #128-131	2.50	2.50

See No. C8.

US Whaling Ships A24

1987, Feb. 20　*Litho.*　*Perf. 14*
132	A24	22c James Arnold, 1854	.50	.50
133	A24	22c General Scott, 1859	.50	.50
134	A24	22c Charles W. Morgan, 1865	.50	.50
135	A24	22c Lucretia, 1884	.50	.50
a.		Block of 4, #132-135	2.00	2.00

Historic and Military Flights A25

Designs: No. 136, Charles Lindbergh commemorative medal, Spirit of St. Louis crossing the Atlantic, 1927. No. 137, Lindbergh flying in the Battle of the Marshalls, 1944. No. 138, William Bridgeman flying in the Battle of Kwajalein, 1944. No. 139, Bridgeman testing the Douglas Skyrocket, 1951. No. 140, John Glenn flying in the Battle of the Marshalls. No. 141, Glenn, the first American to orbit the Earth, 1962.

1987, Mar. 12   Litho.   Perf. 14½

136	A25	33c multicolored	.70	.70
137	A25	33c multicolored	.70	.70
a.		Pair, #136-137	1.40	1.40
138	A25	39c multicolored	.75	.75
139	A25	39c multicolored	.75	.75
a.		Pair, #138-139	1.50	1.50
140	A25	44c multicolored	.80	.80
141	A25	44c multicolored	.80	.80
a.		Pair, #140-141	1.60	1.60
		Nos. 136-141 (6)	4.50	4.50

Souvenir Sheet

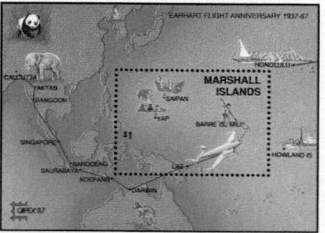

CAPEX '87 — A26

1987, June 15   Litho.   Perf. 14

142	A26	$1 Map of flight	2.50	2.50

Amelia Earhart (1897-1937), American aviator who died during attempted round-the-world flight, 50th anniv. No. 142 has multicolored margin picturing Earhart's flight pattern from Calcutta, India, to the crash site near Barre Is., Marshall Is.

US Constitution Bicentennial — A27

Excerpts from the Marshall Islands and US Constitutions.

1987, July 16   Litho.   Perf. 14

143	A27	14c We,... Marshall	.30	.30
144	A27	14c National seals	.30	.30
145	A27	14c We,... United States	.30	.30
a.		Triptych, #143-145	1.00	1.00
146	A27	22c All we have...	.40	.40
147	A27	22c Flags	.40	.40
148	A27	22c to establish...	.40	.40
a.		Triptych, #146-148	1.25	1.25
149	A27	44c With this Constitution...	.80	.80
150	A27	44c Stick chart, Liberty Bell	.80	.80
151	A27	44c to promote...	.80	.80
a.		Triptych, #149-151	2.50	2.50
		Nos. 143-151 (9)	4.50	4.50

Triptychs printed in continuous designs.

Seashells Type of 1985

1987, Sept. 1   Litho.   Perf. 14

152	A12	22c Magnificent cone	.40	.40
153	A12	22c Partridge tun	.40	.40
154	A12	22c Scorpion spider conch	.40	.40
155	A12	22c Hairy triton	.40	.40
156	A12	22c Chiragra spider conch	.40	.40
a.		Strip of 5, #152-156	2.00	2.00

Copra Industry A28

Contest-winning crayon drawings by Amram Enox; design contest sponsored by the Tubular Copra Processing Co.

1987, Dec. 10   Litho.   Perf. 14

157	A28	44c Planting coconut	.65	.65
158	A28	44c Making copra	.65	.65
159	A28	44c Bottling coconut oil	.65	.65
a.		Triptych, #157-159	2.00	2.00

Biblical Verses A29

1987, Dec. 10

160	A29	14c Matthew 2:1	.25	.25
161	A29	22c Luke 2:14	.40	.40
162	A29	33c Psalms 33:3	.60	.60
163	A29	44c Pslams 150:5	.75	.75
		Nos. 160-163 (4)	2.00	2.00

Christmas.

Marine Birds A30

1988, Jan. 27

164	A30	44c Pacific reef herons	.75	.75
165	A30	44c Bar-tailed godwit	.75	.75
166	A30	44c Masked booby	.75	.75
167	A30	44c Northern shoveler	.75	.75
a.		Block of 4, #164-167	3.00	3.00

Fish — A31

Designs: 1c, Damselfish. 3c, Blackface butterflyfish. 14c, Hawkfish. 15c, Balloonfish. 17c, Trunk fish. 22c, Lyretail wrasse. 25c, Parrotfish. 33c, White spotted boxfish. 36c, Spotted boxfish. 39c, Surgeonfish. 44c, Long-snouted butterflyfish. 45c, Trumpetfish. 56c, Sharp-nosed puffer. $1, Seahorse. $2, Ghost pipefish. $5, Big-spotted triggerfish. $10, Blue jack.

Perf. 14½x14, 14 (#187)

1988-89   Litho.

168	A31	1c multicolored	.25	.25
169	A31	3c multicolored	.25	.25
170	A31	14c multicolored	.25	.25
a.		Booklet pane of 10	3.75	—
171	A31	15c multicolored	.25	.25
a.		Booklet pane of 10	4.50	—
172	A31	17c multicolored	.30	.30
173	A31	22c multicolored	.35	.35
a.		Booklet pane of 10	5.00	—
b.		Bklt. pane, 5 each 14c, 22c	5.00	—
174	A31	25c multicolored	.35	.35
a.		Booklet pane of 10	7.25	—
b.		Bklt. pane, 5 each 15c, 25c	7.25	—
175	A31	33c multicolored	.60	.60
176	A31	36c multicolored	.65	.65
177	A31	39c multicolored	.75	.75
178	A31	44c multicolored	.80	.80
179	A31	45c multicolored	.80	.80
180	A31	56c multicolored	1.00	1.00
181	A31	$1 multicolored	1.90	1.90
182	A31	$2 multicolored	3.50	3.50
183	A31	$5 multicolored	8.00	8.00
184	A31	$10 multi ('89)	16.00	16.00
		Nos. 168-184 (17)	36.00	36.00

Issued: Nos. 170a, 173a, 173b, 3/31/88; 15c, 25c, 36c, 45c, 7/19/; Nos. 171a, 174a, 174b, 12/15; $10, 3/31/89; others, 3/17/88.

A32

1988 Summer Olympics, Seoul — A33

Athletes in motion: 15c, Javelin thrower. 25c, Runner.

1988, June 30   Litho.   Perf. 14

188	A32	15c Strip of 5, #a-e	1.65	1.65
189	A33	25c Strip of 5, #a-e	2.25	2.25

Souvenir Sheet

Pacific Voyages of Robert Louis Stevenson — A34

Stick chart of the Marshalls and: a, *Casco* sailing through the Golden Gate. b, At the Needles of Ua-Pu, Marquesas. c, *Equator* departing from Honolulu and Kaiulani, an Hawaiian princess. d, Chief's canoe, Majuro Lagoon. e, Bronze medallion, 1887, by Augustus St. Gaudens in the Tate Gallery, London. f, Outrigger canoe and S.S. *Janet Nicoll* in Majuro Lagoon. g, View of Apemama, Gilbert Is. h, Samoan outrigger canoe, Apia Harbor. i, Stevenson riding horse Jack at his estate, Vallima, Samoa.

1988, July 19   Litho.   Perf. 14

190		Sheet of 9	6.25	4.50
a.-i.		A34 25c any single	.50	.50

Robert Louis Stevenson (1850-1894), Scottish novelist, poet and essayist.

Colonial Ships and Flags A35

Designs: No. 191, Galleon *Santa Maria de La Victoria*, 1526, and Spanish "Ragged Cross" ensign in use from 1516 to 1785. No. 192, Transport ships *Charlotte* and *Scarborough*, 1788, and British red ensign, 1707-1800. No. 193, Schooner *Flying Fish*, sloop-of-war *Peacock*, 1841, and U.S. flag, 1837-1845. No. 194, Steamer *Planet*, 1909, and German flag, 1867-1919.

1988, Sept. 2   Litho.   Perf. 14

191	A35	25c multicolored	.50	.50
192	A35	25c multicolored	.50	.50
193	A35	25c multicolored	.50	.50
194	A35	25c multicolored	.50	.50
a.		Block of 4, #191-194	2.00	2.00

Christmas — A36

No. 195, Santa Claus riding in sleigh. No. 196, Reindeer, hut and palm trees. No. 197, Reindeer and palm trees. No. 198, Reindeer, palm tree, fish. No. 199, Reindeer and outrigger canoe.

1988, Nov. 7   Litho.   Perf. 14

195	A36	25c multicolored	.50	.50
196	A36	25c multicolored	.50	.50
197	A36	25c multicolored	.50	.50
198	A36	25c multicolored	.50	.50
199	A36	25c multicolored	.50	.50
a.		Strip of 5, #195-199	2.50	2.50

No. 199a has a continuous design.

A37

1988, Nov. 22   Litho.   Perf. 14

200	A37	25c Nuclear threat diminished	.55	.55
201	A37	25c Signing the Test Ban Treaty	.55	.55
202	A37	25c Portrait	.55	.55
203	A37	25c US-USSR Hotline	.55	.55
204	A37	25c Peace Corps enactment	.55	.55
a.		Strip of 5, #200-204	2.75	2.75

Tribute to John F. Kennedy. No. 204a has a continuous design.

US Space Shuttle Program and Kwajalein — A38

No. 205, Launch of *Prime* from Vandenberg Air Force Base downrange to the Kwajalein Missile Range. No. 206, *Prime* X023A/SV-5D lifting body reentering atmosphere. No. 207, Parachute landing and craft recovery off Kwajalein Is. No. 208, Shuttle over island.

1988, Dec. 23   **Litho.**   *Perf. 14*

205	25c multicolored	.50	.50
206	25c multicolored	.50	.50
207	25c multicolored	.50	.50
208	25c multicolored	.50	.50
a.	A38 Strip of 4, #205-208	2.00	2.00

NASA 30th anniv. and 25th anniv. of the Project PRIME wind tunnel tests.
See No. C21.

Links to Japan
A39

Designs: No. 209, Typhoon Monument, Majuro, 1918. No. 210, Seaplane base and railway depot, Djarrej Islet, c. 1940. No. 211, Fishing boats. No. 212, Japanese honeymooners scuba diving, 1988.

1989, Jan. 19   **Litho.**   *Perf. 14*

209	A39 45c multicolored	.75	.75
210	A39 45c multicolored	.75	.75
211	A39 45c multicolored	.75	.75
212	A39 45c multicolored	.75	.75
a.	Block of 4, #209-212	3.00	3.00

Links to Alaska
A40

Paintings by Claire Fejes.

1989, Mar. 31   **Litho.**   *Perf. 14*

213	A40 45c Island Woman	.85	.85
214	A40 45c Kotzebue, Alaska	.85	.85
215	A40 45c Marshallese Madonna	.85	.85
a.	Strip of 3, #213-215	2.55	2.55

Printed in sheets of 9.

Seashells Type of 1985

1989, May 15   **Litho.**   *Perf. 14*

216	A12 25c Pontifical miter	.50	.50
217	A12 25c Tapestry turban	.50	.50
218	A12 25c Flame-mouthed helmet	.50	.50
219	A12 25c Prickly Pacific drupe	.50	.50
220	A12 25c Blood-mouthed conch	.50	.50
a.	Strip of 5, #216-220	2.50	2.50

Souvenir Sheet

In Praise of Sovereigns, 1940, by Sanko Inoue — A41

1989, May 15   **Litho.**   *Perf. 14*

221	A41 $1 multicolored	2.00	2.00

Hirohito (1901-89) and enthronement of Akihito as emperor of Japan.

Migrant Birds
A42

1989, June 27   **Litho.**   *Perf. 14*

222	A42 45c Wandering tattler	.85	.85
223	A42 45c Ruddy turnstone	.85	.85
224	A42 45c Pacific golden plover	.85	.85
225	A42 45c Sanderling	.85	.85
a.	Block of 4, #222-225	3.40	3.40

Postal History
A43

PHILEXFRANCE '89 — A44

Designs: No. 226, Missionary ship *Morning Star V,* 1905, and Marshall Isls. #15 canceled. No. 227, Marshall Isls. #15-16 on registered letter, 1906. No. 228, *Prinz Eitel Friedrich,* 1914, and German sea post cancel. No. 229, Cruiser squadron led by SMS *Scharnhorst,* 1914, and German sea post cancel.
No. 230: a, SMS *Bussard* and German sea post cancel and Germany #32. b, US Type A924 and Marshall Isls. #34a on FDC. c, LST 119 FPO, 1944, US Navy cancel and pair of US #853. d, Mail boat, 1936, cancel and Japan #222. e, Majuro PO f, Marshall Isls. cancel, 1951, and four US #803.
No. 231, Germany #32 and Marshall Isls. cancel, 1889.

1989, July 7

226	A43 45c multicolored	.80	.80
227	A43 45c multicolored	.80	.80
228	A43 45c multicolored	.80	.80
229	A43 45c multicolored	.80	.80
a.	Block of 4, #226-229	3.25	3.25

Souvenir Sheets

230	Sheet of 6	10.00	10.00
a.-f.	A44 25c any single	1.50	1.50
231	A43 $1 multicolored	10.00	3.00

Nos. 230b and 230e are printed in a continuous design.

1st Moon Landing, 20th Anniv.
A45

Apollo 11: No. 232, Liftoff. No. 233, Neil Armstrong. No. 234, Lunar module *Eagle.* No. 235, Michael Collins. No. 236, Raising the American flag on the Moon. No. 237, Buzz Aldrin. $1, 1st step on the Moon and "We came in peace for all mankind."

1989, Aug. 1   *Perf. 13½*

Booklet Stamps

232	A45 25c multicolored	1.25	1.25
233	A45 25c multicolored	1.25	1.25
234	A45 25c multicolored	1.25	1.25
235	A45 25c multicolored	1.25	1.25
236	A45 25c multicolored	1.25	1.25
237	A45 25c multicolored	1.25	1.25

Size: 75x32mm

238	A45 $1 multicolored	7.00	5.00
a.	Booklet pane of 7, #232-238	15.00	
	Nos. 232-238 (7)	14.50	12.50

Decorative inscribed selvage separates No. 238 from Nos. 232-237 and surrounds it like a souvenir sheet margin. Selvage around Nos. 232-237 is plain.

World War II

A46

A47

Anniversaries and events, 1939: No. 239, Invasion of Poland. No. 240, Sinking of HMS *Royal Oak.* No. 241, Invasion of Finland.
Battle of the River Plate: No. 242, HMS *Exeter,.* No. 243, HMS *Ajax,.* No. 244, *Admiral Graf Spee,.* No. 245, HMNZS *Achilles,.*

1989   **Litho.**   *Perf. 13½*

239	A46 25c W1 (1-1)	.60	.45
240	A46 45c W2 (1-1)	1.00	.75
241	A46 45c W3 (1-1)	1.00	.75
242	A46 45c W4 (4-1)	.80	.75
243	A46 45c W4 (4-2)	.80	.75
244	A46 45c W4 (4-3)	.80	.75
245	A46 45c W4 (4-4)	.80	.75
a.	Block of 4, #242-245	3.25	3.00

Issued: No. 239, 9/1; No. 240, 10/13; No. 241, 11/30; No. 245a, 12/13.

1990

1940: No. 246, Invasion of Denmark. No. 247, Invasion of Norway. No. 248, Katyn Forest Massacre. No. 249, Bombing of Rotterdam. No. 250, Invasion of Belgium. No. 251, Winston Churchill becomes prime minister of England. No. 252, Evacuation of the British Expeditionary Force at Dunkirk. No. 253, Evacuation at Dunkirk. No. 254, Occupation of Paris.

246	A46 25c W5 (2-1)	.60	.50
247	A46 25c W5 (2-2)	.60	.50
a.	Pair, #246-247	1.25	1.00
248	A47 25c W6 (1-1)	.50	.50
249	A46 25c W8 (2-1)	.50	.50
250	A46 25c W8 (2-2)	.50	.50
a.	Pair, #249-250	1.00	1.00
251	A46 45c W7 (1-1)	1.00	.90
252	A46 45c W9 (2-1)	1.00	.90
253	A46 45c W9 (2-2)	1.00	.90
a.	Pair, #252-253	2.00	1.80
254	A47 45c W10 (1-1)	1.00	.90

Issued: No. 247a, 4/9; No. 248, 4/16; Nos. 249-251, 5/10; Nos. 252-253, 6/4; No. 254, 6/14.

1990

No. 255, Battle of Mers-el-Kebir, 1940. No. 256, Battles for the Burma Road, 1940-45.
US Destroyers for British bases: No. 257, HMS Georgetown (ex-USS Maddox). No. 258, HMS Banff (ex-USCGC Saranac). No. 259, HMS Buxton (ex-USS Edwards). No. 260, HMS Rockingham (ex-USS Swasey).
Battle of Britain: No. 261, Supermarine Spitfire Mark IA. No. 262, Hawker Hurricane Mark I. No. 263, Messerschmitt Bf109E. No. 264, Junkers JU87B-2. No. 265, Tripartite Pact Signed 1940.

255	A46 25c W11 (1-1)	.60	.50
256	A46 25c W12 (1-1)	.60	.50
257	A46 45c W13 (4-1)	1.00	.90
258	A46 45c W13 (4-2)	1.00	.90
259	A46 45c W13 (4-3)	1.00	.90
260	A46 45c W13 (4-4)	1.00	.90
a.	Block of 4, #257-260	4.00	3.60
261	A46 45c W14 (4-1)	1.00	.90
262	A46 45c W14 (4-2)	1.00	.90
263	A46 45c W14 (4-3)	1.00	.90
264	A46 45c W14 (4-4)	1.00	.90
a.	Block of 4, #261-264	4.00	3.60
265	A46 45c W15	1.00	.90

Issued: No. 255, 7/3; No. 256, 7/18; No. 260a, 9/9; No. 264a, 9/15; No. 265, 9/27.

1990-91

Designs: No. 266, Roosevelt elected to third term, 1940. Battle of Taranto: No. 267, HMS Illustrious. No. 268, Fairey Swordfish. No. 269, RM Andrea Doria. No. 270, RM Conte di Cavour.
Roosevelt's Four Freedoms Speech: No. 271, Freedom of Speech. No. 272, Freedom

---

from Want. No. 273, Freedom of Worship. No. 274, Freedom From Fear. No. 275, Battle of Beda Fomm, Feb. 5-7, 1941.
Germany Invades the Balkans: No. 276, Invasion of Greece. No. 277, Invasion of Yugoslavia.
Sinking of the Bismarck: No. 278, HMS Prince of Wales. No. 279, HMS Hood. No. 280, Bismarck. No. 281, Fairey Swordfish. No. 282, German Invasion of Russia, 1941.

266	A47 25c W16	.60	.50
267	A46 25c W17 (4-1)	.60	.50
268	A46 25c W17 (4-2)	.60	.50
269	A46 25c W17 (4-3)	.60	.50
270	A46 25c W17 (4-4)	.60	.50
a.	Block of 4, #266-270	2.50	2.00
271	A46 30c W18 (4-1)	.65	.60
272	A46 30c W18 (4-2)	.65	.60
273	A46 30c W18 (4-3)	.65	.60
274	A46 30c W18 (4-4)	.65	.60
a.	Block of 4, #271-274	2.60	2.40
275	A46 30c Tanks, W19	.60	.60
276	A47 29c W20 (2-1)	.60	.60
277	A47 29c W20 (2-2)	.60	.60
a.	Pair, #276-277	1.25	1.25
278	A46 50c W21 (4-1)	1.00	1.00
279	A46 50c W21 (4-2)	1.00	1.00
280	A46 50c W21 (4-3)	1.00	1.00
281	A46 50c W21 (4-4)	1.00	1.00
a.	Block of 4, #278-281	4.00	4.00
282	A46 30c Tanks, W22	.60	.60

Issued: No. 266, 11/5/90; No. 270a, 11/11/90; No. 274a, 1/6/91; No. 275, 2/5/91; No. 277a, 4/6/91; No. 281a, 5/27/91; No. 282, 6/22/91.

1991

1941 — Declaration of the Atlantic Charter: No. 283, Pres. Roosevelt and USS Augusta. No. 284, Churchill and HMS Prince of Wales. No. 285, Siege of Moscow.
Sinking of USS Reuben James: No. 286, Reuben James hit by torpedo. No. 287, German U-562 submarine.
Japanese attack on Pearl Harbor: No. 288, American warplanes. No. 289, Japanese warplanes. No. 290, USS Arizona. No. 291, Japanese aircraft carrier Akagi.

283	A47 29c W23 (2-1)	.60	.60
284	A47 29c W23 (2-2)	.60	.60
a.	Pair, #283-284	1.25	1.25
285	A46 29c W24	.60	.60
286	A46 30c W25 (2-1)	.60	.60
287	A46 30c W25 (2-1)	.60	.60
a.	Pair, #286-287	1.25	1.25
288	A46 50c W26 (4-1)	1.00	1.00
a.	Revised inscription	4.75	1.00
289	A47 50c W26 (4-2)	1.00	1.00
290	A47 50c W26 (4-3)	1.00	1.00
291	A47 50c W26 (4-4)	1.00	1.00
a.	Block of 4, #288-291	4.00	4.00
b.	Block of 4, #288a, 289-291	8.50	4.00

Inscriptions read "Peal" on No. 288 and "Pearl" on No. 288a.
Issued: No. 284a, 8/14; No. 285, 10/2; No. 287a, 10/31; No. 291a, 12/7.

1991-92

1941-42: No. 292, Japanese capture Guam. No. 293, Fall of Singapore.
First combat of the Flying Tigers: No. 294, Curtiss Tomahawk. No. 295, Mitsubishi Ki-21 on fire.
No. 296, Fall of Wake Island.
No. 297, Roosevelt and Churchill at Arcadia Conference. No. 298, Japanese tank entering Manila. No. 299, Japanese take Rabaul. No. 300, Battle of the Java Sea. No. 301, Rangoon falls to Japanese. No. 302, Japanese land on New Guinea. No. 303, MacArthur evacuated from Corregidor. No. 304, Raid on Saint-Nazaire. No. 305, Surrender of Bataan / Death March. No. 306, Doolittle Raid on Tokyo. No. 307, Fall of Corregidor.

292	A47 29c W27	.60	.60
293	A46 29c W28	.60	.60
294	A46 50c W29 (2-1)	1.00	1.00
295	A46 50c W29 (2-2)	1.00	1.00
a.	Pair, #294-295	2.00	2.00
296	A46 29c W30	.60	.60
297	A46 29c W31	.60	.60
298	A46 50c W32	1.00	1.00
299	A46 29c W33	.60	.60
300	A47 50c W35	1.00	1.00
301	A46 29c W34	.60	.60
302	A46 29c W36	.60	.60
303	A46 29c W37	.60	.60
304	A46 29c W38	.60	.60
305	A47 29c W39	.60	.60
306	A47 50c W40	1.00	1.00
307	A46 29c W41	.60	.60

Issued: Nos. 292-293, 12/10/91; No. 295a, 12/20/91; No. 296, 12/23/91; No. 297, 1/1/92; No. 298, 1/2/92; No. 299, 1/23/92; No. 300, 2/15/92; Nos. 301-302, 3/8/92; No. 303, 3/11/92; No. 304, 3/27/92; No. 305, 4/9/92; No. 306, 4/18/92; No. 307, 5/6/92.

1992

1942 — Battle of the Coral Sea: No. 308, USS Lexington. No. 309, Japanese Mitsubishi A6M2 Zeros. No. 310, Douglas SBD Dauntless dive bombers. No. 311, Japanese carrier Shoho.

Battle of Midway: No. 312, Japanese aircraft carrier Akagi. No. 313, U.S. Douglas SBD Dauntless dive bombers. No. 314, USS Yorktown. No. 315, Nakajima B5N2 Kate torpedo planes.

No. 316, Village of Lidice destroyed. No. 317, Fall of Sevastopol.

Convoy PQ17 destroyed: No. 318, British merchant ship in convoy. No. 319, German U-boats.

No. 320, Marines land on Guadalcanal. No. 323, Battle of Stalingrad. No. 324, Battle of Eastern Solomons.

No. 321, Battle of Savo Island. No. 322, Dieppe Raid. No. 325, Battle of Cape Esperance. No. 326, Battle of El Alamein.

Battle of Barents Sea: No. 327, HMS Sheffield. No. 328, Admiral Hipper.

308	A46	50c W42 (4-1)	1.00	1.00
a.		Revised inscription	2.00	2.00
309	A46	50c W42 (4-2)	1.00	1.00
a.		Revised inscription	2.00	2.00
310	A46	50c W42 (4-3)	1.00	1.00
a.		Revised inscription	2.00	2.00
311	A46	50c W42 (4-4)	1.00	1.00
a.		Block of 4, #308-311	4.00	4.00
b.		Revised inscription	2.00	2.00
c.		Block of 4, #308a-310a, 311b	8.50	4.00
312	A46	50c W43 (4-1)	1.00	1.00
313	A46	50c W43 (4-3)	1.00	1.00
314	A46	50c W43 (4-2)	1.00	1.00
315	A46	50c W43 (4-4)	1.00	1.00
a.		Block of 4, #312-315	4.00	4.00
316	A46	29c W44	.60	.60
317	A47	29c W45	.60	.60
318	A46	29c W46 (2-1)	.60	.60
319	A46	29c W46 (2-2)	.60	.60
a.		Pair, #318-319	1.25	1.25
320	A46	29c W47	.60	.60
321	A47	29c W48	.60	.60
322	A46	29c W49	.60	.60
323	A47	50c W50	1.25	1.00
324	A46	50c W51	.60	.60
325	A46	50c W52	1.25	1.00
326	A46	29c W53	.60	.60
327	A46	29c W54 (2-1)	.60	.60
328	A46	29c W54 (2-2)	.60	.60
a.		Pair, #327-328	1.25	1.25

Inscription reads "U.S.S. Lexington/Grumman F4F-3 Wildcat" on No. 308a, "Japanese Aichi D3A1 Vals/Nakajima B5N2 Kate" on No. 309a, "U.S. Douglas TBD-1 Devastators" on No. 310a, "Japanese Carrier Shoho/Mitsubishi A6M2 Zeros" on No. 311b.

Issued: No. 311a, 5/8/92; No. 315a, 6/4; No. 316, 6/9/92; No. 317, 7/4; No. 319a, 7/5; No. 320, 8/7; #321, 8/9; Nos. 322-323, 8/19; No. 324, 8/24; No. 325, 10/11; No. 326, 10/23; No. 328a, 12/31.

Vertical pairs, Nos. 312-313 and Nos. 314-315 have continuous designs.

No. 310 incorrectly identifies Douglas TBD torpedo bombers.

1993 **Litho.** *Perf. 13½*

1943 — No. 329, Casablanca Conf. No. 330, Liberation of Kharkov.

Battle of Bismarck Sea: No. 331, Japanese A6M Zeroes, destroyer Arashio. No. 332, U.S. P38 Lightnings, Australian Beaufighter. No. 333, Japanese destroyer Shirayuki. No. 334, U.S. A-20 Havoc, B-25 Mitchell.

No. 335, Interception of Admiral Yamamoto.

Battle of Kursk: No. 336, German Tiger I. No. 337, Soviet T-34.

329	A46	29c W55	.65	.60
330	A46	29c W56	.65	.60
331	A46	50c W57 (4-1)	1.00	1.00
332	A46	50c W57 (4-2)	1.00	1.00
333	A46	50c W57 (4-3)	1.00	1.00
334	A46	50c W57 (4-4)	1.00	1.00
a.		Block of 4, #331-334	4.00	4.00
335	A46	50c W58	1.00	1.00
336	A46	29c W59 (2-1)	.85	.60
337	A46	29c W59 (2-2)	.85	.60
a.		Pair, #336-337	1.70	1.25
		Nos. 239-337 (99)	78.50	74.05

Issued: No. 329, 1/14; No. 330, 2/16; No. 334a, 3/3; No. 335, 4/18; No. 337a, 7/5.

See Nos. 467-524, 562-563.

Christmas
A57

Angels playing musical instruments.

1989, Oct. 25 *Perf. 13½*

341	A57	25c Horn	.80	.80
342	A57	25c Singing carol	.80	.80
343	A57	25c Lute	.80	.80
344	A57	25c Lyre	.80	.80
a.		Block of 4, #341-344	3.25	3.25

Miniature Sheet

Milestones in Space
Exploration — A58

Designs: a, Robert Goddard and 1st liquid fuel rocket launch, 1926. b, *Sputnik*, 1st man-made satellite, 1957. c, 1st American satellite, 1958. d, Yuri Gagarin, 1st man in space, 1961. e, John Glenn, 1st American to orbit Earth, 1962. f, Valentina Tereshkova, 1st woman in space, 1963. g, Aleksei Leonov, 1st space walk, 1965. h, Edward White, 1st American to walk in space, 1965. i, Gemini-Titan 6A, 1st rendezvous in space, 1965. j, 1st Soft landing on the Moon, 1966. k, Gemini 8, 1st docking in space, 1966. l, 1st probe of Venus, 1967. m, Apollo 8, 1st manned orbit of the Moon, 1968. n, Apollo 11, 1st man on the Moon, 1969. o, Soyuz 11, 1st space station crew, 1971. p, Apollo 15, 1st manned lunar vehicle, 1971. q, *Skylab 2*, 1st American manned space station, 1973. r, 1st Flyby of Jupiter, 1973. s, Apollo-Soyuz, 1st joint space flight, 1975. t, 1st Landing on Mars, 1976. u, 1st flyby of Saturn, 1979. v, *Columbia*, 1st space shuttle flight, 1981. w, 1st probe beyond the solar system, 1983. x, 1st untethered space walk, 1984. y, Launch of space shuttle *Discovery*, 1988.

1989, Nov. 24 **Litho.** *Perf. 13½*

345	A58	Sheet of 25	25.00	25.00
a.-y.		45c any single	.90	.90

No. 345 contains World Stamp Expo '89 emblem on selvage.

Birds
A59   A59a

Designs: 1c, Black noddy. 5c, Red-tailed tropic bird. 10c, Sanderling. 12c, Black-naped tern. 15c, Wandering tattler. 20c, Bristle-thighed curlew. 23c, Northern shoveler. 25c, Brown noddy. 27c, Sooty tern. 29c, Wedge-tailed shearwater. 30c, Northern pintail. 35c, Pacific golden plover. 36c, Red footed booby. 40c, White tern. 50c, Great frigate bird. 52c, Great crested tern. 65c, Lesser sand plover. 75c, Little tern. $1, Pacific reef heron. $2, Masked booby.

1990-92 **Litho.** *Perf. 13½*

346	A59	1c multicolored	.25	.25
347	A59	5c multicolored	.25	.25
348	A59	10c multicolored	.25	.25
349	A59	12c multicolored	.25	.25
350	A59	15c multicolored	.30	.30
351	A59	20c multicolored	.40	.40
352	A59	23c multicolored	.45	.45
353	A59	25c multicolored	.50	.50
354	A59	27c multicolored	.55	.55
355	A59a	29c multicolored	.60	.60
356	A59a	29c multicolored	.60	.60
357	A59	30c multicolored	.60	.60
358	A59	35c multicolored	.70	.70
359	A59	36c multicolored	.75	.75
360	A59	40c multicolored	.80	.80
361	A59	50c multicolored	1.00	1.00
a.		Min. sheet of 4 (#347, 350, 353, 361)	2.25	2.00

362	A59	52c multicolored	1.00	1.00
363	A59	65c multicolored	1.25	1.25
364	A59	75c multicolored	1.50	1.50
365	A59	$1 multicolored	2.00	2.00
365A	A59	$2 multicolored	4.00	4.00
		Nos. 346-365A (21)	18.00	18.00

No. 361a for ESSEN '90, Germany Apr. 19-22.

Issued: 5c, 15c, 25c, 50c, 3/8; 30c, 36c, 40c, $1, 10/11; No. 361a, 4/19; No. 355, 20c, 52c, 2/22/91; 27c, 3/8/91; 1c, 12c, 35c, $2, 11/6/91; No. 356, 2/3/92; 10c, 23c, 65c, 75c, 4/24/92.

See Nos. 430-433.

Children's
Games
A60

1990, Mar. 15

366	A60	25c Lodidean	.80	.75
367	A60	25c Lejonjon	.80	.75
368	A60	25c Etobobo	.80	.75
369	A60	25c Didmakol	.80	.75
a.		Block of 4, #366-369	3.25	3.00

Penny
Black, 150th
Anniv.
A61

Designs: No. 370, Penny Black, 1840. No. 371, Essay by James Chalmers. No. 372, Essay by Robert Sievier. No. 373, Essay by Charles Whiting. No. 374, Essay by George Dickinson. No. 375, Medal engraved by William Wyon to celebrate Queen Victoria's first visit to London. $1, Engraver Charles Heath, engraving for master die.

1990, Apr. 6 **Booklet Stamps**

370	A61	25c multicolored	1.00	1.00
371	A61	25c multicolored	1.00	1.00
372	A61	25c multicolored	1.00	1.00
373	A61	25c multicolored	1.00	1.00
374	A61	25c multicolored	1.00	1.00
375	A61	25c multicolored	1.00	1.00

Size: 73x31mm

376	A61	$1 multicolored	4.00	4.00
a.		Booklet pane of 7, #370-376	10.00	—
		Nos. 370-376 (7)	10.00	10.00

Decorative inscribed selvage picturing part of a Penny Black proof sheet separates No. 376 from Nos. 370-375 in pane and surrounds it like a souvenir sheet margin. Selvage around Nos. 370-375 is plain.

Endangered Wildlife — A62

Sea Turtles: No. 377, Pacific green turtle hatchlings entering ocean. No. 378, Pacific great turtle under water. No. 379, Hawksbill hatchling, eggs. No. 380, Hawksbill turtle in water.

1990, May 3

377	A62	25c multicolored	.80	.75
378	A62	25c multicolored	.80	.75
379	A62	25c multicolored	.80	.75
380	A62	25c multicolored	.80	.75
a.		Block of 4, #377-380	3.25	3.00

Stick Chart, Canoe and Flag of the
Republic of the Marshall Islands
A63

1990, Sept. 28 *Perf. 11x10½*

381	A63	25c multicolored	.95	.60

See No. 615, US No. 2507, Micronesia Nos. 124-126.

German Reunification — A64

1990, Oct. 3 *Perf. 13½*

382	A64	45c multicolored	1.25	1.00

Christmas
A65

1990, Oct. 25 **Litho.** *Perf. 13½*

383	A65	25c Canoe, stick chart	.75	.75
384	A65	25c Missionary preaching	.75	.75
385	A65	25c Sailors dancing	.75	.75
386	A65	25c Youths dancing	.75	.75
a.		Block of 4, #383-386	3.00	3.00

Breadfruit — A66

1990, Dec. 15 **Litho.** *Perf. 12x12½*

387	A66	25c Harvesting	.75	.75
388	A66	25c Peeling, slicing	.75	.75
389	A66	25c Preserving	.75	.75
390	A66	25c Kneading dough	.75	.75
a.		Block of 4, #387-390	3.00	3.00

US Space
Shuttle
Flights,
10th Anniv.
A67

1991, Apr. 12 **Litho.** *Perf. 13½*

391	A67	50c 747 ferry	.90	.90
392	A67	50c Orbital release of LDEF	.90	.90
393	A67	50c Lift-off	.90	.90
394	A67	50c Landing	.90	.90
a.		Block of 4, #391-394	3.75	3.75

Flowers — A68

1991, June 10   Litho.   Perf. 13½

395	A68	52c Ixora carolinensis	1.10	1.00
396	A68	52c Clerodendrum in-erme	1.10	1.00
397	A68	52c Messerchmidia argentea	1.10	1.00
398	A68	52c Vigna marina	1.10	1.00
a.		Miniature sheet of 4, #395-398	4.75	4.00
b.		Block of 4, #395-398, without inscription	4.50	4.00

Phila Nippon '91 (No. 398a). Stamps from miniature sheets inscribed C53A.

Operation Desert Storm — A69

1991, July 4   Litho.   Perf. 13½

399	A69	29c multicolored	.80	.60

Birds — A70

1991, July 16   Booklet Stamps

400	A70	29c Red-footed booby	1.25	.60
401	A70	29c Great frigate bird (7-2)	1.25	.60
402	A70	29c Brown booby	1.25	.60
403	A70	29c White tern	1.25	.60
404	A70	29c Great frigate bird (7-5)	1.25	.60
405	A70	29c Black noddy	1.25	.60

Size: 75x33mm

406	A70	$1 White-tailed tropic bird	6.50	2.00
a.		Booklet pane of 7, #400-406	14.00	—
		Nos. 400-406 (7)	14.00	5.60

Decorative selvage separates No. 406 from Nos. 400-405 and surrounds it like a souvenir sheet margin.

Aircraft of Air Marshall Islands — A71

1991, Sept. 10   Litho.   Perf. 13½

407	A71	12c Dornier 228	.25	.25
408	A71	29c Douglas DC-8	.65	.50
409	A71	50c Hawker Siddeley 748	1.10	.85
410	A71	50c Saab 2000	1.10	.85
		Nos. 407-410 (4)	3.10	2.45

Admission to United Nations A72

1991, Sept. 24   Litho.   Perf. 11x10½

411	A72	29c multicolored	.70	.65

Christmas — A73

1991, Oct. 25   Perf. 13½

412	A73	30c multicolored	.75	.75

Peace Corps in Marshall Islands, 25th Anniv. A74

1991, Nov. 26   Litho.   Perf. 11x10½

413	A74	29c multicolored	.75	.60

Ships A75

No. 414, Bulk cargo carrier, Emlain. No. 415, Tanker, CSK Valiant. No. 416, Patrol boat, Ionmeto. No. 417, Freighter, Micro Pilot.

1992, Feb. 15   Litho.   Perf. 11x10½

414	A75	29c multicolored	.80	.45
415	A75	29c multicolored	.80	.45
416	A75	29c multicolored	.80	.45
417	A75	29c multicolored	.80	.45
a.		Strip of 4, #414-417	3.25	2.00

Voyages of Discovery A76

Designs: No. 418, Traditional tipnol. No. 419, Reconstructed Santa Maria. No. 420, Constellation Argo Navis. No. 421, Marshallese sailor, tipnol. No. 422, Columbus, Santa Maria. No. 423, Astronaunt, Argo Navis. $1, Columbus, sailor, and astronaunt.

1992, May 23   Litho.   Perf. 13½
Booklet Stamps

418	A76	50c multicolored	1.00	1.00
419	A76	50c multicolored	1.00	1.00
420	A76	50c multicolored	1.00	1.00
421	A76	50c multicolored	1.00	1.00
422	A76	50c multicolored	1.00	1.00
423	A76	50c multicolored	1.00	1.00

Size: 75x32mm

424	A76	$1 multicolored	4.00	2.00
a.		Booklet pane of 7, #418-424	10.00	

Decorative selvage separates No. 424 from Nos. 418-423 and surrounds it like a souvenir sheet margin.

Traditional Handicrafts — A77

1992, Sept. 9   Litho.   Perf. 13½

425	A77	29c Basket weaving	.60	.60
426	A77	29c Canoe models	.60	.60
427	A77	29c Wood carving	.60	.60
428	A77	29c Fan making	.60	.60
a.		Strip of 4, #425-428	2.40	2.40

Christmas A78

1992, Oct. 29   Litho.   Perf. 11x10½

429	A78	29c multicolored	.70	.60

Bird Type of 1990

1992, Nov. 10   Litho.   Perf. 13½

430	A59	9c Whimbrel	.25	.25
431	A59	22c Greater scaup	.45	.45
432	A59	28c Sharp-tailed sandpiper	.55	.55
433	A59	45c Common teal	.90	.90
		Nos. 430-433 (4)	2.15	2.15

Reef Life — A79

1993, May 26   Litho.   Perf. 13½

434	A79	50c Butterflyfish	1.40	1.00
435	A79	50c Soldierfish	1.40	1.00
436	A79	50c Damselfish	1.40	1.00
437	A79	50c Filefish	1.40	1.00
438	A79	50c Hawkfish	1.40	1.00
439	A79	50c Surgeonfish	1.40	1.00

Size: 75x33mm

440	A79	$1 Parrotfish	5.50	2.00
a.		Booklet pane of 7, #434-440	13.00	
		Nos. 434-440 (7)	13.90	8.00

Decorative selvage separates No. 440 from Nos. 434-439 and surrounds it like a souvenir sheet margin. See No. 1103.

Ships A80

Marshallese Sailing Vessels — A81

Designs: 10c, Spanish galleon San Jeronimo. 14c, USCG Fisheries Patrol vessel Cape Corwin. 15c, British merchant ship Britannia. 19c, Island transport Micro Palm. 20c, Dutch ship Eendracht. 23c, Frigate HMS Cornwallis. 24c, U.S. naval schooner Dolphin. 29c, Missionary packet Morning Star. 30c, Russian brig Rurick. 32c, Spanish sailing ship Santa Maria de la Vittoria. 35c, German warship SMS Nautilus. 40c, British brig Nautilus. 45c, Japanese warships Nagara, Isuzu. 46c, Trading schooner Equator. 50c, Aircraft carrier USS Lexington CV-16. 52c, HMS Serpent. 55c, Whaling ship Potomac. 60c, Coast Guard cutter Assateague. 75c, British transport Scarborough. 78c, Whaler Charles W. Morgan. 95c, US steam vessel Tanager. $1, Walap, Eniwetok. $1, Barkentine hospital ship Tole Mour. $2, Walap, Jaluit. $2.90, Marshall Islands fishing vessels. $3, Schooner Victoria. $5, Tipnol, Ailuk. $10, Racing canoes.

Perf. 11x10½ (A80), 13½ (A81)

1993-95   Litho.

441	A80	10c multicolored	.25	.25
442	A80	14c multicolored	.30	.30
443	A80	15c multicolored	.30	.30
444	A80	19c multicolored	.40	.40
445	A80	20c multicolored	.40	.40
446	A80	23c multicolored	.45	.45
447	A80	24c multicolored	.50	.50
448	A80	29c multicolored	.60	.60
449	A80	30c multicolored	.60	.60
450	A80	32c multicolored	.65	.65
451	A80	35c multicolored	.70	.70
452	A80	40c multicolored	.80	.80
453	A80	45c multicolored	.90	.90
454	A80	46c multicolored	.95	.95
455	A80	50c multicolored	1.00	1.00
456	A80	52c multicolored	1.10	1.10
457	A80	55c multicolored	1.10	1.10
458	A80	60c multicolored	1.25	1.25
459	A80	75c multicolored	1.50	1.50
460	A80	78c multicolored	1.65	1.65
461	A80	95c multicolored	1.90	1.90
462	A80	$1 multicolored	2.00	2.00
463	A81	$1 multicolored	2.00	2.00
464	A81	$2 multicolored	4.00	4.00
465	A80	$2.90 multicolored	5.75	5.75
466	A80	$3 multicolored	6.00	6.00
466A	A81	$5 multicolored	10.00	10.00
466B	A81	$10 multicolored	20.00	20.00
		Nos. 441-466B (28)	67.05	67.05

Souvenir Sheet

Stamp Size: 46x26mm

466C	A81	Sheet of 4, #d.-g.	3.75	3.50

No. 466C contains 15c, 23c, 52c and 75c stamps. Inscription reads "Hong Kong '94 Stamp Exhibition" in Chinese on Nos. 466Cd, 466Cg, and in English on Nos. 466Ce-466Cf.

Issued: 15c, 24c, 29c, 50c, 6/24/93; 19c, 23c, 52c, 75c, 10/14/93; No. 463, 5/29/93; $2, 8/26. 10c, 30c, 35c, $2.90, 4/19/94; $5,

3/15/94; $10, 8/18/94; 20c, 40c, 45c, 55c, 9/23/94; No. 466C, 2/18/94; 14c, 46c, 95c, No. 462, 9/25/95; 32c, 60c, 78c, $3, 5/5/95. See No. 605.

World War II Type of 1989

1943 — Invasion of Sicily: No. 467, Gen. George S. Patton, Jr. No. 468, Gen. Bernard L. Montgomery. No. 469, Americans landing at at Licata. No. 470, British landing south of Syracuse.

Allied bomber raids on Schweinfurt: No. 471, B-17F Flying Fortresses and Bf-109 fighter. No. 472, Liberation of Smolensk. No. 473, Landings at Bougainville. No. 474, Invasion of Tarawa, 1943. No. 475, Teheran Conference, 1943.

Battle of North Cape: No. 476, HMS Duke of York. No. 477, Scharnhorst.

1944 — \No. 478, Gen. Dwight D. Eisenhower, SHAEF Commander. No. 479, Invasion of Anzio. No. 480, Siege of Leningrad lifted. No. 481, U.S. liberates Marshall Islands. #482, Japanese defeated at Truk. No. 483, Big Week, US bombing of Germany.

1993-94   Litho.   Perf. 13½

467	A46	52c W60 (4-1)	1.10	1.10
468	A46	52c W60 (4-2)	1.10	1.10
469	A46	52c W60 (4-3)	1.10	1.10
470	A46	52c W60 (4-4)	1.10	1.10
a.		Block of 4, #467-470	4.50	4.50
471	A46	50c W61	1.00	1.00
472	A47	29c W62	.60	.60
473	A46	29c W63	.60	.60
474	A46	50c W64	1.00	1.00
475	A47	52c W65	1.10	1.10
476	A46	29c W66 (2-1)	.60	.60
477	A46	29c W66 (2-2)	.60	.60
a.		Pair, #476-477	1.25	1.25
478	A46	52c W67	.60	.60
479	A46	50c W68	1.00	1.00
480	A46	52c W69	1.10	1.10
481	A46	29c W70	.60	.60
482	A47	29c W71	.60	.60
483	A46	52c W72	1.10	1.10
		Nos. 467-483 (17)	14.90	14.90

Issued: Nos. 467-470, 7/10/93; No. 471, 8/17/93; No. 472, 9/25/93; No. 473, 11/1/93; No. 474, 11/20/93; No. 475, 12/1/93; Nos. 476-477, 12/26/93; No. 478, 1/16/94; No. 479, 1/22/94; No. 480, 1/27/94; No. 481, 2/4/94; No. 482, 2/17/94; No. 483, 2/20/94.

1994   Litho.   Perf. 13½

1944 — No. 484, Lt. Gen. Mark Clark, Rome falls to the Allies.

D-Day-Allied landings in Normandy: No. 485, Horsa gliders. No. 486, U.S. P-51B Mustangs, British Hurricanes. No. 487, British gun defenses. No. 488, Allied amphibious landing.

No. 489, V-1 flying bombs strike England. No. 490, U.S. Marines land on Saipan.

First Battle of the Philippine Sea: No. 491, Grumman F6F-3 Hellcat.

No. 492, U.S. liberates Guam. No. 493, Warsaw uprising. No. 494, Liberation of Paris. No. 495, U.S. Marines land on Peliliu. No. 496, MacArthur returns to the Philippines. No. 497, Battle of Leyte Gulf.

German battleship Tirpitz sunk: No. 498, Avro Lancaster. No. 499, Tirpitz.

Battle of the Bulge: No. 500, Infantry. No. 501, Armor. No. 502, Aviation. No. 503, Lt. Col. Creighton W. Abrams, Brig. Gen. Anthony C. McAuliffe.

484	A47	50c W73	1.00	1.00
485	A46	75c W74 (4-1)	1.60	1.50
a.		Revised inscription	3.25	1.50
486	A46	75c W74 (4-2)	1.60	1.50
a.		Revised inscription	3.25	1.50
487	A46	75c W74 (4-3)	1.60	1.50
a.		Revised inscription	3.25	1.50
488	A46	75c W74 (4-4)	1.60	1.50
a.		Block of 4, #485-488	6.50	6.00
b.		Block of 4, #485a-487a, 488	12.00	6.00
489	A46	50c W75	1.00	1.00
490	A46	29c W76	.60	.60
491	A46	50c W77	1.00	1.00
492	A46	29c W78	.60	.60
493	A46	50c W79	1.00	1.00
494	A46	50c W80	1.00	1.00
495	A46	29c W81	.60	.60
496	A46	52c W82	1.00	1.00
497	A46	52c multicolored	1.00	1.00
498	A46	50c W84 (2-1)	1.00	1.00
499	A46	50c W84 (2-2)	1.00	1.00
a.		Pair, #498-499	2.00	2.00
500	A47	50c W85 (4-1)	1.00	1.00
501	A47	50c W85 (4-2)	1.00	1.00
502	A47	50c W85 (4-3)	1.00	1.00
503	A47	50c W85 (4-4)	1.00	1.00
a.		Block of 4, #500-503	5.00	4.00
		Nos. 484-503 (20)	21.20	20.80

Inscription reads "Horsa Gliders, Parachute Troops" on #485a, "British Typhoon-1B, U.S. P51B Mustangs" on #486a, "German Gun Defenses, Pointe du Hoc" on #487a.

Issued: No. 484, 6/4; Nos. 485-488, 6/6; No. 489, 6/13; No. 490, 6/15; No. 491, 6/19; No. 492, 7/21; No. 493, 8/1; 494, 8/25; No. 495, 9/15; No. 496, 10/20; No. 497, 10/24; Nos. 498-499, 11/12; Nos. 500-503, 12/16.

1995   Litho.   Perf. 13½

1945 — No. 504, Stalin, Churchill, Roosevelt, Yalta Conference. No. 505, Meissen porcelain, bombing of Dresden, 1945. No. 506, Iwo Jima invaded by US Marines.
No. 507, Remagen Bridge taken by US forces.
No. 508, Okinawa invaded by US forces. No. 509, Death of Franklin D. Roosevelt. No. 510, US/USSR troops meet at Elbe River. No. 511, Russian troops capture Berlin. No. 512, Allies liberate concentration camps.
VE Day: No. 513, German surrender, Rheims. No. 514, Times Square, New York. No. 515, Victory Parade, Moscow. No. 516, Buckingham Palace, London.
UN Charter signed: No. 517, 563, U.S. Pres. Harry S Truman, Veteran's Memorial Hall, San Francisco.
No. 518, Potsdam Conference Convenes. No. 519, Churchill resigns. No. 520, B-29 Enola Gay drops atomic bomb on Hiroshima.
V-J Day: No. 521, Mt. Fuji, ships in Tokyo Bay. No. 522, USS Missouri. No. 523, Adm. Nimitz signs surrender document. No. 524, Japanese delegation.

504	A47	32c W86	.65	.65
505	A47	55c W87	1.10	1.10
506	A47	$1 W88	2.25	2.00
507	A47	32c W89	.65	.65
508	A47	55c W90	1.10	1.10
509	A46	50c W91	1.00	1.00
510	A46	32c W92	.65	.65
511	A46	60c W93	1.25	1.25
512	A46	55c W94	1.10	1.10
513	A46	75c W95 (4-1)	1.60	1.50
514	A46	75c W95 (4-2)	1.60	1.50
515	A46	75c W95 (4-3)	1.60	1.50
516	A46	75c W95 (4-4)	1.60	1.50
a.		Block of 4, #513-516	6.50	6.00
517	A46	32c W96	.65	.65
518	A46	55c W97	1.10	1.10
519	A46	60c W98	1.25	1.25
520	A46	$1 W99	2.25	2.00
521	A46	75c W100 (4-1)	1.75	1.50
522	A46	75c W100 (4-2)	1.75	1.50
523	A46	75c W100 (4-3)	1.75	1.50
524	A46	75c W100 (4-4)	1.75	1.50
a.		Block of 4, #521-524	7.25	6.00
		Nos. 504-524 (21)	28.40	26.50

Issued: No. 504, 2/4/95; No. 505, 2/13/95; No. 506, 2/19/95; No. 507, 3/7/95; No. 508, 4/1/95; No. 509, 4/12/95; No. 516a, 5/8/95; No. 517, 6/26/95; No. 518, 7/7/95; No. 519, 7/26/95; No. 520, 8/6/95; No. 524a, 9/2/95.

Souvenir Sheets

No. 562a, like #303. No. 562b, like #496

1994-95   Imperf.
562		Sheet of 2	2.00	2.00
a.-b.		A40 50c any single	1.00	1.00
563	A46	$1 like #517	2.00	2.00

No. 563 contains one 80x50mm stamp with UN 50th anniv. emblem.
Issued: No. 562, 10/20/94; No. 563, 6/26/95.
Nos. 525-561, 564-566 are unassigned.

Dedication of Capitol Building Complex A82

Designs: No. 567, Capitol building. No. 568, Nitijela (parliament) building. No. 569, Natl. seal, vert. No. 570, Flag over complex, vert.

1993, Aug. 11   Litho.   Perf. 11x10½
567	A82	29c multi (4-1)	.50	.50
568	A82	29c multi (4-2)	.50	.50

Perf. 10½x11
569	A82	29c multi (4-3)	.50	.50
570	A82	29c multi (4-4)	.50	.50
		Nos. 567-570 (4)	2.00	2.00

Souvenir Sheet

Christening of Mobil Super Tanker Eagle — A83

1993, Aug. 25   Perf. 13½
571	A83	50c multicolored	.85	.85

Marshallese Life in 1800's — A84

1993, Sept. 15   Litho.   Perf. 13½
572	A84	29c Woman, breadfruit (4-1)	.60	.60
573	A84	29c Canoes, warrior (4-2)	.60	.60
574	A84	29c Young chief (4-3)	.60	.60
575	A84	29c Drummer, dancers (4-4)	.60	.60
a.		Block of 4, #572-575	2.40	2.40

Christmas A85

1993, Oct. 25   Litho.   Perf. 13½
576	A85	29c multicolored	.60	.60

Souvenir Sheet

Constitution, 15th Anniv. — A86

1994, May 1   Litho.   Perf. 13½
577	A86	$2.90 multicolored	4.50	4.50

Souvenir Sheet

Marshall Islands Postal Service, 10th Anniv. — A87

1994, May 2
578	A87	29c multicolored	.60	.60

1994 World Cup Soccer Championships, U.S. — A88

Design: No. 580, Soccer players, diff.

1994, June 17   Litho.   Perf. 13½
579	A88	50c red & multi (2-1)	1.60	1.00
580	A88	50c blue & multi (2-2)	1.60	1.00
a.		Pair, #579-580	3.25	2.00

No. 580a has a continuous design.

Miniature Sheet

Solar System — A89

Mythological characters, symbols: a, Solar system. b, Sun. c, Moon. d, Mercury. e, Venus. f, Earth. g, Mars. h, Jupiter. i, Saturn. j, Uranus. k, Neptune. l, Pluto.

1994, July 20   Litho.   Perf. 13½
582	A89	50c Sheet of 12, #a.-l.	12.00	12.00

First Manned Moon Landing, 25th Anniv. — A90

Designs: No. 583, First step onto Moon's surface. No. 584, Planting US flag on Moon. No. 585, Astronaut's salute to America, flag. No. 586, Astronaut stepping onto Moon, John F. Kennedy.

1994, July 20
583	A90	75c multi (4-1)	1.10	1.10
584	A90	75c multi (4-2)	1.10	1.10
585	A90	75c multi (4-3)	1.10	1.10
586	A90	75c multi (4-4)	1.10	1.10
a.		Block of 4, #583-586	4.50	4.50
b.		Souvenir sheet of 4, #583-586	4.50	4.50

Souvenir Sheet

Butterflies — A91

1994, Aug. 16   Litho.   Perf. 13½
587	A91	Sheet of 3	3.75	3.75
a.		29c Meadow argus	.60	.60
b.		52c Brown awl	1.10	1.10
c.		$1 Great eggfly	2.00	2.00

PHILAKOREA '94.

Christmas — A92

1994, Oct. 28   Litho.   Perf. 13½
588	A92	29c multicolored	.60	.60

Souvenir Sheet
New Year 1995 (Year of the Boar) — A93

1995, Jan. 2   Litho.   Perf. 13½
589	A93	50c multicolored	1.00	1.00

Marine Life — A94

Designs: a, Meyer's butterflyfish, achilles tang, scuba diver. b, Scuba diver, moorish idols (a, d). c, Pacific green turtle, fairy basslets. d, Fairy basslets, emperor angelfish, orange-fin anemonefish.

1995, Mar. 20   Litho.   Perf. 13½
590		Block of 4	4.50	4.50
a.-d.		A94 55c Any single	1.10	1.10

See Nos. 614, 644.

John F. Kennedy (1917-63), 35th Pres. of US — A95

Designs: a, PT-109. b, Taking presidential oath. c, Peace Corps volunteers. d, US aircraft, naval vessels, Cuban Missile Crisis. e, Signing Nuclear Test Ban Treaty. f, Eternal flame, Arlington Natl. Cemetery.

1995, May 29   Litho.   Perf. 13½
591		Strip of 6	5.25	5.25
a.-f.		A95 55c Any single	1.00	1.00

Marilyn Monroe (1926-1962),
Actress — A96

Various portraits with background color: a,
red. b, green. c, orange. d, violet.

1995, June 1		Litho.	Perf. 13½
592	A96 75c Block of 4, #a.-d.	5.75	5.75

No. 592 was issued in sheets of three
blocks.

Cats — A97

Designs: a, Siamese, exotic shorthair. b,
American shorthair, Persian. c, Maine coon,
Burmese. d, Abyssinian, Himalayan.

1995, July 5		Litho.	Perf. 13½
593	Block of 4	2.50	2.50
	a.-d. A97 32c Any single	.60	.60

Mir-Space Shuttle Docking & Apollo-
Soyuz Link-Up — A98

a, Space station Mir. b, Space shuttle Atlantis. c, Apollo command module. d, Soyuz
spacecraft.

1995, June 29		Litho.	Perf. 13½
594	A98 75c Block of 4, #a.-d.	4.75	4.75

Nos. 594 is a continuous design.

Pacific
Game
Fish — A99

a, Pacific sailfish. b, Albacore. c, Wahoo. d,
Pacific blue marlin. e, Yellowfin tuna. f, Giant
trevally. g, Dolphin fish. h, Mako shark.

1995, Aug. 21		Litho.	Perf. 13½
595	Block of 8	11.00	11.00
	a.-h. A00 60c Any single	1.35	1.35

Island
Legends — A100

Designs: a, Inedel's Magic Kite. b, Lijebake
Rescues Her Granddaughter. c, Jebro's
Mother Invents the Sail. d, Limajnon Escapes
to the Moon.

1995, Aug. 25		Litho.	Perf. 13½
596	Block of 4 + 4 labels	2.50	2.50
	a.-d. A100 32c Any single	.60	.60

See Nos. 612, 643.

Miniature Sheet

Singapore '95 World Stamp
Exhibition — A101

Orchids: a, Paphiopedilum armeniacum. b,
Masdevallia veitchiana. c, Cattleya francis. d,
Cattleya x guatemalensis.

1995, Sept. 1		Litho.	Perf. 13½
597	A101 32c Sheet of 4, #a.-d.	2.25	2.25

Souvenir Sheet

Intl. Stamp & Coin Expo, Beijing
'95 — A102

1995, Sept. 12			
598	A102 50c Suzhou Gardens	.85	.85

Christmas
A103

1995, Oct. 31		Litho.	Perf. 13½
599	A103 32c multicolored	.55	.55

Miniature Sheet

Jet Fighter Planes — A104

a, Me 262-1a Schwalbe. b, Meteor F.MK8.
c, F-80 Shooting Star. d, F-86 Sabre. e, F9F-2
Panther. f, MiG-15. g, F-100 Super Sabre. h,
F-102A Delta Dagger. i, F-104 Starfighter. j,
MiG-21 MT. k, F8U Crusader. l, F-105 Thun-
derbird. m, Saab J35 Draken. n, Fiat G91Y. o,
F-4 Phantom II. p, Saab JA37 Viggen. q,
Mirage F1C. r, F-14 Tomcat. s, F-15 Eagle. t,
F-16 Fighting Falcon. u, Tornado F.MK3. v,
Sukhoi Su-27UB. w, Mirage 2000C. x, Sea
Harrier FRS.MK1. y, F-117 Nighthawk.

1995, Nov. 10			
600	A104 32c Sheet of 25,		
	#a.-y.	16.00	16.00

No. 600 was sold in uncut sheets of 6
panes.

See Nos. 617, 641, 666, 708, 728.

Yitzhak Rabin
(1922-95), Israeli
Prime
Minister — A105

1995, Nov. 10		Litho.	Perf. 14
601	A105 32c multicolored	.55	.55

No. 601 was issued in sheets of 8.

Souvenir Sheet

New Year 1996 (Year of the
Rat) — A106

1996, Jan. 5		Litho.	Perf. 13½
602	A106 50c multicolored	.85	.85

Native Birds
A107

Designs: a, Blue-gray noddy. b, Gray-
backed tern. c, Masked booby. d, Black-footed
albatross.

1996, Feb. 26		Litho.	Perf. 13½
603	Block of 4	2.50	2.50
	a.-d. A107 32c Any single	.60	.60

Wild
Cats — A108

a, Cheetah. b, Tiger. c, Lion. d, Jaguar.

1996, Mar. 8		Litho.	Perf. 13½
604	Block of 4	3.75	3.75
	a.-d. A108 55c Any single	.90	.90

Sailing Ship Type of 1993
Miniature Sheet

Designs: a, like #443. b, like #447. c, like
#448. d, like #455. e, like #444. f, like #446. g,
like #456. h, like #459. i, like #441. j, like #449.
k, like #451. l, like #465. m, Malmel outrigger
sailing canoe. n, like #445. o, like #452. p, like
#453. q, like #457. r, like #450. s, like #458. t,
like #460. u, like #466. v, like #442. w, like
#454. x, like #459A. y, like #462.

1996, Apr. 18		Litho.	Perf. 11x10½
605	A80 32c Sheet of 25, #a.-		
	y.	16.00	16.00

Olympic
Games,
Cent. — A109

First Olympic stamps, Greece: a, #119. b,
#124. c, #123. d, #125.

1996, Apr. 27		Litho.	Perf. 12
606	Block of 4	4.00	4.00
	a.-d. A109 60c Any single	.95	.95

Issued in sheets of 4. A small number were
were overprinted in gold in the margin for
Olymphilex '96.

Miniature Sheet

History of the Marshall Islands — A110

a, Undersea eruptions form island bases. b,
Coral reefs grow. c, Storms bring birds &
seeds. d, Early human inhabitants arrive. e,
Seen by Spanish explorers, 1527. f, Capt.
John Marshall, RN, charts islands, 1788. g,
Islands become German protectorate, 1885.
h, Japan seizes islands, 1914. i, US troops
liberate islands, 1944. j, Bikiniatoll evacuated
for nuclear testing, 1946. k, Islands become
UN Trust Territory, 1947. l, Independence,
1986.

1996, May 2		Litho.	Perf. 13x12
607	A110 55c Sheet of 12,		
	#a.-l.	10.50	10.50

Elvis Presley's First #1 Hit, "Heartbreak Hotel," 40th Anniv. — A111

1996, May 5   *Perf. 10½x11*
608 A111 32c multicolored   .65   .65
Issued in sheets of 20.

Souvenir Sheet

China '96, 9th Asian Intl. Philatelic Exhibition — A112

Design: The Palance Museum, Shenyang.

1996, May 17   *Perf. 13½*
609 A112 50c multicolored   1.00 1.00

James Dean (1931-55), Actor — A113

1996, June 1   Litho.   *Perf. 10½x11*
610 A113 32c multicolored   .65   .65
No. 610 was issued in sheets of 20.

First Ford Automobile, Cent. — A114

Designs: a, 1896 Quadricycle. b, 1903 Model A Roadster. c, 1909 Model T Touring Car. d, 1929 Model A Station Wagon. e, 1955 Thunderbird. f, 1964½ Mustang convertible. g, 1995 Explorer. h, 1996 Taurus.

1996, June 4   Litho.   *Perf. 13½*
611 Sheet of 8   6.00 6.00
a.-h. A114 60c Any single   .75   .75

Island Legends Type of 1995
Designs: a, Kijeek An Letao. b, Mennin Jobwodda. c, Wa Kone, Waan Letao. d, Kouj.

1996, July 19
612 Block of 4 + 4 labels   2.25 2.25
a.-d. A100 32c Any single   .55   .55

Steam Locomotives — A115

Designs: a, Pennsylvania K4, U.S. b, "Big Boy," U.S. c, Mallard, Great Britain. d, RENFE Class 242, Spain. e, DB Class 01, Germany. f, FS Group 691, Italy. g, "Royal Hudson,"

Canada. h, Evening Star, Great Britain. i, SAR 520 Class, Australia. j, SNCF 232.U1, France. k, QJ "Advance Forward," China. l, C62 "Swallow," Japan.

1996, Aug. 23   Litho.   *Perf. 13½*
613 Sheet of 12   11.00 11.00
a.-i. A115 55c Any single   .90   .90

Marine Life Type of 1995
Designs: a, like #590a. b, like #590b. c, like #590c. d, like #590d.

1996, Oct. 21   Litho.   *Perf. 13½*
614 Block of 4   1.75 1.75
a.-d. A94 32c Any single   .40   .40
Taipei '96, 10th Asian Intl. Philatelic Exhibition. Nos. 614a-614b have Chinese inscription, Nos. 614c-614d English.

Stick Chart, Canoe and Flag of the Republic Type of 1990
1996, Oct. 21   *Perf. 11x10½*
615 A63 $3 like No. 381   6.00 6.00
No. 615 inscribed "Free Association United States of America."

Angels from "Madonna and Child with Four Saints," by Rosso Fiorentino A116

1996, Oct. 31   Litho.   *Perf. 13½*
616 A116 32c multicolored   .55   .55
Christmas.

Legendary Planes Type of 1995
Biplanes: a, JN-3 Jenny. b, SPAD XIII. c, Albatros D.III. d, DH-4 Liberty. e, Fokker Dr.1. f, F-1 Camel. g, Martin MB-2. h, MB-3A Tommy. i, Curtiss TS-1. j, P-1 Hawk. k, Boeing PW-9. l, Douglas 0-2H. m, LB-5 Pirate. n, 02U-1 Corsair. o, F8C Heldiver. p, Boeing F4B-4. q, J6B Gerfalcon. r, Martin BM. s, FF-1 Fifi. t, C.R. 32 Cricket. u, Polikarpov I-15 Gull. v, Mk.1 Swordfish. w, Aichi D1A2. x, Grumman F3F. y, SOC-3 Seagull.

1996, Nov. 1
617 A104 32c Sheet of 25,
     #a. y.   16.00 16.00

Native Crafts A117

Designs: a, Fan making. b, Canoe models. c, Carving. d, Basketmaking.

1996, Nov. 7   Litho.   *Perf. 11x10½*
618 Block of 4   1.60 1.60
a.-d. A117 32c Any single   .40   .40
See Nos. 629-630.

Souvenir Sheet

New Year 1997 (Year of the Ox) — A118

1997, Jan. 7   Litho.   *Perf. 13x13½*
619 A118 60c multicolored   1.25 1.25

Amata Kabua (1928-96), President of Marshall Islands — A119

1997, Jan. 27   Litho.   *Perf. 13½*
620 A119 32c multicolored   .65   .65
621 A119 60c multicolored   1.25 1.25
No. 621 has vertical inscriptions in English.

Elvis Presley (1935-77) A120

Designs: a, "Rocking 50's." b, "Soaring 60's." c, "Sensational 70's."

1997, Jan. 8   Litho.   *Perf. 13½*
622 A120 32c Strip of 3, #a.-c.   2.00 2.00

Hong Kong '97 — A121

Hong Kong at sunrise, ships: No. 623: a, Walap. b, Junk.
Hong Kong at night, ships: No. 624: a, Canoe. b, Junk, diff.

1997, Feb. 12   *Perf. 12*
623 Sheet of 2 + 3 labels   1.25 1.25
a.-b. A121 32c Any single   .60   .60
624 Sheet of 2 + 3 labels   1.25 1.25
a.-b. A121 32c Any single   .60   .60

Christianity in Marshall Islands, 140th Anniv. — A122

Apostles: No. 625: a, Andrew. b, Matthew. c, Philip. d, Simon. e, Thaddeus. f, Thomas. g, Bartholomew. h, John. i, James, the Lesser. j, James, the Greater. k, Paul. l, Peter.
$3, The Last Supper, by Peter Paul Rubens.

1997, Mar. 28   *Perf. 13½*
625 Sheet of 12   14.50 14.50
a.-i. A122 60c Any single   1.20 1.20

Souvenir Sheet
Perf. 13x13½
626 A122 $3 multicolored   6.00 6.00
No. 626 contains one 80x50mm stamp.

First Decade of 20th Century — A123

Designs: a, Family of immigrants. b, Dowager Empress, Boxers, China. c, Photography for every man. d, Dr. Walter Reed, mosquito. e, Sigmund Freud. f, Marconi, wireless transmitter. g, Enrico Caruso, phonograph. h, Wright Brothers, Flyer. i, Einstein. j, HMS Dreadnought. k, San Francisco earthquake, 1906. l, Gandhi, non-violent protestors. m, Picasso. n, Dawn of the automobile age. o, Man, camels, oil derrick amid sand dunes.

1997, Apr. 15   Litho.   *Perf. 13½*
627 Sheet of 15   18.00 18.00
a.-o. A123 60c Any single   1.10 1.10
See Nos. 646, 654, 657, 679, 702, 711, 723, 726 and 730.

Deng Xiaoping (1904-97), Chinese Leader — A124

1997, Apr. 21
628 A124 60c multicolored   1.25 1.25

Crafts Type of 1996
Designs: Nos. 629a, 630a, Fan making. Nos. 629b, 630b, Canoe models. Nos. 629c, 630c, Wood carving. Nos. 629d, 630d, Basket making.

1997, May 29   Litho.   *Perf. 11x10½*
Self-Adhesive
629 Block of 4   2.50 2.50
a.-d. A117 32c Any single   .60   .60
Serpentine Die Cut Perf. 11
Self-Adhesive
630 Strip of 4   2.50 2.50
a.-d. A117 32c Any single   .60   .60
No. 629 was issued in sheets of 20 stamps. No. 630 was issued in sheets of 16 stamps. Die cutting does not extend through backing paper on No. 630.

Marshall Islands Stamps, Cent., US Stamps, 150th Anniv. A126

1997, May 29   Litho.   *Perf. 13½*
Booklet Stamps
631 A126 50c No. 1   1.00 1.00
632 A126 50c No. 2   1.00 1.00
633 A126 50c No. 3   1.00 1.00
634 A126 50c No. 4   1.00 1.00
635 A126 50c No. 5   1.00 1.00
636 A126 50c No. 6   1.00 1.00
a.   Booklet pane, #631-636   6.00

Size: 75x32mm
637 A126 $1 US Nos. 1 & 2   2.00 2.00
a.   Booklet pane of 2   2.00
     Complete booklet, #636a, #637a   8.00
PACIFIC 97.

Bristle-thighed Curlew — A127

World Wildlife Fund: a, Walking right. b, On tree branch. c, Standing with mouth open. d, In flight.

1997, June 6
638 Block or strip of 4   4.00 4.00
a.-d. A127 16c Any single   1.00 1.00

Souvenir Sheet

Bank of China, Hong Kong — A128

1997, July 1   Litho.   Perf. 13½
639 A128 50c multicolored   1.00 1.00

Canoes
A129

Designs: a, Pacific Arts Festival canoe, Walap of Enewetak. b, Large Voyaging canoe, Walap of Jaluit. c. Racing canoe. d, Sailing canoe, Tipnol of Ailuk.

1997, July 10   Litho.   Perf. 13½
640 Block or strip of 4   2.50 2.50
a.-d. A129 32c Any single   .60   .60

Legendary Aircraft Type of 1995

Designs: a, C-54 Skymaster. b, B-36 Peacemaker. c, F-86 Sabre. d, B-47 Stratojet. e, C-124 Globemaster II. f, C-121 Constellation. g, B-52 Stratofortress. h, F-100 Super Sabre. i, F-104 Starfighter. j, C-130 Hercules. k, F-105 Thunderchief. l, KC-135 Stratotanker. m, B-58 Hustler. n, F-4 Phanton II. o, T-38 Talon. p, C-141 Star Lifter. q, F-111 Aardvark. r, SR-71 "Blackbird." s, C-5 Galaxy. t, A-10 Thunderbolt II. u, F-15 Eagle. v, F-16 Fighting Falcon. w, F-117 Nighthawk. x, B-2 Spirit. y, C-17 Globemaster III.

1997, July 19
641 A104 32c Sheet of 25,
     #a.-y.   16.00 16.00

USS Constitution, Bicent. — A130

1997, July 21
642 A130 32c multicolored   .65   .65

Island Legends Type of 1995

Designs: a, The Large Pool of Mejit. b, The Beautiful Woman of Kwajalein. c, Sharks and Lowakalle Reef. d, The Demon of Adrie.

1997, Aug. 15   Litho.   Perf. 13½
643 Block of 4 +4 labels   2.50 2.50
a.- A100 32c Any single
d.   .60   .60

Marine Life Type of 1995

Designs: a, Watanabe's angelfish, gray reef shark. b, Raccoon butterflyfish. c, Flame angelfish, d, Square-spot fairy basslets.

1997, Aug. 21
644 Block of 4   4.75 4.75
a.- A94 60c Any single
d.   1.10 1.10

Diana, Princess of Wales (1961-97)
A131

Various portraits, background color: a, violet. b, blue. c, yellow orange.

1997, Sept. 30   Litho.   Perf. 13½
645 Strip of 3   3.75 3.75
a.-c. A131 60c Any single   1.25 1.25

No. 645 printed in sheets with two vertical strips flanking three horizontal strips.

Events of the 20th Century Type

1910-19: a, Women mobilize for equal rights. b, Ernest Rutherford, model of atom. c, Sun Yat-sen. d, Sinking of the Titanic. e, Igor Stravinsky, The Rite of Spring. f, Ford begins assembly line production of autos. g, Archduke Franz Ferdinand, wife Sophie. h, German U-boat sinks Lusitania. i, Soldiers in trenches at Battle of Verdun. j, Patrick Pearse proclaims Irish Republic. k, Jews praying at Wailing Wall. l, Cruiser Aurora. m, Baron Manfred von Richtofen. n, German revolutionary troops, 1918. o, Negotiators write Treaty of Versailles.

1997, Oct. 15   Litho.   Perf. 13½
646 Sheet of 15   18.00 18.00
a.-o. A123 60c Any single   1.20 1.20

Christmas
A132

Cherubs from Sistine Madonna, by Raphael: No. 647, With hand under chin. No. 648, With arms folded under chin.

1997, Oct. 25
647 A132 32c multicolored   .60   .60
648 A132 32c multicolored   .60   .60
a.   Pair, #647-648   1.25 1.25

US State-Named Warships — A133

Designs: a.-z., aa.-ax.: USS Alabama-USS Wyoming in alphabetical order. USS Honolulu shown for Hawaii.

1997, Nov. 1
649 Sheet of 50   20.00 20.00
a.-z.,aa.- A133 20c Any single
ax.   .40   .40

Souvenir Sheet

Shanghai 97, Intl. Stamp and Coin Expo — A134

Treasure ship, Ming Dynasty.

1997, Nov. 19   Litho.   Perf. 13x13½
650 A134 50c multicolored   1.00 1.00

Souvenir Sheet

New Year 1998 (Year of the Tiger) — A135

1998, Jan. 2   Litho.   Perf. 13x13½
651 A135 60c multicolored   1.25 1.25

Elvis Presley's 1968 Television Special
A136

Scenes from special: a, shown. b, Red background. c, Elvis in white suit.

1998, Jan. 8   Perf. 13½
652 Strip of 3   1.75 1.75
a.-c. A136 32c Any single   .55   .55

Sea Shells
A137

a, Chicoreus brunneus. b, Cypraea aurantium. c, Lambis chiragra. d, Tridanca squamosa.

1998, Feb. 13   Litho.   Perf. 13½
653 Strip of 4   2.50 2.50
a.-d. A137 32c Any single   .60   .60

Events of the 20th Century Type

1920-29: a, Radio broadcasting reaches the world. b, Quest for peace lurches forward. c, Architects reshape the world. d, Funerary mask of King Tutankhamen. e, USSR emerges as a Communist State. f, Nations emerge from Ottoman Empire, Kemal Ataturk. g, Arrival of the Jazz Age. h, Age of the rocket launched, Robert Goddard. i, Talkies arrive at the movie theater. j, Scourge of Fascism arrives. k, Man's universe expands. l, Penicillin launches antibiotic revolution. m, First glimmers of television. n, Aviation shrinks the world, Graf Zeppelin. o, World suffers economic depression.

1998, Mar. 16   Litho.   Perf. 13½
654 Sheet of 15   18.00 18.00
a.-o. A123 60c Any single   1.20 1.20

Canoes of the Pacific — A138

a, Pahi Sailing canoe, Tuamotu Archipelago. b, Maori war canoe, New Zealand. c, Wa'a Kaukahi fishing canoe, Hawaii. d, Amatasi sailing canoe, Samoa. e, Ndrua sailing canoe, Fiji. f, Tongiaki voyaging canoe, Tonga. g,

Tipairua traveling canoe, Tahiti. h, Walap sailing canoe, Marshall Islands.

1998, May 21   Litho.   Perf. 13½
655 A138 32c Sheet of 8, #a.-h.   5.00 5.00
     See Nos. 690-698.

Berlin Airlift, 50th Anniv. — A139

Designs: a, Douglas C-54/R4D-5. b, Avro York. c, Watching the flights of freedom. d, Berliners welcoming supplies.

1998, June 26   Litho.   Perf. 13½
656 A139 60c Block of 4, #a.-d.   4.75 4.75

Events of the 20th Century Type

1930-39: a, Economic depression engulfs the world. b, Scientists split the atom. c, Stalin's terror reigns in Soviet Union. d, Fascism becomes rampant. e, Engineers harness nature (Dneproges Dam). f, Streamlined design symbolizes bright future. g, Passengers travel airways in comfort. h, Artists protest the scourges of war. i, Media create indelible memories. j, Japanese agression arouses world opinion. k, Era of appeasement. l, Inventions pave way to future. m, Persecution of Jews portends holocaust. n, World War II begins in Europe. o, Movies cheer audiences.

1998, July 15
657 Sheet of 15   17.50 17.50
a.-o. A123 60c Any single   1.10 1.10

Czar Nicholas II — A140

No. 658, Coronation Czar Nicholas II, 1896. No. 659, Russo-Japanese War and the Cruiser Varyag, 1904-05. No. 660, Czar's Manifesto, 1905. No. 661, Peasant sower, Rasputin, 1905. No. 662, Czar with soldiers at the front, 1915. No. 663, Ipateva House, Ekaterinburg, 1917. $3, Family portrait.

1998, July 17   Perf. 13½
     Booklet Stamps
658 A140 60c multicolored   1.25 1.25
659 A140 60c multicolored   1.25 1.25
660 A140 60c multicolored   1.25 1.25
661 A140 60c multicolored   1.25 1.25
662 A140 60c multicolored   1.25 1.25
663 A140 60c multicolored   1.25 1.25
     Size: 60x54mm
     Perf. 13½ at Top
664 A140 $3 multicolored   6.00 6.00
a. Booklet pane, #658-664   13.50
   Complete booklet, #664a   13.50

George Herman "Babe" Ruth (1895-1948)
A141

1998, Aug. 16   Litho.   Perf. 13½
665 A141 32c multicolored   .65   .65

Legendary Aircraft Type of 1995

US Navy aircraft: a, NC-4. b, PBY-5 Catalina. c, TBD Devastator. d, SB2U Vindicator. e, F4F Wildcat. f, OS2U Kingfisher. g, SBD Dauntless. h, F4U Corsair. i, SB2C Helldiver. j, PV-Ventura. k, TBM Avenger. l, F6F Hellcat. m, PB4Y-2 Privateer. n, A-1J Skyraider. o, F2H Banshee. p, F9F-2B Panther. q, P5M Marlin. r, F-8 Crusader. s, F-4 Phantom II. t, A-6 Intruder. u, P-3 Orion. v, A-7 Corsair II. w, A-4 Skyhawk. x, S-3 Viking. y, F/A-18 Hornet.

1998, Aug. 28
666 A104 32c Sheet of 25,
#a.-y.   16.00 16.00

Chevrolet Automobiles — A142

Designs: a, 1912 Classic Six. b, 1931 Sports Roadster. c, 1941 Special Deluxe. d, 1955 Cameo Carrier Fleetside. e, 1957 Corvette. f, 1957 Bel Air. g, 1967 Camaro. h, 1970 Chevelle SS 454.

1998, Sept. 1
667   Sheet of 8   9.50 9.50
a.-h. A142 60c Any single   1.15 1.15

Marshallese Language and Alphabet — A143

Letter, example of Marshallese word beginning with letter: a, "A," Amata Kabua, first president. b, "A," Aj, to weave. c, "B," butterfly. d, "D," beautiful lady. e, "E," fish. f, "I," Rainbow. g, "J," mat. h, "K," house of government. i, "L," stars. j, "L," Tropicbird. k, "M," breadfruit. l, "M," Arrowroot plant. m, "N," Coconut tree. n, "N," Ocean wave. o, "N," shark tooth. p, "O," Fish net. q, "O," Tattoo. r, "O," Lionfish. s, "P," Visitor's hut. t, "R," Whale. u, "T," outrigger canoe. v, "U," Fire. w, "U," Dorsal fin of whale. x, "W," Woven sail.

1998, Sept. 14
668   Sheet of 24   16.00 16.00
a.-x. A140 33c Any single   .65 .65

New Buildings in Marshall Islands — A144

a, Trust Company of the Marshall Islands, 1998. b, Embassy of the People's Republic of China, 1996. c, Outrigger Marshall Islands Resort, 1996.

1998, Oct. 12
669   Strip of 3   2.00 2.00
a.-c. A144 33c Any single   .65 .65

Christmas A145

1998, Oct. 26
670 A145 32c Midnight angel   .65 .65

(note: image shows stamp captioned "John Glenn's Return to Space A146")

John Glenn's Return to Space A146

No. 671, Friendship 7 launch, 1962. No. 672, Glenn in spacesuit, 1962. No. 673, Mercury capsule in space, 1962. No. 674, Shuttle Discovery Launch, 1998. No. 675, Astronaut and US Senator Glenn, 1998. No. 676, Shuttle Discovery in space, 1998.
$3, US #1193, astrological drawings.

1998, Oct. 29   **Booklet Stamps**
671 A146 60c multicolored   1.25 1.25
672 A146 60c multicolored   1.25 1.25
673 A146 60c multicolored   1.25 1.25
674 A146 60c multicolored   1.25 1.25
675 A146 60c multicolored   1.25 1.25
676 A146 60c multicolored   1.25 1.25
     Size: 75x32mm
677 A146 $3 multicolored   6.00 6.00
a.   Booklet pane, #671-677   13.50
     Complete booklet, #677a   13.50

     Souvenir Sheet

Antonov An-124 Delivering Drought Relief Supplies — A147

1998, Nov. 3   **Litho.**   **Perf. 13½**
678 A147 $3.20 multicolored   6.50 6.50

Events of the 20th Century Type

1940-49: a, Aviation assumes strategic importance. b, State of war becomes global. c, Missiles announce new age of warfare. d, Music raises spirits. e, Determined peoples fight for survival. f, The Holocaust. g, Mankind faces Atomic Age. h, War's end brings hope. i, Computer age dawns. j, Nations unite for peace. k, World demands justice from war criminals. l, A time for rebuilding. m, Transistor opens door to miniaturization. n, World divided by cold war. o, New China is proclaimed.

1998, Nov. 16   **Litho.**   **Perf. 13½**
679   Sheet of 15   17.50 17.50
a.-o. A123 60c Any single   1.15 1.15

(sheet image: HISTORY'S GREATEST FIGHTING SHIPS)

Warships — A148

Designs: a, Trireme Galley. b, Trireme Romano. c, Viking Longship. d, Ming Treasure ship. e, The Mary Rose. f, Nuestra Señora del Rosario. g, Korean Turtle ship. h, Brederode. i, Galera Veneziana. j, Santisima Trinidad. k, Ville de Paris. l, HMS Victory. m, Bonhomme Richard. n, USS Constellation. o, USS Hartford. p, Fijian Ndrua. q, HMS Dreadnought. r, HMAS Australia. s, HMS Dorsetshire. t, Graf Spee. u, Yamato. v, USS Tautog. w, Bismarck. x, USS Hornet. y, USS Missouri.

1998, Dec. 1
680 A148 33c Sheet of 25,
#a.-y.   16.00 16.00

     Souvenir Sheet

New Year 1999 (Year of the Rabbit) — A149

1999, Jan. 2   **Litho.**   **Perf. 13x13½**
681 A149 60c multicolored   1.25 1.25

Birds — A150

1c, Lesser golden plover. 3c, Siberian tattler. 20c, Brown noddy. 22c, Common fairy tern. 33c, Micronesian pigeon. 55c, Long-tailed cuckoo. $1, Christmas shearwater. $10, Eurasian tree sparrow.

1999, Jan. 9   **Perf. 13½**
682 A150 1c multicolored   .25 .25
683 A150 3c multicolored   .25 .25
684 A150 20c multicolored   .40 .40
685 A150 22c multicolored   .45 .45
686 A150 33c multicolored   .65 .65
687 A150 55c multicolored   1.10 1.10
688 A150 $1 multicolored   2.00 2.00
689 A150 $10 multicolored   15.00 15.00
     Nos. 682-689 (8)   20.10 20.10

     See Nos. 714-721.

Canoes of the Pacific Type

Designs: a, like #655a. b, like #655b. c, like #655c. d, like #655f. e, like #655e. f, like #655d. g, like #655g. h, like #655h.

1999, Jan. 25   **Litho.**   **Perf. 13½**
690 A138 33c Sheet of 8, #a.-h. 5.25 5.25
     Self-Adhesive
     Size: 40x25mm
     Perf. 11x10½
691 A138 33c like #690a   .65 .65
692 A138 33c like #690b   .65 .65
693 A138 33c like #690c   .65 .65
694 A138 33c like #690d   .65 .65
695 A138 33c like #690e   .65 .65
696 A138 33c like #690f   .65 .65
697 A138 33c like #690g   .65 .65
698 A138 33c like #690h   .65 .65
a.   Block of 10, #691-697, 3 #698 6.50

     Issued in sheets of 20.

Great American Indian Chiefs — A151

Designs: a, Tecumseh. b, Powhatan. c, Hiawatha. d, Dull knife. e, Sequoyah. f, Sitting Bull. g, Cochise. h, Red Cloud. i, Geronimo. j, Chief Joseph. k, Pontiac. l, Crazy Horse.

1999, Feb. 1   **Perf. 13½**
699   Sheet of 12   14.50 14.50
a.-l. A151 60c Any single   1.15 1.15

National Flag A152

1999, Feb. 5   **Perf. 14**
700 A152 33c multicolored   .65 .65

Flowers of the Pacific A153

Designs: a, Plumeria. b, Vanda. c, Ilima. d, Tiare. e, White ginger. f, Hibiscus.

1999, Feb. 18   **Perf. 13½**
701   Block of 6   4.00 4.00
a.-f. A153 33c Any single   .65 .65

Events of the 20th Century Type

1950-59: a, World enters age of television. b, Cold war battles erupt. c, Vaccines conquer scourge of polio. d, U.S., USSR engage in arms race. e, Science begins to unravel genetic code. f, Conquests reach unconquered heights. g, Pageantry reassures commonwealth. h, Rock 'n' roll reshapes music beat. i, Suns sets on Colonial Empires. j, World condemns racial discrimination. k, Unrest challenges Communism's march. l, Vision of European Union takes form. m, Space race opens space age. n, Jets shrink time and distance. o, Microchip presages computer revolution.

1999, Mar. 15
702   Sheet of 15   18.00 18.00
a.-o. A123 60c Any single   1.20 1.20

     Souvenir Sheet

HMAS Australia — A154

1999, Mar. 19
703 A154 $1.20 multicolored   2.50 2.50
     Australia '99, World Stamp Expo.

Elvis Presley — A155

1999, Apr. 6   **Litho.**   **Perf. 13½**
704 A155 33c multicolored   .65 .65

IBRA '99 World Stamp Exhibition, Nuremberg, Germany A156

Designs: a, #25. b. #24. c. #23. d, #22.

1999, Apr. 27   **Litho.**   **Perf. 13½**
705   Sheet of 4   4.75 4.75
a.-d. A156 60c Any single   1.15 1.15

Marshall Islands Constitution, 20th
Anniv. — A157

1999, May 1   Litho.   Perf. 13½
706 A157 33c Constitution Com-
           mittee   .65   .65

Marshall Islands Postal Service, 15th
Anniv. — A158

Portions of No. 607 and, clockwise: a, #572,
644, 689, 597d (b). b, #668c, 595c, 655h,
597a. c, #381, 570, 574, 668d. d, #597b,
643b, 621.

1999, May 2
707 A158 33c Block of 4, #a.-d.   2.50 2.50

Legendary Aircraft Type of 1995
a, Martin B-10B. b, Northrop A-17A Nomad.
c, Douglas B-18 Bolo. d, Boeing B-17F Flying
Fortress. e, Douglas A-20 Havoc. f, North
American B-25B Mitchell. g, Consolidated B-
24D Liberator. h, North American P-51B Mus-
tang. i, Martin B-26 Marauder. j, Douglas A-
26B Invader. k, Bell P-59 Airacomet. l, Boeing
KC-97 Stratofreighter. m, Douglas A-1J
Skyraider. n, Lockheed P2V-7 Neptune. o,
North American B-45 Tornado. p, Boeing B-50
Superfortress. q, North American AJ-2 Sav-
age. r, Grumman F9F Cougar. s, Douglas A-3
Skywarrior. t, Martin B-57E Canberra. u,
Douglas EB-66 Destroyer. v, Grumman E-2A
Hawkeye. w, Northrop F-5E Tiger II. x,
McDonnell Douglas AV-8B Harrier II. y,
Rockwell B-1B Lancer.

1999, June 1
708 A104 33c Sheet of 25,
                #a.-y.   16.00 16.00

Souvenir Sheet

PhilexFrance 99 — A159

1999, July 2   Litho.   Perf. 13½
709 A159 $1 Astronaut, lunar
             rover   2.00 2.00

Souvenir Sheet

Tanker Alrehab — A160

1999, July 15 Litho. Perf. 13x13½
710 A160 60c multi   1.25 1.25

Events of the 20th Century Type
1960-69: a, Invention of the laser. b, Pill
revolutionizes family planning. c, Gagarin

becomes the Columbus of the cosmos. d,
Communism advertizes failures. e, Planet
Earth endangered. f, Superpowers totter on
precipice of war. g, Spirit of ecumenism
renews Christianity. h, Railways achieve
record speeds. i, Cultural Revolution stuns
China. j, Arab-Israeli War unsettles Middle
East. k, Organ transplants repair human body.
l, America engulfed in Vietnam War. m, Political assassinations shock world. n, Supersonic
travel becomes a reality. o, Mankind leaps
from Earth to Moon.

1999, July 15   Perf. 13½
711   Sheet of 15   18.00 18.00
  a.-o. A123 60c Any single   1.20   1.20

First Manned Moon Landing, 30th
Anniv. — A161

Designs: a, Saluting astronaut, Earth. b,
Flag. c, Astronaut.

1999, July 20
712 A161 33c Sheet of 3, #a.-c.   2.00 2.00

Ships — A162

Designs: a, Galleon Los Reyes, Spain,
1568. b, Frigate Dolphin, Great Britain, 1767.
c, Bark Scarborough, Great Britain, 1788. d,
Brig Rurick, Russia, 1817.

1999, Aug. 26
713 A162 33c Block of 4, #a.-d.   2.75 2.75

Bird Type of 1999
Designs: 5c, Black-tailed godwit. 40c,
Franklin's gull. 45c, Rufous-necked stint. 75c,
Kermadec petrel. $1.20, Purple-capped fruit
dove. $2, Mongolian plover. $3.20, Cattle
egret. $5, Dunlin.

1999, Sept. 16   Litho.   Perf. 13½
714 A150   5c multi   .25   .25
715 A150   40c multi   .80   .80
716 A150   45c multi   .90   .90
717 A150   75c multi   1.50 1.50
718 A150 $1.20 multi   2.40 2.40
719 A150 $2 multi   4.00 4.00
720 A150 $3.20 multi   6.50 6.50
721 A150 $5 multi   10.00 10.00
     Nos. 714-721 (8)   26.35 26.35

Christmas
A163

1999, Oct. 26   Litho.   Perf. 13½
722 A163 33c multi   .65   .65

Events of the 20th Century Type
1970-79: a, Jumbo jets enter transatlantic
service. b, China advances on world stage. c,
Terrorists range the world. d, Space stations
orbit earth. e, Oil crisis strangles world. f,
China unearths underground army. g, Reign of
death devastates Cambodia. h, Superpowers

proclaim era of détente. i, America celebrates
bicentennial. j, Personal computers reach markets. k, Diagnostic tools revolutionize
medicine. l, Automobiles transport millions. m,
Prospect of peace in Middle East. n, Compact
disc revolutionizes recording. o, Islam's
prophets resurgent.

1999, Nov. 15
723   Sheet of 15   18.00 18.00
  a.-o. A123 60c Any single   1.20   1.20

Millennium — A164

Earth and inscriptions: No. 724, "December
31, 1999." No. 725, "January 1, 2000."

1999, Dec. 31   Litho.   Perf. 13½
724 33c multi   .65   .65
725 33c multi   .65   .65
  a. A164 Pair, #724-725   1.30 1.30

Events of the 20th Century Type
1980-89: a, People unite in freedom's quest.
b, Mankind confronts new diseases. c, Royal
romance captivates the world. d, Information
age begins. e, Armed conflicts upset peace. f,
Cell phone revolutionizes communication. g,
Every man a movie maker. h, Space exploration makes headlines. i, Disaster alerts public
to nuclear risks. j, Perestroika signals change.
k, Technology of war advances. l, Terrorism
claims innocent victims. m, World's oceans
endangered. n, Eys of the world on
Tiananmen. o, Events signal "end of history."

2000, Jan. 15
726   Sheet of 15   18.00 18.00
  a.-o. A123 60c Any single   1.20   1.20

Souvenir Sheet

New Year 2000 (Year of the
Dragon) — A165

2000, Jan. 20   Perf. 13x13½
727 A165 60c multi   1.25 1.25

Legendary Aircraft Type of 1995
Designs: a, P-26 Peashooter. b, N2S-1
Kaydet. c, P-35A. d, P-36A Hawk. e, P-40B
Warhawk. f, P-38 Lightning. g, P-39D
Airacobra. h, C-46 Commando. i, P-47D Thun-
derbolt. j, P-61B Black Widow. k, B-29 Super-
fortress. l, F7F-3N Tigercat. m, F8F-2 Bearcat.
n, F-82, Twin Mustang. o, F-84G Thunderjet.
p, FJ-1 Fury. q, C-119C Flying Boxcar. r, F3D-
2 Skynight. s, F-89D Scorpion. t, F-94B
Starfire. u, F4D Skyray. v, F3H-2 Demon. w,
RF-101A/C Voodoo. x, U-2F Dragon Lady. y,
OV-10 Bronco.

2000, Feb. 10   Perf. 13½
728 A104 33c Sheet of 25,
                #a.-y.   16.00 16.00

Roses — A166

Rose varieties: a, Masquerade. b, Tuscany
Superb. c, Frau Dagmar Hastrup. d, Ivory
Fashion. e, Charles De Mills. f, Peace.

2000, Feb. 23
729   Block of 6   4.00 4.00
  a.-f. A166 33c Any single   .65   .65

Events of the 20th Century Type
1990-99: a, Free markets and trade reshape
world economy. b, Coalition expels Iraq from
Kuwait. c, South Africans freed from
apartheid. d, WWW revolutionizes information
superhighway. e, Era of Soviet power ends. f,
A lasting peace in Middle East is promised. g,
Engineering triumphs alter landscape. h, Ethnic conflicts stun world. i, Athletes celebrate
peaceful world competition. j, Scientists probe
secrets of life. k, Hong Kong and Macao return
to China. l, Space exploration captivates millions. m, World mourns global heroines. n,
Architecture shows confidence in the future. o,
World population soars to new record.

2000, Mar. 15   Litho.   Perf. 13½
730   Sheet of 15   18.00 18.00
  a.-o. A123 60c Any single   1.20   1.20

Pandas — A167

a, Adult seated. b, Adult, seated, facing
away, & cub. c, Adult holding cub. d, Two
adults. e, Adult climbing. f, Adult & cub seated.

2000, Mar. 31   Perf. 11¾
731 A167 33c Block of 6, #a-f   4.00 4.00

American Presidents — A168

No. 732: a, 1c, George Washington. b, 2c,
John Adams. c, 3c, Thomas Jefferson. d, 4c,
James Madison. e, 5c, James Monroe. f, 6c,
John Quincy Adams.
No. 733: a, 7c, Andrew Jackson. b, 8c, Mar-
tin Van Buren. c, 9c, William Henry Harrison.
d, 10c, John Tyler. e, 11c, James K. Polk. f,
12c, Zachary Taylor.
No. 734: a, 13c, Millard Fillmore. b, 14c,
Franklin Pierce. c, 15c, James Buchanan. d,
16c, Abraham Lincoln. e, 17c, Andrew Johns-
on. f, 18c, Ulysses S. Grant.
No. 735: a, 19c, Rutherford B. Hayes. b,
20c, James A. Garfield. c, 21c, Chester A.
Arthur. d, 22c, Grover Cleveland. e, 23c, Ben-
jamin Harrison. f, 24c, White House.
No. 736: a, 25c, William McKinley. b, 26c,
Theodore Roosevelt. c, 27c, William H. Taft. d,
28c, Woodrow Wilson. e, 29c, Warren G. Har-
ding. f, 30c, Calvin Coolidge.
No. 737: a, 31c, Herbert C. Hoover. b, 32c,
Franklin D. Roosevelt. c, 33c, Harry S Truman.
d, 34c, Dwight D. Eisenhower. e, 35c, John F.
Kennedy. f, 36c, Lyndon B. Johnson.
No. 738: a, 37c, Richard M. Nixon. b, 38c,
Gerald R. Ford. c, 39c, James E. Carter. d,
40c, Ronald W. Reagan. e, 41c, George H. W.
Bush. f, 42c, William J. Clinton.
Illustration reduced.

2000, Apr. 18 — Perf. 13½

732	A168	Sheet of 6, #a-f	.45	.45
733	A168	Sheet of 6, #a-f	1.25	1.25
734	A168	Sheet of 6, #a-f	1.90	1.90
735	A168	Sheet of 6, #a-f	2.60	2.60
736	A168	Sheet of 6, #a-f	3.25	3.25
737	A168	Sheet of 6, #a-f	4.00	4.00
738	A168	Sheet of 6, #a-f	4.75	4.75
		Nos. 732-738 (7)	18.20	18.20

First Zeppelin Flight, Cent. — A169

Designs: a, Original Zeppelin, 1900. b, Graf Zeppelin I, 1928. c, Hindenburg, 1936. d, Graf Zeppelin II, 1937.

2000, May 11 — Perf. 13½

739 A169 33c Block of 4, #a-d — 2.75 2.75

Sir Winston Churchill — A170

No. 740, War correspondent in South Africa, 1899-1900. No. 741, Engagement and marriage to Clementine Hozier, 1908. No. 742, Young statesman, 1900-14. No. 743, Writer and academic, 1898-1960. No. 744, First Lord of the Admiralty, 1939-40. No. 745, Prime Minister, 1940-45. $1, Appointed knight, Nobel Prize for Literature, 1946-65.

2000, June 16 Litho. Perf. 13½
Booklet Stamps

740	A170	60c multi	1.25	1.25
741	A170	60c multi	1.25	1.25
742	A170	60c multi	1.25	1.25
743	A170	60c multi	1.25	1.25
744	A170	60c multi	1.25	1.25
745	A170	60c multi	1.25	1.25

Size: 87x67mm
Perf. 13½ at Top

746	A170	$1 multi	2.00	2.00
a.		Booklet pane, #740-746	9.50	
		Booklet, #746a	9.50	

US Military, 225th Anniv. A171

No. 747: a, Army. b, Navy, c, Marines.

2000, June 22 — Perf. 13½
747 Horiz. strip of 3 — 2.00 2.00
a.-c. A171 33c Any single — .65 .65

National Government — A172

No. 748: a, National seal. b, Nitijela, horiz. c, National flag. d, Capitol buildijng, horiz.

2000, July 4 Litho. Perf. 13½
748 A172 33c Block of 4, #a-d — 2.75 2.75

Ships — A173

No. 749: a, Half Moon. b, La Grande Hermine. c, Golden Hind. d, Mathew. e, Victoria. f, Sao Gabriel.

2000, July 20
749 A173 60c Block of 6, #a-f — 7.25 7.25

Queen Mother, 100th Birthday — A174

No. 750: a, As child. b, As young wife. c, As Queen. d, As Queen Mother.

2000, Aug. 4
750 A174 60c Block of 4, #a-d — 5.00 5.00
Compare with No. 810.

Reef Life A175

No. 751: a, Green sea turtle. b, Blue-girdled angelfish. c, Clown triggerfish. d, Harlequin tuskfish. e, Lined butterflyfish. f, White-bonnet anemonefish. g, Longnose filefish. h, Emperor angelfish.

2000, Aug. 24
751 Sheet of 8 — 5.50 5.50
a.-h. A175 33c Any single — .65 .65

Butterflies — A176

No. 752: a, Holly blue. b, Swallowtail. c, Clouded yellow. d, Small tortoiseshell. e, Nettle tree. f, Long-tailed blue. g, Cranberry blue.

h, Small heath. i, Pontic blue. j, Lapland fritillary k, Large blue. l, Monarch.

2000, Sept. 14 — Perf. 11¾
752 A176 60c Sheet of 12, #a-l — 14.50 14.50
See also Nos. 776, 798, 821, 876.

Reunification of Germany, 10th Anniv. — A177

2000, Oct. 3 — Perf. 13½
753 A177 33c multi — .65 .65

Submarines — A178

No. 754: a, USS S-44, 1925. b, USS Gato, 1941. c, USS Wyoming, 1996. d, USS Cheyenne, 1997.

2000, Oct. 12
754 A178 33c Block of 4, #a.-d. — 2.75 2.75

Christmas — A179

2000, Oct. 26 — Perf. 10¼x11¼
755 A179 33c multi — .65 .65

Sun Yat-sen — A180

No. 756: a, As youth in Cuiheng village, 1866. b, As student in Honolulu and Hong Kong, 1879. c, As President of Tong Meng Hui, 1905. d, Revolution, 1911. e, President of the Republic of China, 1912. f, Principles of Democracy. g, Sun Yat-sen Memorial, Nanjing and Great Wall of China (87x62mm).

2000, Nov. 12 Litho. Perf. 13½
756 Booklet pane of 7 — 9.50
a.-f. A180 60c Any single — 1.25 1.25
g. A180 $1 multi, perf. 13½ at top — 2.00 2.00
Booklet, #756 — 9.50

Souvenir Sheet

New Year 2001 (Year of the Snake) — A181

2001, Jan. 2 Litho. Perf. 13x13¾
757 A181 80c multi — 1.60 1.60

Flowers of the Month — A182

2001		Stamp + label	Perf. 11¾	
758	A182	34c Carnations	.70	.70
759	A182	34c Violets	.70	.70
760	A182	34c Jonquil	.70	.70
761	A182	34c Sweet pea	.70	.70
762	A182	34c Lily of the valley	.70	.70
763	A182	34c Rose	.70	.70
764	A182	34c Larkspur	.70	.70
765	A182	34c Poppy	.70	.70
766	A182	34c Aster	.70	.70
767	A182	34c Marigold	.70	.70
768	A182	34c Chrysanthemum	.70	.70
769	A182	34c Poinsettia	.70	.70
		Nos. 758-769 (12)	8.40	8.40

Issued: No. 758, 1/5; No. 759, 2/1; No. 760, 3/1; No. 761, 4/3; No. 762, 5/1; No. 763, 6/1; No. 764, 7/3; No. 765, 8/1; No. 766, 9/5; No. 767, 10/1; No. 768, 11/1; No. 769, 12/1.

Sailing Canoes A183

Walaps of: $5, Jaluit. $10, Eniwetok.

2001, Jan. 19 Engr. Perf. 12¼
770 A183 $5 green — 10.00 10.00
771 A183 $10 blue — 20.00 20.00

Famous People — A184

Designs: 34c, Pres. Amata Kabua. 55c, Robert Reimers, entrepreneur. 80c, Leonard Hacker, S. J., humanitarian. $1, Dwight Heine, educator.

2001, Jan. 22 Litho. Perf. 10¼x11¼
772 A184 34c multi — .70 .70
773 A184 55c multi — 1.10 1.10
774 A184 80c multi — 1.60 1.60
775 A184 $1 multi — 2.00 2.00
Nos. 772-775 (4) — 5.40 5.40
See Nos. 784, 817-819.

Butterflies Type of 2000

No. 776: a, Red admiral. b, Moroccan orange tip. c, Silver-studded blue. d, Marbled white. e, False Apollo. f, Ringlet. g, Map. h, Fenton's wood white. i, Grecian copper. j, Pale Arctic clouded yellow. k, Great banded greyling. l, Cardinal.

2001, Feb. 22 — Perf. 11¾
776 A176 80c Sheet of 12, #a-l — 20.00 20.00

Fairy Tales A185

No. 777: a, Tom Thumb. b, Three Little Pigs. c, Gulliver's Travels. d, Cinderella. e, Gallant John. f, Ugly Duckling. g, Fisher and the Goldfish.

2001, Mar. 22 Litho. Perf. 13½
777 Vert. strip of 7 — 5.00 5.00
a.-g. A185 34c Any single — .70 .70

Watercraft Racing — A186

No. 778: a, Canoeing. b, Windsurfing. c, Cruising yachts. d, Sailing dinghy.

2001, Apr. 6
778 A186 34c Block of 4, #a-d   2.75 2.75

Manned Spaceflight, 40th Anniv. A187

No. 779: a, Yuri A. Gagarin. b, Alan B. Shepard, Jr. c, Virgil I. Grissom. d, Gherman S. Titov.

2001, Apr. 12
779   Block of 4 + 4 labels   6.50 6.50
a.-d. A187 80c Any single   1.60 1.60

Stamp Day — A188

2001, May 2
780 A188 34c multi   .70 .70
a.   Tete-beche pair   1.40 1.40

American Achievements in Space — A189

No. 781: a, First U.S. astronaut in space, 1962. b, First US space walk, 1965. c, First man on the Moon, 1969. d, First space shuttle, 1977.

2001, May 15
781   A189 80c Block of 4, #a-d   6.50 6.50

Marine Life — A190

No. 782: a, Longnose butterflyfish, star puffer, starfish. b, Nautilus. c, Raccoon butterflyfish. d, Porkfish, grouper.

2001, June 7
782 A190 34c Block of 4, #a-d   2.75 2.75

Sports — A191

No. 783: a, Basketball. b, Bowling. c, Table tennis. d, Kayaking.

2001, June 26   **Perf. 11¾**
783 A191 34c Block of 4, #a-d   2.75 2.75

Famous People Type of 2001
Design: 57c, Atlan Anien, legislator.

2001, July 9   **Perf. 10¼x11¼**
784 A184 57c multi   1.10 1.10

Zodiac Signs — A192

No. 785: a, Aries. b, Taurus. c, Gemini. d, Cancer. e, Leo. f, Virgo. g, Libra. h, Scorpio. i, Sagittarius. j, Capricorn. k, Aquarius. l, Pisces.

2001, July 17   **Perf. 11¾**
785 A192 34c Sheet of 12, #a-l   8.25 8.25

Phila Nippon '01 — A193

No. 786: a, Black Cat, by Tan Axi. b, Brown Cat, by Tan Axi. c, Cliffs, by Wang Xinhai. d, Boat and Bridge, by Li Yan. e, Rooster, by Wang Xinlan. f, Great Wall, by Liu Zhong. g, Crane, by Wang Lynn. h, Baboon With Basket, by Wang Yani. i, Baboon in Tree, by Wang Yani. j, Umbrella, by Sun Yuan. k, Baboon With Fruit, by Wang Yani. l, Baboon on Ox, by Wang Yani.

2001, Aug. 1   **Litho.**   **Perf. 11¾**
786 A193 80c Sheet of 12,
     #a-l   20.00 20.00

US Naval Heroes in WWII Pacific Theater — A194

No. 787: a, Adm. Raymond A. Spruance. b, Adm. Arleigh A. Burke. c, Adm. Ernest A. King. d, Adm. Richmond K. Turner. e, Adm. Marc A. Mitscher. f, Adm. Chester W. Nimitz. g, Lt. Edward H. O'Hare. h, Adm. William F. Halsey, Jr. i, The Sullivan Brothers.

2001, Aug. 24   **Perf. 13½**
787 A194 80c Sheet of 9, #a-i   14.50 14.50

Classic Cars — A195

No. 788: a, 1916 Stutz Bearcat. b, 1909 Stanley Steamer. c, 1934 Citroen 7CV. d, 1910 Rolls-Royce Silver Ghost. e, 1927 Daimler. f, 1935 Hispano-Suiza Type 68V-12. g, 1928 Lancia Lambda V4. h, 1927 Volvo OV4.

2001, Sept. 11
788 A195 34c Block of 8, #a-h   5.50 5.50
   See also Nos. 796, 809, 823, 828, 865.

Remembrance of Victims of Sept. 11, 2001 Terrorist Attacks — A196

No. 789: a, U.S. flag, "Blessed are those..." b, Statue of Liberty, "United we stand. . ." c, U.S. flag, "An attack on freedom. . ." d, U.S. flag, "In the great struggle. . ." e, Statue of Freedom, "We go forward. . ." f, U.S. flag, "In the face of terrorism. . ." g, American people (75x32mm)

2001, Oct. 11   **Litho.**   **Perf. 13½**
789   Booklet pane of 7   6.25 —
a.-f.   A196 34c Any single   .70 .70
g.   A196 $1 multi   2.00 2.00
    Booklet, #789   6.25

Christmas A197

No. 790: a, Angel on high. b, Adoration of the Magi. c, Nativity scene. d, Adoration of the shepherds.

2001, Oct. 26
790   Strip of 4   2.80 2.80
a.-d.   A197 34c Any single   .70 .70

Airplanes — A198

No. 791: a, Supermarine Sea Eagle. b, Gloster Sea Gladiator. c, DHC-6 Twin Otter. d, Shorts 330. e, Sandringham Flying Boat. f, De Havilland DHC-7. g, Beech Duke B60. h, Fokker Friendship F27. i, Consolidated B-24J Liberator. j, Vickers 953C Merchantman.

      Perf. 11¼x10¼
2001, Nov. 13   **Litho.**
791 A198 80c Block of 10, #a-j   16.00 16.00

Souvenir Sheet

New Year 2002 (Year of the Horse) — A199

2002, Jan. 2   **Perf. 13x13½**
792 A199 80c multi   1.60 1.60

Shells — A200

No. 793: a, Frilled dogwinkle. b, Reticulated cowrie-helmet. c, New England neptune. d, Calico scallop. e, Lightning whelk. f, Hawkwing conch.

2002, Jan. 22   **Perf. 11¾**
793 A200 34c Block of 6, #a-f   4.25 4.25

Souvenir Sheet

Reign of Queen Elizabeth II, 50th Anniv. — A201

2002, Feb. 6   Litho.   Perf. 13x13½
794 A201 80c multi   1.60 1.60

United We Stand — A202

2002, Feb. 11   Perf. 13½
795 A202 34c multi   .70   .70

Classic Cars Type of 2001
No. 796: a, 1909 Le Zebre. b, 1886 Hammel. c, 1902 Wolseley. d, 1899 Eysink. e, 1903 Dansk. f, 1907 Spyker. g, 1913 Fiat Model Zero. h, 1902 Weber.

2002, Feb. 26
796 A195 34c Block of 8, #a-h   5.50 5.50

Corals — A203

No. 797: a, Mixed. b, Chalice. c, Elkhorn. d, Finger.

2002, Mar. 13
797 A203 34c Block of 4, #a-d   2.75 2.75

Butterflies Type of 2000
No. 798: a, Grayling. b, Eastern festoon. c, Speckled wood. d, Cranberry fritillary. e, Bath white. f, Meadow brown. g, Two-tailed pasha. h, Scarce swallowtail. i, Dusky grizzled skipper. j, Provençal short-tailed blue. k, Dryal. l, Comma.

2002, Mar. 25   Perf. 11¾
798 A176 80c Sheet of 12,
          #a-l   20.00 20.00

Horses in Art — A204

No. 799: a, Horses, by Giorgio de Chirico. b, Tartar Envoys Give Horse to Qianlong, by Father Giuseppe Castiglione. c, Gathering Seaweed, by Anton Mauve. d, Mares and Foals, by George Stubbs. e, A Mare and Her Foal in a Spring Meadow, by Wilson Hepple. f, Horse with Child and a Dog, by Natale Attanasio. g, The Horse, by Waterhouse Hawkins. h, Attendants and a Horse, by Edgar Degas. i, Mares and Foals in a Landscape, by Stubbs. j, The Horse, by Guglielmo Ciardi. k, Little Blue Horse, by Franz Marc. l, Sketch for the Set of "Fire Bird," by Pavel Kuznetsov.
80c, Emperor Qianlong Leaving for his Summer Residence, by Castiglione.

2002, Apr. 15   Litho.   Perf. 13½
799 A204 34c Sheet of 12, #a-l 8.25 8.25

Souvenir Sheet
Perf. 13x13½
800 A204 80c multi   1.60 1.60

No. 800 contains one 80x50mm stamp.

Miniature Sheet

Russian Fairy Tale, "The Frog Princess" — A205

No. 801: a, Ivan and his brothers shoot arrows. b, First brother finds a wife. c, Second brother finds a wife. d, Ivan and his Frog Princess. e, Ivan presents shirt to the king. f, Ivan presents bread to the king. g, Princess arrives at the ball. h, Princess dances for the king. i, Princess says goodbye to Ivan. j, Ivan and the little hut. k, Ivan and the Princess reunited. l, Ivan and the Princess on a magic carpet.

2002, Apr. 26   Litho.   Perf. 12½x12¼
801 A205 37c Sheet of 12, #a-l 9.00 9.00

Carousel Figures — A206

No. 802: a, Armored horse and rabbit. b, Zebra and camel. c, Horse, reindeer and angel. d, Horse, frog and tiger.

2002, May 13   Litho.   Perf. 13½
802 A206 80c Block of 4, #a-d   6.50 6.50

Birds — A207

No. 803: a, Lesser golden plover. b, Siberian tattler. c, Brown noddy. d, Common fairy tern. e, Micronesian pigeon. f, Long-tailed cuckoo. g, Christmas shearwater. h, Eurasian tree sparrow. i, Black-tailed godwit. j, Franklin's gull. k, Rufous-necked stint. l, Kermadec petrel. m, Purple-capped fruit dove. n, Mongolian plover. o, Cattle egret. p, Dunlin.

2002, May 29
803 A207 37c Sheet of 16,
          #a-p   12.00 12.00

Benjamin Franklin (1706-90) — A208

No. 804: a, Inventor. b, Scholar.

2002, June 10   Litho.   Perf. 13½
804 A208 80c Horiz. pair, #a-b 3.25 3.25

Sea Turtles — A209

No. 805: a, Loggerhead. b, Leatherback. c, Hawksbill. d, Green.

2002, June 25
805 A209 37c Block of 4, #a-d   3.00 3.00

Intl. Federation of Stamp Dealers' Associations, 50th Anniv. — A210

No. 806: a, Stamp collector. b, First day of issue. c, Father and daughter collectors. d, Young collector. e, Sharing Dad's stamp collection. f, The new generation.

2002, July 2
806 A210 80c Block of 6, #a-f   9.75 9.75

US Navy Ships — A211

No. 807: a, USS Hartford. b, Bon Homme Richard. c, Prince de Neufchatel. d, USS Ohio. e, USS Onkahye. f, USS Oneida.

2002, July 18
807 A211 37c Block of 6, #a-f   4.50 4.50

See No. 827.

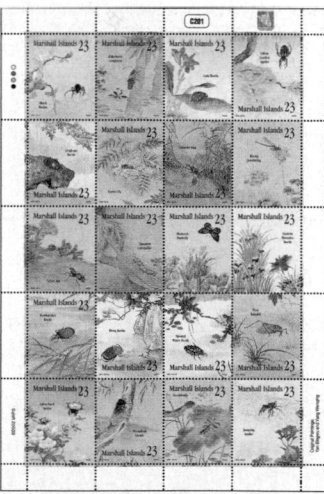

Insects and Spiders — A212

No. 808: a, Black widow spider. b, Elderberry longhorn. c, Ladybug. d, Yellow garden spider. e, Dogbane beetle. f, Flower fly. g, Assassin bug. h, Ebony jewelwing. i, Velvet ant. j, Monarch caterpillar. k, Monarch butterfly. l, Eastern Hercules beetle. m, Bombardier beetle. n, Dung beetle. o, Spotted water beetle. p, True katydid. q, Spiny-back spider. r, Periodical cicada. s, Scorpionfly. t, Jumping spider.

2002, Aug. 2   Litho.   Perf. 13½
808 A212 23c Sheet of 20, #a-t 9.25 9.25

Classic Cars Type of 2001
No. 809: a, 1934 Hotchkiss. b, 1909 De Dion Bouton. c, 1922 Renault. d, 1927 Amilcar Surbaisse. e, 1943 Austin. f, 1913 Peugeot Bebe. g, 1927 O.M. Type 665 Superba. h, 1922 Elizalde Tipo 20C.

2002, Aug. 15
809 A195 80c Block of 8, #a-h   13.00 13.00

Queen Mother Type of 2000 Redrawn

No. 810: a, As child. b, As young wife. c, As Queen. d, As Queen Mother.

2002, Aug. 30
810   A174 80c Block of 4, #a-d   6.50 6.50
Queen Mother Elizabeth (1900-2002).

Souvenir Sheet

Regal Princess — A213

2002, Sept. 10   **Perf. 13¼x13¾**
811   A213 80c multi   1.60 1.60

World War I Heroes — A214

No. 812: a, Adm. William S. Sims. b, Gen. William E. Mitchell. c, Cpl. Freddie Stowers. d, Maj. Gen. Smedley D. Butler. e, Capt. Edward V. Rickenbacker. f, Sgt. Alvin C. York. g, Maj. Gen. John A. Lejeune. h, Gen. John J. Pershing.

2002, Sept. 23   **Perf. 13½**
812   A214 80c Block of 8, #a-h   13.00 13.00

Christmas — A215

Snowman cookies with denomination in: a, Green. b, Red.

2002, Oct. 26   Litho.   Perf. 13½
813   A215 37c Horiz. pair, #a-b   1.50 1.50

Souvenir Sheet

New Year 2003 (Year of the Ram) — A216

2003, Jan. 2   Litho.   Perf. 13x13¾
814   A216 80c multi   1.60 1.60

UN Membership, 12th Anniv. — A217

2003, Jan. 29   **Perf. 11¼x10¼**
815   A217 60c multi   1.25 1.25

Folktales — A218

No. 816: a, Inedel's Magic Kite. b, Lijebake Rescues Her Granddaughter. c, Jebro's Mother Invents the Sail. d, Limajnon Escapes to the Moon.

2003, Jan. 29   **Perf. 13½**
816   A218 50c Block of 4, #a-d, +
                        4 labels   4.00 4.00

Famous People Type of 2001

Designs: 37c, Oscar deBrum (1929-2002), first Chief Secretary. $3.85, Senator Tipne Philippo (1933-2000). $13.65, Senator Henchi Balos (1946-2000).

Perf. 10¼x11¼
2003, Mar. 25   Litho.
817   A184 37c multi   .75   .75
818   A184 $3.85 multi   7.75   7.75
819   A184 $13.65 multi   25.00 25.00
        Nos. 817-819 (3)   33.50 33.50

The denomination of No. 819 was printed in a thermographic ink that changes color when warmed.

Marshallese Culture — A219

No. 820: a, Lagajimi, c. 1870s, by Franz Hernsheim (21x38mm). b, Old-style house with attic-like roof space (46x38mm). c, Tidal lake on Jabwor (46x38mm). d, Kabua, c. 1870s, by Hernsheim (21x38mm). e, Children in mat dresses (21x38mm). f, Jaluit pass, c. 1870s, by Hernsheim (46x38mm). g, Traditional Canoe c. 1870s, by Hernsheim (46x38mm). h, Man in fishing attire (21x38mm).

2003, Mar. 25   **Perf. 13½**
820   A219 37c Block of 8, #a-h   6.00 6.00
        See No. 824.

Butterflies Type of 2000

No. 821: a, False grayling. b, Green hairstreak. c, Purple-shot copper. d, Black-veined white. e, Arctic grayling. f, Greek clouded yellow. g, American painted lady. h, Wall brown. i, Polar fritillary. j, Mountain clouded yellow. k, Camberwell beauty. l, Large white.

2003, May 2   Litho.   Perf. 11¾
821   A176 80c Sheet of 12,
                        #a-l   20.00 20.00

Powered Flight, Cent. — A220

No. 822: a, 1903 Wright Flyer. b, Curtiss JN-3 "Jenny." c, Douglas World Cruiser. d, "Spirit

---

of St. Louis." e, Lockheed Vega. f, Boeing 314 Clipper. g, Douglas C-47 Skytrain. h, Boeing B-50 Superfortress. i, Antonov An-225 Mriya. j, B-2 Spirit.

2003, June 10   **Perf. 13½**
822   A220 37c Block of 10, #a-j   7.50 7.50

Classic Cars Type of 2001

No. 823: a, 1927 Alfa Romeo RLSS. b, 1912 Austro-Daimler Prince Henry. c, 1923 Mors 14/20 HP Tourer. d, 1926 AC Tourer. e, 1903 Scania, 1897 Vabis. f, 1914 Graf und Stift. g, 1919 Pic-Pic. h, 1911 Hispano-Suiza-Alfonso XIII.

2003, July 10   Litho.   Perf. 13½
823   A195 37c Block of 8, #a-h   6.00 6.00

Marshallese Culture Type of 2003

No. 824: a, Kabua's Daughter on Pandanus, c. 1906, by Augustin Krämer (21x38mm). b, Traditional walap (46x38mm). c, Jabwor, Jaluit Atoll (46x38mm). d, Traditional and Modern Dress, by Augustin Erdland (21x38mm). e, Nemedj, c. 1905, by Krämer (21x38mm). f, Typhoon of 1905, by Josef Schmidlin (46x38mm). g, Marshallese Kor Kor, c. 1905, by Richard Deeken (46x38mm). h, Marshallese Grandfather, by Erdland (21x38mm).

2003, Aug. 7   **Perf. 13½x13¼**
824   A219 37c Block of 8, #a-h   6.00 6.00

Christmas Ornaments — A221

No. 825: a, Snowman. b, Jack-in-the-box. c, Toy soldier. d, Reindeer.

2003, Oct. 24   **Perf. 13½**
825   A221 37c Block of 4, #a-d   3.00 3.00

Souvenir Sheet

New Year 2004 (Year of the Monkey) — A222

2004, Jan. 4   Litho.   Perf. 13x13¾
826   A222 $1 multi   2.00 2.00

Ship Type of 2002

No. 827: a, Bonhomme Richard. b, HMS Resolution, denomination at UR. c, HMS Resolution, denomination at UL.

2004, Feb. 14   **Perf. 13½**
827   A211 37c Horiz. strip of 3,
                        #a-c   2.25 2.25

Classic Cars Type of 2001

No. 828: a, 1906 Wolseley-Siddeley. b, 1901 Mors. c, 1908 Hutton. d, 1907 Metallurgique. e, 1902 Benz. f, 1900 Cudell. g, 1906 Peugeot. h, Mercedes 60.

2004, Mar. 15   **Perf. 13½**
828   A195 37c Block of 8, #a-h   6.00 6.00

Greetings — A223

No. 829: a, Thank you! b, Congratulations. c, Happy birthday. d, Best wishes. e, Get well soon. f, Love you, Dad. g, Love you, Mom. h, Best wishes, Get well soon, Love you, Mom, Congratulations, Love you, Dad, Happy birthday, Thank you.

2004, Apr. 15   Litho.   Perf. 13½
829   A223 37c Sheet of 8, #a-h   6.00 6.00

Marshall Islands Postal Service, 20th Anniv. — A224

Messenger and canoe with background colors of: 37c, Prussian blue. 60c, Brown. $2.30, Purple.

2004, May 2
830-832 A224 Set of 3   6.75 6.75

No. 832 printed in sheets of 8 stamps + 8 adjacent certified mail etiquettes. Value is for set with No. 832 with attached etiquette.

Lewis and Clark Expedition, Bicent. — A225

No. 833 — Inscriptions: a, The saga begins. b, Westward bound. c, Endless bison.

2004, May 14
833   A225   Horiz. strip of 3   2.25 2.25
a.-c.   A225   37c Any single   .75   .75

See Nos. 840, 845, 855, 867, 871, 885.

D-Day, 60th Anniv. — A226

No. 834: a, Horsa gliders and parachute troops. b, British Typhoon 1B and US P-51B Mustangs. c, German defenses and Pointe du Hoc. d, Allied amphibious landing.

2004, June 6   Litho.   Perf. 13½
834   A226 37c Block of 4, #a-d   3.00 3.00

Marine Life — A227

No. 835: a, Chambered nautilus, map cowrie, fish, coral, trumpet triton (2-1). b, Marlin spike, fish, coral, turban shell, Toulerei's cowrie (2-2).

2004, July 1
835 A227 37c Horiz. pair, #a-b 1.50 1.50

Pres. Ronald Reagan (1911-2004) A228

2004, July 4
836 A228 60c multi 1.25 1.25

First Manned Moon Landing, 35th Anniv. — A229

No. 837: a, Astronaut floating in space (4-1). b, Astronaut in space (4-2). c, Astronaut floating in orbit (4-3). d, Astronaut and Jupiter (4-4).

2004, July 20
837 A229 37c Block of 4, #a-d 3.00 3.00

Festival of Arts — A230

No. 838: a, Woman showing fan making. b, Woman making baskets. c, Men carving. d,

Children making canoe models. e, White ginger. f, Vanda. g, Tiare. h, Hibiscus. i, Breadfruit. j, Tattooed warrior. k, Young chiefs. l, Drummers and dancers.

2004, July 22
838 A230 37c Sheet of 12, #a-l 9.00 9.00

Aircraft — A231

No. 839: a, 1903 Wright Flyer. b, Blériot XI. c, Curtiss Golden Flyer. d, Curtiss Flying Boat. e, Deperdussin Racer. f, Sikorsky Il'ya Muromets. g, Fokker E1. h, Junkers J1. i, S.E. 5A. j, Handley Page O/400. k, Fokker D VII. l, Junkers F13. m, Lockheed Vega. n, M-130 Pan Am Clipper. o, Messerschmitt BF 109. p, Spitfire. q, Junkers Ju-88. r, A6M Zero. s, Ilyushin Il-2. t, Heinkel He-178. u, C-47 Skytrain. v, Piper Cub. w, Avro Lancaster. x, B-17F Flying Fortress. y, Messerschmitt Me-262. z, B-29 Superfortress. aa, P-51 Mustang. ab, Yak-9. ac, Bell Model 47 helicopter. ad, Bell X-1. ae, Beechcraft Bonanza. af, AN-225 Mriya. ag, B-47 Stratojet. ah, MiG-15. ai, Saab J35 Draken. aj, B-52 Stratofortress. ak, Boeing 367-80. al, U-2. am, C-130 Hercules. an, F-4 Phantom II. ao, North American X-15. ap, Sikorsky S-61 (HH-3E). aq, Learjet 23. ar, SR-71 Blackbird. as, Boeing 747. at, Concorde. au, Airbus A300. av, MiG-29. aw, F-117A Nighthawk. ax, F/A-22 Raptor.

Perf. 10¼x11¼
2004, Aug. 12 *Litho.*
839 Sheet of 50 23.00 23.00
a.-ax. A231 23c Any single .45 .45

Lewis and Clark Type of 2004
No. 840 — Inscriptions: a, First Fourth of July. b, Death of Sgt. Charles Floyd. c, Setting the prairie on fire.

2004, Aug. 24 *Perf. 13½*
840 Horiz. strip of 3 2.25 2.25
a.-c. A225 37c Any single .75 .75

John Wayne (1907-79), Actor — A232

2004, Sept. 9 *Perf. 10¼x11¼*
841 A232 37c multi .75 .75

Miniature Sheet

23rd UPU Congress, Bucharest, Romania — A233

No. 842: a, Great Britain #1. b, Romania #1. c, Marshall Islands #1. d, Marshall Islands #31.

2004, Sept. 15 *Litho.* *Perf. 13½*
842 A233 $1 Sheet of 4, #a-d 8.00 8.00

Miniature Sheet

Marine Life — A234

No. 843: a, Emperor angelfish. b, Pink anemonefish. c, Humphead wrasse, Moorish idol. d, Black-spotted puffer. e, Snowflake moray eel. f, Lionfish. g, Bumphead parrotfish, threadfin butterflyfish. h, Hawksbill turtle. i, Triton's trumpet. j, Oriental sweetlips.

2004, Oct. 1
843 A234 37c Sheet of 10, #a-j 7.50 7.50

Miniature Sheet

Christmas — A235

No. 844: a, Angel with bells. b, God Almighty. c, Appears the Star of Bethlehem. d, Three Wise Men. e, Procession of the poor people. f, Pastors with sheep. g, Flight to Egypt. h, Holy Family. i, Animals adoring Jesus.

2004, Oct. 27
844 A235 37c Sheet of 9, #a-i 6.75 6.75

Lewis and Clark Type of 2004
No. 845 — Inscriptions: a, The interpreters. b, Sacred bison calling. c, Teton Sioux rob men.

2004, Nov. 22
845 Horiz. strip of 3 2.25 2.25
a.-c. A225 37c Any single .75 .75

Battle of the Bulge, 60th Anniv. — A236

No. 846: a, Infantry. b, Armor. c, Aviation. d, Lt. Col. Creighton Abrams and Brig. Gen. Anthony McAuliffe.

2004, Dec. 1
846 A236 37c Block of 4, #a-d 3.00 3.00

United States Presidents — A237

No. 847: a, 1c, George Washington. b, 2c, John Adams. c, 3c, Thomas Jefferson. d, 4c, James Madison. e, 5c, James Monroe. f, 6c, John Quincy Adams. g, 7c, Andrew Jackson. h, 8c, Martin Van Buren. i, 9c, William Henry Harrison. j, 10c, John Tyler. k, 11c, James K. Polk. l, 12c, Zachary Taylor. m, 13c, Millard Fillmore. n, 14c, Franklin Pierce. o, 15c, James Buchanan. p, 16c, Abraham Lincoln. q, 17c, Andrew Johnson. r, 18c, Ulysses S. Grant. s, 19c, Rutherford B. Hayes. t, 20c, James A. Garfield. u, 21c, Chester A. Arthur. v, 22c, Grover Cleveland. w, 23c, Benjamin Harrison. x, 24c, Grover Cleveland. y, 25c, William McKinley. z, 26c, Theodore Roosevelt. aa, 27c, William Howard Taft. ab, 28c, Woodrow Wilson. ac, 29c, Warren G. Harding. ad, 30c, Calvin Coolidge. ae, 31c, Herbert Hoover. af, 32c, Franklin D. Roosevelt. ag, 33c, Harry S Truman. ah, 34c, Dwight D. Eisenhower. ai, 35c, John F. Kennedy. aj, 36c, Lyndon B. Johnson. ak, 37c, Richard M. Nixon. al, 38c, Gerald R. Ford. am, 39c, Jimmy Carter. an, 40c, Ronald W. Reagan. ao, 41c, George H. W. Bush. ap, 42c, William J. Clinton. aq, 43c, George W. Bush. ar, 60c, White House. as, $1, White House.

2005, Jan. 20 *Litho.* *Perf. 13½*
847 A237 Sheet of 45, #a-as 31.00 31.00
No. 847 sold for $15.49.

Souvenir Sheet

New Year 2005 (Year of the Rooster) — A238

2005, Feb. 9 *Litho.* *Perf. 13x13½*
848 A238 $1 multi 2.00 2.00

Rotary International, Cent. — A239

2005, Feb. 23 *Perf. 13½*
849 A239 37c multi .75 .75

Hibiscus Varieties — A240

Designs: 37c, Burgundy Blush. 60c, Fiesta. 80c, June's Joy. $1, Norman Lee.

Perf. 10¼x11¼
2005, Mar. 15   Litho.
850	A240 37c multi	.75	.75
851	A240 60c multi	1.25	1.25
852	A240 80c multi	1.60	1.60
853	A240 $1 multi	2.00	2.00
	Nos. 850-853 (4)	5.60	5.60

See Nos. 860-863, 878-881.

Hans Christian Andersen (1805-75), Author — A241

No. 854: a, The Princess and the Pea. b, Thumbelina. c, The Little Mermaid. d, The Emperor's New Suit.

2005, Apr. 2   Perf. 13½
854	A241 37c Block of 4, #a-d	3.00	3.00

Lewis and Clark Type of 2004
No. 855 — Inscriptions: a, First grizzly confrontation. b, Lewis reaching the Great Falls. c, Sacajawea and her brother reunite.

2005, Apr. 29
855	Horiz. strip of 3	2.25	2.25
a.-c.	A225 37c Any single	.75	.75

American First Day Cover Society, 50th Anniv. — A242

No. 856: a, George W. Linn first day cover for US No. 610 (Harding Memorial stamp). b, First day cover for Marshall Islands Nos. 31-34. c, First day cover of US No. C76 with Moon Landing cancel. d, First day cover for Marshall Islands No. 856.

2005, May 2
856	A242 37c Block of 4, #a-d	3.00	3.00

V-E Day, 60th Anniv. — A243

No. 857: a, German surrender, Reims, France. b, Times Square, New York. c, Victory parade, Moscow. d, Royal family and Winston Churchill, Buckingham Palace, London.

2005, May 9
857	A243 37c Block of 4, #a-d	3.00	3.00

Pope John Paul II (1920-2005) — A244

No. 858: a, Wearing red cape, with arm raised. b, Wearing green vestments. c, Close-

up. d, Holding crucifix, wearing red vestments. e, Wearing miter.

2005, May 18   Litho.   Perf. 13½
858	Vert. strip of 5	3.75	3.75
a.-e.	A244 37c Any single	.75	.75

United Nations, 60th Anniv. — A245

2005, June 26
859	Horiz. pair	2.40	2.40
a.	A245 37c Six people	.75	.75
b.	A245 80c Seven people	1.60	1.60

Hibiscus Varieties Type of 2005
Designs: 1c, Margaret Okano. 24c, Cameo Queen. 39c, Madonna. $4, Estrella Red.

2005, July 13   Perf. 10¼x11¼
860	A240 1c multi	.25	.25
861	A240 24c multi	.50	.50
862	A240 39c multi	.80	.80
863	A240 $4 multi	8.00	8.00
	Nos. 860-863 (4)	9.55	9.55

Space Shuttles A246

No. 864: a, Columbia. b, Discovery. c, Endeavour. d, Challenger. e, Atlantis.

2005, July 26   Perf. 13½
864	Horiz. strip of 5	3.75	3.75
a.-e.	A246 37c Any single	.75	.75

Classic Cars Type of 2001
No. 865: a, 1925 Excelsior (8-1). b, 1912 Adler K (8-2). c, 1920 Thulin (8-3). d, 1913 Palladium (8-4). e, 1926 Minerva (8-5). f, 1922 Elizalde (8-6). g, 1911 Rolls-Royce Silver Ghost (8-7). h, 1931 Invicta (8-8).

2005, Aug. 4
865	Block of 8	6.00	6.00
a.-h.	A195 37c Any single	.75	.75

No. 865b is incorrectly inscribed "1926 Minerva."

V-J Day, 60th Anniv. — A247

No. 866: a, Fujiyama and Tokyo Bay. b, USS Missouri. c, US contingent. d, Japanese delegation.

2005, Sept. 2
866	A247 37c Block of 4, #a-d	3.00	3.00

Lewis & Clark Type of 2004
No. 867 — Inscriptions: a, Crossing the Bitterroots. b, Peace agreement. c, Ocean in view.

2005, Sept. 22
867	Horiz. strip of 3	2.25	2.25
a.-c.	A225 37c Any single	.75	.75

Battle of Trafalgar, Bicent. — A248

No. 868 — Fighting ships: a, Trireme galley. b, Trireme Romano. c, Viking longship. d, Ming treasure ship. e, Mary Rose. f, Nuestra Senora del Rosario. g, Korean turtle ship. h, Brederode. i, Galera Veneziana. j, Santisima Trinidad. k, Ville de Paris. l, HMS Victory. m, Bonhomme Richard. n, USS Constellation. o, USS Hartford. p, Fijian ndrua. q, HMS Dreadnought. r, HMAS Australia. s, HMS Dorsetshire. t, Admiral Graf Spee. u, Yamato. v, USS Tautog. w, Bismarck. x, USS Hornet. y, USS Missouri.

$2, HMS Victory, diff.
Illustration reduced.

2005, Oct. 21   Litho.   Perf. 13½
868	A248 37c Sheet of 25, #a-y	18.50	18.50

Souvenir Sheet
Imperf
869	A248 $2 multi	4.00	4.00

No. 868 contains twenty-five 40x31mm stamps.

Christmas — A249

No. 870 — Angels with: a, Lute. b, Harp, horn and lute. c, Horn. d, Harp.

2005, Nov. 1   Perf. 13½
870	A249 37c Block of 4, #a-d	3.00	3.00

Lewis & Clark Type of 2004
No. 871 — Inscriptions: a, First vote allowed to all. b, Leaving Fort Clatsop. c, At Pompey's Pillar.

2005, Nov. 24
871	Horiz. strip of 3	2.25	2.25
a.-c.	A225 37c Any single	.75	.75

Marshallese Culture A250

No. 872 — Photographs: a, First Catholic Church on Jabwor, Jaluit Atoll, by Josef Schmidlin. b, Women on Jaluit Atoll, by Richard Deeken. c, Canoes in Jaluit Harbor, by Deeken. d, Nelu and His Wife Ledagoba, by Augustin Kramer. e, An Old Man from Ebon Atoll, by Augustin Erdland.

2005, Dec. 1
872	Horiz. strip of 5	3.75	3.75
a.-e.	A250 37c Any single	.75	.75

See also Nos. 886, 901, 929, 950, 973.

Miniature Sheet

Benjamin Franklin (1706-90), Statesman — A251

No. 873 — Franklin: a, Painting by J. S. Duplessis. b, Painting by David K. Stone. c, Painting by Mason Chamberlain. d, Painting by John Trumbull. e, Sculpture, by James Earle Fraser. f, Painting by David Martin. g, Painting by Benjamin West. h, Painting by J. B. Greuze. i, Painting by C. N. Cochin.

2006, Jan. 17   Perf. 13½
873	A251 48c Sheet of 9, #a-i	8.75	8.75

Souvenir Sheet

New Year 2006 (Year of the Dog) — A252

2006, Jan. 27   Perf. 13¼x13½
874	A252 $1 multi	2.00	2.00

Love — A253

2006, Feb. 14   Litho.   Perf. 13½
875	A253 39c multi	.80	.80

Butterflies Type of 2000
No. 876: a, Peacock. b, Southern comma. c, Pale clouded yellow. d, Common blue. e, Wood white. f, Baltic grayling. g, Purple emperor. h, Silky ringlet. i, Peak white. j, Idas blue. k, Cleopatra. l, Chequered skipper.

2006, Mar. 20   Perf. 11¾
876	A176 84c Sheet of 12, #a-l	21.00	21.00

First Spaceflight by Yuri Gagarin, 45th Anniv. — A254

2006, Apr. 12   Litho.   Perf. 11¾
877	A254 39c multi	.80	.80

Hibiscus Varieties Type of 2005
Designs: 10c, Butterscotch Sundae. 63c, Magic Moments. 84c, Joanne Boulin. $4.05, Capsicum Red.

2006, May 2   Perf. 10¼x11¼
878	A240 10c multi	.25	.25
879	A240 63c multi	1.25	1.25
880	A240 84c multi	1.75	1.75
881	A240 $4.05 multi	8.25	8.25
	Nos. 878-881 (4)	11.50	11.50

Miniature Sheet

Washington 2006 World Philatelic
Exhibition — A255

No. 882 — Designs of the United States
1922-25 definitive issue inscribed "Marshall
Islands Postage": a, ½c, Nathan Hale. b, 1c,
Benjamin Franklin. c, 1½c, Warren G. Harding.
d, 2c, George Washington. e, 3c, Abraham
Lincoln. f, 4c, Martha Washington. g, 5c, Theodore Roosevelt. h, 6c, James A. Garfield. i,
7c, William McKinley. j, 8c, Ulysses S. Grant.
k, 9c, Thomas Jefferson. l, 10c, James
Monroe. m, 11c, Rutherford B. Hayes. n, 12c,
Grover Cleveland. o, 14c, American Indian
chief. p, 15c, Statue of Liberty. q, 20c, Golden
Gate, horiz. r, 25c, Niagara Falls, horiz. s, 30c,
Buffalo, horiz. t, 50c, Arlington Amphitheater,
horiz.

2006, May 27	Litho.	Perf. 13½	
882	A255	Sheet of 20, #a-t	4.75 4.75
u.		Souvenir sheet, #882o, 882s, im-	
		perf.	.90 .90

Sharks — A256

No. 883: a, Gray reef shark. b, Silvertip
shark. c, Blacktip reef shark. d, Whitetip reef
shark.

2006, June 16		Perf. 13½	
883	A256	39c Block of 4, #a-d	3.25 3.25

Miniature Sheet

Operations Crossroads, 60th
Anniv. — A257

No. 884: a, Evacuation of Bikinians. b, Navy
preparations. c, "Able" bomb blast. d, "Baker"
bomb blast. e, Ghost fleet. f, Effects on the
Bikinians.

2006, July 1	Litho.	Perf. 13½	
884	A257	39c Sheet of 6, #a-f, +	
		6 labels	4.75 4.75

Lewis and Clark Type of 2004

No. 885 — Inscriptions: a, Leaving Sacagawea and Charbonneau. b, Return to St.
Louis.

2006, Aug. 24			
885		Horiz. pair	1.60 1.60
a.-b.	A225	39c Either single	.80 .80

Marshallese Culture Type of 2005

No. 886 — Photographs: a, Harbor Front of
Jabwor, Jaluit Atoll, by L. Sander. b, Irooj with
Family, Jabwor, Jaluit Atoll, by Richard
Deeken. c, Traditional Voyaging Canoe at
Jaluit Atoll, by Sander. d, Mission Sisters and
Girls Doing Laundry, Jaluit, by Hildegard von
Bunsen. e, Traditional House on Mile Atoll, by
Hans Seidel.

2006, Sept. 22	Litho.	Perf. 13½	
886		Horiz. strip of 5	4.00 4.00
a.-e.	A250	39c Any single	.80 .80

Ships in the Marshallese Maritime and
Corporate Registry — A258

No. 887: a, Cape Norviega. b, Front Cen-
tury. c, Ashley. d, TI Africa. e, Discoverer
Enterprise. f, Genmar Spyridon. g, Rickmers
New Orleans. h, LNG Aquarius. i, Centurion. j,
Barkald.

2006, Oct. 9			
887	A258	39c Sheet of 10, #a-j	8.00 8.00

Christmas
A259

2006, Nov. 1			
888	A259	39c multi	.80 .80

Greetings — A260

No. 889: a, "Happy Birthday." b, "Congratulations." c, "Thank You." d, "Best Wishes."

2007, Jan. 16		Perf. 11¾	
889	A260	39c Block of 4, #a-d	3.25 3.25

Souvenir Sheet

New Year 2007 (Year of the
Pig) — A261

2007, Feb. 19	Litho.	Perf. 13x13½	
890	A261	$1 multi	2.00 2.00

Trains — A262

No. 891: a, Art Deco train. b, Pennsylvania.
c, Santa Fe Chief. d, Hiawatha. e, 20th Century Limited. f, Daylight.

2007, Mar. 26		Perf. 13½	
891	A262	39c Block of 6, #a-f	4.75 4.75

Dolphins — A263

No. 892: a, Spotter dolphins. b, Bottlenose
dolphins. c, Risso's dolphin. d, Common
dolphin.

2007, Apr. 9			
892	A263	39c Block of 4, #a-d	3.25 3.25

Fish
A264

Designs: 26c, Achilles tang. 41c, Regal
angelfish. 52c, Saddled butterflyfish. 61c,
Tinker's butterflyfish.

Perf. 10¼x11¼			
2007, June 12			Litho.
893	A264	26c multi	.55 .55
894	A264	41c multi	.85 .85
895	A264	52c multi	1.10 1.10
896	A264	61c multi	1.25 1.25
		Nos. 893-896 (4)	3.75 3.75

Miniature Sheet

Space Age, 50th Anniv. — A265

No. 897: a, First man in space. b, First man-
made satellite. c, First men on the Moon. d,
First docking in space. e, First woman in
space. f, First manned lunar vehicle. g, First
space walk. h, First landing on Mars. i, First
probe of Venus. j, First American in orbit.

2007, June 12		Perf. 13½	
897	A265	41c Sheet of 10, #a-j	8.25 8.25

Scouting, Cent. — A266

No. 898 — Inscriptions: a, Helping others. b,
Physically strong. c, Mentally awake. d, Fun
and adventure.

2007, June 25			
898	A266	41c Block of 4, #a-d	3.50 3.50

Purple Heart,
225th
Anniv. — A267

2007, July 30	Litho.	Perf. 13½	
899	A267	41c multi	.85 .85

Miniature Sheet

United States Air Force, 60th Anniv. — A268

No. 900: a, C-54 Skymaster. b, B-36 Peacemaker. c, F-86 Sabre. d, B-47 Stratojet. e, C-124 Globemaster II. f, C-121 Constellation. g, B-52 Stratofortress. h, F-100 Super Sabre. i, F-104 Starfighter. j, C-130 Hercules. k, F-105 Thunderchief. l, KC-135 Stratotanker. m, B-58 Hustler. n, F-4 Phantom II. o, T-38 Talon. p, C-141 Starlifter. q, F-111 Aardvark. r, SR-71 Blackbird. s, C-5 Galaxy. t, A-10 Thunderbolt II. u, F-15 Eagle. v, F-16 Fighting Falcon. w, F-117 Nighthawk. x, B-2 Spirit. y, C-17 Globemaster III.

2007, Aug. 7
900 A268 41c Sheet of 25,
#a-y　　　　　　　21.00　21.00

Marshallese Culture Type of 2005

No. 901 — Photographs by J. Debrum: a, Lonkwon Getting Fish from His Trap. b, Alele Style of Fishing at Bilarek. c, Portrait of Lanju and Family. d, Outrigger with Sail. e, Lien and Litublan Collecting Shells.

2007, Sept. 18　Litho.　Perf. 13½
901　　Horiz. strip of 5　　4.25　4.25
a.-e.　A250 41c Any single　　.85　.85

Miniature Sheet

Marshall Islands Yacht Registry — A269

No. 902 — Registered yachts: a, Domani. b, Excellence III. c, Aquasition. d, Perfect Symmetry 5. e, Happy Days. f, Mystique. g, Halcyon Days. h, Man of Steel. i, Marathon. j, Sinbad.

2007, Oct. 8
902 A269 41c Sheet of 10, #a-j　　8.25　8.25

Christmas — A270

No. 903 — Santa Claus: a, Reading list. b, Standing by fireplace. c, Holding gift. d, Waving from sleigh.

2007, Dec. 12
903 A270 41c Block of 4, #a-d　　3.50　3.50

Miniature Sheet

Flower Bouquets — A271

No. 904 — Various bouquets with country name at bottom: a, Scotland. b, Jersey. c, Gibraltar. d, Dominica. e, Canada. f, Cyprus. g, Turks and Caicos Islands. h, Bahamas. i, Montserrat. j, Cayman Islands. k, Bangladesh. l, Falkland Islands. m, Grenada. n, Nevis. o, Jamaica. p, Australia. q, Fiji. r, New Hebrides. s, Pitcairn Islands. t, Cook Islands. u, Tonga. v, Seychelles. w, Zimbabwe. x, Christmas Island. y, Antigua.

2008, Jan. 15　Litho.　Perf. 13½
904 A271 41c Sheet of 25, #a-y　　20.50　20.50
See No. 934.

Miniature Sheet

Chinese New Year Animals and Characters — A272

No. 905: a, Pig. b, Ram. c, Horse. d, Tiger. e, Dog. f, Rabbit. g, Dragon. h, Ox. i, Rooster. j, Monkey. k, Snake. l, Rat.

2008, Feb. 7
905 A272 26c Sheet of 12, #a-l　　6.25　6.25

United States Lighthouses — A273

No. 906: a, St. Augustine Lighthouse, Florida. b, Old Cape Henry Lighthouse, Virginia. c, Cape Lookout Lighthouse, North Carolina. d, Tybee Island Lighthouse, Georgia. e, Morris Island Lighthouse, South Carolina. f, Hillsboro Inlet Lighthouse, Florida.

2008, Mar. 6　Litho.　Perf. 13½
906 A273 41c Block of 6, #a-f　　5.00　5.00

Miniature Sheet

Wild Cats — A274

No. 907: a, Lion family at rest. b, Ocelot mother with cub sitting in grass. c, White Siberian tiger mother with cubs. d, Mother tiger with cubs lying in grass. e, Serval mother with cubs sitting in tall grass. f, North American cougar mother with cubs. g, Lynx mother with cubs. h, Jaguar with cubs at stream. i, Black panther mother with cubs. j, Clouded leopard mother with cubs. k, Cheetah with cubs lying in grass. l, Snow leopard with cubs.

2008, Mar. 26　Litho.　Perf. 13½
907 A274 41c Sheet of 12, #a-l　10.00　10.00

Miniature Sheet

Sailing Ships — A275

No. 908: a, H.M.S. Victory. b, La Grande Hermine. c, U.S.S. Constitution. d, Fram. e, Tovarisch I. f, Ark and Dove. g, Rainbow. h, Great Republic. i, H.M.S. Resolution. j, La Dauphine. k, Kreuzenshtern. l, Golden Hind.

2008, Apr. 2
908 A275 41c Sheet of 12, #a-l　10.00　10.00

Miniature Sheet

Constellations — A276

No. 909: a, Cassiopeia. b, Ursa Major. c, Corvus. d, Camelopardalis. e, Cygnus. f, Andromeda. g, Capricornus. h, Canis Major. i, Dorado. j, Libra. k, Lynx. l, Serpentarius. m, Eridanus. n, Pavo. o, Orion. p, Leo Minor. q, Pegasus. r, Corona Borealis. s, Phoenix. t, Aquarius.

2008, Apr. 29　Litho.　Perf. 13½
909 A276 41c Sheet of 20, #a-t　16.50　16.50
See Nos. 945, 964.

Miniature Sheet

US Marine Corps — A277

No. 910: a, US liberates Marshall Islands. b, John Lejeune. c, Holland Smith. d, Smedley D. Butler. e, Daniel J. Daly. f, Lewis "Chesty" Puller. g, John Basilone. h, Alexander Vandegrift. i, Gregory "Pappy" Boyington. j, Marines raising flag on Iwo Jima.

2008, May 12
910 A277 42c Sheet of 10, #a-j　　8.50　8.50

Tropical Fish A278

Designs: 1c, Banded butterflyfish. 3c, Damselfish. 5c, Pink skunk clownfish. 27c, Copperband butterflyfish. 42c, Threadfin butterflyfish. 60c, Beau Gregory damselfish. 61c, Porkfish. 63c, Goatfish. 94c, Common longnose butterflyfish. $1, Royal gramma. $4.80, Longfin bannerfish. $5, Blue-striped blenny. $16.50, Emperor butterflyfish.

		2008　Litho.　**Perf. 11¼x10¼**	
911	A278	1c multi	.25	.25
912	A278	3c multi	.25	.25
913	A278	5c multi	.25	.25
914	A278	27c multi	.55	.55
915	A278	42c multi	.85	.85
916	A278	60c multi	1.25	1.25
917	A278	61c multi	1.25	1.25
918	A278	63c multi	1.25	1.25
919	A278	94c multi	1.90	1.90
920	A278	$1 multi	2.00	2.00
921	A278	$4.80 multi	9.75	9.75
922	A278	$5 multi	10.00	10.00
923	A278	$16.50 multi	33.00	33.00
	Nos. 911-923 (13)		62.55	62.55

Issued: Nos. 914, 915, 6/24; Nos. 919, 921, 923, 5/12. Nos. 911-913, 916-918, 920, 922, 9/9.

Miniature Sheet

Birds — A279

No. 924: a, Blue-gray tanager. b, St. Vincent parrot. c, Green-throated carib. d, Yellow oriole. e, Blue-hooded euphonia. f, Crested honeycreeper. g, Purple-capped fruit dove. h, Green magpie. i, Bay-headed tanager. j, Bananaquit. k, Cardinal honeyeater. l, Toco toucan. m, Cattle egret. n, Ringed kingfisher. o, Red-necked parrot. p, Purple gallinule. q, Copper-rumped hummingbird. r, Micronesian pigeon. s, Painted bunting. t, Black-naped oriole. u, Channel-billed toucan. v, Saddle-billed stork. w, Blood pheasant. x, Gray-crowned crane. y, Little blue heron.

2008, June 3　Litho.　Perf. 13½
924 A279 42c Sheet of 25, #a-y　21.00　21.00

Miniature Sheet

Dinosaurs — A280

No. 925: a, Camarasaurus. b, Allosaurus. c, Parasaurolophus. d, Ornithomimus. e, Goniopholis. f, Camptosaurus. g, Edmontia. h, Ceratosaurus. i, Stegosaurus. j, Einiosaurus. k, Brachiosaurus. l, Corythosaurus.

2008, June 19
925 A280 42c Sheet of 12, #a-l 10.50 10.50

Miniature Sheet

Fishing Flies — A281

No. 926: a, Lefty's Deceiver (25x35mm). b, Apte Tarpon (25x35mm). c, Royal Wulff (50x48mm). d, Muddler Minnow (25x35mm). e, Jock Scott (25x35mm).

2008, July 20
926 A281 42c Sheet of 5, #a-e 4.25 4.25

Miniature Sheet

Personalities of the Wild West — A282

No. 927: a, Wild Bill Hickok. b, Jim Bridger. c, Geronimo. d, Charles Goodnight. e, Chief Joseph. f, Kit Carson. g, Jim Beckwourth. h, Wyatt Earp. i, Bat Masterson. j, Bill Pickett. k, Bill Tilghman. l, Annie Oakley. m, Buffalo Bill Cody. n, Nellie Cashman. o, Sacagawea. p, John Fremont.

2008, Aug. 14
927 A282 42c Sheet of 16, #a-p 13.50 13.50

Endangered Species — A283

No. 928: a, Blue whale. b, Amazonian manatee. c, Hawaiian monk seal. d, Green turtle. e, Giant clam. f, Killer whale.

2008, Aug. 19 Litho. Perf. 13½
928 A283 42c Block of 6, #a-f 5.25 5.25

Marshallese Culture Type of 2005

No. 929, vert. — Photographs by J. Debrum: a, Lokeinlik Wearing Traditional Mat for Men. b, Limekto Weaving Hat from Kimej. c, Unfinished Outrigger. d, Young Boys in Mejit. e, Lonkoon with Fish Trap.

2008, Sept. 15 Litho. Perf. 13½
929 Horiz. strip of 5 4.25 4.25
a.-e. A250 42c Any single .85 .85

Miniature Sheet

Spacecraft and the Solar System — A284

No. 930: a, Mercury, Mariner 10. b, Uranus, Voyager 2. c, Venus, Mariner 2. d, Pluto, Voyager 2. e, Jupiter, Pioneer 11. f, Earth, Landsat. g, Moon, Lunar Orbiter. h, Saturn, Voyager 2. i, Mars, Viking Orbiter. j, Neptune, Voyager 2.

2008, Oct. 1
930 A284 42c Sheet of 10, #a-j 8.50 8.50

Miniature Sheet

Christmas — A285

No. 931 — Song titles under ornament: a, Silent Night. b, We Three Kings. c, Deck the Halls. d, Hark, the Herald Angels Sing. e, O Little Town of Bethlehem. f, Joy to the World. g, Jingle Bells. h, O Come All Ye Faithful.

2008, Oct. 15 Litho. Perf. 13½
931 A285 42c Sheet of 8, #a-h 6.75 6.75

Owls — A286

No. 932: a, Barn owl. b, Barred owl. c, Burrowing owl. d, Snowy owl. e, Great horned owl. f, Spotted owl.

2008, Nov. 5
932 A286 42c Block of 6, #a-f 5.25 5.25

Souvenir Sheet

First United States Airmail Stamp, 90th Anniv. — A287

2008, Dec. 10 Perf. 13x13½
933 A287 $1 multi 2.00 2.00

Flower Bouquets Type of 2008
Miniature Sheet

No. 934 — Various bouquets with country name at bottom: a, Isle of Man. b, St. Lucia. c, Grenada. d, Bermuda. e, Anguilla. f, Barbados. g, Belize. h, St. Kitts. i, Hong Kong. j, British Virgin Islands. k, St. Vincent. l, Tristan da Cunha. m, St. Helena. n, British Antarctic Territory. o, St. Vincent and the Grenadines. p, New Zealand. q, Papua New Guinea. r, Western Samoa. s, Solomon Islands. t, Brunei. u, Swaziland. v, Botswana. w, Maldives. x, Ghana. y, Sierra Leone.

2009, Mar. 31 Litho. Perf. 13½
934 A271 42c Sheet of 25, #a-y 21.00 21.00

Pres. Abraham Lincoln (1809-65) — A288

No. 935 — Lincoln and: a, "Honesty." b, "Equality." c, "Unity." d, "Liberty."

2009, Apr. 7 Litho. Perf. 13½
935 A288 $1 Block of 4, #a-d 8.00 8.00

Arctic Explorers — A289

No. 936: a, Elisha Kent Kane, ships. b, Robert E. Peary, Matthew A. Henson, dog sled. c, Vilhjalmur Stefansson, ship, dog sled. d, Adolphus Washington Greely, ship.

2009, Apr. 14
936 A289 42c Block of 4, #a-d 3.50 3.50
Peary Expedition to North Pole, cent.

Miniature Sheet

Famous American Indians — A290

No. 937: a, Black Hawk. b, Colorow. c, Looking Glass. d, Dull Knife. e, Mangas Coloradas. f, Red Cloud. g, Little Raven. h, Black Kettle. i, Standing Bear. j, Little Crow. k, Seattle. l, Washakie.

2009, Apr. 21 Litho. Perf. 13½
937 A290 44c Sheet of 12, #a-l 11.00 11.00
See Nos. 960, 987.

Miniature Sheet

US Military Heroes of the Air — A291

No. 938: a, Richard I. Bong. b, Charles "Chuck" Yeager. c, Lauris Norstad. d, William "Billy" Mitchell. e, Curtis E. LeMay. f, Edward Henry O'Hare. g, Claire L. Chennault. h, George C. Kenney. i, James "Jimmy" Doolittle. j, Paul W. Tibbets, Jr. k, Benjamin O. Davis, Jr. l, Carl "Tooey" Spaatz. m, Ira C. Eaker. n, Edward "Eddie" Rickenbacker. o, Henry "Hap" Arnold. p, Map of Marshall Islands, birds, outrigger canoe, dolphin.

2009, Apr. 28
938 A291 44c Sheet of 16, #a-p 14.50 14.50

Souvenir Sheet

Marshall Islands Postal Service, 25th Anniv. — A292

2009, May 2 Litho. Perf. 13x13½
939 A292 44c multi .90 .90

Marine Life A293

Designs: 28c, Masked butterflyfish. 44c, Queen angelfish. 88c, Clownfish. 98c, Starfish. $1.22, Orca whale.

2009, May 11   Litho.   Perf. 11¼x10¼

940	A293	28c multi	.60	.60
941	A293	44c multi	.90	.90
942	A293	88c multi	1.75	1.75
943	A293	98c multi	2.00	2.00
944	A293	$1.22 multi	2.50	2.50
	Nos. 940-944 (5)		7.75	7.75

See No. 965.

Constellations Type of 2008
Miniature Sheet

No. 945: a, Antinous. b, Aquila. c, Cancer. d, Canis Major. e, Leo. f, Ara. g, Sextans Uraniae. h, Cepheus. i, Apus. j, Indus. k, Ursa Minor. l, Grus. m, Centaurus. n, Cetus. o, Piscis Volans. p, Lupus. q, Equuleus. r, Draco. s, Boötes. t, Scorpius.

2009, June 1   Perf. 13½

945	A276	44c Sheet of 20, #a-t	18.00 18.00

2005-09 Rose Varieties of the Year — A294

No. 946: a, Summertime, 2005. b, Champagne Moment, 2006. c, Tickled Pink, 2007. d, Sweet Haze, 2008. e, Lucky!, 2009.

2009, June 18

946		Horiz. strip of 5	4.50 4.50
a.-e.	A294 44c Any single		.90 .90

Hot Air Balloons A295

No. 947: a, Montgolfier's balloon. b, Intrepid. c, Explorer II. d, Double Eagle. e, Contemporary balloons.

2009, July 13

947		Horiz. strip of 5	4.50 4.50
a.-e.	A295 44c Any single		.90 .90

July 22, 2009 Solar Eclipse — A296

No. 948 — Eclipse phases: a, Beginning (shown). b, Totality and near-totality. c, Ending.

2009, July 22

948		Horiz. strip of 3	2.75 2.75
a.-c.	A296 44c Any single		.90 .90

Steam Locomotives — A297

No. 949: a, Samson. b, Best Friend of Charleston. c, John Bull. d, Gowan & Marx. e, Stourbridge Lion. f, Brother Jonathan.

2009, Aug. 6   Litho.   Perf. 13½

949	A297	44c Block of 6, #a-f	5.50 5.50

Marshallese Culture Type of 2005

No. 950 — Photographs by J. Debrum: a, Making Arrowroot Lagoonside. b, Boats in Lagoon, One Capsized for Repair. c, Family Portrait in Front of Wooden Home with Pandanus Roof. d, Man Carrying Fish Trap. e, Portrait of New Year and LemeLali Weaving Baskets.

2009, Sept. 1   Litho.   Perf. 13½

950		Horiz. strip of 5	4.50 4.50
a.-e.	A250 44c Any single		.90 .90

Eagles — A298

No. 951: a, Philippine eagle. b, Tawny eagle. c, Martial eagle. d, Bald eagle. e, African fish eagle. f, Bateleur eagle. g, Golden eagle. h, Harpy eagle.

2009, Sept. 14   Litho.   Perf. 13½

951	A298	44c Block of 8, #a-h	7.25 7.25

Dogs — A299

No. 952: a, Beagle and Boston terrier. b, Chesapeake Bay retriever and Cocker spaniel. c, Alaskan malamute and Collie. d, Water spaniel and Basset hound. e, Coonhound and Foxhound.

No. 953, horiz.: a, Old English sheepdog. b, Irish setter. c, Welsh springer spaniel. d, West Highland terrier.

2009, Oct. 5   Litho.   Perf. 13½

952		Horiz. strip of 5	4.50 4.50
a.-e.	A299 44c Any single		.90 .90
953		Sheet of 4	8.00 8.00
a.-d.	A299 98c Any single		2.00 2.00

Christmas A300

No. 954: a, Chili wreath. b, Christmas wreath. c, Traditional wreath. d, Tropical wreath. e, Colonial wreath.

2009, Oct. 15   Litho.   Perf. 13½

954		Horiz. strip of 5	4.50 4.50
a.-e.	A300 44c Any single		.90 .90

Miniature Sheet

Endangered Species — A301

No. 955: a, Giant anteater. b, Caracal. c, Wild yak. d, Giant panda. e, Black-footed ferret. f, Black rhinoceros. g, Golden lion tamarin. h, African elephant. i, Persian fallow deer. j, Polar bear. k, Ocelot. l, Gorilla.

2009, Nov. 2   Litho.   Perf. 13½

955	A301	44c Sheet of 12, #a-l	11.00 11.00

Prehistoric Animals — A302

No. 956: a, Mastodons on prairie. b, Eohippus. c, Woolly mammoth. d, Saber-toothed cat. e, Mastodons in marsh.

2009, Nov. 24

956		Horiz. strip of 5	4.50 4.50
a.-e.	A302 44c Any single		.90 .90

Shells — A303

No. 957: a, Paper nautilus. b, Giant tun. c, Pilgrim's scallop. d, Gibbula magus.

2009, Dec. 8

957	A303	44c Block of 4, #a-d	3.75 3.75

Miniature Sheet

Signs of the Zodiac — A304

No. 958: a, Aquarius. b, Pisces. c, Aries. d, Taurus. e, Gemini. f, Cancer. g, Leo. h, Virgo. i, Libra. j, Scorpio. k, Sagittarius. l, Capricorn.

2010, Jan. 5   Perf. 11¾

958	A304	44c Sheet of 12, #a-l	11.00 11.00

Miniature Sheet

Waterfowl — A305

No. 959: a, European wigeon. b, Tufted ducks. c, Mallards. d, Gadwall. e, Snow geese. f, Pintail ducks. g, Northern shoveler. h, Canvasback ducks.

2010, Feb. 10   Litho.   Perf. 11¾

959	A305	44c Sheet of 8, #a-h	7.25 7.25

Famous American Indians Type of 2009
Miniature Sheet

No. 960: a, Osceola. b, Lone Wolf. c, Menawa. d, Wabasha. e, Captain Jack. f, Quanah Parker. g, Ouray. h, Mannelito. i, Cochise. j, Satanta. k, Massasoit. l, Red Eagle.

2010, Mar. 4   Litho.   Perf. 13½

960	A290	44c Sheet of 12, #a-l	11.00 11.00

Boy Scouts of America, Cent. — A306

No. 961 — Background color: a, Olive green. b, Red. c, Yellow bister. d, Blue.

2010, Mar. 18   Litho.   Perf. 13½

961	A306	44c Block of 4, #a-d	3.75 3.75

Shells — A307

No. 962: a, Paper nautilus. b, Giant tun. c, Pilgrim's scallop. d, Gibbula magus.

2010, Mar. 29   Litho.   Perf. 13½

962	A307	98c Block of 4, #a-d	8.00 8.00

See Nos. 971-972.

Astronomers
A308

No. 963: a, Nicolaus Copernicus. b, Johannes Kepler. c, Galileo Galilei. d, Sir Isaac Newton. e, Sir William Herschel.

2010, Apr. 7
963   Horiz. strip of 5   4.50 4.50
   a.-e.   A308 44c Any single   .90   .90
No. 963e is incorrectly inscribed "Hirschel."

Constellations Type of 2008
No. 964: a, Columba. b, Virgo. c, Argo Navis. d, Tucana (Toucan). e, Aries. f, Coma Berenices. g, Delphinus. h, Perseus. i, Taurus. j, Monoceros. k, Gemini. l, Vulpecula. m, Lepus. n, Auriga. o, Pisces. p, Sagittarius. q, Crater. r, Lyra. s, Hercules. t, Canes Venatici.

2010, June 1
964   A276 44c Sheet of 20, #a-
                   t   18.00 18.00

Fish Type of 2009
2010, June 1   **Perf. 11¼x10¼**
965   A293 28c Mandarin goby   .60   .60

Marshallese Alphabet — A309

No. 966 — Letters and Marshallese words: a, "A," Amata (first name of first Marshallese president). b, "A with macron," Aj (to weave). c, "B," Babbub (butterfly). d, "D," Deo (beautiful young lady). e, "E," Ek (fish). f, "I," Iokwe (rainbow). g, "J," Jaki (mat). h, "K," Imon Kien (house of government). i, "L," Loktanur (star Capella). j, "L with cedilla," Lokwajek (red-tailed tropic bird). k, "M," Ma (breadfruit). l, "M with cedilla," Makmok (arrowroot plant). m, "N," Ni (coconut tree). n, "N with cedilla," No (ocean wave). o, "N with macron," Niin-pako (shark tooth). p, "O," Ok (fish net). q, "O with cedilla," Eo (tattoo). r, "O with macron," Oo (lionfish). s, "P," Pejak (visitor's hut). t, "R," Raj (whale). u, "T," Tipnol (outrigger sailing canoe). v, "U," Urur (fire). w, "U with macron," Ulin-raj (dorsal fin of whale). x, "W," Wojla (woven pandanus leaf sail).

2010, June 16   Litho.   Perf. 13½
966   Sheet of 24   22.00 22.00
   a.-x.   A309 44c Any single   .90   .90
Miniature Sheet

Statue of Liberty — A310

No. 967 — Statue of Liberty: a, Red clouds and water (9-1). b, Blue background (9-2). c, Brown and gray clouds (9-3). d, American flag (9-4). e, Frederic Bartholdi (9-5). f, Blue background, diff. (9-6). g, White background around head (9-7). h, Torch (9-8). i, Brown background around head (9-9).

2010, June 17   Perf. 11¾
967   A310 44c Sheet of 9, #a-i, +
                   7 labels   8.25 8.25

Miniature Sheet

Classic Cars — A311

No. 968: a, 1935 Duesenberg. b, 1932 Packard. c, 1928 Locomobile. d, 1931 Cord. e, 1929 Pierce Arrow.

2010, July 7
968   A311 44c Sheet of 5, #a-e, +
                   4 labels   4.50 4.50

Carousel Horses — A312

No. 969 — Various carousel horses numberd: a, (6-1). b, (6-2). c, (6-3). d, (6-4). e, (6-5). f, (6-6).

2010, Aug. 12   Perf. 13½
969   A312 44c Block of 6, #a-f   5.50 5.50

US
Warships of
World War
II — A313

No. 970: a, USS Nevada. b, USS Missouri. c, USS Wisconsin. d, USS Oregon. e, USS Massachusetts. f, USS North Carolina. g, USS Texas. h, USS Idaho. i, USS New Jersey. j, USS Colorado. k, USS South Dakota. l, USS New Mexico. m, USS Washington. n, USS Iowa. o, USS Alabama.

2010, Sept. 2   Perf. 13½
970   Sheet of 15   13.50 13.50
   a.-o.   A313 44c Any single   .90   .90

Shells Type of 2010
Designs: 28c, Pilgrim's scallop. 98c, Gibbula magus.

2010, Sept. 20
971   A307 28c multi   .60   .60
972   A307 98c multi   2.00 2.00

Marshallese Culture Type of 2005
No. 973 — Photographs by L. Debrum: a, Church Buildings in Likiep. b, Ijuran Ready to Launch. c, Group of People, One Man Holding Fish Net. d, Lejek with Fish Trap on Korkor in Likiep. e, Landscape with Outrigger and Sailboat.

2010, Sept.14   Perf. 13½
973   Horiz. strip of 5   4.50 4.50
   a.-e.   A250 44c Any single   .90   .90

Christmas — A314

No. 974 — Various depictions of Santa Claus numbered: a, (4-1). b, (4-2). c, (4-3). d, (4-4).

2010, Oct. 18
974   Horiz. strip of 4   3.75 3.75
   a.-d.   A314 44c Any single   .90   .90

Miniature Sheet

Pres. John F. Kennedy (1917-
63) — A315

No. 975 — Various portraits of Kennedy numbered: a, (6-1). b, (6-2). c, (6-3). d, (6-4). e, (6-5). f, (6-6).

2010, Nov. 3
975   A315 44c Sheet of 6, #a-f, +
                   6 labels   5.50 5.50

Miniature Sheet

Orchids — A316

No. 976: a, Psygmorchis purilla. b, Cycnoches spp. c, Aerangis modesta. d, Ansellia africana. e, Vanda coerulea. f, Dendrobium cruentum. g, Phragmipedium korachii. h, Cymbidium ensifolium. i, Laelia milleri.

2010, Nov. 17
976   A316 44c Sheet of 9, #a-i   8.00 8.00

Miniature Sheet

Butterflies — A317

No. 977: a, Monarch. b, Brimstone. c, Blue-spot hairstreak. d, Small tortoiseshell. e, Small skipper. f, Large blue. g, Large copper. h, Eastern orange-tip. i, Red admiral. j, American

---

painted lady. k, Great eggfly. l, Dark green fritillary.

2010, Dec. 8
977   A317 44c Sheet of 12, #a-l 11.00 11.00

Tulips
A318

No. 978 — Inscriptions: a, Yellow tulip. b, Tulips. c, Purple tulips. d, Red and black tulips. e, Yellow and orange tulips. f, Red tulips.

2011, Jan. 11
978   Block of 6   5.50 5.50
   a.-f.   A318 44c Any single   .90   .90

Miniature Sheet

New Year 2011 (Year of the
Rabbit) — A319

No. 979 — Rabbit in: a, Blue. b, Red violet. c, Bister. d, Green.

2011, Feb. 3
979   A319 98c Sheet of 4, #a-d 8.00 8.00

Pres. Ronald
Reagan (1911-
2004)
A320

No. 980 — Inscription: a, Early years. b, Movie actor. c, Governor of California. d, 40th President. e, Elder statesman/late years.

2011, Feb. 6
980   Horiz. strip of 5   4.50 4.50
   a.-e.   A320 44c Any single   .90   .90

Firsts in
Flight
A321

No. 981 — Inscription: a, Centennial of first airmail flight. b, First airmail service in America. c, First U.S. coast-to-coast airmail service. d, First permanent U.S. transcontinental airmail service. e, First international airmail service.

2011, Feb. 18
981   Horiz. strip of 5   4.50 4.50
   a.-e.   A321 44c Any single   .90   .90
See Nos. 988, 994, 1004, 1012.

Turtles
A322

Designs: 1c, Green turtle. 2c, Loggerhead turtle. 5c, Leatherback turtle. $10, Hawksbill turtle.

Perf. 11¼x10¼

2011, Feb. 22				**Litho.**
982	A322	1c multi	.25	.25
983	A322	2c multi	.25	.25
984	A322	5c multi	.25	.25
985	A322	$10 multi	20.00	20.00
	Nos. 982-985 (4)		20.75	20.75

Corals and
Fish — A323

No. 986 — Inscriptions: a, Flora & fauna of the Pacific Ocean. b, Chalice coral. c, Elkhorn coral. d, Brain coral. e, Finger coral.

2011, Mar. 10			**Perf. 13½**	
986		Horiz. strip of 5	3.00	3.00
a.-e.	A323	29c Any single	.60	.60

Famous American Indians Type of 2009

No. 987: a, Pontiac. b, Barboncito. c, Geronimo. d, Victorio. e, Sitting Bull. f, Cornplanter. g, Uncas. h, Little Wolf. i, Crazy Horse. j, Gall. k, Joseph. l, Tecumseh.

2011, Mar. 22				
987	A290	44c Sheet of 12, #a-l	11.00	11.00

Firsts in Flight Type of 2011

No. 988 — Inscriptions: a, First manned flight. b, First manned flight of semi-controlled airship. c, First powered aircraft leaves the ground. d, First manned flight of powered, controlled airship. e, First controlled powered flight.

2011, Apr. 12				
988		Horiz. strip of 5	4.50	4.50
a.-e.	A321	44c Any single	.90	.90

First
Man in
Space,
50th
Anniv.
A324

No. 989: a, Rocket launch, Yuri Gagarin on medal. b, Gagarin wearing space helmet, spacecraft, Earth. c, Monument, Apollo and Soyuz spacecraft docked, medal.

2011, Apr. 12				
989		Strip of 3	6.00	6.00
a.-c.	A324	$1 Any single	2.00	2.00

Printed in sheets containing three strips and seven labels.

Miniature Sheet

Wedding of Prince William and
Catherine Middleton — A325

No. 990 — Various flowers numbered: a, 15-1. b, 15-2. c, 15-3. d, 15-4. e, 15-5. f, 15-6. g, 15-7. h, 15-8. i, 15-9. j, 15-10. k, 15-11. l, 15-12. m, 15-13. n, 15-14. o,15-15.

2011, Apr. 29				
990	A325	44c Sheet of 15,		
		#a-o	13.50	13.50

Miniature Sheet

Apostles of Jesus — A326

No. 991: a, Andrew. b, Philip. c, Simon. d, James the Lesser. e, Paul. f, Matthew. g, James the Greater. h, Thaddeus. i, Peter. j, John. k, Bartholomew. l, Thomas.

2011, May 2				
991	A326	44c Sheet of 12, #a-l	11.00	11.00

Miniature Sheet

Garden Life — A327

No. 992: a, Great eggfly butterfly. b, Passionflower. c, Ladybug. d, Emperor dragonfly. e, Sweet white violet. f, Magpie moth. g, Bluets. h, Katydid. i, Painted lady butterfly. j, Bumblebee. k, Stag beetle. l, Large tortoiseshell butterfly.

2011, May 28				
992	A327	44c Sheet of 12,		
		#a-l	11.00	11.00

Miniature Sheet

Antarctic Treaty, 50th Anniv. — A328

No. 993: a, Penguin and ship (6-1). b, Emperor penguin and juvenile (6-2). c, Penguin and ship (6-3). d, Two penguins on iceberg (6-4). e, King penguin mother and baby (6-5). f, King penguin mothers with babies (6-6). g, Penguin and ship (6-7). h, Two adult Emperor penguins and juvenile (6-8). i, Penguin and ship (6-9).

2011, June 23				
993	A328	98c Sheet of 9, #a-i,		
		+ 7 labels	18.00	18.00

Firsts in Flight Type of 2011

No. 994 — Inscriptions: a, First flight to land on a ship. b, First non-stop North American coast-to-coast flight. c, First non-stop transatlantic flight. d, First round-the-world flight. e, First flight over the North Pole.

2011, July 7				
994		Horiz. strip of 5	4.50	4.50
a.-e.	A321	44c Any single	.90	.90

Outrigger Canoes — A329

Plumeria Flowers — A330

Marshall Islands Flag — A331

Coconut Palm Trees and
Coconuts — A332

Micronesian Pigeons — A333

Triton's Trumpet — A334

2011, July 7				
995	A329	$4.95 multi	10.00	10.00
996	A330	$10.95 multi	22.00	22.00
997	A331	$13.95 multi	28.00	28.00
998	A332	$14.95 multi	30.00	30.00
999	A333	$18.30 multi	37.00	37.00
1000	A334	$29.95 multi	60.00	60.00
	Nos. 995-1000 (6)		187.00	187.00

Miniature Sheet

End of Space Shuttle
Missions — A335

No. 1001 — Space Shuttle: a, And schematic diagrams. b, Lifting off. c, And eagle. d, In orbit. e, On approach for landing. f, Lifting off, U.S. flag in background. g, And planets.

2011, July 21				
1001	A335	44c Sheet of 7, #a-g,		
		+ 8 labels	6.25	6.25

The label on No. 1001 with the names of the Challenger astronauts has the name of "Judith Resnik" misspelled as "Judith Resuik." The sheet was reprinted later in 2011 with the corrected spelling.

Marshallese Culture Type of 2005

No. 1002 — Photographs by L. Debrum: a, Celebration of Alfonso Capelle's Kemen. b, Three Women Making Pandanus Thatch. c, Men Spearfishing on Reef Oceaside of Likiep. d, Men in Boathouse Grinding Arrowroot. e, The Boat Vilma Being Launched at Likiep.

2011, July 22				
1002		Horiz. strip of 5	4.50	4.50
a.-e.	A250	44c Any single	.90	.90

Miniature Sheet

Fish — A336

No. 1003: a, Blue-banded surgeonfish, Bleeker's parrotfish. b, Achilles tang, Oriental sweetlips. c, Regal angelfish, Orangespine unicornfish. d, Coral grouper, Palette surgeonfish. e, Peacock grouper, Coral grouper. f, Bennett's butterflyfish, Picassofish. g, Bleeker's parrotfish, Flame angelfish. h, Orangespine unicornfish, Peacock grouper. i, Flame angelfish, Regal angelfish. j, Palette surgeonfish, Blue-banded surgeonfish. k, Picassofish, Achilles tang. l, Oriental sweetlips, Bennett's butterflyfish.

2011, Aug. 11
1003 A336 44c Sheet of 12,
#a-l 11.00 11.00

Firsts in Flight Type of 2011

No. 1004 — Inscriptions: a, First turbojet flight. b, First jet fighter flight. c, First jet passenger service. d, First Transatlantic jet passenger service. e, First supersonic commercial aircraft.

2011, Aug. 21
1004 Horiz. strip of 5 4.50 4.50
a.-e. A321 44c Any single .90 .90

National Buildings and Symbols A337

Designs: No. 1005, 64c, Capitol Building. No. 1006, 64c, Nitijela Building. No. 1007, 64c, National seal, vert. No. 1008, 64c, National flag, vert.

Perf. 11¼x10¼, 10¼x11¼
2011, Aug. 31 **Litho.**
1005-1008 A337 Set of 4 5.25 5.25

Souvenir Sheet

Marshall Islands No. 411 — A338

2011, Sept. 17 **Litho.** *Perf. 13½*
1009 A338 $4.95 multi 10.00 10.00
Admission to the United Nations, 20th anniv.

Miniature Sheet

Christmas — A339

No. 1010: a, 10c, Christmas shopping. b, 20c, Cutting Christmas tree. c, 30c, Putting wreath on door. d, 40c, Caroling in cathedral at Christmas. e, 50c, Bringing home the tree. f, 60c, A winter sleigh ride. g, 70c, Arrival in sleigh at church. h, 80c, A pause in the sleigh ride. i, 90c, Christmas caroling outside church. j, $1, Sleigh ride to get Christmas tree. k, $1.10, Western Christmas. l, $1.20, Christmas caroling.

2011, Oct. 13
1010 A339 Sheet of 12, #a-l 16.00 16.00

Souvenir Sheet

Compact of Free Association, 25th Anniv. — A340

No. 1011: a, Marshall Islands national seal. b, Walap sailing. c, Marshall Islands flag.

2011, Oct. 21
1011 A340 98c Sheet of 3, #a-c,
+ 3 labels 6.00 6.00

Firsts in Flight Type of 2011

No. 1012 — Inscriptions: a, First man to fly faster than sound. b, First man in space. c, First astronaut in space. d, First man to walk in space. e, First man on the Moon.

2011, Nov. 4
1012 Horiz. strip of 5 4.50 4.50
a.-e. A321 44c Any single .90 .90

Hanukkah — A341

No. 1013 — Various menorahs on: a, Day 1. b, Day 2. c, Day 3. d, Day 4. e, Day 5. f, Day 6. g, Day 7. h, Day 8.

2011, Nov. 20 **Litho.** *Perf. 13½*
1013 A341 44c Block of 8, #a-h 7.25 7.25

Miniature Sheet

American Entry Into World War II, 70th Anniv. — A342

No. 1014 — Inscriptions: a, Burma Road, 717-mile lifeline to China. b, Roosevelt calls for America's first peacetime draft. c, U.S must become "Great Arsenal" to save democracy. d, Lend-Lease Act, aid to our allies. e, Roosevelt, Churchill draft 8 peace aims, joint steps believed changed at parley. f, U.S. Destroyer Reuben James sunk by German U-boat. g, Civil defense mobilizes the U.S.A. h, Kaiser launches Liberty ships. i, War! Oahu bombed by Japanese planes. j, Congress declares war on Japan, 1500 killed in attack on Hawaii.

2011, Dec. 7
1014 A342 44c Sheet of 10, #a-j,
+ 10 labels 9.00 9.00
See Nos. 1035, 1065, 1089.

Miniature Sheet

Stained Glass Windows — A343

No. 1015 — Stained glass windows of: a, Cathedral of Santa Maria del Fiore, Florence, Italy (9-1). b, Nidaros Cathedral, Trondheim, Norway (9-2). c, Canterbury Cathedral, Canterbury, England (9-3). d, Notre Dame Cathedral, Tournai, Belgium (9-4). e, Cathedral of Monaco (9-5). f, St. John's Church, Gouda, Netherlands (9-6). g, St. Florin's Cathedral, Vaduz, Liechtenstein (9-7). h, St. Mary the Crowned Cathedral, Gibraltar (9-8). i, Parish Church of St. Saviour, Jersey (9-9).

2011, Dec. 9
1015 A343 44c Sheet of 9, #a-i 8.00 8.00

Miniature Sheet

Rhododendrons — A344

No. 1016 — Various rhododendrons numbered: a, (9-1). b, (9-2). c, (9-3). d, (9-4). e, (9-5). f, (9-6). g, (9-7). h, (9-8). i, (9-9).

2012, Jan. 10
1016 A344 45c Sheet of 9, #a-i 8.25 8.25

Marine Life — A345

2012, Jan. 22
1017 A345 45c multi .90 .90

Miniature Sheet

New Year 2012 (Year of the Dragon) — A346

No. 1018 — Background color: a, Blue. b, Pink. c, Yellow green. d, Green.

2012, Jan. 23
1018 A346 $1.05 Sheet of 4,
#a-d 8.50 8.50

Whales A347

No. 1019: a, Right whales. b, Killer whales. c, Gervais's whales. d, Blue whales.

2012, Feb. 20 *Perf. 13½*
1019 Horiz. strip of 4 2.60 2.60
a.-d. A347 32c Any single .65 .65

Chuuk War Canoe — A348

Cymbidium Orchid — A349

Arrival of Early Inhabitants — A350

Mandarinfish — A351

Hibiscus Rosa-sinensis — A352

Seahorses — A353

2012, Feb. 27
1020 A348 $5.15 multi 10.00 10.00
1021 A349 $11.35 multi 22.50 22.50
1022 A350 $15.45 multi 31.00 31.00
1023 A351 $16.95 multi 34.00 34.00
1024 A352 $18.95 multi 37.50 37.50
1025 A353 $38 multi 75.00 75.00
Nos. 1020-1025 (6) 210.00 210.00
Compare No. 1020 with No. 1042.

Miniature Sheet

Reign of Queen Elizabeth II, 60th Anniv. — A354

No. 1026 — Stamps of Great Britain depicting Queen Elizabeth II: a, #MH206 (10p). b, #MH211 (20p). c, #MH219 (30p). d, #MH266 (40p). e, #MH385 (50p). f, #MH397 (60p).

2012, Feb. 6
1026   A354 $1.05 Sheet of 6,
                #a-f   13.00 13.00

Birds
A355

Designs: 85c, Black-footed albatross. $1.05, Red-tailed tropic bird.

2012, Feb. 27   *Perf. 11¼x10¼*
1027   A355   85c multi   1.75 1.75
1028   A355 $1.05 multi   2.10 2.10

Chinese Terra Cotta Warriors — A356

No. 1029: a, General figure (6-1). b, Kneeling shooter (6-2). c, Armor warriors (6-3). d, Arrow shooter (6-4). e, General figure (6-5). f, Heavy armor (6-6).

2012, Mar. 15   *Perf. 13½*
1029   A356   45c Block of 6, #a-f   5.50 5.50

Inuits — A357

No. 1030: a, Inuits enjoy a hot drink in their igloo. b, Inuit crafts and sculptures. c, Inuit drummers and dancers. d, Inuit men fishing with harpoons. e, Inuit family in skin tent. f, Inuit hunting.

2012, Mar. 26
1030   A357   45c Block of 6, #a-f   5.50 5.50

Creation of Tobolar Coconut Twine and Rope A358

No. 1031: a, Husking the ripe coconuts after they come off the tree. b, Soaking the husks in sea water under mat and stones. c, Pounding the husks to separate the twine from the meat. d, Making twine and rope from the husk fibers.

2012, Apr. 8
1031   Horiz. strip of 4   3.75 3.75
  a.-d.   A358 45c Any single   .90   .90

Miniature Sheet

Scientists — A359

No. 1032: a, Charles Darwin. b, William Harvey. c, Robert Boyle. d, Johannes Kepler. e, Thomas Edison. f, André-Marie Ampère. g, Michael Faraday. h, Jöns Jacob Berzelius. i, James Watt. j, Galileo Galilei. k, Andreas Vesalius. l, Antoine Lavoisier. m, Dmitry Mendeleyev. n, Carl Gauss. o, Isaac Newton. p, Gregor Mendel. q, John Dalton. r, Carl Linnaeus. s, Robert Fulton. t, William Thomson, Baron Kelvin.

2012, Apr. 23   *Perf. 13½*
1032   A359   45c Sheet of 20,
            #a-t   18.00 18.00

Miniature Sheet

Clouds — A360

No. 1033: a, Altocumulus undulatus. b, Altostratus translucidus. c, Cirrostratus fibratus. d, Cumulus congestus. e, Cumulonimbus incus. f, Cirrus radiatus. g, Cirrocumulus undulatus. h, Cumulonimbus with tornado. i, Cumulus humilis. j, Cumulonimbus mammatus. k, Stratus opacus. l, Altocumulus castellanus. m, Altocumulus stratiformis. n, Altocumulus lenticularis. o, Stratocumulus undulatus.

2012, May 10
1033   A360   45c Sheet of 15,
            #a-o   13.50 13.50

Birds
A361

No. 1034: a, Masked woodswallow. b, Golden-shouldered parrot. c, Regent bowerbird. d, King parrot. e, Rainbow pitta. f, Rainbow bee-eaters on branch. g, White-tailed kingfisher. h, Spotted catbird. i, Rainbow bee-eater in flight. j, Western magpie.

2012, June 18
1034   Block of 10   9.00 9.00
  a.-j.   A361 45c Any single   .90   .90

World War II Type of 2011
Miniature Sheet

No. 1035 — Inscriptions: a, Tokyo bombed! b, Roosevelt praises U.S. rationing effort. c, U.S. wins great naval battle in Coral Sea. d, Corregidor surrenders under land attack after withstanding 300 raids from the air. e, Japanese make landings in Aleutian Islands; U.S. warships attack Attu Island, defeat Japs. f, Codebreaking: Turning the tide in the Pacific. g, Jap fleet smashed by U.S., 2 carriers sunk at Midway. h, Women in the war: "Rosie the Riveter." i, Marines gain hold on Solomon Islands; ships and planes wage fights. j, American forces land in French Africa.

2012, July 3
1035   A342   45c Sheet of 10, #a-j,
           + 10 labels   9.00 9.00

Miniature Sheet

Introduction of Euro Currency, 10th Anniv. — A362

No. 1036 — 1-euro coins of: a, Austria. b, Belgium. c, Finland. d, France. e, Germany. f, Greece. g, Ireland. h, Italy. i, Luxembourg. j, Netherlands. k, Portugal. l, Spain.

2012, July 16
1036   A362   45c Sheet of 12,
            #a-l   11.00 11.00

Miniature Sheet

American Civil War, 150th Anniv. — A363

No. 1037 — U.S. stamps commemorating Civil War centennial: a, #1178 (Fort Sumter, 34x25mm). b, #1179 (Battle of Shiloh, 34x25mm). c, #1180 (Battle of Gettysburg, 34x25mm). d, #1181 (Battle of the Wilderness, 34x25mm). d, #1182 (Surrender at Appomattox, 48x50mm).

2012, July 25
1037   A363   45c Sheet of 5, #a-e   4.50 4.50

American Indian Dances — A364

No. 1038: a, Traditional Dance. b, Raven Dance. c, Fancy Dance. d, Hoop Dance. e, Grass Dance. f, Butterfly Dance.

2012, Aug. 16
1038   A364   45c Block of 6, #a-f   5.50 5.50

Souvenir Sheet

USS Constitution and HMS Guerrière — A365

2012, Aug. 20
1039   A365 $4.95 multi + 4 labels   10.00 10.00

War of 1812, bicent.

Miniature Sheet

Christmas — A366

No. 1040 — Items from carol *The Twelve Days of Christmas*: a, Partridge in a pear tree (12-1). b, Two turtle doves (12-2). c, Three French hens (12-3). d, Four calling birds (12-4). e, Five golden rings (12-5). f, Six geese a-layiing (12-6). g, Seven swans a-swimming (12-7). h, Eight maids a-milking (12-8). i, Nine drummers drumming (12-9). j, Ten pipers piping (12-10). k, Eleven ladies dancing (12-11). l, Twelve lords a-leaping (12-12).

2012, Sept. 28
1040   A366   45c Sheet of 12,
            #a-l   11.00 11.00

Locomotives of the Fifty States — A367

No. 1041 — Steam locomotive from: a, Alabama. b, Alaska. c, Arizona. d, Arkansas. e, California. f, Colorado. g, Connecticut. h, Delaware. i, Florida. j, Georgia. k, Hawaii. l, Idaho. m, Illinois. n, Indiana. o, Iowa. p, Kansas. q, Kentucky. r, Louisiana. s, Maine. t, Maryland. u, Massachusetts. v, Michigan. w, Minnesota. x, Mississippi. y, Missouri. z, Montana. aa, Nebraska. ab, Nevada. ac, New Hampshire. ad, New Jersey. ae, New Mexico. af, New York. ag, North Carolina. ah, North Dakota. ai, Ohio. aj, Oklahoma. ak, Oregon. al, Pennsylvania. am, Rhode Island. an, South Carolina. ao, South Dakota. ap, Tennessee. aq, Texas. ar, Utah. as, Vermont. at, Virginia. au, Washington. av, West Virginia. aw, Wisconsin. ax, Wyoming.

2012, Nov. 3
1041   Sheet of 50   45.00 45.00
  a.-ax.   A367 45c Any single   .90   .90

Chuuk War Canoe A368

2012, Nov. 8   *Perf. 11¼x10¼*
1042   A368 $5.15 multi   10.00 10.00
      Compare No. 1042 and No. 1020.

Birds — A369

No. 1043: a, Great hornbill. b, Peregrine falcon. c, Bald eagle. d, Channel-billed toucan. e, Secretary bird. f, Black-bellied bustard. g, Toco toucan. h, Hyacinth macaw. i, Burrowing owl. j, Bald ibis.

2013, Jan. 10   *Perf. 13½*
1043   A369   45c Sheet of 10, #a-j   9.00 9.00
      See Nos. 1056-1058.

Australia, 225th Anniv. A370

No. 1044 — Stars and: a, Australian settler and land claim. b, Tennis racket, coin showing King George V. c, Sydney Harbour Bridge, Sydney Opera House. d, Cricket player. e, Clipper ship, Southern Cross constellation. f, Clipper ship, sextant markings. g, Australian Parliament, Aboriginal drawings. h, William Shakespeare. i, British Parliament, London. j, Queen Elizabeth II, British coat of arms.

2013, Jan. 25
1044	Sheet of 10	9.50	9.50
a.-j.	A370 46c Any single	.95	.95

Inscription on No. 1044b is incorrect.

Marine Life — A371

Designs: 33c, Raccoon butterflyfish. 46c, Dolphins. $1.10, Long-nosed butterflyfish, horiz. $5.60, Tiger shark, horiz. $12.35, Star puffer, horiz. $16.85, Nassau grouper, horiz. $19.95, Starfish, horiz. $23.95, Porkfish, horiz. $44.95, Grouper, horiz.

2013, Jan. 28   *Perf. 10¼x11¼*
1045	A371	33c multi	.70	.70
1046	A371	46c multi	.95	.95

Perf. 11¼x10¼
1047	A371	$1.10 multi	2.25	2.25
1048	A371	$5.60 multi	11.50	11.50
1049	A371	$12.35 multi	25.00	25.00
1050	A371	$16.85 multi	34.00	34.00
1051	A371	$19.95 multi	40.00	40.00
1052	A371	$23.95 multi	47.50	47.50
1053	A371	$44.95 multi	90.00	90.00

Miniature Sheet

New Year 2013 (Year of the Snake) — A372

No. 1054 — Color of snake: a, Blue (4-1). b, Red Brown (4-2). c, Yellow brown (4-3). d, Green (4-4).

2013, Feb. 10   *Perf. 13½*
1054	A372 $1.10 Sheet of 4, #a-d	9.00	9.00

Camellias — A373

No. 1055 — Number and color of camellias: a, One white (8-1). b, Two red and white (8-2). c, Three pink (8-3). d, One pink (8-4). e, Three dark pink (8-5). f, Two pink (8-6). g, One red (8-7). h, Three pink (8-8).

2013, Feb. 22
1055	A373 46c Block of 8, #a-h	7.50	7.50

Birds Type of 2013
Miniature Sheets

No. 1056: a, Hadada ibis. b, White-face whistling duck. c, Scarlet ibises. d, Fulvous tree duck. e, Knob-billed goose. f, Egyptian goose. g, Baikal teal. h, Humboldt penguins. i, Whooping cranes. j, Red-breasted goose.
No. 1057: a, Caribbean flamingos. b, Dalmatian pelicans. c, Piping plovers. d, Coscoroba swans. e, Hawaiian goose. f, Brown pelican. g, Jabiru. h, King penguins. i, White spoonbill. j, Blue cranes.
No. 1058: a, Golden conure. b, Major Mitchell's cockatoos. c, Eastern bluebirds. d, Giant scops owl. e, Thick-billed parrot. f, Blue-crowned pigeon. g, American kestrels. h, White-breasted silver-eyes. i, St. Lucia amazon. j, California condors.

2013   *Perf. 13½*
1056	A369 46c Sheet of 10, #a-j	9.50	9.50
1057	A369 46c Sheet of 10, #a-j	9.50	9.50
1058	A369 46c Sheet of 10, #a-j	9.50	9.50

Issued: No. 1056, 3/9; No. 1057, 5/16; No. 1058, 10/3.

Cats — A374

No. 1059: a, Four cats, pink flower (6-5). b, Three cats, blue flower, butterflies (6-6). c, Three cats, pink flowers, basket (6-1). d, Three cats looking at grasshopper on basket (6-2). e, Three cats, red and yellow flowers (6-3). f, Three cats, two hummingbirds (6-4).

2013, Mar. 27   *Litho.*   *Perf. 13½*
1059	Horiz. strip of 6	4.25	4.25
a.-f.	A374 33c Any single	.70	.70

Medals — A375

No. 1060 — Inscription below medal: a, George Washington. b, John Adams. c, Thomas Jefferson. d, James Madison. e, James Monroe. f, John Quincy Adams. g, Andrew Jackson. h, Martin Van Buren. i, William H. Harrison. j, John Tyler. k, James K. Polk. l, Zachary Taylor. m, Millard Fillmore. n, Franklin Pierce. o, James Buchanan. p, Abraham Lincoln. q, Andrew Johnson. r, Ulysses S. Grant. s, Rutherford B. Hayes. t, James Garfield. u, Chester Arthur. v, Grover Cleveland. w, Benjamin Harrison. x, Peace and Friendship. y, William McKinley. z, Theodore Roosevelt. aa, William H. Taft. ab, Woodrow Wilson. ac, Warren G. Harding. ad, Calvin Coolidge. ae, Herbert Hoover. af, Franklin Delano Roosevelt. ag, Harry S. Truman. ah, Dwight D. Eisenhower. ai, John F. Kennedy. aj, Lyndon B. Johnson. ak, Richard Milhous Nixon. al, Rerald R. Ford. am, Jimmy Carter. an, Ronald Reagan. ao, Geroge Bush. ap, William Jefferson Clinton. aq, George W. Bush. ar, Presidential Seal. as, The White House.

2013, Apr. 9
1060	Sheet of 45	43.00	43.00
a.-as.	A375 46c Any single	.95	.95

Souvenir Sheet

"Ich Bin Ein Berliner" Speech, by Pres. John F. Kennedy, 50th Anniv. — A376

2013, June 29   *Perf. 13¼x13½*
1061	A376 $2 multi	4.00	4.00

British Steam Locomotives A377

No. 1062: a, No. 43 Calugareni. b, Beyer Peacock 2-6-4T. c, Adam Brown. d, Baldwin 4-6-0. e, 15A Class Garratt. f, Enterprise 1845. g, Grahamstown. h, Flying Scotsman. i, Black Hawthorn. j, LNER "Mallard" 4-6-2.

2013, July 3   *Perf. 13½*
1062	Sheet of 10	9.50	9.50
a.-j.	A377 46c Any single	.95	.95

Indian Headdresses A378

No. 1063 — Inscription: a, Cheyenne Headress. b, Flathead Headress. c, American Indian Headress. d, Shoshone Headress. e, Assiniboine Headress.

2013, Aug. 8
1063	Horiz. strip of 5	4.75	4.75
a.-e.	A378 46c Any single	.95	.95

"Headdress" is spelled incorrectly on Nos. 1063a-1063e.

Miniature Sheet

Landmark Events in American Civil Rights Movement — A379

No. 1064: a, Executive Order 9981, 1948. b, Brown v. Board of Education, 1954. c, Montgomery bus boycott, 1955. d, Little Rock Nine, 1957. e, Lunch counter sit-ins, 1960. f, Freedom Riders, 1961. g, Dr. Martin Luther King's "I Have a Dream" speech, 1963. h, Civil Rights Act, 1964. i, Selma March, 1965. j, Voting Rights Act, 1964.

2013, Aug. 28
1064	A379 46c Sheet of 10, #a-j	9.50	9.50

World War II Type of 2011
Miniature Sheet

No. 1065 — Inscriptions: a, Tenth Fleet: Overcoming the U-boat menace. b, U.S. Medical Service saving lives on the front lines. c, Allies invade Sicily: Patton's Seventh Army drives on Palermo. d, B-24 Liberators bomb Ploesti Oilfields. e, V-Mail — Letters from around the globe. f, Allied forces land at Salerno. g, Back the attack. h, Willie and Joe: A classic portrait of the American GI. i, Gold Star — Remembering those who died for a just cause — Freedom. j, U.S. Marines land on Tarawa Atoll.

2013, Sept. 9   *Perf. 13½*
1065	A342 46c Sheet of 10, #a-j, + 10 labels	9.50	9.50

Traditional Marshallese Children's Games — A380

No. 1066: a, Etobobo (4-1). b, Lejonjon (4-2). c, Lodidean (4-3). d, Didmakol (4-4).

2013, Sept. 27
1066	Horiz. strip of 4	4.00	4.00
a.-d.	A380 46c Any single	.95	.95

Miniature Sheet

Restarting of Space Shuttle Program, 25th Anniv. — A381

No. 1067: a, Launch of Space Shuttle Discovery mission STS-95 (6-1). b, Launch, diff. (6-2). c, Space Shuttle Discoverey and U.S. flag (6-3). d, Space Shuttle Discovery in orbit (6-4). e, Astronaut working outside of Space Shuttle Discovery (6-5). f, U.S. flag, Space Shuttle Discovery on launch pad, Astronaut John Glenn (6-6).

2013, Sept. 29
1007	A381 46c Sheet of 0, #a-f	5.75	5.75

World War II Aircraft — A382

No. 1068: a, F4U Corsair. b, C-46 Commando. c, A6M Zero. d, B-29 Superfortress. e, Bf 109. f, Ju 88. g, P-38 Lightning. h, A-26 Invader. i, B-17 Flying Fortress. j, P-51 Mustang. k, Il-2. l, P-40 Warhawk. m, C-47 Skytrain. n, B-24 Liberator. o, Spitfire. p, B-25 Mitchell. q, PBY Catalina. r, B-26 Marauder. s, TBM-1C Avenger. t, Lancaster. u, Yak-9. v, F6F Hellcat. w, C54 Skymaster. x, PB4Y-2 Privateer. y, P-47 Thunderbolt.

2013, Oct. 14
1068	Sheet of 25	24.00	24.00
a.-y.	A382 46c Any single	.95	.95

Christmas — A383

No. 1069: a, Annunciation (6-1). b, Journey to Bethlehem (6-2). c, Holy Family (6-3). d, Angel and shepherds (6-4). e, Magi (6-5). f, Nativity (6-6).

2013, Oct. 31   *Litho.*   *Perf. 13½*
1069	A383 46c Block of 6, #a-f	5.75	5.75

Miniature Sheet

Gettysburg Address, 150th
Anniv. — A384

No. 1070 — Soldiers and: a, U.S. Pres.
Abraham Lincoln, U.S. flag (34x25mm). b,
Confederate States Pres. Jefferson Davis,
Confederate flag (34x25mm). c, Gen. Ulysses
S. Grant, U.S. flag (34x25mm). d, Gen. Robert
E. Lee, Confederate flag (34x25mm). e, U.S.
and Confederate flags (48x50mm).

2013, Nov. 19   Litho.   Perf. 13½
1070 A384 46c Sheet of 5, #a-e   4.75 4.75

Souvenir Sheet

Declaration of Thanksgiving Day as
U.S. Federal Holiday, 150th
Anniv. — A385

Perf. 13¼x13¾
2013, Nov. 28   Litho.
1071 A385 $2 multi   4.00 4.00

Military Aircraft Diagrams — A386

No. 1072: a, B-24D Liberator. b, F-104
Starfighter. c, KC-135 Stratotanker. d, AV-8B
Harrier II. e, P40-Warhawk. f, F/A-18 Hornet.
g, P-38 Lightning. h, F-100 Super Sabre. i, P-
26 Peashooter. j, F-16 Fighting Falcon. k, TBD
Devastator. l, F-15 Eagle. m, C-130 Hercules.
n, F-105 Thunderchief. o, B-17 Flying
Fortress.

2014, Jan. 12   Litho.   Perf. 13½
1072 A386 46c Sheet of 15,
     #a-o   14.00 14.00
       See Nos. 1082, 1098.

Souvenir Sheet

Marshall Islands Postal Service
Authority, 30th Anniv. — A387

2014, Jan. 22   Litho.   Perf. 13¼x13½
1073 A387 $5.60 multi   11.50 11.50

Shells
A388

Reticulated helmet, New England neptune
and Calico scallop shells, with largest being:
34c, Reticulated helmet. 49c, New England
neptune. $1.15, Calico scallop.

2014, Jan. 26   Litho.   Perf. 11¼x10¼
1074 A388 34c multi   .70   .70
1075 A388 49c multi   1.00 1.00
1076 A388 $1.15 multi   2.40 2.40
     Nos. 1074-1076 (3)   4.10 4.10
    See Nos. 1083-1084, 1090-1094.

Miniature Sheet

New Year 2014 (Year of the
Horse) — A389

No. 1077 — Color of horse: a, Blue (4-1). b,
Red brown (4-2). c, Golden brown (4-3). d,
Green (4-4).

2014, Jan. 31   Litho.   Perf. 13½
1077 A389 $1.15 Sheet of 4, #a-
     d   9.25 9.25

Insects — A390

No. 1078: a, Garden insects, red panels
(10-1). b, Checkered beetle (10-2). c, Lacewing (10-3). d, Red admiral butterfly (10-4). e,
Honey bee (10-5). f, Leaf skeletonizer (10-6).
g, Drone fly (10-7). h, Bumblebee (10-8). i,
Lamellicorn beetle (10-9). j, Garden insects,
blue panels (10-10).

2014, Mar. 1   Litho.   Perf. 13½
1078   Block of 10   10.00 10.00
a.-j. A390 49c Any single   1.00 1.00

Castles in
Great
Britain — A391

No. 1079: a, Carrickfergus Castle, Northern
Ireland (4-1). b, Windsor Castle, England (4-
2). c, Caernarfon Castle, Wales (4-3). d, Edinburgh Castle, Scotland (4-4).

2014, Mar. 15   Litho.   Perf. 13½
1079   Horiz. strip of 4   9.75 9.75
a.-d. A391 $1.15 Any single   2.40 2.40

Miniature Sheet

Historical Flags of the United
States — A392

No. 1080: a, Continental flag (15-1). b, Ben-
nington flag (15-2). c, Forster flag (15-3). d,
Sons of Liberty flag (15-4). e, Brandywine flag
(15-5). f, Pierre L'Enfant flag (15-6). g, Indian
Peace flag (15-7). h, Star Spangled Banner
(15-8). i, Great Star flag (15-9). j, Fort Sumter
flag (15-10). k, Centennial flag (15-11). l, 29-
star flag (15-12). m, 38-star flag (15-13). n, 48-
star flag (15-14). o, 50-star flag (15-15).

2014, Apr. 4   Litho.   Perf. 13½
1080 A392 49c Sheet of 15,
     #a-o, + 9 la-
     bels   15.00 15.00

Miniature Sheet

Traditional Costumes of European
Countries — A393

No. 1081: a, Switzerland (20-1). b, Monaco
(20-2). c, Luxembourg (20-3). d, Spain (20-4).
e, Belgium (20-5). f, Denmark (20-6). g, Italy
(20-7). h, Ireland (20-8). i, Norway (20-9). j,
Great Britain (20-10). k, Portugal (20-11). l,
Turkey (20-12). m, France (20-13). n, Sweden
(20-14). o, Iceland (20-15). p, Germany (20-
16). q, Netherlands (20-17). r, Greece (20-18).
s, Liechtenstein (20-19). t, Finland (20-20).

2014, May 10   Litho.   Perf. 13½
1081 A393 49c Sheet of 20,
     #a-t   20.00 20.00

**Military Aircraft Diagrams Type of
2014**
Miniature Sheet

No. 1082: a, F-80 Shooting Star. b, SR-71
Blackbird. c, U-2. d, F-86 Sabre. e, F-14 Tomcat. f, F6F Hellcat. g, P-47 Thunderbolt. h, F-
117 Nighthawk. i, C-5 Galaxy. j, B-52
Stratofortress. k, F-4 Phantom II. l, P-51 Mustang. m, SBD Dauntless. n, B-1 Lancer. o,
PBY-5 Catalina.

2014, June 2   Litho.   Perf. 13½
1082 A386 49c Sheet of 15,
     #a-o   15.00 15.00

Shells Type of 2014

Various shells with largest being: 4c, Hawk-
winged conch. $19.99, Frilled dogwinkle.

Perf. 11¼x10¼
2014, June 16   Litho.
1083 A388   4c multi   .25   .25
1084 A388 $19.99 multi   40.00 40.00

Trees — A394

No. 1085: a, White willow (6-1). b, Poplar (6-
2). c, Oak (6-3). d, Birch (6-4). e, Maple (6-5).
f, Larch (6-6).

2014, July 7   Litho.   Perf. 13½
1085 A394 49c Block of 6, #a-f   6.00 6.00

Souvenir Sheet

Opening of Panama Canal,
Cent. — A395

2014, Aug. 15   Litho.   Perf. 13x13½
1086 A395 $5.60 multi   11.50 11.50

Miniature Sheet

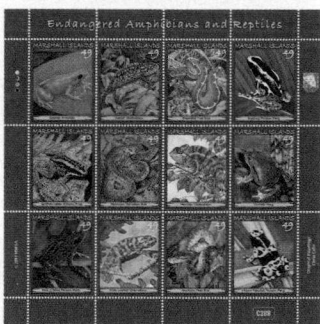

Amphibians and Reptiles — A396

No. 1087: a, Golden mantella frog (12-1). b,
Carpet chameleon (12-2). c, Emerald tree boa
(12-3). d, Dyeing poison dart frog (12-4). e,
Golfodulcean poison frog (12-5). f, Peruvian
rainbow boa (12-6). g, Panther chameleon
(12-7). h, Tomato frog (12-8). i, Red & blue
poison frog (12-9). j, Flap-necked chameleon
(12-10). k, Amazon tree boa (12-11). l, Yellow-
banded poison dart frog (12-12).

2014, Aug. 21   Litho.   Perf. 13½
1087 A396 49c Sheet of 12,
     #a-l   12.00 12.00

Souvenir Sheet

Writing of "The Star-Spangled Banner," 200th Anniv. — A397

2014, Sept. 3   Litho.   Perf. 13x13½
1088 A397 $5.60 multi   11.50 11.50

World War II Type of 2011
Miniature Sheet

No. 1089 — Inscriptions: a, Allied Forces retake New Guinea. b, 2,000 U.S. planes attack Berlin and 2 aircraft plants near city. c, Invasion is on! d, Airborne units spearhead ground attacks. e, Submarine warfare cripple Japan's shipping routes. f, Paris and Rome liberated by Allies. g, Operation Forager. h, Red Ball Express speeds vital supplies to allies. i, Battle for Leyte Gulf. j, Battle of the Bulge.

2014, Sept. 15   Litho.   Perf. 13½
1089 A342 49c Sheet of 10,
            #a-j, + 10 la-
            bels   10.00 10.00

Shells Type of 2014
Various shells.

Perf. 11¼x10¼

			Litho.
2014, Sept. 18			
1090	A388	$5.75 multi	11.50 11.50
1091	A388	$5.95 multi	12.00 12.00
1092	A388	$6.10 multi	12.50 12.50
1093	A388	$12.65 multi	25.50 25.50
1094	A388	$17.90 multi	36.00 36.00
	Nos. 1090-1094 (5)		97.50 97.50

Movie Monsters — A398

No. 1095: a, Count Dracula holding candle (10-1). b, Frankenstein's Monster near stairway (10-2). c, Phantom of the Opera without mask (10-3). d, The Mummy carrying woman (10-4). e, The Wolf Man crouching (10-5). f, Count Dracula at open window (10-6). g, Frankenstein's Monster in laboratory (10-7). h, Phantom of the Opera wearing mask (10-8). i, The Mummy and skull (10-9). j, The Wolf Man and wolf (10-10).

2014, Oct. 14   Litho.   Perf. 13½
1095 A398 49c Block of 10,
            #a-j   10.00 10.00

Christmas — A399

No. 1096: a, Singing angels (6-1). b, Shepherd with flock (6-2). c, Three Kings following star (6-3). d, Three Kings at manger (6-4). e, Mary and Baby Jesus (6-5). f, White doves (6-6).

2014, Oct. 10   Litho.   Perf. 13½
1096 A399 49c Block of 6, #a-f   6.00 6.00

Seahorses — A400

No. 1097: a, Horned seahorse (4-1). b, Lined seahorse (4-2). c, Lined seahorse, diff. (4-3). d, Lined seahorse, diff. (4-4).

2014, Oct. 20   Litho.   Perf. 13½
1097   Horiz. strip of 4   4.00 4.00
  a.-d. A400 49c Any single   1.00 1.00

Military Aircraft Diagrams Type of 2014
Miniature Sheet

No. 1098: a, Fokker D VII. b, J35 Draaken. c, Bf 109. d, Yak 9. e, MiG 29. f, A-10 Thunderbolt II. g, Me 262. h, B-2 Spirit. i, Spitfire. j, B-29 Superfortress. k, X-15. l, Lancaster. m, A6M Zero. n, F/A 22. o, J1 Monoplane.

2014, Oct. 28   Litho.   Perf. 13½
1098 A386 49c Sheet of 15,
            #a-o   15.00 15.00

A401

A402

A403

Space Adventure for Children
A404

2014, Nov. 7   Litho.   Perf. 13½
1099   Strip of 4   4.00 4.00
  a. A401 49c multi   1.00 1.00
  b. A402 49c multi   1.00 1.00
  c. A403 49c multi   1.00 1.00
  d. A404 49c multi   1.00 1.00

Flowers
A405

No. 1100: a, Six flowers including thistle at LL (10-1). b, Lily (10-2). c, Iris (10-3). d, Thistles (10-4). e, Rose (10-5). f, Pansy (10-6). g, Strawberries and blossom (10-7). h, Tulip (10-8). i, Three pansies (10-9). j, Five flowers and strawberry at bottom center (10-10).

2014, Nov. 18   Litho.   Perf. 13½
1100   Block of 10   10.00 10.00
  a.-j. A405 49c Any single   1.00 1.00

Greetings — A406

No. 1101: a, Happy birthday. b, Thinking of you. c, Love. d, Thank you. e, Best wishes. f, Congratulations.

2015, Jan. 5   Litho.   Perf. 13½
1101 A406 49c Block of 6, #a-f   6.00 6.00

Dinosaur Skeletons
A407

No. 1102: a, Triceratops. b, Stegosaurus. c, Protoceratops. d, Tyrannosaurus.

2015, Jan. 15   Litho.   Perf. 13½
1102   Horiz. strip of 4   2.80 2.80
  a.-d. A407 34c Any single   .70 .70

Reef Life Type of 1993
Miniature Sheet

No. 1103: a, Butterflyfish. b, Soldierfish. c, Damselfish. d, Filefish. e, Hawkfish. f, Surgeonfish. g, Parrotfish (75x33mm).

2015, Jan. 28   Litho.   Perf. 13½
1103   Sheet of 7   17.00 17.00
  a.-f. A79 $1 Any single   2.00 2.00
  g. A79 $2.50 multi   5.00 5.00

Berries — A408

No. 1104: a, Blueberries. b, Raspberries. c, Blackberries, raspberries, strawberries and blueberries. d, Strawberries. e, Blackberries.

2015, Feb. 14   Litho.   Perf. 13½
1104   Horiz. strip of 5   5.00 5.00
  a.-e. A408 49c Any single   1.00 1.00

Miniature Sheet

New Year 2015 (Year of the Ram) — A409

No. 1105 — Color of ram: a, Blue (4-1). b, Red brown (4-2). c, Yellow brown (4-3). d, Green (4-4).

2015, Feb. 19   Litho.   Perf. 13½
1105 A409 $1.15 Sheet of 4, #a-
            d   9.25 9.25

SEMI-POSTAL STAMPS

Operation Crossroads, Nuclear Testing at Bikini Atoll, 50th Anniv. — SP1

Designs: a, Evacuation of Bikinians. b, Navy preparations. c, Able. d, Baker. e, Ghost fleet. f, Effects on Bikinians.

1996, July 1   Litho.   Perf. 13½
B1   SP1 32c +8c #a.-f. + 6 la-
          bels   4.75 4.75

Surtax for the benefit of the people of Bikini.

AIR POST STAMPS

Audubon Type of 1985

1985, Feb. 15   Litho.   Perf. 14
C1   A11 44c Booby Gannet,
          vert.   .90 .90
C2   A11 44c Esquimaux Cur-
          lew, vert.   .90 .90
  a. Pair, #C1-C2   1.80 1.80

AMERIPEX Type of 1986

Designs: No. C3, Consolidated PBY-5A Catalina Amphibian. No. C4, Grumman SA-16 Albatross. No. C5, McDonnell Douglas DC-6B Super Cloudmaster. No. C6, Boeing 727-100.

1986, May 22   Litho.   Perf. 14
C3   A20 44c multicolored   .85 .85
C4   A20 44c multicolored   .85 .85
C5   A20 44c multicolored   .85 .85
C6   A20 44c multicolored   .85 .85
  a. Block of 4, #C3-C6   3.50 3.50

Operation Crossroads Type of 1986
Souvenir Sheet

1986, July 1   Litho.   Perf. 14
C7   A21 44c USS Saratoga   4.00 4.00

Statue of Liberty Cent., Intl. Peace Year — AP1

1986, Oct. 28   Litho.
C8   AP1 44c multicolored   1.00 .95

Natl. Girl Scout Movement, 20th Anniv. — AP2

1986, Dec. 8   Litho.
C9   AP2 44c Community ser-
          vice   .75 .75
C10 AP2 44c Salute   .75 .75
C11 AP2 44c Health care   .75 .75
C12 AP2 44c Learning skills   .75 .75
  a. Block of 4, #C9-C12   3.00 3.00

Girl Scout Movement in the US, 75th anniv. (1912-1987).

1987, Jan. 12   Litho.   Perf. 14

C13	AP3	44c	Wedge-tailed shearwater	.75	.75
C14	AP3	44c	Red-footed boo-by	.75	.75
C15	AP3	44c	Red-tailed tropic-bird	.75	.75
C16	AP3	44c	Great frigatebird	.75	.75
a.			Block of 4, #C13-C16	3.00	3.00

CAPEX '87
AP4

Last flight of Amelia Earhart: No. C17, Take-off at Lae, New Guinea, July 2, 1937. No. C18, USCG Itasca cutter at Howland Is. No. C19, Purported crash landing of the Electra at Mili Atoll. No. C20, Recovery of the Electra by the Koshu, a Japanese survey ship.

1987, June 15   Litho.   Perf. 14

C17	AP4	44c	multicolored	.75	.75
C18	AP4	44c	multicolored	.75	.75
C19	AP4	44c	multicolored	.75	.75
C20	AP4	44c	multicolored	.75	.75
a.			Block of 4, #C17-C20	3.00	3.00

Space Shuttle Type of 1988

1988, Dec. 23   Litho.   Perf. 14

C21	A38	45c	Astronaut, shuttle over Rongelap	.85	.85

Aircraft — AP5

1989, Apr. 24   Litho.   Perf. 14x14½

C22	AP5	12c	Dornier Do228	.25	.25
a.			Booklet pane of 10	3.00	—
C23	AP5	36c	Boeing 737	.75	.75
a.			Booklet pane of 10	8.00	—
C24	AP5	39c	Hawker Siddeley 748	.90	.90
a.			Booklet pane of 10	9.00	—
C25	AP5	45c	Boeing 727	1.00	1.00
a.			Booklet pane of 10	10.00	—
b.			Bklt. pane, 5 each 36c, 45c	8.75	—
			Nos. C22-C25 (4)	2.90	2.90

MARTINIQUE

ˌmär-tən-ˈēk

LOCATION — Island in the West Indies, southeast of Puerto Rico
GOVT. — French Colony
AREA — 385 sq. mi.
POP. — 261,595 (1946)
CAPITAL — Fort-de-France

Formerly a French colony, Martinique became an integral part of the Republic, acquiring the same status as the departments in metropolitan France, under a law effective Jan. 1, 1947.

100 Centimes = 1 Franc

Catalogue values for unused stamps in this country are for Never Hinged items, beginning with Scott 196 in the regular postage section, Scott C1 in the airpost section, and Scott J37 in the postage due section.

See France Nos. 1278 and 1508 for stamps inscribed "Martinique."

Stamps of French Colonies 1881-86 Surcharged in Black

Nos. 1, 7   No. 2

No. 3   No. 4

Nos. 5-6, 8   Nos. 9-20

1886-91   Unwmk.   Perf. 14x13½

1	A9	5 on 20c		65.00	55.00
a.		Double surcharge		750.00	750.00
2	A9	5c on 20c		15,000.	15,000.
3	A9	15c on 20c ('87)		275.00	240.00
a.		Inverted surcharge		2,350.	2,500.
4	A9	05c on 20c ('87)		100.00	100.00
a.		Inverted surcharge		1,500.	1,500.
b.		Se-tenant pair, #3-4		475.00	425.00
c.		Se-tenant pair, #3a-4a		4,750.	4,750.
5	A9	01 on 20c ('88)		20.00	19.00
a.		Inverted surcharge		350.00	350.00
6	A9	05 on 20c		16.00	13.00
7	A9	15 on 20c ('88)		200.00	180.00
c.		Inverted surcharge		700.00	750.00
8	A9	015 on 20c ('87)		60.00	65.00
a.		Inverted surcharge		875.00	825.00
9	A9	01c on 2c ('88)		4.75	3.25
a.		Double surcharge		475.00	475.00
10	A9	01c on 4c ('88)		15.00	4.75
11	A9	05c on 4c ('88)		1,500.	1,375.
12	A9	05c on 10c ('90)		120.00	72.50
a.		Slanting "5"		300.00	240.00
13	A9	05c on 20c ('88)		28.00	20.00
a.		Slanting "5"		150.00	120.00
b.		Inverted surcharge		425.00	375.00
14	A9	05c on 30c ('91)		35.00	28.00
a.		Slanting "5"		160.00	150.00
15	A9	05c on 35c ('91)		20.00	16.00
a.		Slanting "5"		160.00	150.00
b.		Inverted surcharge		325.00	300.00
16	A9	05c on 40c ('91)		65.00	47.50
a.		Slanting "5"		260.00	165.00
17	A9	15c on 4c ('88)		12,000.	11,000.
18	A9	15c on 20c ('87)		150.00	120.00
a.		Slanting "5"		500.00	425.00
b.		Double surcharge		700.00	700.00
19	A9	15c on 25c ('90)		32.50	20.00
a.		Slanting "5"		150.00	130.00
b.		Inverted surcharge		325.00	275.00
c.		Double surcharge		450.00	450.00
20	A9	15c on 75c ('91)		210.00	175.00
a.		Slanting "5"		550.00	450.00

French Colonies No. 47 Surcharged

1891

21	A9	01c on 2c brn, *buff*		11.00	11.00

French Colonies Nos. J5-J9 Surcharged

1891-92   Black Surcharge   Imperf.

22	D1	05c on 5c blk ('92)		17.50	17.00
a.		Slanting "5"		72.50	65.00
23	D1	05c on 15c blk		16.00	16.00
a.		Slanting "5"		72.50	65.00
24	D1	15c on 20c blk		20.00	16.00
a.		Inverted surcharge		300.00	300.00
b.		Double surcharge		300.00	300.00
25	D1	15c on 30c blk		20.00	16.00
a.		Inverted surcharge		300.00	300.00
b.		Slanting "5"		80.00	72.50
		Nos. 22-25 (4)		73.50	65.00

Red Surcharge

26	D1	05c on 10c blk		14.50	11.00
a.		Inverted surcharge		300.00	300.00
27	D1	05c on 15c blk		16.00	16.00
28	D1	05c on 20c blk		52.50	45.00
a.		Inverted surcharge		450.00	450.00
		Nos. 26-28 (3)		83.00	72.00

French Colonies No. 54 Surcharged in Black

j   k

1892   Perf. 14x13½

29	A9 (j)	05c on 25c		65.00	65.00
a.		Slanting "5"		300.00	300.00
30	A9 (j)	15c on 25c		36.00	36.00
a.		Slanting "5"		275.00	275.00
31	A9 (k)	05c on 25c		65.00	65.00
a.		"1882" instead of "1892"		675.00	600.00
b.		"95" instead of "05"		850.00	800.00
c.		Slanting "5"		300.00	300.00
32	A9 (k)	15c on 25c		32.50	32.50
a.		"1882" instead of "1892"		600.00	600.00
b.		Slanting "5"		160.00	160.00
		Nos. 29-32 (4)		198.50	198.50

Navigation and Commerce — A15

1892-1906   Typo.   Perf. 14x13½
"MARTINIQUE" Colony in Carmine or Blue

33	A15	1c blk, *lil bl*		1.50	1.40
a.		"MARTINIQUE" in blue		1,000.	1,000.
b.		"MARTINIQUE" omitted		5,500.	
34	A15	2c brn, *buff*		1.75	1.40
35	A15	4c claret, *lav*		2.00	1.50
36	A15	5c grn, *grnsh*		2.40	1.50
37	A15	5c yel grn ('99)		3.50	1.10
38	A15	10c blk, *lav*		11.00	2.00
39	A15	10c red ('99)		5.25	1.50
40	A15	15c blue, quadrille paper		42.50	8.00
41	A15	15c gray ('99)		13.50	2.10
42	A15	20c red, *grn*		20.00	10.00
43	A15	25c blk, *rose*		24.00	3.25
44	A15	25c blue ('99)		16.00	14.50
45	A15	30c brn, *bis*		36.00	19.00
46	A15	35c blk, *yel* ('06)		16.00	9.50
47	A15	40c red, *straw*		36.00	19.00
48	A15	50c car, *rose*		40.00	24.00
49	A15	50c brn, *az* ('99)		42.50	32.50
50	A15	75c dp vio, *org*		32.50	20.00
51	A15	1fr brnz grn, *straw*		32.50	21.00
52	A15	2fr vio, *rose* ('04)		92.50	75.00
53	A15	5fr lil, *lav* ('03)		110.00	95.00
		Nos. 33-53 (21)		581.40	363.25

Perf. 13½x14 stamps are counterfeits.
For surcharges see Nos. 54-61, 101-104.

Stamps of 1892-1903 Surcharged in Black

1904

*54	A15	10c on 30c brn, *bis*		14.50	14.50
a.		Double surcharge		525.00	525.00
b.		Inverted surcharge		1,600.	1,600.
55	A15	10c on 5fr lil, *lav*		16.00	16.00

Surcharged

56	A15	10c on 30c brn, *bis*		24.00	24.00
57	A15	10c on 40c red, *straw*		24.00	24.00
a.		Double surcharge		600.00	600.00
58	A15	10c on 50c car, *rose*		28.00	28.00
59	A15	10c on 75c dp vio, *org*		20.00	20.00
60	A15	10c on 1fr brnz grn, *straw*		24.00	24.00
a.		Double surcharge		350.00	350.00
61	A15	10c on 5fr lil, *lav*		200.00	200.00
		Nos. 54-61 (8)		350.50	350.50

Martinique Woman — A16   Girl Bearing Pineapple in Cane Field — A18

View of Fort-de-France — A17

1908-30   Typo.

62	A16	1c red brn & brn		.25	.25
63	A16	2c ol grn & brn		.30	.25
64	A16	4c vio brn & brn		.30	.30
65	A16	5c grn & brn		1.10	.40
66	A16	5c org & brn ('22)		.50	.40
67	A16	10c car & brn		1.10	.50
68	A16	10c bl grn & grn ('22)		.55	.40
69	A16	10c brn vio & rose ('25)		.55	.40
70	A16	15c brn vio & rose ('17)		.65	.40
71	A16	15c bl grn & gray grn ('25)		.50	.40
72	A16	15c dp bl & red org ('28)		1.60	1.60
73	A16	20c vio & brn		1.40	1.10
74	A17	25c bl & brn		2.25	1.10
75	A17	25c org & brn ('22)		.90	.55
76	A17	30c brn org & brn		2.25	1.10
77	A17	30c dl red & brn ('22)		.75	.65
78	A17	30c rose & ver ('24)		.55	.55
79	A17	30c ol brn & brn ('25)		.55	.55
80	A17	30c sl bl & bl grn ('27)		1.60	1.60
81	A17	35c vio & brn		.90	.65
a.		White chalky paper		4.50	2.75
82	A17	40c gray grn & brn		.90	.65
83	A17	45c dk brn & brn ('22)		.90	.65
a.		White chalky paper		2.00	1.60
84	A17	50c rose & brn		2.25	1.10
85	A17	50c bl & brn ('22)		1.40	1.30
86	A17	50c org & grn ('25)		.90	.40
87	A17	60c dk bl & lil rose ('25)		.75	.75
88	A17	65c vio & ol brn ('27)		2.00	2.00
89	A17	75c slate & brn		1.40	1.10
90	A17	75c ind & dk bl ('25)		.90	.90
91	A17	75c org brn & lt bl ('27)		2.75	2.75
92	A17	90c brn red & brt red ('30)		5.50	5.50
93	A18	1fr dl bl & brn		1.20	1.00
94	A18	1fr dk bl ('25)		1.00	.90
95	A18	1fr ver & ol grn ('27)		2.75	2.75
96	A18	1.10fr vio & dk brn ('28)		3.75	4.50
97	A18	1.50fr ind & ultra ('30)		5.50	5.50
98	A18	2fr gray & brn		4.50	2.00
99	A18	3fr red vio ('30)		9.50	9.50
100	A18	5fr org red & brn		10.50	8.00
		Nos. 62-100 (39)		76.90	64.40

For surcharges see Nos. 105-128, B1.

Nos. 41, 43, 47 and 53 Surcharged in Carmine or Black

1912, Aug.
Spacing between figures of surcharge 1.5mm (5c), 2mm (10c)

101	A15	5c on 15c gray (C)	1.00	1.00
102	A15	5c on 25c blk, *rose* (C)	1.50	1.50
103	A15	10c on 40c red, *straw*	2.40	2.40
104	A15	10c on 5fr lil, *lav*	3.00	3.00
		Nos. 101-104 (4)	7.90	7.90

Two spacings between the surcharged numerals are found on Nos. 101 to 104. For detailed listings, see the *Scott Classic Specialized Catalogue of Stamps and Covers.*

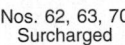

Nos. 62, 63, 70 Surcharged

1920, June 15

105	A16	5c on 1c	2.10	2.10
a.		Double surcharge	45.00	45.00
b.		Inverted surcharge	32.50	32.50
106	A16	10c on 2c	2.10	2.10
a.		Double surcharge	130.00	
b.		Inverted surcharge	45.00	45.00
c.		Double surcharge, one inverted	95.00	
107	A16	25c on 15c	2.25	2.25
a.		Double surcharge	55.00	55.00
b.		Inverted surcharge	55.00	55.00
c.		Double surcharge, one inverted	100.00	
d.		Pair, one stamp without surcharge	160.00	160.00
		Nos. 105-107 (3)	6.45	6.45

No. 70 Surcharged in Various Colors

1922, Dec.

108	A16	1c on 15c (Bk)	.50	.50
a.		Double surcharge	190.00	190.00
109	A16	2c on 15c (Bl)	.50	.50
110	A16	5c on 15c (R)	.65	.65
a.		Imperf., pair	260.00	
		Nos. 108-110 (3)	1.65	1.65

Types of 1908-30 Surcharged

1923-25

111	A17	60c on 75c bl & rose	.65	.65
112	A17	65c on 45c ol brn & brn ('25)	1.45	1.45
113	A17	85c on 75c blk & brn (R) ('25)	1.75	1.75
		Nos. 111-113 (3)	3.85	3.85

Nos. 63, 73, 76-77, 84-85 Surcharged in Brown

Surcharge is horiz. on Nos. 114-115, vert. reading up on Nos. 116, 119 and down on Nos. 117-118.

1924, Feb. 14

114	A16	1c on 2c	3.25	3.25
a.		Double surcharge	550.00	550.00
b.		Inverted surcharge	100.00	100.00
115	A16	5c on 20c	4.00	4.00
a.		Inverted surcharge	100.00	100.00
116	A17	15c on 30c (#76)	16.00	16.00
a.		Surcharge reading down	57.50	57.50
117	A17	15c on 30c (#77)	22.50	22.50
a.		Surcharge reading up	67.50	67.50

118	A17	25c on 50c (#84)	325.00	350.00
119	A17	25c on 50c (#85)	10.50	10.50
a.		Double surcharge	400.00	400.00
b.		Surcharge reading down	47.50	
		Nos. 114-119 (6)	381.25	406.25

Stamps and Types of 1908-30 Surcharged

1924-27

120	A16	25c on 15c brn vio & rose ('25)	.55	.55
121	A18	25c on 2fr gray & brn	.50	.50
122	A18	25c on 5fr org red & brn (Bl)	2.10	1.75
123	A17	90c on 75c brn red & red ('27)	3.75	2.75
124	A18	1.25fr on 1fr dk bl ('26)	1.10	1.00
125	A18	1.50fr on 1fr dk bl & ultra ('27)	2.00	1.10
126	A18	3fr on 5fr dl red & grn ('27)	3.00	3.00
127	A18	10fr on 5fr dl grn & dp red ('27)	12.00	12.00
128	A18	20fr on 5fr org brn & red vio ('27)	18.50	17.50
		Nos. 120-128 (9)	43.50	40.15

Common Design Types pictured following the introduction.

Colonial Exposition Issue
Common Design Types
1931, Apr. 13   Engr.   Perf. 12½
Name of Country in Black

129	CD70	40c deep green	5.25	5.25
130	CD71	50c violet	5.25	5.25
131	CD72	90c red orange	5.25	5.25
132	CD73	1.50fr dull blue	5.25	5.25
		Nos. 129-132 (4)	21.00	21.00

Village of Basse-Pointe — A19

Government Palace, Fort-de-France — A20

Martinique Women A21

1933-40   Photo.   Perf. 13½

133	A19	1c red, *pink*	.25	.25
134	A20	2c dull blue	.25	.25
135	A20	3c sepia ('40)	.35	.35
136	A20	4c olive grn	.25	.25
137	A20	5c dp rose	.35	.35
138	A19	10c blk, *pink*	.35	.35
139	A20	15c blk, *org*	.35	.35
140	A21	20c org brn	.35	.35
141	A19	25c brn vio	.35	.35
142	A20	30c green	.50	.50
143	A20	30c lt ultra ('40)	.40	.40
144	A21	35c dl grn ('38)	1.00	.90
145	A21	40c olive brn	.65	.50
146	A20	45c dk brn	2.00	1.90
147	A20	45c grn ('40)	.65	.65
148	A20	50c red	.50	.30
149	A19	55c brn red ('38)	1.30	1.00
150	A19	60c lt bl ('40)	.95	.95
151	A21	65c red, *grn*	.50	.50
152	A19	70c brt red vio ('40)	.75	.75
153	A19	75c dk brn	1.10	.90
154	A20	80c vio ('38)	.75	.65
155	A19	90c carmine	1.90	1.75

156	A19	90c brt red vio ('39)	.95	.95
157	A20	1fr blk, *grn*	1.90	1.40
158	A20	1fr rose red ('38)	.75	.65
159	A21	1.25fr dk vio	.80	.80
160	A21	1.25fr dp rose ('39)	.75	.75
161	A19	1.40fr lt ultra ('40)	.80	.80
162	A21	1.50fr dp bl	.65	.55
163	A20	1.60fr chnt ('40)	.80	.80
164	A21	1.75fr ol grn	9.50	5.25
165	A21	1.75fr dp bl ('38)	.75	.75
166	A19	2fr dk bl, *grn*	.50	.40
167	A21	2.25fr blue ('39)	.75	.75
168	A19	2.50fr sepia ('40)	.95	.95
169	A21	3fr brn vio	.65	.60
170	A21	5fr red, *pink*	1.30	1.10
171	A19	10fr dk bl, *bl*	1.10	.80
172	A20	20fr red, *yel*	1.35	.95
		Nos. 133-172 (40)	40.05	32.75

For surcharges see Nos. 190-195.
For type A20 without "RF," see Nos. 189A-189E.

Landing of Bélain d'Esnambuc — A22

Freed Slaves Paying Homage to Victor Schoelcher A23

1935, Oct. 22   Engr.   Perf. 13

173	A22	40c blk brn	3.25	3.25
174	A22	50c dl red	3.25	3.25
175	A22	1.50fr ultra	12.00	12.00
176	A23	1.75fr lil rose	12.00	12.00
177	A23	5fr brown	12.00	12.00
a.		5fr ultramarine (error)	950.00	
178	A23	10fr blue grn	9.50	9.50
		Nos. 173-178 (6)	52.00	52.00

Tercentenary of French possessions in the West Indies.

Colonial Arts Exhibition Issue
Common Design Type
Souvenir Sheet
1937   Imperf.

179	CD74	3fr brt grn	8.75	10.50
a.		"MARTINIQUE" omitted	3,100.	
b.		Inscriptions inverted	2,200.	

Paris International Exposition Issue
Common Design Types
1937, Apr. 15   Perf. 13

180	CD74	20c dp vio	2.10	2.10
181	CD75	30c dk grn	1.75	1.75
182	CD76	40c car rose	1.75	1.75
183	CD77	50c dk brn & blk	1.60	1.60
184	CD78	90c red	2.00	2.00
185	CD79	1.50fr ultra	2.00	2.00
		Nos. 180-185 (6)	11.20	11.20

New York World's Fair Issue
Common Design Type
1939, May 10   Perf. 12½x12

186	CD82	1.25fr car lake	1.10	1.10
187	CD82	2.25fr ultra	1.25	1.25

View of Fort-de-France and Marshal Pétain — A23a

1941   Engr.   Perf. 12½x12

188	A23a	1fr dull lilac	.80	
189	A23a	2.50fr blue	.80	

Nos. 188-189 were issued by the Vichy government in France, but were not placed on sale in Martinique.
For surcharges, see Nos. B10A-B10B.

Types of 1933-40 without "RF"
1942-44   Photo.   Perf. 13½

189A	A20	3c sepia	.50
189B	A20	15c blk, *org*	.55
189C	A20	30c yel green	.55
189D	A20	50c red	1.40
189E	A20	1.50fr dp bl	.65
		Nos. 189A-189E (5)	3.65

Nos. 189A-189E were issued by the Vichy government in France, but were not placed on sale in Martinique.

Nos. 134, 135, 136 and 151 Surcharged in Red, Black or Blue

1945   Perf. 13½, 13x13½

190	A20	1fr on 2c dl bl (R)	.65	.65
191	A19	2fr on 4c ol grn	.65	.65
192	A20	3fr on 2c dl bl (R)	.80	.80
193	A21	5fr on 65c red, *grn*	1.40	1.40
194	A21	10fr on 65c red, *grn*	1.50	1.50
195	A20	20fr on 3c sepia (Bl)	1.50	1.50
		Nos. 190-195 (6)	6.50	6.50

> **Catalogue values for unused stamps in this section, from this point to the end of the section, are for Never Hinged items.**

Eboue Issue
Common Design Type
1945   Engr.   Perf. 13

196	CD91	2fr black	.75	.55
197	CD91	25fr Prussian green	1.30	1.00

Victor Schoelcher and View of Town of Schoelcher A24

1945   Unwmk.   Litho.   Perf. 11½

198	A24	10c dp bl vio & ultra	.35	.25
199	A24	30c dk org brn & lt org brn	.35	.25
200	A24	40c grnsh bl & pale bl	.40	.35
201	A24	50c car brn & rose lil	.40	.35
202	A24	60c org yel & yel	.40	.35
203	A24	70c brn & pale brn	.40	.35
204	A24	80c lt bl grn & pale grn	.40	.35
205	A24	1fr bl & lt bl	.40	.35
206	A24	1.20fr rose vio & rose lil	.40	.35
207	A24	1.50fr red org & org	.40	.35
208	A24	2fr blk & gray	.40	.35
209	A24	2.40fr red & pink	1.75	1.00
210	A24	3fr pink & pale pink	.75	.50
211	A24	4fr ultra & lt ultra	.95	.50
212	A24	4.50fr yel grn & lt grn	1.10	.50
213	A24	5fr org brn & lt org brn	.95	.50
214	A24	10fr dk vio & lil	1.10	.65
215	A24	15fr rose car & lil rose	1.50	.75
216	A24	20fr ol grn & lt ol grn	2.25	1.25
		Nos. 198-216 (19)	14.65	9.30

Martinique Girl A25

Mountains A30

Cliffs
A26

Gathering
Sugar
Cane
A27

Mount
Pelée
A28

Tropical
Fruit — A29

1947, June 2   Engr.   Perf. 13

217	A25	10c red brown	.50	.25
218	A25	30c deep blue	.50	.40
219	A25	50c olive brown	.50	.40
220	A26	60c dark green	.55	.50
221	A26	1fr red brown	.55	.35
222	A26	1.50fr purple	.60	.50
223	A27	2fr blue green	1.10	.75
224	A27	2.50fr blk brn	1.10	.65
225	A27	3fr deep blue	1.10	.65
226	A28	4fr dk brown	1.00	.65
227	A28	5fr dark green	1.10	.65
228	A28	6fr lilac rose	1.00	.65
229	A29	10fr indigo	1.75	1.25
230	A29	15fr red brown	1.90	1.25
231	A29	20fr blk brown	2.50	1.50
232	A30	25fr violet	2.50	1.60
233	A30	40fr blue green	3.00	2.00
	Nos. 217-233 (17)		21.25	14.00

SEMI-POSTAL STAMPS

Regular Issue of
1908 Surcharged in
Red

Perf. 13½x14

1915, May 15   Unwmk.

B1	A16	10c + 5c car & brn	2.75	2.00
	Never hinged		4.00	

Curie Issue
Common Design Type

1938, Oct. 24   Perf. 13

B2	CD80	1.75fr + 50c brt ul-tra	13.00	13.00
	Never hinged		17.50	

French Revolution Issue
Common Design Type

Photo.; Name & Value Typo. in Black

1939, July 5

B3	CD83	45c + 25c grn	10.50	10.50
	Never hinged		15.00	
B4	CD83	70c + 30c brn	10.50	10.50
	Never hinged		15.00	
B5	CD83	90c + 35c red org	10.50	10.50
	Never hinged		15.00	
B6	CD83	1.25fr + 1fr rose pink	10.50	10.50
	Never hinged		15.00	
B7	CD83	2.25fr + 2fr blue	10.50	10.50
	Never hinged		15.00	
	Nos. B3-B7 (5)		52.50	52.50

Common Design Type and

Colonial
Infantry
with
Machine
Gun
SP1

Naval
Rifleman
SP2

1941   Photo.   Perf. 13½

B8	SP1	1fr + 1fr red	1.25
B9	CD86	1.50fr + 3fr maroon	1.40
B10	SP2	2.50fr + 1fr blue	1.40
	Nos. B8-B10 (3)		4.05

Nos. B8-B10 were issued by the Vichy government in France, but were not placed on sale in Martinique.

Nos. 188-
189 Srchd.
in Black or
Red

1944   Engr.   Perf. 12½x12

B10A	50c + 1.50fr on 2.50fr blue (R)		.95
B10B	+ 2.50fr on 1fr dull lilac		1.00

Colonial Development Fund.
Nos. B10A-B10B were issued by the Vichy government in France, but were not placed on sale in Martinique.

Red Cross Issue
Common Design Type

1944   Perf. 14½x14

B11	CD90	5fr + 20fr dark green	1.20	1.20

The surtax was for the French Red Cross and national relief.

AIR POST STAMPS

Catalogue values for unused stamps in this section are for Never Hinged items.

Common Design Type
1945 Unwmk. Photo. Perf. 14½x14

C1	CD87	50fr dark green	1.25	.80
C2	CD87	100fr plum	1.75	.80

Two other values, 8.50fr orange and 18fr red brown, were prepared but not issued. Value, $210 each.

Victory Issue
Common Design Type

1946, May 8   Engr.   Perf. 12½

C3	CD92	8fr indigo	1.30	1.00

European victory of the Allied Nations in WWII.

Chad to Rhine Issue
Common Design Types

1946, June 6

C4	CD93	5fr orange	1.00	.90
C5	CD94	10fr slate grn	1.40	1.10
C6	CD95	15fr carmine	1.40	1.20
C7	CD96	20fr chocolate	1.40	1.20
C8	CD97	25fr deep blue	1.75	1.40
C9	CD98	50fr gray blk	1.90	1.50
	Nos. C4-C9 (6)		8.85	7.30

Seaplane and Beach Scene — AP1

Plane over Tropic
Shore — AP2

Albatross — AP3

1947, June 2   Perf. 13

C10	AP1	50fr dk brn vio	6.50	2.75
C11	AP2	100fr dk bl grn	8.00	3.75
C12	AP3	200fr violet	45.00	25.00
	Nos. C10-C12 (3)		59.50	31.50

AIR POST SEMI-POSTAL STAMPS

Nurse with Mother & Child — SPAP1

Unwmk.
1942, June 22   Engr.   Perf. 13

CB1	SPAP1	1.50fr + 3.50fr green		.90
CB2	SPAP1	2fr + 6fr brn & red		.90

Native children's welfare fund.
Nos. CB1-CB2 were issued by the Vichy government in France, but were not placed on sale in Martinique.

Colonial Education Fund
Common Design Type

1942, June 22

CB3	CD86a	1.20fr + 1.80fr blue & red		1.00

No. CB3 was issued by the Vichy government in France, but was not placed on sale in Martinique.

POSTAGE DUE STAMPS

The set of 14 French Colonies postage due stamps (Nos. J1-J14) overprinted "MARTINIQUE" diagonally in red in 1887 was not an official issue.

Postage Due Stamps of
France, 1893-1926
Overprinted

1927, Oct. 10   Perf. 14x13½

J15	D2	5c light blue	1.75	1.75
J16	D2	10c brown	2.10	2.00
J17	D2	20c olive green	2.10	2.00
J18	D2	25c rose	2.75	2.60
J19	D2	30c red	3.75	3.50
J20	D2	45c green	5.25	5.00
J21	D2	50c brn violet	6.50	6.00
J22	D2	60c blue green	6.50	6.00
J23	D2	1fr red brown	8.75	8.25
J24	D2	2fr bright vio	12.00	11.00
J25	D2	3fr magenta	13.00	12.00
	Nos. J15-J25 (11)		64.45	60.10

Tropical Fruit — D3

1933, Feb. 15   Photo.   Perf. 13½

J26	D3	5c dk bl, *green*	.50	.50
J27	D3	10c orange brown	.50	.50
J28	D3	20c dk blue	.95	.95
J29	D3	25c red, *pink*	1.40	1.40
J30	D3	30c dk vio	1.40	1.40
J31	D3	45c red, *yel*	1.10	1.10
J32	D3	50c dk brn	1.75	1.75
J33	D3	60c dl grn	1.75	1.75
J34	D3	1fr blk, *org*	1.75	1.75
J35	D3	2fr dp rose	1.75	1.75
J36	D3	3fr dk blue, *bl*	1.75	1.75
	Nos. J26-J36 (11)		14.60	14.60

Type of 1933 Without "RF"
1943

J36A	D3	10c orange brown	.35
J36B	D3	20c dk blue	.35
J36C	D3	25c red, *pink*	.50
J36D	D3	30c dk vio	.50
	Nos. J36A-J36D (4)		1.70

Nos. J36A-J36D were issued by the Vichy government in France, but were not placed on sale in Martinique.

Catalogue values for unused stamps in this section, from this point to the end of the section, are for Never Hinged items.

Map — D4

1947, June 2   Engr.   Perf. 14x13

J37	D4	10c ultra	.40	.30
J38	D4	30c brt bl grn	.40	.30
J39	D4	50c slate gray	.40	.30
J40	D4	1fr org red	.40	.30
J41	D4	2fr dk vio brn	.90	.75
J42	D4	3fr lilac rose	.95	.80
J43	D4	4fr dk brn	.95	.95
J44	D4	5fr red	1.20	.95
J45	D4	10fr black	2.10	1.60
J46	D4	20fr olive grn	2.40	1.75
	Nos. J37-J46 (10)		10.10	8.00

PARCEL POST STAMP

Postage Due Stamp of
French Colonies
Surcharged in Black

1903, Oct.   Unwmk.   Imperf.

Q1	D1	5fr on 60c brn, buff	550.00	675.00
a.	Inverted surcharge		875.00	950.00

MAURITANIA

mor-ə-ta-nē-ə

LOCATION — Northwestern Africa, bordering on the Atlantic Ocean
GOVT. — Republic
AREA — 398,000 sq. mi.
POP. — 2,581,738 (1999 est.)
CAPITAL — Nouakchott

The Islamic Republic of Mauritania was proclaimed Nov. 28, 1958.
Stamps of French West Africa were used in the period between the issues of the colony and the republic.

100 Centimes = 1 Franc
Ouguiya ("um") (1973)

Catalogue values for unused stamps in this country are for Never Hinged items, beginning with Scott 114 in the regular postage section, Scott B9 in the semipostal section, Scott C6 in the airpost section, Scott J19 in the postage due section, and Scott O1 in the official section.

See French West Africa No. 65 for additional stamp inscribed "Mauritanie" and "Afrique Occidentale Francaise."

General Louis Faidherbe A1

Oil Palms — A2

Dr. Noel Eugène Ballay A3

Perf. 14x13½

			Typo.		Unwmk.

1906-07 Typo. Unwmk.
"Mauritanie" in Red or Blue

1	A1	1c slate	.70	.70
2	A1	2c chocolate	2.10	2.10
3	A1	4c choc, *gray bl*	2.75	2.75
4	A1	5c green	1.40	1.40
5	A1	10c carmine (B)	14.00	7.00
7	A2	20c black, *azure*	27.50	17.50
8	A2	25c blue, *pnksh*	10.00	7.00
9	A2	30c choc, *pnksh*	105.00	62.50
10	A2	35c black, *yellow*	10.00	7.00
11	A2	40c car, *az* (B)	10.00	10.00
12	A2	45c choc, *grnsh* ('07)	10.00	10.00
13	A2	50c deep violet	10.00	7.00
14	A2	75c blue, *org*	10.00	10.00
15	A3	1fr black, *azure*	27.50	27.50
16	A3	2fr blue, *pink*	55.00	55.00
17	A3	5fr car, *straw* (B)	140.00	150.00
		Nos. 1-17 (16)	435.95	377.45

Crossing Desert A4

1913-38

18	A4	1c brn vio & brn	.30	.55
19	A4	2c black & blue	.30	.55
20	A4	4c violet & blk	.30	.55

21	A4	5c yel grn & bl grn	1.00	.70
a.		Chalky paper	2.10	1.40
22	A4	5c brn vio & rose ('22)	.35	.35
23	A4	10c rose & red org	2.50	1.75
a.		Chalky paper	3.50	2.50
24	A4	10c yel grn & bl grn ('22)	.35	.70
25	A4	10c lil rose, *bluish* ('25)	.70	1.00
26	A4	15c dk brn & blk ('17)	.70	.70
a.		Chalky paper	1.00	1.00
27	A4	20c bis brn & org	.70	.70
28	A4	25c blue & vio	1.40	1.00
29	A4	25c grn & rose ('22)	.35	.35
30	A4	30c bl grn & rose	1.40	1.50
31	A4	30c rose & red org ('22)	1.75	2.10
32	A4	30c black & yel ('26)	.35	.35
33	A4	30c bl grn & yel grn ('28)	1.40	1.40
34	A4	35c brown & vio ('38)	.70	.75
35	A4	35c dp grn & lt grn	1.40	1.40
36	A4	40c gray & bl grn	2.75	2.50
37	A4	45c org & bis brn	1.40	1.75
38	A4	50c brn vio & rose	1.00	1.40
39	A4	50c dk bl & ultra ('22)	.70	.70
40	A4	50c gray grn & dp bl ('26)	.35	.70
41	A4	60c vio, *pnksh* ('25)	.70	1.00
42	A4	65c yel brn & lt bl	1.00	1.75
43	A4	75c ultra & brown	1.00	1.40
44	A4	85c myr grn & lt brn ('26)	1.40	1.75
45	A4	90c brn red & rose ('30)	2.10	2.10
46	A4	1fr rose & black	1.00	1.40
47	A4	1.10fr vio & ver ('28)	10.00	14.00
48	A4	1.25fr dk bl & blk brn ('33)	2.10	2.50
49	A4	1.50fr lt bl & dp bl ('30)	1.40	1.40
50	A4	1.75fr bl grn & brn red ('33)	2.10	2.50
51	A4	1.75fr dk bl & ultra ('38)	2.10	2.10
52	A4	2fr red org & vio	1.75	2.10
53	A4	3fr red violet ('30)	2.10	2.10
54	A4	5fr violet & blue	3.00	3.75
		Nos. 18-54 (37)	53.90	63.30

Stamp and Type of 1913-38 Srchd.

1922-25

55	A4	60c on 75c violet, *pnksh*	1.00	1.40
56	A4	65c on 15c dk brn & blk ('25)	1.75	2.10
57	A4	85c on 75c ultra & brn ('25)	1.75	2.10
		Nos. 55-57 (3)	4.50	5.60

Type of 1913-38 Srchd.

1924-27

58	A4	25c on 2fr red org & vio	1.00	1.40
59	A4	90c on 75c brn red & cer ('27)	2.10	2.75
60	A4	1.25fr on 1fr dk bl & ultra ('26)	.70	.70
61	A4	1.50fr on 1fr bl & dp bl ('27)	1.40	1.75
62	A4	3fr on 5fr ol brn & red vio ('27)	7.00	7.00
63	A4	10fr on 5fr mag & bl grn ('27)	7.00	7.75
64	A4	20fr on 5fr bl vio & dp org ('27)	7.00	8.00
		Nos. 58-64 (7)	26.20	29.35

Common Design Types pictured following the introduction.

Colonial Exposition Issue
Common Design Types
Engr.; Name of Country Typo. in Black

1931, Apr. 13   Perf. 12½

65	CD70	40c deep green	7.00	7.00
66	CD71	50c violet	5.00	5.00
67	CD72	90c red orange	5.00	5.00
68	CD73	1.50fr dull blue	5.00	5.00
		Nos. 65-68 (4)	22.00	22.00

Paris International Exposition Issue
Common Design Types

1937, Apr. 15   Perf. 13

69	CD74	20c deep violet	1.75	1.75
70	CD75	30c dark green	1.75	1.75
71	CD76	40c carmine rose	2.10	2.10
72	CD77	50c dk brn & blk	1.40	1.40
73	CD78	90c red	1.40	1.40
74	CD79	1.50fr ultra	2.10	2.10
		Nos. 69-74 (6)	10.50	10.50

Colonial Arts Exhibition Issue
Common Design Type
Souvenir Sheet

1937   Imperf.

75	CD76	3fr dark blue	10.00	14.00

Camel Rider — A5   Mauri Couple — A8

Mauris on Camels A6

Family Before Tent — A7

1938-40   Perf. 13

76	A5	2c violet blk	.25	.25
77	A5	3c dp ultra	.25	.25
78	A5	4c rose violet	.30	.30
79	A5	5c orange red	.30	.30
80	A5	10c brown car	.35	.35
81	A5	15c dk violet	.35	.35
82	A6	20c red	.35	.35
83	A6	25c deep ultra	.35	.35
84	A6	30c deep brown	.25	.25
85	A6	35c Prus green	.35	.70
86	A6	40c rose car ('40)	.35	.35
87	A6	45c Prus grn ('40)	.35	.35
88	A6	50c purple	.35	.50
89	A7	55c rose violet	.70	1.00
90	A7	60c violet ('40)	.35	.35
91	A7	65c deep green	.70	1.00
92	A7	70c red ('40)	.70	.70
93	A7	80c deep blue	1.40	1.40
94	A7	90c rose violet ('39)	.70	.70
95	A7	1fr red	2.75	2.10
96	A7	1fr dp green ('40)	.70	1.00
97	A7	1.25fr rose car ('39)	1.40	1.40
98	A7	1.40fr dp blue ('40)	.70	.70
99	A7	1.50fr violet	.70	1.00
99A	A7	1.50fr red brn ('40)	110.00	
100	A7	1.60fr black brn ('40)	1.75	1.75
101	A8	1.75fr deep ultra	1.40	1.40
102	A8	2fr rose violet	.35	1.00
103	A8	2.25fr dull violet ('39)	.70	.70
104	A8	2.50fr black brn ('40)	1.40	1.40
105	A8	3fr deep green	.35	.90
106	A8	5fr scarlet	.70	1.00
107	A8	10fr deep brown	1.75	1.90
108	A8	20fr brown car	2.10	2.75
		Nos. 76-108 (34)	135.45	28.80

Nos. 91 and 109 surcharged with new values are listed under French West Africa.
For surcharges see Nos. B9-B12.

Caillie Issue
Common Design Type

1939, Apr. 5   Engr.   Perf. 12½x12

109	CD81	90c org brn & org	.35	1.00
110	CD81	2fr brt violet	.35	1.40
111	CD81	2.25fr ultra & dk bl	.35	1.40
		Nos. 109-111 (3)	1.05	3.80

New York World's Fair Issue
Common Design Type

1939, May 10

112	CD82	1.25fr carmine lake	.70	1.40
113	CD82	2.25fr ultra	.70	1.40

Catalogue values for unused stamps in this section, from this point to the end of the section, are for Never Hinged items.

Caravan and Marshal Pétain A9

1941

114	A9	1fr green	.80	1.25
115	A9	2.50fr deep blue	.80	1.25

For surcharges, see Nos. B15A-B15B.

Types of 1938-40 Without "RF"

1943-44

115A	A5	10c brown car	.70	
115B	A5	15c dk violet	1.40	
115C	A6	40c rose car	1.75	
115D	A6	50c purple	1.75	
115E	A7	60c violet	1.75	
115F	A7	1fr dp green	1.75	
		Nos. 115A-115F (6)	9.10	

Nos. 115A-115F were issued by the Vichy government in France, but were not placed on sale in Mauritania.

Islamic Republic

Camel and Hands Raising Flag — A10

Unwmk.

1960, Jan. 20   Engr.   Perf. 13
116 A10 25fr multi, *pink*   .60   .35

Issued to commemorate the proclamation of the Islamic Republic of Mauritania.

Imperforates
Most Mauritania stamps from 1960 onward exist imperforate in issued and trial colors, and also in small presentation sheets in issued colors.

C.C.T.A. Issue
Common Design Type

1960, May 16
117 CD106 25fr bluish grn & ultra   .75   .40

Flag and Map — A11

1960, Dec. 15   Engr.   Perf. 13
118 A11 25fr org brn, emer & sepia   .60   .30

Proclamation of independence, Nov. 28, 1960.

Pastoral
Well — A12

Scimitar-horned
Oryx — A15

Spotted
Hyena
A13

Ore Train
and Camel
Riders
A14

Designs: 50c, 1fr, Well. 2fr, Date harvesting. 3fr, Aoudad. 4fr, Fennecs. 5fr, Millet harvesting. 10fr, Shoemaker. 15fr, Fishing boats. 20fr, Nomad school. 25fr, 30fr, Seated dance. No. 130, Religious student. 60fr, Metalworker.

1960-62   Unwmk.   Perf. 13
119	A12	50c mag, yel & brn ('61)	.25	.25
120	A12	1fr brn, yel brn & grn	.25	.25
121	A12	2fr dk brn, bl & grn	.25	.25
122	A13	3fr bl grn, red brn & gray ('61)	.40	.25
123	A13	4fr yel grn & ocher ('61)	.40	.25
124	A12	5fr red, dk brn & yel brn	.35	.25
125	A14	10fr dk bl & org	.40	.25
126	A14	15fr ver, dk brn, grn & bl	.50	.25
127	A14	20fr grn, sl grn & red brn	.50	.25
128	A12	25fr ultra & gray grn ('61)	.65	.25
129	A12	30fr lil, bis & indigo	.65	.25
130	A12	50fr org brn & grn	1.10	.40
131	A14	50fr red brn, bl & ol ('62)	3.00	.80
132	A12	60fr grn, cl & pur	2.00	.40
133	A15	85fr bl, brn & blk ('61)	4.75	1.90
	Nos. 119-133 (15)		15.45	6.25

An overprint, "Jeux Olympiques / Rome 1960 / Tokyo 1964," the 5-ring Olympic emblem and a 75fr surcharge were applied to Nos. 126-127 in 1962. Two overprint types, varying in size. Values, set: small overprint, $20; large overprint, $22.50.

An overprint, "Aide aux Rèfugiès" with uprooted oak emblem, was applied in 1962 to No. 132 and to pink-paper printings of Nos. 129-130. Two types: type 1, 26 leaves on tree; type 2, 37 leaves on tree. Values, set: type 1, $24; type 2, $8.

Other overprints, applied to airmail stamps, are noted after No. C16.

1963, July 6

Designs: 50c, Striped hyena. 1.50fr, Cheetah. 2fr, Guinea baboons. 5fr, Dromedaries. 10fr, Leopard. 15fr, Bongo antelopes. 20fr, Aardvark. 25fr, Patas monkeys. 30fr, Crested porcupine. 50fr, Dorcas gazelle. 60fr, Common chameleon.

134	A15	50c sl grn, blk & org brn	.25	.25
135	A13	1fr ultra, blk & yel	.25	.25
136	A15	1.50fr ol grn, brn & bis	.35	.25
137	A13	2fr dk brn, grn & dp org	.30	.25
138	A15	5fr brn, ultra & bis	.35	.25
139	A13	10fr blk & bis	.75	.25
140	A13	15fr vio bl & red brn	.75	.25
141	A13	20fr dk red brn, dk bl & bis	.85	.30
142	A15	25fr brt grn, red brn & ol bis	1.25	.30
143	A13	30fr dk brn, dk bl & ol bis	2.40	.30
144	A15	50fr grn, ocher & brn	3.00	.90
145	A13	60fr dk bl, emer & ocher	3.75	1.25
	Nos. 134-145 (12)		14.25	4.80

UN Headquarters, New York, and
View of Nouakchott — A15a

1962, June 1   Engr.   Perf. 13
167	A15a	15fr blk, ultra & cop red	.30	.30
168	A15a	25fr cop red, sl grn & ultra	.45	.35
169	A15a	85fr dk bl, dl pur & cop red	1.25	1.10
	Nos. 167-169 (3)		2.00	1.75

Mauritania's admission to the UN.

African-Malagasy Union Issue
Common Design Type
1962, Sept. 8   Photo.   Perf. 12½x12
170 CD110 30fr multi   .75 .50

Organization Emblem and View of
Nouakchott — A16

1962, Oct. 15   Perf. 12½
171 A16 30fr dk red brn, ultra & brt grn   .70 .50

8th Conf. of the Organization to Fight Endemic Diseases, Nouakchott, Oct. 15-18.

Map, Mechanized and Manual Farm
Work — A17

1962, Nov. 28   Engr.   Perf. 13
172 A17 30fr blk, grn & vio brn   .75 .40

2nd anniversary of independence.

People in European and Mauritanian
Clothes — A18

1962, Dec. 24   Unwmk.
173 A18 25fr multicolored   .40 .25

First anniversary of Congress for Unity.

Weather and WMO
Symbols — A20

1964, Mar. 23   Unwmk.   Perf. 13
175 A20 85fr dk brn, dk bl & org 1.50 .85

UN 4th World Meteorological Day, Mar. 23.

IQSY
Emblem
A21

1964, July 3   Engr.
176 A21 25fr dk bl, red & grn   .60 .45

International Quiet Sun Year, 1964-65.

Striped
Mullet
A22

Designs: 5fr, Mauritanian lobster, vert. 10fr, Royal lobster, vert. 60fr, Maigre fish.

1964, Oct. 5   Engr.   Perf. 13
177	A22	1fr org brn, dk bl & grn	.40	.25
178	A22	5fr org brn, sl grn & choc	.50	.25
179	A22	10fr dk bl, bis & sl grn	.80	.25
180	A22	60fr dk brn, dp grn & dl bl	3.00	.80
	Nos. 177-180 (4)		4.70	1.55

Cooperation Issue
Common Design Type
1964, Nov. 7   Unwmk.   Perf. 13
181 CD119 25fr mag, sl grn & dk brn   .60 .35

Water Lilies
A23

Tropical Plants: 10fr, Acacia. 20fr, Adenium obesum. 45fr, Caralluma retrospiciens.

1965, Jan. 11   Engr.   Perf. 13
182	A23	5fr multi	.25	.25
183	A23	10fr multi, vert.	.25	.25
184	A23	20fr multi	.55	.25
185	A23	45fr multi, vert.	1.00	.50
	Nos. 182-185 (4)		2.05	1.25

Hardine
A24

Musical Instruments: 8fr, Tobol (drums). 25fr, Tidinit (stringed instruments). 40fr, Musicians.

1965, Mar. 8   Perf. 13
186	A24	2fr red brn, brt bl & sep	.25	.25
187	A24	8fr red brn, red & brn	.40	.25
188	A24	25fr red brn, emer & blk	.65	.25
189	A24	40fr vio bl, plum & blk	1.00	.35
	Nos. 186-189 (4)		2.30	1.10

Abraham Lincoln
(1809-1865) — A25

1965, Apr. 23   Photo.   Perf. 13x12½
190 A25 50fr lt ultra & multi   .80 .40

Palms at
Adrar
A26

Designs: 4fr, Chinguetti mosque, vert. 15fr, Clay pit and donkeys. 60fr, Decorated door, Oualata.

1965, June 14   Engr.   Perf. 13
191	A26	1fr brn, bl & grn	.25	.25
192	A26	4fr dk red, bl & brn	.25	.25
193	A26	15fr multi	.35	.25
194	A26	60fr grn, dk brn & red brn	1.10	.55
	Nos. 191-194 (4)		1.95	1.30

Issued for tourist publicity.

Tea Service
in Inlaid
Box — A27

7fr, Tobacco pouch and pipe, vert. 25fr, Dagger, vert. 50fr, Mederdra ornamental chest.

1965, Sept. 13   Unwmk.   Perf. 13
195	A27	3fr gray, choc & ocher	.25	.25
196	A27	7fr red lil, Prus bl & org	.25	.25
197	A27	25fr blk, org red & brn	.50	.25
198	A27	50fr brt grn, brn org & mar	1.00	.40
	Nos. 195-198 (4)		2.00	1.15

Choum Railroad
Tunnel — A28

10fr, Nouakchott wharf, ships & anchor, horiz. 30fr, as 5fr. 85fr, Nouakchott hospital & caduceus, horiz.

1965, Oct. 18   Engr.   Perf. 13
199	A28	5fr dk brn & brt grn	.25	.25
200	A28	10fr dk vio bl, brn red & Prus bl	.25	.25
201	A28	30fr brn red, red & red brn	.70	.25
202	A28	85fr dp bl, rose cl & lil	1.30	.65
	Nos. 199-202 (4)		2.50	1.40

Sculptured
Heads
A29

Designs: 30fr, "Music and Dance." 60fr, Movie camera and huts.

1966, Apr.   Engr.   Perf. 13
203	A29	10fr brt grn, blk & brn	.25	.25
204	A29	30fr brt bl, red lil & blk	.50	.25
205	A29	60fr red, org & dk brn	1.00	.45
	Nos. 203-205 (3)		1.75	.95

Intl. Negro Arts Festival, Dakar, Senegal, Apr. 1-24.

Mimosa — A30

Myrina
Silenus — A31

Flowers: 15fr, Schouwia purpurea. 20fr, Ipomea asarifolia. 25fr, Grewia bicolor. 30fr, Pancratium trianthum. 60fr, Blepharis linariifolia.

1966, Aug. 8   Photo.   Perf. 13x12½
Flowers in Natural Colors
206 A30 10fr dl bl & dk bl   .40   .25
207 A30 15fr dk brn & buff   .50   .35
208 A30 20fr grnsh bl & lt bl   .60   .40
209 A30 25fr brn & buff   .80   .50
210 A30 30fr lil & vio   1.20   .65
211 A30 60fr grn & pale grn   1.60 1.00
    Nos. 206-211 (6)   5.10 3.15

1966, Oct. 3   Photo.   Perf. 12x12½
Various Butterflies
212 A31 5fr buff & multi   1.10   .30
213 A31 30fr bl grn & multi   3.50   .45
214 A31 45fr yel grn & multi   4.75   .65
215 A31 60fr dl bl & multi   6.75 1.10
    Nos. 212-215 (4)   16.10 2.50

Hunter, Petroglyph from Adrar A32

Designs: 3fr, Two men fighting, petroglyph from Tenses (Adrar). 30fr, Copper jug, Le Mreyer (Adrar). 50fr, Camel caravan.

1966, Oct. 24   Engr.   Perf. 13
216 A32 2fr dk brn & brn org   .30   .25
217 A32 3fr bl & brn org   .80   .45
218 A32 30fr sl grn & dk red   1.40   .30
219 A32 50fr mag, sl grn & brn   2.40   .70
    Nos. 216-219 (4)   4.90 1.50

Issued for tourist publicity.

UNESCO, 20th Anniv. A33

1966, Dec. 5   Litho.   Perf. 12½x13
220 A33 30fr multi   .00   .40

Plaza of Three Cultures, Mexico City — A34

Olympic Village, Grenoble A35

Designs: 40fr, Olympic torch and skating rink. 100fr, Olympic Stadium, Mexico City.

1967, Mar. 11   Engr.   Perf. 13
221 A34 20fr dl bl, brn & sl grn   .50   .25
222 A35 30fr dl bl, brn & grn   .60   .40
223 A34 40fr brt bl, dk brn & sep 1.00   .55
224 A35 100fr brn, emer & blk   1.75 1.00
    Nos. 221-224 (4)   3.85 2.20

Nos. 221 and 224 commemorate the 19th Olympic Games, Mexico City; Nos. 222 and 223, the 10th Winter Olympic Games, Grenoble.

Trees — A36   1967 Jamboree Emblem and Campsite — A37

1967, May 15   Engr.   Perf. 13
225 A36 10fr Prosopis   .45   .25
226 A36 15fr Jujube   .60   .25
227 A36 20fr Date palm   .70   .25
228 A36 25fr Peltophorum   .80   .30
229 A36 30fr Baobob   1.10   .35
    Nos. 225-229 (5)   3.65 1.40

1967, June 5
Design: 90fr, 1967 Jamboree emblem and Mauritanian Boy Scouts, horiz.
230 A37 60fr brn, ultra & slate grn .95   .35
231 A37 90fr dl red, bl & slate grn 1.40   .50

12th Boy Scout World Jamboree, Farragut State Park, Idaho, Aug. 1-9.

Weavers A38

10fr, Embroiderer, vert. 20fr, Nurse, mother & infant. 30fr, Laundress, vert. 50fr, Seamstresses.

1967, July 3   Engr.   Perf. 13
232 A38 5fr plum, blk & cl   .25   .25
233 A38 10fr plum, brt grn & blk   .25   .25
234 A38 20fr brt bl, plum & blk   .50   .25
235 A38 30fr dk bl, brn & blk   .60   .30
236 A38 50fr plum, sl & blk   1.00   .30
    Nos. 232-236 (5)   2.60 1.35

Progress made by working women.

Cattle and Hypodermic Syringe — A39

1967, Aug. 21   Engr.   Perf. 13
237 A39 30fr sl grn, brt bl & rose cl .80   .35

Campaign against cattle plague.

Monetary Union Issue
Common Design Type
1967, Nov. 4   Engr.   Perf. 13
238 CD125 30fr gray & orange   .45   .25

Fruit — A40   Human Rights Flame — A41

1967, Dec. 4   Engr.   Perf. 13
239 A40 1fr Doom palm   .35   .25
240 A40 2fr Bito, horiz.   .40   .25
241 A40 3fr Baobob   .50   .25
242 A40 4fr Jujube, horiz.   .60   .25
243 A40 5fr Daye   .75   .40
    Nos. 239-243 (5)   2.60 1.40

For surcharges see Nos. 323-327.

1968, Jan. 8   Photo.   Perf. 13x12½
244 A41 30fr brt grn, blk & yel   .60   .25
245 A41 50fr brn org, blk & yel   .75   .35

International Human Rights Year.

Nouakchott Mosque A42

45fr, Amogjar Pass. 90fr, Cavaliers' Towers.

1968, Apr. 1   Photo.   Perf. 12½x13
246 A42 30fr multi   .35   .25
247 A42 45fr multi   .50   .25
248 A42 90fr multi   .85   .50
    Nos. 246-248 (3)   1.70 1.00

For surcharges see Nos. 332-333.

UPU Building, Bern, Globe and Map of Africa A43

1968, June 3   Engr.   Perf. 13
249 A43 30fr ver, ultra & olive   .60   .25

Mauritania's admission to the UPU.

Symbolic Water Cycle A44

1968, June 24
250 A44 90fr car, lake, grn & sl grn .75   .40

Hydrological Decade (UNESCO), 1965-74.

Land Yacht Racing — A45   Donkey and Foal — A46

40fr, Three land yachts racing, horiz. 60fr, Crew changing wheel of land yacht.

1968, Oct. 7   Engr.   Perf. 13
251 A45 30fr ultra, org & ocher   .55   .25
252 A45 40fr ultra, dp org & plum .70   .30
253 A45 60fr brt grn, dp org & ocher 1.10 .60
    Nos. 251-253 (3)   2.35 1.15

1968, Dec. 16   Photo.   Perf. 13
Domestic Animals: 10fr, Ewe and lamb. 15fr, Camel and calf. 30fr, Mare and foal. 50fr, Cow and calf. 90fr, Goat and kid.
254 A46 5fr ocher & multi   .30   .25
255 A46 10fr multi   .40   .25
256 A46 15fr multi   .45   .25
257 A46 30fr multi   .85   .30
258 A46 50fr pur & multi   1.25   .40
259 A46 90fr multi   2.40   .60
    Nos. 254-259 (6)   5.65 2.05

For surcharge see No. 303.

ILO Emblem and Map — A47   Desert Monitor — A48

1969, Apr. 14   Photo.   Perf. 13x12½
260 A47 50fr dk & lt bl, pur & org .60 .30

ILO, 50th anniversary.

1969, May 5   Photo.   Perf. 13x12½
Reptiles: 10fr, Horned viper. 30fr, Common spitting cobra. 60fr, Rock python. 85fr, African crocodile.
261 A48 5fr brn, pink & yel   .40   .25
262 A48 10fr brn, lt grn & yel   .70   .30
263 A48 30fr dk brn, pink & yel   1.75   .50
264 A48 60fr dk brn, lt bl & yel 3.00 1.40
265 A48 85fr dk brn, yel & red   5.50 1.75
    Nos. 261-265 (5)   11.35 4.20

Lady Beetle Eating Noxious Insects A49

1969, May 26   Engr.   Perf. 13
266 A49 30fr indigo, grn & mar   1.50   .70

Natural protection of date palms.

Development Bank Issue
Common Design Type
1969, Sept. 10   Engr.   Perf. 13
267 CD130 30fr Prus bl, grn & ocher .60 .25

Pendant — A50

Design: 20fr, Rahla headdress, horiz.

1969, Oct. 13   Engr.   Perf. 13
268 A50 10fr dk brn, lil & brn   .25   .25
269 A50 20fr blk, Prus bl & mag   .50   .25

For surcharges see Nos. 309-310.

Desalination Plant A51

Designs: 15fr, Fishing harbor, Nouadhibou. 30fr, Meat refrigeration plant, Kaedi.

1969, Dec. 1   Engr.   Perf. 13
270 A51 10fr brt rose lil, dk bl & red brn .25 .25
271 A51 15fr dk car, blk & dp bl   .25   .25
272 A51 30fr blk, dk bl & rose brn .40   .25
    Nos. 270-272 (3)   .90   .75

Issued to publicize economic progress.

Lenin (1870-
1924)
A52

Sternocera
Interrupta
A53

1970, Feb. 16   Photo.   Perf. 12x12½
273 A52 30fr car, lt bl & blk   1.40   .40

1970, Mar. 16   Engr.   Perf. 13
Insects: 10fr, Anoplocnemis curvipes. 20fr,
Julodis aequinoctialis. 30fr, Thermophilum
sexmaculatum marginatum. 40fr, Plocaederus
denticornis.

274 A53   5fr red brn, buff & blk   .40   .25
275 A53 10fr red brn, yel & brn   .65   .25
276 A53 20fr red brn, lil & dk ol   .85   .30
277 A53 30fr red brn, grn & vio   1.40   .45
278 A53 40fr red brn, lt bl & brn   2.25   .85
     Nos. 274-278 (5)   5.55 2.10

For surcharges see Nos. 311-315.

Soccer Players and
Hemispheres — A54

Hemispheres & various views of soccer
play.

1970, May 11   Engr.   Perf. 13
279 A54   25fr bl, vio bl & dk brn   .45   .25
280 A54   30fr vio bl, brn & ol brn   .45   .25
281 A54   70fr brt pink, mar & dk
                brn   .90   .50
282 A54 150fr brn red, grn & dk
                brn   2.10   .75
     Nos. 279-282 (4)   3.90 1.75

9th World Soccer Championships for the
Jules Rimet Cup, Mexico City, 5/29-6/21.

UPU Headquarters Issue
Common Design Type

1970, May 20   Engr.   Perf. 13
283 CD133 30fr grn, dk brn & red
                  brn   .60   .30

Woman Wearing
"Boubou" — A55

Various Traditional Costumes: 30fr, 70fr,
Men. 40fr, 50fr, Women.

1970, Sept. 21   Engr.   Perf. 12½x13
284 A55 10fr red brn & org   .25   .25
285 A55 30fr ol, red brn & ind   .60   .25
286 A55 40fr red brn, plum & dk
                brn   .85   .35
287 A55 50fr dk brn & brt bl   1.20   .45
288 A55 70fr bl, brn & dk brn   1.50   .65
     Nos. 284-288 (5)   4.40 1.95

People of Various Races — A55a

Design: 40fr, Outstretched hands, vert.

1971, Mar. 22   Engr.   Perf. 13
288A A55a 30fr brn vio, ol & brt
                   bl   .60   .25
288B A55a 40fr brn red, bl & blk   .80   .35
Intl. year against racial discrimination.

Gen. Charles de Gaulle (1890-1970),
President of France — A56

Design: 100fr, De Gaulle as President.

1971, June 18   Photo.   Perf. 13
289 A56   40fr gold, blk & grnsh
                bl   2.00   .75
290 A56 100fr lt bl, gold & blk   4.50 1.50
  a.   Souvenir sheet of 2, #289-290 6.50 6.50

Iron Ore Freight Train of Miferma
Mines — A57

1971, Nov. 8   Photo.   Perf. 12½x12
291   A57   ore cars   1.75   .65
292   100fr engines   4.00 1.60
  a. A57 Pair, #291-292   7.50 7.50

UNICEF
Emblem
and Child
A59

1971, Dec. 11   Litho.   Perf. 13½
293 A59 35fr lt ultra, blk & brn   .50   .25
UNICEF, 25th anniv.

Samuel F. B. Morse
and
Telegraph — A60

Designs: 40fr, Relay satellite over globes.
75fr, Alexander Graham Bell.

1972, May 17   Engr.   Perf. 13
294 A60 35fr lilac, indigo & vio   .55   .25
295 A60 40fr bl, ocher & choc   .60   .25
296 A60 75fr grn, ol grn & Prus
                bl   .90   .45
     Nos. 294-296 (3)   2.05   .95

4th World Telecommunications Day.
For surcharge see No. 343.

Fossil Spirifer Shell — A61

1972, July 31   Litho.   Perf. 12½
297 A61 25fr shown   2.25   .90
298 A61 75fr Phacops rana   4.00 1.25
            Fossil shells.
For surcharges see Nos. 306, 308.

West African Monetary Union Issue
Common Design Type

1972, Nov. 2   Engr.   Perf. 13
299 CD136 35fr brn, yel grn &
                  gray   .75   .25

Mediterranean Monk Seal and
Pup — A63

1973, Feb. 28   Litho.   Perf. 13
300 A63 40fr multi   2.00   .80
See No. C130. For surcharges see Nos.
307, C145.

Food
Program
Symbols
and
Emblem
A64

1973, Apr. 30   Photo.   Perf. 12x12½
301 A64 35fr gray bl & multi   .45   .25
World Food Program, 10th anniversary.

UPU
Monument
and Globe
A65

1973, May 28   Engr.   Perf. 13
302 A65 100fr grn, ocher & bl   1.60   .75
Universal Postal Union Day.

Currency Change to Ouguiya ("um")
No. 258 Surcharged with New Value, 2
Bars, and Overprinted:
"SECHERESSE / SOLIDARITE /
AFRICAINE"

1973, Aug. 16   Photo.   Perf. 13
303 A46 20um on 50fr multi   .90   .40
African solidarity in drought emergency.

African Postal Union Issue
Common Design Type

1973, Sept. 12   Engr.   Perf. 13
304 CD137 20um org, brn &
                  ocher   1.10   .40

INTERPOL
Emblem,
Detective,
Criminal,
Fingerprint
A66

1973, Sept. 24
305 A66 15um brn, ver & vio   .90   .50
50th anniv. of Intl. Criminal Police Org.

**Nos. 297-298, 300 and 268-269
Surcharged with New Value and
Two Bars in Ultramarine, Red or
Black**

1973-74   Litho.   Perf. 12½
306 A61   5um on 25fr (U) ('74)   2.50   .40
307 A63   8um on 40fr (R)   .95   .40
308 A61 15um on 75fr (U) ('74)   7.00 1.75

**Engr.
Perf. 13**
309 A50 27um on 10fr (B) ('74)   1.60   .75
310 A50 28um on 20fr (R) ('74)   1.75   .90
     Nos. 306-310 (5)   13.80 4.20

**Nos. 274-278 Surcharged with New
Value and Two bars in Violet Blue
or Red**

1974, July 29   Engr.   Perf. 13
311 A53   5um on 5fr   1.25   .60
312 A53   7um on 10fr   1.10   .40
313 A53   8um on 20fr   1.25   .45
314 A53 15um on 30fr (R)   1.75   .50
315 A53 20um on 40fr   3.50 1.40
     Nos. 311-315 (5)   8.85 3.35

UPU Emblem and Globes — A67

1974, Aug. 5   Photo.   Perf. 13
316 A67 30um multi   2.10   .80
317 A67 50um multi   3.50 1.40
Centenary of Universal Postal Union.
For overprints see Nos. 321-322.

5-Ouguiya Coin and Bank Note — A68

Designs: 8um, 10-ouguiya coin. 20um, 20-
ouguiya coin. Each design includes picture of
different bank note.

1974, Aug. 12   Engr.
318 A68   7um blk, ultra & grn   .60   .25
319 A68   8um blk, sl grn & mag   .70   .25
320 A68 20um blk, red & bl   1.40   .55
     Nos. 318-320 (3)   2.70 1.05

First anniversary of currency reform.

**Nos. 316-317 Overprinted in Red: "9
OCTOBRE / 100 ANS D'UNION
POSTALE / INTERNATIONALE"**

1974, Oct. 9   Photo.   Perf. 13
321 A67 30um multi   2.25 1.00
322 A67 50um multi   4.00 1.50
Centenary of Universal Postal Union.

**Nos. 239-243 Surcharged with New
Value and Two Bars in Black or
Violet Blue**

1975, Feb. 14   Engr.   Perf. 13
323 A40   1um on 5fr multi (B)   .30   .25
324 A40   2um on 4fr multi (VB)   .30   .25
325 A40   3um on 2fr multi (B)   .35   .25
326 A40 10um on 1fr multi (B)   .95   .25
327 A40 12um on 3fr multi (VB)   1.10   .30
     Nos. 323-327 (5)   3.00 1.30

Hunters, Rock
Carvings — A69

Rock Carvings from Zemmour Cave: 5um,
Ostrich. 10um, Elephant, horiz.

1975, May 26   Engr.   Perf. 13
328 A69   4um lt brn & car   1.00   .25
329 A69   5um red lil   1.25   .30
330 A69 10um blue   1.90   .45
     Nos. 328-330 (3)   4.15 1.00

Europafrica Issue

White and Black Men, Map of Europe and Africa — A70

1975, July 7   Engr.   Perf. 13
331 A70 40um dk brn & red   2.10 .80

Nos. 247-248 Surcharged in Red or Black

1975, Aug. 25   Photo.   Perf. 12½x13
332 A42 15um on 45fr (R)   1.25 .50
333 A42 25um on 90fr   2.00 .80

African solidarity in drought emergency.

Map of Africa with Mauritania, Aljoujt Blast Furnace, Camel — A71

Design: 12um, Snim emblem, furnace, dump truck, excavator.

1975, Sept. 22   Engr.   Perf. 13
334 A71 10um brt bl, choc & org   .90 .30
335 A71 12um brt bl & multi   1.00 .40

Mining and industry: Somima (Société Minière de Mauritanie) and Snim (Société Nationale Industrielle et Minière).

Fair Emblem — A72

1975, Oct. 5   Litho.   Perf. 12
336 A72 10um multi   .60 .30

National Nouakchott Fair, Nov. 28-Dec. 7.

Commemorative Medal — A73

Design: 12um, Map of Mauritania, vert.

1975, Nov. 28   Litho.   Perf. 12
337 A73 10um sil & multi   1.00 .35
338 A73 12um grn, yel & grn   1.00 .35

15th anniversary of independence.

Docked Space Ships and Astronauts — A74

Docked Space Ships and: 10um, Soyuz rocket launch.

1975, Dec. 29   Litho.   Perf. 14
339 A74 8um multi   .70 .25
340 A74 10um multi   .85 .25
Nos. 339-340,C156-C158 (5)   7.15 2.65

Apollo Soyuz space test project, Russo-American cooperation, launched July 15, link-up July 17, 1975.

French Legion Infantryman A75

Uniform: 10um, Green Mountain Boy.

1976, Jan. 26   Perf. 13½x14
341 A75 8um multi   .80 .25
342 A75 10um multi   1.00 .25
Nos. 341-342,C160-C162 (5)   7.30 2.75

American Bicentennial.

No. 296 Surcharged

1976, Mar. 1   Engr.   Perf. 13
343 A60 12um on 75fr multi   .70 .30

Arab Labor Charter, 10th anniversary.

Map of Mauritania with Spanish Sahara Incorporated — A76

1976, Mar. 15   Litho.   Perf. 13x12½
344 A76 10um grn & multi   .80 .30

Reunified Mauritania, Feb. 29, 1976.

LZ-4 over Hangar — A77

75th anniv. of the Zeppelin: 10um, Dr. Hugo Eckener and "Schwaben" (LZ-10). 12um, "Hansa" (LZ-13) over Heligoland. 20um, "Bodensee" (LZ-120) and Dr. Ludwig Dürr.

1976, June 28   Litho.   Perf. 11
345 A77 5um multi   .25 .25
346 A77 10um multi   .60 .25
347 A77 12um multi   .75 .30
348 A77 20um multi   1.25 .40
Nos. 345-348,C167-C168 (6)   9.35 3.85

Mohenjo-Daro — A78

1976, Sept. 6   Litho.   Perf. 12
349 A78 15um multi   1.10 .40

UNESCO campaign to save Mohenjo-Daro excavations, Pakistan.

A. G. Bell, Telephone and Satellite — A79

1976, Oct. 11   Engr.   Perf. 13
350 A79 10um bl, car & red   .80 .25

Centenary of first telephone call by Alexander Graham Bell, Mar. 10, 1876.

Mohammed Ali Jinnah (1876-1948), Governor General of Pakistan — A80

1976, Dec. 25   Litho.   Perf. 13
351 A80 10um multi   .60 .30

NASA Control Room, Houston — A81

Design: 12um, Viking components, vert.

1977, Feb. 28   Perf. 14
352 A81 10um multi   .60 .25
353 A81 12um multi   .75 .25
Nos. 352-353,C173-C175 (5)   7.60 2.15

Viking Mars project.
For surcharge and overprints see Nos. 425-426, C192-C195.

Jackals A82

Designs: 5um, Wild rabbits. 12um, Warthogs. 14um, Lions. 15um, Elephants.

1977, Mar. 14   Litho.   Perf. 12½
354 A82 5um multi   .40 .25
355 A82 10um multi   1.00 .40
356 A82 12um multi   1.40 .50
357 A82 14um multi   1.50 .60
358 A82 15um multi   3.00 .90
Nos. 354-358 (5)   7.30 2.65

For surcharge see No. 577.

Irene and Frederic Joliot-Curie, Chemistry — A83

Nobel prize winners: 15um, Emil A. von Bering, medicine.

1977, Apr. 29   Litho.   Perf. 14
359 A83 12um multi   1.10 .25
360 A83 15um multi   .90 .25
Nos. 359-360,C177-C179 (5)   9.05 2.10

APU Emblem, Member's Flags — A84

1977, May 30   Photo.   Perf. 13
361 A84 12um multi   .65 .40

Arab Postal Union, 25th anniversary.

Oil Lamp A85

Tegdaoust Pottery: 2um, 4-handled pot. 5um, Large jar. 12um, Jug with filter.

1977, June 13   Engr.   Perf. 13
362 A85 1um multi   .25 .25
363 A85 2um multi   .25 .25
364 A85 5um multi   .30 .25
365 A85 12um multi   .80 .30
Nos. 362-365 (4)   1.60 1.05

X-ray of Hand — A86

1977, June 27 Engr. Perf. 12½x13
366 A86 40um multi   2.50 1.25
World Rheumatism Year.

Charles Lindbergh and "Spirit of St. Louis" — A87

History of aviation: 14um, Clement Ader and "Eole!" 15um, Louis Bleriot over channel. 55um, Italo Balbo and seaplanes. 60um, Concorde. 100um, Charles Lindbergh and "Spirit of St. Louis."

1977, Sept. 19
367 A87 12um multi   .65 .25
368 A87 14um multi   .70 .25
369 A87 15um multi   .85 .30
370 A87 55um multi   3.00 .70
371 A87 60um multi   3.50 .75
   Nos. 367-371 (5)   8.70 2.25

Souvenir Sheet
372 A87 100um multi   6.00 1.50

Dome of the Rock, Jerusalem — A88

1977, Oct. 31 Litho. Perf. 12½
373 A88 12um multi   .65 .25
374 A88 14um multi   .85 .40
Palestinian fighters and their families.

Soccer and Emblems — A89

Emblems and: 14um, Alf Ramsey and stadium. 15um, Players and goalkeeper.

1977, Dec. 19 Litho. Perf. 13½
375 A89 12um multi   .55 .25
376 A89 14um multi   .65 .25
377 A89 15um multi   .80 .25
   Nos. 375-377,C182-C183 (5)   7.25 2.05
Elimination Games for World Cup Soccer Championship, Argentina, 1978.
   For overprints see Nos. 399-401, C187-C189.

Helen Fourment and her Children, by Rubens A90

Paintings by Peter Paul Rubens (1577-1640): 14um, Knight in armor. 67um, Three Burghers. 69um, Landscape, horiz. 100um, Rubens with wife and son.

1977, Dec. 26
378 A90 12um multi   .65 .25
379 A90 14um multi   .80 .35
380 A90 67um multi   3.25 .70
381 A90 69um multi   3.50 .85
   Nos. 378-381 (4)   8.20 2.15

Souvenir Sheet
382 A90 100um gold & multi   5.50 1.50

Sable Antelope and Wildlife Fund Emblem — A91

Endangered Animals: 12um, Gazelles, vert. 14um, Manatee. 55um, Aoudad, vert. 60um, Elephant. 100um, Ostrich, vert.

1978, Feb. 28 Litho. Perf. 13½x14
383 A91 5um multi   .80 .30
384 A91 12um multi   1.60 .40
385 A91 14um multi   1.75 .60
386 A91 55um multi   6.00 1.75
387 A91 60um multi   7.00 2.00
388 A91 100um multi   9.00 3.25
   Nos. 383-388 (6)   26.15 8.30

Nouakchott-Nema Road — A91a

1978, June 19 Litho. Perf. 13
388A A91a 12um multicolored   11.00 8.50
388B A91a 14um multicolored   12.50 9.00

Soccer and Games' Emblem — A92

14um, Rimet Cup. 20um, Soccer ball & F.I.F.A. flag. 50um, Soccer ball & Rimet Cup, horiz.

1978, June 26 Photo. Perf. 13
389 A92 12um multi   .60 .25
390 A92 14um multi   .70 .30
391 A92 20um multi   1.10 .30
   Nos. 389-391 (3)   2.40 .85

Souvenir Sheet
392 A92 50um multi   2.50 1.00
11th World Cup Soccer Championship, Argentina, June 1-25.

Raoul Follereau and St. George Slaying Dragon — A93

1978, Sept. 4 Engr. Perf. 13
393 A93 12um brn & dp grn   1.50 .60
25th anniversary of the Raoul Follereau Anti-Leprosy Foundation.

Anti-Apartheid Emblem, Fenced-in People — A94

Design: 30um, Anti-Apartheid emblem and free people, vert.

1978, Oct. 9
394 A94 25um bl, red & brn   1.25 .65
395 A94 30um grn, bl & brn   1.75 .85
   Anti-Apartheid Year.

Charles de Gaulle A95

14um, King Baudouin. 55um, Queen Elizabeth II.

1978, Oct. 16 Litho. Perf. 12½x12
396 A95 12um multi   1.10 .40
397 A95 14um multi   1.10 .40
398 A95 55um multi   2.50 1.00
   Nos. 396-398 (3)   4.70 1.80
Rulers who helped in de-colonization. No. 398 also commemorates 25th anniversary of coronation of Queen Elizabeth II.

Nos. 375-377 Overprinted in Arabic and French in Silver: "ARGENTINE-/ PAYS BAS 3-1"
1978, Dec. 11 Litho. Perf. 13½
399 A89 12um multi   .60 .25
400 A89 14um multi   .65 .30
401 A89 15um multi   .90 .50
   Nos. 399-401,C187-C188 (5)   7.25 3.90
Argentina's victory in World Cup Soccer Championship 1978.

View of Nouakchott — A96

1978, Dec. 18 Litho. Perf. 12
402 A96 12um multi   .65 .30
20th anniversary of Nouakchott.

Flame Emblem — A97   Leather Key Holder — A98

1978, Dec. 26 Perf. 12½
403 A97 55um ultra & red   2.50 1.25
Universal Declaration of Human Rights, 30th anniv.

1979, Feb. 5 Litho. Perf. 13½x14
Leather Craft: 7um, Toothbrush case. 10um, Knife holder.
404 A98 5um multi   .35 .25
405 A98 7um multi   .45 .25
406 A98 10um multi   .65 .30
   Nos. 404-406 (3)   1.45 .80

Farmers at Market, by Dürer — A99

Engravings by Albrecht Durer (1471-1528): 14um, Young Peasant and Wife. 55um, Mercenary with flag. 60um, St. George Slaying Dragon. 100um, Mercenaries, horiz.

Litho.; Red Foil Embossed
1979, May 3 Perf. 13½x14
407 A99 12um blk, buff   .60 .25
408 A99 14um blk, buff   1.00 .25
409 A99 55um blk, buff   2.40 .80
410 A99 60um blk, buff   3.00 .95
   Nos. 407-410 (4)   7.00 2.25

Souvenir Sheet
Perf. 14x13½
411 A99 100um blk, buff   5.00 3.50

Buddha, Borobudur Temple and UNESCO Emblem — A100

UNESCO Emblem and: 14um, Hunter on horseback, Carthage. 55um, Caryatid, Acropolis.

1979, May 14 Photo. Perf. 12½
412 A100 12um multi .70 .35
413 A100 14um multi .90 .40
414 A100 55um multi 2.75 1.25
  Nos. 412-414 (3) 4.35 2.00
Preservation of art treasures with help from UNESCO.

Paddle Steamer Sirius, Rowland Hill — A101

Sir Rowland Hill (1795-1879), originator of penny postage, and: 14um, Paddle steamer Great Republic. 55um, S.S. Mauritania. 60um, M.S. Stirling Castle. 100um, Mauritania No. 8.

1979, June 4 Litho. Perf. 13½x14
415 A101 12um multi .55 .25
416 A101 14um multi .70 .25
417 A101 55um multi 2.40 .55
418 A101 60um multi 2.90 .70
  Nos. 415-418 (4) 6.55 1.75
Souvenir Sheet
419 A101 100um multi 5.00 1.25

Embossed Leather Cushion — A102

30um, Satellite, jet, ship, globe & UPU emblem.

1979, June 8 Litho. Perf. 12½
420 A102 12um multi 1.10 .50
Engr.
Perf. 13
421 A102 30um multi, vert. 3.00 1.40
Philexafrique II, Libreville, Gabon, June 8-17. Nos. 420, 421 each printed in sheets of 10 and 5 labels showing exhibition emblem.

Mother and Children, IYC Emblem — A103

1979, Oct. 2 Litho. Perf. 12½
422 A103 12um multi .55 .25
423 A103 14um multi .70 .35
424 A103 40um multi 2.00 .90
  Nos. 422-424 (3) 3.25 1.50
International Year of the Child

Nos. 352-353 Overprinted in Silver: "ALUNISSAGE / APOLLO XI / JUILLET 1969" and Emblem
1979, Oct. 24 Litho. Perf. 14
425 A81 10um multi .60 .30
426 A81 12um multi .60 .30
  Nos. 425-426,C192-C194 (5) 7.20 3.35
Apollo 11 moon landing, 10th anniversary.

Runner, Moscow '80 Emblem A104

Moscow '80 Emblem and: 14um, 55um, 100um, Running, diff. 60um, Hurdles.

1979, Oct. 26 Litho. Perf. 13½
427 A104 12um multi .55 .25
428 A104 14um multi .75 .25
429 A104 55um multi 2.10 .50
430 A104 60um multi 2.50 .60
  Nos. 427-430 (4) 5.90 1.60
Souvenir Sheet
431 A104 100um multi 4.75 1.25
  Pre-Olympic Year.

Scomberesox Saurus Walbaum — A104a

1979, Nov. 12 Photo. Perf. 14
431A A104a 1um shown .75 .30
431B A104a 5um Trigla lucerna .75 .30
A 20m denomination (Xiphias gladius) also exists. Value $250.

Ice Hockey, Lake Placid '80 Emblem — A105

Various ice hockey plays.

1979, Dec. 6 Litho. Perf. 14½
432 A105 10um multi .50 .25
433 A105 12um multi .65 .25
434 A105 14um multi .65 .30
435 A105 55um multi 2.40 .55
436 A105 60um multi 2.50 .65
437 A105 100um multi 4.25 1.10
  Nos. 432-437 (6) 10.95 3.10
13th Winter Olympic Games. Lake Placid, NY, Feb. 12-24, 1980.
For overprints see Nos. 440-445.

Arab Achievements — A106

1980, Mar. 22 Litho. Perf. 13
438 A106 12um multi .70 .35
439 A106 15um multi .80 .35

Nos. 432-437 Overprinted:
a. Médaille / de bronze / SUÈDE
b. MÉDAILLE / DE BRONZE / SUÈDE
c. Médaille / d'argent / U.R.S.S.
d. MÉDAILLE / D'ARGENT/ U.R.S.S.
e. MÉDAILLE / D'OR / ÉTATS-UNIS
f. Médaille / d'or / ÉTATS-UNIS

1980, June 14 Litho. Perf. 14½
440 A105(a) 10um multi .55 .25
441 A105(b) 12um multi .60 .25
442 A105(c) 14um multi .65 .35
443 A105(d) 55um multi 2.40 .85

444 A105(e) 60um multi 2.50 .95
445 A105(f) 100um multi 4.25 1.50
  Nos. 440-445 (6) 10.90 4.15

Equestrian, Olympic Rings — A107

Designs: Equestrian scenes. 10um, 20um, 70um, 100um, vert.

1980, June Litho. Perf. 14
446 A107 10um multi .45 .25
447 A107 20um multi .85 .25
448 A107 50um multi 2.40 .50
449 A107 70um multi 3.25 .70
  Nos. 446-449 (4) 6.95 1.70
Souvenir Sheet
450 A107 100um multi 5.50 1.75
22nd Summer Olympic Games, Moscow, July 19-Aug. 3.
For overprints see Nos. 464-468.

Armed Forces Day — A108

1980, July 9 Perf. 13x12½
451 A108 12um multi .60 .25
452 A108 14um multi .65 .30

World Red Cross Day — A109

1980, June 14 Perf. 13
453 A109 20um multi 12.00 —

Pilgrimage to Mecca — A110

Design: 50um, Mosque, outside view.

1980
454 A110 10um multi .90 .35
455 A110 50um multi 2.75 1.40

Man with Turban, by Rembrandt A111

Rembrandt Paintings: 10um, Self-portrait. 20um, His mother. 70um, His son Titus reading. 100um, Polish knight, horiz.

1980, July Litho. Perf. 12½
456 A111 10um multi .60 .25
457 A111 20um multi 1.00 .30
458 A111 50um multi 2.60 .50
459 A111 70um multi 3.00 .80
  Nos. 456-459 (4) 7.20 1.85
Souvenir Sheet
460 A111 100um multi 5.50 1.50

Tea Time A112

1980, Mar. 11 Litho. Perf. 12½
460A A112 1um multi .40 .25
461 A112 5um multi .65 .25
462 A112 12um multi 1.00 .30
  Nos. 460A-462 (3) 2.00 .80

Arbor Day — A113

1980, Aug. 29
463 A113 12um multi 1.10 .40

Nos. 446-450 Overprinted with Winner and Country
1980, Oct. Litho. Perf. 14
464 A107 10um multi .45 .25
465 A107 20um multi .85 .30
466 A107 50um multi 2.25 .60
467 A107 70um multi 3.00 .80
  Nos. 464-467 (4) 6.55 1.95
Souvenir Sheet
468 A107 100um multi 4.75 2.50

Mastodont Locomotive, 1850 — A114

Designs: Various locomotives.

1980, Nov. Perf. 12½
469 A114 10um shown .70 .25
470 A114 12um Iron ore train .85 .30
471 A114 14um Chicago-Milwaukee line, 1900 1.10 .40
472 A114 20um Bury, 1837 1.50 .50
473 A114 67um Reseau North line, 1870 5.00 .70
474 A114 100um Potsdam, 1840 7.50 1.10
  Nos. 469-474 (6) 16.65 3.25

20th Anniversary of
Independence — A115

1980, Nov. 27   **Perf. 13**
475 A115 12um multi   .55   .25
476 A115 15um multi   .60   .30

El Haram Mosque — A116

1981, Apr. 13   Litho.   Perf. 12½
477 A116 2um shown   .25   .25
478 A116 12um Medina Mosque   .60   .30
479 A116 14um Chinguetti
            Mosque   .80   .30
      Nos. 477-479 (3)   1.65   .85
Hegira, 1500th anniversary.

Prince Charles and Lady Diana,
Coach — A117

Designs: Coaches.

1981, July 8   Litho.   Perf. 14½
480 A117 14um multi   .60   .25
481 A117 18um multi   .75   .25
482 A117 77um multi   2.75   .90
      Nos. 480-482 (3)   4.10 1.40
            Souvenir Sheet
483 A117 100um multi   4.50 1.10
Royal wedding.
For overprints see Nos. 518-521.

Intl. Year of
the
Disabled
A119

1981, June 29   Litho.   Perf. 13x13½
486 A119 12um multi   .80   .40

Battle of Yorktown Bicentenary
(American Revolution) — A120

1981, Oct. 5   Perf. 12½
487 A120 14um George Wash-
            ington, vert.   .55   .25
488 A120 18um Admiral de
            Grasse, vert.   .80   .30
489 A120 63um Surrender of
            Cornwallis   2.50 1.00
490 A120 81um Battle of Chesa-
            peake Bay   3.50 1.50
      Nos. 487-490 (4)   7.35 3.05

475th Death Anniv. of Christopher
Columbus (1451-1506) — A121

1981, Oct. 5
491 A121 19um Pinta   1.10   .40
492 A121 55um Santa Maria   3.25 1.10

World Food
Day — A122

1981, Oct. 16   Perf. 13
493 A122 19um multi   .80   .40

Kemal Ataturk
Birth
Cent. — A123

1981, Oct. 29   Perf. 12½
494 A123 63um multi   2.50 1.25

Scouting Year — A124

Designs: Boating scenes. 92um vert.

1982, Jan. 20   Litho.   Perf. 12½
495 A124 14um multi   .70   .25
496 A124 19um multi   1.00   .25
497 A124 22um multi   1.10   .25
498 A124 92um multi   4.25   .85
      Nos. 495-498 (4)   7.05 1.60
            Souvenir Sheet
                Perf. 13
499 A124 100um Baden-Powell,
            scout   5.00 1.25

75th Anniv. of Grand Prix — A125

Designs: Winners and their Cars.

1982, Jan. 23   Perf. 13½
500 A125 7um Deusenberg,
            1921   .60   .25
501 A125 12um Alfa Romeo,
            1932   .85   .25
502 A125 14um Juan Fangio,
            1949   .95   .25
503 A125 18um Renault,
            1979   1.10   .25
504 A125 19um Niki Lauda,
            1974   1.25   .30
      Nos. 500-504 (5)   4.75 1.30
            Souvenir Sheet
505 A125 100um Race   6.00 1.75

Birds of
the Arguin
Bank
A126

1981, Dec. 17   Photo.   Perf. 13
506 A126 2um White pelicans   1.00   .25
507 A126 18um Pink flamingoes   3.75   .75

Battle of
Karameh
A127

1982, Dec. 19   Litho.
508 A127 14um Hand holding tat-
            tered flag   .80   .35

Deluth
Turtle — A128

Designs: Sea turtles.

1981, Dec. 21   Photo.   Perf. 14x13½
509 A128 1um shown   1.50   .25
510 A128 3um Green turtle   2.00   .25
511 A128 4um Shell turtle   2.50   .35
      Nos. 509-511 (3)   6.00   .85

APU, 30th
Anniv. — A129

1982, May 14   Litho.   Perf. 13
512 A129 14um org & brn   .65   .30

A130

1982, May 17   Photo.   Perf. 13½x13
513 A130 21um multi   .85   .40
14th World Telecommunications Day.

A131

1982, June 7   Litho.   Perf. 12½
514 A131 14um grnsh bl   .65   .30
UN Conf. on Human Environment, 10th
anniv.

21st Birthday of Princess Diana of
Wales — A132

Portraits.

1982, July   Perf. 14x13½
515 A132 21um multi   .75   .40
516 A132 77um multi   2.50   .85
            Souvenir Sheet
517 A132 100um multi   3.75 1.50

**Nos. 480-483 Overprinted in Blue:
"NAISSANCE ROYALE 1982"**
1982, Aug. 2   Perf. 14½
518 A117 14um multi   .50   .30
519 A117 18um multi   .70   .25
520 A117 77um multi   2.50 1.25
      Nos. 518-520 (3)   3.70 1.90
            Souvenir Sheet
521 A117 100um multi   3.50 1.50
Birth of Prince William of Wales, June 21.

Agricultrual Development — A132a

Designs: 14um, Cattle and camels at watering hole, Hodh el Gharbi. 18um, Irrigation system, Gorgol.

1982, Dec. 13   Litho.   Perf. 14½
521A A132a 14um multi   5.00 2.00
521B A132a 18um multi   7.00 2.50

Manned
Flight
Bicentenary
A133

1982, Dec. 29   Litho.   Perf. 14
522 A133 14um Montgolfiere
            balloon, 1783,
            vert.   .95   .25
523 A133 18um Hydrogen bal-
            loon, 1783   .95   .25
524 A133 19um Zeppelin, vert.   .95   .35
525 A133 55um Nieuport plane   2.50   .50
526 A133 63um Concorde   2.75   .60
527 A133 77um Apollo II, vert.   3.00   .70
      Nos. 522-527 (6)   11.10 2.65

Preservation of Ancient Cities — A134

1983, Feb. 16   Litho.   Perf. 14x14½
528 A134 14um City Wall,
　　　　Ouadane   .70 .25
529 A134 18um Chinguetti   .80 .30
530 A134 24um Staircase,
　　　　panels, Qalata   1.00 .50
531 A134 30um Ruins, Tichitt   1.60 .70
　　　Nos. 528-531 (4)   4.10 1.75

World
Communications
Year — A135

1983, June 21   Litho.   Perf. 13
532 A135 14um multi   .70 .30

30th Anniv. of Customs Cooperation
Council — A136

1983, June 25
533 A136 14um multi   .70 .30

Traditional
Houses
A137

1983, June 14   Photo.   Perf. 13½
534 A137 14um Peule   2.25 .35
535 A137 18um Toucouleur   3.00 .50
536 A137 19um Tent   3.25 .55
　　　Nos. 534-536 (3)   8.50 1.40

Ancient Manuscript
Page — A138

1983, June 15   Photo.   Perf. 12½x13
537 A138 2um shown   .30 .25
538 A138 5um Ornamental scroll-
　　　　work   .50 .25
539 A138 7um Sheath   .65 .25
　　　Nos. 537-539 (3)   1.45 .75

Manned Flight Bicentenary — A139

Early Fliers and their Balloons or Dirigibles.
10um, 14um vert.

1983, Oct. 17   Litho.   Perf. 13½
540 A139 10um F. Pilatre de
　　　　Rozler   .70 .25
541 A139 14um John Wise   .85 .25

542 A139 25um Charles Re-
　　　　nard   1.75 .30
543 A139 100um Henri Julliot   5.50 1.10
　　　Nos. 540-543 (4)   8.80 1.90
Souvenir Sheet
544 A139 100um Joseph
　　　　Montgolfier   6.00 1.25

No. 544 contains one stamp 47x37mm.
Nos. 543-544 airmail.

Mortar — A140

Various prehistoric grinding implements.

1983, Dec. 28   Litho.   Perf. 13
545 A140 10um multi   .85 .35
546 A140 14um multi   1.40 .45
547 A140 18um multi   1.90 .75
　　　Nos. 545-547 (3)   4.15 1.55

Pre-Olympics — A141

1983, Dec. 31   Litho.   Perf. 13½
548 A141 1um Basketball   .25 .25
549 A141 20um Wrestling   .85 .40
550 A141 50um Equestrian   2.00 .70
551 A141 77um Running   3.50 .95
　　　Nos. 548-551 (4)   6.60 2.30
Souvenir Sheet
552 A141 100um Soccer   4.75 1.25

No. 552 contains one stamp 41x36mm.
Nos. 551-552 airmail.

Scouting
Year — A142

Artemis, by Rembrandt — A142a

Events & Annivs.: 14um, Johann Wolfgang
von Goethe. 25um, Virgin and Child, by Peter
Paul Rubens.

1984, Jan. 24
553 A142 5um Flag, Baden-
　　　　Powell   1.00 .50
553A A142 14um multicolored   1.00 .50
553B A142 25um multicolored   1.50 .50
　　　Nos. 553-553B (3)   3.50 1.50
Souvenir Sheet
553C A142a 100um multicolored   4.25 1.50

No. 553C is airmail and contains one
42x51mm stamp.

Sand Rose
A143

1984, Mar.   Litho.   Perf. 14
554 A143 21um multi   15.00 1.50
Inscribed 1982.

Anniversaries and Events — A145

1984, Apr. 26
555 A145 10um Albrecht Durer
　　　　(1471-1528)   .70 .25
556 A145 12um Apollo XI, 15th
　　　　anniv.   .85 .35
557 A145 50um Chess   2.75 1.25
　　　Nos. 555-557 (3)   4.30 1.85

1984, Apr. 16   Litho.   Perf. 13½
　　Designs: 77um, Prince Charles, Princess
Diana. 100um, Prince Charles, Princess
Diana, vert.
557A A145 77um multi   3.75 1.90
Miniature Sheet
557B A145 100um multi   5.50 3.50
　　　Nos. 557A-557B airmail.

Fishing
Industry
A146

1984
558 A146 1um Tuna   .40 .25
559 A146 2um Mackerel   .40 .25
560 A146 5um Haddock   .55 .25
561 A146 14um Black chinchard   1.40 .50
562 A146 18um Boat building   1.75 .60
　　　Nos. 558-562 (5)   4.50 1.85

Nouakchott
Olympic
Complex
A148

1984, Sept. 26   Litho.   Perf. 13½
569 A148 14um multi   1.00 .40

Infant Survival
Campaign
A149

1984, Sept. 26   Litho.   Perf. 12½
570 A149 1um Feeding by glass   .30 .25
571 A149 4um Breastfeeding   .30 .25
572 A149 10um Vaccinating   .90 .25
573 A149 14um Weighing   1.10 .30
　　　Nos. 570-573 (4)   2.60 1.05

Pilgrimage to Mecca — A150

1984, Oct. 3   Litho.   Perf. 13
574 A150 14um Tents, mosque   .70 .40
575 A150 18um Tents, courtyard   1.25 .60

10th Anniv., West African
Union — A151

1984, Nov.   Litho.   Perf. 13
576 A151 14um Map of member
　　　　nations   .85 .40

No. 355 Overprinted "Aide au Sahel
84" and Surcharged

1984   Litho.   Perf. 12½
577 A82 18um on 10um   1.25 .50
Issued to publicize drought relief efforts.

Technical & Cultural Cooperation
Agency, 15th Anniv. — A152

1985, Mar. 20   Litho.   Perf. 12½
578 A152 18um Profiles, emblem   1.00 .45

League of Arab States, 40th
Anniv. — A153

1985, May 7   Perf. 13
579 A150 14um brt yel grn & blk   .75 .40

German Railways 150th
Anniv. — A154

Anniversaries and events: 12um, Adler, 1st
German locomotive, 1835. 18um, Series 10,
1956, last Fed. German Railways locomotive.
44um, European Music Year, Johann Sebastian Bach, composer, and Angels Making
Music, unattributed painting. 77um, George
Frideric Handel. 90um, Statue of Liberty,
cent., vert. 100um, Queen Mother, 85th birthday, vert.

1985, Sept.
580 A154 12um multi   .65 .25
581 A154 18um multi   1.00 .45
582 A154 44um multi   2.00 1.10

583 A154 77um multi 3.50 1.90
584 A154 90um multi 4.00 2.25
Nos. 580-584 (5) 11.15 5.95
Souvenir Sheet
585 A154 100um multi 4.75 2.25

World Food Day — A155

1985, Oct. 16 **Perf. 13x12½**
586 A155 18um multi .70 .40
UN Food and Agriculture Org., 40th anniv.

Fight Against Drought A156

1985, Apr. 10 **Litho.** **Perf. 13**
586A A156 10um Tree planting .50 .30
587 A156 14um Antelope .70 .35
588 A156 18um Oasis .90 .50

Fight Against Desert Encroachment — A157

1985
589 A157 10um Grain harvest, vert. .55 .30
590 A157 14um Brush fire 2.00 .75
591 A157 18um Planting brush 2.00 .75
Nos. 589-591 (3) 4.55 1.80

Natl. Independence, 25th Anniv. — A158

1985, Nov. 27 **Perf. 15x14½**
592 A158 18um multi 1.00 .40

Intl. Youth Year A159

1986, Feb. 13 **Litho.** **Perf. 13**
593 A159 18um Development .80 .40
594 A159 22um Participation 1.00 .50
595 A159 25um Peace, vert. 1.40 .60
Nos. 593-595 (3) 3.20 1.50

Toujounine Satellite Station — A160

1986, May 22 **Litho.** **Perf. 12½**
596 A160 25um multi 1.25 .60

World Wildlife Fund — A161

Monk seal (Monachus monachus).

1986, June 12 **Perf. 13**
597 A161 2um multi 1.50 .35
598 A161 5um multi 2.40 .60
599 A161 10um multi 3.75 1.00
600 A161 18um multi 6.75 2.00
Nos. 597-600 (4) 14.40 3.95
Souvenir Sheet
601 A161 50um multi 15.00 5.00

Weaving — A162

1986, July 20 **Litho.** **Perf. 12½**
602 A162 18um multi .80 .40

Sabra and Chatila Massacre, 4th Anniv. — A163

1986, Oct. 18
603 A163 22um multi .90 .40

A164

Christopher Columbus — A165

Indians, maps on globe and: 2um, Santa Maria. 22um, Nina. 35um, Pinta. 150um, Columbus.

1986, Oct. 14 **Litho.** **Perf. 13½**
604 A164 2um multi .25 .25
605 A164 22um multi .80 .35
606 A164 35um multi 1.25 .55
607 A164 150um multi 5.50 2.25
Nos. 604-607 (4) 7.80 3.40
Souvenir Sheet
608 A165 100um Columbus, Earth 4.50 4.00
Nos. 607-608 are airmail.

US Space Shuttle Challenger Explosion, Jan. 28, 1986 — A166

Crew members and: 7um, Space shuttle. 22um, Canadarm. 32um, Sky, moon. 43um, Memorial emblem.

1986, Oct. 14
609 A166 7um multi .25 .25
610 A166 22um multi .80 .30
611 A166 32um multi 1.25 .50
612 A166 43um multi 1.75 .65
Nos. 609-612 (4) 4.05 1.70
Souvenir Sheet
613 A166 100um Crew, lift-off 4.00 1.50
Nos. 612-613 are airmail.

Fish A167

1986, Oct. 16 **Perf. 13**
614 A167 4um Dorade .50 .25
615 A167 98um Truite de mer 7.50 2.25
See Nos. 631-633.

Birds A168

1986, Oct. 16
616 A168 22um Spatule blanche 2.50 .60
617 A168 32um Sterne bridee 3.00 .80
See Nos. 634-635.

World Food Day A169

1986, Nov. 6 **Perf. 12½**
618 A169 22um multi 1.00 .40

A170

Halley's Comet — A171

Space probes and portraits: 5um, J.H. Dort, Giotto probe. 18um, Sir William Huggins (1824-1910), English astronomer, and launch of Giotto on Ariane rocket. 26um, E.J. Opik, Giotto and Vega. 80um, F.L. Whipple, Planet-A. 100um, Edmond Halley, Giotto.

1986, Oct. 14 **Litho.** **Perf. 13½**
619 A170 5um multi .25 .25
620 A170 18um multi .60 .25
621 A170 26um multi 1.00 .40
622 A170 80um multi 3.25 1.25
Nos. 619-622 (4) 5.10 2.15
Souvenir Sheet
623 A171 100um multi 4.00 2.00
Nos. 622-623 are airmail.

Jerusalem Day — A172

1987, May 21 **Litho.** **Perf. 13½**
624 A172 22um Dome of the Rock 1.00 .40

Cordoue Mosque, 1200th Anniv. A173

1987, Sept. 5 **Litho.** **Perf. 13½**
625 A173 30um multi 1.50 .55

Literacy Campaign A174

1987, Sept. 12
626 A174 18um Classroom .70 .40
627 A174 22um Family reading, vert. .90 .60

World Health Day — A175

1987, Oct. 1 *Perf. 13*
628 A175 18um multi .80 .40

Natl. Population Census A176

1988, Aug. 21 Litho. *Perf. 13½*
629 A176 20um multi .80 .40

WHO, 40th Anniv. — A177

1988, Sept. 19 *Perf. 13*
630 A177 30um multi 1.25 .50

Fish Type of 1986
1988, Sept. 10 Litho. *Perf. 13*
631 A167 1um Rascasse
blanche .60 .25
632 A167 7um Baliste 1.00 .35
633 A167 15um Bonite a ventre
raye 2.75 .75
Nos. 631-633 (3) 5.25 1.35

Bird Type of 1986
1988, Sept. 15
634 A168 18um Grand cormorant 1.40 .60
635 A168 80um Royal tern 6.00 2.75

Arab Scouting Movement, 75th Anniv. — A178

1988, Sept. 29 Litho. *Perf. 13*
636 A178 35um multi 1.60 .60

1st Municipal Elections — A179

1988, Nov. 22 *Perf. 13½*
637 A179 20um Men casting ballots .65 .30
638 A179 24um Woman casting
ballot 1.00 .40

Organization of African Unity, 25th Anniv. (in 1988) — A180

1988, Dec. 7 Litho. *Perf. 13*
639 A180 40um multi 1.25 .65

Intl. Fund for Agricultural Development, 10th Anniv. (in 1988) — A181

1988, Dec. 15
640 A181 35um multi 1.75 .70

Autonomy of Nouakchott (Amitie) Port, 1st Anniv. — A182

1988, Dec. 20 Litho. *Perf. 13*
641 A182 24um multi 1.40 .60

A183

1989, July 7 Litho. *Perf. 13*
642 A183 35um multi 1.60 .60
French Revolution bicent., PHILEXFRANCE '89.

A184

1989, July 17
643 A184 20um multi .90 .40
1990 World Cup Soccer Championships, Italy.

Pilgrimage to Mecca A185

1989, Aug. 26 Litho. *Perf. 13½*
644 A185 20um Mosque .90 .40

African Development Bank, 25th Anniv. — A186

1989, Sept. 2
645 A186 37um lt vio & blk 1.25 .60

Tapestry — A187

1989, Oct. 1 *Perf. 13*
646 A187 50um multicolored 2.25 .85

Locusts, Moths and Ladybugs A188

1989, Dec. 29
647 A188 2um Heliothis
armigera .25 .25
648 A188 5um Locust .50 .25
649 A188 6um Aphis gossypii .25 .25
650 A188 10um Agrotis ypsilon .50 .25
651 A188 20um Chilo .95 .35
652 A188 20um Two locusts,
egg case 1.00 .35
653 A188 24um Locusts
emerging 1.10 .40
654 A188 24um Plitella xylos-
tella 1.10 .40
655 A188 30um Henosepi-
lachna elater-
ii 1.60 .50
656 A188 40um Locust flying 2.25 .70
657 A188 42um Trichoplusia ni 2.00 .70
658 A188 88um Locust, diff. 5.50 1.40
Nos. 647-658 (12) 17.00 5.80

For surcharge see No. 737.

Revolt — A189

1989, Dec. 8 Litho. *Perf. 13*
659 A189 35um multicolored 1.60 .70
2nd Anniv. of the Palestinian Uprising and 1st anniv. of the declaration of a Palestinian State.

Maghreb Arab Union, 1st Anniv. — A190

1990, Feb. 17 Litho. *Perf. 13½*
660 A190 50um multicolored 1.75 .80

Mineral Resources A191

1990, July 27 *Perf. 11½*
661 A191 60um multicolored 2.75 1.60

Intl. Literacy Year — A192

1990, July 27
662 A192 60um multicolored 1.75 1.00

1992 Summer Olympics, Barcelona A193

Litho. & Typo.
1990, Sept. 2 *Perf. 13½*
663 A193 5um Equestrian .25 .25
664 A193 50um Archery 1.90 .75
665 A193 60um Hammer
throw 2.00 1.25
666 A193 75um Field hockey 2.75 1.25
667 A193 90um Handball 3.50 1.50
668 A193 220um Table tennis 8.50 3.25
Nos. 663-668 (6) 18.90 8.25

Souvenir Sheet
669 A193 150um Runner 6.25 2.50
Nos. 668-669 airmail.

A194

1990, July 27 *Perf. 11½*
670 A194 50um multicolored 2.00 .75
Multinational Postal School, 20th anniv.

A195

1990, Nov. 21   Litho.   Perf. 11½
671 A195 85um multicolored   3.75 1.60
Declaration of the Palestinian State, 2nd anniv.

1992 Winter Olympics, Albertville A196

1990, Dec. 10   Litho.   Perf. 13½
672 A196 60um Downhill ski-
            ing   1.75 .75
673 A196 75um Cross-coun-
            try skiing   2.00 .90
674 A196 90um Ice hockey   2.75 1.10
675 A196 220um Pairs figure
            skating   6.25 2.75
     Nos. 672-675 (4)   12.75 5.50

Souvenir Sheet
676 A196 150um Slalom skiing 5.00 2.50
     Nos. 675-676 are airmail.

Release of Nelson Mandela A197

1990, Dec. 10
677 A197 85um multicolored   3.75 1.90

Return of Senegalese Refugees — A198

1990, Dec. 10
678 A198 50um Cooking at en-
            campment   2.00 1.00
679 A198 75um Women sewing 3.00 1.60
680 A198 85um Drawing water 3.50 1.75
     Nos. 678-680 (3)   8.50 4.35

Boy Scouts Observing Nature — A199

Scout: 5um, Picking mushrooms. 50um, Holding mushroom. 60um, Drawing butterfly. 75um, Feeding butterfly. 90um, Photographing butterfly. 220um, Drying mushrooms. No. 687, Using microscope.

1991, Jan. 16   Litho.   Perf. 13½
681 A199 5um multicolored   .40   .25
682 A199 50um multicolored 2.40 .95
683 A199 60um multicolored 2.25 1.10
684 A199 75um multicolored 2.50 1.00
685 A199 90um multicolored 2.50 1.10
686 A199 220um multicolored 5.75 2.75
     Nos. 681-686 (6)   15.80 7.15

Souvenir Sheet
687 A199 150um multicolored 6.00 4.00
Nos. 684 and 687 are airmail. Nos. 683-685 exist in souvenir sheets of 1.

Independence, 30th Anniv. — A200

1991, Mar. 5
688 A200 50um Satellite dish
            antennae   1.90 1.00
689 A200 60um Container ship 2.25 1.40
690 A200 100um Harvesting rice 3.75 1.90
     Nos. 688-690 (3)   7.90 4.30

World Meteorology Day — A201

1991, Mar. 23   Perf. 14x15
691 A201 100um multicolored 3.75 2.10

World Population Day — A202

1991, July 27   Litho.   Perf. 13½
692 A202 90um multicolored 3.50 1.75

Domesticated Animals — A203

1991   Litho.   Perf. 13½
693   A203 50um Cats   2.25 1.00
693A A203 60um Dog   2.75 1.60

Campaign Against Blindness A204

1991, Nov. 10   Litho.   Perf. 13½
694 A204 50um multicolored 2.00 1.00

Doctors Without Borders, 20th Anniv. A205

1991   Litho.   Perf. 13½
695 A205 60um multicolored 2.50 1.25

Installation of Central Electric Service (in 1989) A206

1991, Dec. 29   Litho.   Perf. 13½
696 A206 50um multicolored 2.50 1.00

Mineral Exploration, M'Haoudat A207

1993   Litho.   Perf. 13½
697 A207 50um shown   2.10 1.00
698 A207 60um Desert land-
            scape   2.50 1.40

1994 Winter Olympics, Lillehammer A208

1993
699 A208 10um Bobsled   .40   .25
700 A208 50um Luge   1.75 1.05
701 A208 60um Figure skating 2.10 1.25
702 A208 80um Downhill skiing 2.75 1.75
703 A208 220um Cross-country
            skiing   7.75 4.50
     Nos. 699-703 (5)   14.75 8.80

Souvenir Sheet
704 A208 150um Downhill ski-
            ing, diff.   5.75 3.25
No. 704 is airmail.
No. 700 exists dated "1998."

Intifada, 6th Anniv. — A209

Design: 60um, Palestinian children, horiz.

1993
705 A209 50um multicolored 2.10 1.00
706 A209 60um multicolored 2.50 1.40

First Multiparty Presidential Elections, 1st Anniv. A209a

Design: 60um, Line at polling place.

1993   Litho.   Perf. 13½
706B A209a 60um multi   25.00 —
An additional stamp was issued in this set. The editors would like to examine any example.

Caravans — A210

1993
707 A210 50um blue & multi 1.90 1.00
708 A210 60um violet & multi 2.25 1.40

Hut A210a

1994   Litho.   Perf. 13¼x13½
708A A210a 50um Hut, diff.   —   —
708B A210a 60um multi   —   —
708C A210a 80um Hut, diff.   —   —
             Set of 3   80.00

1994 World Cup Soccer Championships, U.S. — A211

Designs: 10um, Soldier Field. 50um, Foxboro Stadium. 60um, Robert F. Kennedy Stadium. 90um, Stanford Stadium. 220um, Giants Stadium. 150um, Rose Bowl.

1994, Feb. 10   Litho.   Perf. 13
709 A211 10um multicolored .35   .25
710 A211 50um multicolored 1.60 1.05
711 A211 60um multicolored 1.90 1.25
712 A211 90um multicolored 2.75 1.75
713 A211 220um multicolored 7.00 4.50
     Nos. 709-713 (5)   13.60 8.80

Souvenir Sheet
714 A211 150um multicolored 5.75 3.25

Birds of Banc d'Arguin National Park — A211a

Designs: 10 um, Gulls, horiz. 30um, Various birds. 40um, Terns. 50um, Sandpipers.

1994   Litho.   Perf. 13½
714A A211a 10um lt blue & multi — —
714B A211a 30um lt blue & multi — —
714C A211a 40um lt blue & multi — —
714D A211a 50um lt blue & multi — —

UN, 50th Anniv. A212

1995   Litho.   Perf. 11½
715 A212 60um Emblem, #167 1.50 .75

FAO, 50th
Anniv.
A213

1995
716 A213 50um Working in field 1.00 .70
717 A213 60um With fishing boat 1.25 .85
718 A213 90um Planting garden 1.90 1.25
Nos. 716-718 (3) 4.15 2.80

Traditional
Handicrafts — A214

1995, Aug. 14 Litho. Perf. 12
719 A214 50um Weaving rug — —
Perf. 11½x12
720 A214 60um Kettle — —

1996 Summer
Olympics,
Atlanta — A216

Design: 20um, Sprinters crouching at starting line. 40um, Five Runners. 50um, Runners.

1996, July 19 Litho. Perf. 11¾
725 A216 20um pink & multi — —
727 A216 40um blue & multi — —
728 A216 50um yel & multi — —

An additional stamp was issued in this set. The editors would like to examine any example.

Traditional
Games
A218

Design: 90um, Women and sticks.

1996, Oct. 25 Litho. Perf. 11¾
733 A218 90um multi — —

Two additional stamps were issued in this set. The editors would like to examine any examples.

French Pres. Jacques Chirac,
Mauritanian Pres. Maaouya Ould Sid
Ahmed Taya — A219

1997 Litho. Perf. 13¼x13
735A A219 60um multi — —
State visit of Chirac to Mauritania.

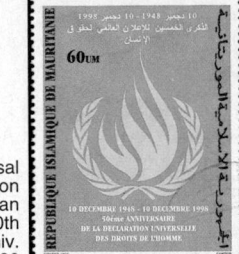

Universal
Declaration
of Human
Rights, 50th
Anniv.
A220

1998 Litho. Perf. 13x13¼
736 A220 60um multi — —

The editors suspect that other stamps were issued in this set and would like to examine any examples.

No. 649
Surcharged

2000 Method and Perf. As Before
737 A188 50um on 6um #649 — —

Indopondonoo, 40th Anniv. A221

2000 Litho. Perf. 13¼
738 A221 50um multi — —

Education
A222

Designs: 50um, Man with tablet, woman at computer. 60um, Open-air class. 90um, Reading class. 100um, Mathematics class.

2000
739-742 A222 Set of 4 — —

Mauritanian postal officials have declared as "illegal" the following items:
Sheets of 9 stamps with 60um denominations depicting Famous actresses (2 different). Classic actresses, Marilyn Monroe, Elvis Presley, The Beatles, Queen, Walt Disney, The Simpsons, Teddy bears.
Sheets of 6 stamps with 80um denominations depicting Birds and Scout emblem (15 different).
Sheets of 6 stamps with 60um denominations depicting Trains (5 different), Penguins and Rotary emblem (2 different), Cats and Rotary emblem (2 different), Elephants and Rotary emblem (2 different), Polar bears and Rotary emblem (2 different), Lighthouses and Rotary emblem (2 different), Firearms and Rotary emblem, Firearms and Scout emblem, Pope John Paul II, Harry Potter, Scooby-Doo.
Sheets of 4 stamps depicting various sports of the Sydney Olympics (2 different).
Souvenir sheet depicting Various sports of the Sydney Olympics.
Se-tenant sets of 4 stamps depicting sports of the Sydney Olympics (2 different).

Flora, Fauna and Mushrooms — A223

No. 743: a, Chelonia mydas. b, Octopus vulgaris. c, Coelacanth.
No. 744: a, Lepiota aspera. b, Lactarius camphoratus. c, Clitocybe gibba.
No. 745: a, Harpa costata. b, Voluta lapponica. c, Tellina variegata.
No. 746: a, Akhal-Teke horse. b, Arabian horse. c, Lipizzaner horse.
No. 747: a, Tibetan dog, Balinese cat. b, Shetland sheepdog, Ragdoll cat. c, Cao de Serra de Aires sheepdog, Abyssinian cat.
No. 748: a, Acraea igati. b, Mylotris humbolti. c, Mylotris ngaziya.
No. 749: a, Zosterops maderaspatana. b, Otus rutilus. c, Nelicurvitus nelicourvi.
No. 750: a, Maxillaria tenuifolia. b, Crotalaria. c, Maxillaria marginata.
No. 751, Russula virescens. No. 752, Black Russian cat.

2000, Nov. 5 Litho. Perf. 13½
743 Horiz. strip of 3 1.60 1.60
a.-c. A223 50um Any single .50 .50
744 Horiz. strip of 3 1.60 1.60
a.-c. A223 50um Any single .50 .50
745 Horiz. strip of 3 1.75 1.75
a.-c. A223 60um Any single .55 .55
746 Horiz. strip of 3 2.75 2.75
a.-c. A223 90um Any single .90 .90
747 Horiz. strip of 3 3.00 3.00
a.-c. A223 100um Any single 1.00 1.00
748 Horiz. strip of 3 6.00 6.00
a. o. A223 200um Any single 2.00 2.00
749 Horiz. strip of 3 7.00 7.00
a.-c. A223 220um Any single 2.25 2.25
750 Horiz. strip of 3 2.75 2.75
a. A223 60um multi .60 .60
b. A223 90um multi .90 .90
c. A223 100um multi 1.00 1.00
Nos. 743-750 (8) 26.45 26.45

Souvenir Sheets
751 A223 300um multi 4.75 4.75
752 A223 300um multi 4.75 4.75

Nos. 746-749 exist in souvenir sheets containing one strip of 3 with light blue frames. No. 750 exists imperf.

2002 World Cup
Soccer
Championships,
Japan and
Korea — A224

No. 753: a, Zinedine Zidane. b, Christian Vieri. c, Alessandro del Piero. d, Lilian Thuram.

No. 754: a, Oliver Bierhoff. b, Jürgen Klinsmann. c, Edgar Davids. d, Dennis Bergkamp.
300um, Jules Rimet Cup, soccer players, horiz.

2000
753 Horiz. strip of 4 14.00 14.00
a.-d. A224 90um Any single 3.00 3.00
754 Horiz. strip of 4 14.00 14.00
a.-d. A224 100um Any single 3.00 3.00
Souvenir Sheet
755 A224 300um multi 4.00 4.00

No. 755 contains one 57x51mm stamp. Souvenir sheets of 4 stamps exist with Nos. 753a-753d and 754a-754d with colored stamp frames.

Theodore Monod
(1902-2000),
Naturalist
A225

2003, Jan. 1 Perf. 13¼x13
756 A225 370um multi 3.50 2.50

Trains
A226

Designs: 100um, Freight train for minerals. 370um, Passenger train. 440um, Desert train.

2003, Jan. 1 Perf. 13x13¼
757-759 A226 Set of 3 10.00 10.00

Tourist
Attractions
A227

Designs: 100um, Sailboats, Banc d'Arguin. 220um, Ben Amera. 370um, Desert warthogs, Diawling Park. 440fr, Palms, Tergit, vert.

2003, Jan. 1 Perf. 13x13¼, 13¼x13
760-763 A227 Set of 4 12.00 7.00

Handicrafts
A228

Designs: 100um, Wooden chest. 220um, Pipes. 310um, Teapot. 370um, Beads.

2003, Jan. 1 Perf. 13x13¼
764-767 A228 Set of 4 10.00 6.00

Historic
Towns
A229

Designs: 100um, Mosque, Chinguetti. 220um, Mosque, Ouadane. 660um, Wall design, Oualata. 880um, Mosque, Tichitt.

2003, Jan. 1
768-771 A229 Set of 4 18.00 12.00

Promotion of Books and Reading
A230

Open book and: 100um, Stack of books, chair. 220um, Camel. 280um, Tower. 370um, Man, construction equipment.

2003, Jan. 1   **Litho.**   *Perf. 13*
772-775   A230   Set of 4   12.50   6.00

Diplomatic Relations Between Mauritania and People's Republic of China, 40th Anniv.
A231

Flags and: 100um, Ships and crane. 370um, Ship and crane, vert.

     Perf. 13x13¼, 13¼x13
2005, July 19   **Litho.**
776-777   A231   Set of 2   6.25   6.25

Independence, 45th Anniv. — A232

Denominations: 100um, 370um.

2005, Nov. 16   *Perf. 13*
778-779   A232   Set of 2   5.00   5.00

World Summit on the Information Society, Tunis
A233

Denominations: 100um, 370um.

2005, Nov. 16
780-781   A233   Set of 2   5.00   5.00

Musical Instruments — A234

Designs: 100um, Tidinit and gambré. 220um, Ardines, vert. 370um, Tom-toms. 440um, Kora and djembé, vert.

2005, Nov. 28
782-785   A234   Set of 4   13.00   13.00

Flora
A235

Designs: 100um, Acacia tree. 220um, Euphorbia, vert. 370um, Jujube tree. 440um, Baobab tree, vert.

2005, Nov. 28
786-789   A235   Set of 4   13.00   13.00

Fauna
A236

Designs: 100um, Starred lizard. 220um, Horned viper, vert. 370um, Lizard. 440um, Scorpion, vert.

2005, Nov. 28
790-793   A236   Set of 4   13.00   13.00

Tourism
A237

Designs: 100um, People, fish and dolphins in water. 220um, Hodh El Gharbi. 370um, Adrar. 440um, Tiris Zemour.

2005, Nov. 28
794-797   A237   Set of 4   13.00   13.00

Jewelry
A238

Designs: 100um, Necklaces. 220um, Khalkhal bracelets. 370um, Strings of beads. 440fr, Bracelets.

2008   **Litho.**   *Perf. 13*
798-801   A238   Set of 4   17.00   17.00

Exploitation of Natural Resources — A239

Designs: 100um, Zouerate iron mine. 280um, Chinguitti oil platform, vert. 310um, Akjoujt copper mine. 370um, Taziast gold mine, vert.

2008
802-805   A239   Set of 4   17.00   17.00

Animals
A240

Designs: 100um, Birds. 220um, Dolphins. 370um, Seal. 440um, Sea turtle.

2009   **Litho.**   *Perf. 13*
806-809   A240   Set of 4   13.50   13.50

Saddles
A241

Saddle for: 100um, Horse. 220um, Cow. 370um, Ass. 440um, Camel.

2009
810-813   A241   Set of 4   13.50   13.50

Gear for Nomads
A242

Designs: 100um, Rifle holster. 150um, Tassoufra. 220um, Powder horns. 370um, Palanquin, vert. 440um, Prayer rug.

2009
814-818   A242   Set of 5   16.50   16.50

Necklaces
A243

Designs: 100um, Ebony necklace. 150um, Agate necklace. 220um, Amber necklace. 370um, Traditional necklace. 440um, Stone necklace.

2010   *Perf. 13¼*
819-823   A243   Set of 5   12.00   12.00

Independence, 50th Anniv. — A244

2010   *Perf. 13*
824   A244   370um multi   7.50   7.50

Fish
A245

Designs: 100um, Daisy stingray (pastenague marguerite). 220um, Guitar fish (raie guitare). 370um, Spinner shark (requin tisserand).

2011
825-827   A245   Set of 3   7.00   7.00

Mammals
A247

Designs: 100um, Hyena. 370um, Fennec.

2011   **Litho.**   *Perf. 13*
832-833   A247   Set of 2   5.00   5.00

2012 Festival of Old Towns, Ouadane — A248

Designs: 100um, Town. 370um, Festival emblem and names of host towns.

2012
834-835   A248   Set of 2   6.00   5.00

Marine Life
A249

Designs: 100um, King mackerel (Maquereau bonite). 150um, Butterfish (Lippe). 220um, Red-banded sea bream (Pagre rayé). 280um, Blue-spotted sea bream (Merou à points bleus). No. 840, 370um, Dogfish (Chien de mer). No. 841, 370um, Cuttlefish (Seiche commune). 440um, Round sardinella (Sardinelle ronde).

2013   **Litho.**   *Perf. 12¾x13*
836-842   A249   Set of 7   —   —

SEMI-POSTAL STAMPS

Nos. 23 and 26 Surcharged in Red

1915-18   **Unwmk.**   *Perf. 14x13½*
B1   A4   10c + 5c rose & red org   1.75   2.10
   a.   Double surcharge   225.00
B2   A4   15c + 5c dk brn & blk ('18)   1.75   2.10
   a.   Double surcharge   190.00
   b.   Inverted surcharge   150.00

Curie Issue
Common Design Type
1938, Oct. 24   *Perf. 13*
B3   CD80   1.75fr + 50c brt ultra   7.75   7.75

French Revolution Issue
Common Design Type
Photo.; Name and Value Typographed in Black
1939, July 5   **Unwmk.**
B4   CD83   45c + 25c grn   8.50   8.50
B5   CD83   70c + 30c brn   8.50   8.50
B6   CD83   90c + 35c red org   8.50   8.50
B7   CD83   1.25fr + 1fr rose pink   8.50   8.50
B8   CD83   2.25fr + 2fr bl   8.50   8.50
   Nos. B4-B8 (5)   42.50   42.50

> **Catalogue values for unused stamps in this section, from this point to the end of the section, are for Never Hinged items.**

Stamps of 1938 Surcharge in Red or Black

1941
B9   A6   50c + 1fr pur (R)   7.00   3.50
B10   A7   80c + 2fr dp bl (R)   14.00   7.00
B11   A7   1.50fr + 2fr vio (R)   14.00   10.00
B12   A8   2fr + 3fr rose vio (Bk)   14.00   10.00
   Nos. B9-B12 (4)   49.00   30.50

Common Design Type and

Moorish Goumier
SP1

White Goumier — SP2

1941 **Photo.** *Perf. 13½*
B13 SP1 1fr + 1fr red 1.00
B14 CD86 1.50fr + 3fr claret 1.00
B15 SP2 2.50fr + 1fr blue 1.00
Nos. B13-B15 (3) 3.00

Nos. B13-B15 were issued by the Vichy government in France, but were not placed on sale in Mauritania.

Nos. 114-115 Surcharged in Black or Red

1944 **Engr.** *Perf. 12½x12*
B15A 50c + 1.50fr on 2.50fr deep blue (R) .80
B15B + 2.50fr on 1fr green .80

Colonial Development Fund.
Nos. B15A-B15B were issued by the Vichy government in France, but were not placed on sale in Mauritania.

Islamic Republic
Anti-Malaria Issue
Common Design Type

1962, Apr. 7 **Engr.** *Perf. 12½x12*
B16 CD108 25fr + 5f light olive grn .80 .80

Freedom from Hunger Issue
Common Design Type

1963, Mar. 21 **Unwmk.** *Perf. 13*
B17 CD112 25fr + 5fr multi .80 .80

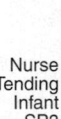

Nurse Tending Infant SP3

1972, May 8 **Photo.** *Perf. 12½x13*
B18 SP3 35fr + 5fr grn, red & brn 1.50 1.50

Surtax was for Mauritania Red Crescent Society.

___

AIR POST STAMPS

Common Design Type
Perf. 12½x12

1940, Feb. 8 **Engr.** **Unwmk.**
C1 CD85 1.90fr ultra .35 .35
C2 CD85 2.90fr dk red .35 .35
C3 CD85 4.50fr dk gray grn .70 .70
C4 CD85 4.90fr yel bister .70 .70
C5 CD85 6.90fr deep org 1.40 1.40
Nos. C1-C5 (5) 3.50 3.50

> Catalogue values for unused stamps in this section, from this point to the end of the section, are for Never Hinged items.

Common Design Types
1942
C6 CD88 50c car & bl .35
C7 CD88 1fr brn & blk .35
C8 CD88 2fr dk grn & red brn .70
C9 CD88 3fr dk bl & scar .70
C10 CD88 5fr vio & brn red 1.00

Frame Engraved, Center Typo.
C11 CD89 10fr ultra, ind & hn 1.40
a. Center inverted 1,400.

C12 CD89 20fr rose car, mag & buff 1.75
a. Center inverted 1,400.
C13 CD89 50fr yel grn, dl grn & org 3.50 3.25
Nos. C6-C13 (8) 9.75

There is doubt whether Nos. C6-C12 were officially placed in use.
No. C11 exists with violet-blue center. Value $300.

Islamic Republic

Flamingoes AP1

Designs: 200fr, African spoonbills. 500fr, Slender-billed gull, horiz.

Unwmk.
1961, June 30 **Engr.** *Perf. 13*
C14 AP1 100fr red org, brn & ultra 3.75 2.00
C15 AP1 200fr red org, sep & sl grn 5.75 3.50
C16 AP1 500fr red org, gray & bl 17.00 8.00
Nos. C14-C16 (3) 26.50 13.50

An overprint, "Europa / CECA / MIFERMA," was applied in carmine to No. C16 in 1962. Two types exist: type 1, no box around "MIFERMA"; box surrounding "MIFERMA". Values: type 1, $35; type 2, $16.
The anti-malaria emblem, including slogan "Le Monde contre le Paludisme," was overprinted on Nos. C14-C15 in 1962. Two types of overprint: type 1, double lines of latitude and longitude on globe; type single lines of latitude and longitude on globe. Values: type 1, $27.50; type 2: $8.

Air Afrique Issue
Common Design Type

1962, Feb. 17
C17 CD107 100fr sl grn, choc & bis 2.50 1.25

UN Headquarters, New York; View of Nouakchott — AP2

1962, Oct. 27 **Engr.** *Perf. 13*
C18 AP2 100fr bluish grn, dk bl & org brn 1.50 1.00

Mauritania's admission to the UN.

Plane, Nouakchott Airport — AP3

1963, May 3 **Unwmk.** *Perf. 13*
C19 AP3 500fr dp bl, gldn brn & slate grn 11.00 4.00

Miferma Open-pit Mine at Zouerate — AP4

Design: 200fr, Ore transport at Port Etienne.

1963, June **Photo.** *Perf. 13x12*
C20 AP4 100fr multi 1.90 .55
C21 AP4 200fr multi 4.75 1.25

African Postal Union Issue
Common Design Type

1963, Sept. 8 **Unwmk.** *Perf. 12½*
C22 CD114 85fr blk brn, ocher & red 1.50 .60

Globe and Telstar — AP5

Design: 150fr, Relay satellite and stars.

1963, Oct. 7 **Engr.** *Perf. 13*
C23 AP5 50fr yel grn, pur & red brn .75 .40
C24 AP5 150fr red brn & sl grn 2.50 1.40

Communication through space.

Tiros Satellite and Emblem of WMO — AP6

1963, Nov. 4
C25 AP6 200fr ultra, brn & grn 4.00 1.75

Space research for meteorology and navigation.

1963 Air Afrique Issue
Common Design Type

1963, Nov. 19 **Photo.** *Perf. 13x12*
C26 CD115 25fr multi .70 .25

UN Emblem, Doves and Sun — AP7

1963, Dec. 10 **Engr.** *Perf. 13*
C27 AP7 100fr vio, brn, & dk bl 1.75 .90

Universal Declaration of Human Rights, 15th anniv.

Europafrica Issue

Symbols of Agriculture and Industry — AP8

1964, Jan. 6 **Photo.**
C28 AP8 50fr multi 1.40 .90

Signing of economic agreement between the European Economic Community and the African and Malgache Union at Yaoundé, Cameroun, July 20, 1963.

Lichtenstein's Sand Grouse — AP9

Birds: 200fr, Long-tailed cormorant. 500fr, Chanting goshawk.

1964, Feb. 3 **Engr.** *Perf. 13*
C29 AP9 100fr ocher, ol & dk brn 3.25 1.10
C30 AP9 200fr blk, dk bl & brn 5.00 1.90
C31 AP9 500fr rose red, grn & sl 15.00 5.75
Nos. C29-C31 (3) 23.25 8.75

Isis, Temple at Philae and Trajan's Kiosk — AP10

1964, Mar. 8 **Unwmk.** *Perf. 13*
C32 AP10 10fr red brn, Prus bl & blk .50 .25
C33 AP10 25fr red brn, ind & Prus bl .80 .40
C34 AP10 60fr blk brn, Prus bl & red brn 1.60 .75
Nos. C32-C34 (3) 2.90 1.40

UNESCO world campaign to save historic monuments in Nubia.

Syncom Satellite, Globe — AP11

1964, May 4 **Engr.**
C35 AP11 100fr red, red brn & ultra 1.50 .75

Issued to publicize space communications.

Horse Race on Bowl — AP12

Sport Designs from Ancient Pottery: 50fr, Runner, vert. 85fr, Wrestlers, vert. 100fr, Charioteer.

1964, Sept. 27　Unwmk.　Perf. 13
C36 AP12　15fr ol bis & choc　　.45　.30
C37 AP12　50fr bl & org brn　　1.10　.55
C38 AP12　85fr crim & brn　　1.90　1.10
C39 AP12　100fr emer & dk red
　　　　　　brn　　2.40　1.40
　a.　Min. sheet of 4, #C36-C39　7.25　7.25
　　　Nos. C36-C39 (4)　5.85　3.35

18th Olympic Games, Tokyo, Oct. 10-25.

Pres. John F.
Kennedy (1917-
1963)
AP13

1964, Dec. 7　Photo.　Perf. 12½
C40 AP13　100fr red brn, bl grn &
　　　　　　dk brn　　1.50　1.50
　a.　Souv. sheet of 4　7.00　7.00

ITU Emblem, Induction Telegraph and
Relay Satellite — AP14

1965, May 17　Engr.　Perf. 13
C41 AP14　250fr multi　　4.75　3.00
ITU, centenary.

Fight Against
Cancer — AP15

1965, July 19　Unwmk.　Perf. 13
C42 AP15　100fr bis, Prus bl &
　　　　　　red　　1.45　.70
Issued to publicize the fight against cancer.

Winston
Churchill — AP16

1965, Dec. 6　Photo.　Perf. 13
C43 AP16　200fr multi　　2.75　1.40
Sir Winston Spencer Churchill (1874-1965), statesman and WWII leader.

Diamant Rocket
Ascending
AP17

French achievements in space: 60fr, Satellite A-1 and earth, horiz.　90fr, Scout rocket and satellite FR-1, horiz.

1966, Feb. 7　Engr.　Perf. 13
C44 AP17　30fr dp bl, red & grn　　.50　.30
C45 AP17　60fr mar, Prus grn &
　　　　　　bl　　1.10　.55
C46 AP17　90fr dp bl, rose cl &
　　　　　　vio　　1.60　.80
　　　Nos. C44-C46 (3)　3.20　1.65

Dr. Albert Schweitzer and
Clinic — AP18

1966, Feb. 21　Photo.　Perf. 12½
C47 AP18　50fr multi　　1.50　.65
Schweitzer (1875-1965), medical missionary to Gabon, theologian and musician.

Thomas P. Stafford, Walter M. Schirra
and Gemini 6 — AP19

Designs: 100fr, Frank A. Borman, James A. Lovell, Jr., and Gemini 7.　200fr, Pavel Belyayev, Alexei Leonov, Voskhod 2.

1966, Mar. 7　Photo.　Perf. 12½
C48 AP19　50fr multi　　.70　.30
C49 AP19　100fr multi　　1.50　.55
C50 AP19　200fr multi　　2.50　1.25
　　　Nos. C48-C50 (3)　4.70　2.10

Issued to honor achievements in space.

Map of Africa
and
Dove — AP20

1966, May 9　Photo.　Perf. 13
C51 AP20　100fr red brn, sl & yel
　　　　　　grn　　1.00　.50
Organization for African Unity.

D-1 Satellite over
Earth — AP21

1966, June 6　Engr.
C52 AP21　100fr bl, dk pur &
　　　　　　ocher　　1.50　.80
Launching of the D-1 satellite at Hammaguir, Algeria, Feb. 17, 1966.

Bréguet 14 — AP22

Planes: 100fr, Goliath Farman, and camel caravan.　150fr, Couzinet "Arc-en-Ciel." 200fr, Latécoère 28 hydroplane.

1966, July 4　Engr.　Perf. 13
C53 AP22　50fr sl bl, dl grn &
　　　　　　ol bis　　1.00　.30
C54 AP22　100fr brt bl, dk grn &
　　　　　　dk red brn　　2.10　.50
C55 AP22　150fr dl brn, Prus bl
　　　　　　& saph　　3.00　.80
C56 AP22　200fr dk red brn, bl &
　　　　　　ind　　4.25　1.25
　　　Nos. C53-C56 (4)　10.35　2.85

Air Afrique Issue
Common Design Type
1966, Aug. 31　Photo.　Perf. 13
C57 CD123　30fr red, blk & gray　　.80　.30

"The Raft of the Medusa," by
Théodore Géricault — AP23

1966, Sept. 5　Photo.　Perf. 12½
C58 AP23　500fr multi　　11.50　7.00
Sinking of the frigate "Medusa" off Mauritania, July 2, 1816.

Symbols of Agriculture and
Industry — AP24

1966, Nov. 7　Photo.　Perf. 13x12
C59 AP24　50fr multi　　1.00　.40

Third anniversary, economic agreement between the European Economic Community and the African and Malgache Union.

Crowned
Crane — AP25

1967, Apr. 3　Perf. 12½x13
C60 AP25　100fr shown　　2.40　.85
C61 AP25　200fr Common egret　4.50　1.25
C62 AP25　500fr Ostrich　　12.00　4.75
　　　Nos. C60-C62 (3)　18.90　6.85
For surcharge see No. C129.

Eye, Globe and
Rockets — AP26

1967, May 2　Engr.　Perf. 13
C63 AP26　250fr brn, Prus bl &
　　　　　　blk　　4.00　1.40
EXPO '67 Intl. Exhibition, Montreal, Apr. 28-Oct. 27.

Emblem of
Atomic Energy
Commission
AP27

1967, Aug. 7　Engr.　Perf. 13
C64 AP27　200fr dk red, brt grn &
　　　　　　ultra　　2.75　1.25
International Atomic Energy Commission.

African Postal Union Issue
Common Design Type
1967, Sept. 9　Engr.　Perf. 13
C65 CD124　100fr brn org, vio brn
　　　　　　& brt grn　　1.25　.60

Francesca da Rimini, by Ingres AP28

Paintings by and of Ingres: 100fr, Young man's torso. 150fr, "The Iliad" (seated woman). 200fr, Ingres in his Studio, by Alaux. 250fr, "The Odyssey" (seated woman).

1967-68		Photo.	Perf. 12½	
C66	AP28	90fr multi	1.75	.60
C67	AP28	100fr multi ('68)	1.75	.70
C68	AP28	150fr multi ('68)	2.50	1.05
C69	AP28	200fr multi	3.00	1.10
C70	AP28	250fr multi ('68)	4.25	1.75
		Nos. C66-C70 (5)	13.25	5.20

Jean Dominique Ingres (1780-1867), French painter.
Issued: 90fr, 200fr, 10/2/67; others, 9/2/68. See No. C79.

Konrad Adenauer AP29

1968, Feb. 5		Photo.	Perf. 12½	
C71	AP29	100fr org brn, lt bl & blk	1.50	.70
a.		Souv. sheet of 4	7.50	6.00

Adenauer (1876-1967), chancellor of West Germany (1949-63).

Gymnast AP30

Sports: 20fr, Slalom, horiz. 50fr, Ski jump. 100fr, Hurdling, horiz.

1968, Mar. 4		Engr.	Perf. 13	
C72	AP30	20fr plum, blk & bl	.35	.25
C73	AP30	30fr dl pur, brt grn & brn	.45	.25
C74	AP30	50fr Prus bl, bis & bl grn	.65	.30
C75	AP30	100fr brn, grn & ver	1.40	.45
		Nos. C72-C75 (4)	2.85	1.25

1968 Olympic Games.

WHO Emblem, Man and Insects — AP31

1968, May 2		Engr.	Perf. 13	
C76	AP31	150fr red lil, dp bl & org red	1.90	.80

WHO, 20th anniversary.

Martin Luther King — AP32

Design: No. C78, Mahatma Gandhi.

1968, Nov. 4		Photo.	Perf. 12½	
C77	AP32	50fr sl bl, cit & blk	1.00	.30
C78	AP32	50fr sl bl, lt bl & blk	1.00	.30
a.		Souv. sheet of 4, 2 each #C77-C78	4.25	4.25

Issued to honor two apostles of peace.

PHILEXAFRIQUE Issue
Painting Type of 1967

Design: 100fr, The Surprise Letter, by Charles Antoine Coypel.

1968, Dec. 9		Photo.	Perf. 12½	
C79	AP28	100fr multi	3.00	1.50

PHILEXAFRIQUE, Phil. Exhib., Abidjan, Feb. 14-23. Printed with alternating brown red label.

2nd PHILEXAFRIQUE Issue
Common Design Type

50fr, Mauritania #89 & family on jungle trail.

1969, Feb. 14		Engr.	Perf. 13	
C80	CD128	50fr sl grn, vio brn & red brn	1.90	.75

Napoleon Installed in Council of State, by Louis Charles Couder AP33

Paintings: 50fr, Napoleon at Council of the 500, by F. Bouchot. 250fr, Farewell at Fontainebleau, by Horace Vernet.

1969, Feb. 24		Photo.	Perf. 12½	
C81	AP33	50fr pur & multi	2.00	.90
C82	AP33	90fr multi	2.50	1.40
C83	AP33	250fr multi	6.75	3.25
		Nos. C81-C83 (3)	11.25	5.55

Napoleon Bonaparte (1769-1821).

Camel, Gazelles, and Tourist Year Emblem — AP34

1969, June 9		Engr.	Perf. 13	
C84	AP34	50fr org, dk brn & lt bl	1.00	.50

Year of African Tourism.

Dancers and Temple Ruins, Baalbek — AP35

1969, June 16
C85	AP35	100fr Prus bl, ol brn & rose car	1.40	.55

International Baalbek Festival, Lebanon.

Apollo 8 and Moon Surface — AP36

Embossed on Gold Foil
1969		Die-cut Perf. 10		
C86	AP36	1000fr gold	20.00	20.00

Man's first flight around the moon, Dec. 21-28, 1968 (US astronauts Col. Frank Borman, Capt. James Lovell and Maj. William Anders).

Mamo Wolde, Ethiopia, Marathon AP37

Designs: 70fr, Bob Beamon, US, broad jump. 150fr, Vera Caslavska, Czechoslovakia, gymnastics.

1969, July 7		Engr.	Perf. 13	
C87	AP37	30fr multi	.40	.25
C88	AP37	70fr multi	.70	.40
C89	AP37	150fr multi	1.90	.90
		Nos. C87-C89 (3)	3.00	1.55

Issued to honor gold medal winners in the 19th Olympic Games, Mexico City.

Map of London-Istanbul Route — AP38

London to Sydney automobile rally: 20fr, Map showing Ankara to Teheran route, and compass rose. 50fr, Map showing Kandahar to Bombay route, arms of Afghanistan and elephant. 70fr, Map of Australia with Perth to Sydney route, and kangaroo.

1969, Aug. 14		Engr.	Perf. 13	
C90	AP38	10fr multicolored	.25	.25
C91	AP38	20fr multicolored	.45	.25
C92	AP38	50fr multicolored	.75	.30
C93	AP38	70fr multicolored	1.10	.40
a.		Min. sheet of 4, #C90-C93	3.00	3.00
		Nos. C90-C93 (4)	2.55	1.20

Palette with World Map, Geisha and EXPO '70 Emblem — AP39

EXPO '70 Emblem and: 75fr, Fan & fireworks. 150fr, Stylized bird, map of Japan & boat.

1969, June 15 Photo. Perf. 12½
|---|---|---|---|---|
1970, June 15 Photo. Perf. 12½
C94	AP39	50fr multi	.70	.25
C95	AP39	75fr multi	1.00	.40
C96	AP39	150fr multi	1.75	.80
		Nos. C94-C96 (3)	3.45	1.45

Issued to publicize EXPO '70 International Exhibition, Osaka, Japan, Mar. 15-Sept. 13.

UN Emblem, Balloon, Rocket, Farm Woman, Tractor, Old and New Record Players — AP40

1970, June 22 Engr. Perf. 13
C97	AP40	100fr ultra, dk brn & grn	1.20	.55

25th anniversary of the United Nations.

Elliott See (1927-1966), American Astronaut AP41

No. C99, Vladimir Komarov (1927-67). No. C100, Yuri Gagarin (1934-68). No. C101, Virgil Grissom (1926-67). No. C102, Edward White (1930-67). No. C103, Roger Chaffee (1935-67).

1970 Engr. Perf. 13
Portrait in Brown
C98	AP41	150fr gray & brt bl	1.75	.80
C99	AP41	150fr gray & org	1.75	.80
C100	AP41	150fr gray & org	1.75	.80
a.		Souv. sheet of 3, #C98-C100	5.50	5.50
C101	AP41	150fr ultra & grnsh bl	1.75	.80
C102	AP41	150fr ultra & org	1.75	.80
C103	AP41	150fr ultra & grnsh bl	1.75	.80
a.		Souv. sheet of 3, #C101-C103	5.50	5.50
		Nos. C98-C103 (6)	10.50	4.80

American and Russian astronauts who died in space explorations.

Apollo 13 Capsule with Parachutes AP42

Gold Embossed
1970, Aug. 17			Perf. 12½	
C104	AP42	500fr gold, crim & bl	7.00	7.00

Safe return of Apollo 13 crew.

Parliament, Nouakchott, and Coat of Arms — AP43

1970, Nov. 28   Photo.   Perf. 12½
C105 AP43 100fr multi   1.25 .50
10th anniversary of Independence.

Hercules Wrestling Antaeus — AP44

1971, Mar. 8   Engr.   Perf. 13
C106 AP44 100fr red lil, brn & ul-
         tra   1.90 .85
Pre-Olympic Year. Design from a vase dec-
oration by Euphronius.

Gamal Abdel Nasser (1918-1970), President of U.A.R. — AP46

1971, May 10   Photo.   Perf. 12½
C109 AP46 100fr gold & multi 1.00 .45

Boy Scout, Emblem and Map of Mauritania AP47

1971, Aug. 16   Photo.   Perf. 12½
C110 AP47 35fr yel & multi   .55   .25
C111 AP47 40fr pink & multi   .60   .25
C112 AP47 100fr multi   1.50 .45
      Nos. C110-C112 (3)   2.65 .95
13th Boy Scout World Jamboree, Asagiri
Plain, Japan, Aug. 2-10.

African Postal Union Issue
Common Design Type

Design: 100fr, Women musicians and
UAMPT building, Brazzaville, Congo.

1971, Nov. 13   Photo.   Perf. 13x13½
C113 CD135 100fr bl & multi   1.20 .65

Letter and Postal Emblem AP48

1971, Dec. 2   Perf. 13
C114 AP48 35fr bis & multi   .65   .30
10th anniversary of African Postal Union.

Mosul Monarch, from Book of Songs, c. 1218 AP49

Designs from Mohammedan Miniatures:
40fr, Prince holding audience, Egypt, 1334.
100fr, Pilgrim caravan, from "Maquamat,"
Baghdad, 1237.

1972, Jan. 10   Photo.   Perf. 13
C115 AP49 35fr gold & multi   .50   .25
C116 AP49 40fr gray & multi   .65   .30
C117 AP49 100fr buff & multi 1.75 .60
      Nos. C115-C117 (3)   2.90 1.15
For surcharges see Nos. C140, C143-C144.

Grand Canal, by Canaletto — AP50

Designs: 45fr, Venice Harbor, by Carlevaris,
vert. 250fr, Santa Maria della Salute, by
Canaletto.

1972, Feb. 14
C118 AP50 45fr gold & multi   .75   .30
C119 AP50 100fr gold & multi 1.90 .70
C120 AP50 250fr gold & multi 4.00 1.10
      Nos. C118-C120 (3)   6.65 2.10
UNESCO campaign to save Venice.

Hurdles and Olympic Rings — AP51

1972, Apr. 27   Engr.   Perf. 13
C121 AP51 75fr org, vio brn &
         blk   .75   .25
C122 AP51 100fr Prus bl, vio brn
         & brn   1.10 .40
C123 AP51 200fr lake, vio brn &
         blk   2.40 .60
   a. Min. sheet of 3, #C121-C123   6.00 6.00
      Nos. C121-C123 (3)   4.25 1.25
20th Olympic Games, Munich, Aug. 26-
Sept. 11.
For overprints see Nos. C126-C128.

Luna 17 on Moon — AP52

75fr, Luna 16 take-off from moon, vert.

1972, Oct. 9
C124 AP52 75fr vio bl, bis & grn .80   .25
C125 AP52 100fr dl pur, sl & ol
         bis   1.10 .40
Russian moon missions, Luna 16, Sept. 12-
14, 1970; and Luna 17, Nov. 10-17, 1970.

**Nos. C121-C123 Overprinted in
Violet Blue or Red:**
   a. 110m HAIES / MILBURN MEDAILLE
       D'OR
   b. 400m HAIES / AKII-BUA MEDAILLE
       D'OR
   c. 3.000m STEEPLE / KEINO MEDAILLE
       D'OR

1972, Oct. 16
C126 AP51(a) 75fr multi (VB)   .90   .40
C127 AP51(b) 100fr multi (R)   1.10 .55
C128 AP51(c) 200fr multi (VB) 2.50 1.05
      Nos. C126-C128 (3)   4.50 2.00
Gold medal winners in 20th Olympic
Games: Rod Milburn, US, John Akii-Bua,
Uganda, and Kipchoge Keino, Kenya.

**No. C62 Surcharged with New
Value, Two Bars and: "Apollo XVII /
December 1972"**

1973, Jan. 29   Photo.   Perf. 12½x13
C129 AP25 250fr on 500fr multi 3.50 1.40
Apollo 17 moon mission, Dec. 7-19, 1972.

Seal Type of Regular Issue
1973, Feb. 28   Litho.   Perf. 13
C130 A63 135fr Seal's head   4.50 1.90
For surcharge see No. C145.

Lion Eating Caiman, by Delacroix — AP53

Painting: 250fr, Lion Eating Boar, by
Delacroix.

1973, Mar. 26   Photo.   Perf. 13x12½
C131 AP53 100fr blk & multi   2.00 .90
C132 AP53 250fr blk & multi   4.50 2.25
For surcharges see Nos. C148-C149.

Villagers Observing Solar Eclipse — AP54

40fr, Rocket take-off & Concord, vert. 140fr,
Scientists with telescopes observing eclipse.

1973, June 20   Engr.   Perf. 13
C133 AP54 35fr grn & pur   .50   .25
C134 AP54 40fr ultra, pur &
         scar   .55   .30
C135 AP54 140fr scar & pur   2.00 .80
   a. Souvenir sheet of 3   3.75 3.75
      Nos. C133-C135 (3)   3.05 1.35
Solar eclipse, June 30, 1973. No. C135a
contains 3 stamps similar to Nos. C133-C135
in changed colors (35fr, 140fr in magenta and
violet blue; 40fr in magenta, violet blue and
orange).
For surcharges see Nos. C141-C142, C146.

Soccer AP55

1973, Dec. 24   Photo.   Perf. 13
C136 AP55 7um multi   .55   .25
C137 AP55 8um multi   .55   .25
C138 AP55 20um multi   1.90 .60
      Nos. C136-C138 (3)   3.00 1.10
Souvenir Sheet
C139 AP55 30um multi   1.75 1.75
World Soccer Cup, Munich, 1974.

**Nos. C115-C117, C130 and C133-
C135 Surcharged with New Value
and Two Bars in Red, Black or
Ultramarine**

1973-74   Photo., Litho. or Engr.
C140 AP49 7um on 35fr (R)
         ('74)   .50   .25
C141 AP54 7um on 35fr (B)   .60   .25
C142 AP54 8um on 40fr (B)   .60   .25
C143 AP49 8um on 40fr (U)
         ('74)   .50   .25
C144 AP49 20um on 100fr (R)
         ('74)   1.75 .70
C145 A63 27um on 135fr (R)   2.50 .80
C146 AP54 28um on 140fr (B)   2.00 .80
      Nos. C140-C146 (7)   8.45 3.30

Winston Churchill (1874-1965) AP56

1974, June 3   Engr.   Perf. 13
C147 AP56 40um blk, brn & hn
         brn   2.00 1.00

**Nos. C131-C132 Surcharged with New
Value and Two Bars in Red**
1974, July 15   Photo.   Perf. 13x12½
C148 AP53 20um on 100fr multi 1.50 .70
C149 AP53 50um on 250fr multi 4.00 1.80

Lenin (1870-1924) AP57

1974, Sept. 16   Engr.   Perf. 13
C150 AP57 40um slate grn & red 3.50 1.25

Women, IWY Emblem AP58

40um, Woman's head and IWY emblems.

1975, June 16   Engr.   Perf. 13
C151 AP58 12um multi   .60   .25
C152 AP58 40um dk brn, lt brn &
         bl   2.25 .90
International Women's Year.

Albert Schweitzer and Patients Arriving — AP59

1975, Aug. 4   Engr.   Perf. 13
C153 AP59 60um multi   3.25 1.60
Schweitzer (1875-1965), medical missionary.

Javelin and Olympic Emblem — AP60

52um, Running and Olympic emblem.

1975, Nov. 17   Engr.   Perf. 13
C154 AP60 50um sl grn, red & ol   2.50 1.40
C155 AP60 52um car, ocher &
           ultra   2.50 1.40
Pre-Olympic Year 1975.

Apollo Soyuz Type, 1975
Docked Space Ships and: 20um, Apollo rocket launch. 50um, Handshake in linked-up cabin. 60um, Apollo splash-down. 100um, Astronauts and Cosmonauts.

1975, Dec. 29   Litho.   Perf. 14
C156 A74 20um multi   .90 .40
C157 A74 50um multi   2.10 .75
C158 A74 60um multi   2.60 1.00
    Nos. C156-C158 (3)   6.00 2.15
Souvenir Sheet
C159 A74 100um multi   4.00 1.75

American Bicentennial Type, 1976
Uniforms: 20um, French Hussar officer. 50um, 3rd Continental Artillery officer. 60um, French infantry regiment grenadier. 100um, American infantryman.

1976, Jan. 26
C160 A75 20um multi   .75 .35
C161 A75 50um multi   2.00 .90
C162 A75 60um multi   2.75 1.00
    Nos. C160-C162 (3)   5.50 1.75
Souvenir Sheet
C163 A75 100um multi   4.50 1.60

Running and Olympic Rings AP61

12um, High jump. 52um, Fencing.

1976, June 14   Engr.   Perf. 13
C164 AP61 10um pur, grn & brn   .80 .25
C165 AP61 12um pur, grn & brn   1.00 .40
C166 AP61 52um pur, grn & brn   3.50 1.50
    Nos. C164-C166 (3)   5.30 2.15
21st Olympic Games, Montreal, Canada, July 17-Aug. 1.

Zeppelin Type, 1976
Designs: 50um, "Graf Zeppelin" (LZ-127) over US Capitol. 60um, "Hindenburg" (LZ-130) over Swiss Alps. 100um, "Führersland" (LZ-129) over 1936 Olympic stadium.

1976, June 28   Litho.   Perf. 11
C167 A77 50um multi   2.75 1.25

C168 A77 60um multi   3.75 1.40
Souvenir Sheet
C169 A77 100um multi   6.00 1.00

Marabou Storks — AP62

African Birds: 50um, Sacred ibis, vert. 200um, Long-crested eagles, vert.

1976, Sept. 20   Litho.   Perf. 13½
C170 AP62 50um multi   3.50 1.10
C171 AP62 100um multi   6.50 1.90
C172 AP62 200um multi   13.00 4.00
    Nos. C170-C172 (3)   23.00 7.00

Viking Type, 1977
Designs: 20um, Viking orbiter in flight to Mars. 50um, Viking "B" in descent to Mars. 60um, Various phases of descent. 100um, Viking lander using probe.

1977, Feb. 28   Perf. 14
C173 A81 20um multi   1.00 .25
C174 A81 50um multi   2.50 .60
C175 A81 60um multi   2.75 .80
    Nos. C173-C175 (3)   6.50 1.40
Souvenir Sheet
C176 A81 100um multi   5.00 1.00
For surcharge & overprints see #C192-C195.

Nobel Prize Type, 1977
14um, George Bernard Shaw, literature. 55um, Thomas Mann, literature. 60um, Intl. Red Cross Society, peace. 100um, George C. Marshall, peace.

1977, Apr. 29   Litho.   Perf. 14
C177 A83 14um multi   .80 .25
C178 A83 55um multi   2.75 .60
C179 A83 60um multi   3.50 .75
    Nos. C177-C179 (3)   8.50 1.40
Souvenir Sheet
C180 A83 100um multi   7.00 2.00

Holy Kaaba — AP63

1977, July 25   Litho.   Perf. 12½
C181 AP63 12um multi   1.75 .50
Pilgrimage to Mecca.

Soccer Type of 1977
50um, Soccer ball. 60um, Eusebio Ferreira. 100um, Players holding pennants.

1977, Dec. 19   Litho.   Perf. 13½
C182 A89 50um multi   2.50 .55
C183 A89 60um multi   2.75 .75
Souvenir Sheet
C184 A89 100um multi   4.50 1.40
For overprints see Nos. C187-C189.

Franco-African Co-operation — AP63a

1978, June 7   Embossed   Perf. 10½
C184A AP63a 250um silver   10.00 10.00
C184B AP63a 500um gold   25.00 25.00

**Philexafrique II — Essen Issue
Common Design Types**
No. C185, Hyena and Mauritania #C60. No. C186, Wading bird and Hamburg #1.

1978, Nov. 1   Litho.   Perf. 12½
C185 CD138 20um multi   1.75 1.10
C186 CD139 20um multi   1.75 1.10
a.   Pair #C185-C186 + label   4.50 4.00

**Nos. C182-C184 Overprinted in
Arabic and French in Silver:
"ARGENTINE- / PAYS BAS 3-1"**
1978, Dec. 11   Litho.   Perf. 13½
C187 A89 50um multi   2.10 1.25
C188 A89 60um multi   3.00 1.60
Souvenir Sheet
C189 A89 100um multi   5.00 5.00
Argentina's victory in World Cup Soccer Championship 1978.

Flyer A and Prototype Plane — AP64

Design: 40um, Flyer A and supersonic jet.

1979, Jan. 29   Engr.   Perf. 13
C190 AP64 15um multi   1.10 .35
C191 AP64 40um multi   2.50 1.00
75th anniversary of first powered flight.

**Nos. C173-C176 Overprinted and
Surcharged in Silver:
"ALUNISSAGE / APOLLO XI /
JUILLET 1969" and Emblem**
1979, Oct. 24   Litho.   Perf. 14
C192 A81 14um on 20um multi   .75 .30
C193 A81 50um multi   2.50 1.05
C194 A81 60um multi   2.75 1.40
    Nos. C192-C194 (3)   6.00 2.45
Souvenir Sheet
C195 A81 100um multi   5.00 5.00
Apollo 11 moon landing, 10th anniversary.

Soccer Players — AP65

Designs: Various soccer scenes.

1980, Sept. 29   Litho.   Perf. 12½
C196 AP65 10um multi   .40 .25
C197 AP65 12um multi   .50 .25
C198 AP65 14um multi   .50 .25
C199 AP65 20um multi   .90 .30
C200 AP65 67um multi   2.50 .70
    Nos. C196-C200 (5)   4.80 1.75
Souvenir Sheet
C201 AP65 100um multi   4.50 1.25
World Soccer Cup 1982.
For overprints see Nos. C212-C217.

Flight of Columbia Space Shuttle — AP66

Designs: Views of Columbia space shuttle.

1981, Apr. 27   Litho.   Perf. 12½
C202 AP66 12um multi   .60 .25
C203 AP66 20um multi   1.00 .25
C204 AP66 50um multi   2.25 .60
C205 AP66 70um multi   3.25 .80
    Nos. C202-C205 (4)   7.10 1.90
Souvenir Sheet
C206 AP66 100um multi   5.00 1.40

Dinard Landscape, by Pablo Picasso — AP67

Picasso Birth Centenary: 12um, Harlequin, vert. 20um, Vase of Flowers, vert. 50um, Three Women at the Well. 100um, Picnic.

1981, June 29   Litho.   Perf. 12½
C207 AP67 12um multi   .70 .25
C208 AP67 20um multi   1.10 .30
C209 AP67 50um multi   2.50 .70
C210 AP67 70um multi   3.50 .95
C211 AP67 100um multi   5.00 1.40
    Nos. C207-C211 (5)   12.80 3.60

**Nos. C196-C201 Overprinted in Red
with Finalists and Score on 1 or 2
Lines**
1982, Sept. 18   Litho.   Perf. 12½
C212 AP65 10um multi   .40 .25
C213 AP65 12um multi   .50 .25
C214 AP65 14um multi   .50 .30
C215 AP65 20um multi   .90 .30
C216 AP65 67um multi   2.50 .75
    Nos. C212-C216 (5)   4.80 1.85
Souvenir Sheet
C217 AP65 100um multi   4.50 1.25
Italy's victory in 1982 World Cup.

25th Anniv. of Intl. Maritime Org. — AP68

1983, June 18   Litho.   Perf. 12½x13
C218 AP68 18um multi   .85 .40

Paul Harris, Rotary Founder AP69

1984, Jan. 20   Litho.   Perf. 13½
C219 AP69 100um multi   4.75 1.10

1984 Summer Olympics — AP70

1984, July 15   **Litho.**   **Perf. 14**

C223	AP70	14um Running, horiz.	.60	.30
C224	AP70	18um Shot put	.75	.40
C225	AP70	19um Hurdles	.85	.40
C226	AP70	44um Javelin	1.75	1.00
C227	AP70	77um High jump	3.75	1.90
		Nos. C223-C227 (5)	7.70	4.00

Souvenir Sheet

C228	AP70	100um Steeplechase	6.00	2.50

Olympics Winners — AP71

1984, Dec. 20   **Litho.**   **Perf. 13**

C229	AP71	14um Van den Berg, sailboard, Netherlands	.85	.30
C230	AP71	18um Coutts, Finn sailing, N.Z.	1.00	.45
C231	AP71	19um 470 class, Spain	1.10	.50
C232	AP71	44um Soling, US	2.50	1.10
		Nos. C229-C232 (4)	5.45	2.35

Souvenir Sheet

C233	AP71	100um Sailing, US	5.75	3.50

PHILEXAFRICA '85, Lome, Togo — AP72

1985, May 23   **Litho.**   **Perf. 13**

C234	AP72	40um Youths, map, IYY emblem	.60	.45
C235	AP72	40um Oil refinery, Nouadhibou	1.75	1.20
a.		Pair, #C234-C235 + label	3.25	3.25

Exists with two labels showing map of Africa or Lome '85 emblem.

1985, Nov. 12   **Perf. 13x12½**

C236	AP72	50um Iron mine, train	2.50	1.00
C237	AP72	50um Boy reading, herding sheep	2.50	1.00
a.		Pair, #C236-C237 + label	6.00	6.00

Audubon Birth Bicentenary AP73

1985, Aug. 14

C238	AP73	14um Passeriformes thraupidae	.80	.30
C239	AP73	18um Larus philadelphia	1.00	.30
C240	AP73	19um Cyanocitta cristata	1.25	.40
C241	AP73	44um Rhyncops nigra	2.75	.80
		Nos. C238-C241 (4)	5.80	1.80

Souvenir Sheet

C242	AP73	100um Anhinga anhinga	8.00	5.00

1st South Atlantic Crossing, 55th Anniv. — AP74

1986, May 19   **Litho.**   **Perf. 13**

C243	AP74	18um Comte de Vaux, 1930	.65	.35
C244	AP74	50um Flight reenactment, 1985	1.75	1.00
a.		Pair, #C243-C244 + label	3.25	3.25

1986 World Cup Soccer Championships, Mexico — AP75

Various soccer plays.

1986, June 19   **Litho.**   **Perf. 13**

C245	AP75	8um No. 279	.30	.25
C246	AP75	18um No. 280	.75	.35
C247	AP75	22um No. 281	.95	.40
C248	AP75	25um No. 282	1.10	.45
C249	AP75	40um Soccer cup	1.75	.80
		Nos. C245-C249 (5)	4.85	2.25

Souvenir Sheet

C250	AP75	100um multi	4.75	3.00

Air Africa, 25th Anniv. — AP76

1986, Oct. 6   **Litho.**   **Perf. 13**

C251	AP76	26um multi	.90	.45

1988 Summer Olympics, Seoul — AP77

1987, Aug. 13   **Litho.**   **Perf. 13**

C252	AP77	30um Boxing	1.25	.50
C253	AP77	40um Judo	1.60	.65
C254	AP77	50um Fencing	1.90	.85
C255	AP77	75um Wrestling	3.25	1.25
		Nos. C252-C255 (4)	8.00	3.25

Souvenir Sheet

C256	AP77	150um Judo, diff.	6.00	2.75

1988 Winter Olympics, Calgary — AP78

1987, Sept.

C257	AP78	30um Women's slalom	1.25	.50
C258	AP78	40um Speed skating	1.60	.65
C259	AP78	50um Ice hockey	1.90	.85
C260	AP78	75um Women's downhill skiing	3.25	1.25
		Nos. C257-C260 (4)	8.00	3.25

Souvenir Sheet

C261	AP78	150um Men's cross-country skiing	6.00	2.75

For overprints see Nos. C267-C271.

1988 Summer Olympics, Seoul AP79

1988, Sept. 17   **Litho.**   **Perf. 13**

C262	AP79	20um Hammer throw	.85	.35
C263	AP79	24um Discus	.90	.40
C264	AP79	30um Shot put	1.25	.50
C265	AP79	150um Javelin	5.75	2.25
		Nos. C262-C265 (4)	8.75	3.50

Souvenir Sheet

C266	AP79	170um Javelin, diff.	6.50	2.75

Nos. C257-C261 Overprinted "Medaille d'or" in Red or Bright Blue and:

a. "Vreni Schneider (Suisse)"
b. "1500 m / Andre Hoffman (R.D.A.)"
c. "U.R.S.S."
d. "Marina Kiehl (R.F.A.)"
e. "15 km / Mikhail Deviatiarov (U.R.S.S.)"

1988, Sept. 18

C267	AP78(a)	30um multi	1.25	.50
C268	AP78(b)	40um multi (BB)	1.75	.65
C269	AP78(c)	50um multi	2.00	.90
C270	AP78(d)	75um multi	3.50	1.40
		Nos. C267-C270 (4)	8.50	3.45

Souvenir Sheet

C271	AP78(e)	150um multi	6.50	3.50

World Cup Soccer Championships, Italy — AP80

Map of Italy and various soccer plays.

1990   **Litho.**   **Perf. 13**

C272	AP80	50um multicolored	2.00	.65
C273	AP80	60um multicolored	2.00	.85
C274	AP80	70um multicolored	2.50	.95

C275	AP80	90um multicolored	3.50	1.25
C276	AP80	150um multicolored	7.50	2.75
		Nos. C272-C276 (5)	17.50	6.45

AIR POST SEMI-POSTAL STAMPS

Maternity Hospital, Dakar — SPAP1

Dispensary, Mopti — SPAP2

Nurse Weighing Baby — SPAP3

Unwmk.

1942, June 22   **Engr.**   **Perf. 13**

CB1	SPAP1	1.50fr + 3.50fr green	.80	5.50
CB2	SPAP2	2fr + 6fr brown	.80	5.50
CB3	SPAP3	3fr + 9fr carmine	.80	5.50
		Nos. CB1-CB3 (3)	2.40	16.50

Native children's welfare fund.

Colonial Education Fund
Common Design Type

1942, June 22

CB4	CD86a	1.20fr + 1.80fr bl & red	.80	5.50

POSTAGE DUE STAMPS

D1   D2

Perf. 14x13½

1906-07   **Unwmk.**   **Typo.**

J1	D1	5c grn, grnsh	3.50	3.50
J2	D1	10c red brn	3.50	3.50
J3	D1	15c dk bl	10.00	7.00
J4	D1	20c blk, yellow	10.00	10.00
J5	D1	30c red, straw	14.00	10.00
J6	D1	50c violet	17.50	17.50
J7	D1	60c blk, buff	14.00	14.00
J8	D1	1fr blk, pinkish	24.00	17.50
		Nos. J1-J8 (8)	96.50	83.00

Issue dates: 20c, 1906; others 1907. Regular postage stamps canceled "T" in a triangle were used for postage due.

1914

J9	D2	5c green	.25	.35
J10	D2	10c rose	.30	.50
J11	D2	15c gray	.35	.70
J12	D2	20c brown	.35	.70
J13	D2	30c blue	.70	1.00
J14	D2	50c black	1.75	1.75
J15	D2	60c orange	1.40	1.40
J16	D2	1fr violet	1.40	1.40
		Nos. J9-J16 (8)	6.50	7.80

Type of 1914 Issue
Surcharged

1927, Oct. 10

J17	D2 2fr on 1fr lil rose	3.50	3.50
a.	Period after "F" omitted	14.00	15.00
J18	D2 3fr on 1fr org brn	3.50	4.25

Catalogue values for unused stamps in this section, from this point to the end of the section, are for Never Hinged items.

Islamic Republic

Oualata Motif — D3

Perf. 14x13½

1961, July 1   Typo.   Unwmk.
Denominations in Black

J19	D3 1fr plum & org yel	.25	.25
J20	D3 2fr red & gray	.25	.25
J21	D3 5fr mar & pink	.25	.25
J22	D3 10fr dk grn & grn	.30	.25
J23	D3 15fr ol & brn org	.30	.25
J24	D3 20fr red brn & lt blue	.50	.50
J25	D3 25fr grn & vermilion	.75	.50
	Nos. J19-J25 (7)	2.60	2.00

Vulture (Ruppell's Griffon) — D4

Birds: No. J27, Eurasian crane. No. J28, Pink-backed pelican. No. J29, Garganey teal. No. J30, European golden oriole. No. J31, Variable sunbird. No. J32, Shoveler ducks. No. J33, Great snipe. No. J34, Vulturine guinea fowl. No. J35, Black stork. No. J36, Gray heron. No. J37, White stork. No. J38, Red-legged partridge. No. J39, Paradise whydah. No. J40, Sandpiper (little stint). No. J41, Sudan bustard.

1963, Sept. 7   Engr.   Perf. 11

J26	D4 50c blk, yel org & red	.25	.25
J27	D4 50c blk, yel org & red	.25	.25
a.	Pair, #J26-J27	.50	.50
J28	D4 1fr blk, red & yel	.25	.25
J29	D4 1fr blk, red & yel	.25	.25
a.	Pair, #J28-J29	.60	.60
J30	D4 2fr blk, bl grn & yel	.25	.25
J31	D4 2fr blk, bl grn & yel	.25	.25
a.	Pair, #J30-J31	.80	.80
J32	D4 5fr blk, grn & red brn	.35	.35
J33	D4 5fr blk, grn & red brn	.35	.35
a.	Pair, #J32-J33	1.25	1.25
J34	D4 10fr blk, red & tan	.70	.70
J35	D4 10fr blk, red & tan	.70	.70
a.	Pair, #J34-J35	2.50	2.50
J36	D4 15fr blk, emer & red	.75	.75
J37	D4 15fr blk, emer & red	.75	.75
a.	Pair, #J36-J37	2.75	2.75
J38	D4 20fr blk, yel grn & red	1.00	1.00
J39	D4 20fr blk, yel grn & red	1.00	1.00
a.	Pair, #J38-J39	3.25	3.25
J40	D4 25fr blk, yel grn & brn	1.50	1.50
J41	D4 25fr blk, yel grn & brn	1.50	1.50
a.	Pair, #J40-J41	4.50	4.50
	Nos. J26-J41 (16)	10.10	10.10
	Nos. J27a-J41a (8)	16.15	16.15

Ornament
D5

1976, May 10   Litho.   Perf. 12½x13

J42	D5 1um buff & multi	.25	.25
J43	D5 3um buff & multi	.25	.25
J44	D5 10um buff & multi	.45	.45
J45	D5 12um buff & multi	.55	.55
J46	D5 20um buff & multi	.95	.95
	Nos. J42-J46 (5)	2.45	2.45

OFFICIAL STAMPS

Catalogue values for unused stamps in this section are for Never Hinged items.

Islamic Republic

Cross of Trarza — O1

Perf. 14x13½

1961, July 1   Typo.   Unwmk.

O1	O1 1fr vio & lilac	.25	.25
O2	O1 3fr red & slate	.25	.25
O3	O1 5fr grn & brown	.25	.25
O4	O1 10fr grn & vio bl	.25	.25
O5	O1 15fr blue & org	.35	.25
O6	O1 20fr sl grn & emer	.45	.25
O7	O1 25fr red org & mar	.50	.30
O8	O1 30fr maroon & grn	.60	.40
O9	O1 50fr dk red & dk brn	1.25	.50
O10	O1 100fr orange & blue	1.90	.90
O11	O1 200fr grn & red org	3.75	1.75
	Nos. O1-O11 (11)	9.80	5.35

Ornament
O2

1976, May 3   Litho.   Perf. 12½x13

O12	O2 1um black & multi	.25	.25
O13	O2 2um black & multi	.25	.25
O14	O2 5um black & multi	.25	.25
O15	O2 10um black & multi	.50	.25
O16	O2 12um black & multi	.70	.30
O17	O2 40um black & multi	2.50	.90
O18	O2 50um black & multi	3.00	1.25
	Nos. O12-O18 (7)	7.45	3.45

MAURITIUS

mo-'ri-sh ē-,əs

LOCATION — Island in the Indian Ocean about 550 miles east of Madagascar
GOVT. — Republic
AREA — 720 sq. mi.
POP. — 1,182,212 (1999 est.)

CAPITAL — Port Louis

12 Pence = 1 Shilling
100 Cents = 1 Rupee (1878)

The British Crown Colony of Mauritius was granted self-government in 1967 and became an independent state on March 12, 1968.

Nos. 1-6, 14-17 unused are valued without gum.

Nos. 3a-8, 14-15 are printed on fragile paper with natural irregularities which might be mistaken for faults.

Very fine examples of Nos. 22-58 will have perforations touching the design on one or more sides. Examples with perfs clear on four sides are scarce and will sell for more. Inferior examples will sell for much reduced prices.

Catalogue values for unused stamps in this country are for Never Hinged items, beginning with Scott 223 in the regular postage section, Scott J1 in the postage due section.

Queen Victoria
A1   A2

1847   Unwmk.   Engr.   *Imperf.*

1	A1 1p orange	1,250,000.	1,150,000.
2	A1 2p dark blue		1,700,000.

Nos. 1 and 2 were engraved and printed in Port Louis. There is but one type of each value. The initials "J. B." on the bust are those of the engraver, J. Barnard.

All unused examples of the 2p are in museums. There is one unused example of the 1p in private hands. There are two used examples of the 1p in private hands, both of which have small faults and are valued thus.

Earliest Impressions

1848   Thick Yellowish Paper

3	A2 1p orange	62,500.	18,000.
4	A2 2p dark blue	57,500.	23,000.
d.	"PENOE"	115,000.	40,000.

Early Impressions
Yellowish White Paper

3a	A2 1p orange	29,000.	7,250.
4a	A2 2p blue	31,000.	8,000.
e.	"PENOE"	57,500.	14,500.

Bluish Paper

5	A2 1p orange	29,000.	7,250.
6	A2 2p blue	31,000.	8,000.
c.	"PENOE"	57,500.	14,500.

Intermediate Impressions
Yellowish White Paper

3b	A2 1p red orange	19,000.	2,850.
4b	A2 2p blue	19,000.	3,750.
f.	"PENOE"	31,500.	7,250.

Bluish Paper

5a	A2 1p red orange	18,500.	2,900.
6a	A2 2p blue	19,000.	3,750.
d.	"PENOE"	32,500.	7,250.
f.	Double impression		—

Worn Impressions
Yellowish White Paper

3c	A2 1p orange red	6,750.	900.
d.	1p brownish red	6,750.	900.

4c	A2 2p blue	8,500.	1,550.
g.	"PENOE"	11,000.	3,150.

Bluish Paper

5b	A2 1p orange red	6,250.	850.
c.	1p brownish red	6,250.	850.
d.	Double impression		
6b	A2 2p blue	8,250.	1,450.
e.	"PENOE"	12,500.	3,000.

Latest Impressions
Yellowish or Grayish Paper

3e	A2 1p orange red	5,250.	725.
f.	1p brownish red	5,250.	725.
4h	A2 2p blue	6,250.	1,050.
i.	"PENOE"	11,500.	2,000.

Bluish Paper

5e	A2 1p orange red	5,250.	725.
f.	1p brownish red	5,250.	725.
6g	A2 2p blue	6,250.	1,050.
h.	"PENOE"	11,500.	2,000.

These stamps were printed in sheets of twelve, four rows of three, and each position differs in details. The "PENOE" error is the most pronounced variety on the plates and is from position 7.

The stamps were in use until 1859. Earliest impressions, Nos. 3-4, show the full background of diagonal and vertical lines with the diagonal lines predominant. Early impressions, Nos. 3a-4a, 5-6, show the full background with the vertical lines predominating. As the plate became worn the vertical lines disappeared, giving the intermediate impressions, Nos. 3b-4b, 5a-6a.

Worn impressions, Nos. 3c-4c, 5b-6b, have little background remaining, and latest impressions, Nos. 3e-4h, 5e-6g, have also lost details of the frame and head. The paper of the early impressions is usually rather thick, that of the worn impressions rather thin. Expect natural fibrous inclusions in the paper of all impressions.

"Britannia"
A3   A4

1849-58

7	A3 red brown, *blue*	26.00	
8	A3 blue ('58)	9.00	
	Nos. 7-8 were never placed in use.		

1858-59

9	A3 (4p) green, *bluish*	550.00	240.00
10	A3 (6p) red	57.50	125.00
11	A3 (9p) magenta ('59)	850.00	240.00

No. 11 was re-issued in Nov. 1862, as a 1p stamp (No. 11a). When used as such it is always canceled "B53." Price so used, $200.

1858   Black Surcharge

12	A4 4p green, *bluish*	1,650.00	525.00

Queen Victoria — A5

1859, Mar.   Early Impressions

14	A5 2p blue, *grayish*	12,500.	2,900.
a.	2p deep blue, *grayish*	14,500.	3,400.
14B	A5 2p blue, *bluish*	12,500.	2,900.
c.	Intermediate impression	8,000.	1,250.
d.	Worn impression	4,250.	850.

Type A5 was engraved by Lapirot, in Port Louis, and was printed locally. There were twelve varieties in the sheet.

Early impressions have clear and distinct background lines. In the intermediate impressions, the lines are somewhat blurred, and white patches appear. In the worn impressions, the background lines are discontinuous, with many white patches. Analogous wear is also obvious in the background of the inscriptions on all four sides. Values depend on the state of wear. One should expect natural fibrous inclusions in the paper on all printings.

A6

A7

1859, Oct.

15	A6	2p blue, *bluish*	190,000.	11,000.

No. 15 was printed from the plate of the 1848 issue after it had been entirely re-engraved by Sherwin. It is commonly known as the "fillet head." The plate of the 1p, 1848, was also re-engraved but was never put in use.

1859, Dec.　　Litho.　　Laid Paper

16	A7	1p vermilion	8,000.	1,350.
a.		1p deep red	13,500.	2,350.
b.		1p red		1,675.
17	A7	2p pale blue	4,500.	850.
a.		2p slate blue	8,500.	1,250.
b.		2p blue	5,000.	950.

Lithographed locally by Dardenne.

"Britannia" — A8

1859　　Wove Paper　Engr.　*Imperf.*

18	A8	6p blue	800.00	57.50
19	A8	1sh vermilion	3,150.	62.50

1861

20	A8	6p gray violet	37.50	67.50
21	A8	1sh green	675.00	160.00

1862　　　　　　　　*Perf. 14 to 16*

22	A8	6p slate	34.00	110.00
a.		Horiz. pair, imperf between	8,500.	
23	A8	1sh deep green	2,900.	400.00

Following the change in currency in 1878, a number of issues denominated in sterling were overprinted "CANCELLED" in serifed type and sold as remainders.

A9

A10

1860-63　　Typo.　　Perf. 14

24	A9	1p brown lilac	375.00	37.50
25	A9	2p blue	400.00	60.00
26	A9	4p rose	400.00	42.50
27	A9	6p green ('62)	1,050.	175.00
28	A9	6p lilac ('63)	425.00	125.00
29	A9	9p dull lilac	190.00	50.00
30	A9	1sh buff ('62)	400.00	100.00
31	A9	1sh green ('63)	900.00	200.00

For surcharges see Nos. 43-45.

1863-72　　　　　　　　Wmk. 1

32	A9	1p lilac brown	85.00	17.50
a.		1p bister brown	160.00	17.00
b.		1p brown	110.00	13.00
33	A9	2p blue	100.00	13.00
a.		Imperf., pair	1,950.	2,350.
34	A9	3p vermilion	90.00	20.00
35	A9	4p rose	100.00	4.00
36	A9	6p lilac ('64)	425.00	45.00
37	A9	6p blue grn ('65)	235.00	7.25
a.		6p yellow green ('65)	285.00	16.75
38	A9	9p green ('72)	200.00	375.00
39	A9	1sh org yel ('64)	365.00	29.00
a.		1sh yellow	285.00	14.50

40	A9	1sh blue ('70)	155.00	28.50
41	A9	5sh red violet	260.00	65.00
a.		5sh bright violet	325.00	65.00
		Nos. 32-41 (10)	2,015.	604.25

For surcharges see Nos. 48-49, 51-58, 87.

1872

42	A10	10p claret	375.00	57.50

For surcharges see Nos. 46-47.

No. 29 Surcharged in Black or Red

a

b

1876　　　　　　　　　Unwmk.

43	A9(a)	½p on 9p	24.00	22.00
a.		Inverted surcharge	800.00	
b.		Double surcharge		2,350.
44	A9(b)	½p on 9p	5,000.	
45	A9(b)	½p on 9p (R)	3,400.	

Nos. 44 and 45 were never placed in use. No. 45 is valued with perfs cutting into the design.

Stamps of 1863-72 Surcharged in Black

c

d

1876-77　　　　　　　　Wmk. 1

46	A10(a)	½p on 10p claret	4.25	27.50
47	A10(c)	½p on 10p cl ('77)	10.00	47.50
48	A9(d)	1p on 4p rose ('77)	23.00	25.00
49	A9(d)	1sh on 5sh red vio ('77)	340.00	125.00
a.		1sh on 5sh violet ('77)	340.00	160.00
		Nos. 46-49 (4)	377.25	225.00

A16

1878　　　　　　　Black Surcharge

50	A16	2c claret	15.50	10.00

Stamps and Type of 1863-72 Surcharged in Black — e

51	A9	4c on 1p bister brn	25.00	9.00
52	A9	8c on 2p blue	90.00	4.00
53	A9	13c on 3p org red	24.00	45.00
54	A9	17c on 4p rose	200.00	4.25
55	A9	25c on 6p sl blue	290.00	7.75
56	A9	38c on 9p violet	45.00	100.00
57	A9	50c on 1sh green	100.00	4.75
58	A9	2r50c on 5sh violet	20.00	24.00
		Nos. 50-58 (9)	809.50	208.75

For surcharge see No. 87.

A18

A19

A20　　　　　A21

A22

A23

A24

A25

A26

1879-80　　　　　　　　Wmk. 1

59	A18	2c red brn ('80)	55.00	25.00
60	A19	4c orange	72.50	4.25
61	A20	8c blue ('80)	37.50	4.50
62	A21	13c slate ('80)	175.00	325.00
63	A22	17c rose ('80)	90.00	9.50
64	A23	25c bister	475.00	17.00
65	A24	38c violet ('80)	200.00	375.00
66	A25	50c green ('80)	5.25	4.50
67	A26	2r50c brn vio ('80)	57.50	85.00
		Nos. 59-67 (9)	1,167.	849.75

Nos. 59-67 are known imperforate.
For surcharges & overprints see Nos. 76-78, 83-86, 122-123.

1882-93　　　　　　　　Wmk. 2

68	A18	1c violet ('93)	2.10	.55
69	A18	2c red brown	38.50	6.00
70	A18	2c green ('85)	4.25	.75
71	A19	4c orange	95.00	5.25
72	A19	4c rose ('85)	4.50	1.25
73	A20	8c blue ('91)	4.25	1.80
74	A23	25c bister ('83)	11.50	3.75
75	A25	50c dp orange ('87)	42.50	18.00
		Nos. 68-75 (8)	202.60	37.35

For surcharges and overprint see Nos. 88-89, 121.

Nos. 63 and Type of 1882 Surcharged in Black

f

g

1883　　　　　　　　　Wmk. 1
Surcharge Measures 14x3½mm

76	A22(f)	16c on 17c rose	180.00	60.00
a.		Double surcharge		2,900.

Surcharge Measures 15½x3½mm

77	A22(f)	16c on 17c rose	190.00	60.00
a.		Double surcharge		3,150.

Surcharge Measures 15½x2¾mm

78	A22(f)	16c on 17c rose	375.00	135.00

Wmk. 2

79	A22(g)	16c on 17c rose	115.00	2.40
		Nos. 76-79 (4)	860.00	257.40

Queen Victoria — A29

1885-94

80	A29	15c orange brown ('92)	9.00	1.50
81	A29	15c blue ('94)	10.00	1.50
82	A29	15c orange brown	9.50	2.75
		Nos. 80-82 (3)	28.50	5.75

For surcharges see Nos. 90, 116.

Various Stamps Surcharged in Black or Red

h

j

1885-87　　　　　　　　Wmk. 1

83	A24(h)	2c on 38c violet	170.00	47.50
a.		Inverted surcharge	1,250.	1,000.
b.		Double surcharge	1,350.	
c.		Without bar		275.00
84	A21(j)	2c on 13c sl (R) ('87)	80.00	130.00
a.		Inverted surcharge	260.00	300.00
b.		Double surcharge	975.00	850.00
c.		As "b," one on back	1,000.	
d.		Double surcharge, both inverted		1,750.

k

l

1891

85	A22(k)	2c on 17c rose	145.00	155.00
a.		Inverted surcharge	575.00	—
b.		Double surcharge	950.00	950.00
86	A24(k)	2c on 38c vio	10.50	14.50
a.		Double surcharge	240.00	260.00
b.		Dbl. surch., one invtd.	260.00	300.00
c.		Inverted surcharge	1,250.	
87	A9(e+l)	2c on 38c on 9p vio	12.50	6.75
a.		Double surcharge	850.00	850.00
b.		Inverted surcharge	625.00	—
c.		Dbl. surch., one invtd	200.00	225.00

Wmk. 2

88	A19(k)	2c on 4c rose	1.80	.85
a.		Double surcharge	95.00	90.00
b.		Inverted surcharge	90.00	—
c.		Dbl. surch., one invtd.	95.00	90.00
		Nos. 85-88 (4)	169.80	177.10

m

n

1893, Jan.

89	A18(m)	1c on 2c violet	2.75	1.35
90	A29(n)	1c on 16c org brown	2.75	4.00

Coat of Arms — A38

1895-1904　　　　　　　Wmk. 2

91	A38	1c lilac & ultra	.90	1.80
92	A38	1c gray blk & black	.60	.25
93	A38	2c lilac & orange	6.75	.60
94	A38	2c dull lil & vio	1.00	.25
95	A38	3c lilac	.85	.60
96	A38	3c grn & scar, *yel*	4.50	1.50
97	A38	4c lilac & green	4.50	.60
98	A38	4c dull lil & car, *yel*	1.80	.50
99	A38	4c gray green & pur	1.90	2.40
100	A38	4c black & car, *blue*	16.00	.75
101	A38	5c lilac & vio, *buff*	10.00	85.00
102	A38	5c lilac & blk, *buff*	3.00	3.00
103	A38	6c grn & rose	5.75	5.00
104	A38	6c violet & scar, *red*	3.50	1.00
105	A38	8c gray grn & blk, *buff*	4.00	12.50
106	A38	12c black & car rose	2.75	2.75
107	A38	15c grn & org	26.00	10.00
108	A38	15c blk & ultra, *blue*	65.00	1.50
109	A38	18c gray grn & ultra	19.00	4.25

110 A38 25c grn & car, *grn,*
chalky paper 5.00 *25.00*
111 A38 50c green, *yel* 20.00 *80.00*
Nos. 91-111 (21) 202.80 *239.25*

The 25c is on both ordinary and chalky paper. Ornaments in lower panel omitted on Nos. 106-111.
Year of issue: Nos. 103, 107, 1899; Nos. 92, 94, 98, 1900; Nos. 96, 99, 101-102, 104-106, 110-111, 1902; Nos. 100, 108, 1904; others, 1895.
See Nos. 128-135. For surcharges and overprints see Nos. 113, 114, 117-120.

Diamond Jubilee Issue

Arms
A39

1898, May 23 **Wmk. 46**
112 A39 36c brown org & ultra 13.00 *25.00*

60th year of Queen Victoria's reign.
For surcharges see Nos. 114 and 127.

No. 109 Surcharged in
Red

1899 **Wmk. 2**
113 A38 6c on 18c 1.50 1.20
a. Inverted surcharge 725.00 340.00

No. 112 Surcharged in Blue

Wmk. 46
114 A39 15c on 36c 3.00 2.10
a. Without bar 525.00

Admiral Mahe de
La Bourdonnais
A40

1899, Dec. **Engr.** **Wmk. 1**
115 A40 15c ultra 30.00 5.00

Birth bicent. of Admiral Mahe de La Bourdonnais, governor of Mauritius, 1734-46.

No. 82 Surcharged in
Black

1900 **Wmk. 2**
116 A29 4c on 16c orange brown 13.50 24.00

No. 109 Surcharged in
Black — r

1902
117 A38 12c on 18c grn & ultra 3.00 *9.00*

Preceding Issues
Overprinted in Black

1902
118 A38 4c lilac & car, *yel* 1.50 .35
119 A38 6c green & rose 1.50 *3.25*
120 A38 15c green & org 6.25 1.35
121 A23 25c bister 8.00 3.25
Wmk. 1
122 A25 50c green 20.00 6.25
123 A26 2r50c brown violet 135.00 *225.00*
Nos. 118-123 (6) 172.25 *239.45*

Coat of
Arms — A41

1902 **Wmk. 1**
124 A41 1r blk & car rose 62.50 60.00
Wmk. 2 Sideways
125 A41 2r50c grn & blk, *bl* 35.00 *160.00*
126 A41 5r blk & car, *red* 100.00 *170.00*
Nos. 124-126 (3) 197.50 *390.00*

No. 112 Surcharged type "r" but with longer bar

1902 **Wmk. 46**
127 A39 12c on 36c 2.00 1.50
a. Inverted surcharge 775.00 *525.00*

Arms Type of 1895-1904

1904-07 **Wmk. 3** **Chalky Paper**
128 A38 1c gray blk & black ('07) 8.75 5.00
129 A38 2c dl lil & vio ('05) 34.00 2.00
130 A38 3c grn & scar, *yel* 22.50 10.50
131 A38 4c blk & car, *blue* 15.00 .25
132 A38 6c vio & scar, *red* ('06) 12.50 .35
133 A38 15c blk & ultra, *bl* 4.50 .40
135 A38 50c green, *yel* 3.00 *5.25*
136 A41 1r black & car rose ('07) 47.50 65.00
Nos. 128-136 (8) 147.75 88.75

The 2c, 4c, 6c also exist on ordinary paper.
Ornaments in lower panel omitted on 15c and 50c.

Arms — A42 Edward VII — A43

1910 **Wmk. 3** **Ordinary Paper**
137 A42 1c black 3.25 .30
138 A42 2c brown 3.00 .25
139 A42 3c green 3.25 .25
140 A42 4c ol grn & rose 4.00 .25
141 A42 5c gray & rose 3.00 *3.25*
142 A42 6c carmine 5.25 .25
143 A42 8c brown orange 3.25 *1.60*
144 A43 12c gray 3.75 *3.00*
145 A42 15c ultramarine 4.00 .25
Chalky Paper
146 A43 25c blk & scar, *yel* 2.25 13.00
147 A43 50c dull vio & blk 2.60 20.00
148 A43 1r blk, *green* 17.75 13.00
149 A43 2r50c blk & car, *bl* 27.50 75.00
150 A43 5r grn & car, *yel* 42.50 100.00
151 A43 10r grn & car, *grn* 165.00 *250.00*
Nos. 137-151 (15) 307.35 *480.40*

Numerals of 12c, 25c and 10r of type A43 are in color on plain tablet.
See Nos. 161-178.

King George V — A44

Die I

For description of dies I and II see "Dies of British Colonial Stamps" in table of contents.
Numeral tablet of 5c, 50c, 1r, 2.50r and 5r of type A44 has lined background with colorless denomination.

1912-22 **Wmk. 3** **Ordinary Paper**
152 A44 5c gray & rose 3.00 *4.50*
153 A44 12c gray 8.00 1.10
Chalky Paper
154 A44 25c blk & red, *yel* .45 1.50
a. 25c gray black & red, *yellow,* Die II 1.10 *25.00*
155 A44 50c dull vio & blk 52.50 *125.00*
156 A44 1r black, *emerald,* die II 2.50 *8.00*
a. 1r black, *emer,* dark blue, die I ('21) 11.50 *60.00*
b. 1r blk, *bl grn,* olive back, die I 6.75 *21.00*
157 A44 2r50c blk & red, *bl* 42.50 *75.00*
158 A44 5r grn & red, *yel* 115.00 *175.00*
a. Die II ('22) 115.00 *200.00*
159 A44 10r grn & red, *emer, die II* ('21) 47.50 *180.00*
a. 10r grn & red, *bl grn,* olive back, die I 1,150.
b. 10r green & red, *emer,* die I 85.00 *200.00*
c. 10r grn & red, *emer,* olive back, die I 145.00 *210.00*
d. 10r grn & red, *grn,* die I 105.00 *210.00*
Surface-colored Paper
160 A44 25c blk & red, *yel* ('16) 2.75 *21.00*
Nos. 152-160 (9) 274.20 *591.10*

1921-26 **Wmk. 4** **Ordinary Paper**
161 A42 1c black 1.10 1.10
162 A42 2c brown 1.10 .25
163 A42 2c violet, *yel* ('25) 3.50 2.00
164 A42 3c green ('25) 3.50 3.50
165 A42 4c ol grn & rose 1.60 *2.00*
166 A42 4c green 1.10 .25
167 A42 4c brown ('26) 4.50 *2.50*
168 A42 6c rose red 13.50 7.25
169 A42 6c violet 1.35 .25
170 A42 8c brown org ('25) 2.50 *24.00*
171 A42 10c gray ('22) 2.25 *3.75*
172 A42 10c rose red ('25) 12.00 6.75
173 A42 12c rose red 1.70 1.60
174 A42 12c gray ('25) 1.90 *5.00*
175 A42 15c ultramarine 6.00 5.50
176 A42 15c dull blue ('25) 1.60 .25
177 A42 20c ultra ('22) 2.25 .90
178 A42 20c dull vio ('25) 9.50 *16.00*
Nos. 161-178 (18) 70.95 *82.85*

Ornaments in lower panel omitted on Nos. 171-178.
For surcharges see Nos. 201-203.

Die II

1922-34 **Ordinary Paper**
179 A44 1c black 2.40 *3.00*
180 A44 2c brown 1.10 .25
181 A44 3c green 2.10 .45
182 A44 4c olive grn & red ('27) 3.25 .30
a. Die I ('32) 18.00 *62.50*
183 A44 4c green, die I ('33) 13.50 .50
184 A44 5c gray & car 1.10 .25
a. Die I ('32) 10.00 6.50
185 A44 6c olive brn ('28) 5.50 .65
186 A44 8c orange 2.10 *15.50*
187 A44 10c rose red ('26) 4.25 .25
a. Die I ('32) 15.50 16.75
188 A44 12c gray, small "c" ('22) 5.00 *23.00*
189 A44 12c gray, "c" larger & thinner ('34) 17.50 .25
190 A44 12c rose red .70 *3.75*
191 A44 15c dk blue ('28) 4.75 .25
192 A44 20c dull vio 4.75 .45
193 A44 20c dk blue ('34) 28.00 .45
a. Die I ('27) 11.00 2.60
194 A44 25c black & red, *yel* 1.10 .25
a. Die I ('32) 7.25 *67.50*
Chalky Paper
195 A44 50c dull vio & blk 8.00 3.75
196 A44 1r blk, *emerald* 6.75 .55
a. Die I ('32) 25.00 *62.50*
197 A44 2r50c blk & red, *bl* 22.00 19.00
198 A44 5r green & red, *yel* 47.50 *95.00*
199 A44 10r green & red, *emer* ('28) 145.00 *340.00*
Nos. 179-199 (21) 326.35 *507.85*

A45

1924
200 A45 50r lilac & green 1,000. *2,750.*

Nos. 166, 173, 177
Surcharged

1925
201 A42 3c on 4c green 8.00 *6.25*
202 A42 10c on 12c rose red .50 *1.60*
203 A42 15c on 20c ultra .65 1.75
Nos. 201-203 (3) 9.15 9.60

Common Design Types
pictured following the introduction.

Silver Jubilee Issue
Common Design Type

1935, May 6 **Engr.** **Perf. 13½x14**
204 CD301 5c gray black & ultra .60 .25
205 CD301 12c indigo & green 5.50 .25
206 CD301 20c blue & brown 6.50 .25
207 CD301 1r brt vio & indigo 35.00 *57.50*
Nos. 204-207 (4) 47.60 *58.25*
Set, never hinged 60.00

Coronation Issue
Common Design Type

1937, May 12 **Wmk. 4** **Perf. 13½x14**
208 CD302 5c dark purple .30 .25
209 CD302 12c carmine .50 2.40
210 CD302 20c bright ultra 1.25 1.10
Nos. 208-210 (3) 2.05 *3.75*
Set, never hinged 3.25

King George VI — A46

1938-43 **Typo.** **Perf. 14**
211 A46 2c gray ('43) .25 .25
a. Perf. 15x14 ('43) .70 .25
212 A46 3c rose vio & car ('43) 1.50 2.15
213 A46 4c green ('43) 3.25 *2.15*
214 A46 5c violet ('43) 2.10 .25
a. Perf. 15x14 ('43) 40.00 .25
215 A46 10c carmine ('43) 1.90 .25
a. Perf. 15x14 ('43) 2.50 2.50
216 A46 12c salmon pink ('43) .70 .25
a. Perf. 15x14 ('43) 40.00 1.35
217 A46 20c blue ('43) .70 .25
218 A46 25c maroon ('43) 6.00 .25
219 A46 1r brown black ('43) 14.00 2.00
220 A46 2.50r pale violet ('43) 25.00 26.00
221 A46 5r olive green ('43) 21.00 42.50
222 A46 10r rose violet ('43) 9.75 *42.50*
Nos. 211-222 (12) 86.15 *118.80*
Set, never hinged 127.00

Nos. 218-222 exist on both chalky and ordinary papers. Values above are for stamps on ordinary paper. For detailed listings, see *Scott Classic Specialized Catalogue of Stamps & Covers.*

> **Catalogue values for unused stamps in this section, from this point to the end of the section, are for Never Hinged items.**

Peace Issue
Common Design Type
Perf. 13½x14

1946, Nov. 20		Engr.		Wmk. 4
223	CD303	5c lilac	.25	.80
224	CD303	20c deep blue	.25	.25

"Post Office"
Stamp of
1847 — A47

1948, Mar. 22				Perf. 11½
225	A47	5c red vio & orange	.25	.55
226	A47	12c green & orange	.25	.25
227	A47	20c blue & dp blue	.25	.25
228	A47	1r lt red brn & dp blue	.35	.35
		Nos. 225-228 (4)	1.10	1.40

Cent. of the 1st Mauritius postage stamps.

Silver Wedding Issue
Common Design Types

1948, Oct. 25		Photo.	Perf. 14x14½
229	CD304	5c violet	.25	.25

Perf. 11½x11
Engraved; Name Typographed
230	CD305	10r lilac rose	17.50	45.00

UPU Issue
Common Design Types
Engr.; Name Typo. on 20c, 35c
Perf. 13½, 11x11½

1949, Oct. 10			Wmk. 4
231	CD306	12c rose carmine	.65	2.10
232	CD307	20c indigo	2.40	2.75
233	CD308	35c rose violet	.65	1.60
234	CD309	1r sepia	.65	.25
		Nos. 231-234 (4)	4.35	6.70

Sugar
Factory — A48

Aloe Plant — A49

Designs: 2c, Grand Port. 4c, Tamarind Falls. 5c, Rempart Mountain. 10c, Transporting cane. 12c, Map and dodo. 20c, "Paul et Virginie." 25c, Statue of Mahe La Bourdonnais. 35c, Government House. 50c, Pieter Both Mountain. 1r, Sambar. 2.50r, Port Louis. 5r, Beach scene. 10r, Arms.

Perf. 13½x14½, 14½x13½

1950, July 1				Photo.
235	A48	1c red violet	.25	.55
236	A48	2c cerise	.25	.25
237	A49	3c yel green	.70	4.50
238	A49	4c green	.25	3.25
239	A48	5c greenish blue	.25	.25
240	A48	10c red	.30	.80
241	A48	12c olive green	1.60	3.25
242	A49	20c brt ultra	1.10	.25
243	A49	25c vio brown	2.15	.45
244	A49	35c rose violet	.45	.25
245	A49	50c emerald	3.00	.55
246	A48	1r sepia	10.00	.25
247	A49	2.50r orange	22.00	17.50
248	A48	5r red brown	23.00	17.50
249	A48	10r gray blue	18.00	37.50
		Nos. 235-249 (15)	83.30	87.10

Coronation Issue
Common Design Type

1953, June 2		Engr.	Perf. 13½x13
250	CD312	10c dk green & black	1.00	.25

Sugar
Factory — A50

Tamarind
Falls — A51

Designs: 2c, Grand Port. 3c, Aloe plant. 5c, Rempart Mountain. 15c, Museum, Mahebourg. 20c, Statue of Mahe La Bourdonnais. 25c, "Paul et Virginie." 35c, Government House. 50c, Pieter Both Mountain. 60c, Map and dodo. 1r, Sambar. 2.50r, Port Louis. 5r, Beach scene. 10r, Arms.

Perf. 13½x14½, 14½x13½

1953-54		Photo.		Wmk. 4
251	A50	2c rose car ('54)	.30	.25
252	A51	3c yel green ('54)	.35	.25
253	A51	4c red violet	.30	.60
254	A50	5c grnsh blue ('54)	.30	.25
255	A51	10c dk green	.30	.25
256	A50	15c scarlet	.30	.25
257	A51	20c violet brown	.30	.25
a.		Imperf., pair		
258	A51	25c brt ultra	1.60	.25
259	A51	35c rose vio ('54)	.30	.25
260	A51	50c emerald	.75	.75
261	A51	60c gray grn ('54)	12.00	.25
262	A51	1r sepia	.35	.25
a.		Imperf., pair		
263	A50	2.50r orange ('54)	16.00	9.25
264	A50	5r red brn ('54)	16.00	9.25
265	A50	10r gray blue ('54)	16.00	1.25
		Nos. 251-265 (15)	65.15	23.60

See Nos. 273-275.

King George III and Queen Elizabeth
II — A52

Wmk. 314

1961, Jan. 11		Litho.	Perf. 13½
266	A52	10c dk red & dk brown	.25	.25
267	A52	20c lt blue & dk blue	.25	.25
268	A52	35c org yel & brown	.30	.30
269	A52	1r yel green & dk brn	.60	.60
		Nos. 266-269 (4)	1.40	1.40

Sesquicentenary of postal service under British administration.

Freedom from Hunger Issue
Common Design Type

1963, June 4		Photo.	Perf. 14x14½
270	CD314	60c lilac	.50	.50

Red Cross Centenary Issue
Common Design Type

1963, Sept. 2			Perf. 13
271	CD315	10c black & red	.25	.25
272	CD315	60c ultra & red	.65	.65

Types of 1953-54
Perf. 14½x13½, 13½x14½

1963-64		Photo.		Wmk. 314
273	A51	10c dark green ('64)	.50	.30
274	A50	60c gray green ('64)	2.75	.30
275	A50	2.50r orange	9.75	11.00
		Nos. 273-275 (3)	13.00	11.60

Gray White-Eye — A53

Birds of Mauritius: 3c, Rodriguez fody. 4c, Olive white-eye. 5c, Mauritius paradise flycatcher. 10c, Mauritius fody. 15c, Rose-ringed parakeet. 20c, Cuckoo shrike. 25c, Mauritian kestrel. 35c, Pink pigeon. 50c, Mauritius olivaceous bulbul. 60c, Mauritius blue pigeon. 1r, Dodo. 2.50r, Rodriguez solitaire. 5r, Van den Broeck's red rail. 10r, Broad-billed Mauritian parrot.

Wmk. 314

1965, Mar. 16		Photo.	Perf. 14½
		Birds in Natural Colors		
276	A53	2c brt yel & brn	.50	.30
a.		Gray (leg, etc.) omitted	210.00	
277	A53	3c brn & dk brn	1.00	.30
a.		Black (eye, beak) omitted	210.00	
278	A53	4c dl rose lil & blk	.35	.30
a.		Rose lilac omitted	55.00	
279	A53	5c gray & ultra	3.25	.30
a.		Wmkd. sideways ('66)	.25	.25
280	A53	10c dl grn & dk brn	.35	.30
281	A53	15c lt gray & dk brn	2.10	.30
a.		Carmine (beak) omitted	160.00	
282	A53	20c pale yel & dk brown	2.10	.30
283	A53	25c gray & brown	2.10	.30
284	A53	35c vio bl & blk	2.75	.30
a.		Wmkd. sideways ('67)	.40	.35
285	A53	50c pale yel & blk	.50	.50
286	A53	60c pale cit & brn	.60	.30
287	A53	1r lt yel grn & blk	5.50	.30
a.		Pale gray (ground) omitted	250.00	
b.		Pale orange omitted	175.00	
288	A53	2.50r pale grn & brn	4.75	6.00
289	A53	5r pale blue & blk	14.00	9.00
290	A53	10r pale grn & ultra	26.00	22.50
		Nos. 276-290 (15)	65.85	41.30

On No. 278 the background was printed in two colors. The rose lilac tint is omitted on No. 278a.
See Nos. 327-332. For overprints see Nos. 306-320.

ITU Issue
Common Design Type
Perf. 11x11½

1965, May 17		Litho.	Wmk. 314
291	CD317	10c dp org & apple grn	.30	.25
292	CD317	60c yellow & violet	.90	.40

Intl. Cooperation Year Issue
Common Design Type

1965, Oct. 25			Perf. 14½
293	CD318	10c lt green & claret	.25	.25
294	CD318	60c lt violet & green	.45	.45

Churchill Memorial Issue
Common Design Type

1966, Jan. 24		Photo.	Perf. 14
		Design in Black, Gold and Carmine Rose		
295	CD319	2c brt blue	.40	.40
296	CD319	10c green	.40	.40
297	CD319	60c brown	1.00	1.00
298	CD319	1r violet	2.25	2.25
		Nos. 295-298 (4)	4.05	4.05

UNESCO Anniversary Issue
Common Design Type

1966, Dec. 1		Litho.	Perf. 14
299	CD323	5c "Education"	.35	.35
300	CD323	10c "Science"	.35	.35
301	CD323	60c "Culture"	1.40	.80
		Nos. 299-301 (3)	2.10	1.50

Red-Tailed Tropic Bird — A54

Birds of Mauritius: 10c, Rodriguez bush warbler. 60c, Newton's parakeet. 1r, Mauritius swiftlet.

1967, Sept. 1		Photo.	Perf. 14½
302	A54	2c lt ultra & multi	.40	.40
303	A54	10c emerald & multi	.40	.40
304	A54	60c salmon & multi	1.25	1.25
305	A54	1r yellow & multi	2.40	2.40
		Nos. 302-305 (4)	4.45	4.45

Attainment of self-government, Sept. 1, 1967.

Bird Issue of 1965-67 and Type Overprinted: "SELF GOVERNMENT 1967"

1967, Dec. 1		Photo.	Wmk. 314
306	A53	2c multicolored	.25	.25
307	A53	3c multicolored	.25	.25
308	A53	4c multicolored	.25	.25
309	A53	5c multicolored	.25	.25
310	A53	10c multicolored	.25	.25
311	A53	15c multicolored	.25	.25
312	A53	20c multicolored	.25	.25
313	A53	25c multicolored	.25	.25
314	A53	35c multicolored	.25	.25
315	A53	50c multicolored	.40	.25
316	A53	60c multicolored	.45	.30
317	A53	1r multicolored	.75	.45
318	A53	2.50r multicolored	2.10	2.25
319	A53	5r multicolored	4.25	4.25
320	A53	10r multicolored	8.00	8.50
		Nos. 306-320 (15)	18.20	18.25

5c, 10c, 35c watermarked sideways.

Independent State

Flag of Mauritius — A55

Designs: 3c, 20c, 1r, Dodo emerging from egg and coat of arms.

Perf. 13½x13

1968, Mar. 12		Litho.	Unwmk.
321	A55	2c brt violet & multi	.25	.25
322	A55	3c red brown & multi	.25	.25
323	A55	15c brown & multi	.25	.25
324	A55	20c multicolored	.50	.25
325	A55	60c dk green & multi	.65	.40
326	A55	1r brt violet & multi	1.00	.65
		Nos. 321-326 (6)	2.90	2.05

Independence of Mauritius.

Bird Type of 1965 in Changed Background Colors
Wmk. 314

1968, July 12		Photo.	Perf. 14½
		Birds in Natural Colors		
327	A53	2c lemon & brown	.30	.25
328	A53	3c ultra & dk brown	.30	.25
329	A53	15c tan & dk brown	.90	.25
330	A53	20c dull yel & dk brn	1.40	.25
331	A53	60c pink & black	3.50	2.50
332	A53	1r rose lilac & black	5.50	4.50
		Nos. 327-332 (6)	11.90	8.00

Domingue Rescuing Paul and Virginie — A56

Designs: 15c, Paul and Virginie crossing river, vert. 50c, La Bourdonnais visiting Madame de 1a Tour. 60c, Paul and Virginie, vert. 1r, Departure of Virginie for Europe. 2.50r, Bernardin de St. Pierre, vert. The designs are from old prints illustrating "Paul et Virginie."

Perf. 13½

1968, Dec. 2		Unwmk.	Litho.
333	A56	2c multicolored	.25	.25
334	A56	15c multicolored	.25	.25
335	A56	50c multicolored	.30	.30
336	A56	60c multicolored	.40	.40
337	A56	1r multicolored	.65	.65
338	A56	2.50r multicolored	1.75	1.75
		Nos. 333-338 (6)	3.60	3.60

Bicent. of the visit of Bernardin de St. Pierre (1737-1814), author of "Paul et Virginie."

Batardé
Fish
A57

Marine Life: 3c, Red reef crab. 4c, Episcopal miter shell. 5c, Bourse fish. 10c, Starfish. 15c, Sea urchin. 20c, Fiddler crab. 25c, Spiny shrimp. 30c, Single and double harp shells. 35c, Argonaut shell. 40c, Nudibranch (sea-slug). 50c, Violet and orange spider shells. 60c, Blue marlin. 75c, Conus clytospira. 1r, Dorad. 2.50r, Spiny lobster. 5r, Sacré chien rouge fish. 10r, Moonfish.

Wmk. 314 Sideways (#339-344, 351-352), others Upright

		1969, Mar. 12	**Photo.**	**Perf. 14**	
339	A57	2c pink & multi	.30	.30
340	A57	3c yellow & multi	.30	.30
341	A57	4c multicolored	.30	.30
342	A57	5c lt blue & multi	.30	.30
343	A57	10c salmon & multi	.30	.30
344	A57	15c pale blue & multi	.30	.30
345	A57	20c pale gray & multi	.30	.30
346	A57	25c multicolored	.30	.30
347	A57	30c multicolored	.30	.40
348	A57	35c multicolored	.30	.40
349	A57	40c tan & multi	.40	.50
350	A57	50c lt vio & multi	.50	.60
351	A57	60c ultra & multi	.70	.75
352	A57	75c lemon & multi	.85	.85
353	A57	1r cream & multi	.90	1.10
354	A57	2.50r lt vio & multi	3.75	4.75
355	A57	5r multicolored	7.75	10.00
356	A57	10r multicolored	13.50	17.50
		Nos. 339-356 (18)	31.35	39.25

For overprints see Nos. 368-369.

Wmk. 314 Upright (#339a-344a, 351a-352a), others Sideways

1972-74

339a	A57	2c multi ('74)	1.00	1.00
340a	A57	3c multi ('74)	1.00	1.00
341a	A57	4c multi ('74)	1.00	1.00
342a	A57	5c multi ('74)	1.00	1.00
343a	A57	10c multicolored	1.00	1.00
344a	A57	15c multi ('74)	1.00	1.00
345a	A57	20c multicolored	1.00	1.00
346a	A57	25c multi ('73)	1.00	1.00
347a	A57	30c multicolored	1.25	1.00
348a	A57	35c multicolored	1.50	1.25
349a	A57	40c multicolored	1.50	1.50
350a	A57	50c multi ('73)	1.50	1.50
351a	A57	60c multi ('74)	2.00	1.50
352a	A57	75c multicolored	2.50	2.00
353a	A57	1r multicolored	3.00	2.50
354a	A57	2.50r multi ('73)	7.50	7.00
355a	A57	5r multi ('73)	15.00	12.50
356a	A57	10r multicolored	29.00	25.00
		Nos. 339a-356a (18)	72.75	63.75

1975-77 | | | **Wmk. 373** |

339b	A57	2c multi ('77)	.75	.75
340b	A57	3c multi ('77)	.75	.75
341b	A57	4c multi ('77)	.75	.75
342b	A57	5c multi ('77)	.75	.75
344b	A57	15c multicolored	.75	.75
345b	A57	20c multi ('76)	.75	.75
346b	A57	25c multicolored	.95	.75
347b	A57	30c multicolored	1.10	.95
348b	A57	35c multi ('76)	1.10	.95
349b	A57	40c multicolored	1.10	1.10
350b	A57	50c multi ('76)	1.50	1.10
351b	A57	60c multi ('77)	1.90	1.50
352b	A57	75c multi ('77)	1.90	1.90
353b	A57	1r multi ('76)	3.00	2.75
354b	A57	2.50r multi ('77)	12.50	7.50
355b	A57	5r multicolored	21.00	16.00
356b	A57	10r multicolored	50.00	32.50
		Nos. 339b-356b (17)	100.55	71.50

Gandhi as Law Student in London — A58

Portraits of Gandhi: 15c, as stretcher bearer during Zulu rebellion. 50c, as member of non-violent movement in South Africa (Satyagrahi). 60c, wearing Indian garment at No. 10 Downing Street, London. 1r, wearing turban in Mauritius, 1901. 2.50r, as old man.

		1969, July 1	**Litho.**	**Perf. 13½**	
357	A58	2c dull org & multi	.30	.30
358	A58	15c brt blue & multi	.30	.30
359	A58	50c multicolored	.30	.30
360	A58	60c brick red & multi	.40	.40
361	A58	1r multicolored	.75	.75
362	A58	2.50r olive & multi	1.90	1.90
a.		Souvenir sheet of 6, #357-362	7.50	7.50
		Nos. 357-362 (6)	3.95	3.95

Mohandas K. Gandhi (1869-1948), leader in India's struggle for independence.

Vertical Cane Crusher (19th Century) A59

Dr. Charles Telfair (1778-1833) A60

Designs: 15c, The Frangourinier, 18th century cane crusher. 60c, Beau Rivage sugar factory, 1867, painting by Numa Desjardin. 1r, Mon Desert-Alma sugar factory, 1969.

Perf. 11x11½, 11½x11

		1969, Dec. 22	**Photo.**	**Wmk. 314**	
363	A59	2c multicolored	.25	.25
364	A59	15c multicolored	.25	.25
365	A59	60c multicolored	.25	.25
366	A59	1r multicolored	.30	.30
367	A60	2.50r multicolored	.60	.60
a.		Souvenir sheet of 5	2.75	2.75
		Nos. 363-367 (5)	1.65	1.65

150th anniv. of Telfair's improvements of the sugar industry.

No. 367a contains one each of Nos. 363-367. The 2.50r in the sheet is imperf., the others are perf. 11x11½.

Nos. 351 and 353 Overprinted: "EXPO '70 / OSAKA"

		1970, Apr. 7		**Perf. 14**	
368	A57	60c ultra & multi	.25	.25
369	A57	1r cream & multi	.40	.40

EXPO '70 Intl. Exhib., Osaka, Japan, Mar. 15-Sept. 13.

Lufthansa Plane over Mauritius — A61

25c, Brabant Hotel, Morne Beach, horiz.

		1970, May 2	**Litho.**	**Perf. 14**	
370	A61	25c multicolored	.25	.25
371	A61	50c multicolored	.40	.40

Lufthansa's inaugural flight from Mauritius to Frankfurt, Germany, May 2, 1970.

Lenin as Student, by V. Tsigal — A62

Design: 75c, Bust of Lenin.

		1970, May 15	**Photo.**	**Perf. 12x11½**	
372	A62	15c dk slate blue & sil	.25	.25
373	A62	75c dk brown & gold	.65	.65

Birth cent. of Lenin (1870-1924), Russian communist leader.

UN Emblem and Symbols of UN Activities — A63

		1970, Oct. 24	**Litho.**	**Perf. 14**	
374	A63	10c blue black & multi	.25	.25
375	A63	60c blue black & multi	.40	.40

25th anniversary of the United Nations.

Mauritius No. 2, and Post Office before 1870 A64

Designs: 15c, General Post Office Building, 1870-1970. 50c, Mauritius mail coach, 1870. 75c, Port Louis harbor, 1970. 2.50r, Arrival of Pierre André de Suffren de St. Tropez in Port Louis harbor, 1783.

		1970, Oct. 15	**Litho.**	**Perf. 14**	
376	A64	5c multicolored	.25	.25
377	A64	15c multicolored	.25	.25
378	A64	50c multicolored	.25	.25
379	A64	75c multicolored	.30	.30
380	A64	2.50r multicolored	1.00	1.00
a.		Souvenir sheet of 5	5.00	5.00
		Nos. 376-380 (5)	2.05	2.05

Centenary of the General Post Office and to show the improvements of Port Louis harbor. No. 380a contains one each of Nos. 376-380 and a label showing map of Mauritius.

Waterfall A65

15c, Trois Mamelles Mountains. 60c, Beach scene with sailboats. 2.50r, Marine life.

		1971, Apr. 12	**Litho.**	**Perf. 14**	
381	A65	10c multicolored	.25	.25
382	A65	15c multicolored	.25	.25
383	A65	60c multicolored	.40	.40
384	A65	2.50r multicolored	1.90	1.90
		Nos. 381-384 (4)	2.80	2.80

Tourist publicity. Each stamp has a different 6-line message printed in black on back.

Mauritius at Crossroads of Indian Ocean — A66

60c, Plane at Plaisance Airport. 1r, Stewardesses on plane ramp. 2.50r, Roland Garros' airplane, Choisy Airfield, 1937.

		1971, Oct. 23	**Wmk. 314**	**Perf. 14½**	
385	A66	15c multicolored	.25	.25
386	A66	60c multicolored	.55	.55
387	A66	1r multicolored	.65	.65
388	A66	2.50r multicolored	2.75	2.75
		Nos. 385-388 (4)	4.20	4.20

25th anniversary of Plaisance Civil Airport.

Princess Margaret Orthopedic Center — A67

75c, Operating room, National Hospital.

		1971, Nov. 2		**Perf. 14x14½**	
389	A67	10c multicolored	.25	.25
390	A67	75c multicolored	.30	.30

3rd Commonwealth Medical Conf., Nov. 1971.

Elizabeth II and Prince Philip — A68

Design: 2.50r, Queen Elizabeth II, vert.

		1972, Mar.	**Litho.**	**Perf. 14½**	
391	A68	15c brown & multi	.30	.30
392	A68	2.50r ultra & multi	2.75	2.75

Visit of Elizabeth II and Prince Philip.

Port Louis Theater and Masks A69

Design: 1r, Interior view and masks of Comedy and Tragedy.

		1972, June 26			
393	A69	10c brown & multi	.25	.25
394	A69	1r multicolored	.45	.45

Sesquicentennial of Port Louis Theater.

Pirate Dhow Entering Tamarind River A70

Perf. 14x14½, 14½x14

		1972, Nov. 17		**Litho.**	
395	A70	15c shown	.30	.30
396	A70	60c Treasure chest, vert.	.85	.85
397	A70	1r Lememe and brig Hirondelle, vert.	2.00	2.00
398	A70	2.50r Robert Surcouf	7.00	7.00
		Nos. 395-398 (4)	10.15	10.15

Pirates and privateers.

Mauritius University — A71

60c, Tea development plant. 1r, Bank of Mauritius.

		1973, Apr. 10		**Perf. 14½**	
399	A71	15c green & multi	.25	.25
400	A71	60c yellow & multi	.25	.25
401	A71	1r red & multi	.30	.30
		Nos. 399-401 (3)	.80	.80

5th anniversary of independence.

OCAM Emblem A72

Design: 2.50r, Handshake, map of Africa; inscriptions in French, vert.

1973, Apr. 25
402	A72	10c multicolored	.25 .25
403	A72	2.50r lt blue & multi	.60 .60

Conference of the Organisation Commune Africaine, Malgache et Mauricienne (OCAM), Mauritius, Apr. 25-May 6.

WHO Emblem A73

Perf. 14½x14
1973, Nov. 20   **Wmk. 314**
404	A73	1r green & multi	.40 .40

25th anniv. of WHO.

Meteorological Station, Vacoas — A74

1973, Nov. 27
405	A74	75c multicolored	.40 .40

Cent. of intl. meteorological cooperation.

Surcouf and Capture of the "Kent" A75

1974, Mar. 21   **Litho.**   **Perf. 14½x14**
406	A75	60c sepia & multi	1.25 1.25

Bicentenary of the birth of Robert Surcouf (1773-1827), French privateer.

Philibert Commerson & Bougainvillaea A76

1974, Apr. 18   **Perf. 14**
407	A76	2.50r slate grn & multi	.70 .70

Philibert Commerson (1727-1773), French physician and naturalist.

FAO Emblem, Woman Milking Cow A77

1974, Oct. 23   **Perf. 14½**
408	A77	60c multicolored	.35 .35

8th FAO Regional Conference, Aug. 1-17.

Mail Train and UPU Emblem A78

1974, Dec. 4   **Litho.**   **Perf. 14½**
409	A78	15c multicolored	.30 .30
410	A78	1r multicolored	.80 .80

Centenary of Universal Postal Union.

Cottage Life, by F. Leroy A79

Paintings: 60c, Milk Seller, by A. Richard, vert. 1r, Entrance to Port Louis Market, by Thuillier. 2.50r, Washerwomen, by Max Boullé, vert.

1975, Mar. 6   **Wmk. 373**
411	A79	15c multicolored	.25 .25
412	A79	60c multicolored	.40 .40
413	A79	1r multicolored	.65 .65
414	A79	2.50r multicolored	1.50 1.50
		Nos. 411-414 (4)	2.80 2.80

Artistic views of life on Mauritius.

Mace, Map and Arms of Mauritius, Association Emblem — A80

1975, Nov. 21   **Litho.**   **Wmk. 373**
415	A80	75c multicolored	.60 .60

French-speaking Parliamentary Association, conf.

Woman and Aladdin's Lamp A81

1975, Dec. 5   **Perf. 14½**
416	A81	2.50r multicolored	.75 .75

International Women's Year.

Parched Land A82

Drought in Africa: 60c, Map of Africa, carcass and desert, vert.

1976, Feb. 26   **Litho.**   **Wmk. 373**
417	A82	50c vermilion & multi	.25 .25
418	A82	60c blue & multi	.30 .30

Pierre Loti, 1953-1970 — A83

Mail Carriers: 15c, Secunder, 1907. 50c, Hindoostan, 1842. 60c, St. Geran, 1740. 2.50r, Maen, 1638.

1976, July 2   **Litho.**   **Wmk. 373**
419	A83	10c multicolored	.65 .65
420	A83	15c multicolored	.65 .65
421	A83	50c multicolored	.95 .95
422	A83	60c multicolored	1.25 1.25
423	A83	2.50r multicolored	5.50 5.50
a.		Souvenir sheet of 5, #419-423	13.50 13.50
		Nos. 419-423 (5)	9.00 9.00

Flame, and "Hindi Carried Across the Sea" A84

Designs: 75c, like 10c. 1.20r, Flame and tablet with Hindi inscription.

1976, Aug. 28   **Perf. 14½x14**
424	A84	10c multicolored	.25 .25
425	A84	75c lt blue & multi	.25 .25
426	A84	1.20r multicolored	.35 .35
		Nos. 424-426 (3)	.85 .85

2nd World Hindi Convention.

Commonwealth Emblem, Map of Mauritius — A85

King Priest and Steatite Pectoral — A86

2.50r, Commonwealth emblem twice.

1976, Sept. 22   **Litho.**   **Perf. 14x14½**
427	A85	1r multicolored	.40 .40
428	A85	2.50r multicolored	.90 .90

22nd Commonwealth Parliamentary Association Conference, Mauritius, Sept. 17-30.

1976, Dec. 15   **Wmk. 373**   **Perf. 14**

Designs: 1r, House with well, and goblet. 2.50r, Terracotta goddess and necklace.
429	A86	60c multicolored	.35 .35
430	A86	1r multicolored	.75 .75
431	A86	2.50r multicolored	1.75 1.75
		Nos. 429-431 (3)	2.85 2.85

UNESCO campaign to save Mohenjo-Daro excavations.

Sega Dance A87

1977, Jan. 20   **Litho.**   **Perf. 13**
432	A87	1r multicolored	.50 .50

2nd World Black and African Festival, Lagos, Nigeria, Jan. 15-Feb. 12.

Elizabeth II at Mauritius Legislative Assembly — A88

Designs: 75c, Queen holding scepter and orb. 5r, Presentation of scepter and orb.

1977, Feb. 7   **Perf. 14½x14**
433	A88	50c multicolored	.25 .25
434	A88	75c multicolored	.25 .25
435	A88	5r multicolored	1.10 1.10
		Nos. 433-435 (3)	1.60 1.60

25th anniv. of the reign of Elizabeth II.

Hugonia Tomentosa — A89

Flowers: 1r, Oehna mauritiana, vert. 1.50r, Dombeya acuntangula. 5r, Trochetia blackburniana, vert.

1977, Sept. 22   **Wmk. 373**   **Perf. 14**
436	A89	20c multicolored	.25 .25
437	A89	1r multicolored	.40 .40
438	A89	1.50r multicolored	.60 .60
439	A89	5r multicolored	1.75 1.75
a.		Souvenir sheet of 4, #436-439	5.00 5.00
		Nos. 436-439 (4)	3.00 3.00

Twin Otter of Air Mauritius — A90

Designs: 50c, Air Mauritius emblem (red-tailed tropic bird) and Twin Otter. 75c, Piper Navajo and Boeing 747. 5r, Air Mauritius Boeing 707 in flight.

1977, Oct. 31   **Litho.**   **Perf. 14½**
440	A90	25c multicolored	.60 .60
441	A90	50c multicolored	.90 .90
442	A90	75c multicolored	1.00 1.00
443	A90	5r multicolored	5.50 5.50
a.		Souvenir sheet of 4, #440-443	12.00 12.00
		Nos. 440-443 (4)	8.00 8.00

Air Mauritius International Inaugural Flight.

Mauritius, Portuguese Map, 1519 — A91

Dutch Occupation, 1638-1710 — A92

Designs: 20c, Mauritius, map by Van Keulen, c. 1700. 25c, 1st settlement of Rodrigues, 1708. 35c, Proclamation, arrival of French settlers, 1715. 50c, Construction of Port Louis, c. 1736. 60c, Pierre Poivre and nutmeg tree. 70c, Map by Belin, 1763. 75c, First coin minted in Mauritius, 1810. 90c, Naval battle of Grand Port, 1810. 1r, Landing of the British, Nov. 1810. 1.20r, Government House, c. 1840. 1.25r, Invitation with No. 1 and ball of Lady Gomm, 1847. 1.50r, Indian immigration in Mauritius, 1835. 2r, Champ de Mars race course, c. 1870. 3r, Place D'Armes, c. 1880. 5r, Postal card commemorating visit of Prince and Princess of Wales, 1901. 10r, Curepipe College, 1914. 15r, Raising flag of Mauritius, 1968. 25r, Raman Osman, first Governor General and Seewoosagur Ramgoolan, first Prime Minister.

1978, Mar. 12   **Wmk. 373**   **Perf. 13½**
444	A91	10c multicolored	.25 .25
445	A92	15c multicolored	.25 .25
446	A92	20c multicolored	.25 .25
447	A91	25c multicolored	.25 .25
448	A91	35c multicolored	.25 .25
b.		Perf. 14½, "1986"	.25 .25
449	A92	50c multicolored	.25 .25
450	A91	60c multicolored	.35 .35
451	A92	70c multicolored	.40 .35
452	A91	75c multicolored	.45 .40
453	A92	90c multicolored	.45 .40
454	A92	1r multicolored	.45 .45
455	A92	1.20r multicolored	.45 .45
456	A91	1.25r multicolored	.45 .45
457	A92	1.50r multicolored	.55 .60
458	A92	2r multicolored	.75 .80

Design: 1r, New General Post Office Building, Port Louis, and UPU emblem.

459	A92	3r multicolored	1.10	1.25
460	A92	5r multicolored	1.90	2.00
461	A92	10r multicolored	3.75	4.00
462	A91	15r multicolored	5.25	6.00
463	A92	25r multicolored	8.75	9.75
		Nos. 448-463 (20)	26.55	28.75

Nos. 448, 452, 456, 458 reprinted inscribed 1983; Nos. 444, 447-449, 452, 454, 456, 460 reprinted inscribed 1985.

1985-89   Wmk. 384   Perf. 14½

446a	A92	20c "1987"	.25	.25
447a	A91	25c "1987"	.25	.25
448a	A91	35c ('85)	.25	.25
449a	A92	50c ('85)	.25	.25
452a	A91	75c ('85)	.25	.25
458a	A92	2r "1987"	.25	.25
459a	A92	3r "1989"	.40	.40
460a	A92	5r "1989"	.70	.70
463a	A92	25r "1989"	3.45	3.45
		Nos. 446a-463a (9)	6.05	6.05

Issued: 20c, 25c, 2r, 1/11/87; 3r-25r, 1/19/89.
Nos. 449a and 458a reprinted inscribed 1989.

Elizabeth II Coronation Anniv. Issue
Common Design Types
Souvenir Sheet

1978, Apr. 21   Unwmk.   Perf. 15

464		Sheet of 6	2.75	2.75
	a.	CD326 3r Antelope of Bohun	.50	.50
	b.	CD327 3r Elizabeth II	.50	.50
	c.	CD328 3r Dodo	.50	.50

No. 464 contains 2 se-tenant strips of Nos. 464a-464c, separated by horizontal gutter with commemorative and descriptive inscriptions and showing central part of coronation procession with coach.

Dr. Fleming, WWI Casualty, Bacteria — A93

1r, Microscope & 1st mold growth, 1928. 1.50r, Penicillium notatum, close-up. 5r, Alexander Fleming & nurse administering penicillin.

Wmk. 373

1978, Aug. 3   Litho.   Perf. 13½

465	A93	20c multicolored	.80	.80
466	A93	1r multicolored	1.60	1.60
467	A93	1.50r multicolored	2.75	2.75
468	A93	5r multicolored	3.75	3.75
	a.	Souvenir sheet of 4, #465-468	11.00	11.00
		Nos. 465-468 (4)	8.90	8.90

Discovery of penicillin by Dr. Alexander Fleming, 50th anniversary.

Citrus Butterfly — A94

Wildlife Protection (Wildlife Fund Emblem and): 1r, Geckos. 1.50r, Flying foxes. 5r, Mauritius kestrels.

1978, Sept. 21   Perf. 13½x14

469	A94	20c multicolored	4.00	2.50
470	A94	1r multicolored	3.50	2.50
471	A94	1.50r multicolored	3.50	2.50
472	A94	5r multicolored	18.50	5.00
	a.	Souvenir sheet of 4, #469-472	110.00	80.00
		Nos. 469-472 (4)	29.50	12.50

Le Reduit — A95

15c, Ornate table. 3r, Reduit gardens.

1978, Dec. 21   Perf. 14½x14

473	A95	15c multicolored	.25	.25
474	A95	75c multicolored	.30	.30
475	A95	3r multicolored	1.00	1.00
		Nos. 473-475 (3)	1.55	1.55

Reconstruction of Chateau Le Reduit, 200th anniversary.

Whitcomb, 1949 — A96

Locomotives: 1r, Sir William, 1922. 1.50r, Kitson, 1930. 2r, Garratt, 1927.

1979, Feb. 1   Perf. 14½

476	A96	20c multicolored	.25	.25
477	A96	1r multicolored	.50	.50
478	A96	1.50r multicolored	.95	.95
479	A96	2r multicolored	1.25	1.25
	a.	Souvenir sheet of 4, #476-479	5.25	5.25
		Nos. 476-479 (4)	2.95	2.95

Father Laval and Crucifix — A97

Designs: 1.50r, Jacques Desire Laval. 5r, Father Laval's sarcophagus, horiz.

1979, Apr. 30   Wmk. 373   Perf. 14

480	A97	20c multicolored	.25	.25
481	A97	1.50r multicolored	.30	.30
482	A97	5r multicolored	1.00	1.00
	a.	Souvenir sheet of 3, #480-482	3.75	3.75
		Nos. 480-482 (3)	1.55	1.55

Beatification of Father Laval (1803-1864), physician and missionary.

Souvenir Booklet

10th Anniv. of Apollo 11 Moon Landing — A98

Imperf. x Roulette 5

1979, July 20   Litho.

Self-adhesive

483	A98	Booklet of 9	8.00
	a.	20c Astronaut and Lunar Module	.20
	b.	3r Neil Armstrong on moon	.90
	c.	5r Astronaut walking on moon	3.75
	d.	Bklt. pane of 3 (20c, 5r, 3r)	5.00
	e.	Bklt. pane of 6 (3 each 20c, 3r)	3.50

No. 483 contains 2 panes printed on peelable paper backing showing map of moon (d) and details of uniform and spacecraft (e).

Rowland Hill and Great Britain No. 23 — A99

Rowland Hill and: 2r, Mauritius No. 261. 3r, Mauritius No. 2. 5r, Mauritius No. 1.

1979, Aug. 29   Perf. 14½

484	A99	25c multicolored	.25	.25
485	A99	2r multicolored	.50	.50
486	A99	5r multicolored	1.25	1.25
		Nos. 484-486 (3)	2.00	2.00

Souvenir Sheet
Perf. 14½

487	A99	3r multicolored	1.75	1.75

Sir Rowland Hill (1795-1879), originator of penny postage. No. 487 contains one stamp.

Infant Vaccination — A100

IYC Emblem and: 25c, Children playing. 1r, Coat of arms, vert. 1.50r, Children in laboratory. 3r, Teacher and student working lathe.

Wmk. 373

1979, Oct. 11   Litho.   Perf. 14

488	A100	15c multicolored	.25	.25
489	A100	25c multicolored	.25	.25
490	A100	1r multicolored	.25	.25
491	A100	1.50r multicolored	.35	.35
492	A100	3r multicolored	.70	.70
		Nos. 488-492 (5)	1.80	1.80

International Year of the Child.

Lienard Obelisk A101

Designs: 25c, Poivre Avenue, 1r, Pandanus. 2r, Giant water lilies, 5r, Mon Plaisir.

1980, Jan. 24   Perf. 14x14½

493	A101	20c multicolored	.25	.25
494	A101	25c multicolored	.25	.25
495	A101	1r multicolored	.25	.25
496	A101	2r multicolored	.40	.40
497	A101	5r multicolored	1.00	1.00
	a.	Souvenir sheet of 5, #493-497	4.25	4.25
		Nos. 493-497 (5)	2.15	2.15

Pamplemousses Botanical Gardens.

"Emirne," 19th Century, London 1980 Emblem — A102

1980, May 6   Litho.   Perf. 14½

498	A102	25c shown	.25	.25
499	A102	1r Boissevain, 1930's	.50	.50
500	A102	2r La Boudeuse, 18th cent.	1.00	1.00
501	A102	5r Sea Breeze, 19th cent.	2.25	2.25
		Nos. 498-501 (4)	4.00	4.00

London 80 Intl. Stamp Exhib., May 6-14.

Helen Keller Reading Braille — A103

1980, June 27   Litho.   Perf. 14½

502	A103	25c Blind men weaving baskets	.25	.25
503	A103	1r Teacher and deaf girl	.50	.50
504	A103	2.50r shown	1.25	1.25

505	A103	5r Keller graduating college	2.00	2.00
		Nos. 502-505 (4)	4.00	4.00

Helen Keller (1880-1968), blind and deaf writer and lecturer.

Prime Minister Seewoosagur Ramgoolan, 80th Birthday — A104

Litho.; Gold Embossed

1980, Sept. 18   Perf. 13½

506	A104	15r multicolored	2.00	2.00

Mauritius Institute, Centenary — A105

1980, Oct. 1   Litho.   Perf. 13

507	A105	25c shown	.25	.25
508	A105	2r Rare Veda copy	.50	.50
509	A105	2.50r Rare cone	.60	.60
510	A105	5r Landscape, by Henri Harpignies	1.25	1.25
		Nos. 507-510 (4)	2.60	2.60

Hibiscus Liliiflorus — A106   Arms of Curepipe — A107

1981, Jan. 15   Litho.   Perf. 14

511	A106	25c shown	.25	.25
512	A106	2r Erythrospermum monticolum	.70	.70
513	A106	2.50r Chasalia boryana	.90	.90
514	A106	5r Hibiscus columnaris	1.75	1.75
		Nos. 511-514 (4)	3.60	3.60

Perf. 13½x13

1981, Apr. 10   Litho.   Wmk. 373

Designs: City coats of arms.

515	A107	25c Beau-Bassin / Rose Hill	.25	.25
516	A107	1.50r shown	.30	.30
517	A107	2r Quatre-Bornes	.40	.40
518	A107	2.50r Vacoas/Phoenix	.50	.50
519	A107	5r Port Louis	1.00	1.00
	a.	Souv. sheet of 5, #515-519, perf. 14	3.25	3.25
		Nos. 515-519 (5)	2.45	2.45

Royal Wedding Issue
Common Design Type

1981, July 22   Litho.   Perf. 14

520	CD331	25c Bouquet	.25	.25
521	CD331	2.50r Charles	.50	.50
522	CD331	10r Couple	2.00	2.00
		Nos. 520-522 (3)	2.75	2.75

Emmanuel Anquetil and Guy
Rozemont — A108

Famous Men: 25c, Remy Ollier, Sookdeo
Bissoondoyal. 1.25r, Maurice Cure,
Barthelemy Ohsan. 1.50r, Guy Forget, Ren-
ganaden Seeneevassen. 2r, Abdul Razak
Mohamed, Jules Koenig. 2.50r, Abdoollatiff
Mahomed Osman, Dazzi Rama. 5r, Thomas
Lewis.

1981, Aug. 13   *Perf. 14½*
523 A108 20c black & red .25 .25
524 A108 25c black & yellow .25 .25
525 A108 1.25r black & green .35 .35
526 A108 1.50r black & vermilion .40 .40
527 A108 2r black & ultra .55 .55
528 A108 2.50r black & red brn .65 .65
529 A108 5r black & blue grn 1.40 1.40
    Nos. 523-529 (7) 3.85 3.85

Chinese
Pagoda
A109

1981, Sept. 16   *Perf. 13½*
530 A109 20c Tamil Women .25 .25
531 A109 2r Swami Sivananda,
    vert. .75 .75
532 A109 5r shown 1.90 1.90
    Nos. 530-532 (3) 2.90 2.90

World Tamil Culture Conference, 1980 (20c).

A110   A111

1981, Oct. 26   Litho.   *Perf. 14*
533 A110 25c Pottery making .25 .25
534 A110 1.25r Dog grooming .25 .25
535 A110 5r Hiking .75 .75
536 A110 10r Duke of Edin-
    burgh 1.50 1.50
    Nos. 533-536 (4) 2.75 2.75

Duke of Edinburgh's Awards, 25th anniv.

1981, Nov. 26   Wmk. 373   *Perf. 14½*
537 A111 25c Holy Ka'aba, Mec-
    ca .30 .30
538 A111 2r Prophet's Mosque .80 .80
539 A111 5r Holy Ka'aba,
    Prophet's Mosque 1.90 1.90
    Nos. 537-539 (3) 3.00 3.00

Hegira, 1,500th anniv.

Scouting
Year — A112

1982, Feb. 25   Litho.   *Perf. 14x14½*
540 A112 25c Emblem .25 .25
541 A112 2r Baden-Powell .60 .60
542 A112 5r Grand howl, sign 1.40 1.40
543 A112 10r Scouts, mountain 2.75 2.75
    Nos. 540-543 (4) 5.00 5.00

Darwin Death Centenary — A113

1982, Apr. 19   Litho.   *Perf. 14*
544 A113 25c Portrait .25 .25
545 A113 2r Telescope .45 .45
546 A113 2.50r Riding elephant .55 .55
547 A113 10r The Beagle 2.25 2.25
    Nos. 544-547 (4) 3.50 3.50

Princess Diana Issue
Common Design Type

1982, July 1   Litho.   *Perf. 13*
548 CD333 25c Arms .25 .25
549 CD333 2.50r Diana .75 .75
550 CD333 5r Wedding 1.50 1.50
551 CD333 10r Portrait 3.00 3.00
    Nos. 548-551 (4) 5.50 5.50

Birth of
Prince
William of
Wales, June
21 — A114

1982, Sept. 22   Litho.   *Perf. 14½*
552 A114 2.50r multicolored 1.10 1.10

Issued in sheets of 9.

TB Bacillus
Centenary — A115

1982, Dec. 15   *Perf. 14*
553 A115 25c Aphloia
    theiformis .25 .25
554 A115 1.25r Central Market,
    Port Louis .55 .55
555 A115 2r Gaertnera
    psychotrioides .85 .85
556 A115 5r Selaginella deli-
    quescens 1.25 1.25
557 A115 10r Koch 3.75 3.75
    Nos. 553-557 (5) 6.65 6.65

A116

1983, Mar. 14   *Perf. 13x13½*
558 A116 25c Flag, arms .25 .25
559 A116 2.50r Satellite view .40 .40
560 A116 5r Sugar cane har-
    vest .85 .85
561 A116 10r Port Louis Harbor 1.75 1.75
    Nos. 558-561 (4) 3.25 3.25

Commonwealth Day.

World Communications Year — A117

1983, June 24   Wmk. 373   *Perf. 14*
562 A117 25c Antique tele-
    phone, vert. .25 .25
563 A117 1.25r Early telegraph
    apparatus .35 .35
564 A117 2r Earth satellite
    station, vert. .50 .50
565 A117 10r 1st hot air bal-
    loon in Maurit-
    us, 1784 2.40 2.40
    Nos. 562-565 (4) 3.50 3.50

Namibia
Day — A118

1983, Aug. 26
566 A118 25c Map .70 .70
567 A118 2.50r Breaking
    chains 1.60 1.60
568 A118 5r Family, village 3.25 3.25
569 A118 10r Diamond min-
    ing 6.00 6.00
    Nos. 566-569 (4) 11.55 11.55

Fishery Resources — A119

1983, Oct. 7
570 A119 25c Fish trap, vert. .25 .25
571 A119 1r Fishermen in boat .40 .40
572 A119 5r Game fishing, vert. 1.75 1.75
573 A119 10r Octopus drying 3.75 3.75
    Nos. 570-573 (4) 6.15 6.15

Swami
Dayananda, Death
Centenary — A120

1983, Nov. 3   Litho.   Wmk. 373
574 A120 25c shown .25 .25
575 A120 35c Last meeting with
    father .25 .25
576 A120 2r Receiving instruc-
    tion .30 .30
577 A120 5r Demonstrating
    strength .80 .80
578 A120 10r Religious gathering 1.75 1.75
    Nos. 574-578 (5) 3.35 3.35

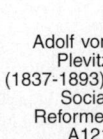

Adolf von
Plevitz
(1837-1893),
Social
Reformer
A121

1983, Dec. 8
579 A121 25c shown .30 .30
580 A121 1.25r Government
    school .65 .65
581 A121 5r Addressing Com-
    mission of En-
    quiry 1.10 1.10
582 A121 10r Indian field work-
    ers 2.50 2.50
    Nos. 579-582 (4) 4.55 4.55

Mauritius
Kestrels
A122

1984, Mar. 26   Wmk. 373   *Perf. 14*
583 A122 25c Courtship
    chase .40 .40
584 A122 2r Side view,
    vert. 2.40 2.40
585 A122 2.50r Fledgling 2.75 2.75
586 A122 10r Bird, diff., vert. 12.00 12.00
    Nos. 583-586 (4) 17.55 17.55

Lloyd's List Issue
Common Design Type

1984, May 23   Litho.   *Perf. 14½x14*
587 CD335 25c Tayeb, Port
    Lewis .35 .35
588 CD335 1r Taher .70 .70
589 CD335 5r East Indiaman
    Triton 2.40 2.40
590 CD335 10r Astor 5.50 5.50
    Nos. 587-590 (4) 8.95 8.95

Palm   Slave
Trees — A123   Sale — A124

1984, July 23   Litho.   *Perf. 14*
591 A123 25c Blue latan .30 .30
592 A123 50c Hyophorbe
    vaughanii .30 .30
593 A123 2.50r Tectiphiala fer-
    ox 1.40 1.40
594 A123 5r Round Isld.
    bottle-palm 2.75 2.75
595 A123 10r Hyophorbe
    amaricaulis 5.75 5.75
    Nos. 591-595 (5) 10.50 10.50

1984, Aug.   *Perf. 14½*
596 A124 25c Woman .30 .30
597 A124 1r shown .95 .95
598 A124 2r Family, horiz. 1.50 1.50
599 A124 10r Immigrant arri-
    val, horiz. 7.50 7.50
    Nos. 596-599 (4) 10.25 10.25

Alliance Francaise Centenary — A125

1984, Sept. 10   *Perf. 14½*
600 A125 25c Production of
    Faust, 1959 .25 .25
601 A125 1.25r Award ceremo-
    ny .65 .65
602 A125 5r Headquarters 2.10 2.10
603 A125 10r Lion Mountain 4.50 4.50
    Nos. 600-603 (4) 7.50 7.50

Queen Mother 85th Birthday
Common Design Type
    Perf. 14½x14

1985, June 7   Wmk. 384
604 CD336 25c Portrait, 1926 .25 .25
605 CD336 2r With Princess
    Margaret .55 .55
606 CD336 5r On Clarence
    House balcony 1.50 1.50
607 CD336 10r Holding Prince
    Henry 2.75 2.75
    Nos. 604-607 (4) 5.05 5.05

Souvenir Sheet

608 CD336 15r On Royal Barge,
    reopening Strat-
    ford Canal,
    1964 6.75 6.75

2nd Annual Indian Ocean Islands Games — A126

Pink Pigeon — A127

1985, Aug. 24   Wmk. 373   Perf. 14½
609 A126 25c High jump .35 .35
610 A126 50c Javelin .75 .75
611 A126 1.25r Cycling 4.75 4.75
612 A126 10r Wind surfing 8.25 8.25
  Nos. 609-612 (4) 14.10 14.10

1985, Sept. 2   Wmk. 384   Perf. 14
613 A127 25c Adult and young 6.25 1.25
614 A127 2r Nest site display 11.00 2.75
615 A127 2.50r Nesting 12.50 4.25
616 A127 5r Preening 20.00 6.00
  Nos. 613-616 (4) 49.75 14.25
  World Wildlife Fund.

World Tourism Org., 10th Anniv. A128

1985, Sept. 20   Perf. 14½
617 A128 25c Patates Caverns .60 .60
618 A128 35c Colored Earth, Chamarel .60 .60
619 A128 5r Serpent Island 2.75 2.75
620 A128 10r Coin de Mire Is. 11.00 11.00
  Nos. 617-620 (4) 14.95 14.95

Port Louis, 250th Anniv. A129

1985, Nov. 22   Perf. 13½
621 A129 25c Old Town Hall .30 .30
622 A129 1r Al-Aqsa Mosque .90 .90
623 A129 2.50r Tamil-speaking Indians, settlement 1.75 1.75
624 A129 10r Port Louis Harbor 6.50 6.50
  Nos. 621-624 (4) 9.45 9.45

Halley's Comet A130

1986, Feb. 21   Wmk. 384   Perf. 14
625 A130 25c Halley, map .55 .55
626 A130 1.25r Newton's telescope, 1682 sighting .75 .75
627 A130 3r Mauritius from space 1.50 1.50
628 A130 10r Giotto space probe 5.00 5.00
  Nos. 625-628 (4) 7.80 7.80

Queen Elizabeth II 60th Birthday
Common Design Type

Designs: 25c, In uniform, Grenadier Guards, 1942. 75c, Investiture of the Prince of Wales, 1969. 2r, State visit with Prince Philip. 3r, State visit to Germany, 1978. 15r, Visiting Crown Agents' offices, 1983.

1986, Apr. 21   Litho.   Perf. 14½x14
629 CD337 25c scar, black & sil .25 .25
630 CD337 75c ultra & multi .25 .25
631 CD337 2r green & multi .40 .40

632 CD337 3r violet & multi .55 .55
633 CD337 15r rose vio & multi 2.25 2.25
  Nos. 629-633 (5) 3.70 3.70

Intl. Events — A131

Designs: 25c, World Food Day. 1r, African Regional Industrial Property Organization, 10th anniv. 1.25r, Intl. Peace Year. 10r, 1986 World Cup Soccer Championships.

1986, July 25   Litho.   Perf. 14
634 A131 25c FAO emblem, corn .30 .30
635 A131 1r ARIPO emblem .65 .65
636 A131 1.25r IPY emblem .95 .95
637 A131 10r Athlete, MFA 7.25 7.25
  Nos. 634-637 (4) 9.15 9.15

Orchids — A132

1986, Oct. 3   Litho.   Perf. 14½
638 A132 25c Cryptopus elatus .65 .65
639 A132 2r Jumellea recta 1.10 1.10
640 A132 2.50r Angraecum mauritianum 1.75 1.75
641 A132 10r Bulbophyllum longiflorum 6.50 6.50
  Nos. 638-641 (4) 10.00 10.00

Bridges A133

1987, May 22   Wmk. 373
642 A133 25c Hesketh Bell .25 .25
643 A133 50c Sir Colville Deverell .60 .60
644 A133 2.50r Cavendish 1.50 1.50
645 A133 5r Tamarin 3.00 3.00
646 A133 10r Grand River North West 6.00 6.00
  Nos. 642-646 (5) 11.35 11.35

The Bar, Bicent. A134

Perf. 14x14½
1987, June 2   Wmk. 384
647 A134 25c Port Louis Supreme Court .25 .25
648 A134 1r Flacq District Court .50 .50
649 A134 1.25r Statue of Justice .55 .55
650 A134 10r Barristers, 1787-1987 3.25 3.25
  Nos. 647-650 (4) 4.55 4.55

Intl. Festival of the Sea — A135

1987, Sept. 5   Wmk. 373
651 A135 25c Dodo mascot, vert. .75 .75
652 A135 1.50r Sailboats 1.75 1.75
653 A135 3r Water-skier 2.75 2.75
654 A135 5r Tall ship Svanen, vert. 4.75 4.75
  Nos. 651-654 (4) 10.00 10.00

Industrialization — A136

1987, Oct. 30   Perf. 14
655 A136 20c Toy .30 .30
656 A136 35c Spinning .30 .30
657 A136 50c Rattan .30 .30
658 A136 2.50r Optical .95 .95
659 A136 10r Stone carving 3.25 3.25
  Nos. 655-659 (5) 5.10 5.10

Art & Architecture A137

Designs: 25c, Maison Ouvriere, Intl. Year of Shelter for the Homeless emblem. 1r, Paul et Virginie, a lithograph. 1.25r, Chateau Rosney. 2r, Old Farmhouse, Boulle. 5r, Three Peaks, watercolor.

1988, June 29   Wmk. 384   Perf. 14½
660 A137 25c multicolored .25 .25
661 A137 1r gray & black .40 .40
662 A137 1.25r multicolored .50 .50
663 A137 2r multicolored .60 .60
664 A137 5r multicolored 1.60 1.60
  Nos. 660-664 (5) 3.35 3.35

Natl. Independence, 20th Anniv. — A138

Designs: 25c, University of Mauritius. 75c, Calisthenics at sunset in stadium. 2.50r, Runners, Sir Maurice Rault Stadium. 5r, Air Mauritius jet at gate, Sir Seewoosagur Ramgoolam Intl. Airport. 10r, Gov.-Gen. Veerasamy Ringadoo and Prime Minister Aneerood Jugnauth.

1988, Mar. 11   Wmk. 373   Perf. 14
665 A138 25c multicolored .25 .25
666 A138 75c multicolored .25 .25
667 A138 2.50r multicolored .90 .90
668 A138 5r multicolored 1.60 1.60
669 A138 10r multicolored 3.25 3.25
  Nos. 665-669 (5) 6.25 6.25

WHO, 40th Anniv. — A139

1988, July 1   Wmk. 373   Perf. 13½
670 A139 20c Breast-feeding .30 .30
671 A139 2r Immunization .90 .90
672 A139 3r Nutrition 1.75 1.75
673 A139 10r Emblem 5.00 5.00
  Nos. 670-673 (4) 7.95 7.95

Mauritius Commercial Bank, Ltd., 150th Anniv. A140

1988, Sept. 1   Wmk. 373   Perf. 14
674 A140 25c Bank, 1981, vert. .30 .30
675 A140 1r Bank, 1897 .40 .40
676 A140 1.25r Coat of arms, vert. .50 .50
677 A140 25r 15-Dollar bank note, 1838 8.00 8.00
  Nos. 674-677 (4) 9.20 9.20

1988 Summer Olympics, Seoul A141

1988, Oct. 1
678 A141 25c shown .25 .25
679 A141 35c Wrestling .35 .35
680 A141 1.50r Running .65 .65
681 A141 10r Swimming 4.00 4.00
  Nos. 678-681 (4) 5.25 5.25

Environmental Protection — A142

Wmk. 384 (20c, 40c, 50c, 1r, 10r), 373 (Others)
1989-97   Litho.   Perf. 14
682 A142 15c Tropical reef .35 .35
  a. Dated "1994" .35 .35
  b. Dated "1995" .35 .35
683 A142 20c like #682 .35 .35
684 A142 30c Greenshank .40 .40
  a. Wmk. 384 .35 .35
  b. As No. 684, dated "1995" .40 .40
685 A142 40c shown .35 .35
  a. Wmk. 373 .35 .35
  b. As a, dated "1994" .35 .35
  c. As a, dated "1997" .35 .35
686 A142 50c Round Island, vert. .35 .35
  a. Dated "1997" .35 .35
687 A142 60c like #685 .35 .35
688 A142 75c Bassin Blanc .35 .35
689 A142 1r Mangrove, vert. .35 .35
  a. Dated "1998" .35 .35
690 A142 1.50r Whimbrel .40 .40
691 A142 2r Le Morne .40 .40
692 A142 3r Fish .75 .75
693 A142 4r Fern tree, vert. 1.00 1.00
  a. Dated "1994" 1.00 1.00
  b. Dated "1998" 1.00 1.00
694 A142 5r Riviere du Poste Estuary 1.00 1.00
  a. Dated "1998" 1.00 1.00
695 A142 6r Ecological scenery, vert. 1.50 1.50
  a. Dated "1998" 1.50 1.50
696 A142 10r Phelsuma ornata, vert. 2.40 2.40
  a. Wmk. 373 ('97) 2.40 2.40
  b. As a, dated "1995" 2.40 2.40
  c. As a, dated "1997" 2.40 2.40
  d. As a, dated "1998" 2.40 2.40
697 A142 15r Benares surf 3.25 3.25
  a. Wmk. 384 3.00 3.00
  b. As No. 697, dated "1998" 3.25 3.25
698 A142 25r Migratory birds, vert. 5.50 5.50
  a. Wmk. 384 ('96) 5.25 5.25
  b. As a, dated "1997" 5.25 5.25
  c. As No. 698, dated "1998" 5.25 5.25
  Nos. 682-698 (17) 19.05 19.05

Issued: 40c, 3r-10r, 3/11/89; No. 685a, 2/19/91; 50c, 75c, 2r, 5r, 15r, 10/4/91; 20c, 60c, 3/96; others, 11/22/90.
For surcharge see No. 781.

A143

French Revolution, Bicent.: 30c, La Tour Sumeire, Place Du Theatre Municipal. 1r, Salle De Spectacle Du Jardin. 8r, Le Comte De Malartic. 15r, Anniv. emblem.

1989, July 14   Wmk. 373

702	A143	30c multicolored	.25	.25
703	A143	1r multicolored	.25	.25
704	A143	8r multicolored	2.00	2.00
705	A143	15r multicolored	3.75	3.75
		Nos. 702-705 (4)	6.25	6.25

A144

Visit of Pope John Paul II: 30c, Cardinal Jean Margeot. 40c, Pope welcoming Prime Minister Aneerood Jugnauth to the Vatican, 1988. 3r, Mother Mary Magdalene of the Cross (1810-1889) and Filles des Marie Chapel, Port Louis, 1864. 6r, St. Francis of Assisi Church, 1756, Pamplemousses. 10r, Pope John Paul II.

1989, Oct. 13   Perf. 14x13½

706	A144	30c multicolored	.30	.30
707	A144	40c multicolored	1.00	1.00
708	A144	3r multicolored	2.00	2.00
709	A144	6r multicolored	4.25	4.25
710	A144	10r multicolored	6.75	6.75
		Nos. 706-710 (5)	14.30	14.30

Jawaharlal Nehru, 1st Prime Minister of India — A145

Designs: 1.50r, Nehru and Indira, Rajiv and Sanjay Gandhi. 3r, With Mahatma Gandhi. 4r, With Nasser and Tito. 10r, With children.

1989, Oct. 13   Wmk. 384   Perf. 14

711	A145	40c shown	1.25	1.25
712	A145	1.50r multicolored	1.50	1.50
713	A145	3r multicolored	3.00	3.00
714	A145	4r multicolored	3.75	3.75
715	A145	10r multicolored	9.00	9.00
		Nos. 711-715 (5)	18.50	18.50

Sugar Cane Industry, 350th Anniv. A146

Perf. 13½x14

1990, Jan. 10   Litho.   Wmk. 384

716	A146	30c Cutting cane	.30	.30
717	A146	40c Refinery, 1867	.30	.30
718	A146	1r Mechanically loading cane	.75	.75
719	A146	25r Modern refinery	12.00	12.00
		Nos. 716-719 (4)	13.35	13.35

Prime Minister Jugnauth's 60th Birthday A147

Jugnauth: 35c, And symbols of the industrial estate. 40c, At his desk. 1.50r, And stock exchange emblem. 4r, And Gov.-Gen. Ramgoolam. 10r, And Pope John Paul II, map.

Wmk. 373

1990, Mar. 29   Litho.   Perf. 14

720	A147	35c multicolored	.35	.35
721	A147	40c multicolored	.35	.35
722	A147	1.50r multicolored	1.60	1.60
723	A147	4r multicolored	3.50	3.50
724	A147	10r multicolored	8.75	8.75
		Nos. 720-724 (5)	14.55	14.55

Mauritian Television, 25th Anniv. A148

Anniversaries and Events: 30c, Death of Desjardins, naturalist, 150th anniversary, vert. 6r, Line barracks, 250th anniversary, vert. 8r, Municipality of Curepipe, centenary.

1990, July 5

725	A148	30c lt orange & multi	.50	.50
726	A148	35c pink & multi	.50	.50
727	A148	6r lt blue & multi	5.25	5.25
728	A148	8r lt green & multi	6.50	6.50
		Nos. 725-728 (4)	12.75	12.75

Intl. Literacy Year A149

Wmk. 373

1990, Sept. 28   Litho.   Perf. 14

729	A149	30c shown	.35	.35
730	A149	1r Blind girl printing braille	1.40	1.40
731	A149	3r Globe, open book	2.50	2.50
732	A149	10r Open book, world map	8.75	8.75
		Nos. 729-732 (4)	13.00	13.00

Elizabeth & Philip, Birthdays
Common Design Types

Wmk. 384

1991, June 17   Litho.   Perf. 14½

733	CD345	8r multicolored	1.75	1.75
734	CD346	8r multicolored	1.75	1.75
a.		Pair, #733-734 + label	3.75	3.75

Port Louis, City Incorporation, 25th Anniv. — A150

Anniversaries and Events: 4r, Col. Draper, 150th death anniv., vert. 6r, Joseph Barnard, engraver of first Mauritius stamps, 175th birth anniv., vert. 10r, Spitfire, Mauritius' contribution to Allied war effort, 1939-1945.

Wmk. 373

1991, Aug. 18   Litho.   Perf. 14

735	A150	40c multicolored	.30	.30
736	A150	4r multicolored	2.10	2.10
737	A150	6r multicolored	3.25	3.25
738	A150	10r multicolored	5.25	5.25
		Nos. 735-738 (4)	10.90	10.90

Phila Nippon '91 — A151

Butterflies: 40c, Euploea euphon. 3r, Hypolimnas misippus, female. 8r, Papilio manlius. 10r, Hypolimnas misippus, male.

Perf. 14x14½

1991, Nov. 15   Litho.   Wmk. 373

739	A151	40c multicolored	.90	.90
740	A151	3r multicolored	2.00	2.00
741	A151	8r multicolored	4.75	4.75
742	A151	10r multicolored	5.50	5.50
		Nos. 739-742 (4)	13.15	13.15

Flora and Fauna From Mauritius A152

Designs: 40c, Chelonia mydas, Tromelin. 1r, Ibis, Agalega. 2r, Takamaka flowers, Chagos Archipelago. 15r, Lambis violacea, St. Brandon.

1991, Dec. 13   Perf. 14

743	A152	40c multicolored	.75	.75
744	A152	1r multicolored	1.25	1.25
745	A152	2r multicolored	1.60	1.60
746	A152	15r multicolored	9.50	9.50
		Nos. 743-746 (4)	13.10	13.10

Republic

Proclamation of the Republic of Mauritius — A153

1992, Mar. 12

747	A153	40c President	.30	.30
748	A153	4r Prime Minister	1.40	1.40
749	A153	8r Mauritian children	3.00	3.00
750	A153	10r President's flag	3.50	3.50
		Nos. 747-750 (4)	8.20	8.20

8th African Track and Field Championships A154

Designs: 40c, Games mascot, Tricolo. 4r, Sir Anerood Jugnauth Stadium, horiz. 5r, High jumper, horiz. 6r, Torch, emblem of games.

1992, June 25   Perf. 13½

751	A154	40c multicolored	.25	.25
752	A154	4r multicolored	.85	.85
753	A154	5r multicolored	1.25	1.25
754	A154	6r multicolored	1.50	1.50
		Nos. 751-754 (4)	3.85	3.85

Anniversaries and Events — A155

Designs: 40c, Flower, vert. 1r, Swami Krishnanandji Maharaj, vert. 2r, Boy and dog.

3r, Building, flags. 15r, Radio telescope antennae.

1992, Aug. 13

755	A155	40c multicolored	.25	.25
756	A155	1r multicolored	.60	.60
757	A155	2r multicolored	.95	.95
758	A155	8r multicolored	1.50	1.50
759	A155	15r multicolored	6.50	6.50
		Nos. 755-759 (5)	9.80	9.80

Fleurir Maurice, 25th anniv. (No. 755). 25th anniv. of Swami Maharaj's arrival (No. 756). Humane education (No. 757). Indian Ocean Commission, 10th anniv. (No. 758). Inauguration of radio telescope project (No. 759).

Bank of Mauritius, Silver Jubilee A156

Designs: 40c, Bank of Mauritius building, vert. 4r, Dodo gold bullion coin. 8r, First bank note issues. 15r, Foreign exchange reserves 1967-1992.

Perf. 14½x14, 14x14½

1992, Oct. 29   Litho.   Wmk. 373

760	A156	40c multicolored	.30	.30
761	A156	4r multicolored	1.60	1.60
762	A156	8r multicolored	3.50	3.50
763	A156	15r multicolored	5.75	5.75
		Nos. 760-763 (4)	11.15	11.15

National Day, 25th Anniv. — A157

30c, Housing development. 40c, Computer showing gross domestic product. 3r, Flag in shape of map of Mauritius. 4r, Ballot box. 15r, Medal for Grand Commander of the Order of the Star & Key of the Indian Ocean.

1993, Mar. 12   Perf. 15x14

764	A157	30c multicolored	.25	.25
765	A157	40c multicolored	.25	.25
766	A157	3r multicolored	.55	.55
767	A157	4r multicolored	.80	.80
768	A157	15r multicolored	2.75	2.75
		Nos. 764-768 (5)	4.60	4.60

Air Mauritius Ltd., 25th Anniv. A158

40c, Bell 206B Jet Ranger. 3r, Boeing 747SP. 4r, ATR 42. 10r, Boeing 767-200ER.

1993, June 14   Perf. 14

769	A158	40c multicolored	.85	.85
770	A158	3r multicolored	1.50	1.50
771	A158	4r multicolored	2.00	2.00
772	A158	10r multicolored	4.75	4.75
a.		Souvenir sheet of 4, #769-772	11.50	11.50
		Nos. 769-772 (4)	9.10	9.10

5th Francophone Summit — A159

Designs: 1r, 1715 Act of French Seizure of Mauritius, 1810 Act of Surrender. 5r, Signs. 6r,

Page from Napoleonic Code. 7r, French publications.

1993, Oct. 16

773	A159	1r multicolored	.25	.25
774	A159	5r multicolored	2.50	2.50
775	A159	6r multicolored	3.00	3.00
776	A159	7r multicolored	3.50	3.50
		Nos. 773-776 (4)	9.25	9.25

Telecommunications — A160

Designs: 40c, SS Scotia, cable laying. 3r, Morse code, Morse key. 4r, Signal mountain station. 8r, Communications satellite.

1993, Nov. 25   *Perf. 13*

777	A160	40c multicolored	.65	.65
778	A160	3r multicolored	1.10	1.10
779	A160	4r multicolored	1.75	1.75
780	A160	8r multicolored	3.50	3.50
		Nos. 777-780 (4)	7.00	7.00

No. 686 Surcharged

1993, Sept. 15   Litho.   *Perf. 14*

781	A142	40c on 75c multi	2.00	2.00

Mammals — A161

Wmk. 384

1994, Mar. 9   *Perf. 14½*

782	A161	40c Mongoose	.30	.30
783	A161	2r Hare	1.25	1.25
784	A161	8r Monkey	4.00	4.00
785	A161	10r Tenrec	4.50	4.50
		Nos. 782-785 (4)	10.05	10.05

Anniversaries and Events — A162

40c, Dr. E. Brown-Sequard (1817-94). 4r, Silhouettes of family. 8r, World Cup trophy, US map. 10r, Control Tower, SSR Intl. Airport.

Wmk. 373

1994, June 16   Litho.   *Perf. 14*

786	A162	40c multicolored	.25	.25
787	A162	4r multicolored	.75	.75
788	A162	8r multicolored	1.60	1.60
789	A162	10r multicolored	2.00	2.00
		Nos. 786-789 (4)	4.60	4.60

Intl. Year of the Family (No. 787). 1994 World Cup Soccer Championships, US (No. 788). ICAO, 50th anniv. (No. 789).

Wreck of the St. Geran, 250th Anniv. A163

Page from Napoleonic Code. 7r, French publications. *(column 2)*

Wmk. 384

1994, Aug. 18   Litho.   *Perf. 14*

790	A163	40c Leaving L'Orient	.35	.35
791	A163	5r In rough seas	1.50	1.50
792	A163	6r Ship's bell	1.75	1.75
793	A163	10r Relics from ship	3.00	3.00
		Nos. 790-793 (4)	6.60	6.60

Souvenir Sheet

794	A163	15r St. Geran, vert.	9.00	9.00

Children's Paintings of Leisure Activities — A164

Designs: 30c, "Ring Around the Rosey." 40c, Playing with balls, jump rope. 8r, Water sports. 10r, "Blindman's Buff."

Wmk. 373

1994, Oct. 25   Litho.   *Perf. 13½*

795	A164	30c multicolored	.25	.25
796	A164	40c multicolored	.25	.25
797	A164	8r multicolored	1.50	1.50
798	A164	10r multicolored	1.90	1.90
		Nos. 795-798 (4)	3.90	3.90

Spices — A165

Perf. 13x14

1995, Mar. 10   Litho.   Wmk. 373

799	A165	40c Nutmeg	.30	.30
800	A165	4r Coriander	.85	.85
801	A165	5r Cloves	1.25	1.25
802	A165	10r Cardamon	2.40	2.40
		Nos. 799-802 (4)	4.80	4.80

End of World War II
Common Design Type

Designs: No. 803, HMS Mauritius. No. 804, Mauritian servicemen, map of North Africa. No. 805, Catalina, Tombeau Bay.

Wmk. 373

1995, May 8   Litho.   *Perf. 14*
Size: 35x28mm

803	CD351	5r multicolored	2.50	2.50
804	CD351	5r multicolored	2.50	2.50
805	CD351	5r multicolored	2.50	2.50
		Nos. 803-805 (3)	7.50	7.50

Anniversaries & Events — A166

1995, May 8

806	A166	40c multicolored	.25	.25
807	A166	4r multicolored	1.25	1.25
808	A166	10r multicolored	2.75	2.75
		Nos. 806-808 (3)	4.25	4.25

Construction of Mare Longue Reservoir, 50th anniv. (No. 806). Construction of Mahebourg Europipe Road, bicent. (No. 007). Great fire of Port Louis, cent. (No. 808).

A167

Designs: Lighthouses.

Perf. 13x14

1995, Aug. 28   Litho.   Wmk. 373

809	A167	30c Ile Plate	1.00	1.00
810	A167	40c Pointe aux Caves	1.00	1.00
811	A167	8r Ile aux Fouquets	4.75	4.75
812	A167	10r Pointe aux Cannonniers	6.00	6.00
a.		Souvenir sheet of 4, #809-812	15.00	15.00
		Nos. 809-812 (4)	12.75	12.75

UN, 50th Anniv.
Common Design Type

Designs: 40c, Silhouettes of children under UNICEF umbrella. 4r, ILO contruction site. 8r, WMO satellite view of hurricane. 10r, Bread, grain representing FAO.

Wmk. 373

1995, Oct. 24   Litho.   *Perf. 14*

813	CD353	40c multicolored	.25	.25
814	CD353	4r multicolored	.65	.65
815	CD353	8r multicolored	1.40	1.40
816	CD353	10r multicolored	1.60	1.60
		Nos. 813-816 (4)	3.90	3.90

A168

1995, Dec. 8   Litho.   *Perf. 13*

817	A168	60c pink & multi	25	25
818	A168	4r blue & multi	.55	.55
819	A168	8r yellow & multi	1.25	1.25
820	A168	10r green & multi	1.40	1.40
		Nos. 817-820 (4)	3.45	3.45

Common Market for Eastern and Southern Africa (COMESA).

Snails A169

Designs: 60c, Pachystyla bicolor. 4r, Gonidomus pagodus. 5r, Harmogenanina implicata. 10r, Tropidophora eugeniae.

Wmk. 373

1996, Mar. 11   Litho.   *Perf. 13*

821	A169	60c multicolored	.35	.35
822	A169	4r multicolored	1.00	1.00
823	A169	5r multicolored	1.25	1.25
824	A169	10r multicolored	2.50	2.50
		Nos. 821-824 (4)	5.10	5.10

Modern Olympic Games, Cent. A170

Wmk. 384

1996, June 26   Litho.   *Perf. 13½*

825	A170	60c Boxing	.30	.30
826	A170	4r Badminton	.75	.75
827	A170	5r Basketball	.95	.95
828	A170	10r Table tennis	2.00	2.00
		Nos. 825-828 (4)	4.00	4.00

Ships A171

Wmk. 373

1996, Sept. 30   Litho.   *Perf. 14*

829	A171	60c SS Zambezia	.30	.30
830	A171	4r MV Sir Jules	.80	.80
831	A171	5r MV Mauritius	1.00	1.00
832	A171	10r MS Mauritius Pride	2.10	2.10
a.		Souvenir sheet of 4, #829-832	5.00	5.00
		Nos. 829-832 (4)	4.20	4.20

Post Office Ordinance, 150th Anniv. — A172

Wmk. 384

1996, Dec. 2   Litho.   *Perf. 13½*

833	A172	60c Pillar box	.30	.30
834	A172	4r Early handstamp cancel	1.10	1.10
835	A172	5r Mobile post office	1.50	1.50
836	A172	10r Carriole	3.00	3.00
		Nos. 833-836 (4)	5.90	5.90

Fruit — A173

Designs: 60c, Vangueria madagascariensis. 4r, Mimusops coriacea. 5r, Syzgium jambos. 10r, Diospyros digyna.

Perf. 14x13½

1997, Mar. 10   Litho.   Wmk. 373

837	A173	60c multicolored	.25	.25
838	A173	4r multicolored	.50	.50
839	A173	5r multicolored	.65	.65
840	A173	10r multicolored	1.40	1.40
		Nos. 837-840 (4)	2.80	2.80

Anniversaries and Events — A174

Designs: 60c, Ile de France, Mahé de La Bourdonnais. 1r, Exploration, La Perouse. 4r, Lady Gomm's Ball, Sir William Maynard Gomm. 6r, Skeleton of the Dodo, George Clark. 10r, Professor Brian Abel-Smith.

Wmk. 373

1997, June 9   Litho.   *Perf. 13½*

841	A174	60c multicolored	.45	.45
842	A174	1r multicolored	.45	.45
843	A174	4r multicolored	.85	.85
844	A174	6r multicolored	1.25	1.25
845	A174	10r multicolored	2.00	2.00
		Nos. 841-845 (5)	5.00	5.00

First Postage Stamps of Mauritius, 150th Anniv. A175

Stamps: 60c, #1. 4r, #2. 5r, #2, #1, gold background. 10r, #1, #2, silver background. 20r, #2, #1 on "The Bordeaux Cover."

Wmk. 373
1997, Sept. 22   Litho.   Perf. 13½
846 A175 60c multicolored   .40   .40
847 A175 4r multicolored   1.25   1.25
  a.   Sheet of 12, 7 #846, 5 #847   6.75   6.75
848 A175 5r multicolored   1.50   1.50
849 A175 10r multicolored   3.25   3.25
    Nos. 846-849 (4)   6.40   6.40

Souvenir Sheet
850 A175 20r multicolored   5.75   5.75

Booklet Panes and Booklets
846a   Booklet pane of 10   3.50
        Complete booklet, #846a   3.50
847b   Booklet pane of 10   11.00
        Complete booklet, #847b   11.00
848a   Booklet pane of 10   14.50
        Complete booklet, #848a   14.50
849a   Booklet pane of 10   30.00
        Complete booklet, #849a   30.00

Local Occupations — A176

Wmk. 373
1997, Dec. 1   Litho.   Perf. 14½
851 A176 60c Wheelwright   .40   .40
852 A176 4r Washerman   .70   .70
853 A176 5r Shipwright   .90   .90
854 A176 15r Quarryman   2.75   2.75
    Nos. 851-854 (4)   4.75   4.75

Geckos A177

Designs: 1r, Phelsuma guentheri. 6r, Nactus serpensinsula. 7r, Nactus coindemirensis. 8r, Phelsuma edwardnewtonii.

Wmk. 373
1998, Mar. 11   Litho.   Perf. 13½
855 A177 1r multicolored   .40   .40
856 A177 6r multicolored   1.25   1.25
857 A177 7r multicolored   1.50   1.50
858 A177 8r multicolored   1.75   1.75
    Nos. 855-858 (4)   4.90   4.90

Inland Transportation — A178

Wmk. 373
1998, June 15   Litho.   Perf. 13½
859 A178 40c Railroad   .60   .60
860 A178 5r Truck   1.25   1.25
861 A178 6r Bus, bicycles,
             cars   1.60   1.60
862 A178 10r Boat   2.50   2.50
    Nos. 859-862 (4)   5.95   5.95

Dutch Landing, 400th Anniv. A179

50c, Maurits van Nassau, landing scene. 1r, Otaheite sugar cane, Frederik Hendrik Fort. 7r, Dutch map, 1670. 8r, Landing fleet. 25r, Ships of landing fleet.

Wmk. 373
1998, Sept. 18   Litho.   Perf. 13½
863 A179 50c multicolored   .35   .35
864 A179 1r multicolored   .35   .35
865 A179 7r multicolored   1.75   1.75
866 A179 8r multicolored   2.25   2.25
    Nos. 863-866 (4)   4.70   4.70

Souvenir Sheet
867 A179 25r multicolored   5.50   5.50

State Visit of South African Pres. Nelson Mandela — A180

1998, Sept. 10   Litho.   Perf. 14
868 A180 25r multicolored   3.25   3.25

Waterfalls — A181

1r, Balfour Falls. 5r, Rochester Falls. 6r, GRSE Falls, vert. 10r, 500-Foot Falls, vert.

1998   Litho.   Wmk. 384   Perf. 13½
869 A181 1r multicolored   .50   .50
870 A181 5r multicolored   1.00   1.00
871 A181 6r multicolored   1.40   1.40
872 A181 10r multicolored   2.10   2.10
    Nos. 869-872 (4)   5.00   5.00

Creation of Presidential Residence "Le Réduit," 250th Anniv. — A182

Designs: 1r, Drawing of floor plan, 1823. 4r, Exterior view, by P.A.F. Thuillier, 1814. 5r, "Le Réduit," by Hassen Edun, 1998. 15r, Commemorative monument, 1998.

1998   Litho.   Wmk. 373   Perf. 14½
873 A182 1r multicolored   .40   .40
874 A182 4r multicolored   .70   .70
875 A182 5r multicolored   .90   .90
876 A182 15r multicolored   2.50   2.50
    Nos. 873-876 (4)   4.50   4.50

Admiral Mahé de la Bourdonnais, 300th Birth Anniv. — A183

Wmk. 373
1999, Feb. 11   Litho.   Perf. 13
877 A183 7r No. 115   1.75   1.75

Native Flowers A184

Designs: 1r, Clerodendron laciniatum. 2r, Senecio lemarckianus. 5r, Cylindrocline commersonii. 9r, Psiadia pollicina.

1999, Mar. 10   Perf. 13½
878 A184 1r multicolored   .40   .40
879 A184 2r multicolored   .40   .40
880 A184 5r multicolored   .70   .70
881 A184 9r multicolored   1.25   1.25
    Nos. 878-881 (4)   2.75   2.75

Paintings — A185

Designs: 1r, "The Washerwomen," by Hervé Masson. 3r, "The Casino," by Gaetan de Rosnay. 4r, "The Four Elements," by Andrée Poilly. 6r, "Coming out of Mass," by Xavier Le Juge de Segrais.

1999, June 18   Perf. 14x15
882 A185 1r multicolored   .50   .50
883 A185 3r multicolored   .60   .60
884 A185 4r multicolored   .70   .70
885 A185 6r multicolored   1.10   1.10
    Nos. 882-885 (4)   2.90   2.90

Old Sugar Mill Chimneys — A186

Wmk. 384
1999, Sept. 17   Litho.   Perf. 14¼
886 A186 1r Alma   .40   .40
887 A186 2r Antoinette   .60   .60
888 A186 5r Belle Mare   .90   .90
889 A186 7r Grande Rosalie   1.00   1.00
  a.   Souvenir sheet of 4, #886-889,
        Wmk. 373   3.25   3.25
    Nos. 886-889 (4)   2.90   2.90

Achievements in the 20th Century — A187

Designs: 1r, Eradication of malaria. 2r, Emancipation of women. 5r, International Conference Center. 9r, Special sugars.

Perf. 13¼x13
1999, Dec. 7   Litho.   Wmk. 373
890 A187 1r multi   .40   .40
891 A187 2r multi   .60   .60
892 A187 5r multi   1.10   1.10
893 A187 9r multi   2.00   2.00
    Nos. 890-893 (4)   4.10   4.10

Chamber of Commerce & Industry, 150th Anniv. — A188

1r, Emblem. 2r, Computer chip. 7r, Francis Channell, 1st sec. 15r, Louis Léchelle, 1st pres.

2000, Jan. 25   Litho.   Perf. 13¼
894 A188 1r multi   .40   .40
895 A188 2r multi   .60   .60
896 A188 7r multi   1.10   1.10
897 A188 15r multi   2.10   2.10
    Nos. 894-897 (4)   4.20   4.20

Insects A189

Designs: 1r, Cratopus striga. 2r, Cratopus armatus. 3r, Cratopus chrysochlorus. 15r, Cratopus nigrogranatus.

Wmk. 373
2000, Mar. 29   Litho.   Perf. 14¼
898 A189 1r multi   .40   .40
899 A189 2r multi   .40   .40
900 A189 3r multi   .50   .50
901 A189 15r multi   2.40   2.40
  a.   Souvenir sheet of 4, #898-901   4.00   4.00
    Nos. 898-901 (4)   3.70   3.70

2000 Summer Olympics, Sydney — A190

Wmk. 373
2000, June 28   Litho.   Perf. 14½
902 A190 1r Handball   .40   .40
903 A190 2r Archery   .60   .60
904 A190 5r Sailing   .80   .80
905 A190 15r Judo   2.40   2.40
    Nos. 902-905 (4)   4.20   4.20

Sir Seewoosagur Ramgoolam, Birth Cent. — A191

Designs: 1r, Ramgoolam with Mother Teresa. 2r, As elected member of legislative council, vert. 5r, As student, 1926, vert. 15r, As Prime Minister, 1968, vert.

Perf. 13¼x13, 13x13¼
2000, Sept. 18   Litho.   Wmk. 373
906-909 A191   Set of 4   4.25   4.25

Fish A192

Designs: 50c, Scarus ghobban. 1r, Cephalopholis sonnerati. 2r, Naso brevirostris. 3r, Lethrinus nebulosus. 4r, Centropyge debelius. 5r, Amphirion chrysogaster. 6r, Forcipiger flavissimus. 7r, Acanthurus leucosternon. 8r, Pterois volitans. 10r, Siderea grisea. 15r, Carcharhinus wheeleri. 25r, Istiophorus platypterus.

Perf. 14½x14¼
2000, Oct. 9   Litho.   Wmk. 373
910 A192 50c multi   .40   .40
911 A192 1r multi   .40   .40
912 A192 2r multi   .40   .40
913 A192 3r multi   .40   .40
914 A192 4r multi   .50   .50
915 A192 5r multi   .60   .60
916 A192 6r multi   .75   .75
917 A192 7r multi   .80   .80
918 A192 8r multi   1.00   1.00
919 A192 10r multi   1.10   1.10
  a.   Souvenir sheet, #914, 917-
        919   3.50   3.50
  b.   As #919, perf. 13½ ('08)   .75   .75
920 A192 10r multi   1.90   1.90
  a.   Souvenir sheet, #913, 915-
        916, 920   3.50   3.50
921 A192 25r multi   2.75   2.75
  a.   Souvenir sheet, #910-912,
        921   3.50   3.50
    Nos. 910-921 (12)   11.00 11.00

No. 919b issued 5/28/08.

Famous People — A193

Designs: 1r, Affan Tank Wen (1842-1900). 5r, Alphonse Ravaton (1900-92), musician. 7r, Dr. Idrice Goumany (1859-89). 9r, Anjalay Coopen (d. 1943), martyr.

Perf. 14¼x14½

2000, Dec. 13   **Wmk. 373**
922-925 A193   Set of 4   3.75 3.75

Textile Industry A194

Designs: 1r, Finished sweater. 3r, Computer-aided machinery. 6r, T-shirt folder. 10r, Embroidery machine.

2001, Jan. 10   **Perf. 14½x14¼**
926-929 A194   Set of 4   3.25 3.25

End of Slavery and Indentured Labor, 166th Anniv. — A195

2001, Feb. 1   **Perf. 14x13½**
930 A195 7r multi   2.00 2.00

Trees A196

Designs: 1r, Foetida mauritana. 3r, Diospyros tessellaria. 5r, Sideroxylon puberulum. 15r, Gastonia mauritana.

2001, Mar. 21   **Wmk. 373**   **Perf. 13½**
931-934 A196   Set of 4   5.00 5.00

Expedition of Nicholas Baudin, Bicent. — A197

Designs: 1r, Ships Géographe and Naturaliste. 4r, Baudin and map of itinerary. 6r, Phedina borbonica. 10r, Napoleon Bonaparte and account of expedition, vert.

Wmk. 373
2001, June 13   **Litho.**   **Perf. 14¼**
935-938 A197   Set of 4   4.00 4.00

20th Century Achievements — A198

Designs: 2r, Hotel School of Mauritius. 3r, Steel bar milling. 6r, Solar energy, Agalega. 10r, Indian Ocean Rim Association for Regional Cooperation.

Wmk. 373
2001, Sept. 12   **Litho.**   **Perf. 13½**
939-942 A198   Set of 4   3.50 3.50

Mahatma Gandhi's Visit to Mauritius, Cent. — A199

2001, Oct. 2   **Perf. 14¾x14**
943 A199 15r No. 361   3.00 3.00

Copra Industry A200

Designs: 1r, Dehusking of coconuts, vert. 5r, Deshelling of coconuts. 6r, Drying copra. 10r, Oil extraction, vert.

2001, Dec. 5   **Perf. 13½**
944-947 A200   Set of 4   4.75 4.75

Republic, 10th Anniv. A201

Designs: 1r, Port development. 4r, Financial services. 5r, Water storage. 9r, Road development.

Perf. 13½x13¾
2002, Mar. 12   **Litho.**   **Wmk. 373**
948-951 A201   Set of 4   4.00 4.00

Cicadas — A202

Designs: 1r, Abricta brunnea. 6r, Fractuosella darwini. 7r, Distantada thomaseti. 8r, Dinarobia claudeae.

Wmk. 373
2002, June 12   **Litho.**   **Perf. 13½**
952-955 A202   Set of 4   3.50 3.50
    a.   Souvenir sheet, #952-955   4.00 4.00

Maps of the Southwest Indian Ocean — A203

Maps by: 1r, Alberto Cantino, 1502. 3r, Jorge Reinel, 1520. 4r, Diogo Ribeiro, 1529. 10r, Gerard Mercator, 1569.

2002, Sept. 18
956-959 A203   Set of 4   5.00 5.00

Constellations A204

Designs: 1r, Orion. 7r, Sagittarius. 8r, Scorpius. 9r, Crux.

Perf. 14¼x14½
2002, Dec. 18   **Litho.**   **Wmk. 373**
960-963 A204   Set of 4   4.00 4.00

2nd U.S. — Sub-Saharan Africa Trade and Economic Forum — A205

Panel color: 1r, Violet blue. 25r, Red.

2003, Jan.   **Perf. 14¼**
964-965 A205   Set of 2   3.25 3.25

Worldwide Fund for Nature (WWF) — A206

Echo parakeet: 1r, Chick. 2r, Fledgling. 5r, Female. 15r, Male.

Wmk. 373
2003, Mar. 19   **Litho.**   **Perf. 13½**
966-969 A206   Set of 4   4.00 4.00

Flowers — A207

Designs: 1r, Trochetia boutoniana. 4r, Trochetia uniflora. 7r, Trochetia triflora. 9r, Trochetia parviflora.

Wmk. 373
2003, June 18   **Litho.**   **Perf. 13½**
970-973 A207   Set of 4   3.75 3.75

Anniversaries and Events — A208

Designs: 2r, Sixth Indian Ocean Games, Mauritius. 6r, Mauritius Chamber of Agriculture, 150th anniv. 9r, Visit of Abbé de la Caille, 250th anniv. 10r, Mauritius Sugar Industry Research Institute, 50th anniv.

2003, Aug. 20
974-977 A208   Set of 4   5.75 5.75

Fortresses — A209

Designs: 2r, Batterie de la Pointe du Diable. 5r, Donjon St. Louis. 6r, Martello tower. 12r, Fort Adelaide,

2003, Dec. 10
978-981 A209   Set of 4   4.00 4.00

Indian Ocean Commission, 20th Anniv. — A210

Wmk. 373
2004, Feb. 16   **Litho.**   **Perf. 13½**
982 A210 10r multi   2.25 2.25

Mountains — A211

Designs: 2r, Le Pouce. 7r, Corps de Garde. 8r, Le Chat et La Souris. 25r, Piton du Milieu.

2004, Mar. 11   **Perf. 14½x14¼**
983-986 A211   Set of 4   6.50 6.50

Traditional Trades — A212

Designs: 2r, Tinsmith. 7r, Cobbler. 9r, Blacksmith. 15r, Basket weaver.

Wmk. 373
2004, June 30   **Litho.**   **Perf. 13½**
987-990 A212   Set of 4   5.00 5.00

24th Southern Africa Development Community Summit — A213

Emblem, woman at computer, building and panel in: 2r, Gray. 50r, Red.

Wmk. 373

2004, Aug. 16   Litho.   Perf. 13½
991-992 A213   Set of 2   7.50 7.50

Rodrigues Regional Assembly — A214

Designs: 2r, Plaine Corail Airport. 7r, Ecotourism. 8r, Agricultural products. 10r, Coat of arms.

Wmk. 373

2004, Oct. 12   Litho.   Perf. 13½
993-996 A214   Set of 4   5.50 5.50

Anthurium Andreanum Varieties A215

Designs: 2r, Acropolis. 8r, Tropical. 10r, Paradisio. 25r, Fantasia.

2004, Dec. 1   Perf. 13¼
997-1000 A215   Set of 4   7.00 7.00

Round Island Flora and Fauna A216

Designs: 2r, Juvenile keel scale boa. 8r, Hurricane palm. 9r, Round Island petrel. 25r, Mazambron.

Wmk. 373

2005, Mar. 18   Litho.   Perf. 13¼
1001-1004 A216   Set of 4   7.00 7.00

Postal Services A217

Designs: 2r, Counter services. 7r, Mail sorting. 8r, Mail distribution. 10r, Mail transfer.

Wmk. 373

2005, July 14   Litho.   Perf. 13¼
1005-1008 A217   Set of 4   4.00 4.00

Stone Buildings — A218

Designs: 2r, Vagrant Depot, Grand River North West. 7r, Postal Museum, Port Louis. 16r, Carnegie Library, Curepipe.

Wmk. 373

2005, Oct. 9   Litho.   Perf. 13½
1009-1011 A218   Set of 3   3.75 3.75

Ship Models — A219

Designs: 7r, 100-gun ship. 8r, Sampan. 9r, Roman galley. 16r, Drakkar. 25r, Drakkar, horiz.

Perf. 13¾x13½
2005, Dec. 20   Litho.
1012-1015 A219   Set of 4   6.00 6.00

Souvenir Sheet
Perf. 13½x13¾
1016 A219 25r multi   4.25 4.25

Mahebourg, Bicent. — A220

Designs: 2r, Market. 7r, Regattas. 8r, Le Lavoir. No. 1020, 16r, Pointe des Régates. No. 1021, vert.: a, 16r, Mahé de la Bourdonnais. b, 16r, Gen. Charles Decaen.

Wmk. 373

2006, Feb. 4   Litho.   Perf. 13½
1017-1020 A220   Set of 4   5.00 5.00

Souvenir Sheet
1021 A220 16r Sheet of 2, #a-b   5.25 5.25

Professor Basdeo Bissoondoyal (1906-91), Educator — A221

Wmk. 373

2006, Apr. 15   Litho.   Perf. 13¾
1022 A221 10r multi   1.10 1.10

Ecological History — A222

Designs: 2r, Biological control of locusts with introduction of mynah birds, 1763. 8r, Fish repopulation with artificial reefs, 1980. 10r, Erosion control with terraces in Rodrigues, 1958. 25r, First captive breeding of giant tortoises, 1881.

2006, June 5   Perf. 13½
1023-1026 A222   Set of 4   5.50 5.50

Crabs — A223

Designs: 2r, Tourloulou crab. 7r, Land crab. 8s, Freshwater crab. 25r, Coconut crab.

Wmk. 373

2006, Oct. 9   Litho.   Perf. 13¼
1027-1030 A223   Set of 4   4.50 4.50

Traditional Children's Activities — A224

Designs: 5r, Sapsiwaye. 10r, Marbles, horiz. 15r, Hop Scotch, horiz. 25r, Kite flying.

Perf. 13¾x13½, 13½x13¾
2006, Dec. 7
1031-1034 A224   Set of 4   3.50 3.50

Corals A225

Designs: 3r, Rodrigues endemic coral. 5r, Soft coral. 10r, Chagos coral. 15r, Head coral. 22r, Table coral. 25r, Tube coral.

Wmk. 373

2007, Apr. 30   Litho.   Perf. 13½
1035-1040 A225   Set of 6   5.25 5.25

Drawings of Dodo Birds — A226

Drawing: 5r, From Journal of the Gelderland, 1601. 10r, By Adrian van de Venne, 1626. 15r, Published by Harrison, 1798. No. 1044, 25r, By J. W. Frohawk, 1905. No. 1045, By Julian Pender Hume, 2001, vert.

Wmk. 373

2007, June 25   Litho.   Perf. 13½
1041-1044 A226   Set of 4   3.50 3.50

Souvenir Sheet
Perf. 13x13¼
1045 A226 25r multi   1.60 1.60

No. 1045 contains one 28x45mm stamp.

24th UPU Congress, Nairobi A227

Wmk. 373

2007, Oct. 9   Litho.   Perf. 13¼
1046 A227 50r multi   3.50 3.50

Due to political unrest in Kenya, the UPU Congress was moved to Geneva, Switzerland.

Anniversaries — A228

Designs: 5r, Ministerial System, 50th anniv. 10r, Arrival in Mauritius of Manilall Doctor, cent., vert. 15r, Scouting, cent., vert. 25r, First

---

meteorological observatory in Mauritius, 175th anniv.

2007, Dec. 4   Perf. 13½
1047-1050 A228   Set of 4   3.75 3.75

Ministerial System, 50th Anniv. (With Corrected Photograph) — A229

2007, Dec. 4   Litho.   Perf. 13½
1051 A229 5r multi   .35 .35

The photo in the LR corner on No. 1051 differs from the photo in the LR corner on No. 1047.

Authors Who Mentioned Mauritius — A230

Author and work: 5r, Bernardin de St. Pierre (1737-1814), Paul et Virginie. 10r, Alexandre Dumas (père) (1802-70), Georges. 15r, Charles Baudelaire (1821-67), A une Dame Creole. 22r, Mark Twain (1835-1910), Following the Equator. 25r, Joesph Conrad (1857-1924), A Smile of Fortune.

Wmk. 406

2008, Dec. 8   Litho.   Perf. 13½
1052-1056 A230   Set of 5   4.75 4.75

Flowers — A231

Designs: 3r, Myonima obovata. 4r, Cylindrocline lorencei. 5r, Crinum mauritianum. 6r, Elaeocarpus bojeri. 7r, Bremeria landia. 8r, Distephanus populifolius. 9r, Gaertnera longifolia. 10r, Dombeya acutangula. 15r, Aphloia theiformis. 22r, Barleria observatrix. 25r, Roussea simplex. 50r, Hibiscus fragilis.

Wmk. 406

2009, Apr. 9   Litho.   Perf. 13½
1057	A231	3r multi	.25	.25
1058	A231	4r multi	.25	.25
1059	A231	5r multi	.30	.30
1060	A231	6r multi	.35	.35
1061	A231	7r multi	.45	.45
a.		Dated "2010"	.50	.50
1062	A231	8r multi	.50	.50
a.		Dated "2010"	.55	.55
1063	A231	9r multi	.55	.55
1064	A231	10r multi	.60	.60
1065	A231	10r multi	.90	.90
a.		Dated "2010"	1.00	1.00
1066	A231	22r multi	1.40	1.40
1067	A231	25r multi	1.50	1.50
a.		Dated "2010"	1.75	1.75
1068	A231	50r multi	3.00	3.00
	Nos. 1057-1068 (12)		10.05	10.05

Extinct Mauritian Giant Tortoises — A232

Designs: 5r, Cylindraspis peltastes. 10r, Cylindraspis vosmaeri, vert. 15r, Cylindraspis inepta. 25r, Cylindraspis triserrata, vert. 50r, Cylindraspis peltastes, diff.

Wmk. 406
2009, July 16   Litho.   Perf. 13½
1069-1072 A232   Set of 4   3.50 3.50
Souvenir Sheet
1073 A232 50r multi   3.25 3.25

New Mauritius Travel Slogan — A233

No. 1074 — New slogan on: a, Yellow background. b, Mountain background.

Perf. 13½x13
2009, Oct. 9   Litho.   Wmk. 406
1074 A233 7r Vert. pair, #a-b   .95 .95

Chinese Chamber of Commerce, Cent. (in 2008) — A234

Dr. Kissoonsingh Hazareesingh, Historian, Birth Cent. — A235

Capture of Rodrigues Island by British, Bicent. — A236

Teeluckpersad Callychurn, Postmaster General, Birth Cent. — A237

Wmk. 406
2009, Nov. 30   Litho.   Perf. 13½
1075 A234 7r multi   .50 .50
1076 A235 14r multi   1.00 1.00
1077 A236 20r multi   1.40 1.40
1078 A237 21r multi   1.50 1.50
    Nos. 1075-1078 (4)   4.40 4.40

Muhammad al-Idrisi (c.1100-c.1165), Geographer and Cartographer A238

Wmk. 406
2010, Aug. 2   Litho.   Perf. 13½
1079 A238 27r multi   1.90 1.90

Mauritius No. 2 — A239

2010, Aug. 20
1080 A239 30r multi   2.00 2.00

Expo 2010, Shanghai.

Battle of Grand Port, Bicent. A240

Designs: 14r, Battle scene. 21r, Ile de la Passe.

2010, Aug. 20
1081-1082 A240   Set of 2   2.25 2.25

Sir Seewoosagur Ramgoolam (1900-85), Prime Minister — A241

Litho. & Embossed With Foil Application
2010, Sept. 18   Wmk. 406
1083 A241 100r multi   6.75 6.75

British Conquest of Isle de France, Bicent. — A242

Designs: 2r, Capitulation document. 7r, British landing on Isle de France, horiz.

Wmk. 406
2010, Dec. 3   Litho.   Perf. 13½
1084-1085 A242   Set of 2   .60 .60

UNESCO World Heritage Sites — A244

Designs: 7r, Steps, Aapravasi Ghat. 14r, Mountain, Le Morne, horiz. 15r, Monument, Le Morne, horiz. 25r, Hospital kitchen, Aapravasi Ghat.

Wmk. 406
2011, Apr. 11   Litho.   Perf. 13½
1087-1090 A244   Set of 4   4.50 4.50
1090a   Souvenir sheet of 4, #1087-1090   4.50 4.50

19th Century Census Form A245

Sir Moilin Jean Ah Chuen (1911-91), Politician — A246

Dr. Maurice Curé (1886-1977), Co-Founder of Labor Party — A247

Médine Sugar Estates, Cent. A248

2011, June 30
1091 A245 7r multi   .50 .50
1092 A246 14r multi   1.00 1.00
1093 A247 21r multi   1.50 1.50
1094 A248 25r multi   1.75 1.75
    Nos. 1091-1094 (4)   4.75 4.75

Observation of Transit of Venus From Rodrigues by Alexandre Guy Pingré — A249

Intl. Year of Forests A251

2011, Sept. 8
1095 A249 11r multi   .80 .80
1096 A250 12r multi   .85 .85
1097 A251 17r multi   1.25 1.25
    Nos. 1095-1097 (3)   2.90 2.90

HIV and AIDS Awareness A252

Post Office in Rodrigues, 150th Anniv. — A253

2011, Oct. 9
1098 A252 7r multi   .50 .50
1099 A253 21r multi   1.50 1.50

Tea Industry — A254

Designs: 7r, Tea flushes. 8r, Tea pickers, horiz. 15r, Loose tea on saucer, spoon, tea bags, horiz. 25r, Tea pot and cup.

2011, Dec. 19
1100-1103 A254   Set of 4   3.75 3.75

Law Day A255

Designs: 7r, Grand Port District Court. 8r, Interior of Court of Justice. 15r, Sir Michel Rivalland, 1967-70 Chief Justice, vert. 20r, Gavel.

2012, Apr. 4   Perf. 13¼
1104-1107 A255   Set of 4   3.50 3.50

Mauritius postal officials have declared sheets of four and six 9r stamps depicting Michael Jackson as "illegal."

Intl. Year of Chemistry — A250

Mauritius Turf Club, 200th Anniv. — A256

Designs: 7r, Horse race. 10r, Aerial view of Champ de Mars Race Track. 14r, Grandstand, 1917. 21r, Emblem of Mauritius Turf Club, vert. 50r, Jockey on horse in paddock.

2012, June 25   ***Perf. 13½***
1108-1111 A256   Set of 4   3.50 3.50
        Souvenir Sheet
1112 A256 50r multi   3.25 3.25

Customs Department — A257

Designs: 7r, Old and new Custom Houses. 8r, Customs officer scanning packages. 20r, Dog sniffing packages, vert. 25r, Customs officers on boat.

2012, Sept. 10
1113-1116 A257   Set of 4   4.00 4.00

Intl. Year of Cooperatives — A258

Diplomatic Relations Between Mauritius and People's Republic of China, 40th Anniv. — A259

Scouting in Mauritius, Cent. — A260

2012, Oct. 9
1117 A258   6r multi   .40 .40
1118 A259   14r multi   .90 .90
1119 A260   21r multi   1.40 1.40
    Nos. 1117-1119 (3)   2.70 2.70

Famous Men — A261

Designs: 6r, Marcel Cabon (1912-72), musician. 10r, Goolam Mahomed Dawjee Atchia, newspaper publisher.

2012, Nov. 9
1120-1121 A261   Set of 2   1.10 1.10

Methods of Mail Conveyance — A262

Early Mauritius Stamps — A263

No. 1122: a, Foot messenger, 1772. b, Packet mail landing, 1915. c, Express letter messenger, 1930. d, Inland mail arrival, 1935. e, Delivery of mail bags by van, 2012.
No. 1123: a, Mauritius #1 and copper plate cliché. b, Mauritius #2 and copper plate cliché.

2012, Dec. 21   ***Perf. 12½x13***
1122   Horiz. strip of 5   2.25 2.25
  a.-e. A262 7r Any single   .45 .45
        Souvenir Sheet
        Perf. 13½
1123 A263 25r Sheet of 2, #a-b, + label   3.25 3.25
Postal services in Mauritius, 240th anniv.

Sites and Monuments — A264

Designs: 5r, Belle Mare Prison. 9r, Bel Ombre Château. 10r, IBL Building, Bowen Square. 18r, Le Batelage.

        Wmk. 406
2013, Apr. 18   **Litho.**   ***Perf. 13½***
1124-1127 A264   Set of 4   2.75 2.75

Intl. Red Cross, 150th Anniv. — A265

2013, May 30
1128 A265 3r multi   .25 .25

63rd FIFA Congress, Mauritius — A266

2013, May 30
1129 A266 18r multi   1.25 1.25

Renewable Energy — A267

Designs: 2r, Solar energy. 6r, Wind energy.

2013, May 30
1130-1131 A267   Set of 2   .55 .55

Flora and Fauna — A268

Designs: 3r, Hurricane palm. 10r, Oeoniella polystachys orchid. 18w, Mascarene swallow.

        Wmk. 406
2013, Aug. 30   **Litho.**   ***Perf. 13½***
1132-1134 A268   Set of 3   2.00 2.00

Famous Men — A269

Designs: 9r, Hervé Masson (1919-90), painter. 26r, Prof. Stanley Alexander de Smith (1922-74), Constitiutional Commissioner of Mauritius.

        Wmk. 406
2013, Dec. 11   **Litho.**   ***Perf. 13½***
1135-1136 A269   Set of 2   2.40 2.40

Flora and Fauna A270

Designs: 7r, Dragonfly. 14r, Roussette de Rodrigues. 25r, Pignon d'Inde, vert.

        Wmk. 406
2014, Mar. 28   **Litho.**   ***Perf. 13½***
1137-1139 A270   Set of 3   3.00 3.00

Father Jacques-Désiré Laval (1803-64), Missionary — A271

Children's Office Ombudsperson, 10th Anniv. — A272

Arrival in Mauritius of Rev. Jean Joseph Lebrun as Missionary, 200th Anniv. — A273

Introduction of Mobile Telephones in Mauritius, 25th Anniv. — A274

        Wmk. 406
2014, May 28   **Litho.**   ***Perf. 13½***
1140 A271   8r multi   .55 .55
1141 A272   14r multi   .95 .95
1142 A273   15r multi   1.00 1.00
1143 A274   25r multi   1.60 1.60
    Nos. 1140-1143 (4)   4.10 4.10

Green Turtle A275

        Unwmk.
2014, Oct. 9   **Litho.**   ***Perf. 14***
1144 A275 14r multi   .90 .90
   See Comoro Islands No. , France No. 4695, French Southern and Antarctic Territories No. 511, Malagasy Republic No. , Seychelles No.

_____

SPECIAL DELIVERY STAMPS

SD1

1903   **Wmk. 1**   ***Perf. 14***
       Red Surcharge
E1 SD1 15c on 15c ultra   14.50 37.50

SD2   SD3

EXPRESS DELIVERY
(INLAND)
15 c   New Setting with Smaller "15c" without period — SD3a

1904

E2	SD2	15c on 15c ultra		62.50	95.00
a.		"INLAND" inverted			3,400.
b.		Inverted "A" in "INLAND"		1,700.	1,250.
E3	SD3	15c on 15c ultra		9.00	3.75
a.		Double surcharge, both inverted		1,875.	1,900.
b.		Inverted surcharge		1,250.	800.00
c.		Vert. pair, imperf between		6,250.	
E3F	SD3a	15c on 15c ultra		840.00	800.00
g.		Inverted surcharge			1,775.
h.		Double surcharge			3,750.
i.		Double surcharge, both inverted		—	5,500.
j.		"c" omitted			2,750.

To make No. E2 the word "INLAND" was printed on No. E1. For Nos. E3 and E3F, new settings of the surcharge were made with different spacing between the words.

SD4   SD5

E4	SD4	15c green & red		18.00	6.25
a.		Double surcharge		800.00	800.00
b.		Inverted surcharge		1,000.	900.00
c.		"LNIAND."			
d.		As "c," double surcharge		900.00	800.00
E5	SD5	18c green & black		3.00	32.50
a.		Exclamation point (!) instead of "I" in "FOREIGN"		800.00	

POSTAGE DUE STAMPS

Catalogue values for unused stamps in this section are for Never Hinged items.

Numeral — D1

Perf. 14½x14

1933-54		**Typo.**	**Wmk. 4**	
J1	D1	2c black	1.50	.60
J2	D1	4c violet	.60	.80
J3	D1	6c red	.70	.95
J4	D1	10c green	.85	2.40
J5	D1	20c ultramarine	.75	2.60
J6	D1	50c dp red lilac ('54)	.65	19.00
J7	D1	1r orange ('54)	.85	19.00
		Nos. J1-J7 (7)	5.90	45.35

1966-68		**Wmk. 314**	**Perf. 14**	
J8	D1	2c black ('67)	2.75	3.75

Perf. 14½x14

J9	D1	4c rose violet ('68)	1.90	8.50
J10	D1	6c dp orange ('68)	7.00	27.50
J11	D1	10c yel green ('67)	.35	2.10
J12	D1	20c ultramarine	2.40	5.75
J13	D1	50c dp red lilac ('68)	.80	13.00
		Nos. J8-J13 (6)	15.20	60.60

Nos. 445-446, 450, 455, 457, 462 Surcharged "POSTAGE/ DUE" and New Value
Wmk. 373

1982, Oct. 25		**Litho.**	**Perf. 13½**	
J14	A92	10c on 15c multi	.25	.25
J15	A92	20c on 20c multi	.25	.60
J16	A91	50c on 60c multi	.35	.35
J17	A92	1r on 1.20r multi	.45	.35
J18	A92	1.50r on 1.50r multi	.60	.85
J19	A91	5r on 15r multi	1.10	2.50
		Nos. J14-J19 (6)	3.00	4.90

MAYOTTE

mä-ˈyät

LOCATION — One of the Comoro Islands situated in the Mozambique Channel midway between Madagascar and Mozambique (Africa)
GOVT. — French Colony
AREA — 144 sq. mi.
POP. — 149,336 (1999 est.)
CAPITAL — Mamoutzou
    See Comoro Islands.

    100 Centimes = 1 Franc
    100 Cents = 1 Euro (2002)

Stamps of Mayotte were replaced successively by those of Madagascar, Comoro Islands and France. Individual issues were resumed in 1975.

See France No. 2271 for French stamp inscribed "Mayotte."

Catalogue values for unused stamps in this country are for Never Hinged items, beginning with Scott 75 in the regular postage section, and Scott C1 in the airpost section.

Navigation and Commerce — A1

Perf. 14x13½

1892-1907		**Typo.**		**Unwmk.**	
Name of Colony in Blue or Carmine					
1	A1	1c blk, lil bl		1.40	.90
2	A1	2c brn, buff		1.90	1.40
a.		Name double		575.00	500.00
3	A1	4c claret, lav		2.40	1.75
4	A1	5c grn, grnsh		4.75	3.25
5	A1	10c blk, lavender		9.00	4.75
6	A1	10c red ('00)		67.50	52.50
7	A1	15c blue, quadrille paper		17.50	10.50
8	A1	15c gray ('00)		125.00	110.00
9	A1	20c red, grn		13.50	10.50
10	A1	25c blk, rose		14.50	9.75
11	A1	25c blue ('00)		16.00	13.50
12	A1	30c brn, bis		22.00	16.00
13	A1	35c blk, yel		11.00	8.00
14	A1	40c red, straw		22.50	16.00
15	A1	45c blk, gray grn ('07)		21.00	20.00
16	A1	50c carmine, rose		32.00	22.50
17	A1	50c brn, az ('00)		30.00	30.00
18	A1	75c dp vio, org		30.00	21.00
19	A1	1fr brnz grn, straw		32.00	22.50
20	A1	5fr red lil, lav ('99)		80.00	45.00
		Nos. 1-20 (20)		623.95	504.80

Perf. 13½x14 stamps are counterfeits.

Issues of 1892-1907 Surcharged in Black or Carmine

1912

22	A1	5c on 2c brn, buff		3.25	4.00
23	A1	5c on 4c cl, lav (C)		2.00	2.00
24	A1	5c on 15c bl (C)		2.00	2.00
25	A1	5c on 20c red, grn		2.00	2.40
26	A1	5c on 25c blk, rose (C)		1.60	1.60
a.		Double surcharge		300.00	
b.		Pair, one stamp without surcharge		1,000.	
27	A1	5c on 30c brn, bis (C)		2.00	2.00
28	A1	10c on 40c red, straw		2.00	2.40
a.		Double surcharge		300.00	
29	A1	10c on 45c blk, gray grn (C)		2.00	2.00
a.		Double surcharge		300.00	325.00
30	A1	10c on 50c car, rose		4.50	5.00
31	A1	10c on 75c dp vio, org		3.50	4.25

32	A1	10c on 1fr brnz grn, straw		3.50	4.25
		Nos. 22-32 (11)		28.35	31.90

Two spacings between the surcharged numerals are found on Nos. 22-32. For detailed listings, see the *Scott Classic Specialized Catalogue of Stamps and Covers.*
Nos. 22-32 were available for use in Madagascar and the entire Comoro archipelago.

Catalogue values for unused stamps in this section, from this point to the end of the section, are for Never Hinged items.

Marianne Type of France Overprinted

1997, Jan. 2		**Engr.**		**Perf. 13**	
Design A1161					
75		10c on #2179		.25	.30
76		20c on #2180		.25	.30
77		50c on #2181		.25	.30
78		1fr on #2182		.55	.55
79		2fr on #2333		1.10	1.10
80		(2.50fr) on #2340		1.25	1.25
81		2.70fr on #2335		1.50	1.50
82		3.80fr on #2337		2.00	2.00
83		5fr on #2194		2.75	2.75
84		10fr on #2195		5.50	5.50
		Nos. 75-84 (10)		15.40	15.55

Ylang Ylang — A5

1997, Jan. 2		**Litho.**	**Perf. 13½x13**	
85	A5	2.70fr multicolored	1.50	1.50

Coat of Arms — A6

1997, Jan. 2			**Perf. 13x13½**	
86	A6	3fr multicolored	1.60	1.60
a.		Sheet of 4	7.25	7.25

No. 86a issued 6/19/99 for Philex France 99.

Le Banga — A7

1997, May 31		**Litho.**	**Perf. 13**	
87	A7	3.80fr multicolored	1.90	1.90

Dzen Dzé Musical Instrument A8

Photo. & Engr.

1997, May 31			**Perf. 12½**	
88	A8	5.20fr multicolored	2.50	2.50

Lemur A9

1997, Aug. 30		**Engr.**	**Perf. 12**	
89	A9	3fr red & dk brown	1.60	1.60

Face of a Woman A10

1997, Aug. 30		**Litho.**	**Perf. 13**	
90	A10	3.50fr multicolored	1.75	1.75

Marine Life — A11

1997, Nov. 29		**Litho.**	**Perf. 13**	
91	A11	3fr multicolored	1.60	1.60

Longoni Port — A12

1998, Jan. 31		**Litho.**	**Perf. 13**	
92	A12	2.70fr multicolored	1.40	1.40

Chelonia Mydas — A13

1998, Jan. 31				
93	A13	3fr multicolored	1.75	1.75

Family Planning — A14

1998, Apr. 1		**Litho.**	**Perf. 13¼x13**	
94	A14	1fr multicolored	.75	.75

**France Nos. 2594, 2595 and 2597
Overprinted "MAYOTTE"**

1997, Aug. 18		**Engr.**	*Perf. 13*	
95	A1409	2.70fr brt grn (#2594)	—	—
96	A1409	(3fr) red (#2495)	—	—
97	A1409	3.80fr blue (#2497)	—	—

France No. 2604 Ovptd. "MAYOTTE"

Die Cut x Serpentine Die Cut 7

1998, Apr. 15		**Engr.**		
		Self-Adhesive		
104	A1409	(3fr) red	1.40	1.40
a.		Booklet pane of 10		14.00

No. 104a is a complete booklet, the peelable backing serves as a booklet cover.

Children's
Carnival
A15

1998, May 30	**Litho.**	*Perf. 13*	
105 A15	3fr multicolored	1.50	1.50

Ferry, "Salama Djema II" — A16

1998, May 30			
106 A16	3.80fr multicolored	1.75	1.75

Mosque of
Tsingoni
A17

1998, Sept. 5	**Litho.**	*Perf. 13*	
107 A17	3fr multicolored	1.50	1.50

Mariama
Salim — A18

Photo. & Engr.

1998, Oct. 3		*Perf. 13*	
108 A18	2.70fr multicolored	1.25	1.25

Traditional Fishing, Djarifa — A19

1998, Nov. 7	**Litho.**	*Perf. 13*	
109 A19	2fr multicolored	1.25	1.25

Pomacanthus — A20

1998, Nov. 7			
110 A20	3fr multicolored	1.50	1.50

See Nos. 121-124.

Agricultural Tools — A21

1998, Dec. 19	**Litho.**	*Perf. 13*	
111 A21	3fr multicolored	1.50	1.50

**France Nos. 2589-2593, 2601, 2603
Ovptd. "MAYOTTE"**

1999, Jan. 1		**Engr.**	*Perf. 13*	
112	A1409	10c brn (#2589)	.25	.25
113	A1409	20c brt bl grn	.30	.30
		(#2590)		
114	A1409	50c purple (#2591)	.50	.50
115	A1409	1fr brt orange	.65	.65
		(#2592)		
116	A1409	2fr brt blue	1.00	1.00
		(#2593)		
117	A1409	5fr brt grn bl	2.25	2.25
		(#2601)		
118	A1409	10fr violet (#2603)	4.75	4.75
		Nos. 112-118 (7)	9.70	9.70

Map of
Mayotte
A22

1999, Feb. 6		*Perf. 12x13*	
119 A22	3fr multicolored	1.50	1.50

Combani
Dam
A23

1999, Feb. 6	**Litho.**	*Perf. 13*	
120 A23	8fr multicolored	3.50	3.50

Fish Type of 1998

Designs: 2.70fr, Cephalopholis miniatus, vert. 3fr, Pterois volitans. 5.20fr, Pygoplites diacanthus. 10fr, Acanthurus leucosternon.

	Perf. 13¼x13, 13x13¼		
1999, Apr. 3		**Litho.**	
121 A20	2.70fr multicolored	1.25	1.25
122 A20	3fr multicolored	1.40	1.40
123 A20	5.20fr multicolored	2.50	2.50
124 A20	10fr multicolored	4.25	4.25
	Nos. 121-124 (4)	9.40	9.40

France No. 2691 Ovptd. "MAYOTTE"

1999, May 25	**Engr.**	*Perf. 13*	
125 A1470	3fr red & blue	1.25	1.25

Founga — A24

Photo. & Engr.

1999, June 5		*Perf. 13*	
126 A24	5.40fr multicolored	2.50	2.50

Baobab
Tree — A25

1999, June 5	**Litho.**	*Perf. 13x13½*	
127 A25	8fr multicolored	3.50	3.50

Dzaoudzi
Prefecture
A26

1999, Sept. 25	**Litho.**	*Perf. 13x13¼*	
128 A26	3fr multicolored	1.40	1.40

Souvenir Sheet

Pirogues — A27

Designs: a, Pirogues on beach, shown. b, Pirogues, vert. c, Pirogues, close-up.

1999, Sept. 25		*Perf. 13*	
129 A27	5fr Sheet of 3, #a.-c.	10.50	10.50

Vanilla
A28

1999, Nov. 6	**Litho.**	*Perf. 13*	
130 A28	4.50fr multi	1.75	1.75

Soulou
Waterfalls — A29

1999, Dec. 11		*Perf. 13½x13*	
131 A29	10fr multi	4.00	4.00

Year 2000
A30

1999, Dec. 11		*Perf. 13*	
132 A30	3fr multi	1.25	1.25

Indian
Ocean
Boat — A31

2000, Feb. 5	**Litho.**	*Perf. 13x13¼*	
133 A31	3fr multi	1.25	1.25

Whales
A32

2000, Feb. 5	**Litho.**	*Perf. 13x13¼*	
134 A32	5.20fr multi	2.50	2.50

Inner Wheel
Rotary
District — A33

2000, Mar. 24		*Perf. 13¼x13*	
135 A33	5.20fr multi	2.50	2.50

Lagoon
A34

2000, Apr. 29	**Litho.**	*Perf. 13x13¼*	
136 A34	3fr multi	1.40	1.40

Souvenir Sheet

Mahoraise Women — A35

Woman in: a, 3fr, red. b, 5.20fr, white.

2000, Apr. 29		*Perf. 13¼x13*	
137 A35	Sheet of 2, #a-b	5.00	5.00

Tire Race
A36

2000, June 24   Perf. 13x13¼
138 A36 3fr multi   1.40 1.40

Tomb of Sultan Andriantsouli — A37

2000, June 24
139 A37 5.40fr multi   2.10 2.10

Souvenir Sheet

Sea Shells — A38

No. 140: a, Cassis cornuta. b, Charonia tritonis. c, Cyraecassis rufa. d, Cyprae mauritania, Cyprae tigris.

2000, Sept. 23   Litho.   Perf. 13x13½
140 A38 3fr Sheet of 4, #a-d   8.00 8.00

Zéna
M'Déré
(1917-99),
Politician
A39

2000, Oct. 27   Perf. 13
141 A39 3fr multi   1.40 1.40

Ylang
Distillery
A40

2000, Nov. 25   Litho.   Perf. 13x13½
142 A40 2.70fr multi   1.40 1.40

New
Hospital — A41

2000, Nov. 25   Perf. 13½x13
143 A41 10fr multi   4.50 4.50

Map of Mayotte — A42

2001, Jan. 1   Litho.   Perf. 13
144 A42 2.70fr grn & blk   1.25 1.25
145 A42 (3fr) red & blk   1.25 1.25

Breastfeeding
A43

2001, Jan. 27   Perf. 13¼x13
146 A43 3fr multi   1.60 1.60

Return of
Pilgrims to
Mecca
A44

2001, Mar. 10   Perf. 13x13¼
147 A44 2.70fr multi   1.40 1.40

Bush Taxi — A45

2001, Mar. 10   Perf. 13
148 A45 3fr multi   1.40 1.40

Soccer — A46

2001, May 26   Litho.   Perf. 13¼x13
149 A46 3fr multi   1.40 1.40

Fish Type of 1998

Design: Pajama fish (gaterin, plectorhinchus orientalis).

2001, May 26   Perf. 13x13¼
150 A20 10fr multi   5.00 5.00

Foreign Legion Detachment in
Mayotte, 25th Anniv. — A47

2001, Apr. 30   Litho.   Perf. 13
151 A47 5.20fr multi   2.75 2.75

Souvenir Sheet

Flying Foxes — A48

No. 152: a, 3fr, Hanging from branch. b, 5.20fr, In flight.

2001, July 7   Litho.   Perf. 13x13½
152 A48   Sheet of 2, #a-b   6.50 6.50

Adapted
Military
Service
Group, 1st
Anniv.
A49

2001, Sept. 1   Litho.   Perf. 13x13½
153 A49 3fr multi   1.40 1.40

Flowers
A50

Designs: 3fr, Shown. 5.40fr, Fruits.

2001, Sept. 22   Perf. 13
154-155 A50   Set of 2   4.00 4.00

Lake Dziani Dzaha — A51

2001, Nov. 17
156 A51 5.20fr multi   2.40 2.40

Mayotte
Post Office
A52

2001, Nov. 17
157 A52 10fr multi   5.00 5.00

100 Cents = 1 Euro (€)

Arms — A53

2002, Jan. 1   Litho.   Perf. 13x13½
158 A53 46c multi   1.75 1.75

France Nos. 2835,
2849-2863 Overprinted

2002, Jan. 1   Engr.   Perf. 13
159 A1583   1c yellow   .25 .25
160 A1583   2c brown   .25 .25
161 A1583   5c brt bl grn   .30 .30
162 A1583   10c purple   .40 .40
163 A1583   20c brt org   .70 .70
164 A1583   41c brt green   1.25 1.25
165 A1409   (46c) red   1.40 1.40
166 A1583   50c dk blue   1.50 1.50
167 A1583   53c apple grn   1.60 1.60
168 A1583   58c blue   1.75 1.75
169 A1583   64c dark org   2.00 2.00
170 A1583   67c brt blue   2.10 2.10
171 A1583   69c brt pink   2.25 2.25
172 A1583   €1 Prus blue   3.00 3.00
173 A1583   €1.02 dk green   3.00 3.00
174 A1583   €2 violet   6.00 6.00
   Nos. 159-174 (16)   27.75 27.75

Athletics — A54

2002, Mar. 23   Litho.   Perf. 13
175 A54 41c multi   1.50 1.50

Kawéni Mangrove Swamp — A55

2002, Mar. 25
176 A55 €1.52 multi   5.00 5.00

Mayotte
Communes, 25th
Anniv. — A56

2002, June 3   Litho.   Perf. 13¼x13
177 A56 46c multi   1.60 1.60

Salt Drying — A57

2002, June 3   Perf. 13x13¼
178 A57 79c multi   3.00 3.00

2002
Census — A58

2002, July 29   Litho.   Perf. 13¼x13
179 A58 46c multi   1.75 1.75

Abandoned Sugar Processing
Equipment — A59

2002, Sept. 21   Litho.   Perf. 13
180 A59 82c multi   2.75 2.75

Miniature Sheet

Birds — A60

No. 181: a, Souimanga. b, Drongo. c,
Oiseau-lunette. d, Foudy.

2002, Sept. 21   Perf. 13x13¼
181 A60 46c Sheet of 4, #a-d   8.50 8.50

Mt.
Choungui — A61

2002, Nov. 16   Litho.   Perf. 13¼x13
182 A61 46c multi   1.75 1.75

Breadfruit — A62

2002, Nov. 16
183 A62 €1.22 multi   4.00 4.00

Vanilla and
Ylang
Museum
A63

2003, Jan. 1   Litho.   Perf. 13x13½
184 A63 46c multi   2.00 2.00

Banana
Tree — A64

2003, Feb. 1   Perf. 13½x13
185 A64 79c multi   2.75 2.75

Holiday
Face
Decorations
A65

2003, Apr. 5   Litho.   Perf. 13
186 A65 46c multi   1.75 1.75

Swordfish — A66

2003, Apr. 5
187 A66 79c multi   3.00 3.00

Gecko — A67

2003, June 14   Litho.   Perf. 13
188 A67 50c multi   2.00 2.00

Mraha Game — A68

2003, June 14   Engr.   Perf. 13x12½
189 A68 €1.52 claret & brown   5.50 5.50

Mtzamboro
College
A69

2003, Sept. 6   Litho.   Perf. 13x13¼
190 A69 45c multi   1.75 1.75

Ziyara de
Pole — A70

2003, Sept. 6   Perf. 13¼x13
191 A70 82c multi   3.00 3.00

Basketball — A71

2003, Nov. 15   Litho.   Perf. 13¼x13
192 A71 50c multi   1.75 1.75

Wadaha
A72

2004, Jan. 3   Perf. 13
193 A72 50c multi   1.75 1.75

**Map Type of 2001 Inscribed "RF"
and With Euro Denominations Only**
2004
194 A42 1c yel & blk   .25   .25
195 A42 2c gray & blk   .25   .25
196 A42 5c greenish bl & blk   .30   .30
197 A42 10c red vio & blk   .30   .30
198 A42 20c org & blk   .50   .50
199 A42 45c green & black   1.25 1.25
200 A42 50c dk bl & blk   1.25 1.25
201 A42 €1 Prus bl & blk   2.40 2.40
202 A42 €2 violet & blk   5.00 5.00
             Nos. 194-202 (9)   11.50 11.50

Issued: 1c, 2c, 50c, €2, 3/10; 5c, 10c, 20c,
€1, 4/17; 45c, 7/17.

Sada Bay — A73

2004, Apr. 3   Litho.   Perf. 13
203 A73 90c multi   2.75 2.75

Souvenir Sheet

Butterflies — A74

No. 204: a, Junonia rhadama. b, Papilio
demodocus. c, Acraea ranavalona. d, Danaus
chrysippus.

2004, Apr. 3   Perf. 13x13¼
204 A74 50c Sheet of 4, #a-d   7.00 7.00

Papaya
and
Papaya
Tree
A75

2004, June 12   Litho.   Perf. 13x13¼
205 A75 50c multi   1.75 1.75

Gold
Jewelry
A76

2004, June 12   Litho.   Perf. 13
206 A76 €2.40 multi   7.50 7.50

Kwalé
River
Bridge
A77

2004, Sept. 25   Litho.   Perf. 13x13¼
207 A77 50c multi   1.75 1.75

Maki and
Young
A78

2004, Sept. 25   Perf. 13
208 A78 75c multi   2.50 2.50

Woman Cooking Food A79

2004, Nov. 13 **Perf. 13x13¼**
209 A79 45c multi 1.50 1.50

Domino Players — A80

2004, Nov. 13 **Perf. 13**
210 A80 75c multi 2.50 2.50

Ylang-ylang Trees — A81

2005, Jan. 3 **Litho.** **Perf. 13**
211 A81 50c multi 2.00 2.00

Traditional Women's Clothing A82

2005, Mar. 14 **Litho.** **Perf. 13**
212 A82 53c multi 2.00 2.00

Breadfruit and Tree — A83

2005, Mar. 14 **Perf. 13¼x13**
213 A83 64c multi 2.00 2.00

Rotary International, Cent. — A84

2005, May 13 **Perf. 13**
214 A84 90c multi 2.75 2.75

Souvenir Sheet

Marine Mammals — A85

No. 215: a, Humpback whale (Baleine à bosse). b, Dolphins. c, Sperm whale (grand cachalot). d, Dugongs.

2005, May 13 **Perf. 13x13¼**
215 A85 53c Sheet of 4, #a-d 8.00 8.00

Stick Figure Drawings A86

2005, July 4 **Perf. 13**
216 A86 48c multi 1.75 1.75

Mamoudzou — A87

2005, Sept. 10 **Litho.** **Perf. 13**
217 A87 48c multi 1.50 1.50

Fisherman in Pirogue A88

2005, Sept. 10
218 A88 75c multi 2.25 2.25

Blacksmith A89

2005, Nov. 12 **Litho.** **Perf. 13x13¼**
219 A89 53c multi 1.75 1.75

Tam-tam Boeuf Celebration — A90

2005, Nov. 12 **Perf. 13**
220 A90 53c multi 1.75 1.75

Woman Grating Coconuts A91

2006, Jan. 14 **Litho.** **Perf. 13x13¼**
221 A91 53c multi 1.75 1.75

Moya Beach — A92

2006, Mar. 18 **Litho.** **Perf. 13**
222 A92 48c multi 1.75 1.75

Souvenir Sheet

Turtle Protection — A93

No. 223: a, Turtle swimming. b, Turtle laying eggs. c, Hatchlings.

2006, Mar. 18 **Perf. 13x13¼**
223 A93 53c Sheet of 3, #a-c 7.50 7.50

Farmer's Market — A94

Ferries — A95

2006, May 15 **Litho.** **Perf. 13x12¾**
224 A94 53c multi 1.50 1.50
225 A95 €1.07 multi 3.50 3.50

Aloe Mayottensis A96

2006, July 3 **Litho.** **Perf. 13¼x13**
226 A96 53c multi 1.75 1.75

Frangipani Shrub and Flowers A97

2006, Sept. 9 **Perf. 13x13¼**
227 A97 53c multi 1.75 1.75

Moulidi Dance — A98

2006, Sept. 9 **Perf. 13**
228 A98 75c multi 2.75 2.75

Tropic Birds A99

2006, Nov. 18 **Litho.** **Perf. 13**
229 A99 54c multi 2.00 2.00

Resumption of Stamp Issues, 10th Anniv. — A100

2007, Jan. 20 **Litho.** **Perf. 13½x13**
230 A100 54c multi 1.75 1.75

Phanelopsis Orchid — A101

2007, Jan. 20 **Perf. 13x13½**
231 A101 54c multi 2.00 2.00

Audit Office, Bicent. A102

2007, Mar. 17   Engr.   Perf. 13¼
232 A102 54c multi   1.75 1.75

Phyllostachys Edulis — A103

2007, Mar. 19   Litho.   Perf. 13¼x13
233 A103 €1.01 multi   4.00 4.00

Traditional House A104

2007, May 14   Perf. 13x13¼
234 A104 54c multi   1.75 1.75

General Council, 30th Anniv. — A105

2007, May 12   Litho.   Perf. 13¼x13
235 A105 54c multi   2.00 2.00

Souvenir Sheet

Corals — A106

No. 236: a, Corail corne d'elan. b, Gorgone eventail. c, Corail corne de cerf. d, Cerveau de Neptune.

2007, June 16   Perf. 13x13¼
236 A106 54c Sheet of 4, #a-d   9.00 9.00

Mangos and Mango Tree A107

2007, Sept. 17   Litho.   Perf. 13x13¼
237 A107 54c multi   1.75 1.75

Chameleon — A108

2007, Sept. 17
238 A108 54c multi   1.75 1.75

Beach Grill and Shelter — A109

2007, Nov. 10   Perf. 13
239 A109 54c multi   1.75 1.75

N'Gouja Beach — A110

2007, Nov. 10   Perf. 13x13¼
240 A110 54c multi   2.00 2.00

Zebu A111

2008, Jan. 28   Litho.   Perf. 13x13½
241 A111 54c multi   1.75 1.75

Coconuts and Coconut Palm — A112

2008, Jan. 28   Perf. 13x13¼
242 A112 54c multi   1.75 1.75

Miniature Sheet

Spices — A113

No. 243: a, Cinnamon (cannelle). b, Nutmeg (muscade). c, Turmeric (curcuma). d, Ginger (gingembre).

2008, Mar. 22   Litho.   Perf. 13x13¼
243 A113 55c Sheet of 4, #a-d   7.75 7.75

Hibiscus — A114

2008, May 26   Perf. 13¼x13
244 A114 55c multi   2.00 2.00

Wedding Ceremony A115

2008, May 26   Perf. 13
245 A115 55c multi   2.00 2.00

Younoussa Bamana (1935-2007), Politician — A116

2008, June 23   Litho.   Perf. 13¼x13
246 A116 55c multi   1.90 1.90

M'Biwi Dance A117

2008, Sept. 22   Litho.   Perf. 13x13¼
247 A117 55c multi   1.75 1.75

Embroidery — A118

2008, Nov. 10   Litho.   Perf. 13x13¼
248 A118 55c multi   1.75 1.75

Mamoudzou Town Hall — A119

2008, Dec. 8   Perf. 13
249 A119 55c multi   1.75 1.75

Longoni Power Station — A120

2009, Jan. 12
250 A120 55c multi   1.75 1.75

Cardinals A121

2009, Jan. 12   Litho.   Perf. 13
251 A121 55c multi   2.00 2.00

Tamarind Tree and Fruit A122

2009, Mar. 9   Perf. 13x13¼
252 A122 56c multi   1.75 1.75

Fishing by Kerosene Lantern — A123

2009, Mar. 9   Perf. 13
253 A123 56c multi   1.75 1.75

Miniature Sheet

Citrus Fruits — A124

No. 254: a, Oranges. b, Grapefruit (pamplemousse). c, Lemons (citron). d, Kaffir limes (combava).

2009, May 18   Perf. 13x13¼
254 A124 56c Sheet of 4, #a-d   7.75 7.75

Souvenir Sheet

Les Quatres Freres — A125

No. 255: a, Close-up view (blue sky). b, Distant view (yellow sky).

2009, June 29 Litho. *Perf. 13x13¼*
255 A125 56c Sheet of 2, #a-b   4.00 4.00

Jasmine Flowers A126

2009, Sept. 21 Litho. *Perf. 13*
256 A126 56c multi   2.00 2.00

Gaboussi Player A127

2009, Nov. 16 *Perf. 13x13¼*
257 A127 56c multi   1.75 1.75

Welcome to Travelers A128

2010, Jan. 11 Litho. *Perf. 13*
258 A128 56c multi   1.75 1.75

Basket Weaver — A129

2010, Mar. 8 Litho. *Perf. 13*
259 A129 56c multi   1.75 1.75

Governor's House — A130

2010, Mar. 8
260 A130 56c multi   1.75 1.75

Sparrow Hawk A131

2010, May 17 Engr. *Perf. 13¼*
261 A131 56c multi   1.40 1.40

Platycerium Alcicorne A132

2010, May 17 Litho. *Perf. 13¼*
262 A132 56c multi   1.40 1.40

Decorated Book Rest A133

2010, July 5 Engr. *Perf. 12¼*
263 A133 58c multi   1.50 1.50

Customs Department Building — A134

2010, July 30 Litho. *Perf. 13x13½*
264 A134 58c multi   1.50 1.50

Chigoma Dance — A135

2010, Sept. 13
265 A135 95c multi   2.60 2.60

Mail Carrier on All-Terrain Vehicle — A136

2010, Nov. 8 *Perf. 13¼x13*
266 A136 58c multi   1.60 1.60

Miniature Sheet

Women's Hairstyles — A137

No. 267 — Various hairstyles of women wearing: a, Lilac clothing, woman facing right. b, Yellow brown clothing. c, Red clothing. d, Lilac clothing, woman facing left.

2011, Jan. 17 *Perf. 13½x13*
267 A137 58c Sheet of 4, #a-d   6.50 6.50

Grand Mosque of Mtsapéré A138

2011, Feb. 14 *Perf. 13¼x13*
268 A138 58c multi   1.75 1.75

Woman Carrying Laundry A139

2011, Mar. 14 *Perf. 13*
269 A139 58c multi   1.75 1.75

Bee-eaters A140

2011, Mar. 14
270 A140 58c multi   1.75 1.75

Mayotte's Association With France, 170th Anniv. — A141

2011, Apr. 4 Engr. *Perf. 13x12¼*
271 A141 58c brown   1.75 1.75

White Sand Island A142

2011, May 16 Litho. *Perf. 13x13¼*
272 A142 58c multi   1.75 1.75

Kingfisher A143

2011, May 16 *Perf. 13¼x13*
273 A143 58c multi   1.75 1.75

Kapok Tree — A144

2011, June 20
274 A144 58c multi   1.75 1.75

Mtzamboro Island Oranges and Orange Tree — A145

2011, June 20
275 A145 58c multi   1.75 1.75

Majlis Ceremony — A146

2011, June 20 *Perf. 13*
276 A146 58c multi   1.75 1.75

Skin Divers — A147

2011, July 4 Litho. *Perf. 13¼x13*
277 A147 60c multi   1.75 1.75

Karehani Lake — A148

2011, July 4
278 A148 60c multi   1.75 1.75

Marketplace — A149

2011, Sept. 5   *Perf. 13x13½*
279   A149   60c multi   1.75   1.75

Flycatchers — A150

2011, Sept. 5
280   A150   60c multi   1.75   1.75

Indian Ocean Philatelic Show A151

2011, Sept. 19   *Perf. 13*
281   A151   60c multi   1.75   1.75

Change of Mayotte's Political Status — A152

2011, Sept. 1
282   A152   60c multi   1.75   1.75

The Overseas Collectivity of Mayotte became France's 101st department on Mar. 31, 2011.

Pottery — A153

2011, Oct. 3   *Perf. 13¼x13*
283   A153   60c multi   1.75   1.75

Aquaculture — A154

2011, Nov. 14   *Perf. 13x13¼*
284   A154   60c multi   1.60   1.60

Padza of Dapani A155

2011, Nov. 14
285   A155   60c multi   1.60   1.60

Fishermen Returning with Catch A156

2011, Dec. 5   *Perf. 13*
286   A156   60c multi   1.60   1.60

Northern Islets A157

2011, Dec. 12   *Perf. 13x13¼*
287   A157   60c multi   1.60   1.60

Ship Marion Dufresne in Mamoudzou Lagoon — A158

2011, Dec. 31   *Perf. 13*
288   A158   60c multi   1.60   1.60

See French Southern & Antarctic Territories No. 453.

Mayotte began to use the postage stamps of France as of Jan. 1, 2012.

AIR POST STAMPS

> **Catalogue values for unused stamps in this section are for Never Hinged items.**

Opening of New Air Terminal — AP1

1997, Mar. 1   *Engr.*   *Perf. 13x12½*
C1   AP1   20fr multicolored   11.00   11.00

First Mayotte-Réunion Flight, 20th Anniv. — AP2

Photo. & Engr.
1997, Nov. 29   *Perf. 13x12½*
C2   AP2   5fr multicolored   3.00   3.00

Pique-boeuf Bird, Zebu — AP3

1998, Apr. 1   *Litho.*   *Perf. 13*
C3   AP3   30fr multicolored   13.00   13.00

Deba Religious Festival — AP4

1999, Nov. 6   *Litho.*   *Perf. 13*
C4   AP4   10fr multicolored   5.00   5.00

Dzaoudzi Aero Club — AP5

2001, July 7   *Litho.*   *Perf. 13*
C5   AP5   20fr multi   9.50   9.50

Dzaoudzi Rock — AP6

2003, Nov. 15   *Litho.*   *Perf. 13*
C6   AP6   €1.50 multi   5.00   5.00

MEMEL

'mā-məl

LOCATION — In northern Europe, bordering on the Baltic Sea
GOVT. — Special commission (see below)
AREA — 1099 sq. mi.
POP. — 151,960

Following World War I this territory was detached from Germany and by Treaty of Versailles assigned to the government of a commission of the Allied and Associated Powers (not the League of Nations), which administered it until January, 1923, when it was forcibly occupied by Lithuania. In 1924 Memel became incorporated as a semi-autonomous district of Lithuania with the

---

approval of the Allied Powers and the League of Nations.

100 Pfennig = 1 Mark
100 Centu = 1 Litas (1923)

> **Excellent counterfeits of all Memel stamps exist.**

Stamps of Germany, 1905-20, Overprinted

Wmk. Lozenges (125)
1920, Aug. 1   *Perf. 14, 14½*

1	A16	5pf green	1.25	9.00
2	A16	10pf car rose	2.75	10.00
3	A16	10pf orange	.30	2.75
4	A22	15pf violet brown	2.75	13.00
5	A16	20pf blue violet	1.20	5.50
6	A16	30pf org & blk, *buff*	1.40	8.75
7	A16	30pf dull blue	.40	3.50
8	A16	40pf lake & blk	.25	3.50
9	A16	50pf pur & blk, *buff*	.30	3.50
10	A16	60pf olive green	1.60	6.50
11	A16	75pf grn & blk	2.75	21.00
12	A16	80pf blue violet	1.60	10.00

Overprinted

13	A17	1m car rose	.40	3.50
14	A17	1.25m green	13.50	52.50
15	A17	1.50m yel brn	4.75	32.50
16	A21	2m blue	2.00	14.50
17	A21	2.50m red lilac	12.00	65.00
		Nos. 1-17 (17)	49.20	265.00

Stamps of France, Surcharged in Black

On A22

On A18

1920   **Unwmk.**   *Perf. 14x13½*

18	A22	5pf on 5c green	.80	3.25
19	A22	10pf on 10c red	.30	2.75
20	A22	20pf on 25c blue	1.25	3.75
21	A22	30pf on 30c org	.40	3.00
22	A22	40pf on 20c red brn	1.25	3.00
23	A22	50pf on 35c vio	.30	2.75
24	A18	60pf on 40c red & pale bl	.35	3.00
25	A18	80pf on 45c grn & bl	1.25	4.00
26	A18	1m on 50c brn & lav	.55	4.00
27	A18	1m 25pf on 60c vio & ultra	1.30	9.00
28	A18	2m on 1fr cl & ol grn	.35	2.75
29	A18	3m on 5fr bl & buff	18.50	67.50
		Nos. 18-29 (12)	26.60	108.75

For stamps with additional surcharges and overprints see Nos. 43-49, C1-C4.

French Stamps of 1900-20 Surcharged like Nos. 24 to 29 in Red or Black

On A18

Type I

Type II

1920-21 Unwmk. Perf. 14x13½
30	A18	3m on 2fr org & pale bl	24.00	67.50
31	A18	4m on 2fr org & pale bl (I) (Bk)	.50	2.75
a.		Type II	52.50	160.00
32	A18	10m on 5fr bl & buff	3.00	16.00
33	A18	20m on 5fr bl & buff	40.00	160.00
		Nos. 30-33 (4)	67.50	246.25

For stamps with additional overprints see Nos. C5, C19.

New Value with Initial Capital
1921
39	A18	60Pf on 40c red & pale bl	4.75	20.00
40	A18	3M on 60c vio & ul-tra	2.40	8.00
41	A18	10M on 5fr bl & buff	2.40	8.00
42	A18	20M on 45c grn & bl	4.75	26.00
		Nos. 39-42 (4)	14.30	62.00

The surcharged value on No. 40 is in italics. For stamps with additional overprints see Nos. C6-C7, C18.

Stamps of 1920 Surcharged with Large Numerals in Dark Blue or Red

No. 43

No. 49

1921-22
43	A22	15pf on 10pf on 10c	.50	2.00
a.		Inverted surcharge	67.50	160.00
44	A22	15pf on 20pf on 25c	.50	3.00
a.		Inverted surcharge	72.50	175.00
45	A22	15pf on 50pf on 35c (R)	.50	3.00
a.		Inverted surcharge	72.50	175.00
46	A22	60pf on 40pf on 20c	.50	2.00
a.		Inverted surcharge	67.50	160.00
47	A18	75pf on 60pf on 40c	.75	3.50
48	A18	1.25m on 1m on 50c	.50	2.75
49	A18	5.00m on 2m on 1fr	1.25	4.25
a.		Inverted surcharge	200.00	625.00
		Nos. 43-49 (7)	4.50	20.50

Stamps of France Surcharged in Black or Red

On A20, A22

1922
50	A22	5pf on 5c org	.25	1.40
51	A22	10pf on 10c red	.80	5.50
52	A22	10pf on 10c grn	.50	1.40
53	A22	15pf on 10c grn	.25	1.40
54	A22	20pf on 20c red brn	8.00	40.00
55	A22	20pf on 25c bl	8.00	40.00
56	A22	25pf on 5c org	.25	1.40
57	A22	30pf on 30c red	1.20	5.50
58	A22	35pf on 35c vio	.25	.80
59	A20	50pf on 50c dl bl	.30	1.40
60	A22	75pf on 15c grn	.25	.80
61	A22	75pf on 35c vio	.30	1.40
62	A22	1m on 25c blue	.25	.80
63	A22	1¼m on 30c red	.30	1.40
64	A22	3m on 5c org	.30	4.50
65	A20	6m on 15c grn (R)	.70	5.50
66	A22	8m on 30c red	.70	13.50

On A18

67	A18	40pf on 40c red & pale bl	.25	1.40
68	A18	80pf on 45c grn & bl	.30	1.40
69	A18	1m on 40c red & pale bl	.30	1.40
70	A18	1.25m on 60c vio & ultra (R)	.30	1.40
71	A18	1.50m on 45c grn & bl (R)	.30	1.40
72	A18	2m on 45c grn & bl	.50	2.25
73	A18	2m on 1fr cl & ol grn	.30	1.40
74	A18	2¼m on 40c red & pale bl	.25	.80
75	A18	2½m on 60c vio & ultra	.45	2.40
76	A18	3m on 60c vio & ultra (R)	1.20	5.50
77	A18	4m on 45c grn & bl	.25	.80
78	A18	5m on 1fr cl & ol grn	.30	1.60
79	A18	6m on 60c vio & ultra	.25	.80
80	A18	6m on 2fr org & pale bl	.35	1.60
81	A18	9m on 1fr cl & ol grn	.40	.80
82	A18	9m on 5fr bl & buff (R)	.40	2.75
83	A18	10m on 45c grn & bl (R)	.70	5.25
84	A18	12m on 40c red & pale bl	.35	2.25
85	A18	20m on 40c red & pale bl	.70	5.25
86	A18	20m on 2fr org & pale bl	.25	2.00
87	A18	30m on 60c vio & ultra	.70	5.25
88	A18	30m on 5fr dk bl & buff	2.75	20.00
89	A18	40m on 1fr cl & ol grn	.70	6.75
90	A18	50m on 2fr org & pale bl	8.50	47.50
91	A18	80m on 2fr org & pale bl (R)	.70	6.75
92	A18	100m on 5fr bl & buff	1.10	13.50
		Nos. 50-92 (43)	45.15	268.90

A 500m on 5fr dark blue and buff was prepared, but not officially issued. Value: unused $950; never hinged $2,400.

For stamps with additional surcharges and overprints see Nos. 93-99, C8-C17, C20-C29.

Nos. 52, 54, 67, 59 Surcharged "Mark"
1922-23
93	A22	10m on 10pf on 10c	.90	8.00
a.		Double surcharge	110.00	275.00
94	A22	20m on 20pf on 20c	.40	4.75
95	A22	40m on 40pf on 40c ('23)	.80	5.25
96	A20	50m on 50pf on 50c	2.40	13.50
		Nos. 93-96 (4)	4.50	31.50

Nos. 72, 61, 70 Srchd. in Red or Black

1922-23
97	A18	10m on 2m on 45c	2.00	13.50
98	A22	25m on 1m on 25c	2.00	13.50
99	A18	80m on 1.25m on 60c (Bk) ('23)	1.20	7.50
		Nos. 97-99 (3)	5.20	34.50

For No. 99 with additional surcharges see Nos. N28-N30.

AIR POST STAMPS

Nos. 24-26, 28, 31, 39-40 Ovptd. in Dark Blue

1921, July 6 Unwmk. Perf. 14x13½
C1	A18	60pf on 40c	40.00	160.00
C2	A18	80pf on 45c	4.00	20.00
C3	A18	1m on 50c	4.75	13.00
C4	A18	2m on 1fr	4.50	16.00
C5	A18	4m on 2fr (I)	4.25	20.00
a.		"Flugpost" inverted	170.00	
b.		Type II	120.00	275.00
		Pair, type I and type II	150.00	

New Value with Initial Capital
C6	A18	60Pf on 40c	4.00	20.00
a.		"Flugpost" inverted	190.00	
C7	A18	3M on 60c	3.50	15.00
a.		"Flugpost" inverted	175.00	
		Nos. C1-C7 (7)	65.00	264.00

The surcharged value on No. C7 is in italics.

Nos. 67-71, 73, 76, 78, 80, 82 Ovptd. in Dark Blue

1922, May 12
C8	A18	40pf on 40c	.40	2.75
C9	A18	80pf on 45c	.40	2.75
C10	A18	1m on 40c	.40	2.75
C11	A18	1.25m on 60c	.80	4.75
C12	A18	1.50m on 45c	.80	4.75
C13	A18	2m on 1fr	.80	4.75
C14	A18	3m on 60c	.80	4.75
C15	A18	5m on 1fr	1.20	4.75
C16	A18	6m on 2fr	1.20	4.75
C17	A18	9m on 5fr	1.20	4.75

Same Overprint On Nos. 40, 31
C18	A18	3m on 60c	130.00	1,100.
C19	A18	4m on 2fr	.80	4.50
		Nos. C8-C17,C19 (11)	8.80	46.00

Nos. 67, 69-71, 73, 76, 78, 80, 82 Ovptd. in Black or Red

1922, Oct. 17
C20	A18	40pf on 40c	1.25	16.00
C21	A18	1m on 40c	1.25	16.00
C22	A18	1.25m on 60c (R)	1.25	16.00
C23	A18	1.60m on 45c (R)	1.25	16.00
C24	A18	2m on 1fr	1.25	16.00
C25	A18	3m on 60c (R)	1.25	16.00
C26	A18	4m on 2fr	1.25	16.00
C27	A10	5m on 1fr	1.25	10.00
C28	A18	6m on 2fr	1.25	16.00
C29	A18	9m on 5fr (R)	1.25	16.00
		Nos. C20-C29 (10)	12.50	160.00

No. C26 is not known without the "FLUGPOST" overprint.

OCCUPATION STAMPS

Issued under Lithuanian Occupation
Surcharged in Various Colors on Unissued Official Stamps of Lithuania Similar to Type O4

On Nos. N1-N6	On Nos. N7-N11

Memel Printing
1923 Unwmk. Litho. Perf. 11
N1	O4	10m on 5c bl (Bk)	1.20	12.00
a.		Double overprint	40.00	275.00
b.		"Memel" and bars omitted	5.75	60.00
N2	O4	25m on 5c bl (R)	1.20	12.00
a.		Double overprint	40.00	160.00
N3	O4	50m on 25c red (Bk)	1.20	12.00
a.		Double overprint	40.00	275.00
N4	O4	100m on 25c red (G)	1.20	12.00
a.		Double overprint	40.00	275.00
N5	O4	400m on 1 l brn (R)	1.60	16.00
a.		Double overprint	40.00	275.00
N6	O4	500m on 1 l brn (Bl)	1.60	16.00
a.		Double overprint	40.00	275.00
		Nos. N1-N6 (6)	8.00	80.00

Kaunas Printing
Black Surcharge
N7	O4	10m on 5c blue	.80	7.25
N8	O4	25m on 5c blue	.80	7.25
N9	O4	50m on 25c red	.80	7.25
N10	O4	100m on 25c red	.95	7.25
N11	O4	400m on 1 l brn	1.60	11.00
		Nos. N7-N11 (5)	4.95	40.00

No. N8 has the value in "Markes," others of the group have it in "Markiu."
For additional surcharge see No. N87.

Surcharged in Various Colors on Unissued Official Stamps of Lithuania Similar to Type O4

1923
N12	O4	10m on 5c bl (R)	1.60	9.50
a.		"Markes" instead of "Markiu"	20.00	110.00
N13	O4	20m on 5c bl (R)	1.60	9.50
N14	O4	25m on 25c red (Bl)	1.60	13.00
N15	O4	50m on 25c red (Bl)	3.25	13.00
a.		Inverted surcharge	40.00	160.00
N16	O4	100m on 1 l brn (Bk)	3.25	17.50
a.		Inverted surcharge	40.00	160.00
N17	O4	200m on 1 l brn (Bk)	4.00	19.00
		Nos. N12-N17 (6)	15.30	81.50

No. N14 has the value in "Markes," others of the group have it in "Markiu."

"Vytis"	
O4	O5

1923, Mar.
N18	O4	10m lt brown	.40	6.75
N19	O4	20m yellow	.40	6.75
N20	O4	25m orange	.40	8.00
N21	O4	40m violet	.40	6.75
N22	O4	50m yellow grn	1.20	14.50
N23	O5	100m carmine	.55	7.25
N24	O5	300m olive grn	6.00	145.00
N25	O5	400m olive brn	.55	7.25
N26	O5	500m lilac	6.00	145.00
N27	O5	1000m blue	1.10	12.00
		Nos. N18-N27 (10)	17.00	359.25

No. N20 has the value in "Markes."
For surcharges see Nos. N44-N69, N88-N114.

No. 99 Surcharged in Green

1923, Apr. 13
N28	A18	100m on No. 99	5.00	72.50
a.		Inverted overprint	110.00	
N29	A18	400m on No. 99	3.75	72.50
a.		Inverted overprint	110.00	
N30	A18	500m on No. 99	5.00	72.50
a.		Inverted overprint	110.00	
		Nos. N28-N30 (3)	13.75	217.50

The normal position of the green surcharge is sideways, up-reading, with the top at the left. Inverted varieties are reversed, with the overprint down-reading.

Ship — O7	Seal — O8

Lighthouse — O9

1923, Apr. 12   Litho.

N31	O7	40m olive grn	4.50	40.00
N32	O7	50m brown	4.50	40.00
N33	O7	80m green	4.50	40.00
N34	O7	100m red	4.50	40.00
N35	O8	200m deep blue	4.50	40.00
N36	O8	300m brown	4.50	40.00
N37	O8	400m lilac	4.50	40.00
N38	O8	500m orange	4.50	40.00
N39	O8	600m olive grn	4.50	40.00
N40	O9	800m deep blue	4.50	40.00
N41	O9	1000m lilac	4.50	40.00
N42	O9	2000m red	4.50	40.00
N43	O9	3000m green	4.50	40.00
		Nos. N31-N43 (13)	58.50	520.00

Union of Memel with Lithuania. Forgeries exist.
For surcharges see Nos. N70-N86.

Nos. N20, N24, N26 Surcharged in Various Colors

1923   Thin Figures

N44	O5	2c on 300m (R)	6.50	16.00
a.		Double surcharge	80.00	400.00
N45	O5	3c on 300m (R)	7.25	20.00
a.		Double surcharge	175.00	475.00
N46	O4	10c on 25m (Bk)	7.25	16.00
a.		Double surcharge	80.00	400.00
b.		Inverted surcharge	110.00	325.00
N47	O4	15c on 25m (Bk)	7.25	16.00
N48	O5	20c on 500m (Bl)	11.00	32.50
N49	O5	30c on 500m (Bk)	8.75	16.00
a.		Double surcharge		
N50	O5	50c on 500m (G)	20.00	32.50
a.		Inverted surcharge	65.00	240.00
b.		Double surcharge	160.00	725.00
		Nos. N44-N50 (7)	68.00	149.00

Nos. N19, N21-N27 Surcharged

N51	O4	2c on 20m yellow	3.25	16.00
N52	O4	2c on 50c yel grn	3.25	16.00
a.		Double surcharge	65.00	325.00
b.		Vert. pair, imperf between	80.00	350.00
N53	O4	3c on 40m violet	4.75	14.50
a.		Double surcharge	65.00	325.00
N54	O5	3c on 300m ol grn	3.25	12.00
a.		Double surcharge	160.00	550.00
N55	O5	5c on 100m car-mine	8.00	12.00
N56	O5	5c on 300m ol grn (R)	4.00	20.00
a.		Double surcharge	110.00	400.00
N57	O5	10c on 400m ol brn	12.00	24.00
N58	O5	30c on 500m lilac	6.50	28.00
a.		Double surcharge	110.00	400.00
b.		Inverted surcharge	120.00	450.00
N59	O5	1 l on 1000m blue	20.00	75.00
a.		Double surcharge	160.00	550.00
		Nos. N51-N59 (9)	65.00	217.50

There are several types of the numerals in these surcharges. Nos. N56 and N58 have "CENT" in short, thick letters, as on Nos. N44 to N50.

Nos. N18-N23, N25, N27 Surcharged

Thick Figures

N60	O4	2c on 10m lt brn	6.50	80.00
N61	O4	2c on 20m yellow	20.00	140.00
N62	O4	2c on 50m yel grn	8.00	95.00
N63	O4	3c on 10m lt brn	20.00	130.00
a.		Double surcharge	160.00	650.00
N64	O4	3c on 40m violet	24.00	225.00
N65	O5	5c on 100m car	12.00	40.00
a.		Double surcharge	110.00	350.00
N66	O5	10c on 400m ol brn	145.00	675.00
N67	O4	15c on 25m orange	145.00	675.00
N68	O5	50c on 1000m blue	6.50	12.00
a.		Double surcharge	110.00	350.00
N69	O5	1 l on 1000m blue	8.00	24.00
a.		Double surcharge	110.00	350.00
		Nos. N60-N69 (10)	395.00	2,096.

No. N69 is surcharged like type "b" in the following group.

Nos. N31-N43 Surcharged

a   b

N70	O7(a)	15c on 40m ol grn	5.50	32.50
N71	O7(a)	30c on 50m brown	5.25	24.00
a.		Double surcharge	65.00	275.00
N72	O7(a)	30c on 80m green	5.25	40.00
N73	O7(a)	30c on 100m red	5.50	16.00
N74	O8(a)	50c on 200m dp blue	6.00	32.50
N75	O8(a)	50c on 300m brn	5.25	20.00
a.		Double surcharge	65.00	275.00
b.		Inverted surcharge	67.50	325.00
N76	O8(a)	50c on 400m lilac	5.50	28.00
a.		Inverted surcharge	72.50	325.00
N77	O8(a)	50c on 500m org	5.50	16.00
a.		Double surcharge	65.00	275.00
N78	O8(b)	1 l on 600m ol grn	5.50	36.00
N79	O9(b)	1 l on 800m dp blue	6.50	36.00
N80	O9(b)	1 l on 1000m lil	6.00	36.00
N81	O9(b)	1 l on 2000m red	6.00	36.00
N82	O9(b)	1 l on 3000m grn	6.50	36.00
		Nos. N70-N82 (13)	74.25	389.00

These stamps are said to have been issued to commemorate the institution of autonomous government.

Nos. N32, N34, N36, N38 Surcharged in Green

1923

N83	O7	15c on 50m brn	275.	2,000.
a.		Thick numerals in surcharge	950.	4,750.
N84	O7	25c on 100m red	150.	1,200.
a.		Thick numerals in surcharge	550.	3,250.
N85	O8	30c on 300m brn	250.	1,300.
a.		Thick numerals in surcharge	725.	3,500.
N86	O8	60c on 500m org	150.	1,200.
a.		Thick numerals in surcharge	550.	2,400.

Surcharges on Nos. N83-N86 are of two types, differing in width of numerals. Values are for stamps with narrow numerals, as illustrated. Stamps with wide numerals sell for two to four times as much. For detailed listing see the *Scott Classic Specialized Catalogue of Stamps & Covers.*

Nos. N8, N10-N11, N3 Surcharged in Red or Green

N87	O4	10c on 25m on 5c bl (R)	35.00	120.00
N88	O4	15c on 100m on 25c red (G)	40.00	350.00
a.		Inverted surcharge	400.00	2,250.
N89	O4	30c on 400m on 1 l brn (R)	17.50	47.50
N90	O4	60c on 50m on 25c red (G)	40.00	325.00
		Nos. N87-N90 (4)	132.50	842.50

Nos. N18-N22 Surcharged in Green or Red

N91	O4	15c on 10m	32.50	210.00
N92	O4	15c on 20m	3.50	32.50
N93	O4	15c on 25m	5.25	65.00
N94	O4	15c on 40m	3.50	32.50
N95	O4	15c on 50m (R)	2.75	24.50
a.		Inverted surcharge	65.00	250.00

N96	O4	25c on 10m	11.00	120.00
N97	O4	25c on 20m	3.50	32.50
a.		Double surcharge	160.00	
N98	O4	25c on 25m	5.25	47.50
N99	O4	25c on 40m	4.50	47.50
a.		Inverted surcharge	60.00	
N100	O4	25c on 50m (R)	2.60	24.50
a.		Inverted surcharge	65.00	
N101	O4	30c on 10m	32.50	200.00
N102	O4	30c on 20m	3.75	40.00
N103	O4	30c on 25m	5.25	65.00
N104	O4	30c on 40m	3.75	24.00
N105	O4	30c on 50m (R)	2.60	24.00
a.		Inverted surcharge	65.00	
		Nos. N91-N105 (15)	122.20	989.50

Nos. N23, N25, N27 Surcharged in Green or Red

N106	O5	15c on 100m	2.75	22.50
a.		Inverted surcharge	60.00	
N107	O5	15c on 400m	2.50	18.50
N108	O5	15c on 1000m (R)	65.00	400.00
a.		Inverted surcharge	200.00	800.00
N109	O5	25c on 100m	2.50	22.50
N110	O5	25c on 400m	2.50	22.50
a.		Double surcharge	160.00	
N111	O5	25c on 1000m (R)	65.00	400.00
a.		Inverted surcharge	200.00	800.00
N112	O5	30c on 100m	2.60	24.50
a.		Inverted surcharge	60.00	
N113	O5	30c on 400m	2.60	24.50
N114	O5	30c on 1000m (R)	65.00	475.00
a.		Inverted surcharge	200.00	800.00
		Nos. N106-N114 (9)	210.45	1,410.

Nos. N96 to N100 and N109 to N111 are surcharged "Centai," the others "Centu."

MESOPOTAMIA

ˌme-s.ə-ˌpə-ˈtā-mē-ə

LOCATION — In Western Asia, bounded on the north by Syria and Turkey, on the east by Persia, on the south by Saudi Arabia and on the west by Trans-Jordan.
GOVT. — A former Turkish Province
AREA — 143,250 (1918) sq. mi.
POP. — 2,849,282 (1920)
CAPITAL — Baghdad

During World War I this territory was occupied by Great Britain. It was recognized as an independent state and placed under British Mandate but in 1932 the Mandate was terminated and the country admitted to membership in the League of Nations as the Kingdom of Iraq. Postage stamps of Iraq are now in use.

16 Annas = 1 Rupee

Watermark

Wmk. 48 —
Diagonal Zigzag
Lines

Issued under British Occupation

Baghdad Issue
Stamps of Turkey 1901-16 Surcharged

N1

N2

N3

N4

N5

The surcharges were printed from slugs which were arranged to fit the various shapes of the stamps.

1917   Unwmk.   Perf. 12, 13½
On Turkey Nos. 254, 256, 258-260

N1	¼a on 2pa red lil	325.00	375.00
a.	"IN BRITISH" omitted	14,000.	
N2	¼a on 5pa vio brown	225.00	250.00
a.	"¼ An" omitted	11,000.	

N3	½a on 10pa green	1,200.	1,400.
N4	1a on 20pa red	800.00	900.00
N5	2a on 1pi blue	375.00	400.00
	Nos. N1-N5 (5)	2,925.	3,325.

On Turkey No. 249

N6	A22 2a on 1pi ultra	700.00	875.00

On Turkey No. 251

N7	A23 ½a on 10pa green	1,850.	2,100.

On Turkey Nos. 272-273

N8	A29 1a on 20pa red	425.	500.
a.	"OCCUPATION" omitted	10,000.	
N9	A30 2a on 1pi blue	5,250.	6,000.

On Turkey Nos. 346-348

N10	A41 ½a on 10pa car, perf 12½	700.00	800.00
N11	A41 1a on 20pa ultra, perf 12½	1,500.	2,000.
a.	"1 An" omitted	13,000.	
N12	A41 2a on 1pi vio & black, perf 13½	190.00	200.00
a.	"BAGHDAD" omitted	9,750.	

On Turkey Nos. 297, 300

N13	A17 ¼a on 5pa purple	10,000.	
N14	A17 2a on 1pi blue	300.	350.

On Turkey No. 306

N15	A18 1a on 20pa car	700.	825.

On Turkey Nos. 329-331

N16	A22 ½a on 10pa bl grn	175.00	190.00
N17	A22 1a on 20pa car rose	650.00	700.00
a.	"1 An" omitted	7,000.	5,750.
N18	A22 2a on 1pi ultra	190.00	200.00

On Turkey No. 337

N19	A22 1a on 20pa car rose	6,000.	7,500.

On Turkey No. P125

N20	A17 1a on 20pa car	—	

On Turkey Nos. B1, B8

Inscription in crescent is obliterated by another crescent handstamped in violet black on Nos. N21-N27.

N21	A18 ½a on 10pa dull grn	200.00	250.00
a.	"OCCUPATION" omitted	12,500.	
N22	A21 1a on 20pa car rose	700.00	750.00

On Turkey No. B29

N23	A21 2a on 1pi ultra	2,500.	2,750.

On Turkey Nos. B33-B34

N24	A22 1a on 20pa car rose	200.00	250.00
N25	A22 2a on 1pi ultra	300.00	350.00
a.	"OCCUPATION" omitted	12,000.	
b.	"BAGHDAD" omitted	11,000.	

On Turkey No. B42

N26	A41 ½a on 10pa car, perf 12½	300.00	325.00
a.	"BAGHDAD" double		

On Turkey No. B38

N27	A11 1a on 10pa on 20pa vio brn	325.00	350.00

Iraq Issue

N28

N29

N30

N31

N32

N33

N34

N35

N36

N37

N38

N39

N40

N41

Turkey Nos. 256, 258-269 Surcharged

1918-20		**Perf. 12**	
N28	¼a on 5pa vio brn	.55	1.10
N29	½a on 10pa grn	.75	.25
N30	1a on 20pa red	.55	.25
N31	1½a on 5pa vio brn	8.75	5.50
N32	2½a on 1pi blue	1.35	1.50
a.	Inverted surcharge	8,500.	
N33	3a on 1½pi car & black	1.60	.25
a.	Double surcharge, red & blk	3,500.	4,500.
N34	4a on 1¾pi slate & red brn	1.60	.30
a.	Center inverted		30,000.
N35	6a on 2pi grn & black	1.75	2.00
N36	8a on 2½pi org & ol grn	2.25	2.25
N37	12a on 5pi dl vio	2.00	5.00
N38	1r on 10pi red brown	2.50	1.50
N39	2r on 25pi ol grn	8.00	2.75

N40		5r on 50pi car	26.00	30.00
N41		10r on 100pi dp blue	92.50	18.50
		Nos. N28-N41 (14)	150.15	71.15

See #N50-N53. For overprints see #NO1-NO21.

Mosul Issue

A13

A14

A15

A16

A17

A18

A19

1919   **Unwmk.**   **Perf. 11½, 12**

N42	A13	½a on 1pi grn & brn red	2.40	2.10
N43	A14	1a on 20pa *rose*	1.50	1.90
a.		"POSTAGE" omitted		
N44	A15	1a on 20pa *rose*	4.50	4.50
a.		Double surcharge	725.00	

Turkish word at right of tughra ("reshad") is large on No. N43, small on No. N44.

Wmk. Turkish Characters
Perf. 12½

N45	A16	2½a on 1pi vio & yel	1.60	1.60
N46	A17	3a on 20pa grn & yel	75.00	100.00

Wmk. 48

N47	A17	3a on 20pa green	1.75	4.25
N48	A18	4a on 1pi dull vio	3.50	3.75
a.		Double surcharge	1,100.	
b.		"4" omitted	2,000.	
c.		As "b," double surcharge		
N49	A19	8a on 10pa claret	4.25	5.50
a.		Double surcharge	700.00	875.00
b.		Inverted surcharge	800.00	1,000.
c.		8a on 1pi dull violet	3,250.	
		Nos. N42-N49 (8)	94.50	123.60

Value for No. 49c is for a stamp with the perfs cutting into the design.

Iraq Issue
Types of 1918-20 Issue

1921   **Wmk. 4**   **Perf. 12**

N50	A28	½a on 10pa green	3.25	2.25
N51	A26	1½a on 5pa dp brn	2.50	1.10
N52	A37	2r on 25pi ol grn	24.00	13.00
		Nos. N50-N52 (3)	29.75	16.35

Type of 1918-20 without "Reshad"
1922   **Unwmk.**

N53	A36	1r on 10pi red brn	220.00	26.00

"Reshad" is the small Turkish word at right of the tughra in circle at top center.
For overprint see No. NO22.

OFFICIAL STAMPS

Nos. N29-N41 Overprinted

1920   **Unwmk.**   **Perf. 12**

NO1	A28	½a on 10pa grn	13.00	2.00
NO2	A29	1a on 20pa red	5.50	.65
NO3	A26	1½a on 5pa vio brown	37.50	2.75
NO4	A30	2½a on 1pi blue	5.50	6.00
NO5	A31	3a on 1½pi car & black	26.00	.85
NO6	A32	4a on 1¾pi sl & red brn	37.50	4.00
NO7	A33	6a on 2pi grn & black	32.50	8.00
NO8	A34	8a on 2½pi org & ol grn	35.00	5.00
NO9	A35	12a on 5pi dull vio	25.00	16.00
NO10	A36	1r on 10pi red brown	32.50	12.00
NO11	A37	2r on 25pi ol green	32.50	17.50
NO12	A38	5r on 50pi car	65.00	48.00
NO13	A39	10r on 100pi dp blue	92.50	120.00
		Nos. NO1-NO13 (13)	440.00	242.75

Same Overprint on Types of Regular Issue of 1918-20
1921-22   **Wmk. 4**

NO14	A28	½a on 10pa grn	1.10	1.10
NO15	A29	1a on 20pa red	7.50	1.10
NO16	A26	1½a on 5pa dp brn	3.00	.75
NO17	A32	4a on 1¾pi gray & red brn	2.25	2.75
NO18	A33	6a on 2pi grn & black	30.00	140.00
NO19	A34	8a on 2½pi org & yel grn	3.50	2.25
NO20	A35	12a on 5pi dl vio	30.00	85.00
NO21	A37	2r on 25pi ol grn	85.00	130.00
		Nos. NO14-NO21 (8)	162.35	362.95

Same Overprint on No. N53
1922   **Unwmk.**

NO22	A36	1r on 10pi red brn	37.50	7.50

MEXICO
'mek-si-ˌkō

LOCATION — Extreme southern part of the North American continent, south of the United States
GOVT. — Republic
AREA — 759,529 sq. mi.
POP. — 100,294,036 (1999 est.)
CAPITAL — Mexico, D.F

8 Reales = 1 Peso
100 Centavos = 1 Peso

> Catalogue values for unused stamps in this country are for Never Hinged items, beginning with Scott 792 in the regular postage section, Scott C143 in the airpost section, Scott E8 in the special delivery section, and Scott G4 in the insured letter section.

District Overprints
Nos. 1-149 are overprinted with names of various districts, and sometimes also with district numbers and year dates. Some of the district overprints are rare and command high prices. Values given for Nos. 1-149 are for the more common district overprints.

Watermarks

Wmk. 150 — PAPEL SELLADO in Sheet

Wmk. 151 — R. P. S. in the Sheet (R.P.S. stands for "Renta Papel Sellado")

Wmk. 152 — "CORREOS E U M" on Every Horizontal Line of Ten Stamps

Wmk. 153 — "R M" Interlaced

Wmk. 154 — Eagle and R M

Wmk. 155 — SERVICIO POSTAL DE LOS ESTADOS UNIDOS MEXICANOS

Wmk. 156 — CORREOS MEXICO

Wmk. 248 — SECRETARIA DE HACIENDA MEXICO

Wmk. 260 — Lines and SECRETARIA DE HACIENDA MEXICO

Wmk. 272 — "S. H. C. P. MEXICO" and Eagle in Circle

Wmk. 279 — GOBIERNO MEXICANO and Eagle in Circle

Wmk. 300 — MEX-MEX and Eagle in Circle, Multiple (Letters 6mm)

Wmk. 350 — MEX and Eagle in Circle, Multiple. Letters 8-9mm

Miguel Hidalgo y Costilla — A1

Handstamped with District Name

1856	Unwmk.	Engr.	Imperf.
1	A1 ½r blue	50.00	40.00
b.	Without overprint	45.00	45.00
2	A1 1r yellow	30.00	5.00
b.	Half used as ½r on cover		10,000.
c.	Without overprint	25.00	30.00
d.	1r green (error)		
3	A1 2r yellow grn	27.50	3.50
a.	2r blue green	275.00	40.00
b.	2r emerald	250.00	50.00
c.	Half used as 1r on cover		600.00
d.	Without overprint	40.00	22.50
e.	As "a," without overprint	250.00	45.00
f.	As "b," without overprint		75.00
	Printed on both sides (yel green)	300.00	
4	A1 4r red	175.00	110.00
a.	Half used as 2r on cover		250.00
b.	Quarter used as 1r on cover		700.00
c.	Without overprint	140.00	160.00
d.	Three quarters used as 3r on cover		12,000.
5	A1 8r red lilac	350.00	200.00
a.	8r violet	300.00	200.00
b.	Without overprint	225.00	225.00
c.	Eighth used as 1r on cover		17,500.
d.	Quarter used as 2r on cover		225.00
e.	Half used as 4r on cover		900.00
	Nos. 1-5 (5)	632.50	358.50

The 1r and 2r were printed in sheets of 60 with wide spacing between stamps, and in sheets of 190 or 200 with narrow spacing.

No. 3a can be distinguished from the other 2r stamps by the horizontal grain of the paper. The plate for No. 3b has framelines.

All values, except the 1r, have been reprinted, some of them several times. The reprints usually show signs of wear and the impressions are often smudgy. The paper is usually thicker than that of the originals. Reprints are usually on very white paper. Reprints are found with and without overprints and with cancellations made both from the original handstamps and from forged ones.

Counterfeits exist.

See Nos. 6-12. For overprints see Nos. 35-45.

1861

6	A1 ½r black, buff	50.00	45.00
a.	Without overprint	34.00	62.50
7	A1 1r black, green	20.00	5.50
a.	Impression of 2r on back		450.00
b.	Without overprint	5.00	22.50
d.	As "b", blk, pink (error)	8,000.	9,000.
f.	Double impression		150.00
8	A1 2r black, pink	15.00	4.50
a.	Impression of 1r on back		0,000.
b.	Half used as 1r on cover		750.00
c.	Without overprint	3.50	22.50
d.	Printed on both sides		2,250.
e.	Double Impression		100.00
f.	As "e," without overprint	—	
9	A1 4r black, yellow	200.00	100.00
a.	Half used as 2r on cover		190.00
b.	Without overprint	50.00	100.00
c.	Quarter used as 1r on cover		700.00
d.	Three-quarters used as 3r on cover		35,000.
10	A1 4r dull rose, yel	200.00	70.00
a.	Half used as 2r on cover		950.00
b.	Without overprint	110.00	140.00
c.	Printed on both sides		9,000.
d.	Quarter used as 1r on cover		10,000.
11	A1 8r black, red brn	375.00	250.00
a.	⅛ used as 1R on cover front		11,000.
b.	Quarter used as 2r on cover		250.00
c.	Half used as 4r on cover		750.00
d.	Without overprint	110.00	225.00
e.	Three quarters used as 6r on cover		45,000.
12	A1 8r grn, red brn	500.00	240.00
a.	Half used as 4r on cover		30,000.
b.	Without overprint	150.00	200.00
c.	Quarter used as 2r on cover		40,000.
d.	Printed on both sides	12,500.	12,500.
	Nos. 6-12 (7)	1,360.	715.00

Nos. 6, 9, 10, 11 and 12 have been reprinted. Most reprints of the ½r, 4r and 8r are on vertically grained paper. Originals are on horizontally grained paper. The original ½r stamps are much worn but the reprints are unworn. The paper of the 4r is too deep and rich in color and No. 10 is printed in too bright red.

Reprints of the 8r can only be told by experts. All these reprints are found in fancy colors and with overprints and cancellations as in the 1856 issue.

Counterfeits exist.

Hidalgo — A3

With District Name

1864			Perf. 12
14	A3 1r red	750.	3,000.
a.	Without District Name	.75	
15	A3 2r blue	1,100.	1,750.
a.	Without District Name	.75	
16	A3 4r brown	1,250.	2,400.
a.	Without District Name	1.25	
b.	Vert. pair, imperf. between		
17	A3 1p black	3,250.	—
a.	Without District Name	2.00	

Nos. 14 to 17 were issued with district overprints of Saltillo or Monterrey on the toned paper of 1864. Overprints on the 1867 white paper are fraudulent. Counterfeits and counterfeit cancellations are plentiful. The 1r red with "½" surcharge is bogus.

Coat of Arms — A4

Overprint of District Name, etc.

Five types of overprints:

I — District name only.

II — District name, consignment number and "1864" in large figures.

III — District name, number and "1864" in small figures.

IV — District name, number and "1865."

V — District name, number and "1866."

1864-66			Imperf.
18	A4 3c brn (IV, V)	1,300.	2,500.
a.	Without overprint	700.00	
b.	Laid paper	4,500.	6,000.
19	A4 ½r brown (I)	400.00	250.00
a.	Type II	2,200.	2,250.
b.	Without overprint	200.00	650.00
20	A4 ½r lilac (IV)	60.00	55.00
a.	Type II	140.00	75.00
b.	Type II	200.00	200.00
c.	Type V		3,000.
d.	½r gray (V)	70.00	80.00
e.	Without overprint	5.75	
f.	½r gray lilac	250.00	100.00
21	A4 1r blue (IV, V)	15.00	9.00
a.	Type III	80.00	40.00
b.	Without overprint	2.50	
c.	Half used as ½r on cover		3,000.
22	A4 1r ultra (I, II)	120.00	30.00
a.	Type III	90.00	40.00
b.	Without overprint	160.00	150.00
c.	Half used as ½r on cover		7,250.
23	A4 2r org (III, IV, V)	10.00	4.00
a.	Type II	20.00	6.00
b.	Type I	50.00	7.00
c.	2r dp org, without ovpt., early plate	175.00	65.00
d.	Without ovpt., late plate	2.00	
e.	Half used as 1r on cover		6,000.
24	A4 4r grn (III, IV, V)	100.00	50.00
a.	Types I, II	160.00	77.50
b.	4r dk grn, without ovpt.	4.75	1,700.
d.	Half used as 2r on cover		700.00
25	A4 8r red (IV, V)	150.00	90.00
a.	Types II, III	175.00	125.00
b.	Type I	400.00	175.00
e.	8r dk red, without ovpt.	7.00	575.00
f.	Quarter used as 2r on cover		15,000.
g.	Three-quarters used as 6r on cover		

The 2r printings from the early plates are 25½mm high; those from the late plate, 24½mm.

Varieties listed as "Without overprint" in unused condition are remainders.

Besides the overprints of district name, number and date, Nos. 18-34 often received, in the district offices, additional overprints of numbers and sometimes year dates. Stamps with these "sub-consignment numbers" sell for more than stamps without them.

Genuine examples of No. 20c should bear Mexico district name overprint, together with consignment numbers 1-1866 or 17-1866. Gray lilac stamps of other consignments are examples of No. 20f.

Value unused for No. 18 is for an example without gum. Examples with original gum sell for more. Examples of No. 18a on laid paper are forgeries.

No. 25g does not exist on full cover.

Faked quarterings and bisects of 1856-64 are plentiful.

The 3c has been reprinted from a die on which the words "TRES CENTAVOS," the outlines of the serpent and some of the background lines have been retouched.

Emperor Maximilian — A5

Overprinted with District Name, Number and Date 1866 or 866; also with Number and Date only, or with Name only

1866			Litho.
26	A5 7c lilac gray	65.00	125.00
a.	7c deep gray	85.00	140.00
b.	Half used as 7c on cover		2,500.
c.	Without overprint	2,500.	
27	A5 13c blue	35.00	35.00
a.	13c cobalt blue	25.00	25.00
b.	Half used as 13c on cover		2,500.
c.	Without overprint	2,500.	
28	A5 25c buff	12.50	9.00
a.	Half used as 13c on cover		2,500.
b.	Without overprint	2,500.	
29	A5 25c orange	12.00	12.00
a.	25c red orange	20.00	27.50
b.	25c red brown	85.00	47.50
c.	25c brown	110.00	85.00
30	A5 50c green	25.00	30.00
	Nos. 26-30 (5)	149.50	211.00

Litho. printings have round period after value numerals.

Overprinted with District Name, Number and Date 866 or 867; also with Number and Date only Engr.

31	A5 7c lilac	450.00	5,500.
a.	Without overprint	3.50	
32	A5 13c blue	12.00	12.00
a.	Without overprint	1.25	
33	A5 25c orange brown	12.00	11.00
a.	Without overprint	1.25	
34	A5 50c green	700.00	70.00
a.	Without overprint	2.50	

See "sub-consignment" note after No. 25. Engraved printings have square period after value numerals.

Varieties listed as "Without overprint" in unused condition are remainders.

1867			
35	A1 ½r blk, buff	2,500.	5,000.
36	A1 1r blk, green	60.00	10.00
37	A1 2r blk, pink	22.50	5.00
a.	Printed on both sides		140.00
38	A1 4r red, yel	625.00	50.00
a.	Printed on both sides		175.00
39	A1 4r red	6,000.	3,250.
40	A1 8r blk, red brn	3,500.	275.00
41	A1 8r grn, red brn		4,000.

Dangerous counterfeits exist of the "Mexico" overprint.

Examples of No. 38 with yellow removed are offered as No. 39.

Same Overprint Thin Gray Blue Paper Wmk. 151

42	A1 ½r gray	275.00	190.00
a.	Without overprint	175.00	175.00
43	A1 1r blue	400.00	65.00
b.	Without overprint	300.00	125.00
44	A1 2r green	200.00	30.00
a.	Printed on both sides	6,000.	3,500.
b.	Without overprint	300.00	50.00
45	A1 4r rose	3,000.	75.00
a.	Without overprint	5,000.	225.00

Most examples of Nos. 42-45 do not show the watermark. Values are for unused stamps. Examples showing the watermark sell for more.

Reprints of the ½r and 4r exist on watermarked paper. Reprints of ½r and 8r also exist in gray on thick grayish wove paper, unwatermarked.

Hidalgo — A6

Overprinted with District Name, Number and Abbreviated Date

1868	Unwmk.	Litho.	Imperf.
46	A6 6c blk, buff	40.00	20.00
47	A6 12c blk, green	45.00	20.00
a.	Period after "12"	65.00	55.00
48	A6 25c bl, pink	75.00	20.00
a.	Without overprint	125.00	
49	A6 50c blk, yellow	600.00	60.00
50	A6 100c blk, brown	775.00	140.00
a.	Half used as 50c on cover		3,000.
51	A6 100c brn, brn	1,750.	500.00

		Perf.	
52	A6 6c blk, buff	35.00	35.00
a.	Without overprint	150.00	
b.	Period after "6"	100.00	75.00
53	A6 12c blk, green	35.00	12.00
a.	Period after "12"	85.00	30.00
b.	Very thick paper	50.00	25.00
c.	Without overprint	110.00	
54	A6 25c blue, pink	55.00	10.00
b.	Without overprint	150.00	
55	A6 50c blk, yellow	325.00	45.00
a.	Half used as 50c on cover		3,000.
56	A6 100c blk, brown	375.00	110.00
a.	Without overprint	350.00	
57	A6 100c brn, brn	1,000.	375.00
a.	Printed on both sides	1,250.	1,000.

Four kinds of perforation are found in the 1868 issue: serrate, square, pin and regular. The narrow spacing between stamps was inadequate for some of these perforation types.

Thick Figures of Value, with Period after Numerals

Overprinted with District Name, Number and Abbreviated Date

58	A6	6c blk, *buff*	9.50	4.50
59	A6	12c blk, *green*	4.25	1.25
a.		Very thick paper		10.00
c.		12c black, *buff* (error)	575.00	575.00
d.		Printed on both sides		3,000.
e.		No period after "12"	—	
61	A6	25c blk, *pink*	8.00	1.25
a.		No period after "25"		90.00
c.		Very thick paper	25.00	6.00
d.		"85" for "25"	75.00	50.00
e.		"35" for "25"		75.00
f.		Printed on both sides	—	
62	A6	50c blk, *yellow*	125.00	15.00
a.		No period after "50"	225.00	35.00
b.		50c blue, *lt pink*	3,000.	2,000.
c.		Half used as 25c on cover		1,000.
d.		Very thick paper		50.00
e.		"30" for "50"	750.00	750.00
64	A6	100c blk, *brown*	150.00	90.00
a.		No period after "100"	175.00	100.00
b.		Very thick paper		75.00
c.		Quarter used as 25c on cover		2,000.
		Nos. 58-64 (5)	296.75	112.00

Perf.

65	A6	6c blk, *buff*	40.00	20.00
a.		Very thick paper	60.00	35.00
66	A6	12c blk, *green*	5.50	5.50
a.		Very thick paper	20.00	15.00
b.		12c black, *buff* (error)	575.00	575.00
c.		No period after "12"	—	
68	A6	25c blue, *pink*	20.00	2.50
a.		No period after "25"	80.00	80.00
c.		Thick paper	30.00	15.00
d.		"85" for "25"	80.00	40.00
69	A6	50c blk, *yellow*	200.00	25.00
a.		No period after "50"	200.00	30.00
b.		50c blue, *lt pink* (error)	2,500.	1,500.
c.		Thick paper		60.00
70	A6	100c blk, *brown*	200.00	60.00
a.		No period after "100"	200.00	60.00
b.		Very thick paper		80.00
		Nos. 65-70 (5)	465.50	113.00

Postal forgeries of Nos. 58-70 were printed from original plates with district name overprints and forged. These include the pelure paper varieties and some thick paper varieties. The "Anotado" handstamp was applied to some of the confiscated forgeries and they were issued, including Nos. 73a and 78a.

Stamps of 1868 Handstamped

Overprinted with District Name, Number and Abbreviated Date Thick Figures with Period

1872   ***Imperf.***

71	A6	6c blk, *buff*	650.00	675.00
72	A6	12c blk, *green*	85.00	75.00
73	A6	25c bl, *pink*	40.00	45.00
a.		Pelure paper	55.00	65.00
b.		"85" for "25"		125.00
74	A6	50c blk, *yellow*	850.00	475.00
a.		No period after "50"	900.00	475.00
75	A6	100c blk, *brown*	1,250.	1,000.
a.		No period after "100"		1,100.

Perf.

76	A6	6c blk, *buff*		750.00
77	A6	12c blk, *green*	90.00	80.00
78	A6	25c blue, *pink*	35.00	42.50
a.		Pelure paper	65.00	90.00
79	A6	50c blk, *yellow*	850.00	600.00
a.		No period after "50"		550.00
80	A6	100c blk, *brown*		

Counterfeit "Anotado" overprints abound. Genuine cancellations other than Mexico City or of the Diligencias de Puebla are unknown. It is recommended that these be purchased accompanied by certificates of authenticity from competent experts.

The stamps of the 1872 issue are found perforated with square holes, pin-perf. 13, 14 or 15, and with serrate perforation.

Counterfeits of the 1868 6c, 12c buff, 50c and 100c (both colors) from new plates have clear, sharp impressions and more facial shading lines than the originals. These counterfeits are found perf. and imperf., with thick and thin numerals, and with the "Anotado" overprint.

Hidalgo — A8

Moiré on White Back Overprinted with District Name, Number and Abbreviated Date White Wove Paper

1872   **Litho.**   **Wmk. 150**   ***Imperf.***

81	A8	6c green	325.00	275.00
82	A8	12c blue	250.00	125.00
a.		Laid paper	2,000.	350.00
83	A8	25c red	400.00	125.00
a.		Laid paper	2,000.	350.00
84	A8	50c yellow	2,000.	850.00
a.		50c blue (error)		3,000.
b.		Laid paper		4,000.
c.		As "a," without ovpt.	130.00	
86	A8	100c gray lilac	1,000.	650.00
		Nos. 81-86 (5)	3,975.	2,025.

Wmk. "LA + F"

81a	A8	6c green	2,000.	1,000.
82b	A8	12c blue	450.00	325.00
83b	A8	25c red	575.00	575.00
c.		Without overprint	500.00	
84d	A8	50c yellow	3,500.	2,000.
86a	A8	100c gray lilac	4,000.	1,500.

1872   **Wmk. 150**   ***Pin-perf.***

87	A8	6c green	2,500.	2,000.
88	A8	12c blue	475.00	175.00
89	A8	25c red	550.00	275.00
b.		Laid paper		1,000.
90	A8	50c yellow	1,500.	950.00
a.		50c blue (error)	1,000.	1,250.
b.		As "a," without overprint	200.00	
92	A8	100c gray lilac	1,200.	1,200.
		Nos. 87-92 (5)	6,225.	4,600.

Wmk. "LA + F"

87a	A8	6c green	2,500.	2,000.
88a	A8	12c blue	450.00	400.00
89a	A8	25c red	950.00	350.00
90c	A8	50c yellow	4,000.	2,500.
92a	A8	100c gray lilac	3,600.	2,750.

The watermark "LA+F" stands for La Croix Frères, the paper manufacturers, and is in double-lined block capitals 13mm high. A single stamp will show only part of this watermark.

Values for Nos. 87-92a are for examples with visible perfs on all sides.

1872   **Unwmk.**   ***Imperf.***

93	A8	6c green	12.50	12.50
a.		Without moiré on back, without overprint	60.00	65.00
b.		Vertically laid paper	3,000.	1,300.
c.		Bottom label retouched	100.00	90.00
d.		Very thick paper	37.50	37.50
94	A8	12c blue	2.00	1.75
a.		Without moiré on back, without overprint	30.00	35.00
b.		Vertically laid paper	350.00	210.00
c.		Thin gray bl paper of 1867 (Wmk 151)		2,000.
95	A8	25c red	8.50	2.00
a.		Without moiré on back, without overprint	30.00	35.00
b.		Vertically laid paper	450.00	500.00
c.		Thin gray bl paper of 1867 (Wmk 151)		1,500.
96	A8	50c yellow	140.00	35.00
a.		50c orange	140.00	35.00
b.		Without moiré on back, without overprint	50.00	70.00
c.		Vertically laid paper		2,000.
d.		50c blue (error)		650.00
e.		As "d," without overprint	45.00	
f.		As "e," without moiré on back	65.00	
g.		Half used as 25c on cover		5,000.
98	A8	100c gray lilac	90.00	50.00
a.		100c lilac	100.00	42.50
b.		Without moiré on back, without overprint	50.00	110.00
c.		Vertically laid paper		1,250.
		Nos. 93-98 (5)	253.00	101.25

Counterfeits of these stamps are 24 ½mm high instead of 24mm. The printing is sharper and more uniform than the genuine. Forged district names and consignment numbers exist.

Pin-perf. and Serrate Perf.

99	A8	6c green	90.00	75.00
100	A8	12c blue	3.50	3.00
a.		Vertically laid paper		350.00
b.		Horiz. pair, imperf. vert.	100.00	100.00
c.		Vert. pair, imperf. between		150.00
101	A8	25c red	3.25	1.50
a.		Vertically laid paper		500.00
b.		Horiz. pair, imperf. vert.	100.00	100.00
102	A8	50c yellow	175.00	50.00
a.		50c orange	160.00	50.00
b.		50c blue (error)	475.00	500.00
c.		As "b," without overprint	45.00	
104	A8	100c lilac	150.00	80.00
a.		100c gray lilac	125.00	80.00
		Nos. 99-104 (5)	421.75	209.50

Values for Nos. 99-104a are for examples with visible perfs on all sides.

A9   A10

Hidalgo

A11   A12

A13   A14

Overprinted with District Name and Number and Date; also with Number and Date only Thick Wove Paper, Some Showing Vertical Ribbing

1874-80   **Unwmk.**   **Engr.**   ***Perf. 12***

105	A9	4c org ('80)	12.50	12.00
a.		Vert. pair, imperf. btwn.	60.00	
b.		Without overprint	6.50	12.50
c.		Half used as 2c on cover		1,000.
106	A10	5c brown	4.50	3.00
a.		Horizontally laid paper	100.00	55.00
b.		Imperf., pair	60.00	
c.		Horiz. pair, imperf. btwn.	50.00	300.00
d.		Vert. pair, imperf. btwn.	110.00	110.00
e.		Without overprint	37.50	37.50
f.		As "a," wmkd. "LACROIX"	1,750.	1,000.
107	A11	10c black	2.00	1.25
a.		Horizontally laid paper	2.50	2.50
b.		Horiz. pair, imperf. btwn.	75.00	75.00
c.		Without overprint	35.00	27.50
d.		Half used as 5c on cover		2,000.
e.		Imperf., pair		
f.		As "a," wmkd. "LACROIX"	350.00	250.00
108	A11	10c org ('78)	2.00	1.25
a.		10c yellow bister	7.50	4.25
b.		Imperf., pair		
c.		Without overprint	55.00	55.00
d.		Half used as 5c on cover		100.00
109	A12	25c blue	.85	.70
b.		Horizontally laid paper	2.25	1.75
c.		Imperf., pair	50.00	25.00
d.		Without overprint	35.00	20.00
e.		Horiz. pair, imperf. btwn.	125.00	
f.		As "b," horiz. pair, imperf. vert.		200.00
g.		As "b," wmkd. "LACROIX"	300.00	250.00
h.		Printed on both sides		1,500.
i.		Half used as 10c on cover		2,000.
110	A13	50c green	13.00	13.00
a.		Without overprint	50.00	
b.		Half used as 25c on cover		2,500.
111	A14	100c carmine	18.00	15.00
a.		Imperf., pair	200.00	200.00
b.		Without overprint	50.00	
c.		Quarter used as 25c on cover		3,000.
		Nos. 105-111 (7)	52.85	46.20

The "LACROIX" watermark is spelled out "LACROIX FRERES" in 2 lines of block capitals without serifs once to a sheet of horiz. laid paper. 6-12 stamps may have a portion of the wmk.

1875-77   **Wmk. 150**

112	A10	5c brown	110.00	70.00
113	A11	10c black	110.00	70.00
114	A12	25c blue	110.00	70.00
115	A13	50c green	650.00	450.00
116	A14	100c carmine	600.00	400.00
		Nos. 112-116 (5)	1,580.	1,060.

1881   **Unwmk.**   **Thin Wove Paper**

117	A9	4c orange	70.00	70.00
a.		Without overprint	20.00	20.00
118	A10	5c brown	10.00	6.50
a.		Without overprint	.50	20.00
b.		As "a," vert. pair, imperf. horiz.	1,000.	
119	A11	10c orange	6.00	3.50
a.		Imperf., pair		
b.		Vert. pair, imperf. horiz.		
c.		Without overprint	.75	4.50
d.		Vert. pair, imperf. btwn.		
e.		Half used as 5c on cover		1,500.
120	A12	25c blue	4.00	2.25
a.		Imperf., pair	100.00	
b.		Without overprint	.50	8.00
c.		Double impression		65.00
d.		Printed on both sides		1,500.

121	A13	50c green	45.00	40.00
a.		Without overprint	4.00	30.00
122	A14	100c carmine	50.00	50.00
a.		Without overprint	6.00	300.00

The stamps of 1874-81 are found with number and date wide apart, close together or omitted, and in various colors.

The thin paper is fragile and easily damaged. Values for Nos. 117-122 are for undamaged, fine examples.

Benito Juárez — A15

Overprinted with District Name and Number and Date; also with Number and Date only Thick Wove Paper, Some Showing Vertical Ribbing

1879   ***Perf. 12***

123	A15	1c brown	4.00	4.00
a.		Without overprint	75.00	140.00
b.		1c gray	20.00	15.00
124	A15	2c dk violet	4.00	4.50
a.		Without overprint	75.00	150.00
b.		Printed on both sides		
c.		2c dark gray	20.00	14.00
125	A15	5c orange	2.25	1.50
a.		Without overprint	75.00	90.00
b.		Double impression		500.00
126	A15	10c blue	3.00	2.50
a.		Without overprint	75.00	150.00
b.		10c ultra	160.00	160.00
127	A15	25c rose	8.00	30.00
a.		Without overprint	1.75	150.00
128	A15	50c green	15.00	50.00
a.		Without overprint	1.25	150.00
b.		Printed on both sides		165.00
129	A15	85c violet	20.00	250.00
a.		Without overprint	2.50	
130	A15	100c black	25.00	75.00
a.		Without overprint	3.00	150.00
		Nos. 123-130 (8)	81.25	417.50

Used values for Nos. 127-130 are for stamps with postal cancellations. Pen cancelled examples are worth the same as unused stamps.

Forged cancellations on Nos. 127-130 are plentiful.

1882   **Thin Wove Paper**

131	A15	1c brown	40.00	37.50
a.		Without overprint	125.00	
132	A15	2c dk violet	27.50	24.00
a.		2c slate	47.50	50.00
b.		Without overprint	110.00	
c.		Half used as 1c on cover		
133	A15	5c orange	9.00	6.00
a.		Without overprint	1.25	
b.		Half used as 2c on cover		
c.		As "a," vert. pair, imperf. btwn.		
134	A15	10c blue	9.00	6.00
a.		Without overprint	1.25	
b.		Half used as 5c on cover		
135	A15	10c brown	9.00	
a.		Imperf., pair	3.00	
136	A15	12c brown	7.50	8.00
a.		Without overprint	2.50	22.50
b.		Imperf., pair	75.00	
c.		Half used as 6c on cover		
137	A15	18c orange brn	9.00	15.00
a.		Horiz. pair, imperf. btwn.	100.00	
b.		Without overprint	2.25	18.00
138	A15	24c violet	9.00	11.00
a.		Without overprint	2.25	17.50
139	A15	25c rose	45.00	250.00
a.		Without overprint	4.50	
140	A15	25c orange brn	5.50	
141	A15	50c green	45.00	75.00
a.		Without overprint	6.25	
142	A15	50c yellow	80.00	350.00
a.		Without overprint	150.00	
143	A15	85c red violet	55.00	
144	A15	100c black	75.00	250.00
a.		Without overprint	5.00	
b.		Vert. pair, imperf. btwn.	165.00	165.00
145	A15	100c orange	95.00	400.00
a.		Without overprint	150.00	
		Nos. 131-145 (15)	520.50	1,432.

No. 135, 140 and 143 exist only without overprint. They were never placed in use.

Used values for Nos. 139, 141, 142, 144 and 145 are for postally used stamps. Forged cancellations are plentiful. Pen cancelled examples are worth the same as unused stamps.

See note on thin paper after No. 122.

A16

Overprinted with District Name, Number and Abbreviated Date

1882-83

146 A16	2c green	11.00	8.00
a.	Without overprint	27.50	20.00
147 A16	3c car lake	11.00	8.00
a.	Without overprint	5.25	8.50
148 A16	6c blue ('83)	30.00	40.00
a.	Without overprint	30.00	50.00
149 A16	6c ultra	6.00	8.50
a.	Without overprint	3.50	6.00
b.	As "a," imperf pair	50.00	
	Nos. 146-149 (4)	58.00	64.50

See note on thin paper after No. 122.

Hidalgo — A17

1884 Wove or Laid Paper   Perf. 12

150 A17	1c green	4.00	.75
a.	Imperf., pair	125.00	
b.	1c blue (error)	600.00	475.00
151 A17	2c green	6.75	2.00
a.	Imperf., pair	200.00	225.00
b.	Half used as 1c on cover		
152 A17	3c green	12.50	2.00
a.	Imperf., pair	200.00	250.00
b.	Horiz. pair, imperf. vert.	225.00	250.00
153 A17	4c green	16.00	2.00
a.	Imperf., pair	200.00	250.00
b.	Half used as 2c on cover		400.00
c.	Horiz. pair, imperf. btwn.	200.00	250.00
154 A17	5c green	17.50	1.50
a.	Imperf., pair	200.00	
c.	Horiz. pair, imperf. btwn.		250.00
d.	Vert. pair, imperf. btwn.		275.00
155 A17	6c green	15.00	1.50
a.	Imperf., pair	200.00	250.00
156 A17	10c green	16.00	.75
a.	Imperf., pair	125.00	150.00
157 A17	12c green	30.00	3.50
a.	Vert. pair, imperf. between	250.00	350.00
b.	Half used as 6c on cover		300.00
158 A17	20c green	90.00	2.50
a.	Diagonal half used as 10c on cover		300.00
b.	Imperf., pair	350.00	350.00
159 A17	25c green	150.00	5.00
a.	Imperf., pair	300.00	300.00
160 A17	50c green	.60	5.00
a.	Imperf., pair	150.00	150.00
b.	Horiz. pair, imperf. btwn.	300.00	
c.	Double impression	200.00	200.00
161 A17	1p blue	.60	11.00
a.	Imperf., pair	250.00	250.00
b.	Vert. pair, imperf. between	100.00	
c.	1p with 1c printed on back	300.00	
d.	Horiz. pair, imperf. btwn.	250.00	
162 A17	2p blue	.60	22.50
a.	Imperf., pair	175.00	200.00
163 A17	5p blue	350.00	300.00
164 A17	10p blue	500.00	225.00
	Nos. 150-162 (13)	359.55	60.00

Imperforate varieties should be purchased in pairs or larger. Single imperforates are usually trimmed perforated stamps.

Beware of examples of No. 150 that have been chemically changed to resemble No. 150b.

Bisects were not officially authorized. Nos. 155 and 160 exist as bisects on piece.

Forged cancels on Nos. 161-162 are plentiful.

Some values exist perf. 11.
See Nos. 165-173, 230-231.

1885

165 A17	1c pale green	35.00	7.00
166 A17	2c carmine	25.00	3.50
a.	Diagonal half used as 1c on cover		350.00
167 A17	3c orange brn	25.00	6.00
a.	Imperf., pair	250.00	250.00
b.	Horiz. pair, imperf. btwn.		300.00
168 A17	4c red orange	42.50	19.00
169 A17	5c ultra	27.50	3.50
170 A17	6c dk brown	32.50	6.00
a.	Half used as 3c on cover		350.00
171 A17	10c orange	27.50	1.50
a.	10c yellow	30.00	1.50
b.	Horiz. pair, imperf. btwn.	250.00	250.00
c.	Imperf., pair	300.00	
172 A17	12c olive brn	57.50	9.00
a.	Printed on both sides	300.00	
173 A17	25c grnsh blue	225.00	22.50
	Nos. 165-173 (9)	497.50	78.00

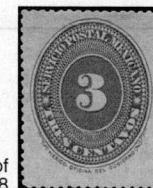

Numeral of
Value — A18

1886   Perf. 12

174 A18	1c yellow green	2.25	.75
a.	1c blue grn	5.50	4.50
b.	Horiz. pair, imperf. btwn.	200.00	200.00
c.	Perf. 11	45.00	45.00
175 A18	2c carmine	2.60	.90
a.	Horiz. pair, imperf. btwn.	80.00	75.00
b.	Vert. pair, imperf. between	200.00	200.00
c.	Perf. 11	45.00	45.00
d.	Half used as 1c on cover		100.00
176 A18	3c lilac	12.00	7.50
177 A18	4c lilac	18.00	5.25
a.	Perf. 11	50.00	55.00
b.	Horiz. pair, imperf. btwn.	450.00	
178 A18	5c ultra	2.25	1.00
a.	5c lilac	2.25	.75
179 A18	6c lilac	30.00	7.50
180 A18	10c lilac	22.50	1.10
a.	Perf. 11		125.00
181 A18	12c lilac	25.00	14.00
182 A18	20c lilac	190.00	110.00
183 A18	25c lilac	75.00	19.00
	Nos. 174-183 (10)	379.60	167.00

Nos. 175, 191, 194B, 196, 202 exist with blue or black surcharge "Vale 1 Cvo." These were made by the Colima postmaster.

1887

184 A18	3c scarlet	1.90	.60
a.	Imperf., pair	75.00	
185 A18	4c scarlet	7.50	2.25
a.	Imperf., pair	500.00	
b.	Horiz. pair, imperf. btwn.	400.00	
186 A18	6c scarlet	12.50	2.25
a.	Horiz. pair, imperf. btwn.	200.00	
187 A18	10c scarlet	2.75	.60
a.	Imperf., pair	75.00	
b.	Horiz. pair, imperf. btwn.	200.00	
188 A18	20c scarlet	18.00	1.50
a.	Horiz. pair, imperf. btwn.	275.00	
b.	Vert. pair, imperf. btwn.	350.00	
189 A18	25c scarlet	15.00	4.00
	Nos. 184-189 (6)	57.65	11.20

Perf. 6

190 A18	1c blue grn	45.00	45.00
191 A18	2c brown car	22.50	42.00
192 A18	5c ultra	15.00	4.50
a.	5c blue	15.00	4.50
193 A18	10c lilac	15.00	4.25
193A A18	10c brown lilac	15.00	3.00
194 A18	10c scarlet	35.00	15.00

Perf. 6x12

194A A18	1c blue grn	62.50	42.50
194B A18	2c brown car	85.00	75.00
194C A18	3c scarlet	300.00	350.00
194D A18	5c ultra	60.00	45.00
194E A18	10c lilac	90.00	75.00
194F A18	10c scarlet	80.00	60.00
194G A18	10c brown lilac	90.00	75.00

Many shades exist.

Paper with colored ruled lines on face or reverse of stamp

1887   Perf. 12

195 A18	1c green	75.00	45.00
196 A18	2c brown car	190.00	47.50
198 A18	5c ultra	110.00	30.00
199 A18	10c scarlet	110.00	25.00

Perf. 6

201 A18	1c green	60.00	20.00
202 A18	2c brown car	60.00	24.00
204 A18	5c ultra	50.00	12.00
205 A18	10c brown lil	42.50	10.00
206 A18	10c scarlet	250.00	40.00
	Nos. 201-206 (5)	462.50	106.00

Perf. 6x12

207 A18	1c green	225.00	140.00
208 A18	2c brown car	325.00	140.00
209 A18	5c ultra	225.00	140.00
210 A18	10c brown lil	290.00	135.00
211 A18	10c scarlet	350.00	225.00
	Nos. 207-211 (5)	1,415.	780.00

1890-95   Wmk. 152   Perf. 11 & 12
Wove or Laid Paper

212 A18	1c yellow grn	.75	.35
a.	1c blue green	.75	.35
b.	Horiz. pair, imperf. btwn.	125.00	125.00
c.	Laid paper	2.50	2.50
d.	Horiz. pair, imperf. vert.	125.00	125.00
213 A18	2c carmine	1.50	.75
a.	2c brown car	1.25	1.00
b.	Vert. pair, imperf. btwn.	150.00	
c.	Imperf., pair	200.00	
214 A18	3c vermilion	1.00	.60
b.	Horiz. pair, imperf. btwn.	200.00	
215 A18	4c vermilion	3.25	2.10
a.	Horiz. pair, imperf. btwn.	200.00	
216 A18	5c ultra	.60	.50
a.	5c dull blue	1.00	.50
217 A18	6c vermilion	3.75	2.75
a.	Horiz. pair, imperf. btwn.	300.00	
218 A18	10c vermilion	.50	.35
b.	Horiz. or vert. pair, imperf. btwn.	175.00	175.00
c.	Horiz. pair, imperf. horiz.	175.00	
d.	Imperf., pair	200.00	
219 A18	12c ver ('95)	14.00	18.00
a.	Horiz. pair, imperf. btwn.	450.00	
220 A18	20c vermillion	3.50	1.50
220A A18	20c dk violet	160.00	190.00
221 A18	25c vermilion	5.00	2.50
	Nos. 212-220,221 (10)	33.85	29.40

No. 219 has been reprinted in slightly darker shade than the original.

1892

222 A18	3c orange	4.00	2.00
223 A18	4c orange	4.25	3.00
224 A18	6c orange	5.75	2.00
225 A18	10c orange	27.50	2.00
226 A18	20c orange	50.00	6.00
227 A18	25c orange	16.00	4.50
	Nos. 222-227 (6)	107.50	19.50

1892

228 A18	5p carmine	1,250.	900.
229 A18	10p carmine	1,900.	1,250.
230 A17	5p blue green	3,500.	1,200.
231 A17	10p blue green	7,000.	2,700.

1894   Perf. 5½, 6

232 A18	1c yellow grn	3.00	3.00
233 A18	3c vermilion	9.00	9.00
234 A18	4c vermilion	40.00	37.50
235 A18	5c ultra	12.50	5.00
236 A18	10c vermilion	7.50	3.00
236A A18	20c vermilion	110.00	110.00
237 A18	25c vermilion	62.50	62.50
	Nos. 232-237 (7)	244.50	230.00

Perf. 5½x11, 11x5½, Compound and Irregular

238 A18	1c yellow grn	7.00	7.00
238A A18	2c brown car	16.00	16.00
238B A18	3c vermilion	47.50	32.50
238C A18	4c vermilion	55.00	55.00
239 A18	5c ultra	17.50	12.50
a.	5c blue	12.50	12.50
239C A18	6c vermilion	75.00	75.00
240 A18	10c vermilion	20.00	7.00
240A A18	20c vermilion	200.00	200.00
241 A18	25c vermilion	62.50	62.50
	Nos. 238-241 (9)	500.50	467.50

The stamps of the 1890 to 1895 issues are also to be found unwatermarked, as part of the sheet frequently escaped the watermark.

Letter
Carrier — A20

Mounted
Courier with
Pack
Mule — A21

Statue of
Cuauhtémoc
A22

Mail Coach
A23

Mail Train — A24

1895   Regular or Pin Perf. 12   Wmk. 152
Wove or Laid Paper

242 A20	1c green	3.00	.75
a.	Vert. pair, imperf. horiz.	175.00	
d.	Watermarked sideway ('97)	125.00	15.00
243 A20	2c carmine	3.75	1.00
a.	Half used as 1c on cover		250.00
c.	Watermarked sideways ('97)	80.00	10.00
244 A20	3c orange brown	3.75	1.00
a.	Vert. pair, imperf. horiz.		250.00
d.	Watermarked sideways ('97)	125.00	10.00
e.	Horiz. or vert. pair, imperf. between		300.00
246 A21	4c orange	12.50	1.50
a.	4c orange red	7.50	1.25
247 A22	5c ultra	7.00	.35
a.	Imperf., pair	175.00	200.00
b.	Horiz. or vert. pair, imperf. between	175.00	200.00
e.	Half used as 2c on cover		400.00
f.	Watermarked sideways ('97)	15.00	5.00
248 A23	10c lilac rose	4.50	1.00
a.	Horiz. or vert. pair, imperf. between		250.00
b.	Half used as 5c on cover		250.00
249 A21	12c olive brown	50.00	12.50
251 A23	15c brt blue	27.50	3.00
b.	Watermarked sideways		100.00
c.	Imperf., pair		300.00
252 A23	20c brown rose	32.50	3.00
b.	Half used as 10c on cover		200.00
c.	Watermarked sideways ('97)	1,000.	750.00
253 A23	50c purple	70.00	16.00
254 A24	1p brown	90.00	35.00
a.	Watermarked sideways ('97)	750.00	900.00
255 A24	5p scarlet	300.00	190.00
256 A24	10p deep blue	650.00	350.00
	Nos. 242-256 (13)	1,254.	615.10

No. 248 exists in perf. 11.

Nos. 242d, 243c, 244d, 247f, 251b, 252c and 254a was a special printing, made in Jan. 1897. The watermark is sideways, the grain of the paper is horizontal (rather than vertical, as appears on Nos. 242-256), and the design is somewhat shorter than the other stamps in this series. The sideways orientation of the watermark is the most easily identifable feature of this printing.

Important: For unwatermarked examples of Nos. 242-256, see the footnote after No. 291.

Perf. 6

242b	A20	1c green	60.00	35.00
243b	A20	2c carmine	125.00	60.00
244b	A20	3c orange brown	90.00	50.00
247c	A22	5c ultra	90.00	50.00
248c	A23	10c lilac rose	125.00	55.00
249a	A21	12c olive brn	100.00	50.00

Perf. 6x12, 12x6 & Compound or Irregular

242c	A20	1c green	30.00	20.00
244c	A20	3c orange brown	35.00	20.00
246b	A21	4c orange	75.00	50.00
247d	A22	5c ultra	75.00	50.00
248d	A23	10c lilac rose	35.00	20.00
249b	A21	12c olive brown	50.00	25.00
251a	A23	15c brt blue	60.00	40.00
252a	A23	20c brown rose	100.00	70.00
253b	A23	50c purple	150.00	100.00

See Nos. 257-291. For overprints see Nos. O10-O48A.

"Irregular" Perfs.

Some stamps perf. 6x12, 12x6, 5½x11 and 11x5½ have both perf. 6 and 12 or perf. 5½ and 11 on one or more sides of the stamp. These are known as irregular perfs.

1896-97   Wmk. 153   Perf. 12

257	A20	1c green	14.00	1.25
c.		Imperf., pair		250.00
258	A20	2c carmine	17.50	1.50
a.		Horiz. pair, imperf. vert.		
259	A20	3c orange brn	20.00	1.50
c.		Horiz. pair, imperf. between		300.00
260	A21	4c orange	32.50	1.75
a.		4c deep orange	30.00	6.00
261	A22	5c ultra	9.00	1.25
a.		Imperf., pair	200.00	200.00
b.		Vert. pair, imperf. btwn.	200.00	
262	A21	12c olive brn	160.00	80.00
263	A23	15c brt blue	200.00	13.00
264	A23	20c brown rose	750.00	275.00
265	A23	50c purple	175.00	110.00
266	A24	1p brown	300.00	250.00
267	A24	5p scarlet	800.00	600.00
268	A24	10p dp blue	900.00	525.00
		Nos. 257-268 (12)	3,378.	1,860.

Perf. 6

257a	A20	1c green	35.00	25.00
259a	A20	3c orange brown	35.00	20.00
260a	A21	4c orange	40.00	25.00
261c	A22	5c ultra	110.00	70.00
263a	A23	15c bright blue	75.00	35.00

Perf. 6x12, 12x6 and Compound or Irregular

257b	A20	1c green	25.00	20.00
258b	A20	2c carmine	50.00	25.00
259b	A20	3c orange brown	40.00	20.00
260b	A21	4c orange	45.00	20.00
261d	A22	5c ultra	40.00	20.00
262a	A21	12c olive brown	125.00	80.00
263b	A23	15c bright blue	250.00	125.00
264a	A23	20c brown rose		
265a	A23	50c purple		

1897-98   Wmk. 154   Perf. 12

269	A20	1c green	20.00	3.00
270	A20	2c scarlet	35.00	4.50
c.		Horiz. pair, imperf. btwn.		250.00
271	A21	4c orange	52.50	3.75
a.		Horizontal pair, imperf. vertical	—	
272	A22	5c ultra	50.00	3.75
a.		Imperf., pair	85.00	
273	A21	12c olive brown	200.00	45.00
275	A23	15c brt blue	275.00	85.00
276	A23	20c brown rose	175.00	15.00
c.		Horiz. pair, imperf. btwn.		300.00
277	A23	50c purple	375.00	75.00
278	A24	1p brown	425.00	200.00
278A	A24	5p scarlet	—	4,000.
		Nos. 269-278 (9)	1,607.	435.00

Perf. 6

269a	A20	1c green	45.00	25.00
270a	A20	2c scarlet	45.00	25.00
272b	A22	5c ultra	60.00	25.00
273a	A21	12c olive brown	110.00	60.00
276a	A23	20c brown rose		650.00

Perf. 6x12, 12x6 and Compound or Irregular

269b	A20	1c green	25.00	15.00
270b	A20	2c scarlet	30.00	22.50
271b	A21	4c orange	65.00	12.50
272c	A22	5c ultra	50.00	15.00
273b	A21	12c olive brown	125.00	65.00
275a	A23	15c bright blue	125.00	65.00
276b	A23	20c brown rose	240.00	30.00
277a	A23	50c purple	125.00	50.00

1898   Unwmk.   Perf. 12

279	A20	1c green	3.00	.50
a.		Horiz. pair, imperf. vert	300.00	
b.		Imperf., pair	250.00	

280	A20	2c scarlet	6.25	.75
a.		2c green (error)	475.00	
281	A20	3c orange brn	6.00	.75
a.		Imperf., pair	250.00	250.00
b.		Pair, imperf. between	80.00	80.00
282	A21	4c orange	30.00	3.00
b.		4c deep orange	37.50	7.00
c.		Imperf., pair		300.00
283	A22	5c ultra	2.00	.50
a.		Imperf., pair	200.00	200.00
b.		Pair, imperf. between	200.00	
284	A23	10c lilac rose	550.00	175.00
285	A21	12c olive brn	80.00	27.50
a.		Imperf., pair	200.00	
286	A23	15c brt blue	175.00	8.00
287	A23	20c brown rose	35.00	3.00
a.		Imperf., pair	250.00	
288	A23	50c purple	150.00	42.50
289	A24	1p brown	175.00	80.00
290	A24	5p carmine rose	550.00	425.00
291	A24	10p deep blue	800.00	575.00
		Nos. 279-291 (13)	2,562.	1,341.

Warning: Sheets of Nos. 242-256 (watermarked "CORREOS E U M") have a column of stamps without watermarks, because the watermark did not fit the sheet size. As a result, be careful not to confuse unwatermarked examples of Nos. 242-256 with Nos. 279-291. This is especialy important for No. 284. Nos. 242-256 and the watermarked 1895-97 overprinted Officials, Nos. O10-O39, have a vertical grain or mesh to the paper. Nos. 279-291 and the unwatermarked 1898 overprinted Officials, Nos. O40-O48B, have a horizontal grain or mesh to the paper. Be careful not to confuse unwatermarked examples of Nos. O10-O39 with Nos. O40-O48B.

Perf. 6

279c	A20	1c green	85.00	35.00
280b	A20	2c scarlet	75.00	30.00
281c	A20	3c orange brown	50.00	35.00
283c	A22	5c ultra	65.00	30.00
287b	A23	20c brown rose	125.00	75.00
291a	A24	10p deep blue		

Perf. 6x12, 12x6 and Compound or Irregular

279d	A20	1c green	25.00	20.00
280c	A20	2c scarlet	25.00	20.00
281d	A20	3c orange brown	30.00	20.00
282a	A21	4c orange	40.00	25.00
283d	A22	5c ultra	20.00	10.00
284a	A23	10c lilac rose	125.00	85.00
285b	A21	12c olive brown	90.00	60.00
286a	A23	15c bright blue	75.00	50.00
287c	A23	20c brown rose	100.00	50.00
288a	A23	50c purple	575.00	575.00

Forgeries of the 6 and 6x12 perforations of 1895-98 are plentiful.

Coat of Arms
A25   A26

A27   A28

A29   A30

A31

Juanacatlán Falls — A32

View of Mt. Popocatépetl A33

Cathedral, Mexico, D. F. — A34

1899, Nov. 1   Wmk. 155   Perf. 14, 15

294	A25	1c green	1.90	.35
295	A26	2c vermilion	4.50	.35
296	A27	3c orange brn	3.00	.35
297	A28	5c dark blue	4.75	.35
298	A29	10c violet & org	6.00	.35
299	A30	15c lav & claret	8.00	.35
300	A31	20c rose & dk bl	9.00	.40
301	A32	50c red lil & blk	35.00	2.25
a.		50c lilac & black	42.50	2.25
302	A33	1p blue & blk	80.00	3.50
303	A34	5p carmine & blk	275.00	12.00
		Nos. 294-303 (10)	427.15	20.25
		Set, never hinged	1,500.	

See Nos. 304-305, 307-309. For overprints see Nos. 420-422, 439-450, 452-454, 482-483, 515-516, 539, 550, O49-O60, O62-O66, O68-O74, O101.

A35

1903

304	A25	1c violet	1.50	.35
305	A26	2c green	2.00	.35
306	A35	4c carmine	5.00	.45
307	A28	5c orange	1.25	.35
308	A29	10c blue & org	5.00	.35
309	A32	50c carmine & blk	75.00	6.50
		Nos. 304-309 (6)	89.75	8.35
		Set, never hinged	350.00	

For overprints see Nos. 451, O61, O67.

Independence Issue

Josefa Ortiz — A36   Leona Vicario — A37

López Rayón — A38   Juan Aldama — A39

Miguel Hidalgo — A40   Ignacio Allende — A41

Epigmenio González A42   Mariano Abasolo A43

Declaration of Independence A44

Mass on the Mount of Crosses A45

Capture of Granaditas A46

1910   Perf. 14

310	A36	1c dull violet	.35	.35
311	A37	2c green	.35	.35
312	A38	3c orange brn	.60	.35
313	A39	4c carmine	2.50	.45
314	A40	5c orange	.35	.35
315	A41	10c blue & org	1.50	.35
316	A42	15c gray bl & cl	8.00	.50
317	A43	20c red & bl	5.00	.40
318	A44	50c red brn & blk	12.00	1.60
319	A45	1p blue & blk	15.00	2.00
320	A46	5p car & blk	57.50	16.50
		Nos. 310-320 (11)	103.15	23.20
		Set, never hinged	325.00	

Independence of Mexico from Spain, cent. For overprints and surcharges see Nos. 370-380, 423-433, 455-465, 484-494, 517-538, 540-549, 551-558, 577-590, O75-O85, O102-O112, O191-O192, O195, RA13, Merida 1.

CIVIL WAR ISSUES

During the 1913-16 Civil War, provisional issues with various handstamped overprints were circulated in limited areas.

Sonora

A47

Seal

Typeset in a row of five varieties. Two impressions placed tête bêche (foot to foot) constitute a sheet. The settings show various wrong font and defective letters, "!" for "1" in "1913", etc. The paper occasionally has a manufacturer's watermark.

a   b   c   d

Four Types of the Numerals.
a — Wide, heavy-faced numerals.
b — Narrow Roman numerals.
c — Wide Roman numerals.
d — Gothic or sans-serif numerals.

Nos. 321-346 Issued Without Gum
Embossed "CONSTITUCIONAL"

1913   Typeset   Unwmk.   Perf. 12

321	A47(a)	5c blk & red	4,250.	800.00
a.		"CENTAVOB"	4,750.	850.00

Colorless Roulette

322	A47(b)	1c blk & red	22.00	25.00
a.		With green seal	1,500.	250.00

323	A47(a)	2c blk & red	18.00	15.00
a.	With green seal		2,000.	2,000.
324	A47(c)	2c blk & red	87.50	72.50
a.	With green seal		5,000.	5,000.
325	A47(a)	3c blk & red	97.50	77.50
a.	With green seal		750.00	750.00
326	A47(a)	5c blk & red	190.00	77.50
a.	"CENTAVOB"		200.00	50.00
327	A47(a)	5c blk & red	1,200.	350.00
a.	With green seal			1,000.
328	A47(b)	10c blk & red	35.00	37.50

Black Roulette

329	A47(d)	5c blk & red	300.00	140.00
a.	"MARO"		87.50	52.50

Stamps are known with the embossing double or omitted.

The varieties with green seal are from a few sheets embossed "Constitucional" which were in stock at the time the green seal control was adopted.

Nos. 322-329 are known with papermakers' watermark ("Peerless Mills" or "Yukon Aurora").

No. 339

Without Embossing
With Green Seal
Colorless Roulette

336	A47(b)	1c blk & red	15.00	10.00
337	A47(a)	3c blk & red	14.50	9.00
a.	Imperf.		350.00	
338	A47(a)	5c blk & red	750.00	250.00
a.	"CENTAVOB"		800.00	275.00
339	A47(b)	10c blk & red	8.00	7.50

Colored Roulette

340	A47(d)	5c brnsh blk & red	25.00	6.00
a.	5c lilac brown & red		75.00	22.50
b.	Double seal			1,250.
c.	Red printing omitted			1,000.

Nos. 336-340 are known with papermaker's watermark ("Peerless Mills" or "Yukon Aurora").

1913-14   *Black Roulette*
With Green Seal

341	A47(a)	1c black & red	4.00	4.00
b.	"erano" ('14)		100.00	60.00
342	A47(d)	2c black & red	4.50	4.00
a.	"erano" ('14)		30.00	35.00
343	A47(a)	3c black & red	4.75	4.00
a.	"CENTAVO"		25.00	25.00
b.	"erano" ('14)		35.00	35.00
344	A47(d)	5c black & red	4.75	4.00
b.	Heavy black penetrating roulette		2.75	1.75
c.	As "b," "MARO"		10.50	5.00
d.	Without green seal		2,250.	
	Nos. 341-344 (4)		18.00	16.00

Stamps without seal are unfinished remainders.

On Nos. 341-344 the rouletting cuts the paper slightly or not at all. On Nos. 344b-344c the rouletting is heavy, cutting deeply into the paper.

1914

345	A47(a)	5c black & red	5.00	5.00
346	A47(b)	10c black & red	4.25	5.00

Coat of Arms — A49

Revenue Stamps Used for Postage

1913		Litho.	*Rouletted 14, 14x7*	
347	A49	1c yellow grn	2.00	2.50
a.	With coupon		7.00	6.00
348	A49	2c violet	3.50	4.00
a.	With coupon		17.50	14.50
349	A49	5c brown	.60	.75
a.	With coupon		2.00	1.50
350	A49	10c claret	2.50	3.50
a.	With coupon		15.00	12.00
351	A49	20c gray grn	3.00	3.50
a.	With coupon		20.00	18.00
352	A49	50c ultra	11.00	16.00
a.	With coupon		60.00	47.50

353	A49	1p orange	45.00	55.00
a.	With coupon		175.00	120.00
	Nos. 347-353 (7)		67.60	85.25
	Set, never hinged		275.00	

For a short time these stamps (called "Ejercitos") were used for postage with coupon attached. Later this was required to be removed unless they were to be used for revenue. Stamps overprinted with district names are revenues. Values above 1p were used for revenue. Imperfs exist of all values, but were not issued.

Many examples do not have gum because of a flood.

Use of typeset Sonora revenue stamps for postage was not authorized or allowed.

Coat of Arms
A50   A51

5c (A50): "CINCO CENTAVOS"
14x2mm

1914			*Rouletted 9½x14*	
354	A50	1c deep blue	.45	.45
355	A50	2c yellow grn	.60	.35
a.	2c green		3.00	1.75
356	A50	4c blue vlo	11.00	2.50
a.	Horiz. pair, imperf. btwn.		250.00	
357	A50	5c gray grn	11.00	3.00
a.	Horiz. pair imperf. btwn.		250.00	
358	A50	10c red	.45	.45
359	A50	20c yellow brn	.60	.60
a.	20c deep brown		2.25	2.25
b.	Horiz. pair, imperf. btwn.		250.00	
360	A50	50c claret	2.50	3.50
a.	Horiz. pair, imperf. btwn.		250.00	
361	A50	1p brt violet	14.00	16.00
a.	Horiz. pair, imperf. btwn.		250.00	
	Nos. 354-361 (8)		40.60	26.85
	Set, never hinged		175.00	

Nos. 354-361 (called "Transitorios") exist imperf. but were not regularly used.

Many examples do not have gum because of a flood.

See Note after No. 465.
See No. 369. For overprints see Nos. 362-368, 559-565.

Overprinted in Black

1914

362	A50	1c deep blue	200.00	175.00
a.	"1912" for "1914"		2,000.	
363	A50	2c yellow green	225.00	200.00
364	A50	4c blue violet	250.00	300.00
365	A50	5c gray green	35.00	50.00
a.	Horiz. pair, imperf. btwn.		550.00	
366	A50	10c red	150.00	150.00
a.	"1912" for "1914"		2,000.	
367	A50	20c yellow brn	2,500.	2,500.
a.	"1912" for "1914"		7,000.	
368	A50	50c claret	3,500.	3,500.

Values are for stamps with design close to, or just touching, the perfs.

Excellent counterfeits of this overprint exist.

Redrawn
"CINCO CENTAVOS" 16x2½mm

1914			*Perf. 12*	
369	A51	5c gray green	1.00	.35

Imperfs are printers' waste.

Regular Issue of 1910 Overprinted in Violet, Magenta, Black or Green

1914			Wmk. 155	*Perf. 14*	
370	A36	1c dull violet	1.50	.60
371	A37	2c green	3.00	1.25
372	A38	3c orange brn	3.00	1.25
373	A39	4c carmine	5.00	2.00
374	A40	5c orange	1.00	.35
375	A41	10c blue & org	6.00	2.00
376	A42	15c gray bl & cl	10.00	3.00
377	A43	20c red & blue	20.00	6.00
378	A44	50c red brn & blk	25.00	8.00

379	A45	1p blue & blk	55.00	11.00
380	A46	5p carmine & blk	190.00	160.00
	Nos. 370-380 (11)		319.50	195.45
	Set, never hinged		1,000.	

Overprinted On Postage Due Stamps of 1908

381	D1	1c blue	27.50	30.00
382	D1	2c blue	27.50	30.00
383	D1	4c blue	27.50	30.00
384	D1	5c blue	27.50	30.00
385	D1	10c blue	27.50	30.00
	Nos. 381-385 (5)		137.50	150.00
	Set, never hinged		375.00	

This overprint is found double, inverted, sideways and in pairs with and without the overprint.

There are two or more types of this overprint.

The Postage Due Stamps and similar groups of them which follow were issued and used as regular postage stamps.

Values are for stamps where the overprint is clear enough to be expertised.

Counterfeits abound.

A52

1914		Unwmk.	Litho.	*Perf. 12*	
386	A52	1c pale blue	.35	.50
387	A52	2c light green	.35	.45
388	A52	3c orange	.50	.50
389	A52	5c deep rose	.50	.35
390	A52	10c rose	.70	.85
391	A52	15c rose lilac	1.20	1.75
392	A52	50c yellow	2.00	2.50
a.	50c ocher		1.75	
393	A52	1p violet	8.50	12.00
	Nos. 386-393 (8)		14.10	18.90
	Set, never hinged		100.00	

Nos. 386-393, are known imperforate.

This set is usually called the Denver Issue because it was printed there.

See Note after No. 465.

For overprints and surcharges see Nos. 566-573, 591-592.

A53

Revenue Stamps Used for Postage

1914, July			*Perf. 12*	
393A	A53	1c rose		40.00
393B	A53	2c lt green		35.00
393C	A53	3c lt orange		75.00
393D	A53	5c red		15.00
393E	A53	10c gray green		70.00
393F	A53	25c blue		150.00
	Nos. 393A-393F (6)			385.00

Nos. 393A-393F were used in the northeast. Values are for examples with postal cancellations.

Unused examples are to be considered as revenues.

Pres. Madero

Stamps in this design, featuring Pres. Madero, within a frame very similar to that of the Denver Issue (Nos. 386-393), were ordered in 1915 by Francisco Villa, to be used by the Constitutionalist government. Five values (1c green, 2c brown, 3c carmine, 5c blue, and 10c yellow) were printed by Ellis Brothers & Co., El Paso, Texas. By the time of the stamps' arrival in Mexico City, the Constitutionalist regime had fallen, and the new Conventionist government returned them to the printer, who later sold the unissued stamps within the philatelic market. Value, set $10.

Background as A55 — A54

Nos. 394-413 Issued Without Gum
1914   *Imperf.*
Values and Inscriptions in Black
Inscribed "SONORA"

394	A54	1c blue & red	.35	.35
a.	Double seal			
b.	Without seal		20.00	
395	A54	2c green & org	.35	.35
a.	Without seal		100.00	
396	A54	5c yellow & grn	.35	.35
a.	5c orange & green		1.50	1.25
b.	Without seal			300.00
397	A54	10c lt bl & red	3.50	1.75
a.	10c blue & red		40.00	15.00
398	A54	20c yellow & grn	1.75	2.00
399	A54	20c orange & bl	15.00	17.50
400	A54	50c green & org	1.25	1.25
	Nos. 394-400 (7)		22.55	23.55

Shades. Stamps of type A54 are usually termed the "Coach Seal Issue."

Inscribed "DISTRITO SUR DE LA BAJA CAL"

401	A54	1c yellow & blue	2.00	30.00
a.	Without seal		50.00	
402	A54	2c gray & ol grn	2.50	25.00
a.	Without seal		50.00	
403	A54	5c olive & rose	2.00	20.00
a.	Without seal		50.00	
404	A54	10c pale red & dl vio	2.00	20.00
a.	Without seal		50.00	
	Nos. 401-404 (4)		8.50	95.00

Counterfeit cancellations exist.

A55

Inscribed "SONORA"

405	A55	1c blue & red	6.00	
a.	Without seal		50.00	
406	A55	2c green & org	.50	
407	A55	5c yellow & grn	.50	2.50
a.	Without seal		75.00	
408	A55	10c blue & red	.50	2.50
409	A55	20c yellow & grn	75.00	15.00
a.	Without seal		95.00	
b.	Double seal		80.00	
	Nos. 405-409 (5)		82.50	20.00

With "PLATA" added to the inscription

410	A55	1c blue & red	1.00	
a.	"PLATA" inverted		60.00	
b.	Pair, one without "PLATA"		15.00	
411	A55	10c blue & red	1.00	
412	A55	20c yellow & grn	2.50	
a.	"PLATA" double		50.00	
413	A55	5c gray grn & org	1.75	
a.	Without seal		1.00	
b.	As "a," "P" of "PLATA" missing		150.00	
	Nos. 410-413 (4)		6.25	

Stamps of type A55 are termed the "Anvil Seal Issue".

Nos. 410-413 were not placed in use.

Oaxaca

Coat of Arms — A56

5c:
Type I — Thick numerals, 2mm wide.
Type II — Thin numerals, 1½mm wide.

1915		Typo.		Unwmk.	
			Perf. 8½ to 14		
414	A56	1c dull violet	2.00	1.25
415	A56	2c emerald	3.00	2.25
a.	Inverted numeral		30.00	
e.	Numeral omitted		35.00	
416	A56	3c red brown	4.00	3.50
b.	Inverted numeral		30.00	
417	A56	5c org (type I)	77.50	77.50
a.	Tête bêche pair		175.00	175.00

418	A56	5c org (type II)	.50	.75
a.		Types I and II in pair	70.00	
419	A56	10c blue & car	4.00	4.00
		Nos. 414-419 (6)	91.00	89.25
		Set, never hinged	275.00	

Many printing errors, imperfs and part perfs exist. Mostly these are printers' waste, private reprints or counterfeits.

Nos. 414-419 printed on backs of post office receipt forms.

Regular Issues of 1899-1910 Overprinted in Black

1914		Wmk. 155		Perf. 14

On Issues of 1899-1903

420	A28	5c orange		
421	A30	15c lav & claret	250.00	250.00
		Never hinged	700.00	
422	A31	20c rose & dk bl	1,000.	500.00

Counterfeits exist.
The listing of No. 420 is being re-evaluated. The Catalogue Editors would appreciate any information on the stamp.

On Issue of 1910

423	A36	1c dull violet	.35	.35
424	A37	2c green	.35	.35
425	A38	3c orange brown	.40	.40
426	A39	4c carmine	.50	.50
427	A40	5c orange	.35	.35
428	A41	10c blue & orange	.35	.35
429	A42	15c gray bl & claret	.70	.60
430	A43	20c red & blue	.75	.70

Overprinted

431	A44	50c red brn & blk	1.75	1.50
432	A45	1p blue & blk	4.00	4.50
433	A46	5p carmine & blk	42.50	32.50
		Nos. 423-433 (11)	56.00	43.10
		Set, never hinged	170.00	

In the first setting of the overprint on 1c to 20c, the variety "GONSTITUCIONALISTA" occurs 4 times in each sheet of 100. In the second setting it occurs on the last stamp in each row of 10.

The overprint exists reading downward on Nos. 423-430; inverted on Nos. 431-433; double on Nos. 423-425, 427.

See Note after No. 465.

For overprints see Nos. 528-538.

Postage Due Stamps of 1908 Overprinted

434	D1	1c blue	4.75	5.00
435	D1	2c blue	6.00	5.00
436	D1	4c blue	25.00	25.00
437	D1	5c blue	25.00	25.00
438	D1	10c blue	5.50	5.00
a.		Double overprint		
		Nos. 434-438 (5)	66.25	65.00
		Set, never hinged	200.00	

Preceding Issues Overprinted

This is usually called the "Villa" monogram. Counterfeits abound.

1915		On Issue of 1899

439	A25	1c green	210.00	
440	A26	2c vermilion	210.00	
441	A27	3c orange brn	175.00	
442	A28	5c dark blue	210.00	
443	A29	10c violet & org	210.00	
444	A30	15c lav & claret	750.00	750.00
445	A31	20c rose & bl	1,000.	—
446	A32	50c red lil & blk	500.00	—

447	A33	1p blue & blk	500.00	—
448	A34	5p car & blk	750.00	—
		Nos. 439-448 (10)	4,515.	

On Issue of 1903

449	A25	1c violet	200.00	
450	A26	2c green	200.00	
451	A35	4c carmine	200.00	
452	A28	5c orange	45.00	
a.		Inverted overprint	75.00	
453	A29	10c blue & org	750.00	—
454	A32	50c car & blk		—
		Nos. 449-453 (5)	1,395.	

In Sept. 1915 Postmaster Hinojosa ordered a special printing of Nos. 439-454 (as valued) for sale to collectors. Earlier a small quantity of Nos. 444-445, 448 and 452-454 was regularly issued. They are hard to distinguish and sell for much more. Counterfeits abound.

On Issue of 1910

455	A36	1c dull violet	.85	1.00
456	A37	2c green	.40	.60
457	A38	3c orange brown	.60	.75
458	A39	4c carmine	4.00	4.50
459	A40	5c orange	.35	.35
460	A41	10c blue & orange	7.00	7.50
461	A42	15c gray bl & cl	3.00	4.00
462	A43	20c red & blue	5.50	7.00
463	A44	50c red brn & blk	13.00	14.00
464	A45	1p blue & blk	17.00	20.00
465	A46	5p carmine & blk	150.00	
		Nos. 455-464 (10)	51.70	59.70
		Nos. 455-464, never hinged 175.00		

Nos. 455-465 are known with overprint inverted, double and other variations. Most were ordered by Postmaster General Hinojosa for philatelic purposes. They were sold at a premium. This applies to Nos. 354-361, 386-393, 431-433 with this monogram as well.

Overprinted On Postage Due Stamps of 1908

466	D1	1c blue	15.00	20.00
467	D1	2c blue	15.00	20.00
468	D1	4c blue	15.00	20.00
469	D1	5c blue	15.00	20.00
470	D1	10c blue	15.00	20.00
		Nos. 466-470 (5)	75.00	100.00
		Set, never hinged	225.00	

Nos. 466 to 470 are known with inverted overprint. All other values of the 1899 and 1903 issues exist with this overprint. See note after No. 465.

Issues of 1899-1910 Overprinted

This is called the "Carranza" or small monogram. Counterfeits abound.

On Issues of 1899-1903

482	A28	5c orange	40.00	20.00
		Never hinged	125.00	
483	A30	15c lav & claret	200.00	80.00
		Never hinged	650.00	

On Issue of 1910

484	A36	1c dull violet	.70	.70
485	A37	2c green	.70	.60
486	A38	3c orange brn	.75	.75
487	A39	4c carmine	2.00	2.00
488	A40	5c orange	.35	.35
489	A41	10c blue & org	1.50	1.50
a.		Double ovpt., one invtd.	25.00	
490	A42	15c gray bl & cl	1.50	1.50
491	A43	20c red & blue	1.50	1.50
492	A44	50c red brn & blk	10.00	10.00
493	A45	1p blue & blk	15.00	15.00
494	A46	5p car & blk	150.00	150.00
		Nos. 484-494 (11)	184.00	183.90
		Set, never hinged	550.00	

All values exist with inverted overprint; all but 5p with double overprint.

Overprinted On Postage Due Stamps of 1908

495	D1	1c blue	22.00	25.00
496	D1	2c blue	22.00	25.00
497	D1	4c blue	22.00	25.00
498	D1	5c blue	22.00	25.00
499	D1	10c blue	22.00	25.00
		Nos. 495-499 (5)	110.00	125.00
		Set, never hinged	325.00	

Nos. 495-499 exist with inverted overprint.

It is stated that, in parts of Mexico occupied by the revolutionary forces, instructions were given to apply a distinguishing overprint to all stamps found in the post offices. This overprint was usually some arrangement or abbreviation of "Gobierno Constitucionalista". Such overprints as were specially authorized or were in general use in large sections of the country are listed. Numerous other handstamped overprints were used in one town or

locality. They were essentially military faction control marks necessitated in most instances by the chaotic situation following the split between Villa and Carranza. The fact that some were often struck in a variety of colors and positions suggests the influence of philatelists.

Coat of Arms
A57

Statue of Cuauhtémoc
A58

Ignacio Zaragoza
A59

José María Morelos
A60

Francisco Madero — A61

Benito Juárez — A62

1915		Unwmk.	Litho.	Rouletted 14

500	A57	1c violet	.25	.25
501	A58	2c green	.25	.25
502	A59	3c brown	.50	.25
503	A60	4c carmine	.50	.25
504	A61	5c orange	.75	.25
505	A62	10c ultra	.35	.30
		Nos. 500-505 (6)	2.60	1.55
		Set, never hinged	4.00	

Nos. 500-505 exists imperf.; some exist imperf. vertically or horizontally; some with rouletting and perforation combined. These probably were not regularly issued in these forms.

See Nos. 506-511. For overprints see Nos. O86-O97.

Map of Mexico — A63

Veracruz Lighthouse
A64

Post Office, Mexico, D.F. — A65

TEN CENTAVOS:
Type I — Size 19½x24mm. Crossed lines on coat.
Type II — Size 19x23½mm. Diagonal lines only on coat.

1915-16				Perf. 12

506	A57	1c violet	.40	.25
507	A58	2c green	.40	.30
508	A59	3c brown	.50	.30
509	A60	4c carmine	.50	.35
a.		"CEATRO"	7.50	7.50
510	A61	5c orange	.75	.35
511	A62	10c ultra, type I	1.00	.35
a.		10c ultra, type II	.50	.25

Engr.

512	A63	40c slate	.75	.35
513	A64	1p brown & blk	1.00	.75
a.		Inverted center	200.00	275.00
514	A65	5p cl & ultra ('16)	12.00	4.00
a.		Inverted center	450.00	
		Nos. 506-514 (9)	17.30	7.00
		Set, never hinged	60.00	

Nos. 507-508, 510-514, exist imperf; Nos. 513-514 imperf with inverted center. These varieties were not regularly issued.

See Nos. 626-628, 647. For overprints see Nos. O92-O100, O121-O123, O132-O133, O142-O144, O153-O154, O162-O164, O174, O188, O193, O207, O222.

Issues of 1899-1910 Overprinted in Blue, Red or Black

On Issues of 1899-1903

1916		Wmk. 155		Perf. 14

515	A28	5c orange (Bl)	125.00	175.00
		Never hinged	400.00	
516	A30	15c lav & cl (Bl)	775.00	775.00
		Never hinged	2,250.	

On Issue of 1910

517	A36	1c dull vio (R)	10.00	10.00
518	A37	2c green (R)	.50	.35
519	A38	3c orange brn (Bl)	.55	.40
a.		Double overprint		500.00
520	A39	4c carmine (Bl)	6.00	8.00
521	A40	5c orange (Bl)	.25	.25
a.		Double overprint	75.00	
522	A41	10c blue & org (R)	1.25	1.50
523	A42	15c gray bl & cl (Bk)		1.75	3.00
524	A43	20c red & bl (Bk)	1.75	3.00
525	A44	50c red brn & blk (R)		8.50	5.00
526	A45	1p blue & blk (R)	15.00	6.50
527	A46	5p car & blk (R)	175.00	175.00
		Nos. 517-527 (11)	220.55	213.00
		Nos. 517-527, never hinged	650.00	

Nos. 519-524 exist with this overprint (called the "Corbata") reading downward and Nos. 525-527 with it inverted. Of these varieties only Nos. 519-521 were regularly issued.

On Nos. 423-430

528	A36	1c dull vio (R)	2.50	4.00
529	A37	2c green (R)	.75	.60
530	A38	3c orange brn (Bl)	.60	.60
531	A39	4c carmine (Bl)	.60	.60
532	A40	5c orange (R)	1.00	.30
533	A41	10c blue & org (R)	.75	.60
534	A42	15c gray bl & cl (Bk)	.80	.80
535	A43	20c red & bl (Bk)	.80	.80

On Nos. 431-433 in Red

536	A44	50c red brn & blk	7.50	6.00
537	A45	1p blue & blk	16.00	16.00
538	A46	5p carmine & blk	150.00	140.00
a.		Tablet inverted	300.00	
		Nos. 528-538 (11)	181.30	170.30
		Set, never hinged	550.00	

Nos. 529 to 535 are known with the overprint reading downward and Nos. 536 to 538 with it inverted.

On No. 482

539	A28	5c orange (Bl)	400.00	400.00

On Nos. 484-494

540	A36	1c dull vio (R)	6.00	6.00
541	A37	2c green (R)	.75	.75
a.		Monogram inverted	100.00	
542	A38	3c orange brn (Bl)	.75	.75
543	A39	4c carmine (Bl)	8.50	10.00
544	A40	5c orange (R)	1.25	.35
545	A41	10c blue & org (R)	2.00	2.50
546	A42	15c gray bl & cl (Bk)		1.75	.75
a.		Tablet double	750.00	750.00
b.		Monogram double		750.00
547	A43	20c red & bl (Bk)	1.75	1.50
548	A44	50c red brn & blk (R)		9.00	10.00
a.		Monogram inverted	75.00	
b.		Tablet inverted	85.00	
549	A45	1p blue & blk (R)	13.00	14.00
a.		Tablet double	200.00	
b.		Monogram inverted	70.00	
		Nos. 539-549 (11)	444.75	446.60
		Set, never hinged	1,300.	

Nos. 541-547 exist with overprint reading downward. A few 5p were overprinted for the Post Office collection.

On No. 452

550	A28	5c orange (Bl)	125.00	125.00

On Nos. 455-462

551	A36	1c dull vio (R)	11.00	15.00
552	A37	2c green (R)	1.50	.90
553	A38	3c org brn (Bl)	3.25	4.50

554	A39	4c carmine (Bl)	13.00	15.00
555	A40	5c orange (Bl)	4.50	6.00
556	A41	10c bl & org (R)	12.00	14.00
a.		Monogram inverted	250.00	
557	A42	15c gray bl & cl (Bk)	12.00	14.00
a.		Monogram inverted	250.00	
558	A43	20c red & bl (Bk)	12.00	14.00
a.		Monogram inverted	250.00	
		Nos. 550-558 (9)	194.25	208.40
		Set, never hinged	650.00	

Stamps of 50c, 1p and 5p were overprinted for the Post Office collection but were not regularly issued.

Issues of 1914
Overprinted

On "Transitorio" Issue
Rouletted 9½x14
Unwmk.

559	A50	1c dp blue (R)	24.00	24.00
		Never hinged	75.00	
560	A50	2c yellow grn (R)	12.00	18.00
		Never hinged	27.50	
561	A50	4c blue vio (R)	425.00	375.00
		Never hinged	1,200.	
562	A50	10c red (Bl)	2.00	6.00
		Never hinged	4.00	
a.		Vertical overprint	125.00	
563	A50	20c yellow brn (Bl)	3.00	6.00
		Never hinged	7.50	
564	A50	50c claret (Bl)	15.00	20.00
		Never hinged	45.00	
565	A50	1p violet (Bl)	24.00	24.00
		Never hinged	100.00	
a.		Horiz. pair, imperf. btwn.		
		Nos. 559-565 (7)	505.00	473.00

Overprinted in Blue On "Denver" Issue
Perf. 12

566	A52	1c pale blue	3.75	
567	A52	2c lt green	3.75	
568	A52	3c orange	.45	5.00
569	A52	5c deep rose	.45	5.00
570	A52	10c rose	.45	5.00
571	A52	15c rose lilac	.45	5.00
572	A52	50c yellow	1.10	15.00
573	A52	1p violet	9.50	25.00
		Nos. 566-573 (8)	19.90	
		Set, never hinged	65.00	

Many of the foregoing stamps exist with the "G. P. DE M." overprint printed in other colors than those listed. These "trial color" stamps were not regularly on sale at post offices but were available for postage and used copies are known.

There appears to have been speculation in Nos. 516, 517, 520, 528, 539, 540, 543, 566, and 567. A small quantity of each of these stamps was sold at post offices but subsequently they could be obtained only from officials or their agents at advanced prices.

Venustiano Carranza — A66

1916, June 1   Engr.   Perf. 12

574	A66	10c blue	1.75	1.00
a.		Imperf., pair	25.00	
575	A66	10c lilac brown	15.00	15.00
a.		Imperf., pair	50.00	
		Nos. 574-575, never hinged	32.50	

Entry of Carranza into Mexico, D.F. Stamps of type A66 with only horizontal lines in the background of the oval are essays.

Coat of Arms — A67

1916

576	A67	1c lilac	.35	.25
		Never hinged	.80	

Issue of 1910
Surcharged in
Various Colors

This overprint is called the "Barril."

1916   Wmk. 155   Perf. 14

577	A36	5c on 1c dl vio (Br)	.50	.50
a.		Vertical surcharge	1.25	1.25
b.		Double surcharge	150.00	
578	A36	10c on 1c dl vio (Bl)	.50	.50
a.		Double surcharge	100.00	
579	A40	20c on 5c org (Br)	.50	.50
a.		Double surcharge	90.00	
580	A40	25c on 5c org (G)	.40	.50
581	A37	60c on 2c grn (R)	27.50	20.00
		Nos. 577-581 (5)	29.40	22.00
		Set, never hinged	100.00	

On Nos. 423-424, 427

582	A36	5c on 1c (Br)	.50	.50
a.		Double tablet, one vertical	100.00	
b.		Inverted tablet	250.00	250.00
583	A36	10c on 1c (Bl)	1.00	1.00
584	A40	25c on 5c (G)	.50	.50
a.		Inverted tablet	225.00	225.00
585	A37	60c on 2c (R)	650.00	425.00
		Nos. 582-584, never hinged	4.50	

No. 585 was not regularly issued. The variety "GONSTITUCIONALISTA" is found on Nos. 582 to 585.

On No. 459

586	A40	25c on 5c org (G)	.25	.25
		Never hinged	.70	

On Nos. 484-485, 488

587	A36	5c on 1c (Br)	15.00	20.00
a.		Vertical tablet	100.00	125.00
588	A36	10c on 1c (Bl)	5.00	7.50
589	A40	25c on 5c (G)	1.00	1.50
a.		Inverted tablet	225.00	
590	A37	60c on 2c (R)	650.00	
		Nos. 587-589, never hinged	60.00	

No. 590 was not regularly issued.

Surcharged on "Denver" Issue of 1914

1916   Unwmk.   Perf. 12

591	A52	60c on 1c pale bl (Br)	3.00	6.00
592	A52	60c on 2c lt grn (Br)	3.00	6.00
a.		Inverted surcharge	1,250.	
		Set, never hinged	18.00	

Postage Due Stamps Surcharged Like Nos. 577-581

1916   Wmk. 155   Perf. 14

593	D1	5c on 1c blue (Br)	2.50	
594	D1	10c on 2c blue (V)	2.50	
595	D1	20c on 4c blue (Br)	2.50	
596	D1	25c on 5c blue (G)	2.50	
597	D1	60c on 10c blue (R)	1.50	
598	D1	1p on 1c blue (C)	1.50	
599	D1	1p on 2c blue (C)	1.50	
600	D1	1p on 4c blue (C)	.80	.80
601	D1	1p on 5c blue (C)	2.50	
602	D1	1p on 10c blue (C)	2.50	
		Nos. 593-602 (10)	20.30	
		Set, never hinged	60.00	

There are numerous "trial colors" and "essays" of the overprints and surcharges on Nos. 577 to 602. They were available for postage though not regularly issued.

Postage Due Stamps
Surcharged

1916

603	D1	2.50p on 1c blue	1.25	1.25
604	D1	2.50p on 2c blue	10.00	
605	D1	2.50p on 4c blue	10.00	250.00
606	D1	2.50p on 5c blue	10.00	
607	D1	2.50p on 10c blue	10.00	
a.		Inverted surcharge	1,500.	
		Nos. 603-607 (5)	41.25	
		Set, never hinged	125.00	

Regular Issue

Ignacio
Zaragoza
A68

Ildefonso
Vázquez
A69

J. M. Pino
Suárez
A70

Jesús
Carranza
A71

Maclovio
Herrera — A72

F. I.
Madero — A73

Belisario
Domínguez
A74

Aquiles Serdán
A75

Rouletted 14½

1917-20   Engr.   Unwmk.
Thick Paper

608	A68	1c dull violet	2.00	1.00
		Never hinged	4.00	
609	A68	1c lilac gray ('20)	5.00	.75
		Never hinged	9.50	
a.		1c gray ('20)	5.00	5.00
610	A69	2c gray green	1.50	.50
		Never hinged	3.00	
611	A70	3c bister brn	1.50	1.00
		Never hinged	3.00	
612	A71	4c carmine	2.50	1.00
		Never hinged	7.50	
613	A72	5c ultra	2.50	.50
		Never hinged	5.00	
a.		Horiz. pair, imperf. btwn.	75.00	
b.		Imperf., pair	35.00	75.00
614	A73	10c blue	4.00	.50
		Never hinged	10.00	
a.		Without imprint	7.50	1.00
		Never hinged	16.00	
615	A74	20c brown rose	40.00	2.00
		Never hinged	90.00	
a.		20c rose	40.00	2.00
		Never hinged	80.00	
616	A75	30c gray brown	90.00	3.00
		Never hinged	200.00	
617	A75	30c gray blk ('20)	100.00	4.00
		Never hinged	250.00	
		Nos. 608-617 (10)	249.00	14.25

Perf. 12
Thick or Medium Paper

618	A68	1c dull violet	35.00	25.00
		Never hinged	100.00	
619	A69	2c gray green	10.00	6.00
		Never hinged	20.00	
620	A70	3c bis brn ('17)	200.00	200.00
		Never hinged	400.00	
622	A72	5c ultra	5.00	.25
		Never hinged	10.00	
623	A73	10c blue ('17)	5.00	.25
		Never hinged	10.00	
a.		Without imprint ('17)	20.00	15.00
		Never hinged	40.00	
624	A74	20c rose ('20)	140.00	3.00
		Never hinged	350.00	
625	A75	30c gray blk ('20)	140.00	2.00
		Never hinged	350.00	

Thin or Medium Paper

626	A63	40c violet	65.00	1.00
		Never hinged	200.00	
627	A64	1p blue & blk	50.00	1.50
		Never hinged	150.00	
a.		With center of 5p	800.00	
b.		1p bl & dark blue (error)	500.00	20.00
c.		Vert. pair, imperf. btwn.		250.00

628	A65	5p green & blk	1.50	10.00
		Never hinged	3.00	
a.		With violet or red control number	25.00	10.00
b.		With center of 1p	800.00	

The 1, 2, 3, 5 and 10c are known on thin paper perforated. It is stated they were printed for Postal Union and "specimen" purposes.

All values exist imperf; these are not known to have been regularly issued. Nos. 627a and 628b were not regularly issued.

All values except 3c have an imprint.

For overprints and surcharges see Nos. B1-B2, O113-O165.

Meeting of
Iturbide and
Guerrero
A77

Entering City
of Mexico
A78

1921

632	A77	10c blue & brn	25.00	3.00
		Never hinged	82.50	
a.		Center inverted		40,000.
633	A78	10p black brn & blk	22.50	37.50
		Never hinged	75.00	

Commemorating the meeting of Agustín de Iturbide and Vicente Guerrero and the entry into City of Mexico in 1821.

For overprint see No. O194.

"El Salto de Agua," Public Fountain
A79

Pyramid of the Sun at Teotihuacán
A80

Chapultepec Castle
A81

Columbus Monument
A82

Juárez Colonnade, Mexico, D. F.
A83

Monument to Josefa Ortiz de Dominguez
A84

Cuauhtémoc Monument — A85

1923   Unwmk.   Rouletted 14½

634	A79	2c scarlet	2.00	.25
635	A80	3c bister brn	2.00	.25
636	A81	4c green	2.50	.75
637	A82	5c orange	5.00	.25
638	A83	10c brown	3.75	.25
639	A85	10c claret	3.50	.25
640	A84	20c dk blue	52.50	1.75
641	A85	30c dk green	52.50	2.00
		Nos. 634-641 (8)	123.75	5.75
		Set, never hinged	300.00	

See Nos. 642-646, 650-657, 688-692, 727A, 735A-736. For overprints see Nos.

O166-O173, O178-O181, O183-O187, O196-O197, O199-O206, O210, O212-O214, O217-O222.

Communications Building — A87

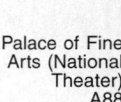

Palace of Fine Arts (National Theater) A88

Type I

Type II

Two types of 1p:
I — Eagle on palace dome.
II — Without eagle.

1923   Wmk. 156   Perf. 12

642	A79	2c scarlet	10.00	10.00
643	A81	4c green	1.40	.30
644	A82	5c orange	10.00	7.00
645	A85	10c brown lake	12.50	6.00
646	A83	30c dark green	.95	.25
647	A63	40c violet	1.25	.25
648	A87	50c olive brn	1.00	.25
649	A88	1p red brn & bl (I)	1.00	1.00
a.		Type II	3.00	10.00
		Nos. 642-649 (8)	38.10	25.05
		Set, never hinged	90.00	

Most of Nos. 642-649 are known imperforate or part perforate but probably were not regularly issued.
For overprints see Nos. O175-O176, O189-O190, O208-O209, O223.

1923-34   Rouletted 14½

650	A79	2c scarlet	.25	.25
651	A80	3c bis brn ('27)	.25	.25
652	A81	4c green	47.50	35.00
653	A82	4c green ('27)	.25	.25
654	A82	5c orange	.25	.25
655	A85	10c lake	.25	.25
656	A84	20c deep blue	.75	.30
657	A83	30c dk green ('34)	.75	.30
		Nos. 650-657 (8)	50.25	36.85
		Set, never hinged	125.00	

Nos. 650 to 657 inclusive exist imperforate.

Medallion A90

Map of Americas A91

Francisco García y Santos — A92

Post Office, Mexico, D. F. — A93

1926   Perf. 12

658	A90	2c red	2.50	1.00
659	A91	4c green	2.50	1.00
660	A90	5c orange	2.50	.75

661	A91	10c brown red	4.00	1.00
662	A92	20c dk blue	4.00	1.25
663	A92	30c dk green	7.50	4.00
664	A92	40c violet	13.50	3.00
665	A93	1p brown & blue	27.50	10.00
a.		1p red & blue	37.50	15.00
		Nos. 658-665 (8)	64.00	22.00
		Set, never hinged	150.00	

Pan-American Postal Congress.
Nos. 658-665 were also printed in black, on unwatermarked paper, for presentation to delegates to the Universal Postal Congress at London in 1929. Remainders were overprinted in 1929 for use as airmail official stamps, and are listed as Nos. CO3-CO10.
For overprints see Nos. 667-674, 675A-682, CO3-CO10.

Benito Juárez — A94

1926

666	A94	8c orange	.30	.25
		Never hinged	.70	

For overprint see No. O182.

Nos. 658-665 Overprinted

1930   Perf. 12

667	A90	2c red	4.00	2.25
a.		Reading down	15.00	15.00
668	A91	4c green	4.00	2.50
a.		Reading down	15.00	15.00
669	A90	5c orange	4.00	2.00
a.		Reading down	15.00	35.00
b.		Double overprint	75.00	75.00
670	A91	10c brown red	7.50	2.50
671	A92	20c dk blue	9.50	3.50
672	A92	30c dk green	8.50	4.00
a.		Reading down	10.00	12.00
673	A92	40c violet	12.50	8.50
a.		Reading down	47.50	50.00
674	A93	1p red brn & bl	11.00	7.00
a.		Double overprint	250.00	
b.		Triple overprint	200.00	
		Nos. 667-674 (8)	61.00	32.25
		Set, never hinged	150.00	

Overprint horizontal on 1p.

Arms of Puebla — A95

1931, May 1   Engr.

675	A95	10c dk bl & dk brn	3.00	.50
		Never hinged	7.50	

400th anniversary of Puebla.

Nos. 658-665a Overprinted

1931

676	A91	4c green	70.00	75.00
a.		Inverted overprint	750.00	
677	A90	5c orange	13.00	17.00
678	A91	10c brown red	13.00	14.00
679	A92	20c dk blue	13.00	18.00
680	A92	30c dk green	22.50	25.00
681	A92	40c violet	32.50	35.00
682	A93	1p brown & bl	30.00	35.00
a.		1p red & blue	42.50	45.00
		Nos. 676-682 (7)	194.00	219.00
		Set, never hinged	475.00	

Overprint horizontal on 1p.
Nos. 676 and 682 are not known to have been sold to the public through post offices.
Forgeries of overprint exist.

Bartolomé de las Casas — A96

1933, Mar. 3   Engr.   Rouletted 14½

683	A96	15c dark blue	.30	.25
		Never hinged	.70	

For overprint see No. O215.

Emblem of Mexican Society of Geography and Statistics — A97

1933, Oct.   Rouletted 14½

684	A97	2c deep green	1.50	.60
685	A97	5c dark brown	1.75	.50
686	A97	10c dark blue	.75	.25
687	A97	1p dark violet	100.00	65.00
		Nos. 684-687 (4)	104.00	66.35
		Set, never hinged	250.00	

XXI Intl. Congress of Statistics and the 1st centenary of the Mexican Society of Geography and Statistics.

Types of 1923 and PT1

1934   Perf. 10½, 11 (4c)

687A	PT1	1c brown	1.00	.30
688	A79	2c scarlet	.35	.25
689	A82	4c green	.35	.25
690	A85	10c brown lake	.35	.25
691	A84	20c dark blue	.75	.75
692	A83	30c dk blue grn	.75	.25
		Nos. 687A-692 (6)	3.80	3.05
		Set, never hinged	9.00	

See 2nd note after Postal Tax stamp No. RA3.

Indian Archer — A99

Indian — A100

Woman Decorating Pottery A101

Peon A102

Potter A103

Sculptor A104

Craftsman A105

Offering to the Gods A106

Worshiper — A107

1934, Sept. 1   Wmk. 156   Perf. 10½

698	A99	5c dk green	10.00	3.00
699	A100	10c brown lake	17.00	4.00
700	A101	20c ultra	30.00	20.00
701	A102	30c black	60.00	42.50
702	A103	40c black brn	37.50	25.00
703	A104	50c dull blue	175.00	160.00
704	A105	1p brn lake & blk	350.00	175.00
705	A106	5p brn blk & red brn	750.00	725.00
706	A107	10p brown & vio	2,000.	2,500.
a.		Unwatermarked	3,250.	
		Never hinged	5,000.	
		Nos. 698-706 (9)	3,429.	3,654.
		Set, never hinged	7,500.	

National University.
The design of the 1p is wider than the rest of the set. Values are for examples with perfs just touching the design.
See Nos. C54-C61, RA13B.

Yalalteca Indian — A108

Tehuana Indian — A109

Arch of the Revolution A110

Tower of Los Remedios A111

Cross of Palenque A112

Independence Monument A113

Independence Monument, Puebla A114

Monument to the Heroic Cadets A115

Stone of Tizoc — A116

Ruins of Mitla — A117

Coat of Arms
A118

Charro
A119

Imprint: "Oficina Impresora de Hacienda-Mexico"

1934-40   Wmk. 156   Perf. 10½
Size: 20x26mm

707	A108	1c orange	.65	.25
a.		Unwmkd.		—
708	A109	2c green	.65	.25
a.		Unwmkd.	3.75	3.75
709	A110	4c carmine	.90	.25
710	A111	5c olive brn	.65	.25
a.		Unwmkd.	400.00	350.00
711	A112	10c dk blue	.80	.25
712	A112	10c violet ('35)	1.25	.25
a.		Unwmkd.	200.00	40.00
713	A113	15c lt blue	4.00	.30
714	A114	20c gray green	1.90	.25
a.		20c olive green	2.00	.25
715	A114	20c ultra ('35)	1.40	.25
a.		Unwmkd.		150.00
716	A115	30c lake	.90	.25
a.		Unwmkd.	350.00	
716B	A115	30c lt ultra ('40)	1.00	.25
717	A116	40c red brown	1.00	.25
718	A117	50c grnsh black	.90	.25
a.		Imperf., pair	2.50	
b.		Unwmkd.		375.00
719	A118	1p dk brn & org	2.50	.25
a.		Imperf., pair	350.00	
720	A119	5p org & vio	7.75	.75
		Nos. 707-720 (15)	26.25	4.30
		Set, never hinged	70.00	

No. 718a was not regularly issued.
The existence of No. 707a has been questioned.
See Nos. 729-733, 733B, 735, 784-788, 795A-800A, 837-838, 840-841, 844, 846-851. For overprints see Nos. 728, O224-O232.

Tractor — A120

1935, Apr. 1   Wmk. 156   Perf. 10½
721	A120	10c violet	4.00	.50
		Never hinged	9.00	

Industrial census of Apr. 10, 1935.

Arms of Chiapas — A121

1935, Sept. 14
722	A121	10c dark blue	.50	.25
		Never hinged	1.40	
a.		Unwmkd.	125.00	100.00

The 111th anniversary of the joining of the state of Chiapas with the federal republic of Mexico. See No. 734.

Emiliano Zapata — A122

1935, Nov. 20   Wmk. 156
723	A122	10c violet	.75	.25
		Never hinged	2.00	

25th anniversary of the Plan of Ayala.

US and Mexico Joined by Highways
A123

Matalote Bridge
A124

View of Nuevo Laredo Highway — A125

1936   Wmk. 248   Perf. 14
725	A123	5c blue grn & rose	.35	.25
726	A124	10c slate bl & blk	.50	.25
727	A125	20c brn & dk grn	1.50	1.00
		Nos. 725-727,C77-C79 (6)	3.60	2.50
		Set, never hinged	8.50	

Opening of the Mexico City - Nuevo Laredo Highway.

Monument Type of 1923

1936   Wmk. 248   Engr.   Perf. 10½
727A	A85	10c brown lake	2,500.	650.00

No. 712 Overprinted in Green

1936, Dec. 15   Wmk. 156
728	A112	10c violet	.60	.50
		Never hinged	1.50	

1st National Congress of Industrial Hygiene and Medicine.

Type of 1934
Redrawn size: 17½x21mm
Imprint: "Talleres de Imp. de Est. y Valores-Mexico"

1937   Photo.   Wmk. 156   Perf. 14
729	A108	1c orange	.60	.25
a.		Imperf., pair	12.50	12.50
		Never hinged	25.00	
730	A109	2c dull green	.60	.25
a.		Imperf., pair	12.50	12.50
		Never hinged	30.00	
731	A110	4c carmine	.90	.25
a.		Imperf., pair	12.50	12.50
		Never hinged	30.00	
732	A111	5c olive brn	.80	.25
a.		Unwmkd.		300.00
733	A112	10c violet	.70	.25
a.		Imperf., pair	10.00	12.50
		Never hinged	12.00	
		Nos. 729-733 (5)	3.60	1.25
		Set, never hinged	9.00	

The imperfs were not regularly issued.

Types of 1934-35
1937   Wmk. 260   Size: 17½x21mm
733B	A111	5c olive brown	4,000.	250.00
		Never hinged	6,000.	

1937   Engr.   Perf. 10½
734	A121	10c dark blue	35.00	35.00
		Never hinged	75.00	

1937   Size: 20x26mm
735	A112	10c violet	350.00	55.00

Types of 1923
1934-37   Wmk. 260   Perf. 10½
735A	A79	2c scarlet	6,000.	
735B	A85	10c brown lake	—	

Forged perforations exist.
The listing of No. 735B is being re-evaluated. The Catalogue Editors would appreciate any information on the stamp.

Rouletted 14½
736	A85	10c claret	5,500.	175.00

Blacksmith A126

Revolutionary Soldier A127

Revolutionary Envoy — A128

Wmk. 156
1938, Mar. 26   Photo.   Perf. 14
737	A126	5c black & brn	.80	.25
738	A127	10c red brown	.35	.25
739	A128	20c maroon & org	6.00	1.00
		Nos. 737-739,C82-C84 (6)	13.15	5.00
		Set, never hinged	32.00	

Plan of Guadalupe, 25th anniv.

Arch of the Revolution A129

Independence Monument A131

Design: 10c, National Theater.

1938, July 1
740	A129	5c bister brn	4.25	.60
741	A129	5c red brown	25.00	2.25
742	A129	10c orange	15.00	11.00
743	A129	10c chocolate	1.00	.25
744	A131	20c brown lake	6.00	4.00
745	A131	20c black	18.00	15.00
		Nos. 740-745 (6)	69.25	33.10
		Nos. 740-745,C85-C90 (12)	129.60	63.30
		Set, never hinged	275.00	

16th Intl. Congress of Planning & Housing.

Arch of the Revolution A132

1939, May 1
746	A132	10c Prus blue	.65	.25
		Nos. 746,C91-C93 (4)	4.75	3.00
		Set, never hinged	11.00	

New York World's Fair.

Indian — A133

1939, May 17
747	A133	10c red orange	.45	.25
		Nos. 747,C94-C96 (4)	5.55	2.80
		Set, never hinged	13.00	

Tulsa World Philatelic Convention.

Juan Zumárraga A134

First Printing Shop in Mexico, 1539 A135

Design: 10c, Antonio de Mendoza.

1939, Sept. 1   Engr.   Perf. 10½
748	A134	2c brown blk	.75	.25
749	A135	5c green	.75	.25
750	A134	10c red brown	.25	.25
		Nos. 748-750,C97-C99 (6)	3.75	1.95
		Set, never hinged	11.50	

400th anniversary of printing in Mexico.

View of Taxco A137

Allegory of Agriculture A138

10c, Two hands holding symbols of commerce.

1939, Oct. 1   Photo.   Perf. 12x13
751	A137	2c dark carmine	1.25	.25
752	A138	5c sl grn & gray grn	.25	.25
753	A138	10c org brn & buff	.25	.25
		Nos. 751-753,C100-C102 (6)	6.25	2.00
		Set, never hinged	14.00	

Census Taking.

"Penny Black" of 1840 — A140

1940, May   Perf. 14
754	A140	5c black & lemon	.90	.50
755	A140	10c dark violet	.25	.25
756	A140	20c lt blue & car	.25	.25
757	A140	1p gray & red org	7.00	4.00
758	A140	5p black & Prus bl	50.00	50.00
		Nos. 754-758,C103-C107 (10)	141.00	116.05
		Set, never hinged	340.00	

Postage stamp centenary.

Roadside Monument — A141

1940   Wmk. 156
759	A141	6c deep green	.50	.25
		Never hinged	1.25	

Opening of the highway between Mexico, D. F., and Guadalajara. See Nos. 789, 842.

Vasco de Quiroga — A142

Melchor Ocampo — A143

College Seal — A144

1940, July 15   Engr.   Perf. 10½

760	A142	2c violet	1.30	.50
761	A143	5c copper red	.80	.25
762	A144	10c olive bister	.80	.30
a.		Imperf., pair	150.00	

Nos. 760-762,C108-C110 (6)   5.10 2.60
Set, never hinged   11.00

Founding of the National College of San Nicolas de Hidalgo, 400th anniv.

Coat of Arms of Campeche A145

1940, Aug. 7   Photo.   Perf. 12x13

763	A145	10c bis brn & dk car	5.00	1.25

Nos. 763,C111-C113 (4)   12.60 6.70
Set, never hinged   30.00

400th anniversary of the founding of Campeche.

Man at Helm A146

1940, Dec. 1

764	A146	2c red org & blk	1.60	.60
765	A146	5c peacock bl & red brn	8.00	3.50
766	A146	10c slate grn & dk brn	4.00	.85

Nos. 764-766,C114-C116 (6)   21.00 9.45
Set, never hinged   45.00

Inauguration of Pres. Manuel Avila Camacho.

Alternated Perforations

Nos. 763-766, 774-779, 792-795, 801-804, 806-811, 813-818, C100-C102, C111-C116, C123-C128, C143-C162, C430-C431 have alternating small and large perforations.

Javelin Thrower — A147

1941, Nov. 4   Perf. 14

767	A147	10c dull yellow grn	5.00	.50

National Athletic Games of the Revolution, Nov. 4-20, 1941.

Serpent Columns, Chichén Itzá A148

Mayan Sculpture A149

Coat of Arms of Merída — A150

1942, June 30

768	A148	2c dk olive bis	1.40	.75
769	A149	5c deep orange	2.25	.60
770	A150	10c dark violet	1.60	.25

Nos. 768-770,C117-C119 (6)   11.50 6.35

400th anniversary of the founding of Merida.

Independence Monument to Hidalgo — A151

Government Palace — A152

View of Guadalajara — A153

1942, Feb. 11   Engr.   Perf. 10x10½

771	A151	2c bl vio & vio brn	.35	.30
772	A152	5c black & cop red	1.25	.50
773	A153	10c red org & ultra	1.25	.40

Nos. 771-773,C120-C122 (6)   7.85 4.20

Founding of Guadalajara, 400th anniv.
No. 773 exists imperf on unwatermarked paper as a color proof.

Black Cloud in Orion A154

Designs: 5c, Total solar eclipse. 10c, Spiral galaxy in the "Hunting Dogs."

1942, Feb. 17   Photo.   Perf. 12x13

774	A154	2c lt vio & indigo	10.00	3.00
775	A154	5c blue & indigo	15.00	2.00
776	A154	10c red org & indigo	15.00	.75

Nos. 774-776,C123-C125 (6)   100.00 17.25

Astrophysics Congress and the inauguration of an observatory at Tonanzintla, Feb. 17, 1942.

"Mother Earth" A157

Sowing Wheat A158

Western Hemisphere Carrying a Torch — A159

1942, July 1

777	A157	2c chestnut	2.00	.40
778	A158	5c turq blue	3.50	1.10
779	A159	10c red orange	1.50	.55

Nos. 777-779,C126-C128 (6)   12.90 5.50

2nd Inter-American Agricultural Conference.

Fuente Academy A160

1942, Nov. 16   Perf. 14

780	A160	10c grnsh black	2.50	.75

75th anniversary of Fuente Academy.

Las Monjas Church — A161

Generalissimo Ignacio José de Allende — A163

Design: 5c, San Miguel Church.

1943, May 11

781	A161	2c intense blue	1.00	.35
782	A161	5c deep brown	1.10	.30
783	A163	10c dull black	3.50	1.00

Nos. 781-783,C129-C131 (6)   10.60 5.35

400th anniv. of the founding of San Miguel de Allende.

Types of 1937

1944		**Photo.**	**Wmk. 272**	
784	A108	1c orange	2.00	.25
785	A109	2c dull green	2.00	.25
786	A110	4c carmine	4.00	.25
787	A111	5c olive brown	4.00	.25
788	A112	10c violet	2.00	.25

Type of 1940

789	A141	6c green	2.00	.25

Nos. 784-789 (6)   16.00 1.50

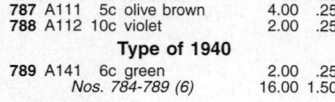

"Liberty" — A164

1944   Photo.

790	A164	12c violet brown	.35	.25

See No. 845.

Juan M. de Castorena — A165

1944, Oct. 12   Engr.   Perf. 10

791	A165	12c dark brown	.60	.25

Third Book Fair. See No. C142.

> **Catalogue values for unused stamps in this section, from this point to the end of the section, are for Never Hinged items.**

Hands Holding Globe Showing Western Hemisphere A166

1945, Feb. 27   Photo.   Perf. 12x13

792	A166	12c dark carmine	.60	.25
793	A166	1p slate green	1.00	.25
794	A166	5p olive brown	5.75	4.50
795	A166	10p black	17.50	8.00

Nos. 792-795,C143-C147 (9)   55.25 33.80

Inter-American Conf. held at Chapultepec, Feb. 1945.

Types of 1934-40
Wmk. 272

1945-46		**Engr.**	**Perf. 10½**	
795A	A113	15c lt grnsh bl ('46)	325.00	60.00
796	A114	20c gray grn	2.50	.25
797	A115	30c lt ultra	3.25	.25
798	A116	40c brown	2.50	.25
799	A117	50c grnsh blk	1.60	.25
800	A118	1p dk brn & org	7.00	.25
b.		Imperf., pair		
800A	A119	5p org & vio ('46)	17.00	6.00

Nos. 795A-800A (7)   358.85 67.25

Theater of Peace, San Luis Potosi A167

1945, July 27   Photo.   Perf. 12x13
801 A167 12c blk & vio brn   .45   .25
802 A167 1p blk & bl gray   .60   .40
803 A167 5p blk & brn lake   5.50   5.00
804 A167 10p blk & grnsh bl   17.00 12.00
   Nos. 801-804,C148-C152 (9) 51.65 35.50

Reconstruction of the Peace Theater (Teatro de la Paz), San Luis Potosi.

Fountain of Diana, the Huntress — A168

1945   Perf. 14
805 A168 3c violet blue   .55   .25
   See No. 839.

Removing Blindfold A169

1945, Nov. 2   Perf. 12x13
806 A169 2c bluish grn   .40   .25
807 A169 6c orange   .40   .25
808 A169 12c ultra   .40   .25
809 A169 1p olive   .60   .25
810 A169 5p gray & pale rose 3.50   3.00
811 A169 10p bl & yel grn   27.50 20.00
   Nos. 806-811 (6)   32.80 24.00
Nos. 806-811,C153-C157 (11)   68.30 55.90

Issued to publicize the national literacy campaign.

M. E. de Almanza — A170

1946   Perf. 14
812 A170 8c black   1.25   .25

Martines Enriquez de Almanza, founder of the Mexican posts. See No. 843.

Allegory of World Peace A171

1946, Apr. 10   Perf. 12x13
813 A171 2c dk olive bis   .35   .25
814 A171 6c red brown   .30   .25
815 A171 12c Prus green   .25   .25
816 A171 1p lt green   .60   .40
817 A171 5p dull red vio   5.50   5.00
818 A171 10p lt ultra   30.00 20.00
   Nos. 813-818 (6)   37.00 26.15
Nos. 813-818,C158-C162 (11)   64.25 40.80

United Nations.

Arms of Zacatecas A173

Monument to Gen. Gonzalez Ortega A174

Ramón Lopez Velarde — A175

Francisco Garcia Salinas — A176

Wmk. 279
1946, Sept. 1   Photo.   Perf. 14
820 A173 2c orange brn   .55   .25
821 A173 12c Prus blue   .25   .25

Engr.
Perf. 10x10½
822 A174 1p lilac rose   .70   .25
823 A175 5p red   5.50   3.00
824 A176 10p dk blue & blk 40.00 10.00
   Nos. 820-824 (5)   47.00 13.75
Nos. 820-824,C163-C166 (9)   68.65 32.20

400th anniversary of the founding of the city of Zacatecas.

A177

1947   Photo.   Perf. 14
825 A177 15c Postman   .25   .25
   a.   Imperf., pair   110.00

A178

10c, F. D. Roosevelt and Stamp of 1st Mexican Issue. 15c, Arms of Mexico and Stamp of 1st US Issue.

1947, May 16
826 A178 10c yellow brown   1.60   1.00
827 A178 15c green   .25   .25
   Nos. 826-827,C167-C169 (5) 4.60   2.40

Cent. Intl. Phil. Exhib., NYC, 5/17-25/47.

Justo Sierra — A180

Communications Building — A181

Perf. 10x10½, 10½x10
1947   Engr.   Wmk. 279
828 A180 10p brown & dl grn 150.00 40.00
829 A181 20p dk green & lil   1.60   2.00

Cadet Juan Escutia — A182

Gen. Manuel Rincón — A186

Flag of San Blas Battalion — A188

Designs: 2c, Cadet Francisco Márquez. 5c, Cadet Fernando Montes de Oca. 10c, Cadet Juan Escutia. 15c, Cadet Agustin Melgar. 1p, Gen. Lucas Balderas.

1947, Sept. 8   Photo.   Perf. 14
830 A182 2c brown black   .45   .25
831 A182 5c red orange   .30   .25
832 A182 10c dk brown   .25   .25
833 A182 15c dk Prus green   .25   .25
834 A186 30c dull olive grn   .35   .25

Engr.
Perf. 10x10½
835 A186 1p aqua   .45   .45
836 A188 5p dk blue & claret 1.90   1.90
   Nos. 830-836 (7)   3.95   3.60
Nos. 830-836,C180-C184 (12)   7.30   6.35

Centenary of the battles of Chapultepec, Churubusco and Molino del Rey.

Types of 1934-46
1947-50   Wmk. 279   Photo.   Perf. 14
837 A108 1c orange   1.00   .30
   a.   Imperf., pair   150.00
838 A109 2c dk green   .60   .25
839 A168 3c violet blue   .60   .25
840 A110 4c dull red   1.90   .25
841 A111 5c olive brown   2.50   .25
842 A141 6c deep green   .45   .25
   a.   Imperf., pair   150.00
843 A179 8c black   .35   .25
844 A112 10c violet   1.90   .25
845 A164 12c violet brn   12.00   .75

Types A108 to A112 are in the redrawn size of 1937.

Size: 19x25mm
Engr.   Perf. 10½
846 A114 20c olive green   1.25   .25
   a.   20c green   3.00   .30
847 A115 30c lt ultra   12.00   .40
848 A116 40c red brown   1.40   .25
849 A117 50c green   1.90   .25
   a.   Imperf., pair   110.00
850 A118 1p dk brn & org   45.00   9.00
851 A119 5p org & vio ('50) 35.00 11.00
   Nos. 837-851 (15)   117.85 23.95

A189

Designs: 3c, Modernistic church, Nuevo Leon. 5c, Modern building, Mexico City. 10c, Convent, Morelos. 15c, Benito Juarez. 20c, Puebla Cathedral. 30c, Indian dancer, Michoacan. 40c, Stone head, Tabasco. 50c, Carved head, Veracruz. 1p, Convent and carved head,

Hidalgo. 5p, Galleon, arms of Campeche. 10p, Francisco I. Madero. 20p, Modern building, Mexico City.

1950-52   Wmk. 279   Photo.   Perf. 14
856 A189 3c blue vio ('51)   .50   .25
857 A189 5c dk red brn   .75   .25
858 A189 10c dk green   3.50   .25
859 A189 15c dk green ('51) 1.75   .25
860 A189 20c blue violet   14.00   .25
861 A189 30c red   .50   .25
862 A189 40c red orange ('51) 1.00 .25
863 A189 50c blue   1.25   .25

Engr.
864 A189 1p dull brown   4.50   .25
865 A189 5p ultra & bl grn 7.00   4.00
866 A189 10p blk & dp ultra
          ('52)   7.00   7.00
867 A189 20p pur & grn ('52) 10.00 10.00
   Nos. 856-867 (12)   51.75 23.25

See Nos. 875-885, 909, 928-931, 943-952, 1003-1004, 1054-1055, 1072, 1076, 1081, 1090-1091, 1094-1102.

Highway Bridge A190

Symbolical of Construction in 1950 — A191

Perf. 10½x10, 10x10½
1950   Engr.
868 A190 15c purple   .60   .25
869 A191 20c deep blue   .40   .25
   Nos. 868-869,C199-C200 (4) 4.30 1.00

Completion of the International Highway between Ciudad Juarez and the Guatemala border.

Railroad Laborer — A192

Design: 20c, Map and locomotive.

Inscribed: "Ferrocarril del Sureste 1950"

1950, May 24   Perf. 10x10½
870 A192 15c chocolate   1.25   .25
871 A192 20c dp carmine   .45   .25
   Nos. 870-871,C201-C202 (4) 2.55 1.00

Opening of the Southeastern Railroad between Veracruz, Coatzocoalcos and Yucatan, 1950.

Postal Service — A193

1950, June 25   Perf. 10x10½
872 A193 50c purple   .40   .25
   Nos. 872,C203-C204 (3)   1.25   .80

75th anniv. (in 1949) of the UPU.

Miguel Hidalgo y
Costilla — A194

Wmk. 300

1953, May 8		**Photo.**	**Perf. 14**
873	A194 20c grnsh bl & dk brn	1.75	.25
	Nos. 873,C206-C207 (3)	3.55	.75

Bicentenary of birth of Miguel Hidalgo y Costilla. See Nos. C206-C207.

Type of 1950-52

Designs as before.

Two types of 5p:
Type I — Imprint ½mm high and blurred.
Type II — Imprint ¾mm high and clear.

1954-67		**Photo.**	**Perf. 14**
875	A189 5c red brown	.50	.25
876	A189 10c green, redrawn	2.50	.25
a.	10c dark green	2.50	.25
877	A189 15c dk green	.40	.25
878	A189 20c bluish blk, white paper, colorless gum ('67)	.60	.25
a.	20c dark blue	3.50	.25
879	A189 30c brown red	.75	.25
a.	30c redsh brn	.75	.25
880	A189 40c red orange	1.50	.25
881	A189 50c lt blue	1.00	.25

Engr.

882	A189 1p olive grn, perf. 11, vert. wmk. ('58)	12.00	.25
a.	1p olive grn, perf. 14	7.00	.25
b.	olive brown	12.00	.25
883	A189 5p ultra & bl grn, I	7.00	1.00
a.	Type II	500.00	7.00
884	A189 10p sl & dp ultra ('56)	9.00	5.00
a.	10p slate green & ultra	35.00	5.00
885	A189 20p purple & grn	11.00	9.00
a.	20p brn vio & yel grn	75.00	20.00
	Nos. 875-885 (11)	46.25	17.00

Nos. 875-881 come only with watermark vertical, and in various shades. Watermark inverted on Nos. 884, 885.

On No. 876, imprint extends full width of stamp.

Vert. pairs, imperf. horiz. of Nos. 878, 880 are noted after No. 1004.

Aztec Messenger of the Sun — A195

1954, Mar. 6			
886	A195 20c rose & bl gray	1.10	.25
	Nos. 886,C222-C223 (3)	2.85	.85

7th Central American and Caribbean Games.

Symbolizing Adoption of National Anthem — A196

1954, Sept. 16			**Photo.**
887	A196 5c rose lil & dk bl	.75	.25
888	A196 20c yel brn & brn vio	.90	.25
889	A196 1p gray grn & cerise	.65	.40
	Nos. 887-889,C224-C226 (6)	3.40	1.65

Centenary of the adoption of Mexico's National Anthem.

Torch-Bearer and Stadium — A197

1955, Mar. 12	**Wmk. 300**		**Perf. 14**
890	A197 20c dk grn & red brn	.85	.25
	Nos. 890,C227-C228 (3)	2.35	.85

Second Pan American Games, 1955.

Aztec Designs A198

1956, Aug. 1			
891	A198 5c "Motion"	.50	.25
892	A198 10c Bird	.50	.25
893	A198 30c Flowers	.40	.25
894	A198 50c Corn	.50	.25
895	A198 1p Deer	.60	.25
896	A198 5p Man	2.25	2.25
a.	Souv. sheet, #891-896, imperf.	75.00	75.00
	Nos. 891-896,C229-C234 (12)	7.90	6.00

Centenary of Mexico's 1st postage stamps. No. 896a sold for 15p.

Stamp of 1856 A199

1956, Aug. 1			
897	A199 30c brn & intense bl	.75	.25

Cent. of 1st Mexican Stamp Intl. Philatelic Exhibition, Mexico City, Aug. 16, 1956.

Francisco Zarco — A200

Portraits: 25c, 45c, Guillermo Prieto. 60c, Ponciano Arriaga.

1956-63			
897A	A200 25c dk brown ('63)	.75	.50
898	A200 45c dk blue green	.35	.25
899	A200 60c red lilac	.35	.35
900	A200 70c violet blue	.40	.25
	Nos. 897A-900,C236-C237A (7)	4.45	2.70

Centenary of the constitution (in 1957). See Nos. C289, 1075, 1092-1093.

"Mexico" — A201

Design: 1p, National Assembly.

1957, Aug. 31		**Photo.**	**Perf. 14**
901	A201 30c maroon & gold	.50	.25
902	A201 1p pale brn & metallic grn	.35	.25
	Nos. 901-902,C239-C240 (4)	1.70	1.00

Constitution, centenary.

Mexican Eagle and Oil Derrick — A202

Design: 5p, Map of Mexico and refinery.

1958, Aug. 30	**Wmk. 300**		**Perf. 14**
903	A202 30c lt blue & blk	.50	.25
904	A202 5p hn brn & Prus grn	6.00	4.00
	Nos. 903-904,C243-C244 (4)	7.15	4.75

20th anniv. of the nationalization of Mexico's oil industry.

UNESCO Building and Eiffel Tower — A203

1959, Jan. 20			
905	A203 30c dull lilac & blk	.50	.25

UNESCO Headquarters opening, Paris, Nov. 9.

UN Headquarters, New York — A204

1959, Sept. 7	**Litho.**		**Perf. 14**
906	A204 30c org yel & bl	.50	.25

Meeting of UNESCO.

Carranza — A205

1960, Jan. 15	**Photo.**		**Wmk. 300**
907	A205 30c pale grn & plum	.35	.25

Birth centenary of Pres. Venustiano Carranza. See No. C246.

Humboldt Statue — A206

1960, Mar. 16	**Wmk. 300**		**Perf. 14**
908	A206 40c bis brn & grn	.35	.25

Cent. of the death (in 1859) of Alexander von Humboldt, German naturalist and geographer.

**Type of 1950-52 Inscribed:
"HOMENAJE AL COLECCIONISTA
DEL TIMBRE DE MEXICO-JUNIO
1960"**

1960, June 8	**Engr.**		**Wmk. 300**
909	A189 10p lil, brn & grn	100.00	75.00

Visit of the Elmhurst (Ill.) Philatelic Society of Mexico Specialists to Mexico, 25th anniv. See No. C249.

Independence Bell & Monument
A207   A208

5p, Bell of Dolores and Miguel Hidalgo.

Wmk. 300

1960, Sept. 15	**Photo.**		**Perf. 14**
910	A207 30c grn & rose red	3.00	.25
911	A208 1p dl grn & dk brn	.50	.25
912	A208 5p maroon & dk bl	5.00	5.00
	Nos. 910-912,C250-C252 (6)	15.50	8.25

150th anniv. of Mexican independence. See US No. 1157.

Agricultural Reform A209

Symbols of Health Education — A210

Designs: 20c, Sailor and Soldier, 1960, and Fighter of 1910. 30c, Electrification. 1p, Political development (schools). 5p, Currency stability (Bank and money).

1960-61	**Photo.**		**Perf. 14**
913	A209 10c sl grn, blk & red org	.75	.25
914	A210 15c grn & org brn	2.75	.50
915	A210 20c brt bl & lt brn ('61)	1.00	.25
916	A210 30c vio brn & sep	.40	.25
917	A210 1p redsh brn & slate	.50	.25
918	A210 5p maroon & gray	6.00	3.50
	Nos. 913-918,C253-C256 (10)	18.80	8.80

50th anniversary (in 1960) of the Mexican Revolution.

Issued: No. 913, 11/20/60; No. 914, 916-918, 12/23/60; No. 915, 3/14/61.

Tunnel — A211

1961, Dec. 7	**Wmk. 300**		**Perf. 14**
919	A211 40c blk & brt grn	.40	.25
	Nos. 919,C258-C259 (3)	1.20	.75

Opening of the railroad from Chihuahua to the Pacific Ocean.

Microscope, Mosquito and Globe — A212

1962, Apr. 7
920 A212 40c dl bl & maroon   .40   .25
WHO drive to eradicate malaria.

President Joao Goulart of Brazil — A213

Wmk. 300
1962, Apr. 11   Photo.   Perf. 14
921 A213 40c brown olive   1.00   .25
Visit of Joao Goulart, president of Brazil, to Mexico.

Insurgent at Marker for Battle of Puebla — A214

1902, May 5
922 A214 40c sepia & dk grn   .35   .25
Centenary of the Battle of May 5 at Puebla and the defeat of French forces by Gen. Ignacio Zaragoza. See No. C260.

Draftsman and Surveyor — A215

1962, June 11
923 A215 40c slate grn & dk bl   .90   .25
25th anniversary of the National Polytechnic Institute. See No. C261.

Plumbline — A216

1962, June 21
924 A216 20c dp blue & blk   1.40   .25
Issued to publicize the importance of mental health.

"Space Needle" and Gear Wheels — A217

1962, July 6
925 A217 40c dk grn & gray   .35   .25
"Century 21" International Exposition, Seattle, Wash., Apr. 21-Oct. 12.

Globe — A218

1962, Oct. 1   Perf. 14
926 A218 40c gray & brn   .35   .25
1962 meeting of the Inter-American Economic and Social Council. See No. C263.

Pres. Alessandri of Chile — A219

1962, Dec. 20   Wmk. 300   Perf. 14
927 A219 20c olive black   .75   .25
Visit of President Jorge Alessandri Rodriguez of Chile to Mexico, Dec. 17-20.

Type of 1950-52
Designs as before.

Wmk. 300, Vertical
1962-74   Photo.   Perf. 14

928	A189	1p ol gray ('67)	1.25 .25
a.		1p green	4.00 .25
929	A189	5p dl bl & dk grn	3.50 .75
a.		5p bluish gray & dark green, white paper ('67)	3.50 .50
930	A189	10p gray & bl ('63)	8.50 5.00
a.		10p green & deep blue ('74)	8.50 5.50
931	A189	20p lil & blk ('63)	9.00 7.50
a.		Redrawn, white paper	10.00 10.00
		Nos. 928-931 (4)	22.25 13.50

No. 928 is on thick, luminescent paper. No. 929 is 20½mm high; No. 929a, 20¾mm. Nos. 931a and 1102 (unwmkd.) have more shading in sky and spots on first floor windows.

Pres. Betancourt of Venezuela — A220

1963, Feb. 23   Wmk. 300
932 A220 20c slate   .70   .25
Visit of President Romulo Betancourt of Venezuela to Mexico.

Congress Emblem — A221

1963, Apr. 22   Wmk. 300   Perf. 14
933 A221 40c fawn & blk   .60   .25
19th International Chamber of Commerce Congress. See No. C271.

Wheat Emblem — A222

1963, June 23   Wmk. 300   Perf. 14
934 A222 40c crim & dk bl   .60   .25
FAO "Freedom from Hunger" campaign.

Mercado Mountains and Arms of Durango — A223

1963, July 13   Photo.
935 A223 20c dk bl & choc   .60   .25
400th anniv. of the founding of Durango.

Belisario Dominguez — A224

1963, July 13   Photo.
936 A224 20c dk grn & ol gray   .60   .25
Centenary of the birth of Belisario Dominguez, revolutionary leader.

Mexico. No. 897, depicting Mexico No. 1 — A225

1963, Oct. 9   Wmk. 350   Perf. 14
937 A225 1p int blue & brn   1.25   .75
77th Annual Convention of the American Philatelic Society, Mexico City, Oct. 7-13. See No. C274.

Tree of Life — A226

1963, Oct. 26   Wmk. 350   Perf. 14
938 A226 20c dl bl grn & car   .40   .25
Intl. Red Cross, cent. See No. C277.

José Morelos — A227

1963, Nov. 9
939 A227 40c grn & dk sl grn   .55   .25
150th anniv. of the 1st congress of Anahuac.

Pres. Victor Paz Estenssoro — A228

1963, Nov. 9   Wmk. 350   Perf. 14
940 A228 40c dk brn & dk red brn   .60   .25
Visit of President Victor Paz Estenssoro of Bolivia.

Arms of Sinaloa University — A229

1963   Photo.
941 A229 40c slate grn & ol bister   .60   .25
90th anniversary of the founding of the University of Sinaloa.

Diesel Train, Rail Cross Section and Globe A230

1963, Nov. 29   Photo.
942 A230 20c black & dk brn   .90   .50
11th Pan-American Railroad Congress. See No. C279.

Type of 1950-52
Designs as before.

1963-66   Wmk. 350   Photo.   Perf. 14

943	A189	5c red brn ('65)	.60 .25
944	A189	10c dk green ('64)	.65 .25
945	A189	15c dk green ('66)	.60 .25
946	A189	20c dark blue	.60 .25
948	A189	40c red orange	.70 .25
949	A189	50c blue ('64)	2.00 .25
950	A189	1p olive grn ('64)	4.00 .25
951	A189	5p dl bl & dk grn ('66)	100.00 30.00

952 A189 10p gray & Prus bl
('65)   35.00 25.00
Nos. 943-952 (9)   144.15 56.75

The 20c is redrawn; clouds almost eliminated and other slight variations.

"F.S.T.S.E."
Emblem — A231

1964, Feb. 15
954 A231 20c red org & dk brn   .40   .25

25th anniv. (in 1963) of the Civil Service Statute affecting federal employees.

Academy of Medicine
Emblem — A232

1964, May 18   **Wmk. 350**   *Perf. 14*
955 A232 20c gold & blk   .40   .25

National Academy of Medicine, cent.

José Rizal — A233

40c, Miguel Lopez de Legaspi, Spanish navigator.

1964, Nov. 10   **Photo.**   *Perf. 14*
956 A233 20c dk bl & dp grn   .50   .25
957 A233 40c dk bl & brt vio   .60   .25
Nos. 956-957,C300-C301 (4)   6.10 1.85

Issued to honor 400 years of Mexican-Philippine friendship.

View of
Zacatecas — A234

1964, Nov. 10   **Wmk. 350**
958 A234 40c slate grn & red   .55   .25

50th anniv. of the capture of Zacatecas.

Col. Gregorio
Mendez — A235

1964, Nov. 10
959 A235 40c grysh blk & dk brn   .50   .25

Cent. of the Battle of Jahuactal, Tabasco.

Morelos Theater,
Aguascalientes
A236

1965, Jan. 9   **Photo.**   *Perf. 14*
960 A236 20c dl cl & dk gray   .35   .25

50th anniversary of the Aguascalientes Convention, Oct. 1-Nov. 9, 1914.

Andrés
Manuel del
Río
A237

1965, Feb. 18   **Wmk. 350**   *Perf. 14*
961 A237 30c gray   .40   .25

Bicentenary of the birth of Andrés Manuel del Río, founder of the National School of Mining and discoverer of vanadium.

José Morelos and
Constitution — A238

1965, Apr. 24   **Photo.**   *Perf. 14*
962 A238 40c brt grn & dk red brn .45   .25

Sesquicentennial (in 1964) of the 1st Mexican constitution.

Trees — A239

1965, July 14   **Wmk. 350**   *Perf. 14*
963 A239 20c blue & green   .30   .25

Issued to commemorate Tree Day, July 8.

ICY
Emblem
A240

1965, Sept. 13   **Photo.**
964 A240 40c olive gray & slate
grn   .30   .25

International Cooperation Year, 1965.

Athlete
with Sling,
Clay Figure
A241

Design: 40c, Batter. Clay figures on 20c and 40c found in Colima, period 300-650 A.D.

1965, Dec. 17   **Wmk. 350**   *Perf. 14*
965 A241 20c olive & vio bl   3.25   .25
966 A241 40c pink & black   1.00   .25
Nos. 965-966,C309-C311 (5)   6.70 1.30

19th Olympic Games, Mexico, 1968.

José Morelos by
Diego Rivera — A242

1965, Dec. 22
967 A242 20c lt vio bl & blk   .40   .25

José Maria Morelos y Pavon (1765-1815), priest and patriot in 1810 revolution against Spain.

Emiliano
Zapata — A243

20c, Corn, cotton, bamboo, wheat and cow.

1966, Jan. 10   **Photo.**
968 A243 20c carmine rose   .35   .25
969 A243 40c black   .45   .25

50th anniv. of the Agrarian Reform Law.

Mexican Postal
Service
Emblem — A244

1966, June 24   **Wmk. 300**   *Perf. 14*
970 A244 40c brt green & blk   .40   .25
Nos. 970,C314-C315 (3)   1.00   .75

Congress of the Postal Union of the Americas and Spain, UPAE, Mexico City, June 24-July 23.

Bartolomé de Las
Casas — A245

1966, Aug. 1   **Photo.**   **Wmk. 300**
971 A245 20c black & buff   .40   .25

400th anniv. of the death of Bartolomé de Las Casas (1474-1566), "Apostle of the Indies."

Mechanical
Drawings
and
Cogwheels
A246

1966, Aug. 15   **Photo.**   *Perf. 14*
972 A246 20c gray & grn   .30   .25

50th anniversary of the founding of the School of Mechanical and Electrical Engineering (ESIME).

FAO Emblem — A247

1966, Sept. 30   **Wmk. 300**   *Perf. 14*
973 A247 40c green   .30   .25

FAO International Rice Year.

Wrestling,
by Diego
Rivera
A248

1966, Oct. 15   **Size: 35x21mm**
974 A248 20c Running and
Jumping   1.25   .25
975 A248 40c shown   1.00   .25
   a.   Souvenir sheet   4.00 4.00
Nos. 974-975,C318-C320 (5)   5.70 1.55

Issued to publicize the 19th Olympic Games, Mexico City, D.F., 1968. No. 975a contains 2 imperf. stamps similar to Nos. 974-975 with simulated perforations. Sold for 90c.

First Page of
Constitution — A249

Wmk. 300
1967, Feb. 5   **Photo.**   *Perf. 14*
976 A249 40c black   .50   .25

Constitution, 50th anniv. See No. C322.

Oil Refinery and Pyramid of the Sun — A250

1967, Apr. 2   Wmk. 300   Perf. 14
977 A250 40c lt bl & blk   .35 .25
7th Intl. Oil Congress, Mexico City, Sept. 1967.

Nayarit Indian — A251

1967, May 1   Wmk. 300   Perf. 14
978 A251 20c pale grn & blk   .30 .25
50th anniversary of Nayarit Statehood.

Degollado Theater, Guadalajara — A252

Wmk. 300
1967, June 12   Photo.   Perf. 14
979 A252 40c pink & black   .35 .25
Centenary of the founding of the Degollado Theater, Guadalajara.

Mexican Eagle over Imperial Crown — A253

Perf. 10x10½
1967, June 19   Litho.   Wmk. 350
980 A253 20c black & ocher   .30 .25
Centenary of the victory of the Mexican republican forces and of the execution of Emperor Maximilian I.

Canoeing A254

Designs: 40c, Basketball. 50c, Hockey. 80c, Bicycling. 2p, Fencing.

Wmk. 300
1967, Oct. 12   Photo.   Perf. 14
981 A254 20c blue & blk   .50 .25
982 A254 40c brick red & blk   .50 .25
983 A254 50c brt yel grn & blk   .50 .25
  a. Souvenir sheet of 3, #981-983, imperf.   5.00 3.50
984 A254 80c brt pur & blk   1.25 .25
985 A254 2p orange & blk   2.25 .30
  a. Souvenir sheet of 2, #984-985, imperf.   7.00 4.00
  Nos. 981-985,C328-C331 (9)   8.75 2.95
  Nos. 981-985 (5)   5.00 1.15

Issued to publicize the 19th Olympic Games, Mexico City, Oct. 12-27, 1968.

No. 983a sold for 1.50p; No. 985a sold for 3.50p. Both sheets are watermark 350.
See Nos. 990-995, C335-C338.

Artemio de Valle-Arizpe — A255

1967, Nov. 1   Photo.
986 A255 20c brown & slate   .35 .30
Centenary of the Ateneo Fuente, a college at Saltillo, Coahuila.

Pedro Moreno — A256

1967, Nov. 18   Wmk. 300   Perf. 14
987 A256 40c blk & lt bl   .35 .25
Moreno (1775-1817), revolutionary leader.

Gabino Barreda A257   Staircase, Palace of Mining A258

1968, Jan. 27   Photo.   Perf. 14
988 A257 40c dk bl & rose claret   .40 .25
989 A258 40c blk & bl gray   .40 .25
Centenary of the founding of the National Preparatory and Engineering Schools.

Type of Olympic Issue, 1967
20c, Wrestling. 40c, Pentathlon. 50c, Water polo. 80c, Gymnastics. 1p, Boxing. 2p, Pistol shoot.

1968, Mar. 21   Wmk. 300   Perf. 14
990 A254 20c olive & blk   .75 .25
991 A254 40c red lil & blk   .75 .25
992 A254 50c brt green & blk   .75 .25
  a. Souvenir sheet of 3, #990-992, imperf.   7.00 4.00
993 A254 80c brt pink & blk   1.00 .25
994 A254 1p org brn & blk   4.00 3.50
995 A254 2p gray & blk   5.50 3.50
  a. Souvenir sheet of 3, #993-995, imperf.   7.50 4.00
  Nos. 990-995,C335-C338 (10)   15.45 9.90

19th Olympic Games, Mexico City, Oct. 12-27. No. 992a sold for 1.50p; No. 995a sold for 5p. Both sheets are watermark 350.

Map of Mexico, Peace Dove — A259

Symbols of Cultural Events A260

40c, University City Olympic stadium. 50c, Telecommunications tower. 2p, Sports Palace. 10p, Pyramid of the Sun, Teotihuacan, & Olympic torch.

Wmk. 350
1968, Oct.   Photo.   Perf. 14
996 A259 20c blue, yel & grn   .75 .25
997 A259 40c multicolored   .75 .25
998 A259 50c multicolored   .75 .25
  a. Souv. sheet of 3, #996-998, imperf.   20.00 10.00
999 A260 2p multicolored   4.00 .50
1000 A260 5p silver & blk   10.00 1.25
  a. Souv. sheet of 2, #999-1000, imperf.   25.00 20.00
1001 A259 10p multicolored   7.50 2.00
  Nos. 996-1001,C340-C344 (11)   32.35 8.40

19th Olympic Games, Mexico City, Oct. 12-27 (Nos. 996-1000). Arrival of the Olympic torch in Veracruz (No. 1001).
#998a sold for 1.50p. No. 1000a sold for 9p. Issued: Nos.996-1000, 10/12; No. 1001, 10/6.

Arms of Veracruz — A261

1969, May 20   Wmk. 350   Perf. 14
1002 A261 40c multicolored   .35 .25
450th anniv. of the founding of Veracruz.

Type of 1950-52 Coil Stamps
Perf. 11 Vert.
1969   Wmk. 300   Photo.
1003 A189 20c dk blue   4.00 2.00
1004 A189 40c red orange   5.00 3.00
Vert. pairs, imperf. horiz. may be from uncut rolls of coils.

Subway Train — A262

1969, Sept. 4   Wmk. 350   Perf. 14
1005 A262 40c multicolored   .35 .25
Inauguration of Mexico City subway.

Honeycomb, Bee and ILO Emblem — A263

1969, Oct. 18   Photo.   Perf. 14
1006 A263 40c multicolored   .30 .25
50th anniversary of the ILO.

Gen. Allende, by Diego Rivera — A264

1969, Nov. 15   Wmk. 350   Perf. 14
1007 A264 40c multicolored   .30 .25
Gen. Ignacio Allende Unzaga (1769-1811), hero of Mexican independence.

Tourist Issue

Pyramid of Niches at El Tajin, Veracruz, and Dancers Swinging from Pole A265

Anthropology Museum, Mexico City — A266   Deer Dance, Sonora — A267

Designs: No. 1010, View of Puerto Vallarta. No. 1011, Puebla Cathedral. No. 1012, Calle Belaunzaran. No. 1014, Ocotlan Cathedral, horiz.

1969-73   Photo.   Wmk. 350
1008 A265 40c shown   .45 .25
1009 A266 40c shown ('70)   .45 .25
1010 A266 40c Jalisco ('70)   .45 .25
1011 A266 40c Puebla ('70)   .45 .25
1012 A266 40c Guanajuato ('70)   .45 .25

Wmk. 300
1013 A267 40c shown ('73)   .35 .25
1014 A267 40c Tlaxcala ('73)   .35 .25
  Nos. 1008-1014,C354-C358 (12)   6.35 3.15
  Nos. 1008-1014 (7)   2.95 1.40

No. 1010 is inscribed "1970" below the design. Copies inscribed "1969" are from an earlier, unissued printing. Value $500.
Issued: No. 1008, 12/13/69; Nos. 1009-1012, 1/17/70; Nos. 1013-1014, 3/6/73.

Luminescence
Fluorescent stamps include Nos. 1013-1014, 1035, 1038, 1041, 1043-1045, 1047-1050, 1054-1059. (See Luminescence note over No. C527.)

"How Many, Who and What are We?" — A268

40c, "What, How & How Much do we produce?" (horse's head & symbols of agriculture).

1970, Jan. 26   Wmk. 350   Perf. 14
1024 A268 20c multicolored   .30 .25
1025 A268 40c blue & multi   .30 .25
Issued to publicize the 1970 census.

Human Eye and Spectrum A269

1970, Mar. 8   Photo.   Wmk. 350
1026 A269 40c multicolored   .30 .25
  21st International Congress of Ophthalmology, Mexico City, Mar. 8-14.

Helmets of 1920 and 1970 A270

1970, Apr. 11   Wmk. 350   Perf. 14
1027 A270 40c dk car rose, blk & lt
          brn   .30 .25
  50th anniversary of the Military College.

José Maria Pino Suarez — A271

1970, Apr. 25   Photo.
1028 A271 40c black & multi   .30 .25
  Centenary of the birth of José Maria Pino Suarez (1869-1913), lawyer, poet and Vice President of Mexico.

Coat of Arms of Celaya — A272

1970, Oct. 12   Photo.   Perf. 14
1029 A272 40c black & multi   .30 .25
  City of Celaya, 400th anniversary.

Eclipse of Sun — A273

1970, Nov. 27   Wmk. 350   Perf. 14
1030 A273 40c black & gray   .30 .25
  Total eclipse of the sun, Mar. 7, 1970.

Spheres with Dates 1970-1770 A274

1971, June 26   Photo.   Perf. 14
1031 A274 40c emerald & blk   .30 .25
  Bicentenary of National Lottery.

Vasco de Quiroga, Mural by O'Gorman A275

1971, July 10   Photo.
1032 A275 40c multicolored   .30 .25
  500th anniversary of the birth of Vasco de Quiroga (1470-1565), Archbishop of Michoacan, founder of hospitals and schools.

Amado Nervo (1870-1919), Poet — A276

1971, Aug. 7   Wmk. 350   Perf. 14
1033 A276 40c multicolored   .30 .25

Waves and Transformer A277

1971, Oct. 8
1034 A277 40c blk, lt bl & lt grn   .30 .25
  50th anniversary of Mexican radio.

Pres. Lazaro Cardenas (1895-1970) — A278

1971, Oct. 19   Wmk. 300
1035 A278 40c blk & pale lil   .30 .25

Keyboard and Lara's Signature A279

1971, Nov. 6   Wmk. 350
1036 A279 40c blk, buff & pale bl   .30 .25
  Agustin Lara (1900-70), composer.

Arms of Monterrey — A280

1971, Dec. 18
1037 A280 40c black & multi   .30 .25
  375th anniv. of the founding of Monterrey.

Cardiology Institute and WHO Emblems — A281

1972, Apr. 8   Wmk. 300
1038 A281 40c multicolored   .30 .25
  "Your heart is your health," World Health Day 1972. See No. C395.

Gaceta de Mexico, Jan. 1, 1722 A282

1972, June 24   Wmk. 350
1039 A282 40c multicolored   .30 .25
  250th anniv. of 1st Mexican newspaper.

Lions Intl. Emblem — A283

1972, June 28
1040 A283 40c black & multi   .30 .25
  55th Lions International Convention.

Sailing Ship Zaragoza — A284

1972, July 1
1041 A284 40c blue & multi   .30 .25
  75th anniv. of the Naval School of Veracruz.

Olive Tree and Branch — A285

1972, July 18   Wmk. 350   Perf. 14
1042 A285 40c lt grn, ocher & blk   .30 .25
  a.   40c light green, yellow & black 3.00 3.00
  Centenary of Chilpancingo as capital of Guerrero State.

Margarita Maza de Juárez — A286

Design: 40c, Benito Juárez, by Diego Rivera.

1972, Sept. 15   Photo.   Wmk. 300
1043 A286 20c pink & multi   .40 .25
1044 A286 40c dp yellow & multi   .40 .25
  Nos. 1043-1044,C403-C405 (5) 1.65 1.25
  Benito Juárez (1806-1872), revolutionary leader and president of Mexico.

Emperor Justinian I, Mosaic A287

1972, Sept. 30   Wmk. 300
1045 A287 40c multicolored   .65 .25
  Mexican Bar Association, 50th anniv.

Caravel — A288

1972, Oct. 12   Wmk. 350
1046 A288 80c buff, pur & ocher   .40 .25
  Stamp Day of The Americas.

Olympic Emblems A289

1972, Dec. 9   Wmk. 300
1047 A289 40c multicolored   1.00 .25
  20th Olympic Games, Munich, Aug. 26-Sept. 11. See Nos. C410-C411.

Library, Book Year Emblem — A290

1972, Dec. 16
1048 A290 40c black & multi   .30 .25
  International Book Year 1972.

Fish in Clean Water A291

1972, Dec. 16
1049 A291 40c blk & lt bl   .40 .25
  Anti-pollution campaign. See No. C412.

Metlac Railroad Bridge — A292

1973, Feb. 2   **Perf. 14**
1050 A292 40c multicolored   .85 .25
   Centenary of Mexican railroads.

Cadet — A293

1973, Oct. 11   **Photo.**   **Wmk. 300**
1051 A293 40c black & multi   .45 .25
   Sesquicentennial of Military College.

Madero, by Diego Rivera — A294

1973, Nov. 9   **Wmk. 350**   **Perf. 14**
1052 A294 40c multicolored   .30 .25
   Pres. Francisco I. Madero (1873-1913).

Antonio Narro — A295

1973, Nov. 9   **Photo.**
1053 A295 40c steel gray   .35 .25
   50th anniversary of the Antonio Narro Agriculture School in Saltillo.

Type of 1950-52

Designs as before.

1973   **Unwmk.**   **Perf. 14**
1054 A189 20c blue violet   5.00 2.00
1055 A189 40c red orange   5.00 2.00
   Fluorescent printing on back (or on front of 40c) consisting of network pattern and diagonal inscription.

Unsaturated Hydrocarbon Molecule — A296

Wmk. 300
1973, Dec. 7   **Photo.**   **Perf. 14**
1056 A296 40c blk, dk car & yel   .30 .25

Pointing Hand Emblem of Foreign Trade Institute — A297

1974, Jan. 11   **Photo.**   **Wmk. 300**
1057 A297 40c dk green & blk   .30 .25
   Export promotion.

A298

1974, Jan. 18   **Litho.**   **Wmk. 300**
1058 A298 40c black   .30 .25
   EXMEX 73 Philatelic Exhibition, Cuernavaca, Apr. 7-15. See No. C424.

Manuel M. Ponce at Keyboard A299

1974, Jan. 18   **Photo.**   **Wmk. 300**
1059 A299 40c gold & multi   .30 .25
   Manuel M. Ponce (1882-1948), composer.

Silver Statuette of Mexican Woman — A300

1974, Mar. 23   **Photo.**   **Perf. 14**
1060 A300 40c red & multi   .30 .25
   First World Silver Fair.

Mariano Azuela A301

1974, Apr. 26   **Wmk. 300**   **Perf. 14**
1061 A301 40c multicolored   .30 .25
   Mariano Azuela (1873-1952), writer.

Dancing Dogs, Pre-Columbian A302

1974, Apr. 10
1062 A302 40c multicolored   .30 .25
   6th Traveling Dog Exhibition, Mexico City, Nov. 23-Dec. 1.

Aqueduct, Tepotzotlan — A303

1974, July 1   **Photo.**   **Wmk. 300**
1063 A303 40c brt blue & blk   .45 .25
   National Engineers' Day, July 1.

Dr. Rodolfo Robles A304

1974, July 19   **Perf. 14**
1064 A304 40c bister & grn   .30 .25
   25th anniv. of WHO (in 1973).

EXFILMEX 74 Emblem — A305

1974, July 26   **Perf. 13x12**
1065 A305 40c buff, grn & blk   .30 .25
   EXFILMEX 74, 5th Inter-American Philatelic Exhibition honoring UPU cent, Mexico City, 10/26-11/3. See No. C429.

Demosthenes A306

1974, Aug. 2   **Photo.**   **Perf. 14**
1066 A306 20c green & brn   .35 .25
   2nd Spanish-American Cong. for Reading and Writing Studies, Mexico City, May 7-14.

Map of Chiapas and Head A307

1974, Sept. 14   **Wmk. 300**   **Perf. 14**
1067 A307 20c black & grn   .30 .25
   Sesquicentenary of Chiapas statehood.

Law of 1824 — A308

1974, Oct. 11   **Wmk. 300**
1068 A308 40c gray & grn   .30 .25
   Sesquicentennial of the establishment of the Federal Republic of Mexico.

Sebastian Lerdo de Tejada — A309

1974, Oct. 11   **Photo.**
1069 A309 40c black & lt bl   .30 .25
   Centenary of restoration of the Senate.

UPU Monument, Bern A310

1974, Dec. 13   **Wmk. 300**   **Perf. 14**
1070 A310 40c ultra & org brn   .30 .25
     Nos. 1070,C437-C438 (3)   .80 .75
   Cent. of UPU.

Types of 1950-56

Designs (as 1951-56 issues): 80c, Michoacan dance of the Moors. 2.30p, Guillermo Prieto. 3p, Modernistic church, Nuevo Leon. 50p, Benito Juarez.

1975   **Photo.**   **Wmk. 300**   **Perf. 14**
1072 A189   80c green   .55 .25
1075 A200 2.30p dp violet bl   .85 .35
1076 A189   3p brick red   .85 .35
1081 A189   50p orange & grn   10.00 7.50
     Nos. 1072-1081 (4)   12.25 8.45
   See No. 1097 for unwmkd. 3p with no shading under "Leon."

Handicrafts
A509

100p, Lacquerware tray, Uruapan, Michoacan. 200p, Blanket, Santa Ana Chiautempan, Tlaxcala. 230p, Lidded jar, Puebla, Pue.

1987, May 29   Photo.   Perf. 14
1480	A509 100p multicolored	.30	.25
1481	A509 200p multicolored	.60	.35
1482	A509 230p multicolored	1.00	.50
	Nos. 1480-1482 (3)	1.90	1.10

Genaro Estrada,
(1887-1937) Political
Reformer — A510

1987, June 2
1483	A510 100p pale pink, blk & pale rose	.30	.25

See Nos. 1509, 1568-1569.

Native Traders, 1961, Mural by P.
O'Higgins — A511

1987, June 8
1484	A511 100p multicolored	.30	.25

Nat'l. Bank of Int'l. Commerce, 50th anniv.

Publication of the 1st Shipbuilding
Manual in the Americas, by Diego
Garcia Palacio, 400th Anniv. — A512

1987, June 15
1485	A512 100p multicolored	.30	.25

Nat'l. Food
Program,
50th. Anniv.
A513

1987, June 22
1486	A513 100p multicolored	.30	.25

Rotunda of Illustrious Men Type of 1986

1987, June 22
1487	A498 100p multicolored	.30	.25

Leandro Valle (1833-1861), General.

Paintings by Saturnino Herran (1887-
1918) — A514

1917 paintings: No. 1488, Self-portrait with Skull. No. 1489, The Offering. No. 1490, Creole Woman with Mantilla.

1987, July 9
1488	A514 100p black & red brn	.35	.25
1489	A514 100p multicolored	.35	.25
1490	A514 400p multicolored	1.10	.75
	Nos. 1488-1490 (3)	1.80	1.25

Export Type of 1975

Designs: 10p, Meat cuts marked on steer. 20p, Bicycle. 50p, Tomatoes. 300p, Motor vehicle. 500p, Petroleum valves. 600p, Jewelry. 700p, Film. 800p, Construction materials. 900p, Pistons. 1,000p, Agricultural machinery. 2,000p, Wrought iron. 3,000p, Electric wiring. 4,000p, Honey. 5,000p, Cotton.

1987-88   Photo.   Unwmk.   Perf. 14
1491	A320 10p brt carmine	.25	.25
1492	A320 20p black & org	.25	.25
1493	A320 50p ver & yel grn	.45	.25
1494	A320 300p chalky blue & scar, type I	.45	.25
1495	A320 300p Prus blue & brt rose	.55	.25
a.	Thin paper	1.10	.25
b.	Brt blue & brt rose	.60	.25
1496	A320 500p dark gray & Prus blue	.90	.25
1497	A320 600p multicolored	1.75	.30
a.	Thin paper	1.50	.25
1498	A320 700p brt yel grn, dark red & blk	1.50	.75
a.	Brt yel grn, lilac rose & blk	1.75	.85
1499	A320 800p dark red brn & golden brn	2.50	1.25
1500	A320 900p black	5.00	2.10

Wmk. 300
Granite Paper
Type I Burelage in Gray
1501	A320 1000p dk red & blk	6.00	1.10
1502	A320 2000p black	5.50	1.75
1503	A320 3000p gray blk & org	5.50	1.75
1504	A320 4000p yel org & red brn	5.00	2.50
1505	A320 5000p apple grn & org	6.50	3.25
	Nos. 1491-1505 (15)	42.10	16.25

Issue years: 10p-50p, 1987; others, 1988.

A515

10th Pan American Games,
Indianapolis — A516

Unwmk.

1987, Aug. 7   Photo.   Perf. 14
1506	A515 100p multicolored	.30	.25
1507	A516 200p blk, brt grn & dk red	.30	.25

Federal Power Commission, 50th
Anniv. — A517

1987, Aug. 14   Photo.   Perf. 14
1508	A517 200p multicolored	.40	.25

Art and Science Type of 1987

Design: J.E. Hernandez y Davalos (1827-1893), historian.

1987, Aug. 25   Perf. 14
1509	A510 100p buff, blk & dull red brn	.30	.25

Pre-Hispanic Art Type of 1980

Designs: 100p, Xolotl (d. 1232), king of Amaquemecan. 200p, Nezahualpilli (1460-1516), king of Texcoco, conqueror. 400p, Motecuhzoma Ilhuicamina (Montezuma I d. 1469), emperor of Tenochtitlan (1440-1469).

1987, Aug. 31   Perf. 14
1510	A361 100p multicolored	.30	.25
1511	A361 200p multicolored	.50	.30
1512	A361 400p multicolored	.90	.35
	Nos. 1510-1512 (3)	1.70	.90

Tourism Type of 1979

Designs: 100p, Central Public Library, Mexico State. No. 1514, Patzcuaro Harbor, Michoacan. No. 1515, Garcia Caverns, Nuevo Leon. No. 1516, Beach resort, Mazatlan, Sinaloa.

1987   Perf. 14
1513	A353 100p multicolored	.30	.25
1514	A353 150p multicolored	.30	.25
1515	A353 150p multicolored	.30	.25
1516	A353 150p multicolored	.30	.25
	Nos. 1513-1516 (4)	1.20	1.00

Issue dates: 100p, Sept. 11; others, Oct. 19.

Formula 1 Grand Prix Race, Oct.
18 — A518

1987, Sept. 11
1517	A518 100p multicolored	.30	.25

13th Intl. Cartography
Conference — A519

1987, Oct. 12
1518	A519 150p Map, 16th cent.	.30	.25

Discovery
of America,
500th
Anniv. (in
1992)
A520

Design: Santa Maria, emblem of the Discovery of America Festival to be held in 1992.

1987, Oct. 12   Perf. 14
1519	A520 150p multicolored	3.50	.25

For overprint see No. 1698.

Illuminated Codices Type of 1982

Mendocino Codex (c. 1541): No. 1520, Founding of Tenochtitlan by the Aztecs, 1324. No. 1521, Pre-Hispanic wedding. No. 1522, Montezuma's Council.

1987, Nov. 3
1520	A408 150p multicolored	.35	.25
1521	A408 150p multicolored	.35	.25
1522	A408 150p multicolored	.35	.25
	Nos. 1520-1522 (3)	1.05	.75

Christmas
1987
A521

1987, Nov. 6
1523	A521 150p brt pink	.30	.25
1524	A521 150p dull blue	.30	.25

World Post
Day
A522

Documents: 150p, Ordinance for expediting mail by sea, 1777. 600p, Roster of correspondence transported by coach, 1857.

1987, Nov. 12
1525	A522 150p pale gray & slate gray	.30	.25

Size: 129x102mm
Imperf
1526	A522 600p rose lake & yel bis	3.00	1.00

Meeting of Eight Latin American
Presidents, 1st Anniv. — A523

1987, Nov. 26   Perf. 14
1527	A523 250p shown	.40	.25
1528	A523 500p Flags, peace doves	.60	.40

Dualidad 1964, by Rufino Tamayo (b. 1899) — A524

1987, Dec. 9
1529 A524 150p multicolored .35 .25

Nationalization of Mexican Railroads, 50th Anniv. — A525

1987, Dec. 15
1530 A525 150p Metlac Bridge 1.00 .25

Antonio Stradivarius (c. 1644-1737), Italian Violin Maker — A526

1987, Dec. 18   *Perf. 14*
1531 A526 150p bluish lilac .40 .25

Constitutional Tribunal of the Supreme Court, Plenum Hall, Jan. 15 — A527

Design: Statue of Manuel Rejon, author of the Mexican constitution.

1988, Jan. 15   **Photo.**   *Perf. 14*
1532 A527 300p multicolored .50 .30

Fauna A528

1988, Feb. 29   **Photo.**   *Perf. 14*
1533 A528 300p Ambystoma
     mexicanum 1.00 .40
1534 A528 300p Trichechus
     manatus 1.00 .40

A529

Nationalization of the Petroleum Industry, 50th Anniv. — A530

1988, Mar. 18
1535 A529 300p blue & blk .30 .25
1536 A530 300p PEMEX em-
     blem, vert. .30 .25
1537 A530 500p shown .40 .35
     Nos. 1535-1537 (3) 1.00 .85

Vaccination, Detroit, 1932, Mural (detail) by Diego Rivera — A531

1988, Apr. 7
1538 A531 300p olive grn & hen-
     na brn .35 .25
World Health Day: child immunization.

The People in Pursuit of Health, 1953, by Diego Rivera — A532

1988, Apr. 7
1539 A532 300p multicolored .35 .25
World Health Organization, 40th anniv.

Vallejo in Repose (Large) — A533

Vallejo in Repose (Small) — A534

1988, Apr. 15
1540 A533 300p shown .35 .25
1541 A533 300p Portrait, diff.
     (large) .35 .25
   a. Pair, #1540-1541 + label 3.25 3.25
   b. Bklt. pane of 4 (2 each
     #1540-1541) + label 250.00
1542 A534 300p shown .35 .25
1543 A534 300p As #1541
     (small) .35 .25
   a. Pair, #1542-1543 + label 3.25 3.25
     Nos. 1540-1543 (4) 1.40 1.00

Cesar Vallejo (1892-1938), Peruvian poet. Stamps of the same type printed se-tenant in sheets of 20 stamps containing 10 pairs plus 5

---

labels between inscribed with various Vallejo quotes or commemorative text.
     Issued: No. 1541b, 11/9/90. Label in No. 1541b is overprinted in red with Mexican Chicagopex '90 souvenir cancel, and had limited distribution.

Sketch of Carlos Pellicer Camara (1897-1977), Poet, by Fontanelly — A535

1988, Apr. 23
1544 A535 300p pale vio, blk &
     sal .35 .25

MEPSIRREY '88 Philatelic Exhibition, Monterrey, May 27-29 — A536

1988, May 27
1545 A536 300p Youth collectors .35 .25
1546 A536 300p Handstamped
     cover .35 .25
1547 A536 500p Alfa Planetarium .55 .50
     Nos. 1545-1547 (3) 1.25 1.00

Mexico-Elmhurst Philatelic Society Intl. (MEPSI).

1988 Formula I Grand Prix of Mexico — A537

Design: Layout of Hermanos Rodriguez race track, Mexico City, and car.

1988, May 28   **Photo.**   *Perf. 14*
1548 A537 500p multicolored .50 .35

A538

Ramon Lopez Velarde (1888-1921), Poet — A539

1988, June 15
1549 A538 300p multicolored .30 .25
1550 A539 300p multicolored .30 .25
   a. Bklt. pane of 4 + label 250.00

     Issue date: No. 1550a, Nov. 9, 1990. Label in No. 1550a is overprinted in red with Mexican Chicagopex '90 souvenir cancel, and had limited distribution.

University Military Pentathlon, 50th Anniv. — A540

1988, July 9   **Photo.**   *Perf. 14*
1551 A540 300p multicolored .30 .25

1st Mexico-Japan Friendship, Commerce and Navigation Treaty, Cent. — A541

1988, Aug. 16
1552 A541 500p multicolored .50 .35

Joint Oceanographic Assembly, Acapulco, Aug. 23-31 — A542

1988, Aug. 23
1553 A542 500p multicolored .50 .35

1988 Summer Olympics, Seoul — A543

1988, Aug. 31   **Photo.**   *Perf. 14*
1554 A543 500p multicolored 1.00 .35
     Size: 71x55mm
     Imperf
1555 A543 700p Emblems,
     Olympic flame 3.50 .60

World Boxing Council, 25th Anniv. A544

1988, Sept. 9
1556 A544 500p multi .50 .35

Intl. Red Cross and Red Crescent Organizations, 125th Annivs. — A545

1988, Sept. 23   **Photo.**   **Perf. 14**
1557 A545 300p blk, gray & scar   .30   .25

Jose Guadalupe Posada (1852-1913), Painter, Illustrator — A546

1988, Sept. 29
1558 A546 300p sil & blk   .30   .25

World Wildlife Fund — A547

Various monarch butterflies, *Danaus plexippus.*

1988, Sept. 30   **Perf. 14**
1559 A547 300p shown   3.00   .65
1560 A547 300p Three adults   3.00   .65
1561 A547 300p Larva, adult,
             pupa   3.00   .65
1562 A547 300p Five adults   3.00   .65
     Nos. 1559-1562 (4)   12.00 2.60

Rotunda of Illustrious Men Type of 1986

Portrait and eternal flame: Manuel Sandoval Vallarta (1899-1977), physicist.

1988, Oct. 5
1563 A498 300p multi   .30   .25

World Post Day A548

1988, Oct. 9   **Perf. 14**
1564 A548 500p World map   .50   .35
     Size: 75x44mm
        Imperf
1565 A548 700p Envelope,
          doves, Earth   3.50 1.00

Discovery of America, 500th Anniv. (in 1992) — A549

Illuminations: Aztec painter Tlacuilo from the Mendocine Codex, 1541, and Dominican scribe from the Yanhuitlan Codex, 1541-50.

1988, Oct. 12   **Perf. 14**
1566 A549 500p multi   .50   .35

World Food Day A550

1988, Oct. 16   **Perf. 14**
1567 A550 500p multi   .50   .35

Art and Science Type of 1987

No. 1568, Alfonso Caso (1896-1970), educator, founder of the Natl. Museum of Anthropology. No. 1569, Vito Alessio Robles (1879-1957), historian.

1988, Oct. 24   **Perf. 14**
1568 A510 300p gray & blk   .30   .25
1569 A510 300p pale yel, blk &
          red brn   .30   .25

Act of Independence, 175th Anniv. — A551

1988, Nov. 9
1570 A551 300p claret brn &
          fawn   .30   .25

Art Type of 1986

Paintings by Antonio M. Ruiz (1895-1964): No. 1571, *Parade*, 1936. No. 1572, *La Malinche*, 1939. No. 1573, *Self-portrait*, 1925, vert.

1988, Nov. 21   **Perf. 14**
1571 A490 300p multi   .30   .25
1572 A490 300p multi   .30   .25
1573 A490 300p multi   .30   .25
     Nos. 1571-1573 (3)   .90   .75

Tempera and Oil Paintings by Jose Reyes (b. 1924) A552

1988, Nov. 25   **Perf. 14**
1574 A552 300p Feast   .30   .25
1575 A552 300p Pinata, vert.   .30   .25
     Christmas.

Municipal Workers' Trade Union, 50th Anniv. A553

1988, Dec. 5   **Perf. 14**
1576 A553 300p pale bister & blk   .30   .25

Flora — A554

1988, Dec. 20   **Perf. 14**
1577 A554 300p Ustilago maydis   .30   .25
1578 A554 300p Mimosa
          tenuiflora   .30   .25

Exporta Type of 1975

Designs: 40p, 1400p, Chemistry flasks. 200p, Citrus fruit. 450p, Circuit board. 750p, Film. 950p, Pistons. 1000p, Agricultural machinery. 1100p, Minerals. 1300p, Strawberries. 1500p, Copper vase. 1600p, Steel pipes. 1700p, Tequila. 1900p, Abalone. 2000p, Wrought iron. 2100p, Bicycles. 2500p, Overalls. 5000p, Cotton.
Nos. 1588A, 1589, 1592, 1598A, 1599, 1601, 1603 have gray burelage Type I.

1988-92   **Photo.**   **Unwmk.**   **Perf. 14**
          Design A320
1583   40p black   .25   .25
1584   200p emer & brt yel   .50   .25
   a.   Thin paper   1.10   .40
1585   450p yel bister & lil
          rose   .75   .25
   a.   Thin paper   1.25   .40
1586   750p brt yel grn, dark
          red & dark
          gray   2.00   .40
1587   950p indigo   1.75   .60
   a.   Thin paper   2.25   .75
1588   1000p dark red & blk   1.10   .25
1588A 1000p dark red & blk,
          type 1   2.50   .25
1589   1100p dark gray, type I   1.75   .40
1590   1100p dark gray   2.25   .50
1591   1300p red & grn   2.25   .55
1592   1300p red & grn, type I   2.00   .55
   a.   Thin paper   3.00   .75
1593   1400p black   1.75   .50
1594   1500p tan   1.75   .60
   a.   1500p orange brown   1.75   .60
1595   1600p red orange   1.60   .55
1596   1700p dk grn & yel grn   1.60   .60
1597   1900p bl grn & bl   1.75   .65
1598   2000p black   2.75   .75
1598A 2000p black, type 1   2.25   .25
1599   2100p black & orange,
          type I   4.00   .85
1600   2100p black & ver   7.50 1.00
1601   2500p dark blue, type I   4.00 1.00
1602   2500p slate blue   4.00   .90
1603   5000p apple grn & org,
          type I   4.50 1.90
     Nos. 1583-1603 (23)   54.55 13.80

Issued: 40p, 1/5/88; 200p, 2/27/89; 450p, 2/10/89; No. 1585a, 950p, No. 1587a, 1589, 3/30/89; 1,000p, 1989; Nos. 1590, 1599, 1601, 1991; Nos. 1600, 1602, 5000p, 1992; others, 1990.

Graphic Arts Workshop, 50th Anniv. A555

1989, Feb. 9   **Photo.**   **Perf. 14**
1604 A555 450p yel bis, red &
          blk   .45   .35

Coat of Arms and *E Santo Domingo*, the Natl. Hymn — A556

1989, Feb. 27
1605 A556 450p multicolored   .45   .35
     Dominican Republic independence, 145th anniv.

Intl. Border and Territorial Waters Commission of Mexico and the US, Cent. — A557

1989, Mar. 1
1606 A557 1100p multi   1.25   .80

10th Intl. Book Fair A558

1989, Mar. 4
1607 A558 450p UNAM School
         of Engineering   .45   .35

Lyricists and Composers Soc., 25th Anniv. A559

1989, Mar. 17
1608 A559 450p multi   .45   .35

World Day for the Fight Against AIDS — A560

1989, Apr. 7
1609 A560 450p multi   .45   .35

Leona Vicario (1779-1842), Heroine of the Independence Movement — A561

1989, Apr. 20   **Photo.**   **Perf. 14**
1610 A561 450p blk, sepia &
          golden brn   .45   .35

Alfonso Reyes (1889-1959), Author, Educator — A562

1989, May 17
1611 A562 450p multi   .45   .35

Formula 1 Grand Prix of
Mexico — A563

1989, May 28   *Perf. 14*
1612 A563 450p multi   .45   .35

14th Tourism
Congress,
Acapulco — A564

1989, June 11   *Perf. 14*
1613 A564 1100p multi   1.10   .80

14th Intl. Gerontology
Congress,
Mexico — A565

Statue: The god Huehueteotl as an old man
bearing the weight of the world on his
shoulders.

1989, June 18
1614 A565 450p multi   .45   .35

Battle of Zacatecas, 75th
Anniv. — A566

1989, June 23
1615 A566 450p black   .45   .35

Baseball Hall of Fame of
Mexico — A567

1989, June 25
1616 A567 550p Umpire,
                 catcher   3.00   .45
1617 A567 550p Batter   3.00   .45
  a.   Pair, #1616-1617 + label   15.00   15.00
  No. 1617a has continuous design.

35th World Archery Championships,
Lausanne, Switzerland, July 4-
8 — A568

1989, July 2
1618 A568 650p Bows and ar-
                 rows   1.50   .50
1619 A568 650p Arrows, target   1.50   .50
  a.   Pair, #1618-1619 + label   15.00   15.00
  No. 1619a has continuous design.

Tijuana,
Cent.
A569

1989, July 11   Photo.   *Perf. 14*
1620 A569 1100p Municipal arms   .90   .70

French
Revolution,
Bicent.
A570

1989, July 14
1621 A570 1300p blue, blk &
                  dark red   1.40   .80

Gen. Francisco Xavier Mina (1789-
1817), Independence Hero — A571

1989, Sept. 7
1622 A571 450p green, blk &
                 dark red   .50   .30

Natl. Museum of Anthropology,
Chapultepec, 25th Anniv. — A572

1989, Sept. 17   *Perf. 14*
1623 A572 450p multicolored   .50   .30

7th Mexico City Marathon — A573

1989, Sept. 24
1624 A573 450p multicolored   .50   .30

Printing in America, 450th
Anniv. — A574

1989, Sept. 28
1625 A574 450p multicolored   .50   .30

World Post
Day
A575

1989, Oct. 9   Photo.   *Perf. 14*
1626 A575 1100p multicolored   1.10   .65

Sovereign Revolutionary Convention of
Aguascalientes, 75th Anniv. — A576

1989, Oct. 10
1627 A576 450p multicolored   .90   .25

Exploration and Colonization of the
Americas by Europeans — A577

1989, Oct. 12
1628 A577 1300p multicolored   2.00   .75

America Issue — A578

UPAE emblem and symbols like those produced on art by pre-Columbian peoples.

1989, Oct. 12
1629 A578 450p shown   .50   .25
1630 A578 450p multi, diff., vert.   .50   .25

Natl. Tuberculosis
Foundation, 50th
Anniv. — A579

1989, Nov. 10
1631 A579 450p multicolored   .35   .25

Mask of the
Bat God,
Zapoteca
Culture, c.
200-300
A580

1989, Nov. 28
1632 A580 450p multicolored   .50   .25

Serfin
Commercial
Bank of
Mexico,
125th
Anniv.
A581

1989, Nov. 29
1633 A581 450p deep blue, gold
                 & blk   .50   .25

Pres. Adolfo Ruiz Cortines (1889-
1973) — A582

1989, Dec. 3
1634 A582 450p multicolored   .50   .25

Christmas
A583

1989, Dec. 11
1635 A583 450p Candlelight vigil   .50   .25
1636 A583 450p Man sees star,
                 vert.   .50   .25

Natl. Institute of Anthropology and
Natural History, 50th Anniv. — A584

1989, Dec. 13
1637 A584 450p dark red, gold &
              black   .60   .25

Nationalization of the Railway System
in Mexico, 80th Anniv. — A585

1989
1638 A585 450p multicolored   .70   .25

**Issue dates for some 1990-1991
issues are based on First Day
cancels. Original printings were
small. Later printings, made in 1991,
were distributed to the stamp trade
and seem to be the ones used for
"First Day Covers."**

Tampico Bridge — A586

1990, Jan. 11   Photo.   Perf. 14
1639 A586 600p gold, blk & red   .80   .30

Eradication of Polio — A587

1990, Feb. 1
1640 A587 700p multicolored   .70   .35

Natl.
Census
A588

1990, Mar. 12
1641 A588 700p lt grn & yel   .75   .35

Mexican Philatelic Assoc., 10th
Anniv. — A589

1990, Apr. 19
1642 A589 700p multicolored   .75   .35

Natl. Archives, Bicentennial — A590

1990, Apr. 24
1643 A590 700p pale violet   .75   .35

Intl. Conf. of Advertising
Agencies — A591

1990, Apr. 27
1644 A591 700p multicolored   .75   .35

Stamp
World
London
'90 — A592

1990, May 3
1645 A592 700p multicolored   .80   .35

First Postage Stamps, 150th
Anniv. — A593

1990, May 6
1646 A593 700p lake, gold & blk   .80   .35

15th Tourism
Exposition — A594

1990, May 6
1647 A594 700p multicolored   .75   .35

Visit
of
Pope
John
Paul II
A595

1990, May 6
1648 A595 700p multicolored   .80   .35

Health of
Young
Mothers
A596

1990, May 10
1649 A596 700p multicolored   .75   .35

Fight Against
Smoking — A597

1990, May 31
1650 A597 700p multicolored   .75   .35

World Environment Day — A598

1990, June 5
1651 A598 700p multicolored   .75   .35

Formula 1 Grand Prix of
Mexico — A599

1990, June 24
1652 A599 700p grn, red & blk   .75   .35

Airport & Auxiliary Services, 25th
Anniv. — A600

1990, June 25   Photo.   Perf. 14
1653 A600 700p multicolored   .70   .35

Fight Against Drugs — A601

1990, June 26
1654 A601 700p multicolored   .75   .35

Protection of Rain Forests — A602

1990, July 6
1655 A602 700p multicolored   .90   .35

Solidarity with Poor People — A603

1990, Aug. 8
1656 A603 700p multicolored   .70   .35

   Solidarity is a governmental social program
of Pres. Salinas de Gortari. See No. 1704.

Voyages of Discovery A647

Discovery of America, 500th Anniv. (in 1992) A648

Design: No. 1708, Sailing ship, storm.

1991, Oct. 12
1707 A647 1000p multicolored 1.75 .60
1708 A647 1000p multicolored 1.75 .60
a. Pair, #1707-1708 4.00 1.25
1709 A648 1000p multicolored 2.50 .60
Nos. 1707-1709 (3) 6.00 1.80

No. 1708a has continuous design. Printed in sheets of 20+5 labels.

Christmas A649

Christmas A650

1991, Nov. 26
1710 A649 1000p multicolored .85 .60
1711 A650 1000p multicolored .85 .60

Carlos Merida, Birth Cent. A651

1991, Dec. 2 Photo. Rouletted 6½
1712 A651 1000p multicolored .85 .60

Wolfgang Amadeus Mozart, Death Bicent. A652

1991, Dec. 5
1713 A652 1000p multicolored .85 .60

Self-sufficiency in Corn and Bean Production — A653

1991, Dec. 11 Photo. Rouletted 6½
1714 A653 1000p multicolored .80 .55

City of Morelia, 450th Anniv. A654

1991, Dec. 13
1715 A654 1000p multicolored .80 .55

Merida, 450th Anniv. A655

1992, Jan. 6 Photo. R
1716 A655 1300p multicolored

1992, Jan. 15
1717 A656 1300p blue & red

1992 Summer Olympics, Barcelona A657

Design: No. 1719, Stylized

1992 Photo. P
1718 A657 2000p multicolore
1719 A657 2000p multicolore
Issued: No. 1718, Feb. 10; No

Guadalajara, 450th Ann

No. 1720: a, 1300p, Coat of
Municipal buildings. c, 1300
Cathedral. d, 1900p, Allego
founding. e, 1900p, Anniver

1992, Feb. 14
1720 A658 Strip of 5, #a.-e.

Healthy
Develop

1992, Feb. 26
1721 A659 2000p multicolor

Formula 1 Grand Prix of Mexico A660

1992, Mar. 22
1722 A660 1300p multicolo

Introduction of the wheel a horses to America, 500th ann

Oaxaca Cultural Heritage — A604

1990, Aug. 10
1657 A604 700p multicolored .75 .35

Nature Conservation — A605

1990, Aug. 21
1658 A605 700p blk, gray & org .85 .35

Mexican Institute of Petroleum, 25th Anniv. A606

1990, Aug. 23
1659 A606 700p black & blue .75 .35

8th Mexico City Marathon — A607

1990, Aug. 24
1660 A607 700p blk, red & grn .75 .35

University of Colima, 50th Anniv. A608

1990, Sept. 16
1661 A608 700p gray, bister, rod & grn .70 .35

Mexico City Advisory Council, Founded in 1929 — A609

1990, Sept. 17
1662 A609 700p sil, yel, blk & org .70 .35

Nationalization of Electric Industry, 30th Anniv. — A610

1990, Sept. 27
1663 A610 700p gray, grn, red & blk .75 .35

City of Campeche, 450th Anniv. A611

1990, Oct. 4
1664 A611 700p multicolored 70 .35

Silvestre Revueltas (1899-1940), Musician — A612

1990, Oct. 4
1665 A612 700p multicolored .60 .35

Plan of San Luis, 80th Anniv. A613

1990, Oct. 5
1666 A613 700p multicolored .60 .35

14th World Conference of Supreme Counselors — A614

1990, Oct. 8
1667 A614 1500p vio, sil, gold & grn 1.10 .80

Discovery of America, 498th Anniv. — A615

1990, Oct. 12
1668 A615 700p multicolored .50 .35

Mexican Archaeology, Bicentennial — A616

1990, Nov. 18
1669 A616 1500p multicolored 1.50 .80

16th Central American and Caribbean Games — A617

1990, Nov. 20
1670 A617 750p shown .75 .40
1671 A617 750p Mayan ball player .75 .40
1672 A617 750p Mayan ball player, vert. .75 .40
1673 A617 750p Ball court, stone ring, vert. .75 .40
a. Strip of 4, #1670-1673 4.50 4.50
Nos. 1670-1673 (4) 3.00 1.60

Christmas
A618 A619

1990, Dec. 3
1674 A618 700p Poinsettias .70 .35
1675 A619 700p Candles .70 .35

Mexican Canine Federation, 50th Anniv. A620

1990, Dec. 9
1676 A620 700p multicolored .80 .35

World Post Day A621

1990, Oct. 9 Photo. Perf. 14
1677 A621 1500p multicolored 1.50 .80

America Issue A622

No. 1678, Flowers, galleon. No. 1679, Galleon, parrot.

1990, Oct. 12
1678 A622 700p multicolored .85 .35
1679 A622 700p multicolored .85 .35
a. Pair, #1678-1679 + blank label 2.75 2.75

No. 1679a has continuous design.

Mexican Brewing Industry, Cent. — A623

1990, Nov. 8 Perf. 14
1680 A623 700p multicolored .75 .35

National Chamber of Industrial Development, 50th Anniv. — A624

1990, Dec. 5 Perf. 14
1601 A624 1500p multicolored 1.40 .80

Naval Secretariat, 50th Anniv. A625

1991, Jan. 4 Photo. Perf. 14
1682 A625 1000p bl, blk & gold .90 .50

Prevent Transportation Accidents — A626

1991, Jan. 11   Photo.   Perf. 14
1683 A626 700p multicolored   .75 .40

Natl. Consumers Institute, 15th Anniv. — A627

1991, Feb. 11
1684 A627 1000p multicolored   .80 .55

Voter Registration A628

1991, Feb. 13   Perf. 14
1685 A628 1000p org, blk & grn   .80 .55

Olympic Basketball — A629

1991, Feb. 25   Perf. 14
1686 A629 1000p black & yellow   1.00 .55

Campaign Against Polio — A630

1991, Mar. 8
1687 A630 1000p multicolored   1.25 .55

Nos. 1688-1691, 1697 with "NP" and Post Office eagle head logo or just the logo, are specimens.

Childrens' Day for Peace and Development — A631

Salud e Integración Familiar

1991, Apr. 16
1688 A631 1000p multicolo...
1689 A632 1000p multicolo...

Mining in Mexico, 500th Anniv. — A633

1991, Apr. 25
1690 A633 1000p multicol...

Promotion of Breastf...

1991, May 10
1691 A634 1000p multico...

16th ... Expos...

1991, May 12
1692 A635 1000p brt grr... grn

Rotary Intl. Convention A636

1991, June 2
1693 A636 1000p blue &...

Inte... Com... Tran... Sys... Cen...

Designs: No. 1695a, 1... 1500p, Airport control t... machine. d, 1500p, Upp... quarters. e, 1000p, Co... 1500p, Satellite. g, 100... earth. h, 1000p, Boxcar... tives. j, 1000p, People... 1500p, Lower floors, S... 1000p, Hillside road, ... bridge. m, 1500p, Cen... bridge. n, 1000p, Right... 1000p, Cranes loading ... Bow of cargo ship. q, 1... era. r, 1500p, Bus. s, 1... Trailers passing through... Bridge construction. Co...

1991, June 11
1694 A637 1000p gray...
1695 A637 Block of 2...

1996, Aug. 6   Litho.   Perf. 13½
Color of Film Cells
1986 A812 1.80p grn, ocher & vio   .45 .35
1987 A812 1.80p pur, grn & red   .45 .35
  a. Pair, #1986-1987   2.25 2.25

Justice Dept., 60th Anniv. A813

1996, Aug. 18
1988 A813 1.80p multicolored   .75 .35

14th Mexico City Marathon A814

1996, Aug. 20
1989 A814 2.70p multicolored   .90 .50

City of Zacatecas, 450th Anniv. A815

1996, Sept. 8
1990 A815 1.80p multicolored   .90 .35

Natl. Council to Promote Education, 25th Anniv. A816

1996, Sept. 17
1991 A816 1.80p multicolored   .90 .35

Souvenir Sheet

City of Monterrey, 400th Anniv. — A817

1996, Sept. 20
1992 A817 7.40p multicolored   4.50 4.50

Family Planning — A818

1996, Sept. 26
1993 A818 1.80p multicolored   .90 .35

Independence, 175th Anniv. — A819

1996, Sept. 27
1994 A819 1.80p multicolored   .90 .35

Endangered Species — A820

Designs show a wide variety of species, one from each stamp is: a, Aguila arpia. b, Tortola serrana. c, Monarch butterflies. d, Venado bura. e, Guacamaya roja. f, Quetzal. g, Venado cola blanca. h, Puma. i, Coyote. j, Jaguar. k, Martucha. l, Woodpecker. m, Cuco canelo. n, Lince. o, Oso hormiguero. p, Ocelote. q, Encino. r, Chachalaca. s, Liebre. t, Tapir. u, Crocodile. v, Armadillo. w, Pecari. x, Cacomixtle.

1996, Oct. 2
Sheet of 24
1995 A820 1.80p #a.-x. + label 24.00 24.00
See US No. 3105.

World Post Day — A821

1996, Oct. 9
1996 A821 2.70p multicolored   .90 .50

Salvador Zubirán Natl. Nutrition Institute, 50th Anniv. A822

1996, Oct. 12
1997 A822 1.80p multicolored   .90 .35

Radio in Mexico, 75th Anniv. — A823

1996, Oct. 13
1998 A823 1.80p multicolored   .90 .35

Paintings in Viceregal Gallery A824

Designs: a, 1.80p, Portrait of a Woman, by Baltasar de Echave Ibia. b, 2.70p, Archangel Michael, by Luis Juarez. c, 1.80p, Portrait of young Joaquín Manuel Fernández of Santa Cruz, by Nicolas Rodriguez Xuarez. d, 2.70p, The Virgin of the Apocalypse, by Miguel Cabrera. e, 1.80p, Portrait of Dona Maria Luisa Gonzaga Foncerrada y Labarrieta, by Jose Maria Vazquez.

1996, Oct. 14   Perf. 14
1999 A824 Strip of 5, #a.-e.   4.75 4.75

World Food Day — A825

1996, Oct. 31   Perf. 13½
2000 A825 2.70p multicolored   .90 .50

Mexican Science A826

1996, Sept. 2
2001 A826 1.80p multicolored   .90 .35

Intl. Subway Conference A828

1996, Nov. 12   Litho.   Perf. 13½
2003 A828 2.70p multicolored   .90 .50

Christmas A829

1996, Nov. 14   Litho.   Perf. 13½
2004 A829 1p Star pinata   .35 .25
2005 A829 1.80p Man carrying pinatas   .55 .30

Andres Henestrosa, Writer — A830

1996, Nov. 23   Litho.   Perf. 14
2006 A830 1.80p multicolored   .90 .30

Natl. Cancer Institute, 50th Anniv. A831

1996, Nov. 25   Litho.   Perf. 13½
2007 A831 1.80p multicolored   .90 .30

Paisano Program — A832

1996, Nov. 28   Litho.   Perf. 13½
2008 A832 2.70p multicolored   .90 .50

David Alfaro Siqueiros (1896-1974), Painter — A833

1996, Dec. 5   Litho.   Perf. 13½
2009 A833 1.80p multicolored   .90 .30

32nd Natl. Assembly of Surgeons A834

Dr. José Ma. Barceló de Villagrán

1996, Dec. 6   Litho.   Perf. 13½
2010 A834 1.80p multicolored   .90 .30

Wildlife Conservation — A835

1996, Dec. 11   Litho.   Perf. 14
2011 A835 1.80p Black bear, cubs   2.25 .75

UNICEF, 50th Anniv. A836

1996, Dec. 11   Litho.   Perf. 13½
2012 A836 1.80p multicolored   .90 .30

Palafoxiana Library, Puebla, 350th Anniv. — A837

1996, Dec. 17   Litho.   Perf. 13½
2013 A837 1.80p multicolored   .90 .30

Natl. Institute of Nuclear Research A838

1996, Dec. 19 Litho. Perf. 13½
2014 A838 1.80p multicolored   .90 .30

A839   A840

1996, Dec. 19 Litho. Perf. 13½
2015 A839 1.80p multicolored   .90 .30
Intl. Day for Preservation of the Ozone Layer.

1996, Dec. 20 Litho. Perf. 13½
2016 A840 1.80p multicolored   .90 .30
30 year career of plastic arts sculptor Sebastian.

Mexican Diplomats A841

Design: Isidro Fabela (b. 1882), lawyer, and Genaro Estrada (1887-1977), journalist, politician.

1996, Oct. 24 Litho. Perf. 13½
2017 A841 1.80p multicolored   .90 .30

Carlos Pellicer (1897-1977), Poet, Museum Founder — A842

1997, Jan. 16
2018 A842 2.30p multicolored   1.00 .40

Andres Eloy Blanco (1896-1955), Poet — A843

1997, Feb. 6 Litho. Perf. 13½
2019 A843 3.40p multicolored   1.40 .60

A844   A845

1997, Feb. 10
2020 A844 3.40p multicolored   1.40 .60
UNESCO Intl. Summit on Education, Confederation of American Educators.

1997, Feb. 14
2021 A845 3.40p multicolored   1.40 .60
Treaty of Tlatelolco prohibiting nuclear weapons in Latin America & Caribbean.

Souvenir Sheet

Mexican Central Post Office, 90th Anniv. — A846

1997, Feb. 20
2022 A846 7.40p multicolored   6.00 6.00

A847   A848

Generals: No. 2023, Francisco L. Urquizo. No. 2024, Mariano Escobedo. No. 2025, Jacinto B. Trevino Gonzalez. No. 2026, Felipe Angeles. No. 2027, Candido Aguilar Vargas. No. 2028, Joaquin Amaro Dominguez.

1997, Mar. 5
2023 A847 2.30p multicolored   .90 .40
2024 A847 2.30p multicolored   .90 .40
2025 A847 2.30p multicolored   .90 .40
2026 A847 2.30p multicolored   .90 .40
2027 A847 2.30p multicolored   .90 .40
2028 A847 2.30p multicolored   .90 .40
  Nos. 2023-2028 (6)   5.40 2.40

1997, Mar. 8
2029 A848 2.30p multicolored   .80 .40
Intl. Women's Day.

1st Intl. Congress for Spanish Language A849

Painting: Allegory, "La Gramatica," by Juan Correa.

1997, Apr. 7 Litho. Perf. 13½
2030 A849 3.40p multicolored   .90 .40

Dr. Ignacio Chávez, Pres. of Natl. Academy of Medicine, Birth Cent. A850

1997, Apr. 23
2031 A850 2.30p multicolored   .80 .40

Mexican Constitution, 80th Anniv. — A851

1997, Apr. 29
2032 A851 2.30p Venustiano Carranza   .80 .40

First Edition of "Al Filo Del Agua," by Agustín Yáñez, 50th Anniv. A852

1997, May 9
2033 A852 2.30p multicolored   .80 .40

Prof. Rafael Ramírez (1855-1959), Educator — A853

1997, May 15
2034 A853 2.30p green & gray   .80 .40

Japanese Emigration to Mexico, Cent. A854

1997, May 12
2035 A854 3.40p multicolored   1.75 .60
See Japan No. 2569.

A855   A856

1997, May 31
2036 A855 2.30p multicolored   .80 .40
Autonomous University of Baja California, 40th Anniv.

1997, June 26
Intl. Day to Stop Use of Illegal Drugs: a, 2.30p, Dove, clouds, sunlight. b, 3.40p, Man with one hand on bars, one hand raised

toward sky. c, 3.40p, Dove in window behind bars.
2037 A856 Strip of 3, #a.-c. + label   5.50 5.50

Sigmund Freud — A857   Naval Military School, Cent. — A858

1997, June 28
2038 A857 2.30p multicolored   .80 .40

1997, July 1
2039 A858 2.30p multicolored   .80 .40

Natl. Bank of Foreign Commerce, 60th Anniv. A859

1997, July 4 Litho. Perf. 13½
2040 A859 3.40p multicolored   1.25 .60

United for Conservation — A860

1997, July 16
2041 A860 2.30p Vaquita. calf   2.00 .90

Mexican College of Aviation Pilots, 50th Anniv. A861

1997, July 17
2042 A861 2.30p multicolored   .90 .40

15th Mexico City Marathon — A862

1997, Aug. 6
2043 A862 3.40p multicolored   1.25 .60

Juarez Hospital of Mexico, 150th Anniv. A863

1997, Aug. 18
2044 A863 2.30p multicolored   .90 .40

Battles of 1847
A864

No. 2045, Battle of Padierna. No. 2046, Battle of Churubusco. No. 2047, Battle of Molino del Rey. No. 2047A, Defense of the Castle of Chapultepec.

1997
2045	A864	2.30p multicolored	.90	.40
2046	A864	2.30p multicolored	.90	.40
2047	A864	2.30p multicolored	.90	.40
2047A	A864	2.30p multicolored	.90	.40
		Nos. 2045-2047A (4)	3.60	1.60

Issued: No. 2045, 8/19; No. 2046, 8/20; No. 2047, 9/8; No. 2047A, 9/13.

A865　　　A866

1997, Sept. 3
2048	A865	2.30p multicolored	.90	.40

Guillermo Prieto, poet, death cent.

1997, Sept. 12　Litho.　Perf. 13½
2049	A866	3.40p multicolored	1.25	.60

Battalion of St. Patrick, 150th anniv. See Ireland No. 1085.

A867　　　A868

1997, Oct. 6
2050	A867	2.30p multicolored	.90	.40

Reproductive health for adolescents month.

1997, Oct. 9
2051	A868	3.40p Stamp Day	1.25	.60

Heinrich von Stephan (1831-97)
A869

1997, Oct. 9
2052	A869	3.40p multicolored	1.25	.60

Manuel Gómez Morin (1897-1949), Politician — A870

1997, Oct. 14
2053	A870	2.30p multicolored	.90	.40

Dr. Manuel Gea González General Hospital, 50th Anniv. A871

1997, Oct. 14
2054	A871	2.30p multicolored	.90	.40

Mexican Bar Assoc. College of Law, 75th Anniv. — A872

1997, Oct. 30
2055	A872	2.30p multicolored	.90	.40

Christmas
A873

Children with piñatas: No. 2056, By Ana R. Botello. No. 2057, By Adrián Laris.

1997, Nov. 19
2056	A873	2.30p multicolored	.90	.40
2057	A873	2.30p multicolored	.90	.40

New Law on Social Security — A874

1997, Dec. 10
2058	A874	2.30p multicolored	.90	.40

Central University Hospital, Chihuahua, Cent. — A875

1997, Dec. 5　Litho.　Perf. 13½
2059	A875	2.30p multicolored	.90	.40

Dr. Mario Jose Molina Henriquez, 1995 Nobel Prize Recipient in Chemistry
A876

1997, Dec. 8
2060	A876	3.40p multicolored	1.25	.55

Baking Industry Granary, 50th Anniv. A877

Baked goods and: a, Storage shelves. b, Man working at oven. c, Basic ingredients, man working with dough.

1997, Dec. 10
2061	A877	2.30p Vert. strip of 3, #a.-c. + label	4.00	4.00

A878　　　A879

Modern Mexican art, by Jose Chavez Morado.

1997, Dec. 19
2062	A878	2.30p multicolored	.90	.40

Cervantes Festival, Guanajuato, 45th anniv.

1997, Dec. 20
2063	A879	2.30p multicolored	.90	.40

City of Loreto, 300th anniv.

Military School of Arms, 50th Anniv. A880

1998, Mar. 1　Litho.　Perf. 13½
2064	A880	2.30p multicolored	.90	.40

Intl. Mother's Day A881

1998, Mar. 8
2065	A881	2.30p multicolored	.90	.40

Cinco de Mayo — A882

1998, Apr. 16
2066	A882	3.50p multicolored	1.25	.60

See US No. 3203.

1998 World Cup Soccer Championships, France — A883

Eiffel Tower, national colors of France and Mexico and: No. 2067, Soccer player. No. 2068, Mexican Eagle mascot.
No. 2069: a, 8.60p, like #2067. b, 6.20p, like #2068.

1998
2067	A883	2.30p multicolored	1.50	1.50
2068	A883	2.30p multicolored	1.50	1.50

Souvenir Sheet
2069	A883	Sheet of 2, #a.-b.	8.00	8.00

Issued: No. 2067, 4/20; No. 2068, 5/11; No. 2069, 5/25. No. 2069 contains two 24x40mm stamps with a continuous design.

Justo Sierra, Educator, 150th Birth Anniv. — A884

1998, Apr. 23
2070	A884	2.30p multicolored	.90	.40

Dr. Salvador Zubiran, Birth Cent. A885

1998, Apr. 24
2071	A885	2.30p multicolored	.90	.40

Organization of American States, 50th Anniv. — A886

1998, Apr. 27
2072	A886	3.40p multicolored	1.00	.55

University of Puebla, 25th Anniv. A887

1998, May 6
2073	A887	2.30p multicolored	.90	.40

Teacher's Day — A888

1998, May 15
2074	A888	2.30p Soledad Anaya Solorzano	.90	.40

State of Tamaulipas (New Santander), 250th Anniv. — A889

1998, May 31
2075	A889	2.30p multicolored	.90	.40

Sports Lottery, 20th Anniv. A890

1998, June 2
2076 A890 2.30p multicolored .90 .40

Universal Declaration of Human Rights, 50th Anniv. A891

1998, June 5 Litho. Perf. 13½
2077 A891 3.40p multicolored 1.00 .35

Federico García Lorca (1898-1936), Poet — A892

1998, June 5
2078 A892 3.40p multicolored 1.00 .35

Philippine Independence, Cent. — A893

3.40p, Mexican flag, sailing ship. 7.40p, Mexican, Philippine flags, sailing ship.

1998, June 3 Litho. Perf. 13½
2079 A893 3.40p multicolored 1.00 .55
Souvenir Sheet
2080 A893 7.40p multicolored 4.75 4.75
See Philippines Nos. 2537-2539, Spain No. 2949.

Intl. Day Against Drugs — A894

1998, June 26
2081 A894 2.30p multicolored .90 .35

Chapultepec Zoological Park, 7th Anniv. — A895

Design: Alfonso L. Herrera, jaguar.

1998, July 6
2082 A895 2.30p multicolored .90 .35

Arbor Day — A896

1998, July 9
2083 A896 2.30p multicolored .90 .35

Opening of the Philatelic Museum, Oaxaca — A897

Designs: No. 2084, Convent of St. Peter and St. Paul, Teposcolula. No. 2085, Burnished vase with carving. No. 2086, San Bartolo Coyotepec, "El Camino," by Francisco Toledo. No. 2087, Golden breast plate from Tomb 7, Monte Alban.

1998, July 9
2084 A897 2.30p multicolored .90 .35
2085 A897 2.30p multicolored .90 .35
2086 A897 3.40p multicolored 1.75 .75
2087 A897 3.40p multicolored 1.75 .75
  Nos. 2084-2087 (4) 5.30 2.20

Precinct in Natl. Palace Honoring Benito Juárez (1806-72) A898

1998, July 18 Perf. 14
2088 A898 2.30p multicolored .90 .35

Santo Domingo Cultural Center, Oaxaca — A899

a, Entire complex. b, Portals of museum. c, Francisco da Burgoa Library. d, Ethnobotanical Garden.

1998, July 24 Perf. 13½
2089 A899 2.30p Block of 4, #a.-d. 4.25 4.25

Marine Life A900

a, Frigatebird, gray whale. b, Albatross. c, Whale's tail flukes. d, Dolphins, flamingos. e, Turtles. f, Sea lions. g, Elegant swallows, dolphin. h, Killer whale. i, Flamingos. j, Alligator. k, Sardines. l, Squid, loggerhead turtle. m, Bluefin tuna, jellyfish. n, Barracudas. o, Manatee. p, Garibaldi. q, Hammerhead shark. r,

Huachinango, shrimp, ray. s, Octopus, mero. t, Blowfish, turtle. u, Crab, sandollars. v, Seahorse, angelfish. w, Crab, turtle, moray eel. x, Mariposa de cuatro ojos. y, Shark, coral.

1998, Aug. 14 Sheet of 25
2090 A900 2.30p #a.-y. 25.00 25.00
  No. 2090 is a continuous design showing many different species of marine life, aquatic birds, and surrounding vegetation. Just a few species from each stamp are described in the above design note.

16th Mexico City Marathon A901

1998, Aug. 19 Litho. Perf. 13½
2091 A901 3.40p multicolored 1.00 .55

World Tourism Day A902

1998, Sept. 25
2092 A902 3.40p multicolored 1.00 .55

Natl. Archives, 175th Anniv. A903

1998, Sept. 29 Perf. 14
2093 A903 2.30p multicolored .90 .35

A904   A905

1998, Oct. 1 Perf. 13½
2094 A904 3.40p multicolored 1.00 .55
  Interpol, 75th Anniv.

1998, Oct. 5
2095 A905 2.30p multicolored .60 .35
  Reproductive Health Month.

Luis Nishizawa (b. 1918), Painter — A906

1998, Oct. 9
2096 A906 2.30p multicolored .60 .35

World Post Day A907

1998, Oct. 9
2097 A907 3.40p multicolored 1.00 .55

Heroic Military College, 175th Anniv. A908

1998, Oct. 11
2098 A908 2.30p multicolored .60 .35

District of Tamaulipas, 250th Anniv. A909

1998, Oct. 12
2099 A909 2.30p multicolored .60 .35

United for Conservation — A910

1998, Oct. 13
2100 A910 2.30p Aguila real .60 .35

World Food Day A911

1998, Oct. 16
2101 A911 3.40p multicolored 1.00 .55

Natl Mexican Migration Week A912

1998, Oct. 19
2102 A912 2.30p multicolored .60 .35

José Alfredo Jiménez (1926-72), Composer A913

1998, Nov. 11
2103 A913 2.30p multicolored .60 .35

College of Petroleum Engineers, 25th Anniv. — A914

1998, Nov. 11
2104 A914 3.40p multicolored 1.00 .55

Cultural and Economic Cooperation
Between Mexico and France — A915

1998, Nov. 12
2105 A915 3.40p multicolored 1.00 .55

City of
Colima,
475th
Anniv.
A916

1998, Nov. 16
2106 A916 2.30p multicolored .60 .35

Christmas
A917

Children's drawings: 2.30p, Nativity scene.
3.40p, Pinata, candy, vert.

1998, Nov. 17 Self-Adhesive
2107 A917 2.30p multicolored .60 .35
2108 A917 3.40p multicolored 1.00 .55

Latin American Civil
Aviation Commission,
25th Anniv. — A918

1998, Dec. 14 Litho. Perf. 13½
2109 A918 3.40p multicolored 1.00 .55

Natl.
Institute of
Native
People,
50th Anniv.
A919

1998, Dec. 4
2110 A919 2.30p multicolored .60 .35

Federation
of Govt.
Workers,
60th Anniv.
A920

1998, Dec. 7
2111 A920 2.30p multicolored .60 .35

State University of
Sinaloa, 125th
Anniv. — A921

1998, Dec. 18
2112 A921 2.30p multicolored .60 .35

Mexico's
Natl.
Program for
Women
A922

1999, Mar. 8 Litho. Perf. 13½
2113 A922 4.20p multicolored 1.25 .45

A923

1999, Feb. 9
2114 A923 3p multicolored .90 .35
Carnaval '99, Veracruz.

A924

1999, Feb. 27
2115 A924 3p Hammock .65 .35
2116 A924 4.20p Divers .90 .45
  a. Pair, #2115-2116 4.00 4.00
Acapulco, 200th Anniv.

Launching
of SATMEX
5 — A925

1999, Feb. 9
2117 A925 3p multicolored .90 .35

Souvenir Sheet

Visit of Pope John Paul II — A926

1999, Jan. 22
2118 A926 10p multicolored 5.00 5.00

Tourism Type of 1993
Denomination Shown As $
Unwmk.

1999-2001		**Photo.**	**Perf. 14**	
2119	A683	50c Coahuila	.75	.25
2120	A683	70c Yucatan	.75	.25
2121	A683	1.50p Chiapas	1.00	.25
2122	A683	2p Coahuila	1.00	.25
2123	A683	2.50p Yucatan	1.25	.25
2124	A683	2.60p Colima	2.00	.30
2125	A683	3p Michoa-can, vert.	1.75	.30
2126	A683	3.60p Coahuila	1.75	.40
2127	A683	4.20p Guana-juato	1.75	.45
2128	A683	4.20p Zacatecas, vert.	3.00	.45
2129	A683	4.50p Mexico	3.00	.50
2130	A683	4.90p Sonora	3.00	.50
2131	A683	5.30p Michoa-can, vert.	3.75	.55
2132	A683	5.90p Quereta-ro	3.50	.55
2133	A683	6p Sinaloa	3.50	.70
2134	A683	6p Michoa-can, vert.	4.00	.70
2135	A683	6.50p Quereta-ro	4.50	.70
2136	A683	7p Coahuila	4.50	.75
2137	A683	8p Zacatecas, vert.	9.00	.85
2138	A683	8p Sinaloa	4.75	.85
2139	A683	8.50p Chiapas	4.75	.90
2139A	A683	8.50p Chiapas, denomi-nation upright	5.50	1.10
2140	A683	8.50p Zacatecas, vert.	4.75	.95
2141	A683	10p Campeche	18.00	1.10
2141A	A683	10p Chiapas	7.50	1.10
2141B	A683	10.50p Michoa-can, vert.	7.00	1.10
2141C	A683	11.50p Quereta-ro	8.50	1.25
2141D	A683	30p Quereta-ro	19.00	3.25
Nos. 2119-2141D (28)			133.50	20.55

Issued: Nos. 2122, 2124, 2126, 2127, 2130-2133, 2137, 1999; No. 2120, 2000; Nos. 2119, 2121, 2123, 2125, 2128, 2129, 2134-2136, 2138-2141D, 2001.
The denomination of No. 2139 is in italics.

Natl. Commission to Distribute Free
Textbooks, 40th Anniv. — A927

1999, Mar. 11 Litho. Perf. 13½
2142 A927 3p gold & multi 1.00 .35
See Nos. 2155-2156, 2172.

Natl. Population Commission, 25th
Anniv. — A928

1999, Mar. 26
2143 A928 3p multicolored 1.00 .35

Souvenir Sheet

Ponciano Díaz Salinas (1856-99),
Bullfighter — A929

Sheet Size: 95x240mm

1999, Apr. 17
2144 A929 10p sheet of 1 5.00 5.00

Ceniceros
de Pérez
(1908-68),
Teacher
A930

1999, May 15
2145 A930 3p multicolored .90 .35
Teacher's Day.

AAA
Mexican
Baseball
League,
75th Anniv.
A931

Designs: a, Skeleton pitcher, skeleton bat-ter. b, Stylized pitcher. c, Pitcher lifting up large foot, sun. d, Catcher.

1999, May 31
2146 A931 3p Block of 4, #a.-d. 5.00 5.00
Also available in strip of 4 + label.

National Bank of Mexico, 115th
Anniv. — A932

Designs: No. 2147, Old, new bank buildings. No. 2148, 10p bill.

1999, June 2
2147 A932 3p multicolored .90 .35
2148 A932 3p multicolored .90 .35

World Dog
Show — A933

a, 4.20p, Chihuahua. b, 4.20p, Xoloitzcuin-tle. c, 3p, German shepherd. d, 3p, Rottweiler.

1999, June 2
2149 A933 Sheet of 4, #a.-d. 7.50 7.50

A934   A935

Perf. 13¼x13½
1999, June 25 Litho.
2150 A934 4.20p multicolored 1.25 .45
Intl. Day Against Illegal Drugs.

1999, July 2 Litho. Perf. 13¼x13½
2151 A935 3p multicolored .90 .35
National Bank, 65th anniv.

Arbor Day
A936

1999, July 26   **Perf. 13½x13¼**
2152 A936 3p multicolored   .90   .35

Civil Register, 140th Anniv.
A937

1999, July 27
2153 A937 3p multicolored   .90   .35

17th Mexico City Marathon
A938

1999, Aug. 11
2154 A938 4.20p multicolored   1.75   .45

Free Textbook Type of 1999

Designs: No. 2155, Children, book, flag, cacti. No. 2156, "Tsuni tsame."

1999   **Litho.**
2155 A927 3p green & multi   .90   .35
2156 A927 3p orange & multi   .90   .35

Issued: No. 2155, 8/23; No. 2156, 10/28.

Self portrait, by Rufino Tamayo (1899-1991) — A939

1999, Aug. 28   **Perf. 13¼x13½**
2157 A939 3p multicolored   .90   .35

City of Toluca, Bicent.
A940

1999, Sept. 12   **Perf. 13½x13¼**
2158 A940 3p copper & brown   .90   .35

State of Mexico, 175th Anniv.
A941

1999, Sept. 14
2159 A941 3p multicolored   1.00   .35

Union of Latin American Universities, 50th Anniv. — A942

1999, Sept. 22   **Perf. 13¼x13½**
2160 A942 4.20p multicolored   1.25   .45

Institute of Security & Social Services of State Workers, 40th Anniv.
A943

1999, Oct. 1   **Perf. 13½x13¼**
2161 A943 3p multicolored   1.00   .35

State of Baja California Sur, 25th Anniv.
A944

1999, Oct. 4
2162 A944 3p multicolored   1.00   .35

Family Planning, 25th Anniv.
A945

1999, Oct. 4
2163 A945 3p multicolored   1.00   .35

Nature Conservation — A946

1999, Oct. 5
2164 A946 3p Harpy eagle   1.00   .35

State of Quintana Roo, 25th Anniv. — A947

1999, Oct. 8   **Litho.**   **Perf. 13¼x13½**
2165 A947 3p multicolored   1.00   .35

UPU, 125th Anniv. — A948   World Post Day — A949

1999, Oct. 9
2166 A948 4.20p multicolored   1.50   .45
1999, Oct. 9
2167 A949 4.20p multicolored   1.50   .45

12th General Assembly of the Int'l Council on Monuments and Sites
A950

1999, Oct. 17   **Perf. 13½x13¼**
2168 A950 4.20p multicolored   1.50   .45

Carlos Chavez (1899-1978) & Silvestre Revueltas (1899-1940), Composers — A951

1999, Oct. 21
2169 A951 3p multicolored   1.00   .35

Autonomous Metropolitan University, 25th Anniv. — A952

1999, Oct. 25   **Perf. 13¼x13½**
2170 A952 3p multicolored   1.00   .35

State of Guerrero, 150th Anniv.
A953

1999, Oct. 27   Litho.   Perf. 13½x13¼
2171 A953 3p multicolored   1.00   .35

Free Textbook Type of 1999

Design: "Ciencias Naturales."

Perf. 13¼x13½
1999, Nov. 12   **Litho.**
2172 A927 3p multi   1.00   .35

Christmas
A954   A955
1999, Nov. 29
2173 A954 3p multi   1.00   .35
2174 A955 4.20p multi   1.75   .45

Natl. Commission of Professional Education, 20th Anniv. — A956

1999, Dec. 1   **Perf. 13½x 13¼**
2175 A956 3p multi   1.00   .35

Scientific Voyage of Alexander von Humboldt to Americas, Bicent.
A957

1999, Dec. 1
2176 A957 3p multi   1.00   .35

The 20th Century
A958

Education: a, 3p, Natl. Autonomous University of Mexico. b, 3p, Justo Sierra, José Vasconcelos. c, 3p, Natl. Poytechnic Institute. d, 3p, Free text books. e, 4.20p, Reading programs.

Litho. & Embossed
1999, Dec. 15   **Perf. 14x14½**
2177 A958 Sheet of 5, #a.-e.   10.00 10.00

Nos. 2177c-2177d are 79x25mm, No. 2177e is oval-shaped and 39x19mm.
See Nos. 2180-2181, 2191-2196.

A959   A960

2000, Jan. 24   Litho.   Perf. 13¼x13½
2178 A959 3p multi   1.00   .35
2000 census.

2000, Mar. 8   Litho.   Perf. 13¼x13½
2179 A960 4.20p multi   1.50   .45
International Women's Day.

The 20th Century Type of 1999

Building Democracy — No. 2180: a, 3p, Mexican presidents from Porfirio Díaz to Lázaro Cárdenas, Mexican Constitution. b, 3p, Pancho Villa, Emiliano Zapata. c, 3p, Mexican presidents from Manuel Avila Camacho to Gustavo Díaz Ordaz. d, 3p, Political figures, protestors, newspaper boy. e, 4.20p, Voter registration card, child at ballot box.
10p, People writing and at computers.

Litho. & Embossed
2000, Mar. 16   **Perf. 14x14½**
2180 A958 Sheet of 5, #a-e   10.00 10.00
Souvenir Sheet
Litho.
Perf. 13½
2181 A958 10p multi   7.50   7.50

Nos. 2180a and 2180b are 79x25mm, and No. 2180e is oval-shaped and 39x49mm.

Natl. Assoc. of Universities and Institutions of Higher Learning, 50th Anniv.
A961

Perf. 13½x13¼
2000, Mar. 24   **Litho.**
2182 A961 3p multi   1.00   .35

25th Mexican Travel Trade Show, Acapulco A962

2000, Apr. 9
2183 A962 4.20p multi   1.50   .45

Discovery of Brazil, 500th Anniv. A963

2000, Apr. 22
2184 A963 4.20p multi   1.50   .45

Teacher's Day — A964

2000, May 15   Perf. 13¼x13½
2185 A964 3p Luis Alvarez Barret 1.00   .35

Stampin' the Future Children's Stamp Design Contest Winners A965

Art by: 3p, Alejandro Guerra Millán. 4.20p, Carlos Hernández García.

2000, May 17   Perf. 13½x13¼
2186 A965   3p multi   1.00   .35
2187 A965   4.20p multi   1.50   .45

Fourth Meeting of Telecommunications Ministers and Information Industry Leaders — A966

2000, May 24
2188 A966 4.20p multi   1.50   .45

Intl. Day Against Illegal Drugs — A967

**   Perf. 13¼x13½**
2000, June 26   Litho.
2189 A967 4.20p multi   1.50   .45

National Worker's Housing Fund Institute — A968

No. 2190, Sculptures: a, 3p, Pre-Hispanic building. b, 3p, Pre-Hispanic building with stairway. c, 10p, Pre-Hispanic natives in circle.

2000, June 27   Perf. 14¼x13½
2190 A968   Sheet of 3, #a-c   7.00 7.00

The 20th Century Type of 1999

Cultural Idenity and Diversity — No. 2191: a, Xóchitl Incuícatl. b, Corre y se va. c, Tercera llamada. . . Cácado! d, Al Hablar como al guisar, su granito de sal. e, Children.

Health — No. 2192: a, Six men, certificate, man in tuberculosis prevention truck. b, Children on line. c, Nine men, posters. d, Poster showing tractor, health care. e, Modern medical equipment.

Art — No. 2193: a, El sello de la casa. b, Espíritu del siglo. c, La luz de México. d, Los nostros en que nos reconocemos. e, Building dome, artists and artwork.

Photography — No. 2194: a, Colchón enrollado, by Manuel Alvarez Bravo. b, Roses, by Tina Modotti. c, Four vertical photos, four horizontal photos. d, Two vertical photos, six horizontal photos. e, Three photos.

Commercial Development and Industrialization — No. 2195: a, Tractor. b, Truck cab. c, Store. d, Automobile. e, Globe.

Communications — No. 2196: a, Telephones and telegraph. b, Roads and bridges. c, Postal services. d, Railroads. e, Satellite, satellite dish, train.

Litho. & Embossed
2000   Perf. 14x14¼
2191   Sheet of 5   10.00 10.00
a.-d.   A958 3p Any single   1.00   .30
e.   A958 4.20p multicolored 1.50   .45
2192   Sheet of 5   10.00 10.00
a.-d.   A958 3p Any single   1.00   .30
e.   A958 4.20p multicolored 1.50   .45
2193   Sheet of 5   10.00 10.00
a.-d.   A958 3p Any single   1.00   .30
e.   A958 4.20p multicolored 1.50   .45
2194   Sheet of 5   10.00 10.00
a.-d.   A958 3p Any single   1.00   .30
e.   A958 4.20p multicolored 1.50   .45
2195   Sheet of 5   10.00 10.00
a.-d.   A958 3p Any single   1.00   .30
e.   A958 4.20p multicolored 1.50   .45
2196   Sheet of 5   10.00 10.00
a.-d.   A958 3p Any single   1.00   .30
e.   A958 4.20p multicolored 1.50   .45
            Nos. 2191-2196 (6)   60.00 60.00

Issued: No. 2191, 7/18; No. 2192, 10/24; No. 2193, 11/10; No. 2194, 12/9; No. 2195, 12/20; No. 2196, 12/21.

Nos. 2191c-2196c, 2191d-2196d are 79x25mm and Nos. 2191e-2196e are oval shaped and 39x49mm.

Natl. Program for Development of Handicapped People, 5th Anniv. — A969

2000, Aug. 2 Litho. Perf. 13¼x13½
2197 A969 3p multi   1.00   .35

Latin American Integration Association, 20th Anniv. — A970

2000, Aug. 11   Perf. 13½x13¼
2198 A970 4.20p multi   1.50   .45

Restoration of the Senate, 125th Anniv. — A971

2000, Aug. 17   Perf. 13¼x13½
2199 A971 3p multi   1.00   .35

Souvenir Sheets

Expo 2000, Hanover — A972

a, 1p, Mexican soul. b, 1p, Natl. mosaic. c, 1.80p, Future construction. d, 1.80p, Plaza pyramid. e, 2p, Creation of towns. f, 2p, Millennial construction. g, 3p, Naturea. h, 3p, Humanity. i, 3p, Technology. j, 3.60p, Expo 2000, Hanover. k, 4.20p, Emblem.

Litho. & Embossed
2000, Aug. 20   Perf. 14½x14
2200 A972   Sheet of 11, #a-k 12.50 12.50

No. 2200k is oval shaped and 39x49mm.

Bank of Mexico, 75th Anniv. — A973

2000, Aug. 23   Litho.   Perf.
2201 A973 10p multi   5.00 5.00

Stamp is oval-shaped and 49x39mm.

18th Mexico City Marathon A974

2000, Aug. 24   Perf. 13½x13¼
2202 A974 4.20p multi   1.50   .45

2000 Summer Olympics, Sydney A975

2000, Sept. 15
2203 A975 4.20p multi   1.50   .45

Paisano Program A976

2000, Sept. 21
2204 A976 4.20p multi   1.50   .45

2nd Intl. Memory of the World Conference A977

2000, Sept. 12
2205 A977 4.20p multi   1.50   .45

Women's Reproductive Health Month — A978

2000, Oct. 5   Perf. 13¼x13½
2206 A978 3p multi   1.00   .35

Ciudad Victoria, 250th Anniv. A979

2000, Oct. 6   Perf. 13½x13¼
2207 A979 3p multi   1.00   .35

World Post Day — A980

2000, Oct. 9   Perf. 13¼x13½
2208 A980 4.20p multi   1.50   .45

Natl. Human Rights Commission, 10th Anniv. — A981

2000, Oct. 23   Perf. 13½x13¼
2209 A981 3p multi   1.00   .35

World Meteorological Organization, 50th Anniv. — A982

2000, Oct. 27
2210 A982 3p multi   1.00 .35

Intl. Diabetes Federation, 50th Anniv. A983

2000, Nov. 6
2211 A983 4.20p multi   1.50 .45

Telegraphy in Mexico, 150th Anniv. A984

2000, Nov. 11
2212 A984 3p multi   1.00 .35

Luis Buñuel (1900-83), Film Director A985

2000, Nov. 21
2213 A985 3p multi   1.00 .35

Electrical Research Institute, 25th Anniv. A986

2000, Nov. 25
2214 A986 3p multi   1.00 .35

Customs Administration, Cent. — A987

2000, Nov. 28
2215 A987 3p multi   1.00 .35

Christmas A988

2000, Nov. 29
2216 A988   3p shown   1.00 .35
2217 A988 4.20p Poinsettias   1.50 .45

Television in Mexico, 50th Anniv. A989

2000, Nov. 30
2218 A989 3p multi   1.00 .35

Souvenir Sheet

Postal Headquarters — A990

No. 2219: a, 3p, Adamo Boari (1863-1928), architect. b, 3p, Roofline. c, 3p, Gonzalo Garita y Frontera (1867-1922), engineer. d, 10p, Headquarters building.

Litho. & Embossed
2000, Nov. 30   *Perf. 14¼x13½*
2219 A990   Sheet of 4, #a-d   9.00 9.00

Pre-Hispanic City of El Tajín — A991

Perf. 13½x13¼
2000, Dec. 14   *Litho.*
2220 A991 3p multi   1.00 .35

Nature Conservation — A992

2000, Dec. 15
2221 A992 3p Manatee   1.00 .35
   Stamps inscribed 'Aquila Real / Unidos Para Conservacion' with white, yellow or gray backgrounds and 20c denominations have no postal validity.

Francisco Sarabia (1900-39), Aviator — A993

2000, Dec. 20   *Perf. 13¼x13½*
2222 A993 3p multi   1.00 .35

Law Faculty of National Autonomous University of Mexico, 50th Anniv. A994

2001, Mar. 7   *Litho.*   *Perf. 13½x13¼*
2223 A994 3p multi   1.00 .30

Intl. Women's Day A995

2001, Mar. 8
2224 A995 4.20p multi   1.50 .45

National Cement Council, 53rd Anniv. A996

2001, Mar. 27
2225 A996 3p multi   1.00 .30

Teacher's Day A997

2001, May 15   *Perf. 14*
2226 A997 3p José Vasconcelos   1.00 .30

World Refugee Day — A998   Frida Kahlo (1907-54), Painter — A999

2001, June 20
2227 A998 4.20p multi   1.50 .45

2001, June 21
2228 A999 4.20p multi   1.50 .45

Intl. Day Against Illegal Drugs — A1000

2001, June 26
2229 A1000 4.20p multi   1.50 .45

Mario de la Cueva, Educator, Cent. of Birth — A1001

2001, July 11   *Litho.*   *Perf. 14*
2230 A1001 3p multi   1.00 .30

Intl. Volunteers Year A1002

2001, July 25
2231 A1002 4.20p multi   1.50 .45

Souvenir Sheet

Rodolfo Morales (1925-2001), Painter — A1003

2001, Aug. 4   *Perf. 14¼x13½*
2232 A1003 10p multi   4.50 4.50

Federal Fiscal and Administrative Justice Tribunal, 65th Anniv. — A1004

2001, Aug. 23   *Perf. 14*
2233 A1004 3p multi   1.00 .30

University of Mexico, 450th Anniv. A1005

2001, Sept. 3
2234 A1005 3p multi   1.00 .30

Adela Formoso de Obregón Santcilia (1907-81), Woman's Rights Activist — A1006

2001, Sept. 6
2235 A1006 3p multi   1.00 .30

Daniel Cosío Villegas (1898-1976), Historian — A1007

2001, Sept. 6
2236 A1007 3p multi   1.00 .30

Mexican Pharmacies A1008

2001, Sept. 27   *Litho.*   *Perf. 14*
2237 A1008 3p multi   1.00 .30

Intl. Day of the Elderly A1009

2001, Oct. 1
2238 A1009 3p multi   1.00 .30

Year of Dialogue Among Civilizations — A1010

2001, Oct. 9
2239 A1010 3p multi 1.00 .30

World Post Day — A1011

2001, Oct. 9
2240 A1011 3p multi 1.00 .30

Women's Health Day — A1012

2001, Oct. 31
2241 A1012 3p multi 1.00 .30

Ophthalmology Institute, 25th Anniv. — A1013

2001, Nov. 23
2242 A1013 4.20p multi 1.50 .45

United for Conservation — A1014

2001, Nov. 26
2243 A1014 5.30p Chara pinta 2.50 .90

Christmas A1015

2001, Dec. 3
2244 A1015 3p shown 1.00 .30
2245 A1015 4.20p Candles 1.50 .45

Souvenir Sheet

Souvenir Sheet

Fund for Indigenous People's Health and Education — A1016

2001, Dec. 4 Perf. 13½x14¼
2246 A1016 3p multi 1.50 1.50

Souvenir Sheet

National Scholarship Fund — A1017

2001, Dec. 4
2247 A1017 3p multi 1.50 1.50

Children's Protection A1018 / World Food Day A1019

2001, Dec. 11 Perf. 14
2248 A1018 3p multi 1.00 .30

2001, Dec. 17
2249 A1019 3p multi 1.00 .30

United For Conservation — A1020

2002, Jan. 24 Litho. Perf. 14
2250 A1020 6p Borrego cimarrón 2.50 .90

Manuel Alvarez Bravo, Photographer, Cent. of Birth — A1021

2002, Feb. 3
2251 A1021 6p gray & blk 2.25 .70

Mexico — People's Republic of China A1022

Designs: No. 2252, green panel at UL and brown panel at LL. No. 2252A, Like #2252, but with brown panel at UL, green panel at LL.

2002, Feb. 14 Litho. Perf. 14
2252 A1022 6p multi 2.00 .65
2252A A1022 6p multi 2.00 .65
b. Vert. pair, #2252-2252A 5.00 5.00

Conservation — A1023

Designs: 50c, Mangrove swamps. No. 2254, Rivers. No. 2255, Forests. 1.50p, No. 2267, Land mammals. No. 2257, Rain forests. No. 2258, Cacti. 4.50p, Birds. No. 2260, Sea turtles. No. 2261, Reptiles. No. 2262, Butterflies. No. 2263, Eagles. 7p, Reefs. 8.50p, 12p, Tropical forests. No. 2266, Marine mammals. No. 2268, Orchids. No. 2269, Cats. No. 2270, Oceans. No. 2271, Coastal birds. No. 2273, Deserts. No. 2274, Lakes and lagoons.

2002, Feb. 18 Litho. Perf. 14
2253 A1023 50c multi .25 .25
2254 A1023 1p multi .25 .25
2255 A1023 1p multi .35 .25
2256 A1023 1.50p multi .50 .25
2257 A1023 2p multi .70 .25
2258 A1023 2p multi .70 .25
2259 A1023 4.50p multi 1.50 .50
2260 A1023 5p multi 1.75 .55
2261 A1023 5p multi 1.75 .55
2262 A1023 6p multi 2.00 .65
2263 A1023 6p multi 2.00 .65
2264 A1023 7p multi 2.40 .75
2265 A1023 8.50p multi 2.75 .95
2266 A1023 10p multi 3.50 1.10
2267 A1023 10p multi 3.50 1.10
2268 A1023 10.50p multi 3.50 1.25
2269 A1023 10.50p multi 3.50 1.25
2270 A1023 11.50p multi 3.75 1.25
2271 A1023 11.50p multi 3.75 1.25
2272 A1023 12p multi 4.00 1.25
2273 A1023 30p multi 10.00 3.25
2274 A1023 30p multi 10.00 3.25
Nos. 2253-2274 (22) 62.40 21.05

2003 Perf. 13x13¼
2253a A1023 50c multi .40 .25
2254a A1023 1p multi 1.10 .25
2255a A1023 1p multi 1.10 .25
2259a A1023 4.50p multi 3.50 .40
2260a A1023 5p multi 1.75 .45
2261a A1023 5p multi 1.75 .45
2262a A1023 6p multi 2.50 .55
2263a A1023 6p multi 2.00 .55
2264a A1023 7p multi 2.50 .65
2265a A1023 8.50p multi 3.75 .75
2266a A1023 10p multi 4.00 .90
2267a A1023 10p multi 4.25 .90
2268a A1023 10.50p multi 5.00 .95
2269a A1023 10.50p multi 4.25 .95
2270a A1023 11.50p multi 6.00 1.00
2271a A1023 11.50p multi 6.00 1.00
Nos. 2253a-2271a (16) 49.85 10.25

See Nos. 2321-2330, 2362-2377, 2394-2436, 2452-2473.

2002 Winter Olympics, Salt Lake City A1024

2002, Feb. 20 Litho. Perf. 14
2275 A1024 8.50p multi 2.75 .95

Veracruz Port Modernization, Cent. — A1025

2002, Mar. 4
2276 A1025 6p multi 2.25 .70

Mexico — South Korea Diplomatic Relations, 40th Anniv. A1026

2002, Mar. 5
2277 A1026 8.50p multi 2.75 .95

Council for the Restoration of Historic Central Mexico City — A1027

2002, Mar. 7
2278 A1027 6p multi 2.25 .70

Natl. Women's Institute A1028 / José Guadalupe Posada (1851-1913), Printmaker A1029

2002, Mar. 8
2279 A1028 8.50p multi 2.75 .95

2002, Mar. 18
2280 A1029 6p gold & black 2.25 .65

Justo Sierra Mendez (1848-1912), Writer — A1030

2002, May 15 Litho. Perf. 14
2281 A1030 6p multi 2.25 .65

UN General Assembly Special Session on Children A1031

2002, May 27
2282 A1031 6p multi 2.25 .65

Discovery of the Tomb of Pakal, 50th Anniv. A1032

2002, June 14
2283 A1032 6p multi 2.25 .65

2002 World Cup Soccer Championships, Japan and Korea — A1033

2002, June 15
2284 A1033 8.50p multi 2.75 .85

Intl. Day Against Illegal Drugs — A1034

2002, June 26
2285 A1034 6p multi 2.25 .65

5th Mexico-Central American Summit — A1035

2002, June 27
2286 A1035 6p multi 2.25 .65

Intl. Year of Mountains A1036

2002, July 24   Litho.   Perf. 14
2287 A1036 6p multi 2.25 .65

Intl. Day of Indigenous People A1037

2002, Aug. 9   Perf. 13x13¼
2288 A1037 6p multi 2.25 .65

Federal Electricity Commission A1038

2002, Aug. 14   Perf. 14
2289 A1038 6p multi 2.25 .65

Natl. Blood Donor Day — A1039

2002, Aug. 23   Perf. 13¼x13
2290 A1039 6p multi 2.25 .65

Campaign Against Corruption A1040

2002, Sept. 12   Litho.   Perf. 13x13¼
2291 A1040 6p multi 2.25 .60

Code of Ethics for Public Servants — A1041

2002, Sept. 12   Perf. 13¼x13
2292 A1041 6p multi 2.25 .60

World Tourism Day A1042

2002, Sept. 27   Perf. 13x13¼
2293 A1042 8.50p multi 2.75 .85

Natl. Organ Transplant and Donation Week — A1043

2002, Oct. 7   Perf. 13¼x13
2294 A1043 6p multi 2.25 .60

World Post Day A1044

2002, Oct. 9   Perf. 13¼x13
2295 A1044 8.50p multi 2.75 .85

State of Baja California, 50th Anniv. A1045

2002, Nov. 1
2296 A1045 6p multi 2.25 .60

Luis Barragan (1902-88), Architect — A1046

2002, Nov. 7   Perf. 13¼x13
2297 A1046 6p multi 2.25 .60

Renewal of Diplomatic Relations Between Mexico and Spain, 25th Anniv. A1047

2002, Nov. 19   Perf. 13x13¼
2298 A1047 8.50p multi 2.75 .85

Mexico City Intl. Airport, 50th Anniv. — A1048

Details from mural "The Conquest of the Air by Man": a, Indian chief at left, Montgolfier balloon flight at right. b, Charles Lindbergh at left, parachutist at center. c, Wright Brothers at left, Mexico City at center.

2002, Nov. 19   Perf. 13¼x13
2299   Horiz. strip of 3   7.50 7.50
a.-b. A1048 6p Either single   2.25 .60
c. A1048 8.50p multi   2.75 .85

Information Technology Development in Mexico, 75th Anniv. — A1049

2002, Nov. 21
2300 A1049 6p multi 1.75 .60

Anti-Violence Campaign — A1050

2002, Nov. 25   Perf. 13¼x13
2301 A1050 8.50p multi 2.50 .85

Pan-American Health Organization, Cent. — A1051

2002, Dec. 2   Perf. 13¼x13
2302 A1051 8.50p multi 1.75 .85

Acolmiztli Nezahualcóyotl (1402-72), Poet — A1052

2002, Dec. 10
2303 A1052 6p multi 1.75 .60

Christmas A1053

Children's art: 6p, Nativity, by Sara Elisa Miranda Alcaraz. 8.50p, Children with Nativity Scene, by Alejandro Ruíz Sampedro.

2002, Dec. 19   Perf. 13x13¼
2304 A1053 6p multi 1.75 .60
2305 A1053 8.50p multi 2.50 .80

Powered Flight, Cent. A1054

2003, Mar. 6   Litho.   Perf. 13x13¼
2306 A1054 8.50p multi 2.50 .80

Iberoamerican University, 60th Anniv. — A1055

2003, Mar. 7   Perf. 13¼x13
2307 A1055 6p multi 1.75 .55

Intl. Women's Day — A1056

2003, Mar. 8
2308 A1056 8.50p multi 2.50 .80

Mexicali, Cent. A1057

2003, Mar. 14   Perf. 13¼x13
2309 A1057 6p multi 1.75 .55

Mexican Chamber of Industry and Construction, 50th Anniv. — A1058

2003, Mar. 26
2310 A1058 6p multi 1.75 .55

Federico Gomez Children's Hospital, 60th Anniv. A1059

2003, Apr. 30   Litho.   Perf. 13x13¼
2311   A1059   6p multi   1.75   .60

Miguel Hidalgo y Costilla (1753-1811), Independence Leader — A1060

2003, May 8   Perf. 13¼x13
2312   A1060   6p multi   1.75   .60
    a.   Perf 14   350.00   350.00

Gregorio Torres Quintero (1866-1934), Educator — A1061

2003, May 15
2313   A1061   6p multi   1.75   .55
    a.   Perf. 14   150.00   —

Natl. Astronomical Observatory, 125th Anniv. — A1062

2003, May 20   Perf. 13x13¼
2314   A1062   6p multi   1.75   .55

World Day Against Tobacco — A1063

2003, May 30   Perf. 13¼x13
2315   A1063   8.50p multi   2.50   .80

Inauguration of Satellite Internet Network — A1064

2003, June 5
2316   A1064   6p multi   1.75   .55

Intl. Day Against Illegal Drugs A1065

2003, June 26   Litho.   Perf. 13x13¼
2317   A1065   8.50p multi   2.50   .80

Mexican Baseball Hall of Fame, 30th Anniv. A1066

2003, July 21
2318   A1066   6p multi   1.75   .55

Xavier Villaurrutia (1903-51), Poet A1067

2003, July 24
2319   A1067   6p multi   1.75   .55

Veterinary Medicine Education in Mexico, 150th Anniv. A1068

2003, Aug. 16
2320   A1068   6p multi   1.75   .55

Conservation Type of 2002

Designs: 50c, Oceans. 1p, Reptiles. No. 2323, Land mammals. No. 2324, Rain forests. No. 2325, Coastal birds. 4.50p, Orchids. 6p, Rivers. 8.50p, Cacti. No. 2329, Lakes and lagoons. No. 2330, Sea turtles.

Perf. 13x13¼, 13½ (#2328)
2003-04   Litho.
2321   A1023   50c multi ('04)   .50   .25
2322   A1023   1p multi ('04)   .50   .25
2323   A1023   2.50p multi   1.25   .25
2324   A1023   2.50p multi   1.25   .25
2325   A1023   2.50p multi ('04)   1.25   .25
2326   A1023   4.50p multi ('04)   2.00   .40
2327   A1023   6p multi ('04)   2.75   .55
2328   A1023   8.50p multi ('04)   3.50   .75
2329   A1023   10.50p multi ('04)   4.00   .95
2330   A1023   10.50p multi ('04)   4.50   .95
        Nos. 2321-2330 (10)   21.50   4.85

National Pedagogical University, 25th Anniv. — A1069

2003, Aug. 29   Litho.   Perf. 13¼x13
2331   A1069   6p multi   1.75   .55

Federico Silva Museum, San Luis Potosí A1070

2003, Sept. 18   Perf. 13x13¼
2332   A1070   6p multi   1.75   .55

National Organ and Tissue Donation Week A1071

2003, Sept. 26
2333   A1071   6p multi   1.75   .55

World Post Day A1072

2003, Oct. 9   Perf. 13¼x13
2334   A1072   8.50p multi   2.25   .75

2003, Oct. 16
2335   A1073   6p multi   1.50   .55

Health Ministry, 60th Anniv. A1074

2003, Oct. 23   Perf. 13x13¼
2336   A1074   6p multi   1.50   .55

Juarez Theater, Cent. A1075

2003, Oct. 27
2337   A1075   6p multi   1.50   .55

Teaching of Law in the Americas, 450th Anniv. — A1076

2003, Nov. 4   Perf. 13¼x13
2338   A1076   8.50p multi   2.25   .80

Central Power and Light, Cent. A1077

2003, Nov. 18   Litho.   Perf. 13x13¼
2339   A1077   6p multi   1.50   .55

Christmas A1078

Children's drawings of Nativity by: 6p, Valeria Báez. 8.50p, Octavio Alemán.

2003, Dec. 3
2340   A1078   6p multi   1.50   .55
2341   A1078   8.50p multi   2.25   .75

A1079   A1080

2003, Dec. 5   Perf. 13¼x13
2342   A1079   6p multi   1.50   .55
       Children's rights.

2003, Dec. 11
2343   A1080   8.50p multi   2.25   .75
       Intl. Year of Fresh Water.

National Technical Education College, 25th Anniv. A1081

2003, Dec. 15   Perf. 13x13¼
2344   A1081   6p multi   1.50   .55

First Visit of Pope John Paul II to Mexico, 25th Anniv. A1082

2004, Jan. 28   Litho.   Perf. 13x13¼
2345   A1082   6p multi   1.10   .55

Agustín Yáñez (1904-80), Novelist A1083

2004, May 4
2346   A1083   8.50p multi   1.50   .75

Enrique Aguilar González — A1084

2004, May 15   Perf. 13¼x13
2347   A1084   8.50p multi   1.50   .75
       Teacher's Day.

Cable Television in Mexico, 50th Anniv. — A1085

2004, May 19
2348   A1085   6p multi   1.10   .55

Mexican Geological Society, Cent. A1086

2004, June 2   *Perf. 13x13¼*
2349 A1086 8.50p multi   1.50   .75

Intl. Day Against Illegal Drugs — A1087

2004, June 25   *Perf. 13¼x13*
2350 A1087 8.50p multi   1.50   .75

Salvador Novo (1904-74), Poet A1088

2004, July 30   *Perf. 13x13¼*
2351 A1088 7p multi   1.25   .60

Gilberto Owen (1905-52), Poet A1089

2004, Aug. 8   Litho.   *Perf. 13x13¼*
2352 A1089 7p multi   1.25   .60

FIFA (Fédération Internationale de Football Association), Cent. — A1090

2004, Aug. 11
2353 A1090 11.50p multi   2.00 1.00

Mexican Cartooning — A1091

2004, Aug. 13   *Perf. 13¼x13*
2354 A1091 6p multi   1.00   .50

2004 Summer Olympics, Athens — A1092

2004, Aug. 13
2355 A1092 10.50p multi   1.90   .95

Celestino Gorostiza (1904-67), Writer A1093

2004, Aug. 16   Litho.   *Perf. 13x13¼*
2356 A1093 7p multi   1.25   .60

Fresnillo, 450th Anniv. — A1094

2004, Sept. 2   *Perf. 13¼x13*
2357 A1094 7p multi   1.25   .60

Economic Culture Fund, 70th Anniv. A1095

2004, Sept. 6   *Perf. 13x13¼*
2358 A1095 8.50p multi   1.50   .75

Autonomy of National Autonomous University of Mexico, 75th Anniv. — A1096

2004, Sept. 6   *Perf. 13¼x13*
2359 A1096 11.50p multi   2.00 1.00

Autonomous University of Chihuahua, 50th Anniv. — A1097

2004, Sept. 8   *Perf. 13x13¼*
2360 A1097 7p multi   1.25   .60

Palace of Fine Arts, 70th Anniv. A1098

2004, Sept. 29
2361 A1098 7p multi   1.25   .60

Conservation Type of 2002

Designs: 50c, Cats. No. 2363, Oceans. No. 2364, Rain forests. 2.50p, No. 2374, Reefs. 4.50p, Forests. 5p, No. 2370, Land mammals.

Nos. 2368, 2376, Reptiles. No. 2369, Birds. Nos. 2371, 2375, Deserts. No. 2372, Cacti. No. 2373, Tropical forests. No. 2377, Coastal birds.

2004		Litho.	*Perf. 13x13¼*	
2362	A1023	50c multi	.45	.25
2363	A1023	1p multi	2.50	.25
2364	A1023	1p multi	.45	.25
2365	A1023	2.50p multi	1.25	.25
2366	A1023	4.50p multi	1.25	.40
2367	A1023	5p multi	1.90	.45
2368	A1023	6p multi	1.90	.55
2369	A1023	6p multi	1.75	.55
2370	A1023	6p multi	2.00	.55
2371	A1023	7p multi	2.00	.60
2372	A1023	7p multi	2.00	.60
2373	A1023	10p multi	3.50	.90
2374	A1023	10p multi	3.50	.90
2375	A1023	10.50p multi	3.50	.95
a.		Microprinting at top in black	4.25	1.00
2376	A1023	30p multi	8.00	2.25
2377	A1023	30p multi	8.00	2.25
Nos. 2362-2377 (16)			43.95	11.95

Microprinting at top on No. 2375 is in gray.

State Workers' Institute of Social Services and Security — A1099

2004, Oct. 1   Litho.   *Perf. 13¼x13*
2378 A1099 6p multi   1.10   .55

Termination of Walled District of Campeche, 300th Anniv. — A1100

2004, Oct. 6   *Perf. 13x13¼*
2379 A1100 6p multi   1.10   .55

National Anthem, 150th Anniv. A1101

2004, Oct. 8
2380 A1101 6.50p multi   1.25   .60

World Post Day A1102

2004, Oct. 11
2381 A1102 6p bright rose lilac   1.10   .55

Admission to UPU, 125th Anniv. A1103

2004, Oct. 29
2382 A1103 8.50p multi   1.50   .75

Channel 11 Television — A1104

2004, Nov. 10   *Perf. 13¼x13*
2383 A1104 8.50p multi   1.50   .75

Superior Federation Audit, 180th Anniv. — A1105

2004, Nov. 16
2384 A1105 6.50p multi   1.25   .60

Health Secretary's Building, 75th Anniv. A1106

2004, Nov. 22   *Perf. 13x13¼*
2385 A1106 8.50p multi   1.60   .80

Culture on the Radio — A1107

2004, Nov. 30   *Perf. 13¼x13*
2386 A1107 6.50p multi   1.25   .60

Natl. Communications and Transportation Department Center, 50th Anniv. — A1108

2004, Nov. 30   *Perf. 13¼x13*
2387 A1108 6.50p multi   1.25   .60

     Souvenir Sheet
     Perf. 14¼x14
2388 A1108 7.50p multi   1.40   .70

Town of General Escobedo, 400th Anniv. A1109

2004, Dec. 3   *Perf. 13x13¼*
2389 A1109 8.50p multi   1.60   .80

Natl. Free Textbook Commission, 45th Anniv. — A1110

2004, Dec. 6

2390	A1110	10.50p multi	1.90	.95

A1111

Christmas — A1112

2004, Dec. 13   *Perf. 13x13¼*

2391	A1111	7.50p multi	1.40	.70

Perf. 13¼x13

2392	A1112	10.50p multi	1.90	.95

Traffic Accident Prevention — A1113

2004, Dec. 17   Litho.   *Perf. 13¼x13*

2393	A1113	8.50p multi	1.60	.80

Conservation Type of 2002

Designs: Nos. 2394, 2404, Deserts. Nos. 2395, 2406, 2408, 2411, Orchids. Nos. 2396, 2410, 2419, 2435, Sea turtles. Nos. 2397, 2416, Birds. Nos. 2398, 2401, 2421, 2433, Marine mammals. Nos. 2399, 2425, Oceans. Nos. 2400, 2402, 2424, Cats. Nos. 2403, 2430, Rain forests. Nos. 2405, 2412, Eagles. Nos. 2407, 2415, Lakes and lagoons. Nos. 2409, 2436, Butterflies. Nos. 2413, 2423, Tropical forests. Nos. 2414, 2431, Rivers. Nos. 2417, 2429, Reefs. Nos. 2418, 2427, Forests. Nos. 2420, 2434, Coastal birds. No. 2422, Reptiles. Nos. 2426, 2428, Land mammals. No. 2432, Mangrove swamps.

2004-05   Litho.   *Perf. 13½x13¼*
Inscribed "ROMO" at Lower Right

2394	A1023	50c multi	.50	.25
2395	A1023	1p multi	.50	.25
2396	A1023	2.50p multi	1.00	.50
2397	A1023	6.50p multi	2.00	1.00
2398	A1023	6.50p multi	150.00	—
2399	A1023	7p multi	3.00	1.50
2400	A1023	7.50p multi	3.00	1.50
2401	A1023	8.50p multi	3.50	1.75
		Complete booklet, 6 #2401	21.00	
2402	A1023	10.50p multi	6.50	3.25
		Complete booklet, 6 #2402	39.00	
2403	A1023	13p multi	10.00	5.00

Inscribed "TIEV" at Lower Right
Perf. 13x13¼

2404	A1023	50c multi	.50	.25
2405	A1023	50c multi	.50	.25
2406	A1023	50p multi	.75	.40
2407	A1023	1p multi	.40	.25
2408	A1023	1p multi	.40	.25
a.		Perf. 14	1.75	.80
2409	A1023	2p multi	.80	.40
2410	A1023	2.50p multi	.90	.45

2411	A1023	2.50p multi	.90	.45
2412	A1023	2.50p multi	1.00	.50
2413	A1023	5p multi	1.75	.90
2414	A1023	5p multi	1.75	.90
2415	A1023	5p multi	1.75	.90
2416	A1023	6.50p multi	1.75	.90
2417	A1023	6.50p multi	1.75	.90
2418	A1023	6.50p multi	1.75	.90
2419	A1023	6.50p multi	2.00	1.00
2420	A1023	6.50p multi	2.00	1.00
2421	A1023	6.50p multi	1.75	.90
2422	A1023	6.50p multi	1.75	.90
2423	A1023	7p multi	1.75	.90
2424	A1023	7.50p multi	2.25	1.10
2425	A1023	7.50p multi	2.25	1.10
2426	A1023	7.50p multi, denomination in black	2.50	1.25
a.		Denomination in gray	9.00	4.50
2427	A1023	8.50p multi	3.00	1.50
2428	A1023	10.50p multi	4.00	2.00
2429	A1023	10.50p multi	4.00	2.00
2430	A1023	13p multi	5.50	2.75
2431	A1023	13p multi	5.50	2.75
2432	A1023	13p multi	5.50	2.75
2433	A1023	14.50p multi	5.50	2.75
2434	A1023	14.50p multi	5.50	2.75
2435	A1023	30.50p multi	7.25	3.75
2436	A1023	30.50p multi	7.25	3.75
		Nos. 2394-2436 (43)	265.90	58.50

Issued: Nos. 2401, 2402, 2004. Others, 2005. Colors are duller on stamps inscribed "TIEV" than those on similar stamps inscribed "ROMO."

Mexico General Hospital, Cent. — A1114

2005, Feb. 4   Litho.   *Perf. 13¼x13*

2437	A1114	6.50p multi	1.25	.60

Intl. Women's Day A1115

2005, Mar. 8   *Perf. 13x13¼*

2438	A1115	6.50p multi	1.25	.60

Publication of Pedro Paramo by Juan Rulfo, 50th Anniv. A1116

2005, Mar. 13

2439	A1116	6.50p multi	1.25	.60

Natl. University Games A1117

World Without Polio A1118

2005, Apr. 18   *Perf. 13¼x13*

2440	A1117	7.50p multi	1.40	.70

2005, Apr. 29

2441	A1118	10.50p multi	1.90	.95

Eulalia Guzmán A1119

2005, May 15   *Perf. 13x13¼*

2442	A1119	6.50p multi	1.25	.60

Teacher's Day.

Souvenir Sheet

Publication of Don Quixote, 400th Anniv. — A1120

No. 2443: a, 6.50p, Silhouette of Don Quixote. b, 10.50p, Crowd, horse and rider. c, 10.50p, Don Quixote.

2005, May 23   *Perf. 13¼x13*

2443	A1120	Sheet of 3, #a-c	5.25	5.25

Intl. Year of Physics — A1121

2005, May 26

2444	A1121	7.50p multi	1.40	.70

Natl. Human Rights Commission — A1122

2005, June 5   *Perf. 13x13¼*

2445	A1122	6.50p multi	1.25	.60

Society of Mexican Architects, Cent. — A1123

2005, June 8   *Perf. 13¼x13*

2446	A1123	6.50p multi	1.25	.60

Intl. Day Against Illegal Drugs — A1124

2005, June 24

2447	A1124	10.50p multi	2.00	1.00

Baseball — A1125

2005, June 27

2448	A1125	7.50p multi	1.40	.70

Information Access and Transparency — A1126

2005, June 27

2449	A1126	6.50p multi	1.25	.60

Memin Pinguin, by Yolanda Vargas Dulche — A1127

Memin Pinguin: a, And comic book page. b, Holding flower. c, Holding open comic book. d, Wearing tuxedo. e, Holding closed book.

2005, June 28   *Perf. 13*

2450		Horiz. strip of 5	9.50	9.50
a.-e.	A1127	6.50p Any single	1.90	.95

Multiple Self-portrait, by Juan O'Gorman (1905-82) — A1128

2005, June 29   *Perf. 13¼x13*

2451	A1128	7.50p multi	1.40	.70

Conservation Type of 2002

Designs: No. 2452, Butterflies. Nos. 2453, 2473, Sea turtles. No. 2454, Coastal birds. Nos. 2456, 2463, Marine mammals. Nos. 2457, 2459, Rivers. Nos. 2458, 2462, 2466, Oceans. No. 2460, Lakes and lagoons. Nos. 2461, 2469, Cats. No. 2464, Reptiles. No. 2465, Mangrove swamps. No. 2467, Birds. No. 2468, Cacti. No. 2470, Reefs. No. 2471, Eagles. No. 2472, Tropical forests.

2005   Litho.   *Perf. 13¼x13*
Inscribed "TIEV" at Lower Right

2452	A1023	50c multi	.25	.25
2453	A1023	50c multi	.25	.25
2454	A1023	1p multi	.25	.25
2456	A1023	1p multi	.25	.25
2457	A1023	2.50p multi	.50	.25

2458	A1023	5p multi	.95	.50
2459	A1023	6.50p multi	1.25	.60
2460	A1023	6.50p multi	1.25	.60
2461	A1023	6.50p multi	1.25	.60
2462	A1023	7p multi	1.40	.70
2463	A1023	7p multi	1.40	.70
2464	A1023	7.50p multi	1.40	.70
2465	A1023	7.50p multi	1.40	.70
2466	A1023	10.50p multi	2.00	1.00
2467	A1023	10.50p multi	2.00	1.00
2468	A1023	13p multi	2.50	1.25
2469	A1023	13p multi	2.50	1.25
2470	A1023	13p multi	2.50	1.25
2471	A1023	14.50p multi	2.75	1.40
2472	A1023	30.50p multi	5.75	2.75

Inscribed "ROMO" at Lower Right
Booklet Stamp

2473	A1023	(15.75p) multi	3.00	1.50
a.		Booklet pane of 4	12.00	—
		Complete booklet, 4 #2473	12.00	

Nos. 2452-2473 (21) 34.80 17.75

See No. 2399 for 7p Oceans stamp with "ROMO" inscription. No. 2473 is inscribed "Porte mundial" at lower left.

Minerals — A1129

No. 2474: a, Silver. b, Argentite. c, Marcasite, quartz and galena. d, Allende meteorite. e, Gold. f, Galena. g, Pyrargyrite. h, Gypsum. i, Manganocalcite. j, Barite. k, Stephanite. l, Red calcite. m, Calcite. n, Asbestos. o, Valencianite. p, Livingstoneite. q, Beryl. r, Smithsonite. s, Fluorite. t, Amethyst quartz. u, Azurite. v, Hemimorphite. w, Apatite. x, Pyromorphite. y, Actinolite with talc.

2005, Aug. 3   Perf. 13¼x13

2474		Sheet of 25	32.50	32.50
a.-y.	A1129 6.50p Any single		1.25	.60

Ignacio L. Vallarta (1830-94), Chief Justice A1130

2005, Aug. 23   Perf. 13x13¼

2475	A1130	7.50p multi	1.40	.70

Judicial Anniversaries — A1131

Designs: No. 2476, Federal Justice Council, 10th anniv. No. 2477, Supreme Court, 180th anniv. 10.50p, Supreme Justice Tribunal, 190th anniv.

2005, Aug. 23

2476	A1131	6.50p multi	1.25	.60
2477	A1131	6.50p multi	1.25	.60
2478	A1131	10.50p multi	2.00	1.00
a.		Souvenir sheet, #2476-2478	4.50	4.50

Expo 2005, Aichi, Japan — A1132

2005, Sept. 15   Perf. 13¼x13

2479	A1132	13p multi	2.40	1.25

Federal District Superior Court, 150th Anniv. — A1133

No. 2480 — Buildings from: a, 1855. b, 2005. c, 1964.

2005, Oct. 6

2480		Horiz. strip of 3	4.00	4.00
a.-b.	A1133 6.50p Either single		1.25	.60
c.	A1133 7.50p multi		1.40	.70

World Post Day — A1134

2005, Oct. 10

2481	A1134	10.50p multi	2.00	1.00

United Nations Day A1135

2005, Oct. 24   Perf. 13x13¼

2482	A1135	10.50p multi	2.00	1.00

Jalisco Philatelic Organization, Cent. — A1136

2005, Oct. 27

2483	A1136	6.50p multi	1.25	.60

Lebanese in Mexico, 125th Anniv. — A1137

2005, Nov. 11   Perf. 13¼x13

2484	A1137	10.50p multi	2.00	1.00

Rodolfo Usigli (1905-79), Playwright — A1138

2005, Nov. 15

2485	A1138	7.50p multi	1.50	.75

San Juan de Ulua, Last Spanish Redoubt — A1139

2005, Nov. 23

2486	A1139	7.50p multi	1.50	.75

Gómez Palacio, Cent. — A1140

2005, Nov. 24

2487	A1140	6.50p multi	1.25	.60

Folk Art — A1141

Designs: 50c, Legged earthen pot. 1p, Lacquered wooden chest. 1.50p, Horn comb. 2p, Black clay jug. 2.50p, Paper bull. 5p, Silk shawl. No. 2494, Model. No. 2495, Glazed basin. No. 2496, Vase. No. 2497, Wooden mask. No. 2498, Tin rooster. 7p, Doll. 7.50p, Copper jar. 9p, Embroidered tablecloth. 10.50p, 11.50p, Woven basket. 13p, 13.50p, Silver pear. 14.50p, 15p, Amber marimba. 30.50p, Obsidian and opal turtle.

2005, Nov. 30   Litho.   Perf. 13¼x13

2488	A1141	50c multi	.25	.25
a.		Dated "2006"	.25	.25
b.		Dated "2007"	.25	.25
c.		Dated "2008"	.25	.25
d.		Magenta panel, dated "2010"	.25	.25
e.		Dated "2011"	.25	.25
f.		Dated "2012"	.25	.25
g.		Dated "2013"	.25	.25
h.		Dated "2014"	.25	.25
2489	A1141	1p multi	.25	.25
a.		Dated "2006"	.25	.25
b.		Dated "2007"	.25	.25
c.		Dated "2008"	.25	.25
d.		Dated "2010"	.25	.25
e.		Dotod "2011"	.25	.25
f.		Dated "2012"	.25	.25
g.		Dated "2013"	.25	.25
h.		Dated "2014"	.25	.25
2490	A1141	1.50p multi	.30	.25
a.		Dated "2006"	.30	.25
b.		Dated "2007"	.30	.25
c.		Dated "2008"	.30	.25
d.		Dated "2009"	.25	.25
e.		Dated "2010"	.25	.25
f.		Dated "2011"	.25	.25
g.		Dated "2012"	.25	.25
h.		Dated "2013"	.25	.25
i.		Dated "2014"	.25	.25
2491	A1141	2p multi	.40	.25
a.		Dated "2006"	.40	.25
b.		Dated "2007"	.40	.25
c.		Dated "2008"	.30	.25
d.		Dated "2009"	.30	.25

e.		Dated "2010"	.35	.25
f.		Dated "2011"	.30	.25
g.		Dated "2012"	.30	.25
h.		Dated "2013"	.30	.25
i.		Dated "2014"	.30	.25
2492	A1141	2.50p multi	.50	.25
a.		Dated "2006"	.45	.25
b.		Dated "2007"	.45	.25
c.		Dated "2008"	.40	.25
d.		Dated "2010"	.40	.25
e.		Dated "2011"	.40	.25
f.		Dated "2012"	.35	.25
g.		Dated "2013"	.40	.25
h.		Dated "2014"	.40	.25
2493	A1141	5p multi	.95	.50
a.		Dated "2006"	.95	.50
b.		Dated "2007"	.95	.50
c.		Dated "2008"	.75	.35
d.		Dated "2009"	.80	.40
e.		Dated "2010"	.85	.40
f.		Dated "2011"	.80	.40
g.		Dated "2012"	.70	.35
h.		Dated "2013"	.80	.40
i.		Dated "2014"	.75	.35
2494	A1141	6.50p multi	1.25	.60
a.		Dated "2006"	1.25	.60
b.		Dated "2007"	1.25	.60
c.		Dated "2008"		
2495	A1141	6.50p multi	1.25	.60
a.		Dated "2006"	1.25	.60
b.		Dated "2007"	1.25	.60
c.		Dated "2008"		
2496	A1141	6.50p multi	1.25	.60
a.		Dated "2006"	1.25	.60
b.		Dated "2007"	1.25	.60
c.		Dated "2008"		
2497	A1141	6.50p multi	1.25	.60
a.		Dated "2006"	1.25	.60
b.		Dated "2007"	1.25	.60
c.		Dated "2008"		
2498	A1141	6.50p multi	1.25	.60
a.		Horiz. or vert. strip of 5, #2494-2498	6.25	3.00
b.		Dated "2006"	1.25	.60
c.		Horiz. or vert. strip of 5, #2494a, 2495a, 2496a, 2497a, 2498b	6.25	3.00
d.		Dated "2007"	1.25	.60
e.		Horiz. or vert. strip of 5, #2494b, 2495b, 2496b, 2497b, 2498d	6.25	3.00
f.		Dated "2008"	—	—
g.		Horiz. or vert. strip of 5, #2494c, 2495c, 2496c, 2497c, 2498f	—	—
2499	A1141	7p multi	1.40	.70
a.		Dated "2006"	1.40	.70
b.		Dated "2007"	1.40	.70
c.		Dated "2008"	1.10	.55
d.		Dated "2010"	1.25	.60
e.		Dated "2011"	1.10	.55
f.		Dated "2012"	1.00	.50
g.		Dated "2013"	1.10	.55
2500	A1141	7.50p multi	1.50	.75
a.		Dated "2006"	1.40	.70
b.		Dated "2007"	1.40	.70
c.		Dated "2008"	1.10	.55
d.		Dated "2009"	1.25	.60
e.		Dated "2010"	1.25	.60
f.		Dated "2011"	1.25	.60
g.		Dated "2012"	1.10	.55
h.		Dated "2013"	1.25	.60
i.		Dated "2014"	1.00	.55
2501	A1141	9p multi	1.75	.85
a.		Dated "2010"	1.50	.75
b.		Dated "2011"	1.40	.70
c.		Dated "2012"	1.25	.65
d.		Dated "2013"	1.40	.70
e.		Dated "2014"	1.25	.60
2502	A1141	10.50p multi	2.00	1.00
a.		Dated "2006"	2.00	1.00
b.		Dated "2007"	2.00	1.00
c.		Dated "2008"	1.60	.80
d.		Dated "2009"	1.60	.80
2502E	A1141	11.50p multi	1.90	.95
f.		Dated "2011"	1.75	.85
g.		Dated "2012"	1.75	.85
h.		Dated "2013"	1.75	.85
i.		Dated "2014"	1.75	.85
2503	A1141	13p multi	2.50	1.25
a.		Dated "2006"	2.40	1.25
b.		Dated "2007"	2.40	1.25
c.		Dated "2008"	1.90	.95
2503D	A1141	13.50p multi	2.25	1.10
e.		Dated "2011"	2.10	1.10
f.		Dated "2012"	1.90	.95
g.		Dated "2013"	2.10	1.10
2504	A1141	14.50p multi	2.75	1.40
a.		Dated "2006"	2.75	1.40
b.		Dated "2007"	2.75	1.40
c.		Dated "2008"	2.10	1.10
2504D	A1141	15p multi	2.50	1.25
e.		Dated "2011"	2.40	1.25
f.		Dated "2012"	2.25	1.10
g.		Dated "2013"	2.40	1.25
h.		Dated "2014"	2.25	1.10
2505	A1141	30.50p multi	6.00	3.00
a.		Dated "2006"	5.75	2.75
b.		Dated "2007"	5.75	2.75
c.		Dated "2008"		
d.		Dated "2012"	4.50	2.25

Nos. 2488-2505 (22) 33.70 17.25

Nos. 2502E, 2503D and 2504D are dated "2010."

Christian Brothers in Mexico, Cent. — A1142

2005, Dec. 2   Perf. 13¼x13

2506	A1142	6.50p multi	1.25	.60

Jews in Mexico, Cent. — A1143

2005, Dec. 6
2507 A1143 7.50p multi   1.40 .70

Indigenous Popular Culture A1144

2005, Dec. 16   *Perf. 13x13¼*
2508 A1144 6.50p multi   1.25 .60

A1145

Christmas A1146

2005, Dec. 20
2509 A1145 6.50p multi   1.25 .60
2510 A1146 7.50p multi   1.40 .70

Souvenir Sheet

National Polytechnic Institute, 70th Anniv. — A1147

2006, Feb. 27   Litho.   *Perf. 13¼x13*
2511 A1147 10.50p multi   2.00 1.00

Wolfgang Amadeus Mozart (1756-91), Composer — A1148

2006, Mar. 31
2512 A1148 7.50p multi   1.40 .70

Central Library of National Autonomous University of Mexico, 50th Anniv. — A1149

2006, Apr. 5
2513 A1149 6.50p multi   1.25 .60

Latin American Tower, 50th Anniv. A1150

2006, Apr. 26   *Perf. 13x13¼*
2514   6.50p multi   1.25 .60
2515   10.50p multi   2.00 1.00
   a. A1150 Vert. pair, #2514-2515   3.25 1.60

Isidro Castillo Pérez, Educator — A1151

2006, May 15   *Perf. 13¼x13*
2516 A1151 6.50p multi   1.25 .60

Vasconcelos Library — A1152

2006, May 16
2517 A1152 6.50p multi   1.25 .60

Intl. Women's Day A1153

2006, May 31   *Perf. 13x13¼*
2518 A1153 6.50p multi   1.25 .60

2006 World Cup Soccer Championships, Germany — A1154

2006, June 9   *Perf. 13¼x13*
2519 A1154 13p multi   2.40 1.25

Souvenir Sheet

President Benito Juarez (1806-72) — A1155

2006, June 22   *Perf. 13¼x13*
2520 A1155 13p multi   2.40 1.25

Navy Qualification Center, 50th Anniv. — A1156

2006, Aug. 11   Litho.
2521 A1156 6.50p multi   1.25 .60

Popular Television Characters — A1157

No. 2522: a, El Chayo del Ocho and barrel. b, El Chapulín Colorado with arms crossed. c, El Chayo del Ocho, door and window d, El Chapulín Colorado with arms spread. e, El Chayo del Ocho holding suspenders.

2006, Aug. 21   *Perf. 13¼x13*
2522   Horiz. strip of 5   9.75 4.75
   a. A1157 6.50p multi   1.25 .60
   b. A1157 7.50p multi   1.40 .70
   c. A1157 10.50p multi   1.90 .95
   d. A1157 13p multi   2.40 1.25
   e. A1157 14.50p multi   2.60 1.25

Intl. Year of Deserts and Desertification — A1158

2006, Sept. 20
2523 A1158 6.50p multi   1.25 .60

Souvenir Sheet

Dinosaurs — A1159

No. 2524: a, 6.50p, Muzzy (40x24mm). b, 7.50p, Sabinosaurus (40x48mm). c, 10.50p, Aramberri Monster (40x48mm).

2006, Sept. 29   *Perf. 13¼x13*
2524 A1159 Sheet of 3, #a-c   4.50 2.25

Engineering Institute of National Autonomous University of Mexico, 50th Anniv. — A1160

2006, Oct. 5   *Perf. 13¼x13*
2525 A1160 6.50p multi   1.25 .60

Miniature Sheet

First Mexican Stamps, 150th Anniv. — A1161

No. 2526 — Miguel Hidalgo y Costilla and inscription: a, Aguascalientes. b, Colima. c, Edo. de México. d, Michoacán. e, Nayarit. f, Quintana Roo. g, Tamaulipas. h, Baja California. i, Chiapas. j, Guanajuato. k, Morelos. l, Nuevo León. m, San Luis Potosí. n, Tlaxcala.

o, Baja California Sur. p, Chihuahua. q, Guerrero. r, Oaxaca. s, Sinaloa. t, Veracruz. u, Campeche. v, Distrito Federal. w, Hidalgo. x, Puebla. y, Sonora. z, Yucatán. aa, Coahuila. ab, Durango. ac, Jalisco. ad, Querétaro. ae, Tabasco. af, Zacatecas. ag, Estados Unidos Mexicanos (70x22mm).

Litho., Litho. & Embossed (50p)
2006, Oct. 9
2526	A1161	Sheet of 33	65.00	65.00
a.-g.		6.50p Any single	1.25	.60
h.-n.		7.50p Any single	1.40	.70
o.-t.		9p Any single	1.75	.85
u.-z.		10.50p Any single	1.90	.95
aa.-af.		13p Any single	2.40	1.25
ag.		50p multi	9.25	4.75

World Post
Day — A1162

2006, Oct. 9　　　　　　　**Litho.**
2527	A1162	13p multi	2.40	1.25

Popular Television
Characters — A1163

Xavier López "Chabelo": 6.50p, Boy with ice cream cone. 10.50p, Man seated.

2006, Oct. 30
2528		6.50p multi	1.25	.60
2529		10.50p multi	2.00	1.00
a	A1163	Horiz. pair, #2528-2529	3.25	1.60

Letter Carrier's Day — A1164

2006, Nov. 10
2530	A1164	6.50p multi	1.25	.60

Transformation of the Autonomous Scientific and Literary Institute, Autonomous University of the State of Mexico, 50th Anniv. — A1165

2006, Nov. 17　　　　**Perf. 13x13¼**
2531	A1165	10.50p multi	1.90	.95

"Children,
The Future
of Mexico"
A1166

2006, Nov. 22
2532	A1166	10.50p multi + label	1.90	.95

Andrés Henestrosa,
Writer, Cent. of
Birth — A1167

2006, Nov. 23　　　　**Perf. 13¼x13**
2533	A1167	9p multi	1.75	.85

Edmundo
O'Gorman
(1906-95),
Historian
A1168

2006, Nov. 28　　　　**Perf. 13x13¼**
2534	A1168	10.50p multi	1.90	.95

Mexico in Intl.
Telecommunications
Union,
Cent. — A1169

2006, Nov. 30　　　　**Perf. 13¼x13**
2535	A1169	7p multi	1.40	.70

Christmas
A1170

Children's art by: 7.50p, Ricardo Salas Pineda. 10.50p, María José Goytia.

2006, Dec. 6　　**Litho.**　**Perf. 13¼x13**
2536		7.50p multi	1.40	.70
2537		10.50p multi	2.00	1.00
a.		A1170 Pair, #2536-2537	3.40	1.70

El Universal Newspaper, 90th
Anniv. — A1171

2006, Dec. 22　　　　**Perf. 13¼x13**
2538	A1171	10.50p multi + label	2.00	1.00

Teacher's
Day — A1172

2007, May 15
2539	A1172	7.50p multi	1.40	.70

Frida Kahlo
(1907-54),
Painter
A1173

2007, June 13　　　　**Perf. 13x13¼**
2540	A1173	13p multi	2.40	1.25

Scouting, Cent. — A1174

Designs: 6.50p, Dove and compass. 10.50p, Centenary emblem, compass.

2007, June 30　　　　**Perf. 13¼x13**
2541		6.50p multi	1.25	.60
2542		10.50p multi	2.00	1.00
a.		A1174 Pair, #2541-2542	3.25	1.60

Miniature Sheet

Chichén Itzá — A1175

No. 2543: a, Pelota ring, Jaguar Temple, serpent head. b, Colonnade. c, Observatory. d, Castillo, jaguar head. e, Chac Mool.

2007, July 13
2543	A1175	Sheet of 5 + label	9.25	4.75
a.-b.		6.50p Either single	1.25	.60
c.		10.50p multi	1.90	.95
d.-e.		13p Either single	2.40	1.25

State of Colima, 150th
Anniv. — A1176

2007, July 19
2544	A1176	10.50p multi	1.90	.95

Miniature Sheet

Postal Headquarters Building,
Cent. — A1177

No. 2545: a, Nude boy writing (40x23mm). b, Nude boy touching item on pedestal (40x23mm). c, Two nude boys, chalice (40x23mm). d, Two nude boys, press (40x23mm). e, Boy, gear (40x23mm). f, Clock and machinery (40x23mm). g, Sculpture of UPU emblem, photographs (80x23mm). h, Mercury and caduceus (40x23mm). i, Two nude boys (40x23mm). j, Two nude boys, diff. (40x23mm). k, Seated nude boy with arms extended, holding bird (40x23mm). l, Seated nude boy holding bird (40x23mm). m, Stairway (40x48mm). n, Glass ceiling (40x48). o, Stairways (80x48mm). p, Building exterior (80x48mm).

2007, Aug. 1　　　　**Perf. 13x13¼**
2545	A1177	Sheet of 16	35.00	35.00
a.-b.		5.50p Either single	1.00	.50
o.-g.		6.50p Any single	1.25	.00
h.-i.		9p Either single	1.75	.85
j.		10.50p multi	1.90	.95
k.-l.		13p Either single	2.40	1.25
m.-n.		14.50p Either single	2.75	1.40
o.		15.50p multi	3.00	1.50
p.		39.50p multi	7.25	3.50

Torreón,
Cent.
A1178

No. 2546: a, Locomotive, Torreón Station Museum. b, Bridge, church spires. c, Isauro Martínez Theater. d, Statue of Jesus Christ. e, Bilbao Dunes, Tower.

2007, Sept. 5
2546		Horiz. strip of 5	8.75	4.50
a.		A1178 5p multi	.90	.45
b.-c.		A1178 6.50p Either single	1.25	.60
d.-e.		A1178 14.50p Either single	2.60	1.25

Cultural
Forum,
Monterrey
A1179

No. 2547: a, Dove and hand. b, Child and books. c, Children, windmill, hand picking orange. d, Woman and artist. e, Sculpture and figurines.

2007, Aug. 20 **Litho.** **Perf. 13x13¼**

2547		Horiz. strip of 5	9.00	4.50
a.	A1179 7p multi		1.25	.60
b.-c.	A1179 7.50p Either single		1.40	.70
d.-e.	A1179 13p Either single		2.40	1.25

Central University City Campus of National Autonomous University of Mexico World Heritage Site — A1180

No. 2548: a, Olympic Stadium and artwork. b, University building, University Library. c, Rectory Building.

2007, Sept. 21

2548	Horiz. strip of 3	5.25	2.75
a.	A1180 6.50p multi	1.25	.60
b.	A1180 9p multi	1.60	.80
c.	A1180 13p multi	2.40	1.25

University of Baja California, 50th Anniv. A1181

2007, Oct. 1

2549	A1181 7.50p multi	1.40	.70

Ozone Layer Protection A1182

No. 2550: a, Doves, tree, leaves. b, Doves, Earth in hands.

2007, Oct. 1

2550	A1182	Vert. pair	4.00	2.00
a.	7p multi		1.25	.60
b.	14.50p multi		2.75	1.40

St. Christopher, by Nicolás Rodríguez Juárez — A1183

2007, Oct. 3

2551	A1183 6.50p multi	1.25	.60

Autonomous University of Coahuila, 50th Anniv. — A1184

2007, Oct. 4 **Perf. 13¼x13**

2552	A1184 7.50p multi	1.40	.70

World Post Day A1185

No. 2553 — Envelope with denomination in: a, Yellow. b, Black.

2007, Oct. 9 **Perf. 13x13¼**

2553	A1185	Vert. pair	3.25	1.60
a.	7p multi		1.25	.60
b.	10.50p multi		2.00	1.00

Rights of People With Disabilities A1186

2007, Oct. 11

2554	A1186 6.50p multi	1.25	.60

Miniature Sheet

Francisco Gabilondo Soler (1907-90), Composer of Children's Songs — A1187

No. 2555: a, Turtle, giraffe, peacock (Caminito de la Escuela). b, Dog, camel, mouse (Caminito de la Escuela). c, Duck and ducklings (La Patita). d, Girl and mouse (La Muñeca Fea). e, Cat with guitar (Gato de Barrio). f, King and cakes (Bombón I). g, Three pigs and cakes (Cochinitos Dormilones). h, Three pigs in bed (Cochinitos Dormilones). i, Old woman and cat (Di Por Que). j, Mouse in cowboy's clothes (El Ratón Vaquero). k, Boy eating watermelon (Negrito Sandía). l, Cricket holding stick (Cri-Cri). m, Soler. n, Cricket at music stand (Cri-Cri). o, Ant and fountain (El Chorrito).

2007, Oct. 11 **Perf. 13¼x13**

2555	A1187	Sheet of 15	18.50	18.50
a.-b.	5p Either single		.90	.45
c.-k.	6.50p Any single		1.25	.60
l.-n.	7p Any single		1.25	.60
o.	7.50p multi		1.40	.70

Degrees in Administration, 50th Anniv. — A1188

2007, Oct. 19 **Perf. 13x13¼**

2556	A1188 7.50p multi	1.40	.70

Cuauhtemoc Sailing School — A1189

2007, Nov. 4 **Perf. 13¼x13**

2557	A1189 7.50p multi	1.40	.70

A1190

A1191

Letter Carrier's Day — A1192

No. 2559: a, Girl writing letter, letter carrier on bicycle. b, Girl mailing letter in mailbox. c, Letter carrier on bicycle. d, Letter carrier delivering letter.

No. 2560: a, Female letter carrier. b, Letter carrier on bicycle. c, Letter carrier on motorcycle. d, Letter carrier with mail bag. e, Three letter carriers. f, Five letter carriers. g, Letter carriers on rowboat. h, Horse-drawn carriage. i, Letter carrier and mail bag on railway hand car.

2007, Nov. 12 **Perf. 13**

2558	A1190 10.50p multi	2.00	1.00
2559	A1191 Block of 4	5.00	2.50
a.-d.	6.50p Any single	1.25	.60
2560	A1192 Sheet of 9	13.50	13.50
a.-c.	6.50p Any single	1.25	.60
d.-f.	7p Any single	1.25	.60
g.-i.	10.50p Any single	2.00	1.00

Mountains — A1193

Designs: No. 2561, Mt. Minya Konka, People's Republic of China. No. 2562, Popocatépetl, Mexico.

2007, Nov. 22 **Litho.** **Perf. 13¼x13**

2561	A1193 6.50p multi	1.25	.60
2562	A1193 6.50p multi	1.25	.60

See People's Republic of China Nos. 3635-3636.

Intl. Day Against Violence Towards Women — A1194

2007, Nov. 26

2563	A1194 7p multi	1.40	.70

Mariano Otero (1817-50), Judicial and Constitutional Reformer — A1195

2007, Nov. 27 **Perf. 13x13¼**

2564	A1195 10.50p multi	2.00	1.00

Trials of Amparo, legal protection of individual constitutional guarantees in federal courts.

Miniature Sheet

Monte Albán Archaeological Site — A1196

No. 2565: a, Scribe of Cuilapan. b, Head with jaguar helmet. c, Building II, Cocijo urn. d, Building I, Central Plaza, Cocijo urn. e, Observatory, Southern Platform, Central Plaza.

2007, Dec. 11 **Perf. 13¼x13**

2565	A1196	Sheet of 5 + label	9.50	4.75
a.-b.	6.50p Either single		1.25	.60
c.	10.50p multi		2.00	1.00
d.-e.	13p Either single		2.40	1.25

Christmas A1197

2007, Dec. 12   *Perf. 13*
2566   Horiz. strip of 5   10.00   5.00
   a. A1197 6.50p Candle   1.25   .60
   b. A1197 7p Bell   1.40   .70
   c. A1197 10.50p Angel   2.00   1.00
   d. A1197 13.50p Magi   2.50   1.25
   e. A1197 14.50p Holy Family   2.75   1.40

Miniature Sheet

Dogs — A1198

No. 2567: a, Two English bulldogs. b, Two rottweilers. c, Two boxers. d, Two beagles. e, Head of English Bulldog. f, Head of Rottweiler. g, Head of boxer. h, Head of beagle. i, English bulldog. j, Rottweiler. k, Boxer. l, Beagle.

2007, Dec. 14
2567   A1198   Sheet of 12   19.00   9.50
   a.-d.   6.50p Any single   1.25   .60
   e.-h.   7p Any single   1.40   .70
   i.-l.   10.50p Any single   2.00   1.00

See Nos. 2762-2763.

Jesús García Corona (1883-1907), Heroic Railroad Engineer — A1199

2007, Dec. 17   *Perf. 13¼x13*
2568 A1199 10.50p multi   2.00   1.00

Satélite Towers, Naucalpan, 50th Anniv. A1200

2007, Dec. 19   *Perf. 13x13¼*
2569 A1200 6.50p multi   1.25   .60

El Cajón Dam — A1201

Aerial view of: 7p, Open spillway. 13p, Dam.

2007, Dec. 28   *Perf. 13¼x13*
2570 A1201   7p multi   1.40   .70
2571 A1201   13p multi   2.40   1.25

Letter and Heart A1202

2008, Jan. 29 Litho.   *Perf. 13½x13¼*
2572 A1202 6.50p multi   1.25   .60

Mother's Day A1203

2008, May 2   *Perf. 13x13¼*
2573 A1203 6.50p multi   1.25   .60

Pres. Miguel Alemán Valdés (1900-83) A1204

2008, May 14   *Perf. 13x13¼*
2574 A1204 6.50p multi   1.25   .60

The Fruits, by Diego Rivera A1205

2008, May 15
2575 A1205 6.50p multi   1.25   .60

Teacher's Day.

Miniature Sheet

El Santo and El Hijo del Santo — A1206

No. 2576: a, El Santo wearing silver mask and robe. b, El Santo in ring. c, El Hijo del Santo with hands outstretched. d, El Santo with automobile. e, El Hijo del Santo in ring. f, El Hijo del Santo with arms crossed.

2008, June 17   *Perf. 13*
2576 A1206   Sheet of 6   7.50   3.75
   a.-f.   6.50p Any single   1.25   .60

El Santo (Rodolfo Guzmán Huerta, 1917-84), El Hijo del Santo (Jorge Guzmán), wrestling legends and film stars.

2008 Summer Olympics, Beijing A1207

Designs: No. 2577, Rowing. No. 2578, Weight lifting. No. 2579, Rhythmic gymnastics.

2008, Aug. 8   *Perf. 13*
2577 A1207 6.50p multi   1.25   .60
2578 A1207 6.50p multi   1.25   .60
2579 A1207 6.50p multi   1.25   .60
   Nos. 2577-2579 (3)   3.75   1.80

Electoral Justice — A1208

2008, Aug. 19 Litho.   *Perf. 13¼x13*
2580 A1208 6.50p multi   1.25   .60

Mexico Post Emblem — A1209

2008, Sept. 8
2581 A1209 6.50p multi   1.25   .60

Fight for Mexican Independence, Bicent. — A1210

Designs: No. 2582, Ignacio Allende (1769-1811), revolutionary leader. No. 2583, Josefa Ortíz de Dominguez (1768-1829), revolutionary leader. No. 2584, José María Morelos y Pavón (1765-1815), revolutionary leader. No. 2585, Battle of Monte de las Cruces, 1810, horiz. No. 2586, Battle of Alhóndiga de Grandaitas, 1810, horiz. No. 2587, Meeting of Miguel Hidalgo and Morelos, horiz. No. 2588, Querétaro Conspiracy, horiz. No. 2589, Francisco Primo de Verdad y Ramos (1760-1808), promoter of Mexican independence, horiz. No. 2590, Miguel Hidalgo and Cry of Independence. No. 2591, Crowd on Mexico City Alameda.

2008, Sept. 15   *Perf. 13x13¼*
2582 A1210   6.50p multi   1.25   .60
2583 A1210   6.50p multi   1.25   .60
2584 A1210   6.50p multi   1.25   .60

    Perf. 13¼x13
2585 A1210   6.50p multi   1.25   .60

    Size: 71x30mm
2586 A1210   6.50p multi   1.25   .60
2587 A1210   6.50p multi   1.25   .60
2588 A1210   6.50p multi   1.25   .60
2589 A1210   6.50p multi   1.25   .60
   Nos. 2582-2589 (8)   10.00   4.80

    Imperf
    Size:80x80mm
2590 A1210   10.50p multi   1.90   .95
2591 A1210   10.50p multi   1.90   .95

See Nos. 2627-2636.

Miniature Sheet

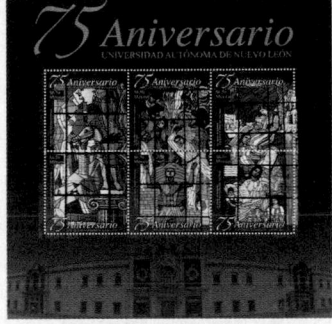

Autonomous University of Nuevo León, 75th Anniv. — A1211

No. 2592 — Stained-glass windows by Roberto Montenegro: a, Top of "La Historia." b, Top of "La Agricultura." c, Top of "La Ciencia y la Sabiduría." d, Bottom of "La Historia." e, Bottom of "La Agricultura." f, Bottom of "La Ciencia y la Sabiduría."

2008, Sept. 25   *Perf. 13*
2592 A1211   Sheet of 6   7.50   7.50
   a.-f.   6.50p Any single   1.25   .60

World Post Day A1212

2008, Oct. 9   *Perf. 13x13¼*
2593 A1212 10.50p multi   1.60   .80

Flowers — A1213

No. 2594: a, Hylocereus undulatus. b, Curcubita pepo.

2008, Oct. 10   *Perf. 13*
2594 A1213   Horiz. pair   2.00   1.00
   a.-b.   6.50p Either single   1.00   .50

Juarez Autonomous University of Tabasco, 50th Anniv. — A1214

2008, Nov. 3 Litho.   *Perf. 13x13¼*
2595 A1214 6.50p multi   1.00   .50

Miniature Sheet

Letter Carrier's Day — A1215

No. 2596: a, Letter carrier with large shoulder pouch. b, Letter carrier on bicycle. c, Letter carrier on motorcycle with sidecar. d, Letter carrier on motor scooter. e, Postal service automobile. f, Postal truck. g, Letter carriers, bicycles and truck. h, Postal van, letter carrier on bicycle.

2008, Nov. 12   ***Perf. 13***
2596   A1215   Sheet of 8   7.75   7.75
a.-h.   6.50p Any single   .95   .50

National Employment
Service — A1216

2008, Nov. 19   ***Perf. 13¼x13½***
2597   A1216   6.50p multi   .95   .50

Mexican
Revolution,
Cent. (in
2011)
A1217

Designs: No. 2598, José María Pino Suárez (1869-1913), politician. No. 2599, Aquiles Serdán (1876-1910), politician. No. 2600, Ricardo Flores Magón (1874-1922), anarchist, and Regeneración Newspaper. No. 2601, Mexican Liberal Party. No. 2602, Cananea Strike. No. 2603, Railway system. No. 2604, Rio Blanco Strike. No. 2605, Revolutionary Junta of Puebla.

No. 2606, Triumphal Entry of Francisco I. Madero. No. 2607, Tienda de raya (company store).

2008, Nov. 20   ***Perf. 13x13¼***
2598   A1217   6.50p multi   .95   .50
2599   A1217   6.50p multi   .95   .50
2600   A1217   6.50p multi   .95   .50

Size: 71x30mm
Perf. 13¼x13
2601   A1217   6.50p multi   .95   .50
2602   A1217   6.50p multi   .95   .50
2603   A1217   6.50p multi   .95   .50
2604   A1217   6.50p multi   .95   .50
2605   A1217   6.50p multi   .95   .50
     Nos. 2598-2605 (8)   7.60   4.00

Imperf
Size: 80x80mm
2606   A1217   10.50p multi   1.60   .80
2607   A1217   10.50p multi   1.60   .80
     See Nos. 2647-2656.

Parque La Venta Archaeological
Museum, La Venta — A1218

2008, Dec. 4   ***Perf. 13***
2608   A1218   6.50p multi   .95   .50

Christmas
A1219

Designs: 6.50p, Adoration of the Shepherds, by Cristóbal de Villalpando. 10.50p, Adoration of the Magi, by unknown artist.

2008, Dec. 10   ***Perf. 13x13¼***
2609   A1219   6.50p multi   1.00   .50
2610   A1219   10.50p multi   1.60   .80
a.   Horiz. pair, #2609-2610   2.60   1.30

Dr. Gonzalo Aguirre Beltrán (1908-96),
Anthropologist — A1220

2008, Dec. 16   ***Perf. 13¼x13***
2611   A1220   6.50p multi   .95   .50

Miniature Sheet

Palenque Archaeological Site — A1221

No. 2612: a, Mayan hieroglyphic cartouches, tomb, seated figure. b, Jade mask, skull mask, tablet. c, Palace and tower. d, Temple of the Sun, Temples 14 and 15. e, Temple of Inscriptions, incense holder.

2008, Dec. 19   ***Litho.***
2612   A1221   Sheet of 5 + label   7.25   7.25
a.-b.   6.50p Either single   .95   .50
c.   10.50p multi   1.50   .75
d.-e.   13p Either single   1.90   .95

Mexican Academy of
Film Ariel Awards,
50th Anniv. — A1222

2008, Dec. 24   ***Perf. 13¼x13***
2613   A1222   6.50p multi   .95   .50

St. Valentine's
Day — A1223

2009, Feb. 9   ***Litho.***   ***Perf. 13x13¼***
2614   A1223   6.50p multi   .90   .45

Veracruz
Carnival
A1224

2009, Feb. 18
2615   A1224   6.50p multi   .90   .45

Miniature Sheet

Tajín Archaeological Site — A1225

No. 2616: a, Yoke, eagle-shaped hatchet. b, Decorated panel. c, Terracotta pelota player and pelota pyramid. d, Pyramid, bird's head hatchet, lightning bolt. e, Temple, temple diagram, decorated handle.

2009, Mar. 21   ***Perf. 13¼x13***
2616   A1225   Sheet of 5 + label   7.50   3.75
a.-b.   6.50p Either single   .95   .50
c.   10.50p multi   1.60   .80
d.-e.   13p Either single   1.90   .95

Channel 11 Television, 50th
Anniv. — A1226

2009, Mar. 27
2617   A1226   6.50p multi   .95   .50

Teacher's
Day
A1227

2009, May 15   ***Perf. 13x13¼***
2618   A1227   6.50p multi   1.00   .50

Miniature Sheet

National Bank of Mexico, 125th
Anniv. — A1228

No. 2619: a, Palacio de los Condes de San Mateo de Valparaiso, Mexico City. b, Main patio, Palacio de los Condes de San Mateo de Valparaiso. c, Column and main door, Palacio de Iturbide, Mexico City. d, Casa Montejo, Mérida. e, Doors, Casa del Mayorazgo de la Canal, San Miguel de Allende. f, Main patio, Palacio de los Condes del Valle de Súchil, Durango.

2009, June 2   ***Perf. 13***
2619   A1228   Sheet of 6   6.00   3.00
a.-f.   6.50p Any single   1.00   .50

World Environment Day — A1229

2009, June 5   ***Perf. 13¼x13***
2620   A1229   10.50p multi   1.60   .80

Aguascalientes Autonomous
University — A1230

2009, June 19
2621   A1230   10.50p multi   1.60   .80

Gymnogyps Californianus — A1231

2009, July 27   ***Perf. 13¼x13***
2622   A1231   10.50p multi   1.60   .80

Intl. Day of Indigenous People A1232

2009, Aug. 11
2623 A1232 6.50p multi   1.00 .50

The Country, by Jorge González Camarena — A1233

2009, Aug. 20   Litho.   Perf. 13¼x13
2624 A1233 6.50p multi   1.00 .50
National Free Textbook Commission, 50th anniv.

Preservation of Polar Regions and Glaciers — A1234

Designs: 10.50p, Mts. Popocatépetl and Iztaccíhuatl. 13p, Mt. Citlaltépetl.

2009, Sept. 14   Perf. 13
2625   10.50p multi   1.60 .80
2626   13p multi   1.90 .95
   a. A1234 Vert. pair, #2625-2626   3.50 1.75

Fight For Mexican Independence Type of 2008

Designs: No. 2627, Congress of Chilpancingo. No. 2628, Establishment of the Supreme Junta. No. 2629, Leona Vicario (1789-1842), supporter of independence movement, and husband, Andrés Quintana Roo (1787-1851), independence movement leader and politician. No. 2630, Execution of José María Morelos y Pavón, horiz. No. 2631, Capture of Miguel Hidalgo and insurgents, horiz. No. 2632, Execution of Hidalgo, horiz. No. 2633, Siege of Cuautla, horiz. No. 2634, Constitution of Apatzingán, horiz.
No. 2635, Map of campaign of Morelos, portraits of compatriots Hermenegildo Galeana, Mariano Matamoros, Pablo Galeana, and Nicolás Bravo. No. 2636, Abolition of slavery.

2009, Sept. 16   Perf. 13¼x13
2627 A1210 6.50p multi   1.00 .50
2628 A1210 6.50p multi   1.00 .50
2629 A1210 6.50p multi   1.00 .50
Perf. 13¼x13
2630 A1210 6.50p multi   1.00 .50
2631 A1210 6.50p multi   1.00 .50
2632 A1210 6.50p multi   1.00 .50
Size: 71x30mm
2633 A1210 6.50p multi   1.00 .50
2634 A1210 6.50p multi   1.00 .50
   Nos. 2627-2634 (8)   8.00 4.00
Imperf
Size: 80x80mm
2635 A1210 10.50p multi   1.60 .80
2636 A1210 10.50p multi   1.60 .80

UNI Global Union Post and Logistics Conference, Mexico City — A1235

2009, Sept. 30   Perf. 13x13¼
2637 A1235 6.50p multi   1.00 .50

Autonomous University of San Luis Potosí Scientific and Literary Institute, 150th Anniv. — A1236

2009, Oct. 5   Perf. 13¼x13
2638 A1236 6.50p multi   1.00 .50

World Post Day A1237

2009, Oct. 9   Perf. 13x13¼
2639 A1237 10.50p multi   1.60 .80

City of Chihuahua, 300th Anniv. — A1238

2009, Oct. 12   Perf. 13¼x13
2640 A1238 6.50p multi   1.00 .50

Day of the Dead (All Souls' Day) — A1239

Figurines: No. 2641, Woman honoring dead. No. 2642, Ferris wheel with skeleton riders.

2009, Nov. 2   Perf. 13
2641   6.50p multi   1.00 .50
2642   6.50p multi   1.00 .50
   a. A1239 Horiz. pair, #2641-2642   2.00 1.00

Juan Bosch (1909-2001), President of Dominican Republic — A1240

2009, Nov. 4   Perf. 13x13¼
2643 A1240 10.50p multi   1.60 .80

Wilderness Areas A1241

No. 2644: a, El Carmen Mountains, Mexico. b, Nahanni National Park, Canada. c, Zion National Park, US. d, Kronotsky Reserve, Russia. e, Baviaanskloof Reserve, South Africa.

2009, Nov. 6   Litho.   Perf. 13
2644   Horiz. strip of 5   8.50 4.25
   a. A1241 6.50p multi   1.00 .50
   b.-c. A1241 10.50p Either single   1.60 .80
   d. A1241 13p multi   2.00 1.00
   e. A1241 14.50p multi   2.25 1.10

Letter Carrier's Day — A1242

Letter carrier on: No. 2645, Bicycle. No. 2646, Motorcycle.

2009, Nov. 12   Perf. 13
2645   6.50p multi   1.00 .50
2646   6.50p multi   1.00 .50
   a. A1242 Horiz. pair, #2645-2646   2.00 1.00

Mexican Revolution Type of 2008

Designs: No. 2647, Emiliano Zapata (1879-1919), General of Liberation Army of the South. No. 2648, Pres. Francisco I. Madero (1873-1913). No. 2649, Proclamation of the Plan of Ayala. No. 2650, Taking of Zacatecas, horiz. No. 2651, Women revolution fighters, horiz. No. 2652, Francisco "Pancho" Villa (1878-1923), General of the Division of the North, horiz. No. 2653, Railroads in the revolution, horiz. No. 2654, The "Ten Tragic Days," horiz.
No. 2655, Venustiano Carranza (1859-1920), revolution leader, and proclamation of Plan of Guadalupe. No. 2656, Revolutionaries, painting by David Alfaro Siqueiros.

2009, Nov. 20   Perf. 13x13¼
2647 A1217 6.50p multi   1.10 .55
2648 A1217 6.50p multi   1.10 .55
2649 A1217 6.50p multi   1.10 .55
Perf. 13¼x13
2650 A1217 6.50p multi   1.10 .55
2651 A1217 6.50p multi   1.10 .55
Size: 71x30mm
2652 A1217 6.50p multi   1.10 .55
2653 A1217 6.50p multi   1.10 .55
2654 A1217 6.50p multi   1.10 .55
   Nos. 2647-2654 (8)   8.80 4.40
Imperf
Size: 80x80mm
2655 A1217 10.50p multi   1.75 .85
2656 A1217 10.50p multi   1.75 .85

Traffic Safety A1243

2009, Nov. 23   Perf. 13¼x13
2657 A1243 6.50p multi   1.10 .55

Jaíme Sabínes (1926-99), Poet — A1244

2009, Nov. 27   Litho.
2658 A1244 6.50p multi   1.10 .55

Federal Fiscal Auditor, 50th Anniv. — A1245

2009, Nov. 30
2659 A1245 6.50p multi   1.10 .55

Christmas
A1246   A1247

2009, Dec. 1   Perf. 13¼x13
2660 A1246 6.50p Melchior   1.10 .55
2661 A1246 6.50p Gaspar   1.10 .55
2662 A1246 6.50p Balthazar   1.10 .55
2663 A1247 6.50p Santa Claus   1.10 .55
   Nos. 2660-2663 (4)   4.40 2.20

Oportunidades Human Development Program — A1248

2009, Dec. 15   Perf. 13x13¼
2664 A1248 6.50p multi   1.00 .50

Energy Conservation — A1249

No. 2665 — Children's drawings: a, Child connecting power cord from house to sun. b, Light bulbs in daytime and nighttime. c, Light bulb people in room.

2009, Dec. 16   Perf. 13¼x13
2665   Horiz. strip of 3   3.00 1.50
   a.-c. A1249 6.50p Any single   1.00 .50

Paisano Program A1250

2009, Dec. 18   *Perf. 13x13¼*
2666 A1250 6.50p multi   1.00   .50

Pres. Venustiano Carranza (1859-1920) — A1251

2009, Dec. 21
2667 A1251 6.50p multi   1.00   .50

Aviation in Mexico, Cent. — A1252

2010, Jan. 8   Litho.   *Perf. 13¼x13*
2668 A1252 7p multi   1.10   .55

State Workers' Security and Social Services Institute, 50th Anniv. — A1253

2010, Jan. 19
2669 A1253 7p multi   1.10   .55

St. Valentine's Day — A1254

2010, Feb. 3
2670 A1254 7p multi   1.10   .55

New Year 2010 (Year of the Tiger) A1255

2010, Feb. 11   *Perf. 13x13¼*
2671 A1255 7p multi   1.10   .55

Mexican Red Cross, Cent. A1256

2010, Feb. 21   *Perf. 13*
2672 A1256 10.50p multi   1.75   .85

Inter-America Development Bank Assembly of Governors, Cancun — A1257

2010, Mar. 19   *Perf. 13x13¼*
2673 A1257 11.50p multi   1.90   .95

Souvenir Sheet

Mexico City Red Devils Baseball Players — A1258

No. 2674: a, José Luis Sandoval. b, Miguel Ojeda. c, Roberto Saucedo.

2010, Apr. 11   *Perf. 13*
2674 A1258   Sheet of 3   3.50 1.75
   a.-c.   7p Any single   1.10   .55

Mother's Day A1259

2010, Apr. 23   *Perf. 13x13¼*
2675 A1259 7p multi   1.10   .55

Teacher's Day A1260

2010, May 15
2676 A1260 7p multi   1.10   .55

2010 World Cup Soccer Championships, South Africa — A1261

No. 2677 — 2010 World Cup emblem and: a, Mexican team. b, Gerardo Torrado, Giovani Dos Santos. c, Andrés Guardado, Guillermo Ochoa.

2010, May 15   *Perf. 13¼x13*
2677   Horiz. strip of 3   4.00 2.00
   a.-b.   A1261 7p Either single   1.10   .55
   c.   A1261 11.50p multi   1.75   .90

Intl. Mother Language Day — A1262

2010, May 21
2678 A1262 11.50p multi   1.75   .90

Pres. Adolfo López Mateos (1909-69) — A1263

2010, May 26
2679 A1263 7p multi   1.10   .55

Natl. Human Rights Commission — A1264

2010, June 7   Litho.
2680 A1264 7p multi   1.10   .55

Scouting in Mexico, 90th Anniv. A1265

2010, July 17   *Perf. 13*
2681 A1265 7p multi   1.10   .55

Grandparent's Day — A1266

2010, Aug. 16
2682 A1266 7p multi   1.10   .55

Mexican Petroleum Institute — A1267

2010, Aug. 23   *Perf. 13¼x13*
2683 A1267 7p multi   1.10   .55

Mexican Independence, Bicent. — A1268

Designs: No. 2684, Pres. Guadalupe Victoria (1789-1843). No. 2685, Pedro Moreno (1775-1817), revolutionary leader. No. 2686, Father Servando Teresa de Mier (1765-1827), politician. No. 2687, Xavier Mina (1789-1817), revolutionary leader. No. 2688, Vicente Guerrero (1783-1831), soldier and politician. No. 2689, Flag of the Army of the Three Guarantees. No. 2690, Gen. Manuel de Mier y Terán (1789-1832), Nicolás Bravo (1786-1854), soldier and politician, horiz. No. 2691, Ignacio López Rayón (1773-1832), leader of revolutionary government, Gen. Ramón Rayón (1775-1839), horiz. No. 2692, O'Donojú Conference, horiz.

No. 2693, Miguel Hidalgo y Costilla (1753-1811), revolutionary leader; Lieutenant Colonel Mariano Jiménez (1781-1811); Juan Aldama (1774-1811), soldier; Leona Vicario (1789-1842), revolution supporter; José María Morelos y Pavón (1765-1815), revolutionary leader; Ignacío Allende (1769-1811), revolutionary leader; Josefa Ortiz de Domínguez (1768-1829), revolution supporter; and Miguel Domínguez (1756-1830), revolutionary leader. No. 2694, Entrance into Mexico City of the Army of the Three Guarantees.

2010, Sept. 16   *Perf. 13x13¼*
2684 A1268   7p multi   1.10   .55
2685 A1268   7p multi   1.10   .55
2686 A1268   7p multi   1.10   .55
2687 A1268   7p multi   1.10   .55
2688 A1268   7p multi   1.10   .55
2689 A1268   7p multi   1.10   .55

    Perf. 13¼x13
2690 A1268   7p multi   1.10   .55
2691 A1268   7p multi   1.10   .55
2692 A1268   7p multi   1.10   .55
   Nos. 2684-2692 (9)   9.90 4.95

    Imperf
    Size: 80x80mm
2693 A1268 11.50p multi   1.90   .95
2694 A1268 11.50p multi   1.90   .95

Miniature Sheet

National University of Mexico, Cent. — A1269

No. 2695: a, University founder Justo Sierra, opening of National University. b, National Preparatory School, College of San Ildefonso. c, National School of Law, Academy of San Carlos, National School of Higher Studies. d, Murals by José Clemente Orozco and David Alfaro Siqueiros. e, National University of Mexico Symphonic Orchestra in Nezahualcoyotl Hall, Olympic Stadium, Dancers of National

University of Mexico Choreographic Studio. f, University Museum of Contemporaneous Art.

2010, Sept. 21   Litho.   Perf. 13
2695   A1269   Sheet of 6   6.75   3.50
a.-f.   7p Any single   1.10   .55

Girl Guides of Mexico A1270

2010, Sept. 25
2696   A1270   7p multi   1.10   .55

Plenipotentiary Conference of the Intl. Telecommunications Union, Guadalajara — A1271

2010, Oct. 4   Perf. 13¼x13
2697   A1271   11.50p multi   1.90   .95

World Post Day A1272

2010, Oct. 9   Perf. 13x13¼
2698   A1272   11.50p multi   1.90   .95

Souvenir Sheet

Temples — A1273

No. 2699: a, Pyramid of the Sun, Teotihuacan, Mexico. b, Ateshgah, Baku, Azerbaijan.

2010, Oct. 12
2699   A1273   Sheet of 2   2.25   1.10
a.-b.   7p Either single   1.10   .55

See Azerbaijan No. 934.

National Center for Disaster Prevention, 20th Anniv. A1274

2010, Oct. 13
2700   A1274   7p multi   1.25   .60

All Souls' Day (Day of the Dead) — A1275

2010, Oct. 25
2701   A1275   7p multi   1.25   .60

A1276

Christmas A1277

Designs: No. 2702, Santa Claus, children, Christmas tree, toys.
No. 2703 — Red ribbon and: a, Holy Family and angel. b, Candle, children hitting piñata. c, Three Magi.

2010, Nov. 4   Litho.   Perf. 13
2702   A1276   7p multi   1.25   .60
2703   Horiz. strip of 3   3.75   1.90
a.-c.   A1277 7p Any single   1.25   .60

Letter Carrier's Day — A1278

Designs: 7p, Postman and old postal truck. 11.50p, Postman on motorcycle, row of postal trucks.

2010, Nov. 11
2704   7p multi   1.25   .60
2705   11.50p multi   1.90   .95
a.   A1278 Horiz. pair, #2704-2705   3.25   1.60

Rodolfo Neri Vela, First Mexican in Space, 25th Anniv. A1279

Neri Vela and: No. 2706, Space equipment. No. 2707, Mexican flag, Space Shuttles.

2010, Nov. 16   Perf. 13x13¼
2706   7p multi   1.25   .60
2707   7p multi   1.25   .60
a.   A1279 Vert. pair, #2706-2707   2.50   1.25

Palace of Fine Arts, Mexico City — A1280

2010, Nov. 19   Perf. 13¼x13
2708   A1280   7p multi   1.25   .60

Mexican Revolution, Cent. A1281

Designs: No. 2709, Pres. Venustiano Carranza (1859-1920), Carranza and crowd. No. 2710, Luis Cabrera (1876-1954), politician, and Agricultural Law. No. 2711, 1917 Constitution, detail of painting by Jorge González Camarena depicting Pres. Carranza and papers. No. 2712, 1917 Constitution, by Camarena, detail depicting Constitutional Congress and eagle. No. 2713, The Convention of Aguascalientes, detail of painting by Oswaldo Barra Cunningham, horiz. No. 2714, Battle of Celaya, horiz. No. 2715, Provisional Presidents Eulalio Gutiérrez (1881-1939), Roque González Garza (1885-1962), and Francisco Lagos Cházaro (1878-1932), Provisional Government one-peso banknote, horiz. No. 2716, Women fighters in the Mexican Revolution, horiz.
No. 2717, Revolution leaders Carranza, Francisco "Pancho" Villa (1878-1923), and Emiliano Zapata (1879-1919) on horseback. No. 2718, 1910 Revolution, detail of mural by Diego Rivera depicting revolution leaders.

2010, Nov. 20   Perf. 13x13¼
2709   A1281   7p multi   1.25   .60
2710   A1281   7p multi   1.25   .60
2711   A1281   7p multi   1.25   .60
2712   A1281   7p multi   1.25   .60

Perf. 13¼x13
2713   A1281   7p multi   1.25   .60
2714   A1281   7p multi   1.25   .60

Size: 71x30mm
2715   A1281   7p multi   1.25   .60
2716   A1281   7p multi   1.25   .60
Nos. 2709-2716 (8)   10.00   4.80

Imperf
Size: 80x80mm
2717   A1281   11.50p multi   1.90   .95
2718   A1281   11.50p multi   1.90   .95

Monumental Clock, Pachuca, Cent. — A1282

2010, Nov. 25   Perf. 13
2719   A1282   7p multi   1.25   .60

Campaign Against Violence Towards Women — A1283

2010, Dec. 1   Perf. 13¼x13
2720   A1283   11.50p multi   1.90   .95

2010 United Nations Climate Change Conference, Cancún — A1284

2010, Dec. 6   Perf. 13x13¼
2721   A1284   7p multi   1.25   .60

National Council of Science and Technology (CONACYT), 40th Anniv. — A1285

2010, Dec. 9   Perf. 13¼x13
2722   A1285   7p multi   1.25   .60

Awarding of Nobel Prize for Literature to Octavio Paz, 20th Anniv. — A1286

2010, Dec. 10   Litho.
2723   A1286   7p multi   1.25   .60

Letter
Carrier's
Day
A1323

2011, Nov. 11
2761 A1323 7p multi   1.10 .55

Dogs Type of 2007

Designs: 7p, German shepherd (Pastor Alemán). 13.50p, English cocker spaniel (Cocker spaniel Inglés).

2011, Nov. 17   **Perf. 13**
2762 A1198   7p multi   1.10 .55
2763 A1198 13.50p multi   2.00 1.00

Christmas — A1324

Designs: No. 2764, Santa Claus, letters, silhouette of Santa's sleigh in front of Moon. No. 2765, vert.: a, Children, Christmas piñata. b, Creche, candle, fruit and cup. c, Letters, Magi, Christmas gifts.

2011, Nov. 18   **Perf. 13¼x13**
2764 A1324 11.50p multi   1.75 .85
2765   Vert. strip of 3   4.75 2.25
  a.   A1324 7p multi   1.10 .55
  b.-c. A1324 11.50p Either single   1.75 .85

Veracruz Delegation of Mexican Social
Security Institute, 50th Anniv.
A1326

2011, Nov. 30   **Perf. 13x13¼**
2766 A1326 7p multi   1.10 .55

Intl. Day for
Elimination of
Violence Toward
Women — A1327

2011, Nov. 30   **Perf. 13¼x13**
2767 A1327 11.50p multi   1.75 .85

National
Voluntary
Action and
Solidarity
Prize
A1328

2011, Dec. 7   **Perf. 13x13¼**
2768 A1328 11.50p multi   1.75 .85

Mexican Urban UNESCO World
Heritage Sites — A1329

2011, Dec. 8   **Perf. 13¼x13**
2769 A1329 11.50p multi   1.75 .85

State
Workers'
Security
and Social
Services
Institute,
50th Anniv.
A1330

2011, Dec. 16   **Perf. 13x13¼**
2770 A1330 7p multi   1.10 .55

Diplomatic Relations Between Mexico
and South Korea, 50th
Anniv. — A1331

Designs: No. 2771, Adult gray whale, denomination at left. No. 2772, Juvenile gray whale, denomination at right.

2012, Jan. 26 Litho. Perf. 13¼x13
2771   13.50p multi   2.10 1.10
2772   13.50p multi   2.10 1.10
  a.   A1331 Horiz. pair, #2771-2772   4.25 2.25

See South Korea No. 2377.

St. Valentine's Day — A1332

2012, Feb. 2   **Perf. 13**
2773 A1332 7p multi   1.10 .55

Intl.
Women's
Day
A1333

2012, Mar. 8   **Perf. 13x13¼**
2774 A1333 11.50p multi   1.75 .90

World Down Syndrome Day — A1334

2012, Mar. 21   **Perf. 13¼x13**
2775 A1334 13.50p multi   2.10 1.10

National Bioethics Commission, 20th
Anniv. — A1335

2012, Mar. 27   **Litho.**
2776 A1335 7p multi   1.10 .55

Campaign
Against
Human
Trafficking
A1336

2012, Mar. 29   **Perf. 13x13¼**
2777 A1336 7p multi   1.10 .55

Linares, 300th Anniv. — A1337

2012, Apr. 10   **Perf. 13¼x13**
2778 A1337 7p multi   1.10 .55

Mother's
Day
A1338

Designs: No. 2779, Mother receiving card and breakfast from two children. No. 2780, Mothers and children.

2012, Apr. 26   **Perf. 13**
2779 A1338 7p grn & multi   1.10 .55
2780 A1338 7p pink & multi   1.10 .55

Interior Stairway
of Postal Palace
(Main Post
Office), Mexico
City — A1339

2012, May 4   **Perf. 13x13¼**
2781 A1339 7p multi   1.00 .50

Souvenir Sheet

Battle of Puebla, 150th
Anniv. — A1340

No. 2782: a, Map of Mexico, flags of France, Great Britain and Spain. b, General Ignacio Zaragoza, soldiers. c, Army of the East.

2012, May 5   **Perf. 13**
2782 A1340   Sheet of 3   3.00 1.50
  a.-c.   7p Any single   1.00 .50

Teacher's
Day
A1341

2012, May 15   **Perf. 13¼x13**
2783 A1341 7p multi   1.00 .50

Traditional
Foods of
Mexico
and Brazil
A1342

Designs: No. 2784, Pozole. No. 2785, Milho e mandioca.

2012, June 1   Litho.   Perf. 13
2784   13.50p multi   1.90 .95
2785   13.50p multi   1.90 .95
  a.   A1342 Horiz. pair, #2784-2785   3.80 1.90

See Brazil No. 3217.

Mexican Wolves — A1343

2012, June 4   **Perf. 13¼x13**
2786 A1343 11.50p multi   1.75 .85

World Anti-Tobacco Day — A1344

2012, July 5   **Perf. 13¼x13**
2787 A1344 7p multi   1.10 .55

Escuela Libre de Derecho (Law School), Mexico City, Cent. — A1345

2012, July 24   **Litho.**
2788 A1345 7p multi   1.10 .55

Grandparent's Day — A1346

2012, Aug. 13   **Perf. 13**
2789 A1346 7p multi   1.10 .55

Miniature Sheet

Federal Electricity Commission, 75th Anniv. — A1347

No. 2790: a, El Cajón Dam, Nayarit. b, Guaycora Solar Farm, Sonora. c, La Venta Wind Generators, Oaxaca. d, Lineman and electrical lines. e, National Energy Control Center. f, Transmission towers, Colima.

2012, Aug. 14   **Perf. 13**
2790 A1347 Sheet of 6   6.75 3.50
   a.-f.   7p Any single   1.10 .55

Mexican Petroleum Congress A1348

Designs: No. 2791, PEMEX Refinery, Ciudad Madera. No. 2792, PEMEX offshore oil platform.

2012, Sept. 9   **Perf. 13x13¼**
2791   7p multi   1.10 .55
2792   7p multi   1.10 .55
   a.   A1348 Vert. pair, #2791-2792   2.20 1.10

40th Intl. Cervantes Festival, Guanajuato — A1349

2012, Sept. 25   **Perf. 13¼x13**
2793 A1349 13.50p multi   2.10 1.10

National Polytechnic Institute Center for Research and Advanced Studies (CINVESTAV), Saltillo, 50th Anniv. — A1350

2012, Oct. 2
2794 A1350 7p multi   1.10 .55

University of Sonora, 70th Anniv. A1351

No. 2795: a, Rector's Building (denomination at UR). b, Stained-glass window depicting Don Quixote. c, University Library and Museum (denomination at UL).

2012, Oct. 2   **Perf. 13x13¼**
2795   Horiz. strip of 3   3.50 1.75
   a.-c.   A1351 7p Any single   1.10 .55

World Post Day A1352

2012, Oct. 9   **Perf. 13¼x13**
2796 A1352 11.50p multi   1.75 .90

Minaret, Agua Caliente — A1353

2012, Oct. 11
2797 A1353 11.50p multi   1.75 .90

School Counseling, 20th Anniv. A1354

2012, Oct. 15   **Perf. 13x13¼**
2798 A1354 7p multi   1.10 .55

Sacred Art of the Viceroys   A1355

Paintings by unknown artists of crowned nuns: No. 2799, Sister María Engracia Josefa del Santísimo Rosario (holding candlestick with flowers). No. 2800, Sister from Order of the Immaculate Conception (with round breastplate).

2012, Oct. 25
2799   7p multi   1.10 .55
2800   7p multi   1.10 .55
   a.   A1355 Horiz. pair, #2799-2800   2.20 1.10

All Souls' Day (Day of the Dead) A1356

2012, Oct. 29   **Perf. 13¼x13**
2801 A1356 7p multi   1.10 .55

Miniature Sheet

Tulum Archaeological Site — A1357

No. 2802: a, Interior of Temple of the Paintings. b, View of cliffs and the side of the Castillo. c, Front view of the Castillo. d, Temple of the Paintings. e, Building ruins and sculpture

of Itzamná from corner of Temple of the Paintings.

2012, Oct. 31   **Litho.**
2802 A1357   Sheet of 5 + label   8.25 4.25
   a.-b.   7p Either single   1.10 .55
   c.   11.50p multi   1.75 .90
   d.-e.   13.50p Either single   2.10 1.10

Christmas A1358

No. 2803: a, Elves packing toys in boxes. b, People celebrating Christmas. c, Magi on camels.

2012, Nov. 8   **Perf. 13**
2803   Horiz. strip of 3   5.25 2.75
   a.-c.   A1358 11.50p Any single   1.75 .90

Letter Carrier's Day A1359

2012, Nov. 12   **Perf. 13x13¼**
2804 A1359 7p multi   1.10 .55

Lebanese Center, Mexico City, 50th Anniv. — A1360

2012, Nov. 13   **Perf. 13¼x13**
2805 A1360 13.50p multi   2.10 1.10

Public Housing Authority (FOVISSSTE), 40th Anniv. — A1361

2012, Nov. 28   **Perf. 13x13¼**
2806 A1361 7p multi   1.10 .55

University of Guanajuato, 280th Anniv. — A1362

2012, Dec. 3   **Perf. 13¼x13**
2807 A1362 7p multi   1.10 .55

Justo Sierra (1848-1912),
Writer — A1363

2012, Dec. 7 Litho.
2808 A1363 7p multi 1.10 .55

Sacred Mayan Canoe
Crossing — A1364

No. 2809 — Rowers at: a, Rear of canoe. b,
Center of canoe. c, Front of canoe.

2012, Dec. 21 Perf. 13¼x13
2809 Horiz. strip of 3 5.25 2.75
 a. A1364 7.50p multi 1.25 .60
 b. A1364 11.50p multi 1.90 .95
 c. A1364 13.50p multi 2.10 1.10

St.
Valentine's
Day
A1365

2013, Feb. 8 Perf. 13
2810 A1365 7p multi 1.10 .55

President's Day — A1366

2013, Feb. 15 Perf. 13¼x13
2811 A1366 7p multi 1.10 .55

Iberoamericana University, Mexico
City, 70th Anniv. — A1367

No. 2812: a, Statue and building. b, Buildings. c, Covered steps.

2013, Mar. 7 Perf. 13x13¼
2812 A1367 Horiz. strip of 3 3.30 1.65
 a.-c. 7p Any single 1.10 .55

National Association
of Supermarkets and
Department Stores,
30th Anniv. — A1368

2013, Mar. 13 Perf. 13¼x13
2813 A1368 7p multi 1.25 .60

Intl. Mother Language Day — A1369

2013, Mar. 13
2814 A1369 11.50p multi 1.90 .95

Expropriation of Foreign-Owned
Petroleum Rights and Facilities, 75th
Anniv. — A1370

2013, Mar. 17 Litho.
2815 A1370 7p multi 1.25 .60

Guillermo
Haro
Barraza
(1913-88),
Astronomer
A1371

2013, Mar. 21 Perf. 13x13¼
2816 A1371 7p multi 1.25 .60

Promulgation of Plan of Guadalupe,
Cent. — A1372

2013, Mar. 26 Perf. 13¼x13
2817 A1372 7p multi 1.25 .60

Diplomatic Relations Between Mexico
and Indonesia, 60th Anniv. — A1373

Designs: No. 2818, Neofelis diardi borneen-
sis. No. 2819, Panthera onca.

2013, Apr. 6 Perf. 13
2818 15p multi 2.50 1.25
2819 15p multi 2.50 1.25
 a. A1373 Horiz. pair, #2818-2819 5.00 2.50

See Indonesia No. 2345.

Mexican
Army, Cent.
A1374

2013, Apr. 17 Perf. 13x13¼
2820 A1374 7p multi 1.25 .60

Federico Gómez
Children's Hospital,
Mexico City, 70th
Anniv. — A1375

2013, Apr. 30 Litho. Perf. 13¼x13
2821 A1375 7p multi 1.25 .60

Children's Day — A1376

2013, Apr. 30 Litho. Perf. 13¼x13
2822 A1376 7p multi 1.25 .60

Mother's
Day
A1377

2013, May 10 Litho. Perf. 13
2823 A1377 11.50p multi 1.90 .95

Teacher's
Day
A1378

2013, May 15 Litho. Perf. 13¼x13
2824 A1378 7p multi 1.10 .55

Mexican Army, Cent. — A1379

2013, Aug. 13 Litho. Perf. 13¼x13
2825 A1379 7p multi 1.10 .55

Veterinary Education in Mexico, 160th
Anniv. — A1380

2013, Aug. 16 Litho. Perf. 13¼x13
2826 A1380 7p multi 1.10 .55

Manuel Acuña (1849-73),
Writer — A1381

2013, Aug. 27 Litho. Perf. 13¼x13
2827 A1381 7p multi 1.10 .55

Grandparent's Day — A1382

2013, Aug. 28 Litho. Perf. 13
2828 A1382 7p multi 1.10 .55

First Congress of Anáhuac, 200th
Anniv. — A1383

2013, Sept. 5 Litho. Perf. 13¼x13
2829 A1383 7p multi 1.10 .55

Metropolitan Cathedral, Mexico City,
200th Anniv. — A1384

2013, Sept. 11 Litho. Perf. 13x13¼
2830 A1384 7p multi 1.10 .55

Confederation of Industrial Chambers
of Mexico, 95th Anniv. — A1385

2013, Sept. 20   Litho.   *Perf. 13¼x13*
2831 A1385 7p multi   1.10   .55

Miniature Sheet

Autonomous University of Nuevo León,
80th Anniv. — A1386

No. 2832: a, Las Informantes de Sahagún,
by Federico Cantú (head at center top facing
right). b, Las Informantes de Sahagún (head
at center top facing left). c, Espejos Comunicantes, by Guillermo Ceniceros (compass
rose at right). d, Espejos Comunicantes
(heads at right). e, Einstein, by Sebastián Xavier Treviño (head of Albert Einstein). f, Einstein
(faceless figure and geometric shapes).

2013, Sept. 25   Litho.   *Perf. 13*
2832 A1386 Sheet of 6   6.75 3.50
 a.-f.   7p Any single   1.10   .55

World Post
Day — A1387

2013, Oct. 9   Litho.   *Perf. 13¼x13*
2833 A1387 13.50p multi   2.10 1.10

Woman
Suffrage in
Mexico,
60th Anniv.
A1388

2013, Oct. 11   Litho.   *Perf. 13x13¼*
2834 A1388 7p multi   1.10   .55

Secretary
of Health,
70th Anniv.
A1389

2013, Oct. 18   Litho.   *Perf. 13x13¼*
2835 A1389 7p multi   1.10   .55

All Souls' Day (Day of the
Dead) — A1390

2013, Oct. 22   Litho.   *Imperf.*
2836 A1390 15p multi   2.25 1.10

Gran Café de la Parroquia Restaurant,
Veracruz, 205th Anniv.
A1391

2013, Oct. 23   Litho.   *Perf. 13x13¼*
2837 A1391 7p multi   1.10   .55

Bilateral Relations Between Mexico
and South Africa, 20th Anniv.
A1392

2013, Oct. 24   Litho.   *Perf. 13x13¼*
2838 A1392 15p multi   2.25 1.10

National Institute for Rural
Development, 40th Anniv. — A1393

2013, Nov. 5   Litho.   *Perf. 13x13¼*
2839 A1393 7p multi   1.10   .55

Federal
Conciliation
and
Arbitration
Tribunal,
50th Anniv.
A1394

2013, Nov. 8   Litho.   *Perf. 13x13¼*
2840 A1394 7p multi   1.10   .55

Letter
Carrier's
Day
A1395

2013, Nov. 12   Litho.   *Perf. 13x13¼*
2841 A1395 7p multi   1.10   .55

Casino
Español
Restaurant,
Mexico City,
150th
Anniv.
A1396

2013, Nov. 14   Litho.   *Perf. 13x13¼*
2842 A1396 13.50p multi   2.10 1.10

Mexican Army, Cent. — A1397

2013, Nov. 15   Litho.   *Perf. 13¼x13*
2843 A1397 7p multi   1.10   .55

Interior of
Postal
Palace
(Main Post
Office),
Mexico City
A1398

2013, Nov. 19   Litho.   *Perf. 13x13¼*
2844 A1398 7p multi   1.10   .55

San Matías Jalatlaco Temple, Former
Convent of San Pablo, Historical
Center of Oaxaca UNESCO World
Heritage Site — A1399

2013, Nov. 21   Litho.   *Perf. 13¼x13*
2845 A1399 15p multi   2.40 1.25
 a.   Tete-beche pair   4.80 2.50

Migrant's
Protection
Program
A1400

2013, Nov. 27   Litho.   *Perf. 13x13¼*
2846 A1400 7p multi   1.10   .55

Christmas — A1401

Poinsettia and: No. 2847, Magi. No. 2848,
Santa Claus. 11.50p, Christmas tree. 13.50p,
Holy Family.

2013, Nov. 28   Litho.   *Perf. 13*
2847 A1401   7p multi   1.10   .55
2848 A1401   7p multi   1.10   .55
2849 A1401   11.50p multi   1.75   .80
 a.   Pair, #2847, 2849   3.00 1.40
2850 A1401   13.50p multi   2.10 1.10
 a.   Pair, #2848, 2850   3.25 1.75
       Nos. 2847-2850 (4)   6.05 3.00

Morelos State
Autonomous
University, 60th
Anniv. — A1402

2013, Dec. 6   Litho.   *Perf. 13¼x13*
2851 A1402 7p multi   1.10   .55

National
Education
Worker's
Union, 70th
Anniv.
A1403

2013, Dec. 7   Litho.   *Perf. 13x13¼*
2852 A1403 7p multi   1.10   .55

Mexican
Institute of
Industrial
Property,
20th Anniv.
A1404

2013, Dec. 12   Litho.   *Perf. 13x13¼*
2853 A1404 7p multi   1.10   .55

National Commission for Sports and
Physical Culture, 25th Anniv. — A1405

2013, Dec. 13   Litho.   *Perf. 13¾x13*
2854 A1405 7p multi   1.10   .55

Paintings by Francisco Eppens (1913-90), Stamp Designer A1406

No. 2855: a, La Danza de la Media Luna, 1984. b, Alcatraces, 1988. c, Cactáceas, 1988. d, Guerrero Aguila y Guerrero Tiger, 1980. e, Caballos de Colores, 1985.

2013, Dec. 13 Litho. *Perf. 13x13¼*
2855   Horiz. strip of 5   8.50 4.50
a.-b. A1406 7p Either single   1.10 .55
c.   A1406 11.50p multi   1.75 .90
d.   A1406 13.50p multi   2.10 1.10
e.   A1406 15p multi   2.40 1.25

Promotion of philately.

Industrial Labor Training Centers, 50th Anniv. A1407

2013, Dec. 17 Litho. *Perf. 13x13¼*
2856 A1407 7p multi   1.10 .55

Federal Police, 85th Anniv. A1408

2013, Dec. 19 Litho. *Perf. 13x13¼*
2857 A1408 7p multi   1.10 .55

Pipe Organs — A1409

No. 2858 — Organs in Oaxaca: a, Santa Maria Tiltepec Temple. b, San Jerónimo Tlacochahuaya Church. c, San Andrés Zautla Church. d, Santa María de la Natividad Tamazulapan. e, Santo Domingo Yanhuitlán Church. f, Oaxaca Cathedral.

2013, Dec. 20 Litho. *Perf. 13¼x13*
2858   Horiz. strip of 6   10.00 5.00
a.-b. A1409 7p Either single   1.10 .55
c.-d. A1409 11.50p Either single   1.75 .85
e.-f. A1409 13.50p Either single   2.10 1.10

National Water Commission, 25th Anniv. — A1410

No. 2859: a, Weir at Los Mochis, Abelardo Rodríguez Dam, Rosales Canal. b, San Pedro

Piedra Gorda Dam, San José I Dam. c, Francisco I. Madero Dam, "El Manantial," sculpture by José Sacal. d, Los Berros Water Purification Plant, La Principal Water Treatment Plant. e, Water tunnel, Atotonilco Water Treatment Plant.

2014, Jan. 16 Litho. *Perf. 13x13¼*
2859   Horiz. strip of 5   5.50 2.75
a.-e. A1410 7p Any single   1.10 .55

St. Valentine's Day A1411

2014, Jan. 31 Litho. *Perf. 13*
2860 A1411 7p multi   1.10 .55

National Chamber of the Mexican Publishing Industry, 50th Anniv. — A1412

2014, Feb. 28 Litho. *Perf. 13¼x13*
2861 A1412 7p multi   1.10 .55

Octavio Paz (1914-98), 1990 Nobel Laureate in Literature A1413

2014, Mar. 20 Litho. *Perf. 13x13¼*
2862 A1413 7p multi   1.10 .55

National Fund for Tourism Development, 40th Anniv. — A1414

2014, Apr. 1 Litho. *Perf. 13¼x13*
2863 A1414 7p multi   1.10 .55

Second Battle of Torreón, Cent. — A1415

2014, Apr. 3 Litho. *Perf. 13¼x13*
2864 A1415 7p multi   1.10 .55

Mexican Pres. Adolfo López Mateos and French Pres. Charles de Gaulle A1416

2014, Apr. 11 Litho. *Perf. 13x13¼*
2865 A1416 13.50p multi   2.10 1.10

Visit of Pres. de Gaulle to Mexico, 50th anniv.

Miniature Sheet

American Occupation of Veracruz, Cent. — A1417

No. 2866: a, Veracruz citizens face the intervention. b, Naval Academy cadets. c, General Rubio Navarrete prepares to contain the American advance. d, Venustiano Carranza makes his triumphal entry into Mexico City. e, Cadet José Virgilio Uribe Robles, Lieutenant Luis Felipe José Azueta Abad. f, Naval Academy parade after the intervention.

2014, Apr. 21 Litho. *Perf. 13*
2866 A1417   Sheet of 6   6.75 3.50
a.-f.   7p Any single   1.10 .55

City of General Escobedo, 410th Anniv. A1418

2014, Apr. 25 Litho. *Perf. 13x13¼*
2867 A1418 7p multi   1.10 .55

Intl. Day of Intellectual Property A1419

2014, Apr. 28 Litho. *Perf. 13x13¼*
2868 A1419 15p multi   2.40 1.25

Children's Day A1420

2014, Apr. 30 Litho. *Perf. 13*
2869 A1420 7p multi   1.10 .55

City of Misantla, 450th Anniv. — A1421

2014, May 3 Litho. *Perf. 13¼x13*
2870 A1421 7p multi   1.10 .55

Mother's Day A1422

2014, May 9 Litho. *Perf. 13*
2871 A1422 11.50p multi   1.75 .90

National Fund for Workers Consumption (FONACOT), 40th Anniv. — A1423

2014, May 14 Litho. *Perf. 13¼x13*
2872 A1423 7p multi   1.10 .55

Autonomous University of the State of Mexico, 70th Anniv. — A1424

2014, May 14 Litho. *Perf. 13x13¼*
2873 A1424 7p multi   1.10 .55

Laura Mendez de Cuenca (1853-1928), Teacher and Writer — A1425

2014, May 15 Litho. *Perf. 13¼x13*
2874 A1425 7p multi   1.10 .55

Teacher's Day.

Mexican National Soccer Team — A1426

2014, May 27 Litho. *Perf. 13¼x13*
2875 A1426 7p multi   1.10 .55

Diplomatic Relations Between Mexico and Portugal, 150th Anniv. — A1427

Mexican and Portuguese flags with denomination color of: No. 2876, White. No. 2877, Black.

2014, June 6   Litho.   Perf. 13
2876   13.50p multi   2.10 1.10
2877   13.50p multi   2.10 1.10
  a.   A1427 Horiz. pair, #2876-2877   4.20 2.20

See Portugal Nos. 3605-3606.

Signing of the Treaties of Teoloyucan, Cent. A1428

2014, Aug. 13   Litho.   Perf. 13x13¼
2878   A1428 7p multi   1.10 .55

National Association of Engineering Schools, 50th Anniv. — A1429

2014, Aug. 22   Litho.   Perf. 13¼x13
2879   A1429 7p multi   1.10 .55

Firefighter's Day — A1430

2014, Aug. 22   Litho.   Perf. 13¼x13
2880   A1430 7p multi   1.10 .55

Technological Institute of Ciudad Juárez, 50th Anniv. — A1431

2014, Sept. 4   Litho.   Perf. 13x13¼
2881   A1431 7p multi   1.10 .55

Greetings — A1432

No. 2882: a, Graduates and diploma. b, Doves and stained-glass window. c, Flowers. d, Clown candle. e, Cupcakes.

2014, Sept. 5   Litho.   Perf. 13¼x13
2882   Horiz. strip of 5   7.00 3.50
  a.-c.   A1432 7p Any single   1.10 .55
  d.-e.   A1432 11.50p Either single 1.75 .85

National Bank of Mexico, 130th Anniv. A1433

2014, Sept. 9   Litho.   Perf. 13
2883   A1433 11.50p multi   1.75 .85

Veracruz University, 70th Anniv. — A1434

2014, Sept. 10   Litho.   Perf. 13¼x13
2884   A1434 7.50p multi   1.10 .55

Postal Palace (Main Post Office), Mexico City A1435

2014, Sept. 11   Litho.   Perf. 13¼x13
2885   A1435 7p multi   1.10 .55

La Jornada Newspaper, 30th Anniv. — A1436

2014, Sept. 18   Litho.   Perf. 13¼x13
2886   A1436 7p multi   1.10 .55

Palace of Fine Arts, 80th Anniv. A1437

2014, Sept. 29   Litho.   Perf. 13¼x13
2887   A1437 7p multi   1.10 .55

Resolution of Chamizal Border Dispute With United States, 50th Anniv. A1438

2014, Sept. 30   Litho.   Perf. 13x13¼
2888   A1438 11.50p multi   1.75 .85

Creation of State of Quintana Roo, 40th Anniv. A1439

2014, Oct. 1   Litho.   Perf. 13x13¼
2889   A1439 7p multi   1.10 .55

Autonomous Metropolitan University, 40th Anniv. — A1440

2014, Oct. 8   Litho.   Perf. 13¼x13
2890   A1440 7p multi   1.10 .55

World Post Day A1441

2014, Oct. 9   Litho.   Perf. 13¼x13
2891   A1441 13.50p multi   2.00 1.00

2014 Latin American Integration Association Expo, Montevideo, Uruguay A1442

2014, Oct. 10   Litho.   Perf. 13¼x13
2892   A1442 13.50p multi   2.00 1.00

Battle of Zacatecas, Cent. — A1443

2014, Oct. 14   Litho.   Perf. 13¼x13
2893   A1443 7p multi   1.10 .55

Institute of Epidemiological Diagnosis and Reference, 75th Anniv. — A1444

2014, Oct. 17   Litho.   Perf. 13x13¼
2894   A1444 7p multi   1.10 .55

Dated 2012.

Air Traffic Controller's Day — A1445

2014, Oct. 20   Litho.   Perf. 13¼x13
2895   A1445 7p multi   1.10 .55

Constitution of Apatzingán, 200th Anniv. — A1446

2014, Oct. 22   Litho.   Perf. 13¼x13
2896   A1446 7p multi   1.10 .55

Philips Mexico, 75th Anniv. A1447

2014, Oct. 22   Litho.   Perf. 13¼x13
2897   A1447 13.50p multi   2.00 1.00

Miniature Sheet

Paquimé Archaeological Site — A1448

No. 2898: a, Pottery, denomination at LR. b, Pottery, denomination at LL. c, Casa de los Cráneos. d, Casa de las Guacamayas, denomination at UR. e, Casa de las Guacamayas, denomination at UL.

2014, Oct. 25   Litho.   Perf. 13¼x13
2898   A1448   Sheet of 5 + label 8.00 4.00
  a.-b.   7p Either single   1.10 .55
  c.   11.50p multi   1.75 .85
  d.-e.   13.50p Either single   2.00 1.00

All Souls' Day (Day of the Dead) A1449

2014, Oct. 29   Litho.   Perf. 13¼x13
2899   A1449 11.50p multi   1.75 .85

First Performance of Mexican National
Anthem, 160th Anniv. — A1450

2014, Oct. 30   **Litho.**   ***Perf. 13x13¼***
2900   A1450   13.50p multi   2.00   1.00

Inventor's Day — A1451

2014, Nov. 4   **Litho.**   ***Perf. 13¼x13***
2901   A1451   7p multi   1.10   .55

Souvenir Sheet

Alberto Córdova Stadium, Autonomous
University of Mexico State, 50th
Anniv. — A1452

No. 2902: a, Aerial view of area, stadium in
inset. b, Hill overlooking decorated stadium
seats. c, Aerial view of stadium and other
buildings.

2014, Nov. 5   **Litho.**   ***Perf. 13x13¼***
2902   A1452   Sheet of 3   3.30   1.75
a.-c.   7p Any single   1.10   .55

Letter Carrier's Day — A1453

2014, Nov. 10   **Litho.**   ***Perf. 13¼x13***
2903   A1453   7p multi   1.00   .50

Crabs — A1454

Designs: 13.50p, Isostichopus fuscus. 15p,
Danielum ixbauchac.

2014, Nov. 18   **Litho.**   ***Perf. 13¼x13***
2904   13.50p multi   1.90   .95
2905   15p multi   2.10   1.10
a.   A1454 Horiz. pair, #2904-2905   4.00   2.10

Ciudad Madero Technological Institute,
60th Anniv. — A1455

2014, Nov. 19   **Litho.**   ***Perf. 13¼x13***
2906   A1455   7p multi   1.00   .50

Intl. Year of
Crystallography
A1456

2014, Nov. 19   **Litho.**   ***Perf. 13¼x13***
2907   A1456   13.50p multi   1.90   .95

Ministry of Health, 85th
Anniv. — A1457

2014, Nov. 20   **Litho.**   ***Perf. 13¼x13***
2908   A1457   7p multi   1.00   .50

World Food
Day
A1458

Designs: 7p, Shrimp boat, hand holding
shrimp. 13.50p, Hand holding tilapia.

2014, Nov. 24   **Litho.**   ***Perf. 13¼x13***
2909   7p multi   1.00   .50
2910   13.50p multi   1.90   .95
a.   A1458 Vert. pair, #2909-2910   3.00   1.50

Anáhuac
University,
50th Anniv.
A1459

No. 2911: a, Building and plaza. b, Commemorative pillar, building.-c, Fountain.

2014, Nov. 26   **Litho.**   ***Perf. 13¼x13***
2911   Horiz. strip of 3   3.00   1.50
a.-c.   A1459 7p Any single   1.00   .50

Autonomous University of Chihuahua,
60th Anniv. — A1460

2014, Dec. 3   **Litho.**   ***Perf. 13¼x13***
2912   A1460   11.50p multi   1.60   .80

Christmas — A1461

Designs: No. 2913, Magi. No. 2914, Santa
Claus. 11.50p, Christmas tree. 13.50p, Holy
Family, shepherd and lambs.

2014, Dec. 5   **Litho.**   ***Perf. 13***
2913   A1461   7p multi   .95   .45
2914   A1461   7p multi   .95   .45
2915   A1461   11.50p multi   1.60   .80
a.   Pair, #2913, 2915   2.60   1.25
2916   A1461   13.50p multi   1.90   .95
a.   Pair, #2914, 2916   3.00   1.40
     Nos. 2913-2916 (4)   5.40   2.65

General Eulalio Gutiérrez (1881-1939),
Provisional President — A1462

2014, Dec. 8   **Litho.**   ***Perf. 13x13¼***
2917   A1462   7p multi   .95   .45
Sovereign Revolutionary Convention, cent.

Latin American
Parliament, 50th
Anniv. — A1463

2014, Dec. 9   **Litho.**   ***Perf. 13¼x13***
2918   A1463   13.50p multi   1.90   .95

Fernando Hiriart Balderrama (1914-
2005), Secretary of Energy, Mines and
State Industry — A1464

2014, Dec. 10   **Litho.**   ***Perf. 13x13¼***
2919   A1464   7p multi   .95   .45

Taking
of San
Pedro,
Cent.
A1465

2014, Dec. 11   **Litho.**   ***Perf. 13¼x13***
2920   A1465   7p multi   .95   .45

National College of Professsional
Technical Education, 35th
Anniv. — A1466

2014, Dec. 11   **Litho.**   ***Perf. 13¼x13***
2921   A1466   7p multi   .95   .45

North American Free Trade
Agreement, 20th Anniv. — A1467

2014, Dec. 18   **Litho.**   ***Perf. 13¼x13***
2922   A1467   11.50p multi   1.60   .80

Diplomatic Relations Between Mexico
and Iran, 50th Anniv. — A1468

2014, Dec. 18   **Litho.**   ***Perf. 13¼x13***
2923   A1468   15p multi   2.10   1.10

Philately and Postal Culture — A1469

2014, Dec. 19   Litho.   Perf. 13¼x13
2924   A1469 7p multi   .95   .45

SEMI-POSTAL STAMPS

Nos. 622, 614
Surcharged in Red

1918, Dec. 25   Unwmk.   Perf. 12
B1   A72 5c + 3c ultra   20.00 25.00

Rouletted 14½
B2   A73 10c + 5c blue   25.00 25.00
Set, never hinged   57.50

AIR POST STAMPS

Eagle
AP1

Unwmk.
1922, Apr. 2   Engr.   Perf. 12
C1   AP1 50c blue & red brn   67.50 50.00
   Never hinged   160.00
 a. 50c dark blue & claret ('29) 90.00 90.00
   Never hinged   200.00

See Nos. C2-C3. For overprints and surcharges see Nos. C47-C48, CO1-CO2B, CO18-CO19, CO29.

1927, Oct. 13   Wmk. 156
C2   AP1 50c dk bl & red brn   .75   .25
   Never hinged   2.50
 a. 50c dark blue & claret ('29)   .75   .25
   Never hinged   3.00
 b. Vert. strip of 3, imperf. btwn. 7,500.

The vignettes of Nos. C1a and C2a fluoresce a bright rose red under UV light.

1928
C3   AP1 25c brn car & gray brn   .45   .25
C4   AP1 25c dk grn & gray brn   .45   .25
Set, never hinged   2.50

On May 3, 1929, certain proofs or essays were sold at the post office in Mexico, D. F. They were printed in different colors from those of the regularly issued stamps. There were 7 varieties perf. and 2 imperf. and a total of 225 copies. They were sold with the understanding that they were for collections but the majority of them were used on air mail sent out that day.

Capt. Emilio Carranza and his
Airplane "México Excelsior"
AP2

1929, June 19
C5   AP2 5c ol grn & sepia   1.10   .65
C6   AP2 10c sep & brn red   1.25   .70
C7   AP2 15c vio & dk grn   3.00 1.25
C8   AP2 20c brown & blk   1.25   .75

C9   AP2 50c brn red & blk   7.50 5.00
C10 AP2 1p black & brn   15.00 10.00
   Nos. C5-C10 (6)   29.10 18.35
Set, never hinged   75.00

1st anniv. of death of Carranza (1905-28). For overprints see Nos. C29-C36, C40-C44.

Coat of
Arms and
Airplane
AP3

1929-34   Perf. 11½, 12
C11 AP3 10c violet   .35   .25
C12 AP3 15c carmine   1.35   .25
C13 AP3 20c brown olive   37.50 1.25
C14 AP3 30c gray black   .25   .25
C15 AP3 35c blue green   .35   .25
 a. Imperf., pair   1,200.
C16 AP3 50c red brn ('34)   1.25   .65
C17 AP3 1p blk & dk bl   1.25   .65
C18 AP3 5p claret & dp bl   4.00 3.50
C19 AP3 10p vio & ol brn   6.00 7.00
   Nos. C11-C19 (9)   52.30 14.05
Set, never hinged   130.00

1930-32   Rouletted 13, 13½
C20 AP3 5c lt blue ('32)   .35   .25
C21 AP3 10c violet   .35   .25
C22 AP3 15c carmine   .35   .25
 a. 15c rose carmine   .40   .25
C23 AP3 20c brown olive   1.50   .25
 a. 20c brown   .50   .25
 b. 20c yellow brown   .50   .25
 c. Horiz. pair, imperf. btwn.
C24 AP3 25c violet   .95   .80
C25 AP3 50c red brown   .90   .75
   Nos. C20-C25 (6)   4.40 2.55
Set, never hinged   13.00

Trial impressions of No. C20 were printed in orange but were never sold at post offices.
See Nos. C62-C64, C75. For overprints and surcharges see Nos. C28, C38-C39, C46, C49-C50, CO17, CO20-CO28, CO30.

Plane over
Plaza,
Mexico
City — AP4

1929, Dec. 10   Wmk. 156   Perf. 12
C26 AP4 20c black violet   1.25 1.00
C27 AP4 40c slate green   85.00 75.00
Set, never hinged   210.00

Aviation Week, Dec. 10-16.
For overprint see No. CO11.

No. C21 Overprinted in Red

1930, Apr. 20   Rouletted 13, 13½
C28 AP3 10c violet   2.00 1.25
   Never hinged   5.50

National Tourism Congress at Mexico, D. F., Apr. 20-27, 1930.

Nos. C5 and C7 Overprinted

1930, Sept. 1   Perf. 12
C29 AP2 5c ol grn & sepia   5.50 4.50
 a. Double overprint   225.00 250.00
C30 AP2 15c violet & dk grn   9.00 7.75
Set, never hinged   45.00

Nos. C5-C10 Overprinted

1930, Dec. 18
C31 AP2 5c ol grn & sepia   7.00 6.50
C32 AP2 10c sep & brn red   3.50 4.00
 a. Double overprint   60.00 60.00
C33 AP2 15c vio & dk grn   7.50 7.00
C34 AP2 20c brown & blk   7.00 5.50
C35 AP2 50c brn red & blk   14.00 10.00
C36 AP2 1p black & brn   4.00 2.75
   Nos. C31-C36 (6)   43.00 35.75
Set, never hinged   130.00

Plane
over
Flying
Field
AP5

1931, May 15   Engr.   Perf. 12
C37 AP5 25c lake   4.00 4.50
   Never hinged   11.00
 a. Imperf., pair   80.00 72.50
   Never hinged   175.00

Aeronautic Exhibition of the Aero Club of Mexico. Of the 25c, 15c paid air mail postage and 10c went to a fund to improve the Mexico City airport.
For surcharge see No. C45.

Nos. C13 and C23 Srchd. in Red

1931
C38 AP3 15c on 20c brn ol   32.50 35.00
   Never hinged   80.00

Rouletted 13, 13½
C39 AP3 15c on 20c brn ol   .30   .25
   Never hinged   1.00
 a. Inverted surcharge   150.00 200.00
 b. Double surcharge   150.00 200.00
 c. Pair, one without
   surcharge   350.00

Nos. C5 to
C9
Overprinted

1932, July 13   Perf. 12
C40 AP2 5c ol grn & sep   6.00 5.00
 a. Imperf., pair   60.00 60.00
C41 AP2 10c sep & brn red   5.00 3.00
 a. Imperf., pair   60.00 60.00
C42 AP2 15c vio & bk grn   6.00 4.00
 a. Imperf., pair   60.00 60.00
C43 AP2 20c brn & blk   5.00 2.75
 a. Imperf., pair   60.00 60.00
C44 AP2 50c brn red & blk   35.00 35.00
 a. Imperf., pair   60.00 60.00
   Nos. C40-C44 (5)   57.00 49.75
Set, never hinged   170.00
Set, C40a-C44a never
hinged   650.00

Death of Capt. Emilio Carranza, 4th anniv.

No. C37 Surcharged

1932
C45 AP5 20c on 25c lake   .70   .30
   Never hinged   2.50
 a. Imperf., pair   72.50 72.50
   Never hinged   150.00

No. C13 Surcharged

C46 AP3 30c on 20c brn ol   30.00 30.00
   Never hinged   75.00

Similar Surcharge on Nos. C3 and C4

C47 AP1 40c on 25c (#C3)   .90   .90
   Never hinged   3.00
 a. Inverted surcharge   11,000.
C48 AP1 40c on 25c (#C4)   50.00 50.00
   Never hinged   125.00

Surcharged on Nos. C23 and C24
Rouletted 13, 13½
C49 AP3 30c on 20c brn ol   .35   .25
   Never hinged   1.00
 a. Inverted surcharge   2,750.
C50 AP3 80c on 25c dl vio   1.75 1.25
   Never hinged   5.00
   Nos. C45-C50 (6)   83.70 82.70

Palace of
Fine Arts
AP6

1933, Oct. 1   Engr.   Perf. 12
C51 AP6 20c dk red & dl vio   3.50 1.40
C52 AP6 30c dk brn & dl vio   7.00 6.00
C53 AP6 1p grnsh blk & dl
   vio   72.50 70.00
   Nos. C51-C53 (3)   83.00 77.40
Set, never hinged   190.00

21st Intl. Cong. of Statistics and the cent. of the Mexican Soc. of Geography and Statistics.

National University Issue

Nevado de
Toluca
AP7

Pyramids
of the Sun
and Moon
AP8

View of
Ajusco
AP9

Volcanoes Popocatepetl and
Iztaccíhuatl — AP10

Bridge over
Tepecayo
AP11

Chapultepec Fortress — AP12

Orizaba Volcano (Citlaltépetl) AP13

Mexican Girl and Aztec Calendar Stone AP14

1934, Sept. 1   Wmk. 156   Perf. 10½

C54	AP7	20c orange	15.00	10.00
C55	AP8	30c red lilac & vio	20.00	20.00
C56	AP9	50c ol grn & bis brn	20.00	25.00
C57	AP10	75c blk & yel grn	25.00	25.00
C58	AP11	1p blk & pck bl	30.00	30.00
C59	AP12	5p bis brn & dk bl	225.00	250.00
C60	AP13	10p indigo & mar	550.00	525.00
C61	AP14	20p brn & brn lake	1,800.	1,800.

Nos. C54-C61 (8)   2,685.   2,685.
Set, never hinged   4,750.

Type of 1929-34

1934-35   Perf. 10½, 10½x10

C62	AP3	20c olive green	.35	.25
a.		20c slate	500.00	500.00
		Never hinged	600.00	
C63	AP3	30c slate	.40	.40
C64	AP3	50c red brn ('35)	2.00	2.00

Nos. C62-C64 (3)   2.75   2.65
Set, never hinged   7.00

Symbols of Air Service AP15

Tláloc, God of Water (Quetzalcóatl Temple) — AP16

Orizaba Volcano (Citlaltépetl) AP17

"Eagle Man" AP18

Symbolical of Flight AP19

Aztec Bird-Man — AP20

Allegory of Flight and Pyramid of the Sun AP21

"Eagle Man" and Airplanes AP22

Natives Looking at Airplane and Orizaba Volcano — AP23

Imprint: "Oficina Impresora de Hacienda-Mexico"
Perf. 10½x10, 10x10½

1934-35   Wmk. 156

C65	AP15	5c black	.45	.25
a.		Imperf., pair		
C66	AP16	10c red brown	.90	.25
C67	AP17	15c gray green	1.25	.25
a.		Imperf., pair	400.00	
C68	AP18	20c brown car	3.00	.25
a.		20c lake	4.00	.25
b.		Imperf., pair		
C69	AP19	30c brown olive	.70	.25
C70	AP20	40c blue ('35)	1.25	.25
C71	AP21	50c green	2.50	.25
a.		Imperf., pair	275.00	
C72	AP22	1p gray grn & red brn	3.50	.25
C73	AP23	5p dk car & blk	7.25	.70

Nos. C65-C73 (9)   20.80   2.70
Set, never hinged   45.00

See Nos. C76A, C80, C81, C132-C140, C170-C177A. For overprint see No. C74.

No. C68 Overprinted in Violet

1935, Apr. 16

C74	AP18	20c lake	3,250.	4,000.
		Never hinged	6,000.	

Amelia Earhart's goodwill flight to Mexico. No. C74 with "Muestra" to left of "Mexico" was not issued for postage.

Arms-Plane Type of 1929-34

1935   Wmk. 248   Perf. 10½x10

C75	AP3	30c slate	3.00	5.00
		Never hinged	5.00	

Francisco I. Madero AP24

1935, Nov. 20   Wmk. 156

C76	AP24	20c scarlet	.30	.25
		Never hinged	.75	

Plan of San Luis, 25th anniv. See No. C76B.

Eagle Man Type of 1934-35

1936   Wmk. 260

C76A	AP18	20c lake	4,500.	60.00
		Never hinged	7,500.	

Madero Type of 1935

C76B	AP24	20c scarlet	12,500.

Tasquillo Bridge AP25

Corona River Bridge AP26

Bridge on Nuevo Laredo Highway AP27

Wmk. 248

1936, July 1   Photo.   Perf. 14

C77	AP25	10c slate bl & lt bl	.35	.25
C78	AP26	20c dl vio & org	.35	.25
C79	AP27	40c dk bl & dk grn	.55	.50

Nos. C77-C79 (3)   1.25   .90
Set, never hinged   2.75

Opening of Nuevo Laredo Highway.

Eagle Man Type of 1934-35
Perf. 10½x10

1936, June 18   Engr.   Unwmk.

C80	AP18	20c brown carmine	10.00	7.00
		Never hinged	25.00	

Imprint: "Talleres de Imp. de Est. y Valores-Mexico"

1937   Wmk. 156   Photo.   Perf. 14

C81	AP18	20c rose red	1.25	.25
		Never hinged	2.50	
a.		20c brown carmine	1.50	.25
		Never hinged	3.00	
b.		20c dark carmine	2.00	.25
		Never hinged	4.50	
c.		Imperf., pair	37.50	50.00
		Never hinged	75.00	

There are two sizes of watermark 156. No. C81c was not regularly issued.

Cavalryman AP28

Early Biplane over Mountains AP29

Venustiano Carranza on Horseback AP30

1938, Mar. 26

C82	AP28	20c org red & bl	.50	.25
C83	AP29	40c bl & org red	.75	1.00
C84	AP30	1p bl & bis brn	4.75	2.25

Nos. C82-C84 (3)   6.00   3.45
Set, never hinged   18.00

Plan of Guadalupe, 25th anniversary.

Reconstructed edifices of Chichén Itzá — AP31

Designs: Nos. C85, C86, The Zócalo and Cathedral, Mexico City. Nos. C89, C90, View of Acapulco.

1938, July 1

C85	AP31	20c carmine rose	.35	.25
C86	AP31	20c purple	20.00	10.00
C87	AP31	40c brt green	10.00	5.00
C88	AP31	40c dark green	10.00	5.00
C89	AP31	1p light blue	10.00	5.00
C90	AP31	1p slate blue	10.00	5.00

Nos. C85-C90 (6)   60.35   30.25
Set, never hinged   130.00

16th Intl. Cong. of Planning & Housing.

Statue of José María Morelos — AP34

1939   Engr.   Perf. 10½

C91	AP34	20c green	.70	.50
		Never hinged	1.00	
C92	AP34	40c red violet	2.00	1.25
		Never hinged	5.00	
C93	AP34	1p vio brn & car	1.40	1.00
		Never hinged	1.75	

Nos. C91-C93 (3)   4.10   2.75
Set, never hinged   9.50

New York World's Fair. Released in New York May 2, in Mexico May 24.

Type of 1939 Overprinted in Cerise

1939, May 23

C93A	AP34	20c blue & red	425.00	425.00
		Never hinged	800.00	

Issued for the flight of Francisco Sarabia from Mexico City to New York on May 25.

Statue of Pioneer Woman, Ponca City, OK — AP35

1939, May 17

C94	AP35	20c gray brown	1.00	.40
		Never hinged	2.00	
C95	AP35	40c slate green	2.50	1.25
		Never hinged	7.00	
C96	AP35	1p violet	1.60	.90
		Never hinged	3.00	

Nos. C94-C96 (3)   5.10   2.55
Set, never hinged   12.00

Tulsa World Philatelic Convention.

First Engraving Made in Mexico, 1544 — AP36

First Work of Legislation Printed in America, 1563 — AP37

Designs: 1p, Reproduction of oldest preserved Mexican printing.

1939, Sept. 7   **Wmk. 156**
C97	AP36	20c slate blue	.25 .25
a.		Unwmkd.	50.00 25.00
C98	AP37	40c slate green	.65 .25
a.		Imperf., pair	700.00
C99	AP37	1p dk brn & car	1.10 .70
		Nos. C97-C99 (3)	2.00 1.10
		Set, never hinged	8.00

400th anniversary of printing in Mexico.

Alternated Perforations
Nos. 763-766, 774-779, 792-795, 801-804, 806-811, 813-818, C100-C102, C111-C116, C123-C128, C143-C162, C430-C431 have alternating small and large perforations.

Transportation — AP39

Designs: 40c, Finger counting and factory. 1p, "Seven Censuses."

Perf. 12x13, 13x12

1939, Oct. 2   **Photo.**
C100	AP39	20c dk bl & bl	1.00 .25
C101	AP39	40c red org & org	.75 .25
C102	AP39	1p ind & vio bl	2.75 .75
		Nos. C100-C102 (3)	4.50 1.20
		Set, never hinged	10.00

National Census of 1939-40.

Penny Black Type of Regular Issue, 1940

1940, May   **Perf. 14**
C103	A140	5c blk & dk grn	.65 .55
C104	A140	10c bis brn & dp bl	.55 .25
C105	A140	20c car & bl vio	.40 .26
C106	A140	1p car & choc	6.00 1.00
C107	A140	5p gray grn & red brn	75.00 55.00
		Nos. C103-C107 (5)	82.60 61.00
		Set, never hinged	200.00

Issue dates: 5c-1p, May 2; 5p, May 15.

Part of Original College at Pátzcuaro AP43

College at Morelia (18th Century) — AP44

College at Morelia (1940) AP45

1940, July 15   **Engr.**   **Perf. 10½**
C108	AP43	20c brt green	.45 .25
C109	AP44	40c orange	.50 .30
C110	AP45	1p dp pur, red brn & org	1.25 1.00
		Nos. C108-C110 (3)	2.20 1.50
		Set, never hinged	5.00

400th anniv. of the founding of the National College of San Nicolas de Hidalgo.

Pirate Ship AP46

Designs: 40c, Castle of San Miguel. 1p, Temple of San Francisco.

Perf. 12x13, 13x12

1940, Aug. 7   **Photo.**
C111	AP46	20c red brn & bis brn	1.10 .70
C112	AP46	40c blk & sl grn	1.50 .75
C113	AP46	1p vio bl & blk	5.00 4.00
		Nos. C111-C113 (3)	7.60 5.45
		Set, never hinged	20.00

400th anniversary of Campeche.

Inauguration Type of Regular Issue, 1940

1940, Dec. 1   **Perf. 12x13**
C114	A146	20c gray blk & red org	1.90 1.00
C115	A146	40c chnt brn & dk sl	2.00 1.50
C116	A146	1p brt vio bl & rose	3.50 2.00
		Nos. C114-C116 (3)	7.40 4.50
		Set, never hinged	20.00

Tower of the Convent of the Nuns AP50

Casa de Montejo — AP51

1p, Campanile of Cathedral at Mérida.

1942, Jan. 2   **Perf. 14**
C117	AP50	20c Prus blue	1.50 .75
C118	AP51	40c grnsh blk (C)	2.25 2.00
a.		Without overprint	7.50 7.50
C119	AP50	1p carmine	2.50 2.00
		Nos. C117-C119 (3)	6.25 4.75

400th anniversary of Mérida. No. C118 bears the overprint "Servicio Aereo" in carmine.

Church of Zapopan AP53

Our Lady of Guadalupe Church AP54

Guadalajara Arms — AP55

1942, Feb. 11   **Engr.**   **Perf. 10½x10**
C120	AP53	20c green & blk	1.60 .75
C121	AP54	40c ol & yel grn	1.75 1.00
C122	AP55	1p purple & sepia	1.65 1.25
		Nos. C120-C122 (3)	5.00 3.00

400th anniversary of Guadalajara.

Astrophysics Type of Regular Issue

Designs: 20c, Spiral Galaxy NGC 4594. 40c, Planetary Nebula in Lyra. 1p, Russell Diagrams.

1942, Feb. 17   **Photo.**   **Perf. 12x13**
C123	A154	20c dk grn & ind	20.00 3.00
C124	A154	40c car lake & ind	15.00 4.00
C125	A154	1p orange & blk	25.00 4.50
		Nos. C123-C125 (3)	60.00 11.50

Corn AP59

1942, July 1
C126	AP59	20c shown	1.90 .70
C127	AP59	40c Coffee	1.50 .75
C128	AP59	1p Bananas	2.50 2.00
		Nos. C126-C128 (3)	5.90 3.45

2nd Inter-American Agricultural Conf.

View of San Miguel de Allende AP62

Designs: 40c, Birthplace of Allende. 1p, Church of Our Lady of Health.

1943, May 18   **Perf. 14**
C129	AP62	20c dk slate grn	1.00 .60
C130	AP62	40c purple	1.25 .60
C131	AP62	1p dp carmine	2.75 2.50
		Nos. C129-C131 (3)	5.00 3.70

400th anniversary of the founding of San Miguel de Allende.

Types of 1934-35

1944   **Photo.**   **Wmk. 272**
C132	AP18	20c brown carmine	.75 .25

Perf. 10½x10

1944-46   **Engr.**   **Wmk. 272**
C133	AP15	5c black	.50 .25
C134	AP16	10c red brn ('45)	1.25 .25
C135	AP17	15c gray grn ('45)	.85 .25
C136	AP19	30c brown ol ('45)	12.50 .75
C137	AP20	40c gray bl ('45)	1.10 .25
C138	AP21	50c green	.85 .25
C139	AP22	1p gray grn & red brn ('45)	6.00 1.50
C140	AP23	5p dk car & blk ('46)	4.75 2.00
		Nos. C133-C140 (8)	27.80 5.50

Symbol of Flight AP65

Microphone, Book and Camera AP66

1944   **Photo.**   **Perf. 14**
C141	AP65	25c chestnut brown	.35 .25
		See No. C185.	

1944, Nov. 8   **Wmk. 272**
C142	AP66	25c dull slate grn	.65 .25

Issued to commemorate the third Book Fair.

> Catalogue values for unused stamps in this section, from this point to the end of the section, are for Never Hinged items.

Globe-in-Hands Type

1945, Feb. 27   **Perf. 12x13**
C143	A166	25c red orange	.40 .25
C144	A166	1p brt green	.50 .30
C145	A166	5p indigo	2.50 2.00
C146	A166	10p brt rose	7.00 5.25
C147	A166	20p brt vio bl	20.00 13.00
		Nos. C143-C147 (5)	29.75 20.75

Theater Type

1945, July 27
C148	A167	30c slate & ol	.35 .25
C149	A167	1p slate & lil	.50 .35
C150	A167	5p slate & blk	3.25 2.50
C151	A167	10p sl & lt ultra	6.00 4.25
C152	A167	20p blk & gray grn	18.00 10.50
		Nos. C148-C152 (5)	26.35 17.80

Blindfold Type

1945, Nov. 21
C153	A169	30c slate green	.25 .25
C154	A169	1p brown red	.50 .30
C155	A169	5p red brn & pale bl	3.75 2.50
C156	A169	10p sl blk & pale lil	6.00 5.00
C157	A169	20p grn & lt brn	25.00 24.00
		Nos. C153-C157 (5)	33.55 32.00

Torch, Laurel and Flag-decorated ONU — AP70

1946, Apr. 10
C158	AP70	30c chocolate	.25 .25
C159	AP70	1p slate grn	.50 .30
C160	AP70	5p chnt & dk grn	2.00 1.25
C161	AP70	10p dk brn & chnt	6.50 4.00
C162	AP70	20p sl grn & org red	18.00 9.00
		Nos. C158-C162 (5)	25.15 14.75

Issued to honor the United Nations.

Father Margil de Jesus and Plane over Zacatecas AP71

Zacatecas scene and: 1p, Genaro Codina. 5p, Gen. Enrique Estrada. 10p, Fernando Villalpando.

Perf. 10½x10

1946, Sept. 13   **Engr.**   **Wmk. 279**
C163	AP71	30c gray	.25 .25
C164	AP71	1p brn & Prus grn	.40 .35
C165	AP71	5p red & olive	3.00 3.00
C166	AP71	10p Prus grn & dk brn	18.00 15.00
		Nos. C163-C166 (4)	21.60 18.55

400th anniversary of Zacatecas.

Franklin D. Roosevelt and Stamp of 1st Mexican Issue AP72

30c, Arms of Mexico & Stamp of 1st US Issue.

1947, May 16   **Photo.**   **Perf. 14**
C167	AP72	25c lt violet bl	.90 .50
C168	AP72	30c gray black	.60 .25
a.		Imperf., pair	325.00
C169	AP72	1p blue & carmine	1.25 .40
		Nos. C167-C169 (3)	2.75 1.15

Centenary International Philatelic Exhibition, New York, May 17-25, 1947.

Type of 1934-35
Perf. 10½x10, 10x10½

1947		Engr.	Wmk. 279	
C170	AP15	5c black	1.50	.25
C171	AP16	10c red brown	3.00	.30
C172	AP17	15c olive grn	3.00	.30
C173	AP19	30c brown ol	2.00	.25
C174	AP20	40c blue gray	2.00	.25
C175	AP21	50c green	12.50	.30
a.		Imperf., pair	450.00	
C176	AP22	1p gray grn & red brn	3.50	.25
a.		Imperf., pair	500.00	
C177	AP23	5p red & blk	9.00	1.25
c.		5p dark car & black	200.00	3.00

Perf. 14

C177A	AP18	20c brown car	2.75	.50
b.		Imperf., pair	250.00	
	Nos. C170-C177A (9)		39.25	3.65

Emilio Carranza
AP74

Douglas DC-4
AP75

1947, June 25 Engr. Perf. 10½x10

C178	AP74	10p red & dk brn	1.75	1.50
a.		10p dark carmine & brown		8.00
C179	AP75	20p bl & red brn	2.75	2.75

Cadet Vicente Suárez
AP76

Chapultepec Castle — AP78

30c, Lieut. Juan de la Barrera. 1p, Gen. Pedro M. Anaya. 5p, Gen. Antonio de Leon.

1947, Sept. 8 Photo. Perf. 14

C180	AP76	25c dull violet	.25	.25
C181	AP76	30c blue	.25	.25

Engr.
Perf. 10x10½

C182	AP78	50c deep green	.35	.25
C183	AP78	1p violet	.50	.25
C184	AP78	5p aqua & brn	2.00	2.00
a.		Imperf. pair	600.00	
	Nos. C180-C184 (5)		3.35	2.80

Centenary of the battles of Chapultepec, Churubusco and Molino del Rey.

Flight Symbol Type of 1944

1947 Wmk. 279 Photo. Perf. 14

C185	AP65	25c chestnut brown	.50	.25
a.		Imperf., pair	250.00	

Puebla, Dance of the Half Moon
AP81

Designs: 5c, Guerrero, Acapulco waterfront. 10c, Oaxaca, dance. 20c, Chiapas, musicians (Mayan). 25c, Michoacan, masks. 30c, Cuauhtemoc. 35c, Guerrero, view of Taxco. 40c, San Luis Potosi, head. 50c, Chiapas, bas-relief profile, Mayan culture. 80c, Mexico City University Stadium. 5p, Queretaro, architecture. 10p, Miguel Hidalgo. 20p, Modern building.

Two types of 20p:
Type I — Blue gray part 21¼mm wide. Child's figure touching left edge.

Type II — Blue gray part 21¾mm wide; "LQ" at lower left corner. Child's figure 1mm from left edge.

Imprint: "Talleres de Impresion de Estampillas y Valores-Mexico"
Perf. 10½x10

1950-52		Wmk. 279	Engr.	
C186	AP81	5c aqua ('51)	.50	.25
C187	AP81	10c brn org ('51)	2.75	.50
C188	AP81	20c carmine	1.25	.25
C189	AP81	25c redsh brown	1.25	.25
C190	AP81	30c olive bister	.50	.25
C191	AP81	35c violet	2.75	.25
a.		Retouched die	19.00	.30
b.		As "a," imperf., pair	300.00	
C192	AP81	40c dk gray bl ('51)	2.25	.25
a.		Imperf., pair	300.00	
C193	AP81	50c green	3.75	.25
C194	AP81	80c claret ('52)	2.25	.50
a.		Imperf., pair	300.00	
C195	AP81	1p blue gray	1.40	.25
C196	AP81	5p dk brn & org ('51)	5.00	1.00
a.		Imperf., pair		1,800.
C197	AP81	10p blk & aqua ('52)	95.00	20.00
C198	AP81	20p car & bl gray, I ('52)	8.50	9.00
a.		Type II	400.00	100.00
	Nos. C186-C198 (13)		127.15	33.00

No. C191a: A patch of heavy shading has been added at right of "MEXICO;" lines in sky increased and strengthened. On Nos. C191, C191a, the top of the highest tower is even with the top of the "o" in "Guerrero," and has no frame line at right. No. C220C has frame line at right and tower top is even with "Arquitectura."

Many shades exist of Nos. C186-C198.

See Nos. C208-C221, C249, C265-C268, C285-C288, C290-C298, C347-C349, C422, C444, C446-C450, C471-C480.

Pres. Aleman and Highway Bridging Map of Mexico
AP82

Design: 35c, Pres. Juarez and map.

1950, May 21 Engr.

C199	AP82	25c lilac rose	3.00	.25
C200	AP82	35c deep green	.30	.25

Completion of the Intl. Highway between Ciudad Juarez and the Guatemala border.

Trains Crossing Isthmus of Tehuantepec — AP83

Design: 35c, Pres. Aleman and bridge.

1950, May 24

C201	AP83	25c green	.50	.25
C202	AP83	35c ultra	.35	.25

Opening of the Southeastern Railroad between Veracruz, Coatzcoalcos and Yucatan, 1950.

Aztec Courier, Plane, Train
AP84

80c, Symbols of universal postal service.

1950, June 15

C203	AP84	25c red orange	.35	.25
C204	AP84	80c blue	.50	.30

75th anniv. (in 1949) of the UPU.

Miguel Hidalgo
AP86

Design: 35c, Hidalgo and Mexican Flag.

Wmk. 300

1953, May 8 Photo. Perf. 14

C206	AP86	25c gray bl & dk red brn	.90	.25
C207	AP86	35c slate green	.90	.25
a.		Wmk. 279		

Bicentenary of birth of Miguel Hidalgo y Costilla (1753-1811), priest and revolutionist.

Type of 1950-52

Designs as before.

Imprint: "Talleres de Impresion de Estampillas y Valores-Mexico"
Wmk. 300, Horizontal

1953-56		Engr.	Perf. 10½x10	
C208	AP81	5c aqua	.50	.25
C209	AP81	10c orange brn	5.50	3.50
a.		10c orange	11.50	2.50
C210	AP81	30c gray olive	18.00	10.00
C211	AP81	40c gray bl ('56)	18.00	1.50
C212	AP81	50c green	350.00	250.00
C213	AP81	80c claret	100.00	10.00
C214	AP81	1p blue gray	3.00	.30
C215	AP81	5p dk brn & org	2.75	.60
C216	AP81	10p black & aqua	6.25	1.25
C217	AP81	20p car & bl gray (II) ('56)	75.00	8.00
	Nos. C208-C211,C213-C217 (9)		229.00	35.40

Printed in sheets of 30.

Type of 1950-52

Designs as in 1950-52. 2p, Guerrero, view of Taxco. 2.25p, Michoacan, masks.

Two types of 2p:
I — No dots after "Colonial". Frame line at right broken near top.
II — Three dots in a line after "Colonial". Right frame line unbroken.

Wmk. 300, Vertical

1955-65			Perf. 11½x11	
		Design AP81		
C218		5c bluish grn ('56)	.25	.25
		Perf. 11		
C219		10c orange brn ('60)	.35	.25
a.		Perf. 11½x11	1.10	.40
C220		20c carmine ('60)	.35	.25
k.		Perf. 11½x11 ('57)	1.60	.25
C220A		25c vio brn, perf. 11½x11	1.75	.25
C220B		30c olive gray ('60)	.35	.25
l.		Perf. 11½x11	.90	.25
C220C		35c dk vio, perf. 11½x11	.90	.25
C220D		40c slate bl ('60)	.35	.25
m.		Perf. 11½x11	10.00	.25
C220E		50c green, perf. 11½x11	.90	.25
n.		Perf. 11 ('60)	1.10	.25
o.		50c yellow green	1.10	.25
C220F		80c claret ('60)	5.00	.70
p.		Perf. 11½x11	5.00	.60
C220G		1p grn gray ('60)	1.10	.30
q.		Perf. 11½x11	12.50	.30
C220H		2p dk org brn, II ('63)	1.10	.60
i.		2p lt org brn, perf. 11½x11 ('65)	150.00	40.00
j.		2p org brn, I, perf. 11	8.50	1.25
C221		2.25p maroon ('63)	.65	.70
	Nos. C218-C221 (12)		13.05	4.30

Printed in sheets of 45 and 50. Nos. C218-C221 have been re-engraved.

No. C218 has been redrawn and there are many differences. "CTS" measures 7mm; it is 5½mm on No. C208.

Nos. C208-C221 exist in various shades.

For No. C220C, see note after No. C198.

No. C220En was privately overprinted in red: "25vo Aniversario / Primer Cohete Internacional / Reynosa, Mexico-McAllen, U.S.A. / 1936-1961."

Mayan Ball Court and Player
AP87

Design: 35c, Modern Stadium, Mexico.

1954, Mar. 6 Photo. Perf. 14

C222	AP87	25c brn & bl grn	1.00	.35
C223	AP87	35c dl sl grn & lil rose	.75	.25

7th Central American & Caribbean Games.

Allegory
AP88

1954, Sept. 15

C224	AP88	25c red brn & dp bl	.50	.25
C225	AP88	35c dk bl & vio brn	.30	.25
C226	AP88	80c blk & bl grn	.30	.25
	Nos. C224-C226 (3)		1.10	.70

Centenary of national anthem.

Aztec God Tezcatlipoca and Map — AP89

Design: 35c, Stadium and map.

1955, Mar. 12

C227	AP89	25c dk Prus grn & red brn	.75	.30
C228	AP89	35c carmine & brn	.75	.30

2nd Pan American Games, 1955.

Ornaments and Mask, Archeological Era — AP90

Designs: 10c, Virrey Enriquez de Almanza, bell tower and coach, colonial era. 50c, Jose Maria Morelos and cannon, heroic Mexico. 1p, Woman and child and horse back rider, revolutionary Mexico. 1.20p, Sombrero and Spurs, popular Mexico. 5p, Pointing hand and school, modern Mexico.

Perf. 11½x11

1956, Aug. 1		Engr.	Wmk. 300	
C229	AP90	5c black	.40	.25
C230	AP90	10c lt brown	.40	.25
C231	AP90	50c violet brn	.30	.25
C232	AP90	1p blue gray	.40	.25
C233	AP90	1.20p magenta	.40	.25
C234	AP90	5p blue grn	1.25	1.25
a.		Souv. sheet of 6, #C229-C234, perf. 10½x10	60.00	60.00
	Nos. C229-C234 (6)		3.15	2.30

Centenary of Mexico's 1st postage stamps. No. C234a sold for 15 pesos.

Paricutín Volcano
AP91

1956, Sept. 5 Photo. Perf. 14

C235	AP91	50c dk violet bl	.50	.25

20th Intl. Geological Cong., Mexico City.

Valentin Gomez Farias and Melchor Ocampo
AP92

1.20p, Leon Guzman and Ignacio Ramirez.

1956-63   Wmk. 300   Perf. 14

C236 AP92 15c intense blue   .50   .25
C237 AP92 1.20p dk grn & pur   .85   .35
    b.   Dark green omitted   110.00
    c.   Purple omitted   125.00
C237A AP92 2.75p purple ('63)   1.25   .75
    Nos. C236-C237A (3)   2.60   1.30

Centenary of the constitution (in 1957). See Nos. C289, C445, C451, C471A.

Map AP93

1956, Dec. 1

C238 AP93 25c gray & dk bl   .35   .25

4th Inter-American Regional Tourism Congress of the Gulf of Mexico and the Caribbean (in 1955).

Eagle Holding Scales AP94

1p, Allegorical figure writing the law.

1957, Aug. 31   Photo.   Perf. 14

C239 AP94 50c metallic red brn & green   .35   .25
C240 AP94 1p metallic lilac & ultra   .50   .25

Centenary of 1857 Constitution.

Globe, Weights and Measure AP95

1957, Sept. 21

C241 AP95 50c metallic bl & blk   .40   .25

Centenary of the adoption of the metric system in Mexico.

Death of Jesus Garcia AP96

1957, Nov. 7   Wmk. 300   Perf. 14

C242 AP96 50c car rose & dk vio   .35   .25

50th anniversary of the death of Jesus Garcia, hero of Nacozari.

Oil Industry Symbols AP97

Design: 1p, Oil refinery at night.

1958, Aug. 30

C243 AP97 50c emerald & blk   .25   .25
C244 AP97 1p car & bluish blk   .40   .25

Nationalization of Mexico's oil industry, 20th anniv.

Independence Monument Figure — AP98

1958, Dec. 15   Engr.   Perf. 11

C245 AP98 50c gray blue   .35   .25

10th anniversary of the signing of the Universal Declaration of Human Rights.

Pres. Venustiano Carranza AP99

1960, Jan. 15   Photo.   Perf. 14

C246 AP99 50c salmon & dk bl   .35   .25

Centenary of the birth of President Venustiano Carranza.

Alberto Braniff's 1910 Plane, Douglas DC-7 and Mexican Airlines Map AP100

1960, May 15   Wmk. 300   Perf. 14

C247 AP100 50c lt brn & vio   .50   .25
C248 AP100 1p lt brn & bl grn   .40   .25

50th anniversary of Mexican aviation.

Type of 1950-52 inscribed: "HOMENAJE AL COLECCIONISTA DEL TIMBRE DE MEXICO JUNIO 1960"

1960, June 8   Engr.   Perf. 10½x10

C249 AP81 20p lil, brn & lt grn   100.00   100.00

See note below No. 909.

Flag AP101

Designs: 1.20p, Bell of Dolores and eagle. 5p, Dolores Church.

Wmk. 300

1960, Sept. 16   Photo.   Perf. 14

C250 AP101 50c dp grn & brt red   .40   .25
C251 AP101 1.20p grnsh bl & dk brn   .60   .25
C252 AP101 5p sepia & green   6.00   2.25
    Nos. C250-C252 (3)   7.00   2.70

150th anniversary of independence.

Aviation (Douglas DC-8 Airliner) AP102

Designs: 1p, Oil industry. 1.20p, Road development. 5p, Water power (dam).

1960, Nov. 20   Photo.   Perf. 14

C253 AP102 50c gray bl & blk   .40   .25
C254 AP102 1p dk grn & rose car   .50   .25
C255 AP102 1.20p dk grn & sep   .50   .30
C256 AP102 5p blue & lilac   6.00   3.00
    Nos. C253-C256 (4)   7.40   3.75

50th anniversary of Mexican Revolution.

Count de Revillaggigedo AP103

1960, Dec. 23

C257 AP103 60c dk car & blk   .60   .25

80th census and to honor Juan Vicente Güemez Pacheco de Padilla Horcasitas, Count de Revillagigedo, who conducted the 1st census in America, 1793.

Railroad Tracks and Map AP104

Design: 70c, Railroad bridge.

1961, Nov.   Wmk. 300   Perf. 14

C258 AP104 60c chlky bl & dk grn   .40   .25
C259 AP104 70c dk blue & gray   .40   .25

Opening of the railroad from Chihuahua to the Pacific Ocean.

Gen. Ignacio Zaragoza and View of Puebla AP105

1962, May 5

C260 AP105 1p gray grn & slate grn   .60   .25

Centenary of the Battle of May 5 at Puebla and the defeat of French forces by Gen. Ignacio Zaragoza.

Laboratory AP106

1962, June 11

C261 AP106 1p olive & vio bl   .60   .25

National Polytechnic Institute, 25th anniv.

Pres. John F. Kennedy AP107

1962, June 29

C262 AP107 80c brt blue & car   1.75   .40

Commemorates visit of President John F. Kennedy to Mexico, June 29-30.

Globe AP108

1962, Oct. 20

C263 AP108 1.20p violet & dk brn   .60   .25

Inter-American Economic and Social Council meeting.

Balloon over Mexico City, 1862 — AP109

1962, Dec. 21   Wmk. 300   Perf. 14

C264 AP109 80c lt blue & blk   1.60   .60

Cent. of the 1st Mexican balloon ascension by Joaquin de la Cantolla y Rico.

Type of 1950-52

Designs as before.

Two sizes of 80c:
   I — 35½x20mm.
   II — 37x20½mm.

Imprint: "Talleres de Imp. de Est. y Valores-Mexico"

Wmk. 300, Vertical

1962-72   Photo.   Perf. 14

C265 AP81 80c cl, I ('63)   1.40   .30
   a.   Perf. 11½x11, size II ('63)   4.00   .35
   b.   Perf. 11, size II ('63)   3.50   .30
   c.   Perf. 11, size I ('72)   2.50   .25
C266 AP81 5p dk brn & yel org   4.00   1.00
C267 AP81 10p blk & lt grn ('63)   7.00   3.75
C268 AP81 20p car & bl gray   15.00   3.50
   a.   20p carmine & aqua   17.00   4.75
    Nos. C265-C268 (4)   27.40   8.55

Vert. pairs, imperf. horiz. of No. C265, perf. 11, may be from uncut rolls of No. C348.

ALALC Emblem AP110

1963, Feb. 15   Wmk. 300

C269 AP110 80c orange & dl pur   1.10   .30

2nd general session of the Latin American Free Trade Assoc. (ALALC), held in 1962.

Mexican Eagle and Refinery AP111

1963, Mar. 23

C270 AP111 80c red org & slate   .60   .25

Nationalization of the oil industry, 25th anniv.

Polyconic Map AP112

1963, Apr. 22   Photo.   Perf. 14

C271 AP112 80c blue & blk   .85   .30

19th Intl. Chamber of Commerce Congress.

EXMEX Emblem and Postmark AP113

1963, Oct. 9   Wmk. 350   Perf. 14

C274 AP113 5p rose red   2.75   1.75

77th Annual Convention of the American Philatelic Society, Mexico City, Oct. 7-13.

Marshal Tito AP114

1963, Oct. 15   Wmk. 350   Perf. 14
C275 AP114 2p dk grn & vio   2.00   .70
Visit of Marshal Tito of Yugoslavia.

Modern Architecture — AP115

1963, Oct. 19
C276 AP115 80c dk blue & gray   .70   .25
Intl. Architects' Convention, Mexico City.

Dove AP116

1963, Oct. 26
C277 AP116 80c dl bl grn & car   1.25   .35
Centenary of the International Red Cross.

Don Quixote by José Guadalupe Posada AP117

1963, Nov. 9   Engr.   Perf. 10½x10
C278 AP117 1.20p black   1.75   .50
50th anniversary of the death of José Guadalupe Posada, satirical artist.

Horse-drawn Rail Coach, Old and New Trains — AP118

Wmk. 350
1963, Nov. 29   Photo.   Perf. 14
C279 AP118 1.20p violet bl & bl   .90   .35
11th Pan-American Railroad Congress.

Eleanor Roosevelt, Flame and UN Emblem AP119

1964, Feb. 22   Wmk. 350   Perf. 14
C280 AP119 80c lt ultra & red   .85   .25
15th anniversary (in 1963) of the Universal Declaration of Human Rights and to honor Eleanor Roosevelt.

Gen. Charles de Gaulle AP120

1964, Mar. 16   Photo.
C281 AP120 2p dl vio bl & brn   2.50   .80
Visit of President Charles de Gaulle of France to Mexico, Mar. 16-18.

Pres. John F. Kennedy and Pres. Adolfo López Mateos and Map AP121

1964, Apr. 11   Photo.
C282 AP121 80c vio bl & gray   .85   .25
Ratification of the Chamizal Treaty, returning the Chamizal area of El Paso, Texas, to Mexico, July 18, 1963.

Queen Juliana AP122

1964, May 8   Wmk. 350   Perf. 14
C283 AP122 80c bister & vio bl   1.25   .25
Visit of Queen Juliana of the Netherlands.

Lt. José Azueta and Cadet Virgilio Uribe AP123

1964, June 18   Wmk. 350   Perf. 14
C284 AP123 40c dk brn & blk   .55   .25
50th anniversary of the defense of Veracruz (against US Navy).

Types of 1950-62
Designs as before.

Perf. 11 (20c, 40c, 50c, 80c, 2p); 14
Photo.; Engr. (C296-C298)
1964-73   Wmk. 350
C285 AP81 20c carmine ('71)   .75   1.25
C286 AP81 40c gray bl ('71)   125.00 100.00
C287 AP81 50c green ('71)   .50   .50
C288 AP81 80c claret, I ('73)   .50   .50
C289 AP92 1.20p dk grn & pur   6.50   2.50
C290 AP81 2p red brn, II ('71)   1.75   1.40
C296 AP81 5p brn & org ('66)   11.00   9.00
C297 AP81 10p black & aqua   35.00 17.50
C298 AP81 20p car & bl gray   55.00 40.00
Nos. C285-C290, C296-C298 (9)   236.00 172.65

National Emblem, Cahill's Butterfly World Map, Sword and Scales of Justice AP124

1964, July 29   Photo.
C299 AP124 40c sepia & dp bl   .60   .25
10th conference of the International Bar Association, Mexico City, July 27-31.

Galleon AP125

Map Showing 16th Century Voyages Between Mexico and Philippines — AP126

1964, Nov. 10   Wmk. 350   Perf. 14
C300 AP125 80c ultra & indigo   2.25   .35
C301 AP126 2.75p brt yel & blk   2.75 1.00
400 years of Mexican-Philippine friendship.

Netzahualcoyotl Dam, Grijalva River — AP127

1965, Feb. 19   Photo.   Perf. 14
C302 AP127 80c vio gray & dk brn   .50   .25

Radio-electric Unit of San Benito, Chiapas — AP128

80c, Microwave tower, Villahermosa, Tabasco.

1965, June 19   Wmk. 350   Perf. 14
C303 AP128 80c lt bl & dk bl   .65   .30
C304 AP128 1.20p dk grn & blk   .70   .30
Centenary of the ITU.

Campfire, Tent and Scout Emblem AP129

1965, Sept. 27   Photo.   Perf. 14
C305 AP129 80c lt ultra & vio bl   .65   .30
20th World Scout Conference, Mexico City, Sept. 27-Oct. 3.

King Baudouin, Queen Fabiola and Arms of Belgium AP130

1965, Oct. 18   Wmk. 350   Perf. 14
C306 AP130 2p slate grn & dl bl   1.00   .40
Visit of the King and Queen of Belgium.

Mayan Antiquities and Unisphere AP131

1965, Nov. 9   Photo.
C307 AP131 80c lemon & emerald   .50   .25
Issued for the NY World's Fair, 1964-65.

Dante by Raphael — AP132

Perf. 10x10½
1965, Nov. 23   Wmk. 350   Engr.
C308 AP132 2p henna brown   1.25   .65
700th anniv. of the birth of Dante Alighieri.

Runner in Starting Position, Terra Cotta Found in Colima, 300-650 A.D. AP133

Designs: 1.20p, Chin cultic disk, ball game scoring stone with ball player in center, Mayan culture, c. 500 A.D., found in Chiapas. 2p, Clay sculpture of ball court, players, spectators and temple. Pieces on 80c and 2p from 300-650 A.D.

1965, Dec. 17   Photo.   Perf. 14
Size: 35x21mm
C309 AP133 80c orange & sl   .80   .25
C310 AP133 1.20p bl & vio bl   .90   .30
 a.   Souv. sheet of 4, #965-966, C309-C310, imperf.   3.50 3.50
Size: 43x36mm
C311 AP133 2p brt bl & dk brn   .75   .25
 a.   Souv. sheet, imperf.   3.50 3.50
Nos. C309-C311 (3)   2.45   .80
19th Olympic Games, Mexico, 1968. No. C310a sold for 3.90p. No. C311a sold for 3p. Nos. C310a and C311a have large watermark of national arms (diameter 54mm) and "SECRETARIA DE HACIENDA Y CREDITO PUBLICO." Issued without gum.

Ruben Dario — AP134

1966, Mar. 17   Wmk. 350   Perf. 14
C312 AP134 1.20p sepia   .60   .35
Ruben Dario (pen name of Felix Ruben Garcia Sarmiento, 1867-1916), Nicaraguan poet, newspaper correspondent and diplomat.

Father Andres de Urdaneta and Compass Rose AP135

Perf. 10½x10
1966, June 4   Engr.   Wmk. 350
C313 AP135 2.75p bluish blk   1.25   .60
4th centenary of Father Urdaneta's return trip from the Philippines.

UPAE Type of Regular Issue
Designs: 80c, Pennant and post horn. 1.20p, Pennant and UPAE emblem, horiz.

Wmk. 300
1966, June 24   Photo.   Perf. 14
C314 A244   80c magenta & blk   .25   .25
C315 A244   1.20p lt ultra & blk   .35   .25

U Thant and UN Emblem AP136

1966, Aug. 24   Photo.   Wmk. 300
C316 AP136 80c black & ultra   .75   .25
Visit of U Thant, Secretary General of the UN.

AP137

1966, Aug. 26   Perf. 14
C317 AP137 80c green & red   .25   .25
Issued to publicize the year of friendship between Mexico and Central America.

Olympic Type of Regular Issue
Designs by Diego Rivera: 80c, Obstacle race. 2.25p, Football. 2.75p, Lighting Olympic torch.

1966, Oct. 15   Wmk. 300   Perf. 14
Size: 57x21mm
C318 A248   80c org brn & blk   .55   .25
C319 A248   2.25p green & blk   .90   .35
C320 A248   2.75p dp pur & blk   2.00   .45
  a.   Souvenir sheet of 3   3.00   3.00
  Nos. C318-C320 (3)   3.45   1.00
Issued to publicize the 19th Olympic Games, Mexico City, D.F., 1968. No. C320a contains 3 imperf. stamps similar to Nos. C318-C320 with simulated perforations. Sold for 8.70p.

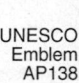

UNESCO Emblem AP138

Litho. & Engr.
1966, Nov. 4   Perf. 11
C321 AP138 80c blk, car, brt grn & org   .50   .25
  a.   Perf. 10½   5.00   2.00
  b.   Perf. 10½x11   25.00
  c.   Perf. 11x10½   12.50   5.00
UNESCO 20th anniv. The 4th color varies from yellow to orange. A number of perforation varieties exist on the perf 11 stamps.

Venustiano Carranza AP139   Tiros Satellite over Earth AP140

1967, Feb. 5   Photo.   Perf. 14
C322 AP139 80c dk red brn & ocher   .35   .25
Constitution, 50th anniv. Venustiano Carranza (1859-1920), was president of Mexico 1917-20.

1967, Mar. 23   Photo.   Wmk. 300
C323 AP140 80c blk & dk bl   .50   .25
World Meteorological Day, Mar. 23.

Medical School Emblem AP141   Captain Horacio Ruiz Gaviño AP142

1967, July 10   Wmk. 300   Perf. 14
C324 AP141 80c black & ocher   .35   .25
Mexican Military Medical School, 50th anniv.

1967, July 17   Photo.
Design: 2p, Biplane, horiz.
C325 AP142 80c black & brown   .25   .25
C326 AP142 2p black & brown   .45   .25
50th anniv. of the 1st Mexican airmail flight, from Pachuca to Mexico City, July 6, 1917.

Marco Polo and ITY Emblem — AP143

1967, Sept. 9   Wmk. 300   Perf. 14
C327 AP143 80c rose cl & blk   .25   .25
Issued for International Tourist Year, 1967.

Olympic Games Type of Regular Issue, 1967
Designs: 80c, Diving. 1.20p, Runners. 2p, Weight lifters. 5p, Soccer.

1967, Oct. 12   Photo.   Perf. 14
C328 A254   80c dp lil rose & blk   .45   .25
C329 A254   1.20p brt grn & blk   .45   .25
  a.   Souv. sheet of 2, #C328-C329, imperf.   5.50   3.75
C330 A254   2p yellow & blk   1.25   .40
C331 A254   5p olive & blk   1.60   .75
  a.   Souv. sheet of 2, #C330-C331, imperf.   7.50   4.00
  Nos. C328-C331 (4)   3.75   1.55
No. C329a sold for 2.50p; No. C331a sold for 9p. Both sheets are watermark 350.

Heinrich Hertz and James Clerk Maxwell AP144

1967, Nov. 15   Photo.   Wmk. 300
C332 AP144 80c brt grn & blk   .30   .25
2nd Intl. Telecommunications Plan Conf., Mexico City, Oct. 30-Nov. 15.

EFIMEX Emblem, Showing Official Stamp of 1884 — AP145

1968, Feb. 24   Wmk. 300   Perf. 14
C333 AP145 80c black & grn   .45   .25
C334 AP145 2p black & ver   .45   .25
EFIMEX '68, International Philatelic Exhibition, Mexico City, Nov. 1-9, 1968.

Olympic Games Type of Regular Issue, 1967
Designs: 80c, Sailing. 1p, Rowing. 2p, Volleyball. 5p, Equestrian.

1968, Mar. 21   Photo.   Perf. 14
C335 A254   80c ultra & blk   .25   .25
C336 A254   1p brt bl grn & blk   .35   .25
  a.   Souv. sheet of 2, #C335-C336, imperf.   3.50   2.75
C337 A254   2p yellow & blk   .70   .30
C338 A254   5p red brn & blk   1.40   1.10
  a.   Souv. sheet of 2, #C337-C338, imperf.   7.50   4.50
  Nos. C335-C338 (4)   2.70   1.80
No. C336a sold for 2.40p; No. C338a sold for 9p. Both sheets are watermark 350.

Martin Luther King, Jr. — AP146

1968, June 8   Photo.   Wmk. 300
C339 AP146 80c black & gray   .35   .25
Rev. Dr. Martin Luther King, Jr. (1929-1968), American civil rights leader.

Olympic Types of Regular Issue, 1968
Designs: 80c, Peace dove and Olympic rings. 1p, Discobolus. 2p, Olympic medals. 5p, Symbols of Olympic sports events. 10p, Symbolic design for Mexican Olympic Games.

1968, Oct. 12   Wmk. 350   Perf. 14
C340 A259   80c green, lil & org   .35   .25
C341 A259   1p green, bl & blk   .45   .25
C342 A259   2p multicolored   .90   .50
  a.   Souvenir sheet of 3, #C340-C342, imperf.   20.00   17.50
C343 A260   5p multicolored   4.00   1.40
C344 A260   10p black & multi   2.90   1.50
  a.   Souvenir sheet of 2, #C343-C344, imperf.   20.00   17.50
  Nos. C340-C344 (5)   8.60   3.80
19th Olympic Games, Mexico City, Oct. 12-27. No. C342a sold for 5p. No. C344a sold for 20p.

Souvenir Sheet

EFIMEX Emblem — AP147

1968, Nov. 1   Photo.   Imperf.
C345 AP147 5p black & ultra   3.50   2.50
EFIMEX '68 International philatelic exhibition, Mexico City, Nov. 1-9. No. C345 contains one stamp with simulated perforations.

Father Francisco Palóu (See footnote) AP148

1969, July 16   Wmk. 350   Perf. 14
C346 AP148 80c multicolored   .40   .25
Issued to honor Father Junipero Serra (1713-1784), Franciscan missionary, founder of San Diego, Calif. The portrait was intended to be that of Father Serra. By error the head of Father Palóu, his coworker, was taken from a painting (c. 1785) by Mariano Guerrero which also contains a Serra portrait.

Type of 1950-52 Redrawn
Imprint: "T.I.E.V."
Coil Stamps
Wmk. 300 Vert.
1969   Photo.   Perf. 11 Vert.
C347 AP81 20c carmine   2.75   2.00
Imprint: "Talleres de Imp de Est y Valores-Mexico"
C348 AP81 80c claret   4.00   2.00

Imprint: "T.I.E.V."
C349 AP81 1p gray grn   4.00   2.25
  Nos. C347-C349 (3)   10.75   6.25

Soccer Ball AP149

Design: 2p, Foot and soccer ball.

1969, Aug. 16   Wmk. 350   Perf. 14
C350 AP149 80c red & multi   1.25   .25
C351 AP149 2p green & multi   1.25   .25
9th World Soccer Championships for the Jules Rimet Cup, Mexico City, May 30-June 21, 1970.

Mahatma Gandhi AP150   Astronaut's Footprint AP151

1969, Sept. 27   Photo.   Perf. 14
C352 AP150 80c multicolored   .30   .25
Mohandas K. Gandhi (1869-1948), leader in India's fight for independence.

1969, Sept. 29   Photo.
C353 AP151 2p black   .50   .25
Man's 1st landing on the moon, July 20, 1969. See note after US No. C76.

Tourist Issue
Type of Regular Issue, 1969-73 and

"Sound and Light" at Pyramid, Teotihuacan — AP152

Designs: No. C355, Acapulco Bay. No. C356, El Caracol Observatory, Yucatan. No. C357, Dancer with fruit basket, Oaxaca. No. C358, Sports fishing, Lower California, horiz.

1969-73   Wmk. 350   Perf. 14
C354 AP152 80c shown   .90   .30
C355 AP152 80c multicolored   .90   .30
C356 AP152 80c multicolored   .90   .30
Wmk. 300
C357 A267 80c multicolored   .35   .25
C358 A267 80c multicolored   .35   .25
  Nos. C354-C358 (5)   3.40   1.35
Issue dates: Nos. C354-C356, Nov. 1, 1969. Nos. C357-C358, Mar. 16, 1973.

Red Crosses AP154

1969, Nov. 8   Photo.   Wmk. 350
C370 AP154 80c black & multi   .35   .25
  a.   Red omitted   150.00
50th anniv. of the League of Red Cross Societies.

AP155   AP156

1969, Dec. 6   **Wmk. 350**   *Perf. 14*
C371 AP155 80c multicolored   .35   .25

Installation of the ground station for communications by satellite at Tulancingo, Hidalgo.

1970, May 31   **Wmk. 350**   *Perf. 14*

Design: 80c, Soccer Ball, and Mexican Masks. 2p, Pre-Columbian sculptured heads and soccer ball.

C372 AP156 80c blue & multi   1.25   .25
C373 AP156 2p multicolored   1.25   .25

World Soccer Championships for the Jules Rimet Cup, Mexico City, May 30-June 21, 1970. The design of Nos. C372-C373 is continuous.

SPORTMEX '70 Emblem — AP157

1970, June 19   *Rouletted 13*
C374 AP157 2p gray & car   5.00 3.00

SPORTMEX '70 philatelic exposition devoted to sports, especially soccer, on stamps. Mexico City, June 19-28. The 2p stamp of No. C374 is imperf.

Ode to Joy and Beethoven's Signature AP158

1970, Sept. 26   **Wmk. 350**   *Perf. 14*
C375 AP158 2p multicolored   .50   .25

200th anniversary of the birth of Ludwig van Beethoven (1770-1827), composer.

UN General Assembly Floor Plan AP159

1970, Oct. 24   **Photo.**   *Perf. 14*
C376 AP159 80c multicolored   .30   .25

25th anniversary of United Nations.

Isaac Newton AP160

1971, Feb. 27   **Wmk. 350**   *Perf. 14*
C377 AP160 2p shown   .45   .25
C378 AP160 2p Galileo   .45   .25
C379 AP160 2p Johannes Kepler   .45   .25
   Nos. C377-C379 (3)   1.35   .75

Mayan Warriors, Dresden Codex AP161

Designs: No. C381, Sister Juana, by Miguel Cabrera (1695-1768). No. C382, José Maria Velasco (1840-1912), self-portrait. No. C383, El Paricutin (volcano), by Gerardo Murillo ("Dr. Atl," 1875-1964). No. C384, Detail of mural, Man in Flames, by José Clemente Orozco (1883-1949).

Imprint includes "1971"

1971, Apr. 24   **Photo.**   **Wmk. 350**
C380 AP161 80c multicolored   .30   .25
C381 AP161 80c multicolored   .30   .25
C382 AP161 80c multicolored   .30   .25
C383 AP161 80c multicolored   .30   .25
C384 AP161 80c multicolored   .30   .25
   Nos. C380-C384 (5)   1.50 1.25

Mexican art and science through the centuries. See Nos. C396-C400, C417-C421, C439-C443, C513-C517, C527-C531.

Stamps of Venezuela, Mexico and Colombia AP162

1971, May 22   **Photo.**   **Wmk. 350**
C385 AP162 80c multicolored   .35   .25

EXFILCA 70, 2nd Interamerican Philatelic Exhibition, Caracas, Venezuela, Nov. 27-Dec. 6, 1970.

Francisco Javier Clavijero AP163

1971, July 10   **Wmk. 350**   *Perf. 14*
C386 AP163 2p lt ol bis & dk brn   .50   .25

Francisco Javier Clavijero (1731-1786), Jesuit and historian, whose remains were returned from Italy to Mexico in 1970.

Waves AP164   Mariano Matamoros, by Diego Rivera AP165

1971, Aug. 7   **Wmk. 350**   *Perf. 14*
C387 AP164 80c multicolored   .25   .25

3rd World Telecommunications Day, May 17.

1971, Aug. 28   **Photo.**
C388 AP165 2p multicolored   .45   .25

Bicentenary of the birth of Mariano Matamoros (1770-1814), priest and patriot.

Vicente Guerrero AP166   Circles AP167

1971, Sept. 27
C389 AP166 2p multicolored   .40   .25

Vicente Guerrero (1783-1831), independence leader, president of Mexico. Painting by Juan O'Gorman.

1971, Nov. 4   **Wmk. 300**
C390 AP167 80c grnsh bl, dk bl &   blk   .30   .25

25th anniv. of UNESCO.

Stamps of Venezuela, Mexico, Colombia and Peru AP168

1971, Nov. 4
C391 AP168 80c multicolored   .45   .25

EXFILIMA '71, 3rd Interamerican Philatelic Exhibition, Lima, Peru, Nov. 6-14.

Faces and Hand AP169

1971, Nov. 29
C392 AP169 2p blk, dk bl & pink   .45   .25

5th Congress of Psychiatry, Mexico City, Nov. 28-Dec. 4.

Ex Libris by Albrecht Dürer AP170

1971, Dec. 18
C393 AP170 2p blk & buff   .65   .25

Albrecht Dürer (1471-1528), German painter and engraver.

Retort, Pulley and Burner AP171   Scientists and WHO Emblem AP172

1972, Feb. 26   **Wmk. 300**   *Perf. 14*
C394 AP171 2p lilac, blk & yel   .35   .25

Anniversary of the National Council on Science and Technology.

1972, Apr. 8
C395 AP172 80c multicolored   .25   .25

World Health Day 1972. Stamp shows Willem Einthoven and Frank Wilson.

Art and Science Type of 1971

Designs: No. C396, King Netzahuacoyotl (1402-1472) of Texcoco, art patron. No. C397, Juan Ruiz de Alarcon (c. 1580-1639), dramatist. No. C398, José Joaquin Fernandez de Lizardi (1776-1827), author. No. C399, Ramon Lopez Velarde (1888-1921), writer. No. C400, Enrique Gonzalez Martínez (1871-1952), poet.

Imprint includes "1972"

1972, Apr. 15   **Wmk. 350**
Black Inscriptions
C396 AP161 80c ocher   1.25   .25
C397 AP161 80c green   1.25   .25
C398 AP161 80c brown   1.25   .25
C399 AP161 80c carmine   1.25   .25
C400 AP161 80c gray blue   1.25   .25
   Nos. C396-C400 (5)   6.25 1.25

Mexican art and science through the centuries.

Rotary Emblem AP173

1972, Apr. 15
C401 AP173 80c multicolored   .30   .25

Rotary Intl. in Mexico, 50th anniv.

Tire Treads AP174

1972, May 11   **Wmk. 300**
C402 AP174 80c gray & blk   .30   .25

74th Assembly of the International Tourism Alliance, Mexico City, May 8-11.

Benito Juárez AP175

Designs: 80c, Page of Civil Register. 1.20p, Juárez, by Pelegrin Clavé.

1972   **Photo.**   *Perf. 14*
C403 AP175 80c gray bl & blk   .25   .25
C404 AP175 1.20p multi   .25   .25
C405 AP175 2p yellow & multi   .35   .25
   Nos. C403-C405 (3)   .80   .60

Benito Juárez (1806-1872), revolutionary leader and president of Mexico.

Issue dates: 80c, 2p, July 18; 1.20p, Sept. 15.

Atom Symbol, Olive Branch — AP176

1972, Oct. 3   Photo.   Wmk. 300
C406 AP176 2p gray, bl & blk   .40   .25
16th Conference of the Atomic Energy Commission, Mexico City, Sept. 26.

"Over the Waves," by Juventino Rosas AP177

1972, Oct. 16   Perf. 14
C407 AP177 80c olive bister   .25   .25
28th Intl. Cong. of the Societies of Authors and Composers, Mexico City, Oct. 16-21.

Child with Doll, by Guerrero Galvan, UNICEF Emblem — AP178

1972, Nov. 4
C408 AP178 80c multicolored   .75   .25
25th anniv. (in 1971) of UNICEF.

Pedro de Gante, by Rodriguez y Arangorti — AP179

1972, Nov. 22   Perf. 14
C409 AP179 2p multicolored   .35   .25
Brother Pedro de Gante (Pedro Moor or van der Moere; 1480?-1572), Franciscan brother who founded first school in Mexico, and writer.

Olympic Games Type of Regular Issue, 1972

Designs: 80c, Olympic emblems and stylized soccer game. 2p, Olympic emblems, vert.

1972, Dec. 9   Photo.   Wmk. 300
C410 A289 80c green & multi   .35   .25
C411 A289 2p yel grn, blk & bl   .65   .25
20th Olympic Games, Munich, Aug. 26-Sept. 11.

Anti-pollution Type of Regular Issue

80c, Bird sitting on ornamental capital, vert.

1972, Dec. 16
C412 A291 80c lt blue & blk   .25   .25
Anti-pollution campaign.

Map of Americas with Tourists' Footprints — AP180

1972, Dec. 23
C413 AP180 80c black, yel & grn   .25   .25
Tourism Year of the Americas.

Mexico #O1, Brazil #992, Colombia #130, Venezuela #22, Peru #C320 AP181

1973, Jan. 19   Perf. 14
C414 AP181 80c multicolored   .25   .25
4th Interamerican Philatelic Exhibition, EXFILBRA 72, Rio de Janeiro, Brazil, Aug. 26-Sept. 2, 1972.

Aeolus, God of Winds — AP182

1973, Sept. 14   Photo.   Wmk. 300
C415 AP182 80c brt pink, blk & bl   .60   .25
Cent. of intl. meteorological cooperation.

Nicolaus Copernicus — AP183

Wmk. 300
1973, Oct. 10   Photo.   Perf. 14
C416 AP183 80c slate green   .30   .25
500th anniversary of the birth of Nicolaus Copernicus (1473-1543), Polish astronomer.

Art and Science Type of 1971

Designs: No. C417, Aztec calendar stone. No. C418, Carlos de Sigüenza y Gongora (1645-1700), mathematician, astronomer. No. C419, Francisco Diaz Covarrubias (1833-1889), topographer. No. C420, Joaquin Gallo (1882-1965), geographer, astronomer. No. C421, Luis Enrique Erro (1897-1955), founder of Tonanzintla Observatory.

Imprint includes "1973"

1973, Nov. 21   Wmk. 350
C417 AP161 80c car & sl grn   .25   .25
C418 AP161 80c multicolored   .25   .25
C419 AP161 80c multicolored   .25   .25
C420 AP161 80c multicolored   .25   .25
C421 AP161 80c multicolored   .25   .25
      Nos. C417-C421 (5)   1.25   1.25

Type of 1950-52

Design: Mexico City University Stadium.

Imprint: "Talleres de Imp. de Est. y Valores-Mexico"
1973   Unwmk.   Perf. 11
C422 AP81 80c claret, I   3.00   .95
Fluorescent printing on front or back of stamps consisting of beehive pattern and diagonal inscription.

San Martin Monument — AP184

Wmk. 350
1973, Dec. 14   Photo.   Perf. 14
C423 AP184 80c orange, indigo & yel   .25   .25
Erection of a monument to San Martin in Mexico City, a gift of Argentina.

Palace of Cortes, Cuernavaca — AP185

Wmk. 300
1974, Feb. 22   Litho.   Perf. 14
C424 AP185 80c black & multi   .25   .25
EXMEX 73 Philatelic Exhibition, Cuernavaca, Apr. 7-15.

Gold Brooch, Mochica Culture AP186

1974, Mar. 6   Photo.   Wmk. 300
C425 AP186 80c gold & multi   .25   .25
Exhibition of Peruvian gold treasures, Mexico City, 1973-74.

Luggage — AP187

1974, Mar. 22   Perf. 14
C426 AP187 80c multicolored   .25   .25
16th Convention of the Federation of Latin American Tourist Organizations (COTAL), Acapulco, May 1974.

CEPAL Emblem AP188

1974, Mar. 22
C427 AP188 80c black & multi   .25   .25
a.   Red omitted   100.00
25th anniversary (in 1973) of the Economic Commission for Latin America (CEPAL).

"The Enameled Casserole," by Picasso — AP189

1974, Mar. 29   Wmk. 300
C428 AP189 80c multicolored   .35   .25
Pablo Ruiz Picasso (1881-1973), painter and sculptor.

EXFILMEX Type of 1974
1974, July 26   Perf. 13x12
C429 A305 80c buff, red brn & blk   .25   .25
See note after No. 1065.

Biplane — AP190

Perf. 13x12
1974, Aug. 20   Photo.   Wmk. 300
C430 AP190 80c shown   .25   .25
C431 AP190 2p Jet plane   .25   .25
50th anniversary of Mexican Airlines (MEXICANA).

Transmitter and Waves Circling Globe — AP191

1974, Oct. 4   Wmk. 300   Perf. 14
C432 AP191 2p multicolored   .25   .25
First International Congress of Electric and Electronic Communications, Sept. 17-21.

Volleyball
AP192

1974, Oct. 12   *Perf. 13x12*
C433 AP192 2p orange, bis & blk   .25 .25
8th World Volleyball Championship. Perforation holes are of two sizes.

Souvenir Sheet

Mexico #O1, Colombia #130,
Venezuela #22, Peru #C320, Brazil
#992, Mexico #123 — AP193

Wmk. 300
1974, Oct. 26   Photo.   *Imperf.*
C434 AP193 10p multicolored   3.50 1.50
EXFILMEX 74, 5th Inter-American Philatelic Exhibition, Mexico City, Oct. 26-Nov. 3. Exists with red omitted.

Felipe Carrillo Puerto
AP194

1974, Nov. 8   *Perf. 14*
C435 AP194 80c grn & gldn brn   .25 .25
Birth centenary of Felipe Carrillo Puerto (1874-1924), politician and journalist.

Mask, Bat and Catcher's Mitt — AP195

1974, Nov. 29   Wmk. 350   *Perf. 14*
C436 AP195 80c multi   .25 .25
Mexican Baseball League, 50th anniversary.

Man's Face, Mailbox, Colonial Period AP196

Design: 2p, Heinrich von Stephan, contemporary engraving.

1974, Dec. 13   Photo.   Wmk. 300
C437 AP196 80c multicolored   .25 .25
C438 AP196 2p green & ocher   .25 .25
Centenary of Universal Postal Union.

Art and Science Type of 1971
Designs: No. C439, Mayan mural (8th century), Bonampak, Chiapas. No. C440, First musical score printed in Mexico, 1556. No. C441, Miguel Lerdo de Tejada (1869-1941), composer. No. C442, Silvestre Revueltas (1899-1940), composer (bronze bust). No. C443, Angela Peralta (1845-1883), singer.

Imprint includes "1974"
1974, Dec. 20   **Wmk. 300**
C439 AP161 80c multi   .25 .25
C440 AP161 80c multi   .25 .25
C441 AP161 80c multi   .25 .25
C442 AP161 80c multi   .25 .25
C443 AP161 80c multi   .25 .25
Nos. C439-C443 (5)   1.25 1.25

Types of 1950-56
Designs (as 1950-56 issues): 40c, San Luis Potosi, head. 60c, Leon Guzman and Ignacio Ramirez. 1.60p, Chiapas, Mayan bas-relief. 1.90p, Guerrero, Acapulco waterfront. 4.30p, Oaxaca, dance. 5.20p, Guerrero, view of Taxco. 5.60p, Michoacan, masks. 50p, Valentin Gomez Farias and Melchor Ocampo.

Engraved (40c), Photogravure
Perf. 11 (40c, 1.60p), 14
1975   **Wmk. 300**
C444 AP81 40c bluish gray   .35 .25
C445 AP92 60c yellow grn   .90 .30
C446 AP81 1.60p red   3.00 .35
C447 AP81 1.90p rose red   3.00 .35
C448 AP81 4.30p ultra   1.00 .25
C449 AP81 5.20p purple   1.75 .40
C450 AP81 5.60p blue grn   2.25 .50
C451 AP92 50p dk bl & brick
                      red   15.00 3.50
Nos. C444-C451 (8)   27.25 5.90

Women's Year Emblem — AP199

1975, Jan. 3   Wmk. 300   *Perf. 14*
C456 AP199 1.60p brt pink & blk   .25 .25
International Women's Year 1975.

Declaration, UN Emblem, Mexican Flag AP200

1975, Feb. 7   Photo.   Wmk. 300
C457 AP200 1.60p multi   .25 .25
Declaration of Economic Rights and Duties of Nations.

Balsa Raft "Acali" — AP201

1975, Mar. 7   Wmk. 300   *Perf. 14*
C458 AP201 80c multicolored   .25 .25
Trans-Atlantic voyage of the "Acali" from Canary Islands to Yucatan, May-Aug. 1973.

Dr. Miguel Jimenez, by I. Ramirez — AP202

1975, Mar. 24   Unwmk.   Perf. 14
C459 AP202 2p multicolored   .25 .25
Fifth World Gastroenterology Congress.

Miguel de Cervantes — AP203

1975, Apr. 26   Photo.   Unwmk.
C460 AP203 1.60p bl blk & dk car   .25 .25
Third International Cervantes Festival, Guanajuato, Apr. 26-May 11.

Four-reales Coin, 1535 — AP204

1975, May 2
C461 AP204 1.60p bl, gold & blk   .25 .25
Intl. Numismatic Convention, Mexico City, Mar. 28-30, 1974.

Salvador Novo, by Roberto Montenegro — AP205

1975, May 9
C462 AP205 1.60p multi   .25 .25
Salvador Novo (1904-1974), author.

Mural, Siqueiros — AP206

1975, May 16
C463 AP206 1.60p multi   .25 .25
David Alfaro Siqueiros (1896-1974), painter.

UN and IWY Emblems AP207

1975, June 19
C464 AP207 1.60p ultra & pink   .25 .25
International Women's Year World Conference, Mexico City, June 19-July 2.

Mexico City Coat of Arms AP208

Unwmk.
1975, Aug. 1   Photo.   Perf. 14
C465 AP208 1.60p multi   .25 .25
650th anniv. of Tenochtitlan (Mexico City).

Domingo F. Sarmiento AP209

Teachers' Monument AP210

Unwmk.
1975, Aug. 9   Photo.   Perf. 14
C466 AP209 1.60p brown & sl grn   .25 .25
1st International Congress of Third World Educators, Acapulco, Aug. 5-9. Domingo Faustino Sarmiento (1811-1888), Argentinian statesman, writer and educator.

1975, Aug. 9
C467 AP210 4.30p green & ocher   .35 .25
Mexican-Lebanese friendship. The monument in Mexico City, by I Naffa al Rozzi, shows Cadmus, a mythical Phoenician, teaching the alphabet.

7th Pan American Games' Emblem AP211

1975, Aug. 29
C468 AP211 1.60p multi   .25 .25
Pan American Games, Mexico City, Oct. 13-26.

Dr. Atl, Self-portrait AP212

Unwmk.

1975, Oct. 3   Photo.   Perf. 14
C469 AP212 4.30p multi   .35 .25

Geraldo Murillo ("Dr. Atl," 1875-1924), painter and writer, birth centenary.

Globe and Traffic Circle — AP213

1975, Oct. 17
C470 AP213 1.60p bl, blk & gray   .25 .25

15th World Road Congress, Mexico City, Oct. 12-26.

Type of 1950-52

Designs: 40c, San Luis Potosi, head. 60c, Leon Guzman & Ignacio Ramirez. 80c, Mexico City University stadium. 1p, Puebla, Half Moon dance. 1.60p, Chiapas, Mayan bas-relief. 5p, Queretaro, architecture. 5.60p, Michoacan, masks. 10p, Miguel Hidalgo. 20p, Modern building.

Engraved (40c, 1p), Photogravure
Perf. 11 (40c, 80c, 1p, 1.60p), 14
1975-76   Unwmk.

C471	AP81	40c bluish gray	.35	.35
C471A	AP92	60c yel grn	1,200.	
C472	AP81	80c claret, II	.60	.50
C473	AP81	1p grysh grn	1.00	.80
C474	AP81	1.60p red	1.75	1.00
C476	AP81	5p dk brn & org ('76)	1.50	1.00
a.		5p dark brown & red orange	2.00	2.00
C477	AP81	5.60p bluish grn ('76)	4.75	3.25
C479	AP81	10p blk & grn ('76)	4.00	2.50
C480	AP81	20p red & dl grn ('76)	7.50	4.00
	Nos. C471, C472-C480 (8)		21.45	13.40

Bicycle and Export Emblem AP214

Designs: Export Emblem and 30c, Copper vase. 80c, Overalls. 1.90p, Oil valves. 2p, Books. 4p, Honey. 4.30p, Strawberry. 5p, Motor vehicles. 5.20p, Farm machinery. 5.60p, Cotton. 20p, Film. 50p, Cotton thread.

1975-82   Unwmk.   Photo.   Perf. 14

C486	AP214	30c copper ('76)	.25	.25
C489	AP214	80c dull blue ('76)	.25	.25
C491	AP214	1.60p black & org	.35	.25
a.		Thin paper ('81)	1.00	.25
C492	AP214	1.90p ver & dk grn	.35	.25
C493	AP214	2p ultra & gold ('76)	.65	.25
C495	AP214	4p yel bis & brn ('82)	1.25	.25
C496	AP214	4.30p brt pink & ol	.50	.25
C497	AP214	5p dk bl & ocher ('76)	1.50	.25
C498	AP214	5.20p red & blk ('76)	.75	.40
C499	AP214	5.60p yel grn & org ('76)	.35	.25
C503	AP214	20p multi, thin paper ('81)	1.00	.25
C508	AP214	50p multi ('82)	4.00	2.00
	Nos. C486-C508 (12)		11.20	4.90

See Nos. C594-C603.

Art and Science Type of 1971

Designs: No. C513, Title page of "Medical History of New Spain," by Francisco Hernandez, 1628. No. C514, Alfonso L. Herrera (1868-1942), biologist. No. C515, Title page, Aztec Herbal, 1552. No. C516, Arturo S. Rosenblueth (1900-1970). No. C517, Alfredo Augusto Duges (1826-1910) French-born naturalist.

Imprint includes "1975"

1975, Nov. 21   Unwmk.   Perf. 14

C513	AP161	1.60p buff, red & blk	.25	.25
C514	AP161	1.60p vio bl & multi	.25	.25
C515	AP161	1.60p black & multi	.25	.25
C516	AP161	1.60p gray & multi	.25	.25
C517	AP161	1.60p green & multi	.25	.25
a.		Thin paper	400.00	
	Nos. C513-C517 (5)		1.25	1.25

Telephone AP216

60-peso Gold Coin, Oaxaca, 1917 AP217

1976, Mar. 10   Photo.
C518 AP216 1.60p gray & blk   .25 .25

Centenary of first telephone call by Alexander Graham Bell, Mar. 10, 1876.

1976, Mar. 25   Photo.   Unwmk.
C519 AP217 1.60p black, ocher & yel   .25 .25

4th International Numismatic Convention, Mexico City, March 1976.

Rain God Tlaloc and Calles Dam AP218

1976, Mar. 29   Perf. 14
C520 AP218 1.00p vio brn & dk grn   .25 .25

12th International Great Dams Congress, Mar. 29-Apr. 2.

Perforation Gauge AP219

1976, May 7   Photo.   Unwmk.
C521 AP219 1.60p blk, red & bl   .25 .25

Interphil 76 International Philatelic Exhibition, Philadelphia, Pa., May 29-June 6.

Rainbow over City — AP220

1976, May 31   Unwmk.   Perf. 14
C522 AP220 1.60p black & multi   .25 .25

Habitat, UN Conf. on Human Settlements, Vancouver, Canada, May 31-June 11.

Liberty Bell — AP221

1976, July 4   Photo.   Perf. 14
C523 AP221 1.60p ultra & red   .25 .25

American Bicentennial.

"Peace" — AP222

Design: "Peace" written in Chinese, Japanese, Hebrew, Hindi and Arabic.

1976, Aug. 3   Photo.   Perf. 14
C524 AP222 1.60p multi   .25 .25

30th Intl. Cong. of Science and Humanities of Asia and North Africa, Mexico, Aug. 3-8.

Television Screen AP223

1976, Aug. 24   Photo.   Unwmk.
C525 AP223 1.60p multi   .25 .25

1st Latin-American Forum on Children's Television.

Luminescence

Fluorescent airmail stamps include Nos. C265, C265c, C288, C357-C358, C390-C415, C422-C423.

Airmail stamps issued on both ordinary and fluorescent paper include Nos. C220, C220D-C220E, C220G-C220H, C265b, C266-C268, C286.

Sky, Sun, Water and Earth AP224

1976, Nov. 8   Photo.   Perf. 14
C526 AP224 1.60p multi   .25 .25

World Conservation Day.

Art and Science Type of 1971

Designs: No. C527, Coatlicue, Mother of Earth, Aztec sculpture. No. C528, El Caballito, statue of Charles IV of Spain, by Manuel Tolsá. No. C529, Chief Tlahuicole, bronze statue by Manuel Vilar. No. C530, Today's God, Money, seated ceramic figure, by L. Ortiz Monasterio. No. C531, Signal, abstract sculpture by Angela Gurria.

Imprint includes "1976"

1976, Dec. 10   Photo.   Perf. 14

C527	AP161	1.60p black & yel	.25	.25
C528	AP161	1.60p blk & red brn	.25	.25
C529	AP101	1.00p black & multi	.25	.25
C530	AP161	1.60p car & multi	.25	.25
C531	AP161	1.60p carmine & blk	.25	.25
	Nos. C527-C531 (5)		1.25	1.25

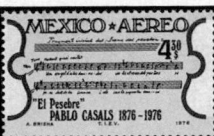

Score for El Pesebre by Casals AP225

1976, Dec. 29
C532 AP225 4.30p lt bl, blk & brn   .35 .25

Pablo Casals (1876-1973), cellist and composer, birth centenary.

Mankind Destroyed by Nuclear Power AP226

1977, Feb. 14   Photo.   Perf. 14
C533 AP226 1.60p multi   .25 .25
a.   Wmk. 300   50.00 40.00

10th anniv. of the Agreement of Tlatelolco, banning nuclear arms in Latin America.

Soccer AP227

Anniversary Emblem — AP228

1977, Aug. 23   Wmk. 300   Perf. 14
C534 AP227 1.60p multicolored   .25 .25
C535 AP228 4.30p black, bl & yel   .35 .25

Mexican Soccer Fed., 50th anniv.

Hands and Scales AP229

1977, Sept. 23   Photo.   Perf. 14
C536 AP229 1.60p org, brn & blk   .25 .25

Federal Council of Reconciliation and Arbitration, 50th anniversary.

Arms of Mexico and Spain AP230

1.90p, Maps of Mexico & Spain. 4.30p, Pres. José Lopez Portillo & King Juan Carlos.

1977, Oct. 8   Perf. 14

C537	AP230	1.60p dull bl & blk	.25	.25
C538	AP230	1.90p lt grn & maroon	.25	.25
C539	AP230	4.30p tan, grn & brn	.35	.25
	Nos. C537-C539 (3)		.85	.60

Resumption of diplomatic relations with Spain.

Tlaloc, the Rain God
AP231

Ludwig van Beethoven
AP232

Wmk. 300

1977, Nov. 4   Photo.   *Perf. 14*

C540   AP231   1.60p multi   .25   .25

National Central Observatory, centenary.

1977, Nov. 10   Photo.

C541   AP232   1.60p brt grn & brn   .25   .25
C542   AP232   4.30p lilac rose & bl   .30   .25

Tractor and Dam
AP233

1977, Nov. 25   Photo.   *Perf. 14*

C543   AP233   1.60p multi   .25   .25

United Nations Desertification Conference.

Mexico City-Cuernavaca Highway — AP234

1977, Nov. 30

C544   AP234   1.60p multi   .25   .25

25th anniversary of first national highway.

Arms of Campeche — AP235

1977, Dec. 3

C545   AP235   1.60p multi   .25   .25

200th anniv. of the naming of Campeche.

Congress Emblem
AP236

1977, Dec. 9

C546   AP236   1.60p multi   .25   .25

20th World Congress for Education, Hygiene and Recreation, July 18-24, 1977.

Freighter Navimex
AP237

1977, Dec. 16

C547   AP237   1.60p multi   .25   .25

60th anniv. of National Merchant Marine.

Mayan Dancer, Jaina — AP238

Pre-Columbian Sculptures: No. C549, Aztec dance god. No. C550, Snake dancer, bas-relief. No. C551, Monte Alban, bas-relief. No. C552, Totonaca figurine.

1977, Dec. 26   *Perf. 14*

C548   AP238   1.60p sal, blk & car   .25   .25
C549   AP238   1.60p lt & dk bl &   blk   .25   .25
C550   AP238   1.60p yel, blk &   gray   .25   .25
C551   AP238   1.60p bl grn, blk &   grn   .25   .25
C552   AP238   1.60p gray, blk &   red brn   .25   .25
      Nos. C548-C552 (5)   1.25   1.25

Mexican art.

Tumor Clinic, by David A. Siqueiros — AP239

4.30p, La Raza Medical Center, by Diego Rivera.

1978, Jan. 19   Photo.   Wmk. 300

C553   AP239   1.60p multi   .25   .25
C554   AP239   4.30p multi   .30   .25

Mexican Social Security Institute, 35th anniv.

Moorish Fountain — AP240

1978, Mar. 1   Photo.   *Perf. 14*

C555   AP240   1.60p multi   .25   .25

Founding of Chiapa de Corzo, Chiapas, 450th anniv.

Oil Industry Type of 1978

Designs: 1.60p, Gen. Lazaro Cardenas. 4.30p, Offshore oil rig.

Wmk. 300

1978, Mar. 18   Photo.   *Perf. 14*

C556   A343   1.60p brt bl & lil rose   .25   .25
C557   A343   4.30p bl, brt bl & blk   .30   .25

Oil industry nationalization, 40th anniv.

Arms of Diego de Mazariegos
AP241

Wmk. 300

1978, Apr. 3   Photo.   *Perf. 14*

C558   AP241   1.60p pink, blk & pur   .25   .25

400th anniversary of the founding of San Cristobal de las Casas, Chiapas, by Diego de Mazariegos.

Blood Pressure Gauge, Map of Mexico
AP242

Globe, Snake, Hand Holding Stethoscope
AP243

1978, Apr. 7

C559   AP242   1.60p dk bl & car   .25   .25
C560   AP243   4.30p org & dk bl   .30   .25

Drive against hypertension and World Health Day.

X-ABC1 Plane
AP244

1978, Apr. 15

C561   AP244   1.60p ultra & multi   .25   .25
C562   AP244   4.30p ultra & multi   .30   .25

1st Mexican airmail route, 50th anniv.

Globe, Cogwheel, UN Emblem — AP245

4.30p, Globe, flags, cogwheel, UN emblem.

1978, Apr. 21

C563   AP245   1.60p multi   .25   .25
C564   AP245   4.30p multi   .30   .25

World Conference on Technical Cooperation of Underdeveloped Countries.

Soccer — AP246

Designs: 1.90p, Goalkeeper catching ball. 4.30p, Soccer player.

Wmk. 300

1978, June 1   Photo.   *Perf. 14*

C565   AP246   1.60p multi   .25   .25
C566   AP246   1.90p multi   .25   .25
C567   AP246   4.30p multi   .35   .25
      Nos. C565-C567 (3)   .85   .75

11th World Cup Soccer Championship, Argentina, June 1-25.

Francisco (Pancho) Villa
AP247

1978, June 5

C568   AP247   1.60p multi   .25   .25

Pancho Villa (1878-1923), revolutionary leader.

Mexico No. C6, Independence Monument, Washington Monument — AP248

1978, June 11

C569   AP248   1.60p ol gray & red   .25   .25

50th anniversary of flight Mexico to Washington by Emilio Carranza (1905-1928).

Woman and Calendar Stone — AP249

Wmk. 300

1978, July 15   Photo.   *Perf. 14*

C570   AP249   1.60p rose, blk & brn   .25   .25
C571   AP249   1.90p brt grn, blk &   brn   .25   .25
C572   AP249   4.30p org, blk & brn   .35   .25
      Nos. C570-C572 (3)   .85   .75

Miss Universe contest, Acapulco, July 1978.

Alvaro Obregón
AP250

1978, July 17

C573   AP250   1.60p multi   .25   .25

Obregón (1880-1928), president of Mexico.

Geographical Institute Type of 1978

Institute emblem in different arrangements.

1978, July 21   Photo.   Wmk. 300

C574   A344   1.60p emerald & blk   .25   .25
C575   A344   4.30p ocher & blk   .35   .25

Pan-American Institute for Geography and History, 50th anniversary.

Sun Rising over Ciudad Obregón AP251

1978, Aug. 4   *Perf. 14*
C576 AP251 1.60p multi   .25 .25
Founding of the city of Obregón, 50th anniv.

Mayan Figure, Castle and Pawn AP252

Aristotle (384-322 B.C.), Philosopher AP253

1978, Aug. 19   **Photo.**   *Perf. 14*
C577 AP252 1.60p multi   .25 .25
C578 AP252 4.30p multi   .35 .25
World Youth Team Chess Championship, Ajedrez, Aug. 19-Sept. 7.

1978, Aug. 25
Design: 4.30p, Statue of Aristotle.
C579 AP253 1.60p multi   .25 .25
C580 AP253 4.30p multi   .35 .25

Mule Deer AP254

Man's Head, Dove, UN Emblem AP255

1978, Sept. 8   **Photo.**   **Wmk. 300**
C581 AP254 1.60p shown   .25 .25
C582 AP254 1.60p Ocelot   .35 .25
Protected animals.

1978, Sept. 22   *Perf. 14*
4.30p, Woman's head, dove, UN emblem.
C583 AP255 1.60p ver, gray & blk   .25 .25
C584 AP255 4.30p lil, gray & blk   .35 .25
Anti-Apartheid Year.

Emblem — AP256

Wmk. 300
1978, Oct. 23   **Photo.**   *Perf. 14*
C585 AP256 1.60p multi   .25 .25
13th Congress of International Union of Architects, Mexico City, Oct. 23-27.

Dr. Rafael Lucio (1819-1886) AP257

Franz Schubert, "Death and the Maiden" AP258

1978, Nov. 13   **Wmk. 350**
C586 AP257 1.60p yellow grn   .25 .25
11th International Anti-Leprosy Congress.

1978, Nov. 19   **Photo.**   *Perf. 14*
C587 AP258 4.30p brn, grn & blk   .35 .25
Schubert (1797-1828), Austrian composer.

Children, Christmas Decorations AP259

Antonio Vivaldi AP260

Wmk. 350
1978, Nov. 22   **Photo.**   *Perf. 14*
C588 AP259 1.60p multi   .25 .25
Christmas 1978.

1978, Dec. 1
C589 AP260 4.30p multi   .35 .25
Antonio Vivaldi (1675-1741), Italian violinist and composer.

Wright Brothers' Flyer AP261

Design: 4.30p, Flyer, different view.

1978, Dec. 17
C590 AP261 1.60p multi   .25 .25
C591 AP261 4.30p multi   .35 .25
75th anniversary of 1st powered flight.

Einstein and his Equation AP262

Wmk. 300
1979, Apr. 20   **Photo.**   *Perf. 14*
C592 AP262 1.60p multi   .25 .25
Albert Einstein (1879-1955), theoretical physicist.

Rowland Hill — AP263

1979, Apr. 27
C593 AP263 1.60p multi   .25 .25
Sir Rowland Hill (1795-1879), originator of penny postage.

Export Type of 1975
Designs: Export Emblem and 50c, Circuit board. 1.60p, Bicycle. 1.90p, Oil valves. 2.50p, Tomato. 4p, Honey. 5p, Motor vehicles. 10p, Citrus fruit. 50p, Cotton thread.

1979-81   **Photo.**   **Wmk. 300**
C594 AP214   50c ocher & red
               brn   .35 .25
C596 AP214 1.60p black & org   .35 .25
C597 AP214 1.90p ver & dk grn
               ('81)   .50 .40
C599 AP214 2.50p ver & grn   .35 .25
C600 AP214   4p yel bis & brn
               ('81)   .35 .25
C601 AP214   5p dk bl & dl
               org   4.50 .50
C602 AP214 10p grn & yel
               grn ('81)   .90 .75
C603 AP214 50p multicolored   6.00 1.50
    Nos. C594-C603 (8)   13.30 4.15
No. C600 exists with brown omitted.

Children, Child's Drawing — AP264

1979, May 16
C604 AP264 1.60p multi   .25 .25
International Year of the Child.

Registered Letter from Mexico to Rome, 1880 — AP265

Wmk. 300
1979, June 7   **Photo.**   *Perf. 14*
C605 AP265 1.60p multi   .25 .25
MEPSIPEX '79, 3rd Intl. Exhibition of Elmhurst Philatelic Society, Mexico City, 6/7-10.

Sports Type of 1979
Designs: 1.60p, Games emblem. 4.30p, Symbolic flame and birds. 10p, Women gymnasts, horiz.

1979, June 15
C606 A348 1.60p multi   .25 .25
C607 A348 4.30p multi   .35 .25

Souvenir Sheet
Imperf
C608 A348 10p multi   2.00 2.00
No. C608 has simulated perforations.

University Type of 1979
Paintings: 1.60p, The Return of Quetzalcoatl, by Chavez Morado. 4.30p, Students Reaching for Culture, by Alfaro Siqueiros.

Messenger and UPU Emblem AP266

1979, July 10   *Perf. 14*
C609 A350 1.60p multi   .25 .25
C610 A350 4.30p multi   .35 .25

1979, July 27   **Photo.**   **Wmk. 300**
C611 AP266 1.60p multi   .25 .25
Cent. of Mexico's membership in UPU.

Sports Type of 1979
1979, Sept. 2   **Wmk. 300**   *Perf. 14*
C612 A352 1.60p Tennis   .25 .25
C613 A352 5.50p Swimming   .35 .25

Souvenir Sheet
Imperf
C614 A352   10p Various sports 1.75 1.75

Tourism Type of 1979
No. C615, Agua Azul Waterfall, Chiapas. No. C616, King Coliman statue, Colima.

Wmk. 300
1979, Sept. 28   **Photo.**   *Perf. 14*
C615 A353 1.60p multi   .25 .25
C616 A353 1.60p multi   .25 .25

Graphic Design AP267

1979, Oct. 14   **Photo.**   **Wmk. 300**
C617 AP267 1.60p multi   .25 .25
ICSID, 11th Congress and Assembly of the Intl. Industrial Design Council, Oct. 1979.

Mail Service Type of 1979
Designs: 1.60p, Martin Enriquez de Almanza, Viceroy of New Spain. 5.50p, King Philip II of Spain. 10p, Sailing ship, horiz.

1979, Oct. 26
C618 A354 1.60p multi   .25 .25
C619 A354 5.50p multi   .35 .25

Souvenir Sheet
Imperf
C620 A354 10p multi   4.50 1.50
No. C620 contains stamp with simulated perfs.

Early Lamp — AP268

1979, Oct. 21   **Wmk. 300**
C621 AP268 1.60p multi   .25 .25
Centenary of invention of electric light.

Union Emblem AP269

Wmk. 300

1979, Nov. 12　Photo.　Perf. 14
C622　AP269　1.60p multi　　.25　.25
Latin American Universities Union, 8th general assembly.

Christmas Type of 1979

Design: 1.60p, Girl and Christmas tree.

1979, Nov. 15
C623　A355　1.60p multi　　.25　.25

Moon Symbol from Mexican Codex AP270

1979, Nov. 30
C624　AP270　2.50p multi　　.25　.25
Apollo 11 moon landing, 10th anniversary.

Monument Type of 1980

Stone Sculptures: 1.60p, Tlaloc, water god. 5.50p, Coyolxauqui, goddess.

1980, Feb. 16　Photo.　Perf. 14
C625　A356　1.60p multi　　.25　.25
C626　A356　5.50p multi　　.35　.25

16th Century Church, Acolman AP271

16th Century Churches in: No. C628, Actopan Convent. No. C629, Tlayacapan. No. C630, Yanhuitlan. No. C631, Yuriria. No. C628 actually shows Tlayacapan; No. C629, Actopan convent (inscriptions reversed).

1980, Feb. 1
C627　AP271　1.60p multi　　.25　.25
C628　AP271　1.60p multi　　.25　.25
C629　AP271　1.60p multi　　.25　.25
C630　AP271　1.60p multi　　.25　.25
C631　AP271　1.60p multi　　.25　.25
　Nos. C627-C631 (5)　　1.25　1.25

Flora and Fauna Types of 1980

1980, Mar. 8　　　　Perf. 14
C632　A357　1.60p Flamingo　　.25　.25
C633　A358　1.60p Vanilla plant　.25　.25

Jules Verne AP272

Wmk. 300

1980, Mar. 24　Photo.　Perf. 14
C634　AP272　5.50p blk & red brn　.35　.25
Jules Verne (1828-1905) French science fiction writer.

Skeleton Smoking Cigar, UN Emblem AP273

1980, Apr. 7　　　　Perf. 14
C635　AP273　1.60p multi　　.25　.25
World Health Day/Fight against cigarette smoking.

Costume Type

1980, Apr. 26　　　Perf. 14
C636　A359　1.60p Chiapaneca, Chiapas　　.25　.25

Items inscribed "MEXICO" and "correo aereo" picturing Emiliano Zapata are not postage stamps.

AIR POST OFFICIAL STAMPS

Nos. C4 and C3 Overprinted in Black or Red

1929　　Wmk. 156　　Perf. 12
CO1　AP1　25c dk grn & gray brn　　4.50　3.25
　a.　Without period　20.00　20.00
CO2　AP1　25c dk grn & gray brn (R)　　4.00　5.00
　a.　Without period　21.00　21.00
CO2B　AP1　25c brn car & gray brn　　10.00　12.50
　c.　Without period　25.00　25.00
　Nos. CO1-CO2B (3)　18.50　20.75
Set, never hinged　35.00

Types of Regular Issue of 1926 Overprinted in Red

1929, Oct. 15　　　Unwmk.
CO3　A90　2c black　75.00　90.00
CO4　A91　4c black　75.00　90.00
CO5　A90　5c black　75.00　90.00
CO6　A91　10c black　75.00　90.00
CO7　A92　20c black　75.00　90.00
CO8　A92　30c black　75.00　90.00
CO9　A92　40c black　75.00　90.00
　Nos. CO3-CO9 (7)　525.00　630.00
Set, never hinged　1,100.

Horizontal Overprint

CO10　A93　1p black　2,250.　2,250.
　Never hinged　4,000.
Nos. CO3-CO9 also exist with overprint reading up.

No. C26 Overprinted in Black

1930　　　　　Wmk. 156
CO11　AP4　20c black violet　1.10　1.75
　Never hinged　2.25
　a.　Without period　20.00　20.00
　b.　Inverted overprint　18.00　18.00
　c.　As "a," inverted overprint　210.00　210.00
No. CO11 with red overprint is believed not to have been issued for postal purposes.

Plane over Mexico City OA1

1930　　　　　　Engr.
CO12　OA1　20c gray black　6.00　6.00
CO13　OA1　35c lt violet　1.10　1.90
CO14　OA1　40c ol brn & dp bl　1.25　1.75
CO15　OA1　70c vio & ol gray　1.25　1.75
　Nos. CO12-CO15 (4)　9.60　11.40
Set, never hinged　22.50

No. CO12 Surcharged in Red

1931
CO16　OA1　15c on 20c　.85　1.40
　Never hinged　1.60
　a.　Inverted surcharge　140.00
　b.　Double surcharge　140.00

No. C20 Overprinted

1932　　Rouletted 13, 13½
CO17　AP3　5c light blue　.80　.90
　Never hinged　1.75

Air Post Stamps of 1927-32 Overprinted

On No. C1a

1932　　Unwmk.　　Perf. 12
CO18　AP1　50c dk bl & cl　1,000.　1,000.
　Never hinged　2,000.

On Nos. C2, C2a
Wmk. 156

CO19　AP1　50c dk bl & red brn　1.25　1.50
　Never hinged　2.25
　a.　50c dark blue & claret　1.40　1.60
　See note after No. C2.

On Nos. C11 and C12

1932　　　　　　Perf. 12
CO20　AP3　10c violet　22.50　25.00
　Never hinged　45.00
CO21　AP3　15c carmine　350.00　375.00
　Never hinged　700.00

On Nos. C21 to C23
Rouletted 13, 13½

CO22　AP3　10c violet　.35　.55
CO23　AP3　15c carmine　1.40　2.00
CO24　AP3　20c brn olive　1.40　2.00

Nos. C20, C21 C23 and C25 Overprinted

1933-34　　　　Rouletted 13½
CO25　AP3　5c light blue　.30　.55
CO26　AP3　10c violet ('34)　.30　.90
CO27　AP3　20c brown olive　.75　1.25
CO28　AP3　50c red brn ('34)　1.25　1.90

On No. C2
Perf. 12

CO29　AP1　50c dk bl & red brn　1.10　2.00
　a.　50c dark blue & claret　1.60　2.50

On No. C11
Perf. 12

CO30　AP3　10c violet ('34)　140.00　175.00
　a.　Double overprint　325.00
　　Forgeries exist.

SPECIAL DELIVERY STAMPS

Motorcycle Postman SD1

1919　　Unwmk.　Engr.　Perf. 12
E1　SD1　20c red & black　70.00　2.75

1923　　　　　Wmk. 156
E2　SD1　20c blk car & blk　.30　.25
　For overprint see No. E7

Messenger with Quipu — SD2

1934
E3　SD2　10c brn red & blue　.30　.50

Indian Archer — SD3

Imprint: "Oficina Impresora de Hacienda Mexico."

1934　　　　Perf. 10x10½
E4　SD3　10c black violet　1.50　.50
　See Nos. E5-E6, E8-E9.

Redrawn

Imprint: "Talleres de Imp. de Est. y Valores-Mexico."

1938-41　　Photo.　Perf. 14
E5　SD3　10c slate violet　.75　.25
　a.　Unwatermarked　50.00
E6　SD3　20c orange red ('41)　.50　.25
Imperforate examples of No. E6 were not regularly issued.

No. E2 Overprinted "1940" in Violet

1940　　　Engr.　Perf. 12
E7　SD1　20c red & black　.40　.25

> Catalogue values for unused stamps in this section, from this point to the end of the section, are for Never Hinged items.

Redrawn Archer Type of 1941

1944-47　Wmk. 272　Photo.　Perf. 14
E8　SD3　20c orange red　　1.40　.25

Wmk. 279
E9　SD3　20c orange red ('47)　1.75　.25

Special Delivery Messenger SD4

Messengers' Hands Transferring Letter — SD5

1950-51   Photo.   Wmk. 279
E10	SD4	25c bright red	.35	.25
E11	SD5	60c dk bl grn ('51)	2.00	.95

Redrawn
1951
E12	SD4	25c bright red	40.00 5.00

Sharper Impression, heavier shading; motorcycle sidecar ½mm from "s" of "centavos;" imprint wider, beginning under "n" of "inmediata."

Second Redrawing
1952
E13	SD4	25c bright red	15.00 2.00

Design 35½mm wide (33mm on Nos. E10 and E12); finer lettering at left, and height of letters in imprint reduced 50 per cent; three distinct lines in tires.

Redrawn Type of 1951
1954   Wmk. 300
E14	SD4	25c red orange	.45 .25

Type of 1951
1954
E15	SD5	60c dk blue grn	.55 1.10

Hands and Pigeon SD6

Plane Circling Globe SD7

1956   Wmk. 300   Photo.   Perf. 14
E16	SD6	35c red lilac	.25	.25
E17	SD7	80c henna brown	.35	1.40

1962
E18	SD6	50c green	.80	.25
E19	SD7	1.20p dark purple	1.25	1.40

1964   Wmk. 350
E20	SD6	50c green	.65	.25
E21	SD7	1.20p dk purple	1.40	1.00

1973   Unwmk.
E22	SD6	50c green	3.50 3.25

Fluorescent printing on front or back consists of beehive pattern and diagonal inscription.

1975   Wmk. 300
E23	SD6	2p orange	.25	1.00
E24	SD7	5p vio bl	1.25	.90

1976   Unwmk.
E25	SD6	2p red org	.25	40
E26	SD7	5p dk vio bl	.35	1.00

Watch SD8

1976   Unwmk.   Photo.   Perf. 14
E27	SD8	2p org & blk	.25	1.00

INSURED LETTER STAMPS

Insured Letters — IL1

Registered Mailbag — IL2

Safe — IL3

1935   Engr.   Wmk. 156   Perf. 10½
G1	IL1	10c vermilion	1.75	.75
a.		Perf. 10x10½		
G2	IL2	50c dk bl	10.00	.60
G3	IL3	1p turq grn	1.25	.85
		Nos. G1-G3 (3)	13.00	2.20

Nos. G1 and G4 were issued both with and without imprint.

> Catalogue values for unused stamps in this section, from this point to the end of the section, are for Never Hinged items.

1944-45   Wmk. 272   Perf. 10x10½
G4	IL1	10c ver ('45)	12.50	1.50
G5	IL2	50c dk bl	2.00	.50
G6	IL3	1p turq grn	3.50	.65
		Nos. G4-G6 (3)	18.00	2.65

1947   Wmk. 279   Perf. 10x10½
G7	IL1	10c vermilion	9.50	.85
G8	IL2	50c dark blue	12.00	1.50
G9	IL3	1p turq grn	4.00	1.00
		Nos. G7-G9 (3)	25.50	3.35

Vault — IL4

1950-51   Photo.   Perf. 14
G10	IL4	20c blue	3.75	.45
G11	IL4	40c purple	.40	.25
G12	IL4	1p yel grn ('51)	1.75	.50
G13	IL4	5p dk bl & gray grn ('51)	1.40	1.00
G14	IL4	10p car & ultra ('51)	4.00	4.00
		Nos. G10-G14 (5)	11.30	6.20

1954-71   Wmk. 300
G15	IL4	20c blue ('50)	.25	.25
G16	IL4	40c lt pur ('56)	.25	.25
G17	IL4	1p yel grn	.40	.25
a.		Size: 37x20¼mm ('71)	2.00	1.10
G18	IL4	5p bl & grn ('59)	1.25	1.00
G19	IL4	10p car & ultra ('63)	4.75	2.50
		Nos. G15-G19 (5)	6.90	4.25

No. G17 measures 35x19½mm. Vertical measurement excludes imprint.

1967   Wmk. 350   Perf. 14
G21	IL4	40c light purple	2.00	1.50
G22	IL4	1p yellow green	2.00	1.50

1975   Photo.   Wmk. 300
G23	IL4	2p lilac rose	.40	.30
G24	IL4	20p orange & gray	3.25	7.00

Padlock — IL5

1976-81   Unwmk.   Photo.   Perf. 14
G25	IL5	40c black & blue	.30	.30
G26	IL5	1p black & blue	.30	.30
G26A	IL5	2p blk & bl ('81)	.35	.30
G27	IL5	5p black & blue	1.50	.50
G28	IL5	10p black & blue	1.50	.50
G28A	IL5	20p black & blue	2.25	.55
		Nos. G25-G28A (6)	6.20	2.45

1979   Photo.   Wmk. 300
G29	IL5	40c black & blue	.90	.30
G30	IL5	1p black & blue	.90	.30
G31	IL5	5p black & blue	1.50	.45
G32	IL5	10p black & blue	4.00	.40
G33	IL5	20p black & blue	4.00	.75
		Nos. G29-G33 (5)	11.30	2.30

Perf. 14½x14
1983-86   Photo.   Unwmk.
Size of Lock: 20x31mm
G36	IL5	5p black & blue	1.25	.40
G37	IL5	10p black & blue	1.00	.40
G38	IL5	20p black & blue	1.00	.40
G39	IL5	50p black & blue	2.50	.45
G40	IL5	100p blk & bl ('86)	5.00	3.00
		Nos. G36-G40 (5)	10.75	4.65

POSTAGE DUE STAMPS

D1

1908   Engr.   Wmk. 155   Perf. 14
J1	D1	1c blue	1.00	3.00
J2	D1	2c blue	1.00	3.00
J3	D1	4c blue	1.00	3.00
J4	D1	5c blue	1.00	3.00
J5	D1	10c blue	1.00	3.00
		Nos. J1-J5 (5)	5.00	15.00

For overprints and surcharges see Nos. 381-385, 434-438, 466-470, 495-499, 593-607.

PORTE DE MAR STAMPS

These stamps were used to indicate the amount of cash to be paid to the captains of the mail steamers taking outgoing foreign mail.

PM2

PM3

1875   Unwmk.   Litho.   Imperf.
JX9	PM2	2c black	.60	50.00
a.		"5" added to make 25c	12.00	100.00
JX10	PM2	10c black	.80	30.00
JX11	PM2	12c black	.80	50.00
JX12	PM2	20c black	1.00	50.00
JX13	PM2	25c black	3.25	50.00
JX14	PM2	35c black	3.25	60.00
JX15	PM2	50c black	3.00	60.00
JX16	PM2	60c black	3.00	75.00
JX17	PM2	75c black	3.50	75.00
JX18	PM2	85c black	3.25	100.00
JX19	PM2	100c black	4.00	100.00
		Nos. JX9-JX19 (11)	26.45	700.00

Same, Numerals Larger
JX20	PM2	5c black	1.00	50.00
JX21	PM2	25c black	1.65	50.00
JX22	PM2	35c black	250.00	
JX23	PM2	50c black	1.00	50.00
JX24	PM2	60c black	125.00	
JX25	PM2	100c violet	.60	100.00
		Nos. JX20-JX25 (6)	379.25	

In Nos. JX9-JX19 the figures of value are 7mm high and "CENTAVOS" is 7½mm long. On Nos. JX20-JX25 the figures of value are 8mm high and "CENTAVOS" is 9½mm long.

Nos. JX9-JX25 exist with overprints of district names.

Counterfeits exist of Nos. JX9-JX31.

1879
JX26	PM3	2c brown	.50
JX27	PM3	5c yellow	.50
JX28	PM3	10c red	.50
JX29	PM3	25c blue	.50
JX30	PM3	50c green	.50
JX31	PM3	100c violet	.50
		Nos. JX26-JX31 (6)	3.00

Nos. JX26-JX31 were never put in use.

Nos. JX26-JX31 were printed on paper watermarked "ADMINISTRACION GENERAL DE CORREOS MEXICO." Approximately ¾ of the stamps do not show any of the watermark.

Stamps of this design were never issued. Examples appeared on the market in 1884. Value, set, $22.

All were printed in same sheet of 49 (7x7). Sheet consists of 14 of 10c; 7 each of 25c, 35c, 50c; 4 each of 60c, 85c; 3 each of 75c, 100c. There are four varieties of 10c, two of 25c, 35c and 50c.

OFFICIAL STAMPS

Hidalgo — O1

Wove or Laid Paper
1884-93   Unwmk.   Engr.   Perf. 12
O1	O1	red	1.40	1.00
a.		Vert. pair, imperf. betwn.	120.00	
O1B	O1	scarlet ('85)	1.40	1.00
O2	O1	olive brn ('87)	.90	.70
a.		Horiz. pair, imperf. betwn.		
b.		Blue ruled lines on paper		
O3	O1	orange ('88)	2.50	.90
a.		Vert. pair, imperf. betwn.	110.00	
b.		Perf. 11	15.00	12.00
O4	O1	blue grn ('93)	1.40	.80
a.		Imperf., pair	15.00	12.00
b.		Perf. 11	15.00	12.00
		Nos. O1-O4 (5)	7.60	4.40

Pin-perf. 6
O5	O1	olive brown ('87)	100.00	50.00

Wmk. "Correos E U M" on every Vertical Line of Ten Stamps (152)
1894   Perf. 5½
O6	O1	ultra	3.00	2.75
a.		Vert. pair, imperf. horiz.	35.00	
b.		Imperf., pair	45.00	

Perf. 11, 12
O7	O1	ultra	1.75	1.60

Perf. 5½x11, 11x5½
O9	O1	ultra	12.00	8.00
		Nos. O6-O9 (3)	16.75	12.35

Regular Issues with Handstamped Overprint in Black

1895   Wmk. 152   Perf. 12

O10	A20	1c green	17.50	6.00
O11	A20	2c carmine	20.00	6.00
O12	A20	3c orange brn	17.50	6.00
O13	A21	4c red orange	26.00	12.00
a.		4c orange	42.50	14.00
O14	A22	5c ultra	35.00	12.00
O15	A23	10c lilac rose	32.50	3.00
O16	A21	12c olive brn	70.00	30.00
O17	A23	15c brt blue	42.50	18.00
O18	A23	20c brown rose	42.50	18.00
O19	A23	50c purple	90.00	42.50
O20	A24	1p brown	200.00	90.00
O21	A24	5p scarlet	475.00	250.00
O22	A24	10p deep blue	750.00	500.00
	Nos. O10-O22 (13)		1,818.	993.50

Similar stamps with red overprint were not officially placed in use. Nos. O10-O22 have a vertical grain or mesh to the paper.

1896-97   Wmk. 153
Black Overprint

O23	A20	1c green	60.00	10.00
O24	A20	2c carmine	60.00	12.00
O25	A20	3c orange brn	60.00	12.00
O26	A21	4c red orange	60.00	12.00
a.		4c orange	75.00	22.50
O27	A22	5c ultra	60.00	12.00
O28	A21	12c olive brn	80.00	30.00
O29	A23	15c brt blue	100.00	30.00
O29A	A23	50c purple	650.00	650.00
	Nos. O23-O29A (8)		1,130.	768.00

Nos. O23-O29A have a vertical grain or mesh to the paper.

1897   Wmk. 154   Black Overprint

O30	A20	1c green	100.00	30.00
O31	A20	2c scarlet	90.00	35.00
O33	A21	4c orange	125.00	60.00
O34	A22	5c ultra	100.00	35.00
O35	A21	12c olive brn	125.00	42.50
O36	A23	15c brt blue	160.00	42.50
O37	A23	20c brown rose	110.00	18.00
O38	A23	50c purple	150.00	30.00
O39	A24	1p brown	375.00	125.00
	Nos. O30-O39 (9)		1,335.	418.00

Nos. O30-O39 have a vertical grain or mesh to the paper.

1898   Unwmk.   Black Overprint

O40	A20	1c green	35.00	9.50
O41	A20	2c scarlet	35.00	9.50
O42	A20	3c orange brn	35.00	9.50
O43	A21	4c orange	60.00	12.00
O44	A22	5c ultra	60.00	20.00
O45	A23	10c lilac rose	—	—
O46	A21	12c olive brn	125.00	30.00
O47	A23	15c brt blue	125.00	30.00
O48	A23	20c brown rose	225.00	75.00
O48A	A23	50c purple	375.00	150.00
O48B	A24	10p deep blue	5,500.	5,500.
	Nos. O40-O48A (10)		1,075.	345.50

The existence of No. O45 has been questioned by specialists. The editors would like to see authenticated evidence of this stamp. See note following No. 291.

Black Overprint
1900   Wmk. 155   Perf. 14, 15

O49	A25	1c green	37.50	2.50
O50	A26	2c vermilion	50.00	4.00
O51	A27	3c yellow brn	50.00	2.50
O52	A28	5c dark blue	50.00	4.50
O53	A29	10c violet & org	65.00	5.50
O54	A30	15c lavender & cl	65.00	5.50
O55	A31	20c rose & dk bl	75.00	2.50
O56	A32	50c red lil & blk	150.00	25.00
O57	A33	1p blue & blk	300.00	10.00
O58	A34	5p carmine & blk	575.00	75.00
	Nos. O49-O58 (10)		1,417.	152.00

Black Overprint
1903   Black Overprint

O59	A25	1c violet	35.00	4.00
O60	A26	2c green	35.00	4.00
O61	A35	4c carmine	65.00	2.50
O62	A28	5c orange	65.00	13.00
O63	A29	10c blue & org	70.00	4.00
O64	A32	50c carmine & blk	200.00	25.00
	Nos. O59-O64 (6)		470.00	52.50

Regular Issues Overprinted

1910   On Issues of 1899-1903

O65	A26	2c green	175.00	6.50
O66	A27	3c orange brn	175.00	10.00
O67	A35	4c carmine	200.00	10.00
O68	A28	5c orange	225.00	50.00
O69	A29	10c blue & org	200.00	4.00
O70	A30	15c lav & claret	225.00	6.50
O71	A31	20c rose & dk bl	275.00	3.00
O72	A32	50c carmine & blk	375.00	35.00
O73	A33	1p blue & blk	575.00	125.00
O74	A34	5p carmine & blk	200.00	125.00
	Nos. O65-O74 (10)		2,625.	369.00

1911   On Issue of 1910

O75	A36	1c violet	5.00	5.00
O76	A37	2c green	3.75	2.25
O77	A38	3c orange brn	5.00	2.50
O78	A39	4c carmine	5.50	2.25
O79	A40	5c orange	12.50	7.00
O80	A41	10c blue & org	5.50	2.50
O81	A42	15c gray bl & cl	13.00	8.50
O82	A43	20c red & blue	10.00	2.50
O83	A44	50c red brn & blk	35.00	15.00
O84	A45	1p blue & blk	60.00	25.00
O85	A46	5p carmine & blk	300.00	125.00
	Nos. O75-O85 (11)		455.25	197.50

Nos. 500 to 505 Overprinted

1915   Unwmk.   Rouletted 14½

O86	A57	1c violet	1.00	2.00
O87	A58	2c green	1.00	2.00
O88	A59	3c brown	1.25	2.00
O89	A60	4c carmine	1.00	2.00
O90	A61	5c orange	1.00	2.00
O91	A62	10c ultra	1.25	2.00
	Nos. O86-O91 (6)		6.50	12.00

All values are known with inverted overprint. All values exist imperforate and part perforate but were not regularly issued in these forms.

On Nos. 506 to 514
1915-16   Perf. 12

O92	A57	1c violet	1.50	2.00
O93	A58	2c green	1.50	2.00
O94	A59	3c brown	1.50	2.00
O95	A60	4c carmine	1.50	2.00
a.		"CEATRO"	21.00	30.00
O96	A61	5c orange	1.50	2.00
O97	A62	10c ultra, type II	1.50	2.00
a.		Double overprint	475.00	
O98	A63	40c slate	8.00	14.50
a.		Inverted overprint	24.00	25.00
b.		Double overprint	40.00	
O99	A64	1p brown & blk	10.00	14.50
a.		Inverted overprint	27.50	27.50
O100	A65	5p claret & ultra	60.00	60.00
a.		Inverted overprint	80.00	
	Nos. O92-O100 (9)		87.00	101.00

Nos. O98 and O99 exist imperforate but probably were not issued in that form.

Preceding Issues Overprinted in Red, Blue or Black

On No. O74
1916   Wmk. 155

O101	A34	5p carmine & blk	900.00

On Nos. O75 to O85

O102	A36	1c violet	6.50
O103	A37	2c green	1.25
O104	A38	3c orange brn (Bl)	1.75
O105	A39	4c carmine (Bl)	7.00
O106	A40	5c orange (Bl)	1.75
O107	A41	10c blue & org	1.75
O108	A42	15c gray bl & cl (Bk)	1.75
O109	A43	20c red & bl (Bk)	1.90
O110	A44	50c red brn & blk	200.00
O111	A45	1p blue & blk	11.00
O112	A46	5p carmine & blk	3,250.
	Nos. O102-O111 (10)		234.65

No. O102 with blue overprint is a trial color. Counterfeits exist of Nos. O110, O112.

Nos. 608, 610 to 612, 615 and 616 Overprinted Vertically in Red or Black

Thick Paper
1918   Unwmk.   Rouletted 14½

O113	A68	1c violet (R)	60.00	35.00
O114	A69	2c gray grn (R)	65.00	35.00
O115	A70	3c bis brn (R)	60.00	35.00
O116	A71	4c carmine (Bk)	60.00	35.00
O117	A74	20c rose (Bk)	125.00	90.00
O118	A75	30c gray blk (R)	190.00	175.00

On Nos. 622-623
Medium Paper   Perf. 12

O119	A72	5c ultra (R)	40.00	40.00
O120	A73	10c blue (R)	35.00	25.00
a.		Double overprint	400.00	400.00
	Nos. O113-O120 (8)		635.00	470.00

Overprinted Horizontally in Red

On Nos. 626-628
Thin Paper

O121	A63	40c violet (R)	35.00	27.50
O122	A64	1p bl & blk (R)	85.00	70.00
O123	A65	5p grn & blk (R)	575.00	600.00
	Nos. O121-O123 (3)		695.00	697.50

Nos. 608 and 610 to 615 Ovptd. Vertically Up in Red or Black

Thick Paper
1919   Rouletted 14½

O124	A68	1c dull vio (R)	6.00	6.00
a.		"OFICIAN"	70.00	80.00
O125	A69	2c gray grn (R)	9.50	3.50
a.		"OFICIAN"	70.00	80.00
O126	A70	3c bis brn (R)	14.00	6.00
a.		"OFICIAN"	95.00	100.00
O127	A71	4c car (Bk)	29.00	13.00
c.		"OFICIAN"		—
O127A	A72	5c ultra	200.00	125.00
b.		"OFICIAN"	500.00	
O128	A73	10c blue (R)	9.50	2.50
a.		"OFICIAN"	85.00	60.00
O129	A74	20c rose (Bk)	60.00	47.50
a.		"OFICIAN"		140.00

On Nos. 618, 622
Perf. 12

O130	A68	1c dull violet (R)	47.50	47.50
a.		"OFICIAN"	140.00	100.00
O131	A72	5c ultra (R)	47.50	22.50
a.		"OFICIAN"	140.00	100.00

Overprinted Horizontally
On Nos. 626-627
Thin Paper

O132	A63	40c violet (R)	47.50	35.00
O133	A64	1p bl & blk (R)	60.00	50.00
	Nos. O124-O133 (11)		530.50	358.50

Nos. 608 to 615 and 617 Ovptd. Vertically down in Black, Red or Blue

Size: 17½x3mm
1921   Rouletted 14½

O134	A68	1c gray (Bk)	30.00	12.00
a.		1c dull violet (Bk)	17.00	7.00
O135	A69	2c gray grn (R)	5.00	3.00
O136	A70	3c bis brn (R)	8.50	4.50
O137	A71	4c carmine (Bk)	27.50	21.00
O138	A72	5c ultra (R)	25.00	12.00
O139	A73	10c bl, reading down (R)	32.50	12.00
a.		Overprint reading up	60.00	60.00
O140	A74	20c rose (Bl)	47.50	27.50
O141	A75	30c gray blk (R)	25.00	25.00

Overprinted Horizontally
On Nos. 626-628
Perf. 12

O142	A63	40c violet (R)	32.50	32.50
O143	A64	1p bl & blk (R)	25.00	25.00
O144	A65	5p grn & blk (Bk)	600.00	600.00
	Nos. O134-O144 (11)		858.50	774.50

Nos. 609 to 615 Overprinted Vertically Down in Black

1921-30   Rouletted 14½

O145	A68	1c gray	5.00	2.50
a.		1c lilac gray	1.00	.70
O146	A69	2c gray green	1.75	.70
O147	A70	3c bister brn	.80	.70
a.		"OFICAL"	47.50	25.00
b.		"OIFCIAL"	47.50	25.00
c.		Double overprint	140.00	
O148	A71	4c carmine	22.50	2.50
O149	A72	5c ultra	1.00	.70
O150	A73	10c blue	1.00	.70
a.		"OIFCIAL"	50.00	
O151	A74	20c brown rose	9.00	9.50
a.		20c rose	5.00	2.50

On No. 625
Perf. 12

O152	A75	30c gray black	7.25	2.50

Overprinted Horizontally
On Nos. 626, 628

O153	A63	40c violet	7.00	5.00
a.		"OFICAL"	60.00	60.00
b.		"OICIAL"	60.00	60.00
c.		Inverted overprint	90.00	125.00
O154	A65	5p grn & blk ('30)	375.00	375.00
	Nos. O145-O154 (10)		430.30	399.80

Ovptd. Vertically Down in Red On Nos. 609, 610, 611, 613 and 614

1921-24   Rouletted 14½

O155	A68	1c lilac	1.60	1.00
O156	A69	2c gray green	1.50	.90
O157	A70	3c brown	4.00	1.00
O158	A72	5c ultra	1.60	.80
O159	A73	10c blue	35.00	3.50
a.		Double overprint		

On Nos. 624-625
Perf. 12

O160	A74	20c rose	7.25	1.60
O161	A75	30c gray black	19.00	5.00

Overprinted Horizontally
On Nos. 626-628

O162	A63	40c violet	14.00	7.50
a.		Vert. pair, imperf. btwn.		
O163	A64	1p bl & blk	35.00	25.00
O164	A65	5p green & blk	300.00	300.00

Overprinted Vertically Down in Blue on No. 612
Rouletted 14½

O165	A71	4c carmine	7.00	3.50
	Nos. O155-O165 (11)		425.95	349.80

Same Overprint Vertically Down in Red on Nos. 635 and 637
1926-27   Rouletted 14½

O166	A80	3c bis brn, ovpt. horiz.	12.00	12.00
a.		Period omitted	30.00	30.00
O167	A82	5c orange	27.50	30.00

Same Overprint Vertically Down in Blue or Red 0n Nos. 650, 651, 655 and 656
Wmk. 156

O168	A79	2c scarlet (Bl)	20.00	20.00
a.		Overprint reading up	30.00	30.00
O169	A80	3c bis brn, ovpt. horiz. (R)	5.00	5.00
a.		Inverted overprint	60.00	
O170	A85	10c claret (Bl)	35.00	16.00
O171	A84	20c deep blue (R)	14.00	12.00
a.		Inverted overprint	14.00	12.00

Overprinted Horizontally in Red
On Nos. 643, 646-649
Perf. 12

O172	A81	4c green	6.00	6.00
O173	A83	30c dk grn	6.00	6.00
O174	A63	40c violet	16.00	16.00
a.		Inverted overprint	80.00	

O175	A87	50c olive brn	1.50	1.50
a.		50c yellow brown	18.00	18.00
O176	A88	1p red brn & bl	15.00	15.00
		Nos. O168-O176 (9)	118.50	97.50

Same Overprint Horizontally on No. 651, Vertically Up on Nos. 650, 653-656, 666, RA1

1927-31			**Rouletted 14½**	
O177	PT1	1c brown ('31)	.70	1.00
O178	A79	2c scarlet	.70	1.00
a.		"OFICAIL"	30.00	30.00
b.		Overprint reading down	1.50	2.00
O179	A80	3c bis brn	2.00	1.50
		"OFICAIL"	40.00	30.00
O180	A82	4c green	1.50	1.00
		"OFICAIL"	40.00	40.00
b.		Overprint reading down	10.00	2.00
O181	A82	5c orange	4.00	3.00
a.		Overprint reading down	4.00	2.50
O182	A94	8c orange	12.00	8.00
a.		Overprint reading down	7.00	6.00
O183	A85	10c lake	2.00	2.00
		Overprint reading down	2.00	2.00
O184	A84	20c dark blue	10.00	4.00
a.		"OFICAIL"	40.00	40.00
b.		Overprint reading down	20.00	4.00
		Nos. O177-O184 (8)	32.90	21.50

Overprinted Vertically Up on #O186, Horizontally
On Nos. 643 and 645 to 649

1927-33			**Perf. 12**	
O185	A81	4c green	6.00	5.00
a.		Inverted overprint	30.00	30.00
O186	A85	10c brown lake	55.00	45.00
O187	A83	30c dark green	1.40	1.00
a.		Inverted overprint	30.00	30.00
b.		Pair, tête bêche overprints	35.00	35.00
c.		"OFICAIL"	35.00	35.00
O188	A63	40c violet	12.00	8.00
O189	A87	50c olive brn ('33)	3.25	4.00
O190	A88	1p red brn & bl	24.00	20.00
		Nos. O185-O190 (6)	101.65	83.00

The overprint on No. O186 is vertical.

Nos. 320, 628, 633 Overprinted Horizontally

On Stamp No. 320

1927-28		**Wmk. 155**	**Perf. 14, 15**	
O191	A46	5p car & blk (I)	175.00	250.00
O192	A46	5p car & blk (Bl)	175.00	250.00

		Unwmk.	**Perf. 12**	
O193	A65	5p grn & blk (Bk)	375.00	500.00
a.		Inverted overprint		
O194	A78	10p blk brn & blk (Bl)	200.00	300.00

No. 320 Overprinted Horizontally

		Wmk. 155	**Perf. 14**	
O195	A46	5p carmine & blk	300.00	

Nos. 650 and 655 Overprinted Horizontally

1928-29		**Wmk. 156**	**Rouletted 14½**	
		Size: 16x2½mm		
O196	A79	2c dull red	18.00	12.00
O197	A85	10c rose lake	27.50	12.00

Nos. RA1, 650-651, 653-656 Overprinted

1932-33				
O198	PT1	1c brown	.70	1.00
O199	A79	2c dull red	.80	1.00
O200	A80	3c bister brn	3.00	3.00

O201	A82	4c green	10.00	8.00
O202	A82	5c orange	12.00	8.00
O203	A85	10c rose lake	3.25	3.00
O204	A84	20c dark blue	15.00	10.00
a.		Double overprint	200.00	90.00
		Nos. O198-O204 (7)	44.75	34.00

Nos. 651, 646-649 Overprinted Horizontally

1933			**Rouletted 14½**	
O205	A80	3c bister brn	3.00	3.00

			Perf. 12	
O206	A83	30c dk green	8.00	3.00
O207	A63	40c violet	15.00	6.00
O208	A87	50c olive brn	2.50	3.00
a.		"OFICIAL OFICIAL"	50.00	50.00
O209	A88	1p red brn & bl, type I	3.00	3.00
		Type II	2.75	3.50

Overprinted Vertically On No. 656

			Rouletted 14½	
O210	A84	20c dark blue	18.00	10.00
		Nos. O205-O210 (6)	49.50	28.00

Nos. RA1, 651, 653, 654, 683 Overprinted Horizontally

1934-37			**Rouletted 14½**	
		Size: 13x2mm		
O211	PT1	1c brown	5.00	6.00
O212	A80	3c bister brn	.70	.70
O213	A82	4c green	12.00	10.00
O214	A82	5c orange	.70	.70
O215	A96	15c dk blue ('37)	1.00	1.00
		Nos. O211-O215 (5)	19.40	18.40

See No. O217a.

Same Overprint on Nos. 687A-692

1934-37			**Perf. 10½**	
O216	PT1	1c brown ('37)	1.00	1.25
O217	A79	2c scarlet	1.00	1.50
a.		On No. 650 (error)	350.00	
b.		Double overprint	275.00	
O218	A82	4c green ('35)	1.40	1.60
O219	A85	10c brown lake	1.00	1.00
O220	A84	20c dk blue ('37)	1.25	1.25
O221	A83	30c dk bl grn ('37)	2.00	2.00

On Nos. 647 and 649
			Perf. 12, 11½x12	
O222	A63	40c violet	3.00	3.50
O223	A88	1p red brn & bl (I)	5.00	6.00
a.		Type II	4.00	4.00
		Nos. O216-O223 (8)	15.65	18.10

On Nos. 707 to 709, 712, 715, 716, 717, 718 and 719
O224	A108	1c orange	2.00	4.00
O225	A109	2c green	1.25	2.00
O226	A110	4c carmine	1.25	1.40
O227	A112	10c violet	1.25	2.50
O228	A114	20c ultra	1.60	2.50
O229	A115	30c lake	2.00	4.00
O230	A116	40c red brown	2.50	4.00
O231	A117	50c black	2.75	2.75
O232	A118	1p dk brn & org	8.00	12.00
		Nos. O224-O232 (9)	22.60	35.15

PARCEL POST STAMPS

Railroad Train PP1

1941		**Photo.** **Wmk. 156**	**Perf. 14**	
Q1	PP1	10c brt rose	2.75	.35
Q2	PP1	20c dk vio bl	1.75	.35

1944-46			**Wmk. 272**	
Q3	PP1	10c brt rose	1.75	1.00
Q4	PP1	20c dk vio bl ('46)	5.00	2.50

1947-49			**Wmk. 279**	
Q5	PP1	10c brt rose	1.25	.60
Q6	PP1	20c dk vio bl ('49)	1.60	.60

Streamlined Locomotive PP2

1951				
Q7	PP2	10c rose pink	5.00	.40
Q8	PP2	20c blue violet	4.00	.70

1954			**Wmk. 300**	
Q9	PP2	10c rose pink	4.25	.60
Q10	PP2	20c blue violet	4.25	1.50

POSTAL TAX STAMPS

Morelos Monument — PT1

		Rouletted 14½		
1925		**Engr.**	**Wmk. 156**	
RA1	PT1	1c brown	.35	.25
a.		Imperf.	30.00	

1926			**Perf. 12**	
RA2	PT1	1c brown	.75	5.00
a.		Booklet pane of 2	12.00	

1925		**Unwmk.**	**Rouletted 14½**	
RA3	PT1	1c brown	75.00	19.00

It was obligatory to add a stamp of type PT1 to the regular postage on every article of domestic mail matter. The money obtained from this source formed a fund to combat a plague of locusts.

In 1931, 1c stamps of type PT1 were discontinued as Postal Tax stamps. It was subsequently used for the payment of postage on drop letters (announcement cards and unsealed circulars) to be delivered in the city of cancellation. See No. 687A.

For overprints see Nos. O177, O198, O211, O216, RA4.

No. RA1 Overprinted in Red

1929			**Wmk. 156**	
RA4	PT1	1c brown	.35	.25
a.		Overprint reading down	75.00	75.00

There were two settings of this overprint. They may be distinguished by the two lines being spaced 4mm or 6mm apart.

The money from sales of this stamp was devoted to child welfare work.

Mother and Child — PT3

1929		**Litho.**	**Rouletted 13, 13½**	
RA5	PT3	1c violet	.35	.25

PT4

1929		**Size: 18x24½mm**	**Unwmk.**	
RA6	PT4	2c deep green	.40	.25
RA7	PT4	5c brown	.40	.25
a.		Imperf., pair	60.00	60.00

For surcharges see Nos. RA10-RA11.

PT5

Two types of 1c:
Type I — Background lines continue through lettering of top inscription. Denomination circle hangs below second background line. Paper and gum white.
Type II — Background lines cut away behind some letters. Circle rests on second background line. Paper and gum yellowish.

1929		**Size: 19x25¼mm**		
RA8	PT5	1c violet, type I	.35	.25
a.		Booklet pane of 4	10.00	
b.		Booklet pane of 2	18.00	
c.		Type II	.40	.25
d.		Imperf., pair	50.00	50.00
RA9	PT5	2c deep green	.65	.25
a.		Imperf., pair		

The use of these stamps, in addition to the regular postage, was compulsory. The money obtained from their sale was used for child welfare work.
For surcharge see No. RA12.

Nos. RA6, RA7, RA9 Surcharged

1930				
RA10	PT4	1c on 2c dp grn	.75	.40
RA11	PT4	1c on 5c brown	1.00	.60
RA12	PT5	1c on 2c dp grn	2.00	1.00
		Nos. RA10-RA12 (3)	3.75	2.00

Used stamps exist with surcharge double or reading down.

No. 423 Overprinted

1931, Jan. 30		**Wmk. 155**	**Perf. 14**	
RA13	A36	1c dull violet	.40	.40
a.		"PRO INFANCIA" double	50.00	

Indian Mother and Child — PT6

Mosquito Attacking Man — PT7

			Wmk. 156	
1934, Sept. 1		**Engr.**	**Perf. 10½**	
RA13B	PT6	1c dull orange	.30	.25

1939		**Photo.** **Wmk. 156**	**Perf. 14**	
RA14	PT7	1c Prus blue	1.50	.25
a.		Imperf.	3.00	3.00

This stamp was obligatory on all mail, the money being used to aid in a drive against malaria.
See Nos. RA16, RA19.

Miguel Hidalgo y Costilla — PT8

1941				
RA15	PT8	1c brt carmine	.45	.25

Type of 1939

			1944	Wmk. 272	Perf. 14
RA16	PT7	1c Prus blue			1.00 .25

Learning Vowels — PT9

1946 Photo. Wmk. 279

RA17	PT9	1c black brown	.45 .25
a.		1c green black	1.00 1.00

1947 Wmk. 272

RA18	PT9	1c black brown	65.00 5.00

**Type of 1939
Wmk. 279**

RA19	PT7	1c Prus blue	3.50 .30

PROVISIONAL ISSUES

During the struggle led by Juarez to expel the Emperor Maximilian, installed June, 1864 by Napoleon III and French troops, a number of towns when free of Imperial forces issued provisional postage stamps. Maximilian was captured and executed June 19, 1867, but provisional issues continued current for a time pending re-establishment of Republican Government.

Campeche

A southern state in Mexico, comprising the western part of the Yucatan peninsula.

A1

**White Paper
Numerals in Black**

		1876	Handstamped	Imperf.
1	A1	5c gray blue & blue		2,000.
2	A1	25c gray blue & blue		1,100.
3	A1	50c gray blue & blue		4,500.

The stamps printed in blue-black and blue on yellowish paper, formerly listed as issued in 1867, are now known to be an unofficial production of later years. They are reprints, but produced without official sanction.

Chiapas

A southern state in Mexico, bordering on Guatemala and the Pacific Ocean.

A1

1866 Typeset

1	A1	½r blk, gray bl	2,000. 1,300.
2	A1	1r blk, lt grn	850.
3	A1	2r blk, rose	900.
4	A1	4r blk, lt buff	2,000.
a.		Vertical half used as 2r on cover	3,000.
5	A1	8r blk, rose	15,000.
a.		Quarter used as 2r on cover	4,000.
b.		Half used as 4r on cover	5,000.

Chihuahua

A city of northern Mexico and capital of the State of Chihuahua.

A1

A2

1872 Handstamped

1	A1	12(c) black	3,000.
2	A2	25(c) black	3,000.

Cuautla

A town in the state of Morelos.

A1

1867 Handstamped

1	A1	(2r) black	7,000.

All known examples on cover are uncancelled. Examples are known without the "73" inside the oval.

Cuernavaca

A city of Mexico, just south of the capital, and the capital of the State of Morelos.

A1

1867 Handstamped

1	A1	(1r) black	1,750.
2	A1	(2r) black	40,000.

No. 1 was canceled at Cuernavaca with the district name overprint. Supplies of overprinted stamps were sent to the Tetecala and Yquala sub-offices, where they were canceled with the usual local postmarks.

No. 2 was created by doubling the impression of the basic stamp and applying the district name overprint twice.

Unused examples of Nos. 1 and 2 do not exist.

Counterfeits exist.

Guadalajara

A city of Mexico and capital of the State of Jalisco.

A1

**Dated "1867"
1st Printing
Medium Wove Paper**

		1867	Handstamped	Imperf.
1	A1	Medio r blk, white		350.00 250.00
2	A1	un r blk, gray bl		750.00 350.00
a.		Overprinted "Cd. Guzman"		1,000.

3	A1	un r blk, dk bl		450.00
4	A1	un r blk, white		250.00
a.		Overprinted "Cd. Guzman"		750.00
5	A1	2r blk, dk grn	250.00 21.00
a.		Overprinted "Cd. Guzman"		500.00
6	A1	2r blk, white		125.00
a.		Overprinted "Cd. Guzman"		400.00
b.		Double print		250.00
7	A1	4r blk, rose	250.00 300.00
a.		Half used as 2r on cover		500.00
b.		Overprinted "Cd. Guzman"		900.00
8	A1	4r blk, white		500.00
a.		Half used as 2r on cover		2,500.
9	A1	un p blk, lilac	250.00 300.00

Serrate Perf.

10	A1	un r blk, gray bl	400.00
11	A1	2r blk, dk grn	700.00
12	A1	4r blk, rose	350.00
12A	A1	un p blk, lilac	1,750.

**2nd Printing
No Period after "2" or "4"
Thin Quadrille Paper
Imperf**

13	A1	2r blk, green	30.00 20.00
a.		Half used as 1r on cover	400.00

Serrate Perf.

14	A1	2r blk, green	225.00

**Thin Laid Batonné Paper
Imperf**

15	A1	2r blk, green	45.00 24.00

Serrate Perf.

16	A1	2r blk, green	225.00

**3rd Printing
Capital "U" in "Un" on 1r, 1p
Period after "2" and "4"
Thin Wove Paper
Imperf**

16A	A1	Un r blk, white	125.00
17	A1	Un r blk, blue	90.00
17A	A1	Un r blk, lilac	100.00
18	A1	2r blk, rose	50.00
18A	A1	4r blk, blue	500.00 1,000.
18B	A1	Un p blue	1,750.

Serrate Perf.

19	A1	Un r blk, blue	300.00
19A	A1	2r blk, rose	750.00
19B	A1	4r blue	500.00

**Thin Quadrille Paper
Imperf**

20	A1	2r blk, rose	42.50 42.50
21	A1	4r blk, blue	15.00 30.00
22	A1	4r blk, white	200.00
23	A1	Un p blk, lilac	15.00 60.00
24	A1	Un p blk, rose	65.00
24A	A1	Un p blk, white	1,500.

Serrate Perf

24B	A1	2r blk, rose	500.00
25	A1	Un p blk, lilac	750.00 750.00
25A	A1	Un p blk, rose	700.00 300.00

**Thin Laid Batonné Paper
Imperf**

26	A1	Un r blk, green	22.50 17.50
27	A1	2r blk, rose	27.50 22.50
27A	A1	2r blk, green	47.50
28	A1	4r blk, blue	17.50 42.50
29	A1	4r blk, white	100.00
30	A1	Un p blk, lilac	30.00 52.50
31	A1	Un p blk, rose	65.00

Serrate Perf.

32	A1	Un r blk, green	65.00
33	A1	2r blk, rose	400.00 200.00
34	A1	4r blk, blue	425.00
34A	A1	4r blk, white	1,750.
34B	A1	Un p blk, lilac	700.00

**Thin Oblong Quadrille Paper
Imperf**

35	A1	Un r blk, blue	250.00 22.50
35A	A1	Un r blk, white	1,500.
36	A1	4r blk, blue	600.00

Serrate Perf.

37	A1	Un r blk, blue	300.00

**4th Printing
Dated "1868"
Wove Paper**

		1868		Imperf.
38	A1	2r blk, lilac		30.00 14.00
a.		Half used as 1r on cover		500.00
39	A1	2r blk, rose		52.50 65.00

Serrate Perf.

40	A1	2r blk, lilac	52.50
41	A1	2r blk, rose	750.00 95.00

Laid Batonné Paper

42	A1	un r blk, green	12.50 12.50
43	A1	2r blk, lilac	12.50 12.50
a.		Half used as 1r on cover	1,500.
43A	A1	2r blk, rose	750.00

44	A1	un r blk, green	250.00 200.00
44A	A1	2r blk, rose	500.00

**Quadrille Paper.
Imperf**

45	A1	2r blk, lilac	25.00 14.00

Serrate Perf.

46	A1	2r blk, lilac	300.00 300.00

**Laid Paper
Imperf**

47	A1	un r blk, green	13.00 17.00
a.		Watermarked "LA + F"	750.00 1,000.
b.		"nu" instead of "un"	750.00
c.		Dated "1863"	300.00
48	A1	2r blk, lilac	32.50 32.50
49	A1	2r blk, rose	37.50 37.50

Serrate Perf.

50	A1	un r blk, green	750.00 55.00
51	A1	2r blk, rose	475.00

Counterfeits of Nos. 1-51 abound.

Merida

A city of southeastern Mexico, capital of the State of Yucatan.

Mexico No. 521 Surcharged **25**

1916 Wmk. 155 Perf. 14

1	A40	25(c) on 5c org, on cover	500.00

The G.P.DE.M. overprint reads down.

Authorities consider the Monterrey, Morelia and Patzcuaro stamps to be bogus.

Tlacotalpan

A village in the state of Veracruz.

A1

Handstamped Monogram, Value in Manuscript

1856, Oct.

1	A1	½(r) black	30,000.

Research suggests that this stamp was not an officially sanctioned issue, but was instead part of a postal fraud orchestrated by Tlacotalpan postmaster Angel Fernando and his assistant Ignacio Crespo to cover theft of funds in that post office. The initials IMC in the stamp are most likely those of Crespo.

REVOLUTIONARY ISSUES

SINALOA

A northern state in Mexico, bordering on the Pacific Ocean. Stamps were issued by a provisional government.

Coat of Arms — A1

1929 Unwmk. Litho. Perf. 12

1	A1	10c blk, red & bl	5.00
a.		Tête bêche pair	35.00
2	A1	20c blk, red & gray	5.00

Just as Nos. 1 and 2 were ready to be placed on sale the state was occupied by the Federal forces and the stamps could not be used. At a later date a few stamps were canceled by favor.

A recent find included a number of errors or printer's waste.

YUCATAN

A southeastern state of Mexico.

Chalchihuitlicue, Nahuatl Water Goddess — A1

"Casa de Monjas" — A2

Temple of the Tigers — A3

Without Gum

1924 Unwmk. Litho. Imperf.

1	A1	5c violet	10.00	15.00
2	A2	10c carmine	40.00	50.00
3	A3	50c olive green	175.00	

Perf. 12

4	A1	5c violet	50.00	60.00
5	A2	10c carmine	50.00	75.00
6	A3	50c olive green	200.00	

Nos. 3 and 6 were not regularly issued.

Scott Album Accessories

SPECIALTY/NATIONAL SERIES BINDERS

National series pages are punched for 3-ring and 2-post binders. The 3-ring binder is available in two sizes. The 2-post binder comes in one size. All Scott binders are covered with a tough green leatherette material that is washable and reinforced at stress points for long wear.

3-RING BINDERS & SLIPCASES

Scott Specialty 3-Ring Binders have been upgraded and improved in durability and function without losing its style or elegance. The new and improved binder features a metal piano hinge running the full height of the binder, offering unsurpassed durability when opening and closing multiple times. It is the same binder style used by the government for long-term storage. With the three ring binder, pages lay flat and the rings make turning the pages easy. The locking mechanism insure that the rings won't pop open even when the binder is full.

Item			Retail	AA*
ACBR01D	Small 3-Ring Binder	Holds up to 100 pages	$41.99	**$34.99**
ACBR03D	Large 3-Ring Binder	Holds up to 250 pages	$41.99	**$34.99**
ACSR01	Small 3-Ring Slipcase		$32.50	**$26.99**
ACSR03	Large 3-Ring Slipcase		$37.50	**$26.99**
ACC102	3-Ring Black Protector Sheets		$4.99	**$3.99**
ACC107	Glassine Interleaving		$11.99	**$10.25**

LARGE 2-POST BINDER & SLIPCASE

For the traditional Scott collector, we offer the standard hinge post binder. Scott album pages are punched with rectangular holes that fit on rectangular posts. The posts and pages are held by a rod that slides down from the top. With the post binder pages do not lie flat. However, filler strips are available for a minimal cost.

Item			Retail	AA*
ACBS03	Large 2-Post Binder	Holds up to 250 pages	$54.99	**$46.99**
ACSS03	Large 2-Post Slipcase		$37.50	**$26.99**
ACC101	2-Post Green Protector Sheets		$4.99	**$3.99**
ACC107	Glassine Interleaving		$11.99	**$10.25**

SCOTT UNIVERSAL BINDER

The Scott Universal Binder is designed to hold any Scott album page. Two round posts can be mounted to accomodate pages punched to fit 3-ring or 2-post binders. Pages will not lie flat when housed in the Universal Binder. Matches Scott 2-post and 3-ring binders in looks. The Universal Binder will hold approximately 150 pages.

Item			Retail	AA*
ACBU	Universal Binder	Holds up to 150 pages	$39.99	**$32.99**
ACSU	Universal Slipcase		$32.50	**$26.99**

BLANK PAGES

High quality paper developed exclusively for each specific album series. Ideal for developing your own album pages to be integrated with your album.

SPECIALTY/NATIONAL SERIES PAGES (20 PGS PER PACK)

Item		Retail	AA
ACC110	Specialty Blank Pages	$8.99	$6.99
ACC111	Specialty Quadrille*	$13.99	$11.99
ACC120	National Blank Pages	$8.99	$6.99
ACC121	National Quadrille*	$13.99	$11.99

AMOS ADVANTAGE

MICRONESIA

,mī-krə-'nē-zhə

LOCATION — A group of over 600 islands in the West Pacific Ocean, north of the Equator.
GOVT. — Republic
AREA — 271 sq. miles
POP. — 131,500 (1999 est.)
CAPITAL — Palikir

These islands, also known as the Caroline Islands, were bought by Germany from Spain in 1899. Caroline Islands stamps issued as a German territory are listed in Vol. 2 of this Catalogue. Seized by Japan in 1914, they were taken by the US in WWII and became part of the US Trust Territory of the Pacific in 1947. By agreement with the USPS, the islands began issuing their own stamps in 1984, with the USPS continuing to carry the mail to and from the islands.

On Nov. 3, 1986 Micronesia became a Federation as a Sovereign State in Compact of Free Association with the US.

100 Cents = 1 Dollar

Catalogue values for all unused stamps in this country are for Never Hinged items.

Postal Service Inauguration — A1

1984, July 12   Litho.   Perf. 14
1	A1	20c Yap	.45	.45
2	A1	20c Truk	.45	.45
3	A1	20c Pohnpei	.45	.45
4	A1	20c Kosrae	.45	.45
a.		Block of 4, #1-4	1.90	1.90

For surcharges see Nos. 48-51.

Fernandez de Quiros — A2   Men's House, Yap — A3

Designs: 1c, 19c, Pedro Fernandez de Quiros, Spanish explorer, first discovered Pohnpei, 1595. 2c, 20c, Louis Duperrey, French explorer. 3c, 30c, Fyodor Litke, Russian explorer. 4c, 37c, Dumont d'Urville. 10c, Sleeping Lady, Kosrae. 13c, Liduduhriap Waterfall, Pohnpei. 17c, Tonachau Peak, Truk. 50c, Devil mask, Truk. $1, Sokeh's Rock, Pohnpei. $2, Canoes, Kosrae. $5, Stone money, Yap.

1984, July 12   Perf. 13½x13
5	A2	1c Prussian blue	.25	.25
6	A2	2c deep claret	.25	.25
7	A2	3c dark blue	.25	.25
8	A2	4c green	.25	.25
9	A3	5c yellow brown	.25	.25
10	A3	10c dark violet	.25	.25
11	A3	13c dark blue	.25	.25
12	A3	17c brown lake	.25	.25
13	A3	19c dark violet	.30	.30
14	A2	20c olive green	.30	.30
15	A2	30c rose lake	.45	.45
16	A2	37c deep violet	.55	.55
17	A3	50c brown	.75	.75
18	A3	$1 olive	1.75	1.75
19	A3	$2 Prussian blue	3.50	3.50
20	A3	$5 brown lake	8.50	8.50
		Nos. 5-20 (16)	18.10	18.10

See Nos. 33, 36, 38.

Ausipex '84
A4

1984, Sept. 21   Litho.   Perf. 13½
21	A4	20c Truk Post Office	.40	.40
		Nos. 21,C4-C6 (4)	3.00	3.00

Christmas
A5

Child's drawing.

1984, Dec. 20
22	A5	20c Child in manger	.90	.90
		Nos. 22,C7-C9 (4)	3.55	3.55

Ships — A6

1985, Aug. 19
23	A6	22c U.S.S. Jamestown	.55	.55
		Nos. 23,C10-C12 (4)	3.00	3.00

Christmas
A7

1985, Oct. 15   Litho.   Perf. 13½
24	A7	22c Lelu Protestant Church, Kosrae	.75	.60
		Nos. 24,C13-C14 (3)	2.90	2.75

Audubon Birth Bicentenary — A8

1985, Oct. 30   Perf. 14½
25	A8	22c Noddy tern	.60	.60
26	A8	22c Turnstone	.60	.60
27	A8	22c Golden plover	.60	.60
28	A8	22c Black-bellied plover	.60	.60
a.		Block of 4, #25-28	2.60	2.60
		Nos. 25-28,C15 (5)	3.40	3.40

Types of 1984 and

Birds — A9

Tall Ship Senyavin   Natl. Seal
A10   A11

Perf. 13½ (A8a), 13½x13

1985-88   Litho.
31	A9	3c Long-billed white-eye	.25	.25
32	A9	14c Truk monarch	.30	.30
33	A3	15c Liduduhriap Waterfall, Pohnpei	.30	.30
a.		Booklet pane of 10	6.00	—
34	A10	22c bright blue green	.35	.35
35	A9	22c Pohnpei mountain starling	.45	.45
36	A3	25c Tonachau Peak, Truk	.50	.50
a.		Booklet pane of 10	6.50	—
b.		Booklet pane, 5 15c + 5 25c	7.50	—
37	A10	36c ultramarine	.70	.70
38	A3	45c Sleeping Lady, Kosrae	.90	.90
39	A11	$10 bright ultra	15.00	15.00
		Nos. 31-39,C34-C36 (12)	21.75	21.75

Issued: $10, 10/15; No. 34, 4/14/86; 3c, 14c, No. 35, 8/1/88; 15c, 25c, 36c, 45c, 9/1/88.

Nan Madol Ruins, Pohnpei
A16

1985, Dec.   Litho.   Perf. 13½
45	A16	22c Land of the Sacred Masonry	.60	.60
		Nos. 45,C16-C18 (4)	3.00	3.00

Intl. Peace Year — A17

1986, May 16
46	A17	22c multicolored	.65	.60

Nos. 1-4 Surcharged

1986, May 19   Litho.   Perf. 14
48	AI	22c on 20c No. 1	.40	.40
49	A1	22c on 20c No. 2	.40	.40
50	A1	22c on 20c No. 3	.40	.40
51	A1	22c on 20c No. 4	.40	.40
a.		Block of 4, #48-51	1.75	1.75

AMERIPEX '86
A18

Bully Hayes (1829-1877), Buccaneer.

1986, May 22   Perf. 13½
52	A18	22c At ship's helm	.50	.50
		Nos. 52,C21-C24 (5)	4.00	4.00

First Passport
A19

1986, Nov. 4   Litho.   Perf. 13½
53	A19	22c multicolored	.60	.60

Christmas
A20

Virgin and child paintings: 5c, Italy, 18th cent. 22c, Germany, 19th cent.

1986, Oct. 15   Litho.   Perf. 14½
54	A20	5c multicolored	.25	.25
55	A20	22c multicolored	.75	.75
		Nos. 54-55,C26-C27 (4)	3.40	3.40

Anniversaries and Events — A21

1987, June 13   Litho.   Perf. 14½
56	A21	22c Intl. Year of Shelter for the Homeless	.50	.50
		Nos. 56,C28-C30 (4)	3.20	3.20

Souvenir Sheet
57	A21	$1 CAPEX '87	3.25	3.25

Christmas
A22

22c, Archangel Gabriel appearing before Mary.

1987, Nov. 16   Litho.   Perf. 14½
58	A22	22c multicolored	.60	.60
		Nos. 58,C31-C33 (4)	3.30	3.30

Colonial Eras — A23

1988, July 20   Litho.   Perf. 13x13½
59	A23	22c German	.60	.60
60	A23	22c Spanish	.60	.60
61	A23	22c Japanese	.60	.60
62	A23	22c US Trust Territory	.60	.60
a.		Block of 4, #59-62	2.40	2.40
		Nos. 59-62,C37-C38 (6)	4.30	4.30

Printed se-tenant in sheets of 28 plus 4 center labels picturing flags of Spain (UL), Germany (UR), Japan (LL) and the US (LR).

1988 Summer Olympics, Seoul — A24

1988, Sept. 1   Litho.   Perf. 14
63	A24	25c Running	.50	.50
64	A24	25c Women's hurdles	.50	.50
a.		Pair, #63-64	1.00	1.00
65	A24	45c Basketball	.80	.80
66	A24	45c Women's volleyball	.80	.80
a.		Pair, #65-66	1.65	1.65
		Nos. 63-66 (4)	2.60	2.60

Christmas — A25

Children decorating tree: No. 67, Two girls, UL of tree. No. 68, Boy, girl, dove, UR of tree. No. 69, Boy, girl, LL of tree. No. 70, Boy, girl, LR of tree. Se-tenant in a continuous design.

1988, Oct. 28   Litho.   Perf. 14
67	A25	25c multicolored	.45	.45
68	A25	25c multicolored	.45	.45
69	A25	25c multicolored	.45	.45
70	A25	25c multicolored	.45	.45
a.		Block of 4, #67-70	1.90	1.90

Miniature Sheet

Truk Lagoon State Monument — A26

a, Sun and stars angelfish. b, School of fish. c, 3 divers. d, Goldenjack. e, Blacktip reef shark. f, 2 schools of fish. g, Squirrelfish. h, Batfish. i, Moorish idols. j, Barracudas. k, Spot banded butterflyfish. l, Three-spotted damselfish. m, Foxface. n, Lionfish. o, Diver. p, Coral. q, Butterflyfish. r, Bivalve, fish, coral.

1988, Dec. 19   Litho.   Perf. 14
71	A26	Sheet of 18	9.50	9.50
a.-r.		25c any single	.50	.50

Mwarmwarms — A27

1989, Mar. 31   Litho.   Perf. 14
72	A27	45c Plumeria	.65	.65
73	A27	45c Hibiscus	.65	.65
74	A27	45c Jasmine	.65	.65
75	A27	45c Bougainvillea	.65	.65
a.		Block of 4, #72-75	2.75	2.75

Souvenir Sheet

Pheasant and Chrysanthemum, 1830s, by Hiroshige (1797-1858) — A28

1989, May 15   Litho.   Perf. 14½
76	A28	$1 multicolored	1.60	1.60

Hirohito (1901-1989), emperor of Japan.

Sharks A29

1989, July 7
77	A29	25c Whale	.40	.40
78	A29	25c Hammerhead	.40	.40
a.		Pair, #77-78	.80	.80

79	A29	45c Tiger, vert.	.75	.75
80	A29	45c Great white, vert.	.75	.75
a.		Pair, #79-80	1.50	1.50
		Nos. 77-80 (4)	2.30	2.30

Miniature Sheet

First Moon Landing, 20th Anniv. — A30

Space achievements: a, X-15 rocket plane, 1959. b, *Explorer 1* launched into orbit, 1958. c, Ed White, 1st American to walk in space, Gemini 4 mission, 1965. d, Apollo 18 command module, 1975. e, Gemini 4 capsule. f, Space shuttle *Challenger*, 1983-86. g, *San Marco 2*, satellite engineered by Italy. h, Soyuz 19 spacecraft, 1975. i, *Columbia* command module and Neil Armstrong taking man's first step onto the Moon during the Apollo 11 mission, 1969.

1989, July 20   Litho.   Perf. 14
81	A30	Sheet of 9	5.25	4.50
a.-i.		25c any single	.50	.45

Earth and Lunar Module, by William Hanson, 1st Art Transported to the Moon — A31

1989, July 20   Perf. 13½x14
82	A31	$2.40 multicolored	4.50	4.00

First Moon landing, 20th anniv.

Seashells — A32

1989, Sept. 26   Perf. 14
83	A32	1c Horse's hoof	.25	.25
84	A32	3c Rare spotted cowrie	.25	.25
85	A32	15c Commercial trochus	.25	.25
a.		Booklet pane of 10	5.00	
87	A32	20c General cone	.30	.30
88	A32	25c Triton's trumpet	.40	.40
a.		Booklet pane of 10	7.50	
b.		Booklet pane, 5 each 15c, 25c	7.50	—
90	A32	30c Laciniated conch	.45	.45
91	A32	36c Red-mouthed olive	.55	.55
93	A32	45c Map cowrie	.70	.70
95	A32	50c Textile cone	.75	.75
100	A32	$1 Orange spider conch	1.75	1.75
101	A32	$2 Golden cowrie	3.50	3.50
102	A32	$5 Episcopal miter	8.50	8.50
		Nos. 83-102 (12)	17.65	17.65

Booklet panes issued Sept. 14, 1990.

Miniature Sheet

Fruits and Flowers Endemic to Kosrae — A33

Designs: a, Orange. b, Lime. c, Tangerine. d, Mango. e, Coconut. f, Breadfruit. g, Sugar cane. h, Thatched dwelling. i, Banana. j, Girl, boy. k, Pineapple picker. l, Taro. m, Hibiscus. n, Ylang ylang. o, White ginger. p, Plumeria. q, Royal poinciana. r, Yellow allamanda.

1989, Nov. 18   Litho.   Perf. 14
103	Sheet of 18	9.00	9.00
a.-r.	A33 25c any single	.45	.45

Margin inscribed for World Stamp Expo '89.

Christmas — A34

1989, Dec. 14   Litho.   Perf. 14½
104	A34	25c Heralding angel	.50	.50
105	A34	45c Three wise men	.90	.90

World Wildlife Fund A35

Micronesian kingfishers and pigeons.

1990, Feb. 19   Litho.   Perf. 14
106	A35	10c Kingfisher (juvenile)	.55	.55
107	A35	15c Kingfisher (adult)	1.25	1.25
108	A35	20c Pigeon	1.75	1.75
109	A35	25c Pigeon, diff.	2.50	2.50
		Nos. 106-109 (4)	6.05	6.05

Stamp World London '90 — A36

Exhibition emblem, artifacts and whaling vessels: No. 110, Wooden whale stamp, *Lyra*, 1826. No. 111, Harpoons, *Prudent*, 1827. No. 112, Scrimshaw (whale), *Rhone*, 1851. No. 113, Scrimshaw on whale tooth, *Sussex*, 1843. $1, Whalers at kill.

1990, May 3   Litho.   Perf. 14
110	A36	45c multicolored	.80	.80
111	A36	45c multicolored	.80	.80
112	A36	45c multicolored	.80	.80
113	A36	45c multicolored	.80	.80
a.		Block of 4, #110-113	3.25	3.25

Souvenir Sheet
114	A36	$1 multicolored	2.00	2.00

Souvenir Sheet

Penny Black, 150th Anniv. — A37

1990, May 6   Perf. 14
115	A37	$1 Great Britain No. 1	2.00	2.00

Main Building — A38   Fr. Hugh Costigan, School Founder — A39

Designs: No. 117, Fr. Costigan, students. No. 119, Fr. Costigan, Isaphu Samuel Hadley. No. 120, New York City Police Badge.

1990, July 31   Litho.   Perf. 14
116	A38	25c multicolored	.50	.50
117	A38	25c multicolored	.50	.50
118	A39	25c multicolored	.50	.50
119	A38	25c multicolored	.50	.50
120	A38	25c multicolored	.50	.50
a.		Strip of 5, #116-120	2.50	2.50

Pohnpei Agriculture and Trade School, 25th anniversary. Printed in sheets of 15.

Souvenir Sheet

Expo '90, Intl. Garden and Greenery Exposition, Osaka, Japan — A40

1990, July 31   Litho.   Perf. 14
121	A40	$1 multicolored	1.75	1.75

Loading Mail, Pohnpei Airport, 1990 A41

Pacifica Emblem and: 45c, Japanese mail boat, Truk Lagoon, 1940.

1990, Aug. 24
122	A41	25c multicolored	.50	.50
123	A41	45c multicolored	1.25	1.25

Canoe, Flag of Federated States of Micronesia A42

Designs: No. 124, Stick chart, canoe, flag of Marshall Islands. No. 125, Frigate bird, eagle, USS Constitution, flag of US.

1990, Sept. 28   *Perf. 13½*
124 A42 25c multicolored   .55   .55
125 A42 25c multicolored   .55   .55
126 A42 25c multicolored   .55   .55
  a. Strip of 3, #124-126   1.75 1.75
  Compact of Free Association with the US.
Printed in sheets of 15. See No. 253, US No.
2506, Marshall Islands No. 381.

Moths
A43

1990, Nov. 10   **Litho.**   *Perf. 14*
127 A43 45c Gracillariidae   .80   .80
128 A43 45c Yponomeatidae   .80   .80
129 A43 45c shown   .80   .80
130 A43 45c Cosmopterigidae,
            diff.   .80   .80
  a. Block of 4, #127-130   3.25 3.25

Miniature Sheet

Christmas — A44

  Designs: a, Cherub. b, Star of Bethlehem. c,
Cherub blowing horn. d, Goats. e, Nativity
scene. f, Children, outrigger canoe. g, Messenger blowing a conch shell. h, Family walking. i, People carrying bundles.

1990, Nov. 19   **Litho.**   *Perf. 14*
131   Sheet of 9   4.50 4.50
  a.-i. A44 25c any single   .50   .50

Souvenir Sheets

New Capital of Micronesia — A45

1991, Jan. 15   **Litho.**   *Perf. 14x13½*
132 A45   Sheet of 2   1.40 1.40
  a.   25c Executive Branch   .50   .50
  b.   45c Legislative, Judicial Branches .90   .90
133 A45 $1 New Capitol   2.00 2.00

Turtles — A46

1991, Mar. 14   **Litho.**   *Perf. 14*
134 A46 29c Hawksbill on beach   1.10 1.10
135 A46 29c Green   1.10 1.10
  a.   Pair, #134-135   2.25 2.25
136 A46 50c Hawksbill   1.40 1.40
137 A46 50c Leatherback   1.40 1.40
  a.   Pair, #136-137   2.75 2.75
     Nos. 134-137 (4)   5.00 5.00

Operation
Desert
Storm
A47

1991, July 30   **Litho.**   *Perf. 14*
138 A47 29c Battleship Missou-
            ri   .60   .60
139 A47 29c Multiple launch
            rocket system   .60   .60
140 A47 29c F-14 Tomcat   .60   .60
141 A47 29c E-3 Sentry
            (AWACS)   .60   .60
  a. Block or strip of 4, #138-141 2.40 2.40
         Size: 51x38mm
142 A47 $2.90 Frigatebird, flag   5.00 5.00
  a. Souvenir sheet of 1   5.50 5.50
     Nos. 138-142 (5)   7.40 7.40

Miniature Sheets

Phila Nippon '91 — A48

  Ukiyo-e prints by Paul Jacoulet (1902-1960)
— No. 143: a, Evening Flowers, Toloas, Truk,
1941. b, The Chief's Daughter, Mogomog,
1953. c, Yagourouh and Mio, Yap, 1938. No.
144a, Yap Beauty and Orchids, 1934. b, The
Yellow-eyed Boys, Ohlol, 1940. c, Violet Flowers, Tomil, 1937. $1, First Love, Yap, 1937,
horiz.

1991, Sept.   **Litho.**   *Perf. 14*
143   Sheet of 3   2.25 2.25
  a.-c. A48 29c any single   .75   .75
144   Sheet of 3   3.50 3.50
  a.-c. A48 50c any single   1.25 1.25

         Souvenir Sheet
145 A48 $1 multicolored   2.40 2.40

Christmas — A49

  Handicraft scenes: 29c, Nativity. 40c, Adoration of the Magi. 50c, Adoration of the
Shepherds.

1991, Oct. 30   *Perf. 14x13½*
146 A49 29c multicolored   .50   .50
147 A49 40c multicolored   .75   .75
148 A49 50c multicolored   1.00 1.00
     Nos. 146-148 (3)   2.25 2.25

Pohnpei
Rain
Forest
A50

  Designs: a, Pohnpei fruit bat. b, Purple
capped fruit-dove. c, Micronesian kingfisher.
d. Birdnest fern. e, Island swiftlet. f, Long-
billed white-eye. g, Brown noddy. h, Pohnpei
lory. i, Pohnpei flycatcher. j, Caroline ground-
dove. k, White-tailed tropicbird. l, Micronesian
honeyeater. m, Ixora. n, Pohnpei fantail. o,
Gray white-eye. p, Blue-faced parrotfinch. q,
Cicadabird. r, Green skink.

1991, Nov. 18
149   Sheet of 18   13.00 13.00
  a.-r. A50 29c any single   .65   .65

Peace Corps — A51

  Designs: a, Learning crop planting techniques. b, Education. c, John F. Kennedy. d,
Public health nurses. e, Recreation.

1992, Apr. 10   **Litho.**   *Perf. 14*
150 A51 29c Strip of 5, #a.-e.   2.50 2.50
     Printed in sheets of 15.

Discovery of
America, 500th
Anniv. — A52

  Designs: a, Queen Isabella I. b, Santa
Maria. c, Columbus.

1992, May 23   **Litho.**   *Perf. 13½*
151   Strip of 3   5.00 5.00
  a.-c. A52 29c any single   1.65 1.65

Admission
to the UN,
First Anniv.
A53

1992, Sept. 24   *Perf. 11x10½*
152 A53 29c multicolored   1.50 1.50
153 A53 50c multicolored   2.25 2.25
  a. Souvenir sheet of 2, #152-153 3.50 3.50

Christmas
A54

1992, Dec. 4   *Perf. 13½*
154 A54 29c multicolored   1.90 1.90

Pioneers of Flight — A55

  a, Andrei N. Tupolev. b, John A. Macready.
c, Edward V. Rickenbacker. d, Manfred von
Richtofen. e, Hugh M. Trenchard. f, Glenn H.
Curtiss. g, Charles E. Kingsford-Smith. h, Igor
I. Sikorsky.

1993, Apr. 12
155 A55 29c Block of 8, #a.-h.   4.75 4.75
  See Nos. 178, 191, 200, 210, 233, 238, 249.

Fish — A56

  Designs: 10c, Bigscale soldierfish. 19c,
Bennett's butterflyfish. 20c, Peacock grouper.
22c, Great barracuda. 25c, Coral grouper.
29c, Regal angelfish. 30c, Bleeker's parrotfish.
35c, Picassofish. 40c, Mandarinfish. 45c,
Bluebanded surgeonfish. 50c, Orange-striped
triggerfish. 52c, Palette surgeonfish. 75c, Oriental sweetlips. $1, Zebra moray. $2, Foxface
rabbitfish. $2.90, Orangespine unicornfish.

1993-94   **Litho.**   *Perf. 13½*
156 A56 10c multicolored   .25   .25
157 A56 19c multicolored   .35   .35
158 A56 20c multicolored   .35   .35
159 A56 22c multicolored   .40   .40
160 A56 25c multicolored   .45   .45
161 A56 29c multicolored   .55   .55
162 A56 30c multicolored   .55   .55
162A A56 35c multicolored   .65   .65
163 A56 40c multicolored   .70   .70
163A A56 45c multicolored   .75   .75
164 A56 50c multicolored   .90   .90
164A A56 52c multicolored   1.00 1.00
164B A56 75c multicolored   1.40 1.40
165 A56 $1 multicolored   1.75 1.75

166 A56 $2 multicolored   3.50 3.50
167 A56 $2.90 multicolored   5.50 5.50
     Nos. 156-167 (16)   19.05 19.05

  Issued: 19c, 29c, 50c, $1, 5/14/93; 22c, 30c,
40c, 45c, 8/26/93; 10c, 20c, 35c, $2.90,
5/20/94; 25c, 52c, 75c, $2, 8/5/94.
  See Nos. 213-227, 250.

A57

  Sailing Ships: a, Great Republic. b, Benjamin F. Packard. c, Stag Hound. d, Herald of
the Morning. e, Rainbow. f, Flying Cloud. g,
Lightning. h, Sea Witch. i, Columbia. j, New
World. k, Young America. l, Courier.

1993, May 21   **Litho.**   *Perf. 13½*
168 A57 29c Sheet of 12, #a.-l. 15.00 15.00

A59

1993, July 4   **Litho.**   *Perf. 13½*
172 A59 29c multicolored   .80   .80
  Thomas Jefferson, 250th anniv. of birth.

Pacific Canoes — A60

1993, July 21   **Litho.**   *Perf. 13½*
173 A60 29c Yap   .80   .80
174 A60 29c Kosrae   .80   .80
175 A60 29c Pohnpei   .80   .80
176 A60 29c Chuuk   .80   .80
  a. Block of 4, #173-176   3.25 3.25

Local
Leaders — A61

  Designs: a, Ambilos Iehsi, (1935-81), educator. b, Andrew Roboman (1905-92), Yap
chief. c, Joab N. Sigrah (1932-88), first vice-
speaker of Congress. d, Petrus Mailo (1902-
71), Chuuk leader.

1993, Sept. 16   **Litho.**   *Perf. 13½*
177   Strip of 4   2.50 2.50
  a.-d. A61 29c any single   .65   .65
     See Nos. 204-207.

       Pioneers of Flight Type of 1993
  Designs: a, Hugh L. Dryden. b, Theodore
von Karman. c, Otto Lilienthal. d, Thomas
O.M. Sopwith. e, Lawrence B. Sperry. f,
Alberto Santos-Dumont. g, Orville Wright. h,
Wilbur Wright.

1993, Sept. 25   **Litho.**   *Perf. 13½*
178 A55 50c Block of 8, #a.-h.   6.75 6.75

Tourist Attractions, Pohnpei — A62

1993, Oct. 5
179 A62 29c Kepirohi Falls   .75 .75
180 A62 50c Spanish Wall   1.50 1.50

Souvenir Sheet
181 A62 $1 Sokehs Rock   2.00 2.00

No. 181 contains one 80x50mm stamp. See Nos. 187-189.

Butterflies — A63

No. 182: a, Great eggfly female (typical). b, Great eggfly female (local variant). No. 183: a, Monarch. b, Great eggfly male.

1993, Oct. 20   Litho.   Perf. 13½
182   Pair   1.40 1.40
 a.-b. A63 29c Any single   .70 .70
183   Pair   2.00 2.00
 a.-b. A63 50c Any single   1.00 1.00

See No. 190.

Christmas — A64

1993, Nov. 11
184 A64 29c We Three Kings   .75 .75
185 A64 50c Silent Night, Holy
           Night   1.25 1.25

Miniature Sheet

Yap Culture — A65

Designs: a, Baby basket. b, Bamboo raft. c, Baskets, handbag. d, Fruit bat. e, Forest. f, Outrigger canoe. g, Dioscorea yams. h, Mangroves. i, Manta ray. j, Cyrtosperma taro. k, Fish weir. l, Seagrass, fish. m, Taro bowl. n, Thatched house. o, Coral reef. p, Lavalava. q, Dance. r, Stone money.

1993, Dec. 15   Litho.   Perf. 13½x14
186 A65 29c Sheet of 18, #a.-
            r.   12.50 12.50

Tourist Attractions Type of 1993

Sites on Kosrae: 29c, Sleeping Lady Mountain. 40c, Walung. 50c, Lelu Ruins.

1994, Feb. 11   Litho.   Perf. 13½
187 A62 29c multicolored   .55 .55
188 A62 40c multicolored   .75 .75
189 A62 50c multicolored   .95 .95
    Nos. 187-189 (3)   2.25 2.25

Butterfly Type of 1993 with Added Inscription
Souvenir Sheet

a, 29c, like No. 182a. b, 29c, like No. 182b. c, 50c, like No. 183a. d, 50c, like No. 183b.

1994, Feb. 18
190 A63 Sheet of 4, #a.-d.   4.25 4.25

Inscription reads "Hong Kong '94 Stamp Exhibition" in Chinese on Nos. 190a, 190d, and in English on Nos. 190b-190c. Inscriptions on Nos. 190a-190d are in black.

Pioneers of Flight Type of 1993

Designs: a, Edwin E. Aldrin, Jr. b, Neil A. Armstrong. c, Michael Collins. d, Wernher von Braun. e, Octave Chanute. f, T. Claude Ryan. g, Frank Whittle. h, Waldo D. Waterman.

1994, Mar. 4   Litho.   Perf. 13½
191 A55 29c Block of 8, #a.-h.   5.75 5.75

1994 Micronesian Games — A66

Designs: a, Spearfishing. b, Basketball. c, Coconut husking. d, Tree climbing.

1994, Mar. 26   Perf. 13½x14
192   Block of 4   2.75 2.75
 a.-d. A66 29c any single   .70 .70

Native Costumes — A67

a, Pohnpei. b, Kosrae. c, Chuuk. d, Yap.

1994, Mar. 31   Perf. 13½
193   Block of 4, #a.-d.   2.75 2.75
 a.-d. A67 29c any single   .70 .70

Constitution, 15th Anniv. — A68

1994, May 10   Litho.   Perf. 11x10½
194 A68 29c multicolored   1.50 1.50

Flowers — A69

Designs: a, Fagraea berteriana. b, Pangium edule. c, Pittosporum ferrugineum. d, Sonneratia caseolaris.

1994, June 6   Litho.   Perf. 13½
195   Strip of 4   2.75 2.75
 a.-d. A69 29c any single   .70 .70

1994 World Cup Soccer Championships, US — A70

Design: No. 197, Soccer players, diff.

1994, June 17   Litho.   Perf. 13½
196 A70 50c red & multi   2.25 2.25
197 A70 50c blue & multi   2.25 2.25
 a.   Pair, #196-197   4.50 4.50

No. 197a has a continuous design.

Micronesian Postal Service, 10th Anniv. — A71

Stamps: a, #39, 45, 54 (c), 159, 189, 192 (b). b, #58 (d), 151, 161 (d), 176a, 183a (d). c, #4a, 137a, 184 (a), C12 (d), C39, C41. d, #161 (b), 183a (b), 183b, 193, C12, C40, C42.

1994, July 12   Litho.   Perf. 13½
198   Block of 4   5.00 5.00
 a.-d. A71 29c any single   1.25 1.25

No. 198 is a continuous design.

Souvenir Sheet

PHILAKOREA '94 — A72

Dinosaurs: a, 29c, Iguanodons (b). b, 52c, Coelurosaurs (c). c, $1, Camarasaurus.

1994, Aug. 16   Litho.   Perf. 13½
199 A72 Sheet of 3, #a.-c.   5.25 5.25

Pioneers of Flight Type of 1993

a, William A. Bishop. b, Karel J. Bossart. c, Marcel Dassault. d, Geoffrey de Havilland. e, Yuri A. Gagarin. f, Alan B. Shepard, Jr. g, John H. Towers. h, Hermann J. Oberth.

1994, Sept. 20   Litho.   Perf. 13½
200 A55 50c Block of 8, #a.-h.   6.75 6.75

Migratory Birds — A73

Designs: a, Oriental cuckoo. b, Long-tailed cuckoo. c, Short-eared owl. d, Dollarbird.

1994, Oct. 20   Litho.   Perf. 13½
201   Block of 4   2.50 2.50
 a.-d. A73 29c any single   .65 .65

Christmas — A74

1994, Nov. 2
202 A74 29c Doves   .60 .60
203 A74 50c Angels   1.00 1.00

Local Leaders Type of 1993

Pioneers of island unification: No. 204, Johnny Moses (1900-91), Pohnpei. No. 205, Belarmino Hatheylul (1907-93), Yap. No. 206, Anton Ring Buas (1907-79), Chuuk. No. 207, Paliknoa Sigrah (King John) (1875-1957), Kosrae.

1994, Dec. 15   Litho.   Perf. 13½
204 A61 32c multicolored   .65 .65
205 A61 32c multicolored   .65 .65
206 A61 32c multicolored   .65 .65
207 A61 32c multicolored   .65 .65
    Nos. 204-207 (4)   2.60 2.60

Souvenir Sheet

New Year 1995 (Year of the Boar) — A75

1995, Jan. 2
208 A75 50c multicolored   1.00 1.00

Chuuk Lagoon A76

Underwater scenes: a, Photographer with light. b, Various species of fish, coral. c, Diver. d, Two gold fish.

1995, Feb. 6
209   Block of 4   2.50 2.50
 a.-d. A76 32c any single   .65 .65

Pioneers of Flight Type of 1993

Designs: a, Robert H. Goddard. b, Leroy R. Grumman. c, Hugo Junkers. d, James A. Lovell, Jr. e, Louis-Charles Breguet. f, Juan de la Cierva. g, Donald W. Douglas. h, Reginald J. Mitchell.

1995, Mar. 4   Litho.   Perf. 13½
210 A55 32c Block of 8, #a.-h.   5.25 5.25

Dogs A77

a, West Highland white terrier. b, Welsh springer spaniel. c, Irish setter. d, Old English sheepdog.

1995, Apr. 5   Litho.   Perf. 13½
211   Block of 4   2.50 2.50
 a.-d. A77 32c any single   .65 .65

Fish Type of 1993

Designs: 23c, Yellow-fin tuna. 32c, Saddled butterflyfish. 46c, Achilles tang. 55c, Moorish idol. 60c, Skipjack tuna. 78c, Square-spot fairy basslet. 95c, Bluelined snapper. $3, Flame angelfish. $5, Cave grouper.

No. 227: a, like #157. b, like #161. c, like #164. d, like #165. e, like #159. f, like #162. g, like #163. h, like #163A. i, like #156. j, like #158. k, like #162A. l, like #167. m, like #217. n, like #160. o, like #164A. p, like #164B. q, like #166. r, like #214. s, like #218. t, like #222. u, like #225. v, like #213. w, like #219. x, like #223. y, like #226.

1996   Litho.   Perf. 13½
213 A56 23c multicolored   .45 .45
214 A56 32c multicolored   .65 .65
217 A56 46c multicolored   .95 .95
218 A56 55c multicolored   1.10 1.10
219 A56 60c multicolored   1.25 1.25
222 A56 78c multicolored   1.50 1.50
223 A56 95c multicolored   1.90 1.90

225	A56	$3 multicolored	6.00	6.00
226	A56	$5 multicolored	10.00	10.00
		Nos. 213-226 (9)	23.80	23.80

Miniature Sheet

227	A56	32c Sheet of 25, #a.-		
		y.	16.00	16.00

Issued: 32c, 55c, 78c, $3, 5/15/95. 23c, 60c, 95c, $5, 8/4/95; 46c, 4/10/96.

Hibiscus — A78

a, Tiliaceus. b, Huegelii. c, Trionum. d, Splendens.

1995, June 1   Litho.   Perf. 13½

228		Strip of 4	2.50	2.50
a.-d.	A78	32c any single	.65	.65

No. 228 is a continuous design.

Souvenir Sheet

UN, 50th Anniv. — A79

1995, June 26   Litho.   Perf. 13½

229	A79	$1 multicolored	2.00	2.00

Miniature Sheet

Singapore '95 — A80

Orchids: a, Paphiopedilum henrietta fujiwara. b, Thunia alba. c, Lycaste virginalis. d, Laeliocattleya prism palette.

1995, Sept. 1   Litho.   Perf. 13½

230		Sheet of 4	2.60	2.60
a.-d.	A80	32c any single	.65	.65

End of World War II, 50th Anniv. — A81

US warships: a, USS Portland. b, USS Tillman. c, USS Soley. d, USS Hyman.

1995, Sept. 2

231		Block of 4	5.00	5.00
a.-d.	A81	60c any single	1.25	1.25

Souvenir Sheet

Intl. Stamp & Coin Expo, Beijing '95 — A82

1995, Sept. 14

232	A82	50c Temple of Heaven	1.00	1.00

Pioneers of Flight Type of 1993

Designs: a, Hugh C.T. Dowding. b, William Mitchell. c, John K. Northrop. d, Frederick Handley Page. e, Frederick H. Rohr. f, Juan T. Trippe. g, Konstantin E. Tsiolkovsky. h. Ferdinand Graf von Zeppelin.

1995, Sept. 21   Litho.   Perf. 13½

233	A55	60c Block of 8, #a.-h.	9.50	9.50

Christmas Poinsettias A83

1995, Oct. 30   Litho.   Perf. 13½

234	A83	32c gray & multi	.65	.65
235	A83	60c bister & multi	1.25	1.25

Yitzhak Rabin (1922-95), Israeli Prime Minister — A84

1995, Nov. 30   Litho.   Perf. 13½

236	A84	32c multicolored	.65	.65

No. 236 was issued in sheets of 8.

Souvenir Sheet

New Year 1996 (Year of the Rat) — A85

1996, Jan. 5   Litho.   Perf. 13½

237	A85	50c multicolored	1.00	1.00

Pioneers of Flight Type of 1993

Designs: a, James H. Doolittle. b, Claude Dornier. c, Ira C. Eaker. d, Jacob C.H. Ellehammer. e, Henry H. Arnold. f, Louis Blériot. g, William E. Boeing. h, Sydney Camm.

1996, Feb. 21   Litho.   Perf. 13½

238	A55	32c Block of 8, #a.-h.	5.25	5.25

Tourism in Yap — A86

a, Meeting house. b, Stone money. c, Churu dancing. d, Traditional canoe.

1996, Mar. 13   Litho.   Perf. 13½

239		Block of 4	2.50	2.50
a.-d.	A86	32c any single	.65	.65

Sea Stars A87

Designs: a, Rhinoceros. b, Necklace c, Thick-skinned. d, Blue.

1996, Apr. 26   Litho.   Perf. 12

240		Block of 4	4.50	4.50
a.-d.	A87	55c any single	1.15	1.15

Olympic Games, Cent. — A88

First Olympic stamps, Greece: a, #120. b, #122. c, #121. d, #128.

1996, Apr. 27

241		Block of 4	4.75	4.75
a.-d.	A88	60c any single	1.20	1.20

Souvenir Sheet

China '96, 9th Asian Intl. Philatelic Exhibition — A89

Design: The Tarrying Garden, Suzhou.

1996, May 15   Perf. 13x13½

242	A89	50c multicolored	1.00	1.00

Patrol Boats — A90

1996, May 3   Litho.   Perf. 13½

243	A90	32c FSS Palikir	.65	.65
244	A90	32c FSS Micronesia	.65	.65
a.		Pair, #243-244	1.30	1.30

No. 244a is a continuous design.

First Ford Automobile, Cent. — A91

a, 1896 Quadricycle. b, 1917 Model T truck. c, 1928 Model A Tudor Sedan. d, 1932 V-8 Sport Roadster. e, 1941 Lincoln Continental. f, 1953 F-100 Truck. g, 1958 Thunderbird convertible. h, 1996 Mercury Sable.

1996, June 4   Perf. 13½

245		Sheet of 8	8.75	8.75
a.-h.	A91	55c any single	1.10	1.10

Officer Reza, Member of Natl. Police Drug Enforcement Unit — A93

1996, July 31   Litho.   Perf. 13½

247	A93	32c multicolored	.65	.65

Citrus Fruit — A94

a, Orange. b, Lime. c, Lemon. d, Tangerine.

1996, Aug. 24   Litho.   Perf. 13½

248		Strip of 4	4.00	4.00
a.-d.	A94	50c any single	1.00	1.00

Pioneers of Flight Type of 1993

Designs: a, Gianni Caproni. b, Henri Farman. c, Curtis E. LeMay. d, Grover Loening. e, Sergey P. Korolyov. f, Isaac M. Laddon. g, Glenn L. Martin. h, Alliott Verdon Roe.

1996, Sept. 18

249	A55	60c Block of 8, #a.-h.	12.50	12.50

Fish Type of 1993

Designs: a, like #157. b, like #165. c, like #162A. d, like #218.

1996, Oct. 21   Litho.   Perf. 13½

250	A56	32c Block of 4, #a.-d.	2.50	2.50

Taipei '96, 10th Asian Intl. Philatelic Exhibition. Nos. 250a, 250d have English inscriptions. Nos. 250b-250c have Chinese inscriptions.

Magi Following Star to Bethlehem A95

1996, Oct. 30   Litho.   Perf. 13½

251	A95	32c dark blue & multi	.65	.65
252	A95	60c blue & multi	1.25	1.25

Christmas.

Canoe, Flag of Federated States of Micronesia Type of 1990

1996, Nov. 3   Perf. 11x10½

253	A42	$3 like #124	6.00	6.00

No. 253 inscribed "Free Association United States of America."

Deng Xiaoping
(1904-97) — A96

Portraits: a, Wearing white-collared shirt. b, Looking left. c, Looking right. d, Wearing hat. $3, Looking left, diff.

1997   Litho.   Perf. 14
254   Sheet of 4   4.75 4.75
a.-d. A96 60c any single   1.20 1.20
Souvenir Sheet
255 A96 $3 multicolored   6.00 6.00

Souvenir Sheet

Hong Kong — A97

1997
256 A97 $2 multicolored   4.00 4.00

New Year 1997 (Year of the
Ox) — A98

1997   Litho.   Perf. 14
257 A98 32c multicolored   .65   .65
Souvenir Sheet
258 A98 $2 like #257   4.00 4.00

Return of
Hong Kong
to China
A99

Flowers, Victoria Harbor: a, Melia azedarach. b, Sail from ship, Victoria Peak. c, Sail from ship, dendrobium chrysotoxum. d, Bauhinia blakeana. e, Cassia surattensis, Chinese junk. f, Junk, nelumbo nucifera.
$3, Strongylodon macrobatrys, pagoda.

1997, July 1
259   Sheet of 6   7.25 7.25
a.-f. A99 60c any single   1.20 1.20
Souvenir Sheet
260 A99 $3 multicolored   6.00 6.00

Sea Goddesses of the Pacific — A100

a, Giant serpent, woman holding child, Walutahanga of Melanesia. b, Sailing ship in storm, woman holding lantern, Tien-Hou of China. c, Woman swimming to bottom of sea gathering fish into basket, Lorop of Micronesia. d, Woman swimming to man in canoe, Oto-Hime of Japan. e, Woman holding seashell, Nomoi of Micronesia. f, Three women in canoe, Junkgowa sisters of Australia.

1997, May 29   Litho.   Perf. 14
261 A100 32c Sheet of 6, #a.-f. 3.75 3.75
PACIFIC 97.

Paintings by
Hiroshige
(1797-1858)
A101

Whirlpools at Naruto in Awa Province, 1857: No. 262: a, Sailboats in distance. b, Island of trees at left. c, Island of trees at right.
Tale of Genji: Viewing the Plum Blossoms, 1852: No. 263: a, Small evergreen trees in front of woman. b, Woman. c, Trees, house in distance with woman.
Snow on the Sumida River, 1847: No. 264: a, House, river. b, Two women under umbrella. c, Woman with folded umbrella.
Each $2: No. 265, Rapids in Bitchu Province, 1854. No. 266, Fuji from Satta Point, 1858.

1997, July 25   Perf. 13½x14
262   Sheet of 3   1.25 1.25
a.-c. A101 20c any single   .40   .40
263   Sheet of 3   3.00 3.00
a.-c. A101 50c any single   1.00 1.00
264   Sheet of 3   3.50 3.50
a.-c. A101 60c any single   1.20 1.20
Souvenir Sheets
265-266 A101 Set of 2   8.00 8.00

Second Federated States of
Micronesia Games — A102

a, Tennis. b, Discus. c, Swimming. d, Canoeing.

1997, Aug. 15   Litho.   Perf. 14
267 A102 32c Block of 4, #a.-d. 2.50 2.50
No. 267 was issued in sheets of 16 stamps.

Elvis Presley
(1935-77)
A103

Various portraits.

1997, Aug. 16
268   Sheet of 6   6.00 6.00
a.-f. A103 50c any single   1.00 1.00

Ocean
Exploration
A104

No. 269: a, Simon Lake, Argonaut, 1897. b, William Beebe, Bathysphere, 1934. c, Auguste Piccard, Bathyscapho, 1954. d, Harold Edgerton, deep-sea camera, 1954. e, Jacques Piccard, Trieste, 1960. f, Edwin Link, Man-in-Sea Project, 1962. g, Melvin Fisher, search for treasure, 1971. h, Robert Ballard, Alvin, 1978. i, Sylvia Earle, Deep Rover, 1979.
Each $2: No. 270, C. Wyville Thomson, deep-sea dredge, vert. No. 271, Shinkai 6500 exploring bottom of sea, vert. No. 272, Jacques-Yves Cousteau, vert.

1997, Oct. 6   Litho.   Perf. 14
269   Sheet of 9   4.25 4.25
a.-i. A104 32c any single   .45   .45
Souvenir Sheets
270-272 A104 Set of 3   30.00 30.00

Diana, Princess
of Wales (1961-
97)
A105

1997, Nov. 26   Litho.   Perf. 14
273 A105 60c multicolored   1.25 1.25
No. 273 was issued in sheets of 6.

World Wildlife Fund — A106

Butterfly fish: a, Blackback. b, Saddled. c, Threadfin. d, Bennett's.

1997, Nov. 24   Litho.   Perf. 14
274 A106 50c Block of 4, #a.-d. 8.00 8.00
No. 274 was issued in sheets of 16 stamps.

Christmas
Paintings
A107

Christ Glorified in the Court of Heaven, by Fra Angelico: No. 275, Angels playing musical instruments. No. 276, Choir of Angels.
A Choir of Angels, by Simon Marmion: No. 277, Two angels blowing long horns. No. 278, One angel blowing horn.

1997, Nov. 25
275 A107 32c multicolored   .65   .65
276 A107 32c multicolored   .65   .65
a.   Horiz. pair, Nos. 275-276 1.30 1.30
277 A107 60c multicolored   1.25 1.25
278 A107 60c multicolored   1.25 1.25
a.   Vert. pair, Nos. 277-278 2.50 2.50
Nos. 276a, 278a were each issued in sheets of 8 pairs.

Souvenir Sheets

New Year 1998 (Year of the
Tiger) — A108

1998, Jan. 2   Litho.   Perf. 14
279 A108 50c shown   1.00 1.00
280 A108 50c Chinese toy (face) 1.00 1.00

Souvenir Sheet

Micronesia's Admission to United
Nations, 7th Anniv. — A109

1998, Feb. 13   Perf. 13½
281 A109 $1 multicolored   2.00 2.00

Winnie the Pooh — A110

No. 282: a, Rabbit. b, Owl. c, Eeyore. d, Kanga and Roo. e, Piglet. f, Tigger. g, Pooh. h, Christopher Robin.
Each $2: No. 283, Piglet, Pooh, and Tigger. No. 284, Rabbit and Pooh.

1998, Feb. 16   Perf. 14x14½
282   Sheet of 8   5.25 5.25
a.-h. A110 32c any single   .65   .65
Souvenir Sheets
283-284 A110 Set of 2   8.00 8.00

1998 World Cup Soccer
Championships, France — A111

Various soccer plays, color of foreground player's shirt & shorts — No. 285: a, White & black. b, Green & white. c, Yellow & blue, socks with colored stripes. d, Green & black. e, Yellow & black. f, Red & blue. g, Yellow & blue, plain socks. h, Red & white.
Each $2: No. 286, Red & blue. No. 287, Green, black & white.

1998, Mar. 20	Litho.		Perf. 13½	
285	Sheet of 8		5.00	5.00
a.-h. A111 32c any single			.65	.65
Souvenir Sheets				
286-287	A111 Set of 2		8.00	8.00

Souvenir Sheet

Micronesia's Recognition by Intl.
Olympic Committee — A112

1998, Mar. 20				
288	A112 $3 multicolored		6.00	6.00

Old Testament
Bible
Stories — A113

Adam and Eve — No. 289: a, Land of plenty. b, Adam, Eve before the fall. c, Serpent of temptation.
Joseph and his brethren — No. 290: a, Brothers plan to sell Joseph. b, Joseph in his many-colored coat. c, Ishmaelites buy Joseph.
Rebekah — No. 291: a, Rebekah at the well. b, Abraham's servant Eliezer. c, Angel sent to prosper Eliezer's way.
Each $2: No. 292, Adam and Eve sent forth from Eden. No. 293, Joseph forgives his brothers. No. 294, Isaac takes Rebekah to wife.

1998, May 13	Litho.		Perf. 13½x14	
289	Sheet of 3		1.90	1.90
a.-c. A113 32c any single			.65	.65
290	Sheet of 3		2.50	2.50
a.-c. A113 40c any single			.85	.85
291	Sheet of 3		3.50	3.50
a.-c. A113 60c any single			1.20	1.20
Souvenir Sheets				
292-294	A113 Set of 3		12.00	12.00

Israel '98.

Intl. Year of
the Ocean
A114

Deep sea research — No. 295: a, Marine observation satellite. b, Support vessel, Natsushima. c, Research vessel, Kaiyo. d, Deep sea anemone. e, Shinkai 2000. f, Deep tow. g, Tripod fish. h, Towed deep survey system. i, Black smokers.
Each $2: No. 296, Communications satellite. No. 297, Ocean observation buoy, vert. No. 298, Weather satellite.

1998, June 2	Litho.		Perf. 13	
295	Sheet of 9		5.75	5.75
a.-i. A114 32c any single			.65	.65
Souvenir Sheets				
296-298	A114 Set of 3		12.00	12.00

Native Birds — A115

No. 299: a, Kosrae white-eye. b, Chuuk monarch. c, Yap monarch. d, Pohnpei lory.
$3, Pohnpei mountain starling.

1998, June 30			Perf. 14x14½	
299	A115 50c Block or strip of 4,		4.00	4.00
	#a.-d.			
Souvenir Sheet				
300	A115 $3 multicolored		6.00	6.00

No. 299 was issued in sheets of 16 stamps.

Fish — A116

Designs: 1c, White-tipped soldierfish. 2c, Red-breasted wrasse. 3c, Bicolor angelfish. 4c, Falco hawkfish. 5c, Convict tang. 10c, Square-spot fairy basslet. 13c, Orangeband surgeonfish. 15c, Multibarred goatfish. 17c, Masked rabbitfish. 20c, White-spotted surgeonfish. 22c, Blue-girdled angelfish. 32c, Wedge picassofish. 39c, Red parrotfish. 40c, Lemonpeel angelfish. 60c, Humphead wrasse. 78c, Sapphire damselfish. $1, Bluefin travally. $3, Whitespot hawkfish. $5, Spotted trunkfish. $10.75, Pinktail triggerfish.

1998		Litho.	Perf. 14½	
301	A116	1c multi	.25	.25
302	A116	2c multi	.25	.25
303	A116	3c multi	.25	.25
304	A116	4c multi	.25	.25
305	A116	5c multi	.25	.25
306	A116	10c multi	.25	.25
307	A116	13c multi	.25	.25
308	A116	15c multi	.30	.30
309	A116	17c multi	.35	.35
310	A116	20c multi	.40	.40
311	A116	22c multi	.45	.45
312	A116	32c multi	.65	.65
313	A116	39c multi	.75	.75
314	A116	40c multi	.80	.80
315	A116	60c multi	1.25	1.25
316	A116	78c multi	1.50	1.50
317	A116	$1 multi	1.90	1.90
318	A116	$3 multi	5.75	5.75
319	A116	$5 multi	10.00	10.00
319A	A116	$10.75 multi	21.00	21.00
	Nos. 301-319A (20)		46.85	46.85

Issued: $10.75, 9/8; others, 7/20.
See Nos. 328-333.

Fala, Franklin D. Roosevelt's Scottish
Terrier — A117

Designs: a, Roosevelt's hand petting dog. b, Radio at right. c, Radio at left. d, In car with FDR. e, Presidential seal. f, Closeup of Fala looking left.

1998, Aug. 27	Litho.		Perf. 13½	
320	Sheet of 6		3.75	3.75
a.-f. A117 32c any single			.65	.65

Eskimo Madonna – Claire Fejes
Federated States of Micronesia 32c
Christmas 1997

Christmas
A118

Twentieth cent. art — No. 321: a, Eskimo Madonna, by Claire Fejes. b, Madonna, by Man Ray. c, Peasant Mother, by David Siquerios.
No. 322: a, Mother and Child, by Pablo Picasso. b, Gypsy Woman with Baby, by Amedeo Modigliani. c, Mother and Child, by José Orozco.
$2, Detail from The Family, by Marisol, horiz.

1998, Sept. 15	Litho.		Perf. 13½x14	
321	Sheet of 3		1.90	1.90
a.-c. A118 32c any single			.65	.65
322	Sheet of 3		3.75	3.75
a.-c. A118 60c any single			1.25	1.25
Souvenir Sheet				
Perf. 14x13½				
323	A118 $2 multicolored		4.00	4.00

John Glenn's
Return to
Space — A119

Each 60c: No. 324: Various photos of Friendship 7 mission, 1962.
Each 60c: No. 325: Various photos of Discovery space shuttle mission, 1998.
Each 60c: No. 326, Launch of Friendship 7. No. 327, Portrait of Glenn, 1998.

1998, Oct. 29	Litho.		Perf. 14	
Sheets of 8				
324-325	Set of 2		19.00	19.00
a.-h. A119 60c any single			1.20	1.20
Souvenir Sheets				
326-327	A119 Set of 2		8.00	8.00

Fish Type of 1993

Designs: 33c, Black jack. 50c, Whitecheek surgeonfish. 55c, Long-jawed squirrelfish. 77c, Onespot snapper. $3.20, Tan-faced parrotfish. $11.75, Yellow-faced angelfish.

1999		Litho.	Perf. 14½	
328	A116	33c multicolored	.65	.65
329	A116	50c multicolored	1.00	1.00
330	A116	55c multicolored	1.10	1.10
331	A116	77c multicolored	1.50	1.50
332	A116	$3.20 multicolored	6.50	6.50
Perf. 14				
Size: 45x21mm				
333	A116	$11.75 multicolored	22.50	22.50
	Nos. 328-333 (6)		33.25	33.25

Issued: $11.75, 3/31; others, 2/22.

Russian Space
Exploration
A120

No. 334: a, Sputnik 1, 1957. b, Leika in Sputnik 2, 1957. c, Luna 1, 1959. d, Luna 3, 1959. e, Yuri Gagarin in Vostok 1, 1961. f, Venera 1, 1961. g, Mars 1, 1962. h, Valentina Tereshkova in Vostok 6, 1963. i, Voskhod 1, 1964. j, Aleksei Leonov in Voskhod 2, 1965. k, Venera 3, 1966. l, Luna 10. m, Luna 9. n, Luna 16, 1970. o, Luna 17, 1970. p, Mars 3, 1971. q, Leonid Popov, Valeri Ryumin, Soyuz 35, 1980. r, Vega 1, 1985. s, Vega 1, Halley's Comet, 1986. t, Mir, 1986-98.
Each $2: No. 335, Russian Space Station, Mir, 1998. No. 336, Docking of USSR Soyuz 19 and Apollo 18, horiz.

1999, Mar. 15			Perf. 14	
334	Sheet of 20		13.50	13.50
a.-t. A120 33c any single			.70	.70
Souvenir Sheets				
335-336	A120 Set of 2		8.00	8.00

See Nos. 344-346.

"Romance of
the Three
Kingdoms,"
by Lo Kuan-
Chung
A121

No. 337: a, Men, women conferring. b, Four men, one grabbing on clothes of another. c, Two men jousting. d, Four men looking down at one man. e, Man kneeling before another man in wheelchair.
No. 338: a, Mounted warriors approaching drawbridge. b, Warriors fighting in front of fire, banners. c, Warrior fighting off others, smoke. d, Man, woman kneeling before old man. e, Two men looking up at smoke coming from boiling pot.
No. 339, Three men in boat, raging fire.

1999, Mar. 19	Litho.		Perf. 13½	
Sheets of 5				
337	A121 33c #a.-e.		3.25	3.25
338	A121 50c #a.-e.		5.00	5.00
Souvenir Sheet				
339	A121 $2 multicolored		4.00	4.00

No. 339 contains one 52x79mm stamp.

IBRA '99, World Stamp Exhibition,
Nuremberg, Germany — A122

Designs: No. 340, The Leipzig-Dresden Railway, Caroline Islands #4. No. 341, Gölsdorf 4-4-0, Caroline Islands #16.
$2, Exhibition emblem, Caroline Islands #6, vert.

1999, Apr. 27			Perf. 14x14½	
340	A122 55c multicolored		1.10	1.10
341	A122 55c multicolored		1.10	1.10
Souvenir Sheet				
342	A122 $2 multicolored		4.00	4.00

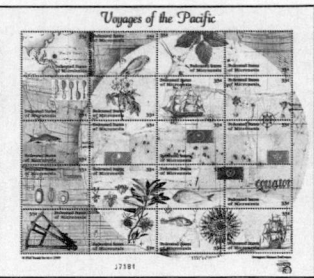

Voyages of the Pacific — A123

Designs: a, Map of Pacific Ocean. b, Parrot. c, Bird in flight, leaves. d, Map, ship's stern. e, Part of ship, various blocks. f, Flower. g, Sailing ship, side view. h, Three flowers, compass rose. i, Fish over ship's drawing. j, Map, flag LL. k, Map, flag UR. l, Map, flag LR. m, Three sections of coconut. n, Three flowers, plant. o, Fish. p, Flag, UL, "Equator." q, Sextant. r, Bottom of plant. s, Fish, compass rose. t, Sailing ship, bow on.

1999, Mar. 19   Litho.   Perf. 13½
343 A123 33c Sheet of 20,
   #a.-t.   13.50 13.50

Space Achievements Type of 1999

US space achievements — No. 344: a, Explorer 1, 1958. b, OSO 1, 1962. c, Mariner 2 to Venus, 1962. d, Mariner 2, 1962. e, Apollo 8, 1968. f, First step onto moon, Apollo 11, 1969. g, First samples from moon, Apollo 11, 1969. h, Apollo 15, 1971. i, Mariner 9, 1971. j, Pioneer 10, 1973. k, Mariner 10, 1974. l, Viking 1, 1976. m, Pioneer 11, 1979. n, STS 1, 1981. o, Pioneer 10, 1983. p, Solar Maximum Mission, 1984. q, Cometary Explorer, 1985. r, Voyager 2, 1989. s, Gallileo to Gaspra, 1992. t, Sojourner, 1997.

Each $2: No. 345, International space station. No. 346, Shuttle mission to repair Hubble Telescope, 1993.

1999, Mar. 15   Litho.   Perf. 14
344 A120 33c Sheet of 20,
   #a.-t.   13.50 13.50

Souvenir Sheets
345-346 A120 Set of 2   8.00 8.00

Illustrations on Nos. 344p and 344q are incorrect.

Earth Day — A124

Endangered, extinct, and prehistoric species — No. 347: a, Black rhinoceros. b, Cheetah. c, Jackass penguin. d, Blue whale. e, Red-headed woodpecker. f, African elephant. g, Aurochs. h, Dodo bird. i, Tasmanian wolf. j, Giant lemur. k, Quagga. l, Steller's sea cow. m, Pteranodon. n, Shonisaurus. o, Stegosaurus. p, Galliminus. q, Tyrannosaurus. r, Archelon. s, Brachiosaurus. t, Triceratops.

Each $2: No. 348, Moa. No. 349, Suchominus tenerensis, horiz.

1999
347   Sheet of 20   13.50 13.50
   a.-t. A124 33c any single   .70   .70

Souvenir Sheets
348-349 A124 Set of 2   8.00 8.00

Nos. 348-349 contain one 50x38mm and one 38x50mm stamp, respectively.

Paintings by Hokusai (1760-1849) A125

Details or entire paintings — No. 350, each 33c: a, Ghost of O-Iwa. b, Horse Drawings (head down). c, Abe Nakamaro. d, Ghost of Kasane. e, Horse Drawings (head up). f, The Ghost of Kiku and the Priest Mitazuki.

No. 351, each 33c: a, Belly Band Float. b, Drawing of Women (facing left). c, Swimmers. d, Eel Climb. e, Drawings of Women (facing right). f, Kimo Ga Imo Ni Naru.

Each $2: No. 352, Whaling off Goto. No. 353, Fishing by Torchlight.

1999, July 20   Litho.   Perf. 13¾x14
Sheets of 6
350-351 Set of 2   8.00 8.00
  a.-f. A125 33c any single .65 .65

Souvenir Sheets
352-353 A125 Set of 2   8.00 8.00

Flowers — A126

Various flowers making up a photomosaic of Princess Diana.

1999   Litho.   Perf. 13¼
354 A126 50c Sheet of 8, #a.-h. 8.00 8.00
See No. 393, 403.

Millennium — A127

No. 355 — Highlights of the 12th Century: a, Death of Emperor Henry IV. b, Taira and Minamoto clans. c, Order of the Knights of the Hospital of St. John founded. d, Nautical compass invented. e, "White Ship" disaster. f, Pope Calixtus and Henry V end dispute. g, Death of Omar Khyyam. h, Death of Duke William IX. i, Roger II crowned King of Sicily. j, Stephen of Blois, Matilda. k, Birth of Maimonides. l, Church condemns Peter Abelard. m, Crusaders defeated at Damascus. n, Fall of city of Tula. o, Completion of Angkor Wat. p, Chimu culture flourishes (60x40mm). q, Honen becomes hermit.

No. 356 — Science and Technology of Ancient China: a, Well drilling. b, Chain pump. c, Magic lantern. d, Seismograph. e, Dial and pointer devices. f, Refined value of pi. g, Porcelain. h, Water mill. i, Stirrup. j, Tea. k, Umbrella. l, Brandy and whiskey. m, Printing. n, Paper money. o, Gunpowder. p, Arch bridge (60x40mm). q, Mercator map projection.

1999, Oct. 4   Perf. 12¾x12½
Sheets of 17
355 A127 20c #a.-q. + label   7.00 7.00
356 A127 33c #a.-q. + label 11.50 11.50

Inscriptions on Nos. 355g, 355o, and perhaps others, are incorrect or misspelled.
See No. 377.

Costumes — A128

Designs: a, French princess gown (head at R). b, As "a," (head at B). c, As "a," (bust). d, As "a," (umbrella). e, Scissors. f, Tools for fabric making. g, Micronesian wedding costume (head at R). h, As "g," (midriff). i, As "g," (feet). j, Japanese fabrics. k, Masai warrior costume (head at L). l, As "k," (head at R). m, African fabric details. n, Kabuki theater costume (head). o, As "n," (midriff). p, French Renaissance costume (head at B). q, Textile patterns. r, As "p," (head at R). s, Rulers. t, Iron.

1999, Nov. 22   Perf. 14¾
357 A128 33c Sheet of 20,
   #a.-t.   13.50 13.50

Vertical strips of 2, 3 or 5 have continuous designs.

Christmas A129

Paintings by Anthony Van Dyck: 33c, Holy Family with St. John. 60c, Madonna with Child. No. 360, The Virgin and Child with Two Donors (detail).
No. 361, The Adoration of the Shepherds.

1999, Dec. 1   Litho.   Perf. 13¾
358 A129 33c multi   .65   .65
359 A129 60c multi   1.25 1.25
360 A129 $2 multi   4.00 4.00
   Nos. 358-360 (3)   5.90 5.90

Souvenir Sheet
361 A129 $2 multi   4.00 4.00

Millennium — A130

Airplanes — No. 362: a, Wright Flyer I. b, Blériot XI. c, Fokker D VII. d, Dornier Komet I. e, Ryan NYP. f, Mitsubishi A6M. g, Boeing B-29. h, Messerschmitt 262A. i, Bell X-1. j, MiG-19. k, Lockheed U-2. l, Boeing 707. m, Concorde. n, McDonnell Douglas DC-10. o, B-2.
No. 363, P38. No. 364, Dornier Do X.

1999, Dec. 9   Perf. 14
362 A130 33c Sheet of 15,
   #a.-o.   10.00 10.00

Souvenir Sheets
Perf. 13¾
363 A130 $2 multi   4.00 4.00
364 A130 $2 multi   4.00 4.00

No. 363 contains one 32x48mm stamp. No. 364 contains one 48x32mm stamp.

Orchids — A131

No. 365: a, Baptistonia echinata. b, Bulbophyllum lobbii. c, Cattleya bicolor. d, Cischweinfia dasyandra. e, Cochleanthes discolor. f, Dendrobium bellatulum.
No. 366: a, Esmeralda clarkei. b, Gomesa crispa. c, Masdevallia elephanticeps. d, Maxillaria variabilis. e, Mitoniopsis roezlii. f, Oncidium cavendishianum.
No. 367: a, Oncidium obryzatum. b, Oncidium phalaenopsis. c, Oncidium pulvinatum. d, Paphiopedilum armeniacum. e, Paphiopedilum dayanum. f, Paphiopedilum druryi.
No. 368, Paphiopedilum hirutissimum. No. 369, Licoglossum oerstedii.

2000, Jan. 5   Perf. 14¼x14
Sheets of 6
365 A131 33c #a.-f.   4.00 4.00
366 A131 33c #a.-f.   4.00 4.00
367 A131 33c #a.-f.   4.00 4.00

Souvenir Sheets
Perf. 14x14¼
368 A131 $1 multi   2.00 2.00
369 A131 $1 multi   2.00 2.00

Nos. 368-369 each contain one 31x53mm stamp.

Leaders of the 20th Century — A132

Designs: a, Martin Luther King, Jr. b, Albert Schweitzer. c, Pope John Paul II. d, Sarvepalli Radhakrishnan. e, Toyohiko Kagawa. f, Mahatma Gandhi. g, Mother Teresa. h, Khyentse Rinpoche. i, Desmond Tutu. j, Chiara Lubich. k, 14th Dalai Lama. l, Abraham Heschel.

2000, Jan. 18   Litho.   Perf. 14¼
370 A132 33c Sheet of 12, #a.-l 8.00 8.00

Souvenir Sheet

New Year 2000 (Year of the Dragon) — A133

2000, Feb. 5　　　　　*Perf. 13¾*
371　A133　$2 multi　　　　4.00　4.00

Butterflies — A134

No. 372: a, Salamis parhassus. b, Morpho rhetenor. c, Danaus plexippus. d, Phyciodes actinote. e, Idea leucone. f, Actinote negra.
No. 373: a, Graphium sarpedon. b, Papilio machaon. c, Ornithoptera priamus. d, Ornithoptera chimaerea. e, Graphium antiphates. f, Pachliopta aristochiae.
Each $2: No. 374, Hamadryas amphinome, vert. No. 375, Colias croceus, vert. No. 376, Butterfly collector, vert.

2000, Feb. 28　Litho.　*Perf. 14*
Sheets of 6
372　A134　20c #a.-f.　　2.40　2.40
373　A134　55c #a.-f.　　6.75　6.75
Souvenir Sheets
374-376　A134　Set of 3　12.00　12.00

Millennium Type of 1999

Highlights of the 1920s: a, Mahatma Gandhi leads non-violent reform in India. b, International Dada Fair in Berlin. c, American women win right to vote. d, Sacco and Vanzetti case. e, Hermann Rorschach develops inkblot test. f, Thomas J. Watson incorporates IBM. g, First successful commercial 35mm camera. h, Scopes "Monkey Trial." i, Charles Lindbergh makes first solo transatlantic flight. j, George Lemaitre develops "Big Bang" theory of cosmology. k, Chiang Kai-shek becomes generalissimo of China. l, Werner Heisenberg states "uncertainty principle" of physics. m, Alexander Fleming isolates Penicillium mold. n, Hirohito enthroned as Japanese emperor. o, Stock market crash starts Great Depression. p, First round-the-world flight (60x40mm). q, "All Quiet on the Western Front" published.

2000, Mar. 13　　*Perf. 12¾x12½*
Sheet of 17
377　A127　20c #a.-q. + label　7.00　7.00
Inscriptions are incorrect or misspelled on Nos. 377a, 377f and 377m.

Millennium Type of 1999 with "Millennium 2000" Inscription
Perf. 13¼x13½
2000, Mar. 13　Litho.
378　A127　33c Like #356o　.65　.65

Peacemakers — A135

a, Mikhail Gorbachev. b, Ending the Cold War. c, Ronald Reagan. d, Le Duc Tho. e, Resolving the conflict in Viet Nam. f, Henry Kissinger. g, Linus Pauling. h, Protest against nuclear weapons. i, Peter Benenson. j, Amnesty Intl. k, Mahatma Gandhi. l, Fasting for peace. m, Initiating the Peace Corps. n, John F. Kennedy. o, Praying for peace. p, The 14th Dalai Lama. q, The UN. r, Cordell Hull. s, F. W. De Klerk. t, Ending apartheid. u, Nelson Mandela. v, Franklin Roosevelt. w, Yalta Conference. x, Winston Churchill.
Illustration reduced.

2000, Mar. 28　　　　*Perf. 14*
379　A135　33c Sheet of 24,
　　　#a-x　　　　16.00　16.00

Philanthropists — A136

a, Andrew Carnegie. b, John D. Rockefeller. c, Henry Ford. d, Madam C. J. Walker. e, James B. Duke. f, Andrew Mellon. g, Charles F. Kettering. h, Robert W. Woodruff. i, Brooke Astor. j, Howard Hughes. k, Jesse H. Jones. l, Paul Mellon. m, J. Paul Getty. n, George Soros. o, Phyllis Wattis. p, Ted Turner.

2000, May 1　　　*Perf. 14¼x14½*
380　A136　33c Sheet of 16,
　　　#a-p　　　　11.00　11.00

Mushrooms — A137

No. 381, each 33c: a, Fairies' bonnets. b, Black bulgar. c, Amethyst deceiver. d, Common morel. e, Bird's nest fungus. f, Trumpet clitocybe.
No. 382, each 33c: a, Bonnet mycena. b, Horse mushroom. c, Velvet boletus. d, Oyster. d, Aztec mandala. e, Fly agaric.
Each $2: No. 383, Magpie ink cap. No, 384, Brown birch bolete.

2000, May 15　　*Perf. 13¾x14¼*
Sheets of 6, #a-f
381-382　A137　Set of 2　8.00　8.00
Souvenir Sheets
383-384　A137　Set of 2　8.00　8.00

Flowers of the Pacific — A138

Wildflowers — A139

No. 385: a, Freycinetia arborea. b, Mount Cook lily. c, Sun orchid. d, Bossiaea ensata. e, Swamp hibiscus. f, Gardenia brighamii.
No. 386: a, Eleagant brodiaea. b, Skyrocket. c, Hedge bindweed. d, Woods' rose. e, Swamp rose. f, Wake robin.
No. 387, Black-eyed Susan. No. 388, Yellow meadow lily.

2000, May 29　　*Perf. 14x13¾*
385　A138　33c Sheet of 6, #a-f　4.00　4.00
386　A139　33c Sheet of 6, #a-f　4.00　4.00
Souvenir Sheets
387　A138　$2 multi　　　4.00　4.00
388　A139　$2 multi　　　4.00　4.00

Souvenir Sheet

2000 Summer Olympics, Sydney — A140

No. 389: a, Henry Taylor. b, Cycling. c, Olympic Stadium, Munich and German flag. d, Ancient Greek wrestling.

2000, July 10　Litho.　*Perf. 14*
389　A140　33c Sheet of 4, #a-d　2.75　2.75

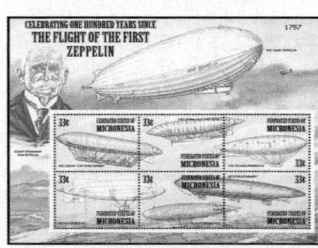

Zeppelins and Airships — A141

No. 390: a, Zodiac Capitaine Ferber. b, Astra Adjutant Reau. c, Italian dirigible IA. d, Astra-Torres XIV. e, Schuttle-Lanz SL3. f, Siemens-Schukert.
Each $2: No. 391, Graf Zeppelin. No. 392, Dupuy de Lome airship.

2000, Aug. 7　Litho.　*Perf. 14*
390　A141　33c Sheet of 6, #a-f　4.00　4.00
Souvenir Sheets
391-392　A141　Set of 2　8.00　8.00
First Zeppelin flight, cent. (Nos. 390, 391).

Flower Photomosaic Type of 1999

Various flowers making up a photomosaic of the Queen Mother.

2000, Sept. 5　Litho.　*Perf. 13¾*
393　A126　33c Sheet of 8, #a-h　5.25　5.25

Souvenir Sheet

2000 Summer Olympics, Sydney — A142

No. 394: a, 33c, Weight lifting. b, 33c, Basketball. c, $1, Weight lifting.

2000, Sept. 11　　　*Perf. 14*
394　A142　Sheet of 3, #a-c　3.50　3.50
Olymphilex 2000, Sydney.

Fish
A143

Designs: No. 395, Rock beauty. No. 396, Bluestreak cleaner wrasse. No. 397, Chevroned butterflyfish (with frame). No. 398, Longfin bannerfish (with frame).
No. 399: a, Mandarinfish. b, Emperor snapper. c, Copper-banded butterflyfish. d, Chevroned butterflyfish (no frame). e, Lemonpeel angelfish. f, Harlequin tuskfish. g, Clown triggerfish. h, Coral hind. i, Longfin bannerfish (no frame).
No. 400: a, Six-spot grouper. b, Common jellyfish. c, Palette surgeonfish. d, Bicolor angelfish. e, Threadfin butterflyfish. f, Clown anemonefish. g, Three-banded demoiselle. h, Reef shark. i, Starfish.
No. 401, Long-nosed butterflyfish. No. 402, Emperor angelfish.

2000, Nov. 1
395-398　A143　33c Set of 4　2.60　2.60
Sheets of 9, #a-i
399-400　A143　33c Set of 2　12.00　12.00
Souvenir Sheets
401-402　A143　$2 Set of 2　8.00　8.00

Flower Photomosaic Type of 1999

Various photos with religious themes making up a photomosaic of Pope John Paul II.

2000, Nov. 1　Litho.　*Perf. 13¾x14*
403　A126　50c Sheet of 8, #a-h　8.00　8.00

Christmas A144

Designs: 20c, The Holy Trinity, by Titian. 33c, The Adoration of the Magi, by Diego Velazquez. 60c, The Holy Nereus, by Peter Paul Rubens. $3.20, St. Gregory With Saints Around Him, by Rubens.

2000, Dec. 1　　　*Perf. 14¼*
404-407　A144　Set of 4　8.75　8.75

Dogs and Cats — A145

No. 408, 33c: a, Afghan hound. b, Yellow Labrador retriever. c, Greyhound. d, German shepherd. e, King Charles spaniel. f, Jack Russell terrier.

No. 409, 33c: a, Siamese. b, Mackerel tabby. c, British shorthair. d, Persian. e, Turkish angora. f, Calico.

No. 410, $2, Dog in field. No. 411, $2, Cat stalking bird.

2000, June 26   Litho.   Perf. 14
Sheets of 6, #a-f
408-409 A145   Set of 2   8.00 8.00
Souvenir Sheets
410-411 A145   Set of 2   8.00 8.00

Souvenir Sheets

New Year 2001 (Year of the Snake) — A146

Designs: No. 412, 60c, Snake on ground. No. 413, 60c, Snake in bamboo, vert.

2001, Jan. 2
412-413 A146   Set of 2   2.40 2.40

Pokémon — A147

No. 414: a, Weepinbell. b, Snorlax. c, Seel. d, Hitmonchan. e, Jynx. f, Ponyta.

2001, Feb. 13   Perf. 13¾
414 A147 50c Sheet of 6, #a-f   6.00 6.00
Souvenir Sheet
415 A147 $2 Farfetch'd   4.00 4.00

Whales — A148

No. 416, 50c: a, Fin. b, Right. c, Pygmy right. d, Humpback. e, Blue. f, Bowhead.

No. 417, 60c: a, True's beaked. b, Cuvier's beaked. c, Shepherd's beaked. d, Baird's beaked. e, Northern bottlenose. f, Pygmy sperm.

No. 418, $2, Killer. No. 419, $2, Sperm.

2001, Feb. 27   Perf. 13¼x13¾
Sheets of 6, #a-f
416-417 A148 Set of 2   13.50 13.50
Souvenir Sheets
418-419 A148 Set of 2   8.00 8.00

Ecology — A149

No. 420: a, Coral reef in peril. b, Galapagos Islands tortoise. c, Tasmanian tiger. d, Yanomani. e, Bird from Florida Keys. f, Eagle, Endangered species act.

No. 421: a, Pollution. b, Deforestation. c, Acid rain. d, Greenhouse effect.

No. 422, $2, Bird in flight. No. 423, Chimpanzee, vert.

Perf. 13¼x13¾, 13¾x13¼
2001, Feb. 27   Litho.
420 A149 34c Sheet of 6, #a-f   4.25 4.25
421 A149 60c Sheet of 4, #a-d   5.00 5.00
Souvenir Sheets
422-423 A149 $2 Set of 2   8.00 8.00

Fish Type of 1998

Designs: 11c, Yellow damselfish. 34c, Rainbow runner. 70c, Whitelined grouper. 80c, Purple queen anthias. $3.50, Eibl's angelfish. $12.25, Blue-spotted boxfish.

2001, Mar. 28   Perf. 14½x14¾
424 A116   11c multi   .25   .25
425 A116   34c multi   .70   .70
426 A116   70c multi   1.40 1.40
427 A116   80c multi   1.60 1.60
428 A116 $3.50 multi   7.00 7.00
429 A116 $12.25 multi   25.00 25.00
        Nos. 424-429 (6)   35.95 35.95

Japanese Art — A150

Designs: No. 430, 34c, Parody of the Allegory of the Sage Chin Kao Riding a Carp, by Suzuki Harunobu. No. 431, 34c, The Courtesan Hinazuru of the Choji-Ya, by Chokosai Eisho. No. 432, 34c, Girl Tying Her Hair Ribbon, by Torii Kiyomine. No. 433, 34c, The Iris Garden, by Kiyonaga Torii. No. 434, 34c, The Courtesan Mayuzumi of the Daimonji-Ya, by Shunsho Katsukawa. No. 435, 34c, Bath House Scene, by Toyokuni Utagawa.

No. 436 — Paintings by Utamaro: a, Dance of a Kamisha. b, The Courtesan Hinazura at the Keizetsuro. c, Toilet Scene. d, Applying Lip Rouge. e, Beauty Reading a Letter. f, The Geisha Kamekichi.

No. 437, $2, Allegory of Ariwara No Narihira, by Kikugawa Eizan, horiz. No. 438, $2, Girl Seated by a Brook, by Harunobu, horiz.

2001, Apr. 20   Perf. 14
430-435 A150   Set of 6   4.25 4.25
436 A150 34c Sheet of 6, #a-f 4.25 4.25
Imperf
Size: 118x88mm
437-438 A150   Set of 2   8.00 8.00
    Phila Nippon '01, Japan (Nos. 436-438).

Toulouse-Lautrec Paintings — A151

No. 439: a, Oscar Wilde. b, Doctor Tapie in a Theater Corridor. c, Monsieur Delaporte. $2, The Clowness Cha-U-Kao.

2001, May 15   Perf. 13¾
439 A151 60c Sheet of 3, #a-c 3.75 3.75
Souvenir Sheet
440 A151 $2 multi   4.00 4.00

Queen Victoria (1819-1901) — A152

Various portraits.

2001, May 15   Perf. 14
441 A152 60c Sheet of 6, #a-f 7.25 7.25
Souvenir Sheet
Perf. 13¾
442 A152 $2 shown   4.00 4.00
    No. 441 contains six 28x42mm stamps.

Queen Elizabeth II, 75th Birthday — A153

No. 443: a, With necklace and brooch. b, Color photograph. c, As girl. d, As child. e, With dog. f, Facing left. $2, Portrait in color.

2001, May 15   Perf. 14
443 A153 60c Sheet of 6, #a-f 7.25 7.25
Souvenir Sheet
444 A153 $2 multi   4.00 4.00

Marine Life — A154

No. 445, 60c, horiz.: a, Striped dolphin. b, Olive Ridley turtle. c, Goldrim tang. d, Blue shark. e, Picasso triggerfish. f, Polkadot grouper.

No. 446, 60c, horiz.: a, Loggerhead turtle. b, Striped marlin. c, Bicolor cherub. d, Clown wrasse. e, Clown triggerfish. f, Japanese tang.

No. 447, $2, Adult and juvenile emperor angelfish. No. 448, $2, Harlequin tuskfish, horiz.

2001, July 16　　　　　*Perf. 14*
Sheets of 6, #a-f
445-446　A154　Set of 2　　14.50 14.50
Souvenir Sheets
Perf. 13¾
447-448　A154　Set of 2　　8.00 8.00

Nos. 445-446 each contain six 42x28mm stamps.

Prehistoric Animals — A155

Designs: No. 449, 60c, Allosaurus (with frame). No. 450, 60c, Psittacosaurus. No. 451, 60c, Triceratops. No. 452, 60c, Archaeopteryx (with frame).

No. 453, 60c: a, Tyrannosaurus. b, Pteranodon. c, Brachiosaurus. d, Spinosaurus. e, Deinonychus. f, Teratosaurus.

No. 454, 60c: a, Parasaurolophus. b, Plateosaurus. c, Archaeopteryx (no frame). d, Allosaurus (no frame). e, Torosaurus. f, Euoplocephalus.

No. 455, $2, Tyrannosaurus. No. 456, $2, Parasaurolophus, horiz.

2001, Aug. 12　　Litho.　　*Perf. 14*
449-452　A155　Set of 4　　4.75 4.75
Sheets of 6, #a-f
453-454　A155　Set of 2　　14.50 14.50
Souvenir Sheets
455-456　A155　Set of 2　　8.00 8.00

Shells — A156

No. 457, 50c: a, Bat volute. b, Horned helmet. c, Troschel's murex. d, Lotorium triton. e, Orange-mouthed olive. f, Phos whelk.

No. 458, 50c, vert.: a, Oblique nutmeg. b, Imperial volute. c, Pontifical miter. d, Eburneus cone. e, Variegated sundial. f, Heart cockle.

No. 459, $2, Eyed auger. No. 460, $2, Geography cone.

2001, Oct. 15　　Litho.　　*Perf. 14*
Sheets of 6, #a-f
457-458　A156　Set of 2　　12.00 12.00
Souvenir Sheets
459-460　A156　Set of 2　　8.00 8.00

On Nos. 485a-458f, the descriptions of the shells are transposed. Our descriptions are those of the stamps as they are printed.

Birds
A157

Designs: 5c, Malleefowl. 22c, Corncrake. 23c, Hooded merganser. $2.10, Purple gallinule.

No. 465, 60c: a, Fairy wren. b, Golden-crowned kinglet warbler. c, Flame-tempered

babbler. d, Golden-headed cisticola. e, White-browed babbler. f, White-breasted dipper.

No. 466, 60c: a, Logrunner. b, Eurasian treecreeper. c, Goldfinch. d, Rufous fantail. e, Orange-billed flowerpecker. f, American goldfinch.

No. 467, $2, Emperor bird of paradise. No. 468, $2, Yellow-eyed cuckooshrike, vert.

2001, Oct. 29　　Litho.　　*Perf. 14*
461-464　A157　Set of 4　　5.25 5.25
Sheets of 6, #a-f
465-466　A157　Set of 2　　14.50 14.50
Souvenir Sheets
467-468　A157　Set of 2　　8.00 8.00

Nobel Prizes, Cent. — A158

No. 469, 60c — Physiology or Medicine laureates: a, Alexis Carrel, 1912. b, Max Theiler, 1951. c, Niels Finsen, 1903. d, Philip S. Hench, 1950. e, Sune Bergström, 1982. f, John R. Vane, 1982.

No. 470, 60c — Laureates: a, Bengt Samuelsson, Physiology or Medicine, 1982. b, Johannes Fibiger, Physiology or Medicine, 1926. c, Theodore Richards, Chemistry, 1914. d, Tadeus Reichstein, Physiology or Medicine, 1950. e, Frederick Soddy, Chemistry, 1921. f, Albert Szent-Györgyi, 1937.

No. 471, $2, Irving Langmuir, Chemistry, 1932. No. 472, $2, Artturi Illmari Virtanen, Chemistry, 1945.

2001, Nov. 12
Sheets of 6, #a-f
469-470　A158　Set of 2　　14.50 14.50
Souvenir Sheets
471-472　A158　Set of 2　　8.00 8.00

Christmas
A159

Santa Claus: 22c, On cat. 34c, Between Christmas trees. 60c, In sleigh. $1, On dog. $2, Entering chimney, vert.

2001, Dec. 5
473-476　A159　Set of 4　　4.50 4.50
Souvenir Sheet
477　A159　$2 multi　　4.00 4.00

Attack on Pearl Harbor, 60th Anniv. — A160

No. 478, 60c: a, Rollover of USS Oklahoma. b, Japanese attack Wheeler Air Field. c, Japanese sailors loading bombs onto planes. d, Destroyer USS Ward sinks a Japanese submarine. e, USS Arizona sunk by Japanese bombs. f, Ewa Marine Base attacked by Japanese.

No. 479, 60c: a, Memorial poster showing attack. b, Japanese Prime Minister Hideki Tojo. c, Rescue at Bellows Field. d, Rescue of USS Arizona crew. e, Admiral Isoroku Yamamoto. f, Memorial poster showing soldier and flag.

No. 480, $2, USS Arizona Memorial. No. 481, $2, Pres. Franklin D. Roosevelt.

2001, Dec. 7
Sheets of 6, #a-f
478-479　A160　Set of 2　　14.50 14.50
Souvenir Sheets
480-481　A160　Set of 2　　8.00 8.00

Souvenir Sheet

New Year 2002 (Year of the Horse) — A161

Various horses.

2002, Jan. 24　　　　*Perf. 13¾x13¼*
482　A161　60c Sheet of 5, #a-e　6.00 6.00

Reign of Queen Elizabeth II, 50th Anniv. — A162

No. 483: a, Queen wearing flowered dress. b, Prince Philip. c, Queen waving, holding flowers. d, Queen with children. $2, Queen wearing scarf.

2002, Feb. 6　　　　　*Perf. 14¼*
483　A162　80c Sheet of 4, #a-d　6.50 6.50
Souvenir Sheet
484　A162　$2 multi　　4.00 4.00

United We Stand — A163

2002, Feb. 20　　　*Perf. 13¾x13¼*
485　A163　$1 multi　　2.00 2.00

Issued in sheets of 4.

2002 Winter Olympics, Salt Lake City — A164

Designs: No. 486, $1, Luge. No. 487, $1, Ice hockey.

2002, Mar. 18　　　　*Perf. 14*
486-487　A164　Set of 2　　4.00 4.00
487a　　Souvenir sheet, #486-487　4.00 4.00

Compare with Nos. 502-503.

Japanese Art — A165

Birds and Flowers of the Twelve Months, by Hoitsu Sakai — No. 488, 60c: a, January. b, February. c, March. d, April. e, May. f, June.

No. 489, 60c: a, July. b, August. c, September. d, October. e, November. f, December.

No. 490, $2, Seashells and Plums by Kiitsu Suzuki. No. 491, Peacock and Peonies, by Rosetsu Nagasawa.

2002, Mar. 25　Litho.　*Perf. 14x14¾*
Sheets of 6, #a-f
488-489　A165　Set of 2　　14.50 14.50
Imperf
490-491　A165　Set of 2　　8.00 8.00

Nos. 488-489 each contain six 77x26mm stamps.

Intl. Year of Mountains — A166

No. 492: a, Matterhorn, Switzerland. b, Maroonbells, U.S. c, Wetterhorn, Switzerland. d, Mt. Tsaranora, Africa. $2, Cerro Fitzroy, South America.

2002, Mar. 30　　　　*Perf. 14*
492　A166　80c Sheet of 4, #a-d　6.50 6.50
Souvenir Sheet
493　A166　$2 multi　　4.00 4.00

Pres. John F. Kennedy (1917-63) — A167

No. 494: a, Dark blue background. b, Lilac background, name at left. c, Tan background, name at left. d, Light blue background.
$2, Purple background.

2002, Mar. 30
494 A167 60c Sheet of 4, #a-d   5.00 5.00
Souvenir Sheet
495 A167 $2 multi   4.00 4.00

Princess Diana (1961-97) — A168

No. 496: a, Wearing wedding veil. b, Wearing tiara and necklace. c, Wearing brimless hat. d, Wearing scarf. e, Hatless. f, Wearing tiara and large collar.
$2, Wearing hat with brim.

2002, Mar. 30
496 A168 60c Sheet of 6, #a-f   7.25 7.25
Souvenir Sheet
497 A168 $2 multi   4.00 4.00

Intl. Year of Ecotourism — A169

No. 498: a, Lizard. b, Canoes. c, Micronesian house. d, Three children in costume. e, Woman. f, Two dancers, house.
$2, Fishermen.

Perf. 13¼x13½
2002, June 17   **Litho.**
498 A169 80c Sheet of 6, #a-f   0.75 0.75
Souvenir Sheet
499 A169 $2 multi   4.00 4.00

20th World Scout Jamboree, Thailand — A170

No. 500: a, Thai temple. b, American scout insignia. c, Scout cap.
$2, Merit badges.

2002, June 17   **Perf. 13½x13¼**
500 A170 $1 Sheet of 3, #a-c   6.00 6.00
Souvenir Sheet
501 A170 $2 multi   4.00 4.00

Winter Olympics Type of 2002 Redrawn With White Panel Behind Olympic Rings

Designs: No. 502, $1, Luge. No. 503, $1, Ice hockey.

2002, July 15
502-503 A164   Set of 2   4.00 4.00
503a   Souvenir sheet, #502-503   4.00 4.00

Xavier High School, 50th Anniv.
A171

2002, July 31   **Perf. 13½x13¾**
504 A171 37c multi   .75 .75

Queen Mother Elizabeth (1900-2002) — A172

No. 505, horiz.: a, At age 7. b, At wedding. c, At birth of Princess Elizabeth. d, At coronation of King George VI, 1937.
$2, As elderly lady.

2002, Aug. 12   **Perf. 14**
505 A172 80c Sheet of 4, #a-d   6.50 6.50
Souvenir Sheet
506 A172 $2 multi   4.00 4.00

Teddy Bears, Cent. — A173

No. 507: a, Burglar bear. b, White bear with heart. c, Blue bear with flowers. d, Brown bear with heart.

2002, Sept. 23   **Litho.**   **Perf. 14**
507 A173 80c Sheet of 4, #a-d   6.50 6.50

Elvis Presley (1935-77) — A174

Presley with: a, Hand below guitar. b, Head on guitar. c, Hat. d, Checked shirt, no hat. e, Arms raised. f, Microphone.

2002, Oct. 7   **Perf. 13¾**
508 A174 37c Sheet of 6, #a-f   4.50 4.50

Christmas
A175

Paintings: 21c, Madonna and Child, by Filippino Lippi, vert. 37c, Madonna and Child, by Giovanni Bellini, vert. 70c, Madonna and Child Between St. Stephen and St. Ladislaus, by Simone Martini, vert. 80c, Holy Family, by Bronzino, vert. No. 513, $2, Holy Family, by Martini, vert.
No. 514, Sacred Conversation, by Bellini, vert.

2002, Nov. 4   **Perf. 14**
509-513 A175   Set of 5   8.25 8.25
Souvenir Sheet
Perf. 14x14¼
514 A175 $2 multi   4.00 4.00

Flora, Fauna and Mushrooms — A176

No. 515, 37c — Moths: a, White-lined sphinx. b, Tropical fruit-piercer. c, Coppery dysphania. d, Large agarista. e, Indian moon moth. f, Croker's frother.
No. 516, 55c — Mushrooms: a, Phellinus robustus. b, Purple coincap. c, Shaggy parasol. d, King bolete. e, Boletus crocipodius. f, Sharp-scaled parasol.
No. 517, 60c — Orchids: a, Eria javanica. b, Cymbidium finlaysonianum. c, Coelogyne asperata. d, Spathoglottis affinis. e, Vanda tricolor. f, Calanthe rosea.
No. 518, 60c — Butterflies: a, Meadow argus. b, Cairns birdwing. c, Large greenbanded blue. d, Beak butterfly. e, Palmfly. f, Broad-bordered grass yellow.
No. 519, 80c — Insects and spiders: a, Stag beetle. b, Honeybee. c, Black widow spider. d, Mosquito. e, Black ant. f, Cicada.
No. 520, $2, Zodiac moth. No. 521, $2, Lepiota acutesquamosa mushroom. No. 522, $2, Dendrobium phalaenopsis orchid. No. 523, $2, Yamfly butterfly. No. 524, $2, Dragonfly, horiz.

2002, Dec. 16   **Perf. 14**
Sheets of 6, #a-f
515-519 A176   Set of 5   35.00 35.00
Souvenir Sheets
520-524 A176   Set of 5   20.00 20.00

Birds — A177

Designs: 3c, Greater flame-backed woodpecker. 5c, Red-tailed tropicbird. 21c, Haircrested drongo. 22c, Pale white-eye. 23c, White-backed munia. 37c, Yap monarch. 60c, Eclectus parrot. 70c, Sulphur-crested cockatoo. 80c, Giant white-eye. $2, Green magpie.

$3.85, Dollarbird. $5, Great frigatebird. $13.65, Micronesian pigeon.

2002, Dec. 30   **Perf. 14¼x14**
525 A177   3c multi   .25 .25
526 A177   5c multi   .25 .25
527 A177   21c multi   .40 .40
528 A177   22c multi   .45 .45
529 A177   23c multi   .45 .45
530 A177   37c multi   .75 .75
531 A177   60c multi   1.25 1.25
532 A177   70c multi   1.40 1.40
533 A177   80c multi   1.60 1.60
534 A177 $2 multi   4.00 4.00
      Perf. 13¾
535 A177 $3.85 multi   7.75 7.75
536 A177 $5 multi   10.00 10.00
537 A177 $13.65 multi   27.50 27.50
   Nos. 525-537 (13)   56.05 56.05

First Non-stop Solo Transatlantic Flight, 75th Anniv. (in 2002) — A178

No. 538: a, Charles Lindbergh, Donald Hall, Spirit of St. Louis. b, Spirit of St. Louis, Apr. 28, 1927. c, Towing of Spirit of St. Louis, May 20. d, Lindbergh taking off from Roosevelt Field, May 20. e, Lindbergh's arrival in Paris, May 21. f, Lindbergh in ticker tape parade, New York.

2003, Jan. 13   **Litho.**   **Perf. 14**
538 A178 60c Sheet of 6, #a-f   7.25 7.25

New Year 2003 (Year of the Ram) — A179

No. 539: a, Black ram facing left, country name at left. b, Black ram facing left, country name at right. c, White ram facing right, country name at left. d, White ram facing forward, country name at right.

2003, Feb. 1   **Litho.**   **Perf. 14¼x14**
539 A179 37c Sheet of 6, #a-b, 2
      each #c-d   4.50 4.50

Astronauts Killed in Space Shuttle Columbia Accident — A180

No. 540: a, Mission Specialist 1 David M. Brown. b, Commander Rick D. Husband. c, Mission Specialist 4 Laurel Blair Salton Clark. d, Mission Specialist 4 Kalpana Chawla. e, Payload Commander Michael P. Anderson. f,

Pilot William C. McCool. g, Payload Specialist Ilan Ramon.

2003, Apr. 7   *Perf. 13½x13¼*
540 A180 37c Sheet of 7, #a-g   5.25 5.25

Coronation of Queen Elizabeth II, 50th Anniv. — A181

No. 541: a, Wearing pearl necklace. b, Wearing sash and tiara. c, Wearing robe.
$2, Wearing crown.

2003, May 13   *Perf. 14x14¼*
541 A181 $1 Sheet of 3, #a-c   6.00 6.00
         Souvenir Sheet
542 A181 $2 multi   4.00 4.00

Prince William, 21st Birthday — A182

No. 543: a, Wearing checked shirt and striped sweater. b, Facing right, wearing sweater, shirt and tie. c, Wearing suit and tie.
$2, Wearing raincoat.

2003, May 14
543 A182 $1 Sheet of 3, #a-c   6.00 6.00
         Souvenir Sheet
544 A182 $2 multi   4.00 4.00

Operation Iraqi Freedom — A183

No. 545, 37c: a, B-52 Bomber. b, F-16 Fighter. c, Cobra Helicopter. d, Apache Helicopter. e, T8000 Tow Missile. f, Bradley Tank.
No. 546, 37c: a, Stealth Fighter. b, AC-130 Cargo plane. c, MH-53j Pave Low II Helicopter. d, Predator. e, Challenger Two Tank. f, Aegis Cruiser.

2003, May 14   *Perf. 14*
       Sheets of 6, #a-f
545-546 A183   Set of 2   9.00 9.00

Tour de France Bicycle Race, Cent. — A184

No. 547: a, Greg LeMond, 1990. b, Miguel Indurain, 1991. c, Indurain, 1992. d, Indurain, 1993.
$2, Marco Pantani, 1998.

2003, July 1   *Perf. 13½*
547 A184 60c Sheet of 4, #a-d   5.00 5.00
         Souvenir Sheet
548 A184 $2 multi   4.00 4.00

Intl. Year of Fresh Water — A185

No. 549: a, Kosrae mangroves. b, Chuuk Lagoon. c, Pohnpei's waterfalls.
$2, Pohnpei Lagoon.

2003, July 21   *Perf. 13½*
549 A185 $1 Sheet of 3, #a-c   6.00 6.00
         Souvenir Sheet
550 A185 $2 multi   4.00 4.00

Powered Flight, Cent. — A186

No. 551: a, Concorde. b, Boeing 757. c, Junkers F13a. d, Martin M-130 China Clipper. e, Handley Page H.P.42W. f, Wright Flyer II.
$2, Boeing 747.

2003, Aug. 7   *Perf. 14*
551 A186 55c Sheet of 6, #a-f   6.75 6.75
         Souvenir Sheet
552 A186 $2 multi   4.00 4.00
   2003 APS Stampshow, Columbus, Ohio (No. 551).

Circus Performers — A187

No. 553, 80c: a, Glen Little. b, Joseph Grimaldi. c, Beverly Rebo Bergeron. d, Coco Michael Polakov.
No. 554, 80c: a, Jana Mandana. b, Maxim Papazov. c, Harry Keaton. d, Giraffe.

2003, Aug. 25   *Perf. 14*
      Sheets of 4, #a-d
553-554 A187   Set of 2   13.00 13.00

Paintings of Boy Scouts by Norman Rockwell (1894-1978) — A188

No. 555: a, Scout with plaid neckerchief, from 1963 Boy Scout Calendar. b, A Scout is Helpful. c, The Scoutmaster. d, Scout with red neckerchief, from 1963 Boy Scout Calendar.
$2, No Swimming.

2003, Sept. 8   *Perf. 14*
555 A188 80c Sheet of 4, #a-d   6.50 6.50
         Imperf
556 A188 $2 multi   4.00 4.00
   No. 555 contains four 28x42mm stamps.

Paintings by Paul Gauguin (1848-1903) — A189

No. 557: a, Vahine No Te Tiare. b, Les Amants. c, Trois Tahitiens Conversation. d, Arearea.
$2, Ta Matete.

2003, Sept. 8   *Perf. 13¾*
557 A189 80c Sheet of 4, #a-d   6.50 6.50
         Imperf
558 A189 $2 multi   4.00 4.00
   No. 557 contains four 51x38mm stamps.

Paintings of James McNeill Whistler (1834-1903) — A190

Designs: 37c, Blue and Silver Blue: Wave, Biarritz. 55c, Brown and Silver: Old Battersea Bridge. 60c, Nocturne in Blue and Silver: The Lagoon, Venice. 80c, Crepuscule in Flesh Color and Green: Valparaiso.
No. 563: a, Symphony in White No. 2: The Little White Girl, vert. b, At the Piano (75x50mm). c, Symphony in White No. 1: The White Girl, vert.
$2, Portrait of Thomas Carlyle: Arrangement in Gray and Black No. 2, vert.

2003, Oct. 6   *Perf. 14¼*
559-562 A190   Set of 4   4.75 4.75
563 A190 $1 Sheet of 3, #a-c   6.00 6.00
      Size: 83x104mm
         Imperf
564 A190 $2 multi   4.00 4.00

Christmas A191

Designs: 37c, Madonna of the Carnation, by Leonardo da Vinci. 60c, Madonna with Yarn Winder, by da Vinci. 80c, Litta Madonna, by da Vinci. $1, Madonna of the Grand Duke, by Raphael.
$2, The Adoration of the Magi, by Giambattista Tiepolo.

2003, Nov. 5   *Perf. 14¼*
565-568 A191   Set of 4   5.75 5.75
         Souvenir Sheet
569 A191 $2 multi   4.00 4.00

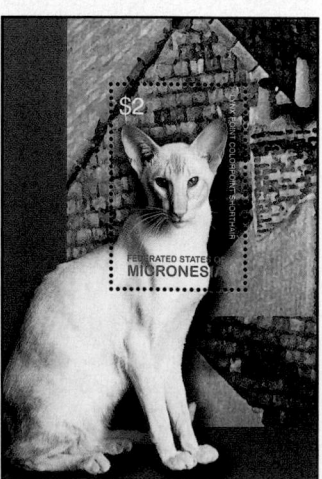

Cats, Dogs, Birds, Reptiles & Amphibians — A192

No. 570, 80c — Cats: a, Ragdoll. b, Calico Shorthaired Japanese Bobtail. c, Blue Mackerel Taffy Exotic Shorthair. d, Dilute Calico.
No. 571, 80c — Dogs: a, Australian shepherd. b, Greyhound. c, English bulldog. d, Schnauzer.

No. 572, 80c, horiz. — Birds: a, Green-winged macaw. b, American flamingo. c, Blue and gold macaw. d, Abyssinian ground hornbill.

No. 573, 80c, horiz. — Reptiles and amphibians: a, Leopard gecko. b, Red-eyed tree frog. c, Panther chameleon. d, Green and black poison frog.

No. 574, $2, Lynx Point Colorpoint Shorthair. No. 575, $2, Toy poodle. No. 576, $2, American flamingo. No. 577, $2, Madagascan chameleon, horiz.

2003, Dec. 22   *Perf. 14*
Sheets of 4, #a-d
570-573 A192   Set of 4   26.00 26.00
Souvenir Sheets
574-577 A192   Set of 4   16.00 16.00

Pres. Bailey Olter (1932-99) — A193

2004, Feb. 16   Litho.   *Perf. 14*
578 A193   37c multi   .75 .75

Paintings by Pablo Picasso (1881-1973) — A194

No. 579: a, Marie-Thérèse Leaning on One Elbow. b, Portrait of Jaime Sabartés. c, Portrait of Emilie Marguerite Walter (Mémé). d, Bust of a Woman Leaning on One Elbow. $2, Seated Bather (Olga).

2004, Mar. 8   *Perf. 14¼*
579 A194   80c Sheet of 4, #a-d   6.50 6.50
Imperf
580 A194 $2 multi   4.00 4.00
No. 579 contains four 37x50mm stamps.

Paintings in the Hermitage, St. Petersburg, Russia A195

Designs: 22c, A Young Lady in a Theatrical Costume, by Alexis Grimou. 37c, Portrait of Mrs. Harriet Greer, by George Romney. 80c, Portrait of Prince Nikolai Yusupov, by Friedrich Heinrich Füger. $1, Portrait of Richard Brinsley Sheridan, by John Hoppner. $2, Spanish Concert (Conversation Espagnole), by Carle Vanloo.

2004, Mar. 8   *Perf. 14¼*
581-584 A195   Set of 4   5.00 5.00
Imperf
Size: 64x81mm
585 A195 $2 multi   4.00 4.00

New Year 2004 (Year of the Monkey) — A196

Designs: 50c, Moon-struck Gibbon, by Gao Qi-feng. $1, Detail from Moon-struck Gibbon.

2004, Mar. 9   *Perf. 13¼*
586 A196   50c multi   1.00 1.00
Souvenir Sheet
Perf. 13¼x13
587 A196 $1 multi   2.00 2.00
No. 587 contains one 30x40mm stamp. No. 586 printed in sheets of four.

Election of Pope John Paul II, 25th Anniv. (in 2003) — A197

No. 588 — Pope John Paul II: a, Visiting Monaco, 1990. b, With Bill and Hillary Clinton, 1999. c, Visiting Ukraine, 2001. d, Visiting Spain, 2003.

2004, Sept. 1   *Perf. 14¼x14*
588 A197   80c Sheet of 4, #a-d   6.50 6.50

2004 European Soccer Championships, Portugal — A198

No. 589: a, Lars Olsen. b, Juergen Klinsmann. c, Peter Schmeichel. d, Nya Ullevi Stadium. $2, 1992 Denmark team, horiz.

2004, Sept. 1   *Perf. 14*
589 A198   80c Sheet of 4, #a-d   6.50 6.50
Souvenir Sheet
Perf. 14¼
590 A198 $2 multi   4.00 4.00
No. 589 contains four 28x42mm stamps.

D-Day, 60th Anniv. — A199

No. 591: a, Landing craft vehicle personnel. b, Destroyer Thompson. c, LST-391. d, Rhino Ferry 2, Rhino Tug 3. e, HMS Mauritius. f, Battleship Arkansas. $2, LCI 1539.

2004, Sept. 1   *Perf. 14*
591 A199   50c Sheet of 6, #a-f   6.00 6.00
Souvenir Sheet
592 A199 $2 multi   4.00 4.00

Souvenir Sheet

Deng Xiaoping (1904-97), Chinese Leader — A200

2004, Sept. 1   Litho.   *Perf. 14*
593 A200 $2 multi   4.00 4.00

Locomotives, Bicent. — A201

No. 594, 80c: a, CFL N5520. b, Inter-region trains. c, SW-600. d, WSOR 3801.
No. 595, 80c: a, Baldwin 2-8-0. b, F-10 #1114 Diesel. c, BNSF locomotive (incorrectly inscribed "Okinawa Hitachi trains". d, Shinkansen.
No. 596, 80c: a, RS-1 #22. b, Diesel class 630. c, Okinawa Hitachi train. d, Eurostar.
No. 597, $2, Eurostar, diff. No. 598, $2, Locomotive 231-065. No. 599, $2, Michigan Central locomotive.

2004, Sept. 1   Sheets of 4, #a-d
594-596 A201   Set of 3   19.50 19.50
Souvenir Sheets
597-599 A201   Set of 3   12.00 12.00

Birds Type of 2002

Designs: 2c, Blue-gray gnatcatcher. 10c, Clapper rail.

2004, Nov. 1   *Perf. 13¼*
600 A177   2c multi   .25 .25
601 A177   10c multi   .25 .25

Miniature Sheet

Intl. Year of Peace — A202

No. 602: a, Nelson Mandela. b, Dalai Lama. c, Pope John Paul II.

2004, Nov. 1   *Perf. 14*
602 A202   80c Sheet of 3, #a-c   5.00 5.00

2004 Summer Olympics, Athens — A203

Designs: 37c, Ancient bronze sculpture of horse and rider. 55c, Pin from 1912 Stockholm Olympics, vert. 80c, Baron Pierre de Coubertin, Intl. Olympic Committee President, vert. $1, Poster from 1968 Mexico City Olympics, vert.

2004, Nov. 1   *Perf. 14¼*
603-606 A203   Set of 4   5.50 5.50

Miniature Sheets

Elvis Presley's First Recording, 50th Anniv. — A204

No. 607, 80c — Presley with: a, Beard. b, Boxing gloves. c, Kaffiyeh. d, Cowboy hat.
No. 608, 80c, vert. — Presley with denomination in: a, Red. b, Purple. c, Blue. d, Orange yellow.

2004, Nov. 1   *Perf. 14*
Sheets of 4, #a-d
607-608 A204   Set of 2   13.00 13.00

Flowers — A205

No. 609, horiz.: a, Epiphytic aeschynanthus. b, Darwinia collina. c, Rhododendron. d, Rhododendron retusum. e, Eucryphia lucida. f, Microporus xanthopus.
$2, Grevillea.

2004, Nov. 1   *Perf. 13¼x13½*
609 A205 55c Sheet of 6, #a-f   6.75 6.75
Souvenir Sheet
Perf. 13½x13¼
610 A205 $2 multi   4.00 4.00

FIFA (Fédération Internationale de Football Association), Cent. — A206

No. 611: a, Herman Crespo. b, Peter Shilton. c, Klaus Augenthaler. d, Bryan Robson.
$2, Ruud Gullit.

2004, Nov. 1   *Perf. 12¾x12½*
611 A206 80c Sheet of 4, #a-d   6.50 6.50
Souvenir Sheet
612 A206 $2 multi   4.00 4.00

National Basketball Association Players — A207

Designs: No. 613, 20c, Dirk Nowitzki, Dallas Mavericks. No. 614, 20c, Vince Carter, Toronto Raptors.

2004   *Perf. 14*
613-614 A207 Set of 2   .80 .80
Issued: No. 613, 11/2; No. 614, 11/3. Each stamp issued in sheets of 12.

When Prehistoric Mammals Walked the Earth...

Prehistoric Animals — A208

No. 615, 80c: a, Indricotheres. b, Hyaenodons. c, Deinotherium. d, Chalicotheres.
No. 616, 80c: a, Apatosaurus. b, Pachyrhinosaurus. c, Kentrosaurus. d, Saltasaurus.
No. 617, 80c, vert.: a, Allosaurus. b, Tyrannosaurus. c, Troodon. d, Carnotaurus.
No. 618, $2, Moeritherium. No. 619, $2, Coelophysis. No. 620, $2, Deinonychus.

Perf. 14½x14, 14x14½
2004, Dec. 13   *Litho.*
Sheets of 4, #a-d
615-617 A208 Set of 3   19.50 19.50
Souvenir Sheets
618-620 A208 Set of 3   12.00 12.00

Fish and Coral — A209

No. 621: a, Clown triggerfish. b, Striped-face unicornfish. c, Firefish. d, Longnose hawkfish. e, Annella mollis. f, Dendronephthya.
$2, Great barracuda.

2004, Nov. 1   *Litho.*   *Perf. 13½*
621 A209 55c Sheet of 6, #a-f   6.75 6.75
Souvenir Sheet
622 A209 $2 multi   4.00 4.00

Reptiles and Amphibians — A210

No. 623: a, Blue coral snake. b, Solomon Islands horned frog. c, Levuka wrinkled ground frog. d, Flying lizard. e, Platymantis vitensis. f, Pacific ground boa.
$2, Loggerhead turtle.

2004, Nov. 1
623 A210 55c Sheet of 6, #a-f   6.75 6.75
Souvenir Sheet
624 A210 $2 multi   4.00 4.00
No. 623c has incorrect inscription as stamp depicts a lizard.

Birds — A211

No. 625, vert.: a, Black-faced woodswallows. b, Brown boobies. c, Rainbow lorikeets. d, Wandering albatross. e, Kagu. f, Great frigatebird.
$2, Golden whistler.

2004, Nov. 1
625 A211 55c Sheet of 6, #a-f   6.75 6.75
Souvenir Sheet
626 A211 $2 multi   4.00 4.00

Christmas A212

Madonna and Child paintings by: 37c, Giovanni Battista Tiepolo. 60c, Raphael. 80c, Jan Gossaert (Mabuse). $1, Fra Filippo Lippi.
$2, Unknown artist.

2004, Dec. 27   *Perf. 14¼*
627-630 A212 Set of 4   5.75 5.75
Souvenir Sheet
631 A212 $2 multi   4.00 4.00

Diplomatic Relations Between Micronesia and People's Republic of China, 15th Anniv. — A212a

Designs: No. 631A, FSM-China Friendship Sports Center. No. 631B, Arms of People's Republic of China and Micronesia.

2004, Dec. 29   *Litho.*   *Perf. 13x13¼*
631A A212a 37c multi   —
631B A212a 37c multi   —
   c.   Horiz. pair, #631A-631B   — —

New Year 2005 (Year of the Rooster) — A213

2005, Jan. 17   *Perf. 12¾*
632 A213 50c multi   1.00 1.00
Printed in sheets of 4.

Basketball Players Type of 2004
Design: Luke Walton, Los Angeles Lakers.

2005, Feb. 24   *Perf. 14*
633 A207 20c multi   .40 .40

Pres. Ronald Reagan (1911-2004) — A214

No. 634: a, With British Prime Minister Margaret Thatcher. b, With Israeli Prime Minister Yitzhak Shamir.

2005, Mar. 21   *Perf. 13¼x13½*
634 A214 55c Horiz. pair, #a-b   2.25 2.25
Printed in sheets containing 3 each Nos. 634a and 634b.

Elvis Presley (1935-2005) — A215

No. 635, 60c — Photos from: a, 1955. b, 1956. c, 1960 (with arm outstretched). d, 1968. e, 1970. f, 1973.
No. 636, 60c — Photos from: a, 1957. b, 1960 (in army uniform). c, 1963. d, 1965. e, 1967. f, 1969.

2005, Mar. 21   *Perf. 13½x13¼*
Sheets of 6, #a-f
635-636 A215 Set of 2   14.50 14.50

End of World War II, 60th Anniv. — A216

No. 637, 60c: a, U.S. soldiers marching in Ireland. b, British troops cross Volturno River, Italy. c, Hawker Typhoon attacks enemy on the Rhine River. d, Damaged Remagen Bridge. e, Meeting of Russian and American armies near Torgau, Germany.
No. 638, 60c: a, Poster remembering Pearl Harbor. b, Chula Beach, Tinian Island. c, Paul Tibbets and the Enola Gay. d, Hiroshima atomic bomb mushroom cloud. e, Newspaper announcing Japanese surrender.

2005, Mar. 31   *Perf. 14*
Sheets of 5, #a-e
637-638 A216 Set of 2   12.00 12.00

Friedrich von Schiller (1759-1805),
Writer — A217

No. 639: a, Wearing red cape. b, Statue. c,
With head on hand.

2005, Mar. 31
639 A217 $1 Sheet of 3, #a-c   6.00 6.00
Souvenir Sheet
640 A217 $2 shown   4.00 4.00

Battle of Trafalgar, Bicent. — A218

Various depictions of ships in battle: 37c,
55c, 80c, $1.
$2, Death of Admiral Horatio Nelson.

2005, Mar. 31   **Perf. 14¼**
641-644 A218 Set of 4   6.60 6.60
Souvenir Sheet
645 A218 $2 multi   4.00 4.00

Pope John Paul II
(1920-2005)
A219

2005, June 27   **Perf. 13½x13¼**
646 A219 $1 multi   2.00 2.00
Printed in sheets of 6.

Rotary International, Cent. — A220

No. 647, vert.: a, Child. b, Emblem. c, 2004-
05 Rotary International President Glenn E.
Estess, Sr.
$2, 2002-03 Rotary International President
Bhichai Rattakul.

2005, July 12   **Perf. 12¾**
647 A220 $1 Sheet of 3, #a-c   6.00 6.00
Souvenir Sheet
648 A220 $2 multi   4.00 4.00

Jules Verne (1828-1905),
Writer — A221

No. 649, vert.: a, Around the World in 80
Days. b, Phineas Fogg in India. c, Phineas
Fogg, explorer and adventurer.
$2, Nautilus.

2005, June 7   **Litho.**   **Perf. 12¾**
649 A221 $1 Sheet of 3, #a-c   6.00 6.00
Souvenir Sheet
650 A221 $2 multi   4.00 4.00

Souvenir Sheet

Expo 2005, Aichi, Japan — A222

No. 651: a, Gray nurse shark. b, Surfer. c,
Krakatoa Volcano. d, Yellow coral.

2005, June 27   **Perf. 12x12¼**
651 A222 80c Sheet of 4, #a-d   6.50 6.50

Boats — A223

No. 652: a, 37c, Papyrus boat. b, 55c, Outrigger canoe. c, 80c, Papyrus sailboat. d, $1,
Arab dhow.
$2, Lateen-rigged Nile riverboat.

2005, June 27   **Perf. 12¾**
652 A223 Sheet of 4, #a-d   5.50 5.50
Souvenir Sheet
653 A223 $2 multi   4.00 4.00

Kosrae Government Building
Complex — A224

Views of various buildings with frame colors
of: 4c, Light yellow. 10c, Light blue. 22c, Pink.
37c, Light green.

2005, July 8   **Perf. 14**
654-657 A224 Set of 4   1.50 1.50

Vatican City
No.
67 — A225

2005, Aug. 9   **Perf. 13x13¼**
658 A225 37c multi   .75   .75
Pope John Paul II (1920-2005). Printed in
sheets of 12.

Worldwide Fund for Nature
(WWF) — A226

No. 659: a, Stephanometra echinus. b,
Oxycomanthus bennetti. c, Alloeocomatella
polycaldia. d, Dichrometra flagellata.

2005, Aug. 31   **Perf. 14**
659 A226 50c Block or vert. strip
           of 4, #a-d   4.00 4.00
   e. Souvenir sheet, 2 each #659a-
       659d   8.00 8.00

Souvenir Sheet

Albert Einstein (1879-1955),
Physicist — A227

No. 660 — Various portraits with "Albert Einstein (1879-1955)" in: a, Orange. b, Blue. c,
Red. d, Black.

2005, Sept. 20   **Perf. 12¾**
660 A227 $1 Sheet of 4, #a-d   8.00 8.00

Bananas
A228

Designs: 4c, Mother feeding banana to
child. 10c, Four bananas. 22c, Bunch of
bananas. 37c, Banana plant.

2005, Oct. 14   **Perf. 14**
661-664 A228 Set of 4   1.50 1.50

Hans Christian Andersen (1805-75),
Author — A229

No. 665: a, Bust of Andersen. b, Statue of
seated Andersen. c, Bust of Andersen on
pedestal.
$2, Statue of standing Andersen.

2005, Nov. 15   **Perf. 12¾**
665 A229 80c Sheet of 3, #a-c   5.00 5.00
Souvenir Sheet
666 A229 $2 multi   4.00 4.00

Pope Benedict
XVI — A230

2005, Nov. 21   **Litho.**   **Perf. 13½**
667 A230 80c multi   1.60 1.60
Printed in sheets of 4.

Christmas — A231

Painting details: 37c, Kanigani Madonna, by
Raphael. 60c, Madonna with the Fish, by
Raphael. 80c, The Holy Family, by Bartolomé
Esteban Murillo. $1, Madonna with the Book,
by Raphael.
$2, The Holy Family, by Murillo, diff.

2005, Dec. 1   **Litho.**   **Perf. 14**
668-671 A231 Set of 4   5.75 5.75
Souvenir Sheet
672 A231 $2 multi   4.00 4.00

Flowers — A232

Designs: 4c, Tecoma stans. 10c, Ipomoea
fistulosa. 22c, Hibiscus rosa-sinensis. 37c,
Gerbera jamesonii. 60c, Helianthus
annuus. $1, Ixora casei.
No. 677, 80c: a, Tapeinochilos ananassae.
b, Bauhinia monandra. c, Galphimia gracilis. d,
Hibiscus rosa-sinensis, diff.
No. 680, $2, Helianthus annuus, diff. No.
681, $2, Phinia variegata.

2005, Nov. 15		Litho.	Perf. 12	
673-678	A232	Set of 6	5.25	5.25
679	A232	80c Sheet of 4, #a-d	6.50	6.50

Souvenir Sheets

| 680-681 | A232 | Set of 2 | 8.00 | 8.00 |

New Year 2006
(Year of the
Dog) — A233

Paintings by Liu Jiyou: 50c, Wolf Dog. $1, Wolf Dog, horiz.

2006, Jan. 3			Perf. 13¼	
682	A233	50c multi	1.00	1.00

Souvenir Sheet

| 683 | A233 | $1 multi | 2.00 | 2.00 |

No. 683 contains one 48x35mm stamp. No. 682 was issued in sheets of 4.

Birds — A234

Designs: No. 684, Glaucous-winged gull. No. 685, Slaty-headed parakeet. No. 686, Harlequin duck. No. 687, Purple sunbird. 75c, Plum-headed parakeet. 84c, Yellow-wattled lapwing. $4.05, Eurasian collared dove, horiz.

2006			Perf. 12	
684	A234	24c multi	.50	.50
685	A234	24c multi	.50	.50
686	A234	39c multi	.80	.80
687	A234	39c multi	.80	.80
688	A234	75c multi	1.50	1.50
689	A234	84c multi	1.75	1.75
690	A234	$4.05 multi	8.25	8.25
		Nos. 684-690 (7)	14.10	14.10

Issued: Nos. 684, 686, 2/21; others, 4/20.

Vice-President
Petrus Tun (1936-
99) — A235

2006, Mar. 19			Perf. 12¾	
691	A235	39c multi	.80	.80

Printed in sheets of 4.

FEDERATED STATES OF
MICRONESIA $2
Rembrandt Harmensz van Rijn (1606 - 1669)

Rembrandt (1606-69), Painter — A236

No. 692: a, Saskia as Flora. b, Young Girl at a Window. c, Girl with a Broom. d, Prodigal Son in the Tavern.
$2, Man in Oriental Costume.

2006, June 22			Perf. 13¼	
692	A236	$1 Sheet of 4, #a-d	8.00	8.00

Imperf

| 693 | A236 | $2 multi | 4.00 | 4.00 |

No. 692 contains four 38x50mm stamps.

Queen Elizabeth II, 80th
Birthday — A237

No. 694 — Dogs and Queen in: a, Red violet dress. b, Beige dress. c, Purple dress. d, Light blue dress.
$2, Green dress.

2006, June 22			Perf. 14¼	
694	A237	84c Sheet of 4, #a-d	6.75	6.75

Souvenir Sheet

| 695 | A237 | $2 multi | 4.00 | 4.00 |

Space Achievements — A238

No. 696 — Various views of Venus Express: a, Text in black. b, Country name in black, denomination in white. c, Country name in white, denomination in black. d, Country name and denomination in red, "Venus Express" at

left. f, Country name and denomination in red, "Venus Express" at right.
No. 697, $1, horiz. — Return to space of Space Shuttle Discovery: a, Denomination in white. b, Shuttle arm. c, Shuttle with cargo bay open. d, Shuttle tail.
No. 698, $1, horiz. — Spacecraft for future trips to: a, Moon, black denomination. b, Moon, blue denomination. c, Mars, red denomination. d, Mars, white denomination.
No. 699, $2, Space Shuttle Discovery astronaut space-walking. No. 700, $2, Mars Reconnaissance Orbiter. No. 701, $2, Stardust probe, horiz.

2006, July 11			Perf. 14¼	
696	A238	75c Sheet of 6, #a-f	9.00	9.00

Sheets of 4, #a-d

| 697-698 | A238 | Set of 2 | 16.00 | 16.00 |

Souvenir Sheets

| 699-701 | A238 | Set of 3 | 12.00 | 12.00 |

Butterflies
A239

Designs: 1c, Papilio euchenor. 2c, Golden birdwing. 4c, Delias henningia. 5c, Bassarona duda. 10c, Common bluebottle. 19c, Arhopala cleander. 20c, Arhopala argentea. 22c, Danaus aspasia. 75c, Arhopala aurea. 84c, Caleta mindaurus. $1, Black and white tit. $4.05, Grand imperial. $5, Jamides abdul. $10, Paralaxita lacoon.

2006, Nov. 15			Perf. 12	
702	A239	1c multi	.25	.25
703	A239	2c multi	.25	.25
704	A239	4c multi	.25	.25
705	A239	5c multi	.25	.25
706	A239	10c multi	.25	.25
707	A239	19c multi	.40	.40
708	A239	20c multi	.40	.40
709	A239	22c multi	.45	.45
710	A239	75c multi	1.50	1.50
711	A239	84c multi	1.75	1.75
712	A239	$1 multi	2.00	2.00
713	A239	$4.05 multi	8.25	8.25
714	A239	$5 multi	10.00	10.00
715	A239	$10 multi	20.00	20.00
		Nos. 702-715 (14)	46.00	46.00

Christmas — A240

Designs: 22c, Christmas tree. 24c, Stocking. 39c, Snowman. 75c, Candle. 84c, Ornament.

2006, Dec. 4			Perf. 13½	
716-720	A240	Set of 5	5.00	5.00

Concorde — A241

No. 721, 75c — Concorde's Jubilee Flypast: a, With statue. b, Without statue.
No. 722, 75c — Concorde 001: a, In flight. b, On ground.

	Perf. 13¼x13½			
2006, Dec. 20			Litho.	
	Pairs, #a-b			
721-722	A241	Set of 2	6.00	6.00

New Year 2007
(Year of the
Pig) — A242

2007, Jan. 3			Perf. 13¼	
723	A242	75c multi	1.50	1.50

Printed in sheets of 4.

Souvenir Sheet

Wolfgang Amadeus Mozart (1756-91),
Composer — A243

2007, Jan. 11				
724	A243	$2 multi	4.00	4.00

Souvenir Sheet

Ludwig Durr (1878-1956),
Engineer — A244

No. 725 — Durr and: a, Walrus Hula airship. b, Walrus heavy transport blimp. c, Hindenburg.

2007, Jan. 11				
725	A244	$1 Sheet of 3, #a-c	6.00	6.00

Souvenir Sheet

Marilyn Monroe (1926-62),
Actress — A245

No. 726: a, Looking right. b, With puckered lips. c, Wearing beret. d, With eyes closed, facing left.

2007, Jan. 11
726 A245 $1 Sheet of 4, #a-d   8.00 8.00

Scouting, Cent. — A246

2007, Jan. 11
727 A246 $1 shown   2.00 2.00

Souvenir Sheet
728 A246 $2 Scouts, flag   4.00 4.00

No. 727 was printed in sheets of 3. No. 728 contains one 37x50mm stamp.

Pope Benedict XVI, 80th Birthday — A247

2007, May 25
729 A247 50c multi   1.00 1.00

Printed in sheets of 8.

Miniature Sheet

Wedding of Queen Elizabeth II and Prince Philip, 60th Anniv. — A248

No. 730 — Queen and Prince: a, Standing, red frame. b, Seated, red frame. c, Seated, white frame. d, Standing, white frame. e, Standing, blue frame. f, Seated, blue frame.

2007, May 25
730 A248 60c Sheet of 6, #a-f   7.25 7.25

Princess Diana (1961-97) — A249

No. 731 — Various portraits with background color of: a, Pink. b, Lilac. c, Bister. d, Light green.
$2, Diana wearing tiara.

2007, May 25
731 A249 90c Sheet of 4, #a-d   7.25 7.25

Souvenir Sheet
732 A249 $2 multi   4.00 4.00

Bananas — A250

Inscriptions: 22c, Utim was. 26c, Utin Iap. 41c, Mangat. 58c, Ipali. 80c, Daiwang. 90c, Akadahn Weitahta, horiz. $1.14, Peleu. $4.60, Utin Kerenis.

Perf. 14x14¾, 14¾x14

2007, June 12
733 A250 22c multi   .45   .45
734 A250 26c multi   .55   .55
735 A250 41c multi   .85   .85
736 A250 58c multi   1.25 1.25
737 A250 80c multi   1.60 1.60
738 A250 90c multi   1.90 1.90
739 A250 $1.14 multi   2.40 2.40
740 A250 $4.60 multi   9.25 9.25
    Nos. 733-740 (8)   18.25 18.25

Miniature Sheet

Elvis Presley (1935-77) — A251

No. 741 — Various portraits with denomination color of: a, Blue (country name in gray). b, Pink. c, Blue (country name in blue). d, Green. e, Buff. f, Lilac.

2007, June 20   Perf. 14¼
741 A251 75c Sheet of 6, #a-f   9.00 9.00

Fish — A252

No. 742: a, Longnose hawkfish. b, Fingerprint sharpnose puffer. c, Ornate butterflyfish. d, Longnose filefish.
$2, Multi barred goatfish.

2007, June 21   Perf. 13¼
742 A252 90c Sheet of 4, #a-d   7.25 7.25

Souvenir Sheet
743 A252 $2 multi   4.00 4.00

Flowers — A253

No. 744: a, White plumeria. b, Yellow plumeria. c, White lily. d, Yellow ginger lily.
$2, Bougainvillea glabra.

2007, June 21
744 A253 90c Sheet of 4, #a-d   7.25 7.25

Souvenir Sheet
745 A253 $2 multi   4.00 4.00

Souvenir Sheet

Peace Corps in Micronesia, 40th Anniv. (in 2006) — A254

No. 746 — Inscriptions: a, Yap State. b, Kosrae State. c, Pohnpei State. d, Chuuk State.

2007, June 22
746 A254 90c Sheet of 4, #a-d   7.25 7.25

Miniature Sheet

Pres. Gerald R. Ford (1913-2006) — A255

No. 747 — Ford: a, With hand raised. b, Seated, reading documents. c, With Pres. Richard Nixon, denomination at UL. d, With Nixon, denomination at UR. e, With wife, Betty. f, Signing Nixon's pardon.

2007, Aug. 7
747 A255 $1 Sheet of 6, #a-f   12.00 12.00

Intl. Polar Year — A256

No. 748: a, African penguins. b, Emperor penguins. c, Galapagos penguin. d, Humboldt penguin. e, Magellanic penguin. f, Rockhopper penguin.
$3.50, Gentoo penguins.

2007, Aug. 7
748 A256 75c Sheet of 6, #a-f   9.00 9.00

Souvenir Sheet
749 A256 $3.50 multi   7.00 7.00

Souvenir Sheet

Micronesian Red Cross, 9th Anniv. — A257

No. 750 — Various pictures of relief efforts with denomination at: a, LR. b, LL. c, UR. d, UL.

2007, Aug. 20
750 A257 90c Sheet of 4, #a-d   7.25 7.25

Cats — A258

Designs: 22c, Scottish Fold. 26c, Munchkin. 41c, Abyssinian. 90c, Somali, horiz. $2, Blue Silver Shaded Tiffanie.

Perf. 13½x13, 13x13½
2007, Sept. 24   Litho.
751-754 A258 Set of 4   3.75 3.75
Souvenir Sheet
Perf. 12½x12¾
755 A258 $2 multi   4.00 4.00

No. 755 contains one 29x42mm stamp.

Christmas A259

Churches: 22c, Mother Church, United Church of Christ, Pohnpei. 26c, St. Mary's Church, Yap, horiz. 41c, Sapore Bethesca Church, Fefan, Chuuk, horiz. 90c, Lelu Congregational Church, Kosrae, horiz.

Perf. 14¼x14¾, 14¾x14¼
2007, Nov. 12
756-759 A259 Set of 4   3.75 3.75

America's Cup Yachting Races, Valencia, Spain — A260

Sails of various sailboats.

2007, Dec. 12   Perf. 13¼
760   Strip of 4   8.50 8.50
  a. A260 26c aquamarine & multi   .50 .50
  b. A260 80c red & multi   1.60 1.60
  c. A260 $1.14 yellow & multi   2.40 2.40
  d. A260 $2 orange & multi   4.00 4.00

First Helicopter Flight, Cent. — A261

No. 761: a, AH-1 Huey Cobra. b, 206 Jet Ranger. c, H-43 Huskie. d, AS-350 Ecureuil. $2.50, Fa 223 Drache.

2007, Dec. 12   *Perf. 13¼*
761 A261 $1 Sheet of 4, #a-d   8.00 8.00

Souvenir Sheet
762 A261 $2.50 multi   5.00 5.00

Princess Diana (1961-97) — A262

Serpentine Die Cut 7¾
2007, Dec. 12   **Litho. & Embossed**
Without Gum
763 A262 $8 multi   16.00 16.00

Miniature Sheet

Pres. John F. Kennedy (1917-63) — A263

No. 764 — Kennedy: a, With curtain at left. b, Color portrait. c, With Presidential Seal. d, At microphones.

2008, Jan. 2   **Litho.**   *Perf. 14*
764 A263 90c Sheet of 4, #a-d   7.25 7.25

New Year 2008 (Year of the Rat) — A264

2008, Jan. 2   **Litho.**   *Perf. 12*
765 A264 90c multi   1.90 1.90
Printed in sheets of 4.

Miniature Sheet

2008 Olympic Games, Beijing — A265

No. 766: a, Cover of book with music from 1904 World's Fair. b, Poster for 1904 Olympic

Games and World's Fair. c, Jim Lightbody. d, Martin Sheridan.

2008, Jan. 8   *Perf. 14*
766 A265 50c Sheet of 4, #a-d   4.00 4.00

Souvenir Sheet

Breast Cancer Awareness — A266

2008, Mar. 12
767 A266 $2 multi   4.00 4.00

Hummer Vehicles — A267

No. 768: a, Front bumper of Hummer H3x, denomination at UR. b, Side view of Hummer H3x, denomination at LR. c, Front view of Hummer H3x, denomination at LR. d, Rear view of Hummer H3x, denomination at UR. $2, Hummer H3.

2008, May 6   *Perf. 13¼*
768 A267 90c Sheet of 4, #a-d   7.25 7.25

Souvenir Sheet
769 A267 $2 multi   4.00 4.00

Jerusalem — A268

2008, May 14   *Imperf.*
770 A268 $3 multi   6.00 6.00
World Stamp Championship, Israel, 2008.

Miniature Sheet

Elvis Presley (1935-77) — A269

No. 771 — Presley: a, With head on hand, buff background. b, Sitting in director's chair, gray background. c, Wearing striped jacket, brown background. d, Wearing brown shirt, red brown background. e, Wearing gray suit, yellow orange background. f, Wearing gray suit, blue gray background.

2008, June 12   *Perf. 13¼*
771 A269 75c Sheet of 6, #a-f   9.00 9.00

Miniature Sheet

Members of Phoenix Suns Basketball Team — A270

No. 772 — Emblem of National Basketball Association and: a, Amare Stodemire. b, Boris Diaw. c, Brian Skinner. d, D. J. Strawberry. e, Shaquille O'Neal. f, Grant Hill. g, Leandro Barbosa. h, Raja Bell. i, Steve Nash.

2008, June 19
772 A270 42c Sheet of 9, #a-i   7.75 7.75

Miniature Sheet

Royal Air Force, 90th Anniv. — A271

No. 773 — Aircraft: a, Tornado. b, Harrier. c, Typhoon. d, Hawk.

2008, May 6   **Litho.**   *Perf. 13¼*
773 A271 90c Sheet of 4, #a-d   7.25 7.25

Miniature Sheet

Visit of Pope Benedict XVI to United States — A272

No. 774 — Pope Benedict XVI and one quarter of Papal arms at: a, LR. b, LL. c, UR. d, UL.

2008, Sept. 9   *Perf. 13¼*
774 A272 94c Sheet of 4, #a-d   7.75 7.75

Miniature Sheets

A273

Muhammad Ali, Boxer — A274

No. 775 — Ali: a, Wearing protective head-gear. b, Receiving adjustment of headgear. c, Looking right. d, In boxing ring, looking right. e, In boxing ring, looking left. f, With trainer, looking at hands.
No. 776 — Ali fighting: a, Throwing left jab. b, Ready to deliver punch. c, With hands in front of his chest. d, With opponent's punch missing.

2008, Sept. 9   *Perf. 11½x11¼*
775 A273 75c Sheet of 6, #a-f   9.00 9.00
         Perf. 13¼
776 A274 94c Sheet of 4, #a-d   7.75 7.75

Star Trek — A275

No. 777: a, U.S.S. Enterprise. b, Mr. Spock and woman. c, Captain Kirk. d, Uhura and Chekov. e, Starbase 11. f, Dr. McCoy and Mr. Spock.
No. 778: a, Scotty. b, Captain Kirk. c, Dr. McCoy and Uhura. d, Chekov.

2008, Sept. 9   *Perf. 12x11½*
777 A275 75c Sheet of 6, #a-f   9.00 9.00
         Perf. 13¼
778 A275 94c Sheet of 4, #a-d   7.75 7.75
No. 778 contains four 38x60mm stamps.

Christmas
A276

Ornaments: 22c, Angel. 27c, Snowflake. 42c, Cross. 94c, Angel, diff.

2008, Sept. 9   *Perf. 14x14¾*
779-782 A276   Set of 4   3.75 3.75

Famous Men — A277

No. 783: a, Ioanis Artui, Palikiri chief. b, Dr. Eluel K. Pretrick, Human Resources Secretary.

2008, Oct. 17   *Perf. 13¼*
783 A277 94c Pair, #a-b   3.75 3.75

Miniature Sheet

Inauguration of US Pres. Barack
Obama — A278

No. 784: a, 42c, Obama facing right. b, 42c,
Obama facing left, one side of shirt collar
showing. c, 42c, Obama facing left, both sides
of shirt collar showing. d, 75c, As "c." e, 75c,
As "b." f, 75c, As "a."

2009, Jan. 20   Litho.   Perf. 11½
784 A278 Sheet of 6, #a-f   7.25 7.25

Miniature Sheet

Marilyn Monroe (1926-62),
Actress — A279

No. 785: a, Monroe in dressing gown. b,
Head of Monroe. c, Monroe in lilac sweater. d,
Monroe in automobile.

2009, Jan. 22
785 A279 94c Sheet of 4, #a-d   7.75 7.75

Surfing — A280

Ocean waves and various surfers. Waves
only on 20c, 22c, 59c, 83c.

2009, Jan. 26   Perf. 14x14¾
786 A280 1c multi   .25 .25
787 A280 2c multi   .25 .25
788 A280 17c multi   .35 .35
789 A280 20c multi   .40 .40
790 A280 22c multi   .45 .45
791 A280 27c multi   .55 .55
792 A280 42c multi   .85 .85
793 A280 59c multi   1.25 1.25
794 A280 72c multi   1.50 1.50
795 A280 83c multi   1.75 1.75
796 A280 94c multi   1.90 1.90
797 A280 $1.17 multi   2.40 2.40
798 A280 $4.80 multi   9.75 9.75
799 A280 $16.50 multi   33.00 33.00
Nos. 786-799 (14)   54.65 54.65

Miniature Sheet

New Year 2009 (Year of the
Ox) — A281

No. 800: a, Denomination next to yellow arc,
three leaves at top. b, Denomination even with
yellow curlicues, two tan arcs going beneath
denomination. c, Denomination next to yellow
arc, one leaf between yellow and pink curlicues at top. d, Denomination even with yellow
curlicues, tip of brown leaf touching "0" in
denomination.

2009, Jan. 26   Perf. 11½
800 A281 94c Sheet of 4, #a-d   7.75 7.75

Peonies
A282

2009, Apr. 10   Perf. 13¼
801 A282 42c multi   .85 .85

Printed in sheets of 6.

Miniature Sheets

A283

China 2009 World Stamp
Exhibition — A284

No. 802 — Olympic sports: a, Triathlon. b,
Diving. c, Equestrian. d, Table tennis.
No. 803 — Tang Dynasty art: a, Portrait of
Emperor Taizong (Li Shih-min). b, Portrait of
Emperor Taizong and his subjects. c, Calligra-
phy of Emperor Taizong. d, Mural of Emperor
Taizong, Dunhuang.

2009, Apr. 10   Perf. 12
802 A283 59c Sheet of 4, #a-d   4.75 4.75
803 A284 59c Sheet of 4, #a-d   4.75 4.75

Souvenir Sheets

A285

A286

A287

Elvis Presley (1935-77) — A288

2009, June 10   Perf. 13¼
804 A285 $2.50 multi   5.00 5.00
805 A286 $2.50 multi   5.00 5.00
806 A287 $2.50 multi   5.00 5.00
807 A288 $2.50 multi   5.00 5.00
Nos. 804-807 (4)   20.00 20.00

Miniature Sheets

A289

Michael Jackson (1958-2009) — A290

No. 808 — Shirt color: a, 28c, Yellow. b,
28c, Black. c, 75c, Yellow. d, 75c, Black.
No. 809 — Shirt color: a, 28c, Tan. b, 28c,
White. c, 75c, Tan. d, 75c, White.

2009, July 7   Litho.   Perf. 13¼x13
808 A289 Sheet of 4, #a-d   4.25 4.25
809 A290 Sheet of 4, #a-d   4.25 4.25

Miniature Sheets

A291

First Man on the Moon, 40th
Anniv. — A292

No. 894 — Princess Diana: a, In beige dress, embracing child. b, In plaid suit, meeting child. c, In blue green suit, meeting child. d, In pink suit.

2010, Aug. 26   Litho.   Perf. 12x11½
894 A319 75c Sheet of 4, #a-d   6.00 6.00

Souvenir Sheet

Issuance of the Penny Black, 170th Anniv. — A320

No. 895: a, Great Britain #1. b, Micronesia #2.

2010, Oct. 6   Perf. 13x13¼
895 A320 $2 Sheet of 2, #a-b   8.00 8.00

Christmas A321

Paintings: 22c, Adoration of the Magi, by Corrado Giaquinto. 28c, Polyptych with the Nativity, by Rogier van der Weiden. 44c, The Nativity, by Federico Barocci. 98c, The Newborn Christ, by Georges de La Tour. $4.95, The Flight into Egypt, by Giotto di Bondone.

2010, Nov. 1   Perf. 13¼x13
896-900 A321   Set of 5   14.00 14.00

Pope John Paul II (1920-2005) A322

2010, Dec. 16   Perf. 12
901 A322 75c multi   1.50 1.50
Printed in sheets of 4.

Miniature Sheet

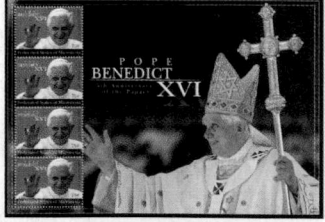

Pope Benedict XVI — A323

No. 902 — Pope Benedict XVI with lower panel: a, In solid black. b, In black and dark gray at LR. c, In brown and black with "d" over black area, finger partially visible at right. d, In brown and black with "of" over black area.

2010, Dec. 16
902 A323 75c Sheet of 4, #a-d   6.00 6.00

Miniature Sheet

Pres. Abraham Lincoln (1809-65) — A324

No. 903 — Lincoln: a, Giving Gettysburg Address. b, With wife, Mary. c, Reading draft of the Emancipation Proclamation. d, Meeting General George McClellan in tent at Antietam.

2010, Dec. 16   Perf. 12½x12
903 A324 75c Sheet of 4, #a-d   6.00 6.00

Miniature Sheets

2010 World Cup Soccer Championships, South Africa — A325

No. 904, 61c: a, Dani Alves. b, Dirk Kuyt. c, Lucio. d, Gregory Van Der Wiel. e, Robinho. f, Mark Van Bommel.
No. 905, 61c: a, Diego Perez. b, Isaac Vorsah. c, Egidio Arevalo. d, Kevin-Prince Boateng. e, Luis Suarez. f, Kwadwo Asamoah.

2010, Dec. 30   Litho.   Perf. 12
Sheets of 6, #a-f
904-905 A325   Set of 2   15.00 15.00

Souvenir Sheet

New Year 2011 (Year of the Rabbit) — A326

2011, Jan. 27
906 A326   Sheet of 2 #906a   6.00 6.00
  a. $1.50 Single stamp   3.00 3.00

Miniature Sheet

Inauguration of Pres. John F. Kennedy, 50th Anniv. — A327

No. 907: a, Kennedy taking oath. b, Kennedy pointing. c, Kennedy on reviewing stand. d, Kennedy with wife, Jacqueline.

2011, Jan. 27
907 A327 75c Sheert of 4, #a-d   6.00 6.00

Miniature Sheet

Elvis Presley (1935-77) — A328

No. 908 — Presley: a, Without guitar. b, Playing guitar, wearing jacket with plain shoulders. c, Holding guitar. d, Playing guitar, wearing shirt with decorated shoulders.

2011, Jan. 27
908 A328 75c Sheert of 4, #a-d   6.00 6.00

Mohandas K. Gandhi (1869-1948) A329

2011, Jan. 27   Perf. 13 Syncopated
909 A329   95c shown   1.90 1.90

Souvenir Sheet
910 A329 $2.50 Gandhi, horiz.   5.00 5.00
Indipex 2011, New Delhi (No. 910). No. 909 was printed in sheets of four.

A330

Beijing 2010 Intl. Philatelic Exhibition — A331

No. 911 — Three Gorges Dam and: a, Reservoir, denomination in red. b, Fountain, denomination in white. c, Denomination in black. d, Boats, denomination in white.
$2, Face of terra cotta warrior, Xi'an.

2011, Jan. 27   Perf. 12
911 A330 75c Sheet of 4, #a-d   6.00 6.00
Souvenir Sheet
912 A331 $2 multi   4.00 4.00

Engagement of Prince William and Catherine Middleton — A332

No. 913: a, Royal arms of the United Kingdom, blue background. b, Arms of Prince William of Wales, blue background. c, Couple, Middleton without hat.
No. 914: a, Royal arms of the Untied Kingdom, brown background. b, Arms of Prince William of Wales, brown background. c, Couple, Middleton with hat.
No. 915, $1.50: a, Couple. b, Royal arms of the Untied Kingdom.
No. 916, $1.50: a, Arms of Prince William of Wales. b, Prince William.

2011, Jan. 27   Perf. 13 Syncopated
913 A332 94c Sheet of 4,
  #913a-913b, 2
  #913c   7.75 7.75
914 A332 94c Sheet of 4,
  #914a-914b, 2
  #914c   7.75 7.75
Souvenir Sheets of 2, #a-b
915-916 A332   Set of 2   12.00 12.00

Miniature Sheets

A333

A334

Travels of U.S. Pres. Barack
Obama — A335

No. 917 — Pres. Obama at United Nations
General Assembly with: a, Viet Nam Pres.
Nguyen Minh Triet, Philippines Pres. Benigno
Aquino III. b, Azerbaijan Pres. Ilham Aliyev. c,
Colombia Pres. Juan Manuel Santos Calde-
rón. d, Kyrgyzstan Pres. Roza Otunbayeva.
No. 918 — Pictures from 2010 G20 Summit
in Seoul: a, Pres. Obama waving. b, Pres.
Obama with France Pres. Nicolas Sarkozy. c,
Pres. Obama with South Korea Pres. Lee
Myung-bak. d, Pres. Obama with Russia Pres.
Dmitry Medvedev.
No. 919 — Pictures from 2010 G20 Summit:
a, Pres. Obama facing right. b, South Korea
Pres. Lee. c, Pres. Obama and others holding
certificate. d, Pres. Obama at lectern, flags in
background.

2011, Jan. 27　Litho.　Perf. 12
917　A333　75c Sheet of 4, #a-d　6.00　6.00
918　A334　75c Sheet of 4, #a-d　6.00　6.00
　　　Perf. 13 Syncopated
919　A335　75c Sheet of 4, #a-d　6.00　6.00
　　　Nos. 917-919 (3)　18.00　18.00

Miniature Sheet

Roald Amundsen's Expedition to the
South Pole, Cent. — A336

No. 920: a, Lake Fryxell, Antarctica. b,
Amundsen. c, Emperor penguins. d, Aurora
Australis at Amundsen-Scott South Pole
Station.

2011, Apr. 6　Perf. 12
920　A336　98c Sheet of 4, #a-d　8.00　8.00

Miniature Sheets

U.S. Civil War, 150th Anniv. — A337

No. 921, 98c — Eagle, shield, Union and
Confederate flags, Commodore George N.
Hollins and Capatin John Pope from Battle of
the Head of Passes, Oct. 12, 1861, and: a,
The CSS Manassas attacks the USS Rich-
mond. b, USS Richmond. c, CSS Manassas.
d, USS Water Witch.
No. 922, 98c — Eagle, shield, Union and
Confederate flags, Colonel Nathan G. Evans
and General Charles F. Stone from Battle of
Ball's Bluff, Oct. 21, 1861, and: a, General
Stone's forces at Ball's Bluff. b, Union artillery
fires shells across Potomac River. c, Battle
map of Ball's Bluff. d, Death of Col. Edward D.
Baker.

2011, Apr. 6　Perf. 13 Syncopated
　　　Sheets of 4, #a-d
921-922　A337　Set of 2　16.00　16.00

U.S. Pres.
Abraham Lincoln
(1809-65)
A338

2011, Apr. 6　Perf. 13 Syncopated
923　A338　75c shown　1.50　1.50
　　　Souvenir Sheet
　　　Perf. 12½
924　A338　$2.50 Lincoln, diff.　5.00　5.00
No. 923 was printed in sheets of 4. No. 924
contains one 38x51mm stamp.

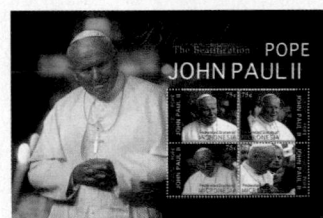

Beatification of Pope John Paul
II — A339

No. 925 — Pope John Paul II: a, With archway in background at left. b, Waving. c, With
man's head in background at left. d, Holding
child.
$2.50, Pope John Paul II wearing miter, vert.

2011, Apr. 6　Perf. 12
925　A339　75c Sheet of 4, #a-d　6.00　6.00
　　　Souvenir Sheet
926　A339　$2.50 multi　5.00　5.00

A340

A341

A342

A343

A344

Elvis Presley (1935-77) — A345

No. 927 — Presley: a, With drums in background. b, Wearing suit with handkerchief in
pocket. c, Playing double-necked guitar. d,
Singing, holding microphone, wearing spotted
and decorated jacket and pants. e, With red
guitar. f, Singing, wearing decorated shirt and
pants.
No. 928 — Presley: a, Wearing Western
shirt with flower on shoulder. b, With hand in
front of mouth. c, Wearing light-colored jacket.
d, Wearing necklaces. e, Singing, with sign in
background. f, With spotlight behind head.

2011　Perf. 13½
927　A340　75c Sheet of 6,
　　　　　#a-f　9.00　9.00
928　A341　75c Sheet of 6,
　　　　　#a-f　9.00　9.00

　　　Souvenir Sheets
　　　Perf. 12½
929　A342　$2.50 multi　5.00　5.00
930　A343　$2.50 multi　5.00　5.00
931　A344　$2.50 multi　5.00　5.00
932　A345　$2.50 multi　5.00　5.00
　　　Nos. 929-932 (4)　20.00　20.00
Issued: Nos. 927-928, 5/16; Nos. 929-932,
4/6.

Wedding of Prince William and
Catherine Middleton — A346

No. 933, 98c — Couple kissing with: a, Light
gray design above denomination, white area to
left of denomination. b, Dark gray design
below and around denomination. c, Light gray
design under and around denomination. d,
White area under and around denomination.
No. 934, 98c — a, Groom, light gray design
above denomination, white area to left of
denomination. b, Bride, dark gray design
under and around denomination. c, Groom,
light gray design under and around denomination. d, Bride, white area under and around
denomination.
$2.50, Couple, diff.

2011, Aug. 29　Perf. 13 Syncopated
　　　Sheets of 4, #a-d
933-934　A346　Set of 2　16.00　16.00
　　　Souvenir Sheet
935　A346　$2.50 multi　5.00　5.00

A347

Princess Diana (1961-97) — A348

No. 936 — Princess Diana wearing: a, Black
dress, holding clutch purse. b, White blouse
covering shoulders. c, Strapless white dress.
d, Purple dress.
No. 937 — Princess Diana: a, As child,
wearing red headband. b, Wearing black and
white dress. c, Wearing red dress and hat. d,
Wearing beige hat and beige checked jacket.

2011, July 14　Perf. 12
936　A347　98c Sheet of 4, #a-d　8.00　8.00
937　A348　98c Sheet of 4, #a-d　8.00　8.00

Reptiles — A349

No. 938: a, Stripe-necked turtle. b, Oceanic gecko. c, Tropical gecko. d, Four-clawed gecko. e, Mourning gecko.
No. 939: a, Marianas blue-tailed skink. b, Green sea turtle.

2011, July 14   **Litho.**
938 A349   50c Sheet of 5, #a-e   5.00 5.00
Souvenir Sheet
939 A349 $1.25 Sheet of 2, #a-b   5.00 5.00

September 11, 2011 Terrorist Attacks, 10th Anniv. — A350

No. 940 — American flag and: a, Silhouette of Pentagon Building. b, World Trade Center in black. c, World Trade Center in gray. d, Map of Stonycreek Township, Pennsylvania. $2.50, World Trade Center, horiz.

2011, Sept. 9   **Perf. 13¼x13**
940 A350   98c Sheet of 4, #a-d   8.00 8.00
Souvenir Sheet
Perf. 12
941 A350 $2.50 multi   5.00 5.00

Miniature Sheets

Japanese Team, Winners of 2011 Women's World Cup Soccer Tournament — A351

Finalists of 2011 Women's World Cup Soccer Tournament — A352

No. 942: a, Two women, woman at right wearing black headband. b, Woman wearing headband. c, Two women, woman at left wearing head bandage, woman at ridght wearing headband. d, Woman wearing yellow and

black uniform. e, Woman in front of players wearing uniform numbers 10 and 7. f, Two women in front of player wearing uniform number 6. g, Woman in front of player wearing uniform number 17. h, Woman in front of woman wearing yellow and black uniform.
No. 943: a, Japan goalie Ayumi Kaihori. b, Team Japan. c, Team USA. d, USA goalie Hope Solo.

2011, Sept. 21   **Perf. 13½x13**
942 A351   50c Sheet of 8, #a-h   8.00 8.00
Perf. 12x12½
943 A352   98c Sheet of 4, #a-d   8.00 8.00

Whales — A353

No. 944: a, Physeter polycyphus. b, Physeter macrocephalus. c, Sei whale.
No. 945: a, Tail of sperm whale. b, Head of sperm whale.

2011, Sept. 21   **Perf. 12½x12**
944 A353 $1 Sheet of 3, #a-c   6.00 6.00
Souvenir Sheet
Perf.
945 A353 $1.25 Sheet of 2, #a-b   5.00 5.00
No. 945 contains two 35mm diameter stamps.

A354

A355

Dr. Sun Yat-sen (1866-1925), President of Republic of China — A355a

No. 946: a, Blue background. b, Pink background.

No. 947: a, Denomination at UR. b, Denomination at UL.
No. 947C: a, Dr. Sun Yat-sen. b, Flag of Wuchang Uprising.

2011, Sept. 27   Perf. 13 Syncopated
946 A354   63c Horiz. pair, #a-b   2.60 2.60
947 A355   63c Pair, #a-b   2.60 2.60
Souvenir Sheet
Imperf
Without Gum
947C A355a $2 Sheet of 2, #d-e 8.00 8.00
No. 946 was printed in sheets containing two pairs. No. 947 was printed in sheets containing three pairs.

Sharks — A356

No. 948: a, Sharpnose seven-gill shark. b, Basking shark. c, Porbeagle. d, Bluntnose six-gill shark.
$2.50, Sand tiger shark.

2011, Oct. 6   **Perf. 13x13¼**
948 A356   75c Sheet of 4, #a-d   6.00 6.00
Souvenir Sheet
949 A356 $2.50 multi   5.00 5.00

Game Fish — A357

No. 950: a, Houndfish. b, Pacific agujon needlefish. c, Keeltail needlefish.
No. 951, $2.50, Swordfish. No. 952, $2.50, Rainbow runner.

2011, Oct. 6   **Perf. 12**
950 A357 $1 Sheet of 3, #a-c   6.00   6.00
Souvenir Sheets
Perf. 13x13¼
951-952 A357   Set of 2   10.00 10.00

Christmas A358

Designs: 22c, Fish and sea anemone. 44c, Perfume flower tree branch. 98c, Palm tree. $4.95, Sea shell.

2011, Nov. 1   **Perf. 12**
953-956 A358   Set of 4   13.50 13.50

Chinese Pottery — A359

No. 957: a, Tang Dynasty ceramic offering plate with six eaves. b, Song Dynasty Celadon

vase. c, Ming Dynasty porcelain plate. d, Qing Dynasty porcelain vase.
$2.50, Ming Dynasty blue and white porcelain plate.

2011, Nov. 7   **Perf. 12**
957 A359 $1.25 Sheet of 4,
                   #a-d   10.00 10.00
Souvenir Sheet
958 A359 $3.50 multi   7.00   7.00
Chinal 2011 Intl. Philatelic Exhibition, Wuxi.

New Year 2012 (Year of the Dragon) — A360

2011, Nov. 7 Embroidered   Imperf.
Self-Adhesive
959 A360 $8 red & yellow   16.00 16.00

Miniature Sheet

Peace Corps, 50th Anniv. — A361

No. 960 — Winning art in children's stamp design contest: a, People in canoe, by Arvin Helgenberger. b, People with sign, by Alex Alexander. c, Trees, people in canoe, and fish, by Ashly-Ann Alfons. d, Ship and flag, by Leonard Klingen.

2011, Nov. 15 Litho. Perf. 12½x12
960 A361   44c Sheet of 4, #a-d   3.75 3.75

Erhart Aten (1932-2004), Governor of Chuuk State — A362

2011, Nov. 28   **Perf. 11¼x11½**
961 A362   44c multi   .90   .90

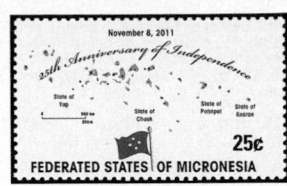

Independence, 25th Anniv. (in 2011) — A363

2012, Mar. 1 **Perf. 12**
962 A363 25c multi .50 .50

Pope Benedict XVI — A364

No. 963: a, Denomination at R. b, Denomination at L.
$3.50, Pope Benedict XVI, vert.

2012, Apr. 4 **Perf. 14**
963 A364 $1.25 Horiz. pair, #a-b 5.00 5.00
Souvenir Sheet
Perf. 12
964 A364 $3.50 multi 7.00 7.00
No. 963 was printed in sheets containing two pairs.

Pres. Ronald Reagan (1911-2004) A365

2012, Apr. 4 **Perf. 12**
965 A365 $1.25 shown 2.50 2.50
Souvenir Sheet
966 A365 $3.50 Reagan, diff. 7.00 7.00
No. 965 was printed in sheets of 4.

Reign of Queen Elizabeth II, 60th Anniv. — A366

No. 967 — Queen Elizabeth II wearing Army uniform in 1945: a, Wearing cap, looking right. b, Wearing cap, looking left. c, Without cap. d, Wearing cap, hands visible.
$3.50, Queen Elizabeth II wearing cap, vert.

2012, Apr. 4 **Perf. 13 Syncopated**
967 A366 $1.25 Sheet of 4,
#a-d 10.00 10.00
Souvenir Sheet
968 A366 $3.50 multi 7.00 7.00

Sinking of the Titanic, Cent. — A367

No. 969, horiz.: a, Titanic sinking. b, People waiting for survivors. c, Last known photograph of the Titanic.
$3.50, Passengers on deck.

2012, Apr. 4 **Perf. 12**
969 A367 $1.25 Sheet of 3, #a-c 7.50 7.50
Souvenir Sheet
970 A367 $3.50 multi 7.00 7.00

Hindenburg Disaster, 75th Anniv. — A368

No. 971 — Hindenburg in color and: a, "D-LZ129" and Olympic rings on side of zeppelin. b, Name "Hindenburg" on side of zeppelin. c, Mooring mast.
$3.50, Hindenburg, diff.

2012, Apr. 4 **Perf. 13 Syncopated**
971 A368 $1.50 Sheet of 3, #a-c 9.00 9.00
Souvenir Sheet
972 A368 $3.50 multi 7.00 7.00

Hybrid Dogs — A369

No. 973: a, Mal-shi. b, Puggle. c, Labradoodle. d, Chiweenie.
$3.50, Schnoodle.

2012, Apr. 4 **Litho.**
973 A369 $1.25 Sheet of 4,
#a-d 10.00 10.00
Souvenir Sheet
974 A369 $3.50 multi 7.00 7.00

Mother Teresa (1910-97), Humanitarian A370

Designs: $1.25, Mother Teresa. $3.50, Mother Teresa holding infant.

2012, Apr. 11 **Perf. 12**
975 A370 $1.25 multi 2.50 2.50
Souvenir Sheet
976 A370 $3.50 multi 7.00 7.00
No. 975 was printed in sheets of 4.

Premiere of Movie "The Three Stooges" — A371

No. 977, vert.: a, Sean Hayes as Larry. b, Chris Diamantopoulos as Moe. c, Will Sasso as Curly. d, Moe grabbing Curly and Larry. e, Stooges on bicycle.
$3.50, Stooges with hands against faces.

2012, Apr. 17 **Perf. 13 Syncopated**
977 A371 $1 Sheet of 5,
#a-e 10.00 10.00
Souvenir Sheet
978 A371 $3.50 multi 7.00 7.00

Miniature Sheet

2012 Summer Olympics, London — A372

No. 979: a, Weight lifting. b, Archery. c, Tennis. d, Equestrian.

2012, May 30 **Perf. 14**
979 A372 80c Sheet of 4, #a-d 6.50 6.50

Turtles — A373

No. 980: a, Hawksbill turtle. b, Leatherback turtle. c, Green sea turtle. d, Olive ridley turtle.
No. 981: a, Loggerhead turtle. b, Flatback turtle.

2012, June 27 **Perf. 13 Syncopated**
980 A373 $1.25 Sheet of 4,
#a-d 10.00 10.00
Souvenir Sheet
981 A373 $1.25 Sheet of 2,
#a-b 5.00 5.00

Souvenir Sheets

Elvis Presley (1935-77) — A374

Presley: No. 982, $3.50, On Heartbreak Hotel record cover. No. 983, $3.50, On Hound Dog record cover. No. 984, $3.50, On Teddy Bear record cover. No. 985, $3.50, Playing guitar. No. 986, $3.50, Wearing striped shirt.

2012, Aug. 7 **Perf. 12½**
982-986 A374 Set of 5 35.00 35.00

Miniature Sheets

A375

Pope Benedict XVI — A376

No. 987 — Pope Benedict XVI: a, Holding Bible. b, Waving, microphone visible. c, With white horizontal panel in background. d, With white vertical panel in background.
No. 988 — Pope Benedict XVI: a, Wearing miter. b, Waving, cross in background. c, With brown, black and gray areas in background. d, Wearing red hat.

2012, Aug. 28 **Perf. 12**
987 A375 $1.25 Sheet of 4,
#a-d 10.00 10.00
988 A376 $1.25 Sheet of 4,
#a-d 10.00 10.00

Space Flight Speech of Pres. John F. Kennedy, 50th Anniv. — A377

No. 989, $1.25: a, Astronaut on Moon. b, Kennedy behind microphones and Presidential seal. c, Mercury capsule. d, Gemini capsule.
No. 990, $1.25: a, Lunar Module orbiting Moon. b, Apollo service and command modules orbiting moon. c, Lunar Module and astronaut on Moon. d, Kennedy and flag.

2012, Aug. 28 **Perf. 12**
Sheets of 4, #a-d
989-990 A377 Set of 2 20.00 20.00

Ranger Moon Program, 50th Anniv. — A378

No. 991, $1.25: a, Atlas Agena rocket lifting off. b, Moon targets. c, Ranger Lander above Moon, denomination at LL. d, Ranger 3 above Moon, country name at bottom.
No. 992, $1.25: a, Ranger 3 above Moon, country name at top. b, Ranger 7. c, Ranger lander above Moon, denomination at LR. d, Ranger 4.

2012, Aug. 28   Perf. 13 Syncopated
Sheets of 4, #a-d
991-992 A378 Set of 2   20.00 20.00

Carnivorous Plants — A379

No. 993: a, Pitcher plant. b, Fairy apron. c, Spoon-leaved sundew. d, Tropical sundew.
No. 994: a, Bladderwort. b, Common swamp pitcher plant.

Perf. 13 Syncopated
2012, Aug. 28   Litho.
993 A379 $1.25 Sheet of 4,
            #a-d   10.00 10.00
Souvenir Sheet
994 A379 $1.25 Sheet of 2,
            #a-b   5.00 5.00

Christmas — A380

Inscriptions: No. 995, 25c, Kosrae. No. 996, 25c, Yap Stone Money, vert. No. 997, 45c, Chuuk. No. 998, 45c, Pohnpei, vert.

2012, Nov. 1   Litho.   Perf. 12½
995-998 A380 Set of 4   2.80 2.80

Miniature Sheet

Octopi — A381

No. 999: a, Longarm octopus. b, Common octopus. c, Giant octopus. d, Red octopus. e, Day octopus.

2012, Nov. 28   Perf. 13¾
999 A381 $1 Sheet of 5, #a-e   10.00 10.00

Raphael Paintings — A382

No. 1000: a, Saint John in the Wilderness. b, The Sistine Madonna. c, Cardinal Bernardo Dovizi da Bibbiena. d, Madonna dell'Impannata.
$3.50, The Transfiguration.

2012, Nov. 28   Perf. 12½
1000 A382 $1 Sheet of 4, #a-
            d   8.00 8.00
Souvenir Sheet
1001 A382 $3.50 multi   7.00 7.00

A383

A384

A385

A386

New Year 2013 (Year of the Snake) A387

2012, Oct. 10   Litho.   Perf. 13¼
1002   Sheet of 20, #1002a-
            1002d, 16 #1002e   8.00 8.00
  a. A383 18c multi   .40   .40
  b. A384 18c multi   .40   .40
  c. A385 18c multi   .40   .40
  d. A386 18c multi   .40   .40
  e. A387 18c multi   .40   .40

Michelangelo's Completion of the Sistine Chapel Ceiling Paintings, 500th Anniv. — A388

No. 1003 — Details from *The Creation of Adam:* a, Adam. b, Hands of Adam and God. c, Head of God. d, Feminine figure.
No. 1004: a, Separation of Land and Water. b, Creation of the Sun, Moon and Earth. c, Separation of Light and Darkness.

2012, Nov. 28   Litho.   Perf. 12½
1003 A388 $1.25 Sheet of 4,
            #a-d   10.00 10.00
Souvenir Sheet
1004 A388 $1.25 Sheet of 3,
            #a-c   7.50 7.50

World Radio Day — A389

No. 1005: a, Alexanderson alternator. b, Brant Rock Radio Tower, Massachusetts. c, Vacuum tube. d, Crystal radio receiver.
$3.50, Telstar communications satellite.

2013, Jan. 8   Litho.   Perf. 12½
1005 A389 $1.25 Sheet of 4,
            #a-d   10.00 10.00
Souvenir Sheet
Perf.
1006 A389 $3.50 multi   7.00 7.00
   No. 1006 contains one 38mm diameter stamp.

Paintings by Vincent van Gogh (1853-90) — A391

No. 1007 — Details from: a, Self-portrait, 1889. b, Starry Night, 1889. c, Still Life: Vase with Irises, 1889. d, Willows at Sunset, 1888.
No. 1008: a, Entrance Hall of Saint-Paul Hospital, 1889. b, Café Terrace at Night, 1888.

---

c, Still Life with Oranges, Lemons and Blue Gloves (Früchtekorb und Handschuhe), 1889. d, Vincent's Bedroom in Arles, 1888.
$3.50, The Painter on His Way to Work, 1888.

2013, Jan. 8   Litho.   Perf. 13¾
1007 A390 $1.20 Sheet of 4, #a-
            d   9.75 9.75
Perf. 12½
1008 A391 $1.20 Sheet of 4, #a-
            d   9.75 9.75
Souvenir Sheet
1009 A391 $3.50 multi   7.00 7.00

Sarah Bernhardt (1844-1923), Actress — A392

No. 1010 — Illustrations by Alfons Mucha showing Bernhardt with: a, Vase. b, Staff. c, Dagger. d, Palm frond.
$3.50, Bernhardt with lilies in hair.

2013, Feb. 20   Litho.   Perf. 12
1010 A392 $1.20 Sheet of 4, #a-
            d   9.75 9.75
Souvenir Sheet
Perf. 12½
1011 A392 $3.50 multi   7.00 7.00
   No. 1011 contains one 38x51mm stamp.

Pres. John F. Kennedy (1917-63) — A393

No. 1012 — Pres. Kennedy: a, Facing right. b, Pointing. c, Facing slightly left, chin above top of diamond. d, Facing slightly left, chin even with top of diamond.
$3.50, Pres. Kennedy, diff.

2013, Apr. 3   Litho.   Perf. 12
1012 A393 $1.20 Sheet of 4, #a-
            d   9.75 9.75
Souvenir Sheet
1013 A393 $3.50 multi   7.00 7.00

Details of Stained Glass Windows by Louis Comfort Tiffany — A394

No. 1014 — Stained-glass window with: a, Green piece of glass just below "MIC." b, Pink and red flower. c, Numerous green pieces of glass. d, Purple and yellow pieces of glass. $3.50, Stained-glass window, vert.

2013, Apr. 4   Litho.   Perf. 13¾
1014 A394 $1.20 Sheet of 4, #a-
                            d   9.75 9.75
Souvenir Sheet
Perf. 12½
1015 A394 $3.50 multi   7.00 7.00
No. 1015 contains one 38x51mm stamp.

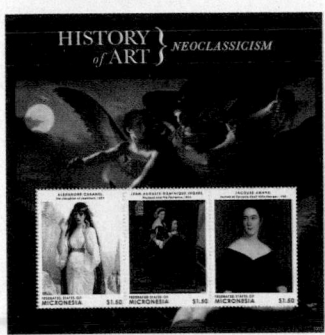
History of Art — A395

No. 1016, $1.50 — Neoclassical paintings: a, The Daughter of Jephthah, by Alexandre Cabanel. b, Raphael and the Fornarina, by Jean Auguste Dominique Ingres. c, Portrait of Cornelia Knott Miltenberger, by Jacques Amans.

No. 1017, $1.50 — Neoclassical paintings: a, Nanna, by Anselm Feuerbach. b, Portrait of Madame de Verninac, by Jacques-Louis David. c, François Marius Gronet, by Ingres.

No. 1018, $3.50, Wanderer Above the Sea of Fog, by Caspar David Friedrich. No. 1019, $3.50, Caspar David Friedrich in his Studio, by Georg Friedrich Kersting, horiz.

2013, Apr. 4   Litho.   Perf. 12½
Sheets of 3, #a-c
1016-1017 A395 Set of 2   18.00 18.00
Souvenir Sheets
1018-1019 A395 Set of 2   14.00 14.00

A396

Resignation of Pope Benedict
XVI — A397

No. 1020 — Pope Benedict XVI: a, Behind lectern. b, Waving, wristwatch visible. c, Kissing person. d, Waving, person wearing red cap in background.

No. 1021 — Pope Benedict XVI: a, Seated in chair. b, Facing forward, white background. c, Waving, grass in background. d, Waving, hand above eyes.

No. 1022, $3.50, In arched doorway, waving. No. 1023, $3.50, Facing right, waving.

Perf. 13 Syncopated
2013, Apr. 29   Litho.
1020 A396 $1.20 Sheet of 4,
                            #a-d   9.75 9.75
1021 A397 $1.20 Sheet of 4,
                            #a-d   9.75 9.75
Souvenir Sheets
1022-1023 A397 Set of 2   14.00 14.00

Dolphins — A398

No. 1024, $1.20: a, Long-beaked common dolphin. b, Short-beaked common dolphin. c, Pygmy killer whale. d, Short-finned pilot whale.

No. 1025, $1.20: Dusky dolphin. b, Hector's dolphin. c, Bottlenose dolphin. d, Pantropical spotted dolphin.

No. 1026, $3.50, Spinner dolphin, horiz. No. 1027, $3.50, Rough-toothed dolphin, horiz.

2012, May 7   Litho.   Perf. 13¾
Sheets of 4, #a-d
1024-1025 A398 Set of 2   19.50 19.50
Souvenir Sheets
1026-1027 A398 Set of 2   14.00 14.00

Fish — A399

No. 1028, $1.20: a, Mandarinfish. b, Neon damselfish. c, Man-of-war fish. d, Banggai cardinalfish.

No. 1029, $1.20: a, Australasian snapper. b, Australian herring. c, Saddletail grouper. d, Tasmanian clingfish.

No. 1030, $3.50, Slender-spined porcupine fish. No. 1031, $3.50, Ocellaris clownfish.

Perf. 13 Syncopated
2013, May 7   Litho.
Sheets of 4, #a-d
1028-1029 A399 Set of 2   19.50 19.50
Souvenir Sheets
1030-1031 A399 Set of 2   14.00 14.00

Dr. Lois Englberger (1948-2011), Acting Director and Research Advisor of Island Food Community
A400

Perf. 13 Syncopated
2013, May 8   Litho.
1032 A400 $1.20 multi   2.40 2.40
Souvenir Sheet
1033 A400 $3.50 multi   7.00 7.00
No. 1032 was printed in sheets of 4.

Mushrooms — A401

No. 1034, $1.25: a, Psilocybe subaeruginosa. b, Gymnopilus luteofolius. c, Gymnopilus junonius. d, Panaeolus cyanescens.

No. 1035, $1.25: a, Psilocybe aucklandii. b, Entoloma hochetottori. c, Amanita citrina. d, Agaricus bernardii.

No. 1036, $3.50, Panaeolus subbalteatus. No. 1037, $3.50, Weraroa novae, vert.

2013, June 3   Litho.   Perf. 12
Sheets of 4, #a-d
1034-1035 A401 Set of 2   20.00 20.00
Souvenir Sheets
1036-1037 A401 Set of 2   14.00 14.00

John De Avila Mangefel (1932-2007), First Governor of Yap — A402

Perf. 13¼x12½
2013, June 13   Litho.
1038 A402 46c multi   .95   .95
No. 1038 was printed in sheets of 4.

Shells — A403

No. 1039: a, Haliotis sorenseni. b, Melongena corona. c, Lyropecten nodosus. d,

Pleurotomaria rumphii. e, Lioconcha castrensis. f, Conus ammiralis.
$3.50, Echinus melo, vert.

2013, July 7   Litho.   Perf. 13¾
1039 A403 $1 Sheet of 6,
                            a-f   12.00 12.00
Souvenir Sheet
Perf. 12½
1040 A403 $3.50 multi   7.00 7.00
No. 1040 contains one 38x51mm stamp.

Wildlife of Thailand — A404

No. 1041: a, Banded pitta. b, Dhole. c, Wrinkled hornbill. d, Nicobar pigeon. e, Lar gibbon. f, Leopard. g, Malaysian tapir. h, Red-footed booby.

No. 1042, vert.: a, Dugong. b, Red-breasted parakeet.

2013, July 7   Litho.   Perf. 13¾
1041 A404 75c Sheet of 8,
                            #a-h   12.00 12.00
Souvenir Sheet
Perf. 12½
1042 A404 $1.75 Sheet of 2,
                            #a-b   7.00   7.00
2013 Thailand World Stamp Exhibition, Bangkok. No. 1042 contains two 38x51mm stamps.

Internet, 30th Anniv. — A405

No. 1043 — Inscriptions: a, The World Wide Web. b, A series of tubes. c, Information super-highway.
3.50, Computer, vert.

2013, Aug. 12   Litho.   Perf. 13¾
1043 A405 $1.50 Sheet of 3, #a-
                            c   9.00   9.00
Souvenir Sheet
Perf. 12½
1044 A405 $3.50 multi   7.00   7.00
No. 1044 contains one 38x51mm stamp.

Souvenir Sheet

Elvis Presley (1935-77) — A406

Litho., Margin Embossed With Foil Application

2013, Aug. 12   **Imperf.**
Without Gum
1045 A406 $10 black   20.00 20.00

Dogs — A407

No. 1046: a, Basset hounds. b, Jack Russell terrier. c, Alaskan huskies. d, Yorkshire terrier. $3.50, Germen shepherds.

2014, Mar. 24   Litho.   Perf. 14
1046 A407 $1.20 Sheet of 4, #a-
            d   9.75 9.75
Souvenir Sheet
Perf. 12
1047 A407 $3.50 multi   7.00 7.00

Parrots — A408

No. 1048: a, Alisterus amboinensis. b, Geoffroyus geoffroyi geoffroyi. c, Loriculus camiguinensis. d, Loriculus calculus. e, Psittacula alexandri alexandri. f, Psittacula alexandri.
$3.50, Alisterus amboinensis, diff.

2014, Mar. 24   Litho.   Perf. 12½
1048 A408 $1 Sheet of 6,
            #a-f   12.00 12.00
Souvenir Sheet
1049 A408 $3.50 multi   7.00 7.00

World War I, Cent. — A409

No. 1050, $1.20: a, Belgian soldier throwing Mills grenade. b, Head of Belgian soldier. c, Head of German soldier. d, German soldier charging.

No. 1051, $1.20, horiz.: a, HMS C1 submarine. b, HMS E5 submarine. c, HMS K17 submarine. d, HMS R3 submarine.
No. 1052, $2: a, King Albert I of Belgium. b, Kaiser Wilhelm II of Germany.
No. 1053, $2, horiz.: a, HMS B11 submarine. b, HMS C27 submarine.

2014, Mar. 24   Litho.   Perf. 14
Sheets of 4, #a-d
1050-1051 A409 Set of 2   19.50 19.50
Souvenir Sheets of 2, #a-b
Perf. 12½
1052-1053 A409 Set of 2   16.00 16.00
No. 1052 contains two 38x51mm stamps.
No. 1053 contains two 51x38mm stamps.

Paintings — A410

No. 1054, $1.50: a, Maria Magdalena, by Carlo Crivelli. b, Madonna of the Goldfinch, by Crivelli. c, The Gentleman in Pink, by Giovanni Battista Moroni.
No. 1055, $1.50: a, Portrait of a Woman with a Winged Bonnet, by Rogier van der Weyden. b, Annunciation, by Peter Paul Rubens. c, St. Augustine, by Caravaggio.
No. 1056, $4, Henry VII, by Hans Holbein the Younger. No. 1057, $4, The Dance Lesson, by Edgar Degas.

2014, Mar. 24   Litho.   Perf. 12½
Sheets of 3, #a-c
1054-1055 A410 Set of 2   18.00 18.00
Size: 100x100
Imperf
1056-1057 A410 Set of 2   16.00 16.00

A411

A412

A413

Pope Francis — A414

No. 1058: a, One ear visible. b, Both ears visible.
No. 1059, Pope wearing zucchetto.
No. 1060: a, Pink area in background. b, White area in background.
No. 1061: a, Denomination in black. b, Denomination in white.

2014, Mar. 24   Litho.   Perf. 14
1058 A411 $1.75 Horiz. pair,
            #a-b   7.00 7.00
1059 A412 $1.75 multi   3.50 3.50
  a. Horiz. pair, #1058b, 1059   7.00 7.00
Souvenir Sheets
Perf. 12
1060 A413 $3.50 Sheet of 2,
            #a-b   14.00 14.00
1061 A414 $3.50 Sheet of 2,
            #a-b   14.00 14.00
No. 1058 and 1059a each were printed in sheets containing two pairs.

A415

Birth of Prince George of
Cambridge — A417

No. 1064: a, Prince George in arms of Duchess of Cambridge. b, Duchess of Cambridge and Prince George. c, Prince George, Duke and Duchess of Cambridge. d, Prince, Duke and Duchess, face of Duchess not visible.
$4, Prince, Duke and Duchess, horiz.

2014, Apr. 29   Litho.   Perf. 13¾
1064 A417 $1.20 Sheet of 4, #a-
            d   9.75 9.75

Souvenir Sheet
Perf. 12½
1065 A417 $4 multi   8.00 8.00
No. 1065 contains one 51x38mm stamp.

Birds — A418

Designs: 1c, Black tern. 2c, Black-headed gull. 4c, Sabine's gull. 5c, Caspian tern. 10c, Common gull. 49c, White-winge black tern. 50c, Wilson's storm petrel. $1, Great skua.

2014, May 8   Litho.   Perf. 13¾
1066-1073 A418 Set of 8   4.50 4.50

Canonization of Pope John Paul
II — A419

No. 1074, $1.20: a, Pope John Paul II in red robe. b, Coat of arms of Pope John Paul II. c, Pope John Paul II wearing miter, color photograph. d, Emblem of the papacy.
No. 1075, $1.20: a, St. Peter's Basilica clock. b, Pope John Paul II wearing miter, black-and-white photograph. c, Papal arms on St. Peter's Basilica. d, Pope John Paul wearing zucchetto.
No. 1076, $2: a, Pope John Paul II in red robe, diff. b, Dome of St. Peter's Basilica.
No. 1077, $2, horiz.: a, Pope John Paul II, color photograph. b, Pope John Paul II, black-and-white photograph.

Perf. 14, 12 (#1077)
2014, May 12   Litho.
Sheets of 4, #a-d
1074-1075 A419 Set of 2   19.50 19.50
Souvenir Sheets of 2, #a-b
1076-1077 A419 Set of 2   16.00 16.00

A420

Nelson Mandela (1918-2013),
President of South Africa — A421

College of Micronesia, 20th
Anniv. — A416

2014, Apr. 5   Litho.   Perf. 12½
1062 A415 49c multi   1.00 1.00
1063 A416 49c multi   1.00 1.00

No. 1078 — Mandela: a, Wearing shirt and sweater. b, Wearing black shirt with white polka dots. c, In black-and-white photograph. d, Wearing suit and tie.

No. 1079 — Mandela: a, On book cover at left, in black-and white photograph at right. b, In black-and-white photograph at left, in color photograph wearing sweater at right. c, Wearing tribal neck covering in black-and-white photograph at left, wearing jacket with Olympic emblem in color photograph at right. d, In two colro photographs.

No. 1080, $7, Mandela wearing green shirt, waving. No. 1081, $7, Mandela wearing blue and white shirt.

2014, May 12   Litho.   Perf. 13¾
1078 A420 $1.75 Sheet of 4, #a-d   14.00 14.00
1079 A421 $1.75 Sheet of 4, #a-d   14.00 14.00
Souvenir Sheets
1080-1081 A421 Set of 2   28.00 28.00

Keitani Graham (1980-2012), Wrestler — A422

Graham: No. 1082, $1, Close-up. No. 1083, $1, With numbered sign in background. No. 1084, $1, Wrestling opponent.

2014, June 4   Litho.   Perf. 14
1082-1084 A422 Set of 3   6.00 6.00

South Korean Tourist Attractions — A423

No. 1085: a, Gwanghwamun Palace, Seoul. b, Seongsan Sunrise Peak, Jeju Island. c, Seorak Mountain, Gangwon Province. d, Bulguksa, Gyeongju.

No. 1086, vert.: a, N Seoul Tower, Seoul. b, Gwangan Bridge, Busan.

2014, June 30   Litho.   Perf. 14
1085 A423 $1.20 Sheet of 4, #a-d   9.75 9.75
Souvenir Sheet
1086 A423 $2 Sheet of 2, #a-b   8.00 8.00

Philakorea 2014 World Stamp Exhibition, Seoul.

A424

A425

A426

Caroline Kennedy, U.S. Ambassador to Japan — A427

Various photographs of Caroline Kennedy, as shown.

2014, June 30   Litho.   Perf. 12
1087 A424 $1.20 Sheet of 4, #a-d   9.75 9.75
1088 A425 $1.20 Sheet of 4, #a-d   9.75 9.75
Souvenir Sheets
1089 A426 $2 Sheet of 2, #a-b   8.00 8.00
Perf. 14
1090 A427 $2 Sheet of 2, #a-b   8.00 8.00

Miniature Sheet

Fruit — A428

No. 1091: a, Strawberries. b, Limes. c, Pears. d, Red currants. e, Blueberries. f, Tomatoes. g, Grapes. h, Oranges. i, Guavas.

2014, July 9   Litho.   Perf.
1091 A428 75c Sheet of 9, #a-i 13.50 13.50

Polar Bears — A429

No. 1092 — Polar bear: a, Underwater, denomination at UR. b, Underwater, head at right, denomination at UL. c, With nose above water, denomination at UR. d, Underwater, head at left, denomination at UL. $2.50, Head of polar bear.

2014, July 31   Litho.   Perf. 14
1092 A429 75c Sheet of 4, #a-d   6.00 6.00
Souvenir Sheet
Perf. 12½
1093 A429 $2.50 multi   5.00 5.00

No. 1093 contains one 51x38mm stamp.

A430

Tropical Fish — A431

No. 1094, 75c: a-d, Various depictions of clownfish in anemone, as shown.

No. 1095, 75c: a, Barcheek unicornfish. b, Discus. c, Old woman angelfish. d, Lined surgeonfish.

No. 1096, $2: a-b, Various depictions of clownfish in anemone, as shown.

No. 1097, $2, vert.: a, Clownfish, anemone at right of fish. b, Clownfish, anemone at left and right of fish

2014, Aug. 27   Litho.   Perf. 14
Sheets of 4, #a-d
1094-1095 A430 Set of 2   12.00 12.00
Souvenir Sheets of 2, #a-b
Perf. 12½
1096-1097 A431 Set of 2   16.00 16.00

Bodyboarding A432

2014, Sept. 6   Litho.   Perf. 14
1098 A432 $2 multi   4.00 4.00

A433

Seaglass — A434

Nos. 1099, 1100, Various depictions of seaglass, as shown.
No. 1101, $4, Seaglass with black rock at left. No. 1102, $4, Seaglass with black rock at top.

Perf. 12, 14 (#1100)

2014, Sept. 15	Litho.		
1099 A433 75c Sheet of 4, #a-d		6.00	6.00
1100 A434 75c Sheet of 6, #a-f		9.00	9.00

Souvenir Sheets

| 1101-1102 A434 | Set of 2 | 16.00 | 16.00 |

A435

Paintings by Qi Baishi (1864-1957) — A436

No. 1103: a, Flowers on branch. b, Flowers and cricket. c, Basket of fruit. d, Mushrooms and flowers.
No. 1104: a, Flowers and beetle. b, Flowers and dragonfly. c, Flowers and dragonfly, diff. d, Flowers and grsasshopper.
No. 1105, $4, Flowers. No. 1106, $4, Rocks and boats.

2014, Sept. 15	Litho.	Perf. 14	
1103 A435 $1.20 Sheet of 4, #a-d		9.75	9.75
1104 A436 $1.20 Sheet of 4, #a-d		9.75	9.75

Souvenir Sheets
Perf. 12

| 1105-1106 A436 | Set of 2 | 16.00 | 16.00 |

Nos. 1105-1106 each contain one 30x50mm stamp.

AIR POST STAMPS

Boeing 727, 1968
AP1

1984, July 12	Litho.	Perf. 13½	
C1 AP1 28c shown		.60	.60
C2 AP1 35c SA-16 Albatross, 1960		.80	.80
C3 AP1 40c PBY-5A Catalina, 1951		1.00	1.00
Nos. C1-C3 (3)		2.40	2.40

Ausipex Type of 1984

Ausipex '84 emblem and: 28c, Caroline Islands No. 4. 35c, No. 7. 40c, No. 19.

1984, Sept. 21	Litho.	Perf. 13½	
C4 A4 28c multicolored		.65	.65
C5 A4 35c multicolored		.85	.85
C6 A4 40c multicolored		1.10	1.10
Nos. C4-C6 (3)		2.60	2.60

Christmas Type

Children's drawings.

1984, Dec. 20			
C7 A5 28c Illustrated Christmas text		.65	.65
C8 A5 35c Decorated palm tree		.90	.90
C9 A5 40c Feast preparation		1.10	1.10
Nos. C7-C9 (3)		2.65	2.65

Ships Type

1985, Aug. 19			
C10 A6 33c L'Astrolabe		.65	.65
C11 A6 39c La Coquille		.80	.80
C12 A6 44c Shenandoah		1.00	1.00
Nos. C10-C12 (3)		2.45	2.45

Christmas Type

1985, Oct. 15	Litho.	Perf. 13½	
C13 A7 33c Dublon Protestant Church		.90	.90
C14 A7 44c Pohnpei Catholic Church		1.25	1.25

Audubon Type

1985, Oct. 31		Perf. 14½	
C15 A8 44c Sooty tern		1.00	1.00

Ruins Type

1985, Dec.	Litho.	Perf. 13½	
C16 A16 33c Nan Tauas inner courtyard		.70	.70
C17 A16 39c Outer wall		.80	.80
C18 A16 44c Tomb		.90	.90
Nos. C16-C18 (3)		2.40	2.40

Halley's Comet
AP2

1986, May 16			
C19 AP2 44c dk bl, bl & blk		1.40	1.25

Return of Nauruans from Truk, 40th Anniv.
AP3

1986, May 16			
C20 AP3 44c Ship in port		1.40	1.25

AMERIPEX '86 Type

Bully Hayes (1829-1877), buccanneer.

1986, May 22			
C21 A18 33c Forging Hawaiian stamp		.55	.55
C22 A18 39c Sinking of the Leonora, Kosrae		.70	.70
C23 A18 44c Hayes escapes capture		.75	.75
C24 A18 75c Biography, by Louis Becke		1.50	1.50
Nos. C21-C24 (4)		3.50	3.50

Souvenir Sheet

| C25 A18 $1 Hayes ransoming chief | | 3.25 | 3.25 |

Christmas Type

Virgin and child paintings: 33c, Austria, 19th cent. 44c, Italy, 18th cent., diff.

1986, Oct. 15	Litho.	Perf. 14½	
C26 A20 33c multicolored		1.00	1.00
C27 A20 44c multicolored		1.40	1.40

Anniversaries and Events Type

1987, June 13	Litho.	Perf. 14½	
C28 A21 33c US currency, bicent.		.60	.60
C29 A21 39c 1st American in orbit, 25th anniv.		1.00	1.00
C30 A21 44c US Constitution, bicent.		1.10	1.10
Nos. C28-C30 (3)		2.70	2.70

Christmas Type

1987, Nov. 16	Litho.	Perf. 14½	
C31 A22 33c Holy Family		.80	.80
C32 A22 39c Shepherds		.90	.90
C33 A22 44c Three Wise Men		1.00	1.00
Nos. C31-C33 (3)		2.70	2.70

Bird Type

1988, Aug. 1	Litho.	Perf. 13½	
C34 A9 33c Great truk white-eye		.55	.55
C35 A9 44c Blue-faced parrotfinch		.70	.70
C36 A9 $1 Yap monarch		1.75	1.75
Nos. C34-C36 (3)		3.00	3.00

Colonial Era Type

1988, July 20		Perf. 13x13½	
C37 A23 44c Traditional skills (boat-building)		.95	.95
C38 A23 44c Modern Micronesia (tourism)		.95	.95
a. Pair, #C37-C38		1.90	1.90

Printed se-tenant in sheets of 28 plus 4 center labels picturing flags of Kosrae (UL), Truk (UR), Pohnpei (LL) and Yap ((LR).

Flags of the Federated States of Micronesia
AP4

1989, Jan. 19	Litho.	Perf. 13x13½	
C39 AP4 45c Pohnpei		.70	.70
C40 AP4 45c Truk		.70	.70
C41 AP4 45c Kosrae		.70	.70
C42 AP4 45c Yap		.70	.70
a. Block of 4, #C39-C42		2.80	2.80

This issue exists with 44c denominations but was not issued.

Aircraft Serving Micronesia
AP5

1990, July 16	Litho.	Perf. 14	
C43 AP5 22c shown		.40	.40
C44 AP5 36c multi, diff.		.65	.65
C45 AP5 39c multi, diff.		.75	.75
C46 AP5 45c multi, diff.		.85	.85
1992, Mar. 27			
C47 AP5 40c Propeller plane, outrigger canoe		.70	.70
C48 AP5 50c Passenger jet, sailboat		.85	.85
Nos. C43-C48 (6)		4.20	4.20

Souvenir Sheet

First Manned Moon Landing, 25th Anniv. — AP6

1994, July 20	Litho.	Perf. 13½	
C49 AP6 $2.90 US #C76		4.25	4.25

MIDDLE CONGO

ˈmi-dəl ˈkäŋˌgō

LOCATION — Western Africa at the Equator, bordering on the Atlantic Ocean
GOVT. — Former French Colony
AREA — 166,069
POP. — 746,805 (1936)
CAPITAL — Brazzaville

In 1910 Middle Congo, formerly a part of French Congo, was declared a separate colony. It was grouped with Gabon and the Ubangi-Shari and Chad Territories and officially designated French Equatorial Africa. This group became a single administrative unit in 1934. See Gabon.

See Congo People's Republic for issues of 1959 onward.

100 Centimes = 1 Franc

See French Equatorial Africa No. 191 for additional stamp inscribed "Moyen Congo" and "Afrique Equatoriale Francaise."

Leopard — A1

Bakalois Woman — A2

Coconut Grove — A3

Perf. 14x13½

1907-22		Typo.		Unwmk.	
1	A1	1c ol gray & brn		.35	.45
2	A1	2c vio & brn		.35	.45
3	A1	4c blue & brn		.70	.85
4	A1	5c dk grn & bl		.70	.70
5	A1	5c yel & bl ('22)		.70	.75
6	A1	10c car & bl		1.00	.70
7	A1	10c dp grn & bl grn ('22)		3.25	3.25
8	A1	15c brn vio & rose ('17)		2.10	1.00
9	A1	20c brown & bl		3.50	2.75
10	A2	25c blue & grn		1.40	1.10
11	A2	25c bl grn & gray ('22)		1.00	1.00
12	A2	30c scar & grn		2.10	1.75
13	A2	30c dp rose & rose ('22)		1.75	2.10
14	A2	35c vio brn & bl		1.75	1.40
15	A2	40c dl grn & brn		1.75	1.75
16	A2	45c violet & red		5.50	3.50
17	A2	50c bl grn & red		2.10	2.10
18	A2	50c bl & grn ('22)		1.75	2.10
19	A2	75c brown & bl		10.00	5.00
20	A3	1fr dp grn & vio		14.00	9.00
21	A3	2fr vio & gray grn		14.00	10.00
22	A3	5fr blue & rose		42.50	37.50
Nos. 1-22 (22)				112.25	89.20

For stamps of types A1-A3 in changed colors, see Chad and Ubangi-Shari. French Congo A4-A6 are similar but inscribed "Congo Francais."
For overprints and surcharges see Nos. 23-60, B1-B2.

Stamps and Types of 1907-22 Overprinted in Black, Blue or Red

1924-30					
23	A1	1c ol gray & brn		.35	.50
a.		Double surcharge		150.00	
24	A1	2c violet & brn		.35	.50
25	A1	4c blue & brn		.35	.50
26	A1	5c yellow & bl		.50	.50
27	A1	10c grn & bl grn (R)		1.10	.35
28	A1	10c car & gray ('25)		.35	.50
29	A1	15c brn vio & rose (Bl)		.70	.50
a.		Double surcharge		110.00	
30	A1	20c brown & blue		.70	.65
31	A1	20c bl grn & yel grn ('26)		.35	.35
32	A1	20c dp brn & rose lil ('27)		1.40	1.00

Nos. 10-22
Overprinted in Black,
Red (R), and Blue
(Bl)

33	A2	25c bl grn & gray	1.00	.40
34	A2	30c rose & pale rose (Bl)	1.40	.70
35	A2	30c gray & bl vio (R) ('27)	.70	.65
36	A2	30c dk grn & grn ('27)	1.75	1.40
37	A2	35c choc & bl	.70	.70
38	A2	40c ol grn & brn	1.40	1.40
a.	Double overprint		275.00	
39	A2	45c vio & pale red (Bl)	1.40	1.00
a.	Inverted overprint		140.00	
40	A2	50c blue & grn (R)	1.40	1.00
41	A2	50c org & blk ('25)	.70	.65
a.	Without overprint		220.00	225.00
42	A2	65c org brn & bl ('27)	2.75	2.10
43	A2	75c brown & blue	1.40	1.40
44	A2	90c brn red & pink ('30)	4.25	3.50
45	A3	1fr green & vio	1.40	1.40
a.	Double overprint		220.00	
46	A3	1.10fr vio & brn ('28)	3.50	4.25
47	A3	1.50fr ultra & bl ('30)	7.00	5.00
48	A3	2fr vio & gray ('30)	2.10	1.40
49	A3	3fr rcd violet ('30)	7.00	5.00
50	A3	5fr blue & rose	5.00	5.00
	Nos. 23-50 (28)		51.00	42.30

Nos. 48 and 50 Surcharged with New Values

1924

51	A3	25c on 2fr vio & gray grn	1.00	1.00
52	A3	25c on 5fr bl & rose (Bl)	1.00	1.00

Types of 1924-27 Surcharged with New Values in Black or Red

1925-27

53	A3	65c on 1fr red org & ol brn	1.00	1.00
a.	Without surcharge		220.00	
54	A3	85c on 1fr red org & ol brn	1.00	1.00
a.	Double surcharge		160.00	
55	A2	90c on 75c brn red & rose red ('27)	2.00	2.40
56	A3	1.25fr on 1fr dl bl & ultra (R)	1.40	1.40
a.	Without surcharge		175.00	175.00
57	A3	1.50fr on 1fr ultra & bl ('27)	2.00	2.00
a.	Without surcharge		175.00	190.00
58	A3	3fr on 5fr org brn & dl red ('27)	4.00	4.00
a.	Without surcharge		275.00	
59	A3	10fr on 5fr ver & bl grn ('27)	13.00	13.00
60	A3	20fr on 5fr org brn & vio ('27)	13.50	13.50
	Nos. 53-60 (8)		37.90	38.30

Bars cover old values on Nos. 56-60.

Common Design Types
pictured following the introduction.

Colonial Exposition Issue
Common Design Types

1931   **Engr.**   **Perf. 12½**
Name of Country in Black

61	CD70	40c deep green	4.00	4.00
62	CD71	50c violet	5.50	5.50
63	CD72	90c red orange	5.50	5.50
64	CD73	1.50fr dull blue	5.50	5.50
	Nos. 61-64 (4)		20.50	20.50

Viaduct at
Mindouli
A4

Pasteur
Institute at
Brazzaville
A5

Government Building, Brazzaville — A6

1933   **Photo.**   **Perf. 13½**

65	A4	1c lt brown	.25	.25
66	A4	2c dull blue	.25	.25
67	A4	4c olive grn	.30	.30
68	A4	5c red violet	.50	.35
69	A4	10c slate	.70	.40
70	A4	15c dk violet	1.40	1.00
71	A4	20c red, *pink*	8.50	6.00
72	A4	25c orange	1.00	1.00
73	A4	30c yellow grn	2.50	1.75
74	A5	40c orange brn	2.50	1.75
75	A5	45c blk, *green*	2.50	1.75
76	A5	50c black violet	.90	.70
77	A5	65c brn red, *grn*	2.50	1.75
78	A5	75c black, *pink*	13.00	9.50
79	A5	90c carmine	2.50	1.75
80	A5	1fr dark red	1.00	.70
81	A5	1.25fr Prus blue	2.10	1.40
82	A5	1.50fr dk blue	14.00	7.00
83	A5	1.75fr dk violet	2.75	1.40
84	A6	2fr grnsh blk	2.10	1.40
85	A6	3fr orange	7.00	4.00
86	A6	5fr slate blue	35.00	25.00
87	A6	10fr black	50.00	35.00
88	A6	20fr dark brown	35.00	27.50
	Nos. 65-88 (24)		188.25	131.90

SEMI-POSTAL STAMPS

No. 6
Surcharged
in Black

1916   **Unwmk.**   **Perf. 14x13½**

B1	A1	10c + 5c car & blue	1.40	1.40
a.	Double surcharge		140.00	140.00
b.	Inverted surcharge		120.00	120.00
e.	As "a," One inverted		175.00	175.00
f.	In pair with unsurcharged stamp		360.00	

A printing with the surcharge placed lower and more to the left was made and used in Ubangi.

No. 6
Surcharged
in Red

B2	A1	10c + 5c car & blue	1.40	1.40

POSTAGE DUE STAMPS

Postage Due Stamps of
France Overprinted

1928   **Unwmk.**   **Perf. 14x13½**

J1	D2	5c light blue	.50	.70
J2	D2	10c gray brn	.60	.70
J3	D2	20c olive grn	1.00	1.40
J4	D2	25c brt rose	1.40	1.75
J5	D2	30c lt red	1.40	1.75
J6	D2	45c blue grn	1.40	1.75
J7	D2	50c brown vio	1.40	1.75
J8	D2	60c yellow brn	2.50	2.75
J9	D2	1fr red brn	2.50	2.75
J10	D2	2fr orange red	3.50	4.00
J11	D2	3fr brt violet	5.00	7.00
	Nos. J1-J11 (11)		21.20	26.30

Village on
Ubangi,
Dance
Mask — D3

Steamer
on Ubangi
River — D4

1930   **Typo.**

J12	D3	5c dp bl & ol	.70	1.40
J13	D3	10c dp red & brn	1.40	1.40
J14	D3	20c green & brn	2.75	2.75
J15	D3	25c lt bl & brn	3.50	3.50
J16	D3	30c bis brn & Prus bl	5.00	5.00
J17	D3	45c Prus bl & ol	6.00	5.50
J18	D3	50c red vio & brn	5.50	6.00
J19	D3	60c gray lil & bl blk	8.50	9.00
J20	D4	1fr bis brn & bl blk	10.00	14.00
J21	D4	2fr violet & brn	14.00	14.00
J22	D4	3fr dk red & brn	12.00	10.00
	Nos. J12-J22 (11)		69.35	72.55

Rubber
Trees and
Djoué
River — D5

1933   **Photo.**   **Perf. 13½**

J23	D5	5c apple green	.70	.70
J24	D5	10c dk bl, *bl*	.70	.70
J25	D5	20c red, *yel*	1.40	1.40
J26	D5	25c chocolate	1.40	1.40
J27	D5	30c orange red	1.75	2.10
J28	D5	45c dk violet	1.75	2.10
J29	D5	50c gray black	2.50	2.75
J30	D5	60c blk, *orange*	3.75	4.00
J31	D5	1fr brown rose	5.50	6.25
J32	D5	2fr orange yel	7.00	8.50
J33	D5	3fr Prus blue	12.00	15.00
	Nos. J23-J33 (11)		38.45	44.90

MOHELI

mo-'ā-lē

LOCATION — One of the Comoro Islands, situated in the Mozambique Channel midway between Madagascar and Mozambique (Africa)
GOVT. — French Colony
AREA — 89 sq. mi.
POP. — 4,000
CAPITAL — Fomboni
     See Comoro Islands

100 Centimes = 1 Franc

Navigation and
Commerce — A1

        Perf. 14x13½

1906-07   **Typo.**   **Unwmk.**
Name of Colony in Blue or Carmine

1	A1	1c blk, *lil bl*	3.75	2.40
2	A1	2c brn, *buff*	2.00	1.75
3	A1	4c claret, *lav*	3.25	2.40
4	A1	5c yellow grn	4.25	2.40
5	A1	10c carmine	5.50	2.40
6	A1	20c red, *green*	13.00	7.25
7	A1	25c blue	13.00	5.50
8	A1	30c brn, *bister*	17.50	14.50
9	A1	35c blk, *yellow*	10.50	4.00
10	A1	40c red, *straw*	17.50	13.50
11	A1	45c blk, *gray grn* ('07)	75.00	60.00
12	A1	50c brn, *az*	24.00	14.50
13	A1	75c dp vio, *org*	26.00	24.00
14	A1	1fr brnz grn, *straw*	24.00	17.50
15	A1	2fr vio, *rose*	35.00	35.00
16	A1	5fr lil, *lavender*	130.00	130.00
	Nos. 1-16 (16)		404.25	337.10

Perf. 13½x14 stamps are counterfeits.
No. 12, affixed to pressboard with animals printed on the back, was used as emergency currency in the Comoro Islands in 1920.

Issue of 1906-07 Surcharged in Carmine or Black

1912

17	A1	5c on 4c cl, *lav* (C)	2.40	3.25
18	A1	5c on 20c red, *grn*	4.00	4.75
19	A1	5c on 30c brn, *bis* (C)	2.75	3.50
20	A1	10c on 40c red, *straw*	2.75	3.50
21	A1	10c on 45c blk, *gray grn* (C)	2.00	2.00
a.	"Moheli" double		475.00	
b.	"Moheli" triple		475.00	
22	A1	10c on 50c brn, *az* (C)	3.50	4.50
	Nos. 17-22 (6)		17.40	21.50

Two spacings between the surcharged numerals are found on Nos. 17 to 22. For detailed listings, see the *Scott Classic Specialized Catalogue of Stamps and Covers.*

The stamps of Mohéli were supposed to have been superseded by those of Madagascar, January, 1908. However, Nos. 17-22 were surcharged in 1912 to use up remainders. These were available for use in Madagascar and the entire Comoro archipelago. In 1950 stamps of Comoro Islands came into use.

MOLDOVA
mäl-'dō-və

(Moldavia)

LOCATION — Southeastern Europe, bounded by Romania and the Ukraine

GOVT. — Independent republic, member of the Commonwealth of Independent States

AREA — 13,012 sq. mi.

POP. — 4,460,838 (1999 est.)

CAPITAL — Chisinau

With the breakup of the Soviet Union on Dec. 26, 1991, Moldova and ten former Soviet republics established the Commonwealth of Independent States.

100 Kopecks = 1 Ruble
100 Bani = 1 Leu (1993)

Catalogue values for all unused stamps in this country are for Never Hinged items.

Coat of Arms — A1

Flag — A2

1991, June 23   Litho.   Imperf.
Without Gum
1	A1	7k grn & multi	.25	.25
2	A1	13k blue & multi	.25	.40
3	A2	30k multi	.40	.40
		Nos. 1-3 (3)	.90	1.05

Codrii Nature Preserve A6

1992, Feb. 8   Litho.   Perf. 12
25	A6	25k multicolored	.40	.40

For surcharge see No. 547.

Natl. Arms — A7

1992, May 24   Photo.   Perf. 13½
26	A7	35k green	.25	.25
27	A7	50k red	.25	.25
28	A7	65k brown	.25	.25
29	A7	1r purple	.25	.25
30	A7	1.50r blue	.25	.25
		Nos. 26-30 (5)	1.25	1.25

Birds — A8

Designs: 50k, Merops apiaster. 65k, Oriolus oriolus. 2.50r, Picus viridis. 6r, Coracias garrulus. 7.50r, Upupa epops. 15r, Cuculus canorus.

1992, Aug. 5   Litho.   Perf. 13½x14
31	A8	50k multicolored	.40	.40
32	A8	65k multicolored	.40	.40
33	A8	2.50r multicolored	.60	.60
34	A8	6r multicolored	1.00	1.00
35	A8	7.50r multicolored	1.30	1.30
36	A8	15r multicolored	2.75	2.75
		Nos. 31-36 (6)	6.45	6.45

No. 31 incorrectly inscribed "ariaster." See Nos. 75-81.

Church of St. Panteleimon, Cent. — A9

1992, Aug. 10   Photo.   Perf. 11½
37	A9	1.50r multicolored	.40	.40

She-Wolf Suckling Romulus and Remus — A10

1992, Aug. 10   Perf. 12x11½
38	A10	5r multicolored	1.00	1.00

Russia Nos. 4598-4599, 5839 Surcharged "MOLDOVA" and New Value in Black or Red
1992, Aug. 31   Litho.   Perf. 12x12½
39	A2138	2.50r on 4k #4599	.40	.40
40	A2139	6r on 3k #4598	.45	.45
41	A2138	8.50r on 4k #4599	.60	.60
42	A2765	10r on 3k #5839 (R)	.70	.70
a.		Black surcharge	.70	.70
b.		Brown red surcharge	.70	.70
		Nos. 39-42 (4)	2.15	2.15

Sheets of Nos. 39, 41 had row 5 inverted. On No. 40 only the 1st 5 stamps of row 5 were inverted. Counterfeit inverts were made using the original plates but with all 100 surcharges inverted. All inverts on No. 42 are fakes.

Russia Nos. 4596-4598 Surcharged in Black, Green or Red

1992, Oct. 20   Litho.   Perf. 12x12½
43	A2138	45k on 2k #4597 (G)	.40	.40
44	A2138	46k on 2k #4597	.40	.40
45	A2138	63k on 1k #4596 (R)	.40	.40
46	A2138	63k on 3k #4598	.70	.70
47	A2138	70k on 1k #4596 (R)	.40	.40
50	A2138	4r on 1k #4596	.70	.70
a.		Red surcharge	.70	.70
		Nos. 43-50 (6)	3.00	3.00

Nos. 45-46 exist with overprint inverted (6th row of sheet).

1992 Summer Olympics, Barcelona — A11

1992, Oct. 24   Litho.   Perf. 13
53	A11	35k High jump	.30	.30
54	A11	65k Wrestling	.35	.35
55	A11	1r Archery	.35	.35
56	A11	2.50r Swimming	.75	.75
57	A11	10r Equestrian	2.50	2.50
a.		Souvenir sheet, #53-57 + label	4.75	4.75
		Nos. 53-57 (5)	4.25	4.25

Nos. 55-56 Ovptd. with Name of Medalist, Medal and Olympic Rings in Bronze or Silver
1992, Oct. 24
58	A11	1r "NATALIA VALEEV / bronz" (BR)	.55	.55
59	A11	2.50r "IURIE BAS-CATOV / argint"	1.00	1.00

Souvenir Sheet

Tudor Casapu, 1992 Weight Lifting Gold Medalist — A12

1992, Oct. 24   Perf. 14½
60	A12	25r multicolored	5.25	5.25

Admission of Moldova to UN — A13

Designs: 12r, UN Headquarters at left, Statue of Liberty, UN emblem, Moldovan flag.

1992, Oct. 24   Perf. 13
61	A13	1.30r multicolored	1.00	1.00
62	A13	12r multicolored	2.00	2.00

Moldovan Participation in Conference on European Security and Cooperation — A14

1992, Oct. 24
63	A14	2.50r Flag, Prague Castle	1.50	1.50
64	A14	25r Helsinki Cathedral, flag	4.00	4.00

Traditional Folk Art — A15

1992, Nov. 21   Perf. 12x11½
65	A15	7.50r Rug, pottery	1.50	1.50

Admission of Moldova to UPU A16

1992, Dec. 26   Perf. 12
66	A16	5r Train, flag, emblem	.30	.30
67	A16	10r Plane, flag, emblem	.60	.60

Discovery of America, 500th Anniv. — A17

1992, Dec. 26   Litho.   Perf. 12
68	A17	1r Galleon	.25	.25
69	A17	6r Carrack	.50	.50
70	A17	6r Caravel	.50	.50
a.		Pair, #69-70	3.25	3.25
		Nos. 68-70 (3)	1.25	1.25

Souvenir Sheet
71	A17	25r Columbus	2.50	2.50

Elaphe Longissima A18

Denominations at: a, UL. b, UR. c, LL. d, LR.

1993, July 3   Litho.   Perf. 13½
72	A18	3r Block of 4, #a.-d.	1.50	1.50
73	A18	15r Natrix natrix	.60	.60
74	A18	25r Vipera berus	.85	.85
		Nos. 72-74 (3)	2.95	2.95

Bird Type of 1992
1993, July 24   Litho.   Perf. 13x13½
75	A8	2r like #31	.30	.30
76	A8	3r like #32	.30	.30
77	A8	5r like #33	.30	.30
78	A8	10r like #34	.30	.30
79	A8	15r like #35	.35	.35
80	A8	50r like #36	.60	.60
81	A8	100r Hirundo rustica	1.25	1.25
		Nos. 75-81 (7)	3.40	3.40

Natl. Arms — A19

1993, Aug. 7   Photo.   Perf. 12x12½
82	A19	2k blue	.25	.25
83	A19	3k purple	.25	.25
84	A19	6k green	.25	.25
85	A19	10k olive & purple	.25	.25
86	A19	15k olive & purple	.25	.25
87	A19	20k gray & purple	.25	.25
88	A19	30k yellow & purple	.25	.25
89	A19	50k pink & purple	.25	.25

Size: 21x32½mm
Perf. 12½x12
90	A19	100k multicolored	.35	.35
91	A19	250k multicolored	.85	.85
		Nos. 82-91 (10)	3.20	3.20

For surcharges see Nos. 558-559.

Butterflies — A20

1993, Dec. 22   Litho.   Perf. 13
94	A20	6b Pyrameis atalanta	.25	.25
95	A20	10b Papilio machaon	.25	.25
96	A20	50b Vanessa jo	.40	.40
97	A20	250b Saturnia pavonia	1.75	1.75
		Nos. 94-97 (4)	2.65	2.65

Flowers — A21

Designs: 6b, Tulipa bibersteiniana. 15b, Convallaria majalis. 25b, Galanthus nivalis. 30b, Paeonia peregrina. 50b, Galanthus plicatus. 90b, Pulsatilla grandis. 250b, Cypripedium calceolus.

1993, Dec. 25   Litho.   Perf. 13½
98	A21	6b multicolored	.25	.25
99	A21	15b multicolored	.25	.25
100	A21	25b multicolored	.30	.30
101	A21	30b multicolored	.35	.35
102	A21	50b multicolored	.40	.40
103	A21	90b multicolored	.65	.65
		Nos. 98-103 (6)	2.20	2.20

Souvenir Sheet
104	A21	250b multicolored	1.80	1.80

No. 104 contains one 30x45mm stamp.

A22

Famous Men: 6b, Dragos Voda. 25b, Bogdan Voda I. 50b, Latcu Voda. 100b, Petru I Musat. 150b, Roman Voda Musat. 200b, Stefan I.

1993, Dec. 29   Litho.   Perf. 13
105	A22	6b multicolored	.25	.25
106	A22	25b multicolored	.25	.25
107	A22	50b multicolored	.25	.25
108	A22	100b multicolored	.30	.30
109	A22	150b multicolored	.45	.45
110	A22	200b multicolored	.75	.75
		Nos. 105-110 (6)	2.25	2.25

Europa (Contemporary art): 3b, History of Man, by M. Grecu. 150b, Springtime, by I. Vieru.

1993, Dec. 29   Litho.   Perf. 13
111	A23	3b multicolored	.50	.50
112	A23	150b multicolored	4.00	4.00
a.		Souvenir sheet, 4 each #111-112 + label	20.00	20.00

1994 Winter Olympics, Lillehammer A24

1994, Feb. 12   Litho.   Perf. 13½
113	A24	3b Biathlete, skiiers	.25	.25
114	A24	150b Biathlete, diff.	1.00	1.00

Russia No. 4596 Surcharged in Dark Blue

1994, Apr. 11   Litho.   Perf. 12x12½
114A	A2138	3b on 1k olive grn	.25	.25
114B	A2138	25b on 1k olive grn	.25	.25
114C	A2138	50b on 1k olive grn	.35	.35
		Nos. 114A-114C (3)	.85	.85

First Manned Moon Landing, 25th anniv. — A25

1994, June 18   Litho.   Perf. 14
Europa: 1b, Gemini space mission, Titan II rocket. 45b, Ed White, Gemini IV. 2.50 l, Lunar landing module.
115	A25	1b multicolored	.50	.50
116	A25	45b multicolored	2.40	2.40
117	A25	2.50 l multicolored	5.25	5.25
		Nos. 115-117 (3)	8.15	8.15

Natl. Arms — A26

1994   Perf. 13½x14
118	A26	1b multicolored	.25	.25
119	A26	10b multicolored	.25	.25
120	A26	30b multicolored	.25	.25
121	A26	38b multicolored	.25	.25
122	A26	45b multicolored	.55	.55
123	A26	75b multicolored	.65	.65
125	A26	1.50 l multicolored	1.20	1.20
126	A26	1.80 l multicolored	1.20	1.20
127	A26	2.50 l multi, size:		
		23½x29mm	1.90	1.90
128	A26	4.50 l multicolored	3.75	3.75
128A	A26	4.50 l multicolored	4.00	4.00
128B	A26	6.90 l multicolored	5.00	5.00

Size: 23½x29mm
128C	A26	7.20 l multicolored	5.00	5.00
129	A26	13 l multicolored	9.25	9.25
130	A26	24 l multicolored	17.50	17.50
		Nos. 118-130 (15)	51.00	51.00

Issued: 1b, 45b, 1.50 l, 4.50 l, 6/11/94; 10b, 20b, 5.40 l, 6.90 l, 13 l, 7/16/94; 38b, 75b, 1.80 l, 2.50 l, 7.20 l, 8/13/94.
This is a expanding set. Numbers may change.

Stamp Card — A27

Designs: 1.50 l, 4.50 l, Map of Moldova.

Rouletted 26 on 2 or 3 Sides
1994, Dec. 22   Litho.
Self-Adhesive
Cards of 6 + 6 labels
131	A27	1.50 l #a.-f., lt vio & multi	6.25
132	A27	4.50 l #a.-f., dp red vio & multi	16.00

Individual stamps measure 70x9mm and have a card backing. Se-tenant labels inscribed "AIR MAIL."

Famous People A28

Designs: 3b, Maria Cibotari (1910-49), singer. 90b, Dumitru Caraciobanu (1937-80), actor. 150b, Eugeniu Coca (1893-1954), composer. 250b, Igor Vieru (1923-83), painter.

1994, June 30   Litho.   Perf. 13½
133	A28	3b multicolored	.25	.25
134	A28	90b multicolored	.30	.30
135	A28	150b multicolored	.40	.40
136	A28	250b multicolored	.70	.70
		Nos. 133-136 (4)	1.65	1.65

Stamp Day A29

Designs: 10b, Designing stamp. 45b, Printing stamps. 2 l, Inspecting finished sheets.

1994, July 22   Litho.   Perf. 14
137	A29	10b multicolored	.30	.30
138	A29	45b multicolored	.75	.75
139	A29	2 l multicolored	2.25	2.25
		Nos. 137-139 (3)	3.30	3.30

Intl. Olympic Committee, Cent. — A30

1994, Aug. 29   Litho.   Perf. 13½x14
140	A30	60b Pierre de Coubertin	.45	.45
141	A30	1.50 l Olympic rings, symbol	1.10	1.10

Moldova's Entrance into NATO — A31

Designs: 60b, Moldova Pres. Mircea Snegur, NATO Secretary General Manfred Worner signing documents. 2.50 l, World map centered on Europe.

1994, Nov. 8   Litho.   Perf. 13½
142	A31	60b multicolored	.85	.85
143	A31	2.50 l multicolored	3.25	3.25

Intl. Year of the Family — A32

1994, Nov. 26   Perf. 14
144	A32	30b Family	.50	.50
145	A32	60b Mother breast-feeding	1.00	1.00
146	A32	1.50 l Child painting	2.00	2.00
		Nos. 144-146 (3)	3.50	3.50

1996 European Soccer Championships, England — A33

Designs: 10b, Handshaking. 40b, Players legs, soccer ball. 1.20 l, Goalie.
No. 150: a, 1.10 l, Soccer federation, German flags. b, 2.20 l, Soccer ball, German, Moldovan flags. c, 2.40 l, Players.

1994, Dec. 10
147	A33	10b multicolored	.25	.25
148	A33	40b multicolored	.45	.45
149	A33	2.40 l multicolored	2.00	2.00
		Nos. 147-149 (3)	2.70	2.70

Souvenir Sheet
150	A33	Sheet of 3, #a.-c.	3.75	3.75

Christmas A34

Paintings of Birth of Christ by: 20b, unknown artist, 18th cent. 3.60 l, Gherasim, 1808.

1994, Dec. 29
151	A34	20b multicolored	.40	.40
152	A34	3.60 l multicolored	3.75	3.75

Mushrooms — A35

1995, Feb. 8
153	A35	4b Russula virescens	.45	.45
154	A35	10b Boletus luridus	.70	.70
155	A35	20b Cantherellus cibarius	1.45	1.45
156	A35	90b Leccinum aurantiacum	4.25	4.25
157	A35	1.80 l Leccinum duriusculum	8.00	8.00
		Nos. 153-157 (5)	14.85	14.85

European Nature Conservation Year — A36

Designs: 4b, Hieraaetus pennatus. 45b, Capreolus capreolus. 90b, Sus scrofa.

1995, Mar. 18   Litho.   Perf. 14
158	A36	4b multicolored	.85	.85
159	A36	45b multicolored	4.00	4.00
160	A36	90b multicolored	8.25	8.25
		Nos. 158-160 (3)	13.10	13.10

Museum of Natural Sciences — A37

Designs: 4b, Jars. 10b+2b, Dinotherium gigantissimum. 1.80 l+30b, Silver coin, 3rd-2nd cent. BC.

1995   **Litho.**   **Perf. 14**
161 A37   4b multicolored   .45   .45
162 A37   10b +2b multi   .90   .90
163 A37   1.80 l +30b multi   6.25   6.25
    Nos. 161-163 (3)   7.60   7.60

Peace & Freedom — A38

Paintings: 10b, May 1945, by Igor Vieru. 40b, Linistea, by Sergiu Cuciuc. 2.20 l, Primavara 1944, by Cuciuc.

1995, May 9   **Litho.**   **Perf. 14**
164 A38   10b multicolored   .40   .40
165 A38   40b multicolored   2.50   2.50
166 A38   2.20 l multicolored   4.75   4.75
    Nos. 164-166 (3)   7.65   7.65

Europa.

A39

Famous People: 90b, Constantin Stere (1865-1936), writer. 10b, Tamara Ceban (1914-90), musician. 40b, Alexandru Plamadeala (1888-1940), sculptor. 1.80 l, Lucian Blaga (1895-1961), writer.

1995, June 17   **Litho.**   **Perf. 14**
167 A39   9b dp cl & gray   .35   .35
168 A39   10b brt mag & gray   .35   .35
169 A39   40b violet & gray   1.40   1.40
170 A39   1.80 l dk grn & gray   6.75   6.75
    Nos. 167-170 (4)   8.85   8.85

A40

Kings of Moldova, reign: No. 171, Alexandru Cel Bun, 1400-32. No. 172, Petru Aron, 1451-52, 1454-57. No. 173, Stefan Cel Mare, 1457-1504. 45 l, Petru Rares, 1527-38, 1541-46. 90 l, Alexandru Lapusneanu, 1552-61, 1564-68. 1.80 l, Ion Voda Cel Cumplit, 1572-74. 5 l, Stefan Cel Mare, 1457-1504.

1995, July 2   **Litho.**   **Perf. 14**
171 A40   10 b multicolored   .40   .40
172 A40   10 b multicolored   .40   .40
173 A40   10 b multicolored   .40   .40
174 A40   45 b multicolored   1.75   1.75
175 A40   90 b multicolored   3.00   3.00
176 A40   1.80 l multicolored   7.00   7.00
    Nos. 171-176 (6)   12.95   12.95

Souvenir Sheet

177 A40   5 l multicolored   3.50   3.50

No. 177 contains one 24x29mm stamp.

Citadels of Moldova A41

1995, July 29
178 A41   10 b Soroca   .30   .30
179 A41   20 b Tighina   .60   .60
180 A41   60 b Alba   1.25   1.25
181 A41   1.30 l Hotin   3.50   3.50
    Nos. 178-181 (4)   5.65   5.65

A42

UN, 50th Anniv. — A43

Designs inside of stylized eye: No. 182, Forest stream. No. 183, Fighter plane. No. 184, Black child, barbed wire fence.
Nos. 185-186: a, 1. b, 2. c, 3. d, 4. e, 5. f, 6. g, 7. h, 8. i, 9. j, 10.

1995, Oct. 24   **Litho.**   **Perf. 14**
182 A42   10b yellow & multi   .40   .40
183 A42   10b blue & multi   .40   .40
184 A42   1.50 l green & multi   5.25   5.25
    Nos. 182-184 (3)   6.05   6.05

Stamp Cards
Rouletted 15 on 2 or 3 Sides
Self-Adhesive
Cards of 10

185 A43   90b #a.-j.   15.00   15.00
186 A43   1.50 l #a.-j.   25.00   25.00

Background color of stamps gradually shifts from light blue (#1) to dark blue (#10). Each stamp is individually numbered.

Motion Pictures, Cent. — A44

Films: 10b, Last Moon of Autumn. 40b, Lautarii. 2.40 l, Dimitrie Cantemir.

1995, Dec. 28   **Litho.**   **Perf. 14**
187 A44   10b red brn & blk   .65   .65
188 A44   40b olive & black   2.00   2.00
189 A44   2.40 l ultra & black   6.50   6.50
    Nos. 187-189 (3)   9.15   9.15

Mushrooms — A45

No. 190, Amanita muscaria. No. 191, Boletus satanas. 65b, Amanita phalloides. 1.30 l, Hypholoma fasciculare. 2.40 l, Amanita virosa.

1996, Mar. 23   **Litho.**   **Perf. 14**
190 A45   10b multicolored   .95   .95
191 A45   10b multicolored   .95   .95
192 A45   65b multicolored   1.45   1.45
193 A45   1.30 l multicolored   2.25   2.25
194 A45   2.40 l multicolored   6.25   6.25
    Nos. 190-194 (5)   11.85   11.85

1996 Summer Olympic Games, Atlanta — A46

1996, Mar. 30
195 A46   10b Weight lifting   .45   .45
196 A46   20b +5b Judo   .45   .45
197 A46   45b +10b Running   .85   .85
198 A46   2.40 l +30b Canoeing   4.75   4.75
    Nos. 195-198 (4)   6.50   6.50

Souvenir Sheet

199 A46   2.20 l Archery   3.00   3.00
a.   With added inscription in sheet margin   3.75   3.75

No. 199 contains one 34x29mm stamp.
No. 199a inscribed "Nicolae JURAVSCHI Victor RENEISCHI / -canoe, argint- / Serghei MUREICO/ -lupte greco-romane,bronz-".

Monasteries A47

1996, Apr. 26
200 A47   10b Rudi, 18th cent.   .45   .45
201 A47   90b Japca, 17th cent.   .80   .80
202 A47   1.30 l Curchi, 18th cent.   1.40   1.40
203 A47   2.80 l Saharna, 18th cent.   3.00   3.00
204 A47   4.40 l Capriana, 16th cent.   4.75   4.75
    Nos. 200-204 (5)   10.40   10.40

Birds — A48

Designs: 9b, Gallinula chloropus. 10b, Anser anser. No. 207, Streptopelia turtur. 4.40 l, Anas platyrhynchos.
No. 209, Phasianus colchicus.

1996, May 17
205 A48   9b multicolored   .35   .35
206 A48   10b multicolored   .35   .35
207 A48   2.20 l multicolored   2.50   2.50
208 A48   4.40 l multicolored   4.25   4.25
    Nos. 205-208 (4)   7.45   7.45

Souvenir Sheet

209 A48   2.20 l multicolored   2.50   2.50

Europa

A49

Famous Women: 10b, Elena Alistar (1873-1955), president of women's league. 3.70 l, Marie Curie (1867-1934), chemist, physicist. 2.20 l, Julia Hasdeu (1869-1888), writer.

1996, June 21   **Litho.**   **Perf. 14**
210 A49   10b multicolored   .60   .60
211 A49   3.70 l multicolored   5.75   5.75

Souvenir Sheet

212 A49   2.20 l multicolored   4.75   4.75

A50

Famous Men: #213, Gavriil Banulescu-Bodoni (1746-1821). #214, Mihail Eminescu (1850-69), poet. 2.20 l, Ion Creanga (1837-89). 3.30 l, Vasile Alecsandri (1821-90). 5.40 l, Petru Movila (1596-1646), theologian.
1.80 l, Eminescu, diff., vert.

1996, July 30   **Litho.**   **Perf. 14**
213 A50   10b gray vio & brn   .35   .35
214 A50   10b lt brn & dk brn   .35   .35
215 A50   2.20 l gray & brn   2.25   2.25
216 A50   3.30 l ol & brn   3.00   3.00
217 A50   5.40 l red brn & brn   5.00   5.00
    Nos. 213-217 (5)   10.95   10.95

Souvenir Sheet

218 A50   1.80 l brn   2.00   2.00

City of Chisinau, 560th Anniv. — A51

Building, year erected: 10b, City Hall, 1902. 1.30 l, Palace of Culture, 1911. 2.40 l, Mazarache Church, 1752.

1996, Oct. 6   **Litho.**   **Perf. 14**
219 A51   10b multicolored   .75   .75
220 A51   1.30 l multicolored   2.50   2.50
221 A51   2.40 l multicolored   5.75   5.75
    Nos. 219-221 (3)   9.00   9.00

A52

Christmas: 10b, Children carrying star. 2.20 l+30b, Mother and child in center of star. 2.80 l+50b, Children decorating Christmas tree.

1996, Dec. 12   **Litho.**   **Perf. 14**
222 A52   10b multicolored   .45   .45
223 A52   2.20 l +30b multicolored   3.25   3.25
224 A52   2.80 l +50b multicolored   4.00   4.00
    Nos. 222-224 (3)   7.70   7.70

A53

Wines of Moldova.

1997, Jan. 17   Litho.   Perf. 14
225 A53 10b Feteasca   .45 .45
226 A53 45b Cabernet-
              Sauvignon   .55 .55
227 A53 65b Sauvignon   .90 .90
228 A53 3.70 l Rara neagra   4.75 4.75
    Nos. 225-228 (4)   6.65 6.65

Easter — A54

Designs: 3.30b, Colored eggs, grass on plate. 5 l, Basket of eggs, food.

1997, Apr. 25   Litho.   Perf. 13½
229 A54 10b multicolored   .45 .45
230 A54 3.30 l multicolored 3.25 3.25
    Souvenir Sheet
231 A54 5 l multicolored   5.50 5.50

Composers — A55

Designs: No. 232, Franz Schubert (1797-1828). No. 233, Gavriil Musicescu (1847-1903). 45b, Sergei Rachmaninoff (1873-1943). 4.40 l, Georges Enescu (1881-1955).

1997, Feb. 22   Litho.   Perf. 14
232 A55 10b slate & bl grn   .35 .35
233 A55 10b slate & bl grn   .35 .35
234 A55 45b slate & bl grn   .60 .60
235 A55 4.40 l slate & bl grn 5.00 5.00
    Nos. 232-235 (4)   6.30 6.30

Stories and Legends A56

Europa: 10b, Man holding up arms, goose flying, arrows from fortress. 2.80 l, Man upside down, church, sun in sky with stars and eye. 5 l, Angel touching flowers during winter.

1997, June 20   Litho.   Perf. 13½
236 A56 10b multicolored   1.00 1.00
237 A56 2.80 l multicolored 6.50 6.50
    Souvenir Sheet
238 A56 5 l multicolored   8.50 8.50

Red Book Insects — A57

Insects on plants, flowers: 25b, Mantis religiosa. 80b, Ascalphus macaronius scop. 1 l, Calosoma sycophanta. 2.20 l, Liometopum microcephalum.
5 l, Scolia maculata drury.

1997, July 26   Litho.   Perf. 14
239 A57 25b multicolored   .35 .35
240 A57 80b multicolored   .95 .95
241 A57 1 l multicolored   1.10 1.10
242 A57 2.20 l multicolored 2.50 2.50
    Nos. 239-242 (4)   4.90 4.90
    Souvenir Sheet
243 A57 5 l multicolored   5.75 5.75

World Post Day — A58

Designs: 10b, Chisinau post office building, 1997. 2.20 l, Mail coach, Chisinaupost office building. 3.30 l, Heinrich von Stephan (1831-97), vert.

1997, Oct. 18   Litho.   Perf. 14
244 A58 10b multicolored   .55 .55
245 A58 2.20 l multicolored 2.50 2.50
246 A58 3.30 l multicolored 5.50 5.50
    Nos. 244-246 (3)   8.55 8.55

Christmas A59

Designs: 10b, Noul Neamt Monastery. 45b, "Adoration of the Shepherds," Noul Neamt Monastery. 5 l, "Nativity," Natl. Museum of Plastic Arts.

1997, Dec. 17   Litho.   Perf. 13½
247 A59 10b multicolored   .25 .25
248 A59 45b multicolored   .30 .30
249 A59 5 l multicolored   3.00 3.00
    Nos. 247-249 (3)   3.55 3.55

A60

Cultural Heritage Sites: 7b, Nicolai Zelinski High School, Tiraspol. No. 251, Railway station, Tighina. No. 252, Cathedral, Balti. 90b, Church, Causeni. 1.30 l, Cathedral, Kagul. 3.30 l, Art Institute, Chisinau.

1997, Dec. 16   Litho.   Perf. 14
250 A60 7b black & lilac   .45 .45
251 A60 10b black & red violet .45 .45
252 A60 10b black & grn blue .45 .45
253 A60 90b black & yel org 1.00 1.00
254 A60 1.30 l black & blue 1.50 1.50
255 A60 3.30 l black & gray 3.50 3.50
    Nos. 250-255 (6)   7.35 7.35

A61

Princes of Moldova, reign: No. 256, Petru Schiopul (1574-77, 78-79, 82-91). No. 257, Ieremia Movila (1595-1606). 45b, Stefan Tomsa (1611-15, 1621-23). 1.80 l, Radu Mihnea (1616-19, 1623-26). 2.20 l, Miron Barnovschi Movila (1626-29, 1633). 2.80 l, Bogdan Orbul (1504-17).
5 l, Mihai Viteazul, 1600.

1997, Dec. 17
256 A61 10b multicolored   .30 .30
257 A61 10b multicolored   .30 .30
258 A61 45b multicolored   .50 .50
259 A61 1.80 l multicolored 2.00 2.00
260 A61 2.20 l multicolored 2.25 2.25
261 A61 2.80 l multicolored 3.00 3.00
    Nos. 256-261 (6)   8.35 8.35
    Souvenir Sheet
262 A61 5 l multicolored   5.50 5.50
    No. 262 contains one 23x29mm stamp.

1998 Winter Olympic Games, Nagano A62

1998, Feb. 28
263 A62 10b Slalom skiing   .45 .45
264 A62 45b Figure skating   .90 .90
265 A62 2.20 l Biathlon   3.75 3.75
    Nos. 263-265 (3)   5.10 5.10

A63

Famous People: 10b, Alexei Mateevici (1888-1917). 40b, Pantelimon Halippa (1883-1979). 60b, Stefan Ciobanu (1883-1950). 2 l, Constantin Stamati-Ciurea (1828-98).
5 l, Nicolae Milescu-Spatarul (1636-1708).

1998, May 9   Litho.   Perf. 14
266 A63 10b multicolored   .25 .25
267 A63 40b multicolored   .45 .45
268 A63 60b multicolored   .60 .60
269 A63 2 l multicolored   1.80 1.80
    Nos. 266-269 (4)   3.10 3.10
    Souvenir Sheet
270 A63 5 l multicolored   4.50 4.50

A64

Monuments and Works of Art: 10b, Monument to Stefan cel Mare, by Alexandru Plamadeala. 60b, The Resurrected Christ, by 19th cent. artist. 1 l, Steel column, by Constantin Brancusi. 2.60 l, Trajan's Column, by Apollodorus of Damascus, Rome.

1998, May 13   Perf. 14½x14
271 A64 10b multicolored   .25 .25
272 A64 60b multicolored   .65 .65
273 A64 1 l multicolored   .90 .90
274 A64 2.60 l multicolored 2.50 2.50
    Nos. 271-274 (4)   4.30 4.30

Natl. Holidays and Festivals A65

Europa: 10b, Eugène Ionesco biennial Theater Festival. 2.20 l, Lurceni ceramics, Nisporeni.
5 l, Music Festival, Martisor.

1998, July 18   Litho.   Perf. 14
275 A65 10b multicolored   .75 .75
276 A65 2.20 l multicolored 4.75 4.75
    Souvenir Sheet
277 A65 5 l multicolored   8.25 8.25

Fruit — A66

1998, Aug. 15
278 A66 7b Cerasus avium   .35 .35
279 A66 10b Prunus domestica .35 .35
280 A66 1 l Malus domestica .90 .90
281 A66 2 l Cydonia oblonga 1.80 1.80
    Nos. 278-281 (4)   3.40 3.40

Diana, Princess of Wales (1961-97) A67

Various portraits: a, 10b. b, 90b. c, 1.80 l. d, 2.20 l. e, 1.80 l.

1998, Aug. 31   Litho.   Perf. 14
282 A67 Sheet of 5, #a.-e. + label 6.00 6.00

First Stamps Used in Moldova, 140th Anniv. A68

Stamps on stamps: 10b, Romania #1-2, Type A2. 90b, Romania #2, #329, Type A177. 2.20 l, Romania #4, Russia #4132, #5916. 2.40 l, Moldova #122, #214, Romania #3.

Photo. & Engr.
1998, Oct. 9   Perf. 14
283 A68 10b multicolored   .25 .25
284 A68 90b multicolored   .45 .45
285 A68 2.20 l multicolored 1.80 1.80
286 A68 2.40 l multicolored 2.25 2.25
    Nos. 283-286 (4)   4.75 4.75

Medieval Fortresses — A69

1998, Sept. 26   Litho.   Perf. 14
287 A69 10b Chilia   .40 .40
288 A69 60b Orhei   .70 .70
289 A69 1 l Suceava   1.10 1.10
290 A69 2 l Ismail   2.40 2.40
    Nos. 287-290 (4)   4.60 4.60

Birds A70

25b, Bubo bubo, vert. 2 l, Anthropoides virgo.

1998, Oct. 31
291 A70 25b multicolored   .55 .55
292 A70 2 l multicolored   3.50 3.50

Regional Costumes A71

1998, Nov. 28   Litho.   Perf. 14
293	A71	25b	Vara	.35	.35
294	A71	90b	Vara, diff.	.80	.80
295	A71	1.80 l	Iarna	1.60	1.60
296	A71	2 l	Iarna, diff.	1.75	1.75
		Nos. 293-296 (4)		4.50	4.50

Annexation of Bessarabia to Romania, 80th Anniv. — A72

1998, Dec. 10
297   A72   90b multicolored   .75   .75

Universal Declaration of Human Rights, 50th Anniv. — A73

1998, Dec. 10
298   A73   2.40 l multicolored   2.75   2.75

UPU, 125th Anniv. A74

1999, Apr. 9   Litho.   Perf. 14
299   A74   25b multicolored   .65   .65

Council of Europe, 50th Anniv. A75

1999, Apr. 9
300   A75   2.20 l multicolored   3.50   3.50

Nature Reserves — A76

Europa: 25b, Prutul de Jos. 2.40 l, Padurea Domneasca. 5 l, Codru.

1999, May 5   Litho.   Perf. 14
301   A76   25b multicolored   .60   .60
302   A76   2.40 l multicolored   3.25   3.25

Souvenir Sheet
303   A76   5 l multicolored   7.00   7.00

Honoré de Balzac (1799-1850), Writer — A77

1999, May 20
304   A77   90b multicolored   1.00   1.00

Aleksandr Pushkin (1788-1837), Poet — A78

1999, June 6
305   A78   65b brown & black   .80   .80

National Sports — A79

1999, June 26   Litho.   Perf. 13¾
306   A79   25b Wrestling   .55   .55
307   A79   1.80 l Oina   2.75   2.75

First Manned Moon Landing, 30th Anniv. A80

1999, July 20   Litho.   Perf. 14
308   A80   25b Michael Collins   .30   .30
309   A80   25b Neil Armstrong   .30   .30
310   A80   5 l Edwin Aldrin   4.75   4.75
      Nos. 308-310 (3)   5.35   5.35

Medals — A81

1999, July 31   Litho.   Perf. 14
311   A81   25b Meritul Militar   .30   .30
312   A81   25b Pentru Vitejie   .30   .30
313   A81   25b Meritul Civic   .30   .30
314   A81   90b Mihai Eminescu   .30   .30
315   A81   1.10 l Gloria Muncii   .90   .90
316   A81   2.40 l Stefan cel Mare 2.25   2.25
      Nos. 311-316 (6)   4.35   4.35

Souvenir Sheet
317   A81   5 l Ordinul Republicii 4.50   4.50

Crafts — A82

1999, Aug. 7
318   A82   5b Wood carving   .25   .25
319   A82   25b Embroidery   .30   .30
320   A82   95b Pottery   .55   .55
321   A82   1.80 l Wicker furniture 1.60   1.60
      Nos. 318-321 (4)   2.70   2.70

Johann Wolfgang von Goethe (1749-1832), German Poet — A83

1999, Aug. 20
322   A83   1.10 l multicolored   1.40   1.40

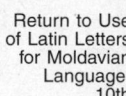

Return to Use of Latin Letters for Moldavian Language, 10th Anniv. — A84

1999, Aug. 31   Perf. 13¾
323   A84   25b multicolored   .30   .30

A85

Metropolitans: 25b, Varlaam (1590-1657). 2.40 l, Gurie Grosu (1877-1943).

1999, Sept. 12   Litho.   Perf. 14
324   A85   25b multicolored   .25   .25
325   A85   2.40 l multicolored   2.50   2.50

A86

Moldavian Rulers, dates ruled: No. 326, Bogdan II (1449-51). No. 327, Bogdan IV (1568-72). No. 328, Constantin Cantemir (1685-93). 1.50 l, Simion Movila (1606-07). 3 l, Duke Gheorghe III (1665-66, 1668-72, 1678-84). 3.90 l, Ilias Alexandru (1666-68). 5 l, Vasile Lupu (1634-53).

1999, Oct. 16   Litho.   Perf. 14¼x14
326   A86   25b multi   .25   .25
327   A86   25b multi   .25   .25
328   A86   25b multi   .25   .25
329   A86   1.50 l multi   .80   .80
330   A86   3 l multi   1.60   1.60
331   A86   3.90 l multi   2.60   2.60
      Nos. 326-331 (6)   5.75   5.75

Souvenir Sheet
Perf. 13¾x14
332   A86   5 l multi   3.75   3.75

No. 332 contains one 24x30mm stamp. Compare with Type A110.

Fauna A87

Designs: 25b, Lutra lutra. 1.80 l, Huso huso. 3.60 l, Rhinolophus ferrumequinum.

1999, Nov. 20   Perf. 14x14¼
333   A87   25b multi   .40   .40
334   A87   1.80 l multi   2.00   2.00
335   A87   3.60 l multi   3.75   3.75
      Nos. 333-335 (3)   6.15   6.15

1999 Women's Chess Championships, Chisinau — A88

1999, Nov. 27   Perf. 13¾
336   A88   25b Woman   .25   .25
337   A88   2.20 l Building   2.50   2.50

A89

Items From National History Museum: 25b, Helmet, candleholder. 1.80 l. Ceramic jug. 3.60 l, Bible.

Perf. 14¼x13¾
1999, Dec. 11   Litho.
338   A89   25b multi   .25   .25
339   A89   1.80 l multi   1.00   1.00
340   A89   3.60 l multi   2.75   2.75
      Nos. 338-340 (3)   4.00   4.00

A90

a, 20b, Raluca Eminovici. b, 5 l, Mihail Eminescu (1850-89), Poet. c, 25b, Gheorghe Eminovici. d, 3 l, Veronica Micle. e, 1.50 l, Iosif Vulcan.

2000, Jan. 15   Litho.   Perf. 13¾x14
341   A90   Sheet of 5, #a.-e., + label   6.00   6.00

Fairy Tales A91

Designs: 25b, Ileana Cosinzeana. 1.50 l, Fat Frumos. 1.80 l, Harap Alb.

2000, Feb. 15   Litho.   Perf. 14
342   A91   25b multi   .25   .25
343   A91   1.50 l multi   1.50   1.50
344   A91   1.80 l multi   1.90   1.90
      Nos. 342-344 (3)   3.65   3.65

Famous People — A92

Designs: No. 345, Henri Coanda (1886-1972), physicist. No. 346, Toma Ciorba (1864-1936), doctor. 2 l, Guglielmo Marconi (1874-1937), physicist. 3.60 l, Norbert Wiener (1894-1964), mathematician.

2000, Feb. 26   Perf. 13¾x14
345   A92   25b multi   .25   .25
346   A92   25b multi   .25   .25
347   A92   2 l multi   1.50   1.50
348   A92   3.60 l multi   2.75   2.75
      Nos. 345-348 (4)   4.75   4.75

Events of the 20th Century A93

Designs: 25b, Moon landing, vert. 1.50 l, Nuclear fission, vert. 3 l, Global computerization, vert. 3.90 l, Reconciliation between Partiarch Teoctist and Pope John Paul II.

2000, Apr. 12   *Perf. 14*
349 A93   25b multi   .25   .25
350 A93   1.50 l multi   1.00 1.00
351 A93   3 l multi   2.00 2.00
352 A93   3.90 l multi   2.75 2.75
     Nos. 349-352 (4)   6.00 6.00

Easter — A94

Religious artwork from: 25b, 1841. 3 l, 19th cent.

2000, Apr. 30   *Perf. 14x13¾*
353 A94   25b multi   .25   .25
354 A94   3 l multi   2.50 2.50

Europa, 2000
Common Design Type
2000, May 9   **Litho.**   *Perf. 14¼x14*
355 CD17   3 l multi   3.50 3.50
     Booklet, 6 #355   19.00

Exhibitions A95

Designs: 25b, Faces, Expo 2000 emblem. 3.60 l+25b, WIPA 2000 Emblem, No. 118.

2000, May 30   **Litho.**   *Perf. 14x13¾*
356 A95   25b multi   .25   .25
357 A95   3.60 l +25b multi   1.50 1.50

Churches and Monasteries — A96

Designs: 25b, Monastery, Tipova, 16th-17th Cent. 1.50 l, Church, Heciul Vechi, 1791. 1.80 l, Church, Palanca, 18th-19th Cent. 3 l, Monastery, Butuceni, 15th-16th Cent.

2000, Aug. 12   **Litho.**   *Perf. 14*
358-361 A96   Set of 4   4.75 4.75

2000 Summer Olympics, Sydney — A97

Olympic flag and: 25b, Judo. 1.80 l, Wrestling. 5 l, Weight lifting.

2000, Sept. 15   **Litho.**   *Perf. 14x13¾*
362-364 A97   Set of 3   5.00 5.00

Teacher's Day A98

25b, Child, teacher, class. 3.60 l, Teacher.

2000, Oct. 5   *Perf. 14x14¼*
365-366 A98   Set of 2   2.75 2.75

Christmas A99

Icons: 25b, Adoration of the Shepherds. 1.50 l, Nativity.

2000, Nov. 11   **Litho.**   *Perf. 13¾*
367-368 A99   Set of 2   1.25 1.25
Souvenir Sheet
Perf. 13¾x14
369 A99   5 l Madonna and Child   3.50 3.50
No. 369 contains one 27x33mm stamp.

UN High Commissioner for Refugees, 50th Anniv. — A99a

2001, Jan. 19   *Perf. 14*
369A A99a   3 l multi   1.25 1.25

Worldwide Fund for Nature (WWF) — A100

Crex crex: a, On rock. b, With mouth open. c, With eggs. d, With chicks.

2001, Mar. 31   **Litho.**   *Perf. 14x14¼*
370 A100   3 l Block of 4, #a-d   6.00 6.00

First Manned Spaceflight, 40th Anniv. — A101

2001, Apr. 12   *Perf. 14*
371 A101   1.80 l Yuri Gagarin   1.25 1.25
     See No. 377.

Famous Women A102

Designs: 25b, Maria Dragan (1947-86), singer. 1 l, Marlene Dietrich (1901-92), actress. 2 l, Ruxandra Lupu (1630?-87). 3 l, Lidia Lipkovski (1884-1958).

2001, Apr. 28   *Perf. 14x14¼*
372-375 A102   Set of 4   4.75 4.75

Europa — A103

2001, May 5   *Perf. 14*
376 A103   3 l multi   2.00 2.00
     Booklet, 6 #376   16.50

Space Anniversary Type of 2001
Design: Dumitru Prunariu, first Romanian cosmonaut.

2001, May 14
377 A101   1.80 l multi   1.25 1.25
     Prunariu's flight, 20th anniv.

Children's Art — A104

Art by: No. 378, 25b, Cristina Mereacre. No. 379, 25b, Ion Sestacovschi. No. 380, 25b, Aliona-Valeria Samburic. 1.80 l, Andrei Sestacovschi.

2001, June 1
378-381 A104   Set of 4   3.50 3.50
Souvenir Sheet

Moldovan Stamps, 10th Anniv. — A105

Pre-independence era stamps: a, 40b, 7c Arms stamp (27x32mm). b, 2 l, 13c Arms stamp (27x32mm). c, 3 l, 30c Flag stamp (42x25mm).

2001, June 23   *Perf. 13¾x14, 14 (3 l)*
382 A105   Sheet of 3, #a-c   3.00 3.00

Animals in Chisinau Zoo — A106

Designs: 40b, Panthera tigris tigris. 1 l Equus quagga. 1.50 l, Ursus arctos. 3 l+30b, Boselaphus tragocamelus. 5 l, Panthera leo.

2001, July 14   *Perf. 13¾*
383-386 A106   Set of 4   5.75 5.75
Souvenir Sheet
387 A106   5 l multi   4.50 4.50

Declaration of Independence, 10th Anniv. — A107

2001, Aug. 27   **Litho.**   *Perf. 14x13¾*
388 A107   1 l multi   1.25 1.25

Musical Instruments — A108

Designs: 40b, Cimpol. 1 l, Fluier. 1.80 l, Nai. 3 l, Taragot.

2001, Oct. 6   Set of 4   *Perf. 14x13¾*
389-392 A108   Set of 4   6.75 6.75

Year of Dialogue Among Civilizations — A109

Designs: 40b, Heads, spacecraft, horiz. 3.60b, Emblem.

2001, Oct. 9   *Perf. 14x14¼, 14¼x14*
393-394 A109   Set of 2   3.25 3.25

A110

Moldavian Rulers — A111

Ruler, dates ruled: No. 395, 40b, Mihai Racovita (1703-05, 1707-09, 1716-26). No. 396, 40b, Nicolae Mavrocordat (1709-10, 1711-15). No. 397, 40b, Constantin Mavrocordat (1733-35, 1741-43, 1748-49, 1769). No. 398, 40b, Grigore Callimachi (1761-64, 1767-69). 1 l, Grigore Alexandru Ghica (1764-67, 1774-77). 3 l, Antion Cantemir (1695-1700, 1705-07). 5 l, Dimitrie Cantemir (1710-11).

2001, Oct. 27   *Perf. 14¼x14*
395-400 A110   Set of 6   3.75 3.75
Souvenir Sheet
Perf. 14x14¼
401 A111 5 l multi   3.25 3.25
Compare with type A86.

Christmas — A112

Designs: 40b, Church, 1821. 1 l, Church, 1841. 3 l, Church, 1636. 3.90 l, Cathedral, 1836.

2001, Nov. 10   *Perf. 13¾x14*
402-405 A112   Set of 4   6.75 6.75

Commonwealth of Independent States, 10th Anniv. — A113

2001, Dec. 14   *Perf. 14¼x14*
406 A113 1.50 l multi   1.25 1.25

2002 Winter Olympics, Salt Lake City — A114

Designs: 40b, Cross-country skiing. 5 l, Biathlon.

2002, Feb. 8   Litho.   *Perf. 13¾x14*
407-408 A114   Set of 2   3.00 3.00

Dances A115

Designs: 40b, Hora. 1.50 l, Sirba.

2002, Mar. 16   *Perf. 14x14¼*
409-410 A115   Set of 2   4.00 4.00

Paintings A116

Designs: No. 411, 40b, Fetele din Ceadir-lunga, by Mihai Grecu. No. 412, 40b, Meleag Natal, by Eleonora Romanescu. 1.50 l, Fata la Fereastra, by Valentina Rusu-Ciobanu. 3 l, In Doi, by Igor Vieru.

2002, Apr. 20   Litho.   *Perf. 13¾*
411-414 A116   Set of 4   4.00 4.00

Europa — A117

2002, May 9   *Perf. 14*
415 A117 3 l multi   1.50 1.50
     Booklet, 6 #415   9.00 9.00

Souvenir Sheet

Botanical Gardens, Chisinau — A118

No. 416: a, 40b, Rose. b, 40b, Peony. c, 1.50 l, Aster. d, 3 l, Iris.

2002, June 14   *Perf. 13¾x14*
416 A118   Sheet of 4, #a-d   3.75 3.75

Souvenir Sheet

Leonardo da Vinci (1452-1519) — A119

No. 417: a, 40b, Lady with an Ermine. b, 1.50 l, Virgin and Child with St. Anne. c, 3 l, Mona Lisa.

2002, July 25
417 A119   Sheet of 3, #a-c   3.25 3.25

Famous Men — A120

Designs: No. 418, 40b, Grigore Ureche (1590-1647), chronicler. No. 419, 40b, Nicolae Costin (1660-1712). No. 420, 40b, Ion Neculce (1672-1745), chronicler. No. 421, 40b, Nicolae Testemiteanu (1927-86). 1.50 l, Sergiu Radautan (1926-98), scientist. 3.90 l, Alexandre Dumas (father) (1802-70), novelist.

2002, Aug. 24
418-423 A120   Set of 6   5.00 5.00

Horses A121

Designs: 40b, Vladimir. 1.50 l, Orlov. 3 l, Arabian.

2002, Sept. 20   *Perf. 14*
424-426 A121   Set of 3   4.00 4.00

The Post in Children's Art — A122

Art by: 40b, Alexandry Catranji. 1.50 l, Natalia Corcodel. 2 l, Dana Lungu.

2002, Oct. 3   Litho.   *Perf. 14*
427-429 A122   Set of 3   3.00 3.00

Commonwealth of Independent States Summit — A123

CIS emblem and: 1.50 l, National leaders and flags. 3.60 l, Handshake.

2002, Oct. 6   Litho.   *Perf. 13½*
430-431 A123   Set of 2   3.25 3.25

Cricova Wine Industry, 50th Anniv. A124

Designs: No. 432, 40b, Truck in warehouse. No. 433, 40b, Entrance to underground warehouse. 1.50 l, Wine glasses on table, vert. 2 l, Dusty wine bottles, wine cellar, statue. 3.60 l, Wine glasses and bottles, vert.

2002, Oct. 11   *Perf. 13¼x13, 13x13¼*
432-436 A124   Set of 5   5.00 5.00

Dirigibles — A125

Designs: 40b, Tissandier dirigible, France, 1883. 2 l, Ucebnii dirigible, Russia, 1908. 5 l, Graf Zeppelin, Germany, 1928.

2003, Apr. 22   Litho.   *Perf. 13¼*
437-439 A125   Set of 3   4.00 4.00

Butterflies — A126

Designs: 40b, Iphiclides podalirius. 2 l, Callimorpha quadripunctaria. 3 l, Marumba quercus. 5 l, Polyommatus daphnis.

2003, Apr. 30   *Perf. 13¼x13*
440-443 A126   Set of 4   6.50 6.50
443a   Souvenir sheet, #440-443   6.50 6.50
443b   Booklet pane, #441-442, 2
      each #440, 443   11.00 —
     Complete booklet, #443b   11.00

Europa — A127

Poster art: 3 l, Popular Dance Ensemble poster. 5 l, Eminescu Exhibition poster.

2003, June 12   *Perf. 13¼*
444-445 A127   Set of 2   5.00 5.00
445a   Booklet pane, 3 each #444-
     445   15.00
     Complete booklet, #445a   15.00

Souvenir Sheet

Moldovan Europa Stamps, 10th Anniv. — A128

No. 446: a, 1.50 l, Rural landscape. b, 5 l, Chisinau.

2003, June 12   *Perf. 13½*
446 A128   Sheet of 2, #a-b + label   4.00 4.00

Red Cross A129

Emblem and: 40b, Flag. 5 l, Red Cross workers at disaster site.

2003, July 4   *Perf. 13¼x13*
447-448 A129   Set of 2   2.10 2.10

Youth Olympics, Paris — A130

Designs: 40b, Runner. 3 l, Cyclists. 5 l, Gymnast.

2003, July 25   *Perf. 13½*
449-451 A130   Set of 3   4.50 4.50

Battle Against Terrorism A131

Art: 40b, Luminari, by A. Ahlupin, vert. 3.90 l, Pax Cultura, by N. Roerich.

2003, Oct. 21
452-453 A131   Set of 2   2.75 2.75

Dimitrie Cantemir (1673-1723), Historian A132

2003, Oct. 24   *Perf. 13*
454 A132 3.60 l multi   2.25 2.25

Visit of Pres. Vladimir Voronin to European Union — A133

2003, Nov. 5   *Perf. 13½*
455 A133 3 l multi   2.25 2.25

Famous Men — A134

Designs: 40b, Nicolae Donici (1874-1956), astronomer. 1.50 l, Nicolae Dimo (1873-1959), agronomist. 2 l, Nicolai Costenco (1913-93), writer. 3.90 l, Lewis Milestone (1895-1980), film director. 5 l, Vincent van Gogh (1853-90), painter.

2003, Nov. 14
456-460 A134   Set of 5   7.50 7.50

Birds From Red Book of Moldova A135

Designs: 40b, Cygnus olor. 2 l, Egretta alba. 3 l, Aquila rapax, vert. 5 l, Tetrax tetrax, vert.

2003, Dec. 18   Litho.   *Perf. 13¾*
461-464 A135   Set of 4   5.00 5.00
464a   Souvenir sheet, #461-464, perf. 13   5.00 5.00

Famous People — A136

Designs: 40b, Natalia Gheorghiu (1914-2001), surgeon. 1.50 l, Metropolitan Dosoftei (1624-93).

2004, Apr. 30   Litho.   *Perf. 14x14½*
465-466 A136   Set of 2   1.75 1.75

Europa A137

Designs: 40b, Archaeological dig. 4.40 l, Tourists at winery.

2004, June 25   Litho.   *Perf. 14x14½*
467-468 A137   Set of 2   4.50 4.50
468a   Booklet pane, 2 each #467-468   9.00
     Complete booklet, #468a   9.00

Stephen the Great (1437-1504), Prince of Moldavia — A138

Stephen the Great and: 40b, Soroca Fortress. 2 l, Capriana Monastery. 4.40 l, Map of Moldova.

2004, July 2   *Perf. 14½x14*
469-470 A138   Set of 2   1.75 1.75
Souvenir Sheet
471 A138 4.40 l multi + 2 labels   3.00 3.00

FIFA (Fédération Internationale de Football Association), Cent. — A139

No. 472: a, 2 l, Goalie catching ball. b, 4.40 l, Player dribbling ball.

2004, Aug. 14
472 A139   Horiz. pair, #a-b, + central label   3.75 3.75

Souvenir Sheet

Iasi-Chisinau Operation Memorial — A140

2004, Aug. 22
473 A140 2 l multi + label   1.50 1.50
Iasi-Chisinau Operation, 60th anniv.

2004 Summer Olympics, Athens — A141

Designs: 40b, Boxing. 4.40 l, Weight lifting.

2004, Dec. 28   *Perf. 14x14½*
474-475 A141   Set of 2   3.00 3.00

Ancient Jewelry A142

Designs: 40b, Earrings, 4th cent. B.C. 1 l, Necklace, 4th-3rd cent. B.C. 1.50 l, Silver temple earring, 14th-15th cent. 2 l, Bronze bracelet, 4th cent. B.C.

2004, Dec. 28
476-479 A142   Set of 4   3.00 3.00

Flowering Bushes — A143

Designs: 40b, Ephedra distachya. 1.50 l, Pyrus elaeagrifolia. No. 482, 2 l, Padus avium. No. 483, 2 l, Crataegus pentagyna.

2004, Dec. 29   *Perf. 14½x14*
480-483 A143   Set of 4   3.50 3.50

Locomotives — A144

Designs: 60b, ER. 1 l, ChME3. 1.50 l, D 777-3. 4.40 l, 3TE10M.

2005, Apr. 2   Litho.   *Perf. 14x14½*
484-487 A144   Set of 4   4.50 4.50

St. George's Church, Capriana Monastery — A145

2005, May 6   *Perf. 14½x14*
488 A145 40b multi   .75 .75

End of World War II, 60th Anniv. — A146

2005, May 9
489 A146 1.50 l multi   .90 .90

Europa A147

Designs: 1.50 l, Cheese, corn meal mush, pitcher and cup. 4.40 l, Pies, stein and bottle of wine.

2005, May 20   *Perf. 14x14½*
490-491 A147   Set of 2   3.75 3.75
491a   Miniature sheet, 3 each #490-491   14.50 —
No. 491a was sold with, but not attached to, a booklet cover.

European Women's Chess Championships, Chisinau — A148

2005, June 10   *Perf. 14½x14*
492 A148 4.40 l multi   3.00 3.00

Composers — A149

Designs: 40b, Serghei Lunchevici (1934-95). 1 l, Valeriu Cupcea (1929-89). 2 l, Anton Rubinstein (1829-94).

2005, July 1   *Perf. 14x14½*
493-495 A149   Set of 3   3.00 3.00

First Europa Stamps, 50th Anniv. (in 1996) — A150

Designs: No. 496, 1.50 l, Moldovan landmarks, flag and map. 15 l, Vignette of 1956 Europa stamps.
No. 498a, Moldoveanca, by Anatol Silitkii.

2005, July 20   Litho.   *Perf. 14½x14*
496-497 A150   Set of 2   5.00 5.00
Souvenir Sheet
498   Sheet, #497, 498a   5.00 5.00
a.   A150 1.50 l multi   .55 .55

World Summit on the Information Society, Tunis — A151

2005, Sept. 14
499 A151 4.40 l multi   2.50 2.50

Souvenir Sheet

Moldovan Passports, 10th Anniv. — A152

No. 500: a, 40b, Three passport pages with pictures. b, 1.50 l, Two closed passports. c, 4.40 l, Two passport pages with pictures.

2005, Sept. 16
500 A152   Sheet of 3, #a-c   3.75 3.75

Endangered Reptiles and Amphibians — A153

Designs: Nos. 501, 505a, 40b, Emys orbicularis. Nos. 502, 505b, 1 l, Eremias arguta. Nos. 503, 505c, 1.50 l, Pelobates fuscus. Nos. 504, 505d, 2 l, Vipera ursini.

2005, Sept. 29   **Perf. 14x14½**
With White Frames
501-504 A153   Set of 4   3.25 3.25
Souvenir Sheet
Without White Frames
505 A153   Sheet of 4, #a-d, + 2 labels   3.25 3.25

St. Nicholas Church — A154

2005, Oct. 30   **Perf. 14½x14**
506 A154 40b multi   .75 .75

Christmas — A155

Designs: 40b, St. Ierarh Nicolae Church, Falesti. 6 l, Varzaresti Monastery.

2005, Dec. 19   Litho.   Perf. 14x14½
507-508 A155   Set of 2   3.25 3.25

Makler Newspaper, 15th Anniv. — A156

2006, Jan. 20
509 A156 60b multi   .30 .30

2006 Winter Olympics, Turin — A157

Designs: 60b, Luge. 6.20 l, Skiing.

2006, Feb. 10
510-511 A157   Set of 2   3.00 3.00

Buildings — A158

Designs: 22b, Post Office No. 21, Balti. 40b, Saint Gates, Chisinau. 53b, Museum of History, Cahul. 57b, Old Post and Telegraph Office, Soroca. 60b, Adormirea Maicii Domnului Church, Copceac. 3.50 l, National Museum of Fine Arts, Chisinau.

2006, Mar. 23   **Perf. 14½x14**
512 A158 22b dark blue   .75 .75
513 A158 40b brown   .75 .75
514 A158 53b dark blue   .75 .75
515 A158 57b green   .75 .75
516 A158 60b olive green   .75 .75
517 A158 3.50 l red brown   2.50 2.50
   Nos. 512-517 (6)   6.25 6.25

Textile Arts and Native Costumes — A159

Designs: 40b, Crocheting. 60b, Moldavian woman, 19th cent., vert. 3 l, Moldavian man, 19th cent., vert. 4.50 l, Embroidery.

2006, Apr. 14   Perf. 14x14½, 14½x14
518-521 A159   Set of 4   3.25 3.25

Gheorghe Mustea, Conductor — A160

2006, Apr. 28   **Perf. 14x14½**
522 A160 60b multi   .30 .30

Europa
A161

Designs: 60b, Children and town on globe. 4.50 l, Artist and musicians, vert.

2006, May 6   Perf. 14x14½, 14½x14
523-524 A161   Set of 2   2.75 2.75
524a   Miniature sheet, 3 each #523-524   8.25 8.25

No. 524a was sold with, but not attached to, a booklet cover.

37th Chess Olympiad, Turin — A162

2006, May 24   **Perf. 14x14½**
525 A162 4.50 l multi   1.75 1.75

2006 World Cup Soccer Championships, Germany — A163

World Cup, emblem and: 2 l, Players. 3 l, Mascot. 4.50 l, Players, diff.

2006, June 28
526-528 A163   Set of 3   4.00 4.00

Famous People — A164

Designs: 40b, Ion Halippa (1871-1941), archaeologist. 1 l, Eufrosinia Cuza (1856-1910), singer. 2 l, Petre Stefanuca (1906-42), folklorist. 4.50 l, Wolfgang Amadeus Mozart (1756-91), composer.

2006, Aug. 11   **Perf. 14½x14**
529-532 A164   Set of 4   5.00 5.00

Endangered Animals — A165

Designs: 60b, Martes martes. 1 l, Mustela erminea. 2 l, Mustela lutreola. 3 l, Mustela eversmanni. 6.20 l, Felis silvestris, vert.

2006, Aug. 16   **Perf. 14x14½**
533-536 A165   Set of 4   3.00 3.00
Souvenir Sheet
Perf. 14½x14
537 A165 6.20 l multi + label   3.00 3.00

Independence, 15th Anniv. — A166

2006, Aug. 27   **Perf. 14½x14**
538 A166 2.60 l multi   1.25 1.25

Dogs A167

Designs: 40b, German shepherd. 60b, Collie. 2 l, Standard poodle. 6.20 l, Hungarian greyhound.

2006, Sept. 8   **Perf. 14x14½**
539-542 A167   Set of 4   3.75 3.75
542a   Sheet, 2 each #539-542   7.50 7.50

National Wine Day — A168

2006, Oct. 7
543 A168 60b multi   .35 .35

Christmas — A169

Paintings by: 40b, Valerii, Metleaev, 1988. 3 l, Mihail Statnii, 1986, vert. 6.20 l, Elena Bontea, 1973.

Perf. 14x14½, 14½x14
2006, Dec. 12   **Litho.**
544 A169 40b multi   .30 .30
545 A169 3 l multi   .80 .80
546 A169 6.20 l multi   1.90 1.90
  a.   Strip of 3, #544-546   3.00 3.00

Nos. 544 and 545 were each printed in sheets of 10 and in sheets of 9 containing 3 each of Nos. 544-546.

No. 25 Surcharged

Methods and Perfs As Before
2007, Jan. 11
547 A6 85b on 25k #547   1.25 1.25

Portraits in Natl. Art Museum — A170

Designs: 65b, Petrarch, by Raphael Morghen. 85b, Napoleon Bonaparte, by unknown artist. 2 l, Freidrich von Schiller, by Johann Gotthard Muller. 4.50 l, Johann Wolfgang von Goethe by James Hopwood.

2007, Feb. 28   Litho.   Perf. 14½x14
548-551 A170   Set of 4   2.75 2.75

Mushrooms — A171

Designs: 65b, Morchella steppicola. 85b, Phylloporus rhodoxantus. 2 l, Amanita solitaria. 6.20 l, Boletus aereus.

2007, Apr. 23   Litho.   Perf. 14x14½
552-555 A171   Set of 4   3.00 3.00

Europa A172

Designs: 2.85 l, Scouts with pencil and paint brush. 4.50 l, Scouts examining butterfly.

2007, May 8
556-557 A172   Set of 2   2.25 2.25
   Scouting, cent.

No. 83 Surcharged in Blue or Black

Methods and Perfs As Before
2007, June 7
558 A19 25b on 3k #83 (Bl)   .30 .30
559 A19 85b on 3k #83 (Bk)   .30 .30

Cats
A173

Designs: 65b, Mixed breed. 1 l, Siamese, vert. 1.50 l, Birman, vert. 6.20 l, Persian.

Perf. 14x14½, 14½x14
2007, June 20 Litho.
560-563 A173 Set of 4 3.00 3.00

Birds
A174

Designs: 75b, Otis tarda. 1 l, Neophron percnopterus. 2.50 l, Lyrurus tetrix. 5 l, Gyps fulvus. 6.20 l, Tetrao urogallus.

2007, Aug. 14 Litho. **Perf. 14x14½**
564-567 A174 Set of 4 3.25 3.25
Souvenir Sheet
568 A174 6.20 l multi + label 2.25 2.25

Dniester River Fish
Preservation — A175

No. 569: a, Acipenser gueldenstaedtii. b, Zingel zingel.

2007, Sept. 6
569 Horiz. pair + central label 1.25 1.25
  a. A175 1 l multi .30 .30
  b. A175 3 l multi .95 .95

See Ukraine No. 694.

Famous People — A176

Designs: 75b, Ion Luca Caragiale (1852-1912), writer. 1 l, Anastasia Dicescu (1887-1945), opera singer. 3 l, Mircea Eliade (1907-86), historian. 6.20 l, Maria Biesu, opera singer, vert.

2007, Sept. 15 **Perf. 14x14½**
570-572 A176 Set of 3 1.50 1.50
Souvenir Sheet
Perf. 14½x14
573 A176 6.20 l multi + label 2.00 2.00

World Chess Championships,
Mexico — A177

2007, Sept. 29 **Perf. 14x14½**
574 A177 6.20 l multi 1.90 1.90

A178

Christmas — A179

2007, Dec. 1 Litho. **Perf. 14x14½**
575 A178 1 l multi .25 .25
576 A179 4.50 l multi 1.25 1.25
  a. Miniature sheet, 6 #575, 3 #576 5.00 5.00

Covered
Wells — A180

Well in: 10b, Peresecina. 75b, Duruitoarea. 1 l, Ciripcau, vert. 3 l, Ocnita, vert.

2008, Feb. 19 **Perf. 14½x14, 14x14½**
577-580 A180 Set of 4 1.50 1.50

2008 Summer Olympics,
Beijing — A181

Designs: 1 l, Cycling. 6.20 l, Boxing. 15 l, Weight lifting

2008, Mar. 5 **Perf. 14x14½**
581-583 A181 Set of 3 5.75 5.75
For overprint see No. 607.

Europa
A182

Designs: 3.50 l, Post rider, scroll, castle. 4.50 l, Letters, computer screen.

2008, Apr. 30 Litho. **Perf. 14x14½**
584-585 A182 Set of 2 2.00 2.00
585a Sheet, 2 each #584-585 4.00 4.00
No. 585a was sold with, but not attached to, a booklet cover.

First Postage Stamps of Moldavia,
150th Anniv. — A183

Designs: 1 l, Romania #1-2. 3 l, Romania #3-4.

2008, May 23
586-587 A183 Set of 2 1.25 1.25
587a Booklet pane of 4, 2 each #586-587 2.50 2.50
  Complete booklet, #587a 2.50

UEFA Euro 2008 Soccer
Championships, Austria and
Switzerland — A184

2008, June 28
588 A184 4.50 l multi 1.40 1.40

Flowers — A185

Designs: 1 l, Maianthemum bifolium. 3 l, Hepatica nobilis. 5 l, Nymphaea alba.

2008, Aug. 19 Litho. **Perf. 14x14½**
589-591 A185 Set of 3 3.00 3.00
591a Souvenir sheet of 3, #589-591, + 3 labels 3.00 3.00

Famous
People
A186

Designs: 1.20 l, Onisifor Ghibu (1883-1972), teacher. 1.50 l, Ciprian Porumbescu (1853-83), composer. 3 l, Leo Tolstoy (1828-1910), author. 4.50 l, Maria Tanase (1913-63), singer.

2008, Sept. 5
592-595 A186 Set of 4 4.00 4.00

Deer — A187

No. 596: a, Cervus nippon. b, Cervus elaphus sibiricus.

2008, Sept. 18
596 A187 3 l Horiz. pair, #a-b 2.25 2.25
See Kazakhstan No. 577.

Souvenir Sheet

Bender (Tighina), 600th
Anniv. — A188

2008, Oct. 8
597 A188 4.20 l brn & buff + 3 labels 1.60 1.60

Princes — A189

Designs: 1.20 l, Prince Antiokh Cantemir (1708-44). 3 l, Prince Dimitrie Cantemir (1673-1723).

2008, Oct. 27 **Perf. 14½x14**
598 A189 1.20 l brown .45 .45
Souvenir Sheet
599 A189 3 l brown + label 1.10 1.10

Princes — A190

Designs: 85b, Prince Mihail Grigore Sutu (1784-1864). 1.20 l, Prince Grigore Alexandru Ghica (1807-57). 1.50 l, Prince Mihail Sturza (1795-1884). 2 l, Prince Alexandru Ipsilanti (1726-1807). 3 l, Prince Ioan Sandu Sturza (1761-1842). 4.50 l, Prince Scarlat Callimachi (1773-1821). 6.20 l, Prince Alexandru Ioan Cuza (1820-73).

2008, Nov. 14
600-605 A190 Set of 6 4.25 4.25
Souvenir Sheet
606 A190 6.20 l multi + 5 labels 2.00 2.00

No. 582 Overprinted in Bronze

2008, Nov. 21 **Perf. 14x14½**
607 A161 6.20 l multi 2.00 2.00

Souvenir Sheet

Moldovan Presidency of the Central
European Initiative — A191

No. 608 — CEI emblems and map of: a, 1.20 l, Western Europe. b, 4.50 l, Eastern Europe.

2008, Nov. 27 **Perf. 14½x14**
608 A191 Sheet of 2, #a-b 1.90 1.90

A192

Christmas — A193

2008, Dec. 5   Litho.   Perf. 14x14½
609   A192   1.20 l multi   .45   .45
Souvenir Sheet
610   A193   6.20 l multi   2.00   2.00

Universal Declaration of Human
Rights, 60th Anniv. — A194

2008, Dec. 10
611   A194   4.50 l multi   1.50   1.50

Moldavian State, 650th Anniv. — A195

Designs: 1.20 l, Moldovan arms and flag,
Presidential offices. 6.20 l, Bogdan I Voda,
Prince of Moldavia.

2009, Jan. 20
612   A195   1.20 l multi   .45   .45
Souvenir Sheet
613   A195   6.20 l multi + label   2.00   2.00

Ancient Weapons — A196

Weapons from: 1.20 l, 10th-14th cents.
4.50 l, 8th-13th cents.

2009, Feb. 24
614-615   A196   Set of 2   1.90   1.90

Preservation of
Polar Regions and
Glaciers — A197

Question mark, emblem and: 1.20 l, Penguin. 6.20 l, Polar bear.

2009, Mar. 18   Litho.   Perf. 14½x14
616-617   A197   Set of 2   2.50   2.50

Easter
A198

Decorated Easter eggs: 1.20 l, In basket. 3 l,
In bowl.

2009, Apr. 2   Perf. 14x14½
618-619   A198   Set of 2   1.25   1.25

Council of Europe,
60th
Anniv. — A199

2009, Apr. 15   Perf. 14½x14
620   A199   4.50 l multi   1.45   1.45

Europa
A200

Designs: 4.20 l, Nicolae Donici (1874-1956),
astrophysicist, observatory, planetary diagram
and eclipse. 4.50 l, Galileo Galilei (1564-
1642), astronomer, armillary sphere and star.

2009, May 7   Perf. 14x14½
621-622   A200   Set of 2   2.00   2.00
622a   Sheet. 3 each #621-622   6.00   6.00

Intl. Year of Astronomy. No. 622a was sold
with, but not attached to, a booklet cover.

Children's Art — A201

Children's art on clean environment theme
by: 1.20 l, Olesea Curteanu. 1.50 l, Iulia
Struta, vert. 5 l+20b, Irina Simion, vert.

2009, June 1   Perf. 14x14½, 14½x14
623-625   A201   Set of 3   2.25   2.25

Flowers
A202

Designs: 1.20 l, Viola suavis. 1.50 l, Adonis
vernalis. 3 l, Campanula persicifolia.
4.50 l, Papaver rhoeas.

2009, June 18   Perf. 13 Syncopated
626-628   A202   Set of 3   1.50   1.50
Souvenir Sheet
629   A202   4.50 l multi + label   1.25   1.25
a.   Sheet of 4, #626-629, + 2 labels   2.75   2.75

Insects
A203

Designs: 1.20 l, Bombus paradoxus. 1.50 l,
Xylocopa valga. 3 l, Carabus clathratus. 4.50 l,
Coenagrion lindeni.

Perf. 13 Syncopated
2009, Sept. 24   Litho.
630-633   A203   Set of 4   2.75   2.75

A204

 (Personalizable stamp, Moldova 1.20 L with statue)

Personalizable Stamps — A205

Designs: No. 636, Statue of Prince Stephen
the Great. No. 637, Cathedral. No. 638,
Roses, wedding rings. No. 639, Basket of
flowers.

2009, Aug. 5   Perf. 13 Syncopated
634   A204   1.20 l   lt bl & dk bl   2.00   2.00
635   A204   1.20 l   red & dk red   2.00   2.00
636   A205   1.20 l   multi + label   2.00   2.00
637   A205   1.20 l   multi + label   2.00   2.00
638   A205   1.20 l   multi + label   2.00   2.00
639   A205   1.20 l   multi + label   2.00   2.00
         Nos. 634-639 (6)   12.00 12.00

Vignettes of Nos. 634-635 and labels of
Nos. 636-639 could be personalized. The
vignette image shown in illustration A204 and
label image shown in illustration A205 are
generic.

Nuts and
Fruit — A206

Designs: 50b, Walnuts. 85b, Mulber-
ries.1.20 l, Pears. 5 l, Apricots.

2009, Aug. 28   Perf. 14½x14
640-643   A206   Set of 4   2.00   2.00

Houses
A207

House in: 1.20 l, Briceni. 4.50 l, Comrat. 7 l,
Orhei.

2009, Oct. 1   Perf. 14x14½
644-646   A207   Set of 3   3.25   3.25

Moldova
Grapes — A208

2009, Oct. 9   Perf. 14½x14
647   A208   4.50 l multi   1.25   1.25

European Day Against Human
Trafficking — A209

2009, Oct. 18   Perf. 14x14½
648   A209   4.50 l multi   1.25   1.25

Famous
People
A210

Designs: No. 649, 1.20 l, Eugene Ionescu
(1909-94), playwright. No. 650, 1.20 l,
Eufrosinia Kersnovskaia (1907-95), writer.
4.50 l, Nicolai Gogol (1809-52), writer. 7 l,
Charles Darwin (1809-92), naturalist.

2009, Nov. 26   Litho.   Perf. 14x14½
649-652   A210   Set of 4   4.00   4.00

Christmas — A211

Designs: 1.20 l, Capra. 4.50 l, Plugusorul.

2009, Dec. 1
653-654   A211   Set of 2   1.40   1.40

Famous
People
A212

Designs: No. 655, 1.20 l, Grigore Vieru
(1935-2009), writer. No. 656, 1.20 l, Natalia
Dadiani (1865-1903), founder of school for
girls. 5.40 l, Ivan Zaikin (1880-1948), wrestler
and aviator. 7 l, Maria Cebotari (1910-49),
singer and actress.
4.50 l, Mihai Eminescu (1850-89), writer,
vert.

2010, Jan. 15   Litho.   Perf. 14x14½
655-658   A212   Set of 4   4.00   4.00
Souvenir Sheet
Perf. 14½x14
659   A212   4.50 l multi + label   1.50   1.50

2010 Winter Olympics,
Vancouver — A213

Designs: 1.20 l, Alpine skiing. 8.50 l, Biathlon, vert.

2010, Feb. 12   *Perf. 14x14½, 14½x14*
660-661   A213   Set of 2   2.50 2.50

Jewelry in National Museum of Archaeology and History — A214

Designs: 1.20 l, Shell necklace, 5th cent. B.C. 7 l, Headband and pendant, 5th cent. B.C.

2010, Feb. 23   *Perf. 13 Syncopated*
662-663   A214   Set of 2   2.25 2.25

Frédéric Chopin (1810-49), Composer — A215

2010, Mar. 1   *Perf. 14x14½*
664   A215   5.40 l multi   1.40 1.40

Mushrooms A216

Designs: 1.20 l, Lactarius piperatus. 2 l, Amanita pantherina. 5.40 l, Russula sanguinea. 7 l, Coprinus picaceus.

2010, Mar. 27   *Perf. 14½x14*
665-668   A216   Set of 4   4.50 4.50
668a   Souvenir sheet, #665-668   4.50 4.50

Birds — A217

Designs: 85b, Carduelis carduelis. 1 l, Passer domesticus. 1.20 l, Strix uralensis. 4.50 l, Pica pica. 8.50 l, Columba livia.

2010, Apr. 8   *Perf. 13 Syncopated*
669-672   A217   Set of 4   2.50 2.50
Souvenir Sheet
673   A217   8.50 l multi   2.75 2.75

Europa A218

Children's books: 1.20 l, Punguta cu doi Bani, by Ion Creanga. 5.40 l, Guguta Si Prietenii Sai, by Spiridon Vangheli.

2010, Apr. 30   *Perf. 14x14½*
674-675   A218   Set of 2   1.75 1.75
675a   Sheet, 3 each #674-675   5.25 5.25

No. 675a was sold with, but unattached to, a booklet cover.

End of World War II, 65th Anniv. — A219

2010, May 9   *Perf. 14½x14*
676   A219   4.50 l multi   1.40 1.40

2010 World Cup Soccer Championships, South Africa — A220

Soccer player and: 1.20 l, Mascot. 8.50 l, Emblem, vert.

Perf. 14x14½, 14½x14
2010, June 11
677-678   A220   Set of 2   2.50 2.50

Campaign Against AIDS — A221

2010, July 1   *Perf. 14x14½*
679   A221   1.20 l multi   .40 .40

Paintings Depicting Flowers A222

Designs: 1 l, Flowers, by Ion Tabirta. 1.20 l, Bouquet of Poppies, by Oleg Cojocari. 2 l, Flowers, by Mihail Statnii. 5.40 l, Chrysanthemums, by Leonid Grigorasenco.

2010, Aug. 6   *Perf. 13 Syncopated*   **Litho.**
680-683   A222   Set of 4   2.50 2.50

Dances — A223

Designs: 85b, Moldovanesca. 5.40 l, Calusarii, vert.

Perf. 14x14½, 14½x14
2010, Sept. 18
684-685   A223   Set of 2   1.60 1.60

Feteasca Grapes — A224

2010, Oct. 9   *Perf. 14½x14*
686   A224   4.50 l multi   1.20 1.20

National Symbols A225

Perf. 13 Syncopated at Top
2010, Nov. 3
687   A225   1.20 l   Arms   .25 .25
  a.   Perf. 13, syncopation at sides   .25 .25
688   A225   4.50 l   Flag   1.00 1.00
  a.   Perf. 13, syncopation at sides   1.00 1.00
  b.   Sheet of 6, 3 each #687a, 688a   3.75 3.75

Prehistoric Animals — A226

Designs: 85b, Mammuthus. 1 l, Ursus spelaeus. No. 691, 1.20 l, Panthera leo spelaea. 4.20 l, Bison.
  No. 693: a, 1.20 l, Pontoceros. b, 1.50 l, Anancus. c, 5.40 l, Stephanorhinus. d, 8.50 l, Homotherium.

2010, Nov. 30   **Litho.**   *Perf. 14x14½*
689-692   A226   Set of 4   1.50 1.50
Souvenir Sheet
693   A226   Sheet of 4, #a-d, + 2 labels   3.50 3.50

Christmas A227

Designs: 1.20 l, Child at window, angel holding gift. 5.40 l, Cathedral.

2010, Dec. 7   *Perf. 13 Syncopated*
694   A227   1.20 l multi   .25 .25
Souvenir Sheet
695   A227   5.40 l multi   1.10 1.10

Items in National Museum of Archaeology and History A228

Designs: 85b, Amphora with lid, 5th cent. B.C. 1.20 l, Vessel with animal design, 4th cent. B.C. 8.50 l, Vessel depicting person, 4th cent. B.C.

2011, Jan. 25
696-698   A228   Set of 3   2.50 2.50
698a   Sheet of 4, #696, 698, 2
           #697 + 2 labels   2.75 2.75

Buildings — A229

Designs: 10b, Ralli family house, 19th cent., Dolna. 25b, Mirzoian family house, 19th cent., Hincesti. 85b, Balioz family house, 1847, Ivancea. 1 l, High school, 1916, Soroca. 1.20 l, Pommer family house, 20th cent., Taul. 1.50 l, Hasnas family house, 19th cent., Sofia.

2011, Feb. 15   *Perf. 14½x14*
699   A229   10b chocolate   .25 .25
700   A229   25b deep blue   .25 .25
701   A229   85b greenish blue   .25 .25
702   A229   1 l plum   .25 .25
703   A229   1.20 l dark blue   .25 .25
704   A229   1.50 l dark green   .30 .30
       Nos. 699-704 (6)   1.55 1.55

Handicrafts A230

Designs: 1.20 l, Decorated rope, by Ludmila Berezin. 4.20 l, Straw head, by Natalia Cangea. 7 l, Rug, by Ecaterina Popescu.

2011, Mar. 1
705-707   A230   Set of 3   3.25 3.25

Self-Portraits A231

Self-portrait of: 85b, Eugenia Malesevschi (1866-1942). 1.20 l, Nicolae Grigorescu (1838-1907). 2 l, Alexandru Piamadeala (1888-1940). 5.40 l, Mihail Grecu (1916-98).

2011, Apr. 1   *Perf. 13 Syncopated*
708-711   A231   Set of 4   2.50 2.50

Miniature Sheet

First Manned Space Flight, 50th Anniv. — A232

No. 712 — Pioneer cosmonauts and astronauts: a, 1.20 l, Yuri Gagarin. b, 5.40 l, Gherman Titov. c, 7 l, Virgil I. Grissom. d, 0.50 l, Alan B. Shepard, Jr.

2011, Apr. 9   *Perf. 14½x14*
712   A232   Sheet of 4, #a-d, + 2 labels   6.00 6.00

Europa — A233

Designs: 4.20 l, Leaf depicting forest fire, healthy forest and buck. 5.40 l, Owl, forest, cut tree.

2011, May 7   *Perf. 13 Syncopated*
713-714 A233   Set of 2   2.40 2.40
714a   Sheet of 6, 3 each #713-714   7.50 7.50

No. 714a was sold with, but unattached to, a booklet cover.

Flowers — A234

2011, May 20   *Perf. 14x14½*
715 A234   70b Hyacinth   .25 .25
716 A234   85b Tulips   .25 .25
717 A234   1.20 l Narcissi   .30 .30
718 A234   2 l Violas   .45 .45
   Nos. 715-718 (4)   1.25 1.25

Deportation of Moldovans to Siberia by the Soviet Union, 70th Anniv. — A235

2011, June 12   *Perf. 14½x14*
719 A235   1.20 l multi   .30 .30

Souvenir Sheet

First Moldovan Stamps, 20th Anniv. — A236

No. 720: a, 85b, Moldova #1. b, 1.20 l, Moldova #2. c, 4.20 l, Moldova #3.

2011, June 23   *Perf. 13 Syncopated*
720 A236   Sheet of 3, #a-c   1.50 1.50

Mammals and Birds — A237

Designs: No. 721, 85b, Meles meles. No. 722, 1.20 l, Erinaceus europaeus. 3 l, Canis lupus. 4.20 l, Vulpes vulpes.
No. 725: a, 85b, Plegadis falcinellus. b, 1.20 l, Pelecanus onocrotalus. c, 5.40 l, Platalea leucorodia. d, 8.50 l, Aythya nyroca.

2011, July 29
721-724 A237   Set of 4   2.10 2.10
725 A237   Sheet of 4, #a-d, + 2 labels   3.75 3.75

Souvenir Sheet

Independence, 20th Anniv. — A238

2011, Aug. 27   *Perf. 14½x14*
726 A238   4.20 l multi + 2 labels   1.10 1.10

Campaign Against Smoking — A239

2011, Sept. 10
727 A239   1.20 l multi   .30 .30

Diplomatic Relations Between Moldova and Romania, 20th Anniv. A240

Designs: 1.20 l, Holy Gates, Chisinau. 4.50 l, Arch of Triumph, Bucharest, Romania.

2011, Oct. 11   *Perf. 13 Syncopated*
728-729 A240   Set of 2   1.50 1.50
729a   Sheet of 2, #728-729, + 4 labels   1.50 1.50

See Romania Nos. 5301-5302.

Miniature Sheet

Chisinau, 575th Anniv. — A241

No. 730: a, 85b, Palace of Culture. b, 1.20 l, National Opera and Ballet Theater. c, 2 l, Mihai Emenscu National Theater. d, 3.85 l, National Palace. e, 5.40 l, Patria Movie Theater.

2011, Oct. 13   *Perf. 14x14½*
730 A241   Sheet of 5, #a-e, + label   3.50 3.50

UN High Commisioner for Refugees, 60th Anniv. — A242

2011, Nov. 25   *Perf. 14½x14*
731 A242   1.20 l multi   .25 .25

A243

Christmas — A244

2011, Dec. 3   *Perf. 14½x14*
732 A243   1.20 l multi   .25 .25
Souvenir Sheet
Perf. 14x14½
733 A244   4.50 l multi   1.10 1.10

Famous People — A245

Designs: 85b, Magda Isanos (1916-44), poet. 1.20 l, Nicolae Sulac (1936-2003), musician. 3 l, Cleopatra Hrsanovschi (1861-1939), musician. 4.50 l, Franz Liszt (1811-86), composer.

2011, Dec. 17   *Perf. 14x14½*
734-737 A245   Set of 4   2.25 2.25

Paintings Depicting Children A246

Designs: 85b, Pokrovka Boy, by Igor Vieru. 1.20 l, Orphan, by Pavel Piscariov. 2.85 l, Portrait of a Child, by Lidia Arionescu-Baillayre. 4.50 l, Boy with Hat, by Constantin Kitaika.

2012, Feb. 4   *Perf. 13 Syncopated*
738-741 A246   Set of 4   2.25 2.25

Souvenir Sheet

Ion (1954-92) and Doina (1958-92) Aldea-Teodorovici, Musicians — A247

2012, Mar. 3   *Perf. 14x14½*
742 A247   7 l multi + label   1.75 1.75

Souvenir Sheet

Mihai Dolgan (1942-2008), Musician — A248

2012, Mar. 14   *Perf. 14½x14*
743 A248   4.50 l multi + label   1.10 1.10

Traditional Costumes — A249

Designs: 85b, Woman. 1.20 l, Man. 3 l, Woman, diff. 8.50 l, Man and woman.

2012, Apr. 7
744-746 A249   Set of 3   1.25 1.25
Souvenir Sheet
747 A249   8.50 l multi + label   1.90 1.90

Regional Communications Commonwealth, 20th anniv.

Europa A250

Designs: 4.20 l, Curchi Monastery. 5.40 l, Winery.

2012, Apr. 18   *Perf. 14½x14*
748 A250   4.20 l multi   .90 .90
a.   Souvenir sheet of 3 + label   2.75 2.75
749 A250   5.40 l multi   1.25 1.25
a.   Souvenir sheet of 3 + label   3.75 3.75

Nos. 748a and 749a were sold with, but unattached to, a booklet cover.

Medieval Military Scenes — A251

Designs: 85b, Battering ram. 1.20 l, Soldier with spear and shield, vert. 1.50 l, Military commander on horseback, vert. 5.40 l, Catapult.

Perf. 14x14½, 14½x14

2012, May 31 Litho.
750-753 A251 Set of 4 2.25 2.25

Pigeons — A252

Designs: 85b, Jucator de Chisinau. 1.20 l, Jucator de Balti. 3 l, Jucator basarbean. 4.20 l, Roller de Chisinau.

2012, June 21 Perf. 14x14½
754-757 A252 Set of 4 2.25 2.25

2012 Summer Olympics, London — A253

Designs: 4.50 l, Wrestling. 5.40 l, Cycling.

2012, July 21
758-759 A253 Set of 2 2.50 2.50

Rose Varieties A254

Designs: 85b, Mildred Scheel. 1.20 l, Friesia. 3 l, Priscilla. 4.20 l, Caribia.

2012, Aug. 10 Perf. 13 Syncopated
760-763 A254 Set of 4 1.90 1.90
763a Sheet of 6, #762-763, 2 each #760-761 2.40 2.40

Famous Men A255

Designs: 85b, Eugeniu Ureche (1917-2005), actor. 1.20 l, Spiridon Mocanu (1932-2007), dancer. 4.50 l, George Emil Palade (1912-2008), 1974 Nobel laureate for Physiology or Medicine. 8.50 l, Jean-Jacques Rousseau (1712-78), political philosopher.

2012, Aug. 27 Perf. 14x14½
764-767 A255 Set of 4 3.25 3.25

Maria Biesu (1935-2012), Opera Singer — A256

2012, Sept. 7 Litho.
768 A256 1.20 l multi .25 .25

Natural Monuments — A257

Designs: 1.20 l, Cheile Butesti Canyon. 4.20 l, Suta de Movile. 7 l, Emil Racovita Caves.

2012, Sept. 21 Perf. 14x14½
769-771 A257 Set of 3 2.50 2.50

Christmas A258

Icons from: 1.75 l, 1903. 5.40 l, 19th cent.

2012, Dec. 1 Perf. 13 Syncopated
772-773 A258 Set of 2 1.50 1.50
Nos. 772-773 each were printed in sheets of 8 + central label.

Zero Kilometer Marker, Chisinau — A259

2012, Dec. 12 Perf. 14½x14
774 A259 1.75 l multi .40 .40

Paintings Depicting Mihai Eminescu (1850-89), Poet — A260

Designs: 1.75 l, Mihai Eminescu, by Emil Childescu. 5.75 l, Dedication, by Vasile Nascu.

2013, Jan. 15 Perf. 13 Syncopated
775-776 A260 Set of 2 1.60 1.60
Nos. 775-776 each were printed in sheets of 8 + label.

Regional Communications Commonwealth Emblem, Communications Tower, Map of Moldova — A261

2013, Feb. 28 Perf. 14½x14
777 A261 4.50 l multi .95 .95

Berries — A262

Designs: 55b, Ribes uva-crispa. 1.50 l, Vaccinium myrtillus. No. 780, Rubus idaeus. No. 781, Viburnum opulus. 2 l, Hippophae rhamnoides. 4 l, Ribes rubrum.

2013, Mar. 30 Perf. 14x14½
778 A262 55b multi .25 .25
779 A262 1.50 l multi .30 .30
780 A262 1.75 l multi .35 .35
781 A262 1.75 l multi .35 .35
782 A262 2 l multi .40 .40
783 A262 4 l multi .80 .80
Nos. 778-783 (6) 2.45 2.45

Europa A263

Postal vehicles: 4.50 l, Van. 5.75 l, Horse-drawn carriage.

2013, Apr. 30
784 A263 4.50 l multi .95 .95
a. Souvenir sheet of 4 4.00 4.00
785 A263 5.75 l multi 1.25 1.25
a. Souvenir sheet of 4 5.00 5.00
Nos. 784a and 785a were sold with, but unattached to, a booklet cover.

Animals in the Chisinau Zoo — A264

Designs: 1.75 l, Panthera uncia. 2 l, Macropus rufogriseus, vert. 5.75 l, Pavo cristatus.

2013, May 18 Perf. 14x14½, 14½x14
786-787 A264 Set of 2 .75 .75
Souvenir Sheet
788 A264 5.75 l multi + label 1.25 1.25

Illustrations From Guguta Stories by Spiridon Vangheli — A265

Designs: No. 789, 1.75 l, Cusma. No. 790, 1.75 l, Datoria.

2013, June 1 Perf. 14½x14
789-790 A265 Set of 2 .70 .70

Folk Traditions — A266

Designs: No. 791, 1.75 l, Cleaning of the well. No. 792, 1.75 l, Rain dance, vert.

Perf. 14x14½, 14½x14
2013, June 20
791-792 A266 Set of 2 .70 .70

Butterflies — A267

Designs: 1 l, Thysania agrippina. No. 794, 1.75 l, Papilio blumei. No. 795, 1.75 l, Salamis temora. 5.75 l, Cymothoe excelsa.

Perf. 13 Syncopated

2013, July 5 Litho.
793-796 A267 Set of 4 2.10 2.10
796a Souvenir sheet of 8, 2 each #793-796, + label 4.25 4.25

Famous People A268

Designs: No. 797, 1.75 l, Adrian Paunescu (1943-2010), poet and politician. No. 798, 1.75 l, Anton Crihan (1893-1993), politician. No. 799, 1.75 l, Ion Bass (1933-2005), folk singer. No. 800, 1.75 l, Angela Paduraru (1938-95), folk singer. 4.50 l, Giuseppe Verdi (1813-1901), composer. 5.40 l, Richard Wagner (1813-83), composer.

2013 Litho. Perf. 14x14½
797-802 A268 Set of 6 3.50 3.50
Issued: Nos. 797-798, 7/20; Nos. 799-802, 8/2.

Souvenir Sheet

Alexei Mateevici (1888-1917), Poet — A269

2013, Aug. 28 Litho. Perf. 14½x14
803 A269 5.75 l multi + label 1.10 1.10

Muscat Grapes — A270

2013, Sept. 13 Litho. Perf. 14½x14
804 A270 1.75 l multi .35 .35

Urban Mass Transportation — A271

Designs: 1.75 l, Bus. 3 l, Trolleybus. 5.75 l, Tram.

2013, Oct. 12   Litho.   Perf. 14x14½
805-806 A271   Set of 2   .95   .95
Souvenir Sheet
807   A271   5.75 l multi + label   1.10 1.10
First tram in Chisinau, cent. (No. 807).

Christmas — A272

2013, Nov. 22   Litho.   Perf. 14x14½
808   A272   1.75 l multi   .35   .35

Forget-me-nots — A273

Tree of Life Embroidery
Design — A274

A275

A276

2013, Dec. 20   Litho.   Perf. 14x14½
809   A273   1.75 l multi + label   .35   .35
810   A274   1.75 l multi + label   .35   .35
Perf. 13 Syncopated
811   A275   1.75 l multi   .35   .35
812   A276   1.75 l multi   .35   .35
        Nos. 809-812 (4)   1.40 1.40

Nos. 809-810 each were printed in sheets of 8 + 8 labels that could be personalized. The labels shown are generic.

Nos. 811-812 each were printed in sheets of 8 stamps + 4 labels that could not be personalized. The image areas of Nos. 811-812 could be personalized. Illustrations show a generic image in the image area.

The frame portion of No. 811 has eight slightly different types. Values are for any of the frame types.

Traditional Crafts — A277

Designs: 1.20 l, Pottery. 1.75 l, Basket weaving. 5.75 l, Carpet weaving.

2014, Jan. 18   Litho.   Perf. 14x14½
813-815 A277   Set of 3   1.60 1.60

2014 Winter Olympics, Sochi,
Russia — A278

Designs: 4.50 l, Skiing, bobsledding, snowboarding. 5.40 l, Ice hockey, figure skating, biathlon.

2014, Feb. 7   Litho.   Perf. 14x14½
816-817 A278   Set of 2   1.90 1.90

Europa
A279

Musical instruments: 3 l, Tambal (dulcimer). 5.75 l, Cobza (lute).

2014, Mar. 22   Litho.   Perf. 14x14½
818-819 A279   Set of 2   1.75 1.75
818a   Sheet of 3 + label   1.90 1.90
819a   Sheet of 3 + label   3.50 3.50

Nos. 818a and 819a were sold with, but unattached, to a booklet cover.

Easter — A280

Perf. 13 Syncopated
2014, Apr. 5   Litho.
820   A280   1.75 l multi   .35   .35
No. 820 was printed in sheets of 8 + central label.

Museums — A281

Designs: 1.20 l, National Museum of Ethnography and Natural History. 2 l, National History Museum. 4 l, National Art Museum.

2014, May 3   Litho.   Perf. 14x14½
821-823 A281   Set of 3   1.40 1.40

Nos. 821-823 each were printed in sheets of 10 + 5 labels.

Arrival of German Settlers in
Bessarabia, 200th Anniv. — A282

2014, May 15   Litho.   Perf. 14x14½
824   A282   1.75 l multi   .35   .35

Famous
People — A283

Designs: 1.20 l, Tamara Ceban (1914-90), singer. 1.75 l, Dumitru Matcovschi (1939-2013), writer. 3 l, Toma Ciorba (1864-1936), physician. 8.50 l, Elena Cernei (1924-2000), opera singer.

Perf. 13 Syncopated
2014, June 7   Litho.
825-828 A283   Set of 4   2.60 2.60

Souvenir Sheet

Mihai Eminescu and Ion Creanga,
Painting by Mihai Grecu — A284

Perf. 13 Syncopated
2014, June 14   Litho.
829   A284   5.75 l multi   1.10 1.10

Deportation of Germans from
Bessarabia, 65th Anniv. — A285

2014, July 5   Litho.   Perf. 14x14½
830   A285   1.75 l multi   .35   .35

Association Agreement Between
Moldova and European Union — A286

2014, Aug. 9   Litho.   Perf. 14x14½
831   A286   1.75 l multi   .35   .35

Sheep
Breeds — A287

Designs: 1.20 l, Karakul sheep. 5.75 l, Tigaie sheep.

Perf. 13 Syncopated
2014, Aug. 16   Litho.
832-833 A287   Set of 2   1.25 1.25

Traditional Dishes — A288

Designs: 1 l, Fried fish with garlic sauce. 1.20 l, Bean soup with thyme. 4 l, Cheese and dill pies. 5.75 l, Chicken broth with parsley.

2014, Sept. 30   Litho.   Perf. 14x14½
834-837 A288   Set of 4   2.25 2.25

Fauna — A289

Designs: 1.20 l, Helix pomatia. 1.50 l, Ciconia ciconia (46x28mm). 1.75 l, Stizostedion lucioperca (46x28mm). 2 l, Cyprinus carpio (46x28mm). 3 l, Viviparus viviparus. 8.50 l, Motacilla flava (46x28mm).

2014, Nov. 7   Litho.   Perf. 14x14½
838-843 A289   Set of 6   3.00 3.00
843a   Souvenir sheet of 6, #838-   3.00 3.00
          843

Famous
Men In
World
War I
A290

Designs: 1.75 l, Dimitrie Bogos (1889-1946), politician. 4 l, General Constantin Braescu (1873-1927). 5.75 l, Marshal Alexandru Averescu (1859-1938).

2014, Nov. 22   Litho.   Perf. 14x14½
844-846 A290   Set of 3   1.90 1.90

New Year
2015 — A291

Designs: 1.75 l, Snowman. 5.75 l, Santa Claus in sleigh.

2014, Dec. 12   Litho.   Perf. 14½x14
847-848 A291   Set of 2   1.25 1.25

AIR POST STAMPS

TU-144 — AP1

1992-93   Litho.   Perf. 12
C1   AP1   1.75r maroon   .40   .40
C2   AP1   2.50r red vio   .45   .45
C3   AP1   7.75r blue   1.50 1.50
C4   AP1   8.50r blue green   1.90 1.90
C5   AP1   25r red brown   .45   .45
C6   AP1   45r brown   .75   .75
C7   AP1   50r olive green   .90   .90
C8   AP1   90r blue   1.90 1.90
      Nos. C1-C8 (8)   8.25 8.25
Issued: #C1-C4, 7/20/92; #C5-C8, 7/24/93.

POSTAGE DUE STAMPS

Dove, Envelope — D1

1994, Nov. 12   Litho.   Perf. 14
J1   D1   30b lt olive & brown   .55   .55
J2   D1   40b pale vio & slate   .65   .65

In use, Nos. J1-J2 were torn apart, one half being affixed to the postage due item and the other half being pasted into the postman's record book. Values are for unused and canceled-to-order pairs.

MONACO

ˈmä-nə-ˌkō

LOCATION — Southern coast of France, bordering on the Mediterranean Sea
GOVT. — Principality
AREA — 481 acres
POP. — 31,842 (2001 est.)
CAPITAL — Monaco

100 Centimes = 1 Franc
100 Cents = 1 Euro (2002)

Catalogue values for unused stamps in this country are for Never Hinged items, beginning with Scott 182 in the regular postage section, Scott B51 in the semi-postal section, Scott C2 in the air-post section, Scott CB1 in the air-post semi-postal section, and Scott J28 in the postage due section.

Values for unused stamps are for examples with original gum as defined in the catalogue introduction. Very fine examples of Nos. 1-181, B1-B50, C1 and J1-J27 will have perforations clear of the design and/or frameline. Very well centered are worth more than the values quoted.

Prince Charles III — A1

1885 Unwmk. Typo. Perf. 14x13½

1	A1	1c olive green	25.00	17.50
2	A1	2c dull lilac	57.50	27.50
3	A1	5c blue	70.00	35.00
4	A1	10c brown, *straw*	85.00	40.00
5	A1	15c rose	350.00	18.00
6	A1	25c green	700.00	75.00
7	A1	40c slate, *rose*	85.00	45.00
8	A1	75c black, *rose*	275.00	125.00
9	A1	1fr black, *yellow*	1,750.	500.00
10	A1	5fr rose, *green*	3,000.	2,000.

Prince Albert I — A2

1891-1921

11	A2	1c olive green	.70	.70
12	A2	2c dull violet	.80	.80
13	A2	5c blue	50.00	6.00
14	A2	5c yellow grn ('01)	.40	.35
15	A2	10c brown, *straw*	100.00	16.00
16	A2	10c carmine ('01)	3.25	.70
17	A2	15c rose	175.00	10.00
a.		Double impression	1,400.	
18	A2	15c vio brn, *straw* ('01)	3.00	1.00
19	A2	15c gray green ('21)	2.00	2.50
20	A2	25c green	275.00	32.50
21	A2	25c deep blue ('01)	15.00	5.00
22	A2	40c slate, *rose* ('94)	3.50	2.40
23	A2	50c violet brown (shades), *orange*	7.00	4.75
24	A2	75c vio brn, *buff* ('94)	27.50	18.00
25	A2	75c ol brn, *buff* ('21)	20.00	24.00
26	A2	1fr black, *yellow*	19.00	11.00
27	A2	5fr rose, *grn*	100.00	87.50
c.		Double impression	1,500.	
28	A2	5fr dull violet ('21)	200.00	250.00
29	A2	5fr dark green ('21)	22.50	27.50
		Nos. 11-29 (19)	1,024.	500.70

The handstamp "OL" in a circle of dots is a cancellation, not an overprint.
For shades, see the *Scott Classic Specialized Catalogue of Stamps and Covers.*

See No. 1782. For overprints and surcharges see Nos. 30-35, 57-59, B1.

Stamps of 1901-21 Overprinted or Surcharged

1921, Mar. 5

30	A2	5c lt green	.70	.70
31	A2	75c brown, *buff*	5.25	6.25
32	A2	2fr on 5fr dull vio	32.50	52.50
		Nos. 30-32 (3)	38.45	59.45

Issued to commemorate the birth of Princess Antoinette, daughter of Princess Charlotte and Prince Pierre, Comte de Polignac.

Stamps and Type of 1891-1921 Surcharged

1922

33	A2	20c on 15c gray green	1.10	1.40
34	A2	25c on 10c rose	.70	.90
35	A2	50c on 1fr black, *yel*	6.00	6.50
		Nos. 33-35 (3)	7.80	8.80

Prince Albert I — A5   Oceanographic Museum — A6

"The Rock" of Monaco — A7

Royal Palace — A8

1922-24   Engr.   Perf. 11

40	A5	25c deep brown	4.00	4.75
41	A6	30c dark green	.90	.90
42	A6	30c scarlet ('23)	.50	.45
43	A6	50c ultra	4.25	4.25
44	A7	60c black brown	.35	.35
45	A7	1fr black, *yellow*	.25	.25
46	A7	2fr scarlet ver	.50	.45
47	A8	5fr red brown	32.50	37.50
48	A8	5fr green, *bluish*	10.50	10.50
49	A8	10fr carmine	14.00	18.00
		Nos. 40-49 (10)	67.75	77.40

Nos. 40-49 exist imperf.
For shades, see the *Scott Classic Specialized Catalogue of Stamps and Covers.*

Prince Louis II
A9   A10

St. Dévote Viaduct ("Bridge of Suicides") A11

1923-24   Engr.

50	A9	10c deep green	.35	.55
51	A9	15c car rose ('24)	.45	.70
52	A9	20c red brown	.35	.55
53	A9	25c violet	.25	.45
a.		Without engraver's name	27.50	27.50
54	A11	40c orange brn ('24)	.65	.55
55	A10	50c ultra	.35	.45
		Nos. 50-55 (6)	2.40	3.25

The 25c comes in 2 types, one with larger "5" and "c" touching frame of numeral tablet.
Stamps of the 1922-24 issues sometimes show parts of the letters of a papermaker's watermark.
The engraved stamps of type A11 measure 31x21½mm. The typographed stamps of that design measure 36x21½mm.
See #86-88. For surcharges see #95-96.

Stamps and Type of 1891-1921 Surcharged

1924, Aug. 5   Perf. 14x13½

57	A2	45c on 50c brn ol, *buff*	.50	.70
a.		Double surcharge	775.00	775.00
58	A2	75c on 1fr blk, *yel*	.50	.70
a.		Double surcharge	550.00	550.00
59	A2	85c on 5fr dk green	.50	.70
a.		Double surcharge	650.00	650.00
		Nos. 57-59 (3)	1.50	2.10
		Set, never hinged	2.25	

Grimaldi Family Coat of Arms — A12

Prince Louis II — A13

Louis II — A14

View of Monaco A15

1924-33   Typo.

60	A12	1c gray black	.25	.25
61	A12	2c red brown	.25	.25
62	A12	3c brt violet ('33)	2.75	1.90
63	A12	5c orange ('26)	.35	.30
64	A12	10c blue	.25	.25
65	A13	15c apple green	.25	.25
66	A13	15c dull vio ('29)	2.75	1.90
67	A13	20c violet	.25	.25
68	A13	20c rose	.35	.25
69	A13	25c rose	.25	.25
70	A13	25c red, *yel*	.25	.25
71	A13	30c orange	.25	.25
72	A13	40c black brown	.25	.25
73	A13	40c lt bl, *bluish*	.35	.35
74	A13	45c gray black ('26)	.90	.70
75	A14	50c myrtle grn ('25)	.25	.25
76	A13	50c brown, *org*	.25	.25
77	A14	60c yellow brn ('25)	.25	.25
78	A13	60c ol grn, *grnsh*	.25	.25
79	A13	75c ol grn, *grnsh* ('26)	.70	.35
80	A13	75c car, *straw* ('26)	.35	.25
81	A13	75c slate	.90	.55
82	A13	80c red, *yel* ('26)	.40	.30
83	A13	90c rose, *straw* ('26)	2.00	1.60
84	A13	1.25fr bl, *bluish* ('26)	.25	.25
85	A13	1.50fr bl, *bluish* ('27)	3.75	1.90

Size: 36x21½mm

86	A11	1fr blk, *orange*	.25	.25
87	A11	1.05fr red violet ('26)	.25	.25
88	A11	1.10fr blue grn ('27)	8.00	6.00
89	A15	2fr vio & ol brn ('25)	2.75	1.00
90	A15	3fr rose & ultra, *yel* ('27)	25.00	12.00

91	A15	5fr green & rose ('25)	8.50	6.00
92	A15	10fr yel brn & bl ('25)	25.00	17.50
		Nos. 60-92 (33)	88.80	56.85
		Set, never hinged	175.00	

Nos. 60 to 74 and 76 exist imperforate.
For surcharges see Nos. 93-94, 97-99, C1.

Type of 1924-33 Surcharged in Black

1926-31

93	A13	30c on 25c rose	.30	.25
94	A13	50c on 60c ol grn, *grnsh* ('28)	1.50	.35
95	A11	50c on 1.05fr red vio ('28)	1.10	.70
a.		Double surcharge	65.00	
96	A11	50c on 1.10fr bl grn ('31)	14.00	8.75
97	A13	50c on 1.25fr bl, *bluish* (R) ('28)	1.60	.65
98	A13	1.25fr on 1fr bl, *bluish*	.80	.50
99	A15	1.50fr on 2fr vio & ol brn ('28)	7.00	5.25
		Nos. 93-99 (7)	26.30	16.45
		Set, never hinged	40.00	

Princes Charles III, Louis II and Albert I A17

1928, Feb. 18   Engr.   *Perf. 11*

100	A17	50c dull carmine	2.50	*4.75*
101	A17	1.50fr dark blue	2.50	*4.75*
102	A17	3fr dark violet	2.50	*4.75*
		Nos. 100-102 (3)	7.50	14.25
		Set, never hinged	18.00	

Nos. 100-102 were sold exclusively at the Intl. Phil. Exhib. at Monte Carlo, Feb., 1928. One set was sold to each purchaser of a ticket of admission to the exhibition which cost 5fr. Exist imperf. Value, set $27.50.

Old Watchtower A20

Royal Palace A21

Church of St. Dévote — A22

Prince Louis II — A23

"The Rock" of Monaco A24

Gardens of Monaco A25

Fortifications and Harbor — A26

1932-37   *Perf. 13, 14x13½*

110	A20	15c lilac rose	.80	.25
111	A20	20c orange brn	.80	.25
112	A21	25c olive blk	1.10	.35
113	A22	30c yellow grn	1.40	.35
114	A23	40c dark brown	3.25	1.40
115	A24	45c brown red	3.50	1.10
a.		45c red	425.00	425.00
116	A23	50c purple	3.25	.85
117	A25	65c blue green	3.50	1.10
118	A26	75c deep blue	4.00	1.75
119	A23	90c red	9.50	3.25
120	A22	1fr red brown ('33)	27.50	7.75
121	A26	1.25fr rose lilac	6.75	4.50
122	A23	1.50fr ultra	40.00	10.50
123	A21	1.75fr rose lilac	35.00	9.50
124	A21	1.75fr car rose ('37)	24.00	13.00
125	A24	2fr dark blue	13.50	4.75
126	A20	3fr purple	20.00	9.00
127	A21	3.50fr orange ('35)	47.50	32.50
128	A22	5fr violet	27.50	20.00
129	A21	10fr deep blue	125.00	70.00
130	A25	20fr black	175.00	140.00
		Nos. 110-130 (21)	572.85	332.15
		Set, never hinged	1,150.	

Postage Due Stamps of 1925-32
Surcharged or Overprinted in Black

1937-38   *Perf. 14x13*

131	D3	5c on 10c violet	1.00	1.00
132	D3	10c violet	1.00	1.00
133	D3	15c on 30c bister	1.00	1.00
134	D3	20c on 30c bister	1.00	1.00
135	D3	25c on 60c red	1.50	1.50
136	D3	30c bister	2.40	2.40
137	D3	40c on 60c red	2.40	2.40
138	D3	50c on 60c red	2.40	2.40
139	D3	65c on 1fr lt bl	2.25	2.00
140	D3	85c on 1fr lt bl	5.00	4.50
141	D3	1fr light blue	7.75	7.75
142	D3	2.15fr on 2fr dl red	7.75	7.75
143	D3	2.25fr on 2fr dl red ('38)	19.00	19.00
144	D3	2.50fr on 2fr dl red ('38)	29.00	29.00
		Nos. 131-144 (14)	83.45	82.70
		Set, never hinged	175.00	

Grimaldi Arms — A27

Prince Louis II — A28

1937-43   Engr.

145	A27	1c dk vio brn ('38)	.25	.25
146	A27	2c emerald	.25	.25
147	A27	3c brt red violet	.25	.25
148	A27	5c red	.25	.25
149	A27	10c ultra	.25	.25
149A	A27	10c black ('43)	.25	.25
150	A27	15c violet ('39)	1.75	1.50
150A	A27	30c dull green ('43)	.25	.25
150B	A27	40c rose car ('43)	.25	.25
150C	A27	50c brt violet ('43)	.25	.25
151	A28	55c red brown ('38)	5.75	2.25
151A	A27	60c Prus blue ('43)	.25	.25
152	A28	65c violet ('38)	30.00	13.00
153	A28	70c red brown ('39)	.35	.35
153A	A27	70c red brown ('43)	.25	.25
154	A28	90c violet ('39)	.35	.30
155	A28	1fr rose red ('38)	18.50	10.50
156	A28	1.25fr rose red ('39)	.35	.35
157	A28	1.75fr ultra ('38)	18.50	10.50
158	A28	2.25fr ultra ('39)	.35	.25
		Nos. 145-158 (20)	78.65	41.75
		Set, never hinged	150.00	

Nos. 151, 152, 155, 157 exist imperf.

Souvenir Sheet

Prince Louis II — A29

1938, Jan. 17   Unwmk.   *Imperf.*

159	A29	10fr magenta	65.00	65.00
		Never hinged	175.00	

"Fête Nationale" 1/17/38. Size: 99x120mm.

Cathedral of Monaco — A30

St. Nicholas Square — A31

Palace Gate — A32

Palace of Monaco — A34

Panorama of Monaco A33

Harbor of Monte Carlo A35

1939-46   *Perf. 13*

160	A30	20c rose lilac	.25	.25
161	A31	25c gldn brown	.45	.30
162	A32	30c dk blue grn	.35	.30
162A	A32	30c brown red ('40)	.35	.25
163	A31	40c henna brn	.70	.50
164	A33	45c brt red vio	.50	.50
165	A34	50c dk blue grn	.35	.25
166	A32	60c rose carmine	.40	.35
166A	A32	60c dk green ('40)	.90	.70
166B	A35	70c brt red vio ('41)	.40	.25
167	A35	75c dark green	.40	.25
167A	A30	80c dull green ('43)	.25	.25
168	A34	1fr brown black	.40	.25
168A	A33	1fr claret ('43)	.25	.25
168B	A31	1.20fr ultra ('46)	.25	.35
168C	A34	1.30fr brown blk ('41)	.40	.35
168D	A31	1.50fr ultra ('46)	.40	.40
169	A31	2fr rose violet	.40	.30
169A	A35	2fr lt ultra ('43)	.25	.25
169B	A34	2fr green ('46)	.35	.25
170	A33	2.50fr red	27.50	17.50
171	A35	2.50fr dp blue ('40)	1.75	1.75
172	A35	3fr brown red	.45	.35
172A	A31	3fr black ('43)	.25	.25
172B	A30	4fr rose lilac ('46)	1.25	.55
172C	A34	4.50fr brt violet ('43)	.25	.25
173	A30	5fr Prus blue	5.25	4.00
173A	A32	5fr deep green ('43)	.25	.25
173B	A34	6fr lt violet ('46)	.70	.55
174	A33	10fr green	1.40	*1.60*
174A	A30	10fr deep blue ('43)	.25	.25
174B	A35	15fr rose pink ('43)	.40	.25
175	A32	20fr brt ultra	1.60	1.25
175A	A33	20fr sepia ('43)	.40	.25
175B	A35	25fr blue green ('46)	1.40	1.25
		Nos. 160-175B (35)	51.10	36.85
		Set, never hinged	100.00	

See Nos. 214-221, 228-232, 274-275, 319-320, 407-408, 423, 426, 428-429, B36-B50.

Louis II Stadium A36

1939, Apr. 23   Engr.

176	A36	10fr dark green	100.00	*110.00*
		Never hinged	175.00	

Inauguration of Louis II Stadium.

Louis II Stadium A37

1939, Aug. 15

177	A37	40c dull green	1.25	1.25
178	A37	70c brown black	1.60	1.60
179	A37	90c dark violet	2.25	2.25
180	A37	1.25fr copper red	3.00	3.00
181	A37	2.25fr dark blue	4.25	4.25
		Nos. 177-181 (5)	12.35	12.35
		Set, never hinged	22.50	

8th International University Games.

Imperforates

Many Monaco stamps from 1940 to 1999 exist imperforate. Officially 20 sheets, ranging from 25 to 100 subjects, were left imperforate.

> **Catalogue values for unused stamps in this section, from this point to the end of the section, are for Never Hinged items.**

Prince Louis II — A38

1941-46   *Perf. 14x13*

182	A38	40c brown carmine	.65	.50
183	A38	80c deep green	.65	.50
184	A38	1fr rose violet	.25	.25
185	A38	1.20fr green ('42)	.25	.25
186	A38	1.50fr rose	.25	.25
187	A38	1.50fr violet ('42)	.25	.25
187A	A38	2fr lt green ('46)	.65	.35
188	A38	2.40fr red ('42)	.25	.25
189	A38	2.50fr deep ultra	1.10	*1.25*
190	A38	4fr blue ('42)	.25	.25
		Nos. 182-190 (10)	4.55	4.10

Prince Louis II — A39

1943   *Perf. 13*

191	A39	50fr purple	2.00	1.10

A40

Prince Louis II — A41

1946   Unwmk.   Engr.   *Perf. 14x13*

192	A40	2.50fr dk blue green	.70	.25
193	A40	3fr brt red violet	.70	.25
194	A40	6fr brt red	.70	.35
195	A40	10fr brt ultra	.70	.35

Perf. 13

196	A41	50fr dp Prus green	4.00	2.10
197	A41	100fr red	5.25	2.75
	Nos. 192-197 (6)		12.05	6.05

Nos. 196-197 exist imperforate.
See Nos. 222-227, 233-236. For overprints see Nos. C8-C9.

Franklin D. Roosevelt — A42

Harbor of Monte Carlo A43

Palace of Monaco A44

Map of Monaco — A45   Prince Louis II — A46

1946, Dec. 13   Unwmk.   Perf. 13

198	A42	10c red violet	.50	.45
199	A43	30c deep blue	.50	.45
200	A44	60c blue black	.50	.45
201	A45	1fr sepia	1.50	1.25
202	A45	3fr lt violet	2.25	1.75
	Nos. 198-202,B93,C14-C15,CB6 (9)		10.35	8.65

Issued in tribute to the memory of Franklin D. Roosevelt.

1947, May 15

203	A46	10fr dark blue green	4.50	4.50

25th anniv. of the reign of Prince Louis II.
See Nos. B94, C20a.

Hurdler A47

Runner — A48

Designs: 2fr, Discus thrower. 2.50fr, Basketball. 4fr, Swimmer.

1948, July 1   Perf. 13

204	A47	50c blue green	.25	.25
205	A48	1fr rose brown	.25	.25
206	A48	2fr grnsh blue	1.25	.85

207	A48	2.50fr vermilion	3.50	2.50
208	A48	4fr slate gray	4.00	3.25
	Nos. 204-208,CB7-CB10 (9)		91.25	89.10

Issued to publicize Monaco's participation in the 1948 Olympic Games held at Wembley, England, during July and August.

Nymph Salmacis A49

Hercules — A50   Aristaeus — A51

Hyacinthus A52

François J. Bosio and Louis XIV Statue — A53

1948, July 12

209	A49	50c dark green	.55	.35
210	A50	1fr red	.55	.35
211	A51	2fr deep ultra	1.90	.75
212	A52	2.50fr deep violet	4.75	2.25
213	A53	4fr purple	4.75	2.50
	Nos. 209-213,CB11-CB14 (9)		94.50	88.20

Issued to honor François J. Bosio (1768-1845), sculptor. No. 213 inscribed "J F Bosio."

Scenic Types of 1939

1948   Engr.

214	A30	50c sepia	.35	.25
215	A31	60c rose pink	.35	.25
216	A32	3fr violet rose	1.10	.35
217	A31	4fr emerald	1.10	.35
218	A34	8fr red brown	4.25	2.00
219	A34	10fr brown red	6.00	2.00
220	A33	20fr carmine rose	1.50	.65
221	A35	25fr gray black	35.00	17.50
	Nos. 214-221 (8)		49.65	23.35

Louis II Type of 1946

1948, July   Perf. 14x13

222	A40	30c black	.30	.25
223	A40	5fr orange brown	.45	.30
224	A40	6fr purple	5.00	1.75
225	A40	10fr orange	.45	.30
226	A40	12fr deep carmine	6.00	2.50
227	A40	18fr dark blue	9.50	6.00
	Nos. 222-227 (6)		21.70	11.10

Scenic Types of 1939

1949   Perf. 13

228	A33	5fr blue green	.85	.35
229	A35	10fr orange	1.75	.65
230	A32	25fr blue	52.50	16.00
231	A30	40fr brown red	9.25	4.75
232	A30	50fr purple	5.75	1.00
	Nos. 228-232 (5)		70.10	22.75

Louis II Type of 1946

1949, Mar. 10   Perf. 14x13

233	A40	50c olive	.35	.25
234	A40	1fr dk violet bl	.25	.25
235	A40	12fr dk slate gray	10.00	7.00
236	A40	15fr brown carmine	10.00	3.75
	Nos. 233-236 (4)		20.60	11.25

Hirondelle I A54

Cactus Plants — A55

Designs: 4fr, Oceanographic Museum. 5fr, Princess Alice II at Spitzbergen. 6fr, Albert I Monument. 10fr, Hirondelle II. 12fr, Albert I whaling. 18fr, Bison.

1949, Mar. 5   Perf. 13

237	A54	2fr brt blue	.25	.25
238	A55	3fr dark green	.25	.25
239	A54	4fr blk brn & bl	.25	.25
240	A54	5fr crimson	1.10	1.10
241	A55	6fr dark violet	1.00	1.00
242	A54	10fr black brown	1.25	1.25
243	A54	12fr brt red violet	2.75	2.75
244	A54	18fr dk brn & org brn	4.00	4.00
	Nos. 237-244 (8)		10.85	10.85

See Nos. C21-C26.

Palace, Globe and Pigeon A56

1949-50   Engr.   Unwmk.

245	A56	5fr blue green	.60	.60
245A	A56	10fr orange	7.00	7.00
246	A56	15fr carmine	.60	.60
	Nos. 245-246,C30-C33 (7)		21.35	21.35

75th anniversary of the UPU.
Nos. 245, 245A and 246 exist imperf.
Issued: 5fr, 15fr, 12/27; 10fr, 9/12/50.

Prince Rainier III A57   A58

1950, Apr. 11

247	A57	10c red & blk brn	.25	.25
248	A57	50c dp yel & dk brn	.25	.25
249	A57	1fr purple	.45	.35
250	A57	5fr dark green	3.50	1.90
251	A57	15fr carmine	5.25	5.25
252	A57	25fr ultra, ol grn & ind	5.25	5.25
	Nos. 247-252,C34-C35 (8)		33.70	30.25

Enthronement of Prince Rainier III.

1950, Apr.   Engr.   Perf. 14x13

253	A58	50c purple	.35	.25
254	A58	1fr orange brown	.35	.30
255	A58	8fr blue green	9.00	2.40
256	A58	12fr blue	2.25	.50
257	A58	15fr crimson	4.25	.70
	Nos. 253-257 (5)		16.20	4.15

1951, Apr. 31   Typo.

258	A58	5fr emerald	12.00	4.75
259	A58	10fr orange	20.00	7.75

See Nos. 276-279.

Statue of Prince Albert I — A59

1951, Apr. 11   Engr.   Perf. 13

260	A59	15fr deep blue	11.00	6.50

Edmond and Jules de Goncourt A60

1951, Apr. 11

261	A60	15fr violet brown	11.00	6.50

50th anniversary of the foundation of Goncourt Academy.

St. Vincent de Paul — A61

Judgment of St. Dévote — A62

Symbolizing Monaco's Adoption of Catholicism — A63

Mosaic of the Immaculate Conception A64

Blessed Rainier of Westphalia A65

Holy Year, 1951: 50c, Pope Pius XII. 12fr, Prince Rainier III at Prayer. 15fr, St. Nicholas de Patare. 20fr, St. Roman. 25fr, St. Charles Borromée. 40fr, Cross, arms and Roman Coliseum. 50fr, Chapel of St. Dévote.

Inscribed: "Anno Santo"

1951, June 4 Unwmk. *Perf. 13*

262 A61 10c ultra & red .25 .25
263 A61 50c dk rose lake & pur .25 .25
264 A62 1fr brown & dk grn .30 .30
265 A63 2fr vio brn & ver .35 .35
266 A64 5fr blue green .45 .45
267 A63 12fr rose violet .70 .70
268 A63 15fr vermilion 4.50 4.50
269 A63 20fr red brown 6.50 6.50
270 A63 25fr ultra 9.00 9.00
271 A63 40fr dk car rose & pur 10.50 10.50
272 A63 50fr ol grn & dk vio brn 14.00 14.00
273 A65 100fr dk violet brn 27.50 27.50
Nos. 262-273 (12) 74.30 74.30

Scenic Types of 1939-46

1951, Dec. 22 *Perf. 13*

274 A31 3fr deep turq green 2.75 .90
275 A32 30fr slate black 8.50 3.50

Rainier Type of 1950

1951, Dec. 22 *Perf. 14x13*

276 A58 6fr blue green 1.75 .75
277 A58 8fr orange 1.75 .75
278 A58 15fr indigo 2.50 .45
279 A58 18fr crimson 6.25 1.50
Nos. 276-279 (4) 12.25 3.45

Radio Monte Carlo — A66

Knight in Armor — A67

1951, Dec. 22 *Perf. 13*

280 A66 1fr blue, car & org 1.10 .35
281 A66 15fr pur, car & rose vio 4.25 1.25
282 A66 30fr indigo & red brn 21.00 6.50
Nos. 280-282 (3) 26.35 8.10

1951, Dec. 22

283 A67 1fr purple 1.25 .55
284 A67 5fr gray black 3.75 2.25
285 A67 8fr deep carmine 7.75 3.75
286 A67 15fr emerald 12.50 7.50
287 A67 30fr slate black 21.00 15.00
Nos. 283-287 (5) 46.25 29.05

See Nos. 328-332, 2025-2026.

Nos. B96-B99a Surcharged with New Values and Bars in Black

1951, Dec. *Perf. 13½x13, Imperf.*

288 SP51 1fr on 10fr + 5fr 12.50 12.50
289 SP52 3fr on 15fr + 5fr 12.50 12.50
290 SP52 5fr on 25fr + 5fr 13.00 12.50
291 SP51 6fr on 40fr + 5fr 13.00 12.50
b. Block of 4, #288-291 51.00 50.00

Gallery of Hercules, Royal Palace A68

1952, Apr. 26 Engr. *Perf. 13*

292 A68 5fr red brn & brn 2.25 .55
293 A68 15fr purple & lil rose 2.75 .75
294 A68 30fr indigo & ultra 3.25 .90
Nos. 292-294 (3) 8.25 2.20

Opening of a philatelic museum at the royal palace, Apr. 26, 1952.

Basketball — A69

2fr, Soccer. 3fr, Sailing. 5fr, Cyclist. 8fr, Gymnastics. 15fr, Louis II Stadium.

1953, Feb. 23 Unwmk. *Perf. 11*

295 A69 1fr dk purple & mag .25 .25
296 A69 2fr dk grn & sl bl .25 .25
297 A69 3fr blue & lt blue .25 .25
298 A69 5fr dk brn & grnsh blk .90 .45
299 A69 8fr brown lake & red 2.25 1.00
300 A69 15fr bl, brn blk & dk grn 1.25 .90
Nos. 295-300,C36-C39 (10) 78.15 53.10

Issued to publicize Monaco's participation in the Helsinki Olympic Games.

Books, Pens and Proof Pages A70

1953, June 29 *Perf. 13*

301 A70 5fr dark green .55 .45
302 A70 15fr red brown 3.75 .70

Publication of a first edition of the unexpurgated diary of Edmond and Jules Goncourt.

Physalia and Laboratory Ship Hirondelle II — A71

1953, June 29

303 A71 2fr Prus green, pur & choc .25 .25
304 A71 5fr dp mag, red & Prus grn .90 .40
305 A71 15fr ultra, vio brn & Prus grn 3.25 1.75
Nos. 303-305 (3) 4.40 2.40

50th anniversary of the discovery of anaphylaxis by Charles Richet and Paul Portier.

Frederic Ozanam — A72

Nun — A73

1954, Apr. 12 Engr. *Perf. 13*

306 A72 1fr bright red .25 .25
307 A73 5fr dark blue .50 .50
308 A72 15fr black 2.10 1.90
Nos. 306-308 (3) 2.85 2.65

Centenary of the death of Frederic Ozanam, founder of the Society of Saint Vincent de Paul.

Jean Baptiste de la Salle
A74 A75

1954, Apr. 12

309 A74 1fr dark carmine .25 .25
310 A75 5fr black brown .50 .50
311 A74 15fr bright ultra 2.10 1.90
Nos. 309-311 (3) 2.85 2.65

Jean Baptiste de la Salle, founder of the Christian Brothers Institute and saint.

A76

A77

Grimaldi Arms — A78

Various Forms of Grimaldi Arms in Black and Red or Black, Red and Deep Plum (5fr)

Perf. 13½x14, 14x13½

1954, Apr. 12 Typo.

312 A76 50c black & mag .25 .25
313 A77 70c black & aqua .25 .25
314 A76 80c black, red & dk grn .25 .25
315 A77 1fr violet blue .25 .25
316 A77 2fr black & dp org .25 .25
317 A77 3fr black & green .25 .25
318 A78 5fr black & lt grn .25 .25
Nos. 312-318 (7) 1.75 1.75

Scenic Types of 1939-46

1954, Apr. 12 Engr. *Perf. 13*

319 A34 25fr bright red 3.75 .75
320 A31 75fr dark green 25.00 8.50

Knight in Armor — A79

1954, Apr. 12 Unwmk. *Perf. 13*

321 A79 4fr dark red 1.50 .40
322 A79 8fr dark green 1.50 .80
323 A79 12fr dark purple 6.00 1.75
324 A79 24fr dark maroon 11.00 4.75
Nos. 321-324 (4) 20.00 7.70

Nos. 321-324 were issued precanceled only. Values for precanceled stamps in first column are for those which have not been through the post and have original gum. Values in the second column are for postally used, gumless stamps.

See Nos. 400-404, 430-433, 466-469.

Lambarene Landing, Gabon — A80

Dr. Albert Schweitzer — A81

Design: 15fr, Lambarene hospital.

1955, Jan. 14 *Perf. 11x11½*

325 A80 2fr ol grn, bl grn & ind .30 .25
326 A81 5fr dk grnsh bl & grn 1.40 1.40
327 A81 15fr dk bl grn, dp cl & brn blk 3.75 3.00
Nos. 325-327 (3) 5.45 4.65

Issued to honor Dr. Albert Schweitzer, medical missionary. See No. C40.

Knight Type of 1951

1955, Jan. 14 *Perf. 13*

328 A67 5fr purple 3.50 1.10
329 A67 6fr red 6.25 2.25
330 A67 8fr red brown 6.25 3.25
331 A67 15fr ultra 15.00 5.00
332 A67 30fr dark green 25.00 15.00
Nos. 328-332 (5) 56.00 26.60

Automobile and Representation of Eight European Cities — A82

1955, Jan. 14 Unwmk.

333 A82 100fr dk brown & red 90.00 65.00

25th Monte Carlo Automobile Rally.

Prince Rainier III — A83

1955, June 7 Engr. *Perf. 13*

334 A83 6fr green & vio brn .70 .40
335 A83 8fr red & violet .70 .40
336 A83 12fr carmine & green .70 .40
337 A83 15fr purple & blue 1.40 .40
338 A83 18fr orange & blue 4.50 .40
339 A83 30fr ultra & gray 14.00 7.75
Nos. 334-339 (6) 22.00 9.75

See Nos. 405-406, 424-425, 427, 462-465, 586, 603-604A, 725-728, 730, 789, 791.

"Five Weeks in a Balloon" — A84

"A Floating City" and Jules Verne — A85

"Michael Strogoff" A86

"Around the World in 80 Days" — A87

USS Nautilus and Verne — A88

Designs (Scenes from Jules Verne's Books): 3fr, The House of Vapors. 6fr, The 500 Millions of the Begum. 8fr, The Magnificent Orinoco. 10fr, A Journey to the Center of the Earth. 25fr, Twenty Thousand Leagues under the Sea.

1955, June 7

340 A84	1fr red brn & bl gray	.25	.25
341 A85	2fr blue, ind & brn	.25	.25
342 A85	3fr red brn, gray & sl	.25	.25
343 A86	5fr car & blk brn	.25	.25
344 A84	6fr blk hrn & bluish gray	.45	.45
345 A86	8fr ol grn & aqua	.35	.35
346 A85	10fr indigo, turq & brn	1.25	1.00
347 A87	15fr rose brn & ver	1.00	.70
348 A85	25fr bl grn, grn & gray	2.50	1.75
349 A88	30fr violet, turq & blk	6.25	5.25
Nos. 340-349,C45 (11)		40.30	35.50

50th anniv. of the death of Jules Verne.

Virgin by Francois Brea A89

Rotary Emblem, World Map — A91

1955, June 7

353 A91	30fr blue & orange	1.10	1.10

50th anniv. of the founding of Rotary Intl.

George Washington A92

Franklin D. Roosevelt — A93

Dwight D. Eisenhower — A94

Palace of Monaco, c. 1790 — A95

Palace of Monaco, c. 1750 — A96

Designs: 3fr, Abraham Lincoln. 30fr, Columbus landing in America. 40fr, Prince Rainier III. 100fr, Early Louisiana scene.

1956, Apr. 3   Engr.   Perf. 13

354 A92	1fr dark purple	.25	.25
355 A93	2fr claret & dk pur	.30	.30
356 A93	3fr vio & dp ultra	.30	.30
357 A94	5fr brown lake	.40	.40
358 A95	15fr brn blk & vio brn	1.00	1.00
359 A95	30fr ind, blk & ultra	3.75	2.00
360 A94	40fr dk brn & vio brn	6.00	2.50
361 A96	50fr vermilion	6.00	2.50
362 A96	100fr Prus green	6.00	3.50
a.	Strip of 3, #360-362	19.00	19.00
Nos. 354-362 (9)		24.00	12.75

5th Intl. Phil. Exhib. (FIPEX), NYC, Apr. 28-May 6, 1956.

Ski Jump, Cortina d'Ampezzo — A97

Design: 30fr, Olympic Scenes.

1956, Apr. 3

363 A97	15fr brn vio, brn & dk grn	1.10	.55
364 A97	30fr red orange	2.25	1.60

Issued to publicize Monaco's participation in the 1956 Olympic Games.

"Glasgow to Monte Carlo" A98

1956, Apr. 3   Unwmk.

365 A98	100fr red brn & red	25.00	25.00

The 26th Monte Carlo Automobile Rally. See Nos. 411, 437, 460, 483, 500, 539, 549, 600, 629.

Princess Grace and Prince Rainier III — A99

1956, Apr. 19   Engr.   Perf. 13
Portraits in Black

366 A99	1fr dark green	.25	.25
367 A99	2fr dark carmine	.35	.25
368 A99	3fr ultra	.45	.35
369 A99	5fr brt yellow grn	1.00	.55
370 A99	15fr redsh brown	1.40	1.40
Nos. 366-370,C46-C48 (8)		10.05	8.65

Wedding of Prince Rainier III to Grace Kelly, Apr. 19, 1956.

Nos. J41-J47, J50-J56 Overprinted with Bars and Surcharged in Indigo, Red or Black
Unwmk.

1956, Apr. 3   Engr.   Perf. 11

Designs: Early Transportation.

371 D6	2fr on 4fr (I)	.50	.45
a.	Pair, #371, 381	1.00	1.00
372 D6	3fr (R)	.50	.45
a.	Pair, #372, 382	1.00	1.00
373 D6	5fr on 4fr	.70	.70
a.	Pair, #373, 383	1.40	1.40
374 D6	10fr on 4fr (R)	1.40	1.10
a.	Pair, #374, 384	2.75	2.75
375 D6	15fr on 5fr (I)	1.75	1.75
a.	Pair, #375, 385	3.50	3.50
376 D6	20fr (R)	2.75	2.75
a.	Pair, #376, 386	5.50	5.50
377 D6	25fr on 20fr	5.00	5.00
a.	Pair, #377, 387	10.00	10.00
378 D6	30fr on 10fr (I)	9.50	9.50
a.	Pair, #378, 388	19.00	19.00

379 D6	40fr on 50fr (R)	13.50	13.50
a.	Pair, #379, 389	27.00	27.00
380 D6	50fr on 100fr (R)	16.00	16.00
a.	Pair, #380, 390	32.00	32.00

Designs: Modern Transportation.

381 D7	2fr on 4fr (I)	.50	.50
382 D7	3fr (R)	.50	.45
383 D7	5fr on 4fr	.70	.70
384 D7	10fr on 4fr (R)	1.40	1.10
385 D7	15fr on 5fr (I)	1.75	1.75
386 D7	20fr (R)	2.75	2.75
387 D7	25fr on 20fr	5.00	5.00
388 D7	30fr on 10fr (I)	9.50	9.50
389 D7	40fr on 50fr (R)	13.50	13.50
390 D7	50fr on 100fr	16.00	16.00
Nos. 371-390,C49-C50 (22)		124.20	123.45

Pairs se-tenant at the base.

Princess Grace — A100

1957, May 11   Engr.   Perf. 13

391 A100	1fr blue violet	.25	.25
392 A100	2fr lt olive grn	.25	.25
393 A100	3fr yellow brown	.25	.25
394 A100	5fr magenta	.35	.25
395 A100	15fr pink	.35	.25
396 A100	25fr Prus blue	1.10	.65
397 A100	30fr purple	1.10	.90
398 A100	50fr scarlet	1.75	.90
399 A100	75fr orange	3.00	2.50
Nos. 391-399 (9)		8.40	6.20

Birth of Princess Caroline of Monaco.

Knight Type of 1954

1957   Unwmk.   Perf. 13

400 A79	5fr dark blue	.40	.25
401 A79	10fr yellow green	.30	.25
402 A79	15fr brt orange	1.40	.90
403 A79	30fr brt blue	2.00	.90
404 A79	45fr crimson	3.25	1.75
Nos. 400-404 (5)		7.35	4.05

Nos. 400-404 were issued only. See note after No. 324.

Types of 1955 and 1939-46

1957

405 A83	20fr greenish blue	2.00	.50
406 A83	35fr red brown	4.00	1.00
407 A33	65fr brt violet	10.00	6.50
408 A30	70fr orange yellow	9.50	6.00
Nos. 405-408 (4)		25.50	14.60

Princesses Grace and Caroline A101

1958, May 15   Engr.   Perf. 13

409 A101	100fr bluish black	8.50	6.00

Birth of Prince Albert Alexander Louis, Mar. 14.

Order of St. Charles — A102

1958, May 15

410 A102	100fr carmine, grn & bis	2.25	2.00

Cent. of the Natl. Order of St. Charles.

Blessed Rainier — A90

Marian Year: 10fr, Pieta by Louis Brea.

1955, June 7

350 A89	5fr vio brn, gray & dk grn	.25	.25
351 A89	10fr vio brn, gray & dk grn	.40	.35
352 A90	15fr black brn & org brn	.60	.55
Nos. 350-352 (3)		1.25	1.15

Rally Type of 1956

Design: 100fr, "Munich to Monte Carlo."

1958, May 15
411 A98 100fr red, grn & sepia   8.00 7.00
27th Monte Carlo Automobile Rally.

Virgin Mary, Popes Pius IX and XII — A103

Bernadette Soubirous A104

Tomb of Bernadette, Nevers A105

Designs: 3fr, Shepherdess Bernadette at Bartres. 5fr, Bouriette kneeling (first miracle). 8fr, Stained glass window showing apparition. 10fr, Empty grotto at Lourdes. 12fr, Grotto with statue and altar. 20fr, Bernadette praying. 35fr, High Altar at St. Peter's during canonization of Bernadette. 50fr, Bernadette, Pope Pius XI, Mgr. Laurence and Abbe Peyramale.

1958, May 15   **Unwmk.**
412 A103 1fr lilac gray & vio brn   .25 .25
413 A104 2fr blue & violet   .25 .25
414 A104 3fr green & sepia   .25 .25
415 A104 5fr gray brn & vio bl   .25 .25
416 A104 8fr blk, ol bis & ind   .35 .25
417 A105 10fr multicolored   .35 .35
418 A105 12fr ol, ol bis & ol grn   .45 .25
    a.   Strip of 3, #416-418   3.50 3.50
419 A104 20fr dk sl grn & rose   .45 .35
420 A104 35fr ol, gray ol & dk sl
              grn   .55 .45
421 A103 50fr lake, ol grn & ind   .90 .55
422 A105 65fr indigo & grnsh bl   1.25 .85
    Nos. 412-422,C51-C52 (13)   9.55 7.95

Centenary of the apparition of the Virgin Mary at Lourdes.
Sizes: Nos. 413-415, 419-420 26x36mm. No. 416 22x36mm. Nos. 417-418 48x36mm. No. 422 36x26mm.

Types of 1939-46 and 1955

1959   **Engr.**   **Perf. 13**
423 A32   5fr copper red   1.10 .55
424 A83   25fr orange & blk   1.10 .55
425 A83   30fr dark violet   4.25 2.10
426 A34   35fr dark blue   8.50 3.25
427 A83   50fr bl grn & rose cl 5.50 2.10
428 A31   85fr dk carmine rose   12.50 6.50
429 A33   100fr brt grnsh blue   12.50 6.50
    Nos. 423-429 (7)   45.45 21.55

Knight Type of 1954

1959
430 A79   8fr deep magenta   .75 .35
431 A79   20fr bright green   1.40 1.25
432 A79   40fr chocolate   2.75 1.10
433 A79   55fr ultra   4.50 2.75
    Nos. 430-433 (4)   9.40 5.45

Nos. 430-433 were issued precanceled only. See note after No. 324.

Princess Grace Polyclinic — A106

1959, May 16
434 A106 100fr gray, brn & grn   3.75 2.25
Opening of Princess Grace Hospital.

UNESCO Building, Paris, and Cultural Emblems — A107

50fr, UNESCO Building, children of various races.

1959, May 16
435 A107 25fr multicolored   .30 .30
436 A107 50fr ol, bl grn & blk brn .40 .40
Opening of UNESCO Headquarters in Paris, Nov. 3, 1958.

Rally Type of 1956

Design: 100fr, "Athens to Monaco."

1959, May 16
437 A98 100fr vio bl, red & sl
              grn, bl   6.50 5.50
28th Monte Carlo Automobile Rally.

Carnations — A108

Bougainvillea — A109

Flowers: 10fr on 3fr, Princess Grace Carnations. 15fr on 1fr, Mimosa, vert. 25fr on 6fr, Geranium, vert. 35fr, Oleander. 50fr, Jasmine. 85fr on 65fr, Lavender. 100fr, Grace de Monaco Rose.

1959, May 16
438 A108 5fr brn, Prus grn
              & rose car   .25 .25
439 A108 10fr on 3fr brn, grn
              & rose   .35 .25
440 A109 15fr on 1fr dk grn &
              cit   .35 .25
441 A109 20fr ol grn & mag   .90 .55
442 A109 25fr on 6fr yel grn
              & red   1.25 .75
443 A109 35fr dk grn & pink   2.50 1.75
444 A109 50fr brn & dk
              grn   3.00 2.10

445 A109 85fr on 65fr ol grn
              & gray vio   3.50 3.00
446 A108 100fr green & pink   4.75 4.25
    Nos. 438-446 (9)   16.85 13.15

Nos. 439-440, 442 and 445 were not issued without surcharge.

View of Monaco and Uprooted Oak Emblem — A110

1960, June 1   Unwmk.   Perf. 13
447 A110 25c bl, olive grn & sepia   .35 .25
World Refugee Year, 7/1/59-6/30/60.

Entrance to Oceanographic Museum — A111

Museum and Aquarium — A112

Designs: 15c, Museum conference room. 20c, Arrival of equipment, designed by Prince Albert I. 25c, Research on electrical qualities of cephalopodes. 50c, Albert I and vessels Hirondelle I and Princesse Alice.

1960, June 1   Engr.   Perf. 13
448 A111 5c blue, sepia & cl   .55 .25
449 A112 10c multicolored   .70 .35
450 A112 15c sep, ultra & bis   .70 .35
451 A112 20c rose lil, blk & bl 1.10 .55
452 A112 25c grnsh blue   2.25 1.60
453 A112 50c lt ultra & brown   2.50 1.75
    Nos. 448-453 (6)   7.80 4.85

Inauguration of the Oceanographic Museum of Monaco, 50th anniv. See #475.

Horse Jumping — A113

Sports: 10c, Women swimmers. 15c, Broad jumper. 20c, Javelin thrower. 25c, Girl figure skater. 50c, Skier.

1960, June 1
454 A113 5c dk brn, car & emer .25 .25
455 A113 10c red brn, bl & grn .25 .25
456 A113 15c dl red brn, ol &
              mag   .35 .35
457 A113 20c black, bl & grn   2.75 2.75
458 A113 25c dk grn & dull pur .90 .90

459 A113 50c dk bl, grnsh bl & dl
              pur   1.10 1.10
    Nos. 454-459 (6)   5.60 5.60

Nos. 454-457 for the 17th Olympic Games, Rome, Aug. 25-Sept. 11; Nos. 458-459 for the 8th Winter Olympic Games, Squaw Valley, Feb. 18-29.

Rally Type of 1956

Design: 25c, "Lisbon to Monte Carlo."

1960, June 1
460 A98 25c bl, brn & car, bluish 2.25 2.00
29th Monte Carlo Automobile Rally.

Stamps of Sardinia and France, 1860, and Stamp of Monaco, 1885 A114

1960, June 1   Engr. & Embossed
461 A114 25c violet, blue & ol   .80 .70
75th anniv. of postage stamps of Monaco.

Prince Rainier Type of 1955

1960   Engr.   Perf. 13
462 A83 25c orange & blk   .55 .25
463 A83 30c dark violet   .55 .25
464 A83 50c bl grn & rose lil 2.25 .35
465 A83 65c yel brn & slate 14.00 4.25
    Nos. 462-465 (4)   17.35 5.10

Knight Type of 1954

1960
466 A79 8c deep magenta   1.60 .55
467 A79 20c brt green   2.75 .55
468 A79 40c chocolate   4.50 1.10
469 A79 55c ultra   6.75 1.60
    Nos. 466-469 (4)   15.60 3.80

Nos. 466-469 were issued only precanceled. See note after No. 324.

Sea Horse — A115

#471 Cactus (Cereanee). #472, Cactus (Nopalea dejecta) #473, Scorpion fish, horiz.

1960, June 1
470 A115 15c org brn & sl grn   .80 .25
471 A115 15c ol grn, yel & brn .95 .25
472 A115 20c maroon & ol   .95 .25
473 A115 20c brn, red brn, red &
              ol   .80 .35
    Nos. 470-473 (4)   3.50 1.10

See Nos. 581-584.

Type of 1960 and

Palace of Monaco A116

Designs: 10c, Type A111 without inscription. 45c, Aerial view of Palace. 85c, Honor court. 1fr, Palace at night.

1960, June 1   Engr.
474 A116 5c green & sepia   .25 .25
475 A111 10c dk bl & vio brn .55 .35
476 A116 45c dl bl, sep & grn 6.75 .70
477 A116 85c slate, gray & bis 8.75 2.10
478 A116 1fr bl, red brn &
              sl grn   1.10 .40
    Nos. 474-478 (5)   17.40 3.80

See #585, 602, 729, 731, 731A, 790, 792.

Sphinx of Wadi-es-Sebua — A117

1961, June 3   Unwmk.   Perf. 13
479 A117 50c choc, dk bl &
ocher   1.25 .80
Issued as publicity to save historic monuments in Nubia.

Murena, Starfish, Sea Urchin, Sea Cucumber and Coral — A118

1961, June 3
480 A118 25c vio buff & dk red   .25 .25
Issued to commemorate the World Congress of Aquariology, Monaco, Nov. 1960.

Medieval Town and Leper — A119

1961, June 3
481 A119 25c ol gray, ocher & car .25 .25
Issued to honor the Sovereign Order of the Knights of Malta.

Hand and Ant A120

1961, June 3
482 A120 25c magenta & dp car .40 .40
Issued to publicize "Respect for Life."

Rally Type of 1956
Design: 1fr, "Stockholm to Monte Carlo."

1961, June 3
483 A98 1fr multicolored   1.50 1.50
30th Monte Carlo Automobile Rally.

Turcat-Mery, 1911 Winner, and 1961 Car — A121

1961, June 3
484 A121 1fr org brn, vio & rose
red   1.60 1.60
50th anniv. of the founding of the Monte Carlo Automobile Rally.

Chevrolet, 1912 A122

Automobiles (pre-1912): 2c, Peugeot. 3c, Fiat. 4c, Mercedes. 5c, Rolls Royce. 10c, Panhard-Levassor. 15c, Renault. 20c, Ford. 25c, Rochet-Schneider. 30c, FN-Herstal. 45c, De Dion Bouton. 50c, Buick. 65c, Delahaye. 1fr, Cadillac.

1961, June 13   **Engr.**
485 A122 1c org brn, dk brn
& grn   .25   .25
486 A122 2c org red, dk bl &
brn   .25   .25
487 A122 3c multicolored   .25   .25
488 A122 4c multicolored   .25   .25
489 A122 5c ol bis, sl grn &
car   .25   .25
490 A122 10c brn, sl & red   .25   .25
491 A122 15c grnsh bl & dk sl
grn   .25   .25
492 A122 20c pur, blk & red   .25   .25
493 A122 25c dk brn lil & red   .45   .45
494 A122 30c ol grn & dl pur 1.10 1.10
495 A122 45c multicolored 2.10 2.10
496 A122 50c brn blk, red &
ultra   2.10 2.10
497 A122 65c multicolored 3.25 3.25
498 A122 1fr brt pur, ind &
red   3.75 3.75
Nos. 485-498 (14)   14.75 14.75
See Nos. 648-661.

Bugatti, First Winner, and Course — A123

1962, June 6   Unwmk.   Perf. 13
499 A123 1fr lilac rose   1.50 1.50
20th Automobile Grand Prix of Monaco.

Rally Type of 1956
Design: 1fr, "Oslo to Monte Carlo."

1962, June 6
500 A98 1fr multicolored   1.50 1.50
31st Monte Carlo Automobile Rally.

Louis XII and Lucien Grimaldi A124

50c, Document granting sovereignty. 1fr, Seals of Louis XII & Lucien Grimaldi.

1962, June 6   **Engr.**
501 A124 25c ver, blk & vio bl   .30 .30
502 A124 50c dk bl, brn & mag   .45 .45
503 A124 1fr dk brn, grn & car   .70 .70
Nos. 501-503 (3)   1.45 1.45
450th anniversary of Monaco's reception of sovereignty from Louis XII.

Mosquito and Swamp A125

1962, June 6
504 A125 1fr brn ol & lt grn   .60 .60
WHO drive to eradicate malaria.

Aquatic Stadium at Night A126

1962, June 6
505 A126 10c dk bl, ind & grn   .25 .25

Sun, Flowers and Hope Chest A127

1962, June 6
506 A127 20c multicolored   .25 .25
Issued to publicize the National Multiple Sclerosis Society of New York.

Wheat Harvest A128

1962, June 6
507 A128 25c dk bl, red brn &
brn   .50 .30
508 A128 50c ind, ol bis & dk bl
grn   .50 .35
509 A128 1fr red lil & olive bister 1.00 .65
Nos. 507-509,C61 (4)   4.00 2.30
Europa. See No. C61.

Blood Donor's Arm and Globe A129

1962, Nov. 15   Engr.   Perf. 13
510 A129 1fr dk red, blk & orange .90 .90
3rd International Blood Donors' Congress, Nov. 15-18 at Monaco.

Yellow Wagtails — A130

Birds: 10c, European robins. 15c, European goldfinches. 20c, Blackcaps. 25c, Great spotted woodpeckers. 30c, Nightingale. 45c, Barn owls. 50c, Common starlings. 85c, Red crossbills. 1fr, White storks.

1962, Dec. 12   **Unwmk.**
511 A130 5c green, sep & yel   .25 .25
512 A130 10c bis, dk pur &
red   .25 .25
513 A130 15c multicolored   .35 .35
514 A130 20c mag, grn & blk   .45 .35
515 A130 25c multicolored   .55 .45
516 A130 30c brn, sl grn & bl   .85 .65
517 A130 45c vio & gldn brn 1.40 1.25
518 A130 50c bl grn, blk & yel 2.25 1.40
519 A130 85c multicolored 2.75 2.00
520 A130 1fr blk, grn & red 3.25 2.25
Nos. 511-520 (10)   12.35 9.20
Protection of useful birds.

Divers A131

10c, Galeazzi's turret, vert. 25c, Williamson's photosphere, 1914 & bathyscape "Trieste," 1962. 45c, Diving suits. 50c, Diving chamber. 85c, Fulton's "Nautilus," 1800 and modern submarine. 1fr, Alexander the Great's underwater chamber and bathysphere of the N. Y. Zoological Society.

1962, Dec. 12
521 A131 5c bluish grn, vio &
blk   .25 .25
522 A131 10c multicolored   .25 .25
523 A131 25c bis, bluish grn & sl
grn   .25 .25
524 A131 45c green, ind & blk   .45 .45
525 A131 50c cit & dk bl   .70 .70
526 A131 85c Prus grn & dk vio
bl   1.25 1.25
527 A131 1fr dk bl, dk brn & dk
grn   2.00 2.00
Nos. 521-527 (7)   5.15 5.15
Issued in connection with an exhibition at the Oceanographic Museum "Man Under Water," showing ancient and modern methods of under-water exploration.

Dancing Children and UN Emblem — A132

Children on Scales A133

Designs: 10c, Bird feeding nestlings, vert. 20c, Sun shining on children of different races, vert. 25c, Mother and child, vert. 50c, House and child. 95c, African mother and child, vert. 1fr, Prince Albert and Princess Caroline.

1963, May 3　　Unwmk.　　Perf. 13
528 A132　5c ocher, dk red & ul-
　　　tra　　　　　　　　　　.25　.25
529 A133　10c vio bl, emer & ol
　　　gray　　　　　　　　　　.25　.25
530 A133　15c ultra, red & grn　　.25　.25
531 A133　20c multicolored　　　.25　.25
532 A133　25c blue, brn & pink　.25　.25
533 A133　50c multicolored　　　.70　.45
534 A133　95c multicolored　　1.25　.70
535 A132　1fr multicolored　　2.00　1.25
　　Nos. 528-535 (8)　　　　5.20　3.65
　Publicizing the UN Children's Charter.

Figurehead with
Red Cross, Red
Crescent and Red
Lion and
Sun — A134

　1fr, Centenary emblem, Gustave Moynier,
Henri Dunant and Gen. Henri Dufour, horiz.

1963, May 3　　　　　　Engr.
536 A134　50c bluish grn, red & red
　　　brn　　　　　　　　.50　.50
537 A134　1fr blue, sl grn & red　.75　.75
　Centenary of International Red Cross.

Racing
Cars on
Monte
Carlo
Course
and Map of
Europe
A135

1963, May 3
538 A135　50c multicolored　　　.70　.45
　European Automobile Grand Prix.

Rally Type of 1956
　Design: 1fr, "Warsaw to Monte Carlo."

1963, May 3
539 A98　1fr multicolored　　1.50　1.50
　32nd Monte Carlo Auto Race.

Lions International Emblem — A136

1963, May 3
540 A136　50c bis, lt vio & bl　　.75　.60
　Issued to commemorate the founding of the
Lions Club of Monaco, Mar. 24, 1962.

Hôtel des Postes, Paris, and UPU
Allegory — A137

1963, May 3
541 A137　50c multicolored　　　　.60　.40
　1st Intl. Postal Conference, Paris, 1863.

Globe and
Telstar
A138

1963, May 3
542 A138　50c grn, dk pur & maroon .75　.50
　1st television connection of the US and
Europe through the Telstar satellite, July 11-
12, 1962.

Holy Spirit
over St.
Peter's and
World
A139

1963, May 3
543 A139　1fr grn, red brn & bl　　.75　.60
　Vatican II, the 21st Ecumenical Council of
the Roman Catholic Church.

Wheat
Emblem
and Dove
Feeding
Nestlings
A140

1963, May 3　　　　　　Engr.
544 A140　1fr multicolored　　　.80　.80
　FAO "Freedom from Hunger" campaign.

Henry Ford
and 1903
Model
A — A141

1963, Dec. 12　　Unwmk.　　Perf. 13
545 A141　20c slate grn & lil rose　.75　.50
　Centenary of the birth of Henry Ford, American automobile manufacturer.

Bicycle
Racer in
Town
A142

　Design: 50c, Bicyclist on country road.

1963, Dec. 12
546 A142　25c bl, sl grn & red brn　.50　.50
547 A142　50c bl, gray grn, & blk
　　　brn　　　　　　　　.50　.50
　50th anniv. of the Bicycle Tour de France.

Pierre de
Coubertin
and
Myron's
Discobolus
A143

1963, Dec. 12
548 A143　1fr dp cl, car & ocher　.75　.75
　Baron Pierre de Coubertin, organizer of the
modern Olympic Games, birth cent.

Rally Type of 1956
　Design: 1fr, "Paris to Monte Carlo."

1963, Dec. 12
549 A98　1fr multicolored　　1.10　1.10
　33rd Monte Carlo Automobile Rally.

Children
with Stamp
Album and
UNESCO
Emblem
A144

1963, Dec. 12
550 A144　50c dp ultra, red & vio　.45　.45
　International Philatelic and Educational
Exposition, Monaco, Nov.-Dec., 1963.

Europa Issue

Woman, Dove and
Lyre — A145

1963, Dec. 12
551 A145　25c brn, grn & car　1.50　.35
552 A145　50c dk brn, bl & car　2.00　.60

Wembley Stadium and British Football
Association Emblem — A146

Overhead
Kick
A147

Soccer
Game,
Florence,
16th
Century
A148

Tackle
A149

　Designs: 3c, Goalkeeper. 4c, Louis II Stadium and emblem of Sports Association of
Monaco, with black overprint: "Championnat
/1962-1963/Coupe de France." 15c, Soule
Game, Brittany, 19th century. 20c, Soccer,
England, 1827. 25c, Soccer, England, 1890.
50c, Clearing goal area. 95c, Heading the ball.
1fr, Kicking the ball.

1963, Dec. 12
553 A146　1c grn, vio & dk red　.25　.25
554 A147　2c black, red & grn　.25　.25
555 A147　3c gray ol, org & red　.25　.25
556 A146　4c bl, red, grn, pur &
　　　blk　　　　　　　　.25　.25
557 A148　10c dk bl, car & sep　.25　.25
558 A148　15c sepia & car　　　.25　.25

559 A148　20c sepia & dk bl　　.25　.25
560 A148　25c sepia & lilac　　.25　.25
　a.　　Block of 4　　　　1.00　1.00
561 A149　30c green, sep & red　.45　.45
562 A149　50c sepia, grn & red　.70　.70
563 A149　95c sepia, grn & red　1.00　1.00
564 A149　1fr sepia, grn & red　1.25　1.25
　a.　　Block of 4　　　　4.00　4.00
　Nos. 553-564 (12)　　　5.40　5.40
　Cent. of British Football Assoc. (organized
soccer). No. 556 also for the successes of the
soccer team of Monaco, 1962-63 (overprint
typographed). No. 556 was not regularly
issued without overprint. Value $750.
　The 4 stamps of No. 560a are connected by
an 1863 soccer ball in red brown; the stamps
of No. 564a by a modern soccer ball.

Design from 1914 Rally Post
Card — A150

Farman Biplane over Monaco — A151

　Designs: 3c, Nieuport monoplane. 4c,
Breguet biplane. 5c, Morane-Saulnier monoplane. 10c, Albatros biplane. 15c, Deperdussin monoplane. 20c, Vickers-Vimy biplane and
map (Ross Smith's flight London-Port Darwin,
1919). 25c, Douglas Liberty biplane (first
American around-the-world flight. 4 planes,
1924). 30c, Savoia S-16 hydroplane (De
Pinedo's Rome-Australia-Japan-Rome flight,
1925). 45c, Trimotor Fokker F-7 monoplane
(first aerial survey of North Pole, Richard E.
Byrd and James Gordon Bennett, 1925). 50c,
Spirit of St. Louis (first crossing of Atlantic,
New York-Paris, Charles Lindbergh, 1927).
65c, Breguet 19 (Paris-New York, Coste and
Bellonte, 1930). 95c, Laté 28 hydroplane (first
South Atlantic airmail route, Dakar-Natal,
1930). 1fr, Dornier DO-X, (Germany-Rio de
Janeiro, 1930).

1964, May 22　　Engr.　　Perf. 13
565 A150　1c green, bl & ol　　.25　.25
566 A151　2c bl, bis & red brn　.25　.25
567 A151　3c olive, grn & bl　　.25　.25
568 A151　4c red brn, bl &
　　　Prus grn　　　　　.25　.25
569 A151　5c gray ol, vio &
　　　mag　　　　　　　.25　.25
570 A151　10c violet, bl & ol　.25　.25
571 A151　15c blue, org & brn　.25　.25
572 A151　20c brt grn, blk & bl　.35　.25
573 A151　25c red, bl & ol　　.35　.35
574 A151　30c bl, sl grn & dp cl　.45　.45
575 A151　45c red brn, grnsh bl
　　　& blk　　　　　.75　.55
576 A151　50c purple, ol & bis　.90　.75
577 A151　65c steel bl, blk &
　　　red　　　　　1.20　1.00
578 A151　95c ocher, sl grn &
　　　red　　　　　1.60　1.25
579 A151　1fr sl grn, bl & vio
　　　brn　　　　　2.25　1.60
　Nos. 565-579,C64 (16)　12.35　10.70
　50th anniv. of the 1st airplane rally of Monte
Carlo. Nos. 565-571 show planes which took
part in the 1914 rally, Nos. 572-579 and C64
show important flights from 1919 to 1961.

Ancient Egyptian Message
Transmitters and Rocket — A152

1964, May 22 — Unwmk.
580 A152 1fr dk bl, indigo & org   .70 .70

Issued to publicize "PHILATEC", International Philatelic and Postal Techniques Exhibition, Paris, June 5-21, 1964.

Types of 1955-60
1c, Crab (Macrocheira Kampferi), horiz. 2c, Flowering cactus (Selenicereus Gr.). 12c, Shell (Fasciolaria trapezium). 18c, Aloe ciliaris. 70c, Honor court of palace (like #477). 95c, Prince Rainier III.

1964, May 19 — Perf. 13
581	A115	1c lt bl grn & dk red	.25 .25
582	A115	2c dk grn & multi	.25 .25
583	A115	12c vio & brn red	.50 .25
584	A115	18c grn, yel & car	.55 .25
585	A116	70c lt grn, choc & red org	.70 .40
586	A83	95c ultra	1.50 .50
		Nos. 581-586 (6)	3.75 1.90

Rainier III Aquatic Stadium — A153

1964-67 — Engr. — Perf. 13
587	A153	10c dk car, rose, bl & blk	1.75 .25
587A	A153	15c dk car, rose, brt bl & blk ('67)	1.00 .25
588	A153	25c dl grn, dk bl & blk	1.00 .25
589	A153	50c lil, bl grn & blk	1.75 1.00
		Nos. 587-589 (4)	5.50 1.75

Nos. 587-589 were issued precanceled only. See note after No. 324. The "1962" date has been obliterated with 2 bars. See Nos. 732-734, 793-796, 976-979.

Common Design Types pictured following the introduction.

Europa Issue, 1964
Common Design Type
1964, Sept. 12
Size: 22x34½mm
590	CD7	25c brt red, brt grn & dk grn	1.00 .25
591	CD7	50c ultra, ol bis & dk red brn	1.50 .45

Weight Lifter — A154

1964, Dec. 3 — Unwmk. — Perf. 13
592	A154	1c shown	.25 .25
593	A154	2c Judo	.25 .25
594	A154	3c Pole vault	.25 .25
595	A154	4c Archery	.25 .25
		Nos. 592-595 (4)	1.00 1.00

18th Olympic Games, Tokyo, 10/10-25. See #C65.

Pres. John F. Kennedy and Mercury Capsule — A155

1964, Dec. 3
596 A155 50c brt bl & indigo   .60 .60

Pres. John F. Kennedy (1917-63).

Television Set and View of Monte Carlo A156

1964, Dec. 3
597 A156 50c dk car rose, dk bl & brn   .50 .50

Fifth International Television Festival.

Frédéric Mistral, (1830-1914), Provençal Poet — A157

1964, Dec. 3 — Engr.
598 A157 1fr gray olive & brn red   .55 .55

Scales of Justice and Code A158

1964, Dec. 3
599 A158 1fr gldn brn & slate grn   .60 .60

Universal Declaration of Human Rights.

Rally Type of 1956
Design: 1fr, "Minsk to Monte Carlo."
1964, Dec. 3
600 A98 1fr bl grn, ocher & brn   1.00 1.00

34th Monte Carlo Automobile Rally.

International Football Association Emblem — A159

1964, Dec. 3
601 A159 1fr red, bl & ol bister   .85 .85

60th anniv. of FIFA, the Federation Internationale de Football (soccer).

Types of 1955 and 1960
Designs: 40c, Aerial view of palace. 60c, 1.30fr, 2.30fr, Prince Rainier III.

1965-66 — Engr. — Perf. 13
602	A116	40c sl grn, dl cl & brt grn	.75 .25
603	A83	60c sl grn & blk	1.10 .35
604	A83	1.30fr dk red & blk	3.25 .75
604A	A83	2.30fr org & rose lil ('66)	2.75 .75
		Nos. 602-604A (4)	7.85 2.10

Telstar and Pleumeur-Bodou Relay Station — A160

Alexander Graham Bell and Telephone A161

Designs (ITU Emblem and): 5c, Syncom II and Earth. 10c, Echo II and Earth. 12c, Relay satellite and Earth, vert. 18c, Lunik III and Moon. 50c, Samuel Morse and telegraph. 60c, Edouard Belin, belinograph and newspaper. 70c, Roman signal towers and Chappe telegraph. 95c, Cable laying ships; "The Great Eastern" (British, 1858) and "Alsace" (French, modern). 1fr, Edouard Branly, Guglielmo Marconi and map of English Channel.

1965, May 17
605	A161	5c vio bl & slate grn	.25 .25
606	A161	10c dk bl & sepia	.25 .25
607	A161	12c gray, brn & dk car	.25 .25
608	A161	18c ind, dk car & plum	.25 .25
609	A160	25c vio, ol & rose brn	.25 .25
610	A161	30c dk brn, ol & bis brn	.35 .35
611	A161	50c groon & indigo	.35 .35
612	A161	60c dl red brn & brt bl	.70 .70
613	A160	70c brn blk, org & dk bl	.85 .85
614	A160	95c indigo, blk & bl	1.00 1.00
615	A160	1fr brn, blk & ultra	1.40 1.40
		Nos. 605-615,C66 (12)	10.65 10.65

International Telecommunication Union, cent.

Europa Issue, 1965
Common Design Type
1965, Sept. 25 — Engr. — Perf. 13
Size: 36x22mm
616	CD8	30c red brn & grn	1.25 .65
617	CD8	60c violet & dk car	2.00 1.00

Palace of Monaco, 18th Century A162

Views of Palace: 12c, From the Bay, 17th century. 18c, Bay with sailboats, 18th century. 30c, From distance, 19th century. 60c, Close-up, 19th century. 1.30fr, Aerial view, 20th century.

1966, Feb. 1 — Engr. — Perf. 13
618	A162	10c vio, dl grn & ind	.25 .25
619	A162	12c bl, bis brn & dk brn	.25 .25
620	A162	18c blk, grn & bl	.25 .25
621	A162	30c vio bl, sep & red	.35 .35
622	A162	60c bl, grn & brn	.70 .70
623	A162	1.30fr dk grn & red brn	1.25 1.25
		Nos. 618-623 (6)	3.05 3.05

750th anniversary of Palace of Monaco.

Dante Alighieri — A163

Designs: 60c, Dante facing Panther of Envy. 70c, Dante and Virgil boating across muddy swamp of 5th Circle. 95c, Dante watching the arrogant and Cross of Salvation. 1fr, Invocation of St. Bernard; Dante and Beatrice.

1966, Feb. 1
624	A163	30c crimson & dp grn	.40 .40
625	A163	60c dl grn, Prus bl & ind	.75 .75
626	A163	70c black, sep & car	.90 .90
627	A163	95c red lilac & blue	1.40 1.40
628	A163	1fr ultra & bluish grn	1.50 1.50
		Nos. 624-628 (5)	4.95 4.95

700th anniv. (in 1965) of the birth of Dante (1265-1321), poet.

Rally Type of 1956
Design: 1fr, "London to Monte Carlo."
1966, Feb. 1
629 A98 1fr purple, red & indigo   .95 .75

The 35th Monte Carlo Automobile Rally.

Nativity by Gerard van Honthorst A164

1966, Feb. 1
630 A164 30c brown   .25 .25

Issued to honor the World Association for the Protection of Children.

Casino, Monte Carlo A165

View of La Condamine, 1860, and Francois Blanc — A166

Designs: 12c, Prince Charles III, vert. 40c, Charles III monument, Bowling Green Gardens. 60c, Seaside Promenade and Rainier III. 70c, René Blum, Sergei Diaghilev and "Petroushka". 95c, Jules Massenet and Camille Saint-Saens. 1.30fr, Gabriel Fauré and Maurice Ravel.

1966, June 1 — Engr. — Perf. 13
631	A165	12c dp blue, blk & mag	.25 .25
632	A165	25c multicolored	.25 .25
633	A166	30c bl, plum, grn & org	.25 .25
634	A165	40c multicolored	.25 .25
635	A166	60c multicolored	.45 .45
636	A166	70c rose cl & ind	.45 .45
637	A165	95c purple & blk	.75 .75
638	A165	1.30fr brn org, ol bis & brn	1.10 1.10
		Nos. 631-638,C68 (9)	6.50 6.50

Centenary of founding of Monte Carlo.

Europa Issue, 1966
Common Design Type
1966, Sept. 26 — Engr. — Perf. 13
Size: 21½x35½mm
639	CD9	30c orange	.75 .25
640	CD9	60c light green	1.25 .40

Prince Albert I, Yachts Hirondelle I and Princess Alice — A167

1966, Dec. 12   Engr.   Perf. 13
641 A167 1fr ultra & dk vio brn   .85 .85

1st Intl. Congress of the History of Oceanography, Monaco, Dec. 12-17. Issued in sheets of 10.

Red Chalk Drawing by Domenico Zampieri — A168

1966, Dec. 12
642 A168 30c brt rose & dk brn   .25 .25
643 A168 60c brt bl & yel brn   .35 .35

20th anniv. of UNESCO.

Television Screen and Cross over Monaco — A169

1966, Dec. 12
644 A169 60c dk car rose, lil & red   .35 .25

10th meeting of "UNDA," the International Catholic Association for Radio and Television.

Precontinent III and Divers on Ocean Floor — A170

1966, Dec. 12
645 A170 1fr Prus bl, yel & dk brn   .60 .35

First anniversary of the submarine research station Precontinent III.

WHO Headquarters, Geneva — A171

1966, Dec. 12
646 A171 30c dp bl, ol brn & dp bl grn   .25 .25
647 A171 60c dk grn, crim & dk brn   .35 .35

Opening of WHO Headquarters, Geneva.

Automobile Type of 1961
Automobiles (Previous Winners): 1c, Bugatti, 1931. 2c, Alfa Romeo, 1932. 5c, Mercedes, 1936. 10c, Maserati, 1948. 18c, Ferrari, 1955. 20c, Alfa Romeo, 1950. 25c, Maserati, 1957. 30c, Cooper-Climax, 1958.

40c, Lotus-Climax, 1960. 50c, Lotus-Climax, 1961. 60c, Cooper-Climax, 1962. 70c, B.R.M., 1963-66. 1fr, Walter Christie, 1907. 2.30fr, Peugeot, 1910.

1967, Apr. 28   Engr.   Perf. 13x12½
648 A122 1c ind, red & brt bl   .25 .25
649 A122 2c green, red & blk   .25 .25
650 A122 5c red, ind & gray   .25 .25
651 A122 10c violet, red & ind   .25 .25
652 A122 18c indigo & red   .45 .25
653 A122 20c dk grn, red & ind   .25 .25
654 A122 25c ultra, red & ind   .35 .25
655 A122 30c brown, ind & grn   .45 .35
656 A122 40c car rose, ind & grn   .55 .45
657 A122 50c lilac, ind & grn   .75 .45
658 A122 60c carmine, ind & grn   1.00 .55
659 A122 70c dl yel, bl grn & ind   1.25 1.00
660 A122 1fr brn red, blk & gray   1.50 1.10
661 A122 2.30fr multicolored   2.75 2.25
Nos. 648-661,C73 (15)   12.70 10.30

25th Grand Prix of Monaco, May 7.

Dog, Egyptian Statue — A172

1967, Apr. 28   Perf. 12½x13
662 A172 30c dk grn, brn & blk   .50 .40

Congress of the International Dog Fanciers Federation, Monaco, Apr. 5-9.

View of Monte Carlo — A173

1967, Apr. 28   Perf. 13
663 A173 30c slate grn, brt bl & brn   .40 .40

International Tourist Year, 1967.

Chessboard and Monte Carlo Harbor — A174

1967, Apr. 28
664 A174 60c brt bl, dk pur & blk   .85 .85

International Chess Championships, Monaco, Mar. 19-Apr. 1.

Melvin Jones, View of Monte Carlo and Lions Emblem — A175

1967, Apr. 28
665 A175 60c ultra, slate bl & choc   .60 .40

50th anniversary of Lions International.

Rotary Emblem and View of Monte Carlo — A176

1967, Apr. 28
666 A176 1fr brt bl & lt ol grn   .60 .50

Issued to publicize the Rotary International Convention, Monaco, May 21-26.

EXPO '67 Monaco Pavilion — A177

1967, Apr. 28
667 A177 1fr multicolored   .55 .45

EXPO '67, International Exhibition, Montreal, Apr. 28-Oct. 27, 1967.

Map of Europe A178

1967, Apr. 28
668 A178 1fr choc, lemon & Prus bl   .55 .45

Issued to publicize the International Committee for European Migration, CIME.

Europa Issue, 1967
Common Design Type

1967, Apr. 28   Perf. 12½x13
669 CD10 30c brt car, rose lil & brt vio   1.00 .30
670 CD10 60c grn ol & bl grn   1.75 .40

Skier and Olympic Emblem — A179

1967, Dec. 7   Engr.   Perf. 13
671 A179 2.30fr red brn, gray & brt bl   1.50 1.10

10th Winter Olympic Games, Grenoble, France, Feb. 6-18, 1968.

Sounding Line and Map — A180

1967, Dec. 7
672 A180 1fr dk bl, grn & ol   .55 .45

9th International Hydrographic Conference, Monte Carlo, April-May, 1967.

Marie Curie, Chemical Apparatus and Atom Symbol — A181

1967, Dec. 7
673 A181 1fr brn, ultra & ol   .70 .50

Marie Curie (1867-1934), discoverer of radium and polonium.

Princes of Monaco Issue

Rainier I, by Eugene Charpentier — A182

#675, Lucien Grimaldi, by Ambrogio di Predis.

1967, Dec. 7   Perf. 12x13
674 A182 1fr multicolored   .90 .90
675 A182 1fr multicolored   .90 .90

See Nos. 710-711, 735-736, 774-775, 813-814, 860-861, 892-893, 991-992, 1035-1036, 1093, 1135-1136, 1187-1188, 1246-1247, 1302-1303.

Shot Put — A183

Sport: 30c, High jump. 60c, Gymnast on rings. 70c, Water polo. 1fr, Wrestling. 2.30fr, Gymnast.

1968, Apr. 29   Engr.   Perf. 13
676 A183 20c brt bl, grn & brn   .25 .25
677 A183 30c vio bl, sep & brn vio   .25 .25
678 A183 60c car, brt rose lil & dp bl   .35 .35
679 A183 70c ocher, brn org & Prus bl   .35 .35
680 A183 1fr brn org, brn & ind   .55 .55
681 A183 2.30fr dk car, vio bl & ol   1.10 1.10
Nos. 676-681,C74 (7)   4.60 4.60

19th Olympic Games, Mexico City, 10/12-27.

St. Martin and the Beggar A184

1968, Apr. 29
682 A184 2.30fr brn red, Prus bl & blk brn 1.25 1.00

Red Cross of Monaco, 20th anniversary.

Anemones, by Raoul Dufy — A185

1968, Apr. 29 Photo. Perf. 12x13
683 A185 1fr lt blue & multi .75 .60

International Flower Show in Monte Carlo. See Nos. 766, 776, 815-816, 829, 865.

Arms of Pope Pius IX and Prince Charles III — A186

St. Nicholas — A187

Designs: 30c, St. Benedict. 60c, Benedictine Monastery, Subiaco (Italy). 1fr, Church of St. Nicholas, Monaco, 13th century, horiz.

Perf. 12½x13, 13x12½
1968, Apr. 29 Engr.
684 A186 10c red & brown .25 .25
685 A187 20c sl grn, ocher & car .35 .25
686 A187 30c ultra & ol grn .35 .25
687 A187 60c lt bl, brn & dk grn .35 .35
688 A187 1fr ind, bl & ol bis .55 .45
Nos. 684-688 (5) 1.75 1.55

Centenary of the elevation of St. Nicholas Church to an Abbey *Nullius*, directly subject to the Holy See.

Europa Issue, 1968
Common Design Type
1968, Apr. 29 Perf. 13
Size: 36x22mm
689 CD11 30c dp orange & car .90 .25
690 CD11 60c carmine & ultra 2.25 .30
691 CD11 1fr green & red brn 2.25 .40
Nos. 689-691 (3) 5.40 .95

Locomotive 030, 1868 — A188

Locomotives and Views: 30c, Type "C"-220, 1898. 60c, Type 230-"C", 1910. 70c, Type 231-"F," 1925. 1fr, Type 241-"A", 1932. 2.30fr, Type "BB," 1968.

1968, Dec. 12 Engr. Perf. 13
692 A188 20c vio bl, brn & blk .70 .35
693 A188 30c dk ol grn, bl & blk .70 .55
694 A188 60c bl, bis & blk 1.10 1.00
695 A188 70c vio, red brn & blk 2.10 1.40
696 A188 1fr bl, brn red & blk 3.25 2.40
697 A188 2.30fr sal pink, brt bl & blk 5.00 3.50
Nos. 692-697 (6) 12.85 9.20

Centenary of the Nice-Monaco Railroad.

Chateaubriand and Combourg Castle — A189

Scenes from Chateaubriand Novels: 20c, The Genius of Christianity. 25c, René. 30c, The Last Abencerage. 60c, The Martyrs. 2.30fr, Atala.

1968, Dec. 12
698 A189 10c dk grn, grn & pur .25 .25
699 A189 20c brt bl, vio & mag .25 .25
700 A189 25c slate, pur & brn .25 .25
701 A189 30c dp brn, brn & pur .25 .25
702 A189 60c brn red, bl grn & dk brn .35 .35
703 A189 2.30fr dk bl, ol & mag 1.10 1.10
Nos. 698-703 (6) 2.45 2.45

Vicomte François René de Chateaubriand (1768-1848), novelist and statesman.

"France" and "Fidelity" by Bosio — A190

François Joseph Bosio (1768-1845), Sculptor — A191

25c, Henri IV as a boy. 60c, Louis XIV on horseback, Place des Victoires. 2.30fr, Busts of Louis XVIII, Napoleon I and Charles X.

1968, Dec. 12
704 A190 20c brown .25 .25
705 A191 25c sal pink & dk brn .25 .25
706 A191 30c slate & vio bl .25 .25
707 A191 60c dk ol grn & gray grn .55 .35
708 A190 2.30fr black & slate 1.00 .90
Nos. 704-708 (5) 2.30 2.00

WHO Emblem — A192

1968, Dec. 12 Photo.
709 A192 60c multicolored .35 .25

World Health Organization, 20th anniv.

Princes of Monaco Type of 1967

Designs: 1fr, Charles II (1581-89). 2.30fr, Jeanne Grimaldi (1596-1620).

1968, Dec. 12 Engr. Perf. 12x13
710 A182 1fr multicolored .70 .70
711 A182 2.30fr multicolored 1.10 1.10

Faust and Mephistopheles — A193

Scenes from "Damnation of Faust" by Berlioz: 10c, Rakoczy March. 25c, Auerbach's Cellar. 30c, Dance of the Sylphs. 40c, Dance of the Sprites. 50c, Faust and Marguerite. 70c, Woods and Meadows. 1fr, The Ride to the Abyss. 1.15fr, Heaven.

1969, Apr. 26 Engr. Perf. 13
712 A193 10c bl grn, pur & org brn .25 .25
713 A193 20c mag, dk ol & lt brn .25 .25
714 A193 25c ind, brn & mag .25 .25
715 A193 30c yel grn, sl & blk .25 .25
716 A193 40c org red, sl & blk .25 .25
717 A193 50c ol, plum & sl .35 .25
718 A193 70c dp grn, sl & lt brn .45 .35
719 A193 1fr mag, blk & ol bis .45 .45
720 A193 1.15fr Prus bl, blk & ultra .70 .70
Nos. 712-720,C75 (10) 4.45 4.25

Hector Berlioz (1803-69), French composer.

St. Elizabeth and Husband, Louis IV, Landgrave of Thuringia A194

1969, Apr. 26
721 A194 3fr dk red, slate & gray 1.60 1.40

Issued for the Red Cross.

See Nos. 767, 812, 830, 905, 963, 1037, 1094, 1189.

Europa Issue, 1969
Common Design Type
1969, Apr. 26
Size: 36x26mm
722 CD12 40c scarlet & purple 2.00 .30
723 CD12 70c brt blue & blk 4.25 .85
724 CD12 1fr yel bis, brn & bl 4.25 .85
Nos. 722-724 (3) 10.50 2.00

Prince Rainier Type of 1955 and Palace Type of 1960

Designs: 80c, Aerial view of Palace. 1.15fr, 1.30fr, Honor Court.

1969-70 Engr. Perf. 13
725 A83 40c olive & rose red .70 .25
726 A83 45c slate & ocher .70 .25
727 A83 50c ocher & mar .70 .35
728 A83 70c dk pur & brt vio bl 1.40 .70
729 A116 80c bl, red brn & grn 1.90 .70
730 A83 85c dk vio & brt grn 1.90 1.25
731 A116 1.15fr blk, bl & mar 2.75 1.60
731A A116 1.30fr ol brn, lt bl & dl grn ('70) 1.50 1.50
Nos. 725-731A (8) 11.55 6.60

Aquatic Stadium Type of 1964-67, "1962" Omitted

1969 Perf. 13
732 A153 22c choc, brt bl & blk .50 .25
733 A153 35c Prus bl, brt bl & blk .50 .25
734 A153 70c black & vio bl .80 .35
Nos. 732-734 (3) 1.80 .85

Nos. 732-734 were issued precanceled only. See note after No. 324.

Princes of Monaco Type of 1967

Designs: 1fr, Honoré II (1604-1662), by Philippe de Champaigne. 3fr, Louise-Hippolyte (1697-1731), by Pierre Gobert.

1969, Nov. 25 Engr. Perf. 12x13
735 A182 1fr multicolored .60 .60
736 A182 3fr multicolored 1.25 1.25

Woman's Head, by Leonardo da Vinci — A195

Drawings by Leonardo da Vinci: 40c, Self-portrait. 70c, Head of old man. 80c, Study for head of St. Magdalene. 1.15fr, Man's head. 3fr, Professional soldier.

1969, Nov. 25 Perf. 13
737 A195 30c dull brown .25 .25
738 A195 40c brn & rose red .35 .25
739 A195 70c gray green .35 .25
740 A195 80c dk brown .45 .35
741 A195 1.15fr orange brn .75 .55
742 A195 3fr olive brown 1.75 1.20
Nos. 737-742 (6) 3.90 2.85

Leonardo da Vinci (1452-1519), Florentine painter, sculptor and scientist.

Alphonse Daudet and Scenes from "Letters from My Windmill" — A196

Various Scenes from "Letters from My Windmill" (Lettres de Mon Moulin).

1969, Nov. 25
743 A196 30c blue grn & multi .25 .25
744 A196 40c brn, vio bl & ol .35 .35
745 A196 70c pur, brn & ol gray .45 .35
746 A196 80c sl grn, vio bl & mar .55 .45
747 A196 1.15fr ocher, sep & blk .70 .70
Nos. 743-747 (5) 2.30 2.10

Centenary of publication of "Letters from My Windmill," by Alphonse Daudet (1840-1897).

ILO
Emblem
A197

1969, Nov. 25   Perf. 13x12½
748 A197 40c dk blue & dk pur   .35 .30
50th anniv. of the ILO.

World Map
and JCI
Emblem
A198

1969, Nov. 25
749 A198 40c olive, dk bl & bl   .35 .25
25th anniversary of the Junior Chamber of Commerce in Monaco.

Television
Camera
and View
of Monte
Carlo
A199

1969, Nov. 25
750 A199 40c red brn, lil & bl   .35 .25
10th International Television Festival in 1970.

King Alfonso
XIII, Prince
Albert I and
Underwater
Scene — A200

1969, Nov. 25   Perf. 12½x13
751 A200 40c dk brn, blk & grnsh bl .45 .45
50th anniv. of the International Commission for the Scientific Exploration of the Mediterranean.

Congress
Building,
Princes
Albert I
and
Rainier
III — A201

1970, Feb. 21   Engr.   Perf. 13
752 A201 40c gray & carmine   .35 .25
Meeting of the Interparliamentary Union, Monaco, Mar. 30-Apr. 5.

EXPO '70
Emblem,
Japanese
Scroll — A202

Designs (EXPO '70 Emblem and): 30c, Red-crowned crane. 40c, Torii. 70c, Cherry blossoms, horiz. 1.15fr, Palace and arms of Monaco, Osaka Castle and arms, horiz.

1970, Mar. 16
753 A202 20c brn, yel grn & car   .25 .25
754 A202 30c brn, yel grn & buff   .25 .25
755 A202 40c olive bis & pur   .35 .35
756 A202 70c lt gray & red   .70 .70
757 A202 1.15fr red & multi   .75 .75
    Nos. 753-757 (5)   2.30 2.30

Issued to publicize EXPO '70 International Exposition, Osaka, Japan, Mar. 15-Sept. 13.

Harbor
Seal Pup
A203

1970, Mar. 16
758 A203 40c red lil, bl & gray   .75 .55
Protection of seal pups.

Doberman
Pinscher
A204

1970, Apr. 25
759 A204 40c ocher & black   1.65 .75
International Dog Show, Monte Carlo, Apr. 25. See No. 996.

Basque
Ponies
A205

Designs: 30c, Parnassius Apollo butterfly. 50c, Harbor seal in Somme Bay. 80c, Pyrenean chamois, vert. 1fr, Whitetailed sea eagles, vert. 1.15fr, European otter, vert.

1970, May 4
760 A205 30c Prus bl & multi   .40 .25
761 A205 40c blue & multi   .65 .35
762 A205 50c grnsh bl, bis & brn   .90 .50
763 A205 80c gray grn, sl bl & brn   1.90 1.00
764 A205 1fr gray, brown & bis   2.50 2.00
765 A205 1.15fr dk brn, lt bl & yel grn   3.25 2.25
    Nos. 760-765 (6)   9.60 6.35

20th anniversary of the International Federation of Animal Protection.

Flower Type of 1968
Roses and Anemones, by Vincent van Gogh.

1970, May 4   Photo.   Perf. 12x13
766 A185 3fr black & multi   2.00 1.75
International Flower Show, Monte Carlo.

Red Cross Type of 1969
3fr, St. Louis giving alms to the poor.

1970, May 4   Engr.   Perf. 13
767 A194 3fr dk gray, ol gray & slate grn   1.50 1.50
Issued for the Red Cross.

Europa Issue, 1970
Common Design Type

1970, May 4
Size: 26x36mm
768 CD13 40c deep rose lilac   .85 .30
769 CD13 80c bright green   2.75 .90
770 CD13 1fr deep blue   2.75 .90
    Nos. 768-770 (3)   6.35 2.10

UPU Headquarters and Monument,
Bern — A206

1970, May 4
771 A206 40c brn ol, gray & bl grn .25 .25
New UPU Headquarters in Bern opening.

Plaque and Flag on the Moon,
Presidents Kennedy and
Nixon — A207

Design: 80c, Astronauts and landing module on moon, and Apollo 11 emblem.

1970, May 4   Photo.
772 A207 40c multicolored   .60 .50
773 A207 80c multicolored   .80 .70

Man's first landing on moon, July 20, 1969. US astronauts Neil A. Armstrong and Col. Edwin E. Aldrin, Jr., with Lt. Col. Michael Collins piloting Apollo 11.

Princes of Monaco Type of 1967
Designs: 1fr, Louis I (1662-1701), by Jean Francois de Troy. 3fr, Charlotte de Gramont (1639-1678), by Sebastian Bourdon.

1970, Dec. 15   Engr.   Perf. 12x13
774 A182 1fr multicolored   .55 .55
775 A182 3fr multicolored   1.25 1.25

Painting Type of 1968
Design: 3fr, Portrait of Dédie, by Amedeo Modigliani (1884-1920).

1970, Dec. 15
776 A185 3fr multicolored   2.75 2.00

Beethoven
and "Ode
to Joy"
A208

1970, Dec. 15
777 A208 1.30fr brown & maroon 2.25 1.10
Ludwig van Beethoven (1770-1827), composer.

Dumas and Scene from "Three
Musketeers" — A209

Designs: 40c, Henri Rougier and biplane over Monaco. 80c, Alphonse de Lamartine and scenes from his works.

1970, Dec. 15
778 A209 30c blue, brown & gray   .35 .25
779 A209 40c blue, sepia & gray   .35 .25
780 A209 80c multicolored   .45 .35
    Nos. 778-780 (3)   1.15 .85

Alexandre Dumas, père (1802-70), novelist; 1st flight over the Mediterranean by Henri Rougier, 60th anniv.; publication of "Méditations Poétiques" by Alphonse de Lamartine (1790-1869), poet, 150th anniv.

Camargue
Horse
A210

Horses: 20c, Anglo-Arabian thoroughbred. 30c, French saddle horse. 40c, Lippizaner. 50c, Trotter. 70c, English thoroughbred. 85c, Arabian. 1.15fr, Barbary.

1970, Dec. 15   Engr.   Perf. 13
781 A210 10c ol, ol bis & dk bl   .35 .25
782 A210 20c vio bl, brn & ol   .35 .25
783 A210 30c blue, brn & grn   .70 .45
784 A210 40c gray, ind & ol bis   1.40 .70
785 A210 50c blue, dk brn & ol   1.75 1.00
786 A210 70c dk grn, ol brn & red brn   3.25 2.00
787 A210 85c dk grn, ol & sl   3.25 2.25
788 A210 1.15fr blue, emer & blk   3.25 2.25
    Nos. 781-788,C77 (9)   16.30 11.15

**Prince Rainier Type of 1955 and
Palace Type of 1960**
90c, Honor Court. 1.40fr, Aerial view of Palace.

1971   Engr.   Perf. 13
789 A83 60c plum & blk   2.75 .70
790 A116 90c dk car, ultra & blk   2.75 .75
791 A83 1.10fr gray & ultra   3.25 1.60
792 A116 1.40fr pur, org & grn   3.25 2.40
    Nos. 789-792 (4)   12.00 5.45

**Aquatic Stadium Type of 1964-67,
"1962" Omitted**
1971
793 A153 26c pur, ultra & blk   .45 .25
794 A153 30c cop red, bl, lil & blk   .55 .25
795 A153 45c sl grn, vio bl & blk   .90 .35
796 A153 90c ol, Prus bl & blk   1.40 .55
    Nos. 793-796 (4)   3.30 1.40

Nos. 793-796 were issued precanceled only. See note after No. 324.
For surcharges, see Nos. 976-979.

Europa Issue, 1971
Common Design Type

1971, Sept. 6
797 CD14 50c carmine rose   2.50 .50
798 CD14 80c brt blue   6.25 .80
799 CD14 1.30fr slate green   6.25 1.50
    Nos. 797-799 (3)   15.00 2.80

Old Bridge at Sospel — A211

80c, Roquebrune Castle. 1.30fr, Grimaldi Castle. 3fr, Roman Monument, La Turbie, vert. All views in Alpes-Maritimes Department, France.

1971, Sept. 6
800 A211 50c sl grn, bl & ol brn   .25 .25
801 A211 80c sl grn, sl & brn   .45 .25
802 A211 1.30fr brn, sl grn & red   .55 .45
803 A211 3fr brt bl, sl & olive   1.50 1.10
    Nos. 800-803 (4)   2.75 2.05

Protection of historic monuments.

Theodolite, Underwater Scene and
Coast Line — A212

1971, Sept. 6
804 A212 80c blue grn & multi .55 .45
International Hydrographical Bureau, 50th
anniv.

Sea Bird
Covered with
Oil — A213

1971, Sept. 6
805 A213 50c dp blue & indigo .55 .45
Against pollution of the seas.

"Arts" (Organ Pipes and
Michelangelo's Creation of
Adam) — A214

"Science"
(Alchemist,
Radar and
Rocket) — A215

Design: 80c, "Culture" (medieval scholar,
book, film and television).

1971, Sept. 6   Engr.   Perf. 13
806 A214 30c brt bl, pur & brn .25 .25
807 A215 50c slate & brn org .35 .25
808 A214 80c emerald & brn .35 .35

Prince Pierre of
Monaco — A216

1971, Sept. 6 Photo.   Perf. 12½x13
809 A216 1.30fr gray green .70 .45
Nos. 806-809 (4) 1.65 1.30
25th anniv. of UNESCO.

Cocker
Spaniel
A217

1971, Sept. 6   Perf. 13x12½
810 A217 50c multicolored 2.50 1.60
Intl. Dog Show. See Nos. 826, 879, 910.

Hand
Holding
Blood
Donor
Emblem
A218

1971, Sept. 6   Engr.   Perf. 13
811 A218 80c red, violet & gray .45 .45
7th International Blood Donors Congress,
Monaco, Oct. 21-24.

Red Cross Type of 1969
3fr, St. Vincent de Paul appearing to
prisoners.

1971, Sept. 6
812 A194 3fr bl grn, ol grn & dp
grn 1.40 1.25

Princes of Monaco Type of 1967
Designs: 1fr, Antoine I (1701-1731), by
Hyacinthe Rigaud. 3fr, Marie de Lorraine
(1674-1724), French School.

1972, Jan. 18   Perf. 12x13
813 A182 1fr multicolored .70 .70
814 A182 3fr multicolored 1.40 1.40

Painting Type of 1968
Designs: 2fr, The Cradle, by Berthe
Morisot. 3fr, Clown, by Jean Antoine Watteau.

1972, Jan. 18
815 A185 2fr green & multi 1.60 1.00
816 A185 3fr multicolored 2.25 1.60
No. 815 issued for 25th anniv. (in 1971) of
UNICEF.

Christ
Before
Pilate, by
Dürer
A219

1972, Jan. 18   Perf. 13
817 A219 2fr lt brown & blk 1.40 1.10
500th anniv. of the birth of Albrecht Dürer
(1471-1528), German painter and engraver.

La Fontaine and
Animals — A220

Saint-Saens and "Samson et
Dalila" — A221

1.30fr, Charles Baudelaire, nudes and cats.

1972, Jan. 18
818 A220 50c brn, grn & sl grn .65 .35
819 A221 90c dk brn & yel brn .60 .45
820 A220 1.30fr blk, red & vio
brn .95 .70
Nos. 818-820 (3) 2.20 1.50
350th anniv. of the birth of Jean de La Fontaine (1621-1695), fabulist; 50th anniv. of the death of Camille Saint-Saens (1835-1921), composer; 150th anniv. of the birth of Charles Baudelaire (1821-1867), poet.

Father Christmas
A222

1972, Jan. 18
821 A222 30c bis, slate bl & red .25 .25
822 A222 50c vio brn, grn & red .25 .25
823 A222 90c ocher, indigo & red .55 .35
Nos. 821-823 (3) 1.05 .85
Christmas 1971.

Battle of Lepanto — A223

1972, Jan. 18
824 A223 1fr dull bl, red & brn .65 .45
400th anniversary of the Battle of Lepanto
against the Turks.

Steam and Diesel Locomotives, UIC
Emblem — A224

1972, Apr. 27   Engr.   Perf. 13
825 A224 50c dk car, lilac & choc 1.00 .75
50th anniversary of the founding of the International Railroad Union (UIC).

Dog Type of 1971
1972, Apr. 27 Photo.   Perf. 13x12½
826 A217 60c Great Dane 2.50 1.60
International Dog Show.

Serene Landscape, Pollution,
Destruction — A225

1972, Apr. 27   Engr.   Perf. 13
827 A225 90c grn, brn & blk .70 .45
Anti-pollution fight.

Ski Jump, Sapporo '72
Emblem — A226

1972, Apr. 27
828 A226 90c bl grn, dk red & blk .70 .55
11th Winter Olympic Games, Sapporo,
Japan, Feb. 3-13.

Flower Type of 1968
3fr, Flowers in Vase, by Paul Cezanne.

1972, Apr. 27   Photo.   Perf. 12x13
829 A186 3fr multicolored 0.25 2.75
International Flower Show, Monte Carlo.

Red Cross Type of 1969
3fr, St. Francis of Assisi comforting poor
man.

1972, Apr. 27   Engr.   Perf. 13
830 A194 3fr dk purple & brn 1.75 1.40
For the Red Cross.

Europa Issue 1972
Common Design Type

1972, Apr. 27   Perf. 12½x13
Size: 26x36mm
831 CD15 50c vio blue & org 1.75 .60
832 CD15 90c vio blue & emer 3.25 .80

Church of
Sts. John
and Paul
(detail), by
Canaletto
A227

Designs: 60c, Church of St. Peter of Castello, by Francesco Guardi. 2fr, St. Mark's Square, by Bernardo Bellotto.

1972, Apr. 27   Perf. 13
Sizes: 36x48mm (30c, 2fr);
26½x48mm (60c)
833 A227 30c rose red .40 .25
834 A227 60c brt purple .50 .35
835 A227 2fr Prus blue 1.90 1.25
Nos. 833-835 (3) 2.80 1.85
UNESCO campaign to save Venice.

A259

Floral
Arrangements
A260

1974, Nov. 12   **Perf. 13x12½**
931 A259 70c multicolored   1.00 .70
932 A260 1.10fr multicolored   1.60 1.10

International Flower Show, Monte Carlo,
May 1975. See Nos. 1003-1004, 1084-1085.

Prince
Rainier III — A261

1974-78		**Engr.**	**Perf. 13**	
933	A261	60c slate green	1.25	.35
934	A261	80c red	1.25	.45
935	A261	80c brt green	.55	.25
936	A261	1fr brown	3.25	1.10
937	A261	1fr scarlet	.75	.25
938	A261	1fr slate green	.60	.25
939	A261	1.20fr violet bl	7.75	2.50
940	A261	1.20fr red	.70	.25
941	A261	1.25fr blue	1.40	1.00
942	A261	1.50fr black	.90	.70
943	A261	1.70fr dp blue	1.00	.70
944	A261	2fr dk purple	2.75	1.60
945	A261	2.10fr olive bister	1.40	.75
946	A261	2.50fr indigo	2.25	1.60
947	A261	9fr brt violet	5.50	3.50
		Nos. 933-947 (15)	31.30	15.25

Issued: 60c, #934, 936, 939, 2fr, Dec. 23;
#935, 937, 1.25fr, 2.50fr, Jan. 10, 1977; #938,
940, 1.50fr, 1.70fr, 2.10fr, 9fr, Aug. 18, 1978.
See Nos. 1200-1204, 1255-1256.

Monte
Carlo
Beach
A262

Prince Albert I
Statue and
Museum — A264

1974-77
948	A262	25c shown	2.50	.55
949	A264	50c Clock tower	2.50	.55
950	A262	1.10fr Like #948 ('77)	2.10	1.10
951	A264	1.40fr shown	3.25	1.00
952	A262	1.70fr All Saints' Tower	4.50	2.40
953	A264	3fr Fort Antoine	6.50	2.50
954	A262	5.50fr La Condamine (view)	9.25	5.00
		Nos. 948-954 (7)	30.60	13.10

Issue: 1.10fr, Jan. 10; others, Dec. 23.
See Nos. 1005-1008, 1030-1033, 1069-
1072, 1095-1098, 1138-1152.

Haageocereus
A265

1974, Dec. 23   **Photo.**   **Perf. 12½x13**
955	A265	10c shown	.25	.25
956	A265	20c Matucana	.35	.25
957	A265	30c Parodia	.55	.35
958	A265	85c Mediolobivia	2.25	1.10
959	A265	1.90fr Matucana	3.75	2.50
960	A265	4fr Echinocereus	6.00	4.25
		Nos. 955-960 (6)	13.15	8.70

Plants from Monaco Botanical Gardens.

Europa Issue

Sailor, by
Philibert
Florence — A266

St. Dévote, by
Ludovic
Brea — A267

1975, May 13   **Engr.**   **Perf. 13**
961	A266	80c brt red lilac	1.75	.50
962	A267	1.20fr brt blue	2.25	.85
a.		Souv. sheet, 5 ea #961-962	40.00	20.00

Red Cross Type of 1969

Design: St. Bernardino of Siena (1380-
1444) burying the dead.

1975, May 13
963 A194 4fr pur & Prus bl   2.75 1.75

For the Red Cross.

Carmen, at
the Tavern
A268

Scenes from Carmen: 30c, Prologue, vert.
80c, The smugglers' hide-out. 1.40fr, Entrance
to bull ring.

1975, May 13
964	A268	30c multicolored	.25	.25
965	A268	60c multicolored	.40	.25
966	A268	80c multicolored	.85	.45
967	A268	1.40fr multicolored	1.25	.90
		Nos. 964-967 (4)	2.75	1.85

Centenary of first performance of opera
Carmen by George Bizet (1838-1875).

Louis de Saint-
Simon
A269

Albert Schweitzer
A270

1975, May 13
968 A269 40c bluish black   .40 .30
969 A270 60c black & dull red   .85 .40

300th birth anniversary of Louis de Saint-
Simon (1675-1755), statesman and writer, and
birth centenary of Albert Schweitzer (1875-
1965), medical missionary.

ARPHILA 75 Emblem, G Clef — A271

1975, May 13
970 A271 80c sepia & org brn   .70 .45

ARPHILA 75 International Philatelic Exhibition, Paris, June 6-16.

Seagull and
Rising Sun
A272

1975, May 13   **Photo.**
971 A272 85c multicolored   .85 .65

Oceanexpo 75, International Exhibition, Okinawa, July 20, 1975-Jan. 1976.

Charity
Label and
"1f"
Destroying
Cancer
A273

1975, May 13   **Engr.**
972 A273 1fr multicolored   .85 .60

Fight against cancer.

Jesus with Crown
of Thorns, Holy
Year
Emblem — A274

1975, May 13
973 A274 1.15fr lilac, bis & ind   1.00 .70

Holy Year 1975.

Villa
Sauber, by
Charles
Garnier
A275

1975, May 13
974 A275 1.20fr multicolored   1.10 .70

European Architectural Heritage Year 1975.

Woman,
Globe, IWY
Emblem
A276

1975, May 13
975 A276 1.20fr multicolored   1.10 .70

International Women's Year.

Nos. 793-796 Surcharged

1975, Apr. 1   **Engr.**   **Perf. 13**
976	A153	42c on 26c multi	2.50	1.10
977	A153	48c on 30c multi	3.25	1.75
978	A153	70c on 45c multi	3.75	2.25
979	A153	1.35fr on 90c multi	5.75	3.00
		Nos. 976-979 (4)	15.25	8.10

Nos. 976-979 were issued
only. See note after No. 324.

Rolls Royce "Silver Ghost"
1907 — A277

1975, Nov.   **Engr.**   **Perf. 13**
980	A277	5c shown	.25	.25
981	A277	10c Hispano Suiza, 1926	.25	.25
982	A277	20c Isotta Fras-chini, 1928	.25	.25
983	A277	30c Cord L. 29	.35	.25
984	A277	50c Voisin, 1930	.90	.70
985	A277	60c Duesenberg, 1933	1.00	.75
986	A277	80c Bugatti, 1938	1.75	1.25
987	A277	85c Delahaye, 1940	2.25	2.00
988	A277	1.20fr Cisitalia, 1946	3.25	2.75
989	A277	1.40fr Mercedes Benz, 1955	4.25	3.00
990	A277	5.50fr Lamborghini, 1974	13.00	9.50
		Nos. 980-990 (11)	27.50	20.95

Development of the automobile.

Princes of Monaco Type of 1967

Paintings (Unknown Artists): 2fr, Prince
Honoré III (1733-1795). 4fr, Princess Catherine de Brignole (1759-1813).

1975, Nov.
991 A182 2fr multicolored   1.90 1.10
992 A182 4fr multicolored   3.75 3.00

Caged Dog
A278

Designs: 80c, Cat chased up a tree, vert.
1.20fr, Horses pulling heavy load.

1975, Nov.
993	A278	60c black & brown	1.10	.70
994	A278	80c blk, gray & brn	1.60	1.00
995	A278	1.20fr mag & sil grn	2.10	1.60
		Nos. 993-995 (3)	4.80	3.30

125th anniv. of the Grammont (J. P. Delmas
Grammont) Law against cruelty to animals.

Dog Type of 1970

1975, Nov.
996 A204 60c Poodle   4.50 3.25

International Dog Show, Monte Carlo.

Maurice Ravel — A279

1.20fr, Johann Strauss and dancers.

1975, Nov.
997 A279 60c maroon & sepia 1.00 .60
998 A279 1.20fr maroon & indigo 2.10 1.40

Maurice Ravel (1875-1937), birth centenary, and Johann Strauss (1804-1849), sesquicentennial of birth, composers.

Clown — A280

1975, Nov.   Photo.   Perf. 12½x13
999 A280 80c multicolored 1.25 .55

2nd Intl. Circus Festival, Monte Carlo, Dec. 1975.

Honoré II Florin, 1640 — A281

1975, Nov.   Engr.   Perf. 13
1000 A281 80c slate & gray .75 .55

See Nos. 1040, 1088, 1234.

Ampère and Ampère Balance A282

1975, Nov.
1001 A282 85c ultra & indigo .75 .60

André Marie Ampère (1775-1836), physicist, birth bicentennial.

Lamentation for the Dead Christ, by Michelangelo — A283

1975, Nov.
1002 A283 1.40fr black & ol gray 1.25 .80

Michelangelo Buonarroti (1475-1564), Italian sculptor, painter and architect.

Flower Types of 1974
Designs: Floral arrangements.

1975, Nov.   Photo.   Perf. 13x12½
1003 A259 60c multicolored 1.10 .60
1004 A260 80c multicolored 1.60 .85

Intl. Flower Show, Monte Carlo, May 1976.

Clock Tower Type, 1974
1976, Jan. 26   Engr.   Perf. 13
1005 A263 50c brown lake .65 .35
1006 A263 60c olive green .75 .50
1007 A263 90c purple 1.10 .75
1008 A263 1.60fr brt blue 1.60 1.40
   Nos. 1005-1008 (4) 4.10 3.00

Nos. 1005-1008 were issued precanceled only. See note after No. 324.

Prince Pierre — A284

André Maurois and Colette — A285

Portraits: 25c, Jean and Jerome Tharaud. 30c, Emile Henriot, Marcel Pagnol, Georges Duhamel. 50c, Philippe Heriat, Jules Supervielle, L. Pierard. 60c, Roland Dorgeles, M. Achard, G. Bauer. 80c, Franz Hellens, A. Billy, Msgr. Grente. 1.20fr, Jean Giono, L. Pasteur-Vallery-Radot, M. Garcon.

1976, May 3   Engr.   Perf. 13
1009 A204 10c black .25 .25
1010 A285 20c red & slate .35 .25
1011 A285 25c red, dk bl & blk .35 .25
1012 A285 30c brown .55 .45
1013 A285 50c brn, red & vio bl .55 .45
1014 A285 60c grn, brn & lt brn .70 .45
1015 A285 80c black & magenta 1.10 .90
1016 A285 1.20fr blk, vio & cl 1.75 1.50
   Nos. 1009-1016 (8) 5.60 4.50

Literary Council of Monaco, 25th anniv.

Dachshunds — A286

1976, May 3   Photo.
1017 A286 60c multicolored 8.00 4.25

International Dog Show, Monte Carlo.

Bridge Table, Coast A287

1976, May 3   Engr.
1018 A287 60c multicolored .70 .45

Fifth Bridge Olympiade, Monte Carlo.

A. G. Bell, Telephone, 1876, Satellite Dish A288

1976, May 3
1019 A288 80c multicolored .55 .35

Centenary of first telephone call by Alexander Graham Bell, Mar. 10, 1876.

Federation Emblem — A289

1976, May 3
1020 A289 1.20fr multicolored .85 .55

International Federation of Philately (F.I.P.), 50th anniversary.

US Liberty Bell Type of 1926 — A290

1976, May 3
1021 A290 1.70fr carmine & blk 1.40 .95

American Bicentennial.

Fritillaria, by Vincent van Gogh A291

1976, May 3   Photo.   Perf. 12x13
1022 A291 3fr multicolored 9.00 5.50

Intl. Flower Show, Monte Carlo, May 1976.

Plate with Lemon Branch — A292

Europa: 1.20fr, The Peddler, 19th century figurine, and CEPT emblem.

1976, May 3   Perf. 12½x13
1023 A292 80c salmon & multi 1.25 .35
1024 A292 1.20fr ultra & multi 1.75 .50
a.   Souv. sheet of 10, 5 each #1023-1024 32.50 25.00

21st Summer Olympic Games, Montreal, Canada — A293

60c, Diving. 80c, Athlete on parallel bars. 85c, Hammer throw. 1.20fr, Rowing, horiz. 1.70fr, Boxing, horiz.

1976, May 3   Engr.   Perf. 13
1025 A293 60c multicolored .35 .35
1026 A293 80c multicolored .45 .35
1027 A293 85c multicolored .55 .45
1028 A293 1.20fr multicolored .80 .60
1029 A293 1.70fr multicolored 1.40 1.10
a.   Souv. sheet of 5, #1025-1029, perf. 14 4.25 4.25
   Nos. 1025-1029 (5) 3.55 2.85

Clock Tower Type, 1974
1976, Sept. 1   Engr.   Perf. 13
1030 A263 52c bister .45 .25
1031 A263 62c red lilac .55 .45
1032 A263 95c scarlet 1.10 .55
1033 A263 1.70fr blue green 1.75 1.00
   Nos. 1030-1033 (4) 3.85 2.25

Nos. 1030-1033 were issued precanceled only. See note after No. 324.

Princes of Monaco Type of 1967
Paintings: 2fr, Honoré IV (1815-1819), by Francois Lemoyne. 4fr, Louise d'Aumont-Mazarin (1750-1826), by Marie Verroust.

1976, Nov. 9   Perf. 12½x13
1035 A182 2fr violet brown 2.25 1.60
1036 A182 4fr multicolored 3.25 2.25

Red Cross Type of 1969
Design: St. Louise de Marillac and children.

1976, Nov. 9   Perf. 13
1037 A194 4fr grn, gray & plum 2.50 2.00

St. Vincent de Paul, View of Monaco A294

1976, Nov. 9
1038 A294 60c multicolored .55 .45

St. Vincent de Paul Conference, Monaco, July 31, 1876, centenary.

Marquise de Sevigné — A295

1976, Nov. 9
1039 A295 80c multicolored .55 .35

Marie de Rabutin-Chantal, Marquise de Sevigné (1626-1696), writer.

Coin Type of 1975
Design: 80c, Honoré II 2-gros coin.

1976, Nov. 9
1040 A281 80c grn & steel bl .75 .45

Richard E. Byrd, Roald Amundsen, North Pole — A296

1976, Nov. 9
1041 A296 85c olive, blk & bl   1.75 1.25
1st flights over the North Pole, 50th anniv.

Gulliver Holding King, Queen and Enemy Fleet — A297

1976, Nov. 9
1042 A297 1.20fr indigo, bl & brn   .80 .55
250th anniversary of the publication of Gulliver's Travels, by Jonathan Swift.

Child and Christmas Decorations A298

1976, Nov. 9   **Perf. 13x12½**
1043 A298 60c multicolored   .40 .25
1044 A298 1.20fr multicolored   .85 .50
Christmas 1976.

"Trapped by Drugs" A299

1976, Nov. 9
1045 A299 80c grn, ultra & org   .60 .35
1046 A299 1.20fr red brn, vio & car   .85 .50
Fight against drug abuse.

Floral Arrangement A300

Design: 1fr, Floral arrangement. Designs by Princess Grace.

1976, Nov. 9 Photo. Perf. 13½x13
1047 A300 80c yellow grn & multi 1.50 .90
1048 A300 1fr lt blue & multi   2.25 1.50
International Flower Show, Monte Carlo, May 1977. See Nos. 1124-1125, 1191.

Clown and Circus Acts — A301

1976, Nov. 9
1049 A301 1fr multi   1.90 1.10
3rd Intl. Circus Festival, Dec. 26-30.

L'Hirondelle I — A302

Prince Albert I — A303

Designs (Gouaches by Louis Tinayre): 30c, Crew of L'Hirondelle. 80c, L'Hirondelle in Storm. 1fr, The Helmsman, vert. 1.25fr, L'Hirondelle in Storm. 1.40fr, Shrimp Fishermen in Boat. 1.90fr, Hauling in the Net, vert. 2.50fr, Catching Opah Fish.

1977, May 3   Engr.   Perf. 13
1050 A302 10c multicolored   .25 .25
1051 A303 20c multicolored   .25 .25
1052 A302 30c multicolored   .30 .25
1053 A302 80c multicolored   .45 .45
1054 A302 1fr multicolored   .75 .55
1055 A302 1.25fr multicolored   1.10 .90
1056 A302 1.40fr multicolored   1.60 .25
1057 A302 1.90fr multicolored   2.75 2.25
1058 A302 2.50fr multicolored   2.25 1.50
   Nos. 1050-1058 (9)   9.70 6.65
75th anniversary of publication of "The Career of a Sailor," by Prince Albert I. See Nos. 1073-1081.

Pyreneean Mountain Dogs — A304

1977, May 3   Photo.
1059 A304 80c multicolored   6.25 3.75
International Dog Show, Monte Carlo. See No. 1199.

Motherhood, by Mary Cassatt — A305

1977, May 3   Engr.
1060 A305 80c multicolored   1.10 .90
World Association of the Friends of Children.

Archers, Target and Monte Carlo — A306

1977, May 3
1061 A306 1.10fr multicolored   .80 .55
10th Intl. Rainier III Archery Championships.

Spirit of St. Louis and Lindbergh — A307

1977, May 3
1062 A307 1.90fr multicolored   1.75 1.25
50th anniversary of first transatlantic flight by Charles Lindbergh.

The Dock at Deauville, by Dufy — A308

1977, May 3   Photo.
1063 A308 2fr multicolored   4.50 3.00
Raoul Dufy (1877-1953), painter, birth centenary.

Young Girl, by Rubens — A309

Rubens Paintings: 1fr, Duke of Buckingham. 1.40fr, Rubens' son Nicolas, 2 years old.

1977, May 3   Engr.
1064 A309 80c multicolored   .75 .55
1065 A309 1fr multicolored   1.10 .70
1066 A309 1.40fr multicolored   2.00 1.25
   Nos. 1064-1066 (3)   3.85 2.50
Peter Paul Rubens (1577-1640).

Helmet Tower, Monaco — A310

Europa: 1.40fr, St. Michael's Church, Menton.

1977, May 3
1067 A310 1fr multicolored   1.25 .50
1068 A310 1.40fr multicolored   3.00 .80
  a. Souv. sheet, 5 each #1067-1068   35.00 25.00

Clock Tower Type of 1974

1977, Apr. 1   Engr.   Perf. 13
1069 A263 54c brt green   .45 .35
1070 A263 68c orange   .55 .45
1071 A263 1.05fr olive   1.10 .55
1072 A263 1.85fr brown   1.75 1.00
   Nos. 1069-1072 (4)   3.85 2.35
Nos. 1069-1072 were issued precanceled only. See note after No. 324.

Career of a Sailor Types of 1977

Designs (Gouaches by Louis Tinayre): 10c, Yacht Princess Alice II, Kiel harbor. 20c, Laboratory on board ship. 30c, Yacht amidst ice floes. 80c, Crew in arctic outfits. 1fr, Yacht in polar region. 1.25fr, Yacht in snow storm. 1.40fr, Building camp on ice. 1.90fr, Yacht under steam amidst ice floes. 3fr, Yacht passing iceberg.

1977, Nov.   Engr.   Perf. 13
1073 A302 10c blk & brt bl   .25 .25
1074 A302 20c Prus blue   .25 .25
1075 A302 30c blk & brt bl   .25 .25
1076 A303 80c multicolored   .55 .45
1077 A302 1fr brt grn & blk   .70 .55
1078 A302 1.25fr vio, sep & blk   1.00 .75
1079 A302 1.40fr ol, bl & pur   1.60 1.25
1080 A302 1.90fr blk & brt bl   2.75 2.25
1081 A302 3fr dk grn, ol & brt bl   4.00 3.00
   Nos. 1073-1081 (9)   11.35 9.00
75th anniversary of publication of "The Career of a Sailor," by Prince Albert I.

Santa Claus A311

1977, Nov.
1082 A311 80c multicolored   .60 .25
1083 A311 1.40fr multicolored   .80 .40
Christmas 1977.

Flowers Types of 1974

Designs: 80c, Snapdragons and bellflowers. 1fr, Ikebana arrangement.

1977, Nov. Photo. Perf. 13½x13
1084 A259 80c multicolored   1.25 .70
1085 A260 1fr multicolored   1.75 1.10
Intl. Flower Show, Monte Carlo, May 1978.

Face (Van Gogh), Syringe, Hallucination Pattern — A312

1977, Nov.   Engr.   Perf. 13
1086 A312 1fr multicolored   .75 .45
Fight against drug abuse.

Clown, Flags of Participants A313

1977, Nov. Photo. Perf. 13½x13
1087 A313 1fr multicolored   1.75 1.25
Fourth International Circus Festival. Monte Carlo, December 1977.

Coin Type of 1975

Design: 80c, Doubloon of Honoré II, 1648.

1977, Nov.   Engr.   Perf. 13
1088 A281 80c lil & brn   .70 .45

Mediterranean Landscape and
Industrial Pollution — A314

1977, Nov.
1089 A314 1fr multicolored .85 .50
Protection of the Mediterranean. Meeting of
the UN Mediterranean Environmental Protection Group, Monte Carlo, Nov. 28-Dec. 6.

Men Spreading Tar, Dr. Guglielminetti,
1903 Car — A315

1977, Nov.
1090 A315 1.10fr multicolored .80 .45
75th anniversary of first tarred roads,
invented by Swiss Dr. Guglielminetti.

View of Monaco and Tennis
Emblem — A316

First Match at Wimbledon and
Stadium — A317

1977, Nov.
1091 A316 1fr multicolored 1.40 .70
1092 A317 1.40fr multicolored 1.50 1.00
Lawn Tennis Federation of Monaco, 50th
anniv. and cent. of 1st intl. tennis match at
Wimbledon.

Prince of Monaco Type of 1967
Honoré V (1819-1841), by Marie Verroust.

1977, Nov. *Perf. 12½x13*
1093 A182 6fr multicolored 4.50 3.25

Red Cross Type of 1969
Design: 4fr, St. John Bosco and boys.

1977, Nov. *Perf. 13*
1094 A194 4fr multicolored 2.50 2.00

Nos. 1069-1072 Surcharged
1978, Jan. 17
1095 A263 58c on 54c brt grn .55 .40
1096 A263 73c on 68c orange .90 .55
1097 A263 1.15fr on 1.05fr olive 1.25 .90
1098 A263 2fr on 1.85fr brn 2.10 1.40
Nos. 1095-1098 (4) 4.80 3.25
See note after No. 324.

Illustrations, Novels by Jules
Verne — A318

5c, Shipwreck. 25c, The Abandoned Ship,
from "Mysterious Island". 30c, Secret of the
Island. 80c, Robur, the Conqueror. 1fr, Master
Zacharius. 1.40fr, The Castle in the Carpathi-
ans. 1.70fr, The Children of Capt. Grant.
5.50fr, Jules Verne and allegories.

1978, May 2 **Engr.** *Perf. 13*
1099 A318 5c multicolored .25 .25
1100 A318 25c multicolored .30 .25
1101 A318 30c multicolored .30 .25
1102 A318 80c multicolored .55 .50
1103 A318 1fr multicolored 1.00 .60
1104 A318 1.40fr multicolored 1.20 .85
1105 A318 1.70fr multicolored 1.75 1.40
1106 A318 5.50fr multicolored 4.25 3.25
Nos. 1099-1106 (8) 9.60 7.35
Jules Verne (1828-1905), science fiction
writer, birth sesquicentennial.

Congress
Center and
Monte
Carlo
A319

1.40fr, Congress Center, view from the sea.

1978, May 2
1107 A319 1fr multicolored .60 .50
1108 A319 1.40fr multicolored .80 .50
Inauguration of Monaco Congress Center.

Soccer Players and Globe — A320

1978, May 2
1109 A320 1fr multicolored .75 .75
11th World Soccer Cup Championship,
Argentina, June 1-25.

Vivaldi and St.
Mark's Place,
Venice — A321

1978, May 2
1110 A321 1fr dk brown & red .90 .80
Antonio Vivaldi (1675?-1741), Italian violinist and composer.

Control Ship and
Grimaldi
Palace — A322

1fr, Map of coastal area and city emblems.

1978, May 2 **Size: 26x36mm**
1111 A322 80c multi .60 .50
Size: 48x27mm
1112 A322 1fr multi, horiz. .60 .50
Protection of the environment, signing of
"Ra Mo Ge" agreement for the protection of
the Mediterranean Coast between Saint-
Raphael, France, and Genoa, Italy (including
Monaco).

Monaco
Cathedral
A323

Europa: 1.40fr, View of Principality from
East.

1978, May 2 *Perf. 12½x13*
1113 A323 1fr multicolored 1.75 .40
1114 A323 1.40fr multicolored 3.25 .70
  a. Souv. sheet, 5 each #1113-
       1114 40.00 25.00

Cinderella — A324

Mother Goose Tales: 25c, Puss in Boots.
30c, Sleeping Beauty. 80c, Fairy tale princess.
1fr, Little Red Riding Hood. 1.40fr, Bluebeard.
1.70fr, Tom Thumb. 1.90fr, Riquet with the Tuft
of Hair. 2.50fr, The Fairies.

1978, Nov. 8 **Engr.** *Perf. 13*
1115 A324 5c multicolored .25 .25
1116 A324 25c multicolored .25 .25
1117 A324 30c multicolored .25 .25
1118 A324 80c multicolored .60 .50
1119 A324 1fr multicolored .80 .60
1120 A324 1.40fr multicolored 1.00 .85
1121 A324 1.70fr multicolored 1.25 1.10
1122 A324 1.90fr multicolored 1.75 1.25
1123 A324 2.50fr multicolored 2.40 1.75
Nos. 1115-1123 (9) 8.55 6.80
Charles Perrault (1628-1703), compiler of
Mother Goose Tales.

Flower Type of 1976
Van Gogh Paintings: 1fr, Sunflowers. 1.70fr,
Iris.

1978, Nov. 8 **Photo.** *Perf. 12½x13*
1124 A300 1fr multicolored 2.75 2.25
1125 A300 1.70fr multicolored 3.75 2.25
Intl. Flower show, Monte Carlo, May 1979,
and 125th birth anniv. of Vincent van Gogh
(1853-1890), Dutch painter.

Afghan
Hound
A325

Design: 1.20fr, Russian wolfhound.

1978, Nov. 8 *Perf. 13x12½*
1126 A325 1fr multicolored 3.00 2.40
1127 A325 1.20fr multicolored 4.50 3.00
International Dog Show, Monte Carlo.

Child Holding Gift
of Shoes — A326

1978, Nov. 8 **Engr.** *Perf. 12½x13*
1128 A326 1fr multicolored .80 .50
Christmas 1978.

Catherine and William Booth,
Salvation Army Band — A327

1978, Nov. 8 **Engr.** *Perf. 13*
1129 A327 1.70fr multicolored 1.20 1.00
Centenary of founding of Salvation Army.

Trained
Seals
A328

1fr, Lions, vert. 1.40fr, Equestrian act.
1.90fr, Monkey music band. 2.40fr, Trapeze
act.

1978, Nov. 8 *Perf. 13x12½*
1130 A328 80c multicolored .70 .50
1131 A328 1fr multicolored 1.00 .80
1132 A328 1.40fr multicolored 1.40 1.00
1133 A328 1.90fr multicolored 2.40 2.00
1134 A328 2.40fr multicolored 3.50 2.40
Nos. 1130-1134 (5) 9.00 6.70
5th Intl. Circus Festival, Monte Carlo.

Princes of Monaco Type of 1967
Paintings: 2fr, Florestan I (1841-1856), by
G. Dauphin. 4fr, Caroline Gilbert de Lametz
(1793-1879), by Marie Verroust.

1978, Nov. 8 **Engr.** *Perf. 12½x13*
1135 A182 2fr multicolored 2.00 1.40
1136 A182 4fr multicolored 3.50 3.00

Souvenir Sheet

Henri Dunant and Battle
Scene — A329

1978, Nov. 8 **Engr.** *Perf. 13*
1137 A329 5fr multicolored 4.25 4.25
Henri Dunant (1828-1910), founder of Red
Cross.

View Types of 1974

1978-80

1138	A262	25c All Saints' Tower	.35	.35
1139	A262	65c Monte Carlo Beach	.35	.35
1140	A263	70c Exotic Garden, cacti ('80)	.70	.55
1142	A262	1.10fr Palais de Justice ('80)	.75	.55
1144	A263	1.30fr Cathedral	.75	.45
1145	A264	1.50fr Prince Albert Statue and Museum ('80)	1.25	1.10
1146	A262	1.80fr La Condamine	1.25	1.00
1148	A262	2.30fr Palace ('80)	2.25	1.60
1152	A262	6.50fr Monte Carlo Auditorium	3.75	2.75
		Nos. 1138-1152 (9)	11.40	8.70

Convention Center, Monte Carlo A330

1978-79

1154	A330	61c vermilion	.40	.25
1155	A330	64c green	.40	.25
1156	A330	68c brt blue	.40	.25
1157	A330	78c dp rose lilac	.55	.25
1158	A330	83c violet blue	.45	.25
1159	A330	88c orange	.45	.25
1160	A330	1.25fr brown	.90	.45
1161	A330	1.30fr purple	.75	.45
1162	A330	1.40fr brt yel grn	.70	.40
1163	A330	2.10fr violet blue	1.10	.80
1164	A330	2.25fr brown org	1.25	.75
1165	A330	2.35fr lilac rose	1.40	.75
		Nos. 1154-1165 (12)	8.75	5.10

Issued precanceled only. See note after No. 324.

Issue dates: 61c, 78c, 1.25fr, 2.10fr, July 10, 1978. Others, 1979.

Souvenir Sheet

Prince Albert — A331

1979, Apr. 30   Engr.   Perf. 12½x13
1166 A331 10fr multicolored   8.25 8.25
21st birthday of Hereditary Prince Albert.

The Juggler of Notre Dame, by Jules Massenet A332

1.20fr, Hans, the Flute Player, by Gaston L. Ganne. 1.50fr, Don Quichotte, by Massenet. 1.70fr, L'Aiglon, by Jacques Ibert & Arthur Honegger, vert. 2.10fr, The Child & the Sorcerer, by Maurice Ravel. 3fr, Monte Carlo Opera & Charles Garnier, architect.

1979, Apr. 30   Perf. 13
1167	A332	1fr multicolored	.55	.45
1168	A332	1.20fr multicolored	.75	.55
1169	A332	1.50fr multicolored	1.10	.90
1170	A332	1.70fr multicolored	1.40	1.25

1171	A332	2.10fr multicolored	2.25	2.00
1172	A332	3fr multicolored	3.25	3.00
		Nos. 1167-1172 (6)	9.30	8.15

Centenary of the Salle Garnier, Monte Carlo Opera.

Flower, Bird, Butterfly, IYC Emblem A333

Children's Drawings (IYC Emblem and): 1fr, Horse and child. 1.20fr, Children shaking hands, and heart. 1.50fr, Children of the world for peace. 1.70fr, Children against pollution.

1979, Apr. 30
1173	A333	50c multicolored	.25	.25
1174	A333	1fr multicolored	.65	.50
1175	A333	1.20fr multicolored	.85	.80
1176	A333	1.50fr multicolored	1.50	1.25
1177	A333	1.70fr multicolored	1.75	1.60
		Nos. 1173-1177 (5)	5.00	4.40

International Year of the Child.

Armed Messenger, 15th-16th Centuries A334

Europa (designs similar to 1960 postage dues); 1.50fr, Felucca, 18th cent. 1.70fr, Arrival of 1st train, Dec. 12, 1868.

1979, Apr. 30
1178	A334	1.20fr multicolored	1.25	.40
1179	A334	1.50fr multicolored	5.00	.60
1180	A334	1.70fr multicolored	5.00	.85
a.		Souv. sheet of 6, 2 each #1178-1180, perf. 13x12½	27.50	18.00
		Nos. 1178-1180 (3)	11.25	1.85

Les Biches, by Francis Poulenc A335

Ballets: 1.20fr, Les Matelots, by George Auric. 1.50fr, Le Spectre de 1a Rose, by Carl Maria Weber, vert. 1.70fr, Gaieté Parisienne, by Jacques Offenbach. 2.10fr, Dance of Salomé, by Richard Strauss, vert. 3fr, Instrumental Music, ceiling decoration of Salle Garnier.

1979, Nov. 12
Size: 26x36mm, 36x26mm
1181	A335	1fr multicolored	.70	.50
1182	A335	1.20fr multicolored	.85	.65
1183	A335	1.50fr multicolored	1.25	1.00
1184	A335	1.70fr multicolored	1.60	1.40
1185	A335	2.10fr multicolored	2.75	2.25

Size: 48x27mm
1186	A335	3fr multicolored	4.00	3.25
		Nos. 1181-1186 (6)	11.15	9.05

Salle Garnier, Monte Carlo Opera, cent.

Princes of Monaco Type of 1967

Paintings: 3fr, Charles III (1856-1889). 4fr, Antoinette de Merode (1828-1864).

1979, Nov. 12   Perf. 12½x13
1187	A182	3fr multicolored	2.25	1.75
1188	A182	4fr multicolored	3.25	2.40

Red Cross Type of 1969

5fr, St. Peter Claver preaching to slaves.

1979, Nov. 12   Perf. 13
1189 A194 5fr multicolored   3.25 2.40

Princess Grace Orchid — A336

1979, Nov. 12   Photo.
1190 A336 1fr multicolored   2.75 1.75
Intl. Orchid Exhibition, Monte Carlo, Apr. 1980.

Flower Type of 1976

Design: 1.20fr, Princess Grace rose.

1979, Nov. 12
1191 A300 1.20fr multicolored   2.75 1.75
Intl. Flower Show, Monte Carlo, May 1980.

Clown Balancing on Globe — A337

1979, Nov. 12
1192 A337 1.20fr multicolored   2.00 1.25
6th International Circus Festival, Monte Carlo, Dec. 6-10.

Rowland Hill, Penny Black — A338

1979, Nov. 12   Engr.   Perf. 13
1193 A338 1.70fr multicolored   1.00 .65
Sir Rowland Hill (1795-1879), originator of penny postage.

Albert Einstein, Equations A339

1979, Nov. 12
1194 A339 1.70fr multicolored   1.40 .80
Albert Einstein (1879-1955), theoretical physicist.

St. Patrick's Cathedral, New York City, Cent. — A340

1979, Nov. 12
1195 A340 2.10fr multicolored   1.25 .75

Nativity A341

1979, Nov. 12
1196 A341 1.20fr multicolored   .80 .65
Christmas 1979.

Bugatti, Monte Carlo, 1929 Winner A342

1979, Nov. 12
1197 A342 1fr multicolored   1.10 .70
50th anniv. of Grand Prix auto race, Monte Carlo.

Arms of Charles V and Monaco, View of Monaco — A343

1979, Nov. 12
1198 A343 1.50fr multicolored   .90 .65
Emperor Charles V visit to Monaco, 450th anniversary.

Dog Type of 1977

Design: 1.20fr, Setter and pointer.

1979, Nov. 12   Photo.
1199 A304 1.20fr multicolored   5.00 3.50
International Dog Show, Monte Carlo.

Prince Rainier Type of 1974

1980, Jan. 17   Engr.   Perf. 13
1200	A261	1.10fr emerald	.70	.25
1201	A261	1.30fr rose red	.70	.25
1202	A261	1.60fr dk blue gray	1.25	.55
1203	A261	1.80fr grnsh blue	2.00	1.90
1204	A261	2.30fr red lilac	2.50	1.40
		Nos. 1200-1204 (5)	7.15	4.35

Chestnut Branch in Spring A344

Designs of 1980, 1981 stamps show chestnut branch. 1982 stamps show peach branch. 1983 stamps show apple branch.

1980-83   Engr.   Perf. 13x12½
1205	A344	76c shown	.50	.40
1206	A344	88c Spring ('81)	.50	.40
1207	A344	97c Spring ('82)	.50	.40
1208	A344	99c Summer	.80	.60
1209	A344	1.05fr Spring ('83)	.80	.60
1210	A344	1.14fr Summer ('81)	.80	.60
1211	A344	1.25fr Summer ('82)	.80	.60
1212	A344	1.35fr Summer ('83)	.85	.60
1213	A344	1.60fr Autumn	1.25	.85
1214	A344	1.84fr Autumn ('81)	1.25	.85
1215	A344	2.03fr Autumn ('82)	1.25	.85
1216	A344	2.19fr Autumn ('83)	1.40	1.00
1217	A344	2.65fr Winter	1.75	1.20
1218	A344	3.05fr Winter ('81)	1.60	1.25
1219	A344	3.36fr Winter ('82)	1.75	1.25
1220	A344	3.63fr Winter ('83)	1.60	1.60
		Nos. 1205-1220 (16)	17.40	13.05

Issued precanceled only. See note after No. 324. See Nos. 1406-1409, 1457-1460.

Gymnast — A345

1980, Apr. 28
1221	A345	1.10fr shown	.40	.25
1222	A345	1.30fr Handball	.50	.35
1223	A345	1.60fr Shooting	.65	.45
1224	A345	1.80fr Volleyball	.85	.60
1225	A345	2.30fr Ice hockey	1.00	.85
1226	A345	4fr Slalom	1.60	1.25
		Nos. 1221-1226 (6)	5.00	3.75

22nd Summer Olympic Games, Moscow, July 19-Aug. 3; 13th Winter Olympic Games, Lake Placid, NY, Feb. 12-24.

Colette, Novelist — A346

Europa: 1.80fr, Marcel Pagnol (1895-1974), French playwright.

1980, Apr. 28   *Perf. 12½x13*
1227	A346	1.30fr multicolored	1.00	.35
1228	A346	1.80fr multicolored	1.50	.35
a.		Souv. sheet, 5 each #1227-1228	15.00	10.00

The Source, by Ingres A347

1980, Apr. 28
1229	A347	4fr multicolored	8.00	5.50

Jean Auguste Dominique Ingres (1780-1867).

Michel Eyquem de Montaigne A348

1980, Apr. 28   *Perf. 13*
1230	A348	1.30fr multicolored	.70	.45

Essays of Montaigne (1533-1592), 400th anniversary of publication.

Guillaume Apollinaire (1880-1918), French Writer — A349

1980, Apr. 28
1231	A349	1.10fr multicolored	.70	.45

Paul P. Harris, Chicago Skyline, Rotary Emblem — A350

1980, Apr. 28
1232	A350	1.80fr multicolored	.75	.55

Rotary International, 75th anniversary.

Convention Center, Map of Europe, Kiwanis Emblem — A351

1980, Apr. 28
1233	A351	1.30fr multicolored	.70	.50

Kiwanis International, European Convention, Monte Carlo, June.

Coin Type of 1975

Design: 1.50fr, Honoré II silver ecu, 1649.

1980, Apr. 28
1234	A281	1.50fr multicolored	.75	.55

Lhasa Apso and Shih-Tzu — A352

1980, Apr. 28   *Photo.*
1235	A352	1.30fr multicolored	5.00	3.25

International Dog Show, Monte Carlo.

The Princess and the Pea — A353

Hans Christian Andersen (1805-1875) Fairy Tales: 1.30fr, The Little Mermaid. 1.50fr, The Chimneysweep and the Shepherdess. 1.60fr, The Brave Little Tin Soldier. 1.80fr, The Little Match Girl. 2.30fr, The Nightingale.

1980, Nov. 6   *Engr.*   *Perf. 13*
1236	A353	70c multicolored	.50	.25
1237	A353	1.30fr multicolored	.70	.60
1238	A353	1.50fr multicolored	1.00	.85
1239	A353	1.60fr multicolored	1.40	.85
1240	A353	1.80fr multicolored	1.40	1.10
1241	A353	2.30fr multicolored	2.00	1.20
		Nos. 1236-1241 (6)	7.00	4.85

Women on Balcony, by Van Dongen — A354

Paintings from 1905 Paris Fall Salon: 2fr, The Road, by de Vlaminck. 4fr, Woman Reading, by Matisse. 5fr, Three Figures Sitting on the Grass, by André Derain.

1980, Nov. 6   *Perf. 13x12*
1242	A354	2fr multicolored	2.50	1.75
1243	A354	3fr multicolored	3.75	2.50
1244	A354	4fr multicolored	5.00	4.25
1245	A354	5fr multicolored	6.00	5.00
		Nos. 1242-1245 (4)	17.25	13.50

Princes of Monaco Type of 1967

Paintings: No. 1246, Prince Albert I (1848-1922), by Leon Bonnat. No. 1247, Princess Alice (1857-1925), by L. Maeterlinck.

1980, Nov. 6   *Perf. 12½x13*
1246	A182	4fr multicolored	3.00	2.40
1247	A182	4fr multicolored	3.00	2.40

Sun and Birds, by Perrette Lambert — A355

1980, Nov. 6   *Perf. 13*
1248	A355	6fr multicolored	4.00	3.25

Red Cross.

7th International Circus Festival — A356

1980, Nov. 6   *Perf. 13x12½*
1249	A356	1.30fr multicolored	2.00	1.25

Christmas 1980 A357

1980, Nov. 6
1250	A357	1.10fr multicolored	.55	.35
1251	A357	2.30fr multicolored	1.20	.75

Princess Stephanie of Monaco Rose — A358

1980, Nov. 6   *Photo.*   *Perf. 12½x13*
1252	A358	1.30fr shown	1.40	.65
1253	A358	1.80fr Ikebana	2.25	1.40

International Flower Show, Monte Carlo, May 1981.

Prince Rainier Type of 1974

1980   *Engr.*   *Perf. 13*
1255	A261	1.20fr bright green	1.10	.25
1256	A261	1.40fr red	1.25	.25

Issue dates: 1.20fr, Aug. 19; 1.40fr, Aug. 11.

Paramuricea Clavata — A359

5c-20c, 40c, 50c, vert.

1980, Nov. 6   *Perf. 13x12½*
1259	A359	5c Spirographis spallanzanii	.25	.25
1260	A359	10c Anemonia sulcata	.25	.25
1261	A359	15c Leptosammia pruvoti	.25	.25
1262	A359	20c Pteroides	.25	.25
1263	A359	30c shown	.25	.25
1264	A359	40c Alcyonium	.35	.25
1265	A359	50c Corallium rubrum	.55	.45
1266	A359	60c Caliactis parisitica	1.00	.65
1267	A359	70c Cerianthus membranaceus	1.25	.90
1268	A359	1fr Actinia equina	1.25	.90
1269	A359	2fr Protula	2.50	1.10
		Nos. 1259-1269 (11)	8.15	5.50

See Nos. 1316-1321, 1380.

25th Wedding Anniversary of Prince Rainier and Princess Grace — A360

1981, May 4   *Perf. 13*
1270	A360	1.20fr green & blk	1.50	1.00
1271	A360	1.40fr carmine & blk	2.00	1.50
1272	A360	1.70fr olive grn & blk	2.50	1.90
1273	A360	1.80fr brown & blk	2.75	2.25
1274	A360	2fr brt blue & blk	3.75	2.75
		Nos. 1270-1274 (5)	12.50	9.40

Mozart with his Father and Sister, by Carmontelle — A361

Wolfgang Amadeus Mozart (1756-1791), 225th Birth Anniversary (Paintings): 2fr, Portrait, by Lorenz Vogel (26x36mm). 3.50fr, Conducting his Requiem Two Days Before his Death, by F.C. Baude.

1981, May 4   *Engr.*   *Perf. 13½x13*
1275	A361	2fr multicolored	1.65	1.50
1276	A361	2.50fr multicolored	2.40	2.00
1277	A361	3.50fr multicolored	3.25	2.50
a.		Strip of 3, #1275-1277	8.50	8.50

Cross of Palms — A362

Europa (Palm Sunday Traditions): 2fr, Children with palms at benediction.

1981, May 4   **Perf. 12½x13**
1278	A362	1.40fr multicolored	.75	.35
1279	A362	2fr multicolored	1.25	.55
a.		Souv. sheet, 5 ea #1278-1279	18.00	9.00

European Soccer Cup, 25th Anniversary A363

1981, May 4   **Perf. 13**
1280	A363	2fr black & blue	1.25	.85

International Year of the Disabled — A364

1981, May 4
1281	A364	1.40fr brt grn & bl	1.00	.60

Monegasque National Pavilion Centenary — A365

1981, May 4
1282	A365	2fr multicolored	1.25	.85

Oceanographic Institute, Monaco and Museum, Paris — A366

1981, May 4
1283	A366	1.20fr multicolored	.95	.80

75th anniversary of the Oceanographic Institute (Monaco-France).

50th Anniversary of the International Hydrographic Bureau — A367

1981, May 4
1284	A367	2.50fr multicolored	1.75	1.25

Rough Collies and Shetland Sheepdogs — A368

1981, May 4   **Photo.**
1285	A368	1.40fr multicolored	5.50	4.00

International Dog Show, Monte Carlo.

Marine Life Preservation A369

1981, Mar. 21   **Photo.**
1286	A369	1.20fr multicolored	1.00	.70

Prince Rainier III and Herediatry Prince Albert — A370

1981-84   **Engr.**   **Perf. 13**
1287	A370	1.40fr dark green	1.00	.25
1288	A370	1.60fr carmine	1.40	.25
1289	A370	1.60fr olive grn ('82)	.75	.25
1290	A370	1.70fr bluish grn ('84)	1.00	.25
1291	A370	1.80fr magenta ('82)	.95	.25
1292	A370	2fr red ('83)	1.10	.25
1293	A370	2.10fr red ('84)	1.10	.25
1294	A370	2.30fr blue	3.50	2.75
1295	A370	2.60fr violet bl ('82)	2.25	1.90
1296	A370	2.80fr steel bl ('83)	2.25	1.60
1297	A370	3fr sky blue ('84)	2.25	1.60
1298	A370	4fr brown	1.75	.75
1299	A370	5.50fr black	2.10	1.50
		Nos. 1287-1299 (13)	21.40	11.85

See Nos. 1505-1515.

Hauling Ice Floes, 17th Cent. Map Arctic A371

1981, Oct. 5
1301	A371	1.50fr multicolored	1.60	1.25

First Intl. Arctic Committee Congress, Rome, Oct. 5-9.

Princes of Monaco Type of 1967

Paintings by P.A. de Laszlo, 1929: 3fr, Prince Louis II. 5fr, Princess Charlotte.

1981, Nov. 5   **Engr.**   **Perf. 12½x13**
1302	A182	3fr multicolored	2.50	1.25
1303	A182	5fr multicolored	3.50	2.40

Ettore Bugatti, Auto Designer and Racer, Birth Centenary A372

1981, Nov. 5   **Perf. 13**
1304	A372	1fr multicolored	1.25	.85

George Bernard Shaw (1856-1950) A373

2.50fr, Fernand Leger, painter, birth cent.

1981, Nov. 5
1305	A373	2fr multicolored	1.25	1.00
1306	A373	2.50fr multicolored	1.25	1.00

Self-portrait, by Pablo Picasso (1881-1973) — A374

#1308, Self-portrait, by Rembrandt (1606-69).

1981, Nov. 5   **Perf. 12½x13**
1307	A374	4fr multicolored	4.50	3.25
1308	A374	4fr multicolored	4.50	3.25

Ikebana, Painting by Ikenobo, 1673 — A375

Intl. Flower Show, Monte Carlo, 1982: 1.40fr, Elegantines, morning glories.

1981, Nov. 5   **Photo.**   **Perf. 12½**
1309	A375	1.40fr multicolored	1.40	1.00
1310	A375	2fr multicolored	2.25	1.75

Catherine Deneuve Rose A376

1981, Nov. 5   **Perf. 13x12½**
1311	A376	1.80fr multicolored	4.00	2.50

First Intl. Rose Competition, Monte Carlo, June 12-14.

8th Intl. Circus Festival, Monte Carlo, Dec. 10-14 — A377

1981, Nov. 5   **Engr.**   **Perf. 13**
1312	A377	1.40fr multicolored	2.50	1.40

Christmas 1981 A378

1981, Nov. 5
1313	A378	1.20fr multicolored	.75	.60

50th Monte Carlo Auto Race — A379

1981, Nov. 5
1314	A379	1fr Lancia-Stratos	1.50	1.10

Souvenir Sheet

Persimmon Branch in Different Seasons — A380

1981, Nov. 5   **Perf. 13x12½**
1315		Sheet of 4	8.50	8.50
a.	A380	1fr Spring	.80	.80
b.	A380	2fr Summer	1.50	1.50
c.	A380	3fr Autumn	2.50	2.50
d.	A380	4fr Winter	3.00	3.00

Coral Type of 1980

Exotic Plants. 1.40fr, 1.60fr, 2.30fr vert.

Perf. 12½x13, 13x12½

1981-82   **Photo.**
1316	A359	1.40fr Hoya bella	3.25	1.60
1317	A359	1.60fr Bolivicereus samaipatanus	2.75	1.10
1317A	A359	1.80fr Trichocereus grandiflorus	2.25	1.10
1318	A359	2.30fr Euphorbia milii	2.75	1.10
1319	A359	2.60fr Echinocereus fitchii	2.75	1.10
1320	A359	2.90fr Rebutia heliosa	2.75	1.10
1321	A359	4.10fr Echinopsis multiplex	3.25	2.75
		Nos. 1316-1321 (7)	19.75	9.85

Issued: 1.80fr, June 7; others Dec. 10.

Miniature Sheet

1982 World Cup — A381

Designs: Various soccer players.

1982, May 3   *Perf. 13*
1322		Sheet of 4	8.00	8.00
a.	A381	1fr multicolored	.75	.75
b.	A381	2fr multicolored	1.50	1.50
c.	A381	3fr multicolored	2.25	2.25
d.	A381	4fr multicolored	2.75	2.75

Mercantour Natl. Park Birds — A382

1982, May 3   *Perf. 12½x13, 13x12½*
1323	A382	60c Nutcracker	1.00	.85
1324	A382	70c Black grouse	1.20	1.10
1325	A382	80c Rock partridge	1.20	1.10
1326	A382	90c Wall creeper, horiz.	2.25	1.75
1327	A382	1.40fr Ptarmigan, horiz.	3.00	2.40
1328	A382	1.60fr Golden eagle	3.75	2.40
		Nos. 1323-1328 (6)	12.40	9.60

Europa — A383

1982, May 3   *Perf. 12½x13*
1329	A383	1.60fr Guelph attacking Fortress of Monaco, 1297	1.50	.40
1330	A383	2.30fr Treaty of Peronne, 1641	1.50	.50
a.		Souv. sheet, 5 ea #1329-1330	18.00	9.00

Fontvieille Landfill Project A384

1982, May 3   *Perf. 13x12½*
1331	A384	1.40fr Old coastline	1.00	.50
1332	A384	1.60fr Landfill site	1.00	.60
1333	A384	2.30fr Completed site	1.50	1.00
		Nos. 1331-1333 (3)	3.50	2.10

Fontvieille Stadium — A385

1982, May 3   *Perf. 13*
1334	A385	2.30fr multicolored	1.25	1.00

PHILEXFRANCE '82 Stamp Exhibition, Paris, June 11-21 — A386

1982, May 3
1335	A386	1.40fr multicolored	1.00	.80

Intl. Dog Show, Monte Carlo A387

1982, May 3   Photo.   *Perf. 13x12½*
1336	A387	60c Old English sheepdog	3.25	1.75
1337	A387	1fr Briard terrier	3.25	1.75

See Nos. 1366, 1431, 1479, 1539, 1676, 1704, 1756, 1806, 1855, 1900, 1940, 1990, 2035, 2069A, 2108.

Monaco Cathedral, Arms of Pope John Paul II and Monaco A388

1982, May 3   Engr.
1338	A388	1.60fr multicolored	.85	.80

Creation of archbishopric of Monaco, July 25, 1981.

800th Birth Anniv. of St. Francis of Assisi — A389

1982, May 3   *Perf. 12½x13*
1339	A389	1.40fr multicolored	1.00	.80

TB Bacillus Cent. — A390

1982, May 3
1340	A390	1.40fr multicolored	1.00	.85

Scouting Year — A391

1982, May 3
1341	A391	1.60fr dk brown & blk	1.60	1.00

Intl. Hunting Council, 29th Meeting — A392

1982, June 11   Photo.   *Perf. 12½*
1342	A392	1.60fr St. Hubert	1.20	1.00

Intl. Bibliophile Assoc. General Assembly — A393

1982, Sept. 30   Engr.   *Perf. 13*
1343	A393	1.60fr multicolored	.80	.60

Monte Carlo and Monaco During the Belle Epoch (1870-1925), by Hubert Clerissi — A394

1982, Nov. 8   Engr.   *Perf. 13x12½*
1344	A394	3fr Casino, 1870	1.75	1.25
1345	A394	5fr Palace, 1893	3.75	2.00

See Nos. 1385-1386, 1436-1437, 1488-1489, 1546-1547, 1605-1606, 1638-1639, 1695-1696.

Nicolo Paganini (1782-1840), Composer and Violinist — A395

1.80fr, Anna Pavlova (1881-1931), ballerina. 2.60fr, Igor Stravinsky (1882-1971), composer.

1982, Nov. 8   Engr.   *Perf. 12½x13*
1346	A395	1.00fr multicolored	1.25	1.00
1347	A395	1.80fr multicolored	1.75	1.20
1348	A395	2.60fr multicolored	2.00	1.40
		Nos. 1346-1348 (3)	5.00	3.60

In a Boat, by Manet (1832-1883) — A396

Design: No. 1350, Les Poissons Noir, by Georges Braque (1882-1963).

1982, Nov. 8   Engr.   *Perf. 13x12½*
1349	A396	4fr multicolored	4.00	3.00
1350	A396	4fr multicolored	4.00	3.00

Intl. Flower Show, Monte Carlo — A397

Designs: Various floral arrangements.

1982, Nov. 8   Photo.   *Perf. 12½x13*
1351	A397	1.60fr multicolored	2.10	1.25
1352	A397	2.60fr multicolored	2.10	1.25

Bouquet — A398

1982   *Perf. 13*
1353	A398	1.60fr multicolored	2.50	1.75

Christmas 1982 — A399

1982, Nov. 8   Engr.   *Perf. 12½x13*
1354	A399	1.60fr Three Kings	.60	.35
1355	A399	1.80fr Holy Family	.75	.35
1356	A399	2.60fr Shepherds	1.10	.50
a.		Souv. sheet of 3, #1354-1356	3.25	3.25
		Nos. 1354-1356 (3)	2.45	1.20

Intl. Polar Year Centenary — A400

1982, Nov. 8   Engr.   *Perf. 13*
1358	A400	1.60fr Prince Louis, Discovery	2.25	1.60

Discovery of Greenland Millenium — A401

1982, Nov. 8
1359 A401 1.60fr Erik the Red's longship 2.25 1.60

Death Bimillenium of Virgil — A402

1982, Nov. 8
1360 A402 1.80fr Scene from Aeneid, Book 6 2.25 1.60

50th Anniv. of Botanical Garden A403

1983, Feb. 11 Photo. Perf. 12½x13
1361 A403 1.80fr Cacti, vert. 1.50 1.10
1362 A403 2fr Exotic plants, vert. 1.75 1.20
1363 A403 2.30fr Intl. exhibits, vert. 2.00 1.75
1364 A403 2.60fr Cave 2.50 1.75
1365 A403 3.30fr Prehistoric Anthropology Museum 3.50 2.75
Nos. 1361-1365 (5) 11.25 8.55

Monte Carlo Dog Show Type
1983, Apr. 13 Perf. 13x12½
1366 A387 1.80fr Alaskan malamute 7.25 4.75

Souvenir Sheet

Princess Grace (1929-1982) — A405

1983, Apr. 19 Engr. Perf. 13
1367 A405 10fr black 8.25 8.25

Europa — A406

1983, Apr. 27 Perf. 12½x13
1368 A406 1.80fr Montgolfiere balloon flight, 1783 1.75 .35
1369 A406 2.60fr Columbia space shuttle 1.75 .50
a. Souv. sheet, 5 ea #1368-1369 20.00 8.00

St. Charles' Church, Monte Carlo, Cent. — A407

1983, Apr. 27 Engr.
1370 A407 2.60fr St. Charles Borromeo 1.00 .90

Franciscan College Centenary A408

1983, Apr. 27 Perf. 13x12½
1371 A408 2fr Church, medallion .90 .70

Fontvielle Stadium Interior — A409

1983, Apr. 28 Perf. 13
1372 A409 2fr multicolored .90 .70

Automobile Centenary — A410

1983, Apr. 27
1373 A410 2.90fr Benz, 1883, Formula One racer 3.25 1.90

Save the Whales Campaign — A411

1983, Apr. 27
1374 A411 3.30fr Blue whale 3.75 3.00

World Communications Year — A412

1983, Apr. 27
1375 A412 4fr lil rose & brn vio 1.60 1.20

Souvenir Sheet

Fig Branch in Different Seasons — A413

1983, Nov. 9 Engr. Perf. 13x12½
1376 Sheet of 4 8.00 8.00
a. A413 1fr Spring .75 .75
b. A413 2fr Summer 1.40 1.40
c. A413 3fr Autumn 2.25 2.25
d. A413 4fr Winter 2.75 2.75

Exotic Plant Type of 1980
1983, Nov. 9 Photo. Perf. 13
1380 A359 2fr Argyroderma roseum 1.75 .65

Belle Epoch Type of 1982
Paintings by Hubert Clerissi: 3fr, Thermes Valentia from the Beach, 1902. 5fr, Cafe de Paris and Place du Casino, 1905.

1983, Nov. 9 Engr. Perf. 13x12½
1385 A394 3fr multicolored 3.00 2.40
1386 A394 5fr multicolored 4.25 3.50

Portrait of a Young Man, by Raphael (1483-1520) — A414

Passage Cottin, by Maurice Utrillo (1883-1955) — A415

1983, Nov. 9 Engr. Perf. 13
1387 A414 4fr multicolored 3.25 2.40
1388 A415 4fr multicolored 3.25 2.40

Johannes Brahms (1833-1897), Composer — A416

#1390, Giacomo Puccini (1858-1924), composer, scene from Madame Butterfly.

1983, Nov. 9 Engr. Perf. 13½x13
1389 A416 3fr multicolored 1.40 1.20
1390 A416 3fr multicolored 1.60 1.20

9th Intl. Circus Festival, Monte Carlo, Dec. 8-12 — A417

1983, Nov. 9 Perf. 13
1391 A417 2fr multicolored 1.75 1.40

Intl. Flower Show, Monte Carlo — A418

1983, Nov. 9 Photo.
1392 A418 1.60fr Pansies, convolvulus, carnations 1.50 1.00
1393 A418 2.60fr Oriental poppies 2.25 1.50

Christmas 1983 — A419

1983, Nov. 9 Photo.
1394 A419 2fr Provencal creche figures 1.60 1.10

Alfred Nobel (1833-1896), Literature Medal — A420

1983, Nov. 9 Engr.
1395 A420 2fr multicolored 1.00 .80

Sesquicentenary of Society of St. Vincent de Paul — A421

1983, Nov. 9 Engr.
1396 A421 1.80fr F. Ozanam, founder, Paris headquarters 1.00 .60

A422

1983, Nov. 9
1397 A422 5fr Offshore petroleum plant 2.25 1.25

19th Cent.
Figurines, Galea
Toy Collection
A423

1983, Nov. 9 Photo. Perf. 12½x13
1398	A423	50c Water pipe smoker	.25	.25
1399	A423	60c Clown with yo-yo	.40	.25
1400	A423	70c Smoking monkey	.40	.25
1401	A423	80c Farmer and pig	.50	.50
1402	A423	90c Buffalo Bill	.60	.60
1403	A423	1fr Snake charmer	.60	.60
1404	A423	1.50fr Piano and harp player	1.00	.80
1405	A423	2fr Girl powdering her face	1.75	1.00
		Nos. 1398-1405 (8)	5.50	4.25

Quince
Branch in
Spring
A424

1984, May 10 Photo. Perf. 13x12½
1406	A424	1.14fr shown	.80	.50
1407	A424	1.47fr Summer	.85	.60
1408	A424	2.38fr Autumn	1.50	1.00
1409	A424	3.95fr Winter	1.90	1.50
		Nos. 1406-1409 (4)	5.05	3.60

Issued precanceled only. See note after No. 324.

Place de la
Visitation, by
Hubert
Clerissi — A425

Drawings by Hubert Clerissi: 10c, Town Hall. 15c, Rue Basse. 20c, Place Saint-Nicolas. 30c, Quai du Commerce. 40c, Rue des Iris. 3fr, Bandstand. 6fr, Opera House.

1984, May 10 Engr. Perf. 12½x13
1410	A425	5c brown	.25	.25
1411	A425	10c claret	.25	.25
1412	A425	15c violet	.25	.25
1413	A425	20c dark blue	.25	.25
1414	A425	30c deep blue	.25	.25
1415	A425	40c dark green	.70	.25
1416	A425	3fr red brown	2.25	.90
1417	A425	6fr yellow green	1.25	1.10
		Nos. 1410-1417 (8)	5.45	3.50

See #1516-1524, 1750-1755, 1821-1825.

Souvenir Sheet

1984 Los Angeles Olympics — A426

Rhythmic Gymnastics.

1984, May 10 Perf. 13
1418		Sheet of 4	7.50	7.50
a.	A426	2fr Ball	.95	.95
b.	A426	3fr Clubs	1.40	1.40
c.	A426	4fr Ribbon	1.75	1.75
d.	A426	5fr Hoop	2.40	2.40

1984 Winter Olympics — A427

1984, May 10
| 1422 | A427 | 2fr Rink, speed skater | .90 | .55 |
| 1423 | A427 | 4fr Skater, snowflake | 1.60 | 1.10 |

Europa
(1959-84)
A428

1984, May 10 Perf. 13x12½
1424	A428	2fr blue	1.50	.40
1425	A428	3fr yel grn	2.50	.85
a.		Souv. sheet, 4 ea #1424-1425	20.00	8.50

Butterflies
and Rare
Flowers,
Mercantour
Natl. Park
A429

1.60fr, Boloria graeca tendensis, ranunculus montanus. 2fr, Zygaena vesubiana, saxifraga aizoides. 2.80fr, Erebia aethiopella, myosotis alpestris. 3fr, Parnassius phoebus gazeli, rhododendron ferrugineum. 3.60fr, Papilio alexanor, myrrhis odorata. Nos. 1426-1428 vert.

Perf. 12½x13, 13x12½
1984, May 10 Photo.
1426	A429	1.60fr multicolored	1.50	1.25
1427	A429	2fr multicolored	2.40	1.40
1428	A429	2.80fr multicolored	2.25	1.75
1429	A429	3fr multicolored	3.00	2.25
1430	A429	3.60fr multicolored	4.00	2.50
		Nos. 1426-1430 (5)	13.15	9.15

Monte Carlo Dog Show Type
1984, May 10 Perf. 13x12½
| 1431 | A387 | 1.60fr Auvergne pointer | 4.00 | 2.50 |

Sanctuary of Our
Lady of
Laghet — A431

1984, May 10 Engr. Perf. 12½x13
1432 A431 2fr Statue, rosary, pilgrimage sanctuary .90 .45

Auguste Piccard,
Birth
Cent. — A432

1984, May 10
| 1433 | A432 | 2.80fr Stratosphere balloon | 1.10 | .60 |
| 1434 | A432 | 4fr Bathyscaphe | 1.50 | .85 |

25th Anniv.
of Princely
Palace
Concerts
A433

1984, May 10 Perf. 13x12½
1435 A433 3.60fr Orchestra 1.60 .90

Belle Epoch Type of 1982

Paintings by Hubert Clerissi: 4fr, Rue Grimaldi, 1908. 5fr, Train Entering Monte Carlo Station, 1910.

1984, Nov. 8 Engr. Perf. 12½x13
| 1436 | A394 | 4fr multicolored | 3.50 | 2.40 |
| 1437 | A394 | 5fr multicolored | 5.50 | 3.75 |

25th Intl. Television Festival, Monte
Carlo, Feb. 1985 — A434

1984, Nov. 8 Engr. Perf. 13
| 1438 | A434 | 2.10fr Lights | 1.00 | .60 |
| 1439 | A434 | 3fr Golden nymph (prize) | 1.40 | .85 |

Intl. Flower Show,
Monte
Carlo — A435

1984, Nov. 8 Photo. Perf. 12½x13
| 1440 | A435 | 2.10fr Mixed bouquet | 1.60 | 1.00 |
| 1441 | A435 | 3fr Ikebana | 2.40 | 1.25 |

See Nos. 1491-1492, 1552-1553.

Pharmaceuticals,
Cosmetics
Industry — A436

1984, Nov. 8 Engr. Perf. 13
1442 A436 2.40fr multicolored 1.10 .85

Illustration from Gargantua, by
Rabelais — A437

Francois Rabelais (1490-1553), 17th
Cent. Drawing — A438

1984, Nov. 8 Perf. 13x12½, 12½x13
1443	A437	2fr With animals	1.10	.60
1444	A437	2fr With sheep of Panurge	1.10	.60
1445	A438	4fr multicolored	2.50	1.25
		Nos. 1443-1445 (3)	4.70	2.45

Souvenir Sheet

10th Intl. Circus Festival, Dec. 6-
10 — A439

1984, Nov. 8 Photo. Perf. 13
1446 A439 5fr Poster 4.00 4.00

La Femme
a la
Potiche, by
Degas
A440

1984, Nov. 8 Engr. Perf. 12x13
1447 A440 6fr multicolored 5.00 2.75

Christmas
1984 — A441

Figurines from Provence.

1984, Nov. 8 Perf. 12½x13
1448	A441	70c Shepherd	.45	.40
1449	A441	1fr Blind man	.55	.50
1450	A441	1.70fr Happy man	1.20	1.00
1451	A441	2fr Woman spinning	1.25	1.10
1452	A441	2.10fr Angel	1.40	1.20
1453	A441	2.40fr Garlic seller	1.60	1.40
1454	A441	3fr Drummer	1.90	1.60
1455	A441	3.70fr Knife grinder	2.40	2.00

1456 A441   4fr Elderly coup-
                le   2.75   2.40
     Nos. 1448-1456 (9)   13.50 11.60
  See Nos. 1737-1739, 1766-1768, 1838-
1840, 1883-1885, 1919-1921, 1976-1978.

Cherry Tree
A442

1985, Mar. 1   Engr.   Perf. 13
1457 A442 1.22fr Spring   .80   .50
1458 A442 1.57fr Summer   1.00   .60
1459 A442 2.55fr Fall   1.60 1.10
1460 A442 4.23fr Winter   2.10 1.75
     Nos. 1457-1460 (4)   5.50 3.95
  Issued precanceled only. See note after No.
324.

No. 1 in
Green
A443

1985, Mar. 25
1461 A443 1.70fr shown   .85   .50
1462 A443 2.10fr #1 in scarlet 1.00   .25
1463 A443   3fr #1 in lt peacock
               bl   1.20   .85
     Nos. 1461-1463 (3)   3.05 1.60
  Stamp centenary, Natl. Stamp Exhibition,
Dec. 5-8, Monte Carlo.

Europa
1985 — A444

  Portraits: 2.10fr Prince Antoine I (1661-
1731), Founder of Monaco Palace, music
library. 3fr, Jean-Baptiste Lully (1632-1687),
composer, violinist, superintendent of music to
King Louis XIV.

1985, May 23   Perf. 12½x13
1464 A444 2.10fr brt blue   1.75   .50
1465 A444   3fr dark carmine   3.00   .75
  a. Souv. sheet, 5 #1464, 5
        #1465   25.00 15.00

Flowers in
Mercantour
Park
A444a

  1.70fr, Berardia subacaulis. 2.10fr, Saxifraga florulenta, vert. 2.40fr, Fritillaria mog-
gridgei, vert. 3fr, Sempervivum allionii, vert.
3.60fr, Silene cordifolia, vert. 4fr, Primula
allionii.

Perf. 13x12½, 12½x13
1985, May 23   Photo.
1466 A444a 1.70fr multi   .85   .80
1467 A444a 2.10fr multi   1.00   .85
1468 A444a 2.40fr multi   1.20 1.00
1469 A444a   3fr multi   1.75 1.20
1470 A444a 3.60fr multi   2.40 1.60
1471 A444a   4fr multi   3.00 2.00
     Nos. 1466-1471 (6)   10.20 7.45

Japanese
Medlar
A445

1985, May 23   Engr.   Perf. 13x12½
1472   Sheet of 4   6.50 6.50
  a. A445 1fr Spring   .55   .55
  b. A445 2fr Summer   1.25 1.25
  c. A445 3fr Autumn   1.90 1.90
  d. A445 4fr Winter   2.40 2.40

Nadia Boulanger
(1887-1979),
Musician,
Composer,
Conductor
A446

  Portraits, manuscripts and music: 2.10fr,
Georges Auric (1899-1983), composer of film,
ballet music, Music Foundation council
president.

1985, May 23   Perf. 13
1473 A446 1.70fr brown   1.00   .60
1474 A446 2.10fr brt ultra   1.25   .90
  Prince Pierre de Monaco Music Foundation
composition prize, 25th anniv.

Natl. Oceanographic Museum, 75th
Anniv. — A447

1985, May 23
1475 A447 2.10fr brt bl, grn & blk 1.00   .80

Graphs, Fish, Molecular Structures,
Lab Apparatus — A448

1985, May 23
1476 A448 3fr dk bl grn, blk & dk
               rose lil   1.25   .70
  Prince Rainier III Scientific Research
Center, 25th anniv.

Intl. Athletic Championships, May 25-
26 — A449

1985, May 23
1477 A449 1.70fr Running   .70   .55
1478 A449 2.10fr Swimming   1.00   .55
  Opening of Louis II Stadium, May 25.

Monte Carlo Dog Show Type
1985, May 3   Photo.   Perf. 13x12½
1479 A387 2.10fr Boxer   3.25 2.00

Intl. Youth
Year
A450

1985, May 23   Engr.   Perf. 13
1480 A450 3fr fawn, sepia & dp
              grn   1.25   .75

Fish, Natl.
Oceanographic
Museum
Aquarium
A451

1985, Aug. 13   Photo.   Perf. 12½x13
1481 A451 1.80fr Pygoplites
                diacanthus   1.40 1.10
1482 A451 2.20fr Acanthurus
                leucos-
                ternon   1.40 1.10
1483 A451 3.20fr Chaetodon
                collare   2.25 1.60
1484 A451 3.90fr Balistoides
                conspicillum   2.75 2.25
        Size: 40x52mm
         Perf. 13
1485 A451   7fr Aquarium   4.75 3.50
     Nos. 1481-1485 (5)   12.55 9.55
  See Nos. 1560-1561, 1610-1615.

Souvenir Sheet

Transatlantic Yachting Race, Oct.
13 — A452

  Yacht classes: a, Catamaran. b, Mono-
coque. c, Trimaran.

1985, Oct.   Engr.   Perf. 13
1486   Sheet of 3   6.00 6.00
  a.-c. A452 4fr, any single   1.75 1.75
  Monaco-New York competition.

ITALIA '85, Rome, Oct. 25-Nov.
3 — A453

  Design: Exhibition emblem, St. Peter's
Cathedral and Temple of Castor ruins.

1985, Oct. 25   Perf. 13½x13
1487 A453 4fr int blk, brt grn &
              red rose   1.75 1.00

Belle Epoch Type of 1982
Illustrations by Hubert Clerissi.

1985, Nov. 7   Engr.   Perf. 13x12½
1488 A394 4fr Port of Monaco,
              1912   3.00 1.75
1489 A394 6fr La Gare Vers Ave-
              nue, 1920   3.50 3.00

11th Intl. Circus
Festival, Dec. 5-
9 — A454

1985, Nov. 7   Photo.   Perf. 13
1490 A454 1.80fr multi   1.50 1.10

Intl. Flower Show Type of 1984
1985, Nov. 7
1491 A435 2.20fr Roses, tulips,
                jonquils   1.40 1.00
1492 A435 3.20fr Ikebana of
                chrysanthe-
                mums, bryony   2.10 1.90
      Dated 1986.

Factory, Ship,
Fish,
Crustaceans
A455

1985, Nov. 7   Engr.   Perf. 13x13½
1493 A455 2.20fr brt bl, dp brn &
              dk grnsh bl   1.00   .60
  Monagasque fishing industry, Fontvieille
District. See No. 1555.

Christmas
1985 — A456

1985, Nov. 7   Photo.   Perf. 12½x13
1494 A456 2.20fr multi   1.25   .50

EUTELSAT Orbiting Earth — A457

1985, Nov. 7   Engr.   Perf. 13
1495 A457 3fr int blk, dp rose lil
              & dk bl   1.40 1.00
  European Telecommunications Satellite Org.

Sacha Guitry (1885-1957), Actor,
Dramatist — A458

  Authors, composers: 4fr, Brothers Grimm.
5fr, Frederic Chopin and Robert Schumann,
composers. 6fr, Johann Sebastian Bach and
George Frideric Handel, composers.

1985, Nov. 7

1496	A458	3fr brn blk & gldn brn	1.50	1.20
1497	A458	4fr dp rose lil, sep & turq bl	2.00	1.20
1498	A458	5fr stl bl, dp bl & grnsh bl	2.50	1.90
1499	A458	6fr blk, brn & stl bl	3.00	2.40
		Nos. 1496-1499 (4)	9.00	6.70

Souvenir Sheet

Natl. Postage Stamp Cent. — A459

Altered designs: a, Type A1. b, Type A2. c, Type A13. d, Type A83.

1985, Dec. 5

| 1500 | | Sheet of 4 | 8.00 | 8.00 |
| a.-d. | A459 5fr, any single | | 2.00 | 2.00 |

Rainier and Albert Type of 1981-84

1985-88   Engr.   Perf. 13

1505	A370	1.80fr brt grn	1.10	.25
1506	A370	1.90fr ol grn ('86)	1.90	.55
1507	A370	2fr emer grn ('87)	1.25	.25
1508	A370	2.20fr red rose	1.25	.25
1509	A370	2.50fr dk brn	1.50	.75
1510	A370	3.20fr brt bl	2.75	2.25
1511	A370	3.40fr ind ('86)	4.25	2.25
1512	A370	3.60fr dp ultra ('87)	2.75	1.25
1513	A370	10fr claret ('86)	4.75	1.10
1514	A370	15fr dk bl grn ('86)	9.25	2.25
1515	A370	20fr brt blue ('88)	11.00	2.75
		Nos. 1505-1515 (11)	41.75	13.90

Views of Old Monaco Type of 1984

Illustrations by Hubert Clerissi: 50c, Port of Monaco. 60c, St. Charles Church. 70c, Promenade. 80c, Harbor, olive trees. 90c, Quay. 1fr, Palace Square. 2fr, Ships, harbor mouth. 4fr, Monaco Tram Station. 5fr, Mail coach.

1986, Jan. 23

1516	A425	50c red	.25	.25
1517	A425	60c Prus blue	.25	.25
1518	A425	70c orange	.55	.35
1519	A425	80c brt yel grn	.35	.25
1520	A425	90c rose violet	.35	.25
1521	A425	1fr brt blue	.45	.25
1522	A425	2fr black	.95	.45
1523	A425	4fr ultramarine	1.90	.75
1524	A425	5fr olive green	2.40	.75
		Nos. 1516-1524 (9)	7.45	3.55

Hazel Nut Tree A460

1986, Feb. 24   Engr.   Perf. 13x12½

1525	A460	1.28fr Spring	.70	.45
1526	A460	1.65fr Summer	.90	.55
1527	A460	2.67fr Fall	1.40	1.00
1528	A460	4.44fr Winter	2.00	1.60
		Nos. 1525-1528 (4)	5.00	3.60

Nos. 1525-1528 known only precanceled. See note after No. 324.
See Nos. 1580-1583, 1616-1619, 1685-1688, 1719-1722, 1809-1812.

Port of Monaco, 18th Cent. A461

1986, Feb. 24

| 1529 | A461 | 2.20fr ultra, gray & brown | 1.10 | .45 |

Publication of Annales Monegasques, 10th anniv.

Europa 1986 — A462

1986, May 22   Engr.   Perf. 12½x13

1530	A462	2.20fr Ramoge Nature Protection Treaty	1.75	.40
1531	A462	3.20fr Natl. marine reserve	2.25	.75
a.	Souv. sheet, 5 each #1530-1531		25.00	14.00

Souvenir Sheet

1986 World Cup Soccer Championships, Mexico — A463

1986, May 22

1532		Sheet of 2	6.50	6.50
a.	A463 5fr Player		2.50	2.50
b.	A463 7fr Goalie		3.50	3.50

Ovis Musimon A464

1986, May 22   Perf. 13x12½

1533	A464	2.20fr shown	1.25	.60
1534	A464	2.50fr Capra ibex	1.25	1.00
1535	A464	3.20fr Rupicapra rupicapra	1.75	1.60
1536	A464	3.90fr Marmota marmota	2.50	2.00
1537	A464	5fr Lepus timidus varronis	3.00	2.75
1538	A464	7.20fr Mustela erminea	3.75	3.25
		Nos. 1533-1538 (6)	13.50	11.20

Nos. 1536-1538 vert.

Monte Carlo Dog Show Type

1986, May 22   Photo.   Perf. 13x12½

| 1539 | A387 | 1.80fr Terriers | 5.00 | 3.25 |

Prince Albert I, Parliament — A465

1986, May 22   Perf. 13

| 1540 | A465 | 2.50fr brn & ol grn | 1.10 | .75 |

First Constitution, 75th anniv.

Serge Diaghilev, Founder — A466

1986, May 22   Perf. 13

| 1541 | A466 | 3.20fr brn blk, carm rose & blk | 1.90 | 1.60 |

Diaghilev's first permanent ballet company, 75th anniv., and creation of Monte Carlo Ballet Company, 1986.

1st Monte Carlo Auto Rally, 75 Anniv. — A467

Winner Henri Rougier and Turcat-Mery, 1911.

1986, May 22

| 1542 | A467 | 3.90fr rose mag & car | 2.50 | 2.00 |

Statue of Liberty, Cent. — A468

1986, May 22

| 1543 | A468 | 5fr multi | 2.00 | 1.40 |

Halley's Comet — A469

1986, May 22

| 1544 | A469 | 10fr Sightings, 1986, 1352 | 4.25 | 3.00 |

AMERIPEX '86, Chicago, May 22-June 1 — A470

1986, May 22

| 1545 | A470 | 5fr US flag, skyline | 2.00 | 1.20 |

Belle Epoch Type of 1982

Illustrations by Hubert Clerissi.

1986, Oct. 28   Engr.   Perf. 12½x13

| 1546 | A394 | 6fr Pavilion, 1920, vert. | 4.00 | 2.40 |
| 1547 | A394 | 7fr Beau Rivage Avenue, 1925, vert. | 5.75 | 3.00 |

Premiere of El Cid, by Pierre Corneille, 350th Anniv. — A471

1986, Oct. 28   Engr.   Perf. 13

| 1548 | A471 | 4fr Scenes | 1.75 | 1.20 |

Franz Liszt, Composer — A472

1986, Oct. 28

| 1549 | A472 | 5fr dk red brn & brt ultra | 2.00 | 1.40 |

The Olympic Diver, 1961, by Emma de Sigaldi A473

1986, Oct. 28   Perf. 12½x13

| 1550 | A473 | 6fr multi | 2.50 | 1.60 |

Intl. Insurers Congress, Monte Carlo, Sept. 30 — A474

1986, Oct. 28   Perf. 13½x13

| 1551 | A474 | 3.20fr brn, dp grn & brt bl | 1.50 | 1.00 |

Intl. Flower Show Type of 1984

2.20fr, Bouquet of roses, acidenthera. 3.90fr, Ikebana of lilies, beech branches.

1986, Oct. 28   Photo.   Perf. 12½x13

| 1552 | A435 | 2.20fr multi | 1.90 | .80 |
| 1553 | A435 | 3.90fr multi | 2.75 | 1.75 |

Dated 1987.

12th Intl. Circus Festival, Dec. 4-8 — A475

1986, Oct. 28   Perf. 13

| 1554 | A475 | 2.20fr multi | 1.75 | 1.00 |

Industries Type of 1985

Design: 3.90fr, Plastics industry.

1986, Oct. 28   Engr.

| 1555 | A455 | 3.90fr dk red, dk gray & bl grn | 1.75 | 1.20 |

Christmas
A476

1986, Oct. 28 Photo. Perf. 12½x13
1556	A476	1.80fr Holly	.85	.30
1557	A476	2.50fr Poinsettia	1.25	.50

Ascent of Mt. Blanc by J. Balmat and
M.G. Paccard, Bicent. — A477

1986, Oct. 28 Engr. Perf. 13
1558	A477	5.80fr red, brt bl & slate bl	2.50	1.75

Miniature Sheet

Arbutus Tree — A478

1986, Oct. 28 Perf. 13x12½
1559		Sheet of 4	9.50	9.50
a.	A478	3fr Spring	1.25	1.25
b.	A478	4fr Summer	1.90	1.90
c.	A478	5fr Fall	2.75	2.75
d.	A478	6fr Winter	2.50	2.50

See Nos. 1645, 1680, 1736, 1775, 1804,
1852, 1934, 1943.

Aquarium Type of 1985
1986, Sept. 25 Photo. Perf. 12½x13
1560	A451	1.90fr like No. 1481	2.25	1.00
1561	A451	3.40fr like No. 1483	4.00	2.50

Prince Rainier
III — A479

Villa Miraflores, Seat of the Philatelic
Bureau — A480

#1562b, Prince Louis II, founder of the
bureau.

1987, Apr. 23 Engr. Perf. 12½x13
1562		Strip of 3	8.50	8.50
a.	A479	4fr bright blue	1.90	1.90
b.	A479	4fr dark red	1.90	1.90
c.	A480	8fr black	3.75	3.75

Philatelic Bureau, 50th anniv.
See No. 1607.

Louis II
Stadium
A481

1987, Apr. 23 Perf. 13x12½
1563	A481	2.20fr Exterior	1.75	.40
1564	A481	3.40fr Interior	2.00	.75
a.		Min. sheet, 5 each #1563-1564	25.00	13.00

Europa 1987.

Insects — A482

1987, Apr. 23 Photo.
1565	A482	1fr Carabe de solier	.55	.55
1566	A482	1.90fr Guepe dorec	1.00	.90
1567	A482	2fr Cicindele	1.25	1.00
1568	A482	2.20fr Grande aeschne	1.50	1.00
1569	A482	3fr Chrysomele	2.40	1.75
1570	A482	3.40fr Grande sauter- elle verte	3.25	2.50
		Nos. 1565-1570 (6)	9.95	7.70

Nos. 1565, 1567 and 1569 horiz.

St. Devote Parish,
Cent. — A483

1987, Apr. 23 Engr. Perf. 12½x13
1571	A483	1.90fr black	.90	.45

Monaco Diocese,
Cent. — A484

1987, Apr. 23
1572	A484	2.50fr dk yellow grn	1.00	.55

50th Intl.
Dog Show,
Monte
Carlo
A485

1987, Apr. 23 Perf. 13x12½
1573	A485	1.90fr Dog breeds	2.00	1.25
1574	A485	2.70fr Poodle	3.50	1.90

Stamp Day — A486

1987, Apr. 23 Perf. 13
1575	A486	2.20fr multi	1.00	.45

Red Curley Tail, Mobile by Alexander
Calder (1898-1976), Sculptor — A487

1987, Apr. 23 Photo.
1576	A487	3.70fr multi	1.60	1.00

Sculpture Exhibition, Monte Carlo.

2nd Small European Countries
Games, May 14-17 — A488

1987, Apr. 23 Engr.
1577	A488	3fr Tennis	2.00	1.60
1578	A488	5fr Windsurfing	2.50	1.75

Miniature Sheet

Grape Vines — A489

1987, Apr. 23 Perf. 13x12½
1579		Sheet of 4	12.00	12.00
a.	A489	3fr Spring	1.60	1.60
b.	A489	4fr Summer	2.25	2.25
c.	A489	5fr Autumn	3.25	3.25
d.	A489	6fr Winter	3.75	3.75

Four Seasons Type of 1986
Life cycle of the chestnut tree.

1987, Mar. 17 Engr. Perf. 13x12½
1580	A460	1.31fr Spring	.70	.45
1581	A460	1.69fr Summer	.90	.70
1582	A460	2.74fr Fall	1.40	1.10
1583	A460	4.56fr Winter	2.00	1.60
		Nos. 1580-1583 (4)	5.00	3.85

Nos. 1580-1583 known only precanceled.
See note after No. 324.

The Life of
St. Devote,
Patron
Saint of
Monaco
A490

Text: 4fr, Born in 283, in Quercio, Devote
was martyred in Mariana, Corsica. 5fr,
Devote's nurse teaches the saint about
Christianity.

1987, Nov. 13 Photo. Perf. 13x12½
1584	A490	4fr multi	1.90	.85
1585	A490	5fr multi	2.40	1.40

Red Cross of Monaco.

See Nos. 1643-1644, 1692-1693, 1714-
1715, 1776-1777, 1836-1837.

Philately
A491

Butterflies and butterflies on simulated
stamps.

1987, July 28 Engr.
1586	A491	1.90fr brt grn & dk gray	.90	.40
1587	A491	2.20fr rose red & rose lake	.95	.50
1588	A491	2.50fr red lil & vio	1.25	.80
1589	A491	3.40fr brt bl & bluish blk	1.90	.85
		Nos. 1586-1589 (4)	5.00	2.55

13th Int'l. Circus
Festival, Monte
Carlo, Jan. 28-
Feb. 1 — A492

1987, Nov. 13 Photo. Perf. 12½x13
1590	A492	2.20fr multi	2.10	1.00

1988 Int'l Flower
Show — A493

1987, Nov. 13
1591	A493	2.20fr Ikebanas	1.25	.60
1592	A493	3.40fr multi, horiz.	2.10	1.20

Dated 1988. See Nos. 1651, 1749.

Christmas
A494

1987, Nov. 13 Engr. Perf. 13x12½
1593	A494	2.20fr crimson	1.00	.50

5-Franc
Prince
Honoré V
Coin
A495

1987, Nov. 13 Perf. 13
1594	A495	2.50fr scar & dk gray	1.10	.45

Recapture of the Mint, 150th anniv.

Electronics Industry — A496

1987, Nov. 13
1595 A496 2.50fr henna brn, vio bl
& grn 1.10 .80

Int'l. Marine Radioactivity Laboratory,
25th Anniv. — A497

Design: Monaco Oceanographic Museum
and Int'l. Agency of Atomic Energy, Vienna.

1987, Nov. 13
1596 A497 5fr brt bl, red brn &
blk 2.25 1.40

Louis
Jouvet
(b.1887),
French
Actor
A498

1987, Nov. 16   *Perf. 13x12½*
1597 A498 3fr black 1.25 1.10

A499

1987, Nov. 16
1598 A499 3fr The River Crossing 1.25 1.10

Paul and Virginia, by Bernardin de Saint-
Piorro, firot odition boont. (in 1088).

Marc Chagall (1887-1985),
Painter — A500

1987, Nov. 16   *Perf. 13*
1599 A500 4fr terra cotta & bl
gray 2.25 1.25

Jean Jenneret (Le Corbusier, 1887-
1965), French Architect — A501

1987, Nov. 16
1600 A501 4fr Architect,
Ronchamp Chap-
el 1.90 1.20

Newton's Theory of Gravity, 300th
Anniv. — A502

Invention of the Telegraph by Samuel
Morse, 150th Anniv. — A503

1987, Nov. 16
1601 A502 4fr magenta & dk bl 2.10 1.10
1602 A503 4fr brt vio, turq bl &
brn 2.10 1.10

Don Juan, Opera by Mozart,
Bicent. — A504

Mass of the Dead, by Berlioz — A505

1987, Nov. 16
1603 A504 5fr ind, vio brn &
sage grn 2.50 1.50
1604 A505 5fr sl grn, vio brn & bl 2.50 1.50

Belle Epoch Type of 1982
Illustrations by Hubert Clerissi. 6fr, 7fr vert.

1987, Nov. 16   **Engr.**   *Perf. 12½x13*
1605 A394 6fr Rampe Major 3.75 2.50
1606 A394 7fr Old Monte Carlo
Station 5.00 3.75

Philatelic Bureau Type of 1987
1907, Nov. 13   **Engr.**   *Perf. 12½x13*
1607 Sheet of 3 8.00 8.00
a. A479 4fr blk vio, like #1562a 1.90 1.90
b. A479 4fr blk vio, like #1562b 1.90 1.90
c. A480 8fr blk vio, like #1562c 3.75 3.75

Postage Due Arms Type of 1985
Booklet Stamps
1987-88   Photo.   *Perf. 13 on 3 Sides*
Size: 17x23mm
1608 D10 2fr multi ('88) 1.00 .40
a. Bklt. pane of 10 11.00
1609 D10 2.20fr multi 1.00 .60
a. Bklt. pane of 10 11.00

Issued: 2fr, Jan. 15; 2.20fr, Nov. 13.

Aquarium Type of 1985
Perf. 13x12½, 12½x13
1988, Jan. 15   **Photo.**
1610 A451 2fr Bodianus rufus 1.25 .80
1611 A451 2.20fr Chelmon
rostratus 1.75 .50
1612 A451 2.50fr Oxymona-
canthus
longirostris 2.00 1.10
1613 A451 3fr Ostracion
lentigi-
nosum 1.50 .80
1614 A451 3.70fr Pterois
volitans 2.50 2.10
1615 A451 7fr Thalassoma
lunare,
horiz. 3.50 2.25
Nos. 1610-1615 (6) 12.50 7.55

Four Seasons Type of 1986
Life cycle of the pear tree.

1988, Feb. 15   *Perf. 13x12½*
1616 A460 1.36fr Spring .70 .45
1617 A460 1.75fr Summer .90 .70
1618 A460 2.83fr Fall 1.40 1.10
1619 A460 4.72fr Winter 2.00 1.60
Nos. 1616-1619 (4) 5.00 3.85

Nos. 1616-1619 known only precanceled.
See note after No. 324.

Souvenir Sheet

Biathlon, 1988 Winter Olympics,
Calgary — A506

1988, Feb. 15   **Engr.**   *Perf. 13*
1620 Sheet of 2 13.50 13.50
a. A506 4fr Skiing 5.75 5.75
b. A506 6fr Shooting 6.75 6.75

51st Intl. Dog
Show, Monte
Carlo — A507

1988, Mar. 30   Photo.   *Perf. 12½x13*
1621 A507 3fr Dachshunds 3.00 2.00

World
Assoc. of
the Friends
of Children
(AMADE),
25th Anniv.
A508

1988, Mar. 30   Engr.   *Perf. 13*
1622 A508 5fr dark vio blue, dark
brn & brt olive
grn 2.50 1.75

Europa
1988 — A509

Transport and communication: 2.20fr, Globe
picturing hemispheres, man, brain, telecommunications satellite. 3.60fr, Plane propeller
and high-speed locomotive.

1988, Apr. 21   *Perf. 12½x13*
1623 A509 2.20fr multi 1.50 .50
1624 A509 3.60fr multi 2.75 1.00
a. Souv. sheet, 5 each #1623-
1624 27.50 12.50

Mushrooms
of
Mercantour
Natl. Park
A510

Perf. 13x12½, 12½x13
1988, May 26   **Photo.**
1625 A510 2fr Leccinum
rotundifoliae 1.25 .90
1626 A510 2.20fr Hygrocybe
punicea 1.50 .85
1627 A510 2.50fr Pholiota
flammans 1.60 1.50
1628 A510 2.70fr Lactarius
lignyotus 2.10 1.75
1629 A510 3fr Cortinarius
traganus 2.50 2.25

1630 A510 7fr Russula
olivacea 4.50 4.25
Nos. 1625-1630 (6) 13.45 11.50
Nos. 1629-1630 vert.

Nautical Soc., Cent. — A511

1988, May 26   **Engr.**   *Perf. 13*
1631 A511 2fr dk red, lt blue &
dk grn 1.10 .70

5th Year of
Restoration of
Our Lady of
Laghet Sanctuary
A512

1988, May 26   *Perf. 12½*
1632 A512 5fr multicolored 2.50 1.40

World Health Organization, 40th
Anniv. A513

1988, May 26   *Perf. 13*
1633 A513 6fr brt blue & lake 2.75 1.75

Intl. Red Cross and Red Crescent
Organizations, 125th Annivs. — A514

1988, May 26   Photo.   *Perf. 13x12½*
1634 A514 6fr dull red, blk & gray 2.75 1.75

Jean Monnet
(1888-1979),
Nobel Peace
Prize Winner in
1922 — A515

Maurice Chevalier
(1888-1972),
Actor — A516

1988, May 26   Engr.   *Perf. 12½x13*
1635 A515 2fr brt blue, dark olive
bister & blk 3.50 1.75
1636 A516 2fr blk & dark blue 3.75 1.75

1st Crossing of Greenland by Fridtjof Nansen (1861-1930), Cent. — A517

1988, May 26   *Perf. 13*
1637 A517 4fr bright violet   2.10 1.60

Belle Epoch Type of 1982

Illustrations by Hubert Clerissi.

1988, Sept. 8   Engr.   Perf. 13x12½
1638 A394 6fr Packet in Monte
              Carlo Harbor,
              1910   4.00 2.50
1639 A394 7fr Monte Carlo Sta-
              tion, c. 1910   4.50 3.25

Souvenir Sheet

1988 Summer Olympics, Seoul — A518

Woman wearing Korean regional costume, Games emblem and event: 2fr, Women's tennis. 3fr, Women's table tennis. 5fr, Women's yachting. 7fr, Women's cycling.

1988, Sept. 8   **Engr.**
1640   Sheet of 4   9.50 9.50
  a. A518 2fr blk, light ultra & brown   1.10 1.10
  b. A518 3fr blk, light ultra & brown   1.40 1.40
  c. A518 5fr blk, light ultra & brown   2.40 2.40
  d. A518 7fr blk, light ultra & brown   3.25 3.25

Monte Carlo Congress Center, 10th Anniv. — A519

1988, Sept. 8   *Perf. 13*
1641   2fr dark blue grn   1.00 1.00
1642   3fr henna brn   1.25 1.25
  a. A519 Pair, #1641-1642   2.50 2.50

Monegasque Red Cross Type of 1987

The Life of St. Devote, patron saint of Monaco: 4fr, Devote witnessing the arrival of the governor of Rome. 5fr, Devote and the governor.

1988, Oct. 20   Photo.   Perf. 13x12½
1643 A490 4fr multicolored   2.00 1.00
1644 A490 5fr multicolored   2.50 1.50

Tree Type of 1986

Life cycle of the olive tree.

1988, Oct. 20   Engr.   Perf. 13x12½
1645   Sheet of 4   12.50 12.50
  a. A478 3fr Spring   2.25 2.25
  b. A478 4fr Summer   2.75 2.75
  c. A478 5fr Fall   3.25 3.25
  d. A478 6fr Winter   3.75 3.75

Le Nain and Brothers, Detail of a Painting in the Louvre, by Antoine Le Nain (c. 1588-1648) A521

1988, Oct. 20   Perf. 12½x13
1646 A521 5fr ol brn, dull brn &
              car rose   3.25 1.90

Les Grands Archeologues, Bronze Sculpture by Giorgio De Chirico (1888-1978), Italian Painter and Sculptor — A522

1988, Oct. 20   Perf. 13
1647 A522 5fr ol bis, blk brn &
              dark bl   3.25 1.90

Pierre Carlet de Chamblain de Marivaux (1688-1763), French Playwright, Novelist — A523

1988, Oct. 20
1648 A523 3fr dull ol & ultra   1.75 1.00

Lord Byron (1788-1824), English Poet — A524

1988, Oct. 20
1649 A524 3fr grnsh bl, brn & blk 1.75 .85

14th Intl. Circus Festival, Monte Carlo, Feb. 2-6, 1989 — A525

1988, Oct. 20 Photo. Perf. 12½x13
1650 A525 2fr multi   1.50 1.00

Intl. Flower Show Type of 1987
1988, Oct. 20
1651 A493 3fr Ikebana   2.10 1.25

22nd Intl. Flower Show and Flower Arranging Contest, Monte Carlo.

Textile Industry (Ready-to-Wear Clothes by Bettina and Le Squadra) A526

1988, Oct. 20   Engr.   Perf. 13
1652 A526 3fr blk, yel org & dk ol
              grn   1.40 1.00

Christmas A527

1988, Oct. 20   Litho.   Perf. 12½x13
1653 A527 2fr black & lemon   1.25 .70

Petroglyphs, Mercantour Natl. Park — A528

Perf. 13x12½, 12½x13
1989, Feb. 8   Litho.
1654 A528   2fr multi   1.00 .80
1655 A528 2.20fr multi, diff. 1.00 .80
1656 A528   3fr multi, diff.   1.40 1.20
1657 A528 3.60fr multi, diff. 2.00 1.50
1658 A528   4fr multi, diff.,
              vert.   2.25 1.75
1659 A528   5fr multi, diff.,
              vert.   2.75 2.00
        Nos. 1654-1659 (6)   10.40 8.05

St. Nicolas Place — A528a

1989, Feb. 8   Litho.   Perf. 13½x13
Booklet Stamps
1660   A528a   2fr Rue des
              Spelugues   1.00 .50
  b.   Booklet pane of 10   12.00
1660A A528a 2.20fr shown   1.25 .60
  c.   Booklet pane of 10   14.00
        See Nos. 1702-1703, 1826-1827.

Prince Rainier III — A529

1989-91   Engr.   Perf. 13
1661 A529   2fr pale blue
              grn &
              Prus grn   1.00 .35
1662 A529 2.10fr lt blue &
              Prus blue   1.00 .25
1663 A529 2.20fr pink & rose
              brn   1.10 .25

1664 A529 2.20fr pale green-
              ish bl &
              greenish
              bl   1.00 .35
1665 A529 2.30fr pale pink &
              car lake   1.10 .25
1666 A529 2.50fr pale rose &
              rose lake   1.25 .25
1667 A529 3.20fr pale blue &
              brt blue   1.50 .90
1668 A529 3.40fr lt bl & dk bl 1.75 1.00
1669 A529 3.60fr lt blue &
              sapphire   2.00 1.25
1670 A529 3.80fr pale pink &
              dk lil rose   1.75 .55
1671 A529   4fr pale vio &
              rose vio   1.90 1.25
1672 A529   5fr buff & dark
              vio brn   2.40 .55
1673 A529   15fr dark vio &
              indigo   7.00 1.75
1673A A529   20fr pink & rose
              car   9.50 2.75
1674 A529   25fr pale gray &
              blk   11.50 2.00
        Nos. 1661-1674 (15)   45.75 13.70

Issued: 2fr, #1663, 3.60fr, 5fr, 15fr, 3/14; 2.10fr, 2.30fr, 25fr, 1/11/90; 3.20fr, 3.80fr, 3/15/90; 20fr, 4/26/91; #1664, 2.50fr, 3.40fr, 4fr, 9/24/91.
    See Nos. 1790-1799.

5th Magic Grand Prix, Monte Carlo, Mar. 17-19 A530

1989, Mar. 14   Engr.   Perf. 13x12½
1675 A530 2.20fr multi   1.40 .80

Dog Show Type of 1982
1989, Mar. 14   **Photo.**
1676 A387 2.20fr Yorkshire terrier 2.00 1.10

Our Lady of Mercy Soc., 350th Anniv. A531

1989, Mar. 14   Engr.   Perf. 13
1677 A531 3fr choc, dark red &
              blk   1.25 .75

Theater & Film — A532

Designs: 3fr, Jean Cocteau (1889-1963), French writer, artist. 4fr, Charlie Chaplin (1889-1977), English actor, film producer.

1989, Mar. 14
1678 A532 3fr Prus grn, olive grn
              & dp rose lil   1.40 1.10
1679 A532 4fr dk grn, dk vio &
              dk red   2.75 1.60

Tree Type of 1986

Life cycle of the pomegranate tree.

1989, Mar. 14   Perf. 13x12½
Miniature Sheet
1680   Sheet of 4   10.00 10.00
  a. A478 3fr Spring   1.40 1.40
  b. A478 4fr Summer   2.00 2.00
  c. A478 5fr Fall   2.75 2.75
  d. A478 6fr Winter   3.00 3.00

Souvenir Sheet

Reign of Prince Rainier III, 40th Anniv. — A533

1989, May 9　Engr.　Perf. 13
1681　A533　20fr rose vio　11.00 11.00
　　　See No. 2128.

Europa 1989 — A534

Children's games.

1989, May 9　Perf. 12½x13
1682　A534　2.20fr Marbles　1.50 .40
1683　A534　3.60fr Jumping
　　　　rope　2.75 .70
a.　Souv. sheet, 5 each #1682-
　　1683　27.50 14.00

Souvenir Sheet

French Revolution, Bicent., PHILEXFRANCE '89 — A535

a, Liberty. b. Equality. c, Fraternity.

1989, July 7　Engr.　Perf. 12½x13
1684　A535　Sheet of 3　7.50 7.50
a.　5fr sapphire　2.40 2.40
b.　5fr black　2.40 2.40
c.　5fr dark red　2.40 2.40

Four Seasons Type of 1986

Life cycle of the pear tree.

1989, July 27　Photo.　Perf. 13x12½
1685　A460　1.39fr like No. 1616　.80 .50
1686　A460　1.79fr like No. 1617　1.00 .80
1687　A460　2.90fr like No. 1618　1.60 1.25
1688　A460　4.84fr like No. 1619　2.00 1.75
　　　Nos. 1685-1688 (4)　5.40 4.30

Nos. 1685-1688 known only precanceled. See note after No. 324.

Portrait of the Artist's Mother, by Philibert Florence A536

Regatta at Molesey, by Alfred Sisley (1839-1899) — A537

Paintings: 8fr, *Enclosed Courtyard, Auvers,* by Paul Cezanne (1839-1906), vert.

Perf. 13, 13x12½ (6fr), 12½x13 (8fr)
1989, Sept. 7　Engr.
1689　A536　4fr olive black　2.50 1.75
1690　A537　6fr multi　3.25 2.00
1691　A537　8fr multi　4.25 3.00
　　　Nos. 1689-1691 (3)　10.00 6.75

Birth sesquicentennials of painters.

Monegasque Red Cross Type of 1987

The life of St. Devote, patron saint of Monaco: 4fr, Eutychius refuses to betray Devote to Barbarus and is poisoned. 5fr, Devote is condemned to torture by Barbarus when she refuses to make sacrifices to the Gods.

1989, Sept. 7　Photo.　Perf. 13x12½
1692　A490　4fr multi　1.75 1.20
1693　A490　5fr multi　2.50 1.40

Interparliamentary Union, Cent. — A538

1989, Oct. 26　Engr.　Perf. 13
1694　A538　4fr multi　2.00 1.00

Belle Epoch Type of 1982

Illustrations by Hubert Clerissi.

1989, Oct. 26　Perf. 12½x13
1695　A394　7fr Ship in Monaco
　　　　Port　3.75 2.50
1696　A394　8fr Gaming hall,
　　　　Monte Carlo Casino　4.25 3.00

Souvenir Sheet

Princess Grace Foundation, 25th Anniv. — A539

a, Princess Grace. b, Princess Caroline.

1989, Oct. 26
1697　Sheet of 2　9.25 9.25
a.-b.　A539 5fr any single　3.50 3.50

20th UPU Congress — A540

Design: Views of the Prince of Monaco's palace and the White House.

1989, Oct. 26　Perf. 13
1698　A540　6fr multicolored　2.75 1.75

Christmas A541

1989, Oct. 26　Litho.　Perf. 12½x13
1699　A541　2fr Poinsettia　2.25 .80

15th Intl. Circus Festival, Monte Carlo, Feb. 1-5, 1990 — A542

1989, Dec. 7　Photo.　Perf. 12½x13
1700　A542　2.20fr multicolored　3.50 1.00

Monaco Aid and Presence, 10th Anniv. A543

1989, Dec. 7　Engr.　Perf. 13x12½
1701　A543　2.20fr brown & red　2.25 1.00

Avenues Type of 1989

1990, Feb. 8　Litho.　Perf. 13½x13
1702　A528a　2.10fr The Great
　　　　Stairs　1.00 .50
a.　Bklt. pane of 10 + 2 labels　10.50
1703　A528a　2.30fr Mayoral
　　　　Court of
　　　　Honor　1.25 .50
a.　Bklt. pane of 10 + 2 labels　12.50

Dog Show Type of 1982

1990, Mar. 15　Perf. 13x12½
1704　A387　2.30fr Bearded collie　2.25 1.25

Sir Rowland Hill, Great Britain No. 1 — A544

1990, Mar. 15　Engr.　Perf. 13
1705　A544　5fr royal bl & blk　2.75 2.00

Penny Black, 150th anniv.

Flowers Named for Members of the Royal Family — A545

1990, Mar. 15　Litho.　Perf. 12½x13
1706　A545　2fr Princess Grace　.95 .55
1707　A545　3fr Prince Rainier III　1.40 .70
1708　A545　3fr Grace Patricia　1.40 .90
1709　A545　4fr Principessa Grace　1.90 1.10
1710　A545　5fr Caroline of Mona-
　　　　co　3.25 1.75
　　　Nos. 1706-1710 (5)　8.90 5.00

Intl. Telecommunications Union, 125th Anniv. — A546

1990, Mar. 15　Engr.　Perf. 13
1711　A546　4fr pink, deep vio &
　　　　dull blue grn　2.00 1.50

Antony Noghes (1890-1978), Creator of the Monaco Grand Prix and Monte Carlo Rally — A547

1990, Mar. 15
1712　A547　3fr deep vio, blk &
　　　　dark red　1.50 1.00

Automobile Club, Cent. — A548

1990, Mar. 15
1713　A548　4fr brt pur, sepia &
　　　　brt blue　2.10 1.40

Monegasque Red Cross Type of 1987

The life of St. Devote, patron saint of Monaco: 4fr, Devote tortured to death (whipped). 5fr, Body layed out in a small boat.

1990, Mar. 15　Litho.　Perf. 13x12½
1714　A490　4fr multicolored　1.90 1.25
1715　A490　5fr multicolored　2.50 1.75

Europa — A549

1990, May 3   Engr.   Perf. 12½x12
1716 A549 2.30fr multicolored   1.50   .35
1717 A549 3.70fr multicolored   2.25   .55
a.   Souv. sheet, 4 each, perf.
      12½x13   27.50 13.00

Souvenir Sheet

World Cup Soccer Championships,
Italy — A550

1990, May 3   Perf. 13x12½
1718 A550 Sheet of 4   13.00 13.00
a. 5fr Players, trophy   3.25   3.25
b. 5fr Player dribbling ball 3.25 3.25
c. 5fr Ball   3.25   3.25
d. 5fr Players, stadium   3.25   3.25

Four Seasons Type of 1986
Life cycle of the plum tree.

1990, Sept. 17   Perf. 13
1719 A460 1.46fr Spring   .80   .50
1720 A460 1.89fr Summer 1.00   .80
1721 A460 3.06fr Fall   1.60 1.25
1722 A460 5.10fr Winter   2.25 1.75
    Nos. 1719-1722 (4)   5.65 4.30

Nos. 1719-1722 known only precanceled.
See note after No. 324.

Minerals,
Mercantour
Natl. Park
A551

Perf. 13x12½, 12½x13
1990, Sept. 4   Litho.
1723 A551 2.10fr Anatase 1.00   .50
1724 A551 2.30fr Albite   1.00   .50
1725 A551 3.20fr Rutile   1.50 1.10
1726 A551 3.80fr Chlorite 2.00 1.25
1727 A551 4fr Brookite   2.50 1.75
1728 A551 6fr Quartz   3.25 2.75
    Nos. 1723-1728 (6)   11.25 7.85

Nos. 1727-1728 vert.

Pierrot
Ecrivain — A552

1990, Sept. 4   Engr.   Perf. 12½x13
1729 A552 3fr dark blue   1.50   .80

Helicopter,
Monaco
Heliport
A553

5fr, Helicopters, Monte Carlo skyline.

1990, Sept. 4   Perf. 13
1730 A553 3fr red, brn & blk   1.25 .60
1731 A553 5fr blk, gray bl & brn 2.50 1.40

30th World Congress of Civilian Airports,
Monte Carlo.

C. Samuel Hahnemann (1755-1843),
Physician — A554

1990, Sept. 4
1732 A554 3fr multicolored   1.40 .85

Homeopathic medicine, bicentennial.

Jean-Francois Champollion (1790-
1832), Egyptologist — A555

1990, Sept. 4
1733 A555 5fr blue & brown   2.40 1.25

Offshore Power
Boating World
Championships
A556

6fr, Petanque World Championships.

1990, Sept. 4
1734 A556 2.30fr brt ultra, brn &
            red   1.10 .70
1735 A556 6fr brn org, brn &
            bl   2.75 1.60

Tree Type of 1986
Miniature Sheet
Life cycle of the lemon tree.

1990, Oct. 17   Litho.   Perf. 13x12½
1736 Sheet of 4   9.50 9.50
a. A478 3fr Spring   1.25 1.25
b. A478 4fr Summer   1.75 1.75
c. A478 5fr Fall   2.40 2.40
e. A478 6fr Winter   2.75 2.75

Type of 1984
1990, Oct. 17   Litho.   Perf. 12½x13
1737 A441 2.30fr Miller riding
            donkey   1.25 .45
1738 A441 3.20fr Woman carry-
            ing firewood   1.60 .80
1739 A441 3.80fr Baker   2.10 1.75
    Nos. 1737-1739 (3)   4.95 2.50

The Cathedral, by
Auguste Rodin
(1840-1917)
A558

1990, Oct. 17   Engr.   Perf. 12½
1740 A558 5fr bl & cream   2.25 1.25

La Pie by Claude Monet (1840-
1926) — A559

1990, Oct. 17   Perf. 13x12
1741 A559 7fr multicolored 5.00 4.00

Peter Ilich
Tchaikovsky
(1840-1893),
Composer
A560

1990, Oct. 17   Perf. 12½x13
1742 A560 5fr dark grn & bl 2.25 1.25

16th Intl. Circus
Festival, Monte
Carlo — A561

1991, Jan. 2   Photo.   Perf. 13
1743 A561 2.30fr multicolored 1.50 .85
    See No. 1801.

Intl. Symposium
on Migratory
Birds — A562

Migratory birds and their continents: 2fr,
Ciconia abdimii, Africa. 3fr, Selasphorus
platycercus, America. 4fr, Anas querquedula,
Asia. 5fr, Eurystomus orientalis, Australia. 6fr,
Merops apiaster, Europe.

1991, Feb. 22   Litho.   Perf. 12½x13
1744 A562 2fr multicolored   1.00 .60
1745 A562 3fr multicolored   1.25 1.00
1746 A562 4fr multicolored   2.00 1.25
1747 A562 5fr multicolored   2.50 2.00
1748 A562 6fr multicolored   3.25 2.50
    Nos. 1744-1748 (5)   10.00 7.35

Intl. Flower Show Type of 1987
1991, Feb. 22
1749 A493 3fr Cyclamen   2.00 .85

Views of Old Monaco Type of 1984
Designs: 20c, Cliffs of Monaco, Port de
Fontvieille. 40c, Place du Casino. 50c, Place
de la Cremaillere. 70c, Prince's Palace. 80c,
Avenue du Beau Rivage. 1fr, Place d'Armes.

1991, Feb. 22   Engr.
1750 A425 20c rose violet   .25 .25
1751 A425 40c dk green   .25 .25
1752 A425 50c claret   .25 .25
1753 A425 70c ol green   .25 .25
1754 A425 80c ultramarine   .30 .25
1755 A425 1fr dk blue   .40 .25
    Nos. 1750-1755 (6)   1.70 1.50

Dog Show Type of 1982
1991, Feb. 22   Litho.   Perf. 12
1756 A387 2.50fr Schnauzer   2.25 1.40

Oceanographic
Museum — A563

1991, Feb. 22
1757 A563 2.10fr Phytoplankton 1.25 .80

1992
Olympics
A564

Design: No. 1758b, Cross country skiiers,
diff. No. 1759a, Relay runner receiving baton.
No. 1759b, Runner passing baton.

1991, Apr. 26   Engr.   Perf. 13x12½
1758 Pair   3.50 3.50
a. A564 3fr dark green, blue & olive 1.40 1.25
b. A564 4fr dark green, blue & olive 2.00 1.60
1759 Pair   4.00 4.00
a. A564 3fr brown & Prussian blue 1.40 1.25
b. A564 5fr brown & Prussian blue 2.50 2.00

Nos. 1758 and 1759 have continuous
designs.

Europa
A565

1991, Apr. 26
1760 A565 2.30fr Eutelsat   1.75 .45
1761 A565 3.20fr Inmarsat   3.00 .60
a. Min. sheet, 5 ea. #1760-
    1761   30.00 13.00

25th Intl.
Contemporary Art
Competition
A566

1991, Apr. 26   Engr.   Perf. 12½x13
1762 A566 4fr multicolored   2.00 1.25

Prince Pierre
Foundation, 25th
Anniv. — A567

1991, Apr. 26
1763 A567 5fr multicolored   2.25 1.25

Coral — A568

1991, Apr. 26   **Photo.**   *Perf. 12*
1764 A568 2.20fr shown   1.25 .80
1765 A568 2.40fr Coral necklace   1.25 .85

Christmas Type of 1984
1991, Nov. 7   **Litho.**   *Perf. 12*
1766 A441 2.50fr Consul   1.25 .50
1767 A441 3.50fr Woman from
     Arles   2.00 1.10
1768 A441 4fr Mayor   2.50 1.40
    Nos. 1766-1768 (3)   5.75 3.00

Conifers,
Mercantour
Natl. Park
A569

1991, Nov. 7
1769 A569 2.50fr Epicea   .95 .35
1770 A569 3.50fr Sapin   1.40 .70
1771 A569 4fr Pin a crochets   1.50 .90
1772 A569 5fr Pin sylvestre,
     vert.   1.90 1.10
1773 A569 6fr Pin cembro   2.25 1.50
1774 A569 7fr Meleze, vert.   2.75 1.75
    Nos. 1769-1774 (6)   10.75 6.30

Tree Type of 1986
Miniature Sheet
Life cycle of an orange tree.

1991, Nov. 7   **Engr.**   *Perf. 13x12½*
1775   Sheet of 4   9.50 9.50
  a.   A478 3fr Spring   1.25 1.25
  b.   A478 4fr Summer   1.75 1.75
  c.   A478 5fr Fall   2.50 2.50
  d.   A478 6fr Winter   2.75 2.75

Monagasque Red Cross Type of 1987
Life of St. Devote, Monaco's Patron Saint: 4.50fr, The Storm is Rising. 5.50fr, Arrival of the Rock of Monaco.

1991, Nov. 7   **Photo.**
1776 A490 4.50fr multicolored   2.00 .90
1777 A490 5.50fr multicolored   2.50 1.25

Testudo
Hermanni
A570

1991, Nov. 7   **Litho.**   *Perf. 12*
1778 A570 1.25fr Two crawling
     right   1.40 .80
1779 A570 1.25fr Peering from
     shell   1.40 .80
1780 A570 1.25fr Walking in
     grass   1.40 .80
1781 A570 1.25fr Walking amid
     plants   1.40 .80
  a.   Block or strip of 4, #1778-1781   7.00 7.00

Prince Albert I Type of 1891
Miniature Sheet

1991, Nov. 7   **Engr.**   *Perf. 13*
    Stamp size: 22½x28mm
1782   Sheet of 3   13.00 13.00
  a.   A2 10fr dark red   4.25 4.25
  b.   A2 10fr dark blue green   4.25 4.25
  c.   A2 10fr deep violet   4.25 4.25

Portrait of
Claude
Monet by
Auguste
Renoir
A571

1991, Nov. 7   **Engr.**   *Perf. 12½x13*
1783 A571 5fr multicolored   2.40 1.75

Treaty of
Peronne,
350th
Anniv.
A572

Portraits by Philippe de Champaigne (1602-1674): 6fr, Honore II (1604-1662), Monaco. 7fr, Louis XIII (1610-1643), France.

1991, Nov. 7
1784 A572 6fr multicolored   3.00 2.50
1785 A572 7fr multicolored   3.75 2.50

Princess
Grace
Theatre,
10th Anniv.
A573

1991, Nov. 7   **Litho.**
1786 A573 8fr Princess Grace   5.00 3.75

Prince Rainier III Type of 1989
1991-96   **Engr.**   *Perf. 13*
1790 A529 2.40fr pale
     greenish
     bl & dk
     Prus bl   1.10 .50
1791 A529 2.70fr pale bl
     grn, dk
     bl grn   1.60 .80
1791A A529 (2.70fr) pale &
     Prus grn   1.25 .80
  b.   With strengthened lines in
     military ribbon at LR   1.25 .50
1792 A529 2.80fr pale rose
     & rose
     lake   1.25 .60
1793 A529 3fr pale red,
     red brn   1.75 .90
1793A A529 (3fr) pink & red   1.40 .55
1794 A529 3.70fr pale bl &
     dk bl   1.75 .80
1795 A529 3.80fr pale bl &
     dk bl   2.25 1.10
1796 A529 (3.80fr) pale & dk
     bl   1.75 .70
1797 A529 10fr lt bl grn &
     dp bl grn   4.75 1.90
1799 A529 40fr pale brn
     & dk brn   18.00 8.25
    Nos. 1790-1799 (11)   36.85 16.60

Nos. 1791A, 1793A, 1796 are dated "1999."
Issued: 10fr, 11/7/91; 2.40fr, 2.80fr, 3.70fr, 40fr, 7/28/93; 2.70fr, 3/18/96; 3fr, 3.80fr, 7/8/96; #1791A, 1793A, 1796, 11/28/98. No. 1791Ab, Apr. 2003.
No. 1791Ab sold for 41c on day of issue and has other strengthened lines other than those in the military ribbon.
See No. 1863b.
This is an expanding set. Numbers will change if necessary.

16th Intl. Circus Festival Type
1992, Jan. 6   **Photo.**   *Perf. 12½x13*
1801 A561 2.50fr multicolored   1.60 1.00

1992
Winter and
Summer
Olympics,
Albertville
and
Barcelona
A574

Designs: 7fr, Two-man bobsled. 8fr, Soccer.

1992, Feb. 7   **Engr.**   *Perf. 13*
1802 A574 7fr multicolored   3.25 1.50
1803 A574 8fr multicolored   3.75 2.00

Tree Type of 1986
Miniature Sheet
Life cycle of a cactus plant.

1992, Apr. 24   **Photo.**   *Perf. 13x12½*
1804   Sheet of 4   10.00 10.00
  a.   A478 3fr Spring   1.25 1.25
  b.   A478 4fr Summer   1.75 1.75
  c.   A478 5fr Fall   2.50 2.50
  d.   A478 6fr Winter   3.50 3.50

60th Monte
Carlo Rally
A575

1992, Mar. 13   **Engr.**   *Perf. 13x12½*
1805 A575 4fr dk bl grn, blk &
     red   2.00 1.25

Intl. Dog Show Type of 1982
1992, Mar. 13   **Litho.**   *Perf. 13x12½*
1806 A387 2.20fr Labrador re-
     triever   1.90 1.00

50th Grand
Prix of
Monaco
A576

1992, Mar. 13   **Engr.**
1807 A576 2.50fr vio brn, blk &
     brt bl   1.50 .80

25th Intl. Flower
Show, Monte
Carlo — A577

1992, Mar. 13   **Photo.**   *Perf. 12½x13*
1808 A577 3.40fr multicolored   1.90 1.25
    See No. 1848.

Four Seasons Type of 1986
Life cycle of a walnut tree.

1992, Mar. 13   **Photo.**
1809 A460 1.60fr Spring   .85 .50
1810 A460 2.08fr Summer   1.00 .80
1811 A460 2.98fr Fall   1.50 1.25
1812 A460 5.28fr Winter   2.25 1.75
    Nos. 1809-1812 (4)   5.60 4.30

Nos. 1809-1812 known only precanceled. See the note after No. 324.

Souvenir Sheet

Dolphins — A578

1992, Mar. 13
1813 A578 Sheet of 4   11.50 11.50
  a.   4fr Steno bredanensis   1.90 1.90
  b.   5fr Delphinus delphis   2.40 2.40
  c.   6fr Tursiops truncatus   3.00 3.00
  d.   7fr Stenella coeruleoalba   3.50 3.50
    See Nos. 1853, 1898.

Discovery
of America,
500th
Anniv.
A579

1992, Apr. 24
1814 A579 2.50fr Pinta   1.50 .45
1815 A579 3.40fr Santa Maria   2.75 .80
1816 A579 4fr Nina   4.00 1.25
  a.   Sheet, 2 each #1814-1816   30.00 13.50
    Nos. 1814-1816 (3)   8.25 2.50

Europa.

Ameriflora
Intl. Flower
Show,
Columbus,
Ohio
A580

1992, Apr. 24   **Litho.**   *Perf. 12½x13*
1817 A580 4fr Fruits & vegeta-
     bles   1.90 1.10
1818 A580 5fr Vase of flowers   2.40 1.75

Columbus Exposition, Genoa
'92 — A581

1992, Apr. 24   **Engr.**   *Perf. 13*
1819 A581 6fr multicolored   3.00 1.75

Expo '92, Seville — A582

1992, Apr. 24
1820 A582 7fr multicolored   3.00 2.00

Views of Old Monaco Type of 1984
Illustrations by Hubert Clerissi: 60c, National Council. 90c, Port of Fontvieille. 2fr, Condamine Market. 3fr, Sailing ship. 7fr, Oceanographic Museum.

1992, May 25   **Engr.**   *Perf. 12½x13*
1821 A425 60c dark blue   .25 .25
1822 A425 90c violet brown   .35 .25
1823 A425 2fr vermilion   .95 .40
1824 A425 3fr black   1.40 .60
1825 A425 7fr gray blue & blk   3.25 1.40
    Nos. 1821-1825 (5)   6.20 2.90

Avenues Type of 1989
1992, May 25   **Litho.**   *Perf. 13x13½*
     Booklet Stamps
1826 A528a 2.20fr Porte Neuve,
     horiz.   1.10 .40
  a.   Bklt. pane of 10 + 2 labels   11.00
1827 A528a 2.50fr Placette
     Bosio,
     horiz.   1.10 .45
  a.   Bklt. pane of 10 + 2 labels   11.00

Roses: 3fr, Christopher Columbus. 4fr, Prince of Monaco.

1992, Sept. 18 Litho. *Perf. 12*
1828 A583 3fr multicolored 1.75 1.10
1829 A583 4fr multicolored 1.75 1.10

Gypaetus Barbatus, Mercantour Natl. Park A584

1992, Oct. 20 Engr. *Perf. 13x12½*
1830 A584 2.20fr grn, org & blk 1.25 1.00

Seabus A585

1992, Oct. 20
1831 A585 4fr multicolored 1.75 1.40

Phytoplankton A586

Designs: 2.20fr, Ceratium ranipes. 2.50fr, Ceratium hexacanthum.

1992, Oct. 20 Litho. *Perf. 12*
1832 A586 2.20fr multicolored 1.25 .80
1833 A586 2.50fr multicolored 1.25 .40

Baron de Coubertin's Call for Modern Olympics, Cent. — A587

1992, Oct. 20 Engr. *Perf. 13*
1834 A587 10fr blue 4.75 2.50

Chapel of St. Catherine — A588

Prince of Monaco, the Marquisat of Baux-de-Provence.

1992, Oct. 20 Litho. & Engr.
1835 A588 15fr multicolored 6.50 3.50

Monagasque Red Cross Type of 1987

The life of St. Devote, patron saint of Monaco: 6fr, Fire aboard ship. 8fr, Procession of the reliquary.

1992, Oct. 20 Engr.
Size: 48x36mm
1836 A490 6fr multicolored 2.75 1.75
1837 A490 8fr multicolored 3.50 2.50

Christmas Type of 1984

1992, Oct. 20 Litho. *Perf. 12*
1838 A441 2.50fr Basket maker 1.25 .50
1839 A441 3.40fr Fishmonger 1.90 .85
1840 A441 5fr Drummer 2.50 1.50
Nos. 1838-1840 (3) 5.65 2.85

Miniature Sheet

Postal Museum — A589

Litho. & Engr.
1992, Oct. 20 *Perf. 13*
1841 A589 Sheet of 2 10.50 10.50
a. 10fr Sardinia Type A4 4.75 4.75
b. 10fr France Type A3 4.75 4.75

17th Intl. Circus Festival, Monte Carlo — A590

1993, Jan. 5 Litho. *Perf. 13½x13*
1842 A590 2.50fr multicolored 1.40 .60

Birds, Mercantour Natl. Park — A591

Designs: 2fr, Circaetus gallicus, horiz. 3fr, Falco peregrinus, horiz. 4fr, Bubo bubo. 5fr, Pernis apivorus. 6fr, Aegolius funereus.

Perf. 13x12½, 12½x13
1993, Feb. 15 Engr.
1843 A591 2fr multicolored .95 .55
1844 A591 3fr multicolored 1.40 .70
1845 A591 4fr multicolored 1.90 1.10
1846 A591 5fr multicolored 2.40 1.50
1847 A591 6fr multicolored 2.75 1.75
Nos. 1843-1847 (5) 9.40 5.60

Intl. Flower Show Type of 1992

1993, Mar. 1 Photo. *Perf. 12½x13*
1848 A577 3.40fr multicolored 1.75 .85

10th World Amateur Theater Festival — A592

1993, Mar. 1 Litho. *Perf. 13*
1849 A592 4.20fr multicolored 2.00 .85

Intl. Civil Protection Day — A593

1993, Mar. 1 Engr. *Perf. 12½x13*
1850 A593 6fr multicolored 3.00 1.75

A594

1993, Mar. 24 Engr. *Perf. 13*
1851 A594 5fr Princess Grace 2.40 1.40
See US No. 2749.

Tree Type of 1986
Miniature Sheet

Life cycle of an almond tree: a, Spring. b, Summer. c, Autumn. d, Winter.

1993, Feb. 15 Photo. *Perf. 13x12½*
1852 Sheet of 4 10.50 10.50
a.-d. A478 5fr any single 2.40 2.40

Marine Mammals Type of 1992
Miniature Sheet

1993, Mar. 24
1853 Sheet of 4 11.50 11.50
a. A578 4fr Balaenoptera physalus 1.90 1.90
b. A578 5fr Balaenoptera acutorostrata 2.40 2.40
c. A578 6fr Physeter catodon 3.00 3.00
d. A578 7fr Ziphius cavirostris 3.25 3.25

10th Monte Carlo Open Golf Tournament A595

1993, Mar. 24 Photo. *Perf. 12*
1854 A595 2.20fr multicolored 1.00 .70

Dog Show Type of 1982
1993, Mar. 24 Litho. *Perf. 13x13½*
1855 A387 2.20fr Newfoundland 1.75 1.10

10th Biennial of Antique Dealers of Monte Carlo A596

1993, Mar. 24 *Perf. 12*
1856 A596 7fr multicolored 3.25 1.60

Flowering Cacti — A597

1993, May 4 Engr. *Perf. 13x13½*
Booklet Stamps
1857 A597 2.50fr Echinopsis multiplex 1.10 .70
1858 A597 2.50fr Zygocactus truncatus 1.10 .70
1859 A597 2.50fr Echinocereus procumbens 1.10 .70
1860 A597 2.50fr Euphorbia virosa 1.10 .70
a. Booklet pane, 2 each #1857-1860 9.25
Nos. 1857-1860 (4) 4.40 2.80

See Nos. 1889-1892, 1914-1918, 2007-2009, 2086-2089.

Europa A598

1993, May 4 *Perf. 12½x12*
1861 A598 2.50fr Monte Carlo Ballet .90 .40
1862 A598 4.20fr Sigaldi sculpture 1.25 .70
a. Souvenir sheet, 3 each, #1861-1862, perf. 13x12½ 7.50 7.50

Souvenir Sheet

Admission to the UN — A599

1993, July 28 Engr. *Perf. 13*
1863 A599 Sheet of 3 12.50 12.50
a. 10fr light blue 4.00 4.00
b. 10fr brn vio (Design A529) 4.00 4.00
c. 10fr brown violet & red 4.00 4.00

Intl. Olympic Committee, 101st Session A600

Litho. & Engr.
1993, Sept. 20 *Perf. 13½x13*
Booklet Stamps
1864 A600 2.80fr Coat of arms 1.25 1.25
1865 A600 2.80fr Bobsledding 1.25 1.25
1866 A600 2.80fr Skiing 1.25 1.25
1867 A600 2.80fr Sailing 1.25 1.25
1868 A600 2.80fr Rowing 1.25 1.25
1869 A600 2.80fr Swimming 1.25 1.25
1870 A600 2.80fr Cycling 1.25 1.25
1871 A600 2.80fr shown 1.25 1.25
a. Bklt. pane of 8, #1864-1871 10.00
1872 A600 4.50fr like #1864 2.00 2.00
1873 A600 4.50fr Gymnastics 2.00 2.00
1874 A600 4.50fr Judo 2.00 2.00
1875 A600 4.50fr Fencing 2.00 2.00
1876 A600 4.50fr Hurdles 2.00 2.00
1877 A600 4.50fr Archery 2.00 2.00
1878 A600 4.50fr Weight lifting 2.00 2.00
1879 A600 4.50fr like #1871 2.00 2.00
a. Bklt. pane of 8, #1872-1879 16.00

See No. 1899.

Red Cross of Monaco — A601

Design: 6fr, Red, white crosses.

1993, Nov. 10 Litho. *Perf. 13½x13*
1880 A601 5fr red, black & yellow 2.10 1.25
1881 A601 6fr red & black 2.50 2.00

Monaco Philatelic Union, Cent. A602

1993, Nov. 10   **Perf. 13x13½**
1882 A602 2.40fr multicolored   1.10   .45

Christmas Type of 1984
1993, Nov. 10   **Perf. 13½x13**
1883 A441 2.80fr Donkey   1.25   .50
1884 A441 3.70fr Shepherd   1.75   .85
1885 A441 4.40fr Cow   2.10 1.25
    Nos. 1883-1885 (3)   5.10 2.60

Edvard Grieg (1843-1907), Composer — A603

Joan Miro (1893-1943), Artist — A604

Georges de La Tour (1593-1652), Painter — A605

Litho. (#1887), Engr.
1993, Dec. 10   **Perf. 13**
1886 A603 4fr blue   2.50 1.25
1887 A604 5fr multicolored   2.50 1.60
    Perf. 12x13
1888 A605 6fr multicolored   2.75 1.75

Flowering Cacti Type of 1993
1994, Jan. 7   **Engr.**   **Perf. 13**
1889 A597 20c like #1857   .25 .25
1890 A597 30c like #1858   .25 .25
1891 A597 40c like #1860   .25 .25
1892 A597 4fr like #1859   1.50 .70
    Nos. 1889-1892 (4)   2.25 1.45

18th Intl. Circus Festival, Monte Carlo — A606

1994, Jan. 7   **Litho.**   **Perf. 13½x13**
1893 A606 2.80fr multicolored   1.25 .60

Figurines, Natl. Museum — A607

Designs: No. 1894, Poet. No. 1895, Japanese geisha. No. 1896, Shepherdess with lamb. No. 1897, Parisian woman.

1994, Jan. 7   **Engr.**   **Perf. 12½x13**
1894 A607 2.80fr blue   1.25 .60
1895 A607 2.80fr magenta   1.25 .60
1896 A607 2.80fr purple   1.25 .60
1897 A607 2.80fr blue green   1.25 .60
    Nos. 1894-1897 (4)   5.00 2.40

Marine Mammals Type of 1992
Miniature Sheet
1994, Feb. 11   **Photo.**   **Perf. 13x12½**
1898   Sheet of 4   12.00 12.00
   a.   A578 4fr Orcinus orca   2.10 2.10
   b.   A578 5fr Grampus griseus   2.50 2.50
   c.   A578 6fr Pseudorca crassidens   2.90 2.90
   d.   A578 7fr Globicephala melas   3.50 3.50

Intl. Olympic Committee Type of 1993
Souvenir Sheet
1994, Feb. 11   **Engr.**   **Perf. 13**
1899   Sheet of 2   10.00 10.00
   a.   A600 10fr like #1866   4.50 4.50
   b.   A600 10fr like #1865   4.50 4.50

    1994 Winter Olympics, Lillehammer.

Intl. Dog Show Type of 1982
1994, Mar. 14   **Litho.**   **Perf. 13x13½**
1900 A387 2.40fr King Charles
         spaniel   3.50 .80

27th Intl. Flower Show — A608

1994, Mar. 14   **Perf. 13½x13**
1901 A608 4.40fr Iris   2.50 1.25
    See Nos. 1941, 1989, 2028.

10th Grand Prix of Magic, Monte Carlo A609

1994, Mar. 14   **Engr.**   **Perf. 13x12½**
1902 A609 5fr lake, black & blue   2.50 1.50

25th Conference of the Grand Cordon of French Cuisine A610

1994, Mar. 14   **Perf. 12½**
1903 A610 6fr multicolored   2.75 1.75

Prince Albert I, Research Ship Princess Alice II — A611

Europa: 4.50fr, Opisthoproctus Grimaldii, Eryoneicus Alberti, Oceanographic Museum, Monaco.

1994, May 5   **Engr.**   **Perf. 13x12½**
1904 A611 2.80fr multicolored   1.25 .75
1905 A611 4.50fr multicolored   2.10 1.10
   a.   Min. sheet, 3 each #1904-
        1905   12.00 9.00

Intl. Olympic Committee, Cent. — A612

1994, May 17   **Engr.**   **Perf. 12½x12**
1906 A612 3fr multicolored   1.40 .75

Institute for Preservation of the Sea — A613

1994, May 17   **Litho.**   **Perf. 13**
1907 A613 6fr multicolored   2.75 1.75

Intl. Year of the Family — A614

1994, May 17   **Engr.**   **Perf. 13**
1908 A614 7fr multicolored   3.25 2.00

1994 World Cup Soccer Championships, US — A615

1994, May 17   **Perf. 12½x13**
1909 A615 8fr red & black   3.50 2.25

Intl. Amateur Athletic Federation — A616

1994, June 10   **Perf. 13**
1910 A616 8fr multicolored   3.50 2.25

1903 De Dion Bouton A617

1994, Aug. 22   **Engr.**   **Perf. 13x12½**
1911 A617 2.80fr lil, blk & brn   1.25 .85

Intl. Assoc. of Philatelic Catalogue Editors (ASCAT) — A618

1994, Aug. 22   **Litho.**   **Perf. 13**
1912 A618 3fr blk, lil rose & grn   1.40 .75

21st UPU Congress, Seoul, Korea — A619

1994, Aug. 22
1913 A619 4.40fr bl, red & blk   2.75 1.25

Flowering Cacti Type of 1993
1994, Oct. 17   **Engr.**   **Perf. 13**
1914 A597 50c Selenicereus
         grandiflorua   .25 .25
1915 A597 60c Opuntia basilaris   .30 .25
1916 A597 70c Aloe plicatilis   .35 .25
1917 A597 80c Opuntia hybride   .35 .25
1918 A597 2fr Aporocactus
         flagelliformis   .95 .40
    Nos. 1914-1918 (5)   2.20 1.40

Christmas Type of 1984
1994, Oct. 17   **Litho.**   **Perf. 13**
1919 A441 2.80fr Mary   1.25 .55
1920 A441 4.50fr Christ child   2.10 .90
1921 A441 6fr Joseph   2.75 1.10
    Nos. 1919-1921 (3)   6.10 2.55

Currency Museum — A620

1994, Oct. 17   Engr.   Perf. 12½
1922 A620 3fr Prince Albert   1.40   .85
1923 A620 4fr Arms of Gri-
                  maldi   2.00 1.25
1924 A620 7fr Prince Rainier
                  III   3.25 2.00
       Nos. 1922-1924 (3)   6.65 4.10
Souvenir Sheet
Perf. 12½x13
1925   Sheet of 3   14.00 14.00
  a. A620 10fr like #1922   4.50 4.50
  b. A620 10fr like #1923   4.50 4.50
  c. A620 10fr like #1924   4.50 4.50

Red Cross Campaigns — A621

Designs: 6fr, Fight against cancer. 8fr, Fight against AIDS.

1994, Oct. 17   Litho.   Perf. 13
1926 A621 6fr lake, blue & black   2.75 1.90
1927 A621 8fr lake, grn & blk   3.75 2.50
       See Nos. 1983-1984.

ICAO, 50th Anniv. A622

Helicopters and: 5fr, Monaco Heliport. 7fr, Monaco skyline.

1994, Oct. 17   Engr.   Perf. 13
1928 A622 5fr multicolored   2.40 1.50
1929 A622 7fr multicolored   3.25 2.00

Voltaire (1694-1778), Writer — A623

Sarah Bernhardt (1844-1923), Actress — A624

Publication of Robinson Crusoe, by Daniel Defoe, 275th Anniv. — A625

The Snake Charmer, by Henri Rousseau (1844-1910) — A626

1994, Oct. 17   Engr.   Perf. 13
1930 A623 5fr olive green   2.40 1.25
1931 A624 6fr multicolored   2.75 1.50
Litho.
1932 A625 7fr multicolored   3.25 1.90
1933 A626 8fr multicolored   4.25 2.25
       Nos. 1930-1933 (4)   12.65 6.90

Tree Type of 1986
Miniature Sheet
Life cycle of an apricot tree.

1994, Oct. 17   Photo.   Perf. 13x12½
1934   Sheet of 4   14.00 14.00
  a. A478 6fr Spring   2.75 2.75
  b. A478 7fr Summer   3.25 3.25
  c. A478 8fr Autumn   3.75 3.75
  d. A478 9fr Winter   4.25 4.25

19th Intl. Circus Festival, Monte Carlo — A627

1995, Jan. 3   Litho.   Perf. 13½x13
1935 A627 2.80fr multicolored   1.25   .60

Monte Carlo Television, 35th Festival — A628

1995, Feb. 13   Engr.   Perf. 12½x13
1936 A628 8fr Prince Albert   3.50 1.75

European Nature Conservation Year — A629

1995, Apr. 3   Litho.   Perf. 13x13½
1937 A629 2.40fr multicolored   1.10   .55

Intl. Special Olympics A630

1995, Apr. 3
1938 A630 3fr multicolored   1.40   .80

Rotary Intl. Convention, Nice A631

1995, Apr. 3   Engr.   Perf. 13x12½
1939 A631 4fr blue   2.00 1.00

Intl. Dog Show Type of 1982
1995, Apr. 3   Litho.   Perf. 13x13½
1940 A387 4fr American cocker
                  spaniel   2.75 1.25

Intl. Flower Show Type of 1993
1995, Apr. 3   Perf. 13½x13
1941 A608 5fr Perroquet tulips   2.40 1.25

European Bonsai Congress A632

1995, Apr. 3   Perf. 12
1942 A632 6fr Acer palmatum   2.75 1.40

Tree Type of 1986
Miniature Sheet
Life cycle of a jujube tree.

1995, Apr. 3   Photo.   Perf. 12x12½
1943   Sheet of 4   10.50 10.50
  a. A478 4fr Spring   1.90 1.90
  b. A478 5fr Summer   2.40 2.40
  c. A478 6fr Fall   2.75 2.75
  d. A478 7fr Winter   3.25 3.25

Peace & Liberty A633

Europa: 2.80fr, Dove with olive branch, Alfred Nobel. 5fr, Chain broken over concentration camp, flowers.

Photo. & Engr.
1995, May 8   Perf. 12x12½
1944 A633 2.80fr multicolored   1.25   .80
1945 A633 5fr multicolored   2.40 1.25

50th anniversaries: End of World War II (#1944), liberation of the concentration camps (#1945).

A634

Designs: 5fr, Jean Giono (1895-1970), writer. 6fr, Marcel Pagnol (1895-1974), film producer, writer.

1995, May 8   Engr.   Perf. 12½x13
1946 A634 5fr multicolored   2.40 1.00
1947 A634 6fr multicolored   2.75 1.40

Princess Caroline, Pres. of World Assoc. of Friends of Children — A635

1995, May 8   Photo.   Perf. 13½x13
1948 A635 7fr blue   3.25 2.00

Intl. Council of Wildlife Conservation — A636

1995, May 8   Engr.   Perf. 13
1949 A636 6fr St. Hubert, stag   2.75 1.25

IAAF Track & Field Championships, Louis II Stadium — A637

1995, May 8
1950 A637 7fr multicolored   3.25 1.60

Alps Monument A638

1995, May 8
1951 A638 8fr multicolored   3.75 2.00

Prince Pierre of Monaco (1895-1964) A639

1995, May 8
1952 A639 10fr lake   4.50 2.40

Souvenir Sheet

Stamp & Coin Museum — A640

a, #927. b, Museum entrance. c, #294.

1995, May 8
| 1953 | A640 | Sheet of 3, #a.-c. | 13.50 | 13.50 |
| a.-c. | | 10fr any single | 4.50 | 4.50 |

St. Anthony of Padua (1195-1231) A641

1995, Sept. 25   Litho.   Perf. 13½
| 1954 | A641 | 2.80fr multicolored | 1.25 | .60 |

UN, 50th Anniv. A642

Designs: #1955, 1963a, Soldiers, UN Charter. #1956, 1963b, Grain, child. #1957, 1963c, Childrens' faces. #1958, 1963d, Musical notes, temple of Abu Simbel. #1959, 1963e, UN Security Council. #1960, 1963f, Hand holding grain, field. #1961, 1963g, Letters from various languages. #1962, 1963h, UNESCO Headquarters.

1995, Oct. 24   Engr.   Perf. 13
1955	A642	2.50fr multicolored	1.10	.50
1956	A642	2.50fr multicolored	1.10	.50
1957	A642	2.50fr multicolored	1.10	.50
1958	A642	2.50fr multicolored	1.10	.50
1959	A642	3fr multicolored	1.40	.70
1960	A642	3fr multicolored	1.40	.70
1961	A642	3fr multicolored	1.40	.70
1962	A642	3fr multicolored	1.40	.70
		Nos. 1955-1962 (8)	10.00	4.80

Miniature Sheet
1963		Sheet of 8	16.00	16.00
a.-d.		A642 3fr any single	1.40	1.40
e.-h.		A642 4.50fr any single	2.10	2.10

A643

Flowers: No. 1964, Rose *Grace of Monaco*. No. 1965, Fuschia *Lakeland Princess*. No. 1966, Carnation *Century of Monte Carlo*. No. 1967, Fuschia *Grace*. No. 1968, Rose *Princess of Monaco*. No. 1969, Alstroemeria *Gracia*. No. 1970, Lily *Princess Grace*. No. 1971, Carnation *Princess Caroline*. No. 1972, Rose *Stephanie of Monaco*. No. 1973, Carnation *Prince Albert*. No. 1974, Sweet pea *Grace of Monaco*. No. 1975, Gerbera *Gracia*.

1995, Oct. 24   Litho.   Perf. 13½

Booklet Stamps
1964	A643	3fr multicolored	1.40	.80
1965	A643	3fr multicolored	1.40	.80
1966	A643	3fr multicolored	1.40	.80
1967	A643	3fr multicolored	1.40	.80
1968	A643	3fr multicolored	1.40	.80
1969	A643	3fr multicolored	1.40	.80
1970	A643	3fr multicolored	1.40	.80
1971	A643	3fr multicolored	1.40	.80
1972	A643	3fr multicolored	1.40	.80
1973	A643	3fr multicolored	1.40	.80

1974	A643	3fr multicolored	1.40	.80
1975	A643	3fr multicolored	1.40	.80
a.		Bklt. pane, #1964-1975 + 2 labels	17.00	
		Complete booklet, #1975a	18.00	

Christmas Type of 1984
1995, Oct. 24   Litho.   Perf. 13½x13
1976	A441	3fr Balthazar	1.40	.65
1977	A441	5fr Gaspard	2.40	1.10
1978	A441	6fr Melchior	2.75	1.25
		Nos. 1976-1978 (3)	6.55	3.00

Monagasque Assoc. for Protection of Nature, 20th Anniv. — A644

1995, Oct. 24   Engr.   Perf. 13
| 1980 | A644 | 4fr green, black & red | 1.90 | .85 |

Wilhelm Röntgen (1845-1923), Discovery of X-Rays, Cent. — A645

1995, Oct. 24
| 1981 | A645 | 6fr multicolored | 2.75 | 1.25 |

Motion Pictures, Cent. — A646

1995, Oct. 24
| 1982 | A646 | 7fr dark blue | 3.25 | 1.75 |

Red Cross Campaigns Type of 1994
Designs: 7fr, World fight against leprosy. 8fr, Drs. Prakash and Mandakini Amte, Indian campaign against leprosy.

1995, Oct. 24   Litho.
| 1983 | A621 | 7fr multicolored | 3.25 | 1.50 |
| 1984 | A621 | 8fr multicolored | 3.75 | 1.75 |

Pneumatic Automobile Tires, Cent. — A647

1995, Oct. 24   Engr.
| 1985 | A647 | 8fr claret & dk purple | 3.75 | 1.75 |

Springtime, by Sandro Botticelli (1445-1510) — A648

1995, Oct. 24
| 1986 | A648 | 15fr blue | 9.25 | 5.25 |
| a. | | Souvenir sheet of 1 | 9.25 | 5.25 |

No. 1986 printed in sheets of 10 + 5 labels. No. 1986a inscribed in sheet margin as a winner of the 4th World Cup of Stamps, portrait of Botticelli. Issued 11/6/97.

20th Intl. Circus Festival, Monte Carlo — A649

1996, Jan. 10   Litho.   Perf. 13
| 1987 | A649 | 2.40fr multicolored | 1.10 | .50 |

Magic Festival, Monte Carlo A650

1996, Jan. 10   Engr.
| 1988 | A650 | 2.80fr black & gray | 1.25 | .55 |

Intl. Flower Show Type of 1994
1996, Jan. 26   Litho.
| 1989 | A608 | 3fr Rhododendron | 1.40 | .65 |

Intl. Dog Show Type of 1982
1996, Jan. 26
| 1990 | A387 | 4fr Fox terrier | 2.00 | 1.00 |

Opening of Chapel of Notre Dame of Miséricorde, 350th Anniv. — A651

1996, Jan. 26   Engr.   Perf. 12x13
| 1991 | A651 | 6fr multicolored | 2.75 | 2.00 |

Oceanographic Voyages of Prince Albert I of Monaco and King Charles I of Portugal, Cent. — A652

3fr, Fish in sea, net, Prince Albert I holding binoculars, ship. 4.50fr, Ship, King Charles I holding sextant, microscope, sea life.

1996, Feb. 1   Litho.   Perf. 12
| 1992 | A652 | 3fr multicolored | 1.40 | .70 |
| 1993 | A652 | 4.50fr multicolored | 2.10 | 1.25 |

See Portugal Nos. 2084-2085.

Prince Rainer III Type of 1974
Inscribed "MUSEE DES TIMBRES ET DES MONNAIES"
1996, Mar. 11   Engr.   Perf. 13
1994	AP37	10fr purple	4.50	2.25
1995	AP37	15fr henna brown	7.00	3.50
1996	AP37	20fr ultra	9.50	4.75
		Nos. 1994-1996 (3)	21.00	10.50

Stamp and Currency Museum.

Princess Grace — A653

1996, Apr. 29
| 1997 | A653 | 3fr red & brown | 1.40 | .70 |

Europa.

RAMOGE Agreement Between France, Italy, Monaco, 20th Anniv. A654

Photo. & Engr.
1996, May 14   Perf. 13
| 1998 | A654 | 3fr multicolored | 1.40 | .65 |

See France #2524, Italy #2077.

Annales Monegasques, 20th Anniv. — A655

Famous people: a, Saint Nicolas of Myra, by Louis Brea. b, Guillaume Apollinaire (1880-1918), poet. c, Jean-Baptiste Francois Bosio (1764-1827), painter. d, Francois-Joseph Bosio (1768-1845), sculptor. e, Hector Berlioz (1803-69), composer. f, Niccolo Machiavelli (1469-1527), writer. g, Sidonie-Gabrielle Colette (1873-1954), writer. h, Michael Montaigne (1533-92), essaist.

1996, May 14   Engr.   Perf. 12½x13
1999		Sheet of 8	21.00	21.00
a., e.		A655 3fr any single	1.60	1.60
b., f.		A655 4fr any single	2.00	2.00
c., g.		A655 5fr any single	2.50	2.50
d., h.		A655 6fr any single	3.00	3.00

Souvenir Sheet

CHINA '96, 9th Asian Intl. Philatelic Exhibition — A656

Designs: a, Chinese acrobats in Monaco. b, Fuling Tomb, Shenyang.

1996, May 14   Litho.   Perf. 13
2000 A656 Sheet of 2   5.00 5.00
a.-b. 5fr any single   2.50 2.50

Introduction of Telephone Area Code 377 for Monaco — A657

1996, June 21   Engr.   Perf. 13
2001 A657 3fr dark blue   1.75 .90
2002 A657 3.80fr vermilion   2.25 1.10

1996 Summer Olympic Games, Atlanta — A658

1996, July 19   Litho.   Perf. 13½x13
2003 A658 3fr Javelin, 1896   1.75 .90
2004 A658 3fr Women's softball, 1996   1.75 .90
2005 A658 4.50fr Runners, 1896   2.75 1.40
2006 A658 4.50fr Cycling, 1996   2.75 1.40
      Nos. 2003-2006 (4)   9.00 4.60

Flowering Cacti Type of 1993

Designs: 10c, Bromelia brevifolia. 1fr, Stapelia flavirostris. 5fr, Cereus peruvianus.

1996, Sept. 16   Engr.   Perf. 13
2007 A597 10c multicolored   .25   .25
2008 A597 1fr multicolored   .40   .25
2009 A597 5fr multicolored   2.40 1.00
      Nos. 2007-2009 (3)   3.05 1.50

Tree Type of 1986

Life cycle of thorn (ronce) tree.

1996, Oct. 14   Photo.   Perf. 13
2010 Sheet of 4   11.00 11.00
a. A478 4fr Spring   1.75   1.75
b. A478 5fr Summer   2.25   2.25
c. A478 6fr Fall   2.75   2.75
d. A478 7fr Winter   3.25   3.25

Red Cross Campaigns Type of 1994

Designs: 7fr, Fight against tuberculosis. 8fr, Camille Guérin, Albert-Leon C. Calmette, developers of BCG vaccine against tuberculosis.

1996, Oct. 14
2011 A621 7fr multicolored   3.25 1.50
2012 A621 8fr multicolored   3.75 2.00

UNICEF, 50th Anniv. — A658a

1996, Oct. 14   Engr.   Perf. 12½x13
2013 A658a 3fr multicolored   1.40 .70

Discovery of the Planet, Neptune, 150th Anniv. — A659

Photo. & Engr.
1996, Oct. 14   Perf. 13x12½
2014 A659 4fr multicolored   1.75 .80

René Descartes (1596-1650), Philosopher, Mathematician — A660

1996, Oct. 14   Engr.   Perf. 13
2015 A660 5fr blue & carmine   2.50 1.25

Christmas A661

1996, Oct. 14   Litho.   Perf. 13
2016 A661 3fr Angel   1.40 .65
2017 A661 6fr Angels   2.75 1.25

Self-Portrait, by Corot (1796-1875) — A662

7fr, Self-portrait (detail), by Goya (1746-1828).

Photo. & Engr.
1996, Oct. 14   Perf. 12x13
2018 A662 6fr multicolored   2.75 1.50
2019 A662 7fr multicolored   3.25 1.75

Stamp and Coin Museum — A663

Designs: No. 2020, Printing and engraving stamps. No. 2021, Coins, screw press. 10fr, Front entrance to museum.

1996, Oct. 14   Engr.   Perf. 13
2020 A663 5fr dk olive & violet   2.50 2.50
2021 A663 5fr dk ol & dk bl   2.50 2.50
2022 A663 10fr dk ol & dk bl   4.75 4.75
a. Souvenir sheet, #2020-2022   9.75 9.75
      Nos. 2020-2022 (3)   9.75 9.75

No. 2022 is 48x36mm.

Grimaldi Dynasty, 700th Anniv. A664

No. 2023: a, Francois Grimaldi, 1297. b, Rainier I, d. 1314. c, Charles I, d. 1357. d, Rainier II, 1350-1407. e, Jean I, 1382-1454. f, Catalan, d. 1457. g, Lambert, d. 1494. h, Jean II, 1468-1505. i, Lucien, 1481-1523. j, Augustin, d. 1532. k, Honoré I, 1522-1581. l, Charles II, 1555-1589. m, Hercule I, 1562-1604.
No. 2024: a, Honoré II (1597-1662). b, Louis I (1642-1701). c, Antoine (1661-1731). d, Louise-Hippolyte (1697-1731). e, Jacques I (1689-1751). f, Honoré III (1720-95). g, Honoré IV (1758-1819). h, Honoré V (1778-1841). i, Florestan I (1785-1856). j, Charles III (1818-89). k, Albert I (1848-1922). l, Louis II (1870-1949). m, Rainier III.

1997   Litho.   Perf. 13
2023 Sheet of 13 + 2 labels   35.00 35.00
a. A664 7fr multicolored   3.25 3.25
b.-d. A664 1fr multi, each   .45   .45
e, g. A664 2fr multi, each   .95   .95
f. A664 9fr multicolored   4.25 4.25
h.-j. A664 9fr multi, each   4.25 4.25
k.-m. A664 3fr multi, each   3.25 3.25
2024 Sheet of 13 + 2 labels   35.00 35.00
a.-c. A664 1fr multi, each   .45   .45
d. A664 9fr multi, each   4.25 4.25
e. A664 2fr multicolored   .95   .95
f.-i. A664 9fr multi, each   4.25 4.25
j.-m. A664 7fr multi, each   3.25 3.25

Portions of the designs on Nos. 2023-2024 were applied by a thermographic process producing a shiny, raised effect.
Issued: #2023, 1/8; #2024, 7/3.

Knight in Armor Type of 1951
Inscribed "1297-1997"

1996-97   Engr.   Perf. 13
2025 A67 2.70fr bl, brn & red   1.25   .60
Sheet of 8
2026 2 ea #a.-c., 2025   11.00 11.00
a. A67 2.70fr red   1.50   1.50
b. A67 2.70fr brown   1.50   1.50
c. A67 2.70fr blue   1.50   1.50
Issued: #2025, 12/19/96; #2026, 1/8/97.

Yacht Club of Monaco — A665

1996, Dec. 12   Litho.   Perf. 13
2027 A665 3fr multicolored   1.40 .70

Intl. Flower Show Type of 1993
1996, Dec. 19   Perf. 13½x13
2028 A608 3.80fr Camellia   1.75 .75

Tennis Tournaments in Monaco, Cent. — A666

1997, Feb. 1   Litho.   Perf. 13
2029 A666 4.60fr multicolored   2.10 1.00

Portions of the design on No. 2029 were applied by a thermographic process producing a shiny, raised effect.
For overprint see No. 2049.

37th Festival of Television in Monte Carlo — A667

1996, Dec. 19   Perf. 13½x13
2030 A667 4.90fr multicolored   2.25 1.00

Campanula "Medium" — A668

1996, Dec. 19   Litho.   Perf. 13
2031 A668 5fr multicolored   2.40 1.10

Auto Sports in Monaco — A669

1996, Dec. 19   Litho.   Perf. 13
2032 A669 3fr multicolored   1.40 .65

Philatelic Events A670

Stamp & Coin Museum and: No. 2033, Pictures, engraving tools, picture on stamps. No. 2034, Stamp, magnifying glass, envelopes.

1996, Dec. 19   Engr.   Perf. 13
2033 A670 3fr multicolored   1.40 .60
2034 A670 3fr multicolored   1.40 .60
a. Pair, #2033-2034   3.00 3.00
Monaco Philatelic Office, 60th anniv. (#2033). Monaco Intl. Philatelic Exhibition (#2034).

Dog Show Type of 1982
1996, Dec. 19   Litho.   Perf. 13x13½
2035 A387 4.40fr Afghan hound   2.25 1.00

21st Intl. Circus Festival, Monte Carlo — A671

1996, Dec. 19   Litho.   Perf. 13½x13
2036 A671 3fr multicolored   1.40   .60

Intl. Grand Prix of Philately — A672

1997, Apr. 5   Litho.   Perf. 13
2041 A672 4.60fr multicolored   2.10 1.25

Red Cross Campaign Against Drug Abuse — A673

1997, May 5   Perf. 13½x13
2042 A673 7fr multicolored   3.25 1.60

Europa (Stories and Legends) A674

No. 2043, Legend of St. Devote. No. 2044, Port Hercules named for mythological Hercules.

1997, May 5   Engr.   Perf. 12½x13
2043 A674 3fr multicolored   1.50   .65
2044 A674 3fr multicolored   1.50   .65
  a.   Pair, #2043-2044   3.00 3.00

PACIFIC 97 Intl. Philatelic Exhibition A675

Design: US types A2 & A1, Monaco #1995.

1997, May 29   Perf. 13x12½
2045 A675 4.90fr multicolored   2.25 1.25

Uniforms of the Carabiniers (Palace Guards) A676

Years uniforms used: 3fr, 1997. 3.50fr, 1750-1853. 5.20fr, 1865-1935.

1997, May 31   Litho.   Perf. 13x13½
2046 A676 3fr multicolored   1.40   .50
2047 A676 3.50fr multicolored   1.60   .60
2048 A676 5.20fr multicolored   2.50   .90
       Nos. 2046-2048 (3)   5.50 2.00

No. 2029 Ovptd. "M. RIOS"
1997   Perf. 13
2049 A666 4.60fr multicolored   2.10 1.40

13th Grand Prix of Magic, Monte Carlo — A677

1997   Litho.   Perf. 13½x13
2050 A677 4.40fr multicolored   2.10 1.25

Monaco Soccer Assoc., 1996 French Division 1 Champions — A678

1997   Perf. 13
2051 A678 3fr multicolored   1.40   .80

François Grimaldi, by Ernando Venanzi A679

9fr, Saint Peter and Saint Paul, by Rubens.

1997, Sept. 8   Engr.   Perf. 13½x13
2052 A679 8fr multicolored   3.75 2.00
2053 A679 9fr multicolored   4.25 2.50

Evolution of the Geographic Territory of Monaco — A680

Designs: a, 13th century. b, 15th-19th century. c, Map of western half of Monaco, panoramic view. d, Map of eastern half of Monaco, panoramic view.

1997, Oct. 6   Litho. & Engr.   Perf. 13
2054 A680 5fr Sheet of 4, #a.-d.   9.50 9.50
       Grimaldi Dynasty, 700th anniv.

49th Session of Intl. Whaling Commission — A681

1997, Oct. 20   Photo.   Perf. 13x13½
2055 A681 6.70fr multicolored   3.00 1.75

22nd Intl. Circus Festival, Monte Carlo — A682

1997, Nov. 30   Litho.   Perf. 13½x13
2057 A682 3fr multicolored   1.40   .70

Princess Charlotte (1898-1977) — A683

1997, Nov. 28   Engr.   Perf. 13x12½
2058 A683 3.80fr brown   1.75   .90

A684

Designs by Monagasque Students — A685

Perf. 13½x13, 13x13½
1997, Nov. 29   Litho.
2059 A684 4fr Under 13 group   1.90   .90
2060 A685 4.50fr Over 13 group   2.10   .90

31st Intl. Flower Show — A686

1997, Nov. 30   Perf. 13½x13
2061 A686 4.40fr multicolored   2.10 1.25

1998 Winter Olympic Games, Nagano A687

Designs: No. 2062, 4-Man bobsled, speed skating, ice hockey, figure skating. No. 2063, Downhill skiing, biathlon, luge, ski jumping, slalom skiing.

1997, Nov. 28   Photo.   Perf. 12½
2062 A687 4.90fr multicolored   2.25 1.25
2063 A687 4.90fr multicolored   2.25 1.25
  a.   Pair, #2062-2063   4.50 4.50

Moscow '97 — A688

Ballet Russes de Monte Carlo.

1997, Nov. 28   Photo.   Perf. 13½x13
2064 A688 5fr multicolored   2.40 1.25

J.L. David (1748-1825), Painter — A689

1997, Nov. 30   Engr.   Perf. 12½x13
2065 A689 5.20fr red brn & dk grn   2.40 1.10

Papal Bull for the Parish of Monaco, 750th Anniv. A690

1997, Nov. 30   Perf. 12½x13
2066 A690 7.50fr Pope Innocent IV   3.50 1.90

Prince Albert I (1848-1922) — A691

1997, Nov. 29   Photo.   Perf. 13x12½
2067 A691 8fr multicolored   3.75 2.40

38th Television Festival — A692

1998, Feb. 4 Litho. Perf. 13½x13
2068 A692 4.50fr multicolored 2.10 1.00

Marcel Kroenlein Arboretum, 10th Anniv. — A693

1997, Nov. 28 Photo. Perf. 13
2069 A693 9fr multicolored 4.25 2.50
No. 2069 was issued in sheets of 2.

Dog Show Type of 1987
1998, Mar. 19 Litho. Perf. 13x13½
2069A A387 2.70fr Boxer,
Doberman 1.50 .80

Intl. Academy of Peace A694

1998, Mar. 19 Litho. Perf. 13
2070 A694 3fr green & blue 1.40 .70
Portions of the design of No. 2070 were applied by a thermographic process producing a shiny, raised effect.

15th Spring Arts Festival A695

1998, Mar. 19 Litho. Perf. 13x13½
2071 A695 4fr multicolored 1.75 .90

Pierre and Marie Curie, Discovery of Radium, Cent. A696

1998, Mar. 19 Engr. Perf. 13x12½
2072 A696 6fr lilac & green blue 2.75 1.40

Monegasque Red Cross, 50th Anniv. — A697

Prince Albert, Prince Louis II, Princess Grace, Prince Rainier III.

1998, Mar. 3 Litho. Perf. 13
2073 A697 5fr sepia, red & dk brown 2.40 1.25

Prince Albert I (1848-1922) — A698

1998, May 6 Engr.
2074 A698 7fr dark brown 3.25 1.50

Charles Garnier (1825-98), Architect, Designer of Casino of Monte Carlo — A699

1998, May 6 Litho.
2075 A699 10fr multicolored 4.75 2.25

Festival of St. Dévote — A700

1998, May 6 Litho. Perf. 13x13½
2076 A700 3fr multicolored 1.40 .65
Europa.
Portions of the design on No. 2076 were applied by a thermographic process producing a shiny, raised effect.

Joseph Kessel (1898-1979), Writer and Journalist A701

1998, May 6 Engr. Perf. 13½
2077 A701 3.90fr multicolored 1.75 .90

Expo '98, Lisbon A702

1998, May 6 Litho. Perf. 13x13½
2078 A702 2.70fr multicolored 1.25 .60

1st Formula 3000 Grand Prix in Monaco A703

1998, May 20 Engr. Perf. 12
2079 A703 3fr red & black 1.40 .70

European Conference of the Youth Chamber of Economics A705

1998, May 6 Litho. Perf. 13½x13
2081 A705 3fr multicolored 1.40 .70

World Music Awards — A706

1998, May 6
2082 A706 10fr multicolored 4.25 2.75

Porcelain — A707

1998, June 24 Perf. 13
2083 A707 8fr multicolored 3.75 1.75

Publication of Monaco's Works of Art — A708

1998, June 24
2084 A708 9fr multicolored 4.25 2.00

National Festival — A709

Europa: Prince Albert, Prince Rainier III, national palace.

1998, May 31 Litho. Perf. 13
2085 A709 3fr multicolored 1.40 .70
Portions of the design on No. 2085 were applied by a thermographic process producing a shiny, raised effect.

Flowering Cacti Type of 1993
2.70fr, Opuntia dejecta. 4fr, Echinocereus blanckii. 6fr, Euphorbia milii. 7fr, Stapelia variegata.

			Perf. 13
1998, Aug. 3		**Engr.**	
2086 A597 2.70fr multicolored	1.25	.50
2087 A597 4fr multicolored	1.75	.75
2088 A597 6fr multicolored	2.75	1.10
2089 A597 7fr multicolored	3.25	1.25
Nos. 2086-2089 (4)	9.00	3.60

1998 World Cup Soccer Championships, France — A710

1998, Aug. 3
2090 A710 15fr multicolored 7.00 3.50
No. 2090 contains hexagonal perforated label in center.

Enzo Ferrari (1898-1988), Automobile Manufacturer — A711

1998, Aug. 14 Litho.
2091 A711 7fr multicolored 3.25 1.75

George Gershwin (1898-1937), Composer — A712

1998, Aug. 14 Engr. Perf. 13x12½
2092 A712 7.50fr bl, bl grn & blk 3.50 1.75

Intl. College for Study of Marine Pollution, Marine Environment Laboratory — A713

1998, Sept. 4 Litho. Perf. 13x13½
2093 A713 4.50fr multicolored 2.10 .90

Plenary Assembly of the European Post, Monte Carlo A714

1998, Sept. 4
2094 A714 5fr multicolored 2.40 .90

Expo '98, World Philatelic Exhibition, Lisbon A715

1998, Sept. 4   **Litho. & Engr.**
2095 A715 6.70fr multicolored   3.00 1.50

Intl. Assoc. Against Violence in Sports, 30th Anniv. A716

Photo. & Engr.
1998, Sept. 14   **Perf. 13x13½**
2096 A716 4.20fr multicolored   2.00 1.00

Magic Stars Magic Festival, Monte Carlo — A717

1998, Sept. 26   Litho.   Perf. 13½x13
2097 A717 3.50fr red & bister   1.60 .80
See No. 2140.

Giovanni Lorenzo Bernini (1598-1680), Architect, Sculptor — A718

1998, Sept. 26   Engr.   Perf. 13x12½
2098 A718 11.50fr blue & brown 5.50 3.25

Italia '98, Intl. Philatelic Exhibition, Milan — A719

1998, Oct. 23   **Perf. 12½x13**
2099 A719 4.90fr Milan Cathedral 2.25 1.10

Christmas A720

3fr, Ornament. 6.70fr, Nativity scene, horiz. 15fr, Icon of Madonna and Child, 10th cent.

Perf. 13½x13, 13x13½
1998, Oct. 26   **Litho.**
2100 A720   3fr multicolored   1.40 .50
2101 A720 6.70fr multicolored   3.00 1.25

Souvenir Sheet
Engr.
Perf. 13
2102 A720   15fr multicolored   5.75 5.75
No. 2102 contains one 36x49mm stamp.

23rd Intl. Circus Festival, Monte Carlo — A721

1998, Nov. 20   Litho.   Perf. 13½x13
2103 A721 2.70fr multicolored   1.25 .50

Grimaldi Seamounts A722

1998, Nov. 20   **Perf. 13**
2104 A722 10fr multicolored   4.25 2.00

Souvenir Sheet

Reign of Prince Rainier III, 50th Anniv. — A723

1998, Nov. 20   **Engr.**
2105 A723 25fr red & yel bister 12.00 12.00

Congress Center Auditorium of Monaco, 20th Anniv. A724

1999, Feb. 12   Litho.   Perf. 13x13½
2106 A724 2.70fr multicolored   1.25 .50

39th Intl. Television Festival, Monte Carlo — A725

1999, Jan. 18   Litho.   Perf. 13½x13
2107 A725 3.80fr multicolored   1.75 .80

Dog Show Type of 1982
Cocker spaniel and American cocker spaniel.

1999, Jan. 18   Litho.   Perf. 13x13½
2108 A387 4fr multicolored   2.10 1.10

Geneva Conventions, 50th Anniv. — A726

1999, Jan. 18   Engr.   Perf. 13½x13
2109 A726 4.40fr black & red   2.10 .80

32nd Intl. Flower Show, Monte Carlo — A727

1999, Jan. 18   Litho.   Perf. 13½x13
2110 A727 4.50fr multicolored   2.10 1.10

Monaco '99, Intl. Philatelic Exhibition — A728

Photo. & Engr.
1999, Jan. 18   **Perf. 13x12**
2111 A728 3fr multicolored   1.40 .50

Beginning with No. 2112, denominations are indicated on the stamps in both Francs and Euros. The listing value is shown in Francs.

10th Piano Masters Competition, Monte Carlo — A729

1999, Feb. 12   **Perf. 13x13½**
2112 A729 4.60fr multicolored   2.10 .80

Flowers — A730

Designs: 4.90fr, Prince of Monaco Jubilee Rose. 6fr, Paphiopedilum Prince Rainier III, Prince of Monaco and Grimaldi Roses.

1999   **Litho.   Perf. 13½x13**
2113 A730 4.90fr multicolored   2.25 1.25
2114 A730   6fr multicolored   2.75 1.40
Issued: 4.90fr, 2/14; 6fr, 2/13.

Monaco Charity Assoc., 20th Anniv. A731

1999, Jan. 28   Litho.   Perf. 13
2115 A731 6.70fr multicolored   3.00 1.50

Formula 1 Grand Prix of Monaco, 70th Anniv. — A732

1999, Apr. 16   Photo.   Perf. 12¼
2116 A732 3fr multicolored   1.40 .80

Intl. Grand Prix of Philately, Monaco — A733

1999, Apr. 16   **Perf. 13¼**
2117 A733 4.40fr multicolored   2.00 1.10

Fifth Intl. Show Jumping Championships, Monte Carlo — A734

1999, Apr. 16   Engr.   Perf. 13x12½
2118 A734 5.20fr blk, dk grn & red   2.40 1.50

ASM Sports Club, 75th Anniv. — A735

Cutouts of soccer players over: No. 2119, Palace. No. 2120, Aerial view of city.

1999, Apr. 16   Litho.   Perf. 13x12¾
2119 A735 7fr multicolored   3.25 1.90
2120 A735 7fr multicolored   3.25 1.90
    a.   Pair, #2119-2120   6.50 6.50

Grimaldi Forum A736

1999, Apr. 25   Photo.   Perf. 13¼
2121 A736 3fr multicolored   1.40 .50

Oceanography Museum, Cent. — A737

1999, Apr. 25   Engr.   Perf. 13¼x13
2122 A737 5fr multicolored   2.40 1.25

Philexfrance '99,
Intl Philatelic
Exhibition
A738

France #1, Eiffel Tower, map of France, exhibition emblem, arms of Monaco.

1999, May 5   Engr.   Perf. 13¼
2123 A738 2.70fr multicolored   1.25 .60
See No. 2133.

A739

1999, May 5   Photo.   Perf. 13
2124 A739 3fr Casino, Cliffs   1.50 .65
        Size: 51x28mm
2125 A739 3fr Park in Fontvieille   1.50 .65
   a.   Pair, #2124-2125   3.25 3.25
Europa.

Monegasque Economic
Growth — A740

Chart and: No. 2126, Fontvieille and underground train station. No. 2127, Larvotto and Grimaldi Forum.

1999, May 5   Photo.   Perf. 13x13¼
2126 A740 5fr multi   2.40 .95
2127 A740 5fr multi   2.40 .95
   a.   Pair, #2126-2127   5.00 5.00

Souvenir Sheet

1949   1999

RAINIER III
PRINCE DE MONACO

Reign of Prince Rainier III, 50th
Anniv. — A741

1999, May 9   Engr.   Perf. 13
2128 A741 20fr blue & gold   9.50 9.50
        See No. 1681.

Honoré de
Balzac (1799-
1850),
Writer — A742

Design: 5.20fr, Countess of Ségur (1799-1874), children's storyteller.

1999   Perf. 12¾x13
2129 A742 4.50fr red & blue   2.10 1.10
2130 A742 5.20fr multicolored   2.40 1.25

PRINCIPAUTE DE MONACO

JUBILÉ DE S.A.S LE PRINCE RAINIER III
1949 - 1999

Reign of Prince Rainier III, 50th
Anniv. — A743

Design: #256, 337, 427, 937, 1287, 1669.

1999   Engr.   Perf. 12¾x13
2131 A743 30fr multicolored   14.00 14.00

UNESCO,
50th Anniv.
A744

1999, July 2   Engr.   Perf. 13x12½
2132 A744 4.20fr multicolored   2.00 .80

PhilexFrance Type of 1999
1999, July 2   Engr.   Perf. 13¼
2133 A738 7fr France #4, 92,
            Monaco #3   3.25 1.50

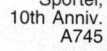

Sportel,
10th Anniv.
A745

1999, July 2   Litho.   Perf. 12¼
2134 A745 10fr multicolored   4.75 2.40

Sovereign
Military
Order of
Malta,
900th
Anniv.
A746

1999, July 2   Engr.   Perf. 11
2135 A746 11.50fr multicolored   5.50 2.75

UPU, 125th
Anniv. — A747

1999, July 2   Engr.   Perf. 13¼
2136 A747 3fr multicolored   1.40 .70

Rose, Iris Named
After Prince
Rainier
III — A748

1999, July 2   Litho.   Perf. 13¼x13
2137 A748 4fr multicolored   1.90 .90

Stamp,
Coin and
Postcard
Show,
Fontvieille
A749

3fr, Aerial photograph, coin obverse, No. 1793A. 6.50fr, Aerial photograph, 100fr coin, #257.

1999   Photo.   Perf. 13¼
2138 A749 3fr multicolored   1.40 .50
        Perf. 13¼x13½
2139 A749 6.50fr multicolored   3.00 1.75
        Jubilee Bourse (#2139).
Issued: 3fr, 7/3; 6.50fr, 9/26.

Magic Stars Type of 1998
Inscribed "99"
Litho. & Typo.
1999, Sept. 6   Perf. 13¼x13
2140 A717 4.50fr red & gold   2.10 1.00

Development Projects — A750

Designs: a, Fontveille 1 & 2. b, La Digue (with jetty). c, Grimaldi Forum. d, La Gare.

1999, Sept. 26   Photo.   Perf. 13
2141   Sheet of 4 + label   20.00 20.00
   a.   A750 4fr multicolored   1.90 1.90
   b.-c. A750 9fr Any single   4.25 4.25
   d.   A750 19fr multicolored   9.00 9.00
        No. 2141d is 80x40mm.

24th Intl. Circus
Festival, Monte
Carlo — A751

1999, Dec. 13   Litho.   Perf. 13¼x13
2142 A751 2.70fr multi   1.25 .55

A752

1999, Dec. 13   Engr.   Perf. 13¼
2143 A752 3fr Christmas   1.40 .60

Holy Year
2000
A753

1999, Dec. 13   Litho.   Perf. 13x13¼
2144 A753 3.50fr multi   1.60 .95

33rd Intl. Flower
Show — A754

1999, Dec. 13   Perf. 13¼x13
2145 A754 4.50fr multi   2.10 1.00

Monaco 2000
Intl. Philatelic
Exposition
A755

1999, Dec. 23   Engr.   Perf. 13¼x13
2146 A755 3fr multi   1.40 .55

Bust of Napoleon,
by Antonio
Canova — A756

Litho. & Embossed

2000, Jan. 17   Perf. 13¼
2147 A756 4.20fr multi   2.00 .90

40th Intl.
Television
Festival, Monte
Carlo — A757

2000, Jan. 17   Litho.   Perf. 13¼x13
2148 A757 4.90fr multi   2.25 .95

The Twelve
Apostles — A758

Saints: 4fr, Peter and James the Great. 5fr, John and Andrew. 6fr, Philip and Bartholomew. 7fr, Matthew and Thomas. 8fr, James the Less and Judas. 9fr, Simon and Matthias.

Engr. with Foil Application

2000, Apr. 3   Perf. 13¼
2149 A758 4fr multi   1.90 .80
2150 A758 5fr multi   2.40 .95
2151 A758 6fr multi   2.75 1.25
2152 A758 7fr multi   3.25 1.50
2153 A758 8fr multi   3.75 2.00
2154 A758 9fr multi   4.25 2.40
     Nos. 2149-2154 (6)   18.30 8.90

Labrador
Retriever
and
Golden
Retriever
A759

2000, Apr. 3   Engr.   Perf. 13¼
2155 A759 6.50fr multi   3.00 1.50

Intl. Dog Show, Monte Carlo.

1993 Intl. Olympic Committee Meeting Awarding 2000 Games to Sydney A760

2000, Apr. 25   Photo.
2156 A760 7fr multi   3.25 1.50

Souvenir Sheet

Art Depicting Monaco and the Sea — A761

Artwork by: a, Adami. b, Arman. c, Cane. d, Folon. e, Fuchs. f, E. De Sigaldi. g, Sosno. h, Verkade.

2000, Apr. 25   Perf. 13x12½
2157   Sheet of 8 + label   25.00 25.00
a.-h. A761 6.55fr Any single   3.00 1.50

2nd Historic
Automobile Grand
Prix — A762

2000, May 9   Litho.   Perf. 13½x13
2158 A762 4.40fr multi   2.10 1.00

Monaco
Pavilion,
Expo 2000,
Hanover
A763

2000, May 9   Perf. 13x13¼
2159 A763 5fr multi   2.40 1.25

Saints Mark, Matthew, John and Luke — A764

2000, May 9   Engr.   Perf. 12¾x13
2160 A764 20fr multi   9.50 6.00

Europa, 2000
Common Design Type and

Flags and Map of Europe — A765

2000, May 9   Litho.   Perf. 13¼x13
2161 CD17 3fr multi   1.40 .70
2162 A765 3fr multi   1.40 .70
a.   Pair, #2161-2162   3.00 3.00

WIPA 2000
Philatelic
Exhibition,
Vienna — A766

2000, May 30   Engr.   Perf. 13¼
2163 A766 4.50fr multi   2.10 1.00

Professional-Celebrity Golf Tournament, Monte Carlo — A767

2000, June 19   Photo.   Perf. 13¼
2164 A767 4.40fr multi   2.10 1.00

Club de Monte
Carlo Exhibition
of Rare Philatelic
Material — A768

2000, June 23
2165 A768 3.50fr multi   1.60 .75

Red
Cross — A769

2000, June 23
2166 A769 10fr multi   4.75 2.00

2000
Summer
Olympics,
Sydney
A770

Olympic rings and: 2.70fr, Fencing, emblem of Monegasque Fencing Federation. 4.50fr, Rowers, flag of Monegasque Nautical Society.

2000, June 23   Engr. & Embossed
2167-2168 A770 Set of 2   3.50 1.75

Automobiles in Prince Rainier III Collection — A771

Woman and: 3fr, 1911 Humber Type Beeston. 6.70fr, 1947 Jaguar 4 cylinder. 10fr, 1956 Rolls-Royce Silver Cloud. 15fr, 1986 Lamborghini Countach.

2000, June 23   Engr.   Perf. 13x13¼
2169-2172 A771 Set of 4   16.00 10.50
     See Nos. 2186-2188.

World Stamp
Expo 2000,
Anaheim — A772

2000, July 7   Litho.   Perf. 13¼x13
2173 A772 4.40fr multi   2.10 .90

Magic Stars
Magic Festival,
Monte
Carlo — A773

2000, Sept. 4   Photo.   Perf. 13¼
2174 A773 4.60fr multi   2.10 1.25

Intl. Mathematics
Year — A774

2000, Sept. 4   Engr.
2175 A774 6.50fr brown   3.00 1.50

Souvenir Sheet

Retable of St. Nicholas, by Ludovic Bréa, Monaco Cathedral — A775

2000, Sept. 4   Photo.
2176 A775 Sheet of 2   14.00 14.00
a.   10fr Two figures, 31x52mm   4.50 1.75
b.   20fr Three figures,
       53x52mm   9.50 4.50

New Aquarium, Oceanographic Museum — A776

2000, Oct. 2   Engr.
2177 A776 3fr multi   1.40 .70

España 2000 Intl. Philatelic Exhibition A777

2000, Oct. 2
2178 A777 3.80fr multi   1.75 .80

Observatory Grotto, 50th Anniv. and Anthropological Museum, 40th Anniv. — A778

2000, Oct. 2
2179 A778 5.20fr multi   2.40 .80

Fish A779

5fr, Fish, coral. 9fr, Fish, starfish, seaweed.

2000, Oct. 2   **Photo.**
2180-2181 A779 Set of 2   6.50 3.00
Fifth Congress of Aquariums (No. 2180), Monegasque Nature Protection Association, 25th anniv. (No. 2181).

Fifth Congress of Aquariums — A780

2000, Nov. 25 Photo. Perf. 13x12¾
2182 A780 7fr multi   3.25 1.75

Christmas A781

2000, Dec. 1 Photo. Perf. 13¼
2183 A781 3fr multi   1.40 .50

Princess Stephanie, President of AMAPEI — A782

2000, Dec. 1   Engr.
2184 A782 11.50fr red & slate   5.50 3.00

Souvenir Sheet

Monaco 2000 Intl. Philatelic Exhibition — A783

2001, Dec. 1   Photo.   Imperf.
2185 A783 Sheet of 2 #2185a   19.00 19.00
  a.   20fr multi   9.50   9.50

Prince's Automobiles Type of 2000
Woman and: 5fr, 1989 Ferrari F1. 6fr, 1955 Fiat 600 Type Jolly. 8fr, 1929 Citroen C4F Autochenille.

2000, Dec. 1 Engr. Perf. 13x13¼
2186-2188 A771 Set of 3   9.00 4.50

Exhibit of Chinese Terracotta Figures, Grimaldi Forum — A784

2000, Dec. 2   Photo.   Perf. 13¼
2189 A784 2.70fr multi   1.25 .40

Postal Museum. 50th Anniv. — A785

2000, Dec. 2
2190 A785 3fr multi   1.40 .50

Coat of Arms — A786

Serpentine Die Cut 11
2000, Dec. 4   Photo.
Booklet Stamp
Self-Adhesive
2191 A786 (3fr) red & black   1.40 .30
  a.   Booklet of 10   14.00
See Nos. 2389, 2410, 2673, 2775. Compare with Type A1076.

Princess Caroline of Monaco Iris — A787

2000, Dec. 2   Photo.   Perf. 13¼
2192 A787 3.80fr multi   1.75 .70
34th Intl. Flower Show.

Sardinian Postage Stamps, 150th Anniv. (in 2001) A788

2000, Dec. 2 Engr. Perf. 13x12½
2193 A788 6.50fr Sardinia #1-3   3.00 1.75

RAMOGE Agreement, 25th Anniv. A789

2000, Dec. 2
2194 A789 6.70fr multi   3.00 1.75

Awarding of ASCAT Grand Prize to Bertrand Piccard — A790

2000, Dec. 2   Photo.   Perf. 13¼
2195 A790 9fr Balloon, #1433   4.25 2.00

Monaco Team, 2000 French Soccer Champions A791

2000, Dec. 3
2196 A791 4.50fr multi   2.10 .90

French, Italian and Monegasque Marine Mammal Sanctuary — A792

2000, Dec. 3
2197 A792 5.20fr multi   2.40 1.25

Neapolitan Creche, Natl. Museum — A793

2000, Dec. 3   Perf. 13x12½
2198 A793 10fr multi   4.75 3.00

25th Intl. Circus Festival, Monte Carlo — A794

No. 2200: a, Clown with guitar. b, Clown. c, Tiger and tent top. d, Acrobats, tiger, lion, horses, clowns. e, Chimpanzee and high-wire acrobat.

2000, Dec. 3   Perf. 13¼
2199 A794 2.70fr shown   1.25 .60
2200 A794 6fr Sheet of 5,
        #a-e + label   14.00 14.00

41st Intl. Television Festival, Monte Carlo — A795

2001, Feb. 5 Photo. Perf. 13½x13
2201 A795 3.50fr multi   1.60 .90

Leonberger and Newfoundland — A796

2001, Apr. 14 Litho. Perf. 13x13¼
2202 A796 6.50fr multi   3.00 1.25

Euroflora Flower Show — A797

2001, Apr. 21 Photo. Perf. 13¼
2203 A797 6.70fr multi   3.00 1.25

Europa — A798

Designs: No. 2204, 3fr, Palace of Monaco, water droplets. No. 2205, 3fr, Wash house.

2001, May 7 Litho. Perf. 13½x13
2204-2205 A798 Set of 2   2.75 1.10

Prince Rainier III Literary Prize, 50th Anniv. — A799

2001, May 14   **Engr.**   **Perf. 13¼**
2206 A799 2.70fr multi   1.25   .45

André Malraux (1901-76), Novelist — A800

2001, May 14   **Litho.**   **Perf. 13¼x13**
2207 A800 10fr black & red   4.75 1.75

Belgica 2001 Intl. Stamp Exhibition, Brussels — A801

2001, June 9   **Engr.**   **Perf. 13¼**
2208 A801 4fr brt blue & red   1.90   .70

2001 Philatelic and Numismatic Bourse — A802

2001, July 2   **Photo.**   **Perf. 13¼**
2209 A802 2.70fr multi   1.25   .45

Princess Grace Dance Academy, 25th Anniv. — A803

2001 July 2   **Photo.**   **Perf. 13¼**
2210 A803 4.40fr multi   2.10   .90

Naval Museum A804

2001, July 2   **Photo.**   **Perf. 13¼**
2211 A804 4.50fr multi   2.10   .90

37th Petanque World Championships — A805

2001, July 2   **Perf. 13x13¼**
2212 A805 5fr multi   2.40   .80

Emile Littré, Denis Diderot, and Reference Books A806

2001, Aug. 1   **Engr.**   **Perf. 13¼**
2213 A806 4.20fr multi   2.00   .95

Prince Albert I Oceanography Prize, 30th Anniv. — A807

2001, Aug. 1   **Engr.**   **Perf. 13¼**
2214 A807 9fr bright blue   4.25 1.50

David, by Michelangelo, 500th Anniv. — A808

2001, Aug. 1   **Engr.**   **Perf. 13**
2215 A808 20fr multi   9.50 6.00

Palace of Monaco — A809

Designs: 3fr, Fireplace, Throne Hall. 4.50fr, Blue Hall. 6.70fr, York Chamber. 15fr, Fresco, ceiling of Throne Hall.

2001, Aug. 1   **Photo.**   **Perf. 13x13¼**
2216-2219 A809   Set of 4   13.50 6.50

A810

Nobel Prizes, Cent. — A811

Designs: 5fr, Alfred Nobel. 8fr, Jean-Henri Dunant, 1901 Peace laureate. 11.50fr, Enrico Fermi, 1938 Physics laureate.

2001, Sept. 3   **Engr.**   **Perf. 13¼**
2220 A810   5fr multi   2.40   .95
2221 A810   8fr multi   3.75 1.50
2222 A811 11.50fr multi   5.50 3.25
   Nos. 2220-2222 (3)   11.65 5.70

36th Meeting of Intl. Commission for Scientific Exploration of the Mediterranean — A812

2001, Oct. 1   **Photo.**   **Perf. 13x13¼**
2223 A812 3fr multi   1.40   .50

Christmas — A813

2001, Oct. 1   **Perf. 13¼**
2224 A813 3fr multi   1.40   .50

100 Cents = 1 Euro (€)

Flora & Fauna A814

Designs: 1c, Arctia caja, vert. 2c, Luria lurida. 5c, Thunbergia grandiflora, vert. 10c, Parus major. 20c, Anthias anthias. 50c, Charaxes jasius, vert. €1, Mitra zonata. €2, Datura sanguinea, vert. €5, Parus cristatus, vert. €10, Macroamphosus scolopax.

2002, Jan. 1   **Engr.**   **Perf. 13¼**
2225 A814   1c multi   .25   .25
2226 A814   2c multi   .25   .25
2227 A814   5c multi   .25   .25
2228 A814   10c multi   .30   .25
2229 A814   20c multi   .60   .25
2230 A814   50c multi   1.50   .75
2231 A814   €1 multi   3.00 1.50
2232 A814   €2 multi   6.00 3.00
2233 A814   €5 multi   15.00 7.50
2234 A814   €10 multi   30.00 15.00
   Nos. 2225-2234 (10)   57.15 29.00

See Nos. 2275, 2323-2324.

Palace of Monaco A815

Designs: 41c, Gallery of Mirrors, vert. 46c, Throne room. 58c, Painting in Gallery of Mirrors.

2002, Jan. 1   **Photo.**
2235-2237 A815   Set of 3   4.25 2.00

26th Intl. Circus Festival — A816

2002, Jan. 1
2238 A816 41c multi   1.25   .60

35th Intl. Flower Show A817

2002, Jan. 1
2239 A817 53c multi   1.50   .75

Souvenir Sheet

Automobile Club of Monaco — A818

No. 2240: a, Old and new cars, emblem of 70th Monte Carlo Rally. b, Racing cars in 3rd Historic Grand Prix and 60th Grand Prix races.

2002, Jan. 16   **Perf. 13¼x13**
2240 A818   Sheet of 2   6.75 6.75
  a.   €1.07 multi   3.00 1.50
  b.   €1.22 multi   3.50 1.75

Prehistoric Anthropology Museum, Cent. — A819

2002, Feb. 8   **Perf. 13¼**
2241 A819 64c multi   1.90   .95

La Carrière d'un Navigateur, by Prince Albert I, Cent. A820

2002, Feb. 8
2242 A820 67c multi   2.00 1.00

2002 Winter Olympics, Salt Lake City — A821

No. 2243: a, Denomination at UL. b, Denomination at UR.

2002, Feb. 8　　　　**Perf. 12¼**
2243　A821　Horiz. pair　1.75　1.75
a.-b.　23c Either single　.85　.40

Jules Cardinal Mazarin (1602-61) A822

2002, Feb. 18
2244　A822　69c multi　2.00　1.00

Legion of Honor, Bicent. — A823

2002, Feb. 18　　　**Perf. 13¼**
2245　A823　70c multi　2.10　1.00

Cetacean Conservation Accord — A824

2002, Feb. 18　　　**Engr.**
2246　A824　75c multi　2.25　1.10

Leonardo da Vinci (1452-1519) — A825

2002, Mar. 21　　　**Photo.**
2247　A825　76c multi　2.25　1.10

St. Bernard and Swiss Bouvier A826

2002, Mar. 21　　　**Engr.**
2248　A826　99c multi　3.00　1.50
Intl. Dog Show. See Nos. 2286, 2491.

Police, Cent. — A827

2002, Apr. 23　　　**Photo.**
2249　A827　53c multi　1.60　.70

European Academy of Philately, 25th Anniv. A828

2002, Apr. 27　　　**Engr.**
2250　A828　58c multi　1.75　.85

20th Intl. Swimming Meet — A829

2002, May 3　**Photo.**　**Perf. 13¼**
2251　A829　64c multi　1.90　.95

Europa — A830

Designs: No. 2252, 46c, Clown on globe, juggler, elephant, tent tops. No. 2253, 46c, "Jours de Cirque," circus acts.

2002, May 3
2252-2253　A830　Set of 2　2.75　1.25

First Experiment with Tar Roads, Cent. A831

2002, May 31　　　**Engr.**
2254　A831　41c multi　1.25　.60

MonacoPhil 2002 Intl. Philatelic Exhibition — A832

2002, May 31
2255　A832　46c multi　1.40　.65

42nd Intl. Television Festival, Monte Carlo — A833

2002, May 31　**Photo.**　**Perf. 13¼x13**
2256　A833　70c multi　2.10　1.00

2002 World Cup Soccer Championships, Japan and Korea — A834

2002, May 31　**Engr.**　**Perf. 13¼**
2257　A834　75c multi　2.25　1.10

"Pelléas et Mélisande," Opera by Claude Debussy, Cent. of Debut — A835

2002, June 21
2258　A835　69c multi　2.10　1.00

Saint Dévote, Dove and Boat A836

2002, June 21
2259　A836　€1.02 multi　3.00　1.50
Red Cross.

Intl. Year of Mountains A837

2002, June 21　**Litho.**　**Perf. 13x13¼**
2260　A837　€1.37 multi　4.00　2.00

Euro Coinage — A838

No. 2261: a, Obverse of 1c, 2c, and 5c coins and reverse. b, Obverse of 10c, 20c, and 50c coins and reverse.
No. 2262: a, Obverse and reverse of €1 coin. b, Obverse and reverse of €2 coin.

Litho. & Embossed
2002, June 21　　　**Perf. 13¼**
2261　A838　Horiz. pair　3.00　3.00
a.-b.　46c Either single　1.40　.70
2262　A838　Horiz. pair　9.25　9.25
a.-b.　€1.50 Either single　4.50　4.50

Victor Hugo (1802-85), Writer — A839

No. 2263: a, Hugo and illustration from *Notre-Dame de Paris*. b, Hugo and illustration from *La Légende de Siécles*.

2002, July 1　　　**Perf. 13¼**
2263　A839　Horiz. pair　3.25　3.25
a.　50c multi　1.50　.75
b.　57c multi　1.75　.85

Alexandre Dumas (Father) (1802-70), Writer — A840

No. 2264: a, Dumas. b, Characters, manuscript.

2002, July 1　　　**Photo.**
2264　A840　Horiz. pair　3.50　3.50
a.-b.　61c Either single　1.75　.85

26th Publication of "Annales Monegasques" A841

2002, July 15
2265　A841　€1.75 multi　5.25　2.50

Christmas — A842

2002, Sept. 2
2266　A842　50c multi　1.50　.75

Debut of Movie "Le Voyage dans le Lune," by Georges Méliès, Cent. — A843

2002, Sept. 2　　　**Perf. 13¼**
2267　A843　76c multi　2.25　1.10

17th Magic Stars Magic Festival, Monte Carlo — A844

2002, Sept. 2
2268 A844 €1.52 multi 4.50 2.25

Awarding of ASCAT Grand Prize to Luis Figo — A845

2002, Nov. 29 **Engr.**
2269 A845 91c multi 2.75 1.25

Automobiles in Prince Rainier III Collection A846

Designs: 46c, 1949 Mercedes 220A Cabriolet. 69c, 1956 Rolls-Royce Silver Cloud I. €1.40, 1974 Citroen DS 21.

2002, Nov. 29 **Photo.**
2270-2272 A846 Set of 3 7.50 3.75

Souvenir Sheet

The Four Seasons, Frescos in Prince's Palace — A847

2002, Nov. 29 **Perf. 13x13¼**
2273 A847 Sheet of 4 15.00 15.00
a. 50c Spring 1.50 .75
b. €1 Summer 3.00 1.50
c. €1.50 Autumn 4.50 2.25
d. €2 Winter 6.00 3.00

Souvenir Sheet

MonacoPhil 2002 Intl. Philatelic Exhibition — A848

No. 2274: a, Monaco attractions. b, Emblem of Club de Monte Carlo.

2002, Nov. 29 **Imperf.**
2274 A848 Sheet of 2 18.00 18.00
a.-b. €3 Either single 9.00 4.50

Flora & Fauna Type of 2002
2002, Nov. 30 **Engr.** **Perf. 13¼**
2275 A814 41c Helix aspersa, vert. 1.25 .60

36th Intl. Flower Show — A849

2002, Nov. 30 **Photo.**
2276 A849 67c multi 2.00 1.00

World Association of Friends of Children, 40th Anniv. (in 2003) A850

2002, Nov. 30
2277 A850 €1.25 multi 3.75 1.75

Martyrdom of St. George, 1700th Anniv. — A851

2002, Dec. 1
2278 A851 53c multi 1.60 .70

Saint Cyr Military School, Bicent. — A852

2002, Dec. 1
2279 A852 61c multi 1.75 .85

27th Intl. Circus Festival — A853

2003, Jan. 2 **Photo.** **Perf. 13¼**
2280 A853 59c multi 1.75 .70

15th New Circus Artists' Festival — A854

2003, Feb. 1
2281 A854 €2.82 multi 8.50 4.00

10th World Bobsled Push Championships, Ilsenberg, Germany — A855

2003, Feb. 3
2282 A855 80c multi 2.40 .95

Monaco Yacht Club, 50th Anniv. — A856

2003, Feb. 5
2283 A856 46c multi 1.40 .60

Intl. Institute for Peace, Cent. — A857

2003, Mar. 3
2284 A857 €1.19 multi 3.50 1.75

Tennis Tournament at Monte Carlo Country Club, 75th Anniv. — A858

2003, Mar. 3
2285 A858 €1.30 multi 4.00 2.00

Dog Show Type of 2002
2003, Mar. 24 Litho. **Perf. 13x13½**
2286 A826 79c Rough collie 2.50 1.25

Junior Economic Chamber of Monaco, 40th Anniv. A859

2003, Apr. 5 **Photo.** **Perf. 13¼**
2287 A859 41c multi 1.25 .60

Monte Carlo Country Club, 75th Anniv. A860

2003, Apr. 12
2288 A860 46c multi 1.40 .70

General Bathymetric Charts of the Oceans, Cent. — A861

No. 2289: a, Prince Albert I, map of Arctic region, chart of Northern hemisphere. b, Oceanographic museum, map of Antarctica, chart of Southern hemisphere.

2003, Apr. 14 **Perf. 13x12½**
2289 A861 €1.25 Vert. pair, #a-b 7.50 7.50

Poster by Alfons Mucha — A862

Poster by Jean-Gabriel Domergue — A863

2003, May 5 **Perf. 13¼**
2290 A862 50c multi 1.50 .75
2291 A863 50c multi 1.50 .75
Europa.

Grand Bourse 2003 — A864

2003, June 2
2292 A864 45c multi 1.40 .70

43rd Intl. Television Festival, Monte Carlo — A865

2003, June 2 **Perf. 13¼x13**
2293 A865 90c multi 2.75 1.25

15th Antiques Biennale — A866

2003, June 2　　*Perf. 13¼*
2294 A866 €1.80 multi　　5.50 2.75

Navigation of Northwest Passage by Roald Amundsen, Cent. A867

2003, June 30
2295 A867 90c multi　　2.75 1.40

Powered Flight, Cent. A868

2003, June 30
2296 A868 €1.80 multi　　5.50 2.75

Hector Berlioz (1803-69), Composer A869

2003, July 21　　*Engr.*
2297 A869 75c red & black　　2.25 1.10

Aram Khatchaturian (1903-78), Composer — A870

2003, July 21
2298 A870 €1.60 multi　　4.75 2.40

Portrait of a Woman, by François Boucher (1703-70) A871

Self-portrait, by Vincent van Gogh (1853-90) — A872

Self-portrait, by Francesco Mazzola, "Il Parmigianino" (1503-40) — A873

2003, Aug. 6　　*Perf. 13¼x13*
2299 A871 €1.30 multi　　4.00 1.90
2300 A872 €3 black & pink　　9.00 4.25
2301 A873 €3.60 black & tan　10.50 5.00
Nos. 2299-2301 (3)　　23.50 11.15

Discovery of Structure of DNA Molecule, 50th Anniv. — A874

2003, Sept. 1　　*Perf. 13¼*
2302 A874 58c multi　　1.75 .85

Nostradamus (1503-66), Astrologer — A875

2003, Sept. 1　　*Photo.*
2303 A875 70c multi　　2.00 1.00

2003 Magic Stars Festival, Monte Carlo — A876

2003, Sept. 1　*Litho.*　*Perf. 13½x13*
2304 A876 75c multi　　2.25 1.10

Discovery of Penicillin by Alexander Fleming, 75th Anniv. — A877

2003, Sept. 1　*Engr.*　*Perf. 13¼*
2305 A877 €1.11 multi　　3.25 1.60

Awarding of Nobel Physics Prize to Pierre and Marie Curie, Cent. A878

2003, Sept. 1　　*Photo.*
2306 A878 €1.20 multi　　3.50 1.75

Conquest of Mt. Everest, by Sir Edmund Hillary, 50th Anniv. A879

2003, Sept. 29　*Engr.*　*Perf. 13¼*
2307 A879 €1 multi　　3.00 1.50

Saint Dévote — A880

No. 2308: a, Kneeling before cross. b, Standing before soldiers. c, Boat and dove. d, Standing in front of church.

2003, Sept. 29
2308 A880 45c Block of 4, #a-d　5.50 5.50

Christmas — A881

2003, Oct. 13　　*Photo.*
2309 A881 50c multi　　1.50 .75

MonacoPhil 2004 Intl. Philatelic Exhibition — A882

2003, Dec. 15
2310 A882 50c multi　　1.50 .75

28th Intl. Circus Festival, Monte Carlo — A883

2003, Dec. 15
2311 A883 70c multi　　2.10 1.00

Beausoleil, France, Cent. A884

2004, Jan. 5　*Photo.*　*Perf. 13¼*
2312 A884 75c multi　　2.25 1.10

Saint Dévote A885

Designs: 50c, Arrest of St. Dévote, vert. 75c, Proceedings against St. Dévote. 90c, Stoning of St. Dévote. €1, St. Dévote in boat, vert. €4, Protection of St. Dévote.

2004, Jan. 5　　*Engr.*
2313 A885 50c red brn & red　1.50 .75
2314 A885 75c brn & orange　2.25 1.10
2315 A885 90c dk brn & brn　2.75 1.50
2316 A885 €1 dk brn & yel brn　3.00 1.50
2317 A885 €4 dk brn & red brn　12.00 6.00
Nos. 2313-2317 (5)　21.50 10.85

6th Monegasque Biennale of Cancerology — A886

2004, Jan. 29　*Photo.*　*Perf. 13¼*
2318 A886 €1.11 multi　　3.25 1.50

Princess Grace Foundation, 40th Anniv. — A887

Princess Grace Irish Library, 20th Anniv. A888

Statue of Princess Grace, by Daphné du Barry — A889

Princess Grace Rose Garden, 20th Anniv. — A890

Photo., Litho. (#2320-2321)
2004, Jan. 29
2319	A887	50c multi	1.50	.75
2320	A888	€1.11 grn & brown	3.25	1.50
2321	A889	€1.45 multi	4.25	2.00
2322	A890	€1.90 multi	5.50	2.75
		Nos. 2319-2322 (4)	14.50	7.00

Flora & Fauna Type of 2002
Designs: 75c, Hyla meridionalis, vert. €4.50, Lacerta viridis, vert.

2004, Mar. 8   Engr.   Perf. 13¼
2323	A814	75c multi	2.25	1.10
2324	A814	€4.50 multi	13.50	6.75

20th Spring of Arts A891

2004, Apr. 2
2325	A891	€1 multi	3.00	1.50

Cathedral Choir School, Cent. — A892

2004, Apr. 5   Photo.
2326	A892	45c multi	1.40	.70

37th Intl. Flower Show — A893

2004, Apr. 5
2327	A893	58c multi	1.75	.85

Dog Show Type of 2002
2004, Apr. 9   Litho.   Perf. 13x13¼
2328	A826	90c Cavalier King Charles Spaniel	2.75	1.40

Monaco Grand Prix, 75th Anniv. A894

2004, Apr. 14   Photo.   Perf. 13¼
2329	A894	€1.20 multi	3.50	1.75

International School of Monaco, 10th Anniv. — A895

2004, Apr. 26   Litho.   Perf. 13x13¼
2330	A895	50c multi	1.50	.75

Europa — A896

Travel posters: No. 2331, 50c, Shown. No. 2332, 50c, Women in bathing suits at beach.

2004, May 3   Photo.   Perf. 13¼
2331-2332	A896	Set of 2	3.00	1.50

Order of Grimaldi, 50th Anniv. — A897

Litho. & Embossed
2004, May 3   Perf. 13¼x13
2333	A897	90c multi	2.75	1.40

2004 Summer Olympics, Athens — A898

No. 2334: a, Stadium, modern runners. b, Stadium, ancient runners.

2004, May 3   Perf. 13x13¼
2334	A898	45c Vert. pair, #a-b	2.75	1.40

Napoleon I and Monegasque Princes in Imperial Army — A899

Stéphanie de Beauharnais, by Baron Gérard — A900

Designs: 75c, Imperial symbols of Napoleon I, horiz. €2.40, Napoleon I, by Gérard.

Perf. 12¼x13, 13x13¼ (75c)
2004, May 28   Photo.
2335	A899	58c multi	1.75	.85
2336	A899	75c multi	2.25	1.10
2337	A900	€1.90 multi	5.75	2.75
2338	A900	€2.40 multi	7.25	3.50
		Nos. 2335-2338 (4)	17.00	8.20

Sergey Diaghilev (1872-1929), George Balanchine (1904-83) and Dancers of Ballet Russes de Monte Carlo — A901

2004, June 14   Engr.   Perf. 13¼
2339	A901	€1.60 multi	4.75	2.40

44th Television Festival, Monte Carlo — A902

2004, June 14   Litho.   Perf. 13¼x13
2340	A902	€1.80 multi	5.50	2.75

Frédéric Mistral (1830-1914), 1904 Nobel Laureate in Literature — A903

2004, June 26   Engr.   Perf. 13¼
2341	A903	45c multi	1.40	.70

23rd UPU Congress, Bucharest, Romania A904

2004, June 26
2342	A904	50c multi	1.50	.75

Marco Polo (1254-1324), Explorer — A905

2004, June 26
2343	A905	50c multi	1.50	.75

Salon du Timbre, Paris A906

2004, June 26
2344	A906	75c multi	2.25	1.10

Translation into French of *A Thousand and One Nights*, 300th Anniv. — A907

Litho. & Silk Screened
2004, June 26   Perf. 13x13¼
2345	A907	€1 deep blue & gray	3.00	1.50

Monte Carlo Beach Hotel, 75th Anniv. A908

2004, July 5   Photo.   Perf. 13¼
2346	A908	45c multi	1.40	.70

FIFA (Fédération Internationale de Football Association), Cent. — A909

2004, Aug. 2
2347	A909	€1.60 multi	4.75	2.40

Magic Stars Magic Festival, Monte Carlo A910

2004, Sept. 6   Litho.   Perf. 13x13¼
2348   A910   45c multi   1.40   .70

Souvenir Sheet

PRINCIPAUTE DE MONACO

Hommage à Grace, Patricia KELLY

Princess Grace (1929-82) — A911

Portraits of Princess Grace engraved by: a, 75c, Pierre Albuisson. b, €1.75, Czeslaw Slania. c, €3.50, Martin Mörck.

2004, Oct. 4   Engr.   Perf. 13¼x13
2349   A911   Sheet of 3 + label   18.00   18.00
  a.   75c green & blue   2.25   1.10
  b.   €1.75 green & blue   5.25   2.50
  c.   €3.50 green & blue   10.50   5.25
    See No. 2367.

Christmas A912

2004, Oct. 4   Photo.   Perf. 13¼
2350   A912   50c multi   1.50   .75

Admission to Council of Europe A913

2004, Oct. 5   Engr.   Perf. 13x12½
2351   A913   50c red & blue   1.50   .75

29th Intl. Circus Festival, Monte Carlo — A914

2004, Dec. 3   Photo.   Perf. 13¼
2352   A914   45c multi   1.40   .70

Louis II Stadium, 20th Anniv. — A915

2004, Dec. 3   Engr.   Perf. 12½x13
2353   A915   50c multi   1.50   .75

University of Paris Student Hostel, 70th Anniv. — A916

2004, Dec. 3   Perf. 13¼
2354   A916   58c multi   1.75   .85

Palace of Justice, 75th Anniv. — A917

2004, Dec. 3   Photo.
2355   A917   75c multi   2.25   1.10

French Alliance of Monaco, 25th Anniv. — A918

2004, Dec. 3
2356   A918   75c multi   2.25   1.10

38th Intl. Flower Show — A919

2004, Dec. 3   Photo.   Perf. 13¼
2357   A919   90c multi   2.75   1.40

Luigi Valentino Brugnatelli (1761-1818), Inventor of Electroplating — A920

Litho. & Engr.
2004, Dec. 3   Perf. 13¼
2358   A920   €1 blk & brn   3.00   1.50

Jean-Paul Sartre (1905-80), Author A921

2004, Dec. 3   Photo.
2359   A921   €1.11 multi   3.25   1.60

Invention of Safety Matches by Johan Edvard Lundstrom, 150th Anniv. A922

2004, Dec. 3
2360   A922   €1.20 multi   3.50   1.75

Publication of Don Quixote, by Miguel de Cervantes, 400th Anniv. — A923

2004, Dec. 3   Engr.
2361   A923   €1.20 multi   3.50   1.75

Léo Ferré (1916-93), Singer A924

2004, Dec. 3   Photo.
2362   A924   €1.40 multi   4.25   2.10

Invention of Hypodermic Syringe by Alexander Wood, 150th Anniv. — A925

2004, Dec. 3   Engr.
2363   A925   €1.60 multi   4.75   2.40

Development of Carbon 14 Dating by Willard F. Libby, 50th Anniv. — A926

2004, Dec. 3   Perf. 12½x13
2364   A926   €1.80 multi   5.50   2.75

Princes and Palace of Monaco — A927

No. 2365: a, Prince Rainier III (30x31mm). b, Palace of Monaco (60x31mm). c, Hereditary Prince Albert (30x31mm).

2004, Dec. 3   Perf. 13¼
2365   A927   50c Horiz. strip of 3,
          #a-c   4.50   2.25

First World Cup Soccer Championships, 75th Anniv. — A928

No. 2366: a, World Cup, goalie catching soccer ball. b, Flag of Uruguay, player dribbling ball.

2004, Dec. 3   Photo.   Perf. 13¼
2366   A928   €1 Horiz. pair, #a-b   6.00   3.00

Princess Grace Type of 2004 in Changed Colors with "MonacoPhil 2004" Added in Sheet Margin
Souvenir Sheet

Designs like No. 2349.

2004, Dec. 3   Engr.   Imperf.
2367   A911   Sheet of 3   18.00 18.00
  a.   75c blue & emerald   2.25   2.25
  b.   €1.75 blue & emerald   5.25   5.25
  c.   €3.50 blue & emerald   10.50 10.50

Rotary International, Cent. — A929

Designs: 55c, Rotary emblem, founder, president, treasurer and secretary of original club. 70c, Rotary emblem, vert.

Litho. & Engr., Litho. (70c)
Perf. 13¼, 13¼x13 (70c)
2005, Feb. 23
2368-2369   A929   Set of 2   3.75   1.90

UNESCO Fine Arts Committee, 50th Anniv. — A930

2005, Mar. 1   Photo.   Perf. 13¼
2370   A930   48c multi   1.40   .70

Publication of Albert Einstein's Theory of Relativity, Cent. — A931

2005, Mar. 1
2371   A931   53c multi   1.60   .80

First Awarding of Diplomas From School of Fine Arts — A932

2005, Mar. 1   Litho.   Perf. 13¼x13
2372   A932   64c black & red   1.90   .95

Dog Show Type of 2002

2005, Mar. 1   Photo.   Perf. 13¼
2373 A826 82c Dachshund (teck-el)   2.50 1.25

Intl. Automobile Federation, Cent. — A933

2005, Apr. 1   Photo.   Perf. 13¼
2374 A933 55c multi   1.60 1.60

21st World Exhibition of Hybrid and Electric Vehicles A934

Designs, 75c, Fetish, first electric sports car. €1.30, Stylized automobile with electric plug.

2005, Apr. 1
2375-2376 A934 Set of 2   6.00 6.00

Tenth Horse Jumping International, Monte Carlo — A935

2005, Apr. 1   Engr.   Perf. 13¼
2377 A935 90c multi   2.75 1.40

Food — A936

No. 2378, 53c: a, Pissaladière. b, Barbaguians.
No. 2379, 55c: a, Tourte de blettes. b, Desserts.

2005, May 3   Photo.
Horiz. Pairs, #a-b
2378-2379 A936 Set of 2   6.50 3.25
Europa (#2378).

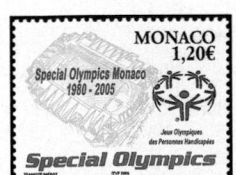

Monegasque Special Olympics, 25th Anniv. — A937

2005, June 3   Litho.   Perf. 13x13¼
2380 A937 €1.20 multi   3.50 1.75

Early 20th Century Advertising Art A938

Advertisements for: 77c, Bains de Mer de Monaco. €2.50, English Sanitary Co. €3.10, Scapini Biscuits.

2005, June 3   Photo.   Perf. 12¼x13
2381-2383 A938 Set of 3   19.00 9.50

Monaco Yacht Show — A939

2005, July 4   Perf. 13¼
2384 A939 82c multi   2.40 1.25

Admission to UPU, 50th Anniv. — A940

2005, July 4   Engr.
2385 A940 €3.03 multi   9.00 4.50

Astronomers A941

Designs: €1.22, Edmond Halley (1656-1742). €1.98, Gerard P. Kuiper (1905-73). €3.80, Clyde Tombaugh (1906-97).

2005, July 4   Perf. 12½x13
2386-2388 A941 Set of 3   21.00 10.50

Coat of Arms Type of 2000
Inscribed "20g Ecopli" at Top
Serpentine Die Cut 11
2005, July 12   Photo.
Booklet Stamp
Self-Adhesive
2389 A786 (48c) grn, blk & red   1.40 1.40
a.   Booklet pane of 10   14.00

10th European Patrimony Day — A942

2005, Sept. 5   Engr.   Perf. 13¼
2390 A942 48c multi   1.40 1.40

20th Magic Stars Festival, Monte Carlo A943

2005, Sept. 5   Litho.   Perf. 13x13¼
2391 A943 €1.45 red, gold & blk 4.25 4.25

Christmas A944

2005, Oct. 3   Engr.   Perf. 13¼
2392 A944 53c blk & red   1.60 1.60

Monte Carlo Bay Hotel and Resort A945

2005, Oct. 7   Photo.
2393 A945 55c multi   1.60 1.60

Nadia Boulanger (1887-1979), Conductor, and Lili Boulanger (1893-1918), Composer — A946

2005, Oct. 21   Engr.
2394 A946 90c multi   2.75 2.75

Miniature Sheet

Restoration of Garnier Hall, Monte Carlo Opera — A947

No. 2395: a, "Song." b, Garnier Hall. c, "Comedy." d, "Dance." e, Charles Garnier (1825-98), architect. f, "Music."

2005, Nov. 16
2395 A947 82c Sheet of 6, #a-f   14.50 14.50

Souvenir Sheet

Prince Rainier III (1923-2005) — A948

2005, Nov. 19   Perf. 13
2396 A948 €4 black   12.00 12.00

Prince Albert II — A949

2005, Nov. 19   Perf. 13x13¼
2397 A949 (48c) green   1.40 1.40
2398 A949 (53c) red   1.60 1.60
2399 A949 (75c) blue   2.25 2.25
Nos. 2397-2399 (3)   5.25 5.25

National Day — A950

No. 2400: a, Fontveille (26x27mm, country name at UL). b, Palace (56x27mm). c, La Condamine and Monte Carlo (26x27mm, country name at UR).

2005, Nov. 19   Photo.   Perf. 13¼
2400 A950 €1.01 Horiz. strip of 3, #a-c   9.00 9.00

MonacoPhil 2006 Philatelic Exhibition A951

2005, Dec. 12
2401 A951 55c multi   1.60 1.60

30th Intl. Circus Festival, Monte Carlo — A952

A952a

No. 2403: a, Charles Rivel, 1974 Golden Clown. b, Fredy Knie, 1977 Golden Clown. c, Alexis Gruss, Sr., 1975 Golden Clown. d, Golden Clown award. e, Georges Carl, 1979 Golden Clown.

2005, Dec. 14
2402 A952 64c shown   1.90 1.90
2403 A952a 75c Sheet of 5,
        #a-e, + label   11.00 11.00

The label on No. 2403 has the same vignette as No. 2402, lacking country name and denomination, but with a gray background.

A953

2006 Winter Olympics, Turin A954

No. 2404: a, Red mascot. b, Blue mascot.

2006, Jan. 9   Photo.   Perf. 13¼
2404 A953 55c Horiz. pair, #a-b   3.25 3.25
2405 A954 82c multi   2.40 2.40

Museum of Postage Stamps and Money, 10th Anniv. A955

2006, Jan. 30   Engr.
2406 A955 53c multi   1.60 1.60

5th Intl. Film and Literature Forum — A956

2006, Feb. 6   Photo.   Perf. 13¼
2407 A956 82c multi   2.40 2.40

Léopold Sédar Senghor (1906-2001), First President of Senegal — A957

2006, Mar. 6   Litho. & Engr.   Perf. 13x13¼
2408 A957 €1.45 multi   4.25 4.25

100th Monte Carlo Tennis Tournament A958

2006, Mar. 8   Photo.   Perf. 13¼
2409 A958 55c multi   1.60 1.60

Coat of Arms Type of 2000
Inscribed "20g Zone A" at Top
Serpentine Die Cut 11
2006, Apr. 6   Photo.
Self-Adhesive
Booklet Stamp
2410 A786 (55c) red & black   1.60 1.60
  a.   Booklet pane of 10   16.00

Monte Carlo Philharmonic Orchestra, 150th Anniv. — A959

2006, Apr. 6   Perf. 13¼
2411 A959 64c multi   1.90 1.90

Arctic Oceanographic Expeditions of Prince Albert I, Cent. — A960

2006, Apr. 10   Litho. & Engr.   Perf. 13x13¼
2412 A960 €1.60 multi   4.75 4.75

Dog Show Type of 2002
2006, Apr. 14   Photo.   Perf. 13¼
2413 A826 64c Special schnau-
        zer   1.90 1.90

39th Intl. Flower Show — A961

2006, Apr. 18
2414 A961 77c multi   2.25 2.25

2006 World Cup Soccer Championships, Germany — A962

No. 2415: a, World Cup, stadium. b, Stadium and 2006 World Cup emblem.

2006, Apr. 18
2415 A962 90c Horiz. pair, #a-b   5.25 5.25

Europa A964

A963

2006, May 5   Photo.   Perf. 13¼
2416 A963 53c multi   1.60 1.60
2417 A964 55c multi   1.60 1.60

RAMOGE Agreement, 30th Anniv. — A965

2006, May 9   Perf. 12¼x13
2418 A965 €1.75 multi   5.25 5.25

Washington 2006 World Philatelic Exhibition A966

2006, May 27   Engr.   Perf. 13¼
2419 A966 90c blue & red   2.75 2.75

John Huston (1906-87), Film Director — A967

2006, May 27   Perf. 13x12¼
2420 A967 €1.80 black & henna
            brn   5.25 5.25

Prince Albert Challenge Sabre Tournament — A968

2006, June 6   Photo.   Perf. 13¼
2421 A968 48c multi   1.40 1.40

Pierre Corneille (1606-84), Dramatist A969

2006, June 17
2422 A969 53c multi   1.60 1.60

46th Intl. Television Festival, Monte Carlo — A970

2006, June 17
2423 A970 82c multi   2.40 2.40

Wolfgang Amadeus Mozart (1756-91), Composer — A971

2006, June 17   Engr.   Perf. 13x12¼
2424 A971 €1.22 org red & blue 3.50 3.50

Prince Pierre Foundation, 40th Anniv. — A972

2006, June 20   Perf. 12½x13
2425 A972 €2.50 multi   7.50 7.50

Dino Buzzati (1906-72), Writer A973

2006, July 17   Photo.   Perf. 13¼
2426 A973 55c multi   1.60 1.60

Cetacean Conservation Accord, 10th Anniv. — A974

2006, July 17   *Perf. 13x12¼*
2427 A974 90c multi   2.75 2.75

Luchino Visconti (1906-76), Film Director A975

2006, July 17   **Engr.**   *Perf. 12¼x13*
2428 A975 €1.75 henna brn   5.25 5.25

Rolls-Royce Automobiles, Cent. — A976

2006, Sept. 4   **Engr.**   *Perf. 13¼*
2429 A976 64c multi   1.90 1.90

2006 Magic Stars Festival, Monte Carlo — A977

2006, Sept. 4   **Photo.**
2430 A977 77c multi   2.25 2.25

Monaco Red Cross — A978

2006, Oct. 2
2431 A978 48c multi   1.40 1.40

Christmas A979

Perf. 13½x13¼
2006, Oct. 2   **Litho. & Engr.**
2432 A979 53c multi   1.60 1.60

Prince Albert II — A980

2006, Dec. 1   **Engr.**   *Perf. 13x13¼*
2433 A980 (49c) green   1.40 1.40
2434 A980 (54c) red   1.50 1.50
    a.   Dated "2009"   1.50 1.50
2435 A980 (60c) blue   1.60 1.60
    Nos. 2433-2435 (3)   4.50 4.50
    Dated 2007.
No. 2434a sold for 56c when issued.

Prince Albert II and Coat of Arms A981

2006, Dec. 1   **Photo.**   *Perf. 13¼x13*
2436 A981 60c multi   1.60 1.60
    Souvenir Sheet
    Perf. 13x13¼
2437 A981 €6 multi   16.00 16.00
    MonacoPhil 2006 Intl. Philatelic Exhibition. Dated 2007.

World AIDS Day A982

2006, Dec. 1   **Litho.**   *Perf. 13x13¼*
2438 A982 49c multi   1.40 1.40
    Dated 2007.

Josephine Baker (1906-75), Singer and Dancer — A983

2006, Dec. 1   *Perf. 13¼x13*
2439 A983 49c multi   1.40 1.40
    Princess Grace Theater, 25th anniv. Dated 2007.

Philatelic Anniversaries A984

2006, Dec. 1   **Photo.**   *Perf. 13¼*
2440 A984 54c multi   1.50 1.50
    Creation of Philatelic Bureau, 70th anniv. (in 2007), Consultative Commission of the Prince's Philatelic Collection, 20th anniv. (in 2007). Dated 2007.

Les Enfants de Frankie Children's Charity, 10th Anniv. (in 2007) — A985

2006, Dec. 1
2441 A985 70c multi   1.90 1.90
    Dated 2007.

Albert Camus (1913-60), 1957 Nobel Literature Laureate — A986

2006, Dec. 1   **Engr.**
2442 A986 84c multi   2.25 2.25
    Dated 2007.

Auguste Escoffier (1846-1935), Chef — A987

2006, Dec. 1
2443 A987 85c multi   2.25 2.25
    Dated 2007.

Daniel Bovet (1907-92), 1957 Nobel Medicine Laureate A988

2006, Dec. 1
2444 A988 86c dk blue & red   2.40 2.40
    Dated 2007.

Cardiothoracic Center, 20th Anniv. (in 2007) — A989

2006, Dec. 1
2445 A989 €1.15 multi   3.25 3.25
    Dated 2007.

Rudyard Kipling (1865-1936), 1907 Nobel Literature Laureate — A990

2006, Dec. 1
2446 A990 €1.57 multi   4.25 4.25
    Dated 2007.

Opening of Institute of Sports Medicine and Surgery A991

2006, Dec. 1
2447 A991 €1.70 multi   4.75 4.75
    Dated 2007.

Meeting of Prince Albert II and Pope Benedict XVI, 1st Anniv. — A992

2006, Dec. 1   **Photo.**   *Perf. 13x13¼*
2448 A992 €1.70 multi   4.75 4.75
    Dated 2007.

Paul-Emile Victor (1907-95), Explorer — A993

2006, Dec. 1   **Engr.**   *Perf. 13x12¼*
2449 A993 €2.11 multi   5.75 5.75
    Dated 2007.

European Philatelic Academy, 30th Anniv. (in 2007) — A994

2006, Dec. 1 Photo. *Perf. 13x13¼*
2450 A994 €2.30 multi   6.25 6.25
Dated 2007.

Awarding of 2006 Grand Prix of Philately to Alexander D. Kroo — A995

2006, Dec. 1 Litho. *Perf. 13¼x13*
2451 A995 €3 multi   8.00 8.00
Dated 2007.

Auto Racing — A996

No. 2452: a, 65th Monaco Grand Prix. b, 75th Monte Carlo Rally.

2006, Dec. 1
2452 A996 60c Horiz. pair, #a-b   3.25 3.25
Dated 2007.

Art in Grimaldi Forum by Nall — A997

No. 2453: a, Purple Flower. b, Yellow Flower

2006, Dec. 1 Photo. *Perf. 13¼*
2453 A997 €1.70 Pair, #a-b   9.25 9.25
Printed in panes of 2 pairs. Dated 2007.

A998

31st Intl. Circus Festival, Monte Carlo — A999

2006, Dec. 1 Photo. *Perf. 13¼*
2454 A998 60c multi   1.60 1.60
Litho.
Perf. 13¼x13
2455 A999 84c multi   2.25 2.25
Dated 2007.

Souvenir Sheet

40th Intl. Flower Show — A1000

No. 2456: a, Classic composition. b, Modern composition. c, Contemporary composition. d, Japanese composition.

2006, Dec. 1 Photo. *Perf. 13¼*
2456 A1000 €1.30 Sheet of 4,
            #a-d   14.00 14.00
Dated 2007.

Stenella Coeruleoalba — A1001

2007, Jan. 2 Litho. *Perf. 13x13¼*
2457 A1001 (36c) multi   .95 .95
Issued precanceled only. See note after No. 324.

Giuseppe Garibaldi (1807-82), Italian Nationalist Leader A1002

2007, Mar. 16 Engr. *Perf. 13¼*
2458 A1002 €1.40 ol brn & red   3.75 3.75

Carlo Goldoni (1707-93), Playwright A1003

Litho. & Silk-screened
2007, Mar. 16 *Perf. 13x13¼*
2459 A1003 €4.54 multi   12.50 12.50

Monaco Olympic Committee, Cent. — A1004

2007, Apr. 2 Photo. *Perf. 13¼*
2460 A1004 60c multi   1.60 1.60

Dalmatian A1005

2007, Apr. 2 *Perf. 13x13¼*
2461 A1005 70c multi   1.90 1.90
Intl. Dog Show.

12th Games of Small European States A1006

2007, Apr. 2 *Perf. 13¼*
2462 A1006 86c multi   2.40 2.40

Princess Grace Exposition, Grimaldi Forum A1007

2007, May 4 Litho. *Perf. 13*
2463 A1007 85c multi   2.40 2.40

First Flight of Helicopter Designed by Maurice Leger, Cent. — A1008

2007, May 4 Engr. *Perf. 12½x13*
2464 A1008 €1.15 multi   3.25 3.25

47th Television Festival, Monte Carlo — A1009

2007, May 4 Litho. *Perf. 13¼x13*
2465 A1009 €2.90 multi   8.00 8.00

Scouting, Cent. — A1010

No. 2466: a, Scouts and campfire. b, Lord Robert Baden-Powell.

2007, May 4 Photo. *Perf. 13¼*
2466 A1010 60c Horiz. pair, #a-b   3.25 3.25

Cartophily, Numismatics and Philately Grand Bourse — A1011

Litho. & Silk-Screened
2007, June 25 *Perf. 13¼x13*
2467 A1011 49c multi   1.40 1.40

22nd Magic Stars Festival, Monte Carlo — A1012

2007, June 25 Litho.
2468 A1012 €1.30 red & black   3.50 3.50

Monaco Harbor — A1013

2007, Oct. 1 Engr. *Perf. 13x12½*
2469 A1013 85c multi   2.40 2.40

Christmas A1014

Litho. & Silk-screened
2007, Oct. 1 *Perf. 13¼x13*
2470 A1014 54c multi   1.60 1.60

32nd Intl. Circus Festival, Monte Carlo — A1015

2007, Oct. 15 Photo. *Perf. 13¼*
2471 A1015 60c multi   1.75 1.75

Giacomo Puccini (1858-1924), Composer A1016

2007, Dec. 7   Engr.   *Perf. 13¼*
2472 A1016 €1.40 blue & red   4.25 4.25

41st Intl. Flower Show — A1017

2008, Jan. 3   Photo.
2473 A1017 49c multi   1.50 1.50

Reformed Church of Monaco, 50th Anniv. — A1018

2008, Jan. 3   Engr.   *Perf. 13¼*
2474 A1018 49c blue & brown   1.50 1.50

Consecration of St. Charles Church, 125th Anniv. — A1019

2008, Mar. 3
2475 A1019 54c gray blue & red   1.60 1.60

Arc de Triomphe du Carrousel Quadriga, Paris, by François Joseph Bosio A1020

2008, Jan. 3
2476 A1020 54c multi   1.60 1.60

Andrea Palladio (1508-80), Architect A1021

2008, Jan. 3   Photo.   *Perf. 13¼*
2477 A1021 60c multi   1.75 1.75

10th Special Session of United Nations Environment Program, Monaco A1022

2008, Jan. 3   Photo.   *Perf. 13¼*
2478 A1022 85c multi   2.50 2.50

Johannes Brahms (1833-97), Composer A1023

2008, Jan. 3   Engr.   *Perf. 13¼*
2479 A1023 €1.15 Prus grn & red   3.50 3.50

Return of Comet Predicted by Edmond Halley, 250th Anniv. A1024

2008, Jan. 3   Photo.   *Perf. 13¼*
2480 A1024 €1.57 multi   4.75 4.75

Marcel Kroenlein Arboretum, Roure, France, 20th Anniv. — A1025

2008, Jan. 3   Engr.   *Perf. 13¼*
2481 A1025 €2.11 multi   6.25 6.25

Poster for Monte Carlo Country Club, by Raymond Gid A1026

Poster for Monte Carlo Beach Hotel, by Raymond Gid A1027

Poster for Monte Carlo Golf Club, by Raymond Gid A1028

Poster for Monte Carlo Tourism, by Louis Rué A1029

Perf. 12¼x13, 13 (#2483)
2008, Jan. 3   Photo., Litho. (#2483)
2482 A1026 70c multi   2.10 2.10
2483 A1027 85c multi   2.50 2.50
2484 A1028 €1.15 multi   3.50 3.50
2485 A1029 €2.90 multi   8.50 8.50
   Nos. 2482-2485 (4)   16.60 16.60

Gen. André Massena (1758-1817) A1030

2008, Jan. 21   Engr.   *Perf. 13¼*
2486 A1030 86c grn & yel brown   2.60 2.60

Apparition at Lourdes, France, 150th Anniv. A1031

2008, Feb. 11   Engr.   *Perf. 13x12¾*
2487 A1031 €1.30 dark blue & blue   4.00 4.00

Introduction of the Ford Model T, Cent. — A1032

2008, Mar. 10   *Perf. 13¼*
2488 A1032 €1.70 multi   5.50 5.50

National Aeronautics and Space Administration, 50th Anniv. — A1033

2008, Mar. 10
2489 A1033 €2.30 multi   7.25 7.25

Alfred Nobel (1833-1906), Inventor and Philantropist A1034

2008, Mar. 10
2490 A1034 €4 blk & claret   12.50 12.50

Dog Show Type of 2002
2008, Mar. 17   Photo.   *Perf. 13¼*
2491 A826 88c Greyhound, vert.   2.75 2.75

Expo Zaragoza 2008 A1035

2008, Mar. 18   Litho.   *Perf. 13x13¼*
2492 A1035 65c multi   2.10 2.10

Mother's Day — A1036

2008, Apr. 8   *Perf. 13¼x13*
2493 A1036 55c multi   1.75 1.75

Stendhal (Marie-Henri Beyle) (1783-1842), Writer — A1037

2008, Apr. 8   Engr.   *Perf. 13¼*
2494 A1037 €1.33 multi   4.25 4.25

Boris Pasternak (1890-1960), Writer — A1038

2008, Apr. 8
2495 A1038 €2.18 multi   7.00 7.00

2008 Summer Olympics,
Beijing — A1039

No. 2496 — Olympic rings and: a, Pagoda, basketball, tennis, javelin. b, Beijing Olympics emblem, baseball, fencing, shooting.

2008, Apr. 8 **Perf. 13x12½**
2496 A1039 Horiz. pair 4.50 4.50
a. 55c red & black 1.75 1.75
b. 85c red & black 2.75 2.75

Cap d'Ail,
France,
Cent.
A1040

2008, Apr. 21 Litho. **Perf. 13x13¼**
2497 A1040 55c multi 1.75 1.75

Exotic
Garden,
75th
Anniv.
A1041

2008, May 2 Engr. **Perf. 13¼**
2498 A1041 50c multi 1.60 1.60

2008 Magic Stars
Festival, Monte
Carlo — A1042

2008, May 5 **Photo.**
2499 A1042 72c multi 2.25 2.25

Europa
A1043

Designs: 55c, Letters encircling globe. 65c, Postmen, letter, means of postal communication.

2008, May 5 **Engr.**
2500-2501 A1043 Set of 2 3.75 3.75

Intl. Skating
Union, 52nd
Congress
A1044

2008, May 16 Litho. **Perf. 13¼x13**
2502 A1044 50c multi 1.60 1.60

Prince
Albert II of
Monaco
Foundation
A1045

Litho. & Engr.
2008, May 16 **Perf. 13x13¼**
2503 A1045 88c multi 2.75 2.75

48th Intl.
Television
Festival, Monte
Carlo — A1046

2008, June 2 Photo. **Perf. 13¼**
2504 A1046 €2.80 multi 9.00 9.00

Monegasque International
Cooperation — A1047

Designs: 65c, Education. €1, Health. €1.25, Campaign against poverty. €1.70, Campaign against desertification.

2008, June 5 **Engr.**
2505-2508 A1047 Set of 4 14.50 14.50

Monaco 2008
Intl. Numismatic
Exhibition
A1048

**Litho. & Embossed With Foil
Application**
2008, June 16 **Perf. 13½x13**
2509 A1048 65c multi 2.10 2.10

Schönbrunn Palace, Vienna — A1049

2008, Sept. 18 Engr. **Perf. 13¼**
2510 A1049 65c multi 1.90 1.90
WIPA 2008 Intl. Philatelic Exhibition, Vienna.

Order of
Saint
Charles,
150th
Anniv.
A1050

**Photo. & Embossed With Foil
Application**
2008, Sept. 18 **Perf. 13x13¼**
2511 A1050 €1.50 multi 4.25 4.25

Coins of
Monaco
A1051

Obverse and reverse of: 50c, 1837 Franc. 55c, 1943 Franc. 72c, 1950 Franc. €1.25, 1960 Franc. €1.64, Euro coinage of 2002. €1.70, Euro coinage of 2006.

**Litho. & Embossed With Foil
Application**
2008, Sept. 18
2512-2517 A1051 Set of 6 17.50 17.50

Christmas
A1052

2008, Sept. 19 Photo. **Perf. 13¼**
2518 A1052 55c multi 1.50 1.50

33rd Intl. Circus
Festival, Monte
Carlo — A1053

2008, Dec. 19 Photo. **Perf. 13¼**
2519 A1053 85c multi 2.40 2.40

Prince Albert I — A1054

Flag of
Monaco
and Intl.
Polar Year
Emblem
A1055

Prince Albert II — A1056

2008, Dec. 19 **Perf. 13x12¼**
2520 Horiz. strip of 3 7.25 7.25
a. A1054 85c multi 2.40 2.40
b. A1055 85c multi 2.40 2.40
c. A1056 85c multi 2.40 2.40

Admiral Robert E. Peary (1856-1920),
Arctic Explorer, and Dog
Sleds — A1057

Peary,
Flag of
US and
Map of
Arctic
Area
A1058

Matthew Henson (1866-1955), Arctic
Explorer and Ship — A1059

Litho. & Engr.
2008, Dec. 19 **Perf. 13¼**
2521 Horiz. strip of 3 7.25 7.25
a. A1057 87c multi 2.40 2.40
b. A1058 87c multi 2.40 2.40
c. A1059 87c multi 2.40 2.40

Monaco
Firefighting
Corps,
Cent.
A1060

Designs: 50c, Railway and road emergency vehicle. 72c, Ladder truck, 1909. 87c, Fireman, ladder truck.

2009, Jan. 5 Photo. **Perf. 13¼**
2522-2524 A1060 Set of 3 5.75 5.75

Princess Grace
Rose Garden,
25th
Anniv. — A1061

2009, Jan. 5 **Perf. 13¼x13**
2525 A1061 €1.25 multi 3.50 3.50

Spring Arts Festival, 25th Anniv. — A1062

2009, Jan. 5
2526 A1062 €1.33 multi 3.75 3.75

First Flight Across English Channel by Louis Blériot, Cent. A1063

Litho. & Engr.
2009, Jan. 29 *Perf. 13x12½*
2527 A1063 87c multi 2.25 2.25

Felix Mendelssohn Bartholdy (1809-47), Composer A1064

2009, Jan. 29 Engr. *Perf. 13¼*
2528 A1064 €1.50 olive grn & blue 4.00 4.00

Beatification of Joan of Arc, Cent. — A1065

2009, Jan. 29
2529 A1065 €2.22 multi 5.75 5.75

MonacoPhil 2009 Philatelic Exhibition A1066

2009, Feb. 7 Litho. *Perf. 13¼x13*
2530 A1066 56c multi 1.50 1.50

Chihuahua and Cavalier King Charles Spaniel A1067

2009, Feb. 7 Photo. *Perf. 13¼*
2531 A1067 72c multi 1.90 1.90
Intl. Dog Show.

2009 Intl. Cat Show A1068

2009, Feb. 7 Litho. *Perf. 13x13¼*
2532 A1068 88c multi 2.25 2.25

Association of Members of the Order of Academic Palms World Conference — A1069

2009, Feb. 7 Engr. *Perf. 13x12½*
2533 A1069 88c multi 2.25 2.25

Barbie Doll, 50th Anniv. — A1070

2009, Feb. 7 Photo. *Perf. 13¼*
2534 A1070 88c multi 2.25 2.25

42nd Intl. Flower Show — A1071

2009, Feb. 7 Photo. *Perf. 13¼*
2535 A1071 89c multi 2.25 2.25

Monaco Fencing and Handgun Club, Cent. — A1072

2009, Feb. 16 Litho. & Engr.
2536 A1072 55c multi 1.40 1.40

Giro d'Italia Bicycle Race, Cent. — A1073

2009, Feb. 16 Photo.
2537 A1073 70c multi 1.75 1.75

Sir Arthur Conan Doyle (1859-1930), Writer — A1074

2009, Feb. 16 Engr. *Perf. 12¼*
2538 A1074 85c multi 2.25 2.25

Edgar Allan Poe (1809-49), Writer — A1075

2009, Feb. 16
2539 A1075 €1.70 red & dark green 4.50 4.50

Coat of Arms — A1076

Serpentine Die Cut 11
2009, Apr. 6 Photo.
Booklet Stamp
Self-Adhesive
2540 A1076 (70c) multi 1.90 1.90
a. Booklet pane of 10 19.00

Louis Notari Library, Cent. A1077

2009, Apr. 29 Engr. *Perf. 13x12½*
2541 A1077 51c red & purple 1.40 1.40

Monaco Grand Prix Auto Race, Cent. — A1078

2009, Apr. 29 Photo. *Perf. 13x13¼*
2542 A1078 70c multi 1.90 1.90

Monaco's Admission to UNESCO, 60th Anniv. — A1079

2009, Apr. 29
2543 A1079 €1.70 multi 4.50 4.50

Louis Braille (1809-52), Educator of the Blind A1080

2009, Apr. 29 Engr. *Perf. 12¼x13*
2544 A1080 €3.80 multi 10.00 10.00

Concerts at the Prince's Palace, 50th Anniv. A1081

2009, May 4 *Perf. 13x13¼*
2545 A1081 51c purple & black 1.50 1.50

Europa A1082

Astronomers: 56c, Francesco Maria Grimaldi (1618-63), map of Moon showing crater named after Grimaldi. 70c, Galileo Galilei (1564-1642), telescope.

Litho. & Engr.
2009, May 4 *Perf. 13x12½*
2546-2547 A1082 Set of 2 3.50 3.50
Intl. Year of Astronomy.

Ballets de Monte-Carlo — A1083

2009, May 11 Photo. *Perf. 13¼x13*
2548 A1083 73c multi 2.10 2.10

Ballets Russes, Cent. A1084

Designs: 89c, Fifteen performers. €1.35, Nine performers.

2009, May 11
2549-2550 A1084   Set of 2   6.25 6.25

Georges Seurat (1859-91), Painter A1085

Litho. & Engr.
2009, May 14   *Perf. 13x13¼*
2551 A1085 73c multi   2.10 2.10

St. Francis of Assisi (c. 1181-1226) A1086

2009, May 14   Engr.   *Perf. 13¼*
2552 A1086 90c blue & black   2.50 2.50
Franciscan Order, 800th anniv.

John Calvin (1509-64), Theologian and Religious Reformer A1087

2009, May 14   *Perf. 13x13¼*
2553 A1087 €1.67 multi   4.75 4.75

49th Intl. Television Festival, Monte Carlo — A1088

2009, May 29   Photo.   *Perf. 13¼*
2554 A1088 €1.60 multi   4.50 4.50

Italian Writers A1089

Emblem of Monaco Dante Alighieri Society and: 70c, Niccolò Machiavelli (1469-1527). 85c, Giovanni Boccaccio (1313-75). €1.30, Francesco Petrarca (Petrarch) (1304-74).

2009, June 3   Engr.   *Perf. 12¼x13*
2555-2557 A1089   Set of 3   8.00 8.00
Monaco Dante Alighieri Society, 30th anniv.

Grande Bourse 2009 — A1090

2009, June 17   Photo.   *Perf. 13¼*
2558 A1090 51c multi   1.50 1.50

Youth Hostels, Cent. A1091

2009, June 17   Litho.   *Perf. 13x13¼*
2559 A1091 90c multi   2.50 2.50

Tuiga, Flagship of Monaco Yacht Club, Cent. A1092

2009, June 18   Photo.   *Perf. 13¼*
2560 A1092 70c multi   2.00 2.00

Start of Tour de France Bicycle Race in Monaco A1093

2009, July 2   Litho.   *Perf. 13¼x13*
2561 A1093 56c multi   1.60 1.60

2009 Magic Stars Festival, Monte Carlo — A1094

2009, Sept. 16   Litho.   *Perf. 13¼x13*
2562 A1094 73c multi   2.25 2.25

Place de la Mairie — A1095

2009, Sept. 16   **Photo.**
2563 A1095 85c multi   2.50 2.50

Big Ben, 150th Anniv. — A1096

2009, Sept. 16   **Engr.**
2564 A1096 €1 red & black   3.00 3.00

Christmas A1097

2009, Oct. 5   *Perf. 13x13¼*
2565 A1097 56c multi   1.75 1.75

2010 Intl. Cat Show — A1098

2009, Dec. 4   Photo.   *Perf. 13¼*
2566 A1098 56c multi   1.75 1.75
Dated 2010.

Jean Anouilh (1910-87), Playwright — A1099

2009, Dec. 4   Engr.   *Perf. 13x12¼*
2567 A1099 73c multi   2.25 2.25
Dated 2010.

Ayrton Senna (1960-94), Race Car Driver — A1100

2009, Dec. 4   Engr.   *Perf. 13x12¼*
2568 A1100 73c multi   2.25 2.25
Dated 2010.

Auguste Rodin (1840-1917), Sculptor — A1101

2009, Dec. 4   Engr.   *Perf. 13x12¼*
2569 A1101 85c multi   2.60 2.60
Dated 2010.

Princess Grace (1929-82) A1102

2009, Dec. 4   Engr.   *Perf. 12¼x13*
2570 A1102 89c red & black   2.75 2.75
Dated 2010.

Gustav Mahler (1860-1911), Composer — A1103

2009, Dec. 4
2571 A1103 90c brown & blue   2.75 2.75
Dated 2010.

2010 Winter Olympics, Vancouver — A1104

No. 2572 — 2010 Winter Olympics emblem and: a, Slalom skier. b, Snowboarder and figure skater.

2009, Dec. 4   Engr.   Perf. 13¼x13½
2572 A1104   Horiz. pair   5.50 5.50
a.-b.   90c Either single   2.75 2.75
Dated 2010.

Monte Carlo Vu de Roquebrune, by
Claude Monet (1840-1926) — A1105

2009, Dec. 4   Photo.   Perf. 13x13¼
2573 A1105   €1.30 multi   4.00 4.00
Dated 2010.

US No.
85A,
Trophy
A1106

2009, Dec. 4   Litho.
2574 A1106   €1.35 multi   4.00 4.00
Awarding of Intl. Association of Stamp Catalogue Publishers Grand Prix for Philately to
William H. Gross. Dated 2010.

The Birth of Venus, by William
Bouguereau (1825-1905) — A1107

2009, Dec. 4   Photo.   Perf. 13¼x13
2575 A1107   €1.60 multi   4.75 4.75
Dated 2010.

Anton Chekhov (1860-1904),
Writer — A1108

2009, Dec. 4   Engr.   Perf. 13x12¼
2576 A1108   €1.67 multi   5.00 5.00
Dated 2010.

Souvenir Sheet

*Exposition Philatélique Internationale
"MonacoPhil 2009", du 4 au 6 Décembre*

Prince Albert II — A1109

Litho. (Margin) & Engr.
2009, Dec. 4   Perf. 13¼x13
2577 A1109   €4 red & black   12.00 12.00
MonacoPhil 2009 Intl. Philatelic Exhibition.
Dated 2010.

Souvenir Sheet

Automobile Club of Monaco, 120th
Anniv. — A1110

No. 2578: a, Race car. b, Formula 1 race
car.

2009, Dec. 4   Photo.   Perf. 13x13¼
2578 A1110   Sheet of 2   9.00 9.00
a.   €1.30 multi   4.00 4.00
b.   €1.70 multi   5.00 5.00
Dated 2010.

34th Intl. Circus
Festival, Monte
Carlo — A1111

2009, Dec. 10   Photo.   Perf. 13¼
2579 A1111   70c multi   2.10 2.10
Dated 2010.

Australian
Shepherd
A1112

2010, Feb. 8   Photo.   Perf. 13¼
2580 A1112   51c multi   1.40 1.40
Intl. Dog Show.

Intl. Flower
Arrangement
Festival — A1113

2010, Feb. 8
2581 A1113   70c multi   1.00 1.00

Five Nations
Rugby
Championships,
Cent. — A1114

2010, Feb. 8   Litho.   Perf. 13¼x13
2582 A1114   70c multi   1.90 1.90

Scenes From "The Seven Samurai,"
Film by Akira Kurosawa (1910-
98) — A1115

2010, Feb. 24   Engr.   Perf. 13x12¼
2583 A1115   51c ol grn & black   1.40 1.40

Monte Carlo
Rolex Masters
Tennis
Tournament
A1116

2010, Mar. 4   Photo.   Perf. 13¼
2584 A1116   85c multi   2.40 2.40

2010 World Cup Soccer
Championships, South Africa — A1117

No. 2585 — Flag of South Africa, players in
stadium with denomination at: a, LL. b, UR.

2010, Mar. 4
2585 A1117   Horiz. pair   5.00 5.00
a.-b.   89c Either single   2.50 2.50

Souvenir Sheet

2008 Monaco Coin — A1118

**Litho. & Embossed With Foil
Application**
2010, Mar. 4   Perf. 13½
2586 A1118   €1 multi   2.75 2.75
Expo 2010, Shanghai.

Miniature Sheet

*Centenaire du Musée océanographique
de Monaco
1910-2010*

Oceanographic Museum of Monaco,
Cent. — A1119

No. 2587: a, Prince Albert I. b, Stuffed
Ursus maritimus. c, Pterapogon kauderni,
horiz. d, Hands pointing at starfish, horiz.

Litho. & Engr.
2010, Mar. 29   Perf. 13¼x13
2587 A1119   Sheet of 4   7.50 7.50
a.   51c multi   1.40 1.40
b.   56c multi   1.50 1.50
c.   73c multi   2.00 2.00
d.   90c multi   2.50 2.50

Miniature Sheet

Les Anciens Fiefs des Grimaldi de Monaco dans le Haut-Rhin

Former Grimaldi Family Fiefs in
France — A1120

No. 2588: a, County of Thann. b, Barony of
Altkirch. c, County of Rosemont. d, County of
Ferrette.

2010, Apr. 23   Photo.   Perf. 13x13¼
2588 A1120   €1 Sheet of 4,
               #a-d   11.00 11.00

Flora and
Fauna — A1121

Designs: 2c, Pinna nobilis, Submarine
Reserve of Larvotto. €2, Lis martagon, Mercantour National Park, France.

2010, Apr. 29   Engr.   Perf. 13¼
2589 A1121   2c multi   .25 .25
2590 A1121   €2 multi   5.50 5.50

Mother Teresa
(1910-97),
Humanitarian
A1122

2010, Apr. 29   Photo.   Perf. 13¼
2591 A1122 €1.70 multi   4.50 4.50

UNAIDS
Program, 15th
Anniv. — A1123

2010, May 5   Photo.   Perf. 13¼
2592 A1123 89c multi   2.25 2.25

Europa
A1124

Map of Europe, books and: 56c, Five children. 70c, One child.

2010, May 5   Engr.   Perf. 13x13¼
2593-2594 A1124 Set of 2   3.25 3.25

London 2010 Festival of
Stamps — A1125

2010, May 7
2595 A1125 €1.30 multi   3.50 3.50

50th Television
Festival, Monte
Carlo — A1126

Litho. With Foil Application
2010, May 26   Perf. 13¼x13
2596 A1126 €2.80 multi   6.75 6.75

Human Paleontology Institute, Paris,
Cent. — A1127

2010, June 1   Engr.   Perf. 13x12¾
2597 A1127 56c multi   1.40 1.40
    See France No. 3821.

Grimaldi
Forum,
10th Anniv.
A1128

2010, June 22   Litho.   Perf. 13x13¼
2598 A1128 75c multi   1.90 1.90

Youth Olympic Games,
Singapore — A1129

2010, June 22   Photo.
2599 A1129 87c multi   2.25 2.25

Maritime and
Airport Police
Division, 50th
Anniv. — A1130

2010, July 1   Engr.   Perf. 13¼
2600 A1130 53c multi   1.40 1.40

Invention
of the
Food
Canning
Process,
by
Nicholas
Appert,
Bicent.
A1131

2010, July 1   Perf. 12¼
2601 A1131 95c red & purple   2.40 2.40

Invention of First Practical Internal
Combustion Engine by Jean-Joseph-
Etienne Lenoir, 150th Anniv. — A1132

2010, July 1
2602 A1132 €1.75 multi   4.50 4.50

Little Africa Gardens,
Monaco — A1133

2010, July 1   Perf. 13x13¼
2603 A1133 €2.30 multi   5.75 5.75

First International Electric Postal
Flight, Monaco to Nice — A1134

2010, Aug. 23   Litho.   Perf. 13
2604 A1134 95c multi   2.50 2.50

Monaco
Scientific
Center,
50th Anniv.
A1135

2010, Sept. 17   Photo.   Perf. 13¼
2605 A1135 58c multi   1.50 1.50

25th Magic Stars
Festival, Monte
Carlo — A1136

2010, Sept. 17   Litho.   Perf. 13¼x13
2606 A1136 €1.40 multi   3.75 3.75

Monaco
Regional
Express
Transport
A1137

2010, Sept. 19   Engr.   Perf. 13x13¼
2607 A1137 €1.35 multi   3.50 3.50

Albert I
High
School,
Cent.
A1138

2010, Oct. 4   Perf. 13x13¼
2608 A1138 75c multi   2.10 2.10

Christmas
A1139

2010, Oct. 4   Photo.   Perf. 13¼
2609 A1139 58c multi   1.60 1.60

35th Intl. Circus
Festival, Monte
Carlo — A1140

2010, Dec. 20   Perf. 13¼
2610 A1140 75c multi   2.00 2.00

Constitution of Monaco,
Cent. — A1141

2011, Jan. 4
2611 A1141 53c multi   1.50 1.50

Egyptian Mau
Cat — A1142

2011, Jan. 4
2612 A1142 87c multi   2.40 2.40
    Intl. Cat Show.

Juan Manuel Fangio (1911-95), Race
Car Driver — A1143

Indianapolis 500, Cent. — A1144

Monte Carlo Rally, Cent. — A1145

2011, Jan. 12   Engr.   Perf. 13x13¼
2613 A1143 95c multi   2.60 2.60
Photo.
2614 A1144 €1.35 multi   3.75 3.75
2615 A1145 €1.40 multi   3.75 3.75
    Nos. 2613-2615 (3)   10.10 10.10

Marine Laboratory of the Intl. Atomic Energy Agency, 50th Anniv. A1146

2011, Jan. 20 **Photo.** **Perf. 13¼**
2616 A1146 87c multi 2.40 2.40

Renewable Energy A1147

2011, Jan. 20 **Litho.** **Perf. 13x13¼**
2617 A1147 €1.80 multi 5.00 5.00

Mission Enfance Association, 20th Anniv. — A1148

2011, Jan. 28
2618 A1148 53c multi 1.50 1.50

Labrador Retriever A1149

2011, Feb. 7 **Photo.** **Perf. 13¼**
2619 A1149 53c multi 1.50 1.50
Intl. Dog Show.

A1150

Sculptors and Their Sculptures — A1151

No. 2620: a, Antoine Bourdelle (1861-1929). b, Horse's head from Monument to General Alvear.
No. 2621: a, Aristide Maillol (1861-1944). b, The Night.

2011, Feb. 21 **Engr.** **Perf. 13¼**
2620 A1150 Horiz. pair 4.25 4.25
a.-b. 75c Either single 2.10 2.10
2621 A1151 Horiz. pair 5.50 5.50
a.-b. 95c Either single 2.75 2.75

State Visit of Prince Albert II to Ireland A1152

2011, Feb. 21 **Photo.** **Perf. 13¼**
2622 A1152 €1.40 multi 4.00 4.00

Monte Carlo Rolex Masters Tennis Tournament A1153

2011, Mar. 2
2623 A1153 75c multi 2.10 2.10

Napoleon II (1811-32), Titular King of Rome — A1154

2011, Mar. 2 **Engr.**
2624 A1154 €1 brown & blue 2.75 2.75

44th Intl. Flower Show, Monte Carlo — A1155

Chelsea Flower Show, London — A1156

Japanese Garden of Monaco A1157

Photo., Litho. (#2626)
2011, Mar. 24 **Perf. 13¼**
2625 A1155 95c multi 2.75 2.75
Perf. 13¼x13
2626 A1156 €1.75 multi 5.25 5.25
Perf. 13x13¼
2627 A1157 €2.35 multi 6.75 6.75
Nos. 2625-2627 (3) 14.75 14.75

Consecration of Monaco Cathedral, Cent. — A1158

2011, Mar. 31 **Engr.** **Perf. 13x13¼**
2628 A1158 58c red & black 1.75 1.75

Lions Club of Monaco, 50th Anniv. A1159

2011, Mar. 31 **Photo.** **Perf. 13¼**
2629 A1159 75c multi 2.25 2.25

Souvenir Sheet

Former Grimaldi Family Fiefs in Provence — A1100

No. 2630: a, Saint-Rémy-de-Provence. b, Les Baux-de-Provence.

2011, Apr. 4 **Perf. 13x13¼**
2630 A1160 Sheet of 2 10.50 10.50
a. €1.75 multi 5.25 5.25
b. €1.80 multi 5.25 5.25

Aquilegia Bertolonii, Mercantour National Park — A1161

2011, Apr. 20 **Photo.** **Perf. 13¼**
2631 A1161 3c multi .25 .25
Engr.
Perf. 13¼x13
2632 A1162 €2.30 multi 6.75 6.75

Tarentola Mauritanica A1162

Europa — A1163

Designs: 58c, Alpine forest. 75c, Mediterranean forest.

2011, May 3 **Photo.** **Perf. 13¼**
2633-2634 A1163 Set of 2 4.00 4.00
Intl. Year of Forests.

Winning Artwork in Environment and Ecology in Monaco Children's Stamp Design Contest — A1164

2011, May 18 **Litho.** **Perf. 13x13¼**
2635 A1164 53c multi 1.60 1.60

A1165

Wedding of Prince Albert II and Charlene Wittstock — A1166

Engr. With Foil Application
2011, July 1 **Perf. 13x13¼**
2636 A1165 55c black & green 1.60 1.60
2637 A1165 60c black & red 1.75 1.75
2638 A1165 77c black & purple 2.25 2.25
2639 A1165 89c black & blue 2.50 2.50
2640 A1165 €4.10 brn, gold & red 11.50 11.50
Nos. 2636-2640 (5) 19.60 19.60
Souvenir Sheet
Photo.
2641 A1166 €5 multi 14.00 14.00

Prince's Company of Carabiniers — A1167

2011, July 18 **Photo.** **Perf. 13¼**
2642 A1167 77c multi 2.25 2.25

Monte Carlo Golf Club, Cent. — A1168

2011, Aug. 9　Litho.　Perf. 13¼
2643　A1168　60c multi　　　1.75　1.75

Monegasque Alpine Club, Cent. — A1169

2011, Aug. 9　Photo.
2644　A1169　60c multi　　　1.75　1.75

2011 Grande Bourse, Salle du Canton — A1170

2011, Aug. 12
2645　A1170　60c multi　　　1.75　1.75

Zeus Faber — A1171

2011, Aug. 16　Litho.
2646　A1171　(39c) multi　　1.10　1.10

No. 2646 was issued precanceled only. See note after No. 324.

MonacoPhil 2011 Intl. Philatelic Exhibition A1172

2011, Aug. 29　　　Perf. 13¼
2647　A1172　55c multi　　　1.50　1.50

Paris Institute of Oceanography, Cent. — A1173

2011, Sept. 19　Engr.　Perf. 13x13¼
2648　A1173　77c multi　　　2.10　2.10

Exotic Garden, Monaco A1174

2011, Sept. 28　Photo.　Perf. 13¼
2649　A1174　75c multi　　　2.10　2.10

First Man in Space, 50th Anniv. A1175

2011, Sept. 28　Engr.　Perf. 13x13¼
2650　A1175　€2.78 blue　　7.75　7.75

Georges Méliès (1863-1938), Film Maker — A1176

2011, Sept. 28
2651　A1176　€1.45 multi　　4.00　4.00

Franz Liszt (1811-86), Composer — A1177

2011, Oct. 10　　　Perf. 13x12¼
2652　A1177　€1 multi　　　2.75　2.75

Théophile Gautier (1811-72), Poet — A1178

2011, Oct. 10　Litho.　Perf. 13
2653　A1178　€1.75 multi　　4.75　4.75

Prince Antoine I (1661-1731) — A1179

Litho. & Embossed With Foil Application
2011, Oct. 10
2654　A1179　€1.80 multi　　5.00　5.00

Henri Troyat (1911-2007), Writer — A1180

2011, Oct. 10　Engr.　Perf. 12¼x13
2655　A1180　€2.40 multi　　6.75　6.75

Christmas A1181

2011, Oct. 17　Litho.　Perf. 13¼
2656　A1181　60c multi　　　1.75　1.75

25th Telethon A1182

2011, Dec. 2
2657　A1182　60c multi　　　1.60　1.60

Intl. Association of Philatelic Catalogue Editors (ASCAT) Grand Prix — A1183

2011, Dec. 2　　　　Photo.
2658　A1183　78c multi　　　2.10　2.10

Souvenir Sheet

Prince Albert II and Princess Charlene — A1184

2011, Dec. 2
2659　A1184　€5 multi　　13.50　13.50
MonacoPhil 2011 Intl. Philatelic Exhibition.

36th Intl. Circus Festival, Monte Carlo — A1185

2011, Dec. 19
2660　A1185　77c multi　　　2.00　2.00

Intl. Flower Arrangement Festival — A1186

2012, Jan. 10　　　　Litho.
2661　A1186　55c multi　　　1.50　1.50

2012 Intl. Cat Show — A1187

2012, Jan. 10　Photo.　Perf. 13¼
2662　A1187　77c multi　　　2.10　2.10

St. Martin's Gardens A1188

2012, Jan. 10
2663　A1188　89c multi　　　2.40　2.40

Miniature Sheet

Frescoes of the Monte Carlo Opera — A1189

No. 2664: a, Comedy, by Frédéric Lix. b, Music, by Gustave Boulanger. c, Dance, by Georges Clairin. d, Song and Eloquence, by François Feyen-Perrin.

2012, Jan. 25　　　Perf. 13x13¼
2664　A1189　€1.45 Sheet of 4,
　　　　#a-d　　　15.50　15.50

2012 Monte Carlo Rolex Masters Tennis Tournament A1190

2012, Feb. 2   *Perf. 13¼*
2665 A1190 89c multi   2.40 2.40

Collie — A1191

2012, Feb. 2   **Engr.**
2666 A1191 89c multi   2.40 2.40
Intl. Dog Show.

Florestan Company, 25th Anniv. — A1192

2012, Feb. 20   **Litho.**   *Perf. 13¼*
2667 A1192 55c multi   1.50 1.50

Recognition by France of Monaco's Independence, 500th Anniv. — A1193

2012, Feb. 20   **Engr.**   *Perf. 13x13¼*
2668 A1193 55c red & black   1.50 1.50

Carabine de Monaco (Rifle Shooting Association), Cent. — A1194

2012, Feb. 20
2669 A1194 €1.35 multi   3.75 3.75

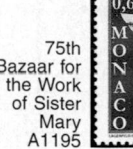

75th Bazaar for the Work of Sister Mary A1195

2012, Mar. 16   **Litho.**   *Perf. 13¼*
2670 A1195 60c multi   1.60 1.60

70th Monaco Grand Prix A1196

2012, Mar. 20   **Engr.**   *Perf. 13x13¼*
2671 A1196 77c multi   2.10 2.10

First Seaplane Competition, Cent. — A1197

2012, Mar. 20
2672 A1197 €1.80 multi   4.75 4.75

Coat of Arms Type of 2000
Inscribed "20g écopli" at Top
Serpentine Die Cut 11
2012, Apr. 20   **Photo.**
Booklet Stamp
Self-Adhesive
2673 A786 (55c) blue & multi   1.50 1.50
  a.   Booklet pane of 10   15.00

Arrival of PlanetSolar Boat in Monaco — A1198

2012, Apr. 20   **Engr.**   *Perf. 13x13¼*
2674 A1198 77c multi   2.10 2.10

Expo 2012, Yeosu, South Korea A1199

2012, Apr. 20   **Photo.**   *Perf. 13¼*
2675 A1199 78c multi   2.10 2.10

Europa A1200

Rooms in the Prince's Palace: 60c, Louis XV Bedroom. 77c, Mazarin Room.

2012, May 9   **Litho.**
2676-2677 A1200   Set of 2   3.50 3.50

Rotary Club of Monaco, 75th Anniv. A1201

2012, June 9
2678 A1201 77c multi   1.90 1.90

United Nations Rio + 20 Conference on Sustainable Development, Rio de Janeiro — A1202

2012, June 9
2679 A1202 78c multi   1.90 1.90

Prince of Monaco Islands, French Southern and Antarctic Territories — A1203

No. 2680: a, Giant Antarctic petrel. b, Coastline of Prince of Monaco Islands.

2012, June 9   **Litho. & Engr.**
2680 A1203   Sheet of 2   5.00 5.00
  a.-b.   €1 Either single   2.50 2.50
See French Southern and Antarctic Territories No. 467.

Souvenir Sheet

Cabaret on the Banks of the River, by Jan Breughel — A1204

2012, June 25   **Photo.**
2681 A1204 €3 multi   7.50 7.50
Exhibition of philatelic collection of Prince Albert II, Bruges, Belgium. See Belgium No. 2577.

Fort-la-Laffe, Matignon, France — A1205

2012, July 5   **Engr.**   *Perf. 13x13¼*
2682 A1205 €1.75 multi   4.50 4.50
Visit of Prince Albert II to Matignon.

Intl. Association of Athletics Federations, Cent. — A1206

2012, July 17   **Photo.**   *Perf. 13¼*
2683 A1206 89c multi   2.25 2.25

2012 Summer Olympics, London A1207

2012, July 17   **Litho. & Engr.**
2684 A1207 €1.35 multi   3.50 3.50

Tenth World Council of Consuls, Monaco A1208

2012, Aug. 22   **Photo.**   *Perf. 12¼*
2685 A1208 55c multi   1.40 1.40

Claude Debussy (1862-1918), Composer — A1209

2012, Aug. 22   **Engr.**   *Perf. 13x12¼*
2686 A1209 €1 red & black   2.50 2.50

Crucifixion, by Louis Brea — A1210

2012, Aug. 22   **Litho.**   *Perf. 12¼x13*
2687 A1210 €1.35 multi   3.50 3.50

Bird Protection League, Cent. — A1211

2012, Sept. 10   **Engr.**   *Perf. 13¼*
2688 A1211 €1 multi   2.60 2.60

Opening of New National Council Building A1212

2012, Sept. 12   *Perf. 13x13¼*
2689 A1212 78c brown & black   2.00 2.00

Great Organ, Monaco Cathedral A1213

Litho. & Engr.
2012, Sept. 12   *Perf. 13¼*
2690 A1213 €1.80 multi   4.75 4.75

Title of Prince of Monaco, 400th Anniv. A1214

2012, Sept. 12 Engr.   *Perf. 13x13¼*
2691 A1214 €2.40 multi   6.25 6.25

Consecration of St. Charles Church, Monaco, Cent. — A1215

2012, Oct. 19   *Perf. 13¼*
2692 A1215 €1.45 multi   3.75 3.75

Auguste Lumière (1862-1954), Filmmaker — A1216

2012, Oct. 19   *Perf. 12¼*
2693 A1216 €2.35 multi   6.00 6.00

Discovery of Bust of Nefertiti, Cent. — A1217

2012, Oct. 19
2694 A1217 €3.78 multi   9.75 9.75

Timbres Passion 2012 Philatelic Exhibition, Belfort, France — A1218

No. 2695 — Coat of arms and: a, Duchess Louise d'Aumont Mazarin (1759-1826), wife of Prince Honoré IV. b, Prince Honoré IV of Monaco (1758-1819).

2012, Nov. 2   Litho.   *Perf. 13¼*
2695 A1218 Horiz. pair   3.00 3.00
  a.-b.   55c Either single   1.50 1.50

Christmas A1219

2012, Nov. 2   **Photo.**
2696 A1219 60c multi   1.60 1.60

Release of Third Volume of *Adventures of Tintin* — A1220

2012, Nov. 21   *Perf. 13x13¼*
2697 A1220 77c multi   2.00 2.00

Prince Albert II — A1221

Inscription: (56c), Ecopli 20g. (63c), Prioritaire 20g. No. 2700, Europa 20g. No. 2701, Ecopli 50g. (€1.05), Prioritaire 50g.

2012, Dec. 1   Engr.   *Perf. 13x13¼*
2698 A1221   (56c) blue   1.50 1.50
2699 A1221   (63c) red   1.75 1.75
  a.   Dated "2015"   1.90 1.90
2700 A1221   (80c) red violet   2.10 2.10
2701 A1221   (80c) green   2.10 2.10
2702 A1221   (€1.05) black   2.75 2.75
     Nos. 2698-2702 (5)   10.20 10.20

Issued: No. 2699a, 1/2/15. No. 2699a sold for 76c on day of issue.

Painting by Patients of Speranza-Albert II Alzheimer's Disease Day Care Center — A1222

2012, Dec. 3 Photo.   *Perf. 13¼x13*
2703 A1222 €1.35 multi   3.50 3.50

Olympia, by Edouard Manet — A1223

2012, Dec. 3   Litho.   *Perf. 13x13¼*
2704 A1223 €1.80 multi   4.75 4.75

37th Intl. Circus Festival, Monte Carlo — A1224

2013, Jan. 2   Photo.   *Perf. 13¼*
2705 A1224 63c multi   1.75 1.75

Pierre de Coubertin (1863-1937), Founder of Intl. Olympic Committee — A1225

2013, Jan. 2   Engr.   *Perf. 13x13¼*
2706 A1225 €2.55 multi   6.75 6.75

Turkish Angora Cat — A1226

2013, Jan. 16   Photo.   *Perf. 13¼*
2707 A1226 56c multi   1.50 1.50

Intl. Cat Show.

Nautical Society of Monaco, 125th Anniv. — A1227

2013, Jan. 16   **Engr.**
2708 A1227 95c multi   2.60 2.60

Intl. Flower Arrangement Festival — A1228

2013, Jan. 16   **Photo.**
2709 A1228 €1.75 multi   4.75 4.75

French Bulldog — A1229

2013, Feb. 7   **Engr.**
2710 A1229 80c red & black   2.10 2.10

Intl. Dog Show.

Monte Carlo Casino Terraces A1230

2013, Feb. 7   **Photo.**
2711 A1230 80c multi   2.10 2.10

Monte Carlo Rolex Masters Tennis Tournament A1231

2013, Feb. 7
2712 A1231 €1.05 multi   2.75 2.75

World Association of Children's Friends, 50th Anniv. — A1232

2013, Feb. 18
2713 A1232 €1.55 multi   4.00 4.00

Intl. Red Cross, 150th Anniv. A1233

2013, Feb. 18 **Engr.** *Perf. 13x13¼*
2714 A1233 €4.10 red & blk   11.00 11.00

Formula 1 Race Cars A1234

Designs: €1.05, Maserati 250F. €1.75, Tyrrell P34.

2013, Mar. 14 **Litho.** *Perf. 13¼*
2715-2716 A1234 Set of 2   7.25 7.25

Clean Transportation — A1235

No. 2717: a, Solar-powered shuttle boat. b, Electric bicycle.

Litho. & Silk-screened
2013, Apr. 5
2717 A1235 Horiz. pair   9.75 9.75
a.-b. €1.85 Either single   4.75 4.75

Archconfraternity of Misericordia, Bicent. — A1236

2013, Apr. 27 **Photo.** *Perf. 13¼*
2718 A1236 80c multi   2.10 2.10

Junior Chamber International Monaco, 50th Anniv. — A1237

2013, May 10 **Litho.**
2719 A1237 56c multi   1.50 1.50

Europa A1238

2013, May 10
2720 A1238 63c multi   1.75 1.75

Grimaldi Family Coat of Arms and Tower of Crest, France A1239

2013, May 17 **Photo.**
2721 A1239 €1.05 multi   3.00 3.00
Visit of Prince Albert II to Duchy of Valentinois and Crest, France.

Giuseppe Verdi (1813-1901), Composer — A1240

Richard Wagner (1813-83), Composer — A1241

Premiere of *The Rite of Spring*, Ballet by Igor Stravinsky, Cent. — A1242

2013, May 22 **Engr.** *Perf. 13x12¼*
2722 A1240 €1.55 multi   4.25 4.25
2723 A1241 €1.85 multi   5.00 5.00
2724 A1242 €2.55 multi   7.00 7.00
Nos. 2722-2724 (3)   16.25 16.25

Admission to United Nations, 20th Anniv. A1243

2013, May 28 **Litho.** *Perf. 13¼*
2725 A1243 80c multi   2.25 2.25

15th World Festival of Amateur Theater A1244

2013, June 5
2726 A1244 63c multi   1.75 1.75

Larus Michahellis — A1245

2013, June 5
2727 A1245 80c multi   2.25 2.25

Discovery of Otiorhynchus Monoecirupus in Monaco — A1246

2013, June 5
2728 A1246 €1 multi   2.75 2.75

Miniature Sheet

Sharks — A1247

No. 2729: a, Blacktip shark (requin bordé). b, Tiger shark (requin-tigre). c, Whale shark (requin-baleine). d, Great white shark (grand requin blanc).

2013, June 8 **Photo.**
2729 A1247 Sheet of 4   9.50 9.50
a.-b. 63c Either single   1.75 1.75
c.-d. €1.05 Either single   3.00 3.00

Miniature Sheet

Monte Carlo Société des Bains de Mer, 150th Anniv. — A1248

No. 2730 — Monte Carlo Casino with: a, Beige background and white dots. b, Beige background. c, Black background. d, Black background and white dots.

Photo., (Sheet Margin Photo., Silk-screened and Embossed)
2013, July 5
2730 A1248 Sheet of 4   11.50 11.50
a.-b. 80c Either single   2.25 2.25
c. €1.05 multi   3.00 3.00
d. €1.35 multi   3.75 3.75

2013 Grande Bourse — A1249

2013, July 10 **Photo.** *Perf. 13¼*
2731 A1249 63c multi   1.75 1.75

MonacoPhil 2013 Intl. Philatelic Exhibition, Fontveille Terraces — A1250

2013, July 10 **Litho.**
2732 A1250 80c multi   2.10 2.10

First Trans-Mediterranean Flight by Roland Garros, Cent. — A1251

2013, Sept. 23 **Litho. & Engr.**
2733 A1251 €1.35 multi   3.75 3.75

Yachts — A1252

2013, Sept. 23 **Engr.** *Perf. 13x13¼*
2734 A1252 Horiz. pair   7.00 7.00
a. €1 Yacht without sails   2.75 2.75
b. €1.55 Yacht with sails   4.25 4.25

Jules Richard (1863-1945), Director of Monaco Oceanographic Museum A1253

2013, Oct. 9 *Perf. 13¼*
2735 A1253 €1 multi   2.75 2.75

Charles Pathé (1863-1957), Sound Recording and Film Entrepreneur A1254

2013, Oct. 9
2736 A1254 €1.85 pur & black   5.00 5.00

Crossword Puzzles, Cent. A1255

2013, Oct. 9　　**Perf. 13x13¼**
2737 A1255 €2.78 black & red　7.50 7.50

Christmas A1256

2013, Oct. 30　**Photo.**　**Perf. 13¼**
2738 A1256 63c multi　　1.75 1.75

Awarding of 2013 ASCAT Grand Prix of Philately to Jacques Rogge, Pres. of Intl. Olympic Committee A1257

2013, Dec. 5　**Litho.**　**Perf. 13¼**
2739 A1257 95c multi　　2.60 2.60

Automobiles — A1258

No. 2740: a, Sunbeam Alpine. b, ZIL-111V.

2013, Dec. 5　**Litho.**　**Perf. 13**
2740 A1258 Horiz. pair　5.25 5.25
a.-b.　95c Either single　2.60 2.60
See Russia No. 7501.

Miniature Sheet

MonacoPhil 2013 Intl. Philatelic Exhibition — A1259

No. 2741: a, Prince Albert II facing right, country name at LL. b, Prince Albert II facing forward. c, Prince Albert II facing right, country name at bottom center. d, Monogram of Prince Albert II.

Engr. With Foil Application
2013, Dec. 5　　**Perf. 13**
2741 A1259　Sheet of 4　11.00 11.00
a.-d.　€1 Any single　2.75 2.75

38th Intl. Circus Festival, Monte Carlo — A1260

2014, Jan. 6　**Photo.**　**Perf. 13¼**
2742 A1260 83c multi　　2.25 2.25

Posters for Movies Starring Grace Kelly A1261

Designs: €1.38, The Country Girl (Une Fille de la Province). €2.40, Dial M for Murder (Le Crime Etait Presque Parfait).

2014, Jan. 16　**Litho.**　**Perf. 13¼**
2743-2744 A1261　Set of 2　10.50 10.50
See Nos. 2783-2784.

British Shorthair Cat A1262

2014, Jan. 30　**Litho.**　**Perf. 13¼**
2745 A1262 61c multi　　1.75 1.75
Intl. Cat Show.

2014 Winter Olympics, Sochi, Russia A1263

2014, Jan. 30　**Engr.**　**Perf. 13x13¼**
2746 A1263 €1.78 multi　　5.00 5.00

Monte Carlo Rolex Masters Tennis Tournament A1264

2014, Feb. 5　**Photo.**　**Perf. 13¼**
2747 A1264 €1.10 multi　　3.00 3.00

Bull Terrier A1265

2014, Feb. 20　**Litho.**　**Perf. 13¼**
2748 A1265 87c multi　　2.40 2.40
Intl. Dog Show.

Intl. Flower Arrangement Festival — A1266

2014, Feb. 20　**Photo.**　**Perf. 13¼**
2749 A1266 €2.10 multi　　5.75 5.75

Gilles Villeneuve (1950-82), Formula 1 Race Car Driver — A1267

Ayrton Senna (1960-94), Formula 1 Race Car Driver — A1268

No. 2750: a, Villeneuve (31x31mm). b, Villeneuve (52x31mm).
No. 2751: a, Senna (31x31mm). b, Senna (52x31mm).

2014, Mar. 5　**Photo.**　**Perf. 13**
2750 A1267　Horiz. pair　3.80 3.80
a.-b.　66c Either single　1.90 1.90
2751 A1268　Horiz. pair　4.50 4.50
a.-b.　83c Either single　2.25 2.25

Princess Grace Foundation, 50th Anniv. — A1269

2014, Mar. 14　**Litho.**　**Perf. 13¼**
2752 A1269 66c multi　　1.90 1.90

Printemps des Arts Festival (Spring Arts Festival), 30th Anniv. — A1270

2014, Mar. 14　**Litho.**　**Perf. 13¼**
2753 A1270 €1.20 multi　　3.25 3.25

Marsupilami, Comic Book Character by André Franquin — A1271

2014, Apr. 1　**Photo.**　**Perf. 13x13¼**
2754 A1271 83c multi　　2.25 2.25

Diana at the Bath, by Carlo Maratti — A1272

No. 2755: a, 18th cent. engraving of painting (denomination at LR). b, Painting, 1684 (denomination at LL).

2014, Apr. 1　**Litho.**　**Perf. 13¼**
2755 A1272　Horiz. pair　9.00 9.00
a.-b.　€1.65 Either single　4.50 4.50

Monaco Air Rally, Cent. — A1273

2014, Apr. 1　**Engr.**　**Perf. 13¼**
2756 A1273 €2.65 multi　　7.25 7.25

Old Tram and Modern Bus — A1274

Litho. & Silk-Screened
2014, Apr. 30　　**Perf. 13**
2757 A1274 59c multi　　1.75 1.75

Europa A1275

2014, May 7　**Litho.**　**Perf. 13¼**
2758 A1275 83c multi　　2.25 2.25

Souvenir Sheet

Ancient Grimaldi Fiefdoms in France — A1276

No. 2759: a, House of the Princes of Monaco, Vic-sur-Cère, France. b, Rocher de Carlat.

2014, May 14　**Photo.**　**Perf. 13¼**
2759 A1276　Sheet of 2　10.50 10.50
a.　€1.65 multi　　4.50 4.50
b.　€2.10 multi　　5.75 5.75

2014 World
Cup Soccer
Tournament,
Brazil
A1277

2014, May 30   Photo.   Perf. 13
2760 A1277 98c multi   2.75 2.75
Values are for stamp with surrounding
selvage.

Prince Honoré IV (1758-
1819) — A1278

2014, May 30   Engr.   Perf. 13x13¼
2761 A1278 €2.10 multi   5.75 5.75
Treaty of Paris, 200th anniv., which restored
Prince Honoré IV to Monegasque throne.

Souvenir Sheet

Sharks — A1279

No. 2762: a, Blacktip reef shark and diver. b,
Hammerhead shark and diver, horiz. c, Gray
reef sharks.

2014, June 10   Photo.   Perf. 13¼
2762 A1279   Sheet of 3   9.50 9.50
  a.   66c multi   1.90 1.90
  b.   €1.10 multi   3.00 3.00
  c.   €1.65 multi   4.50 4.50

Princess Grace
Rose Garden,
30th
Anniv. — A1280

Litho. & Silk-Screened
2014, June 14   Perf. 13¼
2763 A1280 66c multi   1.90 1.90
No. 2763 is impregnated with a rose scent.

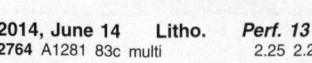

Protea
Flowers
A1281

2014, June 14   Litho.   Perf. 13¼
2764 A1281 83c multi   2.25 2.25

New
Clubhouse
of Yacht
Club of
Monaco
A1282

Litho. & Engr.
2014, June 20   Perf. 13¼
2765 A1282 83c multi   2.25 2.25

Scorpionfish — A1283

2014, June 25   Litho.   Perf. 13¼
2766 A1283 (40c) multi   1.10 1.10
No. 2766 is known only precanceled. See
note after No. 324.

Ceratonia
Siliqua — A1284

2014, July 12   Photo.   Perf. 13¼
2767 A1284 61c multi   1.75 1.75

Princess
Stephanie
and
Elephants
Baby and
Nepal
A1285

2014, July 12   Engr.   Perf. 13x13¼
2768 A1285 €1.10 multi   3.00 3.00
Baby & Nepal Association, 1st anniv.

World War
I, Cent.
A1286

Designs: €1.85, Hotel Alexandra (military
hospital during war). €2.40, Prince Louis II,
volunteer in French Army, and soldiers.

2014, Aug. 1   Engr.   Perf. 13x13¼
2769-2770 A1286   Set of 2   11.50 11.50

2014 Grande
Bourse — A1287

2014, Aug. 22   Litho.   Perf. 13¼x13
2771 A1287 59c multi   1.60 1.60

Opera Set Designed by Eugène Frey
(1864-1930) — A1288

Litho., Silk-Screened & Embossed
2014, Aug. 22   Perf. 13x13¼
2772 A1288 €1.38 multi   3.75 3.75

Sportel Monaco (World Sports Content
Media Convention), 25th
Anniv. — A1289

2014, Sept. 1   Litho.   Perf. 13¼
2773 A1289 59c multi   1.60 1.60

Children's
Day — A1290

2014, Sept. 1   Engr.   Perf. 13¼
2774 A1290 66c multi   1.75 1.75
Intl. Convention on the Rights of the Child,
25th Anniv.

Coat of Arms Type of 2000
Inscribed "20g prioritaire" at Top
Serpentine Die Cut 11
2014, Sept. 17   Photo.
  Booklet Stamp
  Self-Adhesive
2775 A786 (66c) red & black   1.75 1.75
  a.   Booklet pane of 10   17.50

83rd Interpol General Assembly,
Monaco — A1291

2014, Nov. 3   Litho.   Perf. 13¼x13
2776 A1291 66c multi   1.75 1.75

Adoration
of the
Magi, by
Taddeo di
Bartolo
A1292

2014, Nov. 3   Photo.   Perf. 13¼
2777 A1292 66c multi   1.75 1.75
Christmas.

Exhibition on Prince Albert I's
Exploration of Morocco,
Rabat — A1293

No. 2778: a, Hassan Tower, Rabat. b,
Oceanographic Museum, Monaco.

2014, Nov. 7   Photo.   Perf. 13¼
2778 A1293   Horiz. pair   4.25 4.25
  a.   66c multi   1.75 1.75
  b.   98c multi   2.50 2.50
  See Morocco No.

127th
International
Olympic
Committee
Session,
Monaco — A1294

Litho. & Engr.
2014, Dec. 1   Perf. 13¼
2779 A1294 66c multi   1.75 1.75

Fight AIDS
Monaco, 10th
Anniv. — A1295

Litho. & Silk-Screened With
Flocking Application
2014, Dec. 1   Perf. 13¼
2780 A1295 €1 red & black   2.50 2.50

39th Intl. Circus
Festival, Monte
Carlo — A1296

2015, Jan. 7   Photo.   Perf. 13¼
2781 A1296 95c multi   2.25 2.25

Russian Year in Monaco — A1297

No. 2782. a, Text (30x30mm). b, Buildings in
Russia and Monaco (41x30mm).

2015, Jan. 7   Photo.   Perf. 13¼
2782 A1297   Horiz. pair   5.50 5.50
  a.-b.   €1.20 Either single   2.75 2.75

Posters for Movies Starring Grace
Kelly Type of 2014
Designs: €1.50, The Swan (Le Cygne). €2,
To Catch a Thief (La Main au Collet).

2015, Jan. 14   Litho.   Perf. 13¼
2783-2784 A1261   Set of 2   8.00 8.00

Posidonia Oceanica A1298

2015, Jan. 21   Photo.   Perf. 13¼
2785 A1298 68c multi   1.60 1.60

Kiwanis International, Cent. — A1299

2015, Jan. 21   Litho.   Perf. 13¼
2786 A1299 95c multi   2.25 2.25

Princess Antoinette Park A1300

2015, Jan. 21   Photo.   Perf. 13¼
2787 A1300 €1.45 multi   3.25 3.25

German Shorthaired Pointer A1301

2015, Feb. 5   Litho.   Perf. 13¼
2788 A1301 €1.05 multi   2.40 2.40
              Intl. Dog Show.

Monte Carlo Rolex Masters Tennis Tournament A1302

2015, Feb. 5   Litho.   Perf. 13¼
2789 A1302 €1.25 multi   2.75 2.75

Intl. Flower Arrangement Festival — A1303

2015, Feb. 5   Engr.   Perf. 13¼
2790 A1303 €1.45 multi   3.25 3.25

Souvenir Sheet

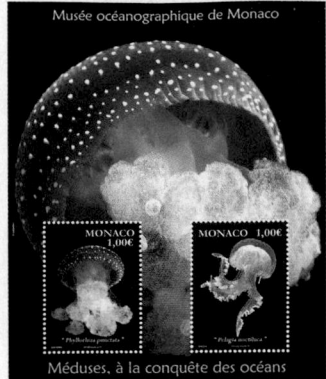

Jellyfish — A1304

No. 2791: a, Phyllorhiza punctata. b, Pelagia noctiluca.

2015, Feb. 25   Photo.   Perf. 13¼
2791 A1304 Sheet of 2   4.50 4.50
  a.-b.   €1 Either single   2.25 2.25

Monaco Pavilion at Expo Milan 2015 A1305

2015, Mar. 5   Litho.   Perf. 13¼
2792 A1305 €1 multi   2.25 2.25

Michele Alboreto (1956-2001), Formula 1 Race Car Driver — A1306

Graham Hill (1929-75), Formula 1 Race Car Driver — A1307

No. 2793: a, Alboreto wearing helmet (31x31mm). b, Alboreto in race car (52x31mm).
No. 2794: a, Hill wearing helmet (31x31mm). b, Hill in race car (52x31mm).

2015, Mar. 5   Engr.   Perf. 13
2793 A1306 Horiz. pair   4.00 4.00
  a.   76c multi   1.75 1.75
  b.   95c multi   2.10 2.10
2794 A1307 Horiz. pair   5.50 5.50
  a.   95c multi   2.10 2.10
  b.   €1.50 multi   3.25 3.25

Monacosat A1308

2015, Mar. 23   Litho.   Perf. 13¼
2795 A1308 76c multi   1.75 1.75

Caritas Monaco, 25th Anniv. — A1309

2015, Mar. 23   Litho.   Perf. 13¼
2796 A1309 76c multi   1.75 1.75

SEMI-POSTAL STAMPS

No. 16 Surcharged in Red

1914, Oct.   Unwmk.   Perf. 14x13½
B1   A2   10c + 5c carmine   8.00 8.00

View of Monaco — SP2

1919, Sept. 20   Typo.
B2   SP2   2c + 3c lilac   32.50   35.00
B3   SP2   5c + 5c green   21.00   20.00
B4   SP2   15c + 10c rose   21.00   20.00
B5   SP2   25c + 15c blue   39.00   40.00
B6   SP2   50c + 50c brn,
              buff   190.00 175.00
B7   SP2   1fr + 1fr blk, yel   300.00 375.00
B8   SP2   5fr + 5fr dull
              red   1,000. 1,200.
      Nos. B2-B8 (7)   1,603. 1,865.

Nos. B4-B8 Surcharged

1920, Mar. 20
B9   SP2   2c + 3c on #B4   40.00   45.00
  a.   "c" of "3c" inverted   1,500. 1,850.
  b.   Pair, Nos. 9, 9a   2,250. 2,600.
B10 SP2   2c + 3c on #B5   40.00   45.00
  a.   "c" of "3c" inverted   1,500. 1,850.
  b.   Pair, Nos. 10, 10a   2,250. 2,600.
B11 SP2   2c + 3c on #B6   40.00   45.00
  a.   "c" of "3c" inverted   1,500. 1,850.
  b.   Pair, Nos. 11, 11a   2,250. 2,600.
B12 SP2   5c + 5c on #B7   40.00   45.00
B13 SP2   5c + 5c on #B8   40.00   45.00

Overprinted

B14 SP2   15c + 10c rose   25.00   25.00
B15 SP2   25c + 15c blue   16.00   16.00
B16 SP2   50c + 50c
              brown,
              buff   55.00   55.00
B17 SP2   1fr + 1fr black,
              yel   75.00   75.00
B18 SP2   5fr + 5fr red   6,500. 6,500.
      Nos. B9-B17 (9)   371.00 396.00

Marriage of Princess Charlotte to Prince Pierre, Comte de Polignac.

Palace Gardens SP3

"The Rock" of Monaco SP4

Bay of Monaco SP5

Prince Louis II — SP6

1937, Apr.   Engr.   Perf. 13
B19 SP3   50c + 50c green   3.00   3.00
B20 SP4   90c + 90c car   3.00   3.00
B21 SP5   1.50fr + 1.50fr blue 6.00   6.00
B22 SP6   2fr + 2fr violet   11.50 11.50
B23 SP6   5fr + 5fr brn red   100.00 100.00
      Nos. B19-B23 (5)   123.50 123.50
      Set, never hinged   250.00

The surtax was used for welfare work.

Pierre and Marie Curie — SP7

Monaco Hospital, Date Palms SP8

1938, Nov. 15   Perf. 13
B24 SP7   65c + 25c dp bl grn   11.00 11.00
B25 SP8   1.75fr + 50c dp ultra 11.00 11.00
      Set, never hinged   40.00

B24 and B25 exist imperforate.
The surtax was for the International Union for the Control of Cancer.

Lucien — SP9

Honoré II — SP10

Louis I — SP11

Charlotte de Gramont — SP12

Antoine
I — SP13

Marie de
Lorraine — SP14

Jacques I
SP15

Louise-Hippolyte
SP16

Honoré III — SP17

"The Rock,"
18th
Century
SP18

1939, June 26

B26	SP9	5c + 5c brown blk	1.90	1.10
B27	SP10	10c + 10c rose vio	1.90	1.10
B28	SP11	45c + 15c brt green	6.75	5.00
B29	SP12	70c + 30c brt red vio	10.00	9.00
B30	SP13	90c + 35c vio	10.00	9.00
B31	SP14	1fr + 1fr ultra	25.00	24.00
B32	SP15	2fr + 2fr brn org	25.00	24.00
B33	SP16	2.25fr + 1.25fr Prus bl	30.00	30.00
B34	SP17	3fr + 3fr dp rose	40.00	42.50
B35	SP18	5fr + 5fr red	75.00	77.50
		Nos. B26-B35 (10)	225.55	223.20
		Set, never hinged	450.00	

Types of Regular
Issue, 1939
Surcharged in Red

1940, Feb. 10   Engr.   Perf. 13

B36	A30	20c + 1fr violet	2.75	2.75
B37	A31	25c + 1fr dk grn	2.75	2.75
B38	A32	30c + 1fr brn red	2.75	2.75
B39	A31	40c + 1fr dk blue	2.75	2.75
B40	A33	45c + 1fr rose car	2.75	2.75
B41	A34	50c + 1fr brown	2.75	2.75
B42	A32	60c + 1fr dk grn	3.50	3.50
B43	A35	75c + 1fr dk grn	3.50	3.50
B44	A34	1fr + 1fr scarlet	4.50	4.50
B45	A31	2fr + 1fr indigo	4.50	4.50
B46	A33	2.50fr + 1fr dk grn	11.00	11.00
B47	A35	3fr + 1fr dk blue	11.00	11.00
B48	A30	5fr + 1fr brn blk	15.00	15.00

B49	A33	10fr + 5fr lt blue	28.00	28.00
B50	A32	20fr + 5fr brn vio	29.00	29.00
		Nos. B36-B50 (15)	126.50	126.50
		Set, never hinged	300.00	

The surtax was used to purchase ambulances for the French government.

> **Catalogue values for unused stamps in this section, from this point to the end of the section, are for Never Hinged items.**

Symbol of
Charity and
View of
Monaco
SP19

Symbol of Charity
and View of
Monaco — SP20

1941, May 15

B51	SP19	25c + 25c brt red vio	3.50	1.75
B52	SP20	50c + 25c dk brown	3.50	1.75
B53	SP20	75c + 50c rose vio	6.50	2.25
B54	SP19	1fr + 1fr dk blue	6.50	2.25
B55	SP20	1.50fr + 1.50fr rose red	6.50	2.25
B56	SP19	2fr + 2fr Prus grn	7.00	3.00
B57	SP20	2.50fr + 2fr brt ultra	8.50	4.00
B58	SP19	3fr + 3fr dl red brn	11.00	4.50
B59	SP20	5fr + 5fr dk bl grn	16.00	6.50
B60	SP19	10fr + 8fr brn blk	24.00	13.00
		Nos. B51-B60 (10)	93.00	41.25

The surtax was for various charities.

Rainier
Grimaldi — SP21

Designs: 5c, Charles II. 10c, Jeanne Grimaldi. 20c, Charles-August Goyon de Matignon. 30c, Jacques I. 40c, Louise-Hippolyte. 50c, Charlotte Grimaldi. 75c, Marie-Charles Grimaldi. 1fr, Honore III. 1.50fr, Honore IV. 2.50fr, Honore V. 3fr, Florestan I. 5fr, Charles III. 10fr, Albert I. 20fr, Marie-Victoire. Frames differ.

1942, Dec. 10

B61	SP21	2c + 3c ultra	.50	.50
B62	SP21	5c + 5c org ver	.50	.50
B63	SP21	10c + 5c blk	.50	.50
B64	SP21	20c + 10c brt grn	.50	.50
B65	SP21	30c + 30c brn vio	.50	.50
B66	SP21	40c + 40c rose red	.50	.50
B67	SP21	50c + 50c vio	.50	.50
B68	SP21	75c + 75c brt red vio	.50	.50
B69	SP21	1fr + 1fr dk grn	.50	.50
B70	SP21	1.50fr + 1fr car brn	.50	.50
B71	SP21	2.50fr + 2.50fr pur	5.50	4.75
B72	SP21	3fr + 3fr turq bl	6.00	4.75
B73	SP21	5fr + 5fr sepia	6.75	6.00
B74	SP21	10fr + 5fr rose lil	7.25	6.75
B75	SP21	20fr + 5fr ultra	8.75	7.75
		Nos. B61-B75 (15)	39.25	35.00

Saint Dévote
SP36

Procession
SP37

Procession
SP38

Church of St.
Dévote — SP39

Burning of
Symbolic
Boat — SP40

Blessing of
the Sea
SP41

Church of
St. Dévote
SP42

Trial of St.
Barbara — SP43

Arrival of St. Dévote at
Monaco — SP44

1944, Jan. 27   Unwmk.   Perf. 13

B76	SP36	50c + 50c sepia	.25	.25
B77	SP37	70c + 80c dp ultra	.25	.25
B78	SP38	80c + 70c green	.25	.25
B79	SP39	1fr + 1fr rose vio	.25	.25
B80	SP40	1.50fr + 1.50fr red	.45	.45
B81	SP41	2fr + 2fr brn vio	.85	.85
B82	SP42	5fr + 2fr violet	.85	.85
B83	SP43	10fr + 40fr royal bl	.85	.85
B84	SP44	20fr + 60fr chlky bl	6.00	6.00
		Nos. B76-B84 (9)	10.00	10.00

Issued in honor of St. Dévote.
Type SP43 is inscribed "Jugement de Sainte Dévote," but actually shows the trial of St. Barbara in 235 A.D.

Needy
Child — SP45

Nurse and
Child — SP46

1946, Feb. 18   Engr.

B85	SP45	1fr + 3fr dp bl grn	.35	.35
B86	SP45	2fr + 4fr rose pink	.35	.35
B87	SP45	4fr + 6fr dk bl	.35	.35
B88	SP45	5fr + 40fr dk vio	1.10	.90
B89	SP45	10fr + 60fr brn red	1.10	.90
B90	SP45	15fr + 100fr indigo	1.60	1.40
		Nos. B85-B90 (6)	4.85	4.25

The surtax was for child welfare.

1946, Feb. 18

B91	SP46	2fr + 8fr brt blue	.75	.70

The surtax was used for prevention of tuberculosis.

19th
Century
Steamer
and Map
SP47

1946

B92	SP47	3fr + 2fr deep blue	.50	.50

Stamp Day, June 23, 1946.

Harbor of
Monte
Carlo
SP48

1946, Dec. 13

B93	SP48	2fr + 3fr dk bluish grn	1.40	1.40

Issued in tribute to the memory of Franklin D. Roosevelt. The surtax was for a fund to erect a monument in his honor.

Prince Louis II Type
Souvenir Sheet
Unwmk.

1947, May 15   Engr.   Imperf.

B94	A46	200fr + 300fr dk red & choc	42.50	24.00

Prince Charles
III — SP50

1948, Mar. 6   Perf. 14x13

B95	SP50	6fr + 4fr dk bl grn, lt bl	.55	.55

Issued for Stamp Day, Mar. 6.

Princess
Charlotte
SP51

Prince Rainier
III
SP52

Perf. 13½x13, Imperf.
1949, Dec. 27   **Engr.**
Cross Typo. in Red
B96	SP51	10fr + 5fr red brown	12.00 12.00
B97	SP52	15fr + 5fr brt red	12.00 12.00
B98	SP52	25fr + 5fr dk vio bl	12.00 12.00
B99	SP51	40fr + 5fr dull green	12.00 12.00
a.		Block of 4, #B96-B99	50.00 50.00

Printed in sheets measuring 151x173mm, perf. and imperf., containing 4 of No. B99a. The surtax was for the Red Cross.
For surcharges see Nos. 288-291.

Hercules Strangling the Lion of Nemea — SP53

Twelve Labors of Hercules: No. B101, Killing the Hydra of Lerna. No. B102, Capturing the Erymanthean boar. No. B103, Killing Stymphalian birds. No. B104, Hercules and the Ceryneian Hind. No. B105, The Augean Stables. No. B106, Hercules and the Cretan Bull. No. B107, Wild horses of Diomedes. No. B108, Hercules and the Oxen of Geryon. No. B109, Hercules and the Belt of Hippolytus. No. B110, Winning the golden apple of Hesperides. No. B111, Battling Cerberus.

1981, Nov. 5   Engr.   Perf. 13
B100	SP53 2.50fr + 50c multi	1.60	1.60
B101	SP53 3.50fr + 50c multi	1.60	1.60

1982, Nov. 8
B102	SP53 2.50fr + 50c multi	1.60	1.60
B103	SP53 3.50fr + 50c multi	1.60	1.60

1983, Nov. 9
B104	SP53 2.50fr + 50c multi	1.60	1.60
B105	SP53 3.50fr + 50c multi	1.60	1.60

1984, Nov. 8
B106	SP53 3fr + 50c multi	1.50	1.50
B107	SP53 4fr + 50c multi	1.90	1.90

1985, Nov. 7
B108	SP53 3fr + 70c multi	1.50	1.50
B109	SP53 4fr + 80c multi	1.90	1.90

1986, Oct. 28
B110	SP53 3fr + 70c multi	1.50	1.50
B111	SP53 4fr + 80c multi	1.90	1.90
	Nos. B100-B111 (12)	19.80	19.80

Surtax on #B100-B111 for the Red Cross.

Monegasque Committee to Fight Tuberculosis and Respiratory Diseases — SP54

1994, Mar. 14   Litho.   Perf. 13½x13
B112	SP54 2.40fr +60c multi	1.25	1.25

AIR POST STAMPS

No. 91 Srchd. in Black

Perf. 14x13½
1933, Aug. 22   Unwmk.
C1	A15 1.50fr on 5fr	25.00	25.00
a.	Imperf., pair	375.00	

> Catalogue values for unused stamps in this section, from this point to the end of the section, are for Never Hinged items.

Plane over Monaco — AP1

Plane Propeller and Buildings — AP2

Pegasus — AP3

Sea Gull — AP4

Plane, Globe and Arms of Monaco AP5

1942, Apr. 15   Engr.   Perf. 13
C2	AP1	5fr blue green	.35	.35
C3	AP1	10fr ultra	.35	.35
C4	AP2	15fr sepia	.70	.70
C5	AP3	20fr henna brown	1.00	1.00
C6	AP4	50fr red violet	5.00	4.00
C7	AP5	100fr red & vio brn	5.00	4.00
		Nos. C2-C7 (6)	12.40	10.40

For surcharges see Nos. CB1-CB5.

Nos. 196-197 Overprinted in Blue

1946, May 20
C8	A41	50fr dp Prus green	4.75	4.25
C9	A41	100fr red	4.75	4.25
a.		Inverted overprint	37,500.	
b.		Double overprint	22,500.	

Douglas DC-3 and Arms AP6

1946, May 20
C10	AP6	40fr red	1.25	.60
C11	AP6	50fr red brown	2.00	.85
C12	AP6	100fr dp blue grn	3.00	1.60
C13	AP6	200fr violet	3.25	2.40
		Nos. C10-C13 (4)	9.50	5.45

Exist imperforate. See Nos. C27-C29.

Harbor of Monte Carlo AP7

Map of Monaco — AP8

1946, Dec. 13
C14	AP7	5fr carmine rose	.65	.65
C15	AP8	10fr violet black	.65	.65

Issued in tribute to the memory of Franklin D. Roosevelt.

Franklin D. Roosevelt Examining his Stamp Collection AP9

Main Post Office, New York City AP10

Oceanographic Museum, Monaco — AP11

Harbor of Monte Carlo — AP12

Statue of Liberty and New York City Skyline — AP13

1947, May 15   Unwmk.
C16	AP9	50c violet	1.25	1.25
C17	AP10	1.50fr rose violet	.55	.55
C18	AP11	3fr henna brown	.55	.55
C19	AP12	10fr deep blue	4.00	4.00
C20	AP13	15fr rose carmine	7.50	7.50
a.		Strip of 3, #C20, 203, C19	16.00	16.00
		Nos. C16-C20 (5)	13.85	13.85

Monaco's participation in the Centenary Intl. Philatelic Exhibition, NYC, May, 1947.

Crowd Acclaiming Constitution of 1911 AP14

Anthropological Museum — AP15

Designs: 25fr, Institute of Human Paleontology, Paris. 50fr, Albert I. 100fr, Oceanographic Institute, Paris. 200fr, Albert I medal.

1949, Mar. 5   Engr.   Perf. 13
C21	AP14	20fr brown red	.75	.75
C22	AP14	25fr indigo	.75	.75
C23	AP15	40fr blue green	2.00	2.00
C24	AP15	50fr blk, brn & grn	2.75	2.75
C25	AP15	100fr cerise	9.25	9.25
C26	AP14	200fr deep orange	15.00	15.00
		Nos. C21-C26 (6)	30.50	30.50

Plane-Arms Type of 1946
1949, Mar. 10
C27	AP6	300fr dp ultra & ind	70.00	70.00
C28	AP6	500fr grnsh blk & bl grn	45.00	45.00
C29	AP6	1000fr black & red vio	75.00	75.00
		Nos. C27-C29 (3)	190.00	185.00

UPU Type of Regular Issue
1949-50
C30	A56	25fr deep blue	.65	.65
C31	A56	40fr red brown & sep	2.50	2.50
C32	A56	50fr dk green & ultra	4.00	4.00
C33	A56	100fr dk car & dk grn	6.00	6.00
		Nos. C30-C33 (4)	13.15	13.15

75th anniv. of the UPU.
Nos. C30-C33 exist imperforate, also No. C30 in deep plum and violet, imperforate. Issued: 25fr, 12/27; others, 9/12/50.

Rainier Type of Regular Issue
1950, Apr. 11   Unwmk.
C34	A57	50fr black & red brn	7.75	6.50
C35	A57	100fr red brn, sep & ind	11.00	10.50

Enthronement of Prince Rainier III.

Runner — AP18

Designs: 50fr, Fencing. 100fr, Target Shooting. 200fr, Olympic Torch.

1953, Feb. 23   Perf. 11
C36	AP18	40fr black	12.00	9.00
C37	AP18	50fr brt purple	15.00	10.00
C38	AP18	100fr dk slate grn	20.00	15.00
C39	AP18	200fr deep carmine	26.00	16.00
		Nos. C36-C39 (4)	73.00	50.00

Issued to publicize Monaco's participation in the Helsinki Olympic Games.

Dr. Albert Schweitzer and Ogowe
River Scene, Gabon — AP19

1955, Jan. 14   *Perf. 13*
C40 AP19 200fr multicolored   42.50 35.00
Dr. Albert Schweitzer, medical missionary.

Mediterranean Sea Swallows — AP20

Birds: 200fr, Sea gulls. 500fr, Albatross.
1000fr, Great cormorants.

1955-57   *Perf. 11*
C41 AP20 100fr dp blue &
            indigo   32.50 13.50
   a.   Perf. 13   32.50 22.00
C42 AP20 200fr bl & blk   32.50 14.50
   a.   Perf. 13   375.00 175.00
C43 AP20 500fr gray & dk
            grn   50.00 32.50
            Perf. 13
C44 AP20 1000fr dk bl grn
            & blk brn   110.00 67.50
   a.   Perf. 11   350.00 225.00
    Nos. C41-C44 (4)   225.00 128.00
Issued: Perf. 11, 1/14/55; Perf. 13, 1957.

"From the Earth to the Moon" and
Jules Verne — AP21

1955, June 7   **Unwmk.**
C45 AP21 200fr dp blue &
           slate   27.50 25.00
50th anniv. of the death of Jules Verne.

Wedding Type of Regular Issue
1956, Apr. 19   **Engr.**
Portraits in Brown
C46 A99 100fr purple   1.25 1.25
C47 A99 200fr carmine   1.60 1.60
C48 A99 500fr gray violet   3.75 3.75
    Nos. C46-C48 (3)   6.60 6.60
Wedding of Prince Rainier III to Grace Kelly,
Apr. 19, 1956.

Nos. J45 and J54 Surcharged and
Overprinted "Poste Aerienne" and
bars
1956, Apr.   *Perf. 11*
C49 D6 100fr on 20fr   10.50 10.50
   a.   Double surcharge   475.00
C50 D7 100fr on 20fr   10.50 10.50
   a.   Double surcharge   475.00
   b.   Pair, #C49, C50   22.50 22.50
    See footnote after No. 390.

Basilica of Lourdes — AP23

200fr, Pope Pius X, underground basilica.

1958, May 15   **Unwmk.**   *Perf. 13*
C51 AP23 100fr dk bl, grn & gray 1.75 1.40
C52 AP23 200fr red brn & sepia 2.50 2.50
   Centenary of the apparition of the Virgin
Mary at Lourdes.

Prince Rainier III
and Princess
Grace — AP24

1959, May 16
C53 AP24 300fr dark purple   14.00 9.25
C54 AP24 500fr blue   20.00 16.00

St. Dévote
AP25

1960, June 1   **Engr.**   *Perf. 13*
C55 AP25 2fr green, bl & vio   1.10 .75
C56 AP24 3fr dark purple   39.00 19.00
C57 AP24 5fr blue   39.00 27.50
C58 AP25 10fr green & brown   6.50 4.00
    Nos. C55-C58 (4)   85.60 51.25

1961, June 3
C59 AP25 3fr ultra, grn & gray ol 2.10 1.10
C60 AP25 5fr rose carmine   4.50 2.10

Europa Issue

Mercury
over Map
of Europe
AP26

1962, June 6   **Unwmk.**   *Perf. 13*
C61 AP26 2fr dk grn, sl grn &
           brn   2.00 1.00

Oceanographic Museum, Atom
Symbol and Princes Albert I and
Rainier III — AP27

1962, June 6
C62 AP27 10fr violet, bl & bis   6.00 6.50
   Establishment of a scientific research center
by agreement with the Intl. Atomic Energy
Commission.

Roland
Garros
AP28

1963, Dec. 12   **Engr.**   *Perf. 13*
C63 AP28 2fr dk blue & dk brn   1.25 1.25
   50th anniversary of the first airplane crossing of the Mediterranean by Roland Garros
(1888-1918).

Type of Regular Issue, 1964
   Design: 5fr, Convair B-58 Hustler (New
York-Paris in 3 hours, 19 minutes, 41 seconds,
Maj. William R. Payne, USAF, 1961).

1964, May 22   **Unwmk.**   *Perf. 13*
C64 A151 5fr brown, blk & bl   2.75 2.75
1st airplane rally of Monte Carlo, 50th anniv.

Bobsledding — AP29

1964, Dec. 3   **Engr.**   *Perf. 13*
C65 AP29 5fr multicolored   2.75 2.75
   9th Winter Olympic Games, Innsbruck, Austria, Jan. 29-Feb. 9, 1964.

ITU Type of Regular Issue
   Design: 10fr, ITU Emblem and Monte Carlo
television station on Mount Agel, vert.

1965, May 17   **Engr.**   *Perf. 13*
C66 A161 10fr bis brn, sl grn & bl 4.75 4.75

Princess Grace with Albert Alexander
Louis, Caroline and Stephanie — AP30

1966, Feb. 1   **Engr.**   *Perf. 13*
C67 AP30 3fr pur, red brn & Prus
           bl   2.25 1.50
Birth of Princess Stephanie, Feb. 1, 1965.

Opera
House
Interior
AP31

1966, June 1   **Engr.**   *Perf. 13*
C68 AP31 5fr Prus bl, bis & dk
          car rose   2.75 2.75
Centenary of founding of Monte Carlo.

Prince Rainier III
and Princess
Grace — AP32

1966-71   **Engr.**   *Perf. 13*
C69 AP32 2fr pink & slate   1.10 .40
C70 AP32 3fr emerald &
           slate   2.10 .80
C71 AP32 5fr lt blue & slate   2.75 1.10
C72 AP32 10fr lemon & sl
           ('67)   5.00 3.50
C72A AP32 20fr orange & brn
           ('71)   42.50 35.00
    Nos. C69-C72A (5)   53.45 40.80
   Issue dates: 10fr, Dec. 7, 1967; 20fr, Sept.
6, 1971. Others, Dec. 12, 1966.

Panhard-Phenix, 1895 — AP33

1967, Apr. 28   **Engr.**   *Perf. 13*
C73 AP33 3fr Prus blue & blk   2.40 2.40
   25th Grand Prix of Monaco.

Olympic Games Type of Regular
Issue
1968, Apr. 29   **Engr.**   *Perf. 13*
C74 A183 3fr Field hockey   1.75 1.75

Berlioz
Monument,
Monte
Carlo — AP34

1969, Apr. 26   **Engr.**   *Perf. 13*
C75 AP34 2fr green, blk & ultra   1.25 1.25
Hector Berlioz (1803-69), French composer.

Napoleon,
by Paul
Delaroche
AP35

1969, Apr. 26   **Photo.**   *Perf. 12x13*
C76 AP35 3fr multicolored   1.60 1.60
   Bicentenary of birth of Napoleon I.

Horses, Prehistoric Drawing from
Lascaux Cave — AP36

1970, Dec. 15   Engr.   Perf. 13
C77 AP36 3fr multicolored   2.00 2.00

Nativity Type of Regular Issue

Design: 3fr, Nativity, Flemish School, 15th
century, vert.

1973, Nov. 12   Engr.   Perf. 12x13
C78 A243 3fr Prus green   2.25 1.75

Prince Rainier
III — AP37

1974, Dec. 23   Engr.   Perf. 12½x13
C81 AP37 10fr dark purple   6.75 3.00
C82 AP37 15fr henna brown   9.25 6.25
C83 AP37 20fr ultra   15.00 8.50
    Nos. C81-C83 (3)   31.00 17.75

See Nos. 1994-1996.

Prince
Rainier and
Hereditary
Prince
Albert
AP38

1982-84   Engr.   Perf. 13x13½
C84 AP38 5fr deep violet   1.60   .60
C85 AP38 10fr red   5.00 1.10
C86 AP38 15fr dk blue grn   6.00 1.75
C87 AP38 20fr brt blue   7.00 2.25
C88 AP38 30fr brown ('84)   11.00 4.50
    Nos. C84-C88 (5)   30.60 10.20

AIR POST SEMI-POSTAL STAMPS

Catalogue values for unused
stamps in this section are for
Never Hinged items.

**Types of 1942 Air Post Stamps
Surcharged with New Values and
Bars
Unwmk.**

1945, Mar. 27   Engr.   Perf. 13
CB1 AP1 1fr + 4fr on 10fr rose
          red   .60   .60
CB2 AP2 1fr + 4fr on 15fr red
          brown   .60   .60
CB3 AP3 1fr + 4fr on 20fr sepia .60   .60
CB4 AP4 1fr + 4fr on 50fr ultra .60   .60
CB5 AP5 1fr + 4fr on 100fr bright
          red violet   .60   .60
    Nos. CB1-CB5 (5)   3.00 3.00

Surtax for the benefit of prisoners of war.

Franklin D. Roosevelt Type

1946, Dec. 13
CB6 A42 15fr + 10fr red   2.40 1.60

The surtax was for a fund to erect a monument in his honor.

1948 Olympic Type

1948, July
CB7   A48 5fr +5fr Rowing   11.00 11.00
CB8   A48 6fr +9fr Skiing   16.00 16.00
CB9   A48 10fr +15fr Tennis   22.50 22.50
CB10 A47 15fr +25fr Sailing   32.50 32.50
    Nos. CB7-CB10 (4)   82.00 82.00

Salmacis
Nymph
SPAP4

Designs similar to regular issue.

1948, July
CB11 A50   5fr + 5fr blk bl   19.00 19.00
CB12 A51   6fr + 9fr dk grn   19.00 19.00
CB13 A52   10fr + 15fr crim   20.00 20.00
CB14 SPAP4 15fr + 25fr red
            brown   24.00 24.00
    Nos. CB11-CB14 (4)   82.00 82.00

François J. Bosio (1769-1845), sculptor.

POSTAGE DUE STAMPS

D1   Prince Albert
                    I — D2

Perf. 14x13½
1905-43   Unwmk.   Typo.
J1   D1 1c olive green   .45   .55
J2   D1 5c green   .45   .55
J3   D1 10c rose   .45   .55
J4   D1 10c brn ('09)   350.00 125.00
J5   D1 15c vio brn, straw   3.50 1.75
J6   D1 20c bis brn, buff
          ('26)   .35   .35
J7   D1 30c blue   .45   .55
J8   D1 40c red vio ('26)   .35   .35
J9   D1 50c brn, org   4.50 4.00
J10   D1 50c blue grn ('27)   .35   .35
J11   D1 60c gray blk ('26)   .35   .65
J12   D1 60c brt vio ('34)   21.00 27.50
J13   D1 1fr red brn, straw
          ('26)   .35   .25
J14   D1 2fr red org ('27)   1.00 1.50
J15   D1 3fr mag ('27)   1.00 1.50
J15A D1 5fr ultra ('43)   .80 1.00
    Nos. J1-J15A (16)   385.35 166.40

For surcharge see No. J27.

1910
J16 D2 1c olive green   .25   .45
J17 D2 10c light violet   .45   .60
J18 D2 30c bister   190.00 160.00

In January, 1917, regular postage stamps
overprinted "T" in a triangle were used as
postage due stamps.

Nos. J17 and J18
Surcharged

1918
J19 D2 20c on 10c lt vio   4.00 7.50
  a.   Double surcharge   1,000.
J20 D2 40c on 30c bister   4.50 8.50

D3

1925-32
J21 D3 1c gray green   .40   .50
J22 D3 10c violet   .40   .55
J23 D3 30c bister   .50   .75
J24 D3 60c red   .70   .75
J25 D3 1fr lt bl ('32)   80.00 80.00
J26 D3 2fr dull red ('32)   80.00 80.00
    Nos. J21-J26 (6)   162.00 162.55

Nos. J25 and J26 have the numerals of
value double-lined.

"Recouvrements" stamps were used to
recover charges due on undelivered or refused
mail which was returned to the sender.

No. J9 Surcharged

1925
J27 D1 1fr on 50c brn, org   .80   .55
  a.   Double surcharge   750.00

Catalogue values for unused
stamps in this section, from this
point to the end of the section, are
for Never Hinged items.

D4

D5

1946-57   Engr.   Perf. 14x13, 13
J28   D4 10c sepia   .25   .25
J29   D4 30c dark violet   .25   .25
J30   D4 50c deep blue   .25   .25
J31   D4 1fr dark green   .25   .25
J32   D4 2fr yellow brn   .25   .25
J33   D4 3fr brt red vio   .30   .30
J34   D4 4fr carmine   .45   .45
J35   D5 5fr chocolate   .35   .35
J36   D5 10fr deep ultra   .65   .65
J37   D5 20fr grnsh blue   .70   .70
J38   D5 50fr red vio & red
          ('50)   55.00 55.00
J38A D5 100fr dk grn & red
          ('57)   12.00 12.00
    Nos. J28-J38A (12)   70.70 70.70

Sailing Vessel — D6

S. S. United States — D7

Early Postal Transport (D6): 1fr, Carrier
pigeons. 3fr, Old railroad engine. 4fr, Old monoplane. 5fr, Steam automobile. 10fr, daVinci's
flying machine. 20fr, Balloon. 50fr, Post rider.
100fr, Old mail coach.
Modern Postal Transport (D7): 1fr, Sikorsky
S-51 helicopter. 3fr, Modern locomotive. 4fr,
Comet airliner. 5fr, Sabre sports car. 10fr,
Rocket. 20fr, Graf Zeppelin. 50fr, Motorcyclist.
100fr, Railroad mail car.

1953-54   Perf. 11
J39 D6 1fr dk grn & brt
         red ('54)   .25   .25
  a.   Pair, Nos. J39, J48   .25   .25
J40 D6 2fr dp ultra & bl
         grn   .25   .25
  a.   Pair, Nos. J40, J49   .40   .40

J41 D6 3fr Prus grn & brn
         lake   .25   .25
  a.   Pair, Nos. J41, J50   .40   .40
J42 D6 4fr dk brn & Prus
         grn   .35   .35
  a.   Pair, Nos. J42, J51   .70   .70
J43 D6 5fr ultra & pur   .85   .85
  a.   Pair, Nos. J43, J52   1.75 1.75
J44 D6 10fr dp ultra & dk
         bl   9.00 9.00
  a.   Pair, Nos. J44, J53   18.00 18.00
J45 D6 20fr indigo & pur   6.00 6.00
  a.   Pair, Nos. J45, J54   12.00 12.00
J46 D6 50fr red & dk brn   12.00 12.00
  a.   Pair, Nos. J46, J55   24.00 24.00
J47 D6 100fr vio brn & dp
         grn   20.00 20.00
  a.   Pair, Nos. J47, J56   40.00 40.00
J48 D7 1fr brt red & dk
         grn ('54)   .25   .25
J49 D7 2fr bl grn & dp ul-
         tra   .25   .25
J50 D7 3fr brn lake &
         Prus grn   .25   .25
J51 D7 4fr Prus grn & dk
         brn   .35   .35
J52 D7 5fr purple & ultra   .85   .85
J53 D7 10fr dk bl & dp ul-
         tra   9.00 9.00
J54 D7 20fr purple & indi-
         go   6.00 6.00
J55 D7 50fr dk brn & red   12.00 12.00
J56 D7 100fr dp grn & vio
         brn   20.00 20.00
    Nos. J39-J56 (18)   97.90 97.90

Pairs se-tenant at the base.
For overprints see Nos. 371-390.

Felucca,
18th
Century
D8

2c, Paddle steamer La Palmaria, 19th cent.
5c, Arrival of 1st train. 10c, Armed messenger,
15th-16th cent. 20c, Monaco-Nice courier,
18th cent. 30c, "Charles III," 1866. 50c, Courier on horseback, 17th cent. 1fr, Diligence,
19th cent.

1960-69   Engr.   Perf. 13
J57 D8 1c bl grn, bis brn & bl   .25   .25
J58 D8 2c sl grn, sep & ultra   .25   .25
J59 D8 5c grnsh bl, gray & red
         brn   .25   .25
J60 D8 10c vio bl, blk & grn   .25   .25
J61 D8 20c blue, brn & grn   .90   .90
J62 D8 30c brn, brt grn & brt bl
         ('69)   1.40 1.40
J63 D8 50c dk bl, brn & sl grn 1.90 1.90
J64 D8 1fr sl grn, bl & brn   2.50 2.50
    Nos. J57-J64 (8)   7.70 7.70

Knight
in
Armor
D9

1980-83   Engr.   Perf. 13
J65 D9 5c red & gray   .25   .25
J66 D9 10c salmon & red   .25   .25
J67 D9 15c violet & red   .25   .25
J68 D9 20c lt green & red   .25   .25
J69 D9 30c blue & red   .25   .25
J70 D9 40c lt brown & red   .35   .35
J71 D9 50c lilac & red   .45   .45
J72 D9 1fr black & blue   .70   .70
J73 D9 2fr dk brn & org ('82)   1.10 1.10
J74 D9 3fr sl bl & rose car
         ('83)   1.60 1.60
J75 D9 4fr red & dk grn ('83)   2.25 2.25
J76 D9 5fr magenta & brn
         ('83)   2.75 2.75
    Nos. J65-J76 (12)   10.45 10.45

Nos. J65-J76 printed in horizontal rows with
princely coat of arms between stamps. Sold in
strips of 3 only.
Issued: #J65-J72, 2/8; #J73, J75, 2/15;
3J74, J76, 1/3.

MONACO
0.05 TIMBRE TAXE

Natl. Coat of Arms — D10

1985-86		Photo.		Perf. 13x12½	
J77	D10	5c multicolored		.25	.25
J78	D10	10c multicolored		.25	.25
J79	D10	15c multicolored		.25	.25
J80	D10	20c multicolored		.25	.25
J81	D10	30c multicolored		.25	.25
J82	D10	40c multicolored		.25	.25
J83	D10	50c multicolored ('86)		.25	.25
J84	D10	1fr multicolored ('86)		.45	.45
J85	D10	2fr multicolored ('86)		.75	.75
J86	D10	3fr multicolored		1.25	1.25
J87	D10	4fr multicolored ('86)		1.60	1.60
J88	D10	5fr multicolored		2.25	2.25
	Nos. J77-J88 (12)			8.05	8.05

See Nos. 1608-1609.

scott/schaubek
u.s. hingeless album

Enjoy the breadth and scope of the Scott National album with the convenience of a hingeless Schaubek album. Published through a joint effort between the two companies, the pages are done in the Schaubek format, while the content appears just as it does in the National album, that means there are spaces for every major U.S. stamp listed in the Scott Catalogue. *(Binders and slipcases sold separately.)*

Item			Retail	AA*
HUSA01	1845 - 1934	97 pgs	$299.95	$224.99
HUSA02	1935 - 1976	108 pgs	$299.95	$224.99
HUSA03	1977 - 1993	110 pgs	$299.95	$224.99
HUSA04	1994 - 2000	116 pgs	$299.95	$224.99
HUSA05	2001 - 2004	62 pgs	$199.95	$148.99
HUSA06	2005 - 2009	88 pgs	$249.99	$179.99
HUSA2010	2010	13 pgs	$54.99	$39.59
HUSA2011	2011	16 pgs	$56.99	$41.39
HUSA2012	2012	17 pgs	$57.99	$46.99
HUSA2013	2013	20 pgs	$59.99	$49.99
HUSA2014	2014	18 pgs	$59.99	$49.99
HRB001	Binders holds	100 pgs	$39.99	$34.99
HRS001	Slipcase		$15.00	$12.99

Call 1-800-572-6885
Visit AmosAdvantage.com

ORDERING INFORMATION
*AA prices apply to paid subscribers of Amos Media titles, or for orders placed online.
Prices, terms and product availability subject to change.

Shipping & Handling:
• United States orders under $10 are only $3.99.
• United States 10% of order over $10 total.
• Minimum Freight Charge $7.99

• Maximum Freight Charge $45.00
• Canada 20% of order total.
• Minimum Freight Charge $19.99
• Maximum Freight Charge $200.00
• Foreign orders are shipped via FedEx Economy International or USPS and billed actual freight.
Brokerage, Customs or duties are the responsibility of the customer.

MONGOLIA

măn-'gōl-yə

(Mongolian People's Republic)

(Outer Mongolia)

LOCATION — Central Asia, bounded on the north by Siberia, on the west by Sinkiang, on the south and east by China proper and Manchuria
GOVT. — Republic
AREA — 604,250 sq. mi.
POP. — 2,617,379 (1999 est.)
CAPITAL — Ulan Bator

Outer Mongolia, which had long been under Russian influence although nominally a dependency of China, voted at a plebescite on October 20, 1945, to sever all ties with China and become an independent nation. See Tannu Tuva.

100 Cents = 1 Dollar

100 Mung = 1 Tugrik (1926)

Catalogue values for unused stamps in this country are for Never Hinged items, beginning with Scott 149 in the regular postage section, Scott B1 in the semi-postal section, Scott C1 in the airpost section, and Scott CB1 in the airpost semi-postal section.

Watermark

Wmk. 170 — Greek Border and Rosettes

Scepter of Indra — A1

1924   Litho.   Unwmk.   Perf. 10, 13½
Surface Tinted Paper

1	A1	1c multi, *bister*	12.00	12.00
2	A1	2c multi, *brnsh*	10.50	5.50
		a. Perf. 13½	47.50	47.50
3	A1	5c multi	40.00	24.00
		a. Perf. 10	47.50	35.00
4	A1	10c multi, *gray bl*	20.00	16.00
		a. Perf. 10	20.00	16.00
5	A1	20c multi, *gray*	27.50	17.50
6	A1	50c multi, *salmon*	40.00	24.00
7	A1	$1 multi, *yellow*	55.00	40.00
		b. Perf. 10	650.00	190.00
		Nos. 1-7 (7)	205.00	139.00

These stamps vary in size from 19x25mm (1c) to 30x39mm ($1). They also differ in details of the design.
Errors of perforating and printing exist.
Some quantities of Nos. 1-2, 4-7 were defaced with horizontal perforation across the center.
The 5c exists perf 11½. Value, $325 unused, hinged $190 used.

Revenue Stamps Handstamp

A2

Sizes: 1c to 20c: 22x36mm
50c, $1: 26x43½mm
$5: 30x45½mm

Overprinted in Violet

1926　　　　　　　　　**Perf. 11**

16	A2	1c blue	12.00	12.00
17	A2	2c orange	16.00	11.00
18	A2	5c plum	16.00	13.00
19	A2	10c green	20.00	17.00
20	A2	20c yel brn	24.00	20.00
21	A2	50c brn & ol grn	190.00	175.00
22	A2	$1 brn & salmon	550.00	475.00
23	A2	$5 red, yel & gray	650.00	—
		Nos. 16-23 (8)	1,478.	723.00

Black Overprint

16a	A2	1c blue	20.00	13.50
17a	A2	2c orange	32.50	20.00
18a	A2	5c plum	36.00	20.00
19a	A2	10c green	47.50	24.00
20a	A2	20c yellow brown	65.00	45.00
21a	A2	50c brown & olive grn	1,200.	325.00
22a	A2	$1 brown & salmon	600.00	400.00
23a	A2	$5 red, yellow & gray	—	—
		Nos. 16a-22a (7)	2,001.	847.50

Red Overprint

16b	A2	1c blue	
17b	A2	2c orange	
18b	A2	5c plum	
19b	A2	10c green	
20b	A2	20c yellow brown	

The preceding handstamped overprints may be found inverted, double, etc. Counterfeits abound.

For overprints and surcharges see #48-61.

A3

A4

Soyombo

TYPE I — The pearl above the crescent is solid. The devices in the middle of the stamp are not outlined.
TYPE II — The pearl is open. The devices and panels are all outlined in black.

1926-29　　　　　　　　**Perf. 11**
Type I
Size: 22x28mm

32	A3	5m lilac & blk	12.00	12.00
33	A3	20m blue & blk	20.00	24.00

Type II
Size: 22x29mm

34	A3	1m yellow & blk	3.25	3.25
35	A3	2m brn org & blk	4.00	3.25
36	A3	5m lilac & blk	4.75	4.00
37	A3	10m lt blue & blk	4.00	2.00
		a. Imperf, pair		
39	A3	25m yel grn & blk	8.00	4.00
		a. Imperf, pair	125.00	110.00

Size: 26x34mm

40	A3	40m lemon & blk	11.00	4.75
41	A3	50m buff & blk	16.00	6.50

Size: 28x37mm

42	A4	1t brown, grn & blk	32.50	12.00
43	A4	3t red, yel & blk	72.50	47.50
44	A4	5t brn vio, rose & blk	95.00	60.00
		Nos. 32-44 (12)	283.00	183.25

In 1929 a change was made in the perforating machine. Every fourth pin was removed, which left the perforation holes in groups of three with blank spaces between the groups. Nos. 44A-44D have only this interrupted perforation. Nos. 37 and 39 are found with both perforations.

For overprints and surcharges see #45-47.

Soyombo — A5

1929, July　　　　**Interrupted Perf 11**

44A	A5	5m lilac & black	25.00	20.00
44B	A5	10m lt grnish blue & black	100.00	65.00
		a. imperf, pair		
44C	A5	20m blue & black	35.00	27.50
		a. imperf, pair		
		b. Horiz. pair, imperf btwn.		—
44D	A5	25m yel grn & black	32.50	27.50
		a. imperf, pair		

See note after No. 44.

Nos. 34, 35, 40 Handstamped With New Values in Black

1930

45	A3	10m on 1m	32.50	30.00
46	A3	20m on 2m	45.00	40.00
47	A3	25m on 40m	52.50	47.50
		Nos. 45-47 (3)	130.00	117.50

Soyombo — A6

Violet Overprint, Handstamped

1931

48	A6	1c blue	24.00	12.00
		a. Blue overprint	87.50	47.50
49	A6	2c orange	27.50	9.50
50	A6	5c brown vio	35.00	9.50
		a. Blue overprint	65.00	22.50
51	A6	10c green	32.50	9.50
		a. Blue overprint	65.00	37.50
52	A6	20c bister brn	47.50	12.00
53	A6	50c brown & ol yel	130.00	120.00
54	A6	$1 brown & salmon	200.00	160.00
		Nos. 48-54 (7)	496.50	332.50

Soyombo — A7

Revenue Stamps Surcharged in Black, Red or Blue

1931

59	A7	5m on 5c brn vio (Bk)	40.00	16.00
		a. Inverted surcharge		35.00
		b. Imperf., pair	225.00	225.00
60	A7	10m on 10c green (R)	55.00	27.50
		a. Inverted surcharge	90.00	50.00
		b. Imperf., pair	225.00	225.00
61	A7	20m on 20c bis brn (Bl)	65.00	35.00
		a. Inverted surcharge		55.00
		b. Imperf., pair	225.00	225.00
		Nos. 59-61 (3)	160.00	78.50

On Nos. 59-61, "Postage" is always diagonal, and may read up or down.

Weaver at Loom — A8

Telegrapher A9

Sukhe Bator A10

Lake and Mountains — A11

Designs: 5m, Mongol at lathe. 10m, Government building, Ulan Bator. 15m, Young Mongolian revolutionary. 20m, Studying Latin alphabet. 25m, Mongolian soldier. 50m, Monument to Sukhe Bator. 3t, Sheep shearing. 5t, Camel caravan. 10t, Chasing wild horses.

Perf. 12½x12
1932   Photo.   Wmk. 170

62	A8	1m brown	3.25	1.50
63	A9	2m red violet	3.25	1.50
64	A8	5m indigo	2.00	.80
65	A8	10m dull green	2.00	.80
66	A9	15m dp brown	2.00	.80
67	A9	20m rose red	2.40	.80
68	A9	25m dull violet	2.40	.80
69	A10	40m gray black	2.00	1.20
70	A10	50m dull blue	2.40	.80

Perf. 11x12

71	A11	1t dull green	2.75	1.20
72	A11	3t dull violet	5.50	2.00
73	A11	5t brown	19.50	12.00
74	A11	10t ultra	40.00	20.00
		Nos. 62-74 (13)	89.45	44.20

Used values are for canceled-to-order stamps.

Nos. 70-74 Handstamped With New Values in Black or Violet

1941　　　　　　**Black handstamp**

74A	A11	5m on 5t	—	—
74B	A10	10m on 50m	—	—
74C	A11	10m on 10t	—	—
74D	A11	15m on 5t	—	—
74E	A11	20m on 1t	—	—
74F	A11	30m on 3t	—	—

Violet handstamp

74G	A11	5m on 5t	—	—
74H	A11	15m on 5t	—	—
74I	A11	20m on 1t	—	—
74J	A11	30m on 3t	—	—

Mongolian Man — A12

Mongolian Woman — A13

Soldier — A14

Camel Caravan A15

Modern School A16

Arms of the Republic — A17

Sukhe Bator — A18

Pasture Scene — A19

Paper with network as in italics

1943		**Typo.**	**Perf. 12½**	
75	A12	5m green, *green*	12.00	10.00
76	A13	10m dp blue, *lt bl*	20.00	11.00
77	A14	15m rose, *lt rose*	22.50	15.00
78	A15	20m org brn, *org*	32.50	27.50
79	A16	25m red brn, *buff*	32.50	32.50
80	A17	30m carmine, *red*	37.50	37.50
81	A18	45m purple, *mauve*	50.00	50.00
82	A19	60m dp green, *grn*	90.00	90.00
	Nos. 75-82 (8)		297.00	273.50

Marshal Kharloin Choibalsan — A21

1945		**Unwmk.**	**Perf. 12½**	
83	A21	1t black brown	60.00	70.00

Choibalsan A22

Victory Medal A24

Sukhe Bator and Choibalsan A23

Designs: #86, Choibalsan as young man. #87, Choibalsan University, Ulan Bator. 1t, Anniversary medal. 2t, Sukhe Bator.

1946, July		**Photo.**	**Perf. 12½**	
84	A22	30m olive bister	6.50	6.50
85	A23	50m dull purple	7.75	7.75
86	A24	60m black	8.00	8.00
87	A23	60m orange brown	14.00	14.00
88	A24	80m dk orange brn	12.50	12.50
89	A24	1t indigo	16.00	16.00
90	A24	2t deep brown	22.50	22.50
	Nos. 84-90 (7)		87.25	87.25

25th anniversary of independence.

New Housing A25

School Children — A26

Mongolian Arms and Flag — A27

Sukhe Bator — A28

Flags of Communist Countries — A29

Lenin — A30

Designs: 15m, Altai Hotel. No. 94, State Store. No. 95, Like 30m. 25m, University. 40m, National Theater. 50m, Pedagogical Institute. 60m, Sukhe Bator monument. Sizes of type A25: Nos. 91, 93-94, 98-99, 32½x22mm. 25m, 55x26mm.

1951, July

91	A25	5m brn, *pink*	6.75	6.75
92	A26	10m dp bl, *pink*	8.25	8.25
93	A25	15m grn, *grnsh*	10.00	10.00
94	A25	20m red org	10.00	10.00
95	A27	20m dk bl & multi	10.00	10.00
96	A25	25m bl, *bluish*	10.00	10.00
97	A27	30m red & multi	10.00	10.00
98	A25	40m pur, *pink*	10.00	10.00
99	A25	50m brn, *grysh*	20.00	20.00
100	A28	60m brn blk	20.00	20.00
101	A29	1t multi	20.00	20.00
102	A28	2t dk brn & org brn	25.00	25.00
103	A30	3t multi	25.00	25.00
	Nos. 91-103 (13)		185.00	185.00

30th anniversary of independence.

Choibalsan — A31

Choibalsan and Farmer — A32

Choibalsan in uniform — A32a

Choibalsan and Sukhe Bator — A33

Designs: No. 108, 30m, Choibalsan and factory worker (47x33mm). 50m, Choibalsan and Young Pioneer. No. 112, 2t, Choibalsan in uniform.

1953, Dec.		**Photo.**	**Perf. 12½**	
104	A31	15m dull blue	5.00	5.00
105	A32	15m dull green	5.00	5.00
106	A31	20m dull green	10.00	10.00
107	A32	20m sepia	10.00	10.00
108	A32	20m violet blue	10.00	10.00
109	A32	30m dark brown	10.00	10.00
110	A33	50m orange brn	10.00	10.00
111	A33	1t carmine rose	10.00	10.00
112	A32a	1t sepia	15.00	15.00
113	A32a	2t red	15.00	15.00
114	A33	3t sepia	20.00	20.00
115	A33	5t red	40.00	40.00
	Nos. 104-115 (12)		160.00	160.00

First anniversary of death of Marshal Karloin Choibalsan (1895-1952).

Arms of Mongolia — A34

1954, Mar.		**Litho.**	**Perf. 12½**	
116	A34	10m carmine	12.00	7.00
117	A34	20m carmine	60.00	50.00
118	A34	30m carmine	12.00	8.00
119	A34	40m carmine	40.00	40.00
120	A34	60m carmine	12.00	10.00
	Nos. 116-120 (5)		136.00	115.00

Sukhe Bator and Choibalsan — A35

Lake Hubsugul A36

Guard with Dog — A37

#122, Lenin Statue, Ulan Bator. 50m, Choibalsan University. 1t, Arms and flag of Mongolia.

1955, June		**Photo.**	**Perf. 12½**	
121	A35	30m green	1.25	1.00
122	A35	30m orange ver	2.50	1.00
123	A36	30m brt blue	2.25	1.25
124	A37	40m dp red lilac	5.00	1.75
125	A36	50m ocher	5.00	2.25
126	A37	1t red & multi	9.00	7.00
	Nos. 121-126 (6)		25.00	14.25

35th anniversary of independence.

1955

Design: 2t, Lenin.

127	A35	2t bright blue	10.00	5.00

85th anniversary of birth of Lenin.

Flags of Communist Countries A38

Arms of Mongolia A39

1955

128	A38	60m blue & multi	5.00	4.00

Fight for peace.

1956		**Photo.**	**Perf. 12½**	
129	A39	20m dark brown	3.00	2.00
130	A39	30m dark olive	4.00	3.00
131	A39	40m bright blue	5.00	4.00
132	A39	60m blue green	6.00	4.50
133	A39	1t deep carmine	10.00	8.00
	Nos. 129-133 (5)		28.00	21.50

Kremlin, Moscow, Train and Sukhe Bator Monument A40

Design: 2t, Flags of Mongolia and USSR.

1956

134	A40	1t dk blue & multi	25.00	15.00
135	A40	2t red & multi	10.00	8.00

Establishment of railroad connection between Moscow and Ulan Bator.

Mongolian Arms and Flag — A41

Hunter with Golden Eagle — A42

Wrestlers A43

Designs: No. 138, 3 children (33x26½mm).

1956, July   Typo.   Perf. 9
136 A41 30m blue   10.00   5.00
137 A42 30m pale brown   50.00 50.00
138 A42 60m orange   20.00 20.00
139 A43 60m yellow green   20.00 20.00
     Nos. 136-139 (4)   100.00 95.00
35th anniversary of independence.

Types A41 and A43 without "XXXV"
1958
140 A41 20m red   5.00   3.00
141 A43 50m brown, *pink*   12.50   3.00
Nos. 140-143 were issued both with and without gum.

Poster — A44

1958, Mar.   Litho.   Perf. 9
142 A44 30m maroon & salmon   5.00   4.00
13th Congress of Mongolian People's Party.

Globe and Dove — A45

1958, May
143 A45 60m deep blue   5.00   4.00
4th Congress of International Democratic Women's Federation, Vienna, June, 1958. Nos. 142-143 exist imperf.

Yak — A46

No. 144, Pelicans, vert. No. 145, Siberian ibex, vert. No. 147, Yak. No. 148, Camels.

1958, July   Typo.   Perf. 9
144 A46 30m lt blue   15.00   3.50
145 A46 30m brt green   4.00   2.50
146 A46 60m orange   4.00   2.50

---

147 A46 1t blue   4.00   3.50
148 A46 1t rose   4.00   3.50
     Nos. 144-148 (5)   31.00 15.50
         Shades exist.

┌─────────────────────────────┐
│   Canceled to Order   │
│ Some quantity of all issues not │
│ printed by the State Printing Works, │
│ Ulan Bator, except Nos. 296-303, │
│ were canceled to order.   │
│ Used values are for c-t-o. Postally │
│ used stamps sell for considerably │
│ more.   │
└─────────────────────────────┘

┌─────────────────────────────┐
│ **Catalogue values for unused** │
│ **stamps in this section, from this** │
│ **point to the end of the section, are** │
│ **for Never Hinged items.** │
└─────────────────────────────┘

Stallion A47

Designs: 5m, 40m, Goat. 10m, 30m, Ram. 15m, 60m, Stallion. 20m, 50m, Bull. 25m, 1t, Bactrian camel.

Perf. 10½x11½
1958, Nov. 11   Litho.
149 A47 5m yellow & brn   .25   .25
150 A47 10m lt grn & brn   .25   .25
151 A47 15m lilac & brn   .35   .25
152 A47 20m lt bl & brn   .35   .25
153 A47 25m rose & brn   .40   .25
154 A47 30m lilac & pur   .50   .25
155 A47 40m lt & dk green   .50   .25
156 A47 50m salmon & brn   .55   .25
157 A47 60m lt blue & ind   .95   .25
158 A47 1t yellow & brn   1.75   .50
     Nos. 149-158 (10)   5.85 2.75

Holy Flame (Tulaga) — A48

1959, May 1   Litho.   Perf. 9
159 A48 1t multi   4.50   3.50
         See No. C36.

Archer — A49

Mongol Sports: 5m, Taming wild horse. 10m, Wrestlers. 15m, Horseback riding. 25m, Horse race. 30m, Archers. 70m, Hunting wild horse. 80m, Proclaiming a champion.

1959, June 6   Photo.   Perf. 11
160 A49 5m multi   .25   .25
161 A49 10m multi   .25   .25
162 A49 15m multi   .25   .25
163 A49 20m multi   .25   .25
164 A49 25m multi   .40   .25
165 A49 30m multi   .55   .25
166 A49 70m multi   .75   .35
167 A49 80m multi   1.10   .55
     Nos. 160-167 (8)   3.80 2.40

Young Wrestlers A50

Youth Festival Emblem — A51

Designs: 5m, Young musician, horiz. 20m, Boy on horseback. 25m, Two opera singers. 40m, Young Pioneers with flags, horiz.

Photo.; Litho. (30m)
1959, July   Perf. 12, 11 (30m)
168 A50 5m vio bl & rose car   .25   .25
169 A50 10m bl grn & brn   .25   .25
170 A50 20m claret & grn   .25   .25
171 A50 25m green & vio bl   .35   .25
172 A51 30m lil & lt bl   .35   .25
173 A51 40m green & pur   1.10   .50
     Nos. 168-173 (6)   2.55 1.75

Mongolian Youth Festival.
The 30m was printed by State Printing Works, Ulan Bator.
Issue dates: 30m, July 11; others July 10.

"Mongol" in Stylized Uighur Script — A52

"Mongol" in Various Scripts: 40m, Soyombo. 50m, Kalmuck. 60m, Square (Pagspa). 1t, Cyrillic.
Printed by State Printing Works, Ulan Bator.

1959, Sept. 1   Litho.   Perf. 11
Size: 29x42½mm
174 A52 30m black & multi   6.50   6.50
175 A52 40m black & multi   6.50   6.50
  a. Horiz. pair, imperf between
      and at right   150.00
176 A52 50m black & multi   8.50   8.50
177 A52 60m black & multi   14.00 14.00
Size: 21x31mm
Perf. 9
178 A52 1t black & multi   17.50 17.50
     Nos. 174-178 (5)   53.00 53.00

1st Intl. Mongolian Language Congress.

Battle Emblem A53

Battle Monument A54

1959, Sept. 15 Photo.   Perf. 12½x12
179 A53 40m yellow, brn & car   .60   .25
180 A54 50m multicolored   .60   .25

Ha-lo-hsin (Khalka) River Battle, 20th anniv.

Congress Emblem A55

Printed by State Printing Works, Ulan Bator.

1959, Dec.   Litho.   Perf. 11
181 A55 30m green   4.50   4.50
2nd meeting of rural economy cooperatives of Mongolia.

Sable — A56

Pheasants — A57

Perf. 15, 11x13
1959, Dec. 21   Photo.
182 A56 5m shown   .25   .25
183 A57 10m shown   .25   .25
184 A56 15m Muskrat   .25   .25
185 A57 20m Otter   .55   .25
186 A56 30m Argali   .55   .25
187 A57 50m Saigas   1.00   .35
188 A57 1t Musk deer   2.00   .75
     Nos. 182-188 (7)   4.85 2.35

Lunik 3 — A58

50m, Lunik 3 with path around moon, horiz.

1959, Dec. 30   Photo.   Perf. 12
189 A58 30m violet & yel grn   .80   .80
190 A58 50m red, dk bl & grn 1.25 1.25

Lunik 3 Russian moon mission, Oct. 7, 1959.

Motherhood Badge — A59

Flower Emblem — A60

1960, Mar. 8   Perf. 11, 12½x11½
191 A59 40m blue & bister .75 .25
192 A60 50m blue, grn & yel 1.10 .40

International Women's Day.

Lenin — A61

1960, Apr. 22   Photo.   Perf. 11½x12
193 A61 40m dk rose car .60 .25
194 A61 50m rose violet .80 .35

90th anniversary, birth of Lenin.

Jacob's-ladder — A62

1960, May 31   Perf. 11½x12
195 A62 5m Larkspur .25 .25
196 A62 10m Tulips .25 .25
197 A62 15m shown .25 .25
198 A62 20m Globeflowers .25 .25
199 A62 30m Bellflowers .35 .25
200 A62 40m Parnassia .65 .25
201 A62 50m Geranium .90 .35
202 A62 1t Begonia 1.25 .80
    Nos. 195-202 (8) 4.15 2.65

For overprints see Nos. 296-303.

Equestrian — A63

Running — A64

1960, Aug. 1   Perf. 15, 11
203 A63 5m shown .25 .25
204 A64 10m shown .25 .25
205 A63 15m Diving .25 .25
206 A64 20m Wrestling .30 .25
207 A63 30m Hurdling .50 .25
208 A64 50m Gymnastics, women's .65 .30

209 A63 70m High jump .80 .35
210 A64 1t Discus, women's 1.25 .40
    Nos. 203-210 (8) 4.25 2.30

17th Olympic Games, Rome, 8/25-9/11.

Red Cross A65

1960, Aug. 29   Perf. 11
211 A65 20m blue, red & yel .80 .40

Newspaper "Unen" (Truth) — A66

1960, Dec. 19   Perf. 12x11½
212 A66 20m red, yel & sl grn .35 .25
213 A66 30m grn, yel & red .45 .25

40th anniversary of Mongolian press.

Golden Orioles — A67

Songbirds: 5m, Rose-colored starling. 10m, Hoopoe. 20m, Black-billed capercaillie. 50m, Oriental broad-billed roller. 70m, Tibetan sandgrouse. 1t, Mandarin duck.
Triangle points down on 5m, 50m, 70m, 1t.

1961, Jan. 3   Perf. 11
214 A67 5m multi .60 .25
215 A67 10m multi .70 .25
216 A67 15m multi .85 .25
217 A67 20m multi 1.00 .25
218 A67 50m multi 1.50 .50
219 A67 70m multi 2.00 .70
220 A67 1t multi 2.10 .85
    Nos. 214-220 (7) 8.75 3.05

Federation Emblem — A68

Design: 30m, Worker and emblem, vert.

Perf. 11½x12, 12x11½
1961, Jan. 29   Photo.
221 A68 30m dk gray & rose .35 .25
222 A68 50m ultra & red .45 .25

World Federation of Trade Unions, 15th anniv.

Patrice Lumumba (1925-1961), Premier of Congo — A69

Bridge A70

Designs: 10m, Shoemaker. 15m, Department Store, Ulan Bator. 20m, Government building. 30m, State Theater, Ulan Bator. 50m, Machinist. 1t, Modern and old buildings.

1961, Apr. 8   Perf. 11½x12
223 A69 30m brown 2.25 1.25
224 A69 50m violet gray 2.75 1.75

1961, Apr. 30   Perf. 11½x12, 15
Sizes: 31½x21mm, 59x20mm (20m)
225 A70 5m emerald .25 .25
226 A70 10m blue .25 .25
227 A70 15m rose red .25 .25
228 A70 20m brown .25 .25
229 A70 30m blue .25 .25
230 A70 50m olive green .35 .25
231 A70 1t violet .60 .35
    Nos. 225-231 (7) 2.20 1.85

40th anniversary of independence; modernization of Mongolia.

Yuri Gagarin and Globe — A71

Designs: 20m, Gagarin with rocket, vert. 50m, Gagarin making parachute descent, vert. 1t, Gagarin wearing helmet, globe.

1961, May 31   Perf. 15
232 A71 20m multi .50 .25
233 A71 30m multi .80 .40
234 A71 50m multi 1.00 .60
235 A71 1t multi 1.50 .65
    Nos. 232-235 (4) 3.80 1.90

Yuri A. Gagarin, 1st man in space, 4/12/61.

Postman on Reindeer A72

15m, #241a, Postman on camel. 10m, 20m, Postman with yaks. 25m, #241c, Postman with ship. 30m, 50m, Diesel train.

1961, June 5   Perf. 15
236 A72 5m multi .25 .25
237 A72 15m multi .25 .25
238 A72 20m multi .25 .25
239 A72 25m multi .25 .25
240 A72 30m multi 4.00 2.00
    Nos. 236-240,C1-C3 (8) 7.00 3.90

Souvenir Sheet
Perf. 11
241   Sheet of 4 6.00 6.00
 a. A72 5m light blue & brown 1.50 1.00
 b. A72 10m green, brown & blue 1.50 1.00
 c. A72 15m green, violet & brown 1.50 1.00
 d. A72 50m violet, green & black 1.50 1.00

40th anniv. of independence; postal modernization. See No. C4b for 25m, perf. 11.

Souvenir Sheet

Ornamental Column — A73

1961, June 20   Perf. 12
242 A73 Sheet of 2 + label 6.00 6.00
 a. 2t blue, red & gold 2.75 2.00

40th anniversary of the Mongolian People's Revolution. No. 242 contains two No. 242a and label, imperf. between.

Herdsman and Oxen — A74

Designs: Herdsmen and domestic animals (except 1t and No. 252a).

1961, July 10   Perf. 13
243 A74 5m Rams .25 .25
244 A74 10m shown .25 .25
245 A74 15m Camels .25 .25
246 A74 20m Pigs and geese .30 .25
247 A74 25m Angora goats .30 .25
248 A74 30m Horses .30 .25
249 A74 40m Sheep .50 .25
250 A74 50m Cows .75 .30
251 A74 1t Combine harvester 1.10 .75
    Nos. 243-251 (9) 4.00 2.80

Souvenir Sheets
Perf. 12
252   Sheet of 3 2.50 2.50
 a. A74 5m Combine harvester .75 .50
 b. A74 15m Angora goats .75 .50
 c. A74 40m Oxen .75 .50
253   Sheet of 3 2.50 2.50
 a. A74 10m Pigs and geese .75 .50
 b. A74 20m Horses .75 .50
 c. A74 30m Cows .75 .50
254   Sheet of 3 3.00 3.00
 a. A74 25m Camels .90 .75
 b. A74 50m Rams .90 .75
 c. A74 1t Sheep .90 .75

40th anniversary of independence. Nos. 252-254 each contain 3 stamps imperf. between.

Horseback Riders — A75

5m, Young wrestlers & instructor. 15m, Camel & pony riders. 20m, Falconers. 30m, Skier. 50m, Archers. 1t, Male dancers.

1961, Aug. 10   Perf. 11
255 A75 5m multi .25 .25
256 A75 10m multi .25 .25
257 A75 15m multi .25 .25
258 A75 20m multi .80 .25
259 A75 30m multi .35 .35
260 A75 50m multi .45 .35
261 A75 1t multi .75 .50
    Nos. 255-261 (7) 3.10 2.20

Independence, 40th anniv.; Mongolian youth sports.

Statue of Sukhe Bator — A76

Designs: 5m, Mongol youth. 10m, Mongol chieftain. 20m, Singer. 30m, Dancer. 50m, Dombra player. 70m, Musicians. 1t, Gymnast. 5m, 10m, 70m, 1t, horiz.

Perf. 12x11½, 11½x12

1961, Sept. 16
262	A76	5m brt grn & red lil	.25	.25
263	A76	10m red & dk brn	.25	.25
264	A76	15m bl & lt brn	.25	.25
265	A76	20m pur & brt grn	.25	.25
266	A76	30m vio bl & car	.30	.25
267	A76	50m ol & vio	.55	.25
268	A76	70m brt lil rose & ol	.65	.35
269	A76	1t dk bl & ver	1.25	.75
		Nos. 262-269 (8)	3.75	2.60

40th anniv. of independence; Mongolian culture.

Arms of Mongolia — A77

1961, Nov. 17   Perf. 11½x12
270	A77	5m multi	.25	.25
271	A77	10m multi	.25	.25
272	A77	15m multi	.25	.25
273	A77	20m multi	.25	.25
274	A77	30m multi	.25	.25
275	A77	50m multi	.35	.25
276	A77	70m multi	.45	.35
277	A77	1t multi	.50	.45
		Nos. 270-277 (8)	2.55	2.30

For surcharges see Nos. 2144A, 2302D.

Congress Emblem A78

1961, Dec. 4   Litho.   Perf. 11½
278	A78	30m vio bl, yel & red	.30	.25
279	A78	50m brn, yel & red	.40	.25

5th World Congress of Trade Unions, Moscow, Dec. 4-16.

UN Emblem and Arms of Mongolia — A79

10m, Globe, map of Mongolia, dove. 50m, Flags of UN & Mongolia. 60m, UN Headquarters, New York. Parliament, Ulan Bator. 70m, UN assembly, UN & Mongolian flags.

1962, Mar. 15   Photo.   Perf. 11
280	A79	10m gold & multi	.25	.25
281	A79	30m gold & multi	.30	.25
282	A79	50m gold & multi	.55	.35
283	A79	60m gold & multi	.65	.35
284	A79	70m gold & multi	.75	.50
		Nos. 280-284 (5)	2.50	1.70

Mongolia's admission to UN.

Soccer — A80

Designs: 10m, Soccer ball, globe and flags. 30m, Soccer players, globe and ball. 60m, Goalkeeper. 70m, Stadium.

1962, May 15   Litho.   Perf. 10½
285	A80	10m multi	.25	.25
286	A80	30m multi	.30	.25
287	A80	50m multi	.45	.30
288	A80	60m multi	.55	.35
289	A80	70m multi	.75	.35
		Nos. 285-289 (5)	2.30	1.50

World Soccer Championship, Chile, 5/30-6/17.

D. Natsagdorji A81   Solidarity Emblem A82

1962, May 15   Photo.   Perf. 15x14½
290	A81	30m brown	.30	.25
291	A81	50m bluish grn	.40	.25

Mongolian writers' congress. For overprints see Nos. 430-431.

1962, May 22   Litho.   Perf. 11½x10½
292	A82	20m yel grn & multi	.30	.25
293	A82	30m bl & multi	.40	.25

Afro-Asian Peoples' solidarity.

Flags of USSR and Mongolia — A83

Perf. 11½x10½

1962, June 25   Litho.
294	A83	30m brn & multi	.30	.25
295	A83	50m vio bl & multi	.40	.25

Mongol-Soviet friendship.

Nos. 195-202 Overprinted

1962, July 20   Photo.   Perf. 11½x12
296	A62	5m multi	.60	.30
297	A62	10m multi	.65	.35
298	A62	15m multi	.75	.35
299	A62	20m multi	.75	.35
300	A62	30m multi	.80	.50
301	A62	40m multi	.90	.50

302	A62	50m multi	1.10	.50
303	A62	1t multi	1.75	.90
		Nos. 296-303 (8)	7.30	3.75

WHO drive to eradicate malaria.

Military Field Emblem — A84

Designs: 30m, Tablets with inscriptions. 50m, Stone column. 60m, Genghis Khan.

1962, July 20   Perf. 11½x12
304	A84	20m blue & multi	1.50	1.50
305	A84	30m red & multi	1.50	1.50
306	A84	50m pink, brn & blk	3.50	3.50
307	A84	60m blue & multi	3.50	3.50
		Nos. 304-307 (4)	10.00	10.00

Genghis Khan (1162-1227), Mongol conqueror.
For overprints see Nos. 1846-1849. For surcharge, see No. 2378A.

River Perch — A85

1962, Dec. 28   Perf. 11
308	A85	5m shown	.25	.25
309	A85	10m Burbot	.25	.25
310	A85	15m Arctic grayling	.25	.25
311	A85	20m Shorthorn sculpin	.25	.25
312	A85	30m Marine zander	.30	.25
313	A85	50m Siberian sturgeon	.30	.30
314	A85	70m Waleck's chub minnow	.40	.35
315	A85	1.50t Cottocomephorid	.65	.35
		Nos. 308-315 (8)	2.65	2.25

Sukhe Bator (1893-1923), National Hero — A86

1963, Feb. 2   Photo.   Perf. 11½x12
316	A86	30m blue	.25	.25
317	A86	60m rose car	.40	.25

Laika and Rocket — A87

Designs: 15m, Rocket launching, vert. 25m, Lunik 2, vert. 70m, Andrian G. Nikolayev and Pavel R. Popovich. 1t, Mars rocket.

1963, Apr. 1   Litho.   Perf. 12½x12

Size: 46x32mm
318	A87	5m multicolored	.25	.25

Size: 20x68mm
319	A87	10m multicolored	.25	.25
320	A87	25m multicolored	.40	.25

Size: 46x32mm
321	A87	70m multicolored	.75	.30
322	A87	1t multicolored	1.00	.60
		Nos. 318-322 (5)	2.65	1.65

Soviet space explorations.

Blood Transfusion — A88

1963, Aug. 15   Perf. 10½
323	A88	20m Packing Red Cross parcels	.25	.25
324	A88	30m shown	.25	.25
325	A88	50m Vaccination	.50	.30
326	A88	60m Ambulance service	.60	.40
327	A88	1.30t Centenary emblem	.90	.50
		Nos. 323-327 (5)	2.50	1.70

Red Cross centenary.

Karl Marx — A89

1963, Sept. 16   Photo.   Perf. 11½x12
328	A89	30m blue	.30	.25
329	A89	60m dk car rose	.40	.30

145th anniversary of birth of Karl Marx.

Mongolian Woman — A90

1963, Sept. 26
330	A90	30m blue & multi	.50	.25

5th Intl. Women's Cong., Moscow, 6/24-29.

Inachis A91

Designs: Mongolian butterflies.

1963, Nov. 7   Litho.   Perf. 11½
331	A91	5m shown	.45	.25
332	A91	10m Gonepteryxrhamni	.50	.25
333	A91	15m Aglais urticae	.70	.25
334	A91	20m Parnassius apollo	.75	.25
335	A91	30m Papilio machaon	1.20	.25
336	A91	60m Agrodiaetus damon	1.75	.50
337	A91	1t Limenitis populi	2.25	.75
		Nos. 331-337 (7)	7.60	2.50

UNESCO Emblem, Globe and
Scales — A92

1963, Dec. 10   Photo.   Perf. 12
338 A92 30m multicolored   .40 .25
339 A92 60m multicolored   .60 .40
Universal Declaration of Human Rights,
15th anniversary.

Coprinus Comatus — A93

Designs: Mushrooms.

1964, Jan. 1   Litho.   Perf. 10½
340 A93 5m shown   .50 .25
341 A93 10m Lactarius tormi-
          nosus   .75 .40
342 A93 15m Psalliota campes-
          tris   .95 .50
343 A93 20m Russula delica   1.10 .55
344 A93 30m Ixocomus granu-
          latus   1.25 .60
345 A93 50m Lactarius
          scrobiculatus   1.50 .75
346 A93 70m Lactarius delici-
          osus   1.75 .90
347 A93 1t Ixocomus varie-
          gatus   2.25 2.10
    Nos. 340-347 (8)   10.05 6.05

Souvenir Sheet

Skier — A94

1964, Feb. 12   Photo.   Perf. 12x11½
348 A94 4t gray   4.50 4.50
9th Winter Olympic Games, Innsbruck, Jan.
29-Feb. 9.

Lenin — A95

1964   Photo.   Perf. 11½x12
349 A95 30m salmon & multi   .60 .25
350 A95 50m blue & multi   .80 .40
60th anniversary of Communist Party. Nos.
349-350 printed with alternating label showing
Lenin quotation.

Javelin — A96

1964, Apr. 30   Litho.   Perf. 10½
351 A96 5m Gymnastics, wo-
          men's   .25 .25
352 A96 10m shown   .25 .25
353 A96 15m Wrestling   .25 .25
354 A96 20m Running, women's   .25 .25
355 A96 30m Equestrian   .40 .25
356 A96 50m Diving, women's   .60 .25
357 A96 60m Bicycling   .80 .30
358 A96 1t Olympic Games
          emblem   1.00 .60
    Nos. 351-358 (8)   3.80 2.40

Souvenir Sheet
Perf. 12x11½
359 A96 4t Wrestling   3.50 3.50
18th Olympic Games, Toyko, Oct. 10-25.
No. 359 contains one horizontal stamp,
37x27½mm. Issued Sept. 1.

Congress Emblem — A97

1964, Sept. 30   Photo.   Perf. 11
360 A97 30m multicolored   .40 .30
4th Mongolian Women's Congress.

Lunik 1 — A98

Space Research: 10m, Vostok 1 and 2.
15m, Tiros weather satellite, vert. 20m, Cosmos circling earth, vert. 30m, Mars probe,
vert. 60m, Luna 4, vert. 80m, Echo 2. 1t,
Radar and rockets.

1964, Oct. 30
361 A98 5m multicolored   .25 .25
362 A98 10m multicolored   .25 .25
363 A98 15m multicolored   .25 .25
364 A98 20m multicolored   .35 .25
365 A98 30m multicolored   .50 .35
366 A98 60m multicolored   .65 .40
367 A98 80m multicolored   .95 .45
368 A98 1t multicolored   1.25 .55
    Nos. 361-368 (8)   4.45 2.75

Rider Carrying
Flag — A99

1964, Nov. 26   Photo.   Perf. 11½x12
369 A99 25m multicolored   .40 .25
370 A99 50m multicolored   .50 .40
40th anniversary of Mongolian constitution.

Weather
Balloon
A100

Designs: 5m, Oceanographic exploration.
60m, Northern lights and polar bears. 80m,
Geomagnetism. 1t, I.Q.S.Y. emblem and Mercator map.

1965, May 15   Photo.   Perf. 13½
371 A100 5m gray & multi   .25 .25
372 A100 10m grn & multi   .25 .30
373 A100 60m blue, blk & pink   .70 .25
374 A100 80m citron & multi   .85 .35
375 A100 1t brt green & multi   1.25 .60
    Nos. 371-375,C6-C8 (8)   7.20 2.85

International Quiet Sun Year.

Horses — A101

Designs: Mares and Foals.

1965, Aug. 25   Perf. 11
376 A101 5m shown   .25 .25
377 A101 10m Falconers   .25 .25
378 A101 15m Taming wild horse   .25 .25
379 A101 20m Horse race   .35 .25
380 A101 30m Hurdles   .50 .35
381 A101 60m Wolf hunt   .65 .40
382 A101 80m Milking a mare   .95 .45
383 A101 1t Mare and foal   1.25 .55
    Nos. 376-383 (8)   4.45 2.75

Girl Holding Lambs — A102

1965, Oct. 10   Photo.   Perf. 11
384 A102 5m shown   .25 .25
385 A102 10m Boy and girl
          drummers   .25 .25
386 A102 20m Camp fire   .30 .25
387 A102 30m Wrestlers   .40 .30
388 A102 50m Emblem   .70 .50
    Nos. 384-388 (5)   1.90 1.55
40th anniv. of Mongolian Youth Org.

Chinese Perch — A103

1965, Nov. 25
389 A103 5m shown   .25 .25
390 A103 10m Lenok trout   .25 .25
391 A103 15m Siberian sturgeon   .25 .25
392 A103 20m Amur salmon   .40 .25
393 A103 30m Bagrid catfish   .60 .25
394 A103 60m Siluri catfish   .95 .25

395 A103 80m Northern pike   1.10 .45
396 A103 1t River perch   1.50 .65
    Nos. 389-396 (8)   5.30 2.60

Marx and
Lenin — A104

1965, Dec. 15   Perf. 11½x12
397 A104 10m red & blk   .35 .25
6th Conference of Postal Ministers of Communist Countries, Peking, June 21-July 15.

Sable — A105

1966, Feb. 15   Photo.   Perf. 12½
398 A105 5m shown   .25 .25
399 A105 10m Fox   .25 .25
400 A105 15m Otter, vert.   .30 .25
401 A105 20m Cheetah, vert.   .30 .25
402 A105 30m Pallas's cat   .40 .25
403 A105 60m Stone marten   .60 .30
404 A105 80m Ermine, vert.   .80 .40
405 A105 1t Woman in mink
          coat, vert.   1.25 .75
    Nos. 398-405 (8)   4.15 2.70

Opening of WHO Headquarters,
Geneva — A106

1966, May 3   Photo.   Perf. 12x11½
406 A106 30m bl grn, bl & gold   .30 .25
407 A106 50m red, bl & gold   .50 .30

For overprints see Nos. 483-484.

Soccer — A107

Designs: 30m, 60m, 80m, Various soccer
plays. 1t, British flag and World Soccer Cup
emblem. 4t, Wembley Stadium, horiz.

1966, May 31   Photo.   Perf. 11
408 A107 10m multicolored   .25 .25
409 A107 30m multicolored   .25 .25
410 A107 60m multicolored   .35 .30
411 A107 80m multicolored   .55 .40
412 A107 1t multicolored   .75 .50
    Nos. 408-412 (5)   2.15 1.70

Souvenir Sheet
Perf. 12½, Imperf.

413 A107   4t gray & brown   2.75 2.00

World Soccer Championship for Jules Rimet
Cup, Wembley, England, July 11-30. No. 413
contains one stamp 61x83mm.

Sukhe Bator, Parliament Building, Ulan
Bator — A108

1966, June 7   Litho.   Perf. 12x12½
414 A108 30m red, bl & brn   .40 .25

15th Congress of Mongolian Communist
Party.

Wrestling
A109

Designs: Various wrestling holds.

1966, June 15   Photo.   Perf. 11½x12
415 A109 10m multicolored   .25 .25
416 A109 30m multicolored   .25 .25
417 A109 60m multicolored   .40 .25
418 A109 80m multicolored   .45 .25
419 A109   1t multicolored   .60 .25
    Nos. 415-419 (5)   1.95 1.25

World Wrestling Championship, Toledo,
Spain.

Emblem and
Map of
Mongolia
A110

Sukhe
Bator,
Grain
and
Factories
A111

Perf. 11½x12, 12x11½
1966, July 11   Litho.
420 A110 30m red & multi   1.10 .80
421 A111 50m red & multi   2.75 1.00

45th anniversary of independence.
For overprints see Nos. 552-553.

Lilium Tenuifolium — A112

1966, Oct. 15 Photo.   Perf. 12x11½
422 A112 5m Physochlaena
             physaloides   .25 .25
423 A112 10m Allium
             polyrrchizum   .30 .25
424 A112 15m shown   .40 .25
425 A112 20m Thermopsis lance-
             olata   .50 .25
426 A112 30m Amygdalus
             mongolica   .60 .30
427 A112 60m Caryopteris
             mongolica   .85 .40
428 A112 80m Piptanthus
             mongolicus   1.00 .55
429 A112   1t Iris bungei   1.25 .75
    Nos. 422-429 (8)   5.15 3.00

Nos. 290-291 Overprinted:
"1906/1966"

1966, Oct. 26 Photo. Perf. 15x14½
430 A81 30m brown   8.00 8.00
431 A81 50m bluish grn   10.00 10.00

60th anniv. of birth of D. Natsagdorji, writer.
50m exists double, one inverted.

Child with
Dove — A113

1966, Dec. 2   Perf. 11½x12, 12x11½
432 A113 10m shown   .25 .25
433 A113 15m Children with rein-
             deer   .35 .25
434 A113 20m Boys wrestling,
             vert.   .40 .25
435 A113 30m Horseback riding   .45 .25
436 A113 60m Children riding
             camel, vert.   .70 .40
437 A113 80m Child with sheep   .95 .50
438 A113   1t Boy archer, vert. 1.25 .75
    Nos. 432-438 (7)   4.35 2.65

Children's Day.

Proton 1 — A114

Perf. 11½x12½, 12½x11½
1966, Dec. 28   Photo.
439 A114 5m Vostok 2, vert.   .25 .25
440 A114 10m shown   .25 .25
441 A114 15m Telstar 1, vert.   .25 .25
442 A114 20m Molniya 1, vert.   .30 .25
443 A114 30m Syncom 3, vert.   .40 .30
444 A114 60m Luna 9   .50 .30
445 A114 80m Luna 12, vert.   .60 .40
446 A114   1t Mariner 4   .80 .50
    Nos. 439-446 (8)   3.35 2.50

Space exploration.

Tarbosaurus — A115

1967, Mar. 31   Perf. 12x11½
447 A115 5m shown   .35 .25
448 A115 10m Talarurus   .40 .25
449 A115 15m Proceratops   .45 .25
450 A115 20m Indricotherium   .45 .25
451 A115 30m Saurolophus   .70 .30
452 A115 60m Mastodon   1.60 .40
453 A115 80m Mongolotherium   1.75 .60
454 A115   1t Mammoth   2.00 .90
    Nos. 447-454 (8)   7.70 3.20

Prehistoric animals.

A116

Congress emblem.

1967, June 9   Litho.   Perf. 12
455 A116 30m lt blue & multi   .40 .25
456 A116 50m pink & multi   .60 .40

9th Youth Festival for Peace and Friendship,
Sofia.

A117

Design: 40m, Sukhe Bator and soldiers.
60m, Lenin and soldiers.

1967, Oct. 25   Litho.   Perf. 11½x12
457 A117 40m red & multi   .45 .25
458 A117 60m red & multi   .75 .35

Russian October Revolution, 50th anniv.

Ice
Hockey
and
Olympic
Rings
A118

1967, Dec. 29   Perf. 12x12½
459 A118 5m Figure skating   .25 .25
460 A118 10m Speed skating   .25 .25
461 A118 15m shown   .35 .25
462 A118 20m Ski jump   .45 .25
463 A118 30m Bobsledding   .75 .35
464 A118 60m Figure skating,
             pair   .90 .40
465 A118 80m Slalom   1.10 .50
    Nos. 459-465 (7)   4.05 2.25

Souvenir Sheet
Perf. 12
466 A118   4t Women's figure
             skating   3.50 3.50

10th Winter Olympic Games, Grenoble,
France, Feb. 6-18.

Bactrian
Camels
A119

1968, Jan. 15   Photo.   Perf. 12
467 A119 5m shown   .25 .25
468 A119 10m Yak   .25 .25
469 A119 15m Lamb   .25 .25
470 A119 20m Foal   .35 .25
471 A119 30m Calf   .40 .25
472 A119 60m Bison   .55 .25
473 A119 80m Roe deer   .80 .35
474 A119   1t Reindeer   1.40 .45
    Nos. 467-474 (8)   4.25 2.30

Young animals.

Black Currants — A120

Berries: 5m, Rosa acicularis. 15m, Goose-
berries. 20m, Malus. 30m, Strawberries. 60m,
Ribes altissimum. 80m, Blueberries. 1t, Hippophae rhamnoides.

Lithographed & Engraved
1968, Feb. 15
475 A120 5m blue & ultra   .25 .25
476 A120 10m buff & brn   .25 .25
477 A120 15m lt grn & grn   .25 .25
478 A120 20m yel & red   .25 .25
479 A120 30m pink & car   .40 .25
480 A120 60m sal & org brn   .45 .25
481 A120 80m pale & dl bl   .80 .30
482 A120   1t lt yel & red   .95 .45
    Nos. 475-482 (8)   3.60 2.25

Nos. 406-407 Overprinted

1968, Apr. 16   Photo.   Perf. 12x11½
483 A106 30m bl grn, bl & gold 6.00 4.00
484 A106 50m red, blue & gold   6.00 4.00

WHO, 20th anniversary.

Human Rights
Flame — A121

1968, June 20   Litho.   Perf. 12
485 A121 30m turq & vio bl   .50 .25

International Human Rights Year.

"Das
Kapital,"
by Karl
Marx
A122

Design: 50m, Karl Marx.

1968, July 1   Litho.   Perf. 12
486 A122 30m blue & multi   .30 .25
487 A122 50m red & multi   .50 .25

Karl Marx (1818-1883).

Artist, by A. Sangatzohyo — A123

Paintings: 10m, On Remote Roads, by Sangatzohyo. 15m, Camel calf, by B. Avarzad. 20m, Milk, by Avarzad. 30m, The Bowman, by B. Gombosuren. 80m, Girl Sitting on Yak, by Sangatzohyo. 1.40t, Cagan Dara Eke, by Janaivajara. 4t, Meeting, by Sangatzohyo, horiz.

1968, July 11   Litho.   Perf. 12
488	A123	5m brown & multi	.25	.25
489	A123	10m brown & multi	.25	.25
490	A123	15m brown & multi	.25	.25
491	A123	20m brown & multi	.40	.25
492	A123	30m brown & multi	.55	.35
493	A123	80m brown & multi	1.10	.55
494	A123	1.40t brown & multi	2.10	1.00

Nos. 488-494 (7)   4.90 2.90

Miniature Sheets
Perf. 11½, Imperf.

495	A123	4t brown & multi	5.00	5.00

Paintings from national museum, Ulan Bator. #495 contains one 54x84mm stamp.

Volleyball — A124

Olympic Rings and: 10m, Wrestling. 15m, Bicycling. 20m, Javelin, women's. 30m, Soccer. 60m, Running. 80m, Gymnastics, women's. 1t, Weight lifting. 4t, Equestrian.

1968, Sept. 1   Litho.   Perf. 12
496	A124	5m multicolored	.25	.25
497	A124	10m multicolored	.25	.25
498	A124	15m multicolored	.25	.25
499	A124	20m multicolored	.25	.25
500	A124	30m multicolored	.35	.25
501	A124	60m multicolored	.50	.30
502	A124	80m multicolored	.70	.35
503	A124	1t multicolored	1.00	.40

Nos. 496-503 (8)   3.55 2.30

Souvenir Sheets
Perf. 11½, Imperf.

504	A124	4t orange & multi	3.50	3.50

19th Olympic Games, Mexico City, Oct. 12-27. #504 contains one 52x44mm stamp.

A125

Hammer, spade & cogwheel.

1968, Sept. 17   Litho.   Perf. 11½
505	A125	50m blue & vermilion	.40	.25

Industrial development in town of Darhan.

A126

1968, Nov. 6   Litho.   Perf. 12
506	A126	60m turquoise & sepia	.40	.25

Maxim Gorki (1868-1936), Russian writer.

Madonna and Child, by Boltraffio A127

Paintings: 10m, St. Roch Healed by an Angel, by Brescia. 15m, Madonna and Child with St. Anne, by Macchietti. 20m, St. John on Patmos, by Cano. 30m, Lady with Viola da Gamba, by Kupetzky. 80m, Boy, by Amerling. 1.40t, Death of Adonis, by Furini. 4t, Portrait of a Lady, by Renoir.

1968, Nov. 20   Litho.   Perf. 12
507	A127	5m gray & multi	.25	.25
508	A127	10m gray & multi	.25	.25
509	A127	15m gray & multi	.30	.25
510	A127	20m gray & multi	.35	.25
511	A127	30m gray & multi	.45	.30
512	A127	80m gray & multi	.85	.40
513	A127	1.40t gray & multi	1.25	.75

Nos. 507-513 (7)   3.70 2.45

Miniature Sheet

514	A127	4t gray & multi	4.00	4.00

UNESCO, 22nd anniv.

Jesse Owens, US — A128

Olympic Gold Medal Winners: 5m, Paavo Nurmi, Finland. 15m, Fanny Blankers-Koen, Netherlands. 20m, Laszlo Papp, Hungary. 30m, Wilma Rudolph, US. 60m, Boris Shakhlin, USSR. 80m, Donald Schollander, US. 1t Akinori Nakayama, Japan. 4t, Jigjidin Munkhbat, Mongolia.

1969, Mar. 25   Litho.   Perf. 12
515	A128	5m multicolored	.25	.25
516	A128	10m multicolored	.25	.25
517	A128	15m multicolored	.25	.25
518	A128	20m multicolored	.25	.25
519	A128	30m multicolored	.30	.25
520	A128	60m multicolored	.50	.30
521	A128	80m multicolored	.75	.50
522	A128	1t multicolored	1.00	.50

Nos. 515-522 (8)   3.55 2.55

Souvenir Sheet

523	A128	4t green & multi	4.00	4.00

Bayit Woman A129

Regional Costumes: 10m, Torgut man. 15m, Dzakhachin woman. 20m, Khalkha woman. 30m, Dariganga woman. 60m, Mingat woman. 80m, Khalkha man. 1t, Bargut woman.

1969, Apr. 20   Litho.   Perf. 12
524	A129	5m multicolored	.25	.25
525	A129	10m multicolored	.25	.25
526	A129	15m multicolored	.30	.25
527	A129	20m multicolored	.50	.25
528	A129	30m multicolored	.60	.25
529	A129	60m multicolored	.70	.25
530	A129	80m multicolored	.90	.40
531	A129	1t multicolored	1.25	.75

Nos. 524-531 (8)   4.75 2.65

Red Cross Emblem and Helicopter — A130

50m, Emblem, Red Cross car, shepherd.

1969, May 15   Litho.   Perf. 12
532	A130	30m multicolored	1.25	.30
533	A130	50m multicolored	1.25	.40

30th anniversary of Mongolian Red Cross.

Landscape and Edelweiss — A131

Mongolian landscapes and flowers.

1969, May 20
534	A131	5m shown	.25	.25
535	A131	10m Pinks	.25	.25
536	A131	15m Dianthus superbus	.30	.25
537	A131	20m Geranium	.30	.25
538	A131	30m Dianthus ramosissimus	.45	.25
539	A131	60m Globeflowers	.55	.25
540	A131	80m Delphinium	.70	.40
541	A131	1t Haloxylon	.90	.45

Nos. 534-541 (8)   3.70 2.35

See No. 1105.

Bull Fight, by Tsewegdjaw — A132

Paintings from National Museum: 10m, Fighting Colts, by O. Tsewegdjaw. 15m, Horseman and Herd, by A. Sangatzohyo. 20m, Camel Caravan, by D. Damdinsuren. 30m, On the Steppe, by N. Tsultem. 60m, Milking

Mares, by Tsewegdjaw. 80m, Going to School, by B. Avarzad. 1t, After Work, by G. Odon. 4t, Horses, by Damdinsuren.

1969, July 11   Perf. 12
542	A132	5m multicolored	.25	.25
543	A132	10m multicolored	.25	.25
544	A132	15m multicolored	.25	.25
545	A132	20m multicolored	.25	.25
546	A132	30m multicolored	.30	.25
547	A132	60m multicolored	.60	.25
548	A132	80m multicolored	.80	.40
549	A132	1t multicolored	1.25	.60

Nos. 542-549 (8)   3.95 2.50

Souvenir Sheet

550	A132	4t multicolored	4.00	4.00

10th anniversary of cooperative movement. No. 550 contains one stamp 65x42mm.

Mongolian Flag and Emblem A133

1969, Sept. 20   Litho.   Perf. 11½
551	A133	50m multicolored	.50	.30

Battle of Ha-lo-hsin (Khalka) River, 30th anniversary.
For surcharge, see No. 2384A.

Nos. 420-421 Overprinted

Perf. 11½x12, 12x11½
1969, Nov. 26   Photo.
552	A110	30m red & multi	8.00	8.00
553	A111	50m red & multi	10.00	10.00

45th anniv. of Mongolian People's Republic.

Mercury 7 — A134

Designs: 5m, Sputnik 3. 10m, Vostok 1. 20m, Voskhod 2. 30m, Apollo 8. 60m, Soyuz 5. 80m, Apollo 12.

1969, Dec. 6   Photo.   Perf. 12x11½
554	A134	5m multicolored	.25	.25
555	A134	10m multicolored	.25	.25
556	A134	15m multicolored	.25	.25
557	A134	20m multicolored	.25	.25
558	A134	30m multicolored	.25	.25
559	A134	60m multicolored	.45	.25
560	A134	80m multicolored	.60	.25

Nos. 554-560 (7)   2.30 1.75

Souvenir Sheet

561	A134	4t multicolored	3.50	2.50

Space achievements of US and USSR.

Wolf — A135

Designs: 10m, Brown bear. 15m, Lynx. 20m, Wild boar. 30m, Moose. 60m, Bobac marmot. 80m, Argali. 1t, Old wall carpet showing hunter and dog.

		1970, Mar. 25	Photo.	Perf. 12	
562	A135	5m multicolored		.25	.25
563	A135	10m multicolored		.25	.25
564	A135	15m multicolored		.35	.25
565	A135	20m multicolored		.40	.25
566	A135	30m multicolored		.45	.25
567	A135	60m multicolored		.75	.40
568	A135	80m multicolored		1.00	.60
569	A135	1t multicolored		1.25	.80
		Nos. 562-569 (8)		4.70	3.05

Lenin and Mongolian Delegation, by Sangatzohyo — A136

Designs: 20m, Lenin, embroidered panel, by Cerenhuu, vert. 1t, Lenin, by Mazhig, vert.

		1970, Apr. 22	Photo. & Litho.		
570	A136	20m multicolored		.30	.25
571	A136	50m multicolored		.50	.25
572	A136	1t lt bl, blk & red		1.25	.90
		Nos. 570-572 (3)		2.05	1.00

Centenary of the birth of Lenin.

Souvenir Sheet

EXPO '70 Pavilion of Matsushita Electric Co. and Time Capsule — A137

		1970, May 26	Photo.	Perf. 12½	
573	A137	4t gold & multi		4.50	4.50

EXPO '70 International Exposition, Osaka, Japan, Mar. 15-Sept. 13.

Sumitomo Fairy Tale Pavilion — A138

		1970, June 5	Photo.	Perf. 12x11½	
574	A138	1.50t multi + label		1.00	1.00

EXPO '70 International Exposition, Osaka. No. 574 printed in sheets of 20 (5x4) with alternating horizontal rows of tabs showing various fairy tales and EXPO '70 emblem.

Soccer, Rimet Cup — A139

		1970, June 20		Perf. 12½x11½	
575	A139	10m multi		.25	.25
576	A139	20m multi		.25	.25
577	A139	30m multi		.25	.25
578	A139	50m multi		.40	.25
579	A139	60m multi		.50	.25
580	A139	1t multi		.90	.25
581	A139	1.30t multi		1.00	.45
		Nos. 575-581 (7)		3.55	1.95

Souvenir Sheet
Perf. 12½

582	A139	4t multi		3.50	3.50

World Soccer Championship for Jules Rimet Cup, Mexico City, May 30-June 21. No. 582 contains one stamp 51x37mm.

Old World Buzzard A140

Birds of Prey: 20m, Tawny owls. 30m, Northern goshawk. 50m, White-tailed sea eagle. 60m, Peregrine falcon. 1t, Old world kestrel. 1.30t, Black kite.

		1970, June 30	Litho.	Perf. 12	
583	A140	10m bl & multi		.75	.25
584	A140	20m pink & multi		1.00	.25
585	A140	30m yel grn & multi		1.10	.25
586	A140	50m bl & multi		1.20	.25
587	A140	60m yel & multi		1.60	.50
588	A140	1t grn & multi		2.00	.50
589	A140	1.30t bl & multi		2.50	.65
		Nos. 583-589 (7)		10.15	2.65

Russian War Memorial, Berlin — A141

		1970, July 11	Litho.	Perf. 12	
590	A141	60m blue & multi		.60	.30

25th anniversary of end of World War II.

Bogdo-Gegen Palace — A142

Designs: 10m, Archer. 30m, Horseman. 40m, "White Mother" Goddess. 50m, Girl in national costume. 60m, Lion statue. 70m, Dancer's mask. 80m, Detail from Bogdo-Gegen Palace, Ulan Bator.

		1970, Sept. 20	Litho.	Perf. 12	
591	A142	10m multi		.35	.25
592	A142	20m multi		.35	.25
593	A142	30m multi		.35	.25
594	A142	40m multi		.35	.30
595	A142	50m multi		.75	.65
596	A142	60m multi		.90	.75
597	A142	70m multi		1.00	.85
598	A142	80m multi		1.25	1.10
a.		Block of 4, #595-598			
		Nos. 591-598 (8)		5.30	4.40

Souvenir Sheet

Recovery of Apollo 13 Capsule — A143

		1970, Nov. 1	Litho.	Perf. 12	
599	A143	4t blue & multi		4.50	4.50

Space missions of Apollo 13, Apr. 11-17, and Soyuz 9, June 1-10, 1970.

Mongolian Flag, UN and Education Year Emblems — A144

1970, Nov. 7

600	A144	60m multi		.60	.30

International Education Year.

Mounted Herald A145

		1970, Nov. 7	Litho.	Perf. 12	
601	A145	30m gold & multi		.50	.30

50th anniv. of newspaper Unen (Truth).

Apollo 11 Lunar Landing Module — A146

Designs: 10m, Vostok 2 & 3. 20m, Voskhod 2, space walk. 30m, Gemini 6 & 7 capsules. 50m, Soyuz 4 & 5 docking in space. 60m, Soyuz 6, 7 & 8 group flight. 1t, Apollo 13 with damaged capsule. 1.30t, Luna 16 unmanned moon landing. 4t, Radar ground tracking station.

		1971, Feb. 25	Litho.	Perf. 12	
602	A146	10m multi		.25	.25
603	A146	20m multi		.25	.25
604	A146	30m multi		.25	.25
605	A146	50m multi		.35	.25
606	A146	60m multi		.45	.25
607	A146	80m multi		.60	.25
608	A146	1t multi		.75	.30
609	A146	1.30t multi		.95	.40
		Nos. 602-609 (8)		3.85	2.20

Souvenir Sheet

610	A146	4t vio bl & multi		3.50	3.50

US and USSR space explorations.

Rider with Mongolian Flag — A147

Designs: 30m, Party meeting. 90m, Lenin with Mongolian leader. 1.20t, Marchers, pictures of Lenin and Marx.

		1971, Mar. 1	Photo.	Perf. 12½	
611	A147	30m gold & multi		.30	.25
612	A147	60m gold & multi		.40	.30
613	A147	90m gold & multi		.50	.40
614	A147	1.20t gold & multi		.60	.50
		Nos. 611-614 (4)		1.80	1.45

Mongolian Revolutionary Party, 50th anniv.

Souvenir Sheet

Lunokhod 1 on Moon — A148

Design: No. 615b, Apollo 14 on moon.

		1971, Apr. 15	Photo.	Perf. 14	
615	A148	Sheet of 2		3.50	3.50
a.-b.		2t any single		1.50	1.50

Luna 17 unmanned automated moon mission, Nov. 10-17, 1970, and Apollo 14 moon landing, Jan. 31-Feb. 9, 1971.

Dancer's Mask A149

Designs: Various masks for dancers.

		1971, Apr. 25	Litho.	Perf. 12	
616	A149	10m gold & multi		.25	.25
617	A149	20m gold & multi		.30	.25
618	A149	30m gold & multi		.40	.25
619	A149	50m gold & multi		.40	.25
620	A149	60m gold & multi		.50	.30
621	A149	1t gold & multi		.90	.40
622	A149	1.30t gold & multi		1.00	.55
		Nos. 616-622 (7)		3.75	2.25

Red Flag and Emblems A150

1971, May 31 Photo. Perf. 12x11½
623 A150 60m bl, red & gold   .40 .25
16th Congress of Mongolian Revolutionary Party.

Steam Locomotive — A151

1971, July 11 Litho. Perf. 12
624 A151 20m shown   .50 .25
625 A151 30m Diesel locomotive   .60 .25
626 A151 40m Truck   .65 .25
627 A151 50m Automobile   .75 .25
628 A151 60m Biplane PO-2   .85 .30
629 A151 80m AN-24 plane   1.00 .40
630 A151 1t Fishing boat   1.75 1.00
    Nos. 624-630 (7)   6.10 2.70
50th anniversary of modern transportation.
For overprints see Nos. 850A-850G.

Arms of Mongolia and Soldier — A152

Design: 1.50t, Arms, policeman and child.

1971, July 11 Litho. Perf. 12
631 A152 60m multi   .50 .25
632 A152 1.50t multi   .65 .30
50th anniversary of the people's army and police.

Mongolian Flag and Emblem — A153

1971, Aug. 25 Photo. Perf. 12x11½
633 A153 60m lt bl & multi   .40 .25
International Year Against Racial discrimination.

Flag of Youth Organization — A154

1971, Aug. 25 Litho. Perf. 12
634 A154 60m org & multi   .60 .30
50th anniversary of Mongolian revolutionary youth organization.

The Woodsman and the Tiger A155

Designs: Various Mongolian fairy tales.

1971, Sept. 15 Litho. Perf. 12
635 A155 10m gold & multi   .25 .25
636 A155 20m gold & multi   .25 .25
637 A155 30m gold & multi   .30 .25
638 A155 50m gold & multi   .35 .25
639 A155 60m gold & multi   .50 .25
640 A155 80m gold & multi   .65 .25
641 A155 1t gold & multi   .90 .35
642 A155 1.30t gold & multi   1.10 .50
    Nos. 635-642 (8)   4.30 2.35

Bactrian Camel — A156

1971, Nov. 1 Litho. Perf. 12½
643 A156 20m Yaks   .25 .25
644 A156 30m shown   .25 .25
645 A156 40m Sheep   .35 .25
646 A156 50m Goats   .40 .25
647 A156 60m Cattle   .55 .35
648 A156 80m Horses   .65 .35
649 A156 1t White horse   1.00 .50
    Nos. 643-649 (7)   3.45 2.20
Mongolian livestock breeding.

Cross-country Skiing — A157

Designs (Sapporo Olympic Emblem and): 20m, Bobsledding. 30m, Women's figure skating. 50m, Slalom. 60m, Speed skating. 80m, Downhill skiing. 1t, Ice hockey. 1.30t, Figure skating, pairs. 4t, Ski jump.

Perf. 12½x11½
1972, Jan. 20   Photo.
650 A157 10m multi   .25 .25
651 A157 20m ol & multi   .25 .25
652 A157 30m ultra & multi   .30 .25
653 A157 50m brt bl & multi   .35 .25
654 A157 60m multi   .45 .25
655 A157 80m grn & multi   .55 .25
656 A157 1t bl & multi   .70 .30
657 A157 1.30t vio & multi   .90 .35
    Nos. 650-657 (8)   3.75 2.15
Souvenir Sheet
Perf. 12½
658 A157 4t lt bl & multi   2.50 2.50
11th Winter Olympic Games, Sapporo, Japan, Feb. 3-13.

Taming Wild Horse A158

Paintings: 20m, Mythological animal in winter. 30m, Lancer on horseback. 50m, Athletes. 60m, Waterfall and horses. 80m, The Wise Musician, by Sarav. 1t, Young musician. 1.30t, Old sage with animals.

1972, Apr. 15 Litho. Perf. 12
659 A158 10m multi   .25 .25
660 A158 20m multi   .25 .25
661 A158 30m multi   .25 .25
662 A158 50m multi   .35 .25
663 A158 60m multi   .40 .25
664 A158 80m multi   .65 .35
665 A158 1t multi   .70 .35
666 A158 1.30t multi   .85 .40
    Nos. 659-666 (8)   3.70 2.35
Paintings by contemporary artists in Ulan Bator Museum.

Calosoma Fischeri A159

Designs: Various insects.

1972, Apr. 30 Litho. Perf. 12
667 A159 10m multi   .25 .25
668 A159 20m multi   .30 .25
669 A159 30m multi   .40 .25
670 A159 50m multi   .50 .25
671 A159 60m multi   .70 .25
672 A159 80m multi   1.00 .50
673 A159 1t multi   1.25 .75
674 A159 1.30t multi   1.75 .95
    Nos. 667-674 (8)   6.15 3.45

UN Emblem A160

1972, Aug. 30 Photo. Perf. 12
675 A160 60m multi   .60 .40
ECAFE (UN Economic Commission for Asia and the Far East), 25th anniv.

Slow Lizard — A161

Designs: 15m, Radd's toad. 20m, Pallas's viper. 25m, Toad-headed agamid. 30m, Siberian wood frog. 60m, Przewalski's lizard. 80m, Taphrometopon lineolatum (snake). 1t, Stoliczka's agamid.

1972, Sept. 5 Litho. Perf. 12
676 A161 10m multi   .25 .25
677 A161 15m multi   .25 .25
678 A161 20m multi   .25 .25
679 A161 25m multi   .40 .25
680 A161 30m multi   .45 .25
681 A161 60m multi   .60 .30
682 A161 80m multi   .95 .45
683 A161 1t multi   1.50 .55
    Nos. 676-683 (8)   4.65 2.55

Symbols of Technical Knowledge — A162

Design: 60m, University of Mongolia.

1972, Sept. 25
684 A162 50m org & multi   .40 .25
685 A162 60m lil & multi   .50 .25
30th anniversary of Mongolian State University.

Virgin and Child with St. John, by Bellini — A163

Paintings by Venetian Masters: 20m, Transfiguration, by Bellini, vert. 30m, Virgin and Child, by Bellini, vert. 50m, Presentation in the Temple, by Bellini, vert. 60m, St. George, by Mantegna, vert. 80m, Departure of St. Ursula, by Carpaccio, vert. 1t, Departure of St. Ursula, by Carpaccio.

1972, Oct. 1
686 A163 10m multi   .25 .25
687 A163 20m multi   .25 .25
688 A163 30m multi   .30 .25
689 A163 50m multi   .50 .25
690 A163 60m multi   .70 .25
691 A163 80m multi   .80 .40
692 A163 1t multi   1.00 .70
    Nos. 686-692 (7)   3.80 2.35
Save Venice campaign. See No. B3.

Manlay Bator Damdinsuren — A164

Designs: 20m, Ard Ayus, horiz. 50m, Hatan Bator Magsarzhav. 60m, Has Bator, horiz. 1t, Sukhe Bator.

1972, Oct. 20 Litho. Perf. 12
693 A164 10m gold & multi   .25 .25
694 A164 20m gold & multi   .30 .25
695 A164 50m gold & multi   .40 .25
696 A164 60m gold & multi   .50 .30
697 A164 1t gold & multi   1.00 .40
    Nos. 693-697 (5)   2.45 1.45
Paintings of national heroes.

Spasski Tower,
Moscow — A165

1972, Nov. 7   Photo.   Perf. 11
698 A165 60m multi + label   .75 .25
50th anniversary of USSR.

Mark Spitz, US, Gold Medal — A166

Designs (Medal and): 10m, Ulrike Meyfarth,
Germany. 20m, Sawao Kato, Japan. 30m,
András Balczó, Hungary. 60m, Lasse Viren,
Finland. 80m, Shane Gould, Australia. 1t,
Anatoli Bondarchuk, USSR. 4t, Khorloo Bai-
anmunk, Mongolia.

1972, Dec. 15   Photo.   Perf. 12½
699 A166 5m grn & multi   .25 .25
700 A166 10m ver & multi   .25 .25
701 A166 20m bl & multi   .30 .25
702 A166 30m multi   .30 .25
703 A166 60m lt vio & multi   .50 .25
704 A166 80m ol & multi   .70 .30
705 A166 1t lem & multi   .90 .40
     Nos. 699-705 (7)   3.20 1.95
                Souvenir Sheet
706 A166 4t red & multi   2.50 2.50
Winners in 20th Olympic Games, Munich.

Chimpanzee on Bicycle — A167

Circus Scenes: 10m, Seal playing ball.
15m, Bear riding wheel. 20m, Woman acrobat
on camel. 30m, Woman equestrian. 50m,
Clown playing flute. 60m, Woman gymnast.
1t, Circus building, Ulan Bator, horiz.

1973, Jan. 29   Litho.   Perf. 12
707 A167 5m multi   .25 .25
708 A167 10m multi   .25 .25
709 A167 15m multi   .30 .25
710 A167 20m multi   .40 .25
711 A167 30m multi   .50 .25
712 A167 50m multi   .60 .25
713 A167 60m multi   .80 .40
714 A167 1t multi   1.00 .70
     Nos. 707-714 (8)   4.10 2.60

Postrider
A168

Designs: 60m, Diesel locomotive. 1t, Truck.

1973, Jan. 31   Photo.   Perf. 12x11½
715 A168 50m brown   .55 .25
716 A168 60m green   2.00 .25
717 A168 1t rose claret   1.00 .30
     Nos. 715-717,C34 (4)   5.15 1.20
For surcharges, see Nos. 2405-2407.

Sukhe Bator
and
Merchants
A169

Paintings of Sukhe Bator: 20m, With elders.
50m, Leading partisans. 60m, With revolutionary council. 1t, Receiving deputation, horiz.

1973, Feb. 2   Photo.   Perf. 11½x12
718 A169 10m gold & multi   .25 .25
719 A169 20m gold & multi   .25 .25
720 A169 50m gold & multi   .40 .25
721 A169 60m gold & multi   .50 .25
722 A169 1t gold & multi   .80 .30
     Nos. 718-722 (5)   2.20 1.30
Sukhe Bator (1893-1923).

Nicolaus
Copernicus
A170

Designs: 60m, 2t, Copernicus in laboratory,
by Jan Matejko, horiz., 55x35mm. Nos. 725,
726b, Portrait. No. 726a, like 50m.

1973, Mar.   Litho.   Perf. 12
723 A170 50m gold & multi   .50 .25
724 A170 60m gold & multi   .60 .30
725 A170 1t gold & multi   1.00 .40
     Nos. 723-725 (3)   2.10 .95
                Souvenir Sheet
726   Sheet of 3   4.00 3.00
a.   A170 1t multi   .60 .60
b.   A170 1t multi   .60 .60
c.   A170 2t multi   1.50 1.50
500th anniversary of the birth of Nicolaus
Copernicus (1473-1543), Polish astronomer.

Marx and
Lenin — A171

1973, July 15   Photo.   Perf. 11½x12
727 A171 60m gold, car & ultra   .75 .40
9th meeting of postal administrations of
socialist countries, Ulan Bator.

Common Shelducks — A172

Designs: Aquatic birds.

1973, Aug. 10   Litho.   Perf. 12x11
728 A172 5m shown   .45 .25
729 A172 10m Arctic loons   .60 .25
730 A172 15m Bar-headed
             geese   1.00 .25
731 A172 30m Great crested
             grebe   1.20 .30
732 A172 50m Mallards   1.60 .40
733 A172 60m Mute swans   1.90 .45
734 A172 1t Greater scaups   2.25 .60
     Nos. 728-734 (7)   9.00 2.50

1973, Aug. 25   Litho.   Perf. 12x11
Designs: Fur-bearing animals.
735 A172 5m Siberian weasel   .25 .25
736 A172 10m Siberian chipmunk   .25 .25
737 A172 15m Flying squirrel   .25 .25
738 A172 20m Eurasian badger   .35 .25
739 A172 30m Eurasian red
             squirrel   .50 .25
740 A172 60m Wolverine   .85 .40
741 A172 80m Mink   1.00 .60
742 A172 1t White hare   1.50 .70
     Nos. 735-742 (8)   4.95 2.95

1973, Dec. 15   Litho.   Perf. 12x11
Designs: Flowers.
743 A172 5m Alpine aster   .25 .25
744 A172 10m Mongolian silene   .25 .25
745 A172 15m Rosa davurica   .25 .25
746 A172 20m Mongolian dande-
             lion   .30 .25
747 A172 30m Rhododendron
             dahuricum   .45 .25
748 A172 50m Clematis tangutica   .75 .35
749 A172 60m Siberian primula   .90 .50
750 A172 1t Pasqueflower   1.50 .65
     Nos. 743-750 (8)   4.65 2.75

Globe and Red
Flag
Emblem — A173

1973, Dec. 10   Photo.   Perf. 12x12½
751 A173 60m gold, red & blue   .60 .25
15th anniversary of the review "Problems of
Peace and Socialism," published in Prague.

Limenitis
Populi
A174

Butterflies: 10m, Arctia hebe. 15m,
Rhyparia purpurata. 20m, Catocala pacta.
30m, Isoceras kaszabi. 50m, Celerio costata.
60m, Arctia caja. 1t, Diacrisia sannio.

1974, Jan. 15   Litho.   Perf. 11
752 A174 5m lil & multi   .30 .25
753 A174 10m brn & multi   .35 .25
754 A174 15m bl & multi   .35 .25
755 A174 20m brn org & multi   .55 .25
756 A174 30m lt vio & multi   .75 .25
757 A174 50m dl red & multi   1.00 .30
758 A174 60m yel grn & multi   1.20 .40
759 A174 1t ultra & multi   1.50 .50
     Nos. 752-759 (8)   6.00 2.45

"Hehe
Namshil"
by L.
Merdorsh
A175

Designs (Various Scenes from): 20m, "Sive
Hiagt," by D. Luvsansharav. 25m, 80m, 1t,
"Edre," by D. Namdag. 30m, "The 3 Khans of
Sara-Gol" (legend). 60m, "Amarsana," by B.
Damdinsuren. 20m and 30m horizontal.

1974, Feb. 20   Litho.   Perf. 12
760 A175 15m sil & multi   .25 .25
761 A175 20m sil & multi   .30 .25
762 A175 25m sil & multi   .40 .25
763 A175 30m sil & multi   .50 .25
764 A175 60m sil & multi   .60 .25
765 A175 80m sil & multi   .80 .30
766 A175 1t sil & multi   1.00 .80
     Nos. 760-766 (7)   3.85 2.35
Mongolian operas and dramas.

Government Building and Sukhe
Bator — A176

1974, Mar. 1   Photo.   Perf. 11
767 A176 60m gold & multi   .75 .40
50th anniv. of renaming capital Ulan Bator.

Juggler
A177

10m, Circus horses, horiz. 30m, Trained elephant. 40m, Yak pushing ball, horiz. 60m,
Acrobats with ring. 80m, Woman acrobat on
unicycle.

1974, May 4   Litho.   Perf. 12
768 A177 10m multi   .25 .25
769 A177 20m multi   .40 .25
770 A177 30m multi   .50 .30
771 A177 40m multi   .80 .40
772 A177 60m multi   1.00 .50
773 A177 80m multi   1.60 .75
     Nos. 768-773,C65 (7)   5.80 3.05
Mongolian Circus. No. 773 has se-tenant
label, with similar design.

Girl on Bronco — A178

Children's Activities: 20m, Boy roping calf. 30m, 40m, Boy taming horse (different designs). 60m, Girl with doves. 80m, Wrestling. 1t, Dancing.

1974, June 2   Litho.   Perf. 12

774	A178	10m dl yel & multi	.25 .25
775	A178	20m lt bl & multi	.25 .25
776	A178	30m grn & multi	.30 .25
777	A178	40m yel & multi	.40 .25
778	A178	60m pink & multi	.60 .25
779	A178	80m bl & multi	.80 .35
780	A178	1t dl bl & multi	1.00 .50
		Nos. 774-780 (7)	3.60 2.10

Children's Day.
For surcharges see Nos. 2577-2578.

Archer — A179

National Sports: 20m, Two horsemen fighting for goatskin. 30m, Archer on horseback. 40m, Horse race. 60m, Riding wild horse. 80m, Rider chasing riderless horse. 1t, Boys wrestling.

1974, July 11   Photo.   Perf. 11

781	A179	10m vio bl & multi	.25 .25
782	A179	20m yel & multi	.25 .25
783	A179	30m lil & multi	.30 .25
784	A179	40m multi	.40 .25
785	A179	60m multi	.60 .25
786	A179	80m multi	.80 .40
787	A179	1t multi	1.00 .60
		Nos. 781-787 (7)	3.60 2.25

Nadom, Mongolian national festival.

Grizzly Bear — A180

1974, July   Litho.   Perf. 12

788	A180	10m shown	.25 .25
789	A180	20m Common panda	.30 .25
790	A180	30m Giant panda	.35 .25
791	A180	40m Two brown bears	.50 .35
792	A180	60m Sloth bear	.75 .35
793	A180	80m Asiatic black bears	1.00 .50
794	A180	1t Giant brown bear	1.50 .75
		Nos. 788-794 (7)	4.65 2.70

Stag in Zuun Araat Wildlife Preserve — A181

1974, Sept.   Litho.   Perf. 12

795	A181	10m shown	.25 .25
796	A181	20m Beaver	.30 .25
797	A181	30m Leopard	.35 .25
798	A181	40m Great black-backed gull	.50 .35
799	A181	60m Deer	.75 .35
800	A181	80m Mouflon	1.00 .50
801	A181	1t Deer and entrance to Bogd-uul Preserve	1.50 .75
		Nos. 795-801 (7)	4.65 2.70

Protected fauna in Mongolian wildlife preserves.

Buddhist Temple, Bogdo Gegen Palace — A182

Mongolian Architecture: 15m, Buddhist Temple, now Museum. 30m, Entrance to Charity Temple, Ulan Bator. 50m, Mongolian yurta. 80m, Gazebo in convent yard.

1974, Oct. 15   Litho.   Perf. 12

802	A182	10m bl & multi	.30 .25
803	A182	15m multi	.35 .25
804	A182	30m grn & multi	.45 .30
805	A182	50m multi	.60 .40
806	A182	80m yel & multi	1.00 .50
		Nos. 802-806 (5)	2.70 1.70

Spasski Tower, Sukhe Bator Statue — A183

1974, Nov. 26   Photo.   Perf. 11½x12

807	A183	60m multi	.75 .40

Visit of General Secretary Brezhnev and a delegation from the USSR to participate in celebration of 50th anniversary of People's Republic of Mongolia.

Sukhe Bator Proclaiming Republic — A184

Designs: No. 808, "First Constitution," symbolic embroidery. No. 809, Flag over landscape, plane and communications tower.

1974, Nov. 28   Litho.

808	A184	60m multi	.65 .25
809	A184	60m multi	.65 .25
810	A184	60m multi	.65 .25
		Nos. 808-810 (3)	1.95 .75

50th anniv. of People's Republic of Mongolia.

Decanter — A185

Designs: 20m, Silver jar. 30m, Night lamp. 40m, Tea jug. 60m, Candelabra. 80m, Teapot. 1t, Silver bowl on 3-legged stand.

1974, Dec. 1   Photo.

811	A185	10m blue & multi	.25 .25
812	A185	20m claret & multi	.30 .25
813	A185	30m multi	.35 .25
814	A185	40m dp bl & multi	.50 .25
815	A185	60m multi	.60 .25
816	A185	80m grn & multi	.80 .40
817	A185	1t lilac & multi	1.00 .50
		Nos. 811-817 (7)	3.80 2.25

Mongolian 19th century goldsmiths' work.

Lapwing (plover) — A186

1974, Dec.   Litho.   Perf. 11

818	A186	10m shown	.35 .25
819	A186	20m Fish	.45 .25
820	A186	30m Marsh marigolds	.55 .25
821	A186	40m White pelican	.75 .25
822	A186	60m Perch	.75 .30
823	A186	80m Mink	.90 .40
		Nos. 818-823,C66 (7)	4.95 2.20

Water and nature protection.

American Mail Coach, UPU Emblem — A187

Designs (UPU Emblem and): 20m, French two-wheeled coach. 30m, Changing horses, Russian coach. 40m, Swedish caterpillar mail truck. 50m, First Hungarian mail truck. 60m, German Daimler-Benz mail truck. 1t, Mongolian dispatch rider.

1974, Dec.   Litho.   Perf. 12

824	A187	10m multi	.25 .25
825	A187	20m multi	.25 .25
826	A187	30m multi	.30 .25
827	A187	40m multi	.40 .30
828	A187	50m multi	.60 .35
829	A187	60m multi	.75 .40
830	A187	1t multi	1.00 .65
		Nos. 824-830 (7)	3.55 2.45

Cent. of the UPU and Stockholmia 74.

Soviet Flag, Broken Swastika A188

1975, May 9   Photo.   Perf. 11½x12

832	A188	60m multi	.75 .40

30th anniversary of the end of World War II and victory over fascism.

Mongolian Woman A189

1975, May

833	A189	60m multi	.75 .45

International Women's Year 1975.

Zygophyllum Xanthoxylon — A190

Medicinal Plants: 20m, Ingarvillea potaninii. 30m, Lancea tibetica. 40m, Jurinea mongolica. 50m, Saussurea involucrata. 60m, Allium mongolicum. 1t, Adonis mongolica.

1975, May 24   Photo.   Perf. 11x11½

834	A190	10m dp org & multi	.25 .25
835	A190	20m grn & multi	.30 .25
836	A190	30m yel & multi	.45 .25
837	A190	40m vio & multi	.60 .25
838	A190	50m brn & multi	.65 .30
839	A190	60m bl & multi	.90 .30
840	A190	1t multi	1.50 .60
		Nos. 834-840 (7)	4.65 2.20

12th International Botanists' Conference.

Shepherd — A191

Puppet Theater: 20m, Boy on horseback. 30m, Boy and disobedient bull calf. 40m, Little orphan camel's tale. 50m, Boy and obedient little yak. 60m, Boy riding swan. 1t, Children's choir.

1975, June 30   Litho.   Perf. 12

841	A191	10m multi	.25 .25
842	A191	20m multi	.30 .25
843	A191	30m multi	.40 .25
844	A191	40m multi	.60 .25
845	A191	50m multi	.70 .30
846	A191	60m multi	.80 .30
847	A191	1t multi	1.25 .50
		Nos. 841-847 (7)	4.30 2.10

For surcharges see Nos. 2575-2576.

Pioneers Tending Fruit Tree — A192

60m, Pioneers studying, and flying model plane. 1t, New emblem of Mongolian Pioneers.

1975, July 15   *Perf. 12x11½*
848	A192	50m multi	.40 .25
849	A192	60m multi	.50 .25
850	A192	1t multi	.70 .40
		Nos. 848-850 (3)	1.60 .90

Mongolian Pioneers, 50th anniversary.

Nos. 624-630 Overprinted

1975, July 15   *Litho.*   *Perf. 12*
850A	A151	20m multi	5.00 5.00
850B	A151	30m multi	5.00 5.00
850C	A151	40m multi	4.00 4.00
850D	A151	50m multi	4.00 4.00
850E	A151	60m multi	5.00 5.00
850F	A151	80m multi	5.00 5.00
850G	A151	1t multi	6.00 6.00
		Nos. 850A-850G (7)	34.00 34.00

Fifty years of communication.

Golden Eagle Hunting Fox — A193

Hunting Scenes: 20m, Dogs treeing lynx, vert. 30m, Hunter stalking marmots. 40m, Hunter riding reindeer, vert. 50m, Boar hunt. 60m, Trapped wolf, vert. 1t, Bear hunt.

1975, Aug. 25   *Litho.*   *Perf. 12*
851	A193	10m multi	.45 .25
852	A193	20m multi	.50 .25
853	A193	30m multi	.60 .25
854	A193	40m multi	.65 .30
855	A193	50m multi	.75 .35
856	A193	60m multi	.85 .40
857	A193	1t multi	1.00 .60
		Nos. 851-857 (7)	4.80 2.40

Hunting in Mongolia.

Mesocottus Haitej — A194

Various Fish: 20m, Pseudaspius leptocephalus. 30m, Oreoleuciscus potanini. 40m, Tinca tinca. 50m, Coregonus lavaretus pidschian. 60m, Erythroculter mongolicus. 1t, Carassius auratus.

1975, Sept. 15   *Photo.*   *Perf. 11*
858	A194	10m multi	.25 .25
859	A194	20m multi	.30 .25
860	A194	30m multi	.45 .25
861	A194	40m bl & multi	.60 .30
862	A194	50m grn & multi	.75 .30
863	A194	60m lil & multi	.90 .40
864	A194	1t vio bl & multi	1.50 .60
		Nos. 858-864 (7)	4.75 2.35

Neck and Bow of Musical Instrument (Morin Hur) — A195

National Handicraft: 20m, Saddle. 30m, Silver headgear. 40m, Boots. 50m, Tasseled Woman's cap. 60m, Pipe and tobacco pouch. 1t, Sable cap.

1975, Oct. 10   *Litho.*   *Perf. 11½x12½*
865	A195	10m multi	.25 .25
866	A195	20m multi	.25 .25
867	A195	30m multi	.30 .25
868	A195	40m multi	.40 .25
869	A195	50m multi	.50 .30
870	A195	60m multi	.60 .30
871	A195	1t multi	1.00 .60
		Nos. 865-871 (7)	3.30 2.20

Revolutionists with Flags — A196

1975, Nov. 15   *Litho.*   *Perf. 11½x12*
872	A196	60m multi	.75 .40

70th anniversary of Russian Revolution.

Ski Jump, Olympic Games Emblem — A197

Winter Olympic Games Emblem and: 20m, Ice hockey. 30m, Skiing. 40m, Bobsled. 50m, Biathlon. 60m, Speed skating. 1t, Figure skating, women's. 4t, Skier carrying torch.

Perf. 11½x12½
1975, Dec. 20   *Litho.*
873	A197	10m multi	.25 .25
874	A197	20m multi	.25 .25
875	A197	30m brn & multi	.30 .25
876	A197	40m grn & multi	.40 .25
877	A197	50m multi	.50 .30
878	A197	60m ol & multi	.60 .30
879	A197	1t multi	1.00 .40
		Nos. 873-879 (7)	3.30 2.00

Souvenir Sheet

880	A197	4t multi	3.00 3.00

12th Winter Olympic Games, Innsbruck, Austria, Feb. 4-15, 1976.

Taming Wild Horse A198

Mongolian Paintings: 20m, Camel caravan, horiz. 30m, Man playing lute. 40m, Woman adjusting headdress, horiz. 50m, Woman wearing ceremonial costume. 60m, Women fetching water. 1t, Woman musician. 4t, Warrior on horseback.

1975, Nov. 30   *Perf. 12*
881	A198	10m brown & multi	.25 .25
882	A198	20m blue & multi	.25 .25
883	A198	30m olive & multi	.35 .25
884	A198	40m lilac & multi	.45 .25
885	A198	50m blue & multi	.55 .30
886	A198	60m lilac & multi	.65 .30
887	A198	1t silver & multi	1.00 .50
		Nos. 881-887 (7)	3.50 2.10

Souvenir Sheet

888	A198	4t bl & multi	4.00 3.50

House of Young Technicians A199

Designs: 60m, Hotel Ulan Bator. 1t, Museum of the Revolution.

1975, Dec. 30   *Photo.*   *Perf. 12x11½*
893	A199	50m ultra	.50 .25
894	A199	60m bl grn	.60 .25
895	A199	1t brick red	1.00 .40
		Nos. 893-895 (3)	2.10 .90

Camels in Gobi Desert — A200

20m, Horse taming. 30m, Herding. 40m, Pioneers' camp. 60m, Young musician. 80m, Children's festival. 1t, Mongolian wrestling.

1976, June 1   *Litho.*   *Perf. 12*
896	A200	10m multi	.25 .25
897	A200	20m multi	.30 .25
898	A200	30m multi	.35 .25
899	A200	40m multi	.50 .25
900	A200	60m multi	.60 .25
901	A200	80m multi	.90 .40
902	A200	1t multi	1.00 .50
		Nos. 896-902 (7)	3.90 2.15

International Children's Day.

Red Star — A201

1976, May 1   *Photo.*   *Perf. 11x12½*
903	A201	60m red, maroon & silver	.75 .40

17th Congress of the Mongolian People's Revolutionary Party, June 14.

Archery, Montreal Games' Emblem, Canadian Flag — A202

20m, Judo. 30m, Boxing. 40m, Vaulting. 60m, Weight lifting. 80m, High Jump. 1t, Target shooting.

1976, May 20   *Litho.*   *Perf. 12½x11½*
904	A202	10m yel & multi	.25 .25
905	A202	20m yel & multi	.25 .25
906	A202	30m yel & multi	.25 .25
907	A202	40m yel & multi	.40 .25
908	A202	60m yel & multi	.55 .30
909	A202	80m yel & multi	.80 .35
910	A202	1t yel & multi	1.00 .50
		Nos. 904-910 (7)	3.50 2.15

21st Olympic Games, Montreal, Canada, July 17-Aug. 1. See No. C81.

Partisans A203

Fighter and Sojombo Independence Symbol — A204

Perf. 12x11½, 11½x12
1976, June 15   *Litho.*
911	A203	60m multi	.60 .30
912	A204	60m multi	.60 .30

55th anniversary of Mongolia's independence. See No. C82.

Souvenir Sheet

Sukhe Bator Medal — A205

1976, July 11   *Perf. 11½*
913	A205	4t multi	4.00 4.00

Mongolian honors medals.

Osprey — A206

Protected Birds: 20m, Griffon vulture. 30m, Bearded lammergeier. 40m, Marsh harrier. 60m, Black vulture. 80m, Golden eagle. 1t, Tawny eagle.

1976, Aug. 16   Litho.   Perf. 12

914	A206	10m multi	.60	.25
915	A206	20m multi	.90	.25
916	A206	30m multi	1.10	.30
917	A206	40m multi	1.40	.30
918	A206	60m multi	1.75	.40
919	A206	80m multi	1.90	.50
920	A206	1t multi	2.25	.60
	Nos. 914-920 (7)		9.90	2.60

"Nadom" Military Game — A207

Paintings by O. Cevegshava: 10m, Taming Wild Horse, vert. 30m, Hubsugul Lake Harbor. 40m, The Steppe Awakening. 80m, Wrestlers. 1.60t, Yak Descending in Snow, vert.

1976, Sept.   Litho.   Perf. 12

921	A207	10m multi	.25	.25
922	A207	20m multi	.25	.25
923	A207	30m multi	.30	.25
924	A207	40m multi	.40	.25
925	A207	80m multi	.70	.30
926	A207	1.60t multi	1.25	.70
	Nos. 921-926 (6)		3.15	2.00

Interlocking Circles, Industry and Transport — A208

1976, Oct. 15   Photo.   Perf. 12x11½

927 A208 60m brn, bl & red   1.25   .30

Soviet-Mongolian friendship.

John Naber,
US Flag,
Gold Medals
A209

Designs: 20m, Nadia Comaneci, Romanian flag. 30m, Kornelia Ender, East German flag. 40m, Mitsuo Tsukahara, Japanese flag. 60m, Gregor Braun, German flag. 80m, Lasse Viren, Finnish flag. 1t, Nikolai Andrianov, Russian flag.

1976, Nov. 30   Litho.   Perf. 12

928	A209	10m multi	.25	.25
929	A209	20m multi	.25	.25
930	A209	30m multi	.25	.25
931	A209	40m multi	.30	.25
932	A209	60m multi	.50	.30
933	A209	80m multi	.75	.40
934	A209	1t multi	.90	.50
	Nos. 928-934 (7)		3.20	2.20

Gold medal winners, 21st Olympic Games, Montreal. See No. C83.

Stone Tablet on   Carved Tablet,
Tortoise   6th-8th Centuries
A210   A211

1976, Dec. 15   Litho.   Perf. 11½x12

935	A210	50m brn & lt bl	1.00	.35
936	A211	60m gray & brt grn	1.50	.40

Intl. Archaeological Conference, Ulan Bator.

R-1 Plane — A212

Designs: Various Mongolian planes.

1976, Dec. 22   Perf. 12

937	A212	10m multi	.25	.25
938	A212	20m multi	.25	.25
939	A212	30m multi	.30	.25
940	A212	40m multi	.35	.25
941	A212	60m multi	.55	.30
942	A212	80m multi	.70	.30
943	A212	1t multi	.80	.50
	Nos. 937-943 (7)		3.20	2.10

Dancers — A213

Folk Dances: 20m, 13th century costumes. 30m, West Mongolian dance. 40m, "Ekachi," or horse-dance. 60m, "Bielge," West Mongolian trunk dance. 80m, "Hodak," or friendship dance. 1t, "Dojarka."

1977, Mar. 20   Litho.   Perf. 12½

944	A213	10m multi	.25	.25
945	A213	20m multi	.30	.25
946	A213	30m multi	.45	.25
947	A213	40m multi	.55	.25
948	A213	60m multi	.75	.25
949	A213	80m multi	1.00	.40
950	A213	1t multi	1.10	.45
	Nos. 944-950 (7)		4.40	2.10

Miniature Sheet

A214 & A215 Designs

a, Path of Pioneer from Earth to Jupiter, deflected by Mars. b, Apple tree. c, Sextant and planets. d, Astronauts in space. e, Isaac Newton. f, Prism and spectrum. g, Rain falling on earth. h, Motion of celestial bodies. i, Pioneer 10 over Jupiter.

1977, Mar. 31   Litho.   Perf. 11½x12

951		Sheet of 9	4.50	2.50
a.	A214	60m multi	.40	.25
b.	A215	60m multi	.40	.25
c.	A214	60m multi	.40	.25
d.	A214	60m multi	.40	.25
e.	A214	60m multi	.40	.25
f.	A214	60m multi	.40	.25
g.	A215	60m multi	.40	.25
h.	A215	60m multi	.40	.25
i.	A214	60m multi	.40	.25

Sir Isaac Newton (1642-1727), English natural philosopher and mathematician.
Nos. 951a-951i arranged in 3 rows of 3. Nos. 951d and 951i inscribed AIR MAIL.

D. Natsagdorji, Writer, and
Quotation — A216

Design: No. 953, Grazing horses, landscape, ornament and quotation.

1977   Perf. 11½x12

952	A216	60m multi	1.00	.50
953	A216	60m multi	1.00	.50

D. Natsagdorji, founder of modern Mongolian literature. Label and vignette separated by simulated perforations.

Primitive Tortoises — A217

Prehistoric Animals: 20m, Ungulate (titanothere). 30m, Beaked dinosaurs. 40m, Entelodon (swine). 60m, Antelope. 80m, Hipparion. 1t, Aurochs.

1977, May 7   Photo.   Perf. 12½

954	A217	10m multi	.35	.25
955	A217	20m multi	.50	.25
956	A217	30m multi	.55	.25
957	A217	40m multi	.75	.30
958	A217	60m multi	1.25	.30
959	A217	80m multi	1.50	.60
960	A217	1t multi	1.75	.90
	Nos. 954-960 (7)		6.65	2.85

Souvenir Sheet

Mongolia,
Type A2 and
Netherlands
No.
1 — A218

1977, May 20

961 A218 4t multi   3.00 2.00

AMPHILEX '77 International Philatelic Exhibition, Amsterdam, May 27-June 5. No. 961 contains one 37x52mm stamp.

Boys on Horseback — A219

20m, Girl on horseback. 30m, Hunter on horseback. 40m, Grazing horses. 60m, Mare & foal. 80m, Grazing horse & student. 1t, White stallion.

1977, June 15   Litho.   Perf. 12

962	A219	10m multi	.25	.25
963	A219	20m multi	.30	.25
964	A219	30m multi	.35	.25
965	A219	40m multi	.45	.25
966	A219	60m multi	.60	.30
967	A219	80m multi	.85	.40
968	A219	1t multi	1.00	.50
	Nos. 962-968 (7)		3.80	2.20

Copper and
Molybdenum
Plant, Vehicles
A220

1977, June 15   Litho.   Perf. 12

969 A220 60m multi   1.50 .50

Erdenet, a new industrial town.

Bucket Brigade Fighting Fire — A221

Fire Fighting: 20m, Horse-drawn fire pump. 30m, Horse-drawn steam pump. 40m, Men in protective suits fighting forest fire. 60m, Modern foam extinguisher. 80m, Truck and ladder. 1t, Helicopter fighting fire on steppe.

1977, Aug.   Litho.   Perf. 12

970	A221	10m multi	.25	.25
971	A221	20m multi	.25	.25
972	A221	30m multi	.40	.25
973	A221	40m multi	.55	.25
974	A221	60m multi	.65	.30
975	A221	80m multi	.85	.35
976	A221	1t multi	1.10	.50
	Nos. 970-976 (7)		4.05	2.15

Radar and
Molniya
Satellite on TV
Screen — A222

1977, Sept. 12   Photo.   Perf. 12x11½

977 A222 60m gray, bl & blk   .50 .30

40th anniversary of Technical Institute.

Lenin Museum, Ulan Bator — A223

1977, Oct. 1   Litho.   Perf. 12

978 A223 60m multi   .60 .30

Inauguration of Lenin Museum in connection with the 60th anniversary of the Russian October Revolution.

Dove,
Globe,
Decree
of Peace
A224

Designs: 50m, Cruiser Aurora and Russian flag, vert. 1.50t, Globe and "Freedom."

Perf. 11½x12, 12x11½

1977, Oct. 1 Photo.
979 A224 50m gold & multi .80 .25
980 A224 60m gold & multi .70 .25
981 A224 1.50t gold & multi 1.25 .60
Nos. 979-981 (3) 2.75 1.10
60th anniversary of the Russian Revolution.

Aporia Crataegi — A225

Moths: 20m, Gastropacha quercifolia. 30m, Colias chrysoteme. 40m, Dasychira fascelina. 60m, Malocosoma neustria. 80m, Diacrisia sanno. 1t, Heodes virgaureae.

1977, Sept. 25 Photo. **Perf. 12½**
982 A225 10m multi .25 .25
983 A225 20m multi .45 .25
984 A225 30m multi .60 .25
985 A225 40m multi .90 .25
986 A225 60m multi 1.20 .30
987 A225 80m multi 1.50 .40
988 A225 1t multi 1.90 .55
Nos. 982-988 (7) 6.80 2.25

Giant Pandas — A226

Pandas: 10m, Eating bamboo, vert. 30m, Female and cub in washtub, vert. 40m, Male and cub playing with bamboo. 60m, Female and cub, vert. 80m, Family. 1t, Male, vert.

1977, Nov. 25 Litho. **Perf. 12**
989 A226 10m multi .25 .25
990 A226 20m multi .30 .25
991 A226 30m multi .45 .25
992 A226 40m multi .60 .30
993 A226 60m multi .90 .35
994 A226 80m multi 1.50 .55
995 A226 1t multi 1.75 .75
Nos. 989-995 (7) 5.75 2.70

Souvenir Sheet

Helen Fourment and her Children, by Rubens — A227

1977, Dec. 5 **Perf. 11½x10½**
996 A227 4t multi 4.50 4.50
Peter Paul Rubens (1577-1640).

Ferrari Racing Car — A228

Experimental Racing Cars: 30m, Ford McLaren. 40m, Madi, USSR. 50m, Mazda. 60m, Porsche. 80m, Russian model car. 1.20t, The Blue Flame, US speed car.

1978, Jan. 28 Litho. **Perf. 12**
997 A228 20m multi .25 .25
998 A228 30m multi .25 .25
999 A228 40m multi .30 .25
1000 A228 50m multi .40 .30
1001 A228 60m multi .60 .30
1002 A228 80m multi .80 .40
1003 A228 1.20t multi 1.25 .50
Nos. 997-1003 (7) 3.85 2.25

Boletus Variegatus — A229

Mushrooms: 30m, Russula cyanoxantha. 40m, Boletus aurantiacus. 50m, Boletus scaber. 60m, Russula flava. 80m, Lactarius resimus. 1.20t, Flammula spumosa.

1978, Feb. 28 Photo. **Perf. 11x11½**
1004 A229 20m yel & multi .35 .25
1005 A229 30m yel & multi .55 .25
1006 A229 40m yel & multi .80 .30
1007 A229 50m yel & multi 1.00 .35
1008 A229 60m yel & multi 1.40 .40
1009 A229 80m yel & multi 1.90 .45
1010 A229 1.20t yel & multi 2.50 .75
Nos. 1004-1010 (7) 8.50 2.75

Young Couple with Youth Flag — A230

1978, Apr. Litho. **Perf. 11½x12**
1011 A230 60m multi .80 .30
17th Congress of Mongolian Youth Organization, Ulan Bator, Apr. 1978.

Soccer, Sugar Loaf Mountain, Rio de Janeiro, Brazil 1950 Emblem — A231

Designs (Various Soccer Scenes and): 30m, Old Town Tower, Bern, Switzerland, 1954. 40m, Town Hall, Stockholm, Sweden, 1958. 50m, University of Chile, Chile, 1962. 60m, Parliament and Big Ben, London, 1966. 80m, Degolladeo Theater, Guadalajara, Mexico, 1970. 1.20t, Town Hall and TV Tower, Munich, Germany.

1978, Apr. 15 **Perf. 12**
1012 A231 20m multi .25 .25
1013 A231 20m multi .25 .25
1014 A231 40m multi .30 .25
1015 A231 50m multi .35 .25
1016 A231 60m multi .45 .30
1017 A231 80m multi .60 .30
1018 A231 1.20t multi .90 .50
Nos. 1012-1018 (7) 3.10 2.15
11th World Cup Soccer Championship, Argentina, June 1-25. See No. C109.

Capex Emblem, Eurasian Beaver and Canada #336 — A232

30m, Tibetan sand grouse & Canada #478. 40m, Red-throated loon & Canada #369. 50m, Argali & Canada #324. 60m, Eurasian brown bear & Canada #322. 80m, Moose & Canada #323. 1.20t, Great black-backed gull & Canada #343.

1978, June Litho. **Perf. 12**
1019 A232 20m multi .25 .25
1020 A232 30m multi .35 .25
1021 A232 40m multi .55 .30
1022 A232 50m multi .75 .40
1023 A232 60m multi .90 .50
1024 A232 80m multi 1.00 .60
1025 A232 1.20t multi 1.50 .80
Nos. 1019-1025 (7) 5.30 3.10
CAPEX '78 International Philatelic Exhibition, Toronto, June 9-18. See No. C110.

Marx, Engels and Lenin A233

1978, July 11 Photo. **Perf. 12x11½**
1026 A233 60m gold, blk & red .70 .30
50th anniversary of publication in Prague of "Problems of Peace and Socialism."

Souvenir Sheet

Outdoor Rest, by Amgalan — A234

Paintings by D. Amgalan: No. 1027b, Winter Night (dromedary and people in snow). No. 1027c, Saddling up.

1978, Aug. 10 Litho. **Perf. 12**
1027 Sheet of 3 3.75 3.75
a.-c. A234 1.50t any single 1.00
Philatelic cooperation between Hungary and Mongolia, 20th anniversary. No. 1027 contains 3 stamps and 3 labels.

Papillon — A235

Dogs: 20m, Black Mongolian sheepdog. 30m, Puli. 40m, St. Bernard. 50m, German shepherd. 60m, Mongolian watchdog. 70m,

Samoyed. 80m, Laika (1st dog in space) and rocket. 1.20t, Cocker spaniel and poodles.

1978, Sept. 25 Litho. **Perf. 12**
1028 A235 10m multi .30 .25
1029 A235 20m multi .30 .25
1030 A235 30m multi .50 .25
1031 A235 40m multi .60 .30
1032 A235 50m multi .80 .30
1033 A235 60m multi .90 .30
1034 A235 70m multi 1.00 .50
1035 A235 80m multi 1.25 .50
1036 A235 1.20t multi 1.50 .80
Nos. 1028-1036 (9) 7.15 3.45

Open Book and Pen — A236

1978, Oct. 20 Photo. **Perf. 12x11½**
1037 A236 60m car & ultra .60 .30
Mongolian Writers' Association, 50th anniversary.

Souvenir Sheets

Paintings — A237

Melancholy, by Dürer — A238

Paintings: No. 1038a, Clothed Maya, by Goya. No. 1038b, "Ta Matete," by Gauguin. No. 1038c, Bridge at Arles, by Van Gogh.

1978, Oct. 30 Litho. **Perf. 12**
1038 Sheet of 3 + 3 labels 4.50 4.50
a.-c. A237 1.50t any single + label 1.25 1.25
  Perf. 11½
1039 A238 4t black 4.50 4.50
Anniversaries of European painters: Francisco Goya; Paul Gauguin; Vincent van Gogh; Albrecht Dürer.

Camel and Calf — A239

Bactrian Camels: 30m, Young camel. 40m, Two camels. 50m, Woman leading pack camel. 60m, Old camel. 80m, Camel pulling cart. 1.20t, Race.

1978, Nov. 30   Litho.   Perf. 12
1040	A239	20m multi	.25 .25
1041	A239	30m multi	.30 .25
1042	A239	40m multi	.45 .30
1043	A239	50m multi	.60 .30
1044	A239	60m multi	.75 .40
1045	A239	80m multi	1.00 .60
1046	A239	1.20m multi	1.40 .75
		Nos. 1040-1046 (7)	4.75 2.85

Flags of Comecon Members, Globe — A240

1979, Jan. 2   Litho.   Perf. 12
1047 A240 60m multi + label   .60 .30

30th anniversary of the Council of Mutual Assistance (Comecon).
Label and vignette separated by simulated perforations.

Silver Tabby — A241

Domestic Cats: 30m, White Persian. 50m, Red Persian. 60m, Cream Persian. 70m, Siamese. 80m, Smoky Persian. 1t, Burmese.

1979, Feb. 10
1048	A241	10m multi	.25 .25
1049	A241	30m multi	.35 .25
1050	A241	50m multi	.50 .25
1051	A241	60m multi	.75 .30
1052	A241	70m multi	.90 .35
1053	A241	80m multi	1.00 .45
1054	A241	1t multi	1.10 .60
		Nos. 1048-1054 (7)	4.85 2.45

Potaninia Mongolica — A242

Flowers: 30m, Sophora alopecuroides. 50m, Halimodendron halodendron. 60m, Forget-me-nots. 70m, Pincushion flower. 80m, Leucanthemum Sibiricum. 1t, Edelweiss.

1979, Mar. 10   Litho.   Perf. 12
1055	A242	10m multi	.25 .25
1056	A242	30m multi	.45 .25
1057	A242	50m multi	.55 .25
1058	A242	60m multi	.65 .25
1059	A242	70m multi	.70 .30
1060	A242	80m multi	.80 .35
1061	A242	1t multi	.90 .50
		Nos. 1055-1061 (7)	4.30 2.15

Finland-Czechoslovakia, Finnish Flag — A243

Ice Hockey Games and 1980 Olympic Emblems: 30m, German Fed. Rep.-Sweden, German flag. 50m, US-Canada, US flag. 60m, USSR-Sweden, Russian flag. 70m, Canada-USSR, Canadian flag. 80m, Swedish goalie and flag. 1t, Czechoslovakia-USSR, Czechoslovak flag.

1979, Apr. 10   Litho.   Perf. 12
1062	A243	10m multi	.25 .25
1063	A243	30m multi	.25 .25
1064	A243	50m multi	.35 .25
1065	A243	60m multi	.45 .25
1066	A243	70m multi	.55 .25
1067	A243	80m multi	.65 .30
1068	A243	1t multi	.90 .40
		Nos. 1062-1068 (7)	3.40 1.95

Ice Hockey World Championship, Moscow, Apr. 14-27.

Lambs — A244

Paintings: 30m, Milking, camels. 50m, Plane bringing supplies in winter. 60m, Herdsmen and horses. 70m, Milkmaids, vert. 80m, Summer Evening (camels). 1t, Landscape with herd. 4t, After the Storm.

Perf. 12x11½, 11½x12
1979, May 3   Litho.
1069	A244	10m multi	.25 .25
1070	A244	30m multi	.25 .25
1071	A244	50m multi	.35 .25
1072	A244	60m multi	.45 .25
1073	A244	70m multi	.50 .30
1074	A244	80m multi	.75 .30
1075	A244	1t multi	.95 .40
		Nos. 1069-1075 (7)	3.50 2.00

Souvenir Sheet
1076 A244 4t multi   3.50 3.50

20th anniv. of 1st agricultural cooperative.

Souvenir Sheet

A245

Designs (Rowland Hill and): No. 1077a, Mongolia No. 4, Bulgaria No. 1, Philaserdica Emblem. No. 1077b, American mail coach. No. 1077c, Mail car, London-Birmingham railroad, 1838. 1077d, Packet leaving Southampton, Sept. 24, 1842, opening Indian mail service.

1979, May 15   Litho.   Perf. 12
1077 Sheet of 4, multi   4.50 4.50
  a.-d. A245 1t any single   1.00 .90

Philaserdica '79, Sofia, May 18-27, and Rowland Hill (1795-1879), originator of penny postage.

Rocket, Manchester, 1829 — A246

Locomotives: 20m, "Adler" Nuremberg-Furth, 1835. 30m, American engine, 1860. 40m, Ulan Bator-Nalajh run, 1931. 50m, Moscow-Ulan Bator run, 1936. 60m, Moscow-Ulan Bator, 1970. 70m, Tokyo-Osaka run, 1963. 80m, Orleans Aerotrain, 1967. 1.20t, Soviet Rapidity, experimental train.

1979, June 8   Litho.   Perf. 12
1078	A246	10m multi	.25 .25
1079	A246	20m multi	.30 .25
1080	A246	30m multi	.45 .25
1081	A246	40m multi	.50 .25
1082	A246	50m multi	.60 .30
1083	A246	60m multi	.65 .30
1084	A246	70m multi	.90 .30
1085	A246	80m multi	.95 .45
1086	A246	1.20t multi	1.00 .60
		Nos. 1078-1086 (9)	5.60 2.95

Intl. Transportation Exhibition, Hamburg. For surcharge see No. 2144B.

Mongolian and Russian Flags — A247

Battle Scene and Emblem A248

1979, Aug. 10   Photo.   Perf. 11½x12
|1087|A247|60m multi|.75 .30|
|1088|A248|60m multi|.75 .30|

Battle of Ha-lo-hsin River, 40th anniversary.

Manuls A249

Wild Cats: 30m, Lynx. 50m, Tigers. 60m, Snow leopards. 70m, Black panthers. 80m, Cheetahs. 1t, Lions.

1979, Sept. 10   Litho.   Perf. 12
1089	A249	10m multi	.25 .25
1090	A249	30m multi	.35 .25
1091	A249	50m multi	.55 .25
1092	A249	60m multi	.60 .25
1093	A249	70m multi	.75 .30
1094	A249	80m multi	.85 .40
1095	A249	1.25	1.25 .50
		Nos. 1089-1095 (7)	4.60 2.20

Souvenir Sheet

A250

a, Brazil No. 1582. b, Brazil #1144 (Pele). c, Mongolia #C1.

1979, Sept. 15   Litho.   Perf. 11
1096 Sheet of 3 + 3 labels   6.75 6.75
  a.-c. A250 1.50t any single + label   2.00 2.00

Brasiliana '79, 3rd World Thematic Stamp Exhibition, Rio de Janeiro, Sept. 15-23.

Cross-Country Skiing, Lake Placid '80 Emblem — A251

30m, Biathlon. 40m, Ice hockey. 50m, Ski jump. 60m, Downhill skiing. 80m, Speed skating. 1.20t, Bobsledding. 4t, Figure skating.

1980, Jan. 20   Litho.   Perf. 11½x12½
1097	A251	20m multi	.25 .25
1098	A251	30m multi	.35 .25
1099	A251	40m multi	.45 .25
1100	A251	50m multi	.60 .25
1101	A251	60m multi	.60 .25
1102	A251	80m multi	.85 .30
1103	A251	1.20t multi	1.00 .40
		Nos. 1097-1103 (7)	4.10 1.95

Souvenir Sheet
1104 A251 4t multi   2.50 2.50

13th Winter Olympic Games, Lake Placid, NY, Feb. 12-24.

Flower Type of 1969
Souvenir Sheet

Design: Landscape and edelweiss.

1980, May 5   Litho.   Perf. 11
1105 A131 4t multi   2.50 2.50

London 1980 Intl. Stamp Exhib., May 6-14. No. 1105 contains one stamp 43x26mm.

Weightlifting, Moscow '80 Emblem — A252

1980, June 2   Litho.   Perf. 12
1106	A252	20m shown	.25 .25
1107	A252	30m Archery	.25 .25
1108	A252	40m Gymnast	.30 .25
1109	A252	50m Running	.40 .25
1110	A252	60m Boxing	.50 .30

1111	A252	80m Judo	.60 .30
1112	A252	1.20t Bicycling	.70 .50
		Nos. 1106-1112 (7)	3.00 2.10

Souvenir Sheet

1113	A252	4t Wrestling	2.50 2.00

22nd Summer Olympic Games, Moscow, July 19-Aug. 3.

Gold Medal, Swimmer, Moscow '80 Emblem — A253

Gold Medal, Moscow '80 Emblem and Number of Medals won by Top Countries: 30m, Fencing. 50m, Judo. 60m, Track. 80m, Boxing. 1t, Weight lifting. 1.20t, Kayak.

1980, Sept. 15   Litho.   Perf. 12½

1114	A253	20m multi	.25 .25
1115	A253	30m multi	.25 .25
1116	A253	50m multi	.30 .25
1117	A253	60m multi	.40 .25
1118	A253	80m multi	.50 .30
1119	A253	1t multi	.70 .40
1120	A253	1.20t multi	.90 .50
		Nos. 1114-1120 (7)	3.30 2.20

See No. C144.

A254

1980, Sept. 17   Perf. 11½x12

1121	A254	60m Jumdshaigiin Zedenbal	.30 .25
1122	A254	60m Zedenbal, 1941, grn	.30 .25
1123	A254	60m Zedenbal, 1979, gray grn	.30 .25
1124	A254	60m with Brezhnev, horiz.	.30 .25
1125	A254	60m with children	.30 .25
1126	A254	60m Sukhe Bator, dk brn	.30 .25
1127	A254	60m Choibalsan, ultra	.30 .25
		Nos. 1121-1127 (7)	2.10 1.75

Miniature Sheet

Benz, Germany, 1885 — A256

Antique Cars: 30m, President, Austria-Hungary, 1897. 40m, Armstrong Siddley, 1904. 50m, Russo-Balt, 1909. 60m, Packard, United States, 1909. 80m, Lancia, Italy, 1911. 1.60t, Marne taxi, France, 1914. 4t, Nami-1, Russia, 1927.

1980, Nov. 20   Litho.   Perf. 12½

1129	A256	20m multi	.25 .25
1130	A256	30m multi	.25 .25
1131	A256	40rn multi	.45 .25
1132	A256	50m multi	.50 .35
1133	A256	60m multi	.60 .40
1134	A256	80m multi	.80 .50
1135	A256	1.60t multi	1.75 .75
		Nos. 1129-1135 (7)	4.60 2.75

Souvenir Sheet

1136	A256	4t multi	3.50 3.50

Penguins A257

1980, Dec. 1   Perf. 12

1137	A257	20m shown	.90 .25
1138	A257	30m Giant blue whale	1.25 .40
1139	A257	40m Albatross	1.50 .50
1140	A257	50m Weddell seals	1.75 .60
1141	A257	60m Emperor penguins	2.00 .70
1142	A257	70m Skua	2.25 .80
1143	A257	80m Grampus	2.75 1.00
1144	A257	1.20t Penguins, Soviet plane	3.25 1.25
		Nos. 1137-1144 (8)	15.65 5.50

Souvenir Sheet

1145	A257	4t World map showing continental drift	7.50 7.50

Antarctic animals and exploration. No. 1145 contains one 44mm circular stamp.

Souvenir Sheet

A258

1980, Dec. 20   Litho.   Perf. 11

1146		Sheet of 2	3.50 2.00
a.		A258 2t shown	1.50 .85
b.		A258 2t Old Marketplace	1.50 .85

The Shepherd Speaking the Truth, IYC Emblem A259

IYC Emblem and Nursery Tales: 30m, Above Them the Sky is Always Clear. 40m, Winter's Joys. 50m, Little Musicians. 60m, Happy Birthday. 80m, The First Day of School. 1.20t, May Day. 4t, The Wonderworking Squirrels.

1980, Dec. 29   Perf. 12

1147	A259	20m multi	.25 .25
1148	A259	30m multi	.25 .25
1149	A259	40m multi	.30 .25
1150	A259	50m multi	.40 .25
1151	A259	60m multi	.50 .30
1152	A259	80m multi	.60 .40
1153	A259	1.20t multi	.75 .50
		Nos. 1147-1153 (7)	3.05 2.20

Souvenir Sheet

1154	A259	4t multi	3.00 2.00

Intl. Year of the Child (1979).

60th Anniversary of People's Army — A260

1981, Jan. 31   Litho.   Perf. 12

1155	A260	60m multi	.75 .30

60th Anniversary of People's Revolutionary Party — A261

1981, Feb. 2

1156	A261	60m multi	.75 .30

Ice Racing — A262

Designs: Various racing motorcycles.

1981, Feb. 28   Perf. 12½

1157	A262	10m multi	.25 .25
1158	A262	20m multi	.25 .25
1159	A262	30m multi	.30 .25
1160	A262	40m multi	.40 .25
1161	A262	50m multi	.40 .25
1162	A262	60m multi	.50 .25
1163	A262	70m multi	.50 .25
1164	A262	80m multi	.60 .30
1165	A262	1.20t multi	.60 .30
		Nos. 1157-1165 (9)	3.80 2.35

Rocket Designer Koroljov — A263

Designs: 20m, Cosmonauts boarding Soyuz 39. 40m, Vostok I, Yuri Gagarin. 50m, Salyut space station. 60m, Satellite photographing earth. 80m, Light crystallization from Salyut spacecraft. 1.20t, Salyut, Kremlin, Sukhe Bator statue. 4t, Soviet and Mongolian cosmonauts.

1981, Mar. 22   Litho.   Perf. 12

1166	A263	20m multi	.25 .25
1167	A263	30m multi	.30 .25
1168	A263	40m multi	.30 .25
1169	A263	50m multi	.40 .30
1170	A263	60m multi	.40 .30
1171	A263	80m multi	.60 .40
1172	A263	1.20t multi	.80 .60
		Nos. 1166-1172 (7)	3.05 2.35

Souvenir Sheet

Perf. 11½

1173	A263	4t multi	2.50 2.50

Intercosmos cooperative space program (Mongolia-USSR). No. 1173 contains one 29x39mm stamp.

A264

1981, Apr. 28   Litho.   Perf. 12

1174		Sheet of 4 + 4 labels	6.00 6.00
a.		A264 1t No. 240, Ulan Bator + label	1.40 1.25
b.		A264 1t Germany #8N4, 8NB10 + label	1.40 1.25
c.		A264 1t Austria #B110 + label	1.40 1.25
d.		A264 1t Japan #827 + label	1.40 1.25

1981 Stamp Exhibitions: Mongolian Natl., Ulan Bator; Naposta, Stuttgart; WIPA, Vienna; Japex, Tokyo.

Star Shining on Factories and Sheep A265

1981, May 5

1175	A265	60m multi	.75 .30

18th Congress of Revolutionary People's Party, May.

Souvenir Sheet

Statue of Sukhe Bator, Mongolian Flag — A266

1981, May 20   Perf. 12½

1176	A266	4t multi	2.50 1.50

Mongolian Revolutionary People's Party, 60th anniv.

Miniature Sheet (continued, below A255)

A255

Cosmonauts from various Intercosmos flights: a, A. Gubarjev. b, Czechoslovakia #2222. c, P. Klimuk. d, Poland #2270. e, V. Bykovsky. f, DDR #1947. g, N. Rukavishnikov. h, Bulgaria #2576. i, V. Kubasov. j, Hungary #C417.

1980, Oct. 10   Litho.   Perf. 12

1128		Sheet of 10	3.50 3.50
a.-j.		A255 40m any single	.30 .30

Intercosmos cooperative space program. See No. 1232.

Sheep Farming (Economic Development) — A267

1981, June 1   *Perf. 12½x11½*
1177	A267	20m shown	.25	.25
1178	A267	30m Transportation	.30	.25
1179	A267	40m Telecommunications	.40	.25
1180	A267	50m Public health service	.50	.35
1181	A267	60m Agriculture	.60	.30
1182	A267	80m Power plant	.80	.40
1183	A267	1.20t Public housing	1.25	.60
		Nos. 1177-1183 (7)	4.10	2.40

Souvenir Sheet

A268

1981, July 11   **Litho**   *Perf. 12½x11½*
1184	A268	4t multi	2.50	2.50

20th anniv. of UN membership.

A269

Designs: Sailing ships. 10m, 20m, horiz.

1981, Aug. 1   *Perf. 12*
1185	A269	10m Egyptian, 15th cent. BC	.25	.25
1186	A269	20m Mediterranean, 9th cent.	.25	.25
1187	A269	40m Hansa Cog, 12th cent.	.35	.30
1188	A269	50m Venitian, 13th cent.	.50	.30
1189	A269	60m Santa Maria	.60	.40
1190	A269	80m Endeavor	.70	.40
1191	A269	1t Poltava, 18th cent.	.85	.45
1192	A269	1.20t US schooner, 19th cent.	1.00	.50
		Nos. 1185-1192 (8)	4.50	2.85

Mongolian-USSR Friendship Pact — A270

1981, Sept. 1   *Perf. 11½x12*
1193	A270	60m multi	.75	.30

Flora, by Rembrandt A271

1981, Sept. 1   *Perf. 11½x12½*
1194	A271	20m shown	.25	.25
1195	A271	30m Hendrickje in the Bed	.35	.25
1196	A271	40m Young Woman with Earrings	.40	.25
1197	A271	50m Young Girl in the Window	.50	.30
1198	A271	60m Hendrickje like Flora	.75	.30
1199	A271	80m Saskia with Red Flower	1.00	.50
1200	A271	1.20t Holy Family with Drape	1.25	.60
		Nos. 1194-1200 (7)	4.50	2.45

Souvenir Sheet
1201	A271	4t Self-portrait with Saskia	4.50	4.50

375th birth anniv. of Rembrandt.

Goat (Pawn) — A272

Designs: Wood chess pieces.

1981, Sept. 30   **Litho.**   *Perf. 12½*
1202	A272	20m shown	.25	.25
1203	A272	40m Cart (castle)	.50	.25
1204	A272	50m Camel (bishop)	.60	.30
1205	A272	60m Horse (knight)	.70	.40
1206	A272	80m Lion (queen)	.95	.50
1207	A272	1.20t Man and dog (king)	1.25	.75
		Nos. 1202-1207 (6)	4.25	2.45

Souvenir Sheet
1208	A272	4t Men playing	4.25	4.25

Camel and Circus Tent A273

1981, Oct. 30   **Litho.**   *Perf. 12*
1209	A273	10m shown	.25	.25
1210	A273	20m Horsemen	.25	.25
1211	A273	40m Wrestlers	.35	.25
1212	A273	50m Archers	.45	.30
1213	A273	60m Folksinger	.55	.35

1214	A273	80m Girl playing jatga	.65	.35
1215	A273	1t Ballet dancers	.95	.50
1216	A273	1.20t Statue	1.10	.60
		Nos. 1209-1216 (8)	4.55	2.85

Wolfgang Amadeus Mozart and Scene from his Magic Flute — A274

Composers and Scenes from their Works.

1981, Nov. 16
1217	A274	20m shown	.30	.25
1218	A274	30m Beethoven, Fidelio	.40	.25
1219	A274	40m Bartok, Miraculous Mandarin	.40	.25
1220	A274	50m Verdi, Aida	.50	.30
1221	A274	60m Tchaikovsky, Sleeping Beauty	.50	.30
1222	A274	80m Dvorak, New World Symphony score	.80	.40
1223	A274	1.20t Chopin, piano	1.25	.50
		Nos. 1217-1223 (7)	4.15	2.25

Ribbon Weaver A275

Designs: Mongolian women.

Perf. 11½x12½

1981, Dec. 10   **Litho.**
1224	A275	20m multi	.25	.25
1225	A275	30m multi	.35	.25
1226	A275	40m multi	.45	.25
1227	A275	50m multi	.50	.25
1228	A275	60m multi	.60	.40
1229	A275	80m multi	.60	.50
1230	A275	1.20t multi	1.25	.75
		Nos. 1224-1230 (7)	4.00	2.65

Souvenir Sheet
1231	A275	4t multi	4.00	4.00

For surcharge, see No. 2728.

Intercosmos Type of 1980

Designs: a, V. Gorbatko. b, Y. Romanenko. c, V. Dzhanibekov. d, L. Popov. e, Vietnamese stamp. f, Cuban stamp. g, No. 1173. h, Romania No. C241.

1981, Dec. 28   *Perf. 12*
1232		Sheet of 8, multi	4.50	4.50
a.-h.	A255	50m, any single	.50	.35

Historic Bicycles A276

1982, Mar. 25   **Litho.**   *Perf. 11*
1233	A276	10m Germany, 1816	.25	.25
1234	A276	20m Scotland, 1838	.25	.25
1235	A276	40m US, 1866	.30	.25
1236	A276	50m France, 1863	.40	.25
1237	A276	60m "Kangaroo", 1877	.50	.30
1238	A276	80m England, 1870	.60	.30
1239	A276	1t 1878	.70	.40
1240	A276	1.20t Modern bike	.80	.40
		Nos. 1233-1240 (8)	3.80	2.40

Souvenir Sheet

Perf. 12½
1241	A276	4t Racing	3.50	3.50

No. 1241 contains one stamp 47x47mm.

1982 World Cup A277

1982, Apr. 20   *Perf. 12*
1242	A277	10m Brazil, 1950	.25	.25
1243	A277	20m Switzerland, 1954	.25	.25
1244	A277	40m Sweden, 1958	.30	.25
1245	A277	50m Chile, 1962	.40	.25
1246	A277	60m England, 1966	.50	.30
1247	A277	80m Mexico, 1970	.60	.30
1248	A277	1t Germany, 1974	.70	.40
1249	A277	1.20t Argentina, 1978	.80	.40
		Nos. 1242-1249 (8)	3.80	2.40

Souvenir Sheet

Perf. 11
1250	A277	4t Spain, 1982	3.00	3.00

No. 1250 contains one stamp 48x48mm.

12th Trade Union Congress, Ulan Bator A278

1982, May 20   **Litho.**   *Perf. 11½x12½*
1251	A278	60m multi	1.40	.50

Souvenir Sheet

PHILEXFRANCE Intl. Stamp Exhibition, Paris, June 11-21 — A279

1982, June 11   *Imperf.*
1252	A279	4t No. B13 design	3.00	3.00

George Dimitrov (1882-1949), First Prime Minister of Bulgaria — A280

1982, June 18   *Perf. 12*
1253	A280	60m gold & blk	.75	.30

Chicks — A281

1982, June 25   **Perf. 11**
1254	A281	10m shown	.25	.25
1255	A281	20m Colt	.25	.25
1256	A281	30m Lamb	.40	.25
1257	A281	40m Fawn	.45	.25
1258	A281	50m Camel calf	.55	.25
1259	A281	60m Kid	.60	.25
1260	A281	70m Calf	.70	.30
1261	A281	1.20t Young boar	.90	.30
		Nos. 1254-1261 (8)	4.10	2.10

Coal Mining Industry — A282

1982, July 5   **Perf. 12**
1262	A282	60m Mine, truck	.75	.30

18th Mongolian
Youth Org.
Congress
A283

1982, Aug. 14   **Perf. 11½x12**
1263	A283	60m multi	.75	.30

Siberian
Pine
A284

1982, Aug. 16
1264	A284	20m shown	.25	.25
1265	A284	30m Abies sibirica	.25	.25
1266	A284	40m Populus diver-sifolia	.40	.25
1267	A284	50m Larix sibirica	.55	.25
1268	A284	60m Pinus silvestris	.65	.25
1269	A284	80m Betula platyphyl-la	.80	.30
1270	A284	1.20t Picea obovata	1.20	.40
		Nos. 1264-1270 (7)	4.10	1.95

60th Anniv. of
Mongolian
Youth
Org. — A285

1982, Aug. 30
1271	A285	60m multi	.75	.30

Iseki-6500 Tractor, Japan — A286

1982, Oct. 1   **Litho.**   **Perf. 12½**
1272	A286	10m shown	.25	.25
1273	A286	20m Deutz-DX-230, Germany	.25	.25
1274	A286	40m Bonser, Gt. Brit-ain	.30	.25
1275	A286	50m Intl.-884, US	.40	.25
1276	A286	60m Renault TX-145-14, France	.50	.30
1277	A286	80m Belarus-611, USSR	.60	.30
1278	A286	1t K-7100, USSR	.70	.40
1279	A286	1.20t DT-75, USSR	.80	.40
		Nos. 1272-1279 (8)	3.80	2.40

Scenes
from The
Foal and
The Hare
Folktale
A287

1983, Jan. 1   **Litho.**   **Perf. 14**
1280	A287	10m multi	.25	.25
1281	A287	20m multi	.25	.25
1282	A287	30m multi	.30	.25
1283	A287	40m multi	.35	.30
1284	A287	50m multi	.45	.30
1285	A287	60m multi	.55	.40
1286	A287	70m multi	.75	.40
1287	A287	80m multi	.95	.40
1288	A287	1.20t multi	1.10	.50
		Nos. 1280-1288 (9)	4.95	3.05

Souvenir Sheet
Imperf
1289	A287	7t multi	4.50	4.50

No. 1289 contains one stamp 58x58mm.

Scenes from Walt Disney's The
Sorcerer's Apprentice — A288

1983, Jan. 1
1290	A288	25m multi	.25	.25
1291	A288	35m multi	.30	.25
1292	A288	45m multi	.35	.25
1293	A288	55m multi	.45	.30
1294	A288	65m multi	.55	.30
1295	A288	75m multi	.65	.30
1296	A288	85m multi	.85	.30
1297	A288	1.40t multi	1.00	.40
1298	A288	2t multi	1.10	.45
		Nos. 1290-1298 (9)	5.50	2.80

Souvenir Sheet
1299	A288	7t multi	4.50	4.50

Fish, Lake Hevsgel — A289

1982, Nov. 30   **Perf. 12**
1300	A289	20m shown	.25	.25
1301	A289	30m Sheep, Zavhan Highlands	.25	.25
1302	A289	40m Beaver, Lake Hovd	.30	.25
1303	A289	50m Horses, Lake Uvs	.40	.35
1304	A289	60m Chamois, Bajanhongor Steppe	.50	.25
1305	A289	80m Mounted hunter, eagle, Rajan-Elgij Highlands	1.40	.45
1306	A289	1.20t Camels, Gobi Desert	1.40	.50
		Nos. 1300-1306 (7)	4.50	2.50

Mongolian Skin Tent (Yurt) — A290

1983, Mar. 30   **Litho.**   **Perf. 14**
1307	A290	20m Antonov AN-24B plane	.30	.25
1308	A290	30m shown	.40	.25
1309	A290	40m Deer	.50	.25
1310	A290	50m Bighorn sheep	.60	.30
1311	A290	60m Eagle	.75	.50
1312	A290	80m Museum of the Khans, Ulan Bator	.90	.55
1313	A290	1.20t Sukhe Bator monument, Ulan Bator	1.10	.60
		Nos. 1307-1313 (7)	4.55	2.70

For surcharge, see No. 2670.

Souvenir Sheet

90th Birth Anniv. of Sukhe
Bator — A291

1983   **Perf. 13x14**
1314	A291	4t multi	4.50	4.50

Local Flowers — A292

1983, Feb. 4   **Photo.**   **Perf. 13**
1315	A292	20m Rose	.25	.25
1316	A292	30m Dahlias	.30	.25
1317	A292	40m Tagetes faula	.35	.25
1318	A292	50m Narcissus	.40	.25
1319	A292	60m Violets	.50	.30
1320	A292	80m Tulips	.65	.30
1321	A292	1.20t Heliopsis helian-thoides	.75	.40
		Nos. 1315-1321 (7)	3.20	2.00

50th Anniv. of
Border
Forces — A293

1983, Feb. 9   **Litho.**   **Perf. 14**
1322	A293	60m multi	.75	.30

Souvenir Sheet

BRASILIANA, Philatelic
Exhibition — A294

1983, July 10   **Litho.**   **Perf. 14**
1323	A294	4t multi	3.00	2.50

Karl
Marx — A295

1983, Oct. 1   **Litho.**   **Perf. 14**
1324	A295	60m gold, dp car & bl	.75	.30

18th Party Congress, Ulan
Bator — A296

1983, Nov. 1   **Litho.**   **Perf. 14**
1325	A296	10m Cattle	.25	.25
1326	A296	20m Coal	.25	.25
1327	A296	30m Garment	.30	.25
1328	A296	40m Agricultural	.40	.30
1329	A296	60m Communications	.60	.30
1330	A296	80m Transportation	1.50	.60
1331	A296	1t Educational Sys-tem	1.00	.60
		Nos. 1325-1331 (7)	4.30	2.55

Souvenir Sheet

Sistine Madonna, by Raphael (1483-1520) — A297

1983, Dec. 15   Litho.   Perf. 14x13½
1332 A297 4t multi   4.00 4.00

A298

Children in Various Activities.

1984, Jan. 1   Photo.   Perf. 13
1333 A298 10m multi   .25 .25
1334 A298 20m multi   .25 .25
1335 A298 30m multi   .30 .25
1336 A298 40m multi   .45 .25
1337 A298 50m multi   .75 .35
1338 A298 70m multi   1.10 .50
1339 A298 1.20t multi   1.50 .75
      Nos. 1333-1339 (7)   4.60 2.60

Rodents — A299

Various rodents.

1984, Jan. 15   Litho.   Perf. 13½x13
1340 A299 20m multi   .30 .25
1341 A299 30m multi   .50 .25
1342 A299 40m multi   .70 .30
1343 A299 50m multi   .80 .40
1344 A299 60m multi   1.00 .50
1345 A299 80m multi   1.25 .75
1346 A299 1.20t multi   1.60 1.00
      Nos. 1340-1346 (7)   6.15 3.45

1984 Winter Olympics — A300

1984, Feb. 15   Litho.   Perf. 14
1347 A300 20m Bobsledding   .25 .25
1348 A300 30m Cross-country
                   skiing   .25 .25
1349 A300 40m Hockey   .35 .25
1350 A300 50m Speed skating   .35 .25
1351 A300 60m Downhill skiing   .50 .25

1352 A300 80m Figure skating   .70 .25
1353 A300 1.20t Biathlon   .75 .40
      Nos. 1347-1353 (7)   3.15 1.90
      Souvenir Sheet
1354 A300 4t Ski jumping   3.25 3.25
      Size of No. 1354: 134x106mm. Nos. 1347-
1352 vert.

Children Feeding Lambs — A301

1984, Mar. 1   Litho.   Perf. 12
1355 A301 20m Ice skating   .25 .25
1356 A301 30m shown   .30 .25
1357 A301 40m Planting tree   .40 .25
1358 A301 50m Playing on
                   beach   .40 .25
1359 A301 60m Carrying pail   .50 .30
1360 A301 80m Dancing   .60 .30
1361 A301 1.20t Dancing, diff. 1.00 .40
      Nos. 1355-1361 (7)   3.45 2.00
      Souvenir Sheet
1362 A301 4t Boy, girl   3.00 3.00
      No. 1362 contains one stamp 48x46mm.
Compare with Type SP3. For surcharges, see
Nos. 2656-2657.

Mail Car, Communications
Emblems — A302

1984, Apr. 15   Perf. 13½x14
1363 A302 10m shown   .25 .25
1364 A302 20m Earth satellite
                   receiving sta-
                   tion   .30 .25
1365 A302 40m Airplane   .40 .25
1366 A302 50m Central PO   .50 .35
1367 A302 1t Radar station   .90 .40
1368 A302 1.20t Train   2.00 1.00
      Nos. 1363-1368 (6)   4.35 2.50
      Souvenir Sheet
      Imperf
1369 A302 4t Dish antenna   4.50 3.50

1984 Summer Olympics — A303

1984, June 1   Photo.   Perf. 14
1370 A303 20m Gymnastics   .25 .25
1371 A303 30m Bicycling   .25 .25
1372 A303 40m Weight lifting   .35 .25
1373 A303 50m Judo   .35 .25
1374 A303 60m Archery   .50 .25
1375 A303 80m Boxing   .50 .25
1376 A303 1.20t High jump   .75 .35
      Nos. 1370-1376 (7)   2.95 1.85
      Souvenir Sheet
1377 A303 4t Wrestling   3.25 2.25

Souvenir Sheet

AUSIPEX '84 and ESPANA
'84 — A304

1984, May   Litho.   Perf. 14
1378 A304 4t Jet   4.00 4.00

Cuban
Revolution, 25th
Anniv. — A304a

1984, June 2   Litho.   Perf. 14
1378A A304a 60m multi   .75 .30

State Bank,
60th Anniv.
A304b

1984, Sept. 25   Perf. 13½x13
1378B A304b 60m Commemora-
                     tive coins,
                     1981   .75 .30

Radio
Broadcasting in
Mongolia, 50th
Anniv. — A304c

1984, Sept. 1   Litho.   Perf. 13x13½
1378C A304c 60m multicolored   .90 .30

Scenes from Walt Disney's Mickey and
the Beanstalk — A305

1984, Dec. 20   Litho.   Perf. 11
1379 A305 25m multi   .30 .25
1380 A305 35m multi   .40 .25
1381 A305 45m multi   .55 .25
1382 A305 55m multi   .65 .25
1383 A305 65m multi   .75 .30
1384 A305 75m multi   .85 .40
1385 A305 85m multi   .95 .50
1386 A305 1.40t multi   1.10 .65
1387 A305 2t multi   1.40 .80
      Nos. 1379-1387 (9)   6.95 3.65
      Miniature Sheet
      Perf. 14
1388 A305 7t multi   4.00 4.00

Fairy Tales — A306

1984, Dec. 20   Litho.   Perf. 13½
1389 A306 10m multi   .25 .25
1390 A306 20m multi   .30 .25
1391 A306 30m multi   .35 .25
1392 A306 40m multi   .40 .25
1393 A306 50m multi   .45 .25
1394 A306 60m multi   .50 .25
1395 A306 70m multi   .60 .35
1396 A306 80m multi   .75 .40
1397 A306 1.20t multi   .90 .55
      Nos. 1389-1397 (9)   4.50 2.80
      Miniature Sheet
1398 A306 4t multi   4.00 4.00

Souvenir Sheet

60th Anniv. of Mongolian
Stamps — A308

1984, Dec. 20   Litho.   Perf. 14
1400 A308 4t No. 1   4.50 3.50

Ulan Bator, 60th
Anniv. — A309

Mongolian
People's
Republic, 60th
Anniv. — A310

1984, Nov. 26   Litho.   Perf. 13x13½
1401 A309 60m multicolored   .75 .40
      Perf. 14
1402 A310 60m multicolored   .75 .40

Mongolian People's Party, 60th Anniv. — A311

1984, Nov. 26   Litho.   Perf. 14
1403 A311 60m multi   .90 .30

Native Masks — A312

1984, Dec. 31   Litho.   Perf. 14
1404 A312 20m multi   .25 .25
1405 A312 30m multi   .30 .25
1406 A312 40m multi   .45 .25
1407 A312 50m multi   .55 .25
1408 A312 60m multi   .75 .30
1409 A312 80m multi   1.00 .30
1410 A312 1.20t multi   1.25 .50
        Nos. 1404-1410 (7)   4.55 2.10
        Souvenir Sheet
1411 A312 4t multi   4.50 4.50

Dogs A313

1984, Dec. 31   Litho.   Perf. 13
1412 A313 20m Collie   .25 .25
1413 A313 30m German Sheep-
               dog   .30 .25
1414 A313 40m Papillon   .45 .25
1415 A313 50m Cocker Spaniel   .55 .25
1416 A313 60m Puppy   .75 .30
1417 A313 80m Dalmatians   1.00 .30
1418 A313 1.20t Mongolian
               Sheepdog   1.25 .50
        Nos. 1412-1418 (7)   4.55 2.10

Cattle — A314

1985, Jan.   Perf. 14
1419 A314 20m Shar tarlan   .25 .25
1420 A314 30m Bor khaliun   .35 .25
1421 A314 40m Sarlag   .45 .25
1422 A314 50m Dornod taliin
               bukh   .50 .25
1423 A314 60m Char tarlan   .60 .25
1424 A314 80m Nutgiin uulderiin
               unee   .80 .35
1425 A314 1.20t Tsagaan tolgoit   .95 .35
        Nos. 1419-1425 (7)   3.90 1.95

1984 Olympic Winners — A315

Gold medalists: 20m, Gaetan Boucher, Canada, 1500-meter speed skating. 30m, Eirik Kvalfoss, Norway, 10-kilometer biathlon. 40m, Marja-Lissa Haemaelainen, Finland, 5-kilometer Nordic skiing. 50m, Max Julen, Switzerland, men's giant slalom. 60m, Jens Weissflog, German Democratic Republic, 70-meter ski jump. 80m, W. Hoppe and D. Schauerhammer, German Democratic Republic, 2-man bobsled. 1.20t, Elena Valova and Oleg Vasiliev, USSR, pairs figure skating. 4t, USSR, ice hockey. Nos. 1430-1432 vert.

1985, Apr. 25
1426 A315 20m multi   .25 .25
1427 A315 30m multi   .30 .25
1428 A315 40m multi   .40 .30
1429 A315 50m multi   .40 .30
1430 A315 60m multi   .60 .40
1431 A315 80m multi   .70 .50
1432 A315 1.20t multi   .80 .60
        Nos. 1426-1432 (7)   3.45 2.60
        Souvenir Sheet
1433 A315 4t multi   3.50 3.00

Souvenir Sheet

Girl, Fawn — A316

1985, Apr. 25
1434 A316 4m multi   4.00 4.00

Birds — A317

1985, May 1   Perf. 12½x13
1435 A317 20m Ciconia nigra   .25 .25
1436 A317 30m Haliaetus albicil-
               la   .35 .25
1437 A317 40m Grus leucoger-
               anus   .50 .25
1438 A317 50m Paradoxornis
               heudei   .60 .25
1439 A317 60m Grus monacha   .80 .30
1440 A317 80m Grus vipio   1.00 .40
1441 A317 1.20t Buteo lagopus   1.25 .50
        Nos. 1435-1441 (7)   4.75 2.20

National Wildlife Preservation Association.

World Youth Festival, Moscow A318

1985, June   Perf. 14
1442 A318 60m Girls in folk cos-
               tumes   .80 .40

Camelus Bactrianus — A319

Panthera Unicias — A320

Cervus Elaphus — A321

Camels, leopards and deer.

1985
1443 A319 50m Adults, young   1.50 .40
1444 A319 50m Facing right   1.50 .40
1445 A319 50m Facing left   1.50 .40
1446 A319 50m Trotting   1.50 .40
1447 A320 50m Hunting   .60 .40
1448 A320 50m Standing in
               snow   .60 .40
1449 A320 50m Female, young   .60 .40
1450 A320 50m Adults   .60 .40
1451 A321 50m Fawn   1.25 .40
1452 A321 50m Doe in woods   1.25 .40
1453 A321 50m Adult male   1.25 .40
1454 A321 50m Adults, fawn   1.25 .40
        Nos. 1443-1454 (12)   13.40 4.80

#1443-1446 show the World Wildlife Fund emblem, #1447-1454 the Natl. Wildlife Preservation emblem. Issue dates: #1443-1446, July 1; #1447-1454, Aug. 1.

UN, 40th Anniv. A322

1985, Aug. 1   Perf. 13½x13
1455 A322 60m Flags, UN build-
               ing   .75 .40

Indigenous Flowering Plants — A323

1985, Aug. 1   Perf. 14
1456 A323 20m Rosa davurica   .25 .25
1457 A323 30m Matricaria
               chamomilla   .35 .25
1458 A323 40m Taraxacum of-
               ficinale   .50 .25
1459 A323 50m Saxzifraga
               hirculus   .60 .25
1460 A323 60m Vaccinium vitis
               idaea   .70 .25
1461 A323 80m Sanguisorba of-
               ficinalis   .90 .35
1462 A323 1.20t Plantago major   1.25 .40
        Nos. 1456-1462 (7)   4.55 2.00
        Souvenir Sheet
1463 A323 4t Hippophae
               rhamnoides   4.00 4.00

A324

1985, Sept. 15   Perf. 13x13½
1464 A324 60m Monument   .75 .30

Defeat of Nazi Germany, 40th anniv.

A325

Various soccer plays. No. 1472 horiz.

1985, Oct. 1   Perf. 14
1465 A325 20m multi   .25 .25
1466 A325 30m multi   .25 .25
1467 A325 40m multi   .25 .25
1468 A325 50m multi   .35 .25
1469 A325 60m multi   .40 .25
1470 A325 80m multi   .50 .25
1471 A325 1.20t multi   .55 .25
        Nos. 1465-1471 (7)   2.55 1.75
        Souvenir Sheet
1472 A325 4t multi   3.00 2.50

1985 Junior World Soccer Championships, Moscow.

Souvenir Sheet

ITALIA '85 — A326

1985, Oct. 1
1473 A326 4t Horseman   3.25 2.50

Conquest of Space — A327

Russian spacecraft.

1985, Nov. 1
1474 A327 20m Soyuz   .25 .25
1475 A327 30m Cosmos   .25 .25
1476 A327 40m Venera 9   .30 .25
1477 A327 50m Salyut   .35 .25
1478 A327 60m Luna 9   .45 .25
1479 A327 80m Train   1.25 .55
1480 A327 1.20t Dish receiver   1.00 .25
     Nos. 1474-1480 (7)   3.85 2.05

Souvenir Sheet
1985, Dec. 15
1481 A327 4t Cosmonaut on space walk   3.25 2.50

Mushrooms — A328

1985, Dec. 1   Perf. 13½
1482 A328 20m Tricholoma mongolica   .35 .25
1483 A328 30m Cantharellus cibarius   .45 .25
1484 A328 40m Armillariella mellea   .55 .25
1485 A328 50m Amanita caesarea   .65 .25
1486 A328 70m Xerocomus badius   .85 .30
1487 A328 80m Agaricus silvaticus   1.10 .30
1488 A328 1.20t Boletus edulis   1.60 .40
     Nos. 1482-1488 (7)   5.55 2.00

Souvenir Sheet

Phalacrocorax Penicillatus — A329

1986, Jan. 15   Perf. 12½x13
1489 A329 4t multi   3.50 3.50

No. 1489 contains one stamp plus 2 labels picturing various bird species.

Young Pioneers
A330

Victory Monument
A331

1985, Dec. 31   Litho.   Perf. 13x13½
1490 A330 60m multi   .70 .30

1985, Dec. 31   Perf. 12½x13
1491 A331 60m multi   .70 .30

Victory over Japan ending WWII, 40th anniv.

Natl. Costumes
A332

1986, Mar. 1   Litho.   Perf. 14
Background Color
1492 A332 60m yel grn, shown   .50 .25
1493 A332 60m red   .50 .25
1494 A332 60m pale yel grn   .50 .25
1495 A332 60m violet   .50 .25
1496 A332 60m ultra   .50 .25
1497 A332 60m bluish grn   .50 .25
1498 A332 60m pale org brn   .50 .25
     Nos. 1492-1498 (7)   3.50 1.75

Ernst Thalmann (1886-1944)
A333

1986, May 15   Litho.   Perf. 14
1499 A333 60m gold, redsh brn & dk brn   .75 .30

Natl. Revolution, 65th Anniv. — A334

1986, May 15
1500 A334 60m Statue of Sukhe Bator   .70 .30

19th Socialist Party Congress
A335

1986, May 15
1501 A335 60m multi   .70 .30

1986 World Cup Soccer Championships, Mexico — A336

FIFA emblem and various soccer plays. Nos. 1502-1503, 1505-1508 vert.

1986, May 31
1502 A336 20m multi   .25 .25
1503 A336 30m multi   .25 .25
1504 A336 40m multi   .35 .25
1505 A336 50m multi   .45 .25
1506 A336 60m multi   .55 .25
1507 A336 80m multi   .65 .25
1508 A336 1.20t multi   .80 .30
     Nos. 1502-1508 (7)   3.30 1.80

Souvenir Sheet
1509 A336   4t multi   1.90

Mink, Wildlife Conservation — A337

1986, June 15
1510 A337 60m Spring   .60 .30
1511 A337 60m Summer   .60 .30
1512 A337 60m Autumn   .60 .30
1513 A337 60m Winter   .60 .30
     Nos. 1510-1513 (4)   2.40 1.20

Flowers — A338

1986, June 1   Litho.   Perf. 14
1514 A338 20m Valeriana officinalis   .25 .25
1515 A338 30m Hyoscymus niger   .30 .25
1516 A338 40m Ephedra sinica   .35 .25
1517 A338 50m Thymus gobica   .40 .25
1518 A338 60m Paeonia anomala   .50 .25
1519 A338 80m Achilea millefolium   .75 .30
1520 A338 1.20t Rhododendron adamsii   1.00 .40
     Nos. 1514-1520 (7)   3.55 1.95

Butterflies — A339

1986, Aug. 1   Perf. 13½
1521 A339 20m Neptis coenobita   .25 .25
1522 A339 30m Colias tycha   .25 .25
1523 A339 40m Leptidea amurensis   .35 .25
1524 A339 50m Oeneis tarpenledevi   .40 .25
1525 A339 60m Mesoacidalia charlotta   .45 .25
1526 A339 80m Smerinthus ocellatus   .55 .30
1527 A339 1.20t Pericalia matronula   .85 .40
     Nos. 1521-1527 (7)   3.10 1.95

Circus — A340

Animal trainers & acrobats. #1531-1534 vert.

1986, Aug. 1   Perf. 14
1528 A340 20m multi   .25 .25
1529 A340 30m multi   .30 .25
1530 A340 40m multi   .35 .25
1531 A340 50m multi   .40 .25
1532 A340 60m multi   .50 .25
1533 A340 80m multi   .75 .25
1534 A340 1.20t multi   1.00 .30
     Nos. 1528-1534 (7)   3.55 1.80

Przewalski's Horses — A341

1986, Aug. 1   Litho.   Perf. 14
1535 A341 50m Two horses, foal   .75 .40
1536 A341 50m One facing left, two facing right   .75 .40
1537 A341 50m Three facing right   .75 .40
1538 A341 50m Four in storm   .75 .40
     Nos. 1535-1538 (4)   3.00 1.60

Pelicans (Pelecanus) — A341a

1986, Sept. 1   Litho.   Perf. 14
1538A A341a 60m Crispus feeding   .80 .50
1538B A341a 60m Crispus wading   .80 .50
1538C A341a 60m Onocrotalus flying   .80 .50
1538D A341a 60m Onocrotalus on land   .80 .50
     Nos. 1538A-1538D (4)   3.20 2.00

Saiga tatarica mongolica — A341b

1986, Sept. 15
1538E	A341b	60m	Spring (doe, fawn)	.75 .40
1538F	A341b	60m	Summer (buck, doe)	.75 .40
1538G	A341b	60m	Fall (buck)	.75 .40
1538H	A341b	60m	Winter (buck, doe)	.75 .40
		Nos. 1538E-1538H (4)		3.00 1.60

Musical Instruments — A342

1986, Sept. 4
1539	A342	20m	Morin khuur	.25 .25
1540	A342	30m	Bishguur	.30 .25
1541	A342	40m	Ever buree	.35 .25
1542	A342	50m	Shudarga	.40 .25
1543	A342	60m	Khiil	.50 .25
1544	A342	80m	Janchir	.75 .30
1545	A342	1.20t	Jatga	1.00 .30
		Nos. 1539-1545 (7)		3.55 1.85

Souvenir Sheet
1546	A342	4t	like 20m, vert.	3.50 3.50

STOCKHOLMIA '86. Nos. 1539-1543 vert.

Intl. Peace
Year — A342a

1986, Sept. 20   Litho.   Perf. 13x13½
1546A	A342a	10m	multicolored	.75 .30

North American Bird Species — A343

1986, Oct. 1
1547	A343	60m	Anthus spinoletta	.80 .50
1548	A343	60m	Aythya americana	.80 .50
1549	A343	60m	Bonasa umbellus	.80 .50
1550	A343	60m	Olor columbianus	.80 .50
		Nos. 1547-1550 (4)		3.20 2.00

Eastern Architecture — A343a

Various two-story buildings.

1986, Oct. 1   Color of Border
1551	A343a	60m	dark grn & blk	.75 .40
1552	A343a	60m	beige & blk	.75 .40
1553	A343a	60m	apple grn & blk	.75 .40
1554	A343a	60m	red brn & blk	.75 .40
		Nos. 1551-1554 (4)		3.00 1.60

Classic Automobiles — A344

1986, Oct. 1   Litho.   Perf. 14
1554A	A344	20m	1922 Alfa Romeo RL Sport, Italy	.25 .25
1554B	A344	30m	1912 Stutz Bearcat, US	.30 .25
1554C	A344	40m	1902 Mercedes Simplex, Germany	.35 .25
1554D	A344	50m	1923 Tatra 11, Czechoslovakia	.40 .25
1554E	A344	60m	1908 Ford Model T, US	.50 .25
1554F	A344	80m	1905 Vauxhall, England	.75 .30
1554G	A344	1.20t	1913 Russo-Baltik, Russia	1.00 .40
		Nos. 1554A-1554G (7)		3.55 1.95

Souvenir Sheet
1554H	A344	4t	like 1.20t	3.00 3.00

Woodpeckers
A344a

1986, Nov. 1
1555	A344a	20m	Picus canus	.25 .25
1556	A344a	30m	Jynx torquilla	.30 .25
1557	A344a	40m	Dryobates major	.35 .25
1558	A344a	50m	Dryobates leucotos	.40 .25
1559	A344a	60m	Dryobates minor	.50 .25
1560	A344a	80m	Dryocopus martius	.75 .30
1561	A344a	1.20t	Picoides tridactylus	1.00 .40
		Nos. 1555-1561 (7)		3.55 1.95

Souvenir Sheet
1562	A344a	4t	Saphopipo noguchi	4.00 4.00

Chess Champions — A345

Portraits and chessmen on boards in match-winning configurations. No. 1562H, Chess champions Gary Kasparov, Jose R. Capablanca, Max Euwe, Vassily Smyslow, Mikhail Tal, Tigran Petrosian, Boris Spasski and Bobby Fischer; W. Menchik, L. Rudenko, E. Bykowa and O. Rubzowa.

1986, Nov. 1   Perf. 14
1562A	A345	20m	Steinitz, Austria	.25 .25
1562B	A345	30m	Lasker, Germany	.25 .25
1562C	A345	40m	Alekhine, France	.25 .25
1562D	A345	50m	Botvinnik, USSR	.35 .25
1562E	A345	60m	Karpov, USSR	.45 .25
1562F	A345	80m	N. Gaprindashvili	.55 .25
1562G	A345	1.20t	M. Chiburdanidze	.90 .30

Size: 110x100mm
Imperf
1562H	A345	4t	multi	4.00 4.00
		Nos. 1562A-1562H (8)		7.00 5.80

Souvenir Sheet

Halley's Comet — A346

1986, Nov. 30   Litho.   Perf. 14
1563	A346	4t	multicolored	4.00 2.50

Ovis Ammon Ammon — A347

1987, Jan. 1
1564	A347	60m	shown	.75 .40
1565	A347	60m	In the mountains	.75 .40
1566	A347	60m	Close-up of head	.75 .40
1567	A347	60m	Male, female, lamb	.75 .40
		Nos. 1564-1567 (4)		3.00 1.60

For surcharges, see Nos. 2779-2782.

Children's
Activities
A348

1987, Feb. 1
1568	A348	20m	Backpacking, hunting butterflies	.25 .25
1569	A348	30m	Playing with calves	.30 .25
1570	A348	40m	Chalk-writing on cement	.35 .25
1571	A348	50m	Playing soccer	.40 .25
1572	A348	60m	Go-cart, model rocket, boat	.45 .25
1573	A348	80m	Agriculture	.55 .25
1574	A348	1.20t	Playing the morin khuur, dancing	.80 .30
		Nos. 1568-1574 (7)		3.10 1.80

Int'l. Peace Year (40m); Child Survival Campaign (50m).

13th Trade Unions Congress — A349

1987, Feb. 15   Perf. 13½x13
1575	A349	60m	multi	1.50 1.00

Equestrian Sports — A350

1987, Mar. 1
1576	A350	20m	Lassoer	.25 .25
1577	A350	30m	Breaking horse	.25 .25
1578	A350	40m	Shooting bow	.30 .25
1579	A350	50m	Race	.40 .25
1580	A350	60m	Retrieving flags	.45 .25
1581	A350	80m	Tug-of-war	.55 .25
1582	A350	1.20t	Racing wolf	.85 .30
		Nos. 1576-1582 (7)		3.05 1.85

Admission into
Comecon, 25th
Anniv. — A351

1987, Apr. 15   Perf. 13x13½
1583	A351	60m	multi	.75 .40

Fruit — A352

A353

1987, June 1   Perf. 13½
1584	A352	20m	Hippophae rhamnoides	.35 .25
1585	A352	30m	Ribes nigrum	.50 .25
1586	A352	40m	Ribes rubrus	.65 .25
1587	A352	50m	Ribes altissimum	.75 .25
1588	A352	60m	Rubus sachalinensis	.90 .25
1589	A352	80m	Padus asiatica	1.00 .25
1590	A352	1.20t	Fragaria orientalis	1.40 .25
		Nos. 1584-1590 (7)		5.55 1.75

Souvenir Sheet
Perf. 14
1591	A353	4t	Malus domestica	3.25 3.25

Soviet-Mongolian Diplomatic Relations, 50th Anniv. — A354

1987, July 1   *Perf. 13x13½*
1592 A354 60m multi   .75 .45

Russian Revolution, 70th Anniv. — A355

1987, July 1
1593 A355 60m multi   .75 .45

Folk Dances — A356

1987, Aug. 1   *Perf. 14*
1594 A356 20m multi   .25 .25
1595 A356 30m multi, diff.   .25 .25
1596 A356 40m multi, diff.   .35 .25
1597 A356 50m multi, diff.   .45 .25
1598 A356 60m multi, diff.   .55 .25
1599 A356 80m multi, diff.   .65 .25
1600 A356 1.20t multi, diff.   .80 .30
   Nos. 1594-1600 (7)   3.30 1.80

Antiques A357

Full costume and accessories.

1987, Aug. 10
1601 A357 20m Folk costumes   .25 .25
1602 A357 30m Gilded nunchaku   .25 .25
1603 A357 40m Brooches   .35 .25
1604 A357 50m Draw-string pouch, rice bowl   .45 .25
1605 A357 60m Headdress   .55 .25
1606 A357 80m Pouches, bottle, pipe   .65 .25
1607 A357 1.20t Sash, brooch   .80 .30
   Nos. 1601-1607 (7)   3.30 1.80

Souvenir Sheet

HAFNIA '87 — A358

1987, Aug. 10
1608 A358 4t multi   3.50 3.00

Swans — A359

1987, Aug. 15
1609 A359 60m Cygnus olor on land   .75 .30
1610 A359 60m Cygnus olor in water   .75 .30
1611 A359 60m Cygnus bewickii   .75 .30
1612 A359 60m Cygnus bewickii, gunus and olor   .75 .30
   Nos. 1609-1612 (4)   3.00 1.20

Domestic and Wild Cats — A360

1987, Oct. 1   *Litho.*   *Perf. 14*
1613 A360 20m multi, vert.   .30 .25
1614 A360 30m multi, vert.   .35 .25
1615 A360 40m multi, vert.   .40 .25
1616 A360 50m shown   .50 .25
1617 A360 60m multi   .60 .25
1618 A360 80m multi   .75 .30
1619 A360 1.20t multi   1.10 .30
   Nos. 1613-1619 (7)   4.00 1.85

Miniature Sheet
1620 A360 4t multi, vert.   4.00 3.00

Disney Cartoons — A362

The Brave Little Tailor (25m-55m, 2t, No. 1637), and The Celebrated Jumping Frog of Calaveras County (65m-1.40t, No. 1638).

1987, Nov. 23   *Perf. 14*
1628 A362 25m multi   .25 .25
1629 A362 35m multi   .35 .25
1630 A362 45m multi   .50 .25
1631 A362 55m multi   .60 .25
1632 A362 65m multi   .70 .25
1633 A362 75m multi   .85 .25
1634 A362 85m multi   .95 .30
1635 A362 1.40t multi   1.10 .50
1636 A362 2t multi   1.40 .75
   Nos. 1628-1636 (9)   6.70 3.05

Souvenir Sheets
1637 A362 7t multi   5.50 5.50
1638 A362 7t multi   5.50 5.50

A363

Tropical Fish — A364

1987, Oct.   *Perf. 13x12½, 12½x13*
1639 A363 20m Betta splendens   .25 .25
1640 A363 30m Carassius auratus   .35 .25
1641 A363 40m Rasbora hengeli   .45 .25
1642 A363 50m Aequidens   .60 .25
1643 A363 60m Xiphophorus macalatus   .70 .25
1644 A363 80m Xiphophorus helleri   .90 .25
1645 A363 1.20t Pterophyllum scalare, vert.   1.00 .30
   Nos. 1639-1645 (7)   4.25 1.80

Miniature Sheet
Perf. 14
1646 A364 4t Crenuchus spilurus   4.25 3.75

19th Communist Party Congress A365

1987, Dec.   *Perf. 14*
1647 A365 60m Family   .40 .25
1648 A365 60m Construction   .75 .25
1649 A365 60m Jet, harvesting, produce   .40 .25
1650 A365 60m Education   .40 .25
1651 A365 60m Transportation   .40 .25
1652 A365 60m Heavy industry   .40 .25
1653 A365 60m Science and technology   .40 .25
   Nos. 1647-1653 (7)   3.15 1.75

Vulpes Vulpes (Fox) — A366

1987, Dec.
1654 A366 60m Adult in snow   .65 .30
1655 A366 60m Adult, young   .65 .30
1656 A366 60m Adult in field   .65 .30
1657 A366 60m Close-up of head   .65 .30
   Nos. 1654-1657 (4)   2.60 1.20

Souvenir Sheet

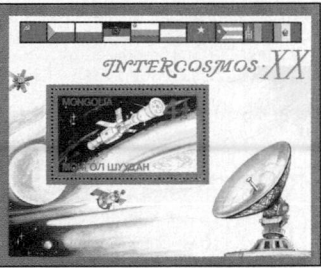

INTERCOSMOS — A367

1987, Dec. 15   *Litho.*   *Perf. 14*
1658 A367 4t multi   3.00 2.50

Souvenir Sheet

PRAGA '88 — A368

1988, Jan. 30
1659 A368 4t 1923 Tatra 11   3.00 2.50

Sukhe Bator — A369

1988, Feb. 2   *Perf. 13x13½*
1660 A369 60m multi   .80 .50

For surcharge, see footnote after No. 2764.

Roses — A370

1988, Feb. 20 — *Perf. 14*
1661 A370 20m Invitation .30 .25
1662 A370 30m Meilland .55 .25
1663 A370 40m Pascali .40 .25
1664 A370 50m Tropicana .50 .25
1665 A370 60m Wendy Cussons .55 .25
1666 A370 80m Blue moon .60 .25
1667 A370 1.20t Diorama .90 .30
Nos. 1661-1667 (7) 3.80 1.80

Souvenir Sheet
1668 A370 4t multicolored 3.25 2.75

19th Communist Youth Congress — A371

1988, Apr. 15 — *Perf. 12½x13*
1669 A371 60m multicolored .80 .50

Puppets — A372

Folk tales.

1988, Apr. 1 — *Litho. Perf. 14*
1670 A372 20m Ukhaant Ekhner .25 .25
1671 A372 30m Altan Everte Mungun Turuut .30 .25
1672 A372 40m Aduuchyn Khuu .40 .25
1673 A372 50m Suulenkhuu .45 .25
1674 A372 60m Khonchyn Khuu .60 .25
1675 A372 80m Argat Byatskhan Baatar .80 .25
1676 A372 1.20t Botgochyn Khuu 1.25 .30
Nos. 1670-1676 (7) 4.05 1.80

1988 Summer Olympics, Seoul — A373

1988, Feb. 15
1677 A373 20m Judo .25 .25
1678 A373 30m Women's archery .25 .25
1679 A373 40m Weight lifting .40 .25
1680 A373 50m Women's gymnastics .45 .25
1681 A373 60m Cycling .50 .25
1682 A373 80m Running .60 .25
1683 A373 1.20t Wrestling 1.00 .30
Nos. 1677-1683 (7) 3.45 1.80

Souvenir Sheet
1684 A373 4t Boxing 3.00 2.50

Soviet Space Achievements A374

1988, May 15
1685 A374 20m Cosmos .25 .25
1686 A374 30m Meteor .25 .25
1687 A374 40m Salyut-Soyuz .40 .25
1688 A374 50m Prognoz-6 .45 .25
1689 A374 60m Molniya-1 .50 .25
1690 A374 80m Soyuz .60 .25
1691 A374 1.20t Vostok 1.00 .25
Nos. 1685-1691 (7) 3.45 1.75

Effigies of Buddhist Deities — A375

Various statues.

1988, June 15 — *Litho. Perf. 14*
1692 A375 20m multi .25 .25
1693 A375 30m multi, diff. .25 .25
1694 A375 40m multi, diff. .35 .25
1695 A375 50m multi, diff. .50 .25
1696 A375 60m multi, diff. .65 .25
1697 A375 70m multi, diff. .85 .25
1698 A375 80m multi, diff. 1.00 .30
1699 A375 1.20t multi, diff. 1.50 .30
Nos. 1692-1699 (8) 5.35 2.10

Wildlife Conservation — A376

Eagles, Haliaeetus albicilla. Nos. 1700-1702 vert.

1988, Aug. 1 — *Litho. Perf. 14*
1700 A376 60m Eagle facing left, diff. .80 .50
1701 A376 60m Landing on branch .80 .50
1702 A376 60m Facing right .80 .50
1703 A376 60m shown .80 .50
Nos. 1700-1703 (4) 3.20 2.00

Souvenir Sheet

Cosmos — A377

1988, Sept. 15 — *Litho. Perf. 14*
1704 A377 4t Satellite links 4.00 4.00

Opera — A378

1988, Oct. 1 — *Litho. Perf. 13x12½*
1705 A378 60m multi + label 1.50 .75

Equus hemionus — A380

1988, May 3
1713 A380 60m Mare, foal .80 .50
1714 A380 60m Ass's head .80 .50
1715 A380 60m Ass galloping .80 .50
1716 A380 60m Ass cantering .80 .50
Nos. 1713-1716 (4) 3.20 2.00

Winners of the 1988 Winter Olympics, Calgary — A381

1988, July 1
1717 A381 1.50t Matti Nykaenen, Finland .70 .30
1718 A381 1.50t Bonnie Blair, US .70 .30
1719 A381 1.50t Alberto Tomba, Italy .70 .30
1720 A381 1.50t USSR hockey team .70 .30
Nos. 1717-1720 (4) 2.80 1.20

Souvenir Sheet
1721 A381 4t Katarina Witt, DDR 3.00 3.00
Nos. 1718-1720 vert.

A382

1988, Sept. 1
1722 A382 10m shown .25 .25
1723 A382 20m Horsemanship .30 .25
1724 A382 30m Archery .35 .25
1725 A382 40m Wrestling .45 .25
1726 A382 50m Archery, diff. .55 .25
1727 A382 70m Horsemanship, diff. .60 .25
1728 A382 1.20t Horsemanship, wrestling, archery .75 .30
Nos. 1722-1728 (7) 3.25 1.80

A383

1988, Dec. 1 — *Perf. 13x13½*
1729 A383 60m multicolored .85 .30
Socialism and Peace.

Goats — A384

Various species.

1989, Jan. 15 — *Perf. 14*
1730 A384 20m multi .30 .25
1731 A384 30m multi .35 .25
1732 A384 40m multi .45 .25
1733 A384 50m multi .50 .25
1734 A384 60m multi .60 .25
1735 A384 80m multi .75 .25
1736 A384 1.20t multi 1.00 .30
Nos. 1730-1736 (7) 3.95 1.80

Souvenir Sheet
1737 A384 4t multi, vert. 3.25 3.25

Souvenir Sheet

Child Survival — A385

1989, Jan. 28 — *Litho. Perf. 14*
1738 A385 4t Drawing by H. Jargalsuren 3.50 2.00

Karl Marx — A386

1989, Feb. 25 — *Litho. Perf. 13x13½*
1739 A386 60m multicolored .75 .30

Miniature Sheet

A387

Mongolian Airline Jet — A388

1989, July 1   *Perf. 14*
1740   Sheet of 3   7.50   7.50
   a. A387 20m Concorde jet   .75   .50
   b. A387 60m TGV high-speed train   2.00   1.75
   c. A387 1.20t Statue of Sukhe Bator   4.50   4.00

Souvenir Sheet

1741 A388   4t multicolored   4.50   4.50
PHILEXFRANCE '89, BULGARIA '89.
For overprint see No. 1756.

World War II
Memorial
A389

1989, Sept. 2
1742 A389   60m multicolored   1.00   .50
For surcharge, see No. 2384B.

Cacti — A390

1989, Sept. 7
1743 A390   20m O. microdasys   .25   .25
1744 A390   30m E. multipiex   .25   .25
1745 A390   40m R. tephra-
     canthus   .45   .25
1746 A390   50m B. haselbergii   .60   .25
1747 A390   60m G. mihanovichii   .70   .25
1748 A390   80m C. strausii   .85   .25
1749 A390   1.20t Horridocactus
     tuberisvicatus   1.10   .30
   Nos. 1743-1749 (7)   4.20   1.80

Souvenir Sheet

1750 A390   4t Astrophytum
     ornatum   4.00   4.00

A391

Winners at the 1988 Summer Olympics,
Seoul.

1989, Oct. 1
1751 A391   60m Kristin Otto, East
     Germany   .75   .30
1752 A391   60m Florence Griffith-
     Joyner, US   .75   .30
1753 A391   60m Gintaoutas
     Umaras, USSR   .75   .30
1754 A391   60m Stefano Cerioni,
     Italy   .75   .30
   Nos. 1751-1754 (4)   3.00   1.20

Souvenir Sheet

1755 A391   4t N. Enkhbat,
     Mongolia   4.00   4.00

**No. 1740 Overprinted for WORLD
STAMP EXPO '89**

1989, Nov. 17   **Miniature Sheet**
1756   Sheet of 3   8.00   8.00
   a. A387 20m multicolored   .75   .50
   b. A387 60m multicolored   2.00   1.50
   c. A387 1.20t multicolored   4.50   4.00

A392

1989, Dec. 1
1757 A392   60m Books, fountain
     pen   .75   .45

Beavers (*Castor fiber birulai*) — A393

1989, Dec. 10
1758 A393   60m Cutting down
     saplings   .70   .30
1759 A393   60m Rolling wood
     across ground   .70   .30
1760 A393   60m Beaver on land,
     in water   .70   .30
1761 A393   60m Beaver and
     young   .70   .30
   Nos. 1758-1761 (4)   2.80   1.20

Medals and Military
Decorations — A394

1989, Dec. 31   *Perf. 13x13½*
1762 A394   60m pink & multi   1.00   .30
1763 A394   60m lt blue grn &
     multi   1.00   .30
1764 A394   60m vio & multi   1.00   .30
1765 A394   60m org & multi   1.00   .30
1766 A394   60m brt blue & multi   1.00   .30
1767 A394   60m ver & multi   1.00   .30
1768 A394   60m vio blue & multi   1.00   .30
   Nos. 1762-1768 (7)   7.00   2.10

Bears and Giant Pandas — A395

1990, Jan. 1   *Perf. 14*
1769 A395   20m Ursus pruinosis   .25   .25
1770 A395   30m Ursus arctos
     syriacus   .25   .25
1771 A395   40m Ursus
     thibetanus   .30   .25
1772 A395   50m Ursus maritimus   .35   .30
1773 A395   60m Ursus arctos
     bruinosus   .55   .45
1774 A395   80m Ailuropus mela-
     noleucus   .75   .60
1775 A395   1.20t Ursus arctos
     isabellinus   1.10   1.00
   Nos. 1769-1775 (7)   3.55   3.10

Souvenir Sheet

1776 A395   4t Ailuropus mela-
     noleucus, diff.   5.00   3.00

Winter
Sports — A396

1990, Jan. 6
1777 A396   20m 4-man bobsled   .25   .25
1778 A396   30m Luge   .25   .25
1779 A396   40m Women's figure
     skating   .35   .25
1780 A396   50m 1-man bobsled   .40   .25
1781 A396   60m Pairs figure
     skating   .45   .25
1782 A396   80m Speed skating   .65   .25
1783 A396   1.20t Ice speedway   .95   .30
   Nos. 1777-1783 (7)   3.30   1.80

Souvenir Sheet

1784 A396   4t Ice hockey   4.00   3.00

Space Exploration — A397

Rockets and spacecraft: 20m, Soyuz,
USSR. 30m, Apollo-Soyuz, US-USSR. 40m,
Columbia space shuttle, US, vert. 50m, *Her-
mes*, France. 60m, *Nippon*, Japan, vert. 80m,
Energy, USSR, vert. 1.20t, *Buran*, USSR, vert.
4t, *Sanger*, West Germany.

1990, Jan. 30
1785 A397   20m shown   .25   .25
1786 A397   30m multicolored   .25   .25
1787 A397   40m multicolored   .35   .25
1788 A397   50m multicolored   .45   .25
1789 A397   60m multicolored   .55   .30
1790 A397   80m multicolored   .75   .30
1791 A397   1.20t multicolored   1.10   .40
   Nos. 1785-1791 (7)   3.70   2.00

Souvenir Sheet

1792 A397   4t multicolored   4.00   4.00

Jawaharlal
Nehru, 1st
Prime Minister
of Independent
India — A398

1990, Feb. 10
1793 A398   10m gold, blk & dark
     red brn   1.50   .75

Statue of Sukhe
Bator — A399

1990, Feb. 27
1794 A399   10m multicolored   1.50   .75

Mongolian Ballet — A400

Dancers in scenes from various ballets.
40m, 80m, 1.20t vert.

1990, Feb. 28
1795 A400   20m shown   .25   .25
1796 A400   30m multi   .25   .25
1797 A400   40m multi   .40   .25
1798 A400   50m multi   .50   .25
1799 A400   60m multi   .60   .25
1800 A400   80m multi   .65   .25
1801 A400   1.20t multi   .90   .30
   Nos. 1795-1801 (7)   3.55   1.80

Automobiles — A401

1990, Mar. 26
1802 A401   20m Citroen, France   .25   .25
1803 A401   30m Volvo 760 GLF,
     Sweden   .25   .25
1804 A401   40m Honda, Japan   .35   .25
1805 A401   50m Volga, USSR   .45   .25
1806 A401   60m Ford Granada,
     US   .50   .25
1807 A401   80m VAZ 21099,
     USSR   .55   .25
1808 A401   1.20t Mercedes Class
     190, West Ger-
     many   .85   .30
   Nos. 1802-1808 (7)   3.20   1.80

Souvenir Sheet

1809 A401   4t like 50m   4.50   3.00

Lenin — A402

1990, Mar. 27   *Perf. 13x13½*
1810 A402   60m gold, black & ver   1.00   .50

Unen
Newspaper,
70th
Anniv. — A403

1990, Apr. 1   *Perf. 14*
1811 A403   60m multicolored   .90   .50

End of World
War II, 45th
Anniv. — A404

1990, Apr. 1
1812 A404 60m multicolored   1.00   .60

Buddhist Deities
(18th-20th Cent.
Paintings)
A405

1990, Apr. 1
1813 A405 20m Damdin Sandub   .25   .25
1814 A405 30m Pagwa Lama   .40   .25
1815 A405 40m Chu Lha   .50   .25
1816 A405 50m Agwanglobsan   .60   .30
1817 A405 60m Dorje Dags Dan   .75   .30
1818 A405 80m Wangchikdorje   .85   .40
1819 A405 1.20t Buddha   1.10   .50
       Nos. 1813-1819 (7)   4.45   2.25
Souvenir Sheet
1820 A405   4t Migjed Jang-
                Rasek   6.50   6.50

A406

Aspects of a Cooperative
Settlement — A407

Paintings: 20m, Animals on plain, rainbow.
30m, Workers, reindeer, dog, vert. 40m, Two
men, mountains, Bactrian camels. 50m, Man,
Bactrian camels. 60m, Huts, animal shelter,
corral. 80m, Breaking horses, vert. 1.20t,
Sheep, shepherd girl on horse. 4t, Wrestling
match.

1990, Apr. 1
1821 A406 20m shown   .25   .25
1822 A406 30m multicolored   .30   .25
1823 A406 40m multicolored   .50   .25
1824 A406 50m multicolored   .60   .30
1825 A406 60m multicolored   .70   .40
1826 A406 80m multicolored   .90   .50
1827 A406 1.20t multicolored   1.40   .55
       Nos. 1821-1827 (7)   4.65   2.50
Souvenir Sheet
1828 A407   4t shown   6.00   6.00

Scenes from Various Mongolian-made
Films — A408

1990, Apr. 1
1829 A408 20m shown   .30   .25
1830 A408 30m multi, diff.   .40   .25
1831 A408 40m multi, diff.   .60   .30
1832 A408 50m multi, diff.   .80   .40
1833 A408 60m multi, diff.   1.10   .50
1834 A408 80m multi, diff.   1.25   .65
1835 A408 1.20t multi, diff.   1.75   1.00
       Nos. 1829-1835 (7)   6.20   3.35
Souvenir Sheet
1836 A408   4t multi, diff., vert. 7.00 7.00

Souvenir Sheet

Stamp World London '90 — A409

1990, Apr. 1
1837 A409   4t multicolored   5.00   5.00

1990 World Cup Soccer
Championships, Italy — A410

Trophy and various athletes.

1990, Apr. 30
1838 A410 20m multicolored   .25   .25
1839 A410 30m multicolored   .25   .25
1840 A410 40m multicolored   .30   .25
1841 A410 50m multicolored   .40   .25
1842 A410 60m multicolored   .45   .25
1843 A410 80m multicolored   .65   .25
1844 A410 1.20t multicolored   .95   .25
       Nos. 1838-1844 (7)   3.25   1.75
Souvenir Sheet
1845 A410   4t Trophy, vert.   4.00   2.50

Nos. 304-307
Ovptd.

1990, May 1   Photo.   Perf. 11½x12
1846 A84 20m multicolored   3.50
1847 A84 30m multicolored   4.00
1848 A84 50m multicolored   5.00
1849 A84 60m multicolored   6.00
       Nos. 1846-1849 (4)   18.50
Coronation of Genghis Khan, 800th anniv.
(in 1989).

Souvenir Sheet

Genghis Khan — A411

1990, May 8   Litho.   Perf. 13½
1850 A411   7t multicolored   7.50   7.50
Stamp World London '90. Exists imperf.
Exists without "Stamp World London '90" and
Great Britain No. 1.

Cranes (Grus vipio pallas) — A412

1990, May 23   Perf. 14
1851 A412 60m brt blue & multi   .90   .60
1852 A412 60m brt rose lil &
               multi   .90   .60
1853 A412 60m red lil & multi   .90   .60
1854 A412 60m car rose & multi   .90   .60
       Nos. 1851-1854 (4)   3.60   2.40
       Nos. 1853-1854 are vert.

Marine Mammals — A413

1990, June 20   Litho.   Perf. 14
1855 A413 20m Balaenoptera
                  physalus   .30   .25
1856 A413 30m Megaptera
                  novaeangliae   .40   .25
1857 A413 40m Monodon mo-
                  noceros   .45   .25
1858 A413 50m Grampus
                  griseus   .55   .30
1859 A413 60m Tursiops trun-
                  catus   .70   .40
1860 A413 80m Lage-
                  norhynchus
                  acutius   .95   .50
1861 A413 1.20t Balaena mys-
                  ticetus   1.40   .55
       Nos. 1855-1861 (7)   4.75   2.50
Souvenir Sheet
1861A A413   4t Killer whale   4.00   4.00

A414

Cultural
Heritage — A415

1990, Aug. 13   Perf. 13x12½
1862 A414 10m shown   .25   .25
1863 A414 10m Like No. 1862,
                arrows at left   .25   .25
1864 A415 40m Fire ring   .45   .25
1865 A415 60m Genghis Khan   .65   .25
1866 A414 60m Tent   .65   .25
1867 A414 60m Horses   .65   .25
1868 A414 80m Royal family
                (green panel)   .95   .40
1869 A414 80m Royal court (dk
                bl panel)   .95   .40
   a. Souv. sheet, #1862-1869 + la-
         bel   8.00   8.00
       Nos. 1862-1869 (8)   4.80   2.30

20th Party
Congress
A416

1990, Mar. 1   Litho.   Perf. 14
1870 A416 60m multicolored   .90   .50

Dinosaurs — A417

1990, Aug. 25
1871 A417 20m shown   .40   .25
1872 A417 30m multi, diff.   .50   .25
1873 A417 40m multi, diff.   .65   .25
1874 A417 50m multi, diff   .75   .30
1875 A417 60m multi, vert.   1.00   .40
1876 A417 80m multi, diff.   1.25   .50
          Size: 60x21mm
              Perf. 13
1877 A417 1.20t multi, diff.   1.75   .55
       Nos. 1871-1877 (7)   6.30   2.50
Souvenir Sheet
1878 A417   4t multi, diff.   6.00   6.00

Giant Pandas — A418

1990, Aug. 15   Litho.   Perf. 14
1879 A418 10m Adult on rock,
                vert.   .25   .25
1880 A418 20m Adult, eating,
                vert.   .30   .25
1881 A418 30m Adult and cub,
                vert.   .45   .25
1882 A418 40m multicolored   .60   .30
1883 A418 50m Adult and cub,
                resting   .70   .40
1884 A418 60m Adult, moun-
                tains   .90   .50
1885 A418 80m Adult and cub,
                playing   1.25   .65
1886 A418 1.20t Adult, in winter 1.75   1.00
       Nos. 1879-1886 (8)   6.20   3.60
Souvenir Sheet
1887 A418   4t Family   6.00   6.00

Pyramids of Egypt — A419

Seven wonders of the ancient world: 20m, Lighthouse of Alexander, vert. 40m, Statue of Zeus, vert. 50m, Colossus of Rhodes, vert. 60m, Mausoleum of Halicarnassus, vert. 80m, Temple of Artemis. 1.20t, Hanging gardens of Babylon, vert. 4t, Pyramids of Egypt, vert.

1990, Sept. 25
1888	A419	20m multicolored	.35	.25
1889	A419	30m shown	.45	.25
1890	A419	40m multicolored	.65	.25
1891	A419	50m multicolored	.75	.25
1892	A419	60m multicolored	1.00	.25
1893	A419	80m multicolored	1.25	.40
1894	A419	1.20t multicolored	1.75	.65
		Nos. 1888-1894 (7)	6.20	2.30

Souvenir Sheet
1895	A419	4t multicolored	6.00	6.00

Moschus Moschiferus — A419a

1990, Sept. 26   Litho.   Perf. 14
1895A	A419a	60m shown	.80	.50
1895B	A419a	60m In snow	.80	.50
1895C	A419a	60m Facing left	.80	.50
1895D	A419a	60m Two, one on ground	.80	.50
		Nos. 1895A-1895D (4)	3.20	2.00

Parrots — A420

1990, Oct. 25   Litho.   Perf. 14
1896	A420	20m shown	.25	.25
1897	A420	30m multi, diff.	.25	.25
1898	A420	40m multi, diff.	.45	.25
1899	A420	50m multi, diff.	.60	.30
1900	A420	60m multi, diff.	.75	.40
1901	A420	80m multi, diff.	1.00	.50
1902	A420	1.20t multi, diff.	1.50	.55
		Nos. 1896-1902 (7)	4.80	2.50

Souvenir Sheet
1903	A420	4t multi, diff.	4.75	4.00

Butterflies — A421

Designs: 20m, Purpurbar. 30m, Grosses nachtpfauenauge. 40m, Grosser C-Falter. 50m, Stachelbeerspanner. 60m, Damenbrett. 80m, Schwalbenschwanz. 1.20t, Aurorafalter. 4t, Linienschwarmer, vert.

1990, Nov. 25   Litho.   Perf. 14
1904	A421	20m multicolored	.25	.25
1905	A421	30m multicolored	.30	.25
1906	A421	40m multicolored	.45	.25
1907	A421	50m multicolored	.60	.30
1908	A421	60m multicolored	.70	.40
1909	A421	80m multicolored	.85	.50
1910	A421	1.20t multicolored	1.20	.55
		Nos. 1904-1910 (7)	4.35	2.50

Souvenir Sheet
1911	A421	4t multicolored	4.25	3.75

Flintstones Visit Mongolia — A422

Designs: 25m, Dino. 35m, Dino, Bamm-Bamm, diff., vert. 45m, Betty, Wilma, Bamm-Bamm, Pebbles. 55m, Fred, Barney, Dino. 65m, Flintstones & Rubbles. 75m, Bamm-Bamm riding Dino. 85m, Fred, Barney, Bamm-Bamm. 1.40t, Flintstones, Rubbles in car. 2t, Fred, Barney. No. 1921, Wilma, Betty & Bamm-Bamm. No. 1922, Bamm-Bamm, Pebbles riding Dino.

1991, Feb. 10   Litho.   Perf. 14
1912	A422	25m multicolored	.30	.25
1913	A422	35m multicolored	.30	.25
1914	A422	45m multicolored	.45	.25
1915	A422	55m multicolored	.50	.25
1916	A422	65m multicolored	.70	.25
1917	A422	75m multicolored	.70	.30
1918	A422	85m multicolored	.85	.30
1919	A422	1.40t multicolored	1.20	.40
1920	A422	2t multicolored	1.75	.40
		Nos. 1912-1920 (9)	6.75	2.65

Souvenir Sheets
1921	A422	7t multicolored	4.50	4.50
1922	A422	7t multicolored	4.50	4.50

The Jetsons A423

Designs: 20m, Jetsons blasting off in space-ship. 25m, Jetsons on planet, horiz. 30m, George, Jane, Elroy & Astro. 40m, George, Judy, Elroy & Astro. 50m, Jetsons in spaceship, horiz. 60m, George, Jane, Elroy & Mr. Spacely, horiz. 70m, George, Elroy wearing jet packs. 80m, Elroy. 1.20t, Elroy, Judy & Astro. No. 1932, Elroy, red flowers. No. 1933, Elroy, blue flowers.

1991, Feb. 10
1923	A423	20m multicolored	.25	.25
1924	A423	25m multicolored	.25	.25
1925	A423	30m multicolored	.35	.25
1926	A423	40m multicolored	.45	.25
1927	A423	50m multicolored	.50	.30
1928	A423	60m multicolored	.55	.30
1929	A423	70m multicolored	.65	.30
1930	A423	80m multicolored	.70	.40
1931	A423	1.20t multicolored	1.10	.40
		Nos. 1923-1931 (9)	4.80	2.70

Souvenir Sheets
1932	A423	7t multicolored	4.50	4.50
1933	A423	7t multicolored	4.50	4.50

Mongolian People's Revolutionary Party, 70th Anniv. — A423a

1991, Mar. 1   Litho.   Perf. 14
1933A	A423a	60m multicolored	.90	.40

A424

Stamp World London '90 — A425

Various birds.

1991, Mar. 3   Litho.   Perf. 14½
1934	A424	25m multicolored	.25	.25
1935	A424	35m multicolored	.35	.25
1936	A424	45m multicolored	.50	.25
1937	A424	55m multicolored	.60	.25
1938	A424	65m multicolored	.75	.25
1939	A424	75m multi, horiz.	.80	.30
1940	A424	85m multicolored	1.00	.40
1941	A424	1.40t multicolored	1.50	.50
1942	A424	2t multicolored	2.25	.55
		Nos. 1934-1942 (9)	8.00	3.00

Souvenir Sheets
1943	A424	7t multicolored	7.00	7.00
1944	A425	7t multicolored	7.00	7.00

Butterflies and Flowers of Mongolia — A426

Designs: 20m, 30m-60m, various butterflies. Others, various flowers.

1991, Mar. 3   Litho.   Perf. 14½
1945	A426	20m multicolored	.45	.25
1946	A426	25m multicolored	.50	.25
1947	A426	30m multicolored	.65	.25
1948	A426	40m multicolored	.85	.25
1949	A426	50m multicolored	1.00	.25
1950	A426	60m multicolored	1.25	.25
1951	A426	70m multicolored	1.50	.30
1952	A426	80m multicolored	1.75	.30
1953	A426	1.20t multicolored	2.25	.40
		Nos. 1945-1953 (9)	10.20	2.50

Nos. 1945-1953 and Types Overprinted

1991, Mar. 3
1954	A426	20m multicolored	.45	.25
1955	A426	25m multicolored	.50	.25
1956	A426	30m multicolored	.65	.25
1957	A426	40m multicolored	.85	.25
1958	A426	50m multicolored	1.00	.25
1959	A426	60m multicolored	1.25	.25
1960	A426	70m multicolored	1.50	.30
1961	A426	80m multicolored	1.75	.30
1962	A426	1.20t multicolored	2.25	.40
		Nos. 1954-1962 (9)	10.20	2.50

Souvenir Sheets
1963	A426	7t Butterfly	10.00	10.00
1964	A426	7t Flower	10.00	10.00

Nos. 1963-1964 were not issued without overprint which appears in sheet margin only.

Mongolian People's Army, 70th Anniv. — A426a

1991, Mar. 18   Litho.   Perf. 14
1964A	A426a	60m multicolored	.90	.40

Birds — A427

1991, Apr. 1   Perf. 14
1965	A427	20m Lururus tetrix	.30	.25
1966	A427	30m Tadorna tadorna	.45	.25
1967	A427	40m Phasianus colchicus	.55	.25
1968	A427	50m Clangula byemalis	.75	.30
1969	A427	60m Tetrastes bonasia	.90	.40
1970	A427	80m Mergus serrator	1.25	.50
1971	A427	1.20t Bucephaia clangula	1.60	.75
		Nos. 1965-1971 (7)	5.80	2.70

Souvenir Sheet
1972	A427	4t Anas crecca, vert.	5.50	5.50

Flowers — A428

1991, Apr. 15
1973	A428	20m Dianthus superbus	.25	.25
1974	A428	30m Gentiana puenmonanthe	.35	.25
1975	A428	40m Taraxacum officinale	.55	.25
1976	A428	50m Iris sibrica	.70	.30
1977	A428	60m Lilium martagon	.70	.40
1978	A428	80m Aster amellus	1.00	.50
1979	A428	1.20t Cizsium rivulare	1.40	.55
		Nos. 1973-1979 (7)	4.95	2.50

Souvenir Sheet
1980	A428	4t Campanula persicifolia	4.50	4.50

Buddhist Effigies — A429

1991, May 1
1981	A429	20m Defend	.25	.25
1982	A429	30m Badmasanhava	.30	.25
1983	A429	40m Avalokitecvara	.50	.25
1984	A429	50m Buddha	.70	.30
1985	A429	60m Mintugwa	.80	.40
1986	A429	80m Shyamatara	1.10	.50
1987	A429	1.20t Samvara	1.20	.55
		Nos. 1981-1987 (7)	4.85	2.50

Souvenir Sheet

1988	A429	4t Lamidhatara	5.00	5.00

a. With Phila Nippon '91 emblem overprinted in sheet margin   —   —

For surcharge, see No. 2658.

Insects — A430

1991, May 22

1989	A430	20m Neolamprima adolphinae	.35	.25
1990	A430	30m Chelorrhina polyphemus	.40	.25
1991	A430	40m Coptolabrus coelestis	.55	.25
1992	A430	50m Epepeotes togatus	.75	.30
1993	A430	60m Cicindela chinensis	.80	.40
1994	A430	80m Macrodontia cervicornis	1.25	.50
1995	A430	1.20t Dynastes hercules	1.50	.55
		Nos. 1989-1995 (7)	5.60	2.50

Souvenir Sheet

1991, May 22   **Litho.**   *Perf. 14*

1995A	A430	4t Cercopis sanguinolenta, vert.	4.50	4.50

African Animals — A431

1991, May 23

1996	A431	20m Zebras	.25	.25
1997	A431	30m Cheetah	.35	.25
1998	A431	40m Black rhinos	.55	.25
1999	A431	50m Giraffe, vert.	.70	.30
2000	A431	60m Gorilla	.80	.40
2001	A431	80m Elephants	1.00	.50
2002	A431	1.20t Lion, vert.	1.25	.55
		Nos. 1996-2002 (7)	4.90	2.50

Souvenir Sheet

2003	A431	4t Gazelle	5.00	5.00

No. 1997 is incorrectly spelled "Cheetan."

Exhibition of Meiso Mizuhara's Mongolian Stamp Collection — A432

1991, June   **Litho.**   *Perf. 13½*

2004	A432	1.20t multicolored	3.00	1.00

Lizards — A433

1991, Oct. 29   *Perf. 14*

2005	A433	20m Iguana iguana	.25	.25
2006	A433	30m Ptychozoon kihli	.30	.25
2007	A433	40m Chlamydosaurus kingii	.45	.25
2008	A433	50m Cordylus cordylus	.60	.30
2009	A433	60m Basiliscus basilisus	.75	.40

2010	A433	80m Tupinambis teguixin	.90	.50
2011	A433	1.20t Amblyrhynchus cristatus	1.60	.55
		Nos. 2005-2011 (7)	4.85	2.50

Souvenir Sheet

2012	A433	4t Varanus bengalensis, vert.	4.50	4.50

Masks and Costumes A434

Various masks and costumes.

1991, Oct. 1

2013	A434	35m multicolored	.40	.25
2014	A434	45m multicolored	.50	.25
2015	A434	55m multicolored	.65	.25
2016	A434	65m multicolored	.75	.30
2017	A434	85m multicolored	1.00	.50
2018	A434	1.40t multicolored	1.65	.80
2019	A434	2t multicolored	2.35	1.00
		Nos. 2013-2019 (7)	7.30	3.35

Souvenir Sheet

2020	A434	4t multicolored	5.50	5.50

Phila Nippon '91 — A435

1991, Oct. 29

2021	A435	1t Pagoda	.55	.50
2022	A435	2t Japanese beauty	.80	.75
2023	A435	3t Mongolian woman	1.10	.75
2024	A435	4t Mongolian building	1.50	1.00
		Nos. 2021-2024 (4)	3.95	3.00

Fantasia, 50th Anniv. A436

Designs: 1.70t, Poster, 1985. 2t, Poster, 1940. 2.30t, Poster, 1982. 2.60t, Poster, 1981. 4.20t, Poster, 1969. 10t, Poster, 1941. 15t, Drawing of Mlle. Upanova, 1940. 16t, Sketch of Mickey as Sorcerer's Apprentice.

No. 2033, Mickey as Sorcerer's Apprentice. No. 2034, Dinosaurs from "The Rite of Spring," horiz. No. 2035, Thistles and orchids from "Russian Dance," horiz. No. 2036, Dancing mushrooms from "Chinese Dance," horiz.

1991, Dec. 31   *Perf. 13½x14, 14x13½*

2025	A436	1.70t multicolored	.40	.25
2026	A436	2t multicolored	.60	.25
2027	A436	2.30t multicolored	.75	.25
2028	A436	2.60t multicolored	1.00	.25
2029	A436	4.20t multicolored	1.25	.40
2030	A436	10t multicolored	1.75	.50
2031	A436	15t multicolored	2.75	1.20
2032	A436	16t multicolored	3.00	1.20
		Nos. 2025-2032 (8)	11.50	4.30

Souvenir Sheets

2033	A436	30t multicolored	7.50	7.50
2034	A436	30t multicolored	7.50	7.50
2035	A436	30t multicolored	7.50	7.50
2036	A436	30t multicolored	7.50	7.50

1992 Winter Olympics, Albertville — A437

1992, Feb. 1   *Perf. 14*

2037	A437	60m Speed skating, vert.	.25	.25
2038	A437	80m Ski jumping, vert.	.35	.25
2039	A437	1t Hockey, vert.	.40	.25
2040	A437	1.20t Figure skating, vert.	.50	.25
2041	A437	1.50t Biathlon	.65	.25
2042	A437	2t Downhill skiing	.90	.25
2043	A437	2.40t Two-man bobsled	1.10	.25
		Nos. 2037-2043 (7)	4.15	1.75

Souvenir Sheet

2044	A437	8t Four-man bobsled, vert.	4.00	2.50

Dogs — A438

Various breeds of dogs.

1991, Dec. 1   **Litho.**   *Perf. 14*

2045	A438	20m multi	.25	.25
2046	A438	30m multi, vert.	.30	.25
2047	A438	40m multi, vert.	.50	.25
2048	A438	50m multi	.65	.30
2049	A438	60m multi	.80	.40
2050	A438	80m multi	.95	.50
2051	A438	1.20t multi	1.50	.70
		Nos. 2045-2051 (7)	4.95	2.65

Souvenir Sheet

2052	A438	4t multi	5.00	5.00

Cats — A439

Various breeds of cats.

1991, Dec. 27

2053	A439	20m multi	.25	.25
2054	A439	30m multi, vert.	.30	.25
2055	A439	40m multi	.50	.25
2056	A439	50m multi, vert.	.65	.30
2057	A439	60m multi, vert.	.80	.40
2058	A439	80m multi, vert.	.95	.50
2059	A439	1.20t multi, vert.	1.50	.70
		Nos. 2053-2059 (7)	4.95	2.65

Souvenir Sheet

2060	A439	4t multi	5.00	5.00

Alces Alces — A440

1992, May 1   **Litho.**   *Perf. 14*

2061	A440	3t Male	1.00	.50
2062	A440	3t Two females	1.00	.50
2063	A440	3t One female, vert.	1.00	.50
2064	A440	3t Male's head, vert.	1.00	.50
		Nos. 2061-2064 (4)	4.00	2.00

Souvenir Sheet

Ferdinand von Zeppelin (1838-1917), Airship Designer — A441

1992, May 1

2065	A441	16t multicolored	4.00	4.00

Souvenir Sheets

People and Events — A442

No. 2066, Pres. Punsalmaagiin Ochirbat visiting Pres. George Bush at White House. No. 2067, Mother Teresa helping poor in Calcutta. No. 2068, Pope John Paul II at mass. Nos. 2069-2070, Boy Scout blowing bugle.

1992, May 22   *Perf. 14x13½*

2066	A442	30t silver & multi	5.00	4.50

Perf. 14

2067	A442	30t silver & multi	5.00	4.50
2068	A442	30t silver & multi	5.00	4.50
2069	A442	30t silver & multi	5.00	4.50
2070	A442	30t silver & multi	5.00	4.50
		Nos. 2066-2070 (5)	25.00	22.50

Nos. 2067-2070 each contain one 43x28mm stamp. Nos. 2069-2070 exist with gold inscription and border. No. 2069, 17th World Boy Scout Jamboree, Korea. No. 2070, 18th World Boy Scout Jamboree, Netherlands, 1995.

Souvenir Sheet

Discovery of America, 500th Anniv. — A443

Designs: a, Columbus. b, Sailing ship.

1992, May 22

2071	A443	30t Sheet of 2, #a.-b.	7.50	6.00

World Columbian Stamp Expo '92, Chicago, Genoa '92.

Miniature Sheets

Railways of the World — A444

Designs: No. 2072a, 3t, Tank locomotive, Darjeeling-Himalaya Railway, India. b, 3t, Royal Scot, Great Britain. c, 6t, Bridge on the River Kwai, Burma-Siam Railway. d, 6t, Baltic tank engine, Burma. e, 8t, Baldwin locomotive, Thailand. f, 8t, Western Railway locomotive, Pakistan. g, 16t, P.36 class locomotive, USSR. h, 16t, Shanghai-Beijing Express, China.

Orient Express: No. 2073a, 3t, 1931 Advertising poster. b, 3t, 1928 poster. c, 6t, Dawn departure. d, 6t, Golden Arrow departing Victoria Station. e, 8t, Waiting at station in Yugoslavia. f, 8t, Turn of the century picture of train. g, 16t, Fleche d'Or locomotive approaching Étaples, France. h, 16t, Arrival in Istanbul, Turkey.

No. 2074, New Tokaido line, Japan. No. 2075, TGV, France. No. 2076a, Emblem of Pullman Car Company. b, Emblem of Intl. Wagons-lits Company. No. 2077, Passengers waiting to board Orient Express.

1992, May 24
2072 A444 Sheet of 8, #a.-h.   12.00 9.00
2073 A444 Sheet of 8, #a.-h.   12.00 9.00
Souvenir Sheets
2074 A444 30t multicolored   6.00 5.00
2075 A444 30t multicolored   6.00 5.00
2076 A444 30t Sheet of 2, #a.-b.   12.00 11.00
2077 A444 30t black & gold   6.00 5.00
Nos. 2074-2075 contain one 58x42mm stamp.

Miniature Sheet

Birds — A445

Various birds: a, 3t. b, 3t, Owl. c, 6t, Gull, horiz. d, 6t, horiz. e, 8t. f, 8t, horiz. g, 16t. h, 16t, horiz.

1992, May 24
2078 A445 Sheet of 8, #a.-h.   15.00 10.00
Souvenir Sheet
Perf. 14x13½
2079 A445 30t Ducks, 30t in UR   4.50 4.50
2080 A445 30t Duck, 30t in LR   4.50 4.50
Nos. 2079-2080 contain one 50x38mm stamp.

Miniature Sheet

Butterflies and Moths — A446

Various butterflies or moths and: a, 3t, Mountains. b, 3t, Desert. c, 6t, Grass. d, 6t, Lake. e, 8t, Mountain, diff. f, 8t, Flowers. g, 16t, Rocks. h, 16t, Lake, diff.

1992, May 24   *Perf. 14*
2081 A446 Sheet of 8, #a.-h.   15.00 10.00
Souvenir Sheet
Perf. 14x13½
2082 A446 30t pink & multi   6.00 5.00
2083 A446 30t blue & multi   6.00 5.00
Nos. 2082-2083 contain one 50x38mm stamp.

1992 Summer Olympics, Barcelona — A447

Designs: a, Gold medal. b, Torch.

1992, Jan. 22   Litho.   Perf. 14
2084 A447 30t Sheet of 2, #a.-b.   8.75 8.75

Souvenir Sheet

Genghis Khan — A448

1992, June 15   Litho.   Perf. 14
2085 A448 16t multicolored   20.00 20.00

Mushrooms — A449

Designs: 20m, Marasmius oreades. 30m, Boletus luridus. 40m, Hygrophorus marzuelus. 50m, Cantharellus cibarius. 60m, Agaricus campester. 80m, Boletus aereus. 1.20t, Amanita caesarea. 2t, Tricholoma terreum. 4t, Mitrophora hybrida.

1991, June 18   Litho.   Perf. 13
2086 A449 20m multicolored   .25 .25
2087 A449 30m multicolored   .30 .25
2088 A449 40m multicolored   .45 .25
2089 A449 50m multicolored   .50 .25
2090 A449 60m multicolored   .60 .30
2091 A449 80m multicolored   .75 .40
2092 A449 1.20t multicolored   1.10 .55
2093 A449 2t multicolored   1.60 .80
Nos. 2086-2093 (8)   5.55 3.05
Souvenir Sheet
2094 A449 4t multicolored   5.50 5.50
Dated 1990. No. 2094 contains one 32x40mm stamp.

Discovery of America, 500th Anniv. — A450

Columbus and: 3t, Two sailing ships. 7t, Natives approaching Santa Maria. 10t, Pinta. 16t, Santa Maria, vert. 30t, Santa Maria, diff. 40t, Santa Maria, dolphins. 50t, Nina. #2102, Ship, vert. #2103, Portrait, vert.

1992, Aug.   Litho.   Perf. 14
2095 A450 3t multicolored   .25 .25
2096 A450 7t multicolored   .50 .25
2097 A450 10t multicolored   .75 .25
2098 A450 16t multicolored   1.00 .30
2099 A450 30t multicolored   1.75 .80
2100 A450 40t multicolored   2.00 1.40
2101 A450 50t multicolored   3.00 1.75
Nos. 2095-2101 (7)   9.25 5.00
Souvenir Sheets
Perf. 13½x14
2102 A450 80t multicolored   5.00 5.00
2103 A450 80t multicolored   5.00 5.00
Nos. 2102-2103 each contain one 38x52mm stamp.

Miniature Sheet

Butterflies A451

#2104: a, 3t, Anthocharis cardamines. b, 8t, Inachis io. c, 10t, Fabriciana adippe. d, 16t, Limenitis reducta. e, 30t, Agrumaenia carniolica. f, 40t, Polyommatus icarus. g, 50t, Parnassius apollo. h, 60t, Saturnia pyri.
No. 2105, Limenitis populi. No. 2106, Heodes virgaureae.

1992, Dec.   Litho.   Perf. 14
2104 A451 Sheet of 8, #a.-h.   12.00 11.00
Souvenir Sheets
Perf. 14x13½
2105 A451 80t multicolored   5.00 4.00
2106 A451 80t multicolored   5.00 4.00
Nos. 2105-2106 each contain one 51x38mm stamp.

1992 Summer Olympics, Barcelona — A452

1993, Jan.   Litho.   Perf. 13½
2107 A452 3t Long jump   .25 .25
2108 A452 6t Pommel horse   .25 .25
2109 A452 8t Boxing   .35 .25
2110 A452 16t Wrestling   .35 .25
2111 A452 20t Archery, vert.   .55 .25
2112 A452 30t Cycling   .60 .25
2113 A452 40t Equestrian   .70 .30
2114 A452 50t High jump   .90 .30
2115 A452 60t Weight lifting   1.10 .40
Nos. 2107-2115 (9)   5.05 2.50
Souvenir Sheet
Perf. 15x14
2116 A452 80t Judo   4.00 3.50
2117 A452 80t Javelin   4.00 3.50
Nos. 2116-2117 contain one 40x30mm stamp.

Miniature Sheet

Birds A453

Designs: No. 2118a, 3t, Tetrae tetrix. b, 8t, Gallinula chloropus. c, 10t, Regulus satrapa. d, 16t, Alcede atthis. e, 30t, Gavia stellata. f, 40t, Ardes cinerea. g, 50t, Upupa epops. h, 60t, Niltava rubeculoides. No. 2119, Gyps fulvus. No. 2120, Podiceps cristatus.

1993, Feb.   Litho.   Perf. 14
2118 A453 Sheet of 8, #a.-h.   11.00 10.00
Souvenir Sheets
Perf. 14x13½
2119 A453 80t multicolored   4.50 4.00
2120 A453 80t multicolored   4.50 4.00
Nos. 2119-2120 each contain one 51x38mm stamp.

Souvenir Sheets

Polska '93 — A454

#2121a, 2122, Copernicus. #2121b, Chopin. #2121c, 2123, Pope John Paul II.

1993, May 1   Litho.   Perf. 13½x14
2121 A454 30t Sheet of 3, #a.-c.   9.00 7.00
2122 A454 80t multicolored   8.00 7.00
2123 A454 80t multicolored   8.00 7.00
Nos. 2121-2123 (3)   25.00 21.00

Animals, Sports, & Transportation — A455

Designs in gold: No. 2124, Cats, dogs. No. 2125, Turtle, bee, wildcat, butterfly. No. 2126, Owl, butterfly, mushroom, dinosaur. No. 2127, Chessmen, archer, baseball player, wrestlers, horse and rider. Nos. 2128, Modern transportation.
No. 2129, Dinosaur, whales, butterflies. No. 2130, Mushroom, turtle, flowers.

1993, Jan. 5   Embossed   Perf. 9
2124-2128 A455 200t Set of 5   75.00 75.00
Nos. 2124-2128 exist in silver and in either gold or silver imperf. souvenir sheets of 1.

Embossed
1993, June 1   *Perf. 8½x9*
Size: 79x53mm
2129 A455 200t silver   15.00 15.00

Souvenir Sheet
Imperf
Litho. & Embossed

2130 A455 200t gold   25.00 20.00

No. 2130, Topex '93, Madison, WI. No. 2129 exists in imperf. souvenir sheet of 1. No. 2130 exists in silver.

Souvenir Sheets

Taipei '93 — A456

1993, Aug. 14   Litho.   Perf. 13½x14

2137 A456 80t Genghis Khan   15.00
2138 A456 80t Sun Yat-Sen   20.00

Dirigible Flight Over Ulan Bator — A457

1993, Aug. 27   Litho.   Perf. 14

2139 A457 80t multicolored   3.00 3.00

No. 2139 has a holographic image. Soaking in water may affect the hologram. Issued in sheets of 4

Buddhist Deities A458

Various statues and paintings.

1993, Oct. 3   Perf. 13½x14

2140 A458 50t multicolored   .35 .25
2141 A458 100t multicolored   .70 .30
2142 A458 150t multicolored   1.00 .50
2143 A458 200t multicolored   1.40 .65
   a.   Miniature sheet of 4   5.25 5.25
    Nos. 2140-2143 (4)   3.45 1.70

Souvenir Sheet

2144 A458 300t multicolored   2.00 2.00

Bangkok '93.

Nos. 276 & 1084 Surcharged

1993   Perfs., Etc. as Before

2144A A77 8t on 70m #276   7.50
2144B A246 15t on 70m
    #1084   15.00

No. 2144A exists with double surcharge. The surcharge on No. 2144B exists with four different type fonts.

New Year 1994 (Year of the Dog) — A459

No. 2146, Stylized dog running, vert.

1994, Jan. 10   Perf. 14x13½, 13½x14

2145 A459 60t multicolored   3.00 .75
2146 A459 60t multicolored   3.00 .75

1994 World Cup Soccer Championships, U.S. — A460

Championship teams: #2147, Uruguay, 1930, 1950. #2148, Italy, 1954. #2149, Brazil, 1959. #2150, West Germany, 1954. #2151, Argentina, 1978, 1986. #2152, Italy, 1938. #2153, Brazil, 1962. #2154, West Germany, 1974. #2155, Brazil, 1970. #2156, Italy, 1982. #2157, West Germany, 1990.

1994, Jan. 15   Perf. 14x13½

2147 A460 150t multicolored   .70 .25
2148 A460 150t multicolored   .70 .25
2149 A460 150t multicolored   .70 .25
2150 A460 150t multicolored   .70 .25
2151 A460 150t multicolored   .70 .25
   a.   Souv. sheet of 2, #2147, 2151   2.00 2.00
2152 A460 200t multicolored   .90 .40
2153 A460 200t multicolored   .90 .40
2154 A460 200t multicolored   .90 .40
2155 A460 200t multicolored   1.20 .55
   a.   Souvenir sheet of 3, #2149, 2153, 2155   3.50 3.50
2156 A460 250t multicolored   1.20 .55
   a.   Souvenir sheet of 3, #2148, 2152, 2156   3.50 3.50
2157 A460 250t multicolored   1.20 .55
   a.   Souvenir sheet of 3, #2150, 2154, 2157   3.50 3.50
   b.   Miniature sheet of 4, #2151, 2155-2157   5.50 6.25
    Nos. 2147-2157 (11)   9.80 4.10

Souvenir Sheet

Punsalmaagiin Ochirbat, First President of Mongolia — A461

1994, Apr. 1   Perf. 14

2158 A461 150t multicolored   2.00 2.00

1994 Winter Olympics, Lillehammer A462

1994, Apr. 10   Litho.   Perf. 13½

2159 A462 50t Biathlon   .35 .25
2160 A462 60t Two-man bob-sled   .45 .25
2161 A462 80t Slalom skiing   .60 .40
2162 A462 100t Ski jumping   .75 .50
2163 A462 120t Pairs figure skating   .80 .55
2164 A462 200t Speed skating   1.10 .90
    Nos. 2159-2164 (6)   4.05 2.85

Souvenir Sheet

2165 A462 400t Ice hockey   4.00 4.00

Souvenir Sheet

Dalai Lama, 1989 Nobel Peace Prize Winner — A463

1994, June 27   Litho.   Perf. 13½

2166 A463 400t multicolored   30.00

A464

People's Army — A465

1994   Litho.   Perf. 14

2167 A464 60m multicolored   .90 .90

Souvenir Sheet

2168 A465 4t multicolored   3.00 3.00

Miniature Sheet of 18

Wildlife — A466

Designs: a, Brown raptor. b, Woodpecker. c, Cranes in flight. d, White raptor. e, Yellow bird on tree branch (i). f, Two birds flying left. g, Raptor perched on rock. h, Two birds flying right. i, Squirrel. j, Dragonfly (f). k, Water bird standing near pond (o). l, Duck in flight over pond. m, Brown bird. n, Ground hog. o, Ladybug on flower. p, Bird's eggs. q, Grasshopper (m). r, Butterfly.

1994, July 15

2169 A466 60t #a.-r. + 2 labels   10.00 7.00

First Manned Moon Landing, 25th Anniv. A467

1994, July 20   Litho.   Perf. 13½

2170 A467 200t Trans-lunar injection   .90 .50
2171 A467 200t Astronaut on moon   .90 .50
2172 A467 200t Space shuttle, earth   .90 .50
2173 A467 200t Astronaut, shuttle   .90 .50
   a.   Miniature sheet of 4, #2170-2173   4.50 2.50
    Nos. 2170-2173 (4)   3.60 2.00

Singpex '94 — A468

1994, Aug. 31
2174 A468 300t Butterfly 1.50 1.00
Souvenir Sheet
2175 A468 400t Dog 6.00 5.00
New Year 1994 (Year of the Dog).

A469

PHILAKOREA
'94 — A470

1994		**Litho.**	**Perf. 14**	
2176	A469	600t Korea #1749	2.50	.75
2177	A469	600t #433	2.50	.75
2178	A470	600t #1	2.50	.75
2179	A470	600t Korea #1	2.50	.75
		Nos. 2176-2179 (4)	10.00	3.00

Souvenir Sheets
Perf. 13½x14
2180 A470 400t #5 .... 4.00 4.00
Perf. 14
2181 A469 600t Yong Sik Hong 4.50 4.00

First Mongolian Stamp, 70th anniv. (#2180).
No. 2180 contains one 34x46mm stamp.
Issued: No. 2180, 11/23, others, 8/16.
For surcharges see #2247C-2247G.

Dinosaurs — A471

1994, Nov. 30			**Perf. 14**	
2182	A471	60t Mammuthus, vert.	.40	.25
2183	A471	80t Stegosaurus, vert.	.50	.30
2184	A471	100t Talararus	.55	.40
2185	A471	120t Gorythosaurus	.75	.55
2186	A471	200t Tyrannosaurus	1.10	.90
		Nos. 2182-2186 (5)	3.30	2.40

Souvenir Sheet
2187 A471 400t Triceratops *1.50 1.50*

Nos. 2182-2187 exist in imperf. sheets of 1.
No. 2182 is misspelled.

Mongolian-Japanese
Friendship — A472

1994, Dec. 15   **Perf. 14x13½**
2188 A472 20t multicolored .... *1.00 .30*

New Year 1995 (Year of the
Boar) — A474

1995, Jan. 1   **Perf. 14x13½, 13½x14**
2190 A474 200t shown .... .85 .30
2191 A474 200t Boar, diff. vert. .85 .30

A475

Litho. & Typo.

1994, July 25   **Perf. 15x14**
Denomination in Black

2192	A475	10t Flower	—	—
2192A	A475	10t Flower, red de-nomination	—	—
2193	A475	18t Ram	—	—
2194	A475	22t Airplane	—	—
2195	A475	22t Airplane, red denomination	—	—
2196	A475	44t like #2193	—	—
2197	A475	44t Ram, blue de-nomination	—	—

Dated 1993.
No. 2192A issued 1994(?).

Religious Masked
Dancing — A476

Various masked dancers in traditional
costumes.

1995, Feb. 25		**Litho.**	**Perf. 14**	
2201	A476	20t multicolored	.25	.25
2202	A476	50t multicolored	.30	.25
2203	A476	60t multicolored	.35	.25
2204	A476	100t multicolored	.60	.30
2205	A476	120t multicolored	.70	.30
2206	A476	150t multicolored	.85	.40
2207	A476	200t multicolored	1.10	.50
		Nos. 2201-2207 (7)	4.15	2.25

Souvenir Sheet
2208 A476 400t multicolored 4.00 4.00

Saiga
Tatarica
A477

1995, Mar. 30		**Litho.**	**Perf. 14**	
2209	A477	40t shown	.40	.25
2210	A477	55t Two adults	.50	.25
2211	A477	70t One running left	.60	.30
2212	A477	200t One up close	1.60	.80
a.		Block of 4, #2209-2212	3.50	3.50

World Wildlife Fund.

Souvenir Sheet

First Philately & Collections Fair, Hong
Kong '95 — A478

Designs: a, Butterfly. b, Flowers.

1995, June 6   **Litho.**   **Perf. 14**
2213 A478 200t Sheet of 2, #a.-
b. + 2 labels 4.25 4.25

Goldfish — A479

Designs: 20t, Yellow oranda. 50t, Red and
white wen-yu. 60t, Brown oranda with red
head. 100t, Calico pearl-scale with phoenix
tail. 120t, Red lion-head. 150t, Brown oranda.
200t, Red and white oranda with narial.
400t, White and gold unidentified fish.

1995, Sept. 1   **Litho.**   **Perf. 14**
2214-2220 A479 Set of 7 .... *5.50 4.00*
Souvenir Sheet
2221 A479 400t multicolored *5.50 4.00*

No. 2221 contains one 50x38mm stamp.

Miniature Sheet

Motion Pictures, Cent. — A480

Various portraits of Marilyn Monroe (1926-
62): No. 2222a, 60t. b, 80t. c, 100t. d, 120t. e,
150t. f, 200t. g, 250t. h, 350t.
No. 2223, In white-collared blouse. No.
2224, With lion. No. 2225, In black lace dress.
No. 2226, In scene from movie, Niagara.

1995, Oct. 20
2222 A480 Sheet of 9, #a.-i. 8.50 7.00
Souvenir Sheets
2223 A480 200t multi 4.50 4.50
2224-2226 A480 300t each 4.50 4.50

Miniature Sheet

UN, 50th Anniv. — A481

Exterior views of UN complexes, Secretar-
ies General: a, Trygve Lie. b, Dag Hammarskjold. c, U Thant. d, Kurt Waldheim. e,
Jose Perez de Cuellar. f, Boutros Boutros-
Ghali.

1995, Oct. 15
2227 A481 60t Sheet of 6, #a.-f. .. 6.50 5.00

Miniature Sheet

Elvis Presley (1935-77) — A482

Various portaits: No. 2228a, 60t. b, 80t. c,
100t. d, 120t. e, 150t. f, 200t. g, 250t. h, 300t. i,
350t.
No. 2229, Wearing yellow sweater. No.
2230, With dancing girl. No. 2231, With guitar.
No. 2232, In army uniform, wife Priscilla.

1995, Oct. 20
2228 A482 Sheet of 9, #a.-i. 9.00 8.00
Souvenir Sheets
2229 A482 200t multi 5.00 5.00
2230 A482 300t multi 5.00 5.00
2231-2232 A482 400t each 6.50 5.00

Miniature Sheet

X-Men Comic Characters — A483

Designs: No. 2233a, 30t, Bishop. b, 50t,
Beast. c, 60t, Rogue. d, 70t, Gambit. e, 80t,
Cyclops. f, 100t, Storm. g, 200t, Professor X.
h, 250t, Wolverine.
No. 2234: a, Wolverine, horiz. b, Magneto,
horiz.

1995, Sept. 15
2233 A483 Sheet of 8, #a.-h. 3.50 3.00
Souvenir Sheet of 2
2234 A483 250t #a.-b. 3.50 3.00

New Year
1996
(Year of
the Rat)
A484

1996, Jan. 1   **Litho.**   **Perf. 14**
2235	A484	150t Rat, diff., vert.	1.00	.60
2236	A484	200t shown	1.50	.85

CHINA
'96 — A485

Designs: a, Monument of Sukhe Bator. b, Temple of Heaven, Beijing. c, Migjed Jang-Rasek. d, Great Wall.

1996, Apr. 25   **Litho.**   **Perf. 13½x14**
2237	A485	65t Sheet of 4, #a.-d.	10.00	10.00

1996
Summer
Olympic
Games,
Atlanta
A486

30t, Cycling. 60t, Women's shooting. 80t, Weight lifting. 100t, Boxing. 120t, Women's archery, vert. 150t, Rhythmic gymnastics, vert. 200t, Hurdles, vert. 350t, Equestrian. 400t, Wrestling.
500t, Basketball. 600t, Judo.

1996   **Litho.**   **Perf. 14**
2238	A486	30t multicolored	.25	.25
2239	A486	60t multicolored	.25	.25
2240	A486	80t multicolored	.25	.25
2241	A486	100t multicolored	.30	.25
2242	A486	120t multicolored	.30	.25
2243	A486	150t multicolored	.40	.25
2244	A486	200t multicolored	.50	.30
2245	A486	350t multicolored	1.00	.70
2246	A486	400t multicolored	1.10	.80
		Nos. 2238-2246 (9)	4.35	3.30

Souvenir Sheets
2246A	A486	500t multicolored	3.50	2.50
2246B	A486	600t multicolored	4.00	4.00

No. 2246A contains one 37x53mm stamp, No. 2246B one 52x39mm stamp.
Olymphilex '96 (#2246A-2246B).

Mongolian postal authorities have declared as "unauthorized" two sheets of nine 350t Train stamps similar to Nos. 2442-2443, two souvenir sheets of one 2000t Train stamps similar to Nos. 2444-2445, and one sheet of six 300t Ferrari stamps similar to No. 2446.

Genghis Khan — A486a

Die Cut Perf. 7½
1996, Aug. 28   **Embossed**
Self-Adhesive
2246C	A486a	10,000t gold	60.00	60.00

CAPEX '96 — A487

Designs: a, 350t, #2. b, 400t, Canada #1.

1996   **Litho.**   **Perf. 12½**
2247	A487	Sheet of 2, #a.-b.	8.00	8.00

No. 2247b is 40x30mm. No. 2247 exists with blue at upper right margin corner and different colored margin picture of CN Tower.

Nos. 2176-2179, 2181 Overprinted

1996, Sept. 8   **Litho.**   **Perf. 14**
2247C	A469	600t On #2176	2.50	2.50
2247D	A469	600t On #2177	2.50	2.50
2247E	A470	600t On #2178	2.50	2.50
2247F	A470	600t On #2179	2.50	2.50
		Nos. 2247C-2247F (4)	10.00	10.00

Souvenir Sheet
2247G	A469	600t On No. 2181	4.00	4.00

Mongolian
National
Democratic
and Social
Democratic
Parties
A487a

1996, Sept. 25   **Litho.**   **Perf. 13¾**
2247H	A487a	100t multicolored	.60	.50

Souvenir Sheet

Taipei '96 — A487b

1996, Oct. 21   **Litho.**   **Perf. 12¾**
2247I	A487b	750t multicolored	5.00	5.00
r.		Overprinted "Taipei 2005" in margin in silver	5.00	5.00

No. 2247Ir issued 8/19/2005.

Children &
Scouting
Emblem — A487c

1996, Dec. 16   **Litho.**   **Perf. 14**
Country Flags
2247J	A487c	250t Mongolia	1.50	.40
2247K	A487c	250t US	1.50	.40
2247L	A487c	250t Germany	1.50	.40
2247M	A487c	250t Russia	1.50	.40
2247N	A487c	250t Japan	1.50	.40
2247O	A487c	250t PRC	1.50	.40
q.		Souvenir sheet, #2247J-2247O	15.00	15.00
		Nos. 2247J-2247O (6)	9.00	2.40

Souvenir Sheet
Perf. 12¾x12¾
2247P	A487c	700t No flag	4.25	4.25

UNICEF (#2247P).

New Year
1997
(Year of
the Ox)
A488

1997   **Litho.**   **Perf. 14**
2248	A488	300t Ox, vert.	1.25	1.00
2249	A488	350t shown	1.50	1.25

Souvenir Sheet

Total Solar Eclipse Over Mongolia,
Mar. 9, 1997 — A489

1997   **Litho.**   **Perf. 12½**
2250	A489	1000t Map of Mongolia	5.00	4.75

Return
of Hong
Kong to
China
A490

Designs: 200t, Former Chinese Pres. Deng Xiaoping, Queen Elizabeth II. 250t, Chinese Pres. Jiang Zemin and Chief Executive of the Special Administrative Region of Hong Kong, Tung Chee-hwa.

1997   **Litho.**   **Perf. 13½**
2251	A490	200t multicolored	1.00	1.00
2252	A490	250t multicolored	1.50	1.50
a.		Pair, #2251-2252	2.50	2.50

Seven Joys — A491

Designs: a, Wheel. b, Gem. c, Minister. d, Queen. e, Elephant. f, Horse. g, General.

1997   **Litho.**   **Perf. 11**
2253	A491	200t Sheet of 7, #a.-g., + 2 labels	6.00	6.00

Souvenir Sheet

Moscow '97 — A492

1997   **Perf. 12½x11½**
2254	A492	1000t No. 264	5.00	5.00
a.		With Irkutsk 2007 emblem and inscription added in sheet margin ('07)	1.75	1.75

No. 2254a issued 6/8/2007.

Monument to
the Politically
Repressed
A493

1997   **Perf. 13x13½**
2255	A493	150t black & gray	.95	.60

Trains
A493a

Designs: 20t, VL-80 electric locomotive. 40t, Japanese high speed electric train. 120t, BL-80 Diesel locomotive. 200t, German steam locomotive. 300t, Lass "FDp" steam locomotive. 350t, 0-6-0 tank locomotive. 400t, Diesel locomotive. 500t, T6-106 Diesel locomotive. 600t, Magnetic train.
No. 2255K, "Rocket." No. 2255L, London-Paris train.

1997, Dec. 5   **Litho.**   **Perf. 14x14¼**
2255A	A493a	20t multi	.45	.25
2255B	A493a	40t multi	.55	.25
2255C	A493a	120t multi	.65	.25
2255D	A493a	200t multi	.85	.30
2255E	A493a	300t multi	.90	.40
2255F	A493a	350t multi	1.00	.60
2255G	A493a	400t multi	1.25	.70
2255H	A493a	500t multi	1.40	.75
2255I	A493a	600t multi	1.75	1.00
j.		Sheet of 9, #2255A-2255I	11.00	11.00
		Nos. 2255A-2255I (9)	8.80	4.50

Souvenir Sheets
Perf. 11¼

2255K	A493a	800t multi	3.75	2.50
2255L	A493a	800t multi	3.75	2.50

Nos. 2255K, 2255L each contain one 59x43mm stamp.

Emperors of Mongolia
A494

a, Genghis Khan. b, Ogadai Khan. c, Guyuk Khan. d, Mangu Khan. e, Kublai Khan.

Perf. 11½x12½

1997, Dec. 25   **Litho.**

2256	A494	1000t Strip of 5,		
		#a.-e.	20.00	20.00

Nos. 2256a-2256e exist in souvenir sheets containing 1 or 2 21x33mm stamps.

New Year 1998 (Year of the Tiger)
A495

Various stylized tigers.

1998, Feb. 1   **Perf. 12**

2257	A495	150t multicolored	1.00	1.00
2258	A495	200t multicolored	1.50	1.50
2259	A495	300t multicolored	2.00	2.00
		Nos. 2257-2259 (3)	4.50	4.50

Design on No. 2259 is oriented point down.

Mongolian Yaks
A496

Various yaks: 20t, Three. 30t, One white. 50t, With carts. 100t, One male. 150t, Female with calf. 200t, Three, campsite. 300t, One with horns, flowing hair. 400t, Brown yak looking back.
800t, Carrying children and supplies.

1998, Mar. 15   **Litho.**   **Perf. 12**

2260	A496	20t multicolored	.25	.25
2261	A496	30t multicolored	.25	.25
2262	A496	50t multicolored	.25	.25
2263	A496	100t multicolored	.35	.35
2264	A496	150t multicolored	.55	.55
2265	A496	200t multicolored	.75	.75

Size: 50x36mm

2266	A496	300t multicolored	1.10	1.10
2267	A496	400t multicolored	1.50	1.50
		Nos. 2260-2267 (8)	5.00	5.00

Souvenir Sheet
Perf. 11

2268	A496	800t multicolored	5.50	5.50

No. 2268 contains one 60x47mm stamp.

Butterflies and Orchids — A497

Designs: 100t, Adonis blue, dendrobium cunninghamii. 150t, Brown hairstreak, oncidium ampliatum. 200t, Large skipper, maxillaria triloris. 250t, Orange tip, calypso bulbosa. 300t, Painted lady, catasetum pileatum. 350t, Purple hairstreak, epidedrum fimbratum. 400t, Red admiral, cleistes rosea. 450t, Small copper, ponthieva maculata. 500t, Small tortoiseshell, cypripeium calceolus.
Each 800t: No. 2278, Red admiral, c. macranthum. No. 2279, Adonis blue, c. guttatum.

1997, Dec. 5   **Litho.**   **Perf. 14**

2269-2277	A497	Set of 9	5.50	3.50

Souvenir Sheets

2278-2279	A497	Set of 2	8.50	5.00

Souvenir Sheet

1998 World Cup Soccer Championships, France — A498

1998, June 1   **Perf. 13**

2280	A498	1000t multicolored	5.00	5.00

Souvenir Sheet

Pres. Natsagyn Bagabandi — A499

1998, July 15   **Litho.**   **Perf. 12½**

2281	A499	1000t multicolored	4.00	3.50

Greenpeace, 26th Anniv. — A500

Designs: 200t, Penguin in snow. 400t, Six penguins, water, mountain. 500t, Two penguins at water's edge. 800t, Large group of penguins.
No. 2286: a, like #2282. b, like #2283. c, like #2284. d, like #2285. e, like #2287.
1000t, Greenpeace ship.

1997, Sept. 15   **Litho.**   **Perf. 13½**

2282-2285	A500	Set of 4	0.25	0.25
2286	A500	Sheet of 5, #a.-e.	7.00	7.00

Souvenir Sheet

2287	A500	1000t multicolored	6.00	6.00

Country name, denominations, "Greenpeace" in red on No. 2286. Nos. 2282-2287 exist imperf.

Diana, Princess of Wales (1961-97)
A501

Various portraits with bister background — #2288: a, 50t. b, 100t. c, 150t. d, 200t. e, 250t. f, 300t. g, 350t. h, 400t. i, 450t.
Various portraits with pale brown background — #2289a, 50t. b, 100t. c, 150t. d, 200t. e, 250t. f, 300t. g, 350t. h, 400t. i, 450t.
Each 1000t: No. 2290, Diana holding infant son. No. 2291, Diana wearing tiara. No. 2292, Diana in pink dress. No. 2293, Diana in white (Mother Teresa in margin).

1997, Dec. 15   **Sheets of 9, #a-i**

2288-2289	A501	Set of 2	12.00	12.00

Souvenir Sheets

2290-2293	A501	Set of 4	14.00	14.00

Nos. 2288-2289 exist imperf.

Genghis Khan's Soldiers
A502

Various soldiers in traditional attire, background color: 100t, tan. 150t, pale violet. 200t, green blue. 250t, green. 300t, gray. 350t, pink. 400t, blue. 600t, pale brown.
Army on the march — #2302: a, 600t, One standing, others on horses. b, 1000t, Leaders riding decorated horses. c, 600t, Two standing, leopards, others on horses.

1997, Dec. 20   **Perf. 12**

2294-2301	A502	Set of 8	8.50	8.50

Souvenir Sheet

2302	A502	Sheet of 3, #a.-c.	8.50	8.50

No. 2302b is 65x56mm.

No. 276 Surcharged

1996, Dec. 25   **Photo.**   **Perf. 11½x12**

2302D	A77	200t on 70m multicolored	10.00	5.00

National Symbols — A503

1998, Jan. 1

2303	A503	300t Natl. flag, horiz.	.90	.75
2304	A503	300t shown	.90	.75

Ursus Arctos Gobiensis
A504

100t, Adult looking forward. 150t, Adult walking left. 200t, Two bears. 250t, Mother, cubs.

1998, July 20

2305-2308	A504	Set of 4	7.00	7.00
2307a		Sheet of 2, #2305, 2307	3.00	3.00
2308a		Sheet of 2, #2306, 2308	4.00	4.00

Fish
A505

Designs: 20t, Lebistes reticulatus. 30t, Goldfish. 50t, Balistes conspicillum. 100t, Goldfish, diff. 150t, Synchirops splendidus. 200t, Auratus. 300t, Xiphophorus helleri. 400t, Pygoplites diacanthus. 600t, Chaetodon auriga.
Various fish, denomination (800t): No. 2318, At top. No. 2319, At bottom.

1998, July 20   **Perf. 12½**

2309-2317	A505	Set of 9	6.00	6.00

Souvenir Sheets
Perf. 11

2318-2319	A505	Set of 2	12.00	12.00

Nos. 2318-2319 each contain one 95x49mm stamp.

Domestic Cats
A506

Designs: 50t, Red Persian. 100t, Manx cat. 150t, Smoke Persian. 200t, Long-haired white Persian. 250t, Silver tabby. 300t, Siamese. 1000t, Kittens, basket.

1998, Sept. 1   **Perf. 12**

2320-2325	A506	Set of 6	5.00	5.00

Souvenir Sheet

2326	A506	1000t multicolored	5.00	5.00

Jerry Garcia (1942-95) and The Grateful Dead
A507

Nos. 2327-2328, Various portraits of Jerry Garcia.
No. 2328A — Black and white photos: f, 100t. g, 150t. h, 50t.
No. 2328B — Blue guitar: i, 150t. j, 200t. k, 100t.
No. 2328C — Red guitar: l, 200t. m, 250t. n, 150t.
No. 2328D — White guitar: o, 200t. p, 250t. q, 150t.
No. 2328E — Dark background: r, 300t. s, 350t. t, 250t.
No. 2329: Various portraits of Garcia: a, 50t. b, 100t. c, 150t. d, 200t. e, 250t. f, 300t. g, 350t. h, 400t. i, 450t.
No. 2330: Various pictures of bears (Grateful Dead emblem) in sports activities: a, 50t. b, Dirt biking. b, 100t, Soccer. c, 150t, Basketball. d, 200t, Golf. e, 250t, Baseball. f, 300t, Roller blading. g, 350t, Ice hockey. h, 400t, Football. i, 450t, Skiing.
Each 1000t: No. 2331, Garcia holding guitar. No. 2331A, Garcia with left hand on guitar, right hand in air.

1998-99   Perf. 12½
2327	A507	100t multicolored	1.00	.50
2328	A507	200t multicolored	1.00	.50

Strips of 3
2328A-2328E	A507	Set of 5	9.00	9.00

Sheets of 9, #a-i
2329-2330M	A507	Set of 2	11.50	11.50

Souvenir Sheets
2331-2331A	A507	Set of 2	5.00	5.00

Nos. 2327-2328 were each issued in sheets of 9. Nos. 2331-2331A contain one 51x76mm.

Dot of "I" in Garcia is a diamond on Nos. 2327-2329, 2331-2331A. "Jerry Garcia" is in pink letters with rose shadowing on Nos. 2328A-2328E.

Issued: No. 2331A, 1/1/99; #2328A-2328E, 1999; others 10/15/98.

See Nos. 2385-2389.

Bob Marley
(1947-81)
A508

Portraits: 200t, Up close. 1000t, At microphone.

1998, Oct. 15
2332	A508	200t multicolored	1.25	1.25

Souvenir Sheet
2333	A508	1000t multicolored	3.00	3.00

No. 2332 was issued in sheets of 9. No. 2333 contains one 51x76mm stamp.

Carlos Santana
A509

1998, Oct. 15
2334	A509	200t multicolored	1.50	1.50

No. 2334 was issued in sheets of 9.

The Three Stooges — A510

Scenes from "The Three Stooges" motion pictures — #2335: a, 50t, Guns, cigars. b, 100t, Road signs. c, 150t, Dynamite. d, 200t, Golf clubs. e, 240t, Medals on uniform. f, 300t, Dove. g, 350t, Flower bouquets. h, 400t, Bright green cap. i. 450t, Whisk broom, cigar.

No. 2336: a, 50t, Doctor's equipment. b, 100t, Musical instruments. c, 150t, Clothes press. d, 200t, Long cord. e, 250t, Vise. f, 300t, Brick wall. g, 350t, Pliers. h, 400t, Turkey. i, 450t, Door.

No. 2337: a, 50t, Union soldiers. b, 100t, French Foreign Legion. c, 150t, Confederate soldiers, women. d, 200t, Horse. e, 250t, Army uniform, grenade. f, 300t, Cannon. g, 350t, Confederate soldiers, whiskey flask. 400t, Army uniforms, officer. 450t, Scarecrow.

Each 800t: No. 2338, like #2335b. No. 2339, like #2336c, vert. No. 2340, With football.

1998, Nov. 25   Litho.   Perf. 13½

Sheets of 9, #a-i.
2335-2337	A510	Set of 3	22.50	22.50

Souvenir Sheets
2338-2340	A510	Set of 3	9.00	9.00

Nos. 2335-2340 exist imperf. Nos. 2338-2340 each contain one 51x41mm stamp.

Eight Offerings of Buddha — A511

#2341, The White Sign of Luck. #2342, The Auspicious Wheel. #2343, The Auspicious Cup. #2344, The White Couch. #2345, The White Umbrella. #2346, The Duaz of Victory. #2347, The White Lotus. #2348, The Auspicious Fish.

1998, Dec. 10   Litho.   Perf. 12
2341-2348	A511	200t Set of 8	5.00	5.00

Howdy Doody Television Show — A512

No. 2349: a, 50t, Chief Thunderthud. b, 100t, Princess Summerfall Winterspring. c, 150t, Howdy in Mexican outfit. d, 150t, Buffalo Bob in gray shirt, Howdy. e, 200t, Buffalo Bob in red and white shirt, Howdy. f, 250t, Howdy, Buffalo Bob rubbing noses. g, 450t, Howdy in military uniform. h, 250t, Clarabell the Clown. i, 450t, Howdy lying down.

Each 800t: No. 2350, Howdy. No. 2351, Buffalo Bob, Howdy, horiz. No. 2352, Howdy, Buffalo Bob.

Perf. 13½x14, 14x13½x14
1999, Apr. 1
2349	A512	Sheet of 9, #a.-i.	6.00	6.00

Souvenir Sheets
Perf. 14 (#2352)
2350-2352	A512	Set of 3	8.00	8.00

No. 2352 contains one 48x61mm stamp.

Prime Ministers of Mongolia — A513

a, T. Namnansuren. b, Badamdorj. c, D. Chagdarjav. d, D. Bodoo. e, S. Damdinbazar. f, B. Tserendorj. g, A. Amar. h, Ts. Jigjidjav. i, P. Genden. j, Kh. Ghoibalsan. k, Yu. Tsedenbal. l, J. Batmunkh. m, D. Sodnom. n, Sh. Gungaadorj. o, D. Byambasuren. p, P. Jasrai. q, M. Enkhsaikhan. r, Ts. Elbegdorj.

1998, Dec. 1   Perf. 12
2353	A513	200t Sheet of 18, #a.-r.	15.00	15.00

Natl. Wrestling Champions
A514

Designs: a, D. Damdin. b, S. Batsuury. c, J. Munkhbat. d, H. Bayanmunkh. e, B. Tubdendorj. f, D. Tserentogtokh. g, B. Baterdne.

1998, Dec. 26   Perf. 12½
2354	A514	200t Sheet of 7, #a.-g.	7.00	7.00

John Glenn's Return to Space
A515

Mercury Friendship 7 — #2355: a, 50t, Mercury capsule in outer space. b, 100t, NASA emblem. c, 150t, Friendship 7 mission patch. d, 150t, Launch of Friendship 7. e, 200t, Glenn, 1962. f, 250th, Recovery of capsule. g, 450t, Moon. h, 250t, Capsule re-entering atmosphere. i, 450t, Stars.

Shuttle Discovery mission — #2356: a, 50t, NASA emblem. b, 100t, Glenn in red launch suit. c, 150t, Discovery mission patch. d, 150t, Launch of Discovery. e, 200t, Glenn, 1998. f, 250t, Discovery landing. g, 450t, Sun. h, 250t, Discovery in outer space. i, 450t, NASA "40" emblem.

1998, Dec. 31   Perf. 14

Sheets of 9
2355-2356	A515	#a.-i., each	11.00	11.00

Postal Delivery — A516

Post office: a, 100t, Brown. b, 200t, Blue. c, 200t, Blue green. d, 400t, Red lilac. e, 400t, Violet.

Electronic services: f, 100t, Blue. g, 200t, Blue green. h, 200t, Red lilac. i, 400t, Violet. j, 400t, Brown.

EMS delivery: k, 100t, Blue green. l, 200t, Red lilac. m, 200t, Violet. n, 400t, Brown. o, 400t, Blue.

Mail train: p, 100t, Red lilac. q, 200t, Violet. r, 200t, Brown. s, 400t, Blue. t, 400t, Blue green.

Jet plane: u, 100t, Violet. v, 200t, Brown. w, 200t, Blue. x, 400t, Blue green. y, 400t, Red lilac.

1998, Nov. 15   Perf. 12
2357	A516	Sheet of 25, #a.-y.	22.50	22.50

Universal Declaration of Human Rights, 50th Anniv. — A517

1998, Dec. 25   Litho.   Perf. 12
2358	A517	450t multi + label	3.50	3.50

New Year 1999 (Year of the Rabbit)
A518

1999, Feb. 17
2359	A518	250t Rabbit, vert.	2.00	2.00
2360	A518	300t shown	2.00	2.00

Buddha Migjed Jankraisig, Ulan Bator
A519

Designs: 200t, Temple.
Each 1000t: No. 2363, Statue. No. 2364, Statue, drawing of Temple.

1999, Apr. 15
2361	A519	200t multicolored	1.00	1.00
2362	A519	400t multicolored	2.00	2.00

Souvenir Sheets
Perf. 11
2363-2364	A519	Set of 2	8.00	8.00

Nos. 2363-2364 each contain one 49x106mm stamp.

Falcons — A520

Falcon: a, 300t, Subbuteo. b, 250t, Naumanni. c, 200t, Tinnunculus. d, 170t, Peregrinus. e, 800t, Rusticolus by nest. f, 600t, Rusticolus in flight. g, 400t, Pelegrinoides over kill. h, 350t, Pelegrinoides on branch. i, 150t, Columbarius. j, 100t, Vespertinus. k, 50t, Cherrug. l, 30t, Amurensis.

1999, Mar. 20   Perf. 12
2365	A520	Sheet of 12, #a.-l.	12.00	12.00

"I Love Lucy" Television Show — A521

Various scenes — #2366: a, 50t. b, 100t. c, 150t. d, 150t. e, 200t. f, 250t. g, 450t. h, 250t. i, 450t.

Each 800t: No. 2367, Lucy talking with woman. No. 2368, Ethel looking at Lucy locked in cold storage locker.

1999, July 15   Litho.   Perf. 13½x14
2366	A521	250t Sheet of 9, #a.-i.	6.00	6.00

Souvenir Sheets
2367-2368	A521	Set of 2	5.50	5.50

Nos. 2367-2368 each contain one 38x51mm stamp.

Betty Boop Cartoon Character
A522

Various pictures of Betty Boop — #2369: a, 50t. b, 100t. c, 150t. d, 150t. e, 200t. f, 250t. g, 450t. h, 250t. i, 450t.

Each 800t: No. 2370, Betty in dog's eyes, horiz. No. 2371, Up close, horiz.

1999, July 15
2369 A522 Sheet of 9, #a.-i.   6.00 6.00
Souvenir Sheets
Perf. 14x13½
2370-2371 A522 Set of 2   4.75 4.75
Nos. 2370-2371 each contain one 51x38mm stamp.

Folk Tales
A523

Designs: 50t, Man, yurt, two demons. 150t, Chess players. 200t, Lion carrying logs. 250t, Flying horse. 300t, Archer, bird, sun. 450t, Horses, cranes.
1000t, Birds, camel in flight.

1999, June 15 Litho. *Perf. 13x13¼*
2372-2377 A523 Set of 6   7.00 7.00
Souvenir Sheet
Perf. 12½
2378 A523 1000t multicolored   7.00 7.00
No. 2378 contains one 41x32mm stamp.

No. 307
Surcharged

Methods and Perfs as Before
1999, June 15
2378A A84 810t on 60m bl & multi   16.00 16.00

Miniature Sheet

Ram — A524

Panel color: a, 250t, Blue. b, 450t, Red.

1999, Aug. 21 Litho. *Perf. 12½*
2379 A524 Miniature sheet of 2, #a.-b.   2.00 2.00
China 1999 World Philatelic Exhibition. No. 2379 is cut from a larger sheet of alternating stamps and labels. The cutting is through the labels along the diagonal axes.

UPU, 125th Anniv. — A525

Designs: No. 2380, Rider, two horses. No. 2381, Rider, one horse. No. 2382, Train and truck. No. 2382, Airplane and computer.
800t, Ogodei Khan (1186-1241).

1999, Oct. 9
2380-2383 A525 250t Set of 4   4.00 4.00
Souvenir Sheet
2384 A525 800t multi   4.50 4.50
No. 2384 contains one 31x41mm stamp.

Nos. 551, 1742 Surcharged

250₮

250₮

Methods and Perfs. as Before
1999, Aug. 25
2384A A133 250t on 50m multi   10.00 10.00
2384B A389 250t on 60m multi   10.00 10.00
Victory in Khalkh-gol War, 60th anniv.

Genghis Khan
A525a

Die Cut Perf. 11½
1999, Sept. 27 Embossed
Self-Adhesive
2384C A525a 15,000t gold & sil   60.00 —

Jerry Garcia Type of 1998

No. 2385 — Rose and blue speckled background: a, 50t. b, 100t. c, 150t.
No. 2386 — Pink-toned vignette extension backgrounds: a, 100t. b, 150t. c, 200t.
No. 2387 — Pink, blue and purple curved line backgrounds: a, 150t. b, 200t. c, 250t.
No. 2388 — Dark blue and purple straight line backgrounds: a, 150t. b, 200t. c, 250t.
No. 2389 — Blue green and green backgrounds: a, 250t. b, 300t. c, 350t.

1999 Litho. *Perf. 12½*
"Jerry Garcia" In Black-Shadowed Letters
2385-2389 A507 Set of 5 strips of 3   9.00 9.00

Stone Carvings
A526

Designs: 50t, Stele with Uigur inscriptions, vert. 150t, Turtle, 13th cent. 200t, Kul Tegin burial site, 7th-8th cent., vert. 250t, Kul Tegin, 8th cent., vert. 300t, Dragon, 8th-9th cent. 450t, Man, 5th-7th cent., vert.

2000, Jan. 17 Litho. *Perf. 12*
2390-2395 A526 Set of 6   5.00 5.00

A527

World Teachers' Day — A528

Academicians: #2396, 2398, Dr. Tsendiin Damdinsuren (1908-86). #2397, 2399, Dr. B. Rinchin (1905-77).

1999, Dec. 5
2396 A527 250t blue & blk   .50 .50
2397 A527 250t grn & blk   .50 .50
2398 A527 450t pur & blk   .85 .85
2399 A527 450t brn & blk   .85 .85
2400 A528 600t multi   1.10 1.10
   Nos. 2396-2400 (5)   3.80 3.80

Souvenir Sheet

Sanjaasuregin Zorig (1962-98), Politician — A529

Designs: a, 600t, Zorig in 1968. b, 1000t, Three people, flag. c, 600t, Zorig in 1998.

1999, Oct. 1 *Perf. 13¼x13*
2401 A529 Sheet of 3, #a.-c.   5.50 5.50
Size of No. 2401b: 59x39mm.

World Intellectual Property Organization, 20th Anniv. — A529a

No. 2401D — e, 250t, Satellite, airplane. f, 450t, Statue, television. g, 250t, Cauldron, toy. h, 250t, Copier, stamps. i, 450t, Camera, yurt, Mongolian couple. j, 250t, Red automobile. k, 250t, Grille of antique auto, bottles, cellular phones, wristwatch. l, 450t, Perfume bottles. m, 250t, Pack of cigarettes, soccer ball, volley ball, basketball, bottle of motor oil, boom box.

1999, Dec. 24 Litho. *Perf. 12*
2401D A529a Sheet of 9, #e-m   8.00 8.00

Souvenir Sheet

Japan-Mongolia Friendship — A530

a, Sumo wrestler. b, Symbols of countries.

1999, Dec. 28 *Perf. 13½*
2402 A530 450t Sheet of 2, #a.-b.   4.50 4.50

New Year 2000 (Year of the Dragon) — A531

Background color: 250t, Red. 450t, Blue, vert.

2000, Jan. 10 Litho. *Perf. 12*
2403-2404 A531 Set of 2   4.00 4.00
For overprint, see Nos. 2733-2734.

Nos. 715-717, C34 Surcharged

Methods and Perfs as Before
2000, Jan. 19
2405 A168 1000t on 50m brn   7.00 7.00
2406 A168 2000t on 60m grn   8.00 8.00
2407 A168 5000t on 1t rose claret   15.00 15.00
2408 AP12 10,000t on 1.50t bl   30.00 30.00
   Nos. 2405-2408 (4)   60.00 60.00

Wolves — A532

Designs: 150t, Pair, one with snout up. 250t, Eating deer. 300t, Nursing young. 450t, Snarling.

2000, Jan. 17 Litho. *Perf. 12*
2409-2412 A532 Set of 4   4.00 4.00
Souvenir Sheet
2413 A532 800t Pair baying   4.00 4.00
No. 2413 contains one 50x30mm stamp.

Sheep — A533

Breeds: 50t, Sumber. 100t, Orkhon. 150t, Baidrag. 250t, Barga. 400t, Uzemchin. 450t, Bayad.

2000, Jan. 20
2414-2419 A533 Set of 6   4.00 4.00
Souvenir Sheet
2420 A533 800t Govi-Altai   4.00 4.00

One Day of Mongolia, by Balduugiin
Sharav — A534

Various parts of painting: a, 50t. b, 100t, c,
150t. d, 200t. e, 250t. f, 300t. g, 350t. h, 450t. i,
600t.

2000, Jan. 24
2421 A534   Sheet of 9, #a-i   9.00 9.00

Huts and
Yurts
A535

Designs: 50t, Hunters returning to hut. 100t,
Mother, daughter, animals near hut. 150t, Yurt
near hill. 250t, Two yurts, motorcycle, and satellite dish. 450t, Yurt construction.
No. 2427, 800t, Yurt's furnishings. No. 2428,
800t, Yurt and wagon.

2000, Jan. 25
2422-2426 A535   Set of 5   4.00 4.00
Souvenir Sheets
2427-2428 A535   Set of 2   8.00 8.00

Union of Mongolian
Production and
Service
Cooperatives, 10th
Anniv. — A536

Panel colors: 300t, Blue. 450t, Green.

2000, Mar. 27   *Perf. 12*
2429-2430 A536   Set of 2   4.00 4.00

A537

A538

A539

A540

A541

A542

A543

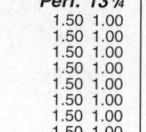

Costumes of
Mongolian
Lords — A544

2000, May 11   *Perf. 13¼*
2431 A537 550t multi   1.50 1.00
2432 A538 550t multi   1.50 1.00
2433 A539 550t multi   1.50 1.00
2434 A540 550t multi   1.50 1.00
2435 A541 550t multi   1.50 1.00
2436 A542 550t multi   1.50 1.00
2437 A543 550t multi   1.50 1.00
2438 A544 550t multi   1.50 1.00
Nos. 2431-2438 (8)   12.00 8.00

Buddhas
A545

No. 2439: a, Jigjid. b, Gombo. c, Tsamba. d,
Jamsran. e, Baldanlkham. f, Ochirvani. g,
Namsrai. h, Gongor. i, Damdinchoijoo. j,
Shalshi.

2000, July 1   *Perf. 13x13½*
2439   Block of 10   15.00 11.00
  a.-j. A545 550t Any single   1.50 1.10

Worldwide Fund for Nature
(WWF) — A546

Two Przewalski's horses: No. 2440a, 300t,
No. 2441a, 100t, Standing apart. No. 2440b,
150t, No. 2441b, 250t, Galloping. No. 2440c,
100t, No. 2441d, 200t, Grazing. No. 2440d,
200t, No. 2441c, 50t, Standing together.

**2000, July 5   Litho.   *Perf. 13½*
2440 A546   Block or strip of 4,
  #a-d   4.50 4.50
Litho. & Holography
Size: 50x35mm
2441 A546   Block of 4, #a-d   5.50 5.50
Illustrations on No. 2441 are mirror images
of those on No. 2440.

Trains — A547

No. 2442: a, 200t, Guaari-Current electric
locomotive, France. b, 400t, 2-10-0 Austerity,
Great Britain. c, 300t, ALG Bo-Bo electric
locomotive, Great Britain. d, 400t, Diesel-electric locomotive, Australia. e, 300t, E-10 Bo-Bo
electric locomotive, Germany. f, 200t, C38
Class Pacific, US. g, 300t, 46 Class electric
locomotive, US. h, 200t, Bo-Bo electric locomotive, New Zealand. i, 400t, Bo-Bo electric
locomotive, Netherlands.
No. 2443: a, 300t, Italian second-clas carriage. b, 400t, Bodmin & Wadebridge Railway
composite carriage. c, 200t, Stephenson 2-2-
2, Russia. d, 200t, 2-2-2 Walt, US. e, 300t, The
General, US. f, 400t, 4-4-0 Washington, US. g,
400t, Braithwaite 0-4-0, Great Britain. h, 200t,
Ross Winans Muddigger locomotive, US. i,
300t, 4-4-0 Ramapo, US.
No. 2444, 800t, The Ringmaster, US. No.
2445, 800t, Deltic electric locomotive, Great
Britain.

**2000, July 7   Litho.   *Perf. 14*
Sheets of 9, #a-i
2442-2443 A547   Set of 2   13.00 13.00
Souvenir Sheets
2444-2445 A547   Set of 2   8.00 8.00

Ferrari Race Cars — A548

No. 2446: a, 1975 312 T. b, 1961 156 F1. c,
1979 312 T4. d, 1964 158 F1. e, 1981 126 CK.
f, 1974 312 B3.

2000, July 15
2446 A548 350t Sheet of 6,
  #a-f   16.00 16.00

2000
Summer
Olympics,
Sydney
A549

Designs: 100t, Boxing. 200t, Wrestling.
300t, Judo. 400t, Shooting.

2000, July 21   *Perf. 13x13¼*
2447-2450 A549   Set of 4   4.00 4.00

Albert Einstein (1879-1955) — A550

Einstein: a, 100t, At blackboard. b, 300t,
Wearing hat. c, 200t, Wearing green sweater.
d, 200t, With violin. e, 550t, Close-up. f, 100t,
At lectern. g, 100t, Holding pipe. h, 400t,
Receiving award. i, 300t, Holding clock.

2000, Aug. 10   *Perf. 12½*
2451 A550   Sheet of 9, #a-i   7.50 7.50

I Love Lucy — A551

No. 2452, vert.: a, 100t, Lucy, wiping hands,
and Ethel. b, 400t, Lucy, reading letter, and
Ethel. c, 200t, Lucy, setting table, and Fred. d,
200t, Lucy on telephone. e, 300t, Lucy with
chin on fist. f, 100t, Lucy with head on hands.
g, 100t, Lucy and Ethel waving. h, 550t, Lucy,

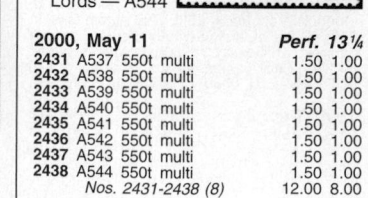

holding bowl, and Ethel. i, 300t, Lucy, wearing brown sweater and holding jar, and Ethel. No. 2453, 800t, Lucy, with mouth open, holding jar, and Ethel. No. 2454, 800t, Lucy. wearing stole, and Ethel.

2000, Aug. 15   Litho.   Perf. 12½
2452 A551   Sheet of 9, #a-i   4.00 4.00
Souvenir Sheets
2453-2454 A551   Set of 2   3.00 3.00

The Three Stooges — A552

No. 2455, horiz.: a, 100t, Moe, Larry and woman. b, 400t, Moe, Shemp and Larry attempting jail escape. c, 300t, Moe, with blow torch, Shemp and Larry. d, 200t, Moe, Larry and Joe Besser with musical instruments. e, 300t, Man knocking together heads of Shemp, Larry and Moe. f, 100t, Man with hammer, Moe, Larry and Shemp. g, 100t, Larry, Joe Besser and Moe in kitchen. h, 550t, Moe, Shemp and Larry with large wrench. i, 200t, Larry, Moe and Shemp in kitchen.
No. 2456, 800t, Moe, with fingers in ears, and Shemp. No. 2457, 800t, Shemp and Larry in army uniforms.

2000, Aug. 17
2455 A552   Sheet of 9, #a-i   8.00 8.00
Souvenir Sheets
2456-2457 A552   Set of 2   3.00 3.00

20th Century Events in Mongolia — A553

No. 2458: a, Independence, 1911. b, National revolution, 1921. c, Declaration of Mongolian People's Republic, 1924. d, Political repression, 1937. e, War years, 1939-45. f, Voting for independence, 1945. g, Agricultural reform, 1959. h, Member of UN, 1961. i, Space flight, 1981. j, Democratic revolution, 1990.

2000, Sept. 13   Litho.   Perf. 13½x13
2458 A553   300t Sheet of 10, #a-j + 2 labels   8.00 8.00
See No. 2482.

Marmota Sidisica — A554

Number of marmots: 100t, One. 200t, Three. 300t, Two. 400t, Three, diff.

2000, Sept. 15   Perf. 13¼x13
2459-2462 A554   Set of 4   6.00 6.00
Souvenir Sheet
Perf. 13x13¼
2463 A554   800t One marmot, horiz.   5.50 5.50

Traditional Patterns A555

Various designs: 50t, 200t, 250t, 300t, 400t, 550t.
50t, 250t, 550t are horiz.

Perf. 13¼x13, 13x13¼
2000, Sept. 20
2464-2469 A555   Set of 6   10.00 10.00

John F. Kennedy, Jr. (1960-99) — A556

2000, Sept. 25   Perf. 14
2470 A556   300t multi   1.50 1.50
Printed in sheets of 6.

Millennium — A557

Exploration: a, 100t, Charles Darwin. b, 200t, Mollusk. c, 300t, HMS Beagle. d, 400t, Peacock. e, 400t, Dinosaur. f, 100t, Clematis. g, 200t, Orchid. h, 300t, Giant tortoise. i, 200t, Reduviid bug. j, 100t, Down House. k, 300t, Duck. l, 550t, The Origin of Species. m, 100t, Chimpanzee. n, 300t, Turkey. o, 550t, Horse. p, 600t, Ram (60x40mm). q, Vormela peregusna.

2000, Oct. 5   Perf. 12¾x12½
2471 A557   Sheet of 17, #a-q + label   17.00 17.00

State Symbols — A558

No. 2472: a, Headdress on spike. b, Horn. c, Bow, arrows and quiver. d, Robe. e, Crossed swords. f, Saddle. g, Belt. h, Seated man. i, Throne.

2000, Oct. 25   Litho.   Perf. 12
2472 A558   300t Sheet of 9, #a-i   15.00 15.00

Queens — A559

No. 2473: a, Oulen. b, Borteujin. c, Turakana. d, Caymish. e, Chinbay.

2000, Oct. 30
2473   Horiz. strip of 5   7.50 7.50
a.-e. A559 300t Any single   1.50 1.50

Trains — A560

No. 2474: a, 200t, TGV, France. b, 100t, X200, Sweden. c, 300t, Regio Runner, Netherlands. d, 100t, Deltic, Great Britain. e, 300t, Type M1200, Burma. f, 200t, ICE, Germany. g, 300t, G Class, Australia. h, 200t, Class E444, Italy. i, 100t, GM F7 Warbonnet, US.
No. 2475: a, 200t, Class 18 4-6-2, Germany. b, 100t, Class GS-4 4-8-4, US. c, 300t, Class 25 4-8-4, South Africa. d, 100t, Class 685 2-6-2, Italy. e, 300t, Class HP, India. f, 200t, Class SY 2-8-2, China. g, 300t, Liner A3 Pacific, Great Britain. h, 200t, Class 231C 4-6-2, France. i, 100t, Class 3700, Netherlands.
No. 2476, 800t, Rocket 0-2-2, Great Britain. No. 2477, 800t, Eurostar, France and Great Britain, vert.

2000, Nov. 25   Perf. 14
Sheets of 9, #a-i
2474-2475 A560   Set of 2   13.50 13.50
Souvenir Sheets
2476-2477 A560   Set of 2   9.00 9.00
Nos. 2474-2475 each contain nine 42x28mm stamps.

Endangered Animals of Gobi Desert — A561

No. 2478: a, 100t, Scarabaeus typhon (40x30mm). b, 400t, Ursus arctos gobiensis (40x40mm). c, 300t, Camelus bactrianus ferus (40x40mm). d, 300t, Saiga tatarica mongolica (40x40mm). e, 550t, Ovis ammon (40x40mm). f, 550t, Uncia uncia (40x40mm). g, 100t, Phrynosephalus helioscopus(40x30mm). h, 200t, Coliber spinalus (40x30mm). i, 200t, Euchoreutes paso (40x30mm). j, 300t, Chlamydotis undulata (40x40mm).

2000, Dec. 25   Perf. 12½
2478 A561   Sheet of 10, #a-j   15.00 15.00

Souvenir Sheet

Advent of New Millennium — A562

Litho. & Embossed with Foil Application
2001, Jan. 1   Perf. 13½
2479 A562   5000t multi   15.00 15.00

New Year 2001 (Year of the Snake) — A563

Color behind snake: 300t, Pink. 400t, green, vert.

2001, Jan. 15   Litho.   Perf. 13¼
2480-2481 A563   Set of 2   4.00 4.00

20th Century Events Type of 2000

World events: a, First World War, 1914. b, October Revolution, 1917. c, Power seized by Fascists, 1933. d, Second World War, 1939. e, Nuclear weapons, 1945. f, Establishment of the United Nations, 1945. g, End of colonialism, 1940. h, Space travel, 1961. i, Downfall of socialism, 1989. j, Establishment of Mongolia, 1911.

2001, Mar. 15   Perf. 13½x13
2482 A553   300t Sheet of 10, #a-j, + 2 labels   8.00 8.00

Armed Forces, 80th Anniv. — A564

Designs: No. 2483, 300t, Marshal G. Demid (blue green). No. 2484, 300t, Marshal J.

Lhagvasuren (dark green). No. 2485, 300t, L. Dandar (olive green).

2001, Mar. 18　　　**Perf. 13¾x13¼**
2483-2485　A564　Set of 3　　3.00　3.00

Souvenir Sheet

Mountaineers — A565

No. 2486: a, Mountaineer waving. b, Mountaineers starting climb.

2001, Apr. 1　　　**Perf. 13¼x13**
2486　A565　400t Sheet of 2　#a-b　4.00　4.00

I Love Lucy — A566

No. 2487, horiz.: a, 100t, Lucy drinking from cup, Hicky reading newspaper. b, 400t, Ricky and Fred. c, 300t, Lucy, Ethel and two candy factory workers. d, 200t, Lucy with arms outstretched, candy factory worker. e, 300t, Lucy looking at candy factory worker. f, 100t, Lucy smearing chocolate on worker's face, g, 100t, Worker smearing Lucy's face with chocolate. h, 550t, Ricky holding stocking, Fred. i, 200t, Ethel and Lucy.

No. 2488, 800t, Lucy wrapping chocolates. No. 2489, 800t, Fred and Ricky preparing dinner.

2001, Apr. 15　　　**Perf. 12½**
2487　A566　Sheet of 9, #a-i　7.00　7.00
Souvenir Sheets
2488-2489　A566　Set of 2　　3.00　3.00

The Three Stooges — A567

No. 2490: a, 100t, Larry. b, 400t, Larry and Shemp inserting instrument into man's mouth. c, 300t, Moe and Shemp. d, 200t, Moe, Larry and Shemp on telephones. e, 300t, Moe with chef's toque, Shemp, Larry. f, 100t, Moe looking in tube. g, 100t, Moe hitting Larry, Shemp. h, 550t, Shemp, Larry, Moe and woman. i, 200t, Moe with gavel, Curly on telephone.

No. 2491, 800t, Shemp and Larry as shown on #2490e. No. 2492, 800t, Shemp as angel, vert.

2001, Apr. 15
2490　A567　Sheet of 9, #a-i　7.00　7.00
Souvenir Sheets
2491-2492　A567　Set of 2　　3.00　3.00

Philatelic Exhibitions — A568

Nomading, by T.S. Minjuur and exhibition emblem of: a, Hong Kong 2001. b, Hafnia 01. c, Phila Nippon '01. d, Belgica 2001.

2001, May 15　　　**Perf. 13½**
2493　A568　400t Sheet of 4, #a-d　4.00　4.00

Souvenir Sheet

Expo 2001, Kitakyushu, Japan — A569

No. 2494: a, Roses from Gobi Dream, by Shosaku Tasaki (52x24mm). b, Dreamer from Gobi Dream, vert. (32x42mm). c, Tarbosaurus (48x25mm). d, Iguanodon, vert. (30x41mm). e, Triceratops (48x25mm).

Serpentine Die Cut 10¾, 12¼
(#2494c-2494e)
2001, July 1
Self-Adhesive
2494　A569　500t Sheet of 5, #a-e　9.00　9.00

Children and Sports — A570

No. 2495: a, Chess. b, Bicycling. c, Baseball.
No. 2496: a, 200t, Mongolian children on horses. b, 350t, Ice hockey. c, 500t, Flag, Mongolian boy on horse. d, 150t, Children playing soccer. e, 300t, Mongolian girl on horse. f, 450t, Boy playing soccer. g, 100t, Mongolian children on horses. h, 250t, Golf. i, 400t, Mongolian children on horses.

2001, Sept. 1　　　**Perf. 12½**
2495　A570　500t Horiz. strip of 3, #a-c　　4.00　4.00
2496　A570　Sheet of 9, #a-i　12.00　12.00

Scouting and Nature — A571

No. 2497: a, 100t, Salpingotus. b, 200t, Uncia uncia. c, 300t, Haliaeetus albicilla. d,

400t, Pandion haliatus. e, 450t, Panciawus colchicus.
No. 2498: a, 50t, Butterfly. b, 100t, Bat. c, 200t, Butterfly, diff. d, 300t, Mushrooms. e, 400t, Dinosaur. f, 450t, Puffin.
No. 2499, vert.: a, 150t, Sea shell. b, 300t, Owl. c, 450t, Sea turtle. d, 100t, Frog. e, 250t, Butterfly. f, 400t, Orchid. g, 50t, Penguins. h, 200t, Elephant. i, 350t, Whale.

2001, Sept. 1
2497　A571　Sheet of 5, #a-e, +　label　5.00　5.00
2498　A571　Sheet of 6, #a-f　5.00　5.00
2499　A571　Sheet of 9, #a-i　7.50　7.50

Modern Transportation — A572

No. 2500: a, 50t, Zeppelin. b, 100t, Balloon. c, 150t, Apollo 11 command module. d, 200t, Apollo Lunar Module. e, 250t, Concorde. f, 300t, Train. g, 350t, Motorcycle. h, 400t, Race car. i, 450t, Sailboat.

2001, Sept. 15
2500　A572　Sheet of 9, #a-i　7.50　7.50

Admission to United Nations, 40th Anniv. — A573

No. 2501: a, Dove, map. b, UN and Mongolian flags.

2001, Oct. 27　　　**Perf. 13**
2501　A573　400t Horiz. pair, #a-b　3.00　3.00

Year of Dialogue Among Civilizations A574

2001, Dec. 20　　　**Perf. 13¼x13**
2502　A574　300t multi　　2.50　2.50

Endangered Species in Steppe Zone — A575

No. 2503: a, 300t, Vespertilio superans (40x40mm). b, 200t, Podoces hendersoni (40x30mm). c, 300t, Capra sibirica (40x40mm). d, 100t, Gazella subgutturosa (40x30mm). e, 400t, Equus przewalskii (40x40mm). f, 300t, Equus hemionus hemionus (40x40mm). g, 550t, Erinaceus dauricus (40x30mm). h, 200t, Papilio machaon (40x30mm). i, 550t, Vormela peregusna (40x30mm). j, 100t, Rana chensinensis (40x30mm).

2001, Dec. 30　　　**Perf. 13½x13¼**
2503　A575　Sheet of 10, #a-j　10.00　10.00

History of Humanity — A576

Prominent features of stamps: a, Leaning Tower of Pisa, Romulus and Remus suckling she-wolf. b, Eagle, warrior with shield. c, Great Wall of China. d, Mosque, warrior on horseback. e, Celtic cross, castle, warrior with shield. f, Mona Lisa, by Leonardo da Vinci, David, by Michelangelo, other sculptures and religious paintings. g, Mask, Easter Island statues, boomerang, native, hut. h, Sir Isaac Newton, telescope, planets, Nicolaus Copernicus. i, Eiffel tower, Napoleon bonaparte on horseback, French flag, Arc de Triomphe. j, Astronaut, Earth, DNA molecule, computer. k, Greek soldier and amphora. l, Taj Mahal, Asoka pillar. m, Statue of Buddha. n, Genghis Khan. o, Yurt, Buddhist statue. p, Jesus Christ, Madonna and Child. q, Globe, ship, Christopher Columbus. r, Statue of Liberty, U.S. Capitol, Indian chief, U.S. flag, George Washington, city skyline. s, Printing press, man on horseback, letters of alphabet. t, Tower Bridge, British flag, Penny Black.

2001, Dec. 30　　　**Perf. 13¼**
2504　　Sheet of 20　20.00　20.00
a.-j.　A576 200t Any single　1.00　1.00
k.-t.　A576 300t Any single　1.00　1.00

New Year 2002 (Year of the Horse) A577

Mane color: 300t, Gray, vert. 400t, Yellow brown.

2002, Feb. 13　**Perf. 13¼x13, 13x13¼**
2505-2506　A577　Set of 2　　4.00　4.00

Birds of Prey — A578

Designs: 100t, Gyps himalayensis. 150t, Gyps fulvus. 300t, Neophron percnopterus. 400t, Aegypius monachus. 550t, Gypaetus barbatus.

2002, Apr. 1　　　**Perf. 12½**
2507-2511　A578　Set of 5　　5.00　5.00

Souvenir Sheets

Mongolia - Japan Diplomatic Relations, 30th Anniv. — A579

No. 2512, 550t: a, Camel. b, Przewalski's horse.
No. 2513, 550t, vert. (38x50mm): a, Rider on horseback. b, Face of cartoon character.

2002, Apr. 27　　　**Perf. 12**
2512-2513　A579　Set of 2　　8.00　8.00

Dogs
A580

Dogs with: 100t, Sheep. 200t, Cattle. 300t, Camel and yurt. 400t, Camels. 800t, Dog.

2002, May 1   **Perf. 13¼x13**
2514-2517 A580   Set of 4   4.00 4.00
Souvenir Sheet
2518 A580 800t multi   3.50 3.50

2002 World Cup Soccer Championships, Japan and Korea — A581

No. 2519: a, 300t, Stadium, Seoul. b, 400t, 1998 French team and flag, World Cup trophy. c, 400t, 1966 English team and flag, Jules Rimet Cup. d, 300t, Stadium, Yokohama.

2002, May 31   **Perf. 12**
2519 A581   Sheet of 4, #a-d   4.50 4.50

Flowers — A582

Designs: 100t, Thermopsis. No. 2521, 150t, Chelidonium. No. 2522, 150t, Hypencum. 200t, Plantago. 250t, Saussurea. 300t, Rosa acicularis. 450t, Lilium.

2002, June 15   **Litho.**   **Perf. 12**
2520-2526 A582   Set of 7   7.00 7.00

Rock Paintings — A583

Various paintings with background colors of: 50t, Pink. 100t, Beige. 150t, Greenish blue. 200t, Green. 300t, Blue. 400t, Blue. 800t, Dark blue.

2002, July 1
2527-2532 A583   Set of 6   6.00 6.00
Souvenir Sheet
2533 A583 800t multi   3.50 3.50

New Year 2003 (Year of the Sheep) — A584

Sheep with background colors of: 300t, Yellow. 400t, Green, horiz.

2003, Jan. 1
2534-2535 A584   Set of 2   4.00 4.00

Mushrooms and Birds
A585

Designs: 50t, Russula aeruginosa, Coccothraustes coccothraustes. 100t, Boletus edulis, Loxia curvirostra. 150t, Boletus badius, Carpodacus erythrinus. 200t, Agaricus campester, Garrulus glandarius. 250t, Marasmius onreades, Luscinia megarhynchos. 300t, Cantharellus cibarius, Locustella certhiola. 400t, Amanita phalloides, Ardea cinerea. 550t, Suillus granulatus, Accipter gentilis.
No. 2544, 800t, Lactarius tormmosus, Aeqithalos caudatus. No. 2545, 800t, Tricholoma pertentosum, Lanius collurio.

2003, Feb. 1   **Perf. 13¼x13**
2536-2543 A585   Set of 8   12.00 12.00
Souvenir Sheets
2544-2545 A585   Set of 2   12.00 12.00
Nos. 2544-2545 each contain one 60x40mm stamp.

Visit Mongolia — A586

No. 2546: a, 100t, Statue of Sukhe Bator. b, 200t, City buildings. c, 300t, Rock formation. d, 400t, Yurts.
No. 2547: a, 100t, Camels. b, 200t, Yaks. c, 300t, Hunter with eagle. d, 400t, Snow leopard.

2003, July 11   **Perf. 12**
Sheets of 4, #a-d
2546-2547 A586   Set of 2   8.00 8.00

Endangered Species in Khangai Zone — A587

No. 2548: a, 300t, Pandion haliaetus (40x30mm). b, 200t, Dryomys nitedula (40x30mm). c, 300t, Rangifer tarandus (40x40mm). d, 100t, Moschus moschiferus (40x40mm). e, 550t, Alces alces pfizenmayeri (40x40mm). f, 400t, Alces alces cameloides (40x40mm). g, 300t, Sus scrofa nigripes (40x40mm). h, 550t, Phasianus colchicus (40x30mm). i, 200t, Lutra lutra (40x30mm). j, 100t, Castor fiber birulai (40x30mm).

2003, Aug. 15   **Perf. 13½**
2548 A587   Sheet of 10, #a-j   10.00 10.00

Birds, Butterflies, Orchids and Mushrooms — A588

No. 2549, 800t — Birds: a, Common bush tanager. b, Black-headed hemispingus. c, Scarlet-rumped tanager. d, Band-tailed seedeater.
No. 2550, 800t — Butterflies: a, Thecla teresina. b, Theritas cypria. c, Theritas coronata. d, Thecla phaleros.
No. 2551, 800t — Orchids: a, Vanda rothschildiana. b, Paphiopedium parishii. c, Dendrobium nobile. d, Cattleya loddigesii.
No. 2552, 800t — Mushrooms: a, Hypholoma fasciculare. b, Marasmiellus ramealis. c, Collybia fusipes. d, Kuehneromyces mutabilis.
No. 2553, 2500t, Andean hillstar. No. 2554, 2500t, Thecla pedusa. No. 2555, 2500t, Barkeria skinnerii. No. 2556, 2500t, Psathyrella multipedata, vert.

Perf. 13¼x13½, 13½x13¼
2003, Dec. 10
Sheets of 4, #a-d
2549-2552 A588   Set of 4   20.00 20.00
Souvenir Sheets
2553-2556 A588   Set of 4   16.00 16.00

Souvenir Sheet

Yang Liwei, First Chinese Astronaut — A589

2003, Dec. 25   **Litho.**   **Perf. 12**
2557 A589 800t multi   4.00 4.00

New Year 2004 (Year of the Monkey) — A590

Monkey and background in: 300t, Blue. 400t, Red.

2004, Feb. 21
2558-2559 A590   Set of 2   4.00 4.00

Peace Mandala — A591

No. 2560: a, 50t, Tushita Heaven. b, 100t, Elephant and Lady Maya. c, 150t, Birth of Buddha. d, 200t, Buddha as prince of Shakya clan. e, 250t, Prince shaving off hair. f, 300t, Buddha beating the devil. g, 400t, Buddha preaching for first time. h, 550t, Great Nirvana Sutra. i, 5000t, Various scenes in Buddha's life.
No. 2561, Central details of No. 2560i.
Size of Nos. 2560a-2560h, 41x38mm; No. 2560i, 132x182mm.

Serpentine Die Cut 10, 6¾ (#2560i, 2561)

2004, June 3   **Litho.**
Self-Adhesive
2560 A591   Sheet of 9, #a-i   18.00 18.00
Souvenir Sheet
Litho. With Foil Application
2561 A591 5000t gold & brn   20.00 20.00

Mammals — A592

Designs: (100t), Equus przewalskii. (300t), Camelus bactrianus ferus. (400t), Ovis ammon. (550t), Capra sibirica.

2004, July 1   **Litho.**   **Perf. 13¼x13**
2562 A592 (100t) multi   .50 .50
2563 A592 (300t) multi   .75 .75
2564 A592 (400t) multi   1.25 1.25
2565 A592 (550t) multi   1.50 1.50
Nos. 2562-2565 (4)   4.00 4.00

Genghis Khan (c. 1162-1227) — A593

Various depictions of Genghis Khan: 200t, 300t, 350t, 550t. 300t is horiz.

2004, July 11   **Perf. 13**
2566-2569 A593   Set of 4   4.00 4.00
Unification of Mongolia, 800th anniv. (in 2006).

2004 Summer
Olympics,
Athens — A594

Designs: 100t, Judo. 200t, Wrestling, horiz.
300t, Boxing. 400t, Pistol shooting, horiz.

2004, Aug. 13   **Perf. 12**
2570-2573 A594   Set of 4   4.00 4.00

UPU, 130th
Anniv. — A595

2004, Sept. 15   **Perf. 12¾**
2574 A595 300t multi   1.50 1.50

Nos. 776, 778, 841, 842 Surcharged

Methods and Perfs as Before
2004, Oct. 5
2575 A191 550t on 10m #841   — —
2576 A191 550t on 20m #842   — —
2577 A178 550t on 30m #776   — —
2578 A178 550t on 60m #778   — —

A596

A597

A598

Soccer
A599

Designs: No. 2581, Goalie making save. No.
2582, Player kicking ball. No. 2583, Three
players. No. 2584, Player and goalie.

2004, Oct. 15   **Litho.**   **Perf. 12¾x13**
2579 A596 50t multi   .25 .25
2580 A597 50t multi   .25 .25
2581 A597 100t multi   .40 .40

2582 A597 100t multi   .40 .40
2583 A597 150t multi   .55 .55
2584 A597 150t multi   .55 .55
2585 A598 200t multi   .80 .80
2586 A599 200t multi   .80 .80
     Nos. 2579-2586 (8)   4.00 4.00

Souvenir Sheet

First Mongolian Stamp, 80th
Anniv. — A600

2004, Dec. 4   **Perf. 13¼x13**
2587 A600 800t multi   3.50 3.50

Miniature Sheets

Insects and Flowers — A601

No. 2588: a, 100t, Mantis religiosa. b, 100t,
Aster alpina. c, 200t, Echinops humilis. d,
200t, Apis mellifera. e, 300t, Angaraeris
barabensis. f, 300t, Nymphaea candida.
No. 2589: a, 100t, Lytta caraganae. b, 100t,
Rosa acicularis. c, 200t, Aguilegia sibirica. d,
200t, Tabanus bovinus. e, 300t, Corizus hyos-
cyami. f, 300t, Lilium pumilum.

2004, Dec. 25   **Perf. 13**
    Sheets of 6, #a-f
2588-2589 A601   Set of 2   10.00 10.00

Women's Headdresses — A602

No. 2590: a, Kazakh headdress, denomination at left. b, Mongol headdress, denomination at right.

2004, Dec. 31   **Perf. 11½x11¾**
2590 A602 550t Horiz. pair, #a-b 5.00 5.00
    See Kazakhstan No. 472.

New Year
2005 (Year
of the
Rooster)
A603

Roosters with frame color of: 300t, Red violet. 400t, Blue, vert.

2005, Jan. 1   **Perf. 12**
2591-2592 A603   Set of 2   4.00 4.00

Souvenir Sheet

Expo 2005, Aichi, Japan — A604

No. 2593: a, 100t, Butterfly on flower. b,
150t, Flower. c, 200t, Puppy. d, 550t, Kitten.

2005, Mar. 25
2593 A604   Sheet of 4, #a-d   4.50 4.50

World
Vision
A605

2005, Apr. 1
2594 A605 550t multi   1.50 1.00

Native Costumes — A606

No. 2595, 200t — Blue frame: a, Man with
white and blue costume. b, Woman with green
and white costume.
No. 2596, 200t — Green frame: a, Man with
stringed instrument. b, Woman with red
costume.
No. 2597, 200t — Rose pink frame: a, Man
with white and blue costume. b, Woman with
green costume.

2005, June 20   **Perf. 13½x13**
    Horiz. pairs, #a-b
2595-2597 A606   Set of 3   5.00 5.00

Maharanza
A607

No. 2595 — Color of face: a, White. b, Blue.
c, Red. d, Yellow brown.

2005, July 8   **Perf. 13x12¾**
2598   Horiz. strip of 4   4.00 4.00
a.-d. A607 400t Any single   1.00 1.00

Souvenir Sheet

Asashorou, Sumo Wrestling
Champion — A608

No. 2599 — Asashorou: a, 600t, Wearing
baseball cap. b, 700t, On horse, vert. c, 800t,
In wrestling loincloth, vert.

2005, July 18   **Perf. 13**
2599 A608   Sheet of 3, #a-c   5.00 5.00

World
Vision
A609

2005, Sept. 20   **Perf. 12**
2600 A609 550t multi   1.50 1.00

Headdresses
A610

People wearing various headdresses: 50t,
100t, 150t, 200t, 250t, 300t.
800t, National headdress.

2005, Oct. 3   **Perf. 12¾x13**
2601-2606 A610   Set of 6   4.00 4.00
    Souvenir Sheet
     Perf. 12
2607 A610 800t multi   3.50 3.50
   No. 2607 contains one 37x56mm stamp.

Souvenir Sheets

Shenzhou VI Space Flight — A611

No. 2608, 800t, Astronauts waving. No.
2609, 800t, Astronauts in spacecraft.

2005, Dec. 9   **Perf. 12**
2608-2609 A611   Set of 2   8.00 8.00

Souvenir Sheet

Coins of the Mongolian
Empire — A612

No. 2610 — Various coins with background
color of: a, Blue. b, Grayish lilac. c, Deep
bister.

2006, Jan. 11   **Perf. 13x12¾**
2610 A612 550t Sheet of 3, #a-c 5.00 5.00

New Year
2006 (Year
of the
Dog)
A613

Mongolian emblem and "Year of the Dog" at:
300t, Right. 400t, Left.

2006, Jan. 27   **Perf. 13x13¼**
2611-2612 A613   Set of 2   3.50 3.50

Miniature Sheet

Europa Stamps, 50th Anniv. — A614

No. 2613: a, Archer. b, Camels. c, Boys herding livestock. d, Goat. e, Rocks. f, Building spire. g, Dinosaur skeleton. h, Circus performers. i, Yurt. j, Two men in native costumes. k, Airplane. l, Ox.

2006, Feb. 1   **Perf. 12½x13**
2613 A614 200t Sheet of 12, #a-l   8.00   8.00
m.   Souvenir sheet, #2613a-2613b, perf. 13   1.50   1.50
n.   Souvenir sheet, #2613c-2613d, perf. 13   1.50   1.50
o.   Souvenir sheet, #2613e-2613f, perf. 13   1.50   1.50
p.   Souvenir sheet, #2613g-2613h, perf. 13   1.50   1.50
q.   Souvenir sheet, #2613i-2613j, perf. 13   1.50   1.50
r.   Souvenir sheet, #2613k-2613l, perf. 13   1.50   1.50

World Vision — A615

No. 2614: a, Children riding ox. b, Child riding horse.

2006, May 5   **Litho.**   **Perf. 12**
2614 A615 550t Horiz. pair, #a-b   3.50   3.50

Souvenir Sheet

Morin Khuur — A616

2006, June 16
2615 A616 550t multi   2.00   2.00

Souvenir Sheet

Pres. Nambaryn Enkhbayar — A617

2006, June 21
2616 A617 800t multi   3.50   3.50

Souvenir Sheet

2006 World Cup Soccer Championships, Germany — A618

No. 2617 — Various stylized players: a, 200t. b, 250t. c, 300t. d, 400t.

2006, June 23
2617 A618   Sheet of 4, #a-d   5.00   5.00

Souvenir Sheet

State Visit of US Pres. George W. Bush — A619

2006, June 30   **Perf. 13x13¼**
2618 A619 600t multi   3.00   3.00

Souvenir Sheets

A620

Famous Mongols — A621

No. 2619 — Various unnamed Mongols: a, 50t (23x33mm). b, 100t (23x33mm). c, 300t (23x33mm). d, 400t (23x33mm). e, 500t (80x56mm).

2006   **Perf. 13, 11½ (#2619e)**
2619 A620 Sheet of 5, #a-e   6.00   6.00
f.   As #2619, with sheet margin overprinted in gold with Mongolian text   1.90   1.90
   Perf. 11½x11¾
2620 A621 3800t shown   12.00   12.00
Mongolian stamps, 85th anniv. (#2619). Issued: No. 2619, 7/8; No. 2619f, 7/16/09. No. 2620, 9/19. Mongolian State, 800th anniv.

Souvenir Sheet

Horse Sculptures — A622

No. 2621: a, 300t, Horse and rider. b, 400t, Horse only.

2006, Sept. 28   **Perf. 12**
2621 A622   Sheet of 2, #a-b   3.50   3.50
See India No. 2167.

Miniature Sheet

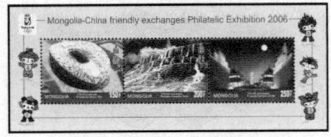

Friendly Exchange Philatelic Exhibition — A623

No. 2622: a, 150t, Olympic Stadium, Beijing. b, 200t, Waterfalls. c, 250t, City street at night.

2006, Oct. 25   **Litho.**   **Perf. 12**
2622 A623   Sheet of 3, #a-c   1.10   1.10

Hucho Taimen Fish — A624

No. 2623 — Various depictions of fish: a, 100t. b, 200t. c, 300t. d, 400t.

2006, Dec. 17
2623 A624   Block of 4, #a-d   1.75   1.75

New Year 2007 (Year of the Pig) — A625

Designs: 300t, Two pigs. 400t, Two pigs, diff.

2006, Dec. 17
2624-2625 A625   Set of 2   1.25   1.25

Dutch Royalty — A625a

No. 2625A: b, Prince Willem-Alexander. c, Prince Willem-Alexander and Princess Máxima. d, Princess Máxima.

2007, Jan. 7   **Perf. 13¼x13½**
2625A   Vert. strip of 3   3.75   3.75
b.-d.   A625a 700t Any single   1.25   1.25
Printed in sheets containing 2 each of Nos. 2625Ab-2625Ad.

Miniature Sheet

Marilyn Monroe (1926-62), Actress — A625b

No. 2625E — Monroe with: f, Background in orange in white, country name and denomination in orange. g, Background and denomination in orange, country name in white. h, Background in rose and white, country name and denomination in white. i, Background in claret, country name and denomination in white.

2007, Jan. 26
2625E A625b 1050t Sheet of 4, #f-i   7.25   7.25

Miniature Sheet

Elvis Presley (1935-77) — A625c

No. 2625J — Presley: k, Facing right, holding microphone. l, Facing forward, country name at top. m, Facing right, without microphone. n, Facing forward, country name at bottom.

2007, Jan. 26   **Perf. 13¼**
2625J A625c 1050t Sheet of 4, #k-n   7.25   7.25

Betty Boop — A625d

No. 2625O — Betty Boop: p, Holding down dress in breeze. q, With both hands in air. r, With hands clasped. s, With one arm raised, parts of "B," "E," and "T" at top. t, Winking, with leg lifted. u, With one arm raised, parts of "B," "O," and "P" at top.

No. 2625V — Betty Boop lifting dress to expose garter: a, Without part of heart to left of "GO" in country name. b, With part of heart to left of "GO" in country name.

2007, Jan. 26   **Perf. 13¼x13½**
2625O   A625d   700t Sheet of 6,
            #p-u   7.25   7.25

Souvenir Sheet
2625V   A625d   1500t Sheet of 2,
            #w-x   5.25   5.25

Souvenir Sheet

Diplomatic Relations Between Mongolia and the United States, 20th Anniv. — A626

No. 2626: a, 400t, Statue of Genghis Khan, Ulan Bator. b, 550t, Statue of Abraham Lincoln, Washington, DC.

2007, Jan. 29   **Perf. 12**
2626   A626   Sheet of 2, #a-b   1.75   1.75

Lama Tsonghapa (1357-1419), Buddhist Teacher — A627

2007, Jan. 30   **Perf. 12¾**
2627   A627   100t multi   .25   .25

Souvenir Sheet

Diplomatic Relations Between Mongolia and Japan, 35th Anniv. — A628

No. 2628: a, 550t, Mt. Fuji, Japan. 700t, Mt. Otgontenger, Mongolia.

2007, Feb. 23   **Perf. 12**
2628   A628   Sheet of 2, #a-b   2.25   2.25

Calligraphy A629

Designs: 50t, Light of wisdom. 100t, Butterfly. 150t, Flower. 200t, Horse. 250t, Spring. 300t, Leaves. 400t, Wow. 550t, Wild camel. 800t, Sky.

2007, Aug. 2   **Perf. 13x12¾**
2629-2636   A629   Set of 8   3.50   3.50
         Souvenir Sheet
         Perf. 12¾
2637   A629   800t multi   1.40   1.40
No. 2637 contains one 43x57mm stamp.

Souvenir Sheets

Modern Art — A630

Art by: No. 2638, 400t, Ts. Tsegmid. No. 2639, 400t, S. Sarantsatsralt. No. 2640, 400t, Ts. Enkhjin. No. 2641, 400t, Do. Bold, horiz. No. 2642, 400t, Sh. Chimeddorj, horiz.

2007, Aug. 21   **Perf. 13**
2638-2642   A630   Set of 5   3.50   3.50

Miniature Sheet

Naotoshi Yamada, Olympic Cheerleader, and Mongolian Sumo Wrestlers — A631

No. 2643 — Yamada and various wrestlers with Mongolian emblem and inscriptions at: a, 500t, Right. b, 500t, Left. c, 600t, Right. d, 600t, Left. e, 700t, Right. f, 700t, Left.

2007, Oct. 3   **Die Cut**
      Self-Adhesive
2643   A631   Sheet of 6, #a-f, +
            10 labels   6.25   6.25

Genghis Khan (c. 1162-1227) — A632

     Perf. 12½x12¾
2007, Nov. 29   **Litho.**
2644   Horiz. strip of 5   5.50   5.50
  a.   A632 230t black   .40   .40
  b.   A632 400t brown   .40   .40
  c.   A632 650t blue   .40   .40
  d.   A632 800t green   .40   .40
  e.   A632 1000t violet   .40   .40

New Year 2008 (Year of the Rat) — A633

No. 2645 — Rat with denomination at: a, UR. b, LL.

2008, Jan. 1   **Perf. 12¾**
2645   A633   800t Vert. pair, #a-b   2.75   2.75

Wedding of Queen Elizabeth II and Prince Philip, 50th Anniv. — A634

No. 2646: a, Queen. b, Queen and Prince.

2008, Jan. 25   **Perf. 13¼**
2646   A634   400t Pair, #a-b   1.40   1.40
Printed in sheets of 6 containing 2 each of Nos. 2646a-2646b.

Princess Diana (1961-97) — A635

No. 2647, vert. — Princess Diana wearing: a, Necklace and black gown. b, Red hat and coat. c, Black and white dress. d, Black and white hat and jacket.
3000t, Prince Charles and Princess Diana.

2008, Jan. 25
2647   A635   1150t Sheet of 4, #a-
           d   8.00   8.00
       Souvenir Sheet
2648   A635   3000t multi   5.25   5.25

First Helicopter Flight, Cent. — A636

No. 2649: a, Belvedere. b, AS 565 Dauphin/Panther. c, Explorer. d, Shark. 3000t, Scout.

2008, Jan. 25
2649   A636   1150t Sheet of 4, #a-
           d   8.00   8.00
       Souvenir Sheet
2650   A636   3000t multi   5.25   5.25

Muhammad Ali, Boxer — A637

No. 2651, 1150t — Ali: a, Wearing shirt. b, Shadow-boxing. c, Punching bag. d, Punching at opponent.
No. 2652, 1150t, horiz. — Ali with: a, Black boxing gloves punching at opponent. b, Red boxing gloves with left arm extended. c, Red boxing gloves, ring rope in background. d, Red boxing gloves, lights and ring rope in background.
No. 2653, 3000t, Ali wearing robe. No. 2654, 3000t, Close-up photograph.

    Perf. 13¼, 11½ (#2652)
2008, Jan. 25
      Sheets of 4, #a-d
2651-2652   A637   Set of 2   16.00   16.00
      Souvenir Sheets
2653-2654   A637   Set of 2   10.50   10.50

Pope John Paul II (1920-2005) — A637a

2008, Jan. 25   Litho.   Perf. 13½x13¼
2654A   A637a   880t multi   1.50   1.50

Miniature Sheet

Photomosaic of Pope Benedict XVI — A638

No. 2655 — Part of photomosaic with frame around it: a, At left and top in green. b, At left in green. c, At left in green and white. d, At left and bottom in white.

2008, Jan. 25		**Perf. 13¼**	
2655	A638	1150t Sheet of 4, #a-d	8.00 8.00

Nos. 1355 and 1359 Surcharged

Methods and Perfs As Before

2008, Feb. 29			
2656	A301	1000t on 20m #1355	1.75 1.75
2657	A301	1000t on 60m #1359	1.75 1.75

No. 1983 Surcharged

Method and Perf. As Before

2008, Mar. 7			
2658	A429	250t on 40m #1983	.45 .45

Campaign Against AIDS — A639

2008, Apr. 10	**Litho.**	**Perf. 12¾x13**	
2659	A639	500t multi	.85 .85

Handcrafted Items A640

Designs: No. 2660, 500t, Pipe and tobacco pouch (shown). No. 2661, 500t, Jar and cloth. No. 2662, 500t, Silver bowls. No. 2663, 500t, Sword and sheath. No. 2664, 500t, Saddle.

2008, June 8		**Perf. 12¾**	
2660-2664	A640	Set of 5	4.50 4.50

Miniature Sheet

2008 Summer Olympics, Beijing — A641

No. 2665: a, Canoe-kayak. b, Fencing. c, Handball. d, Modern pentathlon.

2008, July 8		**Perf. 12¾x12½**	
2665	A641	600t Sheet of 4, #a-d	4.25 4.25

Wild Boars A642

No. 2666: a, Head of boar. b, Sow and piglets. c, Boar. d, Boar and sow.

2008, Sept. 10		**Perf. 12½x12¾**	
2666		Horiz. strip of 4	5.75 5.75
a.-d.	A642	800t Any single	1.40 1.40

New Year 2009 (Year of the Ox) A643

Ox with background color of: 200t, Yellow. 300t, Blue.

2009, Jan. 19		**Perf. 12**	
2667-2668	A643	Set of 2	.75 .75

National Coat of Arms — A644

Great White Banner — A645

National Flag — A646

Soyombo A647

2009, Jan. 28		**Litho.**	
2669		Horiz. strip of 4	4.00 4.00
a.	A644	400t multi	.60 .60
b.	A645	500t multi	.75 .75
c.	A646	800t multi	1.10 1.10
d.	A647	1000t multi	1.50 1.50

No. 1307 Surcharged

Method and Perf. As Before

2009, Apr. 6			
2670	A290	1000t on 20m #1307	1.40 1.40

People in Yurt A648

2009, Apr. 6	**Litho.**	**Perf. 13x12¾**	
2671	A648	1000t multi	1.40 1.40

China 2009 World Stamp Exhibition, Luoyang — A649

No. 2672: a, Giant panda. b, Ursus arctos gobiensis.

2009, Apr. 10		**Perf. 12¾x12½**	
2672	A649	300t Pair, #a-b	.85 .85

Printed in sheets of 14, 7 each Nos. 2672a-2672b, + 2 labels.

Peonies A650

2009, Apr. 23		**Perf. 13½x13¼**	
2673	A650	700t multi	1.00 1.00

Printed in sheets of 6.

Earrings From Korea, 5th-6th Cent. A651

Earrings From Mongolia, 18th-19th Cent. A652

Earring From Kazakhstan, 2nd-1st Cent. B.C. — A653

2009, June 12		**Perf. 12**	
2674		Horiz. strip of 3	3.50 3.50
a.	A651	800t multi	1.10 1.10
b.	A652	800t multi	1.10 1.10
c.	A653	800t multi	1.10 1.10

See Kazakhstan No. 595, South Korea No. 2313.

Battles of Khalkhiin Gol, 70th Anniv. — A654

2009, Aug. 20		**Perf. 13x12½**	
2675	A654	500t lil & pur	.70 .70

Souvenir Sheet

Taras — A655

No. 2676: a, White Tara. b, Green Tara.

2009, Oct. 9		**Perf. 12**	
2676	A655	800t Sheet of 2, #a-b	2.25 2.25

Diplomatic Relations Between Mongolia and People's Republic of China, 60th Anniv. — A656

No. 2677 — Buildings with frame and denomination in: a, Blue. b, Red.

2009, Oct. 9		**Perf. 12¾**	
2677		Horiz. pair with central label	3.00 3.00
a.-b.	A656	1000t Either single	1.50 1.50

APU Company, 85th Anniv. — A657

2009, Dec. 1		**Perf. 12¾x13**	
2678	A657	800t multi	1.10 1.10

Camel Polo A658

2010, Jan. 26	**Litho.**	**Perf. 11½**	
2679	A658	1000t multi	1.40 1.40

A659

A660

A661

A662

A663

A664

Secrets of the Mongols — A665

Designs: No. 2686, Black banner. No. 2687, Five arrows.

2010, Feb. 5   **Perf. 13x12¾**
2680	A659 1000t multi	1.40	1.40
2681	A660 1000t multi	1.40	1.40
2682	A661 1000t multi	1.40	1.40
2683	A662 1000t multi	1.40	1.40
2684	A663 1000t multi	1.40	1.40
2685	A664 1000t multi	1.40	1.40
	Nos. 2680-2685 (6)	8.40	8.40

Souvenir Sheets
Perf. 12
2686	A665 1500t pur & multi	2.10	2.10
2687	A665 1500t grn & multi	2.10	2.10

Compare with Types A677-A683.

New Year 2010
(Year of the
Tiger) — A666

No. 2688 — Tiger with background color of: a, Green. b, Blue.

2010, Feb. 14   **Perf. 12**
2688   A666 1000t Vert. pair, #a-b   3.00   3.00

Children
A667

Children with stringed instruments and: 800t, Horse. 1000t, Camel.

2010, Apr. 20   **Perf. 13½**
2689-2690   A667   Set of 2   2.75   2.75

Mountains — A668

No. 2691: a, Sutai Khairkhan. b, Altan Khokhii. c, Khan Khokhii. d, Suvarga Khairkhan.
No. 2692: a, Burkhan Khaldun. b, Bogd Khairkhan. c, Dariganga, Dari Ovoo. d, Otgontenger.

2010   **Litho.**   **Perf. 13¼**
2691   A668 500t Block or horiz.
      strip of 4, #a-d   3.00   3.00
      Perf. 12
2692   A668 500t Block of 4, #a-d   3.00   3.00
Issued: No. 2691, 5/27; No. 2692, 6/15.

Flag of
Mongolia
A669

2010, June 15   **Perf. 13**
2693   A669 800t multi   1.25   1.25

2010 World Cup Soccer
Championships, South Africa — A670

No. 2694: a, Emblem. b, Mascot.

2010, July 11   **Perf. 13¼x13**
2694   A670 800t Horiz. pair, #a-b,
      + central label   2.40   2.40

Souvenir Sheet

Chingunjav (1710-57), Leader of
Rebellion Against Manchus — A671

2010, Aug. 27   **Perf. 12¼x12**
2695   A671 800t multi   1.25   1.25

Souvenir Sheet

Pres. Tsakhiagiin Elbegdorj — A672

2010, Oct. 22   **Perf. 12½x13**
2696   A672 500t multi   .80   .80

Butterflies
A673

Designs: 100t, Ornithoptera croesus. 200t, Papilio antimachus. 400t, Ornithoptera priamus urvilleanus. 500t, Papilio zalmoxis. 800t, Troides rhadamantius. 1000t, Ornithoptera victoriae epiphanes.

2010, Dec. 8   **Litho.**   **Perf. 12**
2697-2702   A673   Set of 6   5.00   5.00

Souvenir Sheet

Taras — A674

No. 2703: a, Green tara. b, Red tara.

2010, Dec. 8   **Perf. 13x13¼**
2703   A674 800t Sheet of 2, #a-b   2.75   2.75

New Year 2011
(Year of the
Rabbit) — A675

2011, Jan. 12   **Perf. 11½**
2704   A675 1000t multi   1.60   1.60

First Man in
Space, 50th
Anniv.
A676

2011, Apr. 12   **Perf. 13¼**
2705   A676 500t multi   .85   .85
Printed in sheets of 10 + 2 labels.

A677

A678

A679

A680

A681

A682

Secrets of the Mongols — A683

Designs: No. 2712, White banner. No. 2713, Khan's seal of Great Mongol.

2011, May 29 Litho. Perf. 13x12¾
2706	A677	1000t multi	1.60	1.60
2707	A678	1000t multi	1.60	1.60
2708	A679	1000t multi	1.60	1.60
2709	A680	1000t multi	1.60	1.60
2710	A681	1000t multi	1.60	1.60
2711	A682	1000t multi	1.60	1.60
Nos. 2706-2711 (6)			9.60	9.60

Souvenir Sheets
Perf. 12
| 2712 | A683 | 1500t blue & multi | 2.50 | 2.50 |
| 2713 | A683 | 1500t brown & multi | 2.50 | 2.50 |

Compare with Types A659-A665.

Livestock A684

Designs: No. 2714, 1000t, Yak. No. 2715, 1000t, Camel. No. 2716, 1200t, Mongolian horse. No. 2717, 1200t, Reindeer.

2011, June 13 Perf. 13x12¾
| 2714-2717 | A684 | Set of 4 | 7.25 | 7.25 |

Souvenir Sheet

Motor Sports — A685

No. 2718: a, 300t, Road rally. b, 400t, Motorcycle racing. c, 600t, Auto racing.

2011, July 8 Perf. 13x13¼
| 2718 | A685 | Sheet of 3, #a-c | 2.10 | 2.10 |

Miniature Sheet

Mongolian People's Revolution, 90th Anniv. — A686

No. 2719: a, 600t, Kharloin Choibalsan (1895-1952), Prime Minister, 1939-52 (30x30mm). b, 600t, Dogsomyn Bodoo (1895-1922), Prime Minister, 1921-22 (30x30mm). c, 600t, Soliin Danzan (1885-1924), Central Committee chairman (30x30mm). d, 600t, Dambyn Chagdarjav (1880-1922), Prime Minister, 1921 (30x30mm). e, 600t, Dansrabilegiin Dogsom (1884-1939), President, 1936-39

(30x30mm). f, 600t, D. Losol (1898-1940), revolutionist (30x30mm). g, 1200t, Sukhe Bator (1893-1923), leader of revolution (30x40mm).

2011, July 11 Perf. 12
| 2719 | A686 | Sheet of 7, #a-g | 7.75 | 7.75 |

Souvenir Sheets

Reign of Genghis Khan, 805th Anniv. — A687

Designs: No. 2720, 2000t, Genghis Khan (c. 1162-1227). No. 2721, 2000t, Order of Genghis Khan.

2011, July 11 Litho.
| 2720-2721 | A687 | Set of 2 | 6.50 | 6.50 |

Hunnu Culture, 2200th Anniv. — A688

No. 2722: a, Pottery. b, Jewelry depicting horse. c, Jewelry depicting bird. d, Wolf attacking buck. e, Arrowheads.
5000t, Modun Shanyu (c. 234 B.C.-174 B.C.), emperor.

2011, July 25 Perf. 11¾x11½
| 2722 | A688 | 1000t Sheet of 5, | | |
| | | #a-e | 8.25 | 8.25 |

Souvenir Sheet
Perf. 12¾
| 2723 | A688 | 5000t multi | 8.25 | 8.25 |

No. 2723 contains one 60x65mm stamp.

Wildlife A689

Wildlife of: 400t, Antarctic and Arctic regions. 600t, Mongolia. 1000t, Australia. 1200t, Africa.

2011, July 27 Perf. 12
| 2724-2727 | A689 | Set of 4 | 5.25 | 5.25 |

No. 1231 Surcharged in Gold

Method and Perf. As Before
2011, July 28
| 2728 | A275 | 800t on 4t #1231 | 1.40 | 1.40 |

PhilaNippon '11, Intl. Philatelic Exhibition, Yokohama.

Wedding of Prince William and Catherine Middleton A690

Designs: 1200t, Couple.
No. 2730: a, Prince William. b, Catherine Middleton.

2011, Aug. 22 Litho. Perf. 12
| 2729 | A690 | 1200t multi | 2.00 | 2.00 |

Souvenir Sheet
Perf. 13½x13
| 2730 | A690 | 1500t Sheet of 2, | | |
| | | #a-b | 4.75 | 4.75 |

Souvenir Sheet

Education in Mongolia, 90th Anniv. — A691

No. 2731: a, Students, bugler, building. b, Girl, children at computers. c, Mongolian flag, graduates, building.

2011, Sept. 9 Perf. 12
| 2731 | A691 | 1200t Sheet of 3, | | |
| | | #a-c | 5.75 | 5.75 |

Souvenir Sheet

Admission to the United Nations, 50th Anniv. — A692

2011, Oct. 27 Litho. Perf. 12¾
| 2732 | A692 | 1000t multi | 1.60 | 1.60 |

Nos. 2403-2404 Overprinted in Gold

Methods and Perfs As Before
2011, Nov. 11
| 2733 | A531 | 250t multi on #2403 | .40 | .40 |
| 2734 | A531 | 450t multi on #2404 | .70 | .70 |

China 2011 Intl. Philatelic Exhibition, Wuxi.

Souvenir Sheet

Mongolian Diplomatic Service, Cent. — A693

No. 2735: a, Mijiddorjiin Khanddorj (1869-1915), first Mongolian Foreign Minster (30x65mm). b, Flag of Mongolia, United Nations Building, dove (50x38mm). c, Golden gerege (30x65mm).

Perf. 12¾, 13¼ (#2735b)
2011, Dec. 1 Litho.
| 2735 | A693 | 600t Sheet of 3, #a-c | 2.75 | 2.75 |

Souvenir Sheet

United Nations Secretary General Ban Ki-Moon and Mongolian Prime Minister Sukhbaatar Batbold — A694

2011, Dec. 13 Perf. 13x13¼
| 2736 | A694 | 500t multi | .75 | .75 |

Admission to United Nations, 50th anniv.

Souvenir Sheet

Mongolian Government Palace and Flag — A695

2011, Dec. 17 Perf. 12¾
| 2737 | A695 | 1000t multi | 1.50 | 1.50 |

Mongolian government, cent.

Souvenir Sheet

Mongolian Revolution, Cent. — A696

No. 2738: a, Bogdo Jebtsundamba VIII (Bogd Khan, 1869-1924), Emperor. b, Tögs-Ochiryn Namnansuren (1878-1919), Prime Minister.

2011, Dec. 29   **Perf. 13¼x13**
2738 A696 1000t Sheet of 2, #a-
b, + label   3.00 3.00

New Year 2012 (Year of the Dragon) A697

2012, Jan. 1   **Perf. 13x13¼**
2739 A697 600t multi   .90 .90

Souvenir Sheet

Fleet of Kublai Khan — A698

No. 2740: a, 1000t, Kublai Khan (1215-94), Emperor. b, 1200t, Warship.

2012, Mar. 4   **Perf. 12**
2740 A698   Sheet of 2, #a-b   3.50 3.50

Souvenir Sheet

Diplomatic Relations Between Mongolia and Japan, 40th Anniv. — A699

No. 2741: a, Mongolian doll. b, Japanese doll.

2012, Mar. 12   **Perf. 12¾x13**
2741 A699 600t Sheet of 2, #a-b,
+ label   1.90 1.90

Mythological Creatures — A700

Cats — A701

Designs: 100t, Dragon. 200t, Lion. 400t, Tiger. 600t, Khan Garuda.

2012, Apr. 22   **Litho.**   **Perf. 13¼**
2742 A701 100t multi   .25 .25
2743 A701 200t multi   .30 .30
2744 A701 400t multi   .65 .65
2745 A700 600t multi   .95 .95
   Nos. 2742-2745 (4)   2.15 2.15

Souvenir Sheet

Antarctic Explorers — A702

No. 2746: a, Fabian von Bellingshausen (1778-1852). b, Mikhail P. Lazarev (1788-1851).

2012, June 17   **Perf. 13**
2746 A702 800t Sheet of 2, #a-b   2.40 2.40

2012 Summer Olympics, London — A703

No. 2747 — Emblem of 2012 Summer Olympics, British flag and: a, London tourist attractions. b, Athletes.

2012, July 5   **Perf. 13¼**
2747   Pair   2.40 2.40
  a. A703 700t multi   1.10 1.10
  b. A703 800t multi   1.25 1.25

Women in Modern National Costumes A704

Various costumes: 100t, 200t, 300t, 400t, 500t, 600t.
No. 2754: a, 700t. b, 800t.

2012, Aug. 24   **Perf. 12**
2748-2753 A704   Set of 6   3.00 3.00
Souvenir Sheet
   Perf. 13¼x13¼
2754 A704   Sheet of 2, #a-b   2.25 2.25
No. 2754 contains two 38x50mm stamps.

Miniature Sheet

Guardians of the Days — A705

No. 2755 — Guardian and inscription: a, 100t, Moon. b, 200t, Mars. c, 300t, Mercury. d, 400t, Jupiter. e, 500t, Venus. f, 600t, Saturn. g, 700t, Sun.

Self-Adhesive

2012, Oct. 14   **Die Cut Perf.**
2755 A705   Sheet of 7, #a-g   4.00 4.00

Souvenir Sheet

Customs Department, Cent. — A706

No. 2756: a, 800t, Three Mongolian customs officials. b, 1000t, Two modern Mongolian customs officials, flag, horiz. 1200t, Customs dog, marijuana.

2012, Oct. 20   **Perf. 13¼x13**
2756 A706   Sheet of 3, #a-c   4.50 4.50

Souvenir Sheet

Genghis Khan (1162-1227), Mongol Conqueror — A707

No. 2757: a, 350t, Horse. b, 850t, Genghis Khan.

2012, Nov. 14   **Perf. 12**
2757 A707   Sheet of 2, #a-b   1.75 1.75

Birds A708

Designs: 100t, Amazona aestiva, Ara chloroptera, Ara ararauna. 200t, Paradisaea raggiana, Paradisaea rudolphi. 300t, Cygnus atratus, Cygnus olor, Phoenicopterus roseus. 400t, Aix galericulata, Aix sponsa. 800t, Erythrura gouldiae, Pteridophora albertus, Euplectes orix. 1000t, Pavo cristatus, Chrysolophus pictus.

2012, Dec. 24   **Perf. 13¼**
2758-2763 A708   Set of 6   4.00 4.00

Flag and Emblem of Mongolia A709

2012, Dec. 29   **Perf. 13x13¼**
2764 A709 1200t multi   1.75 1.75

No. 1660 with this 500t surcharge in gold, released in Feb. 2013, was produced in limited quantities.

New Year 2013 (Year of the Snake) A710

2013, Feb. 6   **Litho.**   **Perf. 12**
2765 A710 600t multi   .90 .90
No. 2765 was printed in sheets of 16 + 4 labels.

Gazelles A711

Designs: 200t, Gazella subgutturosa. 400t, Procapra gutturosa. 800t, Procapra gutturosa, diff. 1000t, Gazella subgutturosa, diff.

2013, June 4   **Perf. 13x13¼**
2766-2769 A711   Set of 4   3.50 3.50
2769a   Sheet of 8, 2 each #2766-
2769, + central label   7.00 7.00

Miniature Sheet

Falcons — A712

No. 2770: a, 100t, Falcon in flight (60x30mm). b, 200t, Two Falco cherrug in flight (60x30mm). c, 300t, Falcon chicks and eggs (60x30mm). d, 400t, Falcon on rock (60x30mm). e, 800t, Falcon and Mongolian regalia (40x60mm). f, 1000t, Falcon on hand of Mongolian falconer (40x60mm).

Litho., Margin Litho. With Foil Application
2013, June 19   **Perf. 12**
2770 A712   Sheet of 6, #a-f   4.00 4.00

Animals on
Elephant
A713

Musician
A714

Mongolian
Woman
A715

Yurt
A716

2013, July 21 Litho. Perf. 12½x12¾
2771 A713 1000t multi   1.40 1.40
2772 A714 1000t multi   1.40 1.40
2773 A715 1000t multi   1.40 1.40
2774 A716 1000t multi   1.40 1.40
  Nos. 2771-2774 (4)   5.60 5.60

**No. 2363 Srchd. in Red With
Thailand 2013 World Stamp
Exhibition Emblem Added**
Souvenir Sheet

2013, Aug. 2   Perf. 11
2775 A519 1500t on 1000t #2363 2.00 2.00
  Thailand 2013 World Stamp Exhibition,
Bangkok.

Batu Khan (c. 1207-55), Mongol
Ruler — A717

2013, Oct. 16   Litho.   Perf. 12
2776 A717 1000t multi   1.25 1.25

The Beatles — A718

No. 2777: a, 500t, Ringo Starr (38x50mm).
b, 500t, John Lennon (38x50mm). c, 1000t,
Paul McCartney and George Harrison
(60x50mm).

2013, Dec. 6   Litho.   Perf. 13
2777 A718 Sheet of 3, #a-c 2.40 2.40

New Year
2014 (Year
of the
Horse)
A719

No. 2778 — Horse facing: a, Right. b, Left.

2013, Dec. 22 Litho. Perf. 13xx12¾
2778   Horiz. pair + central la-
        bel   1.60 1.60
a.-b.   A719 650t Either single   .80 .80

Nos. 1564-1567 Surcharged

Methods and Perfs As Before
2014, Jan. 6
2779 A347 1300t on 60m #1564 1.60 1.60
2780 A347 1300t on 60m #1565 1.60 1.60
2781 A347 1300t on 60m #1566 1.60 1.60
2782 A347 1300t on 60m #1567 1.60 1.60
  Nos. 2779-2782 (4)   6.40 6.40

Mongolian postage stamps, 90th anniv.

Flowers
A720

Designs: 200t, Lilium dahuricum, Cypripedium calceolus and bee. 300t, Saussurea
involucrata and bird. 400t, Iris sibirica, Lilium
pumilum and butterfly. 900t, Trollius asiaticus,
Tulipa uniflora and dragonfly. 1000t, Cypripedium macranthum, Adonis sibirica and
ladybug.

2014, Feb. 15   Litho.   Perf. 13x12¾
2783-2787 A720 Set of 5   3.25 3.25
2787a   Sheet of 10, 2 each #2783-
             2387, + 2 central labels 6.50 6.50

Scientists — A721

Designs: No. 2788, 100t, Charles Darwin
(1809-82), naturalist. No. 2789, 100t, Albert
Einstein (1879-1955), physicist. No. 2790,
300t, Leonardo da Vinci (1452-1519). No.
2791, 300t, Isaac Newton (1642-1727), physicist. No. 2792, 500t, Galileo Galilei (1564-

1642), astronomer. No. 2793, 500t, Niels Bohr
(1885-1962), physicist.

2014, Mar. 25   Litho.   Perf. 13¼x13
2788-2793 A721 Set of 6   2.10 2.10

No. 1400 Surcharged in Metallic Red

Method and Perf. As Before
2014, May 16
2794 A308 2000t on 4t #1400   2.25 2.25
  Mongolian postage stamps, 90th anniv.

Threatened Species From Red Book
of Mongolia — A722

Designs: 200t, Lynx pardinus. 300t,
Podoces hendersoni. 400t, Phasianus
colchicus. 500t, Vormela peregusna.

2014, May 16   Litho.   Perf. 12
2795-2798 A722 Set of 4   1.60 1.60
2798a   Souvenir sheet of 4,
             #2795-2798   1.60 1.60

Souvenir Sheet

Bank of Mongolia, 90th Anniv. — A723

No. 2799: a, Mongolian man. b, Bank of
Mongolia emblem.

2014, May 30   Litho.   Perf. 13¼x13
2799 A723 2000t Sheet of 2, #a-
            b   4.50 4.50

A724

A725

A726

A727

A728

A729

A730

Items at Bogd
Khan Palace
Museum
A731

Design: 2000t, Bogd Khan (1869-1924), 8th
Jebtsundamba, Khagan of Mongolia.

2014, June 13   Litho.   Perf. 13x13¼
2800 A724 1000t multi   1.10 1.10
2801 A725 1000t multi   1.10 1.10
2802 A726 1000t multi   1.10 1.10
2803 A727 1000t multi   1.10 1.10
2804 A728 1000t multi   1.10 1.10
2805 A729 1000t multi   1.10 1.10
2806 A730 1000t multi   1.10 1.10
2807 A731 1000t multi   1.10 1.10
  Nos. 2800-2807 (8)   8.80 8.80

Souvenir Sheet
2808 A731 2000t multi   2.25 2.25
  No. 2808 contains one 40x60mm stamp.

Tarbosurus Bataar — A733

A732

Designs: No. 2809, 1000t, Tarbosaurus bataar. No. 2810, 1000t, Tarbosaurus bataar skeleton.

No. 2811: a, 200t, Tarbosaurus bataar, diff. b, 400t, Tarbosaurus bataar skull. c, 500t, Tarbosaurus bataar skeleton, diff. d, 800t, Tarbosaurus bataar, map of Mongolia highlighted on globe.

2014, July 24   Litho.   Perf. 13x13¼
2809-2810 A732   Set of 2   2.25 2.25

Miniature Sheet
Perf. 12
2811 A733   Sheet of 4, #a-d   2.10 2.10

Souvenir Sheets

Visits to Mongolia by World Leaders — A734

No. 2812: a, Mongolia Pres. Tsakhiagiin Elbegdorj. b, Xi Jinping, President of People's Republic of China.
No. 2813a, Russian Pres. Vladimir Putin

2014   Litho.   Perf. 12¾
2812 A734 800t Sheet of 2, #a-b   1.75 1.75
2813 A734   Sheet of 2, #2812a,
                       2813a   1.75 1.75
  a.   800t multi   .85   .85

Issued: No. 2812, 8/21, No. 2813, 9/3.

Genghis Khan (c. 1162-1227) — A735

2014, Aug. 28   Litho.   Perf. 12½
2814 A735 100t brn & multi   .25   .25
2815 A735 1300t red & multi   1.50 1.50

Battles of Khalkhiin Gol, 75th Anniv. — A736

2014, Aug. 28   Litho.   Perf. 13¼
2816 A736 750t multi   .85   .85

Souvenir Sheet

Mongolian Postage Stamps, 90th Anniv. — A737

No. 2817: a, Mongolian flag, Mongolia #7. b, Great White Banner, Mongolia #1-6.

Litho., Sheet Margin Litho. With Foil Application
2014, Oct. 7   Perf. 13¼x13
2817 A737 1000t Sheet of 2, #a-
               b   2.25 2.25

Souvenir Sheet

Ulan Bator, 375th Anniv. — A738

2014, Oct. 27   Litho.   Perf. 13¼
2818 A738 1000t multi   1.10 1.10

New Year 2015 (Year of the Ram) A739

No. 2819 — Ram with head at: a, Right. b, Left.

2014, Dec. 28   Litho.   Perf. 13x12½
2819   Horiz. pair + central la-
             bel   1.40 1.40
  a.-b. A739 650t Either single .70   .70

SEMI-POSTAL STAMPS

Vietnamese Mother and Child — SP1

1967, Dec. 22   Photo.   Perf. 12x11½
B1   SP1 30m + 20m multi   .60   .30
B2   SP1 50m + 30m multi   .60   .30

Solidarity with Vietnam.

Save Venice Type of Regular Issue
Souvenir Sheet
Departure of St. Ursula, by Carpaccio.

1972, Oct. 1   Litho.   Perf. 12
B3   A163 3t + 1t multi   4.00 4.00

Save Venice Campaign. No. B3 contains one horizontal stamp.

Girl Feeding Lambs SP2

UNICEF Emblem and: 20m+5m, Boy playing flute and dancing girl. 30m+5m, Girl chasing butterflies. 40m+5m, Girl with ribbon. 60m+5m, Girl with flowers. 80m+5m, Girl carrying bucket. 1t+5m, Boy going to school.

1977, June 1   Litho.   Perf. 12
B4   SP2 10m + 5m multi   .25   .25
B5   SP2 20m + 5m multi   .25   .25
B6   SP2 30m + 5m multi   .35   .25
B7   SP2 40m + 5m multi   .45   .30
B8   SP2 60m + 5m multi   .65   .35
B9   SP2 80m + 5m multi   .85   .55
B10 SP2 1t + 5m multi   1.10   .70
     Nos. B4-B10 (7)   3.90 2.65

Surtax was for Mongolian Children's Village. See No. CB1.

Boys on Horseback — SP3

Children and IYC Emblem: 30m+5m, Raising chickens. 50m+5m, With deer. 60m+5m, With flowers. 70m+5m, Planting tree. 80m+5m, Studying space project. 1t+5m, Dancing. 4t+50m, Girl on horseback.

1979, Jan. 10
B11 SP3 10m + 5m multi   .30   .25
B12 SP3 30m + 5m multi   .30   .25
B13 SP3 50m + 5m multi   .45   .25
B14 SP3 60m + 5m multi   .50   .25
B15 SP3 70m + 5m multi   .65   .35
B16 SP3 80m + 5m multi   .80   .40
B17 SP3 1t + 5m multi   1.10   .65
     Nos. B11-B17 (7)   4.10 2.40

Souvenir Sheet
B18 SP3 4t + 50m multi   3.25 3.25

International Year of the Child. Compare with Type A301.

1998 Winter Olympic Games, Nagano — SP4

1998   Litho.   Perf. 12
B19 SP4 150t +15t Speed skat-
             ing   .65   .50
B20 SP4 200t +20t Ski jumping .80   .60
B21 SP4 300t +30t Snowboard-
             ing   1.30 1.00
B22 SP4 600t +60t Freestyle
             skiing   2.25 1.75
     Nos. B19-B22 (4)   5.00 3.85

Ulan Bator, 360th Anniv. — SP5

Designs, 300t +30t each: No. B23, Flags and arms. No. B24, Seated man. No. B25, Arms.
No. B26, Various views of Ulan Bator.

1999   Litho.   Perf. 12½
B23-B25 SP5 Set of 3   3.00 3.00
Sheet of 9
Perf. 12½x12¼
B26 SP5 200t +20t #a.-i.   8.00 8.00

No. B26 contains nine 45x27mm stamps.

Unity Against Terrorism — SP6

World Trade Center, Statue of Liberty, American flag and country name in: 300t+50t, Red. 400t+50t, Blue.

Perf. 13½x13¼
2001, Nov. 11   Litho.
B27-B28 SP6 Set of 2   3.00 3.00

AIR POST STAMPS

Postal Modernization Type of Regular Issue

Designs: 10m, 20m, Postman with horses. 25m, Postman with reindeer. 30m, 50m, Plane over map of Mongolia. 1t, Post horn and flag of Mongolia.

1961, June 5   Photo.   Perf. 15
C1   A72 10m multicolored   .30   .25
C2   A72 50m multicolored   .60   .25
C3   A72 1t multicolored   1.10   .40
     Nos. C1-C3 (3)   2.00   .80

Souvenir Sheet
Perf. 11
C4   Sheet of 4   3.50 3.50
  a.   A72 20m lt blue grn & multi .80 .80
  b.   A72 25m light blue & multi   .80 .80
  c.   A72 30m light green & multi .80 .80
  d.   A72 1t rose carmine & multi .80 .80

40th anniversary of independence; postal modernization. No. C4b is not inscribed Airmail.

Souvenir Sheet

Austria Type SP55, Austrian and Mongolian Stamps Circling Globe — AP1

1965, May 1   Engr.   Perf. 11½
C5   AP1 4t brown carmine   4.50 3.50

Vienna Intl. Philatelic Exhibition, WIPA, June 4-13. #C5 contains one 61x38mm stamp.

Weather Satellite AP2

Designs: 20m, Antarctic exploration. 30m, Space exploration.

1965, May 15   Photo.   Perf. 13½
C6 AP2 15m lilac, gold & blk   .50   .25
C7 AP2 20m blue & multi   2.75   .60
C8 AP2 30m rose & multi   .65   .25
Nos. C6-C8 (3)   3.90 1.05
International Quiet Sun Year, 1964-65.

ITU Emblem — AP3

Design: 4t, Communications satellite.

1965, Dec. 20   Perf. 11½x12
C9 AP3 30m blue & bister   1.00   .50
C10 AP3 50m red & bister   1.00   .50
Souvenir Sheet
Perf. 11, Imperf.
C11 AP3 4t gold, bl & blk   4.00 3.00
ITU, centenary. No. C11 contains one stamp, 38x51mm. Exists imperf. Values: unused $5.50; used $4.50.

Souvenir Sheet

Luna 10, Moon and Earth — AP4

1966, July 10   Photo.   Imperf.
C12 AP4 4t multicolored   4.50 3.50
Luna 10 Russian moon mission, Apr. 3, 1966.

Souvenir Sheet

Astronaut and Landing Module — AP5

1969, Aug. 20   Litho.   Perf. 11½
C13 AP5 4t ultra & multi   4.00 3.00
Apollo 11 US moon mission, first man landing on moon.

Souvenir Sheet

Apollo 16 — AP6

Perf. 12½x11½
1972, Apr. 16   Photo.
C14 AP6 4t multicolored   4.00 3.00
Apollo 16 moon mission, Apr. 15-27.

Souvenir Sheet

Mongolian Horse — AP7

1972, May 10   Photo.   Perf. 12½
C15 AP7 4t multicolored   4.00 3.00
Centenary of the discovery of the Przewalski wild horse, bred in captivity in Berlin Zoo.

Telecommunication — AP8

Designs: 30m, Horse breeding. 40m, Train and plane. 50m, Corn and farm machinery. 60m, Red Cross ambulance and hospital. 80m, Actors. 1t, Factories.

1972, July 11   Litho.   Perf. 12
C16 AP8 20m olive & multi   .40   .35
C17 AP8 30m violet & multi   .40   .35
C18 AP8 40m rose & multi   .40   .35
C19 AP8 50m red & multi   .40   .35
C20 AP8 60m multicolored   .70   .35
C21 AP8 80m lt blue & multi   .70   .35
C22 AP8 1t green & multi   1.00   .90
Nos. C16-C22 (7)   4.00 3.00
Mongolian Achievements.

Mongolian Flag, Globe and Radar — AP9

Perf. 12½x11½
1972, July 20   Photo.
C23 AP9 60m olive & multi   1.00   .50
Intl. Telecommunications Day, May 17, 1972.

Running and Olympic Rings — AP10

Olympic Rings and: 15m, Boxing. 20m, Judo. 25m, High jump. 30m, Rifle shooting. 60m, Wrestling. 80m, Weight lifting. 1t, Mongolian flag and sport emblem. 4t, Woman archer, vert.

Perf. 12½x11½
1972, July 30   Photo.
C24 AP10 10m multicolored   .30   .30
C25 AP10 15m multicolored   .30   .30
C26 AP10 20m multicolored   .30   .30
C27 AP10 25m multicolored   .30   .30
C28 AP10 30m multicolored   .30   .30
C29 AP10 60m multicolored   .50   .30
C30 AP10 80m multicolored   .65   .50
C31 AP10 1t multicolored   .90   .70
Nos. C24-C31 (8)   3.55 3.00
Souvenir Sheet
Perf. 11½x12½
C32 AP10 4t orange & multi   3.50 3.00
20th Olympic Games, Munich, 8/26-9/11.

U.S./U.S.S.R. Space Achievements — AP11

Astrological Signs of the Eastern Calendar and Space Project: a, Snake, Mars 1. b, Dragon and Mariner 2. c, Hare, Soyuz 5. d, Monkey, Explorer 6. e, Cook, Venera 1. f, Rat, Apollo 15. g, Horse, Apollo 8. h, Boar, Cosmos 110. i, Tiger, Gemini 7. j, Sheep, Electron 2. k, Dog, Ariel 2. l, Ram, Venera 4.

1972, Dec. 4   Photo.   Perf. 12
C33   Sheet of 12   7.00 5.00
a.-f. AP11 60m any single, size: 55x35mm   .50   .40
g.-l. AP11 60m any single, size: 35x35mm   .50   .40

Airliner — AP12

1973, Jan.   Photo.   Perf. 12
C34 AP12 1.50t blue   1.60   .40
For surcharge, see No. 2408.

Weather Satellite, Earth Station, WMO Emblem — AP13

1973, Feb.   Photo.   Perf. 12x11½
C35 AP13 60m multicolored   1.00   .50
Intl. meteorological cooperation, cent.

Holy Flame Type of 1959
Souvenir Sheet
1973, Apr. 15   Photo.   Perf. 12½
C36 A48 4t gold & multi   4.00 3.00
IBRA München 1973 Intl. Stamp Exhibition, Munich, May 11-20. No. C36 contains one 40x63mm stamp in redrawn design of A48

with simulated perforations and wide gold margin.

Mongolia #236 — AP14

Designs: Stamps (with mail-connected designs) of participating countries.

1973, July 31   Litho.   Perf. 12½
C37 AP14 30m Russia No. 3100   .50   .30
C38 AP14 30m shown   .50   .30
C39 AP14 30m Bulgaria #1047   .50   .30
C40 AP14 30m Hungary #B202   .50   .30
C41 AP14 30m Czechoslavia #C72   .50   .30
C42 AP14 30m German Dem. Rep. #369   .50   .30
C43 AP14 30m Cuba #C31   .50   .30
C44 AP14 30m Romania #2280   .50   .30
C45 AP14 30m Poland #802   .50   .30
Nos. C37-C45 (9)   4.50 2.70
Conference of Permanent Committee for Posts and Telecommunications of Council for Economic Aid (COMECON), Ulan Bator, Aug. 1973.

Launching of Soyuz Spacecraft — AP15

1973, Oct. 26   Litho.   Perf. 12½
C46 AP15 5m shown   .30   .25
C47 AP15 10m Apollo 8   .30   .25
C48 AP15 15m Soyuz 4 & 5 docking   .30   .25
C49 AP15 20m Apollo 11 lunar module   .30   .25
C50 AP15 30m Apollo 14 splashdown   .50   .25
C51 AP15 50m Soyuz 6, 7 & 8   .60   .25
C52 AP15 60m Apollo 16 moon rover   .70   .50
C53 AP15 1t Lunokhod 1 on moon   1.00   .75
Nos. C46-C53 (8)   4.00 2.75
Souvenir Sheet
C54 AP15 4t Soyuz and Apollo 4.50 3.50
US and Russian achievements in space.

Comecon Building, Moscow — AP16

1974, Feb. 28   Photo.   Perf. 11½x12
C55 AP16 60m blue & multi   .75   .30
25th anniversary of the Council of Mutual Economic Assistance.

Souvenir Sheet

Mongolia No. 4 — AP17

1974, Mar. 15   Photo.   Perf. 12½
C56 AP17 4t multicolored   4.00 3.00

50th anniv. of 1st stamps of Mongolia.

Postrider and UPU Emblem — AP18

UPU emblem & means of transportation.

1974, Apr.   Litho.   Perf. 12
C57	AP18	50m shown	.65	.35
C58	AP18	50m Reindeer post	.65	.35
C59	AP18	50m Mail coach	.65	.35
C60	AP18	50m Balloon post	.65	.35
C61	AP18	50m Steamship and AN-2 plane	.65	.35
C62	AP18	50m Train, truck and city	.65	.35
C63	AP18	50m Rocket over North Pole	.65	.35
		Nos. C57-C63 (7)	4.55	2.45

Souvenir Sheet
C64 AP18   4t Globe and post horn, vert.   10.00 9.00

Centenary of Universal Postal Union.

Circus Type of 1974

Design: 1t, Two women contortionists.

1974, May 4   Litho.   Perf. 12
C65 A177 1t multicolored   1.25 .60

No. C65 has se-tenant label, with similar design.

Nature Type of Regular Issue

1t, Scientist checking water, globe. 4t, Wild rose.

1974, Dec.   Litho.   Perf. 11
C66 A186 1t multicolored   1.20 .50

Souvenir Sheet
Perf. 12½
C67 A186 4t multicolored   4.00 3.00

UPU Type of 1974
Souvenir Sheet

Design: UPU Emblem, vert.

1974, Dec.   Perf. 11½x12
C68 A187 4t multicolored   4.50 4.50

Soyuz on Launching Pad, Project Emblem — AP19

Project Emblem and: 20m, Radar and Apollo. 30m, Apollo, Soyuz and earth. 40m, Spacecraft before docking. 50m, Spacecraft after docking. 60m, Soyuz circling earth. 1t, Spacecraft, space station and earth. 4t, Russian and American astronauts.

1975, June 14   Litho.   Perf. 12
C69	AP19	10m blue & multi	.25	.25
C70	AP19	20m multicolored	.25	.25
C71	AP19	30m sepia & multi	.25	.25
C72	AP19	40m silver & multi	.45	.30

C73	AP19	50m multicolored	.65	.40
C74	AP19	60m multicolored	.80	.40
C75	AP19	1t multicolored	1.20	.80
		Nos. C69-C75 (7)	3.85	2.65

Souvenir Sheet
C76 AP19   4t black & multi   2.75 2.75

Apollo Soyuz space test project (Russo-American space cooperation), launching July 15; link-up July 17.

Mongolian Mountain Sheep — AP20

1975, Aug. 4   Litho.   Perf. 12
C77 AP20 1.50t multi + label   2.00 1.00

South Asia Tourism Year.

Satellite over Weather Map of Mongolia — AP21

1976, Mar. 20   Perf. 12x11½
C78 AP21 60m blue & yellow   1.00 .30

40th anniversary of meteorological service.

Souvenir Sheet

Girl with Books and Flowers — AP22

1976, Mar. 30   Perf. 12
C79 AP22 4t multicolored   3.50 3.00

30th anniversary of UNESCO.

Souvenir Sheet

The Wise Musician, by Sarav — AP23

1976, May 3   Litho.   Perf. 11½x12½
C80 AP23 4t multicolored   3.50 3.00

Interphil 76 Phil. Exhib., Philadelphia, Pa., May 29-June 6.

Olympic Games Type of 1976
Souvenir Sheet

1976, May 20   Perf. 12½x11½
C81 A202 4t Wrestling   3.00 2.50

Independence Type of 1976

60m, Progress in agriculture and industry.

1976, June 20   Litho.   Perf. 12x11½
C82 A203 60m multicolored   .70 .30

Olympic Medalists Type, 1976
Souvenir Sheet

Design: 4t, Oidov Zeveg, Mongolian flag.

1976, Nov. 30   Litho.   Perf. 11x11½
C83 A209 4t multicolored   3.00 2.50

Mounting Carrier Rocket with Bell-shaped Gear — AP24

Designs: 20m, Launching of Intercosmos 3. 30m, Marine Observatory Gagarin (ship). 40m, Satellite observation of lunar eclipse. 60m, Observatory with multiple antenna system. 80m, Examination of Van Allen Zone, magnetosphere. 1t, Meteorological earth satellite. 4t, Intercosmos satellite with lines showing participating countries on globe.

1977, June 20   Litho.   Perf. 12
C84	AP24	10m multicolored	.25	.25
C85	AP24	20m multicolored	.25	.25
C86	AP24	30m multicolored	.35	.25
C87	AP24	40m multicolored	.45	.25
C88	AP24	60m multicolored	.65	.40
C89	AP24	80m multicolored	.90	.50
C90	AP24	1t multicolored	1.10	.60
		Nos. C84-C90 (7)	3.95	2.50

Souvenir Sheet
Perf. 12½
C91 AP24   4t multicolored   3.50 2.50

11th anniv. of Intercosmos program, cooperation of 9 socialist countries for space research. No. C91 contains one stamp 58x37mm.

Trade Union Emblem, Factory and Sheep AP25

1977, June   Perf. 12x11½
C92 AP25 60m multicolored   1.00 .30

11th Cong. of Mongolian Trade Unions, May 12.

Montgolfier's Balloon — AP26

Dirigibles: 30m, Zeppelin over North Pole, 1931. 40m, Osoaviahim, Russian Arctic cargo. 50m, North, Russian heavy duty cargo. 60m, Aeron-340, Russian planned. 80m, Machinery transport, Russian planned. 1.20t, Flying crane, French planned. 4t, Russia No. C26 (stamp) and Sukhe Bator statue.

1977, Dec.   Perf. 12
C93	AP26	20m multicolored	.25	.25
C94	AP26	30m multicolored	.25	.25
C95	AP26	40m multicolored	.35	.25
C96	AP26	50m multicolored	.45	.30
C97	AP26	60m multicolored	.65	.30
C98	AP26	80m multicolored	.90	.50
C99	AP26	1.20t multicolored	1.40	.60
		Nos. C93-C99 (7)	4.25	2.45

Souvenir Sheet
Perf. 12½x11½
C100 AP26   4t multicolored   4.00 3.00

History of airships.

A. F. Mozhaiski and his Plane, 1884 — AP27

Designs: 30m, Henry Farman and his plane, 1909. 40m, Geoffrey de Havilland and D. H. 66 Hercules, 1920's. 50m, Charles A. Lindbergh, Spirit of St. Louis and route New York to Paris, 1927. 60m, Mongolian pilots Shagdarsuren and Demberel and plane over Altai Mountains, 1935. 80m, Soviet aviators Chkalov, Baidukov, Beliakov, plane and route Moscow to Vancouver, 1937. 1.20t, A. N. Tupolev, supersonic plane TU 154, route Moscow to Alma-Ata, 1968. 4t, Wilbur and Orville Wright and their plane.

1978, Mar. 25   Litho.   Perf. 12½x11
C101	AP27	20m multi	.25	.25
C102	AP27	30m multi	.30	.25
C103	AP27	40m multi	.35	.25
C104	AP27	50m multi	.45	.30
C105	AP27	60m multi	.55	.30
C106	AP27	80m multi	.70	.40
C107	AP27	1.20t multi	1.10	.60
		Nos. C101-C107 (7)	3.70	2.35

Souvenir Sheet
C108 AP27   4t multi   3.50 3.50

75th anniversary of first powered flight, Wright brothers, 1903.

Soccer Type of 1978
Souvenir Sheet

Design: 4t, Two soccer players.

1978, Apr. 15   Perf. 11½
C109 A231 4t multi   3.75 3.75

World Soccer Championships, Argentina 78, June 1-25. #C109 contains 1 45x38mm stamp.

Souvenir Sheet

Canada No. 553 and Mongolia No. 549 — AP28

1978, June   Litho.   Perf. 12½
C110 AP28 4t multi   3.50 3.50

CAPEX '78, Intl. Phil. Exhibition, Toronto, June 9-18.

Map of Cuba, Ship, Plane and Festival Emblem — AP29

1978, July 28   Litho.   Perf. 12
C111 AP29 1t multicolored   1.50 .30

11th World Youth Festival, Havana, 7/28-8/5.

Souvenir Sheet

Aleksei Gubarev and Vladimir Remek, PRAGA '78 Emblem — AP30

1978, Sept. 5   Litho.   Perf. 12
C112 AP30 4t multicolored   3.50 3.50
PRAGA '78 Intl. Phil. Exhib., Prague, Sept. 8-17, and Russian-Czechoslovak space cooperation, Intercosmos.

DDR Flag, TV Tower, Berlin, Satellite AP31

1979, Oct. 9   Litho.   Perf. 11½x12
C113 AP31 60m multicolored   .75 .40
German Democratic Republic, 30th anniv.

Demoiselle Crane AP32

Protected Birds: 30m, Hawk warbler. 50m, Ruddy shelduck. 60m, Blue magpie. 70m, Goldfinch. 80m, Titmouse. 1t, Golden oriole.

1979, Oct. 25
C114 AP32 10m multi   .40 .25
C115 AP32 30m multi   .60 .25
C116 AP32 50m multi   .75 .25
C117 AP32 60m multi   1.00 .25
C118 AP32 70m multi   1.10 .30
C119 AP32 80m multi   1.25 .30
C120 AP32 1t multi   1.50 .35
    Nos. C114-C120 (7)   6.60 1.95

Venera 5 and 6 — AP33

American and Russian Space Missions: 30m, Mariner 5. 50m, Mars 3. 60m, Viking 1 and 2. 70m, Luna 1, 2 and 3. 80m, Lunokhod 2. 1t, Apollo 15. 4t, Apollo 11, astronauts on moon.

Perf. 12½x11½
1979, Nov. 24   Litho.
C121 AP33 10m multi   .25 .25
C122 AP33 30m multi   .25 .25
C123 AP33 50m multi   .35 .25
C124 AP33 60m multi   .45 .25
C125 AP33 70m multi   .55 .30

C126 AP33 80m multi   .65 .40
C127 AP33 1t multi   .80 .40
    Nos. C121-C127 (7)   3.30 2.10
Souvenir Sheet
C128 AP33 4t multi   3.50 3.50
Apollo 11 moon landing, 10th anniversary.

Andrena Scita — AP34

Insects: 30m, Paravespula germanica. 40m, Perilampus ruficornis. 50m, Bumblebee. 60m, Honey bee. 80m, Stilbum cyanurum. 1.20t, Ruby tail.

1980, Feb. 25   Litho.   Perf. 11x12
C129 AP34 20m multi   .25 .25
C130 AP34 30m multi   .30 .25
C131 AP34 40m multi   .45 .30
C132 AP34 50m multi   .55 .30
C133 AP34 60m multi   .65 .40
C134 AP34 80m multi   .85 .50
C135 AP34 1.20t multi   1.25 .60
    Nos. C129-C135 (7)   4.30 2.60

Z-526 AFS Stunt Planes, Czechoslovakia — AP35

1980, Aug. 4   Litho.   Perf. 12
C136 AP35 20m shown   .25 .25
C137 AP35 30m RS-180 "Sportsman," Germany   .25 .25
C138 AP35 40m Yankı-Anu, US   .35 .25
C139 AP35 50m MJ-2 "Tempete," France   .45 .25
C140 AP35 60m "Pits," Canada   .55 .30
C141 AP35 80m "Acrostar," Switzerland   .65 .40
C142 AP35 1.20t JAK-50, USSR   1.00 .55
    Nos. C136-C142 (7)   3.50 2.25
Souvenir Sheet
C143 AP35 4t JAK-52, USSR   3.00 2.50
10th World Aerobatic Championship, Oshkosh, Wisconsin, Aug. 17-30. No. C143 contains one 50x43mm stamp.

Olympic Type of 1980
Souvenir Sheet

1980, Sept. 15   Litho.   Perf. 12½
C144 A253 4t Wrestlers   3.50 3.50
J. Davaajav, Mongolian silver medalist, 22nd Summer Olympic Games, Moscow. Inscribed "Los Angeles '84".

Souvenir Sheet

AP36

1980, Dec. 10   Litho.   Perf. 11½x11
C145 AP36 4t multi   3.50 3.50
Johannes Kepler (1571-1630), German astronomer.

AP37

Graf Zeppelin and: 20m, Germany #C40, sea eagle. 30m, Germany #C41, polar fox. 40m, Germany #C42, walrus. 50m, Russia #C26, polar bear. 60m, Russia #C27, snowy owl. 80m, Russia #C28, puffin. 1.20t, Russia #C29, seal. 4t, Icebreaker Maligin.

1981, Oct. 5   Litho.   Perf. 12x11½
C146 AP37 20m multi   .50 .25
C147 AP37 30m multi   .60 .25
C148 AP37 40m multi   .30 .40
C149 AP37 50m multi   .90 .30
C150 AP37 60m multi   1.00 .40
C151 AP37 80m multi   1.40 .60
C152 AP37 1.20t multi   1.75 .70
    Nos. C146-C152 (7)   6.45 2.90
Souvenir Sheet
C153 AP37 4t multi   4.50 4.00
Graf Zeppelin polar flight, 50th anniv. No. C153 contains one stamp 36x51mm.

ITU Plenipotentiaries Conference, Nairobi, Sept. — AP38

1982, Sept. 27   Litho.   Perf. 12
C154 AP38 60m Map   .80 .30

2nd UN Conference on Peaceful Uses of Outer Space, Vienna, Aug. 9-21 — AP39

1982, Dec. 15   Litho.   Perf. 12
C155 AP39 60m Sputnik 1   .50 .30
C156 AP39 60m Sputnik 2   .50 .30
C157 AP39 60m Vostok 1   .50 .30
C158 AP39 60m Venera 8   .50 .30
C159 AP39 60m Vostok 6   .50 .30
C160 AP39 60m Voskhod 2   .50 .30
C161 AP39 60m Apollo 11   .50 .30
C162 AP39 60m Soyuz 6   .50 .30
    Nos. C155-C162 (8)   4.00 2.40
Souvenir Sheet
Perf. 12½x12
C163 AP39 4t Soyuz 39, Salyut 6   3.50 3.50

Balloon Flight Bicentenary AP40

1982, Dec. 31   Perf. 11½x12½
C164 AP40 20m Montgolfiere, 1783   .25 .25
C165 AP40 30m Blanchard, 1785   .30 .25
C166 AP40 40m Royal-Vauxhall, 1836   .40 .25
C167 AP40 50m Oernen, 1897   .50 .25
C168 AP40 60m Gordon Bennett Race, 1906   .65 .25
C169 AP40 80m Paris, 1931   .90 .30
C170 AP40 1.20t USSR-VR-62, 1933   1.40 .40
    Nos. C164-C170 (7)   4.40 1.95
Souvenir Sheet
C171 AP40 4t Mongolia, 1977   3.50 3.50

Souvenir Sheet

Revolutionary Mongolia Monument — AP41

1983   Litho.   Imperf.
C172 AP41 4t multi   3.50 3.50

Concorde — AP42

1984, Aug. 15   Litho.   Perf. 14
C173 AP42 20m DC-10, vert.   .25 .25
C174 AP42 30m Airbus A-300 B-2   .30 .25
C175 AP42 40m shown   .40 .30
C176 AP42 50m Boeing 747   .50 .40
C177 AP42 60m IL-62   .60 .40
C178 AP42 80m TU-154   .80 .50
C179 AP42 1.20t IL-86   1.20 .60
    Nos. C173-C179 (7)   4.05 2.70
Souvenir Sheet
C180 AP42 4t Yak-42   3.50 3.50

1988 Winter Olympics, Calgary AP43

1988, Jan. 20   Litho.   Perf. 14
C181 AP43 20m Bobsled   .25 .25
C182 AP43 30m Ski jumping   .25 .25
C183 AP43 40m Downhill skiing   .35 .25
C184 AP43 50m Biathlon   .40 .25
C185 AP43 60m Speed skating   .55 .30
C186 AP43 80m Women's figure skating   .65 .30
C187 AP43 1.20t Ice hockey   .75 .40
    Nos. C181-C187 (7)   3.20 2.00
Souvenir sheet
C188 AP43 4t Cross-country skiing   3.25 2.50

Souvenir Sheet

Hong Kong '94 — AP44

1994, Feb. 18　Litho.　Perf. 14½x15
C189　AP44　600t multicolored　4.00　4.00
　a.　　With Hong Kong '97 em-
　　　　blem in sheet margin　4.00　4.00
　　　Issued: #C189a, 1/12/97.

No. C163 Surcharged in Red
Souvenir Sheet

2001, Mar. 22　Litho.　Perf. 12½x12
C190　AP39　400t on 4t multi　25.00　25.00
　　Joint Soviet-Mongolian space flight, 20th
anniv.

AIR POST SEMI-POSTAL STAMP

> **Catalogue values for unused stamps in this section are for Never Hinged items.**

UNICEF Type of 1977
Souvenir Sheet

Design: 4t+50m, Balloon with Mongolian flag, children and UNICEF emblem.

1977, June 1　Litho.　Perf. 12
CB1　SP2　4t + 50m multi　4.00　4.00
　　First balloon flight in Mongolia. Surtax was
for Children's Village.

MONTENEGRO
ˌmän-tə-'nē-ˌgrō

LOCATION — Southern Europe, bordering on the Adriatic Sea
GOVT. — Republic in southern Europe.
AREA — 5,415 sq. mi.
POP. — 620,145 (2003)
CAPITAL — Podgorica

Montenegro maintained a precarious independence from the Ottoman Turks during the 16th-19th centuries as a theocracy, under a succession of bishop princes. In 1852 it became an independent principality. On December 1, 1918, Montenegro, along with Bosnia and Herzegovina, Croatia, Dalmatia and Slovenia, was absorbed by Serbia to form the Kingdom of the Serbs, Croats and Slovenes, which became the Kingdom of Yugoslavia in 1929.

During World War II, an Italian satellite regime was established in an enlarged Montenegrin state, but after the war, Montenegro became one of the constituent republics of the Socialist Federal Republic of Yugoslavia.

In 1992, with the dissolution of the greater Yugoslav republic, only Montenegro remained associated with Serbia, first in the Federal Republic of Yugoslavia and, after 2002, in the looser federation of Serbia & Montenegro.

On May 21, 2006, Montenegrins endorsed independence and complete separation from Serbia in a national referendum, and the Republic of Montenegro declared independence on June 3. On June 7, Serbia officially recognized Montenegro's independence.

100 Novcic = 1 Florin
100 Helera = 1 Kruna (1902)
100 Para = 1 Kruna (1907)
100 Para = 1 Perper (1910)
100 cents = 1 euro (2003)

Canceled to Order
Used values for Nos. 1-110, H1-H5, J1-J26, and stamps issued under German occupation (Nos. 3N1-3NCB6) are for canceled-to-order stamps. Postally used examples sell for considerably more.

Watermarks

Wmk. 91 — "BRIEF-MARKEN" (#1-14) or "ZEITUNGS-MARKEN" (#15-21) in Double-lined Capitals once across sheet

Wmk. 140 — Crown

Prince Nicholas I — A1

Early Printings
Narrow Spacing (2-2½mm)
Perf. 10½ Large Holes, pointed teeth

1874		Typo.	Wmk. 91	
1	A1	2n yellow	40.00	40.00
2	A1	3n green	55.00	40.00
3	A1	5n rose red	50.00	40.00
4	A1	7n lt lilac	50.00	32.50
5	A1	10n blue	120.00	80.00
6	A1	15n yel bister	135.00	120.00
7	A1	25n lilac gray	280.00	210.00
		Nos. 1-7 (7)	730.00	562.50

Middle Printings (1879)
Narrow spacing
Perf. 12, 12½, 13 and Compound

8	A1	2n yellow	10.00	7.00
a.		Perf. 12-13x10½	65.00	65.00
9	A1	3n green	7.50	5.50
10	A1	5n red	7.50	5.50
11	A1	7n rose lilac	7.50	5.50
a.		7n lilac	19.00	14.00
12	A1	10n blue	16.00	11.00
a.		Perf. 12-13x10½	65.00	52.50
13	A1	15n bister brn	19.00	11.00
14	A1	25n gray lilac	25.00	16.00
		Nos. 8-14 (7)	92.50	61.50

Late Printings (1893?)
Narrow and wide spacing (2¾-3½mm)
Perf. 10½, 11½ Small holes, broad teeth
(Perf. 11½ also with pointed teeth)

15	A1	2n yellow	4.00	2.75
a.		Perf. 11 ('94)	27.50	20.00
16	A1	3n green	4.00	2.75
17	A1	5n red	4.75	3.25
18	A1	7n rose	2.75	2.00
a.		Perf. 11 ('94)	12.00	9.00
19	A1	10n blue	4.00	2.75
20	A1	15n brown	4.00	3.25
21	A1	25n brown violet	4.75	3.00
		Nos. 15-21 (7)	28.25	19.75

Dates of issue of the late printings are still being researched.

Types of 1874-93 Overprinted in Black or Red

1893			Perf. 10½, 11½	
22	A1	2n yellow	35.00	6.50
a.		Perf. 11	35.00	35.00
23	A1	3n green	6.50	3.25
24	A1	5n red	2.40	1.60
25	A1	7n rose	4.00	2.50
a.		Perf. 12	60.00	50.00
b.		7n rose lilac	5.00	3.00
c.		7n lilac, perf. 12	125.00	
d.		Perf. 11	40.00	30.00
26	A1	10n blue	4.00	3.25
27	A1	10n blue (R)	6.00	4.00
28	A1	15n brown	4.50	3.25
a.		Perf. 12	50.00	42.50
29	A1	15n brown (R)	2,400.	1,600.
30	A1	25n brown violet	4.00	2.40
31	A1	25n brn vio (R)	6.00	4.00
a.		Perf. 12½		225.00
		Nos. 22-28,30-31 (9)	72.40	30.75

Introduction of printing to Montenegro, 400th anniversary.

This overprint had many settings. Several values exist with "1494" or "1495" instead of "1493," or with missing letters or numerals due to wearing of the clichés. Double and inverted overprints exist. Some printings were made after 1893 to supply a philatelic demand, but were available for postage.

The 7n with red overprint was not issued.

1894-98		Wmk. 91	Perf. 10½, 11½	
32	A1	1n gray blue	.40	.40
33	A1	2n emerald ('98)	.40	.40
34	A1	3n carmine rose ('98)	.40	.40
35	A1	5n orange ('98)	2.40	.55
36	A1	7n gray lilac ('98)	.50	.50
37	A1	10n magenta ('98)	.50	.50
38	A1	15n red brown ('98)	.40	.40
39	A1	20n brown orange	.40	.40
40	A1	25n dull blue ('98)	.40	.40
41	A1	30n maroon	.40	.25
42	A1	50n ultra	.55	.55
43	A1	1fl deep green	.80	.80
44	A1	2fl red brown	1.25	1.25
		Nos. 32-44 (13)	8.80	6.80

Monastery at Cetinje (Royal Mausoleum) A3

		Perf. 10½, 11½		
1896, Sept. 1		Litho.	Unwmk.	
45	A3	1n dk blue & bis	.40	.40
46	A3	2n magenta & yel	.40	.40
47	A3	3n org brn & yel grn	.40	.40
48	A3	5n bl grn & bis	.40	.40
49	A3	10n yellow & ultra	.40	.40
50	A3	15n dk blue & grn	.40	.40
a.		Perf. 11½	60.00	60.00
51	A3	20n bl grn & ultra	.40	.40
a.		Perf. 11½	40.00	40.00
52	A3	25n dk blue & yel	.50	.50
53	A3	30n magenta & bis	.55	.55
54	A3	50n red brn & gray bl	.55	.55
55	A3	1fl rose & gray bl	1.00	1.00
56	A3	2fl brown & black	1.40	1.40
		Nos. 45-56 (12)	6.80	6.80

Bicentenary of the ruling dynasty, founded by the Vladika, Danilo Petrovich of Nyegosh.
Inverted centers and other errors exist, but experts believe these to be printer's waste.
Perf. 11½ counterfeits are common.

Prince Nicholas I — A4

Perf. 13x13½, 13x12½ (2h, 5h, 50h, 2k, 5k), 12½ (1h, 25h)
1902, July 12

57	A4	1h ultra	.40	.40
58	A4	2h rose lilac	.40	.40
59	A4	5h green	.40	.40
60	A4	10h rose	.40	.40
61	A4	25h dull blue	.55	.55
62	A4	50h gray green	.80	.80
63	A4	1k chocolate	.80	.80
64	A4	2k pale brown	.80	.80
65	A4	5k buff	.95	.95
		Nos. 57-65 (9)	5.50	5.50

The 2h black brown and 25h indigo were not issued. The 25h, perf. 12½, probably was never issued.

Constitution Issue

Same Overprinted in Red or Black "Constitution" 15mm

1905, Dec. 5

66	A4	1h ultra (R)	.40	.40
67	A4	2h rose lilac	.40	.40
68	A4	5h green (R)	.80	.80
69	A4	10h rose	.95	.95
70	A4	25h dull blue (R)	.55	.55
71	A4	50h gray green (R)	.55	.55
72	A4	1k chocolate (R)	.55	.55
73	A4	2k pale brown (R)	.80	.80
74	A4	5k buff	1.25	1.25
		Nos. 66-74 (9)	6.25	6.25

Overprints in other colors are proofs.

1906		"Constitution" 16½mm		
66a	A4	1h ultra (R)	.55	.55
67a	A4	2h rose lilac	.55	.55
68a	A4	5h green (R)	.80	.80
69a	A4	10h rose	1.25	1.25
70a	A4	25h dull blue (R)	.80	.80
71a	A4	50h gray green (R)	.80	.80
72a	A4	1k chocolate (R)	1.25	1.25
73a	A4	2k pale brown (R)	1.25	1.25
74a	A4	5k buff	1.25	1.25
		Nos. 66a-74a (9)	8.50	8.50

Three settings of Nos. 66a-74a containing four types of "YCTAB": I, 9¾mm, II, 11¼mm, III, 10¼mm, IV, 8½mm. Type IV occurs only in one setting, at two positions. Nos. 67a, 69a-74a exist in type IV.

Two errors occur: "Constitutton" and "Coustitution." Many other varieties including reversed color overprints exist.

Values are for types I and II.

Prince Nicholas I — A5

1907, June 1　Engr.　Perf. 12½

75	A5	1pa ocher	.45	.45
76	A5	2pa black	.45	.45
77	A5	5pa yellow green	1.40	.45
78	A5	10pa rose red	2.25	.45
79	A5	15pa ultra	.45	.45
80	A5	20pa red orange	.45	.45
81	A5	25pa indigo	.45	.45
82	A5	35pa bister brown	.55	.45
83	A5	50pa dull violet	.80	.50
84	A5	1kr carmine rose	.80	.50
85	A5	2kr green	.80	.80
86	A5	5kr red brown	1.75	1.20
		Nos. 75-86 (12)	10.60	6.60

Many Montenegro stamps exist imperforate or part perforate. Experts believe these to be printer's waste.

King Nicholas I as a Youth — A6

King Nicholas I and Queen Milena — A7

King Nicholas I — A11

Prince Nicholas — A12

5pa, 10pa, 25pa, 35pa, Nicholas in 1910. 15pa, Nicholas in 1878. 20pa, King and Queen, diff.

1910, Aug. 28   **Engr.**

87	A6	1pa black	.65	.65
88	A7	2pa purple brown	.65	.65
89	A6	5pa dark green	.65	.65
90	A6	10pa carmine	.65	.65
91	A6	15pa slate blue	.65	.65
92	A7	20pa olive green	.65	.65
93	A6	25pa deep blue	.65	.65
94	A6	35pa chestnut	1.20	.80
95	A11	50pa violet	1.20	.80
96	A11	1per lake	.65	.80
97	A11	2per yellow green	1.30	.80
98	A12	5per pale blue	1.60	1.25
		Nos. 87-98 (12)	10.50	9.00

Proclamation of Montenegro as a kingdom, the 50th anniv. of the reign of King Nicholas and the golden wedding celebration of the King and Queen.

King Nicholas I — A13

1913, Apr. 1   **Typo.**

99	A13	1pa orange	.65	.65
100	A13	2pa plum	.65	.65
101	A13	5pa deep green	.65	.65
102	A13	10pa deep rose	.65	.65
103	A13	15pa blue gray	.65	.65
104	A13	20pa dark brown	.65	.65
105	A13	25pa deep blue	.65	.65
106	A13	35pa vermilion	.65	.65
107	A13	50pa pale blue	.80	.80
108	A13	1per yellow brown	.80	.80
109	A13	2per gray violet	.80	.80
110	A13	5per yellow green	.80	.80
		Nos. 99-110 (12)	8.40	8.40

SERBIA & MONTENEGRO

100 Cents=1 Euro

Yugoslavia became Serbia & Montenegro Feb. 4, 2003, with each section of the country maintaining and operating their own postal service, and each having their own currency. After a referendum on independence on May 21, 2006, Montenegro seceded from Serbia and Montenegro, declaring independence on June 3. Serbia formally recognized Montenegro's independence on June 7.

The stamps below are inscribed only with euro denominations, used solely within Montenegro. Stamps inscribed with dinar denominations, issued for use in Serbia, and those denominated in both dinar and euro currencies, for use in either region, are found under the Serbia listings.

Budva A20

Durmitor A21

2003, Sept. 15   **Litho.**   **Perf. 12½**

120	A20	25c multi	1.25	1.25
121	A21	40c multi	2.25	2.25

Christmas — A22

2003, Nov. 21   **Perf. 13¼**

122	A22	25c multi	1.75	1.75
		Complete booklet, 10 #122	17.50	

National Symbols A23

Small coat of arms, outline map of Europe and: 25c, Map of Montenegro. 40c, Parliament Building and map of Montenegro. 50c, Large coat of arms and map of Montenegro. 60c, Flag and map of Montenegro.

2005, Dec. 15   **Litho.**   **Perf. 13**

123-126	A23	Set of 4	9.50	9.50

See Nos. 140-142.

Europa A24

Designs: 25c, Fish, shrimp, and mussels. 50c, Meat, olives, cheese and fruit.
No. 128C: d, 25c, Bee, honeycomb and honey. e, 50c, Grapes, grapevine, wine.

2005, Dec. 30   **Perf. 13½x13¾**

127	A24	25c multicolored	5.50	5.50
a.		As #127, perf. 13½ x 13¾x 13½x imperf.	18.00	18.00
128	A24	50c multicolored	11.00	11.00
a.		As #128, perf. 13½x imperf. x 13½x 13¾	25.00	25.00
b.		Souvenir sheet, #127a, 128a	45.00	45.00

Souvenir Sheet
Perf. 13½x13¾

128C	A24	Sheet of 2, #d-e	45.00	45.00

A25

Europa Stamps, 50th Anniv. — A26

No. 129: a, Montenegro #100, common vignette of 1960 Europa stamps. b, Montenegro #101, common vignette of 1961-62 Europa stamps. c, Montenegro #102, bee and honeycomb. d, Montenegro #105, common vignette of 1956 Europa stamps.
No. 129E: f, Like #129a. g, Like #129b. h, Like #129c. i, Like #129d.

2006, Jan. 3   **Litho.**   **Perf. 13½x13¾**
Stamps with Frames

129		Horiz. strip of 4	20.00	20.00
a.		A25 50c multi	1.25	1.25
b.		A25 €1 multi	3.00	3.00
c.-d.		A25 €2 Either single	5.75	5.75

Souvenir Sheet
Stamps Without Frames

129E	A25	Sheet of 4, #f-i	21.00	21.00

Litho. with Foil Application
Imperf
Size: 103x76mm

130	A26	€5.50 multi	15.00	15.00

No. 129E exists imperf. Value, $70.

2006 Winter Olympics, Turin A27

Designs: 60c, Figure skating. 90c, Ski jumping.

2006, Feb. 7   **Litho.**   **Perf. 13½x13¾**

131-132	A27	Set of 2	5.75	5.75

Flowers A28

Designs: 25c, Petteria ramentacea. 50c, Viola nikolai.

2006, Mar. 15

133-134	A28	Set of 2	2.75	2.75

Introduction of Perper Currency, Cent. — A29

Central Bank of Montenegro and: 40c, 1906 1-para coin. 50c, 1906 20-para coin.

2006, Apr. 27   **Litho.**   **Perf. 13½x13¾**

135-136	A29	Set of 2	3.50	3.50

2006 World Cup Soccer Championships, Germany — A30

Designs: No. 137, 60c, Players in match. No. 138, 90c, Players in match, diff. No. 139: a, 60c, Players, empty stadium in background. b, 90c, Players, empty stadium in background, diff.

2006, May 30   **Perf. 13¾x13½**

137-138	A30	Set of 2	5.75	5.75

Souvenir Sheet

139	A30	Sheet of 2, #a-b	5.00	5.00

National Symbols Type of 2005
Redrawn With "Posta Crne Gore"
Under Postal Emblem

Designs as before.

2006, June   **Litho.**   **Perf. 13¾**

140	A23	25c multi	1.00	1.00
a.		Perf. 13	1.00	1.00
141	A23	40c multi	1.50	1.50
a.		Perf. 13	1.50	1.50
142	A23	60c multi	2.50	2.50
		Nos. 140-142 (3)	5.00	5.00

Nos. 140a and 141a are dated "2005," while Nos. 140-142 are dated "2006."

Independent Republic

Tourism A31

Designs: 25c, Durmitor. 50c, Sveti Stefan.

2006, July 5   **Perf. 13½x13¾**

143-144	A31	Set of 2	2.75	2.75

Independence Referendum of May 21 — A32

2006, July 13

145	A32	50c multi	2.00	2.00

Europa — A33

Designs: No. 146, 60c, Women linking chain. No. 147, 90c, People and sun, horiz. No. 148: a, 60c, Man with suitcase. b, 90c, People of different races.

2006, Aug. 30   **Perf. 13¾**

146-147	A33	Set of 2	6.00	6.00

Souvenir Sheet

148	A33	Sheet of 2, #a-b	5.75	5.75

Capt. Ivo Visin (1806-68), Circumnavigator, and Ship, Splendido — A34

2006, Sept. 5   **Perf. 13½x13¾**

149	A34	40c multi	1.60	1.60

Stamp Day — A35

2006, Oct. 2   **Perf. 13¾**
150 A35 25c multi   1.00 1.00

Mona Lisa, by Leonardo da Vinci, 500th Anniv. — A36

2006, Oct. 18   **Perf. 13¾x13½**
151 A36 50c multi   2.00 2.00

Cultural Heritage A37

Designs: No. 152, 25c, Ruins, Dukla Archaeological Site. No. 153, 25c, Glassware.

2006, Nov. 3   **Perf. 13¾x13½**
152-153 A37 Set of 2   2.00 2.00

Tara River A38

     Perf. 13½x13¾
2006, Nov. 15   **Litho.**
154 A38 40c multi   1.50 1.50

Gregorian Calendar, 425th Anniv. A39

2007, Jan. 4   **Perf. 13¾x13**
155 A39 50c multi   2.00 2.00
Printed in sheets of 8 + label.

Wildlife Protection A40

2007, Feb. 7
156 A40 50c multi   2.00 2.00
Printed in sheets of 8 + label.

Europa — A41

Map of Montenegro and: Nos. 157, 159a, 60c, Montengro Scouting emblem. Nos. 158, 159b, 90c, Tent and campfire.

2007, Apr. 20   **Litho.**   **Perf. 13¾**
157 A41 60c multi   2.25 2.25
158 A41 90c multi   3.00 3.00
   a.   Souvenir sheet, #157-158   5.50 5.50

    Perf. 13¾ (Imperf. Between Stamps)

159   Sheet of 2   5.50 5.50
   a.   A41 60c multi, 42x28mm   2.00 2.00
   b.   A41 90c multi, 42x28mm   2.75 2.75

Nos. 157 and 158 were each printed in sheets of 8 + label. No. 159 was sold with but not attached to a booklet cover.

Birds — A42

No. 160: a, 25c, Gull. b, 50c, Eagle.

2007, May 11   **Litho.**   **Perf. 13¾**
160 A42   Pair, #a-b   3.00 3.00

Migration of Montenegrins to Istria, 350th Anniv. — A43

2007, June 21   **Perf. 13¾**
161 A43 60c multi   2.10 2.10
Printed in sheets of 8 + label.

Postal History A44

Glagolithic Text — A45

Mountains A46

Stylized Butterfly A47

2007, July 3
162 A44 25c multi   .90 .90
163 A45 40c multi   1.40 1.40
164 A46 50c multi   1.75 1.75
165 A47 60c multi   2.25 2.25
   Nos. 162-165 (4)   6.30 6.30

Petar Lubarda (1907-74), Painter A48

2007, July 27   **Perf. 13¾**
166 A48 40c multi   1.50 1.50

Ship — A49

2007, Aug. 1
167 A49 60c multi   2.10 2.10
Printed in sheets of 8 + label.

Joy of Europe — A50

2007, Oct. 2
168 A50 50c multi   1.90 1.90

Regional Telephone Service, Cent. — A51

Designs: 25c, Telephone dial. 50c, Telephone dial and red dots.

2007, Nov. 9   **Litho.**   **Perf. 13¾**
169-170 A51   Set of 2   2.75 2.75

New Year's Day — A52

Designs: No. 171, 25c, Twisted ribbon. No. 172, 25c, Christmas ornament on tree branch. 50c, Wreath and bells. €1, Lit candle.

2007, Dec. 5   **Perf. 14x13¾**
171-174 A52 Set of 4   7.25 7.25

Stabilization and Association Agreement Between Montenegro and the European Union — A53

Jigsaw puzzle pieces with: 60c, Montenegro coat of arms and European Union ring of stars.

No. 176: a, 40c, Montenegro coat of arms. b, 50c, European Union ring of stars.

2008, Feb. 1   **Litho.**   **Perf. 13¾**
175 A53 60c multi   2.10 2.10

     Souvenir Sheet
176 A53   Sheet of 2, #a-b   3.25 3.25

Flowers — A54

Designs: 25c, Draba bertiscea. 40c, Edraianthus wettsteinii. 50c, Protoedriantus tarae. 60c, Dianthus nitidus.

2008, Feb. 20
177-180 A54 Set of 4   6.50 6.50
Nos. 177-180 each were printed in sheets of 5 + label.

2008 Summer Olympics, Beijing A55

Stylized athletes, Beijing Olympics emblem and: 60c, Map of Montenegro. 90c, Montenegro coat of arms.

2008, Mar. 26
181-182 A55 Set of 2   5.75 5.75

Europa — A56

Designs: No. 183, 60c, Boy, envelope with stamp. No. 184, 90c, Girl, letter.

No. 185: a, 60c, Boy, right half of envelope.
b, 90c, Girl, left half of envelope.

2008, Apr. 2
183-184 A56   Set of 2   5.75 5.75
        Souvenir Sheet
185   A56   Sheet of 2, #a-b   5.75 5.75
   Nos. 183-184 each were printed in sheets of
8 + label.

Marko Miljanov (1833-1901),
Writer — A57

2008, Apr. 24
186   A57   60c multi   2.25 2.25

Battle of Grahovac, 150th
Anniv. — A58

2008, Apr. 29
187   A58   25c multi   .95   .95

Tourism
A59

   Designs: 25c, Hillside hut. 40c, Fortress.
50c, Pier and boats. 60c, Boat on lake.

2008, May 21
188-191 A59   Set of 4   6.00 6.00
191a   Sheet of 4, #188-191   6.00 6.00

Chess
Olympics,
Dresden,
Germany
A60

2008, June 18   Litho.   Perf. 13¾
192   A60   60c multi   2.25 2.25

Ship
Jadran,
75th
Anniv.
A61

2008, July 16
193   A61   50c multi   2.00 2.00

Victory of Montenegrin Team at
European Water Polo Championships,
Malaga, Spain — A62

2008, Sept. 15
194   A62   50c multi   2.00 2.00
   Printed in sheets of 8 + label.

Roman Art — A63

   No. 195: a, 25c, Frieze depicting faces. 50c,
Mosaic depicting angel.

2008, Sept. 17
195   A63   Horiz. pair, #a-b   2.75 2.75

Stamp
Day A64

2008, Oct. 2
196   A64   60c multi   2.40 2.40

Automobile
A65

Hourglass, Map
of Montenegro
A66

Eagle and
Angel — A67

2008, Oct. 20   Perf. 13¾x13¼
197   A65   40c multi   1.60 1.60
198   A66   50c multi   1.75 1.75
199   A67   60c multi   2.40 2.40
        Nos. 197-199 (3)   5.75 5.75

Alfred Nobel (1833-96), Inventor and
Philanthropist — A68

2008, Oct. 21   Perf. 13¾
200   A68   50c multi   1.90 1.90

A69

A70

A71

A72

A73

First Railway in Montenegro,
Cent. — A74

2008, Nov. 2
201   A69   25c multi   .95   .95
202   A70   25c multi   .95   .95
203   A71   25c multi   .95   .95
204   A72   25c multi   .95   .95
205   A73   25c multi   .95   .95
206   A74   25c multi   .95   .95
   a.   Souvenir sheet of 6, #201-206   5.75 5.75
        Nos. 201-206 (6)   5.70 5.70
   Nos. 201-206 each were printed in sheets of
5 + label.

Joy of
Europe — A75

   Designs: 25c, Shown. 40c, Towers and
bridge, horiz.

2008, Nov. 20
207-208 A75   Set of 2   2.50 2.50
   Nos. 207-208 each were printed in sheets of
8 + label.

Universal Declaration of Human
Rights, 60th Anniv. — A76

2008, Dec. 11   Perf. 13¾
209   A76   50c multi   1.90 1.90
   Printed in sheets of 8 + label.

Louis
Braille
(1809-52),
Educator
of the
Blind
A77

2009, Jan. 30
210   A77   60c multi   2.25 2.25

Kotor Churches Honoring St. Tryphon,
1200th Anniv. — A78

   No. 211 — St. Tryphon and denomination in:
a, Black. b, White.

2009, Feb. 3   Perf. 14
211   A78   50c Horiz. pair, #a-b   3.75 3.75

First Theatrical Performance in Niksic,
125th Anniv. — A79

Vita Nikolic (1934-
94), Poet — A80

Zetski Dom Theater, Cetinje, 125th Anniv. A81

Crnojevic Monastery, 525th Anniv. — A82

2009　　　**Litho.**　　　**Perf. 13¾**
212　A79　25c multi　　　　　　.90　.90
213　A80　40c multi　　　　　　1.25　1.25
214　A81　50c multi　　　　　　1.50　1.50
215　A82　60c multi　　　　　　1.75　1.75
　　　Nos. 212-215 (4)　　　　4.75　4.75

Arts through the ages. Issued: 25c, 2/16; others, 4/8.

Fish A83

Designs: 25c, Alburnus scoranza. 40c, Thymallus thymallus. 50c, Salmothymus obtusirostris zetensis. 60c, Cyprinus carpio.

2009, Apr. 16
216-219　A83　Set of 4　　　　6.00　6.00

Nos. 216-219 each were printed in sheets of 5 + label.

Europa A84

Designs: No. 220, 60c, Boy and girl looking at celestial objects. No. 221, 90c, Boy looking through telescope.
No. 222, vert.: a, 60c, Planets and constellations. b, 90c, Comet, asteroids and constellations.

2009, Apr. 16
220-221　A84　Set of 2　　　　4.00　4.00
　　　　　Souvenir Sheet
222　A84　Sheet of 2, #a-b　　5.00　5.00

Intl. Year of Astronomy.

Tourism A85

Designs: 25c, Water skiing. 40c, Rock climbing in Nevidio Canyon. 50c, Paragliding. 60c, Rafting on the Tara River.

2009, Apr. 16
223-226　A85　Set of 4　　　　6.00　6.00
226a　　　Souvenir sheet of 4, #223-226　　　　　　　　　6.00　6.00

Nos. 223-226 each were printed in sheets of 5 + label.

25th Universiade, Belgrade — A86

2009, June 4　　　　　**Perf. 13¾**
227　A86　50c multi　　　　　1.75　1.75

Printed in sheets of 8 + label.

Prince Vasilije Petrovic-Njegos (1709-66), Bishop — A87

2009, June 4　　　　　**Perf. 13¾x13**
228　A87　40c multi　　　　　1.40　1.40

Vicko Bujovic (1660-1709), Military Leader, and Ship — A88

2009, July 10　　　　　**Perf. 13¾**
229　A88　60c multi　　　　　2.00　2.00

Printed in sheets of 8 + label.

Nature Protection A89

Bandaged plants and: 25c, Lake Plav. 50c, Lake Crno.

2009, July 10　　　　　**Litho.**
230-231　A89　Set of 2　　　2.50　2.50

Nos. 230-231 each were printed in sheets of 8 + label.

Stamp Day — A90

2009, Oct. 2　　　　　**Perf. 13x13¾**
232　A90　25c multi　　　　　1.00　1.00

Joy of Europe — A91

Children's art with: 40c, Dialogue balloon. 50c, Thought balloon.

2009, Nov. 20　　　　　**Perf. 13¾**
233-234　A91　Set of 2　　　3.00　3.00

Nos. 233-234 each were printed in sheets of 8 + label.

Valtazar Bogisic (1834-1908), Jurist — A92

2009, Dec. 7　　　　　**Perf. 13x13¾**
235　A92　50c multi　　　　　1.60　1.60

700-Year-Old Historical Document in Kotor Archives — A93

2009, Dec. 20　　　　　**Perf. 13¾x13**
236　A93　25c multi　　　　　.95　.95

Dado Duric (1933-2010), Painter — A94

St. Elias, Fresco in Moraca Monastery A95

2010, Jan. 28　　　　　**Perf. 13x13¾**
237　A94　50c multi　　　　　1.50　1.50
238　A95　50c multi　　　　　1.50　1.50

2010 Winter Olympics, Vancouver A96

Designs: €1, Speed skater. €1.50, Snowboarder.

2010, Feb. 12　　　　　**Perf. 13¾**
239-240　A96　Set of 2　　　8.00　8.00

Nos. 239-240 each were printed in sheets of 8 + label.

Danilo Kis (1935-89), Writer — A97

2010, Feb. 22　　　　　**Perf. 13¾x13**
241　A97　50c multi　　　　　1.75　1.75

Flora — A98

Designs: 25c, Salvia officialis. 50c, Satureja subspicata. 60c, Tilia tomentosa. €1, Epilobium angustifolium.

2010, Mar. 18　　　　　**Litho.**
242-245　A98　Set of 4　　　7.75　7.75

Nos. 242-245 each were printed in sheets of 5 + label.

Europa — A99

Stack of books and: No. 246, 60c, Girl, butterfly, castle, rainbow. No. 247, 90c, Boy, car, star, rope ladder.
No. 248: a, 60c, Books, fairy, crown, dress. b, 90c, Books, ship, ladder.

2010, Apr. 22　　　　　**Perf. 13¾**
246-247　A99　Set of 2　　　5.25　5.25
　　　　　Souvenir Sheet
248　A99　Sheet of 2, #a-b　　5.25　5.25

St. Basil of Ostrog (1610-71) A100

2010, May 12　　　　　**Perf. 13x13¾**
249　A100　50c multi　　　　1.75　1.75

2010 World Cup Soccer Tournament, South Africa — A101

2010, June 11　　　　　**Perf. 13¾**
250　A101　€1.50 multi　　　4.75　4.75

Printed in sheets of 8 + label.

Tourism A102

Designs: 25c, Canoe and trees. 50c, Mountains. 60c, Waterside straw hut. €1, Beach.

2010, June 24　　　　　**Litho.**
251-254　A102　Set of 4　　8.00　8.00
254a　　　Souvenir sheet of 4, #251-254　　　　　　　　8.00　8.00

Nos. 251-254 each were printed in sheets of 5 + label.

Ship A103

2010, July 8
255　A103　25c multi　　　　1.00　1.00

Printed in sheets of 8 + label.

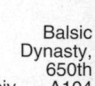

Balsic
Dynasty,
650th
Anniv. — A104

2010, July 15 *Perf. 13x13¾*
256 A104 25c multi .95 .95

First Electric
Power Network
in Montenegro,
Cent. — A105

2010, Aug. 19
257 A105 25c multi .95 .95

Kingdom of
Montenegro,
Cent. — A106

2010, Aug. 28
258 A106 50c multi 1.75 1.75

Bozidar
Vukovic (c.
1466-c. 1540),
Printer
A107

2010, Sept. 16 *Litho.*
259 A107 50c multi 1.75 1.75

Stamp
Day — A108

2010, Oct. 2 *Perf. 13¾x13*
260 A108 30c multi 1.00 1.00

Joy of
Europe
A109

2010, Oct. 21 *Perf. 13¾*
261 A109 90c multi 3.25 3.25

Printed in sheets of 8 + label.

Pasha Husein
Mosque,
Pljevlja — A110

Ivan
Mazuranic
(1814-90),
Poet — A111

Reverse of
Roman Reduced
Sestertius Found
in Duklja
(Podgorica)
A112

Miroslav
Gospels — A113

Perf. 13¾x13, 13x13¾
2010, Nov. 12
262 A110 30c multi 1.00 1.00
263 A111 40c multi 1.25 1.25
264 A112 80c multi 2.50 2.50
265 A113 90c multi 2.75 2.75
Nos. 262-265 (4) 6.70 6.70

Art through the ages.

Nature
Protection — A114

Umbrella over: 30c, Waterfall. 40c,
Mountains.

2010, Dec. 16 *Perf. 13¾x13*
266-267 A114 Set of 2 2.25 2.25

Painting by
Vojo Stanic
A115

Jovan
Ivanisevic
(1860-89),
Composer
A116

2011, Jan. 31 *Litho.* *Perf. 13*
268 A115 30c multi .95 .95
269 A116 40c multi 1.25 1.25

Tripo Kokolja
(1661-1713),
Painter
A117

2011, Feb. 22
270 A117 30c multi .95 .95

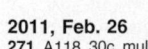

Vuk Vrcevic
(1811-82), Poetry
Translator
A118

2011, Feb. 26
271 A118 30c multi .95 .95

Fauna
A119

Map of Montenegro and: No. 272, 30c, Pina
nobilis. No. 273, 30c, Triturus alpestris
montenegrinus. 40c, Pelecanus crispus. 90c,
Phalacrocorax pygmaeus.

2011, Mar. 17
272-275 A119 Set of 4 6.00 6.00

Europa
A120

Designs: No. 276, 90c, "EU" in foliage. No.
277, 90c, Map of Europe with leaf veins, white
background.
No. 278, 90c, vert.: a, "EU" in foliage. b,
Map of Europe with leaf veins, green
background.

2011, Apr. 21 *Perf. 13¼x13*
276-277 A120 Set of 2 5.75 5.75
Souvenir Sheet
Perf. 13x13¼
278 A120 90c Sheet of 2, #a-b 5.75 5.75

Intl. Year of Forests.

Tourism
A121

Designs: No. 279, 30c, Mountains and valley, "Turizam" at left. No. 280, 30c, Mountains
and lake, "Turizam" at right. 40c, Mountains
and valley, diff. 90c, Beach.

2011, May 12 *Perf. 13*
279-282 A121 Set of 4 5.75 5.75
282a Sheet of 4, #279-282 5.75 5.75

No. 282a was sold with a booklet cover but
was not attached to it.

Environmental Protection — A122

Butterfly, flowers and: 30c, House, oscillo-
scope wave pattern. 40c, Smiling face.

2011, May 21
283-284 A122 Set of 2 2.25 2.25

Kazansky Cathedral, St. Petersburg,
Russia — A123

Russian Diplomatic Mission,
Cetinje — A124

2011, May 26 *Perf. 13¼x13*
285 A123 30c multi 1.00 1.00
286 A124 30c multi 1.00 1.00
a. Horiz. pair, #285-286 2.25 2.25

Nos. 285-286 each were printed in sheets of
8 + label. See Russia No. 7272.

Games of Small European States,
Liechtenstein — A125

Designs: 30c, Volleyball. 90c, Tennis ball.

2011, June 9
287-288 A125 Set of 2 3.75 3.75

Nos. 287-288 each were printed in sheets of
8 + label.

Belvedere Demonstrations, 75th
Anniv. — A126

2011, June 25 *Perf. 13*
289 A126 30c multi .90 .90

Ship
"Brindisi"
A127

2011, July 7 *Perf. 13¼x13*
290 A127 40c multi 1.25 1.25

Printed in sheets of 8 + label.

Concordat
Between
Montenegro
and Vatican
City, 125th
Anniv.
A128

2011, Oct. 7 *Perf. 13*
291 A128 30c multi .95 .95

Joy of
Europe
A129

2011, Oct. 21 *Perf. 13¼x13*
292 A129 90c multi 2.75 2.75

Printed in sheets of 8 + label.

Fresco of King Michael A130

Crnogorac, First Montengrin Newspaper A131

Zabljak Crnojevica Fortified Town — A132

Josip Slade (1828-1911), Architect A133

2011, Nov. 11 **Perf. 13**
293 A130 30c multi .90 .90
294 A131 40c multi 1.25 1.25
295 A132 50c multi 1.50 1.50
296 A133 90c multi 2.75 2.75
Nos. 293-296 (4) 6.40 6.40

Stamp Day — A134

2011, Dec. 15 **Litho.**
297 A134 40c multi 1.25 1.25

Sculptures by Risto Stijovic (1894-1974) A135

Montenegrin Man, by Ilija Sobajic (1876-1953) A136

Painting by Nikola Vujosevic A137

Montenegrin Army Musicians A138

2012, Jan. 27 **Perf. 13**
298 A135 30c multi .90 .90
299 A136 40c multi 1.25 1.25
300 A137 80c multi 2.25 2.25
301 A138 95c multi 2.75 2.75
Nos. 298-301 (4) 7.15 7.15

Ilovik Nomocanon, 750th Anniv. — A139

2012, Feb. 23
302 A139 30c multi .90 .90

Enthronement of Durad Balsic as Lord of Zeta, 650th Anniv. — A140

2012, Feb. 27
303 A140 30c multi .90 .90

Flora A141

Designs: 30c, Nettles (kopriva). 90c, Vranac grapes (vinova loza).

2012, Mar. 16
304-305 A141 Set of 2 3.50 3.50
Nos. 304-305 each were printed in sheets of 5 + label.

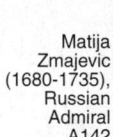

Matija Zmajevic (1680-1735), Russian Admiral A142

2012, May 10
306 A142 30c multi .80 .80

Tourism A143

Designs: No. 307, 30c, Directional arrows on pole. No. 308, 30c, Ship, sun, town names. 80c, Suitcase with blue handle decorated with travel symbols. 95c, Suitcase with red handle decorated with travel symbols.

2012, May 14
307-310 A143 Set of 4 6.50 6.50
310a Souvenir sheet of 4, #307-310 7.00 7.00
No. 310a was sold with, but unattached to, a booklet cover.

Environmental Protection A144

Life preserver on: 30c, Duck. 95c, Frog.

2012, May 21 **Litho.** **Perf. 13**
311-312 A144 Set of 2 3.25 3.25

2012 Summer Olympics, London A145

Designs: 90c, Rhythmic gymnastics. 95c, Discus thrower.

2012, June 8 **Litho.** **Perf. 13¼x13**
313-314 A145 5.00 5.00
314a Souvenir sheet of 2, #313-314 5.00 5.00
Nos. 313-314 each were printed in sheets of 8 + central label.

Battle of Carev Laz, 300th Anniv. — A146

2012, June 25 **Perf. 13**
315 A146 30c multi .80 .80

Accession Negotiations with the European Union — A147

2012, June 29
316 A147 95c multi 2.50 2.50

Lighthouses A148

Designs: No. 317, 30c, Verige Lighthouse. No. 318, 30c, Volujica Lighthouse.

2012, July 6 **Perf. 13x13¼**
317-318 A148 Set of 2 1.60 1.60
Nos. 317-318 each were printed in sheets of 8 + central label.

2012 European Championship of ZRK Buducnost Women's Handball Team — A149

2012, July 27 **Litho.**
319 A149 30c multi .80 .80
No. 319 was printed in sheets of 8 + central label.

Fixing of Montenegrin Boundaries, 175th Anniv. — A150

2012, Oct. 10 **Perf. 13**
320 A150 30c multi .85 .85

Europa A151

Leaves and: 80c, River gorge. 95c, Sveti Stefan.

2012, Oct. 17 **Perf. 13¼x13**
321-322 A151 Set of 2 4.75 4.75
322a Souvenir sheet of 2, #321-322 4.75 4.75
Nos. 321-322 each were printed in sheets of 8 + central label.

Joy of Europe — A152

2012, Oct. 22 **Perf. 13x13¼**
323 A152 90c multi 2.50 2.50
No. 323 was printed in sheets of 8 + central label.

Art in Piva Monastery A153

Hieromonk Makarije Printing Works A154

Legend of Pava and Ahmet — A155

Battle of Tudjemila A156

2012, Nov. 12 **Perf. 13**
324 A153 30c multi .85 .85
325 A154 30c multi .85 .85
326 A155 40c multi 1.25 1.25
327 A156 95c multi 2.75 2.75
Nos. 324-327 (4) 5.70 5.70

Stamp Day — A157

2012, Dec. 14
328 A157 30c multi .80 .80

Success of Montenegro Women's Handball Team — A158

Women's handball team, flag of Montenegro, and: No. 329, 30c, Gold medal from 2012 European championships. No. 330, 30c, Silver medal from 2012 Olympics.

2012, Dec. 28   Litho.   Perf. 13¼x13
329-330 A158   Set of 2   1.60 1.60

Nos. 329-330 each were printed in sheets of 8 + central label.

Camil Sijaric (1913-89), Writer — A160

Pero Pocek (1878-1963), Painter — A161

Traditional Folk Costume — A162

Our Lady of Philerme Icon — A163

2013, Jan. 31   Litho.   Perf. 13
331 A160 30c multi .85 .85
332 A161 40c multi 1.10 1.10
333 A162 80c multi 2.25 2.25
334 A163 95c multi 2.60 2.60
    Nos. 331-334 (4) 6.80 6.80

Prince Petar II Petrovic-Njegos (1813-51) — A164

2013, Feb. 22   Litho.   Perf. 13x13¼
335 A164 30c multi .80 .80

No. 335 was printed in sheets of 8 + central label.

Union of Montenegro and Kotor Bay, 200th Anniv. — A165

2013, Feb. 27   Litho.   Perf. 13
336 A165 30c multi .80 .80

Flora and Fauna — A166

Map of Montenegro and: 80c, Parnassius apollo. 95c, Scabiosa ochroleuca.

2013, Mar. 15   Litho.   Perf. 13
337-338 A166   Set of 2   4.50 4.50

Europa — A167

2013, Apr. 19   Litho.   Perf. 13x13¼
339 A167 95c multi 2.50 2.50

No. 339 was printed in sheets of 8 + central label.

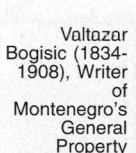

Valtazar Bogisic (1834-1908), Writer of Montenegro's General Property Code — A168

2013, May 10   Litho.   Perf. 13
340 A168 30c multi .80 .80

Tourism A169

Designs: 30c, Two hikers. 40c, Cyclist raising bicycle.

2013, May 14   Litho.   Perf. 13
341-342 A169   Set of 2   1.90 1.90
342a   Souvenir sheet of 2, #341-342   1.90 1.90

Stara Maslina, Old Olive Tree, Stari Bar A170

2013, May 23   Litho.   Perf. 13¼x13
343 A170 30c multi .80 .80

No. 343 was printed in sheets of 8 + central label.

Sports A171

Designs: 80c, Basketball. 95c, "100", emblem of Lovcen soccer team, soccer ball.

2013, June 7   Litho.   Perf. 13
344-345 A171   Set of 2   4.75 4.75
345a   Souvenir sheet of 2, #344-345   4.75 4.75

Participation of Montenegrin team in 2013 Euro Basket tournament, Slovenia (No. 344); Lovcen soccer team, cent. (No. 345).

Edict of Milan, 1700th Anniv. — A172

2013, June 21   Litho.   Perf. 13
346 A172 30c multi .80 .80

Marko Martinovic (1663-1716), Teacher of Naval Navigation — A173

2013, June 28   Litho.   Perf. 13¼x13
347 A173 30c multi .80 .80

No. 347 was printed in sheets of 8 + central label.

First Airplane Flight in Montenegro, Cent. — A174

2013, Sept. 5   Litho.   Perf. 13
348 A174 30c multi .80 .80

Ljubo Cupic (1913-42), Communist Prisoner Executed by Chetniks — A175

2013, Oct. 8   Litho.   Perf. 13
349 A175 30c multi .85 .85

Joy of Europe A176

2013, Oct. 22   Litho.   Perf. 13¼x13
350 A176 95c multi 2.60 2.60

No. 350 was printed in sheets of 8 + central label.

Princess Elena of Montenegro (1873-1952) A177

Map of Stari Bar — A178

2013, Nov. 12   Litho.   Perf. 13
351 A177 30c multi .85 .85
352 A178 40c multi 1.10 1.10

Stamp Day — A179

2013, Dec. 15   Litho.   Perf. 13
353 A179 30c multi .85 .85

Dobrota Lace — A180

Medieval Tombstones A181

2014, Jan. 31   Litho.   Perf. 13
354 A180 30c multi .80 .80
355 A181 95c multi 2.60 2.60

2014 Winter Olympics, Sochi, Russia A182

2014, Feb. 17   Litho.   Perf. 13¼x13
356 A182 95c multi 2.60 2.60

No. 356 was printed in sheets of 8 + central label.

Archbishopric
of Bar, 925th
Anniv. — A183

2014, Feb. 27   Litho.   Perf. 13
357 A183 30c multi   .85 .85

Edraianthus
Wetstainii Ssp.
Lovcenicus
A184

Hypholoma
Fasciculare
A185

2014, Mar. 14   Litho.   Perf. 13
358 A184 30c multi   .85 .85
359 A185 95c multi   2.60 2.60

Gusle — A186

2014, Apr. 18   Litho.   Perf. 13x13¼
360 A186 95c multi   2.60 2.60
  a.   Souvenir sheet of 1   2.60 2.60
  Europa. No. 360 was printed in sheets of 8
+ central label.

Church,
Grahovac, 150th
Anniv. — A187

2014, May 9   Litho.   Perf. 13
361 A187 30c multi   .85 .85

Tourism
A188

Designs: 30c, Porto Montenegro, Tivat. 40c,
Mount Hajla.

2014, May 14   Litho.   Perf. 13
362-363 A188 Set of 2   1.90 1.90

Crna Poda
Forest — A189

2014, May 23   Litho.   Perf. 13x13¼
364 A189 95c multi   2.60 2.60
  No. 364 was printed in sheets of 8 + central
label.

2014 World Cup
Soccer
Championships,
Brazil — A190

2014, June 9   Litho.   Perf. 13
365 A190 95c multi   2.60 2.60
  a.   Souvenir sheet of 1   2.60 2.60

Podgorica
Telegraph
Station,
Cent. — A191

2014, June 20   Litho.   Perf. 13
366 A191 30c multi   .85 .85

Reburial of King Nicholas I and Queen
Milena in Montenegro, 25th
Anniv. — A192

2014, June 27   Litho.   Perf. 13¼x13
367 A192 30c multi   .85 .85
  No. 367 was printed in sheets of 8 + central
label.

ACKNOWLEDGMENT OF RECEIPT STAMPS

Prince Nicholas I
AR1   AR2
Perf. 10½, 11½
1895   Litho.   Wmk. 91
H1 AR1 10n ultra & rose   .95 .95

1902   Unwmk.   Perf. 12½
H2 AR2 25h orange & carmine   .95 .95

Constitution Issue

No. H2 Overprinted in
Black

1905
H3 AR2 25h orange & carmine   1.20 1.20
  a.   "Constitution" 16½mm ('06)   1.60 1.60
           See note after 74a.

AR3

Nicholas
I — AR4

1907   Engr.
H4 AR3 25pa olive   .80 .80

1913   Typo.
H5 AR4 25pa olive green   .80 .80

POSTAGE DUE STAMPS

D1   D2

Perf. 10½, 11, 11½
1894   Litho.   Wmk. 91
J1   D1   1n red   3.25 3.25
J2   D1   2n yellow green   1.10 1.10
J3   D1   3n orange   .85 .80
J4   D1   5n olive green   .55 .55
J5   D1 10n violet   .55 .55
J6   D1 20n ultra   .55 .55
J7   D1 30n emerald   .55 .55
J8   D1 50n pale gray grn   .55 .55
     Nos. J1-J8 (8)   7.95 7.90

1902   Unwmk.   Perf. 12½
J9   D2   5h orange   .40 .40
J10 D2 10h olive green   .40 .40
J11 D2 25h dull lilac   .40 .40
J12 D2 50h emerald   .40 .40
J13 D2   1k pale gray green   .80 .40
     Nos. J9-J13 (5)   2.40 2.00

Constitution Issue
Postage Due Stamps of 1902
Overprinted in Black or Red Like Nos.
66-74

1905
J14 D2   5h orange   .80 .80
J15 D2 10h olive green (R)   .80 .80
J16 D2 25h dull lilac   .80 .80
J17 D2 50h emerald   .80 .80
J18 D2   1k pale gray green   .80 .80
     Nos. J14-J18 (5)   4.00 4.00

The 10h with "Constitution" 16½mm is not
known used. It is an unissued stamp.

D3   D4

1907   Typo.   Perf. 13x13½
J19 D3   5pa red brown   .40 .40
J20 D3 10pa violet   .40 .40
J21 D3 25pa rose   .40 .40
J22 D3 50pa green   .40 .40
     Nos. J19-J22 (4)   1.60 1.60

1913   Perf. 12½
J23 D4   5pa gray   1.20 1.20
J24 D4 10pa violet   .80 .80
J25 D4 25pa blue gray   .80 .80
J26 D4 50pa lilac rose   1.20 1.20
     Nos. J23-J26 (4)   4.00 4.00

ISSUED UNDER AUSTRIAN OCCUPATION

Austrian Military
Stamps of 1917
Overprinted

1917   Unwmk.   Perf. 12½
1N1 M1 10h blue   14.50 12.00
1N2 M1 15h car rose   14.50 12.00

Austrian Military
Stamps of 1917
Overprinted in
Black

1918
1N3 M1 10h blue   40.00
1N4 M1 15h car rose   1.90
  Nos. 1N3-1N4 were never placed in use.
This overprint exists on other stamps of
Austria and Bosnia and Herzegovina, and in
blue or red.

ISSUED UNDER ITALIAN OCCUPATION

Yugoslavia Nos. 142,
144-154 Overprinted

1941   Unwmk.   Typo.   Perf. 12½
2N1   A16 25p black   .80 1.40
2N2   A16   1d yel grn   .80 1.40
2N3   A16 1.50d red   .80 1.40
2N4   A16   2d dp mag   .80 1.40
2N5   A16   3d dull red brn   .80 1.40
2N6   A16   4d ultra   .80 1.40
2N7   A16   5d dark blue   2.25 3.25
2N8   A16 5.50d dk vio brn   2.25 3.25
2N9   A16   6d slate blue   2.25 3.25
2N10 A16   8d sepia   2.25 3.25
2N11 A16 12d brt violet   2.25 3.25
2N12 A16 16d dull violet   2.25 3.25
2N13 A16 20d blue   160.00 210.00
2N14 A16 30d brt pink   50.00 97.50
     Nos. 2N1-2N14 (14)   228.30 335.40
     Set, never hinged   425.00

The 25p, 1d, 3d, 6d and 8d exist with
inverted overprint.

Stamps of Italy,
1929, Overprinted in
Red or Black

1941   Wmk. 140   Perf. 14
2N15 A90   5c ol brn (R)   .80 .95
2N16 A92 10c dark brn   .80 .95
2N17 A93 15c sl grn (R)   .80 .95
2N18 A91 20c rose red   .80 .95
2N19 A94 25c deep grn   .80 .95
2N20 A95 30c ol brn (R)   .80 .95
2N21 A95 50c pur (R)   .80 .95
2N22 A94 75c rose red   .80 .95
2N23 A94 1.25 l dp bl (R)   1.00 .95
     Nos. 2N15-2N23 (9)   7.40 8.55
     Set, never hinged   20.00

Yugoslavia Nos. 144-
145, 147-148, 148B,
149-152 Overprinted
in Black

1942 Unwmk. Typo. Perf. 12½

2N24	A16	1d yel grn	2.00	2.75
2N25	A16	1.50d red	95.00	65.00
2N26	A16	3d dull red brn	2.00	2.75
2N27	A16	4d ultra	2.00	2.75
2N28	A16	5.50d dk vio brn	2.00	2.75
2N29	A16	6d slate blue	2.00	2.75
2N30	A16	8d sepia	2.00	2.75
2N31	A16	12d brt violet	2.00	2.75
2N32	A16	16d dull violet	2.00	2.75
		Nos. 2N24-2N32 (9)	111.00	87.00
		Set, never hinged	220.00	

Yugoslavia Nos. 142 and 146 with this overprint in red were not officially issued.

Red Overprint

2N24a	A16	1d	2.00	2.75
2N25a	A16	1.50d	145.00	200.00
2N26a	A16	3d	2.00	2.75
2N27a	A16	4d	2.00	2.75
2N28a	A16	5.50d	2.00	2.75
2N29a	A16	6d	2.00	2.75
2N30a	A16	8d	2.00	2.75
2N31a	A16	12d	2.00	2.75
2N32a	A16	16d	2.00	2.75
		Nos. 2N24a-2N32a (9)	161.00	222.00
		Set, never hinged	300.00	

Peter Nyegosh and Mt. Lovchen View OS1

Mt. Lovchen Scene OS2

Peter Petrovich Nyegosh — OS3

Designs: 15c, Mountain Church, Eve of Trinity Feast. 20c, Chiefs at Cetinje Monastery. 25c, Folk Dancing at Cetinje Monastery. 50c, Eagle dance. 1.25 l, Chiefs taking loyalty oath. 2 l, Moslem wedding procession. 5 l, Group sitting up with injured standard bearer.

Perf. 14.

1943, May 9 Unwmk. Photo.

2N33	OS1	5c deep violet	2.40	4.00
2N34	OS2	10c dull olive grn	2.40	4.00
2N35	OS1	15c brown	2.40	4.00
2N36	OS1	20c dull orange	2.40	4.00
2N37	OS1	25c dull green	2.40	4.00
2N38	OS1	50c rose pink	2.40	4.00
2N39	OS1	1.25 l sapphire	2.40	4.00
2N40	OS1	2 l blue green	3.60	4.00
2N41	OS2	5 l dark red, *sal*	8.00	14.00
2N42	OS3	20 l dark vio, *gray*	20.00	27.50
		Nos. 2N33-2N42 (10)	48.40	73.50
		Set, never hinged	82.50	

Quotations from national poem on backs of stamps.

For overprints and surcharges see Nos. 3N10-3N14, 3NB3-3NB8.

OCCUPATION AIR POST STAMPS

Yugoslavia Nos. C7-C14 Overprinted Like Nos. 2N1-2N14

Perf. 12½, 11½x12½, 12½x11½

1941 Photo. Unwmk.

2NC1	AP6	50p brown	0.50	7.50
2NC2	AP7	1d yel grn	4.50	7.50
2NC3	AP8	2d blue gray	4.50	7.50
2NC4	AP9	2.50d rose red	6.50	7.50
2NC5	AP6	5d brn vio	35.00	55.00
2NC6	AP7	10d brn lake	35.00	55.00
2NC7	AP8	20d dark grn	72.50	92.50
2NC8	AP9	30d ultra	40.00	55.00
		Nos. 2NC1-2NC8 (8)	204.50	287.50
		Set, never hinged	500.00	

Italy No. C13 Overprinted in Red Like Nos. 2N15-2N23

1941 Wmk. 140 Perf. 14

2NC9	AP3	50c olive brn	1.10	1.10
		Never hinged		2.75

Yugoslavia Nos. C7-C14 Overprinted in Black

a

b

Perf. 12½, 11½x12½, 12½x11½

1942, Jan. 9 Unwmk.

2NC10	AP6(a)	50p brown	12.00	15.00
2NC11	AP7(a)	1d yel grn	12.00	15.00
2NC12	AP8(b)	2d blue gray	12.00	15.00
2NC13	AP9(b)	2.50d rose red	12.00	15.00
2NC14	AP6(a)	5d brn vio	12.00	15.00
2NC15	AP7(a)	10d brn lake	12.00	15.00
2NC16	AP8(b)	20d dk grn	210.00	250.00
2NC17	AP9(b)	30d ultra	35.00	60.00
		Nos. 2NC10-2NC17 (8)	317.00	400.00
		Set, never hinged	700.00	

Nos. 2NC10-2NC17 exist with red overprints. Value, each $80 unused, $150 used.

c

Overprints a, b or c were applied in 1941-42 to the following Yugoslavia stamps under Italian occupation:
  a. or b. Nos. B120-B123 (4 values) in black and in red.
  c. Nos. B116-B119 (4 values) in black and in red.

Cetinje AP1

Mt. Durmitor — AP6

Designs: 1 l, Seacoast. 2 l, Budus. 5 l, Mt. Lovchen. 10 l, Rieka River.

1943 Unwmk. Photo. Perf. 14

2NC18	AP1	50c brown	6.00	8.00
2NC19	AP1	1 l ultra	6.00	8.00
2NC20	AP1	2 l rose pink	6.00	8.00
2NC21	AP1	5 l green	6.00	12.00

2NC22	AP1	10 l lake, *rose buff*	16.00	20.00
2NC23	AP6	20 l indigo, *rose*	27.50	35.00
		Nos. 2NC18-2NC23 (6)	69.50	91.00
		Set, never hinged	175.00	

For overprints and surcharges see Nos. 3NC1-3NC5, 3NCB1-3NCB6.

OCCUPATION POSTAGE DUE STAMPS

Yugoslavia Nos. J28-J32 Overprinted Like Nos. 2N1-2N14

1941 Unwmk. Typo. Perf. 12½

2NJ1	D4	50p violet	4.00	5.50
2NJ2	D4	1d deep magenta	4.00	5.50
2NJ3	D4	2d deep blue	4.00	5.50
2NJ4	D4	5d orange	110.00	120.00
2NJ5	D4	10d chocolate	12.00	15.00
		Nos. 2NJ1-2NJ5 (5)	134.00	151.50
		Set, never hinged	300.00	

Postage Due Stamps of Italy, 1934, Overprinted in Black Like Nos. 2N15-2N23

1942 Wmk. 140 Perf. 14

2NJ6	D6	10c blue	2.75	4.50
2NJ7	D6	20c rose red	2.75	4.50
2NJ8	D6	30c red orange	2.75	4.50
2NJ9	D6	50c violet	2.75	4.50
2NJ10	D7	1 l red orange	2.75	4.50
		Nos. 2NJ6-2NJ10 (5)	13.75	22.50
		Set, never hinged	28.00	

ISSUED UNDER GERMAN OCCUPATION

Yugoslavia Nos. 147-148 Surcharged

1943 Unwmk. Typo. Perf. 12½

3N1	A16	50c on 3d	6.00	14.50
3N2	A16	1 l on 3d	6.00	14.50
3N3	A16	1.50 l on 3d	6.00	14.50
3N4	A16	2 l on 3d	10.00	28.00
3N5	A16	4 l on 3d	10.00	28.00
3N6	A16	5 l on 4d	10.00	28.00
3N7	A16	8 l on 4d	24.00	57.50
3N8	A16	10 l on 4d	32.50	90.00
3N9	A16	20 l on 4d	65.00	200.00
		Nos. 3N1-3N9 (9)	169.50	475.00
		Set, never hinged	375.00	

Montenegro Nos. 2N37-2N41 Ovptd.

1943 Photo. Perf. 14

3N10	OS1	25c dull green	18.00	100.00
3N11	OS1	50c rose pink	18.00	100.00
3N12	OS1	1.25 l sapphire	18.00	100.00
3N13	OS1	2 l blue green	18.00	100.00
3N14	OS2	5 l dk red, *sal*	250.00	1,250.
		Nos. 3N10-3N14 (5)	322.00	1,650.
		Set, never hinged	625.00	

Counterfeits exist.

SEMI-POSTAL STAMPS

Yugoslavia Nos. 147-148 Surcharged

1944 Unwmk. Typo. Perf. 12½

3NB1	A16	15pf + 85pf on 3d	18.00	100.00
3NB2	A16	15pf + 85pf on 4d	18.00	100.00

Montenegro Nos. 2N37-2N40 Surcharged

d

1944 Photo. Perf. 14

3NB3	OS1	15pf +85pf on 25c	18.00	100.00
3NB4	OS1	15pf +1.35m on 50c	18.00	100.00
3NB5	OS1	25pf +1.75m on 1.25 l	18.00	100.00
3NB6	OS1	25pf +1.75m on 2 l	18.00	100.00
		Nos. 3NB1-3NB6 (6)	108.00	600.00
		Set, never hinged	240.00	

Surtax on Nos. 3NB1-3NB6 aided refugees.

Montenegro Nos. 2N37-2N38 and Yugoslavia Nos. 147-148 Surcharged

e

f

1944

3NB7	OS1	15pf + 85pf on 25c (e)	15.00	80.00
3NB8	OS1	15pf + 1.35m on 50c (e)	15.00	80.00
3NB9	A16	50pf + 2.50m on 3d (f)	15.00	80.00
3NB10	A16	50pf + 2.50m on 4d (f)	15.00	80.00
		Nos. 3NB7-3NB10 (4)	60.00	320.00
		Set, never hinged	130.00	

The surtax on Nos. 3NB7-3NB10 aided the Montenegro Red Cross.

AIR POST STAMPS

Montenegro Nos. 2NC18-2NC22 Overprinted Like Nos. 3N10-3N14

1943 Unwmk. Photo. Perf. 14

3NC1	AP1	50c brown	18.00	100.00
3NC2	AP1	1 l ultra	18.00	100.00
3NC3	AP1	2 l rose pink	18.00	100.00
3NC4	AP1	5 l green	18.00	100.00
3NC5	AP1	10 l lake, *rose buff*	3,200.	11,000.
		Nos. 3NC1-3NC5 (5)	3,272.	11,400.
		Set, never hinged	6,250.	

Counterfeits exist.

AIR POST SEMI-POSTAL STAMPS

Montenegro Nos. 2NC18-2NC20 Surcharged Type "d"

1944 Unwmk. Photo. Perf. 14

3NCB1	AP1	15pf +85pf on 50c	18.00	100.00
3NCB2	AP1	25pf +1.25m on 1 l	18.00	100.00

3NCB3	AP1	50pf +1.50m on 2 l	18.00	*100.00*
		Nos. 3NCB1-3NCB3 (3)	54.00	*300.00*
		Set, never hinged	80.00	

The surtax aided refugees.

Same Surcharged Type "e"

1944

3NCB4	AP1	25pf +1.75m on 50c	15.00	*80.00*
3NCB5	AP1	25pf +2.75m on 1 l	15.00	*80.00*
3NCB6	AP1	50pf +2m on 2 l	15.00	*80.00*
		Nos. 3NCB4-3NCB6 (3)	45.00	*240.00*
		Set, never hinged	100.00	

The surtax aided the Montenegro Red Cross.

MONTSERRAT

ˌmän̲t̲·sə-'rat

LOCATION — West Indies southeast of Puerto Rico
GOVT. — British Crown Colony
AREA — 39 sq. mi.
POP. — 12,853 (1999 est.)

Montserrat was one of the four presidencies of the former Leeward Islands colony until it became a colony itself in 1956.

Montserrat stamps were discontinued in 1890 and resumed in 1903. In the interim, stamps of Leeward Islands were used. In 1903-56, stamps of Montserrat and Leeward Islands were used concurrently.

12 Pence = 1 Shilling
20 Shillings = 1 Pound
100 Cents = 1 Dollar (1951)

> Catalogue values for unused stamps in this country are for Never Hinged items, beginning with Scott 104 in the regular postage section, Scott B1 in the semipostal section, Scott O45 in the officials section.

Watermark

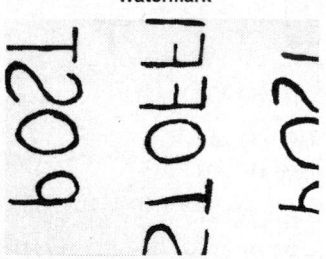

Wmk. 380 — "POST OFFICE"

Values for unused stamps are for examples with original gum as defined in the catalogue introduction. Very fine examples of Nos. 1-2, 6 and 11 will have perforations touching the design on at least one side due to the narrow spacing of the stamps on the plates. Stamps with perfs clear of the framelines on all four sides are scarce and will command higher prices.

Stamps of Antigua Overprinted in Black — a

1876   Engr.   Wmk. 1   *Perf. 14*

1	A1	1p red	30.00	19.00
a.		Vert. or diag. half used as ½p on cover		1,650.
c.		"S" inverted	1,250.	875.00
2	A1	6p green	75.00	50.00
a.		Vertical half used as 3p on cover		—

---

b.	Vertical third used as 2p on cover		6,500.	
c.	"S" inverted	1,900.	1,350.	
d.	6p blue green	1,350.		
e.	As "d," "S" inverted	13,000.		

Some experts consider Nos. 2d, 2e to be from a trial printing.

Queen Victoria — A2

1880   **Typo.**

3	A2	2½p red brown	300.00	225.00
4	A2	4p blue	160.00	47.50
		See Nos. 5, 7-10.		

1884   **Wmk. 2**

5	A2	½p green	1.25	11.00

Antigua No. 18 Overprinted type "a"

1884   **Engr.**

6	A1	1p rose red	27.00	20.00
a.		Vert. half used as ½p on cover		1,550.
b.		"S" inverted	1,100.	1,100.

Type of 1880

1884-85   **Typo.**

7	A2	2½p red brown	275.00	77.50
8	A2	2½p ultra ('85)	27.50	22.50
9	A2	4p blue	2,100.	300.00
10	A2	4p red lilac ('85)	6.00	3.50

Antigua No. 20 Overprinted type "a"

1884   **Engr.**   *Perf. 12*

11	A1	1p red	82.50	65.00
a.		"S" inverted	2,350.	1,550.
b.		Vert. half used as ½p on cover		1,900.

Symbol of the Colony — A3

King Edward VII — A4

1903   Wmk. 2   Typo.   *Perf. 14*

12	A3	½p gray green	.90	19.00
13	A3	1p car & black	.90	.50
14	A3	2p brown & black	6.50	50.00
15	A3	2½p ultra & black	1.75	2.10
16	A3	3p dk vio & brn orange	7.50	50.00
17	A3	6p ol grn & vio	12.50	65.00
18	A3	1sh vio & gray grn	12.00	22.00
19	A3	2sh brn org & gray green	37.50	24.00
20	A3	2sh6p blk & gray grn	26.00	60.00

Wmk. 1

21	A4	5sh car & black	160.00	225.00
		Nos. 12-21 (10)	265.55	517.60

1904-08   Wmk. 3   **Chalky Paper**

22	A3	½p grn & gray grn ('06)	1.00	1.25
a.		Ordinary paper	12.00	3.25
23	A3	1p car & blk ('07)	17.00	30.00
24	A3	2p brown & black ('06)	2.50	1.40
a.		Ordinary paper	2.00	11.00
25	A3	2½p ultra & blk ('05)	3.00	7.75
26	A3	3p dk vio & brn orange ('08)	11.00	2.75
a.		Ordinary paper	10.00	8.00
27	A3	6p ol grn & vio ('08)	13.00	6.50
a.		Ordinary paper	9.50	40.00
28	A3	1sh violet & gray grn ('08)	11.50	8.50
29	A3	2sh brn org & gray grn ('08)	60.00	52.50
30	A3	2sh6p blk & gray grn ('08)	65.00	57.50
31	A4	5sh car & blk ('07)	160.00	180.00
		Nos. 22-31 (10)	344.00	348.15

1908-13   **Ordinary Paper**

31A	A3	½p deep green	11.50	1.10
32	A3	1p carmine	1.75	.35
33	A3	2p gray	2.00	20.00
34	A3	2½p ultramarine	2.50	4.25

Chalky Paper

35	A3	3p vio, *yellow*	1.10	22.50
36	A3	6p red vio & gray vio	12.00	60.00
37	A3	1sh blk, *green*	10.00	55.00
38	A3	2sh bl & vio, *bl*	47.50	67.50
39	A3	2sh6p car & blk, *blue*	37.50	87.50
40	A4	5sh grn & scar, *yel*	65.00	92.50

Surface-colored Paper

41	A3	3p vio, *yel* ('13)	4.50	40.00
		Nos. 31A-41 (11)	195.35	450.70

King George V	
A5	A6

1913   **Chalky Paper**

42	A5	5sh green & scar, *yel*	90.00	160.00

1916-22   Wmk. 3   *Perf. 14*

Ordinary Paper

43	A6	½p green	.45	2.75
44	A6	1p scarlet	2.00	.90
45	A6	2p gray	2.25	5.00
46	A6	2½p ultramarine	2.50	26.00

Chalky Paper

47	A6	3p violet, *yel*	1.40	21.00
48	A6	4p blk & red, *yel* ('22)	7.00	42.50
49	A6	6p dl vio & red violet	3.50	35.00
50	A6	1sh blk, *bl grn, ol back*	3.50	40.00
51	A6	2sh vio & ultra, *bl*	20.00	55.00
52	A6	2sh6p blk & red, *bl*	35.00	85.00
53	A6	5sh grn & red, *yel*	55.00	90.00
		Nos. 43-53 (11)	132.60	403.15

For overprints see Nos. MR1-MR3.

1922-29   Wmk. 4   **Ordinary Paper**

54	A6	¼p brown	.35	6.25
55	A6	½p green ('23)	.30	.30
56	A6	1p dp violet ('23)	.80	.70
57	A6	1p carmine ('29)	1.10	1.75
58	A6	1½p orange	2.50	11.00
59	A6	1½p rose red ('23)	.60	5.00
60	A6	1½p fawn ('29)	2.25	.55
61	A6	2p gray	.80	2.25
62	A6	2½p ultramarine	9.25	18.00
63	A6	2½p orange ('23)	2.75	21.00
64	A6	3p ultra ('23)	.80	18.00

Chalky Paper

65	A6	3p vio, *yel* ('26)	2.00	5.50
66	A6	4p black & red, *yel* ('23)	1.75	14.00
67	A6	5p dull vio & ol grn	4.75	11.00
68	A6	6p dull vio & red vio ('23)	3.50	8.50
69	A6	1sh blk, *emer* ('23)	3.50	8.00
70	A6	2sh vio & ultra, *bl*	8.00	18.00
71	A6	2sh6p blk & red, *bl* ('23)	14.00	60.00
72	A6	3sh green & vio	14.00	21.00
73	A6	4sh black & scar	17.50	42.50
74	A6	5sh grn & red, *yel* ('23)	35.00	60.00
		Nos. 54-74 (21)	125.50	333.30

Tercentenary Issue

New Plymouth and Harbor A7

1932, Apr. 18   **Engr.**

75	A7	½p green	.85	15.00
76	A7	1p red	.85	6.50
77	A7	1½p orange brown	1.40	2.75
78	A7	2p gray	1.90	22.50
79	A7	2½p ultra	1.40	20.00
80	A7	3p orange	1.90	21.00
81	A7	6p violet	2.50	37.50
82	A7	1sh olive green	14.50	50.00
83	A7	2sh6p lilac rose	52.50	87.50
84	A7	5sh dark brown	115.00	200.00
		Nos. 75-84 (10)	192.80	462.75
		Set, never hinged	400.00	

300th anniv. of the colonization of Montserrat.

Common Design Types pictured following the introduction.

Silver Jubilee Issue
Common Design Type

1935, May 6   *Perf. 11x12*

85	CD301	1p car & dk blue	1.25	4.25
86	CD301	1½p gray blk & ultra	2.00	3.75
87	CD301	2½p ultra & brn	2.75	4.25
88	CD301	1sh brn vio & ind	4.25	18.00
		Nos. 85-88 (4)	10.25	30.25
		Set, never hinged	20.00	

Coronation Issue
Common Design Type

1937, May 12   *Perf. 13½x14*

89	CD302	1p carmine	.25	1.50
90	CD302	1½p brown	.40	.35
91	CD302	2½p bright ultra	.35	1.50
		Nos. 89-91 (3)	1.00	3.35
		Set, never hinged	1.75	

Carr's Bay — A8

Sea Island Cotton — A9

Botanic Station A10

1941-48   *Perf. 14*

92	A8	½p dk grn ('42)	.25	.25
93	A9	1p car ('42)	.40	.35
94	A9	1½p rose vio ('42)	.40	.55
95	A10	2p red orange	1.20	.80
96	A9	2½p brt ultra ('43)	.40	.35
97	A8	3p brown ('42)	1.50	.45
98	A10	6p dull vio ('42)	2.00	.70
99	A8	1sh brn lake ('42)	1.75	.35
100	A10	2sh6p slate bl ('43)	13.50	3.00
101	A8	5sh car rose ('42)	16.00	3.50

Perf. 12

102	A10	10sh blue ('48)	10.00	30.00
103	A8	£1 black ('48)	10.00	35.00
		Nos. 92-103 (12)	57.40	75.30
		Set, never hinged	85.00	

1938, Aug. 2   *Perf. 13*

92a	A8	½p	2.50	2.00
93a	A8	1p	2.50	.40
94a	A9	1½p	11.00	1.00
95a	A10	2p	11.00	1.00
96a	A9	2½p	1.25	1.50
97a	A8	3p	3.00	3.25
98a	A10	6p	11.50	1.25
99a	A8	1sh	11.50	1.25
100a	A10	2sh6p	20.00	1.00
101a	A8	5sh	24.00	1.00
		Nos. 92a-101a (10)	98.25	22.65
		Set, never hinged	200.00	

> Catalogue values for unused stamps in this section, from this point to the end of the section, are for Never Hinged items.

Peace Issue
Common Design Type

1946, Nov. 1   Engr.   *Perf. 13½x14*

104	CD303	1½p deep magenta	.25	.25
105	CD303	3p brown	.25	.25

Silver Wedding Issue
Common Design Types

1949, Jan. 3   Photo.   *Perf. 14x14½*

106	CD304	2½p brt ultra	.25	.25

Engraved; Name Typographed
Perf. 11½x11

107	CD305	5sh rose carmine	9.00	18.00

UPU Issue
Common Design Types
Engr.; Name Typo. on 3p and 6p
Perf. 13½, 11x11½

1949, Oct. 10 — Wmk. 4
108	CD306	2½p ultramarine	.45	1.00
109	CD307	3p chocolate	1.10	.75
110	CD308	6p lilac	.75	.85
111	CD309	1sh rose violet	1.10	1.25
		Nos. 108-111 (4)	3.40	3.85

University Issue
Common Design Types
1951, Feb. 16 — Engr. — *Perf. 14x14½*
112	CD310	3c rose lil & gray blk	.25	.60
113	CD311	12c violet & black	.60	.90

Government House
A11

Designs (portrait at right on 12c, 24c and $2.40): 2c, $1.20, Cotton field. 3c, Map of Presidency. 4c, 24c, Picking tomatoes. 5c, 12c, St. Anthony's Church. 6c, $4.80, Badge of Presidency. 8c, 60c, Cotton ginning.

Perf. 11½x11
1951, Sept. 17 — Engr. — Wmk. 4
114	A11	1c gray	.30	.30
115	A11	2c green	.30	.30
116	A11	3c orange brown	.30	.30
117	A11	4c rose carmine	.30	.30
118	A11	5c red violet	.30	.30
119	A11	6c dark brown	.40	.40
120	A11	8c dark blue	.60	.60
121	A11	12c red brn & blue	1.25	1.25
122	A11	24c emer & rose carmine	1.75	1.75
123	A11	60c rose car & gray black	3.50	3.50
124	A11	$1.20 dp bl & emer	11.00	11.00
125	A11	$2.40 dp grn & gray black	14.00	14.00
126	A11	$4.80 pur & gray blk	28.00	28.00
		Nos. 114-126 (13)	62.00	62.00

Coronation Issue
Common Design Type
1953, June 2 — *Perf. 13½x13*
127	CD312	2c dark green & black	.65	.50

Type of 1951 with Portrait of Queen Elizabeth II
½c, 3c, "Map of Presidency." 48c, Cotton field.

1953-57 — *Perf. 11½x11*
128	A11	½c violet ('56)	.30	.25
129	A11	1c gray black	.30	.25
130	A11	2c green	.30	.25
131	A11	3c orange brown	.75	.65
132	A11	4c rose car ('55)	.30	.25
133	A11	5c red vio ('55)	.30	.25
134	A11	6c dk brown ('55)	.80	.70
135	A11	8c dp ultra ('55)	.30	.25
136	A11	12c red brn & blue ('55)	.30	.25
137	A11	24c emer & rose car ('55)	.90	.80
138	A11	48c rose violet & olive ('57)	1.75	1.50
139	A11	60c rose car & blk ('55)	2.25	1.75
140	A11	$1.20 bl & emer ('55)	4.50	3.50
141	A11	$2.40 dp green & blk ('55)	9.25	7.00
142	A11	$4.80 pur & gray black ('55)	40.00	40.00
		Nos. 128-142 (15)	62.30	47.65

See Nos. 146-149, 156.

West Indies Federation
Common Design Type
Perf. 11½x11
1958, Apr. 22 — Engr. — Wmk. 314
143	CD313	3c green	.45	.25
144	CD313	6c blue	.65	.45
145	CD313	12c carmine rose	1.25	.65
		Nos. 143-145 (3)	2.35	1.35

Type of 1953-57
As before, but inscribed: "Map of the Colony" (½c, 3c) "Badge of the Colony" (6c, $4.80).

1958 — Wmk. 4 — *Perf. 11½x11*
146	A11	½c violet	.65	.25
147	A11	3c orange brown	.65	.75
148	A11	6c dark brown	.30	.25
149	A11	$4.80 pur & gray blk	14.50	9.00
		Nos. 146-149 (4)	16.10	10.25

Freedom from Hunger Issue
Common Design Type
Perf. 14x14½
1963, June 4 — Photo. — Wmk. 314
150	CD314	12c lilac	.55	.45

Red Cross Centenary Issue
Common Design Type
1963, Sept. 2 — Litho. — *Perf. 13*
151	CD315	4c black & red	.25	.25
152	CD315	12c ultra & red	.75	.55

Shakespeare Issue
Common Design Type
1964, Apr. 23 — Photo. — *Perf. 14x14½*
153	CD316	12c slate blue	.35	.25

Type of 1953-57
Perf. 11½x11
1964, Oct. 30 — Engr. — Wmk. 314
156	A11	2c green	1.20	.25

ITU Issue
Common Design Type
Perf. 11x11½
1965, May 17 — Litho. — Wmk. 314
157	CD317	4c ver & lilac	.25	.25
158	CD317	48c emer & rose red	1.00	.90

Pineapple — A12

Wmk. 314 Upright
1965, Aug. 16 — Photo. — *Perf. 15x14*
159	A12	1c shown	.30	.25
160	A12	2c Avacado	.30	.25
161	A12	3c Soursop	.30	.25
162	A12	4c Peppers	.30	.25
163	A12	5c Mango	.30	.25
164	A12	6c Tomatoes	.30	.25
165	A12	8c Guava	.30	.25
166	A12	10c Okra	.30	.25
167	A12	12c Limes	.30	.25
168	A12	20c Oranges	.40	.25
169	A12	24c Bananas	.65	.40
170	A12	42c Onion	1.30	1.25
171	A12	48c Cabbage	1.75	1.40
172	A12	60c Papayas	1.75	1.60
173	A12	$1.20 Pumpkin	2.10	2.75
174	A12	$2.40 Sweet potato	5.50	6.00
175	A12	$4.80 Eggplant	11.00	12.00
		Nos. 159-175 (17)	27.15	27.90

For surcharges see Nos. 193-198.

1969 — **Wmk. 314 Sideways**
159a	A12	1c	.25	.25
160a	A12	2c	.45	.50
161a	A12	3c	.30	.40
162a	A12	4c	.75	.40
163a	A12	5c	.90	1.00
166a	A12	10c	1.75	2.00
168a	A12	20c	2.10	2.40
		Nos. 159a-168a (7)	6.50	6.95

Intl. Cooperation Year Issue
Common Design Type
1965, Oct. 25 — Litho. — *Perf. 14½*
176	CD318	2c lt green & claret	.25	.25
177	CD318	12c lt violet & green	.55	.40

Churchill Memorial Issue
Common Design Type
1966, Jan. 24 — Photo. — *Perf. 14*
Design In Black, Gold and Carmine Rose
178	CD319	1c bright blue	.25	.25
179	CD319	2c green	.25	.25
180	CD319	24c brown	.35	.30
181	CD319	42c violet	.75	.75
		Nos. 178-181 (4)	1.60	1.55

Royal Visit Issue
Common Design Type
Perf. 11x12
1966, Feb. 4 — Litho. — Wmk. 314
182	CD320	14c violet blue	.60	.25
183	CD320	24c dk carmine rose	1.10	.75

WHO Headquarters Issue
Common Design Type
1966, Sept. 20 — Litho. — *Perf. 14*
184	CD322	12c multicolored	.25	.25
185	CD322	60c multicolored	.75	.75

UNESCO Anniversary Issue
Common Design Type
1966, Dec. 1 — Litho. — *Perf. 14*
186	CD323	4c "Education"	.25	.25
a.		Orange omitted	60.00	
187	CD323	60c "Science"	.40	.40
188	CD323	$1.80 "Culture"	1.75	1.75
		Nos. 186-188 (3)	2.40	2.40

On No. 186a, the squares of the lowercase letters appear in yellow.

Sailing and ITY Emblem A13

ITY Emblem and: 15c, Waterfall, Chance Mountain, vert. 16c, Beach scene. 24c, Golfers.

1967, Dec. 29 — Photo. — Wmk. 314
189	A13	5c multicolored	.35	.35
190	A13	15c multicolored	.35	.35
191	A13	16c multicolored	.45	.45
192	A13	24c multicolored	1.10	1.10
		Nos. 189-192 (4)	2.25	2.25

Issued for International Tourist Year.

Nos. 167, 169, 171, 173-175 and Type Surcharged

1968, May 6 — *Perf. 15x14*
193	A12	15c on 12c multi	.25	.25
a.		Wmkd. sideways ('69)	1.50	1.75
194	A12	25c on 24c multi	.25	.25
a.		Wmkd. sideways ('69)	2.50	3.00
195	A12	50c on 48c multi	.45	.45
a.		Wmkd. sideways ('69)	5.25	6.00
196	A12	$1 on $1.20 multi	.70	.70
197	A12	$2.50 on $2.40 multi	1.50	1.50
198	A12	$5 on $4.80 multi	3.00	3.00
		Nos. 193-198 (6)	6.15	6.15

The surcharge bars are slightly thinner on the "Wmkd. sideways" varieties.

Woman Runner A14

Designs: 25c, Weight lifter. 50c, Athlete on rings. $1, Runner and Toltec sculptures, vert.

Perf. 14½x14, 14x14½
1968, July 31 — Photo. — Wmk. 314
199	A14	15c gold, brt grn & rose claret	.25	.25
200	A14	25c gold, org & blue	.25	.25
201	A14	50c gold, ver & green	.25	.25
202	A14	$1 multicolored	.30	.30
		Nos. 199-202 (4)	1.05	1.05

19th Olympic Games, Mexico City, 10/12-27.

Albert T. Marryshow — A15

Portraits and Human Rights Flame: 5c, Alexander Hamilton. 25c, William Wilberforce. 50c, Dag Hammarskjold. $1, Rev. Martin Luther King, Jr.

1968, Dec. 2 — Photo. — *Perf. 14x14½*
203	A15	5c multicolored	.25	.25
204	A15	15c multicolored	.25	.25
205	A15	25c multicolored	.25	.25
206	A15	50c multicolored	.25	.25
207	A15	$1 multicolored	1.25	1.25
		Nos. 203-207 (5)		

International Human Rights Year.

The Two Trinities, by Murillo — A16 | Map of Caribbean — A17

Christmas: 15c, 50c, The Adoration of the Magi, by Botticelli.

1968, Dec. 16 — *Perf. 14½x14*
208	A16	5c red & multi	.25	.25
209	A16	15c dk green & multi	.25	.25
210	A16	25c purple & multi	.25	.25
211	A16	50c brown & multi	.25	.25
		Nos. 208-211 (4)	1.00	1.00

1969, May 27 — Photo. — *Perf. 14*
Design: 35c, 50c, "Strength in Unity," horiz.
212	A17	15c green & multi	.25	.25
213	A17	20c brown & multi	.25	.25
214	A17	35c dp carmine & multi	.25	.25
215	A17	50c multicolored	.25	.25
		Nos. 212-215 (4)	1.00	1.00

First anniversary of CARIFTA (Caribbean Free Trade Area).

Telephone and Map — A18

Development Projects (Map and): 25c, Book and "New Schools." 50c, Planes (air transport service). $1, Pylon and power lines.

Wmk. 314
1969, July 29 — Litho. — *Perf. 13½*
216	A18	15c multicolored	.25	.25
217	A18	25c multicolored	.25	.25
218	A18	50c multicolored	.25	.25
219	A18	$1 multicolored	.25	.25
		Nos. 216-219 (4)	1.00	1.00

Dolphin A19

Fish: 15c, Atlantic sailfish. 25c, Blackfin tuna and fishing boat. 40c, Spanish mackerel.

1969, Nov. 1 — Photo. — *Perf. 13x14*
220	A19	5c multicolored	.25	.25
221	A19	15c multicolored	.35	.35
222	A19	25c multicolored	.70	.70
223	A19	40c multicolored	1.25	1.25
		Nos. 220-223 (4)	2.55	2.55

King Caspar, Virgin and Child (Stained-glass Window) — A20

Christmas: 50c, Nativity, by Leonard Limosin, horiz.

Perf. 12½x13, 13x12½

1969, Dec. 10　Litho.　Wmk. 314
224	A20	15c violet & multi	.25	.25
225	A20	25c red & multi	.25	.25
226	A20	50c orange & multi	.25	.25
		Nos. 224-226 (3)	.75	.75

Red Cross and Distribution of Hearing Aids — A21

Red Cross and: 3c, Fund raising sale and invalid. 15c, Car bringing handicapped to work. 20c, Instruction for blind worker.

1970, Apr. 13　Litho.　*Perf. 14½*
227	A21	3c multicolored	.25	.25
228	A21	4c multicolored	.25	.25
229	A21	15c multicolored	.25	.25
230	A21	20c multicolored	.25	.25
		Nos. 227-230 (4)	1.00	1.00

Centenary of British Red Cross Society.

Red-footed Booby A22

Birds: 2c, Killy hawk, vert. 3c, Frigate bird, vert. 4c, White egret, vert. 5c, Brown pelican, vert. 10c, Bananaquit, vert. 15c, Common ani. 20c, Tropic bird. 25c, Montserrat oriole. 50c, Greenthroated carib, vert. $1, Antillean crested hummingbird. $2.50, Little blue heron, vert. $5, Purple-throated carib. $10, Forest thrush.

Wmk. 314 Upright on Horiz. Stamps, Sideways on Vert. Stamps
Perf. 14x14½, 14½x14

1970-74　　　　Photo.
231	A22	1c yel org & multi	.25	.25
232	A22	2c lt vio & multi	.25	.25
233	A22	3c multicolored	.25	.25
234	A22	4c lt grn & multi	.25	.25
235	A22	5c bister & multi	.25	.25
236	A22	10c gray & multi	.25	.25
237	A22	15c multicolored	.50	.40
238	A22	20c rose brn & multi	.65	.55
239	A22	25c brown & multi	.85	.70
240	A22	50c lt vio & multi	1.75	1.40
241	A22	$1 multicolored	3.00	2.40
242	A22	$2.50 dl bl & multi	6.75	5.50
243	A22	$5 multicolored	13.50	11.00
243A	A22	$10 black & multi	26.00	22.50
		Nos. 231-243A (14)	54.50	45.95

Issued: $10, 10/30/74; others 7/2/70.
For surcharges and overprints see Nos. 314, 317, 337-339, O1-O4.

Wmk. Sideways on Horiz. Stamps, Upright on Vert. Stamps

1972-74
231a	*A22*	*1c multicolored*	*.80*	*1.10*
232a	*A22*	*2c multicolored*	*1.00*	*1.10*
233a	*A22*	*3c multicolored*	*1.00*	*1.10*
234a	*A22*	*4c multicolored*	*1.50*	*1.50*
235a	*A22*	*5c multicolored*	*2.00*	*1.75*
237a	*A22*	*15c multicolored*	*5.00*	*4.50*
238a	*A22*	*20c multicolored*	*7.00*	*7.50*
239a	*A22*	*25c multicolored*	*9.75*	*9.50*
		Nos. 231a-239a (8)	*28.05*	*28.05*

Issued: 1c, 2c, 3c, 7/21/72; 5c, 15c, 3/8/73; 20c, 10/2/73; 4c, 2/4/74; 25c, 5/17/74.

"Madonna and Child with Animals," after Dürer — A23

Christmas: 15c, $1, Adoration of the Shepherds, by Domenichino (Domenico Zampieri).

1970, Sept. 21　Litho.　Perf. 14
244	A23	5c lt blue & multi	.25	.25
245	A23	15c red orange & multi	.25	.25
246	A23	20c ol green & multi	.25	.25
247	A23	$1 multicolored	.50	.50
		Nos. 244-247 (4)	1.25	1.25

War Memorial, Plymouth — A24

Tourist Publicity: 15c, Fort St. George and view of Plymouth. 25c, Beach at Carrs Bay. 50c, Golf Course.

1970, Nov. 30　Litho.　*Perf. 14*
248	A24	5c multicolored	.25	.25
249	A24	15c multicolored	.40	.40
250	A24	25c multicolored	.70	.70
251	A24	50c multicolored	1.50	1.50
	a.	Souvenir sheet of 4, #248-251	7.25	7.25
		Nos. 248-251 (4)	2.85	2.85

Girl Guide — A25

Girl Guides' 60th Anniv.: 15c, 25c, Brownie.

1970, Dec. 31
252	A25	10c orange & multi	.25	.25
253	A25	15c lt blue & multi	.25	.25
254	A25	25c lilac & multi	.25	.25
255	A25	40c multicolored	.30	.30
		Nos. 252-255 (4)	1.05	1.05

"Noli me Tangere," by Orcagna (Andrea di Cione) — A26

Easter: 5c, 20c, Descent from the Cross, by Jan van Hemessen.

Perf. 13½x13

1971, Mar. 22　Photo.　Wmk. 314
256	A26	5c orange brn & multi	.25	.25
257	A26	15c multicolored	.25	.25
258	A26	20c green & multi	.25	.25
259	A26	40c blue green & multi	.25	.25
		Nos. 256-259 (4)	1.00	1.00

Distinguished Flying Cross and Medal — A27

Highest Awards for Military Personnel: 20c, Military Cross and Medal. 40c, Distinguished Service Cross and Medal. $1, Victoria Cross.

Perf. 14½x14

1971, July 8　Litho.　Wmk. 314
260	A27	10c gray, vio & silver	.25	.25
261	A27	20c green & multi	.25	.25
262	A27	40c lt bl, dk bl & sil	.25	.25
263	A27	$1 red, dk brn & gold	.40	.40
		Nos. 260-263 (4)	1.15	1.15

50th anniversary of the British Commonwealth Ex-services League.

"Nativity with Saints" (detail), by Romanino A28

Christmas (Paintings): 15c, $1, Angels' Choir, by Simon Marmion.

1971, Sept. 16　　　Perf. 14x13½
264	A28	5c brown & multi	.25	.25
265	A28	15c emerald & multi	.25	.25
266	A28	20c ultra & multi	.25	.25
267	A28	$1 red & multi	.40	.40
		Nos. 264-267 (4)	1.15	1.15

Piper Apache, First Landing at Olveston Airfield — A29

Designs: 10c, Beech Twin Bonanza. 15c, De Havilland Heron. 20c, Britten Norman Islander. 40c, De Havilland Twin Otter. 75c, Hawker Siddeley 748 and stewardesses.

1971, Dec. 16　　　Perf. 13½x14
268	A29	5c multicolored	.25	.25
269	A29	10c multicolored	.30	.30
270	A29	15c multicolored	.45	.45
271	A29	20c multicolored	.65	.65
272	A29	40c multicolored	1.25	1.25
273	A29	75c multicolored	2.00	2.00
	a.	Souvenir sheet of 6, #268-273	16.00	16.00
		Nos. 268-273 (6)	4.90	4.90

14th anniversary of Leeward Islands Air Transport (LIAT).

Chapel of Christ in Gethsemane, Coventry Cathedral — A30

Easter: 10c, 75c, The Agony in the Garden, by Giovanni Bellini.

1972, Mar. 9　Litho.　Perf. 13½x13
274	A30	5c red & multi	.25	.25
275	A30	10c blue & multi	.25	.25
276	A30	20c emerald & multi	.25	.25
277	A30	75c lilac & multi	.75	.75
		Nos. 274-277 (4)	1.50	1.50

Iguana A31

Designs: 15c, Spotted ameiva (lizard), vert. 20c, Frog ("mountain chicken"), vert. $1, Redfoot tortoises.

1972, June 8　Litho.　Perf. 14½
278	A31	15c lilac rose & multi	.60	.60
279	A31	20c black & multi	.70	.70
280	A31	40c blue & multi	1.50	1.50
281	A31	$1 green & multi	3.00	3.00
		Nos. 278-281 (4)	5.80	5.80

Madonna of the Chair, by Raphael A32

Christmas (Paintings): 35c, Virgin and Child with Cherubs, by Bernardino Fungai. 50c, Magnificat Madonna, by Botticelli. $1, Virgin and Child with St. John and Angel, by Botticelli.

1972, Oct. 18　　　Perf. 13½
282	A32	10c violet & multi	.25	.25
283	A32	35c brt red & multi	.25	.25
284	A32	50c red brown & multi	.30	.30
285	A32	$1 olive & multi	.50	.50
		Nos. 282-285 (4)	1.30	1.30

Silver Wedding Issue, 1972
Common Design Type

Design: Queen Elizabeth II, Prince Philip, tomatoes, papayas, limes.

Perf. 14x14½

1972, Nov. 20　Photo.　Wmk. 314
286	CD324	35c car rose & multi	.25	.25
287	CD324	$1 ultra & multi	.30	.30

Passionflower A33

Designs: 35c, Passiflora vitifolia. 75c, Passiflora amabilis. $1, Passiflora alata caerulea.

1973, Apr. 9　Litho.　Perf. 14x13½
288	A33	20c purple & multi	.40	.40
289	A33	35c multicolored	.75	.75
290	A33	75c brt blue & multi	1.10	1.10
291	A33	$1 multicolored	2.00	2.00
		Nos. 288-291 (4)	4.25	4.25

Easter. Black backprinting gives story of passionflower.

Montserrat Monastery, Spain — A34

35c, Columbus aboard ship sighting Montserrat. 60c, Columbus' ship off Montserrat. $1, Arms and map of Montserrat & neighboring islands.

1973, July 16　Litho.　Perf. 13½x14
292	A34	10c multicolored	.40	.40
293	A34	35c multicolored	.90	.90
294	A34	60c multicolored	1.40	1.40

295	A34	$1 multicolored	2.10	2.10
a.		Souvenir sheet of 4, #292-295	20.00	20.00
		Nos. 292-295 (4)	4.80	4.80

480th anniversary of the discovery of Montserrat by Columbus.

Virgin and Child, Studio of David — A35

Christmas (Paintings): 35c, Holy Family with St. John, by Jacob Jordaens. 50c, Virgin and Child, by Bellini. 90c, Virgin and Child by Carlo Dolci.

1973, Oct. 15   Litho.   Perf. 14x13½

296	A35	20c blue & multi	.25	.25
297	A35	35c ol bister & multi	.30	.30
298	A35	50c brt green & multi	.40	.40
299	A35	90c brt rose & multi	.55	.55
		Nos. 296-299 (4)	1.50	1.50

Princess Anne's Wedding Issue
Common Design Type

1973, Nov. 14   Perf. 14

| 300 | CD325 | 35c brt green & multi | .25 | .25 |
| 301 | CD325 | $1 multicolored | .40 | .40 |

Masqueraders A36

1974, Apr. 8

302	A36	20c Steel band, horiz.	.25	.25
303	A36	35c shown	.25	.25
304	A36	60c Girl weaving	.25	.25
305	A36	$1 University Center, horiz.	.40	.40
a.		Souvenir sheet of 4, #302-305	4.50	4.50
		Nos. 302-305 (4)	1.15	1.15

University of the West Indies, 25th anniv. For surcharge see No. 316.

Hands Holding Letters, UPU Emblem A37

Designs: 2c, 5c, $1, Hands and figures from UPU Monument, Bern; UPU emblem. 3c, 50c, like 1c.

1974, July 3   Litho.   Perf. 14

306	A37	1c violet & multi	.25	.25
307	A37	2c red & black	.25	.25
308	A37	3c olive & multi	.25	.25
309	A37	5c orange & black	.25	.25
310	A37	50c brown & multi	.25	.25
311	A37	$1 grnsh blue & black	.40	.40
		Nos. 306-311 (6)	1.65	1.65

Centenary of Universal Postal Union. For surcharges see Nos. 315-318.

Churchill, Parliament, Big Ben — A38

Churchill and Blenheim Palace — A39

Perf. 13x13½

1974, Nov. 30   Unwmk.

312	A38	35c ocher & multi	.25	.25
313	A39	70c brt green & multi	.30	.30
a.		Souvenir sheet of 2, #312-313	.75	.75

Sir Winston Churchill (1874-1965).

Nos. 241, 304, 310-311 Surcharged

Perf. 14x14½, 14

1974, Oct. 2   Photo., Litho.   Wmk. 314

314	A22	2c on $1 multi	.30	.30
315	A37	5c on 50c multi	1.40	1.40
316	A36	10c on 60c multi	3.75	3.75
317	A22	20c on $1 multi	1.25	1.25
a.		One bar in surcharge	2.75	2.75
318	A37	35c on $1 multi	2.75	2.75
		Nos. 314-318 (5)	9.45	9.45

Carib Carbet (House) A40

Carib Artifacts: 20c, Necklace (caracoli). 35c, Club. 70c, Canoe.

Wmk. 314

1975, Mar. 3   Litho.   Perf. 14

319	A40	5c dk red, ocher & blk	.25	.25
320	A40	20c blk, och & dk red	.25	.25
321	A40	35c blk, dk red & och	.25	.25
322	A40	70c ocher, dk red & blk	.35	.35
a.		Souvenir booklet	3.50	
		Nos. 319-322 (4)	1.10	1.10

No. 322a contains 2 self-adhesive panes printed on peelable paper backing with bicolored advertising on back. One pane of 6 contains 3 each similar to Nos. 320-321; the other pane of 4 contains one each similar to Nos. 319-322. Stamps are Imperf. x roulette. Panes have commemorative marginal inscription.

One Bitt A41

Old Local Coinage (1785-1801): 10c, Eighth of a dollar. 35c, Quarter dollars. $2, One dollar.

1975, Sept. 1   Litho.   Perf. 14

323	A41	5c ultra, silver & blk	.25	.25
324	A41	10c brown org, sil & blk	.25	.25
325	A41	35c green, silver & blk	.35	.35
326	A41	$2 brt rose, sil & blk	1.20	1.20
a.		Souvenir sheet of 4, #323-326	2.25	2.25
		Nos. 323-326 (4)	2.05	2.05

Explanation and description of coinage printed in black on back of souvenir sheet.

Montserrat Nos. 1 and 2 — A42

10c, Post Office, Montserrat & #1a with AO8 cancel. 40c, Cover with #1, 1b. 55c, #A4 (G.B. #27 with AO8 cancel) & #2. 70c, 2 #1, 1 #1a with AO8 cancels. $1.10, Packet "Antelope" & #2.

1976, Jan. 5   Perf. 13½

327	A42	5c multicolored	.25	.25
328	A42	10c multicolored	.25	.25
329	A42	40c multicolored	.50	.50
330	A42	55c multicolored	.65	.65
331	A42	70c multicolored	.85	.85
332	A42	$1.10 multicolored	1.25	1.25
a.		Souvenir sheet of 6, #327-332	4.25	4.25
		Nos. 327-332 (6)	3.75	3.75

Centenary of Montserrat's postage stamps.

Trinity, by Orcagna — A43

Paintings by Orcagna (Andrea di Cione): 40c, Resurrection. 55c, Ascension. $1.10, Pentecost.

Perf. 14x13½

1976, Apr. 5   Litho.   Wmk. 373

333	A43	15c multicolored	.25	.25
334	A43	40c multicolored	.25	.25
335	A43	55c multicolored	.25	.25
336	A43	$1.10 multicolored	.30	.30
a.		Souvenir sheet of 4	1.90	1.90
		Nos. 333-336 (4)	1.05	1.05

Easter 1976. Nos. 333-336 were prepared, but not issued in 1975. Stamps are surcharged with new values; date "1975" obliterated with heavy bar. No. 336a contains one each of Nos. 333-336; "1975" in margin obliterated with heavy bar.

Nos. 235-236, 233 Surcharged

Perf. 14½x14

1976, Apr. 12   Photo.   Wmk. 314

337	A22	2c on 5c multi	.35	.35
338	A22	30c on 10c multi	.70	.70
339	A22	45c on 3c multi	1.20	1.20
		Nos. 337-339 (3)	2.25	2.25

For overprints see Nos. O3-O4.

White Frangipani — A44

Designs: Flowering trees of Montserrat.

Perf. 13½x14

1976, July 5   Litho.   Wmk. 373

340	A44	1c shown	.25	.25
341	A44	2c Cannonball tree	.25	.25
342	A44	3c Lignum vitae	.25	.25
343	A44	5c Malay apple	.25	.25
344	A44	10c Jacaranda	.25	.25
345	A44	15c Orchid tree	.25	.25
346	A44	20c Manjak	.25	.25
347	A44	25c Tamarind	.25	.25
348	A44	40c Flame of the Forest	.25	.25
349	A44	55c Pink cassia	.30	.30
350	A44	70c Long John	.35	.35
351	A44	$1 Saman	.50	.50
352	A44	$2.50 Immortelle	1.25	1.25
353	A44	$5 Yellow poui	2.50	2.50
354	A44	$10 Flamboyant	5.00	5.00
		Nos. 340-354 (15)	12.15	12.15

For surcharges and overprints see Nos. 374-376, 420, 435-440, O10-O44.

Mary and Joseph on Road to Bethlehem — A45

Christmas (Map of Montserrat and): 20c, Shepherds. 55c, Virgin and Child. $1.10, Three Kings.

1976, Oct. 4   Perf. 14½

355	A45	15c vio blue & multi	.25	.25
356	A45	20c green & multi	.25	.25
357	A45	55c lilac & multi	.25	.25
358	A45	$1.10 multicolored	.40	.40
a.		Souvenir sheet of 4, #355-358	2.00	2.00
		Nos. 355-358 (4)	1.15	1.15

Hudson River Review of Opsail 76 — A46

Designs: 40c, Raleigh. 75c, HMS Druid (Raleigh attacking Druid, 1776).

1976, Dec. 13   Litho.   Perf. 13

359		15c multicolored	.30	.30
a.	A46	Pair, #359, 362	1.90	1.90
360		40c multicolored	.65	.65
361		75c multicolored	1.10	1.10
a.	A46	Pair, #360-361	1.75	1.75
362		$1.25 multicolored	1.60	1.60
a.	A46	Souvenir sheet of 4, #359-362, perf. 14x13½	4.00	4.00
		Nos. 359-362 (4)	3.65	3.65

American Bicentennial.

Queen Arriving for 1966 Visit, Yacht Britannia — A48

Designs: 45c, Firing of cannons at Tower of London. $1, The crowning.

1977, Feb. 7

363	A48	30c multicolored	.25	.25
364	A48	45c multicolored	.25	.25
365	A48	$1 multicolored	.30	.30
		Nos. 363-365 (3)	.80	.80

25th anniv. of the reign of Elizabeth II. #363-365 were issued also in booklet panes of 4.

Epiphyllum Hookeri — A49

Flowers of the Night: 15c, Ipomoea alba, vert. 55c, Cereus hexagonus. $1.50, Cestrum nocturnum, vert.

1977, June 1   Litho.   Perf. 14
366	A49	15c multicolored	.25	.25
367	A49	40c multicolored	.30	.30
368	A49	55c multicolored	.40	.40
369	A49	$1.50 multicolored	1.25	1.25
a.		Souvenir sheet of 4, #366-369	3.25	3.25
		Nos. 366-369 (4)	2.20	2.20

Princess Anne at Ground-breaking Ceremony, Glendon Hospital — A50

Designs: 40c, New deep-water jetty, Plymouth. 55c, Glendon Hospital. $1.50, Freighter unloading at new jetty.

1977, Oct. 3   Wmk. 373   Perf. 14½
370	A50	20c multicolored	.25	.25
371	A50	40c multicolored	.25	.25
372	A50	55c multicolored	.30	.30
373	A50	$1.50 multicolored	.80	.80
a.		Souvenir sheet of 4, #370-373	2.50	2.50
		Nos. 370-373 (4)	1.60	1.60

Development.

Nos. 349-350, 352 Surcharged with New Value and Bars and Overprinted: "SILVER JUBILEE 1977 / ROYAL VISIT / TO THE CARIBBEAN"

1977, Oct.   Litho.   Perf. 13½x14
374	A44	$1 on 55c multi	.30	.30
375	A44	$1 on 70c multi	.30	.30
376	A44	$1 on $2.50 multi	.30	.30
		Nos. 374-376 (3)	.90	.90

Caribbean visit of Queen Elizabeth II. Surcharge has bars of differing thickness and length. No. 374 has two settings.

"Silent Night, Holy Night" — A51

Christmas Carols and Map of Montserrat: 40c, "We Three Kings of Orient Are." 55c, "I Saw Three Ships Come Sailing In." $2, "Hark the Herald Angels Sing."

1977, Nov. 14   Litho.   Perf. 14½
377	A51	5c blue & multi	.25	.25
378	A51	40c bister & multi	.25	.25
379	A51	55c lt blue & multi	.25	.25
380	A51	$2 rose & multi	.50	.50
a.		Souvenir sheet of 4, #377-380	1.25	1.25
		Nos. 377-380 (4)	1.25	1.25

Four-eye Butterflyfish — A52

Fish: 40c, French angelfish. 55c, Blue tang. $1.50, Queen triggerfish.

1978, Feb. 27   Wmk. 373   Perf. 14
381	A52	30c multicolored	.40	.40
382	A52	40c multicolored	.50	.50
383	A52	55c multicolored	.70	.70
384	A52	$1.50 multicolored	2.00	2.00
a.		Souvenir sheet of 4, #381-384	5.50	5.50
		Nos. 381-384 (4)	3.60	3.60

Elizabeth II and St. Paul's, London — A53

Designs: 55c, Chichester Cathedral. $1, Lincoln Cathedral. $2.50, Llandaff Cathedral, Cardiff.

1978, June 2   Perf. 13½
385	A53	40c multicolored	.25	.25
386	A53	55c multicolored	.25	.25
387	A53	$1 multicolored	.25	.25
388	A53	$2.50 multicolored	.50	.50
a.		Souvenir sheet of 4, #385-388	1.25	1.25
		Nos. 385-388 (4)	1.25	1.25

25th anniversary of coronation of Elizabeth II, Defender of the Faith. Nos. 385-388 printed in sheets of 10 stamps and 2 labels.
#385-388 also issued in bklt. panes of 2.

Alpinia — A54   Private, 1796 — A55

Flowering Plants: 55c, Allamanda cathartica. $1, Blue tree petrea. $2, Amaryllis.

1978, Sept. 18   Litho.   Perf. 13½x13
389	A54	40c multicolored	.25	.25
390	A54	55c multicolored	.35	.35
391	A54	$1 multicolored	.65	.65
392	A54	$2 multicolored	1.25	1.25
		Nos. 389-392 (4)	2.50	2.50

1978, Nov. 20   Litho.   Perf. 14½

Uniforms: 40c, Corporal, 1831. 55c, Sergeant, 1837. $1.50, Officer, 1784.
393	A55	30c multicolored	.25	.25
394	A55	40c multicolored	.25	.25
395	A55	55c multicolored	.35	.35
396	A55	$1.50 multicolored	1.00	1.00
a.		Souvenir sheet of 4, #393-396	2.10	2.10
		Nos. 393-396 (4)	1.85	1.85

See Nos. 401-404.

Cub Scouts A56

Boy Scouts: 55c, Signaling. $1.25, Cooking, vert. $2, Flag folding ceremony, vert.

1979, Apr. 2   Litho.   Perf. 14
397	A56	40c multicolored	.25	.25
398	A56	55c multicolored	.30	.30
399	A56	$1.25 multicolored	.70	.70
400	A56	$2 multicolored	.75	.75
a.		Souvenir sheet of 4, #397-400	2.75	2.75
		Nos. 397-400 (4)	2.00	2.00

50th anniversary of Scouting in Montserrat.

Uniform Type of 1978

30c, Private, 1783. 40c, Private, 1819. 55c, Officer, 1819. $2.50, Highlander officer, 1830.

1979, July 4   Wmk. 373   Perf. 14
401	A55	30c multicolored	.25	.25
402	A55	40c multicolored	.25	.25
403	A55	55c multicolored	.25	.25

404	A55	$2.50 multicolored	1.25	1.25
a.		Souvenir sheet of 4, #401-404	2.50	2.50
		Nos. 401-404 (4)	2.00	2.00

IYC Emblem, Learning to Walk — A56a

1979, Sept. 17   Litho.   Perf. 13½x14
405	A56a	$2 brown org & black	.60	.60
a.		Souvenir sheet	1.50	1.50

International Year of the Child.

Hill, Penny Black, Montserrat No. 1 — A57

Designs: 55c, UPU Emblem, charter. $1, UPU Emblem, cover. $2, Hill, Post Office regulations.

1979, Oct. 1   Perf. 14
406	A57	40c multicolored	.25	.25
407	A57	55c multicolored	.25	.25
408	A57	$1 multicolored	.35	.35
409	A57	$2 multicolored	.70	.70
a.		Souvenir sheet of 4, #406-409	2.75	2.75
		Nos. 406-409 (4)	1.55	1.55

Sir Rowland Hill (1795-1879), originator of penny postage; UPU membership, centenary.

Tree Lizard A58

1980, Feb. 4   Litho.   Perf. 14
410	A58	40c Tree frog	.30	.30
411	A58	55c shown	.45	.45
412	A58	$1 Crapaud	.80	.80
413	A58	$2 Wood slave	1.60	1.60
		Nos. 410-413 (4)	3.15	3.15

Marquis of Salisbury, 1817; Postmarks, 1838, London 1980 Emblem — A59

Ships or Planes, Stamps of Montserrat: 55c, H.S. 748, #349. #416, La Plata, 1901, type A4. #417, Lady Hawkins, 1929, #84. #418, Avon, 1843, Gt Britain #3. #419, Aeronca, #140.

1980, Apr. 14   Litho.   Perf. 14½
414	A59	40c multicolored	.25	.25
415	A59	55c multicolored	.30	.30
416	A59	$1.20 multicolored	.55	.60
417	A59	$1.20 multicolored	.55	.60
418	A59	$1.20 multicolored	.55	.60
419	A59	$1.20 multicolored	.55	.60
a.		Souvenir sheet of 6, #414-419	3.00	3.00
		Nos. 414-419 (6)	2.75	2.95

London 1980 Intl. Stamp Exhib., May 6-14. For surcharges see Nos. 736-740.

No. 352 Overprinted: 75th Anniversary of / Rotary International
1980, July 7   Litho.   Perf. 13½x14
420	A44	$2.50 multicolored	1.10	1.10

Discus Thrower, Stadium, Olympic Rings — A60

Flags of Host Countries: 40c, Greece, 1896; France, 1900; U.S., 1904. 55c, Great Britain, 1908; Sweden, 1912; Belgium, 1920. 70c, France, 1924; Netherlands, 1928; US, 1932. $1, Germany, 1936; Great Britain, 1948; Finland, 1952. $1.50, Australia, 1956; Italy, 1960; Japan, 1964. $2, Mexico, 1968,; Fed. Rep. of Germany, 1972; Canada, 1976.

1980, July 7   Litho.   Perf. 14
421	A60	40c multicolored	.25	.25
422	A60	55c multicolored	.25	.25
423	A60	70c multicolored	.30	.30
424	A60	$1 multicolored	.40	.40
425	A60	$1.50 multicolored	.50	.50
426	A60	$2 multicolored	.70	.70
427	A60	$2.50 multicolored	.90	.90
a.		Souv. sheet of 7, #421-427 + 2 labels	3.50	3.50
		Nos. 421-427 (7)	3.30	3.30

22nd Summer Olympic Games, Moscow, July 19-Aug. 3.

Lady Nelson, 1928 A61

1980   Litho.   Perf. 14
428	A61	40c multicolored	.25	.25
429	A61	55c Chignecto, 1913	.40	.40
430	A61	$1 Solent, 1878	.75	.75
431	A61	$2 Dee, 1841	1.40	1.40
		Nos. 428-431 (4)	2.80	2.80

Plume Worm — A62

1980   Litho.   Perf. 14
432	A62	40c shown	.50	.50
433	A62	55c Sea fans	.70	.70
434	A62	$2 Coral, sponges	1.75	1.75
		Nos. 432-434 (3)	2.95	2.95

Nos. 340, 342, 345, 348 Surcharged
1980, Sept. 30   Litho.   Perf. 14
435	A44	5c on 3c (#342)	.25	.25
436	A44	35c on 1c (#340)	.25	.25
437	A44	35c on 3c (#342)	.25	.25
438	A44	35c on 15c (#345)	.25	.25
439	A44	55c on 40c (#348)	.25	.25
440	A44	$5 on 40c (#348)	1.25	1.40
		Nos. 435-440 (6)	2.50	2.65

Zebra Butterfly — A63

1981, Feb. 2   Wmk. 373
441	A63	50c shown	.75	.50
442	A63	65c Tropical checkered skipper	.90	.55
443	A63	$1.50 Large orange sulphur	1.10	1.00
444	A63	$2.50 Monarch	1.60	1.40
		Nos. 441-444 (4)	4.35	3.45

Spadefish — A64

Wmk. 373

1981, Mar. 20   Litho.   Perf. 13½

445	A64	5c	shown	.25	.25
446	A64	10c	Hogfish	.25	.25
447	A64	15c	Creole wrasse	.25	.25
448	A64	20c	Yellow damselfish	.25	.25
449	A64	25c	Sergeant major	.25	.25
450	A64	35c	Clown wrasse	.25	.25
451	A64	45c	Schoolmaster	.40	.40
452	A64	55c	Striped parrotfish	1.25	1.25
453	A64	65c	Bigeye	.55	.55
454	A64	75c	French grunt	.60	.60
455	A64	$1	Rock beauty	.85	.85
456	A64	$2	Blue chromis	1.75	1.75
457	A64	$3	Fairy basslet, blueheads	2.75	2.75
458	A64	$5	Cherubfish	4.25	4.25
459	A64	$7.50	Longspine squirrelfish	4.75	4.75
460	A64	$10	Longsnout butterflyfish	7.25	7.25
		Nos. 445-460 (16)		25.90	25.90

For surcharges and overprints see Nos. 507-508, 511-512, 515, O45-O55, O95-O97.

Inscribed 1983

1983   Wmk. 380

445a	A64	5c	.30	.25
446a	A64	10c	.35	.25
449a	A64	25c	.40	.25
450a	A64	35c	.45	.30
454a	A64	75c	.65	.55
455a	A64	$1	.85	.70
458a	A64	$5	3.75	3.75
460a	A64	$10	6.75	6.75
		Nos. 445a-460a (8)	13.50	12.80

Fort St. George (National Trust) — A65

1981, May 18   Wmk. 373   Perf. 13½

461	A65	50c	shown	.30	.30
462	A65	65c	Bird Sanctuary, Fox's Bay	.30	.30
463	A65	$1.50	The Museum	.70	.80
464	A65	$2.50	Bransby Point Battery	1.40	1.50
		Nos. 461-464 (4)		2.70	2.90

Prince Charles, Lady Diana, Royal Yacht Charlotte A66

Prince Charles and Lady Diana — A67

Wmk. 380

1981, July 13   Litho.   Perf. 14

465	A66	90c	shown	.35	.35
	a.	Booklet pane of 4, perf. 12		1.75	
466	A67	90c	shown	1.25	1.25
467	A67	$3	Portsmouth	.85	.85
468	A67	$3	like #466	2.10	2.10
	a.	Booklet pane of 2, perf. 12		3.50	
469	A66	$4	Britannia	1.10	1.10
470	A67	$4	like #466	2.40	2.40
		Nos. 465-470 (6)		8.05	8.05

Royal wedding. Each denomination issued in sheets of 7 (6 type A66, 1 type A67).
For surcharges and overprints see Nos. 509-510, 513-514, 578-579, O56-O61.

Souvenir Sheet

1981, Dec.   Perf. 12

471	A67	$5 multicolored	3.00 3.00

50th Anniv. of Airmail Service A68

1981, Aug. 31   Wmk. 373   Perf. 14

472	A68	50c	Seaplane, Dorsetshire	.40 .40
473	A68	65c	Beechcraft Twin Bonanza	.50 .50
474	A68	$1.50	DeHaviland Dragon Rapide	1.00 1.00
475	A68	$2.50	Hawker Siddeley Avro 748	1.60 1.60
		Nos. 472-475 (4)		3.50 3.50

Methodist Church, Bethel — A69

Christmas (Churches): 65c, St. George's Anglican, Harris. $1.50, St. Peter's Anglican, St. Peter's. $2.50, St. Patrick's Roman Catholic, Plymouth.

1981, Nov. 16   Litho.   Perf. 14

476	A69	50c	multicolored	.25 .25
477	A69	65c	multicolored	.30 .30
478	A69	$1.50	multicolored	.50 .50
479	A69	$2.50	multicolored	.90 .90
	a.	Souvenir sheet of 4, #476-479		2.75 2.75
		Nos. 476-479 (4)		1.95 1.95

Wild Flowers First Discovered on Montserrat — A70

1982, Jan. 18   Litho.   Perf. 14½

480	A70	50c	Rondeletia buxifolia, vert.	.25 .25
481	A70	65c	Heliotropium ternatum	.25 .25
482	A70	$1.50	Picramnia pentandra, vert.	.50 .50
483	A70	$2.50	Diospyros revoluta	1.25 1.25
		Nos. 480-483 (4)		2.25 2.25

350th Anniv. of Settlement of Montserrat by Sir Thomas Warner — A70a

Jubilee Type of 1932.

Wmk. 373

1982, Apr. 17   Litho.   Perf. 14½

483A	A70a	40c	green	.25 .25
483B	A70a	55c	red	.25 .25
483C	A70a	65c	brown	.30 .30
483D	A70a	75c	gray	.30 .30
483E	A70a	85c	ultra	.35 .35
483F	A70a	95c	orange	.40 .40
483G	A70a	$1	purple	.40 .40
483H	A70a	$1.50	olive	.60 .60
483I	A70a	$2	car rose	.75 .75
483J	A70a	$2.50	sepia	1.05 1.05
		Nos. 483A-483J (10)		4.65 4.65

A70b

1982, June   Wmk. 380   Perf. 14

484	A70b	75c	Catherine of Aragon, 1501	.30 .30
485	A70b	$1	Aragon arms	.30 .30
486	A70b	$5	Diana	1.40 1.40
		Nos. 484-486 (3)		2.00 2.00

21st birthday of Princess Diana, July 1.
For surcharges and overprints see Nos. 574, O62-O64.

A71

1982, Sept. 13   Litho.   Perf. 14

487	A71	$1.50	Scout	.80 .80
488	A71	$2.50	Baden-Powell	1.20 1.20

Scouting Year.

Christmas A72

1982, Nov. 18   Wmk. 373   Perf. 14

489	A72	35c	Annunciation	.25 .25
490	A72	75c	Shepherds' vision	.35 .35
491	A72	$1.50	Virgin and Child	.65 .65
492	A72	$2.50	Flight into Egypt	1.25 1.25
		Nos. 489-492 (4)		2.50 2.50

Dragonflies — A73

1983, Jan. 19   Litho.   Perf. 13½x14

493	A73	50c	Lepthemis vesiculosa	.55 .55
494	A73	65c	Orthemis ferruginea	.70 .70
495	A73	$1.50	Triacanthagyna trifida	1.50 1.50
496	A73	$2.50	Erythrodiplax umbrata	2.10 2.10
		Nos. 493-496 (4)		4.85 4.85

Blue-headed Hummingbird A74

1983, May 24   Wmk. 373   Perf. 14

497	A74	35c	shown	.90 .90
498	A74	75c	Green-throated carib	1.25 1.25
499	A74	$2	Antillean crested hummingbird	3.25 3.25

500	A74	$3	Purple-throated carib	4.50 4.50
		Nos. 497-500 (4)		9.90 9.90

Arms — A75

1983, July 25   Litho.   Perf. 14½

501	A75	$12	red & black	5.00 7.50
502	A75	$30	blue & red	15.00 20.00

Manned Flight Bicentenary — A76

Designs: 35c, Montgolfiere, 1783, vert. 75c, De Havilland Twin Otter 310, 1981. $1.50, Lockheed Vega's around the world flight, 1933. $2, British R34 airship transatlantic flight, 1919.

1983, Sept. 19   Litho.   Perf. 14

503	A76	35c	multicolored	.30 .30
504	A76	75c	multicolored	.40 .40
505	A76	$1.50	multicolored	.60 .60
506	A76	$2	multicolored	.90 .90
	a.	Souvenir sheet of 4, #503-506		3.00 3.00
		Nos. 503-506 (4)		2.20 2.20

For surcharges see Nos. 573, 577.

Nos. 449, 446, 467-468, 453-454, 469-470, 456 Surcharged

Wmk. 373 (A64), 380

1983, Aug. 15   Litho.   Perf. 13½x14

507	A64	40c on 25c multi	.55 .55
508	A64	70c on 10c multi	.85 .85
509	A66	70c on $3 multi	.75 .75
510	A67	70c on $3 multi	1.75 1.75
511	A64	90c on 65c multi	.95 .95
512	A64	$1.15 on 75c multi	1.20 1.20
513	A66	$1.15 on $4 multi	.95 .95
514	A67	$1.15 on $4 multi	2.25 2.25
515	A64	$1.50 on $2 multi	1.50 1.50
		Nos. 507-515 (9)	10.75 10.75

Christmas Carnival 1983 A77

1983, Nov. 18   Wmk. 380   Perf. 14

516	A77	55c	Clowns	.25 .25
517	A77	90c	Star Bursts	.25 .25
518	A77	$1.15	Flower Girls	.30 .30
519	A77	$2	Masqueraders	.45 .45
		Nos. 516-519 (4)		1.25 1.25

See Nos. 547-550.

Nos. 503-506 were overprinted "INAUGURAL FLIGHT Montserrat — Nevis — St. Kitts." These exist on souvenir covers with first day cancel of Dec. 15, 1983. No announcement of this set was made nor were mint stamps generally available.

1984 Summer Olympics — A78

1984, Mar. 6   Litho.   *Perf. 14*

520	A78	90c Discobolus	.40	.40
521	A78	$1 Torch	.50	.50
522	A78	$1.15 Stadium	.55	.55
523	A78	$2.50 Flags	.90	.90
a.		Souvenir sheet of 4, #520-523	3.00	3.00
		Nos. 520-523 (4)	2.35	2.35

Cattle Egret A79

1984, May 11

524	A79	5c shown	.45	.35
525	A79	10c Carib grackles	.45	.35
526	A79	15c Common gallinule	.45	.35
527	A79	20c Brown boobys	.60	.35
528	A79	25c Black-whiskered vireos	.60	.50
529	A79	40c Scaly-breasted thrashers	.90	.55
530	A79	55c Laughing gulls	1.10	.35
531	A79	70c Glossy ibis	1.40	.50
532	A79	90c Green heron	1.50	.70
533	A79	$1 Belted kingfisher	1.90	.90
534	A79	$1.15 Bananaquits	2.40	1.60
535	A79	$3 Sparrow hawks	5.00	6.00
536	A79	$5 Forest thrush	7.00	8.00
537	A79	$7.50 Black-crowned night heron	9.00	14.50
538	A79	$10 Bridled quail doves	10.50	15.00
		Nos. 524-538 (15)	43.25	50.00

For surcharges see Nos. 651-655, 663-666.
For overprints see Nos. O65-O78.

Packet Boats A80

1984, July 9   Wmk. 380   *Perf. 14*

539	A80	55c Tagus, 1907	.30	.30
540	A80	90c Cobequid, 1913	.45	.45
541	A80	$1.15 Lady Drake, 1942	.55	.55
542	A80	$2 Factor, 1948	.90	.90
a.		Souvenir sheet of 4, #539-542	4.25	4.25
		Nos. 539-542 (4)	2.20	2.20

Marine Life A81

1984, Sept.   Wmk. 380   *Perf. 14*

543	A81	90c Top shell & hermit crab	1.60	1.60
544	A81	$1.15 Rough file shell	2.00	2.00
545	A81	$1.50 True tulip snail	3.00	3.00
546	A81	$2.50 West Indian fighting conch	4.00	4.00
		Nos. 543-546 (4)	10.60	10.60

Christmas Carnival Type of 1983

1984, Nov. 12

547	A77	55c Bull Man	.65	.65
548	A77	$1.15 Masquerader Captain	1.60	1.60
549	A77	$1.50 Carnival Queen contestant	1.75	1.75
550	A77	$2.30 Contestant, diff.	2.75	2.75
		Nos. 547-550 (4)	6.75	6.75

National Emblems — A82   Indigenous Orchids — A83

1985, Feb. 8   Litho.   *Perf. 14*

551	A82	$1.15 Mango	.40	.60
552	A82	$1.50 Lobster Claw	.50	1.00
553	A82	$3 Montserrat Oriole	.75	2.25
		Nos. 551-553 (3)	1.65	3.85

1985, May 9   Wmk. 380   *Perf. 14*

554	A83	90c Oncidium urophyllum	.60	.70
555	A83	$1.15 Epidendrum difforme	.60	.75
556	A83	$1.50 Epidendrum ciliare	.70	.85
557	A83	$2.50 Brassavola cucullata	.85	1.00
a.		Souvenir sheet of 4, #554-557	7.00	7.00
		Nos. 554-557 (4)	2.75	3.30

Queen Mother, 85th Birthday — A84

#558a, 564a, Facing right. #558b, 564b, Facing forward. #559a, Facing right. #559b, Facing left. #560a, Facing right. #560b, Glancing right. #561a, 563a, Facing right. #561b, 563b, Facing left. #562a, Facing right. #562b, Facing forward.

1985-86   Unwmk.   *Perf. 12½*

558	A84	55c Pair, #a.-b.	.45	.45
559	A84	90c Pair, #a.-b.	.75	.75
560	A84	$1.15 Pair, #a.-b.	.85	.85
561	A84	$1.50 Pair, #a.-b.	1.20	1.20
		Nos. 558-561 (4)	3.25	3.25

Souvenir Sheets of 2

562	A84	$2 #a.-b.	1.75	1.75
563	A84	$3.50 #a.-b.	3.50	3.50
564	A84	$6 #a.-b.	5.50	5.50

Issued: #563-564, 1/10/86; others, 8/7/85.
For surcharges see No. 575.

Cotton Industry A85

1985, Sept. 23   Unwmk.   *Perf. 15*

569	A85	90c Cotton plants	.25	.30
570	A85	$1 Carding	.25	.35
571	A85	$1.15 Automated loom	.25	.35
572	A85	$2.50 Hand loom	.40	.50
a.		Souvenir sheet of 4, #569-572	4.50	4.50
		Nos. 569-572 (4)	1.15	1.50

Nos. 504, 485, 560, 505, 469-470 Ovptd. or Surcharged "CARIBBEAN ROYAL VISIT 1985" in 2 or 3 Lines
Perf. 14, 12½ ($1.15)
Wmk. as Before

1985, Nov. 14   Litho.

573	A76	75c multi	4.75	4.75
574	A70b	$1 multi	6.75	6.75
575	A84	$1.15 Pair, #a.-b.	14.50	14.50
577	A76	$1.50 multi	9.25	9.25
578	A66	$1.60 on $4 multi	4.75	4.75
579	A67	$1.60 on $4 multi	17.00	17.00
		Nos. 573-579 (6)	57.00	57.00

No. 579 surcharged but not overprinted.

Audubon Birth Bicentenary — A86

Illustrations of North American bird species by John J. Audubon: #580a, Black-throated blue warbler, #580b, Palm warbler. #581a, Bobolink. #581b, Lark sparrow. #582a, Chipping sparrow. #582b, Northern oriole. #583a, American goldfinch. #583b, Blue grosbeak.

Christmas A87

1985, Nov. 29   Unwmk.   *Perf. 12½*

580	A86	15c Pair, #a.-b.	.25	.25
581	A86	30c Pair, #a.-b.	.25	.25
582	A86	55c Pair, #a.-b.	.40	.40
583	A86	$2.50 Pair, #a.-b.	1.40	1.40
		Nos. 580-583 (4)	2.30	2.30

1985, Dec. 2   Wmk. 380   *Perf. 15*

588	A87	70c Angel of the Lord	.25	.25
589	A87	$1.15 Three wise men	.35	.35
590	A87	$1.50 Caroling, Plymouth War Memorial	.40	.40
591	A87	$2.30 Our Lady of Montserrat	.70	.70
		Nos. 588-591 (4)	1.70	1.70

A set of 8 stamps for the 1986 World Cup was printed but not issued. Stamps became available with the liquidation of the printer.

Girl Guides, 50th Anniv. — A88

#592a, Lord Baden-Powell. #592b, Guide giving oath. #593a, Lady Baden-Powell. #593b, Guide cutting hair. #594a, Lord and Lady Baden-Powell. #594b, Guides in public service. #595a, Troop inspection, 1936. #595b, Guides saluting.

1986, Apr. 11

592	A88	20c Pair, #a.-b.	.25	.25
593	A88	75c Pair, #a.-b.	.75	.75
594	A88	90c Pair, #a.-b.	.85	.85
595	A88	$1.15 Pair, #a.-b.	1.10	1.10
		Nos. 592-595 (4)	2.95	2.95

For overprints see Nos. 966-967.

Queen Elizabeth II, 60th Birthday — A89

Various portraits.

1986, Apr. 11   Unwmk.   *Perf. 12½*

600	A89	10c multicolored	.25	.25
601	A89	$1.50 multicolored	.35	.35
602	A89	$3 multicolored	.55	.55
603	A89	$6 multi, vert.	.85	.85
		Nos. 600-603 (4)	2.00	2.00

Souvenir Sheet

604	A89	$8 multicolored	5.00	5.00

Halley's Comet — A90

Designs: 35c, 40c (No. 613a,) Bayeux Tapestry (detail), 1066 sighting. 50c, $1.75 (No. 613b), Adoration of the Magi, by Giotto. 70c, $2 (No. 613c), Edmond Halley, trajectory diagram, 1531 sighting. $1, $3 (No. 613d), Sightings, 1066 and 1910. $1.15, 55c (No. 614a), Sighting, 1910. $1.50, 60c (No. 614b), Giotto space probe, comet, diagram. $2.30, 80c (No. 614c), U.S. Space Telescope, comet. $4, $5 (No. 614d), Computer picture of photograph, 1910.

1986   *Perf. 14*

605-612	A90	Set of 8	3.75	3.75

Souvenir Sheets

613	A90	Sheet of 4, #a.-d.	2.75	2.75
614	A90	Sheet of 4, #a.-d.	2.75	2.75

Issued: #613-614, 10/10; others, 5/9. For overprints see Nos. 656-657.

A91

Wedding of Prince Andrew and Sarah Ferguson — A92

No. 615: a, Andrew, vert. b, Sarah, vert.
No. 616: a, Andrew wearing cowboy hat. b, Sarah wearing fur hat.

1986   Litho.   *Perf. 12½x13, 13x12½*

615	A91	70c Pair, #a.-b.	.70	.70
616	A91	$2 Pair, #a.-b	1.00	1.00
c.		Souvenir booklet	5.00	

Souvenir Sheet

617	A92	$10 multicolored	5.00	5.00

#616c contains 2 imperf panes. One pane contains 2 #615; the other 2 #616.
Issued: #617, 10/15; others, 7/23.
For overprints see Nos. 628-629.

Clipper Ships A93

1986, Aug. 29   *Perf. 14*

618	A93	90c Antelope, 1793	1.90	1.25
619	A93	$1.15 Montagu, 1840	3.00	3.00
620	A93	$1.50 Little Catherine, 1813	3.25	3.25
621	A93	$2.30 Hinchingbrook, 1813	4.25	4.75
a.		Souvenir sheet of 4, #618-621	12.50	12.50
		Nos. 618-621 (4)	12.40	12.25

Communications — A94

Designs: 70c, Radio Montserrat, near Dagenham. $1.15, Radio Gem ZGM-FM 94, Plymouth. $1.50, Radio Antilles, O'Garro's, $2.30, Cable & Wireless telegraph office, Plymouth.

1986, Sept. 29   Wmk. 380   Perf. 14

622	A94	70c multicolored	1.10	.65
623	A94	$1.15 multicolored	1.60	1.25
624	A94	$1.50 multicolored	1.90	1.90
625	A94	$2.30 multicolored	2.40	3.00
		Nos. 622-625 (4)	7.00	6.80

Nos. 615-616 Ovptd. in Silver
"Congratulations to T.R.H. The Duke &
Duchess of York"
Perf. 12½x13, 13x12½

1986, Nov. 14   Litho.

628	A91	70c Pair, #a.-b.	1.75	1.75
629	A91	$2 Pair, #a.-b.	4.00	4.00

Christmas — A95

1986, Dec. 12   Unwmk.   Perf. 14

632	A95	70c Christmas rose	.85	.85
633	A95	$1.15 Candle flower	1.40	1.40
634	A95	$1.50 Christmas tree kalanchoe	2.00	2.00
635	A95	$2.30 Snow on the mountain	3.00	3.50
a.		Souvenir sheet of 4, #632-635, perf. 12x12½	11.00	11.00
		Nos. 632-635 (4)	7.25	7.75

Souvenir Sheets

Statue of Liberty, Cent. — A96

1986, Nov. 18   Litho.   Perf. 14

636	A96	$3 Statue, pedestal	1.75	1.75
637	A96	$4.50 Head	2.40	2.40
638	A96	$5 Statue, NYC	2.75	2.75
		Nos. 636-638 (3)	6.90	6.90

Sailing
A97

1986, Dec. 10   Perf. 15

639	A97	70c shown	.55	.60
640	A97	$1.15 Golf	.80	1.25
641	A97	$1.50 Plymouth Public Market	.80	1.50
642	A97	$2.30 Air Studios	1.60	2.75
		Nos. 639-642 (4)	3.75	6.10

For surcharge see No. B3.

Sharks
A98

1987, Feb. 2   Wmk. 380   Perf. 14

643	A98	40c Tiger	1.75	.50
644	A98	90c Lemon	3.00	1.25
645	A98	$1.15 White	3.50	2.00
646	A98	$3.50 Whale	7.00	8.50
a.		Souvenir sheet of 4, #643-646, perf. 12½x12	16.00	16.00
		Nos. 643-646 (4)	15.25	12.25

Butterflies
A99

1987, Aug. 10   Wmk. 380   Perf. 14

647	A99	90c Straight-line sulpher	2.25	2.25
648	A99	$1.15 Red rim	3.00	3.00
649	A99	$1.50 Hammock skipper	3.75	3.75
650	A99	$2.50 Mimic	6.00	6.00
		Nos. 647-650 (4)	15.00	15.00

Nos. 531, 527, 525, 532 and 535
Surcharged

1987, Apr. 6

651	A79	5c on 70c multi	.80	1.10
652	A79	$1 on 20c multi	2.60	1.10
653	A79	$1.15 on 10c multi	3.25	1.60
654	A79	$1.50 on 90c multi	3.75	2.25
655	A79	$2.30 on $3 multi	5.50	6.50
		Nos. 651-655 (5)	15.90	12.55

Nos. 613-614 Ovptd. for CAPEX '87 in
Red and Black
Souvenir Sheets of 4

1987, June 13   Unwmk.

656	A90	#a.-d.	3.50	3.50
657	A90	#a.-d.	3.50	3.50

Orchids — A100

1987, Nov. 13   Unwmk.   Perf. 14

658	A100	90c Oncidium variegatum, vert.	1.00	1.00
659	A100	$1.15 Vanilla planifolia	1.25	1.25
660	A100	$1.50 Gongora quinquenervis, vert.	1.75	1.75
661	A100	$3.50 Brassavola nodosa	4.25	4.25
		Nos. 658-661 (4)	8.25	8.25

Souvenir Sheet

662	A100	$5 Oncidium lanceanum	17.00	17.00

Christmas.

Nos. 525, 528-529 and 532
Surcharged "40th Wedding
Anniversary / HM Queen Elizabeth II /
HRH Duke of Edinburgh / November
1987." and New Value

Wmk. 380

1987, Nov. 20   Litho.   Perf. 14

663	A79	5c on 90c No. 532	.55	.55
664	A79	$1.15 on 10c No. 525	.70	.70
665	A79	$2.30 on 25c No. 528	1.60	1.60
666	A79	$5 on 40c No. 529	3.25	3.25
		Nos. 663-666 (4)	6.10	6.10

Exists spelled "Edingburgh." Value, set $45.

Tropical
Bats — A101

1988, Feb. 8   Wmk. 380   Perf. 14

667	A101	55c Free-tailed bat	1.00	1.00
668	A101	90c Fruit bat	1.75	1.75
669	A101	$1.15 Fisherman bat	2.25	2.25
670	A101	$2.30 Fruit bat, diff.	4.50	4.50
		Nos. 667-670 (4)	9.50	9.50

Souvenir Sheet

671	A101	$2.50 Funnel-eared bat	10.50	10.50

Marine
Birds — A102

1988, Apr. 2   Unwmk.

672	A102	90c Magnificent frigatebird	1.00	1.00
673	A102	$1.15 Caribbean elaenia	1.25	1.25
674	A102	$1.50 Glossy ibis	1.50	1.50
675	A102	$3.50 Purple-throated carib	3.25	3.25
		Nos. 672-675 (4)	7.00	7.00

Souvenir Sheet

676	A102	$5 Brown pelican	5.50	5.50

Easter.

1988 Summer Olympics,
Seoul — A103

Eastern architecture and events: 90c,
Women's discus. $1.15, High jump. $3.50,
Women's 200-meter and Seoul university
building. $5, Single scull rowing, pagoda.

Unwmk.

1988, July 29   Litho.   Perf. 14

677	A103	90c multicolored	.95	.95
678	A103	$1.15 multicolored	1.00	1.00
679	A103	$3.50 multicolored	3.25	3.25
		Nos. 677-679 (3)	5.20	5.20

Souvenir Sheet

680	A103	$5 multicolored	5.25	5.25

Sea
Shells
A104

1988, Aug. 30

681	A104	5c Golden tulip	.30	.25
682	A104	10c Little knobby scallop	.30	.25
683	A104	15c Sozoni's cone	.30	.25
684	A104	20c Globular coral shell	.30	.25
685	A104	25c Sundial	.30	.25
686	A104	40c King helmet	.45	.45
687	A104	55c Channeled turban	.55	.60
688	A104	70c True tulip choll	.70	.75
689	A104	90c Music voluto	.90	.90
690	A104	$1 Flame auger	1.00	1.10
691	A104	$1.15 Rooster-tail conch	1.25	1.40
692	A104	$1.50 Queen conch	1.50	1.75
693	A104	$3 Teramachi's slit shell	3.50	3.50
694	A104	$5 Florida crown conch	5.00	5.50
695	A104	$7.50 Beau's murex	7.50	8.50
696	A104	$10 Triton's trumpet	10.50	11.50
		Nos. 681-696 (16)	34.35	37.30

For surcharges see Nos. 698-701, 767-770.
For overprints see Nos. O79-O94.

University of the
West Indies,
40th
Anniv. — A105

1988, Oct. 4   Litho.   Perf. 14

697	A105	$5 multicolored	4.00	4.00

Nos. 687, 690, 693 and 694
Surcharged

Unwmk.

1988, Nov. 4   Litho.   Perf. 14

698	A104	40c on 55c No. 687	.50	.50
699	A104	90c on $1 No. 690	1.50	1.50
700	A104	$1.15 on $3 No. 693	1.75	1.75
701	A104	$1.50 on $5 No. 694	2.50	2.50
		Nos. 698-701 (4)	6.25	6.25

Intl.
Red
Cross,
125th
Anniv.
A106

1988, Dec. 16

702	A106	$3.50 multicolored	2.10	2.10

Christmas — A107

Birds.

1988, Nov. 28   Perf. 14x13½

703	A107	90c Spotted sandpiper	1.00	1.00
704	A107	$1.15 Ruddy turnstone	1.25	1.25
705	A107	$3.50 Red-footed booby	3.75	3.75
		Nos. 703-705 (3)	6.00	6.00

Souvenir Sheet
Perf. 13½x14

706	A107	$5 Aububon's shearwater	6.00	6.00

Uniforms
A108

1989, Feb. 24   Litho.   Perf. 14

707	A108	90c Drum major	1.10	1.10
708	A108	$1.15 Fatigue clothing	1.25	1.25
709	A108	$1.50 Khaki uniform	1.60	1.60
710	A108	$3.50 Dress uniform	4.25	4.25
		Nos. 707-710 (4)	8.20	8.20

Souvenir Sheet

711 A108 $5 Cadet (girl), wo-
man   6.25 6.25
Defense Force, 75th anniv.

Easter
Lilies
A109

1989, Mar. 21   Litho.   Perf. 14
712 A109 90c Amazon   .75 .75
713 A109 $1.15 Salmon blood,
vert.   .90 .90
714 A109 $1.50 Amaryllis, vert. 1.10 1.10
715 A109 $3.50 Amaryllis, diff.,
vert.   3.00 3.00
Nos. 712-715 (4)   5.75 5.75

Souvenir Sheet

716 A109 $5 Resurrection,
vert.   7.25 7.25

Ships Built in Montserrat — A110

Designs: 90c, Schooner Morning Prince,
1942-1948. $1.15, Cargo boat Western Sun.
$1.50, Cargo boat Kim G under construction.
$3.50, Cargo and passenger boat MV
Romaris.

1989, June 30 Litho. Perf. 13½x14
717 A110 90c multicolored   1.50 1.50
718 A110 $1.15 multicolored   1.75 1.75
719 A110 $1.50 multicolored   2.25 2.25
720 A110 $3.50 multicolored   5.00 5.00
Nos. 717-720 (4)   10.50 10.50

For surcharges see Nos. B1-B2.

Making of the Film The Wizard of Oz,
50th Anniv. — A111

1989, Sept. 22   Litho.   Perf. 14
721 A111 90c Scarecrow   .95 .95
722 A111 $1.15 Cowardly Lion   1.10 1.10
723 A111 $1.50 Tin Man   1.50 1.50
724 A111 $3.50 Dorothy   3.25 3.25
Nos. 721-724 (4)   6.80 6.80

Souvenir Sheet

725 A111 $5 shown   7.00 7.00
Nos. 721-724 vert.

1st Moon Landing, 20th
Anniv. — A112

Designs: $1.15, Armstrong on ladder,
descending from lunar module. $1.50, Eagle,
astronaut on lunar surface. $3.50, Recovery of
command module after splashdown. $5,
Astronaut on the Moon, vert.

Perf. 13½x14, 14x13½
1989, Dec. 19   Litho.
726 A112 90c shown   .70 .70
727 A112 $1.15 multicolored   .90 .90
728 A112 $1.50 multicolored   1.20 1.20
729 A112 $3.50 multicolored   2.50 2.50
Nos. 726-729 (4)   5.30 5.30

Souvenir Sheet

730 A112 $5 multicolored   7.50 7.50
For overprints see Nos. 847-850.

World
War II
Battle
Ships
A113

1990, Feb. 12   Litho.   Perf. 14
731 A113 70c I.J.N. Yamato   2.25 2.25
732 A113 $1.15 USS Arizona   4.25 4.25
733 A113 $1.50 K.M. Bismarck
on fire   5.50 5.50
734 A113 $3.50 HMS Hood   12.50 12.50
Nos. 731-734 (4)   24.50 24.50

Souvenir Sheet

735 A113 $5 K.M. Bis-
marck, map   20.00 20.00

Nos. 414-418 Surcharged in Bright Rose Lilac

1990, May 3   Perf. 14½
736 A59 70c on 40c #414   1.10 1.10
737 A59 90c on 55c #415   1.40 1.40
738 A59 $1 on $1.20 #416   1.50 1.50
739 A59 $1.15 on $1.20 #417   1.75 1.75
740 A59 $1.50 on $1.20 #418   2.25 2.25
Nos. 736-740 (5)   8.00 8.00

Stamp World London '90.

Penny
Black,
150th
Anniv.
A114

Designs: 90c, Montserrat #5, General P.O.
$1.15, Montserrat #1, postal workers sorting
mail, vert. $1.50, Great Britain #1, man and
woman mailing letters, vert. $3.50, Great Brit-
ain #2, mailman delivering to residence. $5,
Chateau Barrack cover of 1836, Great Britain
#1, landscape.

1990, June 1   Perf. 13½x14, 14x13½
741 A114 90c shown   1.25 1.25
742 A114 $1.15 multicolored   1.60 1.60
743 A114 $1.50 multicolored   1.90 1.90
744 A114 $3.50 multicolored   4.50 4.50
Nos. 741-744 (4)   9.25 9.25

Souvenir Sheet

745 A114 $5 multicolored   10.00 10.00

Stained-glass Windows — A115

1990, Apr. 12   Litho.   Perf. 14x15
746 A115 Strip of 3   7.00 7.00
  a. $1.15 The Empty Tomb   1.25 1.25
  b. $1.50 The Ascension   1.75 1.75

---

  c. $3.50 Risen Christ with Disciples 3.75 3.75

Souvenir Sheet

747 A115 $5 The Crucifixion   7.50 7.50

World Cup Soccer Championships,
Italy — A116

Designs: 90c, Montserrat vs. Antigua.
$1.15, U.S. vs. Trinidad. $1.50, Montserrat
team. $3.50, West Germany vs. Wales. $5,
World Cup trophy.

1990, July 8   Litho.   Perf. 14
748 A116 90c multicolored   .90 .90
749 A116 $1.15 multicolored   1.25 1.25
750 A116 $1.50 multicolored   1.60 1.60
751 A116 $3.50 multicolored   3.75 3.75
Nos. 748-751 (4)   7.50 7.50

Souvenir Sheet

752 A116 $5 multicolored   8.75 8.75

Spinner
Dolphin
A117

1990, Sept. 25   Litho.   Perf. 14
753 A117 90c shown   2.10 1.10
754 A117 $1.15 Common
dolphin   2.50 1.60
755 A117 $1.50 Striped
dolphin   3.50 3.25
756 A117 $3.50 Atlantic spot-
ted dolphin   5.75 6.25
Nos. 753-756 (4)   13.85 12.20

Souvenir Sheet

757 A117 $5 Atlantic white-
sided dolphin 15.00 15.00

Fish
A118

1991, Feb. 7   Litho.   Perf. 14
758 A118 90c Spotted goatfish   1.75 1.75
759 A118 $1.15 Cushion star-
fish   2.25 2.25
760 A118 $1.50 Rock beuaty   3.00 3.00
761 A118 $3.50 French grunt   6.50 6.50
Nos. 758-761 (4)   13.50 13.50

Souvenir Sheet

762 A118 $5 Trunkfish   14.00 14.00

For surcharges and overprints see Nos.
O98-O99, O104, O107.

Birds
A119

1991, Apr. 17   Litho.   Perf. 14
763 A119 90c Duck   1.00 1.00
764 A119 $1.15 Hen, chicks   1.40 1.40
765 A119 $1.50 Rooster   1.60 1.60
766 A119 $3.50 Helmeted guinea
fowl   4.00 4.00
Nos. 763-766 (4)   8.00 8.00

For surcharges and overprints see Nos.
O100, O102, O105, O108.

Nos. 684-685, 692, 695 Surcharged

1991   Litho.   Perf. 14
767 A104 5c on 20c #684   .40 .40
768 A104 5c on 25c #685   .40 .40
769 A104 $1.15 on $1.50 #692   4.75 4.75
770 A104 $1.15 on $7.50 #695   4.75 4.75
Nos. 767-770 (4)   10.30 10.30

Mushrooms
A120

1991, June 13   Litho.   Perf. 14
771 A120 90c Panaeolus antillarum   1.50 1.50
772 A120 $1.15 Cantharellus
cinnabarinus   1.90 1.90
773 A120 $1.50 Gymnopilus
chrysopellus   2.50 2.50
774 A120 $2 Psilocybe
cubensis   3.50 3.50
775 A120 $3.50 Leptonia
caeruleo-
capitata   5.75 5.75
Nos. 771-775 (5)   15.15 15.15

Lilies — A121

1991, Aug. 8
776 A121 90c Red water lily   .95 .95
777 A121 $1.15 Shell ginger   1.25 1.25
778 A121 $1.50 Early day lily 1.50 1.50
779 A121 $3.50 Anthurium   3.50 3.50
Nos. 776-779 (4)   7.20 7.20

For surcharges and overprints see Nos.
O101, O103, O106, O109.

Frogs and
Toads — A122

1991, Oct. 9   Litho.   Perf. 14
780 A122 $1.15 Tree frog   2.75 2.75
781 A122 $2 Crapaud toad   5.00 5.00
782 A122 $3.50 Mountain
chicken   8.00 8.00
Nos. 780-782 (3)   15.75 15.75

Souvenir Sheet
Perf. 14½x14

783 A122 $5 Sheet of 1   14.50 14.50

No. 783 contains one 81x48mm stamp that
incorporates designs of Nos. 780-782.

Cats
A123

1991, Dec. 5
784 A123 90c Black British
shorthair   1.90 1.90
785 A123 $1.15 Seal point sia-
mese   2.50 2.50
786 A123 $1.50 Silver tabby
persian   3.25 3.25
787 A123 $2.50 Birman temple
cat   5.25 5.25
788 A123 $3.50 Egyptian mau   7.00 7.00
Nos. 784-788 (5)   19.90 19.90

Discovery of America, 500th Anniv. A124

No. 789: a, $1.50, Navigating instruments. b, $1.50, Coat of arms, Columbus. c, $1.50, Columbus, Bahamian natives. d, $1.50, Queen Isabella, Columbus with petition. e, $1.50, Exotic birds. f, $1.50, Exotic plants. g, $3.00, Santa Maria, Nina & Pinta.

1992, Jan. 16   *Perf. 14*
789 A124 Sheet of 7, #a.-g.   17.50 17.50

No. 789g is 85x28mm. See No. 829.

Dinosaurs A125

1992, Aug. 1   Litho.   *Perf. 14*
790 A125 $1 Tyrannosaurus   2.10 2.10
791 A125 $1.15 Diplodocus   2.40 2.40
792 A125 $1.50 Apatosaurus   3.00 3.00
793 A125 $3.45 Dimetrodon   7.00 7.00
   Nos. 790-793 (4)   14.50 14.50

Souvenir Sheet
794 A125 $4.60 Owen with bone, vert.   12.50 12.50

Sir Richard Owen, cent. of death.

1992 Summer Olympics, Barcelona A126

1992, Apr. 10
795 A126 $1 Torch bearer   1.25 1.25
796 A126 $1.15 Flags   1.50 1.50
797 A126 $2.30 Olympic flame, map   2.75 2.75
798 A126 $3.60 Various events   4.50 4.50
   Nos. 795-798 (4)   10.00 10.00

Montserrat Oriole — A127

1992, June 30   Litho.   *Perf. 13½x14*
799 A127 $1 Male   1.50 1.50
800 A127 $1.15 Male, female   1.75 1.75
801 A127 $1.50 Female feeding chicks   2.25 2.25
802 A127 $3.60 Map, male   5.50 5.50
   Nos. 799-802 (4)   11.00 11.00

Insects A128

1992, Aug. 20   Litho.   *Perf. 15x14*
803 A128 5c Grasshopper   .30 .30
804 A128 10c Field cricket   .30 .30
805 A128 15c Dragonfly   .30 .30
806 A128 20c Red skimmer   .30 .30
807 A128 25c Pond skater   .30 .30
808 A128 40c Leaf weevil   .40 .45
809 A128 55c Leaf cutter ants   .55 .60
810 A128 70c Paper wasp   .70 .75
811 A128 90c Bee fly   .95 1.10
812 A128 $1 Lacewing   1.10 1.20
813 A128 $1.15 Orange-barred sulphur   1.20 1.30

814 A128 $1.50 Painted lady   1.50 1.75
815 A128 $3 Bella moth   3.00 3.50
816 A128 $5 Plume moth   5.00 5.75
817 A128 $7.50 White peacock   8.00 8.75
818 A128 $10 Postman   10.50 12.00
   Nos. 803-818 (16)   34.40 38.65

For overprints see #871-872, O110-O125.

A used example of No. 806 with a 10c surcharge was shown to the editors, but Montserrat Postal officials were unable to provide any information about it stating "this was prior to the appointment of the present manager." The editors would like to receive information from any knowledgeable source about this stamp, an example of No. 810 with a 5c surcharge, and the possible existence of other similar surcharges.

Christmas — A129

Designs: $1.15, Adoration of the Magi. $4.60, Angel appearing before shepherds.

1992, Nov. 26   Litho.   *Perf. 13½x14*
819 A129 $1.15 multicolored   1.75 1.75
820 A129 $4.60 multicolored   7.25 7.25

Coins and Bank Notes — A130

Designs: $1, One-dollar coin, twenty-dollar notes. $1.15, Ten-cent, twenty-five cent coins, ten-dollar notes. $1.50, Five-cent coin, five-dollar notes. $3.60, One-cent, two-cent coins, one-dollar notes.

1993, Feb. 10   *Perf. 14x13½*
821 A130 $1 multicolored   1.60 1.60
822 A130 $1.15 multicolored   1.75 1.75
823 A130 $1.50 multicolored   2.25 2.25
824 A130 $3.60 multicolored   5.50 5.50
   Nos. 821-824 (4)   11.10 11.10

Discovery of America, 500th Anniv. (in 1992) — A131

1993, Mar. 10   Litho.   *Perf. 14*
825 A131 $1 Coming ashore   2.25 2.25
826 A131 $2 Natives, ships   4.25 4.25

Organization of East Caribbean States.

Coronation of Queen Elizabeth II, 40th Anniv. — A132

Designs: $1.15, Queen, M.H. Bramble. $4.60, Queen riding in Gold State Coach.

1993, June 2   *Perf. 13½x14*
827 A132 $1.15 multicolored   1.50 1.50
828 A132 $4.60 multicolored   5.50 5.50

Columbus Type of 1992 with Added Text

No. 829: a, $1.15, like #789a. b, $1.15, like #789b. c, $1.15, like #789c. d, $1.50, like #789d. e, $1.50, like #789e. f, $1.50, like #789f. g, $3.45, like #789g.

1993, Sept. 7   Litho.   *Perf. 14*
829 A124 Sheet of 7, #a.-g.   27.50 27.50

Nos. 829a-829g each have different added text.

Royal Air Force, 75th Anniv.
Common Design Type

Designs: 15c, Boeing Sentry, 1993. 55c, Vickers Valiant, 1962. $1.15, Handley Page Hastings, 1958. $3, 1943 Lockheed Ventura, 1943.

No. 834: a, Felixstowe F5, 1921. b, Armstrong Whitworth Atlas, 1934. c, Fairey Gordon, 1935. d, Boulton Paul Overstrand, 1936.

Wmk. 373
1993, Nov. 17   Litho.   *Perf. 14*
830 CD350 15c multicolored   .30 .30
831 CD350 55c multicolored   .80 .80
832 CD350 $1.15 multicolored   1.75 1.75
833 CD350 $3 multicolored   4.25 4.25
   Nos. 830-833 (4)   7.10 7.10

Souvenir Sheet
834 CD350 $1.50 Sheet of 4, #a.-d.   7.25 7.25

Beetles A133

Perf. 15x14
1994, Jan. 21   Litho.   Unwmk.
835 A133 $1 Ground beetle   1.25 1.25
836 A133 $1.15 Click beetle   1.60 1.60
837 A133 $1.50 Harlequin beetle   1.90 1.90
838 A133 $3.45 Leaf beetle   4.50 4.50
   Nos. 835-838 (4)   9.25 9.25

Souvenir Sheet
839 A133 $4.50 Scarab beetle   6.00 6.00

Hibiscus Flowers and Fruits — A134

Designs: 90c, Cotton. $1.15, Sorrel. $1.50, Okra. $3.50, Hibiscus rosa sinensis.

1994, Mar. 22   Litho.   *Perf. 14x13½*
840 A134 90c multicolored   1.25 1.25
841 A134 $1.15 multicolored   1.60 1.60
842 A134 $1.50 multicolored   2.00 2.00
843 A134 $3.50 multicolored   5.00 5.00
   Nos. 840-843 (4)   9.85 9.85

Aquatic Dinosaurs A135

No. 844: a, $1, Elasmosaurus. b, $1.15, Plesiosaurus. c, $1.50, Nothosaurus. d, $3.45, Mosasaurus.

1994, May 6   Litho.   *Perf. 15x14*
844 A135 Strip of 4, #a.-d.   12.50 12.50

1994 World Cup Soccer Championships, U.S. — A136

No. 845: a, 90c, Montserrat youth soccer. b, $1, 1990 World Cup, US vs. England. c, $1.15, Rose Bowl Stadium, Pasadena, Calif., US. d, $3.45, German team, 1990 World Cup Winners.

No. 846: a, Jules Rimet. b, Bobby Moore, England Team Captain, 1966. c, Lew Jaschin. d, Sepp Herberger, German trainer.

1994, May 20   *Perf. 14*
845 A136 Vert. strip of 4, #a.-d.   10.00 10.00

Souvenir Sheet
Perf. 14x14½
846 A136 $2 Sheet of 4, #a.-d. 11.00 11.00

No. 845 printed in sheets of 2 strips + 4 labels.

Nos. 726-729 Ovptd. in Red or Srchd. in Red and Black

Inscribed "Space Anniversaries" and: 40c, "Yuri Gagarin / First man in space / April 12, 1961." $1.15, "First Joint US / Soviet Mission / July 15, 1975." $1.50, "25th Anniversary / First Moon Landing / Apollo XI-July 20, 1994." $2.30, "Columbia / First Space Shuttle / April 12, 1981."

1994, July 20   *Perf. 13½x14*
847 A112 40c on 90c multi   .75 .75
848 A112 $1.15 multi   3.00 3.00
849 A112 $1.50 multi   3.50 3.50
850 A112 $2.30 on $3.50 multi   5.75 5.75
   Nos. 847-850 (4)   13.00 13.00

Obliterator on Nos. 847, 850 is black.

Woodstock Festival, 25th Anniv. A137

1994, Oct. 20   *Perf. 12½*
851 A137 $1.15 1969 Poster   1.90 1.90
852 A137 $1.50 1994 Poster   2.10 2.10

Souvenir Sheets
853 A137 $4.50 like #851   6.00 6.00
854 A137 $4.50 like #852   6.00 6.00

Sea Vegetation A138

1995, Feb. 14   *Perf. 14x15*
855 A138 $1 Sea fan   .85 .85
856 A138 $1.15 Sea lily   1.00 1.00
857 A138 $1.50 Sea pen   1.40 1.40
858 A138 $3.45 Sea fern   3.25 3.25
   Nos. 855-858 (4)   6.50 6.50

Souvenir Sheet
859 A138 $4.50 Sea rose   4.50 4.50

Motion
Pictures,
Cent.
A139

No. 860: a.-i., Various portraits of Marilyn
Monroe.
$6, Marilyn Monroe & Elvis Presley.

1995, June 13   Litho.   Perf. 12½
860 A139 $1.15 Sheet of 9,
            #a-i,   11.50 11.50

Souvenir Sheet
861 A139 $6 multicolored   7.50 7.50

No. 861 contains one 51x57mm stamp.

1995 IAAF World
Track & Field
Championships,
Gothenburg,
Sweden — A140

No. 862: a, Jesse Owens, U.S. b, Eric Lem-
ming, Sweden. c, Rudolf Harbig, Germany. d,
Montserrat youth.

1995, Aug. 3   Perf. 14
862 A140 $1.50 Sheet of 4, #a-d 7.50 7.50

End of
World
War II,
50th
Anniv.
A141

No. 863: a, Atmospheric sounding experi-
ments using V-2 rockets. b, Space Shuttle
Challenger.
No. 864: a, 1st successful nuclear reactor.
b, Calder Hall Atomic Power Station, England.
No. 865: a, Ju88G-7a nightfighter equipped
with SN2 radar. b, NATO Boeing E6 AWACS.
No. 866: a, Gloster Meteor III jet aircraft. b,
British Airways Concorde.

1995, Aug. 15
863 A141 $1.15 Pair, #a.-b.   3.50 3.50
864 A141 $1.15 Pair, #a.-b.   3.50 3.50
865 A141 $1.50 Pair, #a.-b.   4.75 4.75
866 A141 $1.50 Pair, #a.-b.   4.75 4.75
            Nos. 863-866 (4)   16.50 16.50

Nos. 812,
818 Ovptd.

1995   Litho.   Perf. 15x14
871 A128 $1 multicolored   1.25 1.25
872 A128 $10 multicolored   11.00 11.00

UN, 50th
Anniv. — A142

1995, Sept. 4   Litho.   Perf. 14
873 A142 $1.15 Food   1.25 1.25
874 A142 $1.50 Education   1.50 1.50
875 A142 $2.30 Health   2.50 2.50
876 A142 $3 Peace   3.25 3.25
            Nos. 873-876 (4)   8.50 8.50

Souvenir Sheet
877 A142 $6 Justice   7.00 7.00

Natl.
Trust,
25th
Anniv.
A143

Designs: $1.15, Headquarters building.
$1.50, 17th cent. cannon, Bransby Point.
$2.30, Painting of original Galways sugar mill,
vert. $3, Great Alps Falls, vert.

1995, Nov. 15   Litho.   Perf. 14
878-881 A143 Set of 4   12.50 12.50

Scavengers of the Sea — A144

1996, Feb. 14   Litho.   Perf. 15x14
882 A144 $1 Bull shark   1.20 1.20
883 A144 $1.15 Sea mouse   1.40 1.40
884 A144 $1.50 Bristleworm   1.75 1.75
885 A144 $3.45 Prawn xiphocaris 3.75 3.75
            Nos. 882-885 (4)   8.10 8.10

Souvenir Sheet
886 A144 $4.50 Man o'war   6.25 6.25

Radio,
Cent. (in
1995)
A145

Designs: $1.15, Guglielmo Marconi, trans-
mitting equipment, 1901. $1.50, Wireless labo-
ratory, Marconi's yacht, Elettra. $2.30, First
transatlantic radio message, Newfoundland,
1901. $3, First air/ground radio station, Croy-
don, 1920.
$4.50, First radio telescope, Jodrell Bank,
Cheshire, England.

1996, Mar. 19   Litho.   Perf. 14
887-890 A145 Set of 4   8.75 8.75

Souvenir Sheet
891   A145 $4.50 multi   5.25 5.25

1996
Summer
Olympic
Games,
Atlanta
A146

1896 Medalists: $1.15, Paul Masson,
cycling. $1.50, Robert Garrett, discus. $2.30,
Spiridon Louis, marathon. $3, John Boland,
tennis.

1996, June 24   Litho.   Perf. 14
892-895 A146 Set of 4   7.50 7.50

Mythical
Creatures — A147

1996, Aug. 15   Litho.   Perf. 14
896 A147 5c Leprechaun   .25   .25
897 A147 10c Pegasus   .25   .25
898 A147 15c Griffin   .25   .25
899 A147 20c Unicorn   .25   .25
900 A147 25c Gnome   .25   .25
901 A147 40c Mermaid   .40   .40
902 A147 55c Cockatrice   .50   .50
903 A147 70c Fairy   .65   .65
904 A147 90c Goblin   .80   .80
905 A147 $1 Faun   .90   .90
906 A147 $1.15 Dragon   1.00 1.00
907 A147 $1.50 Giant   1.25 1.25
908 A147 $3 Elf   2.40 2.40
909 A147 $5 Centaur   4.00 4.00
910 A147 $7.50 Phoenix   6.00 6.00
911 A147 $10 Erin   7.50 7.50
            Nos. 896-911 (16)   26.65 26.65

For overprints see Nos. O126-O140.

James Dean (1931-55), Actor — A148

Various portraits.

1996, June 28   Litho.   Perf. 12½
912 A148 $1.15 Sheet of 9,
            #a.-i.   11.50 11.50

Souvenir Sheet
913 A148 $6 multicolored   7.50 7.50

No. 913 contains one 51x57mm stamp.
For overprint see No. 921.

Dancing Bears, Emblem of "The
Grateful Dead" — A149

Jerry Garcia
A150

No. 914 — Color of bears: a, blue violet,
green. b, yellow. c, orange, pink.

1996, Oct. 21   Litho.   Perf. 12½
914 A149 $1.15 Strip of 3, #a.-c. 3.75 3.75
915 A150 $6 multicolored   6.75 6.75

For overprint and surcharge see #920A,
928. Compare with #955-956 and #970-83.

Scavenger
Birds
A151

1997, Jan. 28   Litho.   Perf. 14½x14
916 A151 $1 Turkey vulture   1.00 1.00
917 A151 $1.15 American crow   1.25 1.25
918 A151 $1.50 Great skua   1.50 1.50
919 A151 $3.45 Kittiwake   3.50 3.50
            Nos. 916-919 (4)   7.25 7.25

Souvenir Sheet
920 A151 $4.50 King vulture   5.25 5.25

No. 914 Overprinted "Hong Kong '97"
Across Strip in Dark Blue

Methods and Perfs as before
1997, Mar. 26
920A A149 $1.15 Strip of 3,
            #b-d   4.00 4.00

No. 912 Overprinted

Hollywood Legend

Overprints are placed over vertical perfs
separating each column of stamps. Each
stamp in the left and right columns has only
half the overprint. The stamps in the center
column contains two incomplete halves of the
overprint. The overprints also appear twice in
sheet margin.

1997, June 2   Litho.   Perf. 12½
921 A148 $1.15 Sheet of 9,
            #a.-i.   12.50 12.50

Eruption of Mt. Soufriere, Endangered
Species — A152

No. 922: a, Heavy ash eruption, Plymouth,
1995. b, First pyroclastic flow entering sea. c,
Double venting at Castle Peak. d, Mangrove
cuckoo. e, Nocturnal lava flow, Soufriere Hills,
1996. f, Antillean crested hummingbird. g, Ash
cloud engulfing Plymouth. h, Lava spine
extruded, Soufriere Hills, 1996. i, New land
created from pyroclastic flows.

1997, June 23   *Perf. 14*
922 A152 $1.50 Sheet of 9,   12.50 12.50
     #a.-i.
j.   Additional inscription in sheet
    margin   12.50 12.50

    No. 922j is inscribed in sheet margin: "MUSIC FOR" and "IN AID OF THE VICTIMS OF SOUFRIERE HILLS VOLCANO," "ROYAL ALBERT HALL LONDON" and "15th SEPTEMBER 1997."

Elvis Presley
(1935-77)
A153

    American rock stars: No. 924, Jimi Hendrix (1942-70). No. 925, Jerry Garcia (1942-95). No. 926, Janis Joplin (1943-70).

1997, Aug. 29   Litho.   *Perf. 12½*
923 A153 $1.15 multicolored   2.50 2.50
924 A153 $1.15 multicolored   2.50 2.50
925 A153 $1.15 multicolored   2.50 2.50
926 A153 $1.15 multicolored   2.50 2.50
     Nos. 923-926 (4)   10.00 10.00

Abstract
Art — A154

1997, Aug. 29   Litho.   *Perf. 12½*
927 A154 $1.50 multicolored   2.50 2.50

No. 915
Surcharged
in Gold and
Black

1997   Litho.   *Perf. 12½*
928 A150 $1.50 on $6 multi   3.00 3.00

Medicinal
Plants — A155
               A156

1998, Mar. 30   Litho.   *Perf. 15*
929 A155 $1   Prickly pear   .75 .75
930 A155 $1.15 Pomme coolie   .85 .85
931 A155 $1.50 Aloe   1.10 1.10
932 A155 $3.45 Bird pepper   2.75 2.75
     Nos. 929-932 (4)   5.45 5.45

1998, May 18   Litho.   *Perf. 12½*
    Famous People of the 20th Cent.: No. 933, Jean-Henri Dunant. No. 934, Mohandas Gandhi. No. 935, Pablo Picasso. No. 936, David Ben-Gurion. No. 937, Dwidght D. Eisenhower. No. 938, Wernher von Braun. No. 939, Eva & Juan Perón. No. 940, Konrad Adenauer. No.

941, Mao Tse-tung. No. 942, Lord Mountbatten. No. 943, Charles Lindbergh. No. 944, Anne Frank. No. 3, John F. Kennedy.

933 A156 $1.15 multicolored   2.00 2.00
934 A156 $1.15 multicolored   2.00 2.00
935 A156 $1.15 multicolored   2.00 2.00
936 A156 $1.15 multicolored   2.00 2.00
937 A156 $1.15 multicolored   2.00 2.00
938 A156 $1.15 multicolored   2.00 2.00
939 A156 $1.15 multicolored   2.00 2.00
940 A156 $1.50 multicolored   2.75 2.75
941 A156 $1.50 multicolored   2.75 2.75
942 A156 $1.50 multicolored   2.75 2.75
943 A156 $1.50 multicolored   2.75 2.75
944 A156 $1.50 multicolored   2.75 2.75
     Nos. 933-944 (12)   27.75 27.75

Souvenir Sheet
945 A156 $3 multicolored   5.00 5.00

    No. 945 contains one 51x38mm stamp. Issued in sheets of 4 with illustrated right margin.

1998, May 18   Litho.   *Perf. 12½*
    Royalty of the 20th cent.: No. 946, Grand Duchess Charlotte (1896-1985) & Felix, Luxembourg. No. 947, Leopold III (1901-83) & Astrid, Belgium. No. 948, Wilhelmina (1880-1962), Netherlands. No. 949, Gustav V (1858-1950), Sweden. No. 950, Alfonso XIII (1886-1931), Spain. No. 951, Christian X (1870-1947), Denmark. No. 952, Haakon VII (1872-1957) & Olav, Denmark. No. 953, George VI (1895-1952), Great Britain.

946 A156 $1.15 multicolored   1.40 1.40
947 A156 $1.15 multicolored   1.40 1.40
948 A156 $1.50 multicolored   1.60 1.60
949 A156 $1.50 multicolored   1.60 1.60
950 A156 $1.50 multicolored   1.60 1.60
951 A156 $1.50 multicolored   1.60 1.60
952 A156 $1.50 multicolored   1.60 1.60
953 A156 $1.50 multicolored   1.60 1.60
     Nos. 946-953 (8)   12.40 12.40

    Issued in sheets of 4 with illustrated right margin.

Bob Marley
(1947-81)
A157

Various portraits.

1998, Aug. 6
954 A157 $1.15 Sheet of 8,   14.00 14.00
     #a.-h. + label

Jerry Garcia
(1947-95)
A158

Various portraits.

1998, Aug. 6
955 A158 $1.15 Sheet of 9,   14.00 14.00
     #a.-i.
Souvenir Sheet
956 A158 $5 multicolored   8.00 8.00

    No. 956 contains one 51x76mm stamp. Compare with #914-915 and #970-983.

Eclipse of the Sun, Feb. 26,
1998 — A159

    Views of Mt. Soufriere volcano: No. 957, Homes near water. No. 958, Looking across mountain tops. No. 959, Ash on mountainside, home. No. 960, Ash, steam rising in air. $6, View of eclipse, vert.

1998   Litho.   *Perf. 12½*
957 A159 $1.15 multicolored   2.00 2.00
958 A159 $1.15 multicolored   2.00 2.00
959 A159 $1.15 multicolored   2.00 2.00
960 A159 $1.15 multicolored   2.00 2.00
     Nos. 957-960 (4)   8.00 8.00

Souvenir Sheet
961 A159 $6 multicolored   7.75 7.75

Diana,
Princess of
Wales
(1961-97)
A160

1998   Litho.   *Perf. 12½*
962 A160 $1.15 As bride   1.90 1.90
963 A160 $1.50 Princess of charities   2.25 2.25
964 A160 $3 At Royal Ascot   4.25 4.25
     Nos. 962-964 (3)   8.40 8.40
Souvenir Sheet
965 A160 $6 Rose, Diana   8.00 8.00

    No. 965 contains one 51x38mm stamp.

Nos. 592-593 Ovptd. in Red with
emblem and "13th WORLD
JAMBOREE MONDIALE CHILE 1999"
Wmk. 380

1998, Dec. 29   Litho.   *Perf. 15*
966 20c Pair, #a.-b.   .75 .75
967 75c Pair, #a.-b.   2.75 2.75

Nos. 873-874
Overprinted

Unwmk.
1999, Apr. 27   Litho.   *Perf. 14*
968 A142 $1.15 on #873   2.75 2.75
969 A142 $1.50 on #874   3.25 3.25

Jerry Garcia (1947-95) — A161

    Garcia: No. 970, $1.15, Wearing purple shirt, microphone at right, light blue background. No. 971, $1.15, In red light, dark blue background. No. 972, $1.15, Wearing purple shirt, microphone at left. No. 973, $1.15, Like #971, blue green background. No. 974, $1.15, Wearing black shirt, playing guitar. No. 975, $1.15, Wearing red shirt. No. 976, $1.15, Wearing blue shirt, microphone at right, vert. No. 977, $1.15, Wearing blue shirt, microphone to left of face, vert. No. 978, $1.15, Wearing blue shirt, microphone partially covering face, vert. No. 979, $1.15,

---

Wearing black shirt, orange rectangular frame, vert. No. 980, $1.15, Wearing blue shirt, orange and blue frame, vert. No. 981, $1.15, Wearing black shirt, orange and blue frame, vert.
    No. 982, $6, Vignette of #980. No. 983, $6, Wearing black shirt, vert.

1999   Litho.   Unwmk.   *Perf. 12½*
970-981 A161   Set of 12   20.00 20.00
Souvenir Sheets
982-983 A161   Set of 2   20.00 20.00

    Issued in sheets of 9 containing 3 each of Nos. 970-972, 973-975, 976-978, 979-981 respectively. Nos. 982-983 contain one 76x51mm or 51x76mm stamp, respectively. Compare with #914-915 and #955-956.

Fruit
A162

1999   Litho.   Wmk. 380   *Perf. 12½*
984 A162 $1.15 Mango   1.10 1.10
985 A162 $1.50 Breadfruit   1.50 1.50
986 A162 $2.30 Papaya   2.40 2.40
987 A162 $3 Lime   3.00 3.00
988 A162 $6 Akee   6.25 6.25
a.   Sheet of 5, #984-988 +label   15.00 15.00
     Nos. 984-988 (5)   14.25 14.25

Dogs
A163

1999
989 A163 70c Yorkshire terrier   1.30 1.30
990 A163 $1 Welsh corgi   2.25 2.25
991 A163 $1.15 King Charles spaniel   2.25 2.25
992 A163 $1.50 Poodle   3.25 3.25
993 A163 $3 Beagle   6.25 6.25
a.   Sheet of 5, #989-993 + label   15.00 15.00
     Nos. 989-993 (5)   15.30 15.30

World Teachers'
Day — A164

    World map and: $1, Ruler, scissors, compass, pencil, paint brush. $1.15, Teacher lecturing. $1.50, Compass, flag, camera, globe, plumb bob, theodolite. $5, Pen, flask, funnel, thermometer, calipers, microscope.

1999   Litho.   *Perf. 12½*
994-997 A164   Set of 4   14.00 14.00

Worldwide
Fund for
Nature
A165

    No. 998 — Great hammerhead shark: a, Pair swimming. b, Pair near ocean floor. c, Trio swimming. d, One swimming.

           Perf. 13¼
1999, Nov. 29   Litho.   Unwmk.
998   Horiz. strip of 4   4.00 4.00
a.-d. A165 50c Any single   .80 .80

Millennium — A166

2000, Jan. 1   **Unwmk.**
999 A166 $1.50 multi   3.50 3.50

100th Test Cricket
Match at Lord's
Ground — A167

Designs: $1, Alfred Valentine. $5, George
Headley.
$6, Lord's Ground, horiz.

2000, May 5   **Litho.**   **Perf. 13½x13¼**
1000-1001 A167   Set of 2   7.50 7.50
Souvenir Sheet
Perf. 13¼x13½
1002 A167 $6 multi   10.00 10.00

The
Stamp
Show
2000,
London
A168

Battle of Britain, 60th anniv.: 70c, Scramble.
$1.15, Hurricane Mk.1 overhaul. $1.50, Hurricane Mk. 1 and enemy plane. $5, Spitfire Mk.
1a of Flight Lt. Frank Howell.
$6, Plane in air.

Wmk. 373
2000, May 22   **Litho.**   **Perf. 14**
1003 A168   70c multi   .70 .70
1004 A168 $1.15 multi   1.10 1.10
1005 A168 $1.50 multi   1.50 1.50
1006 A168 $5 multi   5.00 5.00
     Nos. 1003-1006 (4)   8.30 8.30
Souvenir Sheet
1007 A168 $6 multi   7.00 7.00

Millennium — A169

People of Montserrat and: 90c, Statue of
Liberty. $1.15, Great Wall of China. $1.50, Eif-
fel Tower. $3.50, Millennium Dome, Great
Britain.

Perf. 13½
2000, July 3   **Litho.**   **Unwmk.**
1008-1011 A169   Set of 4   7.25 7.25

Queen
Mother,
100th
Birthday
A170

Queen Mother and various buildings. Panel
color under country name in: 70c, Yellow.
$1.15, Purple. $3, Green. $6, Orange.

2000, Aug. 4   **Perf. 13½x13**
1012-1015 A170   Set of 4   11.50 11.50
   1015a   Souvenir sheet, #1012-
       1015   13.50 13.50

Christmas
A171

Designs: $1, The three Magi. $1.15, Cavalla
Hill Methodist Church. $1.50, Shepherds. $3,
$6, Mary and Joseph arriving in Bethlehem.

Perf. 14x14¾
2000, Nov. 29   **Wmk. 373**
1016-1019 A171   Set of 4   7.25 7.25
Souvenir Sheet
1020 A171 $6 multi   8.00 8.00

Birds
A172

Designs: $1, Golden swallow, vert. $1.15,
Crested quail dove. $1.50, Red-legged thrush.
$5, Fernandina's flicker, vert.
$8, St. Vincent parrot.

2001, Mar. 26   **Litho.**   **Perf. 13¼**
1021-1024 A172   Set of 4   12.00 12.00
Souvenir Sheet
1025 A172 $8 St. Vincent par-
         rot   10.00 10.00

Philatelic Personalities — A173

Designs: $1, Edward Stanley Gibbons,
Charles J. Phillips. $1.15, John Lister. $1.50,
Theodore Champion and 19th cent. French
postilion. $3, Thomas de la Rue.
$8, Sir Rowland Hill, Bruce Castle.

2001, Apr. 30   **Perf. 13¼**
1026-1029 A173   Set of 4   9.00 9.00
Souvenir Sheet
1030 A173 $8 multi   10.00 10.00

Queen Elizabeth
II, 75th
Birthday — A174

Dress color: 90c, Black. $1.15, Yellow.
$1.50, Pink. $5, Green.
$6, Lilac.

2001, June 22   **Perf. 13¼**
1031-1034 A174   Set of 4   10.00 10.00
Souvenir Sheet
1035 A174 $6 multi   9.00 9.00

Buildings — A175

Designs: 70c, Lookout community. $1, St.
John's Hospital. $1.15, Tropical Mansion
Suites. $1.50, Montserrat Secondary School.
$3, Golden Years Home.

2001, Aug. 15   **Litho.**   **Perf. 13½**
1036-1040 A175   Set of 5   10.00 10.00

Fruit
A176

Designs: 5c, West Indian cherries. 10c
Mammee apples. 15c, Limes. 20c,
Grapefruits. 25c, Orange. 40c, Passion fruits.
55c, Bananas. 70c, Papayas. 90c,
Pomegranates. $1, Guavas. $1.15, Mangos.
$1.50, Sugar apple. $3, Cashews. $5, Sour-
sops. $7.50, Watermelon. $10, Pineapple.

2001, Oct. 10   **Litho.**   **Perf. 13½x13¼**
1041 A176   5c multi   .25 .25
1042 A176   10c multi   .25 .25
1043 A176   15c multi   .25 .25
1044 A176   20c multi   .25 .25
1045 A176   25c multi   .25 .25
1046 A176   40c multi   .40 .40
1047 A176   55c multi   .50 .50
1048 A176   70c multi   .65 .65
1049 A176   90c multi   .85 .85
1050 A176 $1 multi   1.00 1.00
1051 A176 $1.15 multi   1.10 1.10
1052 A176 $1.50 multi   1.40 1.40
1053 A176 $3 multi   3.00 3.00
1054 A176 $5 multi   4.75 4.75
1055 A176 $7.50 multi   7.50 7.50
1056 A176 $10 multi   9.75 9.75
    Nos. 1041-1056 (16)   32.15 32.15

Butterflies — A177

Designs: $1, Common long-tail skipper.
$1.15, Straight-line skipper. $1.50, Giant hairstreak. $3, Monarch.
$10, Painted lady.

2001, Dec. 20   **Litho.**   **Perf. 13¼**
1057-1060 A177   Set of 4   8.50 8.50
Souvenir Sheet
1061 A177 $10 multi   12.50 12.50

2002 Winter Olympics, Salt Lake
City — A178

No. 1062: a, $3, Downhill skiing. b, $5,
Bobsled.

2002, Mar. 12   **Litho.**   **Perf. 13¼**
1062 A178   Horiz. pair, #a-b   9.50 9.50

Fish
A179

Designs: $1, Sergeant major. $1.15, Mutton
snapper. $1.50, Lantern bass. $5, Shy hamlet.
$8, Queen angelfish.

Perf. 13¼
2002, July 29   **Litho.**   **Unwmk.**
1063-1066 A179   Set of 4   11.50 11.50
Souvenir Sheet
1067 A179 $8 multi   10.50 10.50

Nos. 1012-1015 Overprinted

2002, Sept. 23   **Litho.**   **Perf. 13½x13**
1068 A170   70c on #1012   .75 .75
1069 A170 $1.15 on #1013   1.25 1.25
1070 A170 $3 on #1014   3.25 3.25
1071 A170 $6 on #1015   6.75 6.75
    Nos. 1068-1071 (4)   12.00 12.00

Wild Flowers — A180

Designs: 70c, Allamanda cathartica. $1.15,
Lantana camara. $1.50, Leonotis nepetifolia.
$5, Plumeria rubra.
$8, Alpinia purpurata.

Perf. 13¼
2002, Nov. 29   **Litho.**   **Unwmk.**
1072-1075 A180   Set of 4   12.00 12.00
Souvenir Sheet
1076 A180 $8 multi   11.00 11.00

Coronation of Queen Elizabeth II, 50th
Anniv. — A181

No. 1077: a, Queen wearing crown. b,
Crown on pillow. c, Queen wearing tiara and
purple sash.
$6, Queen wearing crown, diff.

2003, Apr. 30   **Perf. 14**
1077 A181 $3 Sheet of 3, #a-c   9.50 9.50
Souvenir Sheet
1078 A181 $6 multi   5.50 5.50

Powered Flight, Cent. — A182

No. 1079: a, Wright Flyer II in blue. b, Wright
Flyer II in brown. c, Wright Brothers. d, Wright
Flyer I.
$6, Wright Flyer II.

2003, June 30   **Litho.**   **Perf. 14**
1079 A182 $2 Sheet of 4, #a-d   9.25 9.25
Souvenir Sheet
1080 A182 $6 multi   8.00 8.00

Prince William, 21st Birthday — A183

No. 1081 — Prince William in suit and tie with: a, Frame obscured at LL and LR by portrait. b, Frame obscured at LL by portrait. c, Frame not obscured.
$6, Wearing sweater and shirt with open collar.

2003, Aug. 20
1081 A183 $3 Sheet of 3, #a-c   10.00 10.00
Souvenir Sheet
1082 A183 $6 multi   8.00 8.00

Fauna — A184

No. 1083: a, Piping frog. b, Land hermit crab. c, Spix's pinche. d, Dwarf gecko. e, Green sea turtle. f, Indian mongoose.
$6, Sally Lightfoot crab.

2003, Nov. 28
1083 A184 $1.50 Sheet of 6,
     #a-f   10.00 10.00
Souvenir Sheet
1084 A184 $6 multi   7.00 7.00

Mushrooms — A185

No. 1085: a, Slimy lead milk cap. b, Rosy spike cap. c, Stump puffball. d, Parasol. e, Crab russula. f, Scaly vase chanterelle.
$6, Fly agaric.

2003, Nov. 28
1085 A185 $1.50 Sheet of 6,
     #a-f   10.00 10.00
Souvenir Sheet
1086 A185 $6 multi   7.25 7.25

Birds A186

Designs: 90c, Belted kingfisher. $1.15, Yellow warbler. No. 1089, $1.50, Hooded warbler. $5, Cedar waxwing.
No. 1091: a, Roseate spoonbill. b, Laughing gull. c, White-tailed tropicbird. d, Bare-eyed thrush. e, Glittering-throated emerald. f, Lesser Antillean grackle.
$6, Bananaquit.

2003, Nov. 28
1087-1090 A186   Set of 4   12.00 12.00
1091 A186 $1.50 Sheet of 6,
     #a-f   9.50 9.50
Souvenir Sheet
1092 A186 $6 multi   7.00 7.00

2004 Summer Olympics, Greece A187

Designs: 90c, 1932 Los Angeles Olympics poster. $1.15, 1972 Munich Olympics pin. $1.50, 1976 Montreal Olympics poster. $5, Pankration, horiz.

2004, June 30   Litho.   Perf. 13¼
1093-1096 A187   Set of 4   9.25 9.25

Butterflies — A188

No. 1097: a, Lacewing. b, Swallowtail. c, Shoemaker. d, White peacock.
$6, Flashing astraptes.

2004, July 6   Litho.   Perf. 14
1097 A188 $2.30 Sheet of 4,
     #a-d   9.25 9.25
Souvenir Sheet
1098 A188 $6 multi   5.00 5.00

Cats — A189

Designs: $1.15, Singapura. $1.50, Burmese. $2, Abyssinian. $5, Norwegian.
$6, Russian Blue.

2004, Aug. 23
1099-1102 A189   Set of 4   10.50 10.50
Souvenir Sheet
1103 A189 $6 multi   9.00 9.00

Fish — A190

No. 1104: a, Blue-girdled angelfish. b, Regal angelfish. c, Emperor angelfish. d, Blotch-eyed soldierfish.
$6, Banded butterflyfish.

2004, Sept. 30
1104 A190 $2.30 Sheet of 4,
     #a-d   9.50 9.50
Souvenir Sheet
1105 A190 $6 multi   8.00 8.00

Locomotives, 200th Anniv. — A191

No. 1106: a, Austerity. b, Deli Vasut. c, Class 424 No. 424.247/287. d, L-1646. e, Steam locomotive 324.1564. f, Class Ia.
No. 1107: a, Old Class TV. b, Class Va 7111. c, Class 424 No. 424.009. d, Class III.
$6, Class QR1.

2004, Oct. 29   Perf. 14½x14
1106 A191 $1.50 Sheet of 6,
     #a-f   7.75 7.75
1107 A191 $2 Sheet of 4,
     #a-d   6.75 6.75
Souvenir Sheet
1108 A191 $6 multi   5.00 5.00

World AIDS Day — A192

2004, Dec. 1   Perf. 13½
1109 A192 $3 multi   2.50 2.50
Printed in sheets of 4.

D-Day, 60th Anniv. A193

Designs: $1.15, Air assault begins. $1.50, Troops assault beaches of Normandy. $2, Field Marshal Montgomery. $5, HMS Belfast.

2004, Dec. 24   Perf. 14
1110-1113 A193   Set of 4   9.00 9.00

National Soccer Team — A194

2004, Dec. 24   Litho.   Perf. 12
1114 A194 $6 multi   5.00 5.00

Nos. 1036-1040 Overprinted

THE VISIT OF
HRH THE PRINCESS ROYAL
FEBRUARY 2005

2005, Feb. 21   Litho.   Perf. 13½
1115 A175 70c multi   .60 .60
1116 A175 $1 multi   .80 .80
1117 A175 $1.15 multi   .95 .95
1118 A175 $1.50 multi   1.25 1.25
1119 A175 $3 multi   2.50 2.50
   Nos. 1115-1119 (5)   6.10 6.10

Birds — A195

No. 1120: a, Brown pelican. b, Red-billed tropicbird. c, Galapagos Island cormorant. d, Waved albatross.
$6, Common tern.

2005, Apr. 25   Litho.   Perf. 13¼x13½
1120 A195 $2.30 Sheet of 4,
     #a-d   7.75 7.75
Souvenir Sheet
1121 A195 $6 multi   5.50 5.50

Orchids — A196

No. 1122: a, Cattleya lueddemanniana. b, Cattleya luteola. c, Cattleya trianaei. d, Cattleya mossiae.
$6, Cattleya mendelii.

2005, Apr. 25
1122 A196 $2.30 Shoot of 4,
     #a-d   7.75 7.75
Souvenir Sheet
1123 A196 $6 multi   5.00 5.00

Molluscs and Shells A197

Designs: $1.15, Liguus virgineus. $1.50, Liguus fasciatus testudineus. $2, Liguus fasciatus. $5, Cerion striatella. $6, Liguus fasciatus, vert.

2005, June 1　　　　**Perf. 13¼x13½**
1124-1127 A197　Set of 4　　　8.25 8.25
　　　　Souvenir Sheet
　　　　Perf. 13½x13¼
1128 A197　$6 multi　　　　5.50 5.50

Miniature Sheet

Soufriere Hills Volcanic Eruption, 10th Anniv. — A198

No. 1129: a, Dome glow. b, Explosion. c, Tar River Delta. d, Belham River. e, MVO Building. f, Pyroclastic flow entering the sea. g, Blackburne Airport, destroyed in 1997. h, Helicopter maintenance and monitoring. i, Instruments used for monitoring.

2005, July 18　Litho.　**Perf. 14**
1129 A198　$2 Sheet of 9, #a-i　16.00 16.00

Rotary International, Cent. — A199

Emblem and: $1, Shamrock. $1.15, Heliconia flower. $1.50, Lady and the Harp. $5, Map of Montserrat.
$6, Medical care for children, horiz.

2005, Sept. 12　　　　**Perf. 12¾**
1130-1133 A199　Set of 4　　8.00 8.00
　　　　Souvenir Sheet
1134 A199　$6 multi　　　　5.50 5.50

Battle of Trafalgar, Bicent. — A200

No. 1135: a, Napoleon Bonaparte. b, Admiral Horatio Nelson. c, Battle of the Nile. d, Battle of Trafalgar.
$6, Nelson, diff.

2005, Nov. 4　Litho.　**Perf. 12**
1135 A200　$2 Sheet of 4, #a-d　8.00 8.00
　　　　Souvenir Sheet
1136 A200　$6 multi　　　　6.00 6.00

Hans Christian Andersen (1805-75), Author — A201

No. 1137: a, Thumbelina. b, The Flying Trunk. c, The Buckwheat.
$6, The Little Mermaid.

2005, Dec. 23　　　　**Perf. 12¾**
1137 A201　$3 Sheet of 3, #a-c　8.00 8.00
　　　　Souvenir Sheet
　　　　Perf. 12
1138 A201　$6 multi　　　　6.00 6.00
No. 1137 contains three 39x25mm stamps.

Famous People A202

Designs: No. 1139, $1.15, William Henry Bramble (1901-88), first chief minister. No. 1140, $1.15, Michael Simmons Osborne (1902-67), merchant and parliamentarian. No. 1141, $1.15, Robert William Griffith (1904-96), union leader. No. 1142, $1.15, Patricia Griffin (1907-86), social worker. No. 1143, $1.15, Lilian Cadogan (1907-92), nurse. No. 1144, $1.15, Samuel Aymer (1911-79), folk musician.

2005, Dec. 5　Litho.　**Perf. 12¾**
1139-1144 A202　Set of 6　　6.00 6.00
1140a　Inscribed "Symmons" instead
　　　of "Simmons"　　　1.00 1.00
1144a　Souvenir sheet, #1139,
　　　1140a, 1141-1144　　6.00 6.00

Nos. 1022, 1058-1059, 1072 and 1075 Overprinted

Methods and Perfs As Before
2006, Apr. 1
1145 A180　70c on #1072　　.60 .60
1146 A172　$1 on #1022　　.85 .85
1147 A177　$1.15 on #1058　1.00 1.00
1148 A177　$1.50 on #1059　1.25 1.25
1149 A180　$5 on #1075　　4.00 4.00
　　　Nos. 1145-1149 (5)　　7.70 7.70
Overprint is on four lines on No. 1146.

Marine Life — A203

No. 1150: a, Giant Caribbean anemone. b, Beadlet anemone. c, Golden crinoid. d, Oval cup coral.
$6, Tube-dwelling anemone.

2006, May 2　Litho.　**Perf. 12**
1150 A203　$2.30 Sheet of 4, #a-d
　　　　　　　　　9.00 9.00
　　　　Souvenir Sheet
1151 A203　$6 multi　　　　5.75 5.75

Moths — A204

No. 1152: a, Cecropia moth. b, Madagascan sunset moth. c, Great peacock moth. d, Zodiac moth.
$6, White-lined sphinx moth.

2006, May 2
1152 A204　$2.30 Sheet of 4, #a-
　　　　　　　　　9.00 9.00
　　　　Souvenir Sheet
1153 A204　$6 multi　　　　5.75 5.75

Dogs — A205

Designs: $1.15, Rottweiler. $1.50, Boxer. $2, Corgi. $5, Great Dane.
$6, St. Bernard.

2006, Aug. 16
1154-1157 A205　Set of 4　　8.50 8.50
　　　　Souvenir Sheet
1158 A205　$6 multi　　　　5.50 5.50

Worldwide Fund for Nature (WWF) — A206

No. 1159 — Various depictions of Mountain chicken frog: a, 70c. b, $1. c, $1.15. d, $1.50.

2006, Aug. 16　　　　**Perf. 13¼**
1159 A206　Block of 4, #a-d　3.75 3.75
　　e.　Miniature sheet, 2 #1159　7.50 7.50

Souvenir Sheet

2006 World Cup Soccer Championships, Germany — A207

No. 1160 — World Cup, emblem and: a, $1.15, FIFA World Cup Stadium, Hanover. b, $1.50, Sir Stanley Matthews, England team uniform. c, $2, Sir Ralph "Dixie" Dean, England team uniform. d, $5, Bobby Moore, England team uniform.

2006, Aug. 31　　　　**Perf. 12**
1160 A207　Sheet of 4, #a-d　8.00 8.00

Christopher Columbus (1451-1506), Explorer — A208

Designs: $1.15, Map of North and South America, Columbus's vessels. $1.50, Columbus and map of voyage. $2, Ship, Earth, Columbus. $5, Columbus, vert.
$6, Earth, Columbus and crew with flag, vert.

2006, Oct. 27　　　　**Perf. 12¾**
1161-1164 A208　Set of 4　　8.00 8.00
　　　　Souvenir Sheet
1165 A208　$6 multi　　　　5.00 5.00

A209

Queen Elizabeth II, 80th Birthday — A210

No. 1166: a, Queen wearing crown, country name in black. b, Queen wearing crown, country name in white. c, Queen wearing tiara. d, Queen wearing tiara and sash.

2006, Oct. 27　　　　**Perf. 13¼**
1166 A209　$2.30 Sheet of 4, #a-
　　　　　　d　　　　　7.00 7.00
　　　　Souvenir Sheet
1167 A210　$8 shown　　　　6.00 6.00

2007 Cricket World Cup, West Indies — A211

Designs: $3, 2007 Cricket World Cup emblem, map and flag of Montserrat. $5, Cricket team, horiz.
$8, 2007 Cricket World Cup emblem.

2007, Mar. 9　Litho.　**Perf. 13¼**
1168-1169 A211　Set of 2　　6.25 6.25
　　　　Souvenir Sheet
1170 A211　$8 multi　　　　6.25 6.25

Scouting, Cent. — A212

No. 1171, horiz. — Scouts: a, Looking at flower. b, Working at construction site. c, In sailboat. d, Feeding goat. e, Making campfire. f, Installing birdhouse.
$6, Lord Robert Baden-Powell.

2007, Mar. 9
1171 A212 $2 Sheet of 6, #a-f   9.50 9.50
Souvenir Sheet
1172 A212 $6 multi   4.75 4.75

Flowers — A213

Designs: 10c, Poinsettia. 30c, Periwinkle. 35c, Bougainvillea. 50c, Ixora. 70c, Heliconia. 80c, Morning glory. 90c, Poinciana. $1, Cup of gold. $1.10, Chenille plant. $1.50, Oleander. $2.25, Hibiscus. $2.50, Frangipani. $2.75, Bird of paradise. $5, Madagascar jasmine. $10, Yellow poui. $20, Rose.

2007, May 14   Litho.   Perf. 12½
1173 A213 10c multi   .25   .25
1174 A213 30c multi   .25   .25
1175 A213 35c multi   .25   .25
1176 A213 50c multi   .40   .40
1177 A213 70c multi   .55   .55
1178 A213 80c multi   .60   .60
1179 A213 90c multi   .70   .70
1180 A213 $1 multi   .75   .75
1181 A213 $1.10 multi   .85   .85
1182 A213 $1.50 multi 1.10 1.10
1183 A213 $2.25 multi 1.75 1.75
1184 A213 $2.50 multi 1.90 1.90
1185 A213 $2.75 multi 2.10 2.10
1186 A213 $5 multi   3.75 3.75
1187 A213 $10 multi   7.50 7.50
1188 A213 $20 multi   15.00 15.00
Nos. 1173-1188 (16)   37.70 37.70

Princess Diana (1961-97) — A214

No. 1189 — Diana wearing tiara and: a, Blue dress. b, Black dress. c, White dress. d, White dress with high neck.
$7, Diana without tiara.

2007, Aug. 8   Litho.   Perf. 13¼
1189 A214 $3.40 Sheet of 4,
            #a-d   12.00 12.00
Souvenir Sheet
1190 A214 $7 multi   6.00 6.00

Turtles — A215

No. 1191: a, Hawksbill turtle. b, Green turtle. c, Leatherback turtle. d, Loggerhead turtle.
$7, Kemp's Ridley sea turtle.

2007, Aug. 8   Perf. 13¼x13½
1191 A215 $3.40 Sheet of 4,
            #a-d   11.50 11.50
Souvenir Sheet
1192 A215 $7 multi   6.00 6.00

Parrots — A216

No. 1193: a, Green-winged macaw. b, Mitred conure. c, Sun conure. d, Blue-and-yellow macaw.
$7, Hyacinth macaw.

2007, Oct. 11   Litho.   Perf. 13½x13¼
1193 A216 $3.40 Sheet of 4,
            #a-d   13.50 13.50
Souvenir Sheet
1194 A216 $7 multi   9.00 9.00

Lilies — A217

No. 1195, horiz.: a, Hippeastrum puniceum. b, Hymenocallis caribaea. c, Zephyranthes puertoricensis. d, Belamcanda chinensis.
$7, Crinum erubescens.

2007, Oct. 11   Perf. 13¼x13½
1195 A217 $3.40 Sheet of 4,
            #a-d   11.50 11.50
Souvenir Sheet
Perf. 13½x13¼
1196 A217 $7 multi   6.00 6.00

Miniature Sheet

Charles Wesley (1707-88), Hymn Writer — A218

No. 1197: a, Portrait of Wesley by unknown artist. b, Portrait of Wesley by John Russell. c, Engraving of Wesley by Jonathan Spilsbury. d, Bethany Methodist Church.

2007, Dec. 18   Litho.   Perf. 13¼
1197 A218 $2.50 Sheet of 4, #a-
            d   8.00 8.00

Whales — A219

No. 1198: a, Sperm whale. b, Minke whale. c, Cuvier's beaked whale. d, Humpback whale.
$7, Blue whale.

2008, May 2   Perf. 12¾
1198 A219 $3.55 Sheet of 4,
            #a-d   13.00 13.00
Souvenir Sheet
1199 A219 $7 multi   8.00 8.00

Space Exploration, 50th Anniv. — A220

No. 1200, vert.: a, Explorer I on Juno I launch rocket. b, Dr. James Van Allen, Explorer I. c, Explorer I. d, Drs. William Pickering, James Van Allen and Wernher von Braun with Explorer I model.
$7, Explorer I, diff.

2008, May 29   Perf. 13¼
1200 A220 $3.55 Sheet of 4,
            #a-d   12.00 12.00
Souvenir Sheet
1201 A220 $7 multi   6.00 6.00

Endangered Animals — A221

No. 1202, vert.: a, African elephant. b, Bald eagle. c, Sumatran tiger. d, Hawksbill turtle. e, Indian rhinoceros. f, Western gorilla.
$7, Rock iguana.

2008, July 3
1202 A221 $2.25 Sheet of 6,
            #a-f   11.00 11.00
Souvenir Sheet
1203 A221 $7 multi   6.00 6.00

Miniature Sheet

Early Postal History — A222

No. 1204: a, "Lady McLeod" stamp, early paddle packet boat. b, Early Montserrat postal card. c, Great Britain #U1-U2. d, Great Britain #1, Sir Rowland Hill. e, Montserrat #1-2. f, Montserrat cancels.

2008, July 31   Litho.   Perf. 13½
1204 A222 $2.75 Sheet of 6,
            #a-f   13.50 13.50

Miniature Sheets

Royal Air Force, 90th Anniv. — A223

No. 1205, $3.55: a, English Electric Lightning P3. b, Hurricane IIC. c, Jet Provost T3A. d, Jaguar GR3A.
No. 1206, $3.55: a, Westland Sea King HAR3 helicopter. b, Gloster Javelin FAW9. c, P-66 Pembroke C1. d, Chinook HC2 helicopter.

2008, Sept. 5   Litho.   Perf. 13¼
Sheets of 4, #a-d
1205-1206 A223 Set of 2   25.00 25.00

University of the West Indies, 60th Anniv. — A224

Designs: $2, Building on Montserrat campus. $5, University arms, diploma.

2008, Sept. 30
1207-1208 A224 Set of 2   6.00 6.00

Miniature Sheets

Orchids — A225

No. 1209, $2.75: a, Cattleya labiata. b, Phalaenopsis cultivar with pink spots. c, Cymbidium annabelle. d, Phalaenopsis taisuco.
No. 1210, $2.75: a, Phalaenopsis amabilis. b, Cattleya aurantiaca. c, Phalaenopsis cultivar with pink lines. d, Dendrobium nobile.

2008, Nov. 27   Perf. 13¼
Sheets of 4, #a-d
1209-1210 A225 Set of 2   19.00 19.00

Dolphins — A226

No. 1211: a, Common dolphin. b, Bottlenose dolphin. c, Pantropical spotted dolphin. d, Long-snouted spinner dolphin.
$7, Risso's dolphin.

2008, Nov. 27   Perf. 12¾
1211 A226 $3.55 Sheet of 4,
            #a-d   12.50 12.50
Souvenir Sheet
1212 A226 $7 multi   5.75 5.75

Miniature Sheet

New Year 2009 (Year of the Ox) — A227

No. 1213: a, Yellow orange ox facing right. b, Black ox facing left. c, Gray ox facing right. d, White ox facing left.

2009, Feb. 2   Litho.   Perf. 12¾
1213 A227 $3.55 Sheet of 4, #a-d   13.00 13.00

Miniature Sheets

Dr. Martin Luther King, Jr. (1929-68), Civil Rights Leader — A228

No. 1214, $2.50: a, King. b, King at desk. c, King wearing hat. d, King's wife, Coretta.
No. 1215, $2.50, horiz.: a, March on Washington crowd. b, King meeting Malcolm X. c, King with Pres. John F. Kennedy and other civil rights leaders. d, King waving to March on Washington crowd.

2009, Feb. 26   Perf. 13½
Sheets of 4, #a-d
1214-1215 A228 Set of 2   16.00 16.00

Birds — A229

No. 1216: a, Smooth-billed ani. b, American kestrel. c, Common moorhen. d, Cattle egret.
$7, Male Montserrat oriole.

2009, Apr. 1
1216 A229 $2.75 Sheet of 4, #a-d   9.00 9.00
Souvenir Sheet
1217 A229 $7 multi   6.50 6.50

Corals — A230

Designs: $1.10, Staghorn coral. $2.25, Zoanthid coral. $2.50, Blade fire coral. $2.75, Brain coral.
$7, Orange tube coral, vert.

2009, Apr. 29
1218-1221 A230 Set of 4   7.00 7.00
Souvenir Sheet
1222 A230 $7 multi   6.00 6.00
No. 1222 contains one 37x51mm stamp.

Charles Darwin (1809-82), Naturalist — A231

No. 1223, vert.: a, Darwin. b, Coenobita clypeatus. c, Anolis lividus. d, Epidendrum montserratense.
$7, Darwin, waterfall, emblem of Montserrat Centre Hills Project.

2009, July 28
1223 A231 $2.75 Sheet of 4, #a-d   8.50 8.50
Souvenir Sheet
1224 A231 $7 multi   6.00 6.00

Rain Forest Animals — A232

No. 1225: a, $1.10, Green iguana. b, $2.25, Galliwasp. c, $2.50, Black snake. d, $2.75, Common agouti.
$5, Yellow-shouldered bat.

2009, Sept. 25   Litho.   Perf. 13¼
1225 A232   Sheet of 4, #a-d   7.50 7.50
Souvenir Sheet
1226 A232 $5 multi   4.25 4.25

Trees — A233

Designs: $1.10, Tamarind. $2.25, Dwarf coconut. $2.50, Breadfruit. $2.75, Calabash. $5, Geiger.

2009, Oct. 30   Perf. 14¼x14¾
1227-1231 A233 Set of 5   10.50 10.50

Miniature Sheet

Naval Aviation, Cent. — A234

No. 1232 — Aircraft carriers: a, 70c, HMS Ark Royal II. b, $1.10, HMS Furious. c, $2.25, HMS Argus. d, $2.50, HMS Illustrious. e, $2.75, HMS Ark Royal IV. f, $5, HMS Invincible.

2009, Dec. 4   Litho.   Perf. 11½x11¼
1232 A234   Sheet of 6, #a-f   11.00 11.00

A235

Christmas — A236

Designs: $1.10, Snowflake bush. $2.25, Carnival troupe. $2.50, Masquerade. $2.75, St. Patrick's Roman Catholic Church.
$6, Creche figurines of Holy Family.

2009, Dec. 18   Perf. 12¾
1233-1236 A235 Set of 4   6.75 6.75
Souvenir Sheet
1237 A236 $6 multi   5.25 5.25

Marine Life A237

Designs: $1.10, Basket star. $2.25, Spiny lobster. $2.50, Spotted drum. $2.75, Sea anemone, vert. $5, Batwing coral crab.

2010, Mar. 15   Perf. 14¼
1238-1242 A237 Set of 5   10.50 10.50

Miniature Sheets

World Landmarks — A238

No. 1243: a, $1.10, Jin Mao Tower, Shanghai, China. b, $2.25, Montserrat Cultural Center, Little Bay, Montserrat. c, $2.50, Assumption Cathedral, Moscow, Russia. d, $2.75, Brooklyn Bridge.
No. 1244: a, $1.10, Fishing villages in Shanghai and Hong Kong. b, $2.25, Camelot Villa, Montserrat. c, $2.50, Buildings at Zaanse Schans Windmill Village, Zaandam, Netherlands. d, $2.75, Reichstag, Berlin, Germany.

2010, Apr. 19   Perf. 14¼
Sheets of 4, #a-d
1243-1244 A238 Set of 2   15.00 15.00

Miniature Sheets

A239

Michael Jackson (1958-2009), Singer — A240

No. 1245 — Jackson: a, Wearing sunglasses. b, Wearing red jacket and white shirt. c, With microphone near mouth. d, Wearing high-collared red jacket.
No. 1246 — Jackson: a, Facing right, no microphone. b, Facing left, holding microphone. c, Wearing black jacket, holding microphone. d, Facing forward, no microphone.

2010, June 25   Perf. 13½
1245 A239 $2.50 Sheet of 4, #a-d   8.50 8.50
1246 A240 $2.50 Sheet of 4, #a-d   8.50 8.50

A241

Flowers — A242

Designs: $1.10, Wild marigold. $2.25, Shrubby toothedthread. $2.50, Wild sweet pea. $2.75, Rosy periwinkle. $5, Measle bush.
$7, Pribby.

2010, Aug. 18
1247-1251 A241 Set of 5   12.00 12.00
Souvenir Sheet
1252 A242 $7 multi   6.50 6.50

Worldwide Fund for Nature
(WWF) — A243

No. 1253 — Reddish egret: a, $1.10, Two
birds in water. b, $2.25, Two birds in flight. c,
$2.50, Bird preening feathers. d, $2.75, Bird
running in water.

2010, Oct. 29   Litho.
1253 A243   Block or strip of
             4, #a-d   7.50 7.50
   e.   Souvenir sheet of 8, 2 each
             #a-d   15.00 15.00

Giant Panda — A244

No. 1254 — Panda: a, Eating, brown in
background. b, Resting on tree. c, Eating,
green in background. d, Walking.
$7, Panda, diff.

2010, Nov. 22   Litho.   Perf. 12
1254 A244 $2.50 Sheet of 4,
             #a-d   3.00 3.00
        Souvenir Sheet
     Perf. 13 Syncopated
1255 A244 $7 multi   4.50 4.50

Beijing 2010 Intl. Philatelic Exhibition.

Shells
A245

Designs: $1.10, Beaded periwinkle. $2.25,
Green star shell. $2.50, Smooth Scotch bon-
net. $2.75, Calico scallop. $5, Hawk wing
conch.
$7, Atlantic partridge tun, vert.

2011, Jan. 10   Perf. 13 Syncopated
1256-1260 A245 Set of 5   10.50 10.50
        Souvenir Sheet
1261 A245 $7 multi   5.25 5.25

        Miniature Sheet

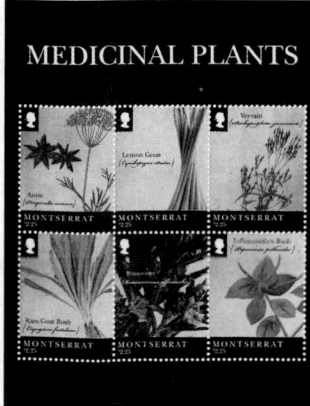

Medicinal Plants — A246

No. 1262: a, Anise. b, Lemon grass. c, Ver-
vain. d, Ram goat bush. e, Rosemary. f,
Inflammation bush.

2011, Mar. 15   Perf. 12x11½
1262 A246 $2.25 Sheet of 6,
            #a-f   10.00 10.00

Engagement of Prince William and
Catherine Middleton — A247

No. 1263: a, Couple, door at left. b, Middleton. c, Prince William. d, Couple, picture frame
in background.
No. 1264: a, Middleton, diff. b, Prince William, diff.

2011, Mar. 31   Perf. 13¼
1263 A247 $2.75 Sheet of 4,
            #a-d   8.25 8.25
        Souvenir Sheet
1264 A247 $5 Sheet of 2,
            #a-b   7.50 7.50

Livestock
A248

Designs: $2.25, Barbados black belly
sheep. $2.50, Boer goat, horiz. $2.75, Black
donkey. $5, Red cattle, horiz.
$7, Arabian horse.

2011, June 6   Perf. 12
1265-1268 A248 Set of 4   9.25 9.25
        Souvenir Sheet
1269 A248 $7 multi   5.25 5.25

Wedding of Prince William and
Catherine Middleton — A249

No. 1270: a, Groom wearing hat. b, Couple,
groom without hat. c, Bride looking left. d,
Groom without hat. e, Couple, groom with hat.
f, Bride looking right.
$7, Couple kissing.

2011, June 29   Perf. 13x13¼
1270 A249 $2.25 Sheet of 6,
            #a-f   10.00 10.00
        Souvenir Sheet
1271 A249 $7 multi   5.25 5.25

we will never forget.

Sept. 11, 2001 Terrorist Attacks, 10th
Anniv. — A250

No. 1272: a, Tribute in Washington Square,
New York City, Sept. 14, 2001. b, American
flag, chain-link fence, message on piece of
wood. c, Messages on pillar in Union Square,
New York City, Sept. 13, 2001. d, Memorial,
Stonycreek Township, Pennsylvania.
$6, Keithroy Maynard (1971-2001), New
York City firefighter killed in attacks.

2011, Sept. 11   Perf. 12
1272 A250 $2.75 Sheet of 4, #a-
            d   8.25 8.25
        Souvenir Sheet
1273 A250 $6 multi   4.50 4.50

Alphonsus
Cassell (1949-
2010), Calypso
and Soca
Singer — A251

Designs: $2.25, Color photograph of Cas-
sell. $2.50, Color photograph, diff.
No. 1276, horiz. — Cassell singing: a, With
spotlights in background. b, Wearing head-
phones. c, With hand raised above head: d,
Not holding microphone.

2011, Oct. 15   Perf. 14
1274-1275 A251 Set of 2   3.50 3.50
                  Perf. 12
1276 A251 $2.75 Sheet of 4, #a-
            d   8.25 8.25

Statue of Liberty, 125th Anniv. — A252

No. 1277 — View of: a, $1.10, Head. b,
$1.10, Torch. c, $2.25, Head, diff. d, $2.25,
Tablet. e, $2.50, Entire statue. f, $2.50, Head
and tablet.
$6, Entire statue and base.

2011, Oct. 28   Perf. 12
1277 A252   Sheet of 6, #a-f 8.75 8.75
        Souvenir Sheet
1278 A252 $6 multi   4.50 4.50
No. 1278 contains one 30x80mm stamp.

        Miniature Sheets

Flora and Fauna of China — A253

No. 1279 — Flora: a, $1.10, Chinese plum.
b, $2.25, Opium poppy. c, $2.50, Japanese
camellia. d, $2.75, Pomegranate.
No. 1280 — Fauna: a, $1.10, Purple heron.
b, $2.25, Indian elephant. c, $2.50, Snub-
nosed monkey. d, $2.75, Royal Bengal tiger.

2011, Nov. 11   Perf. 12
        Sheets of 4, #a-d
1279-1280 A253 Set of 2   13.00 13.00

China 2011 Intl. Philatelic Exhibition, Wuxi.

Christmas
A254

Designs: $2.25, Choral group Voices. $2.50,
Emerald Community Singers. $2.75, Volpan-
ics. $5, New Ebenezer Seventh Day Adventist
Church.

2011, Dec. 6   Perf. 14
1281-1284 A254 Set of 4   9.25 9.25

Ducks — A255

No. 1285: a, Northern pintail. b, Green-
winged teal. c, Fulvous whistling duck. d, Blue-
winged teal.
$6, Northern shoveler.

2012, Feb. 28   Perf. 14
1285 A255 $3.50 Sheet of 4,
            #a-d   10.50 10.50
        Souvenir Sheet
           Perf. 12
1286 A255 $6 multi   4.50 4.50

Cacti — A256

No. 1287: a, Queen of the night. b, Old
man's whiskers. c, Devil cholla. d, Century
plant.
No. 1288: Prickly pear cactus. b, Prickly
pear fruit.

2012, Feb. 10
1287 A256 $2.75 Sheet of 4, #a-
            d   8.25 8.25
        Souvenir Sheet
1288 A256 $3.50 Sheet of 2, #a-
            b   5.25 5.25

Reign of Queen Elizabeth II, 60th Anniv. — A257

No. 1289: a, Head of Queen Elizabeth II. b, Queen Elizabeth II waving, two men in background. c, Queen Elizabeth II on throne. d, Queen Elizabeth II and Prince Philip.
$7, Queen Elizabeth II, vert.

2012, Apr. 18   *Perf. 12*
1289 A257 $3.50 Sheet of 4, #a-d   10.50 10.50
Souvenir Sheet
Perf. 14
1290 A257 $7 multi   5.25 5.25

Bridges — A258

No. 1291, vert.: a, Sydney Harbour Bridge. b, Brooklyn Bridge. c, Golden Gate Bridge.
$6, Tower Bridge, London.

2012, June 8   *Perf. 14*
1291 A258 $4 Sheet of 3, #a-c   9.00 9.00
Souvenir Sheet
1292 A258 $6 multi   4.50 4.50

Marine Life — A259

No. 1293: a, Yellow tang. b, Spotted dolphin. c, Manatee. d, Green sea turtle.
$6, Blue-spotted grouper.

2012, June 26   *Litho.*
1293 A259 $3 Sheet of 4, #a-d   9.00 9.00
Souvenir Sheet
1294 A259 $6 multi   4.50 4.50

Ferns — A260

No. 1295: a, Argyrochosma jonesii. b, Danaea kalevala. c, Lastreopsis effusa. d, Asplenium serratum.

$6, Phlebodium aureum, vert.

2012, Aug. 20   *Perf. 14*
1295 A260 $3 Sheet of 4, #a-d   9.00 9.00
Souvenir Sheet
Perf. 12½
1296 A260 $6 multi   4.50 4.50
No. 1296 contains one 38x51mm stamp.

Scenes From China — A261

No. 1297 — Great Wall of China: a, Tower at right, denomination in black. b, Four towers, denomination in black. c, Wall turrets, denomination in white. d, Wall walkway, denomination in white.
No. 1298: a, Gate of Heavenly Peace. b, Forbidden City. c, Summer Palace, large rock at LL. d, Summer Palace, stairway at LL. e, Pudong skyline. f, Li River, Quangxi Province.
No. 1299, $5, Sanqingshan National Park, vert. No. 1300, $5, Dragon carving on a temple facade, vert.

2012, Nov. 15   *Perf. 13¾*
1297 A261 $2.25 Sheet of 4, #a-d   6.75 6.75
1298 A261 $2.50 Sheet of 6, #a-f   11.50 11.50
Souvenir Sheets
Perf. 12½
1299-1300 A261   Set of 2   7.50 7.50
Beijing 2012 Intl. Philatelic Exhibition. Nos. 1299-1300 each contain one 38x51mm stamp.

Minerals — A262

No. 1301: a, Amber. b, Chrysoberyl. c, Garnet. d, Microcline. e, Sunstone. f, Lapis lazuli.
$6, Orpiment, vert.

2013, Jan. 31   *Perf. 13¾*
1301 A262 $2.50 Sheet of 6, #a-f   11.50 11.50
Souvenir Sheet
Perf. 12¾
1302 A262 $6 multi   4.50 4.50
No. 1302 contains one 38x51mm stamp.

Butterflies — A263

Designs: 10c, Pygmy fritillary. 30c, Cloudless sulphur. 35c, Gulf fritillary. 50c, St. Christopher's hairstreak. 70c, Nyctelius skipper. 80c, Cassius blue. 90c, Antillean crescent. $1,

Polydamas swallowtail. $1.10, Flambeau. $1.50, Bronze hairstreak. $2.25, Caribbean buckeye. $2.50, Red rim. $2.75, White peacock. $5, Stub-tailed skipper. $10, Zebra. $20, Manuel's skipper.

2013, Mar. 5   *Perf. 12*
1303 A263 10c multi   .25 .25
1304 A263 30c multi   .25 .25
1305 A263 35c multi   .25 .25
1306 A263 50c multi   .40 .40
1307 A263 70c multi   .55 .55
1308 A263 80c multi   .60 .60
1309 A263 90c multi   .70 .70
1310 A263 $1 multi   .75 .75
1311 A263 $1.10 multi   .85 .85
1312 A263 $1.50 multi   1.10 1.10
1313 A263 $2.25 multi   1.75 1.75
1314 A263 $2.50 multi   1.90 1.90
1315 A263 $2.75 multi   2.10 2.10
1316 A263 $5 multi   3.75 3.75
1317 A263 $10 multi   7.50 7.50
1318 A263 $20 multi   15.00 15.00
Nos. 1303-1318 (16)   37.70 37.70

Globe Theater Fire, 400th Anniv. — A264

No. 1319 — Plays by William Shakespeare (1564-1616): a, Hamlet. b, Julius Caesar. c, Macbeth. d, Romeo and Juliet.
$7, Shakespeare, vert.

2013, May 29   *Perf. 13¾*
1319 A264 $2.75 Sheet of 4, #a-d   8.25 8.25
Souvenir Sheet
Perf. 12½
1320 A264 $7 multi   5.25 5.25
No. 1320 contains one 38x51mm stamp.

New Year 2014 (Year of the Horse) — A265

No. 1321 — Horse: a, Grazing. b, Pacing, with one front leg lifted. c, Walking, with no feet lifted. d, Galloping, with two front legs lifted.
$7, Horse, diff.

2013, July 17   *Perf. 13¾*
1321 A265 $2.75 Sheet of 4, #a-d   8.25 8.25
Souvenir Sheet
1322 A265 $7 multi   5.25 5.25

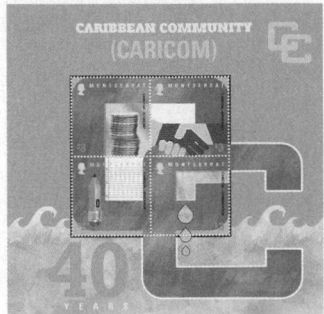

Caribbean Community, 40th Anniv. — A266

No. 1323: a, Economy. b, Diplomacy. c, Education. d, Conservation.
$7, 40th anniv. emblem.

2013, July 31
1323 A266 $3 Sheet of 4, #a-d   9.00 9.00
Souvenir Sheet
1324 A266 $7 multi   5.25 5.25

Flowers — A267

No. 1325: a, $2.75, Black pirate. b, $2.75, Cape blue water lily. c, $3, Angel's trumpet. d, $3, Emerald vine.
$7, Moon vine.

2013, Aug. 27   *Litho.*   *Perf. 12½*
1325 A267   Sheet of 4, #a-d   8.50 8.50
Souvenir Sheet
1326 A267 $7 multi   5.25 5.25

Thailand 2013 World Stamp Exhibition, Bangkok — A268

No. 1326: a, $2.75, Coconut trees. b, $2.75, Sanphet Prasat Palace. c, $3, Buddha statues. d, $3, Erawan Waterfall.
$7, Elephant and riders.

2013, Sept. 2   *Litho.*   *Perf. 13¾*
1327 A268   Sheet of 4, #a-d   8.50 8.50
Souvenir Sheet
1328 A268 $7 multi   5.25 5.25

Birth of Prince George of Cambridge — A269

No. 1329 — Prince George and: a, Duchess of Cambridge. b, Duke and Duchess of Cambridge.
$7, Prince George and Duke of Cambridge.

2013, Sept. 22   *Litho.*   *Perf. 14*
1329 A269 $2.75 Pair, #a-b   4.25 4.25
Souvenir Sheet
1330 A269 $7 multi   5.25 5.25
No. 1329 was printed in sheets containing 2 each of Nos. 1329a and 1329b.

Kittens — A270

No. 1331: a, Bicolor tabby. b, Brown-and-white mackerel tabby. c, Calico. d, Gray-and-white mackerel tabby.
$7, Mackerel tabby, diff.

2013, Nov. 7   Litho.   Perf. 13¾
1331 A270 $3 Sheet of 4, #a-d   9.00 9.00
Souvenir Sheet
1332 A270 $7 multi   5.25 5.25

Pres. John F. Kennedy (1917-63) — A271

No. 1333 — Pres. Kennedy: a, Sitting in rocking chair. b, Facing right. c, Facing forward, picture frame in background. d, Signing paper.
$7, Pres. Kennedy at microphone.

2013, Nov. 22   Litho.   Perf. 13¾
1333 A271 $2.25 Sheet of 4, #a-d   6.75 6.75
Souvenir Sheet
1334 A271 $7 multi   5.25 5.25

Reptiles — A272

No. 1335: a, Red-footed tortoise. b, Iguana. c, Brown anole. d, House gecko.
$7, Blue-headed anole.

2013, Dec. 23   Litho.   Perf. 12
1335 A272 $2.75 Sheet of 4, #a-d   8.25 8.25
Souvenir Sheet
1336 A272 $7 multi   5.25 5.25

War Memorial, Plymouth — A273

Montserrat Coat of Arms — A274

2014, Feb. 7   Litho.   Perf. 12
1337 A273 $50 multi   37.50 37.50
1338 A274 $100 multi   75.00 75.00

World War I, Cent. — A275

No. 1339: a, Female munitions worker welding, 1915. b, Nurse ironing bandages, 1915. c, Woman at Southwark Hall Army Recruiting Office, London, 1915. d, Delivery woman, 1914. e, Woman cleaning railway car door, 1914. f, Miss D. Milman of the Women's Sevice League, 1918.
$7, French Red Cross poster, 1915, vert.

2014, Feb. 26   Litho.   Perf. 13¾
1339 A275 $2.25 Sheet of 6, #a-f   10.00 10.00
Souvenir Sheet   Perf. 12¾x12½
1340 A275 $7 multi   5.25 5.25
No. 1340 contains one 38x51mm stamp.

Hummingbirds — A276

No. 1341: a, Bronze-tailed plumeleteer. b, White-bellied mountaingem. c, Olivaceous thornbill. d, White-bellied emerald.
No. 1342: a, Chestnut-breasted coronet. b, Collared Inca.

2014, Apr. 22   Litho.   Perf. 13¾
1341 A276 $3 Sheet of 4, #a-d   9.00 9.00
Souvenir Sheet
1342 A276 $3.50 Sheet of 2, #a-b   5.25 5.25

Astronomy — A277

No. 1343 — Various illustrations of Moon by Galileo Galilei, as shown.
$7, Galileo Galilei (1564-1642), astronomer.

2014, June 5   Litho.   Perf. 14
1343 A277 $3 Sheet of 4, #a-d   9.00 9.00
Souvenir Sheet
1344 A277 $7 multi   5.25 5.25

Vegetables — A278

No. 1345: a, Lettuce. b, Corn. c, Eggplants. d, Sweet potatoes.
No. 1346: a, Cauliflower. b, Carrots.

2014, June 24   Litho.   Perf. 13¾
1345 A278 $3 Sheet of 4, #a-d   9.00 9.00
Souvenir Sheet
1346 A278 $3.50 Sheet of 2, #a-b   5.25 5.25

Paintings — A279

No. 1347: a, Still Life Vase with Twelve Sunflowers, by Vincent van Gogh. b, Young Woman in the Garden, by Henri Lebasque. c, Dancer Arranging Her Hair, by Edgar Degas. d, The Fruit Seller, by Frederick Childe Hassam.
$7, At the Market, by Félix Vallotton.

2014, Aug. 6   Litho.   Perf. 12½
1347 A279 $3.50 Sheet of 4, #a-d   10.50 10.50
Souvenir Sheet
1348 A279 $7 multi   5.25 5.25

Dogs — A280

No. 1349: a, Siberian husky. b, French bulldog. c, Chihuahua. d, Basset hound.
$7, Dalmatian.

2014, Aug. 27   Litho.   Perf. 12
1349 A280 $3 Sheet of 4, #a-d   9.00 9.00
Souvenir Sheet
1350 A280 $7 multi   5.25 5.25

Sports — A281

No. 1351: a, Hurdling. b, Relay race. c, Shot put. d, Soccer.
$7, Cricket.

2014, Oct. 13   Litho.   Perf. 12½x12
1351 A281 $3.50 Sheet of 4, #a-d   10.50 10.50
Souvenir Sheet
1352 A281 $7 multi   5.25 5.25

Famous People — A282

No. 1353: a, Benjamin Franklin. b, Dr. Martin Luther King, Jr. c, Nelson Mandela. d, Sir Winston Churchill.
$7, Mahatma Gandhi.

2014, Dec. 4   Litho.   Perf. 12x12½
1353 A282 $3.25 Sheet of 4, #a-d   9.75 9.75
Souvenir Sheet   Perf. 13½
1354 A282 $7 multi   5.25 5.25
No. 1354 contains one 38x51mm stamp.

Tropical Fish — A283

No. 1355: a, Blue-girdled angelfish. b, Foxface rabbitfish. c, Powder blue tang. d, Clown triggerfish.

$7, Sixspine butterflyfish.

2014, Dec. 22   Litho.   Perf. 12½x12
1355 A283 $3.25 Sheet of 4, #a-
       d   9.75 9.75

Souvenir Sheet
1356 A283 $7 multi   5.25 5.25

International Year of Light — A284

No. 1357: a, Prism and spectrum. b, Sir
Isaac Newton (1643-1727), physicist. c,
Wavelengths of violet, blue and green light. d,
Wavelengths of yellow, orange and red light.
$7, Wavelengths of ultraviolet and infrared
light.

2015, Jan. 29   Litho.   Perf. 12x12½
1357 A284 $3.25 Sheet of 4, #a-
       d   9.75 9.75

Souvenir Sheet
Perf. 13½
1358 A284 $7 multi   5.25 5.25

No. 1358 contains one 38x51mm stamp.

SEMI-POSTAL STAMPS

> Catalogue values for unused
> stamps in this section, from this
> point to the end of the section, are
> for Never Hinged items.

Nos. 719-720 Surcharged

1989, Oct. 20   Litho.   Perf. 13½x14
B1 A110 $1.50 +$2.50 multi   3.00 3.00
B2 A110 $3.50 +$2.50 multi   4.50 4.50
Surcharge for hurricane relief.

No. 642 Surcharged

1995, Dec. 29   Litho.   Perf. 15
B3 A97 $2.30 +$5 multi   9.00 9.00
Surcharge for volcano relief.

WAR TAX STAMPS

No. 43 Overprinted in
Red or Black

1917-18   Wmk. 3   Perf. 14
MR1 A6 ½p green (R)   .25 1.75
MR2 A6 ½p green ('18)   .25 2.00

Type of Regular Issue
of 1919 Overprinted

1918
MR3 A6 1½p orange & black   .30 .35
Denomination on No. MR3 in black on white
ground. Two dots under "d."

OFFICIAL STAMPS

Nos. O1-O44 used on Post Office
and Philatelic Bureau mail. Not sold to
public, used or unused.

Nos. 235-236,
338-339
Overprinted

Perf. 12½x14
1976, Apr. 12   Photo.   Wmk. 314
O1 A22 5c multicolored   1.90
O2 A22 10c multicolored   2.50
O3 A22 30c on 10c multi   5.00
O4 A22 45c on 3c multi   6.00
    Nos. O1-O4 (4)   15.40

Nos. 243-243A also received this overprint.

Nos. 343-347, 349-351, 353-354 Overprinted

Perf. 13½x14
1976, Oct. 1   Litho.   Wmk. 373
O10 A44 5c multicolored   .25
O11 A44 10c multicolored   .25
O12 A44 15c multicolored   .25
O13 A44 20c multicolored   .25
O14 A44 25c multicolored   .25
O15 A44 55c multicolored   .40
O16 A44 70c multicolored   .50
O17 A44 $1 multicolored   .70
O18 A44 $5 multicolored   3.50
O19 A44 $10 multicolored   7.00
    Nos. O10-O19 (10)   13.35

Nos. 343-347, 349-351, 353-354 Overprinted

1980, Sept. 30   Perf. 14
O20 A44 5c multicolored   .25
O21 A44 10c multicolored   .25
O22 A44 15c multicolored   .25
O23 A44 20c multicolored   .25
O24 A44 25c multicolored   .25
O25 A44 55c multicolored   .35
O26 A44 70c multicolored   .45
O27 A44 $1 multicolored   .65
O28 A44 $5 multicolored   3.00
O29 A44 $10 multicolored   6.00
    Nos. O20-O29 (10)   11.70

Nos. 341-351, 353-354 Overprinted or Surcharged

1980, Sept. 30   Litho.   Perf. 14
O30 A44 5c multicolored   .25
O31 A44 5c on 3c multi   .25
O32 A44 10c multicolored   .25
O33 A44 15c multicolored   .25
O34 A44 20c multicolored   .25
O35 A44 25c multicolored   .25
O36 A44 30c on 15c multi   .25
O37 A44 35c on 2c multi   .40
O38 A44 40c multicolored   .30
O39 A44 55c multicolored   .45
O40 A44 70c multicolored   .60
O41 A44 $1 multicolored   .80
O42 A44 $2.50 on 40c multi   2.00
O43 A44 $5 multicolored   4.00
O44 A44 $10 multicolored   8.00
    Nos. O30-O44 (15)   18.30

> Catalogue values for unused
> stamps in this section, from this
> point to the end of the section, are
> for Never Hinged items.

Fish Issue of 1981
Nos. 445-449,
451, 453, 455,
457-458, 460
Overprinted

1981, Mar. 20   Litho.   Perf. 13½
O45 A64 5c multicolored   .25 .25
O46 A64 10c multicolored   .25 .25
O47 A64 15c multicolored   .25 .25
O48 A64 20c multicolored   .25 .25
O49 A64 25c multicolored   .25 .25
O50 A64 45c multicolored   .35 .35
O51 A64 65c multicolored   .50 .50
O52 A64 $1 multicolored   .75 .75
O53 A64 $3 multicolored   2.25 2.25
O54 A64 $5 multicolored   3.75 3.75
O55 A64 $10 multicolored   7.50 7.50
    Nos. O45-O55 (11)   16.35 16.35

Nos. 465-470 Surcharged

1982, Nov. 17   Litho.   Perf. 14
O56 A66 45c on 90c (#465)   .40 .40
O57 A67 45c on 90c (#466)   .40 .40
O58 A66 75c on $3 (#467)   .70 .70
O59 A67 75c on $3 (#468)   .70 .70
O60 A66 $1 on $4 (#469)   .90 .90
O61 A67 $1 on $4 (#470)   .90 .90
    Nos. O56-O61 (6)   4.00 4.00

Princess Diana
Issue, Nos. 484-
486 Overprinted
or Surcharged

1983, Oct. 19   Litho.   Perf. 14
O62 A70b 70c on 75c (#484)   1.50 1.50
O63 A70b $1 (#485)   1.90 1.90
O64 A70b $1.50 on $5 (#486)   2.50 2.50
    Nos. O62-O64 (3)   5.90 5.90

Nos. 524-536, 538 Overprinted

1985, Apr. 12   Wmk. 380   Perf. 14
O65 A79 5c multicolored   .50 .25
O66 A79 10c multicolored   .50 .25
O67 A79 15c multicolored   .50 .25
O68 A79 20c multicolored   .50 .25
O69 A79 25c multicolored   .50 .25
O70 A79 40c multicolored   .80 .40
O71 A79 55c multicolored   .90 .45
O72 A79 70c multicolored   1.25 .65
O73 A79 90c multicolored   1.60 .80
O74 A79 $1 multicolored   1.90 .90
O75 A79 $1.15 multicolored   2.00 1.00
O76 A79 $3 multicolored   5.25 2.50
O77 A79 $5 multicolored   9.25 4.75
O78 A79 $10 multicolored   17.50 9.00
    Nos. O65-O78 (14)   42.95 21.70

Nos. 681-694 and 696 Overprinted

Unwmk.
1989, May 9   Litho.   Perf. 14
O79 A104 5c multicolored   .25 .25
O80 A104 10c multicolored   .25 .25
O81 A104 15c multicolored   .25 .25
O82 A104 20c multicolored   .25 .25
O83 A104 25c multicolored   .25 .25
O84 A104 40c multicolored   .40 .40
O85 A104 55c multicolored   .60 .55
O86 A104 70c multicolored   .75 .70
O87 A104 90c multicolored   .95 .90
O88 A104 $1 multicolored   1.00 .95
O89 A104 $1.15 multicolored   1.25 1.25
O90 A104 $1.50 multicolored   1.60 1.40
O91 A104 $3 multicolored   3.00 2.75
O92 A104 $5 multicolored   5.25 4.75
O94 A104 $10 multicolored   10.50 9.50
    Nos. O79-O94 (15)   26.55 24.40

Nos. 446, 454a
and 456
Surcharged

1989   Wmk. 373   Perf. 13½
O95 A64 70c on 10c multi   1.75 1.75
O96 A64 $1.15 on 75c multi   3.25 3.25
O97 A64 $1.50 on $2 multi   4.00 4.00
    Nos. O95-O97 (3)   9.00 9.00

Nos. 758-761, 763-766, 776-779
Surcharged or Overprinted "OHMS"

1992		**Litho.**		**Perf. 14**
O98	A118	70c on 90c #758	1.50	1.50
O99	A118	70c on $3.50 #761	1.50	1.50
O100	A119	70c on 90c #763	1.50	1.50
O101	A121	70c on 90c #776	1.50	1.50
O102	A119	$1 on $3.50 #766	2.00	2.00
O103	A121	$1 on $3.50 #779	2.00	2.00
O104	A118	$1.15 on #759	2.25	2.25
O105	A119	$1.15 on #764	2.25	2.25
O106	A121	$1.15 on #777	2.25	2.25
O107	A118	$1.50 on #760	3.00	3.00
O108	A119	$1.50 on #765	3.00	3.00
O109	A121	$1.50 on #778	3.00	3.00
		Nos. O98-O109 (12)	25.75	25.75

Nos. 803-816, 818 Ovptd. "OHMS" in Red

1993, Apr. 14		**Litho.**		**Perf. 15x14**
O110	A128	5c multicolored	.30	.30
O111	A128	10c multicolored	.30	.30
O112	A128	15c multicolored	.30	.30
O113	A128	20c multicolored	.30	.30
O114	A128	25c multicolored	.30	.30
O115	A128	40c multicolored	.50	.50
O116	A128	55c multicolored	.75	.75
O117	A128	70c multicolored	.85	.85
O118	A128	90c multicolored	1.05	1.05
O119	A128	$1 multicolored	1.20	1.20
O120	A128	$1.15 multicolored	1.40	1.40
O121	A128	$1.50 multicolored	1.75	1.75
O122	A128	$3 multicolored	3.75	3.75
O123	A128	$5 multicolored	6.00	6.00
O125	A128	$10 multicolored	12.00	12.00
		Nos. O110-O125 (15)	30.75	30.75

A number has been reserved for an additional value in this set.

Nos. 896-909, 911 Ovptd. "O.H.M.S." In Red

1997		**Litho.**		**Perf. 14**
O126	A147	5c multicolored	.25	.25
O127	A147	10c multicolored	.25	.25
O128	A147	15c multicolored	.25	.25
O129	A147	20c multicolored	.25	.25
O130	A147	25c multicolored	.25	.25
O131	A147	40c multicolored	.40	.40
O132	A147	55c multicolored	.50	.50
O133	A147	70c multicolored	.70	.70
O134	A147	90c multicolored	.90	.90
O135	A147	$1 multicolored	.95	.95
O136	A147	$1.15 multicolored	1.10	1.10
O137	A147	$1.50 multicolored	1.40	1.40
O138	A147	$3 multicolored	3.00	3.00
O139	A147	$5 multicolored	4.75	4.75
O140	A147	$10 multicolored	9.75	9.75
		Nos. O126-O140 (15)	24.70	24.70

Nos. 1041-1054, 1056 Overprinted

Perf. 13½x13¼

2002, June 14				**Litho.**
O141	A176	5c multi	.30	.30
O142	A176	10c multi	.30	.30
O143	A176	15c multi	.30	.30
O144	A176	20c multi	.30	.30
O145	A176	25c multi	.30	.30
O146	A176	40c multi	.35	.35
O147	A176	55c multi	.45	.45
O148	A176	70c multi	.90	.90
O149	A176	90c multi	1.20	1.20
O150	A176	$1 multi	1.40	1.40
O151	A176	$1.15 multi	1.75	1.75
O152	A176	$1.50 multi	2.25	2.25
O153	A176	$3 multi	4.75	4.75
O154	A176	$5 multi	7.50	7.50
O155	A176	$10 multi	15.00	15.00
		Nos. O141-O155 (15)	37.05	37.05

Nos. 1173-1186, 1188 Overprinted

2007, May 14		**Litho.**		**Perf. 12½**
O156	A213	10c multi	.25	.25
O157	A213	30c multi	.25	.25
O158	A213	35c multi	.25	.25

O159	A213	50c multi	.40	.40
O160	A213	70c multi	.55	.55
O161	A213	80c multi	.60	.60
O162	A213	90c multi	.70	.70
O163	A213	$1 multi	.75	.75
O164	A213	$1.10 multi	.85	.85
O165	A213	$1.50 multi	1.10	1.10
O166	A213	$2.25 multi	1.75	1.75
O167	A213	$2.50 multi	1.90	1.90
O168	A213	$2.75 multi	2.10	2.10
O169	A213	$5 multi	3.75	3.75
O170	A213	$20 multi	15.00	15.00
		Nos. O156-O170 (15)	30.20	30.20

Size and location of overprint varies.

MOROCCO

mə-'rä-ˌkō

LOCATION — Northwest coast of Africa
GOVT. — Kingdom
AREA — 171,953 sq. mi.
POP. — 29,661,636 (1999 est.)
CAPITAL — Rabat

A powerful kingdom from the 8th century, during the Middle Ages, Morocco ruled large areas of northwest Africa and Spain. By the turn of the 20th century, it had contracted to roughly its present borders and was the focus of an intense rivalry between France and Germany, who actively competed for control of the country. In 1912 most of Morocco became a French protectorate, with Spain acting as protector of zones in the extreme northern and southern parts of the country. Tangier was designated an international zone, administered by France, Spain, Britain and, later, Italy.

In 1956 the three zones of Morocco, French, Spanish and Tangier, were united to form an independent nation. Nos. 1-24 and C1-C3 were intended for use only in the southern (French currency) zone. Issues of the northern zone (Spanish currency) are listed after Postage Due stamps.

For earlier issues see French Morocco and Spanish Morocco.

400 Moussonats = 1 Rial (1912)
100 Centimes = 1 Franc (1950)
100 Centimes = 1 Dirham (1962)

> Catalogue values for all unused stamps in this country are for Never Hinged items, except for Nos. A1-A14.

Aissaouas Mosque, Tangier — A1a

On White Paper
Narrow Margins

1912, May 25		**Litho.**		**Perf. 11**
A1	A1a	1m light gray	8.00	8.00
A2	A1a	2m lilac	9.00	8.00
A3	A1a	5m blue green	12.00	8.00
A4	A1a	10m vermilion	20.00	8.50
A5	A1a	25m blue	29.00	24.00
A6	A1a	50m violet	42.50	35.00
		Nos. A1-A6 (6)	120.50	91.50

On Nos. A1-A12, the 5m and 10m values always have the name of the engraver beneath the design, while the 1m, 25m and 50m always lack name, and the 2m value exists both with and without name.

Aissaouas Mosque, Tangier — A1b

On Lightly Tinted Paper

1913, Feb.			**Wide Margins**	
A7	A1b	1m gray	1.75	1.75
A8	A1b	2m brown lilac	1.75	1.75
A9	A1b	5m blue green	2.00	2.00
A10	A1b	10m vermilion	2.00	2.00
A11	A1b	25m blue	4.25	4.25
A12	A1b	50m gray violet	4.25	4.25
		Nos. A7-A12 (6)	16.00	16.00

No. A6 Surcharged

1913, Nov.				
A13	A1a	.05 on 50c violet	1,750.	2,000.
A14	A1a	.10 on 50c violet	1,750.	2,000.

Sultan Mohammed V — A1   Men Reading — A2

1956-57		**Unwmk. Engr.**		**Perf. 13**
1	A1	5fr brt bl & indigo	.30	.25
2	A1	10fr bis brn & choc	.25	.25
3	A1	15fr dp grn & magenta	.35	.25
4	A1	25fr purple ('57)	1.10	.25
5	A1	30fr green ('57)	1.90	.25
6	A1	50fr rose red ('57)	2.75	.25
7	A1	70fr dk brn & brn red ('57)	4.25	.80
		Nos. 1-7 (7)	10.90	2.30

For surcharges see Nos. B1-B5, B8-B9.

1956, Nov. 5

Campaign against illiteracy: 15fr, Girls reading. 20fr, Instructor and pupils. 30fr, Old man and child reading. 50fr, Girl pointing out poster.

8	A2	10fr pur & vio	1.75	1.20
9	A2	15fr car & rose lake	2.25	1.50
10	A2	20fr bl grn & grn	2.60	2.40
11	A2	30fr rose lake & brt red	4.25	2.75
12	A2	50fr dp bl & bl	8.25	5.25
		Nos. 8-12 (5)	19.10	13.10

Sultan Mohammed V — A3   Prince Moulay el Hassan — A4

1957, Mar. 2		**Photo.**		**Perf. 13½x13**
13	A3	15fr blue green	1.50	1.10
14	A3	25fr gray olive	2.00	1.10
15	A3	30fr deep rose	4.00	1.90
		Nos. 13-15 (3)	7.50	4.10

Anniversary of independence.

1957, July 9				**Perf. 13**
16	A4	15fr blue	1.50	1.00
17	A4	25fr green	1.90	1.50
18	A4	30fr car rose	3.00	2.10
		Nos. 16-18 (3)	6.40	4.60

Designation of Prince Moulay el Hassan as heir to the throne.

King Mohammed V — A5

1957, Nov.				**Perf. 12½**
19	A5	15fr blk & brt grn	1.40	.70
20	A5	25fr blk & rose red	1.50	.95
21	A5	30fr blk & vio	2.90	1.25
		Nos. 19-21 (3)	5.80	2.90

Enthronement of Mohammed V, 30th anniv.

Morocco Pavilion, Brussels World's Fair — A6

1958, Apr. 20		**Engr.**		**Perf. 13**
22	A6	15fr brt grnsh bl	.40	.25
23	A6	25fr carmine	.40	.30
24	A6	30fr indigo	.55	.35
		Nos. 22-24 (3)	1.35	.90

World's Fair, Brussels.

UNESCO Building, Paris, and Mohammed V — A7

1958, Nov. 23				
25	A7	15fr green	.40	.25
26	A7	25fr lake	.40	.25
27	A7	30fr blue	.55	.30
		Nos. 25-27 (3)	1.35	.80

UNESCO Headquarters opening, Paris, Nov. 3.

Ben Smin Sanatorium A8

1959, Jan. 18		**Unwmk.**		**Perf. 13**
28	A8	50fr dk brn, car & slate grn	.90	.50

Red Cross-Red Crescent Society.

Mohammed V — A9   Princess Lalla Amina — A10

1959, Aug. 18		**Engr.**		**Perf. 13**
29	A9	15fr dk car rose	.60	.40
30	A9	25fr brt bl	.85	.55
31	A9	45fr dk grn	1.10	.60
		Nos. 29-31 (3)	2.55	1.55

50th birthday of King Mohammed V.

1959, Nov. 17				
32	A10	15fr blue	.40	.25
33	A10	25fr green	.50	.25
34	A10	45fr rose lil	.55	.30
		Nos. 32-34 (3)	1.45	.80

Issued for International Children's Week.

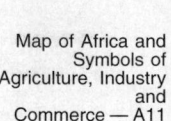

Map of Africa and Symbols of Agriculture, Industry and Commerce — A11

1960, Jan. 31 *Perf. 13*
35 A11 45fr vio, ocher & emer 1.10 .65

Issued to publicize the meeting of the Economic Commission for Africa, Tangier.

Refugees and Uprooted Oak Emblem A12

45fr, Refugee family and uprooted oak emblem.

1960, Apr. 7 *Unwmk.* *Perf. 13*
36 A12 15fr ocher, blk & grn .30 .30
37 A12 45fr blk & grn .50 .50

World Refugee Year, July 1, 1959-June 30, 1960.

Marrakesh A13

1960, Apr. 25 *Engr.* *Perf. 13*
38 A13 100fr grn, bl & red brn 1.40 .90

900th anniversary of Marrakesh.

Lamp — A14

Designs: 25fr, Fountain and arched door. 30fr, Minaret. 35fr, Ornamented wall. 45fr, Moorish architecture.

1960, May 12 *Perf. 13½*
39 A14 15fr rose lil .50 .50
40 A14 25fr dk bl .55 .55
41 A14 30fr org red 1.25 .65
42 A14 35fr black 1.40 1.10
43 A14 45fr yel grn 2.00 1.50
  Nos. 39-43 (5) 5.70 4.30

1,100th anniv. of Karaouiyne University, Fez.

Arab League Center, Cairo and Mohammed V — A15

1960, June 28 *Photo.* *Perf. 12½*
44 A15 15fr grn & blk .60 .25

Opening of the Arab League Center and the Arab Postal Museum, Cairo.

Wrestlers — A16

Sports: 10fr, Gymnast. 15fr, Bicyclist. 20fr, Weight lifter. 30fr, Runner. 40fr, Boxers. 45fr, Sailboat. 70fr, Fencers.

1960, Sept. 26 *Engr.* *Perf. 13*
45 A16 5fr ol, vio bl & plum .25 .25
46 A16 10fr org brn, bl & brn .25 .25
47 A16 15fr emer, bl & org brn .30 .25
48 A16 20fr ultra, ol & brn .35 .25
49 A16 30fr vio bl, mar & sep .40 .25
50 A16 40fr grnsh bl, dk pur & red brn .65 .25
51 A16 45fr grn, plum & ultra .80 .30
52 A16 70fr dk brn, bl & gray 1.10 .40
  Nos. 45-52 (8) 4.10 2.20

17th Olympic Games, Rome, 8/25-9/11.

Runner A17

1961, Aug. 30 *Unwmk.* *Perf. 13*
53 A17 20fr dk grn .25 .25
54 A17 30fr dk car rose .50 .25
55 A17 50fr brt bl .65 .40
  Nos. 53-55 (3) 1.40 .90

3rd Pan-Arabic Games, Casablanca.

Post Office, Tangier — A18

View of Tangier and Gibraltar A19

Design: 30fr, Telephone operator.

1961, Dec. 8 *Litho.* *Perf. 12½*
56 A18 20fr red vio .40 .25
57 A18 30fr green .55 .25
57A A19 90fr lt bl & vio bl 1.00 .50
  Nos. 56-57A (3) 1.95 1.00

Conference of the African Postal and Telecommunications Union, Tangier.

Mohammed V and Map of Africa — A20

Patrice Lumumba and Map of Congo — A21

1962, Jan. 4 *Unwmk.* *Perf. 11½*
58 A20 20c buff & vio brn .30 .25
59 A20 30c lt & dk bl .45 .25

1st anniv. of the conference of African heads of state at Casablanca.

1962, Feb. 12 *Perf. 12½*
60 A21 20c bis & blk .30 .25
61 A21 30c dl red brn & blk .45 .25

1st death anniv. of Patrice Lumumba, Premier of Congo Democratic Republic.

Moroccan Students — A22

Arab League Building, Cairo — A23

1962, Mar. 5 *Engr.*
62 A22 20fr multi .55 .30
63 A22 30fr multi .55 .40
64 A22 90fr gray grn, indigo & brn .90 .70
  Nos. 62-64 (3) 2.00 1.40

Issued to honor the nation's students.

1962, Mar. 22 Photo. *Perf. 13½x13*
65 A23 20c red brn .55 .25

Arab Propaganda Week, 3/22-28. See #146.

Malaria Eradication Emblem and Swamp A24

50c, Dagger stabbing mosquito, vert.

1962, Sept. 3 *Engr.* *Perf. 13*
66 A24 20c dk grn & grnsh blk .35 .25
67 A24 50c dk grn & mag .50 .30

WHO drive to eradicate malaria.

Fish and Aquarium — A25

1962, Nov. 5 *Unwmk.* *Perf. 13*
68 A25 20c shown .60 .25
69 A25 30c Moray eel .75 .25

Casablanca Aquarium.

Courier and Sherifian Stamp of 1912 A26

Designs: 30c, Courier on foot and round Sherifian cancellation. 50c, Sultan Hassan I and octagonal cancellation.

1962, Dec. 15 *Unwmk.*
70 A26 20c Prus grn & redsh brn .75 .25
71 A26 30c dk car rose & blk .75 .40
72 A26 50c bl & bister 1.10 .50
  Nos. 70-72 (3) 2.60 1.15

Stamp Day; 1st National Stamp Exhibition, Dec. 15-23; 75th anniv. of the Sherifian Post and the 50th anniv. of its reorganization.

Boy Scout — A27

King Hassan II — A28

1962, Aug. 8 *Litho.* *Perf. 11½*
73 A27 20c vio brn & lt bl .55 .25

5th Arab Boy Scout Jamboree, Rabat.

1962 *Engr.* *Perf. 13½x13*
75 A28 1c gray olive .25 .25
76 A28 2c violet .25 .25
77 A28 5c black .25 .25
78 A28 10c brn org .25 .25
79 A28 15c Prus grn .25 .25
80 A28 20c purple .25 .25
81 A28 30c dp yel grn .30 .25
82 A28 50c vio brn .60 .25
83 A28 70c deep blue .90 .25
84 A28 80c magenta 1.50 .25
  Nos. 75-84 (10) 4.80 2.50

"Mazelin" (designer-engraver) reads down on Nos. 75-84. See Nos. 110-114.

King Moulay Ismail — A29

Al Idrissi, Geographer — A30

1963, Mar. 3 *Perf. 12½*
85 A29 20c sepia .55 .25

Tercentenary of Meknes as Ismaili capital.

1963-66 *Engr.*

#87, 88A, Ibn Batota, explorer. #88, Ibn Khaldoun, historian and sociologist.

86 A30 20c dk sl grn .50 .30
87 A30 20c dk car rose .50 .30
88 A30 20c black .50 .30
88A A30 40c dk vio bl ('66) .60 .30
  Nos. 86-88A (4) 2.10 1.20

Famous medieval men of Morocco (Maghreb). No. 88A also marks the inauguration of the ferryboat "Ibn Batota" connecting Tangier and Malaga.
Issued: #86-88, 5/7/63; #88A, 7/15/66.

Sugar Beet and Sugar Refinery, Sidi Slimane A31

1963, June 10 *Unwmk.* *Perf. 13*
89 A31 20c shown .45 .25
90 A31 50c Tuna fisherman, vert. .80 .35

FAO "Freedom from Hunger" campaign.

Heads of Ramses II, Abu Simbel A32

Designs: 30c, Isis, Kalabsha Temple, vert. 50c, Temple of Philae.

1963, July 15   Engr.   Perf. 11½
91 A32 20c black   .30 .30
92 A32 30c vio, grysh   .55 .30
93 A32 50c maroon, buff   .75 .40
   Nos. 91-93 (3)   1.60 1.00

Campaign to save historic monuments in Nubia.

Agadir Before Earthquake — A33

30c, Like 20c, with "29 Février 1960" and crossed bars added. 50c, Agadir rebuilt.

Engr.; Engr. & Photo. (No. 95)
1963, Oct. 10   Perf. 13½x13
94 A33 20c bl & brn red   .45 .30
95 A33 30c bl, brn red & red   .50 .40
96 A33 50c bl & brn red   1.00 .60
   Nos. 94-96 (3)   1.95 1.30

Issued to publicize the rebuilding of Agadir.

Centenary Emblem and Plan of Agadir Hospital — A34

1963, Oct. 28   Photo.   Perf. 12½x13
97 A34 30c blk, dp car & sil   .55 .25

Centenary of the International Red Cross.

Arms of Morocco and Rabat — A35

1963, Nov. 18   Perf. 13x12½
98 A35 20c gold, red, blk & emer   .55 .25

Installation of Parliament.

Hands Breaking Chain — A36

1963, Dec. 10   Engr.   Perf. 13
99 A36 20c dk brn, grn & org   .55 .25

15th anniversary of the Universal Declaration of Human Rights.

Flag — A37

1963, Dec. 25   Photo.   Perf. 13x12½
100 A37 20c blk, dp car & grn   .60 .25

Evacuation of all foreign military forces from Moroccan territory.

Moulay Abd-er-Rahman, by Delacroix — A38

1964, Mar. 3   Engr.   Perf. 12x13
101 A38 1d multi   3.00 2.00

Coronation of King Hassan II, 3rd anniv.

Weather Map of Africa and UN Emblem — A39

30c, World map and barometer trace, horiz.

1964, Mar. 23   Photo.   Perf. 11½
Granite Paper
102 A39 20c multi   .50 .25
103 A39 30c multi   .55 .40

UN 4th World Meteorological Day. See No. C10.

Children on Vacation — A40

30c, Heads of boy and girl, buildings.

1964, July 6   Litho.   Perf. 12½
104 A40 20c multi   .40 .40
105 A40 30c multi   .50 .50

Issued for vacation camps for children of P.T.T. employees.

Olympic Torch — A41

1964, Sept. 22   Engr.   Perf. 13
106 A41 20c car lake, dk pur & grn .35 .25
107 A41 30c bl, dk grn & red brn   .55 .35
108 A41 50c grn, red & brn   .70 .60
   Nos. 106-108 (3)   1.60 1.20

18th Olympic Games, Tokyo, Oct. 10-25.

Cape Spartel Lighthouse, Sultan Mohammed ben Abd-er-Rahman — A42

Perf. 12½x11½
1964, Oct. 15   Photo.
109 A42 25c multi   .55 .25

Centenary of the Cape Spartel lighthouse.

King Type of 1962
1964-65   Engr.   Perf. 12½x13
Size: 17x23mm
110 A28 20c purple (redrawn)   2.00 .30
Perf. 13½x13
Size: 18x22mm
111 A28 25c rose red ('65)   .35 .25
112 A28 35c slate ('65)   .55 .25
113 A28 40c ultra ('65)   .55 .25
114 A28 60c red lilac ('65)   .85 .25
   Nos. 110-114 (5)   4.30 1.30

The Arabic inscription touches the frame on No. 110. "Mazelin" (designer-engraver) reads up on No. 110, down on Nos. 111-114. No. 110 is a coil stamp with red control numbers on the back of some copies.

Iris — A43   Mohammed V Arriving by Plane — A44

1965   Photo.   Perf. 11½
Granite Paper
115 A43 25c shown   .85 .50
116 A43 40c Gladiolus segetum   1.10 .60
117 A43 60c Capparis spinosa, horiz. 1.40 1.25
   Nos. 115-117 (3)   3.35 2.35

Printed in sheets of 10. Five tête-bêche pairs in every sheet; vertical stamps arranged 5x2, horizontal stamps 2x5. See Nos. 129-131.

1965, Mar. 15   Litho.   Perf. 12½
118 A44 25c lt bl & dk grn   .50 .30

10th anniv. of the return of King Mohammed V from exile and the restoration of the monarchy.

ITU Emblem, Punched-Tape Writer and Telegraph Wires — A45

Design: 40c, ITU emblem, TIROS satellite, radio waves and "ITU" in Morse code.

Perf. 13x14
1965, May 17   Unwmk.   Typo.
119 A45 25c multi   .50 .25
120 A45 40c lt bl, dp bl & bis   .60 .25

ITU, centenary.

ICY Emblem A46

1965, June 14   Engr.   Perf. 13
121 A46 25c slate grn   .30 .25
122 A46 60c dk car rose   .50 .25

International Cooperation Year.

Royal Prawn A47

#123, Triton shell. #124, Varnish shell (pitaria chione). #125, Great voluted shell (cymbium neptuni). #126, Helmet crab, vert. 40c, Mantis shrimp, vert.

1965   Photo.   Perf. 11½
Granite Paper
123 A47 25c vio & multi   1.00 .40
124 A47 25c lt bl & multi   1.00 .40
125 A47 25c org & multi   1.00 .40
126 A47 25c lt grn & multi   1.00 .40
127 A47 40c bl & multi   1.75 .60
128 A47 1d yel & multi   2.50 1.25
   Nos. 123-128 (6)   8.25 3.45

Printed in sheets of 10. Nos. 126-127 (5x2); others (2x5). Five tête bêche pairs in every sheet.

Flower Type of 1965
Orchids: 25c, Ophrys speculum. 40c, Ophrys fusca. 60c, Ophrys tenthredinifera (front and side view), horiz.

1965, Dec. 13   Photo.   Perf. 11½
Granite Paper
129 A43 25c yel & multi   .90 .50
130 A43 40c dl rose & multi   1.75 .50
131 A43 60c lt bl & multi   2.25 1.50
   Nos. 129-131 (3)   4.90 2.50

Note on tête bêche pairs after No. 117 also applies to Nos. 129-131.

Grain — A48

40c, Various citrus fruit. 60c, Olives, horiz.

1966   Photo.   Perf. 11½
Granite Paper
133 A48 25c blk & bister   .50 .25
136 A48 40c multi   .50 .25
137 A48 60c gray & multi   .55 .25
   Nos. 133-137 (3)   1.55 .75

For surcharge see No. 231.

Flag, Map and Dove A49

1966, Mar. 2   Typo.   Perf. 14x13
139 A49 25c brt grn & red   .50 .25

Tenth anniversary of Independence.

King Hassan II — A50

1966, Mar. 2   Engr.   Perf. 13
140 A50 25c red, brt grn & indigo .50 .25

Coronation of King Hassan II, 5th anniv.

Cross-country Runner — A51

1966, Mar. 20   Engr.   Perf. 13
141 A51 25c blue green   .50 .25

53rd International Cross-country Race.

WHO Headquarters from West — A52

40c, WHO Headquarters from the East.

1966, May 3   Engr.   Perf. 13
142 A52 25c rose lil & blk   .30 .25
143 A52 40c dp bl & blk   .50 .25

Inauguration of the WHO Headquarters, Geneva.

Crown Prince Hassan Kissing Hand of King Mohammed V — A53

25c, King Hassan II and parachutist.

Perf. 12½x12
1966, May 14   Photo.   Unwmk.
144 A53 25c gold & blk   .40 .25
145 A53 40c gold & blk   .55 .30
a.   Strip of 2, #144-145 + label 1.10 .75

10th anniv. of the Royal Armed Forces.

Type of 1962 Inscribed: "SEMAINE DE LA PALESTINE"
1966, May 16   Perf. 11x11½
146 A23 25c slate blue   .50 .25

Issued for Palestine Week.

Train — A54

1966, Dec. 19   Photo.   Perf. 13½
147 A54 25c shown   1.00 .30
148 A54 40c Ship   .95 .40
149 A54 1d Autobus   1.20 .55
       Nos. 147-149 (3)   3.15 1.25

Twaite Shad A55

Fish: 40c, Plain bonito. 1d, Bluefish, vert.

1967, Feb. 1   Photo.   Perf. 11½
Granite Paper
150 A55 25c yel & multi   .75 .30
151 A55 40c yel & multi   .85 .30
152 A55 1d lt grn & multi   1.90 .90
       Nos. 150-152 (3)   3.50 1.50

Printed tête bêche in sheets of 10. Nos. 150-151 (2x5); No. 152 (5x2).

Ait Aadel Dam — A56

1967, Mar. 3   Engr.   Perf. 13
153 A56 25c sl grn, Prus bl & gray .50 .25
154 A56 40c Prus bl & lt brn   .70 .25

Inauguration of Ait Aadel Dam.

Rabat Hilton Hotel, Map of Morocco and Roman Arch — A57

1967, Mar. 3
155 A57 25c brt bl & blk   .40 .25
156 A57 1d brt bl & pur   .90 .25

Opening of the Rabat Hilton Hotel.

Torch, Globe, Town and Lions Emblem — A58

1967, Apr. 22   Photo.   Perf. 12½
157 A58 40c gold & saph bl   .40 .25
158 A58 1d gold & slate grn   1.10 .25

Lions International, 50th anniversary.

Three Hands Holding Pickax — A59

1967, July 9   Engr.   Perf. 13
159 A59 25c slate green   .50 .25

Community Development Campaign.

Intl. Tourism Year Emblem A60

1967, Aug. 9   Photo.   Perf. 12½
160 A60 1d lt ultra & dk bl   .90 .35

Arrow and Map of Mediterranean A61

1967, Sept. 8   Perf. 13x12
161 A61 25c dk bl, ultra, red & tan .50 .25
162 A61 40c blk, bl grn, red & tan   .55 .25

Mediterranean Games, Tunis, Sept. 8-17.

Steeplechase — A62

1967, Oct. 14   Photo.   Perf. 12½
163 A62 40c yel grn, blk & brt rose lilac .50 .25
164 A62 1d lt ultra, blk & brt rose lilac .80 .35

International Horseshow.

Cotton — A63

1967, Nov. 15   Photo.   Perf. 12½
165 A63 40c lt bl, grn & yel   .50 .25

Human Rights Flame — A64

1968, Jan. 10   Engr.   Perf. 13
166 A64 25c gray   .40 .25
167 A64 1d rose claret   .50 .25

International Human Rights Year.

King Hassan II — A65

1968-74   Litho.   Perf. 13
Portrait in Magenta, Brown and Black
Size: 23x30mm
169 A65 1c cream & blk   .25 .25
170 A65 2c lt grnsh bl & blk   .25 .25
171 A65 5c lt ol grn & blk   .25 .25
172 A65 10c pale rose & blk   .25 .25
173 A65 15c gray bl & blk   .25 .25
174 A65 20c pink & blk   .25 .25
175 A65 25c white & blk   .25 .25
176 A65 30c pale rose & blk   .30 .25
177 A65 35c bl & blk   .50 .30
178 A65 40c gray & blk   .50 .25
179 A65 50c lt bl & blk   .60 .25
180 A65 60c salmon & blk   .85 .25
181 A65 70c gray & blk   3.50 .90
182 A65 75c pale yel ('74)   1.00 .30
183 A65 80c ocher & blk   1.00 .30

Perf. 13½x14
Size: 26x40mm
184 A65 90c lt bl grn & blk   1.40 .45
185 A65 1d tan & blk   1.75 .30
186 A65 2d lt ultra & blk   2.50 .60
187 A65 3d bluish lil & blk   5.25 1.10
188 A65 5d apple grn & blk   8.50 3.25
       Nos. 169-188 (20)   29.40 10.25

For overprints & surcharges see #224, B17-B18.

Nurse and Child — A66   Pendant — A67

1968, Apr. 8   Engr.   Perf. 13
189 A66 25c ultra, red & olive   .30 .25
190 A66 40c slate, red & olive   .50 .25

WHO, 20th anniv.

1968, May 15   Photo.   Perf. 11½
191 A67 25c shown   .80 .25
192 A67 40c Bracelet   1.25 .30
a.   Pair, #191-192, vertically tête-bêche 4.00 2.40

Moroccan Red Crescent Society. See Nos. 373-374.

Map of Morocco and Rotary Emblem — A68

1968, May 23   Perf. 13
193 A68 40c multi   .65 .25
194 A68 1d ultra & multi   .95 .30

Rotary Intl. District Conference, Casablanca, May 24-25.

Ornamental Design A69

Designs: Various patterns used for sashes.

1968, July 12   Photo.   Perf. 11½
195 A69 25c multi   2.00 .90
196 A69 40c multi   2.40 1.20
197 A69 60c multi   3.50 2.10
198 A69 1d multi   6.50 3.25
       Nos. 195-198 (4)   14.40 7.45

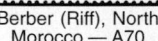

Berber (Riff), North Morocco — A70   Princess Lalla Meryem — A71

Regional Costumes: 10c, Man from Ait Moussa ou Ali. 15c, Woman from Ait Mouhad. No. 200, Bargeman from Rabat Salé. No. 201, Citadin man. 40c, Citadin woman. 60c, Royal Mokhazni. No. 204, Zemmours man. No. 204A, Man from Meknassa. No. 206, Msouffa woman, Sahara.

1968-74   Litho.   Perf. 13x12½
198A A70 10c multi ('69)   .75 .50
199   A70 15c yel & multi   1.25 .70
200   A70 25c bis & multi   1.25 .75
201   A70 25c tan & multi ('69)   1.40 .75
202   A70 40c lt bl & multi   1.50 1.10
203   A70 60c emer & multi   2.10 1.40
204   A70 1d lt bl & multi   2.75 1.90
204A A70 1d gray & multi ('69)   2.50 1.25

Perf. 15
205   A70 1d bis & multi   1.75 1.00
206   A70 1d grn & multi   1.75 1.00
a.   Souvenir sheet of 10, #198A-206, perf. 13 20.00 20.00
b.   As "a," with red overprint & surcharge   22.50 20.00
       Nos. 198A-206 (10)   17.00 10.35

No. 206a issued June 30, 1970, for the opening of the National P.T.T. Museum, Rabat. Sold for 10d.

No. 206b issued Nov. 22, 1974, for the 8th Cong. of the Intl. Fed. of Blood Donors. Each stamp overprinted vertically "8eme Congres de la F.I.O.D.S." and blood container emblem. Black marginal inscription partially obliterated with lines, new Arabic inscription and price added. Sold for 20d.

1968, Oct. 7   Litho.   Perf. 13½

Children's Week: 40c, Princess Lalla Asmaa. 1d, Crown Prince Sidi Mohammed.

207	A71 25c red & multi	.55	.25
208	A71 40c yel & multi	.70	.40
209	A71 1d lt bl & multi	.85	.70
	Nos. 207-209 (3)	2.10	1.35

Wrestling, Aztec Calendar Stone and Olympic Rings — A72

1968, Oct. 25   Photo.   Perf. 12x11½

210	A72 15c shown	.35	.25
211	A72 20c Basketball	.50	.25
212	A72 25c Cycling	.70	.30
213	A72 40c Boxing	.90	.30
214	A72 60c Running	1.40	.30
215	A72 1d Soccer	2.50	.50
	Nos. 210-215 (6)	6.35	1.90

19th Olympic Games, Mexico City, 10/12-27.

10 Dirham Coin of Tetuan, 1780 — A73

Coins: 25c, Dirham, Agmat, c. 1138 A.D. 40c, Dirham, El Alya (Fes), c. 840 A.D. 60c, Dirham, Marrakesh, c. 1248 A.D.

1968, Dec. 17   Photo.   Perf. 11½
Granite Paper

216	A73 20c dp plum, sil & blk	.40	.25
217	A73 25c dk rose brn, gold & blk	.50	.35
218	A73 40c dk grn, sil & blk	1.00	.45
219	A73 60c dk red, gold & blk	1.25	.65
	Nos. 216-219,C16-C17 (6)	17.40	9.30

Issued with tabs.

Women from Zagora A74

Design: 25c, Women from Ait Adidou.

1969, Jan. 21   Litho.   Perf. 12

220	A74 15c multi	1.25	.65
221	A74 25c multi	1.60	.95
	Nos. 220-221,C15 (3)	5.25	2.85

Painting by Belkahya — A75

1969, Mar. 27   Litho.   Perf. 11½x12
222 A75 1d lt grnsh bl, blk & brn   .65 .40

International Day of the Theater.

King Hassan II — A76

1969, July 9   Photo.   Perf. 11½
223 A76 1d gold & multi   1.25 .55

40th birthday of King Hassan II. A souvenir sheet contains one No. 223. Size: 75x105mm. Sold for 2.50d.

No. 185 Overprinted

1969, Sept. 22   Litho.   Perf. 13
224 A65 1d tan & multi   5.25 3.25

First Arab Summit Conference, Rabat.

Mahatma Gandhi — A77

1969, Oct. 16   Photo.   Perf. 11½
225 A77 40c pale vio, blk & gray   1.00 .40

Mohandas K. Gandhi (1869-1948), leader in India's struggle for independence.

ILO Emblem A78

1969, Oct. 29
226 A78 50c multi   .50 .25

ILO, 50th anniv.

King Hassan II on Way to Prayer — A79

1969, Nov. 20   Photo.   Perf. 11½
227 A79 1d multi   1.00 .55

1st Arab Summit Conference, Rabat, Sept. 1969. For overprint see No. 311.

Spahi Horsemen, by Haram al Glaoui A80

1970, Jan. 23   Engr.   Perf. 12x13
228 A80 1d multi   1.00 .55

Main Sewer, Fez — A81

1970, Mar. 23   Litho.   Perf. 12
229 A81 60c multi   .50 .25

50th Congress of Municipal Engineers, Rabat, Mar. 1970.

Guedra Dance, by P. C. Beaubrun A82

1970, Apr. 15
230 A82 40c multi   .55 .25

Folklore Festival, Marrakesh, May 1970.

No. 137 Overprinted "1970", "Census" in Arabic in Red and Surcharged in Black

1970, July 9   Photo.   Perf. 11½
231 A48 25c on 60c multi   .50 .25

Issued to publicize the 1970 census.

Radar Station at Souk El Arba des Sehoul, and Satellite — A83

Ruddy Shelduck — A84

1970, Aug. 20
232 A83 1d lt ultra & multi   1.10 .30

Revolution of King and People, 17th anniv.

1970, Sept. 25   Photo.   Perf. 11½

233	A84 25c shown	1.20	.40
234	A84 40c Houbara bustard	1.60	.45

Campaign to save Moroccan wildlife.

Man Reading Book, Intl. Education Year Emblem — A85

1970, Oct. 20   Litho.   Perf. 12x11½
235 A85 60c dl yel & multi   .55 .25

Symbols of Peace, Justice and Progress A86

1970, Oct. 27   Perf. 13½
236 A86 50c multi   .50 .25

United Nations, 25th anniversary.

Arab League Countries and Emblem A87

1970, Nov. 13   Photo.   Perf. 11½
237 A87 50c multi   .50 .25

Arab League, 25th anniversary.

Olive Grove, Tree and Branch A88

1970, Dec. 3   Litho.   Perf. 12
238 A88 50c red brn & grn   .80 .40

International Olive Year.

Es Sounna
Mosque,
Rabat
A89

1971, Jan. 5   Engr.   Perf. 13
239 A89 60c ol bis, bl & sl grn   .55   .30
Restoration of Es Sounna Mosque, Rabat,
built in 1785.

Heart and
Horse — A90

1971, Feb. 23   Photo.   Perf. 12x12½
240 A90 50c blk & multi   .50   .25
European heart research week, Feb. 21-28.

Dam and
Hassan
II — A91

1971, Mar. 3   Perf. 11½
241 A91 25c multi   .50   .25
  a.   Souv. sheet of 4   2.50 2.00
Accession of King Hassan II, 10th anniv.
No. 241a issued Mar. 24. Sold for 2.50d.

Black and
White
Hands with
Dove and
Emblem
A92

1971, June 16   Photo.   Perf. 13
242 A92 50c brn & multi   .50   .25
Intl. Year against Racial Discrimination.

Children Around
the World — A93

Shah
Mohammed Riza
Pahlavi of
Iran — A94

1971, Oct. 4   Litho.   Perf. 13x14
243 A93 40c emer & multi   .50   .25
International Children's Day.

1971, Oct. 11   Photo.   Perf. 11½
244 A94 1d bl & multi   .70   .45
  2500th anniv. of the founding of the Persian
empire by Cyrus the Great.

Mausoleum of Mohammed V — A95

  50c, Mausoleum, close-up view, and
Mohammed V. 1d, Decorated interior wall.

1971, Nov. 10   Litho.   Perf. 14
245 A95 25c multi   .35   .25
246 A95 50c multi   .45   .25
247 A95 1d multi, vert.   .75   .25
      Nos. 245-247 (3)   1.55 .75

Soccer Ball
and
Games
Emblem
A96

1971, Nov. 30   Photo.   Perf. 13x13½
248 A96 40c shown   .55   .25
249 A96 60c Runner   .80   .25
Mediterranean Games, Izmir, Turkey, Oct.
6-17.

Arab Postal
Union
Emblem
A97

1971, Dec. 23   Litho.   Perf. 13x12½
250 A97 25c dk & lt bl & org   .50   .25
  25th anniv. of the Conference of Sofar, Lebanon, establishing APU.

Sun over
Cultivated Sand
Dunes — A98

1971, Dec. 30   Photo.   Perf. 12½
251 A98 70c blk, bl & yel   .50   .25
  Sherifian Phosphate Office (fertilizer production and export), 50th anniversary.

Torch and Book
Year
Emblem — A99

1972, Jan. 12   Perf. 11½
252 A99 1d silver & multi   .55   .25
International Book Year.

National
Lottery — A100

1972, Feb. 7   Photo.   Perf. 13
253 A100 25c tan, blk & gold   .50   .25
Creation of a national lottery.

Bridge
of
Sighs — A101

  Designs: 50c, St. Mark's Basilica and
waves, horiz. 1d, Lion of St. Mark.

1972, Feb. 25
254 A101 25c multi   .25   .25
255 A101 50c red, blk & buff   .60   .25
256 A101 1d lt bl & multi   .50   .35
      Nos. 254-256 (3)   1.35 .85
UNESCO campaign to save Venice.

Bridge, Road, Map of Africa — A102

1972, Apr. 21   Perf. 13
257 A102 75c blue & multi   .55   .25
2nd African Road Conf., Rabat, Apr. 17-22.

Morocco
No.
223 — A103

1972, Apr. 27   Perf. 11½
258 A103 1d lt ultra & multi   .65   .25
Stamp Day.

The
Engagement
of Imilchil, by
Tayeb Lahlou
A104

1972, May 26   Litho.   Perf. 13x13½
259 A104 60c blk & multi   .90   .50
Folklore Festival, Marrakesh, May 26-June 4.

Map of Africa,
Dove and OAU
Emblem — A105

1972, June 12   Photo.   Perf. 11½
260 A105 25c multi   .50   .25
  9th Summit Conference of Organization for
African Unity, Rabat, June 12-15.

Landscape, Environment
Emblem — A106

1972, July 20   Photo.   Perf. 12½x12
261 A106 50c bl & multi   .50   .25
  UN Conference on Human Environment,
Stockholm, June 5-16

Olympic
Emblems,
Running
A107

1972, Aug. 29   Photo.   Perf. 13x13½
262 A107 25c shown   .25   .25
263 A107 50c Wrestling   .35   .25
264 A107 75c Soccer   .60   .25
265 A107 1d Cycling   .75   .50
      Nos. 262-265 (4)   1.95 1.25
20th Olympic Games, Munich, 8/26-9/11.

Sow
Thistle — A108

Mountain
Gazelle — A109

1972, Sept. 15   Litho.   Perf. 14
266 A108 25c shown   .50   .25
267 A108 40c Amberboa crupi-
          noides   .65   .25
      See No. 305-306.

1972, Sept. 29   Photo.   Perf. 11½
268 A109 25c shown   .80   .35
269 A109 40c Barbary sheep   1.10   .40
Nos. 266-269 issued for nature protection.

Rabat
Rug — A110

  25c, High Atlas rug. 70c, Tazenakht rug.
75c, Rabat rug, different pattern.

Perf. 13½ (25fr, 70fr), 11½
1972-73 **Photo.**
270   A110 25c multi   .90 .25
270A A110 50c multi   1.00 .25
271   A110 70c multi   1.40 .50
271A A110 75c multi   1.50 .50
   Nos. 270-271A (4)   4.80 1.50
Issued: 50c, 75c, 10/27; 25c, 70c, 12/28/73.
See Nos. 326-327.

Child and
UNICEF
Emblem — A111

1972, Dec. 20 Photo. *Perf. 13½x13*
272   A111 75c brt grn & bl   .50 .25
International Children's Day.

Symbolic
Letter
Carrier and
Stamp
A112

1973, Jan. 30 Photo. *Perf. 13x13½*
273   A112 25c brn & multi   .25 .25
Stamp Day.

Weather Map,
Northern
Hemisphere
A113

1973, Feb. 23 Photo. *Perf. 13*
274   A113 70c silver & multi   .55 .30
Intl. meteorological cooperation, cent.

King Hassan II,
Coat of
Arms — A114

1973-76 Photo. *Perf. 14*
275   A114 1c pale yel & multi   .25 .25
276   A114 2c pale bl & multi   .25 .25
277   A114 5c pale ol & multi   .25 .25
278   A114 10c brn org & multi   .25 .25
279   A114 15c vio gray & multi   .25 .25
280   A114 20c pink & multi   .25 .25
281   A114 25c pale bl & multi   .25 .25
282   A114 30c rose & multi   .25 .25
283   A114 35c org yel & multi   .35 .25
284   A114 40c lt gray & multi   4.00 .35
285   A114 50c ultra & multi   .50 .25
286   A114 60c sal & multi   .60 .25
287   A114 70c yel grn & multi   .50 .25
288   A114 75c lem & multi   .45 .25
289   A114 80c multi   .50 .30
290   A114 90c brt grn & multi   .55 .25
291   A114 1d beige & multi   1.75 .25
292   A114 2d gray & multi   3.50 .50
293   A114 3d lt lil & multi   4.50 .75
294   A114 5d lt brn & multi ('75)   3.50 1.00
294A A114 5d pink & multi ('76)   3.50 1.00
   Nos. 275-294A (21)   26.20 7.65

Nos. B26-B27
Surcharged to
Obliterate Surtax

1973, Mar. 13 *Perf. 11½*
295   SP1 25c multi   2.50 2.50
296   SP1 70c multi   2.75 2.75
   a. Pair, #295-296, vert. tête-bêche 7.25 7.25
Tourism Conference 1973. Arabic overprint
and date on one line on No. 296.
See Nos. 351-352.

Holy
Ka'aba,
Mecca,
Mosque
and
Minaret,
Rabat
A115

1973, May 3 Photo. *Perf. 13½x14*
297   A115 25c lt bl & multi   .25 .25
Mohammed's 1,403rd birthday.

Roses and
M'Gouna
A116

1973, May 14 *Perf. 13*
298   A116 25c bl & multi   .25 .25
Rose Festival of M'Gouna.

Hands, Torch,
OAU
Emblem — A117

1973, May 25 Photo. *Perf. 14x13*
299   A117 70c deep claret & multi   .50 .25
OAU, 10th anniversary.

Dancers with Tambourines — A118

Design: 1d, Dancer with handbells, Marrakesh Minaret, Atlas Mountain.

1973, May 30 *Perf. 12½x13*
300   A118 50c multi   .50 .25
301   A118 1d multi   .65 .30
Folklore Festival, Marrakesh.

Copernicus
A119

1973, June 29 *Perf. 13x13½*
302   A119 70c Heliocentric sys-
              tem   1.25 .30

Microscope, WHO
Emblem, World
Map — A120

1973, July 16 Photo. *Perf. 13x12½*
303   A120 70c multi   .55 .25
WHO, 25th anniversary.

INTERPOL
Emblem,
Fingerprint
A121

1973, Sept. 12 Photo. *Perf. 13x13½*
304   A121 70c brn, sil & bl   .50 .25
50th anniv. of Intl. Criminal Police Org.

Flower Type of 1972
1973, Oct. 12 Litho. *Perf. 14*
305   A108 25c Daisies, horiz.   .65 .25
306   A108 1d Thistle   1.25 .50
Nature protection.

Berber
Hyena
A122

Design: 50c, Eleonora's falcon, vert.

1973, Nov. 23 Photo. *Perf. 14*
307   A122 25c multi   1.25 .25
308   A122 50c multi   2.50 .40
Nature protection.

Map and
Colors of
Morocco,
Algeria and
Tunisia
A123

1973, Dec. 7 *Perf. 13x13½*
309   A123 25c gold & multi   .50 .25
Maghreb Committee for Coordination of
Posts and Telecommunications.

Fairway and Drive
over Water
Hazard — A124

1974, Feb. 8 Photo. *Perf. 14x13*
310   A124 70c multi   .25 .25
International Golf Grand Prix for the Hassan
II Morocco trophy.

No. 227
Overprinted
in Red

1974, Feb. 25 *Perf. 11½*
311   A79 1d multi   2.75 1.50
Islamic Conference, Lahore, India, 1974.

Map of Africa,
Scales, Human
Rights
Flame — A125

1974, Mar. 15 Photo. *Perf. 14x13½*
312   A125 70c gold & multi   .50 .25
25th anniversary of the Universal Declaration of Human Rights.

Vanadinite
A126

1974-75 Photo. *Perf. 13*
313   A126 25c shown   2.25 .60
313A A126 50c Aragonite   2.00 .35
314   A126 70c Erythrine   4.00 .75
314A A126 1d Agate   4.00 1.00
   Nos. 313-314A (4)   12.25 2.30
Issued: 25c, 70c, 4/30/74; 50c, 1d, 2/14/75.

Minaret,
Marrakesh
Mosque, Rotary
Emblem — A127

1974, May 11 Photo. *Perf. 14*
315   A127 70c multi   .55 .25
District 173 Rotary International annual
meeting, Marrakesh, May 10-12.

UPU Emblem,
Congress
Dates — A128

1d, Scroll with UPU emblem, Lausanne coat
of arms & 17th UPU Congress emblem, horiz.

1974, May 30 Photo.
316   A128 25c lt grn, org & blk   .30 .25
317   A128 1d dk grn & multi   .70 .25
Centenary of Universal Postal Union.

Drummer and Dancers — A129

Design: 70c, Knife juggler and women.

1974, June 7   Photo.   Perf. 14
318 A129 25c multi   .50 .25
319 A129 70c multi   1.25 .35

National folklore festival, Marrakesh.

Environment Emblem, Polution, Clean
Water and Air — A130

1974, June 25   Perf. 13
320 A130 25c multi   .40 .25

World Environment Day.

Simulated
Stamps,
Cancel and
Magnifier
A131

1974, Aug. 2   Photo.   Perf. 13
321 A131 70c sil & multi   .50 .25

Stamp Day.

No. J5 Surcharged

1974, Sept. 25   Photo.   Perf. 14
322 D2 1d on 5c multi   2.00 1.40

Agricultural census.

World Soccer
Cup — A132

Double-spurred
Francolin — A133

1974, Oct. 11
323 A132 1d brt bl & multi   .95 .65

World Cup Soccer Championship, Munich,
June 13-July 7.
    A stamp similar to No. 323, also issued Oct.
11, has gold inscription: "CHAMPION: R.F.A."
in French and Arabic, honoring the German
Federal Republic as championship winner.
Value $32.50.

Perf. 14x13½, 13½x14
1974, Dec. 5   Photo.
324 A133 25c green & multi   .60 .25
325 A133 70c Leopard, horiz.   1.25 .35

Nature protection.

Zemmour Rug
A134

Columbine
A135

Design: 1d, Beni Mguilo rug.

1974, Dec 20   Perf. 13
326 A134 25c multi   .55 .25
327 A134 1d multi   1.20 .30

See Nos. 349-350, 398-400.

1975   Photo.   Perf. 13½
328 A135 10c Daisies   .25 .25
329 A135 25c Columbine   .50 .25
330 A135 35c Orange lilies   .55 .25
331 A135 50c Anemones   .65 .25
332 A135 60c White starflower   .80 .35
333 A135 70c Poppies   .85 .35
334 A135 90c Carnations   1.20 .50
335 A135 1d Pansies   1.10 .60
        Nos. 328-335 (8)   5.90 2.80

Issued: 25c, 35c, 70c, 90c, 1/10; others,
4/29.

Water Carrier,
by Feu Tayeb
Lahlou
A136

1975, Apr. 3   Perf. 13
338 A136 1d multicolored   1.20 .50

Stamp Collector,
Carrier Pigeon,
Globe — A137

1975, May 21   Photo.   Perf. 13
339 A137 40c gold & multi   .50 .25

Stamp Day.

Musicians and
Dancers — A138

1975, June 12 Photo. Perf. 14x13½
340 A138 1d multicolored   .95 .30

16th Folklore Festival, Marrakesh, 5/30-6/15.

Guitar and
Association
for the
Blind
Emblem
A139

1975, July 8   Perf. 13x13½
341 A139 1d purple & multi   .90 .50

Week of the Blind.

Animals in
Forest — A140

1975, July 25 Photo. Perf. 13x13½
342 A140 25c multicolored   .50 .25

Children's Week.

Games' Emblem, Runner, Weight
Lifter — A141

1975, Sept. 4   Photo.   Perf. 13
343 A141 40c gold, maroon & buff .50 .25

7th Mediterranean Games, Algiers, 8/23-9/6.

Bald Ibis
A142

1975, Oct. 21   Photo.   Perf. 13
344 A142 40c shown   1.25 .40
345 A142 1d Persian lynx, vert. 1.60 .80

Nature protection.

King Mohammed V Greeting Crowd,
Prince Moulay Hassan at Left — A143

King Hassan II
A144

#348, King Mohammed V wearing fez.

1975, Nov. 21   Photo.   Perf. 13½
346 A143 40c blk, sil & dk bl   .55 .25
347 A144 1d blk, gold & dk bl   .80 .50
348 A144 1d blk, gold & dk bl   .80 .50
    a.   Sheet of 3, #346-348 12.50 12.50

20th anniversary of independence.

Rug Type of 1974
25c, Ouled Besseba. 1d, Ait Ouaouzguid.

1975, Dec. 11
349 A134 25c red & multi   .90 .50
350 A134 1d orange & multi   1.40 .55

A number of issues have been
printed se-tenant in sheets of 10 (5x2)
arranged vertically tête bêche.

Nos. B29-B30
Surcharged
in Green to Obliterate
Surtax

1975   Perf. 11½
351 SP1 25c blue & multi   2.50 2.50
352 SP1 70c orange & multi   2.75 2.75
    a.   Pair, #351-352, vertically tête-
          bêche   7.25 7.25

March of Moroccan people into Spanish
Sahara, Dec. 1975.

"Green March of
the
People" — A145

1975, Dec. 30 Photo. Perf. 13½x13
353 A145 40c multicolored   .45 .25

March of Moroccan people into Spanish
Sahara, Dec. 1975.

Copper Coin,
Fez, 1883-
84 — A146

Coins: 15c, 50c, silver coin, Rabat, 1774-
75. 35c, 65c, Gold coin, Sabta, 13th-14th centuries. 1d, Square coin, Sabta, 12th-13th
centuries.

1976   Photo.   Perf. 14x13½
354 A146 5c dull rose & multi   .25 .25
355 A146 15c brown & multi   .25 .25
356 A146 35c gray & multi   .50 .25
357 A146 40c ocher & multi   .70 .25
358 A146 50c ultra & blk   .80 .25
359 A146 65c yellow & multi   .95 .30
360 A146 1d multicolored   1.25 .45
        Nos. 354-360 (7)   4.70 2.00

Issued: #354-356, 4/26; #357-360, 1/20.

1976, Sept. 9

Designs: Various Moroccan coins.

361 A146 5c green & multi   .25 .25
362 A146 15c dp rose & multi   .25 .25
363 A146 20c lt bl & multi   .35 .25
364 A146 30c lil rose & multi   .45 .25
365 A146 35c green & multi   .60 .25
366 A146 70c orange & multi   .80 .25
        Nos. 361-366 (6)   2.70 1.50

See Nos. 403-406A, 524B-524C.

Family — A147

1976, Feb. 12   **Perf. 14x13½**
367 A147 40c multicolored   .50 .25
Family planning.

Arch, Ibn Zaidoun
Mosque — A148

40c, Hall, Ibn Zaidoun Mosque, horiz.

Perf. 13½x14, 14x13½
1976, Feb. 12   **Photo.**
368 A148 40c multicolored   .35 .25
369 A148 65c multicolored   .60 .25
Ibn Zaidoun Mosque, millennium.

Medersa bou Anania, Fez
A149

1976, Feb. 26   **Perf. 13x14½**
370 A149 1d multicolored   .65 .25

Borobudur Temple — A150

Design: 40c, Bas-relief, Borobudur.

1976, Mar. 11   **Photo.**   **Perf. 13**
371 A150 40c multicolored   .40 .25
372 A150 1d multicolored   .80 .25
UNESCO campaign to save Borobudur Temple, Java.

Islamic Conference, 6th
Anniv. — A151

1976   **Litho.**   **Perf. 13½x13**
372A A151 1d Dome of the Rock   .65 .25

Jewelry Type of 1968

Designs: 40c, Pendant. 1d, Breastplate.

1976, June 29   **Photo.**   **Perf. 14x13½**
373 A67 40c blue & multi   .50 .25
374 A67 1d olive & multi   .95 .30
   a.   Pair, #373-374, vertically tête-bêche   1.75 1.75

Moroccan Red Crescent Society.

Bicentennial Emblem, Flags and Map
of US and Morocco — A152

Design: 1d, George Washington, King Hassan, Statue of Liberty and Royal Palace, Rabat, vert.

1976, July 27   **Photo.**   **Perf. 14**
375 A152 40c multicolored   .50 .25
376 A152 1d multicolored   .90 .35
American Bicentennial.

Wrestling
A153

1976, Aug. 11   **Perf. 13x13½**
377 A153 35c shown   .25 .25
378 A153 40c Cycling   .25 .25
379 A153 50c Boxing   .50 .30
380 A153 1d Running   .95 .45
   Nos. 377-380 (4)   1.95 1.25
21st Olympic Games, Montreal, Canada, July 17-Aug. 1.

Old and New Telephones,
Radar — A154

1976, Sept. 29   **Photo.**   **Perf. 14**
381 A154 1d gold & multi   .65 .25
Centenary of first telephone call by Alexander Graham Bell, Mar. 10, 1876.

Blind Person's
Identification
A155

1976, Oct. 12   **Photo.**   **Perf. 13½x14**
382 A155 50c multicolored   .50 .25
Week of the Blind.

Chanting
Goshawk
A156

1976, Oct. 29   **Perf. 13x13½**
383 A156 40c shown   1.40 .40
384 A156 1d Purple gallinule   2.00 .70
Nature protection.

King Hassan,
Star, Torch, Map
of
Morocco — A157

1976, Nov. 19   **Photo.**   **Perf. 12½x13**
385 A157 40c multicolored   .55 .25
Green March into Spanish Sahara, 1st anniv.

**Nos. B34-B35 Ovptd. with 2 Bars
over Srch. and 4-line Arabic
Inscription**

1976, Nov. 29   **Photo.**   **Perf. 13½**
386 SP1 25c ultra, blk & org   2.00 2.00
387 SP1 70c red, blk & org   2.40 2.40
   a.   Pair, #386-387, vert. tête-bêche   5.50 5.50
5th African Tuberculosis Conference, Rabat.

Globe and
Dove
A158

1976, Dec. 16   **Perf. 13**
388 A158 1d blue, blk & red   .55 .25
5th Summit Meeting of Non-aligned Countries, Colombo, Aug. 9-19, and 25th anniv. of Org. of Non-aligned Countries.

Africa Cup — A159

1976, Dec. 29   **Photo.**   **Perf. 14**
389 A159 1d multicolored   .70 .25
African Soccer Cup.

Letters
Circling
Globe,
Postmark
A160

1977, Jan. 24   **Photo.**   **Perf. 13½**
390 A160 40c multicolored   .50 .25
Stamp Day.

Aeonium
Arboreum
A161

Malope
Trifida — A162

1d, Hesperolaburnum platyclarpum.

Perf. 13x13½, 14 (A162)
1977, Feb. 22
391 A161 40c multicolored   .55 .40
392 A162 50c multicolored   1.00 .50
393 A161 1d multicolored   1.20 .65
   Nos. 391-393 (3)   2.75 1.55

Ornamental Lamps, View of
Salé — A163

1977, Mar. 24   **Photo.**   **Perf. 14**
394 A163 40c multicolored   .55 .25
Candle procession of Salé.

No. J6 Surcharged in
Orange

1977, May 11   **Photo.**   **Perf. 14**
395 D2 40c on 10c multi   .80 .40
Cherry Festival.

Map of
Arab
Countries,
Emblem
A164

1977, June 2   **Photo.**   **Perf. 14**
396 A164 50c multicolored   .55 .25
5th Congress of Organization of Arab Cities.

APU
Emblem,
Members'
Flags
A165

1977, June 20
397 A165 1d multicolored   .55 .25
Arab Postal Union, 25th anniversary.

Rug Type of 1974

Designs. 35c, No. 399A, Marmoucha rug, diff. No. 399, Ait Haddou rug. 1d, Salé rug.

Perf. 11½x12, 13½ (#399A)
1977-79   **Photo.**
398 A134 35c multicolored   .45 .25
399 A134 40c multicolored   .55 .25
399A A134 40c multicolored ('79)   1.00 .25
400 A134 1d multicolored   1.00 .40
   Nos. 398-400 (4)   3.00 1.15

Issued: #399A, 3/8/79; others, 7/21/77.

Cithara — A166

1977, Aug. 18   Photo.   Perf. 14
401 A166 1d multi   .90   .30
        Week of the Blind.

Ali Jinnah and
Map of
Pakistan — A167

1977, Oct. 10   Photo.   Perf. 13½x13
402 A167 70c multi   .55   .25
    Mohammed Ali Jinnah (1876-1948), first
Governor General of Pakistan.

Coin Type of 1976
Designs: Various Moroccan coins.

1977-81   Perf. 14x13½
403   A146 10c gray & multi   .35   .25
403A A146 25c ap grn & multi
                ('81)   1.40   .35
404   A146 60c dk red & multi
                ('78)   1.00   .25
405   A146 75c citron & multi   .70   .25
405A A146 80c pale vio & mult
                ('81)   7.00   .50
406   A146 2d yel grn & multi   1.75   .35
406A A146 3d beige & multi
                ('81)   14.00 1.75
        Nos. 403-406A (7)   26.20 3.70

Marcher with
Flag, Map of
Morocco and
Spanish
Sahara — A168

1977, Nov. 6   Photo.   Perf. 14
407 A168 1d multi   .65   .25
    Green March into Spanish Sahara, 2nd
anniv.

Chamber of Representatives — A169

1977, Nov. 6   Perf. 13½
408 A169 1d multi   .65   .25
  a.   Souvenir sheet   3.00   3.00
    Opening of Chamber of Representatives.
No. 408a sold for 3d.

Enameled Silver
Brooch — A170

Copper
Vessel — A171

1977, Dec. 14   Photo.   Perf. 11½
409 A170 1d multi   2.50   .25
    Moroccan Red Crescent Society.

1978, Jan. 5   Photo.   Perf. 13
    1d, Standing filigree copper bowl with cover.
410 A171 40c gold & multi   .40   .25
411 A171 1d gold & multi   .90   .25
  a.   Pair, #410-411, vert. tête-bêche 2.00   2.00

Map of Sahara,
Cogwheel
Emblem — A172

    1d, Map of North Africa, fish in net, camels.

1978, Feb. 27   Photo.   Perf. 14
412 A172 40c multi   .40   .25
413 A172 1d multi, horiz.   .80   .25
    Promotion of the Sahara. See Nos. 441-442
for similar stamps overprinted.

Covered
Jar — A173

1978, Mar. 27   Perf. 13½x13
414 A173 1d shown   .90   .50
415 A173 1d Vase   .90   .50
        Week of the Blind.

Red
Crescent,
Red Cross,
Arab
Countries
A174

1978, Apr. 14   Perf. 13x13½
416 A174 1d multi   .80   .30
    10th Conference of Arab Red Crescent and
Red Cross Societies, Apr. 10-15.

View of Fez,
Rotary
Emblem — A175

1978, Apr. 22   Photo.   Perf. 14
417 A175 1d multi   .65   .30
    Rotary Intl. Meeting, Fez, District 173.

Dome of the Rock,
Jerusalem — A176

1978, May 29   Perf. 14½
418 A176 5c multi   .30   .25
419 A176 10c multi   .30   .25
    Palestinian fighters and their families. For
overprints see Nos. 502-502A.

Folk Dancers and
Flutist — A177

1978, June 15   Perf. 13½x13
420 A177 1d multi   2.00   .50
    National Folklore Festival, Marrakesh.

Sugar
Cane
Field, and
Conveyor
Belt
A178

1978, July 24   Photo.   Perf. 13
421 A178 40c multi   .45   .25
        Sugar industry.

Games
Emblem — A179

1978, Aug. 25
422 A179 1d multi   .90   .25
    World sailing championships.

Bird, Tree, Tent,
Scout
Emblem — A180

1978, Sept. 26   Photo.   Perf. 13
423 A180 40c multi   1.00   .50
    Pan-Arab Scout Jamboree, Rabat.

View of
Fez
A181

1978, Oct. 10
424 A181 40c multi   .45   .25
    Moulay Idriss the Great, Festival, Fez.

Flame
Emblem — A182

1978, Dec. 21   Photo.   Perf. 14
425 A182 1d multi   .70   .25
    30th anniversary of Universal Declaration of
Human Rights.

Houses,
Agadir — A183

1979, Jan. 25   Photo.   Perf. 12
426 A183 40c shown   .40   .25
427 A183 1d Old Fort, Marrakesh   .80   .25

Soccer
and Cup
A184

1979, Mar. 2   Perf. 13
428 A184 40c multi   .55   .25
    Mohammed V Soccer Cup.

Vase — A185

1979, Mar. 29   Photo.   Perf. 14
429 A185 1d multi   .95   .25
        Week of the Blind.

Procession
A186

    1d, Festival, by Mohamed Ben Ali Rbati,
horiz.

1979, Apr. 18 *Perf. 13x13½, 13½x13*
430 A186 40c multi .45 .25
431 A186 1d multi .75 .25

Brass Containers, Red Crescent A187

Perf. 13x13½, 13½x13
1979, May 16 *Photo.*
432 A187 40c shown .30 .25
433 A187 1d Heated coffee urn, vert. .80 .30

Red Crescent Society.

Dancers — A188

1979, June 1 *Photo.* *Perf. 13*
434 A188 40c multi .55 .25

National Festival of Marrakech.

Silver Daggor A180

1979, June 20 *Perf. 14*
435 A189 1d multi .80 .25

King Hassan II, 50th Birthday — A190

1979, July 9 *Photo.* *Perf. 14*
436 A190 1d multi .65 .25

4th Arab Youth Festival, Rabat A191

1979, July 30 *Photo.* *Perf. 13½x14*
437 A191 1d multi .65 .25

King Hassan II and Crowd — A192

1979, Aug. 20 *Perf. 14x13½*
438 A192 1d multi .50 .25

Revolution of the King and the People, 25th anniv.

Intl. Bureau of Education, 50th Anniv. — A193

1979, Sept. 28 *Photo.* *Perf. 13x13½*
439 A193 1d multi .65 .25

Pilgrimage to Mecca, Mt. Arafat, Holy Ka'aba A194

1979, Oct. 25 *Perf. 13½*
440 A194 1d multi .65 .25

No. 413 Redrawn in Smaller Size and Ovptd. in Red

1979, Nov. 7 *Litho.* *Perf. 14*
Size: 33x23mm
441 A172 40c multi .55 .25
442 A172 1d multi 1.10 .40

Return of Oued Eddahab province, Aug. 14.

Leucanthemum Catanance — A195

1979, Nov. 21 *Photo.* *Perf. 14½*
443 A195 40c Centaurium .30 .25
444 A195 1d shown .80 .25

Children, Globe, IYC Emblem — A196

1979, Dec. 3 *Perf. 14*
445 A196 40c multi .90 .30

International Year of the Child.

Otter — A197

1979, Dec. 18 *Perf. 13½x13*
446 A197 40c shown .70 .25
447 A197 1d Redstart 1.50 .25

Traffic Signs and Road — A198

1980, Jan. 3 *Photo.* *Perf. 14*
448 A198 40c shown .25 .25
449 A198 1d Children at curb .55 .25

Fortress A199

1980, Jan. 29 *Perf. 13x13½*
450 A199 1d multi .55 .25

Copper Bowl and Lid, Red Crescent — A200

Red Crescent Soc.: 70c, Copper kettle, brazier.

1980, Feb. 28 *Photo.* *Perf. 14*
451 A200 50c multi .50 .25
452 A200 70c multi .70 .25
a. Pair, #451-452, vert. tête-bêche 1.75 1.75

Week of the Blind — A201

1980, Mar. 19 *Photo.* *Perf. 14*
453 A201 40c multi .50 .25

Rabat Mechanical Sorting Office — A202

1980, Apr. 17
454 A202 40c multi .55 .25

Stamp Day.

Rotary Intl., 75th Anniv. — A203

1980, May 14 *Photo.* *Perf. 14*
455 A203 1d multi .55 .25

Cloth and Leather Goods — A204

1980, May 31 *Photo.* *Perf. 13½x13*
456 A204 1d multi .65 .25

4th Textile and Leather Exhibition, Casablanca, May 2-9.

Gypsum — A205   Falcon — A206

1980, June 19 *Photo.* *Perf. 13½x13*
457 A205 40c multi 1.25 .25

See Nos. 477-478.

1980, July 26 *Perf. 11½*
458 A206 40c multi 1.75 .30

Hunting with falcons.

Fight against Heart Disease A207

1980, Aug. 7 *Photo.* *Perf. 13x13½*
459 A207 1d multi .65 .25

A208

1980, Aug. 18 *Perf. 14*
460 A208 40c shown .60 .25
461 A208 1d Emblems, diff. 1.10 .25

United Nations Decade for Women.

Ornamental Saddle and Harness A209

1980, Sept. 3   *Perf. 14½*
462 A209 40c Saddle, harness,
     diff.   .35 .25
463 A209 1d shown   .90 .25

A210

1980, Sept. 18
464 A210 40c multi   .55 .25

World Meteorological Day.

Hand
Holding
Dry Gas
Pump
A211

1980, Oct. 6   *Photo.*   *Perf. 14*
465 A211 40c Light bulb, gas can   .30 .25
466 A211 1d shown   .65 .25

Energy conservation.

World Tourism
Conference,
Manila, Sept.
27 — A212

1980, Oct. 22   *Perf. 11½x12*
467 A212 40c multi   .55 .25

Symbolic
Tree
Rooted in
Europe
and Africa
A213

1980, Oct. 30   *Perf. 14*
468 A213 1d multi   .80 .25

Straits of Gibraltar linking Europe and Africa.

5th Anniversary of the Green
March — A214

1980, Nov. 6
469 A214 1d multi   .65 .25

Holy
Ka'aba — A215

1980, Nov. 9
470 A215 40c shown   .25 .25
471 A215 1d Mecca Mosque   .70 .25
    a. Souv. sheet of 2, #470-471   2.00 2.00

No. 471a sold for 3d.

Senecio
Antheuphorbium
A216

1980, Dec. 4   *Perf. 13*
472 A216 50c shown   .70 .25
473 A216 1d Periploca laevigata   1.25 .40

Leaves, by   Nejjarine
Mahjoubi   Fountain,
Aherdan — A217   Fes — A218

Design: 40c. Untitled painting by Mahjoubi
Aherdan (23x38mm).

1980, Dec. 18   *Perf. 12*
474 A217 40c multi   .30 .25
475 A217 1d multi   .75 .25

1981, Jan. 22   *Perf. 14x13½*
476 A218 40c multi   .50 .25

Mineral Type of 1980

1981, Feb. 19   *Photo.*   *Perf. 13½x13*
477 A205 40c Onyx   1.00 .25
478 A205 1d Malachite-azurite   2.25 .40

Inscribed 1980.

King Hassan
II — A219

1981, Mar. 2   *Perf. 14*
479 A219 60c shown   .30 .25
480 A219 60c Map of Morocco   .30 .25
481 A219 60c King Mohammed V   .30 .25
    a. Strip of 3, #479-481   1.25 .75

25th anniv. of independence.

25th Anniv. of King Hassan II
Coronation — A220

1981, Mar. 3
482 A220 1.30d multi   .65 .25

The Source, by Jillali
Gharbaoui — A221

1981, Apr. 8   *Perf. 13x12½*
483 A221 1.30d multi   1.00 .35

Anagalis   Army
Monelli — A222   Badge — A223

1981, Apr. 23   *Perf. 13*
484 A222 40c shown   .50 .25
485 A222 70c Bubonium intri-
     catum   1.00 .25

1981, May 14   *Photo.*   *Perf. 14x13½*
   Moroccan Armed Forces, 25th Anniv: No.
486, King Hassan II as army major general;
No. 488, King Mohammed V.
486 A223 60c multi   .30 .25
487 A223 60c multi   .30 .25
488 A223 60c multi   .30 .25
    a. Strip of 3, #486-488   1.10 .75

13th World Telecommunications
Day — A224

1981, May 18   *Perf. 14x13*
489 A224 1.30d multi   .65 .25

Hand-painted
Plate — A225

1981, June 5   *Perf. 14*
490 A225 50c shown   .35 .25
491 A225 1.30d Plate, diff.   .80 .25

Week of the Blind.

22nd Marrakesh
Arts
Festival — A226

1981, June 18   *Perf. 13½x13*
492 A226 1.30d multi   .90 .25

For overprint see No. 579.

Seboula Dagger,
Oujda — A227

1981, Sept. 7   *Photo.*   *Perf. 13½*
493 A227 1.30d multi   1.10 .25

Copper Mortar
and Pestle, Red
Crescent — A228

1981, Sept. 24   *Perf. 14*
494 A228 60c shown   .45 .25
495 A228 1.30d Tripod   1.20 .30

Intl. Year of the
Disabled — A229

1981, Oct. 15   *Perf. 13½*
496 A229 60c multi   .55 .25

Iphiclides
Feisthamelii
A230

1981, Oct. 29   *Perf. 13½x13*
497 A230 60c shown   2.00 .50
498 A230 1.30d Zerynthia rumina   3.50 1.00

See Nos. 528-529.

6th Anniv. of Green March — A231

1981, Nov. 6   *Perf. 13x13½*
499 A231 1.30d multi   .55 .25

Intl. Palestinian Solidarity Day — A232

1981, Nov. 22   *Perf. 13½x13*
500 A232 60c multi   .55 .25

Congress Emblem — A233

1981, Nov. 22   *Perf. 13½*
501 A233 1.30d multi   .65 .33

World Federation of Twin Cities, 10th Congress, Casablanca, Nov. 15-18.

Nos. 418-419 Overprinted

1981, Nov. 25   **Photo.**   *Perf. 14½*
502 A176 40c on 5c multi   8.50 6.00
502A A176 40c on 10c multi   6.50 3.75

First Anniv. of Mohammed V Airport — A234

1981, Dec. 8   **Photo.**   *Perf. 14x13*
503 A234 1.30d multi   .65 .25

Al Massirah Dam Opening A235

1981, Dec. 17   *Perf. 11½*
504 A235 60c multi   .40 .25

King Hassan II — A236

1981, Dec. 28   *Perf. 13x12½*
505	A236	5c multi	.25	.25
506	A236	10c multi	.25	.25
507	A236	15c multi	.25	.25
508	A236	20c multi	.25	.25
509	A236	25c multi	.25	.25
510	A236	30c multi	.25	.25
511	A236	35c multi	.25	.25
512	A236	40c multi	.40	.25
513	A236	50c multi	.25	.25
514	A236	60c multi	.25	.25
515	A236	65c multi	.25	.25
516	A236	70c multi	.25	.25
a.		Perf 12x11¾, granite paper	.25	.25
517	A236	75c multi	.25	.25
518	A236	80c multi	.30	.25
519	A236	90c multi	.50	.25

No. 516a is dated 1999 and has the denomination and "Postes" closer to the shoulder than to the chin.

1983, Mar. 1   **Photo.**   *Perf. 14½*
         Size: 25x32mm
520	A236	1d multi	.30	.25
521	A236	1.40d multi	.40	.25
522	A236	2d multi	.45	.25
523	A236	3d multi	.75	.25
524	A236	5d multi	1.10	.45
524A	A236	10d multi	2.25	.80
e.		Perf 11½, granite paper	2.00	1.00
		Nos. 505-524A (21)	9.45	6.00

No. 524Ae is dated 1999 and has the denomination and "Postes" closer to the shoulder than to the chin.

See Nos. 566-575, 715-724.

Coin Type of 1976
1979-81   **Photo.**   *Perf. 12½*
         Size: 18x23mm
524B	A146	40c ocher & multi	.60	.25
d.		Bklt. pane of 10	6.00	
524C	A146	50c brt bl, blk & dk brn ('81)	.60	.25

Equestrian Sports A237

1981, Dec. 29   *Perf. 13x13½*
525 A237 1.30d multi   1.25 .40

Traditional Carpet Design — A238

1982, Jan. 21
526 A238 50c Glaoua pattern   .25 .25
527 A238 1.30d Ouled Besseba pattern   .65 .25

Butterfly Type of 1981
1982, Feb. 25   *Perf. 13½x13*
528 A230 60c Celerio oken lineata   1.60 .55
529 A230 1.30d Mesoacidalia aglaja lyauteyi   3.50 .85

World Forest Day — A240

1982, Apr. 8   *Perf. 14*
531 A240 40c multi   .55 .25

Blind Week — A241

1982, May 10
532 A241 1d Jug   .55 .25

Folk Dancers, Rabat — A242   Copper Candlestick, Red Crescent — A243

1982, June 3
533 A242 1.40d multi   .65 .25

1982, July 1
534 A243 1.40d multi   .65 .25

Women in Traditional Clothing, by M. Mezian — A244

1982, Aug. 16   **Photo.**   *Perf. 14*
535 A244 1.40d multi   .65 .30

Natl. Census A245

1982, Sept. 6   **Photo.**   *Perf. 11½*
536 A245 60c multi   .40 .25

ITU Conf., Nairobi, Sept. — A246

1982   *Perf. 13½x13*
537 A246 1.40d multi   .55 .25

TB Bacillus Centenary A247

1982, Sept. 30
538 A247 1.40d multi   .80 .30

World Food Day — A248

1982, Oct. 16   *Perf. 14*
539 A248 60c multi   .55 .25

Unity Railroad A249

1982, Nov. 6   *Perf. 13x13½*
540 A249 1.40d multi   1.40 .50

30th Anniv. of Arab Postal Union A250

1982, Nov. 17   *Perf. 14*
541 A250 1.40d multi   .55 .25

Intl. Palestinian Solidarity Day — A251

1982, Nov. 29   *Perf. 14*
542 A251 1.40d sil & multi   .55 .25

Red Coral, Al-Hoceima A252

1982, Dec. 20   *Perf. 13½*
543 A252 1.40d multi   1.00 .30

Stamp
Day — A253

1983, Jan. 26 *Perf. 13½x13*
544 A253 1.40d Nos. 3, 178 .55 .25

Week of the
Blind — A254

1983, Apr. 20 Photo. *Perf. 14*
545 A254 1.40d multi .65 .25

Popular
Arts
A255

1983, June 27 Photo. *Perf. 14*
546 A255 1.40d multi .90 .25

Wrought-Iron
Lectern — A256

1983, July 7 Litho. *Perf. 13½*
547 A256 1.40d multi .90 .25

Economic Commission for Africa, 25th
Anniv. — A257

1983, July 18 Photo. *Perf. 14*
548 A257 1.40d multi .55 .25

Moroccan
Flora — A258

1983, Aug. 1 Litho. *Perf. 14*
549 A258 60c Tecoma .50 .25
550 A258 1.40d Strelitzia 1.00 .30

Kings Mohammed V and Hassan
II — A259

1983, Aug. 20 Litho. *Perf. 14*
551 A259 80c multi .55 .25
  a. Souvenir sheet of 1 2.40 2.40
King and People's Revolution, 30th Anniv.
No. 551a sold for 5 dinars.

Mediterranean
Games — A260

1983, Sept. 3 Photo. *Perf. 14*
552 A260 80c Stylized sportsmen .40 .25
553 A260 1d Emblem .55 .30
554 A260 2d Stylized runner, horiz. 1.60 .45
  a. Souv. sheet of 3, #552-554, imperf. 3.00 3.00
    Nos. 552-554 (3) 2.55 1.00
No. 554a sold for 5d.

Touiza
A261

1983, Sept. 30 Photo. *Perf. 13*
555 A261 80c Tractors .55 .25

Palestinian
Solidarity — A262

1983, Nov. 10 Photo. *Perf. 13½x13*
556 A262 80c multi .45 .25

8th Anniv.
of the
Green
March into
Spanish
Sahara
A263

1983, Nov. 17 *Perf. 13x13½*
557 A263 80c multi .55 .25

Ouzoud
Waterfall — A264

1983, Nov. 28 *Perf. 14*
558 A264 80c multi .45 .25

Children's
Day — A265

1983, Dec. 5 Photo. *Perf. 13½x13*
559 A265 2d multi .65 .25

Zemmouri
Carpet — A266

Various carpets.

1983, Dec. 15 *Perf. 13½*
560 A266 60c multi .45 .25
561 A266 1.40d multi .90 .25

World Communications Year — A267

1983, Dec. 20 *Perf. 14*
562 A267 2d multi 1.20 .25

Twin Cities,
Jerusalem
and Fez
A268

1984, Jan. 16 Photo. *Perf. 13x13½*
563 A268 2d multi 1.00 .25

Desert Fox — A269

1984, Feb. 13 *Perf. 11½x12, 12x11½*
564 A269 80c shown 1.00 .40
565 A269 2d Jumping mouse, vert. 2.25 .80

King Hassan II Type of 1981
1984-88 Photo. *Perf. 14½*
Size: 25x32mm
566 A236 1.20d multi ('88) .30 .25
567 A236 1.25d multi .30 .25
568 A236 1.60d multi ('87) .45 .25
569 A236 2.50d multi ('87) .65 .35
570 A236 3.60d multi ('88) 1.25 .40
571 A236 4d multi 1.10 .65
572 A236 5.20d multi ('88) 1.75 .75
573 A236 6.50d multi ('87) 1.75 1.10
574 A236 7d multi ('87) 1.90 1.25
575 A236 8.50d multi ('87) 2.25 1.60
  Nos. 566-575 (10) 11.70 6.85
Dated 1986: 1.60d, 2.50d, 6.50d, 7d, 8.50d.
Issued: 1.20d, 3.60d, 5.20d, Dec. 26, 1988.

39th
Anniv. of
Arab
League
A270

1984, May 24 *Perf. 14½x14*
578 A270 2d Emblem .65 .25

No. 492
Overprinted

1984, June 12 *Perf. 13½x13*
579 A226 1.30d multi .90 .25
25th Anniv. of Marrakesh Arts Festival.

Local
Plants — A271

1984, June 13 *Perf. 14*
580 A271 80c Mentha viridis .30 .25
581 A271 2d Aloe .90 .40
See Nos. 602-603.

Week of
the Blind
A272

1984, July 10 *Perf. 13x13½*
582 A272 80c Painted bowl .50 .25

Red
Crescent — A273

1984, July 16 *Perf. 14*
583 A273 2d Octagonal brass container .80 .35

1984 Summer
Olympics — A274

1984, Aug. 8 *Perf. 13½x13*
584 A274 2d Sports .90 .35

Intl. Child Victims' Day — A275

1984, Aug. 22   *Perf. 14*
585 A275 2d Children held by dove   .80 .35

UPU Day — A276

1984, Oct. 9   Photo.   *Perf. 13½*
586 A276 2d multi   .65 .25

World Food Day — A277

1984, Oct. 16   *Perf. 14*
587 A277 80c multi   .55 .25

Intl. Civil Aviation Org., 40th Anniv. — A278

1984, Oct. 20   *Perf. 13½*
588 A278 2d multi   1.10 .50

Green March, 9th Anniv. — A279

1984, Nov. 6   *Perf. 14*
589 A279 80c Scroll, text   .55 .25

Palestinian Solidarity — A281

1984, Nov. 29   *Perf. 13½*
591 A281 2d Arab Revolt flag,
    1918-19   1.00 .50

UN Human Rights Declaration, 36th Anniv. — A282

1984, Dec. 10   *Perf. 14*
592 A282 2d multi   .65 .35

Native Dogs — A283

1984, Dec. 21   Photo.   *Perf. 14*
593 A283 80c Aidi   .70 .25
594 A283 2d Sloughi   1.40 .40

UN Child Survival Campaign A284

1985, Mar. 5   Photo.   *Perf. 14*
595 A284 80c Growth monitoring   .55 .25

1st SOS Children's Village in Morocco A285

1985, Mar. 11   *Perf. 13x13½*
596 A285 2d multi   .65 .25

Sherifian Hand Stamp, 1892 — A287

1985, Mar. 25   Photo.   *Perf. 14*
597 A287 2d dl pink, blk & gray   .65 .25

Souvenir Sheet
Perf. 13½
598   Sheet of 6   4.00 4.00
a.   A207 00c green, black & gray   .55 .40
b.   A287 80c yellow, black & gray   .55 .40
c.   A287 80c blue, black & gray   .55 .40
d.   A287 80c red, black & gray   .55 .40
e.   A287 80c purple, black & gray   .55 .40
f.   A287 80c brown, black & gray   .55 .40

Stamp Day. #598 sold for 5d.
See #615-616, 633-634, 668-669, 684-685, 701-702, 733-734, 756-757, 790-791, 806-807, 821-822, 835-836, 906-907.

World Environment Day — A288

1985, June 5   *Perf. 13*
599 A288 80c Emblem, ecosystem   .55 .25

Susi Dancers from Marrakesh and Kutabia, Minaret A289

1985, June 7   *Perf. 13x13½*
600 A289 2d multi   .95 .40

Folk Arts Festival.

Week of the Blind — A290

1985, June 24   *Perf. 14*
601 A290 80c Ceramic bowl   .50 .25

See type A316.

Flower Type of 1984
1985, July 1
602 A271 80c Bougainvillea   1.10 .30
603 A271 2d Red hibiscus   1.90 .50

Berber Woman — A291

1985, July 15   *Perf. 14*
604 A291 2d multi   3.00 .35

Red Crescent Society.

6th Pan-Arab Games — A292

1985, Aug. 2   *Perf. 14½x13½*
605 A292 2d Torch, emblem, map   .90 .35

UN, 40th Anniv. — A293

1985, Oct. 7   *Perf. 13*
606 A293 2d multi   2.00 .75

Intl. Youth Year — A294

1985, Oct. 21
607 A294 2d multi   2.25 .75

Green March, 10th Anniv. — A295

1985, Nov. 6   *Perf. 14½x13½*
608 A295 2d Commemorative
    medal   .65 .25

Palestinian Solidarity A296

1985, Nov. 29   *Perf. 13½*
609 A296 2d multi   .80 .25

Butterflies A297

1985, Dec. 16   Photo.   *Perf. 14*
610 A297 80c Euphydryas
    desfontainii   1.60 .65
611 A297 2d Colotis evagore   4.00 1.60

Accession of King Hassan II, 25th Anniv. — A298

Perf. 13x13½, 13½x13

1986, Mar. 3   **Litho.**
612 A298 80c Natl. arms, vert.   .30 .25
613 A298 2d shown   .70 .40
a.   Souv. sheet of 2, #612-613, im-
       perf.   1.25 1.25

26th Intl. Military
Medicine and
Pharmaceutical
Congress
A299

1986, Mar. 24   **Photo.**   **Perf. 14**
614 A299 2d multi   .60 .45

Hand Stamp Type of 1985

Sherifian postal seals of Maghzen-Safi,
1892.

1986, Apr. 7
615 A287 80c orange & blk   .30 .25
616 A287 2d green & blk   .70 .30

Week of the
Blind — A300

1986, Apr. 21
617 A300 1d multi   1.00 .35

1986 World Cup
Soccer
Championships,
Mexico — A301

1986, May 31   **Perf. 13½**
618 A301 1d Emblems, horiz.   .60 .25
619 A301 2d Soccer cup, em-
       blems   1.10 .35

Red Crescent
Soc. — A302

1986, June   **Perf. 14**
620 A302 2d multi   .90 .35

Popular
Arts
A303

1986, June
621 A303 2d Folk band, dancers   1.00 .30

Flowers — A304

1986, July 21   **Photo.**   **Perf. 14**
622 A304 1d Warionia saharae   1.40 .35
623 A304 2d Mandragora
        autumnalis   2.75 .65

Intl. Peace
Year — A305

1986, Aug. 4   **Perf. 13**
624 A305 2d multi   1.10 .40

18th Skydiving
Championships
A306

1986, Aug. 18   **Perf. 13½x13**
625 A306 2d multi   1.40 .40

Horse
Week
A307

1986, Oct. 10   **Perf. 13**
626 A307 1d multicolored   1.40 .25

Green March,
11th
Anniv. — A308

1986, Nov. 6   **Photo.**   **Perf. 14**
627 A308 1d multicolored   1.40 .25

World Food
Day — A309

1986, Nov. 12
628 A309 2d multicolored   .60 .40

Aga Khan
Architecture
Prize
A310

1986, Nov. 24   **Litho.**   **Perf. 13**
629 A310 2d multicolored   2.50 .75

Operation Grain:
One Million
Hectares — A311

1986, Dec. 8
630 A311 1d multicolored   .55 .25

Butterflies
A312

1986, Dec. 22   **Perf. 14**
631 A312 1d Elphinstonia
          charlonia   1.25 .55
632 A312 2d Anthocharis belia   3.25 1.50

Hand Stamp Type of 1985

Stamp Day: Sherifian postal seals of
Maghzen-Tetouan, 1892.

1987, Jan. 26   **Photo.**
633 A287 1d blue & blk   .75 .35
634 A287 2d red & black   1.50 .65

King Mohammed V, Flag,
1947 — A313

1987, Apr. 9   **Photo.**   **Perf. 13½x13**
635 A313 1d shown   .55 .25
636 A313 1d King Hassan II,
        1987   .55 .25
a.   Souvenir sheet of 2, Nos. 635-
       636   1.20 1.20

Tangiers Conf., 40th anniv. #636a sold for
3d.

Red Crescent
Society — A314

1987, May 1   **Photo.**   **Perf. 14**
637 A314 2d Brass lamp   .80 .35

UN Child Survival
Campaign
A315

1987, May 25   **Perf. 12½x13**
638 A315 1d Oral rehydration   .55 .30
      See Nos. 647, 687.

Week of the
Blind — A316

1987, June 8   **Perf. 14**
639 A316 1d Porcelain cup   .55 .30

Flowering
Plants — A317

1987, July 6   **Photo.**
640 A317 1d Zygophyllum fontanesii .35 .25
641 A317 2d Otanthus maritimus   .70 .35
      See Nos. 661-662.

US-Morocco
Diplomatic
Relations, 200th
Anniv. — A318

1987, July   **Litho & Engr.**
642 A318 1d lt bl, blk & scar   .50 .25
      See United States No. 2349.

Give
Blood — A319

1987, Aug. 20   **Photo.**   **Perf. 13x13½**
643 A319 2d King Hassan II, map   .80 .45

Desert
Costumes, the
Sahara — A320

1987, Sept. 14   *Perf. 13*
644 A320 1d Woman from Melhfa   .50   .25
645 A320 2d Man from Derraa   1.00   .50
    See Nos. 711-712, 740-741.

13th Intl. Cong. on Irrigation and Drainage — A321

1987, Sept. 21
646 A321 1d multi   .55   .30

UN Child Survival Type of 1987
1987, Sept. 28
647 A315 1d Universal immunization   .55   .30

Congress on Mineral Industries, Marrakesh A322

1987, Oct.
648 A322 1d Azurite   .75   .25
649 A322 2d Wulfenite   1.00   .50
    See No. 769.

Green March, 12th Anniv. — A323

1987, Nov. 6   *Photo.*   *Perf. 14*
650 A323 1d multicolored   .55   .25
    See Nos. 667, 683, 695, 727, 750, 769, 802, 820, 834, 848, 862, 885.

Royal Armed Forces Social Services Month A324

1987, Nov. 13   *Perf. 13x12½*
651 A324 1d multicolored   .55   .25

Birds — A325

1987, Dec. 1   *Litho.*   *Perf. 14*
652 A325 1d Passer simplex saharae   .75   .30
653 A325 2d Alectoris barbara   1.50   .45

Natl. Postage Stamp 75th Anniv. — A326

Design: Postmark and Sherifian postage stamp (French Morocco) of 1912.

1987, Dec. 31   *Photo.*   *Perf. 14x13½*
654 A326 3d pale lil rose, blk & blue grn   1.25   .70

Cetiosaurus Mogrebiensis — A327

1988, Jan. 18   *Photo.*   *Perf. 13½*
655 A327 2d multicolored   3.50   .95

A328

1988, Feb. 16   *Litho.*   *Perf. 14*
656 A328 2d multicolored   .65   .45
    Intl. Symposium on Mohammed V, Aug. 16-Nov. 20, 1987.

A329

Perf. 14½x13½
1988, Mar. 13   *Photo.*
657 A329 3d multi   1.00   .75
    16th Africa Cup Soccer Championships.

Horse Week A330

1988, Mar. 20   *Litho.*   *Perf. 14*
658 A330 3d multi   1.75   .75

Intl. Red Cross and Red Crescent Orgs., 125th Annivs. — A331

1988, Apr. 30   *Photo.*   *Perf. 12½x13*
659 A331 3d pink, blk & dark red   .95   .65

Week of the Blind — A332

1988, May 25   *Litho.*   *Perf. 14*
660 A332 3d Pottery bottle   .90   .65

Flower Type of 1987
1988, June 27   *Litho.*   *Perf. 14*
661 A317 3.60d Citrullus colocynthis   1.25   .75
662 A317 3.60d Calotropis procera   1.25   .75

UN Child Survival Campaign A333

1988, July 18   *Litho.*   *Perf. 12½x13*
663 A333 3d multi   .90   .60

1988 Summer Olympics, Seoul — A334

Perf. 14½x13½
1988, Sept. 17   *Litho.*
664 A334 2d multi   .80   .50

Birds — A335

1988, Oct. 26   *Litho.*   *Perf. 14*
665 A335 3.60d Grande outarde   1.75   .75
666 A335 3.60d Flamant rose   1.75   .75

Green March Anniv. Type of 1987
1988, Nov. 6
667 A323 2d multi   .65   .40
    Green March, 13th anniv.

Hand Stamp Type of 1985
    Sherifian postal seals of Maghzen-El Jadida, 1892: No. 668, Octagonal. No. 669, Circular.

1988, Nov. 22   *Photo.*   *Perf. 14*
668 A287 3d olive bister & blk   1.10   .60
669 A287 3d violet & blk   1.10   .60
    Stamp Day.

Housing of the Ksours and Casbahs A336

1989, Jan. 23   *Perf. 13x13½*
670 A336 2d multi   .65   .40

Royal Chess Federation, 25th Anniv. — A337

1989, Apr. 17   *Litho.*   *Perf. 14*
671 A337 2d multi   .80   .40

Red Crescent Society — A338

1989, May 29   *Litho.*   *Perf. 14x13½*
672 A338 2d multi   1.10   .40

Week of the Blind — A339

1989, June 12   *Perf. 14*
673 A339 2d multi   .55   .40

A340

1989, July 9   *Litho.*   *Perf. 13x13½*
674 A340 2d multi   .75   .40
675 A340 2d King Hassan II, diff.   .75   .40
    a.   Souvenir sheet of 2, #674-075, imperf. & embossed   15.00   15.00
    King Hassan II, 60th birthday. No. 675a sold for 5d.

A341

Flowering plants.

1989, Sept. 11   Litho.   Perf. 14
676 A341 2d Narcissus
            papyraceus   .80 .45
677 A341 2d Cerinthe major   .80 .45
      See Nos. 709-710, 742-743.

World Telecommunications
Day — A342

1989, Sept. 25   Perf. 13x12½
678 A342 2d multicolored   .60 .45

13th World
Congress on
Fertility and
Sterility — A343

1989, Oct. 6   Perf. 14
679 A343 2d multicolored   .60 .45

Birds
A344

1989, Oct. 16   Perf. 14
680 A344 2d Desert beater   .70 .45
681 A344 3d Gorget lark   1.00 .70

Interparliamentary Union,
Cent. — A345

1989, Oct. 27
682 A345 2d multicolored   .60 .45

Green March Anniv. Type of 1987
1989, Nov. 6
683 A323 3d multicolored   .90 .70
      Green March, 14th anniv.

Hand Stamp Type of 1985
   Sherifian postal seals of Maghzen-Casa-
blanca, 1892: 2d, Circular. 3d, Octagonal.

1990, Jan. 15   Photo.   Perf. 14
684 A287 2d orange & blk   .65 .45
685 A287 3d green & blk   1.00 .70

Maghreb
Union, 1st
Anniv.
A346

1990, Feb. 17   Perf. 13½x14
686 A346 2d multicolored   .60 .45
   a.   Souv. sheet of one, perf. 13½   .95 .95
      No. 686a sold for 3d.

UN Child Survival Type of 1987
1990   Perf. 12½x13
687 A315 3d Breast feeding   .95 .70

3rd World
Olive Day
A347

1990, May 14   Litho.   Perf. 14
688 A347 2d Olive press   .50 .35
689 A347 3d King Hassan II   .75 .55

Week of
the Blind
A348

1990, May 28   Litho.   Perf. 14
690 A348 2d multicolored   .70 .50

Red
Crescent
Society
A349

1990, June 11
691 A349 2d multicolored   .55 .35

A350

1990, Sept. 17   Litho.   Perf. 14
692 A350 3d blk, yel grn & grn   1.10 .80
      Intl. Literacy Year

Birds
A351

1990, Oct. 26
693 A351 2d Tourterelle, vert.   .85 .50
694 A351 3d Huppe fasciee   1.25 .80

Green March Anniv. Type of 1987
1990, Nov. 5
695 A323 3d multicolored   1.10 .80
      Green March, 15th anniv.

A353

1990, Nov. 18
696 A353 3d multicolored   1.10 .80
      Independence, 35th anniv.

Dam
A354

1990, Nov. 26
697 A354 3d multicolored   1.10 .80

A355

1990, Dec. 28   Litho.   Perf. 14
698 A355 3d multicolored   1.00 .75
   Royal Academy of Morocco, 10th anniv.

A356

Opening of Postal Museum, 20th Anniv.:
No. 699, Telegraph machine. No. 700, Horse-
drawn mail carriage fording river.

1990, Dec. 31   Litho.   Perf. 13½x13
699 A356 2d multicolored   .65 .50
700 A356 3d multicolored   1.00 .75
   a.   Souv. sheet of 2, #699-700, im-
          perf.   2.10 2.10
   No. 700a sold for 6d, has simulated
perforations.

Hand Stamp Type of 1985
   Sherifian postal seals of Maghzen-Rabat,
1892: 2d, Circular. 3d, Octagonal.

1991, Jan. 25   Perf. 14
701 A287 2d ver & blk   .65 .50
702 A287 3d blue & blk   1.00 .75

A357

1991, Feb. 18
703 A357 3d multicolored   1.00 .75
      UN Development Program, 40th anniv.

A358

1991, Mar. 3   Litho.   Perf. 14½x13
704 A358 3d shown   1.25 .35
705 A358 3d Wearing business
            suit   1.25 .35
   a.   Souv. sheet of 2, #704-705, im-
          perf.   3.00 2.35
   Coronation of King Hassan II, 30th anniv.
Nos. 704-705 exist tete beche. No. 705a has
simulated perforations and sold for 10d.

A359

1991, Mar. 28   Litho.   Perf. 14
706 A359 3d multicolored   1.00 .75
      Phosphate Mining, 70th anniv.

Week of the
Blind — A360

1991, May 15   Photo.   Perf. 14
707 A360 3d multicolored   1.00 .75

Red Crescent
Society — A361

1991, May 27   Litho.   Perf. 14
708 A361 3d multicolored   .95 .70

Flowering Plants Type of 1989
1991, June 27   Litho.   Perf. 14
709 A341 3d Pyrus mamorensis   1.00 .70
710 A341 3d Cynara humilis   1.00 .70

Desert Costumes Type of 1987
   Costumes of Ouarzazate.

1991, July 31   Photo.
711 A320 3d Woman   1.00 .70
712 A320 3d Man   1.00 .70

King Hassan II Type of 1981
1991-98   Photo.   Perf. 14½
            Size: 25x32mm
715 A236 1.35d multicolored   .45 .25
717 A236 1.70d multicolored   .40 .25
719 A236 2.30d multicolored   .50 .25
   a.   Perf 11½, granite paper   .50 .25
722 A236 5.50d multicolored   1.25 1.00
   a.   Perf 11½, granite paper   2.00 1.00
723 A236 6d multicolored   1.25 .95
724 A236 20d multicolored   5.00 3.50
         Nos. 715-724 (6)   8.85 6.20

   Issued: 1.35d, Sept. 2; 1.70d, 1994; 2.30d,
6d, 1998.

This is an expanding set. Numbers will change if necessary.
Nos. 719a and 722a are dated 1999, and have the denomination and "Postes" closer to the shoulder than to the chin.

A362

1991, Sept. 23   Litho.   *Perf. 14*
725 A362 3d multicolored   .95   .70

19th World Congress on Roads, Marrakesh.

A363

1991, Oct. 30   Litho.
726 A363 3d multicolored   .95   .70

4th Session of the Council of Presidents of the Maghreb Arab Union.

Green March Anniv. Type of 1987
1991, Nov. 6   Photo.   *Perf. 14*
727 A323 3d multicolored   .95   .70

Green March, 16th anniv.

Birds — A364

1991, Nov. 20   Litho.   *Perf. 14*
728 A364 3d Merops apiaster   1.75   .50
729 A364 3d Ciconia ciconia   1.75   .50

See Nos. 748-749.

Fight Against AIDS — A365

1991, Dec. 16
730 A365 3d multicolored   1.00   .80

Organization of the Islamic Conference, 20th Anniv. — A366

1991, Dec. 16
731 A366 3d multicolored   1.00   .80

A367

1991   Litho.   *Perf. 14*
732 A367 3d multicolored   1.00   .80

African Tourism Year.

Hand Stamp Type of 1985
Sherifian postal seals of Maghzen-Essaouira, 1892: No. 733, Circular. No. 734, Octagonal.

1992, Jan. 13
733 A207 3d olive & blk   1.00   .80
734 A287 3d purple & blk   1.00   .80

A368

1992, Feb. 17
735 A368 3d multicolored   1.00   .80

Intl. Space Year.

Week of the Blind — A369

1992, Mar. 19   Photo.   *Perf. 14*
736 A369 3d multicolored   1.00   .80

Red Crescent Society — A370

1992, Mar. 30
737 A370 3d multicolored   1.00   .80

Minerals — A371

1992, May 11   Litho.   *Perf. 14*
738 A371 1.35d Quartz   .50   .40
739 A371 3.40d Calcite   1.25   1.00

Desert Costumes Type of 1987
Costumes of Tata.

1992, May 25   Photo.   *Perf. 14*
740 A320 1.35d Woman   .50   .40
741 A320 3.40d Man   1.25   1.00

Flowering Plants Type of 1989
1992, July 13
742 A341 1.35d Campanula afra   .50   .40
743 A341 3.40d Thymus broussonetii   1.25   1.00

A372

1992, July 24
744 A372 3.40d multicolored   1.25   1.00

1992 Summer Olympics, Barcelona.

Modes of Transportation and Communications, Map of Africa — A373

1992, Sept. 14   Litho.   *Perf. 14*
745 A373 3.40d multicolored   1.40   .75

Expo '92, Seville — A374

1992, Oct. 12
746 A374 3.40d multicolored   1.40   .75

Discovery of America, 500th Anniv. A375

1992, Oct. 12
747 A375 3.40d multicolored   1.40   .75

Bird Type of 1991
1992, Oct. 26   Litho.   *Perf. 14*
748 A364 3d Gyps fulvus   1.50   .65
749 A364 3d Ganga cata, horiz.   1.50   .65

Green March Anniv. Type of 1987
1992, Nov. 6   Litho.   *Perf. 14*
750 A323 3.40d multicolored   .95   .75

Green March, 17th anniv.

Sherifian Post, Cent. A377

Designs: 3.40d, Octagonal Sherifian postal seal, scroll, Sultan Moulay Hassan I. 5d, Scroll, various circular and octagonal Sherifian postal seals, Sultan.

1992, Nov. 22   Litho.   *Perf. 14*
751 A377 1.35d multicolored   .55   .25
752 A377 3.40d multicolored   .95   .75

Size: 165x115mm
Imperf
753 A377 5d multicolored   2.00   1.00
   Nos. 751-753 (3)   3.50   2.00

Intl. Conference on Nutrition, Rome — A378

1992, Dec. 7   Litho.   *Perf. 14*
754 A378 3.40d multicolored   1.40   .75

Al Massira Airport, Agadir — A379

1992, Dec. 21   Litho.   *Perf. 14*
755 A379 3.40d multicolored   1.25   .80

Hand Stamp Type of 1985
Sherifian postal seals of Maghzen-Tanger, 1892: 1.70, Circular. 3.80d, Octagonal.

1993, Jan. 29   Litho.   *Perf. 14*
756 A287 1.70d green & black   .45   .35
757 A287 3.80d orange & black   1.00   .80

Stamp Day.

Week of the Blind A380

1993, Mar. 15   Litho.   *Perf. 14*
758 A380 4.40d multicolored   1.25   1.00

World Meteorology Day — A381

1993, Mar. 23
759 A381 4.40d multicolored   1.25   1.00

A382

1993, Apr. 26   Litho.   *Perf. 14*
760 A382 4.40d multicolored   1.25   1.00

Red Crescent Society.

A383

1993, June 14
761 A383 4.40d multicolored　　1.25　1.00
World Telecommunications Day.

A384

Argania spinosa.

1993, July 26　　Litho.　　Perf. 14
762 A384 1.70d Extracting oil　　.60　.35
763 A384 4.80d Tree branch　　1.75　1.00

A385

1993, Aug. 21
764 A385 4.80d multicolored　　1.25　1.00
Prince Sidi Mohammed, 30th birthday.

Inauguration of
the Hassan II
Mosque
A386

1993, Aug. 30　　　　Perf. 13
765 A386 4.80d multicolored　　1.25　1.00

A387

1993, Sept. 30　　Litho.　　Perf. 14
766 A387 4.80d multicolored　　1.25　1.00
King and People's Revolution, 40th Anniv.

A388

1993, Oct. 15
767 A388 4.80d multicolored　　1.25　1.00
World Post Day.

New Islamic
University — A389

1993, Nov. 1　　Litho.　　Perf. 14
768 A389 4.80d multicolored　　1.25　1.00

Green March Anniv. Type of 1987
1993, Nov. 6
769 A323 4.80d multicolored　　1.25　1.00
Green March, 18th anniv.

Water
Birds
A390

1993, Dec. 13　　Litho.　　Perf. 14
770 A390 1.70d Sarcelle marbree　　.75　.30
771 A390 4.80d Foulque a crete　　1.75　.85

Manifest of
Independence,
50th
Anniv. — A391

1994, Mar. 31　　Litho.　　Perf. 14
772 A391 4.80d multicolored　　2.50　.85

A392

General
Agreement on
Tariffs and Trade
(GATT), 1994
Summit,
Marrakech
A393

No. 774Ab, 1.70d, like #773. c, 4.80d, like
#774.

1994, Apr. 29　　Litho.　　Perf. 14
773 A392 1.70d multicolored　　.50　.30
774 A393 4.80d multicolored　　1.25　.80

Sheet of 2
Rouletted
774A A393　#b.-c.　　3.50　3.00

Buildings and background are all in shades
of claret on Nos. 774b-774c. No. 773 has
building and background in shades of green.
No. 774 has black building with claret background. No. 774A sold for 10d.

Week of the
Blind — A394

1994, May 9
775 A394 4.80d multicolored　　3.00　1.10

Red Crescent
Society — A395

1994, May 18
776 A395 4.80d multicolored　　1.40　.85

Natl. Conference
on Children's
Rights — A396

1994, May 25
777 A396 1.70d shown　　.50　.30
778 A396 4.80d Boy, girl under
　　　　sun　　1.25　.85

1994 World Cup Soccer
Championships, US — A397

1994, June 17　　　　Perf. 13
779 A397 4.80d multicolored　　2.50　1.00

King
Hassan II,
65th
Birthday
A398

Designs: 1.70d, Wearing business suit.
4.80d, Wearing traditional costume, vert.

1994　　　　Perf. 13x12½, 12½x13
780 A398 1.70d multicolored　　.90　.30
781 A398 4.80d multicolored　　2.25　1.00

A399

1994, June 27　　　　Perf. 12½x13
782 A399 4.80d multicolored　　1.75　.60
Intl. Olympic Committee, Cent.

A400

1994
783 A400 4.80d multicolored　　1.20　.60
Death of Antoine de Saint-Exupery, 50th
anniv.

Flowers
A401

1994　　Perf. 13x12½, 12½x13
784 A401 1.70d Chamaelon gum-
　　　　mifer　　.60　.30
785 A401 4.80d Pancratium mari-
　　　　timum, vert.　　1.25　.60

Water
Birds
A402

1994, Oct. 24　Photo.　Perf. 13x13½
786 A402 1.70d Courlis a bec
　　　　grele　　1.50　.60
787 A402 4.80d Goeland
　　　　d'audouin　　4.50　2.00

A403

Green March, 19th Anniv.: 4.80d, Marchers,
map, inscription.

1994, Nov. 6　　Litho.　　Perf. 12½
788 A403 1.70d multicolored　　.40　.30
789 A403 4.80d multicolored　　1.10　.80

Hand Stamp Type of 1985
Sherifan postal seals of Maghzen-Mar-
rakesh: 1.70d, Circular. 4.80d, Octagonal.

1994, Nov. 22　　　　Perf. 12½
790 A287 1.70d blue & black　　.60　.30
791 A287 4.80d vermilion & black　1.40　.80
Stamp Day.

A404

1995, Feb. 27   Litho.   Perf. 13½
792 A404 4.80d multicolored   2.00   .80
Week of the Blind.

A405

1995, Mar. 22   Litho.   Perf. 13½
793 A405 4.80d multicolored   1.40   .80
Arab League, 50th anniv.

A406

1995, Apr. 24   Litho.   Perf. 13½x13
794 A406 4.80d multicolored   1.40   .80
Red Crescent Society.

Flowers — A407

1995, May 29   Litho.   Perf. 13½x13
795 A407 2d Malva hispanica   .50   .35
796 A407 4.80d Phlomis crinita   1.40   .85

Birds — A408

1995, Sept. 18   Litho.   Perf. 13½x13
797 A408 1.70d Coracias garru-
                lus   .45   .30
798 A408 4.80d Carduelis
                carduelis   1.10   .85
See Nos. 818-819, 832-833, 846-847.

FAO, 50th
Anniv.
A409

1995, Oct. 16   Photo.   Perf. 13½
799 A409 4.80d multicolored   1.40   .85

UN, 50th
Anniv.
A410

1.70d, "50," Moroccan, UN flags. 4.80d,
Moroccan flag, UN emblem, map of Africa.

1995, Oct. 24   Perf. 12½
800 A410 1.70d multicolored   .75   .30
801 A410 4.80d multicolored   2.25   .85

**Green March Anniv. Type of 1987
and**

Green March,
20th
Anniv. — A411

1995, Nov. 6   Photo.   Perf. 12½
802 A323 1.70d multicolored   .40   .30
803 A411 4.80d multicolored   1.10   .85

A412

Independence, 40th anniv.: 4.80d, Crown,
national flag. 10d, King Mohammed V, crown
over flag, King Hassan II.

1995, Nov. 18   Litho.   Perf. 12½
804 A412 4.80d multicolored   1.25   .85
Size: 112x83mm
Imperf
805 A412 10d multicolored   2.75 2.00

Hand Stamp Type of 1985
Sherifan postal seals of Maghzen-Meknes,
1892: 1.70d, Circular. 4.80d, Octagonal.

1995, Nov. 22   Photo.   Perf. 12½
806 A287 1.70d olive & black   .40   .30
807 A287 4.80d violet & black   1.10   .85
Stamp Day.

A413

1996, Mar. 3   Litho.   Perf. 13½
808 A413 2d Natl. arms   .45   .35
809 A413 5.50d King Hassan II   1.25   .95
Size: 134x86mm
Imperf
810 A413 10d Crown, King   2.75 1.75
Accession of King Hassan II, 35th anniv.

Traditional
Crafts — A414

1996, Mar. 25   Photo.   Perf. 13½x13
811 A414 5.50d Pottery   1.25 1.00
812 A414 5.50d Copper   1.25 1.00

Flowers — A415

1996, Apr. 25
813 A415 2d Cleonia lusitani-
                ca   .50   .40
814 A415 5.50d Tulipa sylvestris 1.25 1.00

A416

King Hassan II: 2d, In uniform. 5.50d, Wearing traditional headpiece.

1996, May 14   Photo.   Perf. 13x13½
815 A416 2d multicolored   .60   .40
816 A416 5.50d multicolored   1.40 1.00
Royal Armed Forces, 40th anniv.

A417

1996, July 19   Photo.   Perf. 13½x13
817 A417 5.50d multicolored   1.25 1.00
1996 Summer Olympics, Atlanta.

Bird Type of 1995
1996, Oct. 21   Photo.   Perf. 13½x13
818 A408 2d Pandion
                haliaetus   1.40   .40
819 A408 5.50d Egretta garzetta   3.00 1.00

Green March Anniv. Type of 1987
1996, Nov. 6   Litho.   Perf. 13½
820 A323 5.50d multicolored   1.50 1.00
Green March, 21st anniv.

Hand Stamp Type of 1985
Sherifan postal seals of Maghzen-Fes,
1892: 2d, Circular. 5.50d, Octagonal.

1996, Nov. 22   Photo.   Perf. 13½
821 A287 2d orange & black   .45   .35
822 A287 5.50d green & black   1.40 1.00
Stamp Day.

UNICEF,
50th Anniv.
A418

1996, Dec. 11   Perf. 13x13½
823 A418 5.50d multicolored   1.25 1.00

Moroccan
Pottery
A419

1997, Feb. 24   Photo.   Perf. 13x13½
824 A419 5.50d multicolored   1.25   .90

Flowers — A420

1997, Mar. 24   Photo.   Perf. 13½x13
825 A420 2d Lupinus luteus   .90   .25
826 A420 5.50d Silybum mari-
                anum   2.50   .60

A421

Speakers, 1947: No. 827, Crown Prince
Hassan. No. 828, Sultan Mohammed V.

1997, Apr. 9   Photo.   Perf. 13½x13
827 A421 2d multicolored   .70   .25
828 A421 2d multicolored   .70   .25
Speech in Tangier by King Hassan II, 50th
anniv.

World Reading
and Copyright
Day — A422

1997, Apr. 23
829 A422 5.50d multicolored   1.25   .60

Intl. Meeting on Ibn Battuta (1304-77?), Traveler and Writer — A423

1997, May 9　　　　*Perf. 13x13½*
830　A423　5.50d multicolored　　1.25　.60

Moroccan Copper — A424

1997, July 21　Photo.　*Perf. 13½*
831　A424　5.50d multicolored　　1.25　.55

Bird Type of 1995
Designs: 2d, Anthropoides virgo. 5.50d, Parus caeruleus ultramarinus.

1997, Oct. 20　Photo.　*Perf. 13½x13*
832　A408　multicolored　　　.50　.25
833　A408　5.50d multicolored　1.40　.60

Green March Anniv. Type of 1987
1997, Nov. 6　　　*Perf. 13½*
834　A323　5.50d multicolored　　1.20　.60
　　Green March, 22nd anniversary.

Hand Stamp Type of 1985
Sherifan postal seals of Maghzen-Larache, 1892: 2d, Circular. 5.50d, Octagonal.

1997　　Photo.　　*Perf. 13½*
835　A287　2d blue & black　　　.50　.25
836　A287　5.50d vermilion & black 1.25　.60

Flowers — A425

1998　Photo.　*Perf. 13½x13*
837　A425　2.30d Rhus pentaphylla　.65　.30
838　A425　6d Orchis papilion-
　　　　　acea　　　　　　　1.60　.80

A426

1998
839　A426　6d multicolored　　1.60　.80
　　25th Intl. Road Transportation Congress.

A427

1998
840　A427　6d Copper ornament　1.60　.80

A428

1998
841　A428　6d multicolored　　1.60　.80
　　1998 World Cup Soccer Championships, France.

Pottery A429

1998
842　A429　6d multicolored　　1.60　.80

Intl. Year of the Ocean A430

1998
843　A430　6d multicolored　　1.60　.80

King & People's Revolution, 45th Anniv. A431

1998
844　A431　6d multicolored　　1.60　.80

World Stamp Day — A432

1998　Photo.　*Perf. 13½x13*
845　A432　6d multicolored　　1.60　.80

Bird Type of 1995
Designs: 2.30d, Luscinia megarhynchos. 6d, Struthio camelus.

1998　　　　　　　Photo.
846　A408　2.30d multicolored　　.65　.30
847　A408　6d multicolored　　1.60　.80

Green March Anniv. Type
1998, Nov. 6　　　*Perf. 13½*
848　A323　6d multicolored　　1.60　.80
　　Green March, 23rd anniv.

A433

1998　Litho.　*Perf. 13½x13*
849　A433　6d multicolored　　1.60　.80
　　Public Liberties, 40th anniv.

A434

1998　　　　　　　Photo.
850　A434　6d multicolored　　1.60　.80
　　Universal Declaration of Human Rights, 50th anniv.

A435

1999　Litho.　*Perf. 13¼*
851　A435　6d multi　　　1.50　.75
　　World Theater Day.

A436

Flora: 2.30d, Eryngium triquetrum. 6d, Viscum cruciatum.

1999
852　A436　2.30d multi　　　.60　.30
853　A436　6d multi　　　1.50　.75

Bab Mansour Laalej — A437

1999　　　　*Perf. 13x13¼*
854　A437　6d multi　　　1.50　.75

Jewelry A438

1999　　　　　*Perf. 13¼*
855　A438　6d multi　　　1.50　.75

A439

1999
856　A439　2.30d On throne　　.60　.30
857　A439　6d In robes　　　1.50　.75
　a.　Souvenir sheet, #856-857, im-
　　　perf, without gum　　2.25　1.10
　　King Hassan II, 70th birthday.

A440

1999
858　A440　6d multi　　　1.50　.75
　　World Environment Day.

UPU, 125th Anniv. — A441

1999, Oct. 9　Photo.　*Perf. 13¼*
859　A441　6d multi　　　1.25　.60

FAO Medal Awarded by King Hassan II — A442

1999, Oct. 16
860　A442　6d multi　　　1.60　.60
　　See No. 964.

Anti-poverty Week — A443

1999, Nov. 11   Photo.   Perf. 11¾
Granite Paper
861 A443 6d multi   1.40 1.00
Compare with type A461.

Green March Anniv. Type of 1987
1999, Nov. 6   Photo.   Perf. 13¼
862 A323 6d multi   1.60 .60
Green March, 24th anniv.

Fish
A444

Designs: 2.30d, Diplodus cervinus. 6d, Lampris guttatus.

1999, Nov. 29   Photo.   Perf. 13¼
863 A444 2.30d multi   .65 .25
864 A444 6d multi   1.50 .75

Miniature Sheet

Morocco Year in France — A445

No. 865: a, Stork on nest. b, People in robes. c, Mandolin, pillars. d, Boat at dock.

1999, Dec. 13   Perf. 13¼x13
865   Sheet of 4   6.25 3.00
a.-d. A445 6d Any single   1.50 .75

African Cup Soccer
Tournament — A446

2000, Jan. 25   Perf. 11¾x11½
Granite Paper
866 A446 6d multi   1.50 .75

Year 2000
A447

2000, Jan. 31   Granite Paper
867 A447 6d multi   1.50 .75

Reconstruction of Agadir, 40th
Anniv. — A448

2000, Feb. 29   Photo.   Perf. 11¾
Granite Paper
868 A448 6.50d multi   1.60 .80

Islamic Development Bank — A449

2000, Mar. 6   Photo.   Perf. 11¾x11½
Granite Paper
869 A449 6.50d multi   1.60 .80

Natl. Day of the Handicapped — A450

2000, Mar. 30   Granite Paper
870 A450 6.50d multi   1.60 .80

Flora
A451

Designs: 2.50d, Jasione montana. 6.50d, Pistorica breviflora.

2000, Apr. 27   Photo.   Perf. 11¾
Granite Paper
871-872 A451 Set of 2   2.50 1.10

World Meteorological Organization,
50th Anniv. — A452

2000, May 15   Granite Paper
873 A452 6.50d multi   1.60 .80

Marrakesh
Arts
Festival
A453

2000, June 5   Photo.   Perf. 11¾
Granite Paper
874 A453 6.50d multi   1.60 .80

Intl. Peace
Year
A454

2000   Photo.   Perf. 11¾
Granite Paper
875 A454 6.50d multi   1.60 .80

Enthronement of
King Mohammed
VI, 1st
Anniv. — A455

King in: 2.50d, Business suit. 6.50d, Robe.

2000, July 30   Photo.   Perf. 11¾
Granite Paper
877-878 A455 Set of 2   2.10 1.00
878a   Souvenir sheet of 2, #877-
        878, imperf.   2.50 1.25
No. 878a sold for 10d.

Intl.
Festival,
Volubilis
A456

2000, Sept. 8   Perf. 11¾
Granite Paper
879 A456 6.50d multi   1.90 1.60

2000 Summer
Olympics,
Sydney — A457

2000, Sept. 15   Granite Paper
880 A457 6.50d multi   1.90 1.60

SOS Children's
Villages — A458

2000, Oct. 12   Granite Paper
881 A458 6.50d multi   1.75 .80

World Teacher's
Day — A459

2000, Oct. 25   Photo.   Perf. 11¾
Granite Paper
882 A459 6.50d multi   1.75 .80

Anti-poverty Week — A461

2000, Nov. 1   Photo.   Perf. 11¾
Granite Paper
884 A461 6.50d multi   1.75 .80

Compare with type A443. Value is for stamp with surrounding selvage. See Nos. 911, 928, 953, 997, 1027, 1048, 1076, 1098, 1117, 1144, 1159.

Green March Anniv. Type of 1987 and

Map and
Inscription
A462

2000, Nov. 6   Photo.   Perf. 11¾
Granite Paper
885 A323 2.50d multi   .65 .25
886 A462 6.50d multi   1.75 .80
Green March, 25th anniv.

Antoine de Saint-Exupéry (1900-44), Aviator, Writer — A463

2000, Nov. 13　Photo.　Perf. 11¾
Granite Paper
887　A463　6.50d multi　　2.00　.80

Independence, 45th Anniv. — A464

2000, Nov. 18　　Granite Paper
888　A464　6.50d multi　　1.60　.80

Fish A465

Designs: 2.50d, Apogon imberbis. 6.50d, Scorpaena loppei.

2000, Dec. 25　　Granite Paper
889-890　A465　Set of 2　　2.75　1.25

El Gharbi Gate A466

2001, Mar. 22　Photo.　Perf. 11¾
Granite Paper
891　A466　6.50d multi　　1.75　1.00

World Water Day — A467

2001, Mar. 30　　Granite Paper
892　A467　6.50d multi　　1.75　1.00

Armed Forces, 45th Anniv. — A468

Designs: 2.50d, Soldier and insignia. 6.50d, Soldier in frame.

2001, May 16　Litho.　Perf. 14¼x13¾
893-894　A468　Set of 2　　2.40　1.25

Flora — A469

Designs: 2.50d, Euphorbia rigida. 6.50d, Glaucium flavum.

2001, June 7　Photo.　Perf. 11¾
Granite Paper
895-896　A469　Set of 2　　2.75　1.25

Houses of Worship — A470

Designs: 2.50d, Koekelberg Basilica, Belgium. 6.50d, Hassan II Mosque, Casablanca.

2001, June 10　　Granite Paper
897-898　A470　Set of 2　　2.25　1.50
See Belgium Nos. 1855-1856.

Natl. Diplomacy Day — A471

Perf. 14¼x13¾
2001, June 29　　　Litho.
899　A471　6.50d multi　　1.75　.70

A472

A473

A474

King Mohammed VI A475

Perf. 12¾x13¼, 13¼x12¾
2001, July 31　　　　Litho.
Size: 24x33mm
900　A472　2.50d multi　　.55　.25
901　A473　6d multi　　1.40　.55
902　A474　6.50d multi　　1.50　.60

Size: 32x24mm
Arms 14mm Tall
903　A475　10d multi　　2.40　.85
　　Nos. 900-903 (4)　　5.85　2.25
　Compare type A472 with type A687; type A473 with types A572 and A688; type A475 with type A573.
　See Nos. 934A-934B, 940-943, 960-962, 1007A-1007B, 1020, 1029A.

Marine Life — A476

Designs: 2.50d, Lophius budegassa. 6.50d, Monachus monachus, horiz.

2001, Sept. 28　Litho.　Perf. 11¾
Granite Paper
904-905　A476　Set of 2　　2.25　.95

Hand Stamp Type of 1985
Hand stamps of Ksar el Kebir, 1892: 2.50d, Round. 6.50d, Octagonal.

2001, Oct. 9　Litho.　Perf. 14¼x13¾
906　A287　2.50d olive & black　　.70　.25
907　A287　6.50d violet & black　　1.75　.70

World Day to Combat Desertification A477

2001, Oct. 29　Litho.　Perf. 13¼
908　A477　6.50d multi　　1.40　.60

7th UN Climate Change Conference A478

2001, Oct. 29
909　A478　6.50d multi　　1.40　.60

Green March, 26th Anniv. A479

2001, Nov. 7　Photo.　Perf. 13x13¼
910　A479　6.50d multi　　1.40　.60

Anti-Poverty Week Type of 2000 and

Anti-Poverty Week A480

2001, Nov. 8　　　Perf. 12½
911　A461　6.50d multi　　1.60　.60

Perf. 13x13¼
912　A480　6.50d multi　　1.60　.60
　Value of No. 911 is for stamp with surrounding selvage.

Year of Dialogue Among Civilizations A481

2001, Dec. 14　　　Perf. 13¼x13
913　A481　6.50d multi　　1.40　.60

Fountains — A482

Designs: 2.50d, Wallace Fountain, Paris. 6.50d, Nejjarine Fountain, Fez.

2001, Dec. 14　　　Perf. 13¼
914-915　A482　Set of 2　　2.25　.85
See No. 963. See France Nos. 2847-2848.

Chellah Gate A483

2002, Feb. 28　　　Perf. 13x13¼
916　A483　6.50d multi　　1.60　.60

Intl. Women's Day — A484

2002, Mar. 8　　　Perf. 13¼x13
917　A484　6.50d multi　　1.60　.60

Cedar Tree — A485

2002, Mar. 29
918　A485　6.50d multi　　1.60　.60

2nd World Assembly on the Elderly A486

2002, Apr. 30　　　Perf. 13x13¼
919　A486　6.50d multi　　1.60　.60

Special Session of
UN General
Assembly on
Children — A487

2002, May 8   **Perf. 13¼x13**
920   A487   6.50d multi   1.60   .60
     Dated 2001.

Flora — A488

Designs: 2.50d, Linaria bipartita. 6.50d,
Verbascum pseudocreticum.

2002, June 5   **Photo.**   **Perf. 13¼x13**
921-922   A488   Set of 2   2.75   .80

Intl. Telecommunications Union
Plenipotentiary Conference,
Marrakesh — A489

2002, Sept. 23   **Photo.**   **Perf. 13¼**
923   A489   6.50d multi   1.60   .60
     Size: 120x90mm
     Imperf
     Without Gum
924   A489   10d multi   2.75   1.50

Palestinian
Intifada
A490

2002, Sept. 28   **Perf. 13¼**
925   A490   6.50d multi   1.60   .70

Intl. Year of
Ecotourism
A491

2002, Sept. 30
926   A491   6.50d multi   1.60   .70

Green March, 27th
Anniv. — A492

2002, Nov. 7
927   A492   6.50d multi   1.60   .70

Anti-Poverty Week Type of 2000 and

Anti-Poverty
Week — A493

2002, Nov. 8   **Perf. 12½**
928   A461   6.50d multi   1.40   .70
     Perf. 13¼
929   A493   6.50d multi   1.40   .70
    Value of No. 928 is for stamp with surround-
ing selvage.

Maghzen
Post, 110th
Anniv.
A494

Sultan Moulay Hassan I and: 2.50d, Circular
postal seal. 6.50d, Octagonal postal seal.

2002, Nov. 22   **Perf. 12½, 13 (6.50d)**
930-931   A494   Set of 2   2.50   .95
    Value of Nos. 930-931 are for stamps with
surrounding selvage. No. 931 is ocatagonally
shaped.

UN Year for
Cultural
Heritage
A495

2002, Dec. 18   **Perf. 13¼x13**
932   A495   6.50d multi   1.75   .70

Fish
A496

Designs: 2.50d, Alosa alosa. 6.50d,
Epinephelus marginatus.

2002, Dec. 30   **Perf. 13¼**
933-934   A496   Set of 2   2.75   .95

King Mohammed VI Type of 2001
2002   **Litho.**   **Perf. 11½**
     Granite Paper
     Size: 24x30mm
934A   A472   2.50d multi   .75   .35
934B   A473   6d multi   2.00   1.00

Bab el
Okla,
Tetuan
A497

2003, Feb. 28   **Photo.**   **Perf. 13¼**
935   A497   6.50d multi   1.60   .70

Fir Trees
A498

2003, Mar. 28
936   A498   6.50d multi   1.75   .70

Intl. Year of Fresh
Water — A499

2003, Apr. 28   **Perf. 13¼x13**
937   A499   6.50d multi   1.75   .70

Flora — A500

Designs: 2.50d, Limonium sincatum. 6.50d,
Echinops spinosus.

2003, May 30   **Perf. 13¼**
938-939   A500   Set of 2   2.75   1.25

King Mohammed VI Type of 2001
2003   **Litho.**   **Perf. 13¼x12¾**
940   A475   70c lt bl & multi   .25   .25
941   A475   80c pur & multi   .25   .25
942   A475   5d yel & multi   1.50   .50
943   A475   20d lil & multi   6.00   2.10
    Nos. 940-943 (4)   8.00   3.10
    Coat of arms on Nos. 940 and 941 is 14mm
tall. See Nos. 1007A-1007B for stamps with
coat of arms 11mm tall.

Salé Grand Mosque, 1000th
Anniv. — A501

2003, July 11   **Photo.**   **Perf. 13x12¼**
944   A501   6.50d multi   1.60   .90

World Youth
Congress
A502

2003, Aug. 12   **Perf. 13¼**
945   A502   6.50d multi   1.00   .90

Revolution
of the King
and People,
50th Anniv.
A503

2003, Aug. 20
946   A503   6.50d multi   1.60   .90

King Mohammed
VI, 40th
Birthday — A504

Designs: Nos. 947, 949a, 2.50d, King in suit
and tie. Nos. 948, 949b, 6.50d, King in robe.

2003, Aug. 21
947-948   A504   Set of 2   2.50   1.40
     Souvenir Sheet
     Stamps With Pink Frames
949   A504   Sheet of 2, #a-b   2.75   2.75
    No. 949 sold for 10d.
    Compare with type A545.

Fish
A505

Designs: 2.50d, Sparisoma cretense. 6.50d,
Anthias anthias.

2003, Sept. 30   **Photo.**   **Perf. 13¼**
950-951   A505   Set of 2   2.50   1.40

World Post
Day — A506

2003, Oct. 9
952   A506   6.50d multi   1.90   .95

Anti-Poverty Week Type of 2000 and

King Mohammed VI Visiting Sick
Child — A507

2003, Oct. 31   **Photo.**   **Perf. 12¾**
953   A461   6.50d multi   1.90   .95
954   A507   6.50d multi   1.90   .95

Green March, 28th
Anniv. — A508

2003, Nov. 5   **Photo.**   **Perf. 13¼**
955   A508   6.50d multi   1.90   .95

Rabat, 2003 Arab Culture
Capital — A509

2003, Dec. 19   Litho.   Perf. 13x13¼
956   A509   6.50d multi   2.00   1.00

Philately at
School
A510

2003, Dec. 29   Perf. 13¼
957   A510   6.50d multi   2.00   1.00

UN Literacy Decade — A511

2003, Dec. 29   Perf. 13x13¼
958   A511   6.50d multi   2.00   1.00

Morocco - People's Republic of China
Diplomatic Relations, 45th
Anniv. — A512

2003, Dec. 31   Perf. 12
959   A512   6.50d multi   2.00   1.00

**Types of 2001 Redrawn With Added
Frame Lines**
2002-03   Litho.   Perf. 11½
            Size: 24x30mm
960   A474   6.50d multi   2.50   2.50
            Size: 32x23mm
           Arms 11mm Tall
961   A475   10d multi   4.00   4.00
         Booklet Stamps
         Self-Adhesive
     Serpentine Die Cut 11
            Size: 20x23mm
962   A472   2.50d multi ('03)   .70   .40
   a.   Booklet pane of 10   7.00
963   A482   6.50d Like #915 ('03)   1.75   1.00
   a.   Booklet pane of 10   17.50

   Issued: 6.50d, 10d, 2002. 2.50d, 6.50d,
9/3/03.
   On No. 903, arms are 9mm tall.

FAO Medal Type of 1999
2003, July   Photo.   Perf. 13x13¼
            Size: 48x38mm
964   A442   6d multi   5.00   5.00

Ibn Battutah (1304-68), Traveler and
Author — A513

2004, Feb. 24   Photo.   Perf. 13x12¼
965   A513   6.50d multi   2.00   1.00

Bab Agnaou,
Marrakesh
A514

2004, Mar. 18   Perf. 13¼
966   A514   6.50d multi   2.00   1.00

Flowers — A515

   Designs: 2.50d, Linaria gharbensis. 6.50d,
Nigella damascena.

2004, Mar. 29
967-968   A515   Set of 2   2.75   1.25

16th World Military Equestrian
Championships, Témara — A516

2004, Apr. 18
969   A516   6.50d multi   2.00   1.00

Hassan II Tennis
Grand Prix, 20th
Anniv. — A517

2004, May 14
970   A517   6.50d multi   2.25   1.00

10th World
Sacred
Music
Festival,
Fez
A518

2004, May 28   Perf. 12¼x13
971   A518   6.50d multi   2.00   1.00

Caftan — A519

2004, June 18   Perf. 13¼
972   A519   6.50d multi   2.00   1.00

Dinosaur
Fossils
Found in
Tazouda
A520

2004, July 12
973   A520   6.50d multi   2.00   1.00

30th Intl. Military
History Congress
A521

2004, July 29
974   A521   6.50d multi   2.00   1.00

Enthronement of
King Mohammed
VI, 5th
Anniv. — A522

   Designs: Nos. 975, 977a, 2.50d, King in
suit. Nos. 976, 977b, 6d, King in robe.

2004, July 30
975-976   A522   Set of 2   2.75   2.75
       Souvenir Sheet
   Stamps With Yellow Frames
977   A522   Sheet of 2, #a-b   3.00   3.00
     No. 977 sold for 10d.

Intl. Peace
Day — A523

2004, Sept. 21   Photo.   Perf. 13¼
978   A523   6d multi   1.90   .95

Anti-Poverty Week Type of 2000 and

Anti-Poverty Week — A524

2004, Oct. 22   Perf. 12¾
979   A461   6.50d multi   2.00   1.00
            Perf. 13¼
980   A524   6.50d multi   2.00   1.00
   Value for No. 979 is for stamp with surrounding selvage.

Green March,
29th
Anniv. — A525

2004, Nov. 6   Photo.   Perf. 13¼
981   A525   6d multi   2.00   1.00

Marine Life
A526

   Designs: 2.50d, Xiphias gladius. 6.50d,
Octopus vulgaris.

2004, Nov. 16   Photo.   Perf. 13¼
982-983   A526   Set of 2   2.75   1.25

World Children's
Day — A527

2004, Nov. 24
984   A527   6.50d multi   2.00   1.00

Rotary International, Cent. — A528

2005, Feb. 23   Perf. 13x13¼
985   A528   6.50d multi   2.00   1.00

Arab League, 60th Anniv. — A529

2005, Mar. 22   *Perf. 13¼x13*
986   A529   6.50d multi   2.00   1.00

Bab Boujloud, Fez
A530

2005, Mar. 30   *Perf. 13¼*
987   A530   6.50d multi   2.00   1.00

Amnesty International
A531

2005, May 6   Photo.   *Perf. 13¼*
988   A531   6.50d multi   2.00   1.00

Flora — A532

Designs: 2.50d, Erodium sebaceum. 6.50d, Linaria ventricosa.

2005, May 26   Photo.   *Perf. 13¼*
989-990   A532   Set of 2   2.50   1.00

Rock Carvings, Iourarhane
A533

2005, May 31
991   A533   6.50d multi   2.00   1.00

13th World Neurosurgery Congress, Marrakesh
A534

2005, June 19
992   A534   6.50d multi   2.00   1.00

Phosphates Office, 80th Anniv. — A535

2005, Aug. 31   Photo.   *Perf. 13¼*
993   A535   6.50d multi   2.00   1.00

United Nations, 60th Anniv. — A536

2005, Oct. 24
994   A536   6.50d multi   2.00   1.00

Green March, 30th Anniv.
A537

Marchers and "30" in: 2.50d, Light blue. 6d, Green.

2005, Nov. 6
995-996   A537   Set of 2   2.75   2.75

Anti-Poverty Week Type of 2000 and

Anti-Poverty Week — A538

2005, Nov. 7   *Perf. 12¾*
997   A461   6.50d multi   2.00   1.00
    Perf. 13¼
998   A538   6.50d multi   2.00   1.00

Values for No. 997 are for stamps with surrounding selvage.

Friendship of Morocco and the Netherlands, 400th Anniv. — A539

Designs: No. 999, 6.50d, Five tourist attractions. No. 1000, 6.50d, Arch and waterway, vert.

2005, Nov. 14   *Perf. 13¼*
999-1000   A539   Set of 2   4.00   1.90

World Summit on the Information Society, Tunis
A540

2005, Nov. 16
1001   A540   6d multi   2.00   1.00

Return from Exile of King Mohammed V, 50th Anniv. — A541

Country name in: No. 1002, Red. No. 1003a, Green.

2005, Nov. 16   *Perf. 13¼x13*
1002   A541   6.50d multi   1.90   1.00
Souvenir Sheet
1003   Sheet, #1002, 1003a   4.00   2.25
   a.   A541   6.50d multi   1.75   .75

Souvenir Sheet

Children's Art — A542

No. 1004: a, Children and flower, by Kaoutar Azizi Alaoui. b, Children and dove, by Sara Bourquiba. c, House and trees, by Mohcine Kahyouchat. d, Sun on horizon, by Anise Anico.

2005, Nov. 21   *Perf. 13x13¼*
1004   A542   2.50d Sheet of 4, #a-d   3.00   2.00

Intl. Year of Microcredit
A543

2005, Nov. 30   *Perf. 13¼*
1005   A543   6.50d multi   2.00   1.00

Marine Life
A544

Designs: 2.50d, Sparus aurata. 6d, Sepia officinalis.

2005, Dec. 22
1006-1007   A544   Set of 2   2.70   1.00

King Mohammed VI Type of 2001 Redrawn With Smaller Coat of Arms
2005   Litho.   *Perf. 11½*
Coat of Arms 11mm Tall
1007A   A475   70c multi   5.00   1.00
1007B   A475   80c multi   5.00   1.00

Nos. 1007A and 1007B are dated 2005. Coat of arms is 14mm tall on Nos. 940 and 941.

King Mohammed VI — A545

Designs: No. 1008, King in suit and tie. No. 1009, King in robe.

2005   Litho.   *Serpentine Die Cut 11*
Booklet Stamps
Self-Adhesive
1008   A545   2.50d multi   .75   .75
1009   A545   2.50d multi   .75   .75
   a.   Booklet pane, 5 each #1008-1009   7.50

Compare type A545 with A504. See Nos. 1054A-1054B.

Bustard
A546

Melierax Metabates
A547

Egretta Garzetta
A548

Pandion Haliaetus
A549

Alectoris Barbara
A550

Porphyrio Porphyrio
A551

Carduelis Carduelis
A552

Bird
A553

Duck
A554

Falcon
A555

Self-Adhesive
2005   *Serpentine Die Cut 11*
1010   Booklet pane of 10   8.50
   a.   A546   2.50d multi   .85   .40
   b.   A547   2.50d multi   .85   .40
   c.   A548   2.50d multi   .85   .40
   d.   A549   2.50d multi   .85   .40
   e.   A550   2.50d multi   .85   .40
   f.   A551   2.50d multi   .85   .40
   g.   A552   2.50d multi   .85   .40
   h.   A553   2.50d multi   .85   .40
   i.   A554   2.50d multi   .85   .40
   j.   A555   2.50d multi   .85   .40

Two Women
A556

Ait Mouhad
A557

Saharaoui
Derraa
A558

Two Women
A559

Citadin
A560

Saharaoui
Melhfa
A561

Tata Woman
A562

Tata Man
A563

Meknassa
A564

Mokhazni
du Roi
A565

Self-Adhesive

2005   *Serpentine Die Cut 11*
1011 Booklet pane of 10   20.00
a. A556 6d multi   2.00 1.10
b. A557 6d multi   2.00 1.10
c. A558 6d multi   2.00 1.10
d. A559 6d multi   2.00 1.10
e. A560 6d multi   2.00 1.10
f. A561 6d multi   2.00 1.10
g. A562 6d multi   2.00 1.10
h. A563 6d multi   2.00 1.10
i. A564 6d multi   2.00 1.10
j. A565 6d multi   2.00 1.10

Traffic Safety
Day — A566

2006, Feb. 18 Photo. *Perf. 13½x13*
1012 A566 6.50d multi   2.00 1.00

OPEC Intl. Development Fund, 30th
Anniv. — A567

2006, Feb. 28   *Perf. 13¼*
1013 A567 6.50d multi   2.00 1.00

Bab
Marshan,
Tangiers
A568

2006, Mar. 30
1014 A568 6.50d multi   1.90 1.00

Foreign
Affairs
Ministry,
50th
Anniv.
A569

2006, Apr. 26
1015 A569 6d multi   1.75 1.00

Flowers — A570

Designs: 2.50d, Narcissus cantabricus.
6.50d, Paeonia mascula.

2006, Apr. 28
1016-1017 A570 Set of 2   2.50 2.50

Royal
Armed
Forces,
50th
Anniv.
A571

Kings Mohammed VI, Hassan II, and
Mohammed V, anniversary emblem, airplanes
and: 2.50d, Tank. 6.50d, Ships.

2006, May 14
1018-1019 A571 Set of 2   2.50 1.10
1019a Souvenir sheet, #1018-1019 2.75 2.75
No. 1019a sold for 10d.

Type of 2001 With Added Frameline and

A572

King
Mohammed
VI — A573

2006, July 1   Litho.   *Perf. 11½*
              Granite Paper
1020 A472 3.25d blue & multi   .90   .50
1021 A572 7.80d lt grn & multi 2.40 1.20
1022 A573 13d lilac & multi   3.75 1.90
   Nos. 1020-1022 (3)   7.05 3.60

Designs size of No. 1020: 25x32mm.
See No. 1029A for stamp similar to No.
1020, with 22x32mm design without frameline.
See No. 1054D for stamp similar to No.
1021, with 22x32mm design, with country

name in white, inscribed "Phil@poste" at bottom. Compare types A572 with types A473
and A688.
   Compare type A573 with types A475 and
A599a.

Barbary
Ape — A574

Atlas
Lion — A575

2006, July 31   *Perf. 13¼x13*
1023 A574 3.25d multi   .90   .50
1024 A575 7.80d multi   2.25 1.10

Green
March,
31st Anniv.
A576

Designs: No. 1025, 7.80d, King Mohammed
VI waving to crowd. No. 1026, 7.80d, Mohammed VI Mosque, Boujdour.

2006, Nov. 7   Photo.   *Perf. 13¼*
1025-1026 A576 Set of 2   4.50 2.25

Anti-Poverty Week Type of 2000
2006, Nov. 10
1027 A461 7.80d multi   2.25   .95
   Values are for stamps with surrounding
selvage.

Stamp
Day — A577

2006, Nov. 22
1028 A577 7.80d multi   2.25 1.10
   Values are for stamps with surrounding
selvage.

Admission to the
United Nations,
50th
Anniv. — A578

2006, Nov. 24
1029 A578 7.80d multi   2.25 1.10

King Mohammed VI Type of 2001
2006, Nov.   Litho.   *Perf. 13¼*
              Size: 22x32mm
1029A A472 3.25d blue & multi 1.10 1.10
   No. 1020 has a frame line around design
while No. 1029A does not. No. 1029A has a
printer's imprint of "Phil@poste."

World
AIDS Day
A579

2006, Dec. 1   Litho.   *Perf. 13¼*
1030 A579 7.80d multi   2.25 1.10

Diplomatic
Relations
Between
Morocco
and Japan,
50th Anniv.
A580

Designs: 3.25d, Dove, maps and flags.
7.80d, Flags, arches, pottery.

2006, Dec. 20   Photo.   *Perf. 13¼*
1031-1032 A580 Set of 2   3.25 1.50

Fish
A581

Designs: 3.25d, Thunnus thynnus. 7.80d,
Sardina pilchardus.

2006, Dec. 25
1033-1034 A581 Set of 2   3.25 1.50

African Soccer Confederation, 50th
Anniv. — A582

2007, Feb. 26   Litho.   *Perf. 13¼*
1035 A582 7.80d multi   2.40 1.10
   Values are for stamps with surrounding
selvage.

Mohammed V
University, 50th
Anniv. — A583

2007, Mar. 15
1036 A583 3.25d multi   1.00   .50

Ibn Khaldun (1332-1406),
Philosopher — A584

2007, Mar. 28
1037 A584 7.80d multi 2.40 1.10

Souvenir Sheet

Intl. Agricultural Exhibition,
Meknès — A585

No. 1038: a, Palm trees. b, Argans. c, Cattle, horiz. d, Olives, horiz.

Perf. 12¾x13¼, 13¼x12¾ (horiz. stamps)
2007, Apr. 19
1038 A585 Sheet of 4 7.00 7.00
a.-b. 3.25d Either single 1.00 .50
c.-d. 7.80d Either single 2.40 1.25
No. 1038 sold for 24d.

Couscous
A586

2007, June 1 **Perf. 13¼x13**
1039 A586 7.80d multi 2.40 1.10

Andalusian Music — A587

2007, June 8 **Perf. 13x13¼**
1040 A587 7.80d multi 2.40 1.10

Souvenir Sheet

Paintings — A588

No. 1041: a, Fulgurance, by M. Qotbi, vert. b, Horses and Riders, by, H. Glaoui. c, Symphonie d'Eté, by Qotbi. d, Horses, by Glaoui.

2007, June 21 **Perf. 13**
1041 A588 3.25d Sheet of 4, #a-d 4.00 4.00

Scouting,
Cent. — A589

2007, Aug. 7 Litho. Perf. 13¼
1042 A589 7.80d multi 2.40 1.10

Buildings — A590

Designs: 3.25d, Silves Castle, Portugal. 7.80d, Tower, Arzila, Morocco.

2007, Sept. 26
1043-1044 A590 Set of 2 3.50 1.75
See Portugal Nos. 2955-2956.

World Post Day
A591

2007, Oct. 9
1045 A591 3.25d multi 1.25 .90

Fez, 2007 Islamic Cultural Capital A592

2007, Oct. 30
1046 A592 7.80d multi 2.40 1.10
Compare with Type A618.

Green March, 32nd Anniv. A593

2007, Nov. 6
1047 A593 7.80d multi 2.40 1.10

Anti-Poverty Week Type of 2000
2007, Nov. 8
1048 A461 7.80d multi 2.40 1.10
Values are for stamps with surrounding selvage.

National Quality Week — A594

2007, Nov. 12
1049 A594 7.80d multi 2.40 1.10

World Children's Day — A595

2007, Nov. 20
1050 A595 7.80d multi 2.40 1.10

Supreme Court, 50th Anniv. — A596

2007, Nov. 21
1051 A596 3.25d multi 1.00 .50

Bab Lamrissa — A597

2007, Dec. 7 Litho. Perf. 13¼
1052 A597 7.80d multi 2.40 1.10

Royal Air Morocco, 50th Anniv. A598

2007, Dec. 19
1053 A598 7.80d multi 2.40 1.10

"Morocco of Champions" — A599

2007, Dec. 28
1054 A599 7.80d multi 2.40 1.10
Values are for stamps with surrounding selvage.

King Mohammed VI Types of 2005, 2006 (Redrawn) and

King Mohammed VI — A599a

Booklet Stamps
Self-Adhesive

Designs: No. 1054A, King in suit and tie. No. 1054B, King in robe.

2007 Litho. Serpentine Die Cut 11
1054A A545 3.25d multi 1.00 1.00
1054B A545 3.25d multi 1.00 1.00
c. Booklet pane, 5 each #1054A-1054B 10.00

Size: 22x32mm
Country Name in White
Water-Activated Gum
Perf. 13
1054D A572 7.80d multi 2.25 1.10
f. Dated 2009 2.25 1.00
g. Dated 2010 2.25 .95
Compare with No. 1021, which is wider and has country name in blue.

Size: 31x23mm
1054E A599a 13d pink & multi 3.50 1.75
Compare with No. 1022, which is taller and has a lilac background.

Moroccan Travel Market A600

2008, Jan. 17
1055 A600 7.80d multi 2.40 1.10

Africa Cup of Nations Soccer Championships — A601

2008, Jan. 31
1056 A601 7.80d multi 2.40 1.10

Export Trophy — A602

2008, Apr. 4   Litho.   Perf. 13¼
1057 A602 3.25d multi   1.00 .50

Fez, 1200th Anniv. — A603

2008, Apr. 5
1058 A603 3.25d multi   1.00 .50

Flowers — A604

Designs: 3.25d, Calendula stellata. 7.80d, Convolvulus tricolor.

2008, Apr. 30   Litho.   Perf. 13¼
1059-1060 A604 Set of 2   3.25 1.60

Buildings in Morocco and Iran — A605

No. 1061: a, 3.25d, Flags of Morocco and Iran, Kasbah, Oudayas, Morocco, and Falak-Ol-Aflak Castle, Iran. b, 3.25d, Scroll and Falak-Ol-Aflak Castle. c, 7.80d, Scroll and Kasbah, Oudayas, Morocco.

2008, May 12   Litho.   Perf. 13¼
1061 A605 Horiz. strip of 3, #a-
                              c   4.25 2.25
See Iran No. 2955.

Children's Art — A606

No. 1062: a, Earth, by Narjiss Lasfar. b, House and trees, by Chaimae Abbaich, horiz. c, Polluted sphere, by Ahmed Anas Bennis, vert. d, House and sun, by Wassim Chakou, vert.

2008, May 26
1062 A606 Horiz. strip of 4   4.00 2.00
  a.-d. A606 3.25d Any single   .95   .45

World Environment Day — A607

2008, June 5
1063 A607 7.80d multi   2.40 1.10

Rug From Salé A608

Rug From Marmoucha A609

Rug From Ouled Besseba A610

Rug From Haut Atlas A611

Rug From Ait Haddou A612

Rug From Tazenakht A613

Rug From Marmoucha A614

Rug From Rabat A615

Rug From Ait Ouaouzguid A616

Rug From Rabat A617

Self-Adhesive

2008   Serpentine Die Cut 11
1064   Booklet pane of 10   25.00
  a.   A608 7.80d multi   2.50 1.10
  b.   A609 7.80d multi   2.50 1.10
  c.   A610 7.80d multi   2.50 1.10
  d.   A611 7.80d multi   2.50 1.10
  e.   A612 7.80d multi   2.50 1.10
  f.   A613 7.80d multi   2.50 1.10
  g.   A614 7.80d multi   2.50 1.10
  h.   A615 7.80d multi   2.50 1.10
  i.   A616 7.80d multi   2.50 1.10
  j.   A617 7.80d multi   2.50 1.10

Fez, 1200th Anniv. A618

2008, June 23   Perf. 13¼
1065 A618 7.80d multi   2.40 1.10
Compare with Type A592.

Bouregreg Valley Light Rail Line — A619

No. 1066: a, 3.25d, Train, bridge. b, 7.80d, Train, fortress.

2008, July 21
1066 A619 Horiz. pair, #a-b   3.25 1.60

2008 Summer Olympics, Beijing — A620

No. 1067 — Olympic rings and: a, Four runners. b, Three hurdlers. c, Boxers. d, Runner.

2008, Aug. 8   Photo.   Perf. 13¼
1067   Horiz. strip of 4   4.00 2.00
  a.-d. A620 3.25d Any single   1.00   .45

Arab Post Day — A621

No. 1068 — Emblem and: a, World map, pigeon. b, Camel caravan.

2008, Aug. 28   Litho.   Perf. 12¾
1068   Sheet of 2   4.50 2.25
  a.-b. A621 7.80d Either single   2.25 1.10

Marine Life A622

Designs: 3.25d, Isurus oxyrinchus. 7.80d, Haliotis tuberculata.

2008, Sept. 18   Perf. 13¼
1069-1070 A622 Set of 2   3.25 1.60

Miniature Sheet

Art and Culture — A623

No. 1071: a, Musicians. b, Ezzellij tiles. c, Haïk (white garment). d, Koran school.

2008, Oct. 10   Photo.   Perf. 13¼x13
1071 A623 3.25d Sheet of 4, #a-
                              d   4.00 2.00

Diplomatic Relations Between Morocco and People's Republic of China — A624

Designs: 3.25r, Vases and flags of Morocco and People's Republic of China. No. 1073, 7.80d, Intertwined arabesque and Chinese emblem. No. 1074, 7.80d, Arabic archway and Great Wall of China, vert.

2008, Oct. 30   Photo.   Perf. 12
1072-1074 A624 Set of 3   4.50 2.25

Green March, 33rd Anniv. A625

2008, Nov. 6   Litho.   Perf. 13¼
1075 A625 3.25d multi   1.00 .35

Anti-Poverty Week Type of 2000
2008, Nov. 12   Photo.   Perf. 13¼
1076 A461 7.80d multi   2.00 .95

Natl. Cancer Prevention Day — A626

2008, Nov. 22   Perf. 13¼
1077 A626 3.25d multi   1.00 .35

Universal Declaration of Human Rights, 60th Anniv. A627

2008, Dec. 10   Litho.   Perf. 13
1078 A627 7.80d multi   2.00 .95

Bab Al Marsa, Essaouira A628

2008, Dec. 26   Photo.   Perf. 13¼
1079 A628 7.80d multi   2.00 1.00

Louis Braille
(1809-52),
Educator of the
Blind — A629

2009, Jan. 16
1080 A629 7.80d multi   2.00 .95

Insurance for Artisans and the Self-
Employed — A630

2009, Feb. 16   **Perf. 13x13¼**
1081 A630 3.25d multi   1.00 .35

25th Hassan II
Grand Prix Tennis
Tournament
A631

2009, Apr. 6   **Perf. 13¼**
1082 A631 3.25d multi   1.00 .40

Cadi
Ayyad
University,
Marrakesh,
30th Anniv.
A632

2009, Apr. 20
1083 A632 3.25d multi   1.00 .40

Sugar
Industry — A633

2009, Apr. 22   **Photo.**
1084 A633 3.25d multi   1.00 .40

Leopard With Mail Bag — A633a

2009, May 6 **Litho.** **Perf. 13x13¼**
1084A A633a 5.90d multi   2.00 .75

Natl.
Theater
Day
A634

2009, May 14 **Photo.** **Perf. 13¼**
1085 A634 3.25d multi   1.00 .40

Intl. Year
of
Astronomy
A635

2009, May 15
1086 A635 7.80d multi   2.50 1.00

Protection
for Children
Using
Computers
A636

2009, May 17 **Litho.** **Perf. 13x13¼**
1087 A636 7.80d multi   2.50 1.00

Al-Maghrib
Bank, 50th
Anniv.
A637

2009, July 2 **Photo.** **Perf. 13¼**
1088 A637 3.25d multi   1.00 .40

A638

Enthronement of King Mohammed VI,
10th Anniv. — A639

King Mohammed VI: 3.25d, On horse.
7.80d, Wearing suit.
15d, With images of Kings Mohammed V
and Hassan II.

**Photo. & Embossed With Foil
Application**
2009, July 30   **Perf. 13¼**
Granite Paper (#1089-1090)
1089 A638 3.25d multi   1.00 .40
1090 A638 7.80d multi   2.50 1.00

**Souvenir Sheet
Litho. with Three-Dimensional
Plastic Affixed
Serpentine Die Cut 9½
Self-Adhesive**
1091 A639 15d multi   6.50 6.50
Nos. 1089-1090 have gold frames with an
orange cast. A souvenir sheet containing Nos.
1089-1090 having gold frames with a yellow
cast sold for 36d.

Jerusalem,
Capital of Arab
Culture — A640

2009, Aug. 3 **Litho.** **Perf. 13¼**
1092 A640 3.25d multi   1.00 .40

Natl. Women's
Day — A641

2009, Oct. 10
1093 A641 3.25d multi   1.00 .40

Mohammedia School of Engineering,
50th Anniv. — A652

2009, Oct. 24 **Litho.** **Perf. 13¼**
1095 A652 3.25d multi   1.00 .40

Mehdia
Gate
A653

2009, Oct. 30 **Photo.** **Perf. 13¾**
1096 A653 7.80d multi   2.50 1.10

Green March,
34th
Anniv. — A654

2009, Nov. 6 **Litho.** **Perf. 13¼**
1097 A654 3.25d multi   1.10 .55

Anti-Poverty Week Type of 2001
2009, Nov. 15 **Photo.** **Perf. 13**
1098 A461 7.80d multi   2.50 1.10
Value is for stamp with surrounding selvage.

Port of Tangiers — A655

No. 1099 — Ship in port, gear wheels in: a,
3.25d, Gray. b, 7.80d, Brown.

2009, Dec. 7 **Litho.** **Perf. 13¼**
1099 A655 Horiz. pair, #a-b   3.50 1.50

Caisse de Dépot
et de Gestion,
50th
Anniv. — A656

2009, Dec. 19
1100 A656 7.80d dk blue & gold 2.50 1.00

Fish
A657

Designs: No. 1101, 7.80d, Sarda sarda. No.
1102, 7.80d, Oblada melanura.

2009, Dec. 28
1101-1102 A657 Set of 2   5.00 2.00

Children's
Art
A658

No. 1103: a, Horses. b, Trees. c, Lake,
mountain and trees. d, Building with
smokestacks.

2009, Dec. 31
1103   Vert. strip of 4   4.00 1.75
a.-d. A658 3.25d Any single   .85 .40

Rosa Damascena
A659

Orange
Blossoms
A660

2010, Jan. 14   **Perf. 13¼x13**
1104 A659 7.80d multi   2.50 1.00
          Perf. 13x13¼
1105 A660 7.80d multi   2.50 1.00
Nos. 1104-1105 are each impregnated with
the scent of the depicted flower.

Reconstruction of Agadir, 50th
Anniv. — A661

2010, Feb. 28   *Perf. 13¼*
1106 A661 7.80d multi   2.50   .95

Earth
Day — A662

2010, Apr. 22
1107 A662 3.25d multi   1.00   .40

Alfalfa
A663

2010, Apr. 22   Litho. & Embossed
1108 A663 10d multi   3.50 1.25
No. 1108 has a circle of adhesive tape covering a small embossed circle containing
alfalfa seeds.

Miniature Sheet

Art and Culture — A664

No. 1109 — Paintings of casbahs in: a,
Ibeghouzen. b, Oudaias. c, Ait ben Haddou. d,
Tinzouline.

2010, May 12   *Perf. 13x13¼*
1109 A664 3.25d Sheet of 4, #a-
                d   5.00 1.50

Level A Quality
Certification for
Morocco
Post — A665

2010, May 26   *Perf. 13¼*
1110 A665 3.25d multi   1.00   .35

National
Day of
Resistance
A666

2010, June 18
1111 A666 3.25d multi   1.00   .35

Bab al Bahr,
Abilah — A667

2010, July 10
1112 A667 7.80d multi   2.50   .95

OCP Groupe, 90th Anniv. — A668

2010, Aug. 7   *Perf. 12¼*
1113 A668 7.80d multi   2.50   .95

Intl. Year of
Biodiversity
A669

2010, Oct. 11   Litho.   *Perf. 13¼*
1114 A669 7.80d multi   2.50 1.00

Souvenir Sheet

Green March, 35th Anniv. — A670

No. 1115: a, Marchers. b, Hand holding
Moroccan flag.

2010, Nov. 6   Litho.   *Perf. 14*
1115 A670 7.80d Sheet of 2,
                #a-b   5.00 5.00
Grains of sand were applied to portions of
the design by a thermographic process.

Sciaena
Umbra
A671

2010, Nov. 16   Photo.   *Perf. 13¼*
1116 A671 7.80d multi   2.50   .95

Anti-Poverty Week Type of 2001
2010, Nov. 19   Photo.   *Perf. 13*
1117 A461 7.80d multi   2.50   .95
Value is for stamp with surrounding selvage.

Numeric 2013
Plan — A672

2010, Nov. 30   Litho.   *Perf. 13¼x13*
1118 A672 7.80d multi   2.50   .95

Tenth Marrakesh
Intl. Film
Festival — A673

2010, Dec. 3   Photo.   *Perf. 13¼*
1119 A673 7.80d multi   2.50   .95

Train
A674

2010, Dec. 14
1120 A674 3.25d multi   1.00   .40

Greetings
A675

Inscriptions: No. 1121, 3.25d, Bonheur
(happiness). No. 1122, 3.25d, Prospérité
(prosperity). No. 1123, 3.25d, Santé (health).

2010, Dec. 20
1121-1123 A675 Set of 3   3.00 1.25

King Mohammed VI Type of 2007
and

A687   A688

2011, Feb. 1   Litho.   *Perf. 13x13¼*
1126 A687 3.50d brn org &
                multi   1.25   .40
1127 A688 8.40d lilac & multi   2.75 1.10
                Perf. 13¼x13
1128 A599a 20d lt green &
                multi   6.50 2.50
        Nos. 1126-1128 (3)   10.50 4.00
Compare type A687 with type A472, and
type A688 with types A473 and A572.

Leopard With Mail Bag — A690

2011, Apr. 20   Litho.   *Perf. 13x13¼*
1130 A690 6.40d multi   2.25   .85

Miniature Sheet

Tom and Jerry Cartoons — A691

No. 1131: a, Jerry hitting tennis ball through
Tom's racquet. b, Tom and Jerry in hammocks
on desert island. c, Jerry shooting tennis balls
at Tom with machine. d, Tom swimming with
Jerry on his chest. e, Tom hitting tennis net
with racquet. f, Wave approaching Tom and
Jerry. g, Jerry holding tennis ball for Tom. h,
Jerry listening to shell, Tom collecting shells. i,
Tom slipping on tennis balls thrown by Jerry. j,
Tom and Jerry building sand castles.

2011, May 4   *Perf. 13¼*
1131 A691 3.50d Sheet of 10,
                #a-j   12.00 12.00

Turkeys — A692

Henna
Plant — A693

2011, May 30
1132 A692 3.50d multi   1.25   .45
1133 A693 8.40d multi   2.75 1.10

A694   A695

A696   A697

A698   A699

A700   A701

Copperware
A702   A703

Serpentine Die Cut 11

2011, June 16   **Self-Adhesive**
1134   Booklet pane of 10   25.00
  a. A694 8.40d multi   2.50   1.10
  b. A695 8.40d multi   2.50   1.10
  c. A696 8.40d multi   2.50   1.10
  d. A697 8.40d multi   2.50   1.10
  e. A698 8.40d multi   2.50   1.10
  f. A699 8.40d multi   2.50   1.10
  g. A700 8.40d multi   2.50   1.10
  h. A701 8.40d multi   2.50   1.10
  i. A702 8.40d multi   2.50   1.10
  j. A703 8.40d multi   2.50   1.10

Al Barid Bank
A704

2011, June 27   **Perf. 13¼**
1135 A704 3.50d multi   1.25   .45

Famous Men
A705

No. 1136: a, Moulay Abderrahmane Ben Zidane (1873-1946), historian. b, Abou Chouaib Doukkali Essadiki (1878-1938), scientist. c, Mohamed Ben Larbi Alaoui Lamdaghri (1880-1964), Justice Minister. d, Mohamed El Mokhtar Soussi (1900-63), religious scholar. e, Abdellah Ben Abdessamad Guennoune (1908-89), first governor of Tangiers.

2011, June 30   **Litho.**
1136   Horiz. strip of 5   6.00   6.00
  a.-e. A705 3.50d Any single   1.00   .50

Campaign Against AIDS — A706

2011, July 27
1137 A706 8.40d multi   2.75   1.10

National Artisan's Week — A707

2011, Sept. 8   **Perf. 13¼**
1138 A707 3.50d multi   1.25   .45

First Air Mail in Morocco, Cent. A708

No. 1139 — Airplane and monument in: a, Color. b, Black-and-white.

2011, Sept. 19
1139 A708 8.40d Vert. pair, #a-b   5.00   3.00

Miniature Sheet

Coins — A709

No. 1140: a, Obverse of 1893 bronze 8-fels coin (showing star). b, As "a," reverse (showing "1131" date). c, Obverse of 1609 gold dinar (26mm diameter coin with 20mm diameter inner circle, no horizontal lines). d, As "c," reverse (with long horizontal lines inside inner circle). e, Obverse of gold Almohades dinar (29mm coin with inner square, no long horizontal lines inside square). f, As "e," reverse (with long horizontal line inside square). g, Obverse of 1145 gold dinar (25mm coin with 15mm inner circle, with long horizontal lines inside inner circle). h, As "g," reverse (without long horizontal lines inside inner circle). i, Obverse of 790 silver dirham (Arabic script around edge of coin). j, As "i," reverse (five dots around edge of coin).

Litho. & Embossed
2011, Oct. 20   **Perf. 13¼x13¾**
1140 A709 3.50d Sheet of 10, #a-j   12.00   12.00

National Campaign on Millennial Development Objectives A710

2011, Oct. 24   **Litho.**   **Perf. 13¼**
1141 A710 8.40d multi   2.75   1.10

Children's Art — A711

No. 1142 — Various works of children's art inscribed: a, L'Ecole (school), by Ibtissam Gariate. b, L' Environnement (environment), by Ramah Damach. c, La Sante (health), by Hanane Aliouan. d, L'Enfance (childhood), by Kenza Najdaoui, horiz.

2011, Oct. 25
1142 A711 3.50d Horiz. strip of 4, #a-d   5.00   5.00

Green March, 36th Anniv. — A712

2011, Nov. 6   **Photo.**
1143 A712 8.40d multi   2.75   1.10

Anti-Poverty Week Type of 2001
2011, Nov. 28   **Photo.**   **Perf. 13**
1144 A461 8.40d multi   2.75   1.10
  Values are for stamps with surrounding selvage.

Miniature Sheet

Folding Screens — A713

No. 1145 — Screen art by: a, 3.50d, Paula Cardozo. b, 3.50d, Abdellah Yacoubi. c, 8.40d, Yukako Fukuda-Ota, vert. d, 8.40d, Miki Tica, vert.

Perf. 13x13¼, 13¼x13 (vert. stamps)
2011, Dec. 1
1145 A713   Sheet of 4, #a-d   7.00   7.00

National Statistics and Applied Economics Institute, 50th Anniv. — A714

2011, Dec. 15   **Perf. 13¼**
1146 A714 3.50d multi   1.25   .40

Animals in Rabat Zoo A715

No. 1147: a, Mouflons. b, Oryx. c, Lions, vert. d, Ibises, vert.

2012, Jan. 9   **Photo.**   **Perf. 13¼**
1147   Strip of 4   7.00   7.00
  a.-b. A715 3.50d Either single   1.00   .40
  c.-d. A715 8.40d Either single   2.25   1.00
  e. Souvenir sheet of 4, #1147a-1147d   7.00   7.00

2012 African Cup of Nations Soccer Tournament, Equatorial Guinea and Gabon — A716

2012, Jan. 23   **Litho.**   **Perf. 13¾**
1148 A716 3.50d multi   1.25   .50
  Values are for stamps with surrounding selvage.

Mohammed V Theater, Rabat, 50th Anniv. A717

2012, Mar. 27   **Perf. 13x13¼**
1149 A717 3.50d multi   1.25   .40

Moroccan Postage Stamps, Cent. — A718

No. 1150: a, 3.50d, Anniversary emblem. b, 8.40d, Horses and riders.

2012, May 22   **Perf. 13¼x14**
1150 A718   Vert. pair, #a-b   3.75   3.75

Arab Post Day — A719

2012, Aug. 3   **Perf. 13x13¼**
1151 A719 8.40d multi   2.75   .95

2012 Summer Olympics, London A720

Perf. 13¼ Syncopated
2012, Aug. 17
1152 A720 8.40d multi   2.75   1.00

15th National
Quality
Prize — A721

2012, Sept. 27   **Litho.**
1153 A721 8.40d multi   2.75 1.00

Retirement
Allowance
Collective
Plan, 35th
Anniv.
A722

2012, Oct. 4   Perf. 13¼ Syncopated
1154 A722 3.50d multi   1.25 .40

El Jadida
Horse
Show
A725

Perf. 13¼ Syncopated
2012, Oct. 17   **Photo.**
1157 A725 8.40d multi   2.75 1.00

Anti-Poverty Week Type of 2001
2012, Nov. 7   Photo.   Perf. 13¼
Dated "2012"
1159 A461 8.40d multi   2.75 1.00
Values are for stamps with surrounding
selvage.

Maghzen Post, 120th Anniv. — A728

No. 1161 — Sherifian postal seals and their
impressions: a, Purple circular. b, Purple
octagonal. c, Blue green circular. d, Blue
green octagonal. e, Blue circular. f, Blue
octagonal. g, Red circular. h, Red octagonal. i,
Black circular. j, Black octagonal. k, Orange
circular. l, Orange octagonal.

Perf. 13¼x13 Syncopated
2012, Nov. 22   **Photo.**
1161   Sheet of 12 + 12 la-
            bels   15.00 15.00
a.-l. A728 3.50d Any single + label 1.00 .45

Intl. Year of
Renewable
Energy — A729

Perf. 13¼ Syncopated
2012, Dec. 24   **Photo.**
1163 A729 8.40d multi   2.75 1.00

SEMI-POSTAL STAMPS

Nos. 1-5
Surcharged

1960, Mar. Unwmk. Engr. Perf. 13
B1 A1 5fr + 10fr brt bl & ind   .45 .40
B2 A1 10fr + 10fr bis brn & choc   .55 .55
B3 A1 15fr + 10fr dp grn & mag   1.25 1.10
B4 A1 25fr + 15fr purple   1.40 1.15
B5 A1 30fr + 20fr green   2.25 2.25
            Nos. B1-B5 (5)   5.90 5.45
The surtax aided families whose members
consumed adulterated cooking oil with crip-
pling or fatal results.

French Morocco
Nos. 321 and 322
Surcharged

1960, Sept. 12
B6 A71 15fr + 3fr on 18fr dk grn   .80 .80
B7 A71 20fr + 5fr brown lake   1.25 1.25

Nos. 1 and 6
Surcharged in Red
or Black

1963, Jan. 28   Engr.   Perf. 13
B8 A1 20c + 5c on 5fr brt bl & ind
                      (R)   .70 .70
B9 A1 30c + 10c on 50fr rose red .80 .45
The surtax was for flood victims.

Moroccan
Brooch — SP1

Design: 40c+10c, Brooch with pendants.

1966, May 23   Photo.   Perf. 11½
Granite Paper
B10 SP1 25c + 5c ultra, sil, blk &
            red   .90 .55
B11 SP1 40c + 10c mag, sil, blk,
            ultra & bl   1.40 .70
a.   Pair, #B10-B11, vertically tête-
      bêche   3.25 3.25
Meeting in Morocco of the Middle East and
North African Red Cross-Red Crescent Semi-
nar. The surtax was for the Moroccan Red
Crescent Society.
See Nos. B12-B13, B15-B16, B19-B22,
B26-B27, B29-B30, B34-B35.

1967, May 15   Granite Paper
Designs: 60c+5c, Two brooches, by silver
drapery. 1d+10c, Two bracelets.
B12 SP1 60c + 5c yel bis & multi   .95 .95
a.   Pair, vertically tête-bêche   3.00 3.00
B13 SP1 1d + 10c emer & multi   1.90 1.90
a.   Pair, vertically tête-bêche   4.75 4.75
Surtax for the Moroccan Red Crescent
Society.

Hands Reading Braille and Map of
Morocco — SP2

1969, Mar. 21   Photo.   Perf. 12½
B14 SP2 25c + 10c multi   .60 .25
Week of the Blind, Mar. 21-29.

Jewelry Type of 1966
Designs: 25c+5c, Silver earrings. 40c+10c,
Gold ear pendant.

1969, May 9   Photo.   Perf. 11½
Granite Paper
B15 SP1 25c + 5c gray grn &
            multi   1.25 .65
B16 SP1 40c + 10c tan & multi   1.60 .80
a.   Pair, #B15-B16, vert. tête-bêche 6.00 6.00
50th anniv. of the League of Red Cross
Societies. Surtax was for Moroccan Red Cres-
cent Society.

Nos. 173-174
Surcharged

1970, Feb. 26   Litho.   Perf. 13
B17 A65 10c + 25c multi   3.50 3.50
B18 A65 15c + 25c multi   3.50 3.50
The surtax was for flood victims.

Jewelry Type of 1966
Designs: 25c+5c, Necklace with pendants.
50c+10c, Earring with 5 pendants.
1970, May 25   Photo.   Perf. 11½
Granite Paper
B19 SP1 25c + 5c gray & multi   1.10 .90
B20 SP1 50c + 10c brt vio &
            multi   1.50 1.25
a.   Pair, #B19-B20, vert. tête-bêche 4.00 4.00
Surtax for Moroccan Red Crescent Society.

1971, May 10   Granite Paper
25c+5c, Brooch. 40c+10c, Stomacher.
B21 SP1 25c + 5c gray & multi   1.10 .65
B22 SP1 40c + 10c yel & multi   1.90 1.00
a.   Pair, #B21-B22, vertically tête-
      bêche   3.25 3.25

Globe and
Map of
Palestine
SP3

1971, Apr. 30   Perf. 13
B23 SP3 25c + 10c multi   .60 .30
Palestine Week, May 3-8.

String Instrument and Bow — SP4

1971, June 28   Photo.   Perf. 12
B24 SP4 40c + 10c multi   .60 .40
Week of the Blind.

Mizmar (Double
Flute) — SP5

1972, Mar. 31   Photo.   Perf. 13x13½
B25 SP5 25c + 10c multi   .60 .55
Week of the Blind.

Jewelry Type of 1966
Designs: 25c+5c, Jeweled bracelets.
70c+10c, Rectangular pendant with ball drop.
1972, May 8   Photo.   Perf. 11½
Granite Paper
B26 SP1 25c + 5c brn & multi   .80 .80
B27 SP1 70c + 10c dp grn &
            multi   1.25 1.25
a.   Pair, #B26-B27, vert. tête-bêche 3.25 3.25
For overprints see Nos. 295-296.

Drums
SP6

1973, Mar. 30   Photo.   Perf. 13x14
B28 SP6 70c + 10c multi   .65 .50
Week of the Blind.

Jewelry Type of 1966
25c+5c, Silver box pendant. 70c+10c,
Bracelet.
1973, June 15   Photo.   Perf. 11½
B29 SP1 25c + 5c bl & multi   1.50 .80
B30 SP1 70c + 10c org & multi   2.25 .95
a.   Pair, #B29-B30, vert. tête-bêche 4.50 4.50
Moroccan Red Crescent Society. For overprints see Nos. 351-352.

Pistol — SP7   Erbab
                      (Fiddle) — SP8

70c+10c, Decorated antique powder box.

1974, July 8   Photo.   Perf. 14x13½
B31 SP7 25c + 5c multi   .80 .80
B32 SP7 70c + 10c multi   1.25 1.25
a.   Pair, #B31-B32, vert. tête-bêche 2.50 2.50
Moroccan Red Crescent Society.

1975, Jan. 10   Photo.   Perf. 13
B33 SP8 70c + 10c multi   1.20 .50
Week of the Blind.

Jewelry Type of 1966

25c+5c, Silver pendant. 70c+10c, Earring.

1975, Mar. 13   Photo.   *Perf. 13½*
B34 SP1 25c + 5c multi   .80 .80
B35 SP1 70c + 10c multi   1.25 1.25
  a. Pair, #B34-B35, vert. tête-bêche 2.50 2.50

Moroccan Red Crescent Society. For overprints see #386-387.

AIR POST STAMPS

Sultan's Star   King Hassan II
over Casablanca   AP2
AP1

Unwmk.
1957, May 4   Engr.   *Perf. 13*
C1 AP1 15fr car & brt grn   1.40 1.10
C2 AP1 25fr brt grnsh bl   2.10 1.40
C3 AP1 30fr red brn   3.00 1.90
  Nos. C1-C3 (3)   6.50 4.40

Intl. Fair, Casablanca, May 4-19.

1962
C5 AP2 90c black   .70 .25
C6 AP2 1d rose red   1.00 .25
C7 AP2 2d deep blue   1.15 .60
C8 AP2 3d purple   2.25 1.00
C9 AP2 5d purple   4.50 1.60
  Nos. C5-C9 (5)   9.60 3.70

Meteorological Day Type of Regular Issue

1964, Mar. 23   Photo.   *Perf. 11½*
Granite Paper
C10 A39 90c Anemometer & globe 1.10 .70

Intl. Fair, Casablanca, 20th
Anniv. — AP3

1964, Apr. 30   Photo.   *Perf. 12½*
C11 AP3 1d bl, bis & org   1.10 .70

Moroccan
Pavilion
and
Unisphere
AP4

1964, May 25   Unwmk.   *Perf. 12½*
C12 AP4 1d dk grn, red & bl   1.10 .80
New York World's Fair, 1964-65.

Ramses II and
UNESCO
Emblem — AP5

Litho. & Engr.
1966, Oct. 3   *Perf. 12x11½*
C13 AP5 1d magenta, *yel*   1.25 .80
UNESCO, 20th anniv.

Jet Plane — AP6

Perf. 12½x13½
1966, Dec. 19   Photo.
C14 AP6 3d multi   4.50 2.00

Costume Type of Regular Issue

Design: 1d, Women from Ait Ouaouzguit.

1969, Jan. 21   Litho.   *Perf. 12*
C15 A74 1d multi   2.40 1.25

Coin Type of Regular Issue, 1968

Coins: 1d, King Mohammed V, 1960. 5d, King Hassan II, 1965.

1969, Mar. 3   Photo.   *Perf. 11½*
Granite Paper
C16 A73 1d brt bl, sil & blk   4.75 1.60
C17 A73 5d vio blk, sil & blk   9.50 6.00

King
Hassan II — AP7

1983, Mar. 1   Photo.   *Perf. 12*
Granite Paper
C18 AP7 1.40d multi   .60 .25
C19 AP7 2d multi   .65 .25
C20 AP7 3d multi   .90 .30
C21 AP7 5d multi   1.40 .50
C22 AP7 10d multi   3.00 .95
  Nos. C18-C22 (5)   6.55 2.25

No. C19
Overprinted

1987, Mar. 23   Photo.   *Perf. 12*
Granite Paper
C23 AP7 2d multi   1.10 .65
1st World Congress of Friday Preachers, Al Joumouaa.

No. C18
Overprinted

1989, Mar. 27   Photo.   *Perf. 12*
Granite Paper
C24 AP7 1.40d multi   .50 .40
Maghreb Union, agreement between Morocco, Algeria and Tunisia.

No. C18
Surcharged

2000, July 6   Photo.   *Perf. 12*
Granite Paper
C25 AP7 6.50d on 1.40d multi   1.25 .60
Intl. Colloquium on King Hassan II.

POSTAGE DUE STAMPS

D1   Oranges — D2

1965   Unwmk.   Typo.   *Perf. 14x13½*
J1 D1 5c green   21.00 3.50
J2 D1 10c bister brown   1.00 .30
J3 D1 20c red   1.00 .30
J4 D1 30c brown black   1.50 .65
  Nos. J1-J4 (4)   24.50 4.75

See French Morocco Nos. J27-J34, J46-J56.

1974-96   Photo.   *Perf. 14*
J5 D2 5c shown   .30 .25
J6 D2 10c Cherries   .45 .25
J7 D2 20c Grapes   .60 .25
J8 D2 30c Peaches, horiz.   .90 .25
J9 D2 40c Grapes ('78)   .35 .25
J10 D2 60c Peaches, horiz.
       ('78)   1.10 .25
J11 D2 80c Oranges ('78)   1.40 .25
J12 D2 1d Apples ('86)   .50 .25
J13 D2 1.20d Cherries ('84)   .90 .25
J14 D2 1.60d Peaches ('85)   .90 .25
J15 D2 2d Strawberries ('86)   .90 .35

Litho.
J16 D2 5d like #J12 ('96)   2.10 1.00
  Nos. J5-J16 (12)   10.40 3.85

For surcharges see Nos. 322, 395.

Strawberries — D3

Strawberries — D3a

Grapes   Apples
D4   D5

Cherries — D6

2003   Photo.   *Perf. 13x13½*
J17 D3 1.50d multi
J17A D3a 1.50d multi   .90 .75
J18 D4 2d multi
J19 D5 5d multi   3.25 2.75
J20 D6 2d multi   1.20 1.10
  Nos. J17-J20 (5)   5.35 4.60

Fruit Type of 1974-96

2005 ?   Litho.   *Perf. 14*
J21 D2 60c Peaches

No. J21 has a background of solid color. No. J10 has a background of dots. The text is thicker and heavier on No. J10 than on No. J21.

NORTHERN ZONE

100 Centimos = 1 Peseta

All Northern Zone issues except Nos. 21-22 were also sold imperforate in limited quantities.

Sultan Mohammed
V — A1

Villa
Sanjurjo
Harbor
A2

Designs: 25c, Polytechnic school. 50c, 10p, Institute of Culture, Tetuan.

Perf. 13x12½, 12½x13
1956, Aug. 23   Photo.   Unwmk.
1 A1 10c deep rose   .30 .25
2 A2 15c yellow brn   .30 .25
3 A2 25c dk bl gray   .30 .25
4 A1 50c dark olive   .40 .25
5 A1 80c brt green   .90 .90
6 A2 2p brt red lil   7.50 7.50
7 A2 3p brt blue   15.00 15.00
8 A1 10p green   32.50 45.00
  Nos. 1-8 (8)   57.20 69.40

Value, set of Nos. 1-8 as imperf. pairs $2,500.

A3   Sultan
            Mohammed
            V — A4

1957, Mar. 2   *Perf. 13½x13*
9 A3 80c blue green   .75 .75
10 A3 1.50p gray olive   1.90 1.90
11 A3 3p deep rose   4.00 4.00
  Nos. 9-11 (3)   6.65 6.65

1st anniv. of independence. See Morocco Nos. 13-15. Value, set of Nos. 9-11 as imperf. pairs $500.

1957   Engr.   *Perf. 13*
12 A4 30c brt bl & indigo   .25 .25
13 A4 70c bis, brn & choc   .35 .25
14 A4 80c brt violet   1.50 .35
15 A4 1.50p dp grn & mag   .50 .30
16 A4 3p green   .75 .65
17 A4 7p rose red   5.00 1.50
  Nos. 12-17 (6)   8.35 3.30

Value, set of Nos. 12-17 as imperf. pairs $600.

Prince Moulay el Hassan — A5

1957, July 15   Photo.   *Perf. 13*
18	A5	80c blue	.60	.60
19	A5	1.50p green	1.50	1.50
20	A5	3p carmine rose	4.50	4.50
		Nos. 18-20 (3)	6.60	6.60

Value, set of Nos. 18-20 as imperf. pairs $600.

Nos. 13 and 15 Surcharged in Carmine or Black

1957   Engr.
21	A4	15c on 70c (C)	.75	.75
22	A4	1.20p on 1.50p (Bk)	1.25	1.25

King Mohammed V — A6

1957, Nov.   Photo.   *Perf. 12½*
23	A6	1.20p blk & brt grn	.65	.65
24	A6	1.80p blk & rose red	.65	.65
25	A6	3p black & violet	2.00	2.00
		Nos. 23-25 (3)	3.30	3.30

Enthronement of Mohammed V, 30th anniv.
Value, set of Nos. 23-25 as imperf. pairs $750.

NORTHERN ZONE AIR POST STAMPS

Plane over Lau Dam AP1

1.40p, 4.80p, Plane over Nekor bridge.

Perf. 12½x13

1956, Dec. 17   Photo.   Unwmk.
C1	AP1	25c rose violet	.35	.35
C2	AP1	1.40p lilac rose	.90	.90
C3	AP1	3.40p org vermilion	1.90	1.90
C4	AP1	4.80p dull violet	3.25	3.25
		Nos. C1-C4 (4)	6.40	6.40

Value, Nos. C1-C4 as set of imperf. pairs $750.

MOZAMBIQUE

mō-zəm-'bēk

LOCATION — Southeastern Africa, bordering on the Mozambique Channel
GOVT. — Republic
AREA — 308,642 sq. mi.
POP. — 16,542,800 (1997)

CAPITAL — Maputo

Formerly a Portuguese colony, Mozambique, or Portuguese East Africa, was divided into eight districts: Lourenco Marques, Inhambane, Quelimane, Tete, Mozambique, Zambezia, Nyassa and the Manica and Sofala region formerly administered by the Mozambique Company. At various times the districts issued their own stamps which were eventually replaced by those inscribed "Mocambique."

Mozambique achieved independence June 25, 1975, taking the name People's Republic of Mozambique.

1000 Reis = 1 Milreis
100 Centavos = 1 Escudo (1913)
100 Centavos = 1 Metical (1980)

> **Catalogue values for unused stamps in this country are for Never Hinged items, beginning with Scott 330 in the regular postage section, Scott C29 in the airpost section, Scott J51 in the postage due section, and Scott RA55 in the postal tax section.**

Portuguese Crown — A1

Perf. 12½, 13½
1877-85   Typo.   Unwmk.
1	A1	5r black	2.00	1.00
a.		Perf. 13½	3.00	1.60
2	A1	10r yellow	18.00	4.50
3	A1	10r green ('81)	1.50	.60
4	A1	20r bister	1.50	.75
a.		Perf. 13½	3.00	2.00
5	A1	20r rose ('85)	300.00	125.00
6	A1	25r rose	1.00	.35
a.		Perf. 13½	6.75	1.60
7	A1	25r violet ('85)	3.00	2.00
8	A1	40r blue	25.00	15.00
9	A1	40r yel buff ('81)	2.00	1.60
a.		Perf. 12½	3.50	3.00
10	A1	50r green	60.00	20.00
a.		Perf. 13½	125.00	60.00
11	A1	50r blue ('81)	.75	.40
12	A1	100r lilac	1.00	.50
13	A1	200r orange	2.00	1.40
a.		Perf. 12½	5.25	4.50
14	A1	300r chocolate	2.25	2.00
		Nos. 1-4,6-14 (13)	120.00	50.10

The reprints of the 1877-85 issues are printed on a smooth white chalky paper, ungummed, with rough perforation 13½, also on thin white paper, with shiny white gum and clean-cut perforation 13½.

King Luiz — A2

Typographed and Embossed
1886   *Perf. 12½*
15	A2	5r black	1.50	.60
16	A2	10r green	1.50	.70
17	A2	20r rose	2.00	1.50
18	A2	25r dull lilac	9.00	1.40
19	A2	40r chocolate	1.75	.85
20	A2	50r blue	2.25	.50
21	A2	100r yellow brn	2.50	.50
22	A2	200r gray violet	4.25	1.75
23	A2	300r orange	4.50	2.00
		Nos. 15-23 (9)	29.25	9.80

Perf. 13½
15a	A2	5r	4.00	2.75
16a	A2	10r	4.25	2.75
17a	A2	20r	13.00	6.00
18a	A2	25r	13.00	6.00
19a	A2	40r	15.00	9.50
20a	A2	50r	16.00	4.50
22a	A2	200r	15.00	12.50
		Nos. 15a-22a (7)	80.25	44.00

Nos. 15, 18, 19, 20, 21 and 23 have been reprinted. The reprints have shiny white gum and clean-cut perforation 13½. Many of the colors are paler than those of the originals.

For surcharges and overprints see Nos. 23A, 36-44, 46-48, 72-80, 192, P1-P5.

No. 19 Surcharged in Black

Type I   Type II

Type III

There are three varieties of No. 23A:
I — "PROVISORIO" 19mm long, numerals 4½mm high.
II — "PROVISORIO" 19½mm long, numerals 5mm high.
III — "PROVISORIO" 19½mm long, numerals of both sizes.

1893, Jan.   *Perf. 12½*
Without Gum
23A	A2	5r on 40r choc	125.00	50.00

King Carlos I — A3

1894   Typo.   *Perf. 11½, 12½*
24	A3	5r yellow	.50	.45
25	A3	10r red lilac	.50	.35
26	A3	15r red brown	1.25	.75
27	A3	20r gray lilac	1.25	.50
28	A3	25r blue green	1.25	.25
29	A3	50r lt blue	5.00	1.50
a.		Perf. 12½	7.50	2.00
30	A3	75r rose	1.75	1.25
31	A3	80r yellow grn	2.00	1.00
32	A3	100r brown, *buff*	1.75	1.25
33	A3	150r car, *rose*	8.00	4.00
a.		Perf. 11½		
34	A3	200r dk blue, *blue*	5.00	3.00
35	A3	300r dk blue, *salmon*	7.00	3.00
		Nos. 24-35 (12)	35.25	17.30

Nos. 28 and 31-33 have been reprinted with shiny white gum and clean-cut perf. 13½.
For surcharges and overprints see Nos. 45, 81-92, 193-198, 201-205, 226-228, 238-239.

Stamps of 1886 Overprinted in Red or Black

1895, July 1   *Perf. 12½*
Without Gum
36	A2	5r black (R)	11.00	5.50
37	A2	10r green	12.50	6.50
38	A2	20r rose	14.00	6.00
39	A2	25r violet	16.00	6.50
a.		Double overprint	200.00	
40	A2	40r chocolate	20.00	7.50
41	A2	50r blue	20.00	7.50
a.		Perf. 13½	80.00	55.00
42	A2	100r yellow brown	20.00	8.25
43	A2	200r gray violet	30.00	13.00
a.		Perf. 13½	100.00	65.00
44	A2	300r orange	40.00	17.50
		Nos. 36-44 (9)	183.50	78.25

Birth of Saint Anthony of Padua, 7th cent.

No. 35 Surcharged in Black

1897, Jan. 2   *Perf. 12½*
Without Gum
45	A3	50r on 300r dk bl, *sal*	150.00	40.00

Nos. 17, 19 Surcharged

a   b

c

1898   Without Gum
46	A2	(a) 2½r on 20r rose	42.50	11.00
47	A2	(b) 2½r on 20r rose	30.00	10.00
a.		Inverted surcharge	55.00	45.00
48	A2	(c) 5r on 40r choc	40.00	10.00
a.		Inverted surcharge	90.00	45.00
		Nos. 46-48 (3)	112.50	31.00

King Carlos I — A4

Name and Value in Black except 500r
1898-1903   Typo.   *Perf. 11½*
49	A4	2½r gray	.25	.25
50	A4	5r orange	.25	.25
51	A4	10r lt green	.25	.25
52	A4	15r brown	2.00	1.50
53	A4	15r gray grn ('03)	.70	.55
54	A4	20r gray violet	.85	.40
55	A4	25r sea green	.85	.40
56	A4	25r carmine ('03)	.70	.30
57	A4	50r dark blue	1.50	.50
58	A4	50r brown ('03)	2.00	1.50
59	A4	75r dull blue ('03)	18.00	12.00
60	A4	75r rose	7.00	2.75
61	A4	75r red lilac ('03)	3.00	1.75
62	A4	80r violet	6.00	3.25
63	A4	100r dk blue, *bl*	2.00	1.00
64	A4	115r org brn, *pink* ('03)	10.00	5.00
65	A4	130r brown, *straw* ('03)	10.00	5.00
66	A4	150r brown, *straw*	10.00	2.75
67	A4	200r red lilac, *pnksh*	2.00	1.40
68	A4	300r dk blue, *rose*	8.00	3.25
69	A4	400r dl bl, *straw* ('03)	13.00	7.50
70	A4	500r blk & red, *bl* ('01)	20.00	8.00
71	A4	700r vio, *yelsh* ('01)	25.00	9.00
		Nos. 49-71 (23)	143.35	68.55

For overprints and surcharges see Nos. 94-113, 200, 207-220.

Stamps of 1886-94 Surcharged

On Stamps of 1886
Red Surcharge
1902   *Perf. 12½, 13½*
72	A2	115r on 5r blk	5.00	2.00

Black Surcharge
73	A2	65r on 20r rose	5.00	2.50
a.		Double surcharge	50.00	50.00
74	A2	65r on 40r choc	6.00	4.00
75	A2	65r on 200r violet	5.00	1.75
76	A2	115r on 50r blue	2.00	1.00
77	A2	130r on 25r red vio	3.00	.90
78	A2	130r on 300r orange	3.00	.90
79	A2	400r on 10r green	7.50	3.25
80	A2	400r on 100r yel brn	40.00	25.00
		Nos. 72-80 (9)	76.50	41.30

The reprints of Nos. 74, 75, 76, 77, 79 and 80 have shiny white gum and clean-cut perforation 13½.

On Stamps of 1894
Perf. 11½
81	A3	65r on 10r red lil	3.50	2.00
82	A3	65r on 15r red brn	3.50	2.00
a.		Pair, one without surcharge		

83	A3	65r on 20r gray lil	3.75	2.00
84	A3	115r on 5r yel	4.00	2.00
a.		Inverted surcharge		
85	A3	115r on 25r bl grn	3.50	2.00
86	A3	130r on 75r rose	4.00	2.25
87	A3	130r on 100r brn, buff	6.00	5.00
88	A3	130r on 150r car, rose	4.00	2.00
89	A3	130r on 200r bl, bl	5.00	3.50
90	A3	400r on 50r lt bl	1.00	1.40
91	A3	400r on 80r yel grn	1.00	1.40
92	A3	400r on 300r bl, sal	1.00	1.40

On Newspaper Stamp of 1893
Perf. 13½

93	N3	115r on 2½r brn	2.00	2.25
		Nos. 81-93 (13)	42.25	29.20

Reprints of No. 87 have shiny white gum and clean-cut perforation 13½.

Overprinted in Black

On Stamps of 1898
Perf. 11½

94	A4	15r brown	2.00	.85
95	A4	25r sea green	2.50	.85
96	A4	50r blue	3.00	1.75
97	A4	75r rose	5.00	1.75
		Nos. 94-97 (4)	12.50	5.45

No. 59 Surcharged in Black

1905

98	A4	50r on 65r dull blue	3.00	2.00

Stamps of 1898-1903 Overprinted in Carmine or Green

1911

99	A4	2½r gray	.30	.25
a.		Inverted overprint	15.00	15.00
100	A4	5r orange	.30	.25
101	A4	10r lt green	2.00	.50
102	A4	15r gray grn	.30	.25
103	A4	20r gray vio	2.00	.40
104	A4	25r carmine (G)	.30	.25
a.		25r gray violet (error)		
105	A4	50r brown	.50	.25
106	A4	75r red lilac	1.00	.50
107	A4	100r dk blue, bl	1.00	.50
108	A4	115r org brn, pink	1.50	.85
109	A4	130r brown, straw	1.50	.85
a.		Double overprint		
110	A4	200r red lil, pnksh	3.00	.70
111	A4	400r dull bl, straw	3.50	.85
112	A4	500r blk & red, bl	4.00	.85
113	A4	700r vio, straw	4.50	.85
		Nos. 99-113 (15)	25.70	8.10

King Manuel II — A5

Overprinted in Carmine or Green

1912   **Perf. 11½x12**

114	A5	2½r violet	.25	.25
115	A5	5r black	.25	.25
116	A5	10r gray grn	.25	.25
117	A5	20r carmine (G)	.55	.40
118	A5	25r vio brn	.25	.25
119	A5	50r dp blue	.50	.35
120	A5	75r bis brn	.50	.35
121	A5	100r brn, lt grn	.50	.35
122	A5	200r dk grn, salmon	1.00	.70
123	A5	300r black, azure	1.00	.70

Perf. 14x15

124	A5	500r ol grn & vio brn	2.00	1.25
		Nos. 114-124 (11)	7.05	5.10

Vasco da Gama Issue of Various Portuguese Colonies Common Design Types Surcharged

1913   **On Stamps of Macao**

125	CD20	¼c on ½a bl grn	1.50	1.50
126	CD21	½c on 1a red	1.50	1.50
127	CD22	1c on 2a red vio	1.50	1.50
128	CD23	2½c on 4a yel grn	1.50	1.50
a.		Double surcharge	50.00	50.00
129	CD24	5c on 8a dk bl	2.50	2.50
130	CD25	7½c on 12a vio brn	2.00	2.00
131	CD26	10c on 16a bis brn	1.75	1.50
132	CD27	15c on 24a bis	1.50	1.50
		Nos. 125-132 (8)	13.75	13.50

On Stamps of Portuguese Africa

133	CD20	¼c on 2½r bl grn	1.25	1.25
134	CD21	½c on 5r red	1.25	1.25
135	CD22	1c on 10r red vio	1.25	1.25
a.		Inverted surcharge	45.00	45.00
136	CD23	2½c on 25r yel grn	1.25	1.25
137	CD24	5c on 50r dk bl	1.25	1.25
138	CD25	7½c on 75r vio brn	1.75	1.75
139	CD26	10c on 100r bis brn	1.50	1.50
140	CD27	15c on 150r bis	1.50	1.50
		Nos. 133-140 (8)	11.00	11.00

On Stamps of Timor

141	CD20	¼c on ½a bl grn	1.50	1.50
142	CD21	½c on 1a red	1.50	1.50
143	CD22	1c on 2a red vio	1.50	1.50
144	CD23	2½c on 4a yel grn	1.50	1.50
145	CD24	5c on 8a dk bl	1.50	1.50
146	CD25	7½c on 12a vio brn	3.00	3.00
147	CD26	10c on 16a bis brn	1.50	1.50
148	CD27	15c on 24a bis	2.00	2.00
		Nos. 141-148 (8)	14.00	14.00
		Nos. 125-148 (24)	38.75	38.50

Ceres — A6

1914   **Typo.**   **Perf. 15x14**
Name and Value in Black
Chalky Paper

149	A6	¼c olive brown	.35	.25
150	A6	½c black	.35	.25
151	A6	1c blue green	.35	.25
152	A6	1½c lilac brown	.35	.25
153	A6	2c carmine	.40	.25
154	A6	2½c lt vio	.40	.25
155	A6	5c deep blue	.40	.25
156	A6	7½c yel brn	1.45	.75
157	A6	8c slate	1.45	.75
158	A6	10c org brn	1.45	.75
159	A6	15c plum	3.00	1.40
160	A6	20c yellow green	1.45	.95
161	A6	30c brown, grn	1.50	1.10
162	A6	40c brn, pink	1.25	.85
163	A6	40c brn, pink	1.25	.85
164	A6	50c org, salmon	2.75	3.00
165	A6	1e grn, bl,	18.00	7.00
		Nos. 149-165 (16)	34.90	18.30

1919-26   **Ordinary Paper**

166	A6	¼c olive brown	.25	.25
a.		Name and value printed twice	12.00	
b.		Name and value printed triple	—	
167	A6	½c black	.25	.25
168	A6	1c blue green	.25	.25
169	A6	1½c lilac brown	.25	.25
170	A6	2c carmine	.25	.25
171	A6	2½c lt vio	.25	.25
172	A6	3c org ('21)	.25	.25
a.		Name and value printed twice	—	
173	A6	4c pale rose ('21)	.25	.25
174	A6	4½c gray ('21)	.25	.25
175	A6	5c deep blue	.25	.25
176	A6	7c ultra ('21)	.25	.25
177	A6	7½c yel brn	.25	.25
178	A6	8c slate	.25	.25
179	A6	10c org brn	.25	.25
180	A6	30c deep green ('21)	.75	.50
181	A6	1e rose	1.40	.85
		Nos. 166-181 (16)	5.65	4.85

Perf. 12x11½

182	A6	¼c olive brown	.30	.25
183	A6	½c black	.25	.25
184	A6	1c blue green	.50	.25
a.		Name and value printed twice	16.00	
185	A6	1½c lilac brown	.25	.25
186	A6	2c carmine	.25	.25
187	A6	2c gray ('26)	.25	.25
188	A6	2½c lt vio	.25	.25
189	A6	3c org ('21)	.25	.25
190	A6	4c pale rose ('21)	.25	.25
191	A6	4½c gray ('21)	.25	.25

191A	A6	6c lilac ('21)	.25	.25
a.		Name and value printed twice		
191B	A6	7c ultra ('21)	.25	.25
191C	A6	7½c yel brn	.25	.25
191D	A6	8c slate	.25	.25
191E	A6	10c org brn	.25	.25
191F	A6	12c gray brn ('21)	.25	.25
191G	A6	12c blue grn ('22)	.25	.25
191H	A6	15c plum	.65	.35
191I	A6	15c brn rose ('22)	.25	.25
191J	A6	20c yel grn	.25	.25
191K	A6	24c ultra ('26)	4.50	2.00
191L	A6	25c choc ('26)	1.50	1.25
191M	A6	30c deep green ('21)	1.00	.90
191N	A6	40c turq blue ('22)	1.00	.30
191O	A6	50c lt violet ('26)	.50	.25
191P	A6	60c dk blue ('22)	1.00	.30
191Q	A6	60c rose ('26)	1.00	.25
191R	A6	80c brt rose ('22)	1.60	1.25
191S	A6	80c rose ('22)	1.00	.25
191T	A6	1e rose ('22)	1.60	.50
		Nos. 182-191T (30)	20.50	11.70

For surcharges see Nos. 232-234, 236-237, 249-250, J46-50.

1921   **Chalky Paper**

191U	A6	40c brown, pink ('21)	1.25	.85
191V	A6	60c red brn, pink	1.00	.60
191W	A6	80c dk brn, bl ('21)	1.40	.60
191X	A6	1e grn, bl,	1.40	.60
191Y	A6	2e brt vio, pink	1.40	.60

Perf. 15x14

191Z	A6	30c gray bl, pink ('21)	1.50	1.25
		Nos. 191U-191Z (6)	7.95	4.50

Stamps of 1902 Overprinted Locally in Carmine

1915

On Provisional Stamps of 1902

192	A2	115r on 5r black	175.00	100.00
193	A3	115r on 5r yellow	1.25	.75
194	A3	115r on 25r bl grn	1.25	.75
195	A3	130r on 75r rose	1.25	.75
196	A3	130r on 100r brn, buff	1.25	.75
197	A3	130r on 150r car, rose	1.25	.75
198	A3	130r on 200r bl, bl	1.25	.75
199	N3	115r on 2½r brn	.80	.40

On No. 97

200	A4	75r rose	1.50	1.10
		Nos. 192-200 (9)	184.80	106.00

Stamps of 1902-05 Overprinted in Carmine

1915

On Provisional Stamps of 1902

201	A3	115r on 5r yellow	.80	.50
202	A3	115r on 25r bl grn	.80	.55
203	A3	130r on 75r rose	.80	.55
204	A3	130r on 150r car, rose	1.00	.50
205	A3	130r on 200r bl, bl	1.00	.50
206	N3	115r on 2½r brn	1.00	.50

On No. 96

207	A4	50r blue	1.00	.50

On No. 98

208	A4	50r on 65r dull blue	1.00	.50
		Nos. 201-208 (8)	7.40	4.10

Stamps of 1898-1903 Overprinted Locally in Carmine Like Nos. 192-200

1917

209	A4	2½r gray	20.00	17.50
210	A4	15r gray grn	15.00	12.50
211	A4	20r gray vio	15.00	12.50
212	A4	50r brown	14.00	11.00
213	A4	75r red lilac	32.50	25.00
214	A4	100r blue, bl	6.00	7.00
215	A4	115r org brn, pink	8.00	3.00
216	A4	130r brown, straw	7.50	3.00
217	A4	200r red lil, pnksh	7.50	2.50
218	A4	400r dull bl, straw	7.50	3.00
219	A4	500r blk & red, bl	7.00	2.50
220	A4	700r vio, yelsh	15.00	6.00
		Nos. 209-220 (12)	155.00	101.00

War Tax Stamps of 1916-18 Surcharged

1918   **Rouletted 7**

221	WT2	2½c on 5c rose	2.50	1.50

Perf. 11, 12

222	WT2	2½c on 5c red	1.10	.70
a.		"PETRIA"	3.00	2.00
b.		"PEPUBLICA"	3.00	2.00
c.		"1910" for "1916"	9.00	4.00

War Tax Stamps of 1916-18 Surcharged

1919   **Perf. 11**

224	WT1	1c on 1c gray grn	.75	.40
a.		"PEPUBLICA"	4.75	4.00
b.		Rouletted 7	300.00	100.00

Perf. 12

225	WT2	1½c on 5c red	.40	.35
a.		"PETRIA"	3.00	2.00
b.		"PEPUBLICA"	3.00	2.50
c.		"1910" for "1916"	7.50	3.75

Stamps of 1902 Overprinted Locally in Carmine Like Nos. 192-200

1920

226	A3	400r on 50r lt blue	1.25	1.25
227	A3	400r on 80r yel grn	1.25	1.25
228	A3	400r on 300r bl, sal	1.25	1.25
		Nos. 226-228 (3)	3.75	3.75

War Tax Stamp of 1918 Surcharged in Green

1920   **Perf. 12**

229	WT2	6c on 5c red	.60	.50
a.		"1910" for "1916"	9.00	5.00
b.		"PETRIA"	2.50	2.00
c.		"PEPUBLICA"	2.50	2.00

Lourenco Marques Nos. 117, 119 Surcharged in Red or Bue

1921   **Perf. 15x14**

230	A4	10c on ½c blk (R)	.75	.40
231	A4	30c on 1½c brn (Bl)	1.25	.70

Same Surcharge on Mozambique Nos. 150, 152, 155 in Red, Blue or Green

232	A6	10c on ½c blk (R)	1.00	.85
233	A6	30c on 1½c brn (Bl)	1.10	.70
a.		Double surcharge	30.00	30.00
234	A6	60c on 2½c vio (G)	1.50	.80
		Nos. 230-234 (5)	5.60	3.45

War Tax Stamp of 1918 Surcharged in Green

1921   **Perf. 12**

235	WT2	2e on 5c red	1.00	.50
a.		"PETRIA"	2.50	2.25
b.		"PEPUBLICA"	4.25	2.50
c.		"1910" for "1916"	9.00	6.50

No. 157 Surcharged

1923   **Perf. 12x11½**
236 A6 50c on 4c pale rose   1.00 .55

No. 183 Overprinted in
Green

1924
237 A6 80c bright rose   1.00 .60
4th centenary of the death of Vasco da
Gama.

Nos. 90 and 91
Surcharged

1925   **Perf. 11½**
238 A3 40c on 400r on 50r   .70 .70
239 A3 40c on 400r on 80r   .60 .50
a.   "a" omitted   42.50 42.50

Glazed Paper
1922-26   **Perf. 12x11½**
240 A6 1e blue ('26)   1.60 .65
241 A6 2e dk violet ('22)   1.00 .35
242 A6 5e buff ('26)   8.00 2.50
243 A6 10e pink ('26)   15.00 5.00
244 A6 20e pale turq ('26)   40.00 17.50

Postage Due Stamp
of 1917 Overprinted
in Black and Bars in
Red

1929, Jan.   **Perf. 12**
247 D1 50c gray   .85 .55

No. 188 Surcharged

1931   **Perf. 11½**
249 A6 70c on 2e dk vio   1.00 .50
250 A6 1.40e on 2e dk vio   1.50 .50

"Portugal" Holding
Volume of the
"Lusiads" — A7

Wmk. Maltese Cross (232)
1933, July 13   Typo.   Perf. 14
Value in Red or Black
251 A7 1c bister brn (R)   .25 .25
252 A7 5c black brn   .25 .25
253 A7 10c dp violet   .25 .25
254 A7 15c black (R)   .25 .25
255 A7 20c light gray   .25 .25
256 A7 30c blue green   .25 .25
257 A7 40c orange red   .25 .25
258 A7 45c brt blue   .40 .25
259 A7 50c dk brown   .30 .25
260 A7 60c olive grn   .25 .25
261 A7 70c orange brn   .25 .25
262 A7 80c emerald   .25 .25
263 A7 85c deep rose   1.00 .25
264 A7 1e red brown   .75 .25
265 A7 1.40e dk blue (R)   7.00 1.10

266 A7 2e dk violet   2.00 .35
267 A7 5e apple green   3.00 .50
268 A7 10e olive bister   7.00 1.00
269 A7 20e orange   22.50 2.00
   Nos. 251-269 (19)   46.45 8.70
   See Nos. 298-299.

Common Design Types
pictured following the introduction.

Common Design Types
Perf. 13½x13
1938, Aug.   Engr.   Unwmk.
Name and Value in Black
270 CD34 1c gray green   .25 .25
271 CD34 5c orange brn   .25 .25
272 CD34 10c dk carmine   .25 .25
273 CD34 15c dk vio brn   .25 .25
274 CD34 20c slate   .25 .25
275 CD35 30c rose vio   .25 .25
276 CD35 35c brt green   .30 .25
277 CD35 40c brown   .40 .25
278 CD35 50c brt red vio   .40 .25
279 CD36 60c gray black   .50 .25
280 CD36 70c brown vio   .50 .25
281 CD36 80c orange   .75 .25
282 CD36 1e red   .70 .25
283 CD37 1.75e blue   1.75 .30
284 CD37 2e brown car   1.50 .30
285 CD37 5e olive green   3.50 .50
286 CD38 10e blue vio   9.00 1.00
287 CD38 20e red brown   22.50 1.40
   Nos. 270-287 (18)   43.30 6.75

For surcharges see Nos. 297, 301.

No. 258 Surcharged in
Black

1938, Jan. 16   Wmk. 232   Perf. 14
288 A7 40c on 45c brt blue   2.50 1.40

Map of Africa —
A7a

Perf. 11½x12
1939, July 17   Litho.   Unwmk.
289 A7a 80c vio, pale rose   1.50 1.25
290 A7a 1.75e bl, pale bl   4.00 2.75
291 A7a 3e grn, yel grn   7.00 4.00
292 A7a 20e brn, buff   35.00 50.00
   Nos. 289-292 (4)   47.50 58.00

Presidential visit.

New Cathedral,
Lourenço
Marques — A8

Railroad
Station
A9

Municipal
Hall — A10

1944, Dec.   Litho.   Perf. 11½
293 A8 50c dk brown   .70 .40
294 A8 50c dk green   .70 .40
295 A9 1.75e ultra   4.00 .85
296 A10 20e dk gray   8.50 .85
   Nos. 293-296 (4)   13.90 2.50
4th cent. of the founding of Lourenço Marques. See No. 302. For surcharge see No.
300.

No. 283 Surcharged
in Carmine

1946   Engr.   Perf. 13½x13
297 CD37 60c on 1.75e blue   1.00 .40

Lusiads Type of 1933
1947   Wmk. 232   Typo.   Perf. 14
Value in Black
298 A7 35c yellow grn   4.00 2.00
299 A7 1.75e deep blue   4.50 2.00

No. 296
Srchd. in
Pink

1946   Unwmk.   Perf. 11½
300 A10 2e on 20e dk gray   1.40 .40
No. 273 Surcharged with New Value
and Wavy Lines
Perf. 13½x13
301 CD34 10c on 15c dk vio brn   .70 .40
a.   Inverted surcharge   30.00

Cathedral Type of 1944
Commemorative Inscription Omitted
1948   Litho.   Perf. 11½
302 A8 4.50e brt vermilion   1.75 .40

Antonio Enes — A11

1948, Oct. 4   Perf. 14
303 A11 50c black & cream   1.00 .35
304 A11 5e vio brn & cream   3.00 .85

Birth centenary of Antonio Enes.

Gogogo
Peak — A12

Zambezi River
Bridge — A13

Zumbo River
A14

Waterfall at
Nhanhangare
A15

Lourenço
Marques
A16

Plantation,
Baixa
Zambezia
A17

Pungwe River
at Beira — A18

Lourenço
Marques
A19

Polana
Beach — A20

Malema
River — A21

Perf. 13½x13, 13x13½
1948-49   Typo.   Unwmk.
305 A12 5c orange brn   .25 .50
306 A13 10c violet brn   .25 .25
307 A14 20c dk brown   .25 .25
308 A12 30c plum   .25 .25
309 A14 40c dull green   .25 .25
310 A16 50c slate   .25 .25
311 A15 60c brown car   .25 .25
312 A16 80c violet blk   .25 .25
313 A17 1e carmine   .35 .25
314 A13 1.20e slate gray   .35 .25
315 A18 1.50e dk purple   .50 .25
316 A20 1.75e dk blue ('49)   .75 .25
317 A18 2e brown   .50 .25
318 A19 2.50e dk slate ('49) 1.50 .25
319 A20 3e gray ol ('49)   1.00 .25
320 A15 3.50e olive gray   1.10 .25
321 A17 5e blue grn   1.10 .25
322 A19 10c choc ('49)   2.50 .35
323 A21 15e dp carmine ('49) 7.25 1.75
324 A21 20e orange ('49)   12.00 1.75
   Nos. 305-324 (20)   30.90 8.35
On No. 320 the "$" is reversed.

Lady of Fatima Issue
Common Design Type
1948, Oct.   Litho.   Perf. 14½
325 CD40 50c blue   1.00 .50
326 CD40 1.20e red violet   3.00 1.00
327 CD40 4.50e emerald   6.00 1.50
328 CD40 20e chocolate   10.00 1.50
   Nos. 325-328 (4)   20.00 4.50

Symbols of the
UPU — A21a

1949, Apr. 11   **Perf. 14**
329 A21a 4.50e ultra & pale gray   1.00 .50
75th anniversary of UPU.

> Catalogue values for unused
> stamps in this section, from this
> point to the end of the section, are
> for Never Hinged items.

Holy Year Issue
Common Design Types
1950, May   **Perf. 13x13½**
330 CD41 1.50e red orange   .75 .30
331 CD42 3e brt blue   1.00 .55

Spotted
Triggerfish
A22

Pennant Coral
Fish — A22a

Fish: 10c, Golden butterflyfish. 15c, Orange
butterflyfish. 20c, Lionfish. 30c, Sharpnose
puffer. 40c, Porky filefish. 50c, Dark brown
surgeonfish. 1.60e Rainbow wrasse. 2e,
Orange-spotted gray-skin. 2.50e, Kasmir
snapper. 3e, Convict fish. 3.50e, Stellar triggerfish. 4e, Cornetfish. 4.50e, Vagabond but-
torflyfish. 5e, Mail-cheeked fish. 8e, Pinnate
batfish. 8e, Moorish idol. 9e, Triangulate
boxfish. 10e, Flying gurnard. 15e, Redtooth
triggerfish. 20e, Striped triggerfish. 30e,
Horned cowfish. 50e, Spotted cowfish.

Photogravure and Lithographed
1951   **Unwmk.**   **Perf. 14x14½**
Fish in Natural Colors
332	A22	5c dp yellow	.30	.75
333	A22	10c lt blue	.25	.50
334	A22	15c yellow	.80	1.00
335	A22	20c pale olive	.40	.25
336	A22	30c gray	.40	.25
337	A22	40c pale green	.30	.25
338	A22	50c pale buff	.30	.25
339	A22a	1e aqua	.30	.25
340	A22	1.50e olive	.25	.25
341	A22	2e blue	.30	.25
342	A22	2.50e brnsh lilac	.60	.25
343	A22	3e aqua	.60	.25
344	A22	3.50e olive grn	.60	.25
345	A22	4e blue gray	1.40	1.00
346	A22	4.50e green	1.25	2.00
347	A22	5e buff	1.25	.25
348	A22a	6e salmon pink	1.25	.25
349	A22a	8e gray blue	2.10	.25
350	A22	9e lilac rose	4.50	.30
351	A22	10e gray lilac	13.50	2.00
352	A22	15e gray	40.00	8.75
353	A22	20e lemon	25.00	4.00
354	A22	30e yellow grn	25.00	5.50
355	A22	50e gray vio	42.50	12.00
		Nos. 332-355 (24)	163.15	41.05
		Set, hinged	100.00	

Holy Year Extension Issue
Common Design Type
1951, Oct.   **Litho.**   **Perf. 14**
356 CD43 5e carmine & rose +
       label   2.25 1.00
No. 356 without label attached sells for less.

Victor Cordon — A23

1951, Oct.   **Perf. 11½**
357 A23 1e dk brown   1.75 .40
358 A23 5e black & slate   6.50 1.10
Centenary of the birth of Victor Cordon,
explorer.

Medical Congress Issue
Common Design Type
Design: Miguel Bombarda Hospital.
1952, June 19   **Litho.**   **Perf. 13½**
359 CD44 3e dk bl & brn buff   1.10 .55

Plane and
Ship — A24

1952, Sept. 15   **Unwmk.**
360 A24 1.50e multi   .65 .45
4th African Tourism Congress.

Missionary — A25

1953
361 A25 10c red brn & pale vio   .25 .25
362 A25 1e red brn & pale yel
       grn   .80 .25
363 A25 5e blk & lt bl   1.60 .45
    Nos. 361-363 (3)   2.65 .95
Exhibition of Sacred Missionary Art, held at
Lisbon in 1951.

> **Canceled to Order**
> Certain issues, including Nos. 364-
> 383, were canceled to order under
> Republican administration.

Papilio
Demodocus
A26

Various Butterflies and Moths in Natural Colors
Photogravure and Lithographed
1953, May 28   **Perf. 13x14**
364	A26	10c lt blue	.40	.25
365	A26	15c cream	.40	.25
366	A26	20c yellow grn	.40	.25
367	A26	30c lt violet	.40	.25
368	A26	40c brown	.40	.25
369	A26	50c bluish gray	.40	.25
370	A26	80c brt blue	.40	.25
371	A26	1e gray bl	.40	.25
372	A26	1.50e ocher	.55	.25
373	A26	2e orange brn	5.00	.50
374	A26	2.30e blue	5.00	.35
375	A26	2.50e citron	7.25	.35
376	A26	3e lilac rose	2.60	.25
377	A26	4e light blue	.50	.25
378	A26	4.50e orange	.50	.25
379	A26	5e green	.50	.25
380	A26	6e pale vio	.70	.25
381	A26	7.50e buff	5.50	.30
382	A26	10e pink	8.75	1.25
383	A26	20e grnsh gray	11.00	1.25
		Nos. 364-383 (20)	51.05	7.50

Value of set canceled-to-order, $1.00. For
overprints see Nos. 517, 527.

Stamps of
Portugal and
Mozambique
A27

Stamp of Portugal
and Arms of
Colonies
A27a

1953, July 23   **Litho.**   **Perf. 14**
384 A27 1e multicolored   .95 .40
385 A27 3e multicolored   3.25 .85
Issued in connection with the Lourenço Marques philatelic exhibition, July 1953.

Stamp Centenary Issue
1953   **Photo.**   **Perf. 13**
386 A27a 50c multicolored   .70 .55

Map — A28

1954, Oct. 15   **Litho.**
Color of Colony
387	A28	10c pale rose lilac	.25	.25
388	A28	20c pale yellow	.25	.25
389	A28	50c lilac	.25	.25
390	A28	1e orange yel	.25	.25
391	A28	2.30e white	.65	.40
392	A28	4e pale salmon	.65	.25
393	A28	10e lt green	2.00	.25
394	A28	20e brown buff	2.60	.35
		Nos. 387-394 (8)	6.90	2.25

For overprints see Nos. 516, 530.

Sao Paulo Issue
Common Design Type
1954, July 2
395 CD46 3.50e dk gray, cream &
       ol   .40 .30

Arms of Beira
A29

Mousinho de
Albuquerque
A30

Paper with network as in parenthesis
Arms in Silver, Gold, Red and Pale Green
1954, Dec. 1   **Perf. 13x13½**
396 A29 1.50e dk bl (bl)   .40 .30
397 A29 3.50e brn (buff)   1.00 .35
Issued to publicize the first philatelic exhibition of Manica and Sofala.

1955, Feb. 1   **Litho.**   **Perf. 11½x12**
2.50e, Statue of Mousinho de Albuquerque.
398 A30 1e gray, blk & buff   .75 .35
399 A30 2.50e ol bio, blk & bl   1.40 .65
100th anniversary of the birth of Mousinho
de Albuquerque, statesman.

A31

Eight Races Holding Arms of Portugal
1956, Aug. 4   **Unwmk.**   **Perf. 14½**
Central Design in Multicolored
400 A31 1e pale yellow & multi   .40 .25
401 A31 2.50e lt blue & multi   .80 .40
Issued to commemorate the visit of President Antonio Oscar de Fragoso Carmona.

A32

1957, Aug. 15   **Litho.**
402 A32 2.50e View of Beira   .80 .30
50th anniversary of the city of Beira.

Brussels Fair Issue

Exhibition Emblems
and View — A32a

1958, Oct. 8   **Unwmk.**   **Perf. 14½**
403 A32a 3.50c blk, grn, yel, red &
       bl   .30 .25

Tropical Medicine Congress Issue
Common Design Type
Design: Strophanthus grandiflorus.
1958, Sept. 14   **Perf. 13½**
404 CD47 1.50e sal brn, grn &
       red   4.00 .85

Caravel — A33

1960, June 25   **Litho.**   **Perf. 13½**
405 A33 5e multicolored   .65 .25
500th anniversary of the death of Prince
Henry the Navigator.

Technical
Instruction
A34

1960, Nov. 21   **Unwmk.**   **Perf. 14½**
406 A34 3e multicolored   .55 .25
Commission for Technical Co-operation in
Africa South of the Sahara (C.C.T.A.), 10th
anniv.

Arms of Lourenço
Marques — A35

Arms of various cities of Mozambique.

1961, Jan. 30   Litho.   Perf. 13½
**Arms in Original Colors; Black,
Ultramarine and Red Inscriptions**

407	A35	5c salmon	.25	.25
408	A35	15c pale green	.25	.25
409	A35	20c lt vio gray	.25	.25
410	A35	30c buff	.25	.25
411	A35	50c bluish gray	.25	.25
412	A35	1e pale ol	.25	.25
413	A35	1.50e lt blue	.25	.25
414	A35	2e pale pink	.40	.25
415	A35	2.50e lt bl grn	1.25	.25
416	A35	3e beige	.45	.25
417	A35	4e yellow	.45	.25
418	A35	4.50e pale gray	.45	.25
419	A35	5e pale bluish grn	.45	.25
420	A35	7.50e rose	1.00	.40
a.		"CORREIOS 7$50" omitted	1.60	.40
421	A35	10e lt yel grn	1.60	.40
422	A35	20e beige	3.50	.55
423	A35	50e gray	7.25	1.60
		Nos. 407-423 (17)	18.55	6.20

Sports Issue
Common Design Type

50c, Water skiing. 1e, Wrestling. 1.50e, Woman gymnast. 2.50e, Field hockey. 4.50e, Women's basketball. 15e, Speedboat racing.

1962, Feb. 10   Unwmk.   Perf. 13½
Multicolored Designs

424	CD48	50c gray green	.30	.25
425	CD48	1e dk gray	.85	.25
426	CD48	1.50e pink	.40	.25
427	CD48	2.50e buff	.70	.25
428	CD48	4.50e gray	1.00	.45
429	CD48	15e gray green	1.75	1.00
		Nos. 424-429 (6)	5.00	2.45

For overprints see Nos. 522, 526, 529.

Anti-Malaria Issue
Common Design Type

Design: Anopheles funestus.

1962, Apr. 5   Perf. 13½
430	CD49	2.50e multicolored	1.40	.40

Planes over
Mozambique
A36

Lourenço Marques
1887 and 1962
A37

1962, Oct. 15   Litho.   Perf. 14½
431	A36	3e multicolored	.80	.25

25th anniversary of DETA airlines.

1962, Nov. 1   Perf. 13
432	A37	1e multicolored	.45	.25

75th anniversary of Lourenço Marques.

Vasco da Gama
Statue and
Arms — A38

1963, Apr. 25   Unwmk.   Perf. 14½
433	A38	3e multicolored	.40	.25

Founding of Mozambique City, 200th anniv.

Airline Anniversary Issue
Common Design Type

1963, Oct. 21   Litho.   Perf. 14½
434	CD50	2.50e brt pink & multi	.40	.25
		Nos. 434 (1)	.40	.25

Barque,
1430 — A39

Caravel,
1436 — A40

Development of Sailing Ships: 30c, Lateen-rigged caravel, 1460. 50c, "Sao Gabriel," 1497. 1e, Dom Manuel's ship, 1498. 1.50e, Warship, 1500. 2e, "Flor de la Mar," 1511. 2.50e, Redonda caravel, 1519. 3.50e, 800-ton ship, 1520. 4e, Portuguese India galley, 1521. 4.50e, "Santa Tereza," 1639. 5e, "Nostra Senhora da Conceiçao," 1716. 6e, "Nostra Senhora do Bom Sucesso," 1764. 7.50e, Launch with mortar, 1788. 8e, Brigantine, 1793. 10e, Corvette, 1799. 12.50e, Schooner "Maria Teresa," 1820. 15e, "Vasco da Gama," 1841. 20e, Frigate "Dom Fernando II," 1843. 30e, Training Ship "Sagres," 1924.

1963, Dec. 1   Litho.   Perf. 14½
435	A39	10c multicolored	.25	.25
436	A40	20c multicolored	.25	.25
437	A40	30c multicolored	.25	.25
438	A40	50c multicolored	.25	.25
439	A40	1e multicolored	.55	.25
440	A40	1.50e multicolored	.45	.25
441	A40	2e multicolored	.45	.25
442	A39	2.50e multicolored	.50	.25
443	A40	3.50e multicolored	.45	.30
444	A39	4e multicolored	.60	.25
445	A40	4.50e multicolored	1.10	.25
446	A40	5e multicolored	10.00	.30
447	A39	6e multicolored	1.00	.30
448	A39	7.50e multicolored	1.10	.40
449	A39	8e multicolored	1.10	.40
450	A39	10e multicolored	1.25	.60
451	A39	12.50e multicolored	1.40	.75
452	A39	15e multicolored	1.75	.70
453	A40	20e multicolored	2.75	.70
454	A40	30e multicolored	4.00	1.40
		Nos. 435-454 (20)	28.95	8.35

National Overseas Bank Issue

Modern Bank
Building,
Luanda
A40a

1964, May 16   Perf. 13½
455	A40a	1.50e bl, yel gray & grn	.40	.25

National Overseas Bank of Portugal, cent.

Pres. Americo
Rodrigues
Thomaz — A41

1964, July 23   Litho.   Perf. 13½x12½
456	A41	2.50e multicolored	.40	.25

Visit of Pres. Americo Rodrigues Thomaz of Portugal to Mozambique, in July.

Royal
Barge of
King John
V, 1728
A42

Designs: 35c, Barge of Dom Jose I, 1753. 1e, Customs barge, 1768. 1.50e, Sailor, 1780, vert. 2.50e, Royal barge, 1780. 5e, Barge of

---

Dona Carlota Joaquina, 1790. 9e, Barge of Dom Miguel, 1831.

1964, Dec. 18   Litho.   Perf. 14½
457	A42	15c multicolored	.25	.25
458	A42	35c lt bl & multi	.25	.25
459	A42	1e gray & multi	.50	.25
460	A42	1.50e gray & multi	.30	.25
461	A42	2.50e multicolored	.25	.25
462	A42	5e multicolored	.40	.25
463	A42	9e multicolored	1.00	.65
		Nos. 457-463 (7)	2.95	2.15

ITU Issue
Common Design Type

1965, May 17   Unwmk.   Perf. 14½
464	CD52	1e yellow & multi	.40	.25

National Revolution Issue
Common Design Type

Design: 1e, Beira Railroad Station, and Antonio Enes School.

1966, May 28   Litho.   Perf. 11½
465	CD53	1e multicolored	.50	.30

Harquebusier,
1560 — A42a

30c, Harquebusier, 1640. 40c, Infantry soldier, 1777. 50c, Infantry officer, 1777. 80c, Drummer, 1777. 1e, Infantry sergeant, 1777. 2e, Infantry major, 1784. 2.50e, Colonial officer, 1788. 3e, Infantry soldier, 1789. 5e, Colonial sergeant, 1801. 10e, Colonial officer, 1807. 15e, Colonial infantry soldier, 1817.

1967, Jan. 12   Photo.   Perf. 14
466	A42a	20c multicolored	.25	.25
467	A42a	30c multicolored	.25	.25
468	A42a	40c multicolored	.25	.25
469	A42a	50c multicolored	.25	.25
470	A42a	80c multicolored	.50	.25
471	A42a	1e multicolored	.40	.25
472	A42a	2e multicolored	.40	.25
473	A42a	2.50e multicolored	.60	.25
474	A42a	3e multicolored	.60	.25
475	A42a	5e multicolored	.80	.30
476	A42a	10e multicolored	1.00	.40
477	A42a	15e multicolored	1.40	.60
		Nos. 466-477 (12)	6.70	3.55

Navy Club Issue
Common Design Type

Designs: 3e, Capt. Azevedo Coutinho and gunboat (stern-wheeler) Tete. 10e, Capt. Joao Roby and gunboat (paddle steamer) Granada.

1967, Jan. 31   Litho.   Perf. 13
478	CD54	3e multicolored	.40	.25
479	CD54	10e multicolored	.80	.40

Virgin's Crown,
Presented by
Portuguese
Women — A43

1967, May 13   Litho.   Perf. 12½x13
480	A43	50c multicolored	.25	.25

50th anniversary of the appearance of the Virgin Mary to 3 shepherd children at Fatima.

Cabral Issue

Raising the
Cross at Porto
Seguro — A44

Designs: 1.50e, First mission to Brazil. 3e, Grace Church, Santarem, vert.

1968, Apr. 22   Litho.   Perf. 14
481	A44	1e multicolored	.25	.25
482	A44	1.50e multicolored	.30	.25
483	A44	3e multicolored	.65	.25
		Nos. 481-483 (3)	1.20	.75

500th birth anniv. of Pedro Alvares Cabral, navigator who took possession of Brazil for Portugal.

Admiral Coutinho Issue
Common Design Type

Design: 70c, Adm. Coutinho and Adm. Gago Coutinho Airport.

1969, Feb. 17   Litho.   Perf. 14
484	CD55	70c multicolored	.25	.25

Luiz Vaz de
Camoens — A45

Sailing Ship,
1553 — A46

Designs: 1.50e, Map of Mozambique, 1554. 2.50e, Chapel of Our Lady of Baluarte, 1552. 5e, Excerpt from Lusiads about Mozambique (1st Song, 14th Stanza).

Perf. 12½x13, 13x12½
1969, June 10   Litho.
485	A45	15c multicolored	.25	.25
486	A46	50c multicolored	.25	.25
487	A45	1.50e multicolored	.25	.25
488	A46	2.50e multicolored	.25	.25
489	A45	5e multicolored	.50	.30
		Nos. 485-489 (5)	1.50	1.30

Visit to Mozambique of Luiz Vaz de Camoens (1524-80), poet, 400th anniv.

Vasco da Gama Issue

Map Showing
Voyage to
Mozambique
and
India — A47

1969, Aug. 29   Litho.   Perf. 14
490	A47	1e multicolored	.25	.25

Vasco da Gama (1469-1524), navigator.

Administration Reform Issue
Common Design Type

1969, Sept. 25   Litho.   Perf. 14
491	CD56	1.50e multicolored	.25	.25

King Manuel I Issue

Illuminated
Miniature of
King's
Arms — A48

1969, Dec. 1   Litho.   Perf. 14
492	A48	80c multicolored	.25	.25

500th anniversary of the birth of King Manuel I.

Marshal Carmona Issue
Common Design Type

5e, Antonio Oscar Carmona in marshal's uniform.

1970, Nov. 15   Litho.   Perf. 14
493	CD57	5e multicolored	.40	.25

Fossil
Fern
A49

Fossils and Minerals: 50c, Fossil snail. 1e, Stibnite. 1.50e, Pink beryl. 2e, Dinosaur. 3e, Tantalocolumbite. 3.50e, Verdelite. 4e, Zircon. 10e, Petrified wood.

1971, Jan. 15   Litho.   Perf. 13

494	A49	15c gray & multi	.25	.25
495	A49	50c lt ultra & multi	.25	.25
496	A49	1e green & multi	.30	.25
497	A49	1.50e multicolored	.40	.25
498	A49	2e multicolored	.75	.25
499	A49	3e lt bl & multi	1.50	.25
500	A49	3.50e lilac & multi	2.00	.25
501	A49	4e multicolored	3.00	.30
502	A49	10e dl red & multi	4.00	.85
	Nos. 494-502 (9)		12.45	2.90

For overprints see Nos. 525, 528.

Mozambique
Island — A49a

1972, May 25   Litho.   Perf. 13

503	A49a	4e ultra & multi	.40	.25

4th centenary of publication of The Lusiads by Luiz Camoens.

Olympic Games Issue
Common Design Type

3e, Hurdles and swimming, Olympic emblem.

1972, June 20   Perf. 14x13½

504	CD59	3e multi	.30	.25

For overprint see No. 523.

Lisbon-Rio de Janeiro Flight Issue
Common Design Type

1e, "Santa Cruz" over Recife harbor.

1972, Sept. 20   Litho.   Perf. 13½

505	CD60	1e multi	.25	.25

Sailboats
A50

Designs: Various sailboats.

1973, Aug. 21   Litho.   Perf. 12x11½

506	A50	1e multi	.25	.25
507	A50	1.50e multi	.25	.25
508	A50	3e multi	.40	.25
	Nos. 506-508 (3)		.90	.75

World Sailing Championships, Vauriens Class, Lourenço Marques, Aug. 21-30.
For overprints see Nos. 519-520, 524.

WMO Centenary Issue
Common Design Type

1973, Dec. 15   Litho.   Perf. 13

509	CD61	2e rose red & multi	.30	.25

For overprint see No. 521.

Radar
Station
A51

1974, June 25   Litho.   Perf. 13

510	A51	50c multi	.25	.25

Establishment of satellite communications network via Intelsat among Portugal, Angola and Mozambique.
For overprint see No. 518.

"Bird" Made of Flags of Portugal and Mozambique — A52

1975, Jan.   Litho.   Perf. 14½

511	A52	1e pink & multi	.25	.25
512	A52	1.50e yel & multi	.25	.25
513	A52	2e gray & multi	.25	.25
514	A52	3.50e lem & multi	.40	.30
515	A52	6e lt bl & multi	.90	.30
a.	Souv. sheet of 5, #511-515 + label		4.50	4.50
	Nos. 511-515 (5)		2.05	1.35

Lusaka Agreement, Sept. 7, 1974, which gave Mozambique independence from Portugal, effective June 25, 1975.
No. 515a sold for 25c.
For overprints see Nos. 543-545.

Republic
Issues of 1953-74 Overprinted in Red or Black

a

b

1975, June 25

516	A28 (a)	10c (R; #387)	.40	.40
517	A26 (a)	40c (B; #368)	.25	.25
518	A51 (b)	50c (B; #510)	.30	.25
519	A50 (b)	1e (B; #506)	.50	.40
520	A50 (b)	1.50e (B; #507)	.95	.80
521	CD61 (a)	2e (B; #509)	2.75	2.75
522	CD48 (b)	2.50e (B; #427)	.55	.45
523	CD59 (a)	3e (R; #504)	.65	.55
524	A50 (b)	3e (B; #508)	.70	.65
525	A49 (b)	3.50e (B; #500)	2.75	2.75
526	CD48 (b)	4.50e (B; #428)	3.75	1.75
527	A26 (a)	7.50e (R; #381)	.90	.45
528	A49 (b)	10e (B; #502)	1.75	.60
529	CD48 (b)	15e (B; #429)	2.10	1.75
530	A28 (a)	20e (R; #394)	2.40	1.40
	Nos. 516-530,C35-C38 (19)		25.25	18.85

Workers,
Farmers
and
Children
A53

Designs: 30c, 50c, 2.50e, like 20c. 4.50e, 5e, 10e, 50e, Dancers, workers, armed family.

1975   Litho.   Perf. 12x11½

531	A53	20c pink & multi	.25	.25
532	A53	30c bis & multi	.25	.25
533	A53	50c bl & multi	.25	.25
534	A53	2.50e grn & multi	.25	.25
535	A53	4.50e brn & multi	.40	.25
536	A53	5e bis & multi	.55	.25
537	A53	10e bl & multi	1.00	.45

538	A53	50e yel & multi	4.50	2.25
a.	Souvenir sheet of 8		7.50	7.50
	Nos. 531-538 (8)		7.45	4.20

No. 538a contains 8 stamps similar to Nos. 531-538 with simulated perforation. Sold for 75e.
For overprint see No. 554.

Farm
Woman — A54

1976, Apr. 7   Litho.   Perf. 14½

539	A54	1e shown	.25	.25
540	A54	1.50e Teacher	.25	.25
541	A54	2.50e Nurse	.30	.25
542	A54	10e Mother	1.10	.90
	Nos. 539-542 (4)		1.90	1.45

Day of the Mozambique Woman, Apr. 7.

Nos. 513-515 Overprinted in Red:
"PRESIDENTE KENNETH KAUNDA / PRIMEIRA VISITA 20/4/1976"

1976, Apr. 20   Litho.   Perf. 14½

543	A52	2e gray & multi	.25	.25
544	A52	3.50e lem & multi	.40	.25
545	A52	6e lt bl & multi	.80	.50
	Nos. 543-545 (3)		1.45	1.05

Visit of President Kaunda of Zambia.

Pres. Machel's
Arrival at
Maputo — A55

Mozambique No.
1 — A56

Designs: 1e, Independence proclamation ceremony. 2.50e, Pres. Samora Moises Machel taking office. 7.50e, Military parade. 20e, Flame of Unity and festival.

1976, June 25

546	A55	50c multi	.25	.25
547	A55	1e multi	.25	.25
548	A55	2.50e multi	.30	.25
549	A55	7.50e multi	.80	.30
550	A55	20e multi	2.25	1.25
	Nos. 546-550 (5)		3.85	2.30

First anniversary of independence.

1976, July   Perf. 11½x12

551	A56	1.50e ocher & multi	.25	.25
552	A56	6e red & multi	.55	.30

Centenary of Mozambique postage stamps.

Flag and
Weapons
A57

1976, Sept. 25   Litho.   Perf. 14½

553	A57	3e multi	.40	.25

Army Day 1976.

No. 534 Overprinted in Silver:
"FACIM"

1976   Litho.   Perf. 12x11½

554	A53	2.50e multi	.70	.30

FACIM, Industrial Fair.

Bush Baby — A58

Animals: 1e, Honey badger. 1.50e, Pangolin. 2e, Steinbok. 2.50e, Guenon (monkey). 3e, Cape hunting dog. 4e, Cheetah. 5e, Spotted hyena. 7.50e, Wart hog. 8e, Hippopotamus. 10e, Rhinoceros. 15e, Sable antelope. 1e, 2e, 3e, 4e, 7.50e, 8e, 10e horiz.

1977, Jan.   Litho.   Perf. 14½

555	A58	50c multi	.25	.25
556	A58	1e multi	.25	.25
557	A58	1.50e multi	.25	.25
558	A58	2e multi	.25	.25
559	A58	2.50e multi	.30	.25
560	A58	3e multi	.30	.25
561	A58	4e multi	.50	.25
562	A58	5e multi	.70	.25
563	A58	7.50e multi	1.10	.30
564	A58	8e multi	1.20	.40
565	A58	10e multi	1.20	.40
566	A58	15e multi	1.75	.95
	Nos. 555-566 (12)		8.05	4.05

Congress
Emblem — A59

Monument in
Maputo — A60

Design: 3.50e, Monument in Macheje, site of 2nd Frelimo Congress, horiz.

1977, Feb. 7   Perf. 14½

567	A59	3e multi	.40	.25

Perf. 12x11½, 11½x12

568	A60	3.50e multi	.30	.30
569	A60	20e multi	2.10	.95
	Nos. 567-569 (3)		2.80	1.50

3rd FRELIMO Party Congress, Maputo, Feb. 3-7.

Women, Child's
Design — A61

Worker and
Farmer — A62

1977, Apr. 7   Litho.   Perf. 14½

570	A61	5e dp org & multi	.30	.25
571	A61	15e lt grn & multi	1.40	.55

Mozambique Women's Day 1977

1977, May 1   Litho.   Perf. 14½

572	A62	5e red, blk & yel	1.00	.30

Labor Day.

People, Flags and
Rising Sun — A63

1977, June 25   Litho.   Perf. 11½x12
573 A63   50c multi   .25   .25
574 A63   1.50e multi   .25   .25
575 A63   3e multi   .30   .25
576 A63   15e multi   1.10   .45
      Nos. 573-576 (4)   1.90 1.20

2nd anniversary of independence.

Bread Palm
A64

1977, Dec. 21   Litho.   Perf. 12x11½
577 A64   1e shown   .45   .25
578 A64   10e Nyala   1.10   .55

Nature protection and Stamp Day.

Chariesthes Bella
Rufoplagiata
A65

Beetles: 1e, Tragocephalus variegata.
1.50e, Monochamus leuconotus. 3e, Pros-
pocera lactator meridionalis. 5e, Dinocepha-
lus ornatus. 10e, Tragiscoschema nigroscrip-
tum maculata.

1978, Jan. 20   Litho.   Perf. 11½x12
579 A65   50c multi   .45   .30
580 A65   1e multi   .45   .30
581 A65   1.50e multi   .60   .30
582 A65   3e multi   .70   .30
583 A65   5e multi   .90   .45
584 A65   10e multi   1.50   .45
      Nos. 579-584 (6)   4.60 2.10

Violet-crested
Touraco — A66

Birds of Mozambique: 1e, Lilac-breasted
roller. 1.50e, Weaver. 2.50e, Violet-backed
starling. 3e, Peter's twinspot. 15e, European
bee-eater.

1978, Mar. 20   Litho.   Perf. 11½
585 A66   50c multi   .60   .30
586 A66   1e multi   .60   .30
587 A66   1.50e multi   .80   .30
588 A66   2.50e multi   .95   .30
589 A66   3e multi   1.10   .30
590 A66   15e multi   2.50   .55
      Nos. 585-590 (6)   6.55 2.05

Mother and
Child, WHO
Emblem
A67

1978, Apr. 17   Perf. 12
591 A67   15e multi   .80   .40

Smallpox eradication campaign.

Crinum
Delagoense
A68

Flowers of Mozambique: 1e, Gloriosa
superba. 1.50e, Eulophia speciosa. 3e,
Erithrina humeana. 5e, Astripomoea
malvacea. 10e, Kigelia africana.

1978, May 16   Perf. 11½x12
592 A68   50c multi   .45   .30
593 A68   1e multi   .45   .30
594 A68   1.50e multi   .45   .30
595 A68   3e multi   .45   .30
596 A68   5e multi   .90   .30
597 A68   10e multi   1.20   .60
      Nos. 592-597 (6)   3.90 2.10

No. 1, Canada
No. 1 — A69

1978, June 9
598 A69   15e multi   .80   .55

CAPEX Canadian International Philatelic
Exhibition, Toronto, Ont., June 9-18.

National
Flag — A70

1.50e, Coat of arms. 7.50e, Page of Constitution people. 10e, Music band & natl.
anthem.

1978, June 25   Perf. 11½x12
599 A70   1e multi   .30   .30
600 A70   1.50e multi   .30   .30
601 A70   7.50e multi   .45   .30
602 A70   10e multi   .70   .40
a.   Souvenir sheet of 4   2.40 2.40
      Nos. 599-602 (4)   1.75 1.30

3rd anniversary of proclamation of indepen-
dence. No. 602a contains 4 stamps similar to
Nos. 599-602 with simulated perforations.
Sold for 30e.

Soldiers, Festival
Emblem — A71

2.50e, Student. 7.50e, Farmworkers.

1978, July 28
603 A71   2.50e multi   .25   .25
604 A71   3e multi   .25   .25
605 A71   7.50e multi   .55   .40
      Nos. 603-605 (3)   1.05   .90

11th World Youth Festival, Havana, 7/28-8/5.

Czechoslovakia No. B126 and PRAGA
'78 Emblem — A72

1978, Sept. 8   Litho.   Perf. 12x11½
606 A72   15e multi   .95   .55
a.   Souvenir sheet   3.50 3.50

PRAGA '78 International Philatelic Exhibition, Prague, Sept. 8-17.
No. 606a contains one stamp with simulated
perforations. Sold for 30e.

Soccer
A73

Stamp Day: 1.50e, Shotput. 3e, Hurdling.
7.50e, Fieldball. 12.50e, Swimming. 25e,
Roller skate hockey.

1978, Dec. 21   Litho.   Perf. 12x11½
607 A73   50c multi   .25   .25
608 A73   1.50e multi   .25   .25
609 A73   3e multi   .25   .25
610 A73   7.50e multi   .55   .40
611 A73   12.50e multi   .80   .55
612 A73   25e multi   1.75 1.25
      Nos. 607-612 (6)   3.85 2.95

Carrier
Pigeon,
UPU
Emblem
A74

1979, Jan. 1   Litho.   Perf. 11x11½
613 A74   20e multi   2.25 1.00

Membership in Universal Postal Union.

Soldier Giving Gourd to
Woman — A75

Edward
Chivambo
Mondlane
A76

Designs: 3e, Frelimo soldiers. 7.50e,
Mozambique children in school.

1979, Feb. 3   Perf. 11½x11, 11x11½
614 A75   1e multi   .25   .25
615 A75   3e multi   .25   .25
616 A75   7.50e multi   .55   .40
617 A76   12.50e multi   .80   .60
      Nos. 614-617 (4)   1.85 1.50

Dr. Edward Chivambo Mondlane (1920-
1969), educator, founder of Frelimo Party.

Shaded Silver
Cat — A77

Cats: 1.50e, Manx. 2.50e, English blue.
3e, Turkish. 12.50e, Long-haired Mid-East
tabby. 20e, African wild cat.

1979, Mar. 27   Litho.   Perf. 11
618 A77   50c multi   .40   .25
619 A77   1.50e multi   .45   .25
620 A77   2.50e multi   .45   .25
621 A77   3e multi   .55   .25
622 A77   12.50e multi   1.20   .60
623 A77   20e multi   1.75 1.00
      Nos. 618-623 (6)   4.80 2.60

Wrestling and Moscow '80
Emblem — A78

Sport and Moscow '80 Emblem: 2e, Running. 3e, Equestrian. 5e, Canoeing. 10e,
High jump. 15e, Archery.

1979, Apr. 24   Litho.   Perf. 11
624 A78   1e gray grn & blk   .25   .25
625 A78   2e brt bl & blk   .25   .25
626 A78   3e lt brn & blk   .35   .25
627 A78   5e multi   .50   .25
628 A78   10e grn & blk   .60   .40
629 A78   15e lil rose & blk   1.25   .70
      Nos. 624-629 (6)   3.20 2.10

Souvenir Sheet
Imperf
630 A78   30e rose & dk brn   3.50 3.50

22nd Olympic Games, Moscow, July 10-
Aug. 3, 1980. No. 630 contains one 47x37mm
stamp.

Garden
and IYC
Emblem
A79

Children's Drawings and IYC Emblem:
1.50e, Dancers. 3e, City. 5e, Farmers. 7.50e,
Village. 12.50e, Automobiles, train and
flowers.

1979, June 1   Litho.   Perf. 11
631 A79   50c multi   .30   .30
632 A79   1.50e multi   .30   .30
633 A79   3e multi   .30   .30
634 A79   5e multi   .40   .30
635 A79   7.50e multi   .55   .30
636 A79   12.50e multi   1.25   .55
      Nos. 631-636 (6)   3.10 2.05

International Year of the Child.

Flight from Colonialism — A80

Designs: 2e, Founding of FRELIMO and Pres. Eduardo Chivambo Mondlane. 3e, Advance of armed strruggle and death of Mondlane. 7.50e, Final fight for liberation. 15e, Proclamation of victory, Pres. Samora Moises Machel, flag and torch. Designs after mural in Heroes' Square, Maputo. 30e, Building up the country.

1979, June 25

637	A80	50c multi	.25	.25
638	A80	2e multi	.25	.25
639	A80	3e multi	.25	.25
640	A80	7.50e multi	.45	.30
641	A80	15e multi	.95	.70
b.		Strip of 5, #537-641	3.25	3.25

Souvenir Sheet
Imperf

641A	A80	30e multi	6.25	6.25

4th anniversary of independence. No. 641A contains one stamp with simulated perforations. No. 641b has continuous design.

Scorpion Fish A81

Tropical Fish: 1.50e, King fish. 2.50e, Gobius inhaca. 3e, Acanthurus lineatus. 10e, Gobuchthys lemayi. 12.50e, Variola louti.

1979, Aug. 7   Litho.   Perf. 11

642	A81	50c multi	.45	.30
643	A81	1.50e multi	.45	.30
644	A81	2.50e multi	.45	.30
645	A81	3e multi	.45	.30
646	A81	10e multi	1.20	.30
647	A81	12.50e multi	1.30	.45
		Nos. 642-647 (6)	4.30	1.95

For surcharge see No. 1254.

Quartz A82

Mozambique Minerals.

1979, Sept. 10

648	A82	1e shown	.50	.30
649	A82	1.50e Beryl	.75	.30
650	A82	2.50e Magnetite	1.00	.30
651	A82	5e Tourmaline	1.50	.30
652	A82	10e Euxenite	1.75	.45
653	A82	20e Fluorite	2.50	.80
		Nos. 648-653 (6)	8.00	2.45

Citizens Gathering Arms — A83

1979, Sept. 25

654	A83	5e multi	.45	.25

15th anniversary of independence.

Locomotive — A85

Designs: Historic Locomotives.

1979, Nov. 11   Litho.   Perf. 11

656	A85	50c multi	.25	.25
657	A85	1.50e multi	.25	.25
658	A85	3e multi	.40	.25
659	A85	7.50e multi	.70	.25
660	A85	12.50e multi	1.10	.40
661	A85	15e multi	1.30	.55
		Nos. 656-661 (6)	4.00	1.95

For surcharge see No. 1298.

Dalmatian — A86

Perf. 11½x11, 11x11½

1979, Dec. 17   Litho.

662	A86	50c Basenji, vert.	.40	.30
663	A86	1.50e shown	.40	.30
664	A86	3e Boxer	.50	.30
665	A86	7.50e Blue gasconha braco	.75	.30
666	A86	12.50e Cocker spaniel	1.10	.45
667	A86	15e Pointer	1.50	.65
		Nos. 662-667 (6)	4.65	2.30

For surcharge see No. 1299.

Nireus Lyaeus — A87

Butterflies: 1.50e, Amauris ochlea. 2.50e, Pinacopterix eriphia. 5e, Junonia hierta cebrene. 10e, Nephronia argia. 20e, Catacroptera cloanthe.

1979, Dec. 21

668	A87	1e multi	.40	.30
669	A87	1.50e multi	.40	.30
670	A87	2.50e multi	.55	.30
671	A87	5e multi	.75	.30
672	A87	10e multi	1.25	.35
673	A87	20e multi	2.50	.90
		Nos. 668-673 (6)	5.85	2.45

Dermacentor Rhinocerinus, Rhinoceros — A88

Ticks and Animals: 50c, Dermacentor circumguttatus cunhasilvai, elephant. 2.50e, Green tick, giraffe. 3e, Red tick, antelope. 5e, Ambloymma theilerae, cattle. 7.50e, Buffalo tick, buffalo.

1980, Jan. 29   Litho.   Perf. 11½x11

674	A88	50c multi	.25	.25
675	A88	1.50e multi	.40	.25
676	A88	2.50e multi	.40	.25
677	A88	3e multi	.65	.25
678	A88	5e multi	1.00	.25
679	A88	7.50e multi	1.50	.30
		Nos. 674-679 (6)	4.20	1.55

Ford Hercules, 1950 — A89

Public Transportation: 1.50e, Scania Marcopolo, 1978. 3e, Bussing Nag, 1936. 5e, Articulated Ikarus, 1978. 7.50e, Ford taxi, 1929. 12.50e, Fiat 131 taxi, 1978.

1980, Feb. 29   Litho.   Perf. 11

680	A89	50c multi	.25	.25
681	A89	1.50e multi	.25	.25
682	A89	3e multi	.30	.25
683	A89	5e multi	.35	.25
684	A89	7.50e multi	.60	.25
685	A89	12.50e multi	.80	.40
		Nos. 680-685 (6)	2.55	1.65

Marx, Engels, and Lenin A90

1980, May 1   Litho.   Perf. 11

686	A90	10e multi	1.10	.30

Workers' Day.

"Heads," by Malangatana, London 1980 Emblem — A91

Paintings by Mozambique Artists: 1.50e, Crowded Market, by Moises Simbine. 3e, Heads with Helmets, by Malangatana. 5e, Women with Goods, by Machiana. 7.50e, Crowd with Masks, by Malangatana. 12.50e, Man and Woman with Spear, by Mankeu.

1980, May 6

687	A91	50c multi	.25	.25
688	A91	1.50e multi	.25	.25
689	A91	3e multi	.25	.25
690	A91	5e multi	.40	.25
691	A91	7.50e multi	.55	.25
692	A91	12.50e multi	.75	.35
		Nos. 687-692 (6)	2.45	1.60

London 1980 Intl. Stamp Exhibition, 5/6-14.

World Telecommunications Day — A92

1980, May 17   Litho.   Perf. 12

693	A92	15e multi	1.00	.45

Mueda Massacre, 20th Anniv. — A93

1980, June 16   Litho.   Perf. 11

694	A93	15e multi	1.00	.45

People with Weapons and Flag — A94

1980, June 25

695	A94	1e Development projects, 1975	.25	.25
696	A94	2e shown	.25	.25
697	A94	3e Arms, flags, 1977	.25	.25
698	A94	4e Raised fists, 1978	.35	.25
699	A94	5e Hand holding grain, flags, 1979	.35	.25
700	A94	10e Year banners, 1980	.80	.30
		Nos. 695-700 (6)	2.25	1.55

Souvenir Sheet
Imperf.

700A	A94	30e Soldiers	3.50	3.50

5th anniv. of independence. No. 700A contains one stamp with simulated perforations.

Gymnast, Moscow '80 Emblem — A95

1980, July 19

701	A95	50c shown	.25	.25
702	A95	1.50e Soccer	.25	.25
703	A95	2.50e Running	.25	.25
704	A95	3e Volleyball	.30	.25
705	A95	10e Bicycling	.65	.25
706	A95	12.50e Boxing	.90	.40
		Nos. 701-706 (6)	2.60	1.65

22nd Summer Olympic Games, Moscow, July 19-Aug. 3.

Soldier, Map of Southern Africa Showing Zimbabwe — A96

1980, Apr. 18

707	A96	10e multi	.65	.30

Establishment of Independent Zimbabwe, Apr. 18.

Narina Trogon — A97

1980, July 30   **Litho.**   **Perf. 11**

708	A97	1m shown	.25	.25
709	A97	1.50m Crowned crane	.50	.25
710	A97	2.50m Red-necked francolin	.75	.25
711	A97	5m Ostrich	1.25	.25
712	A97	7.50m Spur-winged goose	1.50	.30
713	A97	12.50m Fish eagle	2.00	.40
		Nos. 708-713 (6)	6.25	1.70

For surcharges see Nos. 1253A, 1255.

First Census, Aug. 1-15 A98

1980, Aug. 12   **Perf. 11**

714	A98	3.5m multi	.40	.25

Brush Fire Control Campaign — A99

1980, Sept. 7

715	A99	3.5m multi	.80	.25

Harpa Major A100

1980, Dec. 12   **Litho.**   **Perf. 11**

716	A100	1m shown	.35	.25
717	A100	1.50m Lambis chiragra	.40	.25
718	A100	2.50m Murex pecten	.50	.25
719	A100	5m Architectonia perspectiva	.60	.25
720	A100	7.50m Murex ramosus	.75	.25
721	A100	12.50m Strombus aurisdinae	1.25	.40
		Nos. 716-721 (6)	3.85	1.65

Pres. Machel and Symbols of Industry and Transportation — A101

Decade of Development, 1981-1990 (Pres. Machel and): 7.50m, Soldiers. 12.50m, Symbols of education.

1981, Jan. 1   **Litho.**   **Perf. 11x11½**

722	A101	3.50m red & bl	.50	.25
723	A101	7.50m grn & red brn	1.00	.25
724	A101	12.50m dk bl & lil rose	1.75	.45
		Nos. 722-724 (3)	3.25	.95

Bilbao Soccer Stadium, Soccer Player — A102

Soccer players and various stadiums.

1981, Jan. 30   **Litho.**   **Perf. 11**

725	A102	1m multi	.25	.25
726	A102	1.50m multi	.25	.25
727	A102	2.50m multi	.25	.25
728	A102	5m multi	.35	.25
729	A102	7.50m multi	.60	.25
730	A102	12.50m multi	.95	.40
c.		Souvenir sheet of 6	2.40	2.40
		Nos. 725-730 (6)	2.65	1.65

Souvenir Sheets
Imperf

730A	A102	20m multi	3.50	3.50
730B	A102	20m multi	3.50	3.50

ESPANA '82 World Cup Soccer Championship. No. 730c contains Nos. 725-730 with simulated perforations. Sizes: No. 730A, 105x85mm; 730B, 141x111mm.
For surcharge see No. 1303.

Giraffe — A103

1981, Mar. 3   **Perf. 11**

731	A103	50c shown	.35	.25
732	A103	1.50m Tsessebe	.40	.25
733	A103	2.50m Aardvark	.60	.25
734	A103	3m African python	.65	.25
735	A103	5m Loggerhead turtle	.70	.25
736	A103	10m Marabou	.90	.35
737	A103	12.50m Saddlebill stork	1.10	.50
738	A103	15m Kori bustard	1.75	.60
		Nos. 731-738 (8)	6.45	2.70

Pankwe A104

1981, Apr. 8   **Litho.**   **Perf. 11**

739	A104	50c Chitende, vert.	.25	.25
740	A104	2m shown	.25	.25
741	A104	2.50m Kanyembe, vert.	.30	.25
742	A104	7m Nyanga	.50	.30
743	A104	10m Likuti and m'petheni	1.10	.45
		Nos. 739-743 (5)	2.40	1.50

International Year of the Disabled — A105

1981, Apr. 18

744	A105	5m multi	.55	.25

African Buffalo and Helicopter, Exhibition Emblem — A106

1981, June 14   **Perf. 11**

745	A106	2m shown	.40	.25
746	A106	5m Hunters, blue kids	.60	.25
747	A106	6m Hunter, impala	.75	.25
748	A106	7.50m Hunters shooting	.90	.25
749	A106	12.50m Elephants	1.10	.35
750	A106	20m Trap	2.35	.65
a.		Souv. sheet of 6, #745-750, imperf.	6.50	6.50
		Nos. 745-750 (6)	6.10	2.00

World Hunting Exhibition, Plovdiv, Bulgaria. No. 750a sold for 60m.
For surcharge see No. 1258.

50-centavo Coin, Obverse and Reverse A107

First Anniversary of New Currency (Coins on stamps of matching denomination).

1981, June 16

751	A107	50c multi	.25	.25
752	A107	1m multi	.30	.25
753	A107	2.50m multi	.40	.25
754	A107	5m multi	.45	.25
755	A107	10m multi	.70	.30
756	A107	20m multi	1.50	.75
a.		Souv. sheet of 6, #751-756, imperf.	3.25	3.25
		Nos. 751-756 (6)	3.60	2.05

No. 756a sold for 40m.

Crops — A108

Designs: 50c, Sunflower (Helianthus annus). 1m, Cotton (Gossypium spp.). 1.50m, Sisal (Agave sisalana). 2.50m, Cashews (Anacardium occidentale). 3.50m, Tea (Camellia sinensis). 4.50m, Sugar cane (Saccharum officianum). 10m, Castor oil plant (Ricinus communis). 12.50m, Coconuts (Cocos nucifera). 15m, Tobacco (Nicotiniana tabacum). 25m, Rice (Oryza sativa). 40m, Corn (Zea mays). 60m, Peanut (Arachis hypogaea).

1981, July 24   **Litho.**   **Perf. 14½**

757	A108	50c red & org	.25	.25
758	A108	1m red & black	.25	.25
759	A108	1.50m red & Prus bl	.25	.25
760	A108	2.50m red & bis	.25	.25
761	A108	3.50m red & gray grn	.25	.25
762	A108	4.50m red & gray	.30	.25
763	A108	10m red & blue	.75	.25
764	A108	12.50m red & dk brn	1.00	.35
765	A108	15m red & ol grn	1.20	.40
766	A108	25m red & yel grn	1.50	.80
767	A108	40m red & org brn	2.50	1.10
768	A108	60m red & brn	3.75	1.75
		Nos. 757-768 (12)	12.25	6.15

For surcharges see Nos. 1034A, 1185, 1216, 1218, 1252, 1300, 1399, 1420.

9th Cent. Persian Bowl, Chibuene Excavation Site — A109

1981, Aug. 30   **Perf. 11**

769	A109	1m Manyikeni Museum	.25	.25
770	A109	1.50m Hand ax, Massingir Dam	.25	.25
771	A109	2.50m shown	.25	.25
772	A109	7.50m Pot, Chibuene, 9th cent.	.50	.25
773	A109	12.50m Gold beads, Manyikeni	.85	.45
774	A109	20m Iron, Manyikeni, 15th cent.	1.40	.75
		Nos. 769-774 (6)	3.50	2.20

For surcharge see No. 1213.

Sculptures A110

1981, Sept. 25   **Litho.**   **Perf. 11**

775	A110	50c Mapiko mask	.25	.25
776	A110	1m Suffering woman	.25	.25
777	A110	2.50m Mother and child	.25	.25
778	A110	3.50m Man making fire	.25	.25
779	A110	5m Chietane	.50	.30
780	A110	12.50m Chietane, diff.	.50	.50
		Nos. 775-780 (6)	2.00	1.80

World Food Day A111

1981, Oct. 16   **Litho.**   **Perf. 11**

781	A111	10m multi	.80	.40

Ocean Tanker Matchedje — A112

1981, Nov. 22   **Litho.**   **Perf. 11**

782	A112	50c shown	.25	.25
783	A112	1.50m Tugboat Macuti	.25	.25
784	A112	3m Prawn trawler Vega 7	.25	.25
785	A112	5m Freighter Linde	.40	.25
786	A112	7.50m Ocean freighter Pemba	.70	.40
787	A112	12.50m Dredger Rovuma	1.25	.75
		Nos. 782-787 (6)	3.10	2.15

Chinaman Crab — A113

1981, Dec. 6
788	A113	50c Portunus Pelagieus	.50	.25
789	A113	1.50m Scylla serrata	.50	.25
790	A113	3m Penaeus indicus	.50	.25
791	A113	7.50m Palinurus delagoae	.80	.25
792	A113	12.50m Lusiosquilla maculata	1.25	.50
793	A113	15m Panulirus ornatus	1.60	.60
		Nos. 788-793 (6)	5.15	2.10

For surcharges see Nos. 1214, 1219, 1253, 1392.

Hypoxis Multiceps A114

1981, Dec. 21   Litho.   Perf. 11
794	A114	1m shown	.25	.25
795	A114	1.50m Pelargonium luridum	.25	.25
796	A114	2.50m Caralluma melananthera	.25	.25
797	A114	7.50m Ansellia gigantea	.50	.35
798	A114	12.50m Stapelia leendertsiae	1.00	.60
799	A114	25m Adenium multiflorium	2.00	1.10
		Nos. 794-799 (6)	4.25	2.80

For surcharges see Nos. 1215, 1217, 1251, 1301, 1390.

First Anniv. of Posts and Telecommunications Dept. — A115

1982, Jan. 1   Litho.   Perf. 11
800	A115	6m Phone, globe	.45	.25
801	A115	15m Envelope	1.25	.80

Gasoline Conservation — A116

1982, Jan. 25
802	A116	5m Piston	.35	.30
803	A116	7.50m Car	.55	.40
804	A116	10m Truck	.75	.60
		Nos. 802-804 (3)	1.65	1.30

Sea Snake A117

1982, Feb. 27   Litho.   Perf. 11
805	A117	50c shown	.65	.25
806	A117	1.50m Mozambique spitting cobra	.65	.25
807	A117	3m Savanna vine snake	.65	.25
808	A117	6m Black mamba	.70	.25
809	A117	15m Boomslang	1.50	.50
810	A117	20m Bitis arietans	2.10	.80
		Nos. 805-810 (6)	6.25	2.30

TB Bacillus Centenary — A118

1982, Mar. 15   Litho.   Perf. 11
811	A118	20m multi	2.00	1.10

ITU Plenipotentiary Conference, Nairobi, Sept. 28-Nov. 5 — A119

1982, Mar. 31   Perf. 13½
812	A119	20m multi	1.60	.80

1982 World Cup — A120

Designs: Various soccer players.

1982, Apr. 19   Litho.   Perf. 13½
813	A120	1.5m multi	.25	.25
814	A120	3.5m multi	.30	.25
815	A120	7m multi	.50	.25
816	A120	10m multi	.85	.35
817	A120	20m multi	1.40	1.00
		Nos. 813-817 (5)	3.30	2.10

Souvenir Sheet
Imperf
818	A120	50m multi	4.00	4.00

Souvenir Sheet

Two Tahitian Women, by Gauguin — A121

1982, June 11   Litho.   Imperf.
819	A121	35m multi	5.25	5.25

PHILEXFRANCE '82 Intl. Stamp Exhibition, Paris, June 11-21.

Natl. Liberation Front, 20th Anniv. — A122

1982, June 25   Perf. 13
820	A122	4m Pres. Mondland addressing crowd	.30	.25
821	A122	8m Guarded fields	.60	.30
822	A122	12m Procession	.90	.45
		Nos. 820-822 (3)	1.80	1.00

Vangueria Infausta A123

Designs: Fruits.

1982, Sept. 13   Perf. 11
823	A123	1m shown	.25	.25
824	A123	2m Mimusops caffra	.25	.25
825	A123	4m Sclerocarya caffra	.30	.25
826	A123	8m Strychnos spinosa	.60	.30
827	A123	12m Salacia kraussi	.90	.50
828	A123	32m Trichilia emetica	2.10	1.10
		Nos. 823-828 (6)	4.40	2.65

25th Anniv. of Sputnik I Flight A124

1982, Oct. 4   Litho.   Perf. 11
829	A124	1m Sputnik, 1957	.25	.25
830	A124	2m Yuri Gagarin's flight, 1961	.25	.25
831	A124	4m A. Leonov's spacewalk, 1965	.30	.25
832	A124	8m Apollo 11, 1969	.60	.30
833	A124	16m Apollo-Soyuz, 1975	1.25	.90
834	A124	20m Salyut-6, 1978	1.60	.90
a.		Min. sheet of 6, #829-834	4.50	4.50
		Nos. 829-834 (6)	4.25	2.85

People's Vigilance Day — A125

1982, Oct. 11   Perf. 13½
835	A125	4m multi	.40	.25

Caique — A126

Traditional boats. 4m, 8m, 12m, 16m horiz.

1982, Nov. 29
836	A126	1m shown	.25	.25
837	A126	2m Machua	.25	.25
838	A126	4m Calaua	.40	.25
839	A126	8m Chitatarro	.75	.30
840	A126	12m Cangaia	1.00	.45
841	A126	16m Chata (flatboat)	1.75	.75
		Nos. 836-841 (6)	4.40	2.25

Marine Life — A127

1982, Dec. 21   Litho.   Perf. 11
842	A127	1m Ophiomastix venosa	.50	.25
843	A127	2m Protoreaster lincki	.50	.25
844	A127	4m Tropiometra carinata	.50	.25
845	A127	8m Holothuria scabra	.80	.25
846	A127	12m Prionocidaris baculosa	1.20	.45
847	A127	16m Colobocentrotus atnatus	1.60	.50
		Nos. 842-847 (6)	5.10	1.95

Frelimo Party 4th Congress — A128

1983, Jan. 17
848	A128	4m Map, soldier	.25	.25
849	A128	8m Voters	.40	.25
850	A128	16m Farm workers	1.00	.65
		Nos. 848-850 (3)	1.65	1.15

Seaweed A129

1983, Feb. 28   Litho.   Perf. 11
851	A129	1m Codium duthierae	.25	.25
852	A129	2m Halimeda cuncata	.25	.25
853	A129	4m Dictyota liturata	.30	.25
854	A129	8m Encorachne bing hamiae	.65	.25
855	A129	12m Laurencia flexuosa	1.00	.40
856	A129	20m Acrosorium sp.	1.25	.75
		Nos. 851-856 (6)	3.70	2.15

1984 Olympic Games, Los Angeles A130

1983, Mar. 31   Litho.   Perf. 11
857	A130	1m Diving	.25	.25
858	A130	2m Boxing	.25	.25
859	A130	4m Basketball	.25	.25
860	A130	8m Handball	.60	.25
861	A130	12m Volleyball	.80	.40
862	A130	16m Running	1.10	.50
863	A130	20m Sailing	1.25	.80
		Nos. 857-863 (7)	4.50	2.70

Souvenir Sheet
Imperf
864	A130	50m Discus	3.25	3.25

For surcharge see No. 1257.

Steam Locomotives — A131

1983, Apr. 29   Litho.   Perf. 11
865 A131 1m 1912   .50 .25
866 A131 2m 1947   .50 .25
867 A131 4m 1923   .50 .25
868 A131 8m 1924   .60 .30
869 A131 16m 1924, diff.   1.40 .40
870 A131 32m 1950   2.75 1.25
      Nos. 865-870 (6)   6.25 2.70

20th
Anniv. of
Org. of
African
Unity
A132

1983, May 25   Litho.   Perf. 11
871 A132 4m multi   .25 .25

Mammals
A133

1983, May 30
872 A133 1m Petrodromus te-
                tradactylus   .50 .25
873 A133 2m Rhabdomys
                pumilio   .50 .25
874 A133 4m Paraxerus vincenti   .50 .25
875 A133 8m Cryptomys hot-
                tentotus   .90 .25
876 A133 12m Pronolagus cras-
                sicaudatus   1.25 .45
877 A133 16m Eidolon helvum   1.50 .60
      Nos. 872-877 (6)   5.15 2.05

Souvenir Sheet

Marimba Players — A134

1983, July 29   Litho.   Perf. 11
878 A134 30m multi   4.00 4.00

BRASILIANA '83 Intl. Stamp Show, Rio de
Janeiro, July 29-Aug. 7.

World Communications Year — A135

1983, Aug. 26   Litho.   Perf. 11
879 A135 8m multi   .60 .25

Fishing Techniques — A136

1983, Oct. 29   Litho.   Perf. 11
880 A136 50c Line fishing   .25 .25
881 A136 2m Chifonho   .25 .25
882 A136 4m Momba   .25 .25
883 A136 8m Gamboa   .50 .30
884 A136 16m Mono   1.40 .50
885 A136 20m Lema   1.60 .75
      Nos. 880-885 (6)   4.25 2.30

World Communications Year, Stamp
Day — A137

1983, Dec. 21   Litho.
886 A137 50c Horn   .25 .25
887 A137 1m Drum   .25 .25
888 A137 4m Native mail carri-
                ers   .45 .25
889 A137 8m Boat   1.10 .25
890 A137 16m Truck   2.00 .55
891 A137 20m Train   3.00 .75
      Nos. 886-891 (6)   7.05 2.30

2nd Anniv. of Mozambique Red Cross
(July 10) — A138

1983, Oct. 29   Litho.   Perf. 11
892 A138 4m Flood relief   .25 .25
893 A138 8m Rescue truck   .55 .25
894 A138 16m First aid   1.25 .50
895 A138 32m Field first aid 2.25 1.00
      Nos. 892-895 (4)   4.30 2.00

Olympic Games
1984, Los
Angeles
A139

1984, Jan. 2   Litho.   Perf. 11
896 A139 50c Swimming   .25 .25
897 A139 4m Soccer   .40 .25
898 A139 8m Hurdles   .60 .30
899 A139 16m Basketball   1.25 .50
900 A139 32m Handball   2.60 1.50
901 A139 60m Boxing   4.25 2.10
      Nos. 896-901 (6)   9.35 4.90

Indigenous Trees — A140

1984, Mar. 30   Litho.   *Perf. 11*
902 A140 50c Trichilia emetica   .25 .25
903 A140 2m Brachystegia
                spiciformis   .25 .25
904 A140 4m Androstachys
                johnsonii   .30 .25
905 A140 8m Pterocarpus
                angolensis   .65 .25
906 A140 16m Milletia stuhlman-
                nii   1.10 .55
907 A140 50m Dalbergia mela-
                noxylon   3.25 1.75
      Nos. 902-907 (6)   5.80 3.30

Nkomati
Accord, Mar.
16 — A141

1984, Mar. 16
908 A141 4m Dove   .40 .25

Natl.
Arms
A142

1984, May 1
909 A142 4m shown   .30 .25
910 A142 8m Natl. flag   .65 .30

Traditional
Dances
A143

1984, May 9
911 A143 4m Makway   .25 .25
912 A143 8m Mapiko   .50 .25
913 A143 16m Wadjaba   1.50 .65
      Nos. 911-913 (3)   2.25 1.15

LUBRAPEX '84, May 9-17.

Museums and Artifacts — A144

Designs: 50c, Nampula Museum, African
carrying water jar, wooden statue. 4m,
Museum of Natural History, preserved bird.
8m, Revolution Museum, guerrilla fighter
statue. 16m, Colonial Occupation Museum,
fort and cannon. 20m, Numismatic Museum,
coins. 30m, Palace of St. Paul, char, 19th cent.

1984, June 25
914 A144 50c multi   .25 .25
915 A144 4m multi   .35 .25
916 A144 8m multi   .60 .30
917 A144 16m multi   1.25 .60
918 A144 20m multi   1.40 .80
919 A144 30m multi   2.25 1.10
      Nos. 914-919 (6)   6.10 3.30

Freshwater Fish — A145

1984, Aug. 24
920 A145 50c Alestes imberi .25 .25
921 A145 4m Labeo congoro   .40 .25
922 A145 12m Syndontis
                zambezensis   1.00 .45
923 A145 16m Notobranchius
                zachovii   1.00 .60
924 A145 40m Barbus paludi-
                nosus   2.75 1.40
925 A145 60m Barilius
                zambezensis   3.75 2.10
      Nos. 920-925 (6)   9.15 5.05

For surcharge see No. 1311.

Intl. Fair,
Maputo —
A145a — 925A

1984, Aug. 24   Litho.   Perf. 11
925A A145a 16m multicolored 1.75 .60

Traditional
Weapons
A146

1984, Sept. 25
926 A146 50c Knife, cudgel   .30 .25
927 A146 4m Axes   .40 .25
928 A146 8m Shield, assagai .45 .25
929 A146 16m Bow and arrow 1.60 .45
930 A146 32m Muzzleloader   2.00 1.10
931 A146 50m Assagai, arrow 3.25 1.75
      Nos. 926-931 (6)   8.00 4.05

Natl. Revolution, 20th anniv.
For surcharge see No. 1256.

Natl. Trade
Unions, 1st
Anniv. — A147

1984, Oct. 13   Perf. 13½
932 A147 4m Workers, emblem .40 .25

Stamp Day — A149

Cancellations on altered stamps and stationery: 4m, Barue cancel on 1885 20r postal
card. 8m, Zumbo cancel on design similar to
No. 52. 12m, Mozambique Co. cancel on
design similar to Mozambique Company Type
API. 16m, Macequece cancel on design similar to Mozambique Company No. 190.

1984, Dec. 21 — Perf. 11½x11

936	A149	4m multi	.35	.25
937	A149	8m multi	.90	.35
938	A149	12m multi	1.50	.60
939	A149	16m multi	1.75	.75
		Nos. 936-939 (4)	4.50	1.95

African Development Bank, 20th Anniv. — A150

1984, Sept. 16 Photo. Perf. 11½x11
940	A150	4m multi	.40	.25

Apiculture A151

1985, Feb. 3
941	A151	4m Beekeeper	.30	.25
942	A151	8m Bee gathering pollen	.70	.30
943	A151	16m Entering nest	1.40	.60
944	A151	20m Building honeycomb	2.00	.90
		Nos. 941-944 (4)	4.40	2.05

OLYMPHILEX '85, Lausanne A152

1985, Mar. 18 — Perf. 11
945	A152	16m Shot putter	1.50	.60

World Meteorology Day — A153

1985, Mar. 23 Litho. Perf. 11
946	A153	4m multi	.45	.25

Southern African Development Coordination Conference, 5th Anniv. — A154

1985, Apr. 1
947	A154	4m Map	.35	.25
948	A154	8m Map, transmission tower	1.00	.35
949	A154	16m Industry	2.00	.75
950	A154	32m Flags	3.25	1.25
		Nos. 947-950 (4)	6.60	2.60

Independence, 10th Anniv. — A155

Colonial resistance battles: 1m, Mujenga, 1896. 4m, Mungari, 1917. 8m, Massangano, 1868. 16m, Marracuene, 1895, and Gungunhana (c. 1840-1906), resistance leader.

1985, June 25 Litho. Perf. 11
951	A155	1m multi	.25	.25
952	A155	4m multi	.30	.25
953	A155	8m multi	.75	.25
954	A155	16m multi	1.60	.65
		Nos. 951-954 (4)	2.90	1.40

UN, 40th Anniv. — A156

1985, June 26
955	A156	16m multi	1.40	.70

Traditional Games — A157

1985, Aug. 28 Litho. Perf. 11
956	A157	50c Mathaouzana	.25	.25
957	A157	4m Mudzobo	.25	.25
958	A157	8m Muravarava	.50	.30
959	A157	16m N'Tshuwa	1.10	.60
		Nos. 956-959 (4)	2.10	1.40

Frogs and Toads A158

1985, Oct. 25 Litho. Perf. 11
960	A158	50c Rana angolensis	.25	.25
961	A158	1m Hyperolius pictus	.40	.25
962	A158	4m Ptychadena porosissima	.55	.25
963	A158	8m Afrixalus formasinii	1.10	.25
964	A158	16m Bufo regularis	2.25	.60
965	A158	32m Hyperolius marmoratus	3.75	1.10
		Nos. 960-965 (6)	8.30	2.70

Medicinal Plants — A159

1985, Nov. 28 Litho. Perf. 11
966	A159	50c Aloe ferox	.25	.25
967	A159	1m Boophone disticha	.25	.25
968	A159	3.50m Gloriosa superba	.30	.25
969	A159	4m Cotyledon orbiculata	.45	.25
970	A159	8m Homeria breyniana	1.10	.30
970A	A159	50m Haemanthus coccineus	6.00	1.75
		Nos. 966-970A (6)	8.35	3.05

Stamp Day A160

Stamps: 1m, Mozambique Company No. 126. 4m, Nyassa Type A6. 8m, Mozambique Company No. 110. 16m, Nyassa No. J2.

1985, Dec. 21
971	A160	1m multi	.25	.25
972	A160	4m multi	.45	.25
973	A160	8m multi	1.00	.25
974	A160	16m multi	2.00	.65
		Nos. 971-974 (4)	3.70	1.40

Halley's Comet — A161

Comet and: 4m, Space probe. 8m, Trajectory diagram. 16m, Newton's telescope, observatory, probe. 30m, Earth.

1986, Jan. 2
975	A161	4m multi	.25	.25
976	A161	8m multi	.60	.25
977	A161	16m multi	1.25	.60
978	A161	30m multi	2.50	1.25
		Nos. 975-978 (4)	4.60	2.35

1986 World Cup Soccer Championships, Mexico — A162

Players.

1986, Feb. 28 Litho. Perf. 11½x11
979	A162	3m Vicente	.25	.25
980	A162	4m Coluna	.25	.25
981	A162	8m Costa Pereira	.45	.30
982	A162	12m Hilario	.85	.45
983	A162	16m Matateu	1.25	.60
984	A162	50m Eusebio	3.75	1.75
		Nos. 979-984 (6)	6.80	3.60

Intl. Peace Year — A163

1986, Mar. 18 — Perf. 11
985	A163	16m multi	1.25	.50

Mushrooms A164

1986, Apr. 8
986	A164	4m Amanita muscaria	.45	.25
987	A164	8m Lactarius deliciosus	.30	.30
988	A164	16m Amanita phaloides	1.75	.75
989	A164	30m Tricholoma nudum	3.50	1.25
		Nos. 986-989 (4)	6.00	2.55

Souvenir Sheet

Statue of Liberty, Cent. — A165

1986, May 22 — Imperf.
990	A165	100m multi	6.75	6.75

AMERIPEX '86. #990 has simulated perfs.

Traditional Women's Hair Styles — A166

1986, June Litho. Perf. 11½x11
991	A166	1m Tanzanian	.25	.25
992	A166	4m Miriam	.30	.25
993	A166	8m Estrelinhas	.60	.25
994	A166	16m Toto	1.60	.70
		Nos. 991-994 (4)	2.75	1.45

Marine Mammals — A167

1986, Aug. — Perf. 11
995	A167	1m Dugongo dugon	.25	.25
996	A167	8m Delphinus delphis	.80	.25
997	A167	16m Neobalena marginata	2.75	.80
998	A167	50m Balaenoptera physalus	7.75	2.25
		Nos. 995-998 (4)	11.55	3.55

Continuing Youth Education Organization, 1st Anniv. — A168

1986, Sept. 16 Litho. *Perf. 11½x11*
999 A168 4m multi .45 .25

Natl. Savings Campaign — A169

Bank notes, front and back.

1986, Oct. 22 Litho. *Perf. 11½x11*
1000 A169 4m 50m note .30 .25
1001 A169 8m 100m note .60 .25
1002 A169 16m 500m note 1.75 .60
1003 A169 30m 1000m note 3.00 1.50
Nos. 1000-1003 (4) 5.65 2.60

For surcharge see No. 1302.

Stamp Day A170

Post offices.

1986, Dec. 21 Litho. *Perf. 11*
1004 A170 3m Quelimane .30 .25
1005 A170 4m Maputo .70 .25
1006 A170 8m Beira 1.25 .35
1007 A170 16m Nampula 2.75 .75
Nos. 1004-1007 (4) 5.00 1.60

Minerals A171

1987, Jan. 2 *Perf. 11x11½*
1008 A171 4m Pyrite .80 .25
1009 A171 8m Emerald 1.50 .35
1010 A171 12m Agate 2.25 .45
1011 A171 16m Malachite 2.75 .60
1012 A171 30m Garnet 4.75 1.50
1013 A171 50m Amethyst 7.00 2.10
Nos. 1008-1013 (6) 19.05 5.15

For surcharges see #1304-1305.

Frelimo Party, 10th Anniv. — A172

1987, Feb. 3 *Perf. 11*
1014 A172 4m multi .45 .25

Pequenos Libombos Dam — A173

1987, Feb. 17 *Perf. 11½x11*
1015 A173 16m multi 1.75 .75

World Health Day A174

1987, Apr. 7 Litho. *Perf. 11x11½*
1016 A174 50m multi 1.20 .50

Birds — A175

1987, Apr. 27 Litho. *Perf. 11½x11*
1017 A175 3m Granatina granatina .25 .25
1018 A175 4m Halcyon senegalensis .30 .25
1019 A175 8m Mellittophagus bullockoides .60 .35
1020 A175 12m Perinestes minor .95 .50
1021 A175 16m Coracias naevia mosambica 1.25 .75
1022 A175 30m Cimmyris neergardi 2.50 1.25
Nos. 1017-1022 (6) 5.85 3.35

For surcharge, see No. 1299A.

Souvenir Sheet

CAPEX '87, Toronto, June 13-21 — A176

1987, June *Imperf.*
1023 A176 200m multi 4.25 4.25

No. 1023 contains one stamp having simulated perforations.

1988 Summer Olympics, Seoul — A177

1987, May Litho. *Perf. 11½x11*
1024 A177 12.50m Soccer players and ball .30 .30
1025 A177 25m Runner's legs .40 .30
1026 A177 50m Volleyball .75 .45
1027 A177 75m Chess 1.20 .70
1028 A177 100m Basketball 1.50 .80
1029 A177 200m Swimming 3.25 1.20
Nos. 1024-1029 (6) 7.40 3.75

Tapestries — A178

1987, Aug. *Perf. 11*
1030 A178 20m Incomplete pattern on loom .30 .25
1031 A178 40m Diamond-shaped pattern .60 .25
1032 A178 80m Landscape pattern 1.20 .40
1033 A178 200m Oriental pattern 2.75 1.00
Nos. 1030-1033 (4) 4.85 1.90

Maputo City A179

Early Portuguese map of Lourenco Marques.

1987, Nov. 10 Litho. *Perf. 11*
1034 A179 20m multi .55 .25

No. 762 Surcharged in Silver and Dark Red

1987 Litho. *Perf. 14½*
1034A A108 4m on 4.50m multi 1.40 1.40

1988 Summer Olympics, Seoul — A180

1988, Feb. 10 Litho. *Perf. 11*
1035 A180 10m Javelin .25 .25
1036 A180 20m Baseball .25 .25
1037 A180 40m Boxing .40 .40
1038 A180 80m Field hockey .80 .80
1039 A180 100m Gymnastic rings 1.20 1.20
1040 A180 400m Cycling 1.60 1.60
Nos. 1035-1040 (6) 4.50 4.50

Nos. 1036-1040 horiz.

Flowering Plants — A181

1988, Mar. 18 *Perf. 11½x11*
1041 A181 10m Heamanthus nelsonii .25 .25
1042 A181 20m Crinum polyphyllum .40 .30
1043 A181 40m Boophane disticha .55 .40
1044 A181 80m Cyrtanthus contractus 1.20 .65
1045 A181 100m Nerine angustifolia 1.60 .80
1046 A181 400m Cyrtanthus galpinnii 2.25 2.25
Nos. 1041-1046 (6) 6.25 4.65

World Health Organization, 40th Anniv. — A182

1988, Apr. 7
1047 A182 20m multi .45 .45

Anti-smoking campaign.

Wickerwork — A183

1988, June 16 Litho. *Perf. 11*
1048 A183 20m Mat .25 .25
1049 A183 25m Lidded container .30 .30
1050 A183 80m Market basket .65 .30
1051 A183 100m Fan .80 .35
1052 A183 400m Flat basket 2.00 1.60
1053 A183 500m Funnel basket 2.75 2.00
Nos. 1048-1053 (6) 6.75 4.80

Souvenir Sheet

FINLANDIA '88 — A184

1988, June 12 Litho. *Imperf.*
1054 A184 500m multi 3.75 3.75

Stamp in No. 1054 has simulated perfs.

Souvenir Sheet

State Visit of Pope John Paul II, Sept. 16-19 — A185

1988	Litho.	Perf. 13½		
1055	A185 500m multi		5.00	5.00

Horses A186

1988, Sept. 20	Litho.	Perf. 11		
1056	A186	20m Percheron	.40	.30
1057	A186	40m Arab	.80	.30
1058	A186	80m Thoroughbred	1.75	.40
1059	A186	100m Pony	2.50	.50
	Nos. 1056-1059 (4)		5.45	1.50

Pres. Samora Machel (1933-1986) A187

1988, Oct. 19	Litho.	Perf. 11		
1060	A187 20m multi		.30	.30

Stamp Day A188

1988, Dec. 21	Perf. 11x11½, 11½x11			
1061	A188	20m P.O. trailer	.30	.30
1062	A188	40m Mailbox, vert.	.30	.30

Ports A189

1988, Nov. 30		Perf. 11		
1063	A189	25m Inhambane	.30	.30
1064	A189	50m Quelimane, vert.	.30	.30
1065	A189	75m Pemba	.50	.30
1066	A189	100m Beira	.60	.30
1067	A189	250m Nacala, vert.	1.50	.45
1068	A189	500m Maputo	3.50	.90
	Nos. 1063-1068 (6)		6.70	2.55

5th Frelimo Party Congress — A190

1989, Jan. 19				
1069	Strip of 5		3.00	3.00
a.	A190 25m Corn		.30	.30
b.	A190 50m Axe		.30	.30
c.	A190 75m Abstract shapes		.30	.30
d.	A190 100m 2 ½ Gearwheels		.40	.40
e.	A190 250m ½ Gearwheel		1.00	1.00

Printed se-tenant in a continuous design.

French Revolution Bicent. — A191

Designs: 100m, *Storming of the Bastille,* by Thevenin. 250m, *Liberty Guiding the People,* by Delacroix. 500m, *Declaration of the Rights of Man and the Citizen,* a print by Blanchard.

1989, Feb. 16		Perf. 11		
1070	A191 100m multi		.40	.30
1071	A191 250m multi		1.20	.45

Souvenir Sheet

| 1072 | A191 500m multi | | 2.40 | 2.40 |

No. 1072 is a continuous design.

Eduardo Chivambo Mondlane (1920-1969), Frelimo Party Founder, 20th Death Anniv. — A192

1989, Feb. 3	Litho.	Perf. 11		
1073	A192 25m blk, gold & dark red		.30	.30

Venomous Species — A193

1989, Mar. 23				
1074	A193	25m Pandinus	.30	.30
1075	A193	50m Naja haje	.30	.30
1076	A193	75m Bombus	.60	.30
1077	A193	100m Paraphysa	1.00	.30
1078	A193	250m Conus marmoreus	1.75	.45
1079	A193	500m Pterois volitans	3.50	.75
	Nos. 1074-1079 (6)		7.45	2.40

Coral A194

1989, May 2	Litho.	Perf. 11		
1080	A194	25m Acropora pulchra	.35	.30
1081	A194	50m Eunicella papilosa	.35	.30
1082	A194	100m Dendrophyla migrantus	.60	.30
1083	A194	250m Favia fragum	1.40	.55
	Nos. 1080-1083 (4)		2.70	1.45

1990 World Cup Soccer Championships, Italy — A195

Athletes executing various plays.

1989, June 22	Litho.	Perf. 11½x11		
1084	A195	30m multi	.25	.25
1085	A195	60m multi	.25	.25
1086	A195	125m multi	.40	.25
1087	A195	200m multi	.60	.35
1088	A195	250m multi	.80	.40
1089	A195	500m multi	1.75	.90
	Nos. 1084-1089 (6)		4.05	2.40

Lighthouses A196

1989, July 24	Litho.	Perf. 11		
1090	A196	30m Macuti	.25	.25
1091	A196	60m Pinda	.25	.25
1092	A196	125m Cape Delgado	.40	.25
1093	A196	200m Isle of Goa	.80	.35
1094	A196	250m Caldeira Point	1.00	.40
1095	A196	500m Vilhena	1.60	.90
	Nos. 1090-1095 (6)		4.30	2.40

Filigree Workmanship in Silver — A197

1989, Aug. 30	Litho.	Perf. 11x11½		
1096	A197	30m shown	.25	.25
1097	A197	60m Flower on band	.25	.25
1098	A197	125m Necklace	.40	.25
1099	A197	200m Decorative box	.75	.35
1100	A197	250m Utensils	.90	.40
1101	A197	500m Butterfly	1.50	.90
	Nos. 1096-1101 (6)		4.05	2.40

Natl. Liberation War, 25th Anniv. A198

1989, Sept. 25				
1102	A198 30m multicolored		.25	.25

Meteorological Instruments A199

Designs: 30m, Rain gauge. 60m, Weather system on radar. 125m, Instrument shelter. 200m, Computer monitor and keyboard.

1989, Oct. 12		Perf. 11½x11		
1103	A199	30m multicolored	.25	.25
1104	A199	60m multicolored	.30	.25
1105	A199	125m multicolored	.45	.25
1106	A199	200m multicolored	.90	.35
	Nos. 1103-1106 (4)		1.90	1.10

Souvenir Sheet

World Stamp Expo '89, Washington, DC — A200

1989, Nov. 17		Perf. 13½		
1107	A200 500m Washington Monument		3.00	3.00

Stamp Day — A201

1989, Dec. 21		Perf. 11½x11		
1108	A201	30m UPU emblem	.25	.25
1109	A201	60m P.O. emblem	.25	.25

Southern African Development Coordination Conf. (SADCC), 10th Anniv. — A201a

1990, Jan. 31		Perf. 11½x11		
1109A	A201a 35m multicolored		.30	.25

Textile Designs A202

1990, Feb. 28	Litho.	Perf. 11x11½		
1110	A202	42m multi, diff.	.25	.25
1111	A202	90m multi, diff.	.35	.25
1112	A202	150m multi, diff.	.50	.30
1113	A202	200m multi, diff.	.65	.35
1114	A202	400m multi, diff.	1.40	.65
1115	A202	500m multi, diff.	1.75	.90
	Nos. 1110-1115 (6)		4.90	2.70

Forts A203

1990, Mar. 20		Perf. 11x11½		
1116	A203	45m Sena	.25	.25
1117	A203	90m Santo Antonio	.35	.25
1118	A203	150m Santo Sebastiao	.50	.30
1119	A203	200m Santo Caetano	.65	.35

1120 A203 400m Our Lady of
　　　　　　Conceicao　　1.40　.65
1121 A203 500m Santo Luis　1.75　.90
　　Nos. 1116-1121 (6)　　4.90 2.70

Souvenir Sheet

Penny Black, Mozambique No.
1 — A204

1990, May 3　Litho.　Perf. 11½x11
1122 A204 1000m red, blk & bl　4.00 4.00
　Penny Black, 150th anniversary. Stamp
World London '90.

Bank of Mozambique, 15th
Anniv. — A205

1990, May 17　Litho.　Perf. 11x11½
1123 A205 100m multicolored　.40 .25

Natl.
Independence,
15th
Anniv. — A206

1990, June 25　　　Perf. 11
1124 A206 42.50m Eduardo
　　　　　　Mondlane　　.25 .25
1125 A206 150m Samora
　　　　　　Machel　　.45 .25

Endangered Species — A207

1990, Aug. 20　Litho.　Perf. 11x11½
1126 A207 42.50m Ceratotherium
　　　　　　simum　　　.40 .25
1127 A207 100m Dugong du-
　　　　　　gong　　　.55 .25
1128 A207 150m Loxodonta
　　　　　　africana　　.80 .30
1129 A207 200m Acinonix
　　　　　　jubatus　　1.00 .35
1130 A207 400m Lutra
　　　　　　maculicollis　2.25 .65
1131 A207 500m Eretmochelys
　　　　　　imbricata　　2.75 .90
　　Nos. 1126-1131 (6)　　7.75 2.70

Trees and
Plants — A208

1990, Oct. 15　Litho.　Perf. 11½x11
1132 A208 42.50m Dichrostachys
　　　　　　cinerea　　.25 .25
1133 A208 100m Queimadas　.35 .25
1134 A208 150m Casuariana
　　　　　　equisetifolia　.50 .30
1135 A208 200m Rhizophora
　　　　　　muronata　　.65 .35
1136 A208 400m Estrato
　　　　　　herbaceo　1.40 .65
1137 A208 500m Atzelia
　　　　　　cuanzensis　1.75 .90
　　Nos. 1132-1137 (6)　　4.90 2.70

Stamp
Day — A209

No. 1138: a, Pick-up at letter box. b, Canceling letters. c, Letter carrier. d, Delivery to
recipient.

1990, Dec. 21　Litho.　Perf. 11½x11
1138　　　　Strip of 4　　.80 .80
a.-d. A209 42.50m any single　.25 .25

Governmental
Departments
A210

Designs: No. 1139, Post Office Dept., 10th
anniv. No. 1140, Telecommunications Dept.

1991, Jan. 2
1139 A210 50m dk bl, red & blk　.25 .25
1140 A210 50m grn, blk & brn　.25 .25

Flowers — A211

1991, Feb. 25　Litho.　Perf. 11½x11
1141 A211 50m Strilitzia reginae　.25 .25
1142 A211 125m Anthurium an-
　　　　　　draeanum　　.40 .30
1143 A211 250m Zantedeschia
　　　　　　pentlandii　　.80 .60
1144 A211 300m Canna indica　1.00 .70
　　Nos. 1141-1144 (4)　　2.45 1.85

Alcelaphus
Lichtensteini
A212

1991, Mar. 27　　　　Perf. 14
1145　　　Strip of 4　　11.00 11.00
a. A212 50m Two adults　　.60 .40
b. A212 100m Adult　　　.90 .40
c. A212 250m Adult grazing　2.25 .90
d. A212 500m Nursing calf　3.75 2.25

Fountains of
Maputo — A213

Designs: 50m, Mpompine. 125m,
Chinhambanine. 250m, Sao Pedro-Zaza.
300m, Xipamanine.

1991, Apr. 15　Litho.　Perf. 11½x11
1146 A213 50m multicolored　.25 .25
1147 A213 125m multicolored　.30 .25
1148 A213 250m multicolored　.60 .30
1149 A213 300m multicolored　.75 .40
　　Nos. 1146-1149 (4)　　1.90 1.20

For surcharge see No. 1394.

Paintings by
Mozambican
Artists — A214

1991, May 18　Litho.　Perf. 11½x11
1150 A214 180m Samale　　.45 .25
1151 A214 250m Malangatana　.60 .30
1152 A214 560m Malangatana,
　　　　　　diff.　　1.40 .70
　　Nos. 1150-1152 (3)　　2.45 1.25

1992 Summer
Olympics,
Barcelona
A215

1991, June 25　Litho.　Perf. 11½x11
1153 A215 10m Swimming　　.25 .25
1154 A215 50m Roller hockey　.25 .25
1155 A215 100m Tennis　　.30 .25
1156 A215 200m Table tennis　.55 .30
1157 A215 500m Running　1.30 .60
1158 A215 1000m Badminton　2.75 1.30
　　Nos. 1153-1158 (6)　　5.40 2.95

For surcharges, see Nos. 1393, 1393A,
1395-1396.

British-Portuguese Agreement on
Mozambique Borders, Cent. — A216

1991, Oct. 9　Litho.　Perf. 11½x11
1159 A216 600m Map of 1890　1.00 .45
1160 A216 800m Map of 1891　1.25 .70

Souvenir Sheet

Phila Nippon '91 — A217

1991, Nov. 15　Litho.　Perf. 11½x11
1161 A217 1500m Map of Japan　3.00 3.00

Children's
Games — A218

1991, Dec. 21
1162 A218 40m Jumping rope　.25 .25
1163 A218 150m Spinning top　.25 .25
1164 A218 400m Marbles　　.55 .30
1165 A218 900m Hopscotch　1.30 .70
　　Nos. 1162-1165 (4)　　2.35 1.50

Stained Glass Windows — A219

No. 1166 — Various designs: a, 40m. b,
150m. c, 400m. d, 900m.

1992, Jan. 22
1166 A219 Block of 4, #a.-d.　1.90 1.90

Plants — A220

1992, Mar. 23　Litho.　Perf. 11½x11
1167 A220 300m Rhisophora
　　　　　　mucronata　　.60 .30
1168 A220 600m Cymodocea
　　　　　　ciliata　　1.25 .60
1169 A220 1000m Sophora in-
　　　　　　hambanensis　2.00 1.00
　　Nos. 1167-1169 (3)　　3.85 1.90

Traditional Tools — A221

1992, May 9
1170	A221	100m Spear, spear-thrower	.25	.25
1171	A221	300m Pitch forks	.60	.30
1172	A221	500m Hatchet	1.00	.55
1173	A221	1000m Dagger	2.00	1.00
		Nos. 1170-1173 (4)	3.85	2.10

Lubrapex '92, Lisbon.

A222

Birds: 150m, Chalcomitra amethystina. 200m, Ceropis senegalensis. 300m, Cossypha natalensis. 400m, Lamprocolius chloropterus. 500m, Malaconotus poliocephalus. 800m, Oriolus auratus.

1992, July 24   Litho.   Perf. 11½x11
1174	A222	150m multicolored	.40	.25
1175	A222	200m multicolored	.45	.25
1176	A222	300m multicolored	.70	.30
1177	A222	400m multicolored	.95	.45
1178	A222	500m multicolored	1.20	.45
1179	A222	800m multicolored	1.90	.90
		Nos. 1174-1179 (6)	5.60	2.60

Eduardo Mondlane University, 30th Anniv. — A223

1992, Aug. 21
1180	A223	150m grn, brn & blk	.40	.25

Traditional Musical Instruments A224

1992, Sept. 18
1181	A224	200m Phiane	.45	.25
1182	A224	300m Xirupe	.60	.25
1183	A224	500m Ngulula	1.10	.35
1184	A224	1500m Malimba	3.25	1.10
a.		Souvenir sheet of 4, #1181-1184, imperf.	4.00	4.00
		Nos. 1181-1184 (4)	5.40	1.95

Genoa '92. #1184a has simulated perfs.

No. 757 Surcharged

1992, Oct.   Litho.   Perf. 14½
1185	A108	50m on 50c #757	.70	.45

Intl. Conference on Nutrition — A225

1992, Oct. 16
1186	A225	450m multicolored	.90	.45

Parachuting A226

Various parchutists descending from sky.

1992, Nov. 10   Litho.   Perf. 11½x11
1187	A226	50m multicolored	.25	.25
1188	A226	400m multicolored	.60	.40
1189	A226	500m multicolored	.80	.45
1190	A226	1500m multicolored	2.40	1.30
		Nos. 1187-1190 (4)	4.05	2.40

No. 690 Surcharged

Methods and Perfs As Before
1992
1190A	A91	200m on 5e #690	—

Medals — A227

1993, Feb. 3   Litho.   Perf. 11½x11
1191	A227	400m Order of Peace & Amity	.30	.25
1192	A227	800m Baga moyo	.60	.40
1193	A227	1000m Order of Eduardo Mondlane	.85	.40
1194	A227	1500m War veterans	1.20	.60
		Nos. 1191-1194 (4)	2.95	1.65

Pollution A228

1993, Apr. 8   Perf. 11x11½
1195	A228	200m Deforestation	.40	.25
1196	A228	750m Factory smoke	1.10	.40
1197	A228	1000m Oil spill from ship	1.50	.45
1198	A228	1500m Automobile exhaust	2.25	.70
		Nos. 1195-1198 (4)	5.25	1.80

Natl. Parks A229

Park, animal, map: 200m, Gorongosa, lion. 800m, Banhine, giraffes. 1000m, Bazaruto, manatees. 1500m, Zinave, ostriches.

1993, May 25   Litho.   Perf. 11x11½
1199	A229	200m multicolored	.30	.25
1200	A229	800m multicolored	.85	.40
1201	A229	1000m multicolored	1.10	.45
1202	A229	1500m multicolored	1.75	.70
		Nos. 1199-1202 (4)	4.00	1.80

Natl. Conference on Culture — A230

1993, Sept. 27   Litho.   Perf. 11½x11
1203	A230	200m multicolored	.45	.25

Union of Portuguese Speaking Capitals A231

1993, July 30   Litho.   Perf. 11x11½
1204	A231	1500m multicolored	2.40	.60

Brasilana '93.

Forest Plants — A232

Designs: 200m, Cycas cercinalis. 250m, Cycas revoluta. 900m, Encephalartos ferox. 2000m, Equisetum ramosissimum.

1993, Dec. 29   Litho.   Perf. 11½x11
1205	A232	200m multicolored	.25	.25
1206	A232	250m multicolored	.25	.25
1207	A232	900m multicolored	.70	.40
1208	A232	2000m multicolored	1.60	.80
		Nos. 1205-1208 (4)	2.80	1.70

Medicinal Plants — A233

1994   Litho.   Perf. 11½x11
1209	A233	200m Anacardium occidentale	.25	.25
1210	A233	250m Sclerocarya caffra	.30	.25
1211	A233	900m Annona senegalensis	1.00	.30
1212	A233	2000m Crinum delagoense	2.25	.70
		Nos. 1209-1212 (4)	3.80	1.50

Nos. 699, 763-764, 772, 791-792, 797-798 Surcharged

1994
Perfs. and Printing Methods as Before
1212A	A94	50m on 5e #699	—	
1213	A109	50m on 7.50m #772	.40	.25
1214	A113	50m on 7.50m #791	.40	.25
1215	A114	50m on 7.50m #797	.40	.25
1216	A108	100m on 10m #763	.55	.25
1217	A114	100m on 12.50m #798	.55	.25
1218	A108	200m on 12.50m #764	1.10	.25
1219	A113	250m on 12.50m #792	1.30	.25
		Nos. 1213-1219 (7)	4.70	1.75

Size and location of surcharge varies. Surcharge on Nos. 1214-1215, 1219 does not contain an obliterator.
For additional surcharge, see No. 1391.

PHILAKOREA '94 — A234

Reptiles: 300m, Ichnotropis squamulosa. 500m, Lepidachelys olivacea. 2000m, Prosyma frontalis. 3500m, Rampholeon marshalli. 4000m, Snake eating a lizard.

1994, Aug. 16   Litho.   Perf. 11½x11
1220	A234	300m multicolored	.25	.25
1221	A234	500m multicolored	.40	.25
1222	A234	2000m multicolored	1.50	.45
1223	A234	3500m multicolored	2.60	.85
		Nos. 1220-1223 (4)	4.75	1.80

Souvenir Sheet
1224	A234	4000m multicolored	4.25	4.25

ICAO, 50th Anniv. A235

Designs: 300d, Crop dusting. 500m, Airport terminal. 2000m, Passenger jet in flight. 3500m, Maintenance man inspecting jet engine.

1994, Oct. 12   Litho.   Perf. 11x11½
1225	A235	300m multicolored	.25	.25
1226	A235	500m multicolored	.40	.25
1227	A235	2000m multicolored	1.50	.60
1228	A235	3500m multicolored	2.75	1.10
		Nos. 1225-1228 (4)	4.90	2.20

World Food Day — A236

1994, Oct. 24   Perf. 11½x11
1229	A236	2000m multicolored	2.25	.60

Lubrapex '94.

National Elections — A237

1994, Oct. 26
1230 A237 900m multicolored   1.10   .40

Fight Against Illegal Drugs — A238

Designs: 500m, Couple using drugs. 1000m, Hypodermic needle, couple tied in rope, skeleton. 2000m, Man with drug dependency. 5000m, Dog apprehending man with contraband.

1994, Dec. 7
1231 A238   500m multicolored   .45   .25
1232 A238 1000m multicolored   .85   .30
1233 A238 2000m multicolored   1.60   .70
1234 A238 5000m multicolored   4.25   1.75
    Nos. 1231-1234 (4)   7.15   3.00

Lusaka Accord, 20th Anniv. — A239

1994, Nov. 9
1235 A239 1500m multicolored   2.25   .45

Basketry — A240

1995, Apr. 15   Litho.   Perf. 11½x11
1236 A240   250m shown   .25   .25
1237 A240   300m Two-handled basket   .25   .25
1238 A240 1200m Round purse   .85   .35
1239 A240 5000m Purse, diff.   3.50   1.25
    Nos. 1236-1239 (4)   4.85   2.10

Clothing — A241

Various styles of women's traditional clothing.

1995, May 25
1240 A241   250m blue & multi   .25   .25
1241 A241   300m pink & multi   .25   .25
1242 A241 1200m blue & multi   .85   .35
1243 A241 5000m red & multi   3.50   1.25
    Nos. 1240-1243 (4)   4.85   2.10

Inauguration of Pres. Joaquim A. Chissano, Dec. 9, 1994 — A242

No. 1244: a, 900m, Natl. arms. b, 5000m, Pres. Chissano. c, 2500m, Natl. flag.

1995, June 25   Litho.   Perf. 11½x11
1244 A242   Strip of 3, #a.-c.   4.00   2.00
No. 1244 has a common inscription across the bottom.

Wild Animals — A243

Designs: 500m, Crassicadautus lombergi. 2000m, Tragelaphus strepsceros, horiz. 3000m, Potamochoerus porcus nyasae, horiz. 5000m, Tragelaphus scriptus.

Perf. 11½x11, 11x11½
1995, Aug. 29   Litho.
1245 A243   500m multicolored   .25   .25
1246 A243 2000m multicolored   .95   .30
1247 A243 3000m multicolored   1.50   .40
1248 A243 5000m multicolored   2.50   .70
    Nos. 1245-1248 (4)   5.20   1.65

FAO, 50th Anniv. — A244

1995, Oct. 16   Perf. 11½x11
1249 A244 5000m multicolored   1.50   .85

UN, 50th Anniv. — A245

1995, Oct. 24
1250 A245 5000m blue & black   1.50   .85

Nos. 647, 711, 713, 749, 763, 792, 798, 862, 929 Surcharged

Perfs. and Printing Methods as Before

1995, Oct. 4
1251 A114   250m on 12.50m #798   .25   .25
1252 A108   300m on 10m #763   .25   .25
1253 A113   500m on 12.50m #792   .25   .25
1253A A97   600m on 5m #711   —   —

1254 A81   900m on 12.50m #647   .45   .25
1255 A97   1000m on 12.50m #713   .45   .25
1256 A146 1500m on 16m #929   .80   .25
1257 A130 2000m on 16m #862   .95   .30
1258 A106 2500m on 12.50m #749   1.20   .40
    Nos. 1251-1258 (9)   4.60   2.20

UNICEF, 20th Anniv. — A246

1995, Nov. 22   Litho.   Perf. 11½
1259 A246 5000m multicolored   1.50   .85

Mozambique-South Africa Soccer Match — A247

Various soccer plays.

1996, Apr. 5   Litho.   Perf. 11x11½
1260 A247 1000m multicolored   .25   .25
1261 A247 2000m multicolored   .45   .30
1262 A247 4000m multicolored   .95   .55
1263 A247 6000m multicolored   1.50   .85
    Nos. 1260-1263 (4)   3.15   1.95

Masks — A248

Various masks.

1996, July 2   Litho.   Perf. 11½x11
1264 A248 1000m multicolored   .25   .25
1265 A248 2000m multicolored   .45   .30
1266 A248 4000m multicolored   .95   .55
1267 A248 6000m multicolored   1.50   .85
    Nos. 1264-1267 (4)   3.15   1.95

Red Cross of Mozambique, 15th Anniv. — A249

1996, July 10
1268 A249 5000m multicolored   1.20   .85

Endangered Wildlife — A250

1996, Sept. 3   Litho.   Perf. 11½x11
1269 A250 1000m Loxodona africana   .40   .25
1270 A250 2000m Ceratotherum simum   .70   .30

1271 A250 4000m Panthera pardus   1.40   .55
1272 A250 6000m Scotopelia peli   2.25   .85
    Nos. 1269-1272 (4)   4.75   1.95

Removal of Land Mines — A251

Designs: 2000m, Mine, tripwire across path. 6000m, Warning sign posted. 8000m, Using mine detector. 10,000m, Removing mine.

1996, Nov. 9   Litho.   Perf. 11½x11
1273 A251   2000m multicolored   .45   .25
1274 A251   6000m multicolored   1.30   .80
1275 A251   8000m multicolored   1.90   1.10
1276 A251 10,000m multicolored   2.40   1.30
    Nos. 1273-1276 (4)   6.05   3.45

Keep The City Clean Campaign A252

1996, Dec. 16   Litho.   Perf. 11½x11
1277 A252 2000m multicolored   .60   .30

Mozambique Postage Stamps, 120th Anniv. — A253

1996, Dec. 16   Litho.   Perf. 11½x11
1278 A253 2000m No. 1   .60   .30

Mozambique Boats — A254

1997, Apr. 10   Litho.   Perf. 11x11½
1279 A254   2000m Mitumbui   .45   .30
1280 A254   6000m Muterere   1.30   .95
1281 A254   8000m Lancha   1.90   1.30
1282 A254 10,000m Dau   2.40   1.60
    Nos. 1279-1282 (4)   6.05   4.15

Children's Day A255

1997, June 1   Litho.   Perf. 11x11½
1283 A255 2000m multicolored   .60   .30

Aquatic Birds A256

Designs: 2000m, Mycteria ibis. 4000m, Himantopus himantopus. 8000m, Calidris subminuta. 10,000m, Pelecanus onocrotalus.

Perf. 11½x11, 11x11½
1997, June 10

1284	A256	2000m multi, vert.	.70	.30
1285	A256	4000m multi, vert.	1.75	.60
1286	A256	8000m multi	3.00	1.30
1287	A256	10,000m multi, vert.	3.50	1.75
	Nos. 1284-1287 (4)		8.95	3.95

Independence of India, 50th Anniv. — A258a

1997   Litho.   Perf. 11x11½

1287A	A258a	2000m multi	1.20	.55

Insects A257

Designs: 2000m, Enaretta conifera. 6000m, Zographus heiroglyphicus. 8000m, Tragiscoschema bertolonii. 10,000m, Tragocephala ducalis.

1997, July 5   Litho.   Perf. 11x11½

1288	A257	2000m multicolored	.70	.30
1289	A257	6000m multicolored	2.00	.95
1290	A257	8000m multicolored	2.75	1.30
1291	A257	10,000m multicolored	3.25	1.60
a.	Souvenir sheet, #1288-1291		8.75	8.75
	Nos. 1288-1291 (4)		8.70	4.15

Labrapex '97 (#1291a).

Joao Ferreira dos Santos Group, Cent. — A258

1997, Sept. 5   Litho.   Perf. 11x11½

1292	A258	2000m multi	16.00	8.00

Protection of the Ozone Layer — A259

1997, Sept. 16   Litho.   Perf. 11½x11

1293	A259	2000m multicolored	.45	.30

Peace Accord, 5th Anniv. — A260

1997, Oct. 4   Litho.   Perf. 11½x11

1294	A260	2000m multi	.55	.30

Souvenir Sheet

Anhinga — A261

1997   Litho.   Perf. 11½x11

1295	A261	5000m multi	22.50	—

Food Products A262

1998, June 1   Litho.   Perf. 11x11½

1296	A262	2000m multicolored	.80	.40

Expo '98, Lisbon A263

1998, May 22

1297	A263	2000m Coelacanth	.95	.40

Nos. 660, 666, 730, 764, 797, 1002, 1009, 1011, 1021 Surcharged

Printing Methods and Perfs as before
1998 (?)

1298	A85	2000m on 12.50e #660	2.75	2.75
1299	A86	2000m on 12.50e #666	2.75	2.75
1299A	A175	2000m on 16m #1021	—	—
1300	A108	4000m on 12.50m #764	1.90	1.90
1301	A114	6000m on 7.50m #797	3.25	3.25
1302	A169	7500m on 16m #1002	3.50	3.50
1303	A102	10,000m on 12.50m #730	2.50	2.50
1304	A171	12,500m on 8m #1009	5.50	5.50
1305	A171	12,500m on 16m #1011	2.75	2.75
	Nos. 1298-1305 (8)		24.90	24.90

For surcharges, see Nos. 1400-1400A.

Diana, Princess of Wales (1961-97) A264

Nos. 1306-1308: Various portraits.
No. 1309, 30,000m, Wearing Red Cross vest. No. 1310, 30,000m, Wearing purple dress.

1998   Litho.   Perf. 13½

1306	A264	2000m Sheet of 9, #a.-i.	5.75	5.75
1307	A264	5000m Sheet of 9, #a.-i.	10.00	10.00
1308	A264	8000m Sheet of 9, #a.-i.	13.00	13.00

Souvenir Sheets

1309-1310	A264	Set of 2	12.00	12.00

Nos. 1309-1310 each contain one 42x60mm stamp.

No. 923 Surcharged in Silver

1998   Litho.   Perf. 14

1311	A145	500m on 16m multi	—	—

Promotion of Breast Feeding — A265

1998   Litho.   Perf. 11½x11

1312	A265	2000m multi	.95	.30

Mother Teresa (1910-97) A266

1998   Perf. 11x11½

1313	A266	2000m multi	.95	.30

UPAP, 18th Anniv. A267

1998, Oct. 9   Perf. 11½x11

1314	A267	2000m multi	.80	.40

Mother's Day — A268

Designs: 2000m, Breast feeding. 4000m, Teacher. 8000m, Using computer. 10,000m, Woman in field.

1998, June 25   Perf. 11½x11

1315-1318	A268	Set of 4	8.00	8.00

For surcharge, see No. 1417.

Plants — A269

Designs: 2000m Garcinia livingstonei. 7500m, Tabernaemontana elegans. 12,500m, Ximenia caffra. 25,000m, Syzygium guineense. 50,000m, Uapaca kirkiana.

1998, Oct. 9   Perf. 11¾x12

1319-1322	A269	Set of 4	12.00	12.00

Souvenir Sheet

1323	A269	50,000m multi	12.00	12.00

For surcharges, see Nos. 1418-1419, 1741-1742.

Dwellings A270

Various dwellings: 2000m, 4000m, 6000m, 8000m, 10,000m, 15,000m, 20,000m, 30,000m, 50,000m, 100,000m.

1998   Litho.   Perf. 11x11¼

1324-1333	A270	Set of 10	20.00	20.00

For surcharges, see Nos. 1399A, 1418-1419.

Souvenir Sheets

I Love Lucy — A270a

Designs: No. 1333A, 35,000m, Lucy wearing hat. No. 1333B, 35,000m, Lucy as ballet dancer.

1999   Litho.   Perf. 13½

1333A-1333B	A270a	Set of 2	12.00	12.00

A271

Diana, Princess of Wales (1961-97) — A272

No. 1334: a, purple, shown. b, Dull brown, looking left. c, Orange brown, wearing pearls. d, Olive green. e, Purple, wearing feathers & hat, looking right. f, Red brown, wearing round earring.

No. 1335 — Diana with: a, Large white collar, earring (purple vignette). b, Hat, looking left (red violet vignette). c, White dress (red brown vignette). d, Dangling earrings (brown vignette). e, Patterned dress (blue violet vignette). f, Flower bouquet (olive green vignette).

1999   **Perf. 14**
1334 A271 6500m Sheet of 6,
    #a.-f.   8.00 8.00
1335 A271 6500m Sheet of 6,
    #a.-f.   8.00 8.00
Litho. & Embossed
Die Cut Perf. 7
1336 A272 25,000m gold & multi   9.50 9.50
Issued: #1336, 6/30.

The Three Stooges — A272a

No. 1336A: b, Joe Besser, Larry, Moe, frying pan. c, Shemp wearing hat. d, Moe and Larry putting pan on Joe Besser's head. e, Moe with pipe. f, Larry and Moe pouring liquids on Curly's head. g, Larry wearing hat. h, Joe Besser and Larry, pulling Moe's tooth. i, Curly. j, Shemp, Larry and Moe.
No. 1336K, 35,000m, Larry in pink shirt. No. 1336L, 35,000m, Larry holding shovel.

1999   **Litho.**   **Perf. 13½**
1336A A272a 5000m Sheet of
    9, #b-j   7.00 7.00
Souvenir Sheets
1336K-1336L A272a   Set of
     2   12.00 12.00

Trains — A273

2000m, DE-AC Blue Tiger, Germany. #1338, 2500m, DB 218 (red & black), Germany. #1339, 3000m, Mt. Pilatus inclined railroad car, Switzerland. 3500m, Berlin subway train, Germany.
No. 1341: a, DB V200, Germany. b, Union Pacific, US. c, Class 613, Germany. d, Canadian Pacific 4242, Canada. e, Duchess of Hamilton, Great Britain. f, Pacific Delhi, India. g, ISA, South Africa. h, DR VT 18-16-07, Germany. i, DB-DE, Australia.

No. 1342: a, DB 218 (green & yellow), Germany. b, QJ Class 2-10-2, China. c, 232 232.9, Germany. d, Flying Scotsman, Scotland. e, WR 360 CH, Germany. f, Henschel 2-8-2. g, Santa Fe 39C, US. h, Balkan Express, Greece. i, DB 218 (red & white), Germany.
No. 1343, 25,000m, Steam 2-8-2, Germany. No. 1344, 25,000m, DMU, Germany.

1999, Oct. 12   **Litho.**   **Perf. 14**
1337-1340 A273 Set of 4   2.10 2.10
1341 A273 2500m Sheet of 9,
    #a.-i.   4.00 4.00
1342 A273 3000m Sheet of 9,
    #a.-i.   4.75 4.75
Souvenir Sheets
1343-1344 A273   Set of 2   10.00 10.00

Betty Boop — A273a

No. 1344A: b, Seated on motorcycle, winking, wearing cap. c, Seated on motocycle, winking, without cap. d, Wearing cap. e, Seated on motorcycle, wearing cap, not winking. f, Hands folded across handlebars. g, Riding motorcycle. h, Hitchhiking. i, Seated on motorcycle, wearing bandana. j, Seated on motorcycle, hand raised.
No. 1344K, 35,000m, Seated on motorcycle, hand raised. No. 1344L, 35,000m, Seated next to motorcycle.

1999   **Litho.**   **Perf. 13½**
1344A A273a 3500m Sheet of
    9, #b-j   6.50 6.00
Souvenir Sheets
1344K-1344L A273a   Set of
     2   12.00 12.00

Cats — A274

No. 1345, 4000m: a, Chartreux. b, Australian Mist. c, Egyptian Mau. d, Scottish Fold. e, Cornish Rex. f, Abyssinian.
No. 1346, 4000m: a, Himalayan. b, Balinese. c, Persian. d, Turkish Van. e, Norwegian Forest Cat. f, Maine Coon Cat.
No. 1347, 25,000m, Ragdoll. No. 1348, 25,000m, Siamese.

2000, Mar. 29   **Litho.**   **Perf. 14**
Sheets of 6, #a-f
1345-1346 A274 Set of 2   9.50 9.50
Souvenir Sheets
1347-1348 A274 Set of 2   9.50 9.50
Dated 1999.

Dogs — A275

No. 1349, 4500m, vert.: a, Shetland sheepdog. b, Basenji. c, Poodle. d, St. Bernard. e, Shar Pei. f, Spinone Italiano.
No. 1350, 4500m, vert.: a, Jack Russell terrier. b, Schweizer Laufhund. c, Japanese Spitz. d, Australian Shepherd. e, Saluki. f, Siberian Husky.
No. 1351, 25,000m, Border Collie. No. 1352, 25,000m, Eurasier.

2000, Mar. 29   **Litho.**   **Perf. 14**
Sheets of 6, #a-f
1349-1350 A275 Set of 2   10.00 10.00
Souvenir Sheets
1351-1352 A275 Set of 2   9.50 9.50
Dated 1999.

Dinosaurs — A276

No. 1353, 3000m: a, Pteranodon. b, Bothriospondylus. c, Iguanodon. d, Stegosaurus. e, Nodosaurus. f, Elaphrosaurus. g, "Petrolaccisaurus." h, Procompsognathus. i, Dimetrodon.
No. 1354, 3000m: a, Plesiosaur. b, "Ceresiosaurus." c, Cryptoclidus. d, Placochelys. e, Plotosaurus. f, Ichthyosaurus. g, Platecarpus. h, Archelon. i, Mosasaur.
No. 1355, 20,000m, Tyrannosaurus Rex. No. 1356, 20,000m, "Honodus."

2000, Apr. 28
Sheets of 9, #a-i
1353-1354 A276 Set of 2   9.50 9.50
Souvenir Sheets
1355-1356 A276 Set of 2   6.50 6.50
Dated 1999.

A277

Butterflies — A278

Designs: 2000m, Palla ussheri. 2500m, Euschemon rafflesia. No. 1359, 3000m, Buttus philenor. No. 1360, 3000m, Hypolimnas bolina. 3500m, Lycorea cleobaea. 4000m, Dynastor napoleon. No. 1363, 4500m, Callimorpha dominula. 5000m, Pereute leucodrosime.
No. 1365, 4500m: a, Tisiphone abeone. b, Pseudacraea boisduvalii. c, Mylothris chloris. d, Papilio glaucus. e, Mimacraea marshalli. f, Gonepteryx cleopatra.
No. 1366, 4500m: a, Palla ussheri, diff. b, Hypolimnas salmacis. c, Pereute leucodrosime, diff. d, Anteos clorinde. e, Colias eurytheme. f, Hebomoia glaucippe.
No. 1367, 4500m, horiz.: a, Thauria aliris. b, Catocala ilia. c, Colotis danae. d, Agrias claudia. e, Euploe core. f, Scoptes alphaeus.
No. 1368, 4500m, horiz.: a, Phoebis philea. b, Anteos clorinde, diff. c, Arhopala amantes. d, Mesene phareus. e, Euploea mulciber. f, Heliconius ricini.
No. 1369, 4500m, vert.: a, Euphaedra neophorn. b, Catopsilia florella. c, Charaxes bohemani. d, Junonia orithya. e, Colotis danae, diff. f, Eurytela dryope.
No. 1370, 4500m, vert.: a, Papilio demodocus. b, Kallimoides rumia. c, Danaus chrysippus. d, Palla ussheri, diff. e, Hypolimnas salmacis, diff. f, Zinina otis.
No. 1371, 20,000m, Papilio glaucus, diff. No. 1372, 20,000m, Delias mysis, horiz. No. 1373, 20,000m, Mylothris chloris, horiz. No. 1374, 20,000m, Loxura atymnus, horiz. No. 1375, 20,000m, Hemiolaus coeculus. No. 1376, 20,000m, Euxanthe wakefieldii.

2000, Apr. 28
1357-1364 A277 Set of 8   4.75 4.75
Sheets of 6, #a-f
1365-1368 A277 Set of 4   19.00 19.00
1369-1370 A278 Set of 2   9.50 9.50
Souvenir Sheets
1371-1374 A277 Set of 4   16.00 16.00
1375-1376 A278 Set of 2   6.50 6.50
Dated 1999.

Worldwide Fund for Nature — A279

No. 1377: a, Two adult gnus. b, Adult and juvenile gnus. c, Lion catching gnu. d, Adult gnu.
Illustration reduced.

2000, Apr. 28
1377 A279 6500m Block of 4,
    #a-d   4.75 4.75
Dated 1999.

Wild Cats — A280

No. 1378, 3000m: a, Leptailurus several. b, Panthera onca. c, Panthera tigris corbetti. d, Puma concolor. e, Panthera leo persica. f, Felis pardina. g, Lepardus pardalia. h, Acinonyx jubatus. i, Felis wrangeli.

No. 1379, 3000m: a, Felis silvestris grampia b, Felis ourata. c, Panthera tigris tigris. d, Panthera uncia. e, Felis caracal. f, Panthera pardus. g, Panthera tigris amoyensis. h, Panthera onca (spotted). i, Neofelis nabuloso.

No. 1380, 25,000m, Panthera tigris altaica. No. 1381, 25,000m, Panthera tigris, horiz.

2000, Apr. 28
Sheets of 9, #a-i
1378-1379 A280 Set of 2 9.50 9.50
Souvenir Sheets
1380-1381 A280 Set of 2 8.00 8.00
Dated 1999.

Flowers — A281

No. 1382, 3000m: a, Laetiocattleya. b, Papaver oriental. c, Anemone blanda. d, Ipoema alba. e, Phalaenopsis luma. f, Iris ensata. g, Coenagrion puella. h, Rosa raubritter. i, Iris x daylilies hybridizers.

No. 1383, 3000m: a, Lilium auratum. b, Oncidium macianthum. c, Dendrobium. d, Cobaea scandens. e, Paphiopedilum gilda. f, Papaver nudicaule. g, Colocasia esculenta. h, Carinatum tricolor. i, Phalaenopsis.

No. 1384, vert.: a, Euanthe sanderiana. b, Torenia fourleri. c, "Amor Perfeito." d, Borboleto matizada. e, Dendrobium primulinum. f, "Lasurstern" Clematite. g, Helianthus annuus. h, Jacinto grana.

No. 1385, 20,000m, Viola x wittrockiana. No. 1386, 20,000m, Nelimbo nucifera. No. 1387, 20,000m, Gerbera jamesonii. No. 1388, 20,000m, Narcissuses and anemones. Illustration reduced.

2000, Apr. 28
Sheets of 9, #a-i
1382-1383 A281 Set of 2 9.50 9.50
1384 A281 3500m Sheet of 8,
          #a-h 5.50 5.50
Souvenir Sheets
1385-1388 A281 Set of 4 12.50 12.50
Dated 1999.

Nos. 792, 797, 1147, 1153, 1154, 1156, 1214 Surcharged

2000 Methods & Perfs. As Before
1390 A114 10,000m on 7.50m
          #797 — —
1391 A113 10,000m on 50m on
          7.50m
          #1214 — —
1392 A113 10,000m on 12.50m
          #792 — —
1393 A215 17,000m on 10m
          #1153 — —
1393A A215 17,000m on 50m
          #1154 — —
1394 A213 17,000m on 125m
          #1147 — —
1395 A215 17,000m on 200m
          #1156 — —
1396 A215 17,000m on 1000m
          #1158 — —

No. 1393A and 1396 lack "2000" date in surcharge. No. 1391 contains "Correios — 2000) in surcharge.

The editors suspect that other surcharges may exist and would like to examine any examples.

No. 763   No. 764
Surcharged in   Surcharged in
Black and Blue   Black and
                  Brown

2000 Litho. Perf. 14½
1398 A108 2000m on 10m #763 —
1399 A108 2000m on 12.50m
          #764 —

No. 1325
Overprinted

2000 Method and Perf. as Before
1399A A270 4000m on #1325 — —

Nos. 1300, 1301
Ovptd. in Brown or
Black

2000 Litho. Perf. 14½
1400 A108 4000m on 12.50m
          #1300 (BR) — —
1400A A114 6000m on 7.50m
          #1301 —

Sports and Chess — A282

No. 1401, 6500m: a, Cycling. b, Volleyball. c, Boxing. d, Weight lifting. e, Fencing. f, Judo.

No. 1402, 9000m — Chess pieces: a, Six pieces, red queen at left. b, Six pieces, gray bishop fifth from left. c, Five knights. d, Six rooks, elephant rook at left. e, Six pawns. f, Six pawns, spearholder pawn at right.

No. 1403, 9500m — Chess champions: a, Paul Morphy. b, Mikhail Botvinnik. c, Emanuel Lasker. d, Wilhelm Steinitz. e, José Raul Capablanca. f, Howard Staunton.

No. 1404, 12,500m: a, Cricket batsmen and bowler. b, Three cricket batsman, one fielder. c, Polo, rider with red shirt at left. d, Polo, player wearing #1 at right. e, Golf, flag stick at right. f, Golf, woman golfer at right.

No. 1405, 14,000m: a, Tennis, woman with headband at right. b, Table tennis, players with blue shirts. c, Table tennis, player with pink shirt in center. d, Tennis, two men at left. e, Tennis, man with cap at left. f, Table tennis, player with red shirt at left.

No. 1406, 35,000m, Table tennis. No. 1407, 35,000m, Chess player Garry Kasparov.

2000 Litho. Perf. 13¼
Sheets of 6, #a-f
1401-1405 A282 Set of 5 40.00 40.00
Souvenir Sheets
1406-1407 A282 Set of 2 17.50 17.50
Nos. 1401-1405 each contain six 59x29mm stamps.

A283

Marine Life — A284

No. 1408: a, Threadfin butterflyfish. b, Common clownfish. c, Regal tang. d, Regal angelfish. e, Copperbanded butterflyfish. f, Blue-girdled angelfish. g, Sharpnosed pufferfish. h, Humbug damselfish. i, Tailbar lionfish. j, Forcepsfish. k, Powder blue surgeon. l, Moorish idol.

No. 1409, 9500m: a, Oceanic whitetip shark. b, Gray reef shark. c, Tiger shark. d, Silky shark. e, Basking shark. f, Epaulette shark.

No. 1410, 9500m: a, Sperm whale. b, Giant squid. c, Killer whale. d, Great white shark. e, Manta ray. f, Octopus.

No. 1411, 9500m: a, Blue whale. b, Dolphinfish. c, Hammerhead shark. d, Whale shark. e, Leatherback turtle. f, Porkfish.

No. 1412, 35,000m, Wimple fish. No. 1413, 35,000m, Queen angelfish.

No. 1414, 35,000m, Phryniethys wedli. No. 1415, 35,000m, Bull shark. No. 1416, 35,000m, Spotted trunkfish.

2001, Aug. 8 Perf. 14
1408 A283 4550m Sheet of 12,
          #a-l 8.00 8.00
Sheets of 6, #a-f
1409-1411 A284 Set of 3 24.00 24.00

Souvenir Sheets
1412-1413 A283 Set of 2 9.50 9.50
1414-1416 A284 Set of 3 14.50 14.50

Nos. 763, 1316-
1317, 1329 and
1330 Surcharged

Methods and Perfs As Before
2001 ?
1416A A268 3000m on 4000m
          #1316 — —
1417 A268 3000m on 8000m
          #1317 — —
1418 A270 3000m on 15,000m
          #1329 — —
1419 A270 3000m on 20,000m
          #1330 — —
1420 A108 5000m on 10m #763 — —

2000 European Soccer
Championships — A285

No. 1421, 10,000m: a, Luis Figo dribbling ball. b, Fernando Couto. c, Figo diving. d, Sergio Conceicao. e, Nuno Gomes. f, Rui Costa.

No. 1422, 17,000m: a, Nicolas Anelka. b, Didier Deschamps. c, Emmanuel Petit. d, Thiorry Henry. e, Marcel Desailly. f, Zinedine Zidane.

No. 1422G, 75,000m, Zinedine Zidane. No. 1422H, 75,000m, Rivaldo.

2001 Litho. Perf. 13¼x12¾
Sheets of 6, #a-f
1421-1422 A285 Set of 2 17.50 17.50
Souvenir Sheets
1422G-1422H A285 Set of 2 16.00 16.00

2000 Summer Olympics
Medalists — A286

No. 1423, 8500m: a, Domenico Fioravanti. b, Stacy Dragila. c, Pieter van den Hoogenband. d, David O'Connor. e, Venus Williams. f, Maurice Greene. g, Joy Fawcett. h, Marion Jones. i, Patricio Ormazabal and Jeff Agoos.

No. 1424, 10,000m: a, Agnes Kovacs. b, Yuulia Raskina. c, Kong Linghui and Liu Guoliang. d, Nicolas Gill. e, Anky van Grunsven. f, Brian Olson. g, Wang Nan. h, Megan Quann. i, Venus Williams.

No. 1425, 17,000m: a, Vince Carter. b, Blaine Wilson. c, Steve Keir. d, Wen Xiao Wang and Chris Xu. e, Venus and Serena Williams. f, Gu Jun and Ge Fei.

No. 1426, 20,000m: a, Clara Hughes. b, Martina Hingis. c, Otilla Badescu. d, Isabel Fernandez. e, Coralie Simmons. f, Mia Hamm.

No. 1427, 28,000m: a, Patrick Rafter. b, Tadahiro Nomura. c, Seiko Iseki. d, Michael Dodge. e, Ann Dow. f, David Beckham.

No. 1428, 50,000m, Andre Agassi. No. 1429, 50,000m, Chang Jun Gao and Michelle Do. No. 1430, 50,000m, Kong Linghui. No.

1431, 100,000m, Michelle Do. No. 1432, 100,000m, Serena Williams. No. 1433, 100,000m, Christophe Legout.

2001   **Litho.**
Sheets of 9, #a-i
1423-1424	A286	Set of 2	22.50	22.50

Sheets of 6, #a-f
1425-1427	A286	Set of 3	25.00	25.00

Souvenir Sheets
1428-1433	A286	Set of 6	47.50	47.50

Chess Champions — A287

No. 1434, 10,000m: a, Mikhail Botvinnik. b, Garry Kasparov. c, Wilhelm Steinitz. d, Emanuel Lasker. e, Paul Morphy. f, Anatoly Karpov. g, Tigran Petrossian. h, Mikhail Tal. i, José Raul Capablanca.
No. 1435, 10,000m: a, Judith Polgar (wearing brown sweater). b, Xie Jun. c, Zsuza Polgar. d, Nana Ioseliani. e, Alisa Galliamova. f, Judith Polgar (head in hands). g, Judith Polgar (wearing blouse). h, Monica Calzetta. i, Anjelina Belakovskaia.
No. 1436, 100,000m, Kasparov. No. 1437, 100,000m, Judith Polgar.

2001   **Perf. 13¼x12¾**
Sheets of 9, #a-i
1434-1435	A287	Set of 2	20.00	20.00

Souvenir Sheets
1436-1437	A287	Set of 2	22.00	22.00

2002 Winter Olympics, Salt Lake City — A288

No. 1438, 17,000m: a, Martin Brodeur. b, Svetlana Vysokova. c, Ray Bourque and Patrik Elias. d, Rachel Belliveau. e, Scott Gomez and Janne Laukkanen. f, Sonja Nef.
No. 1439, 20,000m: a, Rusty Smith. b, Sandra Schmirler. c, Totmianina and Marinin. d, Brigitte Obermoser. e, Roman Turek. f, Jennifer Heil.
No. 1440, 28,000m: a, Kovarikova and Novotny. b, Li Song. c, Armin Zoeggeler. d, Michael von Gruenigen. e, Tami Bradley. f, Chris Drury, Turner Stevenson and Greg de Vries.
No. 1441, 50,000m, Armin Zoeggeler. No. 1442, 75,000m, Tommy Salo. No. 1443, 100,000m, Jayne Torvill and Christopher Dean.

2001   **Litho.**
Sheets of 6, #a-f
1438-1440	A288	Set of 3	40.00	40.00

Souvenir Sheets
1441-1443	A288	Set of 3	24.00	24.00

On illustrated sheets lacking design information the lettering of minors starts with the upper left stamp, goes right and down and ends with the lower right stamp.

2002 World Cup Soccer Championships, Japan and Korea — A289

No. 1444: a, Filippo Inzaghi. b, Georghe Hagi. c, Gabriel Batistuta pointing. d, Mateja Kezman. e, Ivan Zamorano. f, Michael Owen wearing blue uniform.
No. 1445: a, Marcio Amoroso. b, Alessandro Nesta. c, Robbie Keane. d, Michel Owen kicking ball. e, Stefan Effenberg. f, Oliver Kahn.
No. 1446: a, Zinedine Zidane without ball. b, Zoran Mirkovic. c, Robbie Fowler with fist raised. d, Romario wearing red jersey. e, Francesco Totti. f, Ryan Giggs.
No. 1447: a, Javier Saviola. b, Alan Smith. c, Raul Gonzalez. d, Dwight Yorke. e, Joe Cole. f, David Beckham wearing red jersey.
No. 1448: a, Angelo Peruzzi. b, Jaap Stam. c, Jamie Redknapp. d, Rivaldo with ball at feet. e, Alan Shearer. f, Boudewijn Zenden.
No. 1449: a, Hernan Jorge Crespo. b, Gianluigi Buffon. c, Arnold Bruggink. d, Antonio Cassano. e, Mohamed Kallon. f, Jonathan Bachini.
No. 1450: a, Didier Deschamps. b, Cafu wearing green jersey. c, Dennis Bergkamp. d, Lilian Thuram. e, David Beckham wearing red jersey, diff. f, Francesco Totti, diff. g, Carsten Jancker. h, Martin Palermo. i, Andy Cole running left.
No. 1451: a, David Beckham sitting on ball. b, Edgar Davids wearing orange shirt. c, Michael Owen with hands on ball. d, Andy Cole with one leg raised. e, Ronaldo sitting. f, Emmanuel Petit with ball. g, Rivaldo with ball at chest. h, Robbie Fowler looking at ball. i, Romario wearing blue jacket.
No. 1452: a, César Manuel Rui Costa. b, Hidetoshi Nakata. c, Luis Figo. d, Michael Owen. e, Leonardo. f, Thierry Henry. g, Fabien Barthez. h, Oliver Kahn. i, Antonio Conte.
No. 1453: a, Shinji Ono. b, Rigobert Song. c, Matias Jesus Almeyda. d, Ronaldinho. e, Gabriel Batistuta wearing striped jersey. f, Rivaldo sitting on ground. g, Thierry Henry. h, Zinedine Zidane kicking ball. i, Ronaldo with ball.
No. 1454: a, Florain Maurice. b, Nicolas Anelka. c, Zinedine Zidane without ball, wearing striped jersey. d, Kazuyoshi Miura. e, Patrick Vieira. f, Gianfranco Zola. g, Emmanuel Petit without ball. h, Roberto Carlos. i, Teddy Sheringham.
No. 1455, 75,000m, Fabien Barthez. No. 1456, 75,000m, Edgar Davids wearing striped shirt. No. 1457, 75,000m, Cafu wearing red shirt.
No. 1458, 100,000m, Ronaldo wearing striped uniform. No. 1459, 100,000m, Romario wearing yellow shirt. No. 1460, 100,000m, Rivaldo dribbling ball. No. 1461, 100,000m, Nwankwo Kanu. No. 1462, 100,000m, Michael Owen wearing yellow shirt. No. 1463, 100,000m, Franz Beckenbauer. No. 1464, 100,000m, Pelé. No. 1465, 100,000m, Diego Maradona.

2001   **Litho.**   **Perf. 13¼x12¾**
Sheets of 6, #a-f
1444	A289	5000m	multi	3.25	3.25
1445	A289	10,000m	multi	6.75	6.75
1446	A289	12,000m	multi	8.00	8.00
1447	A289	15,000m	multi	10.00	10.00
1448	A289	17,000m	multi	11.50	11.50
1449	A289	20,000m	multi	13.50	13.50
Nos. 1444-1449 (6)				53.00	53.00

Sheets of 9, #a-i
1450	A289	5000m	multi	5.25	5.25
1451	A289	5000m	multi	5.25	5.25
1452	A289	5000m	multi	5.25	5.25
1453	A289	8500m	multi	8.75	8.75
1454	A289	8500m	multi	8.75	8.75
Nos. 1450-1454 (5)				33.25	33.25

Souvenir Sheets
1455-1457	A289	Set of 3	3.25	3.25
1458-1465	A289	Set of 8	115.00	115.00

On illustrated sheets lacking design information, the lettering of minors starts with the upper left stamp, continues right and down and ends with the lower right stamp.

Paintings

Madonna Paintings — A290

Alfred Sisley — A291

Hieronymus Bosch — A292

Pieter Brueghel — A293

Paul Cézanne — A294

Salvador Dali — A295

Henri Matisse — A296

Michelangelo — A297

Vincent van Gogh — A298

Johannes Vermeer — A299

Michelangelo — A300

Amadeo Modigliani — A301

Paintings of Angels — A302

Gustav Klimt — A303

Perf. 13¼x12¾

2001, Dec. 28				**Litho.**

Sheets of 6, #a-f

1466	A290	5000m multi	3.25	3.25
1467	A291	10,000m multi	6.75	6.75
1468	A292	12,000m multi	8.00	8.00
1469	A293	12,000m multi	8.00	8.00
1470	A294	12,000m multi	8.00	8.00
1471	A295	12,000m multi	8.00	8.00
1472	A296	12,000m multi	8.00	8.00
1473	A297	12,000m multi	8.00	8.00
1474	A298	12,000m multi	8.00	8.00
1475	A299	12,000m multi	8.00	8.00
1476	A300	15,000m multi	10.00	10.00
1477	A301	15,000m multi	10.00	10.00
1478	A302	17,000m multi	12.00	12.00
1479	A303	28,000m multi	19.00	19.00
	Nos. 1466-1479 (14)		125.00	125.00

Paintings

Marc Chagall — A304

Salvador Dali — A305

Edgar Degas — A306

Paul Delvaux — A307

Paul Gauguin — A308

Pablo Picasso — A309

Pierre Auguste Renoir — A310

Henri de Toulouse-Lautrec — A311

Vincent van Gogh — A312

Pablo Picasso — A313

Individual stamps depicting various works of art lack titles. On Nos. 1489-1512 artist name is in margin.

No. 1489, Pieter Breughel. No. 1490, Lucas Cranach. No. 1491, Paul Delvaux. No. 1492, El Greco. No. 1493, Wassily Kandinsky. No. 1494, Gustav Klimt. No. 1495, Johannes Vermeer. No. 1496, Paul Cézanne. No. 1497, Marc Chagall. No. 1498, Albrecht Dürer. No. 1499, Thomas Gainsborough. No. 1500, Francisco de Goya. No. 1501, Edouard Manet. No. 1502, Claude Monet. No. 1503, Henri Matisse. No. 1504, Camille Pissarro. No. 1505, Vincent van Gogh. No. 1506, Salvador Dali. No. 1507, Paul Gauguin. No. 1508, Joan Miró. No. 1509, Amadeo Modigliani. No. 1511, Picasso, diff. No. 1512, Henri de Toulouse-Lautrec. No. 1513, Religious icon.

Perf. 13¾x12¾

2001, Dec. 28				**Litho.**

Sheets of 9, #a-i

1480	A304	10,000m multi	8.75	8.75
1481	A305	10,000m multi	8.75	8.75
1482	A306	10,000m multi	8.75	8.75
1483	A307	10,000m multi	8.75	8.75
1484	A308	10,000m multi	8.75	8.75
1485	A309	10,000m multi	8.75	8.75
1486	A310	10,000m multi	8.75	8.75
1487	A311	10,000m multi	8.75	8.75
1488	A312	10,000m multi	8.75	8.75
	Nos. 1480-1488 (9)		78.75	78.75

Souvenir Sheets

1489	A313	50,000m multi	4.00	4.00
1490	A313	50,000m multi	4.00	4.00
1491	A313	50,000m multi	4.00	4.00
1492	A313	50,000m multi	4.00	4.00
1493	A313	50,000m multi	4.00	4.00
1494	A313	50,000m multi	4.00	4.00
1495	A313	50,000m multi	4.00	4.00
1496	A313	75,000m multi	6.25	6.25
1497	A313	75,000m multi	6.25	6.25
1498	A313	75,000m multi	6.25	6.25
1499	A313	75,000m multi	6.25	6.25
1500	A313	75,000m multi	6.25	6.25
1501	A313	75,000m multi	6.25	6.25
1502	A313	75,000m multi	6.25	6.25
1503	A313	75,000m multi	6.25	6.25
1504	A313	75,000m multi	6.25	6.25
1505	A313	75,000m multi	6.25	6.25
1506	A313	100,000m multi	8.25	8.25
1507	A313	100,000m multi	8.25	8.25
1508	A313	100,000m multi	8.25	8.25
1509	A313	100,000m multi	8.25	8.25
1510	A313	100,000m shown	8.25	8.25
1511	A313	100,000m multi	8.25	8.25
1512	A313	100,000m multi	8.25	8.25
1513	A313	100,000m multi	8.25	8.25
	Nos. 1489-1513 (25)		156.50	156.50

Souvenir Sheet

Lance Armstrong, Cyclist — A314

2001	**Litho.**		**Perf. 13¼x12¾**	
1514	A314	100,000m multi	11.00	11.00

2004 Olympic Games, Athens.

New Year 2002 (Year of the Horse) — A315

No. 1515 — Chinese characters in: a, Yellow. b, Purple. c, Pink. d, Brown. 22,000m, Maroon, vert.

2002, May 6	**Litho.**		**Perf. 13¼**	
1515	A315	11,000m Sheet of 4, #a-d	5.25	5.25

Souvenir Sheet

Perf. 13½x13¼

1516	A315	22,000m multi	2.75	2.75

No. 1516 contains one 28x42mm stamp.

2002 Winter Olympics, Salt Lake City A316

Designs: 10,000m, Freestyle skiing. 17,000m, Freestyle skiing, vert.

Perf. 13¼x13½, 13½x13¼

2002, May 6				
1517-1518	A316	Set of 2	2.75	2.75

Intl. Year of Mountains A317

Designs: No. 1519, 17,000m, Mt. Namuli. No. 1520, 17,000m, Mt. Binga.

No. 1521: a, Mt. Kenya, Kenya. b. Mt. Cook, New Zealand. c. Mt. Ararat, Turkey. d. Mt. Paine, Chile. e. Mt. Everest, Nepal. f. Mt. Kilimanjaro, Tanzania. 50,000m, Zugspitze, Germany.

2002, May 6   **Perf. 13¼x13½**
1519-1520 A317 Set of 2   3.25 3.25
1521 A317 17,000m Sheet of 6, #a-f   9.50 9.50

Souvenir Sheet
1522 A317 50,000m multi   4.75 4.75

20th World Scout Jamboree, Thailand — A318

No. 1523, horiz.: a, 1933 Jamboree patch. b, 19th World Jamboree patch. c, Patch and mascot. d, Jamboree emblem, scout. No. 1524, Scout.

2002, May 6   **Perf. 13¼x13½**
1523 A318 28,000m Sheet of 4, #a-d   11.50 11.50

Souvenir Sheet
Perf. 13½x13¼
1524 A318 28,000m multi   3.00 3.00

Amerigo Vespucci (1452-1512), Explorer — A319

No. 1525, horiz.: a, Vespucci observing stars. b, Brotogeris chiriri, ship. c, Huts, ship. 50,000m, Map of voyages to South America.

2002, May 6   **Perf. 13¼x13½**
1525 A319 30,000m Sheet of 3, #a-c   8.75 8.75

Souvenir Sheet
Perf. 13½x13¼
1526 A319 50,000m multi   4.75 4.75

Ships — A320

No. 1527, 13,500m: a-f, Various unnamed ships (shown).
No. 1528, 13,500m: a, Viking ship. b, Kayak. c, Gondola, bridge. d, Fishing boat. e, Light ship. f, Tugboat.
No. 1529, 40,000m, Aircraft carrier. No. 1530, 40,000m, Ship's figurehead, vert.

Perf. 13¼x13½, 13½x13¼
2002, May 6
Sheets of 6, #a-f
1527-1528 A320 Set of 2   14.50 14.50
Souvenir Sheets
1529-1530 A320 Set of 2   7.50 7.50

2002 World Cup Soccer Championships, Japan and Korea — A321

No. 1531, 28,000m: a, Zico. b, 1958 World Cup poster. c, Flag, player from Nigeria. d, Flag, player from Morocco. e, Gwangju Stadium, Korea, horiz. (56x42mm).
No. 1532, 28,000m: a, 1966 World Cup poster. b, Paolo Rossi. c, Flag, player from Denmark. d, Flag, player from Colombia. e, Inchon Munhak Stadium, Korea, horiz. (56x42mm)
No. 1533, 50,000m, Pele. No. 1534, 50,000m, Morlock, horiz.

Perf. 13½x13¼, 13¼x13½
2002, May 6   **Sheets of 5, #a-e**
1531-1532 A321 Set of 2   27.50 27.50
Souvenir Sheets
1533-1534 A321 Set of 2   9.50 9.50

A322

A323

Princess Diana (1961-97) — A324

No. 1538, 50,000m, Brown background. No. 1539, 50,000m, Purple background. No. 1540, 50,000m, Pink lilac background.

2002, May 6   **Perf. 13½x13¼**
1535 A322 28,000m Sheet of 4, #a-d   11.00 11.00
1536 A323 28,000m Sheet of 4, #a-d   11.00 11.00
1537 A324 28,000m Sheet of 4, #a-d   11.00 11.00
Nos. 1535-1537 (3)   33.00 33.00
Souvenir Sheets
1538-1540 A324 Set of 3   14.50 14.50

Butterflies — A325

Designs: 5000m, Papilio demoleus. No, 1542, 10,000m, Euschemom rafflesia. 17,000m, Liphyra brassolis. 28,000m, Mimacraea marshalli.
No. 1545, 10,000m: a, Eurema brigitta. b, Loxura atymunus. c, Arhopala amantes. d, Junonia coenia. e, Eurides isabella. f, Hiliconius ricini. g, Zipaetis scylax. h, Cepheuptychia cephus. i, Philaethria dido.
No. 1546, 10,000m: a, Parides coon. b, Delias mysis. c, Troides brookiana. d, Syrmatia dorilas. e, Danis danis. f, Lycaena dispar. g, Mesene phareus. h, Kallima inachus. i, Morpho rhetenor.
No. 1547, 50,000m, Papilio cresphontes. No. 1548, 50,000m, Ornithoptera alexandrae caterpillar.

2002, June 17   **Perf. 14**
1541-1544 A325 Set of 4   5.25 5.25
Sheets of 9, #a-i
1545-1546 A325 Set of 2   16.00 16.00
Souvenir Sheets
1547-1548 A325 Set of 2   11.00 11.00

Fauna, Flora and Mushrooms — A326

No. 1549, 10,000m: a, Pandion haliaetus. b, Flying squirrel. c, Fox squirrel. d, Agelaius phoeniceus. e, Papilio polyxenes. f, Didelphus virginiana. g, Hyla crucifer. h, Odocoileus virginianus, standing. i, Procyon lotor.
No. 1550, 10,000m: a, Heraclides cresphontes. b, Tyto alba. c, Drocopus pileatus. d, Cypripedium parviflorum, Archilochus colobris. e, Vulpes vulpes. f, Odocoileus virginianus. g, Enallagma sp. h, Amanita muscaria. i, Tamiasciurus hudsonicus.

2002, June 17   **Perf. 14**
Sheets of 9, #a-i
1549-1550 A326 Set of 2   16.00 16.00

Flowers — A327

No. 1551, 10,000m: a, Viola jeannie, Viola cultivar. b, Sunflower Moonshadow. c, Momo botan. d, Schomburgkia orchid. e, Dahlia hybrid. f, Sparaxis elegans harlequin. g, Dianhus. h, Camassia leichtlinii, Tulipa saxatilis. i, Pansy hybrid.
No. 1552, 10,000m, horiz.: a, Hemerocallis. b, Narcissus (Nazcissys). c, Hybrid tea rose. d, Rainbow Promised Cayenne Capers and flying insect. e, Anemone cordnazia. f, Hymenocallis narcissiflora. g, Hymenocallis. h, Tulipa. i, Lachenalia aloides, Meconopsis poppies.
No. 1553, 10,000m, horiz.: a, Narcissus. b, L. bulbiferun var. Croceum. c, Iris purpureobractea. d, Neomarica caerulea. e, Peonia lactiflora, Primula chungensis, Viola cornuta. f, Rainbow Promised Cayenne Capers and beetle. g, Iris purpureobractea (puzpuzeobractea). h, Tuberous begonia cultivar. i, Oriental hybrid lily.

2002, June 17   **Perf. 14**
Sheets of 9, #a-i
1551-1553 A327 Set of 3   16.00 16.00

Dogs, Cats and Horses — A328

No. 1554, 17,000m — Dogs: a, Labrador retriever. b, Bulldog. c, Cocker spaniel. d, Golden retriever. e, Boxer. f, Bloodhound.
No. 1555, 17,000m — Cats: a, Maine Coon. b, Cornish Rex. c, La Perm. d, Sphynx. e, Siamese. f, Persian.
No. 1556, 17,000m — Horses: a, Hanoverian. b, Haflinger. c, Nonius. d, Belgian heavy drafts. e, Australian-bred Arab. f, Thoroughbred.
No. 1557, 40,000m, Basset hound. No. 1558, 50,000m, Chestnut Oriental Longhair cat. No. 1559, 50,000m, Don horses.

2002, June 17   **Perf. 13¼**
Sheets of 6, #a-f
1554-1556 A328 Set of 3   19.00 19.00
Souvenir Sheets
1557-1559 A328 Set of 3   15.00 15.00

Dinosaurs
A329

Designs: 5000m, Protosaurus. No. 1561, 10,000m, Psittacosaurus. 17,000m, Torosaurus. 28,000m, Triceratops.
No. 1564, 10,000m: a, Diplodocus head. b, Pterosaurs. c, Diplodocuses. d, Afrovenator. e, Parasaurolophus. f, Ramphorhynchus. g, Lambeosaur. h, Euoplocephalus. i, Cynodont.
No. 1565, 10,000m: a, Brachiosaur. b, Monoclonius. c, Homalocephalus. d, Pterodactyl. e, Deinonychus. f, Archaeopteryx. g, Cretaceous landscape. h, Hypsilophodon. i, Lystrosaur.
No. 1566, 50,000m, Baryonyx. No. 1567, 50,000m, Styracosaurus, vert.

2002, June 17   Perf. 14
1560-1563 A329   Set of 4   5.25   5.25
Sheets of 9, #a-i, + 3 labels
1564-1565 A329   Set of 2   11.00 11.00
Souvenir Sheets
1566-1567 A329   Set of 2   11.00 11.00

A330

Birds — A331

Designs: No. 1568, 5000m, Tachymarptis melba. No. 1569, 5000m, Falco tinnunculus. No. 1570, 10,000m, Pitta angolensis. No. 1571, 10,000m, Ardea cinerea. No. 1572, 17,000m, Corythaeola cristata. No. 1573, 28,000m, Butastur rufipennis.
No. 1574, 5000m, Creagrus furcatus. No. 1575, 10,000m, Larosterna inca. No. 1576, 17,000m, Pelecanus crispus. No. 1577, 28,000m, Morus bassanus.
No. 1578, 10,000m: a, Phaeton aethereus. b, Catharacta maccormicki. c, Diomedea bulleri. d, Puffinus iherminieri. e, Oceanites oceanicus. f, Pterodroma hasitata. g, Fregata magnificens. h, Sula nebouxii. i, Uria aagle.
No. 1579, 17,000m: a, Psittacus erithacus. b, Ficedula hypleuca. c, Tchagra senegala. d, Oriolus oriolus. e, Luscinia megarhynchos. f, Halcyon malimbica.
No. 1580, 17,000m: a, Coracias garrulus. b, Estrilda astrild. c, Upupa epops. d, Merops apiaster. e, Ploceus cucullatus. f, Clamator glandarius.
No. 1581, 50,000m, Falco subbuteo. No. 1582, 50,000m, Strix varia. No. 1583, 50,000m, Butorides striatus. No. 1584, 50,000m, Actophilornis africanus, horiz.
No. 1585, 50,000m, Spheniscus demersus. No. 1586, 50,000m, Rhynchops niger, horiz.

2002, June 17
1568-1573 A330   Set of 6   6.50   6.50
1574-1577 A331   Set of 4   5.25   5.25
1578 A331 10,000m Sheet of
         9, #a-i   7.75   7.75
Sheets of 6, #a-f
1579-1580 A330   Set of 2   17.50 17.50
Souvenir Sheets
1581-1584 A330   Set of 4   17.00 17.00
1585-1586 A331   Set of 2   8.50   8.50

For surcharges see Nos. 1740, 1748.

Worldwide Fund for Nature (WWF)
A332

African savannah elephant: Nos. 1587a, 1588a, Herd. Nos. 1587b, 1588b, And birds. Nos. 1587c, 1588c, With juvenile. Nos. 1587d, 1588d, With rainbow.

2002, Sept. 20   Perf. 13¼x13½
Size: 40x26½mm
Large Year
1587   Strip of 4   8.50   8.50
a.-d. A332 19,000m Any single   1.90   1.75
Size: 39x25mm
Small Year
1588   Miniature sheet of 4
            + 4 labels   12.00 12.00
a.-d. A332 19,000m Any single   2.50   2.25

Princess Diana — A333

Pope John Paul II — A334

Elvis Presley — A335

Marilyn Monroe — A336

Marilyn Monroe — A337

Lord Robert Baden-Powell, Scout Emblem, Mushrooms and Flowers — A338

Astronauts and the Concorde — A339

Composers — A340

Louis Pasteur and Dogs — A341

Robert Stephenson and Locomotives — A342

Pope John Paul II — A343

Pope John Paul II, Madonna and Child — A344

Pope John Paul II, Madonna and Child — A345

Robert Stephenson — A346

Robert Stephenson — A347

No. 1593 — Famous men: a, Henri Dunant. b, Theodore Roosevelt. c, Albert Einstein. d, Ernest Hemingway. e, Thomas Nast. f, Albert Camus.

No. 1594 — Egyptian rulers: a, Seti I. b, Djedefre. c, Smekhkare. d, Seti II. e, Senusret III. f, Tutankhamun.

No. 1597: a, Michael Collins. b, Concorde. c, John Glenn. d, Concorde, diff. e, Neil Armstrong. f, Concorde, diff.

No. 1598 — Chess players and pieces: a, Tigran Petrosian, Lions emblem. b, Robert Fischer, Rotary emblem. c, Boris Spassky, Lions emblem. d, Raul Capablanca, Rotary emblem. e, Max Euwe, Lions emblem. f, Emanuel Lasker, Rotary emblem.

No. 1599 — Nobel Prize winners: a, Albert Einstein. b, Dalai Lama. c, Winston Churchill. d, Hideki Yukawa. e, Albert Schweitzer. f, Linus Pauling.

No. 1600 — Scout emblem and: a, Lord Robert Baden-Powell. b, Morpho aega, Baden-Powell. c, Prepona meander, Baden-Powell. d, Charaxes bernardus, Baden-Powell. e, Hypolimnas salmacis, Baden-Powell. f, Morpho rhetenor, Baden-Powell.

No. 1601 — Egyptian rulers: a, Netjenkhet Djoser. b, Tutankhamun. c, Neferefre. d, Amenhotep III. e, Pepi I. f, Amenmesses.

No. 1602 — Composers: a, Antonio Vivaldi. b, Franz Liszt. c, Ludwig van Beethoven. d, Wolfgang Mozart.

No. 1603 — Famous Men: a, Che Guevara. b, Pope John Paul II (blue gray background). c, Dr. Martin Luther King, Jr. d, Mao Zedong.

No. 1604 — Princess Diana and Pope John Paul II: a, Princess Diana in deep blue dress. b, Diana holding flowers. c, Pope John Paul II, hand showing. d, Pope John Paul II.

No. 1605 — Nelson Mandela and: a, Heulandite. b, Adamite. c, Wulfenite. d, Hemimorphite.

No. 1606 — Auto racing: a, Ayrton Senna. b, Modern race car. c, Old race car. d, Juan Manuel Fangio.

No. 1607 — Egyptian queens (tan background): a, Nefertiti facing right. b, Cleopatra VII. c, Nefertiti facing left. d, Nefertiti facing forward.

No. 1608 — Egyptian rulers (gray background): a, Nefertari. b, Tutankhamun. c, Tuthmosis. d, Nefertiti.

No. 1609 — Egyptian rulers (green background): a, Amenhotemp II. b, Merenptah. c, Amenophis IV. d, Tuthmosis.

No. 1610 — Famous people: a, Dalai Lama. b, Mother Teresa. c, Pope John Paul II. d, Mahatma Gandhi.

No. 1611 — Explorers: a, Vasco da Gama. b, Ferdinand Magellan. c, Christopher Columbus. d, Amerigo Vespucci.

No. 1612 — Aviation: a, Antoine de Saint-Exupéry. b, Charles Lindbergh standing. c, Lindbergh seated. d, Concorde.

No. 1613 — Lions and Rotary Founders: a, Paul Harris (color picture), Rotary emblem. b, Melvin Jones (sepia picture), Lions emblem. c, Harris (sepia picture), Rotary emblem. d, Jones (color picture), Lions emblem.

No. 1614 — Film personalities: a, Charlie Chaplin. b, Frank Sinatra. c, Alfred Hitchcock. d, Walt Disney.

No. 1615: a, Scipionyx. b, Beipiaosaurus. c, Haroun Tazieff and vanadinite. d, Tazieff and adamite.

No. 1616 — Famous men: a, Winston Churchill. b, John F. Kennedy. c, Konrad Adenauer. d, Charles de Gaulle.

No. 1619 — Scientists: a, Charles Darwin, Byronosaurus. b, Alexander Fleming, Tricholoma terreum. c, Fleming, Boletus edulis. d, Darwin, Irratator.

No. 1620 — Famous men: a, Albert Schweitzer. b, Claude Bernard. c, Henri Dunant. d, Raoul Follerau.

No. 1621: a, John J. Audubon. b, Audubon, Aix sponsa. c, Audubon, Toxastoma montanum, Ixoreus naevius. d, Audubon, Loxia leucoptera.

No. 1625, John Glenn. No. 1626, Lord Robert Baden-Powell. No. 1627, Victor Hugo. No. 1628, John F. Kennedy. No. 1629, Princess Diana. No. 1630, Wolfgang Mozart. No. 1631, Alexander Fleming. No. 1632, Garry Kasparov. Nos. 1633, 1634, Marilyn Monroe. No. 1635, Mother Teresa. No. 1636, Henri Dunant. No. 1637, Nelson Mandela. No. 1638, Elvis Presley. No. 1639, Vasco da Gama. No. 1640, Paul Émile Victor. No. 1641, Tutankhamun. No. 1642, Nefertiti. No. 1643, John J. Audubon, Patagioenas leucophal. No. 1644, Audubon, Quiscalus quiscula.

2002, Sept. 30   Perf. 13¼x12¾
Sheets of 6, #a-f

1589	A333	15,000m multi	8.50	8.50
1590	A334	15,000m multi	8.50	8.50
1591	A335	15,000m multi	8.50	8.50
1592	A336	15,000m multi	8.50	8.50
1593	A336	15,000m multi	8.50	8.50
1594	A336	15,000m multi	8.50	8.50
1595	A337	17,000m multi	9.50	9.50
1596	A338	17,000m multi	9.50	9.50
1597	A339	17,000m multi	9.50	9.50
1598	A339	17,000m multi	9.50	9.50
1599	A339	17,000m multi	9.50	9.50
1600	A339	17,000m multi	9.50	9.50
1601	A339	17,000m multi	9.50	9.50

Sheets of 4, #a-d

1602	A340	5000m multi	1.90	1.90
1603	A340	20,000m multi	7.75	7.75
1604	A340	20,000m multi	7.75	7.75
1605	A340	20,000m multi	7.75	7.75
1606	A340	20,000m multi	7.75	7.75
1607	A340	20,000m multi	7.75	7.75
1608	A340	20,000m multi	7.75	7.75
1609	A340	20,000m multi	7.75	7.75
1610	A340	22,000m multi	8.50	8.50
1611	A340	22,000m multi	8.50	8.50
1612	A340	22,000m multi	8.50	8.50
1613	A340	25,000m multi	9.25	9.25
1614	A340	25,000m multi	9.25	9.25
1615	A340	25,000m multi	9.25	9.25
1616	A340	25,000m multi	9.25	9.25
1617	A341	25,000m multi	9.25	9.25
1618	A342	25,000m multi	9.25	9.25
1619	A342	33,000m multi	12.50	12.50
1620	A342	33,000m multi	12.50	12.50
1621	A342	33,000m multi	12.50	12.50
		Nos. 1589-1621 (33)	292.15	292.15

Souvenir Sheets

1622	A343	88,000m shown	8.50	8.50
1623	A344	88,000m shown	8.50	8.50
1624	A345	88,000m shown	8.50	8.50
1625	A345	88,000m multi	8.50	8.50
1626	A345	88,000m multi	8.50	8.50
1627	A345	88,000m multi	8.50	8.50
1628	A345	88,000m multi	8.50	8.50
1629	A345	88,000m multi	8.50	8.50
1630	A345	88,000m multi	8.50	8.50
1631	A345	88,000m multi	8.50	8.50
1632	A345	88,000m multi	8.50	8.50
1633	A345	88,000m multi	8.50	8.50
1634	A345	110,000m multi	10.50	10.50
1635	A345	110,000m multi	10.50	10.50
1636	A345	110,000m multi	10.50	10.50
1637	A345	110,000m multi	10.50	10.50
1638	A345	110,000m multi	10.50	10.50
1639	A345	110,000m multi	10.50	10.50
1640	A345	110,000m multi	10.50	10.50
1641	A345	110,000m multi	10.50	10.50
1642	A345	110,000m multi	10.50	10.50
1643	A345	110,000m multi	10.50	10.50
1644	A345	110,000m multi	10.50	10.50
1645	A346	110,000m shown	10.50	10.50
1646	A347	110,000m shown	10.50	10.50
		Nos. 1622-1646 (25)	238.50	238.50

World of the Sea

Ships — A348

Aircraft — A349

Sea Lions — A350

Polar Bears — A351

Killer Whales — A352

Whales — A353

Dolphins — A354

Fish — A355

Fish — A356

Fish — A357

Fish — A358

Sea Horses — A359

Penguins — A360

Penguins — A361

Sea Birds — A362

Sea Birds — A363

Sea Birds — A364

Crustaceans — A365

Snails — A366

Jellyfish — A367

Coral — A368

Submarines — A369

Lighthouses — A370

Ship — A371

Ship — A372

Fish — A373

Fish — A374

Sea Horse — A375

Sea Horse — A376

Penguin — A377

Penguin — A378

Sea Bird — A379

Sea Bird — A380

Sea Bird — A381

No. 1668 — Marine invertebrates: a, Phyllidia elegans. b, Phyllidia coelestis. c, Hypselodoris bullocki. d, Glossodoris hikuerensis. e, Glossodoris cruentus. f, Chromodoris leopardus.

No. 1669 — Shells: a, Murex brassica (showing shell opening). b, Cassis cornuta. c, Strombus gigas. d, Rapana rapiformis (showing shell opening). e, Chicoreus ramosus. f, Bursa bubo.

No. 1670 — Shells: a, Chicoreus virgineus. b, Tonna galea. c, Murex erythrostomus. d, Strombus gigas. e, Murex brassica (showing front of shell). f, Rapana rapiformis (showing front of shell).

No. 1671 — Tubeworms and seaweed: a, Kallymenia cribosa. b, Ulva lactuca. c, Chondrus crispus. d, Gigartina disticha. e, Palmaria palmata. f, Filogranella elatensis.

No. 1685, Seal flensing. No. 1686, Polar bear. No. 1687, Killer whale breaching surface. No. 1688, Whales underwater. No. 1689, Dolphins with open mouths. No. 1690, Lobster. No. 1691, Jellyfish. No. 1692, Coral and fish. No. 1693, Filogranella elatensis. No. 1694, Chromodoris leopardus. No. 1695, Tonna galea. No. 1696, Turbo marmoratus. No. 1697, Submarine. No. 1698, Christopher Columbus.

Perf. 12¾x13¼, 13¼x12¾
2002, Nov. 1
Sheets of 6, #a-f

1647	A348	5000m multi	3.25	3.25
1648	A349	17,000m multi	9.50	9.50
1649	A350	17,000m multi	9.50	9.50
1650	A351	17,000m multi	9.50	9.50
1651	A352	17,000m multi	9.50	9.50
1652	A353	17,000m multi	9.50	9.50
1653	A354	17,000m multi	9.50	9.50
1654	A355	17,000m multi	9.50	9.50
1655	A356	17,000m multi	9.50	9.50
1656	A357	17,000m multi	9.50	9.50
1657	A358	17,000m multi	9.50	9.50
1658	A359	17,000m multi	9.50	9.50
1659	A360	17,000m multi	9.50	9.50
1660	A361	17,000m multi	9.50	9.50
1661	A362	17,000m multi	9.50	9.50
1662	A363	17,000m multi	9.50	9.50
1663	A364	17,000m multi	9.50	9.50
1664	A365	17,000m multi	9.50	9.50
1665	A366	17,000m multi	9.50	9.50
1666	A367	17,000m multi	9.50	9.50
1667	A368	17,000m multi	9.50	9.50
1668	A368	17,000m multi	9.50	9.50
1669	A368	17,000m multi	9.50	9.50
1670	A368	17,000m multi	9.50	9.50
1671	A368	17,000m multi	9.50	9.50
1672	A369	20,000m multi	12.00	12.00
1673	A370	33,000m multi	20.00	20.00
Nos. 1647-1673 (27)			263.25	263.25

Souvenir Sheets

1674	A371	110,000m shown	11.00	11.00
1675	A372	110,000m shown	11.00	11.00
1676	A373	110,000m shown	11.00	11.00
1677	A374	110,000m shown	11.00	11.00
1678	A375	110,000m shown	11.00	11.00
1679	A376	110,000m shown	11.00	11.00
1680	A377	110,000m shown	11.00	11.00
1681	A378	110,000m shown	11.00	11.00
1682	A379	110,000m shown	11.00	11.00
1683	A380	110,000m shown	11.00	11.00
1684	A381	110,000m shown	11.00	11.00
1685	A350	110,000m multi	11.00	11.00
1686	A351	110,000m multi	11.00	11.00
1687	A352	110,000m multi	11.00	11.00
1688	A353	110,000m multi	11.00	11.00
1689	A354	110,000m multi	11.00	11.00
1690	A365	110,000m multi	11.00	11.00
1691	A367	110,000m multi	11.00	11.00
1692	A368	110,000m multi	11.00	11.00
1693	A368	110,000m multi	11.00	11.00

1694	A368	110,000m multi	11.00	11.00
1695	A368	110,000m multi	11.00	11.00
1696	A368	110,000m multi	11.00	11.00
1697	A369	110,000m multi	11.00	11.00
1698	A369	110,000m multi	11.00	11.00
	Nos. 1674-1698 (25)		275.00	275.00

Zeppelins — A382

No. 1699, 28,000m, horiz.: a, Ferdinand von Zeppelin, brown and yellow background. b, LZ-2 in flight. c, LZ-10 in flight. d, LZ-1, purple background.

No. 1700, 28,000m, horiz.: a, LZ-1, blue and yellow background. b, LZ-2 tethered. c, LZ-10 above sheep. d, Ferdinand von Zeppelin with binoculars.

No. 1701, 50,000m, Ferdinand von Zeppelin, in military uniform. No. 1702, 50,000m, Ferdinand von Zeppelin, in suit.

2002, Nov. 18   *Perf. 13¼x13½*
Sheets of 4, #a-d

1699-1700	A382	Set of 2	15.00	15.00

Souvenir Sheets
Perf. 13½x13¼

1701-1702	A382	Set of 2	6.75	6.75

Locomotives — A383

No. 1703, 17,000m, horiz.: a, London, Midland and Scottish Railway, England. b, Great Northern Railway, Ireland. c, Southern Railway, England. d, Great Northern Railway, US. e, Chicago, Milwaukee, St. Paul and Pacific Railroad, US. f, London and Northeastern Railway, England.

No. 1704, 17,000m, horiz.: a, Great Southern Railway, Spain. b, Shantung Railway, China. c, Shanghai-Nanking Railway, China. d, Austrian State Railway. e, Victorian Government Railways, Australia. f, London and Northwester Railways, England.

No. 1705, 17,000m, horiz.: a, Western Railways, France. b, Netherlands State Railway (green locomotive on bridge). c, Great Indian Peninsula Railway. d, Paris-Orleans Railway, France. e, Madras and Southern Mahratta Railway, India. f, Netherlands State Railway (green locomotive).

No. 1706, 50,000m, London, Brighton and South Coast Railway, England. No. 1707, 50,000m, New York Central, US.

2002, Nov. 18   *Perf. 13¼x13½*
Sheets of 6, #a-f

1703-1705	A383	Set of 3	20.00	20.00

Souvenir Sheets

1706-1707	A383	Set of 2	6.75	6.75

A384

Automobiles — A385

No. 1708, 13,000m: a, 1912 Bentley. b, 1914 Delage Grand Prix. c, 1949, Healey Silverstone. d, 1922 Duesenberg. e, Delage 1500cc Grand Prix. f, 1961 Ferrari 375/F1.

No. 1709, 13,000m: a, 1906 Mercedes. b, 1951 Morgan. c, 1912 Sunbeam. d, 1922 Sunbeam. e, 1925 Sunbeam Tiger. f, 1908 Austin 100hp.

No. 1710, 17,000m: a, 1937, Bugatti Type 57 Alalante coupe. b, 1948 Tucker Torpedo. c, 1966 Honda S 800m. d, 1946 Cisitalia 202 GT. e, 1958 Chevrolet Impala. f, 1934 Cadillac LaSalle convertible.

No. 1711, 17,000m: a, 1908 Austin. b, 1937 Studebaker coupe. c, 1930 Bugatti Type 40GP. d, 1931 Ford Model A roadster. e, 1937 Alfa Romeo 2900B. f, 1937 Cord 812.

No. 1712, 40,000m, 1931 Alfa Romeo. No. 1713, 40,000m, 1911 Marmon Wasp.

No. 1714, 50,000m, 1957 Plymouth Fury. No. 1715, 50,000m, 1928 Mercedes-Benz SSK.

Perf. 13¼x13½, 13½x13¼
2002, Nov. 18
Sheets of 6, #a-f

1708-1709	A384	Set of 2	10.00	10.00
1710-1711	A385	Set of 2	12.50	12.50

Souvenir Sheets

1712-1713	A384	Set of 2	5.50	5.50
1714-1715	A385	Set of 2	6.75	6.75

Pottery — A386

Designs: 1000m, Pote. 2000m, Chaleira. 4000m, Taças. 5000m, Cantaro. 17,000m, Panela. 28,000m, Alguidar. 50,000m, Jarra. 100,000m, Bilhas.

2002, Dec. 2   *Perf. 12¾*

1716-1723	A386	Set of 8	8.00	8.00

Dated 2001.
For surcharge see No. 1739.

Justino Chemane, Composer of National Anthem — A387

2003, July 11

1724	A387	6000m multi	.55	.55

Minerals — A388

Designs: 5000m, Bauxite. 14,000m, Marble. 19,000m, shown. 33,000m, Gold.

2004, Apr. 30

1725-1728	A388	Set of 4	6.00	6.00

Dated 2003.

Paintings by Jean-Auguste Ingres — A389

Paintings by James Tissot — A390

Paintings by Pierre-Auguste Renoir — A391

Paintings by Edgar Degas — A392

Various unnamed paintings.

2004, June 17   Litho.   *Perf. 13½x13*

1729	A389	6500m	Sheet of 6, #a-f	9.50	9.50
1730	A390	6500m	Sheet of 6, #a-f	9.50	9.50
g.			Souvenir sheet, #1730e	1.60	1.60
1731	A391	10,000m	Sheet of 6, #a-f	11.50	11.50
1732	A392	17,000m	Sheet of 6, #a-f	13.00	13.00
	Nos. 1729-1732 (4)			43.50	43.50

Diplomatic Relations Between Mozambique and People's Republic of China, 30th Anniv. — A395

No. 1735: a, Flags, buildings and animals. b, Arms, Admiral Zheng He, building, vase, sculpture.
Illustration reduced.

2005, June 25   Litho.   *Perf. 13¼*

1735	A395	33,000m	Pair, #a-b	5.50	5.50

Exists imperf.

Southern African Development Community, 25th Anniv. — A396

2005, Aug. 11   *Perf. 11¼x11*

1736	A396	8000m multi	.65	.65

Traditional African Medicine Day A397

2005, Aug. 31   *Perf. 11x11¼*

1737	A397	8000m multi	.65	.65

World Summit on the Information Society, Tunis — A398

2005, Oct. 9   *Perf. 11¼x11*

1738	A398	8000m multi	.65	.65

Nos. 1320, 1576, 1717 Surcharged Like No. 1417 and

No. 1321
Surcharged in
Black and Silver

Methods and Perfs as Before 2005 ?

1739	A386	6000m on 2000m #1717	.50	.50
1740	A331	8000m on 17,000m #1576	.70	.70
1741	A269	33,000m on 7500m #1320	2.75	2.75
1742	A269	33,000m on 12,500m #1321 (B&S)	2.75	2.75
		Nos. 1739-1742 (4)	6.70	6.70

Mozambique Telecommunications
Company, 25th Anniv. — A399

2006, June 10   Litho.   Perf. 11½x11
1743 A399 8000m multi   .65   .65

No. 1743 also has denomination expressed in revalued meticals, which were put into service on July 1.
For surcharge, see No. 1747.

Presidential Initiative Against
AIDS — A400

Pres. Armando Guebuza: 8m, Holding gavel. 16m, Behind microphones. 33m, With arm raised.

2006, Oct. 9   Perf. 11x11½
1744-1746 A400 Set of 3   4.50   4.50

World Vision —
A400a

2006   Litho.   Perf. 11½x11
1746A A400a 33m multi   —

An additional stamp was issued in this set. The editors would like to examine any example.

No. 1743
Surcharged

2006   Litho.   Perf. 11½x11
1747 A399 33m on 8000m #1743   —

The following items inscribed "Moçambique Correios" have been declared "illegal" by Mozambique postal officials:
Sheet of nine stamps of various denominations depicting Princess Diana;
Sheet of six 5000m stamps depicting the art of Paul Delvaux;
Sheet of six 17,000m stamps depicting the art of Edgar Degas;
Stamps depicting the art of Lucas Cranach;
Six different 15,000m souvenir sheets of one depicting Pope John Paul II;
Souvenir sheet of one 30,000m stamp depicting French Pres. Nicolas Sarkozy.
A set of 12 stamps with denominations of 5,000m, 19,000m, and 33,000m depicting Europa stamps, 50th anniv.
Stamps depicting Wolfgang Amadeus Mozart; Pierre Auguste Renoir; Jean Auguste Ingres Bessieres; Marilyn Monroe; Rotary International; Lions International; Formula 1 Racing; Astronauts; 2007 Rugby World Cup.

No. 1575
Surcharged

Methods and Perfs As Before 2006 ?
1748 A331 33m on 10,000m #1575   6.75   6.75

Cahora
Bassa
Dam
A401

Designs: 8m, Dam and reservoir. 20m, Dignitaries shaking hands. 33m, Dam and flag of Mozambique.

2007, Nov. 26   Litho.   Perf. 11x11¼
1749-1751 A401 Set of 3   4.75   4.75

Reign of Aga
Khan, 50th
Anniv. — A402

Designs: 8m, Building. No. 1753, 20m, People on beach. No. 1754, 20m, People under shelter. No. 1755, 33m, Polana Serena Hotel. No. 1756, 33m, Students in classroom, vert. (30x40mm).

Perf. 12¾, 11¼x11 (#1756)
2007, Nov.
1752-1756 A402 Set of 5   9.00   9.00

Fauna, Flora and Minerals — A403

No. 1757 — Map of Africa and wild cats: a, 8m, Acionyx jubatus. b, 8m, Panthera leo with closed mouth. c, 8m, Panthera leo with open mouth. d, 33m, Male Panthera leo. e, 33m, Female Panthera leo, diff. f, 33m, Panthera pardus.
No. 1758 — Map of Africa and elephants: a, 8m, Loxodonta cyclotis facing right. b, 8m, Loxodonta africana. c, 8m, Loxodonta cyclotis facing left. d, 33m, Loxodonta africana facing right. e, 33m, Loxodonta cyclotis, diff. f, 33m, Loxodonta africana facing left.
No. 1759 — Lighthouses and marine mammals: a, 8m, Sousa teuszii. b, 8m, Stenella frontalis. c, 8m, Stenella clymene. d, 33m, Sotalia fluviatilis. e, 33m, Stenella longirostris. f, 33m, Tursiops truncatus.
No. 1760 — Map of Africa and birds of prey: a, 8m, Haliaeetus leucocephalus. b, 8m, Terathopius ecaudatus. c, 8m, Accipiter gentilis. d, 33m, Buteo lagopus. e, 33m, Head of Aquila verreauxii. f, 33m, Aquila verreauxi on branch.
No. 1761 — Hummingbirds and orchids: a, 8m, Tachybaptus. b, 8m, Malaxis uniflora. b, 8m, Fregata magnificus, Coryanthes speciosa. c, 8m, Gallinula, Calochilus robertsonii. d, 33m, Veniliornis, Stanhopea. e, 33m, Basilinna leucotis, Habaneria saccata. f, 33m, Actitis macularia, Diuris filifolia.
No. 1762 — Map of Africa and bees: a, 8m, Polubia. b, 8m, Apis mellifera scutellata. c, 8m, Pompilus. d, 33m, Tiphiidae. e, 33m, Vespula vulgaris. f, 33m, Scoliidae.
No. 1763 — Map of Africa and butterflies: a, 8m, Danaus chrysippus. b, 8m, Libytheana carineta. c, 8m, Papilio morondavana. d, 33m, Danaus gilippus. e, 33m, Amblypodia tyrannus. f, 33m, Lycaena cupreus.
No. 1764 — Map of Africa and crocodiles: a, 8m, Crocodylus porosus. b, 8m, Crocodylus novaeguineae. c, 8m, Crocodylus rhombifer. d, 33m, Crocodylus niloticus. e, 33m, Osteolaemus tetraspis. f, 33m, Crocodylus siamensis.
No. 1765 — Map of Africa and frogs: a, 8m, Gastrotheca. b, 8m, Mantella. c, 8m, Rana esculenta. d, 33m, Litoria rubella. e, 33m, Dendrobatidae. f, 33m, Pyxicephalus.
No. 1766 — Dinosaurs: a, 8m, Aublysodon. b, 8m, Ornithomimus. c, 8m, Coelurus. d, 33m, Velociraptor. e, 33m, Abelisaurus. f, 33m, Saurornithoides.
No. 1767 — Map of Africa and cacti: a, 8m, Hoodia gordonii. b, 8m, Hoodia officinalis. c, 8m, Hoodia ruschii. d, 33m, Hoodia flava. e, 33m, Hoodia officinalis, diff. f, 33m, Hoodia currorii.
No. 1768 — Fruit: a, 8m, Citrus vulgaris. b, 8m, Cola acuminata. c, 8m, Cocos nucifera. d, 33m, Citrus limonum. e, 33m, Cocos nucifera, diff. f, 33m, Citrus bergamia.
No. 1769 — Map of Africa, diamonds and minerals: a, 8m, Fluorite, quartz. b, 8m, Elbalte tourmaline, quartz. c, 8m, Staurolite. d, 33m, Fluorite, pyrite. e, 33m, Benitoite, neptunite. f, 33m, Celestine.
No. 1770, 20m — Map of Africa and primates: a, Cebidae. b, Nomascus leucogenys. c, Borneo proboscis monkey. d, Symphalangus syndactylus. e, Pan troglodytes. f, Cercopithecidae.
No. 1771, 20m — Lighthouses and whales: a, Balaenoptera borealis. b, Orcinus orca. c, Eschrichtius robustus. d, Balaenoptera physalus. e, Three Orcinus orca. f, Megaptera novaeangliae.
No. 1772, 20m — Map of Africa and owls: a, Strix woodfordii. b, Tyto capensis. c, Phodilus badius on thin branch. d, Phodilus badius on thick branch. e, Tytonidae. f, Otus senegalensis.
No. 1773, 20m — Map of Africa and parrots: a, Psittacopes. b, Serudaptus. c, Pseudasturidae. d, Quercypsittidae. e, Xenopsitta. f, Palaeopsittacus.
No. 1774 — Butterflies or moths and unnamed flowers: a, Inachis io. b, Saturnia pavonia. c, Papilio xuthus. d, Prepona praeneste. e, Speyeria cybele. f, Nymphalidae.
No. 1775, 20m — Map of Africa and fish: a, Scorpaenidae. b, Balistodae. c, Antennarius. d, Triglidae. e, Hydrocynus. f, Lophius.
No. 1776, 20m — Map of Africa and marine life: a, Birgus latro. b, Panulirus. c, Gecarcoidea natalis. d, Loligo opalescens. e, Genus ocypode. f, Hapalochlaena.

No. 1777, 20m — Map of Africa and reptiles: a, Vaanus niloticus. b, Chamaeleo jacksonii. c, Veranus exanthematicus. d, Scincus. e, Brookesia. f, Furcifer pardalis.
No. 1778, 20m — Map of Africa and turtles: a, Natator depressus. b, Eretmochelys imbricata. c, Lepidochelys olivacea with dark neck. d, Lepidochelys olivacea with light neck. e, Caretta caretta. f, Chelonia mydas.
No. 1779, 20m — Map of Africa and snakes: a, Bitis nasicornis. b, Bitis gabonica. c, Ophiophagus hannah. d, Thelolornis kirtlandii. e, Dendroaspis angusticeps. f, Atheris.
No. 1780, 20m — Dinosaurs: a, Therizinosaurus. b, Heterdontosaurus. c, Prosaurolophus. d, Melanorosaurus. e, Megalosaurus. f, Proceratosaurus.
No. 1781, 20m — Trees: a, Punica granatum, fruit split, and on branch. b, Elaeis guineensis. c, Cola acuminata. d, Areca catechu. e, Hevea brasiliensis. f, Punica granatum, flowers on branches and split.
No. 1782, 20m — Map of Africa and orchids: a, Purple Cattleya lueddemanniana. b, Paphiopedilum delenatii. c, Vanda coerulea. d, Pink Cattleya lueddmanniana. e, Paphiopedilum. f, Spathoglottis.
No. 1783, 20m — Map of Africa and minerals: a, Carrollite. b, Ettringite. c, Cerrusite, barite. d, Malachite. e, Carrollite, calcite. f, Dioptase.
No. 1784, 132m, Map of Africa and Nomascus nasutus. No. 1785, 132m, Map of Africa and Panthera leo. No. 1786, 132m, Loxodonta africana. No. 1787, 132m, Stenella logirostris, diff. No. 1788, 132m, Orcinus orca and lighthouse, diff. No. 1789, 132m, Lepidocolaptes, Spathoglottis plicata. No. 1790, 132m, Pulchrapollia. No. 1791, 132m, Accipiter nisus. No. 1792, 132m, Map of Africa and Polubia. No. 1793, 132m, Arctia hebe. No. 1794, 132m, Papilio homerus, Caladeria reptans. No. 1795, 132m, Map of Africa and Thassophryninae. No. 1796, 132m, Map of Africa and Chauliodus. No. 1797, 132m, Map of Africa and Dendroaspis polylepis. No. 1798, 132m, Map of Africa and Pogona vitticeps. No. 1799, 132m, Map of Africa and Crocodylus niloticus, diff. No. 1800, 132m, Map of Africa and Eretmochelys imbircata, diff. No. 1801, 132m, Map of Africa and Pychicephalus adspersus. No. 1802, 132m, Hadrosaurus. No. 1803, 132m, Adansonia tree. No. 1804, 132m, Map of Africa and Euphorbia enopla. No. 1805, 132m, Map of Africa, Diuris filifolia, Malaxis uniflora. No. 1806, 132m, Cirtus vulgaris, diff. No. 1807, 132m, Vanadinite, poldervaartite. No. 1808, 132m, Malachite, barite and malachite.

Perf. 12¾x13¼
2007, Dec. 10   Litho.
Sheets of 6, #a-f
1757-1769 A403 Set of 13 125.00 125.00
1770-1783 A403 Set of 14 130.00 130.00
Souvenir Sheets
Perf. 13¼ Syncopated
1784-1808 A403 Set of 25 260.00 260.00

Minerva
Central
Publishers,
Cent.
A404

Background color: 8m, Red. 20m, Olive green. 33m, Purple.

2008, Apr. 10   Litho.   Perf. 11x11¼
1809-1811 A404 Set of 3   4.75   4.75

Second Frelimo
Party Congress,
40th
Anniv. — A405

2008, July 25   Perf. 11¼x11
1812 A405 8m multi   .65   .65

Miniature Sheets

2008 Summer Olympics, Beijing — A406

No. 1813 Surcharged

Nos. 1813 and 1814: a, Soccer. b, Basketball. c, Swimming. d, Running.

2008   *Perf. 13¼x12¾*
1813 A406 8m Sheet of 4, #a-d   5.00 5.00
1814 A406 8m on 8m Sheet of 4,
     #a-d   2.50 2.50

No. 1813 shows an incorrect abbreviation for the currency, which was corrected by the surcharge.

Food — A407

Designs: 8m, Bolo de milho (corn cake). 20m, Mathapa com carangueijo (cassava with crab). 33m, Quiabo com camarao (Okra and shrimp).

2008, Oct. 9   *Perf. 11¼x11*
1815-1817 A407 Set of 3   4.75 4.75

Maria de Lurdes Mutola, 800-Meter Gold Medalist in 2000 Summer Olympics A408

2009, Jan. 21   *Perf. 11x11¼*
1818 A408 8m multi   .65 .65

Mozambique postal officials have declared as "illegal" stamps dated 2008 depicting chess grandmaster Bobby Fischer.

Eduardo Mondlane (1920-69), President of Mozambique Liberation Front — A409

2009, June 20   **Litho.**   *Perf. 11¼x11*
1819 A409 33m black & red   2.40 2.40

Transportation — A410

No. 1820, 33m — Transportation with animals: a, Elephants and howdah. b, Reindeer pulling sled. c, Camel and rider. d, Horse-drawn carriage. e, Donkey and rider. f, Dog sled.

No. 1821, 33m — Two-wheeled transportation: a, Rickshaw. b, Bicycle. c, Motor scooter. d, Motorcycle. e, Foot-powered scooter. f, Segway.

No. 1822, 33m — Old automobiles: a, Citroen BL 11. b, Jaguar XK-140. c, Chrysler Imperial. d, Dodge Royal Lancer. e, Mercedes-Benz 300 SL. f, Ford Custom.

No. 1823, 33m — Modern automobiles: a, Hyundai QuarmaQ. b, Lamborghini Murcielago. c, Buick Invicta. d, Ford Verve. e, Mazda RX-8. f, Cadillac CTS Sport Wagon.

No. 1824, 33m — Modern electric automobiles: a, Mitsubishi iMiEV Sport. b, Opel Meriva. c, Pickup truck (incorrectly identified as InterCity 225). d, Nissan Navara. e, Opel Insignia. f, Tesla Roadster.

No. 1825, 33m — Ancient sailing vessels: a, Phoenician bark. b, Egyptian wooden ship. c, Arab ship. d, Chinese junk. e, Greek galley. f, Roman galley.

No. 1826, 33m — Ships and maps: a, Independence, map of United States. b, Great Harry, map of Great Britain and Ireland. c, Vespucci, map of Spain. d, Norske Lowe, map of Denmark. e, Brederoe, map of Netherlands. f, Madre di Dio, map of Italy.

No. 1827, 33m — Steam-powered ships: a, SS Martha's Vineyard. b, SS America. c, SS Statendam. d, SS Brazil. e, SS Ryndam. f, SS Nieuw Amsterdam.

No. 1828, 33m — Warships: a, Warrior. b, Merrimack. c, Dreadnought. d, Lightning. e, MEKO frigate. f, Yamato.

No. 1829, 33m — Warships: a, HMS Astute. b, NS Yamal. c, USS Harry S Truman. d, Trafalgar. e, Vaygach. f, Nimitz class aircraft carrier.

No. 1830, 33m — Modern ships: a, Surcouf. b, Sea Shadow. c, Skjold class patrol boat. d, MS Radiance of the Seas. e, MS Pacific Princess. f, MS Mariner of the Seas.

No. 1831, 33m — Early locomotives: a, Trevithick. b, Blenkinsop. c, Marc Seguin. d, Puffing Billy. e, Rocket. f, Liverpool.

No. 1832, 33m — Locomotives: a, Evening Star. b, LMS Princess Royal Class. c, Russian 2TE10U. d, Atlantis. e, Cock o' the North. f, LMS Compound 4-4-0.

No. 1833, 33m — Locomotives: a, ALCO RS-1 (bister panel). b, British Rail Class 03. c, 643 Class. d, 661 Class. e, 641 Class. f, Hudswell Clarke 0-4-2ST.

No. 1834, 33m — Locomotives: a, ALCO RS-1 (gray panel). b, Re420. c, TAGAB Re2. d, EuroSprinter DB AG Class 182. e, SKODA 109. f, Re4.

No. 1835, 33m — High-speed trains: a, Thalys. b, Eurostar. c, InterCity 225. d, ICE. e, TGV. f, Pendolino.

No. 1836, 33m — High-speed trains: a, JR-Maglev. b, KTX. c, Maglev. d, 100 Series Shinkansen. e, E1 Series Shinkansen. f, N700 Series Shinkansen.

No. 1837, 33m — Pioneer aircraft: a, 1868 Albatros II glider of Jean-Marie LeBris. b, 1852 Henry Giffard balloon. c, 1849 glider of George Cayley. d, 1897 Avion III airplane of Clément Ader. e, 1874 monoplane of Félix du Temple. f, 1901 flying machine of Traian Vuia.

No. 1838, 33m — Pioneer aircraft: a, 1902 Number 21 airplane of Gustave Whitehead. b,

---

1904 Wright Flyer II. c, 14 Bis, 1906. c, 1908 Henry Farman biplane. d, 1909 Louis Blériot monoplane. f, 1910 Rumpler Taube.

No. 1839, 33m — Airplanes: a, Fokker D.1. b, Handley Page. c, Winstead Special. d, Boeing P26-B. e, Mitsubishi Ki-15. f, Nakajima Ki-27.

No. 1840, 33m — Military airplanes: a, Messerschmitt Bf-109. b, B-29 Superfortress. c, Yak-9. d, Avro Lancaster. e, Kawasaki Ki-61. f, Northrop P-61 Black Widow.

No. 1841, 33m — Military airplanes: a, Saab J35J. b, Sukhoi SU-30MKI. c, A-7 Corsair. d, Boeing 747 carrying Space Shuttle. e, Myasishchev M-55. f, Aero L-39 Albatros.

No. 1842, 33m — Supersonic airplanes: a, TU-144. b, F-105 Thunderbird. c, North American XB-70A. d, SR-71 Blackbird. e, Concorde 102. f, F16XL.

No. 1843, 33m — Fire vehicles: a, 1963 Magirus-Deutz Mercur 126 DL. b, 1979 Mercedes-Benz LA 1113 BR. c, 1958 Magirus-Deutz V6 Ladder. d, 1976 Dodge K1050 Somati MONIA. e, 2002 Scania 91 G310 Rosenbauer. f, 1984 Renault G300-17 Riffaul.

No. 1844, 33m — Ambulances: a, 1942 Morris Y Series. b, 1974 Citroen HB2AS 1600. c, 1942 Dodge WC54. d, 1981 Land Rover. e, 1966 Cadillac S&S48. f, 1955 Ford Kaiser V8.

No. 1845, 33m — Spacecraft: a, Sputnik I. b, Vostok I. c, Explorer I. d, Skylab. e, Mir. f, Apollo 11.

No. 1846, 33m — Spacecraft: a, Venture Star. b, Ares V. c, Space Shuttle Discovery. d, Dawn. e, SpaceShip One. f, Phoenix.

No. 1847, 175m, Camels and rider. No. 1848, 175m, Rickshaw and Segway. No. 1849, 175m, Cadillac Eldorado. No. 1850, 175m, Citroen 2CV. No. 1851, 175m, Renault Z17. No. 1852, 175m, Egyptian canoe. No. 1853, 175m, Portuguese carrack Santa Catarina do Monte Sinai and map of Portugal. No. 1854, 175m, SS Great Britain. No. 1855, 175m, Italian battleship Littorio. No. 1856, 175m, PFS Polarstern. No. 1857, 175m, F261 Magdeburg. No. 1858, 175m, North Star locomotive. No. 1859, 175m, Pannier locomotive. No. 1860, 175m, 10000 locomotive. No. 1861, 175m, CC7102 locomotive. No. 1862, 175m, Thalys, diff. No. 1863, 175m, KTX, diff. No. 1864, 175m, Triplane of John Stringfellow. No. 1865, 175m, Nieuport 28. No. 1866, 175m, Aichi D3A. No. 1867, 175m, Corsair F4U. No. 1868, 175m, EF-111. No. 1869, 175m, A2 airplane. No. 1870, 175m, 1996-2001 Mercedes Unimog 2450 L38 fire truck. No. 1871, 175m, 1956 Gurkha Red Cross Ambulance. No. 1872, 175m, Salyut 1 and Telstar. No. 1873, 175m, V-2 rocket and SS-6 Sapwood. Nos. 1847-1873 are vert.

       Perf. 12¾x13¼
2009, Sept. 30   **Litho.**
     Sheets of 6, #a-f
1820-1846 A410 Set of 27 425.00 425.00
     Souvenir Sheets
    Perf. 13¼ Syncopated
1847-1873 A410 Set of 27 375.00 375.00

Nos. 1847-1873 each contain one 37x38mm stamp.

Famous People and Events — A411

No. 1874, 8m — Year of the Tiger (in 2010): a, Tiger with head at bottom, Temple of Heaven. b, Tiger running, Forbidden City. c, Tiger with head at top, Temple of Heaven. d, Tiger walking, Forbidden City. e, Tiger, Yong He Gong Lama Temple. f, Tiger, Great Wall of China.

No. 1875, 8m — Shen Chou (1427-1509), painter: a, Painting of forest, sketch of tree branch with calligraphy. b, Shen Chou at R, painting at L. c, 14x19mm landscape and 13x26mm landscape. d, 17x21mm landscape and 16x20mm landscape. e, Shen Chou at L, painting at R. f, 13x15mm landscape and 16x23mm painting of man on bridge.

No. 1876, 8m — Pope John Paul II (1920-2005) and: a, Arms, sculpture. b, Dove, St. Peter's Basilica. c, Arms, dome interior. d, Arms, St. Peter's Basilica. e, Dove in flight, St. Peter's Square. f, Arms, buildings in distance.

No. 1877, 8m — Mohandas Gandhi (1869-1948) and: a, Ganesha. b, Spinning wheel. c, Taj Mahal. d, Naja naja (cobra). e, Meditating woman. f, Panthera tigris tigris (tiger).

No. 1878, 8m — Chinese film personalities: a, Sun Daolin. b, Zhao Dan. c, Ge You. d, Bai Yang. e, Ruan Lingyu. f, Zhang Yu.

No. 1879, 8m — People's Republic of China, 60th Anniv.: a, Hand holding Chinese

---

flag, Chinese soldiers. b, Mao Zedong. c, Qian Sanqiang, Tianwan Nuclear Center. d, Deng Xiaoping, Great Wall of China. e, Hu Jintao, fireworks above Olympic Stadium. f, Jiang Zemin, Hong Kong skyline, ruins of St. Paul's Church, Macao.

No. 1880, 20m — Charlie Chaplin (1889-1977), actor, in scene from film from: a, 1915. b, 1925 (clapboard in background). c, 1918 (film reel in background). d, 1925 (film reel in background). e, 1918 (strip of film in background). f, 1925 (standing next to actress).

No. 1881, 20m — Hirohito (1901-89), emperor of Japan, in suit and tie, and in background: a, Japanese flag, Hirohito in military uniform. b, Hirohito, waving, standing next to Empress Nakano. c, Japanese flag. d, Hirohito as child, pagoda. e, Hirohito on horse, Japanese flag. f, Hirohito and Empress Nakano in gown.

No. 1882, 20m — Pres. John F. Kennedy (1917-63) and: a, Astronaut on moon. b, Kennedy at typewriter. c, Kennedy presidential campaign button. d, Family. e, Wife, Jacqueline, holding baby. f, Wedding photo.

No. 1883, 20m — Marilyn Monroe (1926-62), actress: a, Wearing costume from 1954 movie, wearing striped blouse. b, Wearing swimsuit, wearing green coat. c, Wearing top hat, wearing necklace. d, Wearing blue shorts. e, Looking through ship's porthole. f, Wearing short skirt and wearing red dress.

No. 1884, 20m — Elvis Presley (1935-77): a, Wearing white jacket and lei. b, Wearing red jacket, and jumping in air wearing cape. c, With four women. d, With arms raised, and with arms at neck. e, On telephone, wearing blue striped jacket. f, With guitar.

No. 1885, 20m — Michael Jackson (1958-2009), singer: a, Holding on to rail. b, Wearing top hat. c, Holding woman. d, As boy, with brothers. e, Speaking into microphone. f, Behind lectern, raising both arms.

No. 1886, 20m — Pope Benedict XVI: a, Facing forward, wearing miter, holding cross, arms at left. b, Wearing red hat, dove in flight. c, Facing left, wearing miter, holding cross, arms at left. d, Waving censer, arms at UR. e, With arms extended, dove on pedestal. f, Wearing red stole and zucchetto, arms at left.

No. 1887, 20m — Expo 2010, Shanghai: a, Nepal Pavilion. b, Africa Pavilion, with text beginning with "O tema." c, United Kingdom Pavilion. d, Romania Pavilion. e, African Pavilion, with text beginning with "A fachada." f, Japan Pavilion.

No. 1888, 33m — Galileo Galilei (1564-1642), astronomer, and: a, Leaning Tower of Pisa. b, Three people around telescope. c, Gear mechanism. d, Galileo's telescope. e, Telescope on wooden stand. f, Globe.

No. 1889, 33m — Johannes Kepler (1571-1630), astronomer, and: a, Moon. b, Kepler's model of the solar system and book, Mysterium Cosmographicum. c, Austrian coin depicting Kepler. d, Horoscope for General Wallenstein. e, Model of solar system. f, Model inscribed with Kepler's name.

No. 1890, 33m — George Frideric Handel (1685-1759), composer, and: a, Bust. b, Sculpture of Handel. c, Musical notes and orchestra hall in background. d, Engraving of Handel. e, Sculpture of lyre player. f, Handel's house in London.

No. 1891, 33m — William Kirby (1759-1850), entomologist: a, Kirby and Hypochrysops epicurus. b, Nicrophorus vespillo and Dytiscus marginalis. c, Kirby and unnamed butterfly. d, Kirby and Delias ninus. e, Polistes dominula and Philanthus triangulum. f, Kirby and Chilasa agestor.

No. 1892, 33m — Napoleon Bonaparte (1769-1821), emperor of France, and: a, French army. b, Battle of the Pyramids, 1798. c, Battle of Borodino, 1812. d, Imperial arms. e, Napoleon's bed. f, Battle of Arcola Bridge, 1796.

No. 1893, 33m — Joseph Haydn (1732-1809), composer, and: a, Haydn's house, Eisenstadt, Germany. b, Haydn's birthplace. c, Piano. d, Musicians. e, Esterházy Theater. f, Pianist.

No. 1894, 33m — Charles Darwin (1809-82), naturalist, and: a, Mimus trifasciatus. b, Allosaurus. c, Darwin's notes and sketches. d, Desmodus d'Orbignyi. e, Lesothosaurus. f, Microraptor gui.

No. 1895, 33m — Louis Braille (1809-52), educator of the blind: a, Braille, at left, and blind boy reading book, at right. b, Braille Institute. c, Braille, at right, and blind boy writing in Braille, at left. d, Woman and seeing-eye dogs. e, Hands and book in Braille, at left, Braille, at right. f, Braille alphabet.

No. 1896, 33m — Katsushika Hokusai (1760-1849), artist: a, Poppies, ocean waves. b, Man, red mountain. c, Sumo wrestlers. d, Man on horseback. e, Palanquin carriers. f, Man and falcon.

No. 1897, 33m — Alexander von Humboldt (1769-1859), naturalist, and: a, Simia melanocephala. b, Rhexia speciosa. c, Simia leonina. d, Hibiscus. e, Convolvulus. f, Melastoma.

No. 1898, 33m — Georges-Pierre Seurat (1859-91), painter, and paintings on tripod: a, Young woman Powdering Herself (Muher jovem a maquilhar-se). b, The Reaper (O debulhador). c, The Stonebreaker. d, Chahut

(O Chabut). e, A Sunday Afternoon on the Island of La Grande Jatte (Tarde de Domingo na Ilha da Grande Jatte). f, The Bridge - View of the Seine (A vista da ponte de Seine).

No. 1899, 33m — Sir Peter Scott (1909-89), founder of Worldwide Fund for Nature: a, Scott holding dog, painting of birds in flight. b, Scott feeding ducks, painting of ducks in flight. c, Scott facing left, painting of birds in flight. d, Scott with camera, painting of birds in flight. e, Scott facing forward, painting of birds in flight. f, Scott with binoculars, painting of ducks on water.

No. 1900, 33m — First man on the Moon, 40th anniv.: a, Moon, Apollo 11 on launch pad, b, Neil Armstrong, Moon, Apollo 11 in flight. c, Apollo 11 Lunar Module above Moon. d, Apollo 11 above Moon, Edwin E. Aldrin. e, Apollo 11, astronaut and American flag on Moon. f, Apollo 11 Command Module, Michael Collins.

No. 1901, 33m — International Polar Year: a, Iceberg and Odobenus rosmarus. b, Map of Antarctica, Belgium's Princess Elisabeth Antarctic Station. c, Map of Arctic Ocean and CCGS Amundsen. d, Intl. Polar Year emblem, iceberg, Ovibos moschatus. e, Map of Antarctica, Georg von Neumayer (1826-1909) and Karl Weyprecht (1838-81), polar explorers. f, Intl. Polar Year emblem, iceberg, Ursus maritimus.

No. 1902, 175m, Tiger and Forbidden City. No. 1903, 175m, Shen Chou and painting. No. 1904, 175m, Pope John Paul II giving communion to man. No. 1905, 175m, Gandhi. No. 1906, 175m, Xie Jin (1923-2008), Chinese film director. No. 1907, 175m, Ceremony of founding of the People's Republic of China. No. 1908, 175m, Chaplin. No. 1909, 175m, Emperor Hirohito, Empress Nakano and Queen Elizabeth II. No. 1910, 175m, Pres. Kennedy, White House. No. 1911, 175m, Monroe. No. 1912, 175m, Presley. No. 1913, 175m, Jackson and Slash. No. 1914, 175m, Pope Benedict XVI. No. 1915, 175m, Chinese Pavilion at Expo 2010, Shanghai. No. 1916, 175m, Galileo Galilei and men around globe. No. 1917, 175m, Kepler, telescope, planets. No. 1918, 175m, Handel. No. 1919, 175m, Kirby and Psuedotergumia pisidice. No. 1920, 175m, Map, Napoleon on horse. No. 1921, 175m, Haydn, harpsichord. No. 1922, 175m, Darwin and Rhea darwinii. No. 1923, 175m, Braille, teacher and blind students. No. 1924, 175m, Hokusai paintings of server of sake and mountain. No. 1925, 175m, Humboldt and specimens of flora and fauna. No. 1926, 175m, Artist's palette, Bathers at Asniers, by Seurat. No. 1927, 175m, Scott with camera on tripod, painting of birds in flight. No. 1928, 175m, Astronauts on moon, American flag. No. 1929, 175m, Iceberg, Alopes lagopus.

Perf. 12¾x13¼

2009, Nov. 30   **Litho.**
Sheets of 6, #a-f

1874-1901 A411   Set of 28   375.00   375.00

Souvenir Sheets
Perf. 13¼ Syncopated

1902-1929 A411   Set of 28   375.00   375.00

On Nos. 1874-1901, stamps "a," "c," "d" and "f" are 37x38mm, stamps "b" and "e" are 50x38mm. Nos. 1902-1929 each contain one 50x38mm stamp.

Worldwide Fund for Nature (WWF) — A412

No. 1930 — Hippotragus equinus: a, Adult. b, Adult and juvenile. c, Adults at watering hole. d, Adults in grass.
175m, Adult grazing.

2010, Jan. 30   **Perf. 13x13¼**
1930 A412   33m Block or strip
    of 4, #a-d   10.50   10.50
  e.   Souvenir sheet of 8, 2 each
     #1930a-1930d + 2 labels   21.00   21.00

Souvenir Sheet
Perf. 12¾x13¼

1931 A412   175m multi   13.50   13.50

No. 1931 contains one 37x38mm stamp.

Meio Ambiente — Girafas

The Natural World — A413

No. 1932, 8m — Giraffes (Giraffa camelopardalis): a, Two giraffes, giraffe at right on ground. b, Herd of giraffes. c, Two giraffes, giraffe at left on ground. d, Adult and juvenile giraffes. e, Two giraffes, giraffe at left with front legs extended. f, Two adult giraffes standing.

No. 1933, 8m — Wild pigs: a, Sus scrofa facing right. b, Brown Sus scrofa facing left. c, Gray Sus scrofa facing left. d, Phacochoerus aethiopicus. e, Potamochoerus porcus. f, Phacochoerus africanus.

No. 1934, 8m — Zebras: a, Two Equus quagga boehmi with heads pointed to left. b, Two Equus quagga burchellii standing. c, Three Equus quagga burchellii. d, Two Equus quagga crawshayi. e, Two Equus quagga burchellii, zebra on left on ground. f, Two Equus quagga boehmi, zebra at right facing right.

No. 1935, 8m — Squirrels: a, Heliosciurus gambianus. b, Atlantoxerus getulus. c, Funisciurus isabella. d, Funisciurus pyrropus. e, Funisciurus substriatus. f, Geosciurus princeps.

No. 1936, 8m — Elephants (Loxodonta africana): a, Juvenile at left with trunk raised, adult at right. b, Adult at left, juvenile at right facing right. c, Adult facing right. d, Adult facing left. e, Juvenile at left with trunk down, adult at right. f, Adult at left, juvenile at right facing forward.

No. 1937, 20m — Peonies: a, Paeonia lactiflora and Paeonia moutan. b, Paeonia albiflora and Paeonia foemina. c, Paeonia peregrina and Paeonia moutan. d, Paeonia moutan and Paeonia tenuifolia. e, Paeonia nezhnyi and Paeonia officinalis. f, Paeonia arborea and Paeonia mascula.

No. 1938, 20m — Tropical birds and plants: a, Apaloderma vittatum, Sesuvium portulacastrum. b, Corythaeola cristata, Premna leucostoma. c, Lyblus bidentatus, Ehretia rigida. d, Ceyx picta, Tamarind. e, Trachyphonus erythrocephalus, Pterocarpus indicus. f, Indicator indicator, Dracaena fragrans.

No. 1939, 20m — Pigeons: a, Columba arquatrix on branch that extends to right. b, Columba guinea. c, Streptopelia senegalensis on bare branch. d, Streptopelia senegalensis on branch with foliage. e, Columba livia. f, Columba arquatrix on branch that extends to bottom.

No. 1940, 20m — Rabbits and hares: a, Oryctolagus cuniculus, three paws visible. b, Poelagus rupestris, four paws visible. c, Poelagus marjorita. d, Lepus capensis. e, Oryctolagus cuniculus, two paws visible. f, Poelagus rupestris, two paws visible.

No. 1941, 20m — Wild dogs and hyenas: a, Crocuta crocuta. b, Hyaena brunnea. c, Hyaena hyaena facing right. d, Lycaon pictus. e, Proteles cristata. f, Hyaena hyaena facing left.

No. 1942, 20m — Wild cats: a, Acinonyx jubatus. b, Panthera leo. c, Leptailurus serval. d, Profelis aurata. e, Panthera pardus. f, Felis caracal.

No. 1943, 20m — Aardvarks (Orycteropus afer): a, Facing right, tail extending to left of "2." b, Facing left, tip of ear at left under "c" of "Orycteropus." c, Facing right, tip of tail below "20." d, Facing left, snout in air, tip of ear at left under "p" of "Orycteropus." e, Facing right, tip of tail under decimal point in denomination. f, Facing left, snout on ground, tip of ear at left under "p" of "Orycteropus."

No. 1944, 20m — Bats: a, Two Rousettus aegyptiacus, bat at right with wing tip under last "0" in denomination. b, Two Rousettus aegyptiacus, bat at left hanging onto branch. c, Eidolon helvum. d, Otonycteris hemprichii. e, Two Rousettus aegyptiacus hanging onto branches. f, Barbastella barbastellus.

No. 1945, 20m — Rhinoceroses: a, Ceratotherium simum facing left. b, Diceros bicornis facing left, with all legs on ground. c, Ceratotherium simum facing right. d, Diceros bicornis with front legs raised. e, Ceratotherium simum facing forward. f, Diceros bicornis facing right.

No. 1946, 20m — Antelopes and gazelles: a, Tragelaphus buxtoni. b, Taurotragus derbianus. c, Kobus megaceros. d, Damaliscus lunatus. e, Alcelaphus buselaphus. f, Connochaetes gnou.

No. 1947, 33m — Marine birds: a, Morus capensis. b, Rynchops flavirostris. c, Thalasseus bergii. d, Sterna dougallii. e, Larus dominicanus. f, Leucophaeus pipixcan.

No. 1948, 33m — Parrots: a, Psittacus erithacus. b, Agapornis nigrigenis. c, Psittacula krameri. d, Agapornis personatus. e, Poicephalus gulielmi. f, Poicephalus senegalus.

No. 1949, 33m — Birds of prey: a, Circaetus gallicus. b, Terathopius ecaudatus. c, Melierax metabates. d, Melierax canorus. e, Pandion haliatetus. f, Elanus caeruleus.

No. 1950, 33m — Hippopotami (Hippopotamus amphibius): a, Juvenile at left, adult at right with mouth open. b, Adult at left with mouth open, juvenile at right. c, Juvenile at left, adult at right with mouth closed. d, Adult and juvenile facing right. e, Adult. f, Adult at left facing forward, juvenile at right facing right.

No. 1951, 33m — Pangolins: a, Phataginus tricuspis in ball and facing right. b, Manis gigantea facing right. c, Manis gigantea facing left. d, Uromanis tetradactyla. e, Smutsia temminckii. f, Phataginus tricuspis on branch.

No. 1952, 33m — Seals and sea lions: a, Mirounga leonina. b, Gray Monachus monachus, head at left, denomination at right. c, Monachus monachus, denomination at left. d, Brown Monachus monachus, denomination at right. e, Gray Monachus monachus, head at upper right, denomination at left. f, Hydrurga leptonyx.

No. 1953, 33m — Dolphins: a, Delphinus delphis. b, Tursiops truncatus. c, Grampus griseus. d, Stenella coeruleoalba, denomination at right. e, Stenella coeruleoalba, denomination at left. f, Delphinus capensis.

No. 1954, 33m — Whales: a, Eubalaena australis. b, Balaenoptera musculus, denomination at right. c, Caperea marginata. d, Kogia simus, Kogia breviceps. e, Balaenoptera musculus, denomination at left. f, Balaenoptera edeni.

No. 1955, 33m — Monkeys: a, Piliocolobus kirkii. b, Colobus angolensis. c, Cercopithecus solatus. d, Papio cynocephalus. e, Cercocebus torquatus. f, Cercopithecus denti.

No. 1956, 33m — Orchids: a, Neobenthamia gracilis. b, Aeranga distincta. c, Disa cardinalis. d, Mystacidium venosum. e, Phalaenopsis equestris. f, Vanda luzonica.

No. 1957, 33m — Volcanoes: a, Cattle near volcanoes. b, Lava tunnel. c, Robot exploring volcano. d, Mt. Vesuvius, Italy. e, Volcanic island. f, Sadiman Volcano, Tanzania, Goddess Pélé.

No. 1958, 33m — Global warming: a, Iceberg, Ursus maritimus. b, Haliaeetus vocifer, smokestacks. c, Panthera tigris sumatrae, forest fire. d, Sterna paradisaea, iceberg. e, Pandion haliaetus, smokestacks. f, Canis rufus, forest fire.

No. 1959, 175m, Giraffa camelopardalis, diff. No. 1960, 175m, Potamochoerus porcus, diff. No. 1961, 175m, Equus quagga boehmi, diff. No. 1962, 175m, Heliosciurus rufobrachium, Funisciurus lemniscatus. No. 1963, 175m, Three Loxodonta africana. No. 1964, 175m, Paeonia tenuifolia. No. 1965, 175m, Vidua paradisaea, Dracaena fragrans. No. 1966, 175m, Columba livia, diff. No. 1967, 175m, Pronolagus randensis. No. 1968, 175m, Lycaon pictus, diff. No. 1969, 175m, Panthera leo, diff. No. 1970, 175m, Orycteropus afer, diff. No. 1971, 175m, Eidolon helvum, diff. No. 1972, 175m, Ceratotherium simum, diff. No. 1973, 175m, Syncerus caffer. No. 1974, 175m, Pelecanus rufescens. No. 1975, 175m, Psittacus erithacus, diff. No. 1976, 175m, Haliaeetus vocifer, diff. No. 1977, 175m, Hippopotamus amphibius, diff. No. 1978, 175m, Smutsia gigantea. No. 1979, 175m, Hydrurga leptonyx, diff. No. 1980, 175m, Delphinus delphis, diff. No. 1981, 175m, Megaptera novaeangliae. No. 1982, 175m, Theropithecus gelada, Mandrillus sphinx. No. 1983, 175m, Dendrobium gonzalesii. No. 1984, 175m, Piton de la Fournaise Volcano, Reunion. No. 1985, 175m, Copenhagen Congress Center, Little Mermaid Statue, Copenhagen.

2010, Jan. 30   **Perf. 13¼x12¾**
Sheets of 6, #a-f

1932-1958 A413   Set of 27   300.00   300.00

Souvenir Sheets
Perf. 12¾x13¼

1959-1985 A413   Set of 27   375.00   375.00

Miniature Sheet

2010 FIFA WORLD CUP SOUTH AFRICA

2010 World Cup Soccer Championships, South Africa — A414

No. 1986 — Soccer players wearing: a, Dark blue shirt, orange shirt. b, Pink shirt, Light green shirt. c, Lilac shirt, light blue shirt. d, Red shirt, white shirt.

2010, Mar. 31   **Perf. 13¼x13**
1986 A414   33m Sheet of 4,
    #a-d   10.50   10.50

[Sports illustration with DESPORTO — Estádios de Futebol África do Sul 2010]

Sports — A415

No. 1987, 8m — 2010 World Cup venues, South Africa: a, Green Point Stadium, Cape Town. b, Nelson Mandela Bay Stadium, Port Elizabeth. c, Ellis Park Stadium, Johannesburg. d, Free State Stadium, Mangaung-Bloemfontein. e, Soccer City Stadium, Johannesburg. f, Royal Bafokeng Stadium, Rustenburg.

No. 1988, 20m — 2010 Men's Winter Olympic Gold Medalists: a, Alexei Grishin, Freestyle skiing aerials. b, Felix Loch, Luge. c, Bill Demong, Large hill Nordic combined skiing. d, Jung-Su Lee, 1500-meter short-track speed skating. e, Jon Montgomery, Skeleton. f, Jasey Jay Anderson, Snowboard.

No. 1989, 20m — 2010 Women's Winter Olympic Gold Medalists: a, Lydia Lassila, Freestyle skiing aerials (incorrectly inscribed Alexei Grishin). b, Canadian team, Ice hockey. c, Amy Williams, Skeleton. d, Tatjana Huefner, Luge. e, Nicolien Sauerbreij, Snowboard. f, Martina Sablikova, 3000- and 5000-meter long track speed skating.

No. 1990, 20m — Female Table Tennis players: a, Wang Nan, denomination at left. b, Zhang Yining, denomination at right. c, Zhang Yining, denomination at left. d, Guo Yue. e, Li Xiaoxia. f, Wang Nan, denomination at right.

No. 1991, 20m — Female Cyclists: a, Linda Villumsen. b, Marianne Vos. c, Nicole Cooke. d, Victoria Pendleton. e, Simona Krupeckaite. f, Jeannie Longo.

No. 1992, 20m — Female Chess players: a, Antoaneta Stefanova. b, Xu Yuhua. c, Pia Cramling. d, Alexandra Kosteniuk. e, Viktorija Cmilyte. f, Judit Polgar.

No. 1993, 33m — Male Chess players: a, Garry Kasparov. b, Viswanathan Anand. c, Vasily Smyslov. d, Bobby Fischer. e, Anatoly Karpov. f, Veselin Topalov.

No. 1994, 33m — Male Table Tennis players: a, Wang Hao. b, Ma Lin, denomination at right. c, Ma Lin, denomination at left. d, Jorg Rosskopf. e, Wang Liqin. f, Jean-Philippe Gatien.

No. 1995, 33m — 2010 Men's Winter Olympic Gold Medalists: a, Didier Defago, Downhill skiing. b, Evgeny Ustyugov, 15-kilometer biathlon. c, Andre Lange and Kevin Kuske, two-man bobsled. d, Petter Northug, 50-kilometer cross-country skiing. e, Canadian team, Curling. f, Evan Lysacek, Figure skating.

No. 1996, 33m — 2010 Women's Winter Olympic Gold Medalists: a, Maria Riesch, Slalom and Super Combined skiing. b, Magdalena Neuner, 10-kilometer biathlon. c, Kaillie

Humphries and Heather Moyse, bobsled. d, Justyna Kowalczyk, 30-kilometer cross-country skiing. e, Kim Yu-Na, Figure skating. f, Canadian team, Curling.

No. 1997, 33m — Golfers: a, Angel Cabrera. b, Padraig Harrington. c, Vijay Singh. d, Tiger Woods. e, Phil Mickelson. f, Ernie Els.

No. 1998, 33m — Tennis players: a, Dinara Safina. b, Caroline Wozniacki. c, Roger Federer wearing blue shirt. d, Rafael Nadal. e, Novak Djokovic. f, Serena Williams.

No. 1999, 33m — Baseball players: a, Ichiro Suzuki. b, Doug Mientkiewicz. c, Hideo Nomo. d, Ryan Franklin. e, Nomar Garciaparra. f, Adam Everett.

No. 2000, 33m — Ice Hockey players: a, Alexander Ovechkin. b, Sidney Crosby. c, Teemu Selanne. d, Steve Yzerman. e, Mats Sundin. f, Mario Lemieux.

No. 2001, 33m — Male Cyclists: a, Cadel Evans. b, Jan Ullrich. c, Bernard Hinault. d, Mario Cipollini. e, Marco Pantani. f, Miguel Indurain.

No. 2002, 33m — Judo: a, Alina Alexandra Dumitru. b, Ole Bischof. c, Tong Wen. d, Irakli Tsirekidze. e, Masae Ueno. f, Kosei Inoue.

No. 2003, 33m — Taekwondo: a, Cha Dong-Min. b, Guillermo Perez. c, Hadi Saei. d, Lim Su-Jeong. e, Maria Espinoza. f, Son Tae-Jin.

No. 2004, 33m — Polo players: a, Hilario Ulloa. b, Bartolomé Castagnola. c, Juan Martin Nero. d, Gonzalo Pieres. e, Nacho Figueras. f, Charles, Prince of Wales.

No. 2005, 33m — Horse racing: a, Horse #14 and rival horse. b, Horses #8 and #10. c, Horse #2. d, Horse #3. e, Horse #9 and rival horse. f, Horses #4 and #1.

No. 2006, 33m — Dog racing: a, Dog #9. b, Dog #8. c, Dog without visible number. d, Dogs #3 and #4. e, Dog #2. f, Dog #6.

No. 2007, 33m — Rugby players: a, Richie McCaw. b, Matt Giteau. c, Sergio Parisse. d, Bryan Habana. e, Victor Matfield. f, Juan Smith.

No. 2008, 33m — African soccer players: a, Player with orange shirt. b, Player with blue shirt. c, Player #17 in red shirt, player #19 in white shirt. d, Player #15 in white shirt, player in red shirt. e, Player #8 in red shirt, player #20 in blue green shirt. f, Player #5 in orange shirt. player in white shirt.

No. 2009, 33m — Soccer players: a, Samuel Eto'o. b, Kaka. c, Cesc Fabregas. d, Wayne Rooney. e, Cristiano Ronaldo. f, Lionel Messi wearing #70 on pants.

No. 2010, 33m — Lionel Messi, soccer player, dribbling soccer ball, and wearing: a, Red shirt with wide blue vertical stripe in center, at left. b, Red and blue vertically striped shirt with wide stripes, at right. c, Dark blue shirt with white trim, at left. d, Horizontally striped shirt, at right. e, Light blue shirt, at left. f, Red and blue vertically striped shirt with narrow stripes, at right.

No. 2011, 33m — Roger Federer, tennis player, with two images: a, Wearing black shirt at left, white shirt at right. b, Black shirt with blue trim at left and right. c, White shirt at left, red shirt at right. d, White shirt at left, black shirt at right. e, White shirt at left and right. f, Black shirt at left, red shirt at right.

No. 2012, 33m — Alberto Contador, cyclist, on bicycle at left, and wearing, at right: a, White shirt with blue trim. b, Yellow shirt with collar buttoned. c, Yellow shirt with open collar. d, White shirt with blue and red trim. e, Yellow shirt and blue cap. f, Yellow shirt and cap, sunglasses on cap.

No. 2013, 33m — Valentino Rossi, motorcyclist: a, Wearing blue racing uniform at left, on motorcycle at right. b, On motorcycle at left, wearing green racing uniform at right. c, On motorcycle at left, facing right. d, On motorcycle, facing left. e, On motorcycle at left, wearing yellow sun visor at right. f, Wearing horizontally striped shirt at left, on motorcycle at right.

No. 2014, 175m, Loftus Versfeld Stadium, Tshwane-Pretoria. No. 2015, 175m, Mark Tuitert, 1500-meter long track speed skating gold medalist. No. 2016, 175m, Torah Bright, Halfpipe gold medalist. No. 2017, 175m, Guo Yue. No. 2018, 175m, Jeannie Longo, diff. No. 2019, 175m, Alexandra Kosteniuk, diff. No. 2020, 175m, Vasily Smyslov, diff. No. 2021, 175m, Wang Liqin, diff. No. 2022, 175m, Evgeny Ustygov, diff. No. 2023, 175m, Marit Bjoergen, Individual sprint and cross-country skiing gold medalist. No. 2024, 175m, Tiger Woods, diff. No. 2025, 175m, Roger Federer (one image), diff. No. 2026, 175m, Ken Griffey, Jr., baseball player. No. 2027, 175m, Wayne Gretzky, hockey player. No. 2028, 175m, Lance Armstrong, cyclist. No. 2029, 175m, Choi Min-Ho, judo. No. 2030, 175m, Wu Jingyu, taekwondo. No. 2031, 175m, Pablo MacDonough, polo player. No. 2032, 175m, Two race horses. No. 2033, 175m, Dog #8, diff. No. 2034, 175m, Shane Williams, rugby player. No. 2035, 175m, Soccer players wearing red and white shirts. No. 2036, 175m, Didier Drogba, soccer player. No. 2037, 175m, Messi, diff. No. 2038, 175m, Federer (two images), diff. No. 2039, 175m, Contador, diff. No. 2040, Rossi, diff.

2010, Mar. 30   *Perf. 13¼x12¾*
Sheets of 6, #a-f

1987-2013 A415   Set of 27   375.00   375.00

Souvenir Sheets
Perf. 12¾x13¼

2014-2040 A415   Set of 27   375.00   375.00

Mozambique Airlines, 30th Anniv. — A416

Denominations: 8m, 20m, 33m.

2010, Apr. 14   *Perf. 11x11¼*
2041-2043 A416   Set of 3   4.75   4.75

Rock Art — A417

No. 2044: a, Rock art, Tanum, Sweden (38x39mm). b, Altamira cave drawings, Spain (50x39mm). c, Nazca Lines, Peru (39x39mm). d, Rock art, Tadrart Acacus, Libya (38x39mm). e, Vézère Valley Caves rock art, France (50x39mm). f, Ubirr National Park rock art, Australia (38x39mm).
175m, Altamira cave drawing, Spain.

2010, June 30   *Litho.*   *Perf. 13x13¼*
2044 A417   8m Sheet of 6,
      #a-f   3.75   3.75

Souvenir Sheet
Perf. 13¼ Syncopated

2045 A417   175m multi   13.50   13.50
No. 2045 contains one 50x39mm stamp.

French Castles — A418

No. 2046 — Castle at: a, Chenonceau (38x39mm). b, Berzé (50x39mm). c, Montaner (38x39mm). d, Chaumont (38x39mm). e, Amboise (50x39mm). f, Brissac (38x39mm).
175m, Chambord Castle.

2010, June 30   *Perf. 13x13¼*
2046 A418   33m Sheet of 6,
      #a-f   15.50   15.50

Souvenir Sheet
Perf. 13¼ Syncopated

2047 A418   175m multi   13.50   13.50
No. 2047 contains one 50x39mm stamp.

Bridges — A419

No. 2048: a, Beipanjiang Railroad Bridge, Guizhou, People's Republic of China (38x39mm). b, Sydney Harbour Bridge (50x39mm). c, Apollo Bridge, Bratislava, Slovakia (38x39mm). d, Millau Viaduct, Millau, France (50x39mm). e, Tsing Ma Bridge, Hong Kong (50x39mm). f, Coronado Bridge, San Diego, California (38x39mm).
175m, Tower Bridge, London.

2010, June 30   *Perf. 13x13¼*
2048 A419   33m Sheet of 6,
      #a-f   15.50   15.50

Souvenir Sheet
Perf. 13¼ Syncopated

2049 A419   175m multi   13.50   13.50
No. 2049 contains one 50x39mm stamp.

UNESCO World Heritage Sites — A420

No. 2050, 20m — Sites in Africa: a, Rock-hewn church, Lalibela, Ethiopia (38x39mm). b, Great Zimbabwe National Monument (50x39mm). c, Old towns of Djenné, Mali (38x39mm). d, Stone Circles of Senegambia, Gambia and Senegal (38x39mm). e, Timgad, Algeria (50x39mm). f, Carthage, Tunisia (38x39mm).

No. 2051, 20m — Sites in South America: a, Tiwanaku, Bolivia (38x39mm). b, Sacsayhuamán, Cuzco, Peru (50x39mm). c, Chan Chan, Peru (38x39mm). d, Rapa Nui, Chile (38x39mm). e, Machu Picchu, Peru (50x39mm). f, Jesuit Block and Estancias of Cordoba, Argentina (38x39mm).

No. 2052, 20m — Sites in Asia: a, Kathmandu Valley, Nepal (38x39mm). b, Buddhist ruins, Takht-i-Bati, Pakistan (50x39mm). c, Horyu-ji, Japan (38x39mm). d, Nemrut Dag, Turkey (38x39mm). e, Mogao Caves, People's Republic of China (50x39mm). f, Orkhon Valley Cultural Landscape, Mongolia (38x39mm).

No. 2053, 20m — Sites in Europe: a, Olympia, Greece (38x39mm). b, Bend of the Boyne Archaeological Site, Ireland (50x39mm). c, Trulli of Alborello, Italy (38x39mm). d, Delos, Greece (38x39mm). e, Santiago de Compostela, Spain (50x39mm). f, Paphos, Cyprus (38x39mm).

No. 2054, 33m — Sites in Africa: a, Osun-Osogbo Sacred Grove, Nigeria (38x39mm). b, Carthage, Tunisia, diff. (38x39mm). c, Gorée Island, Senegal (38x39mm). d, El Jem Amphitheater, Tunisia (38x39mm). e, Dougga, Tunisia (50x39mm). f, Gebel Barkal, Sudan (38x39mm).

No. 2055, 33m — Sites in Africa: a, Cyrene, Libya (38x39mm). b, Leptis Magna, Libya (50x39mm). c, Aksum, Ethiopia (38x39mm). d, Dougga, Tunisia, diff (38x39mm). e, Sabratha, Libya (50x39mm). f, Thebes, Egypt (38x39mm).

No. 2056, 33m — Sites in North America: a, Palenque, Mexico (38x39mm). b, Uxmal, Mexico (50x39mm). c, Mesa Verde National Park, U.S. (38x39mm). d, Mayan Ruins of Copan, Honduras (38x39mm). e, Teotihuacan, Mexico (50x39mm). f, Chichen-Itza, Mexico (38x39mm).

No. 2057, 33m — Sites in South America: a, Historic Center of Santa Ana de los Ríos de Cuenca, Ecuador (38x39mm). b, Machu Picchu, Peru, diff. (50x39mm). c, Rapa Nui, Chile, diff. (38x39mm). d, Tiwanaku, Bolivia, diff. (38x39mm). e, Rapa Nui, Chile, diff. (50x39mm). f, Sacsayhuamán, Cuzco, Peru, diff. (38x39mm).

No. 2058, 33m — Sites in Asia: a, Palmyra, Syria (38x39mm). b, Persepolis, Iran (50x39mm). c, Ruins of the Buddhist Vihara, Bangladesh (38x39mm). d, Nemrut Dag, Turkey, diff. (38x39mm). e, Tyre, Lebanon (50x39mm). f, Prambanan Temples, Indonesia (38x39mm).

No. 2059, 33m — Sites in Asia: a, Koguryo Tombs, North Korea (38x39mm). b, Palmyra, Syria, diff. (50x39mm). c, Polonnaruwa, Sri Lanka (38x39mm). d, Ayutthaya, Thailand (38x39mm). e, Bosra, Syria (50x39mm). f, Borobudur, Indonesia (38x39mm).

No. 2060, 33m — Sites in Europe: a, Grand-Place, Belgium (38x39mm). b, Historic Center of Rome, Italy (50x39mm). c, Rila Monastery, Bulgaria (38x39mm). d, Gardens and Castle at Kromeriz, Czech Republic (38x39mm). e, Piazza del Duomo, Pisa, Italy (50x39mm). f, Acropolis, Athens, Greece. (38x39mm).

No. 2061, 33m — Sites in Europe: a, Paphos Castle, Cyprus, diff. (38x39mm). b, Roman Monuments, Arles, France (50x39mm). c, Las Médulas, Spain (38x39mm). d, Megalithic Temples of Malta (38x39mm). e, Pont du Gard, France (50x39mm). f, Segovia Aqueduct, Spain (38x39mm).

No. 2062, 175m, Abu Simbel Temple, Egypt. No. 2063, 175m, Volubilis, Morocco. No. 2064, 175m, Sabratha, Libya. No. 2065, 175m, Monte Albán, Mexico. No. 2066, 175m, Sacsayhuamán, Cuzco, Peru, diff. No. 2067, 175m, Rapa Nui, Chile, diff. No. 2068, 175m, Sanchi Buddhist Monuments, India. No. 2069,

---

175m, Lakshmana Temple, Khajuraho Group of Monuments, India. No. 2070, 175m, Lesahn Giant Buddha, People's Republic of China. No. 2071, 175m, Mérida, Archaeological Complex, Spain. No. 2072, 175m, Pompeii, Italy. No. 2073, 175m, Olympia, Greece, diff.

2010, June 30   *Perf. 13x13¼*
Sheets of 6, #a-f
2050-2061 A420   Set of 12   160.00   160.00

Souvenir Sheets
Perf. 13¼ Syncopated
2062-2073 A420   Set of 12   162.50   162.50
Nos. 2062-2073 each contain one 50x39mm stamp.

Museums and Art — A421

No. 2074, 20m — Museum of Modern Art, New York, and work of art by: a, Terry Winters (38x39mm). b, Lisa Yuskavage (50x39mm). c, Ken Price (38x39mm). d, Philip Guston (38x39mm). e, Vincent van Gogh (50x39mm). f, Robert Colescott (38x39mm).

No. 2075, 33m — Metropolitan Museum of Art, New York, and work of art by: a, Bernhard Strigel (38x39mm). b, Johannes Vermeer (50x39mm). c, Thomas Couture (38x39mm). d, Jean Baptiste Greuze (38x39mm). e, Giovanni Bellini (50x39mm). f, Adolphe-William Bouguereau (38x39mm).

No. 2076, 33m — Prado Museum, Madrid, and work of art by: a, Diego Velázquez (38x39mm). b, Francisco de Goya (50x39mm). c, Fra Angelico (38x39mm). d, Hieronymus Bosch (38x39mm). e, Bernaert van Orley (50x39mm). f, Raphael (38x39mm).

No. 2077, 33m — Uffizi Gallery (Galeria dos Ofícios), Florence, Italy, and work of art by: a, Fra Filippo Lippi (38x39mm). b, Leonardo da Vinci (50x39mm). c, Andrea del Verrocchio (38x39mm). d, Sandro Botticelli (38x39mm). e, Giovanni Bellini (50x39mm). f, Raphael (38x39mm).

No. 2078, 33m — Orsay Museum, Paris, and work of art by: a, Claude Monet (38x39mm). b, Paul Signac (50x39mm). c, Edgar Degas (38x39mm). d, Paul Gauguin (38x39mm). e, Berthe Morisot (50x39mm). f, Vincent van Gogh (38x39mm).

No. 2079, 33m — Louvre Museum, Paris, and work of art by: a, Michelangelo Merisi de Caravaggio (38x39mm). b, Hyacinthe Rigaud (50x39mm). c, Quentin Massys (38x39mm). d, Nicolas Poussin (38x39mm). e, Johannes Vermeer (50x39mm). f, Rogier van der Weyden (38x39mm).

No. 2080, 33m — National Gallery, London, and work of art by: a, Antonello da Messina (38x39mm). b, Jan van Eyck (50x39mm). c, Raphael (38x39mm). d, Thomas Gainsborough (38x39mm). e, Hans Holbein the Younger (50x39mm). f, Joseph Mallord William Turner (38x39mm).

No. 2081, 33m — National Museum, Amsterdam, and work of art by: a, Pieter Saenredam (38x39mm). b, Pieter Aertsen (50x39mm). c, Pieter de Hooch (38x39mm). d, Floris van Dijck (38x39mm). e, Jan van Scorel (50x39mm). f, Frans Hals (38x39mm).

No. 2082, 33m — Kunsthistorisches Museum, Vienna, and work of art by: a, Lucas Cranach the Elder (38x39mm). b, Jan Steen (50x39mm). c, Giuseppe Arcimboldo (Fogo, 1566) (38x39mm). d, Arcimboldo (Agua, 1566) (38x39mm). e, Pieter Bruegel the Elder (50x39mm). f, Giorgione (38x39mm).

No. 2083, 33m — Alte Pinakothek, Munich, and work of art by: a, Frans Hals (38x39mm). b, Fritz Schider (50x39mm). c, Hans Wertinger (38x39mm). d, Juan Pantoja de la Cruz (38x39mm). e, Philips Koninck (50x39mm). f, Jean Baptiste Siméon Chardin (38x39mm).

No. 2084, 33m — Gemäldegalerie, Berlin, and work of art by: a, Albrecht Dürer (38x39mm). b, Konrad Witz (50x39mm). c, Rogier van der Weyden (38x39mm). d, Raphael (38x39mm). e, Andrea Mantegna (50x39mm). f, Martin Schongauer (38x39mm).

No. 2085, 33m — Pushkin Museum of Fine Arts, Moscow, and work of art by: a, Maurice de Vlaminck (38x39mm). b, Jan Gossaert (50x39mm). c, Albert Marquet (38x39mm). d, Edgar Degas (38x39mm). e, Gustave Courbet (50x39mm). f, André Derain (38x39mm).

No. 2086, 33m — Hermitage State Museum, St. Petersburg, and work of art by: a, Thomas Gainsborough (38x39mm). b, Pieter Hendricksz de Hooch (50x39mm). c, Leonardo da Vinci (38x39mm). d, Paul Cézanne (38x39mm). e, Louis Le Nain (50x39mm). f, Unknown Egyptian sculptor (38x39mm).

No. 2087, 175m, Museum of Modern Art, work of art by Marlene Dumas. No. 2088, 175m, Metropolitan Museum of Art, work of art by Bartolomé Esteban Murillo. No. 2090, 175m, Uffizi Gallery (Galeria dos Oficios), work of art by Agnolo Bronzino. No. 2091, 175m, Orsay Museum, work of art by Maurice Denis. No. 2092, 175m, Louvre Museum, work of art by Jan van Eyck. No. 2093, 175m, National Gallery, London, work of art by William Hogarth. No. 2094, 175m, National Museum, Amsterdam, work of art by Rembrandt. No. 2095, 175m, Kunsthistorisches Museum, work of art by Pieter Bruegel the Elder. No. 2096, 175m, Alte Pinakothek, work of art by Gerard ter Borch. No. 2097, 175m, Gemäldegalerie, work of art by Hans Holbein the Younger. No. 2098, 175m, Pushkin Museum of Fine Arts, work of art by Paul Cézanne. No. 2099, 175m, Hermitage State Museum, work of art by Vincent van Gogh.

2010, June 30   *Perf. 13x13¼*
Sheets of 6, #a-f
2074-2086 A421   Set of 13 195.00 195.00

Souvenir Sheets
Perf. 13¼ Syncopated
2087-2099 A421   Set of 13 175.00 175.00

Nos. 2087-2099 each contain one 50x39mm stamp.

Association of Portuguese-Speaking Postal and Telecommunications Organizations, 20th Anniv. — A422

2010, Nov. 10   Litho.   *Perf. 11x11½*
2100 A422 92m multi   7.25 7.25

People, Anniversaries and Events — A423

No. 2101, 66m — Jean-Henri Dunant (1828-1910), founder of Red Cross, world map, Red Cross and: a, Red Cross nurse holding child. b, Red Cross workers moving supplies. c, Red Cross worker tending to injured child. d, U.S. Naval Hospital Ship Comfort.

No. 2102, 66m — Katharine Hepburn (1907-2003), actress, and scene from: a, Sea of Grass, 1947. b, Mary of Scotland, 1936. c, A Woman Rebels, 1936. d, The Philadelphia Story, 1940.

No. 2103, 66m — Jonh Lennon (1940-80), singer, and: a, Beatles, peace sign. b, Yoko Ono, protest sign. c, Yoko Ono, guitar. d, Cat.

No. 2104, 66m — Lech Kaczynski (1949-2010), President of Poland, Polish flag, and: a, Wife, Maria, and heraldic eagle. b, Pope Benedict XVI. c, Tupelov Tu-154M. d, Wife, Maria.

No. 2105, 66m — Vasily Smyslov (1921-2010), chess player, and chess board with: a, Brown red squares. b, Blue gray squares. c, Dark blue squares, cat. d, Gray squares.

No. 2106, 66m — Marshall Warren Nirenberg (1927-2010), biochemist, and: a, Macrolepiota procerea. b, Boletus luidus. c, Agaricus albus. d, Agaricus nitidus.

No. 2107, 66m — Tsutomu Yamaguchi (1916-2010), survivor of Hiroshima and Nagasaki nuclear blasts, and: a, Mushroom cloud. b, Enola Gay over Hiroshima. c, Ruins of Hiroshima. d, Mushroom cloud, statue.

No. 2108, 66m — Republic of India, 60th anniv.: a, Mother Teresa, crowd, Hindu god Ganesh. b, Statue of Ganesh, people bathing in the Ganges River. c, Cow, Taj Mahal, mangos. d, Lotus flowers, Bengal tiger.

No. 2109, 66m — Armand Razafindratandra (1925-2010), Archbishop of Antananarivo, Madagascar, and: a, St. Peter's Basilica, cross on rosary. b, Church in Madagascar. c, St. Peter's Square. d, Pope John Paul II.

No. 2110, 66m — 2010 Visit of Pope Benedict XVI to Portugal: a, Pope, cardinals. b, Pope, Papal arms. c, Pope, crowd. d, Pope waving from balcony.

No. 2111, 66m — Paintings of Johannes Vermeer (1632-1675): a, Milkmaid, 1660, and Lacemaker, 1669. b, View of Delft, 1660-61, and Girl with a Pearl Earring, 1675. c, The Art of Painting (detail), 1673, painting of a city, d, The Girl with a Wine Glass, 1659-60, The Astronomer, 1668.

No. 2112, 66m — Mask paintings of James Ensor (1860-1949) from: a, 1892, 1925-29. b, 1898, 1892. c, 1888, 1927. d, 1892, 1908.

No. 2113, 175m, Dunant, world map, Red Cross flag. No. 2114, 175m, Hepburn, scene from The Iron Petticoat, 1956. No. 2115, 175m, Lennon and Yoko Ono, diff. No. 2116, 175m, Kaczynski, cross. No. 2117, 175m, Smyslov, chessboard. No. 2118, 175m, Nirenberg, Cortinarius torvus, diagram of ribonucleic acid molecule. No. 2119, 175m, Yamaguchi, mushroom cloud. No. 2120, 175m, Mohandas K. Gandhi, Indian flag, Nelumbo nucifera. No. 2121, 175m, Razafindratandra, arms. No. 2122, 175m, Pope Benedict XVI, crowd, diff. No. 2123, 175m, The Procuress, 1656, and Girl with a Red Hat, 1666, by Vermeer. No. 2124, 175m, Mask paintings from 1890 and 1888 by Ensor.

2010, Nov. 30   *Perf. 12¾x13½*
Sheets of 4, #a-d
2101-2112 A423   Set of 12 250.00 250.00

Souvenir Sheets
Perf. 13¼ Syncopated
2113-2124 A423   Set of 12 162.50 162.50

Nos. 2113-2124 each contain one 50x39mm stamp.

People, Anniversaries and Events — A424

No. 2125 — 70th birthday of Pelé, wearing New York Cosmos soccer jersey: a, 16m, And jacket with green collar, denomination at UR. b, 16m, Dribbling ball, denomination at UR. c, 16m, Scissor kicking, denomination at UL. d, 66m, Playing against players in green and yellow jerseys. e, 66m, Playing against player in blue, white and green uniforms. f, 66m, Playing against player In blue, orange and white uniforms.

No. 2126 — Athletes of Ninth South American Games: a, 16m, Yari Alvear. b, 16m, Facundo Argüello. c, 16m, Gustavo Tsuboi. d, 66m, Betsi Rivas. e, 66m, Mariana Pajon Londoño. f, 66m, Myke Carvalho.

No. 2127 — Princess Diana (1961-97) and: a, 16m, Tower Bridge, London. b, 16m, London Eye. sons William and Harry. c, 16m, Buckingham Palace. d, 66m, Houses of Parliament, sons William and Harry. e, 66m, Arms and British flag. f, 66m, St. Paul's Cathedral, Mother Teresa.

No. 2128 — Wedding of Prince William and Catherine Middleton: a, 16m, Windsor Castle, Prince William, Catherine Middleton. b, 16m, Princes William and Harry, Buckingham Palace. c, 16m, Palace of Westminster, Prince William, Catherine Middleton. d, 66m, Prince William, map of Great Britain. e, 66m, Prince William, Catherine Middleton, Princess Diana. f, 66m, Prince William, Catherine Middleton, Westminster Abbey.

No. 2129 — Alfred Hitchcock (1899-1980), movie director, and scene from: a, 16m, Vertigo, 1958. b, 16m, Dial M for Murder, 1954. c, 16m, Spellbound, 1945. d, 66m, Rear Window, 1954. e, 66m, Rebecca, 1940. f, 66m, The Birds, 1963.

No. 2130 — Japanese high-speed trains: a, 16m, Joetsu Shinkansen E4 Max Toki. b, 16m, Tohoku Akita Shinkansen Komachi. c, 16m, Nagano Shinkansen E2 Asama. d, 66m, Tokaido Shinkansen 700 Nozomi. e, 66m, Tokaido Shinkansen 700 Nozomi. f, 66m, Tokaido Shinkansen N700 Nozomi.

No. 2131 — European high-speed trains: a, 16m, ICE Bombardieer, Germany. b, 16m,

Thalys, Belgium. c, 16m, Eurostar, Great Britain. d, 66m, Eurostar, Italy. e, 66m, 103 Velaro E Siemens, Spain. f, 66m, TGV, France.

No. 2132 — Paintings by Amedeo Modigliani (1884-1920) from: a, 16m, 1915-16 and 1898-1920. b, 16m, 1918 and 1916. c, 16m, 1917 and 1918. d, 66m, 1917 and 1898-1920. e, 66m, 1915 and 1918. f, 66m, 1909 and 1898-1920.

No. 2133 — Vitaly Sevastyanov (1935-2010), cosmonaut: a, 16m, Wearing suit and tie, with Soyuz TMA-9. b, 16m, Wearing space suit, with Soyuz TMA-18 in space. c, 16m, Wearing suit, with Soyuz TMA-18 in space. d, 66m, Wearing space suit, with Soyuz TMA-18 in space. e, 66m, Wearing suit and tie, with Soyuz TMA-9 being prepared for launch. f, 66m, Wearing suit with military medals, with Salyut 6.

No. 2134 — IKAROS experimental spacecraft: a, 16m, In space, with text over Venus. b, 16m, With H-IIA rocket lifting off. c, 16m, In space, with Venus cut off at top. d, 66m, With rocket H-IIA lifting off, diff. e, 66m, In space, with Venus partially obscured. f, 66m, Akatsuki Vesus orbiter and Earth.

No. 2135 — World development of electrical energy: a, 16m, Earth and stylized birds. b, 16m, Greek philosopher Thales. c, 16m, Silhouettes of people, clouds. d, 66m, Hand with antique map. e, 66m, Inventor Thomas Alva Edison and lightbulb. f, 66m, Chinese Premier Sun Yat-sen and dam.

No. 2136, 175m, Pelé. No. 2137, 175m, Santiago Botero, cyclist. No. 2138, 175m, Princess Diana with youths, Red Cross. No. 2139, 175m, Prince William, Catherine Middleton, engagement ring. No. 2140, 175m, Hitchcock, scene from Psycho, 1960. No. 2141, 175m, 320 km Shinkansen train, 2011. No. 2142, 175m, ALSTOM AGV, France. No. 2143, 175m, Paintings by Modigliani from 1919 and 1918. No. 2144, 175m, Sevastyanov and Salyut 4. No. 2145, 175m, IKAROS and H-IIA rocket lifting off, diff. No. 2146, 175m, Luigi Galvani, and diagram of his experiments with frogs.

2010, Nov. 30   *Perf. 12¾x13½*
Sheets of 6, #a-f
2125-2135 A424   Set of 11 210.00 210.00

Souvenir Sheets
Perf. 13¼ Syncopated
2136-2146 A424   Set of 11 150.00 150.00

People, Anniversaries and Events — A425

No. 2147, 16m — New Year 2011 (Year of the Rabbit): a, Rabbit sitting, facing right, Chinese character to right or rabbit. b, Rabbit facing left, Chinese character to left of rabbit. c, Rabbit running left, Chinese character above rabbit. d, Rabbit running right, chinese character to right of rabbit, below head, text at UL. e, Rabbit with front legs raised, Chinese character to right of rabbit. f, Rabbit leaping, Chinese character below rabbit's hind legs. g, Rabbit standing, facing left, Chinese character to left of rabbit. h, Rabbit standing, facing right, Chinese character to right of rabbit, text at LH.

No. 2148, 16m — Views of Ocean Park, Hong Kong and: a, Ailurus fulgens. b, Zalophus californianus. c, Delphinus delphis. d, Ailuropoda melanoleuca. e, Ramphastos toco. f, Chrysaora fusescens. g, Phoenicopterus roseus. h, Ara ararauna.

No. 2149, 16m — 2010 Commonwealth Games, Delhi, India: a, Achanta Sharath Kamal, table tennis player. b, Allan Davis, cyclist. c, Anastasia Rodionova, tennis player. d, Christine Girard, weight lifter. e, Paddy Barnes, boxer. f, Alicia Coutts, swimmer. g, Alison Shanks, cyclist. h, Azhar Hussain, wrestler.

No. 2150 — Details from paintings by Caravaggio (1571-1610) dated: a, 16m, 1594-95

and 1593-94. b, 16m, 1600-04 and 1593-94. c, 16m, 1607-08 and 1593-94. d, 16m, 1596 and 1601. e, 16m, 1597 and 1595-96. f, 16m, 1598 and 1596-98. g, 92m, 1598-99 and 1599. h, 92m, 1603 and 1608.

No. 2151 — Tony Curtis (1925-2010), actor, and scenes from: a, 16m, Houdini, 1953. b, 16m, Son of Ali Baba, 1952. c, 16m, The Defiant Ones, 1958. d, 16m, The Black Shield of Falworth, 1954. e, 16m, The Great Race, 1965. f, 16m, Wild and Wonderful, 1964. g, 92m, Some Like it Hot, 1959. h, 92m, Sweet Smell of Success, 1957.

No. 2152 — BP Deepwater Horizon oil spill: a, 16m, Bird standing, burning oil rig. b, 16m, Turtle in net, oil boom on water, burning rig. c, 16m, Bird in flight, ships near burning rig. d, 16m, Pelican, boat with oil boom in oil slick. e, 16m, Bird with head raised in oily water. f, 16m, Ship, bird on piling, oil burning on water's surface. g, 92m, Bird, cleanup workers on beach. h, 92m, Birds, burning rig, map of Gulf of Mexico coastline.

No. 2153 — Details of religious paintings by: a, 16m, Titian, from 1535 and 1540 . b, 16m, Alessandro Botticelli, from 1490 and 1470. c, 16m, El Greco, from 1600 and 1590-95. d, 16m, Giotto, from 1295-1300 and 1304. e, 16m, Rogier van der Weyden, from 1445 and 1435-40. f, 16m, Antonio da Correggio, from 1525 and 1520. g, 92m, Piero della Francesca, from 1450-63 and 1454-69. h, 92m, Giovanni Bellini, from 1465 and 1464-68.

No. 2154, 175m, Rabbit and Chinese character, diff. No. 2155, 175m, Stegostoma fasciatum in Ocean Park tank. No. 2156, 175m, Somdev Devvarman, tennis player. No. 2157, 175m, Painting details by Caravaggio, from 1609 and 1593-94. No. 2158, 175m, Curtis, scene from movie. No. 2159, 175m, Bird in flight near burning BP Deepwater Horizon oil rig. No. 2160, 175m, Painting details by Lorenzo Lotto from 1508 and 1530.

2010, Nov. 30   *Perf. 12¾x13½*
Sheets of 8, #a-h
2147-2153 A425   Set of 7 120.00 120.00

Souvenir Sheets
Perf. 13¼ Syncopated
2154-2160 A425   Set of 7 95.00 95.00

Intl. Year of Forests — A426

No. 2161 — Sheet inscribed "Gibao de maos brancas": a, 16m, Hylobates lar sitting on tree branch. b, 16m, Hylobates lar hanging from tree branch. c, 16m, Hylobates lar walking. d, 16m, Hylobates lar, leaves of palm tree beneath denomination. e, 66m, Hylobates lar seated. f, 66m, Hylobates lar seated on stump.

No. 2162 — Sheet inscribed "Lémur": a, 16m, Lemur catta facing left with tail raised. b, 16m, Lemur catta, tail at bottom. c, 16m, Lemur catta facing right with tail raised. d, 16m, Lemur catta with tail over shoulder. e, 66m, Lemur catta with tail around head. f, 66m, Lemur catta with tail hanging.

No. 2163 — Sheet inscribed "Preguiça": a, 16m, Choloepus didactylus. b, 16m, Bradypus pygmaeus. c, 16m, Choloepus hoffmanni. d, 16m, Bradypus variegatus. e, 66m, Choloepus hoffmanni, diff. f, 66m, Choloepus didactylus, diff.

No. 2164 — Sheet inscribed "Rinoceronte-de-sumatra": a, 16m, Dicerorhinus sumatrensis facing right with head near ground. b, 16m, Dicerorhinus sumatrensis facing right with head raised. c, 16m, Dicerorhinus sumatrensis facing left with head near ground. d, 16m, Dicerorhinus sumatrensis facing left with head raised. e, 66m, Dicerorhinus sumatrensis facing right, diff. f, 66m, Dicerorhinus sumatrensis facing left, diff.

No. 2165 — Sheet inscribed "Morcego-Vampiro": a, 16m, Desmodus rotundus facing right, in flight . b, 16m, Desmodus rotundus on rock, blue area surrounding denomination. c, 16m, Desmodus rotundus on rock, rock under "16". d, 16m, Desmodus rotundus facing left, in flight. e, 66m, Desmodus rotundus in flight, diff. f, 66m, Desmodus rotundus on rock, diff.

No. 2166 — Sheet inscribed "Jaguar": a, 16m, Panthera onca facing left on cut off tree branch. b, 16m, Panthera onca on fallen log. c, 16m, Panthera onca on grass. d, 16m, Panthera onca walking. e, 66m, Panthera onca walking, facing left. f, 66m, Panthera onca walking, facing forward.

No. 2167 — Sheet inscribed "Peixi-boi": a, 16m, Trichechus inunguis, left fin close to frame line at bottom. b, 16m, Two Trichechus senegalensis. c, 16m, One Trichechus manatus. d, 16m, Trichechus inunguis, right fin close to frame line at bottom. e, 66m, Two Trichecus manatus. f, 66m, One Trichechus senegalensis.

No. 2168 — Sheet inscribed "Harpia": a, 16m, Harpia harpyja facing right on tree branch with leaves. b, 16m, Harpia harpyja in flight near tree. c, 16m, Harpia harpyja facing left on branch without leaves. d, 16m, Harpia harpyja facing left on tree branch with leaves. e, 66m, Harpia harpyja in flight, tree in background. f, 66m, Harpia harpyja in flight, no trees in background.

No. 2169 — Sheet inscribed "Borboleta asas de pássaro": a, 16m, Ornithoptera alexandrae on leaf, name at LL. b, 16m, Ornithoptera alexandrae in flight. c, 16m, Ornithoptera alexandrae on leaf, name at UR. d, 16m, Ornithoptera alexandrae on leaf, name at UL. e, 66m, Ornithoptera alexandrae on leaf, diff. f, 66m, Ornithoptera alexandrae in flight, diff.

No. 2170 — Sheet inscribed "Borboleta azul": a, 16m, Morpho menelaus on leaf with wings closed, name at UL. b, 16m, Morpho menelaus on tree with wings open, name at UR. c, 16m, Morpho memelaus on tree with wings partially open, name at UL. d, 16m, Morpho menelaus on rock with wings open, name at LL. e, 66m, Morpho menelaus on leaf, name at UL on two lines. f, 66m, Morpho menelaus on leaf, name in UL on one line.

No. 2171 — Sheet inscribed "Piranha": a, 16m, Pygocentrus ternetzi. b, 16m, Serrasalmus manueli. c, 16m, Pygocentrus nattereri. d, 16m, Pygocentrus cariba. e, 66m, Pygocentrus nattereri, diff. f, 66m, Pygocentrus ternetzi, diff.

No. 2172 — Sheet inscribed "Cobra-papagaio": a, 16m, Corallus caninus on branch, head at top of stamp. b, 16m, Corallus caninus on branch, head at LL. c, 16m, Corallus caninus, head at LR. d, 16m, Corallus caninus on branch, head at bottom center. e, 66m, Corallus caninus on branch, head in center, tail visible. f, 66m, Corallus caninus on branch, head at left, tail not visible.

No. 2173 — Sheet inscribed "Jacaré-açu": a, 16m, Melanosuchus niger in grass. b, 16m, Melanosuchus niger swimming. c, 16m, Melanosuchus niger standing, facing right. d, 16m, Melanosuchus niger standing, facing forward. e, 66m, Juvenile melanosuchus niger in water. f, 66m, Melanosuchus niger with mouth open.

No. 2174 — Sheet inscribed "Ra de olhos vermelhos": a, 16m, Agalychnis callidryas on vine, name at LR. b, 16m, Agalychnis callidryas facing right with rear leg extended at top, name at UR. c, 16m, Agalychnis callidryas facing left, name at UR. d, 16m, Agalychnis callidryas on vine, name at UL. e, 66m, Agalychnis callidryas on vine, name at LL. f, 66m, Agalychnis callidryas on vine, name at LR.

No. 2175 — Sheet inscribed "Tartaruga": a, 16m, Trachemys scripta elegans. b, 16m, Geochelone sulcata. c, 16m, Malaclemys terrapin. d, 16m, Chelus fimbriatus. e, 66m, Chelonoidis carbonaria. f, 66m, Terrepene carolina carolina.

No. 2176 — Sheet inscribed "Jupará": a, 16m, Potus flavus, head at UL, name at UR. b, 16m, Potos flavus, name at UL. c, 16m, Potus flavus, head at LL, name at UR, diff. d, 92m, Potos flavus standing, name at UR, diff. e, 92m, Potos flavus, name at UL, diff. f, 92m, potos flavus in tree, name at UR.

No. 2177 — Sheet inscribed "Gorila": a, 16m, Gorilla beringei graueri, name at LR. b, 16m, Gorilla beringei. c, 16m, Gorilla gorilla diehli. d, 16m, Gorilla beringei graueri, name at UR. e, 92m, Gorilla gorilla. f, 92m, Gorilla gorilla gorilla.

No. 2178 — Sheet inscribed "Ateles": a, 16m, Ateles hybridus, name at right. b, 16m, Ateles chamek. c, 16m, Trichechus manatus. d, 16m, Ateles hybridus, name at UL. e, 92m, Ateles paniscus. f, 92m, Ateles hybridus, diff.

No. 2179 — Sheet inscribed "Társio": a, 16m, Tarsius syrichta, name at UR. b, 16m, Tarsius bancanus. c, 16m, Tarsius syrichta, name at LR. d, 16m, Tarsius tarsier. e, 92m, Tarsius dentatus. f, 92m, Tarsius syrichta, name at UL.

No. 2180 — Sheet inscribed "Tigris de Bengala": a, 16m, Panthera tigris, name at left. b, 16m, Panthera tigris tigris. c, 16m, Panthera tigris in water, name at right. d, 16m, Panthera tigris in grass, name at UR. e, 92m, Panthera tigrist tigris laying down. f, 92m, Panthera tigris tigris walking.

No. 2181 — Sheet inscribed "Calaubicórnico": a, 16m, Buceros bicornis on branch, name at UR. b, 16m, Buceros bicornis in flight, name at LR. c, 16m, Buceros bicornis on branch on tree at left, name at UR. d, 16m, Buceros bicornis on branch, name at LL. e, 92m, Buceros bicornis in flight, name at UL. f, 92m, Buceros bicornis in flight, name at LR, diff.

No. 2182 — Sheet inscribed "Casuario Austral": a, 16m, Casuarius causarius sitting, name at UL. b, 16m, Casuarius causarius standing, name at right. c, 16m, Casuarius causarius standing, name at left. d, 16m, Casuarius casuarius with leg lifted, name at left. e, 92m, Cauarius casuarius, name at LL. f, 92m, Casuaraius casuarius, name at UL.

No. 2183 — Sheet inscribed "Coruja": a, 16m, Tyto multipunctata. b, 16m, Ninox connivens. c, 16m, Glaucidium tephronotum. d, 16m, Asio madagascariensis. e, 92m, Ninox novaeseelandiae. f, 92m, Otus rutilus.

No. 2184 — Sheet inscribed "Papagaio": a, 16m, Lorus garrulus. b, 16m, Trichoglossus chlorolepidotus. c, 16m, Trichoglottus flavoviridis. d, 16m, Trichoglossus euteles. e, 92m, Eos reticulata. f, 92m, Trichoglossus haematodus.

No. 2185 — Sheet inscribed "Quetzal-resplandecente": a, 16m, Pharomachrus mocinno on brach, name at right. b, 16m, Pharomachrus mocinno on branch, name at UR. c, 16m, Pharomachrus mocinno on branch, name at LR. d, 16m, Pharomachrus mocinno on branch, name at LL. e, 92m, Pharomachrus mocinno on branch, name at LR, diff. f, 92m, Pharomachrus mocinno on branch, name at LL, diff.

No. 2186 — Sheet inscribed "Tucano": a, 16m, Ramphastos dicolorus. b, 16m, Ramphastos toco. c, 16m, Ramphastos vitellinus. d, 16m, Ramphastos swainsonii. e, 92m, Ramphastos torquatus. f, 92m, Ramphastos sulfuratus.

No. 2187 — Sheet inscribed "Libélula": a, 16m, Anax Imperator. b, 16m, Libellula depressa. c, 16m, Sympetrum fonscolombii. d, 16m, Libellula quadrimaculata. e, 92m, Ischnura heterosticta. f, 92m, Crocothemis sanguinolenta.

No. 2188 — Sheet inscribed "Borboleta-monarca": a, 16m, Danaus plexippus on flower, antennae near flower, name at right. b, 16m, Danaus plexippus on flower, antennae near denomination, name at right. c, 16m, Danaus plexippus on flower, name at UL, denomination at UR. d, 16m, Danaus plexippus on flower, name below denomination at UL. e, 92m, Danaus plexippus on branch, name at UL. f, 92m, Danaus plexippus on flower, name at LL.

No. 2189 — Sheet inscribed "Dendrobatidae": a, 16m, Epipedobates tricolor. b, 16m, Dendrobates auratus. c, 16m, Dendrobates azureus. d, 16m, Dendrobates leucomelas. e, 92m, Phyllobates terribilis. f, 92m, Oophaga pumilio.

No. 2190 — Sheet inscribed "Víbora do Gabao": a, 16m, Bitis gabonica, head at LL, name at LR. b, 16m, Bitis gabonica in grass, head in center, name at LR. c, 16m, Bitis gabonica, name at UL. d, 16m, Bitis gabonica on parched earth, head in center, name at LR. e, 92m, Bitis gabonica, name at LL. f, 92m, Bitis gabonica, name at UR.

No. 2191, 175m, Hylobates lar, diff. No. 2192, 175m, Lemur catta, diff. No. 2193, 175m, Bradypus variegatus, diff. No. 2194, 175m, Three Dicerorhinus sumatrensis. No. 2195, 175m, Desmodus rotundus, diff. No. 2196, 175m, Panthera onca, diff. No. 2197, 175m, Two Trichechus inunguis. No. 2198, 175m, Harpia harpyja in flght, diff. No. 2199, 175m, Ornithoptera alexandrae on leaf, diff. No. 2200, 175m, Two Morpho menelaus on leaves. No. 2201, 175m, Two Pygocentrus nattereri. No. 2202, 175m, Copralius caninus on tree branch, diff. No. 2203, 175m, Melanosuchus niger, diff. No. 2204, 175m, Agalychnis callidryas, diff. No. 2205, 175m, Geochelone sulcata, diff. No. 2206, 175m, Potos flavus, diff. No. 2207, 175m, Gorilla gorilla, diff. No. 2208, 175m, Ateles hybridus, diff. No. 2209, 175m, Tarsius pumilus, diff. No. 2210, 175m, Panthera tigris, diff. No. 2211, 175m, Buceros bicornis, diff. No. 2212, 175m, Casuarius casuarius, diff. No. 2213, 175m, Asio madagascariensis, diff. No. 2214, 175m, Trichoglossus rubritorquis. No. 2215, 175m, Pharomachrus mocinno, diff. No. 2216, 175m, Ramphastos sulfuratus, diff. No. 2217, 175m, Trithemis kirbyi. No. 2218, 175m, Danaus plexippus on flower, diff. No. 2219, 175m, Dendrobates azureus, diff. No. 2220, 175m, Bitis gabonica, diff.

2011, Jan. 30   *Perf. 12¾x13½*
Sheets of 6, #a-f
2161-2190 A426   Set of 30 525.00 525.00
Souvenir Sheets
Perf. 13½x12¾
2191-2220 A426   Set of 30 400.00 400.00

Television in Mozambique, 30th Anniv. — A427

Denominations: 66m, 92m.

2011, Feb. 28 Litho. *Perf. 11x11¼*
2221-2222 A427   Set of 2   12.50 12.50

People, Events and Anniversaries — A428

No. 2223 — George Clooney, actor, and scenes from his films: a, 16m, Solaris. b, 16m, The American. c, 66m, Ocean's 12. d, 92m, The Good German.

No. 2224 — Elizabeth Taylor (1932-2011), actress: a, 16m, Wearing black dress, wearing white dress holding Oscar. b, 16m, Wearing brown dress, wearing white dress. c, 66m, Holding dog. d, 92m, With Michael Jackson.

No. 2225 — Roald Amundsen (1872-1928), Antarctic explorer and scenes from his 1911 expedition: a, 16m, Witn Norwegian flag at South Pole. b, 16m, With expedition members making scientific observations. c, 66m, Standing in hut. d, 92m, With dog team and Norwegian flag.

No. 2226 — Fridtjof Nansen (1961-1930), polar explorer, and: a, 16m, Arctocephalus gazella. b, 16m, Orcinus orca. c, 66m, Aptenodytes forsteri. d, 92m, Ship named Fridtjof Nansen.

No. 2227 — First airmail flight, cent.: a, 16m, Pilot Henri Pequet, airplane, maps. b, 16m, Pilot Earle Lewis Ovington and airplane. c, 66m, Pilot Fred J. Wiseman and airplane. d, 92m, Airplane of Fred J. Wiseman used in airmail flight from Petaluma to Santa Rosa, California.

No. 2228 — Andor Lilienthal (1911-2010), chess grandmaster, chess board and pieces, and: a, 16m, David Bronstein. b, 16m, Ruslan Ponomariov. c, 66m, Lilienthal playing chess. d, 92m, Lilienthal playing against 121 opponents.

No. 2229 — Maia Chiburdanidze, chess grandmaster, and: a, 16m, Chess board in purple. b, 16m, Chess board in gray blue. c, 66m, Knight. d, 92m, Rook and pawn.

No. 2230 — Japanese earthquake relief: a, 16m, Red Cross worker feeding infant. b, 16m, Workers carrying dead body. c, 66m, Red Cross worker watching fire. d, 92m, Fireman with hose.

No. 2231 — Chiune Sugihara (1900-86), Japanese diplomat who saved Jews in World War II, and: a, 16m, Jews, star of David. b, 16m, Sugihara in chair. c, 66m, Sugihara and his family. d, 92m, Monument to Sugihara in Vilnius, Lithuania.

No. 2232 — Rajiv Gandhi (1944-91), Indian prime minister: a, 16m, With Indians and cow. b, 16m, With family. c, 66m, With Mother Teresa. d, 92m, Standing in automobile.

No. 2233 — Paintings by Lucas Cranach, the Younger (1515-86): a, 16m, Portrait of a Woman, 1539. b, 16m, Prince Elector Moritz of Saxony, 1578. c, 66m, Elector Johann Friedrich of Saxony, 1578. d, 92m, Portrait of a Woman, diff.

No. 2234 — Paintings by Giorgio Vasari (1511-74): a, 16m, Lorenzo de Medici, 1533. b, 16m, Battle of Lepanto. c, 66m, St. Luke Painting the Virgin. d, 92m, Entombment.

No. 2235 — Franz Liszt (1811-86), composer, and: a, 16m, Liszt's house in Weimar, Germany from 1869-86. b, 16m, Budapest Opera House. c, 66m, Liszt's residence from 1863-69, Madonna del Rosario Monastery. d, 92m, Birthplace, Dobroján, Hungary.

No. 2236 — Gustav Mahler (1860-1911), composer, and: a, 16m, Symphony orchestra. b, 16m, Hofoper Building, Vienna. c, 66m, Metropolitan Oper, New York. d, 92m, Symphony orchestra, diff.

No. 2237 — Princess Diana (1961-97), and: a, 16m, Elton John. b, 16m, Baroness Chalker. c, 66m, Prince Charles, Ronald and Nancy Reagan. d, 92m, Michael Jackson.

No. 2238 — Human evolution: a, 16m, Australopithecus africanus. b, 16m, Homo habilis. c, 66m, Homo antecessor. d, 92m, Homo heidelbergensis.

No. 2239, 175m, Clooney, director's chair, projector, film reels. No. 2240, 175m, Taylor, diff. No. 2241, 175m, Amundsen and ship trapped in ice. No. 2242, 175m, Nansen, ship and Ursus maritimus. No. 2243, 175m, Pequet

and airplane.No. 2244, 175m, Lilienthal playing chess, diff. No. 2245, 175m, Chiburdanidze, diff. No. 2246, 175m, Japanese firefighter holding hose at fire at industrial complex. No. 2247, 175m, Sugihara and refugees. No. 2248, 175m, Rajiv Gandhi and children. No. 2249, 175m, The III Matched Lovers, painting by Lucas Cranach, the Younger. No. 2250, 175m, The Walk to Emmaus, painting by Lelio Orsi. No. 2251, 175m, Liszt and Franz Liszt Music Academy, Budapest. No. 2252, 175m, Mahler and symphony orchestra, diff. No. 2253, 175m, Princess Diana, roses, Nepalese children. No. 2254, 175m, Australopithecus afarensis, map of Africa.

2011, Apr. 30   *Perf. 13½x12¾*
Sheets of 4, #a-d
2223-2238 A428   Set of 16 240.00 240.00
Souvenir Sheets
2239-2254 A428   Set of 16 225.00 225.00

People, Events and Anniversaries — A429

No. 2255 — James Gandolfini, actor, and scenes from: a, 16m, Surviving Christmas, 2004. b, 16m, Lonely Hearts, 2006. c, 16m, The Last Castle, 2001. d, 16m, Welcome to the Rileys, 2010. e, 66m, The Sopranos, 1999-2007. f, 92m, In the Loop, 2009.

No. 2256 — Joseph Barbera (1911-2006), cartoon director, and: a, 16m, Abbott and Costello cartoon characters. b, 16m, Top Cat. c, 16m, William Hanna, production drawings of cartoon characters for Magilla Gorilla. d, 16m, Huckleberry Hound and elephant. e, 66m, Motormouse and Autocat. f, 92m, Huckleberry Hound with guitar.

No. 2257 — Ishiro Honda (1911-93), film director and scene from: a, 16m, Ghidorah, the Three-Headed Monster. b, 16m, Battle in Outer Space, 1959. c, 16m, Godzilla, 1954. d, 16m, Destroy All Monsters, 1968. e, 66m, Frankenstein Conquers the World, 1965. f, 92m, Yog: Monster from Space, 1970.

No. 2258 — American Civil War soldiers: a, 16m, Three Union soldiers and flag, 1864. b, 16m, Three Confederate soldiers with guns, 1861. c, 16m, Horse, flag and three Union soldiers, 1863. d, 16m, Three Confederate soldiers (one aiming rifle), 1861. e, 66m, Two Union cavalrymen with horses. f, 92m, Three Union soldiers, 1864, diff.

No. 2259 — Antarctic Treaty: a, 16m, Orcinus orca. b, 16m, Pygoscelis adeliae. c, 16m, Pagodroma nivea nivea. d, 16m, Channichthyidae. e, 66m, Arctocephalus gazella. f, 92m, Balaenoptera musculus.

No. 2260 — Beatification of Pope John Paul II: a, 16m, Pope grasping man around head. b, 16m, Pope pointing. c, 16m, Pope with Mother Teresa. d, 16m, Pope with St. Peter's Basilica in background. e, 66m, Pope greeting people. f, 92m, Pope wearing miter, holding crucifix.

No. 2261 — Automobiles from first Monte Carlo Rally, 1911: a, 16m, Turcat-Mery. b, 16m, Gobron 40 HP. c, 16m, Berliet 16 HP. d, 16m, Gobron-Brillié 40/60 CV. e, 66m, Delaunay-Belleville 15 HP. f, 92m, Dürkopp.

No. 2262 — Juan Manuel Fangio (1911-95), race car driver: a, 16m, Ferrari-Lancia d50. b, 16m, Flipped race car. c, 16m, Maserati 250F. d, 16m, Ferrari 166c. e, 66m, Mercedes-Benz W 196. f, 92m, Ferrari-Lancia d50, diff.

No. 2263 — Madame Tussaud Wax Museum sculptures: a, 16m, Albert Einstein. b, 16m, Princess Diana and Prince William. c, 16m, Mahatma Gandhi. d, 16m, Marilyn Monroe. e, 66m, Pope John Paul II. f, 92m, Elvis Presley.

No. 2264 — Alan B. Shepard, Jr. (1923-98), astronaut, and: a, 16m, Saturn V rocket. b, 16m, Mercury-Redstone rocket. c, 16m, Mercury 3 capsule (Freedom 7). d, 16m, Shephard in space suit. e, 66m, Pres. John F. Kennedy. f, 92m, Shepard in space capsule.

No. 2265 — Space Shuttle Challenger astronauts: a, 16m, Gregory Jarvis. b, 16m, Judith Resnik. c, 16m, Ellison Onizuka. d, 16m, Dick Scobee. e, 66m, Ronald McNair. f, 92m, Michael J. Smith.

No. 2266 — Yuri Gagarin (1934-68), first man in space: a, 16m, Gagarin and drawing of cosmonaut and space capsule. b, 16m, Vostok I. c, 16m, Gagarin and rocket launch. d, 16m, Gagarin and spacecraft in flight. e, 66m, Gagarin in Space helmet Autocat. f, 92m, Gagarin and drawing of rocket and space capsule.

No. 2267 — Mir Space Station, 25th anniv: a, 16m, Mir and rocket launch. b, 16m, Mir in space, denomination at UL. c, 16m, Mir and cosmonauts. d, 16m, Mir in space, denomination at UR. e, 66m, Mir and space shuttle. f, 92m, Mir and pieces descending to Earth.

No. 2268 — Wedding of Prince William and Catherine Middleton: a, 16m, Prince Charles and Princess Diana at UR. b, 16m, Westminster Abbey, denomination at UL. c, 16m, Prince Charles and Princess Diana at UL. d, 16m, Westminster Abbey, denomination at UR. e, 66m, Prince Charles, Princess Diana, horse. f, 92m, Westminster Abbey, denomination at UR, diff.

No. 2269, 175m, Gandolfini and scene from The Man Who Wasn't There. No. 2270, 175m, Barbera, Hanna, Autocat and Fred Flintstone. No. 2271, 175m, Honda and scene from Mothra, 1961. No. 2272, 175m, Six Confederate soldiers. No. 2273, 175m, Hydrurga leptonyx. No. 2274, 175m, Pope John Paul II, Mother Teresa. No. 2275, 175m, Turcat-Mery car in first Monte Carlo Rally. No. 2276, 175m, Fangio and Mercedes-Benz W196, diff. No. 2277, 175m, Wax sculptures of Marie Tussaud. No. 2278, 175m, Shepard, Mercury 3 rocket, Apollo 14 emblem. No. 2279, 175m, Challenger astronaut Christa McAuliffe. No. 2280, 175m, Gagarin and space capsule in flight. No. 2281, 175m, Mir in space, diff. No. 2282, 175m, Prince William, Catherine Middleton, Princess Diana and Prince Charles.

2011, Apr. 30   *Perf. 12¾x13½*
Sheets of 6, #a-f
2255-2268 A429   Set of 14 240.00 240.00
Souvenir Sheets
Perf. 13½x12¾
2269-2282 A429   Set of 14 190.00 190.00

People, Events and
Anniversaries — A430

No. 2283 — Beatification of Pope John Paul II: a, 16m, Pope John Paul II wearing miter at left. b, 16m, Pope John Paul praying at right. c, 66m, Pope John Paul II and St. Peter's Basilica. d, 92m, Pope John Paul II greeting crowd.

No. 2284 — Mohandas K. Gandhi (1869-1948), Indian independence leader, and: a, 16m, Gandhi seated, touching child. b, 16m, Gandhi standing in crowd. c, 66m, Gandhi in crowd. d, 92m, Gandhi seated in chair.

No. 2285 — Famous Indians: a, 16m, Rabindranath Tagore (1861-1941), writer and Mohandas Gandhi. b, 16m, Subhas Chandra Bose (1897-1945), nationalist leader, Bose on horseback. c, 66m, Tagore and Albert Einstein. d, 92m, Bose and Mohandas Gandhi.

No. 2286 — Intl. Year of Chemistry: a, 16m, Marie Curie (1867-1934), and model of Radium atom. b, 16m, Curie and Polonium. c, 66m, Curie and daughter, Irene. d, 92m, Curie in laboratory.

No. 2287 — Sir Alexander Fleming (1881-1955), discoverer of penicillin: and: a, 16m, Molecular model of penicillin. b, 16m, Penicillum sp. c, 66m, Vial and needle of penicillin. d, 92m, Petri dish.

No. 2288 — Princess Diana (1961-97): a, 16m, With child, Big Ben. b, 16m, Exiting automobile. c, 66m, Tower Bridge. d, 92m, And child in hospital bed.

No. 2289 — Henri Matisse (1869-1954), painter, and painting from: a, 16m, 1908. b, 16m, 1918. c, 66m, 1901. d, 92m, 1912.

No. 2290 — René Magritte (1898-1967), painter, and painting from: a, 16m, 1966. b, 16m, 1933. c, 66m, 1964. d, 92m, 1936.

No. 2291 — Ford vehicles: a, 16m, 1908 Model T. b, 16m, 1905 Delivery car. c, 66m, 1930 Model A Deluxe Sedan. d, 92m, 1927 Model T.

No. 2292 — Locomotives: a, 16m, Western Pacific 805-A, 1960, U.S. b, 16m, Alco RS-2, 1946, U.S. c, 66m, Bo-Bo Class EO, 1923, New Zealand. d, 92m, Class 103.158, 1969, Germany.

No. 2293 — World War II warships: a, 16m, HMS Hood. b, 16m, HMAS Sydney. c, 66m, DKM Bismarck. d, 92m, IJN Yamato.

No. 2294 — Jet aircraft and engines: a, 16m, F-86 Sabre, Allison J35 engine. b, 16m, Lockheed F-104 Starfighter, General Electric J79 engine. c, 66m, Grumman F9F Panther, Allison J33 engine. d, 92m, Lockheed P-80 Shooting Star, Halford H-1 engine.

No. 2295, 175m, Pope John Paul II and Mother Teresa. No. 2296, 175m, Gandhi, diff. No. 2297, 175m, Tagore and Gandhi, diff. No. 2298, 175m, Curie, diff. No. 2299, 175m, Fleming, penicillin tablets, Red Cross workers treating injured soldiers. No. 2300, 175m, Princess Diana, diff. No. 2301, 175m, Matisse and painting from 1905. No. 2302, 175m, Magritte and painting from 1941. No. 2303, 175m, Henry Ford and 1910 Model T. No. 2304, 175m, EMD GP9 locomotive, 1949, U.S and Canada. No. 2305, 175m, Admiral Graf Spee. No. 2306, 175m, Heinkel He-178, He S-3 engine.

Perf. 13¼x9¼x13¼x9¼
2011, June 30   Litho.
Sheets of 4, #a-d
2283-2294 A430   Set of 12 165.00 165.00
Souvenir Sheets
2295-2306 A430   Set of 12 152.50 152.50

People, Events and
Anniversaries — A431

No. 2307 — Albert Einstein (1879-1955), physicist, and: a, 16m, Mass-energy equivalence equation, text starting with "Em 1919." b, 16m, Expanding universe, mass-energy equivalence equation. c, 16m, Diagram of photoelectric effect. d, 16m, Binary pulsar. e, 66m, Gravitational field. f, 92m, Circles and arrows.

No. 2308 — Musicians: a, 16m, Elvis Presley (1935-77), teddy bear, Ann-Margret. b, 16m, Frank Sinatra (1915-98), and daughter Nancy. c, 16m, Louis Armstrong (1901-71), and Ella Fitzgerald. d, 16m, Presley and scene from movie, Fun in Acupulco. e, 66m, Frank Sinatra and Gene Kelly. f, 92m, Armstrong and scene from movie.

No. 2309 — Musicians: a, 16m, Michael Jackson (1958-2009). b, 16m, Freddie Mercury (1946-91). c, 16m, The Rolling Stones. d, 16m, Jackson and backup singers. e, 66m, Mercury and members of Queen. f, 92m, The Rolling Stones, diff.

No. 2310 — Film personalities: a, 16m, Alfred Hitchcock (1899-1980), director. b, 16m, James Dean (1931-55), actor. c, 16m, Greta Garbo (1905-90), actress. d, 16m, Grace Kelly (1929-82), actress. e, 66m, Clark Gable (1901-60), actor. f, 92m, Marlon Brando (1924-2004), actor.

No. 2311 — Political leaders: a, 16m, Pres. John F. Kennedy (1917-63), American astronauts. b, 16m, Sir Winston Churchill (1874-1965), British prime minister, and Pres. Franklin D. Roosevelt and Joseph Stalin. c, 16m, Charles de Gaulle (1890-1970), President of France. d, 16m, Kennedy, Lyndon B. Johnson and Sam Rayburn. e, 66m, Churchill. f, 92m, De Gaulle and Gen. George C. Marshall.

No. 2312 — Political leaders: a, 16m, Pres. Theodore Roosevelt (1858-1919), moose. b, 16m, Lech Walesa, Polish President, and Solidarity banners. c, 16m, Mikhail Gorbachev, Pres. of Soviet Union, and Pres. Barack Obama. d, 16m, Roosevelt on Wright Brothers airplane. e, 66m, Walesa, diff. f, 92m, Gorbachev and Pres. Ronald Reagan.

No. 2313 — Pioneers in communications technology: a, 16m, Guglielmo Marconi (1874-1937), radio pioneer. b, 16m, John Logie Baird (1888-1946), television pioneer. c, 16m, Thomas Edison (1847-1931), inventor of Kinetoscope. d, 16m, Alexander Graham Bell (1847-1922), inventor of telephone. e, 66m, Edward Roberts (1941-2010), computer engineer. f, 92m, Tim Berners-Lee, inventor of World Wide Web.

No. 2314 — Humanitarians: a, 16m, Mother Teresa (1910-97). b, 16m, Dr. Martin Luther King, Jr. (1929-68). c, 16m, Nelson Mandela. d, 16m, Mother Teresa and Pope John Paul II. e, 66m, King, diff. f, 92m, Mandela, diff.

No. 2315 — Writers: a, 16m, George Orwell (1903-50). b, 16m, Albert Camus (1913-60). c, 16m, Ernest Hemingway (1899-1961), with John Dos Passos, Joris Ivens and Sidney Franklin. d, 16m, Hemingway and buffalo. e, 66m, Kurt Vonnegut, Jr. (1922-2007). f, 92m, Mikhail Bulgakov (1891-1940).

No. 2316 — Sports personalities: a, 16m, Pelé, soccer player. b, 16m, Michael Jordan,

basketball player. c, 16m, Ayrton Senna (1960-94), race car driver. d, 16m, Babe Ruth (1895-1948), baseball player. e, 66m, Nadia Comenici, gymnast. f, 92m, Jim Thorpe (1888-1953), Olympic track athlete.

No. 2317 — Space exploration: a, 16m, Yuri Gagarin (1934-68), Vostok 1. b, 16m, Space Shuttle. c, 16m, Valentina Tereshkova, Vostok 6. d, 16m, Mir Space Station and Space Shuttle. e, 66m, Sputnik 1. f, 92m, Neil Armstrong (1930-2012).

No. 2318 — World War II personalities: a, 16m, Charles de Gaulle (1890-1970). b, 16m, Gen. Dwight D. Eisenhower (1890-1969). c, 16m, Sir Winston Churchill (1874-1965). d, 16m, Gen. Georgy Zhukov (1896-1974). e, 66m, Harry S Truman (1884-1972). f, 92m, Gen. Bernard Montgomery (1887-1976).

No. 2319 — World War II aircraft: a, 16m, Corsair F4-U. b, 16m, Hawker Hurricane, Messerschmitt Me109, Junkers Ju-87D. c, 16m, Hawker Typhoon, Focke-Wulf Fw 190. d, 16m, Supermarine Spitfire MkXIV, Messerschmitt Me262. e, 66m, Curtiss P-40 Warhawk. f, 92m, Consolidated B-24 Liberator, Focke-Wulf 190D-9.

No. 2320 — American Impressionist painters: a, 16m, J. Ottis Adams (1851-1927), paintings from 1896 and 1901. b, 16m, Reynolds Beal (1866-1951), paintings from 1922 and 1924. c, 16m, Dennis Miller Bunker (1861-90), paintings from 1883 and 1890. d, 16m, Theodore Earl Butler (1861-1936), paintings from 1895 and 1911. e, 66m, Mary Cassatt (1844-1926), paintings from 1869 and 1880. f, 92m, Frank Weston Benson (1862-1951), paintings from 1902 and 1904.

No. 2321 — Pablo Picasso (1881-1973) and painting from: a, 16m, 1905. b, 16m, 1954. c, 16m, 1939. d, 16m, 1921-22. e, 66m, 1923. f, 92m, 1954, diff.

No. 2322 — Salvador Dalí (1904-89) and painting from: a, 16m, 1954. b, 16m, 1946. c, 16m, 1931. d, 16m, 1938. e, 66m, 1936. f, 92m, 1934, diff.

No. 2323 — Wedding of Prince William and Catherine Middleton with: a, 16m, Horses and riders in background. b, 16m, Bride and groom walking down aisle. c, 16m, Bride and groom kissing. d, 16m, Attendant carrying train of bride's dress. e, 66m, Couple in coach. f, 92m, Couple in coach, diff.

No. 2324, 175m, Einstein, diff. No. 2325, 175m, Presley and Frank Sinatra. No. 2326, 175m, The Beatles. No. 2327, 175m, Marilyn Monroe (1926-62), actress. No. 2328, 175m, Kennedy, diff. No. 2329, 175m, Gorbachev and Pope John Paul II. No. 2330, 175m, Berners-Lee, diff. No. 2331, 175m, Dr. Albert Schweitzer (1875-1965). No. 2332, 175m, Camus, diff. No. 2333, 175m, Muhammad Ali, boxer. No. 2334, 175m, Gagarin, diff. No. 2335, 175m, Neville Chamberlain (1869-1940). No. 2336, 175m, Supermarine Spitfire battling German airplanes over Dover. No. 2337, 175m, William Merritt Chase (1849-1916), paintings from 1886 and 1894. No. 2338, 175m, Picasso and painting from 1901. No. 2339, 175m, Dalí and painting from 1947. No. 2340, Wedding of Prince William and Catherine Middleton, diff.

2011, June 30   **Sheets of 6, #a-f**
2307-2323 A431   Set of 17 275.00 275.00
Souvenir Sheets
2324-2340 A431   Set of 17 215.00 215.00

Animals of Mozambique — A432

No. 2341 — Hares: a, 16m, Two Lepus saxitilis, animal name at left. b, 16m, Two Lepus saxitilis, animal name at right. c, 16m, Three

Lepus capensis. d, 16m, One Lepus capensis. e, 66m, Two Lepus capensis. f, 92m, Three Lepus capensis, diff.

No. 2342 — Rodents: a, 16m, Anomalurus derbianus. b, 16m, Hystris africaeaustralis. c, 16m, Pedetes capensis. d, 16m, Heliosciurus mutabilis. e, 66m, Paraxerus palliatus. f, 92m, Graphiurus platyops.

No. 2343 — Pangolins and aardvarks: a, 16m, Two Manis temminckii, animal name at LL. b, 16m, Two Orycteropus afer, animal name at UR. c, 16m, Two Orycteropus afer, animal name at left. d, 16m, Two Manis temminckii, animal name at UR. e, 66m, Two Manis temminckii, diff. f, 92m, Two Orycteropus afer, diff.

No. 2344 — Bovids: a, 16m, Litacranius walleri. b, 16m, Aepyceros melampus and Acinonyx jubatus. c, 16m, Oryx beisa beisa. d, 16m, Connochaetes taurinus. e, 66m, Tragelaphus spekeii. f, 92m, Taurotragus oryx.

No. 2345 — African hunting dogs: a, 16m, Three Lycaon pictus, animal name at LL. b, 16m, Two Lycaon pictus. c, 16m, Lycaon pictus chasing Connochaetes taurinus. d, 16m, Two Lycaon pictus, and animal's head with open mouth. e, 66m, Two Lycaon pictus, diff. f, 92m, Lycaon pictus, and head of animal with closed mouth.

No. 2346 — Hippopotamus amphibius: a, 16m, Animals in water and on shore with open mouths. b, 16m, Animal facing left, animal in water with open mouth, skull. c, 16m, Animals in water and on shore with closed mouths. d, 16m, Three animals. e, 66m, Adult and juvenile. f, 92m, Two animals in water.

No. 2347 — Rhinoceroses: a, 16m, Diceros bicornis, drawing of rhinoceros by Albrecht Dürer. b, 16m, Three Ceratotherium simum. c, 16m, Adult and juvenile Ceratotherium simum. d, 16m, Three Diceros bicornis, skull. e, 66m, Three Ceratotherium simum, diff. f, 92m, Three Diceros bicornis, diff.

No. 2348 — Seals: a, 16m, Two Arctocephalus pusillus, sea gull. b, 16m, Three Mirounga leonina, animal name at UL. c, 16m, Three Mirounga leonina, animal name at left. d, 16m, Three Mirounga leonina, animal name at LL. e, 66m, Three Mirounga leonina, diff. f, 92m, Pod of Arctocephalus pusillus.

No. 2349 — Primates: a, 16m, Otolemur crassicaudatus. b, 16m, Galago nyasae, Otolemur crassicaudatus. c, 16m, Chlorocebus pygerythrus. d, 16m, Cercopithecus mitis. e, 66m, Papio ursinus. f, 92m, Papio cynocephalus with Aepyceros melampus.

No. 2350 — Bats: a, 16m, Rhinolophus blasii. b, 16m, Rousettus aegyptiacus. c, 16m, Taphozous mauritianus. d, 16m, Epomophorus wahlbergi. e, 66m, Eidolon helvum. f, 92m, Nyctalus noctula.

No. 2351 — Panthera leo: a, 16m, Lion, lioness and zebra. b, 16m, Lion, two lionesses, animal carcass. c, 16m, Lion and lioness. d, 16m; Lioness with zebra carcass. e, 66m, Two lionesses. f, 92m, Lionesses, buffalo and carcass.

No. 2352 — Wild cats: a, 16m, Caracal caracal. b, 16m, Acinonyx jubatus. c, 16m, Panthera pardus. d, 16m, Leptailurus serval. e, 66m, Leptailurus serval, diff. f, 92m, Acinonyx jubatus, diff.

No. 2353 — Loxodonta africana: a, 16m, Four elephants near watering hole. b, 16m, Elephant facing left near watering hole. c, 16m, Elephant facing forward. d, 16m, Elephant facing right. e, 66m, Three elephants. f, 92m, Adult and juvenile elephants.

No. 2354 — Two Dugong dugon with animal name at: a, 16m, Center left in white. b, 16m, UL in black. c, 16m, LR in white. d, 16m, Center right in white, under denomination. e, 66m, UR in black. f, 92m, UR in black, under denomination.

No. 2355 — Dolphins: a, 16m, Sousa chinensis chinensis. b, 16m, Stenella coeruleoalba. c, 16m, Stenella longirostris. d, 16m, Steno bredanensis. e, 66m, Tursiops truncatus. f, 92m, Lagenodelphis hosei.

No. 2356 — Whales: a, 16m, Feresa attenuata. b, 16m, Orcinus orca. c, 16m, Megaptera novaeangliae. d, 16m, Physeter macrocephalus. e, 66m, Kogia sima. f, 92m, Balaenoptera borealis.

No. 2357 — Bee-eaters: a, 16m, Merops pusillus. b, 16m, Merops bullockoides. c, 16m, Merops persicus. d, 16m, Merops boehmi. e, 66m, Merops nubicoides. f, 92m, Merops apiaster.

No. 2358 — Albatrosses: a, 16m, Thalassarche melanophrys. b, 16m, Diomedea exulans. c, 16m, Phoebetria palpebrata. d, 16m, Thalassarche cauta. e, 66m, Thalassarche chlororhynchos. f, 92m, Phoebetria fusca.

No. 2359 — Storks: a, 16m, Ciconia episcopus. b, 16m, Mycteria ibis. c, 16m, Anastomus lamelligeris. d, 16m, Ciconia nigra. e, 66m, Ephippiorhynchus senegalensis. f, 92m, Ciconia abdimii.

No. 2360 — Flamingos: a, 16m, Phoenicopterus roseus, bird feeding chick in foreground, animal name at UL. b, 16m, Phoenicopterus minor, animal name at top center. c, 16m, Phoenicopterus minor, animal name at UR under denomination. d, 16m, Phoenicopterus roseus in water, animal name at UL. e, 66m, Phoenicopterus minor in flight. f, 92m, Phoenicopterus roseus, diff.

No. 2361 — Pelecanus onocrotalus: a, 16m, Pelican feeding chick with adult near water, animal name at UR. b, 16m, Three pelicans on tree branch, animal name at LL. c, 16m, Three pelicans, animal name at right. e, 66m, Two pelicans, diff. f, 92m, Four pelicans.

No. 2362 — Struthio camelus: a, 16m, Adult and juvenile ostriches. b, 16m, Two ostriches fighting. c, 16m, Head of ostrich, osctrich with wings spread. d, 16m, Two ostriches, nest with eggs. e, 66m, Ostrich running. f, 92m, Ostrich standing.

No. 2363 — Kingfishers: a, 16m, Alcedes cristata. b, 16m, Ceryle rudis. c, 16m, Halcyon senegalensis. d, 16m, Ispidina picta. e, 66m, Halcyon senegaloides. f, 92m, Halcyon leucocephala.

No. 2364 — Birds of prey: a, 16m, Haliaeetus vocifer. b, 16m, Macheiraphus alcinus. c, 16m, Circaetus cinereus. d, 16m, Aquila rapax. e, 66m, Aquila pomarina. f, 92m, Polyboroides typus.

No. 2365 — Two Pandion haliaetus with animal name at: a, 16m, UR under denomination. b, 16m, Bottom, denomination at UR. c, 16m, Bottom, denomination at UL. d, 16m, UL. e, 66m, Left. f, 92m, UL, diff.

No. 2366 — Owls: a, 16m, Tyto capensis. b, 16m, Ptilopsis granti. c, 16m, Glaucidium perlatum. d, 16m, Strix woodfordii. e, 66m, Bubo capensis. f, 92m, Bubo africanus.

No. 2367 — Butterflies: a, 16m, Papilio dardanus. b, 16m, Charaxes varanes. c, 16m, Pharmacophagus antenor. d, 16m, Papilio phorcas. e, 66m, Papilio nireus. f, 92m, Charaxes pollux.

No. 2368 — Shells: a, 16m, Mauritia arabica. b, 16m, Lambis lambis. c, 16m, Clanculus puniceus. d, 16m, Haliotis ovina. e, 66m, Morula granulata. f, 92m, Chicoreus ramosus.

No. 2369 — Sea turtles: a, 16m, Caretta caretta. b, 16m, Chelonia mydas. c, 16m, Demochelys coriacea. d, 16m, Eretmochelys imbricata. e, 66m, Lepidochelys olivacea. f, 92m, Caretta caretta, diff.

No. 2370 — Lizards: a, 16m, Two Cordylus tropidosternum, one on rock. b, 16m, Cordylus mossambicus. c, 16m, Platysaurus intermedius. d, 16m, Two Cordylus tropidosternum fighting. e, 66m, Platysaurus imperator. f, 92m, Platysaurus imperator, diff.

No. 2371, 175m, Lepus capensis, diff. No. 2372, 175m, Rhabdomys pumilio. No. 2373, 175m, Manis temminckii, diff. No. 2374, 175m, Antidoreas marsupialis. No. 2375, 175m, Lycaeon pictus, diff. No. 2376, 175m, Adult and juvenile Hippopotamus amphibius, diff. No. 2377, 175m, Ceratotherium simum, diff. No. 2378, 175m, Pod of Arctocephalus pusillus. No. 2379, 175m, Cercopithecus mitis, diff. No. 2380, 175m, Eidolon helvum, diff. No. 2381, 175m, Panthera leo, diff. No. 2382, 175m, Panthera pardus, diff. No. 2383, 175m, Loxodonta africana, diff. No. 2384, 175m, Dugong dugon, diff. No. 2385, 175m, Lissodelphis peronii. No. 2386, 175m, Feresa attenuata, diff. No. 2387, 175m, Meops hirundineus. No. 2388, 175m, Thalassarchechlororhynchus, diff. No. 2389, 175m, Mycteria ibis, diff. No. 2390, 175m, Phoenicopterus roseus, diff. No. 2391, 175m, Pelecanus onocrotalus, diff. No. 2392, 175m, Struthio camelus and egg. No. 2393, 175m, Megacerlyle maxima. No. 2394, 175m, Aquila verreauxii. No. 2395, 175m, Pandion haliaetus, diff. No. 2396, 175m, Tyto alba. No. 2397, 175m, Hypolimnas salmacis. No. 2398, 175m, Stellaria solaris, Nerita plicata, Achatina vassei. No. 2399, 175m, Eretmochelys imbricata, diff. No. 2400, 175m, Papilio demodocus, Cordylus mossambicus.

2011, Aug. 30   Sheets of 6, #a-f
2341-2370 A432 Set of 30 500.00 500.00
Souvenir Sheets
2371-2400 A432 Set of 30 400.00 400.00

Art — A433

No. 2401, 66m — Byzantine paintings by: a, Duccio di Buoninsegna from 1285 and 1308-11. b, Giotto di Bondone. c, Andrei Rublev. d, Emmanuel Tzanes.

No. 2402, 66m — Paintings by Dutch artists: a, Pieter Claesz. b, Rembrandt van Rijn from 1655. c, Dirck Hals. d, Jacob van Ruisdael.

No. 2403, 66m — Paintings by African artists: a, George Lilanga. b, Noel Kapanda. c, Saidi Omary. d, Steven Mkumba.

No. 2404, 66m — Paintings by Chinese artists: a, Chen Hongshou. b, Gong Kai. c, Xu Wei. d, Ding Guanpeng.

No. 2405, 66m — Fauvist paintings by: a, André Derain. b, Maurice de Vlaminck. c, Henri Matisse from 1904-05 and 1905. d, Charles Camoin.

No. 2406, 66m — Cubist paintings by: a, Juan Gris. b, Georges Braque. c, Pablo Picasso from 1909 and 1937. d, Paul Cézanne from 1890-94 and 1895.

No. 2407, 66m — Pop art works by: a, Richard Hamilton. b, Andy Warhol. c, David Hockney. d, Claes Oldenburg.

No. 2408, 66m — Modern art works by: a, Roy Lichtenstein from 1961 and 1988. b, Picasso from 1927 and 1932. c, Henri Matisse from 1947. d, Joan Miró from 1917 and 1925.

No. 2409, 175m, Paintings by Duccio di Buoninsegna from 1300-05. No. 2410, 175m, Paintings by Johannes Vermeer from 1668. No. 2411, 175m, Paintings by Eduardo Saidi Tingatinga. No. 2412, 175m, Paintings by Li Gonglin. No. 2413, 175m, Paintings by Kees van Dongen. No. 2414, 175m, Painting by Picasso from 1921. No. 2515, 175m, Paintings by Lichtenstein from 1963 and 1984. No. 2416, 175m, Painting by Picasso from 1935.

2011, Oct. 30   Perf. 12¾x13¼
Sheets of 4, #a-d
2401-2408 A433 Set of 8 160.00 160.00
Souvenir Sheets
2409-2416 A433 Set of 8 110.00 110.00

Art — A434

No. 2417 — Pre-historic paintings from: a, 16m, Chauvet Cave, France. b, 16m, Altamira Cave, Spain. c, 16m, Lascaux Cave, France. d, 66m, Lascaux Cave, diff. e, 66m, Niaux Cave, France. f, 66m, Chauvet Cave, diff.

No. 2418 — Paintings by Dutch artists: a, 16m, Rembrandt from 1633. b, 16m, Maarten van Heemskerck. c, 16m, Marinus van Reymerswaele. d, 66m, Vincent van Gogh from 1888. e, 66m, Lucas van Leyden. f, 66m, Johan Jongkind.

No. 2419 — Egyptian paintings from the Tomb of: a, 16m, Huy. b, 16m, Nebamun (man with tools, two women). c, 16m, Nebamun (man with staff, cattle herder and cattle). d, 66m, Nebamun, diff. e, 66m, Sebekhotep. f, 66m, Horemheb.

No. 2420 — Paintings by Flemish artists: a, 16m, Pieter Bruegel the Elder. b, 16m, Jan van Eyck. c, 16m, Frans Hals. d, 66m, Anthony van Dyck. e, 66m, Hugo van der Goes. f, 66m, Gerard David.

No. 2421 — Paintings by French artists: a, 16m, Edgar Degas from 1890. b, 16m, Paul Cézanne from 1866. c, 16m, Gustave Courbet. d, 66m, Paul Gauguin from 1892. e, 66m, Eugene Delacroix. f, 66m, Henri Matisse from 1928.

No. 2422 — Paintings by German artists: a, 16m, Hans Baldung Grien. b, 16m, Lovis Corinth. c, 16m, Ludolf Bakhuizen. d, 66m, Lucas Cranach the Elder. e, 66m, Otto Dix. f, 66m, Adam Elsheimer.

No. 2423 — Paintings by Indian artists: a, 16m, Nandalal Bose. b, 16m, Raja Ravi Varma. c, 16m, Tyeb Mehta. d, 66m, Jamini Roy. e, 66m, Abanindranath Tagore. f, 66m, S.H. Raza.

No. 2424 — Paintings by Italian artists: a, 16m, Michelangelo Buonarroti from 1508-12. b, 16m, Amadeo Modigliani from 1919. c, 16m, Titian. d, 66m, Sandro Botticelli (Minerva and Centaur, 1480). e, 66m, Tintoretto from 1540-42. f, 66m, Caravaggio.

No. 2425 — Paintings by Japanese artists: a, 16m, Toyokuni Utagawa. b, 16m, Kunimasa Utagawa. c, 16m, Toshun Kano. d, 16m, Kunisada Utagawa. e, 16m, Kiyonobu Torii. f, 66m, Shoen Uemura.

No. 2426 — Paintings by Spanish artists: a, 16m, El Greco. b, 16m, Joan Miró from 1917 and 1922-23. c, 16m, Diego Velázquez. d, 66m, Francisco Goya. e, 66m, Salvador Dalí from 1921 and 1925. f, 66m, Joaquí Sorolla.

No. 2427 — Paintings by Jewish artists: a, 16m, Modigliani from 1918. b, 16m, Moritz Daniel Oppenheim. c, 16m, Chaim Goldberg.

d, 66m, Camille Pissarro from 1901. e, 66m, Maurycy Gottlieb. f, 66m, Samuel Hirszenberg.

No. 2428 — Religious art: a, 16m, Stained-glass window depicting Jesus, 1601 painting by Caravaggio. b, 16m, Statue and fresco depicting Buddha. c, 16m, Menorah, 1638 painting of Moses, by José de Ribera. d, 66m, Ottoman calligraphy and ceiling of Ibn Battuta Mall, Dubai. e, 66m, Sculpture and fresco depicting Buddha. f, 66m, Fresco depicting Jesus, 1405 painting depicting the Annunciation by Andrei Rublev.

No. 2429 — Renaissance art by: a, 16m, Raffaello Sanzio da Urbino (Raphael). b, 16m, Botticelli (The Glorification of Mary, 1480). c, 16m, Tintoretto from 1550-53 and 1592-94. d, 66m, Leonardo da Vinci from 1480 and 1495. e, 66m, Michelangelo from 1508 and 1511. f, 66m, Giotto from 1305 and 1310.

No. 2430 — Impressionist paintings by: a, 16m, Armand Guillaumin. b, 16m, Eva Gonzalès. c, 16m, Alfred Sisley. d, 66m, Eugène Boudin. e, 66m, Stanislas Lépine. f, 66m, Edouard Manet from 1872 and 1882.

No. 2431 — Post-impressionist paintings by: a, 16m, Van Gogh from 1888 and 1889. b, 16m, Georges Seurat. c, 16m, Henri de Toulouse-Lautrec. d, 66m, Gauguin from 1888 and 1893. e, 66m, Cézanne from 1875 and 1892. f, 66m, Matisse from 1905 and 1906.

No. 2432 — Expressionist paintings by: a, 16m, Ernst Ludwig Kirchner. b, 16m, Emil Nolde. c, 16m, Franz Marc. d, 66m, Oskar Kokoscka. e, 66m, Max Beckmann. f, 66m, Wassily Kandinsky.

No. 2433 — Realist paintings by: a, 16m, Jules Breton. b, 16m, Jean-Baptiste-Camille Corot. c, 16m, Honore Daumier. d, 66m, Valentin Serov. e, 66m, Jean-François Millet. f, 66m, Ilya Repin.

No. 2434 — Surrealist paintings: a, 16m, Frida Kahlo. b, 16m, Dalí from 1963. c, 16m, Miró from 1940. d, 66m, Marc Chagall from 1911. e, 66m, Giorgio De Chirico. f, 66m, Max Ernst.

No. 2435, 175m, Pre-historic painting from Altamira Cave, diff. No. 2436, 175m, Painting by Johannes Vermeer from 1659. No. 2437, 175m, Painting from Tomb of Huy, diff. No. 2438, 175m, Painting by Peter Paul Rubens. No. 2439, 175m, Painting by Pierre-Auguste Renoir from 1890. No. 2440, 175m, Painting by Albrecht Dürer. No. 2441, 175m, Painting by Amrita Sher-Gil. No. 2442, 175m, Painting by Leonardo da Vinci from 1489-90. No. 2443, 175m, Painting by Hokusai Katsushika. No. 2444, 175m, Paintings by Picasso from 1901 and 1903. No. 2445, 175m, Painting by Chagall from 1913-14. No. 2446, 175m, 1513 painting depicting Madonna and Child by Raphael, ceiling of Farnese Palace by Annibale Carracci. No. 2447, 175m, Paintings by Leonardo da Vinci from 1489 and 1501. No. 2448, 175m, Paintings by Manet from 1878. No. 2449, 175m, Paintings by Van Gogh from 1886 and 1887. No. 2450, 175m, Paintings by Edvard Munch. No. 2451, 175m, Painting by William-Auguste Bouguereau. No. 2452, 175m, Painting by René Magritte.

2011, Oct. 30   Sheets of 6, #a-f
2417-2434 A434 Set of 18 335.00 335.00
Souvenir Sheets
2435-2452 A434 Set of 18 240.00 240.00

Art — A435

No. 2453 — Art of Ancient Greece: a, 16m, Bull's head rhyton, painting depicting women. b, 16m, Fresco from Knossos Palace, tile fragment. c, 16m, Painting of divers, kylix. d, 16m, Painting, sculpture of horse. e, 16m, Fresco depicting bull, pyxis. f, 16m, Fresco depicting dolphins, obverse and reverse of Athenian tetradrachm. g, 92m, Mask of Agamemnon, painting depicting Dionysius riding panther. h,

92m, Image from kylix, mosaic depicting leopard.

No. 2454 — Expensive paintings by: a, 16m, Jackson Pollock. b, 16m, Willem de Kooning. c, 16m, Gustav Klimt. d, 16m, Vincent van Gogh from 1890. e, 16m, Pierre-Auguste Renoir from 1876. f, 16m, Pablo Picasso from 1905. g, 92m, Picasso from 1832. h, 92m, Van Gogh from 1889.

No. 2455 — American Impressionist paintings by: a, 16m, Frank Weston Benson. b, 16m, Theodore Earl Butler. c, 16m, Mary Cassatt from 1879. d, 16m, Colin Campbell Cooper. e, 16m, Mary Agnes Yerkes. f, 16m, Dennis Miller Bunker. g, 92m, Childe Hassam. h, 92m, William Merritt Chase.

No. 2456 — Impressionist paintings by: a, 16m, Frederic Bazille. b, 16m, Berthe Morisot. c, 16m, Camille Pissarro from 1873. d, 16m, Claude Monet. e, 16m, Cassatt from 1873. f, 16m, Pierre-Auguste Renoir from 1882-83. g, 92m, Paul Cézanne from 1888. h, 92m, Edgar Degas from 1888.

No. 2457, 175m, Ancient Greek urn and painting. No. 2458, 175m, Painting by Picasso from 1941. No. 2459, 175m, Painting by Theodore Robinson. No. 2460, 175m, Painting by Gustave Caillebotte.

2011, Oct. 30   Sheets of 8, #a-h
2453-2456 A435 Set of 4 85.00 85.00
Souvenir Sheets
2457-2460 A435 Set of 4 52.50 52.50

Events, People and Anniversaries — A436

No. 2461, 66m — Horse racing: a, Horses facing right, jockeys in foreground wearing black and red shirts. b, Horses in steeplechase race. c, Horses facing right, jockey in foreground wearing black shirt. d, Horses facing left, passing grandstand, jockey wearing black shirt in lead. e, Horses facing left close to rail, grandstand at left. f, Three horses near gray wall.

No. 2462, 66m — Dan Wheldon (1978-2011), race car driver: a, Wheldon in white short-sleeve shirt. b, Race car with "2012" on rear wing. c, Wheldon in red racing uniform, car #10. d, Race car, race track. e, Wheldon with arms raised, race car. f, Wheldon standing next to race car.

No. 2463, 66m — Marco Simoncelli (1987-2011), motorcycle racer: a, With Valentino Rossi. b, Touching forehead. c, Raising trophy above head. d, With motorcycle's front wheel raised. e, Kneeling next to motorcycle. f, Looking right.

No. 2464, 66m — 2012 European Soccer Championships, Poland and Ukraine: a, Denomination at UL, "2012" in yellow at LR. b, Denomination at UL, "2012" in green at UR. c, Denomination at UR, "2012" in indigo at UL, soccer players wearing red and yellow uniforms. d, Denomination at UR, "2012" in indigo at UL, soccer players wearing blue and orange univorms. e, Denomination at UR, "2012" in yellow at UL. f, Denomination at UL, "2012" in green at LR.

No. 2465, 66m — Chess champions: a, Mikhail Tal. b, Viswanathan Anand. c, Bobby Fischer. d, Vladimir Kramnik. e, Garry Kasparov. f, Boris Spassky.

No. 2466, 66m — Boy Scout: a, Hiking, trefoil at LR. b, One one knee, trefoil at left. c, Cycling, trefoil at LR. d, Inspecting small item, trefoil at LL. e, Cooking, trefoil at LR. f, In boat, trefoil at UR.

No. 2467, 66m — Steve Jobs (1955-2011), computer entrepreneur: a, With Apple II computer. b, With Steve Wozniak and computer components. c, Holding apple. d, With beard, wearing glasses. e, Seated in chair using iPad. f, With three computers.

No. 2468, 66m — Mycologists and fungi: a, Elias Magnus Fries, Crinipellis scabella. b, Heinrich Anton de Bary, Psilocybe semilanceata. c, Charles Horton Peck, Crinipellis zonata. d, Narcisse Théophile Patouillard, inocybe patouillardii. e, Miles Joseph Berkeley, Stephanospora caroticolor. f, Károly Kalchbrenner, Sarcodon fuligineoviolaceus.

No. 2469, 66m — Sir Joseph Dalton Hooker (1817-1911), botanist: a, Hooker, Banksia hookeriana, Delias eucharis. b, Charles Darwin, Pan troglodytes. c, Hooker, Liriodendron tulipifera, Junonia lemonias. d, Hooker, Magnolia campbellii. e, Walter Hood Fitch, flowers and colored pencils. f, Darwin, ship and globe.

No. 2470, 66m — 2011 Nobel laureates: a, Bruce A. Beutler, Physiology or Medicine laureate. b, Ralph M. Steinman, Physiology or Medicine laureate. c, Jules A. Hoffmann, Physiology or Medicine laureate. d, Saul Perlmutter, Physics laureate. e, Brian P. Schmidt, Physics laureate. f, Adam G. Riess, Physics laureate.

No. 2471, 66m — Russian Cosmonauts: a, Valentina Tereshkova, Vostok 6. b, Alexei Leonov, 1965 space walk. c, Pavel Popovich, Vostok 4. d, Gherman Titov, Vostok 2. e, Andriyan Nikolayev, Soyuz 9. f, Pavel Belyayev, Voskhod 2.

No. 2472, 66m — African archaeological sites: a, Altar of Osiris, Philae Island, Egypt. b, Triumphal arch, Lambaesis, Algeria. c, Temple of Minerva, Tébessa, Algeria. d, Triumphal arch, Tébessa. e, Kom Ombo Temple, Egypt. f, Gateway to the Temple of Khonsu, Luxor, Egypt.

No. 2473, 66m — Romy Schneider (1938-82), actress, and scenes from: a, Bocaccio '70, 1962. b, Monpti, 1957. c, Sissi: The Fateful Years of an Empress, 1957. d, Ludwig, 1972. e, Un Amour de Pluie, 1974. f, What's New Pussycat?, 1965.

No. 2474, 66m — Wedding of Prince William and Catherine Middleton: a, Couple and Windsor Castle, Middleton holding flowers. b, Couple, Prince William at left, at Cambridge, Prince William. c, Couple, facing forward, at Cambridge, Middleton. d, Couple facing backwards, at Cambridge, Middleton. e, Couple and Winsor Castle. f, Couple, Pippa Middleton.

No. 2475, 66m — British warships: a, HMS Vindictive. b, HMS Victoria. c, HMS Eurydice. d, HMS Powerful (Poderoso). e, HMS Queen (Rainha). f, HMS Raleigh.

No. 2476, 66m — Sinking of the Titanic, cent. (in 2012), and: a, Captain Edward John Smith, ship officers William Murdoch, Henry Wilde, and Captain Charles Bartlett of the HMHS Britannic. b, Angel. c, Lucy Noel Martha Leslie. d, Margaret (Molly) Brown. e, Captain Smith. f, Iceberg.

No. 2477, 66m — Steam locomotives: a, Cheltenham Flyer with front of locomotive in black. b, Cheltenham Flyer with yellow and red rectangle on front. c, Bombay-Poona mail train. d, Silver Jubilee. e, Royal Scot. f, Scarborough Flyer.

No. 2478, 66m — Red Cross flag and ambulance: a, Ambulance crew member removing ambulance covering. b, Ambulance crew loading person into rear of ambulance. c, Motorcycle ambulance. d, Truck ambulance with two crew members in cab. e, Ambulance with rear doors open. f, Horse entering ambulance.

No. 2479, 66m — Dirigibles: a, British Army dirigible "Baby." b, 1852 dirigible. c, Black British war dirigible. d, French dirigible "Ville de Paris." e, German dirigible "Parseval." f, German dirigible "Clouth."

No. 2480, 66m — Trees: a, Malus spp. b, Crataegus monogyna. c, Betula alleghaniensis. d, Populus alba. e, Populus nigra. f, Aesculus hippocastanum.

No. 2481, 66m — Cacti and reptiles: a, Opuntia ficus-indica, Liolaemus platei platei. b, Copiapoa megarhiza, Conolophus subcristatus. c, Copiapoa cinerea, Sistrurus catenatus edwardsii. d, Stapelia pulchellus, Arizona elegans philipi. e, Echinopsis spachiana, Heloderma suspectum. f, Astrophytum hybrid, Gopherus agassizii.

No. 2482, 66m — Phascolarctos cinereus: a, Denomination at UR, animal name at LR. b, Denomination and animal name at UL, with tree trunk and branch. c, Denomination at UL, animal name at UR. d, Denomination at UR, animal name at UL. e, Denomination and animal name at UL, with tree branch only. f, Denomination at UL, animal name at left.

No. 2483, 66m — Cat breeds: a, Bengal. b, Pixie-bob. c, Abyssinian. d, American curl. e, Ocelot. f, Sokoke.

No. 2484, 66m — Dog breeds: a, Beagle. b, Yellow Labrador retriever. c, Irish setter. d, German shepherd. e, Boston terrier. f, English galgo.

No. 2485, 66m — Sharks: a, Alopias superciliosus, Prionace glauca. b, Eugomphodus taurus, Carcharhinus limbatus. c, Stegostoma fasciatum, Carcharhinus melanopterus. d, Triaenodon obesus, Squatina squatina. e, Isurus oxyrinchus, Triakis semifasciata. f, Scyliorhynus stellaris, Carcharhinus leucas.

No. 2486, 66m — Fishing: a, Gymnura natalensis. b, Coryphaena hippurus. c, Oreochromis mossambicus. d, Wattsia mossambica. e, Xiphias gladius. f, Penaeidae.

No. 2487, 66m — DNA molecules and animals: a, Vulpes zerda. b, Arctocephalus. c, Suricata suricatta. d, Ailuropoda melanoleuca. e, Odobenus rosmarus. f, Panthera leo.

No. 2488, 66m — Endangered animals: a, Lynx rufus. b, Two Ailuropoda melanoleuca. c, Panthera tigris. d, Ovis musimon. e, Loxodonta africana. f, Ceratotherium simum.

No. 2489, 175m — Horses racing, diff. No. 2490, 175m, Wheldon, diff. No. 2491, 175m, Simoncelli, diff. No. 2492, 175m, Soccer players, diff. No. 2493, 175m, Anatoly Karpov, chess player. No. 2494, 175m, Two Scouts, trefoil at LR. No. 2495, 175m, Jobs holding iPhone. No. 2496, 175m, Lucien Quélet, mycologist, and Clavariadelphus truncatus. No. 2497, 175m, Hooker, Vanda cathcarti. No. 2498, 175m, Dan Shechtman, 2011 Nobel Chemistry laureate. No. 2499, 175m, Yuri Gagarin, Russian cosmonaut. No. 2500, 175m, Amphitheater, Timgad, Algeria. No. 2501, 175m, Schneider, scene from Triple Cross, 1966. No. 2502, 175m, Prince William, Catherine Middleton, automobile. No. 2503, 175m, HMS Juno. No. 2504, 175m, Titanic and Captain Smith, diff. No. 2505, 175m, Torbay Express. No. 2506, 175m, Fire truck. No. 2507, 175m, French dirigible "Zodiac." No. 2508, 175m, Carpinus spp. No. 2509, 175m, Copiapoa haseltoniana and snake. No. 2510, 175m, Phascolarctos cinereus, diff. No. 2511, 175m, Siamese cat. No. 2512, 175m, Rottweiler. No. 2513, 175m, Sphyrna mokarran. No. 2514, 175m, Scomberomorus plurilineatus and fishermen. No. 2515, 175m, DNA molecule and Puijila darwini. No. 2516, 175m, Delphinus delphi, Stenella coeruleoalba.

2011, Dec. 30   **Perf. 12¾x13¼**
Sheets of 6, #a-f
2461-2488   A436   Set of 28   835.00   835.00
Souvenir Sheets
Perf. 13¼x12¾
2489-2516   A436   Set of 28   375.00   375.00

Miniature Sheets

Indonesia 2012 Intl. Philatelic Exhibition — A437

No. 2517, 66m — Like No. 2482 with exhibition emblem at: a, LR. b, LL. c, LL. d, LR. e, LL. f, LL.

No. 2518, 66m — Like No. 2488 with exhibition emblem at: a, LR. b, LL. c, LL. d, LL. e, LR. f, LL.

2011, Dec. 30   **Perf. 12¾x13¼**
Sheets of 6, #a-f
2517-2518   A437   Set of 2   60.00   60.00

New Year 2012 (Year of the Dragon) A438

Designs: No. 2519, Dragon and clouds. No. 2520, a, 16m, Dragon dance. b, 16m, Chinese calligraphy by Wang Xizhi. c, 16m, Drogon, guitarist Wang Lee-hom. d, 66m, Bruce Lee and Jackie Chan, actors. e, 66m, People's Republic of China banknote depicting dragon. f, Dragon boat race.
175m, Mural depicting dragons.

2011, Dec. 30   **Perf. 13¼**
2519   A438   66m multi   5.00   5.00
      Perf. 12¾x13¼
2520   A438   Sheet of 6, #a-f   18.50   18.50
Souvenir Sheet
Perf. 13¼x12¾
2521   A438   175m multi   13.50   13.50
No. 2519 was printed in sheets of 4.

People, Events and Anniversaries — A439

No. 2522 — Whitney Houston (1963-2012), singer: a, 16m, Houston and Kevin Costner, actor (50x39mm). b, 16m, Two images of Houston (38x39mm). c, 16m, Houston (38x39mm). d, 66m, Houston and Michael Jackson, singer (38x39mm). e, 66m, Houston with arms raised (50x39mm). f, 66m, Houston and Aretha Franklin, singer (38x39mm).

No. 2523 — Elvis Presley (1935-77), singer: a, 16m, Presley and automobiles (38x39mm). b, 16m, Presley as child and as adult (50x39mm). c, 16m, Presley and woman on motorcycle (38x39mm). d, 66m, Presley with guitar (38x39mm). e, 66m, Presley waving (50x39mm). f, 66m, Presley with guitar and woman (38x39mm).

No. 2524 — 70th birthday of Paul McCartney, singer: a, 16m, McCartney playing guitar (38x39mm). b, 16m, McCartney, neck of guitar (50x39mm). c, 16m, McCartney and microphone (38x39mm). d, 66m, McCartney holding guitar (38x39mm). e, 66m, McCartney playing guitar, diff. (50x39mm). f, 66m, McCartney pointing (38x39mm).

No. 2525 — Ludwig van Beethoven (1770-1827), composer: a, 16m, Beethoven and Georg Frideric Handel, composer (38x39mm). b, 16m, Beethoven conducting (50x39mm). c, 16m, Beethoven and Johann Sebastian Bach, composer (38x39mm). d, 66m, Beethoven and building (38x39mm). e, 66m, Head of Beethoven (50x39mm). f, 66m, Beethoven and Johann Wolfgang von Goethe, writer (38x39mm).

No. 2526 — Joseph Haydn (1732-1809), composer: a, 16m, Haydn, building and statue (38x39mm). b, 16m, Haydn and Wolfgang Amadeus Mozart, composer (50x39mm). c, 10m, Haydn holding quill pen, building and statue (38x39mm). d, 66m, Beethoven, Herbert von Karajan conducting (38x39mm). e, 66m, Haydn, building and statue, diff (50x39mm). f, 66m, Bach and building (38x39mm).

No. 2527 — Gene Kelly (1912-96), actor: a, 16m, Kelly (38x39mm). b, 16m, Kelly and Debbie Reynolds, actress (50x39mm). c, 16m, Kelly and Cyd Charisse, actress (38x39mm). d, 66m, Kelly and Reynolds, diff. (38x39mm). e, 66m, Kelly and Donald O'Connor, actor (50x39mm). f, 66m, Kelly, diff (38x39mm).

No. 2528 — Judy Garland (1922-69), actress: a, 16m, Garland holding Toto in The Wizard of Oz. (38x39mm). b, 16m, Garland and daughter, Liza Minnelli. (50x39mm). c, 16m, Garland and Margaret Hamilton as Wicked Witch of the West (38x39mm). d, 66m, Garland (38x39mm). e, 66m, Garland with Jack Haley as the Tinman and Ray Bolger as the Scarecrow (50x39mm). f, 66m, Garland holding tennis racket (38x39mm).

No. 2529 — Marilyn Monroe (1926-62), actress: a, 16m, Monroe as adult and child (38x39mm). b, 16m, Two images of Monroe (50x39mm). c, 16m, Monroe and actors Tony Curtis and Jack Lemmon in Some Like It Hot (38x39mm). d, 66m, Monroe in pink blouse (38x39mm). e, 66m, Two images of Monroe, diff. (50x39mm). f, 66m, Two images of Monroe, diff. (38x39mm).

No. 2530 — Elizabeth Taylor (1932-2011), actress: a, 16m, Taylor (38x39mm). b, 16m, Taylor and husband, Richard Burton, actor (50x39mm). c, 16m, Taylor in chair (38x39mm). d, 66m, Taylor and Lassie (dog) (38x39mm). e, 66m, Taylor and Burton, diff. (50x39mm). f, 66m, Taylor and James Dean, actor (38x39mm).

No. 2531 — François Truffaut (1932-84), actor and director, and: a, 16m, Scene from The 400 Blows, 1959 (38x39mm). b, 16m, Scene from Close Encounters of the Third Kind, 1977 (50x39mm). c, 16m, Scene from The Last Metro, 1980 (38x39mm). d, 66m, Actress Isabelle Adjani in scene from The Story of Adele H, 1975 (38x39mm). e, 66m, Actress Catherine Deneuve in scene from The Last Metro (50x39mm). f, 66m, Alfred Hitchcock, director (38x39mm).

No. 2532 — 80th birthday of Milos Forman, director: a, 16m, Tom Hulce in Amadeus, 1984 (38x39mm). b, 16m, Scene from One Flew Over the Cuckoo's Nest, 1975 (50x39mm). c, 16m, Hulce and F. Murray Abraham in Amadeus (38x39mm). d, 66m, Scene from Hair, 1979 (38x39mm). e, 66m, Forman (50x39mm). f, 66m, Jim Carrey in Man on the Moon, 1999 (38x39mm).

No. 2533 — Pres. John F. Kennedy (1917-63): a, 16m, Senator Robert F. Kennedy, brother, and detail from painting Washington Crossing the Delaware (38x39mm). b, 16m, Senator Edward M. Kennedy, brother (50x39mm). c, 16m, Pres. Bill Clinton and Indian (38x39mm). d, 66m, Pres. Barack Obama, Dr. Martin Luther King, Jr. (38x39mm). e, 66m, Kennedy and astronaut on Moon (50x39mm). f, 66m, Wife, Jacqueline, and son, John, Jr. (38x39mm).

No. 2534 — Boxers: a, 16m, Marvin Hagler (38x39mm). b, 16m, Joe Frazier (50x39mm). c, 16m, Rocky Marciano (38x39mm). d, 66m, Muhammad Ali (38x39mm). e, 66m, Joe Louis (50x39mm). f, 66m, Mike Tyson (38x39mm).

No. 2535 — St. Joan of Arc (1412-31): a, 16m, Holding lamb (38x39mm). b, 16m, In armor on one knee (50x39mm). c, 16m, Tied to stake, holding crucifix (38x39mm). d, 66m, At coronation of King Charles VII (38x39mm).

e, 66m, In battle on horse (50x39mm). f, 66m, Interrogation by Cardinal Winchester (38x39mm).

No. 2536 — Leonardo da Vinci (1452-1519), artist and inventor: a, 16m, Glider, facing right (38x39mm). b, 16m, Gears (50x39mm). c, 16m, Ornithopter, view of underside (38x39mm). d, 66m, Leonardo holding model of invention (38x39mm). e, 66m, Machine gun (50x39mm). f, 66m, Paddlewheel boat (38x39mm).

No. 2537 — Sir Isaac Newton (1642-1727), physicist and astronomer: a, 16m, Telescopes (38x39mm). b, 16m, Newton and statue (50x39mm). c, 16m, XMM-Newton orbiting observatory (38x39mm). d, 66m, Newton and house (38x39mm). e, 66m, Observatory (50x39mm). f, 66m, Newton and Zosimos of Panopolis, alchemist (38x39mm).

No. 2538 — Thomas Edison (1847-1931), inventor, and: a, 16m, Phonograph, compact disc (38x39mm). b, 16m, Edison's automobile and Infiniti Essence prototype (50x39mm). c, 16m, Motion picture camera (38x39mm). d, 66m, Phonograph, record, speakers (38x39mm). e, 66m, Lightbulb, LED light (50x39mm). f, 66m, Lightbulb, microphone (38x39mm).

No. 2539 — Nobel laureates in Chemistry: a, 16m, Ei-ichi Negishi, 2011 (38x39mm). b, 16m, Jacobus Henricus van 't Hoff, 1901 (50x39mm). c, 16m, Ernest Rutherford, 1908 (38x39mm). d, 66m, Marie Curie, 1911 (38x39mm). e, 66m, Sir William Ramsay, 1904 (50x39mm). f, 66m, Wilhelm Ostwald, 1909 (38x39mm).

No. 2540 — Jean-Jacques Rousseau (1712-78), philosopher: a, 16m, Voltaire, philosopher (38x39mm). b, 16m, Thomas Hobbes, philosopher (50x39mm). c, 16m, Voltaire and statue (38x39mm). d, 66m, Rousseau and statue (38x39mm). e, 66m, Louise d'Epinay, writer, and Denis Diderot, philosopher (50x39mm). f, 66m, Rousseau (38x39mm).

No. 2541 — Scenes from novels by Charles Dickens (1812-70): a, 16m, Group of children (38x39mm). b, 16m, Old man, crowded street (50x39mm). c, 16m, Old man and boy (38x39mm). d, 66m, Boy, people wearing hats (38x39mm). e, 66m, Boy and building (50x39mm). f, 66m, Man eating from bowl, buildings (38x39mm).

No. 2542 — Alexandre Dumas (1802-70), writer: a, 16m, Dumas, Gerard Depardieu as Edmond Dantes in The Count of Monte Cristo (38x39mm). b, 16m, Statue of Dumas, scene from The Three Musketeers (50x39mm). c, 16m, Scene from The Vicomte de Bragelonne (38x39mm). d, 66m, Scene from The Lady of the Camellias, by Alexandre Dumas (1824-95) (38x39mm). e, 66m, Auguste Maquet, writer who collaborated with Dumas, swordsman on horseback (50x39mm). f, 66m, Scene from Queen Margot (38x39mm).

No. 2543 — King Frederick II of Prussia (1712-86): a, 16m, Frederick II, Francesco Algarotti, philosopher (38x39mm). b, 16m, Frederick II on medal, Queen consorr Elisabeth-Christine of Brunswick-Wolfenbüttel-Bevern (50x39mm). c, 16m, Frederick II, St. Hedwig's Cathedral, Berlin (38x39mm). d, 66m, Frederick II and statue (38x39mm). e, 66m, Brandenburg Gate, Berlin (50x39mm). f, 66m, Frederick II, Pope Clement XIV (38x39mm).

No. 2544 — Napoleon III (1808-73), French emperor: a, 16m, Napoleon III, Battle of Solferino (38x39mm). b, 16m, Napoleon III at the Tuileries (50x39mm). c, 16m, Napoleon III and Emir Abdelkader, Algerian rebel leader (38x39mm). d, 66m, Napoleon III, Georges-Eugène Hausmann, Parisian civic planner (38x39mm). e, 66m, Napoleon III on horseback (50x39mm). f, 66m, Empress consort Eugénie de Montijo (38x39mm).

No. 2545 — Buildings designed by Antonio Gaudí (1852-1926): a, 16m, Bellesguard, Barcelona, Josep Fontseré, architect (38x39mm). b, 16m, Sagrada Familia Basilica, Barcelona, Joan Miró, painter (50x39mm). c, 16m, Gaudi, Güell Pavilion, Barcelona (38x39mm). d, 66m, Sagrada Familia Basilica, Henri Matisse, painter (38x39mm). e, 66m, Gaudí's Caprice, Comillas, Spain (50x39mm). f, 66m, Eugène Viollet-le-Duc, architect, Casa Vicens, Barcelona (38x39mm).

No. 2546 — Discovery of bust of Nefertiti, cent.: a, 16m, Photographer (38x39mm). b, 16m, Ludwig Borchardt, discoverer, holding bust (50x39mm). c, 16m, Archaeologists examining sculpted tile (38x39mm). d, 66m, Zahi Hawass, Egyptian Minister of Antiquities, Pyramids (38x39mm). e, 66m, Bust and Egyptian statuary (50x39mm). f, 66m, Borchardt uncovering bust (38x39mm).

No. 2547 — Paul von Hindenburg (1847-1934), German President, and Zeppelin LZ-129 Hindenburg: a, 16m, Denomination in white, Pres. Hindenburg in military uniform at LR (38x39mm). b, 16m, Denomination in black Pres. Hindenburg in military uniform at LL (50x39mm). c, 16m, Denomination in black, Pres. Hindenburg in military uniform at LR (38x39mm). d, 66m, Denomination in black, Pres. Hindenburg in military uniform at LR (38x39mm). e, 66m, Denomination in black, Pres. Hindenburg at LR (50x39mm). f, 66m, Denomination in black, Pres. Hindenburg in military uniform at LL (38x39mm).

No. 2548 — Bombardment of Guernica, Spain, 75th anniv.: a, 16m, Junkers Ju-52, denomination at UL (38x39mm). b, 16m, Messerschmitt Bf-109 (50x39mm). c, 16m, Junkers Ju-52, denomination at UR (38x39mm). d, 66m, Messerschmitt Bf-109, diff. (38x39mm). e, 66m, Heinkel He-111 (50x39mm). f, 66m, Pablo Picasso, artist (38x39mm).

No. 2549 — People involved in strugtgle for black civil rights: a, 16m, John Brown, abolitionist, slaves in field (38x39mm). b, 16m, William Wilberforce, British abolitionist, slave auction (50x39mm). c, 16m, Senator Henry Clay, whipping of slave (38x39mm). d, 66m, Pres. Abraham Lincoln, U.S. Capitol, statue of chained slave (38x39mm). e, 66m, Lincoln, Pres. George Washington, Civil War battle (50x39mm). f, 66m, Frederick Douglass, Pres. John F. Kennedy (38x39mm).

No. 2550 — First solo transatlantic flight of Charles Lindberg, 85th anniv.: a, 16m, Spirit of St. Louis, name of airplane at center bottom (38x39mm). b, 16m, Charles Lindbergh, pilot, Spirit of St. Louis (50x39mm). c, 16m, Spirit of St. Louis, name of airplane at UL (38x39mm). d, 66m, Lindbergh, Solar Impulse airplane (38x39mm). e, 66m, Lindbergh, Bernard Piccard, pilot of Solar Impulse (50x39mm). f, 66m, Lindbergh, with helmet, Spirit of St. Louis (38x39mm).

No. 2551 — Space flight of Friendship 7, 50th anniv.: a, 16m, John Glenn, NASA emblem, X-plane (38x39mm). b, 16m, Glenn in space suit and flight suit, experimental plane (50x39mm). c, 16m, Glenn and XB-70 airplane (38x39mm). d, 66m, Glenn, Friendship 7 emblem, Navy airplane (38x39mm). e, 66m, Glenn in space suit and flight suit, X-15 airplane (50x39mm). f, 66m, Glenn and airplane, diff. (38x39mm).

No. 2552, 175m, Houston, diff. No. 2553, 175m, Presley and Frank Sinatra. No. 2554, 175m, McCartney and other members of the Beatles. No. 2555, 175m, Actor Gary Oldman as Beethoven in *Immortal Beloved*. No. 2556, 175m, Haydn and Beethoven. No. 2557, 175m, Kelly and Charisse, diff. No. 2558, 175m, Garland holding Toto, Hamilton as Wicked Witch of the West, Haley as the Tinman. No. 2559, 175m, Monroe as adult and child. No. 2560, 175m, Taylor with Lassie. No. 2561, 175m, Truffaut, scene from *Jules and Jim*, 1962. No. 2562, 175m, Forman, character from *Hair*, 1979. No. 2563, 175m, Pres. Kennedy and brother, Robert, Lunar Module. No. 2564, 175m, Louis, diff. No. 2565, 175m, St. Joan of Arc, diff. No. 2566, 175m, Leonardo painting the Mona Lisa. No. 2567, 175m, Statue of Newton, XMM-Newton. No. 2568, 175m, Edison, lightbulb. No. 2569, 175m, Van 't Hoff, molecular model, building. No. 2570, 175m, Diderot, statue of Rousseau. No. 2571, 175m, Dickens, building. No. 2572, 175m, Dumas, Scene from *The Count of Monte Cristo*. No. 2573, 175m, Frederick II of Prussia, musical concert. No. 2574, 175m, Napoleon III, diff. No. 2575, 175m, Gaudí, Sagrada Familia Basilica. No. 2576, 175m, Bust of Nefertiti, Henri James Simon, German arts patron. No. 2577, 175m, Hindenburg burning. No. 2578, 175m, Junkers Ju-52 over Guernica. No. 2579, 175m, Douglass, freed slaves. No. 2580, 175m, James Stewart as Lindbergh in *The Spirit of St. Louis*, 1957, Spirit of St. Louis. No. 2581, 175m, Glenn, prehistoric man.

2012, Feb. 28   *Perf. 12¾x13¼*
Sheets of 6, #a-f
2522-2551   A439   Set of 30   550.00   550.00
Souvenir Sheets
2552-2581   A439   Set of 30   390.00   390.00

Souvenir Sheets

Russian Flag, Agathon and Oleg Fabergé, Fabergé Eggs — A440

Litho. & Embossed With Foil Application
2012, Feb. 28   *Perf. 13¼*
2582   A440   175m gold & multi   13.00   13.00
   a.   With Rossica 2013 inscription in sheet margin   13.00   13.00

2583   A440   175m silver & multi   13.00   13.00
   a.   With Rossica 2013 inscription in sheet margin   13.00   13.00

Extinct Animals — A441

No. 2584, 66m — Extinct European animals: a, Coelodonta antiquitatis. b, Deinotherium giganteum. c, Equus ferus ferus. d, Hippopotamus antiquus.

No. 2585, 66m, vert. — Extinct African animals: a, Hippotragus leucophorus. b, Bos primigenius. c, Elephas recki. d, Eudorcas rufina.

No. 2586, 66m, vert. — Extinct bats: a, Nyctimene sanctacrucis. b, Pteropus tokudae. c, Pteropus pilosus. d, Mystacina robusta.

No. 2587, 66m — Extinct birds: a, Chlorostilbon bracei. b, Prosobonia leucoptera. c, Hemignathus sogittirostris. d, Xenicus longipes.

No. 2588, 66m, vert. — Extinct African birds: a, Psittacula exsul. b, Alectroenas nitidissima. c, Raphus cucullatus. d, Porphyrio coerulescens.

No. 2589, 66m, vert. — Extinct parrots: a, Cyanoramphus ulietanus, Psittacula wardi. b, Ara tricolor, Psittacula exsul. c, Psephotus pulcherrimus. d, Mascarene parrot, Nestor productus.

No. 2590, 66m — Extinct reptiles: a, Desmatosuchus. b, Scaphonyx. c, Erythrosuchus. d, Dimetrodon.

No. 2591, 66m — Extinct marine life: a, Ichthyostega. b, Bothriolepsis. c, Henodus chelyops. d, Belemnitida.

No. 2592, 175m, Ursus spelaeus. No. 2593, 175m, Panthera leo leo, vert. No. 2594, 175m, Dobsonia chapmani, vert. No. 2595, 175m, Mascarenotus murivorus, Aplonis mavornata. No. 2596, 175m, Mascarinus mascarinus, vert. No. 2597, 175m, Cyanoramphus zealandicus. No. 2598, 175m, Lystrosaurus. No. 2599, 175m, Monachus tropicalis.

2012, Apr. 30   **Litho.**   *Perf. 13¼*
Sheets of 4, #a-d
2584-2591   A441   Set of 8   155.00   155.00
Souvenir Sheets
2592-2599   A441   Set of 8   105.00   105.00

Extinct and Endangered Animals — A442

No. 2600 — Extinct American animals: a, 16m, Macrauchenia patagonica. b, 16m, Bufo periglenes. c, 16m, Mammuthus columbi. d, 66m, Cuvieronius hyodon. e, 66m, Canis dirus. f, 66m, Dasypus bellus.

No. 2601 — Endangered primates: a, 16m, Pan paniscus holding plant near mouth. b, 16m, Two Pan paniscus. c, 16m, Adult and juvenile Pan paniscus. d, 66m, Two troglodytes. e, 66m, Two Gorilla berengei. f, 66m, Two adult and one juvenile Gorilla berengei.

No. 2602 — Endangered cats: a, 16m, Panthera uncia. b, 16m, Felis planiceps. c,

---

16m, Panthera tigris tigris. d, 66m, Felis iriomotensis. e, 66m, Felis viverrina. f, 66m, Panthera leo persica.

No. 2603 — Endangered dolphins: a, 16m, Pontoporia blainvillei. b, 16m, Orcaella brevirostris. c, 16m, Cephalorhynchus hectori. d, 66m, Tursiops truncatus ponticus. e, 66m, Lipotes vexillifer. f, 66m, Platanista gangetica.

No. 2604 — Endangered birds: a, 16m, Buteo jamaicensis. b, 16m, Harpyhaliaetus coronatus. c, 16m, Gyps indicus. d, 66m, Pithecophaga jefferyi. e, 66m, Gyps bengalensis. f, 66m, Haliaeetus vociferoides.

No. 2605, vert. — Endangered marine birds: a, 16m, Puffinus newelli, Larus bulleri. b, 16m, Ciconia boyciana. c, 16m, Puffinus mauretanicus, Sterna lorata. d, 66m, Platalea minor. e, 66m, Hymenolaimus malacorhynchos. f, 66m, Mitu mitu.

No. 2606, vert. — Extinct birds: a, 16m, Microgoura meeki. b, 16m, Ophrysia superciliosa. c, 16m, Phalacrocorax perspicillatus, foliage in background. d, 66m, Ptilonopus mercierii. e, 66m, Ectopistes migratorius. f, 66m, Ectopistes migratorius, Columba jouyi.

No. 2607, vert. — Extinct birds: a, 16m, Fregilupus varius. b, 16m, Amazona violacea. c, 16m, Myadestes myadestinus. d, 66m, Phalacrocorax perspicillatus on rock. e, 66m, Pezophaps solitaria. f, 66m, Porphyria mantelli.

No. 2608 — Endangered insects: a, 16m, Crotchiella brachyptera. b, 16m, Cicindela marginipennis. c, 16m, Xylotoles costatus. d, 66m, Polyphylla barbata. e, 66m, Cicindela puritana. f, 66m, Polposipus herculeanus.

No. 2609 — Endangered reptiles: a, 16m, Psammobates geometricus. b, 16m, Crocodylus siamensis. c, 16m, Ceratophora tennentii. d, 66m, Varanus komodoensis. e, 66m, Callagur borneoensis. f, 66m, Cyclura pinguis.

No. 2610 — Endangered snakes: a, 16m, Aspidites ramsayi. b, 16m, Paracontias minimus. c, 16m, Montivipera albizona. d, 66m, Paracontias rothschildi. e, 66m, Thamnophis sirtalis. f, 66m, Coluber constrictor priapus.

No. 2611 — Endangered carnivores: a, 16m, Vulpes bengalensis. b, 16m, Puma concolor coryi. c, 16m, Canis lupus rufus. d, 66m, Panthera tigris sumatrae. e, 66m, Leopardus pardalis. f, 66m, Lycaon pictus.

No. 2612 — Endangered marine life: a, 16m, Neophoca cinerea. b, 16m, Phocoena sinus. c, 16m, Thunnus thynnus. d, 66m, Enhydra lutris. e, 66m, Megaptera novaeangliae. f, 66m, Oncorhynchus tshawytscha.

No. 2613 — Extinct animals: a, 16m, Dusicyon australis. b, 16m, Macrotus leucura. c, 16m, Equus quagga quagga. d, 66m, Onychogalea lunata. e, 66m, Thylacinus cynocephalus. f, 66m, Pinuinus impennis.

No. 2614, 175m, Bison antiquus. No. 2615, 175m, Three Gorilla berengei, diff. No. 2616, 175m, Lynx pardinus. No. 2617, 175m, Cephalorhynchus hectori maui, vert. No. 2618, 175m, Neophron percnopterus. No. 2619, 175m, Phalacrocorax featherstoni. No. 2620, 175m, Rhodonessa caryophyllacea. No. 2621, 175m, Ara erythrocephala, vert. No. 2622, 175m, Nicrophorus americanus. No. 2623, 175m, Crocodylus cataphractus, Pseudemys rubriventris bangsi, vert. No. 2624, 175m, Pseudechis porphyriacus. No. 2625, 175m, Carcharodon carcharias, vert. No. 2626, 175m, Monachus schauinslandi. No. 2627, 175m, Panthera leo spelaea.

2012, Apr. 30   **Sheets of 6, #a-f**
2600-2613   A442   Set of 14   255.00   255.00
Souvenir Sheets
2614-2627   A442   Set of 14   180.00   180.00

Extinct and Endangered Animals — A443

No. 2628 — Extinct Asian animals: a, 16m, Panthera tigris balica. b, 16m, Neofelis nebulosa brachyura. c, 16m, Gazella arabica. d, 16m, Megatapirus augustus. e, 16m, Canis lupus hodophilax. f, 16m, Cervus schomburgki. g, 92m, Dicerorhinus sumatrensis lasiotis. h, 92m, Panthera tigris virgata.

No. 2629, vert. — Extinct animals of Oceania: a, 16m, Rattus nativitatis. b, 16m, Onychogalea lunata. c, 16m, Caloprymnus campestris. d, 16m, Prototroctes oxyrhynchus. e, 16m, Peltobatrachus pustulatus. f, 16m, Hoplodactylus delcourti. g, 92m, Macrotis leucura. h, 92m, Mystacina robusta.

No. 2630 — Extinct rodents: a, 16m, Pseudomys gouldii. b, 16m, Peromyscus pembertoni. c, 16m, Orysomys nelsoni. d, 16m, Geocapromys thoracatus. e, 16m, Leporillus apicalis. f, 16m, Microtis bavaricus. g, 92m, Notomys macrotis. h, 92m, Megalomys luciae.

No. 2631 — Endangered ungulates: a, 16m, Equus hemionus. b, 16m, Gazella cuvieri. c, 16m, Hippocamelus bisculus. d, 16m, Equus africanus. e, 16m, Kobus megaceros. f, 16m, Addax nasomaculatus. g, 92m, Nilgiritragus hylocrius. h, 92m, Bubalus depressicornis.

No. 2632, vert. — Extinct birds: a, 16m, Quiscalus palustris. b, 16m, Bowdleria rufescens. c, 16m, Alectroenas nitidissima. d, 16m, Porzana palmeri. e, 16m, Nesoclopeus poecilopterus. f, 16m, Pennula sandwichensis. g, 92m, Moho nobilis. h, 92m, Gallirallus wakensis.

No. 2633, vert. — Extinct birds: a, 16m, Rhodacanthis flaviceps. b, 16m, Aplonis corvina. c, 16m, Chaunoproctus ferreorostris. d, 16m, Chaetoptila angustipluma. e, 16m, Fregilus varius. f, 16m, Chloridops kona. g, 92m, Ciridops anna. h, 92m, Zoothera terrestris.

No. 2634, vert. — Endangered butterflies: a, 16m, Speyeria zerene myrtleae. b, 16m, Manduca blackburni. c, 16m, Icaricia icarioides fenderi. d, 16m, Ornithoptera alexandrae. e, 16m, Papilio chikae. f, 16m, Ornithoptera croesus. g, 92m, Apodemia mormo langei. h, 92m, Pterourus homerus.

No. 2635 — Endangered turtles: a, 16m, Platysternon megacephalum. b, 16m, Batagur trivittata. c, 16m, Pelochelys cantorii. d, 16m, Psammobates geometricus. e, 16m, Caretta caretta. f, 16m, Mauremys sinensis. g, 92m, Dermochelys coriacea. h, 92m, Eretmochelys imbricata.

No. 2636, 175m, Panthera tigris sondaica. No. 2637, 175m, Thylacinus cynocephalus, vert. No. 2638, 175m, Notomys amplus, Rattus macleari, vert.. No. 2639, 175m, Gazella dama. No. 2640, 175m, Rhodacanthis palmeri, vert. No. 2641, 175m, Zosterops strenuus, vert. No. 2642, 175m, Ornithoptera meridionalis, vert. No. 2643, 175m, Chelonia mydas.

2012, Apr. 30   **Sheets of 8, #a-h**
2628-2635   A443   Set of 8   165.00   165.00
Souvenir Sheets
2636-2643   A443   Set of 8   105.00   105.00

People, Events and Anniversaries — A444

No. 2644 — Reign of Queen Elizabeth II, 60th anniv.: a, 16m, Queen waving, personal crest, with red and white areas of flag under country name. b, 16m, As "a," with red, white and blue areas of flag under country name. c, 16m, As "a," with continuation of photograph under country name. d, 66m, Queen in white dress, arms, with red, white and blue areas of flag under country name at left. e, 66m, As "d," with no part of flag under country name. f, 66m, As "d," with red, white and blue areas of flag under country name across entire panel.

No. 2645 — Airbus A380: a, 16m, Of Singapore Airlines. b, 16m, Of Transaero Airlines. c, 16m, Of Etihad Airways. d, 66m, With A380 on vertical stabilizer. e, 66m, Of British Airways. f, 66m, With white vertical stabilizer.

No. 2646 — Wilbur Wright (1867-1912), aviation pioneer, and: a, 16m, Wright Flyer, denomination in white. b, 16m, Wright and passenger seated in Wright Flyer. c, 16m, Wilbur and Orville Wright walking. d, 66m, Wright Flyer, no wheels visible. e, 66m, Wright Flyer with wheels. f, 66m, Wright Flyer, Statue of Liberty.

No. 2647 — Harriet Quimby (1875-1912), aviation pioneer, and: a, 16m, Bleriot XI. b, 16m, Nose of Bleriot XI. c, 16m, Inset photograph of Quimby, tail of airplane. d, 66m, Tail of Bleriot XI, complete Bleriot XI in flight. e, 66m, Nose of airplane, diff. f, 66m, Airplane wing tip at left, Bleriot XI at right.

No. 2648 — Hubert Latham (1883-1912), aviation pioneer: a, 16m, Dark blue Antoinette VII. b, 16m, Gray Antoinette VII. c, 16m, Lilac rose Antoinette VII. d, 66m, Latham at LL, Prussian blue Antoinette VII. e, 66m, Latham at LR, blue Antoinette VII. f, 66m, Latham at LL, gray Antoinette VII.

No. 2649 — Sinking of the Titanic, cent.: a, 16m, Lifeboats near sinking Titanic. b, 16m, Titanic, bird, ship with sails. c, 10m, Titanic and tugboat. d, 66m, Titanic at sea, other boats, lower portion of Titanic Memorial. e, 66m, Titanic hitting iceberg, ship name at LL. f, 66m, Titanic approaching iceberg, ship name at UL.

No. 2650 — Byron Nelson (1912-2006), golfer, and: a, 16m, Nelson holding golf club while walking. b, 16m, Nelson holding trophy. c, 16m, Nelson swinging golf club. d, 66m, Emblem of World Golf Hall of Fame. e, 66m, 1974 Bob Jones Award. f, 66m, Congressional medal commemorating Nelson.

No. 2651 — Marilyn Monroe (1926-62), actress: a, 16m, Holding open umbrella. b, 16m, Lying on bed, wearing white blouse with striped neckline. c, 16m, Wearing black dress. d, 66m, Wearing necklace on wrist. e, 66m, Holding closed umbrella. f, 66m, Holding beach bag.

No. 2652 — Elvis Presley (1935-77), singer: a, 16m, Pointing finger upward. b, 16m, Holding microphone stand. c, 16m, Playing guitar. d, 66m, Playing guitar, diff. e, 66m, Seated. f, 66m, On motorcycle with woman.

No. 2653 — Achille-Claude Debussy (1862-1918), composer, and painting by Claude Monet from: a, 16m, 1904. b, 16m, 1903. c, 16m, 1880. d, 66m, 1893. e, 66m, 1886. f, 66m, 1868-69.

No. 2654 — Famous Russians: a, 16m, Nikolai Rimsky-Korsakov, composer. b, 16m, Modest Mussorgsky, composer. c, 16m, César Cui, composer. d, 66m, Vladimir Stasov, critic. e, 66m, Mily Balakirev, composer. f, 66m, Alexander Borodin, composer.

No. 2655 — Igor Stravinsky (1882-1971), composer, and: a, 16m, Sculpture, score with C clef at left. b, 16m, Sculpture, musical note to left of country name. c, 16m, Sculpture, no musical note to left of country name. d, 66m, Dancers with beards. e, 66m, Dancers, score with G clef at left. f, 66m, Women dancers in red costumes.

No. 2656 — Peacemakers: a, 16m, Pope John Paul II, St. Peter's Square. b, 16m, Princess Diana, Picasso's Peace Dove. c, 16m, Pope John Paul II, Pieta, by Michelangelo. d, 66m, Mother Teresa. e, 66m, Princess Diana, British flag, Picasso's Peace Dove. f, 66m, Mother Teresa, Nobel medal.

No. 2657 — Mohandas K. Gandhi (1869-1948), Indian independence leader, and: a,

16m, Indian anti-corruption "bank note" without value. b, 16m, Lotus flower, quote written by Gandhi. c, 16m, Sun symbol. d, 66m, Gandhi and his possessions. e, 66m, Gandhi Memorial, Kanyakumari. f, 66m, Gandhi's pocket watch.

No. 2658 — Pan-African Women's Organization, 50th anniv.: a, 16m, Wangari Muta Maathai, 2004 Nobel Peace laureate, and text. b, 16m, Maathai, mother carrying infant. c, 16m, Maasai, two women. d, 66m, Assetou Koite, President of Pan-African Women's Organization, five women. e, 66m, Koite, women, tents. f, 66m, Koite, three women.

No. 2659 — Pope John Paul II (1920-2005): a, 16m, Waving. b, 16m, Two images. c, 16m, Holding infant. d, 66m, Seated, and praying. e, 66m, Holding catechism, arms of Pope John Paul II. f, 66m, Kissing icon of angel.

No. 2660 — Alexander Pushkin State Museum of Fine Arts, Moscow, cent.: a, 16m, 1888 painting by Vincent van Gogh. b, 16m, 1899 painting by Edgar Degas. c, 16m, 1901 painting by Pablo Picasso. d, 66m, Pushkin (1799-1837), writer. e, 66m, 1914 painting by Marc Chagall. f, 66m, 1626 painting by Rembrandt.

No. 2661 — Charles Darwin (1809-82), naturalist: a, 16m, Sauropelta. b, 16m, Allosaurus. c, 16m, Darwin and chimpanzee. d, 66m, Ceratosaurus. e, 66m, Darwin, pages from "On the Origin of Species", denomination in black. f, 66m, Darwin, page from "On the Origin of Species", denomination in white.

No. 2662 — Dean Arthur Amadon (1912-2003), ornithologist: a, 16m, Amadon and Haliaeetus leucocephalus. b, 16m, Amadon and Circus cyaneus. c, 16m, Amadon and Buteo magnirostris. d, 66m, Accipiter cooperii, Circus cyaneus. e, 66m, Haliaeetus albicilla. f, 66m, Accipiter gentilis.

No. 2663 — Volcanoes and vulcanologists: a, 16m, Kilauea Volcano, Hawaii, Sir William Hamilton. b, 16m, Sakurajima Volcano, Japan, Alfred Lacroix. c, 16m, Ol Doinyo Lengai Volcano, Tanzania, vulcanologist using camera. d, 66m, Mt. St. Helens, Washington, Déodat Gratet de Dolomieu. e, 66m, Gurung Merapi Volcano, Indonesia, vulcanologist in protective suit. f, 66m, Krakatoa Volcano, Indonesia, Haraldur Sigurdsson.

No. 2664 — Wernher von Braun (1912-77), rocket scientist, and: a, 16m, Apollo 11. b, 16m, Saturn V rocket. c, 16m, Walt Disney. d, 66m, Head of Pres. John F. Kennedy, rocket launch. e, 66m, National Medal of Science, rocket launch. f, 66m, Kennedy and von Braun walking, rocket launch.

No. 2665 — Sally Ride (1951-2012), first American woman astronaut, and: a, 16m, Space Shuttle Challenger with open cargo bay doors. b, 16m, Challenger in flight. c, 16m, Challenger landing. d, 66m, Large picture of launch of Challenger, stars in background. e, 66m, Small picture of launch of Challenger. f, 66m, Challenger in orbit.

No. 2666 — Sergei Krikalev, Russian cosmonaut, and: a, 16m, LIBRAR-1. b, 16m, STS-88. c, 16m, Space Shuttle Endeavour. d, 66m, Soyuz TMA-6. e, 66m, Soyuz TMA-7. f, 66m, Space Shuttle Endeavour, diff.

No. 2667 — Liu Yang, Chinese astronaut: a, 16m, In space suit, waving, rocket. b, 16m, In space suit, saluting, Shenzhou-9, Tiangong-1. c, 16m, In space suit, Shenzhou 9 capsule. d, 66m, In uniform, Shenzhou-9. e, 66m, In uniform, saluting, Shenzhou-9. f, 66m, In uniform, waving, mission emblem.

No. 2668 — Animals of Kruger National Park, South Africa: a, 16m, Syncerus caffer. b, 16m, Hippopotamus amphibius. c, 16m, Tragelaphus strepsiceros. d, 66m, Lycaeon pictus. e, 66m, Equus quagga burchelli. f, 66m, Acinonyx jubatus.

No. 2669 — Death of Lonesome George, Pinta Island tortoise: a, 16m, With head raised. b, 16m, With head lowered, facing forward, large rock at right. c, 16m, Facing left, with head lowered. d, 66m, Facing forward, with head raised and turned left, diff. e, 66m, With head raised, facing right. f, 66m, With head lowered, facing left, diff.

No. 2670 — Paintings by Edouard Manet (1832-83) from: a, 16m, 1876. b, 16m, 1870. c, 16m, 1874. d, 66m, 1868. e, 66m, 1866. f, 66m, 1878.

No. 2671 — Jackson Pollock (1912-56), painter, and paintings from: a, 16m, 1946. b, 16m, 1950. c, 16m, 1942. d, 66m, 1940-41. e, 66m, 1943. f, 66m, 1950, diff.

No. 2672 — Art by Russian painters: a, 16m, Portrait of Konstantin Korovin, by Valentin Serov. b, 16m, Self-portrait of Mikhail Nesterov. c, 16m, Self-portrait of Ivan Kramskoi. d, 66m, Portrait of Alexander Herzen, by Nikolai Ge. e, 66m, Portrait of Ivan Goncharov, by Nikolai Yaroshenko. f, 66m, As "a," with different painting in background.

No. 2673, vert. — Paintings by Gustav Klimt (1862-1918) from: a, 16m, 1913. b, 16m, 1902. c, 16m, 1913, drawing by Egon Schiele. d, 66m, 1905. e, 66m, 1907-08. f, 66m, 1910.

No. 2674, 175m, Queen Elizabeth II, British flag. No. 2675, 175m, Airbus A380, diff. No. 2676, 175m, Wright, Wright Flyer, diff. No. 2677, 175m, Quimby, Bleriot XI, diff. No. 2678, 175m, Latham, Antoinette VII, diff. No. 2679, 175m, Titanic, Sterna paradisaea. No. 2680, 175m, Nelson, Congressional medal, diff. No.

2681, 175m, Monroe, diff. No. 2682, 175m, Presley kissing woman. No. 2683, 175m, Debussy, scene from opera Pelléas et Mélisande. No. 2684, 175m, Balakirev, painting by Serov. No. 2685, 175m, Stravinsky, diff. No. 2686, 175m, Kofi Annan, U.N. emblem, Nobel medal. No. 2687, 175m, Gandhi, actor Ben Kinglsey portraying Gandhi. No. 2688, 175m, Koite, Pan-African Women's Organization leaders. No. 2689, 175m, Pope John Paul II, illustration from Catechism. No. 2690, 175m, Pushkin, Alexander Pushkin State Museum of Fine Arts. No. 2691, 175m, Darwin and Euoplocephalus. No. 2692, 175m, Amadon and Accipiter striatus. No. 2693, 175m, Cross-section of volcano, Katia and Maurice Krafft, vulcanologists. No. 2694, 175m, Von Braun and his concept of circular space station. No. 2695, 175m, Ride, Space Shuttle Challenger on launch pad, STS-7 mission emblem. No. 2696, 175m, Krikalev, photograph of land and water taken from space. No. 2697, 175m, Liu Yang, Tiangong-1. No. 2698, 175m, Diceros bicornis. No. 2699, 175m, Lonesome George, diff. No. 2700, 175m, Manet painting from 1873. No. 2701, 175m, Pollock, painting from 1943, diff. No. 2702, 175m, Self-portrait of Nesterov, diff. No. 2703, 175m, Klimt and painting from 1909.

2012, Sept. 30   *Perf. 13¼*
Sheets of 6, #a-f
2644-2673   A444   Set of 30   515.00   515.00
Souvenir Sheets
2674-2703   A444   Set of 30   375.00   375.00

Ungulani Ba Ka Khosa, Writer A445

2012, Oct. 9   *Perf. 11x11¼*
2704   A445   92m buff & gray   6.25   6.25

Lubrapex 2012 Intl. Philatelic Exhibition, Brazil.

Events, Anniversaries and People — A446

No. 2705 — Mariner 2, 50th anniv., and: a, 16m, Gray vertical line, gray horizontal line at R. b, 16m, Gray horizontal line at L. c, 16m, Gray vertical line. d, 66m, Rocket, Earth. e, 66m, Venus at R. f, 66m, Venus at L.

No. 2706 — Apollo 17, 40th anniv.: a, 16m, Eugene Cernan, astronaut. b, 16m, Base of Lunar Module on Moon. c, 16m, Harrison Schmitt, astronaut. d, 66m, Ronald Evans, astronaut. e, 66m, Lunar Rover. f, 66m, Crew compartment of Lunar Module in space.

No. 2707 — Mars Rover Curiosity: a, 16m, Curiosity on Mars. b, 16m, Curiosity descending to Mars. c, 16m, Interior of Mars. d, 66m, Curiosity, diff. e, 66m, Martian rock. f, 66m, Flight Director Bobak Ferdowsi.

No. 2708 — Alouette 1 satellite, 50th anniv.: a, 16m, Engineers Colin A. Franklin, R.K. Brown and J. Barry, model of Alouette 1. b, 16m, Drs. Leroy Nelms and John Chapman, model of Alouette 1. c, 16m, Franklin and model. d, 66m, Alouette 1, maple leaf at LR. e, 66m, Five scientists studying information. f, 66m, Alouette 1, maple leaf at U.

No. 2709 — Union Pacific Railroad, 150th anniv.: a, 16m, Big Boy No. 4014 locomotive. b, 16m, EMD DDA40X locomotive. c, 16m, Locomotive No. 844. d, 66m, GE AC6000CW locomotive. e, 66m, EMD DDA40X locomotive, diff. f, 66m, Big Boy No. 4019 locomotive.

No. 2710 — Chess match between Bobby Fischer and Boris Spassky, 40th anniv., with: a, 16m, Denomination in black, blue squares at UR. b, 16m, Red and white flag stripes at left. c, 16m, Red and white flag stripes at right. d, 66m, Red and white flag stripes at right. e, 66m, Globe, king's crown over Fischer. f, 66m, Flags of the Soviet Union and U.S.

No. 2711 — Svetozar Gligoric (1923-2012), chess player: a, 16m, Ludek Pachmann. b, 16m, Large magnetic chess board. c, 16m,

Vasily Smyslov. d, 66m, Mark Taimanov. e, 66m, Spassky. f, 66m, Chess board.

No. 2712 — Athletes at 2012 Paralympics, London: a, 16m, Cuiping Zhang. b, 16m, David Weir. c, 16m, Mark Rohan. d, 66m, Alan Fonteles Cardozo Oliveira. e, 66m, Esther Vergeer. f, 66m, Sarah Storey.

No. 2713 — Judo champions: a, 16m, Robert Van de Walle. b, 16m, Yasuhiro Yamashita. c, 16m, Shozo Fujii. d, 66m, Naoya Ogawa. e, 66m, David Douillet. f, 66m, Teddy Riner.

No. 2714 — Maurice Ravel (1875-1937), composer, and: a, 16m, Vaslav Nijinsky, choreographer, at piano. b, 16m, Roland Manuel, composer. c, 16m, Jacques Février, pianist. d, 66m, Ricardo Viñes, pianist. e, 66m, Eva Gauthier, opera singer, and various men. f, 66m, 1895 painting by Henri de Toulouse-Lautrec.

No. 2715 — Musicians: a, 16m, Metallica. b, 16m, Bryan Adams. c, 16m, Beyoncé. d, 66m, Shakira. e, 66m, Sir Elton John. f, 66m, Slash.

No. 2716 — Film stars and scenes from their movies: a, 16m, Johnny Depp. b, 16m, Gérard Depardieu. c, 16m, Nicole Kidman and Hugh Jackman. d, 66m, Angelina Jolie. e, 66m, Morgan Freeman and Jack Nichloson. f, 66m, Nicholson.

No. 2717 — Pope Benedict XVI: a, 16m, And painting by Raphael. b, 16m, Wearing zucchetto. c, 16m, And Vatican City arms. d, 66m, And arms of the Holy See. e, 66m, And arms of Pope Benedict XVI. f, 66m, Wearing red hat.

No. 2718 — Mother Teresa (1910-97), humanitarian, and: a, 16m, Nobel medal. b, 16m, Pope John Paul II. c, 16m, Earth. d, 66m, One child. e, 66m, Two children. f, 66m, Window of building.

No. 2719 — Princess Diana (1961-97), and London landmarks: a, 16m, Big Ben. b, 16m, St. Paul's Cathedral. c, 16m, Tower Bridge. d, 66m, Buckingham Palace. e, 66m, Big Ben, diff. f, 66m, Waterloo Bridge.

No. 2720 — Dr. Christiaan Barnard (1922-2001), first heart transplant surgeon, and: a, 16m, Operating room. b, 16m, Red cross. c, 16m, First heart transplant patient, Louis Washkansky. d, 66m, Hearts, arrow, red crosses. e, 66m, Medical helicopter. f, 66m, Cooler for transplant organs, red crosses.

No. 2721 — Red Cross campaign against AIDS: a, 16m, AIDS virus, mother holding child. b, 16m, Red Cross worker inspecting packages. c, 16m, Red Cross worker handling child. d, 66m, Child washing hands. e, 66m, Woman hugging Red Cross worker. f, 66m, People around large AIDS ribbon.

No. 2722 — Battle of Borodino, 200th anniv.: a, 16m, Napoleon Bonaparte, 1897 painting by Vasily Vereshchagin of battle. b, 16m, Four horsemen. c, 16m, Soldiers flags, one horseman. d, 66m, Horseman in blue uniform. e, 66m, Illustration of battle by unknown artist. f, 66m, Russian Field Marshal Mikhail Kutuzov, 1952 painting by Anatoly Shepelyuk.

No. 2723 — League for the Protection of Birds, cent.: a, 16m, Milvus milvus. b, 16m, Aquila fasciata. c, 16m, Falco naumanni. d, 66m, Pandion haliaetus. e, 66m, Tetrax tetrax. f, 66m, Coragyps atratus.

No. 2724 — Riga Zoo, cent.: a, 16m, Panthera leo. b, 16m, Bubo scandiaca. c, 16m, Cervus albirostris. d, 66m, Ursus arctos middendorffi. e, 66m, Tapirus terrestris. f, 66m, Amphiprion ocellaris.

No. 2725 — Sea shells: a, 16m, Spondylus princeps, Bulla striata. b, 16m, Scafander lignarius, Amusium japonicum. c, 16m, Tapes philippinarum, Murex pecten. d, 66m, Donax variabilis, Ovatella firmini, Haminoea hydalis. e, 66m, Pterynotus elongatus, Hexaplex radix. f, 66m, Hexaplex trunculus, Aplysia depilans, Isaac Lea (1792-1886), conchologist.

No. 2726 — Mary Anning (1799-1847), fossil collector: a, 16m, Dimorphodon macronyx. b, 16m, Anning, Mortoniceras inflatum fossil. c, 16m, Fossil bones. d, 66m, Ichthyosaurus fossils. e, 66m, Plesiosaurus. f, 66m, Anning, Plesiosaurus dolichodeirus fossil.

No. 2727 — Henry John Elwes (1846-1922), lepidopterist: a, 16m, Borboleta monarca. b, 16m, Grande borboleta azul, animal name at UR under denomination. c, 16m, Grande borboleta azul, animal name at UL. d, 66m, Elwes, Borboleta asa-de-pássaro. e, 66m, Borboleta "Morpho" azul. f, 66m, Elwes, Borboleta monarca.

No. 2728 — Tadas Ivanauskas (1882-1970), zoologist, and: a, 16m, Deer, Bubo bubo. b, 16m, Cygnus olor. c, 16m, Accipiter gentilis. d, 66m, Raccoon, Aquila pomarina. e, 66m, Upupa epops. f, 66m, Deer, Strix aluco, mouse.

No. 2729 — Gordon H. Cunningham (1892-1962), mycologist: a, 16m, Cunningham and Hygrophorus lucorum. b, 16m, Lycoperdon perlatum. c, 16m, Leccinum scabrum. d, 66m, Bolbitius psittacinus. e, 66m, Calocerea viscosa. f, 66m, Cunningham, Armillaria gallica.

No. 2730 — Dian Fossey (1932-85), zoologist: a, 16m, Gorilla beringei beringei. b, 16m, Fossey with forillas, head of Gorilla beringei beringei. c, 16m, Fossey with book, two Gorilla beringei beringei. d, 66m, Fossey, two Gorilla beringei beringei. e, 66m, Fossey, one Gorilla beringei beringei. f, 66m, Two Gorilla beringei beringei.

No. 2731 — Gustaf Dalén (1869-1937), 1912 Nobel Physics laureate, and: a, 16m, Celarain Lighthouse, Mexico. b, 16m, Point Stephens Lighthouse, Australia. c, 16m, Peninsula Point Lighthouse, Michigan. d, 66m, Dalén light for lighthouses. e, 66m, Barrenjoey Lighthouse, Australia. f, 66m, Skerryvore Lighthouse, Scotland.

No. 2732 — Charleston Lighthouse, South Carolina, and birds: a, 16m, Aix sponsa. b, 16m, Tringa incana. c, 16m, Larus californicus. d, 66m, Eudocimus albus. e, 66m, Lanus atricilla. f, 66m, Recurvirostra americana.

No. 2733 — UNESCO World Heritage Sites, 40th anniv.: a, 16m, Island of Mozambique. b, 16m, Osun-Osogbo Sacred Grove, Nigeria. c, 16m, Koutammakou, Land of the Battamariba, Togo. d, 66m, Royal Palaces of Abomey, Benin. e, 66m, Stone Circles of Senegambia, Gambia and Senegal. f, 66m, Kunta Kinteh Island, Gambia.

No. 2734 — Expo 2012, Yeosu, South Korea: a, 16m, Sky Tower, Thunnus thynnus. b, 16m, Ocean Pavilion, Tursiops truncatus. c, 16m, Marine Life Pavilion, Manta birostris. d, 66m, Korean Pavilion, Dugong dugon. e, 66m, Big-O, Dendrochirus zebra. f, 66m, Expo Digital Gallery, Phoca vitulina.

No. 2735, 175m, Mariner 2, Venus, diff. No. 2736, 175m, Apollo 17 Lunar Module, Lunar Rover, and astronaut on Moon. No. 2737, 175m, Mars Science Laboratory capsule containing Curiosity. No. 2738, 175m, Chapman and Alouette 1. No. 2739, 175m, Union Pacific No. 119 locomotive. No. 2740, 175m, Fischer and Spassky shaking hands. No. 2741, 175m, Gligoric and Fischer. No. 2742, 175m, Oscar Pistorius, Paralympian. No. 2743, 175m, Riner, diff. No. 2744, 175m, Ravel and Bolero dancers. No. 2745, 175m, U2. No. 2746, 175m, Brad Pitt. No. 2747, 175m, Pope Benedict XVI, crucifix. No. 2748, 175m, Mother Teras holding child. No. 2749, 175m, Princess Diana, Buckingham Palace, diff. No. 2750, 175m, Barnard, heart, crosses. No. 2751, 175m, Africans, map, AIDS ribbon. No. 2752, 175m, Napoleon Bonaparte, 1987 Russian coin commemorating Battle of Borodino. No. 2753, 175m, Ciconia ciconia. No. 2754, 175m, Lemur catta, obverse and reverse of Latvian coin commemorating Riga Zoo. No. 2755, 175m, Lea, Venus verrucosa. No. 2756, 175m, Anning, Plesiosaurus macrocephalus fossil. No. 2757, 175m, Elwes and Borboleta "Morpho" cor-de-rosa. No. 2758, 175m, Ivanauskas, Ciconia nigra. No. 2759, 175m, Cunningham, Plectania melastoma. No. 2760, 175m, Fossey, three Gorilla beringei beringei. No. 2761, 175m, Dalén, Nobel medal. No. 2762, 175m, Charleston Lighthouse, Larus californicus, diff. No. 2763, 175m, Historic Cairo UNESCO World Heritage Site. No. 2764, 175m, Aquarium at Expo 2012.

2012, Oct. 30 **Perf. 13¼**
Sheets of 6, #a-f
2705-2734 A446 Set of 30 500.00 500.00
Souvenir Sheets
2735-2764 A446 Set of 30 360.00 360.00

A447

No. 2765 — Rugby players from: a, 16m, New Zealand and South Africa, denomination at bottom. b, 16m, New Zealand and South Africa, denomination at top. c, 92m, Botswana and Zambia. d, 92m, Mexico and Jamaica.

No. 2766 — Rotary International emblem and cricket players: a, 16m, Adam Gilchrist. b, 16m, Donald Bradman. c, 92m, Viv Richards. d, 92m, Brian Lara.

No. 2767 — Table tennis players: a, 16m, Ding Ning. b, 16m, Wu Yang. c, 92m, Jörgen Persson, denomination at UR. d, 92m, Chinese player misidentified as Jörgen Persson, denomination at UL.

No. 2768 — Gilles Villeneuve (1950-82), race car driver, and: a, 16m, Race car, checkered flag. b, 16m, Race car. c, 92m, Race car, diff. d, 92m, Race car and track diagram.

No. 2769 — Lions International emblem and golfers: a, 16m, Ben Hogan. b, 16m, Jack Nicklaus. c, 92m, Bobby Jones. d, 92m, Arnold Palmer.

No. 2770 — Niels Bohr (1885-1962), physicist, and: a, 16m, Formula. b, 16m, Diagram of atom. c, 92m, Diagram of atom, diff. d, 92m, Albert Einstein.

No. 2771 — 2012 Nobel laureates: a, 16m, Serge Haroche, David J. Wineland, physics. b, 16m, Robert J. Lefkowitz, Brian K Kobilka, chemistry. c, 92m, Shinya Yamanaka, Sir John B. Gurdon, physiology or medicine. d, 92m, Alvin E. Roth, Lloyd S. Shapley, economics.

No. 2772 — Minerals: a, 16m, Beryl. b, 16m, Scapolite. c, 92m, Tourmaline. d, 92m, Beryl, diff.

No. 2773 — Campaign against malaria, 50th anniv. (in 2012): a, 16m, Mosquito, Brazil #C106, Ghana #128. b, 16m, Child receiving medicine, Syria #C267-C268. c, 92m, Child receiving medicine, Tunisia #404-405. d, 92m, Mosquito on globe, Democratic Republic of Congo #414-415.

No. 2774 — Orchids: a, 16m, Stanhopea insignis frost. b, 16m, Angraecum sesquipedale. c, 92m, Lycaste macrophylla. d, 92m, Miltonia vexillaria.

No. 2775 — Cat breeds: a, 16m, Singapura. b, 16m, Toyger. c, 92m, Bombay. d, 92m, Cymric.

No. 2776 — Fish: a, 16m, Signigobius biocellatus. b, 16m, Synchiropus splendidus. c, 92m, Antennarius commersoni. d, 92m, Pterois antennata.

No. 2777 — Dogs in art: a, 16m, Dogs Fighting, by Frans Snyders. b, 16m, Master Pelham, by George Romney. c, 92m, Two Hunting Dogs Tied to a Tree Stump, by Jacopo Bassano. d, 92m, Dog Pointing at a Partridge, by Jean-Baptiste Oudry.

No. 2778 — Paintings and self-portraits of Impressionist painters: a, 16m, Claude Monet. b, 16m, Edgar Degas. c, 92m, Pierre-Auguste Renoir. d, 92m, Freédéric Bazille.

No. 2779 — Paintings by Marc Chagall (1887-1985): a, 16m, The Concert, 1957, and Self-portrait, 1909-10. b, 16m, Chagall, The Madonna of the Village, 1942. c, 92m, Chagall, To My Betrothed, 1911. d, 92m, Cow with an Umbrella, 1946.

No. 2780 — Christmas art: a, 16m, Adoration of the Magi, by Gentile da Fabriano. b, 16m, The Annunciation, by Fra Filippo Lippi. c, 92m, Concert of Angels, by Matthias Grünewald. d, 92m, Adoration of the Shepherds, by Gerard von Honthorst.

No. 2781 — Sculptures by Alberto Chissano (1935-94): a, 16m, Three heads. b, 16m, One head. c, 92m, Chissano and head. d, 92m, One head, diff.

No. 2782 — Hans Werner Henze (1929-2012), composer: a, 16m, Scene from opera *The Hoopoe and the Triumph of Filial Love*. b, 16m, Henze musical notes and clef. c, 92m, Scene from opera *Bajazzo*. d, 92m, Scene from opera *Gogo no Eiko*.

No. 2783 — Niccolò Paganini (1782-1840), composer: a, 16m, Paganini and La Scala Theater, Milan. b, 16m, Napoleon I, violin, score for *Napoleon Sonata*. c, 92m, Sculpture of Paganini by Sutton Betti, The Grand Canal of Venice, by J. M. W. Turner. d, 92m, Bust of Paganini, by Pierre-Jean David, violin.

No. 2784 — Genoese ship construction: a, 16m, 12th cent. Genoese ship, boat builder. b, 16m, Construction of hull. c, 92m, Construction of hull, diff. d, 92m, 11th century ship, boat builder.

No. 2785 — Venetian ship construction: a, 16m, Drawing of Venetian ship by Bernhard von Breidenbach. b, 16m, Ship and cross-section diagram. c, 92m, Drawings and Venetian galley. d, 92m, Ship under construction, boat building tools.

No. 2786 — Submarines: a, 16m, USS Gato (SS-212). b, 16m, Shchuka Class submarine, Russia. c, 92m, Japanese submarine I-506. d, 92m, German submarine U-23.

No. 2787 — Tanks: a, 16m, German Neubaufahrzeug Nr. 3-5 tank. b, 16m, Italian M 13/40 tank. c, 92m, M4 Sherman tank with 105mm howitzer, United States. d, 92m, Soviet T-34/76 tank.

No. 2788 — Japanese Shinkansen high-speed trains: a, 16m, Series N700. b, 16m, Series E6. c, 92m, Series E5. d, 92m, Series E3.

No. 2789 — European high-speed trains: a, 16m, FS Class ETR 500 Frecciarossa. b, 16m, LNER Class A4 4468 Mallard. c, 92m, AVE Class 102 Talgo 350. d, 92m, DRG Class SVT 137 Hamburg.

No. 2790 — Fire-fighting aircraft: a, 16m, Conair Turbo Firecat. b, 16m, Aerospatial AS-350B-2 Ecureuil helicopter. c, 92m, PZL-Swidnik W-3A Sokol helicopter. d, 92m, Canadair CL-215.

No. 2791 — Japanese aircraft: a, 16m, Mitsubishi F-4EJ Kai Phantom. b, 16m, Sikorsky (Mitsubishi) SH-60K (S70B-3) helicopter. c, 92m, ShinMaywa US-1A. d, 92m, Mitsubishi F-2A.

No. 2792 — Drones: a, 16m, Taurus UAV. b, 16m, MQ-1 Predator. c, 92m, Gojjet. d, 92m, MQ-4C BAMS Triton.

No. 2793 — Famous Atlantic hurricanes: a, 16m, Hurricane Katrina, 2005. b, 16m, Hurricane Felix, 2007. c, 92m, Hurricane Wilma, 2005. d, 92m, Hurricane Julia, 2010.

No. 2794 — New Year 2013 (Year of the Snake): a, 16m, Snake and yin-yang. b, 16m, Snake at right, Chinese text. c, 92m, Snake at left, Chinese text. d, 92m, Snake and "2013."

No. 2795, 175m, Percy Montgomery and South African rugby team. No. 2796, 175m, Rotary International emblem, cricket player

Sachin Tendulkar. No. 2797, 175m, Table tennis player Wu Yang. No. 2798, 175m, Villeneuve and Ferrari 312T3 race car. No. 2799, 175m, Golfer Annika Sorenstam. No. 2800, 175m, Bohr, diagram and equation. No. 2801, 175m, Mo Yan, 2012 Nobel Literature laureate. No. 2802, 175m, Scapolite and tourmaline. No. 2803, 175m, Mosquito on globe, Ryukyu Islands #95-96. No. 2804, 175m, Cypripedium orchids. No. 2805, 175m, Asian semi-longhair cat. No. 2806, 175m, Pteroidichthys amboinensis. No. 2807, 175m, The Hunting Party with Tsar Alexander III and Tsarina Maria Fedorovna, by Nikolai Semenovich Samokish. No. 2808, 175m, Garden at Sainte-Adresse, by Monet. No. 2809, 175m, Song of Songs IV, 1958, by Chagall, Portrait of Chagall, 1910, by Yury Pen. No. 2810, 175m, Adoration of the Magi, by Giotto di Bondone. No. 2811, 175m, Chissano and sculpture, diff. No. 2812, 175m, Henze and character from opera *Gisela*. No. 2813, 175m, Paganini and Il Cannone Guarnerius. No. 2814, 175m, Genoese ship under construction, 11th cent. No. 2815, 175m, Venetian galley. No. 2816, 175m, Tench Class submarine, United States. No. 2817, 175m, Soviet T-34/76 tank, diff. No. 2818, 175m, Shinkansen Series E954. No. 2819, 175m, SNCF TGV Thalys PBKA. No. 2820, 175m, Sikorsky S-70A Firehawk helicopter. No. 2821, 175m, Blue Impulse Kawasaki T4-46 5726. No. 2822, 175m, Polar Hawk and Boeing Phantom Ray drones. No. 2823, 175m, Hurricane Sandy. No. 2824, 175m, Snake, yin yand and Chinese text.

2013, Feb. 20 **Litho.** **Perf. 13¼**
Sheets of 4, #a-d
2765-2794 A447 Set of 30 450.00 450.00
Souvenir Sheets
2795-2824 A447 Set of 30 375.00 375.00

Worldwide Fund for Nature (WWF) A448

No. 2825 — Smutsia temmincki (Ground pangolin): a, Pangolin facing right. b, Head of pangolin, pangolin rolled in ball. c, Pangolin on rock. d, Pangolin and juvenile.
175p, Two Smutsia temmincki.

2013, Mar. 25 **Litho.** **Perf. 13¼**
2825	Horiz. strip of 4	15.00	15.00
a.-b.	A448 16m Either single	1.10	1.10
c.-d.	A448 92m Either single	6.25	6.25
e.	Miniature sheet of 8, 2 each #2825a-2825d, perf. 13x13¼	30.00	30.00

Souvenir Sheet
Perf. 13¼ Syncopated
2826	A448 175m multi	12.00	12.00

No. 2826 contains one 50x39mm stamp.

Transportation and Space — A449

No. 2827 — Dog teams: a, 16m, Four Canadian Eskimo dogs in harnesses. b, 16m, Two Siberian huskies in harnesses, leg of front dog behind "OC" of country name. c, 16m, Two Siberian huskies, dog sled. d, 16m, Tamaskan dogs. e, 16m, Alaskan malamute dogs. f, 16m, Two Siberian huskies in harnesses, front leg above "C" in country name.

No. 2828 — Horse transportation: a, 16m, Rider standing on two horses of four-horse team. b, 16m, Horse and sulky. c, 16m, Russian troika. d, 16m, Carriage drawn by two horses. e, 16m, Carriage drawn by six horses. f, 16m, English mail coach drawn by four horses.

No. 2829 — Famous bicycle riders in the Tour de France: a, 16m, Louison Bobet. b, 16m, Jacques Anquetil. c, 16m, Eddy Merckx. d, 16m, Bernard Hinault. e, 16m, Mark Cavendish. f, 16m, Bradley Wiggins.

No. 2830 — Ying Liwei, Chinese astronaut: a, 16m, And Shenzhou 5 re-entry capsule. b, 16m, In military uniform, with Shenzhou 5 rocket, flag of People's Republic of China. c, 16m, In spacesuit, adjusting helmet, Shenzhou 5 in space. d, 16m, In spacesuit, waving, Shenzhou 5 launch. e, 16m, In capsule wearing helmet. f, 16m, In capsule, with two fingers raised.

No. 2831 — Alan B. Shepard, Jr. (1923-98), American astronaut, and: a, 16m, Apollo 14 emblem. b, 16m, Apollo 14 plaque. c, 16m, Re-entry of Apollo 14. d, 16m, Mercury-Redstone 3 rocket. e, 16m, Mercury capsule. f, 92m, Statue of Shepard, by Robert L. Rasmussen.

No. 2832 — Apollo 8: a, 16m, Crew of Apollo 8 and launch. b, 16m, Apollo 8 orbiting Moon. c, 16m, Apollo 8 and Earth. d, 16m, Crew of Apollo 8, Apollo 8 and Earth. e, 16m, Crew in spacesuits, Apollo 8 emblem. f, 92m, Apollo 8 capsule, launch of Apollo 8.

No. 2833 — Iceboats with sail inscriptions of: a, 16m, 300. b, 16m, DM 8133. c, 16m, 44. d, 16m, DM 8931. e, 16m, 313. f, 92m, DM G-887.

No. 2834 — 2012-13 Vendée Globe Regatta: a, 16m, Crewman adjusting sails on sailboat. b, 16m, Boat with red and white sail. c, 16m, Crewman trying to keep sailboat from capsizing. d, 16m, Sailboats in line. e, 16m, Boat with black and yellow sails. f, 92m, Sailboat with blue and green hull.

No. 2835 — Rescue ships: a, 16m, 44-foot boat. b, 16m, United States Coast Guard hydrofoil. c, 16m, 45-foot boat. d, 16m, United States Coast Guard buoy tender No. 277. e, 16m, Severn Class rescue boat. f, 92m, 47-foot boat.

No. 2836 — Icebreakers: a, 16m, MV Paardeberg, Russia. b, 16m, Captain Chlebnikov, Russia. c, 16m, Oden, Sweden. d, 16m, Polarstern, Germany. e, 16m, Tempera, Finland. f, 92m, Polar Pevek, Norway.

No. 2837 — Steam locomotives: a, 16m, London & North Eastern Railway Class B17 4-6-0 Sandringham. b, 16m, London Midland & Scottish Railway 4-4-0. c, 16m, Metropolitan Railway tank locomotive. d, 16m, Johore State Railway 4-6-2. e, 16m, Dublin and South Easter Railway 4-4-2 King George. f, 92m, German State Railways 4-6-2 Pacific Express.

No. 2838 — London Metro cars: a, 16m, From 1938. b, 16m, From 1940. c, 16m, From 1973. d, 16m, From 1986. e, 16m, From 2011. f, 92m, Model of car of the future.

No. 2839 — Monorails: a, 16m, Mark VI. b, 16m, Innovia 300 on bridge. c, 16m, Mumbai monorail. d, 16m, Transrapid 09. e, 16m, Innovia 300, diff. f, 92m, Tama Toshi monorail.

No. 2840 — High-speed trains: a, 16m, ETR-500. b, 16m, TGV Réseau. c, 16m, AVE Talgo 350. d, 16m, Eurostar. e, 16m, KTX 2. f, 92m, Transrapid TR-09.

No. 2841 — Early aviators and their airplanes: a, 16m, Richard "Dick" Read Bentley and DeHavilland Moth. b, 16m, Claude Grahame-White and biplane. c, 16m, Owen Cathcart-Jones and Miles Hawk trainer. d, 16m, Alberto Santos-Dumont and Demoiselle. e, 16m, Ross Macpherson Smith and Vickers Vimy biplane. f, 92m, Alan John Cobham and Short Singapore flying boat.

No. 2842 — Small jet airplanes: a, 16m, Cessna Citation X. b, 16m, Hawker 800. c, 16m, Embraer Phenom 100. d, 16m, Gulfstream G200. e, 16m, Gulfstream G550. f, 92m, Dassault Falcon 2000.

No. 2843 — Last flight of the Concorde, 10th anniv.: a, 16m, Concorde and André Turcat, first French Concorde pilot. b, 16m, Barbara Harmer, first female Concorde pilot. c, 16m, Concorde and Sir Archibald Russell, designer of Concorde. d, 16m, Concorde and Brian Trubshaw, first British Concorde pilot. e, 16m, Concorde on fire, July 25, 2000. f, 92m, Last flight of Concorde, Nov. 26, 2003.

No. 2844 — Military helicopters: a, 16m, Mil Mi-24A. b, Boeing-Sikorsky RAH-66 Comanche. c, 16m, AgustaWestland AW-101. d, 16m, Westland Apache WAH-64D Longbow. e, 16m, Harbin Z-19. f, 92m, Mil Mi-171E.

No. 2845 — Drones: a, 16m, NASA Altair. b, 16m, General Atomics MQ-9 Reaper. c, 16m, UAV X-47B. d, 16m, Lockheed Martin RQ-170 Sentinel. e, 16m, UAV X-47A. f, 92m, General Atomics MQ-1C Gray Eagle.

No. 2846 — Dirigibles: a, 16m, Clouth, Germany. b, 16m, First British military dirigible. c, 16m, Torrres Quevedo, Spain. d, 16m, Ville de Paris, France. e, 16m, Baby, Great Britain. f, 92m, Zodiac type dirigible, France.

No. 2847 — Old race cars: a, 16m, 1954 Maserati 250F. b, 16m, 1951 Cooper Climax T51. c, 16m, 1940 Bugatti T73C. d, 16m, 1960 Lotus 18. e, 16m, 1966 Eagle-Climax T2G. f, 92m, 1952 Cooper Bristol.

No. 2848 — Popemobiles: a, 16m, FCS Star and Pope John Paul II. b, 16m, Metalpar Mercedes-Benz and motorcycle. c, 16m, Mercedes-Benz ML 430 and Pope Benedict XVI. d, 16m, Fiat Nuova Campagnola and Pope John Paul II. e, 16m, Mercedes-Benz M Class and

Pope Benedict XVI. f, 92m, Pope Benedict XVI standing in Mercedes-Benz.

No. 2849 — Ferrari automobiles: a, 16m, Enzo Ferrari (1898-1988) and Auto Avio Costruzione 815. b, 16m, Ferrari 125 S. c, 16m, Ferrari 250 GTO. d, 16m, Ferrari 312 P. e, 16m, Ferrari 512 BB. f, 92m, Enzo Ferrari and Ferrari F40.

No. 2850 — Formula 1 racing champions: a, 16m, Sebastian Vettel in Renault race car. b, 16m, Vettel and Formula 1 Championship Trophy. c, 16m, Michael Schumacher and Formula 1 Championship Trophy. d, 16m, Schumacher in Mercedes race car. e, 16m, Fernando Alonso in Ferrari race car. f, 92m, Alonso and Formula 1 Championship Trophy.

No. 2851 — Motorcycles: a, 16m, 1896 Hildebrand Wolfmuller. b, 16m, 1911 Henderson. c, 16m, 1905 FN. d, 16m, 1925 DKW ZM175. e, 16m, 1920 Megola. f, 92m, 1921 Scott Flying Squirrel.

No. 2852 — Mail transport: a, 16m, English Royal Parcel Mail horse-drawn carriage. b, 16m, Workers and sacks in post office. c, 16m, Railroad mail car. d, 16m, Royal Mail truck. e, 16m, Workers and mail sacks near Royal Mail horse-drawn carriage. f, 92m, Mail sacks loaded on Royal Mail horse-drawn wagon.

No. 2853 — Police and rescue vehicles: a, 16m, Eurocopter AS-365N-3 Dauphin 2 police helicopter. b, 16m, BMW R1200RT-P police motorcycle. c, 16m, Higer KLQ6540 ambulance. d, 16m, Scania 94D fire truck. e, 16m, Lenco Bear Cat SWAT Team vehicle. f, 92m, Holden Rodeo police truck.

No. 2854 — Fire-fighting equipment: a, 16m, 1873 hose wagon. b, 16m, 1841 Paul Hodge steam-driven pumper and firefighter. c, 16m, Firemen on bicycle-chain driven vehicle, 1895 hose and ladder wagon. d, 16m, 1880 Piano pumper wagon. e, 92m, 1910 Electric fire engine, fireman in protective clothing. f, 92m, Fire truck with hoses and ladder.

No. 2855 — Military vehicles: a, 16m, Soldiers carrying kettle near Red Cross ambulance. b, 16m, Truck with open bed pulling gun. c, 16m, Red Cross workers near ambulances. d, 16m, Soldiers and Maxim motorcycle with sidecar. e, 92m, Cargo vehicle on tracks. f, 92m, Truck with ladder.

No. 2856, 175m, Siberian husky, dogs pulling sled. No. 2857, 175m, A Royal Mail Coach on a Flooded Road, by James Pollard. No. 2858, 175m, Henri Desgrange, Tour de France cyclist. No. 2859, 175m Yang Liwei, Shezhou 5, diff. No. 2860, 175m, Shepherd and Apollo 14 capsule. No. 2861, 175m, Apollo 8 orbiting Moon, diff. No. 2862, 175m, Iceboat with 221 on sail. No. 2863, 175m, Boat in Vendée Globe Regatta. No. 2864, 175m, 44-foot United States Coast Guard boat. No. 2865, 175m, Arctic Express icebreaker, Finland. No. 2866, 175m, Great Indian Peninsula Railway 4-6-0 steam locomotive. No. 2867, 175m, London Metro car from 1992. No. 2868, 175m, Mark VII monorail. No. 2869, 175m, ETR-500 train, diff. No. 2870, 175m, Amelia Earhart and Lockheed Vega. No. 2871, 175m, Learjet 65. No. 2872, 175m, Last flight of the Concorde, Nov. 26, 2003, diff. No. 2873, 175m, Boeing CH-47 Chinook helicopter. No. 2874, 175m, Firebird-9 drone. No. 2875, 175m, Capezza dirigible, France. No. 2876, 175m, 1935 Alfa Romeo Bimotore. No. 2877, 175m, Pope Benedict XVI and Mercedes-Benz ML 430 Popemobile. No. 2878, 175m, Enzo Ferrari and Ferrari F430. No. 2879, 175m, Formula 1 race car, Vettel holding Korean Grand Prix trophy. No. 2880, 175m, 1911 Indian motorcycle. No. 2881, 175m, English air mail flight, 1911. No. 2882, 175m, Ziegler Z8 airport foam spraying vehicle. No. 2883, 175m, 1863 fire wagon. No. 2884, 175m, Military truck, diff.

2013, Mar. 25   Litho.   Perf. 13¼
Sheets of 6, #a-f

2827-2855 A449 Set of 29 325.00 325.00

Souvenir Sheets

2856-2884 A449 Set of 29 350.00 350.00

A450

No. 2885 — Coat of arms of Pope Benedict XVI and Pope Benedict XVI: a, 16m, Wearing

miter. b, 16m, Wearing zucchetto, domed ceiling in background. c, 92m, Wearing zucchetto, waving. d, 92m, Wearing zucchetto and red stole.

No. 2886 — Coat of arms of Pope Francis and Pope Francis: a, 16m, Wearing miter. b, 16m, Wearing miter and holding crucifix. c, 92m, Wearing zucchetto. d, 92m, Wearing zucchetto and glasses.

No. 2887 — Marilyn Monroe (1926-62), actress: a, 16m, With husband, Joe DiMaggio. b, 16m, With bird on finger. c, 92m, Blowing bubble. d, 92m, Wearing red dress and earrings.

No. 2888 — Mohandas K. Gandhi (1869-1948), Indian independence leader: a, 16m, And Russia #3639. b, 16m, Sitting with crossed legs. c, 92m, Sitting. d, 92m, Women in background.

No. 2889 — Mao Zedong (1893-1976), Chinese communist leader: a, 16m, Reading papers. b, 16m, Wearing cap. c, 92m, With Chinese text at right. d, 92m, With flag of People's Republic of China at left.

No. 2890 — Prince William: a, 16m, Helicopter at right. b, 16m, Wearing air force uniform and flight helmet. c, 92m, Leaving helicopter, squadron emblem at right. d, 92m, Piloting helicopter.

No. 2891 — Female world chess champions: a, 16m, Zhao Xue, China. b, 16m, Humpy Koneru, India. c, 92m, Kataryna Lahno, Ukraine. d, 92m, Viktorije Cmilyte, Lithuania.

No. 2892 — Scouting trefoil and: a, 16m, Boy Scout on bicycle. b, 16m, Boy Scouts carrying canoe. c, 92m, Boy Scout with model airplane, Inachis io. d, 92m, Boy Scout at campfire, Heteronympha merope.

No. 2893 — Paintings by Raphael (1483-1520): a, 16m, Adoration of the Magi, 1502-04. b, 16m, St. George Slaying the Dragon, 1504. c, 92m, Portrait of Bindo Altoviti, 1515. d, 92m, Young Man with an Apple, 1505.

No. 2894 — Paintings by Eugene Delacroix (1798-1863): a, 16m, Christ on the Sea of Galilee, 1854. b, 16m, Orphan Girl at the Cemetery, 1823. c, 92m, Self-portrait. d, 92m, Arab Horses Fighting in a Stable, 1860.

No. 2895 — Paintings by Vincent van Gogh (1853-90): a, 16m, Memory of the Garden at Etten, 1888. b, 16m, Seascape at Saintes-Maries (Fishing Boats at Sea), 1888. c, 92m, A Pair of Shoes, 1887. d, 92m, Noon: Rest from Work, 1890.

No. 2896 — Paintings by Ivan Aivazovsky (1817-1900): a, 16m, Approximation of the Storm, 1877. b, 16m, Crimea, 1852. c, 92m, Ship Twelve Apostles, 1897. d, 92m, Morning at Sea, 1849, and Ocean, 1896.

No. 2897 — 2014 Winter Olympics, Sochi, Russia: a, 16m, Speed skating. b, 16m, Skiing. c, 92m, Curling. d, 92m, Bobsled.

No. 2898 — Intl. Red Cross, 150th anniv.: a, 16m, Rescue worker wearing gas mask carrying man. b, 16m, Jean-Henri Dunant, founder of Red Cross, and nurse carrying Red Cross flag. c, 92m, Rescue dogs at work. d, 92m, Red Cross workers caring for children.

No. 2899 — Steam locomotives: a, 16m, Empire State Express locomotive. b, 16m, 4MT, England. c, 92m, Porter 0-4-0, United States. d, 92m, Pennsylvania Railroad locomotive 4638.

No. 2900 — Volcanoes and minerals: a, 16m, Popocatépetl, Mexico, emerald and turquoise. b, 16m, Augustine Volcano, Alaska, chrysoprase and tourmaline. c, 92m, Popocatépetl, beryl and sapphire. d, 92m, Mount Bromo, Indonesia, topaz and spinel.

No. 2901 — Lighthouses and birds: a, 16m, White Shoal Lighthouse. Michigan, Rissa tridactyla. b, 16m, Portland Head Lighthouse, Maine, Columbus glacialis. c, 92m, Montauk Point Lighthouse, New York, Anas platyrhynchos. d, 92m, Lindau Harbor Lighthouse, Germany, Numenius americanus.

No. 2902 — Ailuropoda melanoleuca: a, 16m, Two pandas. b, 16m, One panda. c, 92m, Panda in tree. d, 92m, Two pandas, diff.

No. 2903 — Loxodonta africana: a, 16m, Adult and juvenile elephants. b, 16m, One elephant facing left. c, 92m, One elephant facing right. d, 92m, Two elephants, diff.

No. 2904 — Dolphins: a, 16m, Delphinus delphis, Delphinus capensis. b, 16m, Stenella attenuata. c, 92m, Lagenorhynchus obsdurus. d, 92m, Steno bredanensis, Cephalorhynchus commersonii.

No. 2905 — Parrots and plants: a, 16m, Charmosyna papou, Schefflera actinophylla. b, 16m, Polytelis swainsonii, Ara macao, Malus, Attalea maripa. c, 92m, Eclectus roratus, Cacatua moluccensis, Punica granatum. d, 92m, Ara rauna, Ara hyacinthe, Atalea funifera.

No. 2906 — Birds of prey and their prey: a, 16m, Aegypius monachus. b, 16m, Buteo buteo, lemmus lemmus. c, 92m, Buteo jamaicensis, Neotamias minimus. d, 92m, Pandion haliaetus.

No. 2907 — Owls and mushrooms: a, 16m, Surnia ulula, Coprinus comatus. b, 16m, Bubo virginianus, Peziza acetabulum. c, 92m, Tyto alba, Amanita rubescens. d, 92m, Ulula cinerea lapponica, Clitocybe inversa.

No. 2908 — Bees: a, 16m, Anthidium florentinum. b, 16m, Apis florea. c, 92m, Osmia ribifloris. d, 92m, Bombus terrestris.

No. 2909 — Insects and mushrooms: a, 16m, Choeradodis, Phrynus lunatus, Agaricus cervinus. b, 16m, Sphinx nerri, Agaricus dryophilus. c, 92m, Papilio priaunus, Sirex gigas, Cortinarius torvus. d, 92m, Heterosterne buprestoide, Russula.

No. 2910 — Butterflies and orchids: a, 16m, Papilio zelicaon, Calanthe biloba. b, 16m, Troides amphrysus. c, 92m, Alcidees metaurus, Phalaenopsis stuartiana. d, 92m, Ornithoptera victoriae, Gastrochilus spp.

No. 2911 — Marine life and seafood dishes: a, 16m, Mytilus edulis, Feijoada de mariscos. b, 16m, Penaeus monodon, Caril de camarao. c, 92m, Mercenaria mercenaria, Amêijoas em tomate. d, 92m, Callinectes sapidus, Caril de caranguejo.

No. 2912 — Frogs and snails: a, 16m, Dendrobates tinctorius, Arianta arbustorum. b, 16m, Oophaga pumilio, Planorbarius corneus. c, 92m, Phyllobates terribilis, Clea helena. d, 92m, Pelophylax shqipericus, Clithon corona.

No. 2913 — Turtles: a, 16m, Emys trinacris. b, 16m, Indotestudo elongata. c, 92m, Heosemys depressa. d, 92m, Batagur trivittata.

No. 2914 — Dinosaurs: a, 16m, Stegosaurus. b, 16m, Saurolophus. c, 92m, Rubeosaurus. d, 92m, Ankylosaurus.

No. 2915, 175m, Pope Benedict XVI and his coat of arms. No. 2916, 175m, Pope Francis and his coat of arms. No. 2917, 175m, Monroe and signature. No. 2918, 175m, Gandhi, diff. No. 2919, 175m, Mao Zedong, diff. No. 2920, 175m, Prince William in helicopter, diff. No. 2921, 175m, Anna Muzychuk, Ukrainian chess player. No. 2922, 175m, Scouting trefoil, Boy Scout with bicycle. No. 2923, 175m, St. Catherine of Alexandria, by Raphael. No. 2924, 175m, Combat of Giaour and Pasha, by Delacroix. No. 2925, 175m, The Langlois Bridge at Arles with Women Washing, by van Gogh. No. 2926, 175m, The Ninth Wave, by Aivazovsky. No. 2927, 175m, Biathlon. No. 2928, 175m, Dunant, Red Cross flag, joined hands. No. 2929, 175m, The General 4-4-0 locomotive. No. 2930, 175m, Puu Oo Volcano, Hawaii, topaz. No. 2931, 175m, Alcatraz Island Lighthouse, California, Larus argentatus. No. 2932, 175m, Ailuropoda melanoleuca, diff. No. 2933, 175m, Loxodonta africana adult and juvenile, diff. No. 2934, 175m, Sousa teuszii, Steno bredanensis. No. 2935, 175m, Deroptyus accipitrinus, Psittacula eupatria, Anacardium occidentale. No. 2936, 175m, Sarcoramphus papa. No. 2937, 175m, Tyto alba, Psalliota campestris. No. 2938, 175m, Apis mellifera. No. 2939, 175m, Calopteryx splendens, Macrothylacia rubi, Coprinopsis atramentaria. No. 2940, 175m, Papilio aegeus, Erasma pulchella, Prosthechea vitellina. No. 2941, 175m, Mytilus edulis, Arroz con mariscos. No. 2942, 175m, Hyla leucophyllata, Arianta arbustorum. No. 2943, 175m, Geoclemys hamiltonii. No. 2944, 175m, Microraptor gui.

2013, June 25   Litho.   Perf. 13¼
Sheets of 4, #a-d

2885-2914 A450 Set of 30 450.00 450.00

Souvenir Sheets

2915-2944 A450 Set of 30 350.00 350.00

2013 China International Collection Expo (Nos. 2902, 2932).

A451

No. 2945, 46m — James Gandolfini (1961-2013), actor: a, Holding Emmy award in foreground. b, Holding walking stick. c, Wearing suit and tie. d, Holding rifle in background, holding Screen Actors Guild award in foreground.

No. 2946, 46m — Giuseppe Verdi (1813-1901), composer: a, Without hat, clef at LL. b, Wearing hat, clef at LL. c, Wearing hat, clef at LL. d, Without hat, clef at LR.

No. 2947, 46m — Richard Wagner (1813-83), composer: a, Without hat, clef at LL. b,

Wearing hat, clef at LR. c, Wearing hat, clef at LL. d, Without hat, clef at LR.

No. 2948, 46m — Elvis Presley (1813-1901), various images with background color of: a, Blue. b, Red. c, Orange. d, Green.

No. 2949, 46m — Russian royalty: a, Tsar Peter the Great (1672-1725). b, Heir apparent Alexei Nikolayevich (1904-18). c, Empress Catherine I (1684-1727). d, Emperor Alexander I (1777-1825).

No. 2950, 46m — Pope John Paul II: a, With hands clasped above heart, coat of arms at right. b, Holding crucifix, wearing white vestments. c, Waving, holding crucifix, wearing green vestments. d, In prayer, with hands clasped near mouth, coat of arms at right.

No. 2951, 46m — Rotary International emblem and: a, Paul Harris (1868-1947), founder, wearing hat. b, Owl, mortarboard, book, Rotary Youth Exchange emblem. c, Child receiving polio vaccine, polio eradication program emblem. d, Harris, without hat.

No. 2952, 46m — Pierre de Coubertin (1863-1937), founder of modern Olympics movement: a, Coubertin and statue. b, Table tennis. c, BMX bicycling. d, Judo.

No. 2953, 46m — Brazilian soccer players: a, Fred. b, Hulk. c, Julio Cesar. c, David Luiz.

No. 2954, 46m — Paintings depicting chess: a, The Chess Game, by Sofonisba Anguissola. b, The Veterans, by Richard Creifelds. c, Chess Game, by Marcel Duchamp. d, The Great Chess Game, by Paul Klee.

No. 2955, 46m — Post-impressionist paintings: a, Tahitian Women on the Beach, by Paul Gauguin. b, The Dining Room in the Country, by Pierre Bonnard. c, Starry Night Over the Rhone, by Vincent van Gogh. d, At the Moulin Rouge the Clowness Cha u kao, by Henri de Toulouse-Lautrec.

No. 2956, 46m — Paintings by Joan Miró (1893-1983): a, Miró and Vuelo de Pájaraos, 1968. b, Running Man. c, Nord-Sud, 1917. d, Waman in Front of the Sun, 1950.

No. 2957, 46m — Paintings by Pablo Picasso (1881-1973): a, Picasso and Still Life with Bottle of Anis del Mono, 1909. b, Nude Woman in Red Armchair, 1932. c, Portrait of Marie Thérèse Walter, 1937. d, Picasso and Table in a Cafe, 1912.

No. 2958, 46m — Russian art: a, Icon of Madonna and Child, by Dionisius. b, Feodor III, by Bogdan Saltanov. c, Icon of St. Sophia, Faith, Hope and Charity, by Karp Zolotaryov. d, Icon of the Trinity, by Andrej Rublev.

No. 2959, 46m — Ancient Egyptian civilization: a, Model of bark constructed in 18th Dynasty. b, King Tutankhamun and his wife. c, Tomb of King Tutankhamun. d, Bust of Nefertiti.

No. 2960, 46m — World War I: a, German submarine U-155, Winston Churchill. b, Tanks in ruined city. c, Red Cross nurse, soldiers in battle. d, T. E. Lawrence (Lawrence of Arabia), Lawrence on camel.

No. 2961, 46m — Fire trucks: a, 1939 Dennis Light 4. b, 1965 Bedford TK. c, 1961 Magirus-Deutz Merkur F 25A. d, 1959 Opel Blitz LF 8.

No. 2962, 46m — Steam locomotives: a, Stourbridge Lion. b, Norris 4-2-0. c, Type 1 2-4-2. d, Problem Class 2-2-2.

No. 2963, 46m — Chinese high-speed trains: a, China Star. b, CRH2. c, CRH380B. d, CRH1.

No. 2964, 46m — Shenzhou 10: a, Shenzhou 10 in orbit. b, Zhang Xiaoguang. c, Wang Yaping. d, Nie Haisheng.

No. 2965, 46m — Minerals: a, Azurite. b, Garnet and smoky quartz. c, Yellow mineral ore. d, Amethyst and quartz.

No. 2966, 46m — Primates: a, Saguinus imperator. b, Cebus capucinus. c, Tarsius syrichta. d, Gorilla beringei graueri.

No. 2967, 46m — African animals: a, Panthera pardus. b, Loxodonta africana. c, Hippopotamus amphibius. d, Giraffa camelopardalis.

No. 2968, 46m — Whales: a, Megaptera novaeangliae. b, Balaena mysticetus. c, Eschrichtius robustus. d, Physeter macrocephalus.

No. 2969, 46m — Owls: a, Strix leptogrammica. b, Otus sagittatus. c, Strix butleri. d, Tyto soumagnei.

No. 2970, 46m — Butterflies: a, Papilio demoleus malayanus. b, Danaus chrysippus chrysippus. c, Euripus nyctelius euploeoides. d, Cethosia cyane.

No. 2971, 46m — Lighthouses and shells: a, Cape Otway Lighthouse, Australia, Cardium costatum. b, Yaquina Head Lighthouse, Oregon, Nautilides. c, Cape Hatteras Lighthouse, North Carolina, Queen conch. d, White Shoal Lighthouse, Michigan, Babylonia canaliculata.

No. 2972, 46m — Reptiles: a, Dendroaspis angusticeps. b, Agama mwanzae. c, Varanus albigularis. d, Diadophis punctatus.

No. 2973, 46m — Dinosaurs and pre-historic hominids: a, Anchiornis huxleyi. b, Homo habilis. c, Homo floresiensis. d, Velociraptor.

No. 2974, 46m — Birth of Prince George of Cambridge: a, Duke and Duchess of Cambridge, Prince George. b, Prince Charles, Duke of Cambridge holding Prince George. c, Princess Diana holding Prince William, Duke of Cambridge holding Prince George. d, Duchess of Cambridge holding Prince George.

No. 2975, 175m, Gandolfini with arms crossed. No. 2976, 175m, Verdi, diff. No. 2977, 175m, Wagner, diff. No. 2978, 175m, Presley, diff. No. 2979, 175m, Emperor Nicholas II of Russia (1868-1918). No. 2980, 175m, Pope John Paul II and his coat of arms. No. 2981, 175m, Harris, Rotary Youth Exchange emblem. No. 2982, 175m, Equestrian competitors. No. 2983, 175m, Neymar. No. 2984, 175m, The Chess Board, by Juan Gris. No. 2985, 175m, Young Women of Provence at the Well, by Paul Signac. No. 2986, 175m, Miró and Siesta, 1925. No. 2987, 175m, Picasso and House in a Garden, 1908. No. 2988, 175m, Old Jew, by Nikolai Yaroshenko. No. 2989, 175m, Bust of Egyptian Pharaoh Menes and Pyramids. No. 2990, 175m, Baron Manfed von Richthofen and Fokker Dr.I triplane in flight. No. 2991, 175m, 1914 Ford Model T fire engine. No. 2992, 175m, Jupiter locomotive. No. 2993, 175m, CHR380D high-speed train. No. 2994, 175m, Wang Yaping, diff. No. 2995, 175m, Aragonite. No. 2996, 175m, Saimiri sciureus. No. 2997, 175m, Panthera leo. No. 2998, 175m, Eubalaena australis. No. 2999, 175m, Strix nebulosa. No. 3000, 175m, Papilio polytes romulus. No. 3001, 175m, Beachy Head Lighthouse, Great Britain, Anadara corbuliodes. No. 3002, 175m, Furcier pardalis. No. 3003, 175m, Homo habilis making tool. No. 3004, 175m, Duke and Duchess of Cambridge, Prince George, diff.

2013, Sept. 25　　Litho.　　Perf. 13¼
Sheets of 4, #a-d
2945-2974　A451　Set of 30　400.00 400.00
Souvenir Sheets
2975-3004　A451　Set of 30　375.00 375.00

Brasiliana 2013 Intl. Philatelic Exhibition, Rio de Janeiro (Nos. 2953, 2983); Rossica 2013 Intl. Philatelic Exhibition (Nos. 2958, 2988); 2013 China International Collection Expo (Nos. 2963, 2964, 2993, 2994).

SEMI-POSTAL STAMPS

"History" Pointing out to the "Republic" Need for Charity SP1

Nurse Leading Wounded Soldiers SP2

Veteran Relating Experiences — SP3

Perf. 11½

			Unwmk.	
1920, Dec. 1		**Litho.**		
B1	SP1	¼c olive	4.00	3.50
B2	SP1	½c olive blk	4.00	3.50
B3	SP1	1c dp bister	4.00	3.50
B4	SP1	2c lilac brn	4.00	3.50
B5	SP1	3c lilac	4.00	3.50
B6	SP1	4c green	4.00	3.50
B7	SP2	5c grnsh blue	4.00	3.50
B8	SP2	6c light blue	4.00	3.50
B9	SP2	7½c red brown	4.00	3.50
B10	SP2	8c lemon	4.00	3.50
B11	SP2	10c gray lilac	4.00	3.50
B12	SP2	12c pink	4.00	3.50
B13	SP3	18c rose	4.00	3.50
B14	SP3	24c vio brn	4.00	3.50
B15	SP3	30c pale ol grn	4.00	3.50
B16	SP3	40c dull red	4.00	3.50
B17	SP3	50c yellow	4.00	3.50
B18	SP3	1e ultra	4.00	3.50
		Nos. B1-B18 (18)	72.00	63.00

Nos. B1-B18 were used Dec. 1, 1920, in place of ordinary stamps. The proceeds were for war victims.

AIR POST STAMPS

Common Design Type

Perf. 13½x13
1938, Aug.　　Engr.　　Unwmk.
Name and Value in Black

C1	CD39	10c scarlet	.30	.25
C2	CD39	20c purple	.30	.25
C3	CD39	50c orange	.30	.25
C4	CD39	1e ultra	.40	.30
C5	CD39	2e lilac brn	1.00	.30
C6	CD39	3e dk green	1.75	.40
C7	CD39	5e red brown	2.10	.70
C8	CD39	9e rose car	4.25	.75
C9	CD39	10e magenta	7.25	1.25
		Nos. C1-C9 (9)	17.65	4.45

No. C7 exists with overprint "Exposicao Internacional de Nova York, 1939-1940" and Trylon and Perisphere.

No. C7 Surcharged in Black

1946, Nov. 2　　　　Perf. 13½x13
C10	CD39	3e on 5e red brn	6.00	1.75
a.		Inverted surcharge		

Plane — AP1

1946, Nov. 2　　Typo.　　Perf. 11½
Denomination in Black

C11	AP1	1.20e carmine	1.10	.85
C12	AP1	1.60e blue	1.40	.90
C13	AP1	1.70e plum	3.50	1.40
C14	AP1	2.90e brown	3.50	1.90
C15	AP1	3e green	3.00	1.75
		Nos. C11-C15 (5)	12.50	6.80

Inscribed "Taxe perçue" and Denomination in Brown Carmine or Black

1947, May 20

C16	AP1	50c blk (BrC)	.50	.25
C17	AP1	1e pink	.50	.25
C18	AP1	3e green	1.00	.40
C19	AP1	4.50e yel grn	2.50	.75
C20	AP1	5e red brown	2.50	.90
C21	AP1	10e ultra	6.00	1.25
C22	AP1	20e violet	11.00	4.00
C23	AP1	50e orange	15.00	6.00
		Nos. C16-C23 (8)	39.00	13.80

Dangerous counterfeits exist.

Planes Circling Globe — AP2

1949, Mar.

C24	AP2	50c sepia	.30	.25
C25	AP2	1.20e violet	.50	.30
C26	AP2	4.50e dull blue	1.25	.40
C27	AP2	5e blue green	1.75	.50
C28	AP2	20e chocolate	4.00	.85
		Nos. C24-C28 (5)	7.80	2.40

> **Catalogue values for unused stamps in this section, from this point to the end of the section, are for Never Hinged items.**

Oil Refinery, Sonarep AP3

Designs: 2e, Salazar High School, Lourenço Marques. 3.50e, Lourenço Marques harbor. 4.50e, Salazar dam. 5e, Trigo de Morais bridge. 20e, Marcelo Caetano bridge.

1963, Mar. 5　　Litho.　　Perf. 13
C29	AP3	1.50e multi	.60	.25
C30	AP3	2e multi	.30	.25
C31	AP3	3.50e multi	.60	.25
C32	AP3	4.50e multi	.40	.25
C33	AP3	5e multi	.50	.25
C34	AP3	20e multi	1.40	.60
		Nos. C29-C34 (6)	3.80	1.85

Republic

Nos. C31-C34 Overprinted in Red

1975, June 25　　Litho.　　Perf. 13
C35	AP3	3.50e multi	.55	.40
C36	AP3	4.50e multi	.60	.45
C37	AP3	5e multi	1.40	.80
C38	AP3	20e multi	2.00	2.00
		Nos. C35-C38 (4)	3.15	1.00

DeHavilland Dragonfly, 1937 — AP4

Designs: 1.50m, Junker JU-52-3M, 1938. 3m, Lockheed Lodestar L-18-08, 1940. 7.50m, DeHavilland Dove DH-104, 1948. 10m, Douglas Dakota DC-3, 1956. 12.5m, Fokker Friendship F-27, 1962.

1981, May 14　　Litho.　　Perf. 11
C39	AP4	50c multi	.90	.25
C40	AP4	1.50m multi	1.10	.25
C41	AP4	3m multi	1.75	.25
C42	AP4	7.50m multi	2.50	.25
C43	AP4	10m multi	3.00	.40
C44	AP4	12.5m multi	4.50	.55
		Nos. C39-C44 (6)	13.75	1.95

Piper Navajo Over Hydroelectric Dam — AP5

Designs: 40m, De Havilland Hornet trainer, 1936. 80m, Boeing 737, Maputo Airport, 1973. 120m, Beechcraft King-Air. 160m, Piper Aztec. 320m, Douglas DC-10, 1982.

1987, Oct. 28　　Litho.　　Perf. 11
C45	AP5	20m multi	.30	.25
C46	AP5	40m multi	.60	.25
C47	AP5	80m multi	1.25	.40
C48	AP5	120m multi	1.60	.45
C49	AP5	160m multi	2.50	.60
C50	AP5	320m multi	4.00	1.10
		Nos. C45-C50 (6)	10.25	3.05

POSTAGE DUE STAMPS

D1

1904　Unwmk.　Typo.　Perf. 11½x12
Name and Value in Black

J1	D1	5r yellow grn	.40	.25
J2	D1	10r slate	.40	.25
J3	D1	20r yellow brn	.40	.25
J4	D1	30r orange	.80	.70
J5	D1	50r gray brn	.70	.55
J6	D1	60r red brown	3.50	1.75
J7	D1	100r red lilac	3.00	1.75
J8	D1	130r dull blue	1.50	1.20
J9	D1	200r carmine	2.00	1.20
J10	D1	500r violet	2.50	1.20
			15.20	9.10

See J34-J43. For overprints see Nos. 247, J11-J30.

Same Overprinted in Carmine or Green

1911

J11	D1	5r yellow green	.25	.25
J12	D1	10r slate	.40	.25
J13	D1	20r yellow brn	.30	.25
J14	D1	30r orange	.30	.25
J15	D1	50r gray brown	.40	.30
J16	D1	60r red brown	.60	.35
J17	D1	100r red lilac	.80	.55
J18	D1	130r dull blue	1.10	.80
J19	D1	200r carmine (G)	1.20	.95
J20	D1	500r violet	1.60	.95
		Nos. J11-J20 (10)	6.95	4.90

Nos. J1-J10 Overprinted Locally in Carmine

1916

J21	D1	5r yellow grn	4.00	3.25
J22	D1	10r slate	5.50	3.25
J23	D1	20r yellow brn	80.00	60.00
J24	D1	30r orange	22.50	12.50
J25	D1	50r gray brown	80.00	55.00
J26	D1	60r red brown	65.00	45.00
J27	D1	100r red lilac	80.00	60.00
J28	D1	130r dull blue	2.40	2.25
J29	D1	200r carmine	2.75	3.00
J30	D1	500r violet	5.50	4.75
		Nos. J21-J30 (10)	347.65	249.00

War Tax Stamps of 1916 Ovptd. Diagonally

1918　　　　　　　Rouletted 7
J31	WT1	1c gray green	.95	.80
J32	WT2	5c rose	.95	.80
a.		Inverted overprint	8.25	7.50

Perf. 11
J33	WT1	1c gray green	.95	.80
a.		"REPUBLICA"	50.00	40.00
		Nos. J31-J33 (3)	2.85	2.40

Type of 1904 Issue With Value in Centavos

1917　　　　　　　　Perf. 12
J34	D1	½c yellow green	.30	.30
J35	D1	1c slate	.30	.30
J36	D1	2c orange brown	.30	.30
J37	D1	3c orange	.30	.30
J38	D1	5c gray brown	.30	.30
J39	D1	6c pale brn	.30	.30
J40	D1	10c red violet	.30	.30
J41	D1	13c deep blue	.55	.55
J42	D1	20c rose	.55	.55
J43	D1	50c gray	.55	.55
		Nos. J34-J43 (10)	3.75	3.75

Lourenco Marques Nos. 117, 119 Surcharged in Red

1921
J44	A4	5c on ½c blk	1.60	.95
J45	A4	10c on 1½c brn	1.60	.95

Same Surcharge on Mozambique Nos. 151, 155, 157 in Red or Green
J46	A6	6c on 1c bl grn (R)	1.60	.95
J47	A6	20c on 2½c vio (R)	1.00	.85
a.		Inverted surcharge	7.50	7.50
J48	A6	50c on 4c rose (G)	1.00	.85
		Nos. J44-J48 (5)	6.80	4.55

Regular Issues of 1921-22 Surcharged in Black or Red

1924 **Perf. 12x11½**
J49	A6	20c on 30c ol grn (Bk)	1.10	.45
a.		Perf. 15x14	19.00	4.50
J50	A6	50c on 60c dk bl (R)	1.00	1.00

> Catalogue values for unused stamps in this section, from this point to the end of the section, are for Never Hinged items.

Common Design Type
Photo. and Typo.

1952 Unwmk. Perf. 14
Numeral in Red Orange or Red; Frame Multicolored
J51	CD45	10c carmine (RO)	.25	.25
J52	CD45	30c black brn	.25	.25
J53	CD45	50c black	.25	.25
J54	CD45	1e violet blue	.25	.25
J55	CD45	2e olive green	.25	.25
J56	CD45	5e orange brown	.55	.30
		Nos. J51-J56 (6)	1.80	1.55

WAR TAX STAMPS

Coats of Arms of Portugal and Mozambique on Columns, Allegorical Figures of History of Portugal and the Republic Holding Scroll with Date of Declaration of War — WT1

Prow of Galley of Discoveries. Left, "Republic" Teaching History of Portugal; Right "History" with Laurels (Victory) and Sword (Symbolical of Declaration of War) — WT2

1916 Unwmk. Litho. Rouletted 7
MR1	WT1	1c gray green	2.25	.55
a.		Imperf., pair	15.00	
MR2	WT2	5c rose	2.25	.55
a.		Imperf., pair	15.00	

1918 Perf. 11, 12
MR3	WT1	1c gray green	.85	.55
a.		"PEPUBLICA"	8.50	4.75
MR4	WT2	5c red	1.00	.70
a.		"PETRIA"	3.50	3.50
b.		"PEPUBLICA"	3.50	3.50

c.	"1910" for "1916"	11.00	5.50
d.	Imperf., pair		
	Nos. MR1-MR4 (4)	6.35	2.35

For surcharges and overprints see Nos. 221-225, 229, 235, J31-J33.

NEWSPAPER STAMPS

No. 19 Surcharged in Black, Red or Blue

a   b

1893 Unwmk. Perf. 11½, 12½, 13½
P1	A2 (a)	2½r on 40r	200.00	90.00
P2	A2 (a)	5r on 40r	175.00	90.00
P3	A2 (a)	5r on 40r (R)	150.00	75.00
P4	A2 (a)	5r on 40r (Bl)	180.00	75.00
P5	A2 (b)	2½r on 40r	22.50	16.00
		Nos. P1-P5 (5)	727.50	346.00

Nos. P1-P5 exist with double surcharge, Nos. P2-P4 with inverted surcharge.

N3

1893 Typo. Perf. 11½, 13½
P6	N3	2½r brown	.35	.30

For surcharge and overprint see Nos. 93, 199, 206.

No. P6 has been reprinted on chalk-surfaced paper with clean-cut perforation 13½. Value, 50 cents.

POSTAL TAX STAMPS

Pombal Commemorative Issue
Common Design Types
1925 Engr. Perf. 12½
RA1	CD28	15c brown & black	.30	.25
RA2	CD29	15c brown & black	.30	.25
RA3	CD30	15c brown & black	.30	.25
		Nos. RA1-RA3 (3)	.90	.75

Seal of Local Red Cross Society
PT7   PT8
Surcharged in Various Colors

1925 Typo. Perf. 11½
RA4	PT7	50c slate & yel (Bk)	1.60	1.60

1926
RA5	PT8	40c slate & yel (Bk)	3.25	3.25
RA6	PT8	50c slate & yel (R)	3.25	3.25
RA7	PT8	60c slate & yel (V)	3.25	3.25
RA8	PT8	80c slate & yel (Br)	3.25	3.25
RA9	PT8	1e slate & yel (Bl)	3.25	3.25
RA10	PT8	2e slate & yel (G)	3.25	3.25
		Nos. RA5-RA10 (6)	10.50	10.50

Obligatory on mail certain days of the year. The tax benefited the Cross of the Orient Society.

Type of 1926 Issue
1927 Black Surcharge
RA11	PT8	5c red & yel	3.25	3.25
RA12	PT8	10c green & yel	3.25	3.25
RA13	PT8	20c gray & yel	3.25	3.25
RA14	PT8	30c lt bl & yel	3.25	3.25
RA15	PT8	40c vio & yel	3.25	3.25
RA16	PT8	50c car & yel	3.25	3.25
RA17	PT8	60c brown & yel	3.25	3.25
RA18	PT8	80c blue & yel	3.25	3.25

RA19	PT8	1e olive & yel	3.25	3.25
RA20	PT8	2e yel brn & yel	3.25	3.25
		Nos. RA11-RA20 (10)	32.50	32.50

See note after No. RA10.

PT9

1928 Litho.
RA21	PT9	5c grn, yel & blk	4.50	4.50
RA22	PT9	10c sl bl, yel & blk	4.50	4.50
RA23	PT9	20c gray blk, yel & blk	4.50	4.50
RA24	PT9	30c brn rose, yel & blk	4.50	4.50
RA25	PT9	40c cl brn, yel & blk	4.50	4.50
RA26	PT9	50c red org, yel & blk	4.50	4.50
RA27	PT9	60c brn, yel & blk	4.50	4.50
RA28	PT9	80c dk brn, yel & blk	4.50	4.50
RA29	PT9	1e gray, yel & blk	4.50	4.50
RA30	PT9	2e red, yel & blk	4.50	4.50
		Nos. RA21-RA30 (10)	45.00	45.00

See note after RA10.

Mother and Children — PT10

1929 Photo. Perf. 14
RA31	PT10	40c ultra, cl & blk	2.75	2.75

The use of this stamp was compulsory on all correspondence to Portugal and Portuguese Colonies for eight days beginning July 24, 1929.
See Nos. RA39-RA47.

Mousinho de Albuquerque
PT11

1930-31 Perf. 14½x14
Inscribed: "MACONTENE"
RA32	PT11	50c lake, red & gray	3.50	4.00

Inscribed: "COOLELA"
RA33	PT11	50c red vio, red brn & gray	3.50	4.00

Inscribed: "MUJENGA"
RA34	PT11	50c org red, red & gray	3.50	4.00

Inscribed: "CHAIMITE"
RA35	PT11	50c dp grn, bl grn & gray	3.50	4.00

Inscribed: "IBRAHIMO"
RA36	PT11	50c dk bl, blk & gray	3.50	4.00

Inscribed: "MUCUTO-MUNO"
RA37	PT11	50c ultra, blk & gray	3.50	4.00

Inscribed: "NAGUEMA"
RA38	PT11	50c dk vio, lt vio & gray	3.50	4.00
		Nos. RA32-RA38 (7)	24.50	28.00

The portrait is that of Mousinho de Albuquerque, the celebrated Portuguese warrior, and the names of seven battles in which he took part appear at the foot of the stamps. The stamps were issued for the memorial fund bearing his name and their use was obligatory on all correspondence posted on eight specific days in the year.

Type of 1929 Issue
Denominations in Black
No. RA42 Without Denomination

1931 Perf. 14
RA39	PT10	40c rose & vio	4.00	3.25
RA40	PT10	40c ol grn & vio ('32)	5.50	4.50
RA41	PT10	40c bis brn & rose ('33)	5.50	4.50
RA42	PT10	bl grn & rose ('34)	3.75	3.50
RA43	PT10	40c org & ultra ('36)	5.50	4.50
RA44	PT10	40c choc & ultra ('37)	5.50	4.50
RA45	PT10	40c grn & brn car ('38)	7.50	5.50
RA46	PT10	40c yel & blk ('39)	7.50	5.50
RA47	PT10	40c gray brn ('40)	7.50	5.50
		Nos. RA39-RA47 (9)	52.25	41.25

Allegory of Charity
PT12

White Pelican — PT13

1942 Unwmk. Litho. Perf. 11½
Denomination in Black
RA48	PT12	50c rose carmine	8.25	2.00

1943-51 Perf. 11½, 14
Denomination in Black
RA49	PT13	50c rose carmine	17.00	1.25
RA50	PT13	50c emerald	10.00	1.25
RA51	PT13	50c purple	15.00	1.25
RA52	PT13	50c blue	12.00	1.25
RA53	PT13	50c red brown	50.00	1.25
RA54	PT13	50c olive bister	10.00	1.25
		Nos. RA49-RA54 (6)	122.00	7.50

There are two sizes of the numeral on No. RA49.

> Catalogue values for unused stamps in this section, from this point to the end of the section, are for Never Hinged items.

Inscribed: "Provincia de Mocambique"
1954-56 Perf. 14½x14
RA55	PT13	50c orange	1.40	.60
RA56	PT13	50c olive grn ('56)	1.40	.60
RA57	PT13	50c brown ('56)	1.40	.60
		Nos. RA55-RA57 (3)	4.20	1.80

No. RA57 Surcharged with New Value and Wavy Lines
1956
RA58	PT13	30c on 50c brown	.85	.35

Pelican Type of 1954-56
1958 Litho. Perf. 14
Denomination in Black
RA59	PT13	30c yellow	.80	.60
RA60	PT13	50c salmon	.80	.60

Imprint: "Imprensa Nacional de Mocambique"
1963-64
Denomination Typographed in Black
RA61	PT13	30c yellow ('64)	.80	.60
RA62	PT13	50c salmon	.80	.60

Women and
Children
PT14

Lineman on
Pole and Map of
Mozambique
PT15

1963-65   Litho.   Perf. 14
RA63 PT14 50c blk, bis & red   .30 .25
RA64 PT14 50c blk, pink & red ('65) .30 .25
See Nos. RA68-RA76.

1965, Apr. 1   Unwmk.   Perf. 14
30c, Telegraph poles and map of
Mozambique.

Size: 23x30mm
RA65 PT15 30c blk, salmon & lil   .25 .25

Size: 19x36mm
RA66 PT15 50c blk, bl & sepia   .25 .25
RA67 PT15 1e blk, yel & org   .25 .25

The tax was for improvement of the telecommunications system. Obligatory on inland mail.
A 2.50e in the design of the 30c was issued for
use on telegrams.

Type of 1963
1967-70   Litho.   Perf. 14
RA68 PT14 50c blk, lt yel grn &
            red   .40 .25
RA69 PT14 50c blk, lt bl & red
            ('69)   .40 .25
RA70 PT14 50c blk, buff & brt red
            ('70)   .40 .25
      Nos. RA68-RA70 (3)   1.20 .75

1972-73
RA71 PT14 30c blk, lt grn & red   .25 .25
RA72 PT14 50c blk, gray & red
            ('73)   1.00 .25
RA73 PT14 1e blk, bis & red ('73) .25 .25
      Nos. RA71-RA73 (3)   1.50 .75

1974-75
RA74 PT14 50c blue, yel & red   .25 .25
RA75 PT14 1e blk, gray & ver   .85 .25
RA76 PT14 1e blk, lil rose & red
            ('75)   .40 .25
      Nos. RA74-RA76 (3)   1.50 .75

Intl. Year of the
Child — PT16

1979   Litho.   Perf. 14¼
RA77 PT16 50e red   1.50 1.50

POSTAL TAX DUE STAMPS

Pombal Commemorative Issue
Common Design Types

1925   Unwmk.   Perf. 12½
RAJ1 CD28 30c brown & black   .55 .65
RAJ2 CD29 30c brown & black   .55 .65
RAJ3 CD30 30c brown & black   .55 .65
      Nos. RAJ1-RAJ3 (3)   1.65 1.95

MOZAMBIQUE COMPANY

mō-zəm-'bĕk 'kəmp-nē

LOCATION — Comprises the territory
of Manica and Sofala of the
Mozambique Colony in southeastern
Africa
GOVT. — A part of the Portuguese
Colony of Mozambique
AREA — 51,881 sq. mi.

POP. — 368,447 (1939)
CAPITAL — Beira

The Mozambique Company was
chartered by Portugal in 1891 for 50
years. The territory was under direct
administration of the Company until July
18, 1941.

1000 Reis = 1 Milreis
100 Centavos = 1 Escudo (1916)

Mozambique Nos. 15-
23 Overprinted in
Carmine or Black

1892   Unwmk.   Perf. 12½, 13½
1   A2 5r black (C)   3.00 .50
a.   Pair, one without overprint 50.00 22.50
2   A2 10r green   3.00 .50
3   A2 20r rose   3.00 .50
a.   Perf. 13½   45.00 30.00
4   A2 25r violet   3.00 .45
a.   Double overprint   27.50
5   A2 40r chocolate   3.00 .45
a.   Double overprint   20.00
6   A2 50r blue   3.00 .50
7   A2 100r yellow brown   3.00 .75
8   A2 200r gray violet   4.00 .90
9   A2 300r orange   5.00 .90
        Nos. 1-9 (9)   30.00 5.45

Nos. 1 to 6, 8-9 were reprinted in 1905.
These reprints have white gum and clean-cut
perf. 13½ and the colors are usually paler than
those of the originals.

Company Coat of
Arms — A2

Perf. 11½, 12½, 13½
1895-1907   Typo.
Black or Red Numerals
10 A2 2½r olive yellow   .25 .25
11 A2 2½r gray ('07)   1.50 1.50
12 A2 5r orange   .25 .25
a.   Value omitted   15.00
b.   Perf. 13½   2.00 1.10
13 A2 10r red lilac   .40 .30
14 A2 10r yel grn ('07)   2.50 .40
a.   Value inverted at top of stamp 20.00 20.00
15 A2 15r red brown   1.00 .30
16 A2 15r dk green ('07)   2.50 .40
17 A2 20r gray lilac   1.50 .30
18 A2 25r green   .75 .30
a.   Perf. 13½   1.90 1.25
19 A2 25r carmine ('07)   2.50 .60
a.   Value omitted   15.00 10.00
20 A2 50r blue   .90 .30
21 A2 50r brown ('07)   2.50 .60
a.   Value omitted   15.00
22 A2 65r slate blue ('02)   .75 .35
23 A2 75r rose   .70 .30
24 A2 75r red lilac ('07)   5.00 1.00
25 A2 80r yellow green   .50 .30
26 A2 100r brown, buff   1.00 .30
27 A2 100r dk bl, bl ('07)   4.00 1.00
28 A2 115r car, pink ('04)   1.25 .70
29 A2 115r org brn, pink
            ('07)   6.00 1.40
30 A2 130r grn, pink ('04)   1.50 .70
31 A2 130r brn, yel ('07)   6.00 1.40
32 A2 150r org brn, pink   1.00 .60
33 A2 200r dk blue, bl   1.00 .90
a.   Perf. 13½   2.00 1.60
34 A2 200r red lil, pink
            ('07)   7.00 1.40
35 A2 300r dk bl, salmon   1.10 .90
a.   Perf. 13½   2.50 1.40
36 A2 400r brn, bl ('04)   2.50 1.10
37 A2 400r dl bl, yel ('07)   8.00 3.25
38 A2 500r blk & red   1.10 .75
39 A2 500r blk & red, bl
            ('07)   8.00 1.90
a.   500r pur & red, yel (error)
40 A2 700r slate, buff ('04)   8.50 2.00
41 A2 700r pur, yel ('07)   5.00 2.00
42 A2 1000r violet & red   1.50 1.00
        Nos. 10-42 (33)   87.95 28.75

#12b, 18a, 33a, 35a were issued without
gum.
For overprints & surcharges see #43-107,
B1-B7.

**Nos. 25 and 6 Surcharged or
Overprinted in Red**

       b   c

1895   Perf. 12½, 13½
43 A2(b) 25r on 80r yel grn   22.50 16.00
44 A2(c) 50r blue   9.00 4.00

Overprint "c" on No. 44 also exists reading
from upper left to lower right.

Stamps of 1895
Overprinted in Bister,
Orange, Violet,
Green, Black or
Brown

1898   Perf. 12½, 13½
Without Gum
45 A2 2½r olive yel (Bi)   5.00 1.50
a.   Double overprint   40.00 25.00
b.   Red overprint   60.00 50.00
46 A2 5r orange (O)   7.00 1.50
47 A2 10r red lilac (V)   7.00 1.50
48 A2 15r red brown (V)   10.00 3.00
a.   Red overprint
49 A2 20r gray lilac (V)   10.00 3.00
50 A2 25r green (G)   12.00 3.00
a.   Inverted overprint   65.00 40.00
51 A2 50r blue (Bk)   12.00 4.00
a.   Inverted overprint   60.00 40.00
52 A2 75r rose (V)   12.50 4.00
a.   Inverted overprint   75.00 40.00
b.   Red overprint
53 A2 80r yellow grn (G)   17.50 5.00
a.   Inverted overprint
54 A2 100r brn, buff (Br)   17.50 5.00
55 A2 150r org brn, pink
            (O)   17.50 5.00
a.   Inverted overprint   75.00 30.00
b.   Double overprint
56 A2 200r dk blue, bl (Bk)   16.00 7.50
57 A2 300r dk blue, sal
            (Bk)   20.00 10.00
a.   Inverted overprint   60.00 50.00
b.   Green overprint
        Nos. 45-57 (13)   164.00 55.00

Vasco da Gama's discovery of route to
India, 400th anniversary.
No. 57b was prepared but not issued.
Nos. 45 and 49 were also issued with gum.
The "Centenario" overprint on stamps perf.
11½ is forged.

**Nos. 23, 12, 17 Surcharged in Black,
Carmine or Violet**

       e

    f   g

1899   Perf. 12½
59 A2(e) 25r on 75r rose (Bk)   4.00 2.50

1900   Perf. 12½, 12½x11½
60 A2(f) 25r on 5r org (C)   2.10 1.40
61 A2(g) 50r on half of 20r
            gray lil (V)   2.00 1.00
b.   Entire stamp   15.00 9.00

No. 61b is perf. 11½ vertically through
center.

Stamps of 1895-1907
Overprinted Locally
in Carmine or Green

1911   Perf. 11½, 13½
61A A2 2½r gray (C)   7.00 3.00
62   A2 5r orange (G)   6.00 3.00
63   A2 10r yellow grn (C)   .70 .50
64   A2 15r dk green (C)   .90 .50
a.   Double overprint   40.00 20.00
65   A2 20r gray lilac (G)   1.25 .50
a.   Perf. 13½   1.40 .80
66   A2 25r carmine (G)   1.25 .60
67   A2 50r brown (G)   .70 .45
68   A2 75r red lilac (G)   1.10 .45
69   A2 100r dk bl, bl (C)   1.25 .50
70   A2 115r org brn, pink (G) 2.00 1.25
71   A2 130r brn, yel (G)   3.00 1.25
72   A2 200r red lil, pink (G) 3.00 1.25
73   A2 400r dull bl, yel (C)   3.00 .70
74   A2 500r blk & red, bl (C) 4.00 1.40
75   A2 700r pur, yel (G)   4.00 1.40
        Nos. 61A-75 (15)   39.15 16.75

Nos. 63, 67 and 71 exist with inverted overprint; Nos. 63, 72 and 75 with double
overprint.

Overprinted in Lisbon
in Carmine or Green

1911   Perf. 11½, 12½
75B A2 2½r gray   .30 .25
76   A2 5r orange   .30 .25
77   A2 10r yellow grn   .25 .25
78   A2 15r dark green   .35 .25
79   A2 20r gray lilac   .40 .25
80   A2 25r carmine (G)   .35 .25
a.   Value inverted at top of stamp 18.00
81   A2 50r brown   .70 .25
82   A2 75r red lilac   .70 .25
a.   Value omitted   15.00
83   A2 100r dk blue, bl   1.00 .25
84   A2 115r org brn, pink   2.50 .40
85   A2 130r brown, yel   3.00 .40
a.   Double overprint   30.00
86   A2 200r red lil, pink   3.00 .40
87   A2 400r dull bl, yel   5.00 .40
88   A2 500r blk & red, bl   7.50 .40
89   A2 700r pur, yel   5.00 .55
        Nos. 75B-89 (15)   30.35 4.80

Nos. 75B-89
Surcharged

1916   Perf. 11½
90   A2 ¼c on 2½r gray   .25 .25
91   A2 ½c on 5r org   .25 .25
a.   "½c" double   20.00
92   A2 1c on 10r yel grn   .40 .25
93   A2 1½c on 15r dk grn   .40 .25
a.   Imperf., pair   35.00
94   A2 2c on 20r gray lil   .50 .25
95   A2 2½c on 25r car   1.00 .25
96   A2 5c on 50r brn   .40 .25
a.   Imperf., pair   40.00
97   A2 7½c on 75r red lil   .65 .25
98   A2 10c on 100r dk bl, bl   1.25 .95
a.   Inverted surcharge   40.00 40.00
99   A2 11½c on 115r org brn,
            yel   3.50 .95
a.   Inverted surcharge   50.00 50.00
100 A2 13c on 130r brn, yel   6.50 .95
101 A2 20c on 200r red lil,
            pink   5.50 1.10
102 A2 40c on 400r dl bl, yel 6.50 .50
103 A2 50c on 500r blk &
            red, bl (R)   8.00 .70
104 A2 70c on 700r pur, yel   8.00 1.25
        Nos. 90-104 (15)   43.10 8.40

Nos. 87 to 89
Surcharged

1918   *Perf. 11½*
105	A2	½c on 700r pur, *yel*	2.50	1.30
106	A2	2½c on 500r blk & red, *bl* (Bl)	3.50	1.30
107	A2	5c on 400r dl bl, *yel*	4.50	1.30
		Nos. 105-107 (3)	10.50	3.90

Native and Village — A9

Man and Ivory Tusks — A10

Corn — A11

Tapping Rubber Tree — A12

Sugar Refinery — A13

Buzi River Scene — A14

Tobacco Field — A15

View of Beira — A16

Coffee Plantation A17

Orange Tree A18

Cotton Field A19

Sisal Plantation A20

Scene on Beira R. R. — A21

Court House at Beira — A22

Coconut Palm A23

Mangroves A24

Cattle — A25

Company Arms — A26

1918-31   **Engr.**   *Perf. 14, 15, 12½*
108	A9	¼c brn & yel grn	.55	.50
109	A9	¼c ol grn & blk ('25)	.30	.25
110	A10	½c black	.55	.50
111	A11	1c green & blk	.55	.50
112	A12	1½c black & grn	.55	.50
113	A13	2c carmine & blk	.55	.50
114	A13	2c ol blk & blk ('25)	.30	.25
115	A14	2½c lilac & blk	.55	.50
116	A11	3c ocher & blk ('23)	.30	.25
117	A15	4c grn & brn ('21)	.30	.25
118	A15	4c red & blk ('25)	.30	.25
119	A9	4½c gray & blk ('23)	.30	.25
120	A16	5c blue & blk	.55	.50
121	A17	6c claret & bl ('21)	.80	.30
122	A17	6c lilac & blk ('25)	.30	.25
123	A21	7c ultra & blk ('23)	1.00	.50
124	A18	7½c orange & grn	.75	.70
125	A19	8c violet & blk	1.50	1.10
126	A20	10c red org & blk	1.50	1.10
128	A19	12c brn & blk ('23)	1.00	.70
129	A19	12c bl grn & blk ('25)	2.00	.35
130	A21	15c carmine & blk	1.00	.95
131	A22	20c dp green & blk	1.60	.65
132	A23	30c red brn & blk	3.50	.95
133	A23	30c gray grn & blk ('25)	2.00	.55
134	A23	30c bl grn & blk ('31)	3.50	.55
135	A24	40c yel grn & blk	1.90	1.10
136	A24	40c grnsh bl & blk ('25)	.70	.85
137	A25	50c orange & blk	2.25	1.10
138	A25	50c lt vio & blk ('25)	2.25	.80
139	A25	60c rose & brn ('23)	1.50	.80
140	A20	80c ultra & brn ('23)	4.00	.80
141	A20	80c car & blk ('25)	1.10	.80
142	A26	1e dk green & blk	2.25	2.00
143	A26	1e blue & blk ('25)	2.25	.80
144	A16	2e rose & vio ('23)	5.00	1.30
145	A16	2e lilac & blk ('25)	4.00	.80
		Nos. 108-145 (37)	53.30	24.80

Shades exist of several denominations.
For surcharges see Nos. 146-154, RA1.

Nos. 132, 142, 115, 120, 131, 135, 125, 137 Surcharged with New Values in Red, Blue, Violet or Black

h

i

j

1920   *Perf. 14, 15*
146	A23(h)	½c on 30c (Bk)	6.00	5.00
147	A26(h)	1c on 1e (R)	6.00	5.00
148	A14(h)	1½c on 2½c (Bl)	5.00	2.25
149	A16(h)	1½c on 5c (V)	5.00	2.25
150	A14(h)	2c on 2½c (R)	5.00	2.25
151	A22(i)	4c on 20c (V)	5.75	4.50
152	A24(i)	4c on 40c (V)	5.75	4.50
153	A19(j)	6c on 8c (R)	7.00	4.50
154	A25(j)	6c on 50c (Bk)	8.00	4.50
		Nos. 146-154 (9)	53.50	34.75

The surcharge on No. 148 is placed vertically between two bars. On No. 154 the two words of the surcharge are 13mm apart.

Native — A27

View of Beira — A28

Tapping Rubber Tree — A29

Picking Tea — A30

Zambezi River — A31

1925-31   **Engr.**   *Perf. 12*
155	A27	24c ultra & blk	1.25	1.00
156	A28	25c choc & ultra	1.25	1.00
157	A27	85c brn red & blk ('31)	.95	.80
158	A28	1.40e dl bl & blk ('31)	.90	.80
159	A29	5e yel brn & ultra	1.75	.65
160	A30	10e rose & blk	2.75	.95
161	A31	20e green & blk	3.25	1.20
		Nos. 155-161 (7)	12.10	6.40

Ivory Tusks — A32

Panning Gold — A33

1931   **Litho.**   *Perf. 14*
162	A32	45c lt blue	2.50	1.30
163	A33	70c yellow brn	1.40	.70

Zambezi Railroad Bridge — A34

1935   **Engr.**   *Perf. 12½*
164	A34	1e dk blue & blk	8.75	1.60

Opening of a new bridge over the Zambezi River.

Airplane over Beira — A35

1935
165	A35	5c blue & blk	.55	.55
166	A35	10c red org & blk	.55	.40
a.		Comparine pair, imperf. between	50.00	
167	A35	15c red & blk	.55	.40
a.		Square pair, imperf. between	50.00	
168	A35	20c yel grn & blk	.55	.40
169	A35	30c green & blk	.55	.40
170	A35	40c gray bl & blk	.70	.55
171	A35	45c blue & blk	.70	.55
172	A35	50c violet & blk	.70	.70
a.		Square pair, imperf. btwn.	60.00	
173	A35	60c carmine & brn	1.10	.65
174	A35	80c carmine & blk	1.10	.65
		Nos. 165-174 (10)	7.05	5.25

Issued to commemorate the opening of the Blantyre-Beira Salisbury air service.

Giraffe — A36

Thatched Huts — A37

Rock Python — A41

Coconut Palms A50

Zambezi Railroad Bridge A52

Sena Gate — A53

Company Arms — A54

Designs: 10c, Dhow. 15c, St. Caetano Fortress, Sofala. 20c, Zebra. 40c, Black rhinoceros. 45c, Lion. 50c, Crocodile. 60c, Leopard. 70c, Mozambique woman. 80c, Hippopotami. 85c, Vasco da Gama's flagship. 1e, Man in canoe. 2e, Greater kudu.

1937, May 16   *Perf. 12½*
175	A36	1c yel grn & vio	.30	.25
176	A37	5c blue & yel grn	.30	.25
177	A36	10c ver & ultra	.30	.25
178	A37	15c carmine & blk	.30	.25
179	A36	20c green & ultra	.30	.25
180	A41	30c dk grn & ind	.30	.30
181	A41	40c gray bl & blk	.30	.30
182	A41	45c blue & brn	.30	.30
183	A41	50c dk vio & emer	.30	.30
184	A37	60c carmine & bl	.30	.30
185	A36	70c yel brn & pale grn	.30	.30
186	A37	80c car & pale grn	.40	.35
187	A41	85c org red & blk	.50	.40
188	A41	1e dp bl & blk	.50	.40
189	A50	1.40e dk bl & pale grn	.90	.40
190	A41	2e pale lilac & brn	1.50	.50
191	A52	5e yel brn & bl	1.25	.75
192	A53	10e carmine & blk	2.25	1.50
193	A54	20e grn & brn vio	3.00	2.75
		Nos. 175-193 (19)	13.60	10.10

Stamps of 1937 Overprinted in Red or Black

1939, Aug. 28
194	A41	30c dk grn & ind (R)	2.00	.85
195	A41	40c gray bl & blk (R)	2.00	.85
196	A41	45c blue & brn (Bk)	2.00	.85
197	A41	50c dk vio & emer (R)	3.00	1.00
198	A41	85c org red & blk (Bk)	3.00	1.00
199	A41	1e dp bl & blk (R)	3.00	1.25
200	A41	2e pale lil & brn (Bk)	3.50	1.75
		Nos. 194-200 (7)	18.50	7.55

Visit of the President of Portugal to Beira in 1939.

King Alfonso
Henriques
A55

King John IV
A56

1940, Feb. 16   Typo.   Perf. 11½x12
201 A55 1.75e blue & lt blue   1.50   .75

800th anniv. of Portuguese independence.

1941   Engr.   Perf. 12½
202 A56 40c gray grn & blk   .65   .50
203 A56 50c dk vio & brt grn   .65   .50
204 A56 60c brt car & dp bl   .65   .50
205 A56 70c brn org & dk grn   .65   .50
206 A56 80c car & dp grn   .65   .50
207 A56 1e dk bl & blk   .65   .50
    Nos. 202-207 (6)   3.90 3.00

300th anniv. of the restoration of the Portuguese Monarchy.

Mozambique Company's charter terminated July 18th, 1941 after which date its stamps were superseded by those of the territory of Mozambique.

SEMI-POSTAL STAMPS

Lisbon Issue of 1911
Overprinted in Red

1917   Unwmk.   Perf. 11½
B1 A2 2½r gray   9.00 10.50
  a.   Double overprint   75.00 75.00
B2 A2 10r yellow grn   10.00 15.00
B3 A2 20r gray lilac   14.00 20.00
B4 A2 50r brown   20.00 25.00
B5 A2 75r red lilac   65.00 70.00
B6 A2 100r dk blue, bl   75.00 80.00
B7 A2 700r purple, yel   175.00 225.00
    Nos. B1-B7 (7)   368.00 445.50

Nos. B1-B7 were used on July 31, 1917, in place of ordinary stamps. The proceeds were given to the Red Cross.

AIR POST STAMPS

Airplane over
Beira — AP1

1935   Unwmk.   Engr.   Perf. 12½
C1 AP1 5c blue & blk   .25 .25
C2 AP1 10c org red & blk   .25 .25
C3 AP1 15c red & blk   .25 .25
C4 AP1 20c yel grn & blk   .25 .25
C5 AP1 30c green & blk   .25 .25
C6 AP1 40c gray bl & blk   .25 .25
C7 AP1 45c blue & blk   .25 .25
C8 AP1 50c dk vio & blk   .40 .25
C9 AP1 60c car & brn   .40 .25
C10 AP1 80c car & blk   .50 .25
C11 AP1 1e blue & blk   .50 .25
C12 AP1 2e mauve & blk   1.25 .40
C13 AP1 5e bis brn & bl   1.25 .50
C14 AP1 10e car & blk   1.40 .50
C15 AP1 20e bl grn & blk   2.75 1.00
    Nos. C1-C15 (15)   10.20 5.40

POSTAGE DUE STAMPS

D1

1906   Unwmk.   Typo.   Perf. 11½x12
Denominations in Black
J1 D1 5r yellow grn   .70 .40
J2 D1 10r slate   .70 .55
J3 D1 20r yellow brn   1.25 .55
J4 D1 30r orange   1.50 1.00
J5 D1 50r gray brown   1.50 1.00
J6 D1 60r red brown   22.50 9.00
J7 D1 100r red lilac   4.00 2.50
J8 D1 130r dull blue   32.50 12.00
J9 D1 200r carmine   13.00 4.00
J10 D1 500r violet   18.00 5.00
    Nos. J1-J10 (10)   95.65 36.00

Nos. J1-J10
Overprinted in
Carmine or Green

1911
J11 D1 5r yellow grn   .30 .30
J12 D1 10r slate   .30 .30
J13 D1 20r yellow brn   .30 .30
J14 D1 30r orange   .30 .30
J15 D1 50r gray brown   .30 .30
J16 D1 60r red brown   .50 .50
J17 D1 100r red lilac   .50 .50
J18 D1 130r dull blue   2.00 1.40
J19 D1 200r carmine (G)   1.30 1.35
J20 D1 500r violet   2.50 1.40
    Nos. J11-J20 (10)   8.30 6.65

D2

Company
Arms — D3

1916   Typo.
With Value in Centavos in Black
J21 D2 ½c yellow grn   .30 .30
J22 D2 1c slate   .30 .30
J23 D2 2c orange brn   .30 .30
J24 D2 3c orange   .70 .30
J25 D2 5c gray brown   .70 .30
J26 D2 6c pale brown   .70 .35
J27 D2 10c red lilac   .70 .55
J28 D2 13c gray blue   1.40 1.30
J29 D2 20c rose   1.40 1.30
J30 D2 50c gray   3.25 1.50
    Nos. J21-J30 (10)   9.75 6.50

1919   Engr.   Perf. 12½, 13½, 14, 15
J31 D3 ½c green   .25 .25
J32 D3 1c slate   .25 .25
J33 D3 2c red brown   .25 .25
J34 D3 3c orange   .25 .25
J35 D3 5c gray brown   .25 .25
J36 D3 6c lt brown   .50 .50
J37 D3 10c lilac rose   .50 .50
J38 D3 13c dull blue   .50 .50
J39 D3 20c rose   .50 .50
J40 D3 50c gray   .50 .50
    Nos. J31-J40 (10)   3.75 3.75

NEWSPAPER STAMP

Newspaper Stamp of
Mozambique
Overprinted

1894   Unwmk.   Perf. 11½
P1   N3 2½r brown   .65 .55
  a.   Inverted overprint   30.00 30.00
  b.   Perf. 12½   1.50 1.10

Reprints are on stout white paper with clean-cut perf. 13½. Value $1.

POSTAL TAX STAMPS

No. 116
Surcharged in
Black

1932   Perf. 12½
RA1 A11 2c on 3c org & blk   1.40 2.00

Charity — PT2

1933   Litho.   Perf. 11
RA2 PT2 2c magenta & blk   1.40 2.00

PT3

1940   Unwmk.   Perf. 10½
RA3 PT3 2c black & ultra   15.00 16.00

PT4

1941
RA4 PT4 2c black & brt red   15.00 16.00

Vol. 4 Number Additions, Deletions & Changes

Number in 2015 Catalogue	Number in 2016 Catalogue

Jamaica

new	59a
new	MR11a

Jordan

new	392a
new	393a
new	394a
new	395b
new	429a
new	499a
new	534Ba
new	534Ea

Kazakhstan

new	164a
new	174a
new	174b
new	598a
new	697a

Korea, People's Democratic Republic (North Korea)

99b	deleted
3595b	3595d

Laos

1743-1746	deleted

Macao

new	62d
new	75b
new	76b
new	77a
new	144c
new	195a
new	195b
new	197a
new	198b
new	200a
new	202a
new	204a
new	209a

Mauritius

new	1061a

Mexico

new	362a
new	366a
new	367a

Mozambique

1532-1534A	1531-1534

New World of Technology

6-IN-1 LED POCKET MAGNIFIER/ MICROSCOPE (55X)

A powerful LED microscope (up to 55X magnification) teams up with two aspheric Perspex lenses (3X magnification large and 10X magnification small) to examine objects at various levels of detail. Built-in focus wheel ensures clarity. View objects even in low-light conditions with three lighting functions: three LED flashlight, simple UV light, one white LED. Black composite housing.

Item	Retail	AA*
MG61LED	21.95	19.95

5-IN-1 MULTI-FUNCTION POCKET MAGNIFIER 2.5X-10X LED

A sturdy stainless steel frame houses two aspheric lenses: 2.5X rectangular and 10X round, plus three lighting functions: 3-LED side flashlight, 1-LED research light, simple 395nm long-wave UV light. A mini ballpoint pen, available to take notes, tucks inside the acrylic housing. Leatherette case and 3 #LR927 batteries included.

Item	Retail	AA*
MG51	15.95	13.95

3.2X LED ILLUMINATED MAGNIFIER

This 7" aluminum 3.2X magnifier is both beautiful and functional. Six LEDs surround the 1.375" lens to provide glare-free illumination. Zippered protective case and 2 AA batteries included.

Item	Retail	AA*
MG32XL	35.95	31.95

SCHAUBEK 10X LED & UV COMBO MAGNIFIER

This pocket-sized magnifier boasts 10X magnification with both LED and UV longwave light. Battery powered for maximum portability. Handy carrying case protects the 21mm magnifier while on the go.

Item	Retail	AA*
MG10XLUV	39.99	34.99

LIGHTHOUSE DIGITAL CALIPERS 6"

Sliding calipers measure from 1-150mm (0"-6") in .01mm increments with accuracy to 0.3mm. Six-digit LCD display easily switches from millimeters to inches. Batteries and padded case included.

Item	Retail	AA*
LHSL1	49.95	42.95

LHSCOPE

Clip this compact Lighthouse Phonescope lens on your smartphone or tablet to transform it into a powerful digital microscope. See the smallest details and instantly capture high-quality images and videos. The precision macro glass lens offers up to 60X magnification and requires no batteries. Field of view: 1/2" (13mm). Phonescope works with all popular smartphones without scratching display. Image resolution and zoom function dependent upon your device.

Item	Retail	AA*
LHSCOPE	25.99	21.99

ZOOM 20X-40X MICROSCOPE WITH LED

This practical zoom microscope provides what collectors have been waiting for – outstanding clarity and resolution. Magnification is continuously adjustable between 20X and 40X. Powerful LED lighting illuminates the stage (3 #LR44 batteries included). Stand, examination slides, and slide covers also included.

Item	Retail	AA*
LHPM3	29.95	21.95

LIGHTHOUSE DUAL WAVE ULTRAVIOLET LAMP

Examine your collectibles for both fluorescence (long wave) and phosphorescence (short wave) using one versatile ultraviolet lamp. Flip a switch to change quickly and easily between short and long UV rays (254 and 380nm). Short wave exposes tagging, while long wave reveals faults, tears, and repairs. Battery operated; requires 4x AA batteries (not included).

Item	Retail	AA*
LHL81	71.95	59.95

LIGHTHOUSE .1-500G DIGITAL SCALE

This portable-sized digital scale displays weight in six different units: g, oz, ozt, dwt, ct, gn. Illuminated LCD display with tare function is great for gold coins. Weight range 0.1-500 g with +/- 0.03 g tolerance. Requires 2 AA batteries, included.

Item	Retail	AA*
LHDW4	29.95	24.95

ZOOM 20X-200X USB DIGITAL MICROSCOPE, 2.0 MEGAPIXELS

Powered by your computer's USB port, this digital microscope offers amazing 2.0 megapixel resolution. Examine objects, take photos, and shoot short videos all with the same device. 20X-200X magnification enhanced with 8 adjustable LED lights will show the smallest details. Microscope comes complete with CD-ROM software, stand and USB cable. Compatible with Windows 2000 / XP / Vista / Win7 / Win8 and Mac OS X 10.5 and higher. Web based updates available.

Item	Retail	AA*
LHDM1	169.95	137.95

ACC213W

The OttLite DuoFlex has a two-pronged approach to enhance your vision. First, the large 3X-5X magnifier enlarges your subject. Then the energy-efficient 13w "E" bulb spotlights the field. Flexible arms allow nearly infinite positioning. Long-term bulb is rated to last up to 10,000 hours.

Item	Retail	AA*
ACC213W	109.99	59.99

ORDERING INFORMATION: *AA prices apply to paid subscribers of Amos Hobby titles, or for orders placed online. Prices, terms and product availability subject to change.

Call: **1-800-572-6885**
Outside U.S. & Canada Call: **1-800-572-6885**
Visit: **www.amosadvantage.com**

AMOS ADVANTAGE

Illustrated Identifier

This section pictures stamps or parts of stamp designs that will help identify postage stamps that do not have English words on them.

Many of the symbols that identify stamps of countries are shown here as well as typical examples of their stamps.

See the Index and Identifier on the previous pages for stamps with inscriptions such as "sen," "posta," "Baja Porto," "Helvetia," "K.S.A.," etc.

Linn's Stamp Identifier is now available. The 144 pages include more than 2,000 inscriptions and more than 500 large stamp illustrations. Available from Linn's Stamp News, P.O. Box 4129, Sidney, OH 45365-4129.

1. HEADS, PICTURES AND NUMERALS

GREAT BRITAIN

Great Britain stamps never show the country name, but, except for postage dues, show a picture of the reigning monarch.

Victoria

Edward VII   George V   Edward VIII

George VI

Elizabeth II

Some George VI and Elizabeth II stamps are surcharged in annas, new paisa or rupees. These are listed under Oman.

Silhouette (sometimes facing right, generally at the top of stamp)

The silhouette indicates this is a British stamp. It is not a U.S. stamp.

VICTORIA

Queen Victoria

INDIA

Other stamps of India show this portrait of Queen Victoria and the words "Service" (or "Postage") and "Annas."

AUSTRIA

YUGOSLAVIA

(Also BOSNIA & HERZEGOVINA if imperf.)

BOSNIA & HERZEGOVINA

Denominations also appear in top corners instead of bottom corners.

HUNGARY

Another stamp has posthorn facing left

BRAZIL

AUSTRALIA

Kangaroo and Emu

GERMANY

Mecklenburg-Vorpommern

SWITZERLAND

PALAU

2. ORIENTAL INSCRIPTIONS

CHINA

Any stamp with this one character is from China (Imperial, Republic or People's Republic). This character appears in a four-character overprint on stamps of Manchukuo. These stamps are local provisionals, which are unlisted. Other overprinted Manchukuo stamps show this character, but have more than four characters in the overprints. These are listed in People's Republic of China.

Some Chinese stamps show the Sun.

Most stamps of Republic of China show this series of characters.

Stamps with the China character and this character are from People's Republic of China.

人

中国人民郵政
T.34.(5-1)

Calligraphic form of People's Republic of China

(一)	(二)	(三)	(四)	(五)	(六)
1	2	3	4	5	6
(七)	(八)	(九)	(十)	(一十)	(二十)
7	8	9	10	11	12

Chinese stamps without China character

REPUBLIC OF CHINA

PEOPLE'S REPUBLIC OF CHINA

Mao Tse-tung

MANCHUKUO

Temple   Emperor Pu-Yi

The first 3 characters are common to
many Manchukuo stamps.

The last 3 characters are common to
other Manchukuo stamps.

Orchid Crest

Manchukuo
stamp
without
these
elements

JAPAN

Chrysanthemum Crest   Country Name

Japanese stamps without these elements

The number of characters in the
center and the design of dragons on
the sides will vary.

RYUKYU ISLANDS

Country Name

PHILIPPINES
(Japanese Occupation)

Country Name

NETHERLANDS INDIES
(Japanese Occupation)

Indicates Japanese Occupation

Java   Sumatra

Country Name   Country Name

Moluccas, Celebes and
South Borneo

Country Name

NORTH BORNEO
(Japanese Occupation)

Indicates Japanese   Country
Occupation   Name

MALAYA
(Japanese Occupation)

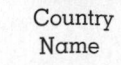

Indicates Japanese   Country
Occupation   Name

BURMA
Union of Myanmar

Union of Myanmar
(Japanese Occupation)

Indicates Japanese Occupation	Country Name

Other Burma Japanese Occupation stamps without these elements

Burmese Script

KOREA

These two characters, in any order, are common to stamps from the Republic of Korea (South Korea) or of the People's Democratic Republic of Korea (North Korea).

This series of four characters can be found on the stamps of both Koreas. Most stamps of the Democratic People's Republic of Korea (North Korea) have just this inscription.

Indicates Republic of Korea (South Korea)

South Korean postage stamps issed after 1952 do not show currency expressed in Latin letters. Stamps wiith " HW," "HWAN," "WON," "WN," "W" or "W" with two lines through it, if not illustrated in listings of stamps before this date, are revenues. North Korean postage stamps do not have currency expressed in Latin letters.

Yin Yang appears on some stamps.

South Korean stamps show Yin Yang and starting in 1966, 'KOREA" in Latin letters

Example of South Korean stamps lacking Latin text, Yin Yang and standard Korean text of country name. North Korean stamps never show Yin Yang and starting in 1976 are inscribed "DPRK" or "DPR KOREA" in Latin letters.

THAILAND

Country Name

King Chulalongkorn

King Prajadhipok and Chao P'ya Chakri

3. CENTRAL AND EASTERN ASIAN INSCRIPTIONS

INDIA - FEUDATORY STATES

Alwar

Bhor

Bundi

Similar stamps come with different designs in corners and differently drawn daggers (at center of circle).

Dhar   Duttia

Faridkot

Hyderabad

Similar stamps exist with different central design which is inscribed "Postage" or "Post & Receipt."

Indore

Jammu & Kashmir

Text varies.

Jasdan

Jhalawar

Kotah

Size and text varies

Nandgaon

Nowanuggur

Poonch

Similar stamps exist
in various sizes with different text

Rajasthan

Rajpeepla

Soruth

Tonk

BANGLADESH

Country Name

NEPAL

Similar stamps are smaller, have squares in
upper corners and have five or nine
characters in central bottom panel.

TANNU TUVA   ISRAEL

GEORGIA

This inscription
is found on other
pictorial stamps.

Country Name

ARMENIA

The four characters are found somewhere
on pictorial stamps. On some stamps only
the middle two are found.

4. AFRICAN INSCRIPTIONS

ETHIOPIA

5. ARABIC INSCRIPTIONS

AFGHANISTAN

Many early Afghanistan stamps show Tiger's head, many of these have ornaments protruding from outer ring, others show inscriptions in black.

Crest of King Amanullah

Arabic Script

Mosque Gate & Crossed Cannons

The four characters are found somewhere on pictorial stamps. On some stamps only the middle two are found.

BAHRAIN

EGYPT

Postage

IRAN

Country Name

Royal Crown

Lion with Sword

Symbol

Emblem

IRAQ

JORDAN

LEBANON

Similar types have
denominations at top
and slightly different
design.

LIBYA

Country Name in various styles

Other Libya stamps show Eagle and
Shield (head facing either direction) or
Red, White and Black Shield (with or with-
out eagle in center).

Without Country Name

SAUDI ARABIA

Tughra (Central design)

← Palm Tree and Swords

SYRIA

Arab Government Issues

THRACE   **YEMEN**

PAKISTAN

PAKISTAN - BAHAWALPUR

Country Name in top panel, star and crescent

TURKEY

 Star & Crescent is a device found on many Turkish stamps, but is also found on stamps from other Arabic areas (see Pakistan-Bahawalpur)

Tughra (similar tughras can be found on stamps of Turkey in Asia, Afghanistan and Saudi Arabia)

Mohammed V

Mustafa Kemal

Plane, Star and Crescent

TURKEY IN ASIA

Other Turkey in Asia pictorials show star & crescent. Other stamps show tughra shown under Turkey.

6. GREEK INSCRIPTIONS

GREECE

Country Name in various styles (Some Crete stamps overprinted with the Greece country name are listed in Crete.)

Lepta

Drachma　　Drachmas　　Lepton

Abbreviated Country Name

Other forms of Country Name

No country name

CRETE

Country Name

Crete stamps with a surcharge that have the year "1922" are listed under Greece.

EPIRUS

Similar stamps have text above the eagle.

IONIAN IS.

7. CYRILLIC INSCRIPTIONS

RUSSIA

Postage Stamp   Imperial Eagle

Postage in various styles

Abbreviation   Abbreviation   Russia
for Kopeck   for Ruble

Abbreviation for Russian Soviet Federated Socialist Republic RSFSR stamps were overprinted (see below)

Abbreviation for Union of Soviet Socialist Republics

This item is footnoted in Latvia

RUSSIA - Army of the North

"OKCA"

RUSSIA - Wenden

RUSSIAN OFFICES IN THE TURKISH EMPIRE

These letters appear on other stamps of the Russian offices.

The unoverprinted version of this stamp and a similar stamp were overprinted by various countries (see below).

ARMENIA

BELARUS

FAR EASTERN REPUBLIC

Country Name

FINLAND

Circles and Dots
on stamps similar
to Imperial
Russia issues

SOUTH RUSSIA

Country Name

BATUM

Forms of Country Name

TRANSCAUCASIAN FEDERATED REPUBLICS

Abbreviation for
Country Name

KAZAKHSTAN

Country Name

KYRGYZSTAN

Country
Name

ROMANIA

TAJIKISTAN

Country Name & Abbreviation

UKRAINE

Country Name in various forms

The trident appears
on many stamps,
usually as
an overprint.

Abbreviation for
Ukrainian
Soviet
Socialist
Republic

WESTERN UKRAINE

Abbreviation for
Country Name

AZERBAIJAN

AZƏRBAYCAN

Country Name

A.C.C.P.　Abbreviation for Azerbaijan
Soviet Socialist Republic

MONTENEGRO

ЦРНЕГОРЕ

ЦРНА ГОРА

Country Name in various forms

ПР.ГОРЕ

Abbreviation
for country
name

No country name
(A similar Montenegro
stamp without coun-
try name has same
vignette.)

SERBIA

СРПСКА　**СРБИЈА**

Country Name in various forms

СРП　**К. С.**

Abbreviation for country name

No country name

MACEDONIA

МАКЕДОНИЈА

МАКЕДОНИЈА

Country Name

МАКЕДОНСКИ ПОШТИ

МАКЕДОНСКИ

Different form of Country Name

SERBIA & MONTENEGRO

YUGOSLAVIA

ЈУГОСЛАВИЈА

Showing country name

No Country Name

BOSNIA & HERZEGOVINA
(Serb Administration)

РЕПУБЛИКА СРПСКА

Country Name

РЕПУБЛИКЕ СРПСКЕ

Different form of Country Name

No Country Name

BULGARIA

Country Name   Postage

Stotinka

Stotinki (plural)   Abbreviation for
Stotinki

Country Name in various forms and styles

No country name

 Abbreviation
for Lev, leva

MONGOLIA

ШУУДАН   тегрег

Country name in   Tugrik in Cyrillic
one word

МОНГОЛ
ШУУДАН   мөнгө

Country name in   Mung in Cyrillic
two words

MONGOLIA
МОНГОЛ ШУУДАН

Mung
in Mongolian

MONGOLIA
МОНГОЛ ШУУДАН

Tugrik
in Mongolian

Arms

No Country Name

Scott International Album

Prices have never been so low on selected album parts. It is a wonderful opportunity to collect internationally. The Ultimate Album for Worldwide Collectors! Pick a period in history and embark on a philatelic adventure. With the International Album, the whole world is divided chronologically into more than 40 parts. From the classic era of philately to present day, the International is one of the broadest and far reaching worldwide albums available. *Binders are sold separately.*

- More than 16,000 pages with spaces for over 220,000 stamps.
- Pages printed on 2 sides.

Item	Part	Binder		Retail	AA*
801A140	1A1	(1840-1940)	Regular	$150.00	$120.00
801A240	1A2	(1840-1940)	Regular	$150.00	$120.00
801B140	1B1	(1840-1940)	Regular	$150.00	$120.00
801B240	1B2	(1840-1940)	Regular	$150.00	$120.00
802P149	2A	(1940-49)	Regular	$150.00	$120.00
802P249	2B	(1940-49)	Regular	$150.00	$120.00
803P155	3A	(1949-55)	Regular	$150.00	$120.00
803P255	3B	(1949-55)	Regular	$150.00	$120.00
804P159	4A	(1956-60)	Regular	$150.00	$120.00
804P259	4B	(1956-60)	Regular	$150.00	$120.00
805P063	5	(1960-63)	Jumbo	$150.00	$120.00
805P165	5A	(1963-65)	Jumbo	$150.00	$120.00
806P066	6	(1965-66)	Jumbo	**$75.00**	**$55.00**
806P168	6A	(1966-68)	Jumbo	**$75.00**	**$55.00**
807P171	7A	(1968-71)	Jumbo	**$75.00**	**$55.00**
807P271	7B	(1968-71)	Jumbo	**$75.00**	**$55.00**
808P173	8A	(1971-73)	Regular	$150.00	$120.00
808P273	8B	(1971-73)	Regular	$150.00	$120.00
809P074	9	(1973-74)	Regular	$150.00	$120.00
810P075	10	(1974-75)	Jumbo	$150.00	$120.00
811P076	11	(1975-76)	Jumbo	$150.00	$120.00
812P077	12	(1976-77)	Jumbo	$150.00	$120.00
813P078	13	(1977-78)	Jumbo	$150.00	$120.00
814P078	14	(1978)	Regular	$150.00	$120.00
815P079	15	(1979)	Regular	$150.00	$120.00
816P080	16	(1980)	Jumbo	$150.00	$120.00
817P081	17	(1981)	Regular	$150.00	$120.00
818P082	18	(1982)	Regular	$150.00	$120.00
819P083	19	(1983)	Regular	$150.00	$120.00
820P084	20	(1984)	Jumbo	**$60.00**	**$44.00**
821P085	21	(1985)	Jumbo	$150.00	$120.00
822P186	22A	(1986)	Regular	**$60.00**	**$44.00**
822P286	22B	(1986)	Regular	**$60.00**	**$44.00**
823P187	23A	(1987)	Regular	**$60.00**	**$44.00**
823P287	23B	(1987)	Regular	$150.00	$120.00
824P188	24A	(1988)	Regular	**$60.00**	**$44.00**
824P288	24B	(1988)	Regular	**$60.00**	**$44.00**
825P189	25A	(1989)	Regular	**$60.00**	**$44.00**
825P289	25B	(1989)	Regular	**$60.00**	**$44.00**
826P190	26A	(1990)	Regular	$150.00	$120.00
826P290	26B	(1990)	Regular	**$60.00**	**$44.00**
827P191	27A	(1991)	Regular	**$60.00**	**$44.00**
827P291	27B	(1991)	Regular	**$60.00**	**$44.00**
828P192	28A	(1992)	Regular	**$60.00**	**$44.00**
828P292	28B	(1992)	Regular	**$60.00**	**$44.00**
829P193	29A	(1993)	Regular	**$60.00**	**$44.00**
829P293	29B	(1993)	Regular	**$60.00**	**$44.00**
830P194	30A	(1994)	Regular	**$60.00**	**$44.00**
830P294	30B	(1994)	Regular	**$60.00**	**$44.00**
831P195	31A	(1995)	Regular	**$60.00**	**$44.00**
831P295	31B	(1995)	Regular	**$60.00**	**$44.00**
832P196	32A	(1996)	Regular	**$60.00**	**$44.00**
832P296	32B	(1996)	Regular	**$60.00**	**$44.00**
833P197	33A	(1997)	Regular	**$60.00**	**$44.00**
833P297	33B	(1997)	Regular	**$60.00**	**$44.00**
834P198	34A	(1998)	Regular	**$60.00**	**$44.00**
834P298	34B	(1998)	Regular	**$60.00**	**$44.00**
835P199	35A	(1999)	Regular	$150.00	$120.00
835P299	35B	(1999)	Regular	$150.00	$120.00
836P100	36A	(2000)	Regular	$150.00	$120.00
836P200	36B	(2000)	Regular	$150.00	$120.00
837P101	37A	(2001)	Regular	$150.00	$120.00
837P201	37B	(2001)	Regular	$150.00	$120.00
838P102	38A	(2002)	Regular	**$60.00**	**$44.00**

Item	Part	Binder		Retail	AA*
838P202	38B	(2002)	Regular	**$60.00**	**$44.00**
839P103	39A	(2003)	Regular	**$60.00**	**$44.00**
839P203	39B	(2003)	Regular	**$60.00**	**$44.00**
840P104	40A	(2004)	Regular	**$60.00**	**$44.00**
840P204	40B	(2004)	Regular	**$60.00**	**$44.00**
841P105	41A	(2005)	Regular	**$60.00**	**$44.00**
841P205	41B	(2005)	Regular	**$60.00**	**$44.00**
842P106	42A	(2006)	Regular	$135.00	$99.99
842P206	42B	(2006)	Regular	$135.00	$99.99
843P107	43A	(2007)	Regular	$99.99	$72.50
843P207	43B	(2007)	Regular	$99.99	$72.50
844P108	44A	(2008)	Jumbo	$135.00	$99.99
844P208	44B	(2008)	Jumbo	$135.00	$99.99
845P109	45A	(2009)	Jumbo	$135.00	$99.99
845P209	45B	(2009)	Jumbo	$135.00	$99.99
846P110	46A	(2010)	Regular	$135.00	$99.99
846P210	46B	(2010)	Regular	$135.00	$99.99
847P111	47A	(2011)	Regular	$135.00	$99.99
847P211	47B	(2011)	Regular	$135.00	$99.99
848P112	48A	(2012)	Regular	$135.00	$99.99
848P212	48B	(2012)	Regular	$135.00	$99.99
849P113	49A	(2013)	Regular	$135.00	$99.99
849P213	49B	(2013)	Regular	$135.00	$99.99
800PC72	People's Republic of China			$49.99	$39.99
800BOH	Bosnia & Herzegovina 1879-2007			$49.99	$39.99

INTERNATIONAL SERIES BINDERS AND SLIPCASES

Attractive, blue two-post binder is available in two sizes. Features distinctive silver embossed spine. **Binder will hold International pages only.** Labels available for all parts. For a complete list see amosadvantage.com

Item		Retail	AA*
800B001	Regular Binder Holds 300 pages	$52.99	$40.99
800B002	Jumbo Binder Holds 400 pages.	$52.99	$40.99
800BC01	Regular Binder Slipcase	$32.99	$26.99
800BC02	Jumbo Binder Slipcase	$32.99	$26.99
8__LB01	International Label(s)	$2.29	$1.69

Call: **1-800-572-6885**

Outside U.S. & Canada Call:

1-800-572-6885

Visit:

www.amosadvantage.com

INDEX AND IDENTIFIER

All page numbers shown are
those in this Volume 4.

Postage stamps that do not have
English words on them are shown
in the Illustrated Identifier.

ScottMounts

PRE-CUT SINGLE MOUNTS

ITEM	W x H (MM)	DESCRIPTION	MOUNTS	RETAIL	AA*
901	40 x 25	U.S. Standard Comm. Hor. Water Activated	40	$3.50	$2.39
902	25 x 40	U.S. Standard Comm. Vert. Water Activated	40	$3.50	$2.39
903	25 x 22	U.S. Regular Issue – Hor. Water Activated	40	$3.50	$2.39
904	22 x 25	U.S. Regular Issue – Vert. Water Activated	40	$3.50	$2.39
905	41 x 31	U.S. Semi-Jumbo – Horizontal	40	$3.50	$2.39
906	31 x 41	U.S. Semi-Jumbo – Vertical	40	$3.50	$2.39
907	50 x 31	U.S. Jumbo – Horizontal	40	$3.50	$2.39
908	31 x 50	U.S. Jumbo – Vertical	40	$3.50	$2.39
909	25 x 27	U.S. Famous Americans/Champions Of Liberty	40	$3.50	$2.39
910	33 x 27	United Nations	40	$3.50	$2.39
911	40 x 27	United Nations	40	$3.50	$2.39
976	67 x 25	Plate Number Coils, Strips of Three	40	$6.25	$3.99
984	67 x 34	Pacific '97 Triangle	10	$3.50	$2.39
985	111 x 25	Plate Number Coils, Strips of Five	25	$6.25	$3.99
986	51 x 36	U.S. Hunting Permit/Express Mail	40	$6.25	$3.99
1045	40 x 26	U.S. Standard Comm. Hor. Self-Adhesive	40	$3.50	$2.39
1046	25 x 41	U.S. Standard Comm. Vert. Self-Adhesive	40	$3.50	$2.39
1047	22 x 26	U.S. Definitives Vert. Self Adhesive	40	$3.50	$2.39
966	Value Pack	(Assortment pre-cut sizes)	320	$23.25	$15.25
975 B	Best Pack	(Assortment pre-cut sizes - Black Only)	160	$14.75	$9.99

PRE-CUT PLATE BLOCK, FDC, POSTAL CARD MOUNTS

ITEM	W x H (MM)	DESCRIPTION	MOUNTS	RETAIL	AA*
912	57 x 55	Regular Issue Plate Block	25	$6.25	$3.99
913	73 x 63	Champions of Liberty	25	$6.25	$3.99
914	106 x 55	Rotary Press Standard Commemorative	20	$6.25	$3.99
915	105 x 57	Giori Press Standard Commemorative	20	$6.25	$3.99
916	127 x 70	Giori Press Jumbo Commemorative	10	$6.25	$3.99
917	165 x 94	First Day Cover	10	$6.25	$3.99
918	140 x 90	Postal Card Size/Submarine Booklet Pane	10	$6.25	$3.99
1048	152 x 107	Large Postal Cards	8	$10.25	$6.99

STRIPS 215MM LONG

ITEM	W x H (MM)	DESCRIPTION	MOUNTS	RETAIL	AA*
919	20	U.S. 19th Century, Horizontal Coil	22	$7.99	$5.25
920	22	U.S. Early Air Mail	22	$7.99	$5.25
921	24	U.S., Vertical Coils, Christmas (#2400, #2428 etc.)	22	$7.99	$5.25
922	25	U.S. Commemorative and Regular	22	$7.99	$5.25
1049	26	U.S. Commemorative and Regular	22	$7.99	$5.25
923	27	U.S. Famous Americans	22	$7.99	$5.25
924	28	U.S. 19th Century, Liechtenstein	22	$7.99	$5.25
925	30	U.S. 19th Century; Jamestown, etc; Foreign	22	$7.99	$5.25
926	31	U.S. Horizontal Jumbo and Semi-Jumbo	22	$7.99	$5.25
927	33	U.S. Stampin' Future, UN	22	$7.99	$5.25
928	36	U.S. Hunting Permit, Canada	15	$7.99	$5.25
929	39	U.S. Early 20th Century	15	$7.99	$5.25
930	41	U.S. Vert. Semi-Jumbo ('77 Lafayette, Pottery, etc.)	15	$7.99	$5.25
931		Multiple Assortment: One strip of each size 22-41 above (SMKB) (2 x 25mm strips)	12	$7.99	$5.25
932	44	U.S. Vertical Coil Pair Garden Flowers Booklet Pane	15	$7.99	$5.25
933	48	U.S. Farley, Gutter Pair	15	$7.99	$5.25
934	50	U.S. Jumbo (Lyndon Johnson, '74 U.P.U., etc.)	15	$7.99	$5.25
935	52	U.S. Standard Commemorative Block (Butterflies)	15	$7.99	$5.25
936	55	U.S. Standard Plate Block - normal margins	15	$7.99	$5.25
937	57	U.S. Standard Plate Block - wider margins	15	$7.99	$5.25
938	61	U.S. Blocks, Israel Tabs, '99 Christmas Madonna Pane	15	$7.99	$5.25

STRIPS 240MM LONG

ITEM	W x H (MM)	DESCRIPTION	MOUNTS	RETAIL	AA*
939	63	U.S. Jumbo Commemorative Horizontal Block	10	$9.25	$5.99
940	66	U.S. CIPEX Souvenir Sheet, Self-Adhesive Booklet Pane (#2803a, 3012a)	10	$9.25	$5.99
941	68	U.S. ATM Booklet Pane, Farley Gutter Pair & Souvenir Sheet	10	$9.25	$5.99
942	74	U.S. TIPEX Souvenir Sheet	10	$9.25	$5.99
943	80	U.S. Standard Commemorative Vertical Block	10	$9.25	$5.99
944	82	U.S. Blocks of Four, U.N. Chagall	10	$9.25	$5.99
945	84	Israel Tab Block, Mars Pathfinder Sheetlet	10	$9.25	$5.99
946	89	Submarine Booklet, Souvenir Sheet World Cup, Rockwell	10	$9.25	$5.99
947	100	U.S. '74 U.P.U. Block, U.N. Margin Inscribed Block	7	$9.25	$5.99
948	120	Various Souvenir Sheets and Blocks	7	$9.25	$5.99

STRIPS 265MM LONG

ITEM	W x H (MM)	DESCRIPTION	MOUNTS	RETAIL	AA*
1035	25	U.S. Coils Strips of 11	12	$9.25	$5.99
949	40	U.S. Postal People Standard Standard & Semi-Jumbo Commemorative Strip	10	$9.25	$5.99
981	44	U.S. Long self-adhesive booklet panes	10	$9.25	$5.99
1030	45	Various (Canada Scott #1725-1734)	10	$9.25	$5.99
1036	46	U.S. Long self adhesive booklet panes of 15	10	$9.25	$5.99

STRIPS 265MM LONG - CONTINUED

ITEM	W x H (MM)	DESCRIPTION	MOUNTS	RETAIL	AA*
950	55	U.S. Regular Plate Block or Strip of 20	10	$9.25	$5.99
951	59	U.S. Double Issue Strip	10	$9.25	$5.99
952	70	U.S. Jumbo Commemorative Plate Block	10	$12.50	$8.50
1031	72	Various (Canada Scott #1305a-1804a)	10	$12.50	$8.50
1032	75	Plate Blocks: Lance Armstrong, Prehistoric Animals, etc.	10	$12.50	$8.50
953	91	U.S. Self-Adhesive Booklet Pane '98 Wreath, '95 Santa	10	$12.50	$8.50
1033	95	Mini-Sheet Plate Blocks w/top header	10	$12.50	$8.50
954	105	U.S. Standard Semi-Jumbo Commemorative Plate Number Strip	10	$12.50	$8.50
955	107	Same as above–wide margin	10	$12.50	$8.50
956	111	U.S. Gravure-Intaglio Plate Number Strip	10	$14.75	$9.99
957	127	U.S. 2000 Space S/S, World War II S/S	10	$17.50	$11.99
958	137	Great Britain Coronation	10	$17.50	$11.99
959	158	American Glass, U.S. Football Coaches Sheets	10	$17.99	$12.50
960	175	Large Block, Souvenir Sheet	5	$12.50	$8.50
961	231	U.S. Full Post Office Pane Regular and Commemorative	5	$17.99	$12.50

SOUVENIR SHEETS/SMALL PANES

ITEM	W x H (MM)	DESCRIPTION	MOUNTS	RETAIL	AA*
962	204 x 153	New Year 2000, U.S. Bicentennial S/S	4	$9.25	$5.99
963	187 x 144	55¢ Victorian Love Pane, U.N. Flag Sheet	9	$15.50	$10.25
964	160 x 200	U.N., Israel Sheet	10	$15.50	$10.25
965	120 x 207	U.S. AMERIPEX Presidential Sheet	4	$6.25	$3.99
968	229 x 131	World War II S/S Plate Block Only	5	$9.25	$5.99
970	111 x 91	Columbian Souvenir Sheet	6	$6.25	$4.75
972	148 x 196	Apollo Moon Landing/Carnivorous Plants	4	$7.99	$5.25
989	129 x 122	U.S. Definitive Sheet: Harte, Hopkins, etc.	8	$10.25	$6.99
990	189 x 151	Chinese New Year	5	$10.25	$6.99
991	150 x 185	Breast Cancer/Fermi/Soccer/'96 Folk Heroes	5	$10.25	$6.99
992	198 x 151	Cherokee Strip Sheet	5	$10.25	$6.99
993	185 x 151	Bernstein/NATO/Irish/Lunt/Gold Rush Sheets	5	$10.25	$6.99
994	198 x 187	Postal Museum	5	$10.25	$6.99
995	156 x 187	Sign Language/Statehood	5	$10.25	$6.99
996	188 x 197	Illustrators, '98 Music: Folk, Gospel; Country/Western	4	$10.25	$6.99
997	151 x 192	Olympic	5	$10.25	$6.99
998	174 x 185	Buffalo Soldiers	5	$10.25	$6.99
999	130 x 198	Silent Screen Stars	5	$10.25	$6.99
1000	190 x 199	Stars Stripes/Baseball/Insects & Spiders/ Legends West/ Aircraft, Comics, '96 Olympics, Civil War	4	$10.25	$6.99
1001	178 x 181	Cranes	4	$10.25	$6.99
1002	183 x 212	Wonders of the Sea, We the People	3	$10.25	$6.99
1003	156 x 264	$14 Eagle	4	$10.25	$6.99
1004	159 x 270	$9.95 Moon Landing	4	$10.25	$6.99
1005	159 x 259	$2.90 Priority/$9.95 Express Mail	4	$10.25	$6.99
1006	223 x 187	Hubble, Hollywood Legends, O'Keefe Sheets	3	$10.25	$6.99
1007	185 x 181	Deep Sea Creatures, Olmsted Sheets	4	$10.25	$6.99
1008	152 x 228	Indian Dances/Antique Autos	5	$10.25	$6.99
1009	165 x 150	River Boat/Hanukkah	6	$10.25	$6.99
1010	275 x 200	Dinosaurs/Large Gutter Blocks	2	$10.25	$6.99
1011	161 x 160	Pacific '97 Triangle Mini Sheets	6	$10.25	$6.99
1012	174 x 130	Road Runner, Daffy, Bugs, Sylvester & Tweety	6	$10.25	$6.99
1013	196 x 158	Football Coaches	4	$10.25	$6.99
1014	184 x 184	American Dolls, Flowering Trees Sheets	4	$10.25	$6.99
1015	186 x 230	Classic Movie Monsters	3	$10.25	$6.99
1016	187 x 160	Trans-Mississippi Sheet	4	$10.25	$6.99
1017	192 x 230	Celebrate The Century	3	$10.25	$6.99
1018	156 x 204	Space Discovery	5	$10.25	$6.99
1019	182 x 209	American Ballet	5	$10.25	$6.99
1020	139 x 151	Christmas Wreaths	5	$10.25	$6.99
1021	129 x 126	Justin Morrill, Henry Luce	8	$10.25	$6.99
1022	184 x 165	Baseball Fields, Bright Eyes	4	$10.25	$6.99
1023	185 x 172	Shuttle Landing Pan Am Invert Sheets	4	$10.25	$6.99
1024	172 x 233	Sonoran Desert	3	$10.25	$6.99
1025	150 x 166	Prostate Cancer	5	$10.25	$6.99
1026	201 x 176	Famous Trains	4	$10.25	$6.99
1027	176 x 124	Canada - Historic Vehicles	5	$10.25	$6.99
1028	245 x 114	Canada - Provincial Leaders	5	$10.25	$6.99
1029	177 x 133	Canada - Year of the Family	5	$10.25	$6.99
1034	181 x 213	Arctic Animals	3	$10.25	$6.99
1037	179 x 242	Louise Nevelson	3	$10.25	$6.99
1038	179 x 217	Library Of Congress	3	$10.25	$6.99
1039	182 x 232	Youth Team Sports	3	$10.25	$6.99
1040	183 x 216	Lucille Ball Scott #3523	3	$10.25	$6.99
1041	182 x 244	American Photographers	3	$10.25	$6.99
1042	185 x 255	Andy Warhol	3	$10.25	$6.99
1043	165 x 190	American Film Making	4	$10.25	$6.99
1044	28 x 290	American Eagle PNC Strips of 11 Available in clear or black backgrounds. Please specify color choice when ordering.	12	$9.25	$5.99

ACCESSORIES

ITEM	W x H (MM)	DESCRIPTION	MOUNTS	RETAIL	AA*
LH180MC		Stamp Mount Cutter 7"		$23.99	$19.99
980RMC		Rotary Mount Cutter		$89.99	$79.99
SG622		Hawid Glue Pen		$7.95	$7.25

Call **1-800-572-6885**

Outside U.S. & Canada Call:

1-937-498-0800

Visit **AmosAdvantage.com**

ORDERING INFORMATION
1. *AA prices apply to paid subscribers of Amos Media titles, or for orders placed online.
2. Prices, terms and product availability subject to change.
3. Shipping & Handling
   United States: Orders under $10 are only $3.99, 10% of order total. Minimum charge $7.99, Maximum charge $45
   Canada: 20% of order total. Minimum charge $19.99, Maximum charge $200
   Foreign orders are shipped via FedEx Intl and billed actual freight.

INDEX TO ADVERTISERS
2016 VOLUME 4

2016
VOLUME 4
DEALER DIRECTORY
YELLOW PAGE LISTINGS

This section of your Scott Catalogue contains advertisements to help you conveniently find what you need, when you need it...!

Accessories

BROOKLYN GALLERY COIN & STAMP, INC.
8725 4th Ave.
Brooklyn, NY 11209
PH: 718-745-5701
FAX: 718-745-2775
info@brooklyngallery.com
www.brooklyngallery.com

Appraisals

DR. ROBERT FRIEDMAN & SONS STAMP & COIN BUYING CENTER
2029 W. 75th St.
Woodridge, IL 60517
PH: 800-588-8100
FAX: 630-985-1588
drbobstamps@comcast.net
www.drbobfriedmanstamps.com

Asia

MICHAEL ROGERS, INC.
Suite 4-1
415 S. Orlando Ave.
Winter Park, FL 32789-3683
PH: 407-644-2290
PH: 800-843-3751
FAX: 407-645-4434
Stamps@michaelrogersinc.com
www.michaelrogersinc.com

THE STAMP ACT
PO Box 1136
Belmont, CA 94002
PH: 650-703-2342
PH: 650-592-3315
FAX: 650-508-8104
thestampact@sbcglobal.net

Auctions

DANIEL F. KELLEHER AUCTIONS LLC
PMB 44
60 Newtown Rd
Danbury, CT 06810
PH: 203-297-6056
FAX: 203-297-6059
info@kelleherauctions.com
www.kelleherauctions.com

DUTCH COUNTRY AUCTIONS
4115 Concord Pike
Wilmington, DE 19803
PH: 302-478-8740
FAX: 302-478-8779
auctions@dutchcountryauctions.com
www.dutchcountryauctions.com

R. MARESCH & SON LTD.
5th Floor - 6075 Yonge St.
Toronto, ON M2M 3W2
CANADA
PH: 416-363-7777
FAX: 416-363-6511
www.maresch.com

Auctions - Public

ALAN BLAIR AUCTIONS, L.L.C.
Suite 1
5405 Lakeside Ave.
Richmond, VA 23228-6060
PH: 800-689-5602
FAX: 804-262-9307
alanblair@verizon.net
www.alanblairstamps.com

British Asia

THE STAMP ACT
PO Box 1136
Belmont, CA 94002
PH: 650-703-2342
PH: 650-592-3315
FAX: 650-508-8104
thestampact@sbcglobal.net

British Commonwealth

ARON R. HALBERSTAM PHILATELISTS, LTD.
PO Box 150168
Van Brunt Station
Brooklyn, NY 11215-0168
PH: 718-788-397
arh@arhstamps.com
www.arhstamps.com

Buying

DR. ROBERT FRIEDMAN & SONS STAMP & COIN BUYING CENTER
2029 W. 75th St.
Woodridge, IL 60517
PH: 800-588-8100
FAX: 630-985-1588
drbobstamps@comcast.net
www.drbobfriedmanstamps.com

Canada

CANADA STAMP FINDER
54 Soccavo Crescent
Brampton, ON L6Y 0W3
PH: 905-488-6109
Toll Free in North America
PH: 877-412-3106
FAX: 323-215-2635
info@canadastampfinder.com
www.canadastampfinder.com

China

MICHAEL ROGERS, INC.
Suite 4-1
415 S. Orlando Ave.
Winter Park, FL 32789-3683
PH: 407-644-2290
PH: 800-843-3751
FAX: 407-645-4434
Stamps@michaelrogersinc.com
www.michaelrogersinc.com

Collections

DR. ROBERT FRIEDMAN & SONS STAMP & COIN BUYING CENTER
2029 W. 75th St.
Woodridge, IL 60517
PH: 800-588-8100
FAX: 630-985-1588
drbobstamps@comcast.net
www.drbobfriedmanstamps.com

Ducks

MICHAEL JAFFE
PO Box 61484
Vancouver, WA 98666
PH: 360-695-6161
PH: 800-782-6770
FAX: 360-695-1616
mjaffe@brookmanstamps.com
www.brookmanstamps.com

German Colonies

COLONIAL STAMP COMPANY
5757 Wilshire Blvd. PH #8
Los Angeles, CA 90036
PH: 323-933-9435
FAX: 323-939-9930
Toll Free in North America
PH: 877-272-6693
FAX: 877-272-6694
info@colonialstampcompany.com
www.colonialstampcompany.com

Germany

JAMES F TAFF
PO Box 19549
Sacramento, CA 95819
PH: 916-454-9007
FAX: 916-454-9009

Great Britain

COLONIAL STAMP COMPANY
5757 Wilshire Blvd. PH #8
Los Angeles, CA 90036
PH: 323-933-9435
FAX: 323-939-9930
Toll Free in North America
PH: 877-272-6693
FAX: 877-272-6694
info@colonialstampcompany.com
www.colonialstampcompany.com

Japan

MICHAEL ROGERS, INC.
Suite 4-1
415 S. Orlando Ave.
Winter Park, FL 32789-3683
PH: 407-644-2290
PH: 800-843-3751
FAX: 407-645-4434
Stamps@michaelrogersinc.com
www.michaelrogersinc.com

THE STAMP ACT
PO Box 1136
Belmont, CA 94002
PH: 650-703-2342
PH: 650-592-3315
FAX: 650-508-8104
thestampact@sbcglobal.net

Kenya, Uganda, Tanzania

COLONIAL STAMP COMPANY
5757 Wilshire Blvd. PH #8
Los Angeles, CA 90036
PH: 323-933-9435
FAX: 323-939-9930
Toll Free in North America
PH: 877-272-6693
FAX: 877-272-6694
info@colonialstampcompany.com
www.colonialstampcompany.com

Kiauchau (German)

COLONIAL STAMP COMPANY
5757 Wilshire Blvd. PH #8
Los Angeles, CA 90036
PH: 323-933-9435
FAX: 323-939-9930
Toll Free in North America
PH: 877-272-6693
FAX: 877-272-6694
info@colonialstampcompany.com
www.colonialstampcompany.com

Korea

MICHAEL ROGERS, INC.
Suite 4-1
415 S. Orlando Ave.
Winter Park, FL 32789-3683
PH: 407-644-2290
PH: 800-843-3751
FAX: 407-645-4434
Stamps@michaelrogersinc.com
www.michaelrogersinc.com

Leeward Islands

COLONIAL STAMP COMPANY
5757 Wilshire Blvd. PH #8
Los Angeles, CA 90036
PH: 323-933-9435
FAX: 323-939-9930
Toll Free in North America
PH: 877-272-6693
FAX: 877-272-6694
info@colonialstampcompany.com
www.colonialstampcompany.com

Liechtenstein

HENRY GITNER PHILATELISTS, INC.
PO Box 3077-S
Middletown, NY 10940
PH: 845-343-5151
PH: 800-947-8267
FAX: 845-343-0068
hgitner@hgitner.com
www.hgitner.com

Luxembourg

HENRY GITNER PHILATELISTS, INC.
PO Box 3077-S
Middletown, NY 10940
PH: 845-343-5151
PH: 800-947-8267
FAX: 845-343-0068
hgitner@hgitner.com
www.hgitner.com

Madagascar (British Issues)

COLONIAL STAMP COMPANY
5757 Wilshire Blvd. PH #8
Los Angeles, CA 90036
PH: 323-933-9435
FAX: 323-939-9930
Toll Free in North America
PH: 877-272-6693
FAX: 877-272-6694
info@colonialstampcompany.com
www.colonialstampcompany.com

Malaya

COLONIAL STAMP COMPANY
5757 Wilshire Blvd. PH #8
Los Angeles, CA 90036
PH: 323-933-9435
FAX: 323-939-9930
Toll Free in North America
PH: 877-272-6693
FAX: 877-272-6694
info@colonialstampcompany.com
www.colonialstampcompany.com

THE STAMP ACT
PO Box 1136
Belmont, CA 94002
PH: 650-703-2342
PH: 650-592-3315
FAX: 650-508-8104
thestampact@sbcglobal.net

Manchukuo

MICHAEL ROGERS, INC.
Suite 4-1
415 S. Orlando Ave.
Winter Park, FL 32789-3683
PH: 407-644-2290
PH: 800-843-3751
FAX: 407-645-4434
Stamps@michaelrogersinc.com
www.michaelrogersinc.com

Mariana Islands (Ger & Sp)

COLONIAL STAMP COMPANY
5757 Wilshire Blvd. PH #8
Los Angeles, CA 90036
PH: 323-933-9435
FAX: 323-939-9930
Toll Free in North America
PH: 877-272-6693
FAX: 877-272-6694
info@colonialstampcompany.com
www.colonialstampcompany.com

Marshall Islands

COLONIAL STAMP COMPANY
5757 Wilshire Blvd. PH #8
Los Angeles, CA 90036
PH: 323-933-9435
FAX: 323-939-9930
Toll Free in North America
PH: 877-272-6693
FAX: 877-272-6694
info@colonialstampcompany.com
www.colonialstampcompany.com

Mauritius

COLONIAL STAMP COMPANY
5757 Wilshire Blvd. PH #8
Los Angeles, CA 90036
PH: 323-933-9435
FAX: 323-939-9930
Toll Free in North America
PH: 877-272-6693
FAX: 877-272-6694
info@colonialstampcompany.com
www.colonialstampcompany.com

Mesopotamia

COLONIAL STAMP COMPANY
5757 Wilshire Blvd. PH #8
Los Angeles, CA 90036
PH: 323-933-9435
FAX: 323-939-9930
Toll Free in North America
PH: 877-272-6693
FAX: 877-272-6694
info@colonialstampcompany.com
www.colonialstampcompany.com

Middle East-Arab

MICHAEL ROGERS, INC.
Suite 4-1
415 S. Orlando Ave.
Winter Park, FL 32789-3683
PH: 407-644-2290
PH: 800-843-3751
FAX: 407-645-4434
Stamps@michaelrogersinc.com
www.michaelrogersinc.com

Natal

COLONIAL STAMP COMPANY
5757 Wilshire Blvd. PH #8
Los Angeles, CA 90036
PH: 323-933-9435
FAX: 323-939-9930
Toll Free in North America
PH: 877-272-6693
FAX: 877-272-6694
info@colonialstampcompany.com
www.colonialstampcompany.com

New Britain

COLONIAL STAMP COMPANY
5757 Wilshire Blvd. PH #8
Los Angeles, CA 90036
PH: 323-933-9435
FAX: 323-939-9930
Toll Free in North America
PH: 877-272-6693
FAX: 877-272-6694
info@colonialstampcompany.com
www.colonialstampcompany.com

New Issues

DAVIDSON'S STAMP SERVICE
PO Box 36355
Indianapolis, IN 46236-0355
PH: 317-826-2620
ed-davidson@earthlink.net
www.newstampissues.com

New Zealand

ARON R. HALBERSTAM PHILATELISTS, LTD.
PO Box 150168
Van Brunt Station
Brooklyn, NY 11215-0168
PH: 718-788-397
arh@arhstamps.com
www.arhstamps.com

COLONIAL STAMP COMPANY
5757 Wilshire Blvd. PH #8
Los Angeles, CA 90036
PH: 323-933-9435
FAX: 323-939-9930
Toll Free in North America
PH: 877-272-6693
FAX: 877-272-6694
info@colonialstampcompany.com
www.colonialstampcompany.com

Niger Coast Protectorate

COLONIAL STAMP COMPANY
5757 Wilshire Blvd. PH #8
Los Angeles, CA 90036
PH: 323-933-9435
FAX: 323-939-9930
Toll Free in North America
PH: 877-272-6693
FAX: 877-272-6694
info@colonialstampcompany.com
www.colonialstampcompany.com

Orange River Colony

COLONIAL STAMP COMPANY
5757 Wilshire Blvd. PH #8
Los Angeles, CA 90036
PH: 323-933-9435
FAX: 323-939-9930
Toll Free in North America
PH: 877-272-6693
FAX: 877-272-6694
info@colonialstampcompany.com
www.colonialstampcompany.com

Proofs & Essays

HENRY GITNER PHILATELISTS, INC.
PO Box 3077-S
Middletown, NY 10940
PH: 845-343-5151
PH: 800-947-8267
FAX: 845-343-0068
hgitner@hgitner.com
www.hgitner.com

Rhodesia

COLONIAL STAMP COMPANY
5757 Wilshire Blvd. PH #8
Los Angeles, CA 90036
PH: 323-933-9435
FAX: 323-939-9930
Toll Free in North America
PH: 877-272-6693
FAX: 877-272-6694
info@colonialstampcompany.com
www.colonialstampcompany.com

Stamp Stores

California

BROSIUS STAMP, COIN & SUPPLIES
2105 Main St.
Santa Monica, CA 90405
PH: 310-396-7480
FAX: 310-396-7455
brosius.stamp.coin@hotmail.com

COLONIAL STAMP COMPANY
5757 Wilshire Blvd. PH #8
Los Angeles, CA 90036
PH: 323-933-9435
FAX: 323-939-9930
Toll Free in North America
PH: 877-272-6693
FAX: 877-272-6694
info@colonialstampcompany.com
www.colonialstampcompany.com

Georgia

STAMPS UNLIMITED OF GEORGIA, INC.
Suite 1460
100 Peachtree St. NW
Atlanta, GA 30303
PH: 404-688-9161
tonyroozen@yahoo.com
www.stampsunlimitedofga.com